W9-AZL-461

Who's Who in American Art™

Who'sWho in American Art™

2007~2008

•

27th Edition

890 Mountain Ave., Ste. 4
New Providence, NJ 07974 U.S.A.
www.marquiswhoswho.com

Who's Who in American Art™

Published by Marquis Who's Who® LLC

For information, contact:
Marquis Who's Who®
890 Mountain Avenue, Suite 4
New Providence, New Jersey 07974
1-908-673-1000
www.marquiswhoswho.com

WHO'S WHO IN AMERICAN ART™ is a trademark of Marquis Who's Who LLC.
Library of Congress Catalog Card Number 36-27014
International Standard Book Number 0-8379-6306-0
International Standard Serial Number 0000-0191

Manufactured in the United States of America.

Table of Contents

Preface

Marquis Who's Who is proud to present the 27th edition of Who's Who in American Art. This biennial directory, first published in 1953, profiles 11,481 contributors to the visual arts in the United States, Canada and Mexico. These representatives from all segments of the art world include artists, administrators, consultants, critics, curators, dealers, historians, educators, lecturers, collectors, librarians and publishers.

CONTENT AND COVERAGE

The main biography section lists entrants alphabetically. Individual biographies may be composed of many elements depending upon the activity of the entrant. These elements can include vital statistics, * professional classifications, education and training, * works in public collections, * commissions, * exhibitions, * publications, positions held in schools, museums and organizations, * memberships in art societies, * honors and awards, research statements, * media, dealer, and mailing address. Elements preceded by an asterisk are limited as to number included. If entrants exceed the limitations, the most current and/or most notable information is selected.

368 new entries appear in the 27th edition. The names of these individuals were obtained from nominations provided by current entrants, art associations, galleries and museums or from citations in professional publications. Each nominee received a questionnaire to fill out. Selection for inclusion in Who's Who in American Art was determined by the information submitted by each nominee. For artists, consideration is given to work in public collections, commissioned works and exhibitions of an international, national and wide regional scope in non-commercial galleries and museums. Inclusion of entrants other than artists is based upon position and experience in the art world. Among those represented are art administrators and curators of major museums, scholars and librarians of prominent institutions and widely published art writers and critics.

INDEXING

To locate entrants by region, check our geographic index that breaks down listings by state and city within the United States and by province and city within Canada. For entrants who reside outside North America, a breakdown by country is included. To locate entrants by area of expertise, consult our professional classification index. A necrology index is also provided, cumulative from 1953.

COMPILATION

All entrants appearing in the 27th edition were mailed their biographies for corroboration and updating before publication in this edition. Information provided by entrants is included as completely as possible within the boundaries of editorial and space restrictions. Every effort was made to update biographies for individuals who did not reply by direct telephone calls and secondary sources and to assure accurate reproduction of the material submitted. The publishers do not assume and hereby disclaim any liability to any party for any loss or damage caused by errors or omissions in Who's Who in American Art, whether such errors or omissions resulted from negligence, accident or any other cause. In case of a publication error, the sole responsibility of the publisher will be the entry of corrected information in succeeding editions.

The editors welcome the submission of artist nominations, suggestions, and comments for future editions. Send all inquiries to The Editors, Who's Who in American Art, 890 Mountain Avenue, Suite 4, New Providence, New Jersey 07974.

Table of Abbreviations

The following abbreviations and symbols are frequently used in this book.

A

abstr—abstract(s)
acad—academia, academic, academica, academie, academique, academy, accademia
acoust—acoustic(s), acoustical
actg—acting
addn—addition, additional
adj—adjunct
Adm—Admiral
admin—administration, administrative
adminr—administrator
admis(s)—admission(s)
adv—adviser(s), advisory
advan—advance(d), advancement
advert—advertisement, advertising
aesthet—aesthetics
affil—affiliate, affiliation
agr—agricultural, agriculture
akad—akedemi, akademia
Ala—Alabama
Alta—Alberta
Am—America, American
anal—analysis, analytic, analytical
analog—analogue
anat—anatomic, anatomical, anatomy
ann—annual
anthrop—anthropological, anthropology
antiq—antiquary, antiquities, antiquity
antiqn—antiquarian
app—appoint, appointed
appl—applied
approx—approximate, approximately
Apr—April
apt—apartment(s)
arch—archive, archiva, archives, archivio, archivo
archeol—archeological, archeologie, archeologique, archeology
archit—architectural, architecture
Arg—Argentina
Ariz—Arizona
Ark—Arkansas
asn—association
asoc—asociacion
assoc(s)—associate(s), associated
asst(s)—assistant(s)
atty—attorney
Aug—August
auth—author
AV—audiovisual
Ave—Avenue

B

b—born
BC—British Columbia
bd—board
Belg—Belgian, Belgium
bibliog—bibliografia, bibliographic, bibliographical, bibliography(ies)
bibliot—biblioteca, bibliotek, bibliotheca, bibliothek, bibliotheque
biog—biographical, biography
bk(s)—book(s)
Bldg—Building(s)
Blvd—Boulevard
br—branch(es)
bro(s)—brother(s)
Brit—Britain, British
bull—bulletin
bur—bureau
bus—business
BWI—British West Indies

C

Calif—California
Can—Canada, Canadian, Canadien, Canadienne
Capt—Captain
Cath—Catholic
CBS—Columbia Broadcasting System
cent—central
Cent Am—Central America
cert—certificate(s), certification, certified
chap—chapter
chmn—chairman
c/o—care of
co—companies, company
Co—County
coauth—coauthor
co-chmn—co-chairman
co-dir—co-director
co-ed—co-editor
co-educ—co-educational
CofC—Chamber of Commerce
Col—Colonel
col(s)—college(s), collegiate
collab—collaboration, collaborative
collabr—collaborator
Colo—Colorado
com—commerce, commercial
comdr—commander
commun—communication(s)
comn(s)—commission(s), commissioned
comnr—commissioner
compos—composition
comt(s)—committee(s)
conf—conference
Cong—Congress, Congressional
Conn—Connecticut
conserv—conservacion, conservation, conservatiore, conservatory
construct—construction
consult—consult, consultant, consultantship, consultation, consulting
contemp—contemporary
contrib—contribute, contributing, contribution
contribr—contributor
conv—convention
coop—cooperating, cooperation, cooperative
coord—coordinate, coordinating, coordination
coordr—coordinator
corp—corporate, corporation
corresp—correspondent, corresponding
coun—council, counsel, counseling
counr—councilor, counselor
CPA—Certified Public Accountant
Ct—Court
ctr—center
cult—cultural, culture
cur—curator
curric—curriculum
Czech—Czechoslovakia

D

DC—District of Columbia
Dec—December
Del—Delaware
deleg—delegate, delegation
demonstr—demonstrator
dept—department, departmental
develop—development, developmental
dict—dictionaries, dictionary
dig—digest
dipl—diplom, diploma, diplomate, diplome
dir(s)—director(s), directory
dist—district
distribr—distributor
div—division, divisional, divorced
doc—document(s), documentary, documentation
Dom—Dominion
Dr—Doctor, Drive

E

E—East
econ—economic(s), economical, economist, economy
ed—edicion, edit, edited, editing, edition, editor(s), editorial, edizione
educ—educate, educated, educating, education, educational
elec—electric, electrical, electricity
elem—elementary
emer—emeriti, emeritus
encyl—encyclopedia
eng—engineering
Eng—England, English
environ—environment(s), environmental
equip—equipment
estab—established, establishment
estud—estudante, estudas, estudiante, estudio, estudo
Europ—European
exam—examination
exec(s)—executive(s)
exhib(s)—exhibit(s), exhibition
exped(s)—expedition(s)
explor—exploration(s), exploratory
expos—exposition
exten—extention

F

fac—faculty
Feb—February
fed—federal
fedn—federation
fel(s)—fellow(s), fellowship(s)
Fla—Florida
for—foreign
found—foundation
Fr—France, French
Ft—Fort
ft—feet, foot

G

Ga—Georgia
gen—general, generale
Ger—German, Germany
Ges—Gesellschaft
gov—governing, governor
govt—government, governmental
grad—graduate, graduated
GtBrit—Great Britain
gym—gymnasium

H

handbk(s)—handbook(s)
hist—historia, historic, historica, historical, historique, historisch(e), history
HM—Her Majesty
hochsch—hochschule
hon(s)—honor(s), honorable, honorary
hosp(s)—hospital(s), hospitalization
hq—headquarters
Hwy—Highway

I

Ill—Illinois
illum—illuminating, illumination
illus—illustrate, illustrated, illustration
illusr—illustrator
Inc—Incorporated
incl—include, included, includes, including
Ind—Indiana
indust(s)—industrial, industries, industry
info—information
inst—institut, instituto
inst(s)—institute(s), institution(s)
instnl—institutional, institutionalized
instr(s)—instruct, instruction, instructors
instrnl—instructional
int—internacional, international, internazionale
introd—introduction
ist—istituto
Ital—Italia, Italian, Italiana, Italiano, Italica, Italien, Italienisch, Italienne(s)

J

J—Journal (title)
Jan—January
jour—journal (descriptive)
jr—junior
juv—juvenile(s)

K

Kans—Kansas
Ky—Kentucky

L

La—Louisiana
lab(s)—laboratories, laboratory
lang—language(s)
lect—lecture(s)
lectr—lecturer(s)
lett—letter(s)
lib—liberal
libr—libraries, library, librerio
librn—librarian
lit—literary, literaure, literatura, literature, littera, litterature
Lt—Lieutenant
ltd—limited

M

mag—magazine
maj—major
Man—Manitoba
Mar—March
Mass—Massachusetts
mat—material(s)
Md—Maryland
med—medical, medicine, medicinal
mem—member(s), membership(s), memoirs
Mem—Memorial
metrop—metropolitan
Mex—Mexican, Mexicano, Mexico
mgr—manager
mgt—management
Mich—Michigan
Minn—Minnesota
Miss—Mississippi
Mo—Missouri
mo—month
mod—modern, moderna, moderne, moderno
monogr—monograph
Mont—Montana
Mt—Mount
munic—municipal, municipalities
mus—musee, museo, museum(s)

N

N—North
nac—nacional
nat—nationaal, national, nationale, nationalis
naz—nazionale
NB—New Brunswick
NC—North Carolina
NDak—North Dakota
Nebr—Nebraska
Neth—Netherlands
Nev—Nevada
New Eng—New England
Nfld—Newfoundland
NH—New Hampshire
NJ—New Jersey
NMex—New Mexico
Norweg—Norwegian
Nov—November
NS—Nova Scotia
NSW—New South Wales
NY—New York
NZ—New Zealand

O

Oct—October
off—office, official
Okla—Oklahoma
Ont—Ontario
oper(s)—operation(s), operational, operative
Ore—Oregon
orgn—organization, organizational

P

Pa—Pennsylvania
Pac—Pacific
Pan-Am—Pan-American
partic—participant, participating
PEI—Prince Edward Island
philos—philosophic, philosophical, philosophy
photog—photographic, photography
photogr—photographer(s)
Pkwy—Parkway
Pl—Place

PO Box—Post Office Box
polytech—polytechnic, polytechnical
Port—Portugal, Portuguese
PQ—Province of Quebec
PR—Puerto Rico
prehist—prehistoric, prehistory
pres—president
Presby—Presbyterian
preserv—preservation
prof—profession, professional, professor, professorial
prog(s)—program(s), programmed, programming
proj(s)—project(s), projection(s), projectional, projective
prom—promotion
prov—province, provincial
pub—public
publ—publication(s), published, publisher(s), publishing
pvt—private

Q

Quart—Quarterly
Que—Quebec

R

Rd—Road
RD—Rural Delivery
rec—record(s), recording
regist—register, registered, registration
registr—registrar
relig—religion, religious
rep—represent, representative
Repub—Republic
res—research
ret—retired
rev—review, revised, revision
RFD—Rural Free Delivery
RI—Rhode Island
Rm—Room
RR—Rural Route
Rte—Route
Russ—Russia, Russian

S

S—South
S Africa—South Africa, South African
S Am—South America, South American
Sask—Saskatchewan
SC—South Carolina
Scand—Scandinavia, Scandinavian
sch(s)—school(s)
scholar—scholarship
sci—science(s), scientific
SDak—South Dakota
sec—secondary
sect—section
secy—secretary
sem—seminar, seminary
Sen—Senator, Senatorial
Sept—September
ser—series
serv—service(s), serving
soc(s)—sociedad, societa, societas, societate, societe, societet, societies, society
Span—Spanish
spec—special
Sq—Square
sr—senior
St—Saint, Street
sta(s)—station(s)
Ste—Sainte
struct—structural, structure(s)
super—superieur, superior, superiore
suppl—supplement, supplemental, supplementary
supt—superintendent
supv—supervising, supervision
Swed—Swedish
Switz—Switzerland
symp—symposium(s)

T

tech—technical, technique
technol—technologic, technological, technology
tel—telegraph(y), telephone
Tenn—Tennessee
Terr—Terrace
Tex—Texas
transp—transparent, transportation
transl—tranlation(s)
translr—translator
treas—treasurer, treasury
Twp—Township

U

UN—United Nations
undergrad—undergraduate
UNESCO—United Nations Educational, Scientific and Cultural Organization
univ(s)—universidad, universite, universities, university
US—United States
USA—United States Army
USAF—United States Air Force
USMC—United States Marine Corps
USN—United States Navy

V

Va—Virginia
var—various
vchmn—vice chairman
Vet—Veteran(s)
VI—Virgin Islands
vis—visiting
voc—vocational
vol(s)—volume(s)
vpres—vice president
Vt—Vermont

W

W—West
Wash—Washington
Wis—Wisconsin
wk—week
WVa—West Virginia
Wyo—Wyoming

Y

yearbk—yearbook
YMCA—Young Men's Christian Association
YMHA—Young Men's Hebrew Association
yr(s)—year(s)
YWCA—Young Women's Christian Association
YWHA—Young Women's Hebrew Association

Who'sWho in American Art™

Biographies

A

AADLAND, DALE LYNN
PRINTMAKER; PAINTER
b Sisseton, SDak, Mar 21, 62. *Study:* Minn State Univ, BFA, 1997. *Comn:* print etching, Dakota Fine Art, Fargo, NDak, 95. *Exhib:* Northern Plains Int Printmaking Exhib, Fifth St Gallery, Bismarck, NDak, 97; Tehawitha Fine Art Ctr, Sisseton, 99. *Teaching:* mentor, Wilmot Pub Sch, SDak, 99-. *Awards:* Artists Grant, SDak Arts Coun, 2000; Career Opportunity Grant, Minn Arts Coun, 96. *Media:* Etching. *Dealer:* Harold Moore PO Box 147 Browns Valley MN 56219. *Mailing Add:* RR2 Box 20 Wilmot SD 57279

ABANY, ALBERT CHARLES
PAINTER, PRINTMAKER
b Boston, Mass, Mar 30, 1921. *Study:* Sch Mus Fine Arts, Boston, M O H Longstreth scholar, 42, dipl, 48; Tufts Univ, BS(educ), 49. *Exhib:* One-man shows, Carl Siembab Gallery, Boston, 56; Clark Univ, 63; Northeastern Univ, 67; Wessell Libr, Tufts Univ, 71; Art Inst Boston, 72. *Teaching:* Art teacher drawing & painting, Boston Ctr Adult Educ, 49-51; art teacher drawing, painting, printmaking & art hist, Art Inst Boston, 65-73; art teacher oil & acrylic painting, Brockton Art Mus, Mass, 75-77; art teacher drawing & painting, Danforth Mus Sch, Framingham, 75-77; teacher drawing, painting & hist art, Quincy Jr Col, 75-76; teacher drawing & painting, S Shore Art Ctr, Cohasset, Mass, 83-. *Media:* Oil, Graphics, Mixed Media. *Mailing Add:* 42 MacArthur Rd Natick MA 01760-2938

ABBE, ELFRIEDE MARTHA
SCULPTOR, PRINTMAKER
b Washington, DC. *Study:* Col Archit, Cornell Univ, BFA, 40. *Work:* Rosenwald Collection, Nat Gallery Art; Mus Fine Arts, Boston; Houghton Libr, Harvard Univ; Sloniker Collection, Cincinnati Art Mus; Mus Fine Arts, Venice, Italy. *Comn:* The Hunter (large statue), NY World's Fair, 39; oak frieze, Mann Libr, Cornell Univ, 55 & bronze sculptures, Clive McCay Mem, 67; Napoleon (bronze head), McGill Univ Libr; The Illuminator (walnut carving), Sterling Mem Hunt Libr, Carnegie-Mellon Univ, 69. *Exhib:* Nat Acad Design, NY; San Diego Fine Arts Gallery, 60; Printing in the USA & United Kingdom, London Chappel Exhib, Eng, 63; Int Botanical Artists, Hunt Libr, Carnegie-Mellon Univ, 68; Nat Arts Club, NY, 69 & 70. *Awards:* Gold Medal, Nat Arts Club, 70 & Acad Artists Asn, Springfield, Mass, 76; Elliot Liskin Cash Award, Salmagundi Club, 79. *Bibliog:* Norman Kent (auth), The Book Art of Elfriede Abbe, Am Artist Mag, 60. *Mem:* fel Nat Sculpture Soc; Nat Soc Mural Painters. *Media:* Wood; Woodcut. *Publ:* Designed, illus & printed, Garden Spice & Wild Pot-Herbs, Cornell Univ, 55, The American Scholar, 56, Seven Irish Tales, 57 & Significance of the Frontier, 58

ABBETT, ROBERT KENNEDY
PAINTER, WRITER
b Hammond, Ind, Jan 5, 1926. *Study:* Purdue Univ, BSc, 46; Univ Mo, BA(art), 48; Chicago Acad Fine Art, 48-50; Am Acad Art, Chicago, 49. *Work:* Cowboy Hall Fame & Western Heritage Ctr, Oklahoma City; Diamond M Mus, Snyder, Tex; Genesee Country Mus, Rochester, NY; Dog Mus Am, St Louis; Nat Bird Dog Mus, Grand Junction, Tenn. *Comn:* Portrait of Mrs Roy Larsen, Audubon Soc, Fairfield, Conn, 73; portrait of Jimmy Stewart, Cowboy Hall Fame, Oklahoma City, 75; portrait of Luther Burbank, Burbank Ctr Arts, Santa Rosa, Calif, 75; portrait of Silver comn by Ann Cox Chambers, US Embassy, Brussels, Belgium, 77; Gens Jackson and Lee, Am Military Collection, 84. *Exhib:* Nat Cowboy Western Heritage Mus, Oklahoma City, 74, 75, 86, 95, 2000, 01, 02 & 03; Artists of Am, Denver Rotary, 82-85 & 90-93; miniature show, Thomas Gilcrease Mus, Tulsa, 84, 85, 88, 95 & 96; Cheyenne Frontier Days, Old West Mus, 85-90; Wildlife & Sporting Art, Legacy Gallery, Jackson, Wyo, 1995-2004. *Teaching:* Instr media, Silvermine Col, New Canaan, Conn, 59-61; instr drawing, Sisters Notre Dame, Wilton, Conn, 70 & Washington Art Asn, Conn, 77; workshop, Scottsdale Artists Sch, Ariz, 86-96; coun, Private Career Counseling, 92-05. *Awards:* Outstanding Work, Artists & Books, Soc Illusr, 65; First Prize, Salmagundi Club, New York, 73; Artist Year, Nat Wildlife Art Collectors Soc, Minneapolis, 84. *Bibliog:* Nick Meglin (auth), Robert Abbett, Am Artist, 7/77; Michael McIntosh (auth), Robert Abbett, Southwest Art, 11/88; Tom Davis (auth), The Magic Show of Robert Abbett, Wildlife Art News, 9-10/88. *Mem:* Soc Illusr; Westport Artists (pres, 67); Soc Animal Artists. *Media:* Oil. *Res:* Writing and researching art subjects for my column, Abbett on Art, For Sporting Classics Magazines. *Interests:* Sporting art, dogs, horses, hunting scenes and fishing. *Publ:* coauth, Outdoor Paintings of Robert K Abbett, Peacock/Bantam, 76; coauth with Michael McIntosh, Abbett Briar Patch Pubs, 89; auth, From behind the easel, column, Wildlife Art News, 85-; Wings from Cover, The Upland Images of Robert K Abbett and Ed Gray, Willow Creek Press, 96; auth, A Season for Painting the Outdoor Art of Robert K Abbett, Collectors Covey, 2001. *Dealer:* Russell Fink Box 250 Lorton VA 22199; Legacy Gallery Scottsdale AZ & Jackson WY; Collectors Covey Gallery Dallas. *Mailing Add:* 168 Henry Sanford Rd Bridgewater CT 06752

ABBOTT, LINDA J
STAINED GLASS ARTIST, INSTRUCTOR
b Hempstead, NY, Oct 10, 43. *Study:* Queensboro Soc Allied Arts & Crafts, 55-59; Fashion Inst Technol, State Univ NY, AAS(design), 63; Art Inst Ft Lauderdale, cert, 97. *Work:* Holocaust Mus, Copper City, Fla. *Comn:* Entry restoration of glass, Paewonsky Mansion-Govt Hill, Charlotte Amalie, Virgin Islands, 85; etched & carved glass, Vanderbilt Estate, Manalapan, Fla, 88; 16 windows, entry & creche, St Matthews Catholic Church, Hallandale, Fla 96; 14 windows, Temple Israel, W Palm Beach, Fla, 97; 45 ft skylight dome, WindJammer Cruises, Miami Beach, Fla, 98. *Exhib:* Glass in the Garden, Denver Colo Gardens, 81; Art Glass Symposium, Salt Lake City Mus Art, Utah, 82; Art Glass Expo, Art Barn Mus, Salt Lake City, Utah, 83-84; Retrospective, Art Serve, Mus Art, Ft Lauderdale, Fla, 97; Designer's Invitational, Miami Conv Ctr, Fla, 98. *Pos:* Coordr, Art Glass Expo, Salt Lake City, 81-83 & Art Glass Am, Tampa, 98; educ seminar coordr, Art Glass Supplies Asn, Chicago, 94-95; freelance consult various manufacturers & art orgns, 93-; instr, Educ Comn, Int Art Glass Supplies Asn, Long Beach, 99. *Teaching:* Instr, Crystal Rainbow Inc, Dania, Fla, 89- & Art Glass Expo, Las Vegas, 94-. *Awards:* Best of Show, Cal City Art Asn, 78. *Bibliog:* Al Lewis (auth), Beautiful entryways, Prof Stained Glass Mag, 94; Staff writer (auth), Clearly Beautiful, Palm Beach Illus, 97; Kay Bain Weiner (auth), Stained Glass - The Tiffany Style, Watkins Guptil, 97. *Mem:* Int Stained Glass Designers Asn (pres, 95 98); Art Glass Guild Artisans (founder & bd mem, 96); Art Glass Supplies Asn (ednl sem com, 2001). *Media:* Stained & Carved Glass; Painted Glass. *Publ:* Auth, bi-monthly articles on various art glass subjects, Glass Craftsman Mag, 95-; coauth, Hot & Wired (with instrnl video), 93, Somethings Fishy, 94, Rainforest, 95 & Image is Everything, 96, Stained Glass Images

ABBOTT, REBECCA PHILLIPS
CURATOR, PHOTOGRAPHER
b Giessen, Ger, Jan 10, 50; US citizen. *Study:* Emory & Henry Col, Va, BA, 73. *Exhib:* C & O Canal, Anton Gallery, Washington, DC, 92, The Wind, 94 & Shadows at 18th & K, 98. *Pos:* Dir, Nat Mus Women Arts, Washington, DC, 89-98. *Mem:* Am Asn Mus; Art Table. *Res:* Picturing Time: Self-Portraits of Andy Warhol; Remedios Varo: A Feminist Vision for a New Metaphysics. *Dealer:* Burton Marinkovich Fine Art 1506 21st St NW Washington DC 20036. *Mailing Add:* 4397 Embassy Park Dr NW Washington DC 20016

ABEL, RAY
ILLUSTRATOR, PRINTMAKER
b Chicago, Ill, Sept 19, 11. *Study:* Univ Chicago, AB; Art Inst Chicago; NY Univ, MA; Art Students League, with Kenneth Hayes Miller, George Grosz, Alexander Brook & Ernest Fiene. *Comn:* Aviation (mural frieze), US Army Air Corps Cafeteria, Mitchel Field, NY, 44-45; bk illustrations, McKay, Prentice-Hall, Grolier, Knopf, Lippincott, Viking & others, 50-; bk jackets, Harper & Row, Putnam, Dodd, Mead, Dutton & others, 50-. *Exhib:* Artists of Chicago & Vicinity, Art Inst Chicago, 43; Nat Acad Design Ann Am Exhib, 42; Ann Exhib Am Art, Mint Mus, 44. *Pos:* Ed publ, Art Students League, The League Mag, 41-43; mem bd control, Art Students League NY, 41-49; art dir, Ray Abel Assoc, 51-; artist-in-residence, Kala Inst, Berkeley, Calif. *Teaching:* Instr, Packer Inst, 51-52, Newark Acad Art, 48-51 & Am Art Sch, 55-58. *Awards:* Hon Mentions, Ill State Mus Ann; Mint Mus Ann, 73; Cert Excellence, Am Observed, Soc Illusr, New York, 72. *Mem:* Soc Illusr; life mem Art Students League NY; Kala Inst. *Media:* Pen and Ink; Etching. *Publ:* Coal: Energy and Crisis, Harvey House, 74; Wylie Sypher (auth), 4 children's novels, Atheneum, 76; Bret Harte (auth), The Outcasts of Poker Flat, Listening Libr, 77; co-illusr, The Complete Illustrated Shakespeare, Crown, 79; illusr, The Seven Ages of Man, Shakespeare, State Univ NY, Purchase, 86. *Mailing Add:* 2550 Dana St Berkeley CA 94704-2878

ABELES, KIM VICTORIA
SCULPTOR
b Richmond Heights, Mo, Aug 28, 52. *Study:* Ohio Univ, BFA(painting), 74; Univ Calif, Irvine, MFA(studio art), 80. *Work:* Washington & Jefferson Col, Washington, Pa; Fashion Inst, Los Angeles, Calif; Cal State Univ; Long Beach Art Mus, Long Beach, Calif; City of Santa Monica, Calif; Mus Contemp Art, Los Angeles, Los Angeles Co Mus of Art; plus others; Calif Science Ctr, Berkeley Art Mus; African Am Mus; US Info Agency. *Comn:* Artistic enhancements for the new Secretary of State/State Archives Building, Sacramento, Calif, 90; Panorama City Pub Libr, 92-93; Los Angeles Hill St Pedestrian Corridor, 94; Marvin Braude SanFernando Constiuency Ctr, Van Nuys, Calif. *Exhib:* Solo shows, Munic Art Gallery, 81, Karl Bornstein Gallery, 81-83, 85 & 87, Los Angeles City Hall, 82, Phyllis Kind Gallery, Chicago & NY, 83, AIR Gallery, NY, 86, Mt St Mary's Col, Los Angeles, 87, Calif Mus Sci & Indust, Los Angeles, 90, Atlanta Pavilion, Atlanta, GA, 90, Santa Monica Art Mus, Calif, 93, The Forum, St Louis, 94 & Fresno Art Mus, 94; ART Inc, NY, 89; Nat Mus Fine Arts, Santiago, Chile, 96; Mus Mod Art, Rio de Janeiro, Brazil, 96; CEPA Gallery, Buffalo, 98; Contemp Art Ctr, Cincinnatti, Ohio, 2000; Intersection, San Francisco, 2001; Arts Resource Tranfer, NY, 2001; Calif Sci Ctr, Los Angeles Calif, 2001, 2003; Elcamino Col, Torrance, Calif, 2003. *Pos:* Associate Prof, Calif State Univ Northridge. *Teaching:* Distinguished vis artist, Calif State Univ, Fullerton, 85-87; vis artist, Claremont Grad Sch, 86, 87, 90 & 93 & Univ Calif, Irvine, 87-89; Calif State Univ, Northridge, 98-. *Awards:* Fel, J Paul Getty Trust Fund Visual Arts, 93; Grant, Pollock-Krasner Found, 90 & US Info Agency, 96; Fel, Calif Arts Coun, 94 & Cult Affairs Dept, Los Angeles, 96; Richard Neutra Award for Professional Excellance, 2001. *Bibliog:* Patterson Sims (essayist), Kim Abeles, ART Press, 89; Andrea Liss (auth), The Insistent Voice, After Image, 3/90; Kim Abeles: Encyclopedia Persona, A 15-Year Survey, Fel Contemp Art, 93; Brandon LaBelle, Ken Ehrlich and Stephen Vitiello (editors) Problematics of Site-Surface Tension. Errant Bodies Press, 2003. *Mem:* Col Art Asn; Mus Contemp Art; Laguna Art Mus. *Media:* Miscellaneous. *Publ:* Contribr, Fiction International, San Diego State Univ, 85; The Image of St Bernadette, pvt publ, 87; High Performance, spring/summer 88; Camerawork, San Francisco Camerawork Inc, 94; Twelve Artists, Art Press, 97; Lewis MacAdams (poetry) and Kim Abeles (images), The Family Trees, Blue Press, 2001. *Mailing Add:* 940 E 2nd St No 1 Los Angeles CA 90012

ABELES, SIGMUND
PRINTMAKER, PAINTER
b New York, NY, Nov 6, 34. *Study:* Pratt Inst; Univ SC, BA, 55; Art Student League; Skowhegan Sch Painting & Sculpture; Brooklyn Mus Sch; Columbia Univ, MFA, 57; Coastal Carolina Univ, DA (hon), 2000. *Hon Degrees:* Hon DFA, Coastal Carolina Univ, Conway, SC, 99. *Work:* Mus Mod Art, NY; Mus Arte, Ponce, PR; Philadelphia Mus Art; Boston Mus Fine Arts; Brit Mus; Albert & Victoria Mus, London, Gt Brit; Smithsonian Inst, Washington, DC; Metrop Mus Art, NY; Nat Acad Design, NY; Whitney Mus Am Art. *Comn:* illustrations, Maggie Girl of the Streets, Limited Editions Club, 74. *Exhib:* One-man exhibs, Mary Ryan Gallery, NY, 83, Isis Gallery, Notre Dame Univ, South Bend, Ind, 88, Brattleboro Mus, Vt, 88, Yeshiva Univ Mus, NY, 88-89, Shaare Zedek Med Ctr, Jerusalem, Israel, 89, Univ WVa Art Galleries, Charlottesville, Starr Gallery, Leventhal-Sidman Jewish Community Ctr, Newton Ctr, 89, Barridoff Galleries, Portland, Maine, 90; With Nothing On, New Orleans Mus Art, La, 90; Am Drawing Invitational, Hastings Col, Nebr, 90; one-man retrospectives, New Eng Col, Henniker, NH, Art & Sci Ctr, Manchester, NH, McKissick Mus, Univ SC, Columbia, Cheekwood Mus, Nashville, Tenn & Fitchburg, Mass, 92-93; Abeles Drawings, Boston Pub Lib, 93; Thomas Williams Fine Arts, London, Eng, 2000; group shows incl Pinkard Gallery, Bunting Ctr, Md, Col Art, Baltimore, 2001, Randall Bryan Art Gallery, 2001; Art 2003, London; Memorials of War, Whitney Mus Am Art, Summer, 2004; Drawings by Sigmund Abeles & Philip Growsman, Union Col, Schenectady, NY, 2004. *Pos:* bd dir, Artist Fel, New York City. *Teaching:* Instr, Swain Sch Design, New Bedford, Mass, 61-64, Wellesley Col, 64-69, Boston Univ, 69-70, Univ NH, 70-; Wellesley Col, 64-69; Boston Univ, 69-70; Univ NH, 70-87; prof emer dept Am Art, Univ NH, 87-; instr, Acad Realist Art, Seattle, Wash, 95 & Art Student League, NY, 97-01. *Awards:* Grant for Graphics, Louis Comfort Tiffany Found, 67; Academic Seminar to Israel, Am Jewish Comt, 81; Summer Sr Fac Fel, Univ NH, 84; Chateau Rochfort en Terra, Britany, France, 2000; Hall of Fame Honoree, Pastel Soc Am Nat Arts Club, 2004. *Bibliog:* Philip Isaacson (auth), Fine Artists Turn Talented Hands to Applied Art (review), Maine Sunday Telegram, 3/25; Louise Dunn Yochim (auth), Michael Weinberg (ed), The Harvest Freedom, Jewish Artists in America, 1930-80's, Am References, Chicago, IL, 90; Sigmund Abeles (monogr), New Eng Col Gallery, 92. *Mem:* Soc Am Graphic Artists (Hall of Fame honoree, 2004); Assoc Nat Acad Design (Leo Meisner prize 1983, acad 1990, mem coun, corr sec 1991-); Pastel Soc Am; Artists Fel. *Media:* Etching, Lithography; Oil, Pastel. *Publ:* Illusr, Maggie, A Girl of the Streets, Limited Ed Press, 75; The Max Drawings, Tom Bolt (auth), Am Artist Mag, 11/87. *Dealer:* Portfolio Gallery Columbia SC; Thomas Williams Fine Arts London Eng; Cheryl Newby Fine Arts Pawley's Island SC; The Old Print Shop New York NY. *Mailing Add:* Box 433 57th Conconcourse Niverville NY 12130

ABELLO , JUAN
COLLECTOR
Pos: pres, AirTel (acquired by Vodafone), formerly; chmn, Grupo Torreal, SA, Madrid, Nueva Compania de Inversiones, SA, Inversiones Naira SIMCAVF, SA; Chmn bd dir, RTL Group, 2000-04; bd dir, Grupo Televisa, SA, 2000-, Banco Santander Central Hispano, 2002-, Sacyr-Vallehermoso, SA, Compania Vinmcola del Norte de Espana, SA. *Awards:* Named one of 200 Top Collectors, ArtNews Magazine, 2004. *Mailing Add:* c/o Banco Santander Central Hispano Edificio Pereda Piso 1 Ave de Cantabria Madrid 28669 Spain

ABER, ITA
ARTIST, HISTORIAN, CONSERVATOR
b Montreal, Que, Mar 27, 32; US citizen. *Study:* Empire State Col, MA; Jewish Theological Sem, NY grad courses. *Work:* Smithsonian Inst, Washington; B'Nai Brith Nat Jewish Mus, Washington; Israel Mus, Jerusalem; Brooklyn Mus; Mobile Mus Art, Ala; Ark Art Ctr, Little Rock; and others. *Comn:* Wall hangings (outdoor/indoor), holy scroll covers & ark curtains throughout US, Can & Israel, 74-; Hebrew Union Col, NY, Cincinnati, Ohio, 9/00-6/01. *Exhib:* Solo exhib, Seltzer Gallery, 88, Empire State Col, 90; traveling exhib, Yeshiva Univ Mus, NY, 93-98; CORE Exhib, Jewish Mus, NY, 93-; Israel Mus, Jerusalem, Israel, 95; B'Nai Brith Nat Jewish Mus, Washington, 95; Hudson River Mus, NY, 97; 55 yr retrospective exhib, Broome St Gallery, NY, 1/01. *Pos:* Cur hist, Hudson River Mus, Yonkers, 1969-70; cur collection, Park Ave Synagogue, NY, 83-2004; cur, Hebrew Home for Aged, Riverdale, NY, 89-93; bd mem, Judaica Mus, Riverdale, NY, 89-; Int Soc Jewish Art, 90-; comr, Yonkers Landmark Bd, 91-94; bd mem, Glenview com Hudson River Mus, 00. *Teaching:* Lecturer at many museums & institutions. *Awards:* Cert Honors, Valentine Mus, 75; Hudson River Mus Grant, N, 97; Grant, Pomegranate Guild of Indaie Needlework, 99 & 2003. *Bibliog:* Video, Yeshiva Univ Mus, 93; Outlook Mag, 93 & 97; Riverdale Press, 96 & 97. *Mem:* Int Soc Jewish Art (bd mem, 90-, treas, 92-95); Textile Study Group NY; NY Artists Equity. *Media:* Judaic Textiles, Mixed Media. *Publ:* The Art of Judaic Needlework, Charles Scribner's Sons, NY, 79; Textile Study Guide, Ind Univ, 85; Woman's Art J, 87; Jewish Art, 87; Jewish Art, Sepharad, 92; monograph, 55 Yrs, 00

ABERNETHY-BALDWIN, JUDITH ANN
PAINTER
b Cincinnati, Ohio, May 15, 42. *Study:* With Philip Pearlstein, Dan'l Greene & Robert Natkin; Cincinnati Art Acad, 70-74; Univ Cincinnati, 75-78. *Work:* Sun Bank NA & Orlando Regional Med Ctr, Orlando, Fla; Scripps-Howard Newspapers, Cincinnati, Ohio; Feldman Group Inc, West Chester, NY; Kennedy Capital Management Inc, St Louis, Mo; Keep Fla Beautiful Inc. *Exhib:* 34th Ann Knickerbocker and Grand Nat Exib, Salmagundi Club, NY, 84; 48th Ann Nat Midyear, Butler Inst Am Art, Youngstown, Ohio, 84; Invitational Exhib, High Mus, Atlanta, Ga, 88; Abernethy At-Large, Brest Mus, Jacksonville Univ, 86; 37th Ann All Fla, Boca Raton Mus, 88; Places Revisited, Brevard Art Mus, Melbourne, Fla, 88; Atlantic Ctr Arts, New Smyrna, Fla, 88; Judith Abernethy, Boca Raton Mus Art, 91; one-person exhib, Hospitality Gallery, Orlando, Fla, 93 & TK Enterprises, Longwood, Fla, 94; Scott Laurent Gallery, Winter Park, Fla, 95; 34th Ann Fine Arts Competition & Exhib, Ridge Art Asn, Winter Haven, Fla, 96; Ryals Gallery, Boca Raton, Fla, 96. *Teaching:* Seminole Community Col, 87. *Awards:* Second Prize, 83 & 88, Judges Award, 84, Ridge Art Asn. *Bibliog:* Chris Schneider (auth), Judith Abernathy, Ctr Stage Mag, 6/86; Jim Runnels (auth), Artist depicts, Lake Sentinal, 11/88; Sally Henderson (auth), Light taking possession, Zelo Mag, 2/89; Keep Fla Beautiful Mag, Cover Spring, 91. *Mem:* Nat Asn Women Artists; Int Women Artists Archive; Women's Caucus Art; Women Artists of West. *Media:* Acrylic. *Dealer:* Albertson-Peterson 329 Park Ave S Winter Park FL 32789. *Mailing Add:* PO Box 4061 Enterprise FL 32725

ABID, ANN B
LIBRARIAN
b St Louis, Mo, Mar 17, 1942. *Pos:* Asst librn, St Louis Art Mus, 63-68, librn, 68-85; head librn, Cleveland Mus Art, 85-. *Mem:* Mus, Arts, & Humanities Div, Spec Libr Asn; Art Libr Soc NAm; Soc Am Archivists; Int Fedn Libr Asns & Insts; Am Libr Asn; Col Art Asn. *Publ:* Auth, Documents of Surrealism: 1918-1942, St Louis Art Mus, 81; ed, Roy Lichtenstein, 81; Max Beckmann Retrospective, 84; auth, Loss liability: risk, responsibility, recovery, Art Doc, winter 91; coauth, Planning for automation of the slide and photograph collections at the Cleveland Mus of Art: a Draft MARC/Visual materials record, VRA Visual Resources Asn Bulletin, summer 92. *Mailing Add:* Cleveland Mus Art 11150 East Blvd Cleveland OH 44106

ABISH, CECILE
ENVIRONMENTAL ARTIST, PHOTOGRAPHER
b New York, NY. *Study:* Brooklyn Col, BFA. *Comn:* Boxed Monuments-3, Multiples, Inc, NY, 69, Field Quartering, Lakeview Ctr Arts, Peoria, Ill, 72; Renaissance Fix, Independent Curators, Inc, NY, 79; Atlanta Arts Festival, Piedmont Park, Ga, 80; Land Marks, Bard Col, NY, 84. *Exhib:* Inst Contemp Art, Boston, Mass, 74; Hudson River Mus, Yonkers, NY, 79; The New Mus, NY, 80; Kunstgebaude, Stuttgart, Ger, 81; Fine Arts Ctr, State Univ NY, Stony Brook, 82; Long Beach Mus, Calif, 83; Ctr Creative Photog, Tucson, Ariz, 84; Mus Mod Kunst, Vienna, Austria, 85; Architektur Zentrum, Vienna, Austria, 93; Artists Space, NY, 94; Islip Art Mus, NY, 95; Books & Co, NY, 96; PSI Contemp Art Ctr, NY, 99; and others. *Teaching:* Instr art, Queens Col, NY; vis artist, Univ Mass, Amherst, Cooper Union, NY & Harvard Univ, Mass. *Awards:* Creative Artists Pub Service Fel, 75; Nat Endowments Arts Fel, 77 & 80; Deutscher Akademischer Austavschdienst, Berlin, 87. *Bibliog:* Lawrence Alloway (auth), article, Arts Mag, 2/77; Jeffrey Keeffe (auth), article, Artforum, 10/78; Donald B Kuspit (auth), article, Art in Am, 1/82. *Mem:* Col Art Asn. *Media:* Varied Media. *Publ:* Firsthand, Photo/work, Wright State Univ, Dayton, Ohio, 78; Situation esthetics, Artforum, 1/80; Greek Gifts, LAICA J, winter 86; Chinese Crossing Photo/work, Conjunctions 9, 86; 99: The New Meaning, Photo/work, Burning Deck, 90. *Mailing Add:* Cooper Sta PO Box 485 New York NY 10276

ABLOW, JOSEPH
PAINTER, WRITER
b Salem, Mass, Aug 16, 28. *Study:* Sch Mus Fine Arts, Boston, Paige Traveling Fel, dipl with highest hons, 51; Bennington Col, BA, 54; Harvard Univ, MA, 55; Fulbright Grant, Paris, 58; advan study in painting with Oskar Kokoschka & in design with Gyorgy Kepes. *Work:* De Cordova Mus, Lincoln, Mass; Univ Mass, Boston; Amherst

Col; Middlebury Col, Vt; Rose Art Mus, Brandeis Univ; Wiggin Coll, Boston Pub Libr, Mass. *Exhib:* 62nd Am Exhib, Art Inst Chicago, 57; retrospectives, Bard Col, 72, Mead Art Gallery, Amherst Col, 76 & 82, Simmons Col, 83 & Fitchburg Art Mus, 87; A Selection of American Art: The Skowhegan Sch, 1946-76, Inst Contemp Art, Boston; one-man shows, Mirski Gallery, 61, 66 & 69, Princeton Gallery, 71, Pucker Gallery, 79, 81, 83, 87, 89, 91, 94 & 2001 & Miami Univ, Oxford, Ohio, 95; and others. *Pos:* Contrib ed, Bostonia Mag, 86-89. *Teaching:* Instr, Middlebury Col, 55-58; asst prof, Bard Col, 59-61 & Wellesley Col, 62-63; chmn div art, Boston Univ, 64-67, prof art, 72-97, prof emer, 97-; vis prof, Mass Inst Technol, 73-75; vis artist, Amherst Col, 75-76, 81. *Awards:* Silver Medal Award, Coun Advan & Support Educ, 87; Res Grant, Boston Univ, 82; Distinguished Fac Award, Boston Univ, 96. *Media:* Oil & Pastel. *Publ:* Auth, Two cheers for realism, 9/78 & Boston expressionism, 2-3/79, New Boston Rev; Gombrich's art and-or illusion, Boston Univ J, Vol XXXV, No 3, 78; Ordered terror: the art of Philip Guston, 9-10/94 & Stuart Davis and all that jazz, 4/97, Bostonia Mag. *Dealer:* Pucker Gallery 171 Newbury St Boston MA 02116. *Mailing Add:* 16 Monmouth Ct Brookline MA 02146

ABLOW, ROSELYN KAROL (ROZ KOYOL ABLOW)
PAINTER, INSTRUCTOR
b Allentown, Pa. *Study:* Bennington Col, BA, 54; Boston Univ Sch Arts, with Walter Murch, 59-61; studied in Europe, 59-60 & 68-69. *Work:* Mobil Corp, Chemical Bank, NY; New Eng Mutual Life Insurance Co, Boston; Conn Gen Life, Hartford; Sears, Roebuck & Co, Chicago; Wiggin Collection, Boston Pub Libr. *Comn:* Diptych mixed media on paper, Broadway Crown Plaza Hotel, NY, 89. *Exhib:* New Am Monotypes, Smithsonian Inst Traveling Exhib, 78-80; Three Grant Recipients, The Bunting Inst, Radcliffe Col, 88; David Brown Gallery, Provincetown, Mass, 88; Contemp Monotypes, Gallery 30, Burlingame, Calif, 93; fac exhib, New Art Ctr, Newton, Mass, 94; New Artists, New Works, Pucker Gallery, 2004; solo exhib, Works on Paper, Lee Gallery, Miami Univ, Oxford, Ohio, 95, Image and Abstraction, Rosenau Gallery Arts Ctr, Old Forge, NY, 02. *Collection Arranged:* Four Sculptors: Public Commisions-Private Works, 85, Watercolor in the 1980s, 86, & Volume and Plane, Wall Sculpture, 91, Newton Arts Ctr; Legacy: Nine Artists Who Studied with Philip Guston, New Art Ctr, Newton, Mass, 94; Paper & Color, Vineyard Studio, 96; Unique Print, Star Gallery, Newton, Mass, 97. *Teaching:* Monotype workshops, Bunting Inst, 88, Newton Arts Ctr, 89-92, New Arts Ctr, 93-95 & 96-97. *Awards:* Fel, Bunting Inst, Radcliffe Col, 88; Mass Arts Lottery Coun Grant, 90-91. *Bibliog:* Robert Taylor (auth), article, Boston Sunday Globe, 6/10/79; Kenneth Baker (auth), Lasting impressions, Boston Phoenix, 2/9/81; Christine Temin (auth), The Work of the Superiors, Boston Globe, 4/24/91. *Media:* Mixed Water Media, Collage on Paper. *Dealer:* Pucker Gallery Boston. *Mailing Add:* 16 Monmouth Ct Brookline MA 02146

ABRAHAM, CAROL JEANNE
ASSEMBLAGE ARTIST, CERAMIST
b Philadelphia, Pa, 49. *Study:* Tyler Sch Art, Philadelphia, 64-67; Boston Mus Sch Fine Arts, 67-71; Tufts Univ, Medford, Mass, BS, 67-71; Rochester Inst Technol, Sch Am Craftsmen, MFA, 73; Penland Sch Crafts, NC, 75, Brooks Inst Photog, dipl, 88. *Work:* Rochester Inst Technol, NY; Mus Ceramics, Bassano Del Grappa, Italy; Renwick Gallery, Smithsonian Inst, Washington, DC; Brigham Young Univ, Provo, Utah; Int Acad Ceramics, Canada; Brooks Inst Photog. *Comn:* Mural, sculpture, Romerbad Hotel, Ger, 84. *Exhib:* Renwick Gallery, Smithsonian Inst, Washington, DC, 75; Tweed Mus Art, Duluth, Minn, 81; Celebration 81, Spokane, Wash; Interfaith Forum Relig, Art & Archit, 81; State Univ Mus Art, University Park, Pa, 81; Fletcher Brownbuilt Pottery Exhib, Auckland, NZ, 81; and many others. *Pos:* Cur, Western States Mus Photog, Santa Barbara, Calif, 85-89. *Teaching:* Silk screening, Boston Pub Sch System (Pilot Sch), 70; instr ceramics, Rochester Inst Technology, NY, 72-73; asst prof ceramics & sculpture, Southern Utah State Col, Cedar City, 75-77; ceramics, El Camino Col, Torrance, Calif, 80-81; ceramics, Ventura Community Col, 82-84; design, Brooks Inst Photog, 89-. *Awards:* Third Prize, Ceramics International 1973, Canada; Grant, Burbank Fine Arts Fedn, 81; Purchase Award, Second Crossing Gallery, 81. *Bibliog:* Hildegard Storr-Britz (auth), Contemp Int Ceramics, 80; Jan Axel & Karen McCready (coauths), Porcelain: Traditions and New Visions, 81; Glen C Nelson (auth), Ceramics, A Potters Handbook, 4th & 5th eds, 78-84. *Media:* Photography, Fiber; Porcelain, Thixotropic Porcelain. *Publ:* Auth, The Mirror Book, Jay & Lee Newman, 78; Crafts Horizons, 8/73, 12/73, 2/76; Ceramics Monthly, 9/73, 5/75, 5/76, 10/76; Decorazione - Ceramica, Nino Caruso, Italy, 88; Egypt: Land of Adventures, 89. *Mailing Add:* 286 Briar Rd Bellingham WA 98225-7712

ABRAM, RUTH J
WRITER
b Calif, Sept 19, 45. *Study:* Sarah Lawrence Col, BA, 67; Florence Hellar Sch, Brandeis Univ, MSW, 70; NY Univ, MA, 83. *Hon Degrees:* Russell Sage Col, Hon D Pub Serv, 99. *Work:* Lower E Side Tenement Mus. *Exhib:* Send Us A Lady Physician: Women Doctors in Am, 1835-1920, Med Col Pa, 85. *Pos:* Prog dir, Am Civil Liberties Union Found, 72-74; exec dir, Women's Action Alliance, 74-79; founder & dir, Lower East Historic Conservancy; founder, Lower East Side Tenement Mus; pres, Paraphrase, Inc. *Awards:* Alvin Brown Fel, Aspen Inst Humanistic Studies; Kenan Fel, NY Univ, 81-82; Camille Mermod Award, Am Med Women's Asn, 87. *Mem:* Am Asn Hist Med; Am Asn State & Local Hist; Am Mus Asn; Organization Am Hist; Independent Sector; Archives Med Col Pa; MAZON; Nat Conf Soviet Jewry; New Israel Fund; Telecommun Coop Network. *Publ:* Auth, Send Us a Lady Physician: Women Doctors in America; Women's Section, Information Please Almanac, 78-79; Poetry in Midwest Poetry Review, Poetry Mag, 81; In Recognition of Sara A Cohen, MD, Women in Health, 82; To Do Something and To Be Something, Philadelphia Co Med Soc J, 85. *Mailing Add:* 110 Riverside Dr No 11B New York NY 10024

ABRAMOVIC, MARINA
ARTIST
b Belgrade, Yugoslavia, 46. *Study:* Art Inst Chicago, PhD(hon), 2004. *Work:* Brooklyn Mus, European Performance Series, NY, 1978, Mus Contemp Art, Chicago, 1982, Artist Body-Pub Body, Mus Contemp Art, Valencia, Spain, 1998, The House with the Ocean View, 2003 (NY Dance & Performance Award, 2003), Directions, Hirschhorn Mus & Sculpture Garden, 2001, Moving Pictures, Soloman R Guggenheim Mus, NY, 2002, exhib in group shows at Whitney Biennial Exhib, Whitney Mus Am Art, 2004. *Exhib:* One-woman shows incl Art must be Beautiful Artist must be Beautiful, Art Festival, Copenhagen, Denmark, 1975, Breathing out/Breathing in (with Ulay), Studenski Kulturni Ctr, Belgrade, 1977, Charged Space (with Ulay), Rest Energy (with Ulay), ROSC 80, Dublin, 1990, Nightsea Crossing (with Ulay), Die Mond der Sonne (with Ulay), The House, Santa Monica, 1987, The Lovers: The Great Wall Walk (with Ulay), The Great Wall China, 1988, Dragon Heads, Kunstmuseum, Bonn, Ger, Sean Kelly Gallery, NY, 1995, The Biography, Schouwburg, Groningen, 1996, Balkan Baroque, Biennale di Venezia, Venice, Italy, 1997, Luminosity, Sean Kelly Gallery, NY, 1997. *Pos:* artist in residence, Atelier Calder, Saché, 2001. *Teaching:* Instr, Acad Fine Arts, Novi Sad, 73—75; vis prof, Académie des Beaux-Arts, Paris, 83; prof, Braunschweig, 97; artist in residence, Atelier Calder, Saché, 2001. *Awards:* Recipient Niedersächsicher Kunstpreis, 2003. *Mailing Add:* c/o Solomon R Guggenheim Mus 1071 5th Ave New York NY 10128

ABRAMOWICZ, JANET
PAINTER, PRINTMAKER
b New York, NY. *Study:* Art Students League, Columbia Univ, Acad delle Belle Arti, Bologna, Italy, BFA & MFA, with Giorgio Morandi. *Work:* Mus Mod Art, Kyoto; Dept of Prints, NY Pub Libr & Metrop Mus Art, NY; Ohara Mus, Kurashiki; Contemp Art, Mus d'Arte Mod, Bologna; Mus d'Arte Mod, La Spezia, Italy; Yale Univ Art Gallery. *Exhib:* Works on Paper, Harvard Sch Design, 74; Abstract Art (sculpture), Boston City Hall, 75; solo exhib, Susan Caldwell Gallery, NY, 80, Nantenshi Gallery, Tokyo, 81 & Galleria del Milione, Milano, Italy, 81; Prints Recently Acquired, RI Sch Design & Metrop Mus Art, NY, 85; 24th Nat Print Exhib, Brooklyn Mus, 86; British 11th Int Print Biennale (invitational), 90-91; Synthetic Century, Yale Univ Art Gallery, (Int catalog), 2002. *Collection Arranged:* Giorgio Morandi (with catalog), Busch-Reisinger Mus, Harvard Univ, 68; L'Opera Grafica di Qiorgio Morande, Rome, 90. *Pos:* Critic, Asahi Evening News, Tokyo & Print Collector's Newsletter; vis artist, Am Acad Rome, 84-85. *Teaching:* Instr, Radcliffe Col, Worcester Art Mus, Acad delle Belle Arti & Univ Ill; lectr art hist, Div Educ, Boston Mus Fine Arts, 58-70; sr lectr painting, printmaking & drawing, Fine Arts Dept, Fogg Art Mus, Harvard Univ, 71-91. *Awards:* Rockefeller Found, Bellagio, 89; Am Coun Learned Soc Fel, 90-91; Guggenheim Fel, 92; Fulbright Fel, 79 & 89; McDowell Colony Fel, 75 & 76. *Mem:* Am Acad Rome; hon mem Accademia Clementina, Bologna, Italy; vis fel, Am Acad, Rome, Italy. *Publ:* Auth, Vision and Technique, The Etchings of Giorgio Morandi, 9/10/82 & A European Sensibility: The Photographs of Andre Kertesz, 9/10/83, Print Collector's Newsletter; Milan: The Liberation of the Object, Art Am, 83; auth, Technique of the Graphic Works of Giorgio Morandi; In memoriam: Kasuo Shimizu, Ahsahi Evening News, Tokyo; La tecnia dell 'arte incisonia di Giorgio Morandi, exhib catalog, Rome, 90; Yale Univ Press, Giorgio-Morandi, The Art of Silence. *Dealer:* Tokyo Nanten Shi Gallery Kyo-Bashi Tokyo. *Mailing Add:* 30 W 15th St New York NY 10011-6816

ABRAMS, EDITH LILLIAN
INSTRUCTOR, SCULPTOR
b New York, NY. *Study:* Brooklyn Col, BA, 74; Pratt Inst, MFA, 78. *Work:* Evansville Mus Arts & Science, Ind; Brookdale Hosp, NY. *Comn:* Many pvt portrait sculpture comn. *Exhib:* Int Sculpture Fair, Sheraton Hotel, NY, 79; 4th & 6th Ann Exhib Painting & Sculpture; Brooklyn Mus, 79-81; Catharine Lorillard Wolfe Art Club, Nat Arts Club, NY, 79-88; Audubon Artists 38th Ann Exhib, NY, 80; ArtExpo, NY Coliseum, NY, 80; Providence Art Club Centennial Exhib Sculpture, RI, 80; Brooklyn Mem Am Soc Contemp Artists, 15th Ann Exhib, 84, Brooklyn Mus; Nat Acad Design, 86-88. *Teaching:* Instr sculpture & ceramics, Sephardic Community Ctr, New York, 82-85. *Awards:* Purchase Award, 1st Prize, Schulman Rehabilitation Inst, Brookdale Hosp, NY, 76; Margaret Hirsch Levine Mem Prize, Audubon Artists 38th Ann, 80; Ann Hyatt Huntington Bronze Medal, Catharine Lorillard Wolfe Art Club 84th Ann, 80 & 89th Ann, Helen McCahill Slottman Mem Award, 85; Charles D Murphy Award, Nat Asn Women Artists, 82. *Mem:* Metrop Painters & Sculptors; New York Artists Equity Asn; Am Soc Contemp Artists (pres, 83-85); Nat Asn Women Artists; Catharine Lorillard Wolf Art Club. *Media:* All. *Mailing Add:* 2820 Ave J Brooklyn NY 11210

ABRAMS, JANE ELDORA
PAINTER
b Eau Claire, Wis, Jan 2, 40. *Study:* Univ Wis-Stout, Menomonie, BS, 62, MS, 67; Ind Univ, Bloomington, with Pozzath & Lowe, MFA(with distinction), 71. *Work:* Ind Univ Mus Fine Arts; Univ Dallas, Tex; Tex Tech Univ; Tamarind Inst; Mus NMex; and others. *Exhib:* Works on Paper traveling exhib, Univ Utah, Salt Lake City, Univ Tex, Houston & Los Angeles Co Mus of Art, Calif, 77; Works on Paper: Southwest 1978, Dallas Mus Fine Arts, 78; Art Inst Chicago, 81; New Mexico Impressions, Mus Fine Arts, Santa Fe; Modes of Expression, State Univ Mus, Potsdam; Common Ground-New Acquisitions, Albuquerque Mus; Retrospective, Fine Arts Gallery, Ind Unv; and many others. *Teaching:* Instr art, Univ Wis-Stout, Menomonie, 67-69; from asst prof to regents prof art, painting, drawing & grad studies, Univ NMex, 71-; guest artist, Ind Univ, Bloomington, 76 & Univ Tex, Austin, 83; and others. *Awards:* Artist-in-Res Grant, Roswell Mus, 85-86; Distinguished Alumni Award, Ind Univ, Bloomington, 91 & Univ Wisc, 92; and others. *Mem:* Col Art Asn Am; Women's

Caucus Art; Los Angeles Print Soc; Soc Am Graphic Artists. *Media:* All Media. *Publ:* Contribr, Colorprints, USA (slide series), 71-72; Two Decades of Change (exhib catalog), Ind Univ, 91; contribr, Clinton Adams, Printmaking in New Mexico. *Mailing Add:* 7811 Guadalupe Tr NW Albuquerque NM 87107

ABRAMS, JOYCE DIANA
PAINTER, SCULPTOR
b New York, NY, Dec 8, 45. *Study:* Cooper Union, New York, BFA, 66; Columbia Univ, MFA, 72. *Work:* Gannett Ctr Media Studies, New York Pub Libr & Franklin Furnace Archives Mus Mod Art, NY; Atlantic Richfield Co, Anchorage, Alaska; Burlington Northern, Inc, Seattle, Wash; Anaconda Co, Denver, Colo; Alberta Gas Trunk Line, Ltd, Calgary, Alta, Can; Citrus Ctr, Orlando, Fla; UCLA, Los Angeles, Calif. *Exhib:* Newscapes Land & City-States of Mind, One Penn Plaza, NY, 84; Painted Constructions-Constructed Paintings, Rockland Ctr Arts, Nyack, NY, 85; Mid Am Biennial, Owensboro Mus Fine Art, Ky, 88; one-person show, Edward Williams Gallery, Fairleigh Dickinson Univ, Hackensack, NJ, 88; Works on Paper, Knoxville Mus Fine Art, Tenn, 89; Spirit of the Object, Humphrey Fine Art, NY, 92; Women of the Book, 98-05. *Pos:* Art consult, Neville Lewis & Assoc, New York, NY, 80-82 & Tokyo Cent Mus, 83, 89-; cur, Orgn Int Artists, New York, 82 & Rockland Ctr Arts, West Nyack, New York, 91. *Teaching:* Instr painting, City Univ New York, 78-81; Univ South Maine, 87; Parsons Sch Design, 89-92. *Awards:* MacDowell Colony Fel, 85 & 87; Fel, Corp Yaddo, 88; Creative Artist Fel, The Japan Found, 99-2000. *Bibliog:* Diana Morris (auth), Summer group show, Arts Mag, 10/83; Steve Bush (auth), See here, now-back to the present, Artspeak, 2/16/86. *Mem:* New York Artists Equity Asn. *Media:* Paint; Wood. *Res:* Now and Then Japan; Fifty Years of Tradition and Change; Comparison Between Japan in the 1950's; Japan at the Turn of the 21st Century, a Visual Essay. *Publ:* Auth, A personal view of the MacDowell experience, Artist's Proof, 4/88; Discarded, Rockland Ctr Arts; Born in a Fire, 94. *Mailing Add:* 100 W 94th St New York NY 10025

ABRAMS, VIVIEN (JOY)
PAINTER
b Cleveland, Ohio, July 26, 46. *Study:* Carnegie-Mellon Univ, BFA, 68; Inst Allende, San Miguel Allende, Mex, MFA, 71. *Work:* Cleveland Mus Art; Aldrich Mus Contemp Art; Columbus Mus Arts & Sci, Ga; Currier Gallery Art, NH; Nat City Bank Cleveland. *Comn:* Memory Structures (constructed painting), AT&T Longlines. *Exhib:* Solo exhibs, Akron Art Inst, Ohio, 76, New Gallery Contemp Art, Cleveland, Ohio, 77 & 80, Luise Ross Gallery, NY, 84, Manhattanville Col, Purchase, NY, 86 & Coup de Grace Gallery, NY, 92; Butler Inst Am Art, 76 & 77; Cleveland Mus Art, 76, 77, 79, 81 & 84; Drawing as Process, Akron Art Inst traveling show, 77; NY Now, Phoenix Mus Art, 79; two-artist show, Soho Ctr Visual Artists, NY, 79; Little Rock Art Mus, Ark, 82; Sculpture Ctr, NY, 83; Aldrich Mus Contemp Art, Ridgefield, Conn, 84 & 86; Cleveland Ctr Contemp Art, 87; Geometric Abstraction: A Cleveland Tradition, Cleveland Inst Art, 88; Squibb Gallery, Princeton, NJ, 88; OIA Salon, NY, 91. *Teaching:* Vis artist, State Univ NY, Purchase, 83; instr design, Manhattanville Col, Purchase, NY, 85-86. *Awards:* MacDowell Colony Fels, 79, 81 & 85; Yaddo Fels, 79 & 82; First Prize Painting, 62nd May Show, Cleveland Mus Art, 81; Athena Found Grant, 84. *Bibliog:* Helen Cullinan (auth), Art: A matter of math and logic, Sunday Plain Dealer Mag, 9/25/77; Stephen Westfall (auth), Arts reviews, Arts Mag, 10/82 & 11/84. *Dealer:* Luise Ross 50 W 57th St New York NY 10019. *Mailing Add:* 133 Delaware Ave Freeport NY 11520

ABRAMSON, ELAINE SANDRA
CARTOONIST, DESIGNER
b Cleveland, Ohio, Aug 27, 42. *Study:* NY Univ, Cert, 90; Kent State Univ, Ohio, BS(art); Cleveland Inst Art, Ohio; Hayim Greenberg Inst, Scholar, Jerusalem, Israel. *Work:* State Capitol, Austin, Tex; Cleveland Mus Art, Ohio; Maryland Pub Television, Baltimore; Kent State, traveling exhibs, Ohio; Times Newspapers, Baltimore, Md. *Comn:* Rapco Inc, Chicago, Ill; Ann Richards Gov Campaign, Austin & Ft Worth, Tex; Paragon Neddle Craft, NY; General Crafts Corp, Baltimore; plus many others. *Exhib:* Invitational Maryland Artists, Baltimore Harbor, 71-75; PCM Hall of Fame, PCM Exhibit, Dallas, Tex, 85; Texas State Artist, 88-90 & Tex Woman's Hall of Fame, 89, State Capitol, Austin; Composers, Authors & Artists of Am, NY & FTW, 91-92; Artists Christmas, 91-92; Solo shows, Palace Art Gallery, Baltimore, Levendale Art Gallery Graphic Arts Show, Baltimore, Portfolio Gallery, Mt Wash, Md, Loyola Fed Savings & Loan, Baltimore, Calvert Savings & Loan Asn, Reisterstown, Md, Design House, Stevenson, Md & Kent State Univ Gallery, Ohio, New Eng Fine Arts Inst, Boston, Mass, Lincoln Center Art Gallery, NY, Butler Inst Art, Youngstown, Ohio; plus many other group exhibs. *Pos:* Owner, Toy & Craft Design, 67-; syndicated columnist, Appraisals by Abramson, currently; Brd of Dir, Nat League of Am Pen Women; Natl Brd of Dir, Graphic Artists Guild; Founding Artist, Sassy Cat Art Gallery. *Teaching:* Art, Cleveland Pub Sch, 65-67. *Awards:* All-expense scholarship, Govt Israel/Hayim Greenberg Inst, Jerusalem, Israel, 60-61; First American Art/Craft Instr to train Israeli publ schl teachers, Israel, 64; Tex Women's Hall of Fame, 91-94; Nobel Prize and Guinness Book of Records Nominee, 91-93; First Woman State Artist, Tex, 93-94; Int Women of Yr in Art, Eng, 93, 95, 96 & 98; Am Express aaart.com licensing, NY, 2000-2002; Outstanding Artist and Designer of 20th Cent, Int Biog Ctr; First Woman/First Cartoonist, State of Texas, 93-94; Editors Choice Award, Int Libr Photography; Nomination, Nat Assembly Local Arts Agencies (bd Dir 1994); Hon Mention, Nat Park Acad of Fine Arts; Outstanding WOman of the 21st Century, Am Biog Inst; Int Commendation of Success, Am Biog Inst. *Bibliog:* B J Hennersdorph, article, Tex Woman, fall 89; Campaigning characters, Greetings Mag, winter/spring 90. *Mem:* Metrop Mus Art; Soc Craft Designers; Nat Enamelists Guild; Am Crafts Coun; Nat League Am Pen Women (pres, 95-); Graphic Artists Guild; Cartoonists Guild; Cleveland Int of Art Alumni Assoc. *Media:* Pen and Ink, Mixed Media Painting. *Interests:* Writing and illustr children's picture books, creating children's plush toys, painting and rug making. *Publ:* Auth, Animation, First Tex Co Camp Fire; SW Art Review, Tarrant Bus, Tex Source Bk; contribr, Baltimore Sun

ABT, JEFFREYY
PAINTER, WRITER
b Kansas City, Mo, Feb 27, 49. *Study:* Drake Univ, Des Moines, BFA, 71; MFA, 77; Jewish Inst of Religion, Hebrew Union Col, Jerusalem, Fel, 71-72. *Work:* Des Moines Art Ctr, Iowa; Minn Mus Art, St Paul; Nelson-Atkins, Mus Art, Kansas City, Mo; Washington & Jefferson Col, Pa; Wichita Art Mus, Kans; Dow Automotive, Mich; Polk Technologies, Mich; Federal Reserve Bank, Detroit. *Comn:* Bas relief, Iowa Jewish Guild, Des Moines, 74; sculpture, Waldinger Found, Des Moines, 75; Detroit Contemporary, 2002. *Exhib:* Dobrick Gallery, Ltd, Chicago, 82; Art/Work, Art Inst Chicago Gallery, 87; Egg Tempera, Contemp Art Workshop, Chicago, 88; Exquisite Visions, Meadowbrook Gallery, Oakland Univ, Rochester, Mich, 92; Jeffrey Abt: Paintings and Drawings, The Cliff Dwellers, Chicago, 97 & Cary Gallery, Rochester, Mich, 98; Washington Arts Coun Gallery, Worthington, Ohio, 2000; Jeffrey Abt, Recent Work, Wayne State Univ, Detroit, MI, 2003. *Pos:* Exhibs coordr, Dept Spec Collections, Univ Chicago Libr, 80-86; asst dir, Smart Mus Art, Univ Chicago, 86-87, acting dir, 87-89. *Teaching:* Assoc prof drawing, painting, criticism, Dept Art & Art Hist, Wayne State Univ, Detroit, 89-. *Awards:* Var grants, Nat Endowment Humanities, Nat Endowment Arts & Inst Mus Servs; Polk Tech Purchase Award; Pub award Hist Soc of Mich; Bd Governors Fac Achievement Award, Wayne State Univ. *Bibliog:* Andy Argy (auth), Art/Work, New Art Examiner, 87; Frank Provenzano (auth), Abt depicts an orderly world, Birmingham Observer & Eccentric, 98; Keri Guten Cohen (auth), Exhib Celebrates Prolific Prof, Detroit Free Press, 88; Jeanne C Fryer-Kohles (auth), Dislocations: Recent Work by Jeffrey Abt, Dialogue: Voicing the Arts, 2000. *Mem:* Col Art Asn; Ragdale Found, Artists Colony (trustee, 85-); Detroit Artists Market (bd dir, 94-); Am Asn Mus, 86-; Wayne State Univ Press (ed bd, 90- & chmn, 96-2001); Asn Mus Hist, (cofounder), 2003-. *Media:* Oil, Drawing. *Res:* The history of museums and exhibitions; artists and museums. *Publ:* Auth, The Printers Craft, 82 & The Book Made Art, 86, Univ Chicago Libr; contribr, Guide to the Collections, Smart Mus Art, 90; Dictionary of Art, MacMillan, 95; article, Art Hist, 96; auth, A Museum on the Verge: a Socioeconomic History of the Detroit Institute of Arts, 1882-2000, Wayne State Univ Press, 2001; article, Blackwells Companion to Museum Studies, 2006. *Mailing Add:* 26881 York Rd Huntington Woods MI 48070

ABULARACH, RODOLFO MARCO
PAINTER, PRINTMAKER
b Guatemala City, Guatemala, Jan 7, 33. *Study:* Nat Sch Plastic Arts, Guatemala City; Art Students League; Pratt Graphic Art Ctr, NY. *Work:* Mus Mod Art, New York Pub Libr & Metrop Mus Art, NY; World Print Council, San Francisco; Philadelphia Mus Art, Pa; and others. *Comn:* Print-engraving-etching, Hommage Aux Prix Nobel, Malmo, Sweden, 77; print edition, etching & engraving, World Print Coun, San Francisco, 80. *Exhib:* Mus Mod Art, NY, 60, 63, 64, 69 & 70; 100 Contemp Graphics, Pratt Graphic Art Ctr at Jewish Mus, NY, 64; 17th Nat Exhib Graphics, Brooklyn Mus, NY, 70; 12 Latin-Am Artists, Ringling Mus, Fla, 71; Biennial PanAm Graphic Arts, Mus Mod Art, La Tertulia, Columbia, 73; Biennial, Firence, Italy, 74; Biennal Prints, Mus Mod Art, Tokyo, Japan, 79; and others. *Teaching:* Instr graphic workshop, Univ Costa Rica, 76; taller nove arte, Bogota, Columbia, 82 & 83. *Awards:* First Prize in Drawing, Panamerican Exhib Graphic Arts, Columbia, 70; Special Ed Prize & Award of Merit, World Print Council, San Francisco, 80; Silver Medal, Buenos Aires, Arg, 87. *Bibliog:* Stuart Preston (auth), 20th century sense & sensibility, New York Times, 5/7/61; John Canaday (auth), New talent in printmaking, New York Times, 5/27/67; Elisabeth Perez Luna (auth), The eyes of Abularach, Hombre Mag, 7/79. *Media:* Oil; Pen & Ink. *Publ:* Tamarind: Homage to Lithography, Mus Mod Art, New York, 69; Biblioteca Luis Angel, Mus Plastic Arts, Bogota, Columbia, 79; The Council House, The Art Collection by Lee Nordness, Perimeter Press Inc, 80; Modern Masters, Galerie Borjeson, Malmo, Sweden, 80; Artists of Am, Rafeal Squirru, Art Editions, Gaglione, 84; Mus Mod Art Latin Am, selections from the permanent collection, Orgn Am States, Washington, DC, 85; Mus Mod Art, La Tertulia, Carvajal, Colombia, 86; The Latin Am Spirit, 1920-1970, Bronx Mus, N Abrams Inc, 88. *Mailing Add:* c/o Anita Shaplsky Gallery 152 E 65 St New York NY 10021

ACCETTA, SUZANNE RUSCONI
PAINTER, INSTRUCTOR
b Cincinnati, Ohio, June 26, 53. *Study:* Univ Cincinnati, BFA, 75, and with Everet Raymond Kinstler, 87, 88 & 89; Otterbein Col, 94-96. *Work:* Vanderbilt Univ Hosp & Northern Telcom Inc, Nashville, Tenn; Cincinnati Bell Tel, Scioto Mem Hosp, Ohio; Franklin Park Conserv, Columbus, Ohio. *Comn:* Portrait of Reggie Williams, NFL Man of the Year, Van Levnans Co, Cincinnati, Ohio; painting, Franklin Park Conserv, Columbus, Ohio,. *Exhib:* Midwest Watercolor Soc, Madison, Wis, 89; Elyria Ohio Art Ctr, 90; Middletown Ohio Art Ctr, 91; Allied Artists Am, NY, 90; Rocky Mountain Nat, Denver, Colo, 89; and others. *Pos:* Chmn bd, Okla Artist Guild, Oklahoma City, Okla, 83-84; dir, Ohio Realist Group, Columbus, Ohio, 87-90; show dir, Ohio Realist Group, 87-; pres, Bexley Art Guild, 90-91; vpres, bd dir, Columbus Children's Theatre. *Teaching:* Instr drawing, Cheekwood Fine Art Ctr, Nashville, Tenn, 81-82, Okla Art Guild, Okla City, 83-85, North Light Art Sch, Cincinnati, Ohio, 86-87, Immaculate Conception Sch, Columbus, Ohio, 86-89, Gahanna Art League, 99; Delaware Art Ctr, Oh, 89-91, Westerville Art League, 89-92 & Dublin Art League, 91; guest artist, Marietta Col, 89-91; Instr drawing & painting, Otterbein Col, 2003-. *Awards:* Jurors Merit Award, Tenn All State Exhib, 81; Best of Show, Oklahoma City Artist Guild, 84; Best of Show, 86-88 & Awards, 89-94, Central Ohio Watercolor Soc. *Bibliog:* Calvin J Goodman (auth), Supplementing Gallery Sales, Am Artist, 6/89; Suzanne Rusconi Accetta (auth), Putting emotion into your art, Am Artist, 91; Bernard Poulin (auth), The Complete Colored Pencil Book, 92. *Mem:* Bexley Area Artist Guild (vpres); Ohio Realist Group (dir, 87-); Cent Ohio Watercolor Soc (chmn com, 96-97); Ohio Watercolor Soc Signature (chmn com, 97-2001); The Artists Fel; Am Watercolor

Soc; Allied Artists Am. *Media:* Watercolor, Colored Pencil. *Publ:* Auth, Capturing emotion, Gallery J Ohio Realist Group, 87. *Dealer:* Madison Rd Gallery 1991 Madison Rd Cincinnati OH 45208; Columbia Portraits 291 S Columbia Ave Columbus OH 43209. *Mailing Add:* 4787 Rustic Bridge Dr Columbus OH 43214

ACCONCI, VITO
SCULPTOR
b New York, NY, Jan 24, 40. *Study:* Holy Cross Col, AB; Univ Iowa, MFA. *Work:* Mus Mod Art, Paris; Mus Mod Art, Whitney Mus Am Art, NY; Los Angeles Co Mus; Williams Col Mus Art, Williamstown, Mass. *Comn:* Coca Cola Co, Atlanta; Lloma Station, Scottsdale, Ariz.; Indoor Park for Departures Terminal, Philadelphia Airport; Billboards for Breda (Neherlands) Garbage Dump; Store Windows for Saks Fifth Ave, New York City; Shibuya Subway Station Entrance, Tokyo. *Exhib:* Sonnabend Gallery, NY, 72, 73, 76, 77, 79 & 80; Eight Contemp Artists, Mus Mod Art, NY, 74; Venice Biennale, 76, 78 & 80; Whitney Biennial, 77, 81 & 91; Stedelijk Mus, Amsterdam, 78; Kunstmuseum Luzern, 78; Mus Contemp Art, Chicago, 80; Kunstverein Koln, 81; Brooklyn Mus, 85; Vienna Festival, 86; LaJolla Mus, Calif, 87; Committed to Print, Mus Mod Art, NY, 88; 15th Ann Exhib, Rhona Hoffman Gallery, Chicago, Ill, 92; solo exhibs, L'Usine, Le consortium, Dijon, France, 94, La Criee Centre d'Art Contemporain, Rennes, France, 95, Dia Ctr Arts, Brooklyn Acad Music, NY, 95, Monika Spruth Gallery, Koln, Ger, 96, Centro Gellego de Art Contemporanea, Santiago de Campostela, Spain, 96, Stroom, The Hague, The Neth, 97 & Barbara Gladstone Gallery, NY, 98 Univ of Arts, Philadelphia, 99, Inst Francais d'Architecture, Paris, 2000, Arnolfini Gallery, Bristol, Eng, Acts of Archit, Milwaukee Art Mus, Wis and Aspen Art Mus, Colo, 2002; group exhibs, Passenger: the Viewer as Participant, Astrup Fearnley Mus of Mod Art, 2002, En Route, Serpentine Gallery, London, Eng, 2002. *Teaching:* Instr art, Sch Visual Arts, NY, 68-71, Nova Scotia Col Art, 71 & 78, Calif Inst Art, 76, Cooper Union, NY, 82 & 86, Chicago Art Inst, 83, Minn Col Art, 84, Univ NC Sch Art, 85, Tyler Sch Arts, Philadelphia, 90, Yale Univ, 91-94 & Bard Col, NY, 94. *Awards:* Nat Endowment Arts Fel, 76, 80 & 83; Guggenheim Fel, 79; ID Mag Award Excellence Design, 98; Sculpture Ctr Award for Lifetime Achievement, 1997; Excellence in Design award, ID Mag, 1998; Spe Citation NY Chap AIAA, 99; Recipient Archit Fel NY Found for Arts, 2000; Nancy Graves grant for Visual Artists, 2001. *Bibliog:* R Pincus-Witten (auth), Vito Acconci & the conceptual performance, Artforum, 4/72; Alan Sondheim (auth), Vito Acconci: Work 1973-74, Arts, 3/75; Mario Diacono (auth), Vito Acconci: Dal Testo-Azione Al Corpo Come Testo, Out-of-London Press, 76; G Celant (auth), Dirty Acconci, Artforum, 11/80; S Platt (auth), Vito Acconci: The sheltering city, Artweek, 9/83; P Phillips (auth), Vito Acconci at Nature Morte, Artforum, 2/85. *Media:* All. *Publ:* Contribr, Conceptual Art, Dutton, 72; Vito Acconci Issue, Avalanche Mag, 72; auth, Pulse: From my mother, Multiplicata, 72; Ten-Point Plan for Video, Video Art, Harcourt-Brace, 76; Think-Leap-Rethink-Fall, Wright State Univ Press, 77; Television, Furniture and Sculpture: The Room with an American View, Stedelijk Mus, Amsterdam, 84; Notes on Vienna, Wienfluss, Austria, 86. *Dealer:* Barbara Gladstone Gallery 515 W 24th New York NY 10011. *Mailing Add:* 20 J St Ste 215 Brooklyn NY 11201

ACEBO, DAVIS TERRY
PRINTMAKER
b Oakland, Calif. *Study:* Calif State Univ, Hayward, BS (nursing), 76; Univ Calif, San Francisco, D (pediatric oncology), 83; San Jose State Univ, BFA (printmaking), 91, MFA (printmaking), 93. *Exhib:* Nat Acad Mus, NY City, 2006. *Pos:* Pediatric transport nurse Lucile Packard Children's Hosp, Stanford, Calif, 76-; principal artist DIWA artists' collective. *Awards:* James D Phelan Award in Printmaking, 97; Radius Award, Palo Alto, Calif, 97. *Mem:* LA Printmaking Soc; Asian Americans Artists Asn. *Mailing Add:* c/o Togonon Gallery Second Floor 77 Geary St San Francisco CA 94108

ACHEPOHL, KEITH ANDEN
PRINTMAKER, PAINTER
b Chicago, Ill, Apr 11, 1934. *Study:* Knox Col, BA, DFA, 96; Univ Iowa, MFA; Pac Lutheran Univ, DFA, 89. *Work:* Nat Gallery Art & Pennell Collection, Libr Cong, Washington; Los Angeles Co Mus, Calif; Art Inst Chicago; Bibliot Nac, Madrid, Spain; and many others; Whitney Mus Am Art; Smithsonian Am Art Mus; Seattle Art Mus. *Comn:* Garden of Stone & Light, paintings, Atrium Durham Ctr, Iowa State Univ, 89. *Exhib:* Nat Print Exhib, Libr Cong, 60, 61, 63 & 69; Brooklyn Mus, 68-74; Utah Mus Fine Arts, 80; Art Inst Chicago, 81; Honolulu Acad Art Exhib, Japan, 90; Egyptian Nat Mus, 90; Gonzaga Univ, 96; Western Ill Univ, 97; Washburn Univ, 97; Davenport Art Mus, 97; Percival Gallery, Des Moines, 97; Printworks Chicago, 03. *Pos:* Dir, Univ Iowa Summer in Venice Prog, 96-. *Teaching:* Instr printmaking, Univ Iowa, 64-67; asst prof, Hope Col, 67-69; vis artist printmaking, Univ Wash, summer 69, Scuola Int di Grafica, Venezia, summer, 92, 93 & 95; vis artist printmaking, Univ Iowa, 72-73, assoc prof, 73-78, prof, 78-. *Awards:* Tiffany Found Award, 66; Fulbright Sr Lectureship Award, Cairo, Egypt, 79-80 & Ankara, Turkey, 84; Gold Medal Printmaking, Mediterranean Biennale, Alexandria, Egypt, 82; Edmondson Award, Des Moines Art Ctr, 90. *Media:* works on Paper. *Res:* Turkish nomad weaving. *Publ:* Auth, Yield from the Sea Transformations with Ink on Paper, 03. *Dealer:* Struve Gallery 309 W Superior Chicago IL 60610; Locus Gallery St Louis MO; Printworks Chicago 311 W Superior Chicago IL. *Mailing Add:* 650 Kirkwood Ave Iowa City IA 52240-4605

ACKERMAN, GERALD MARTIN
HISTORIAN, EDUCATOR
b Alameda, Calif, Aug 21, 1928. *Study:* Univ Calif, BA, 52; Munich Univ, 56-58, with Prof Sedlmayr; Princeton Univ, MFA, 60, PhD, 64, with Prof Lee & Panofsky. *Work:* Life and Work of JL Gerome, 86; American Orientalists, 94; The Barque-Gerome Drawing Course, 2003. *Collection Arranged:* Thiebaud Figures, Stanford Univ Mus, 65; Gerome, Dayton Art Inst, Minneapolis Art Inst, Walters Art Gallery, Baltimore, 72-73; Gerome and Goupil/Art & Industry, Dahesh Mus, New York, NY, 2000; Charles Barque, Dahesh Mus, New York, NY, 2003. *Teaching:* Instr art hist, Bryn Mawr Col, 60-64; asst prof, Stanford Univ, 65-70; assoc prof, Pomona Col, 71-76, prof, 76-89, emer prof, 89- chmn art dept, 72-81; Fulbright prof, Univ Leningrad, USSR, 79; Appleton Eminent Scholar, Fla State Univ, 94. *Res:* American, French & British orientalist painters, in particular academic artists such as Jean Leon Gerome and William Bouguereau; art theory. *Publ:* Lomazzo's treatise on painting, Art Bull, 59; Thomas Eakins and His Parisian Masters, Gerome and Bonnat, Gazette des Beaux Arts, 72; The Life and Works of JL Gerome, New York, 86; American Orientalist, Paris, 94; American Orientalistes, Paris, 94; La Vie et l'Oeuvre de j-l Gerome, 3rd edit, Paris, 2000; The Barque-Gerome Drawing Course, 2003. *Mailing Add:* 360 S Mills Ave Claremont CA 91711-5331

ACKERMAN, JAMES S
HISTORIAN, EDUCATOR
b San Francisco, Calif, Nov 8, 1919. *Study:* Yale Univ, BA, 41; NY Univ, MA, 47, PhD, 52. *Hon Degrees:* Kenyon Col, LHD, 61; Md Inst Art, Hon DFA, 72; Univ Md, Baltimore Co, LHD, 76; Univ Venice, DArch, 84; Mass Col Art, DFA, 84. *Pos:* Ed-in-chief, Art Bulletin, 56-60; co-founder & pres, Univ Film Study Ctr, 67-75; trustee, Am Acad in Rome, 67-84, resident scholar, 74-75; trustee, Artists Found, 77-87, pres, 77-79; coun scholars, Libr of Congress, 80-82; art hist panel, Sr Fulbright fels, 89-92; ed, Annali di Architettura, 92-94, ed bd, 92-. *Teaching:* Lectr, Yale Univ, 46 & 49; asst prof hist art & archit, Univ Calif, 52-56, assoc prof, 56-60; Fel, Coun Humanities, Princeton Univ, 60-61; prof fine arts, Harvard Univ, 61-90, chmn dept, 63-80 & 82-84, Arthur Kingsley Porter prof, emer, 90-; Slade prof fine art, Univ Cambridge, 69-70; Mellon lectr, Nat Gallery Art, 85; SMeyer Schapiro vis prof art hist, Columbia Univ, 88, vis prof, 91; vis prof fine arts, New York Univ, 92; vis prof archit, Mass Inst Tech, 96 & Harvard Univ Sch Design, 97 & 99. *Awards:* Grand Officer in the Order of Merit of the Italian Republic, 78; Fel, Guggenheim Found, 93; Premio Daria Borghese, 95; Paul Oskar Kristeller Lifetime Achievement Award, Renaissance Soc Am, 98; Int Balzan Prize for career achievement in the history of archit and urban planning, 01. *Mem:* Corresp fel Accademia Olimpica Vicenza; corresp fel Brit Acad; corresp fel Royal Acad Uppsala; corresp fel Ateneo Veneto; hon fel Bavarian Acad Sci; Am Philosophical Union; Am Acad of Arts & Scis; Accademia di San Luca, Rome. *Res:* History of architecture; critical and historical theory; interaction of art and science in the period of 1200-1700. *Publ:* The Cortile del Belvedere, Vatican City, 54; The Archit of Michelangelo, London/NY, 61; Art and Archaeology (with Rhys Carpenter), Englewood Cliffs, 62; Auth, Palladio, Penguin, Eng, 66; auth, Palladio the Architect and his Influence in America (film), 80; The Villa: Form & Ideology of Country Houses, Princeton Univ Press, Thames & Hudson, London; Distance Points: Studies in Theory and Renaissance Art and Architecture, Cambridge, Mass, 91 & American Inst of Archits Award in History & Theory, 92; Osservazioni sui progetti di chiese di Leonardo da Vinci, pvt publ, 98; co-ed, Conventions of Architectural Drawing: Representation and Misrepresentation, Harvard Univ, 2000; Origins, Imitation, Conventions, 02. *Mailing Add:* Sackler Mus Harvard Univ 485 Broadway Cambridge MA 02138

ACKERMAN, RUDY SCHLEGEL
PAINTER, EDUCATOR
b Allentown, Pa, Mar 30, 1933. *Study:* Kutztown State Col, BS(art educ), 58; Temple Univ, MS(educ), 63; Pa State Univ EdD, 67. *Work:* Allentown Art Mus, Pa; Pa State Col; Lehigh Univ; Moravian Col, Pa. *Comn:* 14 ft metal sculpture, Pa Power & Light Co, Allentown, 67; tunnel mural, Allentown-Bethlehem-Easton Airport, Pa, 76; murals, The Marketplace, Bethlehem Mall, 78, Civic Ctr, Bethlehem, Pa, 84; Childrens Sculpture Park, Trexlerton, Pa. *Exhib:* The Circle, Allentown Art Mus, 74; Works on Paper, Studio Proposte, Florence, Italy, 79; one-man show, Gallery Doshi, Harrisburg, 79, Lehigh Univ, 80 & Monotypes 81, Alain Bilham Gallery, NY, 81; Allenton Art Mus, 83; Moravian Col, 85, 87, 89, 91, 93, 95 & 97; Muhlenberg Col, 88. *Pos:* Chmn art dept, Moravian Col, 63-; exec dir, Baum Sch Art, Allentown, 65-. *Teaching:* Prof studio art & art hist, Moravian Col, 63-. *Awards:* Distinguished Prof Achievement Award, Kutztown State Univ Alumni, 94. *Mem:* Col Art Asn. *Media:* Oil Paint, Sculptur. *Publ:* Moravian Col Mag, fall 91 & spring 93. *Mailing Add:* 2708 W Washington Allentown PA 18104-9839

ACORD, JAMES See Shie & Acord, Susan & James

ACTON, ARLO C
SCULPTOR
b Knoxville, Iowa, May 11, 1933. *Study:* Wash State Univ, BA, 58; Calif Inst Arts, MFA, 59. *Work:* San Francisco Mus Art. *Exhib:* Some Points of View for '62, Stanford Univ, 62; The Artist's Environment: The West Coast, Ft Worth, Tex, 62; Fifty California Artists, Whitney Mus Am Art, NY, 62-63; California Sculpture, Kaiser Ctr, Oakland, Calif, 63; 3rd Paris Biennial, 63; and many others. *Teaching:* Univ Calif, Berkeley, 63. *Awards:* Edgar Walter Mem Prize, San Francisco Mus Art, 61; Second Prize, Richmond Art Asn Ann, 61; Award, San Francisco Art Asn, 64; plus others. *Bibliog:* Peter Selz (auth), Funk, Univ Calif, Berkeley, 67; Maurice Tuchman (auth), American Sculpture of the Sixties, Los Angeles Co Mus Art, 67. *Mailing Add:* PO Box 75 North San Juan CA 95960

ADAMS, ALICE
SCULPTOR
b New York, NY, Nov 16, 30. *Study:* Columbia Univ, BFA, 53; Fulbright travel grant, 53-54; French govt fel, 53-54; L'Ecole Nat d'Art Decoratif, Aubusson, France. *Work:* Haags Gemeentemuseum, The Hague, Neth; Univ Nebr, Lincoln; Hertz Corp, NY; Am Craft Mus, NY; Chase Manhattan Bank, NY; Edwin I Ulrich Mus, Wichita, Kans; NJ

State Mus, Trenton; City of Denver, Colo; Broward Co, Fla; The State Conn; Univ Del, Newark, Del. *Comn:* Small Park with Arches, Toledo Botanical Garden, Ohio, 83; Glider Park, Bronx, NY, 90; The Roundabout, Philadelphia, Pa, 92; African Garden, Brooklyn, NY, 93; The River, Middletown, Conn, 93; Beaded Circle Crossing, Denver Int Airport, Colo, 94; Healer's Spring, Univ Tex, San Antonio, 97; Scroll Circle, Univ Del, 2001; Habitat, Little Falls, NJ, 2004; Wall fo this tides, Uineland, NJ, 2006; and others. *Exhib:* Contemp Am Sculpture, Whitney Mus Am Art, 70-71 & 73; Am Women Artists, Kunsthaus, Hamburg, Ger, 72; one person exhib, 55 Mercer, NY, 70, 72, 73 & 75, Hal Bromm Gallery, 78, 79 & 81, Artemesia Gallery, Chicago, Ill, 80 & Dag Hammarskjold Plaza, NY, 83; An Int Survey of Painting and Sculpture, Mus Mod Art, NY, 84; Builtwork, Sarah Lawrence Col Gallery, Bronxville, NY, 85; Am Abstract Artists 1936-1986, Brox Mus Arts, NY, 86; House and Garden, Nassau Co Mus Fine Arts, Roslyn, NY, 86; Fiber-Five Decades, Selections from the Permanent Collection, Am Craft Mus, NY, 95; Alice Adams: Pub Projects, Lehman Col Art Gallery, Bronx, NY, 2000. *Collection Arranged:* Haags Gemete Mus, The Hague, Neth; Univ Nebr; Everson Mus, Syracuse, NY; Am Craft Mus, NY City; Edwin Ulrich Mus, Wichita, Kans; Rosenquist Collection, East Hampton, NY; Ryman Collection, NY City; Columbia Univ, NY City; Whitney Mus, NY City. *Pos:* Design Team Artist, Downtown Seattle Transit Project, 88-90, St Louis Metrolink Rail, 92-93, Centro Transit Syst, Birmingham, Eng, 93, NJ Transit, NJ, 2002-2003, Charlotte Area Transit Syst, NC, 2002-2003. *Teaching:* Instr sculpture, Manhattanville Col, 61-79; instr, Pratt Inst, 79-80; instr, Sch Visual Arts, 80-85. *Awards:* MacDowell Colony, MacDowell Found, 67; Nat Endowment Arts Grant, 79 & 84-85; Princeton Univ Fel, 80; Fel, Guggenheim Found, 81-82; Award Sculpture, Am Acad & Inst Arts & Letts, 84; Prize winning entry, Westside Competition, Munic Art Soc, NY; Rockefeller Study and Conference Center, Bellagio, Italy, 2002; and others. *Bibliog:* Barbara Kafka (auth), The Woven Structures of Alice Adams, Craft Horizons, 3/67; Lucy Lippard (auth), The Abstract Realism of Alice Adams, Art Am, 9/79; Elaine Louis (auth), Spaceships? No, just chandeleliers, NY Times, 7/3/97. *Mem:* Am Abstr Artists (secy, 67). *Media:* Wood, Metal, Concrete, Landscape. *Publ:* auth (exhib catalog), Alice Adams: Public Projects, Lehman Col Art Gallery. *Mailing Add:* 3370 Ft Independence St Bronx NY 10463

ADAMS, BOBBI (BARBARA) JEAN AUSTIN
PAINTER, COLLAGE ARTIST
b Plainfield, NJ, July 30, 39. *Study:* Wheaton Col, Ill, BS (high honors), 61; Art Students League, with R Brackman, R Philipp, M Cooper & V Vytlacil, 70-74; Nat Acad Design, New York, 73-74, NY Univ, MA, 98. *Comn:* Two murals, William S Hall Psychiatric Inst, 88; mural, Calhoun Co High Sch, St Matthews, 89; mural, Redcliffe Elem, Aiken, 90; mural, Govs Sch of Math & Sci, 93 & 96; mural, Mayo Magnet High Sch, Darlington, 97; Mural, Lee County Pub Libr, 2006. *Exhib:* Guild SC Artists, Columbia Mus Art, 82; Gallery Exhib, Jimmy Milling, Sumter Daily Item, 86; SC Arts Comn Retrospective, 88; Oil Painters Invitational, 92 & 97; Fausto Lorenzi Contemporanea, Brescia, Italy, 97; Centennial Exhib, SC State Mus, 94; Washington Sq E Galleries, NY, 98; Mus St Paul de Vance, Nice, 2000; Frances Marion Univ, 2002; Winthrop Univ, 2003; Biennale Int del L'arte Contemporanea, 2003; Oils Painter' Invitational, 2004 & 2006. *Pos:* SC artist in res, 80-. *Awards:* Purchase Award, State SC, 80; Westvaco Award, Gibbes Gallery, 80; Cert Merit, Columbia Mus, 81; Cert Merit, SC State Fair, Columbia, 96 & 98. *Bibliog:* The Adams Papers, NJ Music-Arts, 75; Sumter Daily Item, 4/14/86; Contemporanea 8, Brescia, Italy, 97. *Mem:* life mem Art Students League; Sumter Artists Guild. *Media:* Oil, Pigment; Paper. *Collection:* State of SC Art Collection; Cent Carolina Tech Col; Nat Bank of SC; Munic Collection, Brescia, Italy. *Mailing Add:* 215 S Heyward St Bishopville SC 29010

ADAMS, CELESTE MARIE
MUSEUM DIRECTOR, CURATOR
b Cleveland, Ohio, July 4, 47. *Study:* Univ Mich, Ann Arbor, BA, 69; Univ Pa, Philadelphia, AM(art hist), 70; Harvard Univ, AM, 78. *Work:* Cleveland Mus Art, Ohio; Mus Fine Arts, Houston, Tex; Grand Rapids Art Mus, Mich. *Collection Arranged:* Japanese Landscape and Figure Painting (auth, catalog), Am Australian Found Arts, 83 & Visions of the American West (auth, catalog), 86; Mattuas Alter: Journey of an American Painter, Mus Fine Arts, Houston, 97; Quiet Grandeur: Four Centeries of Dutch Art, 98. *Pos:* Asst dir & cur, Mus Fine Arts, Houston, Tex, 80-93; dir, Grand Rapids Art Mus, 97-. *Mailing Add:* 201 W Fulton St Apt 1405 Grand Rapids MI 49503-2678

ADAMS, DENNIS PAUL
SCULPTOR, CONCEPTUAL ARTIST
b Des Moines, Iowa, Nov 15, 48. *Study:* Drake Univ, BFA, 69; Tyler Sch Art, Philadelphia, Pa, MFA, 71. *Work:* Etablissement Public pour L'Amanagement de la Defense & Centre Nat d'Art Contemporain, Paris, France; Mus Mod Art, NY; Gemäldegalerie Staatliche Museen Preussischer Kulturbesitz, Ger; Israel Mus, Jerusalem; Lenbachhaus Städtische Galerie, Munich; Whitney Mus Am Art, NY; Neue Galerie am Landesmuseum, Joanneum, Graz, Austria; Walker Art Ctr, Minneapolis; Westfalisches Landesmuseum fur Kunst und Kulturgeschichte, Munster, Ger; Denver Art Mus; Mus Contemp Art, Chicago; New Mus, NY; Israel Mus, Jerusalem; Queens Mus Art, NY; plus many others. *Comn:* Bus Shelter IV, Skulptur Projekte Münster, WGer, 87; Fallen Angels, Steirischer Herbst, Graz, Austria, 88; Pedestrian Tunnels, Villa Merkel, Esslingen, Ger, 89; Terminus II, de Achterstraat, Hoorn, Holland, 90; Seige, TSWA Four Cities Proj, Derry, Northern Ireland, 90; Emancipation, Boston, 91; Arcadian Blind, Floriadepark, Holland, 92; Réservoir, Musée d'Art Contemporain de Montreal, 92; Port View, Marseille, France, 92. *Exhib:* Solo exhib, Alternative Mus, NY, 87, Portikus, Frankfurt, 93 & Mus Van Hedendaagse Antwerpen, 94; Images Critiques, Musee d'Art Mod de La Ville de Paris, 89 & Passages de L'Image, 90, Magiciens de la Terre, 89, Musee Nat d'Art Mod, Centre Pompidou, Paris, France; Image World: Art & Media Cult, Whitney Mus, NY, 89; Photog of Invention, Nat Mus Am Art, Smithsonian Inst, 89 & Works: The Archive, Hirschhorn Mus, 90, Washington, DC; Images in Transition, Nat Mus Mod Art, Kyoto, Japan, 90; Mus Mod Art, NY, 91; Sala Montcado de la Fundacío "la caixa", Barcelona, 92; plus others. *Pos:* Bd govs, NY Found for Arts, 89-92. *Teaching:* Vis artist sculpture, Tyler Sch Art, Philadelphia, Pa, 87, Cooper Union Sch Art, 88, Parsons Sch, 90-99, NY, Ecole Nationale Superieure des Beaux-Arts, Paris, 92, Rijkakademi, Amsterdam, 92-, Akademie der Bildenden Kuenste, Munich, 93-94 & prof and dir visual arts prog Mass Inst Technol, Boston, 94-2001, NY Found for the Arts, 2004; prof, Cooper Union, 2001-, acting dean, 2004-. *Awards:* Nat Endowment Arts Fel, 84, 88 & 95; Deutscher Akademischer Austauschdienst, WGer, 89. *Bibliog:* Eleanor Heartney (auth), Dennis Adams, Flash Art, summer 89; Daniella Goldmann (auth), Interview with Dennis Adams, Noema Art J, 10-11/91; Lynne Cooke (auth), Dennis Adams, Galeries Mag, 2-3/91. *Media:* All Media. *Publ:* Works--Hirshhorn Mus--Dennis Adams, Hirshhorn Mus, 90; Architecture of Amnesia--Dennis Adams, Kent Fine Art, 90; Dennis Adams: El Pavelló de l'Est, Sala Montcado de la Fundacio "la Caixa", Barcelona, 92; Port of view, L'observatoire/Marseille; Trans/Actions, Mus Van Hedendaagse Kunst Antwerpen. *Dealer:* Kent Gallery 541 W 25th St New York NY 10001. *Mailing Add:* 42 Walker St New York NY 10013

ADAMS, HANK M
CRAFTSMAN
b Philadelphia, Pa, 56. *Study:* RI Sch Design, BFA (painting), 78; Penland Sch, Spruce Pine, NC, 80; Pilchuck Sch, Stanwood, Wash, 81; Tenn Technol Univ, Cookeville, Tenn, 81-84. *Work:* Detroit Inst Art, Mich; Brooks Mus, Memphis, Tenn; Oberglas Mus, Barnbach, Austria; JB Speed Art Mus, Louisville, Ky; Contemp Arts Ctr, Honolulu, Hawaii. *Exhib:* Solo exhibs, Traver Sutton Gallery, Seattle, Wash, 86, Mich Gallery, Detroit, 87, Great Am Gallery, Atlanta, Ga, 87, Dorothy Weiss Gallery, San Francisco, Calif, 87, 89, 92 & 93, Kohler Arts Ctr, Sheboygan, Wis, 88 & Heller Gallery, NY, 88, 90 & 94, The Arts Ctr of the Capital Region, NY, 2001, Elliot Brown Gallery, Wash, 2001, Marx-Saunders Gallery, Chicago, Ill, 2002; Maximizing the Minimum: Small Glass Sculpture, Mus Am, Milville, NJ, 93; Contemp Crafts & the Saxe Collection, Toledo Mus Art, 93; The Art of Contemp Glass, JB Speed Art Mus, 93; Tiffany to Ben Tre, A Century of Glass, Milwaukee Art Mus, 93; The Forest, Elliott Brown Gallery, Seattle, 95; Hokkaido Mus of Modern Art, Sapporo, Japan (traveling to other city museums in Japan and on to Dusseldorf, Ger), 97; Bumbershoot, 2000, Seattle Ctr, 2000, SeaTac Airport, 2001; group exhibs, Primary Colors, Elliot Brown Gallery, Seattle, Wash, 2001, Glass Am, Heller Gallery, 2001, 02, Fire and Form, Norton Mus of Art, W Palm Beach, Fl, 2003. *Pos:* Designer, Benko Glass Co, Milton, WVa, 88-94. *Teaching:* Appalachian Ctr, Smithville, Tenn, 81-85; Pilchuck Sch, Stanwood, Wash, 81; Ctr Creative Studies, Detroit, Mich, 87, 96, 97; vis artist, Univ Hawaii, Honolulu, 82, Toledo Mus Sch, 84, At Park, Lewiston, NY, 85, Univ Ill, Urbana, 86, Univ Ala, Tuscaloosa, 88, Oberglas Barnbach, Austria, 89 & 90 & Cranbrook Educ Community, Bloomfield Hills, Mich, 91, Corning Mus, NY, 2002, Mass Col of Art, Boston, 2002, Calif State Univ at Fullerton, Calif, 2003, San Jose State Univ, Calif, 2003, Calif Col of Arts and Crafts, Oakland, Calif, 2003. *Awards:* Fel, Nat Endowment Arts, 86, 88 & 90; Prize, Simonoseki City Art Mus, 92; Grant, Empire State Crafts Alliance, 93; Wheaton Fel, Creative Glass Ctr of Am, 2001; NY State Arts Fel, 2003. *Bibliog:* Warmus, William (auth.) Castings: Hank Murta Adams, Glass Mag, 97. *Dealer:* Elliott Brown Gallery 619 N 35th St Seattle WA 98103. *Mailing Add:* Fort Orange St Box 6933 Albany NY 12206

ADAMS, JAY H
JEWELER, MEDALIST
b Clinton, Iowa, Sept 11, 1937. *Study:* Lincoln Col, Ill, 58; Ill Wesleyan Univ, BFA, 62; Ill State Univ, MS, 68. *Work:* St Charles Art Ctr, Ill; Park Forest Art Ctr, Ill; Brooks Mem Art Gallery, Memphis, Tenn; Western Ill Univ Art Gallery. *Comn:* Candelabra, Lincoln Col, Ill, 71. *Exhib:* Goldsmith NAm Exhib, Renwick Gallery, Smithsonian Inst, Washington, DC, 74; Prof Jewelry Exhib, Univ Mo Fine Arts Gallery, Columbia, 76; NAm Goldsmith Exhib, Phoenix Art Mus, Ariz, 77; Am Goldsmiths Now, Washington Univ Gallery Art, St Louis, Mo, 78; Pewter Exhib, Tulsa Jr Col, Okla, 79; and others. *Teaching:* Instr jewelry-metals, Ill State Univ, 68-69; assoc prof jewelry-metals, Southwest Mo State Univ, 69-. *Awards:* Best of Show, Mo Crafts Coun Ann Show, 76. *Bibliog:* Edgar A Albin (auth), The Arts, 11/28/71 & View Mag, 10/22/77, Springfield News-Leader & Jay Adams, Art Craft Mag, 12/79-1/80. *Mem:* Am Crafts Coun; Soc NAm Goldsmiths; Mo Crafts Coun. *Media:* Gold; Pewter. *Publ:* Auth, Goldsmiths J, Soc NAm Goldsmiths, 10/79. *Mailing Add:* 910 S Kickapoo Ave Springfield MO 65804-0014

ADAMS, KIM HASTINGS
SCULPTOR
b Dec 17, 51; Can citizen. *Study:* Univ Victoria, BFA, 80. *Work:* Nat Gallery Can, Ottawa, Ont; Art Gallery Ont, Ydessa Hendeles Art Found, Toronto; Art Gallery Windsor, Winnipeg, Man; Winnipeg Art Gallery, Windsor, Ont; Concordia Art Gallery, Musee d' art Contemporain, Montreal; Canada Coun Art Bank, Ottawa; Centraal Mus, Holland; London Regional Art and Hist Mus; MacDonlad Stewart Art Ctr; MacKenzie Art Gallery. *Comn:* Crablegs (outdoor sculpture), Mcdonald Stewart Art Ctr, Guelph, Can, 94; The Studio, Toronto Sculpture Garden, Can, 94. *Exhib:* On Track, Olympic Arts Festival, Calgary, Alta, 88; Canadian Biennial of Contemp Art, Nat Gallery Can, Ottawa, Ont, 89; one-man shows, Shedhalle Zurich, Switz, 90, Winnipeg Art Gallery, Man, 91 & The Power Plant, Toronto, Ont, 92; Unnatural Acts: Contemp Art, Barbican Art Gallery, London, Eng, 91; Mus d'Art Contemp (auth, catalog), Montreal, Quebec, 96; Sculpture Projects (auth, catalog), Munster, Ger, 97; InSite 97, San Diego, Calif, 97; Mus Civilization, Hull, Que, 97; Winnipeg Art Gallery, Manitoba, 98; Dunlop Art Gallery, Regina, 98; Mendel Art Gallery, Saskatoon, 99; Edmonton Art Gallery, 99; Art Gallery of Hamilton, 99; Charles H Scott Gallery, Vancouver, 99;

Vancouver Art Gallery, 2000; Art Grandeur Nature, Paris, 2000. *Bibliog:* Bruce Ferguson (auth), Northern Noises, Winnipeg Art Gallery, 87; Nancy Tousley (auth), Worlds within worlds, Can Art Mag, 88; Gary Garnels & Jack Reynolds (auths), Sculpture at the Point, 88; Madill (auth), Kim Adams, Winnipeg Art Gallery, 91; Sandra Grant Marchand (auth), Kim Adams, 96; Klaus Bussman, Kasper Konig & Florian Matzner (ed), Sculpture Projects, 97; Sara Milroy (auth), Kim Adams, Artnews, 98; Joan Murray (auth), Canadian Art in the Twentieth Century, 99. *Media:* All Media. *Dealer:* Galerie Christine Chassay 372 St Catherine W Montreal PQ H3B 1A2 Canada; Genereux/Grünwald Gallery 21 Morrow Ave Toronto ON M6R 2H9 Canada. *Mailing Add:* RR 2 Grand Valley ON L0N 1G0 Canada

ADAMS, LAURIE SCHNEIDER
HISTORIAN, EDITOR

b New York, NY, Sept 29, 41. *Study:* Tulane Univ, BA, 62; Columbia Univ, MA (art hist), 63, MA (psychology), 64, PhD, 67. *Pos:* Ed, Source: Notes in the History of Art J, 84-. *Teaching:* Prof art hist, John Jay Col, City Univ New York, 67-, Cuny Grad Ctr, 90-. *Mem:* Col Art Asn. *Res:* Renaissance art, art and psychoanalysis, iconography, psychobiography. *Publ:* auth, The Methodologies of Art, Harper Collins, 96; Federico da Montefeltro and Sigismondo Malatesta: The Eagle and the Elephant (with Maria G Pernis), Peter Lang, 96; Art Across Time, McGraw-Hill, 99; A History of Western Art, McGraw-Hill, 2000; Key Monuments of the Italian Renaissance, Westview Press Icon Ed, 2000, Key Monumnets of the Baroque, Westview Press Icon Ed, 2000, Italian Renaissance Art, Westview Press, 2001, Looking at Art, Prentice Hall, 2002; Lucrezia Tornabuoni De'Medici and the Medici Family in the Fifteenth Century (with Maria G. Pernis), Peter Lang, 2006. *Mailing Add:* 224 East 68th St New York NY 10121

ADAMS, LISA KAY
PAINTER

b Bristol, Pa, Aug 3, 55. *Study:* Univ Heidelberg, Ger, 75; Scripps Col, BA, 77; Claremont Grad Univ, MFA, 80. *Work:* Edward Albee Found, Montauk, NY; Weisman Mus, Malibu, Calif; Laguna Mus Art, Laguna Beach, Calif; Nippon Steel, USA Inc & Eli Broad Corp Collection, Los Angeles. *Comn:* BMW N Am, ArtCar, 93. *Exhib:* Solo exhibs, Recent Paintings, William Turner Gallery, Venice, Calif, 94, Col SNev, 95, Miller Fine Art, Los Angeles, 97 & Gallery Paradise, Costa Mesa, Calif, 98; AB Strak Shun, William Turner Gallery, Venice, Calif, 94; Others Among Otheres, Wierzbowski Gallery, Houston, 94; Smoggy Abstraction, Haggerty Mus, Milwaukee, 96; New Image Art, Los Angeles, 98; Patricia Correia Gallery, Santa Monica, 99 & 2002; The Living Room 2000, Sandberg Inst, The Neth, 2000; The Sandbox, Venice, 2003; The Office, 2004; White Box Galley, 2005. *Pos:* Instr painting, Art Ctr Col, Pasadena, Calif, 94 & Claremont Grad Univ, Calif, 94. *Teaching:* Instr drawing, Univ Calif Los Angeles Extension, 88-98; instr painting, Santa Monica Col Design, Art & Archit, 90-98; instr drawing, Univ Southern Calif, Los Angeles, 96; instr painting & drawing, Univ Calif Riverside, 99-2000 & Otis Col Art & Design, 2001-02. *Awards:* Brody Arts Fund Fel, 92; Fulbright Senior Award, 96; Artist in Residence, Nordic Inst Contemp Art, Helsinki, 99; Artist in Residence, Gifu Design, 2000; White Residency, Costa Rica, 2002. *Bibliog:* James Scarborough (auth), Smoggy Abstraction (catalogue essay); Betty Brown (auth), Muses (catalog). *Mem:* Los Angeles Contemp Exhib. *Media:* Acrylic, Oil, Videographer, Installation. *Mailing Add:* PO Box 2456 Venice CA 90294

ADAMS, MAC
SCULPTOR, PHOTOGRAPHER

b South Wales, Gt Brit, 43. *Study:* Cardiff Col Art (nat dipl design), 61-66, ATD, 66-67; Rutgers Univ, MFA, 67-69. *Work:* Brooklyn Mus, Guggenheim Mus, NY; Wallraf Richartz Mus, Cologne, Ger; Univ Iowa Mus; Victoria & Albert Mus, London, Eng; Musee De Toulon, France; Los Angeles Co Mus, Calif; Ga Mus Art, Athens; La Jolla Mus Contemp Art, Calif; Microsoft Corp; Maison Europeenne de la Photographie, Paris; plus others. *Comn:* Sweptaway, N Princeton Develop Ctr, NJ State Coun Arts, Skillmen, 83; Serpent Bearer, Montclair State Col, NJ Governer's Challenge for Excellence Grant, 87; NY Korean War Mem, Battery Park, NY, 91; Mustangs at Noon, Henry Gonzalez Conv Ctr, San Antonio, Tex, 2000; plus others. *Exhib:* One-man shows, Hammerskjold Plaza Sculpture Garden, NY, 84, Galerie Maier-Hahn, Dusseldorf, Ger, 87, Montclair State Col, NJ, 88, La Jolla Mus Contemp Art, Calif, 88-89, Gracie Mansion Gallery, NY, 90,Silence of Shadows, Cardiff Arts Trust, Touring Exhib, UK, 98, Printemps de Cahors, EXTRAetORDINIRE Cahors, France, 99, Serge Aboukrat Gallery, Paris, 2000, plus others; New York Diary: Almost 25 Different Things, PS 1 Mus, Inst Contemp Art, 91; The Seventies, John Gibson Gallery, NY, 92; The Order of Things: Toward a Politic of Still Life, Widner Gallery, Trinity Col & Real Art Ways, Conn, 92; Quotations, The Second Hist of Art, Aldrich Mus Contemp Art & Mus Contemp Art, Wright State Univ, 92; Eclipses, CEAC, Strasbourg, France, 99; plus others. *Pos:* Chmn, State Univ NY, 88-. *Teaching:* Asst prof photog, State Univ NY Col, Old Wesbury, 88-. *Awards:* Nat Endowment Fel Arts, 76, 80, 82; Berlin Artist in Residence Prog, 81; NY State Fel Arts (sculpture), 88. *Bibliog:* Shoichiro Higuchi (auth), Water as Environmental Art, p 148, Kashiwashobo Publ Co, 91; Julia Ballerini (auth), The Surrogate Figure: Intercepted Identities in Contemporary Photography, Ctr Photog, 91; Charles Hagen (auth), NY Times Reviews, 3/92; and many others. *Media:* All. *Dealer:* Stux Gallery Janet Bornew Gallery New York

ADAMS, PAT
PAINTER, EDUCATOR

b Stockton, Calif, July 8, 28. *Study:* Univ Calif, Berkeley, BA, 49; Brooklyn Mus Art Sch, with Max Beckmann & John Ferren, 50-51. *Work:* Whitney Mus; Joseph Hirshhorn Mus; Yale Gallery Art; Brooklyn Mus; Jane Voorhees Zimmerli Mus, Rutgers Univ; Corcoran Gallery Art; Palm Springs Desert Mus; Nat Acad Mus, NY; Berkshire Mus, Mass; Brooks Mus, Memphis, Tenn; and others. *Comn:* TRW Hq, Lyndhurst, Ohio. *Exhib:* One person shows, Zabriskie Gallery Biennial, 54-2006, Survey 1954-79, Cincinnati Contemp Art Ctr, 79, MModA traveling Exh to France, 56-57, Stable Gallery, NY, 56, Zabruskie Gallery, Paris, 80, Columbia Mus Art & Sci, SC, 82, Va Commonwealth, 82, Haggin Mus, Stockton, Calif, 86, NY Acad Sci, 88, Addison-Ripley, Washington, 88, Survey, 68-88, Berkshire Mus, Pittsfield, Mass, 88-89 & Jaffe-Friede Strauss Galleries, Dartmouth Col, 94, Torrant Gallery, Flynn Informing Arts Ctr, Burlington, Vt; Yale Sch Art Fac 1950-1990, Marilyn Pearl, NY, 90; Traditional Sources: Contemp Visions, Webb & Parsons Gallery, Burlington in collaboration with Shelburne Mus, Vt, 91; Bennington Col Collects, Williams Col Mus Art, 91; Nat Acad Mus, 92-95, 2001; Late Modern Drawings 1960-70's, Corcoran Gallery Art, 93; A View of Ones Own: Nat Asn Women Artists Collection, Zimmerli Mus, Rutgers, NJ, 94; Urdang Gallery, Boston, 97; Rider Univ, Lawrenceville, NJ, 97; Silvermine Guild, 98; Helen Day Art Ctr, Stowe, Vt, 98 & 2006; Middlebury Col Art Mus, 2000; Univ Rhode Island, 2000; Decordova Mus, Lincoln, Mass; Block Mus, Northwestern Univ, 2001, Fleming Mus Univ Vt, Burlington, 2002; Nat Acad Mus, Challenging Tradition, 2003; Galeria Nat/Museo de Los Ninos, 2004; Vermont Arts Council, Wood Gallery, Montpelier, Vt, 2005; Zabruskie Gallery, NY, Paris Season, 2005. *Pos:* Bd dir, Vt Coun Arts, 77-81, Yaddo Corp, 81-, vchmn, 85-88, Williamstown Regional Art Conserv Lab, 85-86 & Col Art Asn, 86-90; artist-in-residence, Dartmouth Col, 94. *Teaching:* Art fac painting, Bennington Col, 64-93; vis critic painting, Yale Univ, 71-72; grad sem, Queens Col, 72, RI Sch Design, 81; vis prof, Grad Sch Art, Yale Univ, 83; vis artist, Univ Iowa, Univ NMex, Western Ky Univ, Columbia Univ, Kent State Univ & Cornell Univ, Mills Col; lectr & critic, RI Sch Design, 89, Univ Mass, Amherst, 89 & Skidmore Col, summer 92; lectr, The Not as Yet, Nat Asn Women Artists, NY; sr critic, Grad Prog, Yale Sch Art, 90-95; lectr critique, Vt Studios Ctr, 93, 94, 97, 99, 2000 & 2001, Am Univ, Washington, DC, 2002. *Awards:* Nat Endowment Arts, 68,76 & 87; Hassam Purchase Award, Am Acad Arts & Letters, 83, 85 & 89; Distinguished Teaching Art Award, 84; Govs Award Excellence Arts, Vt Coun Arts, 95; Andrew Carnegie Prize for Painting, Nat Acad Design Exhib, 95; Jimmy Ernst Award for painting, Am Acad Arts & Letters, 96; Ranger Purchase Award, 2005. *Bibliog:* Emmy Donadio (auth), Nightflight to Byzantium: Pat Adams' new work, Arts, summer 86; Debra Bricker Balken (auth), Pat Adams, Paintings, 68-88, Berkshire Mus Pittsfield, Mass, 88; Jed Perl (auth), Gallery Going, 91; Ruth Meyer (auth), Pat Adams Paintings 1954-1979, Cincinnati Art Center; and others. *Mem:* Vt Acad Arts & Sci (elections Fel, 90); Nat Acad Design (assoc, 92, acad, 93); Col Art Asn; Vt Coun Arts; Phi Beta Kappa. *Media:* Oil-Isobutyl Methacrylate, Acrylic, Monoprint, Etching. *Publ:* Auth, Art Now, 6/72; On working, Quadrille, fall 77; Subject and being, Art J (Col Art Asn Am), 82; The Making of Art & the Making of Artists Colloquium, Atlanta Col Art, 87; Zabruskie 50th Anniversary, Ruden Finn, 2005. *Dealer:* Virginia Zabriskie Gallery 41 E 57th New York NY 10019. *Mailing Add:* 370 Elm St Bennington VT 05201

ADAMS, PETER
PAINTER

b Los Angeles, Calif, Aug 27, 50. *Study:* Otis Art Inst, Los Angeles, 70; Art Ctr Col Design, Los Angeles, 70; Lukits Acad Fine Art, Los Angeles, 77. *Work:* Forbes Magazine Coll, New York, NY; Carnegie Art Mus, Oxnard, Calif; Calif Club, Los Angeles; Stephen's Col, Columbia, Mo; Southern Alleghenies Mus Art, Loretto, Pa. *Comn:* 50th Anniversary (painting), Chadwick Sch, Palos Verdes, Calif, 87; Headmaster (portrait), Curtis Sch, Los Angeles, 88; family portrait, comn by Eric & Ronna Hoffman, Portland, Ore, 93; family portrait, comn by Mr & Mrs Robert Warren, Portland, Ore, 94; book cover, Caroline Hudson Firestone, Afghan Story Teller. *Exhib:* The Mystical Paintings of Peter Adams, Carnegie Art Mus, Oxnard, Calif, 98; On Location Malibu, Frederick R Weisman Mus Art, Malibu, Calif, 99 & 2003; Drawn to Yellowstone, Mus Am West, Autry National Ctr, Los Angeles, Calif, 2004. *Pos.* Mem bd trustees, Pac Asia Mus, Pasadena, Calif; coauth, Calif Art Club News, 93-2006; bd dir, Acad Art Univ, San Francisco, currently; pres, California Art Club, 93-; adv bd member, Am Soc Portrait Artists, 2000-. *Awards:* Challacombe Award, Oil Painters of Am, 93; Art Calif Discovery Award, 94-95; Gold Crown Award, vis art, Pasadena Arts Council, 97. *Bibliog:* Berkley Hudson (auth), Art of War, Los Angeles Times, 2/23/89; B Eric Rhoads (auth), Imagination at Work, Plein Air Magazine, 9/04; Paul Soderberg (auth), Peter and Elaine Adams: The Art Bridge Builders of California, Art-Talk, 3/04. *Mem:* Calif Art Club (pres, 93-); signature mem Pastel Soc Am; signature mem Oil Painters Am; signature mem Plain Air Painters Am; hon emer assoc guild mem Am Soc Classical Realism. *Media:* Oil, Pastel. *Publ:* Auth, Moods of the Pacific, Pac Asia Mus, 93; Peter Adams: Eastern Exposure, Southwest Art Mag, 96; auth, Afghanistan Evolving, Caroline Hudson Firestone Publ, 2004; auth, From Sea to Shinging Sea: A Reflection of America, Thomas Haggin Mus Publ, CA, 2004. *Dealer:* American Legacy Fine Arts LLC PO Box 92345 Pasadena CA 91109, web: www.americanlegacyfinearts.com, tel: 626-577-7733. *Mailing Add:* 949 Linda Vista Ave Pasadena CA 91103

ADAMS, PHOEBE
SCULPTOR

b Greenwich, Conn, 53. *Study:* Philadelphia Col Art, Pa, BFA, 76; Skowhegan Sch Painting & Sculpture, Maine, 77; State Univ NY, Albany, MFA, 78. *Work:* Solomon R Guggenheim, Metrop Mus Art, NY; Brooklyn Mus, NY; AT&T, Chicago, Ill; Pa Acad Fine Arts, Philadelphia, Pa Convention Ctr & Philadelphia Mus Art, Pa; Storm King Art Ctr, Mountainville, NY; Prudential Insurance Co; Walker Art Ctr, Minneapolis, Minn; Harn Mus, Fla; others. *Comn:* Sculpture for outdoor garden, Walker Art Ctr, Mineapolis, Minn, 88; Intaglio print, Friends of the Philadelphia Mus Art, Pa, 91; Sculpture, Pa Convention Ctr, Philadelphia, 93. *Exhib:* solo shows, Lawrence Oliver Gallery, Philadelphia, Pa, 84, 86 & 90, Curt Marcus Gallery, NY, 87, 90, & 95, Pence Gallery, Santa Monica, Calif, 88 & 91, Locks Gallery (with catalog), Philadelphia, Pa, 93 & Anna Leonouens Gallery, NS Col Art & Design, 94, Bellas Artes Gallery, Santa Fe, NMex, 99, 2000 & 2001, Nesbit Gallery, Drexel Univ, Philadelphia, 2000; Sculpture Inside/Out (with catalog), Walker Art Ctr, Minneapolis, Minn, traveling, 88;

The Material Imagination, Guggenheim Mus Soho, 95; Subjective Vision, Kipp Gallery, Ind Univ Pa, 96; Contemp Art Ctr of Va, Va Beach, 97; San Francisco Mus Mod Art, 2000; Univ Colo, Denver, 2001. *Teaching:* Asst prof, Kutztown Univ, Pa, 91-; Artist in residence, Kent State Univ, Ohio, Pilchuck Glass Sch Stanwood, Wash, 2001. *Awards:* Pa Coun Arts, 82 & 84; Guggenheim Sculptor in Residence, Chesterwood, Stockbridge, Mass, 86; Nat Endowment Arts Fel Grant, 86. *Bibliog:* Kimberly Davenport (auth), Impossible liberties: contemporary artists on the life of their work, Art J, summer 95; Pepe Karmel (auth), Art in review: Phoebe Adams, NY Times, 2/3/95; Tom Csaszar (auth), In the studio, Phoebe Adams, Sculpture, 1/96; and others. *Mailing Add:* c/o Bellas Artes 653 Canyon Rd Santa Fe NM 87501

ADAMS, ROBERT MCCORMICK
ADMINISTRATOR, WRITER
b Chicago, Ill, July 23, 26. *Study:* Univ Chicago, PhB, 47 AM, 52, PhD, 56; Univ Pittsburgh, Dr Sci, 85; Hunter Col, City Univ New York, LHD, 86; Ill Univ, Edwardsville, LHD, Col William and Mary, LHD, 89; Dartmouth Col, Dr Sci, 89. *Pos:* Trustee, Nat Opinion Res Ctr, 70-95, Russell Sage Found, 78-92, Santa Fe Inst, 84- & George Washington Univ, 86-92; auth, column, Smithsonian Horizons, Smithsonian Mag, 84-94; chief exec, Smithsonian Inst, 84-94. *Teaching:* Instr, Univ Chicago, 55-63, dir Oriental Inst, 62-68 & 81-83, prof, 64-84, dean Social Sci, 70-74 & 79-80, Harold Swift Distinguished Serv Prof, 75-84, provost, 83-84, res assoc dept anthropology, 84-; adj prof, dept anthropology & Near Eastern studies, John Hopkins Univ, formerly. *Mem:* Am Oriental Soc; assoc mem Iraqi Acad; fel Am Acad Arts & Sci; Soc Antiquaries London. *Publ:* Auth, Heartland of Cities: Surveys of Ancient Settlement and Land Use on the Central Floodplain of the Euphrates, Univ Chicago Press, 81; co-ed, Behavioral and Social Science Research: A National Resource, Vol 1 & 2, Nat Acad Press, 82; auth, Change and continuity in faculty, student body and research support: A decade-long perspcetive, Chicago Chronicle, 5/10/84; approx 100 articles & reviews. *Mailing Add:* 9753 Keeneland Row La Jolla CA 92037

ADAMS, SHELBY LEE
PHOTOGRAPHY
b Hazard, Ky, Oct 24, 50. *Study:* Cleveland Inst Art, BFA (photog), 74; Univ Iowa, MA (photog), 75; Mass Col Art, Boston, MFA (photog), 89. *Work:* Art Inst Chicago; Los Angeles Co Mus Art; San Francisco Mus Mod Art; Mus Fine Arts, Houston; Mus Mod Art, NY; Whitney Mus Am Art; and others. *Exhib:* Solo exhibs, Southern Light Gallery, Amarillo, Tex, 84, Harvard Fogg Mus, Cambridge, 89, OK Harris Works of Art, NY, 93 & 95, Robert Koch Gallery, San Francisco, 93, Northern Ill Univ, 94, Etherton Gallery, Tucson, Ariz, 94, Catherine Edelman Gallery, Chicago, 94, Int Ctr Photog, Midtown, NY, 94, FotoGalerie, Amsterdam, The Neth, 95 & Cleveland Mus Art, 95; Devotion, Faith and Fervor - The Faithful and the Damned, 292 Gallery, NY, 94; Workshop Instructor, Anderson Ranch Arts Ctr, Aspen, Colo, 94; A Photog Bestiary, Robert Koch Gallery, San Francisco, 94; Photog Exhib-Three, Cinti Art Acad, 95; Appalachian Legacy (with catalog), Arles Int Photog Festival, France, 99; Stephen Bulger Gallery, Toronto, 2002; Yossi Milo Gallery, NY, 2002. *Pos:* Freelance photogr, 80-87 & 92-98. *Teaching:* Instr photog hist, Northern Ky Univ, Highland Heights, 79; instr camera & studio lighting, Cincinnati Art Acad, 79; head instr photog, Ill Cent Col, East Peoria, 81-84; asst prof & head photog prog, Salem State Col, Salem, Mass, 85-92; instr nat & int workshops, 92-; artist in res, Bennington Col, Vt, 96-97; lectr, Cincinnati Art Mus, Ohio, 98, Dallas Mus Art, Tex, 98. *Awards:* Nat Endowment Arts Fel, 78 & 92; Artist Support Grant, Polaroid Corp, Cambridge, Mass, 89-92; Artist Support Grant, Elizabeth Firestone Graham Found, Akron, Ohio, 1990, Peter S Reed Found, NY, 2000. *Publ:* Illusr, Photographer's Forum (by Gretje Ferguson), 93; View Camera (Elizabeth A Johnson, ed), 93; Appalachian Portraits, Univ Press Miss, Jackson, 93; Camera and Darkroom (by Dean Brierly), 94; Amerika (Frans Zerhagen, ed), Amsterdam, Holland, 94; auth introduction, 80 photogs, Appalachian Legacy, Univ Press Miss, 1998; 80 photogs, Appalachian Lives, Univ Press Miss, introduction by Vicki Goldberg, 2003; Lens Work, (by Brooks Jensen), 2000; ARTForum (by Bob Nickas), 2002; Photovision (by Ellen Rennard), 2001; Documentary film on work & life, New Release (70 mins); True Meaning of Pictures, (film, dir Jennifer Baichwal), Mercury Films, Inc, 2002. *Dealer:* Yossi Milo Gallery, New York; David Fahey/Klein Gallery, Los Angeles. *Mailing Add:* 3 South Church St Pittsfield MA 01201-6103

ADAMSON, JEROME D
ART DEALER, CONSULTANT
b Glendale, Calif, July 14, 44. *Study:* Whittier Col, BA, 67. *Pos:* Dir, Adamson-Duvannes Galleries, 80-. *Mem:* Art Dealers Asn Calif (pres). *Specialty:* 19th and 20th-century American and European painting; Special interest in paintings that focus on grandeur and beauty of the West, its hist, settlement and develop. *Publ:* Auth, With an Eye Toward Collecting California Painting (exhib catalog), 85; American Art 1830-1940: A Century Observed (exhib catalog), 89; The California Vision: Watercolors in the California Style (exhib catalog), 90. *Dealer:* Adamson-Duvannes Galleries. *Mailing Add:* Adamson/Duvannes Galleries 484 S San Vicente Blvd Los Angeles CA 90048

ADAMSON, LINNY J
CURATOR, WEAVER
b Portland, Ore, Jan 4, 52. *Study:* Ore State Univ, 70-73; Portland State Univ, 74; special studies with Britt Warsinki, Norway & Peter Collingwood, Eng. *Work:* Timberline Lodge, Nat Hist Landmark, Ore. *Comn:* Wall hanging (woven), Rankin, McMurry & Osborn Attys, Portland, Ore, 76; office dividers (woven), Wilamette Dental Group, Portland, 77; International Kings Table (wall woven pieces), Eugene, Ore, 78; (wall piece), Clatskanie Ore Savings & Loan, 78. *Exhib:* Ore Artists Under 35, Portland Art Mus, Ore, 74. *Collection Arranged:* LACE Collection, Portland Art Mus, 81; Mountain High IV-Glass, 83; Mountain High V-Metal, Northwest Blacksmiths, 85; Timberline Textiles, Ore Hist Soc, 86; Rachael Griffin Hist Exhib Ctr, 86. *Pos:* Dir, Fibres Gallery, Portland, Ore, 75-77; weaver, Friends of Timberline, 75-78; dir, Timberline Textile Wkshp, 78-80 & 40 volunteer rug hookers, 83-86; cur, Timberline Lodge, 78-86; bd mem, Ore Sch Arts & Crafts, 84-86. *Teaching:* Instr sales & weaving, Wildflowers Fibres, Portland, Ore, 73-76; instr weaving, Portland Parks Bureau, 74-79. *Awards:* First Place, Valley Invitational, Corvallis Art Ctr, 74. *Bibliog:* Portraits in Art, Linda Adamson, Handweaver, Curator (film), Rogers Cable Systems, 84. *Media:* Textiles. *Res:* 1930's Works Progress Administration arts and crafts. *Mailing Add:* c/o Friends Timberline Lodge PO Box 69544 Portland OR 97240

ADAMY, GEORGE E
EDUCATOR, SCULPTOR
b Manchester, Conn, Apr 19, 1925. *Study:* Univ Conn, BS, 48; NY Univ, MBA, 54, PhD credits, 55; New Sch Social Res, with M Borne, 63; Mus Mod Art, with R Carpentier & S Weiner, 63-64; Scarsdale studio workshop with F Dzubas & Knox Martin, 63-65. *Work:* Aldrich Mus of Contemp Art, Ridgefield, Conn; Vatican Art Collection, Vatican City; White Plains Hosp, NY; Mayo Clinic, Minn. *Comn:* Outdoor sculpture environment containing five 5 ft laminated acrylic discs in an 800 sq ft area, 77 Water St, NY, 69-70; Designer & fabricator, Hutchinson Art Garden, Pelham, NY, 87-. *Exhib:* Aldrich Mus of Contemp Art, 65; Neuberger Mus, State Univ NY, Purchase, 75; Hudson River Mus, Yonkers, NY. *Pos:* Owner, art materials innovator and consult to industs & artists, George E Adamy Co & GEA Co, 62-; owner, Adamy's Concrete & Paper Workshops, 79-; founder & pres, Life Reproductions Ltd, 81; sr partner, Impressions, 83. *Teaching:* Instr pvt workshops, 68-; lectr plastics, State Univ NY Col, Purchase, 73-84; vis adj prof, Univ Bridgeport, Conn, 75; lectr, Elizabeth Seton Col, 74, Sarah Lawrence Col, 77; lectr, Parsons Sch Design, 82, Moorhead State Univ, 89, Carleton Col, 90. *Awards:* Numerous awards for sculpture & collage in plastics. *Bibliog:* Luisa Kriesberg & Kathie Beals (auths), articles in Westchester-Rockland newspapers, 63-; Sherri Warner Hunter (auth), Creating With Concrete, LarkBooks.com, 2002. *Mem:* Hudson River Contemp Artists. *Media:* Cement, Paper Pulp. *Publ:* Auth, The POLYADAM Concrete System: State of the Art Construction and Casting & The ADAMATE System of Molding Humans and Delicate Objects, 86. *Mailing Add:* 11-1 Woods Brooke Cir Ossining NY 10562

ADAN, SUZANNE
PAINTER
b Woodland, Calif, Feb 12, 46. *Study:* Calif State Univ, Sacramento, BA, 69, MA, 71. *Work:* Crocker Art Mus, Sacramento; Continental Bank, Houston, Tex; Lexecon, Inc, Chicago, Ill; Impact Commun, Bloomington, Ill; Livingston & Mattesich, Sacremento. *Comn:* Ceramic Tile Mural, Univ Calif Med Ctr, Sacramento, 90; Ceramic Tile Murals, National Station, Folsom Calif, 90. *Exhib:* San Francisco Art Institute Centennial Exhibition, San Francisco Mus Mod Art, 71; Extraordinary Realities, Whitney Mus Art, NY, 73-74; one-person exhibs, Womanspace, Los Angeles, 74, Betsy Rosenfield Gallery, Chicago, 83 & 85, Himovitz-Salomon Gallery, Sacramento, 84, 86 & 93, John Berggruen Gallery, San Francisco, 87 & Susan Cummins Gallery, Mill Valley, 97; two-person show, A Survey, Mem Union Gallery, Univ Calif, Davis, 90; Tribute Exhib: Works on Paper & Sculpture By Crocker Kingsley Artists, Crocker Art Mus, Sacramento, 91; Black & White in Color, Spectrum/Himovitz Gallery, San Francisco, 91; Discovery Contemp Calif Narrations, Am Cult Ctr, Brussels, 92; Ink & Clay, Holmes Fine Art Gallery, San Jose, Calif, 93; The Michael Himovitz Gallery, Crocker Art Mus, Sacramento, 94; Art of Collecting: The Artist as Collector, Mem Union Gallery, Univ Calif, Davis, 94; plus many others. *Teaching:* Instr drawing, Am River Col, Sacramento, Calif, 75-76; artist-in-residence, Calif Arts Coun. *Awards:* Hardison, Komatsu, Ivelich & Tucker Award, Richmond Art Ctr, 80; New Works Grant, Sacramento Metrop Arts Comn, 90 & 96; James D Phelan Art Award, San Francisco Found Kala Inst, Berkeley, 91. *Bibliog:* Ruth Holland & Susan Willoughby (auths), Fifty Years of Crocker Kingsley, Crocker Art Mus, Sacramento, 75; Roger Clisby (auth), Welcome to the Candy Store, Crocker Art Mus, Sacramento, 81; Janice T Dreisbach & Barbara K Gibbs (auths), Michael Himovitz Gallery: An Exhibition at the Crocker Art Mus, Sacremento, 94. *Mem:* Col Art Asn. *Media:* Oil on Canvas. *Mailing Add:* 3977 Rosemary Cir Sacramento CA 95821

ADATO, LINDA JOY
PRINTMAKER, INSTRUCTOR
b Edgware, England, Oct 24, 42; US citizen. *Study:* Hornsey Col Art, Eng, 60-61; Univ Calif, Los Angeles, BA, 66, MA, 67. *Work:* Fine Arts Mus San Francisco, Calif; Corcoran Gallery, Washington DC; DeCordova Mus, Lincoln, Mass; Brit Mus, London, England; NY Pub Libr. *Exhib:* British Int Miniature Prints, City Gallery, London, Eng, 97, 2000; New York City Centennial Portfolio, The Old Print Shop, NY, 98 & 2002; Int Print Biennial, Silvermine Guild Galleries, New Canaan, Conn, 94, 96, 98; City Views, DeCordova Mus, Lincoln, Mass, 98-99; 5th British Int Miniature Prints, 2003-05; NY Soc Etchers & Gallery, Australia Exchange Exhib, 04; Boston Printmakers N Am Print Biennial, Boston Univ, Mass, 05; 6th British Int Miniature Prints, 2006-; Hollar Soc Gallery, Prague, Czech Repub, 2006. *Teaching:* adjunct lectr printmaking, Manhattanville Col, Purchase, NY, 87-2000; instr printmaking, Silvermine Sch Art, New Canaan, Conn, 95-. *Awards:* Gold Medal of Honor, Audubon Artists, NY, 2000; Ralph Fabri Medal of Merit, Audubon Artists, 2002; Art Students League NY Award, Audubon Artists, 2003. *Mem:* Soc Am Graphic Artists (treas, 95-2002); Boston Printmakers; Silvermine Guild Arts Ctr; Audubon Artists. *Media:* Etching. *Dealer:* The Old Print Shop 150 Lexington Ave New York NY 10016; Platt Fine Art LLC 561 West Diversey Parkway Suite 204A Chicago Il 60614. *Mailing Add:* 20 Pratt St New Rochelle NY 10801

ADDISON, BYRON KENT
PAINTER, EDUCATOR
b St Louis, Mo, July 12, 37. *Study:* Washington Univ, St Louis, Mo, BFA, 59; Univ Notre Dame, South Bend, Ind, MA, 60. *Work:* Univ Tulsa Libr, Okla; Maryville Univ Libr, St Louis, Mo; Springfield Art Mus, Springfield, Mo; Neville Pub Mus, Green Bay, Wis; The Evansville Mus Arts & Sci, Ind. *Comn:* Forest Park sculpture, St Louis Award Comt, Mo, 65; entrance wall sculpture, Continental Tel Co, Wentzville, Mo, 67; wall sculpture, Westinghouse Elec Corp, Abington, Va, 71; fountain & sculpture, United Methodist Church, Sun City, Ariz, 74; religious sculpture, St Joseph Church, Manchester, Mo, 80. *Exhib:* Nat Competition, Nat Watercolor Soc, Muckenthaler Cult Ctr, Fullerton, Calif, 92; Nat Exhib Transparent Watercolors, Midwest Watercolor Soc, Neville Pub Mus, Green Bay, Wis, 92; Five State Exhib, Wichita Art Mus, Kans, 92; Rocky Mountain Nat Watermedia Exhib, Foothills Art Ctr, Colo, 92; Watercolor USA, Springfield Art Mus, MO, 92; Ga Watercolor Soc 18th Nat Exhib, Mus Art & Sci, Macon, Ga, 97; Kans Watercolor Soc 26th Ann 7 State Exhib, Wichita Art Mus, Kans, 97; Rocky Mountain Nat Watermedia Exhib, The Foothills Art Ctr, Golden, Colo, 97 & 99; Watercolor USA, Springfield Art Mus, Mo, 98, 99 & 2005; 24th Exhib Nat Watercolor Okla, Kirkpatrick Galleries, Olka City, 98; Midwest Nat Exhib, The Rahr-West Art Mus, Wis, 99; Watercolor USA Hon Soc Exhib, Huntsville (Ala) Mus Art, 2000; Midwest Nat Exhib, The Canton (Ohio) Mus Art, 2000; Kans Watercolor Soc Honor Show, Wichita Ctr Arts, 2000 & 06; MOAK 4 State Exhib, Springfield Art Mus, 2000; Western Colo Watercolor Soc Ann Nat Exhib, Western Colo Ctr Arts, Colo, 2000, 2001; Watercolor USA Honor Soc, 9th Biennial Exhib, Springfield Art Mus, MO, 2003; Ann Kans Watercolor Soc Competition, Wichita Art Mus, Kans, 2004 & 06; Winston Churchhill Meml, Fulton, Mo, 2006; Univ Art & Design Gallery, Springfield, Mo, 2006. *Teaching:* Emer prof art, Maryville Univ, St Louis, Mo, 61-95, chmn, Art Dept, 65-79 & prof drawing, watercolor & sculpture, 80-95. *Awards:* Springfield Art Mus Cash Award, 92; Purchase, Neville Pub Mus, 92; Winsor & Newton Art Award, Adirondack Exhib, 92; Southern Watercolor Soc Award of Distinction, 97, Award of Citation, 97; Watercolor USA Cash Award, 97, John and Beth Raidel Patorn Purchase Award, 98; Kans Watercolor Soc Charles & Ruth Sanderson Cash Award, 97; Context Mo Collection Award, St Louis Artists' Guild, 97; Special Merit Award, Midwest Watercolor Soc, 99, Prof Packers and Shippres Awad, 99; Ecus Paper Award, Ky Watercolor Soc, 2000, Airfloat Award, 2000; Robert E Goodier Memorial Cash Award, Watercolor USA, Springfield Art Mus, Springfield, Mo, 2001; Southwest Mo Mus Asn Purchase for Springfield Art Mus Permanent Col, Springfield, Mo, 2002; Beaver Bend Prairie Naturals Award, Annual Kans Watercolor Soc Competition, Wichita Art Mus, Wichita, Kans, 2004. *Bibliog:* Herbert Gralnick (auth), Alone with His God, St Louis Mag, 3/84; Bebe Raupe (auth), Award Winning Watercolors, Artists' Mag, 8/98; M Stephen Doherty (auth), Recent Images Recent Concerns, Watercolor 90, Am Artist Publ, fall 90; Bebe Raupe (auth), Award Winning Watercolors: The Regional Showcase, Artists Mag, 9/91; Betsy Schein Goldman (auth), Kent & Sharon's Place, Watercolor 95, Am Artist Publ, Premiere issue, winter 95; Watercolor Majic Winter 2002, Maureen Bloomfield (auth), In the Spotlight: Center Stage, 2001. *Mem:* Watercolor USA Honor Soc; Transparent Watercolor Soc Am; Nat Watercolor Soc, Rocky Mountain Nat Watermedia Soc. *Media:* Welded Steel, Watercolor. *Mailing Add:* 17775 Orville Rd Wildwood MO 63005

ADE, IRENE M
PAINTER
Study: Ridgewood Art Inst, studied with John Osborn, Arthur Maynard, Betty Kaytes & Joe Hing Lowe; studied watercolor with Theresa Heidel, Leo Yeni & Terri Jeffries. *Exhib:* Butler Inst Am Art, Youngstown, Ohio; Audubon Art Asn; Suburban Art League. *Pos:* fac, IBM, formerly. *Awards:* WC Tiffany Award, Salmagundi Club; and several others. *Mem:* Salmagundi Club; Allied Artists of Am (bd mem, currently); Rockport Art Asn; Kent Art Asn; Am Artists Prof League (bd mem, currently). *Mailing Add:* 739 Pine Lake Dr Township of Washington NJ 07676

ADELMAN, BUNNY
SCULPTOR
b New York, NY, May 7, 35. *Study:* Mt Holyoke Col, Columbia Univ, BA, 56; Nat Acad Sch Fine Arts, with Stephen Csoka & Evangelos Frudakis, scholar, 76. *Comn:* Figure, comn by A Petaccio, Clifton, NJ, 77; B'Nai Brith Medal, comn by Roger Williams Mint, 78; presidential relief, M H Lamston Inc, NY, 78; Manager of Year Award, M H Lamston Inc, NY, 79; mem relief, W R Thomas Co, Warsaw, Ind, 80. *Exhib:* Allied Artists Am, Nat Acad Design,NY, 74-79 & 81; Nat Acad Ann, Nat Acad Design, NY, 76-78; Salmagundi Club Ann, NY, 78; one-woman show, Bergen Community Mus, Paramus, NJ, 79; Pen & Brush Soc, NY, 81. *Awards:* Gold Medal, Catherine Lorillard Wolfe Ann Show, 74; Coun Am Artists Soc Award, Nat Sculpture Soc, 75; Bronze Casting Award, Pen & Brush Ann, Joel Meisner Foundry, 81. *Mem:* Nat Sculpture Soc (fel); Catherine Lorillard Wolfe Club; Allied Artists Am. *Media:* Bronze. *Mailing Add:* 68 Homestead Rd Tenafly NJ 07670-1109

ADELMAN, DOROTHY (LEE) MCCLINTOCK
PRINTMAKER, INSTRUCTOR
b New York, NY. *Study:* Art Students League, with Roberto Delamonico & Michael Ponce de Leon; with Ruth Bamberger, Paris & Jerusalem; Silvermine Guild Artists, Inc, New Canaan, Conn. *Work:* Nat Mus Am Art, Smithsonian Inst; Hudson River Mus; Beneficial Life Insurance Co; Int Bus Machines; Sears Roebuck. *Exhib:* Katonah Mus; Hudson River Mus; 2nd NH Int Graphic Ann; Nat Arts Club, Juried Show NY; Knickerbocker Artist Juried Exhib, NY. *Teaching:* Instr painting, Am Red Cross, White Plains, 71 & Westchester Art Workshop, 71-82; instr, Elizabeth Seton Col, Yonkers, NY; E Seton Col, Yonkers, NY, 76. *Awards:* Purchase Award, Westchester Art Workshop, 69 & Hudson River Mus, 71; First & Third Award, Mamaroneck Artist Guild, 72; First Award, Westchester Art Soc, 73 & 75. *Bibliog:* Leslie Doo (auth), Int Artist, Architect Engineer, pro of Art. *Mem:* Art Students League; Mamaroneck Artists Guild; Abraxas Art Group; Coun Mem Katonah Mus Katonah, NY. *Media:* Intaglio, Printing. *Publ:* Illusr, Spot Lite Mag, 5/86. *Dealer:* Sound Shore Gallery Inc Port Chester NY; Art Search New York Hastings-on-Hudson NY 10106. *Mailing Add:* 90 Ringgold St Apt 5109 Peekskill NY 10566-3321

ADICKES, DAVID (PRYOR)
PAINTER, SCULPTOR
b Huntsville, Tex, Jan 19, 27. *Study:* Kansas City Art Inst, 48; Sam Houston Univ, Huntsville, Tex, BS, 48; Atelier Fernand Leger, Paris, 48-50. *Work:* Houston Mus Fine Art, Tex; Pa Acad Fine Art, Philadelphia; James A Michener Found Mus, Univ Tex, Austin; Witte Mus Art, San Antonio; World Bank, NY. *Comn:* Permian Basin (tapestry), Petroleum Club, Houston, 61; Spring Trees (tapestry), Hyatt Regency Hotel, Houston, 69; Virtuoso (sculpture monument), Lyric Ctr Bldg, Houston, 83; Pres George Bush (bronze sculpture), Tex A&M Univ, College Station, 92; Sam Houston Monument, Huntsville, Tex, 94. *Exhib:* One-man shows, Mus Fine Art, Houston, 51, New Works, Witte Mus Art, San Antonio, 57 & Laguna Gloria Art Mus, Austin, 57; retrospective, Ft Worth Art Ctr, 66. *Teaching:* Instr painting, Univ Tex, Austin, 55-57. *Awards:* First Purchase Prize, Houston Artists, Contemp Arts Asn, 54; First Purchase Prize, Houston Artists Ann, Mus Fine Arts, Houston, 55; Purchase Prize, Texas Art, DD Feldman, Dallas, 57. *Bibliog:* Campbell Geeslin (auth), Adickes (monograph), James Bute Co, 57; A Cantey (auth), Adickes (monograph), 62 & James A Michener (auth), Adickes, 68, Seix y Barral, Barcelona; Dr Linda Wiley (auth), Making It Happen, Wiley Publ, Huntsville, Tex. *Media:* Oil, Bronze, Portland Cement. *Publ:* Illusr, El Centauro, Seix Barral, 67 & illusr, Ingenioso Caballero Don Quixote de la Mancha: Cervantes, 68. *Dealer:* David Adickes Sculpture Works 2500 Summer St Houston TX 77007. *Mailing Add:* 2409 Kingston St Houston TX 77019

ADKINS, TERRY R
SCULPTOR
b Washington, DC, May 9, 53. *Study:* Fisk Univ, BS, 75; Ill State Univ, MS (printmaking), 77 & Univ Ky, MFA (sculpture), 79. *Work:* Metrop Mus Art, NY; High Mus Art, Atlanta; Hirschhorn Mus & Sculpture Garden, Washington, DC; Washington Post Collection, Washington, DC; TimeBased Media (video archives), Amsterdam, Neth; Blanton Mus Art, Austin, Tex. *Comn:* Percent for Art Program, New York Dept Cult Affairs, Harlem Encore, NY Metropolitian Transportation Authority. *Exhib:* Portfolio, Va Mus Fine Arts, Richmond, 80; Experiments in Paper, Va Mus Fine Arts, Richmond, 83; solo exhibs, Projekt Binz 39, Zurich, Switz, 86, Galerie Emmerich-Baumann, Zurich, Switz, 87, Liz Harris Gallery, Boston, Mass, 88, Galerie Andy Jilien, Zurich, Switz, 89, Miami-Dade Community Col, Fla, 90, Valencia Community Col, Orlando, Fla, 90 & Anderson Gallery, Va Commonwealth Univ, Richmond, 90; Hammonds House Gallery, Atlanta, 95; Other Bloods, Mus Arti Et Amicitiae, Amsterdam, 95; Whitney Mus Am Art, 95; Seamless Robe, William Benton Mus, Stoles, Conn, 97; Material Dialogues, NJ State Mus, Trenton, 97; Later Colefrain, Hamilton Col, Clinton, NY, 98; Muffled Drums, PPOW Gallery, NY, 98; Invisible (slight return), Watermark Cargo Gallery, Kingston, NY, 99; Inst Contemp Art, Phildelphia, 99; Wild Ashes Mute, Finesilver Gallery, San Antonio, 2000; Deeper Still, Harn Mus, Gainsville, Fla, 2001; and many others. *Pos:* Artist-in-residence, Kenkeleba House, NY, 88-89, Koprod, Zurich, Switz, 89. *Teaching:* Asst prof, State Univ NY, New Paltz, 93-96, assoc prof, 96-2000; Assoc prof fine arts, Univ Pa, 2000. *Awards:* Artists Fel, Sculpture, Nat Endowment Arts, 86; Fel, Joan Mitchell Found, 94; Perspectives African Am Art Award, NY Found Arts, 96. *Bibliog:* Peggy Cyphers (auth), New York in review, Arts Mag, 1/90; Carl Hazelwood (auth), Genealogy of Objects, NKAJ Contemp African Art, 97; Barry Schwabsky (auth), Assembling Pieces with a Surprise Quotient, NY Times, 98; Joannas Kover (auth), Through Coletrain - Shape & Sound, Observed Dispatch, 98; Edward J Suzanski (auth), At ICA Review of Relay, Art Papers, 2000. *Media:* Wood, Metal. *Publ:* Auth, Eagle Eyed: The Ethereal Vision of Joseph Egan (catalog), Kunstraum Muchen, Munich, Ger. *Mailing Add:* 383 Grand Ave Brooklyn NY 11238-2405

ADKISON, KATHLEEN (GEMBERLING)
PAINTER
b Beatrice, Nebr. *Study:* With Mark Tobey. *Work:* Seattle Art Mus; Seattle First Nat Bank; Bank Wash, Tacoma & Spokane; Butler Inst Am Art, Youngstown, Ohio; Cheney Cowles Mus, Spokane; Northwest Bell & Boeing, Seattle. *Exhib:* Butler Inst Am Art Ann, 61-69; World's Fair Northwest Artists, Seattle, 62 & 74; Pa Acad Fine Arts 159th Ann, 64; one-person shows, Univ Wash Mus Art, Pullman, 76, Univ Ore Mus Art, Eugene, 77, Wash State Art Mus, Olympia, 77 & Bellevue Art Mus, Wash, 81; Spokane World's Fair Expo 74 Northwest Art, Wash; and others. *Teaching:* Instr painting, Wash State Univ Exten, 55-67. *Awards:* Sun Carnival First Prize, El Paso Mus, 61; Dr Fuller Purchase Award, Northwest Ann, 61; Prize for Winter Retreat, Friends Am Art, 69. *Bibliog:* Twenty five years painting, Bellevue Art Mus, Wash, 81. *Media:* Oil. *Dealer:* Gordon Woodside Gallery 1101 Howell Seattle WA 98101. *Mailing Add:* 1397 Honeysuckle Ave Ventura CA 93004-3579

ADLER, LEE
PAINTER, PRINTMAKER
b New York, NY, June 22, 1934. *Study:* Art Students League, 62-64; Brooklyn Mus Art Sch, 64-65; Pratt Graphics Ctr, New York, 69. *Work:* Metrop Mus Art, NY; Brit Mus, London; Whitney Mus Am Art, NY; Art Inst Chicago; Corcoran Gallery Art, Washington, DC. *Comn:* Graham Gallery, NY, 70; Book-of-the-Month Club, 73; NY Times-Quadrangle Books, 73; Hagley Mus, Wilmington, Del, 74. *Exhib:* Butler Inst Am Art, Youngstown, Ohio, 67, 68 & 77; Nat Acad Design, NY, 69; 17th Nat Print Biennial, Brooklyn Mus, 70; Print Acquisitions, Whitney Mus Art, 70; Mint Mus Art, Charlotte, NC, 78; Weatherspoon Art Gallery, Univ NC, Greensboro, 78; Aldrich Mus Contemp Art, Ridgefield, Conn, 79; Edwin A Ulrich Mus Art, Wichita, Kans, 80; Nat Mus Art, New Delhi, 82; Mus Mod Art, Mexico City, 83. *Collection Arranged:*

Metropolitan Mus Art, NYC; Whitney Mus Am Art, NYC; Brooklyn Mus, NY; British Mus, London; Art Institute Chicago; Corcoran Gallery Art, Washington, DC; Cincinnati Art Mus; Grey Art Gallery & Study Ctr, NYU; Butler Institute Am Art, Youngstown, Ohio; Andrew Dickson White Mus Art, Cornell Univ, Ithaca, NY; Jersey City Mus; Ithaca Mus Art; Syracuse Univ Art Mus, NY; NYCC, Brooklyn; DeCordova Mus, Lincoln, Mass; Federico Castellon Memorial Print Collection, Teachers Col, Columbia Univ, NYC; Indianapolis Mus Art; Albion Col, Mich; Seattle Art Mus; Fogg Art Mus, Harvard Univ, Cambridge, Mass; Hagley Mus, Wilmington, Del; Municipal Art Gallery, Dublin, Eire; Mus Modern Art, Sao Paulo, Brazil; Del Art Mus, Wilmington; Mus Fine Art, Montreal, Quebec; Auckland Art Mus, New Zealand; Fairleigh Dickinson Univ, Madison, NJ; Long Island Univ, Brooklyn; Printmaker's Workshop Collection, NYC; Edwin A Ulrich Mus Art, Wichita State Univ, Kans; Aldrich Mus Contemporary Art, Ridgefield, Conn; Colgate Univ, Picker Art Gallery, Hamilton, NY; Philadelphia Mus Art; Munson-Williams-Proctor Institute, Utica, NY; Nat Academy Health & Safety, Bureau of Mines, Beckley, WVa; NY Public Library; Detroit Institute Art; Mus Contemporary Art, Sao Paulo; Art Gallery of Ontario, Toronto, Canada; Mint Mus Art, Charlotte, NC; Farmington Valley Art Ctr, Avon, Conn; US Int Communications Agency, Washignton, DC; Housatonic Mus Art, Bridgeport, Conn; Weatherspoon Art Gallery, Univ NC, Greensboro; Lyman Allyn Mus, New London, Conn; Municipal Gallery and Mus Modern Art, Udine, Italy; Instituto de Cultura Hispanica, Madrid, Spain; Neuberger Mus, SUNY, Purchase. *Awards:* Grumbacher Award, Jersey City Mus, 68; Purchase Award, Childe Hassam Fund Competition, 69; Federico Castellon Purchase Award, Soc Am Graphic Artists, 79. *Bibliog:* Juan Acha (auth), Lee Adler, Mexico City Mus Mod Art, 76; Jeffrey Hoffeld (auth), Lee Adler, New York, 78; Carlus Dyer (auth), Lee Adler, Arts, 10/78. *Mem:* Soc Am Graphic Artists; Audubon Artists; Allied Artists Am; Painters & Sculptors Soc NJ. *Media:* Oil, Silk Screen Printing. *Dealer:* Allan Stone Gallery 48 E 86th St New York NY 10028. *Mailing Add:* Lime Kiln Farm Climax NY 12042

ADLER, MYRIL
PAINTER, PRINTMAKER

b Vitebsk, Belarus, Sept 22, 20: US citizen. *Study:* Brooklyn Mus Art Sch; Art Students League; Theatre Arts Workshop, NY, with Moi Solotaroff; Pratt Graphics Ctr, 60-64; Mobile Puppet Theatre Social Commentary, NYC, 60-64; Yale Joel Photog Workshop, 65, Computer Generated Imagery via Printmaking, Pratt Ctr, 82. *Work:* NY Pub Libr, Hudson River Mus, Yonkers, NY; Mus Mod Art, Caracas, Venezuela; Univ Calif, Berkeley; Univ RI, Providence; and others. *Comn:* 50 Yrs/50 Faces: 50 Yr Portrait Retrospective (painting, drawing, printmaking), Fine Art Gallery, Westchester Community Col, 91. *Exhib:* Gallerie Berneim Jeune, Paris, 50; Csa Municipale, Merano, Italy, 52; One-person shows, Westbroadway Gallery, NY, 72, 74 & 76, Hudson River Mus, Yonkers, 72 & 74, Katonah Mus Art Gallery, NY, 72, 76 & 80, Ossining Pub Libr, Ossining, NY, 90 & Royal Athena Gallery, NY; High Tech/High Touch: Computer Graphics Printmaking, Pratt Manhattan Gallery, NY, 87; Rubelle & Norman Schafer Gallery, Pratt Inst, Brooklyn, 89; Javitz Ctr, NY, 90; Myths & Mysteries, Temple Israel Northern Westchester, Croton, NY, 93; 30 yr retrospective printmaking, Katonah Libr Gallery, NY, 94; all media, incl puppets, Ossining Arts Coun Gallery 60-Yr Retrospective, 1996; monotype portraits of NY homeless, Articoli Fine Arts, 1999; Ava Fine Arts, White Plains, NY, 2000; Working with Technol, Gallery on the Hudson, Irvington, NY, 2001; Mus Gallery, Univ Colo, Boulder, 44. *Pos:* Dir, Myril Adler Arts Workshop, Briarcliff Manor, NY, 56-; artist-in-residence, Pratt Graphics Ctr, NY, 82-86. *Teaching:* Myril Adler Arts Workshop, 56-; printmaking, Pratt Graphics Ctr, NY, 82-86; various comprehensive art programs. *Awards:* Purchase Award, Hudson River Mus, Yonkers, NY; 100th Ann Award, Nat Asn Women Artists; Abel Silvan Mem Award for Printmaking, 83; Hortense Ferne Mem Award, 89. *Bibliog:* Norman Laliberte & Alex Mogelon (coauths), The Reinhold Book of Art Ideas, Van Nostrand Reinhold, 77; coauth, The Complete Printmaker, Ross, Romand & Ross, Free Press-Macmillan, 90; Jules Heller (auth), Encyclopedia of American Woman Artists, 95; collage, montage assemblage, Laliberte & Mogelon (auths), Demonstrations, Van Nostrand Reinhold. *Mem:* Artists Equity, NY; Nat Asn Women Artists; Abraxas Artists Group (secy, treas). *Media:* Oil; Mixed Media; Intaglio Etching, Monoprinting; Xerox Collages; Multimedia Computer-Generated Works. *Res:* Computer-generated images via photography, etching, silk screen, lithography. *Specialty:* Visual arts in all media from classical to contemporary. *Interests:* Reading, cooking, world travel, gardening. *Publ:* Illusr, Dances of Palestine, B'Nai B'Rith Hillel Foundations, New York, 47. *Dealer:* Images Art Gallery Inc 1157 Pleasantville Rd Briarcliff Manor NY 10510; artsnet.net. *Mailing Add:* 266 Dalmeny Rd Briarcliff Manor NY 10510

ADLER, TRACY L
CURATOR, EDUCATOR

b New York, NY, Apr 5, 68. *Study:* Skidmore Col, BA (art hist) with Prof Harry Gaugh, 90; Hunter Col, CUNY, MA (art hist) with Prof William C Agee, 96. *Collection Arranged:* After Rabin: New Art from Isreal, 99; Giulio Romano: Master Designer, 99; Remnant, 2001; Exotic Representation, 2002; Strange Worlds, 2003; Off the Wall, 2005; and others. *Pos:* dept asst, Dept Prints & Photogs, Metrop Mus Art, NY, 91-92; admin asst, BlumHelman Gallery, NY, 92-93; studio mgr, Shonna Valeska Photog, NY, 94-97; exhib asst, The Jewish Mus, NY, 97-98; cur, Hunter Col Art Galleries, NY, 98-; consultant, Adler Arts, 2003-. *Bibliog:* Sari Carel (auth), Critic's Picks, Off the Wall, Artforum, 2005; Tania Dudina (auth), The Secret Treasure of Hunter College, Hunter Envoy, 2005; John Ewing (auth), Off the Wall, Modern Painters, 2005. *Mem:* New Leadership Associates, Arttable; Am Asn Mus. *Publ:* auth, I wanna tell you something: Omer Fast, Gb Agency, Paris, 2002; auth, Strange Worlds, Hunter Col, NY, 2003; ed, Tracing Tony Smith's Tau, Hunter Col, NY, 2004; contribr, Seeing Red: On Nonobjective Painting & Color Theory, Salon Verlag, Cologne, Ger, 2004; auth, Off the Wall, Hunter Col, NY, 2005. *Mailing Add:* 695 Park Ave New York NY 10021

ADRIAN, BARBARA TRAMUTOLA
PAINTER, COLLECTOR

b New York, NY, July 25, 1931. *Study:* Art Students League, with Reginald Marsh, 47-54; Hunter Col, 51; Columbia Univ, 52-54. *Work:* City Hall, San Juan, PR; Nat Acad Design; Ark Arts Ctr; So Alleghenies Mus Art, Lorreto, Pa; Philamonic Ctr for Arts, Naples, Fla; The Century Asn, NYC. *Exhib:* Butler Inst Am Art, 70; Suffolk Mus, Stony Brook, NY, 71; Whitney Mus, 75; Ranger Fund Exhib, Nat Acad Design, 81; Women in the Making of Art Hist, Art Students League, NY, 82; Seventh Ann Nat Invitational Drawing Exhib, Norman Eprink Gallery, Emporia State Univ, & Univ Kans; Art and the Law, five locations, 86; Nat Acad Design, New York City, 90, 2003-04; Century Asn, New York City, 2003-04. *Pos:* Art consult, R H Macy, NY, 60-61; Saks Fifth Ave, NY, 60; Doyle Dane & Bernbach, NY, 60. *Teaching:* Art instr painting & drawing, Art Student League, 68-. *Awards:* Dorothy Haphman Ferriss Award, Pen & Brush, 83 & Walker Award, 85; Forbes Award, 1990; Cert Merit, Nat Acad Design, 95; Richard H Recchia Meml Prize, 2001; Nat Acad Design, NYC, 2002. *Bibliog:* Painting Techniques, Comprehensive Treatise, 81; Am Artists, 9/90; Maine Bar J Cover, 9/90. *Mem:* Life mem Art Students League; Nat Acad Design; Century Asn. *Media:* Oil, Egg Tempera. *Collection:* Reginald Marsh, John Sloan, Will Barnet, Henry Pearson, Rouault, Versalius, Goya, Martin Lewis. *Publ:* Auth, Art as Image and Ideas, Feldman Publ. *Dealer:* Harmon-Meek Gallery 386 Broad Ave S Naples FL 34102; Gerald Peters Gallery Santa Fe NM. *Mailing Add:* 420 E 64th St New York NY 10021

AEBI, ERNST WALTER
ILLUSTRATOR, PAINTER

b Zurich, Switz, Mar 25, 1938; US citizen. *Study:* Zurich Univ, lic oec publ, 65. *Work:* Montclair Mus & Kasser Found, Montclair, NJ; Adriance Mus, Westchester, NY; Klimastation, Gais, Switz. *Comn:* Roosevelt Raceway (mural in lobby), NY Racing Comn, Long Island, 70; sculpture, Swiss Am Soc, NY, 70; sculpture, Sandoz Inc, Hanover NJ, 74. *Exhib:* NY Artists, Southampton Parrish Mus, 66; Community Art, Brooklyn Mus, 68; Contemp Swiss Art, Prague State Mus, Czech, 69; Biennale Europeenne, Berheim-Jeune, Paris, 69; one-man show, NY Univ, 76. *Collection Arranged:* One Trillion People Falling Off the Edge of the Earth, James Yu, New York, 77. *Pos:* Illusr, New York Times & Harpers Mag, 76-79, Harvard Bus Rev & Times Mag, 77. *Teaching:* Illusr, New York Times & Harpers Mag, 76-79, Harvard Bus Rev & Times Mag, 77. *Bibliog:* Henry J Seldis (auth), Phantasmagoria, Los Angeles Times, 66; Malcolm Preston (auth), The world of Ernst Aebi, Newsday, 70; Stuart Murray (auth), The restless artist, New York Times, 74. *Media:* Pen and Ink; Concrete. *Publ:* Auth, Seasons of Sand, Simon & Schuster, 93. *Dealer:* James Yu 393 W Broadway New York NY 10012. *Mailing Add:* 460 W Broadway New York NY 10012-5311

AFSARY, CYRUS
PAINTER

b Middle East, Oct 18, 40; US citizen. *Study:* Liberal Arts Col, BA(fine arts) & BA(interior design), 70. *Comn:* Murals & portraits, MGM Grand Hotel, Las Vegas, Nev, 81. *Exhib:* C M Russell Show & Auction, C M Russell Mus, Great Falls, Mont, 84-86; Gilcrease Mus Show, Tulsa, Okla, 85; Southwest Fine Art Competition, Mus Fine Arts, Santa Fe, NMex, 85; Northwest Rendevous Show, Helena, Mont, 85-88; Nat Acad Western Art, Cowboy Hall Fame, Oklahoma City, Okla, 86-88. *Awards:* Nat Arts Club Award Exceptional Merit, Pastel Soc Am, 86; Gold Medal in Oil, 87 & Robert Lougheed Mem Award, 88; Gold Medal Oil Painting & Silver Medal Drawing, Nat Acad Western Art, 86; and others. *Mem:* Nat Acad Western Art Northwest Rendezvous. *Media:* Oil, Pastel. *Publ:* Southwest Art, 1/87; Art of the West, 11-12/88; Int Fine Arts Collectors Mag, 3/92. *Mailing Add:* PO Box 3217 Scottsdale AZ 85271

AGAR, EUNICE JANE
PAINTER, WRITER

b Great Barrington, Mass, May 14, 1934. *Study:* Wellesley Col Mass, BA (art hist), 56; Art Students League, 57-60 & 69, study under Jean Liberte, 57-63. *Work:* Columbia-Greene Community Col, Hudson, NY; Le Moyne Art Found, Tallahassee, Fla; Bates Col Mus Art; Columbia Greene Community Col, Hudson, NY; LeMoyne Art Ctr, Tallahassee, Fla. *Comn:* Private Commissions. *Exhib:* One-woman shows, Le Moyne Art Ctr, Tallahassee, Fla, 66, 91 & 96, Albany Inst Hist & Art, NY, 67, Ainilian Gallery, Washington, 85, 87, & 90, Windham Gallery, NY, 86, Columbia-Greene Community Col, Hudson, NY, 88; Dunedin Fine Arts Ctr, Fla, 91; Denise Bibro Fine Art, NY, 95, 98, 99, 2002, 2004; Univ Maine, Machias, 99-2004; Becket Art Ctr, MA, 2000. *Collection Arranged:* Monotypes, The Painterly Print, Catskill Gallery, Catskill, NY, NY State Coun Arts, 86. *Pos:* Asst ed, Am Artist, NY, 58-60, managing ed, 60-63, writer, 80-, contrib ed, 83-. *Teaching:* Instr painting, drawing & printmaking, Simon's Rock Early Col, 69-78, chmn studio arts, 74-78, chmn arts div & studio arts, 75-78. *Bibliog:* Article, Am Artist, 2/84; article, Tallahassee Mag, 4/91; article, The Artful Mind, 3/2000. *Mem:* Life mem Art Students League New York. *Media:* Oil, Casein, Watercolor, All drawing Media. *Specialty:* Representational landscapes, genre figurative painting. *Collection:* Private Collectors. *Publ:* Interview articles, Am Artist. *Dealer:* Denise Bibro Fine Art 584 Broadway New York NY 10012; Yvonne Rapp 2007 Frankfort Ave Louisville KY 40206. *Mailing Add:* 20 Egremont Plain Rd Great Barrington MA 01230

AGEE, ANN G
SCULPTOR, PAINTER

b Philadelphia, Pa, Apr 19, 59. *Study:* Cooper Union Sch Art, New York, BFA(painting), 81; Yale Sch Art, Yale Univ, MFA, 86. *Comn:* men's room, John Micheal Kohler Arts Ctr, Sheboygan, Wis, 98; lobby, Pub Sch 137, Queens, NY, in process. *Exhib:* Solo exhibs, Ann Nathan Gallery, Chicago, 91, John Michael Kohler Art Ctr, Sheboygan, Wis, 93, Arena Gallery, Brooklyn, NY, 94 & Yoshii Gallery, NY,

96 & Rena Bransten Gallery, San Francisco, 98, 2000, PPOW, New York City, 2001; Domestic Exceptions, Elsa Mott Ives Gallery, NY, 96; Douglas Udell Gallery, Vancouver, 96; Millennium Eve Dress, Fabric Workshop, Philadelphia, 96; Eccentricities, Judy Ann Goldman Fine Art at Beth Urdang Gallery, Boston, Mass, 96; Working in the 90's, Col Mainland, Tex City, 96; Domestic Exceptions, Elsa Mott Ives Gallery, NY, 96; Group Exhibition, Douglas Udell Gallery, Vancouver, 96; Codpiece, Griffin Linton, Contemp Exhib, Los Angeles, Calif, 97; Ornament and Landscape: on the Nature of Artifice, Apex Gallery, NY, 97; Felissimo NYFA Design Award Show, Felissimo, NY, 97; The Art Exchange Show, Arena Gallery, NY, 97; Figuring Women's Lives, Kingsborough Community Col Art Gallery, Brooklyn, NY, 97; Pool, Rena Bransten Gallery, San Francisco, Calif, 97; Ordinary/Extradinary, Johnson Co Community Col Art, Kansas City, Mo, 98; Domestic Transformations/Working in Brooklyn, Brooklyn Mus Art, NY, 98-99; Portrait of Our Time II, Revolution, Ferndale, Mich, 99; Pattern, James Graham and Sons, New York City, 99; The Erotic Life of Clay: Sex Pots, Fine Arts Gallery, San Francisco State Univ, 02. *Awards:* Fel, Nat Endowment Arts, 89, 92 & 93; Design Award, Felissimo, NY Found Arts, 97; Tiffany Found Grant, 98. *Bibliog:* Shawn Hill (auth), The body as battlefield, Bay Windows, 2/29/96; Cate McQuaid (auth), Eccentricities' nicely mixes it up, Boston Globe, 3/14/96; Roger Green (auth), Chicago Expo's world acclaim grows, Ann Arbor News, 5/26/96. *Publ:* Auth, Art in a factory, Ceramics Monthly, 10/92; Welcome to the Doll House, NY Times Mag, 12/26/99. *Dealer:* Rena Bransten Gallery 77 Geary St San Francisco CA. *Mailing Add:* 373 DeGraw St Brooklyn NY 11231

AGEE, WILLIAM C
EDUCATOR, HISTORIAN
b New York, NY, Sept 26, 36. *Study:* Princeton Univ, AB, 60; Yale Univ, MA, 63. *Collection Arranged:* Synchromism and American Painting (auth, catalog), 65; Donald Judd (auth, catalog), 68; Modern American Painting: Toward a New Perspective (auth, catalog), 77; Patrick Henry Bruce (auth, catalog), 79; Morton Livingston Schamberg (auth, catalog), 82. *Pos:* Dir, Mus Fine Arts, Houston, 74-82; sr vis scholar, Arch Am Art, Smithsonian Inst, 83-85; ed, Stuart Davis Catalogue Raisonné, 85-; prof art hist, Hunter Col, 90-. *Teaching:* Am Modernism, Hurto Col, 87 & 89. *Mem:* Am Asn Mus; Col Art Asn. *Res:* Modern American and European art. *Publ:* Auth, Ralston Crawford, Twelve Trees Press, 83; Herbert Ferber, Mus Fine Arts, Houston, 83; The Advent of Modernism, High Mus, Atlanta, 86. *Mailing Add:* 157 Alta Ave Yonkers NY 10705-1414

AGID, LUCY BRADANOVIC
SCULPTOR
b San Pedro, Calif, May 5, 29. *Study:* Otis Art, 55. *Work:* Mus Deio Bozzetti, Pietrasanta, Italy; Mus Storico della Resistenza Sant'Anna, Italy; Braille Inst, Los Angeles, Calif; City of Torrance, Calif; Warner Brothers; Univ of Loyola; Marymount Col; and others. *Exhib:* Loyola Marymount Univ, Laband Gallery, Los Angeles, 89; Woman Artist of West, Visalia, Calif, 91; Hands on Exhib, Braille Inst, Los Angeles, 93; Rise & Fall of Man, Fed Bldg, NY, 93; Dance of Life, Mus Deio Bozzetti, Italy, 94; Calif Art Gallery, 99; Marymount Univ, 2000; Univ of Loyola, 2002; many others. *Teaching:* lectr on sculpture, Palos Verdes Art. *Awards:* Madonna Festival, Nat Competition, Wilshire Ebel; Susman Award, Pen & Brush, NY, 1st Place Sculpture Award; First Place, Palos Verdes Art Show, 96; Millard Sheets Gallery award; LA Co Fair Award, 2002. *Bibliog:* Marcia Forsberg (auth), Inspired by Italian Marble, Quadrifoglia; Day with the Artist (film), Torrance Cable, City of Torrance. *Mem:* Nowa NY. *Media:* Marble, Granite, Bronze. *Dealer:* Starry Sheets 1590 S Coast Hwy Laguna Beach CA 92651; Herb Agid Gallery; Leica Art@Verizon.net. *Mailing Add:* 60 Portuguese Bend Rd Rolling Hills CA 90274

AGNEW, ELLEN SCHALL
DIRECTOR
b Pensacola, Fla, Feb 19, 58. *Study:* Randolph-Macon Woman's Col, BA (cum laude), 80; State Univ NY, Binghamton, MA (art hist), 83. *Exhib:* 83d Ann Exhib, Joan Mitchell, 93; The Art of Zelda Fitzgerald: Alice in Wonderland and other Fairy Tales, Maier Mus of Art, 98; 88th Ann Exhib, Louise Bourgeois Prints: 1989-1998, 99, Cleveland Ctr for Contemp Art and Minneapolis Inst of Arts; Fairy Tales, Portrait Paintings by Elena Sisto, Maier Mus Art, 99; Old Dreams, New Dreams: Works by Kathy and Jim Muehlemann, Maier Mus Art, 99; Diana Michener Photographs, with Kathy Muehlemann, Maier Mus Art, 2000; 91st Ann Exhib, Drawing the Line: A Retrospective of Drawings by Brice Marden, 2001; 93d Ann Exhib, A Bend in the Road: Paintings and Works on Paper by Jane Berthot, Philip Guston, Bill Jensen, Pat Passlof, Milton Renick, and Myron Stout, 2003; 94th Ann Exhib, Documenting Poetry: Contemp Latin Am Photog; and many others. *Collection Arranged:* A Celebration of Contemporary American Craft, 85; Artists on Our Wish List, 86; Prints by Our Painters, 88; Focus on Photography, 91; Jennifer Bartlett, 92. *Pos:* Asst registrar, The Chrysler Mus, Norfolk, VA, 81; Cur, Maier Mus Art, Lynchburg, VA, 84-88, dir 88-95, assoc dir 95-98, interim dir 98-99, assoc dir 99-. *Bibliog:* John Wilmerding and David Sokol (coauth) American Art: American Visions, Paintings from a Century of Collecting (exhib catalog), 90; The Art of Zelda Fitzgerald: Alice in Wonderland and Other Fairy Tales, (exhib catalog), Maier Mus of Art, 98; plus others. *Mem:* Southeastern Mus Conf; Am Asn Mus; Va Comn Arts (adv panel 89-90); Va Asn Mus (sec exec coun 89-90 & dir-at-large 91-92). *Publ:* Ed, Maier Mus of Art Newsletter, 84-; The Creative Spirit: A Celebration of Contemporary American Craft (exhib catalog), 85; 75 Years of American Art at Randolph-Macon Woman's College (exhib catalog), 86; The Art Collection on Tour, Randolph-Macon Woman's Col Alumnae Bull, 90; American Art: American Vision, Maier Mus Art, 90; Diana Michener Photographs (catalog), Lynchburg: Maier Mus of Art, 2000; plus others. *Mailing Add:* Assoc Dir - The Maier Mus Randolph-Macon Woman's Col 2500 Rivermont Ave Lynchburg VA 24503

AGUILERA, ALEJANDRO
SCULPTOR
b Holguin, Cuba, May 3, 64. *Study:* Escuela Provincial de Arte, Holguin, Cuba, BA, 83; Inst Superior de Arte, La Habana, higher educ, 88; Mass Col Art, MA, 90. *Work:* Mus Nac de Bellas Artes & Centro de DeSarrollo de las Artes Visuales, Havana, Cuba; Peter Ludwig Museo de Aachen, Ger; Marco & Ramis Barquet, Monterrey, Mex. *Exhib:* Colonizacion y Descolonizacion, Mus Nac de Bellas Artes, Havana, Cuba, 91; 15 Artistas Cubanos, Ninart, Centro de Cultura, Mex, 91; Nuevas Adquisiciones Contemporaneas, Mus Nac de Bellas Artes, Havana, Cuba, 91; Forum Int Arte, Colecion Peter Ludwig, Cologne, 91; Cuba Construye, Euskal Fonda Bilbao, 91; solo exhib, Jos buenos y los malos, Galería Ramos Barquet, Monterrey, Mexico. *Teaching:* Prof sculpture, Inst Superior del Arte, 89-91. *Awards:* Critics Award, Sci Student Journey, High Inst Art, 89. *Bibliog:* Antonio E Tonel (auth), Cuba OK, Stadische Kunstalle, 90; Edward Sullivan (auth), Los Buenos y Los Malos, Galeria Ramis Barquet, 92; Luis Camnitzer (auth), New Art of Cuba, Univ Tex Press, 94. *Media:* All Media. *Dealer:* Ave Real San Agustin No 304 L-2B Residencial San Agustin Garza Garcia N L Mexico 66260. *Mailing Add:* E/T Guarez y Morelos Ave Vasconcelos No 116-10 San Pedro Garza Garcia Monterrey 66200 Mexico

AGUSTIN, HERNANDEZ
ARCHITECT, SCULPTOR
b Mexico City, Mex, Feb 29, 24. *Study:* Escuela Nac De Arquitectura UNAM, Archit, 54; Modern Art Cult Ctr, hons, 54. *Hon Degrees:* Professor International Academy of Architecture, 2001; National Prize of Science and Art, 2004. *Exhib:* Pratt Inst NY, 83; Int Bauausstellung, Berlin, Ger, 84; Miami Univ, 92; Houston Univ, 93; one-man show, Mus De Monterrey, Nuevo Leon, Mex, 94. *Pos:* Chief design comt, Fed Prog Sch Construction, 54-55; dir, Praxis Interdisciplinary Group Design, Mexico City, Mex, 78-. *Teaching:* Prof, Nat Sch Archit, UNAM, 57-68 & dir design, Atelier Sch Archit, 65-68; Design Atelier Chief at the Northern Anahuac Univ, Mex, 1994-. *Awards:* First Prize Gold Medal, II Biennal De Mex, 92; First Prize, Lifetime Professional Achievement Award Federation of the Mexico Republic, Architects Col, 96; Silver Medal, International Trienal of Architecture, Sophia Bulgary, 97; National Prize of Architecture, 98. *Bibliog:* Ministerio de la Vivienda Arquitect, Actual de las Am, 65; Archit Record, 90; Antonio Toca (auth), Mex Nueva Arquitetura, G Dgili, 91. *Mem:* Mex Soc Archits SAM; Mex Acad Archit; acad emer mem Nat Acad Archit; hon mem Nat Col Engineers & Archit; Arts Acad Mex. *Publ:* Contribr, Search for identity, Pratt Inst, 83; auth, Gravedad, Geometria Y Simbolismo, UNAM, 89; coauth, Agustin Hernandez, Arquitectura Y Pensamiento, Louise Noelle, UNAM, 89; Archit Dig, 90; Arquitectura De Agustin Fernandez, Noriega Editores, 94. *Mailing Add:* Bosque de Acacias 61 Bosques De Las Lomas Mexico 117 00 Mexico

AHART, SHOSHANNA MARIE
PAINTER
b Tiffin, Ohio, Mar 3, 62. *Study:* Marietta Col, Ohio, BA (art, hons art), 84; Am Univ, Washington, with Wayne Theibaud, Nathan Oliveira & Charles Cajori, MFA (painting), 90. *Work:* The Watkins Collection, Am Univ, Quadrangle Develop Corp, Washington; and others. *Comn:* Andrews Hall (commemorative print), Marietta Col, Ohio, 93. *Exhib:* S Ahart & B Gillespie: Fels of NFAA Career Advan of Visual Artists Prog, Ground Level Gallery, S Fla Art ctr, Miami Beach, 94; solo exhib, Herman Fine Arts Ctr, Marietta, Ohio, 92; 7th Ann Women in the Visual Arts Exhib, Erector Sq Gallery, New Haven, Conn, 93; Am Painters, Oberpfalzer Kunstlerhaus, Schwandorf, Ger, 95; Architects Art Apart V, Gallery Contemp, Jacksonville, Fla, 96. *Pos:* Graphic designer, Pyramid Paper Co, Urbana, Ill, 84-87; freelance designer, 92-; guest lectr, Nat Bldg Mus, Washington, 96. *Teaching:* Teaching asst, Art Dept, Am Univ, Washington, 89-90; instr drawing, Continuing Educ Prog, Arlington Co, Va, 91-92. *Awards:* Ludwig Vogelstein Award for Visual Arts, Vogelstein Found, Brooklyn, NY, 91; Career Advan of Visual Artists Fel, Nat Found Advan in Arts, Miami Beach, Fla, 92-94; Oberpfalzer Kunstlerhaus Artist-in-Residence, Va Ctr Creative Arts Int Exchange Fels, 95. *Mem:* Col Art Asn; A Salon Ltd (vpres, 92). *Media:* Oil

AHEARN, JOHN
SCULPTOR
b Binghamton, NY, 1951. *Study:* Cornell Univ, Ithaca, NY, BFA, 73. *Work:* Australian Nat Gallery, Canberra; Metrop Mus, NY; Wallrat-Richartz Mus, Mus Ludwig, Cologne; Lannan Found, Lake Worth, Fla; Eli Broad Family Found, Los Angeles; Greenville Co Art Mus. *Exhib:* One-man exhibs, Contemp Arts Mus, Houston, 91-92, Honolulu Adv Gallery, 92, Washington Proj Arts, 92, Baltimore Mus Art, 93-94 & Douglas F Cooley Mem Art Gallery, Reed Col, Portland, Ore, 93-94, Univ Art Gallery, Univ Calif, San Diego, 95 & Alexander & Bonin, NY, 98, Sculpture from East 100th Street, part II, Alexander and Bonin, NY, 2000, Pan Chiao, Alexander Bonin, NY, 2001; After Street Art, Boca Raton Mus Art, 88; The Future Now, Bass Mus Art, Miami, 89; Personae: Contemp Portraiture & Self-Portraiture, Islip Art Mus, NY, 89; The Blues Aesthetic: Black Cult-Modernism, Traveling, 89. *Awards:* Sculpture Fel, 80 & Art in Pub Places, 82, Nat Endowment Arts; Block Grant, Housing & Urban Development, 81. *Bibliog:* Brigitte Engler (auth), Behind the Mask, Paper, 11/89; Jonathan Phillips (auth), Ahearn at Alexander, Art World, 89; Robert C Morgan (auth), John Ahearn, Arts, 1/89; Suzanne Muchnic (auth), Family Puts Art on a Firm Foundation, Los Angeles Times, 12/5/89. *Mailing Add:* c/o Alexander & Bonin 132 10th Ave New York NY 10011

AHERN, MAUREEN J
MUSEUM DIRECTOR, CURATOR
b Salem, Mass, Oct 7, 47. *Study:* Univ Mass, Amherst, BFA, 69; Metrop Mus Art, courses in museology; State Univ NY, Albany, MA, 74. *Exhib:* Currier Gallery Art, Manchester, NH, 2000; Northfield Mt Herman, Bolger Gallery, Northfield, Mass; The McIninch Art Gallery, Southern New Hampshire Univ, 2002; McQuade Gallery,

Merrimack Col, North Andover, Mass; Library Arts Ctr, 2006; Jaffrey Civic Ctr, 2006. *Collection Arranged:* Native American Neighbors (print, paintings & sculpture), 97; Worldviews (photog), 98; Technics: Bauble of Ballast, 2001; New Hampshire: The State of Art, 2005; Art = Body & Mind, 2006. *Pos:* Art dir, Jewish Community Ctr, Boston, 69-70; cur, Albany Inst Hist & Art, 71-81; dir, Thorne-Sagendorph Art Gallery, Keene State Col, 81-. *Awards:* Grant, Internat Partnership, Amonst Mus. *Mem:* NH Visual Arts Coalition (pres, 87-92); Am Asn Mus; New Eng Mus Asn. *Media:* Acrylic, Silver, Pastel. *Specialty:* Historical and contemp art. *Interests:* travel. *Mailing Add:* Thorne-Sagendorph Art Gallery Keene State Col-Wyman Way Keene NH 03535-3501

AHLANDER, LESLIE JUDD
CRITIC, CONSULTANT
b New York, NY. *Study:* Acad Mod, Paris, with Fernand Leger; Pa Acad Fine Arts, with Henry MacCarter, dipl. *Collection Arranged:* Contemporary Religious Imagery (with catalog), 74; Syd Solomon (with catalog), 75; Doris Leeper (with catalog), 75; Continuing Surrealism (with catalog), 76; Latin Am Horizons (with catalog), 76; The Circus in Art (with catalog), 77; Haitian Art (with catalog), 86. *Pos:* Asst to dir, Mus Mod Art, New York, 41-43; dir exhibs, US Off Educ, Washington, DC, 43-44; chief div visual arts, Pan-Am Union, Washington, DC, 44-45; art critic, Washington Post, Washington, DC, 50-63; cur educ, Corcoran Gallery, Washington, DC, 69-70; from dir educ to cur contemp art, John & Mabel Ringling Mus Art, Sarasota, Fla, 71-78; art coordr, Dade Co, Miami, Fla, 78-83; art critic, Miami News, 83-88; Arte en Colombia, Art Nexus, Art News, 88-. *Awards:* Cresson Traveling Scholar, Pa Acad Fine Arts, Philadelphia, 38; Art Critics Award, Col Art Asn Am, 52 & 53; Lifetime Achievement Award, Fla Art Mus Dirs Asn, 93. *Publ:* Auth, Lynn Gelfman, 85, Trevor Bell, 86 & Hal Kaye, 86; Six Cuban painters, 85; Connie Lloveras (auth), Cuba-USA - The First Generation, 90

AHLGREN, ROY B
PAINTER, PRINTMAKER
b Erie, Pa, July 6, 1927. *Study:* Erie Tech Sch; Univ Pittsburgh, BS Ed. *Work:* US Info Agency, Washington, DC; Minn Mus Art, St Paul; Gornoslaskie Mus, Krakow, Poland; Kanagawa Prefectural Gallery, Yokahama, Japan; Butler Art Inst, Youngstown, Ohio; Mus Wroclaw & Silesia, Poland, 86; Mus Contemp Art, Fredrikstad, Norway; and others; McGraw Hill Corp Collection, Columbus, Ohio; Charles Rand Penney Collection, Mem Art Gallery, Rochester, NY; Pres Gerald Ford, The White House Collection, Washington, D.C. *Comn:* Ed of serigraphs, Asn Am Artists, NY, 70; Int Art Guild, Santa Barbara, 74; serigraphs (54), WQLN, public TV stations, 79. *Exhib:* 21st Nat Exhib Prints, Libr Cong, Washington, DC, 69; 7th, 8th, 10th, 11th & 12th Int Print Biennale, Krakow, Poland; Intergrafia, Katowice, Poland, 78, 80, 84, 86 & 88; Int Exhib Graphic Art, Frechen, Ger, 80; Tokyo Met Mus Art, 85; Norwegian Int Print Biennale, 86; 1st Int Print Biennial Invitational, Maastricht, The Neth, 93; Nat Acad Design, NY, 68, 69, 76, 78, 79; Audubon Artists Ann, Nat Gallery, NY, 68, 69, 71, 72; and others. *Pos:* Assoc, Galerie 8, Erie, 67-75; bd mem, Erie Art Ctr, 70-72, NW Penna Artists Comn, currently. *Teaching:* Instr art, Tech Mem High Sch, Erie, 70-90; asst prof printmaking, Edinboro State Col, 74; artist-in-residence, Hope Col, Holland, Mich, 78; Seventh Ann Spring Conf Southern Graphics Coun, Univ Auburn, Ala, 80. *Awards:* Purchase Award, Drawings, USA, Minn Mus Art, St Paul, 70 & 73; Merit Award, 4th Miami Int Graphic, Biennial, Miami, Fla, 80; Prize Winner, Norwegian Int Print Biennale, 86; and others. *Bibliog:* Jane Abrams (auth), Educational slide collection, Univ NMex, 71; Lynwood Kreneck (auth), Colorprint USA filmstrip, Tex Tech Univ, 71; Joseph Cain (auth), Corpus Christi, Tex, Iman show, 73. *Mem:* Boston Printmakers; Northwest Pa Artists Asn; Erie Art Ctr; The Pa Soc; Albright-Knox, Buffalo, NY; Iota Lambda Sigma. *Media:* Acrylic. *Interests:* Photography. *Publ:* Auth, Buyers Guide to Contemporary Art, Artists USA, 70-71; Alliance Art Publ, Cable, Wis. *Dealer:* Benjaman Gallerie Buffalo NY 14222; Kada Gallery Erie PA 16505; Bayfront Gallery Erie, Pa 16501. *Mailing Add:* 1012 Boyer Rd Erie PA 16511

AHLSTED, DAVID R
PAINTER, EDUCATOR
b Minneapolis, Minn, 43. *Study:* Minneapolis Col Art, BFA, 65; Indiana Univ, MFA, 68. *Work:* Whitney Mus Am Art, Mus Mod Art, NY; Aldrich Mus Contemp Art, Ridgefield, Conn; Pepsico Inc, Purchase, NY; State Univ NY, Cortland, NY. *Comn:* 6 murals, NJ State Capitol, Trenton, 95; 7 murals, Rutgers Univ, NJ, 95. *Exhib:* Solo Exhibs, Hawthorn Gallery, Skidmore Col, Saratoga, NY, 71, Art Gallery, State Univ NY, Cortland, 75, SoHo Ctr Visual Arts, NY, 76, Art Gallery, Stockton State Col, Pomona, NJ, 84, Marian Locks Gallery, Philadelphia, Pa, 86 & 89 & Perlow Gallery, NY, 92; David Ahlsted, Art Gallery, State Univ Cortland, NY, 75; Contemp Reflections, Aldrich Mus Art, Ridgefield, Conn, 76; David Ahlsted, SoHo Ctr Visual Arts, NY, 76; David Ahlsted, Art Gallery, Stockton State Col, Pomona, NJ, 84; Nature Morte, Southern Alleghenies Mus Art, Loretto, Pa, 86; David Ahlsted, Marian Locks Gallery, Philadelphia, PA, 86, 89; Fel Exhib, Morris Mus, Morristown, NJ, 87; Philadelphia Mus Art, Pa, 90; Katharina Rich Perlow Gallery, 92, 94, 97 & 2000. *Teaching:* Asst prof painting, Skidmore Col, 69-75; assoc prof painting, State Univ NY, Cortland, 75-76; prof painting, Stockton State Col, 76-. *Awards:* Painting Fel, NJ State Coun Arts, 81 & 85. *Bibliog:* Anne Fabbri (auth), Celebration of NJ Artists The NOYES Mus Art, 83; Anne d'Harnoncourt (auth), Contemp Philadelphia Artists, Philadelphia Mus Art; Gerrit Henry (auth), Art in America, New York, 140-141, 2/2001. *Media:* Oil on Canvas, Oil on Gessoed Paper. *Dealer:* Gross McCleaf Gallery 127 S Sixteenth St Philadelphia PA 19102. *Mailing Add:* 840 W Clarks Landing Rd Egg Harbor City NJ 08215-3900

AHLSTROM, RONALD GUSTIN
COLLAGE ARTIST, PAINTER
b Chicago, Ill, Jan 17, 1922. *Study:* Art Inst Chicago, BFA, with Paul Weighart; Univ Chicago; DePaul Univ. *Work:* Art Inst Chicago, Blue Cross Collection & Ill Bell Telephone, Chicago; Tacoma Art Mus, Wash; Philbrook Art Ctr, Tulsa. *Exhib:* 27th Corcoran Biennial, Washington, DC, 61; Chicago & Vicinity Exhib, Art Inst Chicago, 62; 12 Chicago Artists, McCormick Pl Gallery, 62; 50th Northwest Ann, Seattle Art Mus, 64; 6 American Artists, Touchstone Gallery, NY, 73; Zriny-Hayes Gallery, Chicago, 78; Collection Container Corp, Smithsonian Inst, Washington, DC, 88. *Pos:* Asst dir, McCormick Place Art Gallery, Chicago; dir, Tacoma Art Mus, Wash. *Awards:* Clyde Carr Prize, 55 & William H Bartels Prize, 58, Art Inst Chicago; Purchase Prize, 50th Northwest Ann, Ford Found, 64. *Bibliog:* Meilach & Ten Hoor (auth), Collage and Found Art, 64 & Collage, Trends and Technique, 73, Reinholt Publ; Gerald F Brommer (auth), The Art of Collage, Davis Publ, 78; Gerald Brommer (auth), Collage Techniques, A Guide for Artists & Illustrators, Watson-Guptill, New York, 94. *Media:* Collage & Acrylic; Mixed Media. *Mailing Add:* 121 W Park St Lombard IL 60148

AHO, ERIC
PAINTER
b Melrose, Mass, Oct 20, 1966. *Study:* Mass Col Art, BFA, 88, postgrad, 88; postgrad work at Inst Superior de Arte, Havana, Cuba, 89, Lahti Art Inst, Finland. *Exhib:* Nat Acad Mus, NY City, 2006; represented in permanent collections of Fine Art Mus, San Francisco, Fleming Mus, Univ Vt, US Embassy Helsinki, Fidelity Investment Corp, Boston, Union Bank Scandinavia, NY City, The Uhlmann Corp, Kansas City Mo, Oulu City Art Mus, Finland. *Teaching:* Faculty mem visual arts The Putney Sch, Vt, 89-98, Univ Lapland, Rovaniemi, Finland, 97-; vis lectr Burren Col Art, County Clare, Ireland, 96. *Awards:* Fulbrigth Fellow, 91-92; Am-Scandinavian Found Fellow, 93; Pollock-Krasner Found Fellow, 94; Finlandia Found Grant, NY City, 97; Vt Arts Council Grant, Nat Endowment Arts, 97. *Mailing Add:* PO Box 436 Saxtons River VT 05154-0436

AHO, PAUL RICHARD
PAINTER
b Milwaukee, Wis, Sept 3, 54. *Study:* Fla State Univ, BFA, 77; Univ South Fla, MFA, 79. *Work:* New Orleans Pub Libr; Boca Raton Mus of Art; Univ South Fla, Tampa; Miami Univ, Oxford, Ohio; Palm Beach Int Airport; Fla Atlantic Univ, Boca Raton, Fla. *Comn:* Ruth Among the Rushes, Set Design for Dau Raku Productions, Lake Worth, Fla, 92; Jah Music, Set Design for Ballet Fla, West Palm Beach, 2001. *Exhib:* Ann All Fla Juried Exhib, Boca Raton Mus Art, 2002; Painting Abstraction, NY Studio Sch, 2000; Manif, Seoul 97, Seoul Arts Ctr, 97; New Am Talent, Laguna Gloria Mus, 93, 2004; Tampa Triennial, Fla, 85; Cool Intentions, Somerhill Gallery, Chapelhill, NC; Select, Schmidt Col of Arts Thumanities, Fla; Atlantic Univ, Norte Americanos, Archvte Arte Contemoraneo, San Pedro Garza Farcia, Mex. *Collection Arranged:* Janet Fish - A Sea of Color, Armory Act Ctr, 2003; Thought Through My Eyes, Graham Nickson, 2001; A Sense of Urgency - Sidney Goodman, 85; Armort Art, Conn, 2000; Nelson Shanks, Armory Art Ctr, 2002. *Pos:* chief program officer, Palm Beach Photog Ctr, Delray Beach, Fla, 03; dir visual arts, Palm Beach Co Cult Coun. *Teaching:* Dean Armory Art Ctr, West Palm Beach, 96-; Adj Fac, Palm Beach Com Col, 80-99; ADJ Faculty, Florida Atlantic Univ, 2004-. *Awards:* S Fla Cult Consortium Fel, Boca Mus Art, 95; Jurors Award, Laguna Gloria Mus, 93; Ubertelli Mem award, 87. *Bibliog:* New Am Paintings, Opon Studios Press, #45, 03; Digital Realms, Fla; Atlantic Univ, 97; Culture Mag, 6/87. *Mem:* Nat Asn Schs Art and Design; Coll Art Asn. *Dealer:* Marjory Margolis, Gallery Camino Real, 608 Banyan Trail, Boca Raton, FL, 33431. *Mailing Add:* 717 Forest Hill Blvd West Palm Beach FL 33405

AHRENDT, MARY E
CONCEPTUAL ARTIST
b Chicago, Ill, Oct 19, 40. *Study:* Univ Ill, Chicago, BA(scuplture hons), 78; Art Inst Chicago, Ill, MFA(painting & performance), 80. *Work:* Mus Contemp Art, Chicago, Ill. *Exhib:* Seven Artists, 81 & Alternative Spaces, 84, Mus Contemp Art, Chicago, Ill; Sculpture Today, 1982, Indianapolis Mus Art, Ind; Recent Color, San Francisco Mus Mod Art, Calif, 82; Construction Works, Inst Contemp Art, Va Mus, Richmond, 84; Drawings, Chicago & Vicinity, Art Inst Chicago, Ill, 85; Self-Portraits by Women Artists, Collage Arts Asn, Los Angeles, Calif, 85; Nude, Naked Stripped, Albert & Vera List Visual Ctr, Mass Inst Technol, Boston, 86; Images for Human Conduct (catalog), Mus Contemp Art, Chicago, 86, First Person Singular: Self-Portrait Photog (catalog), High Mus Art, Atlanta, 88, Toward the Future: Contemp Art in Context (catalog), Mus Contemp Art, Chicago, 90. *Pos:* Bd mem, Artemisia Gallery, 78-79 & NAME Gallery, 81-86, Chicago, Ill. *Teaching:* Vis artist painting, Univ Ind, Terre Haute, 83 & Univ Ill, Champaign, 85; vis artist painting & photogr, Minneapolis Col Art & Design, Minn, 83. *Awards:* Ill Artists Grant, 83-87. *Bibliog:* David Elliott (auth), Chicago enjoys it's own eclecticism, Art News, 5/82; Catherine Reeve (auth), The New Photography, Prentice-Hall, 83; Alan G Artner (auth), Arts, Chicago Tribune, 6/15/84. *Media:* Photography, Film

AHRENS, HANNO D
SCULPTOR
b Ft Worth, Tex, 54. *Exhib:* One-man shows, Santa Cruz Art Ctr, 77, Dan McHenrey Libr, Santa Cruz, 79, Deborah Sharpe Gallery, NY, 87 & 88, Kim Foster Gallery, 97 & 98 & Boulder Mus Contemp Art, Colo; Univ Art Gallery, Albany, 89; Farnesworth Mus, Rockport, Maine, 90; David Beitzel Gallery, NY, 90; Frumkin/Adams Gallery, NY, 91; The Returns of the Cadavre Exquis, Drawing Ctr, NY, 93; The Edward R Broida Collection: A Selection of Works, Orlando Mus Art, Fla, 98. *Awards:* Pollock-Krasner Found Grant, 86, 91 & 97; Nat Endowment Arts Grant, 86 & 90; New York Found Arts Grant, 89. *Bibliog:* Corrine Robbins (auth), Hanno Ahrens, Sculpture, 7/8/88; Dan Rubey, Hanno Ahrens, Studio, 2/89; AFC, Mass appeal, Vanity Fair, 1/90. *Mailing Add:* c/o Kim Foster Gallery 529 W 20th St New York NY 10011

AHRENS, KENT
MUSEUM DIRECTOR, HISTORIAN
b Martinsburg, WVa. *Study:* Dartmouth Col, AB, 61; Univ Md, MA, 66; Univ Del, PhD, 72. *Collection Arranged:* The Drawings and Watercolors by Truman Seymour (1824-1891) (auth, catalog), Everhart, 86; Frederic C Knight (1898-1979), Everhart, 87; Edward D Boit (auth, catalog), Oils & Watercolors, Everhart, 90; Cyrus E Dallin: His Small Bronzes and Plasters (auth, catalog), Rockwell Mus, 95; Currier and Ives: Selection from the Nationwide Collection (auth catalog), Kennedy Mus Art, 2000. *Pos:* Assoc cur paintings, Wadsworth Atheneum, 77-78; dir, Everhart Mus, 82-90, Rockwell Mus, 90-95, Civic Fine Arts Ctr, SDak, 96-97 & Kennedy Mus Am Art, Ohio Univ, 97; dir Tiogfa Co Hist Soc Mus, 2000-; mus cons, 2000-. *Teaching:* Fac mem, Fla State Univ, 71-74 & Georgetown Univ, 79-82; fac mem & cur, Randolph-Macon Womans Col, 74-77; adj prof, Ohio Univ, 97-2000. *Awards:* Kress Fel, 68 & Dale Fel, 70, Nat Gallery Art. *Mem:* Mus Asn Pa (chmn, 84-90); Williamstown Regional Art Conserv Lab Inc (trustee, 84-92); Mus West (bd dir, 90-95). *Res:* American art. *Publ:* Auth, The portraits by Robert W Weir, 74 & Henry R Newman (1843-1917), 76, Am Art J; Constantino Brumidi's Apotheosis of Washington, 76 & Nineteenth Century History Painting in the United States Capitol, 80, Rec Columbia Hist Soc; American paintings before 1900 at the Wadsworth Atheneum, Antiques, 78; Jennie Brownscombe, 81 & Priscilla Longshore Garrett, 85, Womans Art J; Cyrus E Dallin: American Sculptor (1861-1944), American Art Review, 95; and others. *Mailing Add:* Tioga County Hist Soc 110 Front St Oweto NY 13827

AHYSEN, HARRY JOSEPH
PAINTER, EDUCATOR
b Port Arthur, Tex, Sept 6, 28. *Study:* Tulane Univ; Univ Houston, BFA, 55; Univ Tex, Austin, MFA, 62. *Work:* Over 150 pvt collections; Southern State Col, Hillsboro, Ohio; Tex Artists Mus; West Palm Beach Mus; Zanesville Mus, Ohio; and others. *Comn:* Fifteen paintings & watercolors, Banker's Land Co, West Palm Beach, Fla, 83; sculpture, Boca Raton, Fla, 84; Pelican, Point Jupiter, Fla, 84; four murals, Casa Thomas, Tex, 85-86; ten paintings, Methodist Hosp Houston; mural 16'x30', Washington Court House, Ohio, 92. *Exhib:* First Nat Bank, Huntsville, 82; Odessa Oil Field Show, 82; All State Artists Show, Senate Chambers, Austin, 82; Tex Artists Mus Soc, Port Arthur, 82; Brazos Valley Art League Show, Bryan, 83; one-man shows, The Drawing Room, Houston, Hearnwood Gallery, Hearne, Honorarium, Texas A & M at Galveston & Allen Acad, Bryan, 85, Tex; Zanesville Mus, Ohio, 88; and 110 others. *Pos:* Bd dir, Tex Artist Mus. *Teaching:* From asst prof to prof oil painting & watercolor, Sam Houston State Univ, 63-; lectr, Univ Houston, 65 & Univ Tex, 85. *Awards:* Italian "Oscar" of Italia, Accade Mia Italia, Italy, 85; Official Coast Guard Artist, 94; and others. *Mem:* Nat Soc Marine Painters, 92; Leesberg Art Guild. *Media:* Oil, Watercolor. *Publ:* Auth, Sketch Workbook: Landscape and Seascape Devices, Kendall Hunt Publ, 78; auth, article, Palette Talk, No 52. *Mailing Add:* 542 Washington Ave Washington Court House OH 43160-2048

AIKEN, WILLIAM A
PAINTER
b Pittsburgh, Pa, May 26, 1934. *Study:* Carnegie-Mellon Univ, BFA, 55. *Work:* City of San Francisco & Embarcadero Ctr, Calif; Carnegie Mellon Univ; ABC, Washington, DC; Univ Santa Clara, Calif; Delaware Mus of Art, Wilmington, Del. *Comn:* Oil painting, Shaklee Corp, Emeryville, Calif, 74. *Exhib:* Paintings, USA, Mus Mod Art, NY, 61; Allied Artists Am, Nat Acad, NY, 74, 80 & 82; 39th Ann Midyear Show, Butler Inst Am Art, Youngstown, Ohio, 75; Sun Carnival Nat Art Exhib, El Paso Mus Art, Tex, 77; one-man show, San Francisco Art Comn Gallery, 78; The New Realists, Mongerson Gallery, Chicago, 82; Nature Interpreted, Cincinnati Mus Nat Hist, 82; and others. *Awards:* Charles F Romans Award for Oil Painting, Allied Artists Am Ann Exhib, 80; John Young-Hunter Mem Award for Oil Painting, 92; Second Place Award for Oil Painting, Yosemite Rennaissance Ann Exhib, 2001. *Bibliog:* Paul Perry (auth), View from the Rorshach Canvas, Southwest Art, 12/77. *Mem:* Allied Artists of Am. *Media:* Oil Paint; Oil Glaze. *Dealer:* Water Street Gallery Saugatuck Michigan. *Mailing Add:* 1587 35th Ave San Francisco CA 94122

AINSWORTH, DIANE
PAINTER
Study: Univ Okla & Univ Tulsa. *Comn:* Evergreen Hosp Med Center, Kirkland, Wash; Providence Everett Med Center, Everett, Wash. *Pos:* Las Cruces Art Guild demo & judging, 1995; Demonstrations & workshops for Daniel Smith, Seattle, Wash, 1995-2001; Sequim arts demo, 2000; Judge for Jefferson Art Alliance Small Expressions show, 2002; Judge for Northwest Pastel Society, 2004. *Mem:* Oil Painter of Am; Northwest Watercolor Society; Taos Art Asn; Society of Taos Watercolorists; Wash Plein Air Painters; Okla Society of Impressionists. *Media:* Watercolor, Oil. *Publ:* Southwest Art Mag, Best of the West, Feb 2001; Artists to Watch, Dec 2001; Rivers & Lakes, Vol I, Int Artist Pub, 2004; Cover story, Peninsula Lifestyle mag, Feb 2006; Gathering Place calendar cover, 2006. *Mailing Add:* 410 S Jacob Miller Rd Port Townsend WA 98368

AISTARS, JOHN
PAINTER, EDUCATOR
b Riga, Latvia, Jun 9, 38; US citizen. *Study:* Sch Art Inst Chicago, BFA, 61; Syracuse Univ, MFA, 65. *Work:* Syracuse Univ, Marine Midland Bank & Crouse-Irving Hosp, Syracuse, NY; Ohio Dominican Col, Columbus; First City Nat Bank, Binghamton, NY. *Exhib:* Sch Art Inst Chicago, Ill, 57, 59, 60 & 61; Everson Regional Exhib, Everson Mus, Syracuse; Regional Exhib, Mem Art Gallery, Rochester, NY, Munson-Williams-Proctor Inst, Utica, NY, Robeson Ctr Arts & Sci, Binghamton, NY; Cooperstown Nat, Cooperstown Art Asn, NY. *Collection Arranged:* Various exhibs for Chapman Art Ctr Gallery, Cazenovia Col; Marine Midland Bank, Syracuse, NY; Crouse-Irving Mem Hosp, Syracuse, NY; First City Nat Bank, Binghamton, NY; Syracuse Univ, Syracuse, NY; Ohio Dominican Col, Columbus, OH. *Pos:* Dir, Chapman Art Ctr Gallery, Cazenovia Col, Studio Art Prog, Cazenovia Col. *Teaching:* Grad asst color & lettering, Syracuse Univ, 64-65; prof painting & drawing, Cazenovia Col, NY, 65-98. *Awards:* First City National Award, Susquehanna Regional, 75; First Prize, Central NY Regional Exhib, 89; M Bevier Prize, Cooperstown Nat, 89; Distinguished Fac Achievement Award, Cazenovia Col, 91; First Prize for Painting, Art & Community Ctr, Rome, NY, 99. *Bibliog:* Articles in numerous publications. *Mem:* Cooperstown Art Asn. *Media:* Oil. *Publ:* Auth & illusr of 70 articles, Laiks, Brooklyn, 81-98; Latvija Amerika, Toronto, ON. *Dealer:* Steuben Park Gallery 25 Hopper St Utica NY 13501. *Mailing Add:* 3999 Oran Delphi Rd Manlius NY 13104

AITKEN, DOUG
VIDEO ARTIST
Study: Marymount Col, Palos Verdes, Calif, 86-87; Art Ctr Col Design, BFA, Pasadena, Calif, 91. *Exhib:* Solo exhibs, Taka Ishii Gallery, Tokyo, Japan, 98, Jiri Svestka Gallery, Prague, Czech Repub, 98, Doug Lawing Gallery, Houston, 99, Victoria Miro Gallery, London, 99 & Dallas Mus Art, Tex, 99, 303 Gallery, NY, 2002, Magasin, Ctr Nat d'Art Contemp de Grenoble, France, 2002, Victoria Miro, London, 2003, Kunsthalle Zurich, Switz, 2003, Fondazione Sandretto Re Rebaudengo, Ital, 2003; Speed, Photogrs Gallery, London, 98; I Love New York - Crossover of Contemp Art (with catalog), Mus Ludwig, Cologne, Ger, 98; Whitney Biennial, Whitney Mus Am Art, NY, 97; New Selections from the Permanent Collection, Walker Art Ctr, Minneapolis, 98; dAPPERTutto, Venice Biennale, Italy, 99; group exhibs, Art Inst of Chicago, Sonic Process, MACBA, Barcelona, Spain, and Ctr Pompidou, Paris, France, 2002, Nat Gallery of Victoria, Melbourne, Australia, Liquid Sea, Mus of Contemp Art, Sydney, 2003; and many others. *Awards:* Internat Prize, Venice Biennale, Ital, 99; Aldrich Award, Aldrich Mus of Contemp Art, Ridgefield, Conn, 2000. *Bibliog:* Bill Arning (auth), rev, Time Out NY, 1/7/99; Jerry Saltz (auth), New channels, Village Voice, 1/12/99; Nicole Krauss (auth), rev, Art Am, 3/99. *Dealer:* 303 Gallery 525 W 22nd St New York NY 10011. *Mailing Add:* 2437 Via Sonoma Palos Verdes Estates CA 90274-2030

AKAWIE, THOMAS FRANK
EDUCATOR, PAINTER
b New York, NY, Feb 22, 1935. *Study:* Los Angeles City Col, 53-56; Univ Calif, Berkeley, BA(art hist), 59, MA(painting), 63. *Work:* Milwaukee Art Ctr, Wis; Ithaca Col Art Mus, NY; Oakland Mus, Calif; Williams Col Mus, Williamstown, Mass. *Exhib:* One-man shows, La Jolla Mus Art, Calif, 67, Calif Palace Legion Hon, San Francisco, 72 & San Jose Mus Art, Calif, 77; Ann Exhib, Whitney Mus Am Art, NY, 69; Painting & Sculpture in Calif, San Francisco Mus Mod Art, 76 & Nat Collection Fine Arts, Smithsonian Inst, Washington, DC, 77; 4th Triennale-India 78 Inc, Thailand & Iran, 78; Calif Visionary Painting, Japan, 78; and others. *Teaching:* Asst prof painting & drawing, Univ Calif, Los Angeles, 65-66; lectr painting & drawing, Univ Calif, Berkeley, 72-73; instr spray-painting & drawing, San Francisco Art Inst, 66-. *Awards:* Los Angeles All-City Exhib Award, City of Los Angeles, Calif, 65; First Prize, Ann Downey Mus Invitational, Calif, 66; First Prize, Jack London Art Exhib, Oakland, Calif, 69. *Bibliog:* Charles Shere & John Coney (auths), Art of Tom Akawie, KQED-TV, 71. *Media:* Acrylic. *Publ:* Contribr, Visions, Pomegranate Publ, 77. *Dealer:* Botanica Fine Art Bozeman MT. *Mailing Add:* 1740 University Ave Berkeley CA 94703-1514

AKERS, ADELA
WEAVER, CRAFTSMAN
b Santiago de Compostela, Spain, 1933. *Study:* Univ Havana, 55; Sch Art Inst Chicago, 57-60; Cranbrook Acad Art, 60,-61 & 62-63. *Work:* W B Saunders Publs, Philadelphia, Pa; Sumitono Bank, NY; Manchester Community Col, Conn; Olympia-York, Toronto, Ont; Chase Manhattan Bank, NY. *Exhib:* Solo exhibs, Bloomsburg State Col, Pa, 77, Fiberworks Gallery, Berkeley, Calif, 80, Triangle Gallery, San Francisco, 81, Mandell Gallery, Los Angeles, 81, Modern Master Tapestries, NY, 84, Pa Acad Fine Arts, Philadelphia, 86 & Patrick King Contemp Art, Indianapolis, Ind, 87; Multiplicity in Clay-Metal-Fiber, Skidmore Col, Saratoga Springs, NY, 84; Inaugural Exhib, Am Crafts Mus, NY, 86; Fiber: The Next Generation, Ill State Univ, Normal, 87; Maple Hill Gallery, Portland, Maine, 88; Pa Acad Fine Arts, 86; Helen Drutt Gallery, New York City, 90; Brown/Gratta Arts, Wilton, Conn, 00; Triangle Gallery, San Francisco, 01; Solomon Dubrick Gallery, San Francisco, 01; Snyderman-Works Galleries, Philadelphia, 98, 02. *Collection Arranged:* Metrop Mus Art, NYC, Renwick Gallery, Washington, DC, Bell Atlantic, Hewlett Packard, and others. *Pos:* Lectr, Ctr for Textile Arts, Berkeley, Calif, 84, NC Weaver's Guild, Charlotte, 86, Philadelphis Textile Soc, Pa, 86, Philadelphia Weaver's Guild, Pa, 88; designer for Oaxaca Loom, cottage industry in Diaz Ordas, Oaxaca, Mex, 87; Seminar leader, Nat Conference Handweaver's Guild of Am, Chicago, 88. *Teaching:* Inst, crafts prog, City of Chicago, 65-67; Penland Sch Crafts, NC, summers 68, 69, & 70; New Sch Social Res, 70-71; Cooper Square Art Ctr, New York, 71; San Francisco State Univ, 81; prof, Tyler Sch Art, Temple Univ, Philadelphia, Pa, 72-. *Awards:* Artist in Residence Penland Sch, 69 & 71, Craftsman's Fel, 74 & 80, Nat Endowment Arts; NJ State Coun Arts Grants, 71; Research Grants, Temple Univ, 75, 79, 84 & 88; Pa Coun Arts Grants, 83. *Bibliog:* Articles in Crafts Horizons Mag, 2/77 & Fiberarts Mag, 3/4/81, 2001; Weaving: A Handbook for Fiber Artists, 80. *Mailing Add:* c/o Snyderman Gallery 303 Cherry St Philadelphia PA 19106

AKERS, GARY
PAINTER, WRITER
b Pikeville, Ky, Feb 22, 51. *Study:* Morehead State Univ, BA (Greenshilds Found Grant), 72, MA, 74. *Work:* Boone Co Pub Libr & Art Gallery & St Luke Hosp, Florence, Ky; Mus Art Ogunquit, Maine; Ky Fried Chicken Corp & Brown/Foreman Corp, Louisville, Ky; Coca Cola Bottling Co, Zaring Nat Corp, Cincinnati Financial

Corp & Proctor & Gamble Corp, Cincinnati, Ohio; USF&G Co, Baltimore, Md; Claypool-Young Art Gallery, Morehead State Univ, Ky; Kemper Mus of Contemp Art, Kansas City, Mo; Ross Collection; McGraw Hill Publications. *Comn:* Egg tempera, comn by pvt collector, Maine; Cincinnati Financial Corp, Ohio; watercolor, Brown-Forman Corp, Louisville, Ky; 3 watercolors, Eastern Ky Univ, Richmond; watercolor for President Reagan, Republican Party, Cincinnati, Ohio; painting for President Reagan, Republican Party, Cincinnati, Ohio. *Exhib:* Ky Art Exhib, JB Speed Art Mus, Louisville, Ky, 86; Asheville Art Mus, NC, 86; Ogunquit Mus Am Art, Maine; Nat Acad Design, NY, 94; Am Watercolor Soc Ann Exhib, NY; Owensboro Mus Fine Art, Ky, 96; Artists of Am, Colo Hist Mus, Denver, 97 & 98; Great Am Artists Exhib, Cincinnati Mus Ctr, Ohio, 98. *Awards:* Friends Ky Watercolor Soc Award, 78; Dale Meyers Cooper Medal Hon, Southern Watercolor Soc Award, 83, Lee Printing Co Award, 84; Top Merit Award, Aqueous, Ky Watercolor Soc, 83, Ky Artist Award, 85; Mario Cooper Award, Am Watercolor Soc, 84. *Bibliog:* Bill R Booth (auth), Painting: Border Brothers Farm, Am Artist, 82 & Pages from a passing scene, Southwest Art, 82; Artist's Mag, 10/84 & 2/88; US Art, July-Aug, 89. *Mem:* Ky Watercolor Soc; Am Watercolor Soc; Southern Watercolor Soc. *Media:* Egg Tempera, Watercolor. *Publ:* Auth, A New Spirit of Watercolor, N Light Bks, 89; Watercolor 90, An Am Artist Publ; The Creative Artist, N Light Bks, 90; Being an Artist, N Light Bks, 92; Kentucky: Land of Beauty, Paintings by Gary Akers, pvt publ, 98; Memories of Maine, 03. *Dealer:* Gary-Lynn Galleries 10100 Meiman Dr Union Ky; The Gary Akers Gallery Green Schoolhouse South 131 South Thomaston ME; Hammer Galleries 33 West 57th St NY; Portnoy Gallery 6th Ave at Dolores Carmel CA; DeBruyne Fine Art 275 Broad Ave S FLA; Tree's Place Gallery Rt 6A Orleans MA. *Mailing Add:* PO Box 100 Union KY 41091

AKIN, GWEN
PHOTOGRAPHER
b New York, NY, July 26, 1950. *Study:* Boston Mus Sch; Tufts Univ. *Work:* San Francisco Mus Mod Art; Los Angeles Co Mus Art; Mus Fine Arts, Houston, Tex; New Orleans Mus Art, La; Kiyosato Mus Photog Arts, Japan; Espace Photographique de Paris, France; Chrysler Mus, Norfolk, VA; Kiyosato Mus Photographic Arts, Kiyosato, Japan. *Exhib:* Mirror Mirror, Wadsworth Athenaeum, Hartford, Conn, 93; Bad Girls, New Mus, NY; Addison Gallery Am Art, Andover, MA, 94; Solo exhibs, Twining Gallery, New York City, 87-, Sha Idai Gallery, Tokyo, 87, Cepa Gallery, Buffalo, 87-, White Columns, New York City, 88-, XYZ Gallery, Ghent, Belgium, 89, Farideh Cadot Gallery, NYC, 88, 90, Pamela Auchincloss Gallery, NY, 94, Gallery 954, Chicago, 94, Gallery at 777, Los Angeles, 94, Cepa Gallery, Buffalo, 95, Chrysler Mus, Norfolk, 95, Hudson River Mus Westchester, Yonkers, NY, 95 & Houston Ctr Photog, Tex, 95; Within Memory, Montage, Rochester, NY, 93; Parko Gallery, Tokyo, 93; Natural Hist Formaldehyde Photog, The Ctr Photog at Woodstock, NY, 93; Narcissicism, Thread Waxing Space, NY, Beyond Ars Medica (catalog), Calif Ctr Arts Mus, Escondido, Calif, 95; Ricco/Maresca Gallery, New York City, 99-2001; In Visible Light, Mus Photog Helskini, Finland, 99; Extra Ordinary Bodies from the Muter Mus, List Gallery, Swarthmore Col, PA, 2005. *Awards:* Materials grant, Polaroid Corp, 86 & 87; Materials grant, Agfa Corp, 90; Nat Endowment Arts, 91; and others. *Bibliog:* Newspaper article in De Cenbenaar, Ghent, Belg, 5/5/89; Kate McQuaid (auth), Photo surrealism, South End News, Boston, 2/15/90; articles in numerous other newspapers, mags & J's; Phptpgraphy Speaks, 150 Photgraphers Speak on their Art, Brooks Johnson, ed, Aperture Foundation & Chrysler Mus, 2004, pp 304-305. *Media:* Photography. *Publ:* Fine Art Photog 95, Graphis Press Corp, Zurich; Contemporary Photography from Chicago Collections, by Nadine Wasserman, Mus Contemp Art, Chicago, Ill, 3/95; Beyond Ars Medica, Charles Hagen, NY Times, 12/95; Ars Medica by John Strausbaugh, New York Press, Vol 8, No 47, 95; A Gallery of Women, by William Zimmer, NY Times, 5/95; and others. *Dealer:* Galerie Farideh Cadot 77 Rue Des Archives 75003 Paris France; Ricco/Maresca Gallery NYC, 529 E 20th St, New York, NY 10011. *Mailing Add:* 55 Prince St New York NY 10012

AKINS, FUTURE RENE
PRINTMAKER, SCULPTOR
b Hampton, Va, Feb 5, 50. *Study:* Tex Tech Univ, Lubbock, BA (art hist), 72, MFA (printmaking), 77. *Work:* Sch of Art Inst Chicago, Ill; World Bank Am, San Francisco; Red River Mus, Moorhead, Minn; Valley Nat Bank, Phoenix, Ariz; Mus Southwest, Midland, Tex. *Comn:* Print ed, Tex Fine Arts Asn, Austin, 81 & The Mus, Tex Tech Univ, Lubbock, 83. *Exhib:* World Print Competition III, Smithsonian Inst, Washington, DC, 76-78; Breaking the Bindings: Am Book Art Now, Univ Wis, Madison, 83; Artists Books, San Antonio Art Inst, Tex, 83; Women Artists of Tex, Nat Mus for Women in the Arts, Washington, DC; solo exhibs, New Paintings & New Prints, James Harris Gallery, Seattle, Wash, 2000, Material Handling, Stephen Wirtz Gallery, 2001 & Deborah Oropallo, San Jose Mus Art, 2001. *Collection Arranged:* Nothin Else to Do (auth, catalog), Music Heritage W Tex, 84; Con Dios, Retabloes, 85; Peter Hurd in Lubbock, Drawings Mural, 86; Honky Tonk Visions (auth, catalog), Art & Music W Tex, 86. *Pos:* Asst to dir, The Mus, Tex Tech Univ, 83-85, cur art, 85-88. *Awards:* Cash Awards, Los Angeles Printmaking Soc, 77 & Brand Gallery, 78; Jurors Award, Objects in Transition, Temari-Book Art, Honolulu, Hawaii, 84. *Mem:* Nat Orgn Women; World Print Coun; Tex Asn Mus. *Dealer:* Charles Adams Gallery Kingsgate North Lubbock TX 79401; Stephen Wirtz Gallery San Francisco CA. *Mailing Add:* 4715 27th St Lubbock TX 79410-2323

AKUTSU, SHOICHI
PAINTER, INSTRUCTOR
b Japan, Jan 18, 56, Japanese Citizen. *Study:* Musashino Art Univ, BFA, 80; The Art Students League NY, 98. *Work:* The Art Students League, NY. *Exhib:* Key West Biennial Contemp Fla Art, Key West Mus Art, Key West, Fla, 2000; NY Classicism Now, Hirschl & Adler Gallery, New York, NY, 2000; The Arts Students League NY Highlights from the Permanent Collection, Owensboro Mus Fine Art, Owensboro, Ky, 2006. *Awards:* Gold Medal, 85th Ann Exhib, The Allied Artists Am, 98; Silver Medal, 59th Ann Exhib, The Audubon Artists, 2001; Juror Award, Small Works, NY Univ, 80 Wash Sq Gallery, 2002-2003. *Mem:* Allied Artists Am. *Media:* Oil. *Publ:* auth, Art in review, NY Times, 2000; auth, Hodgepodge exhibition is classicism - not, NY Observer, 2000. *Dealer:* Allen Sheppard 530 W 25 St New York NY 10001. *Mailing Add:* 215 W 109th St New York NY 10025

ALBANO, PATRICK LOUIS
ART DEALER
b St Louis, Mo, June 19, 47. *Study:* Univ Miss, BA, 69; Univ Iowa, MA, 71. *Pos:* Dir, Aaron Galleries, Chicago, Ill, currently. *Mem:* Int Fine Print Dealers; Am Hist Print Collectors Soc. *Specialty:* American masters of the 19th and 20th centuries. *Publ:* Auth, articles in: Antique Market Report, Bales Publ, 1/86 & 9/86. *Mailing Add:* 50 E Oak St Chicago IL 60611-1236

ALBENDA, RICCI
SCULPTOR, PAINTER
b New York, NY, 66. *Study:* RI Sch Design, BFA, 88. *Comn:* lobby installation, Salud.com, Miami, Fla, 2000. *Exhib:* Fluxus Attitudes, The New Mus Contemp Art, NY, 92; Facing the Millenium: Texas Meets NY, Arlington Art Mus, Tex, 96; Elysian Fields, Ctr Georges Pompidou, Paris, France, 2000; Greater New York, PS1/MOMA, Long Island City, NY, 2000; One-man show, Andrew Kreps Gallery, NY, 99, 2000, Van Laeve Contemp Artwerp, Belgium, 99, 2000. *Awards:* The Louis Comfort Tiffany Biennial Award, Louis Comfort Tiffany Found, 99-2000. *Bibliog:* Ken Johnson (auth), Ricci Albenda, The New York Times, 3/20/98; Bill Arning (auth), Ricci Albenda, Time Out New York, 98; Tim Griffin (auth), Ricci Albenda at Andrew Kreps, Art in America, 99. *Media:* Fiberglass, Acrylic. *Mailing Add:* c/o Andrew Kreps Gallery 516 W 20th St New York NY 10011

ALBERT, CALVIN
SCULPTOR, EDUCATOR
b Grand Rapids, Mich, Nov 19, 18. *Study:* Grand Rapids Art Gallery, with Otto Karl Bach; Art Inst Chicago; Inst Design, with Moholy-Nagy & Gyorgy Kepes; Archipenko Sch Sculpture. *Work:* Metrop Mus, Whitney Mus Am Art & Jewish Mus, NY; Art Inst Chicago; Detroit Inst Arts. *Comn:* Ark Doors & Candelabra, Steinberg House, Park Ave Synagogue, NY, 54; Outdoor Candelabra, Temple Israel, Tulsa, Okla, 55; Crucifix, Tabernacle & Candlesticks, St Paul's Church, Peoria, Ill, 59; Facade Relief, Congregation Emanuel, Grand Rapids, 74. *Exhib:* Unknown Political Prisoner Prizewinners, Mus Mod Art, NY & Tate Gallery, London, 53; le Dessin Contemporains aux Etats Unis, Musee Nat d'Arte Moderne, Paris, 54; Whitney Ann Am Artists, 54-68; Univ Ill Contemp Painting & Sculpture, 57 & 65; 20th Century Masters of Drawing, Mus Mod Art, NY, 64; Benton Gallery, 86; Vered Gallery, 88 & 89; Boca Raton Mus Art, 90 & 04; Arlene Bujese Gallery, E Hampton, NY, 2006. *Teaching:* Instr sculpture & design, Inst Design, Chicago, 42-46; instr color & drawing, Brooklyn Col, 47-49; prof art & head grad sculpture prog, Pratt Inst, 49-85, prof emer. *Awards:* Guggenheim Fel 66; Nat Inst Arts & Lett Award, 75; Nat Acad Design Award, 81. *Media:* Bronze, Terra Cotta. *Interests:* Hiking, movies, reading. *Publ:* Coauth, Figure drawing comes to life, 57. *Mailing Add:* 6525 Brandywine Dr S Margate FL 33063-5538

ALBERTI, DONALD WESLEY
PAINTER
b Ft Eustis, Va, Dec 25, 50. *Study:* Col William & Mary, BA, 71. *Exhib:* Condeso/Lawler Gallery, New York City, 84, 86, Kunsthalle Bielefeld, Ger, 86, G Brownstone & Co, Paris, 88, La Couleur Seule L'Experience De Monochrome, Mus St Pierre, Lyon, France, 88; Mediterranean Abstraction, Fr Inst Naples, Italy, 92; F NY, Mus Modernerkunst, Ottendorf, Ger, 92; F NY, Am House, Berlin, Ger, 93; Konkret Konstruktiv Mus, St Ingbert, Saarland, 96; Pardo View Gallery, New York City, 96; Molloy Coll Art Gallery, NY, 2000. *Teaching:* Guest lectr, Sch Visual Arts, NY, 83-84; vis artist lectr ser, Hartwick Col, Oneonta, NY, 87. *Awards:* Fel, NY Found Arts, 87; Fel, Igor Found, 90. *Bibliog:* Clio Mitchell (auth), Instant myth, Art Int, winter 88; Peter Bellamy (auth), The Artist Project, 91. *Media:* All Media. *Publ:* Dir, Pollock/Beaubourg: 1982 (16mm Film Doc), 86. *Dealer:* Estrada Fine Art Los Angeles Calif. *Mailing Add:* 93 Crosby St New York NY 10012

ALBRECHT, MARY DICKSON
SCULPTOR, DESIGNER
b Dothan, Ala, June 4, 1930. *Study:* Univ Houston; Tex Woman's Univ, BS(sculpture, with hons), 70. *Work:* Okla Art Ctr Mus, Oklahoma City; City Dallas Park & Recreation Dept, Tex; Univ Tex at Arlington; Zilker Botanical Gardens, Austin, Tex. *Comn:* Sculpture, Allied Tower at Fountain Place, comn by Sharon Criswell, Criswell Development Co, 86; The Kim, Dallas Commun Coun, 88; Rosemary-Goddess of Herb Gardens (sculpture) Austin Herb Soc Inc, 2000. *Exhib:* 13th Nat Exhib Prints & Drawings, Okla Art Ctr, 71; 15th Tex Crafts Exhib, Dallas Mus Fine Arts, 71; Tex Fine Arts Asn State Citation Show, 72, 75 & 76 & 61st Ann Nat Exhib, 72, Laguna Gloria Mus, Austin; 14th Midwest Biennial, Joslyn Art Mus, Omaha, Nebr, 76; Tenth Nat Drawing & Small Sculpture Show, Del Mar Col, Corpus Christi, Tex, 76. *Awards:* Juror's Choice & Circuit Merit Awards, Tex Fine Arts Asn State Citation Show, 71, 72 & 76; Purchase Award, Univ Tex, Arlington, 72. *Mem:* Int Sculpture Soc; Smithsonian Inst. *Media:* Steel, Bronze. *Mailing Add:* PO Box 163536 Austin TX 78716-3536

ALDANA, CARL
PAINTER
b Guatemala City, Guatemala; US citizen. *Study:* Self taught. *Work:* USAF, Washington DC; City of Hockaichi Collection, Japan; US Embassy, El Salvador; Auto Club of Calif, Los Angeles; Long Beach Mus Art, Calif. *Comn:* Portrait of Margaret Mead, 69, portrait Dr Jean Mayer, 68, portrait BF Skinner, 73, Psychology Today, San

Diego, Calif; portrait Richard Nixon, Los Angeles Times, Calif, 72; painting, CRM Books, San Diego, Calif, 68. *Exhib:* Arco Ctr for Visual Arts, Los Angeles, 77, Rio Hondo Col, Whittier, 88; Los Angeles As Seen By Los Angeles Artists, Los Angeles Munic Art Gallery, 81; San Diego Mus Art; one-man show, San Bernardino Co Mus, 94, FACES Gallery, Long Beach & Golden W Col, Calif, 98; La Sierra Univ; Texas Tech Univ; 70 Yrs of Westways Covers, Petersen Mus, Los Angeles, 95; Portrait Exhib, Barnsdall Munic Art Gallery, Los Angeles, 96; Los Angeles Skyline, Los Angeles Conservancy Invitational Auction, 97; Archangels, Mus Latin Am Art, 97. *Collection Arranged:* Long Beach Mus of Art; US Naval Art; Calif Hist Soc, AAA. *Teaching:* teaching painting watercolors, Calif State Univ, Long Beach, 67-68, 80-81; instr drawing & painting, Fullerton Col, Calif, 72-77, Santa Monica, 75-78. *Awards:* Gold Medal & Award of Merit, Soc of Illusr, NY, 67. *Bibliog:* article in Cinema Mag, Ger, 7/94; article in Anthem, Eureka/Humbolt Co Calif, 8/94; TV interview with Maria Hall Brown, KOCE-PBS, Channel 50, 2/28/98. *Mem:* Movie Illusr Union (bd dir); Acad Motion Pictures Arts & Sciences (bd mem, currently). *Media:* Oil. *Publ:* art dir, Air Force One (film), Columbia Pictures, 96. *Mailing Add:* 386 Ultimo Long Beach CA 90814

ALDEN, RICHARD
PAINTER
US citizen. *Study:* Pratt Inst, Brooklyn, BA (archit), 66, MA (archit), 68; Archit Asn, Fulbright Grant, 67. *Work:* Milford Fine Arts Coun, Conn; Trenton State Col, NJ. *Exhib:* Salmagundi Club 3rd Ann, NY, 80; Audubon Artists 38th Ann Nat, NY, 80; Springfield Art League 61st Nat, Mass, 80; Nat Print Exhib, Holman Art Gallery, Trenton, NJ, 80; Mamaroneck Artists Guild, Larchmont, NY, 81; and others. *Teaching:* Asst prof design, Pa State Univ, 68-. *Awards:* Third Prizes, 8th Ann, York Art Asn, 78 & Cent Pa Festival Arts, 78; First Prize, 21st Three Rivers Arts Festival, 80. *Media:* Colored Pencil. *Publ:* Fragments of a Total Picture: Beyond Style & Fashion, Alden Publ, 86. *Dealer:* Capricorn Gallery 4849 Rugby Ave Bethesda MD 20014. *Mailing Add:* Penn State Univ/Dept Archit State College PA 16827

ALDEN, TODD
CRITIC, CONCEPTUAL ARTIST
b Oct 7, 63. *Study:* Grad Ctr, City Univ New York, MA(art hist), 91. *Mem:* Col Art Asn; Conceptual Clearinghouse Ltd (dir, 92). *Publ:* Ed & auth, The Library of Babel (exhib catalog), Hallwalls Cont Arts Ctr, Buffalo, NY, 91; auth, Sophie Calle & the Aesthetics of the Uncanny Arts, 91, Louise Lawler: Love for Sale, 91 & coauth, Total Metal, 91, Arts; auth, Marcel Broodthaers: On the tautology of art & merchandise, Print Collector's Newsletter, 92. *Mailing Add:* 225 W 14th St Apt 3E New York NY 10011-7135

ALDERDICE, CYNTHIA LOU
PAINTER, PRINTMAKER
b Des Moines, Iowa, Mar 16, 32. *Study:* Univ Tex, BA, 57; NYU, 81; Acad Jewelry, New York, 85-95. *Work:* Robert C Williams Am Mus Papermaking, Atlanta, Ga; Musee d'Art Contemp, France; Ga Tech Univ, Atlanta; Int Monetary Fund Collection, Washington, DC; Fisher Col Bus, Ohio State Univ, Columbus; Federal Home Loan Morgage Corp, Washington DC; Jane Voorhees Zilmmerli Art Mus, NB, NJ; Fisher Col Bus, Ohio State Univ, Columbus. *Exhib:* A Cult Language, Robert First Ctr for Arts, Ga Tech, Atlanta, 98; World Wide Treinnial Exhib, Musee d'Art Contemp, Chamalieres, France, 91; Prints '97, Corcoran Mus art, Washington, DC, 97; Frequencies Nature, Tallahassee Mus Hist Natural Sci, Fla, 98; A Cult Language, Robert C Williams Am Mus Papermaking, Atlanta, Ga, 98; Beyond Words, Ellen Noel Art Mus, Odessa, Tex, 99; Printers Identity, Am Swedish Hist Mus, Philadelphia, Pa, 2000; An Exhib of Am Vietnamese Artists, Hanoi Col Fine Art, Vietnam, 2000; Surfacetension, Rep River Valley Mus, Vernan, Tex, 2000, Kirkpatric Galleries at Omniplex, Oklahoma City, 2001; Pass Through It, Mill River Gallery, Ellicott City, Md, 2001; Cross Currents, Art Gallery Univ Md, College Park, 2001; solo, Touchstone Gallery, Washington, DC, 2002; solo, Morris Mechanic Theater, Balt, 2002; Impressions-Printmaking, Carla Massoni Gallery, Chestertown, Md, 2002; Pushing Paper, Hand Workshop Art Ctr, Richmond, Va, 2002; solo show: Touchstone Gallery, 2004; Group exhibs: Invitational, past & present bd dirs, Md Fedn Art, Annapolis, Md, 2004, Pulp Painting Exhib, Sandy Spring Mus, Sandy Spring, Md, 2005; Jewelry Fair Invitational, Walters Art Mus, 2005-2006-. *Awards:* Individual Artist Award, Visual Arts, Md State Arts Coun, 92; Annie Award Vis Arts Recipient, Cult Arts Found of Anne Arundel Co, 2004. *Bibliog:* Lynne Allen/Phyllis McGibbon, The Best of Printmaking, Rockport Pub, 97. *Mem:* Md Fedn Art (pres 85-87); Md Printmakers; Pyramid Atlantic (treas 96-2000); Friends of Dard Hunter. *Media:* oil on canvas, printmaking. *Mailing Add:* Annapolis Bus Park 2104 Renard Ct Annapolis MD 21401

ALDRICH, LYNN (BARRON)
SCULPTOR, CONCEPTUAL ARTIST
b Bryan, Tex, Dec 16, 44. *Study:* Univ NC, Chapel Hill, BA, 66; Calif State Univ, Northridge, BA, 84; Art Cen Col Design, MFA, 86. *Work:* Los Angeles Co Mus Art; Mus Contemp Art, Los Angeles; Neuberger Berman, Inc, NYC; Neiman Marcus, Inc, Dallas; Belhaven Col, Jackson, Miss. *Comn:* permanent structural installation, Metro, Los Angeles, Calif, 96. *Exhib:* Made in Calif, Los Angeles Co Mus Art, 2000; Flying Lessons, Santa Monica Mus Art, 93; Forms of Address, San Francisco Art Inst, 94; Intersections: Personal & Social, MOCA, Los Angeles, 95, Altered States, 93; The Garden Show, PICA, Portland, Ore, 97; COLA 2000, UCLA Hammer Mus Art, Los Angeles, 2000; Liquid Art, Long Beach Mus Art, Long Beach, Calif, 2001; The Permanent Collection, 1970-2000, Los Angeles Co Mus Art, 2001; Return Engagement, Copia Ctr for Wine, Food, and the Arts, Napa, Calif, 2002; New Works, New Spaces, Armory Ctr for the Arts, Pasadena, 2002; Los Angeles Post-Cool, San Jose Mus Art, Calif, 2002; Certain Traces, Kampa Mus, Prague, 2004; Contemporaries, Gallery at REDCAT, Disney Concert Hall, Los Angeles, 2004; The Next Generation, Mus of Biblical Art, NYC, 2005; Extreme Materials, Rochester Mem Art Mus, NY, 2006; Swell, NY Ctr Art and Media Studies, NYC, 2006. *Teaching:* instr fine arts, Art Cen Col Design, Pasadena, Calif, 86-98. *Awards:* Purchase Award, Los Angeles Co Mus, 99; Individual Artist Fel Award, City Los Angeles, 99; Individual Artist Fel Award, J Paul Getty Trust Fund, 2000. *Bibliog:* M A Greenstein (auth) Meeting of Disciplines, World Sculpture News, 98; Michael Duncan (auth) Review, Art in America, 2000; Doug Harvey (auth), Stuff: The Sculptures of Lynn Aldrich, LA Weekly, 2003. *Media:* Miscellaneous Media, Plastic. *Dealer:* Carl Berg Gallery, Los Angeles; Art Affairs Gallery, Amsterdam. *Mailing Add:* 2020 N Main St #238 Los Angeles CA 90031

ALEXANDER, ANTHONY K
SCULPTOR
b Granite City, Ill, May 21, 51. *Comn:* Tribal Totem Pole, 88 & Tribal Symbols, 89, Greater Albany Sch Dist, Ore; Caduceus Sculptor, comn by Dr Roger P Setera, Portland, Ore, 90; Northwest Coast Art, Larry Day Assoc, Portland, Ore, 90; sculpture (life-size female Deputy Sheriff), Linn Co, Albany, Ore, 93. *Exhib:* Wildlife & Western Wildlife Exhib, Minneapolis, 90; Roughrider Art Show, Williston, NDak, 91; Jazzed About Art, Newberg, Ore, 91, 92, 93 & 94. *Media:* Bronze, Wood; Silver

ALEXANDER, DIANE DAVENPORT
PAINTER
b New York, NY. *Study:* Studied with Robert Brackman, 46; Yale Univ, BFA, 48. *Work:* Gen Elec Corp Collection, Fairfield, Conn; Reichold Chemical Corp, White Plains, NY; Univ Conn, Conn Collection, Storrs; Town Westport, Westport Libr Collection, Conn. *Exhib:* Twenty Five & Under, Seligman Gallery, NY, 47-49; Nat Acad Design, NY, 73-78; Images in Air Brush, Fairfield Univ, Conn, 80; Spray-1980, Silvermine Gallery, New Canaan, Conn, 80; New Eng Ann, Art NE USA, Silvermine Gallery, New Canaan, Conn, 80-90; Hudson River Mus, NY, 85. *Awards:* J J Newman Medal, Nat Soc Acrylic Partners, 73 & Grumbacher Co Top Award, 78; Lillian Cotton Mem Award, Nat Asn Women Artists, 77. *Mem:* Nat Asn Women Artists. *Media:* Acrylic with Airbrush. *Dealer:* Silvermine Guild of Artists 1037 Silvermine Rd New Canaan CT 06840. *Mailing Add:* 463 Oak Point Rd Osprey FL 34229-9265

ALEXANDER, EDMUND BROOKE
ART DEALER, PUBLISHER
b Los Angeles, Calif, Apr 26, 37. *Study:* Yale Univ, BA, 60. *Pos:* Dir Editions Alecto, New York, 67 & Brooke Alexander, Inc, 68-; owner, Brooke Alexander Gallery & Brooke Alexander Editions Inc, 75-; partner, Galeria Weber, Alexander y Cobo, Madrid, 90; mem gov bd, Yale Univ Art Gallery; bd mem, Chinati Foundation. *Mem:* Art Dealers Asn Am. *Specialty:* Contemp Am prints; contemp paintings, drawings and sculpture. *Publ:* Ed, Robert Motherwell-Selected Prints 1961-1974, 74, Jasper Johns-Screenprints, 77 & Sam Francis--The Litho Shop 1970-1979, 79, pvt publ; Jasper Johns: The Season, 91. *Mailing Add:* c/o Brooke Alexander Gallery 59 Wooster St New York NY 10012

ALEXANDER, JANE
ADMINISTRATOR
b Boston, Mass, Oct 28, 39. *Study:* Sarah Lawrence Col; Univ Edinburgh; various hon degrees from US Cols & Univs, 84-98. *Pos:* Chmn, Nat Endowment Arts, 93-97. *Teaching:* Inst, Adult Theater Workshop, Okla Arts Inst, 91. *Awards:* Emmy Award, Outstanding Performance by an Actress in a Supporting Role, 81; Sara Lee Frontrunner Award, 96. *Mem:* Acad Motion Picture Arts & Sci; Creative Coalition. *Mailing Add:* 15 Gordon Rd Carmel NY 10512

ALEXANDER, KAREN
PATRON
Mem: Art Inst Chicago (vchmn bd trustees, currently); Dept European Decorative Arts & Sculpture & Ancient Art. *Mailing Add:* Art Inst Chicago 111 S Michigan Ave Chicago IL 60603

ALEXANDER, KENNETH LEWIS
CARTOONIST
b Gridley, Calif, June 16, 1924. *Study:* Univ Calif, Berkeley, 42-43; Rutgers Univ, 43-44; Calif Col Arts & Crafts, 46-47. *Pos:* Freelance com artist, 47-58; ed, Pictorial Living Mag, San Francisco Examnr, 58-63, Sunday art dir, 63-66, ed cartoonist, 66-; TV ed cartoonist, KGO-TV, 68-69. *Mem:* Soc Am Ed Cartoonist; Nat Cartoonists Soc; Am Newspaper Guild; Am Fedn TV Radio Artists. *Mailing Add:* 1182 Glen Rd Lafayette CA 94549-3044

ALEXANDER, PETER
SCULPTOR
b Los Angeles, Calif, Feb 27, 39. *Study:* Univ Pa, Univ Park, 57-60; Univ London, Eng, 60-62; Univ Calif, Berkeley, 62-63; Univ Southern Calif, Los Angeles, 63-64; Univ Calif, Los Angeles, BA, 65, MFA, 68. *Work:* Walker Art Ctr, Minneapolis, Minn; Mus Mod Art, Brooklyn Mus, Guggenheim Mus, Metrop Mus Art, NY; Corcoran Gallery Art, Washington, DC; Los Angeles Co Mus Art; San Francisco Mus Mod Art, Calif; Fogg Mus, Harvard Univ, Cambridge, Mass; and others. *Exhib:* Whitney Mus Am Art Ann, 69; Highlights: 1968-1969, Aldrich Mus Contemp Art; Painting & Sculpture in Calif: The Modern Era, San Francisco Mus Mod Art, 76; one-man exhibs, James Corcoran Gallery, Los Angeles, Calif, 81, 85-92, Van Straaten Gallery, Chicago, Ill, 84, Fuller Goldeen Gallery, San Francisco, Calif, 84, Gallery 454 North, West Hollywood, Calif, 88, Work Gallery, Costa Mesa, Calif, 91, Brian Gross Fine Art, San Francisco, 91 & 94, Laguna Art Mus, Calif, 92, Charles Whitchurch Gallery, Huntington Beach, Calif, 92, Barbara Mathes Gallery, (catalogue), NY, 94, Craig

Krull Gallery, Santa Monica, 94 & Gallery at 777 (catalogue), Los Angeles, 95; Brooklyn Mus, 83; Mus Mod Art, NY, 84; Best of the West, Zero One Gallery, Los Angeles, 94; City Art, Millard Sheets Gallery, Pomona, Calif, 94; Shoes or No Shoes, Provincial Mus Mod Art, Oostende, Belg, 94; Paper Presence, Jan Abrams Gallery, Los Angeles, 94; Dennis Ochi Gallery, Ketchum, Idaho, 95; retrospective, Orange Co Mus Art, Newport Beach, Calif, 99; Los Angeles Co Mus Art, 2000. *Pos:* Artist-in-residence, Calif Inst Technol, Pasadena, 70-71, Calif State Univ, Long Beach, 76, Fullerton Col, Calif, 76, Univ Colo, Boulder, 81, Centrum Found, Wash, 82 & Cirrus Publ, Los Angeles, 83. *Awards:* Nat Endowment Arts Fel, 80. *Bibliog:* Monroe Hodder (auth), Unto Caesar: Peter Alexander at Brian Gross Art, Artweek, 10/20/94; Edith Newhall (auth), Peter Alexander at Barbara Mathes, Art News, 12/94; Naomi Vine and Dave Hickey (coauth), Peter Alexander: In This Light, OCMA, 99. *Mailing Add:* 1811 16th St Santa Monica CA 90404-4403

ALEXANDER, VIKKY M
CONCEPTUAL ARTIST

b Jan 30, 59. *Study:* NS Col Art & Design, BFA, 79. *Work:* Vancouver Art Gallery; Winnipeg Art Gallery; Household Finance Corp; Prudential Insurance Co; Progressive Corp. *Exhib:* Window Installation, New Mus Contemp Art, NY, 85; The Castle, Documenta, Kassel, WGer, 87; Art of the Real, De Appel, Amsterdam, The Neth, 87; New Territories in Art: Europe-Am, Fondabione Michetti, Rome, Italy, 87; Past/Future/Tense, Winnipeg Art Gallery, Winnipeg & Vancouver Art Gallery, British Columbia, 90-91; James Welling & Vikky Alexander, Kunsthalle Bern, Switz, 90; Nat Gallery Can, Ottawa, 2000. *Collection Arranged:* Nat Gallery Can; Vancouver Art Gallery; Winnipeg Art Gallery; Mackenzie Art Gallery; Edmonton Art Gallery; Art Gallery Surrey; Art Bank Can; Goldman Sachs Ltd, Toronto, Can; Kenderdine Art Gallery, Univ Saskatoon, Can; many others. *Teaching:* prof photog, New York Univ, 89-92, Univ Victoria, 92-. *Awards:* Visual Arts Grants; Can Coun Visual Arts Grant, 83, 84, 87, 89, 91, 2004; Can Coun Projects Grant, 85; London Life Young Contemporaries Purchase Award, 90; Univ Victoria Faculty Rsch Grant, 92, 94, 95, 96, 97, 98, 2001, 2002, 2004. *Bibliog:* Nancy Tousley (auth), Vikky Alexander, Canadian Arts, 88; Brian Wallis (auth), Vikky Alexander (catalog), Stride Gallery, 89; Bruce Ferguson (auth), GLAS (NOT) Sculpture (catalog), 90; Ian Wallace, Contemp Art Gallery, 00. *Mem:* AAUW; Coll Art Asn; BC Photography & Media Arts Soc; Ctr Experimental & Photographic Arts (aesthetic adv bd 97-). *Media:* Mixed Media. *Publ:* Contribr, Tropical codes, Kunstforum, 86; Thought Objects, JAA, 87; Contemporary photography, Art & Auction, 87; Fabrications, Abbeville Press, 88. *Dealer:* Trepanier Baer Gallery Calgary AB Canada; State Gallery, Vancouver, BC; Lisa Marks, NYC. *Mailing Add:* 1445 Marpole Apt 410 Vancouver BC V6H 1S5 Canada

ALEXANDER, WICK
PAINTER

b San Diego, Calif, Apr 10, 55. *Study:* San Diego State Univ, 73-75; Univ Calif, San Diego, BA, 79, MFA, 83. *Work:* Mission Bay Pump Station, San Diego, Calif; Sushi Gallery, San Diego, Calif; Tijuana River Estuary, Imperial Beach, Calif; Bantt Ctr Arts, Alta, Can; Mus Contp Art, San Diego. *Comn:* Pillars of the Community, Escondido, Calif, 96; Work in Progress, San Diego, Calif, 96; Light is Life (mural), San Diego, Calif, 98; Bird Park, Balboa Park, 99; Banner Project, City of San Diego, 98; Pillars of the Community, South Escondido Blvd, Calif, 99; Moving Pictures, Culver City, Calif, 2000. *Exhib:* Solo exhibs, Java Art Space, San Diego, Calif, 92, Simay Space, San Diego, 93 & Quint Gallery, San Diego, 94, SW Col Art Gallery, Tulla Vista, Calif, 96, Robin Brailsford Gallery, San Diego, 97, San Diego Mesa Col Gallery, 98 & Calif Ctr Arts, 99, RB Stevenson Gallery, San Diego, 2000; retrospective, Installation Gallery, 91; La Calle, Tijuana River Estuary, 91; Orange Co Ctr Contemp Art, 92; Transcending Borders, Centro Cult Tijuana, Mex, 92; San Diego Mus Contemp Art, 95, 96 & 97; Santa Fe Mus Fine Arts, 96; Mus Contemp Art, San Diego, 97; San Diego State Univ, 97; Irvine Art Ctr, 98; Calif Ctr for the Arts, Escondido, 99; Cannon Gallery, Carlsbad, Calif, 2000; RB Stevenson Gallery, San Diego, 2000. *Teaching:* Instr art, Metrop Correctional Ctr, US Dept Justice, San Diego, 83-87 & San Diego State Univ, 89; artist in residence, Young at Art, San Diego City Sch, 91-92; instr painting & drawing, Univ Calif, San Diego, presently. *Awards:* Ford Found Grant, 82; Nat Endowment Arts Fel, 89; CAC Artist Fel Painting, 90; Orchid Award, City San Diego, 96; Artist-in-Residence, Banff Ctr for the Arts, Alberta, Can, 96; Project of the Yr Landscape Design Award, Am Pub Works Asn, 97. *Mailing Add:* 3327 Nile St San Diego CA 92104

ALEXANDER-GREENE, GRACE GEORGE
EDUCATOR, MUSEUM DIRECTOR

b Cleveland, Ohio, Sept 18, 18. *Study:* NJ State Teachers Col, with Sybil Browne, BS, 40; Hunter Col; NY Univ; Queens Col; Univ PR; Columbia Univ. *Exhib:* Lever House, 86. *Pos:* TV producer-broadcaster art, New York City Bd Educ, 65-73, supervisor art, 73-77, dir art, 77-79; bd mem, Inst Study Art in Educ, 78 & 79; freelance TV producer art, 79-; consult, Am Mus Moving Image, 85. *Teaching:* Instr visual literacy, Am Festival in Britain, 73; instr art educ, Queens Col, 71-72; instr art educ, Sch Visual Arts, New York, 79-. *Awards:* Ohio State Award, 63 & 73; Outstanding Alumni Award, Kean Col, 80; Monitor Award, Video Production Asn, 84. *Bibliog:* Barbara Y Newsom (auth), The Art Museum as Educator, Univ Calif, Press, 78; Potell Herbert (ed), Rationale for Art Education in the Eighties, High Points, 80. *Mem:* Nat Art Educ Asn; Univ Coun Art Educ; Am Women Radio & TV; New York City Art Teachers Asn. *Publ:* Auth, Artists in New York, 66 & The Moving Image, 70, New York City Bd Educ; From the Teachers Corner, Am Educ US Dept Health Educ & Welfare, 78. *Mailing Add:* 12 72nd St W New York NY 10023-4167

ALEXENBERG, MEL
CONCEPTUAL ARTIST, EDUCATOR

b Brooklyn, NY, Feb 24, 37. *Study:* Queens Col, City Univ NY, BS, 58; Yeshiva Univ, MS, 59; Art Students League; NY Univ, EdD, 69. *Work:* Metrop Mus Art, NY; Baltimore Mus Art, Md; Israel Mus, Jerusalem; Haags Gemeente Mus, The Hague, Neth; Victoria & Albert Mus, London, Eng. *Comn:* Mem to Six Million, Dachau Death Camp, Ger, 83; Torah Spectrogram, Ramat Hanegev Col, Yeroham, Israel, 84; Pinim/Panim: Biofeedback-computer graphics interactive system, Yeshiva Univ Mus, NY, 87; Faxart Homage to Rembrandt, AT&T, NY, Amsterdam, Jerusalem, Tokyo, Los Angeles, 89; Four Wings of America (environment art work), Miami, San Diego, Seattle, Portland, 96. *Exhib:* Crash: Computer Assisted Hardcopy, Wright Mus Art, Beliot, Wis, 88; Golem, Jewish Mus, NY, 88; Lights/Orot, Yeshiva Univ Mus, NY, 88; Faxart Mem, Mus Het Rembrandthuis, Amsterdam, The Neth, 89; High Tech/High Touch, Miami Univ Art Mus, Oxford, Ohio, 90; Imagenes Norteamericanas, Instituto Chileno Nortamericano de Cultura, Santiago, Chile, 92 & 98; Aesthetic Peace Plan, Nat Jewish Mus, Washington, 94; Four Corners of Am, ArtMiami, 96. *Pos:* Research fel, MIT Ctr Advanced Vis Studies, 84-88; dean, vis arts, New World Sch Arts, Miami, Fla, 90-. *Teaching:* Senior lectr, Tel Aviv Univ, Israel, 69-73; assoc prof art, Columbia Univ, NY, 73-77; assoc prof aesthetic educ, Bar-Ilan Univ, Ramat Gan, Israel, 77-84; prof & chmn fine arts, Pratt Inst, Brooklyn, NY, 85-90. *Awards:* Founder's Day Award, NY Univ, 69; MIT/CAVS Fel, 84-85; NY State Coun on Arts, 87-88. *Bibliog:* Elizabeth Hayt-Atkins (auth), Lights Orot, Art News, 9/88; John Ross, Clare Romano & Tim Ross (auths), The Complete Printmaker, Macmillan, 90; Helen Kohen (auth), Fresh works, Miami Herald, 94. *Mem:* Int Soc Educ Through Art; Nat Art Educ Asn; Israel Soc Painters and Sculptors. *Media:* Multimedia, Electronic Media. *Publ:* Auth, Aesthetic experience in creative process, Bar-Ilan Univ Press, 81; coauth, Lights Orot, MIT/CAVS, 88; ed, The Visual Computer, Springer, 88; auth, Aesthetics in Judaism, Wellsprings, 90; Miami in Ecological Perspective, 94

ALEXICK, DAVID FRANCIS
EDUCATOR, PAINTER

b Philadelphia, Pa, 42. *Study:* Richmond Prof Inst, BFA, 64; Va Commonwealth Univ, MFA, 66; Pa State Univ, PhD, 76. *Work:* private collections. *Exhib:* Va Artists Biennial, Va Mus Fine Arts, Richmond, 64; one-man show, Robinson House, Va Mus Fine Arts, Richmond, 65; Longwood Col Fac Show, Bedford Gallery, Farmville, Va, 71-78; James River Show, Mariners Mus, Newport News, Va, 73; various fac shows, Falk Gallery, Christopher Newport Univ. *Teaching:* Instr art, York Col Pa, 66-68; asst prof art, Longwood Col, Farmville, Va, 71-78; instr art educ, Col William & Mary, Williamsburg, Va, 79-80; asst prof art, Christopher Newport Col, VA, 79-82, dir art, Dept Arts & Communications, 82-88, assoc prof, 82-2003, prof, 2003-. *Awards:* Cert Distinction, Va Mus Fine Arts, 64; 1st Prize, South Eastern Regional, Lynchburg Fine Arts Ctr, 67; Patron Arts Award, Lynchburg Art Festival, 78. *Mem:* Col Art Asn; Nat Art Educ Asn; Va Art Educ Asn. *Media:* Oil, Acrylic, Bronze. *Res:* Programs of art and perceptual awareness for institutionalized retarded children. *Interests:* currency trading, futures and options. *Dealer:* 220 Crittenden. *Mailing Add:* Christopher Newport Univ Ferguson Ctr Arts Rm 119 1 University Pl Newport News VA 23606

ALF, MARTHA JOANNE
PAINTER, WRITER

b Berkeley, Calif, Aug 13, 1930. *Study:* San Diego State Univ, with Everett Gee Jackson, BA, MA (painting), 63; Univ Calif, Los Angeles, with James Weeks, William Brice & Richard Diebenkorn, MFA (pictorial arts), 70. *Work:* Los Angeles Co Mus Art; San Diego Mus Art; Santa Barbara Mus Art; Newport Harbor Art Mus, Newport Beach, Calif; Israel Mus Art, Jerusalem; Chemical Bank & Metrop Mus Art, NY. *Exhib:* Whitney Biennial Contemp Art, Whitney Mus Am Art, 75; The Michael and Dorothy Blankfort Collection, Los Angeles Co Mus Art, Calif, 82; one-person retrospective, Los Angeles Munic Art Gallery & San Francisco Art Inst, 84; Contemp Am Luminism, Henry Gallery, Univ Wash, 85; Martha Alf-Helen Ludenberg: Two Views: 1970-1987, Palos Verdes Art Ctr, Calif, 87; Martha Alf: Survey 1965-1990, Art Inst Southern Calif, Laguna Beach, 91; Recent Drawings, Fresno Art Mus, Calif, 92; Internal Interface: 25 yrs survey, Mt San Antonio Col, Walnut, Calif, 93; Generation of Mentors, Nat Mus of Women in the Arts, Washington, DC, 94 & traveling, 94-95; and many other group and one-person shows. *Pos:* Guest cur, Painting: Color Form & Surface (17 Los Angeles Painters), Lang Art Gallery, Scripps Col, Claremont, Calif. *Teaching:* Instr drawing & painting, Los Angeles Harbor Col, Wilmington, Calif, 71-75; instr, current art in Los Angeles, Univ Calif Extn, Los Angeles, 71-78, inside the art world, 73-79. *Awards:* Nat Endowment Arts Visual Artist Grant for Drawing, 89; Nat Endowment Arts Grant, 79; Kay Nielsen Mem Purchase Award, Los Angeles Co Mus Art, 79; and others. *Bibliog:* Merle Schipper (auth), Martha Alf (Tortue Gallery), Art News, pp 24, 27, 2/87; Wendy Beckett (auth), Martha Alf, pp 18, 19, Contemporary Woman Artists, Phaidon, Oxford, 88; Peter Clothier (auth), Martha Alf: Red Pulse, Artspace, 7/8/92. *Media:* Painting, Photography. *Publ:* Auth, My interest in women artists of the past, Womanspace J, Vol 1, No 2; The psychological world of Joyce Treiman, 3/76, The structural language of Claire Falkenstein, 4/76 & Women artists throughout history, 1/77, Artweek. *Dealer:* Newspace Gallery 5241 Melrose Ave Los Angeles CA 90038. *Mailing Add:* c/o Newspace Gallery 5241 Melrose Ave Los Angeles CA 90038

ALFANO, ANGEL
PAINTER

b Cosenza, Italy, Oct 6, 40. *Study:* Liceo Artistico, Rome, Italy. *Work:* Garibaldi-Meucci Mus, NY; Current Art Boston; W Broadway Gallery, NY; Alternate Space Gallery, NY. *Exhib:* Salon Int De L'Art Libre, Paris, France, 68; 10th Art Exhib, NY, 75; Contemp Art Show, Santa Fe, NMex, 78; Fine Art Gallery, Westchester Community Col, Valhalla, NY, 86; Garibaldi-Meucci Mus, NY, 91; Int Art Show, Rio De Janerio, Brazil, 98; Contemp Art Show, Sharjah Art Mus, United Arab Emirates,

99; Int Art Show, Toledo Univ, Toledo, Ohio, 2000; The 6th Int Ann Miniature Art, Stockholm, Sweden, 2001; and others. *Awards:* Gold Medal Award, Miami, Fla, 65; Prize Special Au Salon Int De L'Art Libre, Paris, France, 65; First Place, Nat Art Show, Naples, Italy, 70. *Media:* Oil, Watercolor. *Publ:* Illusr, Concoa de Amor, Kim Sam Young, 88; Poesie, Teresinka Pereira, 89. *Mailing Add:* 44 Merritt Ave Eastchester NY 10707-3110

ALFOND, BARBARA LAWRENCE
COLLECTOR
Study: BA in Eng, Rollins Col, 68. *Pos:* trustee Mus Fine Arts, Boston, Holderness Sch, NH, 84-, Rollins Col, Fla, 89-. *Awards:* named one of Top 200 Collectors, ARTnews, 2006. *Mailing Add:* 1 Chestnut St Weston MA 02193

ALFOND, TED B
COLLECTOR
b Maine. *Study:* BA Rollins Col, 1968. *Pos:* exec vpres Dexter Shoe Co, 69-99; ltd partner Boston Red Sox, 80-; trustee Boston Mus Fine Arts, Rollins Col. *Awards:* named one of Top 200 Collectors, ARTnews, 2006. *Mailing Add:* 1 Chestnut St Weston MA 02193

ALFORD, GLORIA K
PAINTER, SCULPTOR
b Chicago, Ill, Oct 3, 28. *Study:* Univ Calif, Berkeley, AB; Art Inst Chicago; Penland Sch Crafts, NC; Columbia Univ; Pratt Graphics Ctr. *Work:* Elvehjem Mus, Univ Wis-Madison; CUNA Art Collection, Madison, Wis; Prudential Art Collection, Monterey Mus Art, Calif; Paper construction, Silicon Graphics, Mountain View, Calif. *Comn:* Four paper sculptures, Ask Computer Systems, Inc, 88, TGV Inc Santa Cruz, 94. *Exhib:* In Her Own Image, Philadelphia Mus Art, 74; 19th Ann Print Exhib, Brooklyn Mus, 74; Wis Directions, Milwaukee Art Ctr, 75; solo shows, Monterey Peninsula Mus Art, 80, The Neth Inst Advan Study, Wassenar, 82 & Djurovich Gallery, Sacramento, Calif, 86; Placement-Displacement Sculpture Show, Cabrillo Col, 83; Content Contemp Issues, Euphrat Gallery, 86; The Chaminade Artists Series, Santa Cruz, Calif, 90-94; Computer Technology in the Arts, Sesnon Art Galley, Univ Calif, 90, Galerie Reve, Los Angeles, Calif, 90; Woven Wonders, Pajaro Valley Arts Coun, 94; Oriental Influences, Pope Gallery, 95; Biennale Int dell'Arte Contemp, Florence, Italy; Arte Studio, Via Guelfa; Jofi Gallery, Santa cruz, Calif, 2006. *Pos:* Vis artist, Cult Exchange Prog, France, 76; bd mem & chairperson exhib Comt, Santa Cruz Ctr Arts, 91-94. *Teaching:* Instr monoprints, Univ Calif Extension at Santa Cruz, 91; guest lectr, Printmaking, Univ Calif Santa Cruz, summer 92-94. *Awards:* Top Honors, Univ Wis Art Show, Richland Ctr, 72. *Bibliog:* Donna Maurillo (auth), Gloria Alford of Santa Cruz, Monterey Life Mag, 11/84; Robert Sward (auth), Autobiography Contemporary Authors Autobiography Series (CAAS), Vol 13, 91. *Mem:* Santa Cruz Art League (bd mem, 91); founding Santa Cruz Mus Art and History. *Media:* All Media. *Dealer:* Jofi Gallery Santa Cruz Calif; American Art Gallery Carmel Calif. *Mailing Add:* 435 Meder St Santa Cruz CA 95060

ALGAZE, MARIO A
PHOTOGRAPHER
b Havana, Cuba, Oct 4, 47: US citizen. *Work:* Lowe Art Mus, Coral Gables; Mus Cuevas, Mexico City; Milwaukee Art Mus; Norton Gallery Art, West Palm Beach, Fla; Santa Barbara Mus; and others. *Exhib:* Guayasamin Found, Quito, Ecuador, 91; Int Fototage, Herten, Ger, 93; Houston Phofest, Tex, 94; Magic Moments, Royal Photog Soc, Bath, Eng, 94, Henie-Onstad Art Ctr, Oslo, Sweden, 94 & Montreauk Art Mus Switz, 94; Magic Moments: Celebrating Leica Cameras (traveling 107 countries), 96; Throckmorton Gallery, NY, 97; Peter Federman Gallery, Santa Monica, Calif, 99; Throck Morton Gallery, NY, 99; one man exhibs El Sur, Fundacion Banco del Comercio, Lima, Peru, 89, 45 Imagenes, Mus Antioquia, Medellin, Colombia, 89, Caras, Cuban Mus Arts & Cult, Miami, 89, 40 Images, L'Alliance Francaise au Perou, Lima, 91, Film Festival Portraits, Ambrosino Gallery, Coral Gables, 92, Portfolio Latinoamericano 2, Int Fototage, Herten, Ger, 93, Houston Photofest, 94 & Throck Morton Fine Art Gallery, NY, 97, Fundacion Guaysamin, Quito, Ecuador, 95, Sur, Freites Revilla Gallery, Coral Gables, 98, Peter Fetterman Photog Works of Art, Santa Monica, Calif, 99, John Cleary Gallery, Houston, 99 & Throck Morton Fine Art Gallery, NY, 99. *Pos:* freelance photojournalist, 71-; owner, dir, Gallery Exposures, Coral Gables, Fla, 79-81. *Awards:* Cintas Fel, 89; Nat Endowment Arts/SAF Fel, 91; Nat Endowment Arts Fel, 92. *Dealer:* Throckmorton Gallery New York NY. *Mailing Add:* PO Box 141027 Coral Gables FL 33114

ALHILALI, NEDA
ENVIRONMENTAL ARTIST, PAINTER
b Cheb, Czech, Nov 26, 38. *Study:* St Martin's Sch Art, London, Eng; Kunst Akademie, Munich, WGer; Univ Calif, Los Angeles, BA, 65, MA, 68. *Work:* Banff Art Ctr, Canada; Crocker Art Mus, Sacramento, Calif; Albright Col, Pa; ARAMCO, Houston; Central Mus Textiles, Lodz, Poland; and others. *Comn:* Blue Cross Hq, Los Angeles, 77; Hyatt Regency Hotels, Chicago, 77, also Los Angeles, Columbus, Maui & Palm Beach; Tishman Corp, Los Angeles, 78; Prince Kuhio Hotel, Hawaii, 80; Sheraton Hotel, Crystal City, Va; and others. *Exhib:* Mus of Contemp Art, Chicago, Pac Design Ctr, Los Angeles & Mus of Sci & Indust, Los Angeles, 76; Fiberworks, Cleveland Mus of Art, Ohio, 77; The Americas & Japan--Fiberworks, Nat Mus Mod Art, Tokyo & Kyoto, Japan, 77; one-woman shows, Allrich Gallery, San Francisco, Vanguard Gallery, Los Angeles, 77, Hunsaker Gallery, Los Angeles, Calif, 80 & 82 & Renwick Gallery, Washington, DC; Art Fabric: Mainstream, Am Fedn Arts: Mus Mod Art, San Francisco, Calif. *Collection Arranged:* Fiberworks (auth, catalog), Lang Art Gallery, Scripps Col, Claremont, Calif, 73; Inaugural Exhib, Mano Gallery, Chicago, 76; Paper Art (coauth, catalog), Galleries of the Claremont Cols, 77. *Teaching:* Asst prof art, Univ Calif, Los Angeles Exten, 70-77; from asst prof to assoc prof, Scripps Col & Claremont Grad Sch, 71-, chmn dept art, Scripps Col, 82-. *Awards:* Nat Endowment for the Arts Grants, 74 & 79; First Scripps Col Fac Recognition Award, 81. *Bibliog:* Betty Pawk (auth), Interview with N Al-Hilali, Fiberarts Mag, 7/8/79; Scott Miller (auth), Cassiopeia's Court, Images & Issues, Vol 3, No 1; Nan Hackett (auth), Opposites, Seattle Post Intelligencer, 7/2/82. *Mem:* Artists Equity Asn; Am Crafts Coun; World Crafts Coun. *Media:* Mixed. *Res:* Historic textiles. *Dealer:* Allrich Gallery San Francisco CA; Joyce Munsaker Gallery 812 N La Cienega Blvd Los Angeles CA 90069. *Mailing Add:* 3114 Halm Ave Los Angeles CA 90034

ALI, LAYLAH
PAINTER
b Buffalo, NY, 68. *Study:* Williams Col, BA in Studio Art & English Lit, 91; Whitney Mus Ind, NY, Study prog, 91-92; Skowhegan Sch Painting & Sculpture, Maine, 93; Wash Univ, MFA (painting), 94. *Work:* Mus Contemp Art, Chicago, 1999; Bizzarro World, Cornell Fine Arts Mus, Fla, 1999; The 1999 DeCordova Ann. Exhib, Decordova Mus & Sculpture Park, Mass, 1999; Freestyle, Studio Mus Harlem, NY, 2001; A Work in Progress, New Mus, NY, 2001; Project 75, Mus Modern Art, NY, 2002; Indianapolis Mus Art, Iowa, 2002; Painting in Boston, DeCordova Mus & Sculpture Park, Mass, 2002; First Person Singular, Seattle Art Mus, 2002; Contemp Art Mus, Houston, Tex, 2003; Whitney Biennial Am Art, Whitney Mus Am Art, NY, 2004; Material Witness, Mus Contemp Art, Cleveland, 2004. *Exhib:* One-woman shows, Hallwalls Contemp Arts Ctr, Buffalo, NY, 94, Miller Block Gallery, Boston, 98, Mass MOCA, North Adams, Mass, 2000, 303 Gallery, NY, 2000, Yerba Buena Ctr Arts, San Francisco, 2001, Inst Contemp Art, Boston, 2001, Atlanta Col Art Gallery, Georgia, 2002, Albright-Knox Art Gallery, Buffalo, NY, 2003, 303 Gallery, NY, 2005; group shows, Telling Tales, Atrium Gallery, Univ Conn, 98, Selections Summer '98, Drawing Ctr, NY, 98, Posing, Boston Ctr Arts, 98, Paradise 8, Exit Art, NY, 98; Premio Regione Piemonte, Palazzo Re Rebaudengo, Italy, 2001; Fantasyland, D'Amelio Terras, NY, 2002; Me and More, Kunstmusuem Lucerne, Switz, 2003; Fault Lines: Contemp African Art & Shifting Landscapes, Venice Biennale, Italy, 2003; The 10 Commandments, KW Inst Contemp Art, Berlin, 2004. *Mailing Add:* c/o 303 Gallery 525 W 22nd St New York NY 10011

ALICEA, JOSE
PRINTMAKER
b Ponce, PR, Jan 12, 28. *Study:* Acad Pov, Ponce; Inst PR Cult, with Lorenzo Homar. *Work:* Philadelphia Mus Art; Mus Mod Art, NY; Libr of Cong, Washington, DC; Boston Pub Libr; Mus Arte Ponce. *Comn:* Woodcut mural, Inst PR Cult for Guayanilla High Sch, 70. *Exhib:* 4th Int Exhib of Drawing, Yugoslavia; 10th & 11th Biennalle Int d'Art, Menton, France; 12th Bienal de Sao Paulo, Brazil; 2nd & 3rd Bienal Int de Grafica, Frechen, Ger; and others. *Pos:* Asst to dir, Inst PR Cult Workshop, 58-62, instr, currently. *Teaching:* Instr printmaking, Escuela Artes Plasticas, San Juan, 67-. *Awards:* Prize for Graphic, Ateneo Puertorriqueno, 65; Mildred Boerike Prize, Print Club Philadelphia, 67; Travel Grant, Casa Del Arte, San Juan, 68. *Bibliog:* E Ruiz de la Mata (auth), The art of Jose R Alicea, San Juan Rev Mag, 7/66 & Graphics by Alicea, San Juan Star, 8/9/70; Gloria Borras (auth), El grabado en la vida de Jose R Alicea, El Mundo, 69. *Media:* Miscellaneous. *Publ:* Illusr, Trovas larenas, 68, auth, Rio grande de Loiza (portfolio of prints), 68; Cancion de Baquine (portfolio of prints), 70; En las manos del pueblo, 72; Calambrenas. *Mailing Add:* c/o Galeria Palomas PO Box 9023356 Old San Juan PR 00902

ALIKI, LIACOURAS BRANDENBERG
ILLUSTRATOR, WRITER
b Philadelphia, Pa. *Study:* Philadelphia Mus Col Art, grad. *Work:* Kerlan Collection, Walter Libr, Univ Minn, Minneapolis; de Grummond Collection, Univ Southern Miss, Hattiesburg; Seattle Pub Libr, Wash; Falvey Mem Libr, Villanova Univ, Pa; Rutgers Univ Children's Literature Collection, New Brunswick, NJ; Free Libr Philadelphia; Mazza Collection, Ohio; Arne Nixon Ctr, Study of Children's Books. *Exhib:* Children's Bk Coun Showcase Exhib; Biennale of Illus, Bratislava, Czech, 75; Soc Illusr Exhib, NY; Am Inst Graphic Arts Bk Exhib. *Awards:* Children's Sci Book Award, NY Acad Scis, 77; Zilveren Griffel, Netherlands, 81; Garden State Childrens Book Award, 82, 96; Omar's Book Award, 86; Prix del Libre, Switz, 87; Drexel Univ Free Libr Philadelphia Citation, 91; Pa Sch Librns Asn Award, 91; Jane Addams Picture Book Award, New York, 99. *Bibliog:* Grace Hogarth (auth), Illustrators of Children's Books, Horn Bk Inc, 78; Iris M Tiedt (auth), Exploring Books with Children, Houghton Mifflin, 79; Monson & Sutherlan (auths), Children & Books, Scott, Foresman, 81. *Media:* Watercolor, Crayon. *Res:* Research varies according to current book project. *Interests:* Gardening, cooking, traveling & reading. *Publ:* A Medieval Feast, 83, Digging Up Dinosaurs, 88, Harper/Collins; Feelings, Greenwillow, 84; Marianthe's Story, Greenwillow, 98; William Shakespeare and the Globe, Harper Collins, 99; Ah, Music!, 2003; A Play's the Thing, 2005; and many others. *Mailing Add:* 17 Regent's Park Terr London NW1 7ED United Kingdom

ALINDER, JAMES GILBERT
GALLERY OWNER, PHOTOGRAPHER
b Glendale, Calif, Mar 31, 1941. *Study:* Macalester Col, BA, 62; Univ Minn, 62-64; Univ NMex, MFA, 68. *Work:* Mus Mod Art, NY; Bibliot Nat, Paris; Art Inst Chicago & Mus Contemp Photog, Chicago; Int Mus Photog, George Eastman House, Rochester, NY; Nat Gallery Can, Ottawa; San Francisco Mus Mod Art; Victoria & Albert Mus, London, Eng; Stanford Univ, Ctr for Creative Photog; and others. *Exhib:* Light, Hayden Gallery, Mass Inst Technol, 68; solo exhibs, Sheldon Gallery, Univ Nebr, 69, Camerawork Gallery, San Francisco, 79 & Spiva Art Ctr, Joplin, Mo, 80; Be-Ing Without Clothes, Hayden Art Gallery, Mass Inst Technol, 70; The Diana Show, Wynn Bullock Gallery, Carmel, Calif, 80, Am Photog Today: Univ Colo, 82; Exposed & Developed, Nat Mus Am Art, Washington, 84; Family Portraits, Wright State Univ, 87; Photog Truth: Bruce Mus, 88; retrospective, Int Photog Hall Fame, 92; Image and

Text, Ctr Creative Photog, Univ Ariz, Tucson, 93; Somalia, As it Was, Alinder Gallery, Gualala, 93; Selections from the Permanent Collection, Mus Contemp Art, Los Angeles, 93; On the Road, Mus Fine Arts, Houston, 94; EvenColor, Ctr Arts, Vero Beach, Fla, 94; The Discerning Eye, Santa Cruz Mus Art, 94; The Enduring Illusion, Stanform Univ Mus Art, 95; The Family, Spencer Mus Art, Univ Kans, 97; Looking Back, Clear Sky Gallery, Lincoln, 98; 20/20 Mus NMex, Santa Fe, 2000; Classic Images, Ctr Creative Photog, Tucson, 2002; Edges and Intersections, Nat Stinbeck Ctr, Salinas, 2003. *Collection Arranged:* Wright Morris: Structures & Artifacts, Sheldon Mem Art Gallery, Lincoln, Nebr, 75; Crying for a Vision, 76; Twelve Photographers: A Mid-America Contemporary Document, 78; Jerome Liebling: Retrospective, 78; New Color Work: Divola, Fitch, North, Ollman & Pfahl, 78; Ruth Bernhard Retrospective (with catalog), 79; The Contact Print (with catalog), 82; Ansel Adams Classic Images (with catalog), 86; Light Years, 87. *Pos:* Exec dir, Friends of Photog, Carmel, Calif, 77-87, bd trustees, 87, actg exec dir, 88-89 & juror Ferguson Grant, 92; bd trustees, Monterey Pen Mus Art, 86-, vpres, 87, pres, 88; vis artist, Sheldon Mus Univ Nebr, Lincoln, 1997. *Teaching:* Assoc prof photog & photog hist, Univ Nebr, Lincoln, 68-77; instr, Ansel Adams Yosemite Workshop, 79-81 & workshop, Jackson Hole, Wyo, 2003; lectr, Calif Hist Soc, San Francisco, 94, Stanford Univ Mus Art, 2002 & Joslyn Mus Art, Omaha, 2002. *Awards:* Nat Endowment Arts Fel, 73 & 80; Woods Found Fel, 74. *Bibliog:* N Geske (ed), Photographs, Univ Nebr Press, 77; J Enyeart (ed), Kansas Album, Kans Bankers Asn, 77; J Green (auth), Am Photog, Abrams, 84. *Mem:* Soc Photog Educ (ed Exposure, 73-77, secy, 73-75, vchmn, 75-77, chmn, 77-79); Photog Arts & Sci Found (pres, 85); Monterey Co Cult Coun (chmn, 81-82); Am Asn Mus. *Media:* Photography. *Publ:* Coauth, Ansel Adams: Classic Images, 85 & The Sea Ranch, 2004; intro, Quiet Light, 90; contribr, ViewCamera Mag, 94; ed, Solomon's Temple, 96; auth, Sparkling Harvest, Abrams, 97. *Mailing Add:* Alinder Gallery PO Box 449 Gualala CA 95445

ALINDER, MARY STREET
WRITER, CURATOR
b Bowling Green, Ohio, Sept 23, 46. *Study:* Univ Mich; Univ NMex; Univ Nebr, BA, 76. *Comn:* Authentication of the work of Ansel Adams for mus, auction houses, insurance co and pvt individuals. *Collection Arranged:* Ansel Adams: 80th Birthday Retrospective - 150 Prints (auth, catalog), Monterey Mus Art & Calif Acad Sci, 82; Ansel Adams - 200 prints (auth, catalog), Denver Mus Natural Hist, 83; Ansel Adams - A 125 Print Exhib, Nat Mus Art, Beijing & People's Cultural Palace, Shanghai, People's Repub China; One with Beauty - A 168 print Exhib retrospective of Ansel Adams (auth, catalog), The MH de Young Mem Mus, San Francisco, 87; Ansel Adams: American Artist, The Ansel Adams Ctr, San Francisco, 89; Ansel Adams: Native Californian, State Capitol Bldg, Sacramento, Calif, 2001; Ansel Adams 100th Birthday Celebration (auth catalog), Green Ctr for Music and the Arts. *Pos:* Mgr, Weston Gallery, Carmel, Calif, 78-79; exec asst to Ansel Adams, Carmel, Calif, 79-84; exec ed & bus mgr, Ansel Adams Publ Rights Trust, 84-87; freelance, & co-owner Alinder Gallery, Gualala, Calif, 90-. *Teaching:* Lectr & instr workshops in US, France, Eng and People's Rep China, 82-86; Nat Gallery Art, Washington, 85; Los Angeles Co Mus, MH de Young Mus, Univ Calif, Berkeley, Univ Mich, Univ Cincinnati, Cleveland Mus Natural Hist, Stanford Univ, High Mus Art, Calif Wilderness Collection; visiting artist & lectr, Univ Nebr, 97; speaker, Wallace Stegner Mem Lect, 98; team teacher, Lured to Taos: Artist Pilgrims in the Southwest, Stanford Univ, 2000. *Mem:* Friends of Photog; Ctr Creative Photog. *Res:* Work and life of Ansel Adams; Group f/64; creative photography. *Publ:* Coauth, Seeing Straight: The F-64 Revolution in Photography, Oakland Mus, 92; selector & auth, all biographies, The Focal Encyclopedia of Photography, 3rd ed, Boston & London, 93; Ansel Adams, A Biography, Henry Holt, 96; auth, Motel Mabel: Mabel Dodge Luhan and Photography, View Camera, 98; auth, Ansel Adams and Manzanar, Civilization, 99; Ansel Adams: An Autobiography, 85; Ansel Adam: Letters and Images, 88. *Mailing Add:* PO Box 1146 Gualala CA 95445-1146

ALLAIN, RENE PIERRE
PAINTER, SCULPTOR
b Montreal, Que, Dec 28, 51. *Study:* Loyola Montreal, Que, CEGEP, 71; Univ Ottawa, Ont, BA(fine arts), 81; Hunter Col, City Univ New York, MFA, 86. *Work:* Brooklyn Mus, NY; Nat Gallery Can & Can Coun Art Bank, Ottawa, Ont; London Regional Art & Historical Mus, Ont; Wadsworth Atheneum, Hartford,Conn; Art Gallery Hamilton, Ont; and others. *Comn:* Pub sculpture, City of Ottawa, 82. *Exhib:* Mus Contemp Art, Montreal, Que, 84; selected NY Found Arts Artists, Univ Art Gallery, State Univ NY, Albany, 90; Open Mind: The Lewitt Collection, Wadsworth Atheneum, Hartford, Conn, 91-92; Slow Art: Painting in New York Now, PS 1 Mus, 92; Presence, Ctr Int D'Art Contemporain Montreal (exhib catalog), 93-; The Steel Paintings (traveling), Univ Waterloo Art Gallery, Ont, 96; Steelwork, Littlejohn Contemp, NY, 96; New Paintings, Stefan Stux Gallery, NY, 98; One-woman shows, Galerie de Bellefeuille, Montreal, 98 & 2000, Stefan Stux Gallery, NY, 99, Winchester Galleries, Victoria, Can, 2001 & Roger Ramsay Gallery, Chicago, 2001. *Teaching:* Instr drawing, Sch Visual Arts, New York, 90-. *Awards:* B Grants, Can Coun, 84, 88 & 94; New York Found Arts Fel, 90; Nat Endowment Arts Fel, 91. *Bibliog:* Laurel Berger (auth), In their sights, ARTnews, 3/97; Jean-Jacques Bernier (auth), Aux limites de l'abstraction, Vie des Arts, Spring, 98; Tom McDonough (auth), Review, Art in Am, 4/2000. *Media:* Plaster, Pigments; Steel. *Publ:* Coauth, The Core Island Complex (exhib cat), London Regional Art & Historical Mus, 84. *Dealer:* Stux Gallery 529 W 20th St 9th Flr New York City, NY 10011; Roger Ramsay Gallery Ste 207 325 W Huron St Chicago Il 60610. *Mailing Add:* 139 N 10th St Brooklyn NY 11211

ALLAN, WILLIAM GEORGE
PAINTER, EDUCATOR
b Everett, Wash, Mar 28, 36. *Study:* San Francisco Art Inst, BFA, 58. *Work:* Dallas Mus Art; San Francisco Mus Art; Philadelphia Mus Art; Whitney Mus Am Art, Mus Mod Art, NY. *Exhib:* Carnegie Int Exhib, Pittsburgh, 57; Continuing Surrealism, La Jolla Mus Art, Calif, 71; Whitney Painting Ann, NY, 72; 70th Am Exhib, Art Inst Chicago, 72; Indianapolis Mus Art Exhib, 72; Whitney Mus Am Art, NY, 73-74; Painting & Sculpture in Calif: The Mod Era, San Francisco Mus Mod Art, 76; Chicago Arts Club, 78. *Teaching:* Instr painting, Univ Calif, Davis, 65-67; prof art, Calif State Univ, Sacramento, 68-; instr painting, Univ Calif, Berkeley, 69. *Mem:* Nat Acad. *Media:* Acrylic, Watercolor. *Dealer:* Gallery Paule Anglim 14 Geary St San Francisco CA 94108. *Mailing Add:* 69 Ranch Rd San Rafael CA 94903

ALLARA, PAMELA EDWARDS
EDUCATOR
b Scarsdale, NY, Sept 11, 43. *Study:* Brown Univ, BA, 65; Johns Hopkins Univ, PhD, 71. *Exhib:* Co-existence: Contemp Cult Production in South Africa (Waltham: Rose Art Mus and Cape Town: South African Nat Gallery, 2003). *Pos:* Bd trustees, Inst Contemp Art, Photog Resource Ctr, Boston & Rose Art Mus, Brondeis Univ. *Teaching:* Assoc dean, Mus Sch progs & sr lectr art hist, Fine Arts Dept, Tufts Univ, 73-90; asst prof, Fine Art Dept, Brandeis Univ, Waltham, Mass, 90-. *Awards:* 1998 Choice Outstanding Academic Book Award. *Mem:* Col Art Asn. *Res:* Contemporary art; history of photography; film & women artists. *Publ:* Auth, Expressionism in Boston, de Cordova Mus, 86; Cross Currents/Cross Country, Photog Resource Ctr, Boston, 88; Exterior/Interior: Alice Neel, Tufts Univ Art Gallery, 90; Matter of Fact: Alice Neel's Pregnant Nudes, Am Art, 8/2/94; Pictures of People: Alice Neel's American Portrait Gallery, 98. *Mailing Add:* Brandeis Univ Dept Fine Arts Waltham MA 02254

ALLEN, BRUCE WAYNE
EDUCATOR, SCULPTOR
b Columbia, Mo, Feb 27, 53. *Study:* Centenary Col, La, with Willard Cooper, BA, 75, BS, 77; Acad Der Bildenden Kunst, Stuttgart, WGer, 80-81; Univ Wyo, with David Reif & John van Alstein, MFA, 81. *Work:* Wyo State Mus, Cheyenne; Horizons Gallery, Ft Collins, Colo. *Comn:* Sculpture, Glory Bound, Univ Wyo, Laramie, 82; sculpture, Building Blocks, Red Devil Corp, Cincinnati, Ohio, 86. *Exhib:* Solo Exhib, Wyo State Mus, Cheyenne, 81. *Pos:* cur, Meadows Mus Art, currently. *Teaching:* prof studio & art history, Centenary Col La, 83-90. *Mem:* Art in Action (co-founder, 86); La Artists Inc (pres, 88-90); Int Sculpture Conf; Col Art Asn; Women's Caucus for Arts; Shreveport Regional Arts Coun (vp). *Media:* All Media. *Mailing Add:* Centenary College Dept Art and Visual Culture Turner Art Ctr Rm 104 2911 Centenary Blvd Shreveport LA 71104

ALLEN, CONSTANCE OLLEEN WEBB
PAINTER, JEWELRY DESIGNER
b Camphill, Ala, June 10, 1923. *Study:* George Washington Univ; Inst Allende, San Miguel de Allende, Mex; also with Richard Goetz, Oklahoma City & Roy Swanson, Green Valley, Ariz. *Work:* Jane Brooks Sch Deaf; Chickasha Pub Libr. *Comn:* 20 Indian Portraits, AC Leftwich, Duncan, Okla, 72; Landscapes of Southwest Okla, comn by Susan Johnston, Oklahoma City, 78. *Exhib:* 39th & 41st Ann Miniature Painters, Sculptors & Gravers Soc of Washington, Art Club Washington, 72 & 74; Ann Festival of the Arts, Tubac, Ariz, 85, 87, 88, 89, 90, 92, 93 & 94; Ariz State Exhib, Nat League Am Pen Women, Sedona, 87, Phoenix, 89, Ariz; Mont Miniature Art Soc Ninth Ann Int Show, Billings, Mont, 87. *Teaching:* Instr drawing & painting, Univ Sci & Arts of Okla, Chickasha, 74-76. *Awards:* First Place for Pastel, Chickasha Art Guild, Okla, 73; Merit Award Graphic, Fla Nat Miniature Art Show, Okla, 76; First Place Watercolor, Santa Rita Art League Show, Nogales, Ariz, 87; Hon Mention, Santa Cruz Valley Art Asn, Tubac, Ariz, 86; and others. *Bibliog:* AC Leftwich (auth), Indian Hall of Fame, painted by Mrs Webb, 72 & Mrs NH Welch (auth), Mrs Webb has exhib, 74 Chickasha Daily Express; Dale Parish (auth), Artist paints favorite subjects, Green Valley News, 84. *Mem:* Santa Rita Art League, Ariz (pres, 83-84); Nat League Am Pen Women (pres, Sonora Desert Br, 88-90); Arts & Crafts Asn, Green Valley, Ariz, (vpres, 86-87); Santa Cruz Vallery Art Asn, Tubac, Ariz. *Media:* Watercolor, Pastels, Precious Metals, Gemstones. *Mailing Add:* 2791 S Calle Morena Green Valley AZ 85614

ALLEN, E DOUGLAS
PAINTER, WRITER, SCULPTOR
b Jersey City, NJ, Mar 18, 35. *Study:* Ford Sch, Jersey City, NJ, 1945-1951; Newark Sch of Fine Indust Arts, 1953-1955; WJ Aylward (Howard Pyle pupil), Paul Bransom (summer classes Wyoming), 1960-1961. *Work:* Nat Mus Wildlife Art, Jackson, Wyo; Glenbow Mus, Calgary, Can; Hiram Blauvelt Art Mus, Oradel, NJ; Johnson & Johnson Collection, New Brunswick, NJ; PNC Bank Corp Collection, Philadelphia, Pa. *Comn:* Leather Stocking Tales (mural), Lincoln High Sch, Jersey City, NJ, 1952-1953. *Exhib:* Western Vision, Ann Nat Mus Wildlife Art, Jackson Hole Wyo, 1994-2006; D.A. A Retrospective Exhib 1945-1995, Hiram Blauvelt Art Mus, Oradel, NJ, 1995; Reflections of Nature, Newington Cropsey Art Found, Hastings, NY, 1998; Wildlife for a New Century, Nat Mus Wildlife Art, Jackson, Wyo, 2005; Prix de West, Nat Cowboy & Western Heritage Mus, Okla City, 2005-2006. *Collection Arranged:* Animal Art (assembled), Brandywine River Mus, 1974; Charles Livingston Bull Exhib (co-cur exhibits & wrote artists bio & bibliog for catalog), Hiram Blauvelt Art Mus, Oradel, NJ, 1994. *Pos:* Jury chmn, exec bd, Soc Animal Artists, NY, 1990-2006. *Teaching:* instr, private classes, Somerville, NJ, 1968-1974. *Awards:* Nat Wildlife Fedn, Washington, DC, 1952; Small Exhib Award, Salmagundi Club, 1962; Award of Excellence, Soc Animal Artists, 1985. *Bibliog:* Bonnie Silverstein (auth), Douglas Allen: Echoes of the Brandywine, Am Artist, 1977; Zack Taylor (auth), Outdoor Art of Doug Allen, Sports Afield, 1984; Terry Wieland (auth), Painting Animals Inside Out, Sporting Classics, 1990. *Mem:* Salmagundi Club, NY, 1960-2006; Soc Animal Artists (jury chmn & exec bd), 1961-2006; Du Cret Art Sch (bd mem), Plainfield, NJ, 1990-2006. *Media:* Oil, Metal, Cast. *Specialty:* Hist western art, Taos Painters & contemp sporting art. *Interests:* Spend at least one mo per yr in West, Can Rockies & Africa painting, drawing & photographing animals & landscapes. Continually collect,

write & res the publ works of artist NC Wyeth. Also collect works of Howard Pyle, Carl Rungius, Frederic Remington etc. *Collection:* Works of NC Wyeth, Howard Pyle, Carl Rungius & 19th century animal artists. *Publ:* Illusr, The Big Game Animals of North America, Dutton Outdoor Life, 1961; Illusr, Complete Book of Hunting, Harper Brothers, 1962; coauth, NC Wyeth: Paintings, Illus & Murals, Crown Publ Co, 1972; illusr, Game Birds of North America, Harpers Outdoor Life, 1973; illusr, Game Animals of North America, Crown Outdoor Life, 1978. *Dealer:* JN Bartfield Galleries Michael Frost 30 W 57th St NY 10019. *Mailing Add:* 9 Graig Rd Neshanic Station NJ 08853

ALLEN, EDDA LYNNE
PAINTER, ART DEALER
b Big Spring, Tex, July 29, 1932. *Study:* With Randall Davey, Will Schuster & William Longley, 57-62; Southern Methodist Univ; Tex Tech Univ; Univ NMex; Col Santa Fe, BA(summa cum laude), 68. *Work:* Santa Fe Co Munic Ct, NMex State Capitol, Mayors Off, Santa Fe; NMex State Police Off. *Exhib:* Joslyn Art Mus, Omaha, Nebr, 72; Artist Alpine Holiday, Ouray Arts Asn, Colo, 72; Arts Festival, NMex Art League, Albuquerque, 72-74; Roswell Mus & Art Ctr, NMex, 73; one-man show, NMex State Fair, 75. *Teaching:* Instr tech, Col of Santa Fe, 67-68; lectr Alla Prima tech, Univ NMex, 70-71. *Awards:* Award of Merit, Am Arthritis Found, 75; First in Show, Rio Grande Arts & Crafts, 77-78. *Mem:* Santa Fe Soc Art. *Media:* Oil, Watercolor

ALLEN, HENRY SOUTHWORTH
CRITIC
b Summit, NJ, May 23, 41. *Study:* Hamilton Col, BA, 67. *Pos:* Copy ed, New Haven (Conn) Register, 66; reporter, New York News, New York City, 67-70; reporter, ed, critic, The Wash Post, 70-; Teacher in cult and meaning, Univ Md Honors Prog. *Awards:* Nat Endowment of the Humanities fel for journalists, Univ Mich, 75-76; Recipient Am Soc Newspaper Editors award for commentary, 92; Am Soc of Sunday and Feature Editors prize for creative writing, finalist Pulitzer prize, 94; Pulitzer prize Journalism for Criticism, 2000; Sherwood Media award, Blinded Ams Veterans Found, 2000. *Mem:* Marine Corps Hist Asn. *Publ:* Auth: Fool's Mercy, 1982; Auth: Glare, 1991; Auth: Going Too Far Enough, 1994; What It Felt Like B Living in the Am Century, 2000; writer (articles) NY Review of Books, New Yorker, Forbes, Paris Review, Smithsonian, Vogue, Wilson Quarterly. *Mailing Add:* The Wash Post 1150 15th St Northwest Washington DC 20071-0002

ALLEN, JERE HARDY
PAINTER, EDUCATOR
b Selma, Ala, Aug 15, 1944. *Study:* Ringling Sch Art, Sarasota, Fla, four yr cert, 69, BFA, 70; Univ Tenn, Knoxville, MFA, 72. *Work:* Mobile Mus Art, Ala; Coos Art Mus, Ore; Liberty Corp, Greenville, SC; R I Kahn Gallery, Houston; Meridian Mus Art, Miss; City of Hameln, WGer; Huntsville Mus Art, Hunstville, Ala. *Exhib:* West 79 and 80/The Law, Minn Mus Art, 79 & 80; Der Kunstkreis Hameln, 89; Oldenburger Kunstuerein, 89; Stadtische Galerie, Paderborn, WGer, 90; Brenau Col, Gainsville, Ga, 92; Carol Robinson Gallery, New Orleans, La, 92; Outward Bound, Am Art at the Brink of the Twenty-First Century, Meridian Int Ctr, Washington; plus others. *Teaching:* Instr drawing, Carson-Newman Col, 71-72; prof painting, Univ Miss, 72-2000. *Awards:* Award of Distinction, Mainstreams of Marietta Col, 75; Award, Shreveport Nat, Barnwell Art Ctr, La, 75; Visual Arts Award, Miss Inst Arts & Letts, 93. *Media:* Oil, Mixed Media. *Mailing Add:* c/o Carol Robinson Gallery 840 Napoleon Blvd New Orleans LA 70115

ALLEN, JUDITH S
PHOTOGRAPHER, EDUCATOR
b New York, NY, Jan 21, 56. *Study:* Oberlin Col, BA, 77; Mills Col, MFA, 90. *Exhib:* San Francisco Arts Comn Gallery, 91; Bellevue Art Mus, Wash, 94; Ctr Contemp Art, Seattle, Wash, 94; Photographic Ctr NW, Seattle, Wash, 2002; Tacoma Art Mus, 2004; Ctr Contemp Art, Seattle, Wash, 2006. *Teaching:* lectr photog, San Francisco State Univ, 91-92; assoc prof art, Cornish Col Arts, 92-. *Awards:* Trefethen Award, Mills Col, 89; Visual Artist Fel, Nat Endowment Arts, 90-91; Betty Bowen Memorial-Spec Recognition Award, Seattle Art Mus, 94. *Mem:* Col Art Asn; Soc Photog Educ. *Media:* Mixed Media. *Mailing Add:* 3857 23rd Ave SW No B Seattle WA 98105-1124

ALLEN, KAOLA See Phoenix, Kaola Allen

ALLEN, NANCY SCHUSTER
LIBRARIAN, EDUCATOR
b Buffalo, NY, Jan 10, 48. *Study:* Univ Rochester, BA(fine arts), 71, MA(fine arts), 73; Rutgers Univ, MLS, 73. *Pos:* Reference librn, Mus Fine Arts, Boston, 75-77, head librn, 77-95, dir info serv, 95-. *Teaching:* Lectr, art librarianship, Simmons Col Grad Sch Libr & Info Sci, 84-. *Mem:* Art Libr Soc NAm (exec bd, 82-85, chair, 83-84); Mus Computer Network (chair, Art & Arch Prog Comt, Res Libr Group, 84-87); Int Fedn Art Libr (financial officer, Art Sect, 86-); Fenway Libr Online Inc (vpres, 87-89, pres, 89-91); Comm Preserv & Access, Scholarly Advisory Comt on Art Hist, 90 & Joint Task Force on Text & Image, 89-92. *Res:* Computer applications to accessing art object information, visual resources & bibliographic citations for museum objects, conservation & preservation of art library collections. *Publ:* Auth, Art libr, 1984 American Library Association Yearbook of Library & Information Services, Am Libr Asn, Chicago, 85; The History of Western Language Sources for the Study of Japanese Art, Art Libr J, Vol 11, No 4, 86; Bibliographic systems & their object catalog system counterparts, In: Procedural Guide to Automating an Art Library (ARLIS/NA Occasional Papers, No 7), 87; The museum prototype project of the J Paul Getty Art History & Information Program: A view from the library, In: Linking Art Objects & Art Information (Library Trends, Vol 37, No 2), 88; The Art & Architectural Program of the Research Libraries Group, Vol 13, No 4, Art Libr J, 88, 5-10 & Vol 23, No 3, Inspel, 89, 141-154

ALLEN, PAUL
COLLECTOR
b Seattle, Jan 21, 53. *Study:* Student, Washington State Univ, 71—73. *Pos:* Co-founder Traf-O-Data Co, Seattle, 72-73; progammer Honeywell Int Inc, Waltham, 74-75; co-founder Microsoft Corp (formerly Micro-Soft), Albuquerque, 75; general partner Microsoft Corp, 75-77, vpres, 77-81, exec vpres research & new product devel, 81-83, sr strategy adv, 2000-; founder Asymetrix Corp, Bellevue, Washington, 85, Starwave Corp, Bellevue, 92; co-founder Interval Research Corp, Palo Alto, Calif, 92; founder Vulcan Productions; founder, chmn Vulcan Inc, Seattle; Chief Exec Officer Vulcan Ventures, Bellevue, 87-; owner, chmn bd Portland (Ore) Trail Blazers, 88-; owner, chmn Seattle Seahawks, 97-; chmn Charter Communications Inc, 98-, Charter Investment, Inc, 98-; owner TechTV; sponsor, funder SpaceShipOne Venture, Mojave, Calif, 2003; founder Allen Telescope Array, SETI Inst Univ Calif Berkeley, 2004; bd dir, Egghead Discount Software, Microsoft Corp, 83-2000, Darwin Molecular, Inc; founder Experience Music Project; partner DreamWorks SKG; founder Allen Institute Brain Sci, 2003, Experience Sci Fiction Mus, 2004; Achievements include sponsoring and funding the record flights for Space ShipOne, which won the Ansari X prize on October 4, 2004. *Awards:* Named one of Top 15 Philanthropists in America, Top 200 Collectors, ARTnews Magazine, 2004, 2005, 2006; named to Computer Mus Hall of Fame. *Collection:* Impressionism, Old Masters, pop art, tribal art. *Mailing Add:* Vulcan Inc 505 5th Ave S Ste 900 Seattle WA 98104

ALLEN, PHILIP
b NYC, Jan 15, 1952. *Exhib:* Solo shows at Rosa Esman Gallery, 85, Sorkin Gallery, NY, 90, Eli Marsh Gallery, Amherst Col, 92; group shows include CAPS Painters, 79-80, Rennselaer Polytechnic Inst, 80, Young Painters, 80, Bronx Mus Art, 80, Five from NY, Washington Project Arts, 82; New Talent, AM Sachs Gallery, NY, 82, Paintings, State Univ NY, Purchase, 82, NY to Bennington: Paintings, Susan Lemberg Usdan Gallery, Bennington Col, 83; AVA II, DeCordova and Dana Mus and Park, Lincoln, Mass, 83, Mus Contemp Art Chicago, 83, NYC Painters, Fabian Carlsson Gallery, London, 85; New Response: Contemp Painters of the Hudson River, Albany Inst History and Art, 86, More than Meets the Eye: 9 Painters from NYC, Galleria Carini, Forence, Italy, 86, The Legacy of the Abstract Expressionists, Gallery at Hastings on Hudson, 90, Gallery Artists, German Van Eck Gallery, NY, 92; Maine Coast Artists, Rockport, Maine, 97; Nat Acad Design, 2006; represented in permanent collections of First Nat Bank Chicago, Equitable Life Co, NY, Walter Hopps, Houston, Tex. *Teaching:* Faculty mem Fine Arts Dept, Boston Mus Ch, 92, Parsons Sch Design, 1994-2003; vis artist, RISD vis artist Fordham Univ; vis artist Mass Col Art. *Awards:* Award in Visual Arts, Charlotte, NC, 83; CAPS fel, NY, 80; Nat Endowment Arts fel, Washington, DC, 82; Louis Comfort Tiffany fel, 86

ALLEN, RALPH
PAINTER, EDUCATOR
b Eng, 1926. *Study:* Sir John Cass Sch Art & Slade Sch Fine Arts, London. *Work:* Nat Gallery Can; Art Gallery Toronto; Queen's Univ, Ont; Queen's Park, Toronto; also in pvt collections. *Teaching:* Assoc prof art hist & dir, Agnes Etherington Art Ctr, Queen's Univ, Ont, formerly; retired. *Awards:* Jessie Dow Award, Montreal, 59; Can Coun Scholar, 59 & Sr Fel, 68; Baxter Award, Toronto, 60. *Mem:* Ont Soc Artists; Royal Can Acad Arts. *Mailing Add:* 199 Albert St Kingston ON K7L 3V4 Canada

ALLEN, ROBERTA
CONCEPTUAL ARTIST, PHOTOGRAPHER, COLLAGE ARTIST
b New York, NY, Oct 6, 45. *Work:* Mus Mod Art, NY; Metrop Mus Art, NY; Cooper-Hewitt Mus, NY; Cincinnati Art Mus; Univ Wis-Milwaukee; Stadtische Galerie im Lenbachhaus, Munich. *Exhib:* Solo exhibs, John Weber Gallery, NY, 74, 75, 77 & 79, Kunstforum, Staadtische Gallerie im Lenbachhaus, Munich, 81, Galerie Walter Storms, Munich, 81, Galeria Primo Piano, Rome, 81, Perth Inst Contemp Arts, Australia, 89 & Art Resources Transfer Inc, 2001; Contemp Abstract Art: Works on Paper, Baltimore Mus Art, 76; Abstract Drawings, Albright-Knox Art Gallery, Buffalo, NY, 76; MTL Galerie, Brussels, Belg, 78; and others. *Collection Arranged:* Metrop Mus Art, NY; Biblisteque Nat, Paris; Cincinnati Art Mus; Yale Univ Collection; Wadsworth Atheneum, Conn. *Teaching:* Guest lectr, Corcoran Sch Art, Washington, 75, CW Post Col, Glenvale, NY, 79, Kutztown Univ, 79 & Ctr Fine Arts, Univ W Australia, 89; vis fel, Curtin Univ, Perth, Australia, 89. *Awards:* Residence Fel Yaddo, 83; Fel, Va Ctr for Creative Arts, 85; Artist-in-Residence Fel, Art Gallery W Australia, Perth, 89. *Bibliog:* Jeff Deitch (auth), Roberta Allen, Arts Mag, 2/78; Judith Lopez Cardozo (auth), Roberta Allen, Artforum, 2/78; Holly O'Grady (auth), The paradoxical arrow: Roberta Allen's installations and books, Arts Mag, 2/79. *Media:* Photography, drawing, colllage. *Publ:* Auth, Pointless Arrows, pvt publ, 76; Pointless Acts, Collation Ctr, 77; Possibilities, John Weber Gallery & Parasol Press, 77; Everything in the World There is to Know by Somebody, But Not by the Same Knower, Ottenhausen Verlag, Munich, 81; The Traveling Woman, Vehicle Ed, 86. *Mailing Add:* 18 Pine Grove St Woodstock NY 12498

ALLEN, TERRY
MULTI-MEDIA ARTIST
b Wichita, Kans, May 7, 43. *Study:* Chouinard Art Inst, Los Angeles, BFA, 66. *Work:* Mus Mod Art & Metrop Mus Art, NY; Los Angeles Co Mus Art & Mus Contemp Art, Los Angeles; San Francisco Mus Mod Art, Calif; Dallas Mus Art, Tex; Oakland Mus Art, Calif; plus many others. *Exhib:* Extraordinary Realities (with catalog) & 1973 Biennial Exhib (with catalog), 73 & Whitney Biennial, Whitney Mus, NY, 77; Selections from Cirrus Editions (with catalog), Los Angeles Co Mus Art, Calif, 74; Eight from Calif (with catalog), Nat Collection Fine Arts, Smithsonian Inst, Washington, DC, 75; The Small Scale in Contemp Art (with catalog), Chicago Art Inst, Ill, 75; Painting & Sculpture in California: The Modern Era (with catalog), San

Francisco Mus Mod Art, Calif, traveling, 76; The Modern Era: Bay Area Update, Huntsville Mus Art, Ala, 77; The Record as Artwork (with catalog), Fort Worth Art Mus, Tex, traveling, 77; New Acquisitions Exhib (Prints), Mus Mod Art, NY, 77; Aesthetics of Graffiti, San Francisco Mus Mod Art, Calif, 78; The Southern Voice (with catalog), Ft Worth Art Mus, Tex, 81; Exchange Between Artists 1931-82, Poland-USA (with catalog), Mus Mod Art, Paris, France, 82; Awards in Visual Arts (with catalog), Nat Gallery, Washington, DC, traveling, 82; Site Stradegies (with catalog), Oakland Mus, Calif, 83; Boston Collects: Contemp Painting & Sculpture (with catalog), Boston Mus Fine Arts, Mass, 86; Avant Garde in the Eighties (with catalog), Los Angeles Co Mus Art, Calif, 87; Lost & Found in California: Four Decades of Assemblage Art, James Corcoran Gallery, traveling, 88; Centenary Print Exhib, Mod Mus Ft Worth, Tex, 92; Porfiles II: On Paper (with catalog), Adair Margo Gallery, El Paso, Tex, traveling, 92; Printmaking in Tex: The 1980's, Laguna Gloria Mus, Austin, Tex, 92; La Frontera-The Border (with catalog), Mus Contemp Art, San Diego, Calif, traveling, 93-94; Mapping, UTSA Art Gallery, Univ Tex, San Antonio, traveling, 94; solo shows, Moody Gallery, Houston, Tex, 94 & 96, Blaffer Gallery, Univ Houston, Tex, 94, Blue Star Art Space, San Antonio, Tex, 94, Univ Mo Kansas City Gallery Art, 95, LA Louver Gallery, Venice, Calif, 96, Barry Whistler Gallery, Dallas, Tex, 97 & Michael Solway Gallery, Cincinnati, Ohio, 97; The Prints of Cirrus Edition, Los Angeles Co Mus, Calif, 95; Temporarily Possessed, New Mus, NY, 95; Am Kaleidoscope, Nat Mus Am Art, Washington, DC, 96; Scene of the Crime, Univ Calif Los Angeles, Armand Hammer Mus Art & Cult Ctr, 97; Stephen F Austin State Univ Dept Art, Griffith Gallery, Nacogdoches, Tex, 98; plus many other group & solo shows. *Pos:* Faculty, Calif State Univ, Fresno, 71-79. *Teaching:* Instr drawing, Chouinard Art Inst, Los Angeles, 68-69; guest artist & lectr, numerous univ, mus & institutions, 71-84; assoc prof, 74-77, Calif State Univ, Fresno, prof, 78-79. *Awards:* Nat Endowment Arts Fel, 70, 78 & 85; Bessie Award, NY, 86; Guggenheim Fel, 96; and others. *Bibliog:* Jody Zellen (auth), Terry Allen, Arts Mag, 10/91; Joan Smith (auth), He'll Take it and Make Art, San Francisco Examiner, 10/91; Benjamin Weissman (auth), Terry Allen, Artforum, 11/91. *Publ:* Auth & coauth, numerous theatre & music performance recordings, 68-94; featured on numerous radio progs, 71-93; auth & coauth, numerous videos, 76-94; coauth, A Simple Story (juarez), Wexner Ctr Arts, Columbus, Ohio, 92; Poison Armor, Blue Star Art Space, San Antonio, Tex, 94; and many more. *Dealer:* Moody Gallery 2815 Colquitt Houston TX 77098. *Mailing Add:* Rte 10 Box 88-N Santa Fe NM 87501

ALLEN, WILLIAM J
HISTORIAN, EDUCATOR

b Tuscaloosa, Ala, Nov 8, 45. *Study:* Univ Ala, BA, 68; Johns Hopkins Univ, MA, 73, PhD (Kress Fel, Am Res Inst Turkey Fel), 81. *Teaching:* Vis asst prof, Okla State Univ, 77-79; assoc prof art hist, Ark State Univ, Jonesboro, 79-, chmn art dept, 83-87, dean Col Fine Arts, 87-91, prof art hist, 91- & dir Ctr Learning Technol, 97-. *Mem:* Col Art Asn Am; Hist Photog Group (nat coordr 87-). *Res:* history of photography. *Publ:* Auth, The Spirit of fact in court: Southworth's testimony in Marcy vs Barnes, In: History of Photography, 83 & The Abdul Hamid II collection, 83, Legal Tests of Photography-as-Art: Sarony and Others, 86, History of Photography; Sixty-Nine Istanbul Photographers in Shadow and Substance: Essays on the History of Photography in Honor of Heinz K Henisch, 90; coauth, The McGraw-Hill Guide to Electronic Research in Art, 99 & Teaching Composition Digitally, Visual Resources XV, 99. *Mailing Add:* 1224 S Madison St Jonesboro AR 72401

ALLENTUCK, MARCIA EPSTEIN
HISTORIAN, EDUCATOR

b New York, NY, June 28, 28. *Study:* New York Univ, BA; Columbia Univ, PhD, 64. *Hon Degrees:* Oxford Univ, hon MA, 75. *Pos:* vis scholar, Wolfson Col, 1974- & Burrell Art Collection, Glasgow, Scotland, 1987-88. *Teaching:* Prof hist art, Graduate Ctr, City Univ NY, 1972-88, prof emer, 1988-. *Awards:* Sr Res Fel, Dumbarton Oaks, 1972-73 & Nat Endowment Humanities, 1973-74; Vis Fel, Wolfson Col, Oxford Univ, Eng, 1974; Res Fel Brit Acad, 1980; Inst Advan Studies, Univ Edinburgh, 1983-84; Swann Found Fel, 1989-90. *Mem:* Col Art Asn; Soc Archit Historians Gt Brit; Soc Archit Historians; fel Royal Soc Arts; PEN, Soc of Authors. *Res:* British, American & Canadian art & architectural history. *Publ:* Auth, The work of Henry Needler, Clark Libr, Univ Calif Press, 60; Henry Fuseli: The Artist as Man of Letters & Critic, Univ Microfilm Am, 64; The Achievement of Isaac Bashevis Singer, Southern Ill Univ Press, 69; Rosettis Burd-Alane, Burlington Mag, 12/70; John Graham's System & Dialects of Art, Johns Hopkins Univ Press, 71; Mark Gertler, Apollo, 10/74; Fuseli & Macklin, J of the Warburg & Courtauld Inst, 76. *Mailing Add:* 5 W 86th St Apt 12B New York NY 10024-3665

ALLGOOD, CHARLES HENRY
ART HISTORIAN, PAINTER

b Augusta, Ga, Apr 24, 1923. *Study:* Univ Ga, with Lamar Dodd, Carl Holty, Yasuo Kunyoshi, BFA, MFA; Ecole du Louvre, Paris. *Exhib:* Painting of the Yr, Atlanta, Ga, 63 & 65; Southeastern Art Exhib, Atlanta, 65; Miss Nat Exhib, Jackson, 66; Mid-South Exhib, Memphis, Tenn, 71. *Collection Arranged:* African Art & Artifacts, 74; Egyptian Art & Artifacts, 75. *Pos:* Dir, EH Little Gallery, Memphis State Univ; illusr children's bks, 89. *Teaching:* Prof painting, Judson Col, Marion, Ala, 51-55 & Memphis State Univ, 55-89. *Media:* Oil, Transparent Watercolor. *Mailing Add:* 3886 Healy Rd Memphis TN 38111

ALLING, CLARENCE (EDGAR)
MUSEUM DIRECTOR, CERAMIST

b Dawson Co, Nebr, Jan 28, 1933. *Study:* Washburn Univ, BFA; Ohio State Univ, with Edgar Littlefield; Univ Kans, with Sheldon Carey, MFA. *Work:* Excelsior Ins Co, NY. *Exhib:* One-man shows, Mulvane Art Ctr, Topeka, Kans, 63 & Sioux City Art Ctr, Iowa, 63; Area Artists, Sioux City, 63 & 65 & Des Moines, Iowa, 64; two-man show, L'Atelier, Cedar Falls, Iowa, 65; and others. *Pos:* Dir, Waterloo Mus Art, formerly. *Awards:* Prizes, Designer-Craftsman Show, Lawrence, Kans, 59-61; Purchase award, Ceramic Nat, Everson Mus, Syracuse, NY, 60; Merit award, Sioux City, 65. *Mailing Add:* 1629 Forest Ave Waterloo IA 50702

ALLING, JANET D
PAINTER

b New York, NY Dec 19, 39. *Study:* Skidmore Col, 57-60; Yale Univ Sch Art, MFA, 64; studied with Alex Katz, Neil Welliver, Philip Pearlstein. *Work:* Univ Va Art Mus, Charlottesville; Bellevue Hosp, NY; York Col, City Univ NY & NY City Tech Col; Florists Transworld Deliveries Art Collection, Mich; Security Pac Nat Bank, Los Angeles, Calif. *Comn:* Cape Primrose (painting), comn by Hugh Hardy, NY, 81; Garvins Restaurant, comn by Richard Garvin, NY, 82; Lobelia, comn by Virginia Stein, Somerville, NJ, 88. *Exhib:* Painterly Realists, Art Sch, Art Inst Chicago, 72; Komblee Gallery, 74 & 79; Color Light Image Exhib for United Nations, NY, 75; one-person exhibs, St Mary's Col Md, 90, Vassar Col, Poughkeepsie, NY, 90; Trinity Col Vt, 94; York Col, City Univ NY, 95; Gallery at 17 Peck, Providence, RI, 2006. *Teaching:* instr, oil & watercolor painting, Brooklyn Mus Art School, 73-77; instr, oil painting, Bronxville Adult School, Bronxville, NY, 89-2005. *Awards:* CAPS Award, NY State Coun Arts, 73; Support Grant, Adolph Gottlieb Found, 88; Fel Grant, Nat Endowment Arts, 89. *Bibliog:* Cindy Nemser (auth), The Close Up Vision-Representative Art, Arts Mag, 72; Bob Stone (auth), Janet Alling's Passionate Eye, Am Artist Mag, 10/94. *Media:* Oil, Watercolor. *Interests:* art history, literature & music. *Dealer:* Gallery at 17 Peck Providence RI 02903. *Mailing Add:* 88 Orange St Unit 2B Providence RI 02903

ALLMAN, MARGO
PAINTER, SCULPTOR

b New York, NY, Feb 23, 33. *Study:* Smith Col; Moore Col Art; Univ Pa; Univ Del; with Reginald Marsh & Hans Hofmann. *Work:* Del Art Mus, Wilmington; Philadelphia Mus Art. *Comn:* Travertine sculpture, comn by Mrs Werner Hutz & family, Kennett Square, Pa, 73; cor-ten steel sculpture, comn by Richard Vanderbilt, Chadds Ford, Pa, 74; ferro-cement sculpture, Tidewater Publ Co, Centerville, Md, 75; bronze sculpture, comn by Wesley & Harriet Memeger Jr, Wilmington, Del, 90. *Exhib:* Del Art Mus, 56-81, 93, 2000; Univ Del, 65-72 & 76; one-person shows, Haas Gallery Art, Bloomsburg State Col, Pa, 76 & 77, Moore Col Art, 79 & Del State Art Coun, 81; West Chester Univ, Pa, 94; Del Ctr Contemp Art, 2002 & 05. *Teaching:* Instr, Del Inst Arts Educ, 84-85. *Awards:* Drawing Prize, 51st Ann Show, Del Art Mus, 65; Best Landscape, Wilmington Trust Bank Prize, Del Art Mus, 69; Distinguished Alumnae Award, Moore Col Art & Design, 98. *Bibliog:* Linnette Maxson, Space, Time and Something to Say, Chester Co Press, 10/14/98; Renee Paquin, West Grove woman to exhibit in Biennial 2000, The Kennett Paper, 5/25/00; Victoria Donohoe (auth), Contemplative Works Examine Structure of Life, The Philadelphia Inquirer, 6/2/02. *Mem:* Del Ctr Contemp Arts; Del Art Mus; Nat Mus Women Arts; Syne, a Delaware Valley Consortium of Eight Professional Artists. *Media:* Acrylic, Miscellaneous Media; Carved Concrete, Miscellaneous Media. *Mailing Add:* 202 E State Rd West Grove PA 19390

ALLMOND, CHARLES
SCULPTOR

b Wilmington, Del, Apr 25, 31. *Study:* Univ Del, BS, 53, MS, 57; Sch Law, Temple Univ, JD, 63. *Work:* DuPont-Mitsui Polychemicals, Tokyo; Hercules Inc, NY; Hiram Blauvelt Art Mus, Oradell, NJ; Leigh Yawkey Woodson Art Mus, Wausau, Wis; AstraZeneca, Wilmington, Del; Biggs Mus of Am Art, Dover, DE; Morris Libr Univ of DE, Newark, DE; HRH Crown Princess Victoria of Sweden; Swedish Ambassador to US, Washington, DC. *Comn:* Madonna and Child, Christ in Christmas Committee, Wilmington, 89; Ode to Joy, Class of 1953, Morris Libr, Univ Del, 93; Cantilevers, Frank Lloyd Wright House, Wilmington, 96 & 2002; State of Del for Ambassador of Arts Award, 2004. *Exhib:* Nat Acad Design Ann, NY, 88; Salmagundi Club Ann, NY, 89-93, 95- 2006; Art and the Animal, Ann, 87-2006 & Touring, 90-2006; Woodmere Art Mus, Philadelphia, 94, 95 & 98-2003, 2006; Birds in Art Ann 94-97, 99, 2001-2003 & Touring, 94-95 & 96-99, 2001-2003; The Am Col, Bryn Mawr, Pa, 94 & 98; Hiram Blauvelt Art Mus, Oradell, NJ, 98; Ira Spanierman Gallery, NY, 98; Del Div Arts, Wilmington, 2000; outdoor sculpture exhib, Leigh Yawkey Woodson Art Mus, 2002-2003; Ward Mus Wildfowl Art, Salisbury, Md, 1999, 2000; Biggs Mus Am Art, Dover, Del, 2003; Audubon Artists, NY, 2000-2005; Toad Hall Gallery, Grounds for Sculpture, Hamilton, NJ, 2003-2004. *Pos:* Pres Soc of Animal Artists, 95-2001. *Teaching:* Guest lectr enrichment ser, Acad Lifelong Learning, Univ Del, 88, Gloucester Co Col, Sewell, NJ, 99 & World Wild Life Art Brought to Life Symp, Bjorklunden, Lawrence Univ, Wis, 2000, It's Wild Out There confs, West Valley Art Mus, Surprise, Ariz, 2001. *Awards:* Governor's Award for the Arts (Del), 2004; Soc of Animal Artists Award of Excellence, 87,98, 99, 2000, 2002; Audubon Artists Sculpture Awards, 2001, 2002, 2004, 2005; Woodmere Art Mus Sculpture Awards, 94, 2002; Salmagund: Club Sculpture Awards, 89, 90, 92, 96, 99-2004, 2006. *Bibliog:* Fine Woodworking Design Book Seven, Taunton Press, 96; The Edge of Abstraction, Wildlife Art/Sculpture Forum, 7-8/97; Natural Habitat: Contemporary Wildlife Artists of North America, Spanierman Gallery, LLC, NY; Artistic Elements that Create a Sense of Style; J Brown, Wildlife Art, 2003; dir (film), Charles Allmond, Sculptor, Del

Div Arts, 2004. *Mem:* Soc Animal Artists; Salmagundi Club; Rehoboth Art League; Audubon Artists; Philadelphia Sculptors. *Media:* Stone, Bronze, Wood. *Publ:* Cover illusr, Rehoboth Art League Members Fine Art Show Catalog, 89; contribr, Del Today Mag, 7/91; cover for invitation, Beebe Hosp Dinner & Auction, 94; cover, Rehoboth Art League Calendar, 96; illus, Jeffery Whiting's Owls of North America, Heliconia Press, Clayton, Ontario, 97; Poster Soc of Animal Artists Ann Exhib, 2002. *Dealer:* Shidoni Galleries 1508 Bishops Lodge Rd Tesuque NMex 87574; Somerville Manning Gallery, Breck's Mill, 101 Stone Block Rd, Greenville, DE 19807; Aeric Art Gallery 451/2 Lake St Rehoboth Beach DE 19971. *Mailing Add:* 104 Rowland Park Blvd Wilmington DE 19803

ALLRICH, M LOUISE BARCO
ART DEALER, ART CONSULTANT
b Ft Monroe, Va, Feb 16, 47. *Study:* Univ Calif, Davis, BA, 68; Univ Calif, Berkeley, post-grad work art hist & theory; Univ Calif, Irvine, Appraisal Studies in Fine & Decorative Art. *Pos:* Pres, Allrich Gallery, San Francisco, 71-95; trustee, Fiberworks Ctr for Textile Arts, Berkeley, 72-81; trustee, Old Pueblo Mus, Tucson, Ariz, 88-90. *Teaching:* Lectr, Alta Col Art, 73, Wash State Univ, Pullman, 78, Los Angeles Co Mus, 79, Oakland Mus, 82, Art Inst Chicago, 82 & Portland Art Mus, 83, Sch Art Inst, Chicago, 83, San Jose State Univ, MH de Young Mus, Calif, 97. *Bibliog:* Kuniko Lucy Kato (auth), Tangible Enternity - Magdalena Abakanowicz, Int Art Research, Sapporo, Japan, 91; Jessica Scarborough (auth), From a Gallery Owner's Perspective, an interview with Louise Allrich, Fiberarts Mag, 94; Barbara Mayer (auth), Contemp am Craft Art, Gibbs M Smith, Inc Peregrine, Smith Books, Salt Lake City, 98. *Mem:* Art Table. *Specialty:* Contemp textile art, painting and sculpture. *Publ:* Auth, Center for the Arts, pvt publ, 74; contribr, A look at Fiber, Currant Mag, 76. *Mailing Add:* 236 W Portal Ave Suite 406 San Francisco CA 94127

ALLUMBAUGH, JAMES
SCULPTOR, EDUCATOR
b Dallas, Tex, Jan 27, 1941. *Study:* E Tex State Univ, BS, 63 & MS, 65; N Tex State Univ, EdD, 68. *Work:* Richardson Pub Libr, Tex; Beaumont Art Mus, Tex; Houston Ctr 2, Tex; Tyler Art Mus, Tex; Seaman Collection, Corpus Christi, Tex; MADI Mus, Dallas, Tex. *Exhib:* Solo shows, E Tex State Univ, Commerce, Tex, 92, N Lake Col, Irving, Tex, 92, Del Mar Col, Corpus Christi, Tex, 93, Critics Choice, Dallas Visual Art Ctr, Tex, 96; Americas 2000, Northwest Art Ctr, Minot State Univ, 96; Celebration Am Crafts, Creative Arts Workshop, New Haven, Conn, 97-99; Crafts Nat, Zoller Gallery, The Penn State Univ, 98; LaGrange Nat Biennial, Lamar Dodd Art Ctr, LaGrange, Ga, 98; Meyerson Symphony Ctr, Dallas, Tex, 2000; Black and Blue, MAC Arts Ctr, Dallas, Tex, 2000; La Petite, Alder Gallery, Eugene Ore, 2001, 2002; Oct Int Armory Art Ctr, W Palm Beach, Fla, 2001; Nat Small works, Schoharie Co Art Gallery, Cobleskill, NY, 2001, 2003, 2004; Vision Int, Art Ctr Waco, Waco, Tex, 2002; Am MADI Artists, MADI Mus, Dallas Tex, 2004; Celebration of Geometric Art Salon Barbonico, Naples Italy, 2004; MADI Mus, Dallas Tex, 2005-2006; Art on the Streets, US Bank, Colorado Springs, Colo, 2006; Bath House Cult Ctr, Dallas, Tex, 2006. *Pos:* Dir, Tex Col Sculpture Symposium, Dallas, 77-; photogr and consult, Central Time Zone Sculpture Symposium, Fermilab, Batavia, Ill, 91; photographic liaison, Tex Sculpture Asn, Dallas, 90-2000. *Teaching:* Fel design, N Tex State Univ, 66-68; assoc prof 3-D design, E Tex State Univ, 68-81, prof, 81-99 (now Tex A&M); Instr/Consultant, MADI Mus, 2004-2006. *Awards:* Spanish & Art Mex, Cemanahuac Inst, Cuernavaca; Ice House Cul Ctr, Dallas, 2001; Tex Sculpture Asn, Dallas, 2001-. *Mem:* Int Sculpture Ctr. *Media:* Metal, Photography, Collage. *Publ:* Illusr (cover illus), 16th Ann Invitational Exhib, Longview Arts Ctr, 74 & 45th Ann Exhib, Springfield Art Mus, 75; auth, Cubes Space and Light, Spiral Enterprises, 77; Basic Techniques for Photographing Sculpture, Tex Sculpture Asn, fall journal, 92; American Madi Artists, MADI Mus & Gallery, 2004; 2 Southwestern Artists, MADI Mus 2005. *Dealer:* MADI Mus and Gallery Dallas TX. *Mailing Add:* 2009 St Francis Dallas TX 75228

ALLYN, JERRI
CONCEPTUAL ARTIST, EDUCATOR
b Paterson, NJ, Feb 21, 52. *Study:* Goddard Col, Vt, MA (art & society), 80. *Comn:* Pub Art Fund, NY; MTA Arts for Transit & Creative Time, NY; 3 - New Am Radio, NY. *Exhib:* Sisters of Survival, Nat & European Tour, 82-84; Love Novellas, Franklin Furnace, NY, 83, West Coast Tour, 84; Rape, Univ Gallery, Ohio State Univ, Columbus, 85, Nat Tour, 86-87; Committed to Print, Mus Mod Art, NY, 88, Nat Tour; Am Dining: A Working Woman's Moment, New Mus Contemp Art, NY, 85, Nat Tour, 86-88; Art in the Anchorage, Creative Time, NY, 90; Angels Have Been Sent to Me, Creative Time, NY, 91; Six Moons Over Oaxaca, Bicultural Exchange - Galerie Arte de Oaxaca, Mex & Artists Space, NY, 94-95; High Performance: The First 5 Yrs 1978-1982, Bard Col, NY & LACE Contemp Art Exhibs, Calif, 02-03; A Chair is, Lower Manhattan Cult Coun, NY, 02. *Collection Arranged:* Mus Mod Art; JP Getty Mus, Calif; Wesleyan Univ; Mus Fine Arts, Mass; Smithsonian Inst; pvt collections include Gerardo Barbara, Zebra Davis, David Ehrich III, Aurora Fox, Bill Gordh, Donna Henes, Patricia Spears Jones, Jerry Kearns, Nancy & Alfonso Mayagoitia, Peter McCracken, Dierdre & Fran Resch, Ester Smith & Dikko Faust, Cheryl Swannack. *Pos:* panelist, NY Coun Arts, Visual Arts, 85-86 & Theatre/Solo Performance, 92, Wash State Arts Comn, 89, NY Found Arts, 90, Pittsburgh Filmmakers & Pa Coun Arts, 96, Arts Link Residencies/CEC Int Partners, NY, 98; policy & guideline develop, Nat Endowment Arts, Interarts, 88, Vis Arts & Challenge Prog, Washington, DC, 93; consult, Performance Studies Prog, Syracuse Univ, NY, 86 & Franklin & Marshall Col, Pa, 89; Dir Educ & Pub prog, Bronx Mus Arts, NY, 94-98; mem, Bessies Dance & Performance Art Awards Comn, NY, 87-; entrance examiner, LaGuardia HS of Music, Art & Performing Arts, NY, 97-. *Teaching:* prof, New School for Social Research, NY, 87-92; prof, Western Wash Univ, Bellingham, 87-90; artist-in-residence, Univ Ill, Champagne/Urbana, 87, Cal Col Arts & Crafts, 88, Humbolt Univ, Oakland, Calif, 88, Kutstown Univ, Pa, 89, 90; staff develop, New York City Bd Educ, 98-02. *Awards:* Nat Endowment for the Arts, 81, 85, 87, 89, 90; NY State Coun Arts - Radio, New Tech & Artist Project Grants, 83, 86, 89, 91, 01; Am Int Lila Wallace Readers Digest Residency, Mex, 93-94; Project Arts, Bronx, 99, 00, 01, 02; NY Found Arts/Arts in Educ, 00-01, World Views Studio Spec Project Residency, Lower Manhattan Cult Coun, NY, 00-01; Fund for Creative Communities, NY State Coun Arts, 01-02; Ctr for Arts Educ, NY, 02; Manhattan Graphics Ctr Residency, NY, 02; Rockefeller Fund, Bellagio Conf and Study Ctr, Italy, 02; Joan Mitchell Fund, NY, 02-03. *Bibliog:* Pink Glass Swan, Feminist Essays Art, 95; Mapping the Terrain, New Genre Pub Art, 95; El Guia/Arts Mediterranea (Spain), 96, Pub Art Review, 98; Performance Artists Talking in the Eighties, 00; Parallels & Intersections: A Remarkable History of Woman Artists in California, 1950-2000, 02; Moravic, M, Woman's Building Oral History Project, Smithsonian Archives, 02, Faxen (Austria), 99; High Performance: First 5 Years, 1978-1982, 01; City Folk Morning Prog, Arts Feature, WFUV Radio, 02; Sunday Arts, Staten Island Advance, 02; Sunday Arts & Leisure, NY Times, 02; Cat Radio Café/Arts Mag, WBAI Radio, 02. *Media:* new art forms, Interdisciplinary. *Publ:* Role Confusion, 77; Love Novellas, 84; American Dining Part 1 & 2, 85, 87; Angels Have Been Sent to Me, 90; Six Moons Over Oaxaca, 94; A Chair is a Throne is a Freedom Fighter's Camp Stool, 03. *Mailing Add:* 655 Palms Blvd Venice CA 90291-3846

ALMOND, JOAN
PHOTOGRAPHER
b Los Angeles, Calif, June 3, 35. *Work:* Can Mus Contemp Photog, Ottawa; Brookings Inst, Washington, DC; Santa Barbara Mus Art, Calif. *Exhib:* Solo exhibs, Saiyde Bronfman Ctr, Montreal, 87, Tekeyan Cult Ctr, Montreal, 88, St John's Armenian Church, Southfield, Mich, 89, Soc Contemp Photog, Kansas City, 92, Nile Gallery, Cairo, 92, Schatten Gallery, Emory Univ, Atlanta, Ga, 93, Brooks Inst Photog, Santa Barbara, 94 & Gallery Contemp Photog, Santa Monica, 97, Staton Greenberg Gallery, Santa Barbara, 2004, Cumberlano Gallery, Nashville, TN, 2005, June Batehan Gallery, NYC 2003; Dimensions in Art, Int Design Ctr, Montreal, 88; Visual Concepts, Univ Judaism, Los Angeles, Calif, 90; Celebrating Children, Jacob Javits Conv Ctr, NY, 91. *Collection Arranged:* Canadian Mus Contemp Photography, Ottawa,; Brookings Inst, Washington, DC; Santa Barbara Mus Art, Calif. *Bibliog:* Roberto Tejada (auth), The Past in the Present (monograph) 2002; B & W Magazine, 2004. *Mem:* Women in Photography Int. *Media:* Platinum. *Specialty:* Photographic. *Publ:* Armenians in Jerusalem, Ararat, winter 89; C comme cinema, Art Global, 91; Best of photography, Photographer's Forum, 91; Collector Print Program, Friends of Photography, 98; The Past in the Present, a Catalog of Photographs, 97; The Harvard Jerusalem Studio, MIT Press, 86. *Dealer:* Halted Gallery, Bloomfield Hills, MI; Cumberlano Gallery Nashville, TN; Staton Greenberg Gallery, Santa Barbara, CA; Hochelber Fine Arts, Montreal, Quebec, CDA. *Mailing Add:* 54 Malibu Colony Dr Malibu CA 90265-4637

ALMOND, PAUL
FILMMAKER, WRITER
b Montreal, Que, Apr 26, 31. *Study:* Bishop's Col Sch, 44-48; McGill Univ; Balliol Col, Oxford, BA & MA. *Pos:* Dir & producer, Can Broadcasting Corp, 53-65, BBC, 57, Granada TV, 63. *Awards:* Special Award of Merit for Seven Up, Prague, 63; Canadian Film Awards, Best Motion Picture Dir, 70; Best Television Drama Dir, 79; Officer of the Order of Can, 2001. *Bibliog:* Janet Edsforth (auth), The Flame Within (a study of Paul Almond's Films), Can Film Inst, 71. *Mem:* Dir Guild Am; hon life mem Dir Guild Can; Acad Can Cinema & TV, Royal Can Acad Art; Acad Motion Picture Arts & Sci. *Interests:* birding. *Publ:* Auth, La Vengence des Dieux (Novel); co-auth, High Hopes (memoirs); writer, producer & dir, Isabel (film), 68, Act of the Heart (film), 70, Journey (film), 72, Ups & Downs (film), 82 the Dance Goes On, (film), 91. *Mailing Add:* 54 Malibu Colony Dr Malibu CA 90265-4637

ALPERN, MERRY B
PHOTOGRAPHER
b New York, NY, Mar, 15, 55. *Study:* Grinnel Col, Iowa, 73-77. *Work:* Mus Mod Art, NY; Houston Mus of Fine Arts; Los Angeles Co Mus of Art; Baltimore Mus of Art; Whitney Mus of Am Art, NY. *Exhib:* One-woman shows, Camera Club of NY, 89, Bonni Benrubi Gallery, NY, 95, 99; group Exhib, Mus Mod Art, NY, 91, 92 & 95; The Montreal Mus of Fine Arts, 2000. *Pos:* Photo lab technician, Exposure/Effects, NY, 77-78; staff photog & studio mgr, LGI Photo Agency, 78-80; asst photog ed, Rolling Stone Mag, 80-81; freelance photogr, 81-. *Teaching:* Guest instr, Int Ctr Photog, NY, 89; guest lectr, New Sch, NY, 90; instr, Int Ctr Photog, NY, 94. *Awards:* Second Place, Pictures Yr, Mag Picture Story, 88; Leica Medal Excellence Photojournalism Award, 88; Nat Endowment Arts, Visual Artists Fel Grant, 90. *Bibliog:* Gerri Hershey (auth), Return to Spender, Mirabella, Sept 99; Julie Caniglia (auth), Merry Alpern (review), Artforum, Oct 99; Daphne Merkin (auth), The Last Taboo, NY Times Mag, Dec 2000. *Publ:* Many credits in var newspapers & mags. *Dealer:* Bonni Benrubi 52 E 76th New York NY 10021. *Mailing Add:* 1 Plaza St W Apt 7C Brooklyn NY 11217

ALPERT, BILL (WILLIAM) H
PAINTER, SCULPTOR
b Bronx, NY, Dec 21, 34. *Study:* Univ Calif Los Angeles, BA, 63, grad sch, 63-65. *Work:* Power Gallery Contemp Art, Sydney, Australia. *Exhib:* Orgn Independent Artists Postcard Show, Bologna Art Fair, Italy, 78; Albright-Knox Mus, 78 & 79; Current NY, Joe & Emily Lowe Art Gallery, Syracuse Univ, 80; Color on Structure, W Paterson Col of NJ, Wayne, 81; Col Charleston, SC, 86 & 89; Artists in Paradise, NY Botanical Gardens, Bronx, NY, 93; Dactyl Found Arts & Humanities, New York City, 2005. *Collection Arranged:* Orgn of Independent Artists: Group Show, US Courthouse, 77 & Art in Public Places, 26 Fed Plaza, New York, 77; Six Artists View Development, NY Acad Sci, 78. *Teaching:* Adj prof painting, Cooper Union Sch Art, NY, 79-82; adj instr drawing, Parsons Sch Design, NY, 81-82 & Pratt Inst, Summer

Prog, 81; instr watercolor, Sch Visual Arts, NY, 89-; Yunnan Inst Fine Arts, Kunming, China, 93; Central Acad Fine Arts, Beijing, China, 93; The Green Horse, Ulanbaatar, Mongolia, 98. *Awards:* Creative Artist Pub Serv Prog Finalist, 77-78, 80-81 & 81-82; Tiffany Found Finalist, 79. *Bibliog:* Peter Frank (auth), New York Reviews, Art News, 11/77 & Ellen Lubell (auth), Arts Mag, 11/77; JoAnn Lewis (auth), Sculpture room, Washington Post, 5/27/78; Gregory Battcock (auth), Art Information, 5/81; Nancy S Smith (auth), articles, The News & Courier/The Evening Post, Charleston SC, 2/23/86. *Mem:* NY Artists Equity Asn; Orgn Independent Artists (mem exhib comt, 77-78). *Media:* Watercolor, All Media; Photographs, Chinese Ink. *Publ:* Contribr, New York Art Yearbook, 75-76; Re-View, Vol I, Issue 1, Vered Lieb, 77; The Whitney Counterweight Catalog, 77; Sciences, New York Acad Sci, 3/78; NY Art Rev, 88. *Mailing Add:* 64 Grand St New York NY 10013

ALPERT, GEORGE
PHOTOGRAPHER, PAINTER
b New York, NY, Apr 3, 22. *Study:* NY Univ; NC State Col; Stanford Univ; Univ Calif, Berkeley; Inst Seven Arts, NY. *Work:* Il Diaframma, Milan, Italy; Miller-Plummer Collection, Philadelphia. *Exhib:* One-man shows, Alfred Stieglitz Gallery, Neikrug Gallery, Light Gallery, NY, Period Gallery West, Scottsdale, Ariz, Everson Mus, Heard Mus, Udinotti Gallery & O'Brien Art Emporium, Ariz, C G Rein. *Pos:* Chmn, pres & dir gallery, Sohophoto Found, 70-. *Teaching:* Mem fac creative photog, New Sch Social Res, NY, 74-79. *Bibliog:* George Alpert: paintings, sculpture; George Albert photographs women. *Media:* Acrylic. *Specialty:* Photography, paintings, sculpture. *Publ:* Auth, The Queens, 75 & coauth, Second Chance to Live: The Suicide Syndrome, 75, Da Capo Press; Taos Pueblo, Paradise House, 83

ALPERT, HERB
PAINTER, SCULPTOR
b Los Angeles, Calif, Mar 31, 35. *Study:* Study with Rufino Tamayo & Calvin J Goodman, Univ Southern Calif. *Hon Degrees:* Berk Lee Sch, Hon DMusic, 2000. *Work:* Calif Inst Arts, Valencia; Indian Wells Country Club, Palm Springs, Calif; Vanderbilt Univ Med Ctr, Nashville, Tenn. *Exhib:* Basel Art Fair, Switz, 93; World Contemp Art 98, Los Angeles, 98; Miami Int Art Fair, Fla, 99; MB Modern, NY, 11/2000; Retrospective, Tenn St Mus, 8/2000. *Pos:* Co-chair, Found Communities in Schs, 91; spokesperson, Nat Found Advan Arts, 91. *Awards:* A V Call Achievement Award, Univ Southern Calif, 94. *Bibliog:* Tango Nuevo, The Paintings and Sculpture of Herb Alpert (catalogue), M Barnes Gallery, 98; Peter Frank (auth), Entertainment Today, 11/99. *Media:* Acrylic, Oil; Miscellaneous Media. *Dealer:* Galerie Van der Planken NV Steehouwesvest 13 2000 Antwerp Belgium; MB Modern 41 E 57th New York NY 10022. *Mailing Add:* c/o Molly Barnes Gallery 1414 6th St Santa Monica CA 90401

ALPERT, RICHARD HENRY
VIDEO ARTIST
b Apr 11, 47. *Study:* Univ Pittsburgh, BA, 70; San Francisco Art Inst, MFA(sculpture), 73. *Work:* Mus Conceptual Art, San Francisco; J H Cohn & Co, NY; Va Mus Fine Art, Richmond. *Exhib:* Projekt '74, Kolnischer Kunstverein, Koln, Ger, 74; solo exhibs, La Mamelle Art Ctr, San Francisco, 76 & 80, Los Angeles Inst Contemp Art, 79 & Washington Proj Arts, Washington, DC, 81; Space Time Sound 1970's: A Decade in the Bay Area, San Francisco Mus Mod Art, 79; California Performance Now and Then, Mus Contemp Art, Chicago, 81. *Teaching:* Instr, San Francisco Art Inst, 72-73 & 77 & Calif Col Arts & Crafts, Oakland, 78-79. *Awards:* Artist's Fel Grant, Nat Endowment Arts, 79-80. *Mailing Add:* 2123 Castro St San Francisco CA 94131-2224

ALQUILAR, MARIA
PAINTER, CERAMIST
b Brooklyn, NY, May 25, 38. *Study:* Hunter Col, New York, AB, 59. *Work:* Chase Manhattan Bank, NY & Phoenix; Nat Gallery Am Art, Int Finance Corp-World Bank, Washington; Sacramento Metrop Arts Comn; Redding Mus Art; Dante Mus, Ravenua, Italy; and others; Mus Civico, Padova, Italy. *Comn:* Light Rail Sta, Sacramento, 84; ceramic and metal altar, US Border Sta, San Luis, Ariz, 85; ceramic mural, fountain & waterfall, Water & Sewer Admin Bldg, Sacramento, 86; ceramic mural, Los Viajeros Vienen a San Jose, San Jose Int Airport, Calif, 90; Livermore Central Libr, Livermore, Calif, 2002-2003; 16th St Viaduet Mod Proj, Denver, Colo, 92; Fairbairn Water Treatment Plant, Sacto, Calif, 93; paintings, Int Finance Corp (aka World Bank), 96; cermaic mural, World Bank, Washington DC, 97; Dept Environ Protection, Tallahassee, Fla, 98; Valley Med Ctr, San Jose, 99. *Exhib:* Inedible Renwick Birthday Cake, Smithsonian Inst, 82; Out of the Fire, Betty Rhymer Gallery, Art Inst Chicago, Ill; retrospective exhib, Redding Mus Art, Redding, Calif, 92; The World's Women on Line, Beijing China, Ariz State Univ; Art Mus Santa Cruz Co, Calif; Seventh Ann, John Natsoulis Gallery, Davis, Calif; La Galeria La Mano Magica, Oaxaca, Mex; John Pence Gallery, San Francisco; Mus Civico, Padova, Italy. *Pos:* Dir, Jennifer Pauls Gallery, Sacramento, Calif, 70-85. *Awards:* Residency, John Michael Kohler Art Ctr, Sheboygan, Wis; Hon Award, US Gen Serv Admin, 90. *Bibliog:* Ellen Schlesinger (auth), Sunday woman-artist in residence, Sacramento Bee, 8/83; article, Ceramics Monthly, 5/88. *Media:* Acrylic, Clay. *Interests:* Narrative art and ceramics. *Publ:* Perspective on public art, Ceramics Monthly, 96; Pottery and Ceramics, New Holland, London; Sculpture, Technique, Form, Content, Arthur Williams; Art in Architecture, Our Hispanic Heritage, US Gen Serv Admin. *Dealer:* Guild.com. *Mailing Add:* 703 Darwin St Santa Cruz CA 95062

ALTAFFER, LAWRENCE F, III
ARTIST
b Richmond, Va, Jan 7, 47. *Study:* Univ Va, BA, 1969; MD, 1974. *Work:* McGraw Hill Publ, NYC; Media Gen, Richmond, Va; Galen Capital Group, McLean, Va. *Exhib:* Show Time - Palisades Lake, Oil Painters Am, Carmel, Calif, 2000; Old Rag Mountain, Arts for the Parks, Jackson Hole, Wyo, 2001; Taggart Lake, Oil Painters Am, Chicago, Ill, 2002; Morning on the Potomac, Salmagundi Club, NY, 2002. *Pos:* Physician urologist, pvt practice. *Mem:* Washington Soc Landscape Painters (Am Artist Mar 2002); Salmagundi Club, NY; Oil Painter Am; Allied Artists Am; Am Artists' Prof League. *Interests:* Gardening, hunting, fishing, home. *Mailing Add:* General Delivery Syria VA 22743

ALTEN, JERRY
DIRECTOR, DESIGNER
b Philadelphia, Pa. *Study:* Philadelphia Col Art; Temple Univ, BA(fine arts). *Comn:* SI, NY. *Pos:* art dir, TV Guide Mag, 67; mem staff, Triangle Publ Inc, Radnor, Pa, currently; corp art dir News Corp, 95; art dir, CRR Mag, Egiving Mag, Coventry Health Care; bd dir, Antonelli Col of Art/Photography; creative dir, Giving Mag, 04-. *Teaching:* Lectr, cols in US & Europe. *Awards:* Awards of Excellence & Gold & Silver Medals, NY Art Dirs Club, Soc Publ Designers & Soc Illusr, graphics. *Mem:* Soc Publ Designers; Art Alliance Philadelphia; NY Art Dirs Club; Philadelphia Art Dirs; Philadelphia Col Art Alumni Asn. *Mailing Add:* 10 Wynnedale Cir Narberth PA 19072-1723

ALTERMANN, TONY
ART DEALER
b Dallas, Tex, Aug 10, 40. *Study:* Univ NTex, BA & MS. *Pos:* Dir publicity & pub relations, MGM, Dallas, Tex, 70-72; vpres, Tex Art Gallery, Dallas, 72-78; owner & pres, Altermann Art Gallery, Dallas, Tex, 78- & Altermann & Morris Galleries, Houston, Dallas, Santa Fe & Hilton Head SC; bd dir, Dallas Visual Arts Ctr, Currently. *Mem:* Dallas Art Dealers Asn; Dallas Visual Arts Ctr; Cowboy Artists of Am Mus (life, bd dir); Prix de West Soc of Nat Cowboy Hall of Fame; Western Heritage Ctr; Coll of Arts & Scis/Univ N Tex (chmn adv bd). *Specialty:* Western, wildlife and Americana subjects in all media. *Mailing Add:* c/o Altermann Art Galleries 2727 Routh St Dallas TX 75201

ALTFELD, MERWIN RICHARD
PAINTER, EDUCATOR, ART JUROR
b Elyria, Ohio, Sept 19, 1913. *Study:* Case Western Reserve, BA, 34; Univ Calif, Los Angeles, Art Teaching Credential, 68. *Work:* Queen Mary Ship & Senior Eye Gallery, Long Beach, Calif; Brugger Art Collection, Los Angeles, Calif; Hollywood Press Club, Calif; Univ Calif, Los Angeles. *Comn:* Landmarks of Europe, Postal Press; Landmarks of California, Aaron Bros. *Exhib:* Nat Watercolor 66, 82, 93-95; Am Artists Invitational, Swedish Mus, Stockholm, Sweden, 72; Watercolor USA, Springfield, Art Mus, 72-88, 90-92, 95, 02; Calif Group, Old Bergen Art Guild, 76-88; Artist Influenced by the Circle Traveling Exhib, 78-80; San Diego Int Watercolor, 81, 84, 85, 93, 94, 95, 97, 99, 00, 01, 02. *Pos:* Pres, Los Angeles Art Asn, 91-92. *Teaching:* instr drawing & painting, Los Angeles Adults Schs, 68-73; bd dir, So Calif Contemp Gallery Los Angeles, 87-88; instr creative painting, Univ Judaism, 88. *Awards:* Cash Award for Drawing, Southern Calif Expos, 64; Cash Award, Nat Watercolor Soc, Laguna Beach Mus, 74; Cash Award, San Diego Watercolor Soc Int Exhib, 85, 99, 02. *Bibliog:* David Fessenden (dir), Merwin Altfeld, Malibu (film), 78; Robert Perine (auth), Calif Romantics (art catalogue), 85; Don Hunt (producer), Viewpoint (video), Mountain View Gallery, Pasadena, Calif, 94. *Mem:* Nat Watercolor Soc (pres, 72); Artists Educ Action (bd dir, 78-82); Los Angeles Art Asn (pres, 90); Collage Artists Am; Pacific Palisades Art Asn. *Media:* Acrylic, Watercolor; Mixed. *Publ:* Auth, Canon Laser Creative Ideas, Copyspot Inc, Santa Monica, Calif, 10/90; The Best of Watercolor, 97 & The Best of Drawing, 98, Rockport Publ, 97 & 98; Watercolor Expressions, 99; Strokes of Genius, North Light Books, 2006. *Mailing Add:* 18426 Wakecrest Dr Malibu CA 90265

ALTMAN, EDITH
SCULPTOR, CONCEPTUAL ARTIST
b Altenberg, Ger, May 5, 31; US citizen. *Study:* Wayne State Univ, Detroit, Mich, 49; Marygrove Col, with Paul Weigardt (from the Bauhaus), 56-57. *Work:* Standard Oil Co, Mus Contemp Art, Chicago; State of Ill; Yale Univ Mus; Holocaust Mus; Peace Mus. *Exhib:* Art Inst Chicago Vicinity Exhib, 75, 79, 81 & 85; Mus Contemp Art, Chicago, 76, 81 & 83; solo exhibs, Spertus Mus Gallery Contemp Art (with catalog), 88, Reclaiming The Symbol/The Art of Memory (with catalog), Rockford Art Mus, 89, State of Ill Mus Gallery, Chicago, 92 & Topography of Terror (with catalog), Loyola Univ Fine Arts Gallery, 93; Light Weight Works, Mitchell Mus, Ill, 95; Legacy, Minn Mus Am Art, 95; Drawing in Chicago Now, Columbia Col, Chica, 96; The Spiritual in Contemp Art Today, Hope Col, Mich, 96; Art Chicago 1945-1995, Mus Contemp Art, Chicago, 96-97; Political Vision, Fassbender Gallery, Chicago, Ill, 99; Knoxville Mus Art, Tenn, 98; Spiritual Passport and Transformative Journies, State Ill Art Gallery, Springfield, Ill, 98; Edith Altman Retrospective, Lindenau Mus, Altenburg, Ger, 2001; group exhibs Witness and Legacy, Knowville Mus Art, 98, Polit Visions, Fassbender Gallery, Chicago, 99, Witness and Legacy, Tucson Mus Fine Art, Huntsville Mus, Ala, Decordova Mus, Mass, 2000, Text Cult Ctr, Chicago, 2000, Pedagogy: Beyond Reeling, Writhing, Uglification & Derision, Book & Paper Ctr, Columbia Col, Chicago, 2000, Transcultural Visions: Polish-Am Contemp Art, Hyde Park Art Ctr, Chicago, 2001. *Teaching:* Vis artists & print proj, Univ Omaha, Neb, 84; asst prof painting & grad advisor, Univ Chicago, 84-85; vis asst prof painting, Sch Art Inst Chicago, 85-86; lectr painting, Univ Ill, Columbia Col & Oakton Col, Chicago; lectr, Loyola Univ, 93, Columbus Mus, 93, Notre Dame, 96, Spartus Mus, Chicago, Ill, 98, Depaul Univ, Chicago, Ill & Univ Houston, Tex, 98. *Awards:* Individual Artist Fel, Ill Arts Coun, 84 & 95; Nat Endowment Arts Individual Artist Fel Grant, 90-91; Art Matters, 94. *Bibliog:* V W Jones (auth), Edith Altman at the NAME Gallery, Contemporary American Women Sculptors, The New Art Examiner, ORYK Press, 87; Gloria Feman Orenstein (auth), The Reflowering of the Goddess, Pergamon Press, 90; Claire Krantz (auth), Questions as Model, New Art Examiner, 6/92. *Mem:* Chicago Artist Coalition; founding mem, Comt Artists Rights, 88; hon mem, State of Ill, 92.

Media: Multimedia. *Publ:* Auth, articles in Art in Am, 79 & 87, Artforum, 83, Chicago Tribune, Chicago Sun-Times & New Art Examiner, 92; Positions, NYFAI/Womens Ctr for Learning, 89; Allemenines Lexikon Der Bilden Kunstler, Themel Baecker Publ, Ger, 90. *Mailing Add:* 811 W 16 St Chicago IL 60608

ALTMANN, HENRY S
PAINTER, EDUCATOR
b New York, NY, Dec 4, 1946. *Study:* Pratt Inst, Brooklyn, BFA(art educ), 68; Queens Col, Flushing, NY, MFA(painting), 70; Fulbright Fel painting, 70-71, Fine Arts Acad, Munich, Ger. *Work:* First Nat Bank NY; Skowhegan Sch Painting & Sculpture, NY; Shawmut Bank Boston, Mass. *Comn:* Three stained glass windows & paintings for rear portal (with Maxine Ann Sorokin), Kehillath Jakob Synagogue, Newton, Mass, 73. *Exhib:* One-man shows, First St Gallery, NY & Meetinghouse Gallery, Boston, 73; Young Realist Show, Harbor Gallery, Cold Spring Harbor, Long Island, NY, 72; two-person exhib, Goethe Inst, Boston, 80, Young Adult Ctr, Boston, 84 & Univ Cincinnati, Rose Warner Gallery, 86; Jewish Community Ctr, Southern NJ Gallery, Cherry Hill, 80; One Person Show Framed-In Time Gallery, Framingham, MA, Feb, 2004; group exhib, Shore Road Gallery, Ogunquit, ME, 2005-2006. *Pos:* Exhib chmn, West Roxbury Art Asn, 77-; res comt arch, West Roxbury Hist Soc, 77-, dir visual arts, Jewish Community Ctr, Newton, Mass, 83-. *Teaching:* Instr art, Boston Univ, 71-75; adj assoc prof, Art Inst Boston, 75-; Framingham State Col, Mass, 72-80; visual arts dir, art dept, Leventhal-Sidman JCC, 83-2006; Mass Bay Community Col, 90-91; Fisher College, Boston, MA, Drawing & Painting Instructor, 2004-. *Awards:* Finalist, Mass Found Arts Fel Competition, 83. *Bibliog:* W Rox (auth), Boston Globe article, 5/81; Norman Keyes (auth), Transcript Newspaper article, 81; article, Boston Globe, 96. *Mem:* Boston Vis Artists Union. *Media:* Oil, Pastel, Watercolor. *Dealer:* Shore Road Gallery Ogunquit ME 03907. *Mailing Add:* 61 Perham St West Roxbury MA 02132

ALTMEJD, DAVID
PAINTER, ARTIST
b Can, 74. *Study:* Université du Québec à Montréal, BFA, 98; Columbia Univer, MFA, 2001. *Exhib:* One-man shows, Andrea Rosen Gallery, NY, 2004, Sarah Altmejd, Galerie SKOL, Montreal, 2003, Galerie Optica, Montreal, 2003, Galerie SKOL, Montreal, 2003, Pointe de chute, Galerie de l'UQAM, Montreal, 2002, Interval, Sculpture Ctr, NY, 2002, Clear Structures for a New Generation, Ten in One Gallery, NY, 2002, Mod?s d esprit et jardins int?eurs, Galerie B-312, Montreal, 99, Jennifer, Galerie Clark, Montreal, 98; group shows, Demonclownmonkey, Artist Space, NY, 2002, Material Eyes, LFL Gallery, NY, 2003, 8th Istanbul Biennial, Turkey, 2003, Corp. Profits versus Labor Costs, D'Amelio Terras Gallery, NY, 2003, SCREAM, Anton Kern Gallery, NY, 2004, Whitney Biennial Am Art, Whitney Mus Am Art, 2004. *Mailing Add:* c/o Andrea Rosen Gallery 525 West 24th St New York NY 10011

ALTSHULER, BRUCE J
EDUCATOR, WRITER
b Newark, NJ, Apr 2, 49. *Study:* Princeton Univ, BA, 71; Harvard Univ, MA, 74, PhD, 77. *Collection Arranged:* Isamu Noguchi: Early Abstraction, Whitney Mus Am Art, 94; Isamu Noguchi, Juan March Found, Madrid, Spain, 94. *Pos:* Asst to dir, NY Hist Soc, 83-85; assoc dir, Zabriskie Gallery, NY, 85-89; dir, Isamu Noguchi Garden Mus, Long Island City, NY, 92-98; dir studies, Christie's Educ, NY, 98-2000; dir, Mus Studies Prog, NY Univ, 2001-. *Teaching:* Asst prof philos, Univ Puget Sound, Tacoma, Wash, 77-82; grad fac curatorial studies, Black Ctr for Curatorial Studies, Bard Col, Annandale on Hudson, NY, 94-. *Mem:* Int Asn Art Critics USA (bd dir, 94-2000); Col Art Asn; Am Asn Mus. *Res:* Twentieth century art; contemporary art. *Publ:* (Auth), The Avant-Garde in Exhibition, Harry N Abrams, 94; Isamu Noguchi, Abbeville Press, 94; coauth, Isamu Noguchi: Essays and Conversations, Harry N Abrams, 94; ed, Collecting the New: Museums & Contemporary Art, Princeton Univ Press, 2005. *Mailing Add:* New York Univ Museum Studies Program 240 Greene St Suite 400 New York NY 10003

ALVARADO-JUAREZ, FRANCISCO
PAINTER
Study: State Univ NY, Stony Brook, BA, 1974; Int Ctr Photog, 1975; Md Inst, MFA, 1993. *Work:* Brooklyn Mus of Art, NY; The Bronx Mus of Art, NY; Everson Mus of Art, Syracuse, NY; Museo Publo Serrano, Zaragoza, Spain; Smithsonian Am Art Mus, Washington, DC. *Comn:* Painting, Wash State Art in Pub, Wash, 1995; Serigraph print, Carton de Venezuela, Caracas, 1985; Serigraph print, United Nations Childrens Fund, NY, 1990. *Exhib:* One man show incl: Endangered, The Noyes Mus of Art, Oceanville, NJ, 1998, The Mythology of the Flora and the Fauana, Museo Pablo Serrano, Zaragoza, Spain, 2000, Canto a la Fauna, NY Trophies, NY Fauve, Everson Mus of Art, Syracuse, NY, 2001, Canto a la fauna Am, Museo de Arte Contemp de Oaxaca, Mex, 2002, Erotica of Flora and Fauna, Museo de Arte de Queretaro, Mex, 2005; group exhib incl: Recent Am works on paper, Int tour, Smithsonian Inst Traveling exhib serv, 1985, The Second Biennial of Havana, Museo Nat de Bellas Artes, Cuba, 1986, 19th Sao Paulo Int Biennial, Fundacao Bienal de Sao Paolo, Brazil, 1987, The Awakening, The Discovery Mus, Bridgeport, Conn, 1990, The First Ten Yrs of the Permanent Collection, Islip Art Mus, East Islip, NY, 1996, Object Lessons: Additions to the Collection, Everson Mus of Art, Syracuse, NY, 2003. *Awards:* Artist in Residence Fel, Mid Atlantic Arts Found; Pollock-Krasner Found, Fel; Grant, Gottlieb Found. *Mem:* Bronx Mus of Arts; Brooklyn Mus of Art; Everson Mus of Art; Noyes Mus of Art. *Media:* Painting, installation & video art, photography. *Publ:* Janet Sassi (auth), Crossing landscapes, The Bear Deluxe, 2003; Helen Harrison (auth), A Close Look at the Fragile Beauty & perils of ocean reefs, 1992, ruth Bass (auth), Fransisco Alvarado-Juarez, Art News, 1992. *Mailing Add:* 3647 Broadway Apt 2F New York NY 10031-2506

ALVAREZ, CANDIDA
PAINTER, EDUCATOR
b Brooklyn, NY, Feb 2, 55. *Study:* Fordham Univ, BA, 77, Skowhegan Sch Painting and Sculpture, 81, Yale Univ, MFA, 97. *Work:* Studio Mus Harlem, Whitney Mus Am Art, El Museo Del Barrio & Readers Digest, NY; Univ Del, Newark; German Consulate & Brandywine Workshop, Philadelphia; and many pvt collections. *Comn:* Selected Works by Langston Hughes (mural), CETA Artists proj, NY, 79; drawings, Children's Psychiatric Div, Bellevue Hosp, NY, 84; percent for art, New York, Stained Glass Windows for IS 206A South Bronx, 92. *Exhib:* Recollections, Brooklyn Mus, NY, 79; Books Alive, Met Mus Art, NY, 83; one-man shows, Paintings and Drawings, June Kelly Gallery, NY, 89 & 93, John Street Series, Galerie Schniderei, Cologne, Ger, 90, Paintings and Works on Paper, Queens Mus, Flushing, NY, 91 & Recent Paintings, Bronx Mus Art, NY, 92, Paintings: 1990-1992, Kenyon Col, Ohio, 93, New/Now: Candida Alvarez, New Britain Mus Am Art, Conn, 92; Working on Paper: Contemp Am Drawing, High Mus Art, Atlanta, Ga, 90; Polyptychs, June Kelly Gallery, NY, 93; Contemp Pub Art in the Bronx, Lehman Col Art Gallery, Bronx, NY, 93; Paintings: 1989-92, Olin Art Gallery, Kenyon Col, Gambier, Ohio, 93; Artists Talk Back: Visual Conversations with El Museo; Part 3: Reaffirming Spirituality, El Museo Del Barrio, NY, 95; Creative Artists Network: Selections 1984-96 (with Catalog), Woodmere Art Mus, Philadelphia, 96; Community of Creativity: A Century of MacDowell Colony Artists (with catalog), The Currier Gallery Art, Manchester, NH, 96; Heaven-Private View, PS1 Contemp Art Ctr, Long Island City, NY, 97; Exit Art, New York City-Choice 99, Studio Mus, Harlem, NY; Out of Line: Drawings by Illinois Artists, Chicago Cult Ctr, Ill, 2000. *Pos:* juror, Art Kauai, Hawaii. *Teaching:* Vis artist, Hamilton Col, NY, 91, Sch Mus Fine Arts, Boston, 92-93, Trinity Col, Conn, 93, Univ Wis, Oshkosh, 94, Art Inst Chicago, Ill, 95; artist in residence, Addison Gallery Am Art, Phillips Acad, Mass, 93, Pilchuck Glass Sch, Wash, 98; vis asst prof art, Kenyon Col, Ohio, 94; instr drawing, Penland Sch Arts & Crafts, 96; teaching asst, Yale Univ Sch Art, 97; part time lectr, Mason Gross Sch Arts, Rutgers Univ, New Brunswick, 97-98; asst prof drawing & painting, Sch Art Inst Chicago, 98-; Int artists studio prog, Stockholm, Sweden, 99; dept art, Univ Wis, Madison, 2000 & Vt Studio Ctr, Johnson, 2000; educ adv comt, Smart Mus, Univ Chicago, Chicago, Pub Art Prog, 99-. *Awards:* NY Found Arts Fel, 86; Mid-Atlantic Nat Endowment Arts Reg Fel, 88; Artist Fel, Art Matters, NY, 89; Pollach-Krasner Found Grant, 95. *Bibliog:* Debra Bricker Balken (auth), rev, Art in Am, 4/94; Holland Cotler (auth), NY Times, 4/95; article, The Herald, 5/96; and others. *Mem:* Col Art Asn. *Mailing Add:* 5300 S South Shore Dr Apt 22 Chicago IL 60615-5719

ALVAREZ-CERVELA, JOSE MARIA
EDUCATOR, HISTORIAN
b La Guardia, Spain, Sept 21, 1922. *Study:* Univ Santiago, Spain, BA, 48, Lic en Derecho, 56, PhD(law & artistic works), 68; Middlebury Col, Vt, MA, 65. *Pos:* Dir, Fine Arts Mus, Univ PR, Mayaguez, 58-64. *Teaching:* Prof art & humanities, Univ PR, Mayaguez, 57-. *Awards:* 1983 Citizen of the Year in Mayaguez in Education, 84. *Mem:* PR Acad Arts, Hist & Archaeol. *Res:* Woodcarving of saints in Puerto Rico; mural paintings on ceilings and vaults; funerary art in Puerto Rico. *Publ:* Auth, Signos y Firmas Reales, La Comercial, Santiago, Spain, 57; A Pintura Mitologica e Alegorica nos Tectos e Abobadas do Escorial e do Palacio Real, Ed Imperio, Lisbon, 68; Los Contratos de Obra Artistica de la Catedral de Santiago de Compostela en Siglo XVII, Industrias Graficas Noroeste, Spain, 68; La Arquitectura Clasica Actual en Mayaguez, Antillian Col Press, Mayaguez, 83; El Portico Federico Degetau en UPR Mayaguez, Universidad de Puerto Rico en Mayaguez, 88. *Mailing Add:* c/o Univ Puerto Rico Art Dept PO Box 5000 Mayaguez PR 00381

AMADO, JESSE V
SCULPTOR
b San Antonio, Tex, 51. *Study:* Univ Tex, Austin BA (Eng), 77, Univ Tex, San Antonio, BFA (studio art), 87, MFA (studio art), 90. *Work:* Michael Tracy, pvt collection, San Ygnacio, Tex; Ken Bentley, AIA, pvt collection, San Antonio, Tex; Matthews & Branscomb, Attorneys, corp collection, San Antonio, Tex; Sunbelt Corp, corp collection, San Antonio, Tex. *Exhib:* Solo exhibs, Davis McClain Gallery, Houston, 93 & 95, Bemis Ctr Contemp Art, Omaha, Nebr, 94, Milagros Contemp Art Gallery, San Antonio, 94, San Antonio Mus Art, 95, Carla Stellwig Gallery, NY, 95 & Contemp Art Mus, Houston, 96, McNay Mus Art, San Antonio, Tex, 03; Commissioners Exhib, Tex Comn Arts, Tobin Estates, San Antonio, 94; Putting it on Paper, McNay Art Inst, San Antonio, 94; Low Tech, Ctr Res Contemp Art, Univ Tex, Arlington, 94; Pace Roberts Found Contemp Art, San Antonio, 95; Tres Proyectos Latinos, Austin Mus Art, Tex, 96; Schemata: Drawings by Sculptors, Glassell Sch Art & Mus Fine Art, Houston, Tex, 96-97; Barbara Davis Gallery, Pennzoil Gallery, Kwanglu, S Korea, 97; Art on Paper: Thirty Third Ann Exhib, Weatherspoon Art Gallery, Univ NC, Greensboro; Linc Real Art, San Francisco, 01; Univ Tex, San Antonio, 02; San Antonio Mus Art, 02; San Francisco Arts Comn Gallery, 02; Finesilver Gallery, San Antonio, Tex, 00, 01; and others. *Pos:* Artist-in-residence, Philadelphia Fabric Workshop, 90-91, Bemis Ctr Contemp Arts, Bemis Found, Omaha, Nebr, 94, Pace Roberts Found Contemp Art, San Antonio, Tex, 94-95. *Teaching:* Guest lectr sculpture, Univ Tex, Austin, spring 96. *Awards:* Visual Arts Orgn Grant Artist-in-residence, 90 & Visual Artists Fel Grant (sculpture), Nat Endowment Arts, 90; Visual Arts Fel Grant, Art Matters Inc, NY, 92; Int Artist in Res Prog, City Gallery Kwanglu, S Korea, 97. *Bibliog:* Patricia Johnson (auth), Contemporary Art in Texas, Craftsman House, 94; New Works for a New Space (forward by Robert Storr), Art Pace, San Antonio, 95; Dana Fries-Hansen (auth), Perspectives Series, Contemp Art Mus, Houston, 96; Dan Goddard (auth), Reflecting on Beauty, San Antonio Express News, 2/26/2003. *Dealer:* Davis McClain Gallery 2627 Colquitt Houston TX 77098. *Mailing Add:* c/o Finesilver Gallery 816 Camaron No 1 2 San Antonio TX 78212

AMALFITANO, LELIA
CURATOR, GALLERY DIRECTOR
b New York, NY. *Study:* Calif Inst Arts, Valencia, BFA, 74; Sch Art Inst Chicago, MFA, 78. *Collection Arranged:* New Territory: Art from East Germany, traveling exhib of work by seventeen contemp artists from East Germany (ed & intro, catalog), 90; Between Intuition and Reason (ed, catalog), exhib of work by Jonathan Lasker & St Clair Cemin, 91, Private Visions selected works from pvt collections by Nayland Blake, Cady Noland & Gary Hume, 93, Closed Environments, exhib of work by Jno Cook & Luke Dohner, 94, Self/Conscious Self/Made: Janine Antoni & Bruce Nauman (auth, catalog), selected works, 94, Grossman Gallery, Boston. *Pos:* Vis artist, Art Resources Open to Women, Schenectady, NY, 78; dir & cur, Rathbone Gallery, Russell Sage Jr Col Albany, NY, 83-86; cur, Stux Gallery, Boston & New York, 86-87; cur & dir Exhibs & Vis Artists Progs, Sch Mus Fine Arts, Boston, 86-. *Teaching:* Instr, Women in Art, an art hist survey, Albany Inst Hist & Art, NY, 79; adj prof, Fine Arts Div, Russell Sage Junior Col, Albany, NY, 80-86; instr, Coun Int Educ, Italy, 84. *Bibliog:* Reviews in many publ including, Art New Eng, Boston Globe, Art Am, Boston Phoenix & Albany Times Union. *Publ:* Auth, Self/Made Self/Conscious: Janine Antoni & Bruce Nauman (essay, exhib catalog), Sch Mus Fine Arts, Boston, 94; Carroll Dunhan: Selected Paintings 1990-1995 (essay, exhib catalog), Sch Mus Fine Arts, Boston, 95; Boston School (essay, exhib catalog), Inst Contemp Art, Boston, 95; Social Fictions: Lari Pittman and Andrea Zittel (essay, exhib catalog), Sch Mus Fine Arts, Boston, 96; Lucy Gunning: Persistence of Vision (essay, exhib catalog), Sch Mus Fine Arts, Boston, 96. *Mailing Add:* 441 Shawmut Ave Boston MA 02118-3832

AMANO, TAKA
PAINTER
b Toyama, Japan, Apr 24, 50. *Study:* Ikvei Col, Tokyo, BA, 71; Sch Visual Arts, New York, BFA, 77. *Work:* Solomon R Guggenheim Mus, NY; NY State Univ, Albany; Bronx Mus Arts, NY. *Exhib:* Five-person show, Artists Space, NY, 84; Curators Choice, Bronx Mus Arts, 85; Selections 30, Drawing Ctr, NY, 85; Ten from the Drawing Ctr, NY, 85; Four-person show, Soho Ctr Visual Artists, NY, 87; New Acquisitions, Guggenheim Mus, NY, 87; Group Show, Jilian Pretto Gallery, NY, 89; solo shows, Jilian Pretto Gallery, NY, 89 & 90. *Awards:* Working Space Prog PS 1, Inst for Art & Urban Resources, 77-79; Nat Endowment Arts Regional Fel, Mid-Atlantic Arts Found, 88; Individual Artist Fel, Nat Endowment Arts, 89. *Bibliog:* Kay Larson (auth), article, New York Mag, 10/20/86; Marc Furstenberg (auth), article, Downtown Mag, 4/8/87. *Media:* Watercolor. *Mailing Add:* 6 Greene St New York NY 10013-5814

AMASON, ALVIN ELI
PAINTER
b McKenny, Tex, Apr 6, 48. *Study:* Cent Wash Univ, BA, 73, MA, 74; Ariz State Univ, MFA, 76. *Work:* Nat Collection Fine Arts, Smithsonian Inst, Washington, DC; Nordjyllands Kunstmuseum, Aalborg, Denmark; Alaska State Mus, Juneau; Anchorage Hist & Fine Arts Mus, Alaska; Am Embassy, Brasilia, Brazil. *Comn:* Painting (with Robert Hudson, Sam Francis & Dan Flavin), Govt Serv Admin, Anchorage, 79. *Exhib:* Nat Collection Fine Arts, Washington, DC, 80. *Awards:* Jurors Award, Phoenix Mus Art, 75; Purchase Award, Alaska State Coun Arts, 80. *Bibliog:* Jamake Highwater (auth), The Sweet Grass Lives On, Harper & Row, 80; Sculpture out in the open, Newsweek, 8/18/80; Sandra B Betz (auth), Alvin Eli Amason, Arts & Cult N, 81. *Mem:* Alaska State Coun Arts (councilman, 79-80). *Media:* Oil, Mixed. *Dealer:* Decker Morris Gallery 621 W 6th Ave Anchorage AK 99501-2200. *Mailing Add:* c/o University of Alaska Mus PO Box 756960 Fairbanks AK 99775-1200

AMATO, MICHELE (MICAELA)
PAINTER, SCULPTOR
b New York, NY, July 29, 45. *Study:* Boston Univ, BFA, 68; Univ Colo, Boulder, MFA, 73. *Work:* Chase Manhattan Bank, NY; Nat Mus Women Artists, Washington, DC; Riverdall Collection, Bard Col, NY; Denver Art Mus, Colo; Rose Art Mus, Brandeis Univ; and others. *Exhib:* Painting Invitational, 78 & Print Invitational, 82-88, Denver Art Mus; one person exhibs, Sheldon Art Mus, Univ Nebr, Lincoln, 79, Minneapolis Col Art & Design, Minn, 80 & Marianne Deson Gallery, Chicago, 82-84; The Jewish Mus, NY, 94; Yeshiva Univ, NY, 95; Davidson Col Gallery, NC, 99; Mary Washington Col Mus, Va, 99; 55 Mercer St Gallery, NY, 98, 99 & 2000; Flatfile Gallery, Chicago, Ill, 2000 & 01. *Pos:* Interviewer & reviewer art & dance, Straight Creek J, Denver, 73-75 & Boulder Daily Camera, Colo, 76-77, Ocular Mag 76-79 & Pa State Univ, 88-; cur, Patrick Gallery, Austin, Tex, 83-85. *Teaching:* Grad painting & drawing dept head, Wichita State Univ, Kans, 77-78; vis artist, Minneapolis Col Art & Design, 79-80, Univ Tex, San Antonio, 81-82, Univ Tex, Austin, 84, Univ Colo, 84-85 & E Carolina Univ, NC, 86; Tenured assoc prof art & women's studies, Penn State Univ, 88-. *Awards:* Painting Award, Nat Endowment Art, 87, 88 & 92, New Forms Regional Award, 92; Res & travel grants, Inst Arts & Humanistic Studies, Penn State Univ, 90, 91, 92, 93, 94, 95, 97 & 99; Pollock Krasner Fel, 98-99. *Bibliog:* Lucy Lippard (auth), Tijuana Tavolettas, Lafayette Col Press, Pa,98; William Zimmer (auth), NY Times, 10/6/99; Robert Saltonstall Mattison (auth), Women's Art Jour, 5/2001. *Mem:* Nat Orgn Women Artists; Women's Caucus Art; founding mem Front Range Women, Colo; Col Art Asn. *Media:* All. *Publ:* Auth, In Praise of Paradox & Contradiction, Westminster Col, Pa. *Mailing Add:* 1721 Linden Hall Rd Boalsburg PA 16827

AMAYA, ARMANDO
SCULPTOR
b Puebla, Pue, Mex, Nov 29, 35. *Study:* Escuela Nac Pintura & Escultura La Esmeralda, with Francisco Zuniga. *Work:* Mex Mus, San Francisco, Calif. *Comn:* Benito Juarez (bronze mask), Mex Govt, Santa Ursula, 69. *Exhib:* Pasquale Iannetti Gallery, San Francisco Mus; Mus Contemp Art, Israel; Museo de Arte Latino Americano, Chile; Galeria Tasende, Mex. *Teaching:* Prof art, Escuela Nac Pintura & Escultura La Esmeralda, 69-. *Bibliog:* Mexican Studies, Univ Calif Press, Vol 3, No 2, 87; Diccionario de escultura mexicana del siglo XX, Universidad Nacional Autonoma de Mex, 83. *Media:* Bronze. *Mailing Add:* Cuauh Temoc 168 Col Deo Carmen Coyoacan CP #04100 Mexico

AMBLEY, PAUL
PAINTER - WATERCOLOR
b Ann Arbor, Mich, Feb 14, 48. *Study:* Clemson Univ, SC, BA, 70; Seton Hall Univ, MA, 76. *Exhib:* Purple on Purple, Mus Am Art, NY, 99; Rainbow of Colors, Western Art Gallery, Houston, Tex, 2000; Shades of Purples, Melon Bay Gallery, Santa Fe, Calif, 2001; Purple Unicorns, Merry Way Gallery, Key West, Fla, 2003; Sailing Away, Water Bay Gallery, Key West Fla, 2003. *Pos:* Asst accountant, Edward & Kelcey Archit, Morristown, NJ, 78-80, sr accountant, 80-. *Teaching:* Instr, Nat Watercolor Asn, NJ & NY, currently; instr, painting & drawing, LBI Found, NJ, currently. *Awards:* Best of Show, 100th Ann Watercolor Show, NJ, 2001; Purple Medal Award, NJ Found, 2003; Brightest Watercolor Award, Am Watercolor Exhib, Calif, 2004. *Mem:* NJ Watercolor Asn; Pastels Am Asn; Ocean Watercolor Soc (pres, currently); Nat Watercolor Soc (bd dir, 97-2001). *Media:* Watercolors & Pastels. *Res:* Artists of the world. *Specialty:* Watercolor scenes and sailboats. *Interests:* Sailing the Carribean. *Collection:* Coins. *Dealer:* Waterbay Gallery 1010 Ocean Blvd Key West FL 34444. *Mailing Add:* 101 Barrows Hall Orono ME 04469

AMBROSE, CHARLES EDWARD
PAINTER, EDUCATOR
b Memphis, Tenn, Jan 6, 1922. *Study:* Univ Ala, BFA, 49, MA, 50. *Work:* Univ Southern Miss; Carey Col; Biloxi Art Asn; First Nat Bank, Hattiesburg, Miss. *Comn:* Portrait reliefs, 58 & portraits, 60, Univ Southern Miss; Pat Harrison Waterways Bldg, 65; Carey Col; Miss Archives Bldg, 72. *Exhib:* Mid-Continent Exhib, Mo, 71; Watercolor USA, Springfield, Mo, 73; 1st Ann Bi-State, Meridian, Miss, 73; Central South, Nashville, Tenn, 75; 17th Dixie Ann, Montgomery, Ala, 75. *Teaching:* Assoc prof drawing & painting, Univ Southern Miss, 50-70; head art dept, Miss Univ for Women, 70-82. *Awards:* First Place Watercolor, Miss Art Asn, 68; First Place Drawing, Edgewater Ann, 70; Purchase Award/Drawing, 1st Ann Bi-State, 73. *Mem:* Southeastern Col Arts Conf; Nat Coun Art Adminr; Southern Asn Sculptors; Col Art Asn; Miss Art Asn. *Media:* Watercolor, Oil. *Mailing Add:* 1125 Seventh St N Columbus MS 39701-3409

AMBROSE, RICHARD MICHAEL
DIRECTOR, CURATOR
b Feb 23, 54. *Study:* Univ Ore, BFA, 79; Colo State Univ, MFA, 81. *Collection Arranged:* Ansel Adams: Classic Images, 89; Frank Lloyd Wright: California Architecture, 90; The American Cowboy: From Saddle to the Silverscreen, 92; Stuart Davis and His Contemporaries, 95; Rodin and His Contemporaries, 98; American Accents, Masterpieces from the San Francisco Mus Fine Arts, 2004; Pop Art and its Legacy, 2004. *Pos:* Cur visual art, Sandre de Cristo Arts Ctr, Pueblo, Colo, 84-88; prog dir, Fresno Metrop Mus, Calif, 88-92; deputy dir, Sunrise Mus Inc, Charleston, WVa, 93-; bd mem, Governor's Mansion Historic Preserv, 97-; deputy dir/cur art, Arampato Discovery Mus, Charleston, WV, 2003-. *Teaching:* Drawing instr, WV State Univ, 2005. *Mem:* Pubelo Arts Coun (vpres, 84-88); Fresno Arts Coun (bd mem, 89-91); WVa Arts Advocacy (vpres). *Publ:* Auth, Contemporary Visions of New Mexico (exhib catalog), 85; Shaman of the Prairie: Orlin Helgoe Retrospective (exhib catalog), 85; coauth, Marc Chagall: Les Ames Mortes (exhib catalog), 94; Lee Savage: A Retrospective (exhib catalog), 95; (auth), Color & Light: Selections from Vincent Melzac Collection (exhib catalog), 97; auth, Where Are They Now? (exhib catalog), 98; auth, Appalachian Corridors Juried Exhib (catalog), 2003. *Mailing Add:* Avampato Discovery Museum 300 Leon Sullivan Way Charleston WV 25301

AMBROSE, ROBIN ALLYSON
SCULPTOR
b Rhinebeck, NY, Sept 2, 54. *Study:* Marymount Col, Tarrytown, NY, BA, 76; Univ Ga, Athens, MFA, 89. *Work:* City of Orlando Pub Art Collection, Fla; Maitland Art Ctr, Fla; Valencia Community Col, Orlando, Fla. *Comn:* Faun, comn by Freddy Loef, Athens, 88. *Exhib:* Five from Georgia, Ga Mus Art, Athens, 89; No Mere Mortals, Univ Tenn, Chattanooga, 91; Clay National 94, Dairy Barn Cult Arts Ctr, Athens, Ohio, 94; Orlando Biennial, Terrace Gallery, Orlando City Hall, Fla, 94, The Eight, 94. *Collection Arranged:* Fine Art of Craft, Craft-Nonfunctional, 93; Allan Maxwell: Manipulated Image/Photography, 94; Shared Journey, Installation, 94. *Pos:* Gallery cur, Valencia Community Col, Orlando, Fla, 92- & Seminole Community Col, Sanford, Fla, 93-94; prog dir, Maitland Art Gallery, Maitland, Fla, 96-98. *Teaching:* Adj prof, Valencia Community Col, Orlando, Fla, 90-. *Awards:* Award of Merit Mixed Media, Arts on the Park Inc, 91; Art Servs Coun Fel, 92-94. *Mem:* Col Art Asn; Maitland Art Ctr. *Media:* Ceramic Sculpture, Drawing

AMELCHENKO, ALISON M
PAINTER, INSTRUCTOR
b Summit, NJ, Nov 30, 47. *Study:* Pratt Inst, BFA, 69; Studied with Jochen Seidel. *Comn:* murals, Rohallion Estate, Rumson, NJ, 2000. *Exhib:* One-woman shows, Ocean Co Col, Toms River, NJ, 85 & Georgian Ct Col, Lakewood, NJ, 90; Noyes Mus, Oceanville, NJ, 2001; Georgian Ct Col, Lakewood, NJ, 2001. *Pos:* chmn, Ocean Co Cult & Heritage Comn, 91-99, vice-chair, 2000-2001 & commissioner, 2001-. *Teaching:* dir, instr, Kids Art Studio, Seagirt, NJ, 90-. *Awards:* Best in Show, Ocean Co Artists Guild, 82, 2000. *Mem:* Ocean Co Artist Guild (pres, 87-89). *Media:* Oils. *Dealer:* Thistledown Gallery 1405-1 Third Ave Springlake NJ 07762. *Mailing Add:* Ocean County Cultural& Heritage Comm 126 Osborne Ave Bay Head NJ 08742

AMEN, IRVING
PAINTER, PRINTMAKER
b New York, NY, July 25, 1918. *Study:* Pratt Inst, scholar, 32-39; study in Paris, 50 & Italy, 53. *Work:* Mus Mod Art & Metrop Mus, NY; Butler Inst Am Art; Victoria & Albert Mus, London; Bibliot Nat, Paris; Albertina Mus, Vienna; and others; Bezalel, Jerusalem; Smithsonian Inst, Washington, DC. *Comn:* Peace Medal (commemorating end of Viet Nam War); Twelve Tribes of Israel (12 stained glass windows 16ft high), comn by Agudas Achim Synagogue, Columbus, Ohio. *Exhib:* Master Prints, Mus Mod Art, NY; Int Ausstellung Von Holzschnitten, Zurich, Switz; I Mednarodna Graficna Razstava, Ljubljana, Yugoslavia; L V Biannale di Pittura Americana, Bordighera, Italy; Dessins Americains Contemporains, US Info Serv; Collection of the Butler Inst Am Art, Youngstown, Ohio. *Teaching:* Instr art, Pratt Inst & Univ Notre Dame. *Awards:* Directors Prize, Audubon Artists, NY. *Mem:* Int Inst Arts & Lett; Int Soc Wood Engravers; Acad Fiorentina delle Arti Disegno; Soc Am Graphic Artists; Am Color Print Soc; Audubon Artists; Asca; Artist Fel; Artists Equity, NY. *Media:* Oil, Etching, Woodcut. *Publ:* Print ed, Irving Amen woodcuts 1948-1960, Irving Amen: 1964, Amen: 1964-1968 & Amen: 1968-1970; illusr, Gilgamesh, Ltd Ed Club. *Dealer:* Hillel Gallery Cincinatti. *Mailing Add:* PO Box 812365 Boca Raton FL 33481-2365

AMEND, EUGENE MICHAEL
HISTORIAN, ADVISOR
b Jefferson City, Mo, Oct 31, 50. *Study:* Univ Mo, Columbia, BA, 75, MA, 77; studied with Dr Saul Weinberg, Dr Edzard Baumann, Dr Osmond Overby & Dr Vera Townsend. *Collection Arranged:* Nathan Jones: Works on Paper, Univ Tex, Dallas, 79; Arie Van Selm: Recent Works, Tex Woman's Univ, Denton, 79; Charles Campbell: Retrospective, Longview Mus & Art Ctr, Tex, 79; Auguste Ravier, 1814-1895, Univ Tex, Dallas, 81. *Pos:* Cur & art historian, Stewart Gallery, Dallas, 78-80, art adv & free lance cur, EM Amend & Assoc, Dallas, 80-; dir, Omni Art, Dallas, 84-; consult, Tex Instruments Inc, 87-, Achievement Video Network Inc, 88-89 & Art Alley, 95-98; Raytheon Tech Instit, 98-. *Teaching:* Instr art hist & humanities, Univ Mo, Columbia, 75-76; instr art hist, Richland Col, 80-93; instr humanities, Brookhaven Col, Dallas, Tex, 2002-03. *Mem:* Col Art Asn; Artist Coalition Tex (pres, 79-80); Tex Asn Art Dealers (pres, 93-); candidate mem Am Soc Appraisers. *Res:* American artists and current art patrons and patronage in regional localities; Australian artist, Norman Lloyd (1895-1983). *Mailing Add:* 3130 Chatsworth Dr Dallas TX 75234

AMENOFF, GREGORY
PAINTER
b St Charles, Ill, 48. *Study:* Beloit Col, BA,1970; Mass Col Arts, DFA (hon) 1994. *Hon Degrees:* Mass Col Art, D, 94. *Work:* Albright-Knox Art Gallery, Buffalo, NY; Art Inst of Chicago; Metrop Mus Art, NY; Mus Mod Art, NY; Whitney Mus Am Art; Bklyn Mus Art; Butler Inst Am Art, Youngstown, Ohio; Currier Gallery Art, Manchester, NH; and others. *Exhib:* Works on Paper, Hayden Corridor, Mass Inst Technol, 76; Stephen Wirtz Gallery, San Francisco, 83; Texas Gallery, Houston, 84; The Monotypes, Butler Inst Am Art, Columbus, Ohio, 89; Hirschl & Adler Modern, NY, 90; The Symphony of Trees Project, Art & Cult Ctr Hollywood, Fla, 98; Green Woods and Crystal Water: The Am Landscape Tradition Since 1950, Philbrook Mus Art, Tulsa, 99; Mark Makers: Painterly Abstraction from the Colorado Collection, Univ Col Art Galleries, Boulder, 99; one-man shows, Thirty Views, lLymna Allyn Art Mus, New London, Conn, Lowe Art Gallery, Syracuse Univ, NY, Univ Art Gallery, SUNY, Oswego & Maier Art Mus, Randolph-Macon Women's Col, Lynchburg, Va, 98-2000, Silvermin Guild Arts Ctr, New Canaan, Conn, 99, Paintings, Galerie Vidal St Phalle, Paris, 99, Gregory Amenoff Thirty Views, Nielsen Gallery, Boston, Gregory Amenoff Paintings, Salander O'Reilly Galleries, NY 99, & Gregory Amenoff, Selected Paintings, Drawings and Prints 1987-99, Wright Mus Art, Beloit (Wis) Col, 2000; Invitational Exhib of Painting and Sculpture, Am Acad Arts & Letters, NY, 99; Green Woods and Crystal Water: The Am Landscape Tradition Since 1950, the Philbrook Mus Art, Tulsa, 99; Mark Makers: Painterly Abstraction from the Colorado Collection, Univ Colo Art Galleries,Boulder, 99; After Nature II, Herter Art Gallery, Univ Mass, Amherst, 99; Beyond the Mountains: The Contemp Am Landscape, Lyman Allyn Mus Art, New London, Conn, Ft Wayne (Ind) Mus Art, Boise Art Mus, Polk art Mus, Landeland, Fla, Muskegon Mus Art & Newcomb Art Gallery Tulane U, New Orleans, 99; The Contemp Landscape, Mira Mar Gallery, Sarasota, Fla, 2000; The Poetry of the Earth is Never Dead, 55 Mercer St, NY, 2000; An Homage to Albert Pinkham Ryder, The State of Art Gallery, Brooklyn, 2000; over 65 group exhibs, 74-90. *Pos:* Pres, Nat Acad Design Sch Fine Arts, New York City, 2000-. *Teaching:* Grad painting, Sch Visual Arts, 87; prof art, Columbia Univ, NY, 94-. *Awards:* Mass Bicentennial Painting Award, 76; Nat Endowment Arts, 80, 81 & 89; Tiffany, 80; Recipient Purchase award, Am Acad of Arts and Letters, 1993, 1995, 1996. *Bibliog:* Ed Hallahan (auth), Gregory Amenoff: The Monotypes, Dialogue, 3/4/89; Donald Kuspit (auth), Gregory Amenoff Hirschl Aldler Modern, Art Forum, summer, 93; Eleanor Heartney (auth), Gregory Amenoff at Salander O'Reilly, Art in america, 10/2000; William Zimmer (auth), Foray inot the big forms of land, sea and sky, New York Times, 10/24/99. *Mem:* Nat Acad Design (assoc, 92, acad, 94, pres 2001). *Media:* Oil. *Collection:* Moma, The Metropolitam Museum of Art; The Whitney Museum of American Art; and many others. *Publ:* Notes on identity a look at the landscape in American painting, Napa Contemp Arts Found J, Vol 1, 92; cover art, (Donald Kuspit, auth), The Rebirth of Painting in the Late Twentieth Century, Cambridge U Press, 2000; cover art Full Moon Boat, Graywolf Press, St Paul, Minn, 2000. *Mailing Add:* Nielson Gallery 179 Newbury St Boston MA 02116

AMES, LEE JUDAH
ILLUSTRATOR, WRITER
b New York, NY, Jan 8, 1921. *Study:* Columbia Univ, with Carnahan. *Work:* Many pieces, layouts & finished illus in Univ Ore & Univ Southern Miss permanent collections. *Pos:* Art dir, Weber Assocs, New York, 47-52; pres, Ames Advert, New York, 53-54, Lee Ames & Zak Ltd, 75- & Lee J Ames Enterprises; artist-in-residence, Doubleday Publ Co, New York, 55-60. *Teaching:* Instr comic art, Sch Visual Arts, New York, 48-49; lectr advert art, Dowling Col, 70-72. *Awards:* Garden State Children's Book Award, 86. *Mem:* Nat Cartoonists Soc; Berndt Toast Gang. *Media:* Mixed Media. *Publ:* Auth & illusr, Draw 50 Ser (27 titles), Make 25 Crayon Drawings of the West, Make 25 Felt Tipped Drawings of the Circus & The Dot, Line and Shape Connection, Doubleday; plus illusr for over 100 addn bks. *Mailing Add:* 28071 Via Pedrell Mission Viejo CA 92692-1731

AMES, STEVEN
PATRON
Pos: former partner, Oppenheimer & Co; Pres, Steven Ames & Assoc; adv bd, Guggenheim Mus; trustee, Whitney Mus Am Art. *Mailing Add:* BCE Place 181 Bay St Heritage Bldg Fl 2 Toronto ON M5J 2T3 Canada

AMFT, ROBERT
PAINTER, PHOTOGRAPHER
b Chicago, Ill, Dec 7, 1916. *Study:* Art Inst Sch, grad; Oxbow Sch, Saugatuck, Mich. *Work:* Butler Inst Am Art, Youngstown, Ohio; Brown Foreman, Louisville, Ky. *Exhib:* Pa Acad Ann, 58; Butler Inst Art, 58; One-man shows, Countryside Art Ctr, Arlington Heights, 82, Kans State Univ, Watercolors, 84, Recent Painting, One Ill Ctr, Chicago, 85, Ill Printers, Springfield, 89, Photos, Rotunda Gallery, Highland Park, Ill, 94, Caputo Gallery, Madison, Wisc, 94 & Photos, Int tuitt Gallery, Chicago, 96; Re-Creations, 1800 Clybourn Gallery, 92; New Horizons Ann, Chicago, 92; Pointillism, Color Photos, Rotunda Gallery, Highland Park, Ill, 92; A Place in the World, Alverno Col, Milwaukee, Wis, 93; Genesis, R H Love Gallery, Chicago, 93; Midwestern Sculpture, S Bend Reg Art Ctr, 96; 21st Harper Col, W Ill Univ; Print & Drawing Ann, 97; 1997 Bi-State Exhib, Iowa Mus Art, Davenport, 97; Roadside Attractions, Mus Art, Lafayette, Ind, 97; 8th Int Print Competition, Osaka Triennale, Japan, 97; Int Print Triennial, Cracow, Poland, 2000; Robert Amft:Paintings, A Survey; 1935-2005, Hyde Park Art Ctr. *Awards:* First Prize Painting, 72 & Spec Award, 75, New Horizons; Renaissance Prize, 75th Artists of Chicago, 74; Painting Award, Beverly Art Ctr, 85. *Bibliog:* Great treasures from the Art Institute of Chicago, Chicago Mag, 4/77; Udo Kultermann (auth), Van Gogh in Contemporary Art, Art Voices South, 11-12/78; Alan Artner (auth), rev, Chicago Tribune, 7/24/81. *Mem:* Arts Club Chicago. *Publ:* Illusr, Photographs of sculptor Fred Smith, Life Mag, 11/69; SPOT, Publications of the Houston Ctr for Photography, 91; Reproduction of Amft's Peacock in Chicago, Sun Times, 1/10/92. *Dealer:* Corbett vs Dempsey, Modern Art & Uncommon Objects, John Corbelt, Dusty Groove Building 1120 North Ashland Ave. Chicago, IL, 60622, 773-278-1664. *Mailing Add:* 7340 N Ridge Chicago IL 60645

AMICO, DAVID MICHAEL
PAINTER, INSTRUCTOR
b Rochester, NY, Sept 24, 51. *Study:* Calif State Univ, Fullerton, BA, 74; Hunter Col, New York, 75. *Exhib:* New Figuration in Am, Milwaukee Art Mus, Wis, 82; Sonata, Newport Harbor Art Mus, Newport Beach, Calif, 82; Circus Boy, 87 & Profound Visions, 88, Ace Contemp Exhibs, Los Angeles; Ace Gallery, Los Angeles, 89 & 90, Mexico City, 99, NY, 2000; Los Angeles Munic Gallery, Sociedade Cult Arte Brazil, 90; solo shows, Marc Jancou Galerie, Zurich, Switz, 91, Douglas Lawing Gallery, Houston, 96; Physical Abstraction in Los Angeles, Ace Gallery, Los Angeles, 92 & 94; Ace Gallery, 98; Ace Gallery, Los Angeles, Calif, 200-2004; Claremont Graduate Univ, Claremont, Calif, 2002. *Teaching:* Claremont Grad Univ, Claremont, Calif. *Awards:* Guest Honorarium Cartier Found, Juey es Josas France, 90; Pellack Krasner Found Award, 94, 97; Pres Scholars Distinguished Teacher Award. *Bibliog:* Christopher Knight (auth), Amico's paintings portray private mystery, Los Angeles Herald Examiner, 81; Ralph Rugoff (auth), Hottest new artists, Los Angeles Mag, 85; Lee Wohlfert-Wihldorg (auth), LA's electric, eclectic artists, Town & Country, 86; Margaret Lazzari (auth), Parameters of Meaning, Artweek, 6/90; Lisa Zeitz (auth), The Last Cry in Abstractionism, Kunstmarkt, 2000. *Media:* Oil, Drawing. *Dealer:* Douglas Chrismas 5514 Wilshire Blvd Los Angeles CA 90036; Ace Gallery 275 Hudson St New York NY. *Mailing Add:* 443 S San Pedro No 601 Los Angeles CA 90013

AMINOFF, JUDITH GINTZ
EDITOR, WRITER
b San Diego, Calif, July 9, 1947. *Study:* Univ Calif, Berkeley, BA, 70. *Pos:* Ed & publ, COVER Mag, New York & Paris, 79-83; translr, Mus Mod Art, Paris, 82-; collabr, Editions Territories, Paris, 82-; ed, BHD Buchloh, Thierry de Duve & Mus Mod Art, Paris, 84-; translr & writer, France, 86-. *Awards:* Nat Educ Found Grants, 80-83. *Res:* COVER: a magazine of art presenting new works; artists in their own words and in dialogue with each other, critics, dealers. *Mailing Add:* Mas St Jerome 13810 Eygalieres France

AMISANO, JOSEPH
ARCHITECT
b NY City, Jan 10, 1917. *Study:* Pratt Inst, B (arch), 40, M (arch), 41. *Comn:* Civic Ctr (MARTA Station); Lenox Square Mall, 58; Woodruff Arts Ctr, 68; Two Live Oak Ctr, 69; Peachtree Summit, 75. *Pos:* Registered architect in 14 states including Ga; designer Walter Sanders, NY City, 40-41, Harrison & Fouihoux, NY City, 41-42, Harrison & Abramovitz, NY City, 42-44; structural engineer Pan Am Airport, 44-45; designer Ketchum, Gina & Sharp, 46-49; pres Toombs, Amisano & Wells Architects, Atlanta, 55-; consultant Carlson Group. *Teaching:* Guest lectr Washington Univ, St Louis, 63, Cornell Univ, 64, Ga inst Tech, 85. *Mem:* Nat Acad (assoc, 77, acad, 94); Am Acad Rome (Prix de Rome, 52); Am Inst Planners; fel, Am Inst Architects. *Mailing Add:* Toombs Amisano & Wells 1028 Nawench Dr NW Atlanta GA 30327-1340

AMOROS, GRIMANESA
PAINTER
b July 21, 62. *Study:* The Art Students League, MY, 85-88. *Work:* Univ Vt, Burlington; Doro Productions, Vienna, Austria; Poncidi Press, Rhinbeck, NY; Latin Am Mag, Coltsdale, Ariz; Jack Lowe Visual Arts, NY. *Exhib:* Solo exhibs, Mus Nahin Isaias, Ecuador, 91, Mus Mod Art, Ecuador, 92, Javier Lumbreras Fine Art, Fla, 93, Porter Troupe Gallery, San Diego, 93, Carolyn J Roy Gallery, NY, 94, Mus Mod Art, Sto Domingo Rep Dominican, 95 & Art Renaca Gallery, Chile, 97, Egizio's Project, Timeless Terracotta, NY, 99, Artco Gallery, Installations of Drawings, Lima, Peru, 03; The Body Elecrtic, Spruil Ctr Gallery, Atlanta, 97; K & A Gallery, France, 97. *Awards:* Art Student League, painting fel, 85 & merit scholar, 86; Nat Endowment Arts, 93 & 94; Fel Va Ctr for Creative Arts Residency, 02; Art In Embassies Prog, US State Dept, Lima, Peru, 03. *Bibliog:* Pamela Blume Leonard (auth), Fashion speaks volumns, J Constitution, Art Leisure, 9/97; Michael Carravagio (auth), Body electric, Dunwood Crier, Atlanta, 9/3/97; Pat Worrell (auth), The body electric, Am Syle Mag, Atlanta, 8-9/97; and others; Castro, Juan El Universo, Guayaquil, Ecuador, 01; Trowbridge, Tom KUNM Radio, Santa Fe Art Series, 02. *Dealer:* Porter Troupe Gallery 301 Spruce St San Diego CA 92103; Itturalde Gallery 154 La Brea Ave Los Angeles CA 90069. *Mailing Add:* 117 Hudson St 4th fl New York NY 10013

AMOROSO, NICOLAS ALBERTO AMOROSO BOELCKE
PAINTER, FILMMAKER
b San Miguel de Tucuman, Arg, May 15, 44. *Study:* Faculted de Artes Univ Nac de Tucuman, Artes Plast, 68; Faculted de Bellas Aftes Univ Nac La Plata, Lic Cinematography, 72 & Prof Sup Cinematography, 74 Ar. *Work:* Mus de Arte Contemp Latinoamericano, Punta del Este, Eurguay 4; Mus de Artes y Ciencias, Univ Nac Autonaoma, Mus de Arte Jose Luis Cuevas, Mexico City; Mus Nac de Arte, Managua, Nicaragua; Mus Prov de Bellas Artes, Buenos Aires, Arg. *Comn:* Pintura mural sobre una cupula, comn by Ing Alfredo Sliapnic, Mexico City, 92. *Exhib:* La Seriegrafia en el Arte, Mus de Artes y Ciencias, Mexico City, 84; De su Album Inciertas, Mus de Arte Mod, Mexico City, 85; Las Horas que Pasan, Mus de Arte Mod, Mexico City, 87; Conociendo a Victoria, Mus de Bellas Artes, Tucuman, 91; Carpeta Universitaria, Mus de la Estampa, Mexico City, 93. *Teaching:* Prof & investigador diseno & grafico, Univ Autonoma Metrop de Mex, 82-94. *Awards:* Mencion de Honor, XIII Salon de Artes, 76 & Primer Premio, XV Salon de Artes, 77, Mus de Buenos Aires. *Bibliog:* Silvestre Byron (auth), La Optica Descarnada, Pajaro de Fuego, 78; Santiago Espinosa (auth), Historia de Vida, Revista Universitaria, 87; Raquel Tibol (auth), Memoria y Olivido, Proceso, 91. *Media:* Acrylic, Oil; Video. *Publ:* Auth, La imagen como discurso, Artes Visuales, 79; Tata Dios, Univ Autonoma Metrop de Mex, 88; coauth, Las Artes Plasticas y el Disneo, Trece Ensayos Univ Autonoma Metrop de Mex, 88; Creacion: Contexto de la Idea, Teoria/Arte Univ Autonoma Metrop de Mex, 91; (auth), El Acto de Crear, Univ Autonoma Metrop de Mex, 93. *Dealer:* Galeria Juan Martin Dickens 33B Col Polanco Mex DF 11560 Mexico. *Mailing Add:* Av Centenario 300 Ed 6 Dpto 503 Lomas de Tarango Mexico DF 01620 Mexico

AMORY, CLAUDIA
PAINTER
b Hampton, VA, 53. *Study:* Va Commonwealth Univ, BFA, 76; Md Inst Col Art, MFA, 85. *Comn:* Painting, Steuart Hughes, Williamsburg, Va, 86. *Exhib:* Art in the Bell Tower, Bell Tower Commons, Baltimore, Md, 85; Univ Md, Baltimore Co, 88; Excavations, Arlington Art Ctr, Va, 89; 1989 McDonogh Ann Exhib, Tuttle Gallery, Md, 89. *Pos:* Admin asst, off grad studies, Md Inst, Col Art, 83-85; gallery selection panel mem, Sch 33 Art Ctr, Baltimore, 88-90, dir, 90-. *Teaching:* Art instr, pub sch system, York Co, 76-82; grad inst asst, Mt Royal Grad Sch Art, Md Inst, Col Art, 83-85. *Awards:* Jurors Merit Award, Area Wide Juried Painting Exhib, Arlington Arts Ctr, 85; Fel, Nat Endowment Arts, 87. *Mem:* Arlington Arts Ctr. *Media:* Oil

AMOS, EMMA
PAINTER, PRINTMAKER
b Atlanta, Ga, Mar 16, 38. *Study:* Antioch Col, Yellow Springs, Ohio, BA, 58; London Cent Sch Art, Eng, BFA, 60; New York Univ, MA, 65. *Work:* Mus Mod Art, NY; Wadsworth, Atheneum, Conn; Newark Mus, NJ; NJ State Mus, Trenton; Minn Mus Art, Minn. *Comn:* Mosaic Ceiling, NY Bd Educ, 94; Mosaics, bronzes, landscaping, Ralph David Abernathy Mem, Atlanta, 96. *Exhib:* Committed to Print, Mus Mod Art, NY, 88-90; The Decade Show, Mus Contemp Hispanic Art, NY, 90; Bronx Mus, McIntosh Gallery, Ga; Changing the Subject (traveling exhib), Art in Gen, NY, 94-95; Emma Amos Paintings & Prints 1982-1992 retrospective, Col Wooster Art Mus, 94-95; Bearing Witness, Contemp Works by African Am Women Artists (traveling exhib), Spelman Col, 96-; Solo exhib Art Resources Tranfer (ART), New to NY, recent retrospective exhib, Oct 6-Nov, 2002; Emma Amos, Works on Paper, The Nat Afro-Am Mus and Cult Ctr, Wilberforce, Ohio, 2004; K Caraccio Printmaking Studio, NY, Print Retrospective, April-Oct 2004, Online at www.kcaraccio.com; Emma Amos Works on Paper, Middle Collegiate Church, NY, Jan-Feb, 2005; Flomenhaft Gallery, Emma Amos, Paintings and Prints, Chelsea, NY, 2006; Group Exhib: Academy of Arts and Letters, Ceremonial Exhib, New York City, May, 2003; Crosscurrents in the Mainstream: Transcultural NJ, catalogue, The Jane Voorhees Zimmerli Mus of Art, Rutgers, The State Univ of NJ, April-July, 2004; On Their Own: Transcultural New Jersey, Mason Gross Sch of Arts Galleries, with Melvin Edwards, Fausto Sevila, Hughie Lee Smith, Tashiko Takaezu 2004; and many others. *Pos:* Undergrad dir, Mason Gross Sch Arts, Rutgers Univ, currently; trustee, Richard A Florsheim Art Fund, currently; co-chair bd govs, Skowhegan Sch Painting & Sculpting, Maine, currently. *Teaching:* Prof fine art, Mason Gross Sch Arts, Rutgers Univ, NJ, 80; gov, Skowhegan Sch Painting & Sculpture, 87. *Awards:* Nat Endowment Fel-Drawing, 83; NY Found Fel--Painting, 89; The Jame Van Derzee Award, Kimmel Ctr, PA, 2002; Purchase Award, American Acad of Arts & Letters, NY, 2003; Lifetime Achievement Award, Women 's Caucus for Art, CAA, Seattle, 2004. *Bibliog:* Peter Erickson (auth), Seeing White, Vol 5, No 3, Transition Mag, Oxford Univ Press, NC, fall 95; Art on my mind-visual politics, New Press, New York, 95; Subject: Action Lines, L&M Video, 96; City Paper, Darkness Visible: The BMA Exhib the Sights of Blackness, Lee Gardner, Feb 13, 2002; Nka: Journal of Contemp African Art, Emma Amos, Art Matters, Dr Sharon Patton, pp42-47, Fall-Winter, 2002-2003; Creating their Own Image: African- AM Women Artist, Lisa Farrington, PhD, Amos, Cover Art, Tightrope, Nov Pub, 2004; Creating Black AM, Nell Irvin Painter, Oxford Univ Press, Illustration, Paul Robeson Frieze, 2005. *Mem:* Col Art Asn. *Media:* Acrylic; Mosaic. *Collection:* AZ State Univ Art Mus, Tempe, AZ; Bellevue Hospital Fine Arts Collection, New York, NY; Birmingham Mus of Fine Art, AL; Colgate-Palmolive Collection, NY; The College Board Collection of Prints by AM Artist, New York City; The Columbia Mus, Columbia, SC; Dade County Mus of Art, FL; The Ford Fountain. *Publ:* Coauth, Racism is the issue, Issue 15, 82, & The Art of Education, Issue 25, 90, Heresies Collective; illusr, IKON--Creativity and Change, No 5/6, Ikon Inc, 86; auth & co-host, Show of Hands (ser), WGBH Educ TV, Boston, Mass, 87-88; coauth, M/E/A/N/I/N/G Magazine, Mira Schor & Susan Bee, 90. *Dealer:* McIntosh Gallery 587 Virginia Ave Atlanta GA 30306; Sherry Washington Gallery 1274 Library St Detroit MI 48226. *Mailing Add:* 21 Bond St New York NY 10012-2451

AMOSS, BERTHE
ILLUSTRATOR, PAINTER
b New Orleans, La, Sept 26, 25. *Study:* Newcomb Col, BA; Univ Hawaii; Kunsthalle Bremen, Ger, three yrs; Acad des Beaux Arts, Antwerp, Belg, one yr; Tulane Univ, MA(literature & art). *Work:* La State Libr; De Grummond Collection, Univ Southern Miss, Kerlan; Town of Kerlan, Minn; Tulane Univ. *Exhib:* One person show, Exhib of Illustrators, Howard Tilton Libr, Tulane Univ, 82. *Pos:* Children's bk rev ed, New Orleans Times Picayune, currently; pres, More Than a Card, Inc, currently; pres, Cocodrie Press, currently. *Teaching:* Instr, writing & illustrating children's books, Tulane Univ, 76-82, children's literature & folklore, 82-. *Bibliog:* Selma Lanes (auth), Down the Rabbit Hole, Children's Literature, Stewig. *Media:* Watercolor. *Publ:* Auth & illusr, The Marvelous Catch of Old Hannibal, 70, Old Hasdrubal and the Pirates, 71, Parents Publ; Secret Lives, Atlantic-Little-Brown, 79; The Loup Garou, Pelican, 79; auth, Mockingbird Song, Tom in the Middle, What did you lose Santa, Harper & Row, 87 & 88; auth, More Than a Card, private publ, 88; auth, Draw Yourself into the Ark, WAU Press, 03; auth, Draw Yourself into a Starlit Journey, WAU Press, 03; co-auth rev ed, Writing & Illustrating Childerns Books, Writers Digest Books, 05. *Mailing Add:* 3723 Carondelet St New Orleans LA 70115

ANACKER, JOHN WILLIAM
GALLERY DIRECTOR, PAINTER
b Bozeman, Mont, June 22, 60. *Study:* Mont State Univ, BAA, 83; Univ NC, Chapel Hill, MFA, 86. *Exhib:* 29th Ann Nat Exhib Am Art, Chautauqua Art Asn Galleries, NY, 86; Celebrating Paper, Yellowstone Art Ctr, Billings, Mont, 88. *Pos:* Gallery dir, Haynes Fine Arts Gallery, Bozeman, Mont, 86-. *Teaching:* Instr painting, Mont State Univ Sch Art, 86-. *Mem:* Mont Art Gallery Dirs Asn (treas, 89-90 & pres, 90-). *Media:* Watercolor. *Mailing Add:* 11 Flathead Ave Bozeman MT 59718-6335

ANASTASI, WILLIAM (JOSEPH)
PAINTER, SCULPTOR
b Philadelphia, Pa, Aug 11, 33. *Study:* Univ Pa, 53-61. *Work:* Mus Contemp Art, Los Angeles, Calif; Contemp Mus, Honolulu, Hawaii; Moderna Museet, Stockholm, Sweden; Chrysler Mus, Norfolk, Va; Okla City Art Mus. *Comn:* Viewing a Film of the Period (film), 78, Collapse (photo installation), 81 & Terminus II (photo installation), 81, Whitney Mus Am Art; photo installation, Kunstmus, Dusseldorf, Ger, 79; Terminus I (photo installation), Hudson River Mus, NY, 79. *Exhib:* Menil Collection, Houston, Tex, 94; Mito Tower, Japan, 94; Philadelphia Mus Art, Pa, 95; Niels Borch Jensen Gallery, Berlin, Ger, 2000; Stalke Gallery, Copenhagen, 2000; Anastasi Bradshaw and Cage 2001 Museet for Samtidskunst, Roskelde, Denmark, 2001; Anastasi Bradshaw, Cage and Cunningham, Boyly Art Mus, Univ Va, 2005. *Pos:* Artistic co-adv, Merce Cunningham Dance Co, NY, 84-; artist-in-residence, Sirius Art Ctr, Cork, Ireland, 2000 & Statens Vaerkstedes for Kunst, Copenhagen, 2000. *Teaching:* painting, Sch Visual Arts, NY, 71-86; lectr, Art After Duchamp, Chicago Art Fair, 88, Yale Univ, 91; Alfred Jarry & James Joyce, The Sorbonne, Paris, 95. *Bibliog:* Gregory Battcock (auth), Minimal Art (Introduction), Dutton, 68; Lucy R Lippard (auth), Six Years: The De-materialization of the Art Object, Praeger, 73; Brian O'Doharty, Inside the white cube: Notes on the Gallery Space, Artforum, 3/76; Thomas McEvilley (auth), The Triumph of Anti-Art, McPherson & Co, 2005. *Media:* All Media. *Interests:* Chess. *Publ:* Duchamp on the Jarry Road, Artforum, 9/91; Me Innerman Monophone & Even Haha, Notes on Jarry & Duchamp with Joyce, Anders Tornberg Gallery, Lund, Sweden, 5/92; Jarry, Joyce, Duchamp & Cage, Venice Biennale, 93; Jarry in Joyce, Joyce Studies Ann, 95; Marcel Duchamp in Finnegans Wake Tout Fait, 2003; Aaron Levy & Jean-Michel Rabate (eds), William Anastasi's Pataphysical Society, Jarry, Joyce, Duchamp & Cage, Slought Found, Phila, Pa, 2005. *Dealer:* Anders Tornberg Gallery Lund Sweden; Sandra Gering Gallery New York; Nicholas von Bartha Gallery London Great Britian; Thomas Rehbein Gallery Cologne Germany; Art Agents Gallery Hamburg Germany; Stalke Gallery Copenhagen; Ressle Fine Art New York NY; Baumgartner Gallery New York NY; 360 Degrees Gallery Tokyo Japan. *Mailing Add:* 924 West End Ave New York NY 10025

ANASTASIA, SUSANNA
PAINTER, INSTRUCTOR
b Elizabeth, NJ, July 26, 45. *Study:* Newark Sch Fine & Indsl Art, 66; studied with noted artists. *Work:* Prudential Bache, NY; Wall Twp Bd Edn, NJ; Sea Girt Libr, NJ; Capital Contracting & Design, Plainfield, NJ; Trenton-Mercer Campus Capital Health Syst, Trenton, NJ. *Comn:* painting for Christine Todd Whitman/NJ Gov's Mansion, John R Whitman, Island Beach State Park, 98; guest house watercolor for company

postcard, Conover Guest House, Bay Head, NJ, 99; burro portrait Weidel's Boxwood Farm, Pennington, NJ, 2000; design-graphic collage Brielle Riverview Seniors, Brielle, NJ, 2000; Bohler Engring, Pa. *Exhib:* Monmounth Co Arts Coun Monmouth Mus, Lincroft, NJ, 88, 93, 96, 98, 01, 02, 03, 04, 05 & 06; Millburn/Short Hills Art Asn, Walsh Libr Gallery, Seton Hall Univ, NJ, 98; NJ Watercolor Soc, Renee Fossner Gallery Paper Mill Play House, Millburn, NJ, 98; NJ Watercolor Soc Ann, Monmouth Mus, Lincroft, NJ, 99; Am Artists Profl League, NY Salmugundi Club, 2000; Johnson & Johnson Pharmaceutical, Inc; Seton Hall Univ, Walsh Libr Gallery, 05. *Teaching:* demonstrator/lectr watercolor, Ocean Co Teen Arts Festival Ann, 90-; watercolor demonstrator, NJ Div of the Aging, 99; lectr Wall HS Nat Art Honor Soc Induction, 2000. *Awards:* Best Design award NJ Watercolor Soc Ann, Harry & Ruth Kalish, 93; Grumbacher Gold Medal, Essex WC Club, Grumbacher Corp, 96; Nat Am Artists Profl League Juried award NY Am Artists Profl League, 96; Watercolor Award, Winsor Newton Grand Nat Am Artist Prof League, NY, 2004; Oil and Acrylic Award, Summer Boardwalk Show, Ocean City, NJ, 2004; Alice Berhle Award, Essex Watercolor Club, 2005. *Bibliog:* Tova Novarra (auth), The Nature of Art, Asbury Park Press, NJ, 90; Francis Molinaro (auth), Susanna Anastasia's Flowers in Watercolor, Asbury Park Press, NJ, 98; Desiree A DiCorcia (auth), Into the Woods, The Coast Star, NJ, 2000. *Mem:* Essex Water colorClub NJ (1st vpres 98-03, pres 2005-); Manasquan River Group of Artists/NJ (pres 85-87); Garden State Watercolor Soc; Allied Artists of Am New York City; Audobon Art Soc, NY; Am Artist Prof League, NY; and others. *Media:* Watercolor, Oil. *Publ:* Contrib artist, Long Beach Island Rapsody. *Mailing Add:* 4141 W 18th Ave Farmingdale NJ 07727

ANBINDER, PAUL
ART PUBLISHER, COLLECTOR
b Brooklyn, NY, Apr 19, 40. *Study:* Cornell Univ, AB, 60; Columbia Univ, grad work, 60-61. *Collection Arranged:* Cornell Collects (co-organizer), Hudson River Mus, Yonkers, NY, 76-77. *Pos:* Ed in chief, Shorewood Publ Inc, 64-69; exec ed & vpres, Harry N Abrams Inc, New York, NY, 69-74 & pres, 74-75; dir spec projs, Alfred A Knopf, Random House & ed/vpres, Ballantine Bks, New York, 75-78; pres, Hudson Hills Press, Inc, New York, 78-. *Mem:* Col Art Asn; Friends of Johnson Mus, Cornell Univ (mem exec coun); Century Asn. *Collection:* Contemporary American prints and drawings; Asian decorative art. *Publ:* Auth, Editing the Illustrated Book, Editors on Editing, Harper & Row, New York, 85

ANDELL, NANCY
PAINTER
b Boston, Mass, Nov 14, 53. *Study:* Sch Mus Fine Arts, Boston, Mass, dipl, 74, 5th yr certif, 76; Tufts Univ, Medford, Mass, 75. *Exhib:* Solo exhibs, Flag Gallery, Boston, Mass, 78, Impressions Gallery, Boston, Mass, 79, Impressions Gallery, Boston, Mass, 80, Shaker Mus, Old Chatham, NY, 91 & Vermont Col, Montpelier, 94; Water/Clay/Stone, Smithy Pioneer Gallery, Cooperstown, NY, 92; 20th Anniversary Traveling Exhib; Luminous Emanations, Simon's Rock Col, Great Barrington, Mass, 95; Metrop Mus Art, New Mus Contemp Art, NY; Brooklyn Mus, NY; Worcester Art Mus, Mass; Provincetown Mus Art, Mass; Danforth Mus, Farmingham, Mass. *Teaching:* Fac, Experimental Etching Studio, Boston, Mass, 79-80, McDowell Colony, 1980, Albany Inst Hist & Art, NY, 89-90, Berkshire Mus, Pittsfield, Mass, 89, Renssaeler Co Coun for Arts, Troy, NY, 89-92, Taconic Hills HS, 1990-. *Awards:* Spec Opportunity Stipend: NY Found Arts & Rensselaer Co Coun Arts, 91; Face to Face with the Arts, Columbia Co Initiative Prog, 91; Skidmore Col Fel, Saratoga Springs, NY, 91; Arad Arts Project, Arad, Israel, 1998. *Bibliog:* Lois Tarlow (auth), Profile: Ten Years Later, Art New Eng, 12/89; Lael Locke (auth), Idealized Landscapes, The Paper, 10/91; Meredith Fife Day (auth), Review: Luminous Emanations, paintings on wood, New Eng Art J, 6/96. *Media:* Oil, Mixed Media. *Mailing Add:* PO Box 46 Chatham NY 12037

ANDERSEN, DAVID R L
PAINTER, CURATOR
b Logan, Utah, Sept 30, 57. *Study:* Brigham Young Univ, Provo, Utah, MFA, 88. *Work:* Darthmouth Col, Hanover, NH; Ohio Univ; Utah State Collection; Mauritian Embassy, Washington, DC. *Exhib:* Solo exhibs, Calculations for Future Events, Darthmouth Col, Hanover, NH, 90 & Spiritus Mundi, Grossmont Col, San Diego, Calif, 91; two-person shows, Midland Col, Tex, 90 & Diverse Works Gallery, Houston, Tex, 90; Nat Draw Exhib, Brigham Young Univ, Provo, Utah, 89; Nat Juried Exhib, Natsoulas/Novelozo Gallery, Davis, Calif, 90; Animals, Centennial Mus, El Paso, Tex, 90. *Collection Arranged:* Robert Colescott (paintings), 89; Sera Siempre Asi? (prints; catalog); Sleeping Mutations (sculpture), 89; Cont Graphic Design, 90; Prints From Life, 90. *Pos:* Preparator, Brigham Young Univ, Provo, Utah, 85-88; dir galleries, Univ Tex at El Paso, 88-91; Instr painting/drawing, Brigham Young Univ, Provo, Utah, 85- 88; drawing/design, Univ Tex, El Paso, 88-91. *Awards:* URI Grant, Tex Comn on the Arts. *Media:* Mixed media. *Mailing Add:* c/o Gremillion & Co Fine Art Inc 2501 Sunset Blvd Houston TX 77005

ANDERSEN, LEIF (WERNER)
PAINTER
b Baltimore, Md, Mar 6, 25. *Study:* Art Students League, with Reginald Marsh & Louis Bouche, 46-48. *Work:* Bordighera Mus, Italy. *Exhib:* Am Group Show, Venice, Italy, 52; Nat Acad Design Ann, NY, 57 & 62; Allied Artist Am Ann, Nat Acad Design, 58 & 61; and numerous one-man shows. *Awards:* S J Wallace Truman Award, Nat Acad Design Ann, 57; Margaret Cooper Prize, Allied Artist Am, Nat Acad Design, 61. *Media:* Oil, Acrylic. *Mailing Add:* 246 E 51st St New York NY 10022

ANDERSON, BILL (WILLIAM) MAXWELL
PAINTER, PRINTMAKER
b Mankato, Minn, July 31, 41. *Study:* Mankato State Univ, BS, 59-63; grad studies, 74; Calif State Univ Long Beach, grad studies, 64-68. *Work:* Carnegie Mus Art, Oxnard, Calif; Nat Mus Prints, Mexico City, Mex; Conejo Valley Mus, Thousand Oaks, Calif; Mus Nat De La Acuarela, Mexico City; Bowers Mus, Santa Ana, Calif; Cora Mus, Mexico; The Union Inst, Cincinnati, Ohio. *Comn:* Murals, Mankato State Univ, 90; Painted Mural, Raul Anguiano, East Los Angeles Col, 2002. *Exhib:* Solo shows, Galeria Coyoacan, Mexico City, 80, Geometry & Line, Carnegie Art Mus, Oxnard, Calif, 88, Europe, Univ Calif, Los Angeles, 90, Homecoming, Mankato State Univ, 90, Meeuwis Art Gallery, Oirschot,The Neth, 92, Lodi Art Gallery, Pasadena, Calif, 93 & Sunset Beach, Calif, 96; The Yr of the Horse, Conejo Valley Art Mus, Thousand Oaks, Calif, 90; The Figure and the Horse, Calif State Univ, Los Angeles, 91; 5 Calif Artists in Mexico at Museo Nac De La Acuarela, Mexico City, 93; Primera Bienal Internacidnal De La Acuarela At Mus Nat De La Acuarela, Mexico City, 94; Generations, Six California Artists, Luckman Fine Arts Complex, Calif State Univ, Los Angeles, 96; Southern Exposure-Six Southern California Artists, King Co Art Ctr, Hanford, Calif, 97; 4 Maestros, Raul Anguiano, Vladimir Cora, Felipe Casteneda, Bill Anderson, Cruz Gallery, Santa Ana, Calif, 99; Sculpture by Casteneda, Paintings by Anderson, Sunset Beach, Calif, 2000; Manzanar (group exhib) Manzanar Nat Mus, 2005-2006; Vincent Price Permanent Collection Exhib, E Los Angeles Col, 2006. *Pos:* Art Comn Huntington Beach Calif, 80-94; art curric chmn, Los Alamitos Unified Sch Dist, 84-88; gallery dir, Los Alamitos Unified Sch Dist Gallery, 84-92; owner, Anderson Art Gallery, Sunset Beach, Calif, 95-2000. *Teaching:* Art teacher, gen visual art, Long Beach Unified Sch Dist, Calif, 63-69 & Anaheim & Los Alamitos Sch Dist, Calif, 72-2000, Orange Co High Sch for Arts, 85-94; art teacher printmaking, drawing & painting, Appleton Unified Sch Dist, Wis, 69-72. *Awards:* Teacher of Yr, Anaheim Union HS Dist, 78-79; Huntington Beach, First Outstanding Artist of Yr, 86; Art Mentor, Los Alamitos Unified Sch Dist, 87-88. *Bibliog:* Luis Bruno Ruiz (auth), Estampas Romanticas Caballos en la Pintora Bill Anderson, Excelsior, Mexico City, 80; auth, Anderson, George Zada Publishing, 85; Elaine Craft, The Art of Bill Anderson, cable channel 3, Huntington Beach, 92; James Figmoa (auth) Bill Anderson & Felipe Casteneda, Harbor Sun, 2000; Bill Andersons Line, Kennedy Libr, Calif State Univ at Los Angeles (book/catalog), 98; California Watercolors 1850-1970, Hillcrest Press, 2002. *Mem:* Arts Comn Huntington Beach (pres 81-87); Arts Assocs Huntington Beach; Studio Artists Huntington Beach (founder, 83, pres, 83-87); Cult Task Force Huntington Beach Calif, (94). *Media:* Oils, Watercolor. *Publ:* Illus, Creative Experience, Kendall/Hunt Pub, 89; Raul Anguiano's 75th Anniversary, Excelsior, 90; illus, El Completo de Circe, Eda Mex Pub, 91; Portfolio of Linoleum Cuts, 5 Engravers From USA & Mexico, 94; Primera Bienal Int De La A cuarela, Mus Nat De La Acuarela, 94; coauth with Milford Zornes, Nine Decades with a Master Painter, Earthen Vessel Productions, 2005. *Dealer:* Lodi Art Gallery 230 Lake St Pasadena CA 91101; Anderson Art Gallery 16812 Pacific Coast Hwy Sunset Beach CA90742; Mesa Art 789 W 19th St Ste D Costa Mesa CA 92627. *Mailing Add:* 17831 San Leandro Lane Huntington Beach CA 92647

ANDERSON, BRUCE A
GOLDSMITH, SCULPTOR
b Spokane, Wash, Sept 14, 1948. *Study:* Western Wash State Univ, BA, 73; Syracuse Univ, with Michael Jerry, MFA(metalsmithing), 79. *Exhib:* Young Americans Exhib, Am Craft Mus, NY, 77; Ger-Am Blacksmithing Exhib, Goethe Inst, Atlanta, Ga, 81-82; The First Int Shoebox Sculpture Exhib, Univ Hawaii, Manoa, 82; Jewelry USA, 84 & Am Jewelry, 85, Am Craft Mus, NY. *Mem:* Soc NAm Goldsmiths. *Media:* Metal. *Dealer:* Quadrum Gallery The Mall at Chestnut Hill Chestnut Hill MA. *Mailing Add:* Bulls Head Rd RR 1 Box 308 Stanfordville NY 12581

ANDERSON, BRUCE JAMES
STAINED GLASS ARTIST, VIDEO ARTIST
b Denver, Colo, Nov 18, 1940. *Study:* Ottawa Univ, Kans, BA, 63; Univ Manchester, Eng, 64; Univ Colo, Boulder, MA, 72. *Work:* Agate Community Church, Colo; Holy Mother of God Byzantine Church, Denver; St Stephen Protomartyr Episcopal Church; Brown Palace Hotel. *Comn:* Dutchman Restaurant, Denver, 73; Continental Broker, Denver, 76; six panels, Rik Fulcher, Denver, 79; Blackhawk Hotel, Davenport, Iowa, 79; Lunt Ave Marble Club, Scottsdale, Ariz, 79; and others. *Exhib:* Colo Glass Art, Boulder, 76-78. *Pos:* Owner, dir & designer, Wild Rose Studio & Gallery, 72-86; producer/dir, Lanbdu Report, The Art Seen & other individual productions. *Bibliog:* Joy Overbeck (auth), article, Leisure Living, fall 74; Marjorie Barrett (auth), Home living section, Rocky Mountain News, 10/23/76; Grant Tyson (auth), Gifts worth waiting for, Denver, 11/78. *Media:* Video, Graphic Arts

ANDERSON, CRAIG
PAINTER, SCULPTOR
b Minneapolis, Minn, Aug 22, 46. *Study:* Hamline Univ, BFA, 69; Univ Colo, Boulder, 79. *Exhib:* Small Works, Aspen Art Ctr, Colo, 83; 4th Tex Sculpture Symp, Univ Tex Mus, Austin, 85; Exhib Installation, Southwest Tex Univ, San Marcos, 91; IAIA Fac, Univ Colo, Boulder, 94; IAIA Fac, Inst Am Indian Arts, Santa Fe, 95. *Pos:* Preparator, Minneapolis Art Inst, 69-70; mus tech, Walker Art Ctr, 70-71. *Teaching:* Instr drawing, Univ Colo, Boulder, 78-79, drawing, design, video, Southwest Tex State Univ, 79-82; prof painting, Inst Am Indian Arts, Santa Fe, 89-96. *Awards:* Top 10 Selection, Video Meaning Use, Univ Chicago, 78. *Mem:* Col Art Asn. *Media:* Painting everything. *Mailing Add:* 173A Las Estrellas Santa Fe NM 87501

ANDERSON, CURTIS LESLIE
CONCEPTUAL ARTIST, PAINTER
b Minneapolis, Minn, Oct 5, 56. *Study:* Cooper Union for Advan Sci & Art, BFA, 79. *Work:* Libr Cong, Washington, DC; New York Pub Libr; Mus Atlantico, Tenerife Canary Islands, Spain; Mus des Beaux-Arts de Nantes, France; Toledo Art Mus, Ohio. *Exhib:* Excess in the Techno-Mediacratic Society, Mus Sarret de Grozon Arbois, France, 92; Drawn in the Nineties, Katonah Mus Art, NY, 92; The Return of the Cadavre Exquis, Drawing Ctr, NY, 93; Recent Acquisitions, NY Pub Libr, 93; Drawing the Line Against Aids, Peggy Guggenheim Collection, Venice, Italy, 93.

Bibliog: Martijn van Nieuwenhuyzen (auth), Curtis Anderson/t'Venster, Flashart, 86; Dore Ashton (auth), Curtis Anderson/Catalogue, Galerie Jule Kewenig, 90; Noel Frackman (auth), Curtis Anderson, Arts, 91. *Mem:* Berufsverbandbildenekunstler. *Dealer:* Baron/Boisante 50 W 57th St New York NY 10019. *Mailing Add:* Wormser Strasse 23 Cologne Germany 50677

ANDERSON, DANIEL J
CERAMIST, EDUCATOR
b St Paul, Minn, Nov 2, 45. *Study:* Studied with Renato Bassoli, Milan, Ital 1967-68; Univ Wis-River Falls, BS (art edn, Nat Assn Tobacco Distribrs Scholar), 68; Cranbrook Acad Art, Bloomfield Hills, Mich, MFA (ceramics, Rocco DiMarco Scholar, Sponsored Scholar), 70. *Work:* Carnegie Mus Art, Pittsburgh, Pa, Boise Art Mus, Idaho; Philadelphia Mus Art, Pa; Weisman Art Mus, Minneapolis, MN; Wustum Mus Art, Racine, Wis. *Exhib:* One-man shows, Gail Severn Gallery Sun Valley, 10 Manchester Craftsmen's Guild, Pittsburgh, Pa & Garth Clark Gallery, NY; 52nd Scripps Ceramic Exhib, Claremont, Calif; Ceramics USA 1996, Univ NTex, Denton; SOFA, Navy Pier, Chicago, Ill; Clay/Wood/Fire, Northern Clay Ctr, St Paul, Minn; Clay Ariz Art, N Ariz Univ, Flagstaff, Ariz; Third St Louis Art Fair, Clayton, Mo. *Teaching:* Prof & area head ceramic dept, Southern Ill Univ, Edwardsville, 70-2002; prof emeritus, S Ill Univ; vis instr, Ewha Woman's Univ, Seoul, Korea, 83 & Sch Art Inst, Chicago, Ill, 91; instr, Univ Ga, Cortona, Italy, 90. *Awards:* various grants & awards, Southern Ill Univ, Edwardsville, 70-83, 86, 87, 91, 93, 94, 96 & 99; Ill Arts Coun Grants, 75, 79, 81, 84, 85, 87-89, 91, 96 & 99; Artist Fel, Nat Endowment Arts, 91; and others. *Mem:* NCECA. *Publ:* Ceramics: Art & Perception, Vol 11 & 12. *Mailing Add:* 5519 Old Poag Rd Edwardsville IL 62025

ANDERSON, DAVID
ART DEALER, COLLECTOR
b Buffalo, NY, June 26, 35. *Pos:* Pres & owner, Anderson Gallery Inc, currently. *Specialty:* Art of 20th century since 1945. *Mailing Add:* Anderson Gallery Inc Martha Jackson Pl Buffalo NY 14214

ANDERSON, DAVID C
SCULPTOR, PHOTOGRAPHER
b Jamestown, NY, Mar 10, 31. *Study:* Univ Tulsa, with Alexandre Hogue & Dwayne Hatchett, BA, 64. *Work:* Tulsa S Regional Libr; Univ Tulsa; Okla Educ TV Authority. *Comn:* Sculpture, Price Waterhouse & Co, Houston, 79, Univ Tulsa, 81, Western Nat Bank, Tulsa, 82, Excelsior Hotel, Tulsa, 82 & Royal Bank Can, Dallas, 83. *Exhib:* Oklahoma Sculpture Today, Okla Mus Art, 80; Sculpture in Wood, Wichita Art Mus, 81; Shidoni Ann, Santa Fe, 81 & 82; Art Ann IV, 83 & Okla Sculpture Exhib, 83, Okla Mus Art. *Teaching:* Private lessons sculpture, 78-; adj prof art, Univ Tulsa, 82. *Awards:* Best of Show & First Place Photog, Bartlesville, Okla, 79. *Bibliog:* Clive Cussler (auth), King Dave--from pinstriping to sculpture, Tulsa Mag, 6/78 & David Anderson--Oklahoma Art Gallery, Wall & Wall Publ, 80. *Mem:* Charter mem Okla Sculpture Soc; Int Sculpture Ctr. *Dealer:* 26 East Art Ctr Tulsa OK; Adelle M Fine Arts Dallas TX. *Mailing Add:* 4985 E 26th St Tulsa OK 74114

ANDERSON, DAVID KIMBALL
SCULPTOR
b Los Angeles, Calif, Feb 3, 46. *Study:* San Francisco Art Inst, 67-71; asst to Peter Voulkos, 72-73. *Work:* Mus Mod Art, San Francisco; Mus Fine Arts, Santa Fe; Sheldon Mem Art Mus, Lincoln, Nebr; San Antonio Mus Art, Tex; Art Bank Program, Dept State, Washington, DC. *Comn:* City of Albuquerque. *Exhib:* One-person shows, San Francisco Art Inst, 79, Braunstein Gallery, San Francisco, 75, 78, 80, 83, 85, 87, 90, 94 & 96, Linda Durham Gallery, Santa Fe, 79, 81, 83, 85, 87, 89, 91, 94 & 96, Christopher Grimes Gallery, Santa Monica, Calif, 91, Hokin/Kaufman Gallery, Chicago, 91; Pub Sculpture/Urban Environ, Oakland Mus, Calif, 74; 1975 Biennial Exhib Contemp Art, Whitney Mus, NY, 75; Linda Durham Contemp Art, NY, 2003. *Pos:* San Jose State Univ, 97-. *Teaching:* Sculpture, San Francisco Art Inst, 76-79, Calif Col Arts & Crafts, Oakland, 79 & Univ NMex, 84-94. *Awards:* Nat Endowment Arts Fel Grant, 74, 81 & 88; Pollock-Krasner Found Grant, 86; Artist's Found Grant, 94. *Bibliog:* Art News, 3/86; Artspace, 3-4/90; Art News, 5/94. *Media:* Bronze, Steel. *Dealer:* Linda Durham Contemp Art, New York; Galisteo, NMex. *Mailing Add:* 235 Surfside Ave Cruz CA 95060

ANDERSON, DAWOLU JABARI
ILLUSTRATOR
Study: Tex S Univ, Houston, BFA, 1995; MFA, 2003. *Exhib:* Changing Perspective Mus, 1995; Preventions Collective, Project RowHouse & Commun Arts, 1996; Breaking Into the Mainstream, Irving Arts Ctr, 1996; Artist Board Chooses, Diverse Works, 1997; Bound Books, Brazos, 1998; Sixth Ann African Am Advisory Assn, Mus Fine Arts, 2002; Soul Sonic LustraSilk, Houston Com Coll NE, 2002; Symmetrical Patterns of Def/Collaborative Group Installation, Lawndale Art Ctr, 2004; Who Goliards? Artists at the Turn of the Century, Univ Tex S Univ, 2004; Whitney Biennial, Whitney Mus Am Art, 2006; one-man show: Birth of a Nation: Yo! Bumrush the Show, Art League Houston, 2006. *Pos:* Asst Coord, Project RowHouses, 1995-97; illusr, 1997-. *Awards:* First Prize, Houston Area Exhib, Blaffer Gallery, 2004; grant, Skowhegan Sch Paint & Sculpture, 2006. *Mailing Add:* 602 Sanford Houston TX 77096

ANDERSON, GUNNAR DONALD
PAINTER, ILLUSTRATOR
b Berkeley, Calif, 27. *Study:* Calif Sch Fine Arts, with Clyfford Still; Art Ctr Col Design, BFA, with Lorser Feitelson. *Work:* Brown-Forman Distillers, Louisville, Ky. *Comn:* Gov Lamar Alexander, Tenn; Mr & Mrs Meredith Long, Houston, Tex, 71; Mr & Mrs George Weyerhauser, Tacoma, Wash, 72; Mr & Mrs Charlie Rich, Memphis, Tenn; Mr & Mrs Charles Schulz, Calif. *Exhib:* 5th Winter Invitational, Calif Palace Legion Hon, San Francisco, 64; MH de Young Mem Mus, San Francisco, 25th Ann, Soc Western Artists, 68; Charles & Emma Frye Mus, Seattle, 71; Calif State Fair, Sacramento, 71; Mainstream 72, Grover M Hermann Fine Arts Ctr, Marietta Col, Ohio, 72. *Pos:* Bd Trustees, Soc Western Artists. *Teaching:* instr, Acad Art Col, San Francisco, Calif. *Awards:* Best figure or portrait, 29th Ann, Soc Western Artists, 71 & first place, Ann, 85, 90 & 91; Best Fine Art, Exhib One, Soc Art Ctr, Alumni, 72; Grumbacher Gold Medallion, 86; Best of Show, 53rd Annual Exhib Soc of Western Art, 2003. *Bibliog:* Mrs Linda Hardwick (auth), Collage, educational TV, Memphis Community TV Found, 71-72; TV interview, Memphis, Tenn, 71; Don J Anderson (auth), Paintings of children, Chicago Today, 72. *Mem:* Soc Western Artists; Soc Art Ctr Alumni; Bohemian Club. *Media:* Oil. *Interests:* soaring; flying. *Publ:* Illusr, Oscar Lincoln Busby Stokes, Harcourt, Brace & World Inc, 70. *Dealer:* Mrs. Robert W Sanderson 107 Front St #52 Memphis TN; Mrs. laura Healy 65 Chipstead St London SW6 3SR England. *Mailing Add:* 4583 Belmont Ct Sonoma CA 95476

ANDERSON, HARRY W
COLLECTOR
b Corning, NY. *Study:* Hobart Col, BA, 49. *Pos:* Co-founder Saga Corp food serv, NY, 48; VP, 57-62; vpres, Personnel Officers. Co-founder Harry W and Mary Margaret Anderson Charitable Found, Atherton, Calif; trustee Mount St Scholastica Col, Kans. *Awards:* Named one of Top 200 Collectores, ARTnews Mag, 2004, 2005, 2006. *Collection:* NY Sch Contemporary art. *Mailing Add:* Harry W and Mary Margaret Anderson Chari 62 Faxon Rd Atherton CA 94027-4046

ANDERSON, JOHN S
SCULPTOR
b Seattle, Wash, Apr 29, 28. *Study:* Los Angeles Art Ctr, Pratt Inst. *Work:* Mus Mod Art & Whitney Mus Am Art, NY. *Exhib:* Int Arts Festival, Providence, RI, 65; Albert A List Show, New Sch Social Res, 65; Cummer Gallery Art, Jacksonville, Fla, 66; eight one-man shows, Allan Stone Gallery, NY, 65-74, 77 & 81. *Teaching:* Instr sculpture, Pratt Inst, 59-62; instr sculpture, Sch Visual Arts, 68-70; instr sculpture, Cooper Union, 70-76; vis sculptor, Univ NMex, 69-70 & Univ Conn, 77-78. *Awards:* Guggenheim Found Grant, 65-66; Mini Grant, NJ State Coun Arts, 72. *Media:* All Media. *Mailing Add:* 12 School St Asbury NJ 08802

ANDERSON, KENNETH EDMUND
SCULPTOR, EDUCATOR
b Alameda, Calif, Sept 22, 50. *Study:* Univ Nebr, Omaha, BGS, 77, BFA, 80; Univ Nebr, Lincoln, MFA, 83. *Work:* Sheldon Mem Art Gallery, Lincoln, Nebr. *Exhib:* Great Plains Sculpture Exhib, Sheldon Mem Art Gallery, Lincoln, Nebr, 81; First Int Shoebox Sculpture Exhib, Univ Hawaii, Honolulu, 82; two-person exhib, Joslyn Art Mus, Omaha, 82; 42nd Sioux City Exhib, Sioux City Art Mus, Iowa, 82; Biennial exhib, Joslyn Art Mus, Omaha, 84. *Teaching:* Asst prof art, Peru State Col, Nebr, currently. *Awards:* Second Place, Master's Touch Exhib, Col St Mary's, 80; Merit Award, Great Plains Sculpture Exhib, Nebr Arts Coun, 81. *Bibliog:* Dr Donald Doe (auth), article, Art Express, 9-10/81. *Mem:* Col Art Asn. *Media:* Steel, Wood

ANDERSON, LAURA (GRANT)
PAINTER
b Hartford, Conn, Dec 15, 43. *Study:* Lasell Jr Col, Mass, 63-64; Hartford Art Sch, Univ Hartford, 64-66; RI Sch Design, 88-89. *Work:* Decordova Mus, Lincoln, Mass; Fuller Mus, Brockton, Mass; Mass Mutual Life Insurance Co, Springfield, Mass; Cabot Corp, Boston, Mass; Fleet Nat Bank, RI. *Exhib:* Annual Show, Springfield Mus Art, 89; Realism 94, Parkersburg Art Mus, WVa, 94; In the Grand Tradition, Fairfield Univ Mus, Conn, 94; Get Real: Representational Paintings from the Permanent Collection, DeCordova Mus, Lincoln, Mass, 99. *Awards:* First Prize, Am Artists Golden Ann Exhib, 87; Salzman Award, Nat Arts Club, 93; First Prize, Nat Arts Club, 94. *Bibliog:* Earl Killeen (auth), Acrylic Painting Techniques, North Light Books, 95; Best of Acrylic Painting, Rockport Publs, 96; New American Paintings, A Resource for Collectors, 93. *Mem:* Nat Arts Club, NY; Audubon Artists, NY; Allied Artists of Am, NY; Marion Art Ctr, Mass. *Media:* Acrylic. *Publ:* contrib, Yankee Mag, 8/81, Graphic deFrance & Artists, 6/91. *Mailing Add:* PO Box 105 Marion MA 02738

ANDERSON, LAURIE
CONCEPTUAL ARTIST
b Chicago, Ill, 47. *Study:* Barnard Col, BA(art hist, magna cum laude, 69); Columbia Univ, MFA, 72; San Francisco Art Inst, Hon Inst, Hon Dr, 80; Philadelphia Col Arts, Hon Dr, 87; Art Inst Chicago, Hon Dr, 90; Cal Arts, Hon Dr, 96; Pratt Inst, Hon Dr, 96. *Comn:* Carmen (video), Expo '92, 92; Bridge of Dreams (score), Deutsche Opera, Berlin, 93; New York City for Encyl Brittanica, 2000; Far Side of the Moon (music for Rober LePage theater piece), 2000; Who Am I?, Swiss Expo '02 pavilion, 2001. *Exhib:* Sydney Festival, Australia, 97; solo show, Whirlwind, Artists Space, 98; Handphone Table, Musee Art Contemporain, France, 98; Duets on Ice 1974-75, MOCA Mus, Los Angeles, 98; AE (Amelia Earhart), Am Composers Orch, 99. *Pos:* Art critic, Art Forum, Art News, Art in Am. *Teaching:* Instr art hist, City Col New York, 73-75. *Awards:* Nat Endowment Arts Grant 74-75, 77 & 79; Guggenheim Found Fel, 82; Marlene Award for Performing Arts, Munich, Ger, 96. *Bibliog:* Rose Lee (auth), Laurie Anderson, Abrams, 2000. *Media:* Records; Film & Video. *Publ:* Auth, Empty Places, Harper Collins, 91; Monster in a Box (score), Spalding Gray, 91; Faraway So Close (score), 93; co-producer, Bright Red (record), Warner Brothers, 94; auth, Stories from the Nerve Bible (a retrospective), Harper Perennial, 94); Talk Normal, anthology, Rhino Records, 2000; Life on a String, Nonesuch Records, 2001. *Mailing Add:* Canal Street Communications 530 Canal St New York NY 10013

ANDERSON, LENNART
PAINTER, INSTRUCTOR
b Detroit, Mich, Aug 22, 28. *Study:* Art Inst Chicago, BFA, 46-50; Cranbrook Acad Art, MFA, 50-52; Art Students League, studied with Edwin Dickinson, 54. *Work:* Hirshhorn Mus; Whitney Mus Am Art; Brooklyn Mus, NY; Pa Acad Fine Arts, Philadelphia; Mus Fine Arts, Boston; Weatherspoon Gallery, Univ NC, Greensboro; Minneapolis Inst Arts, Minn; Cleveland Mus Art, Ohio; and others; Hobart & William Smith Cols, Geneva, NY; Mus Art, Penn State Univ, PA; Univ Virginia Art Mus, Charlottesville, VA; Mellon Bank, Pittsburgh, PA; Yale Law Sch, New Haven, Conn; Yale Univ, New Haven, Conn; Harvard Club of New York City, NY; Deleware Art Mus, Wilmington, DE. *Exhib:* Carneige Inst Mus Art, 64 & 67; Whitney Mus Am Art Ann, 67; Vassar Col, 68; Ravinia Festival, Highland Park, Ill, 68; Figurative Realist Art, Artists Choice Mus, NY, 79; Reallegory, Chrysler Mus Art, Norfolk, Va, 83; Drawings by Contemp Artists, Md Inst Col Art, 84; Recent Am Portraits, Robert Schoelkopf Gallery, NY, 85; Form or Formula: Drawing and Drawings, Hudson River Mus, Yonkers, NY, 86; Direct Response: Contemp Landscape Painting, Mem Art Gallery, Univ Rochester, NY, 89; Art with a View, Oglethorpe Univ Art Gallery, Atlanta, Ga, 90; Salander-O'Reilly Galleries, NY, 95; One man shows, Landscapes, Salander-O'Reilly Galleries, NY, 97, 99, 2002 & Three Idylls, Denver Art Mus, Colo, 96; Aspen Art Mus, Colo, 96; Rider Univ, Lawrenceville, NJ, 2000. *Teaching:* Instr,Art Chatham Col, Pittsburgh, 1961-62, Pratt Inst, New York City, 1962-69, Skowhegan Sch, 1965, 67, Art Students League, New York, Yale Univ, 1967, Finch Col, New York City; prof painting and drawing Brooklyn Col, 1974-; Pratt Inst, NY; Yale Univ, New Haven, Conn; American Academy of Art & Letters; Art Students league, NY; Princeton Univ, NY; Intl Sch Art, Montacastello di Vibio, Italy. *Awards:* Nat Coun Arts Award, 66; Guggenheim Fel, 83; Emil and Dines Carlsen Award, Nat Acad Design, 88. *Bibliog:* Mark Strand (ed), Art of the Real: Nine American Figurative Painters, 85; Ronald Pisano (auth), Long Island Landscape Painting Volume II: The Twentieth Century, 90; Lennart Anderson: Recent Paintings, 99, Selander-O'Reilly. *Mem:* Nat Inst Arts & Lett; Nat Acad Design (assoc, 79, acad, 82); Am Acad & Inst Arts & Lett. *Dealer:* Salander-O'Reilly Galleries, New York, NY

ANDERSON, MARGARET POMEROY
APPRAISER, COLLECTION MANAGER
b San Francisco, Calif. *Study:* Univ Calif, Berkeley, BA, 65. *Pos.* Researcher, Pomeroy Galleries, San Francisco, 65-69; archivist, Hoover Gallery, San Francisco, 69-81, consult, 78-; owner, Pomeroy-Anderson, 82-, Accredited Senior Appraiser, 81-. *Teaching:* Lectr art, Westport Arts Ctr, 85-91, Fairfield Univ, Conn, 86-92 & Wadsworth Atheneum, Hartford, 91. *Awards:* Conn Press Club, 89-91. *Mem:* Arch Am Art; West Coast Area Support Comt (chmn, 78-80); Am Soc Appraisers (accredited sr appraiser, 81-, regional gov 93-95); Archives Am Art (NY Area Comt, 83-90); Fairfield Hist Soc (pres, 89-92). *Res:* Life of Marie Laurencin; nineteenth and twentieth century American and European provenance searches; Paul Manship. *Publ:* Contribr, Antiques & the Arts Weekly; Maine Antique Digest; Antiques West Newspaper, New York Correspondent; Antique Monthly; Art & Auction. *Mailing Add:* PO Box 787 Southport CT 06890

ANDERSON, MARK ROBERT
STAINED GLASS ARTIST, SCULPTOR
b Iola, Kans, Aug 14, 48. *Study:* Am Craft Coun, 75-79; Art League Sch, Alexandria, Va, 79-82, Pilchuck Glass Sch, Stanwood, Wash, 79 & 85. *Comn:* Solar Collectors with Stained glass, Brandon Residence, Cabin John, Md, 81-83; Spiral Staircase (sculpture), Torpedo Factory Art Ctr, Alexandria, Va, 84; Stained Glass Window, Bolling Air Force Base Officers Club, Washington, DC, 85; Stained Glass Window, Montgomery Co Pub Schs, Woodlin-Silver Spring, 86; Glass & Neon wall panels, May Ctrs Inc, Ballston Common Ctr, Arlington, Va, 86. *Exhib:* Virginia Craftsmen, Va Mus Fine Arts, Richmond, 80; Studio Glass-Contemp Am Survey, Redding Mus, Calif, 85; Spotlight: Southeast Crafts, Longwood Col, Farmville, Va, 85; Spotlight: Southeast Crafts, Univ Gainesville, Fla, 86; one-man show, Jackie Chalkley Fine Crafts, Washington, DC, 86; New Art Forms I & II: Virginia, Hand Workshop, Richmond Va, 88 & 89; Beyond Function: New Directions in Decorative Arts, Wash Sq Bldg, Washington, DC, 88; Breaking Boundaries: Craft Now, Va Mus Fine Arts, Richmond, 88-91; Creative Craft Coun Winners, Renwick Gallery, Smithsonian, Washington, DC, 89; Rhapsody in Neon, Zenith Gallery, Washington, DC, 89. *Collection Arranged:* High Style, Tomlinson Craft Collection, 83. *Pos:* Exec dir, Friends of Torpedo Factory Art Ctr, Alexandria, Va, 82-84. *Teaching:* Instr stained glass, Art League Sch, Alexandria, Va, 80-. *Awards:* First Prize for Glass, Arlington Arts Ctr, Va, 78; Schwarzschild Award, Schwarzschild Jewelers, 85; First Prize for Glass, Creative Craft Coun, Washington, DC, 86. *Bibliog:* Karen M E Alexis (auth), Washington's fragile world of glass art, Washington Post, 81; Clare Fiore (auth), Which Are Jewels?, Reston Connection, 85; Joseph Porcelli (auth), Profile, Prof Stained Glass, 87; Patricia Dane Rogers (coauth with Cristina Del Sesto), The Move From Down Home to Uptown, Wash Post, 88. *Mem:* Torpedo Factory Artists Asn (vpres, 82-83); Coalition Wash Artists, (steering comt, 86-87); Am Craft Coun. *Media:* Glass. *Dealer:* Glass Arts Collaborative 31 Norfolk Rd Arlington MA 02174. *Mailing Add:* 827 S Quincy St Arlington VA 22204

ANDERSON, MAXWELL L
MUSEUM DIRECTOR, EDUCATOR
b New York, NY, May 1, 56. *Study:* Dartmouth Col, AB, 77; Harvard Univ, AM (hist), 78, PhD (art hist), 81. *Collection Arranged:* The Vatican Collections: The Papacy and Art, 82; Treasures of the Holy Land, 86; Roman Portraits in Context, 88; Radiance in Stone, 89; The Courtauld Collection at the AGO, Art Gallery Ontario, 98; Art in the Age of Van Gogh: Dutch Paintings from the Rijksmuseum, Amsterdam, Arm Gallery of Ontario, 98-99; 2000 Biennial Exhibition, Whitney Mus Am Art, 2000; Tony Oursler: The Darkest Color Infinitely Applied, Whitney Mus Am Art, 2000. *Pos:* asst cur, Metrop Mus Art, 82-87; dir, Emory Univ Mus, Atlanta, 87-95, Michael C Carlos Mus, 98 & Art Gallery Ont, Toronto, 95-98, Whitney Mus Amer Art, 98-2003; dir. and chief exec officer, Indianapolis Mus Art, 2006-; judge, 2000 Business in the Arts Awards, Bus Com for the Arts, Inc & Forbes Mag; mem adv bd NYC 2012 (pvt org seeking to bring Olympic games to New York), 2000; principal, AEA Consulting; lectr in field. *Teaching:* lectr Roman art, Princeton Univ, 85; vis prof, Univ di Roma, 87; adj assoc prof, Emory Univ, 89-. *Awards:* Commendatore Order Merit, Republic of Italy, 90; Cult Laureate New York City Historic Landmarks Preservation Ctr, 99. *Mem:* Am Asn Mus; Col Art Asn; Asn Art Mus Dirs (pres 2002-03); Am Fedn Art (trustee). *Publ:* Coauth, Greece and Rome, Metrop Mus, 87; Pompeian Frescoes in the Metropolitan Museum of Art, Metrop Mus, 87; Roman Portraits in Context, De Luca, 88; Radiance in Stone, De Luca, 89; Intro to The Wired Mus, 97; auth, Preserving the perishable art of the digital age, Arts and Leisure sect, The New York Times, 9/24/2000; preface, Whitney Museum of American Art, Building Blocks series, Princeton Archtl Press, 2000; Online museum coordination, Museum Int, Vol 51, No 4, 10-12/1999; and numerous other articles. *Mailing Add:* Indianapolis Mus Art 4000 Michigan Rd Indianapolis IN 46208-3326

ANDERSON, ROBERT ALEXANDER
PAINTER, ILLUSTRATOR
b Wyandotte, Mich, Jan 26, 46. *Study:* Yale Univ, BA, 64-68, drawing with Bernard Chaet, portrait painting with Deane Keller; Wayne State Univ, 66; Sch Mus Fine Arts, Boston, dipl, 72-75, with Henry Schwartz & John Clift. *Work:* Boston Pub Libr, Mass; Phillips Exeter Acad, NH; Harvard Univ, Cambridge, Mass; Yale Univ, New Haven, Conn; Univ Pa, Philadelphia. *Comn:* Portrait, Sidney Farber & Charles A Dana, Md, Dana Farber Cancer Inst, Boston, Mass, 84; Eleven drawings & portraits, US Postage Stamps, US Postal Serv, Washington, 84-86; portraits, Andrew G DeRocco, Pres Denison Univ, Granville, Ohio & Hon Edward J King, HOn. WmF. Weld, Gov of Massachesetts, Boston, MA, 90 & Rev William Sloane Coffin, Yale Univ, New Haven, Conn, 90, George W. Bush for the Yale Clun of NYC, 93. *Exhib:* Boston Symphony, John F Kennedy Pres Libr & Mus, Dorchester, 81 & Symphony Hall, Boston, 82, Mass; Francesca Anderson Gallery, Boston, Mass, 84-88; Soc Illusrs, NY, 87; St Botolph Club, Boston, Mass, 88; Boston Atheneum, Mass, 89. *Awards:* First Prize, 81 & Grand Prize for best show, 82, Nat Portrait Seminar Nat Competition, 82. *Bibliog:* Crumpled, But Unruffled; The Breck Girl, Advertising Techniques, 10/78; Laura White (auth), A Letter Will Take Two of These, Boston Globe, 2/10/85; John D Beeler (auth), Artist Puts His Stamp on US Mail, Lexington Minute-Man, 2/21/85. *Mem:* Munroe Ctr Arts (chmn bd dir, 93-); Schwamb Mill Preserv Trust (trustee, 85-); St Botolph Club; Yale Club, NY (painter, portrait Pres George W Bush). *Media:* Oil, Pastel. *Publ:* Illusr advertising, (TV & print), Breck Shampoo, 76- & Coca Cola USA, 80; Heath Sci Textbks, DC Heath, 79 & 81; album cover, Karen Kayen; You Don't Have to Take What You Get, Rooster Records, 81. *Dealer:* Portraits Inc 985 Park Ave New York NY 10028. *Mailing Add:* 27 Brush Island Rd Darien CT 06820-5706

ANDERSON, ROBERT DALE
PAINTER, DRAFTSMAN, PRINTMAKER
b Glendale, Calif, Mar 12, 49. *Study:* Pasadena City Col, AA, 70; Calif State Col Long Beach, BA, 72, MFA, 76. *Work:* Blanton Mus Art, Austin, Tex; Albuquerque Mus, NMex; De Young Mus, San Francisco. *Exhib:* Anderson / Dill, Acro Ctr Visual Arts, Los Angeles, 77; Anderson / Alderette, Fine Arts Gallery, Long Beach, Calif, 86; Print Exhib of 6 Calif Artist, Am Center, Uagoya, Japan, 87; 40 Yrs of Calif Assemblage, Wight Gallery, Los Angeles, 89; Obsessed By Magic, ACA Galleries, NY, 97; Crossed Lines, Conduit Gallery, Dallas, Tex, 2000; Dark Ages, Conduit Gallery, Dallas, Tex, 2001; Robert Dale Anderson/Sydney Yeager, D Berman Gallery, Austin, Tex, 2002. *Collection Arranged:* Small World Drawings, Conduit Gallery, Dallas, TX, 2005. *Teaching:* instr, Univ Southern Calif, 76-77 & Pasadena City Col, 77; sr lectr, Univ Tex Austin, 88-. *Bibliog:* Artweek, 2/28/81; Marnie Weber (auth), 40 Years of Calif Assemblage Catalog: Robert Anderson; Robbie Conal (auth), Figural Obsessions. *Mem:* Southern Graphics Coun. *Media:* Graphite, Ink; Lithography; Oil. *Dealer:* Conduit Gallery 1626C Hi Line Dr Dallas TX 75207; d berman Gallery 1701 Guadalupe St Austin TX 78701; ACA Gallery 529 W 20th St 5th Fl New York NY 10011. *Mailing Add:* 2504 Baxter Dr Austin TX 78745-4302

ANDERSON, ROSS CORNELIUS
MUSEUM DIRECTOR, HISTORIAN
b Washington, DC, May 2, 1951. *Study:* Princeton Univ, AB, 73; Harvard Univ, MA, 77. *Pos:* Chief cur, Everson Mus Art, Syracuse, NY, 79-83; dir, Montgomery Mus Fine Arts, Ala, 83-87; Riverside Art Mus, Calif, 87-90, art consult, 91-. *Teaching:* Instr, Syracuse Univ, 81-83. *Res:* 19th and 20th century American painting and sculpture. *Publ:* Contribr, Grueby Pottery, 81, Abbott Handerson Thayer, 82 & American Clay Sculpture 1925-1950, 83, Everson Mus Art; Maurice and Charles Prendergast Raisonne (exhib catalog), Williams Col Mus Art, Prestel, 90. *Mailing Add:* 419 N Larchmont Blvd # 50 Los Angeles CA 90004-3013

ANDERSON, SALLY J
PAINTER, PRINTMAKER
b Rockford, Ill, Feb 5, 42. *Study:* Inst Allende, San Miguel Allende, Mex, 62; Beloit Col, BA, 64; Univ Wis, 67. *Work:* Fed Bldg, Vickers Corp, Oklahoma City; Sunwest Bank, Albuquerque; Saks Fifth Ave, NY; Marriott Hotel Corp, Washington, DC; Product design, Swan/Dolphin Hotel, Orlando, Fla, Connie Chung set, CBS Network, NY, 90. *Exhib:* Solo exhib, Roswell Art Mus, NMex, 70; Southwest Fine Arts Biennial, Mus NMex, Santa Fe, 75 & 79; Convergence 76, Carnegie Inst Mus Art, Pittsburgh, Pa, 76; Ariz Biennial, Phoenix Art Mus, 79; One Space, Three Visions, Albuquerque Mus, 80; and others. *Awards:* First Prize, NMex Crafts Biennial, Mus NMex, Santa Fe, 75; Nat Endowment Arts Grants, 76 & 77. *Bibliog:* Donald Locke (auth), article, Arts Mag, 9/83. *Media:* Acrylic, Oil; Lithography, Product Design. *Dealer:* C G Rein Galleries Edina MN; C G Rein Galleries Scottsdale AZ. *Mailing Add:* 7522 Bear Canyon Albuquerque NM 87109-4464

ANDERSON, SUSAN MARY
PAINTER
b Evanston, Ill. *Study:* St Mary's Col, Notre Dame, Ind, with Norman La Liberté, 60; Marquette Univ, Milwaukee, Wis, BA(english & painting), 65; Art Students League, with Barbara Adrian, Hillary Holmes & Robert Hale, 70-80. *Work:* Housatonic Mus. *Comn:* Lower East Side #1, Am Jewish Comt, 98. *Exhib:* Le Livre dans tous see États, Bibliot Nat, Argenteuil, France, 87 & Beauvais, France, 88; Le Livre Object, Bibliot Nat, Orgeval, France, 88; League at the Cape, Provincetown Mus, Mass, 93; solo exhib, Sound Shore Gallery, Cross River, NY, 96-97 & Stamford Ctr Arts, 99. *Awards:* First & Second Prize, Art Students League, New York, 83. *Bibliog:* Vivien Raynor (auth), Visions in an arcade, NY Times, 8/28/94; Linda Matys O'Connell (auth), Hot tickets: quadrupel vision, Advocate & Village Times, 9/9/94. *Mem:* Life mem, Art Students League. *Media:* Oil. *Dealer:* Mary Udell Sound Shore Gallery 6 Landmark Sq Stamford Ct 06901. *Mailing Add:* 142 Minuteman Cir Allentown NJ 08501

ANDERSON, TROY
PAINTER, SCULPTOR
b Siloam Springs, Ark, Aug 23, 48. *Study:* WTex State Univ, Canyon, BS(art), 70. *Work:* Ark State Bank, Siloam Springs; Bur Indian Affairs, Washington, DC; Five Civilized Tribes Mus, Muskogee, Okla; Capital, State of Ark, Little Rock, Ark. *Comn:* Cherokee Sesquicentennial Trail of Tears Commemorative Gold Medallion, 89. *Exhib:* Denver Mus Natural Hist, 80; Am Indian & Cowboy Artists, San Dimas, Calif, 80-83; Five Civilized Tribes Mus, Muskogee, Okla, 81; Cherokee National History Museum; and others. *Pos:* pres, Am Indian & Cowboy Artist, Inc, formerly. *Awards:* Ambassador of the Year Award, Ctr Am Indian, Kirkpatrick Ctr, Okco; Grand Award Master Artists, Five Civilized Tribes Mus, 82-88; First Place Painting, Cherokee Nat Hist Mus, Tahlequah, Okla, 83-90; Heritage Grand Award, 89; Am Indian & Cowboy Artist Indian Heritage Award, 90. *Bibliog:* Southwest Art, 2/90. *Mem:* Am Indian & Cowboy Artists Inc (vpres, 84-85, pres, 86-87). *Media:* Acrylic, Oil; Mixed Media, Bronze. *Specialty:* Native Am & wildlife. *Publ:* Contrib, Southwest Art, 2/90. *Dealer:* ArtMarket, 9515-D E 51st St, Tulsa, Okla, 74145. *Mailing Add:* c/o Studio of Troy Anderson 23450 Quicks Loop Siloam Springs AR 72761

ANDERSON, WARREN HAROLD
GRAPHIC ARTIST, PAINTER
b Moline, Ill, Sept 27, 25. *Study:* Western Ill Univ, BS, 50; Univ Iowa, MA, 51; Stanford Univ, PhD, 61. *Work:* Joseph H Hirshhorn Collection, Washington; Phoenix Art Mus; Tucson Mus Art; Univ Ariz Mus Art; Western Ill Univ Art Gallery Solo-exhibs. *Exhib:* solo-exhibs, Highway Drawings/Video, Phoenix Art Mus, Ariz, 79, US 80, Drawings, El Paso Mus Art, Tex, 79 & 99, Vanishing Roadside Am (prismacolor drawings), Tucson Mus Art, 82, Tohono Chul Gallery, Tucson, Ariz, 89, Univ NMex, AE Gallery, 91 & Western Ill Univ Gallery, 94; 30 year retrospective, Univ Ariz Mus Art, 86; See the USA, Nat Bldg Mus, Washington, DC, 99, 2000. *Teaching:* Prof art, Univ Ariz, Tucson, 56-86, prof emer, currently. *Awards:* Several state and Southwest regional awards, 58-90; Creative Teaching Award in Art, Ariz Found, 82. *Bibliog:* Vanishing roadside America, Mod Maturity, 9/84; Signs of our Times, Signs of the Times, 5/97 & 5/98; Jesse Greenberg (auth), Art of Warren Anderson: Past Intertwining With Present, Tucson Guide Quar, spring 2001. *Mem:* Soc Com Archeol. *Media:* Prismatic Pencil, Floated Montages. *Res:* Environmental aesthetics; vernacular roadside art forms; cartifacts--artifacts that exist because of cars; vestiges west; ghost town objects and textures. *Specialty:* Realistic Prismatic Pencil; Paintings & Retro ERA; Floated Montages. *Interests:* American & Southwest History. *Publ:* Vanishing Roadside America, Univ Ariz Press, 81. *Dealer:* Vanished Roadside America & Vestiges West Art 6802 N Longfellow Tucson AZ 85718. *Mailing Add:* c/o Univ Ariz Art Dept 108 PO Box 210002 Tucson AZ 85721

ANDERSON, WILLIAM THOMAS
PAINTER, PRINTMAKER
b Minneapolis, Minn, Dec 13, 1936. *Study:* Calif State Univ, Los Angeles, with Leonard Edmondson, Bob Fiedler & Walter Askin; Chaffey Col; El Camino Col, with Charles Blusk. *Work:* Downey Mus Art; Civil Air Patrol, Calif Wing; Humboldt Cult Ctr; Humboldt State Univ; and others. *Comn:* Mural, CAP, Calif Wing; drawing, Kinnebrew Mem. *Exhib:* 18th Ann Nat Printmaking Show, Brooklyn Mus, NY, 73; World Print Competition, San Francisco Mus of Mod Art, 77; Invitational, Univ Puget Sound, 79; Stages/Four Printmakers, Mt St Mary's Col, Los Angeles, 79; Works on a Transparent Support, John Kohler Arts Ctr, Sheboygan, Wis, 79; Invitational, C N Gorman Mus, Univ Calif, Davis, 81; Nat Screenprint Show, Old Dominion Univ, Norfolk, Va, 85-86; and many others. *Pos:* Chief reader, ETS, AP Studio Art; chmn, Art Dept, Humboldt State Univ. *Teaching:* Prof art, Humboldt State Univ, 67-. *Media:* Miscellaneous; Silkscreen. *Mailing Add:* Humboldt State Univ Dept Art Arcata CA 95521

ANDERSON, WILMER (LOUIS)
PAINTER, WRITER
b Houston, Tex, Dec 24, 33. *Study:* Rice Univ, BA, 56; Harvard Univ, AM, 57, PhD, 60. *Work:* Univ Wis Physics dept, Madison. *Exhib:* Riverside Art Mus, Calif, 94; Biennial Exhib, Fed Reserve Gallery, Boston, 98; Rahr-West Mus, Mantiowoc, Wis, 99; Aqueous 2000, Houston, 2000; Nat Arts Club, NY, 2000; Salmagundi Club, NY, 2000; Watercolor West Exhib; New Eng Watercolor Soc; Audubon Artists; Transparent Watercolor Soc Am; Nat Soc Painter. *Pos:* co-founder Madison Watercolor Soc, 83 & pres, 83-89. *Awards:* Edmund A Steinbock Purchase Award, Ky Watercolor Soc, 98; Winsor Newton Award, Audubon Artists, Inc, 99; Maria M Naimir Award, San Diego Watercolor Soc, 2000; Second prize, Pittsburgh Watercolor Soc, 2004; Second prize, Harrisburg Art Asn, 2004; Dirs Award, WASH, 2006. *Mem:* Audubon Artists, Inc; Nat Painters Casein and Acrylic; Western Fedn Watercolor Socs; Transparent Watercolor Soc Am; Watercolor West; Acad Artists Asn. *Media:* Acrylic, Watercolor. *Publ:* coauth, illusr, Electric Circuits and Modern Electronics, Holt Rinehart Winston, 73; auth, Light and Color, Raintree, 78. *Dealer:* Stony Hill Antiques 2140 Regent St Madison WI 53705. *Mailing Add:* 1818 Chadbourne Ave Madison WI 53705

ANDERSON, WINSLOW
DESIGNER, PAINTER
b Plymouth, Mass, May 17, 1917. *Study:* State Univ NY Col Ceramics, Alfred Univ, BFA; Plymouth Pottery, Mass; Hans Hofmann Sch Art, Provincetown, Mass; Pa Acad Fine Arts, Philadelphia; Pratt Graphics Ctr, NY. *Comn:* Triptych mural, Church of St Mary the Virgin Concert Hall, NY. *Exhib:* 5th & 11th Ceramic Exhibs, Syracuse Mus Fine Arts, NY, 40 & 46; Guggenheim Mus Ann, NY, 43-46; Kanawha Artists Asn, Charleston, WVa, 50. *Pos:* Glass designer, Blenko Glass Co, Milton, Va, 46-53; design dir, Lenox China Inc, Trenton, NJ, 53-64, dir dimensional design, 64-80. *Awards:* First Prize for African Mask (sculpture), Nat USA Contest, 44; First Prize for Fish (stained glass), Stained Glass Soc Washington, DC, 53. *Bibliog:* Don Wallace (auth), Shaping America's Products, Reinhold Publ Co, 56. *Media:* Clay, Glass; Pastel, Oil. *Collection:* Haitian primitives. *Publ:* Auth, Offhand design for offhand glass, Am Ceramic Soc J, 4/49. *Mailing Add:* PO Box 606 Milton WV 25541-0606

ANDRADE, BRUNO
PAINTER
b San Antonio, Tex, Nov 3, 47. *Study:* Tex A & I Univ, BS, 70; Univ Mich, MFA, 77. *Work:* Mus Contemp Hispanic Art, NY; Art Mus South Tex, Corpus Christi; Sondra & Charles Gilman Jr Found, NY; McAllen Int Mus, Tex; Mexican Mus, San Francisco, Calif. *Comn:* A H Belo Corp, Dallas, Tex; Pepsi Co Foods Int, Plano, Tex; Compaq Computer, Houston, Tex; Tex Instrument Inc, Houston; B D Holt Co, San Antonio, Tex. *Exhib:* Solo exhibs, Lynn Goode Gallery, Houston, Tex, 89, 91, 93 & 94 & Edith Baker Gallery, Dallas, Tex, 90 & 98; Abstract Visions (with catalog), Mus Contemp Hispanic Art, NY, 87; Confrontacion, Mexio-Arte Mus, Austin, Tex, 92; Bruno Andrade and Michael Lathrop, Barbara Gillman Gallery, Miami Beach, Fla, 93; The Good Earth, Edith Baker Gallery, Dallas, 94; Gallery Artists, Lynn Goode Gallery, Houston, Tex, 95; MB Mod, NY, 96 & 98; MB in LA, Jerry Solomon Gallery, Los Angeles, 97; Art Patterns, Austin Mus Art at Laguna, Gloria, Tex, 97; and others. *Teaching:* Instr painting, Stephens Col, Columbia, Mo, 77-80; prof art painting, Corpus Christi State Univ, Tex, 81-. *Awards:* Artist Fel Grant, Nat Endowment Arts, 80 & 89. *Bibliog:* Diane Armitage (auth), Rediscovering the Landscape of the Americas, The Mag, 9/96; Peter Dellolio (auth), Reviews/New York/Bruno Andrade, NY Arts Mag, Issue No 11, 6/97; Elizabeth B Reese (auth), Mind Mapping Texas Landscapes: Postmodern Pedagogy with or without Computers, Art Educ, Vol 50, No 6, 11/97. *Media:* Oil on Canvas. *Publ:* Contribr, spec issue cover, Contemp Art, Art & Antiques, summer 97. *Dealer:* Edith Baker Gallery Dallas TX; Barbara Gillman Gallery Miami Beach FL

ANDRADE, EDNA WRIGHT
PAINTER, EDUCATOR
b Portsmouth, Va, Jan 25, 17. *Study:* Pa Acad Fine Arts, 33-38; Barnes Foundation 35 & 36; Univ Pa Sch Fine Arts, BFA, 37. *Work:* Yale Art Gallery, New Haven; Montclair Art Mus, NJ; Va Mus Art, Richmond; Edwin A Ulrich Mus, Wichta State Univ; Leeway Found, Phila; Dallas Mus of Art; Houston Mus of Fine Art; Philadelphia Mus Art; Pa Acad Fine Arts; Woodmere Mus, Philadelphia. *Comn:* Mosiac mural, Columbia Br, Free Libr Philadelphia, 62; marble intarsia mural, Welsh Rd Br, Free Libr Philadelphia, 68; granite paving, Salvation Army Div Hq, Philadelphia, 72; poster, Please Touch Mus, Philadelphia, 85; poster, Art Now, Philadelphia, 88. *Exhib:* One-person shows, Marian Locks Gallery, Philadelphia, 71, 74, 77, 83 & 89, Pa Acad Fine Arts, Philadelphia, 93-94, Locks Gallery, Philadelphia, 93, 93-94, 99, 2002-2004, 2006, Inst Contemp Art, Philadelphia, 2003, Print Center, Philadelphia, 2006; two-person show, Rutgers Univ Art Gallery, New Brunswick, NJ, 71; group shows, Woman's Work, Am Art 1974, Philadelphia Civic Ctr, 74; Philadelphia: 300 Yrs of Am Art, 76, Philadelphia Mus Art; In This Acad, Pa Acad Fine Arts, 76; 20th Century Prints, Philadelphia Mus Art, 77; Women's Caucus Art, Port Hist Mus, Philadelphia, 83; Philadelphia Artists: A Juried Exhib, Philadelphia Mus Art, 90; Artists Choose Artists, Inst Contemp Art, Philadelphia, 91; Esther M Klein Gallery, Philadelphia, Pa, 98; Woodmere Art Mus, Philadelphia, Pa, 98; Philadelphia Mus Art, Pa, 2000. *Teaching:* Prof art, Philadelphia Col Art, 57-72, 73-82, prof emer, 82-; prof art, Temple Univ, 72-73; artist-in-residence, Ariz State Univ, 81, adj prof art, 86-; vis critic, Pa Acad Fine Arts, 88. *Awards:* Mayor's Arts & Culture Award, Philadelphia, 91; Samuel S Fleisher Art Mem Founders Award, 93; Dist Teaching Award, Col Art Asn, 96. *Bibliog:* Archives Am Art, Smithsonian Inst; Edna Andrade, Marian Locks Gallery, 1977; A Vision Transformed, Blue Ridge Pub Television, Roanoke, Va, 86; Cool Waves and Hot Blocks: Art of Edna Andrade, Pa Acad of Fine Arts, 1993; Edna Andrade Paintings 1960-1990, Locks Gallery, 1997; Edna Andrade: Optical Paintings 1963-1986, Inst of Contemporary Art, Univ of PA, 03. *Mem:* Pa Acad Fel. *Media:* Oil, Acrylic, Watercolor. *Dealer:* Locks Gallery 600 Washington Sq S Philadelphia PA 19106

ANDRE, CARL
SCULPTOR
b Quincy, Mass, Sept 16, 35. *Study:* Phillips Acad, 51-53; With Patrick & Maud Morgan, Hollis Frampton; Michael Chapman, Frank Stella. *Work:* Nat Gallery Can, Ottawa; Tate Gallery, London; Mus Mod Art, NY; Albright-Knox Art Gallery, Buffalo; Art Inst Chicago; and others. *Comn:* Found Pub Giving, Hartford, Conn. *Exhib:* Multiplicity, Inst Contemp Art, Boston, 66; Cool Art, Aldrich Mus Contemp Art, 68; Art of the Real: USA 1948-88 Traveling Exhib, Mus Mod Art, NY, 68; Directions 1: Options, Milwaukee Art Ctr, 68; Anti-Illusion: Procedures/Materials, Whitney Mus

Am Art, 69; 555,087, Seattle Art Mus, 69; Information, Mus Mod Art, NY, 70; 1970 Ann Exhib: Contemp Am Sculpture, Whitney Mus Am Art, 70; one-person exhibs, Solomon R Guggenheim Mus, 70, Mus Mod Art, NY, 73, Paula Cooper Gallery, 93 & 95, Gagosian Gallery, NY, 95, Syningarsalur Exhib Space, Reykavik, Iceland, 96 & Mus Mod Art, Oxford, Eng, 96; Guggenheim Int Exhib, Solomon R Guggenheim Mus, 72; 1973 Biennial Exhib: Contemp Am Art, Whitney Mus Am Art, 73; 10th Anniversary Exhib, Aldrich Mus Contemp Art, 74; Drawing Now, Mus Mod Art, NY, 76; 72nd Am Exhib Traveling Show, Art Inst Chicago, 76; 200 Yrs Am Exhib, Whitney Mus Am Art, 76; 20th Century Am Drawings: Five Yrs of Acquisition, Whitney Mus Am Art, 78; American Art 1950 to the Present, Whitney Mus Am Art, 78; The Reductive Object, Inst Contemp Art Boston, 79; The Minimal Tradition, Aldrich Mus Contemp Art, 79; Contemp Sculpture: Selections from the Collection of the Mus of Modern Art, Mus Mod Art, NY, 79; Surveying the Seventies, Whitney Mus Am Art, 82; postMINIMALISM, Aldrich Mus Contemp Art, 82; Minimalism x 4, Whitney Mus Am Art, 82; The NY Sch: Four Decades, Solomon R Guggenheim Mus, 82; Contrasts of Form: Geometric Abstract Art, Mus Mod Art, NY, 85; Transformations in Sculpture, Soloman R Guggenheim Mus, 85; Contemp Installation, Mus Mod Art, NY, 86; Immaterial Objects, Whitney Mus Am Art, 91; Manifeste, Mus d'Art Mod, Paris, 92; and many others. *Media:* All. *Publ:* 12 Dialogues 1962-1963, with Hollis Frampton, New York Univ Press, 80. *Mailing Add:* c/o Paula Cooper Gallery 534 W 21st St New York NY 10011

ANDREASON, LEE
SCULPTURE
b Lebanon, Ore, Mar 20, 37. *Study:* Santa Barbara City Col, pvt study with Anthony Priolo, 1980; Pierce Jr Col, 1980; UCLA Art Hist, France, 1985-86. *Work:* US Congressman Sam Farr House of Rep, Wash, DC; Mus of the Horse Ky Horse Park, Lexington, Ky. *Comn:* Man & Horse, Monterey Co Mus of Art, Monterey, 1984; Bust of Client, Colleen Colins, Pebble Beach, Calif, 1993; 5' Bronze Horse Gallery 444 Post, San Francisco, Calif, 1994; 10' Bronze Horse, Reflections Gallery, Santa Fe, NMex, 2000; Hercules II Task Douglas White, Soto Grande, Spain, 2003. *Exhib:* Oh Well Orwell, Monterey Co Mus of Art, Monterey, Calif, 1984; Pacific Grove Art Ctr Mus, Pacific Grove, Calif, 1990; Am Acad, Ky Horse Park, Lexington, Ky, 1994; Gallery Brisomar, Marbella, Spain, 94; Equine Art Ann Juried Ky Horse Park, Lexington, Ky, 1995; Annual Art Show, Juried Churchill Downs Mus, Louisville, Ky, 1995; Galeria Sculptures, Paris, France, 99; Amsteleen Gallery, Amsterdam, 2001; Horse Ponies & Uniforns, Nat Sculpture Soc, NY, 2004; Marin-Price Gallery, Chevy Chase, Md; Galerie Leidel, Munich, Germ; Sammer Gallery, Puerto Banos, Spain, 2006. *Teaching:* instr, Sculpture pvt lessons, Spain, currently; volunteer teacher, Santa Barbara Girls Club, 1980-83. *Awards:* Quendoline May award, Monterey Co, Spain, 1997; Legion of St Francis award, Generic Horse Asn, 1998. *Bibliog:* Susan Lee Hubbard (auth), Alta Vista Mag, Monterey, Calif, 1993; Beth Bueher (auth), Equine Mag, Susan Badger, 1994; Vanesa Mingorance (auth) Prestige Mag, Sam Benat, Spain, Vol X, 2001. *Mem:* Nat Sculpture Soc, NY; Cultural Soc of Soto Grande Spain. *Media:* bronze, terracota. *Interests:* Riding horseback, sailing, foreign cultures, traveling. *Mailing Add:* Lee Anderson Correos Apt #35 Jimena de La Frontera Cadiz 11330 Spain

ANDRES, GLENN MERLE
HISTORIAN, EDUCATOR
b Chicago, Ill, July 15, 41. *Study:* Cornell Univ, BArch, 64; Princeton Univ, MFA, 67, PhD, 71; Am Acad Rome, fel, 67-69. *Collection Arranged:* Builders and Humanists, Univ St Thomas, Houston, 66; Hardy Holzman Pfeiffer Associates: Twenty-Five Years, Middlebury Col, Vt, 93; Hardy Holzman Pfeiffer Associates: Creating Special Places, San Angelo, Mus Art, 99-2000; Tex Tech Univ, 99-2000; Del Mus Art, 99-2000. *Pos:* Assoc dir, Johnson Gallery, Middlebury Col, 76-78. *Teaching:* Asst prof art hist, Middlebury Col, Vt, 70-78, assoc prof, 78-83, prof, 83-, Christian A Johnson prof art, 84-87, 2000-; Fulbright lectr in Am visual cult, Univ Exeter, United Kingdom, 87-88. *Mem:* Sheldon Mus, Middlebury, Vt (trustee, 75-84, 92- & vpres, 78-82); Vt Adv Council for Hist Preservation, 86-; Soc of Architectural Historians; Soc of Fels; Am Acad in Rome. *Res:* 16th century Italian architecture; 19th century American architecture. *Publ:* Auth, A Walking History of Middlebury, Vermont, Addison Press, 75; auth, The Villa Medici in Rome, Garland Press, 76; coauth (with J M Hunisak & A R Turner), The Art of Florence, Abbeville Press, 88; contribr La Villa Medicis, Ecole Francaise de Rome, 91; contribr Hardy Holzman Pfeiffer Associates, Buildings and Projects II, Rizzoli, 99. *Mailing Add:* Dept of History of Art/Arch Middlebury VT 05753

ANDREW, DAVID NEVILLE
PAINTER, EDUCATOR
b Redruth, Eng, Apr 19, 1934; Can citizen. *Study:* Falmouth Sch of Art, 54; Slade Sch of Fine Art, London, 58; influenced by Patrick Heron & Ben Nicholson. *Work:* Kettles Yard Mus, Cambridge Univ, Eng; Art Gallery of Ont, Toronto. *Exhib:* Imprint, Can Nat Exhib (touring), 76; Brit Int Print Biennale, 76 & 78; Premio Int Biella por Incisione, Italy, 76; Int Grafik Biennale, Grenchen, WGer, 76; 9th Burnaby Biennial Print Show, BC, 77; and others. *Pos:* External assessor, Croydon Col of Art, Eng, 73; dir, Falmouth Summer Sch, Cornwall, Eng, 74-77. *Teaching:* Vis artist painting, Portsmouth Col of Art, Eng, 61-70; vis artist painting & print, Bournemouth Col of Art, Eng, 62-69; assoc prof painting & printmaking, Queen's Univ, 71-. *Awards:* Purchase Award, Can Cult Exchange to Hawaii, US Comn on Cult & Arts, 74; Horniansky Award, Imprint, Print & Drawing Coun of Can, 76; Purchase Award, 9th Burnaby Biennial Print Show, Burnaby Art Gallery, 77. *Mem:* Ont Soc Artists; Soc Can Artists; Print & Drawing Coun of Can. *Media:* Collage, Silkscreen. *Dealer:* Mira Godard Gallery 22 Hazleton Ave Toronto ON Can

ANDREWS, BENNY
PAINTER, LECTURER
b Madison, Ga, Nov 13, 30. *Study:* Ft Valley State Col, 48-50; Univ Chicago, 56-58; Chicago Art Inst, BFA, 58. *Work:* Mus Mod Art & Metrop Mus Art, NY; Mus African Art & Hirshhorn Mus, Washington, DC; High Mus, Atlanta; Butler Inst Am Art, Youngstown, Ohio; Brooks Mus, Memphis, Tenn; Detroit Art Inst; Philadelphia Acad Art. *Exhib:* Thirty Contemp Black Am, Minneapolis Inst Arts, Minn, 68; Martin Luther King Mem, Mus Mod Art, 69; Afro-Americans: Boston and NY, Mus Fine Arts, Boston, 70; Symbols, Studio Mus Harlem, NY, 71; Artists as Adversary, Mus Mod Art, 71; NJ State Mus, Trenton, 80; Mus Afro-Am Cult, Philadelphia, Pa, 80; Everson Mus, Syracuse, NY, 81; Albright-Knox Gallery, Buffalo, NY, 82; Newark Mus, NJ, 82; Birmingham Mus, Al, 88; Work on Paper, Wentell St Gallery, Cambridge, Mass, 89; Southland, Deutch Gallery, NY, 90; Recent Works, Gross McCleaf Gallery, 90; Thirty Yrs of Painting, Ratner Gallery, Chicago, Ill, 90; Folk Art of Benny & George Andrews, Brook Mus, Memphis, Tenn, 90; Recent Works, Sherry Wash Gallery, Detroit, Mich, 90; one-man shows, Sherry Wash Gallery, Detroit, Mich, 93, NJ State Mus, 93, Fine Art Mus, Mobile, Ala, 93, Mus Afro-Am Heritage, Tampa, Fla, 93, Ark Art Ctr, Little Rock, 94, McIntosh Gallery, Atlanta, Ga, 94 & Wendell Street Gallery, Cambridge, Mass, 94, Gargo Herne Gallery, Little Rock, 96, Noel Gallery, Charlotte, NC, 98, Sherry Wash Gallery, Detroit, 99, Mus Western Va, 2001. *Pos:* Co-chmn, Black Emergency Cult Coalition, NY, 69-; dir, Visual Arts Prog, Nat Endowment Arts, 82-84 & Nat Arts Productions, 84-86; founder, pres, Benny Andrews Found, Conn, 2001-. *Teaching:* Instr art, New Sch Social Res, 67-70; lectr art, Queens Col, 68-72; Dorne vis prof, Univ Bridgeport, 70; prof art, CUNY Queens Col, New York, 68-97. *Awards:* John Hay Whitney fellow, 1965-67; Dorne Professionship Univ Bridgeport, Conn, 1970; NY State Creative Arts Prog Serv Grant, 71; NY Coun Arts grantee, 1971; NY Coun on Arts, 1971-1981; MacDowell Colony fel, 1973-73, 75-78; Nat Endowment Arts, 74 & 86; fel Nat Endowment for Arts, 1974-81; Elizabeth Cattlett Mora Award for Excellence, 75. *Bibliog:* Samella Lewis & Ruth Waddy (auth), Black artists on art, Contemp Crafts, 71; Elton Fax (auth), 17 Black Artists, Dodd, 71; Barry Schwartz (auth), The New Humanism, Praeger, 74; S Lewis (auth), Art: African American, Harcourt, Brace & Jovanovich, 77; E L Smith (auth), Art of the Seventies, Cornell Univ Press, 80; Dr Richard Gouber (auth), Icons: from Madison to Manhattan, Mus Art Augusta, 99. *Mem:* MacDowell Colony (bd dir, 87); Sculpture Ctr; Nat Acad Art. *Media:* Oil & Collage, Pen & Ink. *Publ:* Auth, A wonderful potpourri of styles and sources, Art J, summer 80; Benny Andrews: An artist's journal, Atlanta Art Papers, 9-10/80; Is there a Black Esthetic?, Art Papers, 12/85; Decentralization: The Greening of America, Art Papers, 4/86; The Mule Is About Keeping On Keeping On, Am Visions, 4/88; illustrator, Sky Sash So Blue, Simon & Schuster, 88; The Hickory Chair, Scholastic Books, 2000

ANDREWS, CHARLEEN KOHL
SCULPTOR
b New York, NY, July 27, 25. *Study:* Univ Southern Calif, BA, 54; Scottsdale Artist Sch with Bruno Luchesi & Ken Bunn, 87 & 89. *Work:* Descanso Gardens, La Canada, Calif; Carnegie Cult Arts Mus, Oxnard, Calif; Los Angeles Arboretum; Whittier City Hall, Calif; Brand Art Gallery. *Comn:* Pelicans, wood sculpture, State Farm Insurance, Los Angeles, 87; Bronze Indian, McDonalds Franchises, Glendora, Calif, 89. *Exhib:* Artists Soc Int, San Francisco, 86; Burbank City Art Competition, Burbank Libr, 87; Anniversary Show, Los Angeles Arboretum, 87; Glendale Arts Coun, Glendale Galleria, 88; Winners Circle, Alhambra City Hall, 88; and others. *Bibliog:* Mary Forgione (auth), For arts sake, Glendale Star, 86; Art highlights, W Art, 89; Bill Youngs (auth), Sculpture in wood, Star/News Herald, 89. *Mem:* Pasadena Soc Artists; Burbank Art Asn; San Gabriel Fine Arts; Int Sculptors Asn & Calif Sculptors Asn. *Media:* Wood. *Mailing Add:* 1278 Upton Pl Eagle Rock CA 90041

ANDREWS, EDWIN C
SCULPTOR
b Emporia, Kans, Dec 16, 56. *Study:* Kans City Art Inst, BFA, 79; Ind Univ, MFA, 82. *Work:* Essex Inst, Salem, Mass; Allegheny Col, Meadville, Pa; Moneta Group Inc, St Louis Sci Ctr, Mark Twain Banks, Patience & Al Jung, St Louis, Mo. *Comn:* Sculpture, Le Frack Commission, Washington; Fed Reserve Bank Plaza, Cincinnati, Ohio; Art Link, Arts in Transit, Light Rail Proj, St Louis, Mo. *Exhib:* Art of the Mask Exhibit, Artists' Found Gallery, Boston, Mass, 91; solo exhib, Dodge Gallery, Northeastern Univ, Boston, 92; The Studio Show, Boston Ctr Arts, Mass, 94; Strokes of Genius, DeCordova Mus & Sculpture Park, Lincoln, Mass, 95; See Through, Mills Gallery, Boston Ctr Arts, 95; Tower of Babel (computer animation), Normandy, France, 96; and others. *Teaching:* Asst prof, Univ Ky, Lexington, 82-86 & Wash Univ, Sch Fine Arts, St Louis, Mo, 86-90; lects at numerous univs and insts, 85-91; assoc prof, Northeastern Univ, Boston, Mass, 90-. *Awards:* Finalist Award in Sculpture, 91; Mass Artists Fel, 91; Lef Found Grant, 95. *Bibliog:* Christine Temin (auth), A haunting last show at NU's art gallery, Boston Globe, 6/92; Robert Duffy (auth), Joyride unusual objects along the new Metrolink route, St Louis Post Dispatch, 7/93; Christine Temin (auth), Arts immediacy is palpable at BCA, Boston Globe, 9/94. *Mailing Add:* c/o Northeastern Univ 239 Ryder Hall Boston MA 02115

ANDREWS, KIM
PAINTER
b Aug 4, 39. *Study:* Univ Alberta, Dipl Art, 61, BFA, 63, Brooklyn Col, City Univ NY, MFA, 68. *Work:* Can Coun Art Bank; Owens Art Gallery, Sackville, NB; Westburne Industries, Montreal; Art Gallery Hamilton, Ont; Art Gallery North York, Ont. *Exhib:* Solo exhibs, Nightingale Gallery, Toronto, 70, Owens Art Gallery, Mt ALison Univ, Sackville, NB, 72, The Gallery, Scarborough Col, Univ Toronto, Olga Korper Gallery, Toronto, 82, 84, 86, 87 & 96, Gallery Wack, Ger, 87 & 92 & Galerie Dr Luise Krohn, Ger, 89; Art Gallery Ont, Traveling Exhib: Owens Art Gallery, Mt Alison Univ, Sackville, NB, 73; Cologne Int Art Fair, Ger, 86 & 87; 15 Anniversary Group Show,

Olga Korper Gallery, Toronto, 88; 49th Parallel, NY, 89; Entschieden & Konsequent, Galerie Dr Luise Krohn, Ger, 91. *Pos:* Course dir, drawing, York Univ, Toronto, 73-74 & 76-77. *Teaching:* spec lectr, Univ Toronto, 75-80, asst prof, drawing & painting, 80-82, assoc prof, 82-. *Dealer:* Olga Korper Gallery 17 Morrow Ave Toronto Ont M6R 2H9. *Mailing Add:* c/o Olga Korper Gallery 17 Morrow Ave Toronto ON M6R 2H9 Canada

ANDREWS, LAWRENCE
VIDEO ARTIST, SCULPTOR
b May 7, 64. *Study:* San Francisco Art Inst, Sobel Scholar, 85, BFA, 87; Corcoran Sch Art, Washington, DC, 82. *Exhib:* Solo exhibs, Western Adition Cult Ctr, San Francisco, 87, New Langton Arts, San Francisco, Calif, 89, Rene Coelho Gallery Monte Video, Amsterdam, 90, The Kitchen, 92 & Washington Project for Arts, 92, Capp ST Proj, San Francisco, Calif, 94 & San Francisco Exploritorium, 95; An I for An I, San Francisco Mus Mod Art, 88; Strategies fro the development of NY, Whitney Biennial, 91; Enlightenment, Revolution Gallery, Ferndale, Mich, 93; The Final Frontier, New Mus Contemp Art, NY, 93; When World Collide, Mus Mod Art, NY, 94; Walker Art Ctr, 94; Flagging the 21st Century, Capp St Proj, 94; Post Colonial Strategies, San Francisco State Univ, Calif, 95; Whitney Biennial, 95; and others. *Pos:* Freelance ed, Bay Area Video Coalition, Video Free Am; bd dir, New Am Makers, 89 & New Langton Arts, 90-; fel panelist visual arts, Nat Endowment Arts, 90; lectr, San Francisco Film Festival, 90, 92 & 93, Mill Valley Film Festival, 92, Pub Art Works, Mill Valley, 92; adv bd, secession Gallery, San Francisco, Calif, 92-; selection panelist, Film Arts Found Grants prog, 92, Seattle Arts Comn Coliseum Proj, 94 & Wash State Pub Schs Video Art Collection; juror, Girbaud Peace Movement Art Exhib; panelist, Creating Democracy: Technology, Pedagogy & the Arts, San Francisco State Univ, 94, Free Media/Accessing Audiences Through Electronic Commons, Capp St Proj, 94. *Teaching:* Asst prof film & electronic media, Univ Calif, Santa Cruz, bd studies theater arts, 91-; artist-in-residence, Rijksacademie Amsterdam, Holland, 89-90; guest lectr & artist-in-residence, Univ Indust Arts, Helsinki, Finland. *Awards:* Fulbright Grant, 89; Visual Arts Fel, Nat Endowment Arts, 89 & 93; Intercultural Media Arts Fel, Rockefeller Found, 93. *Bibliog:* Articles in San Francisco Mag, 1/89, Artweek, 7/1/89, Los Angeles Times, 7/29/89 & High Performance Mag, summer 89; Human Attention/Regaining Control of our senses, Village Voice, 2/4/92; The Body and technology, New York Times, 7/30/93. *Mem:* Bay Area Video Coalition (bd dir, 93-); Acad Standing Comt, 92-93 & 96-97. *Publ:* Shift Mag, Vol 2, No 4, 40-41; Art Week, 2/22/90 & 11/8/90. *Mailing Add:* 376 Capricorn Ave Oakland CA 94611-2058

ANDREWS, MARION
PAINTER
b Norton, Mass. *Study:* Worcester Mus Art Sch; Mass Col Art, Boston, BS; Pratt Inst; Art Students League, studied with Edgar Whitney, Rex Brandt, Donald Jackson & Frank Webb. *Hon Degrees:* Mass Col Art, Hon Fine Arts, 1996. *Work:* Blue Angels, US Air Force, Pensacola, Mus of Navy Yard, Washington, DC; Winds Aloft, The Ninety-Nines Headquarters, Okla City; Air & Space Mus, San Diego, Calif; Smithsonian Inst, Washington, DC; Int Women's Air & Space Mus, Cleve, OH; and others. *Exhib:* Am Watercolor Soc, Salmagundi Club, 1973-; Audubon Artists; Nat Asn of Women Artists; solo exhib, Pen & Brush Club; Nat Arts Club; and others. *Teaching:* instr, Watercolor Painting, Jackson Heights Art Club, formerly; instr, Workshops, Eastern Shore Community Col, 1991. *Awards:* Pen & Brush Club Solo Award; over 100 other awards. *Mem:* Nat Arts Club; Knickerbocker Artists; Salmagundi Club; The Ninety-Nines (women pilots), 1955-; Soc of Scribes, NYC, 1975-; Pen & Brush Club (pres, 1988-92); Audubon Artists (aquamedia dir), 1999; Jackson Heights Art Club. *Media:* Calligraphy, Gilding and Watercolor. *Mailing Add:* 162-11 9th Ave #4B Whitestone NY 11357

ANDREWS, NANCY EVELYN
ARTIST
b Syracuse, NY, Oct 17, 61. *Study:* The Md Inst Col of Art, BFA, 83; Art Inst of Chicago, MFA, 95. *Work:* Mus Modern Art, NY; Biblioteque Nationale, Paris; The Sch of Art Inst of Chicago. *Exhib:* Cineprobe, Mus of Modern Art, NY, 01; MadCat, Berkeley Mus, San Francisco, 02. *Teaching:* adj prof, Sch of Art Inst of Chicago, 95; prof, Col of the Atlantic, Bar Harbor, Me, 99-. *Mailing Add:* PO Box 142 Seal Harbor ME 04675

ANDREWS, RICHARD O
MUSEUM DIRECTOR, ADMINISTRATOR
b Los Angeles, Calif, Nov 8, 49. *Study:* Occidental Col, BA, 71; Univ Wash, BFA, 73, MFA, 75. *Collection Arranged:* Art into Life (Russian constructivism 1914-32; ed, catalog), Rizzoli, 90; James Turrell: Sensing Space (works: 1967-1992; auth & ed, catalog), Henry Art Gallery, 92 & James Turrell: Knowing Light, 2003; Maya Lin: Systematic Landscapes, 2006. *Pos:* Coordr, Art in Pub Places, Seattle Arts Comn, Wash, 78-84; dir, Visual Arts Prog, Nat Endowment Arts, Washington, 85-87 & Henry Art Gallery, Seattle, Wash, 88-. *Mem:* Asn Art Mus Dirs. *Res:* Modern & contemporary art. *Publ:* Contribr, Insights/On Sites, Partners Livable Places, 84; ed, Going Places, Arts Exten Serv, 88; contribr, A Field Guide to Seattle's Public Art, Seattle Arts Comn, 91. *Mailing Add:* c/o Henry Art Gallery Univ Wash Box 351410 Seattle WA 98195

ANDRIULLI, ROBERT
PAINTER, EDUCATOR
b Paterson, NJ, Jan 18, 48. *Study:* William Paterson Col, NJ, BA(painting), 75; Pa State Univ, MFA(painting), 78. *Exhib:* Solo exhibs, Wyckoff Gallery, NJ, 91, Icon Gallery, Brunswick, Maine, 91 & 93, William & Mary Col, Williamsburg, Va, 91, Lebanon Campus, Harrisburg Area Community Col, 92, Lancaster Graphics, Pa, 93, Hemphill Fine Art Gallery, Washington, DC, 94 & Steven Scott Gallery, Baltimore, Md, 94; 33rd Ann Drawing & Sculpture Show, Ball State Univ, Muncie, Ind, 87; Places Near and Far, Wyckoff Gallery, NJ, 94; Expressive Brushwork, Steven Scott Gallery, Baltimore, 94; Summer Skies, Steven Scott Gallery, Baltimore, 94; Through the Woods, Steven Scott Gallery, Baltimore, 94; and others. *Pos:* Dir, Zoller Gallery, Pa State Univ, 79-80. *Teaching:* Instr art, Pa State Univ, 78-82; asst prof art, Bowdoin Col, Brunswick, Maine, 88-90 & Millersville Univ, Millersville, Pa, 90; adj instr art, Seton Hall Univ, 82-86, William Paterson Col, 84-85 & Montclair State Col, 86. *Awards:* NJ State Coun Arts Fel, 79 & 85; Visual Artist Fel, Nat Endowment Arts, 87; Artist-in-Residence Fel, Yaddo Found, NY, 87, Millay Colonie Arts, NY, 87, Fine Arts Ctr, Mass, 87 & Va Ctr Creative Arts, Va, 88-89, 91-92 & 92-93. *Dealer:* Wyckoff Gallery Wyckoff NJ 07481. *Mailing Add:* 448 N Prince St Millersville PA 17551-1406

ANDRY, KEITH ANTHONY
PAINTER, INSTRUCTOR
b Thibodaux, La, June 28, 60. *Study:* Special instruction with Ed Whitney, Robert E Wood, Millard Sheets & Milford Zornes, 73-84; Calif Sch of Art, with Rex Brandt, 86; Nicholls State Univ, AB, 86. *Work:* Fine Arts Mus S, Mobile, Ala; Zigler Mus Art, Jennings, La; Baton Rouge Waterworks, Baton Rouge, La; George's Inc, Springdale, Ark; Andry Interior's, Thibodaux, La. *Comn:* Three paintings, Disney World Dixie Landings Resort, 92. *Exhib:* Georgia Watercolor Soc 3rd Ann, Mus Arts & Sci, Macon, Ga, 82; Georgia Watercolor Soc 6th Ann, Madison-Morgan Cult Ctr, Madison Ga, 85; Rocky Mountain Nat Watermedia Exhib, Foothills Art Ctr, Golden, Colo, 86-87; Nat Watercolor Soc 66th Ann Muckenthaler Cult Ctr, Fullerton, Calif, 87; and othrs. *Pos:* Chmn Arts, 1984 World's Fair, New Orleans, La, 84. *Awards:* Grumbacher Art Award, Grumbacher, 80; Foothills Art Ctr Award, Foothills Art Ctr, 86; Muckenthaler Cult Found, Muckenthaler Cult Ctr, 87. *Bibliog:* Trent Angers (auth), Keith Andry: Watercolorist on a winning streak, Anger's Publ Corp, 83; Sheila Elliot (auth), Keith Andry: Rocky Mountain Watermedia Asn, F & W Publ Corp, 87; Stephen Doherty (auth), Painting on Location - Special Feature, Am Artist Mag, 89. *Mem:* Nat Watercolor Soc signature mem; Ky Watercolor Soc; La Watercolor Soc life mem; Midwest Watercolor Soc life mem; Ga Watercolor Soc signature mem. *Media:* Watercolor. *Publ:* Illusr, The Longest Street, 82; Keith Andry: Watercolorist on a Winning Streak, Anger's Publ Corp, 83; contrib, Louisiana Men are Dinamight, Elm Publ, 84; illusr, Keith Andry: Rocky Mountain National Watermedia Exhibition, F & W Publ Inc, 87; Painting on Location, Stephen Doherty, 89. *Mailing Add:* 16410 Jefferson Hwy Baton Rouge LA 70817

ANGELINI, JOHN MICHAEL
PAINTER, WRITER
b New York, NY, Nov 18, 1921. *Study:* Newark Sch Fine & Indust Art; spec studies in Europe, 61; Fla State Univ, Cert Fla Master Gardener, 98. *Exhib:* Nat Arts Club Watercolor Ann, NY, 64; NJ Pavillion, NY World's Fair, 65; Watercolor USA, Nat Ann & Traveling Exhib, Springfield Mus, Mo, 66; NJ Watercolor Soc Ann, Newark, 74-80; Int Exhib, Nabisco World Hq; Miniature Artists Am Traveling Exhib, 86-98; 1998 Winter Olympics, Nagano, Japan, 98; 2000 Summer Olympics, Sydney; Smithsonion, Wash, DC, 2003; and one-man shows in NY & NJ. *Pos:* Art dir, Berles Carton Co Inc, Paterson, NJ, 50-79; adv bd, NJ Music & Arts, Chatham, 72-78. *Teaching:* Instr, watercolor, private students. *Awards:* Silver Medal for Watercolor, NJ Watercolor Soc, 63; Medal of Honor for Watercolor, Audubon Artists, Nat Acad, 63 & Nat Arts Club, 64; Artist of the Year, Hudson Artists, Inc, NJ, 74; and many other state, regional & nat exhibs. *Bibliog:* L Pessolano (auth), John Angelini--a profile, 70 & R Williams (auth), John Angelini--A W S, 71, NJ Music & Arts; interview & watercolor demonstration, cable TV networks, NY & NJ. *Mem:* Am Watercolor Soc; hon mem Audubon Artists; Fla & NJ Miniature Art Soc; Miniature Artists of Am; Allied Artists Am; Miniature Art Soc Fla Inc. *Media:* Watercolor, Pencil Rendering. *Res:* Renaissance art studies, Italy. *Interests:* Photography, Bonsai. *Collection:* David L Yunich Collection, Bambergers, NJ; Morris Mus of Art, Morristown, NJ; Paterson Main Libr, NJ; Longlines Div, Am Tel & Tel; Morgan Guarantee Trust Co, NY; Lady Laura, Bloomfield Col; Boy Scouts of Am; and others. *Publ:* Contribr, NJ Music & Arts, 70-77; auth, articles in Am Artist, 72; The North Light Art Competition Handbook, North Light Books, 86; Watercolor 86, Am Artist, 86; contribr, 59 More Studio Secrets, North Light Bks, 90; Images, ltd ed bound print portfolio, 2000. *Dealer:* Scalzo Gallery 2617 Jewel Road Belleaire Bluffs FL 33770. *Mailing Add:* 18211 Autumn Lake Blvd Hudson FL 34667-8436

ANGELL, TONY
SCULPTOR, PAINTER
b Los Angeles, Calif, Nov 15, 40. *Study:* Univ Wash, BA, 62. *Work:* Rainier Bank, Safeco Plaza, Seattle; Tacoma Art Mus, Wash; Gilcrease Mus, Tulsa, Okla; Frye Art Mus, Seattle, Wash; Lywam Art Mus, Wausau, Wis. *Comn:* Ascending Eagles, Bellevue, Wash; Trumpeter Swans, Lywam Art Mus, Wausau, Wis; Animal Forms in Stone, Woodland Park Zoo, City Seattle, Wash, 94; Parlament of Owls, Whatcom Col, Wash, 97; Wisdom Seekers, Redmond Pub Libr, Wash, 99; Raven Greet, City of Shoreline, WA; Emissaries, Sleeping Lady Conference Center, 2006. *Exhib:* Nat Acad Western Art, Oklahoma City, 81-98; Artists of Am Show, Denver, 81-97; Tony Angell Retrospective, T Gilcrease Mus, Tulsa, Okla, 86; Animals in Art, Leigh Yawkey Woodson Art Mus, Wasau, Wis, 86-2005; Wildlife Art Am, Univ Minneapolis, Minn, 94; The Artful Animal, Minneapolis Inst Art, 98; Wild at Heart, Nat Mus Wildlife Art, 2005. *Collection Arranged:* Northwest Collection (with catalog), Rainier Bldg, Seattle, 78; Gilcrease Mus, Tulsa, Okla, 86; Northwest Collection, Qwest, Seattle, Wash; Emergence of North West Art, Mus North West Art, Laconner, WA, 2002. *Pos:* Comnr & chair, Visual Arts Comt, King Co Arts Comn, 78-82; adj fac sci illus, Univ Wash Sch Art. *Teaching:* Guest lectr, City of Seattle, 83 & Artists of Am, Denver, 83-88; lectr, Nat Acad Western Art, 93. *Awards:* 50 Best Books Design Award, 86; Blodel Lectr Fel, 94; Master Artist Award, Leigh Yawkey Woodson Art Mus, 2001.

Bibliog: Evening Edition (T Angell), KCTS TV, Seattle, Wash, 87; New York Art Rev, 89; Todd Wilkenson (auth), Spirits from stone, Seattle Mag, 11/96 & Touch stones, Orion Mag, winter 97; A Life in Stone, Pacific Northwest Magazine, Seattle Times, WA, 99. *Mem:* Fel Nat Acad Western Artists; fel Nat Sculpture Soc; Artists Am (designated master). *Media:* Marble, Bronze; Oils, Ink. *Interests:* Natural history & its influence on culture. *Publ:* Auth-illusr, Owls, 74 & Ravens, Crows, Magpies and Jays, 78, Univ Wash; co-auth-illusr, Marine Birds and Mammals of Puget Sound, Nat Oceanic & Atmospheric Admin, 82; illusr, Blackbirds of the Americas, Univ Wash Press, 84; Sea Brothers, 88 & Descent of Love, 95, Univ Pa Press; The Pinyon Jay, TA Poyser, London, 92; In the Company of Crows & Ravens, Yale Univ, 2005; Contemporary Animal Sculptors, Art West Magazine, 7-8/2006; and others. *Dealer:* Foster/White Gallery; Gerald Peters Gallery. *Mailing Add:* 18237 40th Ave NE Seattle WA 98155

ANGELO, SANDRA MCFALL
WRITER, INSTRUCTOR
b St Louis, Mo, Apr 24, 50. *Study:* Seattle Pac Univ, BA, 72; Nat Univ, MBA, 85. *Comn:* Scripps Womens Birthing Ctr, Scripps Hospital, La Jolla, Calif. *Pos:* Nat dir, Discover Art, San Diego, Calif, prod & dir; dir, Int Colored Pencil Symp, 89; contrib ed, Art Mat Today, 93; producer, video/TV. *Teaching:* Teacher art, La Jolla Country Day Sch, 81-86; prof art, US Int Univ, 86-89, Palomar Col, 86-. *Awards:* Fel Award, RI Sch Design, 86; WAVE Award, 95; Award of Excellence, Videographer, 97. *Bibliog:* Tiffany Windsor (dir), Everyone Can Draw, Creative Living TV-TNN, 94; Tiffany Windsor (dir), Fun with Colored Pencil, Creative Living; docs, HGTV (5 shows), summer 98, Discovery Channel, spring 98 & ABC-Good Morning Texas, 2/98. *Mem:* Hobby Indust Am; Soc Decorative Painters; Nat Speakers Asn; Publ Marketing Asn. *Media:* Graphite, Oil, Pastels. *Res:* Drawing methods for new artists lacking natural talent. *Publ:* Auth, Using colored pencil on a colored ground, Am Artist, 93; Colored Pencil Basics, Walter Foster, 94; So You Thought You Couldn't Draw, Discover Art, 94; Combining oil pastels with colored pencils, Drawing Highlights, 94; Painting with colored pencils, Artists Mag, 94; plus many others. *Mailing Add:* PO Box 420551 San Diego CA 92142

ANGELOCH, ROBERT
PAINTER, PRINTMAKER
b Richmond Hill, NY, Apr 8, 22. *Study:* Art Student League; Acad Fine Arts, Florence, Italy; also with Fiske Boyd, Martin Lewis & Y Kuniyoshi. *Work:* Art Student League; Munson-Williams-Proctor Inst, Utica, NY; Russell Sage Col; Western Ky Univ. *Comn:* Murals, NY Bd Educ, Kellogg Corp, Brunswick, NJ & Queensboro Pub Libr. *Exhib:* Metrop Mus; Nat Acad; Libr Congress. *Pos:* Supvr, Woodstock Summer Sch, Art Students League, 60-68; artist-in-residence, Western Ky Univ, 74; dir, Woodstock Sch Art Inc, 80-86, pres, 80-. *Teaching:* Instr, Art Students League, Woodstock Summer Sch, 64-79; instr, Woodstock Sch Art, 68-; instr, Russell Sage Col, 71-72. *Awards:* McDowell Traveling Scholar, Art Students League, 51; Artist in Residence Grant, Nat Endowment Arts, 74; Pollack-Krasner Found Grant, 95. *Bibliog:* S R Day (auth), Creative Woodstock, Mead Mt Press, 66; Fridolf Johnson (auth), Robert Angeloch, Am Artists Mag, 85. *Mem:* Art Student League; Woodstock Artists Asn. *Media:* Oil; Etching. *Publ:* Auth, Basic Oil Painting Techniques, Pitman, 70; Outdoor sketching, Am Artist Mag, 70; contribr, Angeloch: Color Prints, 80. *Dealer:* Paradox Gallery Woodstock NY 12498. *Mailing Add:* PO Box 95 Woodstock NY 12498

ANGER, KENNETH
FILMMAKER, DIRECTOR
Exhib: Producer, dir (films): Escape Episode, 1946; Puce Moment, 1949; Faux d' Artifice, 1953; Inauguration of the Pleasure Dome, 1954; Thelma Abbey, 1955; Scorpio Rising, 1962-64; Kustom Kar Kommandos, 1965; Invocation of My Demon Brother (Lucifer Rising, 1969; Rabbit's Moon, 1971; and others. *Awards:* Fellow, Ford Found, 1964; Whitney Biennial, 2006. *Publ:* auth, Hollywood Babylon, 1959; auth, Hollywood Babylon II, 1984; auth, Ich Will!, 2000; auth, The Man We Want to Hang, 2002; auth, Mouse Heaven, 2004; auth, Anger Sees Red, 2004

ANGULO, CHAPPIE
PAINTER, ILLUSTRATOR
b Mar 3, 28; US citizen. *Study:* Los Angeles City Col, 49; Univ Calif, Los Angeles; Kahn Art Sch; Esmeralda, Inst Nac Bellas Artes, Mexico City, 55; London Art Ctr, Fort Mason, San Francisco, 60. *Work:* Mus Cult, Mexico City; Univ Mus Art, Mexico, DF. *Comn:* Reproduction murals, Bonampak, 57, Chichen Itza & Tomb 7 Oaxaca, 58, Nat Mus Anthrop, Moneda; reproduction mural, Teotihuacan, Ballet Nac, Mex, 59. *Exhib:* One-man shows, Mus Fronterizo, Juarez, Mex, 71, Age Aquarius, Univ Las Americas, Cholula, 73, Gentes y Lugares Mus de las Cult, Mex, Exploraciones, ISSSTE, Cuernavaca, Mor, Mex, 96, Abstracciones, Centro Cult Univ, Morelos, Mex, 97, Ieonoquafias, Museo Caumen, Mex DF, 98, Caminos, Salon Plastica Mex, 98, Aspetos Divevsos, Mus Jalapa, Mex, 99, Centro Cult Coyoaeau, Mex, 2000; 3 decades of Plastic Art-UNAM, Mex, DF, 90; Artistas del Mundo (UNESCO), Tlaxcala, Mex, 96; US Artists in Mexico, Mex DF, 96; Exhib Int Artistas Plasticas, Honduras, 97; Exhib Reapeutuon Col Crisco, 98; Diversidades, Bellas Artes, 2002; 2003 Mus etc Salon de la Plastica Sau Carlos, Salon de la Plastica Sigso XXI; Centos de Alegria, Salon de la Plastica, Mexico, 2006. *Collection Arranged:* Salan Plastica Mexicana, 99, 2000-; Collectivas, 96-2006. *Teaching:* Pvt instr, currently. *Bibliog:* M Vazquez (auth), Museo de las Culturas, Inst Nat Antropologia, 65; A Pastrana (auth), El concreto, Arquitectura Arte & Urbanism Mag, 68; Cirulo de Arte, Mex, 97. *Mem:* Salon de la Plastica, Mex. *Media:* Acrylic; Monotype. *Specialty:* Diverse. *Interests:* Art. *Publ:* Illusr, A Guide to Coatetelco; Iconographic Analysis of Ancient Chalcatzingo, 87; El Axayotl--Un sistema de drenaje aljibe--,Agricultura Indigena, Ciesas, Mex, 90; Aspects of a Culture thru its Pictoric Expression--Section Teotihuacan--Prehispanic Mural Painting in Mexico, Inst Esthetic Investigation, UNAM, Mex, 92; illus, Water Control & Communal Labor, Research in Economic Anthropology, JAI Press, 93. *Dealer:* Salon Plastica Mexicana. *Mailing Add:* A P Postal 21-609 Mexico City Mexico DF 04000

ANKER, SUZANNE C
SCULPTOR, PAINTER
b Brooklyn, NY, Aug 6, 1946. *Study:* Brooklyn Col, BA; Univ Colo, MFA. *Work:* St Louis Art Mus, Mo; Denver Art Mus, Colo; Williams Col Mus Art. *Comn:* Cleveland Art Mus. *Exhib:* New Ways With Paper, Nat Collection Fine Arts, Smithsonian Inst, Washington, DC, 77 & Paper as Medium, 78; Walker Art Ctr, Minneapolis, 79; Richard Gray Gallery, Chicago, 79; Greenberg Wilson Gallery, NY, 88 & 90. *Teaching:* Asst prof experimental printmaking, Washington Univ, St Louis, 76-78. *Awards:* NY Found Grant in Sculpture, 89. *Bibliog:* Meyer Raphael Rubinstein (auth), Suzanne Anker, Arts, 12/88; Carter Ratcliff (auth), Swamp things, Vogue, 4/89; rev, Howard Risatti, Artforum, summer 90. *Mem:* Col Art Asn. *Media:* Paper, Stone. *Mailing Add:* 101 Wooster St Apt 7F New York NY 10012-3895

ANKRUM, JOAN
ART DEALER
b Los Angeles, Calif, 1914. *Collection Arranged:* Of Time & the Image, Calif Artists, Phoenix Mus Art, Ariz, 64; People to People, exhib honoring People's Repub China, 72; The Art of African Peoples, private Black Collections, Ankrum Gallery, 73; Calif Artists Exhib, State Capitol Bldg, Sacramento, 75; Morris Broderson Retrospectives, Univ Ariz Mus Art, 75; Ankrum Gallery, Rochester Nat Tech Inst for the Deaf, 86; Broderson, Ankrum Gallery, 89. *Pos:* Dir, Ankrum Gallery, Los Angeles. *Awards:* Los Angeles City Coun Award, 93. *Bibliog:* H Wurdeman (auth), Los Angeles Galleries, Art in Am, 62; Camilla Snyder (auth), A language without sound, Los Angeles Herald Examr, 5/10/70; Curtis (auth), A woman's place, New York Times, 11/26/71. *Mem:* Art Dealers Asn Southern Calif (bd mem, 70); Am Fedn Arts. *Specialty:* West Coast contemporary artists, primarily Californian, ethnic, including Black, Mexican-Indian (Huichol). *Publ:* Auth & ed, Drawings & Haiku, Janet Lessing, Commun Sci, 65. *Mailing Add:* 327 N Orange Dr Los Angeles CA 90036

ANNIS, NORMAN L
EDUCATOR, SCULPTOR
b Des Moines, Iowa, May 26, 31. *Study:* Univ Northern Iowa, BA, 53; Drake Univ; Univ Iowa, MFA, 59. *Work:* Central Col, Pella, Iowa; Corcoran Gallery Art, DC; Washington & Lee Univ, Lexington, Va. *Comn:* Life-size bronze figure, Gettysburg Col, Pa, 70; life-size welded steel figure, Frey Village, Middletown, 76; life-size cor-ten steel figure, Gettysburg Sr High Sch, 77. *Exhib:* Fourth Dulin Nat Prints, Dulin Gallery, Knoxville, 61; 4th Nat Drawing Exhib, Okla Art Ctr, Oklahoma City, 61; Drawings USA, St Paul Art Ctr, Minn, 61 & 63; 4th Nat Ultimate Concerns, Ohio Univ, Athens, 65; Washington Area Artists Series, Corcoran Gallery Art, DC, 65; Living Am Artists & Human Figure, Pa State Univ Mus Art, State Col, 74. *Teaching:* Instr sculpture, Univ Ill, Champaign, 59-60; prof sculpture, Gettysburg Col, 60-78; prof & head dept art, Southwest Mo State Univ, Springfield, 78-. *Awards:* First Sculpture Award, Fifth Ann Pennational, 62; Purchase Award, St Paul Art Ctr, 63; Anna Hyatt Huntington Award, Corcoran Gallery Art, 63. *Media:* Bronze, Welded Steel. *Dealer:* Michelson Gallery 707 G St NE Washington DC 20002. *Mailing Add:* 108 Round Ridge Rd Mechanicsburg PA 17055-9201

ANNUS, JOHN AUGUSTUS
PAINTER, PHOTOGRAPHER
b Riga, Latvia, Oct 25, 35; US citizen. *Study:* Pratt Inst, with Richard Lindner & Enrico Catellon, BFA, 58; Nat Acad Design, with Louis Bouche, 58-59; Prix de Rome, Am Acad Rome, 59; Acad Belli Arti Liceo Artistico, Rome, 62-64; Circle in Sq Theatre Sch, 70-71. *Work:* Baltimore Mus Fine Art, Md; Ohio Dominican Col, Columbus; Nat Acad Design, NY; Am Acad, Ital Govt, Rome; Henry Ranger Found. *Exhib:* Nat Acad Design Ann, NY, 62, 64, 65, 67, 75, 77, 78, 80, 87, 88, 91 & 2003; one-man shows, Clasing Gallery, Munster, Ger, 81, Julia Black Gallery, Taos, NMex, 82, 83 & 84, Toronto Ctr Art Gallery, 84, Labyrinth of Light, Int Latvian Music & Arts Festival, Munster, Ger, 87, Jakobi Gallery, Hamburg, Ger, 87, Gallery Southwest, Hensley Gallery, Taos, NMex, 89 & Labyrinth of Light, Reitern Gallery, Riga, Latvia, 92; 166th Ann Academicians and--Assoc, Nat Acad Design, 91; Spectrum 5 Gallery, Munster Ger, 92-94; Design-Technic Gallery, Hamburg, Ger, 96; Images, Photokina 96, World Exhib Imaging, Cologne, Ger. *Pos:* Res Asst, Armstrong Circle Theatre CBS, 58-59; art dir & founder, Cine-Centrum Inc, 67-73; art dir feature film, Squeeze Play, 73; production designer feature film, Shadows, 74 & Looking Up, 76; production designer, Linda Yellen Productions, Inc, 75-79. *Awards:* Italian Govt Grant, Ministero Degli Affari Esteri, 61; Gold Medal, Mostra Int di Art Figurative, Rome, 62; J Hallgarten Prize, Nat Acad Design, 64, HW Ranger Prize, 65 & 75, SJ Wallace Truman Prize, 67 & Cert of Merit, 80 & 87. *Bibliog:* Tony Bonavita (auth), La Pazzia di John Annus, Il Vantaggio, 81; Joh Hasenkamp (auth), Visionares in Fabre, Westfalische Nachrichten, 12/30/81; Nikolajs Bulmanis (auth), Dynamic Romantiscism, Laiks, 84; Centennial Dir of Am Acad in Rome, 95. *Mem:* Nat Acad Design (assoc, 96, acad, 79); Soc Fel Am Acad in Rome; Nat Soc Mural Painters; elected academician Nat Acad Design; Nat Asn Broadcast & Television Employees. *Media:* Oils, Multi-media

ANSCHUTZ, PHILIP F
COLLECTOR
Study: Univ Kansas, BS, 1961. *Pos:* Bd mem, Am Petroleum Insti, Nat Petroleum Coun, Nat Hockey League, Kans Univ Endow Assoc, Regal Entertainment Group; dir chmn, QCC, 1993-; founder Anschutz Corp, Denver, 1965; dir chmn, Anschutz Co, 1991-; Chief Exec Officer, dir, Anschutz Corp, 1992-; dir, So Pacific Rail Corp, San

Francisco, 1988-96; chmn, So Pacific Rail Corp, 1988-96; vchmn (merger with So Pacific Rail Corp) Union Pacific, San Francisco, 1996-; dir, Forest Oil Corp, 1995-, Qwest Communications, 1997; chmn, 1997-2002; co-owner Los Angeles Kings, 1995-; owner, Los Angeles Galaxy, 1996-; investor-operator Major League Soccer, 1995-; owner, San Francisco Examiner, The Ind, Grant Printing Co, San Francisco, 2004. *Awards:* Named one of 200 Top Collectors, ARTnews Mag, 2004, 2006. *Interests:* Collecting 19th and 20th century Am. art, especially Western. *Mailing Add:* 555 17th St Ste 2400 Denver CO 80202-3941

ANTEZZO, MATTHEW J
PAINTER
b Harford, Conn, 1962. *Study:* Univ Utah, Salt Lake City, 82-84; Parsons Sch Design, New York, 85-88. *Exhib:* Am Fine Arts, NY, 89; Galerie Georges-Phillipe Vallois, Paris, France, 90 & 91; John Post Gallery, NY, 91; solo exhibs, Galerie Georges-Philippe Vallois, Paris, France, 91 & 93, Basilico Fine Arts, NY, 93 & 94, Interim Art, London, Eng, 94; Backstage, Kunstverein, Hamberg, Ger, 93 & Kuntstmuseum, Luzern, Switz, 94; Pieces a Conviction, FRAC, Langudoc-Roussillon, France, 94; When Attitudes Become Form: Thread Waxing Space, Montclair Art Mus, NJ, 94; Crash, NY, 94; SP-NY, Galerie Camargo, Vilaca, Sao Paolo, Brazil, 94; Pittura Immedia, Neue Galerie am Landesmuseum, Austria, 95; and others. *Bibliog:* Pascale Cassagneau (auth), Matt Antezzo at Galerie Georges-Philippe Vallois, Art Press, 5/91 & 4/93; Melanie Marino (auth), Matthew Antezzo at Basilico Fine, Art in Am, 1/95; James Meyer (auth), Matthew Antezzo at Basilico Fine Arts, Frieze, 1/95. *Dealer:* Basilico Fine Arts 26 Wooster St New York NY 10013. *Mailing Add:* 85 Quay St Brooklyn NY 11222

ANTHONISEN, GEORGE RIOCH
SCULPTOR, PAINTER
b Boston, Mass, July 31, 36. *Study:* Univ Vt, BA, 61; Nat Acad Design, with Douglas Gorsline, 61-62; Art Students League, with Jose De Creeft & John Hovannes, 62-64; Dartmouth Col Med Sch, 67. *Work:* World Health Orgn, Geneva, Switz; James A Michener Art Mus, Doylestown, Pa; Cathedral Heritage Found, Louisville, Ky; Berman Mus Art, Collegeville, Pa; Pa Acad Music, Lancaster, Pa and others. *Comn:* sculpture, Germantown Hosp & Med Ctr, Philadelphia, Pa, 93; sculpture, Philadelphia Col Osteopathic Med, Pa, 94; Doylestown Hosp, Pa; sculpture, Ursinus Col, Collegeville, Pa, 98; sculpture, Please Touch Mus, Philadelphia, Pa, 99. *Awards:* Alaska State Coun Arts, 76; Sculptor in Residence, Augustus St Gaudens Nat Hist Site, US Dept Interior, 71; Exemplary Achievement in Arts Award, Bucks Co C of C, 85. *Bibliog:* Acceptance of the Statue of Senator Ernest Gruening, US Govt Printing Off, 78; I Set Before You This Day (sculpture), James A Michener Art Mus, 90; George Anthonisen: Sculptor, Quest Series, Cable Television Network NJ, Trenton State Col, 93; The Sculpture of George R Anthonisen, Yale Univ Press, 2006. *Mem:* Nat Sculpture Soc; Allied Art Am; Audubon Artists. *Media:* Metal, Cast; Miscellaneous Media. *Publ:* Auth, The Compassionate Spirit: Sculpture and Fresco, Berman Mus Art, 96; auth, Anthonisen, Woodmere Art Mus, Philadelphia, Pa, 92. *Dealer:* Travis Gallery 6089 Lower York Rd New Hope PA 18938; Peter Aaronson 22 Cassway Rd Woodbridge Conn 06525. *Mailing Add:* Box 147 Solebury PA 18963

ANTHONY, AMY ELLEN
CRAFTSMAN, JEWELER
b Concord, Mass, May 11, 55. *Study:* Syracuse Univ, New York, BFA, 77; Sch Am Craftsmen, Rochester Inst Technol, NY, MFA, 85. *Work:* Temple Emmanuel, Woodcliff, NJ. *Exhib:* Table Top, 80, Young Americans, 80 & Approaches to Collecting, 82, Am Craft Mus, NY; Four Jewelry Artists from the States, V&V Gallery, Vienna, Austria, 83; Contemp Metals II, Downey Mus Art, Calif, 87; SNAG 88 Earring Competition, Jean Michilin Collection, NY, 88; One of a Kind: Am Art Jewelry, JoAnne Rapp Gallery, Scottsdale, Ariz, 95. *Teaching:* Lectr, Sch Am Craftsmen, Rochester, NY, 88. *Bibliog:* Susan Grant Lewin (auth), One of a Kind: American Jewelry Today; Deborah Krupenia (auth), The Art of Jewelry Design. *Mem:* Am Crafts Coun. *Media:* Metals. *Publ:* Contribr, Amy Anthony: Studies in aluminum, J Soc NAm Goldsmiths, 85. *Mailing Add:* 9 Tulip Ln Greenfield MA 01301-2718

ANTHONY, LAWRENCE KENNETH
SCULPTOR, PAINTER
b Hartsville, SC, May 27, 1934. *Study:* Washington & Lee Univ, BA; Univ Ga, MFA; study with Lamar Dodd & Howard Thomas. *Work:* Memphis Brooks Mus, Tenn; Vanderbilt Univ, Nashville, Tenn; Ark State Univ, Jonesboro; Gibbes Art Gallery, Charleston, SC; SC Art Comn, Columbia; Audubon Park & Rhodes Col, Memphis. *Comn:* Menorah sculpture, Jewish Community Ctr, Memphis, 67; sculpture, Corinthian Broadcasting Co, NY, 71; wall sculpture, CBS-TV, Sacramento, Calif, 72; Audubon Park, Memphis; Vanderbilt Univ, Nashville. *Exhib:* One-man shows, Columbia Mus Art, 66, Memphis Brooks Mus, 68, Vanderbilt Univ, 72, 74 & Terre Des Hommes, Pavilion, Montreal, 79. *Teaching:* Prof sculpture & drawing, Rhodes Col, Memphis, currently. *Media:* Metal, Plastic. *Mailing Add:* 1111 Ocean Dr Summerland Key FL 33042-4507

ANTHONY, WILLIAM GRAHAM
PAINTER, DRAFTSMAN
b Ft Monmouth, NJ, Sept 25, 1934. *Study:* Yale Univ, BA, 58, with Josef Albers; San Francisco Art Inst, 59-60; Art Student League. *Work:* Whitney Mus Am Art, Metrop Mus Art & Guggenheim Mus, NY; Art Inst Chicago; Corcoran Gallery Art, Washington; plus others. *Exhib:* One man shows, Calif Palace Legion Hon, San Francisco, 62, Frank Marino Gallery, NY, 81, Jane Baum Gallery, NY, 86, Berland-Hall Gallery, NY, 91, Stuart Katz Gallery, Laguna Beach, Calif, 92, Cokkie Snoei Gallery, Rotterdam, The Neth, 95 & Robert Berman Gallery, Santa Monica, 98; Cokkie Snoei Gallery, Rotterdam, The Neth, 99; Dorfman Gallery, NY, 2002 & 2004; Stalke Gallery, Copenhagen, 2004; Christopher Henry Gallery, NY, 2006. *Teaching:* Instr figure drawing, San Francisco Acad Art, 62-63. *Bibliog:* Barry Schwabsky (auth), Bill Anthony, Arts Mag, 1/92; Ken Johnson (auth), William Anthony, NY Times, 10/11/02; Robert Rosenblum (auth), Hilarious Shockers, Art News, 9/04. *Media:* Pencil, Oil. *Publ:* Auth, A New Approach to Figure Drawing, Crown Publ, 65, Odhams, Ltd, Eng, 67 & Bonanza Publ, auth & illusr War is Swell, Smart Art Press, 2000; auth & illusr, Bible Stories, 78 & Bill Anthony's Greatest Hits, 88, Jargon Soc. *Dealer:* Cokkie Snoei Gallery Mauritsweg 55 3012JX Rotterdam Netherlands; Stalke Gallery Kirke Sonnerup Denmark; Christopher Henry Gallery 550 W 29th St New York NY 10001. *Mailing Add:* 903 Westbeth 463 West St New York NY 10014

ANTIC, MIROSLAV
PAINTER, ILLUSTRATOR
b Belgrade, Yugoslavia, June 11, 47. *Study:* Acad of Fine Arts, MFA, 73. *Work:* Rose Art Mus, Brandies Univ, Waltham, Mass; Wellesley Col Art Mus, Mass; De Cordova Mus, Lincoln, Mass; Boca Raton Art Mus, Fla; Chase Manhatton Bank; ITET Corp; Mc Donald Corp; Fidelity Investments; Boston Pub Libr. *Exhib:* Cult Commentaries, Berkshire Mus, Pittsfield, Mass, 85; The Object Found and Perceived, Fitchburg Art Mus, Mass, 91; Shrines, Symbols & Cherished Objects, Fuller Mus Art, Brockton, Mass, 94; Boston Now, Inst Contemp Art, Boston, 94. *Teaching:* Instr, Sch of the Mus of Fine Art, Boston, 80-2000. *Awards:* NEA Fel, 96; Pollock-Krasner Found Grant, 97; Fla Visual Art Fel, 00. *Publ:* Charles Giuliano, Miroslav Antic, New Paintings, Arts Media Mag, 00; Cate McQuaid, Miroslav Antic, The Boston Globe, 00; Mary Sherman, Miroslav Antic, Boston Hearld, 00. *Dealer:* Caeserea Gallery 608 Banyan Tral Boca Raton Fla 33431. *Mailing Add:* 228 Elwa Pl West Palm Beach FL 33405

ANTIN, DAVID A
ART CRITIC, WRITER
b New York, NY, Feb 1, 1932. *Study:* Col City New York, BA, 55; NY Univ, MA, 66. *Teaching:* Prof visual arts, Univ Calif, San Diego, 68-, chmn dept, 70-72, 80-81 & 87-89. *Awards:* Guggenheim Fel, 76-77; Nat Endowment Humanities Fel, 82-83. *Bibliog:* Sherman Paul (auth), In Search of the Primitive, LS Univ Press, 86; Henry Sayice (auth), The Object of Performance, Chicago, 89; William G Doty (ed), Picturing Cultural Values in Postmodern America, Univ Ala, 95; The Beggar and the King, Pacific Coast Philology, Vol 30, No 2, 95; C Carr (auth), review of On the Edge: Performance at the End of the 20th Century, Modernism and Modernity, U Chicago, Vol 2, No 3, 95; Larry McCaffery & Marjorie Perloff (auth), Interview of David Antin, Some Other Frequency, U Pa, 96; Wittgenstein Among the Poets, Modernism and Modernity, Winter 98; I Never Knew What Time It Was, 108, 107, Atlanta, 99; California--the nervous camel, Review of Contemp Fiction, Vol XXI, No 1, Normal, Ill, Spring 2001; An Interview with David Antin, Review of Contemp Fiction, Vol XXI, No 1, Normal, Spring, 2001; The Noise of Time, Boston Rev, MIT, Cambridge, Vol 26, No 2, Apr/May 2001; Fred Garber (auth), Repositionings, Pa State Press, 95; Michael Davidson (auth), Ghostlier Demarcations, U Calif Press, 97. *Mem:* Int Asn Art Critics. *Res:* Studies in modernism and post modernism; history of art criticism and theory; sociology of art; interpretation and meaning in culture and language; theory of narrative. *Publ:* Biography: Representations 16, fall 86; The Stranger at the Door, Genre, Vol XX, No 3-4, fall, winter 87; Selected Poems 1963-1973, Sun & Moon, 89; The real thing, Art Am, 5/81; Tuning, New Directions, 84; What it Means to be Avant-Garde, New Directions, 93; Selected Essays, A Conversation with David Antin, U Chicago, Granary Press, 2001. *Mailing Add:* PO Box 1147 Del Mar CA 92014

ANTIN, ELEANOR
CONCEPTUAL ARTIST, PHOTOGRAPHER
b New York, NY, Feb 27, 35. *Study:* City Col NY, BA; Tamara Daykarhanove Sch for the Stage. *Work:* Whitney Mus Am Art, NY; San Francisco Mus Modern Art; Mus Mod Art, NY; Art Inst Chicago; Los Angeles Co Mus Art. *Exhib:* One-woman exhibs, Mus Mod Art, NY, 73, Everson Mus, Syracuse, NY, 74, Clocktower, NY, 76, M L D'Arc Gallery, NY, 77, Wadsworth Atheneum, Hartford, Conn, 77, Whitney Mus Am Art, NY, 78 & Long Beach Mus Art, Calif, 79; Nurse & the Hijackers, 77, Before the Revolution, 79, Recollections of My Life with Diaghilev, 80, El Desdichado, 83 & Loves of a Ballerina, 86, Ronald Feldman Fine Arts Gallery, NY; Venice Biennale, Contemp Art Mus, Calif, 76; Last Night of Rasputin, Whitney Mus Biennial, 89 & Hirshhorn Mus, Washington, DC, 89; From the Inside Out: Contemp Artists, Jewish Mus, NY, 93; Minetta Lane, A Ghost Story, Ronald Feldman Gallery, NY, 95 & Santa Monica Mus Art, Los Angeles, Calif, 95; Minetta Lane,Ghosts, SE Ctr Contemp Art, Winston-Salem, NC, 96; Eleanor Antin: Selections from the Angel of Mercy, Whitney Mus, NY, 97; Eleanor Antin: An Anthology (retrospective), Los Angeles Co Mus Art, 99; Meade Gallery, Univ Warrwick, UK, 2001; plus others. *Teaching:* Prof visual arts, Univ Calif, San Diego, 75-. *Awards:* Dorothy Arzner Spec Recognition Award, 16th Ann Crystal Awards, Women in Film, 91; Guggenheim Fel, 97; Nat Found Jewish Culture Media Achievement Award, 98; and others. *Bibliog:* Eleanor Munro (auth), Originals: American Women Artists, Simon & Schuster, 79; Frantisck Deak (auth), Eleanor Antin: Before the revolution: Acting as an art paradigm, Images & Issues, 1-2/84; Henry Sayre (auth), The Object of Performance: The American Avante Garde Since 1970, Univ Chicago Press, 89; Howard Fox (auth) Desire and destiny in the art of Eleanor Antin, Eleanor Antin, Los Angeles Co Mus Art, 99; Leah Ollman (auth) Art in Am, 2/2000. *Media:* Performance; Video & Film, Installation Photography. *Publ:* Auth, Autobiography of the artist as an autobiographer, J Los Angeles Inst Contemp Art, 10/74; Some thoughts on autobiography & Olga Feodorova's story, winter 78-79 & A romantic interlude from: Recollections of My Life with Diaghilev, summer 80, Sun & Moon; Being Antinova, Astro Artz Press, 83; Eleanora Antinova Plays, Sun & Moon, 94; 100 Boots, Running Press, 99. *Dealer:* Ronald Feldman Fine Arts 31 Mercer St New York NY 10013; Electronic Arts Intermix New York NY; Milestone Film and Video Harrington Park NJ. *Mailing Add:* PO Box 1147 Del Mar CA 92014

ANTOINETTA, GRECO
PAINTER, PRINTMAKER
b Corigliano Calabro, Italy, Aug 26, 49; US citizen. *Study:* Self taught in Mus of Italy; State Univ NY, BFA, 88; Kington Sch Art, with Nick Buhalis, 92. *Work:* Gen Media Bldg, NY; Marcus Bloom Gallery, New Rochell; Nynex Tel. *Comn:* Family Portrait, Penthouse Publ, NY, 89. *Exhib:* Faber Birren, Stamford Art Asn, 93 & 94; Nat Asn Women Artists, NY, 94; Equestrian Images, Trotting Horse Mus, Goshen, NY, 94; Nat Printmaking traveling exhib, 95; Women Conf, Beijing, China, 96; and others. *Pos:* Exec dir, Mid Hudson Art & Sci Mus, formerly. *Teaching:* Instr, Dutchess Community Col; estab sch fine art for children. *Awards:* Grant, Dutchess Co Art Coun, 93-94. *Bibliog:* Michael McCarthney (interviewer), Media One; Linda LaBrise (auth), Meet the artist, Times Herald-Record, Middletown; Expressions of beauty wonder, Poughkeepsie J. *Mem:* Nat Asn Women Artists; Artists Equity; Orgn Independent Artists. *Media:* Oil, Watercolor. *Publ:* Auth, Art is Missing, Hudson Valley Children, 94

ANTOKAL, GALE
PAINTER
b New York, NY, June 5, 51. *Study:* Long Island Univ, BA, 72; Calif Col Arts & Crafts, BFA, 80, MFA, 84. *Work:* McDonald's Corp, San Jose, Calif; Brobeck, Thlager & Harrington, San Francisco, Calif; Stephen Oliver Collection, Orinda, Calif. *Exhib:* 110 Pots, Untitled, San Francisco, Calif, 91; Weintraub Thomas Gallery, Sacramento, Calif, 95, 98; Couturier Gallery, Los Angeles, Calif, 97, 2000, 01; Patricia Sweetow Gallery, San Francisco, 97, 98, 99; Weintraib Thomas Gallery, Sacramento, Calif, 97. *Teaching:* Instr art, San Jose State Univ, 86-2000; Prof of art, San Jose State Univ, 2002. *Awards:* Visual Art Fel, Nat Endowment Arts, 91-92. *Specialty:* contemporary art. *Dealer:* Patricia Sweetow 46 Geary St San Francisco Calif 94108; Coutuier Gallery Los Angeles Calif 90036. *Mailing Add:* 1054 Spruce St Berkeley CA 94707

ANTOL, JOSEPH (JAY) JAMES
SCULPTOR, CONCEPTUAL ARTIST
b Rexis, Pa, May 2, 47. *Study:* Old Dominion Univ, BFA, 78, MFA, 84; Tamarind Inst, 81. *Work:* Old Dominion Univ, Norfolk, Va. *Exhib:* Still Alive in 85, LAS, Modesto, Calif, 85; Now That We're Home, Art Consortium, Art Ctr, Cincinnati, Ohio, 86; Bookworks, WPA, Washington, DC, 86; Les Hommes, TAG Gallery, D'art Ctr, 87, Va Artists, 88, Peninsula Fine Arts Ctr, 88, Va Comn Arts, 1708 Gallery, 88 & Irene Leach Mem, Chrysler Mus, Va, 88; Visual Arts Home, Ctr UNICEF, Atlanta, Ga, 88. *Teaching:* instr printing drawing, Old Dominion Univ, 81-84; instr lithography, Hampton Univ, 86; instr drawing, Governor's Sch Arts, 88-89. *Awards:* Old Dominion Univ fel, 84; D'art Ctr Fel, 86-87; Va Commission/Arts, State Va, 88. *Bibliog:* Joseph Perrin (auth), Visual Arts for the Home, Southern Homes, 88. *Mem:* Peninsula Fine Art Ctr; Artist Against Hunger; Va Beach Arts Ctr. *Media:* Installation, All Media. *Mailing Add:* 2565 Shore Dr Virginia Beach VA 23451-1452

ANTONAKOS, STEPHEN
SCULPTOR
b Greece, Nov 1, 26; US citizen. *Work:* Whitney Mus Am Art, Mus Mod Art, Guggenheim Mus, NY; Milwaukee Art Ctr, Wis; La Jolla Mus, Calif; Neon for Granpark, Tokyo, 96; Neon Lintel, Neuberger Mus, State Univ NY, Purchase, 97. *Comn:* Neons for Buttonwood, Philadelphia, Pa, 90; Neons for Pershing Sq, Art in Transit Prog, Los Angeles, Calif; Neons for Momochi, Fukuoka City, Japan; Neons for Messe Turm, Frankfurt, 93; Neons for Tachikawa, Tokyo, Japan, 94; and others. *Exhib:* Contemp Am Sculpture Ann, Whitney Mus Am Art, 70; Works in Spaces, San Francisco Mus Art, 73; A Shade of Light, San Francisco Mus Art, Downtown Ctr, 78; Site Sculpture Proj, Joslyn Art Mus, Omaha, 78; Minimal Tradition, Aldrich Mus Contemp Art, Ridgefield, Conn, 79; solo shows, Rose Art Mus, Brandeis Univ, 86, Ileana Tounta Contemp Art Ctr, Athens, Greece, 88 & 92, Galerie d'Art Contemp, Geneva, 90, Macedonian Mus Mod Art, Salonika, Greece, 93, Werner H Kramarsky, NY, 95, Art Inst Boston, 96, Samuel P Harn Mus Art, Gainesville, Fla & Smith Col Mus Art, Northampton, Mass, 97; Neons & Collages, Ileana Tounta Contemp Art Ctr, Athens, 89; Architectural Art, Am Crafts Mus, 88. *Teaching:* Vis artist, Yale Univ, fall 68; artist-in-residence, sculpture, Univ Wis-Madison, spring 71 & Fresno State Col, fall 71. *Awards:* NY State Creative Artists Pub Serv Prog Grant; Individual Artist's Grant, Nat Endowment Arts, 73. *Mem:* Nat Acad. *Media:* Neon. *Mailing Add:* 435 W Broadway New York NY 10012-5902

ANTONI, JANINE
SCULPTOR
b Freeport, Bahamas, Jan 19, 64. *Study:* Sarah Lawrence Col, Bronxville, NY, BA, 86; RI Sch Design, Providence, MFA(sculpture, hons), 89. *Exhib:* Israel Mus, Jerusalem, 92; Whitney Mus Am Art Biennial, 93; Aldrich Mus Contemp Art, 93; Mus Contemp Art, Seoul, Korea, 93; Kunsthaus Zurich, Switz, 94; Joslyn Art Mus, 94; Mus Fine Arts, Boston, 94; solo exhibs, Irish Mus Mod Art, Dublin, 95, Ctr Contemp Arts, Glasgow, Scotland, 95, High Mus Art, 96, Wadsworth Atheneum, 96, Sala Monicada de Fundacio "la Calxa", Barcelona, 96, Whitney Mus Am Art, NY, 98, Luhring Augustine, NY, 99, Aldrich Mus, 01, Woldenberg Art Ctr, Tulane Univ, New Orleans, 02, Site Santa Fe, NMex, 02-03; Glen Dimplex Award Exhib, Irish Mus Mod Art, Dublin, 96; Nowhere, La Mus, Denmark, 96; Hugo Boss Price, Solomon R Guggenheim Mus, 96; Three Legged Race, Harlem Fire House, NY, 96; Rrose is a Rrose is a Rrose, Guggenheim Mus, NY & Andy Warhol Mus, Pittsburgh, Pa, 97; On Life, Beauty, Translations and other Difficulties, 5th Int Istanbul Biennial, Turkey, 97; Looking at Ourselves: Works by Women Artist from the Logan Collection, San Francisco Mus Mod Art, 99; The Am Century: Art & Cult 1950-2000, Whitney Mus Am Art, 99; Open Ends: Minimalism and After, Art at MoMA since 1980, Mus of Modern Art, NY, 2000; Inst Contemp Art, 02-03; Portland Inst Contemp Art, 02, 03; James Cohan Gallery, NY, 03. *Awards:* MacArthur Found Fel, 98; Joan Mitchell Found Painting & Sculptor Grant, 98; New Media Award, ICA, Boston, 99. *Bibliog:* Kay Larson (auth), Women's work (or is it art?) is never done, NY Times, 1/7/96; Holland Cotter (auth), 3 legged race, Janine Antoni, Marcel Odenbach, Nari Ward, NY Times, 9/27/96; Holland Cotter (auth), A Soho sampler: Short list for prize, NY Times, 11/22/96. *Dealer:* Luhring Augustine 531 W 24th St New York NY 10011. *Mailing Add:* Luhring Augustine Gallery 531 W 24th St New York NY 10011

ANTREASIAN, GARO ZAREH
PAINTER, EDUCATOR
b Indianapolis, Ind, Feb 16, 1922. *Study:* Herron Sch Art, BFA, 1948; studied with Stanley William Hayter & Will Barnet; Ind Univ-Purdue Univ at Indianapolis, DFA (hon), 1972. *Hon Degrees:* DFA Indiana/Perdue Univ, Indianapolis, 72. *Work:* Metrop Mus Art, Mus Mod Art, Guggenheim Mus, NY; Art Inst Chicago; Los Angeles Co Mus Art, Calif; Brooklyn Mus; Boston Mus. *Comn:* History of Indiana University, Bloomington, Ind, 54; Lincoln in Indiana (with Ralph Peck), Ind State Off Bldg, Indianapolis, 63. *Exhib:* Tamarind: Homage to Lithography, Mus Mod Art, NY, 69; Pace Gallery, NY, 91; Albuquerque Mus, 91; Worcester Art Mus, 91; Rettig/Martinez Gallery, 81, 91 & 92; Retrospective, Indianapolis Mus Art, 94 & 95; Gerald Peters Gallery, Santa Fe, 2006; Fresno Mus Art, 2006; Cars Antreas an, written on stone catalogue raisonne print, 1994-1995. *Pos:* Tech dir lithography, Tamarind Lithography Workshop, Inc, Los Angeles, 60-61, Tamarind Inst, Univ NMex, 70-72; dir, Col Art Asn Am, 73-80 & World Print Coun, 80-87; bd dir, Albuquerque Mus, 80-90; printmaker, emer Southern Graphics Coun, 1994. *Teaching:* Instr, Herron Sch Art, 48-64; prof art, Univ NMex, 64-87, chmn, Dept Art, 81-84; vis lectr, artist numerous univs; Fulbright vis lectr, Univ São Paulo and Found Armando Alvares Penteado, Brazil, 1985. *Awards:* Visual Artists Grant, Nat Endowment Arts, 82-83; Fulbright lectr, Brazil, 85; NMex Snn Gov's Award, 87; fel Nat Acad Design, New York City, 1993. *Bibliog:* James Waterous (auth), A Century of American Printmaking, 84; Riva Castleman (auth), American Impressions: Prints Since Pollock, 85; Printmaking in New Mexico 1980-1990, Clinton Adams, 91. *Mem:* World Print Coun (bd dir 80-87); Nat Print Coun Am (copress, 80-82); Col Art Asn Am (bd dir 77-80); Nat Acad Design (assoc, 93, acad, 94). *Media:* Painting, Lithography. *Publ:* coauth, The Tamarind Book of Lithography: Art & Techniques, 71; Some thoughts about printmaking & print publications, Art J, Col Art Asn, spring 80; Garo Z Antreasian: A Retrospective 1942-1987, Albuquerque Mus, 88; Garo Z Antreasian: A Retrospective Exhibition of Lithographs, Univ NMex Press, 93. *Dealer:* Lewallen Contemp Art 129 W Palace Santa Fe NM 87501; Spotted Horse Gallery 525 E Cooper Ave Aspen CO 81611; Fenix Gallery 228-B Paseo del Pueblo Norte Taos NM 87571. *Mailing Add:* 9400 Freedon Way NE Albuquerque NM 87109-6311

ANTRIM, CRAIG KEITH
PAINTER, DRAFTSMAN
b Pasadena, Calif, Sept 6, 42. *Study:* Univ Calif, Santa Barbara, Ford Found Experimental Prog Instrs Col, Europ study, 63-65, hons prog, 63-65, BA(art, with hons), 65; Claremont Grad Sch, Calif State Fel, 69-70 & MFA(painting & drawing), 70. *Work:* Mus Mod Art & Whitney Mus Am Art, NY; San Francisco Mus Mod Art; Corcoran Gallery Art, Washington; Los Angeles Co Mus Art, Calif; Palm Springs Desert Mus. *Comn:* Float Light (canvas), Los Angeles Co/Univ Southern Calif Med Credit Union, Los Angeles, 77; Painting, Fairmont Hotel, San Jose, Calif; Painting, Emerald Schaffer Ctr, San Diego, Calif; Los Angeles Co Univ S Calif Med Credit Union, Los Angeles, Calif. *Exhib:* Spiritual in Art/Abstract Painting 1890-1985 (catalog), Los Angeles Co Mus Art, traveling to Haags Gemeentemus, The Neth, 87; solo exhibs, Works Gallery, Long Beach, Calif, 90 & 92, Restaurant Lozano, Sierra Madre, Calif, 93, LACA Gallery, Los Angeles, 93, Pasadena City Col, Calif, 93, Gallery 317, Venice, Calif, 94 & Phoenix Gallery, Santa Monica, Calif, 95; Shape of Abstraction, Luckman Fine Arts Ctr, Los Angeles, 95; Nature Finds/Abstraction, Korean Cult Ctr, Los Angeles, 95; Celebrating New Beginnings, Artworks, Riverside, Calif, 96; Calif Painters, Ash Kenazy Gallery, Los Angeles, 96; Blessings & Beginnings, Skirball Cult Ctr, Los Angeles, 96. *Pos:* Studio Asst, Dockum Mobil-Color Proj System, Altadena, Calif, 68-70. *Teaching:* Instr, Univ Fla, Gainesville, 70-72; asst prof color & design, Scripps Col, Claremont, Calif, 74-76; instr painting & myth, Univ S Cal, Los Angeles, 89-90, instr painting, 91; instr painting, drawing, design & art apprec, El Camino Col, Torrance, Calif, 74-92; instr painting & drawing, Harbor Col, Wilmington, Calif, 75-92; instr adv painting workshop, Otis/Parsons Sch Art, Los Angeles, Calif, 86-92; vis artist/grad supv, Claremont Grad Sch, Claremont, Calif, 75-76, 88 & 92; vis asst prof painting & drawing, Loyola Marymount Univ, Los Angeles, Calif, 92-93. *Bibliog:* Mario Cutajar (auth), The slow growth alternative, Artweek, Vol 22, No 32, 91; Nancy Kapitanoff (auth), Up close & personal, Los Angeles Times, Valley ed, 2/18/94; Edward Lucie-Smith (auth), Artoday, Phaidon, Oxford, Gt Brit, 96; Kinney Littlefield (auth), Meaningful mystery in spiritual objects, Long Beach Press Telegram, 8/25/91; Mario Cutajar (auth), The slow growth alternative, Artweek, Vol 22, No 32, p17, 91; Nancy Kapitanoff (auth), Up Close & Personal, Los Angeles Times, 2/18/94. *Media:* Acrylic, Oil. *Publ:* Auth, Color Consciousness: Seven Los Angeles Artists (catalog), Lang Art Galleries, 78. *Dealer:* John Thomas Gallery 1831 Colorado Ave Santa Monica CA 90404; 317 Gallery 1208 Abbot Kinney Blvd Venice CA 90291. *Mailing Add:* 1129 N LaBrea Ave Inglewood CA 90302

ANUSZKIEWICZ, RICHARD JOSEPH
PAINTER, SCULPTOR
b Erie, Pa, May 23, 30. *Study:* Cleveland Inst Art, BFA, 53; Yale Univ, MFA, 55; Kent State Univ, BSEd, 56. *Work:* Corcoran Gallery Art, Washington, DC; Fogg Art Mus; Mus Mod Art, Guggenheim Mus, Metrop Mus Art & Whitney Mus Am Art, NY; Philadelphia Mus Art; Art Inst Chicago; Albright-Knox Gallery, Buffalo, NY; Smithsonian Inst, Washington, DC. *Comn:* Mural, comn by Univ Medicine &

Dentistry, NJ, 85; Astral Squares, comn by Newark Int Airport, NJ, 88; Chroma Avenue, NJ State Dept Transportation Bldg, Trenton, NJ, 89; Complimentary Reversal-Yellows, Oranges & Reds, Aidekman Ctr Molecular & Behavioral Neurosci, Rutgers Univ, NJ, 92; ASTRAL (mosaic tile floor media medallion, 20' in diameter), Washington Nat Airport, DC, 97. *Exhib:* One-man shows, Brooklyn Mus, 80, Abante Fine Art, Portland, Ore, 92, Ctr Arts, Vero Beach, Fla, 93, Camino Real Gallery, Boca Raton, Fla, 93, Williams Ctr Arts, Lafayette Col, Easton, Pa, 94, Richard Anuszkiewicz: Paintings and Painted Constructions-A Retrospective Survey From 1954 to 1995, Josef Albers Mus, Quadrat im Stadtgarten, Bottrop, Landesmuseum fur Kunst und Kulturgeschichte, Oldenburg & Stadtische Kunstsammlungen, Chemnitz, Ger, 97 & Haus fur konkrete und konstruktive Kunst, Zurich, Switz & Wilhelm Hack Mus, Ludwigshaven, Ger, 98, Okla Harris Gallery, 2000, ACA Gallery, NY, 2003, David Finday Jr Gallery, New York City, 2005; Guggenheim Mus, NY, 82, 87 & 88; Black & White, World Known Constructivist Artists, Cult & Cong Ctr, Ljubljana, Slovenija, 94; Triennale '94 Krakow, Int Print Triennial Soc, Krakow, Poland, 94; Gli Anni Sessanta-Le Immaginial Poteree, Fondazione Mazzotta, Milano, Italy, 96; Paintings from the Permanent Collection, Mus Contemp Art San Diego, La Jolla, Calif, 97; Painting with an Edge, A Historical Perspective, Hunterdon Mus Art, Clinton, NJ, 98. *Teaching:* Artist-in-residence, Dartmouth Col, 67; instr, Univ Wis, 68, Cornell Univ, 68 & Kent State Univ, 68; instr grad painting, Sch Visual Arts, 83-86. *Awards:* Philosopher's Stone Prize, 63 & First Prize, 64, Silvermine Guild; Florsheim Grant, Florsheim Found, 94; Cert Recognition, NY State Art Teachers Asn, 94. *Bibliog:* Karl Lunde (auth), Anuskiewicz, Abrams, 77. *Mem:* Am Abstract Artists; Century Club; Polish Inst Arts & Sci; Nat Acad (assoc, 92, acad, 94). *Media:* All. *Dealer:* David Findlay Jr Gallery New York City; Harmon-Meek Gallery Naples FL; Gallery Carmino Real Boca Raton FL. *Mailing Add:* 76 Chestnut St Englewood NJ 07631

ANZIL, DORIS
PAINTER, SCULPTOR
b Colchester, Vt. *Study:* City Univ New York, BA & MA, 68; NY Univ-Columbia Univ, 68-69; studies in Switz, France & Ger, 70-80. *Work:* Am Cult Inst Gallery in Amerika Haus, Siemens Gallery (Siemens Corp), Haus der Kunst (Mus Contemp Art), Munich, Ger; Brooklyn Mus, NY; Philadelphia Mus Art, Pa. *Comn:* Mural, comn by Dr F Occhionero, Munich, Ger, 81; mural, comn by Dr Von Heusinger, CEO, Siemens Corp, Munich, Ger, 82; mural, Rennert Sch Lang, NY, 84; large painting, comn by RC Archdiocese, Brooklyn, NY, 90; large scale painting, Waverly Sch, Brooklyn, NY, 91. *Exhib:* Solo exhibs, Regensburg Mus, Ger, 80, Maryland Univ Annex, Ger, 81, Am Inst, Munich, Ger, 82, Volker Kundes Mus, Munich, Ger, 84, Wisteria Artspace, Brooklyn, 95; and others; Brooklyn Artists, Brooklyn Mus, NY, 85; Artist Teacher, Lincoln Ctr, Avery Fisher Hall, 94, Cork Gallery, 96; Third Independents Biennial, NY, 96; Art in the Park, Queens Mus, Flushing, 96; Ct St Gallery, Brooklyn, NY, 97; Broom St Gallery, Soho, NY, 97; Avery Fisher Hall, Lincoln Ctr, NY, 97; Growanus Community Arts, Brooklyn, NY, 98; Grand St Gallery, Soho, NY, 98; Independants Biennial IV, NY, 98; Cork Gallery, Lincoln Ctr, NY, 98. *Bibliog:* Dianne Copelon (auth), Doris Anzil: An American artist, Ger Television Film, 81; Doris Schmidt (auth), Review-Doris Anzil, Suddentsche Zeitung, 81; Ingo Glass (auth), Haidhausen Artists, Munich Cultural Affairs Municipality, Lenbach Mus Art-Art Forum, 82. *Mem:* Artists Equity; New York City Artists Teacher Asn. *Media:* All Media. *Mailing Add:* 943 President St Brooklyn NY 11215

AOKI, CAROLE I
CERAMIST
b Salt Lake City, Utah. *Study:* Univ Utah, Salt Lake City, 69-71; Calif Col Arts & Crafts, Oakland, BFA, 77. *Work:* Munic Anchorage Capital Projs, Performing Arts Ctr, Alaska; Everson Mus, Syracuse, NY; Upjohn, Kalamazoo, Mich; IBM, Raleigh, NC; Franklin Mint, Pa; numerous pvt & corp collections. *Exhib:* Solo shows, Joyce Petter Gallery, Sangatuck, Minn, 87, Andrea Schwartz Gallery, San Francisco, Calif, 89, Works Gallery, Philadelphia, Pa, 90 & Worth Gallery, Taos, NMex, 92 & 95; Charles A Wustum Mus Fine Arts, Racine, Wis, 93; Int Ceramics Exhib Ceramic, Czech Repub, 94; NY, NY: Clay, Oslo, Norway, 96; Japanese Ceramics, Arlington Mus Arts, Tex, 96. *Pos:* Dir ceramic dept, Berkeley Parks & Recreation & Ctr Blind, Oakland, Calif, 72-74. *Teaching:* Lect/workshop, var art ctrs, art coun, univ & col, 85-89; instr ceramics, 92nd St Y, 90 & 91; guest lectr, Teacher's Col, Columbia Univ, 91; prof ceramics, Marymount Manhattan Col, NY, 94 & adj prof, 94. *Awards:* Ceramic Art Award, Calif Mus Art, Luther Burbank Ctr Arts, Santa Rosa, 89; Artist-in-residence, Lakeside Studio, Lakeside Group, Mich; Visual Arts Fel, Nat Endowment Arts, 90-91. *Bibliog:* American Craft, Gallery, Vol 52, No 4, 8-9/92; Judy Rowland (auth), The Craftperson Speaks, Greenwood Press, 92; American Craft Gallery, Vol 53, 12/93-1/94. *Media:* Clay, Mixed. *Mailing Add:* 2231 Broadway New York NY 10024

APESOS, ANTHONY
PAINTER, CRITIC
b Newark, NJ, Jan 6, 53. *Study:* Vassar Col, BA, 75; Pa Acad Fine Arts, cert, 79; Bard Col, MFA, 91. *Work:* Summit Art Ctr, NJ; Sacred Heart Hosp, Chester, Pa; Mt Alvernia Col, Reading, Pa; Emerson Col, Boston, Mass; Tufts Univ Med Sch, Boston. *Comn:* Employee's Cafeteria (mural), Meredian Hotel, Boston, 96; numerous portrait commissions. *Exhib:* Sole exhibs, More Gallery, Philadelphia, 83, 85, 86 & 91, M Dunev Gallery, San Francisco, 87 & Fan Gallery, Philadelphia, 92, 94, 95 & 97, 2001, Andrea Marquit, 97 & Univ Mass, Boston, 98; Figure in Landscape, Artists Choice Mus, NY, 85; Myth & Symbol, Pa State Univ, 86; Ann Exhib, Nat Acad Design, NY, 86; Four Contemp Artists, Allentown Art Mus, Pa, 87. *Teaching:* Lectr painting & drawing, Univ of the Arts, 83-86; asst prof, Moore Col Art, 86-92; assoc prof painting, Art Inst Boston, Lesley Univ, 1992-, chair fine arts, 1992-98, acting dir MFA program in visual arts, Art Inst Boston, 2002-. *Awards:* Purchase Prize, Art Quest, 87; Kress Found Traveling Fel, Phila Col Art, 87; New Eng Found Arts Fel, 96; Faculty Dev Grant, Lesley Univ, 99. *Bibliog:* Victoria Donahue (auth), review, Philadelphia Inquirer, 2/4/89; Tom Cezar (auth), review, New Art Examiner, 3-4/93; Edward Sozanski (auth), review, Philadelphia Inquirer, 7/24/94. *Mem:* Col Art Asn; Copley Soc. *Media:* Oil. *Res:* history of artists' techniques. *Interests:* anatomy, botany. *Publ:* Auth, Re-affirming values through the depiction of space, New Art Examiner, 80; The Parkway Madonna, New Art Examiner, 83; Contemporary realist drawing, New Art Examiner, 83; coauth, Raising the reserve: PMA hosts J Johns Show, New Art Examiner, 89. *Dealer:* FAN Gallery, Philadelphia. *Mailing Add:* 366 Arborway Jamaica Plain MA 02130

APGAR, JEAN E
PAINTER, PRINTMAKER
b Rockford, Ill, May 19, 49. *Study:* Northern Ill Univ, BA, 71, MA, 78. *Work:* Swed Am Hosp, Rockford, Ill; Crusader Clinic, Rockford, Ill; Kishwaukee Col, Malta, Ill; Winn Co Title Co, Rockford, Ill; Realism or Not, UIC Community Gallery, Rockford, Ill, 2000, Animal Imagery, 2000; plus others; US Ambassadorial Residence, Niamey, Niger, 99-2002, & Rangoon, Burma, 2002-05. *Comn:* Rose Day (serigraph), Rockford Breakfast Lions, Ill, 80 & 92. *Exhib:* All on Paper Nat, Columbia Green Col, Palenville, NY, 82; Nat Asn Women Artists Traveling Print Exhib, USA, 84-86; Nat Drawing Exhib, Bergen Community Mus, Paramus, NJ, 84; Naturally, Earth, Sea & Sky, Adelphi Univ, NY, 91; Prairie Ctr Arts, Schaumburg, Ill, 92; Int Exhib Animals Art, La State Univ, Baton Rouge, 96; Silk Painters Int, Fairfax, Va, 98; one-woman shows incl Gallery 451, Rockford, Ill, 94 & 95, North Suburban Dist Libr, Loves Park, Ill, 2001; group shows incl Womanspace Traveling Exhib, 2000-01, Animal Imagery, Burpee Nat Hist Mus, Rockford, 2002 & Animals, Wild and Otherwise, Sinsinawa Mounds Center, Wis, 2003; juried shows incl Silk Painters Int, Fairfax, Va, 2000, 26th Ann Fiber and Textile Exhib, Whitewater, Wis, 2002 & Masterpieces of Maturity, Lexington, Ky, 2002, Bead Int '06, Athens, OH, 2006, Silk Painters Int, Santa Fe, NMex, 2006. *Pos:* Chmn, spec events, Beattie Is Festival, Rockford, Ill, 79-80; pres, Images/4, Rockford, Ill, 80-84; partner/publicist, Gallery Ten, Rockford, Ill, 90-94. *Teaching:* Instr drawing painting, Rock Valley Col, Rockford, Ill, 72-79. *Mem:* assoc mem Nat Watercolor Soc; Rockford Area Arts Coun; Silk Painters Int. *Media:* Watercolor, Silk, Embroidery. *Publ:* Approaching Galleries, Art Calendar, 4/92; coauth, Now What? This Art Business (artists' business manual), Jester Publ, 94. *Mailing Add:* 2513 Knight Ave Rockford IL 61101

APP, TIMOTHY
PAINTER, EDUCATOR
b Akron, Ohio, July 5, 47. *Study:* Kent State Univ, BFA, 70; Tyler Sch Art, MFA, 74. *Work:* Univ NMex Art Mus, Albuquerque; Mus Albuquerque, NMex; Roswell Mus & Art Ctr, NMex; Mus Fine Arts, Santa Fe, NMex; Archer M Huntington Gallery, Univ Tex, Austin. *Exhib:* Geometric Formalism in Am Art, Univ NMex, 82; Phoenix Biennial, Phoenix Art Mus, 83; Linda Durham Gallery, 83-92, 20-Year Survey, 89, Santa Fe, NMex; Roswell Mus, NMex, 85; Mus Albuquerque, NMex, 84, 87, 90, 92 & 93; Mus Fine Arts, Santa Fe, 88; Anthony Ralph Gallery, NY, 87-92; Archer M Huntington Gallery, Univ Tex, Austin, 88; Five New Painters, John Davis Gallery, NY, 89; & many others. *Teaching:* Asst prof painting, Pomona Col, 74-78; assoc prof, Univ NMex, Albuquerque, 78-90; prof art, Md Inst Col Art, 90-. *Awards:* Mellon Grant, Pomona Col, 78; Univ NMex Res Grant, 82, 83, 87; Nat Endowment Arts Fel, 87-88. *Bibliog:* Kathleen Sheild (auth), Timothy App at Linda Durham, Art Am, 89; John Dorssey (auth), Art Rev, Baltimore Sun, 94, 97 & 98; & others. *Media:* Acrylic

APPEL, ERIC A
SCULPTOR, PAINTER
b Brooklyn, NY, Dec 26, 1945. *Study:* Pratt Inst, 63-67, BID, 67; Tyler Sch Art, Rome, 67-68; Tyler Sch Art, Temple Univ, Philadelphia, Pa, MFA(painting), 70. *Exhib:* Garden of Delight, Cooper-Hewitt Mus, NY, 81; Spring Garden, Yves Arman Gallery, NY, 81; solo exhibs, Winter Garden, Queens Mus, NY, 81, Joy Horwich Gallery, Chicago, Ill, 83, Field Mus Nat Hist & Chicago Sculpture Int Navy Pier, 83-84 & Windows on Broadway, NY Univ, 85, OK Harris, NY, 91. *Bibliog:* Beth Fallow (auth), Make yourself at home in the mansion gardens, Daily News, 7/24/81; Robin Brentano & Mark Savitt (auth), 112 Workshop, 112 Green St, NY Univ Press, 81. *Media:* Mixed. *Mailing Add:* 102 Christopher St New York NY 10014

APPEL, KEITH KENNETH
SCULPTOR, MURALIST
b Bricelyn, Minn, May 21, 34. *Study:* Mankato State Col, BA, BS & MS; Ohio State Univ, PhD. *Comn:* Sculpture, Alaska Art in Public Places, 81-2002; sculpture, Anchorage C of C, 81; sculpture, Anchorage Art in Public Places; sculpture, Fairbanks Art in Public Places; sculpture, State Courthouse, Fairbanks, 2001; Mural, Lathrop High School, Fairbanks, 99; sculpture, Eilson Air Force Base, Fairbanks, 98; sculpture, Chugiak/Eagle River Middle School, 97. *Exhib:* All Alaska Exhib, 64-80; Alaska Centennial, 67; solo exhibs, Stonington Gallery, Anchorage, 85, Volcano Nat Park, Hawaii, 85, Anchorage Historical & Fine Arts Mus, 70, 75, The Gathering, Ketchikan, Alaska, 80, 82; Alaskan Smithsonian Exhib, 78; Earth, Fire & Fibre Exhibit, Anchorage, 97-99. *Pos:* Chmn art dept, Univ Alaska, Anchorage, 78-81. *Teaching:* Assoc prof art, Univ Alaska, Anchorage, 70-78; retired. *Awards:* Alaska Centennial, 67; All Alaska Juried Exhibition Awards, var times, 67-77. *Mem:* Alaska Artists Guild; Alaska State Arts Coun (mem bd); Nat Art Educ Asn. *Media:* Miscellaneous. *Interests:* architectural scales sculpture, murals. *Mailing Add:* 4705 Malibu Dr Anchorage AK 99517-3273

APPEL, THELMA
PAINTER, INSTRUCTOR
b Tel Aviv, Israel, Jan 6, 40; US citizen. *Study:* St Martins Sch Art, London, dipl art & design, 61; Hornsey Col Art, London, art teacher's dipl, 62. *Work:* Milwaukee Arts Ctr, Wis; Am Tel & Tel Co, NY & Summit, NJ; Chase-Manhattan Bank & Metrop Life Co, NY; Vt State Legislature, Montpelier; Port Authority, NY; IBM Corp,

Lawrence, NJ; Bank of Toyko, NY; Xerox Corp, NY; Cabot Corp, Boston, Mass; Hale & Dore Assocs, Boston; Prudential Collection, NY. *Comn:* Five paintings, Western Corp Bldg, Dallas, Tex, 80; two paintings, Hospital Insurance Co, Grand Prairie, Tex, 85; two paintings, Farm Credit Bank, Austin, Tex, 85. *Exhib:* Solo shows Adelle M Gallery Fine Art, Dallas, Tex, Fischbach Gallery, NY, 79, 82 & Weschester Co Ctr, White Plains, NY, 92, Sacred Spaces, JCC of Greater New Haven, 99, Cabrini Art Gallery Cabrini Hospital, Hastings on Hudson, 2000, Daniels Art Gallery, HRCA, Boston, 2000, 2001; Realism Today, Clary Miner Gallery, Buffalo, NY, 87; Int Art Competition, Pyramid Gallery, NY, 90; Current River View, Hastings Creative Arts Coun, NY, 91; Neighbors, Krasdale Foods Art Gallery in conjunction with Lehman Col Art Gallery, 92; Face to Face, Paramount Ctr Arts, Peekskill, NY, 98; and others. *Teaching:* Instr, Southern Vermont Col, 75-76 & Parsons Sch Art, 76-77; Summer Painting Workshop, Bennington Col, 76-83; Northern Westchester Ctr Arts, 89-95; Putnam Arts Coun, 90-96. *Awards:* Vt Coun Arts Award, 73; Yaddo Residency fel, 74; State of Vt Purchase Award, Vt Coun Arts & Nat Endowment Arts, 78; Jury Award, JCC Greater New Haven, 99. *Bibliog:* Gabrielle V Arnhem (auth), American Romantic Painting, Art Ger, 80; Sunday Times (Westchester Sect), 10/4/92; Judy Birke (auth), New Haven Regist, 5/10/98. *Mem:* Minneapolis Art Inst, Minn, IBM Corp (NJ), Metropolitan Life Corp, MCI Telecommuncations, GTE Corp, Chase Manhattan Bank, Bank of Tokyo, Nyncx Corp, Xerox Corp, Fed Reserve Bank, Boston, RJR Industries, Winston-Salem, NC, Cabot Corp, Ziff-Davis Publishing, NY, Hale & Dorr Attorneys, Richard Greene-The Greene Gallery, Guilford, Conn. *Media:* Oil, Acrylic

APPELSON, HERBERT J
EDUCATOR, PRINTMAKER
b Brooklyn, NY, Dec, 31, 37. *Study:* Brooklyn Col, NY, BA, 59; Univ Wis, Madison, MS, 60, MFA, 61; Columbia Univ, NY, EDD, 72. *Work:* Noyes Mus, Oceanville, NJ; Fairmount Inst, Philadelphia, Pa; NJ Dept Treas, Trenton; Atlantic City Office of Cult Affairs, NJ; Edgewood Col, Madison, Wis; Luther Col, Iowa. *Exhib:* solo exhib, ETS Conant Gallery, Princeton, 85 & Artists' House, Philadelphia, Pa, 95; Malaspina Gallery, Granville Island, Vancouver, BC, Can, 98; Int Miniature Print Competition, Graphic Arts Ctr, Noralle, Conn, 99; Am Color Print Soc Ann, Revsin Gallery, Philadelphia, Pa, 2000; Am Col, Bryn Manor, Pa, 2001; Noyes Mus, Oceanville, NJ, 2001; Am Color Print Soc Exhib, 2004 & 05. *Collection Arranged:* Images of Southern New Jersey from the Heartland to the Seashore (with catalog), Hollybush Invitation Art Exhib, 86; American Artists/Russian Roots (with catalog), Hollybush Arts Festival, 87; Light-Chemistry and a Creative Vision (with catalog), Hollybush Arts Festival, 88; Forms to Figure (with catalog), Hollybush Arts Festival, 89; Abstract Art, Intuition-Invention-Expressionism (with catalog), Hollybush Arts Festival, 90. *Teaching:* Prof printmaking & drawing, Rowan Univ, NJ, 67-. *Awards:* Exib Award, Ann Water Color Exhib, Camden Co Cult & Heritage Comn, 2000; Juror Award, Camden Co Cult & Heritage Comn, 2001; First Prize, Philadelphia Plastic Club, 2002. *Bibliog:* Burton Wasserman (auth), Exploring the visual arts, Davis, Worchester, Mass, 76. *Mem:* Philadelphia Watercolor Club; Am Color Print Soc; Cheltenham Printmakers Guild. *Media:* Relief, Mixed Media. *Collection:* Columbia University, NY, Luther College, IA, Edgewood College, Wis, Univ Wis, Kansas State University, NJ Dept of Treasury, NJ, Noyes Museum, NJ, Camden Cpunty Cultural & Heritage Commissions Art Bank, NJ, Auburn University, Al. *Mailing Add:* 17 Highgate Ln Cherry Hill NJ 08003-1824

APPLE, JACKI (JACQUELINE) B
VISUAL, MEDIA AND PERFORMANCE ARTIST, WRITER, PRODUCER
b New York, NY. *Study:* Syracuse Univ; Parsons Sch Design, BFA. *Work:* Martin Luther King Rehabilitation Ctr, Los Angeles, CA; Little Tokyo Branch Pub Libr, Los Angeles, Calif, 97 2005. *Comn:* Urban Suite (soundtrack), Rudy Perez Performance Ensemble, Los Angeles, 84; Swan Lake (a film noir "ballet" for radio), New Am Radio, 88-89; Palisade 1987, Fluctuations of the Field (performance), Santa Monica Arts Comn, 89; Redefining Democracy in America, Parts 1-6 (radio art), New Am Radio, NY, 91, 92; Pub Arts Comn, City of Los Angeles, 97-99; Oakwaood Community Ctr, Venice, Calif; and many others. *Exhib:* Story Art: Recent Am Narrative Traveling Exhib, Contemp Arts Mus, Houston, 77-78; Mus Mod Art, NY, 78; Schemes: A Decade of Installation Drawings Traveling Exhib, Elise Meyer Gallery, NY, 81-82; Sydney Biennale, Australia, 82; Live to Air, Tate Gallery, London, 82; Sonorita Prospettiche Traveling Exhib, Contemp Art Gallery, Rimini, Italy, 82-83; Whitney Mus Philip Morris, NY, 90; Trnasit Art, ORL Television, Innsbruck, Austria, 93; Outside the Frame: Performance, Object, Cleveland Ctr Contemp Art, Ohio, 94; Sound Culture, Auckland, New Zealand, 99; Gloria: Another Leek at Feminist Art of the 1970's, White Columns, NYC, 2002-03; Birdspace, New Orleans Contemp Art Ctr, Norton Mus Art, West Palm Beach Fla, 2004. *Collection Arranged:* Visual and Sculptural Bookworks, Montclair Mus, NJ & Seibu Mus, Tokyo, 79; Artists Bookworks: Alterations and Transformations, Nelson Gallery, Kansas City, Mo, 80; Alternatives in Retrospect: An Historical Overview 1969-1975, New Mus, New York, 81; Art Lobby, Lower Manhattan Cult Coun, New York, 82. *Pos:* Cur exhibs & performances, Franklin Furnace, 77-80; guest cur, New Mus, NY, 81; producer/host, KPFK-FM, Pacifica Radio, Los Angeles, 82-95; freelance writer, 82-; contrib ed, Artweek, 83-90, Los Angeles Wkly, 85-89, High Performance Mag, 84-95 & Media Arts, 83-90; producer/writer, US EAR, 87-88; co-producer, EARJAM new Music Festival, Los Angeles, Calif, 2000-2004. *Teaching:* Instr, Concordia Univ, Montreal, fall 80, Calif State Univ, Long Beach, spring 83 & Otis Art Inst, Los Angeles, 84-85, 90 & Univ Calif, San Diego, 95-99; Adj Prof, Art Ctr Col of Design, Pasadena, CA, 1983- (Faculty Council Repr 2001-2006). *Awards:* Individual Artist Fel, Nat Endowment Arts, 79 & 81, Inter Arts Prog Grant, 84 & 91-92; Individual Artist Grant, Dept Cult Affairs, Los Angeles, 90; Vesta Award, Los Angeles, 90; Artists Fel, California Arts Council, 96; Faculty Enrichment Grant, Art Ctr Coll Design, 2001; Durfee Found, 2002. *Bibliog:* Steven Durland (auth), Sound Philosophies: The audio art of Jacki Apple, High Performance, 84; Douglas Sadownick (auth), Palisade: exploring love as a high art form, Los Angeles Times, 7/28/87; Colin Gardner (auth), Colonialism and postmodernism, Artweek, 9/7/85; and others. *Mem:* Int Asn Art Critics; Nat Writers Union; Col Art Asn. *Media:* Performance Installation, Photography; Audio, Radio. *Publ:* Auth, The Life & Times of Lin Hixson: The LA Years, Drama Rev, winter 91; Voices in the Dark (CD) Aerial, 92; Thank You for Flying American, Stories and Songs 80-91 & 95 (CD); One Word at a Time, Errant Bodies, 95; Ghost Dances/on the Event Horizon (CD), 96; A (auth), A Different World: A Personal History of Franklin Furnace; The Drama Review, Spring 2005; Resurrecting the Disappeared, Art Journal, 97; and others. *Mailing Add:* 3532 Jasmine Ave Apt 2 Los Angeles CA 90034-4947

APPLEBAUM, LEON
GLASS BLOWER, SCULPTOR
b Toledo, Ohio, Dec 19, 45. *Study:* Peabody Col Vanderbilt, MA, 73; Akrahallskollan Orrefors, Sweden, 74; Rochester Inst Technol, MFA, 75-76. *Work:* Wheaton Mus Glass, Millville, NJ; Smithsonian Nat Air Space Mus, Washington, DC; Corning Mus Glass, NY; McDonauch Collection Am Art, Youngstown, Ohio; Patrick Lannen Art Found, Palm Beach. *Comn:* Seventy wine decantors with state seal of Tenn, Tenn Arts Comn, Nashville, 73. *Exhib:* Saenger Nat Sculpture Exhib; Am Contemp Art Glass, Galerie Verrd Art, Montreal, Can; Butler Inst Am Art, Youngstown, Ohio; Crafts Int, Kanazawa, Japan; Glass Int, Kyoto, Japan; NY Craftsman Show, Smithsonian Inst, Washington, DC; Creative Glass Chap Am Fel Exhib, Snyderman Gallery, Philadelphia; Nat Glass Show, Habitat Gallery, Southfield, Mich. *Pos:* Specialty glass blower, Sonaland, Sweden. *Teaching:* Instr glass, Peabody Col Vanderbilt, Nashville & Rochester Inst Technol, NY. *Awards:* Best of Crafts Gold Medal, Toledo Mus Art, Ohio; Best of Show, Miami Beach Art Festival; Creative Glass Chap Am Fel, Millville, NJ. *Bibliog:* Jacquelin Hall (auth), Hawk Gallery Bedazzling (catalog), Columbus Dispatch, 88; Dan Goddard (auth), Breaking into glass, San Antonio Express News, 5/11/96; article in Ceskolipsko, Czech Repub, 5/28/98. *Mem:* Am Craft Asn. *Media:* Glass. *Mailing Add:* c/o Fanny Garver Gallery 230 State St Madison WI 53703

APPLEBROOG, IDA
PAINTER
b Bronx, NY, Nov 11, 29. *Study:* NY State Inst Appl Arts & Sci, 48-50; Sch Art Inst Chicago, 65-68; Parsons Sch Design, Hon Dr, 97. *Work:* Metrop Mus Art, Mus Mod Art, New Mus Contemp Art, Guggenheim Mus, NY; Denver Mus Art; Sol Lewitt Collection, Wadsworth Atheneum, Hartford, Conn. *Exhib:* Solo exhibs, Whitney Mus Am Art, NY, 78, Realistmus Studio, Berlin, Ger, 92, Everything Is Fine, Brooklyn Mus, 93, Ida Applebroog, Orchard Gallery, Derry, N Ireland, Irish Mus Mod Art, Dublin, Ireland & Cubitt St Gallery, London Eng, 94 & Ida Applebroog: Nothing Personal, Paintings 1987-1997 (with catalog), Corcoran Gallery Art, Washington, DC, Pa Acad Fine Arts & Mus Am Art, Philadelphia, 98, Ida Applebroog, Lowe Gallery, Atlanta, Ga, 99, Galerie Nathalie Parientc, Paris, 2000, Ronald Feldman Fine Arts, New York City, 01, 02; Directions 83, Hirshorn Mus, Washington, DC, 83; 23 Nat Print Exhib, Brooklyn, 83; Mus Mod Art, 84; Documenta 8, Kassel, Ger, 87; Prospects: Selected Work from the Collection and Possible Acquisitions, Bavarian State Collection of Paintings, Munich, Ger, 91; Jersey City Mus, NJ, 92; PS 1 Mus, Long Island City, NY, 92; Devil on the Stairs: Looking Back on the Eighties, ICA, Philadelphia, Pa & Newport Harbor Art Mus, Newport Beach, Calif, 92; Parallel Visions: Modern Artists and Outsider Art, Los Angeles Co Mus Art, 92; The Whitney Biennial, Whitney Mus Am Art, NY, 93; Establishing the Legacy, Nat Mus Women Arts, Washington, DC, 94; 43rd Biennial Exhib Contemp Painting, Corcoran Gallery, Washington, DC, 94; 25 Americans: Painting in the 90's, Milwaukee Art Mus, Wisc, 95; Interstices: A(a)rt the A(a)rtist and the A(a)udience, Duke Univ Mus Art, Durham, NC, 96; Extensions: Aspects of the Figure, Joseloff Gallery Univ Hartford, Conn, 98; Urban Mythologies: The Bronx Represented Since the 1960s, Bronx Mus of the Arts, NY, 99; A Sangre y Fuego, Espai d'Art Contemporani de Castello, Girona, Spain, 99; The Am Century: Art and Cult, 1900-2000, Whitney Mus of Am Art, NY, 99; Kagan Martos Gallery, New York City, 2000; Gallery Contemp Art, Lewis and Clark Col, Portland, Oreg, 01; Bernice Steinbaum Gallery, Miami, 01; Julie Saul Gallery, New York City, 01; Ronald Feldman Gallery Fine Arts, New York City, 02, 03; Paule Anglim Gallery, San Francisco, 02; Lowe Gallery, Santa Monica, 02; Contemp Arts Mus, Houston, 03. *Teaching:* Asst painting, Art Inst Chicago, 62-66; instr painting & sculpture, Univ Calif, San Diego, 73-74. *Awards:* Nat Endowment Arts Grants, 80 & 85; Grant, NY Found Arts, 86 & 90; Guggenheim Fel, 90; MacArthur Found Fel, 98. *Bibliog:* Marilyn Zeitlin, Thomas Sokolowski & Lowery Sims (auth, essay), Ida Applebroog: Happy Families, A Fifteen-Year Survey, Contemp Arts Mus, Houston, Tex, 90; Brigitte Reinhardt, Annelie Pohlen, Robert Storr & Carla Schulz-Hoffmann (auths, essay), Ida Applebroog, Ulmer Mus, Bonner Kunstverein & Realismus Studio de Neven Gassellschaft Fur Bildende Kunst, Ulm, Bonn & Berlin, Ger, 91; Terry Sultan (auth, essay), Ida Applebroog: Innocence versus Realite, Galerie Nathalie Pariente, Paris, France, 98. *Media:* Oil on Canvas. *Publ:* Auth, The I am Heathcliffe, says Catherine, syndrome: Women's humor, Heresies, 5/77. *Mailing Add:* c/o Ronald Feldman Fine Arts 31 Mercer St New York NY 10013

APPLEBY, ANNE L
PAINTER, PRINTMAKER
b Pa, Aug 22, 54. *Study:* Univ Mont, BFA, 77; San Francisco Art Inst, MFA, 89. *Work:* San Francisco Mus Mod Art; Berkeley Art Mus, Calif; Holter Mus Art, Helena, Mont; Yellowstone Art Mus; MH de Young Meml Mus, San Francisco, Calif; San Jose Mus of Art, Calif. *Comn:* Palazzo Ducale, Sassoulo, Italy. *Exhib:* SECA, 1996, San Francisco Mus Mod Art, 96; Towards a New Millienium, Berkeley Mus Art, Calif, 97; Like a Prayer (with catalog), Holter Mus Art, Helena, Mont, 98; Littlejohn Contemp, NY, 98; Greg Kucera Gallery, Seattle, 98; Yellowstone Art Mus, 99; San Jose Mus Art, 2000; Am Acad in Rome, Italy, 2000; Nora Eccles Harrison Mus Art, Logan, Utah,

2000; Berkeley Art Mus, Berkeley, Calif, 2000; and others. *Pos:* bd dir, Mont Artist Refuge, Basin. *Teaching:* Instr, San Francisco Art Inst, 93-96. *Awards:* Pollock Krasner Found Award, 91; Southeastern Ctr Contemp Art Award, San Francisco Mus Mod Art, 96; Western States Arts Found Grant, 96; Louis Tiffany Found Biennale Award, 99. *Bibliog:* David Mabscott (auth), Minimilist Mandelas, World Art, 97; Rick Newby (auth), Like a Prayer: Recent Prints and Paintings Catalogue Essay, Holter Mus Art, 98; Robin Updike (auth), The Color of Memory, The Seattle Times, 98; Kenneth Baker (auth), Memory Fields Catalogue Essay, Greg Kuleva Gallery and Paule Anglim Gallery, 2000; The Panza di Biumo Collection: Works from the 80's and 90's, Am Acad in Rome, 2000; Profs Lester K Little, Linda Blumberg, Marlo Franciolli (auth), Giuseppe Panza Di Biumo, 2000. *Media:* Oil. *Dealer:* Gallery Paul Anglim 14 Geary St San Francisco CA 94108; Greg Kucera Gallery Seattle WA. *Mailing Add:* 1076 N Ewing Helena MT 59601-3456

APT, CHARLES
PAINTER, DESIGNER
b New York, NY, Dec 10, 33. *Study:* Pratt Inst, BFA, 56. *Work:* Chem Bank; Bowery Bank; Celanese Corp; Paine, Webber, NY; Principality of Monaco, France; Am Stock Exchange. *Comn:* Painting, Am Stock Exchange, 68; Loring Gallery, Springfield, Mass, 01. *Exhib:* Allied Artists Am, NY, 64, 65, 67 & 69; Am Watercolor Soc, NY, 65, 66, 68 & 69; Nat Acad Design, NY, 65, 68, 73-81, 83, 85, 87 & 99; Exposition Intercontinentale, Monaco, France, 66 & 68; Mus Fine Art, Springfield, Mass, 66; Nat Mus Racing Ann, Saratoga, NY, 67; One-man shows, Loring Gallery, Cederhurst, NY, 85, 87 & 92; Lorings Gallery, Cedarhurst, NY, 85; and many others. *Teaching:* Instr painting & drawing, Nat Acad Design, 77-81 & Art Students League. *Awards:* Best in Show, Saratoga Mus Racing, 67; 2nd Benjamin Altman Award, Nat Acad Design, 68; Le Prix Prince Souverain, Prince Rainier, Monaco, 68. *Bibliog:* Joan Hess Michael (auth), Charles Apt in Portugal, Am Artist Mag, 4/70; Leonard Kriegel (auth), Charles Apt, Arts Mag, 10/78. *Mem:* Nat Acad Design (assoc, 72, acad, 79); Artists Equity Asn, NY. *Media:* All Media. *Interests:* music, woodworking. *Publ:* Auth, article, House Beautiful, Hearst Publ, 2/85. *Dealer:* Dassin Gallery Los Angeles Calif; Loring Gallery Sheffield Mass. *Mailing Add:* Studio 152 S Almont Dr Los Angeles CA 90048

APTEKAR, KEN
PAINTER
b Detroit, Mich, May 13, 50. *Study:* Univ Mich, BFA, 73, Pratt Inst, MFA, 75. *Work:* Corcoran Gallery Art; Denver Mus Art; Progressive Corp; Jewish Mus, NY; Bell Atlantic Corp, Philadelphia; Meml Art Gallery, Rochester, NY; Kemper Mus Contemp Art; Nat Mus of American Art, Washington, DC; Contemp Art Soc, London, 03; Victoria & Albert Mus, London; Harvard Univ Sch of Bus, Boston. *Comn:* Conrad Hilton, Hong Kong; Victoria and Albert Mus and Serpentine Gallery, London, 01; Meml Art Gallery, Rochester, 02. *Exhib:* Corcoran Biennial of Am Painting, Corcoran Gallery Art, Washington, 93-94; solo exhibs, Jack Shainman Gallery, NY, 94 & 96, Corcoran Gallery Art, Washington, DC, 97-98 & Steinbaum Krauss Gallery, NY, 99 Bernice Steinbaum Gallery, Miami, 2001, Huntington (WVa) Mus. of Art, 2001, Kemper Mus. Contemp Art and Design, Kansas City, Mo, 2001; Rembrandt Redux: The Paintings of Ken Aptekar, Palmer Mus Art, Pa State Univ, 95; Going for Baroque, Walters Art Gallery, Baltimore, 95; Too Jewish? traveling exhib, 96; Masculine Measures, Kohler Art Ctr, Wis, 96; Asheville Art Mus. (NC) and traveling, 98-2000; Skirball Mus and Cult Ctr, Los Angeles, 2000; Metrop Mus, Tokyo, Shizuoka Prefectural Mus, Hiroshima Prefectoral Mus, 2000 and others. *Awards:* Fel, Nat Endowment Arts, 87 & 95; Rockefeller Found, Bellagio Residency, 92; Fel, Mid Atlantic Arts Found, 98; and others. *Bibliog:* Mieke Bal (auth), Semiotica 119-3/4, 98; JoAnn Lewis (auth), The Washington Post, 11/8/97; Scott Heller (auth), Art News, 4/98; Helen Harrison (auth.) N.Y. Times, 98; Stuart Jeffries (auth.) The Guardian, London, 2001; and others. *Dealer:* Bernice Steinbaum Gallery, Miami. *Mailing Add:* 201 W 85th St No 7E New York NY 10024

AQUINO, EDMUNDO
PAINTER, SCULPTOR
b Zimatlan Oaxaca, Mex, June 30, 39. *Study:* Nat Sch Plastics Art, Nat Univ Mex, cert(teacher fine arts), 62; Ecole Nat Superieure Beaux-Arts, Paris, Fr Govt Scholar, 67-69; Slade Sch Fine Arts, London, Brit Coun Scholar, 69. *Work:* Nat Libr Paris; Univ Mass Collection; Mus Mod Art Latin Am, Washington; Nat Inst Fine Arts, Mexico City, Mex; AGPA (Panamerican Graphic Art), Mus Mod Art, NY; and others. *Exhib:* Mus Mod Art, Mexico City, 77-78; Mus Mod Art Latin Am, OAS, Washington, 80; Picasso Mus, Antibes, France, 80; Contemp Latin Am Art and Japan, Nat Mus Art, Osaka, 81; Olympic Mus, Lausanne, Switz, 94; Mex Fine Arts Ctr Mus, Chicago, Ill, 96; Inst Cervantes, Bremen, Ger, 96; Ger Fed Parliament, Bonn, Ger, 97; Museo de las Americas, Denver, Colo, 2000; Sogn og Fjordane Art Mus, Forde, Norway, 03; and others. *Teaching:* Instr drawing & painting & head plastic arts sect, Sch Fine Arts, Oaxaca, Mex, 64-67. *Awards:* First Prize Painting & Drawing, Hotel Monnaie, Paris, 69; Nat Prize, 6th Int Festival Painting, Cagnes-Sur-Mer, France, 74; Third Prize, First Iberoamerican Biennial of Painting, Mexico City, 78; DAAD Fel, Artists in Berlin Prog, Berlin, 86. *Bibliog:* Mariana Frenk-Westheim (auth), article in Unomasuno, Mexico City, 11/83; Antonio Rodriguez (auth), article Excelsior, Mexico City, 7/88; Dr Hans Haufe (auth), article, Albatros viajero-Revista Mexicana de Cultura, 1-3/96. *Media:* All. *Mailing Add:* Calle Ave Maria 60-1 Coyoacan 04000 Mexico DF Mexico

AQUINO, HUMBERTO
PAINTER
b Lima, Peru, Oct 20, 47. *Study:* Nat Sch Fine Arts Lima, Peru, with Alberto Davila, 70; Cardiff Col Art, Wales, Great Britain, 73; Pratt Inst, Brooklyn, NY, 78. *Work:* Smithsonian Inst, Washington, DC; Art Inst Chicago, Ill; Univ Tex Art Mus, Austin; Mus Mod Art Latin Am, Washington, DC; Biblioteca Lvis Angel Arango, Bogota, Columbia. *Exhib:* Latin Am Drawings, Indianapolis Mus Art, 76; Drawings of the 70's, Art Inst Chicago, 77; one-man show, Mus Mod Art Latin Am, Washington, DC, 78; Latin Am Artists in NY Since 1970, Univ Tex Art Mus, 87; Latin Am Drawings Today, San Diego Mus Art, Calif, 4/91. *Pos:* Lectr, Soc of the Americas, NY, 85, Mus of the City of NY, 86. *Awards:* Fulbright Fel, 77; Artist's Fel, NY Found Arts, 85; Mid-Atlantic Regional, Nat Endowment Arts, 88. *Bibliog:* Sebastian Dominguez (auth), Six Artists Working in New York, Visiones - NBC Television, Channel 4, 5/87; Jacqueline Barnitz (auth), Latin Am Artists in New York, Archer M Huntington Art Gallery, 9/87; Framing the Past: essays on art education, Nat Art Educ Asn, 90. *Media:* Oils, Mixed Media. *Dealer:* Odon Wagner 194 Daveport Rd Toronto ON M5R 1J2. *Mailing Add:* c/o Odon Wagner Gallery 196 Davenport Rd Toronto ON M5R 1J2 Canada

ARAI, TOMIE
PRINTMAKER, MURALIST
b New York, NY, Aug 16, 49. *Study:* Philadelphia Col Art, 68. *Work:* Mus Modern Art Libr, Mus Modern Art Print Collection, Chinatown Hist Mus, NY; Libr Cong, Washington. *Comn:* silkscreen prints, Wash State Arts Comn, Seattle; terrazo floor design, Percent for Art Prog, NY Sch Construction Authority, 93; ceramic tile mural, NY Sch Construction Authority, 94; mural, Int Memorialization African Burial Ground, Fed Off Bldg, NY; pub art comn, Morse Sch, Cambridge Arts Coun, Mass, 97-98; glass mural, Riverside Ch, NY, 2000; glass wall syst, Filmore St Bridge, Pub Art Comn, San Francisco Art Comn, San Francisco Redevel Agency, 2000; etched glass mural, Martin Luther King Jr Wing, Riverside Ch, NY, 2000-01. *Exhib:* Committed to Print, Mus Modern Art, NY, 88; Decade Show, New Mus Contemp Art, NY, 91; Framing an Am Identity, Alternative Mus, NY, 92; Breda Fotographica '93, de Beyerd Mus, The Neth, 93; Fables, Fantasies & Everyday Things, Whitney Mus Am Art at Champion, Stamford, 94; Evidence of Memory: Work by Tomie Arai & Lynne Yamamoto, Whitney Mus Am Art; Is it Art? Transgressions in Contemp Art, Katonah Mus, NY; (dis)Oriented: Shifting Identities of Asian Women in Am, Steinbaum Krauss Gallery, NY, 95; Cult Economies: Histories from the Alternative Arts Movement-New York City Drawing Ctr, 96; Precious Objects, Painted Bride Gallery, Philadelphia, Pa, 97; Transferring Cult, LaMama La Galleria, NY, 97; Eye of the Beholder: Photographs From the Avon Collection, Int Ctr Photog, NY, 97; Album: 30 Years at the Lower East Side Printshop, W Chelsea Arts Bldg, NY, 98; Solo shows, Double Happiness, Bronx Mus Arts, NY, 98, Momotary/Peach Boy, Asian Pacific Am Studies Inst, NY Univ, 98, Tomie Arai/New Work, Cheryl McGinness Gallery, NY, 99 & Selected Work, Galeria Otra Vez, Self-Help Graphics & Art, Los Angeles, 2000; Les Reves: Tomie Arai, Nashormeh Lindo, Bomani Gallery, San Francisco, 99; Familiarity, Bronx River Art Ctr and Gallery, NY, 99; Recent Acquisitions from the Permanent Collections, The Bronx Mus Arts, 99; LAtitutudes: A Collaborative Installation, Self Help Graphics and Arts, Los Angeles, 2000; Good Art is the Best Business, Bronx Mus Arts, 2000; A Plurality of Truths, Schick Gallery, Skidmore Col, NY, 2000; Fifteen Asian Am Artists, Staller Arts Ctr, Stonybrook Univ, NY, 2001. *Pos:* Artist in residence art, NY Found Arts, 92-93, Asian Pacific Am Studies Program, NY, 98-99; artist/instr murals, Sites for Students Prog, NY Sch Construction Authority, 94-95; bd dir, Printed Matter Inc, 93-; pres, bd trustees, Chinatown Hist Mus, 94-; cur, Mus Chinese Ams, NY, 98-99; residency, Artists & Communities, Am Creates for the Millennium Artist Residency, 99-2000; Longwood Cyber residency, Bronx Coun Arts, 2000; advisor, artist adv com, NY Found Arts, 97-2001; Guest Speaker,Whitney Mus Am Art, 99. *Awards:* New York Found Arts Fel in Printmaking, 91 & 95; Nat Endowment Arts Visual Arts Fel for Works on Paper, 93-94; Anonymous Was a Woman Award, 97; Phoenix award, New York Asian Women's Ctr, NY, 98; Women's Studio Workshop 21 for 25 Visual Arts Grant, 99. *Bibliog:* Lucy Lippard (auth), Mixed blessings, Pantheon Bks, 90; Kerri Sakamoto (auth), Tomie Arai: Face to face encounters, Alternative Mus, 92; Margo Machida (auth), New feminist criticism: Art identity action, Harper Collins, 94; The Power of Feminist Art, Harry N Abrams Inc, 94; Screenprinting: Water Based Techniques, Watson-Guptill Publ, 94; Edward Wong (auth), Walls stop talking: Political murals are vanishing, The New York Times, 11/26/99; James Prigoff & Robin Dunitz (auths), Walls of Heritage/Walls of Pride African American Murals, Pomengranate Communications, Inc, 2000; Across the color lines, Amerasia Jour, Vol 6, No 3, 2000/2001; Andrea Frohne, Commemorating the Africanburial ground in New York City: Spirituality of space in contemporary art works, Ijele: Art e-Jour of the African World, vol 1,1, 2000. *Media:* All Media. *Publ:* Illusr, Sachiko Means Happiness, Children's Book Press, 92; China's Bravest Girl, Children's Book Press, 93; The NuyorAsian Anthology, Asian American Writings About New York City, 99; Foodculture: Tasting Identities and Geogprahies in Art, XYZ Books, Toronto, 2000. *Mailing Add:* 245 W 107th St Apt 12H New York NY 10025

ARAKAWA, (SHUSAKU)
PAINTER
b Japan, July 6, 36. *Work:* Mus Mod Art, NY; Basel Mus, Switz; Walker Art Ctr, Minneapolis; Japan Nat Mus, Tokyo; Metrop Mus Art, NY; Solomon R Guggenheim Mus, NY; Seibu Mus, Tokyo. *Exhib:* One-person shows, Henie Onstad Mus, Oslo, Norway, 75, Stadisch Kunsthalle, Dusseldorf, Ger, 77, Minneapolis Inst Arts, Minn, 79, Wadsworth Atheneum, Hartford, Conn, 83, Aldrich Mus Contemp Art, Ridgefield, Conn, 84, Seibu Mus, Tokyo, 87, Process in Question, Williams Col Mus, Touko Mus Contemp Art, Joseloff Gallery, Univ Hartford, Conn, 89, 90, Santani Gallery, Tokyo, 91, Gallery Takagi, Nagoya, Japan, 92, Hara Mus Contemp Art, Tokyo, 94, Galerie Busche, Berlin, 95, Kunstsammlung, Düsseldorf, Ger, 95, Ronald Feldman Fine Arts, NY, 97, Guggenheim Mus, 97; Painting & Sculpture Today, Indianapolis Mus Art, Ind & Cincinnati Contemp Arts Ctr, Ohio, 74; Wallraf-Richartz Mus, Cologne, WGer, 74; Kennedy Ctr for Performing Arts, Washington, 74; Nat Mus Mod Art, Tokyo, 91; Nat Mus Kyoto, 92; Busche, Berlin, Ger, 93; Arakawa Drawings 1961-74 (with catalog), Hara Mus Contemp Art, Tokyo, Japan, 94; Reversible Destiny Houses, Galerie Busche, Berlin, Ger, 95; Arakawa Raum (brochure), Kunstsammlung, Nordrhein-Westfalen, Dusseldorf, 95; Reversible Destiny - Arakawa/Gins (with

catalog), Guggenheim Mus, SoHo, NY, 97; Arakawa: Early Drawings and Paintings, 1960-1963, Ronald Feldman Fine Arts, NY, 97; In the Midst of Things, Bournville, Birmingham, UK, 99; and others. *Awards:* Chevalier des Artes et des Lettres, awarded by French Gov, 86; Fel, John Simon Guggenheim, 87-88; Col Art Asn's Artist Award for Exhib of Yr, Distinguished Body of Work, Presentation or Performance Award, 97. *Bibliog:* L Alloway (auth), Introduction to the mechanism of meaning, Bruckman Verlag, 71; N & E Calas (auth), Images & Icons, Dutton, 71; Italo Calvino (auth), The arrow in the mind, Artforum, 9/85 & Blank Arakawa, reprint & interview with Madeline Gins, El Paseante, No 7, 88; Jean Francoise Lyotard (auth), Que Peindre, Paris, Eds de la Difference, 88. *Publ:* Coauth, The Mechanism of Meaning, 71; coauth (with Madeline Gins), Landing Sites/The End of Spacetime, Art & Design, 5-6/93; coauth (with Madeline Gins), Architectural Experiments after Auschwitz-Hiroshima, Acad Ed, 95; coauth (With MadGins) Riverside Destiny: We Have Decided not to Die, Guggenheim Catalog, Abrams In, New York, NY, 97; coauth (with Madeline Gins), Architectural Body, Univ Alabama Press, 2002. *Dealer:* Ronald Feldman Fine Arts Inc 31 Mercer St New York NY 10013. *Mailing Add:* 124 W Houston St New York NY 10012

ARANGO, PLACIDO G, JR
COLLECTOR
Study: Tufts Univ, MA. *Pos:* President Grupo Vips, Madrid; Board trustees Tufts Univ, 87—96. *Awards:* Named one of 200 Top Collectors, ARTnews Magazine, 2004, 2005, 2006. *Collection:* Old Masters, primitive Spanish paintings, modern and contemporary art, Chinese ceramics. *Mailing Add:* Grupo Vips Calle Velazquez Madrid 138 28006 Spain

ARBITMAN, KAHREN JONES
DIRECTOR, HISTORIAN
b Pittsburgh, Pa, May 16, 48. *Study:* Penn State Univ, BA, 69; Univ Pittsburgh, MA, 71; PhD, 80. *Collection Arranged:* Rembrandt Etchings from the Charles J Rosenbloom Collection, 83; Pre-Rembrandt Etchers from the Boymans-van Beuningen Mus, 85; An Englishman Abroad: Watercolors of Edward Lear, 86; Gardens of Earthly Delight: 16th and 17th Century Netherlandish Gardens, 86; At Home in Pittsburgh: Art and Furnishings of Henry Clay Frick, 88; Rembrant Etchings from Carnegie Mus Art, 94; Rembrandt Redux: Paintings of Ken Aptekar, 94; Etchings of Leonard Leibowitz, 94. *Pos:* Cur, Frick Art Mus, 85-89; dir, Palmer Mus Art, Pa State, 90-95 & Cummer Mus Art & Gardens, Jacksonville, Fla, 96-. *Teaching:* Asst prof art history, West Va Univ, Morgantown, 84-5; adj assoc prof art history, Univ Pittsburgh, 85-; vis prof art history, Carnegie Mellon Univ, Pittsburgh, 89-90. *Mem:* Historians of Netherlandish Art (board of dir, 85-88, Pres, 91-93); Am Asn Netherlandish Studies; Am Asn Mus; Col Art Asn. *Res:* 16th and 17th century Netherlandish Art and Iconography. *Publ:* Auth, From These Slopes & Flats: The Paintings of Lee Dittley, PA Council on Humanities, 76; contribr, Landscape Painting in Rome, 1595-1675, Richard Feigen & Co, 85; co-auth, Pre-Rembrandt Etchers (illustrated Bartsch Vol 53) Abaris Books, 85; auth, Gardens of Earthly Delight; co-auth, Clayton, The Pittsburgh Home of Henry Clay Frick, Univ Pittsburgh Press, 88. *Mailing Add:* 829 Riverside Ave Jacksonville FL 32204

ARBUCKLE, LINDA J
CERAMIST, EDUCATOR
b Cleveland, Ohio, Nov 16, 50. *Study:* Cleveland Inst Art, BFA, 81; RI Sch Design, MFA, 83. *Work:* Detroit Inst Art; Stetson Univ; Arrowmont Sch Arts & Crafts; Lamar Dodd Art Ctr; Weisman Mus, Univ Minn; Charles A Wustrum Mus Fine Arts, Racine, Wis; Nations Bank Corporate Hq, Charlotte, NC; Archie Bray Found; Mus Decorative Arts, Ark Art Ctr, Little Rock; Caroline & Dan Anderson, Edwardsville, Iowa; Racine Art Mus, Racine, Wis; City of Orlando, Orlando, Fla; David Demming, President, Cleveland Inst Art, Cleveland, Ohio. *Exhib:* A Tea Party, Nat Mus Ceramic Art, Baltimore, 93; Nat Coun Educ Ceramic Art Clay Nat, Frederick R Weisman Mus, Minneapolis, 95; 4th Ann Strictly Functional Pottery Nat, Market House, Ephrata, Pa, 96; Clay Cup V, Univ Mus, Southern Ill Univ, Carbondale, 96; Madcap Teaparty, Renwick Gallery, Nat Mus Am Art, Washington, 96; Robert Archambeau: Artist, Teacher and Collector, Winnipeg, Manitoba, Canada, 2003; Art to Use: Functional Clay, Thirteen Moons Gallery, Santa Fe, NM, 2004; From Hands to Lips, Canadian Clay and Glass Gallery, Waterloo, ON, Canada, 2004. *Teaching:* Asst prof ceramics, La State Univ, Baton Rouge, 85-90; asst prof, Univ Fla, 93-96, assoc prof ceramics, 96-; vis prof & res fel, Univ Wales Inst Cardiff, fall 2000. *Awards:* Individual Artist Fel, State of Fla, 92; Nat Endowment Arts Fel, 94; Skutt Award, 95. *Bibliog:* Best of Pottery, Rockport Pub, 96; Mathias Ostermann (auth), The New Majolica: Contemporary Approaches to Color & Technique, Tinglaze, A&C Black, London. 2000; Kevin Hluch (auth), Beautiful Use, 2001; Matthias Osterman (auth, Ceramic Surface Decoration: Contemporary Approaches and Techniques, A & C Black, London, Unov Pennsylvania Press, Philadelphia, PA, 2002; Robin Hopper (auth), Making Marks: Discovering the Ceramic Surface, Krause Publ, Iola, WI, 2004. *Mem:* Nat Coun Educ Ceramic Arts; Am Crafts Coun; Clayart; Fla Craftsmen; Am Coun Arts. *Media:* Ceramics, Majolica Glaze on Terracotta. *Publ:* Contribr, The dynamics of useful objects, Ceramics Monthly, Vol 41, No 1, 93; ed, Majolica: Essays, Studio Potter Mag, Vol 24, No 2, 96; contrib, Creative Pottery, Rockport Publ, 98. *Mailing Add:* 14716 SE 9th Terrace Micanopy FL 32667-5276

ARCANGEL , CORY
GRAPHIC ARTIST
Study: Oberlin Col, BA in Technol in Music & Related Arts. *Work:* Am Mus Moving Image, NY, Royal Acad, London, Guggenheim, New Mus Contemp Art, Mus Modern Art, NY, Lothringer13, Make-World Festival, Munich, Migros Mus, Zurich, 2004, exhib in group shows at Whitney Biennial Am Art, Whitney Mus Am Art, 2004. *Exhib:* Cur (distrib on floppy disk, group shows) 1.44 Megs, with Moving Image Gallery & Rhizome.org, (web exhib) Low Level All Stars, Kingdom of Piracy; exhibs incl, NY Underground Film Festival, Fassbender Gallery, Chicago, Deadtech Gallery, Chicago, Foxy Production, Eye Beam, Lothringer13, Make-World Festival, Munich, Leroy Neiman Gallery, Columbia Univ, 2004; exhibs incl, Deitch Projs, 2005. *Pos:* Founding mem, BIEGE Program Ensemble, The 8-bit Construct Set. *Awards:* Grantee, turbulence.org, NY State Coun Arts. *Media:* All Media. *Mailing Add:* c/o Team Gallery 527 West 26th St New York NY 10001

ARCHAMBAULT, LOUIS
SCULPTOR
b Montreal, Que, Apr 4, 15. *Study:* Univ Montreal, BA; Ecole des Beaux-Arts de Montreal, dipl ceramics. *Work:* Nat Gallery Can, Ottawa; Art Gallery Ont, Toronto; Mus Prov Quebec; Mus Int Della Ceramica, Faenza, Italy; Can Imperial Bank Com, Montreal; and others. *Comn:* Mural sculpture, Place de Arts, Montreal, 63; aluminum sculpture, Toronto Airport, 64; 12 steel sculptures, Can Pavilion, Montreal's Expos, 67; bronze sculpture, Queens's Park, Toronto, 70; aluminum structural sculpture, Palais Justice Quebec, 83; and others. *Exhib:* 28th Venice Biennale, 56; Pittsburgh Int, 58; Int Exhib Contemp Sculpture, Expo 67, Montreal, 67; 11th Middelheim Biennale, 71; 10th Int Sculpture Conf, Toronto, 78; and others. *Awards:* Can Gov & Can Coun Fels, 53, 59, 62 & 69; Serv Medal, Order Can, 68; Awards, Ministere de l'Education, Que, 70-72; Diplome d'honneur, Can Conf of the Arts. *Bibliog:* Bill Stephenson (auth), Louis Archambault's wonderful wall, MacLean's, Can, 1/18/58; Guy Robert (auth), Archambault, Vie des Arts, summer 72; Luc Epivent (auth), Vie Arts, Montreal, spring 81. *Mem:* Academician Royal Can Acad Arts. *Media:* Multimedia

ARCHER, CYNTHIA
PRINTMAKER, PAINTER
b New Martinsville, WVa, Mar 28, 53. *Study:* Goucher Col, BA, 75; WVa Univ, MFA, 78. *Work:* Nat Art Gallery, Wellington, New Zealand; Portland Art Mus, Ore; Ill State Mus, Springfield; MacDonald's Corp Hq, Oakbrook, Ill; Danforth Mus, Framingham, Mass; Block Gallery, Northwestern Univ; Benedictine Univ; and others. *Comn:* Chicago Pub Libr, Westlawn Br; Color Lithograph Editions, Lakeside Studio, Lakeside, Mich; edition of hand-painted ceramic plates, Jane Meyer Fine Art, Elburn, Ill, 92; 3D art bench, The Chicago Children's Mus; stained glass window design, Wheller Hall, Southern Ill Univ, Carbondale. *Exhib:* Solo exhibs, Malton Gallery, Cincinnati, Ohio, 87 & 90 & Marcus Gordon Gallery, Pittsburgh, 91; Provenance Inc, Chicago & Kenilworth, Ill, 91-92; New Acquisitions, Col Lake Co, Grayslake, Ill, 92; Open Spectrum, David Adler Cult Ctr, Libertyville, Ill, 92; Art in Mythology, Wood St Gallery, Chicago, 94; Jane Meyer Fine Art, 05; and others. *Pos:* Workshop S, Lakeside Studios, Mich, 77-79; Master lithographer, Plucked Chicken Press, Chicago, 78-; workshops, Shepherd Col, Shepherdstow, WV, 78; vis artist, Southern Ill Univ, Edwardsville, Ill, 84 & Univ Nevada, Reno, 87. *Teaching:* Forum in printmaking, Bradley Univ, Peoria, Ill, 87; artist in residence, Benedictine Univ, Lisle, Ill, 96. *Awards:* Governor's Award, WVa Exhib, Charleston, 79; Merit Award, 6th Bacr Art Competition, Beverly Art Ctr, Chicago, 82; Pres Purchase Award, Bradly Univ, 87. *Media:* Lithography; Acrylic. *Dealer:* Jane Meyer Fine Arts 3 N 692 Highpoint Elburn IL 60119; Jane Meye Fine Arts 205 1/2 State St Geneve Il. *Mailing Add:* 1604 Greenleaf Evanston IL 60202-1159

ARCILESI, VINCENT J
PAINTER, DRAFTSMAN
b St Louis, Mo, May 5, 32. *Study:* Furman Univ, 49-50; Univ Okla, BFA(design), 53; Art Inst Chicago, BFA(painting), 56, MFA, 61. *Work:* Art Inst Chicago Mus; Ill State Mus, Springfield; Fashion Inst Technol, NY; Hirshhorn Mus, Washington, DC; Mus Contemp Art, Chicago; plus pvt collections. *Exhib:* 70th Ann, Art Inst Chicago, 67; Visions/Painting & Sculpture, Distinguished Alumni 1945-Present, Art Inst Chicago Gallery, 76; America 1976 Traveling Exhib, Corcoran Gallery, 76-78; solo shows, Noho Gallery, NY, 81, 85 & 88, Z Gallery, NY, 91; 148 Gallery, NY, 93, Broome St Gallery, NY, 95, 97 & 99 paintings, Carmichael & Carmichael Fine Art, St Paul, Minn, 95, Garden City, NY, Broom St Gallery, NY, 2001, 2003 & 2005, 2/20 Gallery, NY, 96, 2000, 2002, 2004 & 2006; New Art, FIT Galleries, NY, 90; Vincent Arcilesi & Don Perlis, Garrison Art Ctr, NY, 91; Contemp Realism, Farrington-Keith Creative Arts Ctr, Dexter, Mich, 92; Triplex Gallery, Borought of Manhattan City Col, NY, 94; Galleries at FIT, NY, 93, 94, 95 & 96; Ox-Bow Spring Benefit, Sch Art Inst Chicato, 98; The City, Feldman Ctr Gallery, FIT, 98; 5th Ann Small Works Invitational, Blue Mountain Gallery, NY, 98; Media Madness, Westbeth Gallery, NY, 98; Small Works, Wall-to-Wall at Gallery 402, Org Ind Artists, 99; The 4th Ann Loft Pioneer Show, The Puffin Room, NY, 99; Holiday Invitational Exhib, Broome St Gallery, 99 & 2000; Y2K - Aotic: Uncensored All-Media Salon Show, Org Ind Artists, 2000; Artists of the Ideal, Mus Modern & Contemp Art, Palazzo Forti, Verona, Ital, 2002; Whitney Biennial, Whitney Mus Art, NY, 2006; Watercurrents 2006: The Figure, Lori Bookstein Fine Art, NY, 2006. *Teaching:* Asst prof art, Fash Inst Tech, NY, 74-95, assoc prof, 95-99, prof fine art, 99-. *Awards:* American 1976 Grant, US Dept Interior, Washington, 74-75; Creative Artists Pub Serv Prog Fel, 81-82; Nat Endowment Arts Grant, 82. *Bibliog:* Pat Van Gelder (auth), Vincent Arcilesi, Am Artist, 10/83; John Arthur (auth), Spirit of Place, Contemporary Landscape Painting & the American Tradition, Bulfinch Press, Little Brown & Co, 89; Edward Lucie-Smith (auth), American Realism, Harry Abrams, 94; Edward Lucie-Smith (auth), Artist of the Ideal, Palazzo Forti, Verona, Italy, 02. *Mem:* NY Artists' Equity, (bd dir, 86-90 & 2002-2006). *Media:* Oil, Pastel. *Mailing Add:* 116 Duane St New York NY 10007

ARCOMANO, CATHRYN
PAINTER
Study: New Sch Art Workshops. *Work:* Brooklyn Mus, NY; Everson Mus Art, Syracuse, NY; Heckscher Mus, Huntington, NY; Newark Mus, NJ; Snite Mus Art, Univ Notre Dame. *Exhib:* Contemp Reflections 1977-78, Aldrich Mus Contemp Art, Ridgefield, Conn, 78; Mid-Am Exhib, Owensboro Mus Fine Art, Owensboro, Ky, 80;

New Eng Exhib Painting, Drawing & Sculpture, Silvermine, Conn, 81; Mod Drawings from Permanent Col, Snite Mus Art, Univ Notre Dame, Ind, 83; 21st Biennial Art Exhib, Univ Gallery/Mus Studies, Univ Delaware, Newark, Del, 84; Everson Biennial, Everson Mus Art, Syracuse, NY, 86; two-person exhib, Alvin Gallery & Gallery Ninety-Seven, Hong Kong, 88; New Paintings, Univ Cambridge, Eng, Queens Col & Magdalene Col, 98; Galerie Christine Brugger, Bern, Switz, 00, 02, Collaborative Concepts Gallery, Beacon, NY, 01; solo exhibs, Arnot Art Mus, Elmira, NY, 83, Chastein Gallery, Atlanta, Ga, 84, Nauta Dutilh, Amsterdam, 96, Wiard Heijenga, Amsterdam, 97 & Galerie Christine Brugger, Bern, Switz, 97, 00, Univ Cambridge, Eng, Queens Col & Magdalene Col, 98, ADD Gallery, Hudson, NY, 00; Galleria Multigraphic, Venice, Italy, Group Exhib Feb 23-March 20 2004; Hotel ALA-Taranowska's, Venice, Italy, Exhib Jul 16-Sept 30, 2006. *Collection Arranged:* Corporate Collections: Gannett Co, Nordstrom Inc, Pfizer, Ryder Systems, Skadden Alps (law firm). *Awards:* Gertrude Romm Levy Award, New Sch Soc Res, 74; First Award, Painters & Sculptors Soc NJ Ann Exhib, 78; Olaf Oloffson Mem Award, Painters & Sculptors Soc NJ Ann Exhib, 83. *Bibliog:* Astrid Fitzgerald (ed) An Artists Book of Inspiration, Lindisfarne Press, Hudson, NY, 96; Sydney Pollack (dir motion picture) Random Hearts, Columbia Pictures, 99; Peter Anliker (auth) Expressive and forceful, Der Bund, Bern, Switzerland, 6/2000. *Dealer:* The Adamson Gallery 1515 14th St NW Suite 202 Washington DC 20005. *Mailing Add:* 160 Riverside Dr New York NY 10024

ARD, SARADELL
EDUCATOR, PAINTER
b Macon, Ga, Mar 22, 20. *Study:* Asbury Col, AB(art), 42; Univ Mich, MA, 43; Columbia Univ Teachers Col, DEd(art), 70. *Work:* Univ Ill, Edwardsville; Alaska State Mus, Juneau; Alaska Methodist Univ Collection Alaskan Artists, Univ Alaska & Anchorage Mus Hist & Art, Anchorage, Frederick R Weisman Found. *Exhib:* Solo exhibs, Teachers Col Galleries, Columbia Univ, NY, 68 & 70, Alaska State Mus, Juneau, 72 & Anchorage Mus Hist & Art, 76 & 84; Contemp Alaskan Art, Smithsonian Inst, Washington, DC, 78; Univ Alaska Campus Ctr Gallery, Anchorage, 78-83; Alaskaland Gallery, Fairbanks, 83; and others. *Collection Arranged:* 20th Century Alaska Eskimo Art (with catalog), Smithsonian Inst, 82. *Pos:* Dir arts & crafts prog, European Theatre, US Army, 60-62; vchmn bd dir, Visual Arts Ctr, Anchorage, 73-76; mem bd dir, Mayor's Comn, Fine Arts Mus, Anchorage, 73-82. *Teaching:* Prof art, Alaska Methodist Univ, 62-73; prof art, Univ Alaska, Anchorage, 73-85, actg dean, 76-77, prof art emer, 85-. *Awards:* Juror's Choice, Ann All Alaska Art Exhib, 66 & 1st Award Drawing, 67; Gov's Award, 80. *Mem:* Anchorage Mus Asn (pres, 81-82). *Media:* Oil, Acrylic. *Res:* Eskimo art of the Arctic Circle. *Publ:* Auth, Alaskan Eskimo Art Today, 72 & Inuit Sculpture, summer 80, Alaska J; Native Alaskan Art Today, Am Illus, 76; Roots in the past in Inua, Smithsonian Inst Press, 82; Schitz-und gravierkunst der Alaska-Eskimo in geschichte und gegenwart, In: Inuitkunst, Linden Mus, Stuttgart, Ger, 83; and others. *Mailing Add:* 12400 Toilsome Hill Rd Anchorage AK 99516

ARENDT, MARY See DeLoyht-Arendt, Mary Arendt

ARGUE, DOUGLAS
PAINTER
b St Paul, Minn, Jan 21, 62. *Study:* Bemidji State Univ, Minn, 80-82; Univ Minn, 83. *Comn:* Target Corp; Weisman Art Mus. *Exhib:* Solo exhibs, Bockley Gallery, 87, 88, 89 & 90, Minneapolis Inst Arts, 94, Asn Am Artists, NY, 96, Threadwaxing Space, NY, 96, Libr of Babel, Assoc Am Artists, NY, 97, Gallery Co Minneapolis, 04, Sherry Leedy Gallery, Kansas City, 05; Viewpoints: Doug Argue & Jim Lutes, Walker Art Ctr, Minneapolis, 85-86; The Perisistant Figure, Walker Art Ctr, 90; Katherine Nash Gallery, Univ Minn, 92; McKnight Found Exhib, MCAD Gallery, Minneapolis, Minn, 93; Minn Hist Soc, 94; Ann exhib, Am Acad, Rome, Italy, 98; Post Gallery, Los Angeles, 02; Pepperdine Univ, Malibu, Calif, 03; Scope LA, Calif, 04; and many others. *Collection Arranged:* Walker Art Ctr, Minneapolis, Weismann Art Mus, Minneapolis, Minn Inst Arts, Minneapolis, General Mills, and others. *Awards:* McKnight Found Fel, 92; Pollack Krasner Found, 95; Prix de Rome, vis Arts, 97-98. *Bibliog:* Melissa Stang (auth), Doug Argue at Bockley Artpaper, 7/88; Mary Abee (auth), Minneapolis Star Tribune, 4/15/93; Michael Amy (auth), Art in Am, 4/98. *Media:* All. *Dealer:* Weinstein Gallery 908 W 46th St St Paul MN. *Mailing Add:* Doug Argue Studio Bldg 140 2900 Main St Ste 228 Alameda CA 94501

ARGUIMBAU, PETER L
PAINTER, LECTURER
b Stamford, Conn, Oct 22, 51. *Study:* The Loomis Sch, 67-70; Vassar Col, 1970-71; Art Students League, 1973-1981; Classical Study in Venice, Rome and Naples, Italy. *Work:* The Lawrenceville Sch, Bund Libr, Princeton, NJ; Union League (permanent collection), New York, NY; Cheese Bourough Ponds Collection, Greenwich, Conn. *Comn:* Greenwich Panorama (mural), Putnam Trust Bank, Greenwich, Conn, 1989; Chateau Mont Rozier, comn by Claude Cochin, Mt. Rozier, France, 1997; Revelation (ceiling mural), comn by Louis Karcher, New Canaan, Conn, 2000; Hon Gerald Heaney (portrait), 5th Dist Court Bldg, St Paul, MN; Drawing Room, Palace of Prince d' Avalos, Naples, Ital. *Exhib:* Nat Acad Design Show Biannual, New York, NY, 1986; Silvermine Guild New Eng Invitational, Silvermine Guild, New Canaan, Conn, 1987-; 350 years of Greenwich, Greenwich, Conn, 1990; Art's for the Parks Top 100 US Artists, Jackson Hole, Wyo, 1991-93; Mystic Int Exhib, Mystic Maritime Gallery, Mystic, Conn, 1994, 96-98, 2001-02. *Collection Arranged:* Retrospective, The Metrop Club, 1987; Italian Monument Drawing Show, 1992; Retrospective, Union League Club, 1994; NY Harbor Tallship 2000, Wally Findlay Gallery, 2000; Yachting Events of the Present, Harbour Court, Newport, 2005; Nantucket, Gallery Four India Street, 2005. *Teaching:* Oil painting, Darien, Conn, 1985-91; oil painting, Meadows Mus, Dallas, Tex, 1987; oil painting, Omega Inst, Rhinebeck, NY, 1989. *Awards:* Newington Coopsey Award, Hudson River Valley Art Assoc, 1969; Award of Merit, Mystic Intl Competition, 1991. *Bibliog:* Artist brings cause against Michelangelo Restoration, Eden Prairie Sailor, 1984; There is a young Old Master in Darien, Darien News Review, Sept 1993; Nancy Helle (auth), Classicism in a Modern Age, Greenwich Mag, Sept 2003. *Mem:* Nat Soc Mural Painters (vpres, 1996-2000); Art Students League, NY. *Media:* Oil, Flemish Technique. *Specialty:* Marine Art; Classic Yachts; Animal Paintings. *Interests:* oilly -resinous techniques of the Flemish Masters from 1450-1650; classic yachts & workboats of Am waterfront 1850-. *Publ:* Art, The Artist Returns to Art Restoration, American Art's Quarterly, Vol XIII No 3, 1996; art, The Sistine Chapel: Science versus Art, American Art's Quarterly, Vol XV No 23, 1998; art, Impressionism and the Loss of Transperency, American Art's Quarterly, Vol XVIII No 3, 2001. *Dealer:* Linda Lyons PO Box 7674 Greenwich Conn 06830; Harbor Gallery 151 Rowayton Ave Rowayton Conn 06853; Gallery 4 Indid St Nantucket Mass 02554; Wally Findlay Galleries 165 Worth Ave Palm Beach Fla; Mystic Seaport Gallery Mystic Conn 06355; Tilly Pad Gallery Watch Hill RI. *Mailing Add:* 121 E Middle Patent Rd Greenwich CT 06831

ARIAS, SOLEDAD M
CURATOR
b Buenos Aires, Arg. *Study:* Fine Arts, Buenos Aires; Art Students League (Reginald Marsh scholar), NY. *Exhib:* Salon Provincial, Mus De Lujan, Buenos Aires, 90; Small Works, Mus Sivori, Buenos Aires, 91; Nat Show of Fine Arts, Mus Sivori, Buenos Aires, 92. *Awards:* Hommage A Van Gogh Award, Nacion, Buenos Aires; Aim Prog, Bronx Mus Arts, New York, 94. *Bibliog:* Ed McCormick (auth), Art Speak, 4/11/93; Holland Cotter (auth), New York Times, 8/19/94. *Mem:* Art Initiatives. *Media:* Painting. *Mailing Add:* 200 W 70th St New York NY 10023-4323

ARIAS-MISSON, ALAIN
VISUAL POET, GRAPHIC ARTIST
b Brussels, Belg, Dec 11, 39; US citizen. *Study:* Harvard Univ, BA(Greek lit; magna cum laude), 59. *Work:* State Mus (Stedelijk), Amsterdam, Holland; Archive H Sohm, State Gallery, Stuttgart, Ger; Galleria Schwarz, Milan; Cabinet d'Estampes, Bibliotheque Nat, Paris; Dresden Mus; Mus Casabianca, Vicenza; Mus de Senigallia; Liublin Mus, Poland; Jean Brown Collection, Getty Mus, Calif. *Comn:* Public Poem-Beethoven Bicentennial, Bonn, WGer; Public Art, City of Bielefeld, 91. *Exhib:* Galerie Donguy, Paris, 88; Poesia Visiva & Group Art-Documenta 8 Mus Santos Rocha, Portugal, 88; Le Mois de La photographie, Paris, Oct 88; Visual Poetry, Otis Art Inst, Los Angeles, 90; Domus Jani, Int Inst Total Art, Verona, 92, The Lyon Biennale, 93; Emily Harvey Gallery, NY, 98, 01; Galleria Caterina Gualco, Genoa, 99; Leonardo da Vinci, Last Supper, Vinci Mus, Italy, 2001; Emily Harvey Archive, Venice, Italy, 02; Lara Vincy Gallery, Paris, 03. *Teaching:* Creative writing, Columbia Univ, 81-82. *Awards:* NJ State Coun Arts, 85-86; Artists Liaison, 88. *Bibliog:* S H Anderson (auth), When reality becomes superfiction, Int Herald Tribune, 5/75; M Dachy (auth), New York art, Critique, 81, & L'espace Amerique, Change, Paris; and others in Art Vivant, Flashart & Artpress; Infinite, Paris, France, 99. *Mem:* Poets & Writers. *Media:* Shaped Plexiglass and Illumination. *Res:* Shamanic Culture, exp. Maya. *Specialty:* Fluxus. *Publ:* Co-ed, 5 anthologies in Europe & America, 74, Poesia Visiva, Chicago Rev, 76 & Visual poetry, Paris Rev; auth, Confessions of a Murderer, Bomber, Fascist, Rapist, Thief, Chicago Rev Press & Swallow, 75; The Public Poem Book, Arias-Misson, Factotum Press, Italy, 78-79; Verbo-visual Sins of a Literary Saint, Rara Bks, Italy, 92; The Mind Crime of August Saint, Fiction Coll 2. *Dealer:* Emily Harvey Gallery 50 Battery Place 5J New York NY 10280. *Mailing Add:* 15 rue Ambroise Croizat le Manoir Folembray France 02670

ARIAS-MISSON, NELA
PAINTER
b Havana, Cuba, Sept 8, 25; US citizen. *Study:* Art Students League, 55; Hans Hoffman Sch, Provincetown, 56-58. *Work:* State Mus Lindenau, Altenburg, EGer; Circulo de Arte, Cordoba, Spain; Archivo Denza, Brescia, Italy. *Exhib:* Solo exhib, Charlottenborg Gallery-Acad Fine Arts, Copenhagen, Denmark, 62; Kunstmesse-Brescia Gallery, Basel Art Fair, Switz, 73; Phantomas, Mod Mus, Ixelles-Brussels, Belg, 75; Segel der Zeit, State Mus of Lindenau, Altenburg, EGer, 85-86; Ruth Wiseman Gallery, Dallas, 88; St Lifer Art Exchange, 88; Elaine Kaufman Cult Ctr, NY. *Awards:* First Prize, Nat Asn Women Artists, 60. *Bibliog:* Paul de Vree (auth), Nela Arias-Misson, De Periscoop, Belg, 11/68; Adolfo Castaño, Nela Arias-Misson, Estafeta Literaria, Madrid, Spain, 70; Jacques Halber, Artistes Américainà Bruxelles, Annuaire des Beaux-Arts, 72. *Media:* Oil on Canvas. *Publ:* Illusr, The Umbrella, 9/67 & The Tree of Life, 75, Chicago Rev; Table with Bott & Lamp, L'VII (Brussels), No 33, 72; participated in virtual exhib, Artvault.com. *Dealer:* Int Inst for Total Art Verona 37031 Italy

ARIKE, MICHAEL WHITAKER
PRINTMAKER, PAINTER
b Oklahoma City, Okla, Oct 15. 33. *Study:* Okla Stat Univ, with Doel Reed, BFA, 1955; Art Inst Chic, 1956-57; New School with John Ross, New York City. *Work:* British Mus, London, Eng; Portland, Mus, Seattle, Wash; Mus of City of New York, NYC; Fed Reserve Bank, New York City; Nelson-Atkins Mus, Kansas City, Mo. *Comn:* presentation print 2003, Print Club of Albany, 2003; limited edition print, Print Soc of Nelson-Atkins Mus, Kansas City, Mo, 2005. *Awards:* The Wm H Leavin Prize, Nat Acad Design Ann, 2000; Silver Medal in Graphics, Audubon Artist's Ann, 2002; Gold Medal in Graphics, Audubon Artist's Ann, 2004. *Mem:* council mem, Soc Am Graphic Artists (1996-); Audubon Artists; Print Club of Albany; Artist's Fel. *Media:* Miscellaneous Media. *Dealer:* The Old Print Shop 150 Lexington Ave at 30th St New York NY 10016. *Mailing Add:* 331 Prospect Ave Mamaroneck NY 10543

ARION, KATHERINE
PAINTER, MURALIST
b Bucharest, Romania; Romanian & US citizen. *Study:* Tonitza Sch Fine Art, Bucharest, studied composition with Gheorghe Tofan, 71, etching with Gheorghe Ivancenco, BA, 77; Acad Fine Art Nicolae Grigorescu, Bucharest, painting with Eugen Popa, BA, 77. *Work:* Saban Entertainment Co; Romanian Nat Mus Art, Bucharest; Sheriffs Dept Art Collection, Los Angeles; Europ Investment Mgmt; several pvt collections. *Comn:* Painting album cover, Fatha, Quick Silver, Los Angeles, 84; portrait sketches of actress Donna Mills, Overruled Co, Los Angeles, 93; oil portrait, comn by Dr Paul Scrobohaci, Paris, 94; Hora (mural, 2000 sq feet), Metrop Transportation Authority, 97. *Exhib:* UNESCO Conf Show, Bucharest, 75; Bucharest Student Mus, 76; First Ann Art Gallery Show, City West Hollywood, Calif, 93, Second Ann Art Gallery Show, 94; 21st Century Time Capsule Exhib, Bridge Gallery City Hall, Los Angeles, 93; solo shows, Gallery on Rim, 97, Romanian Embassy, Paris, 98, Park La Brea, 98 & Iby Art Gallery, Beverly Hills, 99; Los Angeles Co Mus Art, 98; Hollynock House, Los Angeles & Echo Maya Festival, 98; California 2000 & millennium, Mod Art Gallery, 2000. *Teaching:* Pvt lessons. *Bibliog:* Miriam Tal (art critic), Yehudot Aharonot, 8/79; Edward Golstein (auth), Beverly Hills Today, Len Scholl, 10/92; Rev Braxton Berkley (dir), television interviews, After Thought Productions, 7/94; World Class Beverly Hills Country Club Mag, Constance Franklin Publ. *Mem:* Women in Film; Acad Television Arts & Scis; Los Angeles Press Club. *Media:* Mixed Media; Monoprint on Gold Foil. *Interests:* charitable contributions. *Publ:* Contribr, Gallery Guide, Roger M Peskin, 93; Encyclopedia of Living Artists, Constance Franklin, 93; World Class Beverly Hills Country Club Mag, Ben Nader, 94; Int Newspaper-The Christian Science Monitor, David T Cook, 94; Stock Illustration Source, Ian Gun, 94; and many others. *Dealer:* Iby Fine Art Gallery 9865 Little Santa Monica Blvd Beverly Hills CA 90212

ARISS, HERBERT JOSHUA
PAINTER, ILLUSTRATOR
b Guelph, Ont, Sept 19, 1918. *Study:* Ont Col Art. *Work:* Nat Gallery Can; Art Gallery Ont; Winnipeg Art Gallery; Vancouver Art Gallery; London Art Gallery, Ont; and others. *Comn:* Casein, Huron & Erie Co, Chatham, 58; ceramic, John Labatt Brewery, London, 59; multimedia, Sir Adam Beck Sec Sch, London, 67; multimedia, Ont Govt Bldg, Toronto, 68; mural, Sch Med, Univ Western Ont, London. *Exhib:* 2nd & 3rd Can Biennial, Ottawa, 64-66; Can Soc Graphic Arts, 70; Can Printmakers, Nat Gallery, Can Int Show, 71; Can Soc Painters in Watercolour, London & NY, 72. *Collection Arranged:* Nat Gallery of Canada of Ontario, Vancouver Arts; Caloary Art Gallery Mus, London. *Pos:* Pres, Western Art League, 57-60; mem, London Art Gallery Bd, 68-71; dir, London Art Gallery Asn, 69-72; chmn acquisition comt, London Pub Libr & Art Mus, 70-71. *Teaching:* Instr drawing & painting, Doon Sch Fine Arts, 55-58; head dept art, H B Beal Art Sch, London, Ont, from 65. *Awards:* Can Coun Senior Fel, 60-61; Can Soc Painters in Watercolor Hon Award, 65; Mayor's Hon Award, London, 80. *Bibliog:* Bright lights of London, Time, 68; Barry Lord (auth), How Beal has made London an art centre, Toronto Star, 70; J Bryce (auth), Herb Ariss retrospective, Arts Can, 71. *Mem:* Royal Can Acad Arts; Can Soc Painters in Watercolor. *Media:* Acrylic, Watercolor, Pastel. *Publ:* Illusr, Lectures variees, 58; La double mort de Frederic Belot, 58; Contes d'Aujour d'hui, 63; War, 71; auth, Encounters, London Regional Art Gallery, 82. *Dealer:* Michael Gibson Gallery. *Mailing Add:* 770 Leroy Crescent London ON N5Y 4G7 Canada

ARISS, MARGOT JOAN PHILLIPS
PAINTER, SCULPTOR
b Belleville, Ont, Sept 14, 29. *Study:* London Cent Col, Ont; H B Beal Sec Sch, London, Ont. *Work:* Can Coun Art Bank, Ottawa; London Regional Art Gallery, Ont; London Free Press Newspaper, Ont; Vancouver Art Gallery, BC; McIntosh Art Gallery, London, Ont. *Comn:* Ceramic mural, City of London, Ont; ceramic & fibre mural, City of Kingston, Ont; and many other pvt commissions. *Exhib:* Ceramic Objects, Art Gallery Ontario, 73, Ariss-Hogbin-Hunt, York Univ, 78, Toronto; McIntosh Gallery, Univ Western Ont, 75; Words & Images, Trent Univ, McKenzie Art Gallery, 76; London & Area Artists Part I, 80, Clay & Fibre Show, 86, 40th Ann Western Ontario Exhib, 87, London Regional Art Gallery; Univ Western Ont Collection, Art Gallery, Windsor, 82; one-person show, Univ Waterloo, Ont, 83; Ten Yrs After, Spectrum Art Gallery, London, Ont, 85; Yellow Show, 87, Box Art (touring) 87, Red Show, 88, Blue Show, 89, Book Show, 94, Durham Art Gallery; retrospective, Zen Song, London Regional Art Gallery, 89. *Bibliog:* Articles, Arts Can, 8/69 & Craft Horizons, 10/73 & 6/74; cover & article, Craftsman, 8/78. *Mem:* Royal Can Acad. *Media:* Mixed Media. *Mailing Add:* 770 Leroy Crescent London ON N5Y 4G7 Canada

ARMAJANI, SIAH
SCULPTOR
b Teheran, Iran, 39; US citizen. *Study:* Macalester Col, St Paul, Minn, BA, 63. *Comn:* Gazebo for two architects, Gabriella & Arberto Antolini, Storm King Art Park, Mountainville, NY; The Gazebo for the Irene Hixon Whitney Bridge, Loring Park, Minneapolis, Minn, 93; Bridge/Ramp, City Ctr-Sudwest LB Lautenschlagerstrasse, Stuttgart, Ger, 94; Garden, Villa Arson Mus, Nice, France, 94; The Lighthouse and Bridge, Staten Island, NY, 95; and others. *Exhib:* Architectural Analogues (with catalog), Whitney Mus Am Art, 78; Architectural Sculpture (with catalog), Inst Contemp Art, Los Angeles, 80; Metaphor: New Projects by Contemp Sculptors, Hirshhorn Mus & Sculpture Garden, Smithsonian Inst, 81; Body Language: Figurative Aspects of Recent Art (with catalog), Hayden Gallery, Mass Inst Technol, 81; Biennial (with catalog), Whitney Mus Am Art, 81; Artists' Gardens & Parks, Hayden Gallery, Mass Inst Technol, 81; 74th Ann Am Exhib (with catalog), Art Inst Chicago, 82; Postminimalism (with catalog), Aldrich Mus Contemp Art, 82; Form and Function: Proposals for Pub Art in Philadelphia (with catalog), Pa Acad Fine Arts, 82; New Art (with catalog), Tate Gallery, London, Eng, 83; Directions 1983 (with catalog), Hirshhorn Mus & Sculpture Garden, Smithsonian Inst, 83; Beyond the Monument (with catalog), Hayden Gallery, Mass Inst Technol, 83; An Int Survey of Recent Painting and Sculpture (with catalog), Mus Mod Art, NY 84; Content: A Contemp Focus, 1974-1984, Hirshhorn Mus & Sculpture Garden, Smithsonian Inst, 84; The Artist as Social Designer: Aspects of Public Urban Life Today, Los Angeles Co Mus Art, 86; Second Sight: Biennial IV (with catalog), San Francisco Mus Art, 86; one-person exhibs, Stedelijk Mus, Amsterdam, 87, Kunsthalle Basel, Switz, List Visual Arts Ctr, Mass Inst Technol, 88, Lannan Found, Los Angeles, 92, Storm King Art Ctr, 93, Swiss Inst, NY, 93 & Wright Mus, Beloit Col, Wis, 93; Emerging Artists 1978-1986: Selections from the Exxon Series (with catalog), Solomon R Guggenheim Mus, 87; Avant-Garde in the Eighties, Los Angeles Co Mus Art, 87; View Points: Post-War Painting and Sculpture, Solomon R Guggenheim Mus, 88; Carnegie Int (with catalog), Carnegie Mus Art, Pittsburgh, 88; Cult and Commentary: An Eighties Perspective (with catalog), Hirshhorn Mus & Sculpture Garden, Smithsonian Inst, 90; Enclosures and Encounters (with catalog), Storm King Sculpture Ctr, Mountainville, NY, 91; 20th Century Art, Mus Mod Art, Frankfurt, 91; Century of Sculpture, Stedelijk Mus Amsterdam & Nieuwe Kerk Found, 92; The Open Work, John Good Gallery, NY, 92; Differentes Natures: Visions de l'Art Contemporain (with catalog), Place de la Defense, France, 93; Unpainted to the Last: Moby Dick and the Visual Arts, Spencer Art Mus, Univ Kans, Lawrence, 93; Inside and Out, Roanoke Col, Salem, Va 93; and others. *Bibliog:* Howard Pousner (auth), The olympic cauldron, Atlanta J, 3/25/94; Howard Pousner (auth), Sculpture for olympic flame unveiled, Atlanta J, 3/21/94; Catherine Fox (auth), Armajani's art speaks to American democracy, Atlanta J, 3/24/94. *Mailing Add:* c/o Max Protech Gallery 511 W 22nd St New York NY 10011

ARMSTRONG, BILL HOWARD
PAINTER, EDUCATOR
b Horton, Kans, Dec 13, 1926. *Study:* Bradley Univ, Peoria, Ill, BFA(cum laude), 49; Univ Ill, Urbana, MFA, 55, with Abraham Rattner. *Work:* Brooklyn Mus, NY; San Francisco Mus of Art, Calif; Springfield Art Mus, Mo; Albrecht Gallery, St Joseph, Mo; Art and the Law, West Publ Co, St Paul, Minn. *Comn:* Hist mural, Am Bank, Irving, Tex, 75. *Exhib:* 20th & 24th Print Exhib, San Francisco Mus Art, 56 & 59; Butler Inst Am Art, Youngstown, Ohio, 56-67; Pa Acad Fine Art, Philadelphia, 56-67; 10th Ann Print Exhib, Brooklyn Mus, 59; Soc Am Graphic Artist Int Traveling Exhib, 60; Watercolor USA Nat Exhib, Springfield, Mo, 65-76; Calif Nat Watercolor Soc, Los Angeles, 69-71; Art and the Law, 82-83; watercolor mural, Hamous Hall for the Performing Arts, Springfield, Mo, 92. *Collection Arranged:* Watercolor USA Nat Invitational Exhib, 76. *Pos:* Art adv, Burma Transl Soc, Rangoon, Ford Found, 57-58; co-founder & past pres, Watercolor USA Hon Soc, 85-86. *Teaching:* Asst prof painting, Univ Wis, Madison, 56-63; prof watercolor & graphic design, Southwest Mo State Univ, Springfield, 63-88, emer prof, 88-. *Awards:* Purchase Awards, Watercolor USA, 62-71 & Calif Nat Watercolor Soc, 69 & 70; Purchase Awards, West Publ Co Art & the Law Exhib, 82 & 83; Lifetime Achievement in & Contrib Arts Award, Mo Arts Coun Award, 90. *Media:* Watercolor. *Mailing Add:* 3029 E Wilshire Dr Springfield MO 65804-4149

ARMSTRONG, CAROL
PAINTER
Study: Cent State Univ, Edmond, Okla, BA, 78. *Exhib:* Okla Art Guild Juried Exhib, 82, 85, 86 & 87; Lawton Jr Serv League 15th, 17th & 18th Ann Exhibs, 84, 85 & 87; Nat Watercolor Okla, 86; Tex and Neighbors Art Competition, 86; Art in the Woods, Fifth Juried Exhib, 88. *Teaching:* Painting instr, Norman Woodward's Art & Crafts, Oklahoma City Tabco Hobbies, 80-88 & Firehouse Art Ctr, 89-90. *Bibliog:* Best of Show, Lawton Jr Serv League 18th Ann Exhib, 86. *Mem:* Okla Watercolor Asn; Okla Art Guild. *Mailing Add:* c/o Firehouse Art Ctr 444 S Flood Norman OK 73069

ARMSTRONG, ELIZABETH NEILSON
CURATOR
b Winchester, Mass, June 30, 52. *Study:* Hampshire Col, BA (am studies), 74; Univ Calif, Berkeley, MA (history art), 82. *Collection Arranged:* Jasper Johns: Printed Symbols (auth, catalog), 90; Viewpoints: Hachivie Edgar Heap of Birds, Walker Art Center, Minneapolis, Minn, 90; Ann Hamilton/David Ireland, Walker Art Center, Minneapolis, Minn, 92; Claes Oldenburg: In the Studio, Walker Art Center, Minneapolis, Minn, 92; Robert Motherwell: The Spanish Elegies, Walker Art Center, Minneapolis, Minn, 92; In the Spirit of Fluxus (auth, catalog), Walker Art Center, Minneapolis, Minn, 93; Michael Sommers/Susah Haas: The Question of How, Walker Art Center, Minneapolis, Minn, 93; Duchamp's Leg, Walker Art Center, Minneapolis, Minn, 94; Paul Shambroom: Hidden Places of Power, Walker Art Center, Minneapolis, Minn, 95; Robert Motherwell: Reality and Abstraction, Walker Art Center, Minneapolis, Minn, 96; Peter Fishcli and David Weiss: In a Restless World, Walker Art Center, Minneapolis, Minn, 96; Recent Additions to Collection, Mus Contemp Art, San Diego, Calif, 96; Primarily Paint, Mus Contemp Art, San Diego, Calif, 97; Armando Rascón, Mus Contemp Art, San Diego, Calif, 97; Geoffrey James: Running Fences, Mus Contemp Art, San Diego, Calif, 97; Jay Johnson, Mus Contemp Art, San Diego, Calif, 97; Silvia Gruner, Mus Contemp Art, San Diego, Calif, 98; Double Trouble: The Patchett Collection, Mus Contemp Art, San Diego, Calif, 98; David Reed Paintings: Motion Pictures, Mus Contemp Art, San Diego, Calif, 98; Recent Acquisitions from the Lannan Found, Mus Contemp Art, San Diego, Calif, 99; Marcos Ramirez ERRE: Amor Como Primer Idioma (Love as First Language), Mus Contemp Art, San Diego, Calif, 99; Bertrand Lavier: Walt Disney Productions: Mus Contemp Art, San Diego, Calif, 99; Jean Lowe: The Evolutionary Cul-de-Sac, Mus Contemp Art, San Diego, Calif, 2000; Ultrabaroque: Aspects of Post-Latin American Art, Mus Contemp Art, San Diego, Calif, 2000. *Pos:* Grants adminr, Nat Endowment Humanities, 76-79; asst cur, Walker Art Ctr, 83-86, assoc cur, 86-89 & cur, 89-96; sr

cur, Mus Contemp Art, San Diego, 96-2001; dep dir art, chief cur, Orange Co Mus Art, Newport Beach, Calif, 2001-. *Awards:* Govt Merit Award, Nat Endowment Humanities, 79; Humanities Grad Res Grant, Univ Calif, Berkeley, 81; Mus Profs Fel, Nat Endowment Arts, 89; Int Asn Art Critics award, 1994-95; Spl Exhib Award, Int Asn Art Critics Ger, 98. *Mem:* Coll Art Asn; Print Coun Am. *Res:* Contemporary art; American art. *Publ:* Coauth, First Impressions, Walker/Hudson Hills Press, 89; Double trouble: The Patchett Collection, Mus Contemp Art, 98. *Mailing Add:* Orange County Mus Art 850 San Clemente Dr Newport Beach CA 92660

ARMSTRONG, GEOFFREY
PAINTER, ARCHITECT
b Toronto, Ont, May 27, 28. *Study:* Univ Toronto, BArch, 52. *Work:* Art Gallery Windsor, Ont; Univ Nebr, Fredericton; City North Bay, Ont; Esso Resources, Calgary, Alta; Royal Bank, Toronto. *Exhib:* Art Gallery Hamilton; Montreal Mus Fine Arts; Art Gallery Ont; Trent Univ; Queens Univ, Kingston; Ont Soc Artists Traveling Exhib; Soc Can Artists Traveling Exhib. *Mem:* Royal Archit Inst Can; Soc Can Artists; Ont Soc Artists; Royal Can Acad. *Media:* Acrylic. *Publ:* Contribr, Art Mag, 68-70. *Dealer:* Roberts Gallery 641 Yonge St Toronto ON M4Y 1Z9. *Mailing Add:* 78 B Cresent Rd Toronto ON M4W 1T5 Canada

ARMSTRONG, L C
PAINTER
b Humbolt, Tenn, Dec 18, 54. *Study:* Art Ctr Col Design, BFA, 82; San Francisco Art Inst, BFA, 87. *Work:* Corcoran Gallery Art, Washington, DC; Sony Corp; Univ S Fla, Tampa. *Exhib:* 42nd Biennial, Contemp Am Painters, Corcoran Gallery Art, Washington, DC, 91; Biennial of Sydney, 92; Making & Unmaking, Univ S Fla Contemp Mus, Tampa, 95; Pittura Immedia, Neue Galerie/Landesmuseum, Graz, Austria, 95; L C Armstrong Paintings, Bravin Post Lee, NY, 97; The Corcoran Collects, Corcoran Gallery Art, Washington, DC, 98; Maul Flowers, Gallerie Ausstellungspraum Hubner, Frankfurt, Ger, 98; Life is Beautiful, Laing Art Gallery, Newcastle-Upon-Tyne, Eng, 2002; Flowe Power, Musee des Beaux Arts, Lille, France, 2004; POPulace, Blaffer Gallery, The Art Mus Univ Houston, Tex, 2005; One-person shows Galerie Sophia Ungers, Cologne, Ger, 91, 92, White Columns, New York City, 92, Marsha Mateyka Gallery, Washington, DC, 93, 97, Bravin Post Lee, New York City, 94, USF Contemp Mus, Tampa, Fla, 95, Hofstra Univ, Hempstead, NY, 98, Angeles Gallery, Santa Monica, Calif, 99, Galerie Huebner, Frankfurt, Ger, 2000, Postmasters Gallery, NY, 2001, Marsha Mateyka Gallery, Washington, DC, 2003, others. *Awards:* Pollock Krasner Found Grant, 92. *Bibliog:* Faye Hirsch (auth), L C Armstrong at John Post Lee, Art Am, 94; Ferdinand Protzman (auth), Business is booming, Washington Post, 3/22/97; Barry Schwabsky (auth), The Widening Circle Consequences of Modernism in Contemporary Art, Cambridge Univ Press, 97. *Media:* Acrylic, Bombfuse. *Dealer:* Angles Gallery 2230 Main St Santa Monica CA 90405. *Mailing Add:* 33 Harrison St New York NY 10013

ARMSTRONG, MARTHA (ALLEN)
PAINTER, PHOTOGRAPHER
b Brunswick, Ga, 35. *Study:* Converse Col, under August Cook, 53-56; Heatherly Sch Fine Art, London, Eng, advan painting, 67-69. *Work:* C G Jung Educ Ctr, Rovi Tex Corp, Rapada Corp & Apple Computers, Dallas, Tex; United Energy Resources, Dresdner Bank, Texaco USA, Houston, Tex; Smithsonian Inst, Washington, DC; Lowell Early Childhood Ctr, Fresh Meadows, NY; Enpro Int, Jeddah, Saudi Arabia; and others. *Comn:* Cover art, Performing Arts Mag, 81; cover art, spring brochure, C G Jung Educ Ctr, Houston, 84; cover art, inaugural brochure, Tex Inst Arts Educ, 84; cover art, Houston on Stage Mag, 85. *Exhib:* Houston Mus Fine Arts, Glassell Sch, 78; McMurtrey Gallery, Houston, Tex, 91; Inman Gallery, Houston, Tex, 91; Visual Arts Alliance, 93; Galveston Arts Ctr, 94; Hooks Epsein, Houston, Tex, 94. *Collection Arranged:* 34 Houston Artists Working in their Studios, 77. *Pos:* Visual arts panelist, La State Coun for the Arts, Baton Rouge, 86. *Teaching:* Instr art, All Saints Aids Ctr, Pasadena, Calif, 90-91. *Bibliog:* Patricia Johnson (auth), Martha Armstrong's photography is softly personal, Houston Chronicle, 82; Carol Everingham (auth), New York exhibit features Armstrong photos, Art News, Houston Post, 84; Essays on Texas Women in the Arts, Moore, Sylvia, Midmarch Arts, 88. *Mem:* Cult Arts Coun Houston (bd dir 79-85, vpres, 81, pres, 82, chmn bd, 83); Houston Ctr Photography (trustee, 83-94); Contemp Arts Mus (trustee, 78-80); Fel of Contemp Art, Los Angeles. *Media:* Acrylic, Oil. *Dealer:* McMurtrey Gallery 3508 Lake St Houston TX 77006. *Mailing Add:* 14 Sutton Pl S New York NY 10022

ARMSTRONG, RICHARD
CURATOR, MUSEUM DIRECTOR
b Kans City, Mo, 49. *Study:* Universite de Dijon, cert, 69; Universite de Paris IV, Sorbonne, dipl, 70; Lake Forest Col, (Ill, BA(art hist), 71; Whitney Mus Am Art, Independant Study Prog(Helena Rubinstein Fel), 73-74. *Collection Arranged:* Kim Mac Connel, 76, Manny Farber, 77, The Modern Chair: Its Origins and Evolution, 78 & Richard Art Schwager's Theme(s), 79, La Jolla Mus Contemp Art, Calif; Five Painters in NY, 84, The Sculpture of RM Fischer, 84, Biennial Exhib, 85, 87, 89 & 91, Mechanical Illusions by Robert Cumming, 86, Guy Pene du Bois: The 1920s, 88, Recent Drawings, 88 & Richard Artschwager, 88, Whitney Mus Am Art, NY; David Park: Paintings and Drawings of the 1950s, 89, Craig Kauffman, 89, The New Sculpture 1965-75: Between Geometry and Gesture, 90, Hunt Diederich, 91, Gifts and Acquisitions, 91 & Alexis Smith, 91, Whitney Mus Am Art, New York; Alexis Rockman, 93, Pittsburgh Collects, 93, Andrew Lord, 93, Craigie Horsfield, 93, Andrea Zittel, 94, The Modern Chair, 94, Manny Farber, 94 & Carnegie Int, 95, Carnegie Mus Art. *Pos:* From assoc cur to cur, La Jolla Mus Contemp Art, Calif, 75-80; sr instr, Independant Study Prog, Whitney Mus Am Art, 81-85, adj cur, 84-87, assoc cur, 88-89 & cur, 89-92; cur contemp art, Carnegie Mus Art, 92-96, chief cur, 95-96 & Henry J Heine II dir, 96-. *Mem:* Russell Found, La Jolla, Calif (bd mem, 83-91); Artists Space, New York (bd mem, 85-92); White Columns, New York (bd mem, 86-92). *Publ:* Contribr, Artforum, 79-84. *Mailing Add:* Carnegie Mus Art 4400 Forbes Ave Pittsburgh PA 15213-4080

ARMSTRONG, ROGER JOSEPH
PAINTER, CARTOONIST
b Los Angeles, Calif, Oct 12, 1917. *Study:* Pasadena City Col; Chouinard Art Inst; Art Inst SCalif, Laguna Beach, hon PhD, 90. *Hon Degrees:* Art Inst Southern Calif, PhD, 90. *Work:* City of Santa Fe Springs, Calif; City of Pico Rivera; Banking House of Rothschild, San Francisco; Laguna Beach Art Mus, Calif. *Exhib:* Griswold Gallery, Claremont, Calif, 74; Calif 100 Exhib, Laguna Beach Mus Art, 77; Dana Point Marine Inst, 81; Nat Watercolor Soc Exhib, Brea Civic Cult Ctr, Calif, 84 & 85; Stary Sheets Gallery, Irvine, Calif, 92; Vaguna Art Mus, The Many Faces of Roger Armstrong, Irvine Art Ctr, Nov 04 to Feb 05; one-man show: Retrospective, Works from 1930s to 2005. *Collection Arranged:* Three-man exhib, Keith Finch, Edgar Ewing & Robert Frame, 63; West Coast Figurative, 64; First Ann West Coast Sculpture Exhib, 64; plus others. *Pos:* Bk illusr & cartoonist, Walt Disney Co, 78-88. *Teaching:* Instr cartooning & watercolor painting, Laguna Beach Sch Art, 65-; instr watercolor, Pasadena City Col, 74-78; instr oil painting, Saddleback Community Col, Mission Viejo, 78; instr cartooning, Orange Coast Col, Costa Mesa, Calif, 81-91; So Calif Art Inst, 88-; Irvine Valley Col, Calif, 94-; Art Inst Southern Calif, Laguna Beach, 98-2002. *Awards:* First Purchase Award, First Ann Pio Pico Art Festival, 68; Hon Mention, East Meets West Exhib, Calif Nat Watercolor Soc, 72; Motion Picture Screen Cartoonists (MPSC) Golden Award, 92; Helene Modjeska Cult Legacy Award, Arts Orange Co, 2003. *Bibliog:* Raymond Fisher & John Barnard (auths), Roger Armstrong, triple threat artist, World of Comic Art, winter 66-67; Shel Dorf (auth), Comic Interviews, Roger Armstrong, 86; RC Harvey (auth), Cartoonist Profiles, comics by Roger Armstrong, 91; Gordon T McClelland & Jay Last (auths), California Watercolors 1850-1970. *Mem:* Nat Cartoonists Soc; Comic Artists Professional Soc; Southern Calif Cartoonist Soc; Nat Watercolor Soc (pres, 84-85). *Media:* Watercolor, Ink. *Publ:* Coauth & illusr, Ella Cinders comic strip, United Features Syndicate, 50-61 & Napoleon & Uncle Elby, Los Angeles Times Syndicate, 50-60; auth & illusr, Flintstones, Little Lulu & others, Western Publ, 60-72; comic strip illusr, Scamp, Walt Disney Productions; artist, auth, How to Draw Comic Strips, Walter Foster Publ Co, 90; auth & publ, Favored Nudes (8 vols, 300 paintings). *Dealer:* Anderson Gallery Sunset Beach CA. *Mailing Add:* Roger Armstrong Studio Ste H5 23011 Moulton Parkway Laguna Hills CA 92653

ARMSTRONG, THOMAS NEWTON, III
MUSEUM DIRECTOR EMER
b Portsmouth, Va, July 30, 1932. *Study:* Art Students League, summer 53; Cornell Univ Col Archit, Art & Planning, BFA, 54; Inst Fine Arts, NY Univ, 65-67. *Hon Degrees:* HHD, Hamilton Col. *Pos:* From cur to assoc dir, Abby Aldrich Rockefeller Folk Art Col, Williamsburg, Va, 67-71; dir, Pa Acad Fine Arts, Philadelphia, 71-73; assoc dir, Whitney Mus Am Art, NY, 73-74, dir, 74-90, dir emer, 90-; dir, Andy Warhol Mus, Pittsburgh, 93-95; consultant, 95-; trustee, New York Sch Interior Design; vice chmn, dir The Garden Conservancy, Cold Spring, NY, 91-; mem scholar selection com, Luce Scholars program, Henry Luce Found, Inc, NY, 82-; Garden Committee, Winterthur; trustee, Nat Bldg Mus, Washingtion, 99-; mem adv coun, Mount Vernon, 02; active numerous instns. *Awards:* Faculty Fine Arts Medal, Cornell U, 54; Herbert Adams Mem Award for the Advancement of Sculpture, Nat Sculpture Soc, 77; David L Lawrence Mem Award, Man of the Yr, Pittsburgh, 95; Woodrow Wilson Inst, Woodrow Wilson Fel, 81-85. *Bibliog:* Jean Lipman (auth), Provocative Parallels, EP Dutton & Co, Inc, New York, 74; Peter Jones (auth), The Gardener's Almanac, Houghton Mifflin Co, New York, 97; Wilder Green, New American Filmmakers, Selections from the Whitney Museum of American Art Film Program, Am Fedn Arts, 76. *Publ:* auth, introduction, Pantheon Story of American Art, Pantheon Books, New York, 75; foreword & essay, The Innocent Eye: American Folk Sculpture, David R Godine & Whitney Mus Am Art, Boston, 76; with Susan C Larsen, Art in Place: Fifteen Years of Acquisitions, Whitney Mus Am Art, 89; Amerikanische malerei, 1930-1980, Prestel-Verlag, Munich, 81; American Folk Painters of Three Centuries, Hudson Hills Press, Inc & Whiteny Mus Am Art, New York, 80; foreword,The Aesthetics of American Folk Art, Albright-Knox Art Gallery, 75; 200 Years of American Sculpture, David R Godine & Whitney Mus Am Art, Boston, 76; An American Odyssey, Monacelli Press, 01. *Mailing Add:* 860 United Nations Plaza 23E New York NY 10017

ARNESON, WENDELL H
PAINTER
b Madison, Wis, Sept 10, 46. *Study:* Luther Col, BA, 68; Bowling Green State Univ, MA, 77, MFA, 78. *Work:* Miller Mus Art, Sturgeon Bay, Wis. *Comn:* Univ Wis Hosp, Madison, 82; watercolor triptych, Prudential Life Insurance Corp, Minneapolis, 83; watercolor triptych, Benson Optical Corp, 84; watercolor triptych, 3M Corp, 84; watercolor triptych, IBM Corp, 85. *Exhib:* Minn State Competition Exhib, Rochester Art Ctr, 79; Nat Watercolor Invitational, Clarks Art Ctr, Rockford, Ill, 84. *Teaching:* Prof painting & drawing, St Olaf Col, Northfield, Minn, 78-, chmn dept, 84-91, 94-98. *Awards:* Drawing Award, Toledo Mus Art, 78; Painting Award, Watercolor USA, Springfield Art Mus, 84. *Mem:* Col Art Asn. *Media:* Watercolor, Oil Painting. *Mailing Add:* St Olaf Col Dept Art Northfield MN 55057

ARNETT, JOE ANNA
PAINTER, SCULPTOR
b Jacksonville, Tex, May 9, 50. *Study:* Univ Tex, BFA, 72; Art Students League, New York, 78-82. *Work:* Norwest Bank, Santa Fe, NMex; Blount Corp Collection, Montgomery, Ala; Franklin Mint Corp Collection, Pa; also pvt collections, Mr & Mrs Brian Dennehy, Mr & Mrs Don Meredith, Mr & Mrs Gary Biszantz, Mr & Mrs John

Dobbs, Mr & Mrs Luther Hodges & Mr Roger Ebert. *Comn:* Still Life of Memorable Objects, comn by Sen John Warner, Washington, 92; peppers & brass, comn by James Robinson, NY, 94. *Exhib:* solo exhib, Flowers: A Celebration of Life, 93 & From the Artist's Garden, 95, Zaplin-Lambert Gallery, Santa Fe, NMex; Artists of Am, Denver Hist Soc Mus, Colo, 88-2000; two person show, Catto Gallery, London, 89-92; Albuquerque Art in Miniature, Albuquerque Mus Fine Art, NMex, 89-96; Art Asia, Exhib Ctr, Hong Kong, 94; Prix de West, Nat Cowboy Hall of Fame, 96-2000; Great Am Artists, Cincinnati, Ohio, 97-2000. *Pos:* Art Dir, Young & Rubicam Advert, 76-80. *Teaching:* Inst still life, Scottsdale Artists Sch, Ariz, 91-2000 & La Villa Arrigo, Atelier, Florence, Italy, 98; Fredericksberg Artists Sch, 98-2000. *Awards:* Master Artist, Artist's Am Show; Katherine A Lovell meml Award, Catherine Lorillard Wolfe Art Club, Inc, 84. *Bibliog:* Claire Frankle (auth), Article in Int Herald Tribune, 2/89; Carole Katchen (auth), Painting with Passion, North Light, 94; Vicki Stavice, Art of the west, Art West, fall, 95. *Mem:* Kappa Pi. *Media:* Oil. *Publ:* Auth, The painted flower, Promethena, 95; auth, The Best of Fresh Flowers, 96, Painting Sumptuous Vegetables, Fruits, and Flowers in Oil, 98 & The Best of Flower Painting II, 99, North Light. *Dealer:* Zaplin-Lampert Gallery 651 Canyon Rd Santa Fe NM 87501. *Mailing Add:* PO Box 8022 Santa Fe NM 87504

ARNHEIM, RUDOLF
EDUCATOR, WRITER
b Berlin, Ger, July 15, 1904; US citizen. *Study:* Univ Berlin, PhD, 28; Guggenheim fel, 42-43; RI Sch Design, Hon DFA, 76. *Teaching:* Mem fac psychol art, Sarah Lawrence Col, 43-68; prof, Harvard Univ, 68-74; vis prof, Univ Mich, 74-84. *Awards:* Distinguished Serv Award, Nat Art Educ Asn; Resident, Am Acad Rome, 78; Order of Honor Award, Div 10 Am Psychological Asn; Lifetime Achievement Award, Col Art Asn, 2003. *Mem:* Am Soc Aesthet (pres & trustee); Am Psychol Asn (pres, div arts, 70-72); Col Art Asn. *Publ:* The power of the center, 82 & rev ed, 88; New essays on the psychology of art, 86; Parables of Sun Light, 89; To the Rescue of Art, 92; The Split and the Structure, 96. *Mailing Add:* Glacier Hills Care & Rehab Ctr 1200 Earhart Rd #224 Ann Arbor MI 48105

ARNHOLM, RONALD FISHER
DESIGNER, EDUCATOR
b Barre, Vt, Jan 4, 1939. *Study:* RI Sch Design, BFA(graphic design), 61; Yale Univ, MFA(graphic design), 63. *Work:* Ga Comn Arts Traveling Exhib. *Comn:* Corp design prog (with Jack MacDonald), Am Tube & Controls, West Warwick, RI, 62; typeface: Jenson Roman, Mergenthaler Linotype Co, Plainview, NY, 64; wall mural, Mead Corp, Atlanta, Ga, 65; typefaces: Aquarius series, 70-74, Fovea series, 77-79, Visual Graphics Corp, Tamarac, Fla, Veritas series, 89, World Typeface Ctr, NY, Headline series, 80, Financial & Classified Types, 88, Los Angeles Times, Legacy Series, Int Typeface Corp, NY, 93. *Exhib:* Composing Rm Award Typography Exhib, Gallery 303, NY, 63; one-man show, Ga Mus Art, Athens, 65; 45th Ann Art Dir Club NY Ann Exhib, 66; Southeastern Ann, High Mus Art, Atlanta, 67; Typomundus 20/2 Int Typography Exhib, Stuttgart, Ger, 70. *Pos:* Art dir, The Moderator Mag, New Haven, Conn, 62-63. *Teaching:* From instr to asst prof art, Univ Ga, 63-71, assoc prof, 71-82, prof, 82-. *Awards:* Award of Distinctive Merit, Art Dir Club, New York, 66; Cert of Merit, Typomundus 20/2, 70; Albert Christ-Janer Award, Univ Ga, 94. *Bibliog:* Eugene Ettenberg (auth), The Word Paintings of Ronald Arnholm, Am Artist, 11/70; Edward M Gottschall (auth), The Word Paintings of Ronald Arnholm, Typographic, Vol 3, No 3. *Mailing Add:* Univ Ga Dept Art Athens GA 30602

ARNING, BILL A
CURATOR, ADMINISTRATOR
b New York, NY, Sept 16, 60. *Study:* New York Univ, BA, 84. *Exhib:* Stux Boston, Stux Gallery, NY; The Second Second at Althea Viafora Gallery; The Anti-Masculine, Kimlight Gallery, Los Angeles, 92; Faggots: A Comunique From North Am Gay & Lesbian Artists, F Rojas BA, Argentina. *Pos:* Asst dir, White Columns, 84-85, exec dir, 85-; art ed, Bomb Mag, 91-. *Teaching:* Guest lectr, Pace Univ, 85, Art Inst Chicago, 88, Sch Visual Arts, NY Univ, 90, Snug Harbor, 92, Toronto Col Art, 91, Tyler Sch Art, Philadelphia, 92, Tama Art Univ, Japan, 91, Yale, 94 & Forum Gallery, St Louis. *Publ:* Auth, Update 86, Update 87, Update 88, Update 89, Update 90 & Update 91 & 92 (catalogs), White Columns; Tom Brazelton's fickle abstractions, In: USA Pavilion Catalog, 87; Glittering Prize, 87, Ecuadorian Bienial, 88 & Russel Floersche, 88, Stux Gallery; auth, catalog, Peter Scott, Riverside Studios, London; Jeffrey Jenkins (catalog), Stux Gallery, 89; contribr (with Kirby Gookin), A Naming of the Colors, 93. *Mailing Add:* MIT List Visual Arts Ctr Bldg E15 Atrium level 20 Ames St Cambridge MA 02139

ARNITZ, RICK
PAINTER
b St Louis, Mo, 49. *Study:* Univ Calif, Berkeley, BA, 75, MA, 80, MFA, 82. *Work:* Achenbach Found, Palace Legion Hon, Bank Am, Park Hyatt Hotel, San Francisco Mus Mod Art; Continental Securities, Vancouver; Oakland Mus, Calif; Monterey Mus Art, Calif; San Jose Mus Art; Univ Art Mus, Berkeley, Calif. *Exhib:* One-man shows, Union Gallery, San Jose State Univ, 84, Stephen Wirtz Gallery, San Francisco, 88, 91, 93, 94, 96 & 98, San Francisco Mus Mod Art, 89, Univ Art Mus, Santa Barbara, 90, Plaza Gallery, Bank Am, San Francisco, 93 & Galerie Zenit, Copenhagen, Denmark & As Is, Stephen Wirtz Gallery, 2000, Backdrops: New Paintings, Stephen Wirtz Gallery, San Francisco, Calif, 2002; Old Glory, New Story, Flagging the 21st Century, CAPP St Proj, San Francisco, 92; West Comes East, Miller Block Gallery, Boston, 92; Why Painting-Part I, Susan Cummins Gallery, Mill Valley, 92; Blue, Stephen Wirtz Gallery, San Francisco, 95, Generations, The Lineage of Influence in Bay Area Art, Richmond Art Ctr, Calif, 96; Summer Show, Stephen Wirtz Gallery, San Francisco, Calif, 97; Toward the Millenium: Contemp Works of Art from Northern Calif, Monterey Mus Art, Calif, 97; New Am Talent, 13th Exhib, Univ N Tex Art Gallery, Denton, Tex, 97; In Over Our Heads: The Image of Water in Contemp Art, San Jose Mus Art, Calif, 98; Art from Around the Bay: Recent Acquisitions, San Francisco Mus Mod Art, Calif, 98; Works on Paper, Stephen Wirtz Gallery, San Francisco, Calif, 98; and others. *Awards:* Roslyn Schneider Eisner Award, Univ Calif, Berkeley, 80; Art Space, Support Grant, San Francisco, Calif, 90; Nat Endowment Arts Award, 92. *Bibliog:* Jen Graves (auth), From sea to shining sea, a comprehensive cross-section of American art lands at UNT, Denton Rec Chronicle, 8/28/97; Marcy Freedman (auth), First Thursday report, SF Weekly, Vol 17, No 17, 6/3-9/98; Kenneth Baker (auth), Content tucked in folds of Arnitz's banded work, San Francisco Chronicle, 6/11/98. *Media:* Oil, Acrylic. *Dealer:* Stephen Wirtz Gallery San Francisco CA. *Mailing Add:* c/o Stephen Wirtz Gallery 49 Geary 3rd Flr San Francisco CA 94108

ARNOLD, ANN
ILLUSTRATOR
b San Francisco, 52. *Study:* Univ Calif Santa Cruz, BA, 75. *Exhib:* numerous exhib in London and the US. *Mem:* Nat Acad. *Media:* Oil on wood; Watercolor on paper. *Interests:* Still-Life painting. *Publ:* Illusr (books) Fanny at Chez Panisse, 1992; Stop Smelling My Rose, 1997; The Children's Kitchen Garden: A Book of Gardening, Cooking, and Learning, 1997; Firehouse Max, 1997; auth & illusr, The Adventurous Chef: Alexis Soyer, 2002. *Dealer:* Nath Point Gallery specialists in 19th century Calif painting. *Mailing Add:* c/o Pippin Properties Inc 155 E 38th St ste 2H New York NY 10016

ARNOLD, GLORIA MALCOLM
PAINTER
b Covington, Ga, July 16, 45. *Study:* Univ Ga, BS(educ), 66; study with John Gould, 71-78 & Gunter Korus, 84-98. *Work:* General Electric & Berkshire Bank, Pittsfield, Mass; Beloit Corp, Dalton, Mass; Red Lion Inn/Country Curtains, Stockbridge, Mass; Sweet Brook Care Ctr Inc, Williamstown, Mass. *Comn:* Mt Greylock (painting), Berkshire Bank, Pittsfield, Mass, 87; Water Garden (mural), Sweet Brook Care Ctrs, Williamstown, Mass, 90; Autumn (painting), Beloit Corp, Dalton, Mass, 91. *Exhib:* Copley Soc Boston, Mass, 90-98; Springfield Art League Nat, Mus Fine Art, Springfield, Mass, 91-92; Am Artists Professional League, Salmagundi, Club, NY, 91; Academic Artists, First Church Gallery, Springfield, Mass, 91-93, 95-96 & 98, Oil Painters of Am, Quast Galleries, Taos, NMex & others, 93, 94, 96-98, 99-2002; one-man shows, Western New Eng Col, Springfield, Mass, 94 & Southern Vt Art Ctr, Manchester, Vt, 95, Bethlehem Art Gallery, NY, 99; Arts for the Parks Nat Tour, Jackson, Wyo, 96; Made in Massachusetts Exhib, The Norman Rockwell Mus, Stockbridge, Mass, 99; Art of the Animal Kingdom V, Bennington Ctr for Arts, Vt, 2000; Colonie Art League Nat Exhib, Latham, NY, 2000; Oxford Col of Emory Univ, 2002; Int Exhib Animals in Art, 2003; Exhib Large Works, Workshop Live, Pittsfield, Mass, 2006. *Pos:* Vpres, Pittsfield Art League, Mass, 87-89; mem, Lee Cult Coun, Lee, Mass, 90-98 & 2000; vpres, Kent Art Asn, Conn, 94-96, bd mem, 94-99; bd mem, Academic Artists, 2002-2006. *Teaching:* Oil & watercolor, Gloria Malcolm Arnold Studio, 84-2006; watercolor, Berkshire Mus, Pittsfield, Mass, 90-92. *Awards:* Arts for the Parks Silver Medal & Stamp Artist, Nat Parks Acad Arts, 96; Award Excellence, Oil Painters Am Nat, 97; First in Oils, Intl Nature Fine Arts Competition, 98; Finalist, The Artist's Mag Competition, 96-98 & 2000; Jane Peterson Still life Award, Hudson Valley Art Asoc, 99; Women Artists of the West, Wildlife Art Magazine Award, 2003. *Bibliog:* Timothy Q Cebula (auth), Lee Woman's oil painting receives national honor, Berkshire Eagle, 10/96; Kristin Mally (ed), Showtime, US Art Mag, 12/96; Cristina Adams (auth), Oil Painters America, Southwest Art Mag, 5/98. *Mem:* Copley Soc Boston; fel Am Artists Prof League; Acad Artists (bd mem, 2002-03); Oil Painters Am (signature mem). *Media:* Oil, Watercolor. *Publ:* Auth, Creating a mood, No 71, Palette Talk Mag, 87; contrib, Best of Flower Painting 2, 99, Painting More Creatively: Tips and Techniques From North Light Book Club, 2000, Best of Wildlife Art 2, 99, N Light Bks. *Dealer:* Lenox Gallery Fine Art 69 Church St Lenox MA 01240; The Landmark Gallery 31 Ocean Ave Kennebunkport ME. *Mailing Add:* Studio Fine Art 301 E Center St Lee MA 01238

ARNOLD, JACK
ART DEALER, PUBLISHER
b New York, NY. *Study:* Syracuse Univ, BS, 50. *Pos:* Pres, Collector's Workshop, NY, 76-78; vpres, Gallery Hawaii, Honolulu, 78-80; pres, Falcon Fine Art, NY, 80-82; owner, Jack Arnold Fine Arts, NY, 83-. *Teaching:* Dir lithography, Shorewood Atelier, NY, 72-75. *Specialty:* Contemp paintings, drawings, watercolors & graphics. *Publ:* Contribr, The Contemporary Lithographic Workshop Around the World, Van Nostrand Reinhold Co, 74. *Mailing Add:* 5 E 67th St New York NY 10021

ARNOLD, JOSEPH PATTERSON
PAINTER
b Los Angeles, Calif, May 17, 1954. *Study:* Univ Wyo, pre col art courses, 1972; Philadelphia Col Art, BFA, 1977. *Work:* Univ Wyo Art Mus; Wyo State Mus, Cheyenne; Rock Springs (Wyo) Fine Art Ctr. *Comn:* outdoor mural, Town of Wheatland, Wyo. *Exhib:* Creative Process, Dahl Art Mus, Rapid City, SD, 1997; Western Visions, Nat Mus Wildlife Art, Jackson, Wyo, 2002; Wild Water, Bradford Brinton Mus, Sheridan, Wyo, 2002; Expanded Horizons, Yellowstone Art Mus, Billings, Mont, 2003; Wyoming, High & Wide, Ucross Found Gallery, Clearmont, Wyo, 2004; Painting the American West, Univ Wyo Art Mus, Laramie, Wyo, 2005. *Pos:* cur, Artmobile, Univ Wyo Art Mus, 96-98; roster artist, Wyo Arts Coun, 95-. *Awards:* Purchase award, Defining Line, cur Denver Art Mus, 1994; Best of Show, Int Platform Asn, cur Denver Art Mus, 1994; Fine Arts award, Wheatland Pocket Park, Wyo State Hist Soc, 2000. *Bibliog:* Artist celebrates Wyoming, Am Artist, 90; Bob Budd (auth) Wyoming ranches, Southwest Art, 90; Chase Reynolds (auth) J Arnold, Southwest Art, 93. *Media:* Oil, Pastel. *Mailing Add:* 701 South 4th St Laramie WY 82070

ARNOLD, NANCY ANN
CURATOR, EDUCATOR
b Pasadena, Calif, Mar 3, 67. *Study:* Univ Calif, Santa Barbara, MA (art hist and archit), 98, doctoral studies with Bruce Robertson, 2000. *Collection Arranged:* Obsessions I and II, 97, 99; In the Mood: Early California Photography, 99; Illuminating Pamela Benham, 2000. *Pos:* asst to registr, Univ Art Mus, Santa Barbara, Calif, 97-99; asst to photog cur, Santa Barbara Mus Art, 99; cur, Univ Calif Women's Ctr Art Gallery, Santa Barbara, 97-2000. *Teaching:* teaching asst art hist, Univ Calif, Santa Barbara, 98-2000. *Mem:* Col Art Asn. *Publ:* Auth, Communal Material: The AIDS Memorial Quilt, Univ Calif Santa Barbara, 99. *Mailing Add:* Women's Ctr Art Gallery U Calif Women's Ctr Bldg 434 Santa Barbara CA 93106

ARNOLD, PAUL BEAVER
EDUCATOR, PRINTMAKER
b Taiyuanfu, China, Nov 24, 18; US citizen. *Study:* Oberlin Col, AB, 40, MA, 41; Cleveland Inst Art; Univ Minn, MFA, 55. *Work:* Libr Cong, Washington, DC; Seattle Art Mus, Wash; Baltimore Mus, Md; Dayton Art Inst, Ohio; Cleveland Mus Art, Ohio. *Comn:* Pheasant (color intaglio), Int Graphic Arts Soc, NY, 56; White Peacock (color woodcut), Int Graphic Arts Soc, NY, 57; mural, Gilford Instrument Co, Oberlin, Ohio, 71; Martin Luther King Monument, Oberlin, Ohio, 87. *Exhib:* May Show, Cleveland Mus, 61, 63, 66, 74 & 76; one-man shows, Jersey City State Col, NJ, 66, 78, 86 & 97, Miami Univ, Oxford, Ohio, 68, Univ Kans, Manhattan, 70, Firelands Asn Visual Arts, Oberlin, 85 & 95 & Allen Art Mus, Oberlin, 85, Lorain Co Community Col, 2000, Kendal Gallery, Oberlin, Ohio, 2002; Contemp Prints for Collectors, Columbus Gallery Art, Ohio, 75; two-man show, US Info Serv, US Embassy, Ankara, Turkey, 75; Jane Haslem Gallery, Wash, DC, 90; Intown Club Gallery, Cleveland, 93; Atrium Gallery, Boulder, Colo, 96; group exhib incl: Cleveland Playhouse Gallery, 96, 98, 2001. *Teaching:* From instr to prof art & chmn dept, Oberlin Col, 41-86, Young-Hunter prof, 82-86, prof emer, currently; guest prof, Tunghai Univ, Taiwan, 72, Sarah Lawrence Col, Lacoste, France, 79 & 80 & Lacoste Cleveland Inst Art, 85. *Awards:* Ford Found Fac Fel Prog, 51-52; Audubon Artists Medal of Honor, 57; Great Lakes Cols Asn Res Grant, 65-66; Oberlin Alumni Medal, 85. *Mem:* Nat Asn Schs Art (bd dir, 70-81, vpres, 72-75, pres, 75-78); Col Art Asn (bd dir, 79-, secy, 82-, vpres, 84-86, pres, 86-88); Mid-Am Col Art Asn (bd dir, 89-91). *Media:* Woodcut, Intaglio. *Publ:* Illusr, General chemistry & laboratory experiments in general chemistry, Campbell & Steiner, 55; coauth, The Humanities at Oberlin, 57; auth, Printmaking today, 4/70 & Silkscreen printing, 12/74, Lalit Kala Contemp, New Delhi, India; contribr, Terra cotta army of Quin Shihuangdi, Ceramics Monthly, 11/80. *Mailing Add:* 138 Kendal Dr Oberlin OH 44074

ARNOLD, RALPH MOFFETT
PAINTER, EDUCATOR
b Chicago, Ill, Dec 5, 1928. *Study:* Roosevelt Univ, BA; Art Inst Chicago, with Vera Berdich. *Work:* Whitney Mus Am Art, NY; Fisk Univ, Nashville, Tenn; Rockford Col, Ill; Commonwealth Pa; Ill Bell Tel Co, Chicago. *Comn:* Wall murals, James House, Arthur Rubloff Realty Co, 71. *Exhib:* Violence in Am Art, Mus Contemp Art, Chicago, 69; Am Prints Today, Mus Art, Utica, NY, 70; Afro-Am Arts 1800-1969, Mus Philadelphia Civic Ctr, 70; Contemp Black Artists in Am, Whitney Mus Am Art, 71; Cornell Univ, 75. *Pos:* Adv bd, Arts & Sales & Rental Gallery, Art Inst Chicago; artist adv bd, Ill Arts Coun. *Teaching:* Instr painting, Rockford Col, 69-70; asst prof, Barat Col, Lake Forest, 70-; prof fine arts, Loyola Univ Chicago, 70-, chmn dept, currently. *Awards:* Artists-in-residence to help underprivileged children, Ill Art Coun, 69. *Mem:* Arts Club Chicago. *Mailing Add:* 1858 N Sedgwick St Chicago IL 60614

ARNOLD, ROBERT LLOYD
PAINTER, EDUCATOR
b Buffalo, NY, June 28, 40. *Study:* NY State Univ Col, Buffalo, BS, 66; Fla State Univ, MS, 68; Ind Univ, EdD, 72. *Work:* NY Col Ceramics, Alfred; Nat Art Gallery NZ, Wellington; Fla State Univ, Tallahassee; Ind Univ. *Exhib:* Sign/Symbol, Nat Art Gallery NZ, 77; Artwords & Bookworks, Los Angeles Inst Contemp Art, 78; one-man shows, Ind Univ, Bloomington, 78, Ohio State Univ, 78, Ashland Col, Ohio, 79, Bowling Green State Univ, 80 & Ohio State Univ, Newark, 82; Spangler Cummings Gallery, 86. *Pos:* Assoc provost, Ohio State Univ, 90-94 & vprovost, 94-97. *Teaching:* Prof art & art educ, Ohio State Univ, 70-. *Awards:* Mem Award, Lester C Bush, 74; Battelle Exhib Award, Dollar Savings, 76; Columbus Mus Award, 79. *Bibliog:* Gina Franz (auth), Six in Ohio, New Art Examiner, 78; Robert Pincus-Witten (auth) Six in Ohio, Ohio State Univ/Ohio Arts Coun, 78; Donald Kuspit (auth), Columbus, Art in Am, 79. *Mem:* Ohio Art Educ Asn; Nat Art Educ Asn; Columbus Art League (pres, 79 & 80). *Media:* Acrylic Paint; Canvas. *Res:* Contemporary art; art education. *Publ:* Auth, An analysis of selected teacher preparation programs: 1975, Art Educ, 76; The spoken retrospective: Chris Burden at 30, Midwest Art, 76; The development of a pluralistic avant-garde, Art Educ, 76; An interview with Lawrence Alloway, Midwest Art, 77; Studies in art education (invited ed), 95. *Mailing Add:* 289 Odessa Lane Dublin OH 43017

ARNOLD, SKIP
VIDEO ARTIST, PERFORMANCE ARTIST
b Binghamton, NY. *Study:* State Univ Col, Buffalo, NY, BFA, 80; Univ Calif, Los Angeles, MFA, 84. *Exhib:* One-artist exhibs, Punch (video), Laguna Art Mus, Laguna Beach, Calif, 92, Statue (performance), Kim Light Gallery, Los Angeles, Calif, 93, Living Quarters/Conducting Business, Unfair, Cologne, Ger, 93, Spin (performance), Jack Tilton Gallery, NY, 94, Roger Merians Gallery, NY, 95, 35 rue des Bains, Geneva, 96, Spencer Brownstone Gallery, NY, 97, 99, Galerie Montenay-Giroux, Paris, 99, Aeroplastics, Brussels, Belg, 2000, Shoshana Wayne Gallery, Santa Monica, Calif, 2000, Galerie MXM, Prague, 2000, Roberts and Tilton, Los Angeles, 2000; Let the Artist Live, Exit Art, NY, 94; Courage, New Mus Contemp Art, NY, 94; Persistent Dispositions - Technetronic Identities, Calif Inst Arts, Valencia, 95; Cadeaux Paquets, Galerie Satellite, Paris, 95; Skip Arnold - Sigrid Hackenberg, Roger Merians Gallery, NY, 95; Menu du Jour, Silverstein Gallery, NY, 96; Angel Hair: Ex LA, Dogenhaus Galerie, Leipzig, Ger, 97; The Road Show, Bronwyn Keenan Gallery, NY, 97; Sunshine & Noir: Art from La, 1960-1997, La Mus Art, Humlebaek, Denmark, 97; Identity Crisis, Spencer Brownstone Gallery, New York City, 98; Venus, ARC Galerie, Wien, Austria, 99; Recontre, Int d'Art Performance de Que, Le Lieu, Que, Can, 00; Exit Festival, Helsinki, Finland, 01; Art Unlimited, Art 33 Basel, Switz, 02; and many others. *Teaching:* Vis fac, VUT Acad Art, Brno, Czech, 00; adj fac, Grad Studio Fine Arts and Liberal Arts and Scis, Art Ctr Col Design, Pasadena, Calif, 97-. *Awards:* Brody Arts Found Fel, 92; Art Matters Inc Fel, 92; Nat Endowment Arts Visual Arts Fel Grant, 93; John Simon Guggenheim Mem Found Fel, 95. *Bibliog:* Steve Mikulan (auth), Like a little boy in his fort, Visions, winter 93; Unfair - Art Cologne - Saatchi Collection, Flash Art, Vol XXVII, No 174, 1-2/94; Kateri Butler (auth), Long gone train, LA Weekly, 2/4-10/94; Grady T Turner (auth), Skip Arnold at Spencer Brownstone, 118-119, Art in America, 10/1997; Charlene Roth, Abject Edge: Recent American Figurative Art, 40-45, 12/1999; Shana Nys Dambrot (auth), Pushed to an Abject Edge, 27, dART Int, 2000. *Dealer:* Spencer Brownstone Gallery New York NY; Aeroplastics Brussels Belgium. *Mailing Add:* c/o Musex Editions 3499 Cahuenga Blvd Los Angeles CA 90068

ARNOLDI, CHARLES ARTHUR
SCULPTOR, PAINTER
b Dayton, Ohio, April 10, 46. *Study:* Chouinard Art Inst, Los Angeles, 68. *Work:* Los Angeles Co Mus Art; Mus Mod Art, NY; Chicago Art Inst; Metrop Mus Art, NY; San Francisco Mus Mod Art. *Comn:* Wood relief paintings, Continental Nat Bank, Ft Worth, 81 & First Int Bank, Houston, 82; Hughes Corp, Los Angeles, 85; State of Calif, State Office Bldg, San Francisco, 88; bronze sculpture, City of Beverly Hills, Calif; canvas paintings, 101 2nd St, San Francisco, 99 & Hollywood Renaissance Hotel, Calif, 2001. *Exhib:* solo exhibs, Nicholas Wilder Gallery, 74-75, 77-78 & 79, Seattle Art Mus, 76, Robert Elkon Gallery, NY, 78 & 79, James Corcoran Gallery, Los Angeles, 80-85, Charles Arnoldi: Unique Prints, Los Angeles Co Mus Art, 84, Fuller Goldeen Gallery, San Francisco, 85 & 87, Charles Cowles Gallery, NY, 85-87 & 93-94, Arts Club Chicago, 86, Univ Mo-Kansas City Gallery Art, 86, Univ Art Mus, Calif State Univ, Long Beach, 87, Mus Italo Am, San Francisco, 88, Fred Hoffman Fine Art, Santa Monica, 91 & 96, Tony Shafrazi Gallery, NY, Chac-Mool Gallery, CA, 99 & 2000, Charles Cowles Gallery, NY, 99 & 2000, Ochi Fine Art, Ketchum Idaho, 99 & Busan Metrop Art Mus, South Korea, 2002, Modrnism, San Francisco, 2003, Bobbie Greenfield Gallery, Santa Monica, 2003 & 2004; Whitney Biennial, 81; Am: The Landscape, Contemp Arts Mus, Houston, 81; 38th Biennial, Corcoran Gallery Art, Washington, 83; Am Prints Today, Brooklyn Mus, 86; 70's in 80's: Printmaking Now, Mus Fine Arts, Boston, 86; Prints by Los Angeles Artists, Asahi Shimbun Gallery, Tokyo, 87; The 1980's: A New Generation, Metrop Mus Art, NY, 88; The Unique Print: 70s into 90s, Mus Fine Arts, Boston, 90; Visions/Revisions, Denver Art Mus, 91; The Contemp Mus Collects the First Five Yrs 1988-1993, Contemp Mus, Honolulu, 93; Between Reality & Abstraction: Calif Art at the End of the Century, Art Mus STex, Corpus Christi, 95; Calif Color, Univ Nebr, Lincoln, 96; The View from Denver, Mus Mod Art, Vienna, Austria, 97; Radical Past: Contemp Art and Music in Pasadena 1960-74, Armory Ctr for Arts, 99; Celebrating Modern Art: The Anderson Collection, San Francisco Mus Modern Art, 2000; Lost but Found: Assemblage, Collage & Sculpture, 1920-2002, Norton Simon Mus, Pasadena, Calif, 2004; Paint on Metal, Theson mus Art, 2005. *Awards:* Wittkowsky Award, Art Inst Chicago, 72; Fels, Nat Endowment Arts, 74 & 82 & John Simon Guggenheim Found, 75; Maestro Fel, Calif Arts Coun, 82. *Bibliog:* Fredericka Hunter (auth), Charles Arnoldi: Paintings & Sculpture 1971-1988, Mus Italo Americano, 88; Sam Hunter (auth), Charles Arnoldi, A Mid-Career Survey: 1970-1996, Fred Hoffman Fine Arts, 96; Suzanne Muchnic (auth), Charles Arnoldi at Fred Hoffman, Artnews, 9/96; Fred Hoffman (auth), The Pictorial Journey of Charles Arnoldi, Busan Metrop Art Mus, 2002. *Media:* Bronze; Acrylic, Canvas. *Dealer:* Charles Cowles Gallery 537 W 24th St, New York, NY, 10011. *Mailing Add:* Charles Cowles Gallery 537 W 24th St New York NY 10011

ARONSON, DAVID
PAINTER, SCULPTOR
b Shilova, Lithuania, Oct 28, 23; US citizen. *Study:* Boston Mus Fine Arts Sch, with Karl Zerbe, cert, 45; Nat Soc Arts & Lett grant, 58; Guggenheim fel, 60. *Hon Degrees:* Hebrew Col, Boston, DHL, 93; Boston Univ, DFA, 2005. *Work:* Smithsonian Inst, Washington; Art Inst Chicago; Va Mus Fine Arts, Richmond; Boston Mus Fine Arts; Whitney Mus Am Art, NY. *Comn:* Great Ideas of Western Man, Container Corp Am, 63; Brandeis Univ Libr. *Exhib:* Va Mus Fine Arts Biennial, 45; Nat Collection Fine Arts Opening Exhib, Smithsonian Inst, 65; retrospective exhibs, Brandeis Univ, 79, Jewish Mus, NY, 79 & Mus Am Jewish Hist, Philadelphia, 79; Bronfman Ctr, Montreal, 82; Southeastern Mass Univ, 83; Mickelson Gallery, Wash, 85; retrospecitve, Boston Univ, 2005. *Teaching:* Instr painting, Boston Mus Fine Arts Sch, 43-55; chmn div art, Boston Univ, 55-63, prof art, 62-89, chmn painting dept, 63-89, emer prof art, 89-. *Awards:* Grand Prize, Boston Arts Festival, 52-54; Nat Acad Design, 73, 74 & 75. *Bibliog:* Article, Time Mag, 11/63; Newman (auth), Wax as art form, 66 & Grossman (auth), Art & tradition, 67, Yosellof; David Aronson: Paintings, Drawings, Sculpture Essay, Asher D. Biemann (auth). *Mem:* Nat Acad Design (assoc, 67, acad, 70). *Media:* Pastel; Encaustic, Bronze. *Publ:* Auth, Encaustic, Artist Mag, 62; Real & Unreal: The Double Nature of Art, Boston Univ, 67. *Dealer:* Pucker Gallery 171 Newbury St Boston MA 02116. *Mailing Add:* 137 Brimstone Ln Sudbury MA 01776

ARONSON, GEORGIANNA B See Nyman, Georgianna Beatrice Aronson

ARONSON, SANDA
ASSEMBLAGE ARTIST, SCULPTOR
b New York, NY, Feb 29, 40. *Study:* Oswego State Col, BS, 60; study with J De Creeft & Paul Pollaro at New Sch for Social Res, New York; Tulane Univ, New Orleans; Art Students League. *Work:* NC Print & Drawing Soc. *Comn:* Handprint Harper's Woodcut's, comn by Dr Marvin Oleshanky, 82. *Exhib:* Solo exhibs, Bloomingdale Regional Branch, NY Pub Libr, 74, 75, 95 & 96, Barnard Col, NY, McIntosh Ctr, 85 & Assembled Object, Atlanta Col, Art Gallery, 89; Artists' Soc Int Exhib, ASI Galleries, San Francisco, 87; Tenth Am NDak, Nat Exhib, Minot Art Gallery, 87; Tenth Ann US Print & Drawing Exhib, NC Print & Drawing Soc, 87; Nat Small Works Exhib, Schoharie City Art Coun, Cobbleskill, NY, 87; Winter Solstice Invitational, Ceres Gallery, NY, 87; Am Herstory, Atlanta Col Art Gallery, 88-90; Third Am Int Juried Exhib of Minis, Del Bello Gallery, Toronto; Three Artists, Matrix Gallery, Sacramento, Calif, 88; West Side Art Coalition, Broadway Mall, 99. *Teaching:* Original artist-in-residence Studio in a Sch, 77-79; Artist-in-residence, NY Found Arts, 77-79. *Awards:* Purchase Award, NC Print & Drawing Soc, 87; 2 Pollock-Krasner Found Grants, 86-88; First Place, Sculpture, Emerald City Classic VI, Nepthe Nundi Soc Int Competition, 87; Hon Mention, Emerald City Classic V, 86; Hon Mention, Bodyparts Contest, Lee S McDonald Inc, 88. *Bibliog:* J L Collins (ed), Women Artists in America, Vol II, Univ Tenn at Chattanooga Press, 75; Eleanor Tufts (auth), American Women Artists, Vol II, 89. *Mem:* Disabled Artists' Nework (founder & exec dir, 85-); NY Artists Equity Asn; Women Arts Found (bd-mem-at-large, 75-76). *Media:* Assemblage, Xerographics. *Interests:* Sculpture jewelry. *Publ:* Contribr frontpiece, John Beecher (auth), Hear the Wind Blow, Int Press, 68. *Mailing Add:* PO Box 20781 New York NY 10025

ARSENAULT, KATE WHITMAN See Whitman-Arsenault, Kate

ARTEMIS, MARIA ARTEMIS PAPAGEORGE
SCULPTOR, EDUCATOR
b Greensboro, NC, April 21, 1945. *Study:* Agnes Scott Col, Decatur, Ga, BA, 69; Univ Ga, Athens, MFA, 77; Ga Inst Technol, Col Archit, MS, 91. *Work:* High Mus Art, Atlanta; Huntsville Mus Art, Ala; Columbia Mus Art & Sci, SC. *Comn:* Ctr for Disease Control and Prevention, Environ Health Lab, Gen Serv Admin Art-in Archit, Chamblee, Ga, 99-2001; Mem Proj, Atlanta Detention Ctr, 94; Ex-static (site sculpture), Corp Olympic Develop Atlanta, 95-96; Unknown Remembered Gate (site-specific sculpture), Agnes Scott Col, 96; interfaith chapel, Hartsfield Int Airport, Atlanta, 99-2003. *Exhib:* Avant-Garde/12 in Atlanta, High Mus Art, Ga, 79; Earth Art: Sand & Clay Southeastern Ctr Contemp Art, Winston-Salem, NC, 80; solo exhibs, Nexus Inc 3rd floor Gallery, Atlanta, Ga, 80, Fine Art Gallery, Univ Tenn, Chattanooga, Upstairs Gallery, Tryon, NC, 84, Works on Paper, Univ Central Fla Gallery, Orlando, 87 & Labyrinths: Event, Distillation Artifact, Tulla Found Gallery, Atlanta, 94; Atlanta Women's Art Collective, AIR Gallery, NY, 80; Origins and Evolutions, Part II, Atlanta Col Art Gallery, Mem Art Ctr, Ga, 84; First Atlanta Bienniale, Nexus Gallery, Ga, 84; Avant Garde/12 in Atlanta-Five Yrs Later, Heath Gallery, Ga, 84; Analemma, On Site Work, Atlanta Arts Fest, Piedmont Park, Ga, 85; Contemp Artists in Ga, High Mus Art, Atlanta, 88; New South Group: Installations and Drawings, 112 Greene St, NY, 89; The Women's Path, Permenant Installation, Nexus Art Ctr, 94. *Pos:* Vis artist slides, Univ Wis, Superior, 79; artist-in-residence, Cortona, Italy, 79 & Southeastern Ctr Contemp Art, Winston-Salem, NC, 80; artist fel, Va Ctr Creative Arts, 84 & 91; bd dir, treas, artists initiated projs, New South Group, 89; panel moderator, S Arts Fedn Nat Endowment Arts Regional Fel in Sculpture, 90. *Teaching:* Fac mem sculpture & visual studies, Atlanta Col Art, 79-81; lectr, Atlanta Col Art, spring 83; guest lectr, Ga Inst Technol, Col Archit, Atlanta, Ga, 84; vis prof, Dept Art, Agnes Scott Col, Decatur, Ga, 87-90; adj prof, Atlanta Col Art, 82-. *Awards:* Ga Women in the Visual Arts Award, 97; Mayor's Fel in the Arts Award in Visual Arts, Atlanta, 96; Fulton Co Grant. *Bibliog:* Ann Glenn Crowe (auth), New South Group, Art Papers, 89; Cathy Byrd (auth),Rev of Exhib: Heavy Levity, Sculpture mag, 2000; Anna Bloomfield (auth) 1997 Engaging the Site, Sculpture Mag, Jan/Feb/99; 1997 Comms, Ex-Static, 1/97. *Mem:* Int Sculpture Ctr. *Media:* Mixed. *Publ:* Andy Nasisse: Works off the Wall, Craft Horizon, 78; Art and the Sacred, Art Papers, 11-12/86; auth, Rethinking the Sacred Image, Artpapers, vol IV & V, 90; Public Art in Review, Art in America, 2002. *Dealer:* Sandler Hudson Gallery Atlanta GA. *Mailing Add:* 675 Drewry St Studio 9 Atlanta GA 30306

ARTNER, ALAN GUSTAV
CRITIC
b Chicago, Il, May 14, 47. *Study:* Northwestern Univ, BA 68, MA, 69. *Pos:* Apprentice music critic, Chicago Tribune, 72-73, art critic, 73—; contributing editor, The Art Gallery Mag, 75-76; corr, Artnews Mag, 77-80. *Awards:* Decorated Chevalier de l'ordre des Arts et des Lettres; Rockefeller Found grantee, 71-72. *Publ:* Contribr to Playbill, 1994—. *Mailing Add:* Chgo Tribune Co 435 N Mich Ave Chicago IL 60611-4066

ARTSCHWAGER, RICHARD ERNST
SCULPTOR, PAINTER
b Washington, DC, Dec 26, 1923. *Study:* Cornell Univ, AB; studio study with Amedee Ozenfant. *Work:* Whitney Mus Am Art; Tate Gallery; Chicago Art Inst; Mus Mod Art & Metrop Mus Art; Hirshhorn Mus; pub and pvt collections worldwide. *Comn:* Battery Park City, NY, 88; General Mills Corp, Minneapolis, 88; Elvehjen Mus Art, Madison, Wis, 91. *Exhib:* Cool Art-67, Larry Aldrich Mus, Ridgefield, Conn, 67; Documenta 4, 5, 7, 8 & 9, Kassel, Ger, 68; Radical Realism, Mus Contemp Art, Chicago, 70; Sonsbeek '71, Arnhem/Utrecht, The Neth, 71; Documenta, Kassel, Ger, 68 & 72; Venice Biennale, 76; Two Hundred Yrs of Am Sculpture, Whitney Mus Mod Art, 76; solo exhib, Kunstuerein, Hamburg, 78, Albright-Knox Art Gallery, Buffalo, Inst Contemp Art, Univ Pa, 79, La Jolla Mus Contemp Art, Calif, 80 & Contemp Mus, Houston, Tex, 80; The Destroyed Print, Pratt Manhattan Ctr Gallery, NY, 82; Actual Size, Larry Gagosian Gallery, Los Angeles, 85; An Am Renaissance: Painting and Sculpture Since 1940, Mus Art, Ft Lauderdale, Fla, 85, Retrospective Whitney Mus; Mary Boone Gallery, 90; Kunstnernes Hus, Oslo, 92; Mus Fine Arts, Boston, 92; Found Cartier, Paris, 94; Johnson Mus Art, Cornell Univ, 97; Birth of The Cool, Kunsthalle, Zurich, 97. *Pos:* mem bd Archt League, 80s. *Awards:* Nat Endowment Arts, 71; Archit League New York; Carnegie Prize, 95. *Bibliog:* John Russell (auth), article, NY Times, 79; Roberta Smith (auth), article, Art in Am, 80; Coosje van Bruggen (auth), Richard Artschwajer, Artforum, 9/83. *Publ:* Auth, The hydraulic door check, Arts Mag, 11/67; contribr, Art and Reason, Parkette, No 23, 90. *Mailing Add:* PO Box 23 Hudson NY 12036-0023

ARUM, BARBARA
SCULPTOR
b Des Moines, Iowa, Oct 9, 37. *Study:* With Raymond Rocklin, Vincent Leggiadro, Chaim Gross & Philip Listengart. *Work:* Alan Towers, Inc. *Comn:* Courthouse Annex, Des Moines, Ia. *Exhib:* Hudson River Mus, 82-90; Andre Zarre Gallery, 86; Elaine Benson Gallery, 87; Monmouth Mus Fine Arts, 87; Hammond Mus, 92; and others. *Awards:* Bus Community Award, North Am Sculpture Exhib, Golden, Colo, 87; Dir Max Ellenberg Mem Award, 89 & Gretchen Richardson Freelander Mem Award, 90 & 91, Nat Asn Women Artists, NY; Salvatore Maida Mem Award, Am Soc Contemp Artists, NY, 91. *Bibliog:* Reporters Dispatch, 11/12/82; articles, NY Times, 83, 85 & 87; article, Art World, 10/15/83. *Mem:* Nat Asn Women Artists (sculptor juror, 86-88); Allied Artists (treas, 86); NY Soc Women Artists (pres 90-93); Am Soc Contemp Artists (treas, 92-94); and others. *Media:* Steel; Wood, Bronze. *Publ:* The Guild 9. *Mailing Add:* 20 Hill Rd Accord NY 12404

ASARO, JOHN
PAINTER, ILLUSTRATOR
b San Diego, Calif, Feb 28, 37. *Study:* Apprentice to Donal Hord (sculptor), San Diego, Calif, 52-55; Art Ctr Sch Design, Pasadena, Calif, 55-59; Los Angeles Inst Archit, 79. *Exhib:* Ann Am Watercolor Soc, NY, 83 & 84. *Pos:* Illustr, New Ctr Studios, Detroit, Mich, 60-65; freelance illustr, NY, 65-68 & Los Angeles, 68-70. *Teaching:* Teacher painting, Art Ctr-Col Design, Pasadena, Calif, 74-81, Laguna Beach Sch Art & Design, Calif, 82 & Palomar Col, San Marcos, Calif, 82-85. *Awards:* Excellence Award, NY Art Dirs Club, 68; Cash Award, Ann Am Watercolor Soc, NY, 85. *Bibliog:* J Mathew Fabris (auth), Innocent light, Stepping Out Arts Mag, 11/90; Robert Perine (auth), Asaro, A New Romanticism, Astra Publ, 12/91. *Mem:* Art Students League, NY. *Media:* Oil, Watercolor & Charcoal Drawing. *Publ:* Auth, Painting with Light, Artra Publ, 90. *Dealer:* Marco Fine Arts 201 Nevada St El Segundo CA 90245. *Mailing Add:* 7711 Quitasol St Carlsbad CA 92009-8036

ASAWA, RUTH (ASAWA LANIER)
SCULPTOR, PAINTER
b Norwalk, Calif, Jan 27, 26. *Study:* Milwaukee State Teachers Col, with Robert von Neumann; Black Mt Col, with Josef Albers. *Work:* Whitney Mus Am Art; Chase Manhattan Bank; City of San Francisco; Gov & Mrs Nelson Rockefeller. *Comn:* Two bronze wire sculpture in fountains, Phoenix Civic Plaza; bronze fountain, Ghirardelli Sq; bronze fountain, Hyatt Hotel, San Francisco Union Sq. *Exhib:* Whitney Mus Am Art, 55, 56 & 58; Mus Mod Art, 58; San Francisco Mus Art, 54, 63 & 73; one-man shows, de Young Mem Mus, San Francisco, 60 & Pasadena Mus Art, 65; US Info Agency Junk Art Travel Show, 72-73; plus others. *Pos:* Mem, San Francisco Art Comn, 68-76; co-founder, Alvarado Sch Art Workshop, San Francisco Unified Sch Dist, 68-; mem, Nat Endowment for the Arts Educ Panel, 74-78; mem, Calif Arts Coun, 76-78. *Awards:* Tamarind fel, 65; Purchase Award, San Francisco Art Festival, 66; Dymaxion Award, 66; plus others. *Mailing Add:* 1116 Castro St San Francisco CA 94131

ASCALON, DAVID
SCULPTOR, STAINED GLASS ARTIST
b Tel Aviv, Israel, Mar 8, 45 US Citizen. *Study:* Univ Calif San Fernando Valley, 1965; Pratt Inst, BS, 1974; Bernard Baruch Col, 1974. *Work:* Simon Wiesenthal Ctr, Los Angeles, Calif; Appel Gallery of the Jewish Fed of Southern NJ, Cherry Hill; Science Fiction Mus & Hall of Fame, Seattle, Wash. *Comn:* Holocuast Mem for Buffalo, Temple Beth El, NY, 1986; holocust Mem for Pa, Jewish Community of Greater Harrisburg, Pa, 1994; Tree of Life Monolith, Jewish Fed of Broward Co, Davies, Fla, 1999; Light Monument, Beth Synagogue, Montgomery, Ala, 1999; Holocaust Mem monument, Suburban Torah Ctr, Livingston, NJ, 2000. *Exhib:* Art of the Menorah, The Mus of Am Jewish Hist, Philadelphia, Pa, 1987; Sculpture Retrospective, The Appel Gallery of the Jewish Fed of Southern NJ, 2004. *Pos:* Pres, Ascalon Studios Inc, Berlin, NJ, 1982-; designer, ARi El-Hannani Archit, Tel Aviv, Israel, 1967-68. *Teaching:* lectr, Judaic Art. *Awards:* Litergical Art award, Am Inst of Archit, IFRAA, 1986, 1989; Artists in Residence award, Festival of Art, Music & Culture, 2004. *Bibliog:* Tom Haydon (auth), Message in a Mural, Star Ledger, 4/28/1991; Simon Bronner (auth), Inventing and Invoking Tradition in Holocaust Memorials, Penn St Univ, 10/2000; Jan Heffler (auth), Inside & Outside Sculptor, Philadelphia Inquirer, 10/31/2004. *Mem:* Am Guild Judaic Art (pres, 2004-); Interfaith Forum Religion Art Archit; Am Inst of Archit; Philadelphia Sculptors; Int Sculpture Ctr. *Media:* Sculpture - metal, Stained Glass. *Publ:* Contribr, Synagogues of Am Art Calendar, United Synagogue, 1997-98, 2000-03. *Dealer:* Eric J. Ascalon, Esq. *Mailing Add:* Ascalon Studios 115 Atlantic Ave Berlin NJ 08009-9300

ASCALON, ERIC J
DIRECTOR, ADMINISTRATOR
b NY, Nov 10, 71. *Study:* Rutgers Univ, BA, 93; Am Univ, JD(cum laude), 96. *Comn:* Founders Circle, Science Fiction Mus Hall of Fame, Seattle, Wash. *Collection Arranged:* Metal Crafts of Pal-Bell Co 1939-1956 (trav exhib). *Pos:* atty, Eric J Ascalon, Atty at Law, 97-; Gen Mgr, Ascalon Studios, Berlin, NJ 2001-. *Mem:* Am Guild Judaic art, (treas, 2002-2004); Hist Comn, Cherry Hill, NJ, (voting mem, 2004-). *Interests:* Lawyer specializing in visual arts issues. *Collection:* Mid-Century Design. *Mailing Add:* Ascalon Studios 115 Atlantic Ave Berlin NJ 08009

ASCIAN See Meader, Jonathan (Ascian)

ASHBAUGH, DENNIS JOHN
PAINTER
b Red Oak, Iowa, Oct 25, 46. *Study:* Orange Coast Col, Costa Mesa, Calif, AA, 66; Calif State Univ, Fullerton, BA, 68, MA, 69. *Work:* Rolls Royce Inc, Owens Corning, Inc, Metrop Mus Art, Mus Mod Art, NY; Miami Art Ctr, Fla; Toledo Art Mus, Ohio; Seattle Art Mus, Wash. *Exhib:* One-man shows, Whitney Mus Am Art, 75, Seattle, Art Mus, Wash, 76, Kasmin Gallery, 89 & 90, Margulies-Taplin, Miami, Fla, 91, The Kitchen, NY, 92, Metrop Mus Art Print Gallery, NY, 92, Americas Soc, NY, 92, Goode, Crowley Gallery, Houston, Tex, 93, Marisa del Re Gallery, NY, 93 & Ralls Collection, Washington, DC, 93 Margulies-Taplan Gallery, Miami, 94, Galeri Antoninina Zaru, Capri, Italy, Gallery Twenty Two Eleven, Los Angeles, 01, The Ralls Collection, Washington, 01, and many others; The Painter & His Occasion, Marta Cervera Gallery, NY, 90; Abstraction, Margulies-Taplan Gallery, Boca Raton, Fla, 91; Invisible Body, Rempire Fine Art Gallery, NY, 91; Abstract Painting the '90's, Andre Emmerich, NY; Behind Bars, Thread Waxing Space, NY, 92. *Awards:* Newport Harbor Art Patron's Award, 66; Creative Artists Pub Serv Grant, NY Coun Arts, 75; John Simon Guggenheim Found Fel, 76. *Bibliog:* Guy Martin (auth), Read it Once, Esquire, 5/92; Garvin Edwards (auth), Details, 6/92; Rhonda Lieberman, Artforum, 6/92; and others. *Media:* Oil. *Dealer:* Margulies Taplin Gallery Inc 3310 Ponce De Leon Blvd Coral Gables FL 33134. *Mailing Add:* 67 Greene St New York NY 10012

ASHBERY, JOHN LAWRENCE
CRITIC
b Rochester, NY, July 28, 27. *Study:* Harvard Col, BA (Eng lit), 49; Columbia Univ, MA (Eng lit), 51; New York Univ, 57-58. *Hon Degrees:* Southampton Col, Long Island Univ, DLitt, 79; Harvard Univ, DLitt, 2001. *Pos:* with publicity dept, Oxford Univ Press, New York, 54-55; copywriter, McGraw-Hill Bk Co, New York, 60-65; co-ed, Locus Solus, Lans-en-Vercors, France, 60-62 & Art and Lit, Paris, 64-67; art critic, Art Int, Lugano, Switz, 61-63, New York Mag, 78-80 & Newsweek, New York, 80-85; exec ed, ArtNews, New York, 65-72; poetry ed, Partisan Rev, New York, 76-80. *Teaching:* Prof & co-dir MFA creative writing prog, Brooklyn Col, CUNY, 74-90, distinguished prof, 80-90, distinguished prof emer, 90-; Charles Eliot Norton Prof poetry, Harvard Univ, 89-90; Charles P Stevenson Jr Prof langs & lit, Bard Col, Annandale-on-Hudson, NY, 90-. *Awards:* Spl Citation Lit, Columbia Co Coun Arts, NY, 2001; Wallace Stevens Award, Acad Am Poets, 2001; Officer, Lègion d'Honneur Repub of France, 2002. *Bibliog:* Antoine Cazé (auth), John Ashbery, Voix Américaines, Paris, Berlin, 2000; Poetry and Sense of Panic: Critical Essays on Elizabeth Bishop and John Ashbery, Rodopi, 2000; David Herd (auth), John Ashbery and American Poetry: Fit to Cope with Our Occasions, Manchester Univ Press, 2000, St Martin's, NY, 2001. *Mem:* Am Acad & Inst Arts & Lett; Am Acad Arts & Sci. *Res:* Life & Work of Raymond Roussel. *Publ:* Auth, Girls on the Run, 99; Your Name Here, 2000; Other Traditions, 2000; As Umbrellas Follow Rain, 2001; Chinese Whispers, 2002. *Mailing Add:* c/o Georges Borchardt Inc 136 E 57th St New York NY 10022

ASHCRAFT, EVE
PAINTER
b Pontiac, Mich, Mar 1, 63. *Study:* RI Sch Design, BFA, 85. *Pos:* Owner, Eve Ashcraft Studio, 87; freelance painter, commercial-decorative murals. *Awards:* Nat Endowment Arts Fel, 87. *Mailing Add:* 247 Centre St 7th Fl New York NY 10013

ASHER, ELISE
PAINTER, POET
b Chicago, Ill, 14. *Study:* Art Inst Chicago; Bradford Jr Col; Simmons Col, BS. *Work:* Nat Acad Sci, Washington; Univ Calif Art Mus, Berkeley; John Michael Kohler Arts Ctr, Sheboygan, Wis; Corcoran Gallery, Washington; Provinceton Art Asn Mus, Mass; William Benton Mus, Storrs, Conn; Poets' House, New York. *Comn:* Oil on Plexiglas window, comn by Dr John P Spiegel, Cambridge; cover for Poetry Northwest, autumn-winter 64-65; cover for The Chelsea, No 27, 70; jackets for Stanley Kunitz, The Testing-Tree (poems), Little, Brown, 71; jacket for Passing Through (poem), Norton, 95. *Exhib:* Lettering Traveling Show, Mus Mod Art, NY 67; solo exhibs, Bertha Schaefer Gallery, NY, 73, Univ Richmond, Va, 75, Ingber Gallery, NY, 79, 81 83, 85 & 87, William Benton Mus, 88, June Kelly Gallery (with catalog), NY, 91 & 94, Provincetown Arts Asn & Mus, Mass, 92; Nat Collection Fine Arts, 76 & Nat Acad Sci, 83, Smithsonian Inst; Fine Arts Mus Long Island, 83; Am Acad Arts & Lett, NY, 80 & 89; Pompiddou Ctr, France; Anita Shapolsky Gallery, NY; Retrospective, Provincetown Mus (catalog), 92. *Bibliog:* Eleanor Munro (auth), Originals: American Women Artists, Simon & Schuster, 79 & Avon Press, 82; Rose Slivka (auth), article, Art News, 6/85; Carl Little (auth), Asher at the Ingber, Art Am, 6/87; David Sutton (auth), When Art Becomes Poetry & Poetry Art, Reporter, spring 91; Christopher Busa (auth), Provincetown Arts, 92; Katz (auth), article, Art in Am, 11/94; BH Friedman (auth), book of poems, Provincetown Arts, 95. *Media:* Oil, Pencil & Ink. *Publ:* Auth, The Meandering Absolute, Morris Gallery Press, NY, 55; illusr, This Book is a Movie, 71; contribr, Acrylic for Sculpture & Design, Van Nostrand, 72; Art: A Woman's Sensibility, Calif Inst Arts, 75; auth, The Visionary Gleam, Sheep Meadow Press, 94; auth, Night Train, Sheep Meadow Press, 00. *Dealer:* June Kelly & June Kelly Gallery 591 Broadway New York NY 10012

ASHER, FREDERICK M
HISTORIAN, EDUCATOR
b Chicago, Ill, May 25, 1941. *Study:* Dartmouth Col, BA; Univ Chicago, MA & PhD. *Pos:* Actg dir, Univ Gallery, Univ Minn, 71-72, chair, dept art hist, 78-81; assoc dean, Col Lib Arts, 85-91, chair, dept art hist, 91-. *Teaching:* Instr art hist, Lake Forest Col, 67-70; assoc prof art hist, Univ Minn, Minneapolis, 70-81, prof, 81. *Mem:* Am Comt SAsian Art (treas, 72-74); Am Inst Indian Studies (treas, 87-). *Res:* South Asian art. *Publ:* Various publications pertaining to the art of India. *Mailing Add:* 1776 James Ave S Minneapolis MN 55403-2827

ASHER, LILA OLIVER
PRINTMAKER, PAINTER
b Philadelphia, Pa. *Study:* With Gonippo Raggi, Joseph Grossman & Frank B A Linton; Philadelphia Col Art, grad. *Work:* Corcoran Gallery Art, Georgetown Univ, Howard Univ & Nat Mus Am Art, Washington, DC; Fisk Univ, Nashville; Univ Va, Charlottesville; Nat Mus Women Arts; Gallandet Univ, Washington, DC; Nat Mus History, Taipei, Taiwan; Kastrupgårdsamlingen Kunst Mus, Denmark. *Comn:* Oil paintings, two panels, Congregation Rodeph Shalom, Philadelphia, 40; murals, two rooms, Indian Spring Country Club, Glenmont, Md. *Exhib:* Retrospective Exhib, Howard Univ, 78 & 91; over 50 one-woman shows in US, Japan, India, Taiwan, Denmark, Turkey & Pakistan, var times, 51-85; Univ Calif Los Angeles; Rockville Art Mansion, Md; Cosmos Club, Washington, DC; Franz Bader, Washington, DC, 72; Fisk Univ, Nashville, Tenn, 74; Strathmore Arts Center, Rockville, Md, 2002; and others. *Collection Arranged:* Nat Mus Am Art, Washington, DC Corcoran Gallery Art, Washington, DC Howard Univ, Washington, DC, Univ Va, Charlottesville, Sweet Briar Col, Va, City of Wolfsbang, Germany; David Hyde Kreeger Col, Washington, DC, Ctr for Rsch and Educ, Jerusalem, Embassy of Israel, Tel Aviv, Embassy of US, Mexico City; Fisk Univ, Nashville; Montgomery Community Col Contemp Prints, Md; Georgetown Univ, Washington, DC; Nat Mus Hist Taipei, Taiwan. *Teaching:* Instr art, Howard Univ, 47-51; instr art, Wilson Teachers Col, 53-54; from lectr to prof art, Howard Univ, 61-91; prof emer, Howard Univ. *Awards:* Printmaker of the Year, High Sch Graphics Prog, Nat Mus Am Art, 81. *Bibliog:* American Prints from Wood, Smithsonian Inst; Catalogues, Kastrugårdsamlingen Kunst Mus, Denmark Howard Univ, Washington,; Barnett-Adan Gallery film. *Mem:* Artist Equity Asn (treas, DC Chap, 71-74); Washington Watercolor Asn; Cosmos Club Washington, DC; Washington Print Club; Md Printmakers; and others. *Media:* Wood & Linoleum Block; Oil. *Publ:* Auth, Men I Have Met in Bed, Heritage Press, 2002. *Mailing Add:* 4100 Thornapple St Chevy Chase MD 20815

ASHER, MICHAEL
CONCEPTUAL ARTIST
b Los Angeles, Calif, July 15, 43. *Study:* Orange Coast Col, Costa Mesa, Calif, 61-63; Univ NMex, Albuquerque, 63-64; New York Studio Sch, 64-65; Univ Calif, Irvine, BA(fine arts), 66. *Exhib:* Los Angeles Co Mus Art, Calif, 67, 71, 72, 81, 83; West Coast Now, Portland Art Mus, Ore, 68; The Appearing/Disappearing Image/Object, Newport Harbor Art Mus, Newport Beach, Calif, 69; Whitney Mus Am Art, NY, 69; Seattle Art Mus, Wash, 69; Mus Mod Art, NY, 69-70; Recent Works, Gallery 167, Univ Calif, Irvine, 75; San Francisco Mus Mod Art, Calif, 76; Los Angeles in the Seventies, Fort Worth Art Mus, Tex, 77; one-person exhibs, Mus Contemp Art, Chicago, 79, The Renaissance Soc, Univ Chicago, Ill, 90, Le Nouveau Mus, France, 91, Le Consortium, Dijon, 91, Nat Mus Mod Art, Ctr Georges Pompidou, Paris, 91, Palais des Beaux-Arts, Brussels, Belgium, 92 & Kunsthalle Bern, Switz, 92; Los Angeles in the Seventies, Joslyn Art Mus, Omaha, Nebr, 79; Art Inst Chicago, Ill, 79, 82; L A Hot & Cool: Pioneers, Mass Inst Technol, 87-88; Artists Space, NY, 88; Mus d'Art Mod de la Ville de Paris, traveling, 89; Carnegie Mus Art, Pittsburgh, Pa, 91; Sonsbeek 93, Arnhem, The Neth, 93; Expo 93, Taejon, South Korea, 93; Does the Work Take Place, Witte De With, Rotterdam, The Neth, 94; and many others. *Teaching:* Asst instr sculpture, Univ Calif, Irvine, 66-67, painting instr, 67-68; instr industrial arts, Anaheim Union High Sch District & Garden Grove Sch District, Calif; vis artist, Univ Calif, 73, Calif Inst Arts, Valencia, 73 & 76, NS Col Art & Design, 74 & Otis Art Inst, Los Angeles, 75; instr, Calif Inst Arts, 75-. *Awards:* Art Purchase Award, Contemp Art Coun, Los Angeles Co Mus, 67; John Simon Guggenheim Mem Fel, 74; Artist Fel Grant, Nat Endowment Arts, 75; Aachen Kunstpreis, 2000. *Bibliog:* Corinne Pencenet (auth), Michael Asher: Coup Double, Beaux Arts, 9/91; Sabine B Vogel (auth), Brussels, Artforum, vol XXXI, no 5, 1/93; Maddalena Disch (auth), Michael Asher: Contextual Virtuoso, Rivista D'Arte E Di Cultura, no 31, 93; and many others. *Publ:* Auth, Writings 1973-1983, On Works, 1969-1979, NS Col Art & Design & Mus Contemp Art, Los Angeles, 83. *Mailing Add:* 2270 S Carmelina Ave Los Angeles CA 90064

ASHKIN, MICHAEL
SCULPTOR
b Morristown, NJ, 1955. *Study:* Univ Pa, Philadelphia, BA, 77; Columbia Univ, New York, MA, 80; Sch Art Inst Chicago, MFA(painting & drawing), 93. *Exhib:* Five Different, 1800 N Clybourne, Chicago, 90; Dome Room, Chicago, Ill, 91; Response to War, Artemisia Gallery, Chicago, 91; Migration, Dome Room, Chicago, 92; Ashkin, Fujiwara, Gouch, Levin, Starbuck, Tikka, Gallery 2, Sch Art Inst Chicago, 92; Ambient Spaces/Virtual Reality, Peter Miller Gallery, Chicago, 92; solo shows, Peter Miller Gallery, Chicago, 92 & 94, Bronwyn Keenan Gallery, NY, 96, Feigen Inc, Chicago, 96, Galerie Jousse Sequin, Paris, France 97 & 99, Andrea Rosen Gallery, NY, 98 & 2000, Emily Tsingou Gallery, London, 99; MFA Thesis Show, Sch Art Inst Chicago, 93; The New Pier Show Sculpture Garden, Cityfront Ctr, Chicago, 93; Investigations into the Physical and Metaphorical Hole, Gallery 2, Sch Art Inst Chicago, 94; Mini-Mindus (with catalog), White Columns, NY, 95; Lookin' Good, Feelin' Good, 450 Broadway Gallery, NY, 95; Ooze, Black & Herron Space, NY, 95; Constructions, Michael Klein Gallery, NY, 96; Open Skies, SPAS Gallery, Rochester

Inst Technol, NY, 96; Site Specifics, Carriage House Proj Space (with catalog), Islip Art Mus, NY, 96; Space, Mind, Place, Andrea Rosen Gallery, NY, 96; Currents in Contemp Art, Christie's E, NY, 96; The Lie of the Land (brochure), Univ Art Mus, Univ Calif, Santa Barbara, 96; At the Edge of the Landscape, Galeria Estrany - de la Mota, Barcelona, Spain, 97; Picturing, Ctr Curatorial Studies, Annandale-on-Hudson, NY, 97; Across Lines, Rosenberg Gallery, Hofstra Univ, Hempstead, NY, 97; 20th Ann Benefit Gala & Art Auction, New Mus Contemp Art, NY, 97; 1997 Biennial Exhib (with catalog), Whitney Mus Am Art, NY, 97; Tableaux (with catalog), Mus Contemp Art, Miami, Fla, 97; 24Seven, Galerie Klaus-Peter Goebel, Stuttgart, Ger, 97; Elsewhere: Works by Michael Ashkin, Julie Becker, James Casebere, Miles Coolidge, and Thomas Demand (with catalog), Carnegie Mus Art, 97-98; New Found Landscape, Kerlin Gallery, Dublin, Ireland, 97-98; Where: Allegories of Site in Contemp Art, Whitney Mus Am Art Champion, Stamford, Conn, 98; Sliding Scale, SE Ctr Contemp Art, Winston-Salem, NC, 99; Souvenirs/Documents: 20 Yrs, PS 122 Gallery, NY, 99; Contemp Collections XIV, Mus Contemp Art, San Diego, La Jolla, 99; Landworks Studio, Inc, Salem, Mass, 99; Small World: Dioramas in Contemp Art, Mus Contemp Art, San Diego, 2000; Berardo Collection, Centro Cult de Belem, Lisbon, 2000; 2000 Benefit and Silent Auction, White Columns, NY, 2000, Gallery Patrick Seguin, Paris, 2000; Human/Nature, Caren Golden Gallery, NY, 2000; Picqued Land, Barbara Krakow Gallery, Boston, 2001; Andrea Rosen Gallery, NY, 2000 & 2002. *Pos:* bd trustees, Ft Worth Country Day Sch, 82-87, 88-94; bd adv, art dept, Univ North Tex, 90-; mem, Bush Presdl Libr steering com, Tex A&M Univ, 90-91; mem gov bd, Yale Univ Art Gallery, 91-98; mem vis com, Sherman Fairchild Paintings Conservation Ctr, Metrop Mus Art, NY, 82-; chmn, int bd adv, State Hermitage Mus, 95-2000; vp, Chinati Found, Marfa, Tex, 96-; bd trustees various orgs. *Awards:* Pahlavi Found, 78 Hon Pres Fel, Columbia Univ, 78; Full Merit Scholar, Sch Art Inst Chicago, 91-93; Pollock-Krasner Found, 97; Lily Auchincloss Found Fel Grant, NY Found for the Arts, 99. *Bibliog:* Maia Damianovic (auth), article, Tema Celeste, 9/98; Jennifer Dalton (auth), shake, Rev, Summer 98; Martin Coomer (auth), Time after time, Time Out London, 1/20-27/99. *Mem:* Am Fedn Arts (bd trustees 82-88); Am Friends Hermitage (co-chmn 98-); Asn Art Mus Dirs (bd trustees 89-90); Villa I Tatti Coun (mem adv com 88). *Dealer:* Andrea Rosen Gallery 525 W 24th St New York NY 10011. *Mailing Add:* c/o Andrea Rosen Gallery 625 W 24th St New York NY 10011

ASHTON, DORE
ART CRITIC, WRITER, EDUCATOR
b Newark, NJ, 28. *Study:* Univ Wis, BA; Harvard Univ, MA; Phi Beta Kappa. *Hon Degrees:* Moore Col PhD hc, 75, Hamline Univ, 82, Minneapolis Col Art, 2002. *Pos:* Assoc ed, Art Digest, NY, 52-54; art critic, NY Times, 55-60; contrib ed, Opus Int, Paris, 65-75 & Arts Mag, 74-90; lectr, Pratt Inst, 62-63, head humanities dept Sch Visual Arts, 65-68; mem adv bd John Simon Guggenheim Found, Dedalus Found. *Teaching:* Prof art hist, Cooper Union, 69-; adj prof, Yale Univ. *Awards:* Mather Award Art Criticism, Col Art Asn, 63; Guggenheim Fels, 64 & 69; Ford Found Award, 65; Nat Endowment for Humanities Grant, 80; and others. *Mem:* Int Asn Art Critics; Pen Club. *Res:* Modern art. *Publ:* Auth, Out of the Whirlwind, 87; Fragonard in the Universe of Painting, 88; Noguchi East and West, 92; Terence La Noue, 92; The Delicate Thread: Hiroshi Teshigahara's Life in Art, 97; The Black Rainbow: The Work of Fernando de Szyszlo, 2000; and 20 others. *Mailing Add:* 217 E 11th St New York NY 10003

ASHTON, PAUL
PHOTOGRAPHER
b Key West, Fla, Mar 12, 48. *Study:* Univ Ga, MA, 68, BA, 74. *Comn:* Photog, Digital to Life, comn by Alex Borden, NC, 2001. *Awards:* Best Digital Award, 11th Ann Photog Exhib, 90 & 97; First Place, Nat Photog Asn, 95. *Bibliog:* Janice Barno (auth), Life of a Real Time Photog, Paul Ashton, Lark Publ, 2003; Carl Clapton (auth), Seeing life through Paul Ashton's Work, SoSo Publ, 2004. *Mem:* Nat Photog Asn (bd mem, 90-). *Media:* Black/White & Digital Photography. *Res:* Water and Reefs. *Interests:* Dolphins and Water life. *Publ:* auth, illustr, Pretty Unusual Things, Coral Publ, 2003. *Mailing Add:* 13 Chadwick Ln Lakeland GA 31635-2112

ASHVIL-BIBI, SIGALIT
PAINTER
b Kutaissi,Georgia, USSR, Apr 28, 52; US citizen. *Study:* Acad Music Tbillissi, USSR, BA, 69-73; study with Mordechai-Misha Dzanashvilli, 73-83; NY Acad Art, cert, 91-93. *Work:* Mus Beit Ha'Omamin, Jerusalem, Israel; Mus Yad Le Banim, Hulon, Israel; Yeshiva Univ Mus, NY; White House, Washington, DC. *Exhib:* Father Daughter Team, Brooklyn Mus, 89; The Sepharadic Journey, Yeshiva Univ Mus, Manhattan, 91-92; group exhib, San Francisco, 91; solo exhibs, White House, Washington, DC, 81 & 96, Queens "Y", NY, 96, 97 & 98 & Chassidic Art Inst, Brooklyn, NY, 2000; Brooklyn-Queens Conservatory, 2000 & 2001; Family Group exhib, Jerusalem, Israel. *Teaching:* art & music, currently. *Awards:* Gold Medal, 6th Int Festival between Musicians in USSR, 68. *Bibliog:* Cindy Garfinkel Blaustein (auth), An Investigation, Twentieth Century Observant Jewish Fine Arts, Fla Int Univ, 93; Shivuh Woolfson (auth), Capturing the inner spirit, Chai Mag, 93; Itzhak Atanelov (auth), Jewish-Georgian Spirit, 99; article in Druzhba Mag, 2000. *Mem:* Asn Israeli Artists (bd dir, 79); Am Artist Prof League; Judaic Art. *Media:* Oil, Acrylic & Pastel. *Publ:* Spiritual Leaders (35 portrait exhib), Ben-Rapael, 84; numerous articles in newspapers & mags. *Mailing Add:* 110-01 62nd Dr Apt 2C Forest Hills NY 11375

ASIHENE, EMMANUEL V
EDUCATOR, PAINTER
b Asamankese, Ghana, Dec 1, 37. *Study:* Ohio State Univ, PhD (Art Educ), 73. *Work:* Ohio Pub Libr & Ohio Mus Art, Columbus; Ohio State Univ, Columbus. *Exhib:* One-man show, Afro-Ganza Art Exhib, Mus Fine Art, Columbus, Ohio, 72; Grad Student Show, Ohio State Univ, Columbus, Ohio, 73; Art Fac Show, Atlanta Univ Ctr, Ga, 74; Artists USA, NY, 76; Black Artists South, Huntsville Mus Art, Ala, 79. *Pos:* Chmn art dept, Clark Atlanta Univ, Ga, 73-86. *Teaching:* Prof Art Appreciation & African Art, Clark Atlanta Univ, Ga, 73-. *Awards:* Aggrey & Hazen Found Fel. *Mem:* Nat Art Educ Asn; Ga Alliance Arts Educ; Nat Coun Art Adminr; Dekalb Coun Arts; Am Asn Univ Prof. *Media:* Oil, Watercolor. *Publ:* Auth, Understanding the Traditional Art of Ghana, Assoc Univ Press, 78; Apoo Festival, Ghana Publ Co, 80; Traditional Folk-Tales of Ghana, The Edwin Mullen Press, 97; Guan-Anum-Boso English Dictionary, Apra Svcs Ghana, 98. *Mailing Add:* 2562 Farley St East Point GA 30344

ASKEVOLD, DAVID
CONCEPTUAL ARTIST, INSTRUCTOR
b Conrad, Mont, Mar 30, 40. *Study:* Univ Mont, 58-63; Brooklyn Mus Sch Art, painting cert, 63-64; Kansas City Art Inst, BFA (sculpture), 67-68. *Work:* Van Abbe Mus, Eindhoven, Holland; Nat Gallery Can, Ottawa; Confederation Ctr, PEI; Nat Libr, Ottawa, Ont; Art Gallery of Nova Scotia, Can; Mus Contemp Art, Los Angeles; Vancouver Art Gallery, BC, Can; Art Gallery Windsor, Ont, Can; Art Metropole, Toronto, Can; Can Mus Contemp Photog, Ottawa; Art Ctr Col Design, Pasadena, Calif; Can Coun Art Bank, Ottawa; Long Beach Mus Art, Calif. *Comn:* Can Photographic Portfolio Soc, Vancover, BC, Can, 97. *Exhib:* one-man shows, Van Abbe Mus, 80, Jancar/Kuhlenschmidt Gallery, 81, Coburg Gallery, Vancouver, BC, 84, Anna Leonowens Gallery, Halifax, 85, Clock Tower Gallery, NY, 90, Articule Gallery, Montreal, 94 & Confederation Ctr Art Gallery & Mus, Charlottetown, PEI, 95, Cultural Geographies, Art Gallery Nova Scotia, Halifax, 99, New Pictures & Older Videos, Los Angeles Contemp Exhibs, Calif, 2001, New Works, Wynick/Tuck Gallery, Toronto, 2002, Two Hanks, CANADA, Que, 2003 & Kling & Bang, 2004, Mandarin, 2005; Mus Mod Art, NY, 70 & 71; Documenta, Kassel, Ger, 77; Brian Butler Gallery, Santa Monica, Calif, 92; Whitney Mus Am Art (traveling), 92-95; Terra Firma, Mt St Vincent Univ Art Gallery, Halifax, NS, 93; 1965-1975, Reconsidering the Object of Art, Mus Contemp Art, Los Angeles, 95; Shoshana Wayne Gallery, Santa Monica, Calif, 96; New Pictures and Older Viedos, Los Angeles Contemp Exhibs, 01; New Works, Wynick/Tuck Gallery, toronto, 02; Group Exhibs: Seventies: art in Question, 02; 7th Lyon Biennial Contemp Art, Lyon, France, 2003; Littoral Documents, Confederation Centre Art Gallery, Charlottetown, Prince Edward Island, Can, 2004. *Pos:* Vis artist video & spec topics, Minneapolis Col Art & Design, 84-85. *Teaching:* Asst prof art, NS Col Art & Design, 68-73; vis lectr studio art, Univ Calif, Irvine, 76-77; spec appt photog & post studio art, Calif Inst Arts, Valencia, 77-78; lectr, Art Ctr, Col Design, Pasadena, Calif, 80-81 & Visual Art Dept, York Univ, Downsview, Ont, Can, 81-82; vis artist, Minn Col Art & Design, 84-85; adj prof, Nova Scotia Col Art & Design, 85-88 & 91. *Awards:* Visual Arts A Grant, Can Coun, 93 & 95; Joan Calmers Award, Visual Art, 96. *Bibliog:* Flash Art 38, 74; Red Rider, Halifax: Centre for Art Tapes, 92; Ann Goldstein & Anne Rommimer (coauths), Reconsidering the Object of Art: 1965-75 (exhib catalog), The Mus Contemp Art, Los Angeles, Cambridge, Mass & London, Eng, 96; Holly Myers (auth), Exploring the Dawn of Digital Expression, Los Angeles Times, 2/27/2001. *Mem:* Art Gallery of Nova Scotia (life mem); Nat Art Gallery of Can, Ottawa (life mem). *Media:* Film, Audio, Video. *Dealer:* Wynick/Tuck Gallery 401 Richmond St Toronto ON Canada M5V 5A8; Wynick/Tuck Gallery 55 Chrystie St New York NY 10002; Mandarin 970 N Broadway Suite 213 Los Angeles Calif 90026. *Mailing Add:* 15 Penhorn Dr Dartmouth NS B2Y 3K2 Canada

ASKIN, WALTER MILLER
PAINTER, PRINTMAKER
b Pasadena, Calif, Sept 12, 1929. *Study:* Univ Calif, Berkeley, BA & MA; Ruskin Sch Drawing & Fine Art, Oxford Univ. *Work:* Mus Contemp Art, Chicago; Nat Gallery Art, Washington; San Francisco Mus Art; Los Angeles Co Mus Art; Albright-Knox Gallery, Buffalo; Calif State Univ, Los Angeles; Franco-American Union, Rennes, France; Norton Simon Mus Art, Pasadena, Calif; Whitney Mus, NY; Mus Modern Art, NY; Univ Calif, Berkeley, Calif. *Comn:* Pasadena, Gold Line Innaugural Art Work, Los Angeles Metro Transportation Authority, Calif; Pasadena Playhouse, 2003; Los Angeles City Col, 2005. *Exhib:* One-man shows, La Jolla Mus Art, Calif, 67, Abraxas Gallery, Calif, 79, 80 & 81, Univ Southern Calif, 80 & Kunstlerhaus, Vienna, Austria, 81; Prints by Seven, Whitney Mus Am Art, 70; Int Biennial Graphic Art, Mus Mod Art, Ljubljana, Yugoslavia, 83; Lizardi/Harp Gallery, Pasadena, 88, 90 & 95; Lightside Gallery, Santa Fe, NMex, 95; Univ Kans, Lawernce (traveling), 97; 15th Int Biennial Prints & Drawings, Taipei Art Mus, Taiwan, Repub China, 97-98, 2000-2001; Riverside Art Mus, Calif, 2000; From Paris to Pasadena Norton Simon Mus, 2000-2001; Calif State Univ, Channel Islands, 2002; Brigham Young Univ, 2002; Kimball Art Ctr, Park City, Utah, 2002. *Pos:* Bd trustees, Pasadena Art Mus, 63-68; bd dir, Los Angeles Inst Contemp Art, Los Angeles, 77-81; bd gov, Baxter Art Gallery, Calif Inst Technol, 80-90; artist rep, Graphic Arts Council, Los Angeles Co Mus Art, 80-89; chmn visual arts panel, Nat Art Awards, 81-82; advan placement, studio art exam comt, The Col Bd, 85-, chmn arts adv comt, 86-93; college board commission, Future of the Advanced Placement Program, 98-2000. *Teaching:* Prof art, Calif State Univ, Los Angeles, 56-92, emer prof, 92-; vis prof art, Univ Calif, Berkeley, 68-69, Calif State Univ, Long Beach, 74-75 & Univ Hawaii, 83; vis artist, Kelpra Studio, London, 69 & 73, Tamarind Inst, Univ NMex, 72 & 90, Athens Sch Fine Arts, 73, Cranbrook Acad Art, 79, Ariz State Univ, 80 & 83, Ossabaw Island Found, Ga, 82, Va Ctr Creative Arts, 83 & 86, Vt Studio Colony, 88, & John Michael Kohler Arts Indust Prog, 89; Hambridge Ceneter for Arts and Sciences, Rabun Gap, Georgia, 91; Brigham Young Univ, Provo, Utah, 92. *Awards:* Artist Award, Pasadena Arts Coun, 70; Outstanding Prof Award, Calif State Univ, Los Angeles, 73; First Award Painting, Calif State Fair, 76; Past Presidents' Award, 80th Annual Nat Watercolor Soc, 2000. *Bibliog:* Violante (auth), American Printmakers 74, Graphics Group, 74; Newman (auth), Innovative Printmaking, Crown, 77; Walter Askin 1970-1980, Univ Southern Calif, 80; Roukes (auth), Humor in Art, Davis 97; Roukes (auth), Artful Jesters, Ten Speed Pub, 03. *Mem:* Col Art Asn Am; Los Angeles

Printmaking Soc (pres 2002-2004); Nat Watercolor Soc; Am Print Alliance; Alumni Art Asn Univ Calif Berkeley (hist 2002-). *Media:* bronze, cast iron, steel, screen prints, lithographs. *Res:* Image Making in British Colleges of Art, Bureau of Research, US Office of Educ. *Collection:* Java Wayang Klittiks, Dogon, Baule, Nepal & india, New Guinea, Feininger, Durer, Steinberg, Kimball, Britton, Loran, Crown. *Publ:* Auth, Another Art Book To Cross Off Your List, 84; A Briefer History of the Greeks, 85; The Modern Manifesto Match Game, 98; Contemporary Impressions, Vol 8 #1; Journal of the American Print Alliance, 2000; Womsters & Foozler, 98; How to Become and Artist, 99; The Artists' Man, Dog, Bone Calendar for the Year 2000. *Mailing Add:* PO Box D South Pasadena CA 91031-0120

ASKMAN, TOM K
PAINTER, EDUCATOR
b Leadville, Colo, Oct 27, 41. *Study:* Calif Col Arts & Crafts, BFA; Univ Colo, MFA. *Work:* City Seattle, Wash; Cheney Cowles Art Mus, Spokane, Wash; Ft Worth Art Mus, Tex; Mus Art, Univ Okla, Norman; Mus Art, Univ Colo, Boulder. *Comn:* Columbia River Correctional Inst, Ore Arts Comn, Portland, 94; Tukwilla Park & Ride, Metro Arts Comn, Seattle, Wash, 94; Turnagain Elem Sch, Anchorage, Alaska, 95 & 97; Camino Real Proj, Las Cruces, NMex, 96 & 97; Raccoon River Park, West Des Moines, Iowa, 97. *Exhib:* New Orleans Mus Art, La, 71; Addison Gallery Am Art, Andover, Mass, 71; Minneapolis Art Inst, Minn, 71; Va Mus Fine Arts, Richmond, 72; Extraordinary Realities, Whitney Mus Am Art, NY, 73; Springfield Art Mus, Mo, 73-74; Contemp Arts Ctr, Cincinnati, Ohio, 74; Seattle Art Mus, Wash, 74; Private Views, Henry Gallery, Univ Wash, 80. *Teaching:* Instr, Univ Minn, Minneapolis, 68-70; assoc prof, Nicholls State Univ, Thibodaux, La, 70-72 & Eastern Wash Univ, Cheney, 72-. *Awards:* Cheney Cowles Art Mus, Spokane, 74, 76, 80 & 81; Painting Award, 60th Ann NW Artists, Seattle Art Mus, Wash, 74; State Wash Commissions, 79

ASMAN, ROBERT JOSEPH
PHOTOGRAPHER, PRINTMAKER
b Washington, DC, June 16, 51. *Study:* Cath Univ Am, BA, 73; Rochester Inst Tech, MFA, 76. *Work:* Libr Cong & Nat Gallery Art, Washington, DC; Philadelphia Mus Art; Mus Fine Arts, Houston; Pa State Mus, Harrisburg. *Exhib:* Virginia Collects, Chrysler Mus, Norfolk, 88; photographs, Allentown Art Mus, Pa, 89; Art 21 90 (photo-1980's), Basel, Switz, 90; Artists select Artists, Inst Contemp Art, Philadelphia, 92; Cologne Int Arts Festival, Ger, 96; Basel Int Arts Festival, Switz, 96; Roger LaPelle Gallery, Philadelphia, 02; Philadelphia Mus Art, 02. *Teaching:* Sr lectr photog, Univ Arts, Philadelphia, 97-98, Drexel Univ, 2000; Adj Prof Grad Sch Fine Arts, Univ Pa, 2002. *Awards:* Pa Coun Arts Award, State of Pa, 93; Pew Found Fel, 97. *Media:* Photography. *Publ:* Contribr, Vietnam Veterans Memorial, Crown, 92; Sisters, Mothers, Daughters, Best Friends, Doubleday, 92-94 & 98; Bass Line, Overtime: Photos of Milt Hinton, Temple Univ, 92-96; In Search of Robert E Lee, Combined Books, 96; Excavating Voices & Listening to Voices of Native Americans, Univ Pa Mus, 98. *Dealer:* Galerie Francoise et Alain Paviot 57 Rue Sainte-Anne Paris France 75002. *Mailing Add:* 610 Kimball St Philadelphia PA 19147

ASMAR, ALICE
PAINTER, PRINTMAKER
b Flint, Mich. *Study:* Lewis & Clark Col, BA(magna cum laude); with Edward Melcarth & Archipenko, Univ Wash, MFA; Woolley Fel, Ecole Nat Super des Beaux-Arts, Paris, with M Souverbie; Huntington Hartford Found residence Fels, 61-64; Mac Dowell Colony, Peterboro, NH. *Hon Degrees:* Phi Beta Kappa, Gamma Chapter, Ueuis & Clark col, Portland, Ore, 2000. *Work:* Nat Mus Am Hist Smithsonian Inst, Washington; Pub Int Mus, Gabrova, Bulgaria; Roswell Mus & Art Ctr, NMex; Metro Med Mall, Los Angeles; Kaiser-Permanente, Panorama City, Calif. *Comn:* painting of doves, Bangs Manufacturing Co, Burbank, 92; paintings of Indian dancers, Navarros, Hillsboro, Ore, 92; 45 ink drawings for educ brochures & posters, Small Wilderness Area Preserv, 92; paintings of Calif quail, Maples, San Marino, 93; Los Angeles City-Scape at Sunset (mural), comn by Dr Walter Jayasinghe, 96; Ocean Scenes Comm by Danner corp, Ore, 2000; Mailbu Scenes Comm by Alena Konkol, Malibu, Calif, 2001; Saint Joseph Medical Ctr, Burbank, Calif, 2003. *Exhib:* Seattle Art Mus, 52; Drawings USA, Minn Mus Art Nat Travel Show, 71-73; West 79/The Law, Minn Mus Art, 79-80; solo shows, Mus of Sci & Indust, Los Angeles, 81, Sr Eye Art Gallery, Long Beach, 77 & 82, Circle Gallery Ltd, Houston, 83, Hilton Hotel, 91, Abbott Hall Gallery, William Temple House, Portland, Ore, 92, Descanso Gardens, La Canada Flintridge, Calif, 96 & Gloria Lee Gallery, 96; Sun Cities Art Mus, Ariz, 94; Audubon Art Exhib, Portland, Ore, 94; Walt Disney Sch Art Auction, Burbank, Calif, 94, 95 & 96; Pasadena Showcase, 96; McGroarty Cult Arts Ctr, 96; Rainforest Art Auction, 96; Descanso Gardens Art Gallery, 97; Media Ctr, Burbank Mall, Burbank, Calif, 98; Christmas Echibit, Domazale, Slovania, 2001; solo exhibit, Burbank Media Ctr, 2002; Dorothy Chandler Pavillion, LA, 2003; Aztech Gallery, 2004; Hollenbeck 4th July exhibit, 2005; Future Photo Gallery, Toluca Lake, Calif, 2006. *Collection Arranged:* Millenium Art Collection, The Notherlands, 2000; Burbank Libr, Buena Vista branch, 2002. *Pos:* Eng draftsman, Boeing Aircraft, 52-54; engraver, Nambe Mills, Santa Fe, NMex, 68-; free-lance illusr, Los Angeles Times, 77-81; free-lance illusr for publs, 83-87; art consult, art judging, lectr & demos, var art groups, 88-92; mem, Burbank City Coun, Art in Pub Places, 91-; mem, Site Specific Comt, City of Burbank. *Teaching:* Asst prof painting & drawing, Lewis & Clark Col, 55-58; instr painting, Lennox Adult Educ, Calif, 63-65; part-time, Woodbury Col & Santa Monica City Col, 65-66; watercolor, Descanso Gardens, 88; art instr with admin duties, McGroarty Arts Ctr, Los Angeles Cult Affairs, 88-90; pvt teaching, 90-95, 98-2006 & McGroarty Cult Arts Ctr, 96-97. *Awards:* Sale Cent Purchase Award, NBC, 88; 2000 Notable Am Women, 89; hon mem Nat League Am Pen Women, Washington, 91. *Bibliog:* David Howard (dir), Alice Asmar Documentary (video), Visual Studies, San Francisco, 91; Le-Ann Jolakian (interviewer), Creating World Peace (video), United Artists Production, 91; feature articles, Flowerlover Mag, 95; Edmund Penny & Assoc (video), Alice Asmar, Descanso, 98. *Mem:* Visual Artists & Galleries Asn; Calif Lawyers for Arts; Artists Equity; League of Americas; Int Mus & Artist Registration; Los Angeles co Art Mus; and others. *Media:* Casein, Oil; India Ink, Lithographs. *Publ:* Southwest Arts Mag, 11/78; Los Angeles Times Home Mag, 3/26/78 & 12/3/78; Lewis & Clark J, fall 86; Tolucan, 1/15/92; Flowerlover Mag, 95. *Dealer:* Sachs Gallery Pacific Design Ctr 8687 Melrose Ave Los Angeles CA 90069; Dora Haslett 735 SW St Clair Portland OR 97205. *Mailing Add:* Asmar Studios PO Box 1963 Burbank CA 91507

ASOMA, TADASHI
PAINTER
b Iwatsuki, Japan, Apr 28, 23. *Study:* Saitama Teachers Col, Urawa, MS; Bijitsu Gakko, Tokyo, govt scholar; Grande Chaumiere, Paris, govt scholar; Art Students League. *Work:* Nelson Gallery, Kansas City; Am Express Co, NY; 3M Co, St Paul; Andrew Dickson White Mus, Ithaca, NY; San Diego Mus Art. *Exhib:* One-man shows, David Findlay Galleries, NY, biennially 65-97, Dubins Gallery, Los Angeles, 79 & 85, Foundry Sch Mus NY, 79 & Steckler-Haller Galleries, Scottsdale, Ariz; Tokyo Central Mus, 81 & 84. *Teaching:* Instr art educ, Iwatsuki Jr High Sch, 50-64. *Awards:* Second Prize, Saitama Bijitsu Ten, 55; Second Prize, Nat Exhib Prof Art, 68; People's Westchester Savings Bank Award Best in Show, 20th, 22nd & 24th Ann Fine Art Shows, Putnam Art Coun, Mahopac, NY, 82. *Bibliog:* Articles in Art News, NY Times & NY Post, 65, 67, 69, 79 & 83; and others. *Media:* Oil. *Dealer:* David Findlay Galleries 984 Madison Ave New York NY 10021; John Szoke Graphics Inc 164 Mercer St New York NY 10012. *Mailing Add:* 2 Pondfield Dr N Chappaqua NY 10514-1308

ASPELL, AMY SUZANNE
DIRECTOR, WEAVER
b Chicago, Ill, June 28, 42. *Study:* Knox Col, Galesburg, Ill, BA(art), 63, Univ SFla, Tampa, MA(art educ), 76. *Comn:* Woven relief wall hanging, Caspers Inc, Tampa, Fla, 80. *Pos:* Dir, Tampa Community Design Ctr, 79-81, Ark Arts Coun, 84-87 & Irvine Fine Arts Ctr, 87-. *Teaching:* Univ Calif, Irvine. *Media:* Fiber Art. *Publ:* Auth, Cookbook Weaving I, Craft Publications Inc, 77. *Mailing Add:* 32772 Via Malaga San Juan Capistrano CA 92675-4455

ASTMAN, BARBARA ANNE
PHOTOGRAPHER, PAINTER
b Rochester, NY, July 12, 1950. *Study:* Sch Am Craftsmen, with Albert Paley; Rochester Inst Technol, AA, 70; Ont Col Art, Toronto, Assoc, 73. *Hon Degrees:* Royal Canadian Art. *Work:* Victoria & Albert Mus, London, Eng; Art Gallery Ont, Toronto; Winnipeg Art Gallery; Bibliot Nat, Paris, France; Natl Gallery of Canada, Ottawa. *Comn:* CIL Corp, Toronto, Can; Calgary Winter Olympics, 88; City of Ottawa, Art in Public Places Programme; Cadillac Fairview, Simcoe Place, Toronto, 94; Baycrest Geriatric Ctr, Toronto, 01; Wolfond Ctr for Jewish Studies, Univ Tronto, 04; Can Embassy in Berlin, 04; Loblaws Corp Headquarters, Brampton, Ont, 2006. *Exhib:* Xerography, Art Gallery Ont, Toronto, 77; Contemp Can Photog Portrait, Edmonton Art Gallery, Alta, 78; Winnepeg Perspectives, Winnipeg Art Gallery, 79; Alternative Imageing Systems, Everson Mus, Syracuse, NY, 79; Electroworks, George Eastman House, Rochester, NY, 79-80; one-woman shows, Centre Cult, Paris, France, 82, Sable-Castelli Gallery, Ltd, Toronto, Can, 77-90, Jane Corking Gallery, Toronto, 97, 99, Modern Fuel Gallery, Kingston, Ont, 98, plus others; Generation Polaroid, Forum des Halles, Paris, France, 85; Visual Facts, Third Eye Ctr, Glasglow, Scotland & Mus du Que, Quebec City, 86; Porkkanna Collection, Pro Mus Contemp Art, Helsinki, Finland, 89; Thunder Bay Art Gallery, Ont, 92; 20 Yr Survey Touring Exhib, Art Gallery Hamilton, 95; Corkins Hopland Gallery, Toronto, 1997, 2000, 2001, 2004, 2006; Windsor Art Gallery, ON, 2005; Koffler Art Gallery, Toronto, 2006; plus others. *Pos:* Coordr, Color Xerox Prog, Visual Arts Ont, 77-83; mem, Pub Art Comn, Toronto, currently; bd dir, Toronto Arts Awards Found, 92. *Teaching:* Fac, camera art, Ont Col Art, 75-; Prof, fac art, Ont Col Art & Design, Toronto, 75-. *Awards:* Can Coun Arts Awards Grants, 76, 77, 80, 81, 83, 84, 86 & 88; Prov Ont Coun Arts Grants, 74-82, 84, 92 & 94; Can Coun Sr Arts Awards Grant, 93-94. *Bibliog:* Barbara Astman (catalog), Centre Cult Can, Paris, 82; Astman Places, Nickle Arts Mus, Univ Calgary, Can, 83; Barbara Astman: Personal/Persona, A 20-Year Survey, 95. *Mem:* Univ Art Asn Can; Visual Arts Asn Ont. *Media:* Multi Media, Camera Art. *Interests:* Art & Lit. *Dealer:* Corkin/Shopland Gallery, 55 Mill St, Toronto, Bldng 61. *Mailing Add:* 23 Alcina Ave Toronto ON M6G 2E7 Canada

ASTON, MIRIAM
SCULPTOR, PAINTER
b New York, NY. *Study:* Soc Arts & Crafts, Detroit, with Sarkis Sarkisian, 54-58; Wayne State Univ, BA & MA; Univ Mich, with Gerald Kamrowski; Claremont Grad Sch, Calif. *Work:* Nat Mus Women, Washington. *Comn:* Pvt, nat & int comns. *Exhib:* Detroit Inst Art Ann, 50-72; Calif Mus Science & Industry; Univ Ohio, Athens; Mich Acad Arts, Letters & Sci, Ann Arbor; Riverside Mus Art, NY; Invitational exhib, Women's Conf UN, Nairobi, Kenya, 85; solo exhibs, Wayne State Univ, Detroit, Mich, Los Angeles, Ontario & Calif. *Pos:* Dir develop, Mus Hist & Art, Ontario, Calif. *Teaching:* Instr painting & sculpture, Univ Mich, Dearborn, 68-73; instr sculpture, Calif Polytech Univ, Pomona, 75-; instr drawing, Chaffey Col, Calif; instr painting, Ontario & Claremont, Calif. *Awards:* Gold Medal, 65 & Best Sculpture, Scarab Club; Best Sculpture, Scarab Club; Best Painting, Mich Acad Arts, Lett & Sci. *Mem:* Artists Equity Asn; Women's Caucus Art; hon mem Scarab Club, Detroit, Mich; Sculpture Ctr, Washington; Scripps Col Fine Arts Found, Claremont, Calif. *Media:* Mixed

ASTRUP, HANS RASMUS
COLLECTOR, MUSEUM FOUNDER
Pos: Founder Astrup Fearnley Art Mus, Oslo, 93. *Awards:* Named one of Top 200 Collectors, ARTnews Magazine, 2004. *Collection:* Ccontemporary art. *Mailing Add:* Astrup Fearnley Museum PO Box 1158 Dronningens Gate Oslo 4 0107 Norway

ATKINS, GORDON LEE
DESIGNER, ARCHITECT
b Calgary, Alta, Mar 5, 37. *Study:* Col Archit & Urban Planning, Univ Wash, BArch. *Work:* Royal Can Acad Art; Nat Gallery Can; Massey Found. *Comn:* Studio, comn by Ed Drahanchuk, Bragg Creek, Alta, 68; Mayland Heights Sch, Calgary Pub Sch Bd, 68; Pinebrook Golf & Winter Club, comn by Wilbur Griffith, West of Calgary, 74-75; Stoney Indian Band Admin Bldg, comn by Chief John Snow. *Exhib:* Royal Can Acad Art, Ottawa; Environment '69 & '70, Edmonton & Calgary. *Teaching:* Archit technol, Southern Alta Inst Technol, 61-63; design, Dept Environmental Design, Univ Calgary, 63; interior design, Mount Royal Col, Calgary, 64-66. *Awards:* City Calgary Urban Design Award, 79 & 80; Practice Profile Award, Alberta Asn Architects 75th Anniv, 81; Gov Gen Medal, 82. *Bibliog:* Gordon Atkins/Architect, Cult Develop Br, Dept Prov Cult & South Alta, 70. *Mem:* Alta Asn Archit (pres Calgary chap, 64); Royal Archit Inst Can; academician Royal Can Acad Art. *Publ:* Contribr, Canadian Architecture 1960-1970, 70; auth, Plywood World, 70; Investigation North, Arctic Housing Research for Fed Govt, 75

ATKINS, ROBERT
CRITIC, EDUCATOR, EDITOR
b Cleveland, Ohio. *Study:* Univ Calif, Berkeley, MA(art hist), 76; Univ Calif, Riverside, BA 72, Hon Dr, Phi Beta Kappa, 72. *Collection Arranged:* David Ireland (auth, catalog), New Mus Contemp Art, 84; Between Science & Fiction (auth, catalog), Sao Paulo Biennial, 85; Decoding Gender (auth, catalog), 92; From Media to Metaphor: Art About AIDS (auth, catalog), traveling, 92-94. *Pos:* Art columnist, Village Voice, New York, 88-; Founder, Visual AIDS, New York, 89; Founder, Artists' Survival Workshop, New York, 84; Vpres/ed in chief, Arts Tech entertainment network 96-98; ed: artery The Aids Arts forum, 2000-01; arts ed media channel, 2000-02. *Teaching:* San Francisco State Univ, summers, 84-. *Awards:* Art Critics Fel, Nat Endowment Arts, 81 & Summer Seminar Col Teachers, 81; Manufacturers Hanover Art/World Award Distinguished Art Criticism, 85; Penny McCall Found award in the Visual Arts, for an independent writer/cur, 2001; Penny Mc Call Award for Outstanding Arts Achievement, 2001. *Mem:* Col Art Asn; Visual AIDS. *Publ:* Auth, Artspeak: A Guide To Contemp Ideas, Movements and Buzzwords, 1945-Present, 90 & Artspoke: A Guide to Modern Ideas, Movements and Buzzwords, 1848-1944, 93, Abbeville; co-auth (exhib catalog and book for travelling mus exhib): From Media to Metaphor: Art About AIDS, 1991; "Critic's Choice" Eaton/Shoen Gallery, San Francisco, 1981(also cur); "Apologia" Union Gallery, San Jose State Univ, 1981(also cur); "About TV" Just Above Midtown, NY, 1983(also cur); "Intro: Alan Shepp" Stephen Wirtz Gallery, San Francisco, 1982; "Currents: David Ireland" New Mus of Contemp Art, NY, 1984 (also cur) "; "San Francisco/Science Fiction" San Francisco Art Commission Gallery, Otis-Parsons Gallery (LA), Clocktower Gallery, New York, 1984 (also curator); "Between Science and Fiction" for the 18th Sao Paulo Bienal, Brazil, 1985 (also curator); "What's Happening: Contemporary Art from California, Washington, and Oregon" Alternative Museum, New York, 1984; "Art Against AIDS: Washington, DC" American Foundation for AIDS Research, New York, 1990; "Of Luminosity, Accident and Power Sanders" (for the exhibition Stephen Hannock), James Graham & Sons, New York, 1996; "Rinaldo Hopf: Golden Queers" (for the exhibition of the same name), Wessel + O'Connor Gallery, New York, 1998; "Interactivity and Intervention: Peter d'Agostino's Art of Ideas" (for the exhibition, Peter d'Agostino: Interactivity and Intervention, 1978-99); Lehman College Art Gallery, Bronx, New York, 1999; "Fusion! Artists in a Research Setting" (for the exhibition of the same name), Carnegie Mellon University, Pittsburgh, 2001 (also curator); contribr articles to Advocate, Aperture, Arena (Spain), art + architecture, Art + Text (Australia), Art and Auction, Art Aurea (Ger), Art in America, Art J (Col Art Assoc), Art Paper, ArtByte, Artery: The AIDS-Arts Forum (online), Artforum, ArtLook (CD-Rom), ArtNews, ARTS BT (Japan), Cahier/Witte de With (Neth), Calif, Calif Monthly, Contemporanea, Elle, Esquire (Japan), Flash Art (Italy), Glass Art J, High Performance, Images & Issues, Le Millenium (Japan), Live LA Institute of Contemp Art J, The Media Channel (online), New Art Examiner, Newsday, New West, NY Mag, NY Times, Poz, Print News, San Francisco Bay Guardian, 7 Days, Studio Inter, TalkBack! A Forum for Critical Discourse (online), Vogue, Wired (Japan), Wolkenkrazer (Ger), World Art; cur N.O. Show, South of Market Cultural Ctr (San Francisco), Fashion Moda (the Bronx), 1982; Positive Actions: The Visual AIDS Competition, Clocktower Gallery, DC 37 Union Headquarters, Longwood Gallery (all NY), 1990; From Media to Metaphor: Art About AIDS, (with Thomas Sokolowski), Independent Curs, NY, 1991-1994 (9 mus tour); Decoding Gender, School 33 Art Center, Baltimore, 1992; Peter D'Agostino: Interactivity and Intervention, 1978-99; Lehman Col Art Gallery, Bronx, NY, 1999; Censorship in Camoflauge The New Press, Feb. 2006; and several others

ATKINS, ROSALIE MARKS
PAINTER
b Charleston, WVa, July 21, 1921. *Study:* Mason Col Music & Fine Arts, Charleston, WVa; Morris Harvey Col, Charleston; workshops with Leo Manso & Victor Candell, Provincetown, Mass; also with Bud Hopkins, Truro, Mass. *Work:* WVa Arts & Humanities Permanent Collection. *Exhib:* Nat League Am Pen Women Ann Show, Washington, DC, 72, Univ Charleston, 90, 92 & 94; 39th Ann Exhib Contemp Am Paintings, Four Arts, Palm Beach, Fla, 77; Lighthouse Gallery, Tequesta, Fla, 78-79; Nat League Am Pen Women, Wash, 87; WVa Tech, 98; Univ Charleston, 98; WVa State Col, WVa Juried Exhib. *Collection Arranged:* WVa Div Culture & Hist; Univ Charleston; Rep in many pvt collections. *Awards:* Selected for traveling show, Art in the Embassies Prog, 70 & Nat League Am Pen Women, 72 & 77; Purchase Awards, WVa Arts & Humanities, Allied Artists Award, 72; Purchase Award, Celebration Arts Show, Lighthouse Gallery, Tequesta, Fla; Purchase Award, Exhib 280, Huntington Galleries, WVArts and Humanities Coun. *Bibliog:* Dorothy Seckler (auth), article in Provincetown Painters; article in Artists/USA, 79-80; article, Focus, 5/83. *Mem:* Allied Artists of WVa (vpres, 67); Am Pen Women (pres, Charleston Br, 73-74); Sunrise, Inc; Provincetown Art Asn. *Media:* Acrylic, Oil. *Specialty:* Gallery Eleven, Charleston, WVa. *Publ:* article, Provincetown Painters, Everson Mus Art Syracuse, NY. *Dealer:* Gallery Eleven Charleston WV. *Mailing Add:* 1518 Quarrier St Charleston WV 25311

ATKINSON, CONRAD
SCULPTOR, PAINTER
b Cumbria, Eng, June 15, 40. *Study:* Liverpool Col Art, NDD, ATD, 61; Royal Acad Sch, London, Cert, RAS, Hons, 65; Manchester Col Art, AFD, 67. *Work:* Brooklyn Mus, NY; Pushkin Mus, Moscow; Tate Gallery, Victoria & Albert Mus & Brit Mus, London; Mus Mod Art, NY; Australian Nat Gallery, Canberra. *Comn:* Arts Coun Northern Ireland/Irish Trades Union, Belfast, 75; banners, Gen & Munic Workers Union, Newcastle, Eng, 77; record/sound, comn by Geoff Gordon/Ronald Feldman, NY, 83; painting, Lewisham Borough Coun, London, 85. *Exhib:* Manchester City Art Gallery, Eng, 67; Royal Acad Bicentenary, London, 68; Bienale de Paris, Mus d'Art Mod, Paris, 75; Art for Soc, Whitechapel Art Gallery, London, 78; Messages, Albright-Knox Art Gallery, Buffalo, 80; Victoria & Albert Mus, London, 80, 84, 85 & 87; Tate Gallery, London, 81, 82 & 95; Australian Prints, Nat Gallery, Canberra, 84; Laing Art Gallery, Newcastle, Eng, 86; solo exhibs, Victoria & Albert Mus, London, 89, ICA, Moscow, 93, Ruth Bloom Gallery, Los Angeles, 93, Paule Anglim Gallery, San Francisco, 95 & Univ Art Gallery & Mus, Berkeley, Calif, 95, Tullie House Mus & Art Gallery, Carlisle, Eng, 96, Ronald Feldman Fine Arts, NY, 97, The Atlanta Col of Art Gallery, Atlanta, Ga, 98, Intersection for the Arts, San Francisco, Calif, 2000, Abbot Hall Art Gallery, Kendal Cumbria, 2000; Fractured Fairy Tales (with catalogue), Duke Univ Fine Art Gallery, 96; Ronald Feldman Gallery, NY, 96; Face a l'Histoire, Ctr Georges Pompidou, Paris, France, 96; Campaign to Ban Land Mines, The Very Special Art Gallery, Washington, DC, 97; The Liverpool Biennial of Contemp Art, St Georges Hall, Liverpool, Eng, 99. *Pos:* Vis arts adv, Greater London Coun, 81-86 & Inner London Educ Authority, 86-; chair art & art hist, Univ Calif, Davis. *Teaching:* Lectr fine art, Slade Sch Fine Art, 75-78; artist-in-residence, London Borough of Lewisham, 85; vis prof, Carnegie Melon Univ, Pittsburgh, 89-90; chmn, Univ Calif, Davis, 92-. *Awards:* Churchill Fel, 72; Henry Moore Found Residency, 91-92; Official Artist Award, US Campaign to Ban Landmines, 97. *Bibliog:* Cumbrias, Greatest Living Artist, Cumbria Life Mag, 96; An Interview with Conrad Atkinson: From the Political to the Popular, Sculpture 17, 9/98; Conrad Atkinson at Intersection for the Arts, Artweek 31, 6/2000; Secondhand second thoughts, Guardian 34, 5/2000. *Mem:* Arts Coun Gt Brit; Percent for Art, Nat Steering Comt. *Media:* Multi. *Publ:* Auth, Passive Action/Active Passion, Artforum, 9/80; 1984 in the Light of Guernica, Ronald Feldman Fine Arts, 84; On Practice, Artists on Art, Rudulf Baranik Publ, 86; Desires of Permanence: Dreams of Transience, Huddersfield Art Gallery, 91; Challenging the status quo, The Year of the Visual Arts, Eng, 96. *Mailing Add:* c/o Ronald Feldman Fine Arts 31 Mercer St New York NY 10013

ATKINSON, ERIC NEWTON
PAINTER, EDUCATOR
b Hartlepool, Durham, Eng, July, 23, 28; Brit & Can Citizen. *Study:* Hartlepool Col Art, UK, NDD(hons), 52; Royal Acad Sch, London, UK, 55. *Work:* Contemp Art Soc; Leeds City Art Gallery; Arts Coun, Gt Brit, London; Univ Marburg, Ger; London Regional Art Gallery, Ont; and others. *Exhib:* Figures in their Settings, Tate Gallery, London, Eng, 53; Four Northern Artists, Hatton Gallery, Newcastle, 59; Art from Yorkshire, Stadhausgalerie Mus, Dortmund Ger, 65; Edinburgh 100, Demarco Gallery, Edinburgh, Scotland, 67; British Painting, Corcoran Gallery, Washington, DC, 70; retrospective, Mendel Art Gallery, Saskatoon, Saskatchewan, 80; Lewis Collection, Carnegie Mus Art, Pittsburgh, 80; London (Retrospective), Regional Art Gallery, Ont, 94; Wallace Gallery, Calgary, Alberta, Can, 97; Tate Gallery, St Ives, United Kingdom, 98; Modigliani Ctr, Florence, 2002. *Teaching:* Lectr fine arts, Leeds Col Art, Yorkshire, 56-65, dept head, fine arts, 65-69; dean fac applied arts, Fanshawe Col, London, Ont, 73-82. *Awards:* David Murray Travel Scholar, Royal Acad, London, 52-54; J M Turner, Landscape Bursary, Royal Acad, London, 54. *Bibliog:* Atkinson-Pollock (auth), Artists proof (film), 82; Univ Western Ont, Canadian Art Collection, 84. *Mem:* Royal Canadian Acad Arts. *Media:* Mixed. *Interests:* History. *Publ:* Auth, Alfred Wallis Cornish Primitive, Accent, Leeds, 64; coauth, Art Education at Leeds, Studio Int, 69; auth, Art Education, MASH, Chicago Art Inst, 70; exhib rev, Arts, Can, 76; Forum: Imaginative Use of Space for Arts, London, Ont, 81; Visual education on the back burner, Bulletin Mag, 86; The Incomplete Cirlce, A Scholar Press Book, UK, 2000; plus others. *Dealer:* Mendelson Gallery 5874 Ellsworth Ave Pittsburgh PA 15232; Thielsen Galleries Inc 1038 Adelaide St London ON; Wallace Galleries 500 5th Ave SW Calgary Alberta Can; Moore Gallery LTD, 80 Spadina Ave, Toronto, Ontario. *Mailing Add:* 69 Paddock Green Crescent London ON N6J 3P6 Canada

ATKINSON, LESLIE JANE See Temple, Leslie Alcott (Leslie Jane Atkinson)

ATKINSON, TRACY
CONSULTANT, MUSEOLOGIST
b Middletown, Ohio, Aug 10, 28. *Study:* Ohio State Univ, BFA(summa cum laude), 50; Univ of the Americas, 50; Univ Pa, MA, 51; Bryn Mawr Col, 53. *Collection Arranged:* Pop Art and the American Tradition, 65; The Inner Circle, 66; Botero, 67; Options & The Bradley Collection, 68; Seymour Lipton & A Plastic Presence, 69; Aspects of a New Realism, 70; Portraits Exhibition, 71; Six Painters, 72; The Urban River, 73, Milwaukee Art Mus; Tremaine Collection; Sol Lewitt Wall Drawings; JP Morgan Collector; The Great River, David Bermant Collection, Hartford, Conn. *Pos:* Curatorial asst, Albright-Knox Art Gallery, 55-59; asst dir, Columbus Gallery Fine Arts, 59-61, actg dir, 61-62; dir, Milwaukee Art Ctr, 62-76; dir, Wadsworth Atheneum, 77-88, emer dir, 88-; pvt consultant, 88. *Publ:* Articles in prof journals, nat art news mags & newspapers. *Mailing Add:* 117 Ciderbrook Rd Avon CT 06001

ATLAS, CHARLES
FILMMAKER
b St Louis, Mo, 58. *Exhib:* The Hanged One; Television Dance Atlas, Hail the New Puritan, 87; Superhoney, 94; Merce Cunningham: A Lifetime of Dance, 2000; consulting dir, Art in the 21st Century, 2001; The Legend of Leigh Bowery, 2002. *Pos:* filmmaker in res, Merce Cunningham Dance Co, NY. *Awards:* recipient of multiple Bessie Awards, NY. *Mailing Add:* Merce Cunningham Dance Co 55 Bethune St New York NY 10014

ATLAS, NAVA
WRITER, DESIGNER
b Jaffa, Israel, Apr 29, 55; US citizen. *Study:* Univ Mich, BFA, 77. *Work:* Wichita Art Mus, Kans; New York Pub Libr Print Collection; Col Art Gallery, State Univ NY, New Paltz. *Exhib:* The Radwaste & Stonehenge Series, traveling exhib, collab with Chaim Tabak, 85-89; Humor, Wit & Whimsy, Bowie State Col, MD, 86; Painted Surfaces, Albany Inst Hist & Art, NY, 86; Recent Acquisitions, State Univ NY, New Paltz, 93. *Bibliog:* Howard Dalee Spencer (auth), A Collaborative Exhibition: The Radwaste & Stonehenge Series, Wichita Art Mus, 85. *Publ:* Vegetariana, 93, Vegetarian Express, 95, Vegetarian Celebrations, 96 & Vegetarian Soups for all Seasons, 96, Little Brown; Vegetarian 5 Ingredient Gourmet, Broadway Bks, 2001; Vegetarian Family Cookbook, 2004; Everyday Traditions, 2005. *Mailing Add:* 41 Hombeck Ridge Rd Poughkeepsie NY 12603

ATLEE, EMILIE DES
PAINTER, INSTRUCTOR
b Bethlehem, Pa, July 6, 1915. *Study:* Spring Garden Inst, Philadelphia; also with Roswell Weidner & Joseph & Gertrude Capolino. *Work:* United Airlines, Philadelphia Airport; Palasaides High Sch, Bucks Co, Pa; La Salle Col & Franklin Inst, Philadelphia; Cult Arts Ctr Ocean City, NJ. *Comn:* Portraits, Libr Univ Del & Berks Co Ct House, Pa. *Exhib:* One-woman shows, Little Gallery, 63, Newmans Gallery, Philadelphia, 70 & Arrowroot Natural Foods II, Paoli, Pa, 96; Knickerbocker Artists Ann, NY, 64; Philadelphia Art Teachers Asn, 69-71; Harrisburg Mus, Pa, 71. *Pos:* Critic, 78-. *Teaching:* Instr, 53-69; instr, Main Line Ctr Arts, Bryn Mawr, Pa, 69-77. *Awards:* Hon mention, Nat, Ogunquit Art Ctr, 59 & Nat Benedictine Art Awards, 69; First Prize, Main Line Ctr Arts Members Show, 85. *Bibliog:* Dorothy Grafly (ed), The changing moods of art, Art in Focus, 71. *Mem:* Artists Equity Asn. *Media:* Oil, Pastel. *Dealer:* Newman Galleries 1624 Walnut St Philadelphia PA 19103. *Mailing Add:* 27 Fairview Rd Narberth PA 19072

ATTAL, M GEORGE
ART DEALER, CONSULTANT
b Austin, Tex, Dec 12, 34. *Pos:* Owner, Gen Store Gallery, Austin, Tex, 64-68, Int Fine Arts, HI, 68-79, Austin Galleries, Tex, 79-86 & 89-. *Specialty:* US Agent for the Estate of Joaquin Torrents Llado; 19th and 20th century artists; national and international artists. *Collection:* Modern impressionists paintings. *Mailing Add:* 1219 W 6th St Austin TX 78703

ATTIE, DOTTY
PAINTER
b Pennsauken, NJ, Mar 20, 38. *Study:* Philadelphia Col Art, BFA, 59; Brooklyn Mus Art Sch, Beckmann Fel, 60; Art Students League, 67. *Work:* Allen Mem Art Mus; Mus Mod Art, NY; Whitney Mus Am Art; Brooklyn Mus; Spencer Art Mus; and others. *Exhib:* One-man shows, Air Gallery, NY, 76, OK Harris Gallery, NY, 77, Univ RI, 78, Contemp Arts Mus, Tex, 79, Wadsworth Atheneum, Conn, 80, Pennsylvania Acad Fine Arts, Pa, 81; New Dimensions in Drawing, Aldrich Mus, Ridgefield, Conn, 81; Words as Images, Renaissance Soc, Chicago, 81; Corcoran Biennial, Corcoran Mus, Washington, 93; and other. *Teaching:* Adj prof, NY Univ & Manhattanville Col, 77. *Awards:* Creative Artists Pub Serv Grant, NY State Coun Arts, 76-77; Nat Endowment Arts Grants, 76-77 & 83-84. *Bibliog:* Corinne Robins (auth), Dotty Attie, Arts, 11/78; Susan Putterman (auth), Dotty Attie, Arts, 12/80; Maurice Berger (auth), The Empty Frame, Arts, 9/81; and others. *Media:* Oil Paint. *Dealer:* PPO W 532 Broadway New York NY 10012. *Mailing Add:* 334 E 22nd St New York NY 10010

ATWELL, ALLEN
EDUCATOR, PAINTER
b Pittsburgh, Pa, Oct 19, 25. *Study:* Cornell Univ, BA, 49 & MFA, 51. *Work:* Herbert F Johnson Mus Art, Cornell Univ, Ithaca, NY. *Exhib:* Everson Mus Art, Syracuse, NY, 74; Contemp Reflections, Aldrich Mus Contemp Art, Ridgefield, Conn, 75; Artists of Cent NY, Munson-Williams-Proctor Inst, Utica, NY, 74 & 75, The Abstract Tradition in Cent NY, 79; Herbert F Johnson Mus Art, Cornell Univ, Ithaca, NY, 74, 77 & 79; Art & Frame House, Ithaca, NY 81-88; Kahala Hilton, HI, 89; and others. *Teaching:* From instr art to assoc prof art, 51-64, Cornell Univ, assoc prof art, NY Exten Prog, 64-65; lectr art, New York Univ, 65-66, Manhattan Community Col, 66 & Ithaca Col, NY, 71-77; teaching fel art, Inst Allende, Univ Guanajuato, Mex, 73. *Awards:* Ford Found Fel, India, 53-54; Fulbright Fel, India & Nepal, 61-62; Rockefeller Found Fel, Southeast Asia, Indonesia & Japan, 62-63. *Mem:* Col Art Asn. *Publ:* Auth & illusr, Kuo Hsi's Clearing Autumn Skies Over Mountains & Valleys and Indian Miniature Paintings & The Yama Tanka, 72, Aspen; auth & illusr, Indian art: From multiplicity to unity, Fulbright Newsletter, spring, 74. *Mailing Add:* 2101 Nuvanu Ave Apt 2107 Honolulu HI 96817-1764

ATWOOD PINARDI, BRENDA
PAINTER, INSTRUCTOR
Study: Am Acad Art, Chicago, cert, 56. *Comn:* Dr Raymond Carhart portrait, Northwestern Univ, Evanston, Ill, 73; Nicholas Santucci portrait, comn by Santucci family, Skokie, Ill, 75. *Exhib:* Classic Am Art Show, Beverly Hills, Calif, 85-89; solo exhib, Mus SW, Midland, Tex, 86; Ann Plein Art Show, Catalina Island, Calif, 87-89; Northwest Rendezvous, Holter Mus, Helena, Mont, 88 & 92; Four Am Impressionists, Cincinnati, 91; Am Collectors Invitational, Scottsdale, Ariz, 92; CM Russell Show & Auction, 1993-2003; Artists for Open Space, 1999, 2001, 2003; Miniatures, Albuquerque Mus, 2000-03; Treasure State Invitational, 2000, 02; and others. *Pos:* Dir, founder, Village Art Sch, 66-76, consult, 76-. *Teaching:* instr, Scottsdale Artists' Sch, 1991-2004; instr, Pocatello Art Ctr, 1997, 98; instr, Abbrescia Fine Art & Pottery Studios. *Awards:* Best of Show, Eighth Ann NW Art Show, 78; Artist of Yr, Am Royal Asn, 84; Ashton & Louise Smith Artists' Choice, 94, 2004; Best of Show, CM Russell Mus Show, 1998, 2002, 04; Best Painting, CM Russell Mus Show, 1997; People's Choice award Artists for Open Space, 2001; Artist-in-Residence, Glacier Nat Park, 1998. *Bibliog:* Scott E Dial (auth), Montana's special light, SW Art Mag, 1/77; Susan Hallsten McGarry (auth), Joe Abbrescia, SW Art Mag, 9/86; Lewis Barrett Lehrman (auth), Energize Your Paintings with Color and Freshen Your Paintings With New Ideas, SW Art Mag, 8/95. *Media:* Oil. *Interests:* conservation & restoration, fine art. *Mailing Add:* c/o Abbrescia Inc 12 1st Ave W Kalispell MT 59901-4440

AUBIN, BARBARA
PAINTER, COLLAGE ARTIST
b Chicago, Ill, Jan 12, 28. *Study:* Carleton Col, BA, 49; Art Inst Chicago, BAE, 54, MAE, 55, George D Brown foreign travel fel, France & Italy, 55-56; Buenos Aires Conv Act grant, Haiti, 58-60. *Work:* Ill State Mus; Art Inst Chicago; Ball State Univ; Centre d'Art, Port-au-Prince, Haiti. *Comn:* Collage, 100th Anniversary of the First Exhib of Seurat's Sunday Afternoon on the Island of Grand Jatte, Roy Boyd Gallery, Chicago, 86. *Exhib:* Mid-Year Shows, Butler Inst Am Art, Ohio, 61 & 62; 10th Ann Nat Prints & Drawings Exhib, Okla Art Ctr, 68; Clocktower, NY, 86; Am Hirst: Women & the US Constitution, Atlanta, Ga & traveling, 88; Survey of Contemp Ill Watercolor, Springfield Art Asn & Tarble Art Ctr, Charleston, Ill, 91, 93, 95, 2000, 2001; Women & Surrealism, Womens Caucus Nat Art, Chicago, 92; Three Rivers Arts Festival, Pittsburgh, Pa, 94; Fulbright Nat, Washington, DC, 97; Chicago Women's Caucus Art Ann Show, 98. *Collection Arranged:* Print & Drawing Dept, Art Institute Chicago; Shomer Col, Waukegan, Ill; Kemper Group Collection, Long Grove, Ill; State of Ill Bldg, Chicago. *Pos:* Reporter, Women Artists News, 77-78 & 83-90; critic for var publ; cur, Send a Postcard to Barbara, Loyola Univ & traveling, 79-80; co-cur, Kimo Theatre, Albuquerque, NMex, 97. *Teaching:* Asst prof painting, drawing & watercolor, Sch Art Inst Chicago, 60-68; asst prof painting, drawing & design, Loyola Univ (Chicago), 68-71; lectr painting, drawing & design, St Joseph's Col, 71-74; prof painting, drawing & visual fundamentals, Chicago State Univ, 71-91. *Awards:* Hon Mention for Dana Medal, Pa Acad Fine Arts, 53; Mich Watercolor Soc Award, 65 & 70; Ill Arts Coun Proj Completion grant, 77 & 78; Patron Purchase award, Springfield Art Mus, Mo, 1999; Community Arts Ass Prog Grant, Chicago Dept Current Affairs; SE Ill Arts Coun Access Program. *Mem:* Arts Club Chicago; Chicago Artists Coalition; Women's Caucus Art (vpres, midwest, 82-85, bd mem, Chicago chap); Albuquerque United Artists. *Media:* Waterbased Media, Mixed Media. *Mailing Add:* The Hallmark 2960 N Lake Shore Dr Chicago IL 60657

AUDEAN
PAINTER, ILLUSTRATOR
b Reading, Pa, June 2, 29. *Study:* Philadelphia Mus Sch Industrial Art, 51. *Bibliog:* Article, Am Artist Mag, 5/87; Victoria Mag, 10/90; posters, Frontline Graphics, San Diego. *Media:* Watercolor. *Publ:* Illusr, Soft as a Kitten, Fuzzy as a Puppy, & A B C, Random House. *Dealer:* Craft Haus Vermont. *Mailing Add:* c/o Eleanor Ettinger 119 Spring St New York NY 10012

AUDETTE, ANNA HELD
PAINTER
b New York, NY. *Study:* Smith Col, BA, 60; Sch Art, Yale Univ, BFA, 62 & MFA, 64. *Work:* Fitzwilliam Mus, Cambridge, Eng; Rijksprentenkabinett, Rijksmuseum, Amsterdam, Holland; Metrop Mus Art, NY; Nat Gallery Art & Nat Libr Sci, Washington, DC. *Comn:* Print ed, Barnard Col, NY, 79 & Barbara Gladstone Gallery, NY, 79, 80 & 83; NASA, 90. *Exhib:* Mt Holyoke Col Mus, Mass, 76; Fitzwilliam Mus, Cambridge, Eng, 86; D Berman Gallery, Austin, Tex, 2001; solo shows, Gallery Fikrun Wa Fann, Alexandria, Egypt, 77, Clark Art Inst, Williamstown, Mass, 78, Wesleyan Univ, 82, Munson Gallery, New Haven, 85, 87, 90 & 94 & Marlboro Col, Vt, 97, Paul Mellon Arts Ctr, Wallingford, Conn, 99, 2006 & Southern Vt Art Ctr, Manchester, 2000; City Univ NY/Staten Island, 2002; Nat Acad Sciences, Washington, DC, 2004; Blue Mountain Gallery, New York City, 2006; and others. *Collection Arranged:* In Their Own Image?, Southern Conn State Univ, New Haven, 75, 76 & 78. *Teaching:* Prof art, Southern Conn State Univ, 64-97, emer. *Awards:* fel, Morse Col, Yale Univ. *Bibliog:* Articles, Print Collectors Newsletter, 7-8/79 & Art News, 9/80; Articles, Conn Rev, 88. *Mem:* Conn Acad Arts & Scis; Col Art Asn. *Media:* Painting, Photography. *Publ:* Auth & illusr, The Impress of Anatomy, Pratt Graphic Art Ctr, 65; illusr, Past & Present, The Continuity of Classical Myths, Hakkert, Ltd, Toronto, 72; Song in Stone, 83 & Click, Rumble, Roar, 87, T Y Crowell; auth & illusr, Images Out of Time, Conn Review, 88; auth, The Blank Canvas, Shambhala Publ, Boston, 93; auth/ed, 100 Creative Drawing Ideas, Shambhala Publ, Boston, 2004. *Dealer:* Fenn Gallery 345 Main St South Woodbury CT. *Mailing Add:* 24 Everit St New Haven CT 06511

AUERBACH, RITA ARGEN
PAINTER, INSTRUCTOR
b Buffalo, NY, Mar 28, 33. *Study:* Albright Art Sch, AA, 54; State Univ Col, Buffalo, BS(art educ), 54, MS(art educ), 74. *Work:* Charles Rand Penney Collection, Burchfield-Penney Art Ctr, City Hall Common Coun Chambers & State Univ Col, Buffalo; Acad Art, Riga, Latvia; Chautauqua Inst Sch Art, NY; Castellani Art Mus, Niagara Falls, NY; Roswell Park Cancer Inst, Buffalo. *Comn:* Corp Off (paintings), Del N Companies Inc, Buffalo, NY, 90; cover art (corp collection & ann report), J M

Smucker Co, Orrville, Ohio, 93; prog publ painting, Lockpost Town & Country Club, NY, 98; 75th Anniversary Cover Art, Chautauqua Inst Opera Prog, NY, 99; Canterbury Woods residence, Williamsville, NY. *Exhib:* Adirondacks Nat Exhib Am Watercolors, Old Forge, NY, 84 & 86; Minneapolis City of Lakes, F Styles Gallery, 88 & 89; Nat League Am Pen Women, Pen Arts Bldg, Washington, DC, 88; Watermedia '90 Nat, Mont Watercolor Soc, Missoula, 90; 16th Juried Nat Exhib, Pa Watercolor Soc, Erie, 95; New Work, Chautauqua Ctr Visual Arts, NY, 96; Two Women, Kenan Ctr Art Gallery, Buffalo, NY, 97; Giverny Series, Burchfield-Penny Art Ctr, Buffalo, NY, 97. *Pos:* Judge & juror, Batavia Art Asn, NY, 89; coun mem, Big Orbit Gallery, Buffalo, NY, 90-95; dist art dept chmn, Clarence Cent Schs, NY, 92-94. *Teaching:* Jr & sr high sch instr, Clarence Cent Schs, Clarence, NY, 74-94; watercolor, Chautauqua Inst Sch Arts, NY, 94-. *Awards:* First Place, City of Lakes Nat Exhib, Minneapolis, 88; Best Show, Grumbacher Gold Medialian, Nat League Am Pen Women, 91; Art Educator of the Year, One Western Section, NY State Art Teachers Asn, 93. *Bibliog:* Richard Huntington (auth), Light Show Review, Buffalo News, 6/7/96; Hunter Groninger (auth), Auerbach exhibits: impressionist influence in Giverny Series, Chautauquan Daily, 7/19/97; Ginny Baier, The color orange, Am Artist, winter 98. *Mem:* Niagara Frontier Watercolor Soc (vpres, 85-87); Nat League Am Penwomen; Buffalo Soc Artists (pres, 89 & 91); signature mem Pa Watercolor Soc. *Media:* Watercolor. *Publ:* Auth, Sketches and Reflections of a Journey to Soviet Union, Clarence Graphics, 87; contribr, A Brief History Buffalo Society of Artists, Reflections by President, Partners Press, 91; coauth, New York State Council Arts in Education Grant, Burchfield & Technology, Buffalo State Col, 93; contribr, Living Primetime, Art Strokes, Jerry Flaschner, 96-98; Eclectic Literary Forum Cover Art, ELF Assocs, 97. *Dealer:* Art Dialogue Gallery One Linwood Ave Buffalo NY 14209. *Mailing Add:* 33 Delaware Rd Buffalo NY 14217

AUNIO, IRENE
PAINTER
b Finland; US citizen. *Study:* Art Students League; Brooklyn Mus, studies with John Costigno. *Work:* Evansville Mus Fine Arts, IN; Reading Mus Fine Arts, PA; Art Students League, Dag Hammarskjold Plaza, NY; Katz Commun New York & Int. *Exhib:* one-woman shows, Brooklyn Mus, NY, 66, Suffolk Mus, NY, 74, Gallery Machias, Maine, Grist Mill Gallery, Vt, Jeanne Taylor Gallery, NY, Miriam Perlman Gallery, Ill & Belanthi Gallery, NY. *Teaching:* Instr, watercolor, Prospect Harbor, Maine, 93-; workshops watercolor, Rocky Point, Long Island, NY, currently, Nat Asn Women Artists, NY, Am Watercolor Soc; instr, Elderhostel Program. *Awards:* First Award of Excellence, Independent Art Soc, 92; Best in Show, Nat League Am Pen Women, 98; Ranger Fund Purchase Prize. *Mem:* Am Watercolor Soc, NY; Nat Asn Women Artists; Allied Artists Am; Nat League Am Pen Women. *Media:* Watercolor, Acrylic, Oil. *Publ:* NY Art, Rev, Les Krantz, 88. *Mailing Add:* PO Box 781 Rocky Point NY 11778

AUPING, MICHAEL GRAHAM
CURATOR, HISTORIAN
b Portland, Ore, Oct 17, 1949. *Study:* Santa Ana Col, AA, 69; Calif State Univ, Fullerton, BA(art hist), 71; Calif State Univ, Long Beach, MA(art hist), 75. *Exhib:* Matrix: A Changing Exhib Contemp Art, Univ Art Mus, Berkeley, Calif, 78-80; Francesco Clemente, Walker Art Ctr, Minneapolis, Minn, Dallas Mus Art, Albright-Knox Art Gallery, Buffalo, NY, 85; Hamish Fulton: Selected Walks 1969-1989 (traveling show), Nat Gallery, Ottawa; Jenny Holzer: The Venice Installation, Albright-Knox Art Gallery, Buffalo, NY, Walker Art Ctr, Minneapolis, Minn, traveling, 92; Selected Geometric Abstract Painting in America Since 1945 (traveling show), Milwaukee Art Mus, Wis; Structure to Resemblance: Work by Eight American Sculptors; Drawing Rooms: Jonathan Borofsky, Sol Lewitt, Richard Serra, 94; Arshile Gorky: The Breakthrough Yrs, 95; Tatsuo Miyajima, Big Time, 96; Georg Baselitz: Portraits of Elke, 97; Agnes Martin/Richard Tuttle, 98; House of Sculpture, 99; Natural Deceits, 00; Modern Art Mus of Ft Worth 20000, 2002; Philip Guston Retrospective, 03; and others. *Collection Arranged:* Richard Serra Collection; Robert Irwin Collection; John Chamberlain Collection; Francesco Clemente Collection. *Pos:* Ed, Los Angeles Inst Contemp Art J, 76-78; assoc cur, Univ Art Mus, Berkeley, 78-80; cur 20th century art, John & Mable Ringling Mus Art, Sarasota, Fla, 80-84; prof adv comt, Art Pub Places, Metro-Dade Area, Miami, 84-; chief cur, Albright-Knox Art Gallery, Buffalo, NY, 84-93 & Mod Art Mus Ft Worth, Tex, 93-; var consults, 73-95. *Teaching:* adj lectr art hist, Univ Calif, Santa Barbara, fall 77 & Univ Buffalo, 88-89; lectr, Inst Contemp Art, Boston, Baltimore Mus Art, St Louis Art Mus, Nelson-Atkins Mus Art, Kansas City, Milwaukee Art Mus, Hirshhorn Mus & Sculpture Garden, 89-92, Int Conf, Univ York, Toronto, Can, 91, NC Mus Art, Seattle Art Mus, San Francisco Mus Mod Art, Dallas Mus Art & Boston Mus Fine Arts, 93-94. *Awards:* Comnr, American Pavilion 1990 Venice Biennale, Italy. *Res:* Post-War American and European Art. *Publ:* Auth, Clyfford Still in New York: The Buffalo Project, In: Clyfford Still, Munich: Prestel Verlag, 92; Chuck Close: Face to Face, Artforum, 10/93; Drawing Rooms: Jonathan Borofsky, Sol LeWit, Richard Serra, 94; Arshile Gurky: The Breakthrough Years, 95; Tatsuo Miyajima Big Time, 96. *Mailing Add:* c/o Mod Art Mus Ft Worth 3200 Darnell St Ft Worth TX 76107

AURBACH, MICHAEL LAWRENCE
SCULPTOR, EDUCATOR
b Wichita, Kans, Dec 13, 52. *Study:* Univ Kans, Lawrence, BA, 74, BSJ, 76, MA(art hist), 79, BFA(studio art), 81; Southern Methodist Univ, Dallas, MFA(sculpture), 83. *Work:* Nat Civil Rights Mus, Memphis; Loyola Univ New Orleans. *Exhib:* Southwest 85, NMex Mus Fine Arts, 85; one-man shows, Artemisia Gallery, Chicago, 87, Macon Mus, Ga, 89, Bernice Steinbaum Gallery, NY, 91 & Univ Notre Dame, Southbend, 91, Sothern Meth Univ, Dallas, 93, WVa Univ, Morgantown, 94, ARC/RAW Space, Chicago, 95,N Dakota Mus Art, Grand Forks, NDak, 96, Univ Ga, Athens, 97, Indianapolis Art Ctr, 97, Alexandria (La) Mus Art, 99, First Ctr Visual Arts, Nashville, Tenn, 2001, Spartanburg Mus Art, SC, 2003; Birmingham Biennial IV & V, Birmingham Mus Art, Ala, 87 & 89; Sculpture Tour Nat Invitational, Univ Tenn, 89-90; The Edge of Childhood Nat Invitational, Heckscher Mus, Huntington, NY, 92; Col Art Asn Members Exhib, Atlanta Ctr Contemp Art, Ga, 2005. *Awards:* Outstanding Artistic Achievement, Southeastern Col Art Conf, 95; NEA/Southern Arts Fedn Fel, 87; Art Matters Inc Grant, 89, 92; Tenn Arts Comn Grant, 90, 2003; Puffin Found Grant, 2002; and others. *Bibliog:* Glen Brown (auth), Secrecy and Institutional Power, World Sculpture News, autumn 2000; Dorothy Joiner (auth), review, Metalsmith, spring 2006; Dorothy Joiner (author), review, Sculpture, 2005; Joseph Will (auth), review, Art Papers, March/Apr 2002. *Mem:* Col Art Asn (bd dir, 99-, vpres, external affairs 99-2000, vpres, coms 2000-01, pres 2002-); Southeast Col Art Conf; Int Sculpture Ctr; Founds in Art: Theory and Educ; Mid-Am Col Asn (bd dirs 2005-06). *Media:* Mixed-Media. *Publ:* Auth, Ten in Tennessee review, 12/87 & Jim Poag review, 2/87, New Art Examiner; Primitive elegance: sculpture by D Hall & C Michael, Vol 12, 88 & The Don Evans Case, Vol 17, 93, Art Papers. *Mailing Add:* Vanderbilt Univ Dept Art & Art History Box 1801B Nashville TN 37235

AUSBY, ELLSWORTH AUGUSTUS
PAINTER, INSTRUCTOR
b Portsmouth, Va, Apr 5, 1942. *Study:* Sch Visual Arts, BFA, 75; Pratt Inst. *Work:* Aldrich Mus Contemp Art, Ridgefield, Conn; Cinque Gallery, NY; Rice Univ, Houston; Atlanta Airport. *Comn:* Three pastel paintings, comn by Jean de Mevil, Houston, 71; Space Odyssey (enamel on steel), Howard Johnsons Co, NY, 79-80; Rock Paper Scissor (silkscreen), Path Train Station, NY; Space Odyssey (stainless steel sculpture), NY Technical Col, City Univ NY, 81. *Exhib:* New Black Artist, Brooklyn Mus Fine Arts, 69; Lamp Black, Boston Mus Fine Arts, 70; Black Artist, Whitney Mus Am Art, NY, 71; one-man show, Pa Acad Fine Arts, Philadelphia, 72; Millenium, Mus Philadelphia Civic Ctr, 73; Herbert F Johnson Mus Art, Cornell Univ, Ithaca, NY, 74; Contemp Reflections, Aldrich Mus Contemp Art, 75; Afro-Am Abstractions, Pub Sch 1, Long Island City, 80; Everson Mus, Syracuse, NY, 81. *Collection Arranged:* Some American History (auth, catalog), Rice Univ, 71; Contemporary Reflections (auth, catalog), Am Fedn Art, 75. *Teaching:* Instr painting, Sch Visual Arts, 75-. *Awards:* Comprehensive Employment & Training Act artist grant, 78; Creative Artists Pub Serv Prog painting grant, NY State Coun Arts, 80. *Bibliog:* Barbara Rose (auth), Black artist, 9/70 & Henri Ghent (auth), Quo Vadis black art, 11/74, Art in Am; April Kingsley (auth), Ausby at the Soho Center, Soho Weekly News, 12/75. *Mem:* Cult Coun Found NY; Harlem Cult Coun Found. *Media:* Acrylic, Enamel. *Publ:* Illusr, Slavery (film), Silvermine Productions, 71; illusr, Tuesdays and Every Other Sunday Off, Doubleday, 72; illusr, Black Review Number Two, William Morrow & Co, 72; contribr, Encore Mag, 72; illusr, The Crossroads, Reed, Cannon, Johnson, 75. *Mailing Add:* 63 Steuben St Brooklyn NY 11205-2608

AUSTIN, BARBARA JEAN See Adams, Bobbi (Barbara) Jean Austin

AUSTIN, PAT
PAINTER, PRINTMAKER
b Detroit, Mich, Mar 17, 37. *Study:* Univ Mich, AB, 59; Univ Alaska with Alex Duffs Combs, Jr, 65, MFA, 76; Univ Wash, BFA(art), 71; Univ Alaska, Anchorage, MFA, 77. *Work:* Evergreen State Col, Olympia; Anchorage Hist & Fine Arts Mus, Alaska; Alaska State Coun Arts, Printmakers Alaska Permanent Collection, Anchorage; Anchorage Borough Sch Dist Permanent Print Collection; Visual Arts Ctr, Permanent Print Collection. *Comn:* Providence Hospital Print Project, 86; mural, Family Resource Ctr, 87; mural, Chugach Sr Ctr, Munic Anchorage, 94; 14 series from the Ressurection paintings, St Paul's Episcopal Church, Port Townsend, Wash, 2002; Video of this 30 minute documentary for PT TV (publ television) Glen Paris-Stamm Productions. *Exhib:* All Alaska Juried Exhib, Anchorage, 66-69 & 72-86; 20 Printmakers Touring Invitational, Wash State Artmobile, 71-72; one-man shows, Anchorage Hist & Fine Arts Mus, 75 & 83 & Stoningtor Gallery, Anchorage, 86; Northwest Print Coun, group exhib, 84-86; Silverwater, Port Townsend, Wash, 98; Taylor St Coffee House, Port Townsend, Wash, 2000; group exhib, Quimper Universal Unitarian Church, 2004. *Teaching:* Instr art & Eng, Anchorage Borough Sch Dist, 65-69; instr printmaking & painting, Univ Alaska, 71-87 & Peninsula Col, Wash, 95-97; ret, Univ Alaska, 87; lect, Art of the Print, lect series, Northwind Gallery, 2004; Guy Anderson: Northwest Mystic, lect with his exhib, 2005. *Awards:* Printmaking Award, All Alaska Juried Exhib, 69-74; Mel Kohler Painting Award, 75; Artist Fel, Alaska State Coun Arts, 85. *Bibliog:* Connie Godwin (auth), Pat's art is exploring world, Anchorage Daily Times, 11/3/75; Virginia McKinney (auth), Pat Austin: Printmaker and more, Alaska J, winter 83. *Mem:* Anchorage Hist & Fine Arts Mus Asn; Northwest Print Coun (found, bd mem); Northwind Arts Alliance; Quimper Arts (guild). *Media:* Watermedia, Etching. *Interests:* artists books, writing, non-toxic printmaking. *Publ:* Auth, National Collection of Fine Arts (catalog), Washington, DC, 78; Passing off reproductions as real art, Alaska J, winter 80; auth, Love, Loss, Lust, publ by Knightsmore; auth, poetry, Northwind Readers; auth, poetry, Poetry at Lahani's; auth, poetry, Minstaur. *Mailing Add:* 1309 Ninth St Port Townsend WA 98368-2929

AUTEN, GERALD
PAINTER, EDUCATOR
Study: Univ Iowa, BFA (drawing and painting); Washington Univ, St Louis, MFA (painting); Univ Wis, Milwaukee, (MA archit). *Exhib:* in Teheran, Mexico City, NY and Vancouver; Am Acad Arts and Letters, 2002, 2004; Nat Acad, 2006; represented in permanent collections of Albright Knox Gallery Art, Booz Allen Hamilton, The Hood Mus Art; Inaugural Exhib, Lori Bookstein Fine Art, NY, 2004, In Black and White, 2005. *Teaching:* Sr lectr studio art Dartmouth Col, currently. *Mailing Add:* Dartmouth Coll Dept Studio Art Hinman Box 6081 Hanover NH 03755-3599

AUTH, ROBERT R
PRINTMAKER, PAINTER
b Bloomington, Ill, Oct 27, 26. *Study:* Ill Wesleyan Univ, BFA; Wash State Univ, MFA. *Work:* Salt Lake Art Ctr, Utah; Col Southern Idaho, Twin Falls; Ricks Col, Rexburg, Idaho; Boise Gallery Art, Idaho; Wash State Univ. *Comn:* Five works, Dept Interior-Big Hole Nat Battlefield, Wisdom, Mont; one work, Nat Governor's Conf, 85. *Exhib:* Intermountain Painting & Sculpture 4th Biennial, Salt Lake Art Ctr, 69; Fedn Rocky Mountain States Traveling Exhib, 71-72; Inaugural Exhib, Denver Art Mus, Colo, 71; one-man retrospective, Boise Gallery Art, 80; Sawtooths & Other Ranges of Imagination, Contemp Art from Idaho, Smithsonian Inst, Washington, DC, 83; Calligraphic Letter Art, Smithsonian Nat Postal Mus Exhib, 98-99. *Pos:* Bd dir, Boise Gallery Art, 69-; exec bd dir, Idaho Alliance for the Arts in Educ, 82-; appointment to Mayor's Comn on the Arts, Boise City, 84-. *Teaching:* Instr art, Burley High Sch, Idaho, 60-61; instr art & humanities, Boise High Sch, 61-81; supervisor art, Boise Independent Sch District, 81-87. *Awards:* Allied Arts Coun Artist of Year Award, 72; Governor of Idaho's Medal for Excellence in Arts, 84; Distinguished Citizen Award, The Idaho Statesman, 89. *Mem:* Idaho Art Asn (vpres, 70-72); Boise Art Asn (trustee, 69-). *Media:* All; Acrylic, Oil. *Dealer:* Browns Gallery 1022 Main St Boise ID 83705. *Mailing Add:* PO Box 91 Yellow Pine ID 83677

AUTH, SUSAN HANDLER
CURATOR, EDUCATOR
b New York, NY, June 25, 39. *Study:* Swarthmore Col, BA; Univ London; Univ Mich, MA; Am Sch Classical Studies, Athens, Fulbright Scholar, 64-65; Bryn Mawr Col, PhD, 68. *Work:* Toledo Mus of Art Ohio; Newark Mus NJ. *Collection Arranged:* Myth & Gospel: Art of Coptic Egypt, Newark Mus, 77, Ancient Greece: Life and Art, 80; The Classical Collection, 81 & 89; Coptic Art of Ancient Egypt, Nadler Collection & Newark Mus, NJ, 86; Stepping Into Ancient Egypt: House of the Artist Pashed, 91; The Roman Banquet, 1994; Ancient Adornment, 1997; Artisans of Ancient Rome, 1997; Ancient Galleries 1999-2001; Garden of Remembrance, 2002. *Pos:* Curatorial asst, Toledo Mus Art, Ohio, 67; cur classical collection, Newark Mus, 71-. *Teaching:* Asst prof ancient art & archaeol, Dept Art, Rutgers Univ, Newark, 68-71. *Awards:* Am Numismatic Soc Summer Fel, 63; Travel Grants, Smithsonian Inst, Washington, DC, summer 71, Ford Found Publ, 75, Nat Endowment Arts, Mellon, 91-93, Dodge Found, 97, Mus Loan Network, 2001 & 2003. *Mem:* Archaeol Inst Am; Int Asn Hist Glass; Am Research Ctr, Egypt; Int Asn Egyptologists. *Res:* Ancient glass; Greek, Roman, Egyptian & Coptic art & archaeology. *Publ:* Auth, Ancient Glass at the Newark Mus, from the Eugene Schaefer Collection of Ancient Glass, Newark Mus, 76; var articles, Am J Archaeol, J Glass Studies, Archaeol & Annales Int d'Etude Hist du Verre, Brunildes Ridgway Festschrift, 98, Annales of Int Asn Coptic Studies, 2003; Coptic Glass, The Coptic Encyclopedia, 91; Pottery & Glass, Beyond the Pharaohs, 89. *Mailing Add:* Newark Mus 49 Washington St Newark NJ 07102-3176

AUTH, TONY (WILLIAM ANTHONY), JR
EDITORIAL CARTOONIST
b Akron, Ohio, May 7, 42. *Study:* Univ Calif, Los Angeles, BA(biological illus). *Pos:* Syndicated ed cartoonist, Philadelphia Inquirer, 71- & Universal Press Syndicate, 80-. *Awards:* Sigma Delta Chi Award, Soc of Prof Journalists, 76; Pulitzer Prize, Columbia Univ Trustees, 76; 5 Overseas Press Club Awards received. *Bibliog:* Stephen Hess & Milton Kaplan (co-auth), The Ungentlemanly Art: A History of American Political Cartoons, MacMillan, 75. *Mem:* Soc Illustrators. *Media:* Pen and ink. *Publ:* Auth, Behind the Lines, Houghton-Mifflin, 77; Lost in Space-The Reagan Years, Andrews & McMeel, 88; auth & illusr, Sleeping Babies, Golden Bks, 93; illusr, Tree of Here, Knopf, 93; Sky of Now, Knopf, 95. *Dealer:* Rosenfeld Gallery 113 Arch St Philadelphia PA 19104. *Mailing Add:* Philadelphia Inquirer 400 N Broad St PO Box 8263 Philadelphia PA 19101

AUTIO, (A) RUDY
CERAMIST, EDUCATOR
b Butte, Mont, Oct 8, 26. *Study:* Mont State Univ, BS, 50; Wash State Univ, MFA, 52; Md Inst, Col Art, Baltimore, DFA, 86. *Work:* Renwick Gallery, Smithsonian Mus; Everson Mus, Syracuse, NY; Victoria & Albert Mus, London; Nat Nus, Stockholm; Taideteollisusmuseo, Helsinki. *Comn:* Carved brick relief, First Methodist Church, Great Falls, Mont, 54; ceramic tile relief, Union Bank & Trust Co, Helena, 59-60; metal sculpture, Farm Credit Banks, Spokane, 71; mural, State Security Bank, Polson, Mont, 71; RYA wallhanging, Performing Arts Bldg, Univ Mont, Missoula, 86. *Exhib:* One-man shows, Henry Gallery, Univ Wash, Seattle, 63, Toledo Art Mus, 65, Retrospectives, Am Crafts Mus, NY, 83, John Michael Kohler Art Mus, Sheboygan, Wis, 83, Bellevue Art Mus, Wash, 83 & Montana Horses, Ryijy Tapestry, Taideteollisuusmuseo, Helsinki, Finland, 85; Everson Mus, Syracuse, 64; two-man show, Chicago Art Mus, 68; Am Studio Potters & Victoria & Albert Mus, London, 72; San Francisco Mus Mod Art, 72; Mus Contemp Crafts, NY, 74; Seattle Art Mus, 79; retrospective (with catalog), Am Crafts Mus, NY & Bellevue Mus, Seattle, 84; Western States Arts Found 3rd Ann Exhib, Brooklyn Mus, 86; Contemp Am Ceramics, Nat Mus Mod Art, Seoul, Korea, 87; Am Ceramics Now: 27th Ceramics Nat, Everson Mus, Syracuse, NY, 87; Clay as Art, Gummerson's Konstgalleri, Stockholm, Sweden, 87. *Pos:* Resident artist-dir, Archie Bray Found, 52-56; asst cur, Mont Mus Hist Soc, 56. *Teaching:* Prof ceramics & sculpture, Univ Mont, 57-84. *Awards:* Tiffany Found Award, 63; Purchase Award, Everson Mus, 64; Ceramic Art Award, Am Ceramic Soc, 78; Nat Endowment Award, 80; First Governor's Award in Visual Arts' Most Outstanding Artist, 80; Distinguished Scholar Award, Univ Mont, 84. *Bibliog:* Julie Hall (auth), Tradition and Change, 77 & Clark & Hughto (coauths), A Century of Ceramics in the United States, 79, E P Dutton; Lamar Harrington (auth), Ceramics in the Pacific Northwest: A History, Univ Wash Press, 79; Garth Clark (auth), American Potters, Watson-Guptill Publ, New York, 81; Peter Lane (auth), Studio Ceramics, Chilton Book Co, Radnor, Pa, 83. *Mem:* hon mem Nat Coun Educ Ceramic Arts; fel Am Craftsmen Coun; Archie Bray Found (trustee, 74); Int Ceramic Soc, Geneva; hon mem ORNADO (Finland designers), Helsinki. *Publ:* Auth, About drawing, 12/85 & Figure drawing on clay and other surfaces, 12/87, The Studio Potter. *Dealer:* Dorothy Weiss Gallery 256 Sutter St San Francisco CA 94108

AUTREY, SERGIO
COLLECTOR
Pos: Chmn, Telefonica Autrey (now Principia SA de CV), Mexico City, Satelites Mexicanos SA de CV, Mexico City. *Awards:* Named one of Top 200 Collectors, ARTnews Magazine, 2004, 2005, 2006. *Collection:* Contemporary Mexican art, Old Masters, 19th century European art. *Mailing Add:* Satelites Mexicanos SA de CV Piso 24 Colonia Lomas de Chapultepec Blvd M A Mexico DF 40 11000 Mexico

AUTRY, CAROLYN
PRINTMAKER, EDUCATOR
b Dubuque, Iowa, Dec 12, 40. *Study:* Yale-Norfolk Summer Sch, 62; Univ Iowa, Iowa City, BA, 63, MFA, 65; artist resident, Sch Arts France, Lacoste, fall semesters, 84 & 87. *Work:* Libr Cong, Washington; Philadelphia Mus Art; Worcester Art Mus; Portland Art Mus, Ore; Elvehjem Mus Art, Univ Wis, Madison; and others. *Exhib:* Int Biennial Print & Drawing Exhib, Taipei Fine Arts Mus, Taiwan, 83, 85, 87, 91 & 95; Int Impact Art Festival, Kyoto City Mus, Japan, 90, 91, 92 & 93; Found Mona Bismarck, Paris, 91; Exchanged Impressions, Fine Arts Asn Gallery, Hanoi, Vietnam, 91; Interiors, Mansfield Mus Art, Ohio, 95; New World Gallery, Miami, Printwork '2K; Barrett Art Ctr, Poughkeepsie, NY, 2000; Pacific States Biennial Nat Print Exhib, Univ Hawaii, Hilo, 2000; Int Print Exhib Invitational, Minsk, Belarus, 2002; 69th Nat Juried Exhib, Arts Students League, New York City, 2002; solo exhib, Univ Wyom, Laramie, Univ Dallas, Irving, 2002; NAm Print Exhib, Boston Univ, Mass, 2003; Saga 70th Nat print Exhib, New York City, 2004; The Janet Turner 5th Nat Print Exhib, Calif State Univ, Chico, Calif, 2004; Saga's 90th Ann Show, Arts Students League, NY, 2005; Paper in Particular, Larsen Gallery, Columbia col, Columbia, Mo; Saga mem juried exhib in Prague, Hollar Soc Gallery, Czech Republic. *Teaching:* Instr art & art hist, Baldwin-Wallace Col, Berea, Ohio, 65-66; adj assoc prof art hist, Ctr Visual Arts, Univ Toledo, 66-2001; assoc instr, printmaking, Sch Arts in France, Lacoste, fall semester, 87. *Awards:* Ohio Arts Coun Grant, 79, 89; Ledyard Cogswell Jr Mem Award, Print Club Albany, 95; Artlink Nat Exhib Award, Ft Wayne, Ind, 96 & 97; Counterpoint 2000 Nat Exhib Award, The Hill Country Arts Found, Ingram, Tex, 2000; Janet Turner 5th Nat Print Competition & Exhib Award, Chico, Calif, 2004; The George Sherman Award, Saga's 90th Ann Show, 2005. *Mem:* Soc Am Graphic Artists; Calif Soc Printmakers; Boston Printmakers; Los Angeles Printmakers Soc; Print Club Albany, NY. *Media:* Etching, Aquatint. *Mailing Add:* 26114 W River Rd Perrysburg OH 43551-9786

AVAKIAN, JOHN
PRINTMAKER, INSTRUCTOR
b Worcester, Mass. *Study:* Yale Univ Sch Art & Archit, BFA & MFA. *Work:* Fed Reserve Bank, Boston; Western Mich Univ; Bucknell Univ; Tulsa Civic Ctr, Okla; Boston Pub Libr & Print Dept. *Exhib:* 20th Nat Exhib Prints, Libr Cong, Washington, DC; 38th Int Printmakers Exhib, Seattle Art Mus; one-man show, Higgins Wing, Worcester Art Mus, Mass; 21st Ann Int Exhib, Beaumont Art Mus, Tex, 72; Erector Sq Gallery, New Haven, Conn, 94. *Teaching:* Instr color & design, Northeastern Univ, Mass, 89 & Mt Ida Jr Col, 69-, chmn art dept, 69-83. *Awards:* Blanche E Colman Found Award, 70; Art Patrons League of Mobile Award, 72; Commendation Award, Boston Printmakers NAm Exhib, 93. *Mem:* Col Art Asn Am. *Media:* Monotype, Monoprint. *Mailing Add:* 43 Morse St Sharon MA 02067-2729

AVANT, TRACY WRIGHT
PAINTER, GRAPHIC ARTIST
b Ft Dix, NJ, Dec 15, 60. *Study:* McNay Art Inst, 69; Southwest Tex State Univ, BS, 83; Warren Hunter Acad Art, 90; Coppini Acad Fine Art, 94-95. *Work:* Phil Isley Inc, Tex; Normangee State Bank, Tex; Ocean Wash, USA, Tex. *Comn:* Landscape painting, Minton Oil Co, Tex, 88; bldg painting, Dilley Flower & Gift Shop, Tex, 90; portrait, comn by Dr & Mrs H I Garfield, Tex, 94. *Exhib:* Am Art in Miniature, Thomas Gilcrease, Tulsa, Okla, 94; Oil Painters Am, San Antonio, Tex, 94; Nat Soc Artists, Santa Fe, Tex, 94; Fifth Ann Wildlife Exhib, Colo, 94; Debut '94 Jr Mooney, San Antonio, Tex, 94; Salon Int, Miss, 94; Bridge Nat Juried Expos, NY, 94. *Awards:* Judge's Choice, Oil Painters Am, Heritage Gallery, 94; First Place, Colo Wildlife Expos, Gwendolyn's Gallery, 94; Second Place, Coppini May Garden Show, Coppini Gallery, 94. *Bibliog:* Review, The Current, 94; review, Pleasanton Express, 94; review, The Eagle, 94. *Mem:* Oil Painters Am; Nat Soc Artists; assoc mem Allied Artists Am; Palette & Chisel Acad Fine Art; New Braunfels Art League. *Media:* Oil, Acrylic. *Mailing Add:* PO Box 4 1120 Hwy 81 N Dilley TX 78017-0009

AVEDISIAN, EDWARD
PAINTER, SCULPTOR
b Lowell, Mass, 1936. *Study:* Boston Mus Sch Art. *Work:* Guggenheim Mus, Whitney Mus Am Art & Metrop Mus Art, NY; Los Angeles Co Mus Art; Wadsworth Atheneum; Chicago Art Inst; Cleveland Mus, Ohio. *Comn:* Greens, San Francisco; Desert Cafe, Santa Fe. *Exhib:* John Powers Collection, Larry Aldrich Mus, 66; Robert Rowan Collection, San Francisco Mus Art, 67; Boston Inst Contemp Art, 67-68; Painters Under 40, Whitney Mus Am Art, 68; Six Painters, Albright-Knox Art Gallery, Buffalo, 71; solo exhibs, Gallery Moos, Toronto, 71, Janie C Lee Gallery, Houston, 74, Carriage House Gallery, Buffalo, 75, NY Univ, 77, Nina Freudenheim Gallery, Buffalo, 78, Jason McCoy, New York City, 84 & Baghoomian Gallery, 89; one-man show, Mitchell Algust, 98. *Teaching:* Artist-in-residence, Univ Kans, 69; instr, Sch Visual Arts, NY, 69-70, Univ Calif, Irvine, 72 & Univ La, 73. *Awards:* Guggenheim Found Fel, 67; Nat Coun Arts Award, 68; Paula Krasner Found Grant, 92. *Media:* Acrylic, Oil; All Media. *Dealer:* Vreg Baghoomian 611 Broadway New York NY 10012. *Mailing Add:* 26 Warren Hudson NY 12534

AVEDON, BARRY
PAINTER, EDUCATOR
b Brooklyn, NY, Jan 2, 41. *Study:* Rochester Inst Technol Sch Art, BFA, 62, MFA, 64. *Work:* Eastern Mich Univ, Ypsilanti; Rochester Inst Technol, NY; Bank of Com, Hamtramck, Mich. *Exhib:* Ann Exhib, Albright-Knox Mus Art, 64; Butler Inst Am Art Mid-Year Show, 66; Ball State Nat Drawing Ann, Ball State Univ Gallery, 79; Mich Artists 80/81, Flint Inst Arts, Mich, 81; The Corporation Collects Art, Muskegon Mus Art, Mich, 83; Focus Gallery, Detroit, 85; Battle Creek Art Ctr, 86; Water Street Gallery, Saugatuck, Mich, 96. *Teaching:* Prof painting & drawing, Eastern Mich Univ, 66-. *Awards:* Julius Hallgarten Award, Nat Acad Design Ann, 64; Purchase Award, Ethno-Art '81, Bank of Commerce, Hamtramck, Mich, 81; All Media State Juried Award, Mt Clemens Art Ctr, Mich, 92. *Bibliog:* A Scaglione & B Parker (auth), Detroit Summer III, Park West Galleries, Inc, 82; Robert Iglehart (auth), article, Ann Arbor News, 83. *Mem:* Artists Equity Asn, Mich. *Media:* Oil; Pencil. *Dealer:* Water Street Art Gallery, Saugatuck MI. *Mailing Add:* Dept Art 114 Ford Hall Eastern Mich Univ Ypsilanti MI 48197

AVERBUCH, ILAN
SCULPTOR
b Tel Aviv, Israel, 1953. *Study:* Wimbledon Sch Art, London, Eng, 77-78, Sch Visual Arts, BFA, 79-81, Hunter Col, NY, MFA, 83-84. *Work:* Israel Mus, Jerusalem; Martin Margulies, Coconut Grove, Fla; Vera List, Bryam, Conn; Michael Haas, Toytlof, Berlin, Ger; Ashley D Hoffman, Kings Point, NY. *Exhib:* Solo exhibs, Kunstlerhaus Bethanien, Berlin, Ger, 85, Daadgalerie, Berlin, Ger, 86, Mabat Gallery, Tel Aviv, Israel, 86, Jewish Mus, NY, 86, O K Harris Works of Art, NY, 87, Nancy Hoffman, NY, 89; Peace Biennale, Hamburg, WGer, 85; Sculpture in the Square, Lincoln Ctr, NY, 85-86; Mythos Berlin Concept Show (with catalog), 86; 49th Parallel, NY, 89; Int Contemp Art, Art Gallery Ont, Toronto, 89. *Pos:* Steel instr & coordr sculpture dept, Sch Visual Arts, New York, 80-82; lectr, Brown Univ, Providence, RI, 83, Berlin Technical Univ, 86. *Awards:* DAAD Award, Berlin, WGER. *Bibliog:* Gil Goldfine (auth), Averbuch Sculpture, Jerusalem Post, 10/11/86; Thomas Wulfen (auth), Donald Judd, Carlm Andre, Ilan Averbuch, Tages Spiegel, 6/87; Beatrice V Bismark (auth), Reviews: Ilan Averbuch, Daad Galene, Berlin, Flash Art, winter 86, 87. *Mailing Add:* 1015 48th Ave Long Island City NY 11101-5693

AVERY, FRANCES
PAINTER, PHOTOGRAPHER
b Kitchener, Ont, Aug 23, 10; US citizen. *Study:* John Wickers Art Sch, Detroit; Art Students League, 31-34; Beaux Arts Sch Design; Columbia Univ with Meyer Shapiro; New Sch Social Research with Berenice Abbott, 39. *Comn:* Three easel paintings: Public Sch Noll, Fordham Hosp & New York Public Libr, Public Works Art Proj, NY, 34-35; mural, Lincoln Hosp, Bronx, NY, 36-39. *Exhib:* Group exhibs, Corcoran Gallery, Washington, DC, 40; Mus Mod Art, NY, 42; Whitney Mus Am Art, NY, 54; League at the Cape, 93; Beaux Arts Ann, 93; NY Soc Women Artists, Cork Gallery, Lincoln Ctr, 94; Nat Asn Women Artists Ann, 94; Lever Bros Gallery, NY, 94. *Teaching:* Pvt art class, 46-70; instr painting & drawing, Bergen Sch, NJ, & YWCA, schs in Bronx, Brooklyn, NY, Bergen & Jersey City, NJ, 50 59; asst prof drawing & painting, anatomy, color & media, Adelphi Univ, 59-79; teacher, mural artist, Educ Alliance, 92. *Awards:* Res & Travel Grant, Adelphi Univ, 73 & 77; Ziuta & Joseph Akston Found Prize, Nat Asn Women Artists, 81; Martha Moore Mem Award, Nat Asn Women Artists, 92. *Bibliog:* Lucia A Salemme (auth), The Complete Book of Painting Techniques, 82; Interview, WNYC (radio prog), Works Proj Admin Murals, lost or destroyed, 84. *Mem:* Artists Equity; life mem Art Students League; Nat Soc Mural Artists; Nat Asn Women Artists, 1940-2003; New York Soc Women painters in sculptors, 1939-2003. *Media:* All. *Publ:* Contribr, photographs in Parade, US Camera & other mags; illusr, Aristodemos Kaldis, 94. *Mailing Add:* 14 Horatio St Apt 4 H New York NY 10014-1652

AVLON-DAPHNIS, HELEN BASILEA
PAINTER, SCULPTOR
b New York, NY, June 18, 32. *Study:* Hunter Col, New York, BA, 59, MA, 72; Aspen Mus Sch, 70; Provincetown Sch Fine Arts, Mass, 70-75. *Work:* Gallery I, Westbeth, NY; Cook Gallery, NY. *Comn:* Mural, 250 W 57th Street, NY; The Sea, Provincetown Art Asn Mus. *Exhib:* Solo exhib, Gallery I Mus, Westbeth, NY, 84; Bertha Schaeffer Gallery, NY, 60-65; Provincetown Art Mus, Show of the 60's, 82; Forum Gallery, NY; Baltimore Art Mus. *Bibliog:* Articles in New York Daily News, Art News, Art Digest, Art Speaks and others. *Mem:* Westbeth Workshop Graphics Int. *Media:* Watercolor, Acrylic. *Mailing Add:* 463 West St New York NY 10014-2010

AWALT, ELIZABETH GRACE
PAINTER
b Baltimore, Md, 56. *Study:* Skowhegan Sch Painting, ME, 77; Boston Col, BA, 78; Univ Pa, MA(painting), MFA, 81. *Work:* Boston Pub Libr, Bank Boston, Boston Col Mus Art; Snite Mus Art, Notre Dame, Ind; Prudential Ins Co; Rose Art Mus; AT&T. *Exhib:* Brave New Works, Mus Fine Arts, Boston, 84; solo exhibs, Thomas Segal Gallery, Boston, 85, GW Einstein Co, NY, 88, 90 & 95, Samuelis Baumgarte Galerie, Ger, 93, Seasonal Meditations, GW Einstein, NY, 95 & Salute to Boston, Boston Pub Libr, 98; The Watercolor Show, Loise Ross Gallery, NY, 91; Celebration, GW Einstein Co Inc, 93; Beyond Description: Visions of Nature, GW Einstein Co Inc, NY, 93; Inspired by Nature, Boston Col Mus Art, 95. *Teaching:* Instr painting, drawing, ceramics, Wyncote Acad, Pa, 81; instr art, Boston Col, Newton, Mass, 84-87; instr painting, Waltham Sr Citizen Ctr, Mass, 85-86; instr painting, watercolor, drawing, Danforth Mus Sch, Framingham, Mass, 85-86; instr beginning painting, DeCordova Mus Sch Art, Lincoln, Mass, 86; asst prof, painting & drawing, Boston Col, 85-93, assoc prof, 93-. *Awards:* Mass Artist Fel, Painting, 83; Nat Endowment Arts Grant, Painting, 87; Finalist, Mass Artist Found, 90. *Media:* Oil, Pastel. *Publ:* Contribr, Oil Pastel: Watson-Guptill, 90; Pilgrims & Pioneers: New England Women in the Arts, Faxon & Moore, 87. *Mailing Add:* 40 Hosmer Rd Concord MA 01742-2216

AXELROD, JOHN P
ART DEALER, COLLECTOR
b Boston, Mass, Nov 21, 46. *Study:* Yale Univ, BA, 68; Harvard Law Sch, JD, 72. *Mem:* Mus Fine Arts (bd overseers, 86-94 & 2000-); Wolfsonian Found (found trustee, 92-94). *Specialty:* African-American art; Latin American art; twentieth century American Sculpture, American art deco. *Mailing Add:* 404 Beacon St Boston MA 02115

AYASO, MANUEL
PAINTER, SCULPTOR
b Riviera, Spain, Jan 1, 34; US citizen. *Study:* Newark Sch Fine & Indust Arts, cert. *Work:* Whitney Mus Am Art, NY; Worcester Mus, Mass; Pa Acad Fine Arts, Philadelphia; NJ State Mus, Trenton; Newark Mus, NJ; and others. *Exhib:* 22nd Int Watercolor Biennial, Brooklyn Mus, NY, 63; El Neo-Humanismo en el Dibujo de USA, Ital y Mexico, Univ Mex, 63; American Painting & Sculpture, Pa Acad Fine Arts, 67; Contemp Am Artists, Nat Inst Arts & Lett, 71; Contemp Am Spiritual Art, Mus Contemp Art, Vatican, Rome, 76; The Fine Line: Drawing with Silver in America, circulating exhib, 85 & 86; Objects & Drawings, circulatory exhib, Sanford M & Diane Besser Collection, 92-93; and others; retrospective exhib, Museo del Grabado, Artes-Riveira, Spain, 2002-03. *Collection Arranged:* Whitney Mus Am Art; Neward Mus; NJ State Mus; Butler Inst Am Art; Summer Found for Arts, NJ; St Paul Gallery and Sch of Art, Minn; Norma and John C Marin Jr Col; Ill Weslean Univ; Univ Mass, Amherst; Pa Acad of Fine Arts; Worcester Mus, Mass; Slaten Meml Mus, NMorwich Free Acad, Conn; Am Israel Found; Montclair Art Mus, NJ; Univ Oreg Mus Art, Eugene; Ark Arts Ctr, Little Rock; Samford M and Diane Besser Collection; Casa da Cultura, Ribeira, Spain; Casa de Galicia, Madrid; Centro de Arte Contemporanea, Santiago de Compostela, Spain; Museo Valle Inclan, Puebla del Caraminal, Spain; Museo del Grabado, Artes-Ribeira, Spain. *Awards:* Tiffany Found Scholar in Painting, 62; Ford Found Purchase Award, 64; Childe Hassam Fund Purchase Award, 71. *Bibliog:* Brian O'Doherty (auth), New York Times, 5/31/61; John Canaday (auth), New York Times, 12/8/63; Barry Schwartz (auth), The New Humanism, Praeger Publ, 74. *Mem:* Am Fedn Arts. *Media:* Goldpoint, Mixed Media. *Dealer:* Jean Frank 25 E 83rd St New York NY 10021. *Mailing Add:* 12 Vincent Pl Verona NJ 07044

AYCOCK, ALICE
SCULPTOR
b Harrisburg, Pa, Nov 20, 46. *Study:* Douglass Col, New Brunswick, NJ, BA, 68; Hunter Col, New York, MA, 71, study with Robert Morris. *Work:* Mus Mod Art, Metrop Mus Art, Guggenheim Mus, Whitney Mus Am Art, NY; Mus Ludwig, Cologne, Ger; Kunstmuseum, Basel, Switz; Walker Art Ctr, Minneapolis, Minn. *Comn:* Humanic Corp, Graz, Austria; Roanoke Col, Roanoke, Va; and others. *Exhib:* One-woman exhibs, Abington Art Ctr, Jenkintown, Pa, 90, Yoshiaki Inoue Gallery, Osaka, Japan, 90, Insam Gallery, Vienna, Austria, 91, Percent for Arts, NY, 92, John Weber Gallery, NY, 93 & 94, Sean Kelly Studio, Kansas City, Mo, 93 & Univ Nebr Med Ctr, Omaha, 93; Enclosures & Encounters: Architectural Aspects of Recent Sculpture, Storm King Art Ctr, Mountainville, NY, 91; The Nature of the Machine, Chicago Cult Ctr, 93; Different Natures Traveling Exhib, La Defense, Paris, 93; ICA Benefit, Sonnebend Gallery, NY, 94; Drawings: Reaffirming the Media, Univ Mo-Kansas City Gallery Art, 94. *Pos:* Vol asst, Conserv Dept, Guggenheim Mus, NY, 67; cur, Art Hist Slide Libr, Hunter Col, NY, 69-72. *Teaching:* Instr, Found Sculpture & Advanced Sculpture Courses, Sch Vis Arts, NY, 77-78; vis sculptor & teacher, Princeton Univ, Princeton, NJ, spring semester, 79; vis sculptor & teacher, San Francisco Art Inst, Calif, spring semester, 79; asst prof, Hunter Col, NY, 82-85; teaching res, Kansas City Art Inst, 87; sr critic, Yale Univ, New Haven, Conn, 88-90; teaching res, Atlantic Ctr Arts, New Smyrna Beach, Fla, 89; teaching res, Ecole Nat Superieure des Beaux-Arts, Paris, France, 91; dir grad sculpture studies, Yale Univ, New Haven, Conn, 91-92; sculpture dept, Sch Visual Arts, NY, 92. *Awards:* Nat Endowment Arts Grant, 75, 76 & 80; Creative Artist Pub Serv Grant, 76; City Univ NY Research Grant, 83; Fel, Nat Endowment Arts, 86. *Bibliog:* Howard Fox (auth), Hoodo, Mag Los Angeles Co Mus Art, 14, 7-8/91; Robert Hobbes (auth), Fattoria Celle, Site Specificity in Tuscany, Sculpture, 48-53, 3-4/91; Timothy Porges (auth), Letters/Chicago, Contemporanea, No 24, 25, 1/91. *Media:* Mixed. *Publ:* Five Semi-Architectural Projects, c 7500, Valencia, Calif, 73; New York City orientations, Triquarterly, Evanston, winter 75; The Beginnings of a Complex: Notes, Drawings, Photographs, Lapp Princess, Press Ltd, 77; Work 1972-1974, In: Individuals: Post-Movement Art in America, E P Dutton & Co, Inc, New York, 76; Auth, Making Their Mark, Women Artists Move Into the Mainstream 1970-85, Abbeville Press, 89

AYERS, CAROL LEE
PAINTER, GALLERY DIRECTOR
b Newark, NJ, Dec 25, 29. *Study:* Basically self-taught; studied with David Kwo & Allan Eldredge, 75-76. *Work:* Bicentennial Expos, Everson Mus, Syracuse, NY; Am Telephone & Telegraph Corp Hq, Bedminster, NJ; Westinghouse Corp, Bath, NY; Sterling Drug Corp, New York & Athens, Greece; Trenton Mus; Corning Glass, Corning, NY; and others. *Comn:* Acrylic wall panel, Archdiocese of Rochester, Geneva, NY, 70; mural, comn by B Burley, vpres Sterling Drug Corp, NY, 75; Highland Telephone Corp, Warwick, NY, 86; Mr & Mrs George Plimpton Collection, Southampton, NY, 86-88; First Hope Bank, Hope, NJ, 97. *Exhib:* Silvermine Guild Artists, New Canaan, Conn, 75; Northeast Watercolor Soc, Hall Fame Trotter, Goshen, NY, 84-90, 96 & 98; West Point Acad, 85; Connoisseur Gallery, Rhinebeck, NY 87-90; Springhouse Gallery, Philadelphia, Pa, 90; Dutot Mus, Del Water Gap, Pa, 92; NJ Watercolor Soc, Chester, 98; Buck Hills Falls Art Asn, Pa, 99-2000. *Pos:* Dir, Esperanza Gallery, Yates Co, NY, 68-73, Erincourt Gallery, Penn Yan, NY, 73-79, Gallery-in-the-Gap, Delaware Water Gap, Pa, 80-83 & Sunflower Studio, 83-. *Teaching:* Demonstr acrylic painting, Rotring-Koh-I-Noor, Inc; instr, home studio.

Awards: First Awards, Monroe Co Mus, 83, Chester Art Asn, NJ, 83, Suburban Art League, 83 & Keuka Lake Art Asn, 70, 73-74, 79 & 84-85; Coun Am Artists Soc Award, 93; NE Watercolor Soc Award, 96, 97 & 99; First Award, Buckhill Falls Art Ssn, Pa, 2000. *Bibliog:* Articles in NJ Music & Art Mag, Ridgewood, NJ, 6/77; T Noverro (auth), Save the gallery, Easton Publ Co, Pa, 9/81; articles in NY Art Review, 88 & Am Artist Mag, 89, Watercolor '92 Spring & Fall Issues, The Artist's Mag, 3/92. *Mem:* Signature mem Northeast Watercolor Soc; assoc mem NJ Watercolor Soc; Hunterdon Co Art Ctr, Clinton, NJ; Pocono Mountains Art Group, Pa; Nat Soc of Painters in case in Acrylic, 2003, Assoc mem. *Media:* Watercolor, Liquid Acrylic, Mixed Media. *Specialty:* Original contemporary paintings. *Publ:* Auth, Manuscript on liquid acrylic, Am Artist Mag, 90-91. *Dealer:* Morgan Gallery Fine Art Blakeslee PA; Gallery 23 Blairstown NJ. *Mailing Add:* Sunflower Studio 70 Mt Hermon Rd Blairstown NJ 07825

AYHENS, OLIVE MADORA
PAINTER
b Oakland, Calif, Nov 2, 43. *Study:* San Francisco Art Inst, BFA, 68, MFA, 69. *Work:* Oakland Mus, Calif; Mills Col, Oakland, Calif; Evergreen State Col, Olympia, Wash; Univ Northern Iowa, Cedar Falls; Intercontinental Pac Group, San Francisco, Calif; Watkins Collection, Am Univ; also pvt collections. *Comn:* painting for David Rockefeller Jr, comn by Lower Manhattan Cult Coun, 2000. *Exhib:* Survey Show, San Francisco Mus Art, 75; Passages Calif Women 1945 to present, Fresno Art Ctr & Mus, 87; solo exhibs, San Francisco Mus Mod Art, 89, Michael Himovitz Gallery, 91 & 94, Beall Park Art Ctr, 94; Artists Views on Romance, Monterey Peninsula Mus, 91; Lejauu, Frederick Spratt Gallery San Jose, 96; Earth, Water & Air, DC Moore Gallery, NY, 98; Meaning Method Meaning, Rush Art, NY; Solo Exhib Gary Tatintsian Gallery, New York City, 2002, 2003, 2004, 2005; Group Exhib Am Acad of Artist Letters Invitational & Purchase Award, 2004; Frederieke Taylor Gallery, NY, 2006. *Teaching:* painting & drawing, Univ Tex, Austin, 80-81; Asst prof painting & drawing, Univ Calif, Berkeley, 84-85, Brown Univ, 89-90 & Mont State Univ, 93-94; drawing, Stanford Univ, 91; watercolor, Sarah Lawrence Col, 99-2000; American University, 2004-2005. *Awards:* Marie Walsh Sharpe Art Found Space Grant, 96; Adolph & Esther Gottlieb Individual Support Grant, 96; Pollock Krasner Found Grant, 98; Lower Manhattan Cult Coun World Trade Ctr Residency, 99; Pollock/Krasner, 2001; Guggenheim Fel, 2006; and others. *Bibliog:* Mary Hull Webster (auth), Perils of the Artist Hero, Art Week, 92; Roberta Smith (auth), Aerial Perspectives: Imagination, Reality and Abstraction, New York Times, c 25, Vol CXLVI, 8/21/97; Robert Mahoney (auth), Aerial Perspectives, Imagination, Reality and Abstraction, Time Out New York, Issue 98, 47, 97; Cathy Lebountz Art in America, 2002; Mario Nares New York Observers, 2003-2004; David Cohey NY Sun, 2004; Cynthia Nadelman Art News, 5/2005. *Mem:* Col Art Asn; Artist Equity. *Media:* Painting, Oil; Watercolor, Mixed Media. *Interests:* aesthetics of pollution. *Publ:* DC Moore Gallery, Earth, Water & Air, 98; New York Sun, 2004; Harpers Mag, 2001, 2004; Art In America, 2004; Art News, 2005. *Dealer:* San Francisco Mus Modern Art Artist Gallery Fort Mason. *Mailing Add:* PO Box 320 New York NY 10013-0320

AYLON, HELENE
PAINTER, CONCEPTUAL ARTIST
b New York, NY. *Study:* Dept Art, Brooklyn Col, BA(cum laude), 60; Art Student's League, 60-65; New Sch Social Res, 60-65State Univ San Francisco, MFA, 74; Antioch Col W, MA(performance art). *Work:* Whitney Mus Am Art; Mass Inst Technol, Cambridge; San Francisco Mus Mod Art; Mus Mod Art, NY; A Liberation of God, The NY Jewish Mus. *Comn:* Chapel Libr, John F Kennedy Airport, 66; Lobby, NY Univ Med Ctr, 68. *Exhib:* Lyrical Abstraction, Whitney Mus Am Art, Aldrich Mus Contemp Art & traveling, 69; Season's Highlights, Aldrich Mus Am Art, Ridgefield, Conn, 71; Stretchers, Cleveland Ctr Contemp Art, 89; Aldrich Mus, Conn, 94; two sacs en route, Sony Jumbotron, Times Sq, 95; The Liberation of G-d, Armand Hammer Mus, Los Angeles, 97; The Liberation of G-d, The Contemp, Baltimore, 97. *Teaching:* Instr painting, Brooklyn Mus & Hunter Col, 72-73; instr, San Francisco State Univ, 73-76. *Awards:* New Genre, NY Found Arts, 88 & 93; Installation, two sacs for 1995, NY State Coun Arts, 95; Pollock/Krasner Award. *Bibliog:* Peter Schjeldahl (auth), Art in America, 11/75; Leslie Camhi (auth), Village Voice, 4/2/96; Michael Kimmelman (auth), NY Times, 3/8/96. *Media:* Installation, Environmental Land Art. *Publ:* Too Jewish? Challenging Traditional Identities (exhib catalog), Norman Kleeblat; The SF Jewish Bulletin, 9/96; The Liberation of G-d, Lilith Mag, fall 96; Art in America, 10/99; Bridges Mag, vol 8, 00. *Mailing Add:* 55 Bethune St A808 New York NY 10014-2010

AYOUB, ROULA
PAINTER
b Monrovia, Liberia, West Africa, 64. *Study:* Univ Nebr, 1985; Fla State Univ, 1988. *Work:* Appleton Mus of Art, Ocala, Fla; Mus of Fine Arts, Fla State Univ, Tallahassee, Fla; Sharjah Art Mus, Sharjah, UAE; Istanbul Contemp Art Mus, Istanbul, Turkey; Jordan Nat Gallery of Fine Arts, Amman, Jordan. *Exhib:* Art From the Heartland, Coutts Mem Mus of Art, Eldorado, Kans, 2003; Jordan Nat Gallery of Fine Arts, Amman, Jordan, 2003; Anniversary Invitational, Louisville Art Gallery, Nebr, 2003; Gov's Mansion, Lincoln, Nebr, 2003; Women's Invitational, Louisville Art Gallery, Nebr, 2003; Sharjah Art Mus, Sharjah, UAE, 2004. *Awards:* Third place award, Watercolor Juried Exhib, Union Col, 1986; Special Recognition award, Abstration VI, Period Gallery, 2003. *Bibliog:* Andrea Cranford (auth), Ayoub Paints a Free World on Canvas, Nebr Mag, 2004. *Mem:* Berkeley Art Ctr; Kansas City Artists coalition; Audubon Artists Inc; Nat Oil & Acrylic Painters Soc. *Media:* Acrylic, Oil. *Mailing Add:* 1301 Richmond Ave Apt G2 Houston TX 77006-5404

AYRES, JULIA SPENCER
PAINTER, PRINTMAKER
b Havana, Cuba, Aug 16, 31; US citizen. *Study:* Boston Mus Fine Art Sch, Mass Col Art, 48-49; Art Inst Chicago, 50-52; pvt study with William Maynard, Frederic Taubes & Ralph Love. *Work:* Home Savings Am; Marriott Corp; Unocal Corp, Calif; First Interstate Bank, San Diego; Hilton Corp, Daytona Beach, Fla; Toyota Corp, Calif. *Comn:* Landscapes, seascapes, monotypes & suite of 18 watercolors, Marriott Corp, var locations. *Exhib:* Nat Arts Club Watercolor Ann, NY, 85; Am Artist Prof League Grand Nationals, NY, 85 & 86; Nat Watercolor Soc 64th Ann, Calif; Nat Watercolor Okla, Okla Art Ctr Mus, Oklahoma City, 87; Los Angeles Audubon Nat Art Exhib, Beverly Hills, Calif, 87. *Teaching:* Monotype Workshops Nat; Taught Art Methods, Pasadena, CA, 96-2005; plus many other workshops & studio lessons. *Awards:* Winsor & Newton Award, Nat Watercolor Soc 64th Ann. *Bibliog:* Art Marketing Handbook, Gee Tee Bee, 86; Dorothy Hoyal (auth), Taking oneself seriously as an artist, Am Artist, 6/88; Ayers on Making Monotypes, Am Artist, 88. *Media:* Watercolor, Monotypes. *Publ:* auth, numerous articles, Watercolor, Am Artist, Southwest Art, others; American Artist & Watercolor Mag, Concerning Printmaking, 86-2006; Paper, the critical support, In: Watercolor 87, Am Artist Publ, 87; Making watercolor monotypes, In: Watercolor 88, Am Artist Publ, 88; Julia S Ayres on Monotypes (pictures), Am Artist Mag, 88; Fracoise Gilot's Monotypes, Am Arts Mag, 1/90; Monotype, Medius and Methods of Painterly Printmaking, 91 & Printmaking, Watson Guptill Pub, 93. *Mailing Add:* PO Box 667 Chouteau OK 74337

AYRES, LARRY MARSHALL
HISTORIAN
b Nov 15, 39. *Study:* Dartmouth Col, AB, 64; Univ Oxford, BLitt, 66; Harvard Univ, PhD, 70. *Pos:* Bd dir, Int Ctr Medieval Art, 77-80. *Teaching:* Asst prof art hist, Univ Calif, Santa Barbara, 70-74, assoc prof, 74-79, chmn, 76-88, prof, 79-. *Awards:* Alexander von Humboldt Stiftung Res Fel, 79-80 & 86 & 93; Am Philos Soc Grants, 81 & 82; Prix Rome Res Fel, Am Acad Rome, 83-84. *Mem:* Col Art Asn Am; Mediaeval Acad Am; Southern Calif Art Historians. *Res:* Medieval art; history of the book. *Publ:* Auth, Sources of the lyre drawings, Speculum, 74; English painting and the Continent, Eleanor of Aquitaine: Patron and Politician, 76; Salzburg affliations of a Bible fragment in Vienna, Zeitschrift Kunstgeschichte, 82; Parisian Bibles in Berlin Staatsbibliotek, Pantheon, 82; in Dumbartou Oaks Papers, 87; in Studi Gregoriani, 92; Romanesque Manuscript illumination, Braziller (in prep). *Mailing Add:* Dept Art History Univ Calif Santa Barbara Santa Barbara CA 93106

AYRES, PAMELA GENE
DIRECTOR
b Raleigh, NC, Jan 23, 1967. *Study:* Indiana Univ Pa, BFA in Sculpture, 1991; Long Island Univ, MFA in Sculpture, 1993, studies with Noah Vemisin & Judy Collishan. *Work:* Bur Cable Comms, Dept Pub Works, Pittsburgh; CW Post Pub Art Program, Long Island Univ, Brookville, NY; Nanjing (China) Art Asn; Indiana Univ Pa Alumni Collection. *Comn:* temporary steel constrn, Twin Lakes/Arts Nat, Greensburg, Pa, 1990; temporary sundial installation, Alliquippa (Pa) Arts Festival, 1998-2001; temporary installation piece, Adelphi Univ, Garden City, NY, 2002-03. *Collection Arranged:* permanent collection, Univ Bridgeport, 1997-2000; Stan Brodsky retrospective, Univ Gallery, Univ Bridgeport, Contemporary Visions series, The Millinium Time Capsule, solo exhib Hirokazu Fukawa, Jane Ingram-Allen, Andrea Arroyo & Elizabeth Silver, Invitational Showcase, 1997-2000; Welcome to Bridgeport Exhibition, Remington Art Studios, 2000; public sculpture from Socrates Drawing Exhibition, Univ Gallery, Univ Bridgeport, 2000; others. *Pos:* visual arts dir & sculpture event selection com chair, Festival of the Elements Arts Festival, Bridgeport, 98; Bridgeport arts and community prog dir, Music and Arts Ctr Humanity, Bridgeport, 99-2000 & devel, mktg & pub rels assoc, 2000-01; cons, Artspace Projects, Inc of Conn, Bridgeport, 2000-01; dir galleries, exhib and collections, Bradley Univ Galleries, 2002-. *Teaching:* adj prof sculpture, Univ Bridgeport, 1998, color theory/foundations, 2000; sculpture & environment instr, Weir Farm Nat Historic Trust, Ridgefield, Conn, 2000-01; instr ceramic sculpture, ARTWORKS, Music and Arts Ctr for Humanity, Bridgeport, 2000, instr ceramic sculpture & gallery mgmt, Bridgeport Neighborhood Studios, 2000-01 & instr ceramic sculpture, raku ceramics, gallery mgt & arts resources, 2000-01; adj prof, sculpture, Nassau Community Col, Garden City, 2001; adj prof gallery mgt, Bradley Univ, Peoria, Ill, 2002, 03; numerous lectrs. *Bibliog:* Mark Daniel Cohen (auth), Stamford Mus & Nature Ctr/Stamford, Art New Eng, 8-9/2000; Tori Phelps (auth), Camera Della Donna at Bradely Univ, Arts Alive mag, 2002; Helen A Harrison (auth), Art Review: Evocative works capture land's essence, Outdoor Sculpture Show Adelphi Univ, NY Times, 2002. *Publ:* Auth, MACH Summer Review, Good News, Conn Press, 2000; contribr, Public art, Impact, Bridgeport Regional Bus Coun Publ, 2000. *Mailing Add:* Bradley Univ Heuser Art Center Gallery Slane Coll Commun & Fine Arts Peoria IL 61625

AZACETA, LUIS CRUZ
PAINTER
b Marianao, Cuba, Apr 5, 1942; US citizen. *Study:* Sch Visual Arts, New York, with Leon Golub, Frank Roth & Michael Loew, cert, 69. *Work:* Metrop Mus Art, Mus of Mod Art, NY; Va Mus Fine Arts, Richmond; RI Sch Design Mus; Del Art Mus. *Exhib:* Crimes of Compassion, The Chrysler Mus, Norfolk, Va, 81; The Age of Anxiety: 20th Century Art in the Lila Acheson Wing, Metrop Mus Art, NY, 87; Committed to Print, Mus Mod Art, NY, 88; Large Works NY, Kunst Station, Sankt Peter, Cologne, WGer, 88; and many others. *Teaching:* Vis artist, Univ Calif, Davis, La State Univ, Baton Rouge, Univ Calif, Berkeley & Cooper Union, NY. *Awards:* Nat Endowment Arts, 80-81, 85-86; Guggenheim Mem Found Grant, NY, 85-86; NY Found Arts Grant, 85-86. *Bibliog:* Grace Glueck (auth), article, New York Times, 1/27/84; Ellen

Schlesinger (auth), No room for apathy, Artweek, 84; Linda McGreevy (auth), Painting his heart out, Arts Mag, 6/85; Jose Gomez Sicre (auth), Cuban Artist in Exile, 86. *Media:* Acrylic, Watercolor. *Dealer:* Frumkin/Adams Gallery 50 W 57th St New York NY 10019. *Mailing Add:* c/o Adams Gallery 41 W 57th St 7th Fl New York NY 10019

AZANK, ROBERTO
PAINTER
b Buenos Aires, Arg, Nov 3, 55. *Study:* Sch Archit, Univ Buenos Aires, 74-79. *Comn:* Still Life #34, comn by Ruth & Charles Henri Ford, NY, 97; Still Life #65, comn by Fernando de Martini, NY, 98; Still Life #72, comn by Jorge Quitequi, Buenos Aires, 98; Still Life #73, comn by Beatriz Zobel, Madrid, 98; Still Life #78, comn by Fran Garriguez, Madrid, 98. *Exhib:* One-man shows, 98, Lizan Tops Gallery, East Hampton, Albers Fine Art Gallery, Memphis, Consulate Argentina, NY, M J Alegria Sch Art, PR, Byron Comen Gallery, Kansas City, 2000 & Eleonore Austerer Gallery, San Francisco, 2001, Eleonore Austerer Gallery, Palm Desert, Calif, 2002-, Addison-Ripley Gallery, Wash, DC, 2003, Eleonore Austerer Gallery, San Francisco, Calif, 2003, Plus-One Plus-Two Gallery, London, Eng, 2004 & 2006, The Simmons Gallery, San Francisco, Calif, Unison Arts Center, Ctr of the Earth Gallery, Charlotte, NC; group show, Brewster Arts Ltd, NY, 98 & Va Miller Gallery, Miami, 98. *Bibliog:* Cypherism and the Age of Computation, Inside Art, 8/99; Still Lifes are Still Effective, Kansas City Star, 11/25/99; Big Names in the Summer, Miami Herald, 8/1/99; The Desert Sun, 2001; New York Arts Mag, 2001; When the Subject is Also an Object, Addison-Ripley Gallery, 2003, 2005; Woodstock Times, Moving Stills, 2005. *Mem:* NY Artists Equity Asn. *Media:* Oil on Canvas. *Interests:* Astronomy, Classical Music, Chess, Chi-Kung Bridge. *Collection:* Wash D.C. Conv Ctr, Am Express Financial Advs, Sprint Telecommunications. *Dealer:* Eleonore Austerer Gallery 73-660 El Paseo Palm Desert CA 92260; The Simmons Gallery 565 Sutter St San Francicsco CA 94102; Center of The Earth Gallery 3204 N Davidson St Charlotte NC; Plus One Gallery 91 Pimlico Rd London England. *Mailing Add:* 8 Watch Hill Rd New Paltz NY 12561-2705

AZARA, NANCY J
SCULPTOR, PAINTER
b New York, NY, Oct 13, 39. *Study:* Finch Col, AAS, 59; Art Students League, sculpture with John Hovannes, painting & drawing with Edwin Dickinson, 64-67; Empire State Col, BS(sculpture), 74. *Work:* Sculptors, sound film strip, Harcourt, Brace, Jovanovich; Everson Mus, Syracuse, NY; Univ Southern Ill, Edwardsville; Franklin Furnance, NY; City Col New York, City Univ NY. *Comn:* About the Goddess KALI (wood sculpture), Pamela Oline, S France, 77; Hand Garden/Doctor's Wall, Robert Wood Johnson Univ Hospital, Hamilton, NJ, March 2004. *Exhib:* One-woman shows, AIR Gallery, NY, 89 & 92, Lannon Gallery, Chicago, 90, James Chapel, Union Seminary, 91, E M Donahue & AIR Gallery, 94, Tweed Mus Art, Duluth, 95 & Donahue/Sosinski Gallery, 97, Gwinnett Fine Arts Ctr, Duluth, Ga, 98, Nancy Azara Sculpture, The Art Studio at Woodstock, NY, 98, SACI Gallery, Florence, Italy, 99, Heart Wall & otherworks, Donahue/Sosinski Art, New York City, 2000; From Celestial to Earthly, Paterson Mus, NJ, 95; Chips off the Old Block, Luis Ross Gallery, NY; Healing Art, Mus Fine Arts, The Univ Mont, Missoula, 99; Mirror of the Invisible: Contemp Artists Reflecting on Rumi and Islamic Mysticism, RV Fullerton Art Mus, San Bernardino, Ca, 09/28/2000-11/19/2000. *Teaching:* Lectr art, Sch Contemp Studies, Brooklyn Col, 73-75, lectr sculpture, 75-76; instr sculpture, Brooklyn Mus Sch, 74-77; instr, Col New Rochelle, NY, 79-89; instr, founding mem & mem bd dir, NY Feminist Art Inst, formerly; guest lect numerous schs. *Awards:* Adolph & Esther Gottlieb Found Grant, 85; Bogliasco Found Fel, Genoa, Italy, 2000. *Bibliog:* Harriet Senie (auth), Nancy Azara at Donahue/Sosinski Art, Sculpture Mag, July/Aug 2000; Janet Koplos (auth), Nancy Azara at Donahue/Sosinski, Art in America, 6/2000; Holland Cotter (auth), Nancy Azara, Art in Review, NY Times, 2/18/00; Richard Speer (auth), Going for Gold: Nancy Azara Conjures a Guilded World, Willamette Week, Oct 2004; many others. *Mem:* Art Students League; Womens Caucus Art (adv bd, 80-83); Col Art Asn; Orgn Independent Artists (adv bd, 91-94). *Media:* Wood, Oil; Paper, Paint, gold and silver leaf and encaustic. *Publ:* Auth, Artists in their own image, Ms Mag, 73; The Group, Anandala, Heresies Mag, spring 79; Auth, Spirit Taking Form: Making a Spiritual Practice Out of Making Art, 2002; Auth, Sculpture and the Devine, the Spiritual and Devine in Art, 2002; auth, Spirit Taking Form: a Spiritual Practice of Making Art, Red Wheel/ Weiser, 2002; and others. *Mailing Add:* 91 Franklin St New York NY 10013

AZUA, JON IMANOL
PATRON
Pos: vpres, Basque, formerly; first vpres, econ, affairs, minister, industry & energy, Basque govt; bd trustee, Solomon Guggenheim Mus, New York City. *Mailing Add:* SR Guggenheim Mus Bd Trustees 1071 Fifth Ave New York NY 10128-0173

B

BAAS, JACQUELYNN
DIRECTOR, WRITER
b Grand Rapids, Mich, Feb 14, 48. *Study:* Mich State Univ, with Elizabeth G Holt, BA, 71; Univ Mich, with Charles Sawyer & Joel Isaacson, MA, 73, PhD, 82. *Collection Arranged:* The Artistic Revival of the Woodcut in France 1850-1900 (coauth, catalog), Univ Mich, Ann Arbor 83-84; The Dartmouth Collection (coauth, catalog), 85, Encounter in Space: Double Images in the Graphic Art of Edward Munch (auth, catalog), 86, Mills and Factories of New England, 88 & Hood Mus Art, Dartmouth Col, Hanover, NH; The Independent Group: Postwar Britain & the Aesthetics of Plenty (co-auth, catalog), 91; The Here & the Hereafter: Images of Paradise in Islamic Art, 91; Prints from Van Dycks Iconography, 91; Transformation: The Art of Joan Brown (auth, catalog), Univ Calif Berkeley Art Mus, 98; sixtyslippers: Peter Shelton. *Pos:* Registr, Univ Mich Mus Art, Ann Arbor, 74-78, asst dir, 78-82; chief cur, Hood Mus Art, Dartmouth Col, Hanover, NH, 82-83, acting dir, 84, dir, 85-89; dir, Univ Calif, Berkeley Art Mus & Pac Film Archive, 89-; dir emeritus, 99-; project dir, Awake: Art and Buddhism in America, 2000-. *Teaching:* Hist print media, Univ Mich, 81. *Awards:* Nat Endowment Arts Fel, 88-89. *Mem:* Col Art Asn Am; Am Asn Mus. *Res:* Orozco's Dartmouth mural; Relationship between art and Buddhism in America. *Publ:* auth, Peter Shelton: sixtyslippers, Univ Calif Berkeley Art Mus; Citadels of Inclusive Awareness, Conversations at the Castle: Changing Audiences and Contemporary Culture, 128-135, Mass Inst Technol Press, 98; To Know this Place for the First Time, The Art of Joan Brown (preface & essay), XXXi-XXXii, 189-229, Univ Calif Press, 98; The Epic of American Civilization: The Mural at Dartmouth College, 2002; Smile of the Buddha: Influences in Western Art from Monet to the Present

BABCOCK, JO (JOSEPH) WARREN
PHOTOGRAPHER, SCULPTOR
b St Louis, Mo, Feb 24, 54. *Study:* Univ Calif Los Angeles, with Robert Heinicken, Todd Walker, Bea Nettles, 75; San Francisco Art Inst with, Pirkle Jones, BFA, 76; with Linda Conner, MFA, 79. *Work:* Brooklyn Mus; San Francisco Mod Art; George Eastman House, Rochester, NY; Newport Harbor Art Mus, Newport Beach, Calif; Bibliot, Avignon, France; and others. *Comn:* Photo installation (site specific), Levi Strauss Mus, San Francisco, 90; hist display, Levi Strauss & Co, San Francisco, 91; photos in bus shelters, Arts Comn, San Francisco, 92. *Exhib:* one-man shows, Zwinger Gallery, Berlin, 1987, Chicago Art Inst, 1982, Marcuse Pfeiffer Gallery, New York City, 1988, CEPA, Buffalo, 1988, Artspace, San Francisco, 1989, Visual Studies Workshop, Rochester, NY, 1990, Ctr for Arts, San Francisco, 1995, Oakland Mus, Calif, 1997, Kyle Roberta Gallery, San Francisco, 1992, Addison Gallery Am. Art, Andover, Mass, 1997, and others; California Color, San Francisco Mus Mod Art, 89; de Young Mus, San Francisco, 93; Victoria Room, 94; Luggage Store, 95; San Francisco Ctr Arts, 96; Addison Gallery, Phillips Acad, Mass, 97; Oakland Mus, Calif; MH De Young Memorial Mus; Contemp Arts Mus, Houston; and others. *Pos:* exhib designer, Levi Strauss & Co, 1989-. *Teaching:* Assoc prof new genres in photog, San Francisco Art Inst, 1989-93; vis prof pinhole photog, Visual Studies Workshop, Rochester, NY, 1990. *Awards:* NY State Coun Arts, 88; Art in Transit, Market St Bus Shelter, San Francisco Arts Comn, 92; Fel, Nat Endowment Arts, 90; Fel, San Francisco Arts Comn, 92. *Bibliog:* Kenneth Baker (auth), San Francisco Chronicle, 12/18/2005; Doug Nickel (auth), Low Tech Photography & Sculpture, Invented Camera, 2005; San Francisco Camerawork Quarterly, spring 2006; and others. *Mem:* Primitive Hunting Soc. *Media:* Alternative Photography. *Res:* Pin hole photog. *Specialty:* Fine art. *Publ:* Illusr, Flash Art, 2/88; Low Tech - Camera and Photographs; Newsweek, 8/21/89. *Dealer:* Visual Studies Workshop 31 Prince St Rochester NY 14607. *Mailing Add:* 378 San Jose Ave Apt B San Francisco CA 94110

BABER, BOB
ADMINISTRATOR
b Utica. *Study:* Utica Col, BA in Pub Relations & Journalism; Ball State Univ, MA in News/ed Journalism. *Pos:* Dir, pub relations State Univ of NY Inst Tech, Utica/Rome; dir, commun & devel Pratt at Munson-Williams-Proctor Arts Inst, Utica, NY, 99-2002; dir, commun & interim Dean Sch Art, 2002-03; dean, Sch Art, 2003-. *Teaching:* Instr, journalism Utica Col, Syracuse Univ, Syracuse, NY. *Publ:* Co-auth (with Joe Chilberg): NY Wine Country, 1980. *Mailing Add:* MWP Arts Inst Off of the Dean Pratt 310 Genesee St Utica NY 13502

BABIOR, DANIEL
PHOTOGRAPHER
b Brooklyn, NY, Dec 23, 53. *Study:* State Univ NY, Buffalo, BA, 74; RI Sch Design, MFA, 78. *Work:* Brooklyn Mus, NY; Israel Mus, Jerusalem. *Exhib:* Aldrich Art Mus, Ridgefield, Conn, 91; Crocker Art Mus, Sacramento, Calif, 92. *Teaching:* Acad dean, Marin Acad, 88-. *Awards:* Photog Fel, Nat Endowment Art, 90 & 91; fel, Edward E Ford, 96. *Mailing Add:* 1401 Kains Ave Berkeley CA 94702

BACARELLA, FLAVIA
PAINTER
b Brooklyn, NY. *Study:* New Sch Soc Res, MA, 75; New York Studio Sch Drawing. *Work:* Arthur Andersen, Minneapolis; Va Ctr Creative Arts, Sweet Briar; Bryn Mawr Col. *Exhib:* Prince St Gallery, 85, 88, 91, 95 & 99; Krasdale Galleries, 94. *Teaching:* Asst prof, Herbert H Lehman Col, 85-. *Awards:* Painting Fel, NY Found Arts, 86; Grant, City Univ NY Res Found, 88, 91 & 98. *Mem:* Women's Caucus Art; Col Art Asn. *Media:* Oils. *Mailing Add:* Lehman College Bedford Park Blvd W Bronx NY 10468

BACH, DIRK
PAINTER, EDUCATOR
b Grand Rapids, Mich, Nov 27, 39. *Study:* Univ Denver, BFA(painting), 61, MA(painting), 62; Univ Mich, Ann Arbor, MA(Orient art hist), 64. *Work:* Denver Art Mus, Colo; Hopkins Ctr Art Galleries, Dartmouth Col, Hanover, NH; Lamont Gallery, Phillips Exeter Acad, NH; Loretto-Hilton Gallery, Webster Col, St Louis, Mo; Mus Art, RI Sch Design, Providence; and others. *Comn:* Wall reliefs, Denver Art Mus, 62, NH Comn Arts NH Voc Inst, Berlin, 68 & Grad & Music Schs, Univ NH, 68; St Gaudens Nat Hist Site, Cornish, NH, 72. *Exhib:* New Eng Drawing Exhib, Addison Gallery, Andover, Mass, 70; New Eng Drawing Competition, DeCordova Mus, Lincoln, Mass, 74; Phillips-Exeter Acad, 67, 74 & 79; Newport Art Asn, RI, 76, 77-81; RI Sch Design Mus of Art, Providence, 69-91; Seasons Gallery, Den Haag, The

Neth, 80-81; Susan Cumming Gallery, Mill Valley, Calif, 90; and many others. *Collection Arranged:* One Hundred Years of American Art, 66 & The Rose Art Museum Collection at New Hampshire (with catalog), 69, Scudder Gallery, Durham, NH. *Pos:* Dir, Scudder Gallery, Univ NH, 65-69; adv & contribr, Newport Rev, 79-; coun mem, Art Asn Newport, 80-83. *Teaching:* Asst prof painting, Univ NH, 65-69; assoc prof art hist, RI Sch Design, 69-91, prof, formerly, chmn art hist dept, formerly, chmn fac asn, 89-91; assoc & lectr, Asian Studies, Brown Univ, 70-; dir, RI Sch Design, European Honors Program, Rome, 74-75. *Awards:* Univ NH Cent Univ Res Grant Commemorative Stamp Paintings, 68; Nat Endowment Humanities Travel & Res Grant, Japan, 71; Mellon Fel, Egypt, 84. *Mem:* Col Art Asn Am; Artists Equity Asn; Newport Art Asn; NH Art Asn; NEARI. *Media:* Graphite, Paper. *Res:* Development of Ch'an painting in China; production of cosmic diagrams in the Far East. *Publ:* Contribr, The Painting of Tao Chi, Univ Mich Mus Art, 67; auth, The stamp collection of Dirk Bach, Ramparts, 11/68; Selections From the Oriental Collections, RI Sch Design, 72. *Dealer:* Somerhill Gallery Chapel Hill NC. *Mailing Add:* PO Box 561 Carolina RI 02812-0561

BACH, LAURENCE
PHOTOGRAPHER, EDUCATOR
b Philadelphia, Pa, Jan 2, 47. *Study:* Philadephia Col Art, BFA, 68; Allgemeine Gewerbeschule, Basel, Switz, grad, 70. *Work:* Philadelphia Mus Art; Mus Fine Arts, St Petersburg, Fla. *Exhib:* Three Centuries Am Art, Philadelphia Mus Art, 76; solo exhibs, Modernism Gallery, San Francisco, 79, Robert Samuel Gallery, NY, 81, Photo Ctr Athens, Greece, 82 & Wesleyan Univ, Conn, 83; Group Photographs, Inst Contemp Art, Philadelphia, 80; and others. *Teaching:* Asst prof photog & design, Moore Col Art, 70-72, Philadelphia Col Art, 72-74 & State Univ NY, Purchase, 74-86; prof, Univ Arts, Philadelphia Col Art & Design, currently. *Awards:* Photog Grant, Nat Endowment Arts, 80; Photog Study Grant, Polaroid Corp, 81; NY State Coun Arts Grant, Visual Studies Workshop, 82. *Bibliog:* William Stapp (auth), Three Centuries of American Art (exhib catalog), Philadelphia Mus, 76; Don Ernst (auth), Laurence Bach: Paros shards, Aperture, No 82, 2/79; Owen Edwards (auth), Laurence Bach portfolio, Am Photog, 9/81. *Publ:* Auth, The Paros Dream Book, Visual Studies Workshop Press, 83. *Mailing Add:* 502 E Gorgas Ln Philadelphia PA 19119-1321

BACHARDY, DON
PAINTER, DRAFTSMAN
b Los Angeles, Calif, May 18, 34. *Study:* Chouinard Art Inst, 56-60; Slade Sch Art, London Univ, 61. *Work:* Metrop Mus Art, NY; Nat Portrait Gallery Eng, London; Princeton Univ; Fogg Art Mus; Nat Portrait Gallery, Smithsonian Inst, Washington, DC. *Comn:* Off portrait Calif State Capitol Bldg, Former Gov Edmund G Brown Jr. *Exhib:* Solo exhib, de Young Mem Mus, 64, Los Angeles Munic Art Gallery, 73 & 83 & NY Cult Ctr, 74; Inside-Out: Self Beyond Likeness, Newport Harbor Art Mus, 81; Portland Art Mus, 81; James Corcoran Gallery, Santa Monica, Calif, 87, 91 & 93; Charles Cowles Gallery, NY; de Young Mem Mus, 96; Nat Portrait Gallery, London, Eng, 96; Univ Tex, Austin, 97; Laguna Art Mus, Laguna Beach, 99; Acad of Motion Picture Arts and Sciences, Beverly Hills, Calif, 2000; Huntington Libr, San Marino, Calif, 2004-2005. *Bibliog:* One Hundred Drawings, 83 & Drawings of the male nude, 85, Twelvetrees Press; 70XI, Drawings of Seventy Artists, Illuminati Press, 83; Last Drawings of Christopher Isherwood, Faber & Faber, 91; Stars in My Eyes, Univ Wis Press, 2000. *Media:* Ink, Acrylic. *Publ:* Illusr, Michigan Quart Rev, Univ Mich, winter 80; Paris Rev, Vol 23, No 79, 81; Paris Rev, Vol 25, No 89, 83. *Dealer:* James Cocoran Gallery 1327 Fifth St Santa Monica CA 90401; Charles Cowles Gallery 420 W Broadway New York NY. *Mailing Add:* 145 Adelaide Dr Santa Monica CA 90402

BACHERT, HILDEGARD GINA
ART DEALER
b Mannheim, Ger, Apr 3, 21; US citizen. *Study:* Hunter Col, BA(summa cum laude), 54. *Collection Arranged:* Grandma Moses (contribr, catalog), Nat Gallery Art, Washington, 79; Alfred Kubin, 83; Paula Modersohn-Becker, 83; Kollwitz/Modersohn-Becker traveling exhib, 84-86; Grandma Moses traveling exhib, Japan, 90; Käthe Kollwitz Exhib (auth, catalog), Found Neumann, Gingins & Mus Jenisch, Vevey, Switz, 94. *Pos:* Secy & asst, Nierendorf Gallery, NY, 39-40; exec secy, Galerie St Etienne, NY, 40-78, co-dir, 78-. *Awards:* Decorated Cross of Merit, 1st Class, Ger, 1999; Inductee, Hunter Col Hall of Fame, 2004. *Mem:* Art Dealers Asn Am. *Specialty:* Early 20th century Austrian and German art: Schiele, Klimt, Kokoschka, Kollwitz & Corinth; 19th and 20th century naive art. *Publ:* Contribr, Otto Kallir's Egon Schiele: Oeuvre Catalog of the Paintings, 66 & contribr, Otto Kallir's Egon Schiele: The Graphic Work, 70, Zsolnay, Vienna & Crown; Otto Kallir's Grandma Moses, Crown & Harry N Abrams, 73, Ger transl, DuMont, Cologne, Ger, 79, Jane Kallir's Egon Schiele: The Complete Works, Harry N Abrams, 90, 98; auth, Collecting the Art of Käthe Kollwitz, Käthe Kollwitz by Elizabeth Prelinger, Nat Gallery Art & Yale Univ Press, 92

BACHINSKI, WALTER JOSEPH
PAINTER, PRINTMAKER
b Ottawa, Ont, Aug 6, 1939; Can citizen. *Study:* Ont Col Art, AOCA, 65; printmaking with Frederick Hagen; Univ Iowa, with Mauricio Lasansky, MA(printmaking), 67. *Work:* Montreal Mus Fine Arts, Que; Uffizi Gallery, Florence, Italy; Can Coun Art Bank, Ottawa, Ont; Nat Libr of Canada, Nat Gallery of Canada. *Comn:* Three bas-reliefs on a humanitarian theme, Univ Waterloo, Ont, 75; The Sculptor's Studio (bas-relief), MacLean-Hunter Bldg, College Park, Toronto; Mother and Child (bronze relief), Donald Forster Sculpture Park, MacDonald Stewart Art Gallery, Guelph, Ont, 85; Pastoral (pastel), Cineplex-Odean Theatre, Kiochener, Ont; The Four Seasons (pastel), Mine & Minerals Res Ctr, Laurentian Univ, Sudbury, Ont. *Exhib:* One-man traveling exhibs, Mt St Vincent Univ, 73, Walter Bachinski: Sculpture & Drawing, Art Gallery, Hamilton, 81; Bachinski, A Decade (traveling exhib), Kitchener-Waterloo Art Gallery, 76-77; Approaching Classicism, Selected Works, 1979-89, Kitchener-Waterloo Art Gallery, 91; Still-life, 10 Yrs, McLaren Art Ctr, Barrie, 92. *Teaching:* Prof drawing & printmaking, Dept Fine Arts, Univ Guelph, 67-94. *Awards:* Can Coun Arts Grants, 69, 78, 79 & 82; Arts Coun Ont Grants, 78 & 79; Premio dell Instituto Bancario Si Paolo di Torino, 4th Int Biennale of Graphic Art, Florence, Italy, 74; Can Coun Materials Grant, 78-79; and others. *Bibliog:* Bachinski: A Decade, Kitchener-Waterloo Art Gallery, 76; Walter Bachinski: Sculpture and Drawing, Art Gallery Hamilton, 81; Walter Bachinski: Approaching Classicism, Kiochener-Waterloo Art Gallery, 91. *Mem:* fine Press Book Asn. *Media:* Pastels, All Media. *Publ:* Virgil's The Ecologues, Shanty Bay Press, 99; five poems with pochoir illustrations by Walter Bachinski, Shanty Bay Press, 2002. *Dealer:* Wallace Galleries Ltd Calgary Alberta Can; Galerie de Bellefeuville Montreal Que Can. *Mailing Add:* RR 2 Shanty Bay ON L0L 2L0 Canada

BACHNER, BARBARA L
PAINTER, INSTALLATION SCULPTURE
b Waterville, ME, Sept 14, 34. *Study:* NY Univ Fine Arts, NY BA Magna Cum Laude, 68; Natl Acad Sch Fine Arts, Art Students League, Merit Awards, 75-80; Johnson State Col, Vt Studio, MFA, 2000. *Work:* Robert Blackburn Printmaking Workshop Coll, Libr Congress, Washington, DC, 68; Southwest Minnesota State Univ Coll, Marshall, MN; Kaatsbaan Intl Dance Ctr, Tivoli, NY; Four Seasons Hotel Corp, Las Vegas, NV; Texaco Corp, Houston, TX. *Exhib:* NY State Biennial, NY State Mus, Albany, 98; Biennale d'ELL Arte Contemporanea, Fortezza Da Basso, Florence, Italy, 99; Dream Worlds & Neo-Surrealism, at the Millenium, Attleboro Mus, Attleboro, MA, 2000; solo shows, Memory into Matter, Studio D'ARS, Milan, Italy, 2001, Echoes, AIR Gallery, NY & James Art Ctr, Woodstock, NY, 2004; NY Meets Berlin, May Planck inst for Human Develop, Berlin, Ger, 2004; Point of View, Poughkeepsie Art Mus, Poughkeepsie, NY, 2004; Depth of the Surface, William Whipple Gallery, SW Minnesota State Univ, Marshall, MN, 2004; Recycle/Revisited, Samuel Dorsky Mus Art, State Univ NY, New Paltz, NY, 2005; How we aee China Today, NY Atrs Beijing Gallery, Lhao Yang Qu, Beijing, China, 2006. *Pos:* bd dir, graphics co-chmn, Pen & Brush, New York, NY, 90-95; bd dir, trustee, Woodstock Artists Asn, Woodstock, NY, 90-2002; bd dir, Nat Assn Women Artists, New York, NY, 2000-2002; cur, Woodstock artist assoc & Mus; Woodstock Guild, Kleinert James Gallery. *Teaching:* Instr, Woodtock Sch Art, Woodstock, NY, 2000-2001. *Awards:* Medal of Honor, Annual Exhib, Nat Asn Women Artists, 98; Lorenzo Il Magnifico Metal, Biennale D'Ell Arte Contemporanea, Florence, 99; Travel Grant, NY Meets Berlin, US Embassy, Berlin, 2004. *Bibliog:* Bonnie Langston, Terrorist Attacks Ripple Effect, Daily Freeman, Kingston, NY, 12/4/2000; Silvia Venuti, Memory into Matter, Corriere dell Arte, Milan, Italy, 11/24/2001; Ed McCormack (auth), Barbara Bachner @ Gallery @ 49, Gallery & Studio, April/May, 2002. *Mem:* Col Art Asn; Nat Asn Women Artists, (bd dir, 2000-02); Art Students League, life mem; NY Artists Asn; Woodstock Artists Asn, trustee/dir, juror, cur, painting, printmaking, exhib comt, 90-2002. *Media:* Acrylic, Mixe Media. *Publ:* Behind Closed Eyes, Artist's Book, K Caraccio Printshop Publ, 98. *Dealer:* TAI Gallery, 159 W 25th St, New York, NY. *Mailing Add:* 526 W 26th St Ste 815 New York NY 10001

BACIGALUPA, ANDREA
SCULPTOR, PAINTER
b Baltimore, Md, May 26, 23. *Study:* Art Students League, painting with Arnold Blanch, summer 49; Md Inst Fine Arts, BFA, 50, painting with Jacques Maroger; Acad de Belli Arti, Florence, Italy, PG, painting with Ottone Rosai, 50-51. *Work:* City of Santa Fe, NMex; Basilica Santa Maria del Lauro, Meta di Sorrento, Italy; Cathedral Sta Lawrence, Amarillo, Tex. *Comn:* 14 panels etched glass, St Francis Cathedral, Santa Fe, NMex, 85; Our Lady of Guadalupe (mural), St Johns, Borger, Tex, 88; stained glass, St Thomas More Church, Manhattan, Kans, 90; interior design, Holy Rosary Church, Albuquerque, NMex, 92; Shrine of St Therese, Pueblo, Colo, 94. *Exhib:* One-man show, Mus of NMex, 59; US Church Archit Guild, Pittsburgh, 61; Gov's Gallery, Sante Fe, NMex, 78; Cooper-Hewitt Mus, NY, 81; Group Show, City Hall, Sorrento, Italy, 93, 05; Sonento Holy, 2002. *Pos:* owner, Studio of Gian Andrea, Santa Fe. *Awards:* Bronze Medallion Fine Arts, Md Inst, 50; 1st Prize, Santa Fe Competition, Art in Pub Places, 79; Lerici Pea Int Poetry Award Un Liqure Nel Mondo, Italy, 2002. *Bibliog:* Maurice Lavanoux (auth), Liturgy & art, Liturgical Arts, 73; Clifford Stevens (auth), Sacred arts, Out Sunday Visitor, 74; Denise Kusel (auth), Mem in Old Country, Santa Fe NMex, 10/10/85; Cathy Flores (auth), Dream Realized, Las Cruces, Sun-News, 3/30/86. *Mem:* Santa Fe/Sorretno Sister City Asn (founder emer). *Media:* Bronze; Oil. *Specialty:* Sculpture. *Interests:* Performing Arts, literature and traveling. *Publ:* The Song of Guadalupana, OSV, 79; Franco and Pirata, Pickwick Press, 85; auth, And Come to Dust, Wrtiers Club Press, 2000, Since My Last Confession, 2001, For Having Offended Thee, 2002; Seven Carols, Seven Gifts, Sunstone Press, 2002; Mystical Journey, 05. *Mailing Add:* 626 Canyon Rd Santa Fe NM 87501

BACIGALUPI, DON
MUSEUM DIRECTOR, CURATOR
b New York, NY, Apr 24, 60. *Study:* Univ Houston, BA(art hist), 83; Univ Tex, MA(art hist), 85, PhD(art hist), 93. *Collection Arranged:* Whatley Collection, 90-93; American Photography: A History in Pictures, 94; Synesthesia: Sound & Vision in Contemporary Art (auth, catalog), San Antonio Mus Art, 95; Stella in Studio: The Public Art of Frank Stella, 96; Michael Ray Charles, 1989-1993: An American Artist's Work (auth, catalog), Blaffer Gallery, 97. *Pos:* Cur contemp art, San Antonio Mus Art, Tex 93-95; dir & chief cur, Blaffer Gallery, Univ Houston Art Mus, 95-99; dir, San Diego Mus of Art, 99-2003; dir, Toledo Mus of Art, 2003; AAMD Bd, 2004. *Teaching:* Lectr art hist, Univ Tex, Austin, 88-93; adj prof, Univ Houston, 96-.

Awards: Gold Award Best Catalog, Synethesia: Sound & Vision, Addy Awards, 96; First Prize, Best Catalog, Michael Ray Charles, Am Asn Mus, 98. *Mem:* Tex Asn Mus (co-chmn); Am Asn Mus; Houston Coalition Visual Arts (co-chmn). *Res:* Contemporary American and International art. *Mailing Add:* Toledo Mus Art PO Box 1013 Toledo OH 43697

BACKES, JOAN
PAINTER, ARTIST
b Milwaukee, Wis. *Study:* Univ Iowa, BA, 72; Univ Mo, Kansas City, MA, 83; Northwestern Univ, Evanston, Ill, MFA, 85. *Work:* Aberdeen Art Galleries & Mus, Scotland; Nova Scotia Col of Art and Design, Halifax, NS, Can; Embassy of USA, Reykjavik, Iceland; Boston Publ Libr, Boston, Mass; Wright Mus Art, Beloit Col, Wis; Nelson-Atkins Mus Art, Kansas City, Mo; Milwaukee Art Mus, Wis; SAFN Mus, Reykjavik, Iceland; Reykjavik Art Mus, Iceland; Rauma Art Mus, Finland. *Exhib:* one woman show, Aberdeen Art Galleries & Mus, Scotland, 87 & Museo de Arte Contemporaneo, Santiago, Chile, 96, Nova Scotia Coll Art & Design, Halifax, 99, Braitmayer Art Ctr, Marion, Mass, 2000, Jan Weiner Gallery, Kansas City, MO, 2001, Dartmouth Col, Hanover, NH, 2002, Hafnarborg Inst Cult & Fine Art, 2003, Rauma Art Mus, Finland,2005, SAFN Mus, Reykjavik, Iceland; Primordial Landscape, Hafnarborg Inst Cult & Fine Art, Iceland, 91; Ut Pictora Poesis, Mulvane Art Mus, Topeka, 93; Rocks, Markers, Places, Wustum Mus Fine Art, Racine, Wis, 93; The Landscape Beyond The Landscape, Centro Cult Recoleta, Buenos Aires, Arg, 97; Hafnarborg Inst Cult & Fine Art, 98; Wright Mus Art, Beloit Col, Wis, 2004; Nature Interrupted, New Bedford Art Mus, Mass; Drawing-drawing 2, The Foundry, London Biennial, Eng. *Teaching:* Adj prof painting, Univ Mo, 85-88; vis artist painting, Kansas City Art Inst, 88-95; adj prof, Brown Univ, 97-; adj prof Coll Art Grad Program, Portland, Maine, 2000-; prof painting, Rhode Island Sch Design, Providence, 2006. *Awards:* Nat Endowment Arts & Kans Arts Comn Award, 86 & 92; Sr Fulbright Scholar, Ctr Intl Exchange Scholars, 94-95; Ragdale Found Fel, 98, 99, 2000; Fulbright Hays Award, 2003; US Embassy Grant, Iceland, 2006. *Bibliog:* Eva Grinstein (auth), An Aesthetic View of Inapprehensible Natural Phenomena, Rev El Cronistia, Buenos Aires, Arg, 97; Jon Proppe (auth), Joan Backes Remembering, Hafnarborg Inst, 98; James Yood (auth), Tré, Hafnarborg Inst, 2003; Jon Proppe (auth), Pleasure in the Pathless Wood, Hafnarborg Inst, 2003; Gerald Nordland (auth), Joan Backes, Wright Mus Art, Beloit Col Press, 2004. *Mem:* Col Art Asn. *Media:* Mixed Media. *Publ:* Auth, Letter from the Living, Borderline, Big Blue Prairie Ed, 92; Hafnarborg: 1988-1993, Felagsbokdandid Bokfell, Iceland, 93. *Dealer:* Virginia Lynch Gallery 3883 Main Rd Rte 77 Tiverton RI 02878; Jan Weiner Gallery 4800 Liberty St Kansas City MO 64112; Dean Jensen Gallery 759 N Water St Milwaukee Wis 53202. *Mailing Add:* PO Box 100 Seekonk MA 02771

BACOT, HENRY PARROTT
MUSEUM DIRECTOR, EDUCATOR
b Shreveport, La, Dec 13, 1941. *Study:* Baylor Univ, Waco, Tex, BA, 63; La State Univ, Baton Rouge, 64-65; Attingham Park Summer Sch Study Great English Country Houses, Shropshire, fel, 66; State Univ NY Cooperstown, MA(Scriven Found Fel, Cooperstown Grad Progs), 67. *Collection Arranged:* American Folk Art 1730-1968, 68; Southern Furniture & Silver: The Federal Period 1788-1830, 68; Louisiana Landscape 1800-1969, 69; Natchez-Made Silver of the 19th Century, 70; Sail & Steam in Louisiana Waters, 71; Louisiana Folk Art, 72; Crescent City Silver, 80; Rhoda Stokes: A Retrospective (with catalog), 84; Louisiana Art from the Roger Houston Ogden Collection, 92; France Fobe Rediscovered, 97. *Pos:* Dir, Anglo-Am Art Mus, Baton Rouge, 67-; hist interiors consult, Kings' Tavern, Natchez, Miss, 71-, Kent Plantation House, Alexandria, La, 71- & Magnolia Mound Plantation House, Baton Rouge, 72-; sponsor, Am Friends of Attingham Summer Sch, 77-; exec dir, La State Univ Mus Complex, 82. *Teaching:* Asst prof art hist, La State Univ, 67-84, asst prof hist of interior design, 73, prof art hist, 84-. *Awards:* Ed Bd, J Early Southern Decorative Arts, 97. *Mem:* Soc Archit Historians; Am Victorian Soc; Found Hist La (bd mem, 72-74); Old State Capitol Adv Comt. *Res:* Fine arts, architecture and decorative arts of the Deep South. *Publ:* Coauth, Nineteenth century Natchez-made Silver, 71, Crescent City silver, Historic New Orleans collection, 80; articles, Antiques, 72-97; contribr, Soc Archit Historians J, 74; auth, Nineteenth Century Lighting: Candle-Powered Devices: 1783-1883, Schiffer Pub Ltd, 87

BACZEK, PETER GERARD
PAINTER, PRINTMAKER
b Webster, Mass, June 6, 45. *Study:* San Jose State Univ, BA(art), 70. *Work:* Achenbach Found Graphic Arts, Calif Palace Legion Hon, San Francisco; Brooklyn Mus; Philadelphia Mus Art; Metrop Mus Art Ctr, Coral Gables, Fla; Cooper-Hewitt Mus, New York & Brooklyn Mus Art. *Exhib:* 21st Nat Print Exhib, Brooklyn Mus, 79; Eighth Int Print Biennial, Crakow, Poland, 80; Subjective Realities (with catalog), Calif Palace Legion Hon, San Francisco, 82; Urban Documents: 20th Century Am Prints, Cooper-Hewitt Mus, NY, 83; Rockford Int, Rockford Col, 83; Boston Printmakers 37th Nat Exhib Art Mus, Brandeis Univ, 85; Crocker-Kingsley Ann, Crocker Mus Art, Sacramento, Calif; Ninth British Int Print Biennale, Bradford, Eng, 86. *Awards:* Patron Award, Print Club, Pa, 82; Jurors Spec Mention, Cabo Frio Int Print Biennial, Brazil, 83; Monotype Award, Northern Calif Print Competition, 86. *Bibliog:* Roberta Loach (auth), Book of Hours: A Portfolio of 21 Prints, Visual Dialog, 79; Julie van der Ryn (auth), Shadows and Patterns in the Everyday, City Arts Monthly Mag, 81. *Media:* Oil; Etchings. *Dealer:* Suzy R Locke & Assocs 201 Estates Dr Piedmont CA 94611. *Mailing Add:* 2433 Scenic Ave Oakland CA 94602

BADALAMENTI, FRED L
PAINTER, EDUCATOR
b Long Island, NY, June 25, 1935. *Study:* Pratt Inst, 53-55; State Univ NY Col, New Paltz, BS, 60; Brooklyn Col, MFA(fel), 67; studied with Philip Pearlstein, Carl Holty & Burgoyne Diller. *Work:* Brooklyn Col, NY; State Univ NY, Stony Brook; DBG Properties Corp, New York City; Torrington Mfg Corp, Torrington, Conn; Bellvue Hosp, NYC. *Comn:* Bellevue Hosp, NY. *Exhib:* One-person exhibs, First St Gallery, NY, 76, 80 & 89, Van Loen Gallery, S Huntington, NY, 98; Nassau Co Mus Fine Arts, 87; St Joseph's Col, 87; group exhibs incl: City Univ NY Res Foun Univ Art Gallery, State Univ NY, Stony Brook, 94, 89, Contemp Realist Gallery, San Francisco, Calif, 90, Brooklyn Col Art Gallery, 93, Images Gallery, NY, 95, Gallery N, Setauket, NY, 98, 2003 & 04. *Pos:* Dir, First St Gallery, 78-79; art exhib jurist, Drawing and Painting, various LI locations, 2000-06. *Teaching:* Prof drawing & painting, Brooklyn Col, 69-92, deputy chmn grad art, 72-89, dep chmn undergrad art, 89-92, prof emer, 92-; vis prof drawing & painting, State Univ NY, Stony Brook, 77-78 & summers 78, 80, 81 & 83; adj prof, Brooklyn Col, 92-93, State Univ NY, Stony Brook, 93-99. *Awards:* Fel, Brooklyn Col, 65-67. *Mem:* Col Art Asn; Am Asn Univ Prof. *Media:* Oil, Drawing, Printmaking. *Dealer:* Gallery North Setauket NY 11733. *Mailing Add:* 182 Lower Sheep Pasture Rd Setauket NY 11733

BADEN, KARL
PHOTOGRAPHER, INSTRUCTOR
b New York, NY, 52. *Study:* Syracuse Univ, BA, 74; Univ Ill, MFA, 79. *Work:* Mus Modern Art, NY; Guggenheim Mus, NY; Mus Fine Arts, Boston; Mus Fine Arts, Houston; Santa Barbara Mus Art, Calif. *Exhib:* Contemp Photog or Phantasy, Santa Barbara Mus Art, 82; Karl Baden, Inst Contemp Art, Boston, 84; Reproduction, Mus Fine Arts, Boston, 89; Photographs from the Permanent Collection, Mus Modern Art, New York City, 92; Tradition and the Unpredictable, Mus Fine Arts, Houston, 94; Family Tree, Robert Mann Gallery, New York City, 2000; Photog in Boston 1955-1985, Decordova Mus, Lincoln, Mass, 2000; Get the Picture, Addison Gallery of Am Art, Andover, Mass, 2000. *Teaching:* adj prof photography, Boston Col, 89-. *Awards:* fel NEA, 91; fel Mass Coun for Arts, 99; New Works grantee Mass Photographers Mass Cult Coun, 81. *Bibliog:* Charles Hagan (auth), Karl Baden, The New York Times, 1/6/95; David Bonetti (auth), Karl Baden: Sex, Death, Art News, 89; Gerald Peary (auth), Photography in Boston, Boston Mag, 12/83. *Mem:* Ctr for Visual Arts in the Pub Interest (bd dir 2000-); Photographic Resource Ctr (bd dir 89-97). *Media:* Photography. *Publ:* auth, Some Significant Self-Portraits, Badger Press, 81; auth, How Did I.Get Here?, Light Work Visual Studies, 2000; contbr, Photography in Boston, 1955-1985, MIT Press, 2000; contbr, Pregnant Pictures, Routledge Press, 2000; contbr, The Dog: A Century of Photographs, Chronicle Press, 2000. *Dealer:* Robert Mann Gallery 210 Eleventh Ave New York NY 10001; Howard Yezerski Gallery 14 Newbury St Boston Mass 02116. *Mailing Add:* 44 Alpine St Cambridge MA 02138

BADEN, MOWRY T
SCULPTOR
b Los Angeles, Calif, 36. *Study:* Pomona Col, BA, 58; Stanford, MA, 65. *Work:* Berkeley Art Mus; Oakland Art Mus; San Diego Mus Contemp Art; Vancouver Art Gallery. *Comn:* Univ Calif, Santa Barbara; Exploratorium, San Francisco; Wash Proj for the Arts; Seattle Arts Comm; City of Victoria, BC. *Exhib:* One-man shows, Mercer Union, Toronto, 87, Contemp Art Gallery, Vancouver, BC, 88, Drawing Room, Tucson, Ariz, 88, Alta Col Art Gallery, Calgary, Alta, 89, Capp St Proj, San Francisco, 91, San Diego Mus, La Jolla, Calif, 91, Galerie Christiane Chassay Montreal, 93, 95, 97, 01, Vancouver Art Gallery, 96, 97, Mus Contemp Art, Tokyo, 98, Art Gallery, Otis Col of Art & Design, Los Angeles, 98, Post Gallery, Los Angeles, 99, 01, Blackwood Gallery, Toronto, 00, Montgomer Gallery, Pomona Col, Calif, 01; World Trade Ctr, NY, 90; Un-Natural Traces, Barbican Gallery, London, Eng, 91; Out of Actions, Mus Contemp Art, Los Angeles, 97; Walk Ways, Independent Curators Int, NY, 02. *Awards:* Can Coun Proj Cost Grant, 76-77, 80-81, 81-82, 87, 88 & 89; Nat Endowment Arts Grant, 77-78, 80-81, 84 & 90. *Bibliog:* Robert Hullot-Kentor (auth), Mowry Baden, A Choreography of the Ordinary (exhib catalog), Open Space, Victoria, 98; Liane Davison (auth), Mowry Baden, Sculpture (exhib catalog), Alberta Coll Art, 89; Stephen Horne (auth), Freckled Gyres: Sculpture by Mowry Baden (exhib catalog), Montgomery Art Gallery, Pomona College, Calif, 2001. *Dealer:* Christine Chassay 358 rue Sherbrooke Montreal Quebec Canada H2X 1E6. *Mailing Add:* Post Gallery 1904 E 7th Pl Los Angeles CA 90021

BADGETT, STEVEN
ARTIST
b Ill, 62. *Exhib:* Exhibs incl Highwayscape, Weber State Univ, Ogden, Utah, 1997, An Investigation of Trans-Architecture in Western Am, 1997, Rise Overrun, Plan B Evolving Arts, Santa Fe, 1997, L'Arche, Ecole Nationale d'Art, Cergy, France, 1998, SIMPARCH, Bemis Ctr Contemp Arts, Omaha, 1998, Ship from the Desert, Maschinenhalle, Potsdam, Ger, 1998, Moorings Project, 1998, The Unit, Ctr Land Use Interpretation, Wendover, Utah, 1999, Free Basin, Hyde Park Arts Ctr, Chicago, 2000, Spec, Renaissance Soc, Univ Chicago, 2001, Mood River, Wexner Ctr Arts, Columbus, Ohio, 2002, Documenta XI, Kassel, Ger, 2002, Session the Bowl, Deitch Projects, NY, 2002, Whitney Biennial, Whitney Mus Am Art, NY, 2004, InSITE, San Diego, 2005. *Pos:* Co-found & mem, SIMPARCH, 96-; lectr, Columbus Col Art & Design, Ohio, 2001; Documenta XI, Kassel, Ger, 2002. *Teaching:* lectr, Weber State Univ, Ogden, Utah, 97; resident, Brandenburgischer Kunstverein, Potsdam, Ger, 98; lectr, Univ Utah, Salt Lake City, 99; resident, Ctr Land Use Interpretation, LA, 99, 2003. *Awards:* NMex Arts Coun Grant, 97; Creative Capital Grant, 2002. *Mailing Add:* 3303 S Aberdeen Chicago IL 60607

BAECHLER, DONALD
PAINTER
b Hartford, Conn, 56. *Study:* Maryland Inst Col Art, Baltimore, 74-76; Cooper Union, New York, 77-78; Staatliche Hochschule fuer bildende Kunste, Frankfurt, Ger, 78-79. *Work:* Mus Mod Art, Metrop Mus Art, NY; Philadelphia Mus Art, Pa; Centre Pompidou, Paris, France; William Alan Mus, Oberlin, Ohio. *Exhib:* Solo shows include Sperone Westwater, NY, 93, Paul Kasmin Gallery, NY, 93, Erika & Otto

Friedrich, Bern, Switz, 94, Pace Prints, NY, 94, Stephen Wirtz Gallery, San Francisco, Calif, 94, Laura Carpenter Fine Art, Santa Fe, NMex, 94 & Galerie Thaddaeus Ropac, Paris, 94-95, Maps, Paul Kasmin Gallery, NY, 98, Knowing Children, David Beitzel Gallery, NY, 98, Selected Projects 1985-1990, Baron/Boisante, NY, 99, 2000, Peter Kogler, Ascan Crone, Hamburg, Ger, 99, Road Show, DFN Gallery, NY, 99, Five Easy Pieces, Tony Shafrazi Gallery, NY, 2001, Ironical Instinct, Galleria Cardi, Milan, Ital, 2001, Alain Noirhomme, Brussels, 2002, Recent Paintings, Galerie Bernd Klueser, Munich, 2003, The Enemies of teh Rose, Kunst Meran, Merano, Italy, 2004, Cheim & Read, NY, 2006; group shows include Wadsworth Atheneum, Hartford, Conn, 75; Biennal (with catalog), Whitney Mus Am Art, NY, 89; Parallel Visions: Modern Artists & Outsider Art, Los Angeles Co Mus Art, 92; A Garden, Barbara Krakow Gallery, Boston, 94; The Books, Matthew Marks Gallery, NY, 94; Am Painting Now (with catalog), Eva Menzio, Turin, Italy, 94; Emblems & Contours, Sperone Westwater, NY, 95; The Baseball Show, Curt Marcus, NY, 96; Chanel, ANy Warhol Mus, Pittsburg, Pa, 97; Knowing Children, David Beitzel Gallery, NY; Road Show, DFN Gallery, NY, 99; Painting, Paul Kasmin Gallery, NY, 2000; Mythic Proportions: Painting in the 1980s, MoCA, Miami, 2001; NY Expression, Bergen Kommune, Norway, 2002; Funny Papers: Cartoons and Contemp Drawings, Daniel Weinberg Gallery, LA, 2003; Pop Art and Minimalismus, Albertina, Vienna, 2004; I am the Walrus, Cheim & Read, NY, 2004; represented in permanent colelctions of Mus Modern Art, NY, Whitney Mus Am Art, NY, Guggeheim Mus, NY, NY Public LIbrary, Mus Fine Arts, Boston, Mus Contemp Art, LA, Eli Broad Found, LA, Chase Manhattan Bank, NY, Deutsche Bank, NY, Sony Corp, NY. *Bibliog:* Flower Power, Suddeutsche Zeitung Mag, No 10, 3/3/94; Mark Van De Walle (auth), Donald Baechler: Works on Paper, Santa Fe's Mag Arts, Vol III, No 5, 11/94; Robert Enright (auth), The Incidental Tourist, Border Crossings, Vol 13, No 4, 11/94

BAEDER, JOHN
PAINTER
b South Bend, Ind, Dec 24, 38. *Study:* Auburn Univ, Ala, AB, 60. *Work:* Denver Art Mus; Whitney Mus of Am Art; Mus Mod Art Lending Serv; Cooper-Hewitt Mus; High Mus, Atlanta; and others. *Exhib:* Place, Product, Package, Cooper-Hewitt Mus, Smithsonian Inst, NY, 78; Kunstgewerbemuseum, Zurich, Switz, 79; Danforth Mus, Framingham, Mass, 80; Philbrook Art Ctr, Tulsa, Okla, 80; Real, Really Real, Super Real, San Antonio Mus, 81; Contemp American Realism Since 1960, Pa Acad Fine Arts, 81; Painting NY, Mus City NY, 83-84; and others. *Bibliog:* Gregory Battcock (auth), Super Realism, Dutton, 75; D Filipacchi (auth), Les Hyper Realists Americans. *Media:* Lithography, Oil. *Publ:* Auth, Diners, Harry N Abrams Inc, New York, 78; Gas, Food and Lodging, Abbeville Press, 82. *Dealer:* O K Harris 383 W Broadway New York NY 10012. *Mailing Add:* 1025 Overton Lea Rd Nashville TN 37220-1413

BAER, ADAM
PHOTOGRAPHER
b Mar 16, 69. *Study:* State Univ NY, BFA(photog), 91. *Work:* Art Mus at Princeton Univ; Calif Mus of Photog, Brooklyn Mus of Art. *Exhib:* Taboo, Woman Made Gallery, Chicago, 97; 7th Ann Showcase Exhib, Alternative Mus, NY, 97; Working/Still, Neuberger Mus, NY, 97; Jones Ctr for Contemp Art, Austin, Tex, 97; Expansion Arts: Artists of Our Times II, Alternative Mus, NY, 98; Nat Exhib, Provincetown Art Asn & Mus, Mass, 98; Bonni Benrubi Gallery, NY, 98; The Alternative Mus, NY, 99; PS1 Contemp Art Ctr, NY, 2000; Akus Gallery, Eastern Conn State Univ, 2001; and others; Calif Mus of Photog, 2001; Fifth One Fine Art Photog, Antwerp, 2001; New Photog by Adam Baer, Antwerp, Belg, 2001, Soho Photo, 97, others; Paris Photo, 2002, The Aldrich Mus of Contemp Art, Ridgefield, Conn, 2002. *Awards:* NY Found Arts Fel, 94; Aaron Siskind Found Fel, 95; JS Guggenheim Mem Found Fel, 98. *Bibliog:* Kim Levin (auth), Short List, Village Voice, 1/98; Stewart Klewans (auth), Critics Choice, NY Daily News, 1/17/98; Vince Aletti (auth), Choices, Village Voice, 4/22-28/98; Chris Macleod (auth), Resident, 8/21-27/98; Nadine S Kibanda (auth), Out There: Adam Baer's Surrealist Photographs, www.ps1.org, 2000; Vince Aletti (auth), Choices, Village Voice, 2/2000; Holland Cotter (auth), NY Contemporary, Defined 150 Ways, NY Times (Art Section), 3/6/2000; JS Irons (auth), A Conversation with Adam Baer, Zingmagazine, 2000. *Publ:* Adam Baer: Displaced Perspectives, Catalog: Calif Mus of Photog, 2001. *Dealer:* Fifty One Fine Art Photog, Antwerp, Belgium

BAER, JO
PAINTER, WRITER
b Seattle, Wash, Aug 7, 29. *Study:* Univ Wash; Grad Fac, New Sch Social Res. *Work:* Guggenheim Mus, Mus Mod Art, Whitney Mus Am Art, NY; Stedelijk Mus, Amsterdam; Albright-Knox Art Gallery, Buffalo, NY; Nat Mus, Canberra, Australia; Tate Gallery, London, England; and others. *Exhib:* Systematic Paintings, Guggenheim Mus, 66; Whitney Mus Am Art Biennial, NY, 67, 69, 73 & 75 & solo show, 75; Documenta IV, Mus Friedericianum, Kassel, Ger, 68; 31st Biennial, Corcoran Gallery Art, Washington, DC, 69; one-person shows, Stedelijk Vanabbe Mus, Eindhoven, The Neth, 78 & 86, Galerie Ricke, Cologne, 78, Lisson Gallery, London, 80, Riverside Studios, London, 82, Paley/Levy Gallery, Moore Col, Philadelphia, 93, Paula Cooper Gallery, NY, 95 & Stedelijk Mus, Amsterdam, 98; Ft Worth Mus, Tex, 77; Indianapolis Mus, Ind, 77; Chicago Art Inst, 77; Stadtische Kunsthelle, Dusseldorf, 82; The Window in 20th Century Art, Neuberger Mus, State Univ NY, Purchase, 86-87; La Couleur Seule, Musce St Pierre, Lyon, France, 88; Selected Geometric Abstract Painting in Am since 1945, Albright-Knox Gallery, Buffalo, NY, 89; From Minimal to Conceptual Art, Nat Gallery Art, Washington, 94; Abstraction, Pure & Impure, Mus Mod Art, NY, 96; The Pursuit of Painting, Irish Mus Modern Art, Dublin, 97; Contemp Drawings, Fogg Mus, Cambridge, 97. *Teaching:* Instr painting, Sch Visual Arts, NY, 69-70; guest instr painting, Brighton Tech, England, 82 & Rijksakedemie, Amsterdam, 87-88. *Awards:* Nat Coun Arts Award, 68-69. *Bibliog:* Miriam Seidel (auth), Jo Baer at Moore College of Art, Art in Am, New York, 1/94; Linda Yablonsky, Jo Baer Paintings from the '60s & Early '70s, Time Out, New York, 1/96; Roberta Smith (auth), Philip Johnson & the modern: a loving Marriage, NY Times, 6/7/96. *Media:* Oil. *Publ:* Auth, Radical Attitudes to the Gallery: Statement No 2, Studio Int, London, 80; coauth (with Bruce Robbins), Beyond the pale, Real Life Mag, NY, summer 83; auth, Jo Baer: I am no longer an abstract artist, Art in Am, NY, 83; Jo Baer: Red, White & Blue Gelding Falling to its Right (Doublecross Britanicus/Tricolor Hibernicus), Tis Ill Puddling in the Cockatrice Den (La-Bas), The Rod Reversed (Mixing Memory & Desire) (Catalog), Amsterdam, 90; coauth (with Bruce Robbins), Jo Baer: Four Drawings (catalog), Amsterdam, 93. *Mailing Add:* Rozengracht 207 Amsterdam 1016 LZ Netherlands

BAER, NORBERT S
EDUCATOR
b Brooklyn, NY, June 6, 1938. *Study:* Brooklyn Col, BSc(physical chemistry), 59; Univ Wis, MSc(chemistry), 62; NY Univ, PhD(physical chemistry), 69. *Pos:* Ed adv & assoc ed, Studies in Conservation, J Int Inst for Conserv, 71-; co-chmn, Conserv Ctr, Inst Fine Arts, New York Univ, 75-83, actg dir admin, 78-79; assoc ed, Restaurator, 75-; US exec ed, Conservation in the Arts, Archeol & Archit, Butterworths, 79-; chmn, Adv Comt on Preserv, Nat Archives & Rec Serv, 80-; chmn, Comt Conserv Historic Store Bldgs & Monuments, Nat Mat Adv Bd, Nat Acad Sci, 80-82; mem, Vis Comt Dept Objects Conserv, Metrop Mus Art, 80-. *Teaching:* Instr, Inst Fine Arts, Conserv Ctr, NY Univ, 69-70, asst prof, 70-75, assoc prof, 75-78, prof, 78-86, Hagop Kevorkian prof conserv, 86-. *Awards:* Guggenheim Fel, 83-84. *Mem:* Fel Int Inst Conserv; fel Am Inst Conserv (bd dir, 73-76); fel Am Inst Chemists; Am Chemical Soc; Sigma Xi. *Res:* Application of physico-chemical techniques to the preservation and examination of artistic and historic works. *Publ:* Coauth, Chemical Investigations on Ancient Near Eastern Archaeological Ivory Artifacts: III, Fluorine & Nitrogen Composition & Chemical Aspects of the Conservation of Archaelological Materials, Archeological Chemistry II, Advances in Chemistry, 78; Synthetic Blue Pigments: IX-XVI Centuries, I, Literature, Studies in Conservation, 80; Mechanisms of air pollution-induced damage to stone, Sixth World Congress Air Quality, Paris, Vol 3, 83; and others. *Mailing Add:* 194 Ascan Ave Forest Hills NY 11375

BAER, ROD
CONCEPTUAL ARTIST, SCULPTOR
b Los Angeles, Calif. *Study:* San Diego State Univ, BA; Claremont Grad Sch, MFA. *Work:* Skirball Mus, Los Angeles; Airport Plaza, Van Nuys, Calif; Art/Omi, NY; Armand Hammer Mus, Los Angeles, Calif; Principal Financial Group, Des Moines, Iowa; Jewish Mus, NY. *Comn:* Endless Columns, Carnation Co, Los Angeles, 91; Pocketwatch and Others, Metro-link Train Depot/City Claremont, Calif, 92; Precedent, Zelle & Larson, San Francisco, Calif, 94; Dancing Chairs, St Louis Arts in Transit & St Louis Art Fair, 98; Here Is, Robertson Blvd Public Art Project, Dept Transportation & City of Los Angeles, 98 & 99; All Roads Lead to Westwood, Weyburn Ave Streetscape, Dept Transportation, Los Angeles, Calif, 2001; Palm Tree, Water Drop, Vanowen St Bridge, Aliso Creek, City of Los Angeles, San Fernando Valley, Calif, 2005; Flower, Saticoy St Bridge, Aliso Creek, City of Los Angeles, San Fernando Valley, Calif, 2006; Falling Leaves, Strathern St Bridge, Aliso Creek, City of Los Angeles, San Fernando Valley, Calif, 2006. *Exhib:* Art and Archit, Santa Monica Heritage Mus, 88; Solo exhibs, The Cost of Implosion, Meyers/Bloom Gallery, Santa Monica, 89, Armory Ctr Arts, Pasadena, Calif, 94; Three Sculptors/Three Coasts, Blue Star Art Space, San Antonio, Tex, 90; The Book as Art, The Book in Art, Fendrick Gallery, NY, 90; two-man show, Pima Col, Tucson, Ariz, 92 & Pierce Col, Woodland Hills, Calif, 94; Blessings & Beginnings Inaugural Exhib, Skirball Mus, Los Angeles, Calif, 96; Looking Awry, Coleman Gallery, Albuquerque, NMex, 96; The Book of Lies, New York City Libr & Brooke Alexander Gallery, New York, Armand Hammer Mus, Los Angeles & Art Ctr Sch Design Libr, Pasadena, 96; Got Art, Laguna Art Mus, 97; Unbuilt Southern California, Guggenheim Gallery, Chapman Col, Orange, Calif, 97; The Perpetual Well: Contemp Art from the Jewish Mus (traveling), Samual Harn Mus, Gainesville, Fla, Sheldon Mem Art Gallery, Lincoln, Nebr & Parish Art Mus, Southampton, NY, 2000; Culture & Continuity: the Jewish Journey, Jewish Mus, NY, 2001; 27 Years of Showing Artists, Drudis-Biada Art Gallery, My Saint Mary's Col, Los Angeles, Calif, 2003. *Teaching:* Instr sculpture, Otis Parsons Art Inst, 90-91. *Awards:* Art/Omi Int Residency Fel, New York, 95; Djerassi Found Residency, Calif, 96; Artists Fel Award in New Genre, Calif Arts Coun, 96-97. *Bibliog:* Wesley Pulkka (auth), Sculptors explore, Albuquerque J, 7/28/96; Kathleen Whitney (auth), The body Exhausted, Sculpture, 10/97; Dona Meilach (auth), Direct Metal Sculpture, Schiffer Publ, rev 2nd ed, 2001; Susan Braunstein (auth), Luminous Art, Yale Press, 2004; and others. *Mem:* Int Sculpture Ctr. *Media:* All Media; Text, New Genre. *Mailing Add:* 3803 San Rafael Ave Los Angeles CA 90065

BAGGET, WILLIAM (CARTER), JR
PRINTMAKER, MURALIST
b Montgomery, Ala, Jan 12, 46. *Study:* Auburn Univ, BFA, 68, MFA, 73. *Work:* US Info Agency Embassy Collections, (worldwide); Montgomery Mus Fine Arts, Ala; Univ Miss Mus, Oxford; Vision Nouvelle, Paris, France; IDL Editions Lecureux-Possot, Paris, France; Lauren Rogers Mus Art, Laurel, Miss. *Comn:* Portraits, William Faulkner, Univ Miss, Oxford, 77, TK Mattingly & HM Hartsfield, Auburn Univ, 82; multicolor lithographs, Vision Nouvelle, Paris, 80 & Nahan Ed, New Orleans, 81 & 86; mural, Libr Hattiesburg, Miss, 95; mural, Winfred Wiser Hosp Women & Infants, Univ Miss, Med Ctr, Jackson, 98. *Exhib:* New Orleans Biennial, New Orleans Mus Art, 73; 107th Ann Exhib Am Watercolor Soc, Nat Acad Design, NY, 74; Rocky Mountain Nat Watermedia Exhib, Foothills Art Ctr, Golden, Colo, 74; East/West Echoes, Mokpo Nat Col, Korea, 85; Echo Returns, Dong Duk Art Gallery, Seoul, Korea, 86; solo exhib, Nahan Galleries (with catalog), NY, 91; Les Mois de L'Estampe a Paris, 97. *Teaching:* Asst prof design, Univ Miss, 73-76; assoc prof & coordr visual commun, Auburn Univ, 76-83; prof & chmn dept art, Univ Southern

Miss, 83-86, actg dean, 86-87, prof, 87-. *Awards:* Endowed Professorship, Auburn Univ, 82; Faculty Award of Excellence for Creative Research & Achievement, Univ S Miss, 97; Official Artist of the VIth USA Int Ballet Competition, Jackson, Miss, 98. *Bibliog:* William Baggett's mural for the New Library of Hattiesburg, Mississippi, Nat Forum Mag, spring 96; Southern Expressions (film), Miss Found Pub Broadcasting, 93-95; P Black (auth), Art in Mississippi, Univ Press Miss, 98. *Mem:* Am Inst Graphic Arts. *Media:* Lithography, Egg Tempera. *Mailing Add:* Univ Southern Miss Box 5033 Southern Sta Hattiesburg MS 39406

BAI, QIANSHEN
HISTORIAN, EDUCATOR
Study: Peking Univ, BA, 82; Political Sci, Rutgers Univ, MA, 90; Hist Art, Yale Univ, MA, 92; Hist Art, Yale Univ, MPhil, 93; Hist Art, Yale Univ, PhD, 96. *Pos:* Instr Asian art hist Western Mich Univ, Dept Art, 95, asst prof, Asian art hist, 96-97, Boston Univ, 97-; vis ast prof, Harvard Univ, Dept of Hist of Art and Archit, 2002. *Awards:* Fel Guggenheim Mem Found, 2004. *Mem:* Calligraphy Overview (mem adv bd 87), Canglang Calligraphy Soc (founding mem, 82-92). *Mailing Add:* Boston Univ Art Hist Dept 725 Commonwealth Ave Rm 302 Boston MA 02215

BAILEY, BARBARA ANN
PAINTER, INSTRUCTOR
b Kokomo, Ind, Mar 20, 28. *Study:* Art Inst Pittsburgh; Univ Hawaii; Univ Pittsburgh, BA(cum laude); Seton Hill Col, with Frank Webb & Foster Caddell. *Work:* Air Force Mus Art Collection, Dayton, Ohio; Hoyt Inst Fine Art, New Castle, Pa. *Exhib:* Three Rivers Art Festival, 72, 75 & 83; Hoosier Salon, Indianapolis, 72; Am Artists Prof League Exhib, NY, 74 & 75; Washington & Jefferson Nat Painting Exhib, Washington, Pa, 75 & 81; one-person show, Clarion State Col, Pa, 75 & Pa State Univ, 83; Mus Show Assoc Artists, Butler Inst Am Art, Youngstown, Ohio, 79; Aqueous Open Nat Show, 80 & 82-83; Hoyt Inst Fine Art, 84. *Teaching:* Instr oil painting, Boyce Community Col. *Awards:* Best of Show Award, Indiana Co Fair Art Exhib, Pa, 73; Mus Award, Greensburg Art Asn, Pa, 73; Painting Grant, Monroville Arts Coun, Pa. *Mem:* Pittsburgh Watercolor Soc; E Suburban Artists League, Pittsburgh; Pittsburgh Soc Artists. *Media:* Oil, Pastel. *Publ:* Auth, Create glowing florals in watercolor, Artist's Mag, 8/90

BAILEY, BARRY STONE
SCULPTOR, PAINTER
b High Point, NC, Oct 21, 1952. *Study:* ECarolina Univ, BS(art educ), 75, studies with Norman Keller, MFA(sculpture), 79; studies at Univ Ga, Cortona, Italy prog, 77. *Work:* New Orleans Mus Art; R J Reynolds World Trade Ctr, Winston Salem, NC; Westminster Corp. *Comn:* Welded steel kiosk, Pan Am Life, New Orleans, 82; New Orleans Palms, eight paintings on paper, Hotel Intercontinental, New Orleans, 82; Palm Shrine, Pontchartrain Beach, Contemp Arts Ctr, New Orleans, 83; Rain Pavilion, 2 kinetic bronze sculptures, Hist New Orleans collection, 84; 8' wall sculpture, Saratoga Bldg, Westminster Corp, New Orleans, 85. *Exhib:* Solo exhibs, Louisiana World Expo, New Orleans, 84 & Arthur Roger Gallery, New Orleans, La, 94; Perspectives, Cross Creek Gallery, Malibu, Calif, 87; Seven Sculptors, Alternative Mus, NY, 81; Contemp Arts Ctr, New Orleans, 87; 112 Greene Street, NY, 85; Chicago Int, Navy Pier, 87; Il Via Nazionale, Cortona, Italy, 96; Cole Pratt, New Orleans, 98. *Collection Arranged:* First Louisiana Sculpture Biennial, 81 & The New Louisiana Landscape, 81, Contemp Arts Ctr, New Orleans. *Pos:* Asst cur & supvr exhib artworks, La World Expo, 84. *Teaching:* Teaching fel art appreciation & 3D design, ECarolina Univ, Greenville, NC, 75-77; teaching asst sculpture, Univ Ga abroad, Cortona, Italy, 77; instr sculpture, La State Univ, Baton Rouge, 85, instr, Newcomb Sculpture Dept, Tulane Univ, formerly, assoc prof, currently. *Awards:* Ford Found Fel, 77; Southern Arts Fel, Nat Endowment Arts, 87. *Bibliog:* Roger Green (auth), Environmental influence on shape, Times-Picayune, 7/11/82; Marion Orr (auth), article, in: Gambit, Vol 5, No 37, 9/15/84; Roger Green (auth), Barry Bailey, Randy Ernst at Arthur Roger Gallery, Artnews, 12/86. *Mem:* Young Artists' Movement; Southeastern Col Art Asn; Contemp Arts Ctr. *Media:* Miscellaneous Media. *Dealer:* Cole Pratt Gallery 3800 Magazine St. *Mailing Add:* Tulane Univ Newcomb Art Dept New Orleans LA 70118

BAILEY, CLAYTON GEORGE
SCULPTOR, CERAMIST
b Antigo, Wis, Mar 9, 1939. *Study:* Univ Wis-Madison, BS, 61, MS, 62. *Hon Degrees:* MFA, Fat City Sch Fine Art, 03. *Work:* Oakland Mus, Calif; Mus Contemp Crafts, NY; Addison Gallery Am Art, Andover, Mass; Milwaukee Art Mus; San Francisco Mus Mod Art; and others; San Jose Mus of Art. *Comn:* Exec Teapot, Kohler Co, Kohler, Wis, 79; Sacramento Metrop Light Rail, 86. *Exhib:* Solo exhibs, Milwaukee Art Ctr, 61, Mus Contemp Crafts, NY, 63, MH DeYoung Mus, San Francisco, 75, Triton Mus, Santa Clara, Calif, 81, Monterey Mus Art, Calif, 84 & Henry Gallery, Seattle; Objects USA, Smithsonian traveling exhib, 69; A Decade of Am Ceramics, San Francisco Mus Mod Art, 73; A Century of Ceramics, Syracuse Mus, 79; Am Porcelain, Renwick Gallery, 80; Humor in Art, Los Angeles Co Mus, 81; Ceramic Funic From the Sixties, Ariz, State Univ, Tempe, 2004; and others. *Collection Arranged:* Port Costa Jews Harp Mus, 03. *Pos:* webmaster, www.claytonbailey.com. *Teaching:* Prof ceramics, Wis State Univ, Whitewater, 63-66; prof ceramics, Calif State Univ, Hayward, 68-96, chmn art dept, 79-81, prof emer, 96-. *Awards:* Artists Grants, Louis Comfort Tiffany Found, 63, Am Craftsmen Coun, 63 & Nat Endowment Arts, 79 & 90; Nominated for Nobel Prize, 76; and others. *Bibliog:* Tom Albright (auth), California Art, 86; Donhauser (auth), Am Ceramics, 78; Speight (auth), Hands in Clay, 94; DePaoli (auth) Happenings in the Circus of Life-The Work of Clayton Bailey, 01; Bay area Figuration, Susan Landamer, San Jose Mus of Art 2004. *Mem:* Hon Fel Nat Coun Educ in Ceramic Arts (dir at large, 78-80). *Media:* Clay, Metal. *Res:* Funk Art Practioner, Experimentel Jews Harp Maker. *Interests:* Guns, Jews Harps. *Collection:* San Jose Mus of Art, San Jose, CA. *Publ:* Coauth, My father is a sculptor, Jack & Jill Mag, 70; auth, Wonders of the World Catalog of Kaolithic Curiosities, Artist, 75. *Mailing Add:* PO Box 69 Port Costa CA 94569

BAILEY, MARCIA MEAD
PAINTER
b Hartford, Conn, Jan 10, 47. *Study:* Self-taught. *Exhib:* Henry Ward Ranger Ann Exhib, Nat Acad Design, NY, 80; 39th-45th Ann, Audubon Artists, NY, 81-87 & at Lever House, 86; 68th-74th Ann, Allied Artists Am, NY, 81-87; Dr Maury Leibovitz Exhib, NY, 86; Invitational Traveling Exhib, Allied Artists Am, 2003-05. *Awards:* S J Wallace Truman Prize, Nat Acad Design, New York, 80; Binney and Smith Liquitex Award, Audubon Artists, New York, 81; Gold Medal Honor, Allied Artists Am, 81. *Mem:* Audubon Artists; Allied Artists Am. *Media:* Oil. *Dealer:* Arts Exclusive Inc 690 Hopmeadow St Simsbury CT 06070. *Mailing Add:* 189 Wickham Rd Glastonbury CT 06033

BAILEY, OSCAR
PHOTOGRAPHER, EDUCATOR
b Barnesville, Ohio, July 23, 25. *Study:* Wilmington Col, Ohio, BA; Ohio Univ, Athens, MFA. *Work:* Int Mus Photog, George Eastman House, Rochester, NY; Hist of Photog Collection, Smithsonian Inst, Washington, DC; New Orleans Mus Art, La; Mus Fine Arts, St Petersburg, Fla; Boston Mus Fine Arts. *Exhib:* The Sense of Abstraction in Contemp Photog, Mus Mod Art, NY, 60; Photog USA, De Cordova Mus, Lincoln, Mass & George Eastman House, Rochester, NY, 62; Photog in Fine Arts, Metrop Mus Art, NY, 63 & 76; Four Directions in Photog, Albright-Knox Art Gallery, Buffalo, NY, 64; Photog in the 20th Century, Nat Gallery of Can, Ottawa, 67; Wider View, Int Mus Photog, George Eastman House, 72; Light & Lens, Hudson River Mus, Yonkers, NY, 73; Time & Transformation, Lowe Art Mus, Univ Miami, Fla, 75; Photo/Synthesis, Cornell Univ, Ithaca, NY, 76; The Contemp Am South Traveling Exhib, US Info Agency, SE Asia & Europe, 77; Extended Frame Traveling Exhib, Visual Studies Workshop, Rochester, 78. *Pos:* Artist-in-residence, Artpark, Lewiston, NY, summer 77. *Teaching:* Prof photog, State Univ NY, Buffalo, 58-69 & Univ SFla, Tampa, 69-85. *Awards:* Photog Fel Grant, Nat Endowment Arts, 76. *Bibliog:* John Canaday (auth), New Talent--1960, Art in Am, 60; J Kirk T Varneodoe (ed), Modern Portraits--The Self & Others, Columbia Univ, 76. *Mem:* Founding mem Soc Photog Educ. *Publ:* Coauth, Found Objects, State Univ NY, Buffalo, 65; ed, Silver Bullets, Dept Photog, Univ SFla, 72; contribr, Marcel DuChamp, Mus Mod Art, 73

BAILEY, RICHARD H
SCULPTOR
b Dover, Del, June 24, 1940. *Study:* Del Art Ctr, Wilmington; Art Students League; New Sch Soc Res, New York City; study in Carrara, Italy, Barre, Vt, Goddard Col, Plainfield, Vt; also with Jose DeCreeft, Lorrie Goulet & Leroy Smith. *Work:* Am Mus Natural Hist, NY; Univ Del; Newark Pub Libr; Blue Cross Blue Shield; Bell Tel, Del. *Comn:* Sculpture, comn by Reverend C Jones, 67; sculpture, comn by John Gilbert, 69; sculpture, St Polycarp's Roman Cath Church, 73; medallian, De Trust Co, 76; sculpture, 2nd Baptist Church, 84. *Exhib:* Int Exhib Sculpture, Carrara, Italy; one-man show, Springfield Mus Art, 67, Del Art Mus, 74 & 85 & Baltimore Art Mus, 78; Randall Galleries, NY; Nelson Rockefeller Collections; Peel Gallery Fine Art; Annapolis Marina Art Gallery. *Teaching:* Monitor, New Sch for Soc Res, 68; Rehoboth Art League, 72; YWCA, Newark, 73. *Awards:* Founders Award, Rehoboth Art League, Del, 71 & 75-80 & 86-87; Silvermine Guild Award Sculpture, 72 & 73. *Bibliog:* Del Today Mag, 77; VCR, Day with Bailey, 87; Television special, 10/86. *Mem:* Del Art Mus; Rehoboth Art League. *Media:* Stone; Miscellaneous Media. *Dealer:* Annapolis Marina Gallery Annapolis MD; Carspecken-Scott Gallery Wilmington DE. *Mailing Add:* RR 1 Symina Landing Rd Smyrna DE 19977-3429

BAILEY, WILLIAM
PAINTER
b Council Bluffs, Iowa, Nov 17, 30. *Study:* Univ Kans, Sch Fine Arts, 51; Yale Univ, BFA(Alice Kimball English Traveling Fel), 55, MFA, 57; with Josef Albers; Univ Ut, HHD (hon), 87. *Hon Degrees:* UNW Utah, Hon LHD, 87; Adelphi Univ, Hon OFA, 93; Pa Acad Fine Arts, Hon DFA. *Work:* Joseph Hirshhorn Mus; Mus Mod Art, NY; Hirshhorn Mus, Washington, DC; Chicago Art Inst; Neue Galerie Der Stadt, AA achen; Whitney Mus Am Art, NY; Art Mus San Francisco; Yale Univ Art Gallery; Nat Col Fine Arts, Washington, DC. *Exhib:* Galerie Claude Berward, Paris, 78 & 2000; Galleria Il Gabbiano, Rome, 80, 85, 93 & 97; one-man shows, Am Acad Rome, 84, Donald Morris Gallery, Birmingham, Mich, 91, Andre Emmerich Gallery, NY, 92, 94 & 96 & Betsy Senior Gallery, NY, 94; John Berggruen Gallery, San Francisco, Calif, 88; Alpha Gallery, Boston, 98; Crown Point Gallery, San Francisco, 98; Robert Miller Gallery, 99 & 2003; Palace of the Legion of Honor, San Francisco, 2003; Betty Cuningham Gallery, New York City, 2005. *Pos:* Vis artist, Am Acad Rome, 76. *Teaching:* Prof fine arts, Ind Univ, 62-69; vis prof, Univ Pa, 74; Andrew Carnegie vis prof, The Cooper Union, NY, 75; Meadows distinguished prof, Southern Methodis Univ, Dallas, 82-83; prof art, Yale Univ, 69-78, dean sch art, 74-75 Kingman Brewster prof, 78-95, Kingman Brester emer prof, 95-. *Awards:* Guggenheim Fel, 65; Ingram Merrill Found Grant, 75; Yale Arts Medal for Distinguished Contrib in Painting, 85. *Bibliog:* Mark Stevens (auth), Art Imitates Life: The Revival of Realism, Newsweek, 6/82; Giuliano Briganti & John Hollander (auths), William Bailey, Rizzoli International, 91; Richard Kalina (auth), William Bailey, Arts Mag, 5/91; Hilton Kramer (auth), Emmerichs Bailey show puts museums to shame, New York Observer, 3/21/94; Roger Kimball (auth), William Bailey Selected Works 1964-94, The New Criterion, 4/94; Robert Hughes (auth), Realist as Corn God, Time, 1/72; Mark Strand

(ed), William Bailey, Abrams, 87 & Art of the Real, Clarkson Potter Inc, 83. *Mem:* Am Acad & Inst Arts & Lett; Nat Coun Arts; Tiffany Found (bd dir, currently); Yaddo; Arch of Am Art (trustee); Nat Acad Design (assoc 83, acad, 94); Accademia Nazionale di San Luca, Rome; Accademia di Belle Arti Pietro Vanucci, Perugia. *Media:* Oil. *Dealer:* Betty Cuningham Gallery NY

BAILIN, DAVID
PAINTER, EDUCATOR
b SDak, July 3, 54. *Study:* Univ Colo, Boulder, BFA; Hunter Col, New York, MA. *Work:* Ark Arts Ctr Found Collection, Systematics Inc, Stephens Inc, Mitchell Law Firm, Little Rock, Ark; Klutznick Nat Jewish Mus, Washington; Palmer & Dodge Law Firm, Boston, Mass; Total Systems Serv, Columbus, Ga; Bingham, Dana & Gould, Boston, Mass. *Comn:* Portrait, pvt, 95; portrait, pvt comn, 98; Hot Springs Convention Ctr, Ark, 2000; Hot Springs Nat Park, Ark, 2001; Large scale drawing, Pvt Collection, Los Angeles, Calif, 2005. *Exhib:* One-man shows, Alice Bingham Gallery, Memphis, 88, Territorial Restoration, Little Rock, 89, Snow Fine Arts Gallery, Univ Cent Ark, Conway, 89, Chroma Gallery, Little Rock, 92, Univ Cen Ark, Conway, 96 & Univ Cent Art, Conway, 97 & Strauss Gallery, Ark Arts Ctr, 2000 & Rivermarket Arts Place, 2000, Koplin del Rio Gallery, Los Angeles, Calif, 2002, 2004; 52nd Ann Competition, Butler Inst Am Art, Youngstown, Ohio, 90; Delta Art competition, Ark Arts Ctr, 86-89, 91-93, 96-98, 99 & 2000; group shows, Edith Lambert Gallery, Santa Fe, NMex, 93 & Ark Artists Exhib, Collector Gallery, 93; Hiddened Concealed Revealed, Jewish Community Ctr, Pittsburgh, 97; Kuutznick Nat Jewish Mus, Washington, DC, 97; Adair Margo Gallery, El Paso, Tex, 2000; Portfolio One: Arkansas Masters, Ark Territorial Restoration, Little Rock, 2001; Gescheidle Gallery, Chicago, 2004; 20th Anniversary Celebration of Fellowship Program, Decorative Arts Mus, Little Rock, 2006; New Am Paintings, Open Studio Press, Boston; The Reality Show, Peninsula Fine Arts Ctr, VA, 2005; Art Chicago, Navy Pier; San Francisco Internat Art Expo. *Collection Arranged:* Alltel, Little Rock; Ark Arts Ctr Found Coll, Little Rock; Bingham Dana & Gould Law Offices, Boston; Palmer Dodge, Boston; Stephens Inc, Little Rock; Total Sys Servs, Columbus, Ga; Klutznick Nat Jewish Mus, Washington. *Pos:* Dir, Ark Arts Ctr Mus Sch, Little Rock, 86-96. *Teaching:* Studio & theory classes in painting, drawing, figure drawing & painting, art history & art appreciation; art hist, Hendrix Col, 2006-07; drawing, Univ Ctr Ark, Conway & Univ Ark, Littlerock, 97-2005. *Awards:* Mid-Am Arts Alliance/Nat Endowment Arts, 88; Nat Endowment Arts, 89; Mus Educator of the Year, Ark Art Educ Asn, 94. *Bibliog:* Arkansan Wins 41st Delta, Ark Times, 9/11/98; Art rev, Delta Has Attitude, 9/18/98; Lisa Broadwater (auth), Ark Democrat Gazette, 4/9/2000. *Mem:* Col Art Asn. *Media:* Oil, Charcoal. *Publ:* Designer & auth, The Studio Project, Jonsson Found, Dallas, Tex, 91; A Spectrum Reader, Aug House Publ, Little Rock, Ark, 91; Prophets, Parables, Paradoxes, catalog. *Dealer:* Koplin Del Rio Gallery, Tel: 310-657-9843. *Mailing Add:* 30 Chimney Sweep Ln Little Rock AR 72212-2083

BAKANOWSKY, LOUIS J
SCULPTOR, ARCHITECT
b Norwich, Conn, Oct 8, 30. *Study:* Yale Univ with Joseph Albers, 56; Syracuse Univ, BFA, 57; Harvard Univ, MArch, 61. *Work:* Harvard Univ; Syracuse Univ; Trinity Col; Addison Gallery Am Art; and others. *Comn:* Mem structure, Brunswick, Maine, 73; Mstislav Rostropovich residence, NY, 82. *Exhib:* View, 60 & Selection, 61, Inst Contemp Art, Boston, Mass; one-man show, Siembab Gallery, Boston, 60; Sculpture, DeCordova Mus, Lincoln, Mass, 64; New Eng Art Today, Boston, 65; Immanent Domains, Boston, NY & Philadelphia, 77; Decordova Mus, 87; Paul Pettrick Gallery, Cambridge, Mass, 2006. *Pos:* Archit, Cambridge Seven Assocs, Inc, 62-97. *Teaching:* Asst prof design, Cornell Univ, 61-62; prof design, Grad Sch Design, Harvard Univ, 63-75, prof visual studies, 75- & chmn, Dept Visual & Environ Studies, 75-85; dir, Carpenter Ctr Visual Arts, Harvard Univ, 83-90, Osgood Hooker prof visual arts emer, 98-. *Awards:* Sculpture Prizes, Boston Arts Festival, 58 & Providence Art Festival, 59. *Bibliog:* Sculpture of Louis J Bakanowsky, Connection Mag, 61; article, Kenchiku Bunka Mag, 71. *Mem:* Fel Am Inst Archit. *Media:* Mixed. *Mailing Add:* PO Box 388 Dublin NH 03444

BAKATY, MIKE
PAINTER, SCULPTOR
b Trenton, NJ, Aug 19, 36. *Study:* Miami-Dade Jr Col, Fla, AA, 64; Fla Atlantic Univ, BA, 65; Univ Ore, MFA, 69. *Work:* Colo State Univ, Ft Collins; Miami-Dade Community Col. *Comn:* Outdoor monument, Colo State Univ, 75. *Exhib:* Mike Bakaty, Paley & Lowe Inc, NY, 71-72; Painting & Sculpture Today, 1972, Indianapolis Mus Art, 72; NY Artists, Baltimore Mus Art, Md, 72; Here Comes Tomorrow, Owen Corning Fiberglass Bldg, NY, 73; Mellon Art Ctr, Wallingford, Conn, 74; Am Inst Archit, 74 & Henri Gallery, 74, Washington, DC; and many others. *Teaching:* Adj asst prof art, New York Univ, 71-74; asst prof painting, Fla Int Univ, Miami, 73; adj lectr sculpture, Fiorello LaGuardia Community Col, City Univ NY, 73-78, asst prof, 78-82. *Awards:* State-wide Touring Exhib, State of Fla, 66; Award for Sculpture, Ft Lauderdale Mus Arts, 66. *Bibliog:* Julia Busch (auth), A Decade of Sculpture, Assoc Univ Press, 74; Thelma Newman (auth), Plastics as Sculpture, Chilton Bks, 74; Marcia Tucker (auth), Tatoo, state of the art, Artforum, 5/81. *Media:* Fiberglass; Graphite. *Mailing Add:* 295 Bowery New York NY 10003-7104

BAKER, ALDEN
PAINTER
b New York City, Jan 10, 28. *Study:* Berkeley Secretarial Sch, Cert, 1948; Art Students League, studied with William Draper, Robert Hale & Robert Brackman, 1966-1969; Studied with Henry Hensche, Provincetown, Mass, summers 1967-1973; Studied with S B Baker & Grace Higgins (parents both prof artists). *Hon Degrees:* Master Pastelist, Pastel Soc Am. *Work:* Schering Plough Inc (2 pastels); Westminster Bank (2 pastels). *Exhib:* Xian & Nanchang China (invitation of Chinese Govt), 1997; Copley Gallery, Boston; Lincoln Center & Lever House, Manhattan; Queen, Bergen & Hammond Mus. *Pos:* Critiques chmn, Pastel Soc Am, 1990-2004; pres, Art Center NJ, 1998-2001. *Teaching:* Instr, Pastel Soc Am; instr portraiture, Yard Sch Art, Montclair, NJ. *Awards:* Mr & Mrs Andrew Griffuni Award, Pastel Soc Am Art, 1999; Diane Bernard Silver Medal, Hudson Valley Art Asn, 2004; Dianne Bernhard Gold Medal Award, Salmagundi Club; numerous First Place and Best Show awards. *Bibliog:* Ron Lister (auth), Drawing with Pastel; Charles Movalli (auth), A Conversation with Alden Baker, Am Artist Mag, 5/1995; Ruth Summer (auth), Alden Baker - Seeing True Color is Key to Relationships in Painting, Pastel J, Jan-Feb 2001. *Mem:* Art Center NJ, (first vpres, exhib chmn currently); Pastel Soc Asn (PSA), (corresp secy & critiques chmn, currently); Salmagundi Club; Hudson Valley Art Asn; Am Artists Prof League. *Media:* Pastels. *Publ:* Contribr bk, The Best of Pastel II, 1998; contribr art, Pastelgram, Pastel Soc Am, winter 2005. *Mailing Add:* 49 Druid Hill Rd Summit NJ 07901

BAKER, BLANCHE
SCULPTOR, INSTRUCTOR
b New York, NY. *Study:* Overseas Sch Rome, 1974; Wellesley Col 1978; Parsons Sch Design, with Bruno Lucchessi, 1980. *Work:* Grants Pass Mus Art, Eugene, Ore; Tibet House Mus & Gallery, New York City; Frederick Douglass Mus, Washington, DC. *Comn:* mural, Westchester Coun Arts, 99; sculpture, Tibet House, New York City, 2000; scuplture, comn by Frederick Douglass Mus, Washington, DC, 2001. *Exhib:* One-woman shows Stephen Gang Gallery, New York City, 97, River Gallery, Irvington, NY, 97-98, Gallery at 678, New York City, 98, Westchester Arts Coun, White Palins, NY, 99, Grants Pass Mus Art, Eugene, Ore; group shows at Nat Sculpture Soc, New York City, 2000, The Pen & Brush Club, New York City, 2000, Catharine Lorillard Wolfe Foun, New York City, 2000. *Awards:* Best in Show, Pound Ridge Mus, NY, 98; Leonard Meiselman Award, Pen & Brush Club, New York City, 99; Agop Agopoff Mem Award, Salmujundi Club, New York City, 2000. *Bibliog:* Jenifer Stern (auth), Woman Wins Honorable Mention in War Memorial Design, The Enterpries, 8/18/95; Kirsten A Conover (auth), Art Sparks Dialogue on Race & Religion, The Christian Sci Monitor, 8/14/97; Helaine Chersonsky (auth), Art Show at Museum, Daily Courier, Grants Pass, Ore, 8/7/2000. *Mem:* Jenifer Stern (auth), Woman Wins Honorable Mention in War Memorial Design, The Enterprise, 8/18/95; Hudson Valley Art Asn (sculpture chiar, 98-2001); Catharine Lorillard Wolfe Found (chair annual dinner, 99); Pen & Brush Club; Am Artists Prof League. *Media:* Bronze. *Publ:* illustr, Inkwell Mag, winter 99. *Dealer:* Larry Leckerman The Sculpture Showcase 156 S Main St New Hope PA 18938. *Mailing Add:* 2501 Palesade Ave Bronx NY 10463

BAKER, BLANCHE See Baker, Blanche

BAKER, CORNELIA DRAVES
PRINTMAKER, PAINTER
b Woodbury, NJ, Mar 2, 29. *Study:* Ohio Wesleyan Univ, 47-50; Kunst Stadel Inst, Ger, 50; Univ St Louis, Florence Italy, 92. *Work:* Bergen Mus Art & Sci, Paramus; Berkeley Internat Skiing Fine Arts and Graphics Collection. *Comn:* Oil painting, comn by Paul Nelson, Wyckoff, NJ, 86; gouache work, comn by Jane Gut, Wayne, NJ, 87; monoprint, Stratton Travel Inc, Franklin Lakes, 90. *Exhib:* Solo exhibs, Ramapo Col Gallery, Mahwah, NJ, 86, Sekaikan Gallery, Tokyo, 90, Shimada Mus, Kumamoto, Japan, 90, Presbyterian Church Gallery, Franklin Lakes, NJ, 92 & Bergen Mus Art & Sci, Paramus, NJ, 93, L'Ateliet Inc Gallery, 94, NY Theol Sem, 96, The Gallery Franklin Lakes, 97, Off Congressman SR Rothman, Hackensack, NJ, 97, Lee Hecht Harrison, Paramus, NJ, 98, Willows Cafe, Ramsey NJ, 2000; Bergen Mus Art & Sci, Paramus, NJ, 88 & 90; Nat Asn Women Artists, traveling exhib, India, 89; 100 Years/100 Works, Nat Asn Women Artists, traveling exhib, USA, 89-90; 14th Ann Small Works, S Washington Sq E Gallery, NY, 90; Barn Gallery, Ringwood State Park, NJ, 92. *Pos:* dir The Gallery Franklin Lakes, NJ, 88-97, Marsella Geltman Gallery, New Milford, NJ, 93-96. *Awards:* Women Making Hist in Arts Award, Bergen Co, NJ, 93; Artist showcase award Manhattan Art Internat'l 93; Crabbie Award, Art Calendar, 94; Gold Prize, Riso Edn Found, Japan, 97; Artist Profile Award in the Manhattan Arts Internat'l Her Story Competition, 2003. *Bibliog:* A clearer picture at Bergen Museum, Bergen Record, 1/3/88; At the Bergen Museum Art Show--less is more, Bergen Record, 12/7/89; Monoprints, Nishinippon Simbum, 6/5/90. *Mem:* Nat Asn Women Artists (nominating vchmn, 90-91, chair, printmaking jury, 92-94); Salute to Women in Arts Inc (pres, 89-90); Ringwood Manor Asn of Arts (dir, Ann exhib, 88 & 89); Community Arts Asn (prog chmn, 87); Printmaking Coun of NJ. *Media:* Printmaker, Mixed Media. *Interests:* Travel, mentor artists, organize fund raisers. *Collection:* Pears monoprint, permanent collection of Bergen Mus of Arts & Science; Rendezvous, gouache painting & limited edition print are a part of the Berkeley International skiing & Fine arts col in New Hartford, CT. *Mailing Add:* 293 Green Ridge Rd Franklin Lakes NJ 07417

BAKER, DIANNE ANGELA
ASSEMBLAGE ARTISTS, SCULPTOR
b Buffalo, New York. *Study:* Syracuse Univ, Florence Study, 1964; Syracuse Univ, BA, 1965; State Univ Buffalo, NY, MS, 1969; State Univ at Buffalo, NY, Graduate, 1973-76. *Work:* Charles Rand Penny Collection, Lockport, NY; The Ashford Hollow Found, East Ohio, NY; Roswell Park Cancer Inst, Bufalo, NY; Ridized Metals Corp, Buffalo, NY; Gilda's Club Western New York, Buffalo. *Comn:* Woven/Assemblage Hanging, Econo Lodge Motel, Erie, Pa, 1991; Mixed Media Wall Sculptures, Spikes Restaurant, Buffalo, NY, 1992; Wall Assembly, Wis Arts Bd, Janesville, Wis, 1994; Assemblage, Park Sch, Buffalo, NY, 1998; Environmental Weaving, Lancaster Public Sch, Lancaster, NY, 1978. *Exhib:* The Libr at D Youville Col, Buffalo, NY, 2000; Jewish Community Ctr of Greater Buffalo, Buffalo, NY, 2001; Soc for Contemp Craft, One Mellon Ctr, Pittsburgh, Pa, 2002; Underground Gallery, Ellicottville, NY, 2003; Craft Art Western NY, (Juror: Mark Leach), Burchfield-Penney Art Ctr, Buffalo, NY,

2004; Refuse, Reuse, Redeux, Castellani Art Mus, Niagara Univ, NY, 2003; Refuse, Reuse, Redeux, Castellani Satellite Art Mus, Niagara Falls, NY, 2005; Lost & Found, Nicholas School Gallery, Buffalo, NY, 2006; Prima Materia, McMaster Mus Art, Hamilton, Ontario Can, 2006; Dianne Baker: Sculptor Discover Artworks, Mayville, NY, 2006. *Teaching:* Artist in residence, Buffalo Pub Sch, NY; artist in residence, Lancaster Pub Sch, NY; artist in residence, Park Sch, Amherst, NY. *Awards:* First prize, Tonawanda Art Assoc, Mem Exhib, 1985; Publ work in Nat juried quarterly, Art Calendar Mag, 2000; Honorable mention, WWY Regional, Art Dialogue Gallery, 2003; Honorable mention, Art Dialogue Gallery, 19th Ann Valentine's Show, 2006. *Mem:* Buffalo Soc of Artists; Western NY Artists Group; Collectors Gallery of Albright, Knox Art Gallery, 1978-; Artists in Buffalo, NY; Burchfield, Penney Art Ctr. *Publ:* Artist Beat, Arts Council of Buffalo, 1989; Windrush Gallery, The Republican, Oakland, MD, 1999; Louis Continelli, Unfamiliar Landmarks, The News, Buffalo, NY, 2001. *Mailing Add:* 67 Cleveland Ave Buffalo NY 14222

BAKER, ELIZABETH C
ART EDITOR, CRITIC
b Boston, Mass. *Study:* Bryn Mawr Col, BA; Radcliffe Col, MA. *Pos:* From assoc ed to managing ed, Art News, 63-73; ed, Art in Am, 73-. *Teaching:* Instr art hist, Boston Univ, 58-59, Wheaton Col, Norton, Mass, 60-61 & Sch of Visual Arts, New York, 68-74. *Mailing Add:* 575 Broadway New York NY 10012

BAKER, JILL WITHROW
COLLAGE ARTIST, PAINTER
b Ilion, NY, Oct 12, 42. *Study:* Baylor Univ, BA, 64; Fla State Univ, with Karl Zerbe; Acad di Belle Arti, Florence, Italy, with Silvio Lofreddo; Pratt Inst, MFA, 81. *Work:* Merton Collection, Bellarmine Col, Louisville, Ky; Am Nat Bank, St Thomas Aquinas Chapel, Col Educ Collection, Western Ky Univ, Bowling Green; Goethe House, NY. *Comn:* James Milliken Collection. *Exhib:* Solo shows, US Info Serv, Seoul, Korea, 77, Ward-Nasse Gallery, NY, 80, Long Island Univ, Brooklyn, 81 & Baylor Univ, Waco, Tex, 81; Pratt Alumni Invitational, 85; SOHO/20, NY, 86; Installations One, Los Angeles, 91; Artists Space, 92; Sumner Reg Med Ctr, 10/98. *Collection Arranged:* Target LA, Pasadena, Calif, 83; Thinking Eye Gallery, Calif, 85; Student Art Show, Calif State Univ, Northridge, 86; SPARC Gallery, Venice, Calif, 86. *Pos:* Mem bd dir, Ward-Nasse Gallery, 76-81; western corresp ed, Women Artists News, 84-88; mem, Graphic Arts Coun, Los Angeles Co Mus Art, 85-89; regional vpres, Artists Equity (nat); proprietor & owner, Winchester Cottage Gallery; pres, ART-Sumner. *Teaching:* Instr, adult painting community educ prog, Bowling Green, Ky, 76-81; teaching asst, Pratt Inst, Brooklyn, NY, 78-79; instr, Pierce Col, Woodland Hills, Calif, 84-85, Gallatin Civic Ctr, 96-98 & Nossi Col Art, Goodlettesville, Tenn, 98; istr vis arts, prehistoric, medieval & current art hist Univ Phoenix, Nashville, 2003-. *Awards:* Achievement Award, Bank Am, State Calif, 60; Achievement Trophy, 60; scholar, Southern Women's Club, 63; Awards, Coca Cola Art Show, Elizabethtown, NJ, 78, LA'84, Brand Galleries, 84 & Window to the Future, Scottsdale, Ariz, 84 & Pratt Alumni Invitational, 85. *Bibliog:* Article, Courier-J, Louisville, Ky, 8/17/80; article, Artspeak, NY, 2/4/82 & Gallatin News Examiner, 10/16/98, 3/5/05. *Mem:* Women Artists' Coalition; Los Angeles Visual Artists Guild (mem bd dir, 84-); NY Chap Artists Equity (pres, 94-96); founding mem ART-Sumner (pres, 2000-); Gallatin Arts Coun (pres, 2003-04). *Media:* All, digital. *Specialty:* Fine arts, paintings, prints, digital art. *Interests:* Dancing, swing, ballroom & hustle. *Collection:* Goethe House, NY; Western Ky, University of Education, Bowling Green, KY; Perdue Univ, Lafayette, Ind; Multiple Private Collections & Public Collections. *Publ:* Illusr, The More Things Change, Whippoorwill Press, 71; Songs of Bloody Harlan, Westburg Asn Press, 75; Spring of Violets, 76, Under the Sign of the Waterbearer, 76 & I Knew A Woman, 77, Love St Bks. *Dealer:* Winchester Cottage Gallery. *Mailing Add:* PO Box 452 Gallatin TN 37066

BAKER, KENNETH
CRITIC, WRITER
b Weymouth, Mass, May 3, 46. *Study:* Bucknell Univ, BA, 68. *Pos:* Art critic, Boston Phoenix, Mass, 72-85; sr art critic, San Francisco Chronicle, Calif, 85-. *Teaching:* Adj fac art hist, RI Sch Design, Providence, 79-81 & Boston Col, Chestnut Hill, Mass, 79-85. *Awards:* Distinguished Newspaper Art Criticism Award, Manufacturers Hanover Trust & Art-World, 85; Nominated for Non-fiction Award by Bay Area Book Reviewers Assoc, 90. *Mem:* Int Asn Art Critics; Nat Book Critics Circle. *Res:* Studies in aesthetics, history & criticism of Minimal art. *Publ:* Auth, Giorgio Morandi: Redemption through painting, Des Moines Art Ctr, 81; Julian Opie, Kôlnische Kunstverein, 84; Second generation: Mannerism or momentum & Report from London: The Saatchi museum opens, 85, Art Am; Flashes of understatement: Elmer Bischoff, Artforum, 86; auth, Minimalism, Abbeville Press, 89. *Mailing Add:* c/o San Francisco Chronicle San Francisco CA 94119

BAKER, NANCY SCHWARTZ
PAINTER, PRINTMAKER
b Brooklyn, NY, July 30, 51. *Study:* Sch Visual Arts, New York, BFA, 1975; int study, art residency, Studio Camnitzer, Valdottavo, Italy, 1994-99; art residence, Casa de Mateus, Vila Real, Portugal, 2001. *Work:* NC Mus Art, Raleigh; Bellevue Hosp, NY; Glaxo-Wellcome Corp, Research Triangle Park, NC; TRW Corp, Cleveland; Reynold Industries, Winston Salem, NC. *Exhib:* One-woman shows, Redemptive Spirit, Artspace, Raleigh, NC, 1996, The Hazards of Living, Raleigh Contemp Gallery, 1997, Fed Up, Artspace, 1998, Covered in Thirty Days, The Tire Shop, Raleigh, 1999, Devolution, The Tire Shop, 1999, Alien Stories, Manbites Dog Theatre, Durham, NC, 2000 & The Tire Shop, 2001, Fenómenos de Natureza, Casa de Mateus, Vila Real, Portugal, 2001, Alien Alegations, Artspace, 2002 & 1708 Gallery, Richmond, Va, 2003; Of the Land, Lowe Gallery, Duke Univ Mus Art, Durham, NC, 1997; Valentines, The Tire Shop, 1998; Rage and Resolution, Denver Jewish Ctr, 1999 & Hebrew Union Col, NY, 1999; Deconstructing Santa, The Tire Shop, 2000; When Toys Bite Back, Lump Gallery, Raleigh, 2000; North Carolina Artists Exhibition, NC Mus Art, Raleigh, 2000; A Sense of Place, East Carolina Univ, Greeneville, NC, 2000; North Carolina Fellowship Exhibition, 2001, Wake Forest Univ, Winston Salem, NC, 2001. *Pos:* art critic, Spectator Mag, 96; artist in residence, Cary Acad, NC; owner, dir, The Tire Shop, Raleigh, 97-. *Awards:* Artist Project grant, United Arts Coun, 1997; Visual Arts Fel awrd, NC Arts Coun, 2000; New Works grant, NC Arts Coun, 2001. *Bibliog:* Huston Paschal (auth), NC Mus Artists Exhibn (catalog), 2000; Lissa Brennan (auth), Alien invasion, The Independent, Durham, NC, 2002; Luis Camnitzer (auth), Me alien, You Local (catalog) Alien Allegaions, 2003. *Media:* Acrylic, Oil; Miscellaneous Media. *Dealer:* Joe Rowand Somerhill Gallery 3 Eastgate East Franklin St Chapel Hill NC 27514. *Mailing Add:* 327 Lochside Dr Cary NC 27511

BAKKE, KAREN LEE
ASSEMBLAGE ARTIST, CALLIGRAPHER
b Everett, Wash, Nov 21, 1942. *Study:* Univ Wash; Syracuse Univ, NY, BFA(design), 67, MFA(design), 69. *Work:* Everson Mus, Syracuse. *Comn:* Extensive calligraphy, Syracuse Univ. *Exhib:* Two-person show, Fabric Forms, Kirkland Art Ctr, Clinton, NY, 76; Rubberstamp Invitational, Lightworks Gallery, Syracuse, 81; Calligraphy & Rubberstamps, Everson Mus, 82; Clothing, The Put-On and the Poor Man's Art, Am Home Econ Asn NY State Convention, 82; Suspended in Media, You Are What You See, Cornell Univ, 82; Int Calligraphy Today, Women in Design, 83. *Pos:* Asst cur, Syracuse Univ Art Collection, 67-69; vis artist soft sculpture, NY State Summer Sch of Arts, Fredonia & Chautauqua Inst. *Teaching:* Assoc prof & chairperson dept environ arts, Syracuse Univ, 69-. *Awards:* Hancock Purchase Prize & One-Person Show Award, Cent NY Regional, Everson Mus, 71. *Mem:* Am Crafts Coun; Soc Scribes; Handweavers Guild Am; Women in Design. *Media:* Fabric, Metal. *Publ:* Auth, Sewing Machine as a Creative Tool, Prentice-Hall, 76. *Mailing Add:* 1136 Cumberland Ave Syracuse NY 13210-3413

BAKOIAN, LAUREN
Study: Maine Col Art, BFA (printmaking), 92; Washington Univ, MFA, 94. *Pos:* Dir Lori Bookstein Fine Art, NY, currently. *Teaching:* Vis artist in various NY City public schools. *Mailing Add:* Lori Bookstein Fine Art 3rd Floor 37 West 57th St New York NY 10019

BALABAN, DIANE
PAINTER
b Ogden, Utah, Nov 29, 35. *Study:* With Robert E Wood, Charles Reid, Randal Lake & Valoy Eaton. *Comn:* Painting, St Mary Catholic Church, Park City, Utah, 83; Painting ser, Stein Erikson Lodge, Deer Valley, Utah, 84. *Exhib:* San Diego Art Inst, Calif, 75; Sun Valley Western Art, Idaho, 79; Utah Watercolor Soc, Salt Lake City, 80; one-woman show, Kimball Art Ctr, Park City, Utah; Eccles Art Ctr Invitational, Ogden, Utah. *Pos:* Pres, Park City Artist Asn, 81-83; dir, Kimball Art Ctr, 83-; lectr & judge various art groups. *Teaching:* Instr watercolor workshops, Kimball Art Ctr, Park City, currently. *Awards:* First Place Watercolor, Kimball Art Centennial Exhib, Park City Gallery Asn, 84. *Mem:* Utah Watercolor Soc; Park City Artist's Asn. *Media:* Watercolor, Oil. *Mailing Add:* 38025 S Eagle Dr Tucson AZ 85739-1109

BALAHUTRAK, LYDIA BODNAR
PAINTER
b Cleveland, Ohio, May 6, 51. *Study:* Kent State Univ, BS (art educ), 73; Corcoran Sch Art, 76-77; George Washington Univ, MFA (painting), 77. *Work:* George Washington Univ, Washington, DC; Univ Houston, Transco Energy Co & Baylor Col Med, Houston; Hoyt Inst Fine Arts, New Castle, Pa. *Exhib:* Nat Small Painting & Drawing Competition, Col of Mainland, Texas City, Tex, 83; Solo shows, Univ Houston, 83 & 85, Graham Gallery, Houston, Tex, 88, Galveston Arts Ctr, 93, Dallas Visual Arts Ctr, 95 & Nave Mus Art, 96; Sept Int Competition, Alexandria Mus, La, 84; Hoyt Nat Drawing & Painting Show, Hoyt Inst Fine Arts, 84; 47th Ann Nat Midyear Show, Butler Inst Am Art, 84; Tex Visions Juried traveling show, Transco Art Gallery, Abilene Fine Arts Mus & McAllen Int Mus, 86; Frivolity & Mortality, traveling exhib, 87-89; Int Painters Symp Exhib, Kiev, Ukraine, 93. *Pos:* Art exhibs coordr, Univ Houston, Clear Lake City, 81-82. *Teaching:* Instr drawing & painting, San Jacinto Col, North City, 77-79; lectr drawing 2-D design, Univ Houston, Clear Lake City, 79- 82, 86-87 & 93; guest lectr art, Univ Pittsburgh, 83; vis guest artist, Inst Art, Lviv, Ukraine, 91. *Awards:* La Napoule Art Found Grant, 85; Irex Grant International Research & Exchange, 90; Cult Arts Coun Houston Visual Art Award, 93. *Bibliog:* Donna Tennant (auth), art rev, Houston Chronicle, 12/14/79; Jill Kyle (auth), Lydia Bodnar-Balahutrak: Portrait of a Figure Painter, In Art, 6/85; Robin Longman (auth), Emerging Artists, Am Artist, 8/85; Susan Chadwick (auth), rev, Houston Post, 6/88; Michael Crespo (auth), Watercolor Day By Day, Watson-Guptill, 87. *Media:* Oil, Paint. *Dealer:* Edith Baker Gallery 2404 Cedar Springs Dallas TX 75201. *Mailing Add:* 2528 Dryden Houston TX 77030

BALANCE, JERRALD CLARK
PAINTER
b Ogden, Utah, July 20, 1944. *Study:* Univ Utah, Salt Lake City; mainly self-taught. *Work:* Chrysler Mus at Norfolk, Va; Atlantic City Fine Arts Ctr & Atlantic City Munic Bldg Collection, NJ; Coopers & Lybrand Corp, Washington, DC; US State Dept, Washington, DC; Sperry Corp, Reston, Va. *Exhib:* 19th Area Exhib, Corcoran Gallery Art, Washington, DC, 74; 14th Md Biennial, Baltimore Mus Art, 74; Five Am Abstract Painters, Northeastern Univ Gallery, Boston, 77; Best of NY--A Survey, Root Art Ctr, Hamilton Col, Clinton, 77; one man shows, Genesis Gallery, NY, 78-79 & US State Dept, Washington, DC; Art in the Embassies Prog, Madrid, Spain & Bangkok, Thailand, 78-80. *Awards:* Nat Endowment Grant, Va Commission Arts & Humanities & Emerson Gallery, 76; Washington Cherry Blossom Festival Nat Art Competition

Award in Sculpture, 72. *Bibliog:* Joe Mayer (producer), Beyond Abstract Expressionism: Balance & Chelimsky, Prince Georges Community Col. *Media:* Oil, Enamel; Plastic. *Publ:* Contribr, Washington artists, Artists Equity, 72. *Dealer:* Harriet Lebish Gallery 41 E 57th St New York NY 10022; Jane Hasley Gallery 406 Seventh St Washington DC. *Mailing Add:* 30 Steven Ct Gaithersburg MD 20877-3424

BALAS, IRENE
PAINTER
b Budapest, Hungary, Feb 28, 28; US citizen. *Study:* Acad Fine Arts, Vienna, Austria, MA, 48; studied art therapy with Hans Hoffman & psychiatry with Karl Kaufman. *Work:* Mus Luis Angel Arango, Bogota, Columbia; Mus Vatican, Rome, Italy; Rockefeller Collection, Henry Ford Collection, NY; Mus Atelier; Attila Matyas. *Comn:* Portrait of the Pres, comn by Victor Paz Estenssoro, La Paz, Bolivia, 55; Bolivia Pintoresca, comn by Ger Embassador, La Paz, Bolivia, 55; religious abstracts, Mus el Minuto de Dios, Bogota, Columbia, 67; Birth of Emerald, Banco de Colombia, Bogota, Colombia, 72; Expedition Hungary-USA, Hungarian Air Force, 90; and others. *Exhib:* En Honor del Presidente, Mus Victor Paz, La Paz, Bolivia, 55; solo show, Luis Angel Arango, Bogota, Columbia, 60; South Am, Ed Nacional, Madrid, Spain, 65; The Beauty of Am, Casements, Ormond Beach, Fla, 82; Space, Mus Hist & Art, Palm Beach, Fla, 89; Wings of Ambitions, Art Mus, Budapest, Hungary, 90; and others. *Teaching:* Instr bellas artes, Santiago de Chile, 53-54; Universidad La Javeriana, Bogota, Colombia, 69-71. *Awards:* Nat Prize, Austrian Painters, Kunstlerhaus, 48; Bronze Medal, Salon Oficial, Mus de Bellas Artes, 51; Gold Medal, Concepcion, Univ Medicin, 56. *Bibliog:* Gladys Ostrom (auth), Irene Balas Painter of Presidents, Ann Fabe Isaacs, 77; Tom Elliot (auth), Petit Museum of Irene Balas (film), Fla, 77-78; Lizette Alvarez (auth), Little museum, Miami Herald, 88. *Media:* Oil, Acrylic. *Publ:* Auth, Exposicion del mes, El Correo; Notas de arte, Aramen Dia, 67; The best exhibition; Irene Balas, Andean Times, 69; Irene Balas communicates through her art, Morning J, 82; Artist profile, Directions, 88. *Mailing Add:* 1621 Collins Ave Apt 907 Miami Beach FL 33139

BALAS, JACK J
PAINTER, PHOTOGRAPHER
Study: Sch Archit, Ill Inst Technol, Chicago, 73-74; Inst Design, Ill Inst Technol, Chicago, 74-75; Salzburg Col, Austria, 76; Northern Ill Univ, DeKalb, BA, BFA(sculpture, studio), 78, MA(sculpture), 80, MFA(sculpture), 81. *Work:* San Francisco Mus Art, Calif; US W Commun, Denver, Colo; Hewlett Packard, Fort Collins, Colo. *Exhib:* The New Narratology - Examining the Narrative in Image/Text Art (traveling exhib), Artspace Annex, San Francisco, Calif, 89; Personal/Political: Sexuality Self-Defined, Art Inst Chicago, 90; Rodeo in Fact & Fantasy, Philbrook Mus Art, Tulsa, Okla, 91; Out of Bounds: The Word Becomes Art, Scottsdale Ctr Arts, Ariz, 92; Focus on Colorado/The Front Range: Jack Balas, Wes Hempel & Scott Chamberlin, Aspen Art Mus, Colo, 94; solo shows, Univ Wyo Art Mus, Laramie, 96, Univ Alaska, Anchorage, 97 & Robinson Gallery, Denver, Colo, 98, Mus of the Southwest, Midland, Tex; group exhibs, Egypt of the Mind, Denver Colo, 98, Conceptualisticationism, Brooklyn, NY, 99, The Image of Text, Harrisonburg, Va, 2000, London Biennale, London, Eng. *Teaching:* Artist in Residence, Art Dept, Skidmore Col, NY, 2000. *Awards:* First Place Short Fiction Award, WestWord Mag, Denver, Colo, 89; Creative Fel Photog, Colo Coun Arts & Humanities, 91; Individual Fel Painting, Nat Endowment Arts, Washington, 95. *Bibliog:* Mary Voelz Chandler (auth), Write your own story to go with these pieces, Rocky Mountain News, Denver, Colo, 9/26/93; Hart Hill (auth), Text and texture, WestWord, Denver, Colo, 10/6/93; Marilynne Mason (auth), Not quite on the map: magic & art, Colo Expression, Denver, winter 93. *Media:* Acrylic, Oil. *Publ:* Contribr, Today I drove along the Rio Grande, The Paris Rev, New York, No 120, 121-129, fall 91; The New Censorship, Denver, Colo, Vol 4, No 1, 4/93; High Performance, No 61, 38-39, spring 93; Art & the Law, 20th Annual Exhibition (exhib catalog), West Publ Corp, Minneapolis, Minn, 95. *Dealer:* Robischon Gallery 1740 Wazee St Denver CO 80202. *Mailing Add:* 825 Fourth St PO Box 929 Berthold CO 80513

BALAY, FELICIE
ART DEALER
b New York, NY, June 14, 40. *Study:* New York Univ. *Pos:* Pres, Felicie Inc, New York, 65- & FKH Editions, New York, 74-75. *Specialty:* Works by Joseph Correale, Ralph Fasanella, Oliver Johnson and others

BALCIAR, GERALD GEORGE
SCULPTOR
b Medford, Wis, Aug 28, 42. *Work:* Denver Zoo, Colo; Nat Cowboy Mus, Oklahoma City; Beaver Creek Resort, Avon, Colo; Oklahoma City Zoo; Buffalo Bill Historical Center, Cody, Wyo. *Comn:* Challenge (bronze elk monument), Westminster Sculpture Garden, Westminser, Colo; Centennial (bronze moose monument), Loyal Order of Moose, Mooseheart, Ill; In High Places (bald eagle monument), Univ NTex, Denton, Tex; Bull, Elk, Cow & Two Calves, Beaver Creek Resort, Avon, Colo; Pride (marble cougar), Nat Mus Wildlife Art, Jackson, Wyo; Family Pride (bronze lions), Okla City Zoo, Okla. *Exhib:* Nat Acad Design, NY, 77, 86, 90 & 92; Nat Sculpture Soc, NY, 77-96 & 2002; Allied Artists Am, NY, 77-96 & 2002; Nat Acad Western Art, Cowboy Hall Fame, Oklahoma City, 78, 84 & 2006; Artists of Am, Denver, 85-98. *Awards:* Prix de West & Gold Medal, Nat Acad Western Art, 85; Ellin Speyer Prize, Nat Acad Design, 86; People's Choice Award, Silver Medal, Nat Acad Western Art, 90. *Mem:* Nat Sculpture Soc; Soc Animal Artists; Allied Artist Am; Northwest Rendezvous. *Media:* Marble, Bronze. *Mailing Add:* 12501 Roundup Rd Parker CO 80138

BALDAIA, PETER JOSEPH
CURATOR, DIRECTOR
b Providence, RI, Sept 12, 53. *Study:* RI Col, Providence, BA, 78; Brown Univ, Providence, grad studies, 79; Grad Sch, Boston Univ, Mass, MA(art hist), 82 & dipl(mus studies), 83. *Collection Arranged:* Bunny Harvey, Fuller Mus Art, Brockton, Mass, 88; Henry Schwartz, Fuller Mus Art, Brockton, Mass, 90; Subjective Intentions, Rockford Art Mus, Ill, 93; Harold Gregor, Rockford Art Mus, Ill, 93; Roland Miller: Abandoned in Place (auth, catalog), Huntsville Mus Art, Ala, 94; Breaking the Mold: New Directions in Glass (auth, catalog), Huntsville Mus Art, Ala, 96; Embracing Beauty: Aesthetic Perfection in Contemporary Art (auth, catalog), Huntsville Mus Art, Ala, 97. *Pos:* Cur, Fuller Mus Art, Brockton, Mass, 86-91; cur exhibs & collections, Rockford Art Mus, Ill, 92-94; chief cur, Huntsville Mus Art, Ala, 94-. *Mem:* Am Asn Mus; Southeastern Mus Conf. *Publ:* Auth, Towards Transcendence: The Works of Nan Tull (exhib catalog), Akin Gallery, Boston, Mass, 91; Wrestling with Hist: Trachtman, Erony and the Theme of the Holocaust (exhib catalog), Newton Arts Ctr, Newtonville, Mass, 92; From hand to heart: The art of the American miniature portrait, Am Art Rev, 2-3/96; Breaking the Mold: New Directions in Glass (exhib, catalog), Huntsville Mus Art, Ala, 96; Will Berry: Completely Hatched into Light (exhib catalog essay), Huntsville Mus Art, Ala, 97. *Mailing Add:* c/o Huntsville Mus Art 300 Church St S Huntsville AL 35801

BALDASSANO, VINCENT
PAINTER
b State Island, NY. *Study:* Wagner Col., BA, 1964; Univ of Ore, MFA, 1966; State Univ NY, Painting Fel, 1969-1973. *Work:* Housatonic Mus. of Art, Bridgeport, Conn; Hammond Mus., North Salem, NY; Savannah Col. of Art & Design, Savannah, GA; Sacred Heart Univ. Brigeport, CT; The Children's Mus. of the Arts, New York City. *Exhib:* The Flower in Am Art, Butler Art Inst, Youngstown, Ohio, 1990; Meditations, Hamond Mus, N Salem, NY, 1996 & 2005; Vincent Baldassano, Stamford Mus, Stamford, Conn, 1997; The Energists, Mus of Art, Cagnes Sur Mer, France, 1998; Housatonic Community Col (Faculty Exhib), Housatonic Mus of Art, Bridgeport, Conn, 1998, 2000. *Pos:* Managing Dir, Northern Westchester Ctr for the Arts, Mt Kisco, NY, 1995-1996; Dir, Silvermine Guild Art Gallery, New Canaan, Conn, 1996-2000; Exec Dir, Conn Graphic Arts Ctr, Norwalk, Conn, 1999-2000. *Teaching:* Instr, Silvermine Sch of Art, 1991-2001; Instr, Nat Academy of Design, NYC, 2002-; Instr, Gateway Community Col, 2003-; tchr, Nat Acad Sch Fine Arts, New York City; art history, painting & drawing design, Gateway Community Col, New Haven, Conn, 2004-06; adj prof art appreciation, Univ Conn, Stamford, Conn, 2002 & 04, Quinnipiac Univ, Hamden, Conn, 2004. *Awards:* Va Ctr for Creative Arts Fel, 78; S.O.S. Grant, NY State Coun on Arts, 1999; Creative Arts Public Service, 2002-2006; Gateway Found Grant, 2006. *Bibliog:* Vivien Raynor (auth), Abstract Works to Catch the Adult Eye, NY Times, 1996; Willam Zimmer (auth) Form Color & More, NY Times, 2000; D. Dominick Lombardi (auth), Baldassano, NY Times 2004. *Mem:* New York Artist Equity; Silvermine Guild of Artists; New Haven Art Council; Col Art Assoc. *Media:* All Media. *Mailing Add:* 190 Maple Tree Hill Rd Oxford CT 06478

BALDERACCHI, ARTHUR EUGENE
SCULPTOR, ADMINISTRATOR
b New York, NY, Mar 25, 1937. *Study:* Duke Univ, BA, 60; Univ Ga, MFA, 65. *Work:* Duke Univ, Durham; St Lawrence Univ; State Univ NY Potsdam; Univ Ga, Athens. *Comn:* Seven ft high mem to Dr Martin Luther King, Roland Gibson Art Found, Potsdam, NY. *Exhib:* Numerous solo & group exhibs in the Northeast. *Pos:* Chmn dept arts, Univ NH, 74-80. *Teaching:* Prof art, Univ NH, Durham, 65-. *Mem:* Col Art Asn Am; NH Art Asn. *Media:* Welded Metals, Cast Metals. *Publ:* Coauth (with C Pratt), In the Orchard, Tidal Press, 86; Drawings, 1948, Univ Va Press, 90. *Mailing Add:* 321 Sagamore Ave Portsmouth NH 03801-5530

BALDESSARI, JOHN ANTHONY
CONCEPTUAL ARTIST
b National City, Calif, June 17, 31. *Study:* San Diego State Col, BA, 53, MA, 57; Univ Calif, Berkeley, 54-55; Univ Calif, Los Angeles, 55; Otis Art Inst, Los Angeles, 57-59. *Hon Degrees:* Otis Art Inst, Parsons Sch Design of the New Sch for Social Rsch, D Fine Arts, 90. *Work:* Mus Mod Art, NY; Basel Mus, Switz; Los Angeles Co Mus Art; Chicago Art Inst; Whitney Mus, NY. *Exhib:* Konzeption-Conception, Stadtischen Mus, Leverkusen, Ger, 69; Information, Mus Mod Art, NY, 70; Prosepect, Statischen Kunsthalle, Dusseldorf, Ger, 71; Documenta 5 & 7, Kassel, Ger, 72 & 83; Contemporanea, Rome, 73; Carnegie Inst, Pittsburgh, Pa, 86; John Baldessari: Oeuvres Recentes, Palais des Beaux Arts, Brussels, Belgium, 88, Photoarbeiten, Kestner-Gessellschaft (auth, catalog), Hanover WGer, 88-89, Ni Por Esas/Not Even So (auth,catalog), Ctr de Arte Reina Sofia, Madrid, 89; Bilderstiet, Mus Ludwig in den Rheinhallen der KolnerMesse, Cologne, WGer, 89; Magiciens de la Terre, Ctr Georges Pompidou; and Grande Halle-La Villette, Paris, 89; John Baldessari Retrospective, Mus Contemp Art, Los Angeles, San Francisco Mus Mod Art, Hirshhorn Mus and Sculpture Garden, Walker Art Ctr, Whitney Mus Am Art, Mus d'Art Contemp de Montreal, 90; Spengel Mus, Hannover, Ger, 2000; Museu d'Art Contemporania, Barcelona, Spain, 98; Kunstmalle Basel, Switz, 2000; Monika Spruth/Philomene Magers, Cologne, Ger, 02; Margo Leavin Gallery, Los Angeles, 02; and others. *Teaching:* Asst prof art, Univ Calif, San Diego, 68-70; prof art, Calif Inst Arts, Valencia, 70-87; prof art, Univ Calif, Los Angeles, 96-. *Awards:* Nat Endowment Arts Grants, 73-75; Guggenheim Grant, 86-; Skowhegan Medal, 88; Oscar Kokoschaka Prize, Austria, 96; Govs Award for Lifetime Achievement in the Visual Arts, Calif, 97; Spectrum Int Award for Photography of the Found of Lower Saxony, Ger, 99. *Bibliog:* James Collins (auth), John Baldessari, Artforum, 10/73; Coosje von Bruggen (auth), John Baldessari, Rizzoli, NY, 90; Meg Granston (coauth) While Something is Happening Here, Something Else is Happening There, Sprengel Mus, Hannover and Staatliche Kunstammlungen, Dresden, Germany, 99; Thomas McEvilley (auth) John Baldessari, Tetrad Series, Marian Goodman Gallery, NY, 99, others. *Media:* Photography, Printmaking. *Publ:* Auth, Ingres & Other Parables, 72; Choosing: Green Beans, 72; Throwing Three Balls in the Air to Get a Straight Line (Best of 36 Attempts), 73; Close Cropped Tales, 81; The Telephone Book (with Pearls), 88; coauth The Metaphor Problem Again, Ink Tree Kunsnacht and Mai 36

Galerie, Zurich, Switzerland, 99; A Sentence of Thirteen Parts (with Twelve Alternate Verbs) Ending in Fable, Hamburg, West Germany, 77; Zorro (Two Gestures and One Mark), Octagon Press, 99; plus others. *Dealer:* Marian Goodman Gallery 24 W 57th St New York NY 10019. *Mailing Add:* 2001 1/2 Main St Santa Monica CA 90405-1021

BALDRIDGE, MARK S
GOLDSMITH, EDITOR
b Lyons, NY, Dec 7, 46. *Study:* State Univ NY Col, Buffalo, BS(art educ), 68; Cranbrook Acad Art, Bloomfield Hills, Mich, MFA(metalsmithing), 70. *Exhib:* 10th Piedmont Crafts Exhib, Mint Mus Art, Charlotte, NC, 73; Profiles in US Jewelry, 73, Lubbock, Tex, 73; Va Artists 1973, Va Mus Fine Arts, Richmond, 73; 11th Ann Southern Tier Art & Crafts Show, Corning Glass Ctr, NY, 74; Reprise, Cranbrook Acad Art Mus, Bloomfield Hills, Mich, 75; Objects 75 Designer/Craftsman Show, Grand Junction, Colo, 75; Craft Art & Relig, Vatican Mus, Rome, 76; Marietta Col Crafts Nat, Ohio, 77; Va Craftsmen Biennial, Va Mus Fine Arts, Richmond, 80; SE Metalsmiths, Mint Mus Art; Metalsmith 81, Univ Kans, Lawrence, 81; US Jewelry Invitational, Walker Hill Art Ctr, Seoul, Korea; LeMoyne Arts Found, Tallahassee, Fla; Pensacola Mus of Art; and others. *Pos:* Ed & creator, Goldsmiths J, 74-; co-ed, Metalsmith Mag, 86. *Teaching:* Instr metal-jewelry, Univ Evansville, 70-72; from asst to prof metal-jewelry, Longwood Col, 72-, chmn art dept, 89-93; conduct numerous workshops in field. *Awards:* First Prize-Metal, 40th Nat Cooperstown, NY, 75; First Prize, Lake Superior Int, 75; Merit Award, Goldsmiths 77, Soc NAm Goldsmiths, Phoenix Art Mus, 77. *Mem:* Va Crafts Coun (bd mem, 78-80); Soc NAm Goldsmiths (bd mem, 79-87); SE Am Craft Coun (Va rep & treas, 82-); Richmond Craftsman's Guild (secy, 97-2004, treas 2005). *Media:* Gold, Stained Glass. *Res:* American metalsmithing in the 1940's and 1950's; Glass Casting. *Publ:* Auth, Bi-metal casting to titanium, Metalsmith, Vol 6, No 2, spring 86; Kenneth Bates: Dean of American Enameling, Metalsmith, Vol 8, No 2, spring 88; creator, ed, SNAG newsletter & Goldsmiths Jour; co-ed, assoc ed, Metalsmith Mag; book reviewer, Jeweler's Circular Keystone. *Mailing Add:* 1600 Otterdale Midlothian VA 23114

BALDWIN, GORDON C
CURATOR
b Cleveland, Ohio, Feb 20, 39. *Study:* Amherst Col, AB, 60; Harvard Law Sch; Harvard Grad Sch Design, 63-67. *Collection Arranged:* Photography in Nineteenth-Century Egypt, J Paul Getty Mus, 87; Gustave Le Gray, 88; Grave Testimony: Photographs of the Civil War, 92; Fame & Photography, 93; Roger Fenton: The Orientalist Suite, 96; Jean Gabriel Eyhard: A Life in D Aguerreotypes, 98; Nadar/Warhol: Paris/New York, 99; The Man in the Street, Eugene Atget in Paris, 2000; Gustave Le Gray, Photographer, 2002; Recent Acquistitions. 2004 (co-curator); All the Mighty World The Photographs of Roger Fenton, 2005 (co-curator). *Pos:* Study room supervisor, J Paul Getty Mus, 87-90, asst cur, 90-94, assoc cur, 94-. *Awards:* Rome Prize, Am Acad Rome, 77. *Mem:* Europ Soc Hist Photog; fel Am Acad Rome. *Publ:* Auth, Looking at Photographs: A Guide to Technical Terms, J Paul Getty Mus/British Mus, 91; coauth, Phiz 93; The John Kobal Foundation, Cheatle Gallery, 93; auth, Roger Fenton: Pasha and Bayadére, J Paul Getty Mus, 96; (co-auth) Nador/Warhol, Paris/New York; Photography and Fame, J. Paul Cettty Mus. 99; In Focus; Eugene Atget, J. Paul Getty Mus, 2000; (ed) Gustave Legray, 1820-1884, J. Paul Getty Mus, 2002; co-auth All the Mighty World, The Photographs of Roger Fenton, 1851-1862, Metropolitan Mus of Art, 2004. *Mailing Add:* c/o J Paul Getty Mus 1200 Getty Center Dr Suite 1000 Los Angeles CA 90049-1687

BALDWIN, HAROLD FLETCHER
SCULPTOR, PAINTER
b Lebanon, NH, May 24, 1923. *Study:* Self-taught. *Comn:* Carved map of Northeastern Seaboard, 200 Mormon Missionaries, Cambridge, Mass, 71; The Good Samaritan, Springfield Bicentennial, Vt; Secure Care Prods, Boscausen, NH. *Exhib:* One-man shows, Concord Pub Libr, NH, 71 & Springfield Art & Hist Soc, Vt, 73; Burlington Mall, Mass, 73; NH Art Gallery, Concord; New Eng Woodcarvers' Asn, Concord Gallery, Mass, 73; Herricks Cove Art Gallery, Rockingham, Vt. *Media:* Acrylic. *Mailing Add:* Baldwin Studios 11 Woodland Dr Springfield VT 05156-2138

BALDWIN, RICHARD WOOD
ILLUSTRATOR, SCULPTOR
b Needham, Mass, June 8, 1920. *Study:* Pa Acad Fine Arts, with George Harding; also with Harold Von Schmidt. *Work:* Smithsonian Inst, Washington, DC; Whitney Gallery Western Art; Brown Univ, Libr. *Comn:* Murals, comn by USA, 42-45, now in Smithsonian Inst. *Pos:* Sr master sculptor, Franklin Mint, 70-. *Awards:* Cresson Fel, Pa Acad Fine Arts, 41. *Media:* Oil, Watercolor; Clay, Plaster. *Publ:* Illusr books & periodicals, 46-65. *Mailing Add:* 309 Devon Ln West Chester PA 19380

BALDWIN, RUSSELL W
EDUCATOR, GALLERY DIRECTOR
b San Diego, Calif, May 26, 33. *Study:* San Diego State Univ, BA, 58, MA, 63. *Work:* Joseph Hirshhorn Collection, Washington, DC; San Diego Mus Contemp Art, Calif; Santa Barbara Mus Art; San Francisco Mus Mod Art; Newport Harbor Mus, Calif; Int Paper Co, NY; Kelley Found, Los Angeles. *Exhib:* One-man shows, Santa Barbara Mus Art, 64, San Diego Mus Contemp Art, 64, 73 & 81, Jewish Community Ctr, San Diego, 74 & Casat Gallery, La Jolla, 78; one man retrospective, San Francisco Mus Mod Art, 81; New Works, San Francissco Mus Mod Art, 81; Space Gallery, 82 & 92. *Collection Arranged:* Paintings by John Baldessari, 72; Robert Irwin (installation piece), 75; Photog as a Means, 76; Andy Warhol, 77; Wayne Thiebaud, 78; William Wiley, 78; Masami Tenaoka, 80; Roland Reiss, 81; Star Wars Exhib from Lucas, 86. *Pos:* Dir, Dwight Boehm Gallery. *Teaching:* Assoc prof art, Palomar Col, San Marcos, Calif, 65-. *Awards:* First Painting Award, San Diego Mus Contemp Art, 60; Sculpture Award, Long Beach Mus Art, 73; First Award, Calif-Hawaii Regional, Fine Arts Mus San Diego, 74. *Mem:* San Diego Mus Contemp Art. *Specialty:* Information art. *Publ:* auth, articles in LA Times, San Diego Mag, San Diego Union, Newsweek & Art Week. *Dealer:* Space Gallery Los Angeles CA

BALES, J (JEAN) ELAINE
PAINTER, SCULPTOR
b Pawnee, Okla, Dec 25, 46. *Study:* Okla Col Liberal Arts, BA(art), 69, Univ Sci & Art, BA; prof study, Inst San Miguel de Allende, Mex. *Work:* Southern Plains Indian Mus, Anadarko, Okla; Denver Mus Natural Hist, Colo; US Dept Interior, Washington, DC; Mus Northern Ariz, Flagstaff; Univ Calif at San Diego Med Sch; Lincoln Plaza Ctr; Mus of Western Prairie. *Exhib:* Nat Indian Art Exhib, Heard Mus, Phoenix, 73-79; Am Indian Art Ann, Okla Art Ctr, Oklahoma City, 79-81; Images 80, Denver Mus Natural Hist, Colo, 80; Trail of Tears, Cherokee Nat Mus, Talequah, Okla, 80; Native Am Invitational, Santa Fe Festival Arts, NMex, 81; Circles of the World, Calif Acad Sci, 85; Eye of Man Exhib, San Diego Mus of Man, 85; Fruitland Mus, Harvard, Mass, 87; Kirkpatrick Ctr, Oklahoma City, Okla, 88. *Pos:* Bd dir, Indian Arts & Crafts Asn, 78-79. *Awards:* First in Watercolor, Indian Art Exhib, Heard Mus, 77 & 79; Div Award, Trail of Tears Show, Cherokee Nat Mus, 80; Mountain Bell Award, Gallup Int Tribal Ceremonial Exhib, Mountain Bell, 81; Merit Award, Cherokee Nat Mus, 85, 86, 87 & 88; O'Odham Tash, First & Second Prize, Graphics & Watercolor, Third Prize, Watercolor, 88; Second Prize Prints, Little Classic Art Show. *Bibliog:* Tricia Hurst (auth), Nine major Indian artists, 80 & Crossing bridges, 81, Southwest Art. *Publ:* Illusr, Indian Cultures of Oklahoma, Okla State Dept Educ, 78; Preserving heritage, Lefthander Mag, 10/88; articles in High Plain Lit Rev, spring & fall 88. *Mailing Add:* PO Box 24 Carney OK 74832

BALKA, SIGMUND RONELL
GALLERY DIRECTOR, CURATOR
b Aug 8, 35. *Study:* Williams Col, BA, 1956; Harvard Univ, JD, 1959. *Collection Arranged:* cur, major collection of 20th century mod and contemp arts and Am decorative arts. *Pos:* vpres public & cultural affairs, gen counsel, Krasdale Foods, Inc, Bronx, NY; dir & cur, Krasdale Galleries, Bronx, NY and White Plains, NY; chmn, Hunts Point and White Plains Sculpture, NY, Park Task Force, 88-91; bd dir, Bronx Coun Arts, 80-2004; chmn, fel & mem, Williams Col Mus Art, vis com, 96-99, fel, 2000-; mem adv coun, visual arts, Mason Gross Sch Art, Rutgers Univ; mem exhibs & acquisition com & bd trustees, Queens (NY) Mus Art, 97-98, chmn, 2001-; pres, Print Connoisseurs Soc NY, 74; bd dir, Jewish Repertory Theatre, co-chmn, 2000-01, chmn, 2001-; bd dir, Coun Arts, Longwood Center, 2005; bd dir, Judaica Mus, 2006; numerous cmty and environmental activities. *Awards:* Gala Award, Queens Mus Art, 02. *Mem:* Am Bar Found (fel), 98-; ABA (mem com corp gen counsel, 1974-, planning chmn, 1994-96, mem chmn & sec, 1996-98); Met Corp Counsel (corp counsel adv com); Asn Bar City NY; Am Corp Counsel Fedn (bd dir & treas, 1992-99); Am Corp Counsel Asn (bd dir & chmn Met NY chap, mem pro-bono com); Greater NY Met Food Coun (bd dir, 1986-98). *Specialty:* Mod and Contemp and Am art from all regions of the Country. *Collection:* 20th century American art; American 18th & 19th Century American decorative arts. *Publ:* over 100 catalogues. *Mailing Add:* 70-27 Harrow St Forest Hills NY 11375-5153

BALL, KEN WESTON
ARTIST
b Denver, Colo, June 2, 42. *Study:* Univ Colo, BA, 66. *Work:* The Harmsen Collection, Denver Art Mus; The Gene Autry Western Heritage Mus, Los Angeles. *Comn:* Five Bronze Figures of Native Ams, Aurora Art in Public Places, Colo, 97; Six Bronze Bas Relief Sports Figures, Colo Coun on the Arts, Trinidad, 98. *Exhib:* Iron Eyes Cody Tribute, Washington, DC, 82; Western Reg Exhib, Sangre De Christo Fine Art Center, Pueblo, Colo, 85; Western Art Rendezvous, Morrison, Colo, 92; Sculpture Garden Invitational, Hudson Botanic Gardens, Littleton, Colo, 98; Views of the West, Red Rocks Community Col, Lakewood, Colo, 00. *Awards:* Arts & Humanities Award, Nat Recreation & Park Asn, 98; Best of Show, Arvada Harvest Art Show, 82. *Mem:* Am Soc Landscape Architects. *Publ:* Calfi Art Rev, American References, 89; Xeriscape Programs for Water Utilities, Am Water Works Asn, 90; Water Saving Gardening-Taylors Guide, Houghton-Mifflin, 90. *Mailing Add:* 6786 Salvia Ct Arvada CO 80007

BALL, LILLIAN
SCULPTOR
b Augusta, Maine, Jan 6, 55. *Study:* Inst Bellas Artes, San Miguel Allende, Mex, 71; Nordenfjords Verdens Univ, Copenhagen, BA, 72; Harvard Univ, Cambridge, 75-76; Parsons Sch Design, NY, 78; Columbia Univ, NY, 84-85; New Sch Soc Res, NY, 85. *Work:* Mus Contemp Art, MAMCO, Geneva, Switzerland; Progressive Insurance Corp, Cleveland, Ohio; Bingham, Dana & Gould Attorneys, Boston, MA; Andre Emmerich Sculpture Park, Pawling, NY; William Patterson Col, Patterson, NJ. *Exhib:* Sculpture Forms, Aldrich Mus Contemp Art, 80; solo exhibs, Socrates Sculpture Park, Long Island, NY, 89, Snug Harbor Cult Ctr, Staten Island, NY, 89, Hudson River Mus, Yonkers, NY, 90, Rubin Spangle Gallery, New York, 92 & Sculpture Ctr (with catalog), NY, 95, Support systems, Queens Mus/Bulova, 98, On the Waterfront, Liberty State Park, Jersey City, NJ, 99, Joselyn Naef Fine Art, Lillian Ball, Waterworks, Montreal Canada, 2002; Chateau Chazelles, France, 95; The Transformal, Vienna Secession, Austria, 96; Object Art/Art Object, Elga Wimmer Gallery, NY, 96; Abstract/Real, Mus Mod Art, Vienna, 96; Abstracted & Unfixed, Art in General, NY, 97; Formes du simple, MAMCO Genva, Annemasse, France, 97; Real fiction, Wigmore Fine Art, London, 98; Tick, Tick, Tick, Real Art Ways, Hartford, Conn, 98; 22/21 Vsion, Hofstra Univ, Hempstead, NY, 98; Chromaform, Color in Sculpture, Univ Tex Art Gallery, San Antonio, 98; Achieving Failure Gym Cult, Threadwaxing Space, NY, 2000; many others; Archipeligo, Denver Mus Contemp Art,

2002; Hellsapoppin, Sculpture Exhibition from Coll, MAMCO, Geneva, 2002; Allure Electronica, Wood St Galleries, Pittsburgh, Pa, 2004; 100 Artists See God, Independent Cur Int Contemp Jewish Mus, San Francisco, Ca, 2004; Cuttting Edge, Exploratorium, San Francisco, Ca, 2004. *Pos:* Guest lectr, Boston Univ Prog in Arts, 78, NY Univ Sculpture Dept, 92 & Acad der Kunst, Berlin, 92; asst to Jackie Winsor, NY, 79-80; invited artist, Garner Tullis Monoprints, 87, Santa Barbara, Calif, 87, Urdla Print Publ, Villeurbanne, France, 91 & Int Contemp Art Cruise, France, Spain, Italy, 91; adjudicator, Conn State Sculpture Grants, Hartford, 88; panelist, Dooley Cappelaine Gallery, 92 & Arts Link-Citizen Exchange Coun, NY, 93; collabr, Bioinformatica-Blast 4, X Art Found, 95; artist-in-residence, Pilchuck Glass, Stanwood, Ore, 96; vis artist, guest lectr, UCLA Graduate Dept, Los Angeles, Ca, 2001; grad stud advisor, Maine College Art, Portland, ME, 2002-2003. *Teaching:* vis artist RI Sch Design, 87, NY Univ, 92, Sch Visual Arts, 92, Sch Visual Arts grad dept, New York, 93 & Vt Studio Ctr, Johnson, 93; Instr sculpture, NY Feminist Art Inst, 88-91; visiting artist, guest lectr, RISD, Providence, 98, Vt Studio Ctr, Johnson, 98, The Virutal Life of Sculpture, Mt Holyoke Co, 2000; guest lectr, Col Art Asn, NY, 2000. *Awards:* Sculpture Fel, Nat Endowment Arts, 86-87; Artists Space, Visual Arts Comt, Materials Fund Award, 89; NY Found Arts Grant, 91; John Simon Guggenheim Found Fel in Visual Arts, 99. *Bibliog:* William Zimmer (auth), Mirror of the moment, New York Times, 8/8/98; Edie Newhouse (auth), New York Mag, 8/10/98; Alice Winn (auth), The Female Form, Pulp-Pittsburgh, 2/19/04. *Mem:* NY Artists Equity; Orgn Independent Artists. *Media:* Miscellaneous Media. *Publ:* Auth, Phallus control, Promotional Copy, fall 93; contribr, Time Capsule, NY, 95; auth, The Fantastic, Tema Celeste, spring 96. *Mailing Add:* Seven Harrison St New York NY 10013

BALL, SUSAN L
ADMINISTRATOR, HISTORIAN
b Altadena, Calif, May 25, 47. *Study:* Scripps Col, BA, 69; Univ Calif, Riverside, MA, 74; Yale Univ, PhD, 78. *Collection Arranged:* The Impressionists & the Salon (contribr), Univ Calif, Riverside & LACMA, 74; Richard Brown Baker Collects (contribr), Yale Univ, 75; Rossetti & the Double Work of Art (contribr), Yale Univ, 76. *Pos:* Dir govt & found affairs, Art Inst Chicago, Ill, 85-86; exec dir, Col Art Asn NY, pres, 86-. *Teaching:* Asst prof art hist, Univ Delaware, Newark, 78-81. *Mem:* Am Asn Mus; Art Table; bd mem, Nat Cult Alliance & Nat Humanities Alliance; exec comt mem, Conference Admin Officers Am Coun of Learned Soc. *Res:* Late nineteenth and early twentieth century European painting and architecture. *Publ:* Auth, The impressionists and the salon Los Angeles County Mus, 74; auth, Richard Brown Baker collects (essays), Yale, 75; auth, Works before 1962, Dante Gabriel Rossetti, 76; auth, The early figural paintings of Andre Derain, 1905-1910, Zeitschrift für Kunstgeschichte, 80; auth, Ozenfant and Purism: The evolution of a style 1915-1930, UMI Press, 81. *Mailing Add:* c/o Col Art Asn 275 Seventh Ave New York NY 10001

BALLARD, JAMES A
PAINTER, ARCHITECT
b Monticello, NY, Apr 9, 46. *Study:* Pratt Inst Sch Archit, 63-66; Pratt Inst Sch Fine Art, BFA(cum laude), 71; Columbia Univ, grad studies, 91. *Work:* Mus Mod Art, NY. *Comn:* Studio, Lissom Gallery, London, 97; gallery design, Ricco Manesca Gallery, NY, 97; gallery design, Christine Ruse Gallery, NY, 97; gallery design, John Weber Gallery, NY, 97; renovation, Elizabeth Found Arts, NY, 98. *Exhib:* Untitled V, Mus Mod Art, NY, 72; Art on Paper, Weatherspom, Univ NC, Greensboro, 72; Jusmetched Paintings, Brockton Art Ctr, Mass, 73; one-man shows, Fisch Bach Mus, NY, 73, Race Gallery, Philadelphia, 79, Bova Music Club, NY, 86; Untitled Arc, Fed Plaza, NY, 89; Bird as Critic, Barbara Krakow Gallery, Boston, Mass, 91. *Bibliog:* Jane Coller (auth), review, Art News, 3/73; Nancy Staplen (auth), review, Boston Globe, 7/18/91; David Raymond (auth), review, Art New Eng, 10-11/91. *Media:* Acrylic on Canvas. *Mailing Add:* 315 Church St 3rd Fl New York NY 10013

BALLINGER, JAMES K
MUSEUM DIRECTOR, HISTORIAN
b Kansas City, Mo, July 7, 49. *Study:* Univ Kans, BA, 72, MA(art hist), 74. *Collection Arranged:* Painter in Taos, Eiteljorg Collection, 80; Visitors to Arizona: 1846-80 (auth, catalog), Phoenix Art Mus, 80; Charles M Russell (auth, catalog), The Renner Collection, 81; Dale Eldred: Phoenix Project, 81; Beyond the Endless River Western Am Drawings & Watercolors (auth, catalog), Phoenix Art Mus, 79; Americans in Brittany and Normandy: 1810-1910, 82; Peter Hurd: Insight to a Painter (auth, catalog), 83; Diego Rivera: The Cubist Years, 84; Frank Lloyd Wright Drawings, Frank Lloyd Found, 90; Lucy Drake Marlow Traveling Exhib, 91; Frederic Remington's Southwest Traveling Exhib, Memphis Brooks Mus Art & Joslyn Art Mus, Omaha, Nebr, 92. *Pos:* Gallery coordr, Tucson Art Ctr, 73; registrar, Univ Kans Mus Art, Lawrence, 73-74; cur collections, Phoenix Art Mus, Ariz, 74-81, asst dir & chief cur, 81-82, actg dir, 81-82, Sybil Harrington dir & chief cur, 82-; juror var exhibs, 77-89; lectr var mus, 79-92; bd mem, Balboa Art Conservation Ctr, San Diego, 81-89. *Awards:* Grants, Nat Endowment Arts, 77, 80 & 87; Flinn Found Grant, 88; Nat Arts Stabilization Fund Grant, 89. *Mem:* Western Asn Art Mus; Central Ariz Mus Asn; Am Asn Mus; Am Art Mus Dirs. *Publ:* Auth, American Painting from the Whitney Mus, Phoenix Art Mus, 76; Biennial 1979, Phoenix Art Mus, 79; Frederic Remington, Abrams, 89. *Mailing Add:* 1625 N Central Ave Phoenix AZ 85004

BALLOU, ANNE MACDOUGALL See MacDougall, Anne

BALMACEDA, MARGARITA S
EDUCATOR, VIDEO ARTIST
b Ponce, PR, Dec 30, 33; US citizen. *Study:* Manhattanville Col, Purchase, NY, BFA; Immaculate Heart Col, Hollywood, Calif, teaching cert; Cath Univ of PR, Ponce, MA. *Pos:* Asst dir, Ponce Art Mus, 67-74. *Teaching:* Prof art appreciation & art hist, Univ PR, Ponce, 73-, dir, Humanities Dept, currently. *Awards:* Morell Cambos Award on Art & Cult, Ponce Chamber Com, 94. *Mem:* Sociedad de Autores Puertorriquenos. *Res:* Expressionism; Puerto Rican art. *Publ:* Auth, poems, Tierra y Alma, Ed Ponce de Leon, Spain, 68; dir, Fano (video), 93; Oller Artista (video), 85; Campeche de Ayer, de Hoy y de Siempre (video), 89; auth poems, Un inmenso suspiro, Imprenta Fortuño, Ponce, PR

BALMORI, DIANA
LANDSCAPE ARCHITECT
b Gijon, Spain, Jun 4, 1936. *Study:* Univ Tucuman, Argentina, Diploma in Archit, 60; UCLA, BA in Uban Hist, 68; UCLA, PhD, 73; Radcliffe Univ, student in landscaping, 89. *Pos:* assoc, Cesar Pelli & Assoc, New Haven, 77-81; principal, for landscape and urban design, 81-90; principal, Balmori Assoc, 90-; appointed mem, Comn Fine Arts, 2003; Davenport Chair, of Archit Design Yale Sch of Archit, 2004. *Teaching:* Asst prof, State Univ NY, Oswego, 74-78, assoc prof, 78-79. *Awards:* Grantee Ossabaw Found, 80; res fel NYU, 82; judges Award, Harry Chapin Media Awards, 95. *Mem:* Am Soc Landscape Archits, Catalog of Landscape Records (bd dir, currently); Van Alen Inst (mem exec comt, currently); Am Hist Asn. *Publ:* Auth: Beatrix Farrand, Beatrix Jones Ferrand (1872-1959) Fifty Yrs Of Am Landscape Archit, 1982, Beatrix Farrand's Am Landscapes, 1985, Transitory Gardens, Uprooted Lives, 1993, Redesigning the Am Lawn, 1993, Saarinen House and Garden: A Total Work of Art, 1995; contribr Beatrix Farrand At Dumbarton Oaks: The Design Process of a Garden; co-auth: The Land and Nat Development (LAND) Code: Guidelines for Environmentally Sustainable Land Development. *Mailing Add:* Balmori Assocs Inc 820 Greenwich St 3rd Fl New York NY 10014

BALOSSI, JOHN
SCULPTOR, PAINTER
b Staten Island, NY, May 28, 31. *Study:* Columbia Univ, BFA & MA. *Work:* Mus Mod Art, Finch Col Mus & Chase Manhattan, NY; Ponce Mus, PR; Mus Art, Ft Lauderdale, Fla. *Comn:* Mural, Student Union Bldg, Univ PR, 69; aluminum wall relief, Inst Puerto Rican Cult, 71; mural, CRUV Pub Housing, Manati, PR, 72; mural, Pan Am Games, San Juan, 79. *Exhib:* Sculpture in Clay from Puerto Rico, Mus Fine Arts, Springfield, Mass, 80; Art Mus STex, Corpus Christi, 80; Newark Mus, 81; Bacardi Gallery, Miami, Fla, 81; 39th & 40th Int Competition of Artistic Ceramics, Faenza, Italy, 81 & 82; one-man exhib, paintings, Columbian Quincentennary Celebration, Genoa, Italy, 92. *Teaching:* Assoc prof fine arts, Univ PR, Rio Piedras, formerly. *Awards:* Ateneo Puertorriqueno Award, San Juan, 67; UNESCO Salon Award, San Juan, 74 & 79; R J Reynolds Tobacco Co Award, San Juan, 79. *Bibliog:* Gottfried Borrmann (auth), Keramik der Welt, Kunst & Handwerk, Vertagsanstalt, Dusseldorf, 81; Myrna Rodrigues (auth), Balossi: A Selection of His Work from 1960-1982, 82; Charlotte F Speight (auth), Images in Clay Sculpture, Harper & Row, 83. *Media:* Clay fired; Acrylic on Canvas, Paper. *Dealer:* Studio B 865 49 St SE Reparto Metro San Juan PR 00921. *Mailing Add:* 865 49th St SE Reparto Metro San Juan PR 00921

BALSLEY, JOHN GERALD
PAINTER, SCULPTOR
b Cleveland, Ohio, Apr 15, 1944. *Study:* Univ Americas, 65; Ohio Northern Univ, BA, 67; Northern Ill Univ, MFA, 69. *Work:* St Louis Mus Art, Mo; Nelson-Atkins Gallery, Kansas City, Mo; Des Moines Art Ctr, Iowa; Joslyn Mus Art, Omaha, Nebr; Univ Iowa Art Mus, Iowa City. *Exhib:* Allan Stone Gallery, NY, 72, 74, 76, 78; One-man shows, Madison Art Ctr, Wis, 79, Univ Del, 79, Frumpkin-Struve Gallery, Chicago, Ill, 79 & 80, New Gallery Contemp Art, Cleveland, 80 & Rahr-West Mus, Manitowoc, Wis, 82; Sheldon Mem Art Gallery, Univ Nebr, Lincoln, 82; Yarres Gallery, Scottsdale, Ariz, 83; Birmingham Art Mus, 83, 87 & 88; Painting & Sculpture Today, Indianapolis Mus Art, Ind, 76; Realisms, Ulrich Mus, Wichita State Univ, 76; Chicago Vicinity Show, Art Inst Chicago, 77; Michael Lord Gallery, Milwaukee, Wis, 91; Perimeter Gallery, Chicago, Ill, 91; Morgan Gallery, Kansas City, Mo, 96; SOFA, Chicago, Ill, 99. *Teaching:* Prof sculpture, Univ Wis-Milwaukee, 76-. *Awards:* Louis Comfort Tiffany Found Grant, 72; Nat Endowment Arts Grant, 72 & 80; Univ Wis, Milwaukee Grant, 78; Milwaukee Artists Found Grants, 82 & 87. *Bibliog:* Lou Dunkak (auth), Balsley sculptures explore man and machines, Arts, 12/76; Josh Kind (auth), Model art: The intimate enviroment, New Art Examr, 1/78; Betty Kaufman (auth), John Balsley at Allan Stone, Art World, 1/78; Article in Artspeak, 97. *Mem:* Col Art Asn Am. *Media:* Welded Metal, Wood. *Dealer:* Perimeter Gallery Chicago IL; Michael Lord Gallery Milwaukee WI. *Mailing Add:* 8325 N Cedarburg Rd Milwaukee WI 53209-1526

BALTZ, LEWIS
PHOTOGRAPHER
b Newport Beach, Calif, Sept 12, 45. *Study:* San Francisco Art Inst, BFA, 69; Claremont Grad Sch, MFA, 71. *Work:* Mus Mod Art, Metrop Mus Art, NY; Art Inst Chicago; Los Angeles Mus Contemp Art; Victoria & Albert Mus, London; Nat Gallery Australia, Mod Museet, Stockholm; Palazzo Fortuny, Venice, Italy; Nat Mus Mod Art, Kyoto; and 60 other collections in US, Canada, Australia, Europe & Japan. *Comn:* Courthouse, Joseph E Seagrams Co, 76; American Images, Am Tel & Telgr Co, 78; Nev State Arts Comn, 86; La Mission photographique, Datar, France, 86; Toshiba Project, Japan, 89; Linea di Confine, Reggio Emilia, Italy, 91. *Exhib:* Corcoran Gallery Art, 74-76; Philadelphia Col Art, 75; Mus Fine Arts, Houston, 76; San Francisco Mus Mod Art, 81; RI Sch Design, 83; Univ Art Mus, Univ Calif, Berkeley, 84; Victoria & Albert Mus, London, 85; Ringling Mus, Sarasota, Fla, 91; Des Moines Art Ctr, Iowa, 91; Los Angeles City Mus Art, Calif, 92; solo exhibs, Centre Pompidou, Paris, 92, Galerie Michelle Chomette, Paris, 93, Mus de Cahors, France, 93, Fotomuseum Winterthur, Switz, 93, Mus Art Mod Paris, 93, Janet Borden, Inc, NY, 93 & La Mus Mod Art, Humlebaek, Denmark, 94. *Teaching:* Vis prof, Univ Calif, Riverside, 90; vis art, Calif Inst Arts, 92; vis artist, Yale Univ, 92; vis artist, Ecole des

Beaux Arts, Paris, 92. *Awards:* Nat Endowment Arts Fel, 73 & 77; Guggenheim Mem Found Fel in Photography, 77; Charles Pratt Mem Award, 91. *Bibliog:* Paul Hill (auth), Approaching Photography, Focal Press, London & Boston, 82; Dr Naomi Rosenblum (auth), The World History of Photography, Abbeville Press, NY, 85; Estelle Jussim (coauth Elizabeth Lindquist-Coci), Landscape As Photograph: Reflections on Nature, 85; Ideology, Yale Univ Press, New Haven, 85; Arthur Rothstein (auth), Documentary Photography, p 131, Stoweham, Mass, 86. *Publ:* Auth, Candlestick Point, 89; Giocchi di Simulazione, 91; Rule Without Exception, 91; Ronde de Nuit, 92; Lewis Baltz: 5 Projects, Stedelijk Mus. *Dealer:* Janet Borden Inc 560 Broadway New York NY 10012; Stephen Wirtz Gallery 49 Geary Blvd San Francisco CA 94102. *Mailing Add:* 23 Rue Des Blancs Mantgaux 94966 Paris France 75004

BALZEKAS, STANLEY, JR
MUSEUM DIRECTOR, COLLECTOR
b Chicago, Ill, Oct 8, 24. *Study:* DePaul Univ, BA, 50, MA, 51. *Pos:* Pres, Balzekas Mus Lithuanian Cult, Chicago, Ill, 66-; advisory bd mem, Chicago Dept of Cult Affairs, 79-. *Collection:* 18th-19th century oils by European masters; contemporary graphics and sculptures. *Mailing Add:* c/o Balzekas Museum Lithuanian Culture 6500 S Pulaski Rd Chicago IL 60629

BANANA, ANNA
PUBLISHER, CONCEPTUAL ARTIST
b Victoria, BC, Feb 24, 40. *Study:* Univ BC, Vancouver, BEd, 67. *Work:* Smithsonian Inst Libr, Nat Gallery of Art Serials Libr, Washington; Mus Mod Art Libr, Franklin Furnace, NY Pub Libr, NY; G Pompidou Libr, Paris, France; Nat Libr Can, Nat Postal Mus, Art Bank, Can Coun & Nat Gallery Art, Ottawa; Otis Art Inst, Los Angeles Inst Contemp Art & Jean Brown Collection, Getty Mus; Mus Mod Art, San Francisco. *Comn:* Banana Olympics, Surrey Art Gallery, BC, 80. *Exhib:* Can tour, 15 performances, 14 cities, 80; Univ Calif, Irvine, 80; San Diego State Univ, 80; Inter-Dada Festival, Ukiah, San Francisco, Calif, 80 & 84; Can/USA Tour, 15 performances in 15 cities, incl Vancouver, Edmonton, Toronto, Montreal, Columbia, SC, Dallas & San Jose, Calif, 82; European tour, Copenhagen performance & installation, 86; European Tour (Copenhagen, Umea, Rosenheim, Ghent, Den Hague & London), 86, 89 & 91; Ltd edition artist stamp sheets, Davidson Galleries, Seattle, Wash, 89, 91 & 93, Bumbershoot Arts Festival, Seattle, 90 & Gallery 56, Vancouver, BC, 92; solo exhib, Sarenco Art Club Gallery, Verona, Italy, 98; Popular Art of Postal Parody, Richmond Art Gallery, 99; Open Space, Victoria, BC, 2000; Banana Consciousness Raising Session, New Gallery, Calgary, 2000; Banana Splitz, Banff Ctr Arts, 2001; Tie a Knot on Me, Transportale Event, Norbhnhof Station, Berlin; New Meida: Artwork from the 60s & 70s in Vancouver, Burnaby Art Gallery, 2002; Transportale, Curated Works by 12 Artists, Nordbahnhof Station, Berlin, 2003. *Pos:* Dir, ed & publ, Banana Productions, 72-88; vis artist & lectr, Can cols & univs, 80-; cur, The Color Show (with catalog), Arts, Science & Technol Ctr, Vancouver, 83, Artropolis Show (with catalog), Vancouver, 87, Artistamps from the Mail-Art Network, Sunshine Coast Art Ctr, 98; ed & publ, Int Art Post, 88-, Artistamp News, 91-96. *Teaching:* Instr, New Sch, Vancouver, Can, 66-69. *Awards:* Coord Coun of Lit Mag Assistance Awards, 75, 77 & 79; Can Coun Grants, 80-83, 86, 87, 88, 89, 91, 93, 98, 99, 2000, 2001, 2003. *Bibliog:* Tom Hawthorn (auth), Life's a banana for Anna, The Province, 7/19/92; Bill Hornadge (auth), Cinderella corner/artistamps, Stamp News, 5/92, Australia; Judy Malloy (auth), review of 20 yrs of fooling around with A Banana, Leonardo Electronic News, Vol 2, No 7, 7/15/92, Freya Zabitsky (auth), Still a Banana After All Those Years, Rubberstampmadness, 90. *Mem:* Cent Visual Artists Asn; Sechelt Art Ctr. *Media:* Performance, Collage, Public Events. *Res:* Collection of information on a given topic via the mail-art network on an international basis; grass-roots level of art activity not represented in the art media or establishment; performance and organization of participatory public art events. *Interests:* Recycling Imagery from mass media; artist stamps; public participation in art actions. *Publ:* Ed & publ, About Vile, Vancouver, 83; 20 Years of Fooling Around with A Banana, Banana Productions, 2/90; Encyclopedia Bananica, Vol 1, No 1, 6/90; auth, Performance in Canada 1970-1990, Ed Intervention, 91; Artistamp News, 91-96

BANAS, ANNE
PAINTER, EDUCATOR
b Long Beach, Calif, Dec 9, 48. *Study:* Orange Coast Col, 67-69; Calif State Univ, Fullerton, BA, 71; Claremont Grad Sch, MFA, 74. *Work:* Security Pac Bank, Santa Barbara, Beverly Hills & La Jolla, Calif; Eastern NMex Univ, Roswell; Daytona Beach Int Airport, Barnett Bank, Accordia Corp, Fla; Vistacon, Fla. *Comn:* Profiler's 90 (mural), Daytona Beach Int Airport, Jacksonville, Fla, 92; Jacksonville Jaguars & City of Jacksonville (mural), 94; First Union Bank & Jacksonville Jaguars (mural, 98 x 215), 98. *Exhib:* One woman shows, Grandview Gallery, Los Angeles, 75, Art Rental Gallery, Santa Barbara Mus Art, 78, Alice Benjamin Gallery, Santa Barbara, 80 & Hills Gallery, Santa Fe, 81; Selections from Roswell, Albuquerque Downtown Ctr Arts, 81; Southwest Invitational, Midland Col, Tex, 84; Gallery 88, Jacksonville, Fla, 90; Fla Community Col, Jacksonville, 91; Contemporania Gallery, Jacksonville, Fla, 91 & 93; Orlando Mus Art, 92; Jacksonville Univ, 95 & 97. *Pos:* Founding mem, steering comt, Grandview Gallery, Los Angeles, 73-75; founding mem, Double X, educational art orgn, Los Angeles, 75; dir, art in the community, Santa Barbara Mus, Calif, 77-78. *Teaching:* Instr painting & drawing, West Los Angeles City Col, 75-77; instr painting, drawing, art hist & printmaking, Eastern NMex Univ, Roswell, 82-89; prof art, Fla Community Col, Jacksonville, Fla, 89-. *Bibliog:* Kalliope, Vol XIV, No 2, 5/92. *Media:* Oil. *Mailing Add:* 1775 Forest Blvd Jacksonville FL 32216

BAND, DAVID MOSHE
PAINTER, ART DEALER
b Portland, Maine, Oct 16, 47. *Study:* Self taught. *Work:* First Texas Savings, Dallas, Tex; The Dunnegan Gallery of Art, Bolivar, Mo; Wichita Falls (Tex) Teacher's Credit Union; Davie Mus and Cult Ctr, Wellesley (Mass) Col; Mus Tex Tech Univ, Lubbock; Springfield Art Mus, Mo; and others. *Exhib:* 169th Ann Exhib, Nat Acad Design, 94 & 175th, 2000, 179th, 2004; 79th Ann Exhib Allied Artists Am, Nat Arts Club, Gramercy Park, NY, 92, 81st, 94, 85th, 98, 86th, 99 & 87th, 2000-2004; retrospective, Wichita Falls (Tex) Mus & Art Ctr, 95; Watercolor USA, Springfield (Mo) Mus Art, 99, 2000, 2002, 2004; 63rd Ann Midyear Exhib, Butler Inst Am Art, Youngstown, Ohio, 99 & 64th, 2000, 65th, 2001, 66th, 2002, 67th, 2003, 68th, 2004; Membership Exhib, Nat Watercolor Soc, Glendale, Calif, 2000; 58th Ann Exhib Audubon Aritsts, Salmagundi Club, NY, 2000. *Pos:* Mem bd dir, N Tex Artists Guild, 84-; dir, Eden Gallery, Wichita Falls, Tex, currently; bd mem, Outdoor Painters Soc. *Teaching:* Instr, Wichita Falls Mus & Art Ctr, 73-74 & N Tex Artists Guild, 84-. *Awards:* Adolph and Clara Obrig Pirze for Watercolor by an Am Artist, 175th Ann Exhib, Nat Acad Design, 2000; Robert E Wood Mem Award, Watercolor USA, Springfield Mus Art, 2000; Kent Day Coes Mem Award, Watercolor, 91st annual exhib, Allied Artists of Am, 2004; William A Paton Prize for Watercolor, Nat Acad Design, 2004; Audubon Artists Gold Medal of Honor, 63d Ann Exhib, 2005; Genevieve Cain Award for watercolor, 107th Exhib Nat Arts Club, 2006. *Mem:* assoc mem Am Watercolor Soc; Allied Artists Am; Artists' Fel; Salmagundi Club; assoc mem prof Nat Watercolor Soc; assoc mem Southwestern Watercolor Soc. *Media:* Watercolor, Acrylic. *Specialty:* American prints 1900-1950. *Publ:* Splash II, Americas Best Contemporary Watercolors, North Light & Writer's Dig Bks, 92; auth, Inspirations and Ideas In: Splash II, America's Best Contemporary Watercolors, 93, Splash III, 105 Americas Best Contemporary Watercolors Show and Tell How They Find Their Inspirations and Ideas, North Light & Writer's Dig Bks, 94, Splash IV, America's Best Contemporary Watercolorists, 96; contribr, 10th anniversary issue, Art's Mag, 1/94; Catching the drift of snow, Artists'Mag, 2/95, Landscape basics, Clearing the way to clouds, 10/99, Landscape basics, Shaping reaslistic rocks, 12/99, Landscape basics, The Laws of Light, 7/2000, Landscape basics, Harnessing Nature's elements, 12/2000. *Dealer:* Cole Pratt Gallery New Orleans LA 70115. *Mailing Add:* 1903 Eden Ln Wichita Falls TX 76306

BANDES, SUSAN JANE
MUSEUM DIRECTOR, EDUCATOR
b New York, NY, Oct 18, 51. *Study:* NYU, BA, 71; Bryn Mawr Col, MA, 73, PhD, 78; Mus Mgmt Inst, Berkeley, Calif, 90. *Collection Arranged:* Affordable Dreams: The Goetsch-Winckler House by Frank Lloyd Wright, 90; Maria de Medici Enters Amsterdam: prints by Pieter Nolpe, 95-96; Abraham Rattner in the Tampa Museum of Art Collection (auth, catalog), Tampa Mus Art, 97; Pursuits & Pleasures: Barogue Painting from Detroit Ins of Arts, 2003-04; Circulating Mich Exhib, 2003-04. *Pos:* proj dir, Am Asn Mus, Wash, 83-84; prog officer, J Paul Getty Trust Grant Prog, Los Angeles, 84-86; bd dir, Mich Mus Asn, 87-92; coun, Mich Coun for Humanities, 88-92. *Teaching:* Asst prof, Sweet Briar Col, Va, 78-83; prof & dir, Kresge Art Mus, Mich State Univ, E Lansing, 86-. *Awards:* Whiting Fel, 76-77; Am Philos Soc, 81; Publ Award AIA, 90. *Bibliog:* auth, cur: Pursuits and Pleasures: Baroque Painting from the Detroit Inst of Arts, 2003. *Mem:* Nat Inst for Conserv (treas, 86-90); Mich Mus Asn (bd dir's, 1987-92); Mich Coun for Humanities (coun, 1988-92); Mich Alliance for Conserv (treas, 94-96, pres, 98-2000). *Publ:* editor: The Prints of John S. de Martelly, 1903 1979; Auth & ed, Caring for Collections, 84; Affordable Dreams: The Goetsch-Winckler House and Frank Lloyd Wright, 91; Abraham Rattner (auth), The Tampa Mus of Art Collection, 1997; contribr, articles in prof jour

BANDY, GARY
PAINTER, EDUCATOR
b Pontiac, Mich, May 10, 44. *Study:* Oakland Univ, BA, 65; Columbia Univ, MFA, 68. *Work:* Norton Simon Inc & Muriel Siebert, NY, New Sch Social Res, NY; St Peter's Col, Jersey City, NJ. *Exhib:* Artists Market, Detroit, Mich, 64; Aldrich Mus Contemp Art, Ridgefield, Conn, 74; solo shows, Herbert H Lehman Col Gallery, Bronx, NY, 79 & F Marino Gallery, NY, 82; Large Drawings, Independent Curators Inc traveling, 85-86; and others. *Teaching:* Adj instr art hist, St Peter's Col, Jersey City, NJ, 68-72; lectr & workshop instr, Mus Mod Art, NY, 77-. *Awards:* Artist's Fel, Nat Endowment Arts, 83. *Bibliog:* Review, Art News, 9/74; Palmer Poroner (auth), review, Art Speak, 4/80; Susan Filen Yeh (auth), Gary Bandy, Arts Mag, 4/82. *Media:* Acrylic. *Dealer:* Fawbush Gallery New York NY. *Mailing Add:* 118 W 29th St New York NY 10001-5301

BANDY, MARY LEA
EDITOR, ADMINISTRATOR
b Evanston, Ill, June 16, 43. *Study:* Stanford Univ, BA, 65. *Pos:* Asst ed, Harry N Abrams, New York, 67-73; assoc coordr exhibs, Mus Mod Art, New York, 76-78, dir film dept, 80-. *Publ:* Ed, Rediscovering French film (catalog), Mus Mod Art, 83; Michael Balcon (catalog), Mus Mod Art, 84. *Mailing Add:* Museum Modern Art 11 W 53rd St New York NY 10019

BANDY, RON F
PAINTER, EDUCATOR
b Dayton, Ohio, Feb 18, 36. *Study:* Ohio Univ, Athens, BFA, 62; Univ Fla, Gainesville, MFA, 64; also with Hiram Williams & Enrique Montenegro. *Work:* Weatherhead Found; Ft Wayne Mus, Ind; Owens-Corning Corp, Toledo, Ohio; Hope Colgate Sloane, Bowling Green, Ohio. *Exhib:* Solo exhib, Ft Wayne Mus, Ind, 74; Owens-Corning Collection Show, 76 & Toledo May Show, 81, Toledo Mus, Ohio; Ft Wayne Mus Exhib, Ind, 82; Lady Poverty, Mem Mus, Lima, Ohio, 83. *Teaching:* Prof art, Bowling Green State Univ, 68-. *Bibliog:* Lynn Stevenson (auth), Art from a can, Sunday Mag, Blade, 4/22/73. *Media:* Mixed. *Mailing Add:* 141 S Enterprise St Bowling Green OH 43402

BANE, MCDONALD (MACKEY)
PAINTER, CURATOR
b Bland, Va, Mar 1, 28. *Study:* Va Polytech Inst & State Univ, BS, 49; Univ NC, Greensboro, with Gregory Ivy & John Opper, MFA, 59. *Work:* Mus Mod Art, NY; Weatherspoon Art Gallery, Greensboro, NC; Mint Mus Art, Charlotte, NC; US Dept State, Washington, DC; E Carolina Univ Sch Art. *Comn:* Painting, Philip Morris Co, Salisbury, NC, 82. *Exhib:* Okla Art Ctr, Oklahoma City, 70; Contemp Am Drawings V, Smithsonian Inst, traveling, 71-74; NC Mus Art, Raleigh, NC, 76; Univ Evansville, Ind, 76; solo exhibs, Southeastern Ctr Contemp Art, Winston-Salem, NC, 80 & Univ Ga Art Gallery, Athens, 81. *Collection Arranged:* Collections Arranged Gregory Ivy Watercolors, 1938-1949, Raleigh, Greensboro & Hickory, NC, 96. *Pos:* Cur exhibs, Southeastern Ctr Contemp Art, Winston-Salem, NC, 77-80; exhib coord, The Arts Coun, Winston-Salem, NC, 80-91. *Teaching:* Asst prof, Calif State Univ, Fullerton, 66-68; instr, NC Sch Arts, Winston-Salem, 70-73; asst prof, Southern Ill Univ, Carbondale, 73-76; vis assoc prof, Va Polytech Inst & State Univ, 80. *Awards:* Best Show, Southeastern Ctr Contemp Art 39th Painting & Sculpture Competition, 73. *Media:* Oil. *Publ:* Ed, The Southeast Seven II, 78, Paper Making and Paper Using, 79, Art Patron Art, 79 & Southeast Seven III, 79 (catalogs), Southeastern Ctr Contemp Art, Winston-Salem, NC; auth, Oliver Lee Jackson & The SECCA/WFU/NCSA Prog, Arts J, 80; Corp Art Collections, NC, R J Reynolds Indust, Art J, 83. *Dealer:* Lee Hansley Gallery 225 Glenwood Ave Raleigh NC 27603. *Mailing Add:* 3424 Avent Ferry Rd New Hill NC 27562-9298

BANERJEE, BIMAL
PAINTER, SCULPTOR
b Calcutta, India, Sept 4, 39; US citizen. *Study:* Indian Col Art, Calcutta, DFA(first class hon), 55-60; Col Art, New Delhi, Indian Govt Nat Cult Scholar, 65-67; Atelier 17, Paris, Fr Govt Grant, 67-69; Ecole des Beaux Arts, Paris, Fr Govt Grant & cert of grad study, 67-70; Pratt Inst Exten, NY, inst grants & cert of post grad study, 69 & 70-72; NY Univ, with H W Jensen, 76; Columbia Univ MA, 80, EdM, 81, EdD, 88. *Work:* Mus Mod Art, Paris, France; Mus Fine Arts, Boston; Brooklyn Mus of Art; Nat Gallery Mod Art, New Delhi; Radford Univ Mus, Va; plus many others. *Comn:* Mural with five panels, comn by Mario Manto, Levanto, Italy, 68; mural with three panels, Proj Find Clinton Sr Citizens Ctr, NY, 79; Silk Screen Proj, NY & NJ Port Authority, CCF/CETA Artists Proj, NY, 79; plus others. *Exhib:* Tokyo Biennial, Mus Mod Art, Tokyo, 72; Brooklyn Mus Biennial, 72-73 & 81; World Print Competition, San Francisco Mus Mod Art, 77-79; Inter-Grafik Triennale, Berlin, 84; 42 one-man shows, incl Galerie du Haut Pavé, Paris, 68, Columbia Univ, 78, 79 & 84, Art Heritage Gallery, New Delhi, Chitrakoot Art Gallery, Calcutta, 90 & Bertha Urdang Gallery, NY, 91, Chemould Gallery, Calcutta, 93 & Cité Int des Arts, Paris, 94; Ljubljana Biennial, Mus Mod Art, Ljubljana, Yugoslavia, 87; Kanagawa Biennial, Knagawa, Japan, 90, 92; Cite Int des Art, Paris, 94, 99; Millennium Art Collection Exhib, 2000 Found, Diemen, The Neth, 2000. *Pos:* Therapist, art & educ, St John's Episcopal Hosp, Far Rockaway, NY, 81-83; art consult, New York City Bd Educ, 83-84; founding mem, Bill Clintons presidential Foundation, Little Rock, Ark; founding mem, Wall of Tolerance, Nat Campaign for Tolerance, Montgomery, Ala. *Teaching:* Vis asst teacher graphics, Nat Acad Fine Arts, NY, 69; guest lectr, Parsons Sch Design, NY, 79; lectr philos educ, Bloomfield Col, NJ, 80-81, New Sch Social Res, Parsons Sch Design, NY, 83-88, New York City Bd Educ, 83-2001; Columbia Univ, Teachers' Col, 88. *Awards:* Ctr Cult Int Award, City Univ, Paris, 68; Grant Award, Adolph and Esther Gottueb Found, NY, 89-90; World Cult Prize, Statue of Victory for Arts, Letters & Sciences, Nat Ctr Study & Res, Salsomaggiore, Italy, 84; and others. *Bibliog:* Fumage Works on Paper, catalog for the one-person show of Banerjee, 90, Banerjee's Fumages: Behind the Smoke Screen, Art Heritage Gallery, New Delhi, 90; Arther Jones (auth), Permanent Coll Expo Catalogue, Univ Va, 2000; Basu Chitralekha (auth), Fire & Smoke, Statesman, Calculta, 8/26/2000. *Mem:* Col Art Asn Am, NY; Print Club, Philadelphia; Ancient Art, Paris; MoMA, New York City. *Media:* Fumage; Carbontransfer. *Publ:* Coauth, Mine, 64; contribr, Revolutionist Master-Artist Henri Matisse, 70, Painter Sonia Delaunay, 70, Metaphysical Master-Artist de Chirico, 72 & Picasso, 82; Contemporary Artists of New York, 93; Picasso, 82; and many others; and others. *Dealer:* Bertha Urdang Gallery 23 E 74th St New York NY 10021. *Mailing Add:* Loft 2C 106 Ridge St New York NY 10002-2554

BANEY, RALPH RAMOUTAR
SCULPTOR
b Trinidad, West Indies, Sept 22, 29. *Study:* Brighton Col Art, Eng, 57-62; Univ Md, MFA, 73, PhD, 80; also with Kenneth Campbell & Arthur J Ayres. *Hon Degrees:* Doctor of Letters Univ of the West Indies, St Augustine, Trinidad. *Work:* Nat Mus Art Gallery, Trinidad; Cent Bank, Trinidad; Washington Co Mus, Hagerstown, Md; Univ West Indies; Van Leer Found, Amsterdam, Holland. *Comn:* relief sculpture, Norweg Seamen's Mission, Trinidad, 69; nat coat of arms, Cent Bank Trinidad, 70; mosaic mural (with Vera Baney), Bishop's High Sch, Trinidad, 71; monumental marble sculpture, City Hall, Valjevo, Yugoslavia, 84; mural for Scotiabank Hq, Trinidad. *Exhib:* Sao Paulo Biennial, Brazil, 67 & 69; one-man shows, Sculpture House Gallery, NY, 73, Pan Am Union, Washington, DC, 74 & Washington Co Mus, Hagerstown, Md, 84; Sculptors Guild Mem Ann, Lever House, NY, 74-89; Columbia Art Ctr, Md, 2003; Retrospective, Nat'l Mus, Trinidad, Toyko. *Collection Arranged:* Sculpture in Wood & Bronze, Drawing, Paintings. *Pos:* Free Lance Sculptor. *Teaching:* Supvr art, Ministry Educ & Cult, Trinidad, 63-71; instr art, Univ Md, 72-75; instr art, Smithsonian Inst, 74-79; prof, Dundalk Community Col, 76-. *Awards:* Gold Medal Merit, Govt Trinidad & Tobago, 73; First Prize Sculpture, Ten & 22nd Md Juried Exhib, Easton Acad Md, 74 & 86; First Prize Sculpture, Spanish Am Art Exhib, 74. *Bibliog:* Rod Naylor (auth), Woodcarving Techniques, Batsford, 79; Nicholas Roukes (auth), Masters of Wood Sculpture, Watson Guptill, 80; Anthony Padovano (auth), Sculpture Processes, Doubleday, 81; Robert Bersson (auth), Responding to Art, McGraw Hill. *Mem:* Royal Soc Brit Sculptors (fel); Sculptors Guild; Sculptors' Inc Baltimore; Wash Sculptors Group. *Media:* Wood, Bronze. *Res:* films, clay, glazes. *Interests:* Photog, gardening. *Collection:* Her Majesty, Queen Elizabeth, Nat'l Mus, Trinidad & Tobago. *Publ:* Ralph Baney A Retrospective, Nat'l Mus of Trinidad, A Catalog, 2004. *Mailing Add:* 5203 Talbots Landing Ellicott City MD 21043-6845

BANGERT, COLETTE STUEBE
PAINTER
b Columbus, Ohio, July 7, 1934. *Study:* John Herron Art Inst, BFA, 57; Boston Univ, MFA, 58; Ind Univ; Kans Univ. *Work:* Mulane Art Mus, Topeka, Kans; Mus Mod Art, NY; Univ Okla Mus Art, Norman; Springfield Art Mus, Mo; Sheldon Mem Art Gallery, Lincoln, Nebr; Spencer Art Mus, Univ Kans, Lawrence; Victoria and Albert Mus, London, Eng. *Comn:* Grassland Garden, Topeka Pub Libr, 69 & Landlace: Greening III, Townsite Eatery, 77, Topeka, Kans. *Exhib:* solo exhibs, Sheldon Mem Art Gallery, Lincoln, Nebr, 78 & Albrecht Art Mus, Mo, 84, Krasner Gallery, New York City, 63, 80, The Garden Series: Works on Paper and Thread Pieces, Lawrence Arts Ctr, Kans, 02 & Kans Governor's Offices, Topeka, 2005; Computer Art, Ben Shahn Galleries, Wayne, NJ, 85; ACM Siggraph 86 Art Show: A Twenty Year Computer Art Retrospective, Dallas, Tex & ACM Siggraph 98 Art Show: 25 Year Art Exhib Celebration, Orlando, Fla; Computers and Art, Everson Mus Art, Syracuse, NY & IBM Gallery, NY; Second Emerging Expression Biennial: The Artist and the Computer, Bronx Mus Art, 87; Computer and Video Art, Southern Alleghenies Mus Art, 88; At the Speed of Thought: Two Dimensional Algorithmic Art, Print Club, Philadelphia, Pa, 89; In context: Digital Expressions, Kans State Univ Gallery, Manhattan, 92; A Selection from the Series: The Garden That Was, Kansas City Artists Coalition, Mo, 95; Sumptuous Surfaces/Structured Surfaces, Mulvane Art Mus, Topeka, Kans, 97; Nine Connections, Alice C Sabatini Gallery, & Shawnee Cty Public Libr, Topeka, Kans, 2004. *Teaching:* art instr, Ferry Hall Sch Girls, Lake Forest, Ill, 58-59, Avila Col, Kansas City, Mo, 69-72; drawing instr Univ Mo, Kansas City, 72-74. *Bibliog:* Allan Millstein (auth), Artist abstracts Kansas terrain, Topeka Capital J, 7/14/79; Patrick White (auth), Colette Bangert, New Art Examiner, 5/83; Carolyn McMaster (auth), Personal Visions, Lawrence J World, 9/14/86; Judy Malloy (ed), Women, Art and Technology, 2003; Patric D Prince (auth, MIT pres), Women and The Search for Visual Intelligence, 2003. *Mem:* Kansas City Artists Coalition (pres, 77-78); Imagination & Place Comt, Lawrence, Kans, 2002-. *Media:* Mixed Painting and Drawing, Computer Algorithmic Drawing, Thread Pieces. *Publ:* Coauth, Experiences in making drawings by computer and by hand, Leonardo, 74; illusr, Appreciating Poetry (ed, R P Sugg), Houghton Mifflin, 75; coauth, Computer grass is natural grass, In: Artist and Computer (ed, Ruth Leavitt), Harmony Bks, 76; A short story, In: The Visual Computer (ed, Herbert Franke), Int J Computer Graphics, 86; Colette & Jeff Bangerts Home Page: A Mediation on Computers and Art, Pvt Publ, 94-. *Dealer:* The Fields Gallery Lawrence KS 66044. *Mailing Add:* 721 Tennessee Lawrence KS 66044

BANKER, MAUREEN
DIRECTOR, PRINTMAKER
b Bayonne, NJ. *Study:* Meredith Col, Raleigh, BA, 79; Grad Sch Fine Art, Villa Schifanoia, Florence, Italy, MA(printmaking), 85. *Work:* Munic Bldg Sansepolcro, Italy, Tuscany; Ill Bisonte Graphic Studio & Gallery, Florence, Italy; Meredith Col, Raleigh. *Exhib:* Triennial Int Print Exhib, Clermont-Ferrand, France, 94. *Pos:* Dir galleries, Meredith Col, Raleigh, 90-. *Teaching:* Instr art, Ravenscroft Sch, Raleigh, 80-85; asst prof art & printmaking, Meredith Col, Raleigh, 90-. *Awards:* City Raleigh Emerging Artist Award, 95. *Mem:* United Arts Coun, Raleigh. *Media:* Multiplate Color, Intaglio Etching. *Mailing Add:* Meredith Col 3800 Hillsborough St Raleigh NC 27607-5298

BANKS, ALLAN R
PAINTER
b Dearborn, Mich, Feb 15, 48. *Study:* Sch Fine Arts, Detroit, Mich, 66-68; Atelier of Richard F Lack, Minneapolis, 70-73; R H Ives Gammell Studios, Boston, 76. *Work:* Wadsworth Atheneum, Hartford; Springville Mus Art, Utah; Vixseboxse Galleries, Cleveland Heights, Ohio. *Comn:* Dr James McBride (portrait), Friends of Bowling Green State Univ, Huron, Ohio; two portraits, Hamilton Fish Found, Garrison, NY, 81; five portraits of corporate chairmen, Brush-Wellman Corp, Cleveland, 84; Dr Algalee Adams (portrait), Friends of Bowling Green State Univ, Huron, Ohio, 85. *Exhib:* Butler Inst Am Art, Youngstown, Ohio, 77; Grand Central Art Founders Show, Grand Central Galleries, NY, 81; Art Expo, Nat Coun Jewish Women, Teaneck, NJ, 82; Classical Realism, Amarillo Art Ctr, Tex, 82. *Pos:* Dir, Atelier of Plein Air Studies, 91-. *Awards:* E T Greenshields Award, Greenshields Found, Montreal, 72 & 73; Stacey Award, Stacey Found, NMex, 74; Gold Medal, April Salon, Springville Mus Art, Utah, 82. *Bibliog:* Helen Cullinan (auth) Current day Sargent, Cleveland Plain Dealer, 82; Richard Lack (auth), article, in: Realism in Revolution, Taylor, Dallas, 85; artist subject of film profile, Bowling Green State Univ, Ohio, 85. *Mem:* New Am Acad Art, NY; Soc Classical Realism, Minn; Art Review Ctr. *Media:* Oil. *Publ:* Cover, feature & biog, Am Artist mag, 8/87. *Dealer:* Vixseboxse Art Galleries 12413 Cedar Rd Cleveland Heights OH 44106; Tree's Place Gallery, Cape Cod, MA; REHS Galleries NY NY. *Mailing Add:* PO Box 145 Safety Harbor FL 34695-0145

BANKS, ANNE JOHNSON
PAINTER, EDUCATOR
b New London, Conn, Aug 10, 24. *Study:* Wellesley Col, BA, 46; Honolulu Sch Art, with Willson Stamper, 48-50; George Washington Univ, with Thomas Downing, MFA, 68, sculpture with Jim Sanborn, 78-80. *Exhib:* One-person shows, Lyman Allyn Mus, New London Conn, 64, Alexandria Art League, 73, Foundry Gallery, Washington, 78, 81, 83 & 86 & Gallery 10 Ltd, Washington, 93-97, 99, 2001, 2002, 2005; Hyatt Regency Competition, 81; Va Mus, Richmond, 83; Chrysler Mus, Norfolk, Va, 88; Vartai Gallery, Vilnius, Lithuania, 94, Gallery Riva Sinistra, Florence, Italy, 97;

Phoenix Gallery, NY, 98; Amos Eno Gallery, NY, 2001; Washington Square, Washington, 2000-2002; Venice Prato, Florence, Italy, 2001-2002; and others. *Collection Arranged:* Am Soc Advancement Sci; Northern Va Community Col; Nat Mus of Women in the Arts. *Teaching:* Lectr art, George Washington Univ, summer 68; instr art, George Mason Univ, 68-69; instr art, Northern Va Community Col, 71-72, asst prof, 73-80, chmn dept, 73-89, assoc prof, 80-89, prof emer, 90. *Awards:* Six Merit Awards, Art League, Alexandria, Va, 71-74; Merit Award, Northern Va Fine Arts Asn, 72; Va Ctr Creative Arts Fel, Sweetbriar, 82, 85, 92; Merit Award Arlington Arts Ctr, 2000. *Mem:* Womens Caucus Art; Alexandria Art League; Col Art Asn Am (former mem). *Media:* Drawing, Mixed Media, Painting, Collage, Sculpture. *Res:* hist of design. *Specialty:* contemp fine arts. *Interests:* travel photog. *Publ:* Numerous articles in Northern Va Rev, NY Art Rev & Washington Rev Arts between 81, 87, 98, 2002; Art Criticism: Washington Review of the Arts, Koan, Articulate Mag. *Dealer:* Gallery 10 Ltd Washington DC. *Mailing Add:* The Heights Apt 506 705 New Britain Ave Hartford CT 06106

BANKS, ELLEN
PAINTER
Work: Addison Gallery Am Art, Andover, Mass; Atlanta Pub Libr, Ga; Boston Pub Libr; Citicorp, NY; Chicago Art Inst. *Exhib:* One-person exhibs, McIntosh Gallery, Atlanta, Ga, 89, Soho 20, NY, 90, Akin Gallery, Boston, Mass, 90, Amerika Haus, Berlin, 91, Fine Arts Ctr, Neubrandenburg, Ger, 92, Spandow Gallery, Berlin, Ger, 96 & Artist Haus, Erfreut, Ger, 97; Espace Riquet, 90, Centre de Documentation, 90, CC Gallery, Paris, France, 92; Kennesaw State Col, Marietta, Ga, 91; Stephen Rosenberg Gallery, NY, 91; Donahue/Sosinski, Soho, NY, 97. *Teaching:* Prof painting, Sch Mus Fine Arts, Boston. *Awards:* Nat Endowment Arts, Visual Artist Grant, 87; Nexus Press Bk Grant, 88; Mass Artists Fel, 91. *Bibliog:* Addison Parks (auth), The Christian Science Monitor, 1/91; Alicia Faxon (auth), Women Artists News, winter 91; Renee Schipp (auth), Berliner Morgenpost, 92. *Dealer:* McIntosh Gallery Atlanta GA. *Mailing Add:* 329 Park Place Brooklyn NY 11238

BANKS, HOLLY HOPE
PAINTER
Study: Atelier of Plein-Air Studios, 96; Studio of Daniel Greene, NY, 91; Univ Toledo, BA. *Exhib:* two-person show, Tarpon Springs Cult Ctr, 94; Hilton Head Art League, 97; Catharine Lorillard Wolfe Art Club, 102nd Ann Exhib, Nat Arts Club, NY, 98; Audubon Artists 57th Ann Exhib, NY, 99; 62nd Ann Midyear Exhib, Butler Inst Am Art, Youngstown, Ohio, 2000; 58th Ann Exhib, Audubon Artists, Salmagundi Club, NY, 2000. *Awards:* Art Interests Award, 80; J Paul Dorfmuller Pastel Award, 92; Daler-Rowney Award, Audubon Artists 57th Ann Exhib, Salmagundi Club, NY, 99. *Mem:* Am Soc of Classical Realism; Am Artist Prof League; Audobon Artists; Portrait Soc of Am, Inc; Nat Mus of Women in the Arts. *Media:* Oiil and Pastels, Acrylic, Oil. *Publ:* Cover artist, Masterpieces, 1/97; article Am Artist Mag, 10/98. *Dealer:* Anderson Fine Art Gallery GA; Clare Robbins Portrait Agent FL; Richard Gandy Gallery of Realistic Art Website Gallery. *Mailing Add:* PO Box 233 Safety Harbor FL 34695

BANKS, MARCIA GILLMAN
PAINTER, ILLUSTRATOR
b New York, NY, Feb 20, 34. *Study:* Parsons Sch Design, 55. *Work:* Montclair Art Mus, NJ. *Comn:* Mural, Cotten Entertainment, Dallas, Tex, 93; mural, Melrose Hotel, Dallas, Tex, 94. *Exhib:* Martin Lawrence Gallery, NY. *Awards:* Generoso Pope Award, NY. *Media:* Acrylic on Canvas. *Collection:* Bank of Am. *Mailing Add:* Banks Fine Art 1231 Dragun St Dallas TX 75207

BANKS, ROBERT HARRIS
ART DEALER, PUBLISHER
b New York, NY, Nov 25, 57. *Study:* Fla State Univ, BFA, 78. *Pos:* Dealer, Banks Fine Art, currently. *Mem:* Appraisers Asn Am. *Specialty:* 19th and 20th century American & European paintings. *Mailing Add:* 1231 Dragon St Dallas TX 75207

BANNARD, WALTER DARBY
PAINTER, ART WRITER
b New Haven, Conn, Sept 23, 1934. *Study:* Phillips Exeter Acad; Princeton Univ. *Work:* Whitney Mus Am Art, Guggenheim Mus Mod Art, Metrop Mus Art, NY; Albright-Knox Art Gallery, Buffalo, NY; NJ State Mus; Boston Mus Fine Arts; Houston Mus Fine Arts; Honolulu Mus; plus many others. *Exhib:* Whitney Mus Ann, NY, 72; Abstract Painting in the 70's, Mus Fine Arts, Boston, 72; maj retrospective, Baltimore Mus Art, 73; The Great Decade of American Abstraction, Mus Fine Arts, Houston; Art in America after World War II, Guggenheim Mus, 79; one-man shows, Brush Art Gallery, St Lawrence Univ, 87, Richard Love Gallery, Chicago, Ill, 88, Greenberg Wilson Gallery, NY, 89, Greenberg/Wilson Gallery, New York, 90, Jaffe Baker Gallery, Boca Raton, Fla, 92; retrospectives, Montclair Mus Art (with catalog), 91 & Knoedler Gallery, London, Eng, 91; Salander O'Reilly Galleries, NY, 94; Lowe Art Mus, Miami, 99; and many others. *Pos:* Contrib ed, Artforum Mag, 73-74; deleg, Europ-Am Assembly Art Mus, England, 75; cur, Hans Hofmann, Hirshhorn Mus, Washington, DC, 76; mem, Int Exhib Comt, 78-79; co-chmn, Nat Endowment Arts Int Comt Visual Arts, 79-81. *Teaching:* Lectr at numerous universities; symposium & sem, Princeton Univ, NY Univ, Mus Fine Arts, Boston & others, 66-; grad fac, Sch Visual Arts, NY, 84-89; chmn dept art & art history, Univ Miami, 89-97. *Awards:* Nat Endowment Arts, 68-69; Guggenheim Fel, 68-69; Richard A Florsheim Award, 91. *Bibliog:* K Wilkin (auth), Walter Darby Barnaby, Contemporary Artist, St James Press, 89; W Zimmer (auth), Paintings that Reveal the Alchemy of Creation, NY Times 3/3/91; C Wilkinson (auth), Putting the Paint into 'Painterly Abstraction', Trenton Times, 10/91. *Media:* Acrylic. *Publ:* Auth, Touch and scale, Artforum, 6/71; The Art Museum and the Living Artist, Prentice-Hall, 75; Hans Hofmann, Hirshhorn Mus, 76; auth, The emperor's old clothes, Arts Mag, 9/82; Painting of the 50s, Duke Univ, 83; What It's Like to Be An Artist, Miami Mag, Vol 3, No 2, winter 92; and others. *Dealer:* Greenberg-Wilson Gallery 560 Broadway New York NY 10012. *Mailing Add:* c/o Univ Miami Art Dept PO Box 248106 Coral Gables FL 33124-4410

BANNING, JACK, JR
ART DEALER
b Mt Vernon, NY, June 12, 39. *Study:* Brown Univ, AB, 61. *Pos:* Owner, Banning & Assocs Ltd, 74-; partner, Ubu Gallery, NY, 94-. *Mem:* Poster Soc, Inc (founder, treas & bd mem); New Amsterdam Symphony Orchestra (treas & bd mem); Guggenheim Mus Int Asn; Mus Mod Art, NY. *Specialty:* Avant-garde art movements, 20th Century; Original graphic design & vintage modernist photography. *Publ:* Auth, The New Bauhaus, Sch Design Chicago, 93

BANNISTER, PATI (PATRICIA) BROWN BANNISTER
PAINTER, SCULPTOR
b London, Eng, Oct 29, 29; US citizen. *Study:* Slade Acad, London; Studied with father Harold Brown. *Work:* Daytona Beach Mus Arts & Sci, Fla. *Comn:* portraits, Del Mar Race Track, Turf Paradise Ariz Downs; portrait, Comm by Cambrell Jone. *Exhib:* One-woman show, Daytona Beach Mus, Fla, 79, Southwest Arts Found, Houston, Tex, 83, Rotary Club Art Exhib, Amarillo, Tex; portrait, Comn by, Robert Unsell, 87. *Awards:* Nat Publishing Inst, Award Gold Medal for Color Printing; E Emerson Albright Award. *Bibliog:* Dr Gary Libby (dir), Pati Bannister, SW Art Mag, 4/82; Peggy Samuels (coauth) with Harold Samuels, Pati Bannister, Contemp Western Artists, 82; Dr Gary Libby (dir), Romantic Pati Bannister, Daytona Beach Mus Mag, fall, 84. *Media:* Oil, Acrylic; Bronze. *Publ:* Equestrian illustrations, Riding, London; Various children's books, England. *Dealer:* The Bannister Collection 2301 14th St Gulfport MS 39501. *Mailing Add:* 6518 Mauna Loa Dr Diamondhead MS 39525-3838

BANSEMER, ROGER L
PAINTER, WRITER
b Brockton, Mass, July 25, 48. *Study:* Ringling Sch Art, Sarasota, Fla, BA, 69. *Work:* Sperry Rand Corp, NY; Clearwater Oaks Bank & Barnett Bank, Clearwater, Fla; Rutgers Univ, New Brunswick, NJ; Pioneer Bank, Fla; Forbes, Chateau Balleroy, France. *Comn:* Wall Mural, Spyglass Hotel, Clearwater, 79; etching for Pres Carter, City of Clearwater, 79; mural, City Clearwater, 8; The Rocks (mural), Sydney, Australia, 82; painting for poster, City of Clearwater, 83; mural (20 ft x 30 ft), Home Shopping Network, St Petersburg, Fla, 88; and others. *Exhib:* Infinite Space & Kinetic Color, Adelphi Univ, 77; 15th Ann Maj Fla Artists, Harmon Gallery, Naples, Fla, 77; Pan-Am Bldg, DC, 79; Adelphi Univ, NY, 80; Byways Gallery, Sarasota, Fla, 81; St Petersburg Mus Fine Arts, Fla, 85 & 86; Voorhees Gallery Sarasota, Fla, 88; Upham Gallery, St Petersburg, Fla, 88 & 90; Mystic Seaport Gallery, Conn, 90. *Pos:* Artist-in-residence, City of Clearwater, 78. *Awards:* Int Award of Excellence, Mystic Mus, Conn, 91. *Bibliog:* Review by Gene Shalit Today Show, 89; review, Forbes Mag, 89 & Playboy Mag, 90; feature story, Artist Mag, 89. *Media:* Acrylics; Etching. *Publ:* Auth, Smithsonian, Air & Space Mag, 88, Am Artist Mag, 88, Tampa Tribune, 88, Tampa Bay Life Mag, 88, Homes Mag, 88; The Art of HotAir Ballooning; Southern Shores; Rachael's Splendifilous Adventure; Art Water's Edge, The Birds of Florida; Mountians in the Mist (with foreword by James A Michener). *Mailing Add:* 2352 Alligator Creek Rd Clearwater FL 34625

BANTEL, LINDA
MUSEUM DIRECTOR
b King City, Calif, May 30, 43. *Study:* Inst Fine Arts, New York Univ, MA, 71; Wharton Advand Mgt Prog, Univ Pa, cert, 92. *Pos:* Res assoc, Metrop Mus Art, New York 78-80; assoc to chief cur, Pa Acad Fine Arts, 80-85, dir mus, 85-95. *Mem:* Col Art Asn; Asn Art Mus Dirs; Cosmopolitan Club, Philadelphia. *Publ:* Auth, William Rush, American Sculptor, 82 & introduction, Searching Out the Best, 88, Pa Acad Fine Arts, Philadelphia; coauth, American Paintings in the Metropolitan Museum of Art, Vol II: A Catalog of Works by Artists Born Between 1816-1845, Princeton Univ Press, 85; Raphaelle Peale in Philadelphia, Nat Gallery Art & Pa Acad Fine Arts, 88; The Potamkin collection of American art, Mag Antiques, 8/89; and others. *Mailing Add:* 703 W Phil-Ellena St Philadelphia PA 19119-3513

BAPST, SARAH
CONCEPTUAL ARTIST
b Chicago, Ill, May 21, 50. *Study:* Ind Univ, Bloomington, with Mary Ellen Solt, BA 73; Cranbrook Acad Art, studied with Richard DeVore, MFA, 77. *Exhib:* Affinities: Am Women Artists, Laura Knotts Gallery, Bradford Col, Haverhill, Mass, 2000; Works on Paper, South Shore Art Ctr, Cohasset, Mass, 2000; Small Works, Wash Sq East Gallery, NY Univ, 2001; Drawing the New Millennium: The Challenge of Media and Idea to the Nature of Drawing, Danforth Gallery, Portland, Maine, 2001; Hopscotch: Associative Leaps in the Construction of Narrative, Bride Art Ctr, 2002; Artists Under the Influence, Brickbottom Gallery, Somerville, Maine, 2003; group exhib, Marks, Exhib Contemp Drawing, Target Gallery at Torpedo Factory, Alexandria, Va, 2003, Merry Peace, Sideshow Gallery, Brooklyn, NY, 2004, Second Ann Drawing Faculty Exhib, Brant Gallery, MassArt, 2004, Cambridge Art Asn Nat Prize Show, Mus Contemp Art Chicago, Cambridge Art Asn Gallery, Mass, 2004. *Teaching:* Assoc Prof Studio Foundations, Mass Col Art, Boston, Mass, 84-. *Awards:* Fel Works on Paper, Nat Endowment Arts, 91; Best of Show, Marks Contemp Drawing Exhib, 2003; Second prize, Works on Paper Exhib, South Shore Art Ctr, 2003. *Bibliog:* Ron Jones (auth), The last nat sculpture show, Art Papers, 1-2/83; Mary Sherman (auth), Tenth ann Boston drawing show, Art New Eng, 9/89. *Media:* Paper, Sculpture. *Mailing Add:* 20 Concord Ave No 3 Cambridge MA 02138

BARAN, TRACEY
PHOTOGRAPHER
Exhib: Solo shows: Give and Take, Lievman Magnan, NY, 1999, Still, 2000, Mus Contemporary Photography, Chicago, 2002, Leslie Tonkonow Artworks + Projects, NY, 2004, See Through Me, 2006; Group exhibs: Raise the Roof, White Columns, NY, 1998; Personal Touch, Art in General, NY, 1998; Nature/Culture, Gimpels Fils Gallery, London, 1999, Mommie Dearest, 2000; Female, Wessel + O'Connor Gallery, NY, 1999; Psychosoma, Lombard Fried, NY, 2000; Faces and Figures, Douglas Udell Gallery, Vancouver, British Columbia, 2001; Presence, The Foundation to-Life, Inc, Exhib Space, Mt Kisco, NY, 2004, Signs of Being, 2004, Eccentric Modern, 2005; Extreme Landscape, The Hunterdon Mus, Clinton, NJ, 2003; Rimbaud, I-20 Gallery, NY, 2004; Artists Interrogate: Race and Identity, Milwaukee Art Mus, 2005; A Kiss Isn't Just A Kiss., Contemporary Galleries, Univ Conn, 2005; represented in public collections of Milwaukee Art Mus, Miami Art Mus, The Marieluise Hessel Collection, The Ctr for Curatorial Studies, Bard Col, NY. *Mailing Add:* c/o Leslie Tonkonow Artworks + Projects 6th Floor 535 W 22 St New York NY 10011

BARATZ, ROBIN
PAINTER
b Chicago, IL, July 20, 51. *Study:* Northwestern Univ, BS, 1973; MA, 1974; Studied privately c artist, Joshua Graham, Boston, Mass, 1977-1999. *Exhib:* Am Artists Prof League (NYC), Ann Juried Exhibs, 1990, 1994, 2002-2005; Catherine Lorillard Wolfe Art Club (NYC), Ann Juried Open Exhibs, 1990, 1995-1997, 1999, 2000, 2001, 2003-2005; Salmagundi Club (NYC), Ann Juried Open Exhibs, 1991, 1993, 2002-2004; Audubon Atists (NYC), Ann Juried Exhibs, 1994-1996, 1999-2003, 2005, 2006; Lyme Art Asn (Old Lyme, Conn), Art of New Eng, 2002, 2004. *Awards:* Guilia Palermo Award, Audubon Artists Ann Exhib, 2000; Allied Artists of Am Award, Conn Acad Fine Arts, 2004; Alfred & Mary Crimi Award for Creative Oil, Audubon Artists, 2005. *Bibliog:* J Sanders Eaton (auth), Isle of Skye limned (luminously in oils by Robin Baratz), Gallery & Studio, 2001; Katie Kresser (auth), Boston Weekly Dig, 2003; Jeannie McCormack (auth), Gallery & Studio, 2003. *Mem:* Am Artists Prof League; Audubon Artists; Catharine Lorillard Wolfe Art Club; Oil Painters of Am. *Media:* Oil. *Mailing Add:* 159 Bellevue St Newton MA 02458

BARAZANI, MORRIS
EDUCATOR, PAINTER
b Highland Park, Mich, June 24, 24. *Study:* Inst Design, Cranbrook Acad Art, Bloomfield Hills, Mich. *Work:* Gutenberg Mus, Ger; Blue Cross Blue Shield, Chicago, Ill; Gov's State Univ, Ill. *Exhib:* Art Inst Chicago, 59; Chicago Gallery, Ill, 76; Zriny-Hayes Gallery, Chicago, 77 & 79-81; Gilman Galleries, 83-88; one-man show, Gilman Galleries, 85, 87, 90 & C & D Gallery, 2006; Gruen Galleries, 91-93; and others. *Teaching:* Prof painting, Univ Ill, Chicago, 69-93. *Media:* Oil, Collage. *Dealer:* Corbett & Dempsey Gallery Chicago IL. *Mailing Add:* 5340 N Magnolia Ave Chicago IL 60640

BARBEAU, MARCEL (CHRISTIAN)
PAINTER, SCULPTOR
b Montreal, Que, Feb 18, 1925. *Study:* Ecole Meuble, dipl, 47; with Paul-Emile Borduas. *Work:* Nat Gallery, Can & Washington; Chrysler Mus, Norfolk, Va; Rose Art Mus, Brandeis Univ; British Mus, London; Musee des Beaux-Arts de Lyons & Mus d'Art Contemp, Montreal, Que; Stellejk Mus, Amsterdam; plus others. *Comn:* Nadia or Le saut du tremplin (painted welded aluminum sculpture), Societe du Vieux-Port, Montreal, 76; Liberte, liberte cherie (painted welded steel), Lachine-Marina, Que, 86; Laurentians (acrylic on aluminium mural), Via Rail intercontinental train, 89; Les portes du regard (painted welded steel), City Hall Parc, Montreal-Est, 90; Window on Future (painted welded steel sculpture), McLennan Libr Terr, McGill Univ, 92. *Exhib:* Pen House Show, Mus Mod Art, NY, 65; retrospectives, Winnipeg Art Gallery & Mus Art Contemp, Montreal, 69; Borduas er le Automatist, Grand Palais, Paris, 71; Modern Painting in Canada, Edmonton Art Gallery, 78 & The Contemp Art Society: Montreal 1939-1947, 80, Edmonton Art Gallery; Montreal Mus Fine Arts, 91; Mus d'art Contemporain de Montreal, 92; Canadian Abstract Painting & Design in Fifties, Winnipeg Art Gallery, 92; Modern Sculpture in Quebec: 1947-1960, Mus du Que, 93; Second Jeux de la Francophonie, Paris, 94; The Sixties in Canada, Nat Gallery, Can, 2005; plus others. *Teaching:* Bishop Univ, 78-80. *Awards:* First Prize Sculpture Competition, McDonalds Restaurant, 85; Cert of Excellence, Int Art Competition, NY, 88; Gold Medal (painting), Second Jeux de la Francophonie, Paris, 94; Royal Can Acad, 92, Officer Can Order, 95. *Bibliog:* Carolle Gagnon & Ninon Gauthier, introd by Charles Delloye, Marcel Barbeau: Fugato, CECA Publ, Montreal, 90; Cercle D'Art Paris, 94; Manon Barbeau (film dir, producer), Les Enfants De Refus Global, Ont, 98. *Mem:* Conseil artistes peintres (vpres, 78-79); Fedn artistes arts visuels Que (pres, 78-79); Artist for Peace; Royal Can Acad Arts; Royal Can Acad. *Media:* Acrylic; Welded Metal, Wood. *Interests:* Contemporary Dance & Music, Movies, Poetry. *Publ:* Auth, Grande probite intellectuelle, Devoir, Que, 60; L'artiste devant son oeuvre, Cahiers, Que, 79; and others. *Dealer:* Elliott Louis Gallery Vancouver BC Canada; 1540 West 2nd Avenue Vancouver BC Canada. *Mailing Add:* 11 Rue Sesto Fiorentino Apt 101 Bagnolet France

BARBEE, ROBERT THOMAS
PAINTER, GRAPHIC ARTIST
b Detroit, Mich, Sept 25, 21. *Study:* Cranbrook Acad Art, BA & MFA; Centenary Col; also in Mex. *Work:* Butler Inst Am Art, Youngstown, Ohio; Cranbrook Acad Art, Bloomfield Hills, Mich. *Exhib:* Five shows, Va Mus Fine Arts, Richmond, 53-65 & Traveling Exhibs, 58 & 62; Birmingham Mus Art, 59; Norfolk Mus Art & Sci, 60; Mus Art of Ogunquit, Maine, 62 & 63; Am Fedn Arts, NY, 65; and others. *Teaching:* Instr painting & drawing, Univ Va, assoc prof art, 70-. *Awards:* Prizes, Irene Leach Mem Exhib, Norfolk Mus Arts & Sci, 62 & 64 & Thalheimer's Exhib, Richmond, 63. *Mailing Add:* 1521 Rugby Rd Charlottesville VA 22903-1242

BARBER, BRUCE ALISTAIR
INSTALLATION PERFORMANCE & VIDEO ART, CULT HISTORIAN,
b Auckland, NZ, Dec 11, 50; Can & NZ citizen. *Study:* Auckland Univ Sch Fine Arts, BFA, 73, MFA, 74; NS Col Col Art & Design, Halifax, NS, MFA, 78; European Grad Sch, Leuk-Stadt, Switz, PhD, 2005. *Work:* Ludnizca Centre Poland, AGNS; Halifax & ACAG, Auckland, NZ; Franklin Furnace Archive; Bibliotech Nationale, Paris; Nat Archive Film & Video, NZ. *Exhib:* The Art of Memory-The Loss of Hist (with catalog), New Mus, NY, 85-86; A Different War: Vietnam in Art (catalog), Whatcom Mus, Bellingham De Cordova Traveling, 89-92; Interscop Festival (catalog), Warsaw, Poland, 90; Memory Works (catalog), London Regional Art Gallery, traveling, 90-91; Story Telling/Real Time (catalog), Gdansk, Poland, 91; Reading & writing Room Exhibs, 84, 87, 90, 93, 95, 98, & 2003; Photographers, Wksp Gallery, Toronto, 96; The Seventies, Artspace, Auckland, Govett Browstor, Auckland, 98; Lopdell Art Gallery, Auckland, 98; Gallery, Newcastle Sch Arts, Australia; Room 103, Auckland, NZ; Govett-Brewster, New Plymouth, NZ. *Pos:* ECoast ed, FUSE Mag, Toronto, 84-90; bd mem, Univ Art Asn Can, 89-94, LJB Media ARts Soc, 89 & Can Film Studies Asn, 97-98; Dalhousie Review, 2001; Ed Bd NSCAD Press, 2003; Topie Journal of Can Cult Studies; NZ Journal of Art Hist. *Teaching:* Jr lectr sculpture, Auckland Univ, NZ, 74-75; asst prof fine art, Simon Fraser Univ, 79-81; asst prof intermedia-studio & art hist, NS Col Art & Design, 81-89, assoc prof, 90-95, intermedia coordr & chmn media arts dept, 96-; prof media arts & visual cult studies teaching fel, Univ Kings Col, Halifax, 98-2003; dir MFA prog, NSCAD, U, 90-94, 98, 2005-2006. *Awards:* Queen Elizabeth II Arts Coun, 77 & 79; Social Sci & Humanities Res Coun Can Res Awards, 82, 83, 89, 91, 92 & 96-99; Can Coun B Grant (proj grants), Criticism & Visual Arts, 84, 88 & 90; Ont Critics Grant, 85. *Bibliog:* M Cheetham (auth), Remembering Postmodernism, Oxford Univ Press, Can; L Hutcheon (auth), Splitting Images, Toronto Oxford Univ Press, 91; A M Richard & C Robertson (auths), Performance in Canada 1970-1990, Que Inter/Editeur, 91; M Dunn, NZ Sulpture: A History, 2003. *Mem:* Univ Art Asn Can; Popular Cult Asn Am; Can Film Studies Asn. *Media:* Interdisciplinary, Video, Installation Performance. *Res:* Popular culture, theory & politics, cultural studies. *Publ:* Auth, C Pontbriand (ed), Performance Texts & Documents, Parachute Publ, 81; ed, essays on Performance & Cultural Politicization, Open Letter 5: 5 & 6, 83; D Lander, M Lexier, Sound by Artists, Art Metropole Publ, Toronto, 90; auth, Reading Rooms, Halifax, Eyelevel Pub, 92; co-ed (with S Guilbaut & J O'Brian), Voices of Fire: Art, Rage, Power and The State, Toronto, Univ Toronto Press, 96; Conceptual Art: The NSCAD Connection 1967-1973, 2002. *Mailing Add:* School of Graduate Studies NSCAD Univ 5163 Duke St Halifax NS B3J 3J6 Canada

BARBER, CYNTHIA
SCULPTOR, PRINTMAKER
b Boston, Mass, Dec 12, 39. *Study:* Barnard Col, BA, 61; Brandeis Univ, MA, 63; Richmond Col, Eng, 71-73. *Work:* Albuquerque Mus, NMex; Albuquerque Tech-Vocational Inst, NMex; Duke Univ, Raleigh, NC; Grants Mining Mus, Grants, NMex; George Meany Ctr Labor Studies, Silver Springs, MD. *Comn:* Holocaust Memorial, Gaithersburg Hebrew Congregation, Md, 81; outdoor sculpture for office complex, Shell Plaza, Bakersfield, Calif, 86; Hacienda Towers, Los Angeles, Calif, 90; bronze wall sculpture & lamps, Temple Emanuel, Kensington, MD, 96; outdoor sculpture, Albuquerque Tech-Voc Inst, 96-97. *Exhib:* Asn Int de Defense des Artistes, Amsterdam, 81, traveling throughout Europe, 81-82; Nat Coun Art Jewish Life Judaic Art Exhib, Lever House, NY, 83; Festival Arts: Sculpture for Pub Spaces, Albuquerque, NMex, 85; North Am Sculpture Exhib, Golden, Colo, 86; Art of Albuquerque, Albuquerque Mus, 90; Mile of Sculpture, Gov's Gallery, State of NMex, Santa Fe, 91; Johnson Gallery, Univ NMex, Albuquerque, NMex, 95; Outdoor Installation, NMex Mus Natural Hist, Albuquerque, NMex, 95-98. *Pos:* Founding mem & bd dir, Touchstone Gallery, Washington, DC, 76-77 & Association Internationale de Defense des Artistes, US, 81-85; prog coordr, Tamarind Inst, Alburquerque, NMex, 93-; capitol art found bd, Santa Fe, NMex, 93-96. *Teaching:* Instr humanities, Howard Univ, Washington, DC, 66-70. *Awards:* NMex Art in Pub Places Purchase Awards, Harriet B Samons State Office Bldg, Farmington, NMex, 86; Grants, Mus Mining, NMex, 86. *Bibliog:* Commisions, Sculpture Mag, 11-12/87; Myles Nye (auth), Taos Galleries Have Poetry, Controversy, Albuquerque J, 10/25/92; Wesley Pulka (auth) Space Can't Limit Five Sculptors' Potent Images, Albuquerque J, 8/6/95. *Media:* All; Woodcut. *Mailing Add:* 425 Hermosa Dr SE Albuquerque NM 87108

BARBER, PHILIP JUDD
PAINTER, PRINTMAKER
b Cleveland, Ohio, Sept 27, 51. *Study:* Ohio Univ, BS, 73, BFA, 77. *Work:* Minneapolis Inst Arts; Purdue Univ, Ind; First Banks Systs, Minneapolis; Chemical Bank, NY; Frans Masereel Centrum, Kasterlee, Belg. *Exhib:* Boston Printmakers, DeCordova Mus, Boston, 78; Chautauqua Nat Exhib of Am Art, Chautauqua Art Mus, NY, 83; May Show, Cleveland Mus Art, 83; Small Print Exhib, Purdue Art Mus, Ind, 84; Minn Artists Exhib Prog - 10th Anniversary Exhib, Minneapolis Inst Arts, 86. *Pos:* Studio mgr, Vermillion Ed Ltd, Minn, 78-. *Awards:* First Place, Art Ctr Minn, 85. *Media:* Tempra, Oil; Stick. *Dealer:* Vermillion Ed Ltd 2919 Como Ave SE Minneapolis MN 55414. *Mailing Add:* 2904 Buchanan St NE Minneapolis MN 55418-2209

BARBER, SAM
PAINTER, SCULPTOR
b Naples, Italy, April 9, 43. *Study:* Art Students League, Nat Acad Fine Art, New York, Cape Sch Art, Provincetown, Mass. *Work:* Miss Mus Art, Jackson; New Orleans Mus Art, La; Midwest Mus Am Art, Elkhart, Ind; Hickory Mus Art, NC; Memphis Brooks Mus Art, Tenn. *Exhib:* eleven one-man exhibs, 83-90. *Awards:* Purchase Prize, La Grange Col, Ga, 74; Philip Eisenberg Award, Salmagundi Club, New York, 81. *Media:* Oil. *Dealer:* Cape Cod Guild Fine Arts 248 Stevens Street Hyannis Mass 02601

BARBERA, ROSS WILLIAM
PAINTER
b Brooklyn, NY, Dec 11, 50. *Study:* St John's Univ, Jamaica, NY, BFA, 73; Pratt Inst, Brooklyn, NY, MFA, 75. *Work:* Harley Sch, Wilson Arts Ctr, Rochester, NY; Univ Wis, Milwaukee; La Grange Col, Ga; Chautauqua Arts Ctr, NY. *Comn:* Landscape painting (oil on canvas), Univ Wis, Milwaukee, 85. *Exhib:* One-man shows, Jean Lumbard Gallery, NY, 83 & Clark Whitney Gallery, Lenox, Mass, 89; And the Living is Easy, Visual Arts Mus, NY, 84; The Razor Show, Jayne Baum & Hudson Ctr Galleries, NY, 85; Six Long Island Artists, Islip Art Mus, NY, 85; The Landscape, Columbus Mus Ohio, 87; and others. *Pos:* cur, St John's Univ Gallery, Jamaica, NY, 94. *Teaching:* Asst Prof Fine Art, St John's Univ, Jamaica, NY, 80-; adj asst prof fine art, Nassau Community Col, Garden City, NY, 87-. *Awards:* Creative Artist Pub Serv Painting Fel, NY State, 76; Nat Endowment Arts Painting Fel, 85-86; Grant, Hillwood Mt Mus, Long Island Univ, CW Post. *Bibliog:* Ellen Lubell (auth), Rev, Arts Mag, 10/75; Laurie Hurwitz (auth), Airbrush techniques for landscape painters, Am Artist, 10/87; Eunivce Agar (auth), Painting Expressively with an airbrush, Am Artist, 10/94. *Mem:* Organization of Independent Artists. *Media:* Acrylic, Oil. *Dealer:* Art Exchange Gallery, 60 E. San Francisco, St. Santa Fe NM 87501. *Mailing Add:* 340 Croaton St Ronkonkoma NY 11779-4917

BARBIER-MUELLER, JEAN-PAUL
COLLECTOR, MUSEUM FOUNDER
Pos: Pres, bd, Barbier-Mueller Art Mus, Geneva & Barcelona, 77-; recipient Commandeur de l'Ordee Légion d'Honneur, France, 2002, Commandeur de l'Order des Arts et Lettres, 97. *Awards:* Named one of Top 200 Collectors, ARTnews Mag, 2004, 2005, 2006. *Collection:* Tribal art, Pre-Columbian art, Modern and Contemporary art. *Mailing Add:* Barbier-Mueller Museum Rue Jean-Calvin Geneva 10 1204 Switzerland

BARBOUR, ARTHUR J
PAINTER, WRITER
b Paterson, NJ, Aug 23, 26. *Study:* Newark Sch Fine & Indust Art; and with Avery Johnson, Syd Brown & James Carlin. *Work.* US Navy Dept, Marietta Col; Norfolk Mus Arts & Sci; Prudential Life Ins Co; & many pvt collections. *Comn:* Watercolors, Woman's Day Mag, Ford Motor Co & Essex Chem Corp; mural, Am Artists Christmas Card Group. *Exhib:* Nat Acad Design, NY; Am Watercolor Soc, NY; Am Artists Prof League; one-man show, Beaumont Mus Art, Tex, 65; Wolf Gallery, Franklin, NJ, 73; Fritchman Galleries, Boise, Idaho, 74; and others. *Awards:* Gold Medal, Am Watercolor Soc, 65; Mary S Litt Award, Am Watercolor Soc, 83; Silver Medal Honor, Audubon Artists, 88. *Mem:* Am & NJ Watercolor Socs; Painters & Sculptors Soc NJ; Allied Artists; Nat Soc Painters Casein & Acrylic; Nat Acad. *Media:* Watercolor. *Publ:* Auth, Painting Building in Watercolor 73, Painting the Seasons in Watercolor, 75 & Watercolor: The Wet Technique, 78,; Painting the Seasons in Watercolor, 1980; and others. *Mailing Add:* 29 Voorhis Pl Ringwood NJ 07456

BARBOZA, ANTHONY
PHOTOGRAPHER, PAINTER
b New Bedford, Mass, May 10, 44. *Study:* Self taught. *Work:* Mus Mod Art & Studio Mus Harlem, NY; Oberlin Col, Ohio; Newark Art Mus, NJ; Brooklyn Mus, Brooklyn, NY. *Exhib:* Mirrors & Windows, Mus Mod Art, NY, 78; Nine Contemp Photographers, Witkin Gallery, NY, 79; Polaroids, Photokina, Cologne Ger, 82 & 84; Nude in Photog, Munchner Stadtmuseum, Munich, WGer, 85; Los Angeles Expression, Los Angeles Co Mus Art, 90; Songs of my People, Time Life Worldwide Tour, 90. *Teaching:* Lectr, Int Ctr Photog, New York, 75 & 83, Columbia Col, Chicago, 84 & Rochester Inst Technol, 91. *Awards:* Photog Grants NY State Coun Arts, 74 & 76; Nat Endowment Arts Photog Grant, 80. *Bibliog:* Allen Porter (auth), Portraits, Camera Mag, Switz, 6/80. *Media:* Oil. *Publ:* Auth, Black Borders, pvt publ, 80; Color of Fashion, Stuart, Tabori & Chang/Kodak; African Americans, Viking, 93; Day in the Life of Israel, Viking, 94; Double take, Jazz Portfolio-Duke Univ, fall 95. *Dealer:* Robert Mann Gallery 42 E 76th St New York NY 10021. *Mailing Add:* 915 Gloucester Ct Westburg NY 11590-5301

BARD, GAYLE
PAINTER, SCULPTOR
b Kansas City, Kans. *Study:* DePauw Univ, Univ Chicago, Univ Wis, Milwaukee, Yale Univ, Cornish Col Arts. *Work:* City of Seattle, var collections; Key Corp, Albany, NY; Howard Hughes Properties, Las Vegas, Nev; Microsoft Corp, Federal Home Loan Bank & Safeco Insurance, Seattle; Management Compensation Group, Portland, Ore. *Comn:* Univ Hosp, Univ Wash; Seattle Arts Comn; Wash State Arts Comn; Va Mason Hosp. *Exhib:* First Impressions: Northwest Monotypes, Seattle Art Mus, 89; Linda Hodges Gallery, 98, 99 & 01; From Here to the Horizon: Artists of the Rural Landscape, Whatcom Mus History & Art, Bellingham, Wash, 99; The View from Here: 100Artists/Centennial of Mount Rainier, Kittredge Gallery/Univ Puget Sound and Tokyo, Japan, 99; Self Images, Art Space, Seattle, Wash, 99; Laura Russo Gallery, Portland, Ore, 2000; and others. *Teaching:* Fac, Cornish Inst Arts, Seattle, Wash, 88-90 & NW Col Art, Poulsbo, Wash, 96-97. *Awards:* Fel, Nat Endowment Arts, 87; Fel Printmaking, Centrum Found, 88. *Bibliog:* Ron Glowen (auth), Four directions, Artweek, 5/21/86; Deloris Tarzan (auth), Artists Exhibition offers 'double' vision, Seattle Times, 4/27/86; Christopher Schnoor (auth), Contemporary art, citation & the past, Vision Mag, summer 86; Helen Mershon (auth), Step inside, Oregonian, 3/9/87. *Dealer:* Linda Hodges Gallery 316 First Ave S Seattle WA 98104. *Mailing Add:* 11197 Blue Pond Pl NE Bainbridge Island WA 98110

BARD, JOELLEN
INSTRUCTOR, PAINTER
b Brooklyn, NY, June 19, 42. *Study:* Syracuse Univ Art Sch, 59-62; Brooklyn Col, painting with Philip Pearlstein, MA, 67, adv cert, 87; Brooklyn Mus Art Sch, Max Beckman, scholar class, 70-73; Pratt Inst, Hon BFA; AAS(knitwear design), Fashion Inst Technol, 2001. *Work:* Many pvt & corp collections. *Exhib:* Brooklyn Mus, 73 & 74; one-man shows, Brooklyn Mus Little Gallery, 73, Gallery 91, Brooklyn, 74-76 & Pleiades Gallery, NY, 75, 77, 79 & 82; Windows of Bergdorf Goodman New York City, 89, Brooklyn Botanic Garden, 89. *Collection Arranged:* Tenth St Days--The Co-ops of the 50s. *Pos:* Dir, Asn Artist Run Galleries, 77-. *Teaching:* Art teacher, New York Bd Educ, 64-69 & 78-, Kingsborough Community Col, 79-83 & 86-94. *Bibliog:* Eileen Blair (auth), Mindscapes, Phoenix, 3/21/75; David Shirey (auth), Artists forming sobro, NY Times, 3/75; Helen Thomas (auth), article in Arts Mag, 3/79. *Mem:* Asn Artist Run Galleries; United Fedn Teachers. *Media:* Acrylic on canvas; Plexiglas, Mixed Media; Knitwear

BARDAZZI, PETER
PAINTER
b New York, NY, Mar 5, 43. *Study:* Pratt Inst, BFA, 67; Yale Univ, MFA, 69; also study art & archit, Asia; Alias Technology, Toronto, Canada, Power Animator Certificate in 3D Computer Animation, 91; Silicon Studios, Santa Monica, CA, Digital Masters Certificate, 96. *Work:* Mus Mod Art, NY; Purchase Mus, NY; Corcoran Gallery, Washington, DC; Rockefeller Univ; Neuberger Mus, Purchase, NY; Elder Art Gallery, Wesleyan Univ; Weatherspoon Art Mus, Univ NC; plus many other pvt & public collections. *Exhib:* One-man shows, Cordier & Ekstrom Gallery, 71, 72, 74, 76 & 78 & St Mary's Col, Md, 75; Whitney Mus Am Art Painting Ann, 72; Indianapolis Mus Art Painting & Sculpture Today, 72; Am Acad Arts & Lett, 73; Cordier & Ekstrom, 76; Corcoran Gallery, 76; Univ Tex, Austin, 76; Shriek if You Know What I Did Last Friday the 13th, 99; Curiosity, 2000; Hollywood Goes Digital, 2001; Digital Printmaking Now, 2001; Independent Film Project, NY, 2002; Projects in Hell, Documentary about col student's vision of hell, 2002; DYI Convention, NY; The Exquisite Body (body on the surrealist concept of the Exquisite Corpse), 2003; Scents: Locks: Kisses, Limbburg, Belgium, 2005; Collection of a Lifetime, Neuberger Mus Art, Purchase Col, SUNY, 2006. *Pos:* Guest lectr & artist in residence, St Mary's Col, Md, 75; assoc prof digital arts, NY Univ, 96-; Dir, New Media Development, New York Univ, 2004-06; Dir & co-founder, Ctr for Advanced Digital Applications, NY Univ, 1996-2004; Dir, digital imaging & design master's degree prog, NY Univ, 2000-05; The Art Inst Boston, MFA Mentoring Prog, 2006-; and many others. *Awards:* Fed Work Study Prog Award, 68; Painting Award, New Britain Mus, Conn, 69; Am Accad Arts & Letters Award, painting, 73; Digital Masters Award, Silicon Studios & Graphics, 96; plus many others. *Bibliog:* Hilton Kramer (auth), 10/74 & Vivian Raynor (auth), 5/78, articles, New York Times; Peter Frank (auth), article, Art News Mag, 10/78; and others. *Collection:* Albert Petcavage, NY; Amstar Corp, NY; Armand Deutsch, Beverly Hills, CA; Artco International, Geneva, Switzerland; Chase Manhattan Bank; Corcoran Gallery, Washington, DC; Cordier & Ekstrom, Gallery, NY; Crocker National Bank, NY; Elder Art Gallery, Wesleyan, Univ, NE; French & Company, London; Henry Markus, Chicago, IL; Jan von Haeften, Hambury, Germany; Joseph Barber, NY; Kutztown State College, PA; Mus of Modern Art, NY; Neuberger Mus, Purchase, NY; Rockfeller Univ, NY; Roy Neuberger, NY; Sandra Payson, NY; Singer Corp., NY; Starwood Corp; Willis van Devanter, Upperville, VA; Zao Wou-Ki and Francoise Marquet, Paris France; The Weatherspoon Art Mus at The Univ of North Carolina. *Publ:* Film and Video Mag, Education & Training; Challenge 3, by Iain Blair, Aug 15, 99; Shoot Mag, Second Time Around, by Justine Ellas, Jan, 14, 2000; Millimeter Mag, What CADA Did Last Summer, by Kristinha Mc Cort, May, 1, 2000; New York Times, When A Film Needs a Good Buzz, by Karen W Arenson, Allison Fass, and Jacques Steinberg, November, 29, 2000; Chronicle of Higher Education, Descent Into Darkness, by Jennifer Jacobson, April, 2001; Denver Post, Cinematic Silk Purses Hollywood Portrayals of Historical Women, Unlike Men, Turn Even the Homeliest into Glamour Queens, by William Porter, November, 12, 2002; Los Angeles Times, In Supporting Roles, By Lynn Smith, March, 30, 2003. *Mailing Add:* 210 E15th St Apt 7K New York NY 10003

BAREFORD, DAVID
PAINTER
b Rahway, NJ, 47. *Study:* Wheaton Col, Ill, 1967; Univ Mont, BA, studied with James Dunn, William Hook. *Work:* Sears Corp Collection, Chicago, Ill; Fleet Bank, Boston, Mass; Paine Weber Corp, NY; Otis Elevator Co, Conn. *Exhib:* Nat Acad Design; Am Watercolor Soc Traveling Exhib; Allied Artists Am Nat Shows; Nat Arts Club; solo exhib, Quester Gallery, Stonington, Conn, 1989-2001, Main Street Gallery, Nantucket, Mass, 1980-99. *Awards:* Nat Award, watercolor, Allied Artists of Am, 1975; New Mem Award, Rockport Art Asn. *Mem:* Allied Artists Am, NY; Am Soc Marine Artists; Am Watercolor Soc; Rockport Art Asn, Mass. *Media:* Oil, Watercolor. *Specialty:* Landscapes and marine. *Mailing Add:* 959 Stoning Ton Rd Stonington CT 06378

BAREISS, WALTER
PATRON
b Tubingen, Ger, May 24, 19. *Study:* Yale Univ, BS; Columbia Law Sch. *Work:* Yale; Mus Mod Art; Metrop, NY; Toledo, Ohio Mus Fine Arts; Bavarian State Mus; 20th century art, Yale. *Exhib:* Greek vases, Getty Mus; Greek vases, Metrop Mus; one man show Flinn Gallery, Greenwich Libr. *Pos:* Chmn gov bd, Art Gallery, Yale Univ; comt for prints & illus bks, Mus Mod Art; vis comt 20th century art, Metrop Mus, NY. *Awards:* Medal Yale Univ, 2000. *Mem:* Bavarian State Asn Contemp Art; hon Acad of Fine Arts of Bavaria, Ger. *Media:* African art, contemporary art. *Collection:* Twentieth century art; Greek vases, fifth & sixth centuries, BC; African art 19th & 20th century; contemporary Japanese ceramics; Italian 15th & 16th century ceramics

BARGER, M SUSAN
CONSULTANT, CONSERVATOR
b Tucson, Ariz, Sept 7, 49. *Study:* Immaculate Heart Col, BA, 70; Rochester Inst Technol, MST, 75; Pa State Univ, PhD, 82. *Pos:* Mus consult scientist, 82-; res chemist, Libr of Cong Preserv Lab, 84-86; co dir, Barger & Wilson Collection Serv, Santa Fe, NMex, 96-99 & Barger & Lewis Collection Svcs, 2000; prog mgr, Small Mus Develop Prog, NMex, 2001-04, Mus Develop Assoc, 2005-. *Teaching:* Textiles, M H de Young Mus Art Sch, San Francisco, 71-73; assoc res prof mat sci, Johns Hopkins Univ, 86-92; adj assoc prof, Univ NMex, 90-. *Bibliog:* NM Brown & Gordon Shed (auths), Scattered Images, Research/Penn State 5, 9/84; Quantum, Australian Broadcasting Corp, 9/3/93 & 10/22/93. *Mem:* Am Inst for Conserv Art & Hist Works; Am Asn Mus; Art Table Asn. *Publ:* Auth, Bibliography of Photographic Processes in NSC Before 1880, Graphic Arts Res Group; coauth, Robert Cornelius: Portraits from the Dawn of Photography, 83, The Dagnerreotype: 19th Century Technology & Modern Science, 91, Smithsonian Inst Press, 2d edit, Johns Hopkins Press, 2001. *Mailing Add:* 3 Moya Lane Santa Fe NM 87505

BARKER, AL C
PAINTER, PRINTMAKER
b West Paterson, NJ, June 19, 411. *Study:* WVa Univ, BS, 64; Univ RI, MS, 67; Rutgers Univ, 69-70. *Work:* Sportman's Edge Ltd, NY; Easton Waterfowl, Md; Chesapeake Maritime Mus, Md; NJ Bell Tel; Coun Arts, Easton, Md. *Comn:* NH Ducks Unlimited, 79 & 80; Theodore Gordon Flyfishers, NY, 81-83, 90 & 92; First Nat State Bank, Newark, NJ, 81; NJ State Ducks Unlimited, 81-92 & 95-2004. *Exhib:* Easton Waterfowl Festival, Md, 70-2004; Philadelphia Waterfowl Expos, Mem Hall, 79-81 & 83; Safari Club Int, Am Fac Dallas-Ft Worth Airport, Tex, 80; Tulsa Wildlife Expos, Okla, 80 & 84; Southeastern Wildlife Expos, Charleston, SC, 82-86. *Collection Arranged:* White House, Washington, DC, 2001. *Pos:* Instr painting, Montclair Art Mus, NJ, 91. *Teaching:* Instr forestry, wildlife, Essec Agr Inst, Danvers, Mass, 67-69; instr, Univ RI, Kingston, 67 & NJ State Conserv Sch, Branchville, 69; instr biology, Hightstown High Sch, NJ, 71-78. *Awards:* Whisky Painters Am, Akron, Ohio, 86; Best in Show, Fels Point Nat, Md, 91; SCNY Award & Greata Kempton; Greta Kempton SCNY 92; Hobart Nichols, 94; Frederick S Church, 96; Jane Peterson 2001; Gordon Grant, 2002; Elsie Ject-Key, 2004; Bryam Mem, 2005; Salmagundi Club, NYC. *Mem:* Salmagundi Club, NY (bd dir, 78-81); Miniature Artists Am; Whisky Painters Am; Miniature Art Socs, NJ, Fla, Washington; Artist Fel. *Media:* Watercolor, Oil; Graphics. *Specialty:* Traditional/Representational. *Interests:* Hunting, Fishing, Collectibles. *Publ:* Illusr, Deer Hunting, 82, The Grizzly Book, 82, The Bear Book, 83, Trout Book, 84 & North Light, 85. *Dealer:* Annapolis Marine Annapolis Md; Mystic Seaport Mus Mystic Conn. *Mailing Add:* 224 Prince St PO Box 703 Bordentown NJ 08505

BARKER, WALTER WILLIAM, JR
PAINTER, WRITER
b Coblenz, Ger, Aug 8, 1921; US citizen. *Study:* Washington Univ, BFA, 48, with Horst Janson, Phillip Guston & Max Beckmann; Iowa Univ, with Mauricio Lassansky; Univ Ind, with Alton Pickens & Henry Hope, MFA, 50; Florence, Italy, with Dr Freterick Hart, 56. *Work:* Mus Mod Art & Brooklyn Mus, NY; Hirshhorn Collection, Washington; Boston Mus Fine Arts; James Michener Collection, Univ Tex, Austin; Joseph Pulitzer Jr Collection; and others. *Exhib:* Univ Tex, Austin; Int Exhib Mod Graphic Art, Mus Mod Art, NY, 52; Am Painting, Va Mus Fine Arts, Richmond, 62; Painting & Sculpture Today, Herron Inst Art, Indianapolis, Ind, 67; Weatherspoon Gallery, 75; Univ NC, Greensboro, 77 & 94; one-man retrospective, 1951-1994, Univ NC, Greensboro. *Pos:* Spec corresp, St Louis Post-Dispatch, 62-78. *Teaching:* Lectr art hist, Salem Col, 49-50; instr painting, Washington Univ, 50-62; instr basic found, Brooklyn Mus Sch, 63-66; assoc prof painting, Univ NC, 66-85; prof painting, Univ NC, 85-92, prof emer, 92 & lectr, 92-97. *Awards:* New Talent USA Award, 56; Spec Citation Art Rev, Col Art Asn Am, 66; Distinguished Alumnus, Washington Univ, 72. *Bibliog:* Ernest Smith (auth), Walter Barker, 1958-1968, Webster Col, 68; Joseph Pulitzer, Jr (auth), Walter Barker, Fogg Mus Art, Harvard Univ, 71; Patricia Krebs (auth), On the making of an artist, Greensboro Daily News, 77. *Mem:* Max Beckmann Gesellschaft, Munich, Ger; and others. *Media:* All. *Res:* Max Beckmann's last years in the US. *Publ:* Auth introd, Max Beckmann in America (catalog), Viviano Gallery, 69; auth, Lucian Krokowski & Max Beckmann, Joseph Pulitzer Collection, Vol 3, 71; auth, Max Beckmann's advice to his students, Weatherspoon Gallery Asn Bulletin, Univ NC, 79; auth, Max Beckmann as a Teacher (exhib catalog), Prestel-Verlag, Munich, 84. *Mailing Add:* Dept Art Univ NC Greensboro NC 27412

BARKLEY, JAMES
PAINTER, DESIGNER
b New York City, Apr 19, 1941. *Study:* Sch Visual Arts, full scholar recipient, NY; studied with Robert Weaver, Robe Andrew Parker, Phil Hayes, Bernard Hogarth, John Cabor, Jack Potter & Robert Shore. *Comn:* US Postal Stamp, First Centennial Nat Parks System, Mt McKinley, Alaska; Famous Am Quotes Poster Prog, US Bur of Info; Nat Parks, Artists in the Parks Prog; Prog for Two Hundredth Anniversary, Coast Guard; Art Prog, US Air Force. *Exhib:* The Illustrator and the Environment, Earth Island Inst; Pushing the Envelope, Norman Rockwell Mus, 2000; The Art of the Stamp, Smithsonian Inst, Nat Postal Mus, 2003-04. *Collection Arranged:* US Airforce Permanent Art Collection; US Coast Guard Art Collection for 200th Anniversary; US Bur of Info, Famous Am Quotes Poster Prog, US Embassies, worldwide; US Dept Interior, Nat Parks Art Prog; Mus Am Illus, Permanent Collection. *Pos:* Bd dirs (chmn exhib committee, mem mus committee & permanent collection committee), Soc of Illus; chmn Nat Scholar Competition & Instnl Category for Ann Show, Soc Illus; guest lectr for Lect Series Prog, Soc Ills; lects, Pratt Inst, NY & lects at pub & private schs and various Galleries, mus & Orgns. *Teaching:* Prof, illus, Bridgeport Univ, Bridgeport, CT; Prof, Parsons Sch of Design, NY. *Awards:* Gold Medal, Soc Illusr; Award Excellence, Soc Illusr; Designer's Award, Soc Publ. *Bibliog:* The Postal Service Guide to US Stamps 28th Ed, 1972; 20 Years of Award Winners, Soc Illusr, Hastings House Publ Inc, 1981; Outstanding American Illustrators Today, Graphic Sha Publ Co Ltd, 1984; Frieda Gales (auth), How to Write Illustrate & Design Childrens Books, Lloyd Simone Publ Co, 1986; The Art for Survival, Griphis Press, Zurich Switz, 1992. *Mem:* Soc of Illusrs (chmn, mus comt mem). *Media:* Acrylic, Watercolor. *Publ:* Illus, Sounder Winds; The Drinking Gourd; Why the Wind God Wept; Landis & the Ant; The Minstrel Knight; Cheer the Lonesome Traveler; Silent Night; The Good Earth; Pearl Buck; The India Fan; The Estuary Pilgrim. *Dealer:* The Art Source PO Box 257 Pleasantville, NY 10570. *Mailing Add:* 25 Brook Manor Pleasantville NY 10570

BARKUS, MARIONA
GRAPHIC ARTIST, PAINTER
Study: Art Inst Chicago, Ill, 66; Northwestern Univ, Evanston, Ill, BA, 70; Univ Calif, Los Angeles, 72; Pepperdine Univ, 74. *Work:* Yale Univ Art Gallery; Calif Inst Arts Libr; Mus Mod Art Libr, NY; Art Inst Chicago Libr; Indiana-Purdue Univ; Wexford Arts Center, Ireland; UCLA Medical Center; Getty Res Inst. *Exhib:* Solo exhibs, Founders Gallery, Knox Col, Ill, 79, Freeport Art Mus, Ill, 80, Eastern Wash Univ, 86, Southern Oregon State Col, 89, Univ Calif Berkeley Extension, San Francisco, 91 & SUSHI, San Diego, 91, Munic Art Gallery, 95, Rogue Community Col, ORE, 99, Sinclair Col, Ohio, 99, Univ Tenn, 2002, Univ Nevada, Reno, 2003; Themes: Social & Political, Mount St Mary's Col, Los Angeles, 91; Speaking out, Univ Judaism, 96; Art & the Law, Kresge Art Mus, Univ Miami, Mich, 96; Fun with Dick & Jane, Univ Toledo, Ohio, 97; Indiana-Purdue, Univ, 99; Art Inst, Chicago, 99; SUNY, Buffalo, 2000; Darkroom & Digital, John Wayne Airport, 2001; Univ Richmond Mus, 2002; Universal Warning Sign, Univ Nv, 2002; Angels Gate Cult Ctr, 2004; Berkeley Arts Ctr, 2004; AIR Gallery, NY, 2005; Politick, Los Angeles Munic Gallery, 2006; Gender and Identity, Arts & Literature Lab, 2006; At Work-Art of Calif Labor, PicoHouse Gallery, Los Angeles, 2006; 4th Int Trienniel, Contemp Arts Ctr, Vilnius, Lithunia; and others. *Awards:* Inserts, NY State Coun Arts, Woodstock Times, 90; Earth Banner, Fullerton Mus, Fullerton Cult & Fine Arts Div, Calif, 91; Individual Artist's Grant, Los Angeles Cult Affairs Dept, 91. *Bibliog:* Paul Von Blum (auth), Other Visions, Other Voices, Univ Press Am, 94; Judy Birke (auth), Old Emblems, New Haven Register, 2/19/95; Artworks fusion technology, Satire, Los Angeles times, 7/18/96. *Media:* Graphics; Acrylic, Collage, Digital Prints. *Publ:* Auth, Illustrated History-1981-2006, litikus Press; Visual Satire (catalog), Fla State Univ; Of Nature & Nation (catalog), Security Pac, Los Angeles, 90; Multiples (catalog), Chastain Gallery & Nexus Ctr Contemp Art, Atlanta, 90; Reinventing the Emblem, Yale Univ, 95. *Mailing Add:* PO Box 34785 Los Angeles CA 90034

BARNARD, ROB(ERT) E
CERAMIST, CRITIC
b Lexington, Ky, Dec 16, 49. *Study:* Univ Ky, Lexington, 71-74; Kyoto Univ Fine Arts, Japan, 74-77. *Work:* Renwick Gallery, Smithsonian Inst, Washington, DC; Everson Mus, Syracuse, NY; Dickinson Col, Carlisle, Pa; Millersville Univ, Pa; Mus Ceramic Art, Alfred Univ, NY; Am Craft Mus, NYC; Mint Mus, Charlotte, NC. *Exhib:* Fragile Blossoms, Enduring Earth, Everson Mus, Syracuse, NY, 89; Spirit Material, McLean Project Arts, McLean, Va, 90; Revolving Techniques, James Michner Mus, Doylestown, Pa, 92; Sasakawa Peace Found USA, Washington, DC, 95; Beyond East & West: 20 Yr Retrospective, Sasakawa Peace Found USA, Washington, DC, 95; Rob Barnard Mus, Jan Van Der Togt, Amstelveen, The Neth, 99. *Pos:* Ceramics ed, New Art Examiner, 86-93. *Teaching:* Lectr, Cath Univ Am, Washington, DC. *Awards:* Craftsmen's Fel, 78 & Visual Arts Fel, 90, Nat Endowments Arts. *Bibliog:* Janet Koplos (auth), Rob Barnard, Ichi no Ichi/Mainichi Daily News, Tokyo, 92; John Perreault (auth) Rob Barnard, Am Ceramics, 12/95; Nicolas Fox (auth) Beauty born of fire, 9-10/95. *Media:* Clay. *Publ:* Delivering the promise, Vol 21, No 1, Studio Potter, 12/92; Tradition & the future No 14, Ceramics Art & Perception, 93; The ambiguity of modern craft, issue 98, New Observations, 11-12/93; A basketmaker in rural Japan, Am Craft, 10-11/95; What is Craft For? Vol 23, No 1, Studio Potter, 94; Design Sourcebook: Ceramics, Edmund de Waal, New Holland, London, 99; plus others. *Dealer:* Elizabeth Roberts Gallery 2108 "R" St NW Washington DC 20016; Dai Ichi Gallery 249 E 48th St NYC New York 10017. *Mailing Add:* 597 S Middle Rd Timberville VA 22853

BARNES, CAROLE D
PAINTER
b Bellefonte, Pa, Nov 12, 35. *Study:* Pa State Univ, BA(art ed), 57; also with Edward Betts, Glenn Bradshaw & Alex Nepote. *Work:* IBM, Austin, Tex; Utah State Univ, Logan; United Banks & Midland Savings, Colo. *Exhib:* Rocky Mountain Nat Watermedia Soc, Golden, Colo, 78, 80, 82-84, 86, 87, 89-92; Am Watercolor Soc, NY, 75-78, 83, 86, 89 & 91; Nat Acad Design Ann, NY, 76, 78, 81, 82, 84, 86 & 92; Allied Artists Ann, NY, 76, 77, 81, 83, 85 & 87; Nat Watercolor Soc, Los Angeles, 77, 78, 80, 82, 84 & 87. *Teaching:* Instr, Watercolor Workshops, numerous cities across the US; juror, Nat Watercolor Soc & Am Watercolor Soc. *Awards:* Over 30 Nat Award incl: Ralph Fabri Medal Honor, Nat Soc Painters Casein & Acrylic, 80; Gold Medal, San Diego Nat, Calif, 82; Ford Times Award, Am Watercolor Soc, New York, 83. *Bibliog:* Maxine Masterfield (auth), Painting Spirit of Nature; Marilyn Hughey Phillis (auth), Watercolor Techniques for Releasing the Creative Spirit; Greg Albert (auth), Splash; and others. *Mem:* Am Watercolor Soc; Allied Artists; Nat Watercolor Soc; Nat Soc Painters Casein & Acrylic; Rocky Mountain Nat Watermedia Soc; Audubon Artists. *Media:* Watercolor, Acrylic. *Mailing Add:* 3772 Lakebriar Dr Boulder CO 80304

BARNES, CURT (CURTIS) EDWARD
PAINTER, INSTRUCTOR
b Taft, Calif, Jan 17, 43. *Study:* Univ Calif, Berkeley, BA, 64; Pratt Inst, MFA, 66. *Work:* Mus Contemp Art, Bogota, Columbia; Prudential Insurance Corp Am, Newark, NJ; Franklin Furnace Arch, Mus Mod Art, NY. *Exhib:* Chicago Ann, Art Inst of Chicago, 67; O K Harris Gallery, NY, 70, 72, 79, 85, 88, 97 & 2002; Contemp Reflections, Aldrich Mus Contemp Art, Ridgefield, Conn, 75; Terry Dintenfass Gallery, NY, 89; Gray Gallery, East Carolina Univ, Greenville, NC, 90; Physicality Hunter Col Art Gallery, NY, 91; Defining Spaces, Sigma Gallery, NY, 96. *Teaching:* Instr painting & drawing, Univ Wis, Stevens Point, 66-67; instr drawing, Parsons Sch Design, New York, 67-71; assoc prof painting, drawing & 20th century art hist, Fordham Univ, 69-84; vis assoc prof, Hampshire Col, 79-80 & 84-86; vis adj prof, Pratt Inst, 81; lectr art, Princeton Univ, 91. *Awards:* Yaddo Fel, summer 76 & 88; Grant in Painting, Nat Endowment for Arts, 93-94; Abbey Found Award, British Sch, Rome, 98; Golden Found Grant, 2004. *Bibliog:* John Perreault (auth), Catching up, Soho Weekly News, 3/76; Nancy Grove (auth), Curt Barnes (rev), Arts Mag, 4/76; Joseph Wiltsee (auth), Investing in young artists, Bus Wk, 5/76; Donald Goddard (auth), Curt Barnes: Convex Paintings, New York Art World, 2/2002. *Mem:* Col Art Asn. *Media:* Acrylic, Oil. *Publ:* Auth, Table of Contents, Allesandra Publ, 76; ed & contribr, Col Art Asn, Art J, spring 91. *Mailing Add:* 114 W Houston St New York NY 10012

BARNES, KITT
PAINTER
US citizen. *Study:* Univ NC, Chapel Hill, BFA, 73, MFA, 75. *Work:* Ackland Mus; Sovereign Am Arts Corp; Fayetteville Arts Coun. *Exhib:* Drawing Presentation of MFA Candidates, Corcoran Gallery, 75; Biennial Exhib Piedmont Painting & Sculpture, Mint Mus, 79; Consideration of Line, 20th Century Works On Paper, Stephan Haller Gallery, NY, 95; Textural Integrity, Stephan Haller Gallery, NY, 95; Hudson Guild Invitational NY, 95; Virtuosity, Int Art Fair, The Armory, NY, 95; Aesthetic Makers, Stephen Haller Gallery, NY, 96; Surface Issues, Stephen Haller Gallery, NY, 96; Cult Markers, Stephen Haller Gallery, NY, 96. *Awards:* Grant, NC Arts Coun Exhib, 94. *Bibliog:* Valentin Tatransky (auth), Group show, Arts Mag, 3/83; Carl Schiffman (auth), New York galleries, late fall, New England Review, Vol 17 No 4, 95. *Media:* Oil on Canvas. *Mailing Add:* PO Box 1244 Madison Sq Sta New York NY 10159

BARNES, MARGO
PAINTER
b New York, NY, Sept 3, 47. *Study:* Brooklyn Mus Art Sch, with Isaac Soyer; Boston Univ Sch Fine Arts, BFA, 69. *Exhib:* Solo exhibs, Benson Gallery, Bridgehampton, NY, 76, Meredith Long Contemp Gallery, NY, 78-79, A M Sachs Gallery, NY, 83, Capricorn Galleries, Washington, DC, 84 & Watermill Mus, NY, 85; Waterworks, Heckscher Mus, Huntington, NY, 85; 10 Yr Retrospective (with catalog), Guild Hall Mus, East Hampton, NY, 86; Rease Galleries, NY, 88; Meredith Long Galleries, Houston, 88. *Teaching:* Pvt instruction in studio, NY, 75-. *Awards:* Fulbright Grant, 72; Best in show, Guild Hall Mus Artists Mem Show, East Hampton, NY, 85. *Bibliog:* Gerrit Henry (auth), rev, Art News, 11/79; Nina French-Frazier (auth), rev, Art Int, 12/79; Amei Wallach (auth), Water, water everywhere, Newsday, 10/6/85. *Media:* Oil. *Mailing Add:* 250 E 83rd St Apt 2E New York NY 10028-2817

BARNES, MOLLY
ART DEALER, WRITER
b London, Eng, May 18, 36; US citizen. *Study:* Univ Calif, Berkeley, BA, 57. *Pos:* Owner & dir, Molly Barnes Gallery, 67-85; art critic, KFWB Radio, Los Angeles, 74-78, KPKF Radio, Los Angeles, 80-, KPCC, Pasadena & KSCN Radio, Los Angeles, currently; asst, Frank Perls Gallery, 78; writer, Hollywood Reporter, 78-; art consult, Roger Smith Hotel, NY, 91-95; own, Molly Barnes Gallery, 96-2000; prog dir, New York City Now (formerly Artists Talk on Art), Roger Smith Hotel, NY. *Teaching:* Learning Tree Univ, Chatsworth, Calif, currently. *Awards:* Woman of Yr, Artcore, Los Angeles, 99. *Mem:* Art Critics Am; Mus Contemp Art Los Angeles; AICA; Round Table, New York & Los Angeles. *Specialty:* Contemporary Californians, Robert Cottingham, Don Eddy, John Baldessari, Jack Reilly, Mark Kostabi. *Publ:* Auth, How to Get Hung, Tuttle Publ, 94. *Mailing Add:* Molly Barnes Gallery 474 S Rodeo Dr Beverly Hills CA 90212-4220

BARNES, ROBERT M
PAINTER, EDUCATOR
b Washington, DC, Sept 24, 34. *Study:* Art Inst Chicago, BFA, 56; Univ Chicago, BFA, 56; Columbia Univ, 56; Hunter Col, 57-61; Univ London Slade Sch, Fulbright Grant, 61-63. *Work:* Mus Mod Art, Whitney Mus Am Art, NY; Art Inst Chicago; Pasadena Art Mus, Calif; Nat Gallery Art, Washington; Mus of contemp art, Chicago; and others. *Comn:* Ed lithographs, NY Hilton Hotel, 62. *Exhib:* Mus Civico, Bologna, 65; Galerie Dragon, Paris, 67; Univ Ill, 67; Kansas City Art Inst, 72; Galeria Fanta Spade, Rome, 72; one person exhib, Allan Frumkin Gallery, NY, 83 & 85, Robert Barnes, Struve Gallery, Chicago, Ill, 86, Watercolors, 89, Sources of Power, 92, Blood & Perfume: New Paintings, Sonia Zaks Gallery, Chicago, Ill, 96, Robert Barnes, New Works, 98 & The Ogham, Sonia Zaks Gallery, Chicago, Ill, 2000; and others. *Teaching:* Instr grad painting, Ind Univ, 60-61; vis artist, Kansas City Art Inst, 63-64; asst prof painting & drawing, Ind Univ, Bloomington, 65-70, prof, Dept Fine Arts, 70-, Ruth N Hall prof fine art emeritus, retired, 99. *Awards:* Fulbright Grant, 63; Nat Endowment Arts, 82; Ruth N Halls, prof fine art, Endowed Chmn, 96; Acad Award, Am Acad Arts and Scis, 93. *Bibliog:* Michael Rooks (auth), Seeking the City of Truth: Robert Barnes' Pastels for the Cantos of Ezra Pound, The Smart Mus of Art Bulletin, 96-97, 8-19; Franz Schulze (auth), Fantastic Images Chicago Art Since 1945, Follet Pub Co, 72; Robert Barnes: Work in Progress, interview by L E McCullough, Arts Indiana, 12/90, 28-32. *Mem:* Nat Acad Design. *Media:* Oil/canvas-panel, Casein. *Collection:* Albrecht-Kemper Mus of Art, St. Joseph, MO; Art Ctr Col of Design, Pasadena, Calif; The Art Inst of Chicago; Elvehjem Mus of Art, Univ of Wis, Madison; Fla Int Univ Art Gallery; Ind Univ Art Mus, Bloomington. *Dealer:* Sonia Zaks Gallery 311 W Superior St Chicago IL 60610; Peter Findley Gallery 41 E 57 St New York NY 10021. *Mailing Add:* PO Box 438 Searsport ME 04974

BARNES, WILLIAM DAVID
PAINTER, PRINTMAKER
b Chicago, Ill, Apr 13, 46. *Study:* Drake Univ, Des Moines, Iowa, BFA, 69; Univ Ariz, Tucson, MFA, 74. *Work:* Bowery Gallery, NY; Montgomery Mus, Ala; Lamar Dodd Art Ctr, LaGrange, Ga; Portsmouth Art Ctr, Va; CSX Corp; Washington and Lee Univ, Va; Col William and Mary, Va. *Exhib:* Faculty Show, Muscarelle Mus, Williamsburg, Va, 91, 96 & 2002 (catalog, 2002); solo show, Monotypes, Peninsula Fine Arts Ctr, Newport News, Va, 92, Bowery Gallery, NY, 95 & 98 & John Taylor Art Ctr, Hampton, Va, 96; Paintings and Monotypes, Bowery Gallery, NY, 92; Monotypes, Reynolds Gallery, Richmond, Va, 93; Duo Show, Hermitage Found Mus, Norfolk, Va, 96; Commonwealth Collects, Va Beach Art Ctr, Va, 96; Zenxist-Human Presence, Painting Ctr, NY, 2000. *Teaching:* Instr painting, Univ Ariz, Tucson, 74-75; prof painting, Col William & Mary, Williamsburg, 75-. *Awards:* Cert Distinction, Va Artists, Va Mus, 79; Best in Show, LaGrange Nat, Lamar Dodd Art Ctr, 86; Award of Distinction & Award of Achievement, Peninsula Fine Arts Ctr, 95 & 96. *Bibliog:* PSA Art Showcase Inaugural Exhib Chronicling Time (catalog); Monotypes/William Barnes (catalog), 92. *Mem:* Bowery Gallery, NY; Col Art Asn. *Media:* Oil Paint & Monotype. *Mailing Add:* 716 Jamestown Rd Williamsburg VA 23185

BARNET, WILL
PAINTER, PRINTMAKER
b Beverly, Mass, May 25, 11. *Study:* Boston Mus Fine Arts Sch, with Phillip Hale, 27-30; Art Students League, with Charles Locke, 30-33; Mass Col Art, DFA (hon), 89. *Work:* Boston Mus Fine Arts; Whitney Mus Am Art; Metrop Mus Art; Guggenheim Mus; Cincinnati Art Mus; Boca Raton Mus Art, Fla, 2000; Portland Mus Art, Maine, 2000; Pulmer Mus of Art, 2003. *Exhib:* Inst Contemp Art, Boston; Mus Mod Art; Pa Acad Fine Arts, 70; retrospective, Asoc Am Artists, 72 & Portraits, Terry Dintenfass Gallery, NY, 82, 91 & 94; Ringling Mus, Sarasota, Fla, 80; Wichita Art Mus, 83; Traveling Mus Retrospective, Currier Gallery Art, NH, 84, Huntsville Mus Art, Ala, 84, Minn Mus Art, St Paul, 84-85, Art Gallery Hamilton, Ont, 85 & Farnsworth Libr & Art Mus, Maine, 85, 2002; Butler Art Inst, Ohio, 92; Ark Arts Ctr, 92; Ogunquit Mus Am Art, Maine, 94; Nat Gallery Am Art, 95; Will Barnet: A Timeless world, Motclair Art Mus, 2000; Retrospective Ark Art Ctr, 2001; Harmon-Meek Gallery, Naples, Fla, 2003; Alexander Galeery, 2003. *Teaching:* Instr, Art Students League, 36-; Cooper Union Art Sch, 45-65, prof, 65-; Mont State Col, summer 51; vis critic, Yale Univ, 52 & 53; instr, Univ Ohio, Univ Minn, Duluth, 58 & Univ Wash, 63; Des Moines Art Ctr, Iowa, 65; distinguished vis prof, Pa State Univ, 65-66; instr, Pa Acad Fine Arts, 67-; vis prof, Cornell Univ, 68-69. *Awards:* Benjamin Altman Prize, 77, Proctor Portrait, 84 & Gladys Emerson Cooh Prize, 86, Nat Acad Design; Gold Medal Honor, Nat Arts Club, 90; Butler Medal for Life Achievement in Am Art, 92. *Bibliog:* James T Farrell (auth), Paintings of Will Barnet, Press Eight, New York, 50; Robert Beverly Hale (auth), Will Barnet--27 Paintings Completed 1960-1968, New York, 68; Will Barnet Paintings, Abrams Publ, 84; Gail Stavitsky (auth), Will Barnet: A Timeless World, Rutgers Univ Press, 00. *Mem:* Am Abstr Artists; Nat Acad Design (assoc, 74, acad, 82); Century Asn; Royal Soc Arts, London; Am Acad & Inst Arts & Lett. *Media:* Painter. *Specialty:* Modern 19th Century. *Publ:* Illusr, The World in a Frame, Braziller Pub. *Dealer:* Babcock Gallery NYC 724 Fifth Ave. *Mailing Add:* 15 Gramercy Park New York NY 10003

BARNETT, CHERYL L
SCULPTOR
b Merced, Calif, Feb 24, 56. *Study:* Univ Calif Santa Cruz, BA (art), 77; Calif State Univ Fresno, MA (sculpture), 85. *Comn:* Bronze sculpture, comn by McAuley Family for Mercy / UC Davis Cancer Center, Calif, 2000. *Exhib:* Bay Area Bronze, Civic Arts Ctr, Walnut Creek, Calif, 88; 250 Women, Artworks Foundry and Gallery, Berkeley, Calif, 89; Salute to Arts & Flowers, Arts Comn of San Francisco, 89; one-women show, Merced Col Art Gallery, Calif, 82-94, Fresno Art Mus, Rental Gallery, Calif, 84, Phebe Conley Art Gallery, Calif Stat Univ, Fresno, 85, The Art Circle, Visalia, Calif, 86, Erika Myerovich Gallery, San Francisco, 86-87, Banaker Gallery, Walnut Creek, Calif, 88, Eleonore Austerer Gallery, San Francisco, 90-2001, 04 & The Simmons Gallery, San Francisco, 2005; Life Lines, Mendocino Art Center, Calif, 95 & 97; Speaking of Her, Pac Rim Sulpture Group, San Francisco, 96; The Simmons Gallery, San Francisco, 03-05; Brumley Art Gallery, Bass Lake, Calif, 02-05; Merced Coll Art Gallery, Calif, 82-04; Focus: Sculpture, Elenore Austerer Gallery, Palm Deser, Calif, 2006; and others. *Teaching:* instr art, Merced Col, Calif, 81-86, prof, 88--; instr sculpture, Fresno Art Mus, Calif, 85; instr, sculpture, design & 20th century art hist. *Awards:* Achievement Award in Art, Bank of Am, 74; NISOD Excellence Award for Teaching, Merced Col, Univ Tex, 96; The Frances DeB Henderson Sculpture Prize, Mus Fine Arts, Boston, 98; Nat Prize Show, Cambridge Art Asn, 98; Award of Merit, Santa Clara Biennial Indoor/Outdoor Sculpture Exhib, Calif, 01. *Bibliog:* Cheryl Barnett Exhibits at the Berkeley Art Center, Art Week, 7/23/88; In Three Dimensions: Women Sculptors of the 90's, New House Cen for Contemp Art & Snug Harbor Cultural Ctr, 95; Virtuosity CD-ROM, Art Commun Int, 96. *Mem:* Int Sculpture Ctr, Washington DC; Nat Educators Asn; Am Asn Univ Women; Pac Rim Sculpture Group, San Francisco; Nat Mus Women in the Arts. *Media:* Cast Bronze. *Dealer:* Eleonore Austerer Gallery 73-660 El Paseo Palm Desert CA 92260. *Mailing Add:* 2887 Saint Thomas Ct Merced CA 95348

BARNETT, DAVID J
ART DEALER, PAINTER
b Milwaukee, Wis, Feb 22, 46. *Study:* Lincoln Col; Univ Wis, Milwaukee. *Pos:* Owner, David Barnett Gallery, currently; pres, Van Go Frame & Art America's Gallery to You, currently. *Teaching:* Lectr & adv art acquisition to prof orgn, pvt individuals & corp. *Bibliog:* Art experts can save money & reputation for the wary dealer, Art Bus News, 2/84; Exclusively Yours, For the Love of Art, 4/96; Milwaukee Dealer puts art on wheels in 'gold coast' area, Milwaukee Art Bus News, 9/86; The Renaissance Man, Lifestyle West, 11/01; 6,000 Sq Foot Home Started as Run-Down Wreck, Milwaukee Jour Sentinel, 10/02. *Mem:* Milwaukee Art Mus; Chicago Art Inst; Milwaukee Pub Mus; Appraisers Asn Am. *Media:* Painting; Watercolor. *Specialty:* Nineteenth and twentieth century European and American masters; leading Wisconsin artists; contemporary American artists; American historical prints; International, African, Indonesian & Latin America Art. *Publ:* Auth, Milton Avery-Retrospective (catalog), pvt publ, 12/8/84-1/31/85; Carol Summers woodcuts 1950-1988 (catalog), pvt publ, 88; Milton Avery-The 1930's Period (catalog), pvt publ, summer, 88; Milton Avery-The 1940's Period (catalog), pvt publ, summer, 89; Lester Johnson-Retrospective The 1940's To The Present (catalog), pvt publ, Nov-Dec/89. *Mailing Add:* David Barnett Gallery 1024 E State St Milwaukee WI 53202

BARNETT, EARL D
PAINTER, PORTRAITIST
b Trenton, Tenn. *Study:* Cleveland Sch Art, with Henry G Keller, Viktor Schreckengost, Willard Combes, Kenneth Bates & Frank Wilcox. *Work:* Butler Inst Am Art; Grover M Hermann Fine Arts Ctr, Marietta, Ohio; Dickinson State Univ, NDak. *Comn:* portrait, Hon Robert Downing, Glenview, Ill, 87; 66 past pres portraits, Contracting Plasterers' & Lathers' Int Asn Union Hall, 67-98; portrait, Adm James Ross, Naval Armory, Chicago, 70; Robert Snediker, Chicago Printing, 86; Sam Davidson, pres of Dacor Corp, Northbrook, Ill, 87; 24 portraits, editorial covers, MBE Mag, Los Angeles, 94-00. *Exhib:* Cooperstown Art Asn, NY, 62-72; Allied Artists, NY, 64-73; Butler Inst Am Art, 65-82; Union League Club Ann, Chicago, 67, 68 & 72; Mainstreams, Marietta, 72, 73, 76 & 78; Tex Fine Arts Asn Ann, 73 & 79; Alamo Kiawanas Western Art Show, San Antonio, Tex, 82-85; Dakota 100/88, Montana Water Media, 88-92; Arts for the Parks Top 100/90, 200/91, 100/200, 93, 100/95, 200/98, 99. *Pos:* Art dir, W L Stensgaard & Assocs, Chicago, 45-47; asst art dir & designer, Kling Studios, Chicago, 48-61; vpres & creative dir, JM Callan Co, Chicago, 61-67; vpres & creative dir, Conway Displays, Inc, Niles, Ill, 67-74; merchandise mgr, NCM Int, Arlington Heights, Ill, 74-79; creative dir, Chicago Show Print, Morton Grove, Ill, 79-88. *Awards:* Purchase Award, Dakota 100/88, Dickson, NDak; Special Award, Miss Watercolor Soc, 92. *Mem:* Cowboy Hall of Fame, Oklahoma City, Okla. *Media:* Oil, Watercolor

BARNETT, EMILY
PAINTER, PRINTMAKER
b Brooklyn, NY, Oct 23, 47. *Study:* Queens Col, NY, BFA, 69, Louisiana State Univ, MFA, 76. *Exhib:* Nat Acad Design Ann Juried Exhib, NY, 81, 82 & 90; 33rd New Eng Exhib, Silvermine Ctr Arts, Conn, 82; Ann juried exhib, Fine Arts Mus of Long Island, 88 & 93; Gwenda Jay Gallery, Chicago, 95; Fairleigh Dickinson Univ, NJ, 95; Hutchins Gallery, Long Island Univ, 96; African-Am Mus Nassau Co, 97, 98 & 2000; Parrish Art Mus, 99; Watermark Gallery, Greenport, LI, 2002; Jane Voorhees Zimmerli Art Mus, NJ, 2002; NY Soc Etchers, 2003; Solo exhibs, Heckscher Mus, Bryant Libr, NY, 97, Firehouse Gallery, Nassau Community Coll, NY, 2000, Islip Art Mus Store, NY, 2002, Custer Inst Observatory Gallery, Southold, NY, 2002, Jamaica Wildlife Refuge, NY, 2002; The Catskill Center's Erpf Gallery, 2004; Adelphi Univ, 2004; William Paterson Univ, NJ, 2005; Fashion Inst Tech, NY, 2005-2006; NC Mus Natural Sci, NC, 2006. *Collection Arranged:* Nassau Community Col, NY; Fine Arts Mus Long Island, NY; West Publ Co; Janes Voorhees Zimmerli Art Mus, NJ; City of Seattle, Portable Works Collection, Seattle, Wash. *Teaching:* Instr painting, drawing color theory, color & design, Parsons Sch Design, New York, 80-; adj prof design, Dowling Col, Oakdale, NY, 87; instr drawing painting, Nassau Co Mus Art, 87-; adj prof, Suffolk Community Col, 92-2000, Hofstra Univ, 2000-; Fashion Inst Tech, 2005; Adelphi Univ, 2005-2006; Nassau Community Col, 2006. *Awards:* First Prize, Contemp Portraiture From Northeast, 87; Thomas B Clarke Prize, Nat Acad Design, 90; First Prize, Fine Art Mus Long Island, 95; Purchase Award, West Publ Corp, 95; Irwin Zlowe Award, Nat Asn Women Artists, 2000; Millay Colony Artist Residence Grant, 98; and others. *Bibliog:* The Originals, WLIW-TV, 8-88; Emily Barnett's painting, Life and Art in the Studio (monogr), 88. *Mem:* Nat Asn Women Artists; Inter-Soc Color Coun. *Media:* Oil, Prints. *Dealer:* West Interiors, NY. *Mailing Add:* 222 Carle Pl New York NY 11514

BARNETT, HELMUT
PAINTER, PRINTMAKER
b Stuttgart, Ger, Feb, 16, 46; US citizen. *Study:* Univ Tex, Austin, BFA(studio art) & BA, 73. *Comn:* Mixed media paintings on canvas, Shefelman & Nix, & IBM, Austin, Tex, 84, Am Security Life Insurance Co, San Antonio, 85, Houston Showroom, Hayworth Inc, 85 & Clann, Bell & Murphy, Houston, 85. *Exhib:* Soc Photogrs & Artist Reps National, Shreveport, La, 76; Western Asn Art Mus Traveling Exhib, 79; one-man show, Amdur Gallery, Austin, Tex, 84 & 86; II Ann Exhib, Art Mus S Tex, Corpus Christi, 83; Soho Invitational Show, Works on Paper, Austin, 85; 11th Int Independents Exhib of Prints, Kanagawa Prefectural Gallery, Japan, 85; New Am Talent, Tex Fine Arts Asn, Laguna Gloria Art Mus, Austin, 86. *Media:* Acrylic, Pastel. *Dealer:* Martin/Rathburn Gallery The Blue Star San Antonio TX. *Mailing Add:* 709 Spofford St Austin TX 78704

BARNETT, VIVIAN ENDICOTT
CURATOR, HISTORIAN
b Putnam, Conn, July 8, 1944. *Study:* Vassar Col, AB, 65; Inst Fine Arts, NY Univ, MA, 71; Grad Ctr, City Univ New York. *Collection Arranged:* Kandinsky Watercolors from Solomon R Guggenheim Collection (auth, catalog), 81-82; Vasily Kandinsky (auth, catalog), Art Gallery NSW, 82; Kandinsky in Munich, 82, Kandinsky: Russian and Bauhaus Years, 83, Kandinsky in Paris, 85, Hans Reichel, 88, Guggenheim Mus, Kandinsky Och Sverige, Malmo Kunsthall (auth, catalog), 89; Kandinsky Kleine Freuden, Dusseldorf (auth, catalog), 92. *Pos:* Res asst, Solomon R Guggenheim Mus, 73-77, curatorial asst, 78-79, assoc cur, 80-81, res cur, 81-82, cur, 82-91; dir, Roethel-Benjamin Archive, 91-. *Awards:* John Simon Guggenheim Fel, 90; Inst for Advanced Study, Princeton, 2003-2004. *Mem:* Col Art Asn Am; Am Asn Mus; Int Coun Mus. *Res:* Kandinsky; German Expressionism; Drawings. *Publ:* Kandinsky Watercolors: Catalogue Raisonne, Vol I 1900-1921, 92; The Russian Presence in the 1924 Venice Biennale, The Great Utopia, 92; Kandinsky Watercolors: Catalogue Raisonne, Vol II 1922-1944, 94; Vasily Kandinsky: A Colorful Life, 95; The Blue Four: Feininger, Jawlensky, Kandinsky, and Klee in the New World, 97; Exiles and Emigres, 97; Die Brücke in Dresden, 2001; Mies in America, 2001; The Blue Four Collection at the Norton Simon Museum, 2002; Klee & America, 2006; Kandinsky Drawings: Catalogue Raisonne, Vol I, 2006. *Mailing Add:* Solomon R Guggenheim Mus 1071 Fifth Ave New York NY 10128

BARNEY, MATTHEW
SCULPTOR, FILMMAKER
b San Francisco, Calif, 1967. *Study:* Yale Univ, BA, 89. *Work:* Whitney Mus Am Art, Mus Mod Art, NY; Mus Boymans-van Beuningen, Rotterdam, Holland; Walker Art Ctr, Minneapolis, Minn; Sammlung Goetz, Munich, Ger. *Exhib:* solo exhibs, Tate Gallery, London, 95, Mus Mod Art, San Francisco, 96, Kunsthalle Wien, Austria, 97, Barbara Gladstone Gallery, New York City, 97, Walker Art Ctr, Mpls, 99, San Francisco Mus of Modern Art, 2000, Matthew Barney: The CREMASTER Cycle, Solomon R Guggenheim Mus, NY, 2002-03; Foreign Body, Mus Gegenwartskunst, Basel, Switz, 96; Tenth Biennale, Sydney, Australia, 96; Die Rache der Veronika, Fotosammlung Lambert, Deichtorhallen Hamburg, 98; Global Vision, New Art from the 90's, Dakis Joannou Collection, Desle Found, Athens, 98; Galerie Rudolfino, Prague, 2001; Imperfect Innocence, Contemp Mus, Baltimore, Md, 2003. *Awards:* Europa 2000, XLV Venice Biennale, 93; Hugo Boss Award, Guggenheim Mus, NY, 96; James D Phelan Art award in video, Bay Area Video Coalition, San Francisco Found, 2000. *Bibliog:* Stuart Morgan (auth), Of goats and men, Frieze, 1/95; Norman Bryson (auth), Matthew Barney's Gonadotrophic Cavaleade, Parkett, 12/95; Jerry Saltz (auth), The next sex, Art in Am, 10/96. *Mailing Add:* c/o Barbara Gladstone Gallery 515 W 24th St New York NY 10011

BARNHILL, GEORGIA BRADY
CURATOR, HISTORIAN
b Mt Kisco, NY, 44. *Study:* Wellesley Col, BA(art hist), 66. *Pos:* Cur graphic arts, Am Antiqn Soc, Worcester, Mass, 69-. *Awards:* Fel, First Pub Humanities Inst, Mass Found Humanities & Pub Policy, 82, Bibliog Soc Am, 86, Am Philos Soc, 86 & Huntington Libr, 93; Maurice Rickards Award, Ephemera Soc Am, 87; and others. *Mem:* Fitchburg Art Mus (pres, bd trustees, 91-96); Am Hist Print Collectors Soc (pres, 96-98); Archives Am Art; Arts Worcester (pres 1997-99); New Eng Mus Asn; and others. *Res:* Eighteenth & nineteenth century American prints; American literary illustration. *Interests:* landscape imagery, depictions of national historical events; American Lithography. *Publ:* ed, Prints of New England, Am Antiqn Soc, 91; auth, Wild Impressions: The Adirondacks on Paper, Adirondack Mus & David Godine, 95; Cultivation of American Artists, Am Antiquarian Soc, 97; Illustrations of the Adirondacks in the Popular Press, Adirondack Prints & Printmakers, 98; Depictions of the White Mountains in the Popular Press, Hist NH, Vol 24, 99; auth, Markets for Images from 1670 to 1790 in America, Imprint Vol 25, 2000; many others; ed, Bibliography on American Prints of the Seventeenth to the Nineteenth Centuries, 2006. *Mailing Add:* Am Antiquarian Soc 185 Salisbury St Worcester MA 01609

BARNITZ, JACQUELINE
EDUCATOR, HISTORIAN
b Geneva, Switzerland, Nov 1, 23; US citizen. *Study:* CCNY MPhil, 81, PD, 86. *Teaching:* Lecturer, Latin Am Art SUNY, 69-76; prof, Modern Latin Am Art, Univ Texas, Austin, 81-. *Awards:* spec hon mention, Asn Latin Am Art, 02; Vasari Book Award, Dallas Mus Art, 02. *Mem:* Col Art Asn; Latin Am Studies Asn; Asn Latin Am Art; Am Soc Hispanic Art Historical Studies. *Res:* 19th & 20th Latin American art with specialty in Argentina and Brazil, also contemporary to present. *Publ:* Contribr The School of the South: The Taller Torres-Garcia and Its Legacy, Austin: Archer M Huntington Art Gallery, 92; contribr Latin American Artists of the Twentieth Century, Mus Modern Art, 93; auth Twentieth Century Art of Latin American, Univ Texas Press, 2001. *Mailing Add:* Univ Tex at Austin Dept Art and Art History One University Station D1300 Austin TX 78712-2319

BARNWELL, JOHN L
PAINTER
b Los Angeles, Calif, Mar 17, 22. *Study:* Univ Calif, Berkeley, BA; Newark Sch Fine & Indust Art, NJ; Art Students League, with Frank Reilly; watercolor with Ed Whilney & Ferdinand Petrie. *Work:* Blue Cross, Blue Shield, Rochester, NY. *Exhib:* Jersey City Mus, NJ, 77; Bergen Community Mus, NJ, 77; NJ Watercolor Soc Show, 84, 87, 88 & 89; one-man show, Hamilton, Mass, 87, Bloomfield, NJ 90; West Essex, NJ, 92, 94, 97, 98. *Awards:* Windsor & Newton Award, 90; Community Art Asn Award of Excellence, 93; P Wick Award, Am Artist Prof Soc, 94; NJ State Show, Best in Show, 97, 98. *Mem:* Assoc NJ Watercolor Soc; fel Am Artists Prof League; Miniature Art Soc NJ (pres, 75-80); Art Students League. *Media:* Oil, Watercolor. *Dealer:* Essex Fine Art Gallery 13 S Fullerton St Montclair NJ; Art-on-the-Ave Verona NJ. *Mailing Add:* 11 Kingsland Rd Boonton NJ 07005-9020

BAROFF, JILL (EMILY)
PAINTER, SCULPTOR
b Summit, NJ, Mar 10, 54. *Study:* Antioch Col, BFA, 76; studied, Hunter Col, NYC, 80-81. *Work:* Harvard Univ Art Mus; Werner Kramarsky, NY; Mus of Modern Art, NY; Nat Gallery of Art, Washingotn, DC; Yale Univ Art Mus. *Collection Arranged:* Cleveland Mus Contemp Art; Dayton Art Inst; Harvard Univ Art Mus; Mus Modern Art; Nat Gallery Art, Washington, DC; Progressive Insurance Co, Cleveland; Yale Univ Art Mus. *Awards:* Fel, Pollock-Krasner Found, 87-88 & 92-93; Fel Nat Endowment Arts, 93-94, exchange Fel with Japan, 96; NY Found Arts, 95; Aaron Siskind Found Grant for Photog, 01. *Bibliog:* Anja Chavez (auth), Infinite Possibilities: Serial Imagery in 20th Century Drawings, Davis Mus and Cult Ctr, Wellesley Col, Mass, 2004; Anja Chavez (auth), The Invisible Thread: Buddhist Spirit in Contemp Art, Newhouse Ctr for Contemp Art, New York, 2004; Josef Helfenstein and Jonathan Fineberg (auths), Drawings of Choice from a New York Collection, Kannert Art Mus, Univ Ill, 2002. *Mem:* Orgn Independent Artists; NY Artists Equity. *Media:* Installation, drawing. *Dealer:* Margarete Roeder Gallery 545 Broadway New York City, NY 10012; Josée Bienuenu Gallery New York. *Mailing Add:* 474 Dean St Brooklyn NY 11217

BARONE, MARK
PAINTER
b Chicago, Ill, Aug 25, 59. *Study:* Univ Minnesota, BA, 83; Univ Southern Ill, MFA, 89. *Work:* Evansville Mus Arts and Scis, Ind; Univ Southern Ind, Evansville; Bristol-Meyers Permanent Collection; Williams, Williams & Lentz Accountants, Paducah, Ky; Yeiser Art Center, Paducah; Shawnee Community Coll, Shawnee Town, Ill. *Exhib:* Univ Wis Univ Mus, Madison, 90; Ill Figurative, Bradley Univ, Galesburg, Ill, 90; One-man shows, Northern Ind Arts Asn, Muster, 93, Mercyhurst Coll, Erie, Pa, 94, Murray State Univ, 1995, Ky, Lyons Wier Gallery, Chicago, 97, Van de Griff Gallery, Chicago, 98, Principle Gallery, Alexandria, Va, 2000, numerous others; group shows, Neville Pub Mus, Green Bay, Wis, 94, Eastern Ill Univ, Charleston, Ill, 95, Van de Griff Gallery, Santa Fe, 97, 98, Lyons Wier Gallery, Chicago, 97; Small Works Exhib, Schoharie Arts Coun, Cobleskill, NY, 92; Southeast Ctr Contemp Art, Winston Salem, NC, 94; New Works, Hoyt Nat, New Castle, Pa, 96; Renewal of Spirit, H Lee Moffit Cancer Center, Tampa, Fla, 2000. *Pos:* artist relocation program, Paducah Ky, 2000-. *Teaching:* instr, Galesburg Civic Art Center, Ill, 92; instr, Southern Ill Univ, 86-89. *Awards:* Grumbacher Gold Medallion, Hoyt Inst, 1987; Ill Arts Coun fellow 1991; Wis Arts Bd fellow 1992; Best of Show Award, MPUAG Nat, 1992; Southern Arts Fedn fellow 1994; Ky Arts Coun fellow 1997, 2000; Donors Award, Great Plains Nat, 2000. *Media:* Oil, Panel. *Publ:* artist, New Art Examiner, 94; auth, New American Paintings, Open Studio Press, 97, 99; artist, The Other Side, 11/2000. *Dealer:* Principal Gallery 208 King St Alexandria VA 22314. *Mailing Add:* 3000 Ridgeview Ct Green Bay WI 54301

BARONS, RICHARD IRWIN
EDUCATOR, HISTORIAN
b Bergen, NY, Apr 25, 46. *Study:* State Univ NY Col, New Paltz, BA, 70. *Collection Arranged:* Eighteenth and Nineteenth Century American Folk Pottery (auth, catalog), State Univ NY Col, New Paltz, 68; The American Cooking Hearth: Colonial and Post-Colonial Cooking Tools (auth, catalog), Broome Co Hist Soc, 76; The Folk Arts and Crafts of the Susquehanna and Chenango River Valleys, Roberson Ctr Arts & Sci, 78; Multiples: American Printmaking of the Last Ten Years, 79; Emil Holzhauer: Seventy-Five Years of an Artist's Life (auth, catalog), 80; Severity and Simplicity: The Arts and Crafts Aesthetic in the Northeast 1895-1925 (auth, catalog), Binghamton Univ Mus Art, 94. *Pos:* Cur, Genesee Co Mus, 70-74; cur hist, Roberson Mus & Sci Ctr, 74-79; preservation dir, Bement Billings House, Newark Valley, NY, 83-89; dir, Preservation Asn of the Southern Tier, 86-91 & Binghamton Mus Fine Art, 94-99; dir Southampton Hist Mus, 99-; exec dir, East Hampton Hist Soc, 2006-. *Teaching:* Prof art hist & archit, Broome Community Col, Binghamton, NY, 79-99. *Mem:* Am Asn Mus; Asn State & Local Hist; Mus Am Folk Art; Soc Preserv New Eng Antiquities. *Res:* Eighteenth and nineteenth century American arts, crafts and architecture. *Publ:* Coauth, Franck Taylor Bowers 1875-1932, 77 & auth, The Folk Tradition: The Early Arts and Crafts of the Susquehanna River Valley, 81, Roberson Ctr Arts & Sci; Our Homes, Our Shops: The Early 19th Century Architecture of the Susquehanna Region of New York, Bowers Corners Press, 86; coauth, The Lost Hamptons, Arcadia Books, 2003. *Mailing Add:* 94 Church Lane East Hampton NY 11937

BAROOSHIAN, MARTIN
PAINTER, PRINTMAKER
b Chelsea, Mass, Dec 18, 29. *Study:* Boston Mus Fine Arts Sch, full tuition scholars, dipls with highest hons, 52 & 55; Albert H Whitin Traveling Fel, Europe, 52; Boston Mus Sch Travelling Fel, 52-53; Tufts Univ, BSEd, 53; Boston Univ, MA(art hist), 58; and with Gaston Dorfinant & S W Hayter, Paris. *Work:* Libr & Mus Performing Arts, Lincoln Ctr Mus Mod Art, Metrop Mus Art, NY; Nat Gallery Art, New Delhi, India; Mus Mod Art & Nat Gallery, Yerevan, Armenia; Montreal Art Mus; Boston Pub Libr, Mass. *Exhib:* Boston Printmakers Traveling Exhibs; Soc Am Graphic Artists, NY; First Int Can Graphic Art Exhib, Montreal Mus Fine Art, 71; 1st & 2nd NH Int, 73 & 74; retrospective, Art Complex Mus, Duxbury, Mass, 83 & Firehouse Gallery, Garden City, NY, 93; Julie Heller Gallery, Provincetown, Mass, 2001; Winsor Art Gallery, NY, 2005; multiple group exhibs. *Pos:* Consult, Works on Paper, Swann Galleries, NY; fine arts consult, prints & drawings, 88-95. *Teaching:* Instr lithography Boston Mus Sch, 54-55; instr printmaking workshops, Pratt Inst, NY, 60-69; art instr, Half Hollow Hills Sch, NY, 60-92. *Awards:* Asian Studies Grant, US Dept Educ, 72; Print Prize, Nat Acad Design, 76; USSR Studies Grant, US Dept Educ, 79; and others. *Bibliog:* Helen Terzian (auth), Martin Barooshian, the changing face of art, Ararat, No 21, winter 65; William P Carl (auth), The Inner World of Martin Barooshian, Duxbury Art Complex Mus, Mass, 83; Michael Russo (auth), Discovering the art of Martin Barooshian-surrealist works of the fifties, J of Print World, 2001 & 04. *Mem:* Soc Am Graphic Artists (pres, 72-74); Print Club Albany. *Media:* Oils; Printmaking. *Publ:* Auth, Some Thoughts on Paper & Printmaking, Rising Paper Co, Mass, 86; auth, Reflections on Atelier 17 and Lethography Studios in 1950's, Paris. *Dealer:* Ro Gallery 36th St Long Island City NY 10019; Herbert Halpern Fine Art 1520 St Charles Ave New Orleans LA 70130. *Mailing Add:* 17 West Dr Kings Park NY 11754-3814

BAROWITZ, ELLIOTT
PAINTER
b Westwood, NJ, Aug 22, 36. *Study:* Carnegie-Mellon Univ; RI Sch of Design, BFA; San Francisco Art Inst; Univ Cincinnati; Cincinnati Art Acad, MFA. *Work:* NJ State Mus, Trenton; Rose Mus, Brandeis Univ; Cincinnati Art Mus; Paterson Mus, NJ; Brandeis Mus, Maine; plus others. *Exhib:* San Francisco Art Asn Mus, 61; Nova Zembla Gallery, Hertogebusch, The Neth, 93; Drexel Univ, 93; Cent Conn State Col, Forum Gallery, Jamestown, NY, 94; Regard Parole, Elancourt, France, 94; Exchanging Thought, Univ Thailand, Chiangmai, 96; Spil Cult Ctr, Roselare, Belg, 99; Midrash: Memoirs, Art & Art History, Slifka Ctr, Yale Univ, New Haven, Conn, 2000; restrospective, Leonard Perlstein Gallery, Drexel Univ, 2003; Elder Arts, Napa, Calif, Madelyn Jordon Fine Arts, 2004, plus others. *Pos:* Exec ed, Art & Artist, 80-,. *Teaching:* Prof painting & art theory, Drexel Univ, Philadelphia, 66-2002, prof emer, 2002; instr painting & design, Maine Col Art, Maine, summers 76-99; adj prof contemp art & cultural hist, New York Univ, 1974-present. *Awards:* Grant, NY State Coun Arts. *Bibliog:* Articles, Arts Mag, 69, 80 & 84, Art in Am, 64, Art News 69 & Art in America, 88. *Mem:* Artists Tenants Asn; Found Community Artists (pres bd dir, 78-79); US Comt-Int Asn of Art, Inc (vpres); New York City Loft Board. *Media:* Oil, Photocopy Prints. *Res:* Modern vision & Post-modern vision. *Interests:* Writer on the arts. *Collection:* RI School of Design; Univ of Cincinnati; Paterson NJ Museum; NJ State Museum. *Publ:* Rev, Leon Golub: Existential/Activist Painter by Donald Kuspit, Art & Artists, 86; All's Well that Ends Well Perhaps or Something is Rotten in the State of Denmark-Chicago-USA, Art & Artist, 89; What the Art Student Needs By Golly, 1991 Nat Conf Proceedings, Sch Visual Arts, New York, 91; Conservative Echos in Fins-de-Sieole, Paris Art Criticism, (book review) English Literature in Translation, Univ NC, Greensboro, 93; Italian Art Deco Graphic Design Between The Word (book review), Woman Artist News, 94; Dictionary of the avant-gardes (rev), Woman Artist News, 95; and others. *Dealer:* Madelyn Jordon, Fine Arts. *Mailing Add:* 330 Lafayette St New York NY 10012

BARR, BURT
VIDEO ARTIST, PHOTOGRAPHER
b Lewiston, Maine, Nov 12, 43. *Study:* Boston Univ, BA; San Francisco Art Inst, MFA. *Work:* La Salle Nat Bank, Chicago. *Comn:* La SEPT, Paris; WGBH-TV, Boston. *Exhib:* Solo shows, New Arts Prog, Kutztown, Pa, 91, CAPC Musee, Bordeaux, France, 92, Arteleku, San Sebastian, Spain, 92, Image Forum Festival, Tokyo & Osaka, 93, Paula Cooper Gallery, NY, 93 & 96, Suzanne Dellal Ctr, Tel Aviv, Israel, 93 & Mus Mod Art, NY, 98; Elec Matter Exhib, Philadelphia; Arteleku, San Sebastian, Spain; Suzanne Dellal Ctr, Tel Aviv; Paula Cooper Gallery, NY, 91, 93 & 96; Whitney Biennial, Whitney Mus Am Art, NY, 96, 2001; Lawing Gallery, Houston, Tex, 98; Postmasters Gallery, NY, 2001; Lawing Gallery, Houston, Tex, 2001; Platform Inst Contemp Art Ctr, Istanbul, Turkey, 2002. *Teaching:* NY Univ Grad Sch, Instr of Creative Projects, 2001; Pratt Inst, Instr of Film and Video Projects, 2002; selected lects, Parsons Sch of Design, NY, 2001, RI Sch of Design, 2002, The Reina Sofia Mus, Madrid, 2002, Pratt Inst, Brooklyn, NY, 2002. *Awards:* Nat Endowment Arts Award, 83, 85, 88, 89 & 93; NY State Coun Arts, Individual Artists Prog, 86, 89 & 96; Guggenheim Fel, 98; The Andrea Frank Found, NY, 99; Bellagio, Ital, Recipient, Rockerfeller Found, 2001. *Publ:* Trisha and Carmen (film), 88; The Dogs (film), 89; Aeros (film), 90; The Pool (film), 93; The Hornets, Bob & Evelyn, 94. *Dealer:* Electronic Arts Intermix 536 Broadway New York NY 10012; Patrick Gallery. *Mailing Add:* 541 Broadway New York NY 10012

BARR, DAVID JOHN
SCULPTOR, CONCEPTUAL ARTIST
b Detroit, Mich, Oct 10, 39. *Study:* Wayne State Univ, BFA & MA. *Work:* Detroit Inst Arts; Portland Art Mus; Mich Hist Mus; Flint Airport; and others. *Comn:* Polaris Ring, Lansing, Mich, 88; Fountain, Detroit Zoo, 95; Revolution, Chrysler World Hq, 96; Revolution II, Brussels, Belgium; Synergy, Dennos Mus, Traverse City, Mich, 99; Galileo, Pisa, Italy, 2002; Liberation, Pfizer Corp, Ann Arbor, Mich, 2002; Transcending, Hart Plaza, Detroit, Mich, 2003; Diversity, Mich Legacy Art Park, 2002; and others. *Exhib:* Donald Morris Gallery, 72-96; one-man shows, Richard Gray Gallery, Calif, 78; Dennos Mus, 2000; Vault, Columbus State Community Col, Ohio, 2006; Dawn, Warren, Mich, 2006; and others. *Pos:* founder, artistic dir, Mich Legacy Art Park, Thompsonville, Mich. *Teaching:* Prof sculpture, Macomb Co Col, 64-. *Awards:* Mich Found of the Arts Award, 77; Concerned Citizens Arts Award, 88; Humanity in the Arts Award, Wayne State Univ, 98. *Bibliog:* Realities and Impressions, Brady Production, 88; Arctic Arc, Grace Productions, 88; Tapestry, MCC Prod, 93; Arc of the Umiak, MCC Prod, 93; "Nets", MCC Production, 99. *Mem:* AIA (hon mem). *Media:* Masonite, Steel, Stone. *Publ:* Auth, Notes, 70; Notes III, 72; Structurist, 76; Notes on Celebration, 80; article, CoEvolution Quart, fall 81. *Mailing Add:* 22600 Napier Novi MI 48374

BARR-SHARRAR, BERYL
ART HISTORIAN, PAINTER
b Richmond, Va. *Study:* Mt Holyoke Col, BA; Univ Calif, Berkeley, MA; Inst Fine Arts, NY Univ, MA, PhD. *Work:* Mt Holyoke Col Mus; Los Angeles Saving & Loan Asn; Palmer Mus, Pa State Univ. *Exhib:* Maisons Cult Amiens, Bourges, Mus Avignon, Besancon Montpellier, Nancy & Ste-Etienne, 67; Mus Bordeux, Menton &

le Havre, 68; Sachs Gallery, 73, Livingstone-Learmonth Gallery, 75, NY; Art Galaxy Gallery, NY, 81; Univ Art Mus, State Univ NY, Binghamton, 94; and others. *Pos:* Co-founder, Col Art Study Abroad, Paris, 61, co-dir, 61-68. *Teaching:* Vis lectr painting, Mt Holyoke Col, 68-69; vis lectr art hist, Pratt Inst, 78-79; adj assoc prof art hist, Fordham Univ, 81-82; vis prof art hist, Vassar Col, 82-83; adj prof, New York Univ, 2002-2007. *Awards:* Am Philos Soc Grants, 82 & 96; Ctr Advan Study Visual Arts, Nat Gallery, Washington, 85; Kress Joint Scientific Study Grant, 2000; Prof Dev Grants, NYU, 2005-2006; Hazen Alumnae Grant, Mt Holyoke, 2006. *Mem:* Am Inst Archaeology; Col Art Asn; Asn Ancient Historians. *Media:* Acrylic on Canvas, Paper. *Publ:* The Antikythera Fulcrum attachment: A portrait of Arsinöe III, vol 89, No 4, Am J Archaeology, 10/85; The Hellenistic & Early Imperial Bust, 87; How Important is Provenance? Archaeological & Stylistic Questions in the Attribution of Ancient Bronzes in Small Bronze Sculpture from the Ancient World, Los Angeles, 91; Vergina Tomb II: Dating the Objects in Alexander the Great, VII, The Ancient World, Vol 22, No 2, 91; Earth & Water: Early Traditions & Uses of Ancient Greek Clay in Greek Terracottas of the Hellenistic World, Harvard Univ Art Mus Bull, Vol 1, No 3, Spring 93; Four articles in Das Wrack, Der Antike Schiffsfund von Mahdia, Bonn, 94; Hellenistic Bronze Production on Delos, in Regional Schools in Hell, Sculpture, 98; Cast Bronze Ovoid Situla, Kölner Club, 99. *Mailing Add:* 311 E 72nd St New York NY 10021-4684

BARRA, ROBERT
PAINTER
Study: RI Sch Design; Art Student's League NY. *Exhib:* Blue Heron Gallery, Wellfleet, Mass; Nat Arts Club; Salmagundi Club; James Beard House, New York City; Butler Inst Am Art; Newport Mus, RI; Ridgewood Art Inst, NJ. *Collection Arranged:* Pvt collections: US, Gt Brit, Europe & Mex. *Teaching:* instr, painting, NY Studio, currently. *Mem:* Nat Arts Club; Allied Artists Am (bd mem, currently); Hudson Valley Art Asn; Audubon Artists. *Media:* Miscellaneous Media. *Mailing Add:* 5401 Bayview Dr Fort Lauderdale FL 33308

BARRELL, BILL
PAINTER, COLLECTOR
b London, Eng, Dec 4, 32. *Study:* Pa Acad Fine Art, 56. *Work:* Columbia Univ; Housatonic Mus Art, Conn; NJ State Mus; Jersey City Mus, NJ; Noyes Mus, Oceanville, NJ; and many others. *Exhib:* One-man shows, Dorsky Gallery, NY, Peter Findlay Gallery, NY, David Klein Gallery, Birmingham, Ill, Bhagdad Gallery, St Barth, FWI, Shoe-String Gallery, 94, Chamot Gallery, 97, Halle St Pierre, Paris, France, 98; Ingber Gallery, NY; Jupiter Gallery, NJ; Art Banque, Minneapolis, Minn; The Interior Self, Montclair Mus, NJ, 87; Directors Choice, ARTWORKS, Trenton, NJ, 89; NJ Council on Art Ann, Jersey City Mus, 90; NJ Art Ann, NJ State Mus, Trenton, 94, Six Artists - The Nineties, 96; Artist As Curator, Curator As Artist, Bergen Mus, Paramus, NJ, 96; Art + Suitcase Will Travel, DNA Gallery, Provincetown, Mass, 99; Bagdad Gallery, 2000; Perolas Raras, Portuguese Biennial, 2001; Recent Paintings, Chamot Gallery, NJ, 2002. *Pos:* Owner, Sun Gallery, Provincetown, 59-61. *Teaching:* Vis artist, La State Univ, fall 82; artist-in-residence, Colorado Mountain Col, Vail, Colorado. *Awards:* Harry Devlin Award, NJ State Coun Arts, 83; Rutgers Univ Print fel, 94; Pollock-Krasner fel, 95. *Bibliog:* Barry Barrell (dir), Fruits and Vegetables (film), Barrell Productions, 12/6/67; Peter Schjeldahl (auth), Bill Barrell hits the streets & George Preston (auth), The urbanscape as ideal still life, Potholes, 1/3/78; Herbert E. Reichert (auth), Bill Barrell & The Tree of Life (catalogue), Peter Findlay Gallery, 2000. *Mem:* Orgn Independent Artists. *Media:* Oil-Base Paints; Mixed Media. *Collection:* Red Groom's wood sculpture, Oldenburg's paper collage, Bob Beauchamp's drawings, Mimi Gross Groom's watercolors, Bob Thompson's paintings and drawings and Gandy Brody's gouache. *Publ:* Potholes, Custombook Inc, 78. *Dealer:* Peter Findlay New York NY. *Mailing Add:* c/o Chamot Gallery 111 First St Jersey City NJ 07302-3010

BARRETT, BILL
SCULPTOR
b Los Angeles, Calif, Dec 21, 34. *Study:* Univ Mich, Ann Arbor, BS(design), 58, MS(design), 59, MFA, 60. *Work:* Cleveland Mus Art, Ohio; Aldrich Mus Contemp Art; Norfolk Mus Art, Va; Hakone Open Air Mus, Tokyo; Va Mus Fine Arts, Richmond, Va. *Comn:* Sculpture, New Dorp Sch, NY, 82; sculpture, Rockefeller Reality Group, San Francisco, Calif; sculpture, Criminal Courts Bldg, Hartford, Conn, 86; sculpture, West Group Inc, One Bunker Hill, Los Angeles, Calif, 90; sculpture, Neiman-Marcus, King of Prussia, Pa. *Exhib:* Nat Art Inst Show, San Francisco Mus Art, 64; Whitney Mus Am Art Sculpture Ann, NY, 70; Storm King Art Ctr, NY, 75; one-man show, Sculpture Ctr, NY, 83, Kouros Gallery, NY, 85, 94 & 96, Bellevue Sculpture Garden, 85-86 & Roswitha Benkert Gallery, Zurich, Switz, 86, 90 & 92, De Graaf Gallery, Chicago, 89, Shidoni, Santa Fe, NMex, 90; Cline Gallery, Santa Fe, NMex, 93-96; Mongerson-Wunderlich Gallery, Chicago, Ill, 94; Navy Pier Expo, Sculpture Walk, Chicago, 96. *Pos:* Cur exhib, Sculptors Guild, NY, 90; Cline Fine Art, Santa Fe, 94. *Teaching:* Assoc prof sculpture, Eastern Mich Univ, 60-68; instr, Cleveland Art Inst, 63-64; asst prof, City Col NY, 69-76; lectr, Columbia Univ, 79-; vis artist, Univ Pa, Columbia Univ, & Vt Studio Sch. *Awards:* R S Reynolds Mem Award For Sculpture, 86; Hakone Open Air Mus Award, Japan; Gold Medal of Honor in Sculpture, Audubon Artists, NY. *Bibliog:* Mac McCloud (auth), The Santa Fean, New Mexican, 10/19/90; Guy Cross (auth), article, The Mag, 4/96; Richard Tobin (auth), article, The Mag, 9/96. *Mem:* Sculptors Guild NY (pres, formerly); Audubon Artists, NY; Int Sculpture Ctr, Washington, DC; Century Asn. *Media:* Bronze. *Mailing Add:* 11 Worth St New York NY 10013-2922

BARRETT, LENI MANCUSO See Mancuso, Leni Mancuso Barrett

BARRETT, TERRY M
WRITER, EDUCATOR
b Chicago, Ill, 45. *Study:* Webster Univ, BA, 67; Ohio State Univ, MA, 74, PhD, 83. *Pos:* Ed, Columbus Art, 81-91; sr ed, Studies in Art Educ, 93-95. *Teaching:* Prof art criticism, aesthetics, photog criticism, & Art educ, Ohio State Univ, 83-; vis scholar, Getty Educ Inst Educ Arts, Los Angeles, 95-96; vis prof, Univ Ariz, 97; vis scholar educ, Ctr Creative Photog, Tucson, Ariz, 97; invited art critic, Critic & Artist Residence Series, Colo State Univ, Ft Collins, Colo, 98; vis artist/scholar, Lamar Dodd Sch Art Prog, Univ Ga, Athens, 99; vis artist/scholar, HISK, Antwerp, Belgium, 2002. *Awards:* Honored Educator, Midwest Soc for Photographic Educ, 2001; Outstanding Alumnus, Webster Univ, 2003; Distinguished Fel, Nat Art Education Asn, 2004; Hatcher Mem Award, Ohio State Univ, 2005. *Mem:* Nat Art Educ Asn. *Res:* Teaching art criticism and aesthetics. *Publ:* Auth, Criticizing Photographs, McGraw-Hill, 90, 2nd ed, 95, 3rd ed, 2000; ed, Lessons for Teaching Art Criticism, ERIC: Univ Ind, 95; auth, Talking About Student Art, Davis, 97; Auth, Criticizing Art, McGraw-Hill, 2nd ed, 2000; Auth, Interpreting Art, McGraw-Hill, 2003; auth, Interpreting Art, McGraw Hill, 2003; auth, David Burton, in: Exhibiting Student Art, Teachers College Press, New York, 2005; auth, Teaching Toward Appreciation, in: Handbook of Research of Arts Education, Springer, New York, 2006. *Mailing Add:* 3949 Wynding Dr Columbus OH 43214

BARRETT, THOMAS R
PAINTER, INSTRUCTOR
b Woodhaven, NY, Feb 17, 27. *Study:* Wesleyan Univ, BA; Brooklyn Mus Art Sch; Univ NH, MA. *Work:* Portland Art Mus, Maine; Phillips Exeter Acad, Exeter, NH; Farnsworth Mus, Rockland, Maine; Kresge Collection, Detroit; NH State Art Bank; US Dept State, Washington. *Comn:* Chamber Commerce, Manchester, NH, 88. *Exhib:* Lamont Gallery, Exeter, NH, 79; Deer Isle Art Asn, Maine; Manchester Inst Art & Sci, NH, 86; Art Ctr in Hargate, St Paul's Sch, 86, 87; Le Va-tout Gallery, Waldoboro, Maine, 94; Maine Coast Artist Juried Exhibs, 95-96; Maine at Work, Farnsworth Art Mus, Rockland, Maine, 97; Maine Coast Artists, Rockport, 99; Trinity Gallery, Castine, 2002; Galerie am Neuen Palais, Potsdam, Ger, 2003; Ctr for Maine Contemp Art, 2003-2004; Abbe Mus, Bar Harbor, 2004; Leighton Gallery, Blue Hill, ME, 2005. *Pos:* Dir, Art Ctr-Hargate, St Pauls Sch, Concord, 69-89; pres, Independent Sch Art Inst Asn, 77-80; pres, NH Visual Arts Coalition, 79-81; adv bd visual arts, New Eng Found Arts, 82-85. *Teaching:* Instr painting & art hist & head art dept, St Paul's Sch, Concord, NH; retired. *Awards:* Currier Gallery Art Award, 60 & 62; City of Manchester Award, NH, 65; DeKalb Award, 72. *Mem:* NH Art Asn (pres, 68-69); Asn Am Mus; Col Art Asn; Deer Isle Artists Asn; Union Maine Visual Artists. *Media:* All. *Mailing Add:* PO Box 303 15 Madockawando Rd Castine ME 04421-0303

BARRETT, WILLIAM O
ADMINISTRATOR
b Hartford, Conn, Sept 1, 45. *Study:* RI Sch Design, BFA, 67; New York Univ, MA, 78. *Pos:* Asst Dean, Parsons Sch Design, 79-81; dean, Corcoran Sch Art, Washington, DC, 81-87; pres, San Francisco Art Inst, 87-94; exec dir, Asn Independent Col Art & Design, 94-. *Mem:* Life mem & fel Nat Asn Schs Art & Design. *Mailing Add:* AICAD 3957 22nd St San Francisco CA 94114

BARRIE, DENNIS RAY
MUSEUM DIRECTOR, HISTORIAN
b Cleveland, Ohio, July 9, 47. *Study:* Oberlin Col, BA, MA, 70; Wayne State Univ, PhD, 83. *Exhib:* Body & Soul: Recent Figurative Sculpture, 85; Jenny Holzer & Cindy Sherman: Personae, 86; New Art of Italy: Chia, Clemente, Cucchi, Paladino, 86; The Ties That Bind: Folk Art in Contemp Am Cult, 87; Standing Ground: Sculpture by Am Women, 87. *Collection Arranged:* The New British Painting, 88; Drawings Jim Dine, 1973-87, 88; Mike & Doug Starn: The Starn Twins, 90; The Continuous Presence of Organic Archit, 91; Mechanika, New Kinetic Sculpture, 91; Int Spy Mus, 2002; Bethel Woods Performing Arts Ctr, 2006. *Pos:* Midwest regional dir & contrib ed Jour, Arch Am Art, Smithsonian Inst, Detroit, 72-83; dir, Contemp Arts Ctr, Cincinnati, 83-92, Rock & Roll Hall of Fame & Mus, formerly; pres, Dennis Barrie & Assocs, 92-93; pres, Barrie Consult, Cleveland Heights, Ohio, 96-98; pres, Malrite Co, 98-2005; dir cultural planning, Westlake Reed Leskosky Architects, 2005-; prin, Barrie Project, 2005-. *Awards:* Frederick Weisman Art Found Award; Am Soc Newspaper Eds Award; First Amendment Award, Soc Prof Journalists; Distinguished Alumni Award-Oberlin Col, 2004; Distinguished Alumni Award- Wayne State Univ, 2004. *Bibliog:* Peter Plagens (auth), Mixed signals on obscenity, Newsweek, 10/15/90; Jayne Merkel (auth), Art on Trial, Art in Am, 12/90; James R Petersen (auth), Showdown in Cincinnati, Playboy, 3/91. *Mem:* Am Asn Mus. *Res:* American 20th century art. *Publ:* Auth, The school years 1926-1976, In: Arts and Crafts in Detroit 1906-1970, The Movement, The Society, The School, Detroit Inst Arts, 76; auth & producer TV docs, Artists-in-Residence Portraits of Five Ohio Artists, 80, Artists in America--Portraits of Roger Brown, Richard Hunt, John Hegarty and Marshall Fredericks, 83 & Celebration: The Four Corners--Project of David Barr, 83, Smithsonian Inst; auth, Artists in Michigan in the 20th Century, Wayne State Univ Press, 88. *Mailing Add:* 2709 Berkshire Rd Cleveland OH 44106-3361

BARRIOS, BENNY PEREZ
PAINTER, ART DEALER
b Bisbee, Ariz, Mar 20, 25. *Study:* Sacramento City Col, AA, 48; Chouinard Art Inst, 53; Calif State Univ, Sacramento, BA, 74. *Work:* Crocker Art Gallery, Sacramento; Oakland Art Mus, Calif; Smithsonian Inst, Washington, DC. *Exhib:* One-man shows, Los Angeles Co Mus, 52, San Francisco Mus, 52, De Young Mus, 52, Oakland Mus, 52 & Crocker Art Gallery, 53 & 63; 1st, 2nd & 3rd Invitational, Calif Palace Legion

Hon, San Francisco, 56-58; Butler Inst Am Art, Youngstown, Ohio, 58; Gov Brown Invitational Chicano Art Exhib, Sacramento, 75; group exhib, Instituto Cult Mexicano, Los Angeles, 94. *Pos:* Owner, Barrios Gallery, Sacramento, 59-. *Teaching:* Instr oils & acrylics, San Juan Unified Sch Dist, Sacramento, 62-77, Sacramento Unified Sch Dist, 68-77 & Sacramento City Col, 77-82. *Awards:* Second in Watercolor, Laguna Art Festival, 56; First in Oil, Northern Calif Arts, 58; Second in Oil, Auburn Art Festival, 62. *Bibliog:* Alfred Frankenstein (auth), Wetbacks, San Francisco Chronicle, 54; Charles Johnson (auth), Farm workers plight inspires artist, Sacramento Bee, 75; Peter Moore (auth), Lynton Kistler: The happy printer, Art News, 78. *Media:* Acrylic, Watercolor. *Specialty:* All medias; contemporary artists. *Mailing Add:* 4220 Watkins Dr Fair Oaks CA 95628-7534

BARRON, ROS
PAINTER, VIDEO ARTIST
b Boston, Mass, July 4, 33. *Study:* Mass Col Art, BFA(painting & ceramics); and with Carl Nelson, 48-51; Bunting Inst, Harvard Univ, fel, 66-68. *Work:* Addison Gallery Am Art, Andover, Mass; Worcester Art Mus; Dartmouth Col Collection; Harvard Univ; Boston Mus Fine Arts; and others. *Comn:* Seasons (wall painting), YMCA, Roxbury, Mass, 65; Rainbow, Rocket, Road (wall painting), Lawrence Sch, Brookline, Mass, 67; polarized light painting, comn by SDI, San Francisco, 69; ser wall paintings for Community Ctr, Wilmington, Del, 70; and others. *Exhib:* one-woman shows, De Cordova Mus, Lincoln, 57, Univ Conn, Storrs, 69, Lenore Gray Gallery, Providence, 72, Portland Mus Art, 74 & Helen Shlien Gallery, Boston, 79 & 82; Whitney Ann Am Painting, Salon, 71-72; Surreal Image, De Cordova Mus, 68; UNESCO Art in Architecture, Rotterdam, The Neth; Am Painting & Sculpture, US Info Agency Exhib, Europe; Montevideo Gallery, The Neth, 78; Carnegie Inst, 78; Mus Mod Art, NY, 80; and many others. *Pos:* co-dir, founder, Zone, Visual Theater, 68-. *Teaching:* asst prof art, Univ Mass, Boston, 72-76, assoc prof, 76-; vis artist, de Cordova Mus, Lincoln Mass, 55-58, Univ Mass, 71-72, Univ Colo, Boulder, 83, and others. *Awards:* Guggenheim Found Award for Zone's Yellow Sound, 72; Rockefeller Found Grants, 77-79; Nat Endowment Arts Individual Fel, 75-76; Mass Coun Individual Art Fel in Video, 80-81; and others. *Bibliog:* Frames of reference: Ros Barron (film), co-produced by WGBH Educ Found, 80; Ros Barron: An Artist in Profile, Mass Coun Arts & Humanities, 9/81; Linda Furlong (auth), State of the Art Scan: The Ithaca Video Festival, Afterimage, 1/82. *Mem:* Boston Performance Artists, Mobius Artists Group. *Dealer:* Gilbert Urbano. *Mailing Add:* PO Box 470394 Brookline Village MA 02147

BARRON, STEPHANIE
CURATOR
Study: Barnard Col, Columbia Univ, AB, 72; Studied arts admin, Harvard Inst, 73; Columbia Univ, MA, 74; Grad Ctr, City Univ NY, PhD course work, 75 76. *Collection Arranged:* Degenerate AA, 91; Russian Avant-Garde, 80; David Hockney, 88; Ger Expressionist Sculpture, 82; Made in Calif, 2000. *Pos:* Intern & curatorial asst, Solomon R Guggenheim Mus, 71-72; intern educ, Toledo Mus Art, 73-74; exhib coordr, Jewish Mus, NY, 75-76; assoc cur mod art, Los Angeles Co Mus Art, 76-80, cur twentieth century art, 80-94, coordr curatorial affairs, 93-96, sr cur twentieth century art, 95- & vpres educ & pub progs, 96-2003; Chief cur modern art, 2003. *Awards:* Nat Endowment Arts Fel, 86-87; Best Am Exhib Yr Award, Asn Int Critics Art, 91 & 97; Am Acad Arts & Sci Fel, 97; Alred Barr Award from Col Art Assoc, 92; E L Kirchner Prize, 97; Order of Merrit, Ger Govt, 84; Commanders Curse of the Ger Govt, 2000. *Mem:* Col Art Asn; Am Asn Mus; Int Coun Mus; Bd of Trustees, Scripps, Col. *Res:* Modern & contemp art, Ger Expressionism. *Publ:* Russian Avant Garde, 1910-1930; New Prospectives, LACMA & MIT Press, 80; Ger Expressionist Sculpture, LACMA Press, 82; David Hockney Retrospective, LACMA & Abrams, 88; Degenerate Art, Abrams & LACMA, 91. *Mailing Add:* Los Angeles Co Mus Art 5905 Wilshire Blvd Los Angeles CA 90036

BARRON, SUSAN
COLLAGE ARTIST, PRINTMAKER
b Lake Forrest, Ill, May 15, 47. *Work:* Metrop Mus Art, Pierpont Morgan Libr, Mus Mod Art, NY; Philadelphia Mus Art, Pa; Victoria & Albert Mus, London, Eng; The Getty Mus, Malibu; Fitzwilliam Mus, Cambridge, Eng; Nat Libr France, Paris; Royal Libr of the Neth, Mus Meermanno, Westreenianum; pvt collections of Mr & Mrs Paul Mellon, Lillian Farber, Newfane, Bernard Friedelson, NY, Walter & Naomi Rosenblum Collection, NY, Jacqueline Kennedy Onasis, NY, Ruth & Marvin Sackner Archive, Miami Beach, Fla, Robert & Marjorie Graff, Far Hills, David Grob, London, others. *Comn:* Delivre II (illuminated manuscript), 86 & Twisting Silence (unique book), 91, Sackner Arch, Miami Beach, Fla. *Exhib:* Collage as Intimate Art, Brooklyn Mus, NY, 82; John Cage Collaborations, Whitney Mus Am Art, NY, 82; New Britain Mus Am Art, Conn, 83; solo exhibs, Del Mus Art, Wilmington, 84, Univ of Ill Mus of Art, 93, Newberry Libr, Chicago, 95, Univ Iowa Mus Art, 95, Philadelphia Mus Art, 96-97, Victoria & Albert Mus, London, 97, Drexel Univ Gallery Art, 97 & Ctr Contemp Art, St Louis, 99, Printworks Gallery, 2002; Artists Book, Metrop Mus Art, NY, 86; New Acquisitions, Philadelphia Mus Art, Pa, 87; Dedication Exhib, Israel Mus, Jerusalem, 90; Book Artists Five, Nat Mus Women in Arts, Washington, DC, 92; The Dual Muse (with catalog), Washington Univ, St Louis Int Writers Ctr, 97; The Next Word (with catalog), Newberger Mus Art, 98; Artists Book, Brooklyn Mus Art, NY, 99, New Britain Mus Am Art, Conn, 2003; Smith col, 2005. *Awards:* Artists Grant (photography), NY State Coun on Arts, 81; Dreyfuss Award, MacDowell Fel, 85; Artists Grant (Works on Paper), Nat Endowment for Arts, 93-94. *Bibliog:* Portfolio-Susan Barron, Aperture; The Book Collector, (Spring & Fall) 97; Art on Paper, 2004. *Publ:* coauth (with John Cage), Another Song (monogr), Callaway Ed, 81; Labyrinth of Time, Eleven Vols, pvt publ, 88; Twisting Silence, pvt publ, 91; Jamaica Mistake, pvt publ, 94; The Mirror (braille manuscript scroll), 95. *Dealer:* Elizabeth Phillips 27 Grand Ave Nyack NY 10960; Joshua Heller Rare Books PO Box 34114 Washington DC 20016-9114; Printworks Gallery 311 W Superior Chicago IL 60610. *Mailing Add:* 39 Plaza West Brooklyn NY 11217-3906

BARRON, THOMAS
PAINTER
b Newton, Mass, 49. *Study:* Harvard Univ, 67-70, study painting with Marilyn Powers & Jason Berger, 71-74. *Work:* Boston Mus Fine Arts, Bank of Boston; Rose Art Mus, Brandeis Univ, Waltham, Mass; Duxbury Art Complex Mus, Mass; Mills Col Art Gallery, Oakland, Calif; Tel Aviv Mus Art, Israel; Currier Gallery Art, Manchester, NH; and others. *Comn:* Portrait, Ms Kevin Kling, Paris, France, 77; Ms Catherine Ventura, NY, 80. *Exhib:* The Direct Vision, Fitchburg Art Mus, Mass, 73, Acad Arts, Easton, Md, 76 & Rose Art Mus, Waltham, Mass, 88; Panorama Symposium, Centre d'Arte, Baie St Paul, Quebec, Can, 89; The Drawing Show, Boston Ctr Arts, Boston, Mass, 97; Currier Gallery of Art, Manchester, NH, 97; Le Cri Muet, Centre D'Art Baiest Paul, Quebec, Can, 2000; Abstraction Now, Rensselaer Polytechnical Inst, Troy, NY, 2004. *Pos:* Instr painting & drawing, pvt classes, 75-. *Awards:* Grant, Mass Coun Arts & Humanities, 73 & 75. *Bibliog:* Kenworth Moffett (auth), Abstraction offers most exciting possibilities, Vol 6, Art New Eng, 9/85; Nancy Stapen (auth), Thomas Barron at Andrea Marquit, Art News, 11/96; Piri Halasz (auth), Review of Abstraction Now, From the Mayor's Doorstep, NY, 12/04; Menachem Wecker (auth), The Aesthetic of Mishigaas, Jewish Press Mag, 2004. *Media:* All. *Res:* Included in book by Vicky Perry. *Specialty:* Abstract Painting, Concepts & Techniques. *Publ:* Contribr, drawings, An empty glass house, New Renaissance Mag, spring 86; book cover drawing, Puncturing Our Illusions, Simon & Schuster Press, 99; cover painting, J Current Rsch & Practices in Language Minority Educ, Pearson Custom Publ, 2002; contribr, Communication, Making Connections, Pearson Publishing, 2003. *Dealer:* Andrea Marquit Fine Arts 38 Newbury St Boston MA 02116. *Mailing Add:* 25 Parkman St Brookline MA 02146

BARROW, AMANDA MCLAUGHLIN
PRINTMAKER, COLLAGE ARTIST
b Indianapolis, Ind, Nov 15, 59. *Study:* Colo State Univ, with Richard DeVore & Nilda Getty, BA(humanities), 82. *Work:* Mus Mod Art & Pub Libr, NY; Fine Arts Libr, Harvard Univ; Mus of the Book, The Hague, Neth; Yale Univ, New Haven, Conn. *Exhib:* Modern Tapestries, DeCordora Mus, Lincoln, Maine, 94; Int Kunst Festival, Lokshuppen, Ger, 94; Images of Gotts Island, Wendell Gilley Mus, SW Harbor, Maine, 95; Artist Books, Soc Arts Crafts, Boston, Mass, 97; Look Both Ways, Lawrence Acad, Groton, Mass, 97; Pyramid Atlantic Bk Fair, Corcoran Gallery Art, Washington, DC, 97; Selections Exhib, Univ Mass, Dartmouth, 99; Artist/Author: The Book as Art Since 1980, Am Fedn Arts traveling exhib, USA & Europe, 98-2000. *Awards:* Honorarium, Drawing Ctr, NY, 89; Fulbright Res Grant, India, 92; New England Found Arts Award, 4/98. *Bibliog:* Srimati Lal (auth), Indian art & the big apple, Times India, 94; Judith Hoffberg (auth), Apollo's stage, Umbrella Mag, 97; Clive Phillpot & Cornelia Lauf (auths), Artist/Author: Contemporary Artist's Books, Distributed Art Publ, NY, 98. *Mem:* Womens Caucus Art; Monotype Guild New Eng. *Media:* Artist Books, Works on Paper. *Publ:* Contrib, Tagore Nagar, Dupis Press, 92; Apollo's Stage, Quick Brown Fox, 95. *Mailing Add:* 79 Bridge St Apt 2A Brooklyn NY 11201-7446

BARROW, THOMAS FRANCIS
PHOTOGRAPHER, EDUCATOR
b Kansas City, Mo, Sept 24, 38. *Study:* Kansas City Art Inst, BFA(graphic design), 63; Northwestern Univ, film courses with Jack Ellis, 65; Inst Design, Ill Inst Technol, photog with Aaron Siskind, MS, 67. *Work:* Nat Gallery Can, Ottawa; Mus Mod Art, NY; San Francisco Mus Mod Art, Calif; Philadelphia Mus Fine Arts; Los Angeles Co Mus Art; plus others. *Exhib:* Sharp Focus Realism: A New Perspective, Pace Gallery, NY, 73; Light & Lens: Methods of Photog, Hudson River Mus, Yonkers, NY, 73; one-man show, Light Gallery, NY, 74, 76 & 79; The Extended Document, Int Mus Photog, Rochester, NY, 75; Am Photog: Past & Present, Seattle Art Mus, 76; Contemp Am Photog Works, Mus Fine Arts, Houston, 77; one-man retrospective, San Francisco Mus Mod Art, 86, Los Angeles Co Mus Art, 87. *Collection Arranged:* Light and substance (with Van Deren Coke), 73 & Self as Subject, 83, Univ NMex Art Mus. *Pos:* Asst dir, George Eastman House, Rochester, NY, 71-72; assoc dir, Univ NMex Art Mus, 73-76, actg dir, 85. *Teaching:* Assoc prof, Univ NMex, 73-81, prof art, 81-2001, Presidential Prof, 85-90. *Awards:* Nat Endowment Arts Grant, 73 & 78. *Bibliog:* William Jenkins (auth), The Extended Document, Int Mus Photog, George Eastman House, 74; Inventories and Transformations: The Photographs of Thomas Barrow, Los Angeles Co Mus Art-Univ NMex Press, 86; Geoffrey Batchen (auth), Cancellation in The Last Picture Show, Walker Art Center, 2003. *Mem:* CAA. *Media:* Photography, Lithography. *Publ:* The camera fiend, Image, Vol 14, No 4; contribr, Britannica Encycl Am Art, 73; auth, Three photographers and their books, In: A Hundred Years of Photographic History: Essays in Honor of Beaumont Newhall, 75; ed, Reading Into Photography, Univ NMex Press, 82; Perspectives on Photography: Essays in Honor of Beaumont Newhall, 86; Experimental Vision, Denver Art Mus, 94; The Collectible Moment: Photography in the Norton Simon Mus, 2006. *Dealer:* Andrew Smith 76 E San Francisco St Santa Fe NM 87501; Laurence Miller Gallery 138 Spring St New York NY 10012; Richard Levy Gallery 514 Central Ave Albuquerque NM 87102

BARRY, ANNE MEREDITH
PRINTMAKER, PAINTER
b Toronto, Ont, Aug 31, 32. *Study:* Ont Col of Art, 49-54, with Carl Schaefer & Eric Friefield; also printmaking with N Hornyansky, 63. *Hon Degrees:* Meml Univ of Newfoundland, DHL. *Work:* St Mary's Univ Art Gallery, Halifax, NS; Toronto Dominion Can Collection; Inco Can Collection, Toronto; Arts & Cult Centre, St John's, Nfld; Noreen Can Collection, Toronto; One-person shows include Barry Graphics, MUN Old Harlow, England, 2000, Down North: A Coastal Journey, U of T's Gallery, Toronto & touring 19 Canadian pub art galleries, 95-2000, Images from the Eastern Rim, Atelier d'Art C Bergeron, Ottawa, ON, 97, Gallery One, Toronto,

99-2000, Buschlen Mowatt Gallery, Vancouver, BC, Master Gallery, Calgary, AB, Canada, 93; plus numerous others. *Comn:* Ltd ed seriographs, Dow Chemical Co, Can Ltd, 72, Can Soc Crippled Children, 73 & Gallery Fore, Winnipeg, 75; ltd ed collagraphs, Arts Coun, Brantford Art Gallery, 74; Ont Assoc Art Galleries, 78-79; Toronto Dominion Bank, 82; Dow Chem Co of Can; plus others. *Exhib:* One-person shows, Arts & Cult Centre, St John's, Nfld, 75 & 79, 2000, traveling exhibs; Int Miniature Print Exhib, Pratt Graphic Gallery, NY, 75 & 77; Biennial Am De Artes Graficas, Mus la Tertulia, Cali, SAm, 76; Japan-Can Print Exhib, Japanese Cult Centre, Toronto, 77; Printmaking Experience, traveling pub art galleries, 78-80 & Graphex VII, 79 & 80; Art Gallery Ont, 80, 82 & 83; and others. *Teaching:* Printmaking serigraphy, Mt St Vincent Univ, NS, 74 & 76; Instr workshops, Emily Carr Col Art & Design, 79-84. *Awards:* Merit Award, Art Gallery of Brant, 74. *Bibliog:* Barry and Henry Dunsmore (dirs), Shoreslines (film), 82; Kay Kritzwiser (auth), article, Arts Atlantic, spring 83; John Flood (auth), article, Northward J 28, 83. *Mem:* Print & Drawing Coun of Can; Visual Arts Ont (chmn bd, 76-78); Print & Drawing Coun Can (bd dir, 79-80). *Media:* Woodcut, Collograph; Mixed Media. *Publ:* Auth, Dateline: Newfoundland, 72 & The Collage Print, Art Mag, 73; co-auth, An Introduction to the Collagraph Print, Ont Ministry of Cult & Recreation, 77; illusr, The Private Eye, pvt publ, 77. *Dealer:* Buschlen/Mowatt Gallery 1445 W Georgia St Vancouver BC V6G 2T3. *Mailing Add:* c/o Buschlen Mowatt Gallery 111 1445 W Georgia St Vancouver BC V6G 2T3 Canada

BARRY, ROBERT E
ILLUSTRATOR, EDUCATOR
b Newport, RI, Oct 7, 31. *Study:* Kunstgewerbeschule, Zurich, Switz; RI Sch Design, BFA & MAT. *Work:* Kerlan Collection of Children's Literature & Illus, Univ Minn; Klingspor Mus, Frankfurt, Ger; Mus of the Book, San Juan, PR; Mus of the Virgin Islands, St Thomas. *Pos:* Dir, Art Gallery Southeastern Mass Univ, 77-78; originator & owner, Sportcards, 79-. *Teaching:* Instr art, Averett Col, Danville, Va, 67-68; asst prof art, Tex Woman's Univ, Denton, 68-69; assoc prof art-design, Univ Mass Dartmouth, North Dartmouth, 69-81, prof, 81-97. *Awards:* BK Awards, Boys Club Am, 64 & 67; Award of Merit, NY Soc Illusrs, 65; NY Times Ten Best Illus Books of the Yr, 65. *Mem:* Guild Natural Sci Illusrs. *Publ:* Auth & illusr, Faint George, Houghton Mifflin Co, 63; The Musical Palm Tree, 71 & Ramon and the Pirate Gull, 72, McGraw Hill; auth, Snowman's Secret, MacMillan, 75; Mr Willowby's Christmas Tree, Dell, 92. *Mailing Add:* Driftwood Cliff Ave Newport RI 02840

BARRY, STEVE
SCULPTOR
b Jersey City, NJ, June 22, 56. *Study:* Sch Visual Arts, New York, BFA, 80; Hunter Col, MFA, City Univ New York, 84. *Work:* Albuquerque Mus Art; John Michael Kohler Arts Ctr. *Exhib:* Improbable Machines, Santa Barbara Mus Art, 90; Mechanika, Contemp Arts Ctr, Cincinnati, 91; Visual Arts Awards X, Hirshhorn Mus & Sculpture Garden, Washington, 91; Contemp Art in NMex, Site Santa Fe, 96; Taos, Albuquerque, Santa Fe, Cedar Rapids Mus Art, 98; Stasis, Plan B, Santa Fe, 2000; one-person shows, Contemp Arts Mus, Houston, 92, Ctr Contemp Arts, Santa Fe, 94 & Univ Wyo Art Mus, 95, Albuquerque Contemp Arts Center, 2000; Plan B Santa Fe 2000; Donkey Gallery, Albuquerque, 2004, Univ NMex Art Mus, 2006. *Teaching:* Adj instr sculpture, Hunter Col, New York, 84-89; assoc prof sculpture, Univ NMex, 89-, Regents lectr, 2006-. *Awards:* Fel Nat Endowment Arts, 86, 88 & 90; Awards in the Visual Arts, 90. *Bibliog:* Motion, Motion, Kinetic Art, Perrigrine Press, 89; Contemporary Art in New Mexico, Craftsman House Press, 95; Visual Analogy, MIT Press, 99. *Media:* Steel, Film. *Mailing Add:* PO Box 1046 Corrales NM 87048

BARSANO, RON (RONALD) JAMES
PAINTER, SCULPTOR
b Chicago, Ill, Jan 13, 45. *Study:* Am Acad Fine Art, William Mosby Scholar, 62-67. *Work:* Harwood Found Mus, Taos, NMex; US Army Hq, Washington, DC. *Exhib:* Allied Artists Am, NY 72; Meadowbrook Hall, Mich, 75; Maxwell Gallery, San Francisco, Calif, 75; The Taos 6, Philbrook Mus, Tulsa, Okla, 77; Western Art, Grand Central Art Galleries, NY 78; Am Western Art, Beijing Exhib Palace, China, 81; Pioneer Mus, Colorado Springs, Colo, 85. *Bibliog:* Steve Parks (auth), articles, Profile Mag, 7/78 & Art Lines, 9/81; Brand Shelton (auth), article, SW Profile Mag, 10/83; Tricia Hurst (auth), article, SW Art Mag, 2/85. *Mem:* Fechin Inst, Taos, NMex; Taos Art Asn, NMex. *Media:* Oil, Conte Crayon; Clay. *Publ:* Contribr, Taos Mag, 10/88, NMex Mag, 2/82, Artists of the Rockies Mag, spring 82, Am Artist, 6/82 & Art Gallery Mag, 12/83. *Dealer:* Collins-Pettit Gallery 1 Ledoux St Taos NM 87571. *Mailing Add:* PO Box 590 Arroyo Hondo NM 87513-0590

BARSCH, WULF ERICH
PAINTER, PRINTMAKER
b Reudnitz, Ger, Aug 27, 1943; US citizen. *Study:* Staatliche Hochschule fur Bildende Kunste, Hamburg, 63; Studienatelier K Kaschak, Hamburg, 62; Werkkunstschule, BFA, 68; Brigham Young Univ, MA, 70, MFA, 71. *Work:* Utah Mus of Fine Arts; Utah State Div of Fine Arts; San Francisco Mus of Art; Calif Col of Arts & Crafts, Oakland; States Senate, Hamburg, Ger. *Exhib:* Calif Col Arts & Crafts World Print Competition, San Francisco Mus, 73-76; Mus of Art, Monterey, Calif, 74; Am Acad in Rome, Italy, 76; Smithsonian Inst Traveling Exhib, 77; Corcoran Biennial, 83; 2d Western States Art Found Exhib, Corcoran Gallery Art, Washington, DC, 83; Tamarind, Twenty-five Yrs, 85 & 86; The New West, Colorado Springs Mus Art, 86; solo exhibs, Kimbal Art Ctr, Park City, Utah, 79, Utah Mus Fine Arts, 84, Okla Art Ctr, Scottsdale Ctr Arts, 85, Gremillion Fine Arts, Houston, 86, 87 & 88, Mus Church Hist & Art, Salt Lake City, 86 & River Ctr Gallery, Memphis, Tenn, 88, Dolores Chase Fine Arts, Salt Lake City, 89; 4x4 Western State Printmakers, Nora Eccles Harrison Mus Art, Logan, Utah, 88; Elaine Horwitcz Galleries, Scottsdale, 91; Macon and Co Fine Art, Atlanta, 94, 98, 2000, & 2001; Wyndy Morehead Gallery, New Orleans, 96; Munson Gallery, Santa Fe, 97. *Teaching:* Utah Tech Col, 72, Prof printmaking & painting, Brigham Young Univ, 72-. *Awards:* Special Edition Purchase Award, World Print Competition, San Francisco Mus Modern Art, 1973; Prix de Rome Award, Am Acad, Rome, Italy, 75-76; World Culture Prize-Centro Studie Ricerecke Belle Nazioni, Salromaggiore, Italy, 83; Karl Maeser Res & Creative Arts Award, Karl G Maeser Found, 83; Cliff Lodge Inaugural Exhib, Purchase Award, Utah, 87; Springville Mus of the Arts, Purchase Award, Utah, 86. *Media:* Lithography; Oil. *Publ:* In the Desert (exhib catalog), 85; Looking Toward Home (exhib catalog), 86; Susan Fountleroy (auth), Pasatiempo, Santa Fe Weekly Arts Mag, 10/17/97; All things Testify of Him: Latter Day Saint Inspirational Paintings, Bookcraft, 98; Stephen May (auth), The Reign of Cowboy Art: Western Art in the 1980's, Southwest Art, 10/99. *Mailing Add:* c/o Brigham Young Univ Dept Visual Arts C-502 HFAC Provo UT 84602-6402

BARSNESS, JIM
PAINTER, CARTOONIST
b Bozeman, Mont, 1954. *Study:* Boise State Univ, BA, 79; Boise State Univ, MA, 85; San Francisco Art Inst, MFA, 88. *Exhib:* Solo exhib, San Francisco Art Inst, Calif, 87 & 89, Susan Cummins, Mill Valley, Calif, 90, 91 & 93, Caplan, Santa Monica, Calif, 92, Dominican Col, San Rafael, Calif, 93, George Adams Gallery, NY, 95, 97, 98, 99; group exhib, NY Univ, Small Works, NY, 90, Crocker Art Mus, Sacramento, Calif, 91, Caplan, Santa Monica, Calif, 92, Ark Art Ctr, Collector's Forum, Little Rock, 93, Charles More, Figuatively Speaking, Philadelphia, Pa, 94, Monique Knowlton, NY, 97, Luise Rose, NY, 98, Arkansas Arts Ctr, Little Rock, 98, George Adams Gallery, NY, 2000, Cornell Fine Arts Mus, Rollins Col, Winter Park, Fla, 2000, The Art Mus, Fla Int Univ, Miami, 2000. *Awards:* Binney & Smith Nat Art Achievement Award, San Francisco Art Inst, Calif, 88; Juror's Choice Award, Annual Crocker Art Mus, Sacramento, Calif, 89; Elizabeth Found Grant, 96. *Bibliog:* Terri Cohn (auth), Artweek, 11/28/91; Susan Kandel (auth), Los Angeles Times, 11/12/92; Kenneth Baker (auth), Art News, 3/94; Margaret Shearin (auth), Triad, 5/95; Jonathon Goodman (auth), Art in Am, fall, 98. *Media:* Drawing. *Mailing Add:* 421 Dearing St Athens GA 30605

BART, GEORGIANA CRAY
PAINTER, EDUCATOR
b Wilkes-Barre, Pa, Oct 30, 48. *Study:* Wilkes Col, BA (fine arts, art educ), 70; Univ Pittsburgh, MEd (art educ), 72; Studies with Hope Horn, Scranton, Pa, 94-98. *Work:* MacDonald Art Gallery, Col Misericordia, Dallas, Pa; George B Markie Gallery, Hazleton Art League, Pa; Mill Libr, Nanticoke, Pa. *Comn:* Myzein, pastel painting, Mr & Mrs Lehman, IL; Oil portrait, comn by Mr & Mrs Zoltewicz, Pa. *Exhib:* Homage to Matisse, Everhart Mus, Scranton, Pa, 97; Hoyt Inst Fine Arts Ann, New Castle, Pa, 99; Inaugural Exhibit, Millennium Arts Ctr, Washington DC, 2000; Art of the State: Pa 2000, State Mus Pa, Harrisburg, 2000; Hoyt Inst Fine Arts, 2001; Butler Inst Am Art, Ohio, 2003; Dunedin Fine Arts Ctr, Fla, 2004; Banana Factory, Bethlehem, Pa, 2004; State Mus of PA, Art of the State, Pa, 2004; Ahlum Gallery, Easton, Pa, 2005; Blue Heron Gallery, Wyalusing, Pa, 2005; Broome Street Gallery, 2006; Art of the State, 2006; State Mus, Harrisburg, Pa; and numerous others. *Pos:* bd dir, Wyo Valley Art League, Kingston, Pa, 98-2001. *Teaching:* art teacher, Wyo Valley W Sch, Kingston, Pa, 71-72; assoc prof early childhood art methods, Luzerne Co Community Col, Nanticoke, Pa, 76-78; assoc prof oil painting, Univ Scranton, Pa, 95-96; pvt instr, 2000-; workshops, 2000-; Adj prof drawing & painting, King's Col, Wilkes-Barre, Pa, 2005. *Awards:* Grumbacher Gold Medallion, Wyo Art Soc, 98; PJ Mendoza Mem Award, Am Soc Contemp Artists, 99; Utrecht Award, La Fond Galleries, Pittsburgh, 99; 4th Place Award, Bald Eagle Regional, Williamsport, Pa; Irwin Zlowe Mem Award, 84th Ann Am Soc Contemp Artists, NYC, 2002; Atty Theodore R Laputka Mem Award, Hazleton Art League 48th Ann, Pa, 2006. *Bibliog:* Al Sarkas (auth), Bart Exhibit Impressive, Hazleton Standard Speaker, Pa, 96. *Mem:* Salmagundi Club; Nat Asn Women Artists; PSA; Audubon Artists; Am Soc Contemp Artists; Katharine Lorillard Wolfe Art Club, NYC; Orgn Independent Artists, NYC. *Media:* Oil, Pastel. *Interests:* Reading. *Publ:* contribr, Best of Pastel, 96 & Best of Oil Paint, 96, Rockport Publ, Pastel J, 2002, Am Artist Mag, 2003; Pure Color: The Best of Pastel, North Light Books, 2006; Pastelogram, Pastel Soc Am, 2006. *Dealer:* Morgan Galleries Rte 940 POBox 226 Blakeslee Pa; Laura Craig Gallery 307 Linden St Scranton PA. *Mailing Add:* 37 North River St Wilkes Barre PA 18702

BARTA, DOROTHY ELAINE
PHOTOGRAPHER, WRITER
b Toledo, Ohio, June 23, 24. *Study:* Tex Women's Univ, Denton, 41; Dallas Mus Fine Arts, with Ed Bearden, Chapman Kelley, Stephen Wilder & Roger Winter, 45-49; Art Students League, with Gustav Rehberger, Ray Goodbred, Thomas Fogarty, Ray Froman, Robert E Wood, Ed Whitney, Joseph Magniani, Jan Herring & Charles Reid, 78-80; study with Everett Raymond Kinstler, William Reese, Henry Caselli. *Work:* Russell Daniel Trust, El Paso, 83; John Herring Newcomb Hall, Univ Va, 85; Univ NTex, Denton. *Comn:* Record cover, comn by Maestro Tino Comini, 78; pvt comns by James Babcock, Dallas, 87 & Harriet Ragland, Dallas, 88, Hilary Nicholas, Dallas, 92, Vicki Hummel, 94, Charles McLaughlin, 94, Graham & Caroline Shelby, 94, Charu Shah, 95 & Tom & Dan Sullivan, 96; portrait, Judge Sarah T Hughes for Willis Library, UNT Denton, Tex, 96. *Exhib:* Dallas Mus Fine Arts Co Ann, 56; Southwestern Watercolor Soc, 78, 82 & 83-93; Tex Fine Arts Citation, Dallas, 80 & 83; Pastel Soc Am, 80, 82-84, 88, 91 & 96; Pastel Soc Southwest, 81-85, 87-88, 90-91, 92-94 & 95-96; Knickerbocker 28th Ann, 81; Copley Pastel Exhib, 81; solo exhibs, Artisan's Studio-Gallery, 81-93, Watercolors, Univ Va, 85 & Images of the Ballet, Sheraton Hotel Gallery, Dallas, 88; Okla Art Ann, 82; El Paso Mus Show, 84; Presenting Nine Dallas Women Artists, 85; Artists & Craftsmen, 86-91; Tex Watercolor Soc, 87; Irving Art Asn, 87; Western Fedn Watercolor Socs, 87 & 90; La Watercolor Soc, 87, 90, 91 & 94; Art Focus XC Group, Longview Mus, Dalls, 96 &

Ft Worth, Corpus Christi, Rockport, Tex, 97. *Teaching:* Instr portrait painting, Brookhaven Col, Dallas, Tex; instr life drawing & portrait figure painting, Artisan's Studio-Gallery, Dallas, 81-86; instr, painting workshops nationwide, also international, 90-95. *Awards:* McMurray Grant, 85; Am Artist Achievement Award for pastel artist, 92; Best of Show SWS Signature, 2005. *Bibliog:* Article, Am Artist Mag, 6/92; article, Southwest Art, 12/93 & 96; article, Am Artist, 10/94. *Mem:* Pastel Soc Am, NY; Pastel Soc Southwest, Dallas (founder & pres, 79-83 & 94); Tex Fine Arts Asn, Dallas; Southwestern Watercolor Soc, Dallas; Knickerbocker Artists. *Media:* Various and Mixed, Pastel. *Res:* Horticulture and women in art for magazine and newspaper articles. *Publ:* Today's Dallas Woman, Womans Publ Group, 8/94 7 4/96; auth, The Best of Watercolor, Rockport Publ, 95; American Mothers Magazine Cover, 98, 2001; and others. *Dealer:* Artisan's Studio-Gallery Dallas TX; Barta Originals 3151 Chapel Downs Dallas TX 75229. *Mailing Add:* 3151 Chapel Downs Dr Dallas TX 75229-5834

BARTEK, TOM
SCULPTOR, PRINTMAKER
b Omaha, Nebr, July 25, 32. *Study:* Creighton Univ, Omaha, 50-53; Cooper Union Art Sch, New York, with Robert Gwathmey, 55-56; and studied with Arnold Blanch, 65 & 68. *Work:* Joslyn Art Mus, Omaha; Inst Mex-NAm Relaciones Cult, Mexico City; State Bldgs Iowa; Neville Pub Mus, Green Bay, Wis; Wichita Art Mus, Kans. *Comn:* World Insurance Co, Omaha; 10 murals, executed in glass mosaic by Scuola Mosaici, Murano, Italy. *Exhib:* One-man shows, Inst Mex-NAm Relaciones Cult, Mexico City, 65, Sheldon Gallery, Univ Nebr, Lincoln, 74, Joslyn Art Mus, Omaha, 78, Wesleyan Univ, Nebr, 81, Peter H Davidson Gallery, NY, 88, Artspace, Omaha, Nebr, 91 & 92 & Haydon Gallery, Lincoln, Nebr, 94; A Sense of Place, traveling, 73-74; Nebraska Seen, Sheldon Art Gallery, Univ Nebr, Lincoln & traveling, 78; Mid-Four, Nelson-Atkins Mus, Kansas City, Mo, 78; Sylvia White Gallery, NY & Santa Monica, Calif, 97 & 98; Col St Mary, Omaha, 98. *Pos:* Exhib mgr, Joslyn Art Mus, Omaha, 63-66. *Teaching:* Instr, Col St Mary, Omaha, 64-66; assoc prof, Creighton Univ, Omaha, 66-74, 88-89. *Awards:* Honorable Mentions, Midwest Biennial, Joslyn Art Mus, 62, 64 & 66 & Mid-Four, Atkins Mus Fine Arts, Kansas City, Mo, 78; Purchase Award, Anderson Winter Show, Anderson Fine Arts Ctr, Ind, 85. *Media:* Assemblage; Photography. *Mailing Add:* 400 Center St Omaha NE 68108

BARTEL, TODD HENRY
PAINTER, INSTRUCTOR
b Manitowoc, Wis, July 11, 62. *Study:* RI Sch Design, BFA (painting), 85; Carnegie Mellon Univ, MFA (painting), 93. *Exhib:* One-man show, Juliani Gallery, Mass Bay Community Col, Wellesley, 89 & Reynolds Gallery, Pittsburg, Pa, 90; Exquisite Drawing: Lines of Correspondence, Transmission Gallery, Glasgow, 94; All of a Piece, Katonah Mus, NY, 95; Tontine, Hermen Goode Gallery, Brooklyn, NY, 2000; Fel Artist Exhib 3, Conn Comn Arts, Hartford, 2000. *Teaching:* adj prof, Bridgeport U, Conn, 95-, Manhattanville Col, Purchase, NY, 2000-; art teacher, Vt Col, Montpelier, 99-. *Awards:* Liquitex Art Mat Award, Easton, Pa, 90; Jacob K Javits Fel, US Dept Educ, 90; Artist Fel Grant, Conn Comn Arts, 2000; Purchase Award, Learning Ctr, Rye Brook, NY. *Bibliog:* Alorei Parkhill (auth), An Artist in Residence at the Cambridge School, Wayland-Weston Town Crier, 88; Graham Shearing (auth), Water, Earth, Clay Seeks Spirituality, Pittsburgh Post Gazette, 95; Roger Dell (auth), Tontine, Herman Goode Gallery/Meridan, 2000. *Mem:* Col Arts Asn

BARTELS, PHYLLIS ELAINE
PAINTER
b Joliet, Ill, Mar 8, 30. *Study:* Ray Sch Design, Chicago, 48-49; Gerald Merfeld, 70-92. *Exhib:* Alaskan Wild Life Exhib, Fine Arts Mus, Anchorage, 88-91; Park Forest Art Ctr Show, Ill 80-92; Brookwood Gallery Teachers, New Lenox, Ill, 88-91; Ray Col Design Invitational, Schaumburg, Ill, 90; Akron Soc Artists Grand Exhib, Sheraton Inn, Cuyahoga Falls, Ohio, 91-92; and others. *Teaching:* Pastel painting, Brookwood Gallery, 89-92, Churchmouse Studio, 92-94 & Young Rembrants, 96. *Awards:* Merit Award, Pastel Soc Am, 82; Town Gallery Award, Acad Artists Asn, 84; Julia Lucille Award, Salmagundi Club, 84. *Mem:* Pastel Soc Am; Midwest Pastel Soc; Oil Painters Am. *Media:* Pastel. *Interests:* landscape and still life. *Publ:* Today's Art, Erwin Feldman, Vol 27, 79. *Mailing Add:* 19555 Noel Rd Elwood IL 60421-9542

BARTER, JUDITH A
CURATOR, HISTORIAN
b Chicago, Ill, May 21, 51. *Study:* Ind Univ, Bloomington, BA, 73; Univ Ill, Urbana, MA, 75; Univ Calif, Berkeley; Getty Mus Mgmt Inst, studied museum management, 83; PhD, Univ Mass Amherst, 91. *Collection Arranged:* Currents of Expansion (auth, catalog), St Louis Mus Art, 77; Women Artists 1600-1980: Five College Selections (auth, catalog), 80 & Ideas in Contemporary Papers, 84, Amherst Col; traveling exhibs, Invention and Tradition in Russian Modernist Art (auth, catalog), 81-82 & American Watercolors & Drawings (auth, catalog), Wadsworth Atheneum, 85-86; Prairie Sch, Art Inst Chicago, 96; Mary Cassatt: Modern Woman (with catalog), Art Inst, Chicago, 98. *Pos:* Asst cur, St Louis Art Mus, 75-77; cur collections, Amherst Col, 77-86, assoc dir, 87-92; Field-McCormick cur Am art, Art Inst Chicago, 92-. *Teaching:* Decorative arts, Worcester Art Mus, 80; hist of prints, Amherst Col, 89; Am art & cult, Art Inst Chicago, 94- & Univ Chicago, 98-. *Awards:* Nat Endowment Humanities Grant; Chmn Award, Art Inst Chicago, 95; Getty Trust, 97; Chancellor's Medal, Disting Scholarship, Univ Mass, Amherst, 99. *Mem:* Am Asn Mus; Col Art Asn; Victorian Soc; Decorative Arts Soc (reviewer Choice mag); Am Ceramic Circle. *Res:* 18th-20th Century American paintings & sculptures; decorative arts, prints, drawings & watercolors, particularly 20th Century; corporate support of art. *Mailing Add:* Field-McCormick Curator of Am Arts Art Inst of Chicago 111 S Michigan Ave Chicago IL 60603-6110

BARTH, CHARLES JOHN
EDUCATOR, PRINTMAKER
b Chicago, Ill, Nov 27, 42. *Study:* Chicago State Univ, BEduc; Inst Design, Ill Inst Technol, MS(art educ); Ill State Univ, EdD. *Work:* Art Inst Chicago; Philadelphia Mus Art; Okla Art Ctr, Oklahoma City; Cedar Rapids Mus Art, Iowa; Ma Bolom, San Cristobal, Chiapas, Mex. *Comn:* Two prints & plates, Okla Christian Col, Oklahoma City, 71; 50 intaglio prints, Des Moines Art Ctr Print Club, 97. *Exhib:* Ann Int Open Exhib, The Print Club, Philadelphia, 79, 84, 88 & 94; Muertes Exhib, La Nani Dia de los Nagica, Oaxaoa, Mex, 98, 99, 2000; Iowa Artists Exhib, Des Moines Art Ctr, 93, 94, 95, 97, 98, 99. *Teaching:* Instr art, Lincoln Univ, Jefferson City, Mo, 69-72; from assoc prof art to prof, Mt Mercy Col, Iowa, 72-. *Awards:* Catherine E Eatman Purchase Award, Nat Works Paper, Univ Miss, 90; Best of Show, 41st Iowa Artists Exhib, Des Moines Art Ctr, 92; Gabor Petredi award, 67th Nat Members Print Exhib, Soc Am Concept Artists, New York City, 99. *Mem:* Am Color Print Soc, Philadelphia; Boston Printmakers, Mass; Soc Am Graphic Artists, NY; The Print Consortium, St Joseph, Mo. *Media:* Etching, Collagraph. *Dealer:* Olson-Larson Galleries West Des Moines IA; Campbell/State Gallery Marion IA; La Mano Magica, Oaxaca, Mex. *Mailing Add:* 1307 Elmhurst Dr NE Cedar Rapids IA 52402-4762

BARTH, FRANCES
PAINTER
b Bronx, NY, July 31, 1946. *Study:* Hunter Col, BFA, 68 & MA, 70. *Work:* Whitney Mus, Mus Mod Art, Metrop Mus Art, NY; Albright-Knox Art Gallery, Buffalo; Dallas Mus Fine Art, Tex, Akron Art Inst, Ohio; Milwaukee Art Ctr, Wis. *Comn:* Louisville Ballet, Ky; Atlanta Ballet, Ga. *Exhib:* One-woman shows, Susan Caldwell, Inc, NY, 74, 75, 76, 78, 79 & 83, Jan Cicero Gallery, Chicago, 80, 85, Russian Abecedary, Jersey City Mus, NJ, 83, Nina Freudnheim Gallery, Buffalo, NY, 83, Tomoko Liguori Gallery, NY, 88, 89, Tenri Cult Inst NY, 91, Herter Art Gallery Univ Mass, Amherst, 91, EM Donahue Gallery, NY, 94, Millersville Univ, Pa, 95, Donahue/Sosinski Fine Art, NY, 97, Marcia Wood Gallery, Atlanta, 98, 2001; EM Donahue Gallery, NY, 94 & 97; Charles Cowles Gallery, NY, 96-97; Undoing Geometry, Manhattan Community Col, NY, 96; Landscape as Abstraction, James Graham & Sons, NY, 97 & Trans Hudson Gallery, NY, 97; Marcia Wood Gallery, Atlanta, 98; Jan Cicero Gallery, Chicago, 98, 99 & 2000; Donahue Sosinksi, NY, 2000. *Pos:* Sr critic, Yale Univ, New Haven, current. *Teaching:* Instr, Sarah Lawrence Col, Bennington Col, Princeton Univ, Yale Univ, New Haven. *Awards:* NJ State Council on the Arts Grant, 87; Gottlieb Individual Support Grant, 93; Joan Mitchell Award, 95. *Bibliog:* Hayden Herrera (auth), article, Art in Am, 7-8/78; C Robins (auth), The Pluralist Era, American Art 1968-1981, Harper & Row, 84; W Thompson (auth), Art in Am, 9/89; R Kalina (auth), Art in Am, 10/94; Ken Johnson (auth), article, The New York Times, 11/2000; Mario Naves (auth), article, NY Observer, 11/13/2000; David Moos (auth), Dimension, Art Papers, 3-4, 2000; and others. *Mem:* Col Art Asn. *Media:* Acrylics, Oils. *Publ:* Auth, Art and the Science of Botany 1840-1985 (catalog), Sarah Lawrence Col, 85. *Mailing Add:* 99 Vandam St New York NY 10013

BARTH, JACK ALEXANDER
PAINTER
b Los Angeles, Calif, 1946. *Study:* Calif State Univ, Northridge, BA, 69; Univ Calif, Irvine, MFA, 71. *Work:* Los Angeles Co Mus Art; San Francisco Mus Art; Mus Mod Art, NY; Mead Mus Art; Brown Univ, Providence, RI; and others. *Exhib:* One-man shows, Karen Jaen Bernier Gallery, Athens, 83, Peder Bonnier Gallery, NY, 84, Blum Helman Gallery, NY, 89 & Vaughn & Vaughn, Minneapolis, 90; Points of View: Contemp Landscapes, Univ Gallery, Univ Mass, Amherst, 88; Summer Group Show: Works on Paper, Blum Helman Gallery, NY, 89; The Observatory, Thomas Soloman's Garage, Los Angeles, Calif, 89; Nocturnal Landscapes in Contemp Painting, Whitney Mus Am Art at Equitable Ctr, NY, 89; Harmony & Discord: Am Landscape Today, VA Mus, Richmond, 90; Waterworks, Edward Thorpe Gallery, NY, 94; Paul Kasmin Gallery, NY, 95 & 96; and others. *Teaching:* Instr art, Cooper Union, 83-; Columbia Univ, 93, 95 & 96. *Awards:* Nat Endowment Arts, 84. *Bibliog:* Susan Lubowsky (auth), Nocturnal Visions (exhib pamphlet), Whitney Mus Am Art, New York, 89; Frederick R Brandt (auth), Harmony & Discord: American Landscape Painting Today (exhib catalog), VA Mus Fine Arts, Richmond, 90; Saul Ostrow (auth), Jack Barth, Arts Mag, 2/90. *Media:* Miscellaneous. *Publ:* Auth, Noughts and Crosses, Sculpture, ed 15, A/D Gallery, NY, 91; String of Nights, Granfel Press, NY, 94; Songbirds, Conjunctions, 30th issue, Bard Col, 98; and others. *Mailing Add:* 472 Broome St New York NY 10013

BARTH, UTA
CONCEPTUAL ARTIST, PHOTOGRAPHER
b Berlin, Ger, Jan 29, 58. *Study:* Univ Calif, Davis, BA, 82; Univ Calif, Los Angeles, MFA, 85. *Work:* Mus Mod Art, NY; Los Angeles Co Mus Art, Calif; Whitney Mus Am Art, NY; Mus Contemp Art, Los Angeles; San Francisco Mus Mod Art, Calif; Baltimore Mus of Art, Md; Miami Art Mus, Fla; Seattle Art Mus, Wash. *Exhib:* Deliberate Investigations (with catalog), Los Angeles Co Mus Art, Calif, 89; New Acquisitions, Los Angeles Co Mus Art, Calif, 94; one-person exhibs, London Projects, Eng, 96, Tanya Bonakdar Gallery, NY, 96, Philip Nelson Gallery, Paris, 97, ACME, Santa Monica, 97 & 99, Inst Contemp Art, Portland, 97, Presentation House, Ctr for the Visual & Performing Arts, Vancouver, 97, Mus Contemp Art, Chicago, 97 & (catalog) Henry Art Gallery, Seattle, 2000, Kunstmuseum Wolfsburg, Ger, 2000, Lanna Found, Santa Fe NMex, 2000; Plan (with catalog), Los Angeles Co Mus Art, 95; New Photog II, Mus Mod Art, 95; Painting the Extended Field (with catalog), Magasin 3, Stockholm Konsthall, 96; Malmö, Rooseum, Ctr Contemp Art, Sweden, 96; Just: The Contemp in the Permanent Collection, 1975-96, Mus Contemp Art, 96; Scene of the Crime (with catalog), Armand Hammer Mus Art, Los Angeles, 97; Evidence (with catalog), Wexner Ctr Arts, Columbus, 97; Painting into Photog/Photog into Painting (with catalog), Mus Contemp Art, Miami, 97; New to Houston, Mus

Fine Arts, Houston, 98; Apposite Opposites, Mus Contemp Art, Chicago, 99; In-sites: Interior Spaces in Contemp Art, Whitney Mus Am Art, NY, 2000; Open Ends: White Spectrum, Mus Mod Art, NY, 2000. *Teaching:* Assoc prof art, Univ Calif, Riverside, 90-. *Awards:* Grant, Nat Arts Asn, 83; Nat Endowment Arts Fel, 90-91 & 94-95; Visual Artist Fel, Art Matters, Inc, 92-93 & 95. *Bibliog:* Julia Thrift (auth), Uta Barth, London Time Out, 7/15-24/96; Uta Barth: Nowhere Near, ACME & Tanya Bonakdar Gallery, 99; Uta Barth: And of Time, 2000. *Media:* Mixed. *Publ:* Auth, Artist Project: Field 1996, Blind Spot, 96. *Dealer:* ACME 1800 B Berkeley St Santa Monica CA; Tanya Bonakdar Gallery 521 W 21st St New York NY 10011

BARTLETT, BARRY THOMAS
SCULPTOR
b Detroit, Mich, Dec 15, 52. *Study:* RI Sch Design, Providence (sculpture), 71-73; Kansas City Art Inst, Mo, BFA, 73-75; NY State Col Ceramics, Alfred, MFA, 75-77. *Exhib:* Kansas City Art Inst, Nelson Atkins Mus Art, Mo, 85; Shaw-Guido Gallery, Mich, 91; Jane Hartsbok Gallery, NY, 94; Sch Arts Inst Chicago, 95; Revolution Gallery, Detroit, Mich, 96. *Teaching:* Vis artist ceramics, Camberwell Sch Arts & Crafts, London, Eng, 78 & Arco Sch, Ctr Arts, Lisbon Port, 90; art fac ceramics, Bennington Col, Vt, 87-. *Awards:* Visual Arts Fel, Nat Endowment Arts, 82 & 90. *Media:* Ceramics. *Publ:* Articles, Ceramics Monthly & Am Ceramics. *Mailing Add:* 508 E Sixth St No 1B New York NY 10009-6656

BARTLETT, CHRISTOPHER E
GALLERY DIRECTOR, ILLUSTRATOR
b Stratford-on-Avon, Eng, Dec 11, 44. *Study:* St Paul's Col, Eng, cert educ, 70; Bristol Univ, hon BEd, 71; Syracuse Univ, with James McMullan, Robert Weaver, Tom Allen & Isadore Seltzer, MFA, 78. *Work:* Towson Univ. *Comn:* Illus & design, Van Sant Dugdale Advert, 79, General Electric, 80, Soc Security Admin, Baltimore Sunpapers, Johnson & Higgins, 89. *Exhib:* Int 3-D Illusr Show, NY, 95; Am Soc, Marine Artists Eleventh Ann Juried, Frye Mus, Seattle, 97; Small Sculpture, Gallery Art Club 21, Seoul, Korea; Nat Portrait Gallery, Washington, DC, 93; Illusrs who teach, Soc Illusrs Mus, NY, 98. *Collection Arranged:* Illustrators Invitational, Holtzman Gallery, Towson State Univ, 75, Technol Art Exhib, 76, New Directions in Fabric Design, 77, Function-non-Function, 79 & Low-Fire Clay Sculpture, 81; Clay in the East III, 86. *Pos:* Dean, Md Col Art & Design, 72-74, pres, 73-74; dir, Holtzman Gallery, Towson State Univ, 74-. *Teaching:* Assoc prof illus, Md Col Art & Design, 71-74; from asst prof illus & design to prof, Towson Univ, Baltimore, 74-. *Awards:* Silver Medal and 4 Merit Awards, Three Dimensional Illus, The Best in 3-D Advert and Publ Worldwide, 91; Award Excellence in Illus, Illus only, NY, 95; Excellence in Design Award, Am Graphic Design Awards, 98. *Bibliog:* Barbara Tipton (auth), article in Ceramics Mo, 77; Dr D Blum (auth), article, Chesapeake Bay Mag, 85; Inda Schaenen (auth), Watercolors-The Art, Baltimore Messenger, 89. *Mem:* Am Soc Marine Artists. *Media:* Ceramic Sculpture, Acrylic Painting. *Publ:* auth, Remains to be seen, Ceramics Monthly, 80; article, Royal Col Art, 11/81; Mixed media, Graphics World, London, 2/83; Fable-18M Ceramics: Art & Perception, Australia, 96; Friendship in clay, Ceramics Monthly, 98. *Mailing Add:* 1316 Ivy Hill Rd Cockeysville MD 21030-1414

BARTLETT, JENNIFER LOSCH
PAINTER, WRITER
b Long Beach, Calif, Mar 14, 41. *Study:* Mills Col, BA, 63; Yale Univ, BFA, 64 & MFA, 65, with Jack Tworkov, James Rosenquist, Al Held & Jim Dine. *Work:* Walker Art Ctr, Minneapolis; Mus Mod Art, Metrop Mus Art, Whitney Mus Am Art, NY; Philadelphia Mus Art; Cleveland Mus Art; Fine Art Mus San Francisco; and others. *Comn:* 9-painting series, oil-painted canvas & baked enamel steel plates, Gen Serv Admin; Volvo Corp; Nat Airport, Washington, DC; Sheraton Grand Hotel, Sacramento, Calif; The Mayo Clinic. *Exhib:* Seven Walls, Mus Mod Art, NY, 71; Painting Ann, Whitney Mus Am Art, NY, 72; Painting: New Options, Walker Art Ctr, 72; Contemp Am Drawings, Whitney Mus Am Art, 73; Works on Paper, Va Mus Fine Art, 74; Corcoran Biennial, Corcoran Gallery Art, 75; one-person exhibs, Wadsworth Atheneum, 77, Baltimore Art Mus, Albright-Knox Gallery, 80, Orlando Mus Art, 93, Paula Cooper Gallery, NY, 94, A/D, NY 94 & Baldwin Gallery, Aspen, Colo, 94; Private Images: Photographs by Painters, Los Angeles Co Mus Art, 77; Maps, Mus Mod Art, NY, 77; 1977 Biennial Exhib, Whitney Mus Am Art, 77; 20 Century American Art from Friends' Collections, Whitney Mus Am Art, 77; New Image Painting, Whitney Mus Am Art, 78; Whitney Biennial, Whitney Mus Am Art, 79, 81 & 91; The Decade in Review, Whitney Mus Am Art, 79; 20th Century Recent Acquisitions, Metrop Mus Art, NY, 79; New Dimensions in Drawing, Aldrich Mus Contemp Art, 81; Summer Light, Mus Mod Art, NY; Art in Our Time, Brooks Mem Art Gallery, 82; Block Prints, Whitney Mus Am Art, 82; The American Artists as Printmaker: 23rd National Print Exhib,Brooklyn Mus, 83; Nine Printmakers & the Working Process, Whitney Mus Am Art, 85; 20th Anniversary of the National Endowment for the Arts, Mus Mod Art, 85; Four Printmakers, Whitney Mus Am Art, 86; The 75th American Exhib, Art Inst Chicago, 86; 50th National Midyear Exhib, Butler Inst Am Art, 86; Contemp Diptychs: Divided Visions, Whitney Mus Am Art, 87; New Art On Paper, Philadelphia Mus Art, 88; Nacturnal Visions, Whitney Mus Am Art, 89; Evolutions in Expression: Minimalism & Post-Minimalism From The Permanent Collection of the Whitney Mus of Am Art, Whitney Mus Am Art, 94; Locks Gallery, Philadelphia, 94, 96, 98, 2000-01; Richard Gray Gallery, Chicago, 96, 1999-2001. *Teaching:* Vis artist, Chicago Art Inst, fall 72; instr painting, Sch Visual Arts, NY, 72-77. *Awards:* Am Acad Arts & Letters Award, 83; Harris Prize, Art Inst Chicago, 76, Harris Prize & M V Kohnstamm Award, 86; Am Inst Architects Award, 87. *Bibliog:* Many articles & reviews in Am & Europ publ, incl Eric Gibson (auth), New York reviews, Rhapsody, Art Int, 3/79; Thomas B Hess (auth), Les nouvelle images de la peinture americane, Art Press Int, 5/79; Roberta Smith (auth), Bartlett's Summers, Art in Am, 11/79 & others. *Mem:* NY Inst Humanities; Nat Acad (assoc, 90, acad, 94). *Publ:* Auth, Cleopatra I-IV, Adventures in Poetry Press, 71. *Dealer:* Locks Gallery Philadelphia PA; Richard Gray Gallery Chicago IL. *Mailing Add:* 134 Charles St New York NY 10014

BARTNICK, HARRY WILLIAM
PAINTER, PHOTOGRAPHER, EDUCATOR
b Newark, NJ, July 30, 50. *Study:* Tyler Sch Art, Temple Univ, BFA, 72; Syracuse Univ, MFA, 74. *Work:* Hyde Collection, Glens Falls, NY; DeCordova Mus, Lincoln, Mass; McMullen Mus Art, Boston Col. *Exhib:* Boston (in dialogue) Now, Inst Contemp Art, Boston, Mass, 94; McMullen Mus Art, Boston Col, 95; Lyman Allyn Mus Art, Conn Col, 98; Fuller Mus Art, 98; Palazzo Sertoli, Sondrio, Italy, 2001; Royal Acad Fine Arts, Madrid, 2004; and others. *Collection Arranged:* Contemporary Drawing Invitational, Ctr for Music, Drama & Art, Lake Placid, NY, 76-77. *Teaching:* Instr painting & drawing, Lake Placid Sch Art, 74-78; prof, New Eng Sch Art & Design, Suffolk Univ, 78-; instr painting, Montserrat Col Art, 94. *Awards:* Trustee's Prize, Everson Regional, 74; Creative Artists Pub Serv Grant, 77; Mass Artists Found Grant, 81; Nat Endowment Arts Fel, New Eng Found Arts, 92 & 96; John Simon Guggenheim Grant, 01. *Bibliog:* The Boston art party, Art News, 11/80; article in Christian Sci Monitor, 11/11/94; New Am Paintings, 98, 02; Art in Aviation, Lundwerg Press, Barcelona, 01; Civil Eng and Painting, Royal Acad Fine Arts Press, Madrid, 04. *Media:* Oil, Acrylic on Canvas, Digital Printmaking. *Interests:* European travel; Ital hist and culture. *Mailing Add:* 14 Prospect St Beverly MA 01915

BARTON, BILLIE JO
INSTRUCTOR, PAINTER
b Chridress, Tex, June 23, 26. *Study:* Frank Wiggins Trade Sch, design cert, 43; studied with Gary Jenkins & Tom Lynch, 82-95. *Work:* City of La Palma City Coun Community Ctr, Calif. *Exhib:* Fine Art Inst, Boston, 94; Arts Assocs Gallery, Huntington Beach, Calif, 94; Newport Dunes Festival of Art, Calif, 95; Harbor Festival of Whales, Dana Point, Calif, 95; Cult Arts Comn, Cypress, Calif, 96. *Pos:* News ed, La Palma Art Assoc, 76-78; news ed & Recording secy, Buena Art Guild, Calif, 93-94. *Teaching:* Instr art in oils, Smithys Art Gallery, 76-77, Int Art Studio, 78-79; pvt instr oil painting, 80-96. *Mem:* Fel Nat Mus Women in Arts; fel Nat Asn Fine Art; fel Niguel Art Asn; Buena Art Guild. *Media:* Oil. *Publ:* Auth, The Guidebook for Oil Painters, pvt publ, 93; contribr, Artist of California, Vol III, Mountain Prod Inc, 93. *Mailing Add:* 22873 Road 6 Chowchilla CA 93610

BARTON, JOHN MURRAY
PAINTER, PRINTMAKER
b New York, NY, Feb 8, 21. *Study:* Art Students League; Tschacbasov Sch Art, NY. *Work:* Metrop Mus Art, NY; Mus Mod Art, Haifa, Israel; Butler Inst Am Art, Youngstown, Ohio; Philadelphia Mus Art, Pa; Bibliotheque Nationale, Paris; plus others. *Comn:* Murals (with Lumin Martin Winter), NY Bd Educ; History of Money (oil, with Louise August), SC State Bank, Columbia; oil & lacquer mural, Polyclinic Hosp, NY; acrylic on concrete (with Louise August), Gilbert's Hotel, Fallsburgh, NY. *Exhib:* One-man Shows, Fantasy Gallery, Washington, Hudson Guild, NY, Highgate Gallery, NJ, Glassboro State Col, NJ, Swain Art Gallery, NJ, Fromuth Gallery, Pa, J Walter Thompson, NY. *Pos:* Pres, John Barton Assocs, Inc, 66-85. *Teaching:* Pvt classes at studio on creative expression, 60-65; lectr, creative expression, univ art depts, throughout the East Coast, 60-65. *Media:* Oil; Woodcut. *Publ:* Illusr, Space aeronautics, Print Mag & Printers Ink. *Mailing Add:* 45 Christopher St New York NY 10014

BARTSCHERER, JOSEPH
CONCEPTUAL ARTIST, PHOTOGRAPHER
b New York, NY, Aug 30, 54. *Study:* Harvard Univ, BA, 76; Nova Scotia Col Art & Design, MFA, 79. *Work:* Mus Mod Art, NY; State Libr Archives, Carson City, Nev; San Francisco Mus Mod Art; City of Seattle; Los Angeles Co Mus Art. *Comn:* NW Documents Proj, Seattle Arts Comn, Wash, 84; Nevada, Nev State Coun Arts, Carson City, 93-96; Canal, Pub Art Develop Trust, London, 97-98. *Exhib:* Mus Mod Art, NY, 87 & 95; Mus Contemp Photography, Chicago, 88; San Francisco Mus Mod Art, 96; Inst Contemp Art, Philadelphia, Pa, 2000; and others. *Teaching:* adj prof, MIT, Mass, 94; prof, Bard Col, 88 & 89. *Awards:* Visual Artist Fel Grants, Nat Endowment Arts, 84 & 88; John Simon Guggenheim Fel Grant, 87-88. *Bibliog:* Nancy Princenthal (auth), Joseph Bartscherer at Marian Goodman, Art in Am, 11/95; Tom McDonough (auth), Art in Am, 11/97; Ken Johnson (auth), NY Times, 10/23/98. *Mailing Add:* 71 Hudson St Apt 3 New York NY 10013-2856

BARTZ, JAMES ROSS
PAINTER
b Blufton, Ohio, Feb 20, 42. *Study:* Ohio State Univ, BS, 64, MA(art educ), 70. *Work:* Wichita Art Asn, Wichita Art Mus; Topeka Art Mus, Kans. *Comn:* The Baptism of Christ, Messiah Lutheran Church, Cleveland, Ohio. *Exhib:* Mid-Four, Nelson-Atkins Mus Art, Kansas City, Mo, 83; Smoky Hill Art Exhib, Hays Libr, Kans, 83; Art Ann IV, Okla Art Ctr, Oklahoma City, 83; Fifth Salina Ann, Salina Art Ctr, Kans, 83; Lenox Hill Artists Forum, NY; Regional Artists Biennial, Fort Wayne Mus Art, Ind, 94; Regional Art Ctr, LaCrosse, Wis, 97 & 98; and others. *Teaching:* Asst prof art educ, Wichita State Univ, Kans, 70-78; painting instr figure, Wichita Art Asn, 80-83. *Awards:* Best Show, Second Ann Small Oil Painting, Wichita Art Asn, 82; Best Show, Fifth Salina Ann, Salina Art Ctr, Kans, 83; Best of Show, Smoky Hill Art Exhib, Hays, Kans Art Ctr, 85. *Media:* Acrylic, Oil. *Mailing Add:* 938 Streblow St Onalaska WI 54650-2059

BARUCH, ANNE
ART DEALER, LECTURER
b Chicago, Ill. *Study:* Art Inst Chicago, jr scholar, study with George Beuhr & Dudley Crafts Watson; Gonzaga Univ, Spokane, Wash, PhD. *Collection Arranged:* From Oppression to Freedom: Eastern European Prints and Drawings, Edinboro Univ, Pa, 93; Jiri Balcar, Carlton Col, Northfield, Minn, 93; A Taste of Fiber: The Polish Experience, Univ Southern Ind, New Harmony, 94; Distance of Time: Artists of Three

Generations in Krakow, Northern Ill Univ Art Galleries, De Kalb & Chicago, 94; Dialogue with the Grand Masters: Selected Prints of Jiri Anderle, Nevada Mus Art, Reno, 95; The Distance of Time: Artists of Three Generations in Krakow, Nevada Mus Art, Reno, 95; Jiri Anderle: Dialogues, Univ Mo Kansas City, 97. *Pos:* Pres & dir, Jacques Baruch Gallery Ltd, Chicago, 67-94; pres & dir, Anne & Jacques Baruch Collection Ltd, Chicago, 94-. *Awards:* Medal of Order of Cult Merit, Minister Cult & Fine Arts of Peoples Repub Poland, 87; Silver Medal of Merit, Ministry of Foreign Affairs, Soc Int Relations, Czech, 88; Medal of Nat Artist Karel Plicka, Minister Cult, Czech, 89. *Bibliog:* Kathy Brainard Cook (auth), Gallery owner mixes art with compassion, Spokesman-Review Spokane Chronical, 5/10/87; Cornelia Tuite (auth), Anne Baruch, Today's Chicago Woman, 9/87; Romancing Art, Chicago Tribune, 10/1/89; Marcia Pally (auth), Women, Penthouse, 12/89. *Mem:* Chicago Network; Asn Int Photog Art Dealers; Int Fine Print Dealers Asn; Col Art Asn; Am Asn of Mus. *Specialty:* From Turn-of-the-Century to Contemporary; art from Czechoslovakia, Poland, Slovenia, Croatia, United States and Europe; prints, drawings, photography, tapestry, fiber art; paintings. *Collection:* Outstanding prints, drawings, tapestries, photographs and paintings. *Publ:* Auth, The World of Jan Saudek--Photographs, 79; Jiri Anderle--Master Graphics, 80; Josef Ehm--A Retrospective Exhibition, 90; Twenty Years of Czechoslovak Art: 1968-1988 A Tribute to Jacques Baruch, 90; The Other Side of Frantisek Drtikol, 91. *Mailing Add:* The Anne & Jacques Baruch Collection Ltd 680 N Lake Shore Dr Chicago IL 60611

BARZUN, JACQUES MARTIN
WRITER, ART CRITIC
b Creteil, France, Nov 30, 1907; US citizen. *Study:* Columbia Col, BA, 27; Columbia Univ, MA, 28 & PhD, 32. *Pos:* Lit consult, Charles Scribner's Sons, NY, formerly; retired. *Teaching:* Instr hist, Columbia Col, 29-38; asst prof hist, Columbia Univ, 38-42, assoc prof hist, 42-45, prof hist, 45-75, dean faculties & provost, 55-67. *Mem:* Royal Soc Literature; Am Acad Arts & Letters (past-pres); Am Arts & Sci; Am Philos Soc; Royal Soc Arts. *Res:* Intellectual history and culture. *Publ:* Auth, reviews and articles in Mag of Art, 43-53; articles in Am Scholar, Art Digest & Harper's, 56-; Art--by act of Congress, The Public Interest, fall 65; Museum piece, 67, Mus News, 4/68; The arts to-day; Consolidation or confrontation?, J of Royal Soc Arts, 3/72; The Use & Abuse of Art, Mellon Lectures, Nat Gallery, 73 & Princeton Press, 74; From Dawn to Decadence: 500 Years of Western Cultural Life, 2000; The Modern Researcher (with Henry F Graff), 4th edit, 1985; On Writing, Editing, and Publishing, 1986; Simple and Direct: A Rhetoric for Writers, 1984; A Word or Two Before You Go, 1986; The Culture We Deserve, 1989; An Essay on French Verse for Readers of English Poetry, 1991; Begin Here: The Forgotten Conditions of Teaching and Learning, 1991; A Jacques Banzun Reader, 2002. *Mailing Add:* 18 Wolfeton Way San Antonio TX 78218

BAS, HERNAN
ARTIST
b Miami, Fla, 78. *Study:* New World Sch Art, Miami, Degree. *Work:* It's Super Nat Mus Contemp Art, Miami, 2002, Making Art in Miami:Travels in Hyperreality, Mus Contemp Art, Miami, 2000, Humid, Mus Contemp Art, Chicago, 2001, AOP 2002: 37th Art on Paper Exhib, Weatherspoon Art Mus, Univ NC, 2002, Whitney Biennial Am Art, Whitney Mus Am Art, 2004, Sixth Ann. Altoids Curiously Strong Collection, New Mus Contemp Art, NY, 2004. *Exhib:* One-man shows, Slim Fast, Frances Wolfson Gallery, Miami Dade Community Col, 2000, Hernan's Merit & the Nouveau Sissies, Fredric Snitzer Gallery, Miami, 2001, 2002, Love in Vein, Sandroni Rey, Venice, Calif, 2002, First Comes the Blood, Then Come the Boys, Fredric Snitzer Gallery, Miami, 2002, Sometimes With One I Love, Daniel Reich Gallery, NY, 2004; group shows, at Frank: an adj Connoting.Superfantastic, Baltimore, Md, 97, Fashion Issue: Four Simple Steps Towards Younger Looking Skin, Fredric Snitzer Gallery, Miami, 98, Superfantastic 7, The Dirt Room, Kansas City, Ohio, 99, Departing Perspectives, Espirito Santo Building, Miami, 2000, Ob-la-di-Ob-la-da, Art Ctr/South Fla, 2000, Fast Forward, Projects Nash Hotel Art Fair, Miami Beach, 2001, Champion, Zinc Gallery, Stockholm, Sweden, 2002, Dangerous Beauty, Jewish Community Ctr, Manhattan, 2002, Friends & Family, Lombard-Fried Fine Arts, NY, 2002, In the Place of Revolution, Great Hall of The Cooper Union, 2002, Drawing Conclusions, Buena Vista Building, Miami, 2002, Made in Miami, Fredric Snitzer Gallery, Miami, 2003. *Mailing Add:* c/o MOCA Grand Ave 250 S Grand Ave Los Angeles CA 90012

BASHAM, CHARLES
PAINTER
b Wadsworth, Ohio, 52. *Study:* Kent State Univ, Ohio, BFA, MFA, 72-75; studied with Dougla Unger, William Quinn & Joseph O'Sickley. *Work:* Butler Inst Am Art, Ohio; Hunter Mus Art, Tenn; Mint Mus Art, NC; Coca-Cola Co, Atlanta, Ga. *Exhib:* Butler Inst Am Art, Youngstown, Ohio, 91; Asheville Art Mus, NC; Jerald Melberg Gallery, Charlotte, NC, 2001; US Artists, Philadelphia, Pa, 2001; Solo exhib, David Heath Gallery, Atlanta, Ga, 1989, Butler Inst Am Art, Cudahy's Fine Art Gallery, NY, Knoxville Mus Art, Tenn. *Teaching:* instr, art, Kent State Univ, currently. *Media:* Pastels. *Specialty:* Ohio Farmland Landscapes. *Mailing Add:* 2892 Fixler Ave Medina OH 44256

BASHOR, JOHN W
EDUCATOR, PAINTER
b Newton, Kans, Mar 11, 26. *Study:* Washburn Univ, BA, 49; Univ Iowa, MFA, 53. *Work:* Nelson/Atkins Mus, Kansas City, Mo; Washburn Univ, Topeka, Kans; Springfield Art Mus, Mo; Sandzen Mem Mus, Lindsborg, Kans; Kans State Univ, Manhattan. *Comn:* Murals, Kaw Valley State Bank, Topeka, 64, Bethany Col, Lindsborg, 65 & First Nat Bank, Grand Island, Nebr, 65. *Exhib:* Mid-Am Ann, Nelson/Atkins Mus, 56; Nebr Invitational, Univ Nebr, Lincoln, 62; solo traveling exhib, State Pa, 62-63; Kansas' Artist, Nat Gov Traveling Exhib, 66; Fedn Rocky Mountain States Traveling Exhib, 68. *Teaching:* Assoc prof painting & prints, Bethany Col, 54-66; prof painting, Mont State Univ, 66-, dir sch art, 66-77. *Mem:* Mid-Am Col Art Asn; Col Art Asn Am; Mont Art Educ Asn. *Media:* Acrylic. *Mailing Add:* 10680 Bridger Canyon Rd Bozeman MT 59715-8647

BASQUIN, KIT (MARY SMYTH)
CURATOR, EDUCATOR
b New York, NY, July 3, 41. *Study:* Goucher Col, BA, 63; Ind Univ, Bloomington, MA(art hist), 70; Bread Loaf Writers Conf, Middlebury Col, 83 & 85: Yale Summer Sch, 85; Union Inst, Phd, 2007. *Collection Arranged:* Karl Priebe: A Look at African Americans (galley guide), 90; Francesco Spicuzza: Wisconsin Impressionist (catalog), 92; Images & Death in Contemporary Art (catalog), 1990; Marvin Lowe Retrospective, 1998; The Lunts on Stage in Wisconsin (catalog), 1999. *Pos:* Owner & dir, Washington Gallery, Indianapolis, 77-79 & Kit Basquin Gallery, Milwaukee, 81-83; Wis ed, New Art Examiner, 80; interim cur, Haggerty Mus Art, Milwaukee, 88-89; asst dir collections & pub progs, Haggerty Mus, Marquette Univ, Milwaukee, 89-90, cur ed, 90-95; dir outreach, Milwaukee, Wis Humanities Coun, 95-98; co-producer, documentary video on filmmaker Mary Ellen Bute, 95-; trustee, Ten Chimney Found Inc, Wis, 1997-99; exhib mgr, Auction House, Doyle, NY, 1999-2002; asst, dept drawings and prints, Met Mus of Art, 2000-. *Teaching:* Instr art hist, Fine Arts Sch, Addis Ababa, Ethiopia, 67-68; instr art hist, Concordia Univ Mequon, 92; teacher, Marquette Univ Gaza, 96. *Bibliog:* Holly Day (auth), Indianapolis, Cincinnati, Dayton, Art in Am, 7-8/79; Dean Jensen (auth), Basquin Gallery has different air, Milwaukee Sentinel, 10/2/81. *Mem:* Univ Club Milwaukee; Univ Club, NY; Print Forum (pres, 96-97); Milwaukee Art Mus; Col Art Asn, 2001-. *Res:* Contemporary art by Women and by African Americans. *Publ:* Auth, Mary Ellin Bute's Film Adaptation of Finnegans Wake, James; Dale Chihuly: Reflections in Glass, Sch Arts, 3/92; Susan Rothenberg: Paint & Form, Sch Arts, 2/93; Mary Ellen Bute: Energy in Motion, Angels: Women Working in Film and Video, spring 98; Susan Falkman, Sculpture, summer 98; Ten Chimneys: The Lunts on Stage in Wisconsin, 1998; published by Brooklyn Mus, 95 artists' biographies in Committed to the Image, 2001. *Mailing Add:* 1675 York Ave Apt 19A New York NY 10128

BASS, DAVID LOREN
PAINTER, GALLERY DIRECTOR
b Conway, Ark, July 19, 43. *Study:* Univ NC, Greensboro, MFA; Univ NC, Chapel Hill; Aspen Sch of Contemp Art; Univ Cent Ark, BSE; study with Peter Agostini, Walter Barker, Andrew Martin & Larry Day. *Work:* Mint Mus, Charlotte, NC; Dillard Collection, Weatherspoon Art Gallery, Greensboro, NC; Fayetteville Mus Art, NC; Duke Univ, Durham, NC; US Dept State, Washington, DC; Washington & Lee Univ, Lexington, Va; Art in Public Places, Santa Fe, NM; Mus of the Big Bend, Alpine, TX; Yaddo, Saratoga Springs, NY; Maitland Art Ctr, Maitland, FL. *Exhib:* Biennial Exhib of Piedmont Painting & Sculpture, Mint Mus, Charlotte, 79 & 81; Summer Leisure: Mountains to the Sea, Mint Mus, Charlotte, 82; David Loren Bass: Selected Works, 1983-1989, Theater Art Galleries, High Point, NC, 90; Santa Fe Contemp Art, 98; Watercolor USA 1993, Springfield Mus Art, Mo, 93; Ten By Ten, Addison and Ripley Fine Art, Washington, DC, 99; High Point Theatre Art Gallery, High Point, NC, 2000; one man shows, Morocco Experienced, Bass Fine Art, NMex, 2001, Paintings of the Big Bend, Mus of the Big Bend, Alpine, TX, 2004, Paintings of Tex and NMex, Bass-Thompson Gallery, NMex, 2004; and many others. *Collection Arranged:* Drawings & Sculpture by Peter Agostini, Du Pont Art Gallery, 76 & Prints, Dept of Fine Arts, 76, Du Pont Art Gallery, Washington & Lee Univ. *Pos:* artist-in-residence Greensboro Day Sch, NC, 89. *Teaching:* teacher of art, Kenitra Am HS, 67-73; Instr painting, Washington & Lee Univ, Lexington, Va, 76; instr watercolor, ExploreGuatemala, 2003. *Awards:* Yaddo Residency, Saratoga Springs, NY, 78, 81 & 84; Va Ctr Creative Arts, Sweetbriar, VA, 78; Ossabaw Island Project, Ga, 79; Art in Pub Places, Santa Fe, 93-94. *Bibliog:* Tom Dewey (auth), Southern realism, Miss Mus Art, 79; Douglas Campbell (auth), David Loren Bass, 2005. *Media:* Oil, Watercolor. *Collection:* Peter Agostini, sculpture; Andrew Martin, painting; Suzanne Valodon, Lithograph; Maurice Grosser, Painting; Carol Anthony, painting; Rosemarie Beck, Painting; Isabel McElvain, sculpture. *Dealer:* The Gallery 822 Canyon Rd Santa Fe NM; Kiowa Gallery Alpine TX; William Lester Gallery Point Reyes Station CA. *Mailing Add:* Box 403 Favenida Vista Grande Ste B-7 Santa Fe NM 87508

BASS, JOEL
PAINTER
b Los Angeles, Calif, Dec 23, 42. *Study:* Art Ctr Col Design, BA, 65-67. *Work:* Ft Worth Art Ctr; Mus Mod Art, Whitney Mus Am Art, NY; Albright-Knox Mus Art, Buffalo; San Francisco Mus Art; Metrop Mus Art, NY. *Exhib:* The Structure of Color, Whitney Mus Am Art, NY, 71; Color & Scale: Eight Contemp Calif Painters, Oakland Mus, 71; The State of Calif Painting, Govett-Brewster Art Gallery, New Plymouth, NZ, 72-73; Southern Calif Attitudes, Pasadena Art Mus, Calif, 72; 1973 Biennial Exhib: Contemp Am Art, 73 & Recent Acquisitions Exhib, 73, Whitney Mus, NY; Printsequence, Mus Mod Art, NY, 75; Recent Am Etching, Davison Art Ctr, Wesleyan Univ, Middletown, Conn, 75; solo exhib, Kathryn Markel Fine Arts, NY, 77, Janus Gallery, Los Angeles, 77 & 81 & Burnett Miller Gallery, Los Angeles, 86; and others. *Teaching:* Instr art, Art Ctr Col Design, 76-86 & Otis Art Inst, 86-. *Bibliog:* Jerome Tarshis (auth), article, Artforum, 4/71; Peter Plagens (auth), From school painting to a school of painting in Los Angeles, Art in Am, 3-4/73 & Just another rectangle painter, Artforum, 5/74

BASS, JUDY
PAINTER
b Baltimore, Md, Mar 17, 46. *Study:* Univ Md, College Park, BA, 67; George Washington Univ, MFA, 74. *Work:* The Phillips Collection, Washington, DC; George Washington Univ, Washington, DC; Dept of Health & Human Servs, Washington, DC; Univ NMex, Albuquerque, NMex. *Exhib:* Emerging Artists, Wash Proj for the Arts,

79; one-woman shows, Phillips Collection (with catalog), 81, Cath Univ of Am Art Gallery, Washington, 81, Univ NMex Teaching Gallery, 81, Marsha Mateyka Gallery, Washington, DC, 84, 86 & 88, Mt Vernon Col, Washington, DC, 96 & Galerie Francoise, Balt, Md; Color as Light, Washington Co Mus, Hagerstown, Md, 86; Susan Conway Gallery, 95 & 98; Bird in the Hand Gallery, Washington, DC, 2000; Phillips pvt collection. *Teaching:* Instr art, Mt Vernon Col, Washington, 79-85 & Maryland Inst Col Art, Baltimore, 83-84; vis asst prof painting, Univ NMex, 81-82; assoc prof fine arts, Marymount Univ, Arlington, Va, 84-90, prof, 90-; dir, Barry Art Gallery, Marymount Univ, currently. *Awards:* Cecile R Hunt Mem Prize Painting, Alumni Show, George Washington Univ, Washington, DC, 86. *Bibliog:* Benjamin Forgery (auth), The uptown downtown insider world of Washington Art, Art News, 9/79; Lee Fleming (auth), Washington Iconoclassicism, 8 Washington Women (catalog), 5/82. *Mem:* Col Art Asn; Smithsonian Asn Prog. *Media:* Acrylic Paint; Color Pencils. *Dealer:* Galerie Francoise 2360 W Joppa Rd Lutherville MD 21093. *Mailing Add:* 3318 St James Pl Falls Church VA 22042

BASS, ROBERT MUSE
PATRON
b Ft Worth, Tex, 48. *Study:* Yale Univ, BA, 1970; Stanford Univ, MBA, 1974. *Pos:* Vpres, bd dir, Bass Bros Enterprises Inc, until 1985; pres, Robert M Bass Group Inc (now The Keystone Group), 1985-; founder, Oak Hills Capital Partners; mem collector's comt, Nat Gallery Art; chmn emeritus, Nat Trust Historic Preservation; bd trustees, Stanford Univ, 1989-, chmn, 1996-, Rockefeller Univ, Groton Sch, Middlesex Sch, Amon Carter Mus; commnr, Tex State Hwy and Pub Transp Commn, 1989-87. *Awards:* Named one of world's richest people, Forbes mag. *Mailing Add:* Keystone Inc 201 Main St Ste 3100 Fort Worth TX 76102

BASS, RUTH
EDUCATOR, CRITIC
b Boston, Mass, 38. *Study:* Radcliffe Col, BA(magna cum laude), 60; study with Irving Marantz, Victor Candell, Gabriel Laderman & Maurice Golubov, 60-64; Art Students League, 61-74; NY Univ, MA, 62, PhD, 78. *Exhib:* One-person show, Brata Gallery, NY, 73, Portraits of Women, Rotunda Hall Fame for Great Americans, Bronx, NY, 87; Works on Paper--Women Artists, Brooklyn Mus, NY & Fairleigh Dickinson Univ, 75-76; Shreveport Parks & Recreation Dept Nat, Shreveport, La, 76; Artists Choice Traveling Exhib, 76-77; Women in Definition, First Women's Bank, NY, 83. *Collection Arranged:* Portraits: Form and Content, First Women's Bank, New York, 84; Contemporary Images and Universal Images, 86, John Gundelfinger Paintings, 20 Broad Street, New York, 86. *Pos:* Guest cur, First Women's Bank, NY, 84, The Mendik Co, 86. *Teaching:* Lectr, Univ Bridgeport, Conn, 63-64 & Queens Col, NY, 65-66; from instr to assoc prof art, Bronx Community Col, City Univ NY, 65-81, prof, 81-; instr, New York Univ, 80-81. *Awards:* Women's Res and Develop Fund Award, City Univ New York, 86- 88; Fel, Arts & Soc, funded by Andrew W Mellon Found, Community Col Proj, 82, Humanities, Fel, 90; Borchard Found Grant, 92; and others. *Bibliog:* Lawrence Campbell (auth), review, Art News, 3/73; Michael Brenson (auth), review, NY Times, 6/29/84; Don Gray (auth), article, Art World, 5/87. *Mem:* Am Asn of Univ Prof; Int Asn Art Critics; Art Students League. *Media:* Oil, Charcoal. *Res:* Comedy in Contemporary Art, Contemporary American realist painting, including painterly realism; phenomenological criticism and aesthetics. *Publ:* Auth, The illusion of reality, 12/81 & Bland power, 4/86, Artnews; Minimalism Made Human on Joel Shapiro, Art News, 3/87 & Ordinary People on Ida Applebroog, Art News, 5/88; contribr, Groves Dictionary Art, Vol 34, 96. *Mailing Add:* 125 E 87th St New York NY 10028

BASS, SID R
PATRON
Study: Yale Univ, BA, 65; Stanford Univ, MBA, 69. *Pos:* Founder, Buena Venture Assoc, 98-; vpres & dir, Sid W Richardson Found, currently; vchmn bd trustees, Mus Modern Art, New York City, currently. *Mailing Add:* Buena Venture Assoc 1201 Washington Terrace Fort Worth TX 76107

BASSET, GENE
POLITICAL CARTOONIST
b Brooklyn, NY, 1927. *Study:* Univ Mo; Brooklyn Col, BA(design); Cooper Union; Art Students League; Pratt Inst. *Work:* Syracuse Univ Libr, NY; Wichita State Univ; Univ Mo; Univ Southern Miss; Gustavus Adolphus Col. *Exhib:* Vietnam Drawings, Hilstrom Arts Mus, Gustavos Adolphus Collection. *Pos:* Polit cartoonist, Honolulu-Star Bull, 61-62, Scripps-Howard Newspapers, Washington, DC, 62-81 & United Features Syndicate, 72-; ed cartoonist, Atlanta J, 82-92, Mankazo Free Press, Minn, 93-. *Teaching:* Instr seminar, Gustavus Adolphus Col, Famous Artist Sch; instr cartoon course, Gustaus Adolphus Col, 94. *Awards:* Best Ed Cartoon, Population Inst, 74. *Mem:* Asn Am Ed Cartoonists (pres, 73-74); Nat Cartoonist Soc. *Media:* Ink. *Mailing Add:* 1308 Pine Pointe Curv Saint Peter MN 56082-9804

BASSETTI, FRED FORDE
ARCHITECT
b Seattle, Jan 31, 1917. *Study:* Univ Washington, B (arch), 42; Harvard Univ, M (arch), 46. *Comn:* Col Engineering Bldgs, Univ Washington, 70; Federal Office Bldg, Seattle, 75; US Embassy, Lisbon, Portugal, 77; PACCAR Tech Ctr, Mt. Vernon, Washington, 85; AT&T Gateway Tower, Seattle, 90. *Pos:* Registered architect, Alaska, Idaho, Mont, Oreg and Washington; draftsman Paul Thiry, Seattle, 44, Alvar Aalto, Cambridge, Mass, 46; designer Naramore, Bain, Brady and Johanson, Seattle, 46; principal Bassetti & Morse, 47-62, Fred Bassetti & Co, Seattle, 62-81, Bassetti, Norton, Metler, Seattle, 81-85, Bassetti, Norton, Metler, Rekevics, Seattle, 85-94, Bassetti Architects, Seattle, 94; mem Seattle Design Comt, 76-78; Seattle Landmarks Bd, 78-79; bd dir Discuren Found, Seattle; retired 94. *Awards:* Named Best Local Architect, Seattle Weekly poll, 88. *Mem:* Am Inst Arch (pres Seattle chapter, 67); Nat Acad (assoc, 88, acad, 97); Allied Arts of Seattle and King County (pres 70-72)

BASSIN, JOAN
HISTORIAN, EDUCATOR
b St Louis, Mo, Oct 29, 38. *Study:* Swarthmore Col, BA; Ind Univ, MA & PhD; fel in residence for col teachers, Nat Endowment for Humanities, 78-79; Andrew W Mellon sr fel in humanities, 81. *Exhib:* Curator, GSA Design Awards Exhib, National Building Mus, Washington, DC, 97. *Pos:* Art columnist, City Mag, 78-79; art reviewer, Austin American-Statesman, 82-83; asst to dean, Sch of Archit, New York Inst of Technol, 86-89; exec Dir, Nat Inst Arch Educ, 89-95. *Teaching:* Lectr mod archit, Dartmouth Col, Hanover, NH, 70; instr mod archit & mod sculpture, Kansas City Art Inst, 72-74, asst prof, 74-78, assoc prof, 78-83; assoc prof archit, New York Inst of Technol, 85-89, adj prof, 89-. *Mem:* Landmarks Pres Comm, FT Greene Assoc, Brooklyn, NY, 2005-. *Res:* Nineteenth and twentieth century architecture; Frank Lloyd Wright. *Interests:* NYC Architecture. *Publ:* Auth, The English landscape garden in the eighteenth century: The cultural importance of an English Institution, Albion, Spring 79; Architectural Competitions in 19th Century England, UMI Res Press, 84; Frank Lloyd Wright, BluePrint, 96

BASTIAN, LINDA
PAINTER, EDUCATOR
b Ayer, Mass, Nov 7, 40. *Study:* Antioch Col, BA, 63; Tufts Univ, Boston Mus Sch, MEd, 65; New York Univ, PhD, 72. *Work:* Art in Embassies Prog, US Dept State; Port Authority NY & NJ; Hosp Corp, Bellevue, NY; Temple Univ, Pa. *Exhib:* Works on Paper, Brooklyn Mus, NY, 75 & Weatherspoon Mus, Univ NC, Greensboro, 79; one-woman shows, Soho 20 Gallery, 78, 80, 83, 84, & 86 & Birds, Fish & Flowers, Bronx Mus Arts, 85; Animals in Art, Dept Cult Affairs, NY, 81; Home Work, Women Make Art for the Home, Henry St, Syracuse Univ, 81; Translucency/Transparency, Fordham Univ & Col Art Asn, NY, 82; Artists of Merit, Hudson River Mus, 85. *Teaching:* Chairperson art educ, Sch Visual Arts, New York, 79-. *Awards:* Salamagundi Third Ann Drawing Prize, 80. *Bibliog:* Articles in Arts Mag, 78, Diversion Mag, 82 & House Beautiful, 82. *Media:* Oil, Watercolor. *Dealer:* Soho 20 Gallery 99 Spring St New York NY 10012. *Mailing Add:* 418 Fulton Hill Rd Callicoon NY 12723-4424

BATCHELOR, ANTHONY JOHN
PRINTMAKER, DRAFTSMAN
b Hull, Eng, Sept 3, 44. *Study:* Brighton Col Art, Eng, dipl(art & design), 67-69; Brit Prix Rome, Italy, 72-74. *Work:* S London Gallery, Eng; Glasgow Art Gallery, Scotland; Bradford City Art Gallery, Eng; Ind State Univ; Cincinnati Art Mus, Ohio. *Comn:* Screen printed ceramic mural, Dept of Music, Ohio Univ, 71. *Exhib:* First & Third Brit Int Print Biennale, Bradford, 68 & 72; 8th Tyler Nat, Tyler Mus Art, Tex, 71; Mostra 73 & 74, Brit Acad, Rome, Italy, 73 & 74; one-man show, Cincinnati Art Mus, 75; Cincinnati Comn Arts Gallery, 83; and others. *Teaching:* Lectr, Sunderland Polytechnic, Eng, 69-70; vis asst prof printmaking & basic design, Ohio Univ, Athens, 70-72; instr printmaking & drawing, Art Acad Cincinnati, 75-, chmn found dept, 83-. *Awards:* All-Ohio Graphics Biennale, Ohio Arts Coun, 71; Research Award, Asn Independent Col & Univ Ohio, 89; Award for excellence in teaching, Greater Cincinnati Consortium Col & Univ, 88. *Bibliog:* Articles in Screen Printing Mag, 6/83, 9/83 & 10/87. *Mem:* Col Art Asn; Soc of Rome Scholars; Found Art theory & Educ. *Media:* Water-based Screen Printing, Graphite. *Publ:* Water-based ink in education, Screen Printing, 10/84; Foundation studies in art: reaching the high school audience, FATE in Review, spring, 87; Creativity in the first semester - what's possible? FATE Newsletter, fall, 88; Rasa: The Taste of India, Imprints of India, 96; A Friend of Churchgate, Incliner, Art Acad Cincinnati, 96

BATCHELOR, BETSEY ANN
PAINTER, EDUCATOR
b Wilmington, Del, Dec 12, 52. *Study:* Philadelphia Col Art, BFA, 75; RI Sch Design, MFA, 77. *Work:* Continental Ill Bank & Trust, Chicago; Leif Johnson; CIGNA Corp. *Exhib:* Affect, Effect, Philadelphia Col Art, Pa, 83; solo exhib, Matthews Hamilton Gallery, Philadelphia, Pa, 84, Florence Wilcox Gallery, Swarthmore, Pa, 85, Munson-Williams-Proctor Inst, Utica, NY, Jessica Berwind Gallery, 89 & 92 & Dartmouth Col, 95; Works on Paper, Beaver Col, 89, 90 & 92; Goldey Paley Gallery, Philadelphia, Pa, 89; Woodmere Art Mus, Philadelphia, Pa, 90; solo exhib, Matthews Hamilton Gallery, Philadelphia, Pa, 84, Florence Wilcox Gallery, Swarthmore, Pa, 85, Munson-Williams-Proctor Inst, Utica, NY, 85, Jessica Berwind Gallery, 89 & 92 & Dartmouth Col, 95. *Teaching:* Instr painting, drawing & design, RI Sch Design, 76-80 & Community Col RI, 77-80; asst prof painting & design, Millersville Univ, 83-; asst prof, Munson-Williams-Proctor Inst, 84-85 & Swarthmore Col, 86, Moore Col Art & Design, 86-89, Swarthmore Col, 89-90, Beaver Col, 90-; assoc prof, Beaver Col, 90-. *Awards:* RI State Coun Arts, 80; Pa State Coun Arts, 84; MacDowell Colony Fel. *Bibliog:* Ronald J Onorato (auth), Gallery, Art Express, 3/82; Sid Sachs (auth), Does Philadelphia have an imagist tradition too?, New Art Examiner, 2/83; Edward Sozanski (auth), Philadelphia Inquirer, 6/85, 10/89. *Mem:* Col Art Asn. *Dealer:* Jessica Berwind Gallery 301 Cherry St Philadelphia PA. *Mailing Add:* 709 W Carpenter Ln Philadelphia PA 19119-3407

BATEMAN, ROBERT MCLELLAN
PAINTER
b Toronto, Ont, May 24, 30. *Study:* Univ of Toronto, BA(hon); pvt lessons at Toronto Arts & Lett Club from Gordon Payne; part time studies with Carl Schaeffer; Carlton Univ, Ottawa, hon DSc, 82; Brock Univ, St Catherines, LLD, 82; McMaster Univ, Hamilton, Ont, LHD, Guelph Univ, Ont, DDL, 85. *Work:* Art Gallery of Hamilton, Ont; Toronto Board of Trade; Prince of Wales; Am Artist Col, NY; (The Late) Serene Highness, Princess Grace of Monaco; HRH Prince Philip; Gilcrease Mus, Tulsa, Okla. *Comn:* Polar Bear (silver bowl commemorating endangered species), World Wildlife Fund, 76; Window into Ontario, Toronto Bd Trade, 77; Endangered Species Stamps:

Eastern Cougar, 77, Peregrine Falcon, 78, Bowhead Whale, 79 & Prairie Chicken, 80, Can Post Off; Polar Bear, World Wildlife Fund, 85; Mallard Pair--Early Winter, Wildlife Habitat Can, 85; Snowy Blizzard--Red Tailed Hawk, Art Gallery of Hamilton, 86; Royal Can Mint-Platinum Polar Bear Ser, 90. *Exhib:* Queen Elizabeth Jubilee Show, Tryon Gallery, London, 77; one-man shows, Endangered Species Show, Tryon Gallery, 75 & 79 & Beckett Gallery, Hamilton, Ont, 78, 86 & 91; Smithsonian Inst, Washington, DC, 80 & 87; Images of the Wild, Nat Mus Natural Sci, Ottawa & traveling, Can, USA and Europ, 81-84; Gilcrease Art Mus, Tulsa, Okla, 86; Natural World, Canadian Embassy, Tokyo, 92; Natural Visions, Calif Acad Sci, Los Angeles Mus Natural Hist, Vancouver Mus, Victoria Art Gallery, 92-93; and others. *Pos:* Art consult, Halton Co Bd of Educ, 68-70; art teacher, Lord Elgin High Sch, Burlington, Ont, 70-76; self-employed artist, 77-. *Teaching:* Head dept art, Nelson High Sch, 59-68 & Lord Elgin High Sch, 70-76, Burlington. *Awards:* Merit Award, Soc Animal Artists, 79, 80, 86 & 90; Artist of the Year, Am Artist Mag, 80; Master Artist, Leigh Yawkey Art Mus, Wausau, Wis, 82. *Bibliog:* Norman Lightfoot (dir), Images of the Wild (film), Nat Film Bd of Can, 78; Ramsay Derry (auth), The Art of Robert Bateman, Penguin-Viking Publ, Madison Press, 81, Donnalu Wigmore (prod), Robert Bateman: Artist & Naturalist (film), Can Broadcasting Syst, 84; Ramsay Derry (auth), The World of Robert Bateman, Random House, 85; Rick Archbold (auth), Robert Bateman: An Artist in Nature, Penguin-Viking Publ, Madison Press, 90. *Mem:* Soc Animal Artists; Royal Can Acad Arts; hon life mem Fedn Can Artists; hon life mem Fedn Ont Artists; Brit Soc Wildlife Artists; and others. *Media:* Acrylic and Oils. *Publ:* Illusr, The Nature of Birds, Natural Hist of Can Series, 74. *Dealer:* Mill Pond Press Inc 310 Center Court Venice FL 33595. *Mailing Add:* c/o Mill Pond Press 310 Center Ct Venice FL 34292-3505

BATEMAN, RONALD C
PAINTER
b Caerphilly, Glamorgan, Wales, July 26, 47. *Study:* Cardiff Col of Art, predipl, study with Tom Hudson; Swansea Col of Art, study with William Price; Tyler Sch of Art, Temple Univ, study with David Pease & J Moore, MFA. *Work:* Philadelphia Mus of Art; AT&T, Basking Ridge, NJ; Museo de Ayuntaimento De Pego, Alicante, Spain. *Comn:* Three murals, Wistar Inst, Univ of Pa, Philadelphia, 77; Creative Walls, Inc, Univ Pa. *Exhib:* Pego Ayuntamiento Mus Group Exhib, Alicante Province, Spain, 76; Contemp Artists in Philadelphia, 77; one-man show, Marian Locks Gallery, 77, 82 & 87; About Face, Squibb Gallery, Princeton, NJ; What's Real, Marian Locks Gallery, 81. *Awards:* Elizabeth Greenshields Mem Found Grant, Can, 73; Primero Premio, Certimen de Pintura, Pascual Hermanos, Spain, 76; Mus Purchase, Cheltenham Art Ann, Philadelphia Mus of Art, 76. *Media:* Oil over Acrylic Underpainting on Canvas. *Mailing Add:* c/o Locks Gallery 600 Washington Sq S Philadelphia PA 19106

BATES, DAVID
PAINTER
b Dallas, Tex, 52. *Study:* Southern Methodist Univ, Dallas, BFA, 76 MFA, 77. *Work:* Archer M Huntington Art Gallery, Univ Tex, Austin, Dallas Mus Art, Fort Worth Mus, Tex; Contemp Art Ctr, Honolulu, Hawaii; Metrop Mus Art, NY; New Orleans Mus Art, La; San Francisco Mus Mod Art. *Exhib:* One-person exhib, Charles Cowles Gallery, NY, 84, 85, 86 & 87, Tex Gallery, Houston, 84 & 86, traveling exhib, Fort Worth Mus Art, Tex, 88; The Innovative Still Life, Holly Solomon Gallery, NY, 85; 50th Anniversary Acquistitions, San Francisco Mus Mod Art, 85; The Figure in the Landscape, Art Mus, Fla Int Univ, Miami, 86; Contemp Still Life, Rathbone Gallery, Junior Col Albany, 86; Texas Landscape 1900-1986, Mus Fine Arts, Houston, 86; Sculpture and Works in relief, John Berggruen Gallery, San Francisco, 86; Biennial Exhib, Whitney Mus Am Art, NY, 87. *Awards.* Artist Grant, Dallas Mus Fine Arts, 82; Hassam & Speicher Fund Purchase, Acad & Inst Arts & Letters, 84. *Media:* Oil. *Mailing Add:* 34 Horatio St No 4B New York NY 10014-1622

BATES, KENNETH FRANCIS
ENAMELIST, CRAFTSMAN
b North Scituate, Mass, May 24, 1904. *Study:* Mass Sch Art, BSEduc; also study abroad. *Work:* Cleveland Mus Art, Ohio; Butler Inst Am Art, Youngstown, Ohio; Arch Am Art, Smithsonian Inst. *Comn:* Murals, Campus Sweater Co, Cleveland & Lakewood Pub Libr; ecclesiastical enamels, Univ Notre Dame. *Exhib:* Cleveland Mus Art, 28-79; Smithsonian Inst Traveling Exhib; Nat Syracuse Traveling Exhib; one-man shows, Brooklyn Mus & Art Inst Chicago, 61; plus others. *Teaching:* Instr & lectr, Cleveland Inst Art, 27-71, emer instr, 71-. *Awards:* Silver Medal, Cleveland Mus Art, 49, 57 & 66; Fine Arts Award of Cleveland, 63; Fac Grant Study Abroad, Cleveland Inst Art, 65; Gold Medal, Cleveland Inst Art, 92. *Mem:* Fel Int Inst Arts & Lett. *Publ:* Auth, Enameling, Principles & Practice, 51, Principles & Practice, 60, The Enamelist, 67 & Basic Design, 70, World Publ; Salome's Heritage, Vantage, 77; articles on enameling in Design Mag, Ceramics Mo, Encycl Arts; and others. *Mailing Add:* 7 194th St E Cleveland OH 44119-1027

BATES, LEO JAMES
PAINTER, FILMMAKER
b Pittsburgh, Pa, 44. *Study:* Yale Univ Summer Sch, 65; Carnegie Mellon Univ, BFA, 66. *Work:* Albright-Knox Art Gallery; Brooklyn Mus; Carnegie Mus Art, Pittsburgh; Columbia Mus Art, SC; NJ State Mus, Trenton. *Exhib:* One-person shows, Whitney Mus Art Resources Ctr, NY, 73, Albright-Knox Art Gallery, 75, Picker Art Gallery, Dana Arts Ctr, Colgate Univ, 75 & Harriman Col, 78; All in Line, Joe & Emily Lowe Art Gallery, Syracuse Univ, 80 & Terry Dintenfass Inc, NY, 81; CAPS Grantees in Brooklyn, Brooklyn Mus, 81. *Collection Arranged:* American Management Association, NY; Brooklyn Museum, NY; Columbia Museum of Art, SC; Emerson College, Boston, Mass; Harriman College Art Collection, NY; Pace University, NYC; St. Johns University, NJ; William Penn College, Oskaloosa, IA. *Awards:* Creative Artists Pub Serv Grant, 74. *Bibliog:* Rosemary Mayer (auth), article, Arts Mag, 11/73; Jean Reeves (auth), Bates pastel drawings visual challenge, Buffalo Evening News, 2/3/75; Robyn Brentano (auth), 112 Workshop, NY Univ Press, 81. *Media:* Casein & Rhoplex on Canvas; Film & Computer Animation. *Mailing Add:* 499 11th St Brooklyn NY 11215

BATISTA, KENNETH
PAINTER, EDUCATOR
b Pittsburgh, Pa, Oct 1, 52. *Study:* Columbus Col Art & Design, BFA, 75; Tyler Sch Art, Temple Univ, MFA, 77. *Work:* Westmoreland Co Mus Art, Greensburg, Pa; Grand Rapids Mus Art, Mich; Curtis Inst, Philadelphia, Pa; Hoyt Inst Fine Arts, New Castle, Pa; Erie Art Ctr, Pa. *Exhib:* Pensacola Nat Watermedia Exhib, Pensacola Jr Col, Fla, 82; Nat Watermedia Biennial, Zauer Gallery, Rochester, NY, 82; Am Drawings IV (traveling exhib), Smithsonian Inst, 83-84; Tyler Sch Art Alumni Exhib, Philadelphia, Pa, 87; Perspectives from Pennsylvania, Carnegie Mellon Art Gallery, Pittsburgh, 88. *Pos:* Chmn admin, Univ Pittsburgh, Pa, 87-93. *Teaching:* Instr drawing, Kendall Sch Design, Grand Rapids, Mich, 77-78; assoc prof drawing, Univ Pittsburgh, Pa, 78-. *Awards:* Chancellor's Distinguished Pub Service Award, 97; Purchase Award, Hoyt Nat Painting Show, 82; Jurors Award, Nat Watermedia Biennial, 82. *Mem:* Col Art Asn; Nat Asn Sch Art & Design. *Media:* Watermedia; Drawing. *Dealer:* Rosenfeld Gallery 113 Arch St Philadelphia PA 19106; Concept Gallery 1031 S Braddock Ave Pittsburgh PA 15218. *Mailing Add:* 1217 Milton Ave Pittsburgh PA 15218

BATKIN, JONATHAN
DIRECTOR
b New York, NY, 50. *Study:* Sch Visual Arts, BFA, 77; Teachers Col, Columbia Univ, MA, 83. *Work:* Elizabeth de C Wilson Mus, Manchester, Vt. *Exhib:* Solo exhib, Southern Vt Arts Center, Manchester, 01, 03; Annual invitational, Nat Acad of Design, NY, 90; Urban Nature, Islip Art Mus, Dowling Col, Oakdale, NY, 00. *Pos:* gallery dir, Kingsborough Community Col, CUNY, 2000-. *Teaching:* lectr, Kingsborough Community Col, CUNY, 84-. *Awards:* research grant, CUNY, 98, 02. *Mailing Add:* Wheelwright Mus of Am Indian 704 Camino Lejo Box 5153 Santa Fe NM 87505

BATT, MILES GIRARD
PAINTER, INSTRUCTOR
b Nazareth, Pa, Oct 12, 33. *Work:* Purdue Univ, Calumet, Ind; Ft Lauderdale Mus Arts; Home Savings & Loan Banking Group, Los Angeles; Southeast Banking Group, Miami, Fla; Art & the Law, West Publ, St Paul; plus many others. *Comn:* five paintings, Dade Co Art in Pub Bldg, Miami, Fla; two paintings, Fla State House of Rep, Tallahassee; seven paintings, Hollywood/Ft Lauderdale Int Airport, Broward Co Art in Pub Places; and others. *Exhib:* Nat Exhib of Contemp Painting, Soc of the Four Arts, Palm Beach, Fla, 67-82; Miami Metrop Mus Art Ann, 68-74; Watercolor USA, Springfield, Mo, 68-81; Abstract Real-Real Abstract, Louis K Meisel Gallery, NY, 74; A Change of View, Aldrich Mus, Conn, 75; '77 Photo Realists, Hollywood Cult Ctr, Fla & St Petersburg Mus Fine Arts, Fla, 78; one-man show, Reality's Illusion, Boca Raton Mus Art, 2000; plus others. *Teaching:* Instr watercolor, oil & acrylic, Ft Lauderdale Mus Arts, 69-78; instr watercolor, Norton Gallery & Sch Art, West Palm Beach, 70-73, Miami Art Inst, 74-79 & Hewitt Int Painting Workshops, 79-84; instr, Broward Community Col, 80, 82, 92; vis artist, Ill State Univ, 92. *Awards:* Atwater Kent Award, Soc Four Arts Nat Exhib Contemp Am Painting, 73-81; Purchase Award, Nat Watercolor Soc, 85; Cash & Purchase Award, Watercolor USA, Springfield Mus, 81 & 04; and 170 others. *Bibliog:* Jeanne Wolf (dir), Miles Batt, in Portrait (film), WPBT-2, Miami, 73; Griffin Smith (auth), Why shouldn't a pro win four times in a row, Miami Herald Newspapers, 4/74; Gary Schwan (auth), rev, Boca Raton One-Man Exhib, 8/2000. *Mem:* Nat Watercolor Soc (Los Angeles area rep, 71-05); Am Watercolor Soc; charter mem Fla Watercolor Soc; Rocky Mountain Nat Water Media Soc; Watercolor West, Redlands; and 10 others. *Media:* Acrylic; Watercolor. *Collection:* 450 Public and Private Collections. *Publ:* The Expressive Watercolor, Davis Publ, 81; auth, The Complete Guide to Creative Watercolor, Creative Art Publ, 88; Understanding Watercolor, Davis Publ, 93; Splash III, North Light Publ, 94; Creative Watercolor Step by Step, Rockport Publ, 96; and others. *Dealer:* Tidwell Gallery 325 King St Charleston SC 29401. *Mailing Add:* 2120 Hammock Lane Fort Lauderdale FL 33312

BATTENFIELD, JACKIE
PAINTER
b Pittsburgh, Pa, May 13, 50. *Study:* Pa State Univ, BS, 71; Syracuse Univ, MFA, 78. *Work:* Dow Jones & Co, Inc, Princeton, NJ; US Dept State, Washington; Sasaki Collection, Tokyo, Japan; Montclair Art Mus, NJ; Univ Richmond, Va. *Comn:* Painting, The United States Pharmacopeial Convention, Inc, Rockville, Md; Uzu Maki (set painting) for Janis Brenner & Dancers, Danspace, NY, 94. *Exhib:* Del Mus Art, Wilmington, 78; Selections from the Sasaki Collection, Gallerie Saison, Tokyo, 82; Abstraction, Soho Ctr Vis Artists, NY, 87; Mizu: The Sounds of Water (with catalog), Marsh Gallery, Univ Richmond, Va, 93; solo shows, Erickson & Elins, San Francisco, 94, Addison-Ripley, Washington, 95, 98 & Gwenda Jay Gallery, Chicago, 98. *Pos:* Dir, Rotunda Gallery, Brooklyn, 81-89; proj coordr, Artist in the Marketplace Seminar (AIM), Bronx Mus Arts, 92-99. *Teaching:* Vis artist, Syracuse Univ Col Visual & Performing Arts, 80; adj prof, RI Sch Design, 80-81; adj asst prof, Laguardia Community Col, 87-95; Empire State Col, 89-92 & 95-97. *Awards:* Pollock-Krasner Found, 93; Warren Tanner Mem Award for Painting, OIA, 96. *Bibliog:* Richard Waller (auth), Jackie Battenfield: Mizu, The Sounds of Water, Univ Richmond Press, 93. *Mem:* Am Asn Mus. *Media:* All Media. *Publ:* Auth, Ikat Technique, Van Nostrand Reinhold, 78. *Dealer:* Ericson & Elins 345 Sutter San Francisco; Gwenda Jay Gallery Chicago IL. *Mailing Add:* 158 Franklin St New York NY 10013

BATTIE, DAVID
COLLECTOR
b Oct 22, 42. *Pos:* Dir, Sotheby's, NYC, 76-99; Appraiser, Antique's Road Show, 77-. *Publ:* Price Guide to 19th & 20th C British Porcelain, Sotheby's, 75

BAUER, BETSY (ELIZABETH)
PAINTER, PRINTMAKER
b Mt Holly, NJ, Jan 18, 59. *Study:* Mass Inst Techol with Robert Breer, 79; Philadelphia Col Art, BFA(painting), 76-80; Santa Fe Art Inst with Elizabeth Murray, 95. *Work:* Hallmark Fine Art Collection, Kansas City, Mo; US State Dept, US Embassy, Sarejevo; Nat Acad Sci, Washington, DC; Philadelphia Col Art, Pa; Rohm & Haas Corp, Pa. *Comn:* Painted banner, St Patrick's Cathedral, NY, 84; animated kitchen angels ad, FOX-TV, Albuquerque, 93; painting, Permaculture Drylands J, Tucson, 95; commission poster & notecard set of paintings, Santa Fe Opera, NMex, 96 & 98; cover, Nat Acad Sci Press. *Exhib:* Spacescapes, Visual Arts Mus, NY, 84; solo exhibs, Ceres Gallery, NY, 86 & 88, Hahn Ross Gallery, Santa Fe, NMex, 95, 96 & 98 & Nat Acad Sci, Washington, DC, 97; Women's Sensibilities, Warm Gallery, Minn, 86; The Political Is Personal, NY Feminist Art Inst, NY, 87; The Inspired Garden, Eidilon Gallery, Santa Fe, NMex, 95; Riparte, Int Prints Exhib, Rome, Italy, 95; Botanica, Hand Graphics Gallery, Santa Fe, NMex, 95; Monothon 10, Site Santa Fe, NMex, 96; Spectrum 1996, Hunter Mus, Chattanooga, Tenn, 96; Intimate Prints, Hand Graphics Gallery, Santa Fe, 96; Betsy Bauer Paintings & Prints, Nat Acad Sci, Washington, DC, 97; Organics, Bridgewater/Lustberg Gallery, NY, 97; Read: Text & the Visual, Gallery A, Chicago, 97; Monothon 12, Site Santa Fe, NMex, 98; Fresh, Addison/Ripley Gallery, Washington, DC, 98. *Awards:* Rohm & Haas Painting Award, Rohm & Haas Corp, 80. *Bibliog:* Lis Bensley (auth), Awakening Botanica, Nat Acad Sci, 97; Paula Eastwood (auth), Santa Fean Mag, Santa Fe Opera Collectors ed, 98; Craig Smith (auth), A Marriage of Color & Music, New Mex Pasatiempo, 98. *Mem:* Santa Fe Coun for the Arts. *Media:* Oil Paint, All Media. *Dealer:* Hahn Ross Gallery 409 Canyon Rd Santa Fe NM 87501; Bridgewater/Lustberg Gallery 560 Broadway New York NY 10012. *Mailing Add:* 66 Two Trails Rd Apt 2 Santa Fe NM 87505-9357

BAUER, RUTH KRUSE
PAINTER
b Dallas, Tex, July 26, 1956. *Study:* RI Sch Design, BFA, 78. *Work:* Mass Inst Technol; Graham Gund Found, Boston; Chase Manhattan Bank, NY; Equitable Life, NY; Chemical Bank, NY; DeCordova Mus, Lincoln, Mass. *Exhib:* Solo exhib, Kathryn Markel Gallery, NY, 84; Art of the State, Rose Art Mus, Waltham, 82; Selections 18, Drawing Ctr, NY, 82; Brave New Works, Boston Mus Fine Arts, 83; New Vistas: Contemp Am Landscapes (with catalog), Hudson River Mus & Tucson Mus Art, 84; Landscape of the Spirit, Bruce Mus, Greenwich, Conn & Maxwell Davidson Gallery, NY, 89. *Pos:* Artist-in-residence, City Arts Prog, Dallas, 79-80. *Bibliog:* In a Quiet Way, Art & Antiques, 9/84; Christine Temin (auth), Bauer's landscapes pull in viewer, Boston Globe, 5/86. *Mem:* Women's Caucus Art. *Media:* Oil, Watercolor. *Dealer:* Hokin-Kaufman 210 W Superior Chicago IL 60610. *Mailing Add:* 14 Aber St Beverly MA 01915

BAUER, WILL N
CONCEPTUAL ARTIST, VIDEO ARTIST
b Edmonton, Alta, Dec 12, 60. *Study:* Univ Alta, BSC, 83; Univ Victoria, BC, Can, 85-87. *Work:* Telefonica Found, Madrid, Spain. *Comn:* The Trace, Telefonica Found, Madrid, Spain, 95; Displaced Emperors, ARS Electronic Ctr, Linz, Austria, 97; Re: Positioning Fear, Film & Arc, Graz, Austria, 97. *Exhib:* ARS Electronica, Linz, Austria, 93, 95 & 97; Interactive Media Festival, Los Angeles, Calif, 94; 4 Cyber Conf, Banff Ctr, Alta, Can, 94; ARCO Art Biennale, Madrid, Spain, 95; Film & Arc Biennale, Film & Archit Festival, Graz, Austria, 97. *Pos:* dir media res, APR Inc, 92-; residency, Art & Virtual Environs Prog, Banff Ctr, Alta, Can, 93-94. *Teaching:* adj prof Univ Alberta, 2001-; guest lectr Univ Karlstad Media and Comms Dept, 2000. *Awards:* ARS Electronica Golden Nical (Knowbotic Res), ARS Electronica, 93, (Rafael Lozano-Hemmer), 2000; Best Installation Piece, Int Digital Media Awards, 96. *Bibliog:* Mary Anne Moser (ed), Immersed in Technology, Mass Inst Technol Press, 96; Ole Bouman (auth), Quick space in real time, Archis Mag, No 9, 98; Jen Budney (auth) Artful engineering, Unv Alberta Engineer mag, Fall/99. *Mem:* Edmonton Arts Coun; IEEE. *Media:* Integrated Interactive Electronic Media. *Res:* Theory of Integrated-Media Artwork, Hyper-dimensional Virtual Art Objects, Artistic Bandwidth Measurement Techniques, others. *Publ:* Auth, Integrated Media Manifesto, Wayward Press, 90; coauth, GAMS-An integrated media controller system, Computer Music J, Mass Inst Technol Press, 92; auth, Age of the Data Poets, Flash Art Int, 96. *Dealer:* Relational Art Ciudad Rodrigo # 2 4-Izquierda Madrid Spain 28012. *Mailing Add:* 1803 11027-87 Ave Edmonton AB T6G 2P9 Canada

BAUM, DON
SCULPTOR, CURATOR
b Escanaba, Mich, June 2, 22. *Study:* Univ Chicago, BA, 46; Art Inst Chicago, Hon Dr Fine Arts, 84. *Work:* Arthur Anderson & Co, Chicago, Ill; First Nat Bank Chicago; Ill State Mus, Springfield; Krannert Mus, Univ Ill, Champaign; Milwaukee Art Mus, Wis. *Exhib:* Solo Exhibs, Galerie Darthea Speyer, Paris, France, 85, Betsy Rosenfield Gallery, Chicago, Ill, 87, 89 & 92 & traveling exhib, Madison Art Ctr, 88-89, Art Ctr, Battlecreek, Mich, 89, Rockford Col Art Gallery, Ill 89 & Siena Art Gallery, Adrian, Mich, 90; Face to Face: Self Portraits by Chicago Artists, Chicago Cult Ctr, 92; Assemblage, Southeastern Ctr Contemp Art, Winston-Salem, NC, 92; The Home Show: Objects for and About the Home, Ctr Creative Studies, Detroit, Mich, 92; May 1992, Betsy Rosenfield Gallery, Chicago Int Art Expo, Ill, 92; and others. *Collection Arranged:* Don Baum Says Chicago Needs Famous Artists, 69 & Made in Chicago: Some Resources, 75, Mus Contemp Art, Chicago; Urgent Messages, Chicago Cult Ctr, 88. *Pos:* Bd mem & dir exhibs, Hyde Park Ctr, 56-72; Am comnr US entry Sao Paulo Biennale, Brazil, 73; chmn exhibs, Mus Contemp Art, Chicago, Ill, 74-79, mem bd trustees, 74-86; mem int exhibs comt, Washington, DC, 77-79. *Teaching:* Fac mem art dept, Roosevelt Univ Chicago, 48-84; instr painting, Hyde Park Art Ctr, Chicago, 55-65; grad adv, Art Inst Chicago, 88-92. *Awards:* Pauline Palmer Prize, 80th Exhib Chicago & Vicinity Artists, 84; Visual Arts Fel Award, Nat Endowment Arts, 84; Sidney Yates Arts Advocacy Award, Ill Arts Alliance, 89. *Bibliog:* Barbara Kirshenblatt-Gimblett (auth), Who's bad? accounting for taste, Vol XXX, No 3, 10/91 & James Yood (auth), Don Baum, Vol XXX, No 11, 9/92, Artforum; Sue Taylor (auth), Introductory essay, Don Baum: Domus, Madison Art Ctr, pg 10-23, 9/92. *Media:* Assembled Found Objects. *Mailing Add:* 5530 S Shore Dr 18C Chicago IL 60637-1945

BAUM, JAYNE H
ART DEALER
b Newark, NJ, Dec 3, 54. *Study:* Clark Univ, Mass; NY Univ, BS(fine arts). *Pos:* Assoc & cur, Margo Feiden Galleries, New York, 75-77; dir & consult, Dan Greenblat Assoc, New York, 77-82; owner, Jayne Baum Gallery, New York, currently. *Bibliog:* Gallery exhibs reviewed in Arts Mag, Artnews, Artscribe & Village Voice. *Specialty:* Contemporary photography, paintings, drawings, limited edition prints and sculpture. *Publ:* Auth, Interior design, Whitney Comn Mag Div, 83; Facilities Design and Management, Gralla Publ, 83. *Mailing Add:* 26 Grove St Apt 4C New York NY 10014-5329

BAUM, MARILYN RUTH
PAINTER, PRINTMAKER
b Pittsburgh, Pa, May 24, 39. *Study:* Univ Calif, Los Angeles, BFA, 62, 63-65. *Work:* Mus Mod Art, NY; Nat Mus Am Art; Achenbach Found Graphic Arts, Fine Arts Mus San Francisco; San Jose Mus, Calif; Jacksonville Art Mus, Fla. *Exhib:* Solo exhib, San Jose Mus, 81; California Artists, Oakland Mus, Calif, 81; Recent Acquisitions Part II, Achenbach Found, San Francisco, 83. *Bibliog:* Elise Miller (auth), Marilyn Baum--new paintings, Art Express, 3/82; Jeffrey Weiss (auth), article, Arts, 6/82; Frank Cebulski (auth), The selfish eye, Artweek, 1/83. *Dealer:* Olga Dollar Gallery 126 Post St San Francisco CA 94108. *Mailing Add:* 561 Summit Ave Mill Valley CA 94941-1032

BAUMEL-HARWOOD, BERNICE
PAINTER, PRINTMAKER, SCULPTOR
b Brooklyn, NY. *Study:* 5 Towns Music & Art Asn, NY, with Jacob Lawrence, 57-58; Hofstra Univ, Hempstead, NY, with Pearl Fine, BS(Art Educ), 68-73; Ruth Leaf Studio, Douglastown, NY, 80-85; Pratt Graphics Ctr, NY, 85-86; Studio Camnitzer, Valdottavo, Italy, with David Finkbeiner, 85; Frank Varga Sculpture Studio Fla. *Work:* Am Stock Exchange, NY; IBM, Bethlehem, Pa; Chase Manhattan Bank, NY; Nassau Co Mus Fine Art, Roslyn, NY; Arthur Andersen & Co, St Louis, Mo; Sandoz-Nabisco; & others. *Exhib:* Solo exhib, Etchings & Monoprints, Calkins, Gallery, Hofstra, NY, 85; Nat Asn Women Artists Traveling Print, Greenville Mus Art, NC, 86, Albrecht Mus Art, St Joseph, Mo, 86, & Corcoran Sch Art, Washington, DC, 87; Long Island Artists, Nassau Co Mus, Roslyn, NY, 88; Body Conscious, Elaine Benson Gallery, Bridgehampton, NY, 89; Mari Gallery, Westchester, NY, 90; Norton Gallery Art, West Palm Beach, Fla, 93; Coral Springs Mus of Art, Fla; 6 Person Show, Artists Guild of the Boca Raton Mus of Art. *Pos:* Nassau Co Mus Fine Arts (bd adv 81-88); Graphic Eye Gallery, Port Washington, NY (pres, 86-88); Nat Asn Women Artists (juror graphics, 88-90); Lectr and Print Behonstrations Nassau Co Mus of Art, NY; Cornel Mus of Art, Delray, Fla; Coral Springs Mus of Art, Fla. *Teaching:* Artist in residence, Monoprints, Syosset High Sch, NY, 86. *Awards:* Leila Sawyer Award, Ann Exhib, Nat Asn Women Artists, 83; Award Excellence, Long Beach Mus, Long Beach Art Asn, 85; Sally Carson Award, Norton Gallery, 93. *Bibliog:* Interview with Artist, Art In the World Radio Program Nassau Community College; Article in the Sun Sentinal FL, 2002, On my Life Experiences. *Mem:* Artists Equity Asn, NY; Nat Asn Women Artists (juror, 88-90); Nat Mus Women in the Arts (charter mem); Artists Guild of the Boca Raton Mus of Art. *Media:* Etchings, Monoprints,Watercolors. *Collection:* Queensborough Community College Art Gallery NY; Coral Springs Mus of Art, FL. *Publ:* Illustrator: Five Towns, 62. *Mailing Add:* 41 Windsor Lane Boynton Beach FL 33436

BAUMGARDNER, MATT (MATTHEW) CLAY
PAINTER
b Columbus, Ohio, Feb 5, 1955. *Study:* Univ NC, Chapel Hill, MFA, 82. *Work:* Gibbs Mus, Charleston; Mint Mus, Charlotte; Spartenburg Arts Ctr. *Exhib:* Bienniel Exhib, Mint Mus, Charlotte, 81; Exhibition 280, Huntington Mus, 82; Totem and Taboo, Wessel O'Connor Gallery, NY, 89; solo exhib, Charles Cowles Gallery, NY, 93, Gallery A, Chicago, 95 & 98, Bentley Gallery, Scottsdale, 98, 2000, Md Modern, Houston, 98, Jeffrey Coploff Fine Arts, New York City, 2000, 2001; Visions of Six, Gallery A, Chicago, 94; Pulp Fictions, Gallery A, Chicago, 95; Bentley Gallery, Scottsdale, Ariz, 97; Carrie Secrist Gallery, Chicago, 98; Robert Kidd Gallery, Birmingham, Mich, 99; Jeffrey Coploff Fine Art, New York City, 99; Bemis Ctr, Omaha City, Nebr, 99; Lew Allen Contemp, Santa Fe, 99. *Collection Arranged:* Bear Stearns, Boston; Blank Rome Cominsky & McCauley, Philadelphia; Boston Millennia Partners; Gibbes Mus, Charleston, SC; Hale & Dorr, Boston; Mint Mus, Charlotte, NC; Palmer & Dodge, Boston; Spartenburg Arts Ctr, SC; XL Captial, Pembroke, Bermuda. *Awards:* Visual Artist Fel, Nat Endowment Arts, 93. *Bibliog:* David McCraken (auth), Sampler of Abstraction from New York is down to earth, Chicago Tribune, 2/25/94; interview by Suzy Hendrikx, VTM Belg Television, 97; interview by Richard Hake, WNYC, NPR Radio, 97; Rick Marin (auth), Footloose Where Art Lives, NY Times, 11/21/98. *Media:* Acrylic, Oil

BAUTZMANN, CA-OPA (NANCY ANNETTE)
PAINTER
b Morganton, NC. *Study:* Westminster Col, BA(fine art), 74; study with Hans Axel Walleen, 75-76, Gunter Korus, 92-94. *Work:* J P Adams, Dalton, Mass. *Comn:* Oil painting, comn by David Derry, Pittsfield, Mass, 94; oil portrait, comn by Ed Lewis, Worthington, Mass, 94; watercolor, comn by Mrs Michel Leonart, Tucson, Ariz, 97.

Exhib: Springfield Art League Nat, George Walter Vincent Smith, Mass, 93; Oil Painters of Am Nat, 93, 94, 95, 96 & 98; 18th Ann Art Exhib Nat, Salmagundi Club, NY, 95; Ariz Aqueous Nat, Tubac Ctr Arts, Ariz, 96; Western Fedn Soc Watercolor, Tucson Mus Art, Ariz, 97. *Collection Arranged:* Portfolio of Realism, Berkshire Botanical Garden Ctr, 93; Paintings by Nancy Bautzmann, Pittsfield Art League Co-op Gallery, 94; El Presidio Gallery, Tucson, Ariz, 1995-2003; Granite Mus Gallery, Prescott, Ariz; J&F Fine Arts Gallery, Scottsdale, Ariz. *Pos:* Jury of selection, Kent Art Asn, 92; judge, Cent Berkshire Chamber Com Poster Contest, 94. *Teaching:* Art, Art-for-Children, Berkshire Mus, 88-94, Becket Arts Coun, 89; drawing & watercolor, Pittsfield, Mass & Tucson, Ariz, 1988-2003. *Awards:* Merit Award, 74th Nat Exhib, Springfield Art League, 93; First in Oil, Kent Art Asn, Conn, 94; Merchandise Award, Oil Painters Am, 98; First Place, Southern Ariz Watercolor Guild's Signature Show, 2003. *Bibliog:* Chamber Showing Bautzmann Works, Cent Berkshire Chamber Com, 1/29/92; Janet Jahn (auth), Visiting artist-Nancy Bautzmann, First Congregational Church, 4/16/93. *Mem:* Signature mem Oil Painters Am; signature mem Copley Soc Boston; artist mem Acad Arts Asn; signature mem Southern Ariz Watercolor Guild (show chmn, 97-); Ariz Watercolor Asn. *Media:* Oil, Watercolor. *Publ:* Contribr, The Best of Flower Painting, Northlight, 97; Villages in the spotlight, Casas Adobes Courier, 1999; contribr article and cover Tea A Mag, fall, 2001. *Mailing Add:* 7742 N Harelson Pl Tucson AZ 85704

BAVINGER, EUGENE ALLEN
PAINTER, EDUCATOR
b Sapulpa, Okla, Dec 21, 1919. *Study:* Univ Okla, BFA; Inst Allende, Mex, MFA. *Work:* Addison Gallery Am Art, Andover, Mass; Nelson Gallery, Atkins Mus, Kansas City, Mo; Joslyn Art Mus, Omaha, Nebr; Masur Mus, Monroe, La; Mulvane Art Ctr, Topeka, Kans. *Comn:* Mural, Exxon Oil, Chemical Technol Ctr, Baytown, Tex, 82; mural, Westin Hotel Lobby, Denver, Colo, 86. *Exhib:* Am Painting Today, Metrop Mus Art, NY, 50; 70th Western Ann Invitational-19 artists, Denver Art Mus, Colo, 64; Fifty Artists from Fifty States, Am Fedn Arts Traveling Exhib, 66; one-man shows, Sheldon Art Gallery, Lincoln, Nebr, 67 & retrospective (with catalog), Mus Art, Univ Okla, 86; Razor Gallery, NY, 78. *Teaching:* Prof art, Univ Okla, 47-; retired. *Awards:* First Award, 22nd Ann Exhib, Ft Smith Art Ctr, Ark, 72; Purchase Award, 19th Ann, Ark Art Ctr, Little Rock, 76; Grand Award, Art Ann I, Tulsa, Okla, 80. *Bibliog:* Les Krantz (ed), American Artists, 85. *Media:* Acrylic. *Publ:* Review, Arts Mag, 5/78; Review, Art Voices/South, Susan Caldwell, 9/79. *Dealer:* Rick Moore Gallery Naples FL; Winsois Gallery Diana FL. *Mailing Add:* 730 NE 60th Ave Norman OK 73071-0710

BAXENDELL, JULIE
PAINTER
b New York, NY, Nov 28, 34. *Study:* Philadelphia Col Art, BA, 56. *Exhib:* Nat Spring Open Exhibs, Wayne Art Center, Pa, 99; one-woman show, Rehoboth Art League, De, 02; Mind Scapes, De Div of the Arts, Wilmington, 02. *Pos:* designer & illustrator, Green Scene Mag, 56-94. *Awards:* Fel Grant for Artist, State Office Bldg, De Div of Arts, 02. *Mem:* The Artists Exchange; Del Div of the Arts; The Rehoboth Art League. *Publ:* Green Scene, Pa Horticultural Soc, 1965-94; Jubilee, Am Baptists, 1986-92. *Dealer:* Peninsula Gallery, 520 E Savannah Rd, Lewes, De, 19958. *Mailing Add:* 9255 Shore Dr Prime Hook Beach DE 19963

BAXTER, BONNIE JEAN
PRINTMAKER, PAINTER
b Texarkana, Tex, July 30, 1946. *Study:* Monticello Col, AS, 64-66; Kans Univ, 66-67; Cranbrook Art Acad, BFA, 67-69. *Work:* Mus Mod Art, Montreal; Monticello Col, Godfrey, Ill; Maison de la Cult, Montreal; Galleria Fenwick, Forano, Italy; Maison des Metiers, Rennes, France. *Comn:* Mural, Mich High Sch, Bloomfield Hills, 69; mural for tomb, comn by Gen Paciantiani, Forano, Italy, 73. *Exhib:* Que-Boston Exchange, Experimental Etching Studio, Boston, 82; 171 Artistes Quebecoise, Maison de la Cult, Montreal, 82; Quebec Artists, Maison des Metiers, Rennes, France, 83; Artists Book L'lle, Mus Mod Art, Montreal, 83; l'Atelier de L'lle, Delegation du Que, NY, 83; and others. *Pos:* Owner & dir, Le Scarabee Printing Studio, Val-David, Que, 82-; printer in residence, l'Atelier de L'lle Asn, 80-82, master printer, 82-. *Teaching:* Instr wood-cut, Les Createurs Assoc, Que, 82-83. *Bibliog:* Jacques Gireldeau (dir), Etoile de Aurainegiea (film), Can Nat Film Bd, 78. *Mem:* Conseil Gravare Que; Am Graphics Soc; Les Createur Asn Val-David (pres, 82-); Conseil Regional Cult Laurentides (exec dir, 83-87). *Media:* All. *Publ:* Auth, Atelier d l'lle a Boston, 81 & Atelier d l'lle a New York, 82, Skis-Dite; illusr, L'Ille, Iconia Ed, 82; auth, Bonnie Baxter: Printmaker--fine arts director, Skis-Dite, 82; contribr, Quebec Artists 1970-1983, Iconia Ed, 83. *Mailing Add:* 3224 Ave du Pins CP 375 Val-David PQ J0T 2N0 Canada

BAXTER, DOUGLAS W
ART DEALER
b Ohio, Nov 8, 49. *Study:* Oberlin Col, with Ellen Johnson, BA(art hist), 72. *Exhib:* Cy Twombly: Works on Paper 1957-87, 88; Barnett Newman: The Sublime in Now, 94. *Pos:* Art dealer, Fischbach Gallery, 73-74; art dealer, Paula Cooper Gallery, New York, 74-87; vpres, Pace Gallery, 87- 93 & exec dir, 93-96; exec dir, Pace Wildenstein, 93 & pres, 96-; trustee, Independent Cur Inc, New York, 89-, Chinati Found, Marfa, Tex, 94- & Trisha Brown Dance Co, New York, 97-. *Mem:* Feria de Arte Contemporaneo, Madrid, Spain (mem, org comm, 86-89); Robert Kovich Dance Found, New York (bd mem, 89-93); Art Pro-Choice, Benefit for Nat Abortion Rights Action League (mem, exhib comm, 90). *Specialty:* Contemporary and modern art. *Publ:* Ed, catalogs for Twombly and Newman exhibs, Pace Gallery, New York, 88. *Mailing Add:* Pace Gallery 32 E 57th St New York NY 10022

BAXTER, PAULA ADELL
LIBRARIAN, WRITER
b Hackensack, NJ, Sept 21, 54. *Study:* State Univ MY, Binghamton, BA(art hist), 75, MA, 77; Columbia Univ, MSLS, 79. *Collection Arranged:* Victorian Ornament: Excerpts in Design History, Edna Barnes Salomon Gallery, New York Pub Libr, 89-90 & A change of clothes, 93; Artful Interiors: Rooms with a View, 96-97; Decoration in the Age of Napoleon, 2004-05. *Pos:* Visual arts libr, State Univ NY, Purchase, 81-83; assoc librn reference, Mus Mod Art, NY, 83-87; cur art & archit collection, New York Pub Libr, 87-. *Teaching:* instr, Sch of Libr and Information Sci, Inst on Art Ctions, Pratt Inst, summer 2002. *Mem:* Art Librs Soc NAm (exec bd, 87-88); Col Art Asn. *Res:* Literature and bibliography of art history. *Interests:* British and Native American art; history of decorative arts and design. *Publ:* Navajo and Pueblo Jewelry, 1940-1970, Three Decades of Innovative Design Revisited, Am Indian Art Mag, autumn, 96; Nineteenth-century Navajo and Pueblo silver jewelry, Antiques Mag, 1/98; Encyclopedia of Native American Jewelry, Oryx Pr, 2000; Southwest Silver Jewelry, Schiffer, 2001; The Regency Style's Debt to Napoleon, Antiques Mag, 10/04. *Mailing Add:* New York Pub Libr 42nd St & 5th Ave Rm 313 New York NY 10018

BAXTER, ROBERT CHARLES
PAINTER, EDUCATOR
b Plainfield, NJ, July 21, 30. *Study:* Miami Univ, Ohio, BA, 52; The Chouinard Art Inst (now called, The Calif Inst the Arts), 54-57. *Work:* Chas & Emma Frye Mus, Seattle, Wash; Dept the Interior, US, Washington DC; Town Hall Gallery, Westport, Conn; Fairfield Libr, Fairfield, Conn. *Comn:* oil landscape, Mt Deserts, Dept Interior (soc illusr, New York City), 59. *Exhib:* Nat Acad Design Ann, 5th Ave Gallery, New York, NY, 74, 76 & 78,; Am Watercolor Soc, 5th Ave Gallery, New York, NY, 78 & 97. *Teaching:* adj prof, illus, Fashion Inst Technol, New York City; adj prof, watercolor, Fairfield Univ, Fairfield, Conn; instr, painting, Silvermine Art Sch, N Canaan, Conn. *Awards:* Thos B Clarke Prize, Nat Acad Design, TB Clarke, 72; H Ward Ranger Purchase, Nat Acad Design, Henry Ward Ranger, 78; High Winds Medal, Am Watercolor Soc, 97. *Bibliog:* Gene Thornton (auth), Same place different paintings, Am Artist Mag, 8/91; Elise Maclay (auth), Living the artists life, Westport Mag, 2/2005. *Mem:* Am Watercolor Soc, New York, NY; Allied Artists Am, New York, NY. *Media:* Acrylic, Oil, Watercolor. *Publ:* coauth, 6 Artists Paint a Portrait, Watson-Guptill. *Mailing Add:* 3 Plum Tree Ln Westport CT 06880

BAXTER, ROBERT JAMES
PAINTER
b Milwaukee, Wis, Nov 30, 33. *Study:* Univ Wis, Madison, BS (art), 56, MS (painting) & MFA (painting), 60; studied with John Wilde. *Work:* Vatican Pinacoteca; Hirshhorn Mus, Washington; Whitney Mus Am Art, NY; San Francisco Mus Mod Art; Galleria Nat, Inst Nazionale per la Grafica, Rome. *Comn:* Painting, Vatican, Rome, 77. *Exhib:* Am Drawing Biennial XXII Norfolk Mus Art & Sci, Va, 66; one-man shows, San Francisco Mus Mod Art, Calif, 70, Galleria Nat (Inst Nat Per La Grafica), Rome, 82, Milwaukee Art Mus, Wis, 86, Univ Art Mus, Ariz State Univ, Tempe, 86, Laguna Art Mus, Laguna Beach, Calif, 87 & Norton Mus, Palm Beach, Fla, 87; The Drawing Soc Am, Art Galleries Univ Calif, Santa Barbara, 70; The Fine Line: Drawing with Silver in Am, Norton, Gallery, Palm Beach, Fla, 77; San Paolo Nell'Arte Contemp, Vaticano, Rome, Italy, 77; ACA Galleries, NY, 87 & 90; Perimeter Gallery, Chicago, 94 & 97. *Pos:* Painter in residence, Am Acad, Rome, 69-70 & 71-72. *Teaching:* Prof art, San Diego State Univ, 62-71. *Awards:* Painting Fel, Louis Comfort Tiffany, 72. *Bibliog:* Marilyn Hagberg (auth), Robert Baxter's drawn paintings, Artweek, Vol I, No 36, 10/15/70; Daniel Mendelowitz (auth), A History of American Art, Holt, Reinhart & Winston, 70; Dean Jensen (auth), Robert Baxter's drawings compel with simple power, Milwaukee Sentinel, 6/20/86; and others. *Mem:* Nat Acad. *Media:* Egg Tempera, Oil. *Publ:* In Retrospect: Alfred Sessler, Arts in Society, Edward Kamarch, Vol 3, No 1, Univ Wisc Press, 62. *Dealer:* Perimeter Gallery 210 W Superior Chcago IL 60610

BAXTER, VIOLET
PAINTER, CALLIGRAPHER
b New York, NY, 34. *Study:* Cooper Union Sch Art, New York, Cert, 60, with Morris Kantor, Paul Standard, Robert Gwathmey, Adya Yunkers, Nicholas Carone, 60; Columbia Univ, New York, with Ralph Mayer, 60-61; Pratt Graphic Art Ctr, New York, 81; Hunter Col, New York, 52-54. *Work:* Hon Shunichi Suzuki, Gov Tokyo; Consolidated Edison Co, Oppenheimer Capital Corp, Schroder & Co, NY, Fidelity Investments, Morgan Stanley Trust, Jersey City, NJ; Mus City New York; Savannah Col Art & Design, Ga; SE Mo State Univ Mus; Coun Environment, NY; Jacqueline Casey Hudgens Ctr Arts, Duluth, Ga; and others. *Exhib:* Sharon Creative Arts Found Gallery, Conn, 85-87; Owen Gallery, NY, 95; Park Ave Atrium, NY, 96; Mus City NY, 96; Staten Island Inst Arts Sci (biennial), 96; Forham Univ Lincoln Ctr, NY, 96 & 2000; Butler Inst Am Art, Youngstown, Ohio, 97-98, 2001 & 05; Xian Acad Fine Arts Gallery, Xian, China & Badahsenzi Mem Gallery, Nanchang, 97; Md Fedn Art, Annapolis, 97-98, 2000; Boston Ctr Arts, Artcetera Auction, 98; NYC Tech Col, City Univ NY, 98 & 2000; solo exhibs, Gallery Juno, NY, 99 & Nat Arts Club, NY, 2000 and Southeast Mo State Univ Mus, 2002; The Gallery, Mercer Co Community Col, Trenton, NJ, 2001; David Findlay Jr Fine Art, New York City, 2003; Butler Gallery, Marymount Col & Fordham Univ, 2003; ACA Galleries, New York City, 2006; and many others. *Pos:* guest lectr, Parsons Sch Design, NY, 91 & slide talk, Educ Alliance, NY, 92; bd dir, NY Artists Equity, 88-91, vpres, treas, 91-2002; dir, Fine Arts Federation, NY, 2004-. *Teaching:* Mentor, Integrative Studies (calligraphy), Pratt Inst, NY, 74-75; guest lectr, Sch Practical Philosophy, Pastel Soc Am & Parsons Sch Design, 85 ; instr, drawing, Nat Acad Design, 2001; mem panel, Art Students League, NY, 2003. *Awards:* Gold Medal of Honor, Audubon Artists, NY, 94; Bronze Medal, Audubon Artists, 95 & 97; Jane Peterson Mem Award, Audubon Artists, 96; Vermont Studio Center, Artist Grant, 96; Richard Florsheim Art Fund Grant, 2002. *Bibliog:* Jed

Perl (auth), Real Worlds, Art & Antiques, 1/1992; Katherine Hobson (auth), The Deal of the Art, The Street.com, 10/1999 and The Street's Art Lovers, The New York Observer, 11/1999; Elizabeth Wilson: Interview, Violet Baxter, The Pastel Jour, 12-16, 9-10/2001; F.R. Rivers, Art Review: sub(Urban), Princeton Town Topics, 10/2001; Pat Summers (auth), Three Artists, Vision at Mercer, U.S. 1, 10/2001; Tamara Kerr Art Bank/NY Artists Equity, honoring Placide and George A. Schriever, Univ Mus, exhib catalogue with essay by Stanley I. Grand, Cape Girardeau, Mo, Univ Mus, SE Mo State Univ, 2002; Univ Mus, Violet Baxter: The View from Union Square, exhib catalogue with essay by Stanley I. Grand, Cape Girardeau, Mo Univ Mus, SE Mo State Univ, 2002; Sam Blackwell (auth), Windows on Manhattan, Interview, Arts & Leisure, Southeast Missourian, 10/2002. *Mem:* New York Artists Equity Asn; Audubon Artists; Fedn Mod Painters & Sculptors; Nat Arts Club, New York (hon mem). *Media:* Oil, All Media. *Publ:* Best of Pastel, 96, Landscape Inspirations, 97 & Best of Drawing & Sketching, 99, Rockport Publ; Pure Color: The Best of Pastel, North Light Books, 2006. *Mailing Add:* 333 E 30th St No 18L New York NY 10016

BAYER, ARLYNE
PAINTER, PRINTMAKER
b Washington, DC. *Study:* State Univ NY, Buffalo, BFA; Hunter Col, with Tony Smith, John McCracken & Rosalind Krauss, MA(fine arts). *Work:* Herbert F Johnson Mus Art, Ithaca, NY; Chase Manhattan Bank, Equitable Life Assurance, NY; Prudential Insurance Co, Newark, NJ; Housatonic Mus Art, Bridgeport, Conn. *Comn:* Shearman & Sterling, NY. *Exhib:* Contemp Reflections, Aldrich Mus Contemp Art, 75; 15 New Talents, Aldrich Mus Contemp Art, 79; Solo exhib, Hudson Gallery, NY, 86; Pastel Anthology II, Grace Borgenicht Gallery, NY, 87; Invitational, Richard Green Gallery, Santa Monica, Calif, 91; Activated Walls, Artists Space, NY, 93; Selections, Adam Baumgold Fine Art, NY, 96; and others. *Awards:* Creative Artists Pub Serv Grant, 76-77; MacDowell Colony Fel, 77. *Bibliog:* Jacqueline Moss (auth), article, Arts Mag, 2/80. *Dealer:* Adam Baumgold Gallery 74 E 79th St New York NY 10021. *Mailing Add:* 903 Park Ave No 16C New York NY 10021

BAYLISS, GEORGE
PAINTER, EDUCATOR
b Washington, DC, Oct 14, 31. *Study:* Univ Va; Univ Md, with Herman Maril, BA, 55; Cranbrook Acad Art, with Zoltan Sepeshy, MFA, 56; Corcoran Sch Art. *Work:* Akron Art Inst, Ohio; State Univ NY; Corcoran Gallery Art; Univ Mich; Ford Motor Co; Sloan Kettering Found. *Comn:* Mural, Rural Elect Transmission, Mus Hist & Technol, Smithsonian Inst, 56-57. *Exhib:* Corcoran Biennial Contemp Am Painters, 55 & 59; New Accessions USA, Colorado Springs Fine Arts Ctr, 58; 12 Washington Painters, Univ Ky, 60; Four Washington Artists, Corcoran Gallery Art, 61; Drawings USA, circulated by Smithsonian Inst, 62. *Teaching:* Instr painting & drawing, Sch Akron Art Inst, Ohio, 57-59 & Flint Jr Col, Mich, 59-62; asst prof painting & drawing, State Univ NY Col Potsdam, 62-63; acting dean, Parsons Sch of Design, New York City, 63-67; chmn dept art, State Univ NY Col, Fredonia, 67-72; chmn dept art, Univ Mich, 72-74, dean, Sch Art, 74-84; dean, Tyler Sch Art, 84-89, prof painting, 89-95, prof emeritus, 95-. *Awards:* Principal Purchase Prize, Corcoran Gallery Art, 55; Award of Merit, South Bend Art Asn, Ind, 56; Bundy Co Prize, Bloomfield Hills Art Asn, 56. *Mem:* Col Art Asn; Nat Asn Schs Art & Design (bd dir & pres). *Media:* Oil, Watercolor. *Dealer:* Turtle Gallery Deer Isle Maine. *Mailing Add:* 213 Royal Ave Wyncote PA 19095

BAYNARD, ED
PAINTER, PRINTMAKER
b Washington, DC, Sept 5, 40. *Work:* Chase Manhattan Bank, NY; Wadsworth Atheneum, Hartford, Conn; Whitney Mus Am Art, Mus Mod Art, Metrop Mus Art, NY; Inst Contemp Art, Univ Pa, Philadelphia; Walker Art Ctr, Minneapolis, Minn; High Mus Atlanta, Ga; San Francisco Mus Fine Art, Calif; Ameranda Hess Oil, Woodbridge, NJ; Norton Mus, Palm Beach, Fla. *Exhib:* Landscape, Mus Mod Art, NY, 72; Am Drawing 1963-1973, Whitney Mus Am Art, NY, 73; Tyler Graphics, 80, 81, 88 & 96; Prints from Tyler Graphics, Walker Art Ctr, Minneapolis, 84; solo exhibs, Eleonore Austerer Gallery, San Francisco, 96 & 97, Gallery One, Toronto, Can, 97, Images Gallery, Toledo, 97, Augen Gallery, Portland, 97, Dorothy Blau Gallery, Fla, 97, Irving Gallery, Palm Beach, Fla, 98 & Wright Gallery, NY, 99, Curt Marcus Gallery, NY, 91, 93, 97, Eleonore Austerer Gallery, San Francisco, 2000 & 01, Tyler Graphics: End of and Era, A P Giannini Gallery, San Francisco, 2000, Austerer Crider Gallery, Palm Springs, 2002; Morris/Healy, NY, 95; Eleonore Austerer, San Francisco, Calif, 96; Images Gallery, Toledo, Ohio, 97; Barbicon, London, Eng, 97; Asronson Gallery, Parsons Sch of Design, 99. *Teaching:* Exp art, Ecole des Beaux-Arts, Paris, 68-69. *Awards:* Grants NEA, 80, 82, 86; NY Found for the Arts, 87, 97. *Bibliog:* Roberta Kimmel (auth), In Artists' Homes: The Living Spaces of Contemporary Artists; Ken Johnson (auth), article, NY Times, 2/96; Something different at Tyler Graphics, NY Times Westchester Ed, 2/16/96; Brenson, Michael, New York Times Critics Choice, 83, Tom Butter, 91. *Media:* Oil, Watercolor. *Publ:* Illusr, Somewhere in Ho, Buffalo Press, 72; illusr (cover & frontispiece), Paris Rev, 74; illusr (cover), Miami, Donnes, 75; auth (interview), Arlene Slavin & Ed Baynard, NY Arts J, 76. *Dealer:* Eleonore Austerer 540 Sutter St San Francisco CA 94102

BEACHUM, SHARON GARRISON
PHOTOGRAPHER, GRAPHIC ARTIST
b Oklahoma City, Okla, Dec 1, 53. *Study:* Univ Okla, BFA, 75; Old Dominion Univ & Norfolk State Univ, coop prog, MFA, 86. *Work:* Chrysler Mus, Norfolk, Va; Franklin Furnace, NY. *Exhib:* Why Do Girls Have to Act Like That?, Va Beach Art Ctr, 86; Chromatic Abberations, Washington Ctr Photog, Washington, DC, 88; The Portrait in Am, Chyrsler Mus, Norfolk, Va, 90; solo exhib, Mich State Univ, East Lansing, 90; Light Aberations, Univ Tex, San Antonio, 90; Mid-Atlantic State Photog, James Madison Univ, Harrisonburg, Va, 91. *Pos:* Owner, Swift Graphics, Okla & Va, 77-92; tech illusr, Telemedia, Norfolk, Va, 80-82; graphic designer, Off PR, E Va Med Sch, Norfolk, 82-83. *Teaching:* Assoc prof graphic designs & photog, Hampton Univ, Va, 88-, chmn art dept, 90-94. *Awards:* Mat & Equip Grant, Four Sharp Artists, Copy Data Group, 87; Communs Excellence, Donor Recruitment, 88 & First Place in Nation, Donor Recruitment Campaign, 90, Nat Red Cross; Fulbright-Hays Travel Simihon Award: China, 98; Artist Residency Award, Va Ctr Creative Arts, 98. *Bibliog:* Stephen Perloff (auth), Photo Review, Pa Coun Arts, 87; Brooks Johnson (auth), The Portrait in America, Chrysler Mus, 90. *Mem:* Va Soc Photog Art; Tidewater Artists Asn (bd & publicity, 86-87); Col Art Asn. *Media:* Photo; Collage. *Mailing Add:* Dept Art Hampton Univ Box 6205 Hampton VA 23668

BEAL, GRAHAM WILLIAM JOHN
DIRECTOR, CURATOR
b Stratford-on-Avon, Eng, Apr 22, 47. *Study:* Manchester Univ, BA, 69; Courtauld Inst, London Univ, MA, 72. *Exhib:* Wiley Territory (with catalog), 79; Jim Dine: Five Themes (coauth, catalog), 84; Giacometti: The Last Two Decades (with catalog), 84; Second Sight (with catalog), 86; Recent British Sculpture (with catalog), 87; David Nash: Voyager & Vessels, 94. *Pos:* Dir, Wash Univ Art Gallery, 74-77; chief cur, Walker Art Ctr, Minneapolis, 77-83; dir, Sainsbury Ctr, UK, 83-84; chief cur, San Francisco Mus Mod Art, 84-89; dir, Joslyn Art Mus, Omaha, 89-96 & Los Angeles Co Mus Art, Calif, 96-99; Detroit Inst Arts, 1999-; mem Fed Adv, Comt on Int Exhib, 1991-94; bd trustees, Asn AM Mus Dirs, 2002-05; bd trustees, Am Asn Mus, 2004-. *Mem:* Asn Art Mus Dirs. *Res:* Contemporary art and the surrealist tradition. *Publ:* Auth: (book, exhib catalog) Jim Dine: Five Themes, 1984; co-author: (book, exhib catalog) A Quiet Revolution, 1987, David Nash: Voyages and Vessels, 1994, Sainsbury Collection Catalogue, vol. I, 1997, Joslyn Air Mus: Fifty Favorities, 1994, Joslyn Art Mus: A Bldg Hist, 1998, American Beauty: Am Paintings and Sculpture from the Detroit Inst of Arts, 2002; contrib to Apollo Mag, London, 1989-91. *Mailing Add:* Detroit Inst Arts 5200 Woodward Ave Detroit MI 48202

BEAL, JACK
PAINTER
b Richmond, Va, June 25, 31. *Study:* Norfolk Div, Col William & Mary - Va Polytech Inst, 50-53; Art Inst Chicago, with Briggs Dyer, Isobel MacKinnon & Kathleen Blackshear, 53-56; Art Inst Boston, Hon Doctorate Fine Arts, 92; LHD, Hollins Col, 94. *Work:* Whitney Mus Am Art, Mus Mod Art, NY; Walker Art Ctr, Minneapolis, Minn; Art Inst Chicago; Nat Gallery Art, Wash; San Francisco Mus Art; Philadelphia Mus Art; Hunter Mus Art, Chattanooga, Tenn; and others. *Comn:* Wash & Lee Univ, 74-75; US Dept Interior, 75-76; Hist of Labor in Am (murals), US Labor Bldg, Washington, 75-77; Metrop Trasit Authority, NY, 85-2005; Two Mosaic Murals: Times Sq Subway Station, MTA, New York City, 2000-04. *Exhib:* one-man shows, Galerie Claude Bernard, Paris, 73 & 81, Madison Art Ctr, Wis, travelled to Univ Gallery, Boston Univ & Art Inst Chicago, 77, Reynolds/Minor Gallery, Richmond, 80, Roberson Ctr Arts & Sci, Binghamton, NY, 87-88, Frumkin/Adams Gallery, NY, 88 & 93, Gallery, NY, 88 & 93, Art Mus Western Va, 96 & Oglethorpe Univ Mus, 98, George Adams Gallery, NY, 2001, The Columbus Mus, Ga, 2001, traveled to Yager Mus, Hartwick Col, Oneonta, NY, 2002; Contemp Am Realism, Broden Gallery, Madison, Wis, 92; 40th Anniversary Exhib (with catalog), 92 & Around the House, 94, Frumkin/Adams Gallery, NY; Self-Portrait: The Changing Self, NJ Ctr Visual Arts, Summit, 93; Am Realism & Figurative Painting (with catalog), Cline Fine Art Gallery, Santa Fe, NMex, 94; Galeria Di Arte Moderna, Italy, 99-2003; Polk Mus of Art, Lakeland, Fl, 2003. *Teaching:* Vis lectr at over 100 schls, univs & mus; occupant-endowed chair, Col William & Mary, Va, 92-; fac fel, Hollins Col, Va, 96-. *Awards:* Hermitage Found fel, 1953-56; Recipient Neysa McMein Purchase award Whitney Mus, 65; Nat Endowment Arts Grant, 73; occupant Class of 1939 Endowed Chair Coll William and Mary, 1992; subject of monograph by Eric Shanes, 1993; award Nat Acad & Inst Arts and Letters, 96. *Bibliog:* Mark Strand (auth), Art of The Real, Potter, 83; John Arthur (auth), Realists at Work, Watson-Guptill, 83; Eric Shanes (auth), Jack Beal (monogr), Hudson Hills Press, 93. *Mem:* NY Acad Art; Nat Acad Design (assoc, 76, acad, 83). *Media:* Oil, Pastel. *Dealer:* George/Adams Gallery 41 W 57th St New York NY 10019. *Mailing Add:* c/o George Adams Gallery 41 W 57th St New York NY 10019-3409

BEAL, MACK
SCULPTOR
b Boston, Mass, Apr 20, 24. *Study:* Harvard Univ, BS, 46; grad study, Dept of Art, Univ NH, Durham; apprentice to master blacksmith Joe Tucker, Milford, NH. *Work:* Addison Gallery Am Art, Phillips Acad, Andover, Mass; New Eng Ctr, Univ NH, Durham; Worcester Art Mus, Mass; Permanent Exhib, Symp Lindabruun, Bad Voslau, Austria. *Exhib:* Inst Contemp Art, Boston, 70-73; Addison Gallery Am Art, Phillips Acad, Andover, Mass, 74; Norfolk Art Ctr, Nebr, 79; Nat Ornamental Metal Mus, Memphis, 79; Rowe Gallery, Univ NC, 80; Int Conf Exhib, Hereford, Eng, 80; NH Comn Arts, 81; and many others. *Pos:* Dir, The Sculptors Workshop, Somerville, Mass, 70-80, New Eng blacksmith Asn, NH League Craftsmen's Scholar Awards, NH Coun on The Arts Awards Comt. *Teaching:* Pvt classes at MB's Studio in blacksmithing & sculpture in wood & stone. *Awards:* Silver Medals (2) & Gold Medals (2), Int Teaching Ctr for Metal Design, Aachen, Ger, 86 & 91; FIFI Exhib, Cardiff, Wales, 89; HEFAISTON 90, Int Blacksmiths Prerov, Czech, 90, 99, 2002, 2004 & 2006. *Mem:* NH League Craftsmen; Boston Visual Artists Union; Ogunquit Art Asn; Artist Blacksmith Asn NAm (dir, 76-80); and others. *Media:* Wrought Iron & Stainless Steel, Stone, Wood. *Mailing Add:* PO Box One Jackson NH 03846

BEALE, ARTHUR C
FILMMAKER, CONSULTANT
b Needham, Mass, Apr 12, 40. *Study:* Brandeis Univ, BA, 62; Boston Univ Sch Fine & Appl Arts, 62-64; Harvard Univ Fogg Art Mus, apprentice conserv, 66-68. *Pos:* Conserv, Joint Am Exped Idalion, Cyprus, 71; assoc conserv, Fogg Art Mus, Harvard Univ, 71-74, head conserv, Ctr Conserv & Tech Studies, 75-81, dir, 81-86; conserv,

Kress Collection Renaissance Bronzes & Medals, Nat Gallery Art, 72-75; dir res, Mus Fine Arts, Boston, 86-93; vis comt, J Paul Getty Conserv Inst, 87-92; Nat Mus Serv Bd, 88-95; dir, Objects Conserv & Scientific Res, 93-98 & Conserv & Scientific Res, 98-99, chair Conserv & Collections Mgt, 99-2005. *Teaching:* Asst appl arts, Boston Univ, 62-64; lectr fine arts, Harvard Univ, 74-77 & 87-, sr lectr, 77-86. *Awards:* First Univ Products Award for Distinguished Achievement in the Field of Conserv, 95. *Mem:* Fel Am Inst Conserv; Nat Inst Conserv (pres, 81-82, chmn, 82-85); Int Coun Mus. *Media:* High Definition Video. *Interests:* Native American art. *Publ:* Auth, Technical perspectives on Ital medals, surface characteristics and their interpretation, Studies Hist Art, 87; Scientific Approaches to the Question of Authenticity, small bronze sculpture from the Ancient World, J Paul Getty Mus, 90; Understanding, resorting and conserving ancient bronzes with the aid of science, The fire of hephaistos: Large classical bronzes from North American Collections (ed by Carol C Mattusch), Harvard Univ Art Mus, 96; Little Dancer Aged Fourteen: The Search for the Lost Modele, Degas and the Little Dancer, Joslyn Art Mus, 98. *Mailing Add:* 151 Bullrush Farm Rd Scituate MA 02066-1429

BEALL, DENNIS RAY
PRINTMAKER, EDUCATOR
b Chickasha, Okla, Mar 13, 29. *Study:* Oklahoma City Univ; San Francisco State Univ. *Work:* Achenbach Found for Graphic Arts, San Francisco; San Francisco Mus Mod Art; Mus Mod Art, NY; Libr Cong, Washington, DC; Philadelphia Mus. *Comn:* Lone Star (ed 20, collagraph), C Troup Gallery-Codex Press, Inc, Dallas, 66; Emblem V (ed 75, relief & etching), Univ Calif, Berkeley Mus, 67; Emblem VI (ed 50, collagraph), San Francisco Mus Mod Art, 67; Miz Am (ed 20, etching), Hansen-Fuller Gallery, 68; Ars Medicus (ed 20, etching & screen print), San Francisco Art Comn, 71. *Exhib:* Original Prints, Calif Palace of Legion of Honor, San Francisco, 64; Art in the Embassies Prog, US Dept State, Oakland Art Mus, Calif, 66; one-man show, Achenbach Found Graphic Arts, 68-69; 1st Bienal Int, Segovia, Spain, 73; 11th Biennial Graphic Art, Ljubljana, Yugoslavia, 75; Collagraph, Univ Mont, touring, 87-93; The Stamp of Impulse, Worcester (Mass) Art Mus, 2001; Desert Mus, Palm Springs, Calif, 2003; Int Print Ctr, New York City, 2003; Cummer Mus Art and Gardens, Jacksonville, Fla, 2003; Works on Paper, Tweed Mus Art, Duluth, 2005; Abstract Expressionist Prints, Pollock-Krasner House & Study Ctr, East Hampton, NY, 2006. *Collection Arranged:* Libr Cong, Wash; Mus Mod Art, New York City; Nat Libr Med, Wash; Cleveland Mus; Whitney Mus; Philadelphia Mus; US Embassy Collections, Tokyo, London and other major cities; Victoria & Albert Mus, London; Achenbach Found for Graphic Arts; Calif Palace Legion Hon, San Francisco; Oakland Art Mus; Philadelphia Free Libr; Roanoke Art Ctr, Va; Worcester Art Mus, Mass; and others. *Pos:* Cur, Achenbach Found Graphic Arts, 58 65. *Teaching:* Prof art, San Francisco State Univ, 65-92, emer prof, 92-. *Awards:* Purchase Awards, Ultimate Concerns, Ohio Univ, Athens, 63, 25th & 26th San Francisco Art Festivals, 71 & 72 & 5th Ann Graphics Competition, De Anza Col, Cupertino, Calif, 76. *Bibliog:* Leonard Edmondson (auth), Etching, Van Nostrand, Reinhold, 73; Ross & Romano (coauth), The Complete Collagraph, MacMillian; Una Johnson (auth), American Printmakers, Doubleday. *Mem:* Calif Soc Printmakers (past chmn). *Media:* All media, Watercolor. *Specialty:* Prints. *Interests:* Videography, natural history. *Dealer:* Annex Gallery 604 College Ave Santa Rosa CA 95404. *Mailing Add:* 59 Silvia Dr Cazadero CA 95421

BEALL, JOANNA
PAINTER, SCULPTOR
b Chicago, Ill, Aug 17, 35. *Study:* Yale Sch Fine Art, with Josef Albers, 53-57; Art Inst Chicago, 57. *Comn:* Sculpture (wood), comn by B H Freidman, NY, 63. *Exhib:* Extraordinary Realities, Whitney Mus Am Art, NY, 73; Wadsworth Atheneum Group Exhib, Hartford, Conn, 73; Univ Calif Riverside Group Exhib, 73; Visions, Art Inst Chicago, 76; one-woman shows, James Corcoran Gallery, Los Angeles, 74 & Rebecca Cooper Gallery, Washington, DC, 75; Reality of Illusion, Denver Art Mus, 79, Univ Southern Calif Art Galleries, 79 & Xavier Fourcade, Inc, NY, 79 & 85; plus others. *Pos:* Practicing prof artist. *Teaching:* Vis artist, Univ Colo, Boulder, 79 & 84; Vis artist, Ogden, Utah, 84. *Bibliog:* New Talent USA, Art in Am, New York, 64; Melinda Wortz (auth), The World of Joanna Beall, Art Week, Los Angeles, 74; Dennis Adrian (auth), Visions, Art Inst Chicago, 76. *Mem:* Artists Equity. *Media:* Oil, Watercolor; Wood. *Dealer:* James Corcoran Gallery 8223 Santa Monica Blvd Los Angeles CA 90046. *Mailing Add:* 76 Warren Ave Manchester NH 03102

BEALL, KAREN FRIEDMANN
CURATOR
b Washington, DC. *Study:* Am Univ, BA, 59, grad work, 61-62; Johns Hopkins Univ, grad work, 65-66. *Collection Arranged:* Graphic Landscape, 70, Prints from Eastern Europe, 71 & The Pennell Legacy, 82-83, Libr Cong; Eloquence of the Simple: Shaker & Japanese Craft & The Day of the Dead: A Living Tradition in Mexican Folk Art, Carleton Col, 91; Warren Mackenzie and the Functional Tradition in Clay, 95; Connections: Altars and Objects of Personal Devotion, 96. *Pos:* Cur fine prints, Libr Cong, Washington, DC, 68-82; Res assoc, art hist, Carleton Col, Northfield, Minn, 82-. *Teaching:* Assoc, Kyoto Prog, Kyoto, Japan, 94. *Awards:* Res Grants, Am Philosophical Soc, 66 & 82. *Mem:* Print Coun Am; Col Art Asn; Am Asn Mus. *Res:* Specialist in American graphic arts, 20th century prints of Czechoslovakia, Poland, Yugoslavia and research in ceramics and folk crafts of Japan & Greece. *Publ:* coauth, Viewpoints, Libr Cong, 75; Spectrum of Innovation: Color In American Printmaking, Worcester Art Mus, 90; Graphic Excursions: American Prints in Black & White, Am Fed Arts, 91; Warren MacKenzie and the Functional Tradition in Clay, 95; Connections: Setars and Objects of Personal Devotion, 96; numerous articles in prof jour. *Mailing Add:* 3101 Old Pecos Trail No 610 Santa Fe NM 87505

BEALLOR, FRAN
PAINTER, PRINTMAKER
b New York, NY, Sept 27, 57. *Study:* Pvt study with August Mosca, 71-76; Antioch Col, 74-75; Brooklyn Mus Art Sch, 75-76; also with Charles Pfahl, 76-78. *Work:* PPG Indust, Pittsburgh, Pa; Bellevue Hosp, NY; Texaco Corp, NY; Fidelity Investment, Boston, Mass; Bern Israel-Deaconness Med Ctr, Boston, Mass. *Exhib:* solo exhibs, Nicholas Roerich Mus, NY, 88, Grand Cent Art Galleries, NY, 90 & William Carlos Williams Ctr Arts, Rutherford, NJ, 94, Union Co Col, Cranford, NJ, 97; Am Acad Women Artists, Desert Caballeros Mus, Ariz; group show, Coplan Gallery, Boca Raton, Fla, 98; Midegear Show, Butler Art Inst, Youngstown, Ohio, 97 & 99; Self Reflections, Pfizer, Inc, New York City, 2000. *Pos:* Workshop leader, Int Conf Art & Healing, Ibiza, Spain, 85; Painting, MFA Prog, Norwich Univ, Montpelier, Vt, 90-; guest lectr painting & printmaking, NY, NY & NJ, 93-. *Teaching:* Pvt instr painting & drawing, 78-; Instr painting, MFA Prog, Norwich Univ, Montpelier, Vt, 90-. *Awards:* John F & Anna Lee Stacey Grant, Oklahoma City, 93; Funding Grant Exhib, NJ State Coun Arts, 94; Dealers Choice Exhib (one of 13 artists chosen), Leo Castelli, John Weber & K&E Galleries, Art Initiatives, 96; Honorable Mention Award, Butler Inst Am Art, Ohio, 97. *Bibliog:* Stephen Parks (auth), Top of the line, Art Lines, Taos, NMex, 80; articles, Newsday, NY, 6-8/78, Houston Post, 7/15/84, Miami Herald, 12/7/91 & East Side Resident, New York, 11/4/93; Eunice Agar (auth), Mirror images, Am Artist Mag, 11/94. *Mem:* Artists Equity. *Media:* Oil; Etching, All Media. *Publ:* cover illus, Happy All the Time, Penguin, 85; cover, Art Calendar, 5/91; Hootenanny Ltd Ed, Lit Art J, issues, 3, 4 & 5, 95-96; cover illus, Manhattan Arts Mag, summer 96; exhib catalogue, Butler Inst, Ohio, 97. *Mailing Add:* 839 West End Ave No 6F New York NY 10025-5350

BEAM, MARY TODD
PAINTER
b Dayton, Ohio, Feb 12, 31. *Study:* Cent State Univ, 61-65; Univ Dayton, 62-63; studied with Edward Betts, Maxine Masterfield, Homer Hacker, Edgar Whitney & John Pike. *Work:* Zanesville Art Ctr, Ohio; Bank One & Bank Ohio, Cambridge; Goodyear Corp, Akron, Ohio; Dow Chemical Corp; Fisher Sch Bus, Ohio State Univ. *Comn:* Mt Carmel East Hosp, Columbus, Ohio. *Exhib:* San Diego Watercolor Soc Int Exhib, Hyde Gallery, Grossmont Col, 88; Nat Watercolor Soc Ann, Desert Mus, Muckenthaler Cult Ctr, 88; Am Watercolor Soc Ann, NY, 88, 93 & 96; Keynote Exhib, Shrines & Sacred Places, Albuquerque, NMex, 88; Ohio Watercolor Soc Ann, 89, 90, 91, 92, 93 & 94. *Pos:* Juror, Fla Watercolor Soc 28th Ann, 93, Rocky Mountain Nat Exhib, 94 & St Louis Artists Guild, 94, Watercolor Soc Ore & NC Watercolor; juror of awards, Am Watercolor Soc NY; Juror, New Mexico Watercolor Soc. *Teaching:* Instr art, Zanesville Art Ctr, 79-, experimental workshops, nat & worldwide. *Awards:* Ann Experimental Award, Nat Watercolor Soc, Fullerton, Calif, 88; Silver Medal, Ohio Watercolor Soc, 90 & 94; Gold Medal Hon, Am Watercolor Soc, 96, 2002 & Dolphin Fel; and others; Guernsey County Hall of Fame, 2003. *Bibliog:* Jacqueline Hall (auth), Exuberant paintings show both versatility, dynamics, Columbus Dispatch, 10/81; Mary Carroll Nelson (auth), Shrines & Sacred Spaces, 88; Betsy Schein Goldman (auth), Watercolor "90", Am Artist Mag, 90. *Mem:* Nat Watercolor Soc; Am Watercolor Soc; Soc Layerists Multi-Media; Ohio Watercolor Soc. *Media:* Watercolor, Acrylic. *Publ:* Maxine Masterfieldl (auth), Painting the Spirit of Nature, Marilyn Phillis, Watson-Guptill, 84; Michael Ward (auth), The New Spirit of Painting, 89 & Nita Leland (auth), The Creative Artist, North Light Publ, 90; Watermedia Techniques for Releasing the Creative Spirit (video), Fla Watercolor Soc, 93; The Rounds, Stanford Univ Med Ctr Publ; Celebrating Your Creative Self, F&W Pubs, 2001; From Trash to Treasure (video); plus others. *Dealer:* Art Exchange Columbus OH; Cricket Hollow Gallery; Contemporary Watermedia Gallery. *Mailing Add:* 125 Cricket Hollow Way Cosby TN 37722

BEAM, PATRICE K
ADMINISTRATOR, MUSEUM DIRECTOR
b Los Angeles, Calif, Aug 5, 48. *Study:* Simpson Col, Indianaola, Ind, BA, 78; Iowa State Univ, MA, 88. *Pos:* Asst dir, Davenport Mus Art, 94-96; exec dir, Octagon Ctr Arts, Ames, Iowa, 96-. *Mem:* Victorian Soc Am (v pres, 93-96). *Publ:* Ed, Hope & Glory, IA VSA, 87-93; contribr, Hope & Glory, IA VSA, 92; auth, The last Victorian fair, J West, 94. *Mailing Add:* 2940 Cottage Grove Ave Des Moines IA 50311-3909

BEAMENT, TIB (THOMAS HAROLD)
PAINTER
b Montreal, PQ, Feb 17, 41. *Study:* Fettes Col, Edinburgh, Scotland, O level cert; Ecole Beaux-Arts, Montreal, dipl; Acad Belle Arti, Rome, Italian Govt grant; Ecole Beaux-Arts, Montreal, postgrad studies & teaching cert; Sir George Williams Univ, MA(art educ); also in graphic studios of Shirly Wales, France; Richard Lacroix, Albert Dumouchel & Atelier 838, Montreal. *Work:* Tate Gallery, London; Mus Mod Art, NY; Mus Rio de Janeiro; Nat Gallery Can, Ottawa; Art Inst Chicago. *Exhib:* 4th Biennial Paris, France, 65; Int Exhib Northwest Printmakers, Seattle, Wash, 65; 1st Biennial Graphics, Crakov, Poland, 66; Int Art Fair, Basel, Switz, 74; one-man show, Switz Union Bank, Zurich, 81. *Pos:* Mem exec comt & bd dir, Greenshields Found. *Teaching:* Dir art dept, Edgars & Cramps Sch, Montreal, 66-79; lectr drawing, McGill Univ, 74-82; lectr design & drawing, Concordia Univ, 76-83. *Awards:* Quebec Govt Grant, 66 & 73; Spec Mention, Price Fine Arts Awards, 70; Elizabeth T Greenshields Found Grant, 71 & 75. *Mem:* Royal Can Acad Arts; Print & Drawing Coun Can. *Media:* Acrylic, Lithography. *Dealer:* Walter Klinkhoff Gallery 1200 Sherbrooke St W Montreal PQ Can. *Mailing Add:* RR 1 Ayers Cliff PQ J0B 1C0 Canada

BEARCE, JEANA DALE
PAINTER, PRINTMAKER
b St Louis, Mo. *Study:* St Louis Sch Fine Arts, Washington Univ, with Fred Conway, Fred Becker, Paul Burlin & George Lockwood, BFA, 51; NMex Highlands Univ, MA, 54; Independent study, Italy, France, India. *Work:* St Louis City Art Mus, Mo; Brooklyn Mus Art; Sarasota Art Asn, Fla; Calif Col Arts & Crafts, Oakland; Cornell

Univ; and others. *Comn:* Indian Sand Paint (mural), NMex Highlands Univ, Las Vegas, 54; Seven Gifts (cross), Good Shepherd Church, Brunswick, Maine, 62; Search for Truth (mural), Bowdoin Col Libr, Brunswick, Maine, 65; 14 Stations to the Cross, St Charles Borromeo, Brunswick, Maine, 75; Monumental Mary and Bartholomew, St Bartholomew's, Cape Elizabeth, Maine, 77; and others. *Exhib:* Solo exhibs, Univ Maine, 57, 65, 80, 85, 91 & 95; Print Show, Philadelphia Print Club, 58; St Peter's Church Gallery, NY, 74; India Revisited, Ctr Arts, Bath, 88; Maine to India Series, USM Environ Studies Ctr, 96; and others; The Silk Road: Rome to China and Back. *Teaching:* Instr, drawing, painting & printmaking, Univ Maine, Portland, 65-66, asst prof, 66-70, assoc prof, 70-81; prof, Univ Southern Maine, 81-. *Awards:* Purchase Prize, Sarasota Art Asn, 58; Eight Maine Artists, State of Maine, 64; Sabbatical & Research Awards, India, 80-81, 85, 88 & 93; and others. *Bibliog:* Pat Boyd Wilson (auth), Paintings of the Taj, Christian Sci Monitor, 68; Milldred Burrage (auth), Five Women Artists, Maine Art Gallery, 75. *Media:* Oil, Encaustic; Intaglio. *Dealer:* Benbow Gallery 515 Thane St Newport RI. *Mailing Add:* 327 Maine St Brunswick ME 04011

BEARD, RICHARD ELLIOTT
PAINTER, EDUCATOR
b Kenosha, Wis, June 13, 28. *Study:* Univ Wis-Madison, BS & MA; Ohio State Univ, PhD. *Work:* Ohio State Univ; Univ Ky; Defiance Col; Kankakee Comm Col; Northern Ill Univ. *Comn:* Danube-Main-Rhine mural (9 oil panels), comn by Guillermo Benavides, Laredo, Tex. *Exhib:* Chicago Artists & Vicinity, Chicago Art Inst, 77; one-man shows, Woodstock Opera Gallery, Woodstock, Ill, 88, Vane Co Art Ctr, Geneva, Ill Manhattan Ctr Gallery, NY 91, Gallery Ten, Rockford, Ill, 92 & Acad Animal Satire Series, Northern Ill Univ Mus, 92, Arts Coun, Southeast Mo, Cape Girardeau, 96 & Union Leage Club, Chicago, 99; Nat Exhib, Cooperstown Art Asn, NY, 91 & 94; 42nd Ann Spiva Competition, Joplin, Mo, 92; 10th Ann Art in the Woods, Overland Park, Kans, 93; Gallery Invitational, Chicago Expo, 93 & 94; Rockford Mus, Ill, 95; Ridge Arg Ctr, Winter Haven, Fla, 99; many others. *Teaching:* Asst prof art, Maryville Col, 52-61; asst instr art, Ohio State Univ, 61-63; vis prof art, Univ Ky, 63-64; assoc prof art, Wis State Univ, Stevens Point, 64-66; prof art, Northern Ill Univ, 66-, retired. *Awards:* Purchase Award, Larson Biennial Drawing Competition, Austin Peay State Univ, Tenn, 92; Best in Show, 36th Ann Belcit & Vicinity Exhib, Beloit Col, Wis, 93; 1st Prize, Northern Trust Jury Show, 99, 2nd Prize, 98. *Mem:* Col Art Asn; Mid Am Col Art Asn. *Media:* Oil, Acrylic, Chalk. *Publ:* Collabr, Bells of Lombardy (paintings by artist, poetry by Lucien Stryck), Northern Ill Univ Press. *Dealer:* Expression Graphics Oak Park IL; Hodgell Gallery Sarasota FL

BEARDSLEY, BARBARA H
CONSERVATOR
b New York, NY, Mar 30, 45. *Study:* Elmira Col, BA; Europ Study Prog, Univ Wis, cert; Univ NMex; State Univ NY, Cooperstown, study with Kecks, MA(conserv), cert(advan standing); study with Louis Pomerantz; McCrone Res Inst. *Comn:* Cleveland Mus Art; I Tatti, Harvard Univ, Florence, Italy; Currier Gallery, Manchester, NH; William Hayes Fogg Art Mus, Cambridge, Mass. *Collection Arranged:* Mary Lester Field Collection of Santos, Albuquerque, NMex, 70; Harwood Collection, Span Colonial Art, Taos, NMex, 71; Noyes Collection, Portland, Maine. *Pos:* Conservator, Intermus Conserv Assoc Lab, Oberlin, Ohio, 73-75; conserv intern, Newberry Libr, Chicago, 74-75; guest lectr conserv methods, State Univ NY, Cooperstown, 75-77; conservator, New Eng Coun, Am Asn Mus, six locations, 75-76; chief conservator, Art Conserv Lab Inc, 75-. *Teaching:* Univ NH. *Bibliog:* K Schaal (auth), New life for old masters, NH Profiles, 10/77; J Dueland (auth), Barbara Beardsley's barn, Christian Sci Monitor, 1/78; S Goss (auth), The Art Conservation Laboratory, NH Times, 2/82. *Mem:* Int Coun Mus; Fel Am Inst Conserv Hist & Artistic Works; Nat Conserv Adv Coun; Am Inst Conserv (dir, 76-79); Festival Arts, Waterville Valley, NH (mem, exec bd, 84); Cent for Art (co-chmn, 88-). *Res:* Polarizing pigment analysis, material studies, art history research, Spanish Colonial Santos. *Publ:* Auth, The field collection of Santos, Univ NMex Art Mus Bulletin, 70; The adaptation of an examination microscope, Am Inst Conserv Bulletin, 72; Basic Guide to a Healthy Collection, Art Conserv Lab, rev ed 76; A Flexible Back for the Stabilization of a Botticelli Panel Painting, Oxford Wood Conference, Int Inst Conserv, 78. *Mailing Add:* Dudley Homestead Raymond NH 03077

BEASLEY, BRUCE
SCULPTOR
b Los Angeles, Calif, May 20, 39. *Study:* Dartmouth Col; Univ Calif, Berkeley, BA. *Work:* Mus Mod Art & Solomon R Guggenheim Mus, NY; Los Angeles Co Mus Art; Musee d'Art Moderne, Paris, France; Nat Mus Am Art, Washingotn, DC; Oakland Mus, Calif; Kunsthalle Mannheim, Mannheim, Ger; Fine Arts Mus & Mus Mod Art, San Francisco; Seattle Art Mus, Wash; Santa Barbara Mus Art, Calif; Crocker Art Mus, Sacramento, Calif; Fresno Art Mus, Calif; Wichita Art Mus, Kans; and many more. *Comn:* metal sculpture, City of Dortmund, Ger, 96; Village of Flossmoor, Ill, 2000; Univ Ore Art Mus, 2002; Miami Univ, Oxford, Ohio, 2002; City of Oakland, 2002; La Jolla Crossroads, San Diego, Calif, 2005; City of South San Francisco, 2006. *Exhib:* City Ctr, Dortmund, Ger, 96; Sculpture Invitational, Bad Homburg, Ger, 97; 7th Int Cairo Biennale, Egypt, 98; Mathmatical Sci Res Inst, Berkeley, Calif, 2000; Gail Severn Gallery, Ketchum, Ind, 2001; Solomon Dubnick Gallery, Sacramento, Calif, 2002; 45 yr retrospective, Oakland Mus Calif, 2005. *Awards:* Andre Malraux Purchase Award, Biennale de Paris, 63; Frank Lloyd Wright Mem Purchase Award, Marin Mus Asn, 65; Purchase Prize, San Francisco Arts Festival, 67. *Bibliog:* Donald Thalacker (auth), The Place of Art in the World of Architecture, Chelsea House, 80; Thomas Albright (auth), The Art of the San Francisco Bay Area: 1945 to 1980, Berkeley Univ Calif Press, 85; Artforms, Harper Collins, 5th ed, 94. *Mem:* Int Sculpture Ctr (bd dir). *Media:* Metal, Stone. *Mailing Add:* 322 Lewis St Oakland CA 94607

BEASON, DONALD RAY
EDUCATOR, SCULPTOR
b Camden, Ark, Oct 22, 43. *Study:* Kilgore Col, 63; Stephen F Austin State Univ, BA, 65; Mich State Univ, MFA, 67. *Work:* Cult Exchange Between Italy & US, Rome; Centro Int Ceramica, Rome; Cameron Univ. *Exhib:* Drawing USA, Minn Mus Art, 71; solo exhib, San Antonio Sun Shine, San Antonio Art Inst, 82, Amarillo Sun Set, Amarillo Art Mus, 83 & Midnight Air, Tyler Mus Art, 83; East Texas Show, Tyler Mus Art, 82; Triennial 1983, New Orleans Mus, 83. *Pos:* Mem, fine arts panel, Tex Comn on the Arts, 85-. *Teaching:* Prof art, Stephen F Austin State Univ, 67-, Regents prof, 83-. *Awards:* Fulbright-Hays Fel, 72; Nat Endowment Arts Fel, 82. *Mailing Add:* Stephen F Austin Univ Art Dept Nacogdoches TX 75962

BEATTIE, ELISE MEREDITH
PAINTER, EDUCATOR
b New York City, NY, Jan 4, 58. *Study:* Skidmore Col, 1980; Bellingham Tech Col, 2000; Advan studies with Milford Zornes, Katherine Chang Liu, Glen Bradshaw, Timothy Clarke & Jean Grastorf, 1997-2005. *Work:* Easter Seals Asn, Hemlock Rehabe Ctr, Conn; Ronald McDonald House, Spokane City Bear Neccesities Fund Raiser, Wash. *Comn:* Hawaiian Sun Investments, Mr & Mrs Ron Blanset, Hilo, HI, 1998; Adich Chiropractic Ctr, Dr & Mrs Adich, Bellingham, Wash, 2002; Palma Realty, Mr & Mrs Jim Palma, Anthem, Ariz, 2004; Casitas Mont, Mr & Mrs Jugenheimer, Anthem, Ariz, 2005; Maui Lani Develop, Mr & Mrs Joe Paci, Maui, HI, 2005. *Exhib:* Fla Watercolor Nat Juried Exhib, Dundee Mus, Fla, 1999; Heart to Heart Invitational, Whatcom Mus of Art, Bellingham, Wash, 2000; Northwest Watercolor Int Exhib, Seattle Conv Ctr, Seattle, Wash, 2002; Women Who Happen to Artist, Tex A&M Univ, Tex, 2004; San Diego Int Watermedia Exhib, Showcase Gallery, San Diego, Calif, 2005; Catherine Lorillard Wolfe Nat Exhib, Nat Arts Club, NY, 2005; solo show, Short Stories from the Road Less Traveled by., Nat Asn Women Artists' Gallery, NY, 2006. *Pos:* Chairperson Exhibs, Charlotte Co Art Ctr, 1997-1998; juror, Mont Watercolor Soc Exhib, 2007. *Teaching:* Instr art, Whatcom Community Col, Wash, 2002-2003; Instr, Maricopa Community Col, Scottsdale, Ariz, 2004-2005; instr workshop, Mont Watercolor Soc. *Awards:* Elizabeth Erlanger Mem Award, Nat Asn of Women Artists (family), 2002; Grumbacher Gold Award, Mont Watercolor Soc, Grumbacher co, 2002; Merit Award, Mont Watercolor Soc, St Cuthberts Mill, 2005. *Mem:* Nat Watercolor Soc (assoc mem, 1999-); Nat Assoc of Women Artists (signature mem, 2000-); Fla Watercolor Soc (life mem, 99-); Am Watercolor Soc (assoc mem). *Media:* Watercolor: Acrylics and Mixed media including art school. *Publ:* Contrib, (art), Art Calendar Mag, Carolyn Blakeslee Proeber, 2002. *Mailing Add:* PO Box 31180 Spokane WA 99223

BEATTY, FRANCES FIELDING LEWIS
ART DEALER, CRITIC, COLLECTOR
b New York, NY, Nov 23, 48. *Study:* Vassar Col, BA; Columbia Univ, with Meyer Schapiro & Theodore Reff, MA(art hist; Noble Found Fel), PhD(Vassar Col Fel, Grant). *Pos:* Sr ed, Art-World, 76-84; vpres, Richard L Feigen & Co, currently; dir, Estate of Ray Johnson, currently. *Teaching:* Instr surrealism, Renaissance & 19th & 20th century art hist & lit, Ramapo Col, NJ, 74; instr art hist, Columbia Col, 74-76. *Mem:* The Drawing Ctr (bd dir, chmn bd). *Res:* Work of Andre Masson in the 1920s and its relation to surrealist poetry and prose. *Interests:* Renaissance Medalo, 16th - 20th century, prints and drawings; Contemporary photography. *Publ:* Contribr, Andre Masson (catalog), Mus Mod Art, New York, 76; contribr, Richard Smith (catalog), R L Feigen & Co, NY, 92; introduction, Pierre Roy (catalog), R L Feigen & Co, NY, 93; contribr, Ray Johnson: A Memorial Exhibition (catalog), R L Feigen & Co, NY, 95; co-producer (documentary), How to Draw a Bunny, Ray Johnson, Beckman & Picasso. *Mailing Add:* c/o Richard L Feigen & Co 34 E 69th St New York NY 10021

BEAUDOIN, ANDRE EUGENE
PRESS MANUFACTURER, PHOTOGRAPHER
b Calais, France, Apr 11, 20; US citizen. *Study:* Ecole des Arts de Metiers, Paris, France, machine design & metallurgy; Brown Univ, photog. *Pos:* Owner, designer & constructor of etching & lithographic presses for artist printmakers, Am-French Tool Co, 69-. *Mailing Add:* PO Box 227 Coventry RI 02816

BEAUMONT, MONA
PAINTER, GRAPHIC ARTIST
b Paris, France; US citizen. *Study:* Univ Calif, Berkeley, BA & MA; grad study, Fogg Mus, Harvard Univ, Cambridge, Mass; spec study with Hans Hoffman, NY. *Work:* Oakland Mus Art, Calif; City & Co San Francisco; Hoover Found; Bulart Found, San Francisco. *Exhib:* San Francisco Art Inst, 58, 62-66 & 74, traveling exhib, 64 & 65; Calif Painters & Sculptors, Univ Calif, Los Angeles, 59; Regional Painters, De Young Mem Mus Art, San Francisco, 62; one-person shows, Calif Palace of Legion of Honor, San Francisco, 64, San Francisco Mus Art, 68 & Palo Alto Cult Ctr, Calif, 77; San Francisco Gallery Artists, Stanford Univ Art Mus, 66; Print & Drawing Ann, Richmond Art Ctr, Va, 68; Bell Tel Print-Drawing, Chicago, 69; L'Armitire Gallery, Rouen, France, 72; Honolulu Acad Art, Hawaii, 80; Int Biennial Contemp Art, 98; Trevi Flash Art Mus, Italy; Venice Mask 2 Exhib, Italy, 99; Int Florence Biennale III, Florence, Italy, 2001; plus others. *Awards:* Purchase Award, US Artists Tour of Asia, Grey Found, 63; Purchase & One-Person Show Awards, San Francisco Art Festival Ann, 66 & 75; Ackerman Award, San Francisco Woman Artists Ann, 68; Silver Medal Mask 2 Exhibit, Venice, Italy, 99. *Bibliog:* Andrew De Shong (auth), Works on Paper--San Francisco Art Inst, Art Week Mag, 11/74; Thomas Albright (auth), Art in the San Francisco Bay Area, 85. *Mem:* Arch Am Art; Soc Encouragement Contemp Art. *Media:* Acrylic, Mixed. *Publ:* Contribr, articles in Artforum, 5/64 & 12/64; Frankenstein, San Francisco Chronicle, 66 & 67. *Mailing Add:* 11785 River Rim Rd San Diego CA 92126

BECHTLE, C RONALD
PAINTER, DRAFTSMAN
b Philadelphia, Pa, Nov 14, 24. *Study:* ETenn Univ; Tyler Sch Fine Arts, Temple Univ; Fleisher Mem, Sch Indust Art; also with Benton Spruance, 52-53. *Work:* Munson-Williams-Proctor Inst, Utica, NY; Carnegie Inst Mus Art; Santa Barbara Mus Art, Calif; Columbus Gallery Fine Art, Ohio; Nat Mus Am Art, Washington, DC; Philadelphia Mus Art; Pa Acad Fine Arts; Amherst Col; Akron Art Mus; Butler Inst Am Art, Ohio; San Diego Gallery Fine Arts; many others. *Exhib:* Pa Acad Fine Arts Regional, 65 & 69; one-man shows, Panoras Gallery, NY 1966, Santa Barbara Mus Art, 1967, Miami Mus Mod Art, Fla, 1968 & Philadelphia Art Alliance, 1973, Storelli Gallery, 1974 & E Tenn Univ, 1977, Red Door Gallery, Philadelphia, Fleisher Memorial, Philadelphia, Hugo Storelli Gallery, Philadelphia, others. *Pos:* Pres, Group 55, 56-57; pres, Philadelphia Abstract Artists, 57-63. *Mem:* Am Fedn Arts; Col Art Asn Am. *Media:* Watercolor, Gouache; Crayon, Pencil. *Publ:* Auth, Information theory of art, Mensa J, 61. *Mailing Add:* 26 Strawberry Hill Ave Apt 12B Stamford CT 06902

BECHTLE, ROBERT ALAN
PAINTER
b San Francisco, Calif, May 14, 1932. *Study:* Calif Col Arts & Crafts, BA, 54 & MFA, 58; Univ Calif, Berkeley, 61. *Work:* Whitney Mus Am Art, Mus Mod Art & Guggenheim Mus, NY; San Francisco Mus Art; Metrop Mus Mod Art, NY. *Exhib:* Image, Form & Color: Recent Paintings by 11 Americans, Toledo Mus of Art, Ohio, 75; Aspects of Realism-Du Realisme, Rothmans of Can Ltd, Montreal, 76-77; Illusion & Reality, Australian Gallery Dirs Coun, 77-78; Representations of Am, Pushkin Fine Arts Mus, Moscow, USSR, 78; Contemp Am Realism since 1960, Pa Acad Fine Arts, Philadelphia, 81; Am Realism: The Precise Image, Inetan Mus, Tokyo, Japan, 85; Robert Bechtle: New Work, San Francisco Mus Mod Art, 91; Invitational Exhib Painting & Sculpture, Am Acad Arts & Letters, 95; and many others. *Teaching:* Prof printmaking, Calif Col Arts & Crafts, 57-85; vis artist, Univ Calif, Davis, 66-68; prof art, San Francisco State Univ, 68-76, prof, 76-99, prof emeritus, 99-. *Awards:* Nat Endowment Arts Grant, 77, 82 & 89; Guggenheim Fel, 83, 86; Nat Acad, Nat Acad Design, 93; Acad award Am Acad Arts and Letters, 95. *Bibliog:* G Battcock (auth), Super Realism, A Critical Anthology, Dutton, 75; L Meisel (auth), Photo Realism, Abrams, 80; R Kalina (auth), Painting Snapshots or the Cursory Spectacle, Art in Am, 6/93; C Lindey (auth), Superrealist Painting and Sculpture, William Morrow & Co, 80; and others. *Mem:* Nat Acad Design (assoc, 93, acad, 94). *Media:* Oil, Watercolor. *Dealer:* O K Harris Gallery 383 W Broadway New York NY 10012. *Mailing Add:* c/o Ro Gallery 47-15 36th St Long Island City NY 11101

BECK, DOREEN
WRITER, PRODUCER
b Medomsley, Co Durham, Eng; US & UK citizen. *Study:* Leicester Univ Col, Univ London, BA(hons) in French, 57; NY Univ, film prod; NY Sch Visual Arts, screen writing with Andrew Sarris. *Work:* Symbols of Hope, UN Hdqrs, NY, 91; Plant Man-Madison Ave in Spring, 85; Brownstone Painters, 84; Dining, 2000; Band, 2001; Digging, 2002; July 4th, 14th, etc (latchhook), 77; numerous others. *Comn:* The Sound (quilted, applique wall hanging), Pvt collector, 86. *Exhib:* Quilts & Illustrations, A Husband & Wife Exhib, Soc Illustr, NY, 89; Tactile Archit Exhib, Dectur Carriage House, Washington, 92; Brownstone Painters, 93. *Pos:* Writer & producer AV mat, UN; researcher & writer, Med Newsmag; research, ed & writing, BBC, World Bk Enc (int ed), The Observer, Thames & Hudson, Julian Press, Ved Mehta & New Yorker; free-lance fabric artist. *Awards:* Industrial Design Excellence Award, Human Well Being Exhib, 94-95. *Bibliog:* From Pen & Paper to Glorious Quilts, Creative Quilting Mag, 90; The Artful Home, Guild Sourcebook and Online Commission Ctr, 2003. *Interests:* cello, tennis. *Publ:* Auth, Country & Western Americana, 75; auth & producer, exhibs and related photo books on Visitors Tour Route at UN hq, and in the Public Lobby New York; Common Threads: Indigenous People & The Modern World, 93; A New Agenda for Human Development, 94; and others; auth, Book of American Furniture, 73; auth, Book of Bottle Collecting, 73. *Mailing Add:* 100 W 57th St New York NY 10019

BECK, LONNIE LEE
PAINTER, EDUCATOR
b Marion, Ind, Jan 6, 42. *Study:* Herron Sch Art, Ind Univ, BFA(advan design), 65, BFA(painting), 67; Miami Univ, MFA(painting), 69. *Work:* Herron Sch Art, Ind Univ, Indianapolis. *Exhib:* Indianapolis Mus Art, 68 & 69; Owensboro Mus Fine Arts, Ky, 80; Evansville Mus Art & Sci, Ind, 80; Appalachian State Univ, Boone, NC, 80; Okla Art Ctr, Oklahoma City, 81; Ball State Univ, Muncie, Ind, 82; and many others. *Collection Arranged:* Robert Berkshire Paintings, 75, Rockwell Kent (coauth, catalog), 79, Dean Howell Sculpture, 80, Terrance LaNoue, Jim Sullivan & Frank Owens Paintings, 81 & Dennis Puhalla Paintings, 82, Hiestand Gallery, Miami Univ. *Awards:* Best Show Painting, 500 Festival Arts Comn, 67; Purchase Award, Del Mar Col, 75; Purchase Award, Ball State Univ, 82. *Media:* Oil, Charcoal

BECK, MARTHA ANN
MUSEUM DIRECTOR, CURATOR
b Cleveland, Ohio, June 16, 1938. *Study:* Vassar Col, BA, 60; NY Univ Inst Fine Arts, studied under Erwin Panofsky, 63-67. *Collection Arranged:* The Drawings of Antonio Gaudi, 77; The Travel Sketches of Louis I Kahn, 78; Musical Manuscripts, 78-79; Visionary Drawings of Architecture and Planning, 79; Sculptors' Drawings over Six Centuries, 81; Reading Drawings, A Selection from the Victoria and Albert Mus, 84; Great Drawings from the Royal Institute of British Architects, 83; Drawings from Venice, Masterworks from the Museo Correr, 85; The Northern Landscape: Flemish, Dutch and British Drawings from the Courtauld Collections, 86; Creative Copies: Interpretative Drawings from Michelangelo to Picasso, 88; Inigo Jones: Complete Architectural Drawings, 89; Theatre on Paper-Alexander Schouvaloff, 90. *Pos:* Curatorial asst, Mus Mod Art, New York, 68-75; dir, The Drawing Ctr, 75-90, dir emeritus, 90-; dir, Ctr Int Exhibs Inc, New York, 91-. *Publ:* Coauth, New Drawing in America, The Drawing Ctr, 82; auth, North by Northwest: Hitchcock & Hamlet. *Mailing Add:* 9 Gramercy Park S New York NY 10003

BECK, ROBERT
SCULPTOR, VIDEO ARTIST
b Towson, Md, Dec 9, 59. *Study:* NY Univ, BFA, 83. *Work:* Whitney Mus Am Art, NY; Mus Modern Art, NY; Art Gallery Ont, Toronto, Can; J Paul Getty Mus Art, Los Angeles; Long Beach Mus Art, Calif. *Exhib:* Hindsight: Recent Work from the Permanent Collection, Whitney Mus Am Art, NY, 99. *Teaching:* instr video, Sch Visual Arts, 96-; instr theory and art, Mason Gross Sch Art, Rutgers Univ, 99. *Awards:* Grantee NY Found Art, 95; Grantee Art Matters, Inc, 95; Grantee Louis Comfort Tiffany Found, 99. *Bibliog:* Susanne Leeb (auth), Des einen frued, des anderen leid, Texte zur Kunst, 2000. *Media:* All Media. *Dealer:* CRG Gallery 535 W 22 St New York NY 10011. *Mailing Add:* 304 W 21 St #5A New York NY 10011

BECK, THERESA
PAINTER
b Norfolk, Va, Dec 1, 53. *Study:* Old Dominion Univ, BFA, 75, Northern Ill Univ, MA (painting), 79. *Work:* St Joseph's Hosp & Holland & Knight, Attys, Tampa, Fla; IDS, Chaska, Minn. *Comn:* First Fla Bank, 11/89. *Exhib:* One-woman shows, Fla Gulf Coast Art Ctr Teaching Gallery, Bellair, Fla, 86, Tampa Elec Co, Fla, 87, Osceola Ctr Arts, Kissimmee, Fla, 90; First Fla Bank, Tampa, 89; Beck-Taylor-Edelson-Lurie, Polk Community Col, Winter Haven, Fla, 89; Beck-Hott-Rensel-Smith, Thompson Land Group Property, Ybor City, Tampa, Fla, 92; Mus African-Am Art, 95; Gorilla Theatre, 2000, 01, 05; Stageworks, 2003. *Teaching:* Instr drawing, Renton Parks & Recreation Dept, Wash, 80-81; instr airbrush painting, Cape Coral Art Studio, Fla 84-85, Fla Gulf Coast Art Ctr, Belleair, 86-87, Old Hyde Park Art Ctr, Tampa, Fla, 89-90 & Beach Park Sch, 95-02. *Awards:* Fel, Nat Endowment Arts, 87. *Mem:* Woman's Caucus Art, Fla West Coast Chap (vpres & treas, 87-89); Fla Ctr Contemp Art (exhib comt, 90-91); Arts & Crafts Community Educ Serv (bd mem, 96). *Media:* Acrylic Painting, Muralist. *Interests:* theater scenery, faux finishes, interior design. *Publ:* Art Papers, Photog Installation, Vol 12, No 6, Atlanta, Ga, 11/88; NAAO Directory, Photog Installation, Nat Asn Arts Orgns, 90; Arts News, Illus, Newsletter Arts Coun Hillsborough Co, summer 90; Organica Quarterly, Illus, Vol 11, No 39, spring 92; Tampa Tribune, 95, 2000; St Petersburg Times, 95; Weekly Planet, 98. *Dealer:* The Old Printshop 150 Lexington Ave New York NY 10016. *Mailing Add:* 4606 El Prado Blvd Tampa FL 33629

BECK, URSULA
EDUCATOR
Pos: Founder & Dir, Taos Art Sch, New Mex. *Mailing Add:* Taos Art Sch PO Box 2588 Taos NM 87571

BECKER, DAVID
PAINTER, EDUCATOR
b Milwaukee, Wis, Aug 16, 37. *Study:* Univ Wis-Milwaukee, BS, 61; Univ Ill, Urbana, MFA, 65. *Work:* Libr Cong, Washington, DC; Brooklyn Mus, NY; Mus de Arte Mod, Cali, Colombia; Art Inst Chicago; Detroit Inst Arts, Mich; Nat Mus Am Art, Washington, DC; Portland Art Mus, Ore. *Comn:* Print, Detroit Inst Art Drawing & Print Club, 83. *Exhib:* 30 Yrs of Am Printmaking, Brooklyn Mus, NY, 76; Nat Acad Design Ann Exhib, 87 & 90-94; solo exhib, Jane Haslem Gallery, Washington, DC, 90; Sapporo Int Print Biennale, Sapporo, Japan, 93; First Int Print Biennal Maastright, The Neth, 93; Integrafia, Katowice, Poland, 94; and others; outside Art Fair, New York City, 2002, Arch Chicago, Navy Pier, 2002-03. *Teaching:* Prof art, Wayne State Univ, Detroit, Mich, 65-85; vis prof printmaking, Univ Wis-Madison, 78-79; vis artist, Utah State Univ, Logan, summer 81; prof art, Univ Wis-Madison, 85-87, prof 87-. *Awards:* Cannon Prize, 165th & 168th Ann, 90 & 93; Sponsors Prize, Sapporo Int Print Biennale, Japan, 93; Nat Endowment Arts Visual Artists Fel, 93-94. *Bibliog:* James Watrous (auth), A Century of American Printmaking, Univ Wis Press, 84; John Ross, Clare Romano & Tim Ross (coauths), The Complete Printmaker, Free Press, 89; Warrington Colescott & Arthur Hove (coauth), Progressive Printmakers: Wisconsin Artists and The Print Renaissance, Univ Wisc Press, 99. *Mem:* Nat Acad Design (assoc, 83, acad, 91); fel, MacDowell Colony. *Media:* Oil, Charcoal Drawing. *Dealer:* Ann Nathan Gallery 218 W Superior St Chicago Ill 60610. *Mailing Add:* 2512 Lunde Lane Mount Horeb WI 53572

BECKER, JOHANNA LUCILLE
HISTORIAN, CERAMIST
b Denver, Colo, Dec 17, 21. *Study:* Univ Colo, BFA, 43; Ohio State Univ, MA, 45; Univ Mich, MA, 67, PhD, 74. *Pos:* Cur, permanent collection, Col St Benedict, 81-84. *Teaching:* Chmn dept art, Mayville Col, St Louis, Mo, 45-46; instr studio art & hist, Ill State Univ, Bloomington, 47-48; chmn & prof studio art & hist, Col St Benedict, St Joseph, & St John's Univ, Collegeville, Minn, 57-2001, emer prof, 2001-, chmn art dept, 83-85, 87-90; adj lectr, Dept Art Hist, Univ St Thomas, St Paul, Minn, 95. *Awards:* Fulbright Fel, (res India), US Govt, 63; Am Asn Univ Women Fel (res Japan), 69; Metrop Ctr Far Eastern Studies, Kyoto, Japan, 84. *Mem:* Minneapolis Inst Art, Asian Art (bd dir & acquisitions). *Media:* Ceramics. *Res:* Ceramics; prehistoric through the 17th century Asian ceramics; 17th & 18th century Japanese ceramics. *Publ:* Auth, Karatsu Ceramics of Japan: Origins, Fabrication and Types, Vol I & II, Microfilms, 74; Chinese art under the Mongols: Ceramics and Yuan aesthetics, J Asiatic Soc Japan, 75; Der Karatsu stil und Koreanishe einflusse, Keramos, Rasch Druckerei & Co, Bramsche, 79; Japanese export porcelain at the Princessesdorf, Oriental Art Mag Ltd, London, 82; Karatsu Ware, Kodansha Int, New York & Tokyo, 86. *Mailing Add:* Monastery of St Benedict Saint Joseph MN 56374-0277

BECKER, NATALIE ROSE
PAINTER, INSTRUCTOR
b Philadelphia, Pa. *Study:* Fleisher Art Mem, Philadelphia; Temple Univ, AA; Pa Acad Fine Arts; Art Students League, with Robert Phillip & Henry Gasser. *Work:* Fine Arts Galleries, Carnegie Inst; Bloomfield Col; Slide Photo Archives-Juley Collection, Smithsonian Inst, Nat Mus Am Art. *Exhib:* Audubon Artists Am, 1973-2004; Allied Artists Am, 1974-2004; Nat Arts Club Invitational, 78; Bergen Mus Invitational, 80; Audubon Artists, 1973-2005; Allied Artists, 1974-2005; Butler Inst Am Art, 2001; Attleboro Mus, 2002. *Teaching:* Instr drawing, Union Col, Cranford, NJ. *Awards:* First Prize & Medal of Honor, Audubon Artists Ann Exhib, 80; Katherine Lowell Mem Award, Allied Artists Am Ann Exhib, 95; Pen & Brush Award, 2000; Paul Puzinas Mem Award, Allied Artists Am Ann Exhib, 2000; Len Everett Mem Award, Audubon Artists Ann Exhib, 2001. *Mem:* Audubon Artists (bd mem); Allied Artist Am, (dir oil); Pen & Brush Club; Catharine Lorillard Wolfe Art Club; Nat Asn Women Artists; Fedn Mod Painters & Sculptors. *Media:* Oil, Pen & Ink. *Interests:* Painting on location. *Publ:* Auth, The Best of Oil Painting, 96 & Floral Inspirations, 97, Rockport Publ. *Mailing Add:* 97 Barchester Way Westfield NJ 07090

BECKERMAN, NANCY GREYSON
PAINTER, CRAFTSMAN, STUDIO ART QUILTER
b New York, NY. *Study:* Cornell Univ, 60-62; Hunter Col, BA(magna cum laude & phi beta kappa), 62-64; NY Univ, 65; Boston Univ, 65. *Work:* ABC Collection, NY; numerous pvt collections. *Exhib:* Painted Surfaces, Albany Inst Hist & Art, NY, 86; Out of Time, Art Quilts, San Jose Mus of Textiles, 2000; Threads That Bind, Grants Pass Mus Art, 02; SAQA Invitational Art Quilts, Manhattanville Coll, NY, 02; Quilts for Change, Cincinnati, Ohio, 04; Changing Definitions: The Art Quilt, SAQA Ark Art Ctr, 04; Far Out Fiber, Grants Pass Mus Art, 05. *Awards:* Marion deSola Mendes Mem Award, 79; Juror's Prize, Washington & Jefferson Painting Exhib, 81; First Prize in Contemporary, Pa Nat Quilt Extravaganza, 94. *Bibliog:* Rev, La Revue Moderne, Paris, 80; Robin Bergstrom (dir), Meet the VIP's: Nancy Beckerman, WVIP (radio, cable-tv), 83; Lauren Otis (auth), A powerful presence of women, Artspeak, 86. *Mem:* Nat Asn Women Artists; Artists Equity NY; Studio Art Quilt Assocs; Women in the Arts. *Media:* Acrylic on Canvas; Fabric. *Mailing Add:* 26 White Birch Rd Pound Ridge NY 10576

BECKHARD, ELLIE (ELEANOR)
PAINTER, PHOTOGRAPHER
b Brooklyn, NY. *Study:* Brooklyn Col, 47-51; studied Hans Hoffman Technique with Shirley Gorelick (student of Hoffman) & studied with Leo Manso & Jerry Okimoto, 78. *Exhib:* Silvermine juried show, Silvermine Mus, New Canaan, Conn, 78; 157th Ann, Nat Acad Design, NY, 82; Long Island Invitational, 83 & juried show, 83 & 89, Islip Mus, NY; Fine Arts juried shows, Fine Arts Mus Long Island, Hempstead, NY, 83, 85, 88, 89 & 91; The Expert Eye, Coun Arts N Shore, Glen Cove, NY, 84; Showcase of Excellence III Invitational, Midge Karr Art Ctr, Brookville, NY, 89. *Awards:* Award, Parsons: Leland Bell & Jane Freilicker, 81 & Award Merit, G McCarthy & Irving Sandler, 87 Huntington Township Art League at Heckscher Mus; Ziuta & Joseph Akston Found Award, Nat Asn Women Artists, 86. *Bibliog:* Helen Harrison (auth), Debut of a museum series, 10/83 & Unusual energy mark juried show, 4/87, NY Times; Karin Lipson (auth), Showcase 100 artists, 4/87 & Four gallery exhibition, 6/87, News Day. *Mem:* Nat Asn Women Artists; Huntington Township Art League. *Media:* Acrylic, Pastel. *Publ:* Contribr, Contract Interiors (cover), Donald J Carroll, 9/77; Process Architecture: The Legacy of Marcel Breuer, no 32, p 5, Bunji Murotani, 82; NY Times: Home, section C1, 7/23/81. *Mailing Add:* Red Springs Rd Glen Cove NY 11542

BECKLEY, BILL
POST-CONCEPTUAL ARTIST
b Hamburg, Pa, Feb 11, 46. *Study:* Kutztown State Col, Pa, BFA, 68; Tyler Sch Art, Temple Univ, with Steven Greene & Italo Scanga, MFA, 70. *Exhib:* Stuttgardt Stadt Mus, Ger; Whitney Bienniel Exhib, NY, 79; Morton Neuman Collection, Chicago Art Inst & Los Angeles Co Mus, 79; Image & Text, Chicago Art Inst, 79; Photog Art, Mus Mod Art, Paris, 80; Large Scale Photog, Los Angeles Co Mus, Calif, 88; Image World Art & Media Cult, Whitney Mus Am Art, NY, 89; one-man exhibs, Drawings, Ace Contemp Exhibs, Los Angeles, 91, Pasquale Trisorio Gallery, Naples, 92, Galeria Pedro Oilivera, Porto, 93, Found Chateau de Jau, 94, Hans Mayer, Dusseldorf, 94 & 98 & Anouk Tache & Carole Levy Gallery, Brussels, 99; The Seventies, John Gibson Gallery, 92; Collection of Vicky Remy, Musee d'Art Mod, St Etienne, France, 93; Conceptual Photographs, John Gibson Gallery, 94; Ace Gallery, NY, 95; Ace Gallery, Los Angeles, 96; John Gibson Gallery, NY, 97, 2000; Documenta, 76; Venice Bienniel, 75; Galleria Bilona, 98; Hans Mayer, 98. *Pos:* ed dir, Atlanta Press. *Teaching:* Instr, Sch Visual Arts, 71-. *Awards:* Nat Endowment, 79; Pollard Krasser Found, 96. *Bibliog:* Hervé Gauville (auth), Les acides mesalliances de Beckley, Liberation, Paris, 8/20/94; Exporama, Art Press, No 194, Paris, 9/94; David Shapiro (auth), Bill Beckley: The Art of Liberty 1969-1994 (catalog, essay), Galerie Hans Mayer Dusseldorf & Chateau de Jau, 94; and others. *Media:* Color Photographs. *Specialty:* Conceptual Art. *Publ:* Auth, Pink I think, Art Press, 3/95; The road to Ra, Lingo, 5/96; ed, Uncontrollable Beauty; ed, Sticky Sublime. *Dealer:* John Gibson Gallery 568 Broadway New York NY 10012; Ace Gallery 5541 Wilshire Blvd Los Angeles CA 40036 & New York NY. *Mailing Add:* 155 Wooster St New York NY 10012

BECKMAN, ERICKA
FILMMAKER, PHOTOGRAPHER
b Hempstead, NY, July 7, 51. *Study:* Wash Univ, BFA, 74; Whitney Independent Study Prog, 75; Calif Inst Arts, MFA, 76. *Work:* Inst Contemp Art, London; Am Fedn Arts, NY. *Comn:* DVD, The Walter Art Center, Minneapolis. *Exhib:* Pictures Today, Padligione D'Artes Contemp, Milan, Italy, 80; Whitney Mus Biennial, 83, 85, 89 & 91; Film Screening Cindrella, Walker Art Inst, Minneapolis, Minn, 86; Coeur du Malstrom, Palais Des Beaux Arts, Brussels, 86; Mus Mod Art, Bern, Switz, 92; Mus Mod Art, NY, 93; Wexner Ctr Art, Columbus, Ohio, 94; Gender and Technology, Wexner Ctr Arts, Columbus, Ohio, 95; Cinderella (16mm)-Here and Now Exhib, La Mus Mod Art, 96; Film Retrospective (with catalog), Viper Festival, Lucerne, Switz, 98; We Imitate: We Break-Up (8mm), Big as Life Show, Mus Mod Art, NY, 98; Hiatus (16mm, 40 mins), World Premier, Rotterdam Film Festival, 99; and others; Switch Center, Views from the Avant Garde, NY Film Festival, 2002; Switch Center, Media Scope, MOMA at Gramercy Park Theater, NY, 2003. *Teaching:* asst prof film, Mass Col Art, 83-. *Awards:* Grants, NY State Coun Arts, 88, Jerome Found, 81 & 83 & Nat Endowment Arts, 83 & 94; CAPS Film Grant, Jerome Found Grant, 83; Artist Fel Prog Film Award, NY Found Arts, 87; Experimental Television Ctr projects grant, 99; ArtsLink Collaborative Projects grant, 99; Creative Contact Grant, Harvest Works, NY, 2000. *Bibliog:* J Hoberman (auth), article, 81 & Carrie Rickey (auth), article, 83, Art Forum; Sally Banes (auth), Films by Ericka Beckman, Millenium Film J, 83; J Hoberman (auth), Avant to Live, Village Voice, 6/18/87, Bernice Reynaud (auth), Erika Beckman-Independent America New Film (catalog essay), Am Mus Moving Image, Astoria, Queens, 88. *Publ:* Auth, Chances territory, Effects Mag, 83; The turn-about, Wedge Mag, 83; illusr, The Journal, LAICA, Los Angeles, Calif, 1/85; auth, Polities, Desire & Everyday Life, New Observations, No 45, 87; auth & photogr, The Beanstalk and Jack, Hallwalls Books, Buffalo, NY, 88. *Mailing Add:* 358 Broadway New York NY 10013

BECKMANN, ROBERT OWEN
PAINTER, MURALIST
b Philadelphia, Pa, Mar 20, 1942. *Study:* Col Wooster, BA, 64; Univ Iowa, with Byron Burford, David Proctor, Herbert Katzman, MA, 66, MFA, 67. *Work:* Denver Art Mus, Colo; Amarillo Mus Art, Tex; Bank of Am, Las Vegas; Ringling Sch Art & Design, Sarasota, Fla; plus others. *Comn:* Symbiosis, Friends of Contemp Art, Denver, 72; murals, Lynn Co Courthouse, Las Vegas & Clark Co, Nev, 76-80. *Exhib:* Monumental Propaganda World Financial Ctr, NY, 93; Inst Contemp Art, Moscow, 93; Int Gallery, Smithsonian Inst, Washington, DC, 95; Dunlop Gallery, Regina Pub Libr, Saskatchewan, Can, 95; Contemp Art Mus, Estonia, 95; Lubiljana, Slovenia, 95; Yale Univ Art Gallery, 95; Terrain Gallery, San Francisco, 96 & 97; Bass Mus Art, Miami Beach, Fla, 96; Lenin Mus, Finland, 97; Uppsala Konstmuseum, Sweden, 97; one-man shows, Univ Ala, Tuscaloosa, 97, Bellevue Art Mus, Wash, 97, Ringling Sch Art & Design, Sarasota, Fla, 97, Bowling Green Univ, Ohio, 97 & Sam Francis Gallery, Cross Roads Sch, Santa Monica, Calif, 98; Donna Beam Gallery, Univ Nev, 98; State Mus, The Artists Necropolis, St Petersburg, Russia; plus others. *Pos:* Artist, Beckmann Studio, Denver, 71-77 & 92-; pres, Wallternatives Inc, Las Vegas, 79-92. *Teaching:* Instr studio art, Univ Southern Ala, 67-68; instr life drawing, Northern Ill Univ, Dekalb, 68-71; instr art hist, Kendall Col, summer 69; instr art, Univ Nev, Las Vegas, 77-78. *Awards:* Laura Slobe Mem Prize, Art Inst Chicago, 71; Western States Arts Found Fel, 76; Gov Award, State of Nev, 96. *Bibliog:* Patricia Raymer (auth), Climb aboard the Artrain, Am Educ, 12/73; Duncan Pollock (auth), rev in arts now, Rocky Mountain News, Denver, 9/22/74; Jean Morrison (auth), Project murals, Nevadan, 4/24/77; William L Fox (auth) Mapping the Empty, Univ Nev Press, Reno, 99; Scott Dickensheets (auth) Vegas sublime, Las Vegas Life, 7/2000; plus numerous others. *Media:* Latex, Acrylic

BECKNER, JOY KROEGER
SCULPTOR
b St. Louis, MO, Dec 17, 44. *Study:* Washington Univ Sch of Fine Art (H Rich Duhme), 1962-1964; Fontbonne Univ (Rudi Torrini, 1990; Independent workshops (Tuck Langland, Eugene Daub). *Work:* Ella Carothers Dunnegan Gallery of Art, Bolivar, Mo; Galleries of the Libr of Hattiesburg, Miss; Am Kennel Club Mus of the Dog, St. Louis, Mo; Nat Cosmetology Asn, Chicago, Ill; Matrix Essentials, Solon, Ohio. *Comn:* Fourteen Bronze Bas Relief Portraits, Nat Cosmetology Asn, Chicago, Ill, 1993-1997; Cullen portrait bronze head, Gloria Bahn, Chesterfield, Mo, 2004; Pals, two dog bronze composition, Dr Dennis Birenbaum, Dallas, Tex, 2006; Dear to my Heart, pin & pendant, Lovaine Coxon, Eng, 2006. *Exhib:* Soc of Animal Artists, Nat Mus Tour, 1999-2001, 2003-2006; The Garden of Eden, Memphis Botanic Garden, Sculpture Works, Memphis, Tenn, 2001; Soc of Animal Artists 2000 Encore, Nat Geographic Mus, Washington, DC, 2002; Animals in Art, Miami Metro Zoo, Miami, Fla, 2004; Night of Artists, Nat Western Art Found, San Antonio, Tex, 2005-2006; Masters in Miniature, CM Russell Mus, Great Falls, Mont, 2006; American Art in Miniature, Gilcrease Mus, Tulsa, Okla, 2006; 21st Ann Conservatory Art Classic, Bosque Conservatory, Clifton, Tex, 2006. *Collection Arranged:* co-cur, It's Reigning Cats & Dogs, St Louis Artists Guild, Mo, 2001. *Teaching:* Instr, dog sculpture (workshop), Loveland Acad, Loveland, Colorado, 2001. *Awards:* Silver Medal, John Cavanaugh Prize, Nat Sculpture Soc, 99; Awards Excellence, Soc Animal Artists, 99 & 2003; Lindsey Morris Prize, Allied Artists 88th Ann Exhib, 2001; Am Artists Fund Award, 74th Nat Exhib, Am Artists Prof League, 2002; Polich Art Works Foundry Prize, Nat Sculpture Soc, 2003; Best Animal Sculpture, Viselaya Sculpture Competition, 2003; C Percival Dietsch Prize, Nat Sculpture Soc, 2005; and many others. *Bibliog:* William Secord (auth), A Breed Apart: The Collections of the Am Kennel Club Mus, 2001; Cindy Billhartz (auth), Dachshunds of Bronze, St Louis Post Dispatch, 2004; Jim Schugal (auth), Dog Gone Good Artist, KSDK Channel 5, 2006. *Mem:* Am Women Artists (secy, treas), 2006-; Soc of Animal Artists; Allied Artists of Am; Catharine Lorillard Wolfe Art Club; Nat Sculpture Soc (assoc). *Media:* Metal, Cast; Metal, Precious. *Dealer:* Cavalier Galleries 405 Greenwich Ave Greenwich CT 06830; Bottoms Art Galleries Santa Barbara & Montecito Calif; Chaparral Fine Art 24 W Main Boseman Mont. *Mailing Add:* 15268 Kingsman Cir Chesterfield MO 63017-7412

BEDIA, JOSE
PAINTER, SCULPTOR
b Havana, Cuba, 59; US citizen. *Study:* Sch Art San Alejandro, MA, 76; Super Inst Art, Havanna, BA, 81. *Work:* Hirshhorn Mus & Sculpture Garden, Washington, DC; Ludwig Collection, Ger; Philadelphia Mus Art; Phoenix Art Mus; Whitney Mus Am Art, NY. *Exhib:* Latin Am Artists of the 20th Century, Mus Mod Art, NY, 92-93; Jose Bedia: De Donde Vengo, Inst Contemp Art, Philadelphia, 94-95; Mi Esencialismo (with catalog), Hyde Gallery, Trinity Col, Dublin, Ireland, 95 & Pori Art Mus, Finland, 96 & George Adams Gallery, NY; Cuba Siglo XX: Modernidad y Sincretismo, Centro Atlantico Moderno, Grand Canary Island, 96 & Centre d'Art Santa Monica, Barcelona, Spain, 96; Jose Bedia: The Island, the Hunter & the Prey, Site Santa Fe, NMex, 97; Cronicas Americanas: Obra de Jose Bedia (with catalog), Mus Contemp Art, Monterrey, Mex, 97-98; 20/21: Jose Bedia, Joslyn Art Mus, Omaha, 98; and many others. *Awards:* Gran Premio del Salon del Paisaje, Havana, 82; Premio de la Segunda Bienal de la Habana, 86; Guggenheim Mem Found Int Fel, 94. *Bibliog:* Several articles and reviews in New York Times, Art Nexus, Art in Am, ARTnews, Arts Mag and many others. *Mailing Add:* c/o George Adams Gallery 41 W 57th St 7th Fl New York NY 10019

BEDRICK, JEFFREY K
PAINTER, ILLUSTRATOR
b Providence, RI, Oct 4, 60. *Study:* Studies with Gage Taylor, 77-79; Col Marn, studies with Bill Martin, 79-80; San Francisco State Univ (cinematography & animation), 83. *Work:* Pacific Telesis Corp; Mazda Corp; Syntex Corp; Proctor & Gamble Corp; GTE Corp. *Comn:* Various decorative murals, Renaissance Mural Co, 83; decorative murals for var hotels & restaurants, Elizabeth Weiner & Assocs, Los Angeles, Calif, 86; decorative interior mural, Pacific Telesis Corp, San Francisco, Calif, 88; Valentine Mus mural restoration, John Canning Co, Richmond, Va, 90; decorative interior mural, Peter & Gabrielle Wais, Ross, Calif, 92. *Exhib:* Vision Quest 78 Invitational, Hall of Flowers, Golden Gate Park, San Francisco, Calif, 78; Interfaith Peace Conference, Grace Cathedral, San Francisco, Calif, 83; 100 Vows of the Sun Invitational, Southern Exposure Gallery, San Francisco, Calif, 85; The Environment Invitational, Toyota Amlux Corp Hq, Japan, 91; Collector's Eds/Lyrical Art Co, Tokyo, Japan. *Pos:* Animation prod artist, Colossal Pictures, San Francisco, Calif, 81-91; trade show display muralist, Giltspar Inc, San Francisco, Calif, 92; ad comp artist, Transphere Int Ad Agency, San Francisco, Calif, 92. *Teaching:* Pvt instr painting, 91. *Bibliog:* Michael Bell (auth), Custodian of light, Magical Blend Mag, 90; Jeff Bedrick-Pop Icons, City Mag, 92. *Mem:* San Francisco Soc Illusr. *Media:* Oil on Canvas. *Publ:* Illusr, Line of Fine Art Gift-Cards, titles, Aquamarin Verlag, Ger, 87, The Queens Cards, 91; var book covers, Inner Traditions, Int, 89; Weather, Doubleday, 90; The Lost Continent of Mo, Brotherhood of Life, 90. *Dealer:* Collectors Editions Canoga Park CA. *Mailing Add:* 1040 Cresthaven Dr Los Angeles CA 90042

BEEBE, MARY LIVINGSTONE
ART ADMINISTRATOR
b Portland, Ore, Nov 5, 40. *Study:* The Catlin GablinSch, 45-58; Bryn Mawr Col, Pa, BA, 62; Univ Paris & L'Ecole de Louvre, Paris, 62-63. *Comn:* Commn by Terry Allen, Michael Asher, John Baldessari, Jackie Ferrara & Ian Hamilton Finlay, Richard Fleischner, Tim Hawkinson, Jenny Holzer, Robert Irwin, Elizabeth Murray, Bruce Nauman, Nan June Paik, Niki de Saint Phalle, Alexis Smith, Kiki Smith, William Wegman. *Exhib:* Over 100 exhibs 72-81. *Collection Arranged:* Stuart Col. *Pos:* Mus apprentice, Portland Art Mus, 63-64; asst to registr & secy, Mus Fine Arts, Boston, 65-66; curatorial asst, Fogg Art Mus, Harvard Univ, 66-68, producer, Am Theater Co, Portland, 69-72; exec dir, Portland Ctr Visual Arts, 72-81; dir, Stuart Collection Sculpture, Univ Calif, San Diego, 81-. *Teaching:* instr, Univ Calif, San Diego, formerly. *Awards:* Nat Endowment Arts Fel, 79; AIA Allied Profession Award, 92. *Mem:* Art Matters Inc, New York (bd mem, 1985-); Russell Found, La Jolla (bd mem); Univ Wash (arts adv comt, 89-94); Art Table; UCSF Mission Bay Arts (adv Bd, 99-). *Interests:* Contemporary Art and sculptures; gardening. *Publ:* Landmarks: Sculpture Commissions for the Stuart Collecction at the Univ of Calif-San Diego, 2001. *Mailing Add:* Stuart Collection Univ Calif San Diego-0010 9500 Gilman Dr La Jolla CA 92093-0010

BEECROFT, VANESSA FIONA
PAINTER
b Genoa, Italy, Apr 25, 69; Brit citizen. *Study:* Civico Liceo Artistico Nicolo Barabino, archit, Genoa, Italy, 83-87; Accademia Ligustica Di Belle Arti, painting, Genoa, Italy, 87-88; Academia Di Belle Arti Di Brera, stage design, Milan, Italy, 88-93. *Work:* Castello di Rivoli, Fondazione Sandretto Rerebaudengo, Turin, Italy; Castello di Rivara, Rivara, Italy; Oakis Joannou Collection, Athens, Greece. *Exhib:* Id, Munic Van Abbe Mus Eindhoven, Nfld, 96; Persona, Renaissance Soc, Chicago, 96; Quadriennale d'Arte di Roma, Palazzo Esposizioni, Rome, 96; Traffic, CACP Mus Art Contemp, Bordeaux, France, 96; Conversation Pieces, Inst Contemp Art, Philadelphia, 96; Conversation Pieces, Inst Contemp Art, Boston, 97; Aperto Ital 95, Trevi Flash Art Mus, Italy, 95; Prima Linea (with catalog), Trevi Flash Art Mus, Trevi, Italy, 95; Young and Restless, Mus Mod Art, NY, 96; The Scream (with catalog), Mus Mod Art, Ishoj, Denmark, 96; Fatto in Italia (with catalog), Inst Contemp Art, London, UK, 97; Enterprise (with catalog), Inst Contemp Art, Boston, Mass, 97; Kritische Eleganie, Critical Elegance (with catalog), Musem Dhondt-Dhaenens Deurle, Belgium, 98; Then and Now, Lisson Gallery, London, UK, 98; Helmut Newton, Big Nudes, L'Elac, L'Espacc Lausannois d'Art Contemporian, Geneva, Switz, 98, Wounds Between Democracy and Redemption in Contemp Art (with catalog), Modema Museet, Stockholm, Sweden, 98. *Bibliog:* Visual Images of Today, Monthly Art Mag, Bijutsu Techo BT 9, 9/98; H Kontova & G Politi, Arte (auth), Vanessa Beecroft, Intervista No 14, Polita Editore, 7-8/98; Flash Art XXXI Years, Flash Art Int, Politi Editore, 98. *Media:* Oil, Watercolor. *Publ:* Coauth & illusr, Eh No? - Geapoliti, 96 & coauth, Slownet-Flash Art, summer 96, Politi Editore; contribr, Purple Fashion N2, Purple Inst, 96-97. *Dealer:* Jeffrey Deitch 721 Fifth Ave New York NY 10022. *Mailing Add:* 235 Berry St Brooklyn NY 11211

BEENEN, RICHARD
PHOTOGRAPHER
b Los Angeles, Calif, Nov 23, 53. *Study:* Calif State Univ, Fullerton, MA. *Work:* Holtzman, Wise, Shepard Inc, Phall & Plomkin Inc, Timothy A Geaney Inc, NY; Phylis Lutjeans, Newport Beach, Calif; Cunningham & Assocs, Orange, Calif; Josetta Speglia, Los Angeles, Calif; Lynn Garnier Found, Richard Plumgren Inc, Laguna Beach, Calif. *Exhib:* Series, Gallery Artists, Los Angeles Co Mus, 86; White Columns, NY, 89; Retro Future, Richard/Bennett Gallery, Los Angeles, 89; Ihara Ludens Gallery, NY, 90; Parsons Sch Design, 91, 94 & 95; and others. *Pos:* Prop designer, David Spagnolo Studios Inc, 89-. *Teaching:* Instr, Parsons Sch Design, NY, 86-; fac, Pratt Univ, 87-. *Awards:* Nat Endowment Arts Grant, 89; Pollock-Krasner Found, 90; Esther Gottlieb Award, 91. *Publ:* Conde Nast Publ; Hearst Publ; Newsweek; Delta Airlines. *Mailing Add:* 369 W 36th # 3S New York NY 10018

BEER, KENNETH JOHN
EDUCATOR, SCULPTOR
b Ferndale, Mich, May 4, 32. *Study:* Wayne State Univ, BA & MA. *Work:* Detroit Inst Art; Thalhimers & First Merchants Bank, Richmond & Va Beach Art Ctr, Va. *Comn:* Campus libr relief, Eastern Mennonite Col, Harrisonburg, Va, 69; James Madison Mem (cast bronze), James Madison Univ, Harrisonburg, 77; Arboretum Gates, James Madison Univ, Harrisonburg, 88. *Exhib:* Ann Mich Artists, Detroit Inst Art, 55-62; Va Artists Biennial, Va Mus, Richmond, 65, 67 & 73; Southern Sculpture, Mint Mus, Charlotte, NC, 65, Birmingham Mus, Ala, 66 & Columbus Mus, Ga, 66; solo exhib, Columbia Mus, SC, 69 & Va Mus, 73; Drawing & Sculpture Ann, Ball State Univ Art Gallery, 74 & 76. *Teaching:* Assoc prof sculpture, James Madison Univ, Harrisonburg, 61-. *Awards:* Whitcomb Prize, Mich Artists Ann, Detroit Inst Arts, 61; Best in Show, Thalhimers Invitational, 66; Distinction Award, Va Artists Biennial, Va Mus, 73. *Media:* Bronze, Steel. *Publ:* Auth, Sanctum, The Emergence of a Form, Studies & Res Bull of Madison Col, 64. *Mailing Add:* James Madison Univ School of Art & Art History MSC 7101 Harrisonburg VA 22807

BEERMAN, JOHN THORNE
PAINTER
b Greensboro, NC, Feb 21, 58. *Study:* Skowhegan Sch Painting & Sculpture, 80; RI Sch Design, BFA, 82. *Work:* Metrop Mus Art, NY; Brooklyn Mus; Mus Fine Arts, Houston; Walker Art Ctr, Minneapolis; NC Mus Art, Raleigh. *Exhib:* The New Romantic Landscape, Whitney Mus Am Art, NY, Fairfield Co, Stamford, Conn, 87; The 1980's: A New Generation, Metrop Mus Art, NY; Harmony & Discord: Am Landscape Today, Va Mus Fine Arts, Richmond, 90; Am Narrative Painting & Sculpture 80's, Nassau Co Mus Art, Roslyn, NY, 91; Seeing the Forest Through the Trees, Contemp Arts Mus, Houston, 93; Inspired by Nature, Newberger Mus, Purchase, NY, 94; Changing Horizons, Katonah Mus Art, NY, 96; Divining Nature, Southeastern Mus Contemp Art, Winston-Salem, NC, 98; Bently Gallery, Scottsdale, Ariz, 99; David Beitzel Gallery, NY, 01; Meredith Cory Gallery, Houston, 01; Somerhill Gallery, Chapel Hill, NC, 02; Tibor de Nogy Gallery, NY, 03. *Awards:* Scholar, Skowhegan Sch Painting & Sculpture, Maine, 80; Visual Artist Fel Painting, Yaddo, Saratoga Springs, NY, 84; Subscription Prize, Jane Voorhees Zimmerli Art Mus, Rutgers Univ, New Brunswick, NJ, 86. *Bibliog:* John W Coffey II (auth), Finding the Forgotten Landscape (exhib catalog), NC Mus Art, 91; Vivian Raynor (auth), Surveying realism in celebration of Hopper, NY Times, 96; Ed Bumgardner (auth), Landscape artists tries to capture the magic, Winston-Salem J, 96. *Media:* Oil on Linen. *Dealer:* David Beitzel Gallery 102 Prince St New York NY 10012; Tibor de Nagy, 724 5th Ave, NY, 10014. *Mailing Add:* 278 Piermont Ave South Nyack NY 10960

BEERMAN, MIRIAM BEERMAN-JAFFE
PAINTER
b Providence, RI. *Study:* RI Sch Design, BFA; Art Students League, with Yasuo Kuniyoshi; New Sch Social Res, with Adja Yunkers; New York Univ; Atelier 17, Paris, with Wm Hayter. *Work:* Whitney Mus Am Art, Metrop Mus Art, New Sch Social Res, Brooklyn Mus, Queens Mus & Jewish Mus, NY; Newark Mus, Newark Pub Libr, NJ; Israel Mus, Jerusalem; NJ State Mus, Trenton; Jersey city Mus, NJ; Allan Meml Mus Fine Art, Oberlin, Ohio; Mus Art; Montclair Art Mus; Zimmerli Mus, NJ; Yale Univ, Sterling Art Libr. *Comn:* Mus Art, RI Sch Design, Providence, RI. *Exhib:* Whitney Mus, NY, 58; Brooklyn Mus, NY, 60; Nat Gallery Can, Ottawa, 60; solo exhibs, Am Acad Arts & Letters & Brooklyn Mus, NY, 72, Primal Ground Miriam Beerman: Works from 1983-1987, Montclair, NJ, 87, Works from 1949-1990, NJ State Mus, Trenton, 91, Bergan Mus, Paramus, NJ, 96, Univ Wis, Oshkosh, 2002; one-woman retrospectives, Pratt Inst, NY, 89 & Miriam Beerman: Artist Books, Jersey City Mus, 98; Chicago Art Expo, Ill, 93; Traveling Exhib, Corcoran Gallery Art, Washington, DC, 94; Drawing Invitational, Jersey City Mus, NJ, 95; Queens Mus, NY, 96; Univ Wisconsin, Oshkosh, WI, 2002; Chataqua Ctr for Vis Arts, Chautauqua, NY, 2004. *Collection Arranged:* Israel Mus; NJ StateMus; Bklyn Mus; Whitney Mus Am Art; Met Mus Art; RI Sch Design Mus Art; Jersey City Mus; Allen Meml Mus Art; Montclair Mus; Nat Mus Women in the Arts, Washington, DC; Neuberger Mus, Purchase, NY. *Pos:* Artist-in-Residence, Burston Graphic Ctr, Jerusalem, Israel, 80; guest artist, Rutgers Univ, New Brunswick, NJ, 87 & 97. *Teaching:* Adj prof, Queensborough Community Col, City Univ NY, 72-92; vis artist, Montclair Mus Art Sch, 74-89 & Montclair State Col, 79-89, guest artist, Univ Chicago, 88; lectr art, Rutgers Univ; lectr, guest artist Univ Wis, Oshkosh, 2002.

Awards: Artists Residency, Va Ctr Creative Arts, 85-96, 2000; Artists Residency, Blue Mtn Ctr, 89-96; Mid Atlantic Grant, 96; Fulbright Grant, 2000; Joan Mitchell Award, 2000; Mid-Atlantic Grant, 2000; Pollock-Krasner grant, Women's Studio Workshop, 2000; ED Found grant, Dodge Found, 2000. *Bibliog:* Vivien Raynor (auth), Imaginary Monsters That Dare a Visitor to See the Show, NY Times, 4/14/91; Dimitri Rotov (auth), New Art Examiner, 10/91; John Loughery (auth), Women's Art J, fall 91, winter 92; All Things Considered, Nat Pub Radio, 6/26/94; and many others. *Media:* Oil, Large Drawings. *Interests:* social and political injustice. *Publ:* Ed & illusr, The Enduring Beast, Doubleday, 72. *Mailing Add:* 6 Macopin Ave Montclair NJ 07043

BEERY, ARTHUR O
PAINTER
b Marion, Ohio, Mar 4, 30. *Study:* Self taught. *Work:* Butler Inst Am Art, Youngstown, Ohio; Lessco Data, NY; JM Katz Collection, Pa; Johnson Art Mus, Cornell Univ; Sweet Briar Mus, Sweet Briar Univ; Springfield Art Mus, Springfield, Mo; and others. *Comn:* Murals on canvas of Athens, Greece, Monte Carlo, Stromboli, Rock of Gibralter & Charleston, SC for US Navy Minecraft Base, Charleston, 54. *Exhib:* Solo shows include Galerie Cernuschi, NY, 77, 80, Gallery DeJanout, Cleveland, Ohio, 98, Mahrfield Art Ctr, 2006; group shows include Nat Exhib, Butler Inst Am Art, Youngstown, Ohio, 68, 72, 73, 79; Le Salon De Nations, Paris, France, 83; 28th Ann Chautauga Nat Exhib Am Art, 85; Watercolor USA Hon Soc Biennial Exhib, 87, 89, 91 & 93; Ohio Art League Exhib, Columbus Mus Fine Art, 98 & 2000; Richland Acad, 2000; 23rd Grand Prix, Deauville, France, 72; Contemp Ams, Pavis France, 72; New Am Open, Nat Exhit, 2004; Ohio Curated Exhib, Riffle Gallery, 2005; 61st Ann, Mansfield Art Ctr, Ohio, 2006; and numerous others. *Collection Arranged:* Butler Inst Am Art, Youngstown, OH; J M Katz Collection-P2; Johnson Art Mus, Cornell Univ; Sweet Briar Univ; Sweet Briar Gallery, Sweet Briar, VA. *Awards:* Richard P Stahl Award, Watercolor USA, 71; Purchase Prize, Bulter Inst Am Art, 73; Oscar D'Ital Award, Acad Ital, 85; Mansfield Art Ctr Award, 99; Ohio Art League Exhib awarded Mary Lou Chess Award, 2000; Best in Show, Nat New Am Open, 2004. *Bibliog:* Int Dir Arts, 11th ed, Berlin Ger 72; BF Goodrich (auth), BFG-Today, vol 1 no 4, 77; Roger Schlueter (auth), Saluto to the master, Belleville New Dem, 91; David Breeding (auth), Am art to remember, Marlon Ohio Star, 98; Renne Phillips (auth), Manhattan Arts Int, 2000; Joel Hochman (auth), The Art Crows, 2000; Bill Mayr (auth), Visual Arts, Col Ohio Dispatch, 2004. *Mem:* Mansfield Fine Arts Guild, Ohio; Ohio Art League (Award 2000); Watercolor USA Hon Soc. *Media:* Oils, Watercolor. *Interests:* the creation of beauty by the use of the continuous curve. *Mailing Add:* 452 E Church St Marion OH 43302

BEGININ, IGOR
PAINTER, EDUCATOR
b Susak, Croatia, Aug 31, 1931; US citizen. *Study:* Wayne State Univ, AB, 63, MA, 66. *Work:* Fisher New Ctr, Chrysler Corp, Ford Motor Co, Detroit; Gen Motors, NY; Tung-Hai Univ, Taichong, Taiwan. *Comn:* Detroit Free Press, Mich Med Mag. *Exhib:* Watercolor USA, 68, 73, 93, 98 & 2004; Nat Soc Painters in Casein/Acrylic, New York City, 1969, 94; Kentucky Aqueous, Louisville, 86; Flint Inst Art, 86; Int Watercolor, San Diego, Calif, 88; Okla Nat Exhib, 1993, 98, 2001; Tex Watercolor Soc, 1993 & 2005. *Pos:* Bd mem, Mich Watercolor Soc, 66-70 & 82-91, chmn, 74-77. *Teaching:* Asst prof watercolor, Eastern Mich Univ, 70-77, assoc prof, 77-83, prof, 83-2001, prof emer art. *Awards:* Soc Illusr Award, 68; Mich Watercolor Soc Ann Award, 67, 71, 83, 89, 91, 95 & 2000; Int Exhib, San Diego Watercolor Soc, 88; Watercolor USA, 2004. *Bibliog:* The Daily Sentinel, 70; Ann Arbor News, 73; Associated Newspapers, 87; Observer-Eccentric, 98. *Mem:* Mich Watercolor Soc; Detroit Inst Arts Founders Soc; Watercolor USA Hon Soc. *Media:* Watercolor, Acrylic. *Publ:* Detroit Mag, Detroit Free Press, 65-69 & Michigan Medicine, 69; The Artistic Touch, 95 & The Artistic Touch 2, 97, Creative Art Press; Creative Watercolor, Rockport Publ, 95, Illustrators 10, New York City. *Dealer:* Cary Gallery 226 Walnut Rd Rochester MI 48307. *Mailing Add:* 43524 Bannockburn Dr Canton MI 48187

BEGLEY, J (JOHN) PHILLIP
MUSEUM DIRECTOR
b Akron, Ohio, Mar 21, 47. *Study:* Univ NMex, BFA (hons), 69; Ind Univ, MFA, 75; Mus Management Inst, Getty Trust, AFA, 89. *Collection Arranged:* Traveling Exhibs, Making it in Crafts (auth, catalog), 78, Fiber: State of the Art, 81, Making it in Paper: Twinrocker, 83, Individual Talent (auth, catalog), 84, Kentucky Guild 25th Anniversary Ceremony (auth, catalog), 86 & Contemporary Directions in Fiber (assembled & arranged), 88; Ladies Lunch (producer), 92. *Pos:* Dir, New Harmony Gallery Contemp Art, 75-83; exec dir, Louisville Visual Art Asn, 83-. *Teaching:* Lectr art, Univ Evansville, 76-83 & Univ Louisville, 88-89, adj assoc prof art, Univ Louisville, 97-. *Awards:* Louis Comfort Tiffany Fel, 78. *Media:* All Media Contemporary. *Mailing Add:* 1506 Hepburn Ave Louisville KY 40204-1618

BEHNKE, LEIGH
PAINTER
b Hartford, Conn, Dec 22, 46. *Study:* Pratt Inst, BFA, 69; New York Univ, MA, 76. *Work:* H J Heinz Corp, Pittsburgh, Pa; Deloitte, Haskins, Sells, Marsh & McClennan Co & Xerox Corp, NY; Southeast Banking Corp, Miami, Fla; Currier Mus, Manchester, NH; and others. *Exhib:* Urban Landscape, Wave Hill, NY, 79; New Am Still Life, Westmoreland Mus, Pa; On Paper, Inst Contemp Art, Va Mus, Richmond, 80; Real, Really Real, Super Real, San Antonio Mus, Tex, 81, Carnegie Inst, Pittsburgh, 81 & Indianapolis Mus, Ind, 81; Contemp Am Realist, Univ Art Gallery, Pittsburgh, Pa, 81; Lower Manhattan from Street to Sky, Whitney Mus, 82; Fischbach Gallery, 78-94; Flint Inst Arts, 91; Nassau Co Mus, 92; Nat Acad Sci, 92; Exactitude, Plus One Gallery, London, Eng, 2006. *Pos:* Master teacher & panelist, Nat Foun Adv Arts, 89-93. *Teaching:* Lectr fine art, drawing and painting, Sch Visual Arts, New York, 79-. *Awards:* ED Found grant, 99, 2000. *Bibliog:* New Editions: Leigh Behnke, Art News, 4/82; Christopher Finch (auth), Twentieth Century Watercolors, 88; Roni Cohen (auth), Artforum Mag (rev), 91. *Mem:* Col Art Asn. *Media:* Watercolor, Oil; Silkscreen. *Dealer:* Fischbach Gallery 29 W 57th St New York NY 10019. *Mailing Add:* Dept Fine Arts School of Visual Arts 543 Broadway #3 New York NY 10012

BEHNKEN, WILLIAM JOSEPH
PRINTMAKER, EDUCATOR
b New York, NY, Mar 29, 43. *Study:* City Col NY, BA, 68, MA, 95. *Work:* British Mus, London; Nat Acad Design Mus, NY; NY Pub Libr Print Collection, NY; Brooklyn Mus, NY; Indianapolis Mus Fine Art, Ind; Metrop Mus Art, NY; Fitzwilliam Mus, Cambridge, England; New Orleans Mus, La; Newark Pub Libr Print Div, NJ. *Comn:* print edit, CECO Corp, New York City, 97, 98, 99; print edit, Gallery New World, Dusseldorf, Ger, 96; print edit/portfolio, The Old Print Shop Gallery, New York City, 98; print edit, Print Club of Albany, 2006. *Exhib:* NY at Night, Auburn Col, NY, 89; Small Print Invitational, State Gallery, Lodz, Poland, 96; Drawings Int, Wagner Col, NY, 96; Provincetown Then and Now, St Botolph's Club, Boston, 98; 19th & 20th Century Am Works on Paper, Nat Acad Design, New York City, 99; Parkside Nat Small Print Exhib, Univ Wis, Kenosha, 2000; Prints & Drawings, Old Print Shop Gallery, NY, 2003; Century Asn Invitational, NY, 2003; La Biennale Int d'estampe de Trois-Rirvieres, Que, Can, 2005; Impressions on NY, NY Historical Soc, 2005; SAGA, Hollar Soc Gal, Prague, Czech Rep, 2006; traveling collection, Art Students League NY, 2006-08. *Teaching:* asst prof art, City Col of NY, 70-; vis lectr hist printmaking, CW Post Coll, Long island, NY, 96-97; instr printmaking, Art Students League, NY, 98- & Nat Acad Design, 2001-. *Awards:* Recipient Louis Lozowick awards Audubon Artists Soc, New York City, 1991, 92; Carl Schrag Award, Soc Am Graphic Artists, 97; Graphics Award, Nat Acad Design, 97; John Taylor Arms Purchase Award Albany Print Club, NY, 98; 1st Anniversary Art Career Achievement award City Col Art Alumni Asn, 2004; Ralph Fabri Award, Nat Acad Design, 2003; Audubon Artist Gold Medal Graphics Award, 2003; Silver Medal Graphics Award, Audubon Artists, 2005; Emile & Dines Carlsen Graphics Award, Nat Acad Design. *Bibliog:* Ruth Weisberg (auth), The Best Printmaking, Rockport Pubs, 77; Trudie A Grace (auth), Paper Trail, Nat Acad Design, 97; Marilyn Symmes (auth), Impressions of New York, New York Historical Soc, 2005. *Mem:* Nat Acad Design (mem committeeperson 2000-, Ralph Fabri Graphics prize 2003, instr 2001-); Soc Am Graphic Artists (pres 98-2002); Boston Printmakers, Phi Beta Kappa (pres, City Col of NY Gamma chap 2001); Provincetown Art Asn Mus (sch dir 84-95); Print Coun NY; Audubon Artist (dir graphics 91-92). *Media:* Aquating, Mezzotint, Lithography. *Dealer:* The Old Print Shop 150 Lexington Ave New York NY 10016. *Mailing Add:* 3415 Fort Independence St Bronx NY 10463-4507

BEHR, MARION RAY
PRINTMAKER, WRITER
b Rochester, NY, Sept 12, 39. *Study:* Syracuse Univ, BFA, 61, MFA, 62. *Work:* Jane Voorhees Zimmerli Mus, New Brunswick, NJ, 93, 96 & 2002; Social Sci Res Coun Corp Col, NY, 2005; Nat Mus Am Hist, Smithsonian Inst, Washington, DC; Royal Thai Art Collection, 94; Inst Cult Peruano Norteamericano, Lima, Peru, 99; Bethaniem Gallery, Berlin, 2004; Ben Shahn Gallery, 2006. *Exhib:* Miniature Print Biennial, John Szoke Gallery, NY, 89; Kanagawa Prefectual Gallery, Yokahama, Japan 89; solo exhib, Beamesderfer Gallery, Highland Park, NJ, 92, Hunterton Art Mus, Clinton, NJ, 98, Nat Acad Exhib, NY, 98, Cult Peruano Norteamericano, Lima, Peru, 99, Johnson Gallery, Bedminster, NJ, 2002; Small Works, Wash Sq Gallery, NY, 92; Pac Rim Int Exhib, Univ Hilo, Hawaii, 95; Ann Audubon Artists Exhib, Salmagundi Club, NY, 95 & 97; Zimmerli Art Mus, New Brunswick, NJ 99 & 2005; Grounds for Sculpture, Hamilton, NJ, 2001; Bankgesellschaft Gallery, Berlin, Germ, 2001; Pierro Gallery, NJ, 2004; Deutsche Architektur Zentrum, Berlin, Germ, 2004; World of ElectroEtch, Ortho Gallery, 2006; Redbrick Gallery, Beverly, Mass, 2006. *Collection Arranged:* The World of ElectroEtch, Print Coun NJ, 2005. *Pos:* Pres, Women Working Home Inc, 79-90; partner, ElectroEtch Enterprises, 91-. *Teaching:* vis lectr, Parsons Sch Design, NY, 95; lectr, Stanford Univ, Calif, 99, Holman Island Eskimo Coop, Can, 99, Int Cult Moussem, Asilah, Morocco, 2000, Howard Univ, DC, 2001, Syracuse Univ, NY, 2001; prof, Univ Alaska Juneau, Alaska; prof, Univ Alaska, Fairbanks, Alaska, Druckwerkstatt Bethanien, Berlin, Ger, 2001, Christchurch Polytechnic Univ & UCol, Wanganui, NZ, 2004. *Awards:* Merit Award, Del Bello Gallery, Toronto, Can, 90; Merit Award, Am Artists Prof League, 91; Arts & Humanities Award, Charles A Lindbergh Fund, 93; NY Central Award, Audubon Artists Exhib, 95, Art News Award, 98; NJ Artist of the Month, 8/2005; Purchase Prize, Ben Shahn Gallery, 2006. *Bibliog:* Edmond Andrews (auth), Patent of the week, NY Times, 5/2/92; Eileen Watkins (auth), Weekend guide of arts, Star Ledger, Newark, 11/6/92; Drew Steis (auth), News of the print world, Art Calendar, 10/93; Michele Le Tourneau (auth), News North- Printmaking Innovation in Holman, 10/4/99; Gabriella Wiener (auth), El-Sol, Lima, Peru, 11/4/99; Le Matin (The Morning of Sahara and Morocco-Electrical Etching: A New Non-Toxic Artistic Process, 8/15/2000; Ralph J. Bellantoni (auth), Courier News, 9/11/2002; William Zimmer (auth), New York Times, 1/24/99. *Mem:* Nat Asn Women Artists; Soc Am Graphic Artists; Southern Graphics Coun; Printmaking Coun NJ; Audubon Artists. *Media:* Acid Free Etching, painting, sculpting. *Res:* Co-inventor (with Omri Behr), ElectroEtch, an acid free, environmentally safe graphic etching process. *Publ:* Illusr, Jewish Holiday Book, Doubleday, 77; illusr & coauth, Women Working Home, WWH Press, 81 & 83; Environmentally safe etching, J Print World, 92; Etching & Tone Creation using Low Voltage etc, Leonardo, 93; illusr & auth, ElectroEtch, Printmaking Today, 94; ElectroEtch II, Printmaking Today, Winter, 95. *Mailing Add:* 377 River Rd Somerville NJ 08876-3554

BEHRENS, MARY SNYDER
PAINTER, ASSEMBLAGE ARTIST
b Milwaukee, Wis, Oct 26, 57. *Study:* Mt Mary Col, Milwaukee, 75-77; Minneapolis Col Art & Design, 78-80; Univ Wis, Milwaukee, BFA, 82. *Work:* Pvt collections of Cinncinnati Bell Info Systems, IBM & Thriftway, Cincinnati, Ohio; Hearst Ctr Arts, Cedar Falls, Iowa; Harper Coll, Palatine, Ill. *Comn:* Rivertown Trading Corp, St Paul, Minn. *Exhib:* Celebrating the Stitch, Textile Arts Ctr, Chicago, 91; Newton Arts Ctr, Boston, 92; Fiber Art Int, Pittsburgh Arts Ctr, 99; New Art, Cedar Rapids Mus of Art, 02; Visions Int, Art Ctr, Waco, Tex, 02; Solo exhib, Univ Northern Iowa, 2005. *Awards:* Individual Artists Grant, Ohio Artists Coun, 88 & 90; Proj Grants, Iowa Arts Coun, 97, 98, 99 & 02; Best of Show, Augustana Col Art Gallery Exhib, Rock Island, Il, 02. *Bibliog:* Kate Mattews (auth), Fiberarts Design Book III, Larkbooks, 87; Barbara L Smith (auth), Celebrating the Stitch, Taunton Press, 91; Robbie Steinbach (auth), Lifework: Portraits of Iowa Women Artists, Lifework Arts Found, 98. *Media:* Miscellaneous Media. *Dealer:* Weiderspan Gallery 3413 Mt Vernon Rd SE Cedar Rapids IA 52403. *Mailing Add:* 2022 X Ave Dysart IA 52224-9767

BEHRENS, ROY R
EDITOR, DESIGNER, CURATOR
b Independence, Iowa, June 27, 46. *Study:* Pond Farm Sch, with Bauhaus Potter, M Wildenhain, 64; Univ Northern Iowa, BA, 68; RI Sch Design, MA(art educ), 72. *Exhib:* 8th Ann Ed Design, NY, 73; Commun Arts Ann, Palo Alto, 90; Print Regional, NY, 90; Soc Am Illusrs, NY, 90. *Collection Arranged:* Walter Hamady: Books, Collages and Assemblages, Univ Northern Iowa, 95; Paintings by William Cook: The Man Who Taught Gertrude Stein to Drive, Univ Northern Iowa, 96; Robert Tabor: Four Seasons on an Iowa Farm, Hearst Ctr for Arts, Cedar Falls, Iowa, 99; Art, Design and Camouflage, Univ Northern Iowa, 2000; Modern Design Icons, Univ Northern Iowa, 2001. *Pos:* Design ed, NAm Rev, 72-92, 99-; ed, Ballast Quart Rev, 85-; chmn, Commun Design, Art Acad Cincinnati, 87-90; contrib ed, Print Mag, 92-; corresp ed, Leonardo, 97-; bd adv, Gestalt Theory, 98-. *Teaching:* Assoc prof art design, Univ Northern Iowa, 72-77 & Univ Wis, Milwaukee, 77-87; prof art design, Art Acad Cincinnati, 87-90; prof art design, Univ Northern Iowa, 90-. *Awards:* Res grant, 91, 93, 95, 97, 99, 03 & 05 and Donald McKay Outstanding Res Award, 95, Univ Northern, Iowa; Fac Excellence Award, Iowa Bd Regents, 96 & 2005; Hon Mention Throne/Aldrich Award, State Hist Soc Iowa, 98. *Bibliog:* Steve Heller & Marie Finamore (ed), Design Culture, 97, Steve Heller (ed), The Education of a Graphic Designer, 98; Steve Heller (ed), Graphic Design and Sex Appeal, Allworth, 2000; Hardy Blechman (auth), DPM: Disruptive Pattern Material: An Encyl of Camouflage, Maharishi, 2004. *Mem:* Art Dirs Asn Iowa; Soc Gestalt Theory & Its Applicants. *Media:* collage, digital. *Res:* Camouflage; art and perceptual psychology; history and theory of graphic design. *Publ:* Adelbert Ames, Fritz Heider and the Chair Demonstration, Gesalt Theory, 99; The Hole in Art's Umbrella, Print Mag, 2000; Revisiting Gottschaldt: Embedded Figures in Art, Architecture and Design, Gesalt Theory, 2000; False Colors: Art, Design and Modern Camouflage, Bobolink Books, 2002; Cook Book: Gertrude Stein, William Cook & Le Corbusier, Bobolink Books, 2005. *Mailing Add:* Univ Northern Iowa Dept Art Cedar Falls IA 50614 0362

BEILIN, HOWARD
ART DEALER
Pos: Owner & dir, Howard Beilin Inc, currently. *Specialty:* Nineteenth and 20th century art with a special emphasis on European impressionists and post-impressionists; Norman Rockwell. *Mailing Add:* 510 E 85th St New York NY 10028-7430

BEIRNE, BILL
VIDEO ARTIST, CONCEPTUAL ARTIST
b Brooklyn, NY, Oct 25, 41. *Study:* Pratt Inst, with Louise Bourgeois BFA, 68; Hunter Col, with Robert Morris, MA, 74. *Exhib:* Video as Attitude, Mus Fine Arts Sante Fe, NMex, 83; The Commuter, Fashion Moda, NY, 89; You Connect the Dots, Whitney Mus Am Art, NY, 91; Grief in an Age of Scientific Advance, Int Ctr of Photog, NY, 92; Something's In The Air, Sculpture Ctr, NY, 94; Frames of Reference, List Visual Arts Ctr, Mass Inst Technol, Cambridge, 97; The Gaze of the Other, Nat Ctr Contemp Art, Moscow, 99; Ru Dima's Homework, Contemp Art Ctr, Odessa, Ukraine. *Teaching:* Video, NY Univ, 89-94. *Awards:* Nat Endowment Arts Grant, 80; NY State Coun Arts Fell (video), 79. *Bibliog:* Ann Sargent-Wooster (auth), Formerly formalists, High Performance 14, 91; John G Hanhardt (auth), Understanding television, TV Mag, 80; Elizabeth Hayt-Atkins (auth), megaloculus, 11/92. *Media:* Video Installation & Performance. *Publ:* Auth, A Pedestrian Blockade, Collation Ctr & Wittenbourn Bks, 76. *Mailing Add:* 157 E 72nd St New York NY 10021

BELAG, ANDREA
PAINTER, GRAPHIC ARTIST
b New York, NY, Nov 21, 51. *Study:* New York Studio Sch. *Work:* Newark Mus, NJ; Morris Mus Arts & Sci, Morristown, NJ; Jersey City Mus, NJ; Quaker Oats Corp, Chicago; NJ State Mus, Trenton. *Exhib:* Recent Paintings: Andrea Belag, NJ State Mus, Trenton, 84; Realism & Abstraction: 20th Century Art in the Newark Mus, NJ, 87; After the Fall, Aspects of Abstract Painting Since 1970, Snug Harbor Cutlural Ctr, Staten Isl, NY; one man shows, David Beitzel Gallery, NY, 91 & Richard Anderson Gallery, NY, 92, 93 & 94; Littlejohn Contemp Gallery, NY, 96; Bill Maynes Gallery, NY, 98, 2000, 2002; Galerie Heinz Holtmann, Cologne, Ger, 98, 2000, 2002. *Teaching:* Adj lectr arts, State Univ NY, Purchase, 90-, Maryland Inst, 93, Princeton Univ, 95; instr, Sch Visual Arts, NY, 95-; resident, Bezlagio Study Ctr, Rockefeller Found. *Awards:* Fel, NJ Coun Arts, 84; Individual Fel, Nat Endowment Arts, 87; Guggenheim Fel, 99. *Bibliog:* Robert Edelman (auth), Andrea Belag, Artpress, 9/94; Barry Schwabsky (auth), Andrea Belag, Artforum, 9/94; John Yau (auth), Longing and unbridgable distance, Weidle Verlag, 98; Stephen Westfall (auth), Andrea Belag, Paintings, Calerie Heinz Holtmann, 2000; Sarah Schmerler (auth), Andrea Belag New Paintings and Works on Paper, 2002. *Media:* Oio, Gouache. *Publ:* Auth, Eight Painters, Jersey City Mus, 80; Selected Drawings, Jersey City Mus, 83. *Dealer:* Bill Maynes Gallery New York NY; Galerie Heinz Holtmann Koln. *Mailing Add:* 7 Harrison St New York NY 10013

BELAN, KYRA
PAINTER, WRITER
b China, Apr 22, 47; US citizen. *Study:* Ariz State Univ, BFA, 73; Fla State Univ, MFA, 75; Fla Int Univ, EdD, 92. *Work:* Art & Cult Ctr & Southern Regional Courthouse, Hollywood, Fla; Bass Mus Art, Miami Beach; Metro-Dade Art in Public Places, Miami, Fla; Mus Fine Art, Fla State Univ; Latin Am Art Mus, Coral Gables, Fla; and others. *Comn:* Drawing (color pencil), Broward Co Art in PP, Ft Lauderdale, 81; drawing, site specific sculpture, Metro-Dade Art in Pub Places, Fla, 86; and others. *Exhib:* Women's Mus, Lincoln Ctr, NY, 77; one-person exhibs, The Magic Circle Series 1978-1985, Nova Univ, 85, Great Am Goddess Coatlicue, 85, In Quest of the Am Goddess Coatlicue, 86 & Sun Goddess: Emergence of Myth, 86, Broward Community Col, Great Goddess Chicomecoatl, Art & Cult Ctr, Hollywood, Fla, 87, Cosmic Goddess Chiocomecoatl/Demeter, Dupont Gallery, Washington & Lee Univ, Va, 88, Great Goddess Rhea, Malia, Crete, Greece, 88, Great Goddess Chicomecoatl/Shakti, Rim Inst, Payson, Ala, 88; Mother Earth, Mother God, The 621 Gallery, Tallahassee, Fla, 93; Mother Earth, Changing Woman, Art Gallery, Broward Community Col, 94; Goddess of the World, Art & Cult Ctr, Fla, 96; Celebrating Mother Earth, Rochester Inst Technol, Rochester, NY; Digital Art 98, Spirit Circle, Broward Community Col, 99-2000; Lady Liberty, Broward Community Col, 2004. *Pos:* Pres, Coalition Women's Art Orgn, 85-89 & 96-, vpres 89-; Pres, Southeastern Women's Caucus Art, 85-90. *Teaching:* Prof art, Broward Community Col, 76-. *Awards:* Fla Arts Coun Fel Grant, Tallahassee, 82; Barbara Deming Mem Fund Grant, 86; Int Woman of the Year, Cambridge, Eng, 97-98; and others. *Bibliog:* Patrice Wynn (auth), The Womanspirit Sourcebook, Harper & Row, 88; Gloria Orenstein (auth), The Reflowering of the Goddess, Pergamon Press, 90; Norma Broude & Mary Garrard (auths), The Power of Feminist Art, Harry F Abrams, 94. *Mem:* Col Art Asn Am; South Eastern Art Conference. *Media:* Site-specific Installations, Performance Art; Digital Art. *Interests:* mythology; feminist aesthetics. *Publ:* Auth. Earth, Spirit & Fender, Bent Tree Press, 2005; auth, Lucid Future, Aegina Press, 99; auth, Madonna: From Medieval to Modern, Parkstone Press, 2001. *Mailing Add:* PO Box 6735 Hollywood FL 33081

BELANGER, RON
PAINTER
b Montreal, Que, Apr 13, 41. *Study:* Three Sch Art, 76-80; Royal Ont Mus, 79-82; Ont Col Art, 81-88. *Work:* Mus AOAV, Chatham, Can. *Exhib:* Totem, Royal Ont Mus, Toronto, 87; Celestial Phenomenons, Mus AOAV, Chatham, Can, 89; Theodore Mus Contemp Art, 91; Reves, Relais des Epoques, Montreal, 92; Lumiere Du Ciel, Conviv Art Gallery, Vert St Denis, France, 93; Moment in Time, Connoisseur Gallery, Toronto, 93; Bleu Cid-Galleria Arte, Elemental, Cadiz, Spain, 95; Dreams, Castle San Jorge, Lisbon, Port, 97; Colour Seduc, Gallery 1313, Toronto, Can, 98; Galerie 1040, Montreal, 2005; Espace Contemporain Quebec, 2005-2006; Galerie Alternance, Montreal, 2006; Galerie Mile-End, Montreal, 2006. *Awards:* Gold Medal, Biennale de Lutece, 92; Gold Medal, Grand Prix du Soleil Levant, 92; Gold Medal, Grand Prix des Am, 92. *Bibliog:* Sam Aberg (auth), Passages et Abstraction, Dans L'Art Ed Renaissance; Louis Bruens (auth), 101 Peintres, Ed Poly Inter, 92; Guilde International art Contemporain, France, 2005. *Mem:* Cercle des Artistes du Que; Artistes Ontarios Art Visuel; Bureau de Regroupment des Peintres. *Media:* Acrylic, Watercolor. *Publ:* Cotes des Artistes Peintres et Sculpteurs, Jacques de Roussan, 90; International Art Guide, Semadiras, Paris, 92, 94; Guide Vallee, Mr Vallee, 92, 95; Le Marche de L'Art, Louis Bruens, 93; Magazin Art Guide, 96-98 & 2000-2005. *Dealer:* Gallery 1313 1313A Queen St W Toronto Can M6K 1L8; Galerie Mile-End 5345 Ave du Parc Montreal Que H2V 4G9. *Mailing Add:* PO Box 81 Sta F Toronto ON M4Y 2L4 Canada

BELDNER, LYNN KAREN
SCULPTOR
b Philadelphia, Pa, Feb 2, 54. *Work:* Univ Art Mus, Berkeley, Calif; St Mary's Col, Orinda, Calif; Ohio State Univ, Columbus. *Exhib:* Patricia Correia Gallery, Santa Monica, Calif, 97; Pulliam Deffenbaugh, Portland, Ore, 98; Kiddush Cup, Jewish Mus, San Francisco, 98; Graystone, San Francisco, 98; Traywick Gallery, Berkeley, Calif, 98. *Bibliog:* Cheryl Coon (auth), Process and memory, Art Papers, 98; Alicia Miller (auth), Process and memory, Art Week, 98. *Media:* Mixed Media. *Dealer:* Patricia Correia Gallery Los Angeles CA; Graystone 250 Sutter St San Francisco CA 94108. *Mailing Add:* 5528 Dover St Oakland CA 94609

BELFORT-CHALAT, JACQUELINE
SCULPTOR, PAINTER
b Mt Vernon, NY, Feb 23, 30. *Study:* With Frederick V Guinzburg, 43, Ruth Nickerson, 44, Columbia Univ, sculpture with Oronzio Maldarelli & casting with Ettore Salvatore, 47; Art Students League, life drawing with Klonis, 48; Univ Chicago, AB, 48; Fashion Inst Technol, 48-50; Royal Acad Fine Arts, Copenhagen, Denmark, 60-62. *Work:* Smithsonian Inst, Washington; Govt of Nigeria; Our Lady of Victory, NY; Everson Mus, Syracuse, NY; Jesuit Curia, Rome, Italy; Le Moyne Col, Syracuse, NY. *Comn:* Dr Eugene J Fisher, Washington, 83; Holy Family (terra cotta relief), St Michael's Church, NY, 83; Mary (life-size mixed media), Cathedral Immaculate Conception, Syracuse, NY, 86; Heroic Size Christ, Mixed Media, Most Holy Rosary Church, NY, 92; Dolphin, life-size, Lemoyne Athletic Ctr, Syracuse, 93; and others. *Exhib:* Nat Collection Fine Arts, Washington, 63; Wash Gallery Art, 66; Everson Mus, Syracuse, NY, 72; one-man shows, Everson Mus, 79, City Hall, 81 &

Wilson Gallery, Le Moyne Col, 83, Syracuse; Zurich, Switz, 95; and others. *Teaching:* Prof visual arts, Chair, Le Moyne Col, Syracuse, NY, 1970. *Bibliog:* P Scala (auth), Begotten not made (film), ABC-TV, Syracuse, NY, 74; Idea to Image (video), R Smith, 89. *Mem:* Int Sculpture Ctr; Am Aesthetic Soc; Soc for Art, Relig & Cult; Col Art Asn Am; Int Womens Writers Guild; Womens Bus Owners Connection (WBOC). *Media:* All. *Res:* application of art in a business curriculum. *Publ:* Open Sesame, City New York Bus J, 92; J Funson (dir), Artist's Dance, Cath TV, 94; Holistic or Hole, 97 & Thats Art, 98, NYSA; Idea to Image (essay), Notre Dame Univ, 2004. *Mailing Add:* 321 Hurlburt Rd Syracuse NY 13224

BELGUM, ROLF HENRIK
FILMMAKER
b Minneapolis, Minn, Apr 1, 65. *Study:* Univ Minn, BA, 87; Univ Calif San Diego, MFA, 92. *Work:* Driver 23 (film, 72 minutes), 98; The Atlas Moth (video, 75 minutes), 2001. *Exhib:* Pac Film Arch, Berkeley, Calif, 98; Wexner Ctr for Arts, Columbus, Ohio, 99; Nelson Atkin Mus, 2000; Calif Col Arts & Crafts, 2000; Art Inst Chicago, 2000; Northwest Film Ctr, Portland, Oreg, 2000; Whitney Mus Am Art Bienniel, NY, 2000; Showtime's Sundance Channel, Double film DVD released through Image Entertainment. *Teaching:* teacher design Art Insts Int Minn, 97-. *Awards:* Jacob Javits fel, 88; Best Film Award, Minneapolis/St Paul Int Film Festival, 98, Best Documentary feature, 2001; Cinematic Arts Award Whitney Mus Art Biennial, NYC, 2000; Best Documentary, Chicago Underground, 2001; Film Critics Choice, Village Voice, 2000. *Media:* Film, Video. *Res:* Study at The Darwin Archives, Cambridge, England. *Specialty:* The Proposition, NYC. *Collection:* Art Institute Int, Minn. *Dealer:* The Proposition, Ronald Sosinski, New York NY. *Mailing Add:* 4405 Pleasant Ave Minneapolis MN 55409

BELIAN, GARABED
DEALER, HISTORIAN
b Jerusalem. *Study:* Detroit Inst Musical Art, BM, 68; Wayne State Univ, MA, 75. *Pos:* Pres, Art Ctr Chamber Music Players, 66-68; Dir, Wayne Co Community Col Found, 85-; mem, Mich Coun for Arts, 87-; owner & dir, Belian Art Ctr, Troy, Mich, currently. *Specialty:* Twentieth century American and European sculpture, paintings and graphics, ancient art, African sculpture. *Mailing Add:* Belian Art Ctr 5980 Rochester Rd Troy MI 48098-3333

BELIAN, ISABELLE
ADMINISTRATOR
b Addis Ababa, Ethiopia. *Study:* Beirut Univ Col, BA. *Pos:* Man dir, Belian Art Ctr, Troy, Mich, currently. *Mailing Add:* Belian Art Ctr 5980 Rochester Rd Troy MI 48098

BELL, BYRON
ARCHITECT
b NY City, June 15, 1935. *Study:* Princeton Univ, BA, 57; Columbia Univ, M(arch), 62. *Pos:* Registered architect NY; architect James Byron Bell Assocs, NY City, 64-65, owner 67-78; architect Walker O Cain Assoc, NY City, 56-67; partner Cain, Farrell & Bell, 78-86, Farrell, Bell & Lennard, NY City, 86; sr partner, Bell Larson Architects and Planners, currently. *Awards:* William Kinne Fellows Memorial Fellowship, 63. *Mem:* fel, Am Inst Architects; Am Arbitrator Asn; Nat Inst Archit Educ; World Craft Found; The Century Asn; Tghe Grolier Club; Nat Acad (acad, 95). *Mailing Add:* Bell Larson Architects and Planners 123 West 3rd St New York NY 10012

BELL, DOZIER
PAINTER
b Lewiston, Maine, 1957. *Study:* Smith Col, BA, 81; Skowhegan Sch Painting & Sculpture, 85; Univ Pa, MFA, 86. *Hon Degrees:* Maine Col of Art, DFA, 97. *Work:* Portland Mus Art, Maine; AT&T, NY; Farnsworth Mus, Rockland, Maine; Arthur Andersen & Co, Minneapolis, Minn; Prudential Insurance Co, Newark, NJ; United Talent Agency, Calif; and many others. *Exhib:* One-person show, Ogunquit Mus Art, Maine, 91, Bingham Kurts Gallery, Memphis, Tenn, 91, Schmidt Bingham Gallery, NY, 92, 95 & 2000, The Dissonant Heart (with poet, Wesley McNair), Portland Mus Art, Maine, 95, Schmidt Bingham Gallery, NY, 98 & Dozier Bell: Primary Themes, Lyman Allyn Art Mus, New London, Conn, 98, Chase Gallery, Boston, 99, 2000, 2005, June Fitzpatrick Gallery, Portland, 2000, Aucosisco Gallery, Portland, Maine, 98, 2002, 2004, 2005, Univ Maine, 2003, Hudson River Mus, NY, 2003, Nat Acad Sciences, Washington, DC, 2004, Univ Maine Mus Art, Bangor, 2004, DFN Gallery, NY, 2004, 2006.; Farnsworth Mus Art, Rockland, Maine, 95; Changing Horizons: Landscape on the Eve of the Millennium, Katonah Mus Art, NY, 96; Secrets, Schmidt Bingham Gallery, NY, 97; group exhibs: 2001 Collectors Show, The Ark Arts Ctr, 2001, Arnot Art Mus, Elmira, NY, 2001, Chase Gallery, Boston, Mass, 2001, From Nature, AVC Contemp Arts Gallery, NY, 2002, 9/11: Prelude to an Apocalypse, Art Gallery, Univ of New Eng, Maine, 2002; Seasons of Change: Maine Women Artists and Nature, Payson Gallery, Westbrook Coll, Portland, 98; After Nature, Herter Gallery, Univ of Mass, Amherst, 99; Different Strokes, Farnsworth Mus, Rockland, Maine, 99; Photographing Maine: 1850-2000, Maine Coast Artists, Rockland, 2000; Re-Presenting Represenation V, Arnot Art Mus, NY, 2001-2002; Keenly Observed, Sacred Heart Univ, Conn, 2002; Past, Present and Future: 50th Anniversary Exhibition, Ctr Maine Contemporary Art, Rockport, 2002; Prelude to Apocalypse, Art Gallery Univ New England, Westbrook, Maine, 2002; Facing Reality: The Seavest Collection Contemporary Realism, Neuberger Mus Gallery, NY, 2003-2004; Images of Time and Place: Contemporary Views of Landscape, Lehman Gallery, Bronx, 2004; The Environment of Landscape: Works from the Olivia and Ellwood Straub Collection, Bates Coll Mus Art, Maine, 2005; The Figure in American Painting and Drawing 1985-2005, Ogunquit Mus Am Art, Maine, 2006. *Awards:* Visual Artist Fel Grant, Nat Endowment Arts Grant, 87; Bellagio Study & Conf Ctr Residency, Rockefeller Found, 93; Pollock-Krasher Found Grant, 93; Fulbright Full Grant, residency, Weiman, Ger, 95; Achievement Award, Maine Coll of Art, Portland, 97; Residency at MacDowell Colony, Peterborough, NH, 2000; Pollock-Krasner Found Grant, 2003-04. *Bibliog:* Edgar Allen Beem (auth), True Native Vision: Celeste Roberge and Dozier Bell, Two of Maine's Most Important Artists, Maine Times, 12/2/88, Laurent and Bell in Black and White, Maine Times, 7/12/91 & Two June Shows in July, Maine Times, 7/16/98

BELL, KAREN A
EDUCATOR
b Ithaca, NY, Mar 16, 51. *Study:* State Univ NY, Potsdam, BA, 73; Sarah Lawrence Col, MFA, 80. *Comn:* Free for All (choreography), Univ Memphis, Tenn, 94; Commadeire (choreography), Cornell Univ, Ithaca, NY, 94; I'll Take Five (choreography), comn by Peggy Gaither, Honolulu, 94; More (choreography), comn by Dori Jenks, Waikoloa, Hawaii, 94. *Pos:* Assoc dean, Col Arts, Ohio State Univ, 92-; Northeast regional coordr, Am Col Dance Festival Asn, 92-; chairperson, Dept Dance, Ohio State Univy, 95; assoc dean, Col Arts. Ohio State Univ, 1995-2001, interim dean, 2001-02, dean, 2002-. *Teaching:* Instr dance, Cornell Univ, 74-78; assoc prof dance, Ohio State Univ, 80-. *Awards:* Ohio State Univ Col Arts Res Grant, 83 & 84; Ohio Arts Coun Individual Fel, 85. *Mem:* Am Col Dance Festival Asn. *Media:* Choreography. *Mailing Add:* OSU Col of the Arts Off of the Dean 152 Hopkins Hall 128 No Oval Mall Columbus OH 43210

BELL, LARRY STUART
SCULPTOR
b Chicago, Ill, 39. *Study:* Chouinard Art Inst, Los Angeles, with Robert Irwin, Richards Ruben, Robert Chuey & Emerson Woelfer, 57-59. *Work:* Nat Collection Fine Arts, Wash; Mus Mod Art, Whitney Mus Am Art, Solomon R Guggenheim Mus, NY; Whitney Mus Am Art, NY; Tate Gallery, London, Eng; Menil Collection, Houston, Tex. *Comn:* Gen Elec Corp, Gen Hg Fairfield, Conn; City of Abilene, Abilene Zoological Gardens, Tex; Myers Develop Co, San Francisco; City of Albquerque; Mus Abteiberg, Ger; The Great Eagle Corp, Hong Kong. *Exhib:* solo exhibs, Tampa Mus Art, Fla, 92, Galerie Rolf Ricke, Cologne, Ger, 93, Art Mus Univ NMex, Taos, 2004, Bernard Jacobson Gallery, London, 2005, Pace Wildenstein Gallery, New York City, 2005, Daniel Templon Gallery, Paris, 2006, Annandale Galleries, Sydney, 2006 & and others; Beyond Geometry, LACMA, Los Angeles, Calif, 04; The Big Nothing, Univ Pa, Inst Contemp Art, Philadelphia, Pa, 04; Specific Objects, Mus Contemp Art, San Diego, Calif, 04; Centro Cult Belem, Lisboa, Portugal, 2005; Las Vegas Art Mus, Nev, 2006; Centre George Pompidou, Paris, 2006; Los Angeles County Mus Art, Calif, 2006; Norton Simon Mus, Los Angeles, 2006; and others. *Teaching:* Instr sculpture, Univ SFla, Tampa, Univ Calif, Berkeley & Univ Calif, Irvine, 70-73, Southern Calif Inst Archit, Santa Monica, 88 & Taos Inst Arts, NMex, 89-90; instr, Chouinard, 04-05. *Awards:* Guggenheim Mus Fel, 70; Nat Endowment for Arts Grant, 75; Gov Award for Excellence & Achievement in Arts, Visual Arts, State of NMex, 90. *Bibliog:* Peter Plagens (auth) Ferus, Art Forum Int Best of 2002, 12/2002; James Meyer (auth), Minimalism, Phaidon, 03; Anne Goldstein (auth), A Minimal Future, Los Angeles, 04; Christopher Knight (auth), Max Minimal, LA Times, 04; Terry Berne (auth), In the Age of Monchrome, Art in Am, 05. *Media:* Light. *Mailing Add:* 4101 NDCBU Taos NM 87571

BELL, LILIAN A
SCULPTOR, CONCEPTUAL ARTIST
b London, Eng, Nov 5, 43; US citizen. *Study:* William Morris Tech Sch, London; Linfield Col, McMinnville, Ore, 69-70. *Work:* Portland Art Mus; Visual Art Ctr, Beer Sheva, Israel; Nexus Found Today's Art, Philadelphia; Seattle City Light, Wash; State of Ore Pub Art Collection. *Exhib:* One-man shows, Blackfish Gallery, Portland, Ore, 90 & Nat Mus, San Jose, Costa Rica, 91, Linfield Col, Ore, 96, DNA Dreams, Georgi Velchev Mus, Varna, Bulgaria, 04, Portland Art Inst, Ore, 05; group exhib, Medium: paper, Mus Fine Arts, Budapest, 92; group exhib, Int Fax Art, Int Electrographic Mus, Cuenca, Spain, 92; group exhib, Outside from Within, Univ Arts, Philadelphia, Pa, 94; group exhib, Libros de Artistas, Musee Nacional de Bellas Artes, Buenos Aires, Arg, 96; group exhib, Boundless San Francisco Ctr Bk, 98; group exhib, 3rd Int Triennial of Graphic Art Mus Bitola, Macedonia, 2000, Mus Contemp Art, Miskoki Gallery, Budapest, Hungary, 2004. *Pos:* Guest lectr, US & abroad, 73-; guest cur, Univ Ore Traveling Exhib, 80-82; guest cur, Int Fax Art Events, Enter the Electronic River & Megaliths & Office Machines, Linfield Col, McMinnville, Ore, 94 & 96. *Awards:* Western States Arts Found Visual Arts Fel, 77; Ore Arts Comn Individual Artist Fel, 89. *Bibliog:* Juan Carlos Flores (auth), The death of the icon: The post modern paper sculpture of Lilian A Bell, vol 4 no 2, Reflex, 90; L Robin Rice (auth), Outside from within: paper as sculpture, Hand Papermaking, Vol 9, No 1, 94; David Schlater (auth), University of Idaho Book Arts Gallery, 95. *Mem:* Artists Equity Asn (bd mem Ore chap, 78-79); Digital Art Exchange Global Interconnectivity Initiative, Spokane, Wash; YLEM: Artists Using Sci and Tech. *Media:* Artists Books; Laser Prints. *Publ:* Contribr, The Art of Papermaking, Davis, 83; Sculpture: Technique, Form/Content, Davis, 89; Urgent Images - The Graphic Image of the Fax, Booth-Clibborn Eds, London, 94; Co-Media, Arnyekkotok Electro-Graphic Art, Budapest, Hungary, 92-2003; contribr, Arte Telematica, Itau Cultural, Sao Paulo, Brazil, 2003. *Mailing Add:* PO Box 1235 McMinnville OR 97128-1235

BELL, MARY CATHERINE
ART DEALER
b Richmond, Va, Jan 1, 46. *Study:* Wayne State Univ, Detroit, BA(art hist), 71. *Pos:* Asst sales dir, Samuel Stein Fine Arts, Chicago, 73-76; owner, Mary Bell Galleries, Chicago, 76-. *Bibliog:* Gladys Riskind (auth), Corporate art up and coming, Avenue M Mag, 6/81. *Specialty:* Contemporary American art; Unique paper paintings, sculpture and graphics; Corporate art collections. *Publ:* Auth, Art in the corporate suite, Commerce Mag, 82. *Mailing Add:* 740 N Franklin Chicago IL 60610

BELL, PHILIP MICHAEL
ADMINISTRATOR, HISTORIAN
b Toronto, Ont, Dec 31, 42. *Study:* Univ Toronto, BA & MA(fine art). *Collection Arranged:* W H Coverdale Collection of Canadiana, 73, Western Odyssey, Drawings by S P Hall, 74, Ouebec and Its Environs, Drawings by J P Cockburn (with catalog), 75; Goodridge Roberts: Drawings, 76; William Sawyer: Portrait Painter, 79; Life Forces: Photographs by Carol Marino, Agnes Etherington Art Ctr, 87; Pictorial Incidents: Photographs by William Gordon Shields, Agnes Etherington Art Ctr, 89. *Pos:* Cur paintings, drawings & prints, Pub Archives Can, Ottawa, Ont, 68-73; dir, Agnes Etherington Art Ctr, Queen's Univ, 73-78; visual arts officer, Ont Arts Coun, 78-79; asst dir, Pub Programs, Nat Gallery Can, 79-81, actg dir, 81; dir & chief exec officer, McMichael Can Collection, 81-86; assoc cur, Agnes Etherington Art Ctr, 86-92; dir, Carleton Univ Art Gallery, Ottawa, Ont, 92-. *Teaching:* Instr Can art hist, Queen's Univ, Kingston, Ont, 75-76; assoc prof, Carelton Univ. *Awards:* Governor-General's Award for Non-Fiction for Painters in a New Land, Can Coun, 74. *Mem:* Asn Col & Univ Art Galleries Can (pres, 94-). *Res:* Nineteenth century & Contemp Canadian art. *Publ:* Auth, William Goodridge Roberts 1904-1974: Drawings, 76; The Last Lion, Rambles in Quebec with J P Cockburn, 78; William Sawyer: Portrait Painter, 79; Kanata: Robert Houle's Histories, 93; Colville Being Seen: The Serigraphs, 94. *Mailing Add:* c/o Carleton Univ Art Gallery 1125 Colonel By Dr Ottawa ON K1S 5B6 Canada

BELL, TREVOR
PAINTER
b Leeds, Eng, Oct 18, 30. *Study:* Leeds Col Art, NDD, 49, ATD, 50. *Work:* Tate Gallery, London; Victoria and Albert Mus, London; IBM, Atlanta, NY; Rouse Company, Ohio; Shearson, Lehman, Hutton, NY; Cummer Mus, Fla; Coca-Cola, Atlanta; Arts Coun Great Britain; Contemp Art Soc, London; Balliol, St Annes, St Catherines & Trinity Col, Oxford, Eng; Am Express, Fla. *Comn:* (painting) The Art of Fugue, Phillips Collection, Holland, 64; Southern Light (painting), Lewis State Bank, Fla, 75; Fla Queen (painting), Orlando Aviation Authority, Fla, 81; painting, Tallahassee Civic Ctr, Fla, 82; IBM, NY, 85; Miami Center, Fla, 88. *Exhib:* Retrospective, Demarco, Edinburgh Arts Coun NIreland, Sheffield, Eng, 70; New Work, Corcoran Gallery, Washington & White Chapel Gallery, London, 73; Print Exhib, Tate Gallery, London, 77; Metrop Mus & Gloria Luria Gallery, Miami, 85, 89 & 91; Eves Mannes Gallery, Atlanta, 86 & 90; Cummer Mus, Jacksonville, Fla, 86; New Art Centre, London, 89; Fort Lauderdale Mus, Fla, 89; Lydon Fine Arts, Chicago, 90-92, 93, 94; Gillian Jason Gallery, London, 90; Ctr Arts, Vero Beach, Fla, 90; Ill Ctr, Chicago, 96; Tate Gallery St Ives, 96; Stephen Lacy Gallery, London, 99. *Pos:* Fla Fine Arts Coun Grants Review Panel, 79 & 80. *Teaching:* Head of painting, Winchester Col Art, United Kingdom, 66-70; chairperson art, Fanshawe Col, Ontario, 70-71; prof graduate painting, Fla State Univ, Tallahassee, 72-96, prof emer 96-. *Awards:* Int Painting Prize, Paris Biennale, 59; Gregory Fel, Univ Leeds, United Kingdom, 60-64; Fla Fine Arts Coun Individual Fel, State Fla, 81. *Bibliog:* Patrick Heron (auth), 2 Cultures: Studio Int, 70; John Elderfield (auth), Studio Int, 70; Burlington Mag, 7/2000. *Media:* Acrylic. *Dealer:* Lydon Fine Art 203 W Superior St Chicago IL 60610; Hodgell Gallery Sarasota FL 34236. *Mailing Add:* c/o Fla State Univ Mus Fine Arts Copeland & W Tenn Tallahassee FL 32306

BELL, WILLIAM J, JR
COLLECTOR
Pos: pres, Bell-Phillip TV Productions & Bell Dramatic Serial Co, Los Angeles. *Awards:* Nominated Top 200 Collectors, ARTnews Mag, 2006. *Mem:* Los Angeles Co Mus Art (trustee, 2005-). *Mailing Add:* LA County Museum Art 5905 Wilshire Blvd Los Angeles CA 90036

BELLOSPIRITO, ROBYN SUZANNE
PAINTER, WRITER
b Glen Cove, NY, Sept 11, 64. *Study:* CW Post Col, Long Island Univ, BA(art hist), 86. *Work:* Nat Mus Women Arts, Washington; 1-800-FLOWERS. *Exhib:* Solo exhibs, 1-800-Flowers sponsored exhib, NY, 95 & Manhasset Pub Libr, 96, Inter Media Arts Ctr, Huntington, NY, 2002, Michael Peter Hayes Salon, East Norwich, NY, 2005; Pulse Points, Harvard Univ, Cambridge, Mass, 96; The L-Word, Eighth Floor Gallery, NY, 96; Fine Arts Mus, Long Island, NY, 96; Still Life, Islip Art Mus, NY, 96; Watchung Arts Ctr, NJ, 97-98; Barnes & Noble, NY, 98; Mask Project NY, Westbury, NY, 2000; Soc Illustrators, New York City, 2002. *Pos:* Asst slide libr, Metrop Mus Art, NY, 87-88; asst-classification, Frick Art Ref Libr, NY, 88-89; ed, Exhibitioner Art Mag, 93-96; artistic dir, Sea Cliff Gallery, NY, 94. *Awards:* Award of Merit, NY State Art Teacher's Asn, 82; Puffin Found Grant (multi-media installation), 97. *Bibliog:* Geri Lipschultz (auth), From the personal to the universal, North Shore Woman's Newspaper, 98; Nicole Burdett (auth), Spiritual Reflection, Town Search, 2002; art review, New Island Ear, 2002. *Media:* Oil, Wood. *Publ:* Cover Illus, Manteia, No 15, 11/95; Creations Mag, fall 98, fall 2003; illus, Pentacle Magazine, Eng, 2/2006. *Mailing Add:* PO Box 235 Oyster Bay NY 11771

BELL ZAHN, COCA (MARY) CATLETT
PAINTER
b Weleetka, Okla, Sept 26, 24. *Study:* Univ Okla, BA; painting with Milford Zornes, Edith & Richard Goetz & Charles Reid; drawing with Don Coen & Robert Kaupelis. *Comn:* Oil painting, Gov Mansion, Oklahoma City, 70; three comns, Kerr Conf Ctr, 83; poster, Arts Coun Oklahoma City, 84; watercolor, Omniplex Sci & Arts Ctr, Oklahoma City, 84; Oklahoma City Tree Bank Found, 88; White House, 88. *Exhib:* 14th Ann Eight State Exhib, Okla Art Ctr, 72; 18th Ann Eight State Exhib, 76, four-man show, 77 & two-man shows, 78, 79 & 81, Okla Art Ctr, Oklahoma City; Distinguished Artists of Okla Exhib, Midwestern Gov's Conf, 77; Living Women, Living Art, Gov Gallery, 81; Nat Gov Asn Conf, Okla, 82; Diamond Jubilee Arts Festival, Okla State Capitol, 82; Smithsonian Inst, 88; and others. *Awards:* Fourth Award, 10th Ann Southwestern Watercolor Soc Regional Exhib, 73; Second Award, Watercolor 74, Okla Watercolor Asn, 74. *Bibliog:* Interview, Okla Educ TV, 79. *Mem:* Okla City Mus Art; Okla Art Guild. *Media:* Watercolor, Oil. *Mailing Add:* 6303 Christon Ct Oklahoma City OK 73118

BELOFF, ZOE
VIDEO ARTIST
b Scotland. *Study:* Studied painting & art hist at Edinburg Univ & Col Art; Columbia Univ, MFA. *Exhib:* Mus Mod Art, NY; Pacific Film Archives; Sundance, Berlin, AFI; NY Film Festival; Beyond, Wexner Ctr Arts, Palais de Beaux Arts, Brussels & Whitney Mus Biennial, 97. *Teaching:* Instr film & digital media, City Col & New York Univ. *Awards:* First Prize, Apple Computer, 97; grant, Found Contemp Performance Art, 97. *Publ:* Contrib, Life Underwater (film) Lost (film); CD-Rom Where There There There Where (film); A Mechanical Medium (film). *Mailing Add:* 504 Grand St A35 New York NY 10002-4182

BELTING, HANS
EDUCATOR, WRITER
b Andernach, Ger, 1935. *Study:* Univ Mainz, Ger, PhD, 1959; Courtauld Inst Univ London, LittD (hon), 2003. *Pos:* European Chair, Col de France, 2002-03. *Teaching:* Prof, art hist Univ Heidelberg, Ger, 1970-80, Univ Munich, Ger, 1980-93; prof, art hist and media theory Staatliche Hochschule Fur Gestaltung, Karlsruhe, Ger, 1993-2002, prof emer, Ger, 2002-; Mary Jane Crowe Prof, Art Hist Northwestern Univ, Chicago, 2003; Has held vis appointments Harvard Univ, Columbia Univ; Getty Vis Prof, Buenos Aires, 2002. *Awards:* Recipient Distinguished Lifetime Achievement Award for Writing on Art, Col Art Asn, 2004. *Mem:* Academia Europaea, Heidelberger Akademie der Wissenschaften, Orden pour le merite fur Wissenschaften und Kunste, Ger, Inst Advanced Study, Berlin, Am Acad Arts and Sciences, Medieval Acad Am. *Publ:* Co-auth: Mosaics and Frescoes of St. Mary Pammakaristos (Fethiye Camii) at Istanbul, 1978, Patronage in Thirteenth-Century Constantinople: An Atelier of Late Byzantine Book Illumination and Calligraphy, 1978; auth: The End of the Hist of Art?, 1987, Max Beckmann: Tradition as a Problem in Modern Art, 1990, Likeness and Presence: A Hist of the Image Before the Era of Art, 1993, The Germans and Their Art: A Troublesome Relationship, 1998, The Invisible Masterpiece: The Modern Myths of Art, 2001, Hieronymus Bosch: The Garden of Earthly Delights, 2002, Art History After Modernism, 2003, Image and Its Public in the Middle Ages: Form and Function of Early Paintings of the Passion; others. *Mailing Add:* Northwestern Univ Dept Art Hist Kresge Centennial Hall 1880 Campus Dr Evanston IL 60208-2208

BELTRAN, ELIO (FRANCISCO)
PAINTER
b Regla Habana, Cuba, Dec 3, 29; US citizen. *Study:* Ministry Educ, MA, 53; Fernando Aguardo Rico Sch Arts & Trades, Havana, 55; Cuyahoga Col, Cleveland, Ohio & Temple Univ, Pa, 60-; studied drawing with Prof Matilde Single, San Alejandro Sch Art, Havana; essentially self-taught. *Work:* Inst Art & Educ, NY; Bergen Mus Art & Sci, Paramus, NJ; Mus Mod Art of the Americas, Washington, DC; Jersey City Mus, NJ; Art Mus Fla Int Univ, Miami; and others. *Comn:* Oil painting, comn by C Abril, Madrid, Spain, 92; oil painting, Ed Am, Miami, 93; tribute to Mex painter Refino Tamayo (pvt comn), Princeton, NJ, 97. *Exhib:* Third Biennial Exhib, Newark Mus, NJ, 83; African Currents, Mus Contemp Hispanic Art, NY, 87; Recent Work, Paterson Mus Art, NJ, 89 & Bergen Mus Art & Sci, Paramus, NJ, 95; Cuba USA The First Generation, Mus Contemp Art, Chicago, 91; Discovery Celebration, City Mus NY, 92; First Generation Honor Guest Artist, Mus Fla Int Univ, Miami, 92; Caribbean Connections, Discovery Mus, Bridgeport, 98-99; solo exhib, Jadite Galleries, NY, 98, ARS Atelier, Gustavo Valdes Studio, 99. *Pos:* Judge fel awards, NJ State Coun Art, 85-86. *Teaching:* pvt tutoring. *Awards:* Painting Award, Cinta Found Inst Art & Educ, 83; Priority Winner, NJ State Coun Arts Fel, 83-84; National Outstanding Latino Image Award, NJ Network, 95-96. *Bibliog:* Many articles in newspapers & mags, 81-; Judie Dash (auth & critic), Life Style Mag, Bergen Record, 3/86; Eileen Watkins (auth), Art Section, Star Ledger, Newark, NJ, 10/9/89. *Mem:* PanAm Circle Culture. *Media:* Oil. *Mailing Add:* 242 West Hudson Ave Englewood NJ 07631

BELTRAN, FELIX
PAINTER, PRINTMAKER
b Havana, Cuba, June 23, 38; Mex citizen. *Study:* Sch Visual Arts, New York, NY, 60; New Sch, New York, 61; Am Art Sch, 62. *Work:* Stedelijk Mus, Amsterdam; Kunstgewerbemuseum, Zurich; Moderna Musset, Stockholm; Victoria & Albert Mus, Paris; Ermitage Mus, Leningrad. *Comn:* Murals, Cuban Pavilion, Osaka, 69. *Exhib:* The Art of the Book, Mus der Bilden Kunste, Leipzig, 65; The Art in Cuba, Kunstgewerbemuseum, Zurich, 65; The Art in Cuba, Lunds Konsthall, Lunds, 68; New Prints, Nat Mus, Stockholm, 68; The Art of Cuba, Museo de Arte, Chile, 71; The Art of Cuba, Stedelijk Mus, Amsterdam, 71; New Prints, Ermitage Mus, Leningrad, 73; The Art of Cuba, Altes Mus, Berlin-East, 75. *Pos:* Pres, Union de Artistas de Cuba, Havana, 77-81 & Nat Comt Int Asn Art, Havana, 79-82. *Teaching:* Titular prof fine art, Inst Superior de Arte, Havana, 75-81, Univ Autonoma Metrop, 82- & Univ Iberoamericana, 85-. *Awards:* Excellence Award, Am Inst Graphic Art, New York, 61. *Mem:* Alliance Graphic Int (nat pres, 76); Am Inst Graphic Art; Print Club, Philadelphia. *Media:* All. *Dealer:* Marcela Sotelo-Galeria Trazo-Montanas Rocallosas 508 Lomas de Virreyes Mexico 11000 DF. *Mailing Add:* Apartado De Correos M 10733 Mexico 06000 Mexico

BELVILLE, SCOTT ROBERT
PAINTER, EDUCATOR
b Jan 8, 52; US citizen. *Study:* Ohio Univ, Athens, MFA, 77. *Work:* Hirshhorn Mus, Washington, DC; Ga Mus Art, Athens; Greenville Co Mus Art, SC; Chase Manhattan Bank & Walker Art Ctr, Minneapolis, Minn; First Bank Systems, Minneapolis, Minn. *Exhib:* Solo exhibs, Jus de Pomme Gallery, NY, 86, Greenville Co Mus Art, SC, 88,

Thomas Barry Fine Arts, Minneapolis, 88, 91, Sandler/Hudson Gallery, Atlanta, 90, 94, 95 & 98, Kavesh Gallery, Idaho, 95 & Opelika Art Asn Gallery, Ala, 98; Thomas Barry Fine Arts, Minneapolis, Minn, 88 & 90; Sandler/Hudson Gallery, Atlanta, Ga, 89 & 91; Exploring the Canvas/Int Landscape, Gwinnett Fine Arts Ctr, Ga, 94; Talent, Alan Stone Gallery, NY, 96; Bridgewater/Lustberg Gallery, NY, 96; SEastern Ctr Contemp Art, NC, 97; Greenville Co Mus Art, SC, 97; and others. *Teaching:* Artist-in-residence, Univ Ga, Athens, 77-78, instr painting, 80-81, asst prof, 84-86; instr painting, Converse Col, Spartanburg, SC, 82-84 & 86-88; assoc prof painting, Univ Ga, Athens, 89. *Awards:* Ford Found Fel, Univ Ga, Athens, 77-78; MacDowell Colony Fel, 79; Nat Endowment Arts Grant, 83-84 & 96-97; South Carolina Individual Artist Grant in Painting, 88-89. *Mem:* Col Art Asn. *Media:* Oil. *Dealer:* Thomas Barry Fine Art Minneapolis MN; Sandler/Hudson Gallery 1831A Peachtree Rd Atlanta GA 30309. *Mailing Add:* 230 Milledge Cir Athens GA 30606

BEMAN, LYNN SUSAN
MUSEUM DIRECTOR, HISTORIAN
b Buffalo, NY, Dec 23, 1942. *Study:* Goucher Col, 60-62; Briarcliff Col, BA, 75. *Collection Arranged:* American Watercolors: 1860-1940, Trisdonn Gallery, 82; 19th Century Painters & Paintings of Rockland Co Hopper House, 84; Julian O Davidson: Am Marine Artist, Hist Soc Rockland Co, 86; Elmer Stanley Hader: The GrandView Years, Hopper House, 88; The Ice Horse-Paintings by Thomas Locker, 93; Silent Soliloquy: Paintings by Susan Reddy, 97. *Pos:* Cur, ADC Fine Art Inc, 73-78; dir, Trisdonn Gallery Ltd, 80-84, Beman Galleries Inc, 84-89; cur, Hudson River Maritime Mus, 90, actg dir, 90-91, exec dir, 91-93; exec dir, Amherst Mus, 94-2005; bd dir, Erie & Co Hist Fedn, 94- & WNY Asn Hist Agencies, 95-; comnr, Town of Amherst Historic Preservation Comn, Western Erie Canal Heritage Corridor; exec dir, Mus of Disability Hist, 05-. *Teaching:* lectr art hist, historic preservation & mus studies, Empire State Col. *Awards:* Distinguished Historian, Tappantown Hist Soc, 85; Historical Serv, Lower Hudson Conf, Award for Excellence Hist Agencies & Mus, 87; Award of Merit Western NY Asn Hist Agencies, 98, 99, 2004 & 05. *Mem:* Eric Co Hist Fedn; Am Asn Mus; AASLH; MAAM; WNY Asn Hist Agencies. *Res:* 19th and early 20th-century American art with emphasis on the rediscovery of artists and their work; American marine art. *Publ:* Auth, George Merritt Clark: A Buffalo Bohemian, NY-PA Collector, 83; 19th-Century Painters & Paintings of Rockland Co, NY, Ed Hopper Found, 84; Julian O Davidson (1853-1894): American Marine Artist, Hist Soc Rockland Co, 86; Julian O Davidson A Rediscovery in American Marine Art, Sea Hist Mag, 87; Elmer Stanley Hader (1889-1973): Rediscovered American Impressionist, Nyack Publ, 89. *Mailing Add:* 135 Washington Hwy Amherst NY 14226

BEN-HAIM , TSIPI
CRITIC, EXEC DIR
b USSR; Am & Isreali Citizen. *Study:* Tel-Aviv Univ, BA, 79; NY Univ, MA, 83; Columbia Univ, 87. *Work:* Cityarts Pub Art Catalog, 2002. *Collection Arranged:* Back to Earth (sculpture; catalog), 87; Creative Process (catalog), 87; MozArt (catalog), 91; Cityarts Pieces for Peace Traveling Exhib, 2005-2006. *Pos:* Art critic & NY corresp, Sculpture Mag, 82-; exec & artistic dir, Cityarts Inc, 89-; Art & Culture Writer Yediotlusa, 2006. *Awards:* Am Israel Cult Found, 84; NY Univ, 82-83; Visual Arts Travel Fund, Mid-Atlantic Arts Found. *Bibliog:* Nicole Lyn Pesce (auth), Students Mural Dreams are Coming True, Online News, 7/04; Art Bears an Olive Branch, Daily News, 7/14/06; Christopher Casof (auth), Paint for Peace, NY Post, 7/29/06. *Mem:* Int Sculpture Ctr; Int Art Critics Asn Am; Art Table. *Interests:* Traveling; Reading; Writing; Film; Photog; Dancing; Visial Art. *Publ:* Auth, Cartier Foundation/France/Sculpture Park, 86, Isamu Noguchi - The Cullen Sculpture Park, 86 & Awakening the Brooklyn, 90, Sculpture Mag; The Creative Process (catalog) City Arts, 89 & Charlotto Kotik, Sculpture Mag, 90. *Mailing Add:* 94 Mercer St New York NY 10012-4425

BEN-HAIM, ZIGI
SCULPTOR, PAINTER
b Bagdad, Iraq, Nov 28, 45; US citizen. *Study:* Avni Inst Fine Arts, Tel Aviv, Israel, 66-70; Calif Col Arts & Crafts, Oakland, 71; Calif State Univ, San Francisco, MFA, 74. *Work:* Guggenheim Mus, Jewish Mus & Brooklyn Mus, NY; Israel Mus, Jerusalem; Ghent Mus, Belg; Ursinus Col, Pa; Weisman Found. *Comn:* Wind Hunter (sculpture), Israel Mus, Jerusalem, 84; Blooming Stone (sculpture), Frederick Weisman Found, Los Angeles, 86; Rising Path (sculpture), Snug Harbor, Staten Island, NY, 86; Univ Md (sculpture), College Park, 88; Comment in the Green, Tel-Aviv, 93; and others. *Exhib:* Solo exhibs, Art Gallery Hamilton, Ont, 82 & Israel Mus, Jerusalem, 84, Jewish Mus Sculpture Court, 87; With Paper about Paper, Albright-Knox Gallery, Buffalo, NY, 80; Brooklyn Mus, NY, 85; Walking Field, PS 1, Long Island City, NY, 86; Am Experience, Bass Mus, Miami Beach, Fla, 86; Chelouch Gallery, Tel Aviv Israel, 93; Ann Harper Gallery, NY, 96. *Awards:* Nat Endowment Arts Sculpture Grant, 84; Grant, Pollack Krasner Found, 90 & 95. *Bibliog:* Henry Scarupa (auth), Outdoor Sculpture, 11/13/87; William Zimmer (auth), The importance of imagination, NY Times, 10/9/94; Phyllis Braff (auth), Zigi Ben-Haim at Ann Harper NY, NY Times, 9/8/96. *Mem:* Int Sculpture Ctr, Washington. *Media:* Steel, Wire Mesh, Stainless Steel; Oil, Aluminum, Acrylic, Paper. *Dealer:* Stefan Stux Gallery New York City; Chelouch Gallery Tel-Aviv, Isreal. *Mailing Add:* 94 Mercer St New York NY 10012

BENDELL, MARILYN
PAINTER, INSTRUCTOR
b Grand Ledge, Mich, Sept 19, 21. *Study:* Am Acad Art; and with Arnold E Turtle & Pierre Nuyttens. *Work:* Principia Col, St Louis; Saginaw Mus, Mich; Hadley Sch for Blind, Winnetka, Ill; Huntington Mus Fine Arts, WVa. *Comn:* Juggler of Notre Dame, comn by Sen Schuch, Saginaw Mus, 50; portrait of founder Principia Col, comn by William E Morgan, St Louis, 58; portrait of Helen Keller, Hadley Sch for Blind, 58; portrait of Mrs Paul Schulze, comn by Paul Schulze, Chicago, Ill, 60; David & Kim, Huntington Mus Fine Arts, 65. *Exhib:* Chicago Galleries, Ill, 55; Ill State Fair, Springfield, 58; 16th Ann Mem Exhib, Acad Artists Asn, Springfield, Mass, 64; Famous Fla Artists, Frank Oehlschlaeger Galleries, Sarasota, 64 & 65; Acad Artists Asn Nat Show, Springfield, 72; solo show, Joe Wade Fine Arts, Santa Fe, NMex, 88; Aikens Fine Art, Scottsdale, Ariz, 90; Huntsman Gallery Fine Art, Aspen, Colo, 91; Aidan Flores Gallery Fine Arts, Scottsdale, Ariz, 91. *Teaching:* Instr portrait, figure & still life, Longboat Key Art Ctr, Fla, 52-68; instr still life, Oak Park-River Forest Art League, Ill, 57-59; instr portrait, figure & still life, Cortez Art Sch, Fla, 68-74; pvt art classes, 74-; instr, Bendell Galleries & Art Sch, Fla, 74-82 & Scottsdale Artists Sch, 87-92. *Awards:* Popular Award for Bus Stop, Ill State Fair, 61; First in Portrait for Jeri, 64 & First in Portrait & Figure, Portrait of a Young Woman, 70, Springfield Mus Fine Arts. *Bibliog:* WC Burnett (auth), Two art shows reviewed, Sarasota Herald Tribune, 64; Charles Benbow (auth), She reflects her colorful oil paintings, St Petersburg Times, 11/13/71; Don Jones (auth), 5/82 & Ann Katherine (auth), 5/85, Art Mag; Joy Murphy (auth), Southwest Art Mag, 4/88; Shirley Behrens (auth), Art of the West, 7/90; Vicki Stauig (auth), Art of the West, The Studio, 92; Cecelia Logan (auth), The Artistic Magic of Marilyn Bendell, Int Fine Art Collection, 92; Catherine Butler (auth), The magic of moments, Guest Life Publ, 94, The Romance of the Moment, 95, Moments of Beauty, 98; Candelaria Versace (auth), The Santa Fean, 12/94; Nancy Gillespie (auth), Capturing the Human Spirit, Art of the West Mag,. 2001. *Mem:* Brown Co Art Gallery Asn; Fel Royal Soc Arts; Am Artists Prof League; Acad Artists Asn, Springfield; Sarasota Art Asn. *Media:* Oil. *Dealer:* Mountain Trails, Santa Fe, NM; La Macarena Sante Fe. *Mailing Add:* 46 Loma Blanca Santa Fe NM 87501

BENDER, BILL
PAINTER
b El Segundo, Calif, Jan 5, 19. *Work:* US Air Force Acad, Colorado Springs, Colo; US Navy, Pensacola, Fla; Pentagon, Washington; Living Desert Asn, Palm Desert, Calif; Visitors Ctr, Death Valley, Calif. *Exhib:* Mountain Oyster Contemp Western Art Show, Tucson, Ariz, 72-97; High Plains Heritage Ctr, Spearfish, SDak. *Awards:* Hon Deputy Sheriff, San Bernardino Co. *Bibliog:* Ed Ainsworth (auth), Painters of the desert, Desert Mag, 60; Ed Ainsworth (auth), The Cowboy in Art, World Publ, 69; Peggy & Harold Samuels (auths), Contemporary Western Artists, 83. *Mem:* Life mem Cowboy Hall Fame, Okla; hon life mem, Mountain Oyster Club, Tucson; Death Valley 49ers Inc (hon dir); life mem, Westerners, San Dimas, Calif. *Media:* Oil, Watercolor. *Publ:* Illusr, Christmas cards, stationery & calendars, Leanin' Tree Publ, 60-98; Beckoning Desert, Prentice-Hall, 62; Day I Climb Down from the Horse, Brand Bk 3m, San Diego Westerners, 73; illusr, Paul Bailey (auth), An Unnatural History of Death Valley, 78; auth & illus, The Death Valley 49ers as I Remember Them, 98. *Mailing Add:* 24887 Nat Trails Hwy Oro Grande CA 92368

BENDER, LESLIE MARILYN
PAINTER, MURALIST
b Newark, NJ, Jan 30, 52. *Study:* Art Studies League, 1968-1974; Prat Inst, BFA, 1975; Cobalt Studies (scenic painting), 1995. *Work:* Mus of Mod Art, NYC; Fairview Art Mus, Springville, UT; Dutchess Community Col, Hyde Park, NY; Fins Grafiske Vaerksted, Odense, Denmark; Woodstock Hist Soc. *Comn:* 3 Pub Art Murals, City Arts Workshop, NYC, 1981-1983; Artwork on Paper: Women Chefs, Culinary Inst of Am, Hyde Park, NY, 1990; Mural, St Mark African Am Episcopal Church, Kingston, NY, 1999; Mural, Vassar PEACE Project, Poughkeepsie, NY, 2001. *Exhib:* Meta Manhattan, Whitney Downtown, NYC, 1984; Committed to Print, Mus Mod Art, NYC, 1988; NY Series IX: Message to the Future, Herbert F Johnson Mus, Ithaca, NY, 1991; Hudson-Mohawk Regional, NY State Mus, Albany, NY, 1995-1996, 1998; Chrysler Mus Art, Norfolk, Va, 1998. *Pos:* Mural Artist, various projects, 1981-2006; Scenic Artist, various theaters, 1995-2006. *Teaching:* Mural project coordr, art-in-educ, various schs, 1985-2006. *Awards:* Barbara Bertoli Award for drawing, Woodstock Artists Asn, 1989; Woodstock Artists Grant to Emerging Artists, Woodstock Artists Asn, 1992; Va Center for the Arts, Artist-in-Residence Program, 2000. *Bibliog:* Deborah Wye (auth), Committed to Print, Mus Mod Art, 1990; Angry Graphics, Peregrine Books, 1991. *Media:* Oilpaint, Oilstick, Acrylic, Pastel, Gouache, Graphite. *Dealer:* Chase-Randall Gallery Andes NY 13731. *Mailing Add:* 64 Plains Rd New Paltz NY 12561

BENDER, MAY
PAINTER
b Newark, NJ, Feb 8, 21. *Study:* Art Students League, New York, 45-50, 68-74 & 88-90. *Work:* over 450 oils and many works on paper. *Exhib:* one-woman shows, Middlesex Co Col, Edison, NJ, 93, Temple B'nai Jeshurun, Short Hills, NJ, 93, Tucker Anthony, Princeton, NJ, 94, Johnson & Johnson & Sons Inc, New Brunswick, NJ, 95, Gallery Swan, New York, 96, Georgian Court Col, Lakewood, NJ, 98 & Piscataway Cult Comn, NJ, 98, Northwood Univ, Cedar Hill, Tex, 2002, Full House Productions, New York, 2001-02, Artsforum, New York, 2003; NJ Performing Arts Ctr, Newark, 2000-05; Red River Valley Mus, Tex, 2001; Omniplex Gallery, Oklahoma City, 2001; Estados Unidos de Am, Seville, Madrid, Barcelona, Spain, 2002-03; New Art Ctr, NY, 2003-05; Amsterdam Whitney Gallery, NY, 2004. *Pos:* Creative dir & pres, May Bender Design Assocs, NY & NJ, 68-91. *Teaching:* Instr marketing & package design, Parsons, NY, 80; lectr packaging seminars, Rutgers Univ, Pratt Inst, Long Island Univ & others. *Awards:* Clio Award for packaging, Ann Awards, 77, 78 & 79; Painting Award, Ridgefield Artists Asn. *Mem:* Life mem, NY Art Students League; NY Artists Equity; Visual Artists League, NJ. *Media:* Oil, Ink. *Specialty:* Painting, sculpture and photography. *Interests:* Music, Opera, etc. *Publ:* Auth, Package Design & Social Change, Am Mgt Asn, 75; Package Design in New York, Japanese Publ; numerous articles on package design. *Dealer:* New Art Center New York NY 580 Eigth Ave NYC 10018. *Mailing Add:* 16 Woodland Ave East Brunswick NJ 08816

BENEDICT-JONES, LINDA
PHOTOGRAPHER, CURATOR
b Beloit, Wis, Oct 21, 47. *Study:* Univ Wis-LaCrosse, BS, 69, Univ Lisboa, Portugal, dipl, 72, Mass Inst Tech, MS(visual studies, Arts Coun Gr Brit Grant), 82. *Work:* Bibliotheque Nat, Paris; Mus Cantini, Marseilles, France; Mus Art Hist Fribourg, Switz; Dept Environ, London; Polaroid Collection, Cambridge, Mass. *Exhib:* Imagens de Portugal, Ctr Cult Am, Lisboa, Portugal, 73; solo exhib, Madison Art Gallery, Wis, 76; Serpentine Gallery, London, 78; Quiet Places, Graves Art Gallery, Sheffield, Eng, 79; Les Autoportraits, Ctr Georges Pompidou, Paris, 81; Contemp Self Portraiture, Hayden Gallery, Mass Inst Technol, 83; Latvian Photo Soc, 91. *Pos:* Dir, Clarence Kennedy Gallery, Polaroid Corp, Cambridge, Mass, 84-90, cur, Polaroid Collection, 90-. *Teaching:* Lectr photog, London Col Printing, Eng, 77-79; instr, Mass Inst Technol Creative Photo Lab, 81, DeCordova Mus Sch, Lincoln, Mass, 82-83 & Northeastern Univ, Mass, 83; lectr hist photog, Harvard, 87-. *Bibliog:* Au Coeur d'Elle Meme, Le Nouveau Photo-Cinema, Paris, 76; Roberto Salbitani (auth), Linda Benedict-Jones Progresso Fotografico, Milan, 78; Women on Women, Aurum Press, London, 78. *Mem:* Soc Photog Educ. *Publ:* Auth, biography, Print Letter 24, Switz, 79; Minor White: Contributions & Controversy, Positive, Mass Inst Technol, 81; Lee Friedlander, Positive, Mass Inst Technol, 82; Whither documentary? Ten contemporary British photographers, Positive, Mass Inst Technol, 82; Black British Photographers, Spot, 92. *Dealer:* Galerie Viviane Esders, Paris, France; Photogr Gallery 8-12 Gt Newport St London England. *Mailing Add:* 256 Jefferson Dr Pittsburgh PA 15228-2111

BENEDIKT, MICHAEL
WRITER, CONSULTANT
b New York, NY, May 26, 35. *Study:* NY Univ, BA; Columbia Univ, MA. *Pos:* NY corresp, Art Int Zurich, Switz, 65-67; ed assoc, Art News, NY, 63-72; mem mixed media panels, NY State Coun Arts, 77; consult mem, NY Art Critics Circle, 79-; designated panelist, Nat Endowment Humanities, 82. *Teaching:* Vis prof writing, Sarah Lawrence Col, Bronxville, NY, 69-73; assoc prof, Hampshire Col, Amherst, Mass, 73-75; vis prof writing, Vassar Col, 76-77 & Boston Univ, 77-79. *Awards:* Guggenheim Fel, 68; Creative Artist Pub Serv Prog, NY State Coun Arts Grant, 74; Nat Endowment Arts Fel, 79. *Bibliog:* Benedikt: A Profile (monogr), Logbridge Rhodes, 78. *Mem:* PEN Am Ctr; Am Film Inst. *Res:* 19th century French painting; preparation of revised edition of Modern French Theatre; The Avant Garde, Dada & Surrealism, anthology originally issued by Dutton, 1964; realist tradition in American art, historical and contemporary; links of recent US painting to still photography, film and especially video. *Publ:* Auth, The continuities of Pierre Bonnard, Art News, 64; ed, Theatre Experiment: An Anthology of American Plays from Gertrude Stein to "Happenings", Doubleday, 68; auth, New York Letter on Sculpture as Architecture in Minimal Art (anthology), Dutton, 68; auth, The visionary French Symbolist painters in the Grand Eccentrics (anthology), 71; Notes on Yoko Ono, Art & Artists, 72; The Poetry of Surrealism (anthology), Little Brown, 75; Poetry & Videotape in New Artists Video, Dutton, 78; and others

BENES, BARTON LIDICE
COLLAGE ARTIST, SCULPTOR
b NJ. *Study:* Pratt Inst, painting with Walter Murch, 60-61; Beaux Arts, Avignon, France, graphics, 68. *Work:* Univ Iowa Mus Art; Mus Mod Art, NY; Bibliot Nat, Paris; Nat Mus Am Art, Washington, DC; Art Inst Chicago; Albuquerque Mus Art, Fed Reserve Bd, Washington, DC. *Comn:* Fed Reserve Bd, Washington, DC; UPS, Atlanta, Ga; Artes and Leiloes, Lisbon, Portugal; NDak Mus Art, Grand Forks. *Exhib:* Love and Death, Goteborgs Konst Mus, Goteborg, Sweden, 94; Lennon Weinberg Gallery, NY, 99; Galeria III, Lisbon, Portugal, 2000; Uppsala Konst Mus, Sweden, 2000; Tretyakov Mus, Moscow, Russia, 2000; Galerie Gisele Linder, Basel, Switz, 2003; Musee de la Civilisation Quebec, 2005; Orlando Mus, 2004. *Awards:* Creative Artists Pub Serv Prog grant, 77; Ariana Found Arts Grant, 82; Grant for Graphics, Rutgers Univ, 83; Pollock Krasner Found Grant, 88. *Bibliog:* Jacqueline Brody (auth), On and off the wall with Benes, Print Collectors Newslett, 79; Theatres of the absurd, Art & Antiques, 3/92; Laurel Reuter (auth), Lethal weapons, NDak Mus Art, 94; I am my own curator, by Sam Knight, NY Times, 2/2005. *Media:* Mixed. *Publ:* The Dog Bite, Plainwrapper Press, 70; The Mugging (A Primer of Urban Living), Winterhouse Ltd, 70; I Have Found a Cockroach in Your Product, Wedgepress & Cheese, 82; illusr, Money Matters, Solo Press, 83; Curiosa, Harry Abrams Inc, 2002; Assuary, Mamopritit Workshop, Alexandria, Va, 2004. *Dealer:* Lennon Weinberg Gallery 560 Broadway New York NY; Galeria III Lisbon Portugal; Stefam Andersson Gallery Umea Sweden; Gisele Linder Galerie Basel Switzerland. *Mailing Add:* 463 West St Apt 956H New York NY 10014

BENEZRA, NEAL
MUSEUM DIRECTOR, CURATOR
Study: Univ Calif at Berkeley, BA, 1976; Stanford Univ, MA, 1981; Stanford Univ, PhD, 1983; Ger Acad Exchange Serv, Postgrad, 1983. *Pos:* Assoc cur, The Art Inst Chicago, 1985-86, cur, 1987-91; chief cur, Hirshhorn Mus and Sculpture Garden, Smithsonian Inst, Wash, DC, 1991-1996; asst dir, art and pub prog, 1996; dep dir, Frances and Thomas Dittmer curmodern and contemp art, 2000-2002; dir, San Francisco Mus Modern Art, 2002-; coordr Anderson Collection, Atherton, Calif, 1980-83; asst cur, Des Moines Art Ctr, 1983-84; mem, Smithsonian Coun; art adv bd mem, Univ Calif, San Francisco; art adv panel IRS, Dept Treas. *Teaching:* Vis lectr, Univ Ill, Urbana-Champaign, 1988; vis assoc prof Univ Chicago, 1990. *Awards:* Grad fel Stanford Univ, 1978-81, McCloy fel in Ger art, 1984-85. *Publ:* Cur exhib/auth catalogue: Robert Arneson: A Retrospective, 1986, Ed Paschke: Paintings, 1989, Affinities and Intuitions: The Gerald S. Elliott Collection of Contemp Art, 1990, Martin Puryear, 1991, Bruce Nauman, 1993-94, Stephen Balkenhol, 1995-96. *Mailing Add:* San Francisco Mus Mod Art 151 Third St San Francisco CA 94103

BENGLIS, LYNDA
SCULPTOR, PAINTER
b Lake Charles, La, Oct 25, 41. *Study:* Yale Norfolk Summer Fel, 63; Newcomb Col, Tulane Univ, with Ida Kohlmeyer, Pat Trivigno, Zolton Buki & Halrold Carney, BFA, 64; Brooklyn Mus Art Sch, with Rubin Tam, Max Beckman Scholar, 65. *Hon Degrees:* Hon Dr, Kansas City Art Inst, 2000. *Work:* Whitney Mus Am Art; Solomon R Guggenheim Mus; Am Mus Mod Art, NY; Hokkaido Mus Mod Art, Sapporo, Japan; Gihon Found, Dallas; and others. *Comn:* Adhesive products, Walker Art Ctr, Minneapolis, 71; Hartsfield Int Airport, Atlanta, 80; Leo W O'Brien Fed Bldg, Albany, 81; Fairmont Hotel, Denver, 82; Prudential Life Insurance Co, Parsippanny, NJ, 82; Cadillac Fairview, Dallas, Tex, 84; Crocker Bldg, Crocker Properties, San Francisco, 85. *Exhib:* Painting in Relief, Whitney Mus Am Art, 80; With Paper, About Paper, Albright-Knox Art Gallery, 80; 1981 Whitney Biennial, Whitney Mus Am Art, 81; New Dimensions in Drawing, Aldrich Mus Contemp Art, 81; Developments in Recent Sculpture, Whitney Mus Am Art, 81; 74th Am Exhib, Art Inst Chicago, 82; PostMINIMALISM, Aldrich Mus Contemp Art, Ridgefield Conn; 20th Century Sculpture: Process & Presence, Whitney Mus Am Art, NY, 83; Minimalism to Expressionism: Painting & Sculpture Since 1965 from the Permanent Collection, Whitney Mus Am Art, 83; 20th Anniversary of the National Endowment for the Arts, Mus Mod Art, NY, 86; Made in India, Mus Mod Art, NY, 85; Philadelphia Collects: European & Am Art Since 1940, Philadelphia Mus Art, Pa, 86; Contemp Painting & Sculpture Galleries, Mus Mod Art, NY, 86-87; Structure to Resemblance: Work by Eight Am Sculptors, Albright-Knox Art Gallery, Buffalo, NY, 87; From the LeWitt Collection, Wadsworth Atheneum, 87; Contemp Am Collage Traveling Show, Butler Inst Am Art, 88; La Toilette de Venus: Women and Mirrors, CRG, NY, 96; one-person exhibs, Gallery Chemould, Jehangir Art Gallery, Mumbai, India, 97, Univ NTex, Sch Visual Arts, Denton, 97, Galerie Michael Janssen, Cologne, Ger, 97, Forum Kunst Rottweil, Ger, 98, Contemp Art Mus, Univ SFla, Tampa, 98, Cheim & Read, NY, 98 & 99, Kappatos Gallery, Athens, Greece, 98, Weatherspoon Gallery, Univ NC at Greensboro, 2000, Toomey Turrell Gallery, San Francisco, 01; The Edge of Chaos, Fotouhi Cramer Gallery, NY, 97; After the Fall: Aspects of Abstract Painting Since 1980, Newhouse Ctr Contemp Art, Sang Harbor Cult Ctr, NY, 97; Plastik Wurttembergischer Kunstverein, Stuttgart, Ger, 97; Laying Low, Kunstnernes Hus, Oslo, Norway, 97; Cheim & Read, NY, 97; Gravity-Axis of Contemp Art, Nat Mus Art, Osaka, Japan, 97; Hanging By a Thread, Hudson River Mus, Yonkers, NY, 97; MAI 98 Positions in Contemp Art Since the 1960's, Kunsthalle Koln, 98; Maschile Feeminile per esempio Picasso, Newton, Yoko One e, Centro Internazionale Mostre, Rome, 98; Small Paintings, Cheim & Read, NY, 98; Dreams for the Next Century, Parrish Art Mus, NY, 98; Off the Wall: Eight Contemp Am Sculptors, Asheville Art Mus, NC, 98-99; Afterimage, Drawing Through Process, Mus of Contemp Art, Los Angeles, 99; Am Acad Invitational, NY, 2000; The Am Century: Whitney Mus Modern Art, NY, 2000; Matter, Mus of Modern Art, NY, 01; one man shows, Susanne Hilberry Gallery, Ferndale, Mich, Frank Lloyd Gallery, Santa Monica, Calif, 2005, Linda Benglis: Pleated, Knotted, Poured, Locks Gallery, Philadelphia, Pa, 2006; Contemporary Woman Artists, Univ Art Gallery, Ind State Univ, Terre Haute, Ind, 2005; Women's Work, Greenberg Van Doren, NY, 2006; The Last Time They Met, Stephen Friedman Gallery, London, UK, 2006. *Teaching:* Asst prof sculpture, Univ Rochester, 70-72; asst prof, Hunter Col, 72-73, prof, 80-81; vis prof, Calif Inst Arts, 74 & 76, Princeton Univ, 75, Dept Art, Univ Ariz, 82, fine arts workshop, Sch Visual Arts, 85-96 & Santa Fe Inst Fine Arts, 93, 94 & 96; vis artist, Kent State Univ, 77 & Skowhegan Sch Painting & Sculpture, 79; Col Santa Fe, 94 & 95; sr critic, Yale Univ, 94. *Awards:* Nat Endowment Arts Grant, 79 & 90; Olympiad Art Sculpture Park, Korea, 88; Award of Distinction, Nat Coun Art Adminr, 89. *Bibliog:* Robert Pincus-Witten (auth), The Frozen Gesture & Benglis, Video Medium to Media, In: Post Minimalism, 77; Doug Davis (auth), article, Art Cult, 77; Lynda Benglis (auth), interview in Ocular, summer 79; Michael Brenson (auth), Art, New York Times, 8/3/86; Lisbet Nelson (auth), Chicago's Art Explosion, Artnews, 5/87; Suzanne Muchnic (auth), Lynda Benglisat Margo Leavin, Los Angeles Times 5/22/87; Holland Cotter (auth), Lynda Benglis at Paula Cooper, Art in Am, 7/87; Phyllis Braff (auth), Faculty Show: Range of Ideas, The New York Times, 9/6/87; Robert C Morgan (auth), American Sculpture & the Search for a Referant, Arts Mag, 11/87; and many others

BENGSTON, BILLY AL
PAINTER
b Dodge City, Kans, June 7, 34. *Work:* Mus Mod Art, NY; Art Inst Chicago; San Jose Hilton Collection of Art, Calif; Whitney Mus Am Art, NY; Centre Georges Pompidou, Paris, France. *Comn:* Calif State Off Bldg, Calif Arts Coun, Los Angeles; Los Angeles Chamber Commerce (7 panel painting), 94; Janss Corp (2 Sculptures), Pasadena, Calif, 94; Salik Health Care (mural), Los Angeles, 97. *Exhib:* Chicago Biennial Painting Exhib, Art Inst Chicago, 63 & 72; Eighth Biennial, Sao Paulo, Brazil, also shown Smithsonian Inst, 65; Whitney Ann Painting Exhib, Whitney Mus Am Art, 67, 69 & 79; retrospective, Los Angeles Co Mus Art, 68; Kompas IV, Stekelijk van Abbemuseum, Eindhoven, The Neth, 69; solo exhibs, Honolulu Acad Arts, Hawaii, 80, Corcoran Gallery Art, Washington, DC, 80, San Diego State Univ, Calif, 81 & Galerie Neuendorf, Frankfurt, Ger, 93; Retrospective, Billy II, Paintings of Three Decades, Contemp Arts Mus, Houston, Oakland Mus, Los Angeles Co Mus Art, Contemp Arts Crt, Honolulu, 88. *Pos:* Founder, Artist Studio, Venice, Calif, 60; pres, Westside Strokers, Los Angeles, 78-79 & Pelican Publ, Ltd. *Awards:* Nat Found Arts Grant, 67; Tamarind Fel, Tamarind Lithography Workshop through Ford Found, 68 & 82; Guggenheim Found Fel, 75. *Bibliog:* Fidel Danieli (auth), Billy Al Bengston's Dentos, 5/67 & Peter Plagens (auth), Billy Al Bengston's new paintings, 3/75, Artforum. *Mem:* Outrigger Canoe Club. *Media:* Mixed. *Publ:* Coauth, Business cards, Heavy Indust Publ, 68; auth, Late fifties at the Ferus, Artforum, 1/69; Los Angeles artists' studios, Art in Am, 11-12/70; Paintings of Three Decades, Billy II, Chronicle Books. *Mailing Add:* 805 Hampton Dr Venice CA 90291

BENINI
PAINTER, SCULPTOR
b Imola, Bologna, Italy, Apr, 17, 41. *Study:* Liceo Classico, Cento & Bologna, Italy, 54-57; Enalc, Assisi, Italy, 57-59; also with Morandi, 61-63; Jan Hus Univ (fine art), Hon PhD, 84. *Hon Degrees:* Univ Ark, Hon Dr Art. *Work:* Pensacola Art Ctr & Mus, Fla; Jacksonville Univ, Fla; Brevard Art Ctr & Mus, Melbourne, Fla; Empire Am, Deland, Fla; Thomas Ctr Arts, Gainesville, Fla. *Exhib:* 147 solo exhibs mus, pub insts & univ, Fla State Capitol, 84; Mid-Am Mus, Ark, 91; Ind State Univ, 91; Contemp Art Mus, Rosicrucian Mus, San Jose, 92; Carnegie Art Ctr, Calif, 93; McAllen Int Mus, Tex, 94; Duke Univ, NC, 88; Grace Mus, Abilene, 2000; Michelson Mus, 1999; plus many others. *Media:* Acrylics. *Dealer:* The Benini Found, 377 Shiloh Rd, Johnson City, TX, 78636. *Mailing Add:* 377 Shiloh Rd Johnson City TX 78636

BENJAMIN, ALICE BENJAMIN BOUDREAU
PAINTER, EDUCATOR
b Minneapolis, Minn, May 2, 36. *Study:* Wellesley Col, Mass, 54-56; Univ Minn, Minneapolis, Minn, BA, 58, BS, 63; San Francisco Art Inst, Calif, BFA, 61; State Univ NY, New Paltz, MS, 67; Instituto Allende, San Miguel d'Allende, Mex, 71; Frederic Munoz Workshops, 88-94. *Work:* 3MCo, St Paul, Minn; Univ Art Mus, Northrop auditorium, Minneapolis, Minn; East Cent Reg Libr & Cambridge Ctr Anoka-Ramsey Community Col, Cambridge, Minn; Decision Systems Inc, Minneapolis, Minn; Figures, Portraits, Still Life Spectrum Series, Braden River. *Exhib:* 2 person show, Vern Carver Gallery, Minneapolis, Minn, 93; Local Talent Revealed, Cambridge, Minn, 94; Arts in Harmony, Elk River, Minn, 96; solo exhib, There is Something About France, Iris Gallery, Lindstrom, Minn, 96 & Minn State Fair, 96; Figures, Faces, Unitarian Universalist Church Sarasota, 2005. *Pos:* Illusr zoology dept, Univ Minn, Minneapolis, 58-60. *Teaching:* Instr elem art, Onteora Pub Schs, Boiceville, NY, 63-66; Northrop & Blake Schs, Minneapolis, Minn, 69-75; instr art, drawing, painting & design, Cambridge Ctr, Anoka-Ramsey Community Col, Cambridge, Minn, 78-92; teacher Art League of Manatee Co, Bradenton, Fla. *Awards:* Best of Show, Liberty Studios, White Bear, Minn; Individual Artist's Grant, East Cent Arts Coun, 95; First Place, Art League of Manatee Co, 2001; 2nd place Art Center Manatee, 2005. *Bibliog:* Joanne Frank (auth), Alice Benjamin Boudreau, Minn Rural Artists Asn, 6/86. *Mem:* Nat League Am Pen Women; Art League Mantee Co; Art Ctr Manatee Art Coun of Manatee Co Graphics; Art Ctr Sarasota; Women Contemporary Artists. *Media:* Acrylic. *Mailing Add:* 10816 Forest Run Dr Bradenton FL 34202-9742

BENJAMIN, KARL STANLEY
PAINTER, EDUCATOR
b Chicago, Ill, Dec 29, 25. *Study:* Northwestern Univ; Univ Redlands, BA, 49; Claremont Grad Sch, MA, 60. *Work:* Whitney Mus Am Art, NY; Los Angeles Co Mus Art; San Francisco Mus Art; Wadsworth Atheneum, Hartford, Conn; Nat Collection Fine Arts, Smithsonian Inst, Washington, DC; Mus Contemp Art, Los Angeles; Chicago Art Inst; Seattle Mus Art; Oakland Mus Art, Calif; Sheldon Mem, Lincoln, Nebr. *Exhib:* Painting & Sculpture in Calif: The Modern Era, San Francisco Mus of Mod Art & Nat Collection of Fine Arts, Smithsonian Inst, Washington, 76-77; Los Angeles Hard Edge: The Fifties & the Seventies, Los Angeles Co Mus Art, 77; Am Art from Corp Collections, Corcoran Gallery, Washington, & Ala, Indianapolis & San Diego Mus, 79; Color in Contemp Painting, Henry Gallery, Univ Wash, 82; The Twentieth Century: San Francisco Mus Art Collection, San Francisco Mus Mod Art, 84; Ten California Colorists, Pomona Col, Univ NMex, and others, 85-86; Selected Works 1979-1986 (with catalog), Los Angeles Munic Art Gallery, 86; A Retrospective 1955-1987 (with catalog), Redding Mus, Shasta Col, Univ Pac, & Calif State Univ, Northridge, 89-90; Santa Barbara Mus, Oakland Mus, 90-92; California: Art from the 30's to the Present, San Francisco Mus Art, 93; A Retrospective 1979-1994, Montgomery Gallery, Pomora Col, 94; The Grid in 20th Century Art, Los Angeles Co Mus Art, 96; Eyedazzlers: Color optics from the Navajos to the Present, Univ NMex Art Mus, 97; Elusive Paradise, Mus of Contemp Art (MOCA), 98. *Awards:* Nat Endowment Arts Grant, 83-84 & 89-90; Lifetime Achievement Arts, Los Angeles Art Core, 93. *Bibliog:* Archives Am Art (interview), Smithsonian, Calif Oral Hist Proj; Four Abstract Classicsts, Los Angeles & San Francisco Mus, 59; Karl Benjamin-The Pomona Years (video), Pomona Col, Claremont, Calif, 94. *Media:* Oil. *Specialty:* Painting and Sculptures. *Interests:* Social interests, politics and literature. *Publ:* Karl Benjamin-Paintings 1955-1990 (catalog). *Dealer:* Louis Stern Fine Arts 9002 Melrose Ave West Hollywood Calif 90069; Brian Gross Fine Arts 49 Geary St 5th floor San Francisco Calif 94108. *Mailing Add:* 675 W Eighth St Claremont CA 91711

BENJAMIN, LLOYD WILLIAM, III
HISTORIAN, ADMINISTRATOR
b Painesville, Ohio, Sept 2, 44. *Study:* Emory Univ, BA, 66; Univ NC, Chapel Hill, PhD, 73. *Collection Arranged:* The Art of Designed Environments in the Netherlands (auth, catalog), 83-85. *Pos:* Chmn, Southeastern Col Art Conf, 74-76 & 80-83, dean, 83- & vpres, 91-. *Teaching:* Asst prof art hist, E Carolina Univ, 70-76, chmn dept, 74-76; from asst to assoc prof, Univ Ark, Little Rock, 76-82, chmn dept art, 80-, prof, 83-, dean, Col Fine Arts, 83-88, dean, Col Arts, Humanities & Soc Sci, 88-. *Mem:* Ark Endowment Humanities (bd mem & treas, 77-83); Southeastern Col Art Conf (bd mem, 78-83); Col Art Asn Am; Medieval Acad Am. *Res:* Twentieth century Dutch art and environmental design. *Publ:* Auth, The art of designed environments in the Netherlands, Livability, 82 & Stichting Kunst Bedrijf, 83; coauth, Drawings from the Collection of Herbert and Dorothy Vogel, Univ Ark at Little Rock & Pa State Univ, 86; contribr, Nederlandse opdrachtgebonden kunst in de Verenigde Staten-een primeur: Harmonius Wedding of Art and Technology, Kwartaalblad Kunst en Bedrijf, 87; Public Art in the Netherlands, Dutch Heights: Art and Culture in the Netherlands, 4/88; Painting for the Delectation of the Inner Eye in Sammy Peters: Baser Matter (exhib catalog), 89; and others. *Mailing Add:* 735 Old Johnson Rd Lawrenceville GA 30045-6368

BENNETT, DON BEMCO
PAINTER, PRINTMAKER
b McGlaughlin, SDak, Jan 8, 16. *Study:* Univ Wash; Edison Voc Sch, Seattle; also with the late Eliot O'Hara. *Work:* Cheney-Cowles Fine Arts Mus, Spokane, Wash; Ford Motor Co Collection of Am Art, Dearborn, Mich; Boise Cascade Corp, Boise, Idaho; Valley Nat Bank, Phoenix, Ariz; ITT Sheraton Corp, Boston, Mass. *Exhib:* Fourth Ann Art Exhib, Merchant Seamen UN, Corcoran Gallery, 46; US Info Agency Exhib Contemp Am Artists Worldwide Traveling Exhib, 60; Craftsman Competition, Pac Northwest Painters, Fry Mus, Seattle, 68; 15th Ann Exhib, Acad Artists Asn, Mus Fine Arts, Springfield, Mass, 64; Am Natural Hist Art Show, James Ford Bell Mus, Univ Minn, Minneapolis, 71. *Awards:* First Place in graphics, Acad Artists Asn, 64; Top Twenty Award, Craftsman Press, Seattle, 68; Second Place Award, Representational Watercolor, 28th Ann Exhib Idaho Artists, Boise Art Asn. *Media:* Watercolor, Oil; Lithography. *Publ:* Auth & illusr, Ford Times Mag, 58. *Mailing Add:* PO Box 105 Sun Valley ID 83353

BENNETT, JAMIE
ENAMELIST, SCULPTOR
b Philadelphia, Pa, Oct 6, 1948. *Study:* Univ Ga, BBA & BFA, 70; State Univ NY New Paltz, MFA, 74. *Work:* Ark Decorative Arts Mus, Little Rock; Kunst Industr, Trondheim, Norway; Mus App Arts, Oslow, Finland; Brockton Art Mus, Mass; Renwick Gallery, Smithsonian Inst, Washington; Royal Acad of Art, London, Eng; Philadelphia Mus of Art, Pa. *Exhib:* Solo exhibs, Fergus-Jean Gallery, Cleveland, Ohio, 88, CDK Gallery, NY, 89, Clark Gallery, Boston, Mass, 93 & 95, Helen Drutt Gallery, Philadelphia, Pa, 94 & 95 & Spectrum Gallery, Munich, Ger, 95; Working in Other Dimensions, Drawings and Objects II (catalog), Ark Ctr Arts, Little Rock, Ark, 94; Sculptural Concerns, Spencer Mus Art, Lawrence, Kans, 94; Twelfth Ann Salon Show, Clark Gallery, Lincoln, Mass, 94; Okun Gallery, Santa Fe, NMex, 94; New American Work, Galerie Marze, Nijmegen, The Neth, 95; Five Enamelists, Galerie Trondhorn, Berlin, Ger, 95; Jamie Bennett, Time and Meaning, Clark Gallery, Lincoln, Mass, 95; Jamie Bennett, New Work, Helen Drutt Gallery, Philadelphia, Pa, 96; Recent Visions, Susan Cummins Gallery, San Francisco, Calif, 96; Subjects 96, Int Jewelry Art Exhib, 96; Retretti Art Ctr, Punkaharjy, Finland, 96; James Bennett, Jewelry, Barbara Okun, Tesuque, NMex, 96; Director's Choice, Clark Gallery, Lincoln, Mass, 96; New Times, New Thinking: Jewelry in Europe and America, Crafts Coun, London, Eng, 96 & Nat Mus Wales, Eng, 97; Jewelry: New Thinking, Sybaris Gallery, Royal Oak, Mich, 96; Gold and Silver 96, Am Crafts Mus, NY, 96; Three Generations, Mobilia Gallery, Cambridge, Mass, 97; Danish Mus Decorative Art, Copenhagen, Denmark, 97; Opera Exhib, Susan Cummins Gallery, Mill Valley, Calif, 97; Int Enamel Exhib, Arrowmont Sch, Gatlinburg, Tenn, 97; Jewelry Moves, Nat Mus Scotland, Edinburgh, 98; Jamie Bennett Jurjani Series, Susan Cummins Gallery, Mill Valley, Calif, 98; The River's Edge, Joanne Rapp Gallery, Scottsdale, Ariz, 98; Metals By Five, Clark Gallery, Lincoln, Mass, 2000. *Collection Arranged:* Six at Univ Tex, Arlington, group exhib & symp, 77; Enamelists, Established & Emerging, Chastain Arts Ctr, 77. *Pos:* Artist-in-residence, Kohler Art Ctr, Sheboygan, Wis, 74; vis artist, Penland Sch Crafts, 74, 76, 77 & 80, Fla Int Univ, 77 & Colo Mountain Col, 77 & 78, Boston Univ, 79-80, Carnegie-Mellon Univ, 80 & Haystack, Deer Isle, Maine, 80; adv to bd, Soc Arts & Crafts, Boston, Mass, 89-92. *Teaching:* Instr metal, Bradley Univ, Peoria, Ill, 74-76; asst prof metal & drawing, Memphis Acad Art, Tenn, 76-; assoc prof art, State Univ NY, New Paltz, 85-87, prof, 85-. *Awards:* Fel, Nat Endowment Arts, 73 & 88; Educ Res Grant, State Univ NY, New Paltz, 91 & 97; Am Asn Univ Prof Res Grant, 98; Individual Fel, NY Found for the Arts, 99. *Bibliog:* Sandy Ballatore (auth), Jewelers USA, 3/76 & Enamelists, 11/76, Art News; Lisa Hammel (auth), Enameling, NY Times, 12/76. *Mem:* Soc NAm Goldsmiths. *Media:* Precious Metals; Acrylic, Oil. *Publ:* Contribr, Jewelry Making, Prentice Hall, 74; The Box Book & The Mirror Book, Crown, 76. *Dealer:* Clark Gallery Lincoln Station Lincoln MA 01773. *Mailing Add:* 3392 US Hwy 209 Stone Ridge NY 12484

BENNETT, JOHN M
WRITER, GRAPHIC ARTIST
b Chicago, Ill, Oct 12, 42. *Study:* Wash Univ, St Louis, BA(cum laude), 64, MS, 66; Univ Calif, Los Angeles, PhD, 70. *Exhib:* Solo exhibs, Hopkins Gallery, Ohio State Univ, 74 & 75 & Ten Window on 8th Avenue, NY, 80; Ft Hayes Gallery, Columbus, 88; Cult Arts Ctr, Columbus Sch Fine Arts, Willoughby, 90; Art Gallery, Dayton, Ohio, 91; Mus Poste, Paris, 95; Diana Lowenstein Fine Arts, Miami, Fla, 2003; Minn Center for Book Arts, Minneapolis, Minn, 2004; Gallery Oculus, Tokyo, Japan, 2004; Durban Segnini Gallery, Miami, Fla, 2005; Nave Gallery, Somerville, Mass, 2005. *Pos:* cur, An American Avant Garde: First Wave, Ohio State Univ Libr, 2001, Second Wave, 2002; cur, Avant Writing Coll, Ohio State Univ Libr, 98. *Awards:* Artist Fel, Ohio Arts Coun, 88; Film & Pub Grants, 93-00; Artist fel, Ohio Arts Coun, 97. *Bibliog:* John McClintock (producer), Mail Art Romance (film), 82; Leonard Trawick (auth), John Bennett's Poetry of Beauty and Disgust, The Gamut, 85; Gregory V St Thomasino (auth), Reading John M Bennett, Pudding, 96. *Media:* Wordart. *Publ:* Auth, Infused, 94 & Eddy, 95, Luna Bisonte Prods, Columbus, Ohio; Prime Sway, Texture Press, 96; Ridged, Poeta, 96; coauth (with Sheila E Murphy), Milky Floor, Luna Bisonte Prods, Columbus, Ohio, 96; Mailer Leaves Ham, 99; Rolling Combers, 01; The Peel, 04; Glue, 05; Instruction Book, 06; La Mal, 06; Cantar del Huff, 06. *Dealer:* Volatile Peter Huttinger PO Box 3274 Cincinnati OH 45201. *Mailing Add:* c/o Luna Bisonte Prods 137 Leland Ave Columbus OH 43214

BENNETT, PHILOMENE DOSEK
PAINTER, CERAMIST
b Lincoln, Nebr, Jan 2, 35. *Study:* Univ Nebr, BFA, 56. *Work:* Albrecht Art Mus, St Joseph, Mo; Mushkin Art Mus, Atcheson, Kans; Nelson-Atkins Mus Art, Kansas City, Mo; Mulvane Mus, Washburn Univ, Topeka, Kans; Nat Women's Mus, Washington; Hallmark Collection, Kansas City, Mo; United Mo Bank, Kansas City; Prudential Ins,

NY. *Comn:* Paintings, Crown Ctr Hotel, Kansas City, Mo, 74 & Rockhurst Col Libr, Kansas City, Mo, 75; stained glass windows, St Charles Church, North Kansas City, Mo, 74; 14 Stations of the Cross, Conway Chapel, Rockhurst Col, Kansas City, Mo, 75. *Exhib:* Porcelains, Sheldon Mem Art Gallery, 81; Settings: Inside & Out, Jayne Gallery, Kansas City, Mo, 93, Ann Show, 99, 2000; Myth in the Making, Summerfield Gallery, Santa Fe, NMex, 94; solo show, Walnut St Gallery, Springfield, Mo, 96; Lummiere Gallery, 99; Joyce Petter Gallery, Saugatauck, Mich, 99, 2000; Gallery a, Taos, NMex, 2000. *Pos:* Mem prof bd, Mo Arts Coun, Kansas City, 79-82; art ed, Helicon Nine, 79-; mem bd, Kansas City Arts Council, 82-83. *Teaching:* Artist-in-residence painting, Rockhurst Col, 69-70, Kansas City Art Inst, 83, 84-85 & 90, Univ Ark, 89-; pvt instr painting, Bennett-Marak Studio, Kansas City, Mo, 73-96; instr & lectr, Kans Art Inst, 98. *Awards:* Purchase Award, William Rockhill Nelson Gallery Art, Kansas City, Mo, 62; Award Winner, Univ Mo-Kansas City Women's Caucus for Arts, 77; Eller Outdoor Advert & Kansas City Arts Comn Billboard Award; Alumni award, Univ Nebr; Humanitarian award, Med Missions, Kansas City, Mo, 2003. *Bibliog:* Film-interview, Johnson Co Community Col, 74; Patrick White (auth), article, New Art Examiner, 82; Don Lambert (auth), Images from heaven, Saturday Rev, 1-2/86. *Mem:* Kansas City Artists Coalition (co-founder, vpres, 75, pres, 76, prog chmn, 77); Women's Nat Caucus for Arts; Soc Contemp Photog, Kansas City, Mo; Kansas City Arts Coun (bd mem). *Media:* Acrylic, Oil; Porcelain. *Dealer:* Petter Gallery Sougatuck MI; Hallar Gallery, Kansas City, MO; Gallery Ortiz, San Antonion, TX; Gallery A, Taos, NM. *Mailing Add:* 2400 Red Bridge Terr Kansas City MO 64131

BENNETT, TONY
PAINTER
b Astoria, NY, Aug 3, 26. *Exhib:* Butler Inst Am Art, Youngstown, Ohio, 94. *Mailing Add:* 130 W 57th St Apt 9D New York NY 10019

BENNING, JAMES
FILMMAKER
b Milwaukee, Wis, 42. *Exhib:* Did You Ever Hear That Cricket Sound?, 71; Time and a Half, 72; Ode to Muzak, 72; Art Hist. 101, 72; Michigan Avenue, 73; Honeyland Road, 73; I-94, 74; Gleem, 74; The United States of America, 75; Saturday Night, 75; 3 Minutes on the Dangers of Film Recording, 75; Chicago Loop, 76; A to B, 76; One Way Boogie Woogie, 77; Grand Opera, 78; Four Oil Wells, 78; Oklahoma, 79; Double Yodel, 80; American Dreams, 84; O Panama, 85; Landscape Suicide, 86; Used Innocence, 89; North on Evers, 92; Four Corners, 97; Utopia, 98; Valley Central, El, 2000; Sogobi, 2001; Los, 2004; 13 Lakes, 2004; Ten Skies, 2004; One Way Boogie Woogie/27 Years Later, 2005; Group shows, Whitney Biennial, Whitney Mus Art, 2006

BENNION, JOSEPH W
CERAMIST
b Sept 4, 52; US citizen. *Study:* Tuscarora Pottery Sch, 80; Brigham Young Univ, MFA, 86. *Work:* Pushkin Mus, Moscow, Russ; State Mus Fine Arts, Riga, Latvia; Detroit Inst Art, Mich; Mus Fine Art, Tiumeh, Siberia; Lenigrad Sch Higher Learning, Art & Indust Design, St Petersburg; and others. *Exhib:* Solo exhib, Useful Pottery, Dartmouth Col, Hanover, NH; NCECA Mem Exhib, Taft Mus, Cincinnati; Works in Clay VII, Wichita Falls Mus, Tex; Am Woodfire, Univ Iowa Mus; Kimball Art Ctr, Park City, Utah; Am Pottery, Mogei Gallery, Mashiko, Japan, 97. *Teaching:* Pottery, various workshops & seminars. *Awards:* Nat Endowment Arts Fel Grant, 91; Individual Artist Grant, Utah Arts Coun, 98. *Bibliog:* Gerry Williams (auth), Utah Potters, Studio Potter, 88; Steven Olpin (dir), The Potter's Meal (film), 92. *Mem:* Nat Coun Educ Ceramic Arts. *Media:* Clay. *Publ:* Auth, Social, ethical and environmental responsibilities of ceramic artists, 86 & Emerging talent, 91, Nat Coun Educ for Ceramic Arts; An integration of pots and life, 91 & Eloquent irony, 92, Ceramics: Art & perception. *Mailing Add:* 278 S Main Spring City UT 84662

BENSIGNOR, PAULETTE (MRS PHILIP STEINBERG)
PAINTER, PRINTMAKER
b Philadelphia, Pa, Dec 4, 48. *Study:* Pa Acad Fine Art, 70; Univ Pa, BFA, 71; Temple Univ, Tyler Sch Fine Arts, MEd, 73. *Work:* Bell Atlantic, Dupont Inc, Colonial Penn Insurance, Fidelity Bank, Green Tree Insurance & Mekinsky Co; Delaware Mus Art. *Exhib:* Muse Gallery, 2002; Winterthur Mus, 2003; Moore Col of Art & Design, 2003; Ester Klein Gallery, 2004; Denise Bilbro, 2004-2005. *Collection Arranged:* McGraw Hill Pub Co, London & NYC; Del Mus Art; First Union Bank; Verson, Hilton Corp. NYC & S Korea; Colonial Penn Ins Co; McKinsey Co, Chicago, Ill; Bell Atlantic; many others. *Teaching:* Instr fine art, Pa Sch Dist, 72-88, Gratz Col, 89-; instr, Philadelphia Acad Fine Arts, 91. *Awards:* Pacard Prize, Pa Acad Fine Arts, 70; First Prize, 82 & Edith Emerson Prize, 85, Woodmere Art Mus; Harry Rockower Mem Award, Cheltenham Ctr, Pa, 91; PW Club Award Excellance in Prints, 93; Artist Equity Merit Award, 2005. *Bibliog:* PBS Televesion, Documentary, Artist at Blue Hill, 1996. *Mem:* Fel of Pa Acad Fine Arts (exec bd mem, 79-81); Pa Watercolor Club; Artist Equity; Nat Drawing Soc. *Media:* Oil. *Specialty:* fine art. *Interests:* making art. *Publ:* Auth, Cosmopolitan, Japan Edition, 4/92; An Illustrated Survey of Leading Contemporaries, Am Artist, 91; Phila Inquirer reviews, 2004. *Dealer:* Mary Felton New York NY; Edna Davis Thyme Gallery Havaford PA. *Mailing Add:* 124 Rockland Ave Bala Cynwyd PA 19004-1828

BENSON, MARTHA J
JEWELER, ASSEMBLAGE ARTIST
b Kansas City, Mo, July 30, 28. *Study:* Univ Kansas City; Baker Univ, BA; spec study Kans Univ, Iowa State Univ, Utrecht, Holland, London, Eng, Glasgow & Scotland. *Comn:* Five wood-assemblage panels, St David's Episcopal Church, Ames, 75; six wood-assemblage panels, Chapel, Mary Greeley Hosp, Ames, 77; wall assemblages for pvt homes, Ames, Iowa & Fairmont, Minn; restoration of village oratorio, Bilek, Czech Repub. *Exhib:* 46th Ann Quad-State Juried Exhib, Quincy, Ill, 96; Art of Women, Iowa State Univ, 96; Refined, Nat Silversmithing Exhib, Nacogdoches, Tex, 98; Int Spice Container Exhib, Spertus Mus, Chicago, 98. *Collection Arranged:* Twelve Dutch Potters, 71; Three Chilean Printmakers, 73; Technol & the Artist-Craftsman-A Nat Crafts Exhib, 73-75; The Artists of San Miguel, 74-75; British Ceramics Today, US Tour (auth, catalog), 79; Hand, Mind & Spirit: Crafts Today (auth, catalog), 83; Women in Clay: The Ongoing Tradition (auth, catalog), 84; Legends in Fiber, 86, Textiles of Indian: A Living History, 89; and over 200 other exhibs. *Pos:* found & dir, Octagon Art Ctr, Ames, 68-91; bd dir, British Am Art Asn, Am Asn Mus, Iowa Designers Crafts Asn. *Teaching:* Prof oil painting, Iowa State Univ, 69, basic design, 72. *Awards:* Metal: Octagon Community Artists Exhib, 93; Metal: Octagon Ann (Nat), 95; First Place Metals, Iowa Crafts, MacNider Mus, 95. *Bibliog:* Annabelle Liu (auth), Martha Benson-A Profile, Craft Connection, 75. *Mem:* Am Craft Coun; Am Asn Mus; Art Mus Asn; Iowa Mus Asn; Soc NAm Goldsmiths. *Media:* Wood, Metal. *Dealer:* Mus Shop Nat Mus Women in Arts Washington DC; Octagon Shop Ames IA. *Mailing Add:* 928 Garfield Ames IA 50010

BENTLEY-SCHECK, GRACE MARY
PRINTMAKER
b Troy, NY, Apr 20, 37. *Study:* NY State Col Ceramics Alfred Univ, BFA, 59, MFA, 60. *Work:* Knoxville Mus Art, Tenn; Portland Art Mus; Silvermine Guild Artists, New Canaan, Conn; Newport (RI) Art Mus; Univ NDak, Grand Forks; Microsoft. *Comn:* Theme: the Celebrated Worker (2 prints), State of RI, 92. *Exhib:* Int Print Triennial, Cracow, Poland, 94; Nat Print Biennial, Silvermine Guild Arts Ctr, 96, 98, 2000 & 2003; Univ Gallery, Univ Bridgeport, Conn, 98; Int Print Triennial-Cracow 2000, Bridge to the Future, Poland, Nurnberg, Ger, 2000; solo exhib, Newport Art Mus, 2001 & Arts Exclusive Gallery, Sinsbury, Conn, 2005; Hand-pulled Prints XI, Stonemetal Press, San Antonio, Tex; At Issue: Prints and Social Commentary, Beard Gallery, Wheaton Col, Norton, MA, 2004; Saga, 71st Nat Juried Show, The old Print Shop, NY; Process to Print with Southern News Printmakers Network at Brickbottom Gallery, Somerville, MA, 2004; Saga Exhib in Prague, Hollar Soc Gallery, Czech Republic, 2006; Two-person exhib, The Old Print Shop, 2006. *Collection Arranged:* cur, 3 Printmakers Consider the Environment, Courthouse Center for the Arts, West Kingston, RI, 2002. *Pos:* cur, Hera Gallery, 89, 91 & 94; Vis artist, Univ SDak, Vermillion, 90-. *Awards:* Award, Nat Mem Show, Soc Am Graphic Artists; Juror's Award, 20th Ann Nat Print Exhib, Artlink, Ft Wayne, Ind, 2000; Purchase award, Nat Printmaking, 2003; Robert Conover, 2003; Coll NJ, Ewing; Robert Conover Memorial Award; First Place in Printmaking, Newport Art Mus. *Bibliog:* Buildings cycle reflect our own (rev), Boston Globe, 90; Ordinary is spectacular in art show (rev), Wichita Eagle, 90; and others; The Art of Printmaking at Spring-Bull Gallery, Jour of the Print Works, 2006. *Mem:* Boston Printmakers; Printmaker's Network Southern New Eng; 19 on paper; Soc Am Graphic Artists; Fla Printmakers Soc. *Media:* Collagraph, Collage. *Dealer:* A Clean Well-Lighted Place 863 Bleeker St New York NY 10014; JRS Fine Art 218 Wickenden St Providence RI 02903; Elaine Beckwith Gallery, 3923 Vermont Rt 30 Jamaica Vt 05343; Joyce Petter Gallery 161 Blue Star Saugatuck/Douglas Mich 49406; Esmay Fine Art 1855 Monroe Ave Rochester NY 14618. *Mailing Add:* 63 Sassafras Trail Narragansett RI 02882

BENTON, DANIEL C
PATRON
Study: Colgate Univ, AB, 80; Harvard Univ, MBA. *Pos:* Pres, Pequot, formerly; founder, chmn, Chief Exec Officer, Andor Capital Mgt, Stamford, Conn, 2001-; trustee, Colgate Univ, James B Colgate Soc, 2001-; vpres, Whitney Mus Am Art, currently. *Mailing Add:* Andor Capital Mgmt 153 E 53 St New York NY 10022

BENTON, FLETCHER
SCULPTOR
b Jackson, Ohio, Feb 25, 1931. *Study:* Miami Univ, BFA, 56. *Hon Degrees:* Miami Univ, DFA; Univ Rio Grande, DFA. *Work:* Whitney Mus Am Art, NY; Hirshhorn Mus, Washington, DC; San Francisco Mus Mod Art, Calif; Univ Calif, Los Angeles; Rockefeller Collection, NY; Corcoran Gallery of Art, Washington, DC; Victoria & Albert Mus, London; and others. *Comn:* IBM Corp, Morgan Hill, Calif; Thruman Arnold Bldg, Washington, DC; Univ Calif, Los Angeles; Davies Symphony Hall, San Francisco; public sculpture, City of Offend Bach, WGer; and others. *Exhib:* Solo exhibs, Calif Palace of Legion Honor, San Francisco, 61, San Francisco Mus Art, 65, 70, Milwaukee Art Ctr, 69, Stanford Univ Mus Art, Calif, 71, John Berggrven Gallery, 71, 77, 79, 80, 81, 86, 89 & 96, Phoenix Art Mus, 73, Univ Calif, Davis, 73, Univ Santa Clara, 75, San Jose Mus Art, 78, 82, Newport Harbor Art Mus, Newport Beach, Calif, 80, Oakland Mus, Calif, 80, Portland Art Mus, Ore, 80, Miami Univ Art Mus, Oxford, Ohio, 80, 93, Suermondt-Ludwig Mus, Aachen, WGer, 80, Klingspor Mus, Offenbach, WGer, 81, Calif Int Arts Found, Los Angeles, 86, Harcus Gallery, Boston Mass, 87, Haasner Gallery, Weisbaden, WGer, 87 & 2006, Dorothy Goldeen Gallery, Santa Monica, Calif, 88, Monadnock Bldg, San Francisco, Calif, 89, Gothaer Kunstforum, Cologne, 93, Frankfurt Art Fair, Ger, 97, Sheldon Meml Art Gallery and Sculpture Garden, Univ Nebr, Lincoln, 99, Strategic Air Command Mus, Omaha, Nebr, 99, Art Cologne 2001, Ger, 2001, San Antonio Mus Art, Tex, 2002; Am Pop Cult Today III, Laforet Mus, Jarajuku, Japan, 89; Laforeth Mus, Tokyo, 89; Triton Mus Art, Santa Clara, Calif, 91; Krannert Art Mus, Univ Ill, Urbana-Champaign, 93; Palm Springs Desert Mus, Calif, 93; Neuberger Mus Art, SUNY, Purchase, 93 & 2000; Miami Univ Art Mus, Oxford, Ohio, 96, 98, 2000 & 2002; Nev Mus Art, Reno, 98; San Francisco Mus Modern Art, 2000; Los Angeles Co Mus Art, 2000; Spektrum Kunstlandschaft, Kunsthalle Darmstadt, Ger, 2001; The Art Show, 7th Regiment Armory, NY, 2001; Pasadena Mus Calif Art, 2002. *Teaching:* Instr, Calif Col Arts & Crafts, 59 & San Francisco Art Inst, 64-67; prof art, Calif State Univ, San Jose, 67-86; prof art, San Jose State Univ, 68-. *Awards:* Award in Sculpture for Work of

Distinction, Am Acad & Inst Arts & Letters, 79; President's Scholar Award, San Jose State Univ, Calif; Award of Hon for Outstanding Achievement in Sculpture, San Francisco Art Comn, 82; Ohioana Career Award, Ohioana Libr Asn, 94. *Bibliog:* J Butterfield (auth), Interview with Fletcher Benton, Art Int, 80; Lucie-Smith, Edward and Paul Karlstrom (auth, mongraph), Fletcher Benton, NY, Harry N Abrams, 91; Neubert, George, Peter Selz, Gerhard Kohlberg & Phyllis Tuchman (auth's, monograph), The New Constructivism of Fletcher Benton, Lausanne: Editions Acatos, 2001; Ratcliff Carter and David Finn (auth), Fletcher Benton NY, Ruder Finn Press, 2003; David Finn (auth), Fletcher Benton: The Alphabet NY, Ruder Finn Press, 2005. *Dealer:* Imago Galleries 45-450 Hwy 74 Palm Desert, CA 92260; Neuhoff Gallery 41 E 57th St New York NY 10022; Tasende Gallery 8808 Melrose Ave West Hollywood CA 90069; John Berggruen Gallery 228 Grant Ave San Francisco CA 94108; and others. *Mailing Add:* 250 Dore St San Francisco CA 94103

BENTON, SUZANNE E
SCULPTOR, ART WRITER

b New York, NY, Jan 21, 36. *Study:* Queens Col, New York, BA (fine arts), 56; studies in New York at Art Students League, Columbia Univ, NY Univ, Brooklyn Col, Brooklyn Mus Art Sch, Mus Mod Art; Silvermine Col Art, Conn & Ctr Comtemp Printmaking, Conn. *Work:* Oakton Community Col, Ill; Nat Mus Mod Art, New Delhi, India; Birla Acad, Calcutta, India; Tokyo Sch Fine Arts, Japan; Deree Pierce Col, Athens, Greece; Temple Beth-El, Houston; Cent Conn State Univ; Adams House, Harvard Univ; Am Libr, Kathmandu, Nepal; Andover-Harvard Theol Libr, Harvard Divinity Sch, Cambridge, Mass; Nat Women's Hist Park, Seneca Falls, NY; Fogg Mus, Cambridge, MA; Housatonic Mus, Bridgeport, Conn; Womens Studies Ctr, Univ Conn, Storrs, Conn; numerous others; St Petersburg Mus Art, Fla; Lyman Allyn Mus, New London, Conn; and many others. *Comn:* Sculptured theatre sets, Viveca Lindfor's I Am A Woman Theatre Co, 73; The Sun Queen, large-scale bronze sculpture & Throne of the Sun Queen, bronze & corten steel, Art Park, Lewiston, NY, 75; Constellation (steel & bronze), comn by Wardlaw, 83-84; Ravage: Sun (sheet bronze), 85; Secret Future Work #1, Vivien Leone Collection, 90. *Exhib:* one-person shows, Touching Ritual, Wadsworth Atheneum, Hartford, Conn, 75, Art Park, Lewiston, NY, 75, Hellenic Am Union, Athens, Greece, 76, AB Condon Gallery, NY 81, Korean Cult Ctr, NY, 83, The Great Goddess, Asia Soc, NY, 87 & India Int Ctr, New Delhi, 93, Nineteenth-Century Oberlin Women, Oberlin Col, 1998, Metal Masks and Sculpture, Cabot House, Harvard Univ, 2000, Bosnia and Beyond: An Artist's Commentary on Crisis, Gutman Libr, Harvard Univ, 2001, From Painting to Painting, PMW Gallery, Stamford, Conn, 2002, Spirit of Hope: A Retrospective Exhibition, Silvermine Guild Arts Ctr, New Canaan, Conn, 2003, others; Mystic Works, Nat Mus Am Jewish Hist, 94; 19th Century Women Writers & Feminist Activities, Schlesinger Libr, 94; Journies Through Diverse Worlds: Masks, Monoprints & Secret Future Works, Gallery Contemp Art, Sacred Heart Univ, 95, Univ Dhaka, Bangladesh, 95 & Indigo Gallery, Kathmando, Nepal, 95; 19th Century Women Writers & Feminist Activists, Women's Rights Nat Hist Park, 95-; Adams House, Harvard Univ; KSI Galleries, NY, 97; Director's Choice, Silvermine Guild Artists, Conn, 98; Spiritual Hope, Sil.ermine Guild Art Ctr, Conn; Face and Figure, Queens Col Art Ctr, 2005, Eckerd Col, St Petersburg, Fla, 2006; others. *Collection Arranged:* guest cur Facing East: Asian Masks & Artist Inspired By Them, Hammond Mus, North Salem, NY, 99. *Pos:* Convener-coordr, Arts Festival-Metamorphosis I, New Haven, Conn, 69-70 & Conn Feminists in the Arts, 69-72; performance artist, Mask Ritual Tales, 69-; producer-dir, Four Chosen Women, NY, 72; art consult, Xerox, 73-76; Boeringer Ingelheim Ltd, 80-83; vis artist-in-residence, Adams House, Harvard Univ, 97; artistic, managing dir Positive Power: Women Artists of Conn Forums, 99-2000; co-chair, Salute to Feminist Artists, Veteran Feminists of Am, held at Nat Arts Club, NY, 2003; artist-in-residence Byrdcliffe Artist Colony, Woodstock, NY, 2001, Artist studio, Asilah, Morocco, 2000, Weir Farm Nat Hist Site Trust, Wilton, Conn, 1999. *Teaching:* Instr welded sculpture, Brookfield Craft Ctr, Brookfield, Conn, 72-73, Norwalk Community Col, fall 80 & various art appreciation workshops, mask & all performances & workshops at cols throughout USA, 71- & 19 countries world-wide; Fulbright lectr India, 92-93; guest artist & vis lectr, Oberlin Col, 96; Mask Workshops for Women & Youth, Sarajevo & Zenica, Bosnia through UMCOR; printmaking Armory Art Ctr, 98, 2000, Ctr Contemp Printmaking, Norwalk, Conn, St Petersburg Art Ctr, 2005 & 06 & Helene Wurlitzer Found, Taos, NM, 2006. *Awards:* Fulbright Lectureship to India, 92; Thanks be to Grandmother Winifred, Travel Grant to Africa, 93; Resident Artist, Foundacion Valparaiso, Spain, 96 & 98; Hon assoc Sr Common Room, Adams House, Harvard Univ, 2003-; Pioneer Feminist Award, Veteran Feminists of Am, 1996; US Info Svcs grant to Bulgaria, Bangladesh, India & Pakistan, 1995; to Kenya & Tanzania, 1993. *Bibliog:* LP Steitfeld (auth), Suzanne Benton's Spirit of Hope at Silvermine, Advocate & Greenwich Time, 4/12/2003; Foxy Gwynne (auth), Revisiting the High Priestess of Art, Record Rev, 7/2/2004; Adele Annesi (auth), Artist of the Ages Unmasked, Ridgefield Press, 12/22/2005; others. *Mem:* Women's Caucus Art; Silvermine Guild Artists (mem bd, 88-90); hon mem Nat Korean Sculptress Asn; Nat Asn Women Artists; Col Art Asn. *Media:* Welded Metal, Printmaking; Performance Art. *Publ:* Auth, Beyond the mask: Crossing cultural boundaries, India Mag, 94; Remembering Rachel, Chosen Tales: Stories Told by Jewish Storytellers, Jason Aronson Inc, 95; Myths, symbols and the artist, Art: A Quart J, 95; Spirit poles and flying pigs: Public art and cultural democracy in American communities (review), Women Artist News, Smithsonian Inst Press, 96; The mask, Art: A Quart J, 96; Myths & Masks, Women, Heritage & Violence, Papyros, India, 97; The Art of Welded Sculpture, Van Nostrand Reinhold, 1975; The Journey Letters of a Traveling Artist, Four Blackbirds Press, 2001; Suzanne Benton, Spirit of Hope: Selected works from 1963 to 2003, (exhib catalog) 2003. *Dealer:* Arthaus 1053 Bush St Ste 2 San Francisco CA 94109; Jso Art Assocs 6 Nappa Dr Westport CT 06880. *Mailing Add:* 22 Donnelly Dr Ridgefield CT 06877

BEN TRE, HOWARD B
SCULPTOR, DRAFTSMAN

b Brooklyn, NY, May 13, 49. *Study:* Portland State Univ, BSA, 78; RI Sch Design, MFA, 80. *Work:* Metrop Mus Art, NY; Nat Mus Mod Art, Tokyo, Japan; Nat Mus Am Hist, Smithsonian Inst; Hirshhorn Mus & Sculpture Garden, Washington, DC; Mus Art, RI Sch Design; Los Angeles Co Mus Art, Calif; Philadelphia Mus Art, Pa. *Comn:* Fountains, Post Office Sq Park Redevelop, 91; sculpture, Toledo Mus Art, 92; plaza design & fountains, BankBoston, 98; sculpture, Hunter Mus Am Art, 98; Pedestrianization of Warrington Town Ctr (sculpture & street scheme), Eng, 98. *Exhib:* New Glass Touring Exhib, Corning Mus Glass, Metrop Mus Art & Renwick Gallery, Nat Collection Art, 78-82; Contemp Glass, Nat Mus Mod Art, Kyoto & Tokyo, Japan; Art Gallery Western Australia, Perth, 82; World Glass Now 82, Hokaido Mus Mod Art, Sapporo, Japan, 82; Four Sculptors, Jesse Besser Mus, Alpena, Mich, 82; Columns, Ornament & Sculpture, Cooper Hewitt Mus, NY, 82; solo exhibs, Hadler Rodriguez Galleries, Houston, Tex, 81, 83 & 85, Interior/Exterior, Palm Springs Desert Mus, Calif, 99-02 (traveling), Sculpting Space in the Pub Realm, The Minneapolis Inst of Arts, Minn, 2001, Charles Cowles Gallery, NY, 2001 & 02; Habatat Galleries, Detroit, 81, 83, 84, 85 & 92; Foster/White Gallery, Seattle, Wash, 81 & 83; Clarke Gallery, Lincoln, Mass, 83 & 91; Charles Cowles Gallery, NY, 85, 86, 88, 89, 91, 93 & 96; John Berggruen Gallery, San Francisco, 86; solo exhibs, Fay Gold Gallery, Atlanta, Ga, 87, Dorothy Goldeen Gallery, Santa Monica, Calif, 89 & 91, The Phillips Collection, Washington, DC, 89-90, Carnegie-Mellon Art Gallery, Pittsburgh, Pa, 90, Toledo Mus Art, 92; Brown Univ Bell Gallery, 93; Musee D'Art Moderne et D'Art Contemporain, Nice, France, 94; Cleveland Ctr Contemp Art, 95; Newport Art Mus, 96; Marsh Art Gallery, Richmond, Va, 96; Univ Art Gallery, San Diego, 98; Palmsprings Desert Mus, 99; San Jose Mus Art, 2000; Scottsdale Mus Contemp Art, 2000. *Awards:* Grant, RI State Coun Arts, 79, 84 & 90; Nat Endowment Arts Fel, 80, 84 & 90; Pell Award, 97. *Bibliog:* 100 Selected Works from the Collection, Hokkaido Mus Mod Art, 97; R Pincus (auth), Glassworks, San Diego Union-Tribune, 98; Danto, Arthur & others (auths), Howard Bentre, Hudson Hills Press, 99. *Media:* Cast Glass, Metal. *Mailing Add:* c/o Charles Cowles Gallery 537 W 24th St New York NY 10011

BENTZ, HARRY DONALD
EDUCATOR, PAINTER

b Robesonia, Pa, Dec 2, 31. *Study:* Kutztown State Col, 53; Pa State Univ, with Hobson Pittman, 58; Lehigh Univ, 68; watercolor portraiture with Lester Stone. *Work:* Bank of Pa, Reading. *Comn:* Two murals, Spec Educ Ctr, Reading Sch Dist, 62; 15 display units, Daniel Boone Homestead, Birdsboro, Pa, 63. *Exhib:* Pa Art Educ Exhib, William Penn Mem Mus, 54; Washington Co Mus of Fine Arts Exhib, 65-67; Second Ann Watercolor Exhib, Millersville State Col, 76. *Teaching:* Instr art, Columbia High Sch, 55-60; art supervisor, Reading Sch Dist, 60-71; prof painting, Shippensburg State Col, 70-86, chmn, Dept Art, 71-86; retired. *Awards:* Hayes Art Materials Award, 43rd Ann Cumberland Valley Exhib, 75; Purchase Award, 43rd Ann Cumberland Valley Exhib, Farmers & Merchants Bank, 75; First Prize, Huntingdon Co Arts Festival, Huntingdon Co Arts Coun, 76. *Mem:* Nat Art Educ Asn; Pa Art Educ Asn; Cumberland Valley Arts Coun; Pa Soc Watercolor Painters. *Media:* Watercolor, Oil. *Mailing Add:* 1429 Union St Reading PA 19604-1749

BENZLE, CURTIS MUNHALL
CERAMIST, EDUCATOR

b Lakewood, Ohio, Apr 20, 49. *Study:* Ohio State Univ, BFA, 72; Sch Am Craftmen/RIT, 73; Northern Ill Univ, MA, 78. *Work:* Nat Collection Am Art/Smithsonian Inst, White House, Washington; Int Mus Ceramics, Faenza, Italy; Cleveland Mus Art, Ohio; Los Angeles Co Mus Art, Calif; Everson Mus, Syracuse, NY. *Comn:* Governor's Art Award, State Ohio, Columbus, 82, 01. *Exhib:* Ann, Cleveland Mus Art, Ohio, 71 & 73; Int Competition Artist Ceramics, Faenza, Italy, 81 & 82; Featured Artists, Renwick Gallery/Smithsonian Inst, Washington, 83; Am Porcelain, Suntory Art Mus, Tokyo, Japan, 84; solo exhib, Indianapolis Mus Art, Indiana, 84 & Akaska Green Gallery, Tokyo, Japan, 87 & 90; Ceramic National, Everson Mus Art, Syracuse, NY, 87; Limoges Creative Porcelain Invitational, Limoges, France, 88; Contemp Porcelain, Maggie Banner Ceramics, London, Eng; and others. *Pos:* Pres, Ohio Designer Craftsman, 84-86; pres, Japan/USA Exchange Exhib, 87-91; bd dir, Am Craft Retailer Asn, 90-92; chair, Am Craft Asn/Am Craft Coun, 92-96; exec dir, Ohio Designer Craftsman, 96-. *Teaching:* Instr ceramics, Univ SC, 78-79; Savannah Col Art, 79-80; prof ceramics, CCAD, Columbus, 82-. *Awards:* Fel Grant, Nat Endowment Art Craftsmen, 80; Individual Fel Grant, Ohio Arts Coun, 81, 83, 84 & 88; Individual Fel Grant, Greater Columbus Arts Coun, 87. *Bibliog:* Hideto Satonaka (auth), Patterns & Styles, Honoho Geijutsu, 87; Engracia Schuster (auth), Curtis & Suzan Benzle, Ceramica, 1/88; MJ VanDeventer (auth), Benzle Porcelains, Art Gallery Int, 3/88. *Mem:* Ohio Designer Craftsmen; Japan/USA Exchange Exhib (pres, 87); Ohio Citizens Com Arts; Nat Coun Educ Ceramic Arts; Am Crafts Coun. *Media:* Ceramic. *Publ:* Auth, Edible Art, Sch Arts, 80; The Craft Aesthetic, Dialogue, 81; David Leach, Dialogue, 82; Earning Your Worth, Ceramics Monthly, 88; Robert Eckels, Ceramics Monthly, 93. *Dealer:* Martha Schneider Gallery Inc 2055 Green Bay Rd Highland Park IL 60035. *Mailing Add:* c/o Benzle Porcelain Co 6100 Hayden Run Rd Hilliard OH 43026

BERARDO, JOSE MANUEL
COLLECTOR

b Madeira, Portugal, 44. *Pos:* Co-owner Royal Savoy Resort, Funchal, Madeira, 1988—; other enterprises including mining, media, wine. *Awards:* Named one of Top 200 Collectors, ARTnews Magazine, 2004, 2005, 2006. *Collection:* Post-War and Contemporary Art. *Mailing Add:* Royal Savoy Resort Ave do Inftante Funchal Madeira 9004-542 Portugal

BERD, MORRIS
PAINTER, EDUCATOR
b Philadelphia, Pa, Mar 12, 14. *Study:* Philadelphia Col Art; Univ per Strangeri, Perugia, Italy, cert. *Work:* Philadelphia Mus Art; Pa Acad Fine Arts, Philadelphia; Philadelphia Col Art; Arco Collection, Los Angeles; Barnes Found, Merion, Pa. *Comn:* History of Oil (mural), Sun Oil Co, Franklin Inst; History of Architecture (mural), Gimbel Bros, Philadelphia; Philadelphia Horticultural Soc 1776 Celebration. *Exhib:* Many Pa Acad Fine Arts Ann & Philadelphia Mus Art Regionals; also over 18 one-man shows, incl Wilcox Gallery, Swarthmore Col, 73 & The Four Season, Marian Locks Gallery, 80; Am Col Bryn Mawr, Pa, 88; Ross-Constantine, NY, 90. *Teaching:* Prof painting, Philadelphia Col Art, 36-76, co-chmn dept, 50-71, prof emer, 82. *Awards:* Silver Medal, YMHA Jubilee show; Katzman Prize, Philadelphia Print Club, 62; Philadelphia Col Art Alumni Award, 65. *Bibliog:* Alan Gussow (auth), A Sense of Place, Vol II, 74; William Scott (auth), Four seasons, Am Artist, 2/80; Elizabeth Leonard (auth), Painting the Landscape, 84. *Media:* Oil, Watercolor. *Dealer:* Schmidt/Dean Gallery 1721 Spruce St Philadelphia PA. *Mailing Add:* 350 Howarth Rd Media PA 19063

BERDING, THOMAS G
PAINTER
b Cinncinati, Ohio, Oct 16, 62. *Study:* Edgecliff Col, Xavier Univ, BA(fine arts), 84; RI Sch Design, MFA(painting), 87. *Work:* Hoyt Inst Fine Arts, New Castle, Pa; Lincoln Nat Corp, Mich. *Exhib:* Recent Works, In Vivo Gallery, Indianapolis, 92; Faculty Show, Ind Univ Mus, Bloomington, 93; Struct Group Invitational, New Eng Sch Art & Design, Boston, 94; Regional Artists Biennial, Ft Wayne Mus Art, Ind, 94 & 98; Depauw Univ, Greencastle, Ind, 96; Mus Fine Art, Fla State Univ, 97; Rochester Inst Technol, 98. *Teaching:* Vis asst prof, Dartmouth Col, Hanover, NH, 91 & Ind Univ, Bloomington, 92-93; asst prof painting, Mich State Univ, E Lansing, 93-98 & assoc prof, 98-. *Awards:* Mid-Am Alliance/Nat Endowment Arts Fel, 90; Pollack-Krasner Found Grant, 92; Nat Endowment Art Fel in Painting, 93. *Bibliog:* Marc Pally (auth), Winners, mid-America biennial, Nelson-Atkins Mus Art, 91; Steve Mannheimer (auth), Gallery owners aren't hiding local lights under bushels, Indianapolis Star, 9/27/92; Addison Parks (auth), The artist's conviction marked out in oil, Christian Sci Monitor, 1/26/93. *Media:* Oil, Canvas. *Mailing Add:* 1739 Roseland Ave East Lansing MI 48823

BEREN, STANLEY O
PATRON
b Parkersburg, WVa, Feb 1, 20. *Study:* Harvard Col, AB, 41, Harvard Univ, MBA, 43. *Pos:* Pres, Wichita Art Mus Endowment Asn Inc, 68, chmn bd, 86-88, Wichita Art Mus, 70-72, mem bd, 72-; mem adv bd, JFK Ctr, 70-. *Mem:* Am Asn Mus; Int Coun Mem. *Interests:* Special interest in raising funds for accessions for Wichita Art Mus. *Collection:* Modern painting and pre-Columbian artifacts. *Mailing Add:* 9123 Autumn Chase St Wichita KS 67206

BERG, MICHAEL R
PAINTER, PRINTMAKER
b Portland, Ore, May 19, 48. *Study:* Univ Wash, independent study with Spencer Mosley, BA, 71; Ft Wright Col, Spokane, Wash, scholar prize, BFA, 72; Skowhegan Sch, scholar prize, 72. *Work:* Boulder Mus Contemp Art, Colo; Queens Mus, NY; Neuberger Mus, Purchase, NY. *Comn:* Govt guest house, Peoples Repub China, Fuzhou, 94; 20 Renwick St, comn by Daniel Lazar, NY, 95; PS 3 (wall painting), PS 3, NY, 96; The Days Now Move from Left to Right (wall painting), Denver Found, Boulder, 98; A Walk Across Continents (wall painting), comn by C & A Latham, Seattle, 98. *Exhib:* Painted Light, Reading Mus, Queens Mus, Colby Col & Butler Inst, 83; Vis Artist Show, Sch Art Gallery, La State Univ, Baton Rouge, 85; Interior/Exterior: Architectured Fantasies, Queens Mus, Flushing Park, 87; Inaugural Exhib, Queens Mus & Bulova Corp Ctr, NY, 87; Vis Artists Show, Cantor Art Gallery, Holy Cross Col, Worchester, Maine, 87; Collaboration/Transformation, Montgomery Gallery, Pomona Col & Fred Jones Jr Mus, Univ Okla, 97 & 98; LA Current: Armond Hammer Mus, Los Angeles, 98. *Bibliog:* John Ash (auth), A History of Backward Glances, Art Forum, summer 93; Garrit Henry (auth), Mike Berg at Elaine Kaufman, Art News, 4/96; Michael Petry (auth), A Thing of Beauty, Art & Design, Acad Group Limited, 97. *Media:* All Media. *Dealer:* Gina Fiore Salon Fine Arts 9 McDougal Alley New York NY 10012

BERG, MONA LEA
MUSEUM DIRECTOR
b Los Angeles, Calif, Nov 9, 35. *Study:* Univ Minn, studied with Cameron Booth, BA(art hist & studio), 60; Univ Kans, 69; Univ Okla, MLS(mus studies), 86. *Collection Arranged:* Old Students & Old Masters: The School of Rembrandt, 80, The Geometric Vision: Arts of the Zulu, 83, Renaissance & Baroque Prints, 83, L'Estampe Française, 85, Japanese Packages, 86, Italian Baroque Paintings, 87 & David & Bonnie Ross Collection of Precolumbian Art, 88, Purdue Univ Galleries, Ind. *Pos:* Gallery coordr, Purdue Univ Galleries, Ind, 78-80, dir galleries, 80-. *Mem:* Am Asn Mus; Asn Ind Mus; Asn Col & Univ Mus & Galleries; Midwest Mus Conf. *Res:* 19th & 20th century American art. *Mailing Add:* 231 Tamiami Tr West Lafayette IN 47906-1207

BERG, SIRI
COLLAGE ARTIST, PAINTER
b Stockholm, Sweden; US citizen. *Study:* Inst Art & Archit, Univ Brussels, Belgium, BA; Pratt Graphics Ctr, NY. *Work:* NY Univ, NY; Herbert F Johnson Mus, Cornell Univ; Guggenheim Mus; Jewish Mus, NY; Southwest Minn State Univ Col; others. *Comn:* Kreab-Ann Report Cover, 89-93. *Exhib:* Contemp Reflections, Aldrich Mus, Ridgefield, Conn, 76-77; The Silvia Pizitz Collection, Birmingham Mus, Ala, 80; Yeshiva Univ Mus, NY, 93-98; Thomas Nordenstad Gallery, NY, 95; McLean Gallery, Malibu, Calif, 97; one-woman show, Walter Wickiser Gallery, NY, 97 & 99, Am Swedish Mus, Philadelphia, 99-2000, Mus of Southwest, Midland, Tex, 99, Hallwyl Mus, Stockholm, Sweden, 2000, Rutgers Univ, New Brunswick, NJ, 2000, Consul Gen Sweden, NY, 2002 & Educ Testing Serv Brodsky Gallery, Princeton, NJ, 2003; Workspace, NY, 2002; Monique Goldstrom Gallery, NY, 2002; Martin Gallery, NY, 2002; Workspace, NY, 2002; William Whipple Gallery, Southwest State Univ, Marshall, Minn, 2002 & 2003; Swedish Am Mus, Chicago, 2003; Konstnarshuset, Stockholm, 2003; Berlin Kunstproject, Berlin, 2004; Color Elefante, Valencia, Spain, 2004; Pickled Art Gallery, Beijing, 2005; Nat Maritime Mus, Sydney, Australia, 2005; Year of Swedish Design, Gibson Gallery Art Mus, SUNY, Potsdam, 2006. *Pos:* Mem fac, New Sch - Parsons Sch Design, New York, 77-. *Teaching:* instr color and design, Parson's Sch Design, 77-. *Awards:* Arts Grant, NY State Coun, Artist in Residence, 78; Top Award 8th Ann Works on Paper, Art Gallery City Univ New York, 90; artist in residence, Rutgers Univ, 2000. *Bibliog:* Brandy Schutter (auth), Mater paintings and woodcuts, Impact, 11/2002; Alan Artner (auth), Chicago Tribune, Critics Choice, 9/2003; Chicago Tribune, Visual Logic, Siri Berg, 11/2003; Video of Siri Berg, TV4, Sweden, 2004; Dan Keane (auth), Living History, Nyarts Mag, Nov-Dec/2005; Lina Otterdohl (auth), Datorkonst, PC for Alla, 2/2006; and others. *Mem:* Am Scand Found; Am Scand Soc; Swedish Womens Educ Asn, NY; Am Abstract Artists Assemblage. *Media:* Collage, Oil. *Publ:* Contribr, Contemp Graphic Artists, Vol III, 88; illustrator, It's Only a Paper Moon, Atlanta Jewish Times, 1/97, The Tip of the Siri Berg, Poets, Artists & Madmen, 1/97, Paper Museum, Atlanta Jour, 1/97, Tampa Review, fall 98, Summer House, Metro Source, 99, Siri Berg at The Swedish Museum, Art Matters, 11/99. *Dealer:* Broadway Gallery NYC; Monica Urwitz Gallery Konstruktiv Tendeng Stockholm Sweden; Joyce Pommer Gallery. *Mailing Add:* 93 Mercer Apt 6E New York NY 10012

BERG, TOM
PAINTER
b Aberdeen, SDak, Feb 10, 43. *Study:* Univ Wyo, BA, 66, MA, 68, MFA, 72; Univ Ore, 69. *Work:* Albuquerque Mus, NMex; Palm Springs Desert Mus, Calif; Okla Arts Inst, Oklahoma City; Whitney Mus Am Art, NY; Phillip Morris Collection, NY. *Exhib:* Rosalind Constable Invites Santa Fe Art Festival, 81; Southwest '85, Mus NMex, Santa Fe; Janus Gallery, Santa Fe, 91; Cacciola Gallery, NY, 92, 94 & 96; Munson Gallery, Santa Fe, 93, 95, 97, 99, 2001 & 2003; Hiden Brooks Gallery, 2002, 2006; and others; Price-Dewey Galleries, Santa Fe, NMex, 2005. *Pos:* Vis lectr, Univ Rochester, 71, NMex State Univ, Las Cruces, 89, Univ Okla, Norman, 89 & Okla Arts Inst, Oklahoma City, 89 & 91; artist-in-residence, Univ Maine, Augusta, 72-73 & 87, Wyo Artists in Schs Prog, 73-76 & Delta State Univ, Cleveland, Miss, 76; guest artist Tamarind Found, Univ NMex, Albuquerque, 88, 92. *Teaching:* Instr art, Point Park Col, Pittsburgh, Pa, 69-71; vis lectr painting, Univ Wyo, Laramie, summer 77. *Awards:* Visual Arts Fel Wyo, Western States Arts Found, Denver, 76-77. *Bibliog:* David Bell (auth), Report from Santa Fe, Art in Am, Vol 73, No 9, 9/85; Clinton Adams (auth), New Mexico Impressions: Printmaking from 1880-1990, Univ NMex Press, Albuquerque, 91; Jan Adlman & Barbara McIntyre (auths), Contemporary Art In New Mexico. *Media:* Oil Painting. *Dealer:* Victoria Price Contemp Art 550 S Guadalupe Santa Fe NMex 87501; Hidell Brooks Gallery 1910 S Blvd #130 Charlotte NC 28203; Wade Wilson Art 8853 Inverness Pkwy Houston Tex 77055. *Mailing Add:* 31 Don Bernardo Santa Fe NM 87506

BERGDOLL, BARRY
HISTORIAN, EDUCATOR
b Apr 16, 1955. *Study:* Columbia Univ, PhD, 1986. *Collection Arranged:* Co-cur, Mies in Berlin; cur, Le Panthéon: Symbole des Révolutions, 1989; cur, Les Vaudoyers: une dynastie d'architectes, Paris, 1992. *Teaching:* Faculty mem, Columbia Univ, 1986-, prof, chmn dept art hist and archeol; vis prof art hist, Mass Inst Technol. *Awards:* J P Morgan Berlin Prize,Am Acad Berlin, 2005. *Mem:* Soc Archit Historians (pres). *Publ:* Contributes articles to professional journals, chapters to books; co-auth, Friedrich Weinbrenner, 1984; co-auth, Karl Friedrich Schinkel: An Architecture of Prussia, 1994; co-auth, Mies in Berlin, 2001; co-auth, Mies van der Rohe, 2002; co-auth, The Eiffel Tower, 2002; auth, Léon Vaudoyer: Historicism in the Age of Industry, 1994; European Architecture 1750-1890, 2000. *Mailing Add:* Columbia Univ 909 Schermerhorn Hall 1190 Amsterdam Ave New York NY 10027

BERGE, DOROTHY ALPHENA
SCULPTOR, INSTRUCTOR
b Ottawa, Ill, May 8, 23. *Study:* St Olaf Col, Northfield, Minn, BA, 45; Minneapolis Sch Art, BFA, 50; Ga State Univ, Atlanta, MVA, 76. *Work:* Minneapolis Inst Art, Walker Art Ctr & Univ Minn Gallery, Minneapolis; High Mus Art, Atlanta, Ga. *Comn:* Copper wall sculpture, Mead Packaging Corp, Atlanta, Ga, 66; corten steel sculptures, Great Southwest Indust Park, Atlanta, 68 & 100 Colony Sq, 69; corten steel sculpture, St Olaf Col, comn by Mrs John Oslund, Northfield, Minn, 75; aluminum wall sculpture, Metrop Atlanta Rapid Transit Authority, 80. *Exhib:* Minn Biennial, Minneapolis Inst Art, 54; Recent Sculpture USA, Mus Mod Art, NY, 57; 16 Younger Minn Artists, Walker Art Ctr, Minneapolis, 58; one-person shows, Walker Art Ctr, 59 & High Mus Art, Atlanta, 68; Ga Artists 1, 2 & 6, High Mus Art, Atlanta, 71, 72 & 79. *Pos:* Registr, Walker Art Ctr, Minneapolis, 54-60; coordr circulating exhibs, Mus Mod Art, NY, 60-63. *Teaching:* Instr sculpture, drawing & ceramics, St Olaf Col, Northfield, Minn, 46-48; artist-in-residence sculpture, Nat Endowment Arts, Ga, 71-72. *Awards:* Purchase Award, Ford Found Prog Humanities & Arts, 60. *Media:* Welded Metal. *Dealer:* Heath Gallery 416 E Paces Ferry Rd NE Atlanta GA 30309. *Mailing Add:* 301 Myrtle St W Stillwater MN 55082-4768

BERGEN, JEFFREY B
ART DEALER, DIRECTOR
b New York, NY, Jan 14, 53. *Study:* Antioch Col, Ohio. *Pos:* Owner & dir, ACA Galleries, New York, currently. *Mem:* Art Dealers Asn Am; Threshold Found; Social Venture Network. *Specialty:* 19th and 20th century and contemporary American and European paintings and sculpture. *Mailing Add:* 275 Central Park W No 15 New York NY 10024

BERGEN, JOHN AXEL
SCULPTOR, GRAPHIC ARTIST
b Stockholm, Sweden, Apr 27, 39, US citizen. *Study:* Hamilton Col, with James Penney, BA(hons), 63; Art Student's League, with Jose deCreeft, 64-65; Pratt Inst, with Calvin Albert, MFA, 67. *Work:* Munson-Williams-Proctor Inst, Utica, NY; Lake George Arts Proj, Lake George, NY; Hamilton Col, Clinton, NY; Colgate Univ, Hamilton, NY; Stone Quarry Hill Art Park, Cazenovia, NY. *Comn:* Horace Bushnell Memorial Hall, Hon Aaron Copeland Centenary, Hartford, Conn; Waterfront Recapture, Hartford, Conn; Hamilton Col, Kirkland Gate, Clifton, NY; Temple Beth El, Ark Doors, Utica, NY; Young & Franklin Inc, Grande Comore II, Liverpool, NY. *Exhib:* Prospect Mountain Show: Homage to David Smith, Lake George Arts Proj, Lake George, NY, 79; solo exhib, Munson-Williams-Proctor Inst, Utica, NY, 81 & Art Mus, Colby Col, Waterville, Maine, 87; Roberson Ctr for the Arts & Sci, Binghamton, NY, 82; Richard F Brush Art Gallery, St Lawrence Univ, Canton, NY, 82; Sculpture/Penn's Landing, Port Hist Mus, Philadelphia, 83; Sculpture Space-Recent Trends, Munson-Williams-Proctor Inst, Utica, NY, 84; NY Artists V, Herbert F Johnson Mus, Cornell Univ, Ithaca, NY, 86; retrospective 1970-1992, Edith Barrett Gallery, Utica Col Syracuse Univ, NY, 92; Sculpture Space: Celebrating 20 Yeras, Munson-Williams-Proctor Inst; Farnsworth Art Mus, Rockland, ME, John von Bergen, Marine metaphors, Two Decades of Sculpture, 2003; Stone Quarry Hill Art Park, Cazevonia, NY, Loosely Figurative, 2004. *Pos:* Dir, Kirkland Art Ctr, Clinton, NY, 68-71. *Teaching:* Instr sculpture, Sch Art, Munson-Williams-Proctor Inst, Utica, NY, 72-85; adj prof sculpture, Hamilton Col, Clinton, NY, 73-84; asst prof sculpture, Colgate Univ, Hamilton, NY, 85-89. *Awards:* Fel, Hand Hollow Found, 83; Yaddo Fel, 85; NY Found Arts Fel, 90. *Bibliog:* Hayden Carruth (auth) Essay, John Von Bergen Culpture Kouros Gallery, New York, NY, 96; Suzette McAvoy (auth), Essay, Marien Metaphors, Farnsworth Art Mus, Rockland, ME, 2003; Laurence Karasek (auth), Essay, Loosely Figurative, Stone Quarry Hill Art Park, Cazevonia, NY, 2004. *Mem:* Sculpture Space (co-founder and mem bd 75-); Intl Sculpture Ctr. *Media:* Bronze, Wood. *Interests:* Maritime Art. *Dealer:* Kouros Gallery 23 E 73rd St New York NY 10021

BERGER, JERRY ALLEN
DIRECTOR, CURATOR
b Buffalo, Wyo, Oct 8, 43. *Study:* Univ Wyo, BA, 65, BA(art), 71, MA(art hist), 72. *Pos:* Cur collections, Univ Wyo Art Mus, Laramie, 72-88, actg dir, 84-86, asst dir, 80-83 & 87-88; dir, Springfield Art Mus, Springfield, Mo, 88-. *Mem:* The Nat Arts Club. *Mailing Add:* Springfield Art Museum 1111 E Brookside Dr Springfield MO 65807

BERGER, JOHN PETER
CRITIC, PAINTER, WRITER
b London, Nov 5, 26. *Study:* attended, Central Sch Art; attended, Chelsea Sch Art, London. *Exhib:* Began career as painter, teacher drawing, 48-55; exhib works at Wildenstein Gallery, Redfern Gallery and Leicester Gallery, London. *Teaching:* vis Fel British Film Inst, 90-. *Awards:* Recipient George Orwell Mem prize, 77. *Publ:* art critic Tribune, New Statesman 1951-61; scenario: (with Alain Tanner) La Salamandre, Le Milieu du Monde, Jonas (NY Critics prize for best scenario of Yr 1976), (with Timothy Neat) Play Me Something (BFI), 1989, (film scenario) Isabelle: A Story in Shots, 1998; auth: Marcel Frishman, 1958, (novels) A Painter of Our Time, 1958, Permanent Red, 1960, The Foot of Clive, 1962, Corker's Freedom, 1964, The Success and Failure of Picasso, 1965, Lilac and Flag, 1990, Into Their Labours, 1991, To the Wedding, 1995, King. A Street Story, 1999, (with Patricia Macdonald) Once in Europa, 1999; essays: Keeping a Rendezvous, 1991, (with J. Mohr) A Fortunate Man; the story of a country doctor, 1967; Art and Revolution, 1969, Moments of Cubism and Other Essays, 1969; (essays) The Sense of Sight, 1985 (pub. in England as The White Bird), Photocopies, 1996, (poems) Pages of the Wound: Pocms, Drawings, Photographs 1956-96, 1996, The Shape of a Pocket, 2001, John Berger Selected essays (educated by Geoff Dyer), 2001; essays and articles include: The Look of Things, 1972, G (novel), 1972 (Booker prize 1972, James Tait Black Memorial prize 1972), Ways of Seeing, 1972, (with J. Mohr) The Seventh Man, 1975 (Union of Journalists and Writers of Paris prize for best reportage 1977), Pig Earth (fiction), 1979; About Looking, 1980; (with J. Mohr) Another Way of Telling, 1982, (with Katya Berger) Titian: Nymph and Shepherd, 1996; work for theatre (with Nella Bielski) A Question of Geography, premiere Theatre National de Marseille, 1984, Francisco Goya's Last Portrait, 1989, (with John Christie) I Send You This Cadmium Red, 2000; (non-fiction) And Our Faces, My Heart, Brief as Photos, 1984, Steps Towards a Small Theory of The Visible, 1996; Once in Europa (fiction) 1987 (award 1989); transir: (with A Bostock) Poems on the Theatre (B. Brecht), 1960, Return to My Native Land (Aime Césaire), 1969; writer (screenplay), Jonah Who Will Be 25 in the Yr 2000 and others; numerous TV appearances, incl: Monitor, two series for Granada TV. *Mailing Add:* Quincy Mieussy Taninges 74440 France

BERGER, MAURICE
CULT HISTORIAN & CRITIC
b New York, NY, May 22, 56. *Study:* Hunter Col, City Univ New York, BA(Thomas Hunter Scholar), 78; City Univ New York Grad Ctr, PhD, 88. *Pos:* Asst to dir exhibs, City Univ NY Grad Ctr, 81-; cur, Hunter Col Art Gallery, 83-85, cur, spec projects, 85-; jr fel, NY Inst Humanities, 83-85; cur, Univ Md, Baltimore Co, 92-. *Teaching:* Adj lectr art hist, Hunter Col, NY, 80-84; vis lectr, Queens Col, City Univ NY, 81; vis asst prof, Hunter Col, City Univ, NY, 85-91; vis lectr, Yale Univ, 87; vis lectr, State Univ NY, Stony Brook, 89 & Rutgers Univ, 90; sr fel, New Sch Social Res, 94-. *Awards:* Finalist, Horace Mann Bond Book award, Harvard Univ; Hon Mention, Gustavus Myers Book Award, Boston Univ; Alumni Achievement Award, City Univ NY Grad Ctr. *Mem:* PEN Am Ctr. *Res:* Art Hist, criticicism & critical theory; American Cultural History; race studies. *Mailing Add:* 740 West End Ave Apt 22A New York NY 10025

BERGER, PAT (PATRICIA) EVE
PAINTER, EDUCATOR
b New York, NY. *Study:* Art Ctr Col Design, 48; Univ Calif, Los Angeles, 50-55; studied with Sam Amato, Richard Boyce & John Altoon. *Hon Degrees:* Bravo Award Nominnee-Archievement in the Arts 91-92, 93-94; Nat'l Watercolors Soc, Honorary Life Member, Past Pres, WaterColor USA Honor Soc, Life time Member. *Work:* Long Beach Mus Art; San Diego Mus Art; Palm Springs Desert Mus, Calif; Springfield Art Mus, Mo; Sodertalje Konsthall, Jarnagatan, Sweden; West Publ, St Paul, Minn; and others. *Comn:* Olympic mural, Cent Adult High Sch, Los Angeles, 84; Pac Bell, Exec Floor, Los Angeles, Calif, 89; Northwest Memorial Hospital Chicago, IL, 2000. *Exhib:* Solo exhibs, Light, Illusion & Reality, Riverside Art Ctr & Mus, 83, Paintings of the Homeless, Capitol Bldg, Sacramento & Bridge Gallery, City Hall, 86, Int Contemp Art Fair, Los Angeles, Calif, 86, Jewish Fedn Galleries, Los Angeles, Calif, 88, Univ Judaism, Los Angeles, Calif, 91, Evansville Mus Art & Sci, Ind, 95 & Univ Fairfield, Conn, 96; Am Watercolors, Chateau de Tours, France, 87; Jewish Mus, San Francisco, Calif, 87; travel exhibs, Nat Women Artists Centennial, India, 89, Hunger 1990's, Not by Bread Alone, Carson Sq House Mus, Panhandle, Tex, 90, West Art & The Law, 83, 84, 91, 93 & 96; Inaugural Exhib, Huntington Beach Arts Ctr, 95; Kittakyushn Japan, 2001; Fukuoka Prefectural Mus, Fukyoka, Japan, 2001; Kitakyushn Monicipal Mus, 2005. *Collection Arranged:* Pat Berger's Homelss Series (auth, catalog), Karpeles Manuscript Libr Mus, Buffalo, NY. *Pos:* Muralist, Millard Sheets, Claremont, 75-77. *Teaching:* Instr painting & drawing, Los Angeles Unified Sch Dist, Adult Div, 71-2003; instr murals, Cent Adult High Sch, Los Angeles, 82-85. *Awards:* Purchase Awards, Pa Acad Fine Arts, Ford Found, 64, Los Angeles All City Exhib, Ahmanson Collection, 69 & 76 & Art & the Law, West Publ Co, 91, 93 & 96; Fel, Brody Arts Fund, Calif Community Found, 88; Fel, Julia & David White Artists' Colony, Costa Rica. *Bibliog:* Hazel Harrison (auth), Watercolor School, Quatro Publ, 93; Sandra Knipe (auth), article, Evansville Press, 1/26/95; Phyllis Boros (auth), Artist with a Cause, Conn Post, 1/14/96. *Mem:* Hon life mem Nat Watercolor Soc (pres, 73-74); Watercolor USA Honor Soc (secy, 94); Fine Arts Coun, Univ Judaism; LA Artcore; life mem Watercolor USA Hon Soc; Jewish Initiative Artist of So CA. *Media:* Acrylic, Watercolor. *Specialty:* Landan 20th Century Art-Travel Exhib (contempary Painting and sculpture La Artcore, Los Angeles, CA; Bentley Gallery, Phoenix, AZ. *Interests:* painting, curating, photography, community involvement in arts. *Collection:* Kapeles Manvscript Library Mus, Buffalo, NY; Fred Weisman Mus, Minneapolis, MN; Northwest Memorial Hospital, Chicago, IL. *Publ:* Contribr, Museum Opening Exhibit, Desert Sun, Palm Springs, 70; illusr, Coalescence, 73 & Socrates Jones, 75, Almark Publ Co; contribr, West '84 Art & the Law, West Publ Co, 83, 84, 91, 93 & 96; auth, California Romantics, Harbingers of Watercolorism, Perine, 86. *Dealer:* Landau 20th Century Art 1625 Thayer Ave Los Angeles CA 90024; Mitizi Landan 1525 Selby Ave, Los Angeles, 90024. *Mailing Add:* 2648 Anchor Ave Los Angeles CA 90064

BERGER, PAUL ERIC
COLLAGE ARTIST, PHOTOGRAPHER
b The Dalles, Ore, Jan 20, 48. *Study:* Art Ctr Col Design, Los Angeles, with Tod Walker, 67-69; Univ Calif, Los Angeles, with Robert Heinecken & Robert Fichter, BA, 69-70; Visual Studies Workshop, State Univ NY, Buffalo, with Nathan Lyons, MFA, 70-73. *Work:* Int Mus of Photog/George Eastman House, Rochester, NY; Bibliot Nat, Paris, France; Art Inst Chicago; San Francisco Mus Mod Art; Los Angeles Co Mus Art, Calif. *Exhib:* One-man shows, Photographs, 75-90, Opened Bk, Art Inst Chicago, 75 Mathematics Series, 77, Seattle Subtext, 82, Light Gallery, NY & Cards, USC Altier Gallery, Santa Monica, Calif, Galerie Lichtblick, Cologne, Ger, 96; Works 1976-1989, Seattle Art Mus, Wash; Card Plates, Soho Photo, New York City, 99; Paul Berger: 1973-03, Mus of Contemp Photo, Chicago, 03. *Pos:* Asst prof art, Univ Wash, Seattle, 78, prof art, currently. *Teaching:* Lectr photog, Univ Ill, Champaign, 74-78; from asst to assoc prof photog, Univ Wash, Seattle, 78-. *Awards:* Young Photogr Award, Int Meeting Photog, Arles, France, 75; Nat Endowment Arts photogr fel, 79; Nat Endowment Arts, Visual Artsts Fel, 86. *Bibliog:* Leroy Searle (auth), Paul Berger's mathematics photographs, Afterimage, Rochester, 78; Jim Burns (auth), From Old Images to New, Argus Publ, Seattle, Wash, 79; Rod Slemmons (auth), Paul Berger: Marco Polo in the Land of the Computer, Photo Education (Polaroid Newsletter), 90; Rod Slemmons (auth), Paul Berger: The Machine in the Window, Seattle Art Mus, Wash, 90. *Mem:* Soc Photog Educ (bd dir, 80-84). *Media:* Photography, Digital media. *Collection:* International Museum of Photography, GEH; The Art Institute of Chicago; LA County Museum of Art; San Francisco Museum of Modern Art; Museum of Contempary Photography, Chicago; The Art Museum, Princeton University. *Publ:* Auth, Seattle Subtext, USW and Real Comet Press, 84. *Mailing Add:* Sch of Art Univ Wash Seattle WA 98195

BERGER-KRAEMER, NANCY
PAINTER, SCULPTOR
b New York, NY, Aug 15, 41. *Study:* Adelphi Univ, BA, 63; Queens Col, MS, 68. *Work:* Fordham univ, Lowenstein libr, NY; Johnson & Johnson, NJ; Cali Assocs; AT&T; Nabisco. *Comn:* large collage mixed media box, comn by Mr & Mrs Sandor Hochheiser, West Orange, NJ, 90; large woven wall hanging, comn by Mr & Mrs S Scatcherd, Summit, NJ, 90; fiber, string, paper collage, comn by Mr & Mrs Syd Corn,

Palm Beach, Fla, 95 & 2nd comn, 2002; Dr & Mrs Zacharias, Maplewood, NJ; Mr & Mrs Polon, Tinton Falls, NJ. *Exhib:* Artists of Cent NJ, Middlesex Co Mus, Piscataway, NJ, 90; NJ Fine Arts Ann, Montclair Art Mus, 91; NJ Fine Arts Ann, Noyes Mus, Oceanville, NJ, 92; Five Chinese Elements, Trenton City Mus, NJ, 96; solo exhib, Newark Mus, Bergen Mus, Montclair Art Mus, Trenton State Mus, Trenton City Mus; San Diego Art Inst Int; City Without Walls, Newark, NJ, Skylands Arts Ann Exhib, Sparta, NJ, Ceres, New York City Invitational & many others 2001-2003; Jersey City Mus, NJ; Contemporary Art, The Mill, Lafayette, NJ; Griffin Gallery, Madison, NJ; Court Gallery, Ben Shahn Ctr, Wayne, NJ. *Teaching:* Mixed media weavings, Clinton Elem Sch, Maplewood, NJ, 80-89. *Awards:* Middlesex Co Mus Best of Show, Artists of Cent NJ, 89; Cali Assocs First Place Sculpture, Arts Coun Essex Area Art Exhib, 90; NJ Ctr Visual Art Second Place Award Int Juried Show, 95. *Bibliog:* Dennis C Dougherty (auth), The dichotomy of a creative woman, Essex J-News Rec, NJ, 3/22/90; Nancy Berger-Kraemer fiber sculpture & hangings, Essex J-News Rec, NJ, 2/17/94; Eileen Watkins (auth), Women head field at international show, NJ Star Ledger, 3/15/94; and others. *Mem:* Women's Caucus for Art; Princeton Art Asn; Stamford Art Asn. *Media:* Mixed Assemblage Artist

BERGGRUEN, JOHN HENRY
ART DEALER
b San Francisco, Calif, June 18, 43. *Study:* San Francisco State Col, AB, 67. *Pos:* Pres & owner, John Berggruen Gallery, San Francisco, 70-; mem bd trustees, San Francisco Art Inst. *Mem:* Soc Encouragement Contemp Art; Art Dealers Asn Am. *Specialty:* Paintings, drawings and original prints of the 20th century. *Mailing Add:* 228 Grant Ave 3rd fl San Francisco CA 94108

BERGHASH, MARK W
PHOTOGRAPHER, PAINTER
b Buffalo, NY, Mar 8, 35. *Study:* Univ Buffalo, 52-55; Univ Vienna, Austria, 55-56; Art Students League, with George Grosz, 57-60; with George Tice & Philippe Halsman, 76-78. *Work:* Metrop Mus Art, Jewish Mus & Franklin Furnace Archive, NY; Calif Mus Photography, Riverside; Dayton Art Inst, Ohio; Cameraworks, San Francisco, Calif; Int Ctr Photog, NY. *Exhib:* The Portrait Extended, Mus Contemp Art, Chicago, Ill, 80; Counterparts and Affinities, Metrop Mus Art, NY, 82; Indelible Images, The Jewish Mus, NY, 82; Holocaust Survivors Remembered, Jewish Ctr, Buffalo, NY; one-man shows, Nudes in Parts, Gallery Photog Art, Tel Aviv, 84, Segmented Photogs, Marcuse Pfeifer Gallery, NY, 84, 87 & 89, San Francisco Cameraworks, Calif, 88, CEPA, Buffalo, NY, 88, Trienrak Int de la Photographis, Fribourg, Switz, 88, Art Inst, Chicago, 89, Hilton Hotel, NY, 89 & Port Washington Libr, NY, 89; Jews and Germans: Aspects of the True Self (with catalog), Calif Mus Photog, Riverside, 85; Two to Tango, Int Ctr Photog, NY; Golem, Danger, Deliverance & Art (with catalog), Jewish Mus, NY, 88; The Photographer of Invention (with catalog), Mus Am Art, Washington, DC, Mus Contemp Art, Chicago & Walker Art Ctr, Minneapolis, 89-90; Laurence Miller Gallery, NY, 89; Phyllis Rothman Gallery, Farleigh Dickenson Univ, Madison, NJ, 89; Portraits of Me Rooted and Uprooted, SF Camerawork, San Francisco, Calif, 92. *Pos:* Pres, Twenty-Twenty Serv, Inc. *Bibliog:* Any Grundberg (auth), Why the holocaust defies pictorialization, New York Times, 5/2/82; Zan Dubin (auth), Jews & Germans, Los Angeles Times, 12/2/85; Carol Stevens (auth), Still performances, Print Mag, 3/88; Richard Woodard (auth), Serving up the Poor as Exotic Fare for Voyeurs?, NY Times, 6/89; Catherine Calhoun (auth), Just How Life Is, New York Press, 6/89. *Mem:* Art Students League. *Media:* Silver Emulsion, Color Coupler Print. *Publ:* Coauth, Jews & Germans, CMP, 85. *Mailing Add:* 90 Riverside Dr No 10A New York NY 10002-8261

BERGNER, LANNY MICHAEL
SCULPTOR
b Anacortes, Wash, Dec 4, 52. *Study:* Univ Wash, Seattle, BFA(sculpture), 81; Tyler Sch Art, Philadelphia, Pa, MFA(sculpture), 83. *Work:* Philadelphia Mus Art, Pa; Delaware Art Mus, Wilmington; Walker Hill Art Ctr, Seoul, Korea; Seattle Art Mus, Whatcom Art Mus, Woodenmere Art Mus. *Comn:* Wall Sculpture, Philadelphia Int Airport, Pa, 93. *Exhib:* Biennial 89 & 91, Del Art Mus, Wilmington, 89 & 91; Contemp Philadelphia Artists, Philadelphia Mus Art, Pa, 90; Artists Choose Artists, Inst Contemp Art, Philadelphia, Pa, 91; A New World View, Nat Craft Gallery, Kilkenny, Ireland, 2006; Natures Matrix, Philadelphia Int Airport, Pa, 2006. *Awards:* Sculpture Prize, Contemp Philadelphia artists, Philadelphia Mus Art, 90; Betty Bowen Mem Award, 95; Artist Trust Craft Fellowship, Seattle, 97; Artist Trust Gap Grant, Seattle, 2000; Gold Prize, 4th Cheongju Int Craft Biennial, 2005. *Mem:* Fiber Art Int; Northwest Designer Craftsmen. *Media:* Mixed. *Interests:* music, gardening. *Publ:* 500 Baskets, Lark Books, 2005; Intertwined, ASU Art Mus, 2005; and others. *Dealer:* Snyderman/Works Gallery 303 Cherry St, Philadelphia, PA 19106; Thirteen Moons Gallery 652 Canyon Rd Santa Fe NMex; Cervini Haas Gallery 4222 N Marshall Way Scottsdale Ariz 85251. *Mailing Add:* 7064 Miller Rd Anacortes WA 98221-8321

BERGSTROM, EDITH HARROD
PAINTER
b Denver, Colo. *Study:* Pomona Col, BA, 63; Stanford Univ, MA, 64; Study with Richard Diebenkorn. *Work:* Palm Springs Desert Mus, Calif; San Jose Mus Art, Calif; Utah State Univ, Logan; Achenbach Found for Graphic Arts, Calif, Palace of the Legion of Hon, San Francisco; Claremont Graduate Sch, Calif; Springfield Art Mus, Springfield, Mo; and others. *Comn:* Ten paintings, Hyatt Corp, Houston, Tex. *Exhib:* Am Watercolor Soc,; Rocky Mountain Nat Watermedia Exhib,; Nat Watercolor Soc,; Watercolor USA,; Palm Springs Desert Mus,; Butler Inst Am Art 45th Nat, Youngstown, Ohio, 81 & 86; one-woman shows, Capricorn Galleries, Bethesda, Md, 86, A Gallery, Palm Desert, Calif, 89; Tropical Topics, Monterey Penninsula Mus Art, 88. *Pos:* jury chmn, Nat Watercolor Soc, 87. *Teaching:* Private. *Awards:* Foothill Art Ctr Award, Rocky Mountain Nat Watermedia Exhib, 87; Southwest Mo Mus Asn Purchase Award, Springfield Art Mus, 87; Calif State Fair Award, 87; and others. *Bibliog:* Mary Carhartt (auth), Watercolor: See for Yourself, Grumbacher, 84; Gerald Brommer (auth), Exploring the Art of Painting, Davis Publ, 87; Michael Ward (auth), The New Spirit of Watercolor, N Light Publ, 89. *Mem:* Rocky Mountain Nat Watermedia Soc; Nat Watercolor Soc; Am Watercolor Soc; W Coast Watercolor Soc (past-pres); Watercolor USA Hon Soc. *Media:* Oil, Watercolor. *Specialty:* A Gallery Fine Art-Painting-all Media. *Interests:* Gardening. *Collection:* Many Corp Collections. *Publ:* Auth, article, Am Artist, 1/82; auth, article, Artist's Mag, 7/87. *Dealer:* A Gallery Fine Art 73-956 El Paseo Dr Palm Desert CA 92261. *Mailing Add:* PO Box 126 Palo Alto CA 94302

BERGUSON, ROBERT JENKINS
PAINTER, EDUCATOR
b Blossburg, Pa, Dec 6, 1944. *Study:* Corning Community Col, NY, AA, 64; Univ Iowa, Iowa City, BA, 67, MA, 68, MFA, 70. *Work:* Norfolk Mus Arts & Sci, Va; Univ NDak Art Gallery, Grand Forks; Univ Iowa Sch Art Gallery, Iowa City; Hunter Mus Art, Bluff View, Chattanooga, Tenn; Miss Mus Art, Jackson; La State Univ, Alexandria; New Orleans Mus Art, La; Masur Mus Art, Monroe, La; Concordia Univ, Austin, Tex. *Exhib:* XXIII Am Drawing Biennial, Smithsonian Traveling Exhib Serv, Norfolk Mus Arts & Sci, Va, 69; Louisiana: Major Works 1984, La World Expo, Inc, New Orleans, 84; Louisiana Competition, Baton Rouge, 87 & 90; Fifth Ann Fla Nat, Fla State Univ, Tallahassee, 90; 37th Ann Delta Art Exhib, Little Rock Art Ctr, Ark, 94; Mobile Mus Art Biennial, Ala, 99; Concordia Univ Nat Exhib, Austin, 2001; 25 one-man painting & drawing exhibs; and others. *Teaching:* Asst prof painting & drawing, La Tech Univ, Ruston, 70-76, assoc prof, 77-83, prof, 83-. *Awards:* Purchase Award, XXIII Am Drawing Biennial, Norfolk Art Mus, 69 & 13th NDak Exhib Prints & Drawings, Univ NDak, 70; Merit Award, 16th Hunter Mus Art, Lincoln-Davies, Inc, Bluff View, Chattanooga, Tenn, 77; Honorable Mention, SPAR Nat Art Exhib, Shreveport, La, 82; Cash Award, 80; Louisiana Artist Fel; Louisiana Mini-Grantee, 2001, 2002, 2005. *Mem:* Col Art Asn; Mus Mod Art, NY; Contemp Art Ctr, New Orleans; Found in Art: Theory and Educ. *Media:* Graphite, Acrylic. *Publ:* Auth, article, Art Voices-South, 7-8/79; illusr, Upper & lower case, Int J Typographics, 79. *Dealer:* Cole Pratt Gallery New Orleans, La. *Mailing Add:* 1213 Robinette Dr Ruston LA 71270

BERHANG, MATTIE
SCULPTOR, LECTURER
b New York, NY. *Study:* Tyler Sch Art, BFA; Art Students League, with R B Hale & J DeCreeft; New York Studio Sch, with G Spaventa, R Nakian & M Matter. *Work:* Lannan Found Mus, Los Angeles, Calif; Reich & Tang Inc, Leukemia Soc Am, NY, Sigal Construction Corp, Washington, DC; Albert & Vera List Gallery, Brown Univ, Providence, RI; David Bermant Found, Harrison, NY. *Comn:* Mobile construct, comn by Cermak Plaza Assocs, Berwyn, Ill, 87; mobile construct, comn by Jane Abrams, Palm Beach, Fla, 89; construct, comn by Dr Joseph & Helene Chazan, Providence, RI, 90; crucifix, comn by Grant Nicolson, NY, 96; restoration, comn by Church of St Mary & St Andrew, Ellenville, NY, 2001. *Exhib:* Varfor NY? (with catalog), Stockholm Int Art Expos, Sweden, 83; Sculpture: The Tradition in Steel (with catalog), Nassau Co Mus Fine Arts, Roslyn, NY, 83; Am Women Artists Part II: The Recent Generation (with catalog), Sidney Janis Gallery, NY, 84; Discarded (with catalog), Rockland Ctr Arts, West Nyack, NY, 91; The Big Picture (with catalog), O K Harris Works of Art, NY, 92; and many others. *Teaching:* Guest lectr, Syracuse Univ, 81 & 85, New Sch Social Res, New York, 81, Univ Wis, Eau Claire, 83 & Univ Cincinnati, 84. *Awards:* 1987-88 Artists' Space Individual Artist Grant, Artists' Space, INC, NY; 1989 Artists' Space Individual Artist Grant, Artists Space, Inc, NY. *Bibliog:* The artist framed, Esquire, 4/86; Harvey Stein (auth), Artists Observed, Harry N Abrams, New York, 86; Majory E Bevlin (auth), Design Through Discovery, Holt, Rinehart and Winston, Inc, New York, 89. *Media:* Mixed Materials, Cast Metal. *Mailing Add:* PO Box 92 Ellenville NY 12428-0092

BERK, AMY LYNNE
ARTIST
b Brooklyn, NY, Aug 3, 67. *Study:* San Francisco Art Inst, MFA, 1995; Wesleyan Univ, BA, 1989. *Work:* Oakland Mus, Calif; Children's Television Workshop, NY. *Comn:* Architectonic (Goethe the wall installaton), Goethe the Inst, San Francisco, 1998-99; Market St Art in, San Francisco Art Comn, San Francisco, 1999; Mount Bruce Transit Poster Series, (video series), www.Neighborhood Films Org,. *Exhib:* Getter, San Francisco Arts Comn, San Francisco, Calif, 1999; Needles and Pins, Ctr for the Arts, San Francisco, Calif, 1998; Needle Art, Bedford Gallery, Walnut Creek, 1999; Holy cow! divine bovines, Mus da Republica, Rio De Janeiro, 1999; Following the Tradition, Kraushaar Gallery, New York City, 2003; Revealing Influences, Conversations, Mus of Folk & craft Art, San Francisco, Calif, 2003; Wall Works, Traywick Contemp, Berkeley, 2005; Suell, Tenn Years Later, Meridian Gallery, San Francisco, 2006; Magnes; Magnes Mus, Berkeley, 2006. *Pos:* Co-dir, Meridian Interns Prog, San Francisco, Calif, 1996-2004; co-publ, www.stretcher.org, San Francisco, Calif, 2000-. *Teaching:* instr, Contemp Art San Francisco Adult Community Educ, 1997-2003; instr, San Francisco State, 2000; Instr, UC Berkeley Extension, San Francisco, Calif, 2004-; vis faculty, San Francisco Art Inst, 2006. *Awards:* Artist in Residence, New Pacific Studio, 2001; Purchase Award, 1998. *Mem:* Together we can Defeat Capitalism (TWC DC) 2000-present; San Francisco Art Inst Artists Comt Chair, 1996-1999. *Media:* Painting, Sculpture, Drawing. *Specialty:* Contemp. *Publ:* Article; Margaret Harison & Conrad Atkinson at Refusalon, Art Papers, 2000; Forever on the Move, World Sculpture News, 2000; edit co-publ, Stretcher.org, 2000-; Artist at work, Sabina, Ohio, Art Contemp, 2004; Sarah Ratchye, Marjorie Wood Gallery, 2004. *Dealer:* Katrina Traywick 89 S Colusa Ave Berkeley Calif 94707. *Mailing Add:* 67 29th St San Francisco CA 94110-4910

BERKENBLIT, ELLEN
PAINTER
b Paterson, NJ, 58. *Study:* Cooper Union, BFA, 80. *Comn:* Two fabric designs for spring couture line, comn by Todd Oldham, 93. *Exhib:* Solo exhibs, Club 57, NY, 82, Limbo Lounge, NY, 83, Semaphore East, NY, 84, 85 & 86, White Columns, NY, 92, Galerie Hubert Klocker, Vienna, 93 & Boesky & Callery, NY, 96; East Village Artists, Va Mus Fine Arts, Richmond, 84; Small Wonders, Barry Whistler Gallery, Dallas, 94; Berkenblit, Nares, Prince, Wool, Galleria Bonomo, Rome, 95; Group Hanging, Griffin Linton Fine Arts, Costa Mesa, Calif, 96; Bronwyn Keenan Gallery, NY, 96; and others. *Awards:* NY Found Arts Painting Fel, 92; Nat Endowment Arts Visual Artist Fel, 93. *Bibliog:* Wendy Goodman (auth), Precious nothings, HG, 9/92; Johanna Hofleipner (auth), Rev, Kureir, Vienna, 6/93; Visiting artist, Paper Mag, 4/96

BERKMAN, LILLIAN
COLLECTOR
Study: Univ Philippines, Hon Dr Humanities; Marquette Univ, Hon Dr Fine Arts. *Pos:* Pres, Rojtman Found Inc; fel, Morgan Libr; fel in perpetuity, Metrop Mus Art, NY; overseer, Univ Pa Mus; trustee, Telfair Mus, Savannah, Ga; mem exec bd adv, Inst Fine Arts, NY Univ; trustee Nat Coun, Mem Acquisition Comt Fine Arts Mus, San Francisco; chmn, Asn Am Artists Inc, currently. *Awards:* Pere Marquett Award; Presidential Award for Cult Interchange, Costa Rica; Kyros Award, Marquette Univ. *Mem:* Asia Soc (president's coun); Drawing Soc; Japan Soc, founding mem; Lotos Club, NY; Univ Club NY. *Collection:* Paintings, prints, drawings, sculpture, porcelains; 18th century French furniture; 18th century Chinese jades, archaic Chinese bronzes

BERKON, MARTIN
PAINTER
b Brooklyn, NY, Jan 30, 32. *Study:* Brooklyn Col, BA; New York Univ, MA; Pratt Inst. *Work:* Texaco Inc, White Plains, NY; NASA Gallery of Art, Kennedy Space Ctr, Cape Canaveral, Fla; Pepsico Inc, Somers, NY; Center for the Arts & Vero Beach Mus Art, Vero Beach, Fla; Pfizer Inc, Rye Brook, NY. *Comn:* Painting, NASA, 84 & 87. *Exhib:* One-man shows, Soho Ctr for Visual Artists, NY, 74, Genesis Gallery, NY, 78, Adelphi Univ, 83 & Blue Hill Cult Ctr, Pearl River, NY, 95, Schering Plough Corp Gallery, Madison, NJ, 01; Brooklyn Mus, 58; Butler Inst Am Art Ann Midyear Show, 65, 67 & 69; Contemp Reflections, 74, A Change of View, 75, A Look Back A Look Forward, 82, Aldrich Mus Contemp Art, Ridgefield, Conn; Oakland Univ, Rochester, Mich, 75; Am Fedn Arts Traveling Exhib, 75-76; Kennedy Space Center, Cape Canaveral, Fla, 84 & 87; Visions of Flight: Retrospective From NASA Art Collection, Smithsonian Inst Traveling Exhib World Tour, 1988-91; The Abstract Image, Vero Beach Mus Art, 96; Interpreting the River, Blue Hill Cult Ctr, Pearl River, NY, 97-98. *Teaching:* Instr elements of design, Fairleigh Dickinson Univ, 66-67; lect art, City Col NY, 68-69; guest lectr, Middlebury Col, 77, Nassau Community Col, 82 & St Thomas Acquinas Col, 95. *Bibliog:* Grace Glueck (auth), Art notes, New York Times, 12/1/74; Evalyn E Milman (auth), article, in: Bridgeport Sunday Post, 1/24/82; Merle English (auth), article, in: Newsday, 10/5/84; Shirley Romaine (interviewer), Long Island Artscene, Cox Cable TV, 9/86; Robert Schulman & Lori Dempsey (auth), Visions of Flight: A Retrospective from the NASA Art Collection, catalogue, 88; Genie Carr (auth), Review of NASA Retrospective, color reproduction, in: Winston-Salem J, 9/13/90; color reproduction, Intenet publ, Alison Wright (auth), Nature Art: Imagine Space, 10/2002; color reproductions, Internet publ, Martin Wattenberg (ed), Art and space, Dome News, 9/2002; Julie Clay (auth) NASA's Hospital Visit, Ft. Myers Magazine 6/2005. *Media:* Oil, Acrylic, Watercolor. *Mailing Add:* 503 DeVries Ct Piermont NY 10968

BERKOWITZ, HENRY
PAINTER, DESIGNER
b Brooklyn, NY, Feb 5, 33. *Study:* Brooklyn Mus Art Sch, with Sidney Simon; Workshop Sch Advert & Ed Art; Sch Visual Arts, NY. *Work:* Gutenberg Mus, Main, Ger. *Exhib:* Berkshire Mus, Pittsfield, Mass, 71; Galeries Raymond Duncan, Paris, 74; Art Festival Tours, France, 74; Parrish Art Mus, 75; Surindependants, Paris, 75; The Brooklyn Mus, NY; The New York Coliseum, NY; The Nat Arts Club, NY; The Wilkes Gallery, NY; The Gutenberg Mus, Mainz, Ger; Orlando Mus Art, Fla; Maitland Art Center, Maitland, Fla; plus others. *Pos:* Art dir, Pyramid Publ, New York, 63-77. *Awards:* Award of Merit, New York Coliseum, 70; Am Vet Soc for Artists Award for an Abstract Work of Art, 72; Palmas de Oro, Int Art Festival, Paris, 74; plus others. *Mem:* Am Vet Soc Artists; Huntington Art League; Berkshire Art Asn; Awixa Pond Art Asn; Shore Arts Asn. *Media:* Oil, Mixed Media. *Publ:* Auth & illusr, Fish, Facts and Fancies, 81 & Amphibians & Reptiles, 85, Banyan Books; Dinosaurs, 87, Sharks, 88 & Monsters, 94, Henart Books; Dolphins & Whales, Winner Enterprises, 96. *Dealer:* Ligoa Duncan Gallery 1045 Madison Ave New York NY 10021. *Mailing Add:* 1115 Timberlane Tr Casselberry FL 32707

BERKOWITZ, ROGER M
CURATOR, ADMINISTRATOR
b Denver, Colo, May 30, 44. *Study:* Western Reserve Univ, AB, 66; Univ Mich, MMP, 70, PhD, 77. *Collection Arranged:* El Greco of Toledo, 82; Reinstallation permanent collection, Toledo Mus Art, 83 & 91; Impressionism: Selections from Five Am Mus, 90. *Pos:* Cur, Decorative Arts, Toledo Mus Art, 77- & deputy dir, 86-; bd ed adv, Studies Decorative Arts, Bard Grad Ctr, currently. *Teaching:* Vis lectr art hist, Univ Mich, 73 & 79-. *Awards:* Chester Dale Fel, Nat Gallery Art, 72-73; Award of Achievement, Northern Ohio Live, 91. *Mem:* Ohio Citizens Arts. *Res:* Eighteenth and nineteenth century English silver. *Publ:* Contribr, Toledo Mus Art: European Paintings, 76 & The Museum Collects: Treasures by Sculptors and Craftsmen, 80, Toledo Mus Art; auth, The patriotic fund vases, regency awards to the navy, Apollo, 81

BERKOWITZ, TERRY
INSTALLATION ARTIST
b Brooklyn, NY. *Study:* Sch Visual Arts, New York, cert, 71, Art Inst, Chicago, MFA, 73. *Work:* Mus of Modern Art, NY; pvt collections. *Exhib:* Solo exhibs, People Who Live In Glass Houses, Alternative Mus, NY, 80, Contemp Art Mus, Houston, Tex, 90, Whitney Mus Am Art, 92 & Backseat, Sculpture Ctr, NY (auth, catalog), 94, Metronom, Barcelona, 99; group exhib Schemes, Film as Installation, The Clocktower, NY, 83; El Sueño Imperativo, Circulo De Bellas Artes, Madrid, Spain, 91; Construction in Process, Kodz, Poland, 91; Transition/Dislocation, Cleveland Ctr Contemp Art, 96; Carcel de Amor, Museo Nacional Centro de Arte, Reina Sofia, Madrid, Spain, 2005; EMAP, Korea, 2005; Diva Video Fair, New York City, 2005 & 06; Loop Video Festival, Barcelona, 2006. *Pos:* Artists adv bd, Alternative Mus, NY, 83-86. *Teaching:* prof fine & performing art, Baruch Col/CUNY, 95-. *Awards:* Fel, Nat Endowment Arts, 74; Fel, Creative Artists in Pub Serv, 74; Macdowell Art Colony Fel, Summer, 89; Jerome Found Film/Video Prod Grant, 90 & 96; Fulbright Scholar, 96. *Bibliog:* John Paoletti (auth), At the edge where art becomes media and message becomes polemic: Disinformation at the Alternative Museum, Arts Mag, 5/85; Sue Cramer (auth), Report from Poland: Back to the Future, Art in Am, 3/91; Judy Cantor (auth), El Sueño Imperativo, Art News, 5/91. *Media:* Mixed Media. *Publ:* Auth, Report from behind the scenes, Art Criticism, Vol 2, No 3, 86; Bloodstone, Contemp Arts Mus, Houston, 91. *Mailing Add:* 38 N Moore St New York NY 10013

BERKSON, BILL
CRITIC, POET
b New York, NY, Aug 30, 39. *Study:* Brown Univ, 57-59; New Sch, NY, 59-61; Columbia Univ, 59-60. *Pos:* Assoc prod, Art-New York, WNDT-TV, 64-65; film ed, Kulchur, 62-63; guest ed, Mus Mod Art, 65-69; ed & publ, Best & Co, 69 & Big Sky Mag & Bks, 71-78; consult, Coord Coun Lit Mag, 75; ed, The World Record, St Marks Poetry Proj, 80; corresp, Artforum, 85-91; poetry ed, Video & the Arts, 85-86; coord, Bay Area Consortium Visual Arts, 85-87; contrib ed, Zyzzyva, 87-92; corresp ed, Art in Am, 88-; guest cur, San Francisco Mus Mod Art, 91; cur, Susan Cummins Gallery, 92, Mills Col Art Gallery, 93 & Campbell-Thiebud Gallery, 97; co-cur, Gallery Paule Anglim, 92; interim dean, San Francisco Art Inst, 92, dir, Letters & Sci, 94-98; adj cur, Fine Arts Mus, San Francisco, 95; ed bd, Modern Painters, 2002-. *Teaching:* Assoc prof art hist, Calif Col Arts & Crafts, 83-84; prof art hist, San Francisco Art Inst, 84-. *Awards:* Artspace Art Criticism Award, 90. *Bibliog:* Irving Sandler (co-ed), Alex Katz, 71; Joe LeSueur (co-ed), Homage to Frank O'Hara, 78; Rackstraw Downes (co-ed), Arts J, DeKooning issue, 89. *Mem:* Int Art Critics Asn. *Res:* Contemporary art. *Publ:* Auth, Report from San Francisco, 6/94, In the Heat of the Rose, 3/96, As Ever, de Kooning, 2/97 & The Pollock Effect (rev), 12/97, The Photographist (on Carleton Watkins), 4/2000, Art in Am; About Ernie Gehr (exhib catalog), Walter/McBean Gallery, 95; (exhib cat) Changes Like the Weather, De Young Mas, 95; Shaw Business, 10-11/96 & Nagle Wares, 8-9/97, Am Craft; From the Land of Drawers (exhib catalog), Berggruen Gallery, 1/98; Wayne's World, summer, 98 & A New York Beginner, 9/98, The Portraitist (Elaine de Kooning), spring, 99, What Is There, winter, 99-2000, De Kooning, with Attitude, summer, 2000, Mod Painters; Jackson Pollock/Drawings on Colored Papers, Joan Washburn Gallery; Existing Light in Henry Wessel, Rena Bransten Gallery, 2000; Ceremonial Surfaces: California Art in the Anderson Collection, Univ Calif Press, fall, 2000; The Searcher in Elmer Bischoff, Univ Calif Press, 2001; What the ground looks like in Arial Use: The Art of Yvonne Jacquette, Stanford Art Mus, 2001; The Sweet Singer of Modernism & selected art writings 85-03, Qua Books, 2003. *Mailing Add:* 25 Grand View Ave San Francisco CA 94114

BERLIND, ROBERT
PAINTER, EDUCATOR
b New York, NY, Aug 20, 38. *Study:* Columbia Col, BA, 60; Sch Art & Archit, Yale Univ, BFA, 62, MFA, 63. *Work:* J B Speed Art Mus, Louisville, Ky Neuberger Mus Art, Purchase, NY; Mus of City of NY; Ringling Mus Art, Sarasota, Fla, 2000; Nat Acad Design Painting Ctr, NY City, 2004. *Exhib:* Solo shows, Gallery One, Toronto, 85, Del Valley Arts Asn, 92, Tibor de Nagy Gallery, NY, 94, 96, 98, 01, & 05, Reynolds Gallery, Richmond, 96, Univ Art Galleries, Wright State Univ, Dayton, Ohio, 97, Newberger Mus Art, Purchase, NY, 98, Picker Art Gallery, Colgate Univ, Hamilton, NY, 98 & Alexandre Acque Gallery, Univ Tulsa, 2005; group shows, Bronx Mus Arts, NY, 87, Three River Arts Festival, Pittsburg, Pa, 89, Art Mus Fla Int Univ, Miami, Fla, 89 & 96, Mem Art Gallery Univ Rochester, NY, 89, Md Inst, Col Art, Baltimore, Md, 89, Foundation Mona Bismarck, Paris, France, 91, Neuberger Mus, Purchase, NY, 94, The Police Building, NY, 94, Kunstrarein in Hamburg, Hamburg, Ger, 94; Maier Mus Art, Lynchburg, Va, 96; Lennon, Weinberg, Inc, NY, 98 & Apex Art, 97; Locks Gallery, Philadelphia, 2002. *Teaching:* Asst prof, Minneapolis Sch Art, 64-66 & 69-70; asst prof art hist & humanities, Haarlem, Neth, 66-68; assoc prof & dir grad studies, NS Col Art & Design, 74-76; assoc prof, State Univ NY at Purchase, full prof, 79-. *Awards:* Am Acad Inst Arts & Lett, 92; Nat Endowment Arts Fel Painting, 93; Pollock-Krasner Found Award, 97. *Bibliog:* Ken Johnson (auth), review, NY Times, 6/26/98; Roberta Smith (auth), article, NY Times, 7/17/98; Jonathan Goodman (auth), review, Art in Am, 1/99; Karen Wilkin (auth) article, Partison Review, 02; Karen Wilkin (auth) catalog, Tibor de Nagy Gallery, the First Fifty Years, 1950-00. *Mem:* Nat Acad of Design; Asn International des Critiques d'Art; Col Art Asn. *Media:* Oil. *Publ:* guest ed, Art & Old Age, Art J, spring 94. *Dealer:* Tibor De Nagy Gallery New York NY. *Mailing Add:* 215 W 20th St New York NY 10011

BERLINGIERI, ANNIBALE MARCHESE DE VALLE PERROTTA
COLLECTOR
Awards: Named one of Top 200 Collectors, ARTnews Mag, 2004, 2005, 2006. *Mem:* Asn Italian Hist, Mansions, Rome (pres, Sect Basilicata 2001-). *Collection:* Modern & Contemporary art, especially minimalism. *Mailing Add:* L' associazione Dimore Storiche Italiano L go dei Fiorentini Rome Italy

BERLYN, SHELDON
PAINTER, PRINTMAKER
b Worcester, Mass, Sept 6, 29. *Study:* Yale Norfolk Summer Art Sch, 49-50; Worcester Art Mus Sch, cert, 51; Art Acad Cincinnati with Herbert Barnett, 54-55; State Univ NY, Buffalo, 59-62. *Work:* Worcester Art Mus, Mass; Dayton Art Inst; Albright-Knox Art Gallery, Buffalo, NY; State Univ NY Brockport Gallery Collection; Burchfield-Penny Art Ctr, Buffalo, NY; State Univ NY at Buffalo, Anderson Gallery, NY; and numerous pvt & corp collections. *Exhib:* One-man shows, Dana & Decordova Mus, Lincoln, Mass, 55, Schuman Gallery, Rochester, NY, 65-66 & 70, Albright-Knox Art Gallery, Buffalo, NY, 76, Nancy Kay Gallery, San Diego San Diego, 79, Le Copain Gallery, Buffalo, NY, 81, Castellani Art Mus, Niagara Univ, 97 & Univ Gallery, Ctr for Arts, State Univ NY, Buffalo, 97; Western NY Exhib, Albright-Knox Art Gallery, Buffalo, NY, 58-66 & 77; Drawings Above the Pa Line, Roberson Ctr Arts, Binghamton, NY, 68; Am Drawings, Moore Col Art, Philadelphia, 68; Begegnung-Mass Inst Technol, Auslands Inst, Dortmund, WGer, 76; Anderson Gallery, Buffalo, NY 94; Univ Gallery, State Univ NY, Buffalo, 97; many others. *Teaching:* Assoc prof painting & drawing, State Univ NY Buffalo, 58-, prof emer. *Awards:* Stephen Wilder Traveling Fel, Cincinnati Mus Asn, 55-56; State Univ NY Res Found Fel, 66-70; Sattler Award Painting, Western NY Exhib, Albright Knox Art Gallery, 60 & Reeb Award Drawing, 64. *Bibliog:* Richard Huntington (auth), In Bright Abstract Paintings, Centuries of Possibility, Buffalo News, 4/24/97; Robert Bertholf, Sheldon Berlyn: Caravaggio in New Colors, Artvoice, 5/7/97; Mark Lavatelli, Abstract Expressionism Without the Angst, Artvoice, 5/13/97. *Media:* Acrylic, Oil; Serigraphy. *Mailing Add:* 4598 Vine Rd Penn Yan NY 14527

BERMAN, AARON
ART DEALER, COLLECTOR
b New York, NY, Nov 21, 22. *Study:* Brooklyn Col, BA; Columbia Univ, MA; Bezalel Acad, Jerusalem, dipl painting & sculpture, with Itzhak Danziger. *Pos:* Art dir mod & contemp art, Spencer Enterprises, NY, 57- & Aaron Berman Gallery, 76-; art consult & appraiser, Am Friends Haifa Univ, Israel, 73-; art appraiser, GAB Serv Inc, Interval Video Prog, Chan 13, Sotheby's, IRS & Chai Art Inst. *Teaching:* Lectr contemp art, New Sch for Social Res, NY, 76-, United Jewish Appeal, NY, 88 & Minskoff Ctr, NY. *Bibliog:* Robin Landa (auth), Introduction to Design, Prentice Hall, 83; Les Krantz (auth), Am Art Galleries, Art Biz, (Great books). *Mem:* Art Appraiser's Asoc; fel Nat Acad Design; fel Whitney Mus Art; assoc mem Guggenheim Mus; contrib mem Mus Mod Art. *Specialty:* Modern and contemporary art: American, Israeli and European. *Collection:* Flemish period to modern and contemporary American, Israeli and European art, 19th and 20th centuries. *Publ:* Auth, 13 Mini Retros-Pictures on Exhibit, 4/79; Grace Knowlton, Arts, 9/81; Women's Art-Miles Apart, Valencia Col, 2/82; Auth, Michael Gleizer, Chai Art Inst. *Mailing Add:* Aaron Berman Gallery 660 E 19th St Brooklyn NY 11230

BERMAN, ARIANE R
PAINTER, PRINTMAKER
b Freeport Danzig, Mar 27, 37; US citizen. *Study:* Hunter Col, BFA, 59; Yale Univ, MFA(scholar), 62; Ecole Beaux Artes, Am Asn Univ Women & Fondation Etats-Unis Grants, 62-63; and with Stanley William Hayter & Jacques Desjobert. *Work:* Metrop Mus Art; Philadelphia Mus Art & Philadelphia Art Alliance; Wustum Mus Fine Arts, Duke Univ; Litton Indust; Hearst Corp. *Comn:* Painting, Seventeen Mag, 71; painting, Shipley Sch, Bryn Mawr & Charles E Ellis, Newton Sq, Pa, 71; UNICEF, Philadelphia Child Guidance. *Exhib:* Butler Inst Am Art 36th Ann, 72; Philadelphia Art Alliance, 80; one-man shows, Kornblee Gallery, 82, Phoenix Gallery, NY, 85-87, Concordia Col, Bronxville, NY, 89 & Gallery 84 Inc, NY, 92; Fairleigh Dickinson Univ; Allentown Art Mus; and many others. *Awards:* Artists Equity Award; Purchase Award & Gold Medal, Am Color Print Soc; D L Ferriss Award, Pen & Brush Inc. *Bibliog:* Cover story, Host Mag, 73. *Mem:* Am Color Print Soc; Nat Asn Women Artists; Silvermine Guild Artists; Philadelphia Art Alliance; Artists Equity Asn. *Media:* Acrylic; Serigraphy. *Mailing Add:* 161 W 54th St New York NY 10019

BERMAN, BERNARD
COLLECTOR
b Pennsburg, Pa, Aug 28, 20. *Mem:* Am Asn Mus, Washington, DC (trustee); Allentown Art Mus, Pa (pres bd trustees, 71-). *Collection:* German Expressionist, Italian sculpture, American artists. *Mailing Add:* 2830 Gordon St Allentown PA 18104-4863

BERMAN, ELLEN MERCIL TREW
PAINTER
b Paris, Tex, Dec 5, 1946. *Study:* Univ Tex, Austin, BA(cum laude), 69; Univ Houston, Univ Park, MA, 77; Glassell Sch Art, Mus Fine Arts, Houston, 81-84. *Work:* Tex Commerce Bank, Houston; M Bank, Houston. *Exhib:* one-person show, Adair Margo Gallery, El Paso, 97, McMurtrey Gallery, Houston, 98; group show, Pindar Gallery, NY, 87; Texas Realism, Laguna Gloria Art Mus, Austin, 87; Tex State Exhib, Nat Mus Women Arts, Washington, DC, 88; Recent Paintings, Goethe Inst, Houston, 88; Mid-Am Biennial, Nelson-Atkins Mus Art, Kansas City, Mo, 89; Paintings, Art Mus Southeast Tex, Beaumont, 89; Swimmers' Progress, Col Mainland Art Gallery, Texas City, 89; Recent Paintings, Mexic-Arte Mus, Austin, Tex, 90. *Pos:* Vpres & adv bd, Women's Caucus for Art, 85-90; artists adv bd, Lawndale Art & Performance Ctr, Houston, 88-89. *Awards:* First Place, Houston Jewish Comn Ctr, 87; Best of Show, San Antonio Women's Caucus Art, 88; Mid Am Arts Alliance, Regional Fel, Nat Endowment Arts, 88-89. *Bibliog:* Betty Ann Brown & Arlene Raven (coauths), Exposures: Women and their Art, NewSage Press, 89. *Media:* Oil

BERMAN, FRED J
PAINTER, PHOTOGRAPHER
b Milwaukee, Wis, Nov 3, 26. *Study:* Milwaukee State Teachers Col, BS; Univ Wis-Madison, MS. *Work:* Elvehjem Mus Art, Madison, Wis; Milwaukee Art Mus; Brown Univ, Providence, RI; Haggerty Mus Art, Marquette Univ, Milwaukee; Nelson Atkins Mus Art, Kansas City, Mo; Telfair Mus Art, Savannah, Ga; Frederick M Weisman Mus, Univ Minn, Minneapolis; Mus RI Sch Design, Providence; First Nat Bank Chicago. *Exhib:* Sixth Biennial Contemp Am Paintings, Va Mus Fine Arts, Richmond, 48; Pa Acad Fine Arts Ann, Philadelphia, 51-53; Corcoran Biennials, Corcoran Gallery Art, Washington, DC, 53, 55 & 59; Annual, 59 & Young Am (with catalog), 60, Whitney Mus Am Art, NY; San Francisco Mus Art, 60 & 65; Summer Exhib, Royal Acad Arts, London, 67; one-man exhibs, Bradley Galleries, Milwaukee, 76, Collectors Gallery, Milwaukee, 81, Kresge Art Mus, Mich State Univ, 82, Univ Reading, Eng, 83, Camden Arts Ctr, London, 83, Crescent Art Ctr, Scarborough, Eng, 84, Haggerty Mus Art, Milwaukee, 88, Charles Allis Art Mus, Milwaukee, 90, Mount Mary Col, Milwaukee, 97 & Walls and Windows, Villa Terrace Art Mus, Milwaukee, 2001; Some Photog Uses of Color, Brown Univ, Providence, RI, 84; 100 Yrs of Wisconsin Art, Milwaukee Art Mus, 88; Boite Alert, Boxes by 20th Century Artists, Renee Fotouhi Fine Art, NY, 89; Wisconsin Acad Art, Madison, Wis, 91; The Jewish Contribution to the 20th Century Art, Milwaukee Art Mus, 93; retrospective exhib, 1949-1994, Univ Wis, Milwaukee Art Mus, 94; The Five, Fairfield Pub Gallery, Sturgeon Bay, Wis, 01; group exhib, Paste, Nail, Weld-The Art of Collage, Assemblage and the Found Object, Cardinal Stritch, UNN, Milwaukee, WI, 2003. *Collection Arranged:* Guest cur, Steichen/109, Univ Wis Art Mus, Milwaukee, 88 & Self Portraits: Wisconson Artists, Charles Allis Art Mus, Milwaukee, 96-97; Self and Other Portriats, Wis Artits, Charles Allies Art Mus, Milwaukee, 2002. *Teaching:* Instr painting & printmaking, Layton Sch Art, Milwaukee, Wis, 49-60; prof design & drawing, Univ Wis-Milwaukee, 60-93, prof emer, 93-; exchange lectr, Univ Reading, Eng, 66-67. *Awards:* Milwaukee Art Inst Award, Milwaukee Art Ctr, 47 & 52-56; Joseph Eisendrath Award, Chicago & vicinity, Art Inst Chicago, 50; Wis Union Top Purchase Award, Wis Salon Art, Univ Wis-Madison, 67; Amoco Award for Distinguished Teaching, Univ Wis-Milwaukee, 85. *Bibliog:* Article in Art in Am, 2/56; article in Saturday Review, 5-6/85. *Media:* Oil, Charcoal; Collage. *Interests:* Cubism

BERMAN, VIVIAN
PRINTMAKER
b New York, NY, Aug 28, 28. *Study:* Cooper Union, BFA; Art Students League; Brandeis Univ. *Work:* Libr Cong; Wiggin Collection, Boston Pub Libr, Mass; Pa Acad Art; De Cordova Mus, Lincoln, Mass; Hopkins Art Ctr, Dartmouth Col; United States Information Agency; Fogg Mus, Cambridge, MA. *Exhib:* The Boston Printmakers Ann, 68-2005; Libr Cong Nat Print Exhib, 70; 18th Nat Print Exhib, Brooklyn Mus, 73; Nat Exhib Collagraphs, Pratt Graphic Ctr, NY, 75; British Biennale 1979, Bradford, Eng; The Making of a Print, Delaware Ctr Contemp Art, 90 & Boston Univ, 91. *Pos:* Exec Brd, The Boston Printmakers, Boston, MA; docent, Harvard Mus, Cambridge, MA. *Teaching:* Instr, DeCordova Mus Sch, Lincoln, Mass. *Awards:* Purchase Award, Libr Cong Pennel Fund, 70 & Nat Print Show, Western NMex Univ, 71; MacDowell Colony Fel, 81; and others. *Bibliog:* Wenniger (auth), Collagraph Printmaking, Macmillan, 78; Ross & Romano (auth), The Complete Collagraph, Free Press, 80. *Mem:* Philadelphia Print Club; The Boston Printmakers; Southern Graphics Soc. *Media:* Collagraph, Monoprint. *Dealer:* Spectrom Gallery of Art Brewster Mass; Francesca Anderson Fine Art Lexington MA. *Mailing Add:* 11 Barberry Rd Lexington MA 02173

BERMAN, ZEKE
PHOTOGRAPHER
b New York, NY, 51. *Study:* Philadelphia Col Art, BFA, 74. *Work:* Mus Mod Art, Metrop Mus Art, NY; San Francisco Mus Mod Art; Mus Fine Art, Boston, Mass; Art Inst Chicago; Philadelphia Mus Art. *Exhib:* Counterparts: Form & Emotion in Photographs, Metrop Mus Art, NY, 82, 89 & 93; Mus Mod Art, NY, 82, 84, 85, 90, 92, 93, 2000; Brooklyn Mus, NY, 85; solo exhibs, Art Inst Chicago, 86, Univ Mo Mus, Kansas City, 92, Catherine Edelman Gallery, Chicago, 93, Cleveland Ctr Contemp Art (with catalog), 94, Blue Sky Gallery, Portland, Ore, 95, Julie Saul Gallery, NY, 95 & Portland Sch Art, Maine, 96, Eli Marsh Gallery, Amherst Coll, 97, Inst of Contemp Art, Maine Col of Art, Portland, 97, Laurence Miller Gallery, NY, retrospective -78-83, 2000; Baltimore Mus Art, Md, 87; Mus Fine Arts, Boston, Mass, 89, 94 & 95; Nat Mus Am Art, Washington, 89; Los Angeles Co Mus Art, Calif, 90; Art Inst Chicago, 91 & 93; Mus Fine Arts, Houston, 92 & 93; High Mus Art, Atlanta, Ga, 93; The Perspective Club Show, Gallery Antonia Iannone, Milan, Italy, 95; Paul Kopekin Gallery, Los Angeles, 95; Nelson-Atkins Mus Art (with catalog), Kansas City, Mo, 95; Philadelphia Mus Art, 96; Lawrence Miller Gallery, NY, 97; and many others; Open Ends, Mus Modern Art, NY, 1960-2000. *Teaching:* Instr, Fordham Univ at Lincoln Ctr, NY, 83-, Sch Visual Arts, New York, 86-, City Col NY, 86-87 & NY Univ, 87-88; instr photog, Yale Univ, 93-94. *Awards:* McDowell Colony Residency, 87, 88, 91, 92 & 93; NY Found Arts Fel, 88; Nat Endowment Arts, 88. *Bibliog:* Contemporary American Photography, 95; Terry Barrett (auth), Criticizing Photographs, Mayfield Publ, 96; Photography Speaks, Apperture Press, 96; Graham Clark (auth.) Oxford History of Art, The Photograph, 97; Graphis Fine Art Photography #2. *Dealer:* Laurence Miller Gallery 138 Spring St New York NY 10012

BERMINGHAM, DEBRA PANDELL
PAINTER
b Northhampton, Mass, Sept 18, 53. *Study:* Cornell Univ, Ithaca, NY, BFA, 76; Univ Wash, Seattle, MFA, 79. *Work:* Smith Col Mus; Kalamazoo Inst Arts, Mich; Brooklyn Mus, NY; Art Inst Chicago; and others. *Exhib:* 165th Ann Exhib, Nat Acad Design, 90; New Viewpoints: Contemp Paintings by Distinguished Am Women Artists, organized by Nat Mus Women in the Arts for US pavilion, World's Fair, Seville,

Spain, 91-92; solo exhib, Midtown Payson Galleries, NY, 91 & 93, Augustus Saint-Gaudens Mem, Cornish, NH, 92, Bryn Mawr Col, Pa, 93 & DC Moore Gallery, NY, 98, 99; Illumination and Radiance: Epiphanies in Contemp Painting, Sherry French Gallery, NY, Kalamazoo Inst Arts, Mich, Riverside Art Mus, Calif, Mus Southwest, Midland, Tex & Rahr-West Art Mus, Manitowoc, Wis, 90-92; Invitational Exhib of Painting and Sculpture, Am Acad Arts & Lett, Ny, (2 & 94; Still Life: 1963-1993, Gerald Peters Gallery, Santa Fe, NMex, 93; Invitational Exhib Painting & Sculpture, Am Acad Arts & Lett, NY, 94; The Re-Constructed Figure: The Human Image in Contemp Art, Katonah Mus Art, NY, 95; Am Acad Arts & Lett, NY, 96; Re-Presenting Representation III, Arnot Art Mus, Elmira, NY, 97; Earth, Air, Water, DC Moore Gallery, NY, 98; Art Inst Chicago, 99; Arhot Art Mus, NY, 2001; DC Moore Gallery, NY, 2002; Transforming the Common Place: Masters of Contemp Realism, Susquehanna Art Mus, 2003. *Teaching:* Vis asst prof painting & drawing, Cornell Univ, New York, 96-97& Cornell Univ, NY, 2003. *Awards:* Visual Arts Fel Grant, Nat Endowment Arts, 85-88; Louis Nevelson Award Art, Am Acad Arts & Lett, 96; Constance Saltonstall Found Arts Grant, 97; Ballington Arts Found, Ireland, 2000. *Bibliog:* Debra Bermingham, Still Interiors, 91 (catalogue essay by Carl Little); Debra Bermingham, Across the Blue Room, 93 (catalogue essay by John Gruen); Still Lifes: 1963-1993; 93 (catalogue essay by John Arthur); Debra Bermingham, (catalogue essay by Robert M Murdock), 2002; Beauty Without Regret (catalogue esssay by Robert Kushner), 2001; Contemporary American Realist Drawings-The Jalane & Richard Davidson Collection at The Art Inst of Chicago, The Art Inst of Chicago, 99. *Media:* Oil, Graphite. *Dealer:* DC Moore Gallery 724 5th Ave New York NY 10019. *Mailing Add:* 2700 Vineyard Rd Romulus NY 14541

BERMINGHAM, JOHN C
PAINTER
b Wharton, NJ, Jan 12, 20. *Study:* Univ Notre Dame, Ind, BFA, 42. *Exhib:* Audubon Artists Ann Exhib, Nat Acad Galleries,NY, 73-77 & 81; Allied Artists Ann Exhib, Nat Acad Galleries/Salmagundi Club Galleries, NY, 73-79, 81, 83-87 & 91; Ann Exhib Am Watercolor Soc, Nat Acad Galleries/Salmagundi Club, NY, 73, 74, 76-78, 81, 89, 91, 93, 94 & 95; Am Watercolor Soc Traveling Exhib, 74, 78, 81, 89 & 93; Acad Artists Nat Exhib, Springfield Mus, Mass, 75-82; Ann Exhib Nat Acad Design, Nat Acad Galleries, NY, 76, 80, 82, 84, 88 & 92; Adirondacks Nat Exhib Am Watercolors, 85-87, 92, 95, 96 & 98. *Awards:* Anne Williams Glushien Award, Am Watercolor Soc, 93; Muriel Alvord Award, Hudson Valley Art Assoc, 94; Avery & Nina Johnson Mem Award, NJ Watercolor Soc, 96, Silver Medal of Honor, 97, R & M Price Mem Award, 99, Irving & Frances Phillips Award, 2000; Mary Greca Award, Hudson Valley Art Asn, 99; and others. *Mem:* Allied Artists Am; Am Watercolor Soc; NJ Watercolor Soc (pres, 77-78); Acad Artists; Hudson Valley Art Asn. *Media:* Watercolor. *Mailing Add:* 42 Main St Newton CT 06470-2133

BERMUDEZ, EUGENIA M See Dignac, Geny (Eugenia) M Bermudez

BERMUDEZ, LUIS A
SCULPTOR, EDUCATOR
b Los Angeles, Calif, July 12, 53. *Study:* Calif State Univ, Northridge, BA, 76, MA, 78; Univ Calif, Los Angeles, MFA, 80. *Work:* Los Angeles Co Mus Art; E B Crocker Art Gallery, Sacramento, Calif; Long Beach Mus Art. *Exhib:* Ceramic Conjunction 1976, Long Beach Mus Art, 76; Mandell Gallery, Los Angeles, 80; Elaine Potter Gallery, San Francisco, 84; Tacoma Art Mus, Wash, 86; one-man show, Garth Clark Gallery, Los Angeles, 86; Twentieth Century Ceramics, Los Angeles Co Mus Art, 89, Clay Today, 91-92; Couturier Gallery, Los Angeles, 91; Choice Encounters, LBMA Outdoor Sculpture Garden, Long Beach Mus Art, Calif, 92-93; Suenos From Calif, Art Gallery, Univ Tex, El Paso, 92; Transofrmed From Clay: 14 Southern Calif Artists, Armory Ctr for Arts, Pasadena, Calif, 92; UCLA: Onramps, Offramps, Exchange & Diversity, Lyceum Theatre Gallery, San Diego, 93; Clay Currents, Southwestern Col Art Gallery, Chula Vista, Calif, 93; Fiction, Function, Figuration: The 29th Ceramic National, Newark Mus, NJ, 93-94; Four Sculptors, Jose Drudis-Biada Art Gallery, Mt St Mary's Col, Los Angeles, 94; Calif Sculpture Garden, Venice Art Walk, Westminster Sch, Venice, Calif, 96, 97, 98, 99; Faculty Artists: Images and Dreams, Univ Art Gallery, Calif State Univ, Dominguez Hills, Carson, Calif, 96; The Empowered Object, Hunsaker/Schlesinger, Santa Monica, Calif, 96; Vessels, The Armory Ctr for Arts, Pasadena, Calif, 97; Ceramics Invitational, Art Gallery, Cerritos Col, Norwalk, Calif, 99; The World of Cups, Armory Ctr for Arts, Pasadena, 94; Ceramics Invitational, Art Gallery, Cerritos Col, Norwalk, Calif, 99; 200/2000/20, BGH Gallery, Santa Monica, Calif, 99-2000. *Teaching:* Asst prof, Calif State Univ, Nothridge, 80 & 84; instr, Palos Verdes Art Ctr, Calif, 80; lectr, Univ Calif, Los Angeles, 85-91, vis asst prof, 91-94, adj asst prof, 94-95; lectr, Calif State Univ, Dominquez Hills, 96-, Northridge, 99- & Otis Col Art & Design, Los Angeles, 97-99, Calif State Univ, Northridge, 99; presenter & demonstrator Nat Coun Edn for Ceramic Arts, San Diego, 93; vis artist, NY State Coll Ceramics, Aflred Univ, 94, Pomona Ccl, Claremont, Calif, 96, Saddleback Col, Mission Viejo, Calif, 98; guest artist, Calif State Univ, Northridge, 98. *Awards:* Chancellor's Patent Fund Grant, UCLA, 80; Nat Endowment Arts Visual Arts Fel Grant, 88; Grad Advancement Program Fel, UCLA, 78; Alfredo Orselli Memorial Scholar, UCLA, 78; Pres' Club Scholar, Calif State Univ, Northridge, 75. *Bibliog:* At The Galleries, Los Angeles Times, 4/25/86; Judith Bettelhein (auth), Does a Cultural Crossover Exist Between Japanese and California Ceramists? Pacific Connections, Am Craft, 4-5/86; Catherine Parr (auth), Clay Currents, Ceramics Monthly, 2/94; Reproductions included in numerous art publs,. *Mem:* Nat Coun Educ Ceramic Arts. *Media:* Clay, All Media. *Mailing Add:* 5166 W Adams Blvd Los Angeles CA 90016

BERNARD, DAVID EDWIN
PRINTMAKER, EDUCATOR
b Sandwich, Ill, Aug 8, 1913. *Study:* Univ Ill, BFA; Univ Iowa, MFA; and with Mauricio Lasansky & Humbert Albrizio. *Work:* Wichita Art Mus, Kans; Otis Art Inst, Los Angeles, Calif; Free Pub Libr, Philadelphia, Pa; Joslyn Mus, Omaha, Nebr; Libr Cong, Washington, DC; Portland Art Mus, Ore. *Comn:* free standing tree sculpture (steel), Camp Fire Girls Ore, Wichita Art Mus, Kans, 60; sculpture (steel, wood & brass), Irene Vickers Baker Children's Theatre, Wichita; pair of standing tree shapes, Art Asn Wichita, 71-72; Woodcut the Cannery, City of St Clous, Fla, 2004. *Exhib:* God and Man in Art, Am Fedn Arts Traveling Exhib, 57; First Ann, Otis Art Inst, 61; Univ Nebr Print Exhib, Sheldon Art Gallery, Lincoln, 67; one-man exhib prints, Philbrook Art Ctr, Tulsa, Okla, 67; retrospective, Wichita Art Mus, Kans, 83; A Printmakers Print Collection, Wichita Art Mus, Kans, 96; From the Plains to Palatine: the Prints of David E Bernard, Wichita Art Mus, KS, 2005. *Teaching:* Instr art prog, Maryville Col, 46-48; prof printmaking, Wichita State Univ, 49-83, prof emer, 83. *Awards:* Purchase Award for Hombre y Toro (intaglio), Pennell Collection, Libr Cong, 53; Purchase Award for Calvary (colored intaglio), Mid-Am Ann, Nelson Gallery, 55; Kans Gov's Artist's Award, Kans Arts Comn, Topeka, 82; first award, Printmaking, Osceola Ctr Arts, 96-2003. *Bibliog:* Howard E Wooden (auth), David Bernard: Prints and Sculpture, A Retrospective, 1947-1982, Wichita Art Mus, 83; Stephen Gleissner (cur) Earth Cruiser by David E Bernard, Wichita Art Mus Views, March/April 2005. *Mem:* Soc Am Graphic Artists; Artists Guild Wichita (pres, 56); Wichita Art Mus Mem; Osceola Ctr for the Arts/Kissimmee, Fla; Sandzeri Mem Gallery, Lindsborg, KS. *Media:* Intaglio, Collagraph, Woodcut. *Interests:* Art of the Ancient Maya, Travel, Prints. *Publ:* Auth, The collagraph print, Artists Proof, 62; illusr, A West Wind Rises, 62 & Sun City, 64, Univ Nebr Press; artist & auth, Ten Mayan Gods, (hand made book, original print; Artists: A Kansas Collection, Artists Registry Inc, 89. *Mailing Add:* 3832 Blackberry Circle Saint Cloud FL 34769-1428

BERNAY, BETTI
PAINTER
b New York, NY. *Study:* Pratt Inst; Nat Acad Design, New York, with Louis Bouche; Art Students League, with Frank Mason; also with Robert Brackman. *Work:* Circulo Amistad, Cordoba, Spain; Columbus Mus Arts & Crafts, Ga; Columbia Mus Art, SC; Andre Weil Collection, Paris. *Comn:* Painting, pres of Renault, Madrid, Spain, 64; painting, Children Have No Barriers, IOS Found, Geneva, 69; paintings, Macaws, Seacost E Bldg, Miami Beach, Fla, 69 & mural, Sandy Cove, S Bldg, 70. *Exhib:* Mus Mod Art, Paris, 63; Salon Populiste, Mus Mod Art, Paris, 63; Bacardi Gallery, Miami, Fla, 67; Metrop Mus & Art Ctr, Miami, 75; Rosenbaum Gallery, Palm Beach, Fla, 77; one-man shows - Columbus Mus, GA; Columbia Mus, SC; and many other one-man & group shows. *Awards:* Artistic Merit Medal, City of New York, 42; Prix de Paris, 58; Medal of Honor, Mus Bellas Artes, Malaga, 65; inductee, Library of Human Resources, Am Bicentennial Research Inst, 74. *Mem:* Artists Equity Asn; Am Artists Prof League; Nat Asn Painters & Sculptors Spain; Soc Artistes Francais; Prof Artists Guild; and others. *Media:* Oil, Pastel. *Mailing Add:* Bal Harbour 10155 Collins Ave Apt 1705 Miami FL 33154

BERNECHE, JERRY DOUGLAS
EDUCATOR, PAINTER
b Greentown, Ind, July 24, 32. *Study:* John Herron Art Sch, BFA, 56, studie painting and printmaking with Garo Antreasian; Ohio Univ, MFA, 59, study with Robert Friemark. *Work:* Butler Mus Am Art, Youngstown, Ohio; Springfield Art Mus, Mo; Canton Art Mus & Massillon Mus, Ohio; Mo State Hist Soc, Columbia. *Exhib:* Drawing USA Nat, Walker Art Mus, 62; Mid-Am Nat Exhib, Butler Mus Art, 62-64; Chautauqua Exhib Art, NY, 65-67; Springfield Regional Exhib, 66-75; Watercolor USA Nat, Springfield, 73-74. *Teaching:* Instr art, Cooper Art Sch, Cleveland, Ohio, 62-65 & Mont State Univ, Bozeman, 65-66; assoc prof drawing & painting, Univ Mo, Columbia, 66-81, prof, 81-. *Awards:* Mrs E J Bellinger Award, Chautauqua Nat Exhib, 65 & 67; Watercolor Purchase Award, Watercolor USA, 73; Purchase Award, Mo State Fair, 83. *Media:* Acrylic, Watercolor. *Mailing Add:* 3708 Oakland Rd Columbia MO 65202

BERNHARD, RUTH
PHOTOGRAPHER
b Berlin, Ger, Oct 14, 1905; US citizen. *Study:* Acad Fine Arts, Berlin, 25-27. *Work:* San Francisco Mus Mod Art; Mus Mod Art, NY; Ctr Creative Photog; Bibliot Nat, Paris; George Eastman House, Rochester. *Comn:* Photographs for book, Machine Art, Mus Mod Art, NY, 34. *Exhib:* Inst Cult Relations, Mexico City, 58; Oakland Art Mus, 58; Mus Mod Art, NY, 62; Photog in the Fine Arts, Metrop Mus Art, NY, 67; Friends of Photog, Carmel, Calif, 75; Recollections: Ten Women of Photog, Int Ctr Photog (traveling exhib), 79; Photographers' Gallery, London, Eng, 83; Recontres Int Phtotg, Arles, France, 83; 101 Photographs: Selections from the Steinman Collection, Santa Barbara Mus Art, 84; Das Aktfoto, Mus Art & Cult, Dortmund, WGer, (traveling exhib), 85-86; and many others. *Teaching:* Instr workshops, Univ Calif Exten, San Francisco, 66-74. *Awards:* Distinguished Career Photog, Soc Photog Educ Midwest Regional Conf, Chicago, Ill, 87; Presidential Citation, Utah State Univ, 90; Cyril Magnin Award, San Francisco Chamber Com, 94; Outstanding Achievement Photog, San Francisco Art Comn, 84. *Bibliog:* Ruth Bernhard: The Eternal Body, 1st ed, 86; Photography West Graphics, Carmel, Calif, 2nd ed, 94; Margaretta Mitchell (ed), Chronicle Books, San Francisco, Calif. *Mem:* Friends Photog, Carmel, Calif; Mus Soc, San Francisco. *Publ:* Auth, Growth of a photographer, Contact Mag, 64. *Mailing Add:* 2982 Clay St San Francisco CA 94115-1713

BERNHEIM, STEPHANIE HAMMERSCHLAG
PAINTER, SCULPTOR
b New York, NY. *Study:* Sarah Lawrence Col, BA; NY Univ, MA. *Work:* Cincinnati Mus Book Collection, Ohio; Metrop Mus Book Collection, NY; Princeton Univ Art Mus, NJ; Milwaukee Mus Art, Wis; Yale Univ Art Gallery, New Haven, Conn. *Exhib:* One-person exhibs, Inst for Art & Urban Resources, PS1 Mus, Long Island City, NY, 81, Hinterglasmaleri, AIR Gallery, NY, 94, In the Bag, Delaware Ctr for Contemp Art, Wilmington, 94; PS1 Mus, Long Island, NY, 81; Barbara Mathes Gallery, NY, 86 & 87; Primal Forces, Cooper Union, NY, 90; Burning in Hell, Franklin Furnace, NY, 91; Americana, Tricia Collins/Grand Salon, NY, 95 & 97; Milwaukee Mus Art, 97. *Pos:* Created & organized art events/community panels at Air Gallery, NY, 11/91 & Sarah Lawrence Col, Bronxville, NY, 4/92; vis artist, Parsons Sch Design, 97 & Sarah Lawrence Col, 98. *Teaching:* Lectr, Parsons '96, Panel NY Studio Sch, 95. *Bibliog:* Joseph Ruzicka (auth), Stephanie Bernheim at AIR Gallery, Art in Am, 9/91; Raphael Rubenstein (auth), From End to Beginning (catalog), Hinterrglasmaleri, AIR Gallery, New York, 94; Reagan Upshaw (auth), Stephanie Bernheim at AIR, Art in Am, 10/94. *Mem:* Women's Caucus for Arts; AIR Gallery (exec comt 89-92); Women in Arts Found; Women's Action Coalition; Col Art Asn. *Media:* Acrylic; Mixed Media. *Dealer:* Art Resources Transfer Inc 210 11th Ave New York NY 10001. *Mailing Add:* 50 Walker St Apt 4A New York NY 10013

BERNHEIMER, G MAX
APPRAISER
Study: Classical Civilization, Harvard Univ, MA; Attended, Intercollegiate Center for Classical Studies, Rome; Attended, American Sch of Classical Studies, Athens; Attended, London Institute Archeology. *Pos:* With Christie's, New York City, 92-, specialist in ancient Greek, Roman, Etruscan, Egyptian and Near Eastern Art, sr vpres, into dept head, antiquities. *Bibliog:* (auth): Glories of Ancient Greece, 2001; (co-auth): Ancient Glass from the Collections of Dr. Elie Borowski. *Mailing Add:* Christie's/NY 20 Rockefeller Plz New York NY 10020

BERNS, PAMELA KARI
PAINTER, ADMINISTRATOR
b Sturgeon Bay, Wis, Sept 4, 47. *Study:* Lawrence Univ, Appleton, Wis, BA, 69; Univ Wis, Madison, MFA(painting), 71. *Work:* Bergstrom Art Ctr, Neenah, Wis; Kemper Insurance Co's, Inc, Long Grove, Ill; Miller Art Ctr, Sturgeon Bay, Wis; Andersen Window Corp, Bayport, Minn. *Exhib:* One-person show, Bergstrom Art Ctr, Neenah, Wis, 70; Watercolor Wis, Wustum Mus Art, Racine, 72-79 & 81-82; New Horizons, Chicago, 75; Women in the Arts, West Bend Mus Art, Wis, 76; Art Inst Chicago, 83. *Pos:* Coordr educ programs, Chicago Artists' Coalition, 80-83; publ, Chicago Life Mag, 84-. *Awards:* Second Prizes, Artists Guild Chicago, 76 & Watercolor Wis, 81; Best of Show in Painting, Idea Corp, 79. *Bibliog:* M Tourtelot (auth), Resume--A Selective Guide, The Studios, 75; R Dozer (auth), Recording Door County's Singularity, Chicago Tribune, 75; Door County Creations, Strom Channel 10, 77. *Mem:* Chicago Artists' Coalition (int dir, 79); Wis Watercolor Soc; Wis Painters & Sculptors Asn; Peninsula Arts Asn, Fish Creek, Wis. *Media:* Watercolor, Acrylic. *Dealer:* Edgewood Orchard Gallery Peninsula Players Rd Fish Creek WI 54212. *Mailing Add:* PO Box 11311 Chicago IL 60611

BERNSTEIN, EDWARD I
COLLECTOR
b Philadelphia, Pa, Nov 15, 17. *Work:* Located at Philadelphia Mus Art, Pa Acad Fine Arts, La Salle Col Art Gallery & Dept Art & Hist, Villanova Univ, Pa. *Mem:* Wilson Peale Soc; Pa Acad Fine Art; Haviland Soc; Royal Acad Fine Arts, London, Eng; Philadelphia Mus Art (assoc mem). *Collection:* Contemporary art includes oils, gouche, drawings, prints and sculpture; African paintings and sculpture; Elizabeth Frink. *Mailing Add:* 1810 Rittenhouse Sq Philadelphia PA 19103

BERNSTEIN, JUDITH
PAINTER, PRINTMAKER
b Newark, NJ, Oct 14, 42. *Study:* Pa State Univ, BS & MS, 64; Yale Univ Sch Art, BFA & MFA, 67. *Work:* Mus Mod Art, Brooklyn Mus, NY; Univ Colo Mus, Boulder; Yale Art Gallery, New Haven, Conn; Kronhausen, Lund, Sweden; Colgate Univ Mus, Hamilton, NY; Neuberger Mus Art, Purchase, NY. *Comn:* Two on Site Wall Installation, William N Copley, 77. *Exhib:* One-person shows, AIR Gallery, 73 & 84, State Univ NY, Stony Brook, 77, Brooks Jackson Iolas Gallery, NY, 78 & Univ Ark, Fayetteville, 87; Contemp Women: Consciousness & Content, Brooklyn Mus, NY, 77; Venerezia-Revenice, Titan's Forbidden Fruit, Plazzo Grassi, Venice, Italy, 78; The Great Big Drawing Show, LIC, PS1, NY, 79; Contemp Arte, Hague Geneete Mus, The Neth, Belg & Ger, 79-81; 100 Drawings by Woman, Hillwood Art Mus, Nat Women's Mus, Yale Univ, Crocker Mus, Sacramento, Blum Helman Mus, NY, USIA, Europe, 89-91; Man Revealed, Graham Mod Gallery, NY, 92; Not For Sale, Feminism & Art in the USA-1970's by Laura Cottingham; Seeing Red, White & Blue-Censored in USA, Visual Arts Ctr, Anchorage, Alaska, 92; Coming to Power, David Zwirner, NY, 93; Phallic Symbols, 24 Hours for Life, NY, 95; Sexual Politics: Rewriting Hist (photo catalog), Armand & Hammer Mus Art, Univ Calif, Los Angeles, 96; New Sch, Mus Mod Art, Apex Gallery, NY, 98; Not For Sale, Video Essay, Laura Cottingham, Mus Mod Art, Apex Gallery, New York City, 98; End Papers: 1890-1900 & 1990-2000, Neuberger Mus Art, NY, 2000. *Pos:* Adj prof, sch visual Arts, NY, 99- & Queens Col, NY, 99-. *Teaching:* Pratt Inst; asst prof fine arts, State Univ NY, Stony Brook, 74-78 & State Univ NY, Purchase, 78-; assoc prof fine arts, State Univ NY, Purchase, 78-; Mason Gross Sch Arts, Rutgers Univ, 96-98. *Awards:* Elizabeth Canfield Hicks Mem Scholar, Yale Univ Sch Art & Archit, 64-67; Nat Endowment Arts Grant, 74-75 & 85-86; NY Found for the Arts, 88; Adolph and Esther Gottlieb Found Grant, 2000. *Mem:* Col Art Asn Am; Nat Soc Lit & Arts; Women's Caucus Art. *Media:* Charcoal, Oil. *Mailing Add:* Knickerbocker Sta PO Box 1045 New York NY 10002-0145

BERNSTEIN, SARALINDA
ART DEALER, HISTORIAN
b New York, NY, Jan 7, 51. *Study:* Ecole Pratique des Hautes Etudes, Sorbonne, Paris, 70-71; Swarthmore Col, Pa, BA(magna cum laude), 72; NY Univ Sch Arts, 72; New Sch Social Res, New York, 74, Japan Soc, New York, 82-84. *Collection Arranged:* Edvard Munch: Paradox of Woman (auth, catalog), Aldis Browne Fine Arts, New York, 81; Prints about Prints, 81-82; Nineteenth and Twentieth Century Works on Paper (auth, catalog), 82 & Edgar Chahine: Images of Venice and The Belle Epoque (auth, catalog), 83, Picasso 156, Aldis Browne Fine Arts. *Pos:* Asst to dir, Asn Am Artists, NY, 72-78; exec vpres & dir, Aldis Browne Fine Arts, NY, 78-84; own & dir, Saralinda Bernstein Fine Art, 84-. *Teaching:* Lectr, Soc Ethical Cult, NY, 81. *Res:* Form and function of original prints in society; the concept and definition of form in visual arts, particularly in late 19th through early 20th century European works. *Publ:* Contribr, 10 Jahre Galerie Kühl, Galerie Kühl, 77. *Mailing Add:* 265 Massachusetts Ave Haworth NJ 07641-1809

BERNSTEIN, WILLIAM JOSEPH
DESIGNER, GLASSBLOWER
b Newark, NJ, Dec 3, 1945. *Study:* Philadelphia Col Art, BFA, 68; Penland Sch, NC, 68-70. *Work:* Int Glasmus, Ebeltoft, Denmark; Australian Coun Arts, Sidney; Corning Mus Glass, NY; Renwick Gallery, Nat Mus Am Art, Smithsonian Inst, Washington; Glasmus Frauenau, Bavaria, WGer; Yamaha Corp, Japan; Chrysler Mus, Norfolk, Va; Mint Mus Art, Charlotte, NC. *Exhib:* Baroque '74, Mus Contemp Crafts, NY, 74; In Praise of Hands, 1st World Crafts Exhib, Toronto, Can, 74; Craft Multiples, Renwick Gallery, Smithsonian Inst, Washington, DC, 75; Philadelphia Mus of Art, 77; Am Crafts in the White House, Washington, 77; Victoria & Albert Mus, Eng; USA: Portrait of the South, Palazzo Venezia, Rome, Italy; Am Studio Glass, Isetan Galleries, Japan; Glass from the Corning Collection, Spaso House, Moscow, USSR; one-man exhib, Somerhill Gallery, Chapel Hill, NC, Grohe Glass Gallery, 91, Marx Gallery, Chicago, Ill, 91; Vessels: From Use to Symbol, Am Craft Mus, NY. *Teaching:* Penland Sch Crafts, NC, Univ Southern Calif, Los Angeles, Pilchuck Glass Ctr, Stanwood, Wash & Naples Mill Sch, NY; Summervail Workshop, Vail, Colo. *Awards:* Nat Endowment Arts Fel, 74 & Grant, 76; Louis Comfort Tiffany Found Grant, 75; NC Arts Coun Fel, 83; Masterworks Fel, Creative Glass Ctr Am, 90. *Bibliog:* RL Grover (auth), Contemporary Art Glass, Crown Publ, 75; F Kulasiewicz (auth), Glassblowing, Watson-Guptill, 75; Design in Modern Interiors, Studio Vista, 75; Dan Klein (auth), Glass, A Contemporary Art, Rizzoli. *Publ:* NY Mag, NY Times; Atlanta Constitution Sunday Mag; State Mag NC; Am Craft (portfolio sect); Crafts Report. *Mailing Add:* 250 Chimney Ridge Rd Burnsville NC 28714

BERO, MARY
PAINTER
b Two Rivers, Wis, Mar 2, 49. *Study:* Stout State Univ, BS, 71. *Work:* Milwaukee Art Mus, Wis; Elvejhem Mus Art, Univ Wis, Madison; Minneapolis Inst Arts, Minn; Madeira Threads, United Kingdom; Textilforum, Hannover, Ger. *Exhib:* One-woman show, Octagon Gallery, Evanston, Ill, 81, Triton Mus, Santa Clara, Calif, 81, Mich Technol Univ, 81, Mobilia, Cambridge, Mass, 82 & 96, Kohler Arts Ctr, Sheboygan, Wis, 85, Objects Gallery, Chicago, 91 & 92, The Farrell Collection, Washington, DC, 93, Joanne Rapp Gallery, Scottsdale, Ariz, 95, Tory Folliard Gallery, Milwaukee, Wis, 95, Gallery Design, Univ Wis, 95 & Ann Nathan Gallery, Chicago, Ill, 96 & 99; The Many Faces of Fiber, Barrington Area Arts Coun Gallery, 94; Ann Nathan Gallery, Chicago, Ill, 94; Wall Works in Fiber, Banaker Gallery, San Francisco, 94; Intimate Threads, St Louis, Mo, 95; Threads: Fiber Art in the '90s, NJ Ctr Visual Arts, Summit, 97; Image & Object, Sybaris Gallery, Royal Oak, Mich, 98; The Splendid World of Needle Arts, Art Hall Takashimaya, Tokyo, Japan, 99; Miniatures: 2000, Mus Art & Design, Helsinki, Finland, 2000. *Teaching:* lectr, Renwick Gallery, Smithsonian Inst, Washington, DC, 93, Art Inst Students, Ann Nathan Gallery, 94, SOFA, Chicago, Ill, 97 & Art & Cult Center, Hollywood, Fla, 98. *Awards:* Fel, Arts Midwest NEA Regional Visual Arts, 85; Fel, Nat Endowment Arts, 86 & 92; Fel, Wis Arts Bd, 86 & 92 & Individual Artist Grant, 94; Creative Arts Fel, Dane Co Cult Affairs Comm, 96. *Publ:* New Art Examiner, 4/96; American Craft, 2-3/99; Surface Design Jour, summer 99; Fiberarts Design Book Six, 99; Miniatures, 2000. *Mailing Add:* 2002 Atwood Ave No 215 Madison WI 53704-5368

BERRETH, DAVID SCOTT
MUSEUM DIRECTOR
b Portland, Ore, Oct 10, 49. *Study:* Bowdoin Col, BA, 71; Syracuse Univ, MA, 76. *Pos:* Asst dir, Elvehjem Mus Art, Univ Wis, Madison, 76-79; dir, Miami Univ Art Mus, Oxford, Ohio, 79-88, Madison Art Ctr, Wis, 88-90, Belmont, Gari Melchers Mem Gallery, Fredericksburg, Va, 90-. *Mailing Add:* 224 Wasington St Fredericksburg VA 22405

BERRIDGE, MARY
PHOTOGRAPHER
Study: Univ Mich, BA, 86; Yale Univ Sch Art, MFA, 91. *Exhib:* Ctr Photogr, Woodstock, NY, 91; Pleasures and Terrors of Domestic Comfort (with catalog), Mus Mod Art, NY, 91; Berkshire Mus, Pittsfield, Mass, 92; Family Values, OPSIS Found, NY, 92; solo shows, Col New Rochelle, NY, 93, San Marino Mus Photogr, Repub San Marino, 97, Cathedral of St John the Divine, NY, 97, Univ Mich, 99 & Ctr Doc Studies, Duke Univ, Durham, NC, 99; Midtown Y Photogr Gallery, NY, 93; The Shadow it Casts: AIDS/Four Artists/Four Media, Independent Arts Gallery, Jamaica, NY, 94; Stories From Her, Univ Rochester, NY, 95; Blue Sky Gallery, Portland, Ore, 96; Backyards, Robert Mann Gallery, NY, 97; Soc Contemp Photogr, Kansas City, Mo, 97-98; Mus Fine Arts, Houston, Tex, 97; M D de Young Mem Mus, San Francisco, Calif, 97; Portland Mus Art, Maine, 98; SF Camerwork, San Francisco, Calif, 98; Univ Mich, Ann Arbor, 99. *Teaching:* Adj instr, Concordia Col, Bronxville,

NY, 92, Fairleigh Dickinson Univ, Rutherford, NJ, 92-94, Nassau Community Col, Garden City, NY, 94-96 & Sch Visual Arts, New York, 97; artist in residence & adj instr, Col New Rochelle, NY, 93; lectr, Princeton Univ, NJ, 98-99. *Awards:* Fel Award, Soc Contemp Photog, Kansas City, Mo, 97; Romeo Martinez Int Award, Ministry Cult, Repub San Marino, 97; John Simon Guggenheim Mem Fel, 97. *Bibliog:* River Huston (auth), A Positive Life: Portraits of Women Living with HIV, Running Press, Philadelphia, Pa, 97. *Publ:* The Human Condition/Photography 1995, Graphis Press, New York, 96

BERRIER, WESLEY DORWIN
PAINTER, CONSERVATOR
b Chicago, Ill, July 24, 51. *Study:* Apprentice to Joseph Abbrescia, Village Gallery, 70-74; Col DuPage, AA, 74; George Williams Col, BA(summa cum laude), 80. *Work:* Tesla Mem Soc, Lackawanna, NY. *Comn:* Family portraits, Dr Ned Mandich, HBM Corp, Homewood, Ill, 81-85; restoration of Christ on Mount by Henry Kratzner, First United Methodist Church, Hobart, Ind, 85; portrait, Lou Boudreax (Hall of Fame Baseball Player), 89; restoration 16th century panels, Richard Crowe Collection, Chicago, 92; portrait of Mikola Tesla, Serbian Acad Arts & Sci, Belgrade, 96. *Exhib:* Series of Faust Paintings, Village Art Sch, Skokie, Ill, 90; Serbian-Tesla Mus, Belgrade, 96; Salon Show, Northern Ind Arts Asn, Munster, 97. *Pos:* Own & operator, Berrier Art Studios, Ill, 72-82; restorateur, Village Gallery, Skokie, Ill, 74-; judge art exhibs, NIAA, Munster, Ind, 93-. *Teaching:* Instr oil painting, Berrier Art Studios, Ill, 72-82, Northern Ind Arts Asn, Munster, Ind, 91-; instr aesthetics, Col DuPage, Glen Elyn, Ill, 90-91. *Awards:* Fel, DuPaul Univ, 84-85. *Bibliog:* Northern Ind Arts, Artist at Work Series, Metrovision, 83; This Week in Munster, Munster Cable Studio, Muncab Cable, 92; Berrier, artist & his work, Post Tribune Times, 96. *Mem:* Hogart Arts League; Northern Ind Arts Asn. *Media:* Oil. *Publ:* Auth, Rules for judging, Hogart Arts League, 81. *Mailing Add:* c/o Northern Ind Art Assoc 1040 Ridge Rd Munster IN 46321

BERRY, CAROLYN
PAINTER, ILLUSTRATOR
b Sweet Springs, Mo, June 27, 30. *Study:* Univ Mo, BA, 53; Humboldt Univ, 71; Univ Calif, 85-87. *Work:* Sackner Collection, Miami Beach, Fla; Monterey Peninsula Mus Art, Calif; Nat Mus Women Art; Mus Mod Art Libr; Art Inst Chicago; Museo Internacional De Electrografia, Cuenca, Spain; Univ Calif at Los Angeles; St Stephan Mus, Hungary; Stanford Univ, Stanford, Calif. *Exhib:* Women's Artists Series, Rutgers Univ, 88 & 96; Pacific Rim Exhib, 90-93; Monterey Conf Ctr, 93-94; All Our Lives (with catalog), Women's Caucus for Art, Monterey Bay, 95-96; Lisa Parker Fine Art, NY, 96; Claypoole-Freese, 98; Core Gallery, New Paltz, NY, 2002-03; Walter Avery Gallery, Seaside, Calif, 2004; Int Invitational Mail Art Show, Guy Bleus, Wallen, Belgium, 2005. *Collection Arranged:* Gene McComas Exhib, Monterey Mus Art, 80. *Pos:* Artist-in-residence, Calif Arts Coun. *Teaching:* Instr bk art, Monterey Peninsula Col, 87. *Awards:* First Graphic Award, Monterey Peninsula Mus Art, 74 & 3rd Award, 85; Best in Show, Pac Grove Art Ctr, 97; Lifetime Achievement Award, Women's Caucus for Art, 2006. *Bibliog:* Artists & Their Cats, Midmarch, New York, 90; Mary H Dana (auth), Women Artists Series, Rutgers, 96. *Mem:* Women's Caucus for Art; Montery Mus Art; Nat Mus Women Art; Pac Grove Art Ctr. *Media:* Miscellaneous Media. *Res:* Vinnie Ream, Artist; Gene McComas, Artist; Mildred Walker, Artist; Comenha, The Sorrowing One, Northern Cheyenne, Anna Guy, Chickasaw. *Publ:* Contribr, Zoom Mag, France, 89. *Dealer:* Lisa Parker Fine Art 584 Broadway Suite 308 New York NY 10012; ClayPoole-Freese Gallery. *Mailing Add:* PO Box 51969 Pacific Grove CA 93950-6969

BERRY, GLENN
PAINTER, EDUCATOR
b Glendale, Calif, Feb 27, 29. *Study:* Pomona Col, BA(magna cum laude); Art Inst Chicago, BFA & MFA. *Work:* Storm King Art Ctr, Mountainville, NY; Joseph H Hirshhorn Collection, Washington, DC; Kaiser Aluminum & Chem Corp, Oakland, Calif; Palm Springs Desert Mus, Calif; Calif State Univ, Humboldt. *Exhib:* Phelan Awards Exhib & Artists Behind Artists, Calif Palace Legion Hon, San Francisco, 67; one-man shows, Ankrum Gallery, Los Angeles, 70, Esther Bear Gallery, Santa Barbara, Calif, 71, Col Redwoods, 89 & Humboldt State Univ, 92, Morris Graves Mus of Art, 2000; Six Northern Calif Artists, Henry Gallery, Univ Wash, 75; two-man show, Humboldt Cult Ctr, Eureka, Calif, 77; and others. *Teaching:* Prof painting, Humboldt State Univ, 56-81, prof emer, 81-. *Media:* Acrylic, Oil. *Mailing Add:* PO Box 2241 McKinleyville CA 95521

BERRY, WILLIAM AUGUSTUS
EDUCATOR, GRAPHIC ARTIST
b Jacksonville, Tex, Sept 29, 33. *Study:* Univ Tex, Austin, BFA(summa cum laude), 55; Circolo Artistico, Rome, 56; Univ Southern Calif, MFA, 57. *Work:* Hoyt Inst Fine Arts, New Castle, Pa; Univ N Dak, Grand Forks; Harwell Mus, Bluff, Mo; Stedman Art Gallery, Rutgers Univ, Camden, NJ; Boston Mus Fine Arts; Addison Gallery, Andover, Mass. *Exhib:* Solo Shows, Muscarelle Mus Art, Williamsburg, Va, 84, Galleria Schneider, Rome, Italy, 85, Campbell Gallery, San Francisco, Calif, 87, Brunnier Mus, Ames, Iowa, 88, Harwell Mus, Poplar Bluff, 88 & Traveling exhib sponsored by Mid Am Alliance & NEA, 90-93; more than 300 national juried exhib (group), 79-2005. *Pos:* Freelance illusr, The Reporter, Newsweek, Esquire, Opera News Mag, New York, 60-68; art dir & designer, Tex Mo Mag, 72-73. *Teaching:* Asst prof art, Univ Tex, Austin, 68-74; assoc prof art & chmn graphic design area, Sch Visual Art, Boston Univ, 74-78; vis assoc prof, Grad Summer Sch Teachers, Wesleyan Univ, 76; prof art & dir grad studies visual art, Univ Mo, Columbia, 78-, chmn art dept, 95-99. *Awards:* Artist-in-residence, MacDowell Colony, 84; Artist-in-residence, Rockefeller Found, Bellagio, Italy, 88; Regional fel, Nat Endowment Arts, 94-95. *Bibliog:* Susan E Meyer (auth), William A Berry, illustrator-painter, Am Artist, 3/70; Ruth Seidler (auth), Drawing the Human Form, Libr J, 11/01/77; Betsy Goldman (auth), William A Berry, Am Artist, 2/87. *Mem:* Colored Pencil Soc Am. *Media:* Multimedia, Color Pencils. *Res:* Drawing, technique and theory. *Publ:* Coauth, Paper Construction for Children, Van Nostrand Reinhold, 66; illusr, Carter Wilson's on Firm Ice, Crowell, 69; auth, Visual puns, Print Mag, 9/71; Drawing the Human Form, Simon & Schuster, NY, 77 & 94. *Mailing Add:* 908 Edgewood Ave Columbia MO 65203

BERSHAD, DAVID L
HISTORIAN, EDUCATOR
b San Francisco, Calif, Mar 11, 42. *Study:* Stanford Univ, AB, 62; Univ Calif, Los Angeles, PhD(with distinction), 70. *Teaching:* Asst prof art hist, Ariz State Univ, 70-72; assoc prof art hist, Univ Calgary, 75-85, prof, 85-. *Awards:* Fulbright Fel, 68; Kress Fel, 69; Distinguished Scholar, Univ Lethbridge, 80. *Mem:* Univ Art Asn Can. *Res:* 17th&18th century Italian painting and sculpture, with specific emphasis on Roman art. *Publ:* Auth, A series of papal busts by Domenico Guidi, 70, Domenico Guidi and Nicolas Poussin, 71, The cardinal Marco Bragadino tomb in the church of San Marco in Rome, 77 & auth, New documents concerning Michelangelo's deposition in Florence, 78, Burlington Mag; The tapestries of Raphael and their re-acquisition in 1808, 78 & P E Monnot: Newly discovered sculpture and documents, 84, Antologia di Belle Arti. *Mailing Add:* c/o Univ Calgary Dept Art 2500 University Dr NW Calgary AB T2N 1N4 Canada

BERTHOT, JAKE
PAINTER
b Niagara Falls, NY, Mar 30, 39. *Study:* New Sch for Social Res, NY, 60-61; Pratt Inst, Brooklyn, NY, 60-62. *Work:* Baltimore Mus Art, Md; Va Mus Fine Arts, Richmond; Whitney Mus Am Art, Mus Mod Art & Solomon R Guggenheim Mus, NY; Dallas Mus Fine Arts, Tex; Fogg Art Mus, Cambridge, Mass; Philadelphia Mus Art, Pa; St Louis Mus Art, Mo. *Exhib:* solo shows, Tony Oliver Gallery, Sydney, Australia, 93, McKee Gallery, NY, 94, Nina Nielsen Gallery, Boston, 95, Jaffe-Friede & Strauss Galleries, Dartmouth Col, 95, Nielsen Gallery, 96 & Phillips Collection, Wash, 96, Galleri Gunnar Olsson, Stockholm, Sweden, 97; Ut Pictura Poesis: Berthot, Moskowitz, Twombly, Galleri Gunnar Olsson, Stockholm, Sweden, 96; Founders and Heirs of the NY Sch, Mus Contemp Art, Tokyo, Japan & travels to the Miyagi Mus Art, The Mus Mod Art, Ibaraki, Japan, 97; Galleri Guner Olson, Stockholm, Sweden, 2000; Neilson Gallery, Boston, Mass, 2004; Marist Art Gallery, NY, 2005; Am Acad Invitational Exhib of Painting & Sculpture, 2005. *Teaching:* Instr, Cooper Union, NY, 74-81, Yale Univ, New Haven, Conn, 82; resident artist, Skowhegan Sch, Maine, 82; Sch Visual Arts, New York City, 92-; resident artist, Dartmouth Univ, 95. *Awards:* Guggenheim Fel, 81; Nat Endowment Arts Grant, 83; Academician, Nat Acad Design, 94; Elizabeth Found Grant, 95. *Bibliog:* Joseph Ruzick (auth), Jake Berthot at David McKee, Art in Am, 4/92; Pepe Karmel (auth), Jake Berthot, NY Times, 12/30/94; Nancy Stapen (auth), Jake Berthot paints from palette of emotion, Boston Globe, 4/20/95; and many others. *Mem:* Nat Acad (assoc, 92, Acad, 94). *Dealer:* Betty Cunningham Gallery 541 West 25th St NY NY 10001; Nina Neilsen Gallery 179 Newbury St Boston Mass 02116. *Mailing Add:* Betty Coningham 541 W 25th St New York NY 10001-5501

BERTI, MARY VITELLI
PAINTER
b Brooklyn, NY. *Study:* Suffolk Co Com Col, Selden, NY, AA (honors), 1974; LIU School of Arts, CW Post Ctr, Brookville, NY, BA (summa cum laude), 1975; MA (summa cum laude), 1979. *Work:* Lou Henry Hoover House at Stanford, Univ, Calif; Jin-Hyun Hwang Coll, Samick Park Mansion, Gil-Dong, Seoul, Korea; Dr Kurt Grimm Coll, Untere Augarter, Vienna, Aus; Mr & Mrs G Vlasic Collection, Bloomfield Hills, Mich; Dr & Mrs John L Hennessy Coll Stanford Univ, Calif. *Exhib:* 48th Ann Juried LI Art Exhib, Heckscher Mus Art, Huntington, NY, 1978-2001, 2003; Pastel Soc of Am Juried Ann, Nat Arts Club, New York City, 1980-2005; 27th Parrish Juried Art Exhibit, Parrish Art Mus, Southampton, NY, 1981; Nat Acad of Design Ann Exhib, New York City, 1981,1986, 1988, 1992, 1996; Nat League Am Pen Women Juried Exhib, Vanderbilt Mus, Centerport, NY, 1993; Pastel Invitatioinal, Hermitage Mus, Norfolk, Va, 1999; Master Pastelists, Butler Inst Am Art, Youngstown, Ohio, 2003. *Awards:* Best in Show, Nat League Am Pen Women, Winsor Newton Oils, 1993; Am Artist Mag Award, Pastel Soc of Am, Ann Am Artist Mag, 2001; Award of Excellence, Ann Juried Exhib, Heckscher Mus Art, 2003. *Bibliog:* Rachelle DePalma (auth), Family Portrait, Attenzione Mag Adam Pub, New York City, 1985; R. Tenenbaum (dir), Originals (film), Interview Cable WLIW, Long Island, NY, 1989; Judith Baker (dir), For Art's Sake, Interview Cable, Champaign, Il, 1991. *Mem:* Pastel Soc Am, Natl Arts Club, New York City; Heckscher Mus Art, Huntington, NY; Huntington Arts Coun, Huntington, NY; Art League Long Island, Dix Hills, NY; Friends of Gallery, North Setauket, NY. *Media:* Pastel, Oil, Acrylic. *Publ:* auth, Personal Style, Pastelagram, Pastel Soc of Am, 2003. *Dealer:* Robert Kidd Gallery 107 Towsend St Birmingham, MI 48009. *Mailing Add:* 107 Townsend St Birmingham MI 48009

BERTINE, DOROTHY W
PAINTER
b Madill, Okla, Sep 28, 16. *Study:* Okla State Univ, BS, 1942; Houston Mus Sch Art, with Frances Skinner, 1960-1963; Tex Woman's Univ, MA, 1975. *Work:* Brownsville Mus & Art League, Tex; Laredo Fine Arts Mus & Art League, Tex; Heard Nature Mus Sci, McKinney, Tex; Women's Collection, MBH Libr, Tex Woman's Univ, Denton, Tex; Print Collection, State Mus of NJ. *Comn:* Painting, comn by Mr. & Mrs. Bennett Wooley, Dallas, 1980; Historic Houses remaining in Denton (map), City of Denton, Tex, 1980; watercolor, Lady Love Cosmetics, Dallas, 1993. *Exhib:* Hist Tex Archit & Lect, Tex Woman's Univ Gallery, Denton, Tex, 1975 & 1982; TWU Diamond Jubilee

Exhib, Tex Woman's Univ Gallery, Denton, Tex, 1976; Hist Archit, Ft McIntosh & Nueva Santander Mus Art, Laredo, Tex, 1978; Citation Exhib, Laguna Gloria Art Mus, Austin, Tex, 1979-1981; Southern Watercolor Soc Ann, Columbia Mus Art, Columbia, SC, 1980; Trees and Flowers, Heard Mus of Sci, McKinney, Tex, 1983 & 1989; Goddard Mus Ann, Goddard Mus, Ardmore, Okla, 1984-1987; Hist Tex Archit, Brownsville Art Mus, Tex1984; Southwestern Watercolor Soc 25th Ann Mem Exhib, Mall Gallery, Dallas, 1988; Maj Retrospective, Laredo Art Mus, Tex, 2000. *Pos:* Dept head and instr watercolor & drawing, City of Denton Parks & Recreation, 1975-1985. *Teaching:* Instr watercolor, Brownsville Art Mus, 1965-1970 & 1984-1988; instr watercolor, Tex Woman's Univ, 1974-1975. *Awards:* Grumbacher Medal, Southwestern Watercolor Soc, 1982; Soc Watercolor Artists, Best of Show & Presidents Award, Ft Worth, 1986; Visual Artist of the Year, Int Biog Ctr, 2004. *Bibliog:* Placing Oak Street homes on canvas, Denton Record Chronicle, 1985. *Mem:* Southwestern Watercolor Soc (signature mem 1965-); Assoc Creative Artists, Dallas, Tex (signature mem); Soc Watercolor Artists (signature mem), Ft Worth, Tex; La Watercolor Soc (life mem); Brownsville Art League (life mem & instr). *Media:* Acrylic, Oil, Watercolor, All Media. *Res:* History of ornament used in high Victorian houses. *Interests:* Painting & teaching. *Collection:* Private collection Eastcoast & Calif painters work. *Publ:* Contribr, Best of Watercolor, Painting Light and Shadow, Schleem & Doherty Rockport publ, 1997; Collected Best of Watercolor, Schlemm & Doherty Rockport publ, 2002; Encyclopedia of Living Artists in America, ArtNetWork, 1990 & 2003; Dizionario Enciclopedico Internazionale d'Arte, Alba, Itlay, 2003 & 2005; "Le Mer" Book of Modern & Contemporary Art, Regards d'Arte, Pau, France, 2005. *Dealer:* Craig Wilkerson Gallery Rupp Fine Arts 1025 E 15th St Plano TX 75074. *Mailing Add:* d' Bertine Studio PO Box 2965 Denton TX 76202

BERTMAN, STEPHEN
HISTORIAN, WRITER
b New York, NY, July 20, 37. *Study:* New York Univ, BA, 59; Brandeis Univ, MA, 60; Am Sch Classical Studies, Athens, 62; Columbia Univ, PhD, 65. *Teaching:* Asst prof classics, Fla State Univ, Tallahassee, 63-67; prof langs, lit & culture, Univ Windsor, Ont, 67-2002, emeritus, 02-. *Awards:* Alumni Award Excellence in Univ Teaching, Univ Windsor. *Mem:* Archaeol Inst Am; Col Art Asn Am; Midwest Art History Soc. *Res:* Archeology and ancient art. *Interests:* music. *Publ:* Auth, Art and the Romans, Coronado, 75; Doorways through Time, Jeremy Tarcher-St Martin's Press, 86; Hyperculture, 98 & Cultural Amnesia, 99, Praeger; Handbook of Life in Ancient Mesopotamia, 2003; Facts On File, Climbing Olympus, 2003; sourcebooks

BERTOIA, (MR) VAL
DESIGNER, SCULPTOR
b Santa Monica, Calif, 1949. *Study:* Ind Inst Technol, grad, 71; studied with Dr Harry Bertoia, 72-78; Elizabethtown Col, 86. *Hon Degrees:* Reiki I, Reiki II (Shambala degrees). *Work:* James Allen Ctr, Northwestern Univ, Evanstown, Ill; R Greenberg Assoc, NY; Call Chronicle, Allentown, Pa; J Haight of Allentown Art Mus; Cleveland Pub Lib, Ohio; and others. *Comn:* Wooden playground, Schwenkfelder Church, Palm, Pa, 85; John Smith Memorial, Unitarian Universalists, Pottstown, Pa, 92; wall-mounted sound-sculpture, Alpo Pet Foods, 92; wall-mounted sound-sculpture, Lenox Inc, 93; wind-played sound-sculptures, S Devon, Mich, 93. *Exhib:* Mayfair Juried Show, Muhlenberg Col, 90; 3 Generations of Bertoia, Reading Mus, 90; Wooden 5-Seasons' Gallery, Penn State Univ, 90; Juried Exhib, Hill Sch, 93; Frexberger Gallery, Penn State Berks, 93. *Pos:* pres, Bertoiastudio.com. *Teaching:* Instr, stone sculpture & sculpture jewelry, Wyomissing Inst Fine Arts, 87-88; artist-in-residence, Purnell-Sch, 96. *Awards:* Fourth place sculpture, Festival Arts, Cornerstone, 84; Speaker of the Year, Ind Inst of Tech, 69. *Bibliog:* Marilyn Fox (auth), V Bertoia Sounds Off, Reading Eagle, 87. *Mem:* Pottstown-Area Artists' Guild (pres, 93). *Media:* Bronze, Copper; Nickel, Silver. *Publ:* Auth, James with the Invisible Neck, Boyertown Publ, 85; Optimum Wind-Driven Alternator, Bertoia Studio Ltd, 85; coauth, Bertoia Catalogue, Boyertown Publ, 86; Sonambient CDS, 94; Ecological Sculpture Pathway, Bertoia Studio, 1994; World of Bertoia, Schiffer Publ, 2003. *Dealer:* Khaled of Primaveraart.com; 805-646-7133. *Mailing Add:* Bertoia Studio 644 Main St PO Box 383 Bally PA 19503

BERTOLLI, EUGENE EMIL
SCULPTOR, DESIGNER
b Boston, Mass, Feb 19, 23. *Study:* Boston Col, AB, 43; Hartford Col Grad Sch, cert art educ, 49; pvt study with EG Chandler, 78-83. *Comn:* Stained glass windows, Madigan Convalescent Hosp, Ft Lewis, Wash, 45; sculptured gold pectoral cross, Bishop McGurkin, Tanganyika, Africa, 56; commemorative medal, City of Meriden, Conn, 85; also numerous pvt comns in sculpture & precious jewelry. *Exhib:* One-man shows, Conn Town & Co Asn, Hartford, 80 & Rockport Art Asn, Mass, 85; Nat Exhib, Hudson Valley Arts Asn, Hudson Valley, NY, 83-88; Ann Nat Exhib, Acad Artists Asn, Springfield, Mass, 84-90; Ann Awards Exhib, Guild Boston Artists, Mass, 85. *Pos:* Dir art & educ, Madigan Convent Hosp, Ft Lewis, Wash, 45-47; sr vpres & chief designer, Napier Co, NY, 47-85; pres, Meriden Community Theatre, formerly; pres, Meriden Curtis Mem Libr Bd, formerly; US Army off in charge of the arts and crafts for wounded soldiers WW II; 23 years, Meriden bd of educ for 6 years for pres of Art & Crafts asn Meriden Ctr. *Teaching:* Lectr fine arts; Portraits & figure Sculpture; medallic art sculpture; In the Jewelry design & production (The Napier Co); Lectr on jewelry and its design & production in the USA & Int; Traveled to major department stores as the artist designer of Napier Jewelry: (Stores Lord & Taylor NYC; Lazarus Stores; Marshall Fields, Chicago, Dallas Tex, Disney World Orlando, Hawaii, England, Jordan Marsh, Boston, Etc). *Awards:* Coun Am Artists Soc Award, Acad Artists Asn Nat Exhib, 92; Paul Manship Mem Award Excellence Sculpture, North Shore Arts Asn, 92; Elected, Meriden Hall Fame for Achievements in Art, 95; and others. *Bibliog:* Linda Fridy (auth), kBertolli: Dean of American jewelry designers, Accent Mag, 86. *Mem:* Am Artists Prof League; Guild Boston Artist; Acad Artists Asn (mem, exec comt, Springfield, Mass, 83); Hudson Valley Art Asn; Am Medallic Sculpture Asn; Salmagundi Club; New England Sculptors Asn; FIDEM; Rockport Art Asn, Rockport Mass; North Shore Art Asn, E Gloucestay. *Media:* Metals; All Media. *Publ:* Auth & illusr, Continuity through change: A history of jewelry design, Conn Mag, 60. *Mailing Add:* Bertolli Studios 73 Reynolds Dr Meriden CT 06450

BERTONI, CHRISTINA
CERAMIST, PAINTER
b Ann Arbor, Mich, Jan 15, 45. *Study:* Univ Mich, BFA (painting), 67; Cranbrook Acad Art, MFA (ceramics), 76. *Work:* Brooklyn Mus, Brooklyn, NY; Victoria & Albert Mus, London; Crocker Art Mus, Sacramento, Calif; Mus Fine Arts, Boston, Mass. *Exhib:* Am Potters Today (with catalog), Victoria & Albert Mus, London, Eng, 86; solo exhib, Victoria Munroe Gallery, NY, 87 & 93; Virginia Lynch Gallery, Tiverton, RI, 95 & 97; Sculptural Ceramics in New Eng, Boston Athenium, Mass, 96-97; Painters & Sculptures of the McDowell Colony, Currier Gallery Art, Manchester, NH, 96-97; Power of the Center, Pewabic Pottery, Detroit, Mich, 97. *Teaching:* Assoc prof art, RI Sch Design, Providence, 77-, dean grad studies, currently. *Awards:* Purchase Prize, Crocker Art Mus, Calif, 77; Nat Endowment Arts Craftsman Fel, 79 & 86; Craftsman Grant, RI State Coun Arts, 83. *Bibliog:* Lois Tarlow (auth), Christina Bertoni, Art New Eng, 4/84; James Cobb (auth), article, Am Ceramics, 88; On the spititual art, Agni Rev, fall, 88. *Media:* Clay; Paint. *Dealer:* Siparist Gallery Laurel Oak MI. *Mailing Add:* 152 Laurel Hill Ave Pascoag RI 02859

BESANT, DEREK MICHAEL
PAINTER, INSTRUCTOR
b Ft MacLeod, Alta, July 15, 50. *Study:* Univ Calgary, Alberta Can, BFA, 73. *Work:* De Cordova Mus, Boston, Mass; Metrop Mus, Miami, Fla; Can Coun Art Bank, Ottawa, Ont; Cineplex Odeon Corp, NY; Royal Bank Can. *Comn:* Flatiron mural, A E LePage, Royal Insurance Lavalin Inc, Toronto, Ont, 80; Eau Claire Peel, Bourgeau Developments Sturgets Architects, Calgary, Alta, 82; cardboard windows installation proj, Liberty of London, Eng, 87; paintings, Amoco, Mt Royal Col, Calgary & Bank of Nova Scotia, Toronto. *Exhib:* Boston Printmakers, Boston Ctr Arts, Mass, 78; 8th Int Triennial Color Prints, Grenchen Arts Mus, Switz, 79; Other Realities, Can House London, Eng, Paris, France, 79; Royal Canadian Soc Arts, Mickle Arts Mus, Calgary, Alta, 80; Can Prints, Asn Print Workshops Gt Brit, Edinborough, Scotland, 80; Ten Can Print Artists, Nat Mus Can Japanese Print Coun, Tour Japan Nat Mus, 80-81; Int Print Exhibs Repub China, Taipei, 84; 6th Int Impact Art Festival, Kyoto City Mus, 85; Diagrams, Mira Godard Gallery, Toronto, 86; Asian-Pacific, Univ New Delhi, India, 86; Solo exhib, Woltjen Udell Gallery, Vancouver & Mira Godard Gallery, Toronto, 89, Art Gallery of Hamilton, 90; San Antonio Mus Art, Tex, 92; Sao Paulo, Brazil, 92; Centre de Langues, Brussels, Belg, 92; and others. *Pos:* Exhibs designer, Glenbow Mus, Calgary, 73-77; Alta ed, Artmagazine, Toronto, 74-; drawing chmn, Alta Col Art, 77-; comt mem, Alta Legislature Art Acquisition Comt, 81-82. *Teaching:* Guest artist collaborations, Univ Arts Asn, Univ Alta, 76; guest artist printmaking, Mem Univ, Newfoundland, 77; lectr pub art, Univ Regina, Sask, 81; lectr murals, Red Deer Col, 82 & Southwest Tex State Univ, 89. *Awards:* Canada Coun Grant, 77, 85 & 92; Second Prize, Miami Biennale, Mus Mod Art, 77; Award Winner, Andrew Nelson Wheehead Co, 78; World Cult Prize for Lett, Arts & Sci, 84; Alberta Achievement Award, 84. *Bibliog:* Nancy Tousley (auth), Falls transplanted to Toronto, Calgary Herald, 5/89; Christopher Hume (auth), Huge waterfall graces Scotia Plaza, The Sunday Star, Toronto, 5/89; Patrick McHugh (auth), Toronto Architecture, McClelland & Stewart, Can, 89. *Mem:* Royal Can Acad Arts; Print & Drawing Coun Can (vchmn, 76-78); Can Artists Representation; Visual Arts Ont; World Print Coun. *Media:* Watercolor, Ink. *Res:* Contemporary Canadian. *Publ:* Illusr, The Back Room, Oberon, 80; A Culinary Palette, Merritt, 81; contribr, Artmagazine, 81; Artviews, Visual Arts Ont, 82; Macleans, Maclean Hunter, 82. *Mailing Add:* Dept Art Alberta Col Art 1407 14th Ave NW Calgary AB T2N 1M4 Canada

BESSIRE, MARK HC
MUSEUM DIRECTOR
Study: NYU, BA; Hunter Col, MA in art hist; Columbia Univ, MBA. *Pos:* Dir, Inst Contemp Art, Maine Col Art, 1998—2003; Bates Col Mus Art, Lewiston, Maine, 2003—. *Mailing Add:* Bates Col Mus Art Olin Arts Ctr Rm 202 2 Andrews Rd Lewiston ME 04240-6028

BETANCOURT, CARLOS
PHOTOGRAPHER
b San Juan, Puerto Rico, 1966; arrived in Miami, 1981. *Exhib:* Solo shows include Fracturism, Imperfect Utopia Gallery, Miami Beach, Fla, 94, En la Arena Sabrosa, Meza Fine Art, Coral Gables, Fla, 95, Images of Heaven: New Works, St Thomas Univ Atrium Gallery, Miami, 96, New Works, Galeria Casa Colon, Miami Beach, 1990-2000, Tech Sounds, Symbols Project, Am Found Arts, Miami Beach, 2001, Outdoor Photography Project, Bernice Steinbaum Gallery, Miami, 2001, Recent Photographic Works, Lowe Art Ctr, San Antonio, Tex, 2003, Interventions in Wynwood, Paradises Space, Miami, 2003-2004, Recent Works, Galeria Castellon, Spain, 2004-2005, About the Archaic Substance, Heriard-Cimino Gallery, New Orleans, 2005, Diana Lowenstein Fine Arts, Miami, 2005, Remi Toledo Gallery, NY, 2006, Museo de las Americas, San Juan, PR, 2006, Galeria Casa Colon, Merida, 2006; group shows include Duet in the Sun, Galaxy Gallery, Miami Beach, 90; Sheets, World Gallery, Miami Beach, 92; Feria del Mueblo, Milano, Italy, 92; In Color, Lohman and Busse Gallery, Dortmund, Ger, 93; The Color of Exile, Gallery Natcom, Miami, 95; Art Against Aids VII, Coral Gables, Fla, 98; Lucky 13, South Fla Art Ctr, Miami Beach, 98; Fla-Bra, Tiger Tail Found, Miami, 99; Monster Mash IV, Mus Contemp Art, Miami, 2001; Art Basel Miami, Robert Miller Gallery, 2002; Quinta Gran Subasta, Museo Galeria Banco Santander, San Juan, PR, 2002; Space, Mus Science, Coconut Grove, Fla, 2003; De Cuerpos y Almas, Galeria Carmen de la

Guerra, Madrid, 2003; The Flag Project, The Rubin Mus Art, NY, 2004; Don't Call It Performance/ No Lo Llames Performance, Museo del Barrio, NY, 2004; American Dream, The Ignatian Ctr Arts, Miami, 2004; No Country is an Island, Raritan Valley Community Col, Newark, NJ, 2005; What's New?, Diana Lowenstein Fine Arts, 2005; Chicago Contemp Art Fair, 2005; Art Miami, Galeria de la Guerra, Madrid, 2005; Remi Toledo Gallery, NY, 2005; represented in permanent collections of City Miami Beach, Fla, Transatlantic Bank, Miami, Fla, St Thomas Univ, Miami, Miami-Dade Community Found, Ft Lauderdale Mus Art, Fla, San Antonio Mus Art, Tex, Centro Atlantico de Arte Moderno, Gran Canaria, Spain, Lowe Art Mus, Coral Gables, Fla, Bass Mus Art, Miami Beach Fla, Art Mus, Fla Int Univ, Miami, Nat Portrait Gallery, Smithsonian Inst, Washington, DC, Metrop Mus Art, NY. *Awards:* Nat Cover Award, Dade Community Found, 96; Chivas Regal Order Distinction Award, Plastic Arts, 97; Millennium Cultural Recognition Award, Fla Dept State, 2000; City Miami Beach Arts Council Grant, 99; New Forms Grant, Dade County Cultural Affairs, 99; Cultural Art Council Grant, 2001; Nat Endowment Arts Grant, 2001-2002; Art Walks Grant, City Delray, Fla, 2003-2004. *Mailing Add:* c/o Diana Lowenstein Fine Arts 3080 SW 38th Court Miami FL 33146

BETENSKY, ROSE HART
PAINTER, ART ADMINISTRATOR
b New York, NY 23. *Study:* Painting with Josef Presser. *Work:* Jane Voorhees Zimmerli Art Mus; Nat Asn Women Artists Collection, Rutgers Univ, 96. *Exhib:* Nat Acad Galleries, NY, 60-77; Royal Acad, Edinburgh, Scotland, 63; Norfolk Mus of Arts & Sci, Va, 64; Cult Inst of Tolsa, Guadalajara, Mex, 65; Palazzo Vecchio, Florence, Italy, 72; NY Acad Sci, 92. *Pos:* Pres, NY Soc of Women Artists, 69-70, Nat Asn of Women Artists, 70-72 & Am Soc of Contemp Artists, 77-79. *Teaching:* Painting, Wheatley Sch Old Westbury, Long Island, 63-68. *Awards:* Grumbacher Gold Medal, Nat Asn Women Artists, 87 & Gladys B Blum Mem Award, 97; Sara Winston Mem Award, 98; Award, Am Soc Contemp Artists, 2000. *Mem:* Audubon Artists; Nat Asn Women Artists; NY Asn Women Artists; Am Soc Contemp Artists. *Media:* Acrylic, Canvas & Work on Paper. *Mailing Add:* 100 Harbor View Dr Apt 543 Port Washington NY 11050

BETHEL, DENISE
APPRAISER, COLLECTOR
Pos: Dir, photogrpahy Rare-Book Auction House, 80-90; dir Photography, Sotheby's, 90-. *Mailing Add:* Sotheby's 1334 York Ave New York NY 10021

BETSKY, AARON
MUSEUM DIRECTOR
b Missoula, Mont, 58. *Study:* Yale Univ, BA, 79, MArch, 83. *Comn:* Designer Office of Frank Gehry, 85-87; designer, Hodgetts & Fung Design, 87. *Exhib:* Magnets of Meaning, 97. *Collection Arranged:* Dir, First Int Architecture Biennnale Rotterdam, 2002. *Pos:* Private practice in LA, 87; cur, Architecture and Design San Francisco Mus Modern Art, 1995-2001; cofounder San Francisco Prize, 95; founder, first biannual San Francisco Forum, Architecture of Imagination, 97; dir, Netherlands Architecture Inst, Rotterdam, 2001-2006; dir, Cincinnati Art Mus, 2006-. *Teaching:* Teacher, Univ Cincinnati, 83-85; instr, coordr Special Projects Southern Calif Inst Architecture; adj prof, Calif Col Arts and Crafts. *Publ:* Auth, Violated Perfection: Architecture and the Fragmentation of the Modern, 90; auth, James Gamble Rogers and the Architecture of Pragmatism, 94; auth, Building Sex: Men, Women, Architecture and the Construction of Sexuality; auth, Queer Space: The Spaces of Same Sex Desire, 97; auth, Architecture Must Burn, 2000. *Mailing Add:* Cincinnati Art Museum 953 Eden Park Ave Cincinnati OH 45202

BETTERIDGE, LOIS ETHERINGTON
LECTURER, GOLDSMITH
b Drummonville, Que, Nov 6, 28. *Study:* Ont Col Art, 47-48; Univ Kans, BFA, 51; Cranbrook Acad Art, MFA, 57. *Work:* Royal Scottish Mus, Edinborough; Int Bus Machines, Can; Nat Mus Natural Sci & Nat Mus Man, Ottawa; Cranbrook Acad Art, Mich; R Abramson, Seattle, Wash. *Comn:* Communion set, Christ Church Cathedral, Vancouver, 74; bronze sculptures, IBM Can, 75; desk sets, Provincial Premiers & Prime Minister, Can Pac Railways; bronze sculptures, Imperial Oil Can; ongoing medals, McLuhan Teleglobe Can UNESCO Award. *Exhib:* Contemp Ont Crafts, Agnes Etherington Gallery, Kingston, Ont, 77; Artisans Touring Exhib, Can, 78; solo-exhibs, Reflections in Silver & Gold Traveling Exhib (catalog), 81-83, Recent Works Traveling Exhib (catalog), 88-90 & New Works, Harbinger Gallery, 96; Remains To Be Seen, John Michael Kohler Arts Ctr, Sheboygan, Wis, 82; Silversmithing-Three and a Half Decades, Cranbrook Acad Art, Mich, 82; The Mich Influence, Eastern Mich Univ, Ypsilanti, 82; Masters of Am Metalsmithing, Nat Ornamental Metal Mus, Memphis, 88; Silver: New Forms and Expressions, USA 1990; RCA Canadian Designers, Budapest, Burgundy Edinburgh, 1995; Raised from Tradition; Holloware Past and Present Seafirst Gallery, Seattle, WA, 1998; Benchmarkers; Women in Metal, National Ornamental Metal Mus, Memphis Tenn, 1999; Contemp Images of Ont Lieutenant-Governor's Suite, Queen's Park, 1999; Arts 2000 RCA Stratford, Ont, May 2000; Tribute Exhib at the Macdonald Stewart Art ctr in Guelph in 2000 and at the Nova Scotia Art Gallery, (catalogue). *Collection Arranged:* Pewterworkings Ral End Gallerie, ON Canada. *Pos:* Studio Silversmith. *Teaching:* Lectr design, metal & weaving, Univ Guelph, Ont, 57-61; vis lectr & workshop leader, worldwide, 69-; Holloware instr, Fleming Col, Haliburton Sch Art, Ont, 82; vis artist to Col & Guilds, USA, Can, Europe & Gt Brit. *Awards:* Fel, New Brunswick Craft Sch, 88; Joan M Chalmers 15 Anniversary Award, 91; Hon Fel, Ont Col Art, 92; Citation for Distinguished Professional Achievement, Univ of Kansas, 1975; Saidye Bronfman Award for Excellence in Crafts, 1978; The YMCA, YWCA Women of Distinction Award for Lifetime Achievement, Guelph, 2002; Order of Canada, 97; Queen's Golden Jubilee Medal, 2002. *Mem:* Ont Crafts Coun (mem bd, 72-73); distinguished mem Soc Am Goldsmiths (mem bd, 85-88); Royal Acad Arts; fel Royal Can Acad Arts. *Media:* Silver, Gold. *Res:* my designs. *Specialty:* Holloware, silversmithing. *Publ:* Auth, The Smiths Mandate, Introd, Metalsmith, 4/5/86; David Didur Recent Work, Ont Craft, spring 88; Ken Vickerson & Collen Brzezick, Ont Craft, fall 88; Donald Staurt The Challange of Metals, Metalsmith, summer 94; Gold of Meroe, Royal Ont Mus, Toronto, 94. *Mailing Add:* 9 Kirkland St Guelph ON N1H 4X7 Canada

BETTINSON, BRENDA
PAINTER, PRINTMAKER
b King's Lynn, Eng, Aug 17, 29; US citizen. *Study:* St Martins Sch Art, London, 46-48; Cent Sch Arts & Crafts, London, 48-50, Nat Dipl in Design, 50; Acad de la Grande Chaumiere, Paris, 51; Ecole Pratique des Hautes Etudes, Sorbonne, 51-53, Eleve Titulaire, 52. *Work:* St Anselm's Abbey, Wash; also pvt collections of St Mary's Benedictine Abbey, Morristown, NJ & Dominican House of Studies, Wash; Mus of Art, Bates Col, Maine; Ogunquit Mus of Am Art, Maine. *Comn:* murals, Calvary Hosp, Bronx, 78; and others. *Exhib:* Numerous one-person and group shows in Europe and USA most recently Ogunquit Mus Am Art, 02. *Pos:* Art ed, Riverside Radio WRVR-FM, New York, 61-65; consult, Soc for Renewal of Christian Art, 69-87. *Teaching:* Prof art, Pace Univ, New York, 63-90, chairperson Art & Design, 79-85; lectr art, Katonah Gallery, NY, 72-75, instr Docents' Prog, 88 & 89; prof emer, Pace Univ, 90. *Awards:* Gold Medal, Nat Arts Club, New York, 66. *Bibliog:* Brenda Bettinson: Dancing with buoys, Bob Keyes, Maine Sunday Telegraph, 2002; Brenda Bettinson: from King's Lynn to Barter's Island, Carl Little, Maine Boats Harbors, 2004. *Mem:* Ctr for Maine Contemp Art. *Media:* All Media. *Dealer:* Mathias Fine Art Trevett ME 04571. *Mailing Add:* 10 Mathias Dr Trevett ME 04571

BETTS, EDWARD HOWARD
PAINTER
b Yonkers, NY, Aug 4, 20. *Study:* Art Students League; Yale Univ, BA, 42; Univ Ill, MFA, 52. *Work:* Fogg Mus Art, Cambridge, Mass; Butler Inst Am Art, Youngstown, Ohio; Va Mus Fine Arts, Richmond, Va; Univ Rochester Mem Art Gallery, NY; Indianapolis Art Mus, Ind; Ogunquit Mus of Am Art, 1996?; and others. *Exhib:* Five Corcoran Biennials, Washington, DC, 47-59; Am Painting Today-1950, Metrop Mus Art, NY, 50; Am Watercolor Soc, NY, 50-91; Int Watercolor Exhibs, Brooklyn Mus, NY, 53, 55 & 61; Nat Acad of Design 53-; Watercolor USA, Springfield Art Mus, Mo, 63-71 & 74-75. *Teaching:* Prof painting, Univ Ill, Champaign, 49-84; retired. *Awards:* First Altman Landscape Prize, Nat Acad Design, 57, 59 & 66; Purchase Award, Childe Hassam Purchase Fund Exhib, 66; M Cooper Award, Am Watercolor, Soc, NY, 77; Winsor and Newton award Georgia Water Color Soc, 79. *Bibliog:* A S Weller (auth), Edward Betts, Art in Am New Talent Issue, 2/55. *Mem:* Nat Acad Design (assoc, 58, acad, 61); Am Watercolor Soc; life mem Art Students League. *Media:* Acrylic, Watercolor. *Publ:* Auth, Master Class in Watercolor and Acrylics, Watson-Guptill, 75; Creative Landscape Painting, Watson-Guptill, 78; Creative Seascape Painting, Watson-Guptill, 81; Master Class in Watermedia, Watson-Guptill, 93, 2nd ed, 2000. *Mailing Add:* Two Wonderbrook Dr Kennebunk ME 04043

BETTS, JUDI POLIVKA
PAINTER, INSTRUCTOR
b Western Springs, Ill, July 26, 36. *Study:* Ind U, AB (fine art), 58; La State Univ, MEd, 64; Studied under Barse Miller, Rex Brandt, Millard Sheets & Milford Zornes. *Work:* New Orleans Mus Art, La; Springfield Art Mus, Mo; Loma Linda Univ, Riverside, Calif; State of La Permanent Collection, Baton Rouge; State of Ark Permanent Collection, Little Rock. *Comn:* 10 Hist Bldgs, Commonwealth Mortgage, Houston, Tex, 84; 12 Hist Bldgs, Am Fed Bank, Greenville, SC, 85; religious triptych, DePaul Hosp, New Orleans, La, 85; triptych, dining room, Omni Hotel Chain, Durham, NC, 88; painting, Sen Russell B Long Fed Bldg, Washington, DC, 98. *Exhib:* Nat Acad Design, New York, 90, 92, 94; Signatures Above & Below, Fed Can Artists, Vancouver, 92; In the Grand Tradition, Nat Arts Club, Fairfield, Conn, 94; Nat Taiwan Art Educ Inst, Taipei, 94; Watercolor USA, Springfield Art Mus, Mo; Butler Inst Am Art, Youngstown, Ohio; Art in the Garden, EPCOT Ctr, Orlando, 2000. *Pos:* vpres, La Art & Artists Guild, 65-66, pres, 66-67; owner, Aquarelle Art Sems, 77-. *Teaching:* chair dept art, E Ascension Sr High, Gonzales, La, 66-84; mem watercolor staff, Arrowmont Sch, Univ Tenn, 91-96. *Awards:* Purchase award, Watercolor USA, 80; Mary Pleisner Mem Award, AWS, 86; Obrig Prize, Nat Acad Design, 94. *Bibliog:* George A Magnan (auth), Judi Betts: Watercolors, Today's Art, 79; PJ Gentile (author), Les Ateliers de Judy Betts, Magazin' Art, 90; Randolph Delehanty (auth), Art in the American South, LSU Press, 96. *Mem:* AWS (bd dir 91-); Watercolor USA & Hon Soc; Nat Arts Club; hon mem Fed Can Artists; hon mem Soc Can de l'aquarelle. *Media:* Watercolor. *Publ:* auth, Watercolor.Let's Think About It, Aquarelle Press, 84, The Watercolor Page, Am Artist, 87 & Watercolor Magic-Take It Off!, Artists' Mag, 94; co-auth, Painting.A Quest Toward Xtraord!nary, Aquarelle Press, 99; auth, A Luminous Start, Artists' Mag, 2000. *Dealer:* Taylor Clark Galleries 2623 Government St Baton Rouge LA 70806. *Mailing Add:* PO Box 3676 Baton Rouge LA 70821-3676

BEUZENBURG, RON
SCULPTOR
b Buffalo, NY, 50. *Study:* NY Univ, MA (art), 86; Rochester Inst of Tech, BA (sci), 73. *Exhib:* Butler Inst Am Art, Youngstown, Ohio; Brookgreen Gardens, SC; Wash Ballet; group exhib, Sculptors Alliance The Broome St Gallery, SoHo, NY, 2000, The Allied Artists of Am, Butler Inst Am Art, Youngstown, Ohio, 2001, Angels, Cupids & Creatures of Winged Fantasy, Nat Sculpture Soc, New York City, 2002, The Hudson Valley Art Asn, 2003, 106th Ann Exhib Artist Mem, Exhib of Nat Arts Club, New York, City, 2004. *Awards:* Gold Medal of Hon, Allied Artists Am, 97 & 2003; Nat Sculpture Soc, 99 & 2001; Nat Arts Club, 2001. *Mem:* Nat Sculpture Soc; Nat Arts Club; Audubon Artists; Artists' Fel (bd trustees, currently); Allied Artists Am (dir

sculpture, currently). *Media:* Terra Cotta, Bronze. *Publ:* contribr, 90th Annual (exhib catalog), Allied Artists Am, 2003; contribr, Annual (exhib catalog), Nat Sculpture Soc, 97, 99 & 2001; contribr, 53rd Annual (exhib catalog), Audubon Artists. *Dealer:* 515 Greenwich St Studio 413 NY NY. *Mailing Add:* 405 E 14th St apt 1A New York NY 10009

BEVERIDGE, KARL J
PHOTOGRAPHER
b Ottawa, Ont, Nov 7, 45. *Study:* Ont Col Art, 65-66; New Sch, Toronto, Ont, 66-67. *Work:* Nat Gallery Can & Can Coun Art Bank, Ottawa, Ont; Art Gallery Ont, Toronto; Owens Art Gallery, Sackville, NB; Stedelijk Mus, Amsterdam; Nat Photog Collection, Pub Archives of Can. *Exhib:* Social Criticism & Art Practice, San Francisco Art Inst, Calif, 77; one-man shows, Cepa Gallery, Buffalo, NY, ICA, London, 83, MIA Gallery, Stockholm, 88, Mus Folkswang, Essen, WGer, 88, Hippolyte Gallery, Helsinki, 89, Neue Gesellschaft fur Bildenda Kunst, WBerlin, 89, Museu de Arte Contemporanea, Sao Paulo, Brazil, 94; group exhibs, Lettering in Photog, Centre Nat de la Photographie, Polais de Tokyo, Paris, 89 4eme Triennale Int de la Photographie a Charleroi, Musee de la Photographie, Centre d'Art Contemporain, Charleroi, Belg, 90, Fotobiennal 1990 Vigo, Spain, 90 & Fotografie Biennale Rotterdam, Wilhelminakade, Rotterdam, 90, Pub Domain: Santa Monica Art Centre, Barcelona, 94; Centre Cult Triangle Rennes, France, 91; Museet For Fotokunst Odense, Denmark, 92; Cepa Gallery, Buffalo, NY, 2000; Edmonton Art Gallery, Alberta, Can, 2003; Taxis Pazais, Innsbruck, Austria, 2005; Lewis Glucksman Gallery, Cork, Ireland, 2006; and others. *Pos:* Ed, Fox Mag, New York, 76; ed, Red Herring Mag, New York, 77-78; ed, Centerfold/Fuse Mag, Toronto, 79-80. *Teaching:* Instr, NS Col Art & Design, Halifax, 75-76; Ontario Col Art & Design, 90-2003. *Awards:* Can Coun grants, 68-71, 76, 79, 81-82, 86-87. *Bibliog:* Irene Berggren (auth), New Documentary, Bildtidningen, #41, Stockholm, 89; David Evans & Sylvia Gohl (auths), Photomontage: A Political Weapon, Gordon Fraser, London, 86; Dot Tuer (auth), It's still privileged art, in Nina Felshin (ed), "But is it art", Bay Press, Seattle, 94. *Mem:* Can Artists Representation (chmn, 79-80). *Media:* Digital Photography. *Collection:* It's Still privileged Art, 75, Work in Progress, 80, No Immediate Threat, 85, Free Expression, 89, Non Hábera Nada Para Ninquen, 94, Not a Care, 99, Theatre of Operations, 2000, Calling the Shots, 2002. *Publ:* Auth, Standing Up, Toronto, 86; First Contract, Between the Lines Press, Toronto, 86; Class Work, Communications and Electrical Workers of Canada, Toronto, 90; In the Corporate Shadows, Leonardo, 94; Telling Stories, Questions of Address, Walter Phillips Gallery Publ, Banff Centre. *Mailing Add:* 131 Bathurst St Toronto ON M5V 2R2 Canada

BEVERLAND, JACK E
PAINTER
b Idaho Falls, Idaho, May 15, 39. *Study:* Self taught. *Work:* Oldsmar Arts in Pub Places, Fla; Mus Am Folk Art, OK Harris Gallery, NY; Kennedy Ctr Very Special Arts, Washington, DC & Beverly Hills, Calif; Artists Unlimited, Tampa, Fla; Hillsborough Co, Fla; Mennellon Mus, Orlando, Fla; 5 paintings, Jan Kaminis Platt Regional Libr, Tampa, Fla; Tampa Int Airport, 2005-2006. *Comn:* Painting, City Hall, City of Oldsmar, Fla, 95; painting, Vero Beach Ctr Art, Fla, 96 & 97; painting, Nat Mus Health & Med, Washington, DC, 97; Mennellon Mus, Orlando, Fla; Tampa Mayor's Beautification prog, 2002-2006; poster artist, Art for Life & Project Return, 2006. *Exhib:* African-Am, African Am Mus, Dallas, 95; Minority Enterprises Educ for Tomorrow, Tampa, 95; Juried Exhib, Fla Ctr Contemp Art, Tampa, 95; Benefit, McKee Botanical Garden, Vero Beach, Fla, 96-98; Folk Fest 97, Atlanta, 97; Festival of Arts, Northport, Ala, 97-2006; Challenged Children Art, 97-99; Hillsborough Co, Fla, 98, Mennellon Mus, Orlando, Fla, 2000-06; Tampa Mus of Arts, Fla, 2000; one-man shows, Gov Jeb Bush, Capital Bldg, Tallahassee, Fla, 2002, Cummer Mus, Jacksonville, Fla, 2005 & Thomas Ctr, Gainesville, Fla, 2006. *Teaching:* instr, Art Students Unltd Regional Schs, Hillsborough & Tampa, Fla & Pasco County, Fla. *Awards:* Emerging Artist Grant, Hillsborough Co, 95; Purchase Award, Vero Beach Ctr Arts, 95; Very Special Arts Fla Outstanding Contributions, 98-2000; First Place, Princeton Med Ctr, 2003-2006, Best of Show, 2005-2006. *Bibliog:* Erika Duckworth (auth), One for folk art, St Petersburg Times, 95; Leslie L Neumann, Folk Art Finder, Florence Laffal Publ, 95; Untrained Folk Artists, St Petersburg Times, 99; Life, Tuscaloosa News, 99; Folk Art, Tampa Tribune, 2000; Pasco News, 2000; Kristin G Congdon & Tina Bucuvalas (coauths), Just Above the Water, Univ Press Miss, 2006; Gary Monroe (auth), Extraordinary Interpretations, 2006. *Mem:* Folk Art Soc Am; Very Special Art Nat. *Media:* Acrylic on Board. *Publ:* Contribr, Fla Living Mag, 98; Very Special Arts 25th Anniversary Bk, 99. *Dealer:* Erin Friedbert Art-in-Sight 4837 SW 91 Dr Gainesville FL 32608; Charlotte Terry 3507 Ocean Dr Vero Beach FL 32963

BEVLIN, MARJORIE ELLIOTT
PAINTER, WRITER
b The Dalles, Ore, May 9, 17. *Study:* Univ Colo, BFA; Univ Wash, Col Archit; NY Univ, MS; studied with Jimmy Ernst, 56. *Comn:* Two murals, Otero Jr Col, La Junta, Colo, 55. *Exhib:* Brit Women's Exhib, Liverpool, 64; 8th Ann Prix de Deauville, France, 72; Prix de Rome, 72; one-man shows, Colo, 75, Orcas Island, 81-94. *Pos:* Founding chmn fine arts, Otero Jr Col, 55-75; dir & founder, Ark Valley Sch Arts Festival, 56-75. *Teaching:* Instr fine arts, Otero Jr Col, 55-75. *Awards:* Selectionée de Jury, Prix de Deauville, 72. *Mem:* Nat Asn Women Artists; Delta Phi Delta (vpres Rho Chap, 38). *Media:* Mixed Media, Watercolor, Acrylic. *Res:* All areas of design; drawings at Cabinet des Dessins, The Louvre, Albertina Gallery, Vienna. *Interests:* Illuminated ms gardening. *Publ:* Auth, Design Through Discovery, Harcourt Brace, 6th ed, 93; Design Through Discovery: The Elements and Principles, Harcourt Brace, 2nd Ed, 93; contribr numerous prof journals. *Mailing Add:* 1248 Discovery Way Eastsound WA 98245

BEYER, STEVEN J
SCULPTOR, ADMINISTRATOR
b Minneapolis, Minn, Aug 27, 51. *Study:* Macalester Col, St Paul, Minn, BA, 73. *Work:* Whitney Mus Am Art, NY; Walker Art Ctr & Minneapolis Inst Art, Minn; Newport Harbor Art Mus, Newport Beach, Calif; Madison Art Ctr, Wis; Chicago Art Inst. *Comn:* Sculpture, City St Paul, Park Bd, Minn, 75; sculpture, Spring Hill Conference Ctr, Wayzata, Minn, 77; sculpture, General Mills Corp, Minneapolis, Minn, 78; sculpture, Northern Ill Univ, DeKalb, 81; Pacific Enterprises, Los Angeles, Calif. *Exhib:* Recent Acquisitions, Walker Art Ctr, Minneapolis, Minn, 79; Artists and Printer, Walker Art Ctr, Minneapolis, Minn, 80; Words as Images, Univ Chicago, Ill, 81; Comparaisons, Grand Palais, Paris, France, 84; Mile 4, Chicago Sculpture Int, Chicago, Il, 85; solo & group exhibs, Diane Brown Gallery, 86, 88, 89 & 90; Atlantic Sculpture, Art Ctr, Pasadena, Calif, 87; A Matter of Time, Pa Acad Fine Arts, Philadelphia, 88; Diane Brown Gallery, 86, 88, 89 & 90; Rope, Christian Leigh, Barcelona, Spain, 91; The Fabric Workshop, Philadelphia, 91; Lawrence Oliver, Philadelphia, 91; Kunsthall Gallery, NY, 92. *Collection Arranged:* Sexuality; The play of the World, an Evening of Performance, CAA Ann Conference, New York, 86; Atlantic Sculpture, Art Ctr, Pasadena, Calif, 87. *Pos:* Asst artistic dir, Fabric Workshop & Mus, Philadelphia, currently. *Teaching:* Vis artist sculpture, Kansas City Art Inst, Mo, 79; vis assoc prof sculpture, Univ Iowa, Iowa City, 79-81; instr sculpture, Minneapolis Col Art & Design, 81-82; assoc prof sculpture, Tyler Sch Art, Philadelphia, Pa, 84-90 & head sculpture dept, 86-90. *Awards:* Nat Endowment Arts Fel, 81 & 88; Bush Found Fel, 82; Pew Fels Arts Grant, 91 & 93. *Bibliog:* Articles, Midwest Art & Art Am, 79; Bob Arnold (dir), Family Systems (film), 81. *Mem:* Col Art Asn Am. *Res:* Kitsch as it relates to the Great Sadness with continuing interest in Language, Commerce, & Sexuality. *Publ:* You Must Bend in Order to Go Through the World, (exhib catalog), Diane Brown Gallery, New York, 86; Atlantic Sculpture, Art Ctr, Pasadena, Calif, 87; Angels of Language, (exhib catalog), Crow Wing Press, Philadelphia, Pa, 88

BHAVSAR, NATVAR PRAHLADJI
PAINTER
b Gothava, India, Apr 7, 34. *Study:* Bombay State Higher Art Exam, India, AM, 58, Govt Dipl Art, 59; Gujarat Univ, India, BA, 60; Univ Pa, MFA, 65. *Work:* Whitney Mus Am Art, Metrop Mus Art, NY; Mass Inst Technol, Cambridge; Guggenheim Mus, NY; Australian Nat Gallery, Canberra; Wichita Mus Art; and others. *Exhib:* Whitney Mus Am Art Painting Ann, 70-71; Two Generations of Color Painting, Inst Contemp Art, Univ Pa, Philadelphia, 70; Beautiful Paintings & Sculpture, Jewish Mus, NY, 70; one-man shows, Max Hutchinson Gallery, NY, 71-72, 77-78, Gloria Luria Gallery, Miami, 78 & 92, ACP Vivian Ehrli Gallery, Zurich, Switz, 97& 2000, World Econ Forum, Davos, Switz, 2000 & Sundram Tagore Gallery Exhibits (catalog), 2001-02; Natvar Bhavsar-Color Experiences, 79, Twenty Yrs of Works on Paper (catalog), Wichita Art Mus, Kans, 85. *Teaching:* Art instr, Univ RI, spring semesters 67-69. *Awards:* John D Rockefeller III Fund Fel, 65-66, Guggenheim Fel, 75-76, Vishva Gurjari, Gvjarat, India, 88. *Bibliog:* Elwyn Linn (auth), article, Art Int, 4/77; Dr Irving Sandler (auth, monogr), Natvar Bhavsar, Painting and the Reality of Color, Craftsman House, G & B Arts Int, Sydney, Australia; Robert Morgen (auth, exhib catalog), Sound of Color, 2002. *Media:* Dry Pigment, Acrylic. *Dealer:* ACP Viviane Ehrli Gallery Klingen Strasse 42 8005 Zurich Switzerland; Sundaram Tagore Gallery 137 Greene St New York NY 10012. *Mailing Add:* 131 Greene St New York NY 10012

BIALLER, NANCY
Study: Vassar Col, BA; Yale Univ, MA, MPhil, PhD. *Awards:* Fulbright Fel, Vienna, 72. *Mailing Add:* Sotheby's 1334 York Ave New York NY 10021

BIALOBRODA, ANNA
PAINTER
b Lodz, Poland, 46. *Study:* Otis Art Inst, BFA, 71, MFA, 73; Whitney Mus Am Art Independent Study Prog, 73. *Work:* Albright-Knox Art Gallery, Buffalo, NY; Chemical Bank, DeBevoise & Plimpton, Capitol Holding Group, Neuberger Berman & Atlantic Bell, NY; Europ Fine Art Found, Geneva; Israel Mus, Jerusalem; Arthur Andersen & Co, Chicago, Ill; Nat Mus Warsaw, Poland; and others. *Comn:* GTE Corp, Dallas, Tex, 94. *Exhib:* Patricia Shea Gallery, Santa Monica, Calif, 92; 45th Acad Purchase Exhib, Am Acad Arts & Lett, NY, 93; Jason McCoy Inc, NY, 93; Ars Erotica, Nat Mus Warsaw, Poland, 94; Burnt Whole, traveling, Inst Contemp Art, Boston, Mass & Wash Proj for Arts, Washington, 94; Murder, Asher/Faure Gallery, Santa Monica, Calif, 94; and others. *Awards:* Nat Endowment Arts Grant, 74; NY Found Arts Grant, 91; Rockefeller Found Fel, Bellagio, Italy, 95. *Bibliog:* Eileen Myles (auth), Anna Bialobroda at Jason McCoy, Art in Am, 12/91; David Page (auth), The Hunter Hunted, Los Angeles Times, 12/31/92; Terry Myers (auth), Anna Bialobroda, Flash Art, summer 93. *Media:* Acrylic, Oil. *Publ:* Richard Hertz (auth), Theories of Contemporary Art, Prentice-Hall, Englewood Cliffs, NJ, 85; Barbara Rose, Twentieth Century American Painting, Skira-Rizzoli, Rizzoli Int Publ, New York, 86; Barbara Rose, Autocritique, Essays on Art and Anti-Art 1963-1987, Weidenfeld & Nicholson, New York, 88; Marek Bartelik, Anna Bialobroda-Exits, Galeria Krytykow Pokaz, Warsaw, Poland, 91; John Yau, Anna Bialobroda, Jason McCoy Gallery, New York, 91. *Dealer:* Patricia Shea Gallery 2042 Broadway Santa Monica CA 90404. *Mailing Add:* PO Box 20237 New York NY 10009

BIBLOS, MAHIA
SCULPTOR, DESIGNER
b Buenos Aires, Arg. *Study:* Nat Sch Fine Art, with Prilicliano Pueyrredon, BA; Sch Design, Inst Nat Fine Arts, Mex; Nat Sch Fine Art, Univ Nat Art Mod, Mex, MA. *Work:* Mus Art Contemp José Luis Cuevas, Mex City; Mus Art Contemp, Morelia, Michoacan, Mex; Casa Cult Morelia, Michoacan, Mex. *Exhib:* 4th & 5th Int Triennales of Tapestry, Cent Mus, Lödz, Poland, 81 & 85; Textil Mexicano

Contemporaneo, Ft Mason, San Francisco, 90; Mexico-Polonia-Textil Contemporaneo, Rufino Tamayo, Mex, 91; Coleccion Latino Americana, José Luis Cuevas, Mex, 92. *Pos:* Dept head, textile design & color, Sch Design, Nat Inst Fine Arts, Mex, 76-. *Awards:* Creadores Intelectuales, 91 & Proj Promote Cult, 93, Nat Found Cult Arts. *Bibliog:* Juan Acha (auth), Piel Andina (exhib catalog), Galeria Juan Martin, Mex, 86; Alicia Azuela (auth), La Magia del Tapiz, Banco, BCH, Mex, 88. *Mem:* Agrupación Mex Art Textil (vpres). *Dealer:* Galeria Juan Martin Dickens 33 letra B Col Polanco Mexico DF 11560. *Mailing Add:* Pueblo 126-2 Piso Colonia Roma Mexico DF 06700 Mexico

BICKLEY, GARY STEVEN
EDUCATOR, SCULPTOR
b Lebanon, Va, Apr 25, 53. *Study:* E Carolina Univ, BFA, 76; Univ Ga, MFA, 78. *Work:* Southeastern Ctr Contemp Art, Winston-Salem, NC; Portsmouth Community Arts Ctr, Va; City of Rockville, Md; First Nat Bank, Roanoke, Va. *Exhib:* Painting and Sculpture Today, Indianapolis Mus Art, 78; solo exhibs, Southeastern Ctr Contemp Art, Winston-Salem, NC, 78, 80 & 82; Am Drawing III, Portsmouth Fac & Smithsonian Inst, traveling, 80; Rutgers Nat Works on Paper, Stedman Art Gallery, Camden, NJ, 81; Virginia Painting and Sculpture, Va Mus Fine Arts, Richmond, 81; Clayworks, NY; Exhib 280, Huntington Galleries, WVa; 20 Sculptors Outdoor Exhib, Va Mus Fine Arts. *Teaching:* Asst prof, Va Polytech Inst & State Univ, Blacksburg, 78-; vis prof, Univ Ga, Cortona, Italy, 81. *Awards:* Ford Found Scholar, Univ Ga, 77-78; Summer Stipend, Nat Endowment Humanities, Va Polytech Inst & State Univ, 81; Work Stipend for Clayworks Workshop, Nat Endowment Arts. *Media:* Welded & Cast Metals. *Mailing Add:* Va Tech Dept Art & Art Hist 201 Draper Rd Blacksburg VA 24061-0103

BIDLO, MIKE
PAINTER, CONCEPTUAL ARTIST
b Chicago, Ill, Oct 20, 53. *Study:* Univ Ill, Chicago, BA, 73; Southern Ill Univ, MFA, 75; Teachers Col, Columbia Univ, MA, 78. *Work:* Chase Manhattan Bank & New York Stock Exchange, NY; Sezon Mus, Tokyo; Omaha Nat Bank, Nebr; Mod Mus Stockholm; Fashion Inst Technol, Univ Colo, Boulder; Phila Mus Art. *Exhib:* Grey Art Gallery, NY Univ, 89; Daniel Templon, Paris, 90; Sezon Mus, Japan, 91; Saatchi Collection, London, 91; Bruno Bischofberger Gallery, Zurich, Switz, 92, The Fountain Drawings, 98; Picasso's Women, Leo Castelli Gallery, 88; Astrup Fearnley Mus, Oslo, 02; Nat Gallery Art, Iceland, 03; Erased DeKooning Drawings, Francis Naumann Gallery, NY, 2005; and others. *Teaching:* Guest lectr, Art Ctr, Pasadena, 78, Pratt Inst, NY, 84, Univ Colo, Boulder, 85, Univ Calif, Los Angeles, 88, Otis Art Inst, Los Angeles, 88, Bard Col, 89 & State Univ Calif, Fullerton, 91, The Tate Mus, 99, Pollock Krasner Study Ctr, 99, Univ of Iceland, 03, State Univ of NY, 04. *Awards:* Fel, Nat Endowment Arts. *Bibliog:* Olivier Zahm & Joe Masheck (auths), Not Dechirico (catalog essays), Daniel Templon Gallery, 90; Thomas McEvilley & Francis Naumann (auths), Not Leger (catalogue), Bischofberger Gallery, 92; Francis Naumann, Arthur Danto & Mike Bidlo in Conversation; Robert Rosenblum (auth, Erased DeKooning Drawings (catalog essays), 2005. *Mem:* Am Art Therapy Asn (cert mem). *Media:* All. *Dealer:* Bruno Bischofberger, Zurich. *Mailing Add:* 432 W 38th St New York NY 10018-2816

BIDSTRUP, WENDY
ADMINISTRATOR
b Pittsburgh, Pa, Feb 15, 40. *Study:* Wells Col, BA, 1962. *Work:* Marion Art Ctr, Marion, Mass. *Collection Arranged:* Cecil Clark Davis: A Woman Ahead of Her Time, New Bedford Art Mus, 2002. *Pos:* exec dir, Marion Art Ctr, 84-; cur, New Bedford Art Mus, New Bedford, Mass, summer 2002. *Teaching:* art history lectr, Tabor Acad, Marion, Mass, 74-86. *Bibliog:* David B Boyce (auth) Cecil Clark Davis, The Standard Times, summer, 2002; Paul Kandarian (auth), Cecil Clark Davis, The Boston Globe, 8/2002; John Robeson, Cecil Clark Davis (documentary, in progress). *Mem:* Nat Mus Women in the Arts; Sippican Hist & Preserv Soc. *Mailing Add:* Marion Art Center 80 Pleasant St Box 602 Marion MA 02738

BIEDERMAN, JAMES MARK
PAINTER, SCULPTOR
b New York, NY, Nov 8, 47. *Study:* Whitney Mus Independent Study prog; Yale Univ, MFA, 73. *Work:* Kroller-Muller Riks Mus, Otterlo, Netherlands; Pompidou Ctr, Paris; Mus Mod Art & Metrop Mus Art, NY; Mus Contemp Art, Chicago; Hirshhorn Mus, Washington, DC. *Comn:* Wall sculpture, Home Box Off, NY, 85. *Exhib:* Sculpture, Clocktower Gallery, NY, 81; 2nd Int Jugend, Kunsthalle, Nuremberg, WGer, 82; Choix Pour Aujourd'hui, Ctr Pompidou, Paris, 82; Documenta 7, Kassel, WGer, 82; Kunstmuseum Aalborg & Rander, Denmark, 83; Mus Mod Art, NY; Triennale, Musee Cantonal des Beaux Arts, Lausanne, Switz; Geometric Abstraction, Bronx Mus, NY, 85. *Teaching:* Vis artist sculpture, Boston Mus Sch, 83 & Yale Univ, formerly; painting, NY Univ, 84-86; Hofstra Univ, 98-. *Awards:* Nat Endowment Arts Drawing Award, 79 & Sculpture Award, 82; Painting Award, New York Found Arts, 86; Adolph and Esther Gottlieb Found Grant, 2005. *Bibliog:* Ronnie Cohn (auth), rev, Art Forum, 4/83; Himmel Freeman (auth), New Art, Harry Abrams, 84; Curt Barnes (ed), Constructed PTH, Art J, spring 91; and others. *Media:* Oil on Linen, Oil on Wood. *Dealer:* John Weber Gallery 142 Greene St New York 10012; Galerie Winkelman Neubruckstabe 12 Dusseldorf Fed Repub Ger

BIELER, TED ANDRE
EDUCATOR, SCULPTOR
b Kingston, Ont, July 23, 38. *Study:* Sculpture with Ossip Zadkine, Paris, 53; tapestry with Jean Lurcat, St Cere, France, 54; Slade Sch Art, London, 54; Cranbrook Acad Art, BFA, 61. *Work:* Montreal Mus Fine Arts; Can Coun, Ottawa; Univ Toronto; Agnes Etherington Art Centre, Queen's Univ, Kingston; McMaster Univ; York Univ; Nat Capital Comn, Ottawa, Ont; Univ Windsor, Ont; McMullen Mus, Boston Col, Chestnut Hill, Mass; Georgetown Univ, Lauinger Libr, Washington, DC; New England Col Gallery, Henniker, NH; Sir Wilfred Grenfell Col Art Gallery, Corner Brook, Nfld. *Comn:* Star-Cross'd (sculpture ballet set), comn by Brian MacDonald, Ottawa, 73; stainless steel sculpture, Forensic Sci Bldg, Govt Ont, 75; aluminum tetrahedra sculpture, Portsmouth Harbour, Kingston, Govt Can, 75; sculpture for Govt of Can Bldg, comn by Macy Dubois & Shore Tilbe Henschel Irwin, Architects, Toronto, 77; cast aluminum relief sculpture for Wilson Sta, comn by Spadina Subway Line, Toronto, 78; Boat Bridge (laminated birch relief wall), Govt Ont Bldg, Kingston, 84; Wave Breaking (cast bronze sculpture), Can Chancery, Dept External Affairs, 91; Tower Song (cast aluminum sculpture), Windsor Sculpture Garden, Ont, 98; and others. *Exhib:* Signs & Symbols, Art Gallery Ont Traveling Show, 71; Rehearsal, Harbourfront Art Gallery, Toronto, 77; one-man shows, York Univ, 77, Univ Rochester, 77, Geraldine Davis Gallery, Toronto, 86, Lindsay Gallery, Ont, 89, Vessels: bronze sculptures, Geraldine Davis Gallery, Toronto, 89, Drawings from the Lake, Faculty Club, York Univ, 89; Columns, Valuts, Bridges and Other Sculptures, Glendon Gallery, Toronto, 91; Performance, Harbourfront Art Gallery, Toronto, Ont, 78; Monumental Sculpture, Toronto Dominion Ctr, 78; Artists with their Children, Art Gallery at Harbourfront, Toronto, Ont, 83; York Work, York Univ, Downsview, Ont, 86; The Building of Architectural Vision, City Gallery, NY, 87; Firing the Imagination: Artists & Architects Use Clay, Urban Ctr Gallery, NY & Bennington Col, Vt; Shadows Grow Longer, Ofrenda, Days of the Dead Installation, Harbourfront, Toronto, 94. *Pos:* dir, Graduate Studio Program Visual Arts, York Univ, Toronto, 80-83 & 86-90, chmn, Dept Visual Arts, 87-90; coordr, Odette Ctr for Sculpture, York Univ, 90-91. *Teaching:* Prof fine arts, York Univ, Toronto, 69-. *Awards:* Allied Arts Medal, Royal Archit Asn Can, 69; Can Silver Jubilee Medal. *Bibliog:* L Sabbath (auth), Sculpture in Canada, 62 & H McPherson (auth), Scope of Sculpture, 64, Can Art; William Withrow (auth), Canadian Sculpture, Graph, Montreal, 67; R Burnett & M Schiff (coauths), Contemporary Canadian Art, Hurtig Publ, 83. *Mem:* Royal Can Acad Arts (mem coun, 75-77); Int Sculpture Ctr, Lawrence, Kans; The Sculpture Garden, Toronto (bd dir, 84-). *Mailing Add:* Visual Arts Dept Room 232 CFA York Univ 4700 Keele St North York ON M3J 1P3 Canada

BIELTVEDT, ARNOR G
PAINTER, INSTRUCTOR
b Akureyri, Iceland, May 25, 63. *Study:* Univ Ger, Vordiploma, 1987; Johnson & Wales Univ, BS, MS, 1989; RI Sch of Design, BFA, 1992; Wash Univ, MFA, 1994. *Work:* Reykjavic Art Mus, Reykjavic, Iceland; N Shore Community House, Winnetka, Ill; N Shore Art League, Winnetka, Ill; Embassy of Iceland, Tokyo, Japan; Embassy of Iceland, London, Eng. *Comn:* Homescapes, Anne Loucks Gallery; Portraits of Home & Portraits of People, Glencoe, Ill, 2002-. *Exhib:* 175th Anniversary, Galeri Commeter, Hamburg, Ger, 1996; Viking Celebration, Icelandic Embassy, Wash, DC, 2000; Biennial Int Juried Exhib, Brad Cooper Gallery, Tampa, Fla, 2004; Still Life Contemp Visions, Anne Loucks Gallery, Glencoe, Ill, 2004; Light & Carriers of Light, Icelandic Graphic Mus, Reykjavik, 2005. *Teaching:* Instr art dept head, Logos Sch, St Louis, Mo, 1994-2001; Instr art dept head & Gallery Dir, N Shore Country Day Sch Winnetka, Ill, 2001-. *Bibliog:* Leslie Korengold (auth) Creating Life from Stillness, N Shore Home, 2003; Vala Bergsveinsdotter (auth) Still a Youngster In Art, Morning Paper (Iceland), 2005; Ragna Siguroardottir (auth) Play with Live & Color, Morning Paper (Iceland), 2005. *Mem:* N Shore Art League, Winnetka, Ill. *Mailing Add:* 211 Woodlawn Ave Winnetka IL 60093-1552

BIERBAUM, GRETCHEN ANN
COLLAGE ARTIST, EDUCATOR
b Cheyenne, Wyo, Mar 25, 42. *Study:* Kent State Univ, BA, 64, MA, 68; Pahlavi Univ, Iran, 71-72. *Work:* N Coast Galleries, Hudson, Ohio. *Comn:* Commemorative painting, Hudson Libr & Hist Soc, Ohio, 85; univ campus collage, Kent State Univ, Ohio, 92; biographical collage of the founder of the Akron Conv & Visitors Bur, Ohio, 94; corp collage, Michelin Tire Co, Akron, Ohio, 94; and others. *Exhib:* 42nd Ann Show, Butler Inst Am Art, Youngstown, Ohio, 80; 5th Ann Midwest Watercolor Soc Show, Burpee Mus, Rockford, Ill, 81; Barker Gallery, Palm Beach, Fla, 82; 52nd Ann Exhib, Butler Inst Am Art, Youngstown, Ohio, 90; and others. *Pos:* Docent, Kent State Univ Art Gallery, Ohio, 78-79; auth & ed, North Coast Collage Soc Newslett Quart, 84-90. *Teaching:* Instr watercolor, Univ Akron, Ohio, 79-81; painting at international workshops in Panama & the British West Indies, 93-94. *Awards:* Ruppel Award, Ohio Watercolor Soc Ann, Ruppel's Co, 79; First Place, Solon Show, Anixter-Cleveland Inc, 81; Purchase Award, Westerville Art Festival, Otterbein Col, Marketing Serv Inc, 84. *Bibliog:* Helen Cullinan (auth), North coast: Collage mecca, The Plain Dealer, 89; Don Breedlove (auth), Artists of Ohio the Fine Arts Catalogue, Mountain Productions Inc, 93; Virginia Williams (auth), Creative Collage Techniques, North Light Books, 94. *Mem:* N Coast Collage Soc Inc (founder/pres, 84-); Hudson Soc Artists (pres, 80-81). *Media:* Watercolor. *Mailing Add:* 254 W Streetsboro St Akron OH 44236

BIERMAN, IRENE A
EDUCATOR
b Bogota, NJ. *Study:* Harvard Univ, MA, 66; Univ Chicago, PhD, 80. *Collection Arranged:* The Warp & Weft of Islam (auth catalog), Seattle, Portland & Tocoma, Reno, 79; The Common Cord, Seattle Art Mus, 86; Permanent Near East Collection, Seattle Art Mus. *Teaching:* Vis lectr Islamic art hist, Univ Wash, Seattle, 76-80; prof Islamic art hist, Univ Calif, Los Angeles, 82-. *Awards:* Fel, Ctr for Advanced Study in the Visual Arts, 81-83; Fel, Am Res Ctr Egypt, 80-81; Fulbright-Hays Fel to Egypt & Turkey, 81-82. *Mem:* Col Art Asn; Middle East Studies Asn; Am Oriental Soc; Am Res Ctr Egypt; NAm Hist Islamic Art. *Res:* Public arts in the Islamic world with emphasis on the Mediterranean areas. *Publ:* Coauth, The Warp & Weft of Islam, Univ Washington, 78; auth, The Message of Urban Space: The Case of Crete, Espace et Sociétée; Oriental Carpets, In: Decorative Arts & Household Furnishings Used in Am,

Winterthur Mus, 86; co-auth, Symbols of Islam, Univ Wash Int Studies, 86; auth, The fatimid public text, In: Actes, Congres International de l'Histoire de l'arte XXVI, 86; co-ed, Urban Structure and Social Order: The Ottoman City and its Parts, Caratzas Bros, New York, 91. *Mailing Add:* 1236 Wellesley Ave Los Angeles CA 90095-1139

BIFERIE, DAN (DANIEL) ANTHONY, JR
PHOTOGRAPHER, EDUCATOR
b Miami, Fla, Dec 17, 50. *Study:* Daytona Beach Community Col, AS(with honors), 71; Ohio Univ, BFA(summa cum laude), 72, MFA, 74. *Work:* High Mus; New Orleans Mus Art; Baltimore Mus Art; Santa Barbara Mus Art; Bibliotheque Nationale, Paris; Nat Mus Am Art. *Comn:* Art in Public Places Commission New Smyrna; Beach Regional Libr, 99. *Exhib:* One-man show, Albany Mus Art, 86, Lakeland's Unique Architectural Heritage, Polk Mus Art, Fla, 87, Southeast Mus Photog, 94; Four Photographers, Mass Inst Technol, Boston, 76; Fla Light Invitational, Orlando Mus Art, Fla, 79; Four Southeastern Photographers, Contemp Arts Ctr, New Orleans, La, 81; Contemp Photog as Phantasy (with catalog), Santa Barbara Mus Art, 82-83; Fact & Fiction: The State of Fla Photog (traveling exhib), Norton Gallery Art, West Palm Beach, Fla, 90; Digital Am, Orlando Mus of Art, 98; Dan Biferie, Digital/Photogr Traveling Exhib, 99-2001; Fla Individual Artists Fellowship Program, 25th Ann Traveling Exhib, Cummer Mus of Art, Jacksonville, Fla, 2002-2004. *Pos:* Found, Gallery Fine Arts, Daytona Beach Community Col, Fla, 78-90, chmn visual arts dept, 85-88; pres, Arts Coun Volusia Co, 91-95. *Teaching:* Sr prof, Daytona Beach Community Col, Fla, 75-. *Awards:* Our Children to the South Photo-documentary project Grant, Fla, Int Alliance, 85; Lakelands Architectural Heritage, Photo-documentary Grant, Polk Mus Art; Fla Endowment for the Humantities; Individual Artists Fel, Fla Div of Cult Affairs, 96-97. *Bibliog:* Lakeland's Unique Architectural Heritage (exhib catalog) Polk Mus Art, 87; The New Movement, Focal Point Press, 87; Churchscapes in Black & White (studio photog), 88; Digital Photogr, Greece, 98; Digital Fine Artists Mag, 2000; The Digital Da-Kloom US Art Gallery Mag, 10/2001. *Mem:* Soc Photog Educ (pres 77-84); Daytona Beach Community Col Photog Soc (founder & pres 79-81); Am Asn Mus. *Media:* Silver Print. *Res:* History and criticism of photography, photographic aesthetics. *Interests:* Photogr, Art Education, Film, Antiques, Religious Artifacts. *Collection:* National Mus of Am Art, Smithsonian Inst Washington, DC; Bibliothegue Nationale, Paris, France; New Orleans Mus of Art La; High Mus of Art, Atlanta, Ga. *Publ:* Contribr, Photographic Annual, Middle Tenn State Univ, 75; Florida Light, Loch Haven Art Ctr, 79; Photographers Forum, Darkroom Section, 81; Photography in Florida, Catskill Ctr for Photog Quart Mag, 85; Churchscapes, Studio Photog, 88; Dreaming in B & W Photo's Electronic Imaging Mag, 96. *Mailing Add:* 333 S Dexter Ave Deland FL 32720-5005

BIGELOW, ANITA (ANNE) (EDWIGE LOURIE)
GRAPHIC ARTIST, PRINTMAKER
b Los Angeles, Calif, Mar 3, 46. *Study:* Reed Col, with Lloyd Reynolds & Willard Midgette, BA, 67; San Francisco Art Inst, with Jack Stauffacher & Gerry Gooch: Portland State Univ, MA, 75; Portland Community Col, AA, 85. *Work:* Lloyd Reynolds Collection, Portland Mus Art, Ore. *Comn:* Bookplates (set of 4), comn by Mary Barnard, Vancouver, Wash, 79-81; bookplates (set of 10), Reed Col Libr, Portland, Ore, 81; bookplates (set of 2), Boston Atheneum, Mass, 82. *Exhib:* Contemp Ex-Libris 1980-1982, XIX Int Ex-Libris Cong, Oxford, Eng, 82; The World of Ex Libris, Belgrade, 95. *Mem:* Portland Boat Club; US Rowing. *Media:* Woodcut, Linoleum Cut; Pastel, Pencil. *Publ:* Illusr, Mississippi Mud and various articles-items, Joel Weinstein, 82-86; Time and the White Tigress, B Breitenbush Books, 86. *Mailing Add:* 1825 SE Exeter Dr Portland OR 97202

BIGGS, JOHN HERRON
PATRON
b St Louis, July 19, 36. *Study:* Harvard Univ, AB (magna cum laude), 1958; Wash Univ, PhD, 1983. *Pos:* Vpres, Gen Am Ins Co, 1970-77; vice chancellor for admin and finance, Washington Univ, St Louis, 1977-85; chmn, pres, chief exec officer, Centerre Trust Co, 1985-89; pres, Chief Operating Officer, Teachers Ins and Annuity Asn/Col Retirement Equities Fund, 1989-93, chmn, pres, Chief Exec Officer, 1993-2002; Bd dir, Boeing Co, JP Morgan Chase Co; emer trustee, pres, formerly, Mo Botanical Garden; bd dir, chmn, Nat. Bur Econ Affairs, formerly; trustee Wash Univ; chmn bd trustees, J Paul Getty Trust; emer trustee, Foreign Policy Asn; trustee Danforth Found; bd dir, chmn, United Way New York City, formerly. *Mem:* Soc of Actuaries; Coun Foreign Relations; St Louis Club; Harvard Club NY; Sky Club; Westchester Country Club

BILDER, DOROTHEA A
PRINTMAKER, PAINTER
b Dayton, Ohio, Oct 4, 40. *Study:* Ill Wesleyan Univ, BFA, 62; Southern Ill Univ, Carbondale, MFA, 64. *Work:* Portland Art Inst, Ore; Columbia Col/Mo Arts Coun, Columbia, Mo; Art Inst Chicago, Ill; Fine Arts Mus Long Island, Hempstead, NY; Cincinnati Art Mus, Ohio. *Comn:* Ymagos Atelier di Arte, Ltda, Sao Paulo, Brazil. *Exhib:* Solo shows, Monotypes & Lithographs, Lee Scarfone Gallery, Univ Tampa, Fla, 90, Prints & Works on Paper, Marbeck Ctr Gallery, Bluffton Col, Ohio, 90, Fragments/Painting on Canvas, Gallery 1792, Winter Park, Fla, 93, Hellenic Mus & Cult Ctr, Chicago, 93, Recent Print Work, Expressions Graphics, Oak Park, Ill, 98; 12th Ann Paper in Particular, Nat Exhib Works on/off Paper, Columbia Col & Mo Arts Coun, Columbia, Mo, 91; Look at the World Through Women's Eyes, NGO Forum on Women, United Nat 4th World Conf on Women & Nat Mus Women Arts, Washington, DC, 96; 9th Nat Drawing & Print Competitive Exhib, Col Notre Dame of Md, Gormely Gallery, Baltimore, 97; 10th Ann Nat Exhib Fine Art by Women, Old Courthouse Arts Ctr, NW Area Arts Coun, Woodstock Sq, Ill, 97; Nat Print Exhib Celebrating 200 Yrs of Lithography, Xavier Univ, Dept Art, Cincinnati, Ohio, 98; 15th Nat Biennial Exhib, Los Angels Printmaking Soc, Laband Art Gallery, Loyola Marymount Univ, Los Angeles, 99; over 96 Int & Nat Exhibs. *Pos:* Artist in Residence, Red Deer Col, Alta, Can, 89 & 94. *Teaching:* Prof drawing & printmaking, Northern Ill Univ, De Kalb, 68-; instr printmaking, Penland Sch Crafts, NC, summers 70-80. *Awards:* Merit Award, Emerging Woman Artist Nat, Ind Univ, 87. *Mem:* Col Art Asn; Southern Graphics Coun; Art Inst Alumni Asn; Print Consortium; Chicago Women's Caucas Art. *Media:* Serigraphy, Lithography; Oil, Pastel. *Publ:* Auth & illusr, Silk Screening Printing, In: Art, Fuller & Dees/Times Mirror Co, 74. *Dealer:* Glatt, Sao Paulo & Rio de Janiero Brazil. *Mailing Add:* 2707 Greenwood Acres Dr De Kalb IL 60115

BILLECI, ANDRE GEORGE
SCULPTOR, EDUCATOR
b New York, NY, Dec 2, 33. *Study:* State Univ NY Col of Ceramics, Alfred, BFA(ceramics; cum laude), 60, MFA(ceramic art), 61. *Work:* Corning Mus of Glass, NY; Toledo Mus Art; Australian Nat Gallery, Canberra; Galleries Nat de Prague, Czech; Mus fur Kunsthandwerk, Frankfurt, Ger. *Comn:* Glass sculptures, Penn Mutual Life Insurance, 84 & El Du Pont de Nemours, 85. *Exhib:* One-man shows, Mus Contemp Crafts, NY, 70, Corning Mus Glass, 72, NY State Col Ceramics & Alfred Univ, 80; Reflection, Long Beach Mus Art, Calif, 71; Int Glass Sculpture, Huntington Galleries, WVa, 76; Glassmaking & Purchase Exhib, Corning Mus Glass, 76; and others. *Pos:* Artist-in-residence, Blenko Art Glass Co, Milton, WVa, 71 & Steuben Glass Co, Corning, NY, 72; consult, Mary McFadden Inc, NY, 80 & Corning Mus Glass, India Proj, 86-87, 97 & 99; IESC consult, Vitra Sa, Quetzaltenango, Guatemala, 88 & Argucia & Martinez Crafts, Tegucigalpa, Honduras, 89, UNICEF consult, Blue Glass Proj, Herat, Afghanistan, 93; IESC consult, The Valley Forge, Harare, Zimbabwe, 96. *Teaching:* Prof sculpture & glass, State Univ NY Col, Alfred, 61-89 & Summer Sch, Sheridan Col of Applied Arts & Technol, Toronto, Ont, 7; lectr, Cleveland Art Inst, 78, Carnegie-Mellon Univ, 78, Univ Ill, Champaign-Urbana, 79 & Univ Wis, 81; lectr, Fundacion Centro del Vidrio, La Granja, Spain & Centre del Vidre de Barcelona, Spain, 90; Glass Seminar, Glass Technol for Artists, State Univ NY, Col Ceramics, Alfred, 91, lectr, Elderhostel Prog on Ceramic Arts, 92; retired, currently. *Awards:* Corning Glass Found Grant, 76; Res Grant, Inst Glass Sci & Eng, Mt Athos, Greece, 87; NY State Found Arts Award, 89. *Mem:* Int Sculpture Ctr; Am Ceramic Soc; Int Comn Glass, Comt XVII. *Media:* Glass; Mixed. *Publ:* Auth, Electric Melting Unit for Covered Melting, Corning Mus of Glass, 76; Annealing Glasses & Understanding Glass Calculations, Glass Studio Mag Publ Develop Corp, 78 & 79. *Mailing Add:* 4461 8th Ln Vero Beach FL 32968-4154

BILLIAN, CATHEY R
ENVIRONMENTAL ARTIST, EDUCATOR
b Chicago, Ill. *Study:* Art Inst Chicago, Univ Ariz, BFA; Pratt Inst, fel, MFA (summa cum laude), 78. *Work:* Philadelphia Mus Art; NY Pub Libr Print Collection; Morris Mus; Norton Simon Inc & Chem Bank, NY; Brooklyn Mus; Nat Park Serv; City of Phoenix, Ariz; US Forest Serv; Libr Congress; Smithsonian Inst; pvt collection former vice-pres Al Gore; plus others. *Comn:* Sculpture, Creative Time, Battery Park, NY, 81; light, sculpture & dance environment, Whitney Mus, 84; sculpture, Prospect Park, NY, 85; archit sculpture, US Forest Serv: Southwest Region, 90- & City of Phoenix, 92. *Exhib:* Recent Trends in Light, Morris Mus, 83 & Hofstra Univ (with catalog), 83; Stopped Time, Four Projected Environments, Sculpture Ctr, NY & Rockland Ctr Arts (with catalog), 84; Recent Acquisitions/Louis Comfort Tiffany Found Purchase, Brooklyn Mus, NY; Cathey Billian, Michael Graves, Charles Simonds at Liberty State Park, Jersey City Mus, (with catalog); NY Experimental Glass, Soc Art Craft, Pittsburgh, Pa (with catalog); Luminous Visions, FIT Gallery, NY (with catalog); Four Sculptors from the NY Experimental Glassworks, Nina Owen Ltd, Chicago, Ill; one-woman shows, Cross-Cut Piedra Lumbre, Pratt Inst Gallery, NY, Frozen Moments, Gallery of NY Experimental Glassworks, Future Antiquities, Whitney Mus Sculpture Court, NY, Omi Int Arts Ctr, Fields Sculpture Park, Columbia Co, NY & Mary Boone Gallery, NY. *Collection Arranged:* Knowing Limits, Travelling Exhib of Poetry & Art, 2000-01. *Pos:* Consult, Artpark, NY; NY & NJ State Coun Arts, 82-; artist-in-residence, NY Experimental Glassworks; Bob Blackburn's Printmaking Workshop, NY, Nat Park Serv, Utah, Del Water Gap, Yellowstone Nat Park & Dept Interior, NMex; ed bd & corresp, Pub Art Rev; dir, Wild America; interdisciplinary environmental art initiatives & design rsch with Nat Parks and Arts Cols including Univ Arts & Cooper Union, 97-. *Teaching:* Lectr interdisciplinary environ design, NY State Coun Humanities; instr, Parsons Sch, 80-81, Pratt Inst Grad Dept, 80, Rutgers Univ, 80-82; prof, Pratt Inst, 84-. *Awards:* Sculpture Fel, Nat Endowment Arts, 84; 6 Proj Grants, NY State Coun Arts, Whitney Mus, 85. *Bibliog:* Lucy Lippard (auth), Overlay: Contemporary Art and the Art of Prehistory, 83; Cathey Billian/Frozen Moments, Craft Int, 6/88; Lynn Miller (auth), Lives and Works - 14 Women Artists, 92. *Mem:* Nat Ed Bd, Pub Art Rev; Col Art Asn; fel Hirsch Farm Proj Environ Art; Maine Coast Artists. *Media:* Photography, Environmental Structures & Drawing. *Res:* The intersection of environmental interpretation & public art. *Interests:* Music, Architecture, Nature as they intersect with Visual Art. *Publ:* Guest ed Public Art Review, Nature Trails jour, Fall 2000. *Mailing Add:* 456 Broome St New York NY 10013

BILLS, LINDA
SCULPTOR
b New York, NY, July 22, 43. *Study:* Beaver Col, BFA, 65. *Work:* Am Craft Mus, NY; Nat Mus Am Art; Wustum Mus Fine Arts, Racine, Wis; Del Art Mus, Wilmington; Ark Art Ctr, Little Rock. *Exhib:* Solo exhib, Sybaris Gallery, Royal Oak,Mich, 93 & 96, Villa Julie Coll, Stevenson, Md, 2000; Touch, The Handworkshop, Va Ctr Craft Arts, Richmond, Va, 93; Art Sites 6-, Natural Meaning, Rockville Art Pl, Rockville, Md, 94; Gomez Gallery, Baltimore, Md, 95; In Wood: Material Variations, Md Art Place, Baltimore, 95; Venerable Gardens/Artistes '96, Tudor Pl, Washington, 96; Biennial '96, Del Art Mus, Wilmington, 96; Celebrating Am Craft 1975-1995 (with catalog),

Danish Mus Decorative Art, Copenhagen, Denmark, 97; Poetic Objects: Technique and Vision, Del Art Mus, Wilmington, 97; Biennial 96: Mus Acquisitions, Del Art Mus, Wilmington, 98; Subject To Change, Part I and Part II, Linda Bills, Jann Rosen-Queralt, Jason Swift (with catalog), Md Inst Col Art, Baltimore, 99; Drawing The Line, Philadelphia Art Alliance, Pa, 99; Blurring Boundaries: Objects in Craft Media from the Collection, Del Art Mus, Wilmington, 99; Grandstand Sculpture, Contemp Mus, Baltimore, Md, 99; Nature Re-Bound, Palo Alto Art Ctr, Calif, 2000; Nine Artists/Five Decades: Works by Beaver Coll Alumni Beaver Coll, Glenside, Pa, 2000; Biennial 2000, Del Art Mus, Wilmington, 2000. *Awards:* Swan Prize, Philadelphia Craft Show, Swan Gallery, 87; Visual Artist Fel Grant, Nat Endowment Arts, 88, 90 & 92; Grant-In-Aid, Md State Arts Coun, 87 & Visual Art Fel Grant, 88 & 97; Vt Studio Ctr fel, 99. *Bibliog:* Jack Lenor Larsen cur, The Tactile Vessel, Erie Art Mus, 89; Margo Shermeta (auth), Linda Bills: a balance between strength & delicacy, 9-10/91 & Patricia Malarche (auth), The vessel form, summer 92, Fiber Arts Mag. *Media:* Miscellaneous. *Mailing Add:* Studio 104 2000 Clipper Park Rd Baltimore MD 21211

BILLS, MITCHELL
DESIGNER, VIDEO ARTIST
b Auburn, NY, Dec 23, 50. *Study:* Tyler Sch Art Temple Univ with Joe Scorsone & Peter D'Agostino, MFA, 84. *Work:* Tyler Sch Art Libr, Elkins Park, Pa; Intermedia Arts Minn; Pa State Univ Libr, University Park; Experimental Television Ctr, Owego, NY, 91; UCLA Film & Television Arch, Los Angeles, 92. *Exhib:* Univ & the Arts, Wayne State Univ, Detroit, Mich, 89; 48th Ann Juried Show, Sioux City Fine Arts Ctr, Iowa, 89; Siggraph 92: 19th Int Conf on Computer Graphics & Interactive Techniques, Chicago, 92; About Face, Real Art Ways, Hartford, Conn, 94. *Pos:* Design assoc, Home Viewer Publ, Philadelphia, 85-88. *Teaching:* Asst prof graphic design, SDak State Univ, Brookings, 88-90 & Southern Conn State Univ, 90-. *Awards:* Second Place Award, Prof/Experimental Video, Video 12 regional juried competition, 92. *Mem:* Arts Coun of Greater New Haven/Media Arts Ctr; Col Art Asn; Asn Comput Mach/Siggraph, NY. *Media:* Computer, Video. *Publ:* Auth & illusr, Zero Through One; Poems & Drawings, Moonlight Express, 84; auth, Dog star man, Home Viewer, 88. *Mailing Add:* 53 Hamilton Dr Bethany CT 05624-3414

BILODEAU, DANIEL ALAIN
PAINTER, DRAFTSMAN
b Montreal, Que, Can, US Citizen. *Study:* Ringling Sch Art & Design, BFA, 96-2000; Studio Art Centers Int, study under, Paul Beel, 99; Pa Acad Fine Arts, 2001. *Work:* The Citadel Mus, Canadian, Tex; Univ Tampa Medical Sch, Tampa, Fla; Sarasota Film Festival & E/W Col Medicine, Cynthia O'Donnell, Sarasota, Fla; Semilla Estrella, rainforest ecotourism & preservation, Puerto Jimenez, Costa Rica. *Comn:* mural, Sarasota Film Festival, Sarasota, Fla, 99; large scale painting/installation, Semilla Estrella, rainforest preservation, Puerto Jimenez, Costa Rica, 2005. *Exhib:* Int Juried, Daruma Dolls, Guardian Gallery, Tokyo, Japan, 99; Best of Ringling, Selby Gallery, Sarasota, Fla, 2000; Renaissance 2001, The Franklin Mint Mus, Media, Pa, 2001; solo exhib, Recent Work, Equinox, Sarasota, Fla, 2003, Divine, Dabbert Gallery, Sarasota, Fla, 2006; Galerie Gora, Montreal, Can, 2006. *Awards:* George Sugarman Found Grant, George Sugarman Found, 2004; 2nd Place Juried Award, Drawing, Winterfest, Mountain Valley Arts Coun, Ala, 2004; 3rd Place, Juried Award, Dreams, Art Ctr, Sarasota, Fla, 2006. *Bibliog:* Marty Fugate (auth), Bilodeaus art is divine but down to earth, The Observer, 3/16/6006; Mark Ormond (auth), Work on view by weems, Bilodeau and Reynolds, Pelican Press, 3/30/2006; Brooksie Bergan (auth), Gallery hopping, Style Mag, Sarasota Herald Tribune, 5/2006. *Media:* Oil on Linen, Canvas, Graphite, Mixed Media. *Dealer:* David and Patricia Dabbert Dabbert Gallery 76 S Palm Ave Sarasota Fla 34236; Joseph Gora Galeria Gora 279 Sherbrooke Ouest espace 205 Montreal Que Can H2X 1Y2. *Mailing Add:* 2740 Coconut Bay Ln #2A Sarasota FL 34237

BILOUS, PRISCILLA HALEY See Haley, Priscilla J

BIMPONG, BRIGHT
SCULPTOR
b Takoradi, Ghana, West Africa, 60. *Study:* Univ Sci & Technol, Kumansi, Ghana, West Africa, BA, 87; Johnson Atelier Tech Inst Sculpture, Mercerville, NJ; Skowhegan Sch of Painting & Sculpture, Maine; Mason Gross Sch of Arts, Rutgers Univ, New Brunswick, MFA. *Work:* 1996 Atlanta Olympic Games, Ga; African Art Mus, Smithsonian, Washington, DC; State Forensic Lab, Meriden, Conn; Univ AK, Anchorage. *Exhib:* Skoto Gallery, NY, 2001; Studio Mus, Harlem, NY; Lowell Hist Gallery, Mass; 77th Ann Show, Allied Artists Am, New York City. *Teaching:* instr, bronze casting, Johnson Atelier Tech Inst of Sculpture, 95-98. *Awards:* Elizabeth Greenshields Found, Montreal, Can; Herk Van Tongeren Mem Fund. *Media:* Bronze, Aluminum, Steel and Wood. *Mailing Add:* 111 Alcasar Ave Trenton NJ 08648

BINKS, RONALD C
PHOTOGRAPHER, PAINTER
b Oak Park, Ill, Oct 20, 34. *Study:* George Eastman House, with Minor White, 54; RI Sch Design, BFA, 56; Berlin Art Acad, cert, 58; Yale Univ, MFA, 60. *Work:* Southwest Art Mus, Lubbock, Tex; San Antonio Mus Art, Tex; Ammon Carter Mus, Ft Worth, Tex; Del Mar Col, Corpus Christi, Tex; Springfield Art Mus, Mo; and others. *Comn:* Nature Conservancy Tex. *Exhib:* Fulbright Artists, Whitney Mus Am Art, NY, 58; 20th Century Photog, George Eastman House, Rochester, 60; Abilene Mus Fine Arts, 83; Berlin Fotos, Univ Tex, San Antonio, 98; Sequences, Blue Star Art Ctr, 2005; Binks, 50 Years Photog, Univ Tex San Antonio Gallery, 2006. *Pos:* Ed adv, Photographer's Forum, 79-. *Teaching:* Assoc prof art, RI Sch Design, 62-76, chmn film dept, 68-72; prof, Div Art & Archit, Univ Tex, San Antonio, 76-. *Awards:* Fulbright Fel, 58-60; Prix de Rome, Am Acad Rome, 60-62; Univ Tex, San Antonio, Res Grant, 98; Univ Tex Pres Teaching Award 2004. *Bibliog:* Beaumont Newhall (auth), Young photographers, Art in Am, 60. *Mem:* Soc Photog Educ; Nat Asn Sch Art; Tex Asn Schs Art (bd dir, 80-82); Col Art Asn Am; Nat Coun Art Adminr (chmn, 82-83). *Publ:* Aperture, spring 61; Voices of Art, 2004; Articles, 2006. *Mailing Add:* Dept Art Univ Tex San Antonio One University Circle San Antonio TX 78285

BIOLCHINI, GREGORY PHILLIP
PAINTER
b Peoria, Ill, Mar 24, 48. *Study:* Famous Artist Course, Westport, Conn, 70; Edison Community Col, Ft Myers, Fla, printmaking, 80 & 88; Ringling Art Inst, Sarasota, Fla, figure sculpture, ceramics, workshops in watercolor, pastel & oil, 90. *Work:* State Fla, Capitol Bldg, Tallahassee; Ft Myers Hist Mus, Barbara B Mann Performing Arts Hall, Univ SFla Campus, Harborside Conv Ctr, Edison Mus, Ft Myers, Fla; Embry Riddle Aeronautical Univ, Daytona, Fla. *Comn:* Oil portrait, Mayor Zee Butler, comn by Brent Scheneman, LaBelle Gallery, Sanibel, Fla, 81; oil portraits, J Paul Riddle, 86, T H Embry, 87, Embry-Riddle Univ, Daytona, Fla; oil portrait, Barbara B Mann, comn by Sen Frank Mann, Ft Myers, Fla, 88; bronze portrait, Chief Billy Bowlegs, comn by D J Wilkins, Ft Myers, Fla, 90; Mrs Thomas Alva Edison (oil portrait), The Edison Found, Ft Myers, Fla, 98. *Exhib:* Pastels Only, Nat Arts Club Gallery, NY, 81-2003; solo exhib, Fla Cowboy, Ft Myers Hist Mus, 84; Societee des Pastellistes de France, Paris, 87; Degas Pastel Soc Second Biennial, Nat Exhib, New Orleans, La, 88, 2002; Three Notable Pastelists, Fla Southern Univ, Lakeland, 90; Nat Pastel Soc Master Pastelists, Harmon-Meek Gallery, Naples, Fla, 92; Butler Inst, Youngstown, Ohio, 2003; Fla State Capital Building; and others. *Pos:* Co-founder & vpres, Co-operative Gallery, Bell Tower, Ft Myers, Fla, 83-86. *Awards:* Award for Nude, Pastels Only, Nat Arts Club, Vincent Giffuni, 83; Award for Nude, Pastels Only, Nat Arts Club, Hon & Mrs DiGiovanna, 88; Best of Show, Fla State Wildlife Comn, 2001; Grumbacher Gold Medallion, 2002. *Bibliog:* The Art of Pastel Portraiture (featured artist), Watson-Guptil Publ, 96; The Best of Pastel, Pure Color, Northlight Pub, 2006. *Mem:* Pastel Soc Am (master pastelist status, 88); Degas Pastel Soc; Fla Artists Group; Int Pastel Soc. *Media:* Pastel. *Dealer:* Harmon-Meek Gallery 386 Broad Ave S Naples FL 33940. *Mailing Add:* Studio 412 1617 Hendry St Fort Myers FL 33901

BIONDI, FLORENCE GLORIA
PAINTER, PASTEL
b Sept 25, 24. *Study:* Brooklyn Mus Art Sch, studied with Isaac Soyer, 1968-1975; Art Student League, studied with John H Sanden & Daniel Greene, 1 yr scholar, 1976-1979. *Work:* Princeton Univ, NJ; Harvard Univ, Cambridge, Mass. *Comn:* Portrait John F Kennedy, Italian Execs of Am, NY, 1967; Prehistoric elephant for book, Dr V Maglio, Cambridge, Mass, 1971; Prehistoric man (drawing), Dr V Maglio, Princeton, NJ, 1972. *Exhib:* Salmagundi Club Ann (juried), NYC, 2004; Pastel Soc Am Ann (juried), NYC; Am Artists Prof League Ann (juried), NYC, 2005; Pen & Brush Club Invitational (juried), NYC, 2005; Audubon Artists Ann (juried), NYC, 2005. *Awards:* Pastel Award, CLW Art Club, 2001; Pastel Soc Am Gold Medal, Salmagundi Club, 2004; Audubon Artists Gold Medal, Art Spirit Found, Diane B Bernhard, 2005. *Mem:* Am Artists Prof League; Pastel Soc Am; Catherine Lorillard Wolfe Art Club; Audubon Soc; Art Students League NY. *Media:* Oil. *Publ:* Art, book on prehistoric elephants, Harvard Univ, 1971; art, Contemporary Women Artists Date Book (calendar), Panz Corp, Calif. *Mailing Add:* 426 McDonald Ave Brooklyn NY 11218

BIRBIL, PAUL GREGORY
PAINTER, PRINTMAKER
b Chicago, Ill, 65. *Study:* Univ NMex; Calif Col Arts & Crafts, BFA(hon), 85; Spec course in Salzburg, Bildendkunst with Sandro Chia, cert, 93. *Work:* Museo de Santo Domingo, Mexico City, Mex. *Comn:* Oil painting, Alazraki y Assoc, Mex, 93; painting, Producciones por Marca, Mex, 94; wall painting, New Art Digital, Mex, 94; oil painting, Artes Graficas Panorama, Mex, 96. *Exhib:* Jovenes Nacidos en los 60's (traveling), Mex, 93; solo shows, Mus Contemp Art, Morelia/Michoacan, Mex, 94 & Museo del Chopo, Mex, 96; Contemp Painters from Mexico, Museo de Arte Contemporaneo, Bogata, Colombia, 95. *Awards:* Louis Siegrist Painting Award, 85. *Media:* Oil Paint. *Dealer:* Andres Siegel 40 Veracruz Mexico City Mexico. *Mailing Add:* Madrid 209-Coyoacan 04100 Mexico DF Mexico

BIRCH, WILLIE M
SCULPTOR, PAINTER
b New Orleans, La, Nov 26, 42. *Study:* Southern Univ, BA(painting), 69; Md Inst, Col Art, MFA, 73. *Work:* Pa Acad Fine Arts, Philadelphia; New Orleans Mus Art, La; Harlem Hosp, Hatch-Billops Collection, Health & Hosp Corp, Metrop Mus Art, NY; Miami-Dade Pub Libr, Miami, Fla; Wilfredo Lamb Ctr, Havana, Cuba; Atlanta Life Insurance Co, Ga; and others. *Comn:* Mcpl Collaborative Project for Winston-Salem, NC, 95; Phila Int Airport, Terminal A, 96; New York City Met Transit Auth, Arts for Transit, 135th St and Leroy Ave, 96; Spoffard Juv Detention Ctr, Brooklyn, NY, 97. *Exhib:* Five Md Artists Traveling Exhib, Baltimore Mus Art, 74-75; solo exhibs, Arthur Roger Gallery, NY, 92-93, 95 & 96, Afro-Am Hist & Cult Mus, Philadelphia, 93, York Col Art Gallery, NY, 93, Paa Ya Paa Gallery, Niarobi, Kenya, 93, Sculpture Ctr, NY, 93, Luise Ross Gallery, NY, 94 & 96, SE Ctr Contemp Art, NC, 96; Green Acres: Neo Colonialism in the US, Wash Univ Art Gallery, St Louis, Mo, 92; Bob Blackburn's Printmaking Workshop: Artist of Color, Hillwood Art Gallery, Brookville, NY, 92; Altars, Divinations and Icons, Painted Bride Art Ctr, Philadelphia, 92; Word, Jamaica Arts Ctr, NY, 93; Figurines, Luise Ross Gallery, NY, 93; solo exhibs, Witnessing New Orleans, Arthur Roger Gallery, New Orleans, La, 99, Free to be in Black and White and Color, Luise Ross Gallery, NY, 2000, Black Male, Arthur Roger Gallery, New Orleans, La, 2001; group exhibs, The Rutgers Summer Fest 2000 Exhib, New Brunswick, NJ, 2000, Go Figure, Lew Allen Contemp, Santa Fe, NMex, 2000. *Teaching:* artist in residence, Tamarind Inst, Albuquerque, NMex, 2000;

Spoffard Juvenile Detention Ctr, Brooklyn, NY, 97. *Awards:* NY State Coun Arts Nat Endowment Arts Visual Arts Fel, 89-90; Lila Wallace, Reader's Dig Int Artists Fel, 92; Mid-Atlantic Arts Found Visual Arts Residency Grant, 92; John Guggenheim Sculpture Fel, 93. *Bibliog:* Roberta Smith (auth), Social commentary in works by Willie Birch, NY Times, 4/10/92; Robert Taplin (auth), Review of Exhibitions, Willie Birch at the Sulpture Center, 122-123, 7/91; Michael Brenson (auth) Willie Birch's new paintings at the Luise Ness Gallery, 11/2000. *Mem:* NY Artists Equity Asn. *Media:* All Media. *Publ:* Auth, Knowing Our History, Teaching Our Culture, New Soc Publ, 90. *Dealer:* Luise Ness Gallery 568 Broadway #902 New York NY 10012. *Mailing Add:* c/o Arthur Roger Gallery 432 Julia St New Orleans LA 70130

BIRCHLER, ALEXANDER
FILMMAKER
b Baden, Switz, 62. *Study:* attended, Schule fur Gestaltung, Basel, 83-87; attended, Univ Art & Design, Helsinki, 85; Nova Scotia Col Art & Design, Halifax, MFA, 92. *Work:* Columbus Mus Art, OH; Neues Mus, Nuremberg, Ger; Ulrich Mus Art, Wichita, Kans; Yokohama Mus Art, Japan; and numerous others. *Exhib:* solo shows, Slow Place, Mus fur Gegenwartskunst, Basel, 97; Stripping, Kunstlerhaus Bethanien, Berlin, 89; Gregor's Room, Gallery Bob van Orsouw, Zurich, 99; Motion Pictures, Gallery Barbara Thumm, Berlin, 99; Arsenal, Bonakdar Jancou Gallery, NY, 2000; Tanya Bonakdar Gallery, NY, 2002; ArtPace Found Contemp Art, San Antionio, Tex, 2002; County Line Road, 2003; Single Wide, Whitney Mus Am Art, NY, 2004; Editing the Dark, Kemper Mus Contemp Art, Kansas City, 2005; House with Pool, Miami Art Mus, 2006; Galerie Barbara Thumm, Berlin, 2006; group shows, Nonchalance Revisited, Akademie der Kunste, Berlin, 98; Solitude in Budapest, Kunsthalle, Budapest, 99; Every Time, La Biennale de Montreal, 2000; New Work, Tanya Bonakdar Gallery, NY, 2001; Out of Place: Contemp Art & the Architectural Uncanny, Mus Contemp Art, Chicago, 2002; Adolescence, Reina Sofia Mus, Madrid, 2003; Eight, Centre Culturel Suisse, Paris, 2004; Swiss Experimental Film, Image Forum, Tokyo, 2005; Roaming Memories, Ludwig Forum, Aachen, 2005; Melancholy, Nationalgalerie, Berlin, 2006; Picture Ballot, Kunsthaus, Zurich, 2006; Raised by Wolves, Art Gallery Western Australia, Perth, 2006. *Pos:* lectr at various univs & insts, 92-, including Univ Zurich, 93-94. *Teaching:* core fac mem, Milton Avery Grad Sch, Bard Col, NY, 2005-. *Bibliog:* Dora Imhof (auth), Teresa Hubbard & Alexander Birchler, House with Pool, Kunstforum, Vol 161, 3-4/2004, 504-505; Amoreen Armetta (auth), Teresa Hubbard/Alexander Birchler, Flash Art, 1/2005, 69; Rene Morales, Teresa Hubbard & Alezander Birchler, MAM Portrait: Miami Art Mus, Miami, 7-9/2006, 6; and many others. *Mailing Add:* c/o Tanya Bonakdar Gallery 521 W 21st St New York NY 10011

BIRD, STEPHANIE ROSE
PAINTER, EDUCATOR
b Montclair, NJ, Aug 25, 60. *Study:* Tyler Sch Art Temple Univ, BFA (cum laude), 82; Univ Calif San Diego, MFA, 87. *Comn:* mural, Washington Irving Sch, Oak Park, 95; Harris Bank, Southshore Bank, McCormick Place Navy Pier Exposition Center, Chicago; US Ambassador Pamela Bridgewater Benin, Africa. *Exhib:* Let the Work Speak for Itself, Northern Ill Univ Mus, DeKalb, 90; Re-Making of Myth, Rahr-West Mus, Charles Allis Mus, Appleton Gallery, Wis, 90-91; The Legacy of Africa in the New World, Waterloo Mus, Davenport Mus, Mac Nider Mus, Sioux City Art Ctr, Iowa, 91-92; Black Creativity, Mus of Science & Industry, Chicago, 95, 2001; Earthworks, Chicago State Univ, 98; Int Young Art, Sotheby's, Tel Aviv, Chicago, 99; Everytime I Feel the Spirit, Ind Univ, 2000. *Collection Arranged:* The Literary Impulse Sapphires and Crystals, 97, First Person Pural Australian Aboriginal Art of Chicago, Contemp Sch of the Art Inst, 97; Cleaning House, Woman Made Gallery, Chicago, 99, Autumn Hymn, Gallery EGG, Chicago, 99; Alice & Arthur Baer Competion, Beverly Art Ctr, 2000. *Teaching:* asst prof The Sch of the Art Inst of Chicago, 97-98, adjunct asst prof, 98-2000. *Awards:* Fulbright Senior Scholar Award to Australia, CIES, 93; Faculty Enrichment Grant Ford Found, 96; Pollock-Krasner Found Award, 96. *Media:* Mixed Media. *Dealer:* Murphy Rabb Inc Chicago Ill; Artlink Inc Tel Aviv Israel

BIRDSALL, BYRON
PAINTER
b Buckeye, Ariz, Dec 18, 37. *Study:* Seattle Pacific Col, BA; Stanford Univ, MA. *Work:* Anchorage Hist & Fine Arts Mus; Jean Haydon Territorial Mus, Pago Pago, Am Samoa. *Comn:* Painting, Alaska Bank of Com, Anchorage, 76; Alyeska Pipeline Co, Anchorage, 77; RCA, Anchorage, 77; stone lithos, Anchorage Opera Soc, 85; painting, Anchorage Olympic Organizing Comt, 85; King Co Libr System, 86; and others. *Exhib:* All Alaska Watercolor Exhib, Alaska Watercolor Soc, 75-77; Anchorage Hist & Fine Arts Mus, 76 & All Alaska Exhib, 78; also many one-man shows. *Teaching:* Instr, Makerere Univ, Kampala, Uganda, 66-70; feature prog, art dir, KVZK Television, Pago Pago, Am Samoa, 72-73 & Graphix West Advertising Agency, Anchorage, Alaska, 75-76. *Awards:* Alaska Arts & Crafts League First Prize in Watercolor; Alaska Watercolor Soc First Prize, 76 & Second Prize, 77, Alaska Watercolor Show; Third Prize, All Alaska Art Exhib, 82. *Bibliog:* Lana Johnson (auth), Watercolorist forsakes his palm trees, Anchorage Times, 11/77; Barbara Whipple (auth), Byron Birdsall paints Alaska, Am Artist, 4/81; Janet O'Hara (auth), Byron Birdsall, artist of the world, Wien Air Alaska Flight Time, 9/83. *Mem:* Alaska Watercolor Soc (pres, 76); Alaska Artists Guild. *Media:* Watercolor, Stone. *Publ:* Auth, Letters from Africa, Anchorage Times, 6/81. *Dealer:* Kirsten Gallery 5320 Roosevelt Way NE Seattle WA 98105. *Mailing Add:* c/o Artique Ltd 314 G St Anchorage AK 99501

BIRDSALL, STEPHANIE
ARTIST
b Atlanta, Ga. *Study:* Univ Ga, 1970-1971; Rhodes Col, 1971-1972; City & Guilds London Art Sch, London, Eng, 1972-1976. *Work:* Fla State Art Collection, Fla State Capitol, Tallahassee, Fla; Fla Mus Art & Cult, Avon Park, Fla; Mus of the Everglades, Everglades Nat Monument, Fla. *Exhib:* Seaweed Gallery, Sanibel Island, Fla, 2001; 4th Ann Int Asn Pastel Socs Competition, Chablis Gallery, Placerville, Ga, Gallery on Fifth, Naples, Fla, 2002; Renaissance in Pastel, Nat Exhib W Hartford Art League, W Hartford, Conn, Nat Pastel Exhib, Lone Star Pastel Soc, Amarillo, Tex, 12th Ann Nat Pastel Painting Exhib, Pastel Soc NMex, Albuguerque, NMex, 2003; Eastern Regional Juried Exhib Traditional Oils, Oil Painters Am, Kewaunee, Wis, Southeastern Pastel Soc Int Show, Marietta-Cobb Mus Art, Ga, 2004; 109th Ann Exhib, Catherine Lorillard Wolfe Art Club, NY, 74th Ann Exhib, Hudson Valley Art Asn, Hastings on Hudson, NY, Int Asn Pastel Socs, Art Source Gallery, Raleigh, NC, Putney Painters, Village Arts Gallery, Putney, Vt, 2005; Tucson Plein Air Painters, Northern Trust Bank, Tucson, Ariz, Two Women, Rising Stars, Putney Painters & Friends, Susan Powell Fine Art Gallery, Madison, Conn, 2006; One Women Exhib, Fla Mus Art & Cult, Avon, Fla, Rocky Mountain Plein Air Painters, 5th Ann Show, Elkhorn Gallery, Winter Park, Colo, 2006; Richard Schmid Fine Art Auction, Bellevue, Colo, 2006; and others. *Awards:* Daniel Smith Award, Pastel Soc Northern Fla, 2002; 2nd Place, Nat Pastel Exhib, Lone Star Pastel Soc, 2003; First Place Award of Excellence, Degas Pastel Soc, 2004; 14th Ann Pastel Exhib, Artisan/Santa Fe Award, Pastel Soc NMex, 2005; Exceptional Merit Award, Degas Pastel Soc, 2005; Finalist Artist Art prize Challenge, Int Artist Mag, 2005; and numerous others. *Bibliog:* Lonni Pierson Dunbier (auth), Artist's Blue Book, Am Artists, Mountain Press Publ, 2004; Sara Shlussel & Ron James (coauths), Parks Portrayed in Pen and Paint, 2005; Sylvie Fauvel Cabal (auth), L'Art du Pastel en France, 2006. *Mem:* Pastel Soc Conn (signature mem); Plein Air Soc Fla (signature mem); Pastel Soc Am (signature mem); Nat Asn Women Artists (juried mem); Pastel Soc NMex (signature mem); Catherine Lorillard Wolfe Art Club; and others. *Mailing Add:* 3131 N Deer Track Rd Tucson AZ 85749

BIRENBAUM, CYNTHIA See Barber, Cynthia

BIRK, SANDOW
PAINTER, SCULPTOR
b Detroit, Mich, 62. *Study:* Parsons Sch Design, Otis Art Inst, BFA, 81-88; Am Col Paris, 84; Bath Acad Art, Eng, 85. *Work:* San Francisco Mus Mod Art; Laguna Art Mus, Laguna Beach, Calif; Mus da Republica, Rio de Janeiro, Brazil; Renee di Rosa Mus, Napa, Calif; Sonoma Valley Mus Art, Calif. *Comn:* lobby, Lincoln Properties Bldg, Philadelphia, Pa; City Place Shopping Ctr, City of Long Beach, Calif; Hollenbeck LAPD Station, Los Angles, Calif; Tarzana MTA Station, Tarzana, Calif. *Exhib:* Carioca, Laguna Art Mus, Laguna Beach, Calif, 97, San Jose Mus Art, Calif, 99; When Borders Migrate, Mus Art & Hist, Santa Cruz, Calif, 99; Made in Calif, Los Angeles Co Mus Art, 00; In Smog and Thunder, Laguna Art Mus, Calif, 00; Incarceration, Santa Barbara Contmp Arts Forum, Calif, 01; Sandow Birk's Divine Comedy, San Jose Mus Art, 05; Leading Causes of Death in Am, San Diego Mus Art, 05. *Teaching:* Calif State Univ, Long Beach, 99. *Awards:* the Basil H Alkazzi Award, 98; J Paul Getty Fel for the Visual Arts, 99; Individual Artist Fel, City of Los Angeles, Calif, 01; Guggenheim fel, 95; Int Exchange fel to Mex, NEA, 95; Fulbright fel to Brazil, 97. *Bibliog:* JSM Wittette (auth), Sandow Birk and the killing of Los Angeles, Visions Art Qrtly, 93; Greil Marques (auth), Flotsam and jetsom of California state of mind, NY Times, 98; Claudine Ise (auth), Sly scenes of California Civil War, Los Angeles Times, 98. *Media:* Oil on Canvas. *Interests:* surfing. *Publ:* Gallery - Barry McGee (Twist), Surfers J, 96; Graffiti, 96 & Views of the Getty Museum, 98, Juxtapoz Mag; In Smog and Thunder: The Great War of the Californias, Last Gasp Publ, 2000; Incarcerated: Visions of California in the 21st Century, Last Gasp Publishing, 2001; Dante's Inferno, Chronical Books, 04, Dante's Purgatorio, 05, Dante's Oaradiso, 05. *Dealer:* Koplin Gallery 464 N Robertson Blvd West Hollywood Ca 90048; Catharine Clark Gallery San Francisco CA; Debs & Co Gallery 525 W 26th St 2nd Fl New York NY 10001. *Mailing Add:* Koplin Del Rio Gallery 464 N Robertson Blvd West Hollywood CA 90048

BIRMELIN, ROBERT
PAINTER, DRAFTSMAN
b Newark, NJ, Nov 7, 33. *Study:* Cooper Union Art Sch; Yale Univ, BFA, 56, MFA, 60; RI Col Hon Dr Fine Arts, 96. *Exhib:* One-man shows, Claude Bernard Gallery, NY, 88 & 90, Jersey City Mus, NJ, 97-98, Eugene Olson Gallery, Bethel Col, St Paul, Minn, 98, Lore Degenstein Gallery, Susquehanna Univ, Selinsgrove, Pa, 98, Peter Findlay Gallery, NY, 97 & 2000, Luise Ross Gallery, NY, 99 & Jaff-Friete Gallery, Dartmouth Col, Hanover, NH, 99; Galeria Mara, Buenos Aires, Argentina, 89; Am Imagist and Abstract Painting, Moscow, USSR, 89; Contemp Realist Gallery, San Francisco, 94 & 95; Radix Gallery, NY, 96; Recent Paintings, Bannister Gallery, RI Col, Providence, 96; Powerful Expressions: Drawing Today, Am Acad Design, NY, 96; Sex/Industry, Stefan Stux Gallery, NY, 97; Summer Group Show, Radix Gallery, NY, 97; Re-presenting representation III, Arnot Art Mus, Elmira, NY, 97; 10th Ann Exhib, Hackett-Freedman Gallery, San Francisco, Calif, 97, 2001. *Teaching:* Prof art, Queens Col, NY, 64-, retired. *Awards:* Am Acad Fel, Rome, 61-64; Nat Endowment Arts, 82 & 90; NJ Coun Arts, 88; Nat Endowment of Arts, 1976, 1982, 1989. *Bibliog:* Laurie Hurwitz (auth), Contemporary Masters: Robert Birmelin, Am Artist, 4/90; Robert Berlind (auth), From the corner of the minds eye: the paintings of Robert Birmelin, Art in America, 3/91; Fred Stern (auth), To make the unreal real: the art of Robert Birmelin, Art Leisure, 8/98. *Mem:* Nat Acad Design (assoc, 86, acad, 94). *Media:* Acrylic, Oil. *Dealer:* Hackett-Freedman Gallery 250 Sutter St San Francisco CA 94108; Peter Findlay Gallery 41 E 57th St New York NY 10022. *Mailing Add:* Peter Findlay Gallery 41 E 57th St New York NY 10022

BIRNBAUM, DARA
VIDEO ARTIST
b New York, NY, Oct 29, 46. *Study:* Carnegie Mellon Univ, Pittsburgh, Pa, BA(archit), 69; San Francisco Art Inst, BA, 72; New Sch Social Res, New York, 76. *Work:* Mus Mod Art, NY; Ctr Georges Pompidou, Paris; Mus Contemp Art, Chicago; San Francisco Mus Mod Art; Castello Di Rivoli, Turin, Italy. *Comn:* RIO Videowall, RIO Shopping/Entertainment Complex, Atlanta, Ga; MTV ArtBreak, MTV Network; Fourt Gates, St Polten Kunst & Raum Project, St Polten, Austria. *Exhib:* Whitney Biennial Exhib, Whitney Mus Am Art, NY, 85; solo exhibs, Portikus, Frankfurt, Ger, 94, CAPC Mus Art Contemp Entrepot, Bordeaux, France, 94, X Works at l'Esec, Paris, France, 94, Rena Bransten Gallery, San Francisco, Calif, 94, Paula Cooper Gallery, NY, 94, Norrtalje Konsthall, Swed, 95 & KUNSTHALLEwien, Wien, Austria, 95; L'Effetcinéma, Mus Art Contemp, Montréal, Can, 95; Polyphonix 28, Mus Art Africaine Océanien, Paris, France, 96; Surfing Systems, Mus Fridericianum, Kassel, Ger, 96; 13th Kasseler Dokumetarfilm & Videofest, Filmladen, Kassel, Ger, 96; Women's Work, Greene-Naftali Gallery, NY, 96; and others. *Teaching:* Instr video & post-studio, Calif Inst Arts, Valencia, 82; experimental video instr, Sch Visual Arts, New York, 83-86; Perkins jr fel, Prog Vis Arts, Princeton Univ, 87-88 & vis jr fel Coun Humanities, 87-88; video & media arts, Hunter Col Grad Sch, New York, 90-91; Heinz & Gisela Friedrich-Stiftung guest prof, Stadel-Hochschule for Bildende Kunst & Inst New Media, Frankfurt, Ger, 92. *Awards:* Maya Deren Award for Indep Film & Video Artists, Am Film Inst, 87; Cert, Harvard Univ, 88; Special Jury Prize, Deutcher Videokunstpries Sudwestfunk, 92. *Bibliog:* Dara Birnbaum (monogr), Succes de bedac No 10, Le Coin du Miroir, Dijon, France, 86; Benjamin Buchloh (ed), Rough Edits: Popular Image Video (monogr), Press of Nova Scotia Col Art & Design, 87; Dara Birnbaum (monogr), IVAM, Ctr del Carve, Valencia, Spain, 91. *Mem:* Found Independent Video & Film, NY (bd dir, 83-85); Creative Time (bd dir, 88-96). *Media:* Video, Media Installation. *Publ:* Auth, Playground (The damnation of Faust), Zone, No 1/2, 85; Out of the Blue, in Discourses: Conversations In: Postmodern Art & Culture, Mass Inst Technol Press, 90; The RIO Experience: Video's New Architecture Meets Corporate Sponsorship, In: Illuminating Video: An Essential Guide to Video Art, Aperature Found, New York, 90; Overlapping Signs, In: War after War, City Lights Press, San Francisco, 92; Every TV Needs a Revolution, IMSCHOOT, Uitgevers, Ghent, 92. *Mailing Add:* 140 Thomson St Apt 3A New York NY 10012

BISGYER, BARBARA G (COHN)
SCULPTOR, DESIGNER
b New York, NY, June 7, 33. *Study:* Sarah Lawrence Col; Sculptors & Ceramic Workshop, New York; also indust design with R R Kostellow. *Work:* US Consular Small Sculpture Collection, Smithsonian Inst; Larry Aldrich Mus Contemp Art; Savin Bus Machines Corp. *Comn:* Sculpture, pvt residence, Delray, Fla, 84. *Exhib:* Union Carbide; Aldrich Mus; Avery Fisher Hall, Lincoln Ctr; Hudson River Mus; Pratt Sch Design; Sarah Lawrence Col; and others. *Collection Arranged:* London, 1992; Can, 1999; Switzerland, 1999; Frankfurt, 2001; San Francisco, 2002. *Awards:* Merit Award for Outstanding Design & Craftsmanship in Sculpture, Artist Craftsmen NY; President's Award, Mamaroneck Artists Guild, Westchester Art Soc; Audubon Beaux Arts Award; many others. *Bibliog:* Articles in Art News, Today's Art & La Revue moderne des et de la vie. *Mem:* Artists Craftsmen, NY; Mamaroneck Artists Guild; Artists Equity Asn, NY; Am Soc Contemp Artists; Abraxas. *Media:* Cast Bronze, Welded Steel. *Dealer:* Richard Eyan 35 Newbridge Rd New Milford CT 06766. *Mailing Add:* 1025 Nautilus La Mamaroneck NY 10543

BISHOP, BUDD HARRIS
PAINTER, MUSEUM DIRECTOR
b Canton, Ga, Nov 1, 36. *Study:* Shorter Col, Ga, AB, 58; Univ Ga, MFA, 60, with Lamar Dodd & Howard Thomas; Arts Admin Inst, Harvard Univ, 70. *Work:* Sequatchie Sundown, Bridgestone Collection, Tenn State Mus, 2000. *Comn:* 4 large paintings Fla Landscapes, The Greens Develop, Gainesville. *Exhib:* solo exhib, Arnold Gallery, Shorter Col, Rome, Ga, 2003; solo exhib, Moon Gallery, Berry Col, Mt Berry, Ga, 2003; solo exhib, Parthenon Mus, Nashville, 2003; solo exhib, Deland Mus Art, Fla, 2003; solo exhib, Cumberland Univ, Lebanon, Tenn, 2002. *Collection Arranged:* Tenn State Collection of Sculpture; The First Am Collections of Hunter Mus of Art; Sculpture Collection, Columbus, Mus; Ogilvy Collection Chinese & Japanese Art; Asian Art Collections, Harn Mus Art; Sirak Collection of European Art, Ohio; E Tenn Currents ii, Knoxville Mus Art, 99; Eshib of Shey Private Collection, Harm Mus, 2000. *Pos:* Dir creative serv, Transit Advert Asn, NY, 64-66; dir, Hunter Mus Art, 66-76 & Columbus Mus Art, Ohio, 76-87; dir, Harn Mus Art, Gainesville, Fla, 87-98 & dir emer, 99-; dir, Fla Art Mus Asn, 91-98 & officer at large, 91-93; bd dir, Fla Asn Mus Found Inc, 94-98; indep cur & mus consult, 99-; bd dir, Upper Cumberland Arts Coun, Tenn; bd dir, Friends of Cordell Hull Mus, Tenn. *Teaching:* Lectr art hist, Vanderbilt Univ, 61-62; art dir children's prog, Ensworth Sch, Nashville, Tenn, 61-64; lectr art, Univ Chattanooga, 67-68. *Awards:* Tenn Arts Comt Award, 71; Shorter Col Alumni Award, 79; Lifetime Achievement Mus Service Award, Fla Asn Mus, 97; James R Short Award, SE Mus Conf, 98; Lifetime Achievement Award, Fla Art Mus Asn, 98; Harn Mus Study Ctr renamed Bishop Study Ctr, 98. *Mem:* Am Asn Mus; Tenn Asn Mus (pres, 70-71); Asn Art Mus Dirs; Fla Art Mus Dir Asn. *Media:* landscapes in acrylic, pastel, pencil. *Res:* Early Tennessee artists; early Southern American painting; George Bellows; American and European sculpture. *Publ:* Contribr, Italian Old Master Drawings & Insights and Conclusions: American Master Drawings, Ark Arts Ctr; America's Mirror: Painting in the United States 1850-1950; Inner Eye: Contemporary Art from the Marc and Livia Straus Collection; auth, Linda Howard: Star Flower, 94, Lachaise's Head of a Woman, Harn Mus Art, 96; Shared Treasures: Vero Collects II, Vero Beach Mus Art. *Dealer:* The Arts Co Nashville TN; Gallery 1401 Chattanooga TN. *Mailing Add:* PO Box 258 Livingston TN 38570

BISHOP, JACQUELINE K
PAINTER
b Long Beach, Calif, Oct 1, 55. *Study:* Univ Kansas, Lawrence, 73-75; Univ New Orleans, BA, 76-78; Tulane Univ, MFA, 80-82. *Work:* New Orleans Mus Art, La; Huntsville Mus Art, Ala; City New Orleans - Arts Coun, New Orleans, La; Albrecht-Kemper Mus Art, St Joseph, Mo; Tulane Univ, New Orleans, La. *Exhib:* Bird Space, Hudson River Mus, NY; Terra, Brazil, 96, Albrecht Kemper Mus, 2002; The texture of Memory, Arthur Roger Gallery, New Orleans, La, 2002; Tresspass, Arthur Roger Gallery, New Orleans, La, 2005. *Teaching:* Instr drawing & painting, Newcomb Col, Tulane Univ, New Orleans, 82-84, instr drawing, 93-94; asst prof advan painting, Loyola Univ, New Orleans, La, 90; Loyola Univ, Art & Environment, 2003-2005. *Awards:* La Div Arts Grant. *Bibliog:* D Eric Bookhardt (auth), Color, Time & Space, Gambit Weekly. *Media:* Oil, Mixed Media. *Dealer:* Arthur Roger Gallery 432 Julia St New Orleans LA. *Mailing Add:* 1217 Philip St New Orleans LA 70130

BISHOP, JAMES
PAINTER
b Neosho, Mo, Oct 7, 27. *Study:* Syracuse Univ, New York, BA, 46-50; Wash Univ Sch Fine Arts, 51-54; Black Mountain Col, study with Esteban Vicente, 53; Columbia Univ, 55-56. *Work:* San Francisco Mus of Art; Mus Mod Art, NY; Chase Manhattan, Paris, France; Gillman Paper Co, NY; Brooklyn Mus; and others. *Exhib:* One-man shows, Galerie Jean Fournier, Paris, France, 76, Frank Kolbert Gallery, NY, 80, Anne Marie Verna Gallery, Zurich, Switz, 81, Daniel Weinberg Gallery, San Francisco, Calif, 81, Simon/Neuman Gallery, NY, 87, Kunstmuseum Winterthur, 93, Galerie nationale du Jeu de Paume, Paris, 94 & Landesmuseum, Münster (catalog), 94; Musée d'art moderde de la communauté urbaine de Lille (catalog), 92; Slow Painting, PS1, Inst Art & Urban Resources, Long Island City, NY, 92; Stars Don't Stand Still in the Sky (catalog), Kunstmuseum Winterthur, 92; Galerie de France, Paris, 93; Whitney Biennial, Whitney Mus Am Art, NY, 95. *Pos:* Ed assoc, Art News, 69-72. *Teaching:* Instr, Cooper Union, 69-70, Univ Calif, Irvine, 70, Carnegie-Mellon Inst, 71 & Sch of Visual Arts, New York, 72. *Awards:* Guggenheim Found Fel, 70; Grant, Nat Endowment Arts, 76. *Bibliog:* The Sixties in Abstract (interview), Art in America, 10/83; Carter Ratcliff (auth), Remembering How to See, Artforum, 5/88, 127; Carrie Barker (auth), Contemporary Artists, Third Ed, St James Press, Chicago & London, 89. *Publ:* Contribr, Art Now: New York, vol 4, 72. *Dealer:* Margarete Roeder Gallery 545 Broadway New York NY 10012. *Mailing Add:* One Rue St Vincent Blevy 28170 France

BISHOP, JEFFREY BRITTON
PAINTER, EDUCATOR
b Berkeley, Calif, Feb 18, 49. *Study:* Boston Mus Sch, Dipl(with honors), 73; Tufts Univ, BFA, 74; Univ Wash, MFA, 77. *Work:* Seattle Art Mus, Wash. *Comn:* Large wall installation, City Seattle, Wash, 80. *Exhib:* New Ideas, Seattle Art Mus, Wash, 78; Wash Open, Seattle Art Mus, Wash, 79; one-man shows, Linda Farris Gallery, Seattle, Wash, 80, 82, 88 & 93, Mirage Gallery, Los Angeles, Calif, 81 & Seattle Art Mus, 83, San Diego State Univ Gallery, Calif, 94 & Meyerson & Nowinski Art Assocs, Seattle, Wash, 97; Eight Seattle Artists: Installations, Los Angeles Inst Contemp Art, 80; Wash Yr, Henry Gallery, Univ Wash, Seattle, 81; Collage & Assemblage, Miss Mus Art, Jackson & traveling, 81-83; Bellevue Art Mus, Wash, 83; Betty Bowen Tenth Anniversary Exhib, Seattle, Wash, 88; 20th Anniversary Show, Linda Farris Gallery, Seattle, Wash, 90; Watercolor, Bellevue Art Mus, Wash, 91; Betty Bowen Legacy, Security Pacific Gallery, Seattle, 92; Elizabeth Leach Gallery, Portland, Ore, 94; Vox Populi, NY, 95. *Teaching:* Lectr mod art, Univ Wash, Seattle, 78; program dir, Henry Gallery Lecture Series, Seattle, Wash, 78-82; lectr & instr mod art, drawing & painting, Cornish Inst, Seattle, Wash, 79-82. *Awards:* 66th James William Paige Traveling Fel, Boston Mus Fine Arts, 74; Betty Bowen Award, Seattle Art Mus, 82. *Bibliog:* Mathew Kangas (auth), Seattle, Artforum, 5/79 & Art in Am, 81; Barbara Taylor (auth), Eight Seattle Artists, Los Angeles Inst Contemp Art, 80. *Mem:* Allied Arts of Seattle; founding mem Ctr Contemp Art. *Media:* Water Media, Charcoal. *Publ:* Auth, interview with Susan Sontag, Insight, 82. *Mailing Add:* 240 Carlton Ave Brooklyn NY 11205-4002

BISHOP, JEROLD
EDUCATOR, PAINTER
b Salt Lake City, Utah, Apr 14, 36. *Study:* Southern Utah State Col, Cedar City, AB, 56; Utah State Univ, Logan, BS, 60, MFA, 66. *Work:* Valley Nat Bank, Phoenix; Glendale Community Col, Ariz; Starr Commonwealth Boys, Albion, Mich; Court House Collection, Douglas, Ariz. *Comn:* Ariz Hwy Mag, Phoenix, Ariz, 84-86; Collector Plate Series, Fine Arts Mktg, 85. *Exhib:* Mormon Festival Arts, Brigham Young Univ Art Ctr, Provo, Utah, 77-79; Watercolor USA, Springfield Art Mus, Mo, 77 & 80; Univ Ariz Fac Shows, Mus Art, Tucson, 77-85; Watercolor Biennial, Scottsdale Ctr Arts, Ariz, 80; and others. *Pos:* Art dir, Thiokol Chemical Corp, Brigham City, Utah, 63-64 & 66-67; production artist & art dir, Utah State Univ, Logan, 64-66. *Teaching:* Asst prof art, Univ Ariz, Tucson, 67-72, assoc prof, 72-. *Awards:* Masters Meed Medallion, Tubac Festival Arts, Santa Cruz Valley Art Asn, 76; Special Award, 4th Ann Western Fedn Watercolor Socs Exhib, 79; Silver Medal, 57th Ann Nat, Springville Mus Art, Utah, 81; Merit Award, Ariz Watercolor Asn, Scottsdale, 84; Phippen Family Award, Prescott, Ariz, 85. *Mem:* Western Fedn Watercolor Socs; Southern Ariz Watercolor Guild; Ariz Watercolor Asn. *Media:* Watercolor, Mixed. *Mailing Add:* 9133 E Speedway Blvd Tucson AZ 85710-1818

BISSELL, PHIL
CARTOONIST, ILLUSTRATOR
b Worcester, Mass, Feb 1, 26. *Study:* Sch Practical Art, Boston; Art Instr Inc, Minneapolis, grad. *Work:* Baseball Hall Fame, Cooperstown, NY; Basketball Hall Fame, Springfield, Mass; Football Hall Fame, Canton, Ohio; Hockey Hall Fame, Toronto; Swimming Hall of Fame, Ft Lauderdale; and others. *Comn:* New Eng

Patriots (Nat Football League) insignia; Rourke Bridge Plaques, Lowell, Mass. *Exhib:* Southern Calif Expo, 64; Nat Cartoonists Soc, NY, 71 & Washington, DC, 72-79; Man & His World, Ninth Int Salon Cartoons, Montreal. *Awards:* Best Ed Cartoons, 74-88; Scarlet Quill Award for Outstanding Coverage of Intercollegiate Athletics, 76; Mass Bay Chiefs Award, 81. *Mem:* Hon mem Baseball Writers Asn. *Media:* Ink, Tempera. *Publ:* The World Encyclopedia of Cartoons, Horn, Chelsea House, 80; Sportspot, Tall Tales from Tall Ships. *Mailing Add:* 19 Landmark Ln Rockport MA 01966

BJORKLUND, LEE
PAINTER, EDUCATOR
b Wadena, Minn, June 20, 40. *Study:* Univ Minn, Minneapolis, BA, 69 & MFA, 73. *Work:* Walker Art Ctr, Minneapolis Inst Art, Fed Reserve Bank, Norwest Nat Bank & First Nat Bank, Minneapolis; Amerada Hess Corp, NY. *Comn:* Norwest Bank, Minneapolis, Minn, 78; RAUTI, Rochester, Minn, 87; Mayo Clinic, Scottsdale, Ariz, 87. *Exhib:* Walker Art Ctr, 66, 72 & 75; Univ Gallery, 67, 71 & 81; Minn Inst Arts, 75, 81, 86 & 90; Peter M David Gallery, 80-82 & 85; Kuopio Mus, Kuopio, Finland, 81. *Pos:* Visual art coordr, Minn State Arts Bd, Minneapolis, 74-75, co-founder, Minn Artists Exhib Prog, 75, chmn, Visual Studies Div, 75-78, acad adv, 82 & acting dean students, 85-86. *Teaching:* Instr, Univ Minn, 70-72, Art Ctr Minn, 71-72, Minn Mus Art Sch, St Paul, 72-73, Winona State Univ, 72, Minneapolis Col Art & Design, 73-90, assoc prof. *Awards:* Minn State Arts Bd Grant, 72 & 79; Ford Found Grant, 77; Mellon Found Grant, 82-84; and others. *Bibliog:* Mike Steele (auth), Practitioners explore the modern art mystique, Minneapolis Tribune, 5/18/75; Eleanor Heartney (auth), article, New Art Examiner, summer 81; William Hegeman (auth), article, Art News, 11/81; Margot Kriel Galt (auth), The artists who came in from the cold, Minn Monthly, 1/86. *Mem:* Minneapolis Soc Fine Arts. *Media:* Mixed. *Dealer:* Peter M David Gallery 400 First Ave N Minneapolis, Minn. *Mailing Add:* 326 W Elmwood Pl Minneapolis MN 55419

BLACK, DAVID EVANS
SCULPTOR
b Gloucester, Mass, May 29, 1928. *Study:* Skowhegan Sch, Maine, summer 49; Wesleyan Univ, AB, 50; Ind Univ, Bloomington, MFA, 54. *Work:* Neue Nat Galerie, West Berlin, Ger; Dayton Art Inst; Utsukushi-Ga-Hara Mus, Japan; Kalamazoo Col, Mich; Ft Wayne Mus Art, Ind; Cent Mich Univ Mt Pleasant, Clarkson Univ, Potsdam, NY; Univ Alaska, Fairbanks; Zanesville Art Ctr, Ohio. *Comn:* Island Park, Belmont, Calif, 90; Main Libr Plaza, Tucson, Ariz, 91; Ottawa Park, City of Toledo, Ohio, 94; Univ Circle, Cleveland, Ohio, 95; Flyover (auth, catalog), Wright Brothers Mem, City Dayton, Ohio, 96. *Exhib:* One-man show, Amerika-Haus, W Berlin, 71; Neue Nat Gallerie, Berlin, Ger, 77; Lehmbruck Mus, Duisberg, Ger, 77; Taft Mus (with catalog), Cincinnati, Ohio, 85; Indianapolis Mus Art, 85; Kalamazoo Art Inst (with catalog), Mich, 87. *Pos:* Mem, DAAD Artists Prog, Berlin & WGer Govt, 70-72. *Teaching:* Prof sculpture, Ohio State Univ, 54-84. *Awards:* Fulbright Grant, Italy, 62-63; Nat Endowment Arts Individual Artist Grant, 65; Int Sculpture Prize, Hakone Mus, Japan, 85; Special Award, Nat Coun Engineers Asn, 1999. *Bibliog:* Charlotte Lowe (auth), Sonora, Tucson Citizen, 7/4/91; article, Sculpture Mag, 5/92; article, Competitions Mag, 1/95; Flyover, Dayton Daily News, 1994-96; Black on White (film), Umbrella Films Berlin, 2002. *Media:* Metals, Environments. *Interests:* Reading, classical music, museums. *Publ:* Auth, Flyover (booklet), City of Dayton, Ohio, 97; auth, Sculpture for Urban Space, 2006. *Dealer:* David Black Sculpture1066 Lincoln Rd Columbus OH 43212. *Mailing Add:* 1066 Lincoln Rd Columbus OH 43212

BLACK, HERBERT
COLLECTOR
b Can. *Pos:* Pres, Am Iron & Metal Co, Inc, Montreal, Can, currently. *Awards:* Named one of Top 200 Collectors, ARTnews Mag, 2004. *Collection:* Georgian furniture, Impressionist and Modern Art. *Mailing Add:* Am Iron & Metal Co Inc 9100 Henri-Bourassa Blvd East Montreal PQ H1E 2S4 Canada

BLACK, LEON DAVID
COLLECTOR
Study: Dartmouth Col, AB, 73; Harvard Univ, MBA, 75. *Comn:* Trustee Mus of Modern Art, Mt Sinai Hosp, Lincoln Ctr for Performing Arts, Metrop Mus of Art, Prep for Prep, The Jewish Mus, Cardozo Sch of Law, The Asia Soc, Spence Sch, The Vail Valley Found. *Pos:* With Drexel Burnham Lambert Inc, New York City, 77-90, joined as assoc, financial dept, 77, head mergers and acquisitions, 85-90, Co-head corp financial dept; co-founder The Apollo orgn (incl Apollo Mgt LP, Apollo Advisors LP, Apollo Real Estate Advisors LP), 90-; Bd dir, Vail Resorts Inc, Sequa Corp, United Rentals Inc, Allied Waste Industries Inc, 2000-, AMC Entertainment Inc, 2001-, Sirius Satellite Radio Inc, 2001-, Wyndham Int Inc. *Awards:* Named one of Top 200 Collectors, ARTnews Mag, 2004-2006. *Collection:* Old Masters, Impressionist, Modern and Contemporary Art, and Chinese Sculpture. *Mailing Add:* Apollo Advisors 2 Manhattanville Rd Purchase NY 10577

BLACK, LISA
PAINTER, PHOTOGRAPHER
b Lansing, Mich, June 19, 34. *Study:* Univ Paris, Sorbonne, dipl, 55; Univ Mich, BA, 56. *Work:* Conn Bank & Trust; Stamford Hosp, Stamford, Conn. *Comn:* Mural, Easter Seal Rehabilitation Ctr, 89; Painting, Travel Store, Darien, Conn, 93. *Exhib:* New Haven Paint & Clay Club Art Exhib, Conn, 71-72 & 83; Springfield Art League 53rd Nat Exhib, Mass, 72; 32nd Ann Art Exhib, Cedar City, Utah, 72; 15th Nat Exhib Am Art, Chautauqua, NY, 72; Milford Fine Arts Art Exhib, 83; Stamford Mus Conn Art, 89-90, 92 & 94; Juried Exhib, Rowayton Art Ctr, 94, 97-99; Milford Arts Coun, 99; Greenwich Art Soc, 2003-05; and others. *Pos:* Historian, Greenwich Art Soc, 92-93; bd mem, Rowayton Art Ctr, 2000. *Teaching:* Children's art lessons, pvt studio, 78-79; Art hist 5th grade (volunteer), 97-98. *Awards:* First Prize, Rowayton Arts Ctr, 89, 91, 93, 96 & 98; Fred Kraus Mem Award, Stamford Mus Conn Art, 92; Best in Show, Rowayton Arts, Ctr, 97; Greenwich Art Soc Award, 98, 1st Prize, 99, 2000. *Mem:* Rowayton Arts Ctr; New Haven Paint & Clay Club; Greenwich Art Soc; Nat Mus Women Arts; Art Soc Old Greenwich; NY Inst Photograph; Ctr Contemp Printmakers; Greenwich Art Coun. *Media:* All Media. *Interests:* family, art history, museums. *Dealer:* Wilton Gallery Wilton CT; Ninth Life Fine Art Gallery St Thomas VI; Stone Gallery Stanford CT. *Mailing Add:* 8 Belfor Rd Norwalk CT 06850

BLACK, MARY MCCUNE
CURATOR, PAINTER
b Broadwell, Ohio, Feb 14, 1915. *Study:* Ohio Univ, BS(educ), 37, MFA, 58; Amagansett Sch Art, Sarasota, Fla; workshop study with Charles Burchfield, William Thon, Aaron Bohrod, Paul Sample, Eliot O'Hara & Hilton Leech. *Work:* McJunkin Corp; Kanawha Co Pub Libr; WVa State Col, Permanent Collection; Lutheran Church, Parkersburg, WVa; First Christian Church, Charleston, WVa; Venice (Fla) Art Ctr. *Exhib:* Smithsonian Inst, 63; Nat Exhib, Sacramento, 78; WVa Juried Exhib, 79 & 83; Allied Artists WVa, 82; Duo exhib, WVa State Col, 86; one-woman invitational, Venice Art Ctr, Fla, 94, 2000. *Collection Arranged:* Permanent collection exhibition; Fiber & Fabrics; Collectors Exhib of Kanawha Valley. *Pos:* Dir, Charleston Art Gallery Sunrise, 63-75, cur fine arts Sunrise, 75-77; art juror, Fine Arts Exhib Art & Craft Fair, Cedar Lakes, WVa, 79-88; retired; mem adv bd, Fine Arts Dept, West State Col. *Teaching:* Instr art, Sandusky Jr High Sch, 37-39; instr painting, adult prog, Kanawha Co Bd Educ, 58-64; instr art, Valley Day Sch, 60-63; instr painting, YMCA & Charleston Art Gallery, 63-68. *Awards:* Pat Buster Award, Venice Area Art League, 90 & 96; Purchase Award, Tri-State Asn, Huntington, WVa, 90; Merit Award, WVa Watercolor Soc Juried Exhib, 92 & 96; Best of Show WVa Watercolor Soc Regl Exhib, 99; Winners Circle Award, Venice Art Ctr, 2000; plus others. *Mem:* Allied Artists WVa; Nat League Am Pen Women; Southern Watercolor Soc (signature mem); Venice Area Art League, Fla; charter mem WVa Watercolor Soc. *Media:* Watercolor, Acrylic. *Specialty:* Painting, juried crafts. *Interests:* painting/all media. *Dealer:* Gallery Eleven 1033 Quarrier St Charleston WV 25301. *Mailing Add:* Univ of Charleston Erma Byrd Gallery 2300 MacCorkle Ave Charleston WV 25304

BLACK, SCOTT M
COLLECTOR
Study: Math, Econ, Johns Hopkins Univ, BS; Econ, Harvard Univ, MBA. *Pos:* Various positions to head, corp develop, Merrill Lynch; with Joseph E. Seagram, Xerox, William O'Neill Co, 1978; mgr, Delphi Value Fund; founder, pres, Delphi Mgt Inc, Boston, 80-; adv bd, Portland Mus Art, Mus Fine Arts, Boston, John F Kennedy Sch Govt, Harvard Univ, Boston, Johns Hopkins Univ, Northeastern Univ. *Awards:* Named one of Top 200 Collectors, ARTnews Magazine, 2004-2006. *Collection:* Impressionist and modern art. *Mailing Add:* Delphi Mgmt 50 Rowes Wharf Ste 540 Boston MA 02110

BLACKBURN, DAVID
PAINTER
b Huddersfield, UK, June 22, 39. *Study:* Huddersfield Sch Art, NDD, 59; Royal Col Art, London DesRCA, 62. *Hon Degrees:* U Huddersfield, DLit (hon). *Work:* Fogg Mus, Harvard, Cambridge, Mass; Mus Mod Art, NY; Phillips Collection, Washington; Albertina, Vienna; Nat Gallery Victoria, Melbourne; British Mus, London. *Exhib:* Yale Ctr Brit Art, New Haven, 88; retrospective, Dulwich Picture Gallery, London, 89 & Schloss Cappenberg, Frankfurt, 94; Peter Bartlow Gallery, Chicago, 92; Gallery Bentley, Phoenix, 96; Hart Gallery, London, 94, 96, 98, 00, 02, 04. *Teaching:* Vis prof fine art, Univ Calif, Davis, 79 & Georgetown Univ, Washington, 81; vis artist, Humanities Res Centre, Australian Nat Univ, Canberra, 95. *Bibliog:* R S Phillips (auth), Light & Landscapes, Hart, 92; Peter Fuller (auth), Modern Painters, Methuen, 93; Sasha Grishin (auth), David Blackburn & the Visionary Landscape Tradition, Hart, 95; C Mullins (auth), David Blackburn: The Sublime Landscape, 2002. *Media:* Pastel. *Dealer:* Peter Bartlow Gallery 44 E Superior St Chicago IL. *Mailing Add:* 113 Upper St Islington/London United Kingdom N11QN

BLACKBURN, ED M
PAINTER
b Amarillo, Tex, June 15, 40. *Study:* Univ Tex, BFA, 62; Brooklyn Mus, Beckman Scholar, 63; Univ Calif, Berkeley, MA, 65. *Work:* Ft Worth Art Mus; Dallas Mus Fine Art. *Comn:* Mural on canvas, USAA, San Antonio, 75; Larger Canvas II (billboard), Houston Nat Bank, 78. *Exhib:* Off the Wall, San Antonio Mus Art, 81; solo exhib, Ft Worth Art Mus, 82; Am Still Life 1945-1983, Contemp Arts Mus, Houston, 83; Texas Images and Vision, Univ Tex Huntington Gallery, Austin & Amarillo Art Ctr, 83; 38th Corcoran Biennial & Second Western States, 83-84. *Awards:* Painting Grant, Nat Endowment Arts, 77 & 89-90. *Bibliog:* Ken Harrison (dir), Ed Blackburn (film), PBS, 75. *Media:* Acrylic, Oil. *Dealer:* Moody Gallery 2815 Colquit Houston TX 77098

BLACKBURN, LINDA Z
PAINTER
b Baltimore, Md, July 5, 41. *Study:* Univ Tex, Austin, BFA, 62; Univ Calif, Berkeley, MA, 65. *Work:* Mod Mus Ft Worth, Tex; Longview Mus, Tex; Crescent Collection, Dallas; ARCO, Dallas; Zales, Chicago. *Exhib:* Women of the Am West, Bruce Mus, Greenwich, Conn, 85; solo exhib, Tyler Mus Art, Tex, 89; Texas Women, Nat Mus Women Arts, Washington, DC, 89; Mid Am Biennial, Nelson-Atkins, Kansas City, 89; James Gallery, Houston, 97; and others. *Awards:* Grant, Mid-Am Nat Endowment Arts, 88; Grant, Nat Endowment Arts, 89. *Bibliog:* Susan Freudenheim (auth), A survey of Texas art, Arts & Archit Mag, winter 81; Susan Freudenheim (auth), Linda Blackburn at Mattingly-Baker, Art Am, 1/84; Mark Thistlethwaite (auth), article, Artspace Mag, summer 84. *Media:* All Media. *Dealer:* James Gallery 2930 Revere Suite 200 Houston TX 77098. *Mailing Add:* 3901 Bilglade Ft Worth TX 76109

BLACKBURN, LOREN HAYNER
PAINTER, ILLUSTRATOR
b South Glens Falls, NY, Mar 5, 29. *Study:* Self-taught. *Work:* Coopers Cave Collection Lake George; Summer Youth Theater Group, Lake George, NY; US Air Force Permanent Collection; US Navy Collection. *Comn:* First Nat Bank, Glen Falls; NAm Med Instrument Corp; Champlain Stone Ltd; Garwood Boat Manufacturing; Albany Int. *Exhib:* Solo exhibs, Crandall Libr Mus, Glens Falls, NY, 79, Saratoga Golf & Polo Club, NY, 81, Appleland Gallery, Burnt Hills, NY, 83, Aqueduct Race Track, Jamaica, NY, 83, Smith Opera House, Geneva, NY, 84, Saratoga City Ctr, NY, 84 & 85 & Gallery of Arts Guild, Old Forge, NY, 85, Legends of Lake George, Recent Watercolors, Lake Shore, Gallery Bolton Landing; Fine Arts Pavilion, Worlds Fair, Knoxville, Tenn, 82; Nat Am Watercolor Exhib, Old Forge, NY, 84 & 85; Sarasota Racing Series Paintings, 87 & 88; Saratoga Series, Chapman Hist Mus, 89. *Awards:* Blue Ribbon, 32nd Ann Glens Falls Regional Art Exhib, 79; Second Place & Artists Choice, 12th Ann Old Saratoga Hist Asn Exhib, 80; Best of Watercolors, Lower Adirondack Regional Art Coun Outdoor Show, 80; Todah Moshe Award, Nat Am Exhib, Old Forge, NY, 84. *Bibliog:* Introductions, US Art, 32, 8/97; O Christmas Tree, US Art, 12/97; article, US Art, 9/98. *Mem:* Lower Adirondack Regional Art Coun (mem exec bd, 80-85, pres, 81-82). *Media:* Watercolor, Pastels; Oil. *Specialty:* Lithography & Giclee of org watercolors. *Publ:* Auth, Watercolor page, Am Artist Mag, 3/83. *Dealer:* Blackburn Gallery 261 Bay Rd Glens Falls NY 12801; Primrose Press New Hope PA; Blackburn Gallery 286 Bay Rd Queensbury NY. *Mailing Add:* 38 Fort Amherst Rd Glens Falls NY 12801-2731

BLACKEMORE, AMY
PHOTOGRAPHER
b Tulsa, Okla. *Study:* MFA, 1985. *Exhib:* Jill in Woods, 2005; Group show, Inman Gallery, Houston, Tex. *Pos:* Prof photog, 1986-. *Awards:* Whitney Biennial, Whitney Mus Art, NYC, 2006. *Mailing Add:* 3901 Main St Houston TX 77002

BLACKETER, JAMES RICHARD
PAINTER, ART DEALER
b Laguna Beach, Calif, Sept 23, 31. *Study:* Santa Ana Col; also with Bennett Bradbury. *Exhib:* Laguna Beach Invitational Marine Show, Calif, 59; Los Angeles Co Fair Invitational Exhib, Pomona, Calif, 60; Hunt-Wesson Foods Show, Fullerton, Calif, 72. *Pos:* Art dir, Fed Sign & Signal Corp, Los Angeles, 58-60, Santa Ana, 60-72; owner, The Studio (art gallery), Laguna Beach. *Teaching:* Pvt classes oil painting, 60-. *Awards:* Laguna Beach Art Asn Awards, 51, 58, 59 & 60; Festival of Arts Award, 58; Ebell Club Los Angeles Award, 60. *Mem:* Laguna Beach Art Asn (secy, 60); Am Inst Fine Arts; Laguna Beach Festival Arts, Showcase 21. *Media:* Oil. *Specialty:* Marine oil paintings

BLACKEY, MARY MADLYN
PAINTER, PRINTMAKER
b Glen Cove, NY. *Study:* Albright Art Sch, NY, cert; State Univ NY, Buffalo, BS(art educ); Art Students League; Ruth Leaf Etching Studio; Donn Steward Etching Workshop. *Work:* Columbia Broadcasting Studio, NY; Hofstra Univ; Int Bus Machines; Conoco Oil; Nassau Community Col; James Mitchner Mus. *Exhib:* one-man show, Ariz Aqueous, Tubac, Ariz, 1994, 1999, 2004, Spatial Ventures, Germantown Acad Art Ctr, Pa, 1996 & St Joseph's Col, Philadelphia, Pa, 1997, Planetfest, The Pasadena Center, Los Angeles, 1997, Gloucester Co Col, NJ, 1998, Magical Encounters - Sky and Earth, Pennswood Art Gallery, Pa, 2000 & Reusin Gallery, Philadelphia, Pa, 2000; Project Diomede, Inst Contemp Art, The Clocktower, 89; Positive Actions: Visual Aids, billboard design, Inst Contemp Art, NY, 90; Urban Paradise-Gardens in the City, public art design, Proj of the Pub Art Fund, NY, 93; Three Artist Exhib-Thomas Moser, Philadelphia, Pa, 95; Night of 1000 Drawings, Artists Space, NY, 95; Spiritual Matters, Trenton City Mus, NJ, 95; Works on Paper, Am Col, Pa, 98; Watercolor USA, Springfield Art Mus, Mo, 1999, 2000; A Wintry Mix, Gallery 125, Trenton, NJ, 2005; Spring Exhib, Gallery 125, Trenton, NJ, 2006; Am Color Print Soc Exhib, Philadelphia Sketch Club, Pa, 2006; The Art of Printmaking-Spring, Bull Gallery, Newport, RI, 2006. *Teaching:* Instr watercolor, Jackson Heights Art Club, 71-72, Five Towns Music & Art Found, 77-79, Great Neck Adult Prog, 81-83 & Islip Art Mus, 86. *Awards:* Fourth Prize, Arches Nat Watercolor Competition, 91; Patron Purchase Award, Watercolor, USA, Springfield Art Mus, Mo, 92, 2000; Award Excellence, Aqueous 94, Tubac, Ariz, 94; Crest Award, Philadelphia Watercolor Soc, 2000; Purchase award, Mitchner Mus, Doylestown, Pa, 2001; Jeanne Clair Mem Award-Etching, Am Color Print Soc, Philadelphia, Pa, 2005; Jurors Award, Works on Paper, Artsbridge, Lambertville, NJ, 2006. *Bibliog:* Malcolm Preston (auth), Vision in Space and Form, Newsday, 90; Peter A Juley & Son Collection-Nat Mus Am Art, Smithsonian Inst; The Best of Watercolor, Rockport Publ, 95; Artists of the River Towns-Their Works and their Stories, 2002. *Mem:* Am Watercolor Soc; Nat Soc Painters Casein & Acrylic (bd dir, 82-84); Pa Watercolor Club; Found for Archit, 90-; Philadelphia Watercolor Club, 90-; Am Color Print Soc, 2004-. *Media:* Watercolor, Acrylic; Etching. *Interests:* Walking, travel, archit, local history. *Publ:* The American Medium (watercolor), Am Watercolorists Visual Travel Prog; Watercolor - The Creative Experience, NLight Publ; The Best of Watercolor, Vol 3, Rockport Publ, 95, 99. *Dealer:* Langman Gallery Willow Grove Pa. *Mailing Add:* 1032 Radcliffe St C-15 Bristol PA 19007

BLACKMAN, THOMAS PATRICK
DIRECTOR, PRINTMAKER
b Des Moines, Iowa, May 15, 51. *Study:* Univ Iowa, Iowa City, BFA, 76. *Collection Arranged:* Chicago Sculpture Int-Mile 1, 2, 3, 82-84. *Pos:* Sponger & shop asst, Landfall Press, Chicago, 78-80; intaglio printer, Metropress, Chicago, 80-81; dir, Chicago Int Art Exposition, 81-, Chicago Int Antique Show, 84-91; pres, Thomas Blackman Assoc Inc, Chicago, 92-97. *Mailing Add:* Thomas Blackman Assocs Inc 2550 W Lexington St Chicago IL 60612

BLACKMUN, BARBARA WINSTON
EDUCATOR, CURATOR
b Merced, Calif, June 29, 28. *Study:* Univ Calif, Los Angeles, BA(fine arts; hons), 49 & PhD(art hist), 84; Ariz State Univ, MA(art hist), 71. *Collection Arranged:* Partners of the Soul, San Diego Mus of Art, 03; Decoding design and Disguise, Mesa Coll, 03; Understanding Women in African Art, Mesa Coll, 04; African Arts of Disruption and Cohesion, MEsa Coll, 05; Power and parody: European though African Eyes, Detroit Inst of Art, 02-07; Benin: West African Kingdom, Mus fuer Voelkerkunde Vienna and Ethnologisches Mus Berlin, 04-06. *Pos:* Founding dir, Univ Arts Workshop, Malawi, Africa, 68-69; co-founder & chmn, Pub Arts Adv Coun, Co of San Diego, 76-78; consult, Kingdom of Benin Exhib, Field Mus Natural Hist, Chicago, 91-92, Cleveland Mus Art, 94 & Art Inst Chicago, 95-96; vis cur, San Diego Mus Art, 2003. *Teaching:* Lectr art hist & chmn art subject bd, Univ Malawi, Limbe, Malawi, Africa, 67-69; prof art hist, San Diego Mesa Col, Calif, 71-2000, prof emeritus, 2000, chmn dept visual arts, 76-78 & 83-85; adj asst prof, Univ Calif, San Diego, 87 & 04; adj assoc prof, Univ Calif, Los Angeles, 88; vis prof art history, UCLA, Los Angeles, 2000. *Awards:* Fulbright Hays Doctoral Res Fel, 80; Grant for Advan Area Res on Africa, Am Coun Learned Soc & Social Sci Res Coun, 93; Nat Endowment for Humanities Collab Grant, Cleveland State Univ, 93-98. *Mem:* Col Art Asn; Archaeol Inst Am; African Studies Asn; Art Historians Southern Calif. *Res:* The Nyau masks of the Maravi and their significance in African art; the bronze and terracotta sculpture of Ife, Nigeria, a classification through style analysis; the iconography of carved figural altar tusks from Benin Kingdom, Nigeria; African Ivories; art history of the Kingdom of Benin and its neighbors. *Publ:* auth, Continuity and Change: The Ivories of Ovonranmwen and Eweka II, African Arts 30, 68-79, 94-96; auth, Icons and Emblems in Ivory, The Art Inst Chicago Mus Studies 23; auth, From Time Immemorial: Historicism in the Court Art of Benin, Nigeria, Symbols of Time in the History of Art, Belgium, 2002; auth, The hands of the Artist, Frank Willett, The Art of Life in Metal, Glasgow, 04. *Mailing Add:* 9850 Ogram Dr La Mesa CA 91941

BLACKSTOCK, VIRGINIA HARRIETT
PAINTER
b St Louis, Mo. *Study:* Univ Mo, BS, 1950; Univ Wis, MA, 1952; studied with Frank Webb, Judi Betts, Cheng Khee Chee, Alex Powers & Steve Quiller. *Work:* St Mary's Hosp, Grand Junction, Colo; John Drazek DDS Peridontal Suite, Grand Junctions, Colo; Dr M Kleinsorge Offices, Delta, Colo; Matthew Drbohlav DDS, Hotchkiss, Colo; Craig Cayo DDS, Montrose, Colo. *Comn:* Outdoor Mural, City Delta, Colo, 1995; paintings, Delta Co Mem Hospital, Colo, 2005-2006. *Exhib:* Solo Exhib, 46 and more exhib's; Rocky Mountain Nat Ann Watercolor Exhib, Foothills Art Ctr, Golden, Colo, 1993 & 94; Allied Artists Am, 85th Ann Exhib, Nat Arts Club, NY, 1993 & 1998; Audubon Artists 56th & 58th Ann Exhib, Salmagundi Club, NY, 1995, 1998, 1999 & 2000; Watercolor Soc Ala, 59th Ann Nat Exhib, Wiregrass Mus, Dothan, Ala, 2000; Colo Watercolor Soc, Ann Exhibs, Colo Hist Mus, Denver, Colo, 2003-2006; RI Watercolor Soc, 11th Nat Watercolor Exhib, Nat Register Hist Place, Pawtucket, RI, 2004; Transparent Watercolor Soc of Am, 30th Exhib, Elmhurst, Ill Art Mus, 2006; Kansas Watercolor Soc, Great 8 Exhib, Wichita Art Mus, Kans, 2006. *Pos:* Chmn, Western Colo Watercolor Soc, 1991- 93, 1995, 1998. *Teaching:* Instr, watercolor & drawing, Colo, Ala, Ariz, NMex & Utah, 1995-2005. *Awards:* Honorable Mention, NMex Watercolor Soc, Nat Exhib Chen Khee Chee, 2000; Third place, Wyo Watercolor Soc XVII, Nat Exhib, 2002; First place, Black Canyon Exhib, 44th & 46th Ann, All Media, 2002 & 2004, Second Place, 47th & 48th Ann, 2005-2006; Award of Excellence, 25th Ann Int Exhib, San Diego Watercolor Soc, 2005. *Mem:* Watercolor Soc, La, Mont, Kans, Pa, NMex & Colo (signature mem); Western Colo Watercolor Soc (chmn, 1991-93 & 98, vpres, 2006); San Diego Watercolor Soc; Audubon Artists Inc. *Media:* Watercolor, Acrylic, Oil. *Publ:* Contribr, Creative Watercolor, A Step by Step Guide, Rockport Publ Inc, 1995; contribr, The Artistic Touch I, Ideas & Techniques, Creative Art Press, 1995; contribr, Abstracts in Watercolor, Rockport Publ Inc, 1996; contribr, Exploring Color, North Light Books, 1998; contribr, Artistic Touch III, Works & Inspirations, Creative Art Press, 1999. *Dealer:* Frame Works Gallery 309 Main St Grand Junction Colo 81419. *Mailing Add:* 31045 L Rd Hotchkiss CO 81419-9409

BLACKWELL, TOM (THOMAS) LEO
PAINTER
b Chicago, Ill, Mar 9, 38. *Work:* Currier Gallery Art, Manchester, NH; Guggenheim Mus, Mus Mod Art, Metrop Mus Art, NY; Detroit Inst Fine Art, Mich; Herbert F Johnson Mus, Cornell Univ, Ithaca, NY; Phoenix Mus Art, Ariz; and many others. *Exhib:* Human Concern-Personal Torment, Whitney Mus Am Art, NY, 69; Whitney Mus Am Art Painting Ann, 72; Prospectus, Art in the Seventies, Aldrich Mus Contemp Art, Ridgefield, Conn, 79; Seven Photorealists from NY Collections, Solomon R Guggenheim Mus, NY, 81; Contemp Am Realism since 1960, Pa Acad Fine Art, Philadelphia, Pa, 81-82; solo exhibs, Selected works 1970-1980, Dartmouth Col, Hanover, NH, 80, Univ Ariz Mus Art, Tuscon, 81; Louis K Meisel Gallery, NY, 77, 80, 82 & 91, Currier Gallery Art, Manchester, NH, 85; Carlo Lamagna Gallery, NY, 86; Ten Super Realists, Ft Lauderdale Mus Art, 91-92; Really, Real, Realism, Jack Wright Gallery, Palm Beach, Fla, 93; Photo Realism, The Last Decade, Louis K Meisel Gallery, NY, 93; The Purloined Image, Flint Inst Arts, Mich, 93; Art After Art, Nassau Co Mus, Roslyn, NY, 94; and others. *Teaching:* Artist-in-residence, Dartmouth Col, Hanover, NH, 80; Univ Ariz, Tuscon, 81; instr, Sch Visual Arts, New York, 85-89. *Awards:* Grant, New Hampshire Comn Arts, 85. *Bibliog:* John Russell (auth), Painters from Brussels, New York Times, 5/21/82; Terence Mullaly (auth), Icy reflections of life, London Daily Telegraph, 83; Vivien Raynor (auth), Tom Blackwell, New York Times, 5/2/86. *Media:* Oil. *Publ:* Auth, Photorealism, Harry N Abrams; Photorealism Since 1980, Harry N Abrams; American Watercolors, Abbeville Press; Contemporary American Realism Since 1960, New York Graphic Soc. *Mailing Add:* Thompson Hollow St New Kingston NY 12459

BLACKWOOD, DAVID (LLOYD)
PAINTER, PRINTMAKER
b Wesleyville, Nfld, Can, Nov 7, 41. *Study:* Ont Col Art, Toronto, 59-64. *Work:* Nat Gallery Can; Nat Gallery Australia; Art Gallery Ont; Montreal Mus Fine Arts; NB Mus. *Exhib:* Int Graphics, Montreal Mus Fine Arts, 71; 1st Norweg Biennial, Frederickstad, 72; Biennial Int de l'Estampe, Paris, France, 73. *Pos:* Artist-in-residence, Univ Toronto, 69-75. *Teaching:* Art master, Trinity Col Sch, Port Hope, Ont, 63-75. *Awards:* Ingres Medal, Govt France, 63; Purchase Award Can Biennial, Nat Gallery Can, 64; Hornansky Award Int Graphics, Montreal Mus Fine Arts, 71. *Bibliog:* Rex Bromfield (auth), David Blackwood (film), CBC, 72; Farley Mowat (auth), Survivor, Wake of the Great Sealers, McClelland & Little Brown, 73; Blackwood (film), NFB, 75. *Mem:* Royal Can Acad Art (vpres, 79). *Dealer:* Gallery Quan 112 Scollard St Toronto ON M5R 1G2 Can. *Mailing Add:* 22 King St Port Hope ON L1A 2R5 Canada

BLAGDEN, ALLEN
PAINTER, PRINTMAKER
b New York, NY, Feb 21, 38. *Study:* Hotchkiss Sch; Yale Univ Summer Art Sch; Cornell Univ, BFA. *Work:* Berkshire Mus, Pittsfield, Mass; Garvan Collection, Peabody Mus, New Haven, Conn; New Britain Mus Am Art, Conn; Adirondack Mus, Blue Mountain Lake, NY; Leigh Yawkey Woodson Mus, Wausau, Wis; and others. *Comn:* Many pvt portrait commissions. *Exhib:* Father and Son Show, Mongerson Wunderlich Gallery, Chicago, 89; one-man shows, Rehn Gallery & Kennedy Galleries, NY, Indian Images, Mongerson Wunderlich Gallery, Chicago, 90; Birds in Art, Leigh Yawkey Woodson Art Mus, Wausau, Wis, 90; Artists of Am, Denver, Colo, 90; Howard Godel Fine Arts, NY; and others. *Pos:* Illusr dept ornithology, Smithsonian Inst, Washington, DC, 62-63. *Teaching:* Instr painting, Hotchkiss Sch, 68-69; artist-in-residence, Cornell Univ, 82. *Awards:* Allied Artist Award, 63; Century Club Art Prize, 71; Marine Award, Arts for the Parks, 00. *Mem:* Century Asn, NY; Artists' Fel, NY. *Media:* Watercolor, Oil; Etching, Lithography. *Publ:* Wildlife Painters at Work, Watson-Gupthill. *Dealer:* Mongerson-Wunderlich 704 N Wells St Chicago IL 60610; Howard Godel 39A E 72 New York NY 10021. *Mailing Add:* Box 625 Salisbury CT 06068

BLAGDEN, THOMAS P
PAINTER
b Chester, Pa, Mar 29, 1911. *Study:* Yale Univ, BA, 33; Pa Acad Fine Arts, 33-35; spec study with Henry Hensche & George Demetrios. *Work:* Addison Gallery Am Art, Andover, Mass; Wadsworth Atheneum, Hartford, Conn; Berkshire Mus, Pittsfield, Mass; New Britain Mus Am Art, New Britain, Conn; Neuberger Mus, Purchase, NY; Currier Gallery, Manchester, NH. *Exhib:* Pa Acad Fine Arts, Philadelphia, 38; Corcoran Gallery Art, Washington, DC, 41; Metrop Mus Art, NY, 50; Am Acad Arts & Lett, NY, 61; Loeb Drama Ctr, Harvard Univ, Cambridge, Mass, 71; one-man show, Keene State Col, NH, 79 & 21 other one-man exhibs, incl nine in NY (Milch Galleries & others), St Gaudens Mus, New Britain Mus, American Art. *Teaching:* Instr art, Hotchkiss Sch, Lakeville, Conn, 35-56. *Awards:* Purchase Prize, Wadsworth Atheneum & Berkshire Mus. *Mem:* Century Club, NY; Conn Watercolor Soc. *Media:* Oil, Watercolor. *Mailing Add:* 26 Town Hill Rd Lakeville CT 06039

BLAGG, MARGARET
DIRECTOR
Study: Tex Christian Univ, BA, 70; Univ of Tex at Austin, MA, 75. *Work:* The Old Jail Art Center; The Baltimore Mus Art, Md; Metropolitan Mus Art, NY; Mus of Art, RI Sch of Design, Providence. *Pos:* Exec dir, Tex Asn of Mus, Austin, 1988-94; acct dir, The RISD Mus, Providence, RI, 1998, exec dir, The Old Jail Art Ctr, Albany, Tex, 2001-. *Mem:* AAM; TexAsn Mus. *Mailing Add:* The Old Jail Art Center 201 S Second Albany TX 76430

BLAINE, FREDERICK MATTHEW
SCULPTOR, EDUCATOR
b Baltimore, Md, May 24, 47. *Study:* Univ Miss, BA, 70. *Work:* Blithe Spirit, Frogpond & Japan Phyle, Int Soc Copier Artists; The Tate Gallery, London; Metrop Mus Art, NY; Mus Mod Art, NY; The Smithsonian; Australia Nat Gallery; Pompidou Ctr Gallery, Paris; and others. *Exhib:* 24th, 25th & 26th Ann Nat Show, Acad Arts, Easton, Md, 88; 47th Ann Nat Competition, Lakeworth, Fla, 88; Artist's Equity 3rd & 4th Ann Awards Exhib, Washington, DC, 88; one-man show, DCCA Gallery, Wilmington, Del, 89; Biannual Show Del Art Mus, 89. *Pos:* Bd trustees, Rehoboth Art League, 88-94; chmn art dept, Seaford Sch Dist. *Teaching:* Instr art-sec, Seaford Sch Dist, 70-02; asst prof ceramics & sculpture, Salisbury State Univ, 83-, lectr art, 84-. *Awards:* Jury of Selection Awards, Mont Miniature Internat, (show), 88; First Place Sculpture, RAL 50th Ann Member Show, 88. *Mem:* Del Art Educ Asn; Naval Acad Sailing Squadron; Haiku Soc Am; Brit Haiku Soc. *Media:* All. *Publ:* Contribr, Sculpture: Technique, Form, Content, Davis Publ, 88; auth, Brithespirit, Frogpond, Int Soc Copier Artists. *Dealer:* Art South Philadelphia PA. *Mailing Add:* 908 W St Laurel DE 19956

BLAIR, CARL RAYMOND
PAINTER, ART DEALER
b Atchison, Kans, Nov 28, 32. *Study:* Univ Kans, BFA, 56; Kansas City Art Inst; Sch Design, MFA, 57. *Work:* Mint Mus Art, Charlotte, NC; Greenville Co Mus Art, SC; Greenville Col, Ill; SC Arts Comn, Columbia; Clemson Univ, SC. *Comn:* IBM; McDonalds Inc. *Exhib:* 33rd Butler Ann Painting Exhib, Youngstown, Ohio; Soc Four Arts, Palm Beach, Fla; Piedmont Painting & Sculpture Exhib, Charlotte, 65; Appalachian Corridors I, Charleston, WVa, 68; Int Platform Asn, Washington, DC, 71; Palazzo Venezia, Rome, Italy, 84. *Pos:* Co-founder & pres, Hampton III Gallery, Taylors, SC. *Teaching:* Prof drawing & painting, Bob Jones Univ, 57-98; summer sch, Kansas City Art Inst & Greenville Co Mus Art. *Awards:* Appalachian Corridors I, SC Arts Comn, 68; Int Platform Asn, 68; SC Arts Commission, 88. *Bibliog:* La Revue Moderne, Paris, France, 65-68; Jack A Morris, Jr (auth), Contemporary artists of South Carolina, 70. *Mem:* SC Artists Guild (adv bd, 57-); Upstate Visual Artists. *Media:* Oil; Acrylic. *Specialty:* Painting; Printmaking; Sculpture; Ceramics. *Dealer:* Hampton III Gallery Ltd Gallery Ctr Taylors SC 29687; Larry Elder Gallery Charlotte NC. *Mailing Add:* No 2 Oakleaf Rd Greenville SC 29609

BLAIR, DIKE
PAINTER, SCULPTOR
b New Castle, Pa, Aug 2, 52. *Study:* Univ Colo, 71-75; Skowhegan Sch Painting & Sculpture, 74; Whitney Mus Independent Study Prog, 76; Sch Art Inst Chicago, MFA, 77. *Comn:* Construction (7ft x 30ft), Hosp Corp Am, Nashville, 82; photo glass mural (7 ft x 1/2 ft), Murray Hill Cinema, NY, 90. *Exhib:* Painting & Sculpture Today, Ind Mus Art, 86; Landscape in the Age of Anxiety, Lehman Col Art Gallery, 86; The New Romantic Landscape, Whitney Mus, Fairfield Co, 87; Image World, Whitney Mus Am Art, NY, 89; Bellevue, Mus Mod Art, Vienna, Austria, 89; The Winter of Love, Mus Mod Art, Paris, France; Let's Entertain, The Walker Art Cen, Minneapolis, Minn, 2000; Elysian Fields Cen, Georges Pompidou, Paris, France, 2000. *Pos:* editor, Purple Mag. *Teaching:* adj painting instr, RISD. *Awards:* Fel, Mid-Atlantic Regional, Nat Endowment Arts, 88-89; Louis Comfort Tiffany Found Award, 95. *Bibliog:* Mary Ellen Haus (auth), The Unnatural Landscape, Art News, 1/88; Robert Mahoney (auth), Reviews, Arts Mag, 1/92; Jeff Rian (auth), Ouverture, Flash Art, 97; Tim Griffin (auth) The Intangible Economy, Art & Text, 2000. *Media:* Paint & Photo on Glass. *Publ:* Auth, GFWFQ recalled, Issue No 6, summer 86. *Mailing Add:* c/o Feature Inc 530 W 25th St New York NY 10001

BLAIR, PHILIPPA MARY
PAINTER, EDUCATOR
b Christchurch, NZ, Nov 18, 45; US citizen. *Study:* Univ Canterbury, NZ, Diploma Fine Arts, 67; Massey Univ, NZ, BA English, 68; Auckland Univ, NZ, BA Art Hist, 73-74; Auckland Secondary Teachers Col, Diploma of Art Teaching, 76. *Work:* Long Beach Mus, Calif; Mus of New Zealand (Te Papa), Wellington, NZ; Conn Graphic Arts Ctr, Norwalk; Citicorp/Citibank, NY; Atlantic RIchfield Corp, Los Angeles, Calif; Pfizer Corp, Conn; General Electric Co, NY; Hong Kong & Shanghai Bank. *Comn:* mural, Univ Auckland, NZ, 83; stain glass, Cook Island Church, Auckland, NZ, 83; mural, Auckland City, NZ, 89; After Crazy Horse, Origins Dance Theatre, Auckland, NZ, 90; lithographs, Sky City Hotel & Casino, Auckland, NZ, 95. *Exhib:* Gestural Maps, Post Gallery, Los Angeles, 2000; TransMotion, DoubleVision Gallery, Los Angeles, 2001; Maximal Abstraction, Judith Anderson Gallery, 2001; Trajectories, J Land Gallery, Wellington, NZ, 2001; New Paintings, Pacific Art Gallery, Zug, Switz, 2002; TransMotion, J Land Gallery, Wellington, New Zealand, 2002; Between Heaven and Earth, W Wickiser Gallery, 2003; New Work, Pfizer Global Research Ctr, New London, Conn, 2003; Maps, Fyr Arte Contemporanea, Florence, Italy, 2003; Cutting Loose, D Vision Gallery, La and Janne Land Gallery, NZ, 2004; Eye Blast, Cypress Col, Calif, 2005; Point and Line to Plane, COCA, 2005; Llano Quemado, Fyr Arte Contemporanea, Florence, Ital, 2005; Recent Paintings, Wittenderson Gallery, Auckland, NZ, 2005; Flow Show, Riverside Art Mus, Calif, 2005. *Teaching:* artist in residence, Canberra Sch Art, Australia, 84, Griffis Art Ctr, New London, Conn, 2002 and Rangi Ruru School, Christchurch, NZ, 2005; lectr painting, Univ Canterbury, NZ, 84, Univ Auckland, 87-94 & Otis Col Art & Design, 2001-2004; vis artist, Art Ctr Col Design, Pasadena, Calif, 95-2001; painting instr, Otis Col Art & Design; painting tutor, Santa Reparata Sch of Art, Florence, Italy, 2002 and Santa Repavata School of Art, Florence, Italy, 2005. *Awards:* Arts Coun Grant, Queen Elizabeth II, 80-84; Travel Award, Air NZ / QEII Arts Coun, 87. *Bibliog:* Michael Dunn (auth), Concise History of NZ Painting, 91; Beate Starck (auth), Philippa Blair, Univ of Auckland, 91; W Brown (auth), 100 NZ Paintings, 94; Michael Dunn (auth), Contemp NZ Painting, Craftsman's Press, Australia, 96; Michael Dunn (auth), NZ Painting: A Concise History, 2003. *Mem:* Col Art Asn. *Media:* Oil, Acrylic, Lithography. *Specialty:* Abstract Contemporary Art. *Collection:* Christchurch Gallery, NZ; Long Beach Museum, CA; Auckland City, NZ. *Publ:* auth, Acts of Inclusion, Spirit of P Blairs Recent Painting, Art NZ, 82, Metamorphosis in P Blairs Recent Painting, 86 & Paint for your Life, 94; Micro Organsims: Pacific Circuits, private publ, 96; A Hutchison (auth), Maximal Abstraction, 2001; C Fusco, Transmotion: Drawings & Painting by P Blair, 2002; C Fusco (auth), P Blair at DoubleVision Gallery, Asian Art News, 2002; A Hutchison (auth), Cutting Loose, 2004; A Hutchison (auth), Eye Blast, 2005; P Frank, Flow, Riverside Art Mus, 2005. *Dealer:* Paper Graphica, 192 Bealey Ave, Christchurch NZ; Janne Land Gallery PO Box 6269 Wellington NZ; Warwick Henderson Gallery, 32 Bath St, Parnell, Auckland NZ; Brooke-Gifford Gallery 112 Manchester St Christchurch NZ. *Mailing Add:* 656 Angelus Pl Venice CA 90291

BLAIR, ROBERT NOEL
PAINTER, SCULPTOR
b Buffalo, NY, Aug 12, 12. *Study:* Sch Mus Fine Arts, Boston, Mass. *Work:* Metrop Mus Art, NY; Butler Inst Am Art, Youngstown, Ohio; Munson-Williams-Proctor Inst, Utica, NY; Twain Mus Hist Art; Ford Motor Co Collection, Dearborn, Mich; and others. *Comn:* Sermon on the Mount (oil, tempera), US Army Chapel, Ft McClellan, Ala, 43; Open Hearth (oil), Bethlehem Steel Plant, Lackawanna, NY, 47. *Exhib:* Corcoran Biennial, Corcoran Gallery Art, Washington, DC, 47; Watercolor Int, Art Inst Chicago, Ill, 48; Pa Acad Fine Arts Nat, Philadelphia, 48; Butler Art Inst Nat & Metrop Mus Art Watercolor Nat, 53; one-man retrospective, Community Tribute Exhibition, State Univ NY Col Buffalo, 66, 100 paintings & drawings of World War II - Entitled: A Soldier's Portfolio, Burchfield Art Ctr, Buffalo, NY, 85; and others. *Pos:* Dir, Art Inst Buffalo, 46-49; illusr, Ford Times Mag, 58-61. *Teaching:* Instr painting, Art Inst Buffalo, 38-55, Albright Art Sch, 55 & State Univ NY Col Buffalo, 71. *Awards:* Guggenheim Fels, 46 & 51; Watowsky Prize, Art Inst Chicago, 48; First

Watercolor Prize, Butler Inst Am Art, 53. *Mem:* Buffalo Soc Artists. *Media:* Watercolor, Oil. *Res:* Expansion of technical possibilities in painting. *Publ:* Illusr, St Lawrence Seaway, 57; illusr, Am Artist Mag, 66; illusr, Jeannie's world, 66; illusr & auth, Watercolorists at work, 71. *Mailing Add:* 7703 Olean Rd Holland NY 14080-9709

BLAKE, JANE SALLEY
PUBLISHER, EDITOR
b Tallahassee, Fla, Sept 3, 37. *Study:* Fla State Univ, Tallahassee, BA(fine arts & journalism), 58. *Pos:* Founder, pres & chmn bd, Arts Forum Inc, Louisville, Ky, 78-84; publ, exec ed, Beaux Arts mag, 80-84; pres, Blake Publ Inc, Louisville, Ky, 83-86; pres, principal, J S Blake Commun Group, Louisville, Ky, 86-; pres, principal, Ctr Mag, Inc, 86. *Awards:* 13 Louie Awards, Advert Club, Louisville, Ky, 81-84; 4 Landmarks Excellence Awards, PRSA & IABC, Louisville, Ky; Gov's Arts Award for Media Excellence, 89; Above & Beyond the Call of Duty Award, 90. *Mem:* Sigma Delta Chi Prof Journalism Soc; Pub Relations Soc Am; Women in Commun. *Publ:* Ctr Mag Ky Ctr Arts, 83; Publ, Practical Pub Relations for Non-professionals, 85; Kentucky Marquee, 86. *Dealer:* The Center Magazine Inc PO Box 22312 Louisville KY 40252. *Mailing Add:* PO Box 22312 Louisville KY 40252-0312

BLAKE, JEREMY
ARTIST
Study: Sch Art Inst Chicago, BFA, 1993; Cal-Arts, MFA, 1995. *Work:* Mus Contemp Art, San Diego, 2002, Am Mus Moving Image, Astoria, NY, 2003; Whitney Biennial Am Art, Whitney Mus Am Art, 2000, 2002, 2004; Wadsworth Atheneum Mus Art, Hartford, Conn, 2004. *Exhib:* One-man shows incl One Hit Wonder, Work on Paper Inc, Los Angeles, 1999, Bungalow 8, Contemp Arts Ctr, Cincinnati, 2000, Angel Dust, XYZ, Toronto, Can, 2001, The 59th Minute: Video Art, Time Sq Astrovision, NY City, 2003, Autumn Almanac, Feigen Contemp, NY, 2003, Sister, Los Angeles, 2004, Galerie Ghislaine Hussenot, Paris, 2004, Centro de Arte Caja de Burgos, Spain, 2004; exhib in group shows at Heaven's in the Backseat of My Cadillac, Name Gallery, Chicago, 1995, Hist of Glamour, Works on Paper Inc, Los Angeles, 1998, Fifteen, Lobby Gallery, Deutshe Bank, NY, 1999, Maximal Minimal, Feigen Contemp, NY, 2000, BitStreams, 2001, Looking at Am, Yale Univ Art Gallery, New Haven, Conn, 2002, Animations, Kunst-Werke, Berlin, 2003, Breathtaking, Art Inst Boston, Lesley Univ, 2004, One Channel Only, Atrium Gallery, Univ Conn Sch Fine Arts, 2004, Floor to Ceiling/Wall to Wall. *Awards:* Recipient Interactive Design Rev Medal, ID Mag, 1999; NY Found Arts Fel, 1999; 79th ann Dirs Club Award for Broadcast Design & Animation, 2000. *Mailing Add:* c/o Feigen Contemp Gallery 535 W 20th St New York NY 10011

BLAKE, PETER JOST
ARCHITECT, CRITIC
b Berlin, Ger, Sept 20, 20; US citizen. *Study:* Univ London, 38; Regent St Polytech, Sch Archit, London, 39; Univ Pa, 41; Sch of Archit, Pratt Inst, BArch, 49. *Comn:* Experimental Theaters in NY, Nashville, Tenn, 63-81; Rehabilitation Ctr, Binghamton, NY, 72; Apartment Building for IBA, St Lukes Church, West Berlin, 87-88; Projects for nat & int competition. *Exhib:* Exhibs in Berlin, Moscow & NY, 48-75. *Pos:* Writer, Archit Forum, NY, 42-43, assoc ed, 50-54 & 58-61, managing ed, 61-64, ed, 64-72; cur archit & design, Mus Mod Art, NY, 48-50; partner, Peter Blake & Julian Neski, 58-61; partner, James Baker & Peter Blake, Architects, NY, 64-72; ed-in-chief, Archit Plus, NY, 72-75; chmn, Sch Archit, Boston Archit Ctr, Mass, 75-79; chmn dept archit & planning, Catholic Univ Am, Washington, DC, 79-86; US Delegate for Archit at Helsinki Conf, Budapest, Hungary, 85. *Teaching:* Vis critic/lectr, var US & foreign cols & univs; prof archit, Catholic Univ Am, Washington, DC, 79-91. *Awards:* Archit Critic's Medal, Am Inst Archit, 75; Hon Mention, Vietnam Veterans' Mem Compt, 81; Distinguished Designer Fel, Nat Endowment Arts, 84. *Mem:* Fel Am Inst Architects; Archit League NY (vpres archit, pres, 71-72); Int Design Conf, Aspen, Colo (bd dir, 65-70); Regional Plan Asn. *Publ:* Auth, Master Builders, Knopf, 60; God's Own Junkyard, Holt, Rinehart & Winston, 64; Form Follows Fiasco, Why Modern Architecture Hasn't Worked, Atlantic Monthly Press & Little, Brown & Co, 77; contribr, articles in pop & prof mags & newspapers; auth, No Place Like Utopia, Knopf, 93. *Mailing Add:* Cedar Woods 80 Cedar St Branford CT 06405

BLAKE, PRISCILLA ANN
MURALIST, CERAMIST
b Fall River, Mass, Oct 14, 52. *Study:* Moore Col Art, Philadelphia, Pa, 72; Univ Wis, Madison, BS(textile design), 75. *Work:* Tile Dicarlo Showroom, Chicago, Ill. *Comn:* Jungle design mural, Kwang Herline, Bayside, NY, 86; Trellis mural with leaves, Minchell Residence, Dix Hills, NY, 87; Peacock subject matter, Horvat Residence, Providence, RI, 87; Ocean scene, Padden Residence, Warwick, RI, 88. *Pos:* Textile designer & colorist, Ametex, New York, 77-80; owner, Priscilla Ceramic Tiles, West Yarmouth, Mass, 80-. *Mem:* Am Craft Coun. *Media:* Ceramic Tiles. *Publ:* Darlyn Brewer (auth), Home Section (Art), New York Times, 10/17/85; Kraus Sikes (coauth), The Guild, Kraus & Sikes, 87 & 88

BLAKE, WENDON See Holden, Donald

BLAKELY, GEORGE C
PHOTOGRAPHY, SCULPTOR
b Long Beach, Calif, Apr 7, 51. *Study:* Calif State Univ, Fullerton, MA, 76; Tyler Sch Art, MFA, 78. *Work:* Laguna Art Mus; Fla State Univ; Southwest Ctr Photography. *Exhib:* Solo exhib, San Francisco Mus Mod Art, Calif, 81; Southern Expressions, High Mus Art, Atlanta, Ga, 89; over 250 group exhibs. *Teaching:* Prof art, Fla State Univ, Tallahassee, currently. *Awards:* Grants, Nat Endowment Arts, 81 & 88. *Mem:* Soc Photog Educ. *Media:* Photography. *Mailing Add:* 304 Bradford Rd Tallahassee FL 32303

BLAKENEY, RAE
HISTORIAN, EDITOR
US citizen. *Study:* Wright State Univ, with Dr Eugene Cantelupe, BA, 76; Union Grad Sch, with Dr Barbara Novak, PhD, 87. *Pos:* Guest cur, Tex Humanities Resource Ctr, Austin, 85. *Teaching:* Adj prof urban esthetics, Inst Urban Studies, Univ Tex, Arlington, formerly; adj prof art hist, Dept Art & Art Hist, Univ Tex, formerly. *Mem:* Col Art Asn; Midwest Art Hist Soc; C G Jung Found. *Res:* Psychological basis for meaning of visual form and visual language. *Publ:* Coauth & ed, Rudolf Baranik: Napalm Elegy and Other Works, Wright State Univ Fine Art Galleries, 77; coauth, Alpha, Trans, Chung, A Photographic Model: Semiotics, Film & Interpretation, NFS Press, 78; coauth & ed, Roland Reiss, Psycho-Social Environments, Santa Barbara Mus Art, 81; auth, Image and individuation: Archetypes in the Vervschka Trans-Figurations, SPE Journal, 87

BLANC, (WILLIAM) PETER
SCULPTOR, PAINTER
b New York, NY, June 29, 12. *Study:* Harvard Univ, BA; St John's Univ, LLB; Corcoran Sch Art; Am Univ, MA. *Work:* Va Mus Fine Arts, Richmond; Ft Worth Art Mus, Tex; Tweed Mus, Duluth, Minn; Guild Hall, East Hampton, NY; Harwood Found, Taos, NMex; and others. *Exhib:* Ashawagh Hall, Springs, NY, 71-78, 80, 83-87, 89-93; Goat Alley Gallery, Sag Harbor, NY, 84 & 86, 87-94; Baltimore Mus Art, Md; Brooklyn Mus, NY; Corcoran Gallery, Washington; Fogg Art Mus, Cambridge, Mass; Mus Santa Fe, NMex; Nat Collection Arts, Washington; Va Mus Fine Arts, Richmond, Va; Whitney Mus Am Art, NY; Westbeth Gallery, NY, 88-90; Milleneum Gallery, Easthampton, NY, 95; Clayton Liberatore Gallery, Bridgehampton, NY, 95 & 97; and others. *Pos:* Bd dir, Artists Equity Asn, NY, 63-71. *Teaching:* Pvt classes in painting & drawing, 47-54; instr painting & drawing, Am Univ, 50-53. *Awards:* First Prize for Drawing, Corcoran Gallery Art, 49; Special Award, Wash Watercolor Club, 49 & 52; Hon Mention, Soc Wash Artists, 51 & 53. *Bibliog:* reviews, Newspapers & Art Mags, Washington, DC, New York, East Hampton, NY. *Mem:* Artists Equity Asn, NY; Am Soc Contemp Artists; E Hampton Artist's Alliance. *Media:* Wood; Oil, Charcoal. *Interests:* French & American literature. *Collection:* Virginia Museum Fine Art, Modern Art Museu, Ft Worth, Texas, Tweed Art Museum, Minnesota; Harwood foundation News, Taos, Taos Municipal Schools Collections, New Mexico. *Publ:* Auth, Artist & the atom, Mag of Art, 51, reprinted, Smithsonian Report, 51, Hudson River Mus, 63 & Long Island Univ, 70. *Dealer:* Clayton-Liberatore Gallery Bridgehampton NY. *Mailing Add:* 87 Jermain Ave PO Box 138 Sag Harbor NY 11963

BLANK, MARGOT
PAINTER, PHOTOGRAPHER
b Ger, Jul 31, 25. *Study:* City Col of City Univ of NY, BA, 1966; Col New Rochelle, NY, MA(art educ), 1978. *Work:* Anderson Gallery, Va Commonwealth Univ, Richmond, Va; Charles H Taylor Arts Ctr, Hamton, Va; Joel & Lila Harnett Print Study Ctr, Univ Richmond Mus, Va. *Exhib:* Tredegar Iron Works Exhib II, Fed Arts Coun, Richmond, Va, 1984; Image 86, NC, Ctr for Creative Photog, Durham, NC, 1986; juried exhib, Peninsula Fine Arts Ctr, Newport News, Va, 1992; Hampton Bay Days, 20th Ann Juried Show, The Charles H Taylor Arts Ctr, Hampton, Va, 2002; solo exhib, Charles H Taylor Arts Ctr, Hampton, Va, 2003; 6th Am Print Biennal, Marsh Art Gallery, Univ Richmond Mus, Va, 2004. *Teaching:* Instr, oil painting, YMCA, Macomb, Ill, 1967-68; instr, art, elementary art, NJ Pub Sch, Union City, 1968-69; instr, oil painting, Cult Arts Ctr, Pine Camp, Richmond, Va, 1999-2000. *Awards:* Honorium, Tredegar Iron Works II, Fed Arts Coun, 1984; Thelma Akers Mem Award, Peninsula Fine Arts Ctr, juried exchange, 1992; Best in Show, Purchase Award 20th Annual juried show, Hampton Bay, 2002. *Mem:* Richmond Artists Asn (pres, 1982-84); Va Soc Photographic Arts; Uptown Gallery, Richmond, Va; National Museum of Women in the Arts; Metropolitan Artist Asn, Richmond, Va. *Media:* Oil on canvas, in camera multiexposure, prints on paper. *Publ:* Illustr, Roxbury Chamber Players, Opus One, 1988; illustr, Works by Allan Blank & Margaret Brouwer, Centaur Records Inc, 1993; illustr, New Century, Vol VIII, MMC Recordings Ltd, 1997; illustr, Allan Blank: Music for Bassoon, Centaur Records Inc, 2000; illustr, Chamber Works of Allan Blank, Ariz Univ Recordings, 2000. *Mailing Add:* 2920 Archdale Rd Richmond VA 23235-3208

BLASCO, ISIDRO M
SCULPTOR, ARCHITECT
b Madrid, Spain, Mar 12, 62. *Study:* Sch of Fine Arts of Madrid, BFA, 89, Sch of Arch of Madrid, MArch, 93. *Work:* Mus Modern Art, NY; Mus Modern Art, San Francisco; New Mus, NY. *Comn:* Sculpture, City of ELX, Spain, 92; Public Art, Sculpture Space, Utica, NY, 2000. *Exhib:* Roma, Spanish Acad Rome, 91; Isidro Blasco, Univ Mus, Alicinte, Spain, 98; Isidro Blasco, Contemp Art Mus, San Jose, Calif, 99; Isidro Blasco, Queens Mus, NY, 2000; Insites, Whitney Mus, Stanford, Conn, 2000. *Awards:* Rome Prize, Spanish Acad Rome, 90-91; Pollock-Krainer Award, Pollock Krainer Found, 97-98; Guggenheim Fel, Guggenheim Found, 2000-01. *Media:* All Media. *Dealer:* Stefan Stux, 329 W 20th, 9th Fl, New York NY 10011. *Mailing Add:* 208 W 29th St # 504 New York NY 10001

BLAU, DOUGLAS
ASSEMBLAGE ARTIST
b Los Angeles, Calif, Oct 11, 55. *Study:* Washington Univ, St Louis, AB & BFA, 77. *Work:* Mus Mod Art, NY. *Exhib:* The Naturalist Gathers, Stein Gladstone, NY, 92; Genre: The Conversation Piece, Sperone Westwater, NY, 93; Stills, Mus Mod Art, NY, 94; Biennial Exhib, Whitney Mus Am Art, 97. *Collection Arranged:* Fictions: A Selection of Pictures from the 18th, 19th & 20th Centuries, Kent Fine Art & Curt Marcus Gallery, New York, 87; The Observatory, Thomas Solomon's Garage, Los Angeles, 89; The Times, The Chronicle & the Observer, Kent Fine Art, New York, 90;

The Library, Josh Baer Gallery, New York, 91; The World of Tomorrow, Thomas Solomon's Garage, Los Angeles, 94. *Teaching:* Teacher, Dept Grad Sculpture, Sch Art, Yale Univ, 94-95; teacher, Dept Visual & Environ Studies, Harvard Univ, 95-96. *Bibliog:* Jed Perl (auth), The Gatherers, The New Criterion 3/93; David Humphrey (auth), New York Fax, Art Issues, 1-2/94; Paul Gardner (auth), What Douglas Blau has to do, On Paper, 1-2/98. *Media:* Pictures. *Publ:* Auth & ed, Pictures, Fictions, Kent Fine Art & Curt Marcus, 87; auth & ed, The Observer, The Times, The Chronicle & The Observer, Kent Fine Art, 91; Consider The Sphere, The Library, Josh Baer, NY, 91; contribr, Solid Air, Vija Celmins, Inst Contemp Art, Philadelphia, 92; The Studio, Biennial Exhibition catalog, Whitney Mus Am Art, 97. *Mailing Add:* 200 E 16th St New York NY 10003-3712

BLAUGRUND, ANNETTE
MUSEUM DIRECTOR
Study: Columbia Univ, PhD (art history). *Pos:* Dir, Nat Acad Mus, 1997-. *Teaching:* Tchr, Columbia Univ, formerly. *Publ:* Auth, Paris 1889 American Artists at the Universal Expos, 1989; auth, The Watercolors for the Birds of America, 1998; auth, The Essential Audubon, 1999. *Mailing Add:* Nat Acad Design Mus 1083 5th Ave New York NY 10128

BLAYTON, BETTY BLAYTON-TAYLOR
PAINTER, ADMINISTRATOR
b Williamsburg, Va, July 10, 37. *Study:* Syracuse Univ, BFA, 59; Art Students League, 61; studied with Arnold Prince, 61-62 & Munoru Niizuma, 64-67. *Work:* Studio Mus Harlem, Metrop Mus Art, NY; Fisk Univ; Philip Morris Corp; Chase Manhattan Bank; Spellman Col, Atlanta, GA, Norfolk State Univ, Norfolk VA. *Comn.* Uniwold Group, NY, 98. *Exhib:* Thirty Contemp Black Artists, Minneapolis & traveling, 68; Prof Artist for Young Artists, Metrop Mus Art, NY; Black Am Contemp Artist, Zamoia, Africa, 75; solo exhib, Caravan House Gallery, NY, 75, Fisk Univ, 80, Syracuse Univ, NY, 83, Bedford Stuyvesant Gallery, Brooklyn, NY, 89, Isabel Neal Gallery, Chicago, 90 & Lubin House Gallery, NY, 91; Three Women, Howard Univ Gallery, 76, Brown Univ Gallery, Washington, 87; San Francisco Mus Art; Boston Mus Art; High Mus Art; Minneapolis Inst Art; Everson Mus Art; Milwaukee Art Ctr; Pace Univ Gallery, NY, 94; Cinque Gallery, NY, 97; NCA Int Conference Exhib at the Nat Mus, Accra Ghana, 2001; UFA Gallery, NY, 2001-2003; Parsons Aronson Galleries--African-Am Women Artists, 2004; Smithsonian-The Bob Blackburn Printmaking Workshop Travel Show, 2004; Something to Look Forward To PhillipMuseum Franklin&Marshall Col, Lancaster, 2004. *Pos:* Supv artist graphics & plastics, Harlem Youth Unlimited, 64-67; pres & artistic dir, Children's Art Carnival, New York, 68-98; New York State Comn Educ Curriculum & Assessment Comt Arts & Humanities, 94-95. *Teaching:* Consult, New York City Bd Educ, 72-; prof art educ, City Col New York, 78-. *Awards:* Award Empire State Woman of Yr, 84; Black Women in Arts Award, 88; CBS TV's Martin Luther King, Jr Fulfilling the Dream Award, 95; Woman's Caucus for the Arts Life Time Achievement Award, 2005. *Bibliog:* Five (film), Silvermine Films, 72; Forever Free, Univ Ill Press, 81; Muriel Silverstein (auth), Doing Art Together, 81; African Am Art, The Long Stuggle, Crystal Britton, 96; Collecting African AM Art, Halima Taha, 98; Something to Look Forward to, Exhib Catalog, Franklin & Marshall College, 2004. *Mem:* Arts & Bus Coun (bd mem, 75-96); Printmaking workshop, NY, (bd mem, 79-); founding mem Harlem Textile Works; Advisor, The Bob Blackburn Printmaking workshop, 99. *Media:* Multi Media, Mono Prints,Painting. *Res:* Arts in Education, ages 4 - 21 years, Arts in History. *Specialty:* Picture That LLC Gallery, 84 Courtland Ave, Stanford CT, 06902; Contemportary Visual arts with emphases on Multi Ethnic Artist.; Synchronicity Fine Arts Gallery, Contemp Visual artist nat & international, 1106 West 13th St New York, NY, 10011. *Interests:* Metaphysical Studies, Theatre, Mythology, Anthropology, and Health. *Collection:* The Metropolitan Mus of Art Prints; The Studio Mus, Harlem; The Robert Blackburn Printmaking Workshop; Uniworld Advertising Corp, Phillip Morris Corp, Beatrice Corp; Fisk Univ; Spellman College, Virginia State College, Tugaloo College, The David Rockfeller; The Blanchette Rockfeller, The Reginald Lewis, The Bryon Lewis, The Bettina Hunter & The Evelyn Cunningham; and many others. *Publ:* Auth, People who make things happen, Art Gallery Guide, 69; Making Thoughts Become, 78. *Dealer:* Jan Harrison 509 W 110th St New York NY 10025; Valerie Cooper, Picture That Gallery, LLC, Gallery, 84 Courtland Ave Stanford CT, 06902; John Smith- Amato, Syncronicity Fine Arts, Gallery, 106 West 13th St New York, NY, 10011. *Mailing Add:* 2001 Creston Ave Bronx NY 10453

BLAZEJE, ZBIGNIEW (ZIGGY) BLAZESE
SCULPTOR, PAINTER
b Barnaul, USSR, June 2, 42; Can citizen. *Study:* Royal Conserv Music, Toronto; Ont Col Art. *Work:* Art Gallery Ont, Toronto; Norman McKenzie Art Gallery, Regina, Sask; Confedn Art Gallery, Charlettetown, PEI; Hart House, Univ Toronto; Sir George William Univ, Montreal, PQ. *Comn:* Structural sculpture, Libr-Ross Bldg, York Univ, 72; and others. *Exhib:* Canadian Art, Art Gallery Can Pavillion Expo 67, Montreal; Sculpture 67, City Hall Toronto; Electric Art, Univ Calif, Los Angeles Art Gallery & Phoenix, Ariz, 69; Sensory Perceptions Traveling Exhib, Art Gallery Ont, 70-71; Electronic Paintings, Cybernetic Environment, Hart House Art Gallery, Univ Toronto, 81; and others. *Pos:* Pres & dir, Arts Sake Inc, Inst Visual Art, 79-. *Teaching:* Instr environ, Ont Col Art, 70-81; instr environ, New Sch Art, Toronto, 71-72. *Awards:* Can Coun Jr Grants, 66, 67 & 69; Ont Art Coun Grants, 79 & 81. *Bibliog:* H Malcomson (auth), Sculpture in Canada, Artforum, 10/67; G M Dault (auth), In the galleries Toronto, Artscanada, 6/71; Electric Gallery plus 3, McCurdy-Bursell Films, Toronto, 4/72. *Mem:* Royal Can Acad Arts. *Mailing Add:* 1254 Dundas St W Toronto ON M6J 1X5 Canada

BLEACH, BRUCE R
PRINTMAKER, PAINTER, SCULPTOR
b Monticello, NY, Mar 23, 1950. *Study:* Orange County Community Col, AA, 70; Hartford Art Sch, Univ Hartford, BFA, 72; State Univ NY, New Paltz, MFA, 74. *Work:* Lucent Tech, Orlando Magic, British Airways, Pfizer, Intel, DuPont, Lockhee Martin, AOL, Jackson Nat Life, Motorola, Hyatt, IBM, Merrill Lynch Pierce Fenner Smith Inc & Nat Westminster Bank, NY; Provincial Mus, Taiwan; Southeast Banking Corp, Fla; plus others. *Comn:* XEROX, Novartis, Montefiore Children's Hosp, NY, Triptych, RCA Americom, Princeton, NJ, 80; embossed aluminum, Shulte Inc, NY, 84; monoprint series on hand-made paper, Gallery Sho, Tokyo, Japan, 85; cast paper with multi-media, Fred Dorfman Inc, NY, 86; metal tryptech, comn by Skoke-Koo Gallery for ADP Corp, Calif; Murals for the Pres's Off, 2001; Int Asn of Machinists and Aerospace Workers, 2001; Booz, Allen, and Hamilton, Va, 2000; Johnson and Johnson, Washington, DC, 2000. *Exhib:* Contemp Prints, Nat Prov Mus, Taiwan, 77; Works on Paper, Hudson River Mus, Yonkers, NY, 78; Artists Who Make Prints, Fordham Univ at Lincoln Ctr, NY, 81; Invitational, Cayman Gallery, NY, 83; one-man exhibs, Contemp Ltd Eds, Fla, 85, Hersh Gallery, Long Island, 86, Fred Dorfman Inc, NY, 87, Syd Entel Gallery, Tampa, Fla, 88, Art Forms Gallery, Redbank, NJ, 89, Inner Visions of Georgetown, Washington, DC, 89; Faculty Exhib, Parsons Sch Design, Lake Placid, NY, 84-85; Five Printmakers, Castle Gallery, Col New Rochelle, NY, 85; Zola Fine Art, Los Angeles, 86; Alumni Art, State Univ NY, New Paltz, 87; Los Angeles Expo, 88; NY Expo, 88-90; Save Our Shores, Art Forms Gallery, 88; John Szoke Gallery, NY, Reele Gallery, NY; CS Schulte Gallery, NY, 89. *Pos:* Lead Guitarist, Vocalist in, Boystown. *Teaching:* art prof, Orange Co Community Col, NY (10 yrs). *Awards:* Best of Show, Sullivan Co Art Asn, 73; Directors Award Graphics, Knickerbocker Artists, 75; Drawing Award, Paperworks Exhib, Hastings Gallery, 80; Cover Art for the Guild 8 Designers Source Book. *Bibliog:* Robert Smallman (dir), Printmaking (film), 78. *Media:* Etchings, Monoprints; Mixed Media on Wood & Aluminum, Etched Bronze Wall Sculpture, Collage, Acrylic on Canvas and Wood. *Publ:* Printworld Mag, The Guild Source Book, Art Bus News, NY Gallery Guide, Art in Am, Interior Design Mas, The Village Voice, NY Times. *Dealer:* Innervisions Inc 12211 Folkstone Dr Oak Hill Va 20171. *Mailing Add:* 146 Coleman Rd Goshen NY 10924

BLECHMAN, R O
ILLUSTRATOR, FILMMAKER
b Brooklyn, NY, Oct 1, 30. *Study:* Oberlin Col, BA, 52. *Work:* Mus Mod Art, NY; Libr Cong, Washington; Chase Manhattan Bank, NY. *Comn:* Three murals for US Pavilion, Expo '67, Montreal, 67; illusr for Candide, comn by Olivetti, Milan, Italy, 75; three murals for The Hall of Man, Am Mus Nat Hist, NY, 77; poster based on New Yorker cover, Munic Art Soc, NY, 80; poster, Museum Mile, NY, 82. *Exhib:* One-man shows, Galerie Delpire, Paris, France, 67, Graham Gallery, NY, 78 & Galerie Bartsch & Chariau, Munich, WGer, 82 & 92. *Awards:* Gold Medal, NY Art Dir Club, 68; Gold Medal, Cannes Film Festival, France, 77; Emmy, Outstanding Individual Achievement in Animation Programming, 84. *Bibliog:* Interview, In: Graphic Designers in the USA, Vol 2, Universe Bks, 71; Maurice Sendak (auth), Introduction to R O Blechman: Behind the Lines, Hudson Hills Press, 80. *Mem:* Alliance Graphique Int; Cartoonist Guild; Am Inst Graphic Arts. *Media:* Watercolor. *Publ:* Auth & illusr, The Juggler of Our Lady, Henry Holt, 52; Onion Soup, Odyssey Press, 63; No Room at the Inn, Milano Libri, 70; The Life of St Nicholas, Stewart Tabori & Chang, 96

BLECKNER, ROSS
PAINTER
b New York, NY, 1949. *Study:* NY Univ, BA, 71; Calif Inst Arts, MFA, 73. *Work:* Joslyn Art Mus; J B Speed Art Mus. *Exhib:* 10 Plus 10: Contemp Soviet and Am Painters, Milwaukee Art Mus, Wis, The Corcoran Gallery Art, Washington, Artists' Union Hall of the Tretyakov Embankment, Moscow, USSR & Tsentralnyi Zal Khudozhnikov, Tbilisi, USSR, 90; The Last Decade: Am Artists of the 80's, Tony Shafrazi Gallery, NY, 90; Weitersehen, Mus Haus Esters & Mus Haus Lange, Krefeld, Ger, 90; solo exhibs, Art Gallery, Ontario, Toronto, Can, 90, Galeria Soledad Lorenzo, Madrid, Spain, 90, Heland Wetterling Gallery, Stockholm, Sweden, 90, Kunsthalle, Zurich, Switz, 90, Kolnscher Kunstverein, Koln, WGer, 91, Moderna Museet, Stockholm, Sweden, 91, Galeria Aglutinador, Havana, Cuba, 98, Glenn Horowitz Bookseller, East Hampton, NY, 98, Lehmann Maupin Gallery, NY, 98, Mary Boone Gallery, NY, 98, 01, Baldwin Gallery, Aspen, Colo, 98, Julie M Gallery, Tel Aviv, Israel, 98, Betsy Senior Gallery, NY, 99, Wetterling Gallery, Stockholm, Sweden, 99, Emilio Mazzoli Galleria d'Arte Contemporanea, Modena, Italy, 99, Martin Browne Fine Art, Sydney, Australia, 99, Mario Diacono Gallery, Boston, 2000, Fay Gold Gallery, Atlanta, 2000, Zaknin Schwartz Gallery, Atlanta, 2000, Rebecca Camhi Gallery, Athens, Greece, 2000, Galerie Ernst Beyeler, Basel, Switz, 2000, Inarco Gallery, Italy, 2001; Pintura de los Ochenta en las Americas, Museo de arte contemporaneo de Monterrey, Mex, 91; Carnegie Inst, Mus Art, Pittsburgh, Pa, 88; The Binational/Die Binationale, Kunsthalle Dusseldorf, W Ger, 88; The Image Of Abstraction, Mus Contemp Art, Los Angeles, Calif, 88; solo exhibs, Galerie Daniel Templon, Paris, France, 97, Galerie Ghislaine Hussenot, Paris, France, 97, Bawag Found, Vienna, Austria, 97, Galeria Aglutinador, Havana, Cuba, 98, Lehmann Maupin Gallery, NY, 98, Mary Boone Gallery, New York, 98 & Baldwin Gallery, Aspen, Colo, 98; Stephen Wirtz Gallery, San Francisco, 98; Cleveland Mus Art, 98; Inst Contemp Art, Boston, 99; Katonah Mus Art, NY, 99; Whitney Mus Am Art, NY, 99; Galerie Daniel Templon, Paris, 99; Solomon R Guggenheim Mus, NY, 2000; Victoria Miro Gallery, London, 2000; Chicago Cult Ctr, 2000; Steffany Martz Gallery, NY, 2000; Barbara Gladstone Gallery, NY, 2000; Mus Contemp Art, North Miami, Fla, 2001; Los Angeles Co Mus Art, 2001; and many others. *Bibliog:* Roberta Smith (auth), article, Art in Am, 1/81; Peter Halley (auth), article, 5/82 & Robert Pincus-Witten (auth), Defenestrations, 11/82, Arts Mag; Elizabeth Hess (auth), Celestial Navigations, Village Voice, 88; Kay Larson (auth), article, New York Mag, 11/88; Michael Brenson (auth), article, New York Times, 10/88; Ross Bleckner's Capri Sketchbook, Travel &

Leisure, Mar 98; Annabelle Kerins (auth), An Intimate Exhibition: Bleckner in Miniature, Long Island Newsday, 8/21/98; Rand Gener (auth), Ross Bleckner: A Study in Contrasts, HX Magazine, 11/13/98; Steven Vincent (auth), Bleckner at Mary Boone and Lehmann Maupin, Art and Auction, 11/16/98; Kim Levin (auth), Voice Choices: Ross Bleckner, The Village Voice, 12/1/98; Joyce Korotkin (auth), Ross Bleckner, Cover, Feb 99; Barry Schwabsky (auth), Ross Bleckner, Artforum, Mar 99; Carol Diehl (auth), Ross Bleckner, Art News, Mar 99; Lucy Fremont (auth), Ross Bleckner, Animal Fair, Oct 99; Demetrio Paparoni (auth), Ross Bleckner, Tema Celeste, Jan 2000; Pilar Viladas (auth), Posh Spice, The NY Times, 10/29/2000; Martin Herbert (auth), Ross Bleckner, Tema Celeste, Jan 2001; Elisa Turner (auth), Mythic Proportions, Art News, May 2001. *Media:* Oil on Canvas. *Dealer:* Mary Boone Gallery 745 Fifth Ave New York NY; Lehmann Maupin 39 Greene St New York NY. *Mailing Add:* c/o Mary Boone Gallery 745 5th Ave New York NY 10151

BLEIFELD, STANLEY
SCULPTOR, MEDALIST

b Brooklyn, NY, Aug 28, 24. *Study:* Albert C Barnes Found, Merion, Pa, 42-43; Tyler Sch Art, Temple Univ, BFA, 49, BS(educ), 49, MFA, 50; Lyme Acad Fine Arts, Conn, Doctor of Fine Arts (hon), 97. *Hon Degrees:* Doctor Fine Arts, Honoris Causa, Lyme Acad Fine Arts, Conn, 97. *Work:* New Britain Mus Am Art, New Britain, Conn; Mus City of NY; Westmoreland Mus, Westmoreland, Pa & Pa State Mus; Tampa Bay Art Ctr, Tampa, Fla; Brookgreen Gardens, SC. *Comn:* Vatican Pavilion, NY Worlds Fair, 64-65; Kokomo Pub Libr, Ind, 69; Alberta Family, Calgary, Can, 81; Knights of Columbus Plaza, New Haven, Conn, 82; US Navy Mem, Washington, DC, 82; Navy Mem, Jacksonville, Fla. *Exhib:* Far Gallery, NY, 71, 73 & 77; New Britain Mus Am Art, New Britain, Conn, 74; Images Gallery, Westport, Con, 86; Franz Bader Gallery, Washington, DC 87, 91; 100 Yrs of the Nat Sculpture Soc Italy, 94; and others. *Pos:* Pres, Nat Sculpture Soc Council, 91-94; Coun, Nat Acad Design, 93-, corresp sec, 2000-; Cur, 100 Years NSS, Italy, 94-; chmn ed bd, Sculpture Rev, 94-; adv bd, Portrait Soc Aher, 2000. *Teaching:* Asst prof art, Southern Conn State Col & Western Conn State Col, 53-63; dir Bleifeld Sculpture Group, New Canaan Art Soc, New Canaan, Conn, 66-. *Awards:* Fel, Tyler Sch Fine Arts, Temple Univ, 1967; Silver Medal, Nat Sculpture Soc, 91; Meiselman prize, 97, 98; Henry Hering Mem Medal, 90 & 2000; Internat prize for sculpture, Pietrasanta Versilia in the World, XI edition, 2001; Agopoff prize for Classical Sculpture, 2001. *Bibliog:* Article, Am Artist Mag, 72 & 95, Life, 62; Artists of the Rockies, 81; Sculpture Rev, fall 94. *Mem:* Fel Nat Sculptor Soc (pres 91-93, chmn ed bd, Sculpture Rev, treas 94, John Gregory award 1964, Bronze medal 1970, Proskauer award 1977, Hexter award 1990, Henry Hering award 1990, Silver medal 1991, Bronze medal 1994, Chilmark award 1994, Hexter award 1998, Henry Hering award 2000); Nat Acad Design (assoc, 89, acad, 93, academician council 2001-, corr secy 2001-); Portrait Soc Am (adv bd 2000-, Agopoff prize 2001). *Media:* Bronze, Stone. *Publ:* David Finn & Dena Merriam (auths), Stanley Bleifeld, Madison Books, 96. *Dealer:* Nedra Mattcucci Galleries Santa Fe NM; Eisenhauer Gallery Block Island RI. *Mailing Add:* 27 Spring Valley Rd Weston CT 06883

BLESER, KATHERINE ALICE
PAINTER

b Los Angeles, Calif, Apr 3, 42. *Study:* Northwestern Univ, Evanston, Ill, BA, 73; Ga State Univ, Atlanta, MA, 75. *Work:* Ga Inst Technol & Fed Reserve Bank, Atlanta; Chattahoochee Valley Art Mus, LaGrange, Ga; State of Ga, Atlanta; Springfield Art Mus, Mo; Telfair Mus Art, Savannah, Ga. *Comn:* Six oil paintings, S Trust Bank, Birmingham, Ala, 87; two oil paintings, Anheuser-Busch, Cartersville, Ga, 93; two oil paintings, Kaiser Permanente, Atlanta, Ga, 95; oil painting, Med Ctr, Columbus, Ga, 96; eight oil paintings, Oshner Found Hosp, New Orleans, La, 97. *Exhib:* Am Artists Mag Nat Art Competition, Grand Cent Gallery, NY, 85; Allied Artists Am, Nat Arts Club, NY, 87, 91 & 97; Knickerbocker Artists, Salmagundi Club, NY, 87 & 95, Fine Arts Inst Ann Exhib, San Bernardino Co Mus, Redlands, Calif, 87, 92 & 93; Springfield Art League Ann Exhib, George Walter Vincent Smith Mus, Mass, 88, 90, 94 & 96; Nat Asn Women Artists Exhib to India, Sansker Kendra Mus, Ahmedebad, India, 89-90; Arts for the Parks Ann Competition, Lakeview Mus Arts & Sci, Peoria, Ill & Cincinnati Mus Nat Hist, Ohio, 89-90 & 94-95; South Bend (Ind) Regional Mus Art, 94; Asn Visual Arts Ann Exhibit, Hunter Mus Am Art, Chattanooga, Tenn, 96, 97 & 2000. *Awards:* Hon Mention, Artists Mag Landscape Painting Competition, 87; Catharine Lorillard Wolfe Art Club Medal of Honor, Oil, 90; Merit Award, Springfield Art League Ann Exhib, 88. *Bibliog:* Valerie Rivers (auth), Entering art competition, Am Artists, 9/86; Bebe Raupe (auth), the 1987 landscape painting competition winners, 12/87; Greg Schaber (auth), Entering national competitions, Artist's Mag, 6/96. *Mem:* Catharine Lorillard Wolfe Art Club; Nat Asn Women Artists; Am Artists Prof League; Academic Artists; Audubon Artists. *Media:* Oil. *Publ:* Getting Into - And Staying With - Galleries, Art Calendar, 2/96; Creating a Garden of Hues, Artists Mag, 5/96. *Dealer:* The Little Gallery 6 Bridgewater Plaza Montea VA 24121; Off the Wall Gallery, 123 E Broughton St, Savannah GA; Maralyn Wilson Gallery, 2830 6th Ave, Brimingham AL; Adam Whitney Gallery, 8725 Shamrock Rd, Omaha, NE. *Mailing Add:* PO Box 219 Decatur GA 30031-0219

BLEVINS, JAMES RICHARD
ART ADMINISTRATOR, EDUCATOR

b Feb 1, 34; US citizen. *Study:* David Lipscomb Col, BA, 56; George Peabody Col, MA, 60, PhD, 70; Univ Calif, Los Angeles, 75. *Pos:* Dean, Sch Liberal Arts, Univ Southern Ind, 69-; mem bd dir, Evansville Mus, 70-, chmn, Fine Arts Comt, 76-; chmn, Ohio River Arts Festival, 72; prod, New Harmony Theatre, 88-; prod, Young Abe Lincoln, 89-. *Awards:* Mayors Arts Award, Evansville, 94. *Mem:* Evansville Arts & Educ Coun (vpres, 73); Int Comt Humanities, 80-86 (chmn, 83-84); Nat Fedn State Humanities Couns, 83-85. *Mailing Add:* Univ Southern Ind 8600 University Blvd Evansville IN 47712

BLINDERMAN, BARRY ROBERT
CURATOR, DIRECTOR

b Bethlehem, Pa, June 11, 52. *Study:* Boston Univ, BA(art hist), 75; Univ Pa, MA(art hist), 78. *Collection Arranged:* Jeanne Dunning: Bodies of Work, Univ Galleries, Ill State Univ, 91; Signs of Life: Installations by Kiki Smith, Rebecca Howland, Christy Rupp & Cara Perlman, Univ Galleries, Ill State Univ, 92; Nicholas Africano: Lost Boy, Laughing Man, Univ Galleries, 93; Peep Land: Paintings by Janè Dickson, Univ Galleries, Ill State Univ, 94; Alexis Rockman: Second Nature, Univ Galleries, Ill State Univ, 95. *Pos:* Free-lance writer, Arts Mag & Arts Exchange Mag, 78-82; dir, Semaphore Gallery, NY, 80-87 & Univ Galleries, Ill State Univ, Normal, 87-. *Teaching:* Guest lectr, Tyler Sch Art, Univ Pa, Boston Mus Fine Art, Name Gallery, 79-, Chrysler Mus, Norfolk, Rice Univ, Houston & Univ Ill, Champaign, Ill; lectr art hist & contemp art, Ill State Univ, Normal. *Awards:* Panelist, Ill Arts Coun, Mus Prog Grants, 90. *Res:* Contemporary American Art. *Specialty:* Paintings, drawings, sculpture, and video by contemp artists. *Publ:* Auth, Steve Reich's minimal music, Arts Exchange, 79; Robert Longo's Men in the Cities: Quotes and commentary, 81, Keith Haring's Subterranean Signatures, 81, Modern myths: An interview with Andy Warhol, 81 & Ed Paschke: Reflections and digressions on The Body Electric, 82, Arts Mag; The Veil of the Soul (essay), Mark Innerst: Landscape and Beyond, Exhib & catalogs, 88-89; David Wojnarowicz: The Compression of Time (interview), David Wojnarowicz: Tongues of Flame, catalog, 89; Keith Haring: Future Prime Evaluation, 91. *Mailing Add:* 1109 N Fell Ave Bloomington IL 61701

BLISS, HARRY JAMES
PAINTER, ILLUMINATOR

b May 21, 23; US citizen. *Study:* Studied at Dickinson Jr Col, 47 & Edinboro State Teachers Col, 48; Pratt Inst, cert, 51. *Work:* Lincoln Trust Collection, Rochester, NY; Hartford Insurance Collection, Conn; General Motors Collection; Am Motors Asn Collection, Rochester, NY; Merrill Lynch Pierce Fenner & Smith, Rochester, NY. *Exhib:* Chautauqua Exhib Nat Art, Chautauqua Gallery Art, NY, 90; Finger Lakes Exhib, Memorial Art Gallery, Rochester, NY, 95; Adirondacks Nat Exhib Am Watercolors, Old Forge Gallery, NY, 95; Arts for the Parks, Jackson Hole, Wyo, 95; Cooperstown National, Cooperstown Mus, NY, 96. *Pos:* Art dir & designer, Mel Richmond Studio, Philadelphia, 52-53; designer/illusr, Kilborn Studios, Rochester, NY, 59-61; illusr, Studio 5, Rochester, NY, 63-73; owner, Harry Bliss Gallery, Pittsford, NY, 74-. *Teaching:* Instr watercolor, Rochester Inst Technol, 75-77, instr illus & design, 77-83; instr illus & design, Graphic Careers, 80-87. *Awards:* Robley McCarthy Award, Chautauqua, Exhib National Art, 70; Dale Myers Cooper Medal, Adirondacks Nat Exhib Am Watercolors, 92; Elizabeth Ling Reamer Mem Award, Rochester Finger Lakes Show, 93. *Bibliog:* Pat Hooley (auth), Harry Bliss as fine artist, Pittsford Brighton Post, 82; Teresa Sharp (auth), Artist Harry Bliss creates masterpieces, Pittsford Brighton Post, 84; Judith Reynolds (auth), Heaven's back porch, City Newspaper, 87. *Mem:* Rochester Art Club (v pres). *Media:* Acrylic, Watercolor; Graphite. *Mailing Add:* 581 Marsh Rd Pittsford NY 14534-3331

BLITZ, NELSON, JR
COLLECTOR

Pos: President Nelson Air Device Corp, Maspeth, NY, Nelson Acquisition Corp, Rye. *Awards:* Named one of Top 200 Collectors, ARTnews Magazine, 2004-2006. *Collection:* Viennese furniture, prints and works on paper, especially Munch, Picasso, Kirchner and Johns. *Mailing Add:* Nelson Air Device Corp 46-28 54th Ave Maspeth NY 11378

BLIZZARD, ALAN
PAINTER, EDUCATOR

b Boston, Mass, Mar 25, 39. *Study:* Mass Sch Art, Boston, with Lawrence Kupferman; Univ Ariz, with Andreas Andersen; Univ Iowa, with Stuart Edie, James Lechay & Byron Burford. *Hon Degrees:* Mass Col of Art, BFA. *Work:* Brooklyn Mus, NY; Metrop Mus Art, NY; Art Inst Chicago; Denver Art Mus, Colo; La Jolla Mus Art, Calif; Crocker Mus Art, Sacramento, Calif; Ashland Univ; Columbia Univ; and over 250 other public & pvt collections. *Exhib:* Many exhibs in leading mus, col & univs, incl Oxford Univ, Eng. *Teaching:* Chmn & prof painting, Scripps Col & Claremont Grad Sch, currently; chmn art dept, Scripps Col. *Mailing Add:* Scripps Col Claremont CA 91711

BLOCH, BABETTE
ARTIST, SCULPTOR

b New York City. *Study:* Univ Wis, 1973-1975; Univ Calif, BS 1975-1977; San Francisco Art Inst, summer 1976; Sch of Visual Arts, 1980; Residency Fel, Chateau Rochefort En Terre, Brittany, France, 1996. *Work:* Int Hillel, Washington DC; Temple Soc Concord, Syracuse, NY; Md Inst Art, Baltimore, Md; Hollis Taggart Collection, NY; Douglas Co, Toledo, Ohio, & Winter Park, Fla; Brookgreen Gardens & Sculpture Mus, Murrells Inlet, SC. *Comn:* Lowcountry Sculptures, Brookgreen Gardens, Murrells Inlet, SC; The Pioneers, Hudson Manufacturing, Chicago, Ill for Hudson Heritage Farm, Fennville, Mich; In the Garden, Dolph & Naomi Shayes, Syracuse, NY; Steeloglyph, Boca Rio Golf Club, Boca Raton, Fla; Ark Doors, Eternal Light & Candelabras, Morse Sr Campus, Tradition's Sanctuary, W Palm Beach, Fla. *Exhib:* Connecticut Women, Art Tender Gallery, Bethel, Conn, 1997-1998; solo exhibs, Nat Arts Club, NY, 1999, Harmon Meek Gallery, Naples, Fla, 2001, Soho Arts S, Palm Beach Fla, 2003; Elaine Benson Gallery, Bridgehampton, NY, 2000-2001; Cavalier Galleries, Greenwich, Conn & Nantucket, Mass, 2001-; Chairs, Coins & Candlesticks, Sculpture in Everyday Life, Brookgreen Gardens, Rainey Sculpture Pavilion, Murrells Inlet, SC, 2003; Elaine Baker Gallery, Boca Raton, Fla, 2003-. *Awards:* Dr Max Ellenburg Award, Nat Asn of Women Artists, 1986; Salzman Award for Achievement in Sculpture, Nat Arts Club, 1992; President's Medal of Honor, Nat Arts Club, 1994.

Bibliog: Peggy Keastler (auth), Inform Art, Spring 2002; Parkfield Co Home, 3/2006-4/2006; Redding Pilot, 8/2006. *Mem:* Artist's Fel Inc (pres); Nat Arts Club, Exhibitory Artist Member, (co-chair Roundtab Comt); Salmagundi Club (hon mem). *Mailing Add:* 61 Pheasant Ridge Rd Redding CT 06896

BLOCH, HENRY WOLLMAN
COLLECTOR
b Kansas City, Mo, Jul 30, 22. *Study:* Univ Mich, BS, 44. *Pos:* Trustee, Nelson-Atkins Mus Art. *Collection:* Impressionist and post-impressionist art. *Mailing Add:* H&R Block Inc 4400 Main St Kansas City MO 64111

BLOCH, MILTON JOSEPH
ART ADMINISTRATOR, MUSEUM DIRECTOR
b Bronx, NY, Apr 4, 1937. *Study:* Pratt Inst, Brooklyn, NY, BID, 58; Univ Fla, Gainesville, MFA, 61. *Exhib:* Romare Bearden 1920-1980, 80; Three Centuries of Art in NJ, 71; NJ Arts & Crafts; The Colonial Expression, 73; Romare Bearden, 79; Landon Col Am Art, 80; Ed Budnagurio Paintings, 82; Herb Jackson Paintings, 83; Ida Kohl Meyer, 30 Yrs, 85; Am Masterpieces, 85; Ramesses the Great, 89; Splendors of the New World, 92. *Pos:* Dir, Pensacola Art Ctr, Fla, 64-66; dir, Mus Sci & Natural Hist, Little Rock, Ark, 66-68; dir, Monmouth Mus, Lincroft, NJ, 69-76; dir, Mint Mus, 76-91 & Munson Williams Proctor Inst, 91-. *Teaching:* Instr art & chmn dept, Lake Sumter Col, Fla, 61-63; instr art, Belmont Abbey Col, NC, 79-80. *Mem:* Am Asn Mus; Int Conf Mus; NC Arts Coun; Asn of Art Mus Dirs. *Publ:* Series of six articles on improvised exhibition design, Mus News, 66-68; Articles for Southeastern Mus Conf J, 80-81 & Mus News, 85. *Mailing Add:* Munson-Williams-Proctor Inst 310 Genesse St Utica NY 13502

BLOCK, AMANDA ROTH
PAINTER, PRINTMAKER
b Louisville, Ky, Feb 20, 1912. *Study:* Smith Col; Univ Cincinnati; Art Acad Cincinnati; Art Students League; Herron Sch Art, Ind Univ-Purdue Univ, Indianapolis, BFA; and with Garo Antreasian. *Work:* J B Speed Mus, Louisville, Ky; Cincinnati Art Mus, Ohio; Brooklyn Mus, NY; Tucson Mus of Art, Ariz; Philadelphia Mus Art, Pa. *Exhib:* American Sculpture Show, Chicago Art Inst, Ill, 41; Soc Am Graphic Artists Show, 67-; Philadelphia Print Club; Watercolor, Drawing & Print Biennial, Pa Acad Fine Arts, Philadelphia, 69; Butler Inst Am Art, Youngstown, Ohio; Bus & Corp Collect, Indianapolis Mus of Art, Ind, 77; Retrospective, Indianapolis Art League, Ind, 92. *Teaching:* Lectr lithography & drawing, Herron Sch Art, 69-72; Indianapolis Art League, 72-82. *Awards:* Katherine Mattison Watercolor Award, Indianapolis Mus Art, 63; Watercolor Award, Indiana Artists Exhib, Sheldon Swope Art Gallery, 64; Ben & Beatrice Goldstein Award, Soc Am Graphic Artists Exhib, Kennedy Gallery, New York, 71. *Mem:* Soc Am Graphic Artists. *Media:* Acrylic, Oil; Serigraph, Lithograph. *Dealer:* Editions Limited Gallery 919 Westfield Blvd Indianapolis IN 46220; Editions Limited West San Francisco CA

BLOCK, GAY S
PHOTOGRAPHER
b Houston, Tex, Mar 5, 42. *Study:* Sophie Newcomb, 59-61; Univ Houston, 71-72 & 76; with Geoff Winningham, Garry Winogrand & Anne Tucker, 74-76. *Work:* Mus Fine Arts, Houston, Tex; Ft Worth Art Mus, Tex; Portland Mus Art, Maine; Ctr Creative Photog, Tucson, Ariz; Amon Carter Mus, Ft Worth, Tex; Univ of Tex, Humanities Res, Austin, Tex; Mus Mod Art, NY. *Comn:* Diptychs of Employees at Work and Home, HEB Grocery Co, 85; Ethnics of Houston, Foley's Dept Store: 85-86; Fifty Texas Artists, comn by Chronicle Books, 86. *Exhib:* SECA, San Francisco Mus Mod Art, Calif, 80; Triennial, New Orleans Mus Art, La, 80; Tex Photo Sampler, Washington Project Arts, Washington, DC, 81; Inside-Out: The Self Beyond Likeness, Newport Harbor Art Mus, Calif, 81; One-woman shows, Contemp Art Mus, Houston, Tex, 82; Northlight, Univ of Ariz, 85; Film in the Cities, St Paul, Minn, 86; Western States Biennial, Brooklyn Mus, NY, 86; Visual Studies Workshop, Rochester, NY, 87. *Teaching:* Vis artist photog, Univ Houston, 79-80 & 82-83; instr, Calif Inst Arts, 87. *Awards:* Nat Endowment Arts Photogr Fel Grant, 78; Nat Endowment Arts Survey Grant to Women & Their Work, 81; Tex Hist Found Photogr Survey Grant Tex Sesquicentennial. *Bibliog:* Jon Holmes (auth), Deep in the heart of Texas, Camera Mag, 8/77; Susie Kalil (auth), Portrait of a community, Artweek, 6/16/79; Demetra Bowles (auth), Lone-star tapestry, Artweek, 11/7/81; Margaret Berry (auth), American assignments, Views, Winter, 85. *Mem:* Women's Caucus Art; Houston Arts Coun; Rice Design Alliance; Houston Ctr Photog; Friends of Photog. *Media:* Black & White, Color. *Publ:* Contribr, Self-Portrayal, Friends of Photog, 78; illusr, My Body is Something Special, Union Am Hebrew Congregations, 81

BLOCK, JONATHAN WOLENS
EDUCATOR, WRITER
b Seattle, Wash, June 17, 49. *Study:* Philadelphia Col Art, BS(indust design), 72; Kent State Univ, MA(design & crafts), 73; Wash State Univ, MFA(sculpture), 76. *Work:* Corning Mus Glass, Corning, NY; Fachschule Mus, Zwiesel, Ger; Int Glasmuseum, Frauenan, Ger; Mus Contemp Art, Valencia, Spain; Univ Tex, El Paso. *Exhib:* Cleveland May Show, Cleveland Mus Art, 73; Beaux Arts Biennial, Columbus Mus Fine Arts, Ohio, 73; Collectors, Mus Contemp Crafts, NY, 74; 27th Ceramic & Sculpture Ann, Butler Inst Am Art, 76; Ritual Objects, Seattle Art Mus, 77; solo exhib, Whatcom Mus Art, Bellingham, Wash, 78; New Glass, Corning Mus, NY, 79; Feria Int de Ceramica Vidrio, Palacio Ferial, Valencia, Spain, 83. *Pos:* Dean fac, Whitecliffe Col Art & Design, Auckland, NZ, 92-98. *Teaching:* Assoc prof art, Western Wash Univ, 76-78 & Whitecliffe Col, NZ, 92-98; prof art & design, Parkland Col, Ill, 78-93. *Awards:* Louis Comfort Tiffany Fel, Ger, 73; Am Coun Educ Fel, Mellon Found, 89. *Mem:* Col Art Asn; NZ Acad Fine Arts; Nat Asn Sch Art & Design. *Media:* Mixed Media. *Res:* Technology, pedagogy, values. *Publ:* Coauth, Understanding Three Dimensions, 87 & Design Essentials: A Handbook, 89, Prentice Hall. *Mailing Add:* Symonds St PO Box 8192 Auckland New Zealand

BLOCK, VIRGINIA SCHAFFER
PAINTER, ASSEMBLAGE ARTIST
b Newark, NJ, Apr 24, 46. *Study:* William Paterson Col, Wayne, NJ, BA, 68, MA(visual arts), 69; Rutgers State Univ (serigraphy, advan printmaking), 89, studies with Tom Vincent, 74-78, Jeanne Jaffe, 94. *Work:* Hoesct Celanese, NJ; Mead Data Central, Cincinnati, Ohio; Nabisco Brands USA, Hanover, NJ; Berlex Laboratories, Wayne, NJ; Warner Lambert, NJ; The Quantum Group, NJ; Thacher, Proffitt & Wood, NY; Charles & Lynn Kramer Family Found, NJ; Mutual Benefit Life, NJ; Merrill Lynch, NJ; St. Thomas Univ, Miami, Fla. *Comn:* Canvas, Kimmelman, Wolff & Samson, Roseland, NJ, 86; canvas, Mandelbaum, Salsburg, Gold, West Orange, NJ, 87; canvas/acrylic, Sandoz Pharmaceuticals, Hanover, NJ, 90. *Exhib:* Solo shows, Berlex Lab Corp Gallery, Montville, NJ, Patterns and Placement, 99, Fredrick Clement Gallery, Montclair, NJ, Wavelengths, 01; Juried Nat Exhib: Annual Metro Show of Small Works, City Without Walls, Newark, 97, 2000; The NJ Arts Ann, The Noyes Mus of Art, Oceanville, NJ, 01; Under the Chuppah, Kansas City Jewish Mus, Kans, 02; Group invitation, City Without Walls at Seton Hall Univ Sch Law, Newark, Color and Concept, 03; Int Juried Show, NJ Ctr Visual Arts, Summit, NJ, 04; 68th & 69th Nat Midyear, Butler Inst Am Art, Youngstown, Ohio, 04 & 05; Connection, St. Thomas Univ, Sardiñas Gallery, Miami, Fla, 05. *Pos:* Advert artist, 69; freelance artist, 74-80; co-founder, pres, Studio Montclair Inc, 98-02. *Teaching:* Grad asst fine arts, Wm Paterson Col, Wayne, NJ, 68-69; art teacher, Hanover Twp Pub Sch System, 70-73. *Awards:* Harry & Ruth Kaltish Award for Best Design, NJ Watercolor Soc Open Exhib, 95; Mitsuki Kovac Award, NJ Watercolor Soc Open Exhib, 96; Silver Medal of Honor, Audubon Artists Inc, 2003. *Bibliog:* Intzides, Angelik (auth), Works of the N.A.W.A., Athens, 96; Tu, Hsiao-Ning (auth), Crossing Boundaries (exhib catalog), Noyes Mus Art, 10/2001; Shevchenko, Olya (auth), Connections (exhib catalog), Montclair-Graz Int Cultural Exchange, 2003. *Mem:* Allied Artists Am; Audubon Artists Inc; Nat Asn Women Artists Inc (chmn, traveling painting exhib, USA, 83-85 & for exhibs, 84-85, exec bd, 83-89, newsletter ed, 86-89); NJ Watercolor Soc; Studio Montclair Inc (co-founder, 97, pres, 97-2002). *Media:* All. *Dealer:* Fredrick Clement Gallery 310 E 46th St Suite 3P NY NY 10017; GJ Cloninger & Co 39 E Hanover Ave Morris Plains NJ 07950; Trudy Labell Fine Art 2425 Tamiami Trail N Naples FL 34103. *Mailing Add:* 300 Highland Ave Upper Montclair NJ 07043

BLODGETT, ANNE WASHINGTON
PAINTER
b New York, NY, Apr 17, 1940. *Study:* Smith Col, BA, 61; Boston Mus Sch Fine Arts, 61-62; with George Demetrios, Boston, 63; Sch of Fine Arts, Cambridge, Eng, 64. *Work:* Berkshire Mus, Pittsfield, Mass; Fitzwilliam Col Collection, Cambridge; Corp collections: Wilson Learning Co, Minneapolis; Quixote Co, Chicago; InnerAsia Co, San Francisco; Heublein Co, Hartford, Conn; Mass Gen Hosp Downtown, Boston; Meml Hosp, New York City; Davis, Polk & Wardwell, Inc, New York City. *Comn:* Davis, Polk & Wardwell Co, NY, 81. *Exhib:* One-woman shows, Berkshire Mus, 71, Caravan House Gallery, NY, 71 & 74 & Medici Gallery, London, 73; New Grafton Gallery, London, 72; Bodley Gallery, NY, 80 & 82; Marbella Gallery, NY, 85 & 88; Millbrook Gallery, NY, 88; Saxon Gallery, Southampton, NY, 89. *Bibliog:* Les Krantz (auth), The New York Art Review, 88. *Mem:* Century Asn, 98. *Media:* Oil. *Publ:* Auth, article in Artspeak, 85; Pictures on Exhibit, 89; Miss Porters Sch, Art Issue, 85; Berkshire Eagle, Pittsfield, Mass, 71; Union Leader, 81. *Mailing Add:* 829 Park Ave New York NY 10021-2468

BLOES, RICHARD K
VIDEO ARTIST
b Waterloo, Iowa, Sept 8, 51. *Study:* Univ Iowa Sch Art, BFA, 73, MA, 76, MFA, 77. *Work:* Donnell Media Libr, NY; Port Wash Media Libr, NY. *Comn:* Video production, Jerome Found, Minneapolis, 83; Video production, NY Found Art, 85; Video production, Nat Endowment Art, New Genres, Washington, DC, 87; Video production, NYSCA Media Grant, NY, 88 & 90. *Exhib:* 21st Ann NY Film & Video, Metrop & Brooklyn Mus, NY, 87; Time Spans, Feature, NY, 90; 3rd Emerging Expression Biennial, Bronx Mus Arts, 91; Performance, Video, & Film, Ronald Feldman Gallery, 92; Feature NY, 90, 93, 95-98, 2000 & 2002; Sculpture Ctr, NY, 93; Wexner Ctr Arts, Columbus, Ohio, 93; and many others. *Pos:* Video technician & installer, Whitney Mus, 79-. *Awards:* Special Distinction, Sixth Tokyo Video Fest, 83; Juror's Award, Three Rivers Arts Fest, Video, 87; Guggenheim Fel, 94. *Bibliog:* Helan A Harrison (auth), Sunday NY Times, 90; Brooks Adams (auth), Art in Am, 90; David Reisman (auth), Artscribe, 90. *Mem:* Media Alliance, NY. *Media:* Video Installation Art. *Specialty:* Contemp. *Dealer:* Feature Inc 530 W 25th New York NY 10001. *Mailing Add:* 99 Woodland Dr Carmel NY 10512

BLOMDAHL, SONJA
GLASS BLOWER
b Waltham, Mass, Sept 8, 52. *Study:* Mass Col Art, BFA, 74; Orrefors Glass Skolen, Sweden, 76. *Work:* The White House Permanent Craft Collection, Nat Mus Am Art, Smithsonian Inst, Washington, DC; Kitazawa Contemp Glass Mus, Japan; Mus Decorative Art, Prague, Czechoslovakia; Corning Mus, NY; Am Craft Mus, NY; and many others pub & pvt. *Comn:* Blown Glass window, Everett Pub Libr, Wash; Wash State Gov's Awards, 85. *Exhib:* Solo exhibs, Traver Sutton Gallery, Seattle, Wash, 81-85 & 87, Leedy Voulkos Gallery, Kansas City, Mo, 86 & 91, Edgewood Orchard Galleries, Fish Creek, Wis, 89, William Traver Gallery, Seattle, Wash, 89-92 & 94, Maveety Gallery, Gleneden Beach, Ore, 91, The Glass Gallery, Bethesda, Md, 92 & Daniel Saxon Gallery, Los Angeles, Calif, 92, Butters Gallery, Porland, Ore, 98; History of Am Glass, Corning Mus of Glass at the Hermitage, Leningrad & Moscow, USSR, 89-90; Artists at Work: 25 Northwest Glassmakers, Ceramists & Jewelers, Cheney Cowles Mus, Spokane, Wash & Boise Art Mus, Idaho, 91; Int Exhib Glass Kanazawa, Japan, 92; Clearly Art: Pilchuck's Glass Legacy, Whatcom Co Mus, Bellingham, Wash, traveling, 92-93; Artist Made Building Parts Proj, King Co Arts

Comn, Seattle, Wash, 93; Glass Toady by Am Studio Artists, Boston Mus of Fine Arts, Mass, 97; and others. *Pos:* Partner, Berkshire Blown Glass Works, Stockbridge, Mass, 74-76 & Glass Eye Studios, Seattle, Wash, 79-83; owner & operator, glass blowing studio, Seattle, Wash, 83-; bd adv, Pratt Fine Arts Ctr, Seattle, 1991-94, 1997. *Teaching:* Teaching asst, Pilchuck Sch, Stanwood, Wash, 78-81; instr glass blowing, Pratt Fine Arts Ctr, Seattle, Wash, 80-84; summer instr, Summervail Workshop, Vail, Colo, 83-84, Pilchuck Sch, Stanwood, Wash, 85, Appalachian Ctr, Smithville, Tenn, 86 & Haystack Mountain Sch, Deer Isle, Maine, 88 & 92. *Awards:* Visual Artists Fel Grant, Nat Endowment Arts, 86; Artist's Trust Fel Grant, 87. *Bibliog:* Susan Biskeborn (auth), Artists at Work: 25 Northwest Glassmakers, Ceramists & Jewelers, Alaska Northwest Books, 90; Ellen Nichols (ed), Northwest originals: Washington Women & Their Art; Bonnie Miller (auth), Out of the Fire: Contemporary Glass Artists & Their Work, Chronicle Books, 91; and others. *Publ:* Contribr, Vogue Mag, 1/89; International Crafts, 91. *Dealer:* William Traver Gallery 110 Union St Seattle WA 98101. *Mailing Add:* 1211 Aloha Seattle WA 98109

BLOODGOOD-ABRAMS, JANE MARIE
PAINTER
b Queens, NY, Jan 7, 63. *Study:* Col St Rose, Albany, NY, BS(studio art), 85; State Univ NY, New Paltz, MFA(painting), 87. *Work:* Col St Rose Art Gallery, Albany, NY; Mt St Mary Col, Newburgh, NY; Samuel Dorsky Mus, New Paltz, NY; City of Edinburgh, Scotland. *Comn:* Omni Corp, Albany, NY. *Exhib:* The Art of Nature, N Mus, Lancaster, Pa, 93; Images 94, Pa State Univ Mus, 94; NY State Biennial Invitational, NY State Mus, Albany, 98; Envisioned in a Pastoral Setting, Shelburne Mus, Vt, 98; solo exhib, Allen Sheppard Gallery, Piermont, NY, 98; Landscapes, Carrie Haddard Gallery, Hudson, NY, 2000; Sacred Visions, Austelling, Austria, 2000; Pastel Soc of Am, Nat Arts Club, NY, 2000; Catherine Lorrilard Wolfe Art Club, NY, 2000; Degas Pastel Soc, New Orleans, La, 2000; United Pastelists of Am, Nyack, NY; Florence Int Biennial, Italy. *Awards:* Best of Show, Clermont State Hist Site, 93; Roy Assad Purchase Prize, Pastel Soc Am, 96; Special Opportunity Stipend Award, NY State Coun Arts, 98; Mem of Yr Award, Ulster Co Arts Coun. *Bibliog:* Luminist paintings in Hudson, Northeast Art and Antiques, 12/99; The luminous landscapes of Jane Bloodgood-Abrams, The Country Mag, 11/2000; Luminist pleasure: a marriage of meteorology and physics, Art Ideas, Vol 5, No 3; Back to (the Hudson river) school, Hudson Valley Mag, 4/2002. *Mem:* Signature mem Pastel Soc Am (Award 2000); Hudson Valley Pastel Soc (secy, 95-); Woodstock Art Asn; Nat Asn Women Artists; Catherine Lorillard Wolfe Art Club. *Media:* Oil, Pastel. *Interests:* The Art of George Inness and the Hudson River Sch. *Dealer:* Carrie Haddad Gallery Hudson NY; River Gallery Chattanooga TN; Mark Gruber Gallery New Paltz NY; Charter Oak Gallery Fairfield CT. *Mailing Add:* 30 Staples St Kingston NY 12401

BLOOM, ALAN DAVID
PAINTER, SCULPTOR
b Tucson, Ariz, June 29, 45. *Study:* Univ Ariz, BS, 67; master apprenticeship/gemstone carving with R Lenius, 78; independent study at Rifkind Ctr Ger Expressionist Studies, Los Angeles County Mus Art, 94; Studies at Studio I, Westport, Conn, 72, Mus de Nat, Mexico City, 77, Vatican, Rome, 89. *Work:* Europ Am League Art, Geneva, Switz & San Francisco, Calif. *Comn:* Spirit of Youth in America Mural (20th anniversary repainting with Charles Lobdell), City of San Francisco, 76-96. *Exhib:* Calif Small Works, Calif Mus Art, Santa Rosa, 94; Plein Air Mountainscapes, Rogue Gallery, Rogue Valley Art Community, Medford, Ore, 94; The Spirit of Table Rock Mountain, Wiseman at Rogue Community Col, Grants Pass, Ore, 95; Whispers '97, Gallery on the Rim, San Francisco, 97; Am Passionist Exhib, Humbolt Arts Comn (31st ann), Eureka, Calif, 98; Homage and Inspiration, Sebastopol Ctr for Art, Calif, 98; The Passion Seven, Ore Mus Modern Art, Grants Pass, 99; Jega Art Center, Ashland, Ore, 2000; Quicksilver Mine Co, Front Street Gallery, 2001; US Dept of State, Am Embassy Show File, 2001; Vacant Oasis, Works on Paper at Spring & Wooster, NY, 2001; Linda Penzur Gallery, San Anselmo, Calif, 2002; Catherine Finn Gallery, Tiburon, Calif, 2002; Syder-Highland Found Art Mus, Passion 7, Weaverville, Calif, 2003; Bodega Now, NY in Oil, Bodega, Calif, 2005; UNICEF Int Invitational, Paramount Bldg, San Francisco, Calif, 2005. *Pos:* Co-dir, Work Work Work Inc, 79-81; dir, Love Harmony Inc, 87-98; founder, Studio Bodega, 2002-. *Awards:* Intl Vis Artist of the Yr, 2004; Gold Medal of Excellence, Intl Biographical Soc, Cambridge, Eng; NS Law, Dir Gen. *Bibliog:* doc, Plan Bloom, Pleinnaire Landscapes Abstracted, Ore Pub Television, 1994; Kathleen Ayres (auth), Alan Bloom, Moody Mountains Equals Rock Solid Art, Ore Courier, 95; Edith Decker (auth), Museum Trove of Treasures Bloom, Teases with Tenderness, Grants Pass Courier Entertainment, 99; Si and Ann Frazier (for corresp), Gem Artists, Lapidary J, 25, 99; Biographical Encyclopedia of Am Painters, Sculptors, and Engravers of the United States, Colonial thru Current Yr. *Mem:* signature mem Passion Seven Expressionist Painters; Europe Am League Art. *Media:* Oil, Mixed Media; Gemstone Carving. *Dealer:* Studio Bodega Now Bodega CA. *Mailing Add:* 14201 Bodega Hwy Bodega CA 94922

BLOOM, BARBARA
PHOTOGRAPHER
b Los Angeles, Calif, 1951. *Study:* Calif Inst Arts, BFA, 72. *Work:* Mus Contemp Art & Los Angeles Co Mus Art, Los Angeles, Calif; Mus Mod Art, NY; Stedelijk Mus, Amsterdam, Gemeentemuseum, Arnhem, Groniger Mus, Gronigen, Neth; Art Gallery Ont, Toronto; Australian Nat Gallery, Canberra; Dutch Nat Collection; Groninger Mus, Holland; Israel Mus, Jerusalem; Mus Contemp Art, Helsinki, Finland; San Jose Mus Art, Calif; Yokohama Mus Art, Japan; and many others. *Exhib:* Solo exhibs, Echo, Galerie Sylvana Lorenz, Paris, 92, Never Odd or Even, Carnegie Mus Art, Pittsburgh, Pa, 92, The Gaze, 92 & New Work, 94, S L Simpson Gallery, Toronto, Can, The Passions of Natasha Nokiko, Nanette & Norma, Marstall Bayerisches Staatsschauspiel, Munchen, Ger, 93, Art Metropole, Toronto, Can, 93, The Bridge, Leo Castelli Gallery, NY, 95, Mus Contemp Art, Los Angeles, 96, SL Simpson Gallery, Toronto, Ont, Can, 97, Galleria Raffaela Cortese, Milan, Italy, 99, Galerie Six Friedrich, Munich, Ger, 99, 2002, Parrish Art Mus, Southampton, NY, 2000, Galerie Piece Unique, Paris, 2000, Gorney Bravin + Lee, NY, 2001, Berliner Festspiele, Germ, 2003, UC Berkely Art Mus, Calif, 2004; Pictures of the Real World (catalog), Paula Cooper Gallery, NY, traveling, 94; Shooting Blind, Ezra & Cecile Zilkha Gallery, Wesleyan Univ, Middletown, Conn, 94; Sonnabend Gallery, NY, 94; The Robert Fogelman Collection, Brooks Mus, Memphis Tenn, 94; The Century of the Multiple (catalog), Deichtorhallen Hamburg, Ger, 94; Installations: Selections from the Permanent Collection, Part One, Mus Contemp Art, Los Angeles, 94; The Seven Deadly Sins (installation), Mus Contemp Art, Helsinki, Finland, 95; Hall of Mirrors: Art and Film since 1945 (traveling exhib), Mus Contemp Art, Los Angeles, Wexner Ctr Arts, Columbus, Ohio, Palazzo delle Esposizioni, Rome, Italy & Mus Contemp Art, Chicago, 96; At Home in the Mus, Art Inst Chicago, 98; The Mus as Muse, Mus Mod Art, NY, 99; Now Playing: Audio in Art, Susan Inglett, NY, 2001; Walker Art Ctr, Minneapolis, Minn, 2001; Women's Mus, Washington, DC, 2002; Bellevue Art Mus, Wash, 2002, 03; Margo Leavin Gallery, Los Angeles, Calif, 2003; Henry Art Gallery, Seattle, Wash, 2002. *Teaching:* guest lectr, Cooper Union, NY, Sch Visual Arts, NY, Art Ctr Col of Design, Pasadena, Calif, Yale Univ, New Haven, Conn, Grad Sch Design/Harvard Univ, Cambridge, Mass, Columbia Univ, NY. *Awards:* Louis Comfort Tiffany Found Award, 89; Nat Endowment Arts, 90; Frederick Weisman Found Award, 91; Guggenheim Fel, 98; The Due Mille Prize, Aperto, Venice Biennale, 88. *Bibliog:* Installations: Permanent Collection, The Contemporary, Mus Contemp Art, Los Angeles, fall 94; Holly Brubach (auth), Strengthening the Dollar, New York Times Mag, 10/30/94; Heinz Schutz (auth), Barbara Bloom: Aufgespief te Schmetterlinge, Kunstforum Int, 7-9/94; Joan S Robinson (auth), The Collections of Barbara Bloom, Artforum, 11/27/98; Vicki Goldberg (auth), Eliminating the Distance Between Two Points, NY Times, 11/27/98; Alessandra Pioselli (auth), Barbara Bloom, Flash Art, Feb-Mar, 99; Simon Watson (auth), The Museum as Muse: Artists Reflect, Simon Says, 4/99; Anne Doran (auth), Barbara Bloom: The French Diplomat's Office, Time Out/New York, 4/15/99; Jerry Saltz (auth), Inside Job: The Museum as Muse: Artists Reflect, The Village Voice, 5/18/99; Liz Wood (auth), ArtBeat (Barbara Bloom at the Parrish Museum), The Suffolk Times, 8/17/2000; Phyllis Braff (auth), Art Review: Barbara Bloom "The Gaze", NY Times, 8/20/2000; Peter Nagy (auth), Art Review: Barbara Bloom "The Gaze", Time Out New York, 8/31-9/7/2000; Linda Yablonsky (auth), A Glimpse Through the Walls of Privacy, NY Times, 5/6/2001; Kim Levin (auth), Voice Choice: Art: Barbara Bloom, The Village Voice, 5/15/2001; Holland Cotter (auth), Review: Barbara Bloom "Broken" at Gorney Bravin + Lee, NY Times, 5/18/2001; Martha Schwendener (auth), Review: Barbara Bloom at Gorney Bravin + Lee, Time Out New York, 5/24-31/2001; and numerous others. *Publ:* Auth, Esprit de l'Escalier, 88; Ghost Writer, 88; The Reign of Narcissism, 90; Never Odd or Even, Verlag Silke Schreiber, Munich, Ger & Carnegie Mus Art, Pittsburgh, Pa, 92; Broken, with Abbott Miller, Pentagon, NY, 2001; Vladimir Nabokov, Glenn Horowitz Bookseller, NY, 99; The French Diplomat's Office, with Christian Marclay, Blumarts, Inc, NY, CD (soundtrack), 99; Donna De Salvo (auth), The Collections of Barbara Bloom, exhib brochure, 98; Susan Tallman (auth), Barbara Bloom: Pictures From the Floating World, Sala de Esposiciones Rekalde Erakustaretoa, Bilboa, Spain, 98. *Dealer:* Gorney Bravin + Lee 534 W 26th St New York NY 10001. *Mailing Add:* c/o Jay Gorney Modern Art 534 W 26th St New York NY 10001

BLOOM, DONALD S
PAINTER, ILLUSTRATOR
b Roxbury, Mass, Sept 3, 32. *Study:* Mass Col Art, BFA, 53; Art Students League, 53-55, with Barnet, Levi & Trafton; Inst Allende, San Miguel Allende, Mex, MFA, 57. *Work:* East Brunswick Pub Libr, NJ; South River Pub Libr, NJ; Fairleigh Dickinson Univ, Madison, NJ; Montclair State Col, NJ; Rutgers Univ; Bloomfield NJ College; UPSACA College, East Orange, NJ. *Comn:* mural, Judge Raymond Del Tufo, Newark, NJ, 63. *Exhib:* Whitney Ann Am Painting, Whitney Mus Am Art, NY, 60; Silvermine Guild Ann, New Canaan, Conn, 63; Audubon Artists Ann, Nat Acad Galleries, NY, 63; NJ Pavilion, NY World's Fair, 65; Springfield Watercolor Asn Traveling Show, Mo, 65; NJ State Mus Ann, 66 & 73. *Collection Arranged:* Butler Inst Ann Youngstown, Ohio, 58; four one-man shows at New York City Galleries, 59-64; Charles Press Gallery, Colts Neck, NJ, 70; Art Barn, Mammouth, NJ 73. *Pos:* Staff cartoonist, Sentinel (newspapers), 78-90. *Teaching:* Art instr, Piscataway Schs, 58-92; instr painting & collage, Morris Co Art Asn, NJ, 60-68; instr painting, Bloomfield Col, 65-66; dist chmn art dept, Piscataway Schs, NJ, 66-84; instr watercolor, Summit Art Ctr, 74; instr art, Trenton State Col, 83. *Awards:* Guggenheim Fel Creative Painting, 61; Huntington Hartford Found Fel, 64; Second Place Cachets Award, Am First Day Cover Soc Nat Conv, 98; full scholar to Inst Allende, 56-57. *Bibliog:* E Genauer (auth), rev in NY Herald Tribune, 9/61; J Beck (auth), rev in Art News, 10/61; V Raynor (auth), rev in Arts, 10/61. *Mem:* Nat Cartoonists Soc. *Media:* Oil; Watercolor; Pastel; Ink. *Publ:* Auth, We learned about color & design, Sch Arts Mag, 58; illusr, Seventeen Mag, 61; Country & Western Issue, Billboard Mag, 63; auth, Batik in the classroom & Woodcuts by children, 72 & Two for one, 75, Instructor. *Mailing Add:* 31 Dexter Rd East Brunswick NJ 08816

BLOOM, HYMAN
PAINTER
b Brunoviski, Lithuania, Mar 29, 13. *Study:* West End Community Ctr, Boston, Mass, study with Harold Zimmerman & Denamn W Rott. *Work:* Fogg Art Mus, Harvard Univ; Hirshhorn Mus & Sculpture Garden, Smithsonian Inst, Washington, DC; Kalamazoo Inst Arts, Mich; Mus Mod Art & Whitney Mus Am Art, NY; Minn Mus Art, St Paul; Addison Gallery, Phillips Exeter Acad, Andover, Mass. *Exhib:* Americans 1942, Mus Mod Art, NY; one man exhibs, Whitney Mus Am Art, 45, 54 & 68, Inst Contemp Art, Boston, 49, Albright-Knox Art Gallery, 54, MH De Young Mem Mus, 54, Wadsworth Atheneum, 57, Univ Conn, Mus Art, 69 & Terry Dintenfass Gallery, 72 & 75, Broctoa Mys, 76, Univ NH Mus, 92, Bateo Col Mus, 2001 & Nat

Acad Design, 2002; retrospective, Albright-Knox Art Gallery, Buffalo, NY, 54; Butler Inst Am Art, 72; Esther Robles Gallery, Brentwood Park, 76; Contemp Pastels & Watercolors, Ind Univ Mus, Bloomington, 77; 152 Ann Exhib, Nat Acad Design, 77; The Chosen Object (still life), Joslyn Art Mus, 77; Perceptions of the Spirit in 20th Century American Art (traveling exhib), Ind Mus Art, 77-78; Boston Expressionism, Inst Contemp Art, Boston, 79. *Teaching:* Instr, Wellesley Col, 49-51 & Harvard Univ, 51-53. *Mem:* Am Acad Arts & Lett; Nat Acad Design (assoc, 84, acad, 94). *Media:* Acrylic, Oil. *Mailing Add:* 80 Hills Ferry Rd Nashua NH 03060

BLOOM, MARTHA
COLLAGE ARTIST, PHOTOGRAPHER, EDUCATOR
b Paterson, NJ, Aug 5, 51. *Study:* Green Mountain Col (art maj), 69-70; Art Inst Boston, 70-71, Art Students League, 71-80. *Work:* Assoc Am Artists, NY; Sylvan Cole Gallery, NY; Art Students League; Columbia Mus, Columbia, SC; McNay Mus, San Antonio, Tex; Permanent installation, Art student league children's class etchings, D'Arcy-Massive-Benton-Bowles, NY, 90; Metrop Mus, NY. *Comn:* Union Settlement Asn, NY, 92. *Exhib:* Audubon Soc, Nat Acad Gallery, NY, 74; one-person show, MacDowell Sch, Art Students League, NY, 77; theme shows, Asn Am Artists, 80-85; McNay Ann Collector's Show, McNay Mus, San Antonio, Tex, 84-87; Midtown-Payson Gallery, NY, 89; Book Arts Gallery, NY, 91; Graphics Arts Ctr, Conn, 95 & 97; Salander O'Reilly Gallery, 2002, 2003 & 2004; and others. *Collection Arranged:* Metropolitan Mus of Art; Nat Acad; McNay Mus; Delaware Mus; many private collections. *Teaching:* Lectr, printmaking, Cooper-Hewitt Mus, NY, 80-81; art instr, Art Students League, 85-; Inner City Outreach Prog, NY & Conn, 91-; Silvermine Sch Art, Ct, 92-; Westport Arts Ctr, Ct, 92-; Carrige Barn Ctr, Conn, 97; Whitney Mus Am Art, Champion, Conn; Nat Acad Sch of Fine Arts, NY, 99-; Nat Acad Mus, 2006-. *Awards:* MacDowell Traveling Scholarship, Art Student League, 74-77. *Mem:* Artists Equity Asn, life mem Art Students League (bd control, 3 yrs); Artists Fel Inc; Artists Union Asn; Silvermine Guild; Artist Fellowship Asn. *Media:* Mixed Media. *Interests:* Video; Music; Dance; Singing; Yoga. *Collection:* Metrop Mus of Art; Privately Many; Libr of Cong. *Publ:* Photographs pub in mags and newspapers. *Dealer:* Sylvan Cole Gallery 200 W 57th St New York NY 10019. *Mailing Add:* 322 Green's Farms Rd Westport CT 06880

BLOOM, SUZANNE See Manual, Ed Hill & Suzanne Bloom

BLOOMFIELD, LISA DIANE
PHOTOGRAPHER, CONCEPTUAL ARTIST
b Los Angeles, Calif, Aug 9, 51. *Study:* Univ Calif, Berkeley, BA, 73; Calif Inst Arts, MFA(art & design; scholar), 80. *Work:* J Paul Getty Mus, Malibu, Calif. *Exhib:* Phantasy, Santa Barbara Mus Art, 82; solo show, Arco Ctr Visual Art, 83, Visual Studies Workshop, Rochester, NY, 89; Franklin Furnace, NY; two-person show, Lightwork, Syracuse, NY, 88; Biennial I, Calif Mus Photo, Riverside, 90; Systems, Los Angeles Munic Art Gallery, 90. *Collection Arranged:* Photographs: Griffith Observatory: 1935-1978, Los Angeles, 78; The Theater of Gesture, Los Angeles Ctr Photog Studies, 83. *Teaching:* Instr Otis Art Inst, 81-; lectr, Univ Washington; lectr, Univ Calif Los Angeles, 89; lectr, Univ Calif Riverside & Santa Barbara, 90. *Awards:* Purchase Award, Six State Exhib, Univ NMex, Albuquerque, 82; Calif Arts Coun Grant, 83; Visual Arts Fel, Nat Endowment Arts, 86; Fac Develop Fund, New Sch Soc Res, NY, 89. *Bibliog:* J Hugunin (auth), Mocking objects, Afterimage, 12/80; D Berland (auth), On photography, Los Angeles Times, 5/15/83; J Brumfield (auth), Loaded implications, Art Week, 5/28/83. *Mem:* Friends Photog; Los Angeles Ctr Photog Studies; Soc Photog Educ. *Publ:* Contribr, Impulse Mag, vol 10 #1, 82; Top stories #28, 89; CAA J, 90. *Mailing Add:* 1525 S Stanley Ave Los Angeles CA 90019-3849

BLOOMFIELD, SUZANNE
PAINTER, PRINTMAKER
b Cleveland, Ohio, June 23, 34. *Study:* Ohio Univ, BS, 55; Univ Ariz, ME, 75. *Work:* Pima Coun Aging, Tucson, Ariz; Univ Ariz, Tucson; Albany Print Club, NY; Ariz State Sen Ruth Solomon pvt collection; Nat Asn Women Artists, NYC. *Comn:* Univ Ariz Dept Judaic Studies. *Exhib:* UN World Conf Women, Nairobi, Kenya, 86; Nat Asn Women Artists Centennial Yr, Foreign Exhib Tour India, 89-90; Am Album Res Archives, Nat Mus Women Arts, Washington, DC, 90; Global Focus - UN Fourth World Conf Women, Beijing, China & Moscow, Russ, 95; Galeria Berta Armas, Ensenada, Mex, 97; Mus Contemp Art, Los Angeles, 97; Univ Ariz, Tucson, 98; Traveling Printmaking Exhib USA, 98-00; Millennium Collection, United Nations, New York City, 01; Univ Alaska, Anchorage, 03, Univ Tex, 04. *Collection Arranged:* Univ Ariz; Albany Print Club, NY. *Awards:* Irwin Zlowe Medal Award, 02. *Bibliog:* Calif Art Review, 89; Arizina Illus, KUAT Tv, Tucson, Ariz, 90; Women - Your Voice (doc), Albright Productions, San Antonio, Tex, 92; Into the New Century (exhib catalog), Univ Ariz, 98. *Mem:* Nat Asn Women Artists. *Media:* Encaustics, Oil. *Collection:* Univ Ariz; Albany Print Club. *Mailing Add:* 4270 E Holmes Tucson AZ 87111

BLOSSER, NICHOLAS
PAINTER
b Columbiana, Ohio, Nov 1, 58. *Study:* Ohio State Univ, BFA, 80, MFA, 82. *Work:* Contemp Art Workshop, Chicago. *Exhib:* One-person shows, United Christian Ctr Gallery, Columbus, Ohio, 87, Olin Gallery, Kenyon Col, Gambier, Ohio, 87, Contemp Art Workshop, Chicago, Ill, 87, Bowling Green State Univ Art Gallery, Ohio, 89, Spaces Gallery, Cleveland, Ohio, 89, Jamison/Thomas Gallery, Portland, Ore, 92-94 & Milligan Col, Tenn, 92; Jamison-Thomas Gallery, Portland, Ore, 91 & 92; Montgomery Mus Art, Ala, 92; New Regional Painting II, Moody Gallery Art, Univ Ala, 93; Adam Baumgold Fine Arts, 95, 97 & 2001; PDX Gallery, Portland, 99 & 2002. *Teaching:* Instr art, Mt Vernon Nazarene Col, 85-91, Milligan Col, 91-. *Awards:* Ohio Arts Coun Individual Fel Painting, 83; Rome Prize Fel, Am Acad Rome, 84-87; Nat Endowment Arts Fel, 87 & 92. *Dealer:* Adam Baumgold Fine Art New York. *Mailing Add:* Milligan College PO Box 500 Milligan College TN 37682

BLOVITS, LARRY JOHN
PAINTER, EDUCATOR
b Detroit, Mich, Oct 19, 36. *Study:* Wayne State Univ, Detroit, BFA, 64, MFA, 66; study with Daniel Greene, summers 83-86. *Work:* Muskegon Mus Art, Mich; Battle Creek Art Ctr, Mich; Beta Rho Delta Zeta Nat Sorority Mus, Oxford, Ohio; Mich Supreme Court Chambers, Lansing; Grand Rapids Art Mus, Mich. *Comn:* Pres Martin Essenberg, Covenant Col, Lookout Moutain, Tenn, 88; Pres John Bernhard, Western Mich Univ, Kalamazoo, 90; GW Haworth, Chmn, Haworth Corp, Holland, Mich, 91; Sen Eva M Hamilton, Lansing, Mich, 94; Sen Paul Henry, Allendale, Mich, 95. *Exhib:* Soc Des Pastellistes de France Int, Palais Rameau, Lille, France, 87; OPA 5th Int, Ky Highlands Mus, Ashland, 88; Salmagundi Members Exhib, NY, 88; one-man show, Muskegon Mus Art, Mich, 88; 20th Ann Pastel Soc Ann Nat, Nat Arts Club, NY, 92; and others. *Pos:* Visual arts adv, Mich Coun Arts, Detroit, 76-81; apprentice master teacher, Nat Endowment Arts, Washington, DC, 83; vis artist, Mich Tech Univ, Houghton, 89. *Teaching:* adj instr drawing, Wayne State Univ, Detroit, 66-67; instr drawing & painting, Northern Mich Univ, Marquette, 67; prof art, drawing & painting, Aquinas Col, Grand Rapids, Mich 67-93. *Awards:* Member's Award, 9th Ann Nat, Pastel Soc Am, 81; 9th Ann Salmagundi nat, Metrop Portrait Soc, 86; Outstanding Achievement Portraiture, Nat Portrait Seminar, 91. *Bibliog:* Who's Who Midwest, Marquis, 23rd ed, 91; Madlyn Woolwich (auth), The Art of Pastel Portraiture, Watson-Guptill Books, 96. *Mem:* Am Soc Portrait Artists; Pastel Soc Am; Am Portrait Soc; Midwest Pastel Soc; Salmagundi Club, NY. *Media:* Oil, Pastel. *Publ:* Contribr, Photographing your art, Profile Mag, 84 & Directory of American Portrait Artists, 85, Am Portrait Soc; contribr & coauth, Artist in residence, Larry Blovits multipurpose studio, Am Artists Mag, 90; auth, Pastel Landscape, Technique & Procedure, video, pvt publ, 91; Pastel for the Serious Beginner, Watson-Guptill Books, 96. *Dealer:* Arnold Klein Gallery 4520 N Woodward Royal Oak MI 48072. *Mailing Add:* 0-1835 Luce SW Grand Rapids MI 49504-9503

BLUE, PATT
PHOTOGRAPHER, WRITER
b Paducah, Ky, Apr 27, 1943. *Study:* State Univ NY, Stony Brook, BA(studio art & art hist), 74; Art Inst Chicago, MFA, 87. *Work:* Brooklyn Mus, NY; John F Kennedy Libr, Boston; City Mus New York; Light Work, Syracuse Univ, NY; also pvt collections of David C Ruttenberg & Francis Kohler; NY Pub Libr. *Exhib:* Light Work Retrospective, Everson Mus, Syracuse, NY, 85; solo exhibs, Heart of Man, Sch Art Inst Chicago, 87; Photo Active, Feldman Fine Arts, NY, 88; Myself, My Mother, My Grandmother, (Flesh & Blood), Kilkady Mus, Fotofeis, Scotland, 93, Ansel Adams Ctr Photog, San Francisco, 94; Living on a Dream: Words & Images, Los Angeles Ctr Photog Studies, 94; Life I: Within a Foot, James Howe Gallery, Kean Univ, NJ, 94; Mother's Who Think, 99; Facetime Series: Re-viewing Photog, Univ Arts, Philadelphia, Pa, 2002; and others. *Pos:* Arts & educ adminr, Int Ctr Photog, NY, 75-81; ed photogr, Life Mag, People, Der Stern, Paris Match, and others, 80-86; cur, New Spirit of Photography, Fashion Inst Technol, NY, 85; coordr, Contemp Europ Photog Lect Series, SAIC, Chicago, 87; ed, Findings, Interdisciplinary J Creative Works, 91-92. *Teaching:* Lectr, numerous mus & insts, 82-2003; fac, Int Ctr Photog, 75-81 & NY Univ, 83-84; vis artist, RI Sch Design, Providence, 84; adj fac, Moore Col Art, Philadelphia, 84-85; asst prof photog & resident fac, Kean Univ, Union, NJ, 87-97; grad thesis adv, Sch Visual Arts, NY, 95. *Awards:* Leica Medal of Excellence, 82; W Eugene Smith Found Humanities Photography, 84; Nat Endowment Arts, 88-89; NY Found Arts Fel, 89-90 & 93-94; and others. *Bibliog:* A D Coleman (auth), Documentary solution or problem?, New York Observer, 12/26/88-1/2/89; Review, Sunday Star Ledger, 11/3/91; Ann Marie Rousseau (auth), The larger questions of life: An interview, Photo Rev, Vol 19, No 3, summer 96. *Publ:* Photogr, Babies having babies, Life Mag, 83; John Loengard, Classic Photog, 88; ed, D Friend, The Meaning of Life, Little Brown & Co, 91; Flesh and Blood, George/Heyman/Hoffman, The Picture Project, 92; auth, Living on a Dream: A Marriage Tale, a photog/lit memoir, Univ Press, Miss, 98

BLUE MAN GROUP See Stanton, Phil

BLUE MAN GROUP See Goldman, Matt

BLUE MAN GROUP See Wink, Chris

BLUHM, NEIL GARY
PATRON
Study: Univ Ill, BS; Northwestern Univ, JD. *Pos:* Partner, firm Mayer, Brown & Platt, Chicago, 62-70; pres, JMB Realty Corp, from 70, pres trustee, JMB Realty Trust, 72-; Bd dir, Chicago Cares Inc, Urban Shopping Ctrs Inc, 93-2000; Northwestern Univ, Alzheimer's Disease & Related Disorders Asn; Whitney Mus Am Art; bd trustees, Art Inst Chicago. *Mem:* Bar State Ill; Real Estate Roundtable; Standard Club; Chicago Club. *Mailing Add:* Urban Shopping Ctrs Inc 132 E Delaware St Ste 6501 Chicago IL 60611-1542

BLUM, ANDREA
SCULPTOR
b New York, NY, Apr 6, 50. *Study:* Univ Denver; Boston Mus Sch Fine Arts, BFA, 73; Sch Art Inst Chicago, MFA, 76. *Work:* Art Inst Chicago; AT&T, Chicago; Marina Bank, Chicago; Univ Iowa Mus Art, Iowa City; Nat Collection Fine Arts, Washington, DC. *Exhib:* Boston Mus Sch, 73; Fel Exhib, Art Inst Chicago, 76, Drawings of '70's, 77 & Works on Paper, 78; 3 Sculptors, Northern Iowa Univ Gallery Art, Cedar Falls, 79; Art from Chicago, Koffler Found Collection, Nat Collection Fine Arts, Washington, DC; one-woman show, Marianne Deson Gallery, Chicago, 78 & 80; Beyond Object, Aspen Ctr for Visual Arts, Colo, 80; Creative Time, NY, 81; Installation, Hudson River Mus, NY, 81; DeCordova Mus, Mass, 81; and others.

Teaching: Vis artist & lectr, Univ Iowa, Iowa City, 77, Kalamazoo Inst Art, Mich, 77, Univ Ill, Chicago Circle, 77, Univ Hartford, Conn, 78, Univ Northern Iowa, Cedar Falls, 79 & Univ Chicago, 79; vis artist, Art Inst Chicago, 81. *Awards:* Nat Endowment for Arts individual grants, 76 & 78. *Bibliog:* Franz Schulze (auth), Nothing but abstract, summer 76 & Kay Larson (auth), Rooms with a point of view, 10/77, Art News; C L Morrison (auth), rev in Artforum, 10/76. *Mem:* Col Art Asn Am. *Mailing Add:* 428 Broome St New York NY 10013-3252

BLUM, HELAINE DOROTHY
SCULPTOR, PAINTER
b Cleveland, Ohio. *Study:* Cleveland Art Inst; Western Reserve Univ; Art Students League; Columbia Univ. *Work:* Detroit Inst Art; Israel Mus Art, Jerusalem; Skirball Mus, Los Angeles. *Comn:* Portrait Samuel Golter, City Hope Med Ctr, Duarte, Calif, 72; portrait Marcel Marceau, Friends Marcel Marceau, Paris, 76. *Exhib:* May Show, Cleveland Mus Art, 45-60s; Am Sculpture, Metrop Mus Art, NY, 51; Max Weber Exhib, Jewish Mus, NY, 56; Jewish Art, Smithsonian Inst, 60s; Sculpture, Corcoran Mus, 65; Acad Med, NY, 68; Am Art, Calif Palace Legion Hon, 68; Sculpture, O'Hara Gallery, London, 69. *Awards:* L'Esprit, Silvermine Guild Artists, 59 & 65; Nat Coun Jewish Women Award, 67-82; Nat Asn Women Artists Award, 68. *Bibliog:* Articles, New Yorker, 60, New York Times, 66 & Art News, 71. *Mem:* Artists Equity Asn; Nat Asn Women Artists; Silvermine Guild. *Media:* Bronze. *Mailing Add:* PO Box 93 Santa Monica CA 90406

BLUM, JUNE
PAINTER, SCULPTOR
b Maspeth, NY, Dec 10, 29. *Study:* Brooklyn Col, MA, 59; Brooklyn Mus Art Sch, with Reuben Tam & Tom Doyle, 59-67; New Sch, New York, with Laurie Goulet, 65. *Work:* Brooklyn Col, NY; Okla Art Ctr Mus; Cocoa Beach Libr, Fla. *Comn:* Light Environments (Time-Space), Suffolk Mus, Stony Brook, NY, 70, Okla Art Ctr Mus, Oklahoma City, 72, Hudson River Mus, Yonkers, NY, 73 & Nassau Co Mus Fine Arts, Roslyn, NY, 80. *Exhib:* Works on Paper/Women Artists, Brooklyn Mus, 75; Sons & Others, Queens Mus, Flushing, NY, 76; National Art Club, New York City, 2003; one-woman shows, Paintings, Bronx Mus, NY, 76, Brevard Community Col, Cocoa, Melbourne, Fla, 84, Soho 20 Gallery, NY, 98 & Brevard Mus Art & Sci, Melbourne, Fla, 98; A Woman's Space, Nassau Co Mus Fine Arts, Roslyn, NY, 80; Art to Wear, Barbara Gillman Gallery, Miami, Fla, 81; Brevard Performing Arts Ctr, Melbourne, Fla, 88; Brevard Mus, Cocoa, Fla, 95; Mus Stonybrook, NY, 96. *Collection Arranged:* The Artists Use of Paper, Watercolors, Contemp Outdoor Sculpture, 74, Suffolk Mus; Works on Paper-Women Artists (with catalog), Brooklyn Mus, 75; The Opposite Sex, A Realistic Viewpoint (with catalog), Univ Mo, Kansas City, 79; The Figure of 5 (with catalog), Miami-Dade Community Col, North Campus, 79; Women's Art, Miles Apart, (with catalog), Valencia Col, Orlando, Fla & Aaron Berman Gallery (with catalog), New York, 82; and others. *Pos:* Cur contemp art, Suffolk Mus, Stony Brook, NY, 71-76; dir, Women for Art, 76-. *Awards:* Anne Eisner Putnam Mem Prize, Nat Acad, Nat Asn Women Artists, 68; Hon Mention, White Mountain Festival Arts, Jefferson, NH, 77; Medal of Honor Award, National Arts Club, NY, From Veteran Feminists in the arts, 2003. *Bibliog:* Pam Harbaugh (auth), Artists work reflects how 70's women struggled, Fla Today, 7/98; Ann Samuels (auth), Blum in bloom, Spacecoast Press, 8/98; Lyn Dowling (auth), Artist displays work on women's subject, Cocoa Beach Current, 9/98; Benita Budd (auth) June Blum, environmental images, Women Artists News, Spring 85; plus others. *Mem:* Women's Caucus for Art (nat chap); Col Art Asn Am. *Media:* Oil, Fabric. *Publ:* Auth, Metamorphosis of June Blum, 76, Betty Friedan ser, 76, Female connection, 78 & A woman's space, 80, Women for Art; Women's Art, Miles Apart (catalog intro), Valencia Community Col, Fla, 82; June Blum, Fiberarts, 3/86. *Dealer:* NN Gallery Seattle WA. *Mailing Add:* 120 Boca Ciega Rd Cocoa Beach FL 32931

BLUMBERG, RON
PAINTER
b Reading, Pa. *Study:* Nat Acad Design; Art Students League, New York; Acad Grande Chaumiere, Paris, France. *Work:* Joseph Hirshorn Mus, Washington; Los Angeles Co Mus Art, Calif; Exec Mansion, State of Calif, Sacramento; Bonita Granville; Mrs Mel Blanc. *Exhib:* Dallas Mus Fine Arts, Tex, 35-36; Los Angeles Co Mus Art, Calif, 55-58; MH DeYoung Mem Mus, San Francisco, 67; Art LA 88 & 89, Feingarten Galleries, Los Angeles, 88 & 89; Armory Show, NY, 89 & 90. *Teaching:* Westwood Studio, 50-78. *Mem:* Calif Confederation Arts (bd dir, 80-81); Artist Economic Action (chmn). *Media:* Oil. *Dealer:* Trigg Ison Fine Art West Hollywood CA; La Jolla CA; Feingarten Gallery Los Angeles CA. *Mailing Add:* 17561 Castellammare De Pacific Palisades CA 90272

BLUME, PETER F
MUSEUM DIRECTOR
b Syracuse, NY, Jun 5, 46. *Study:* Syracuse Univ, BFA, 1967; Syracuse Univ, 1973; Attingham Summer Sch, Eng, 1976; Mus Mg Inst, Berkeley, Calif, 1986. *Collection Arranged:* Gustav Grunewald 1805-1878, Allentown Art Mus, Pa, 92; Joan Snyder: Works with Paper, Allentown Art Mus, Pa, 93; Charles Sheeler in Doylestown: American Modernism and the Pennsylvania Tradition, Allentown Art Mus, Pa, 97; All That Jazz: Printed Fashion Silks of the 20's and 30's, Allentown Art Mus, Pa, 99; John Clem Clarke: Comforts, Near Disasters, and Pentimenti, Allentown Art Mus, Pa, 99; Honoring Tradition: Perspectives of Three Asian-American Artists, Indira Freitas Johnson, Naoko Matsubara, Komelia Hongia Okim, Ball State Univ Mus Art, Muncie, Ind, 2004. *Pos:* Cur, Allentown (Pa) Art Mus, 1974-84, dir, 1984-2002; Ball State Univ Mus Art, Ind, 2003-. *Awards:* Rockefeller Found fel Metrop Mus Art, New York City, 1973-74. *Mem:* Mus panel Pa Coun on Arts, Harrisburg (mem, 1983-87); Rotary. *Publ:* Auth exhib catalogs; Auth, George Bellows Dawn Of Peace, Am Art Rev, fall 93. *Mailing Add:* Ball State Univ Mus Art Ball State Univ Muncie IN 47306

BLUMENTHAL, ARTHUR R
MUSEUM DIRECTOR, HISTORIAN
b Cleveland, Ohio, May 25, 42. *Study:* Kent State Univ, BS(art educ), 64; Ford Found Fel Mus Training, 65-67; Inst Fine Arts, NY Univ, MA(art hist), 66, PhD(fine arts), 84; Mus Training Cert, Metrop Mus, 68; Travel grant, Am Coun Learned Socs, 79; Mus Mgt Prog, Univ Colo, Boulder, 94; Rollins Col, Program for Effective Leadership, 2000. *Exhib:* Cubist Prints, Collection Dr Abraham Melamed, 72; Portraits at Dartmouth, Dartmouth Col, 78; Theater Art of the Medici (auth, catalog), Dartmouth Col, 80; Treasures of Cornell Fine Arts Mus (auth, catalog), 93-; Italian Renaissance & Baroque Paintings in Fla Mus (auth, catalog); Cornell Fine Arts Mus, 91; Degas to Delaunay: Masterworks from Robert & Maurine Rothschild Family Collection (auth, catalog), Cornell Fine Arts Mus, 99; Cosimo Rosselli: Painter of the Sistine Chapel (auth, catalog), 2001; Honoré Daumier! Paintings, Sculpture, & Prints from the UCLA Hammer Mus. *Pos:* Cur art, Hood Mus, Dartmouth Col, 76-82; dir, The Art Gallery, Univ Md, 82-84 & Cornell Fine Arts Mus, Rollins Col, Winter Park, Fla, 88-; cur, Elvehjem Mus Art, Univ Madison, Wis. *Awards:* Spec Proj Grant, Eng Speaking Union-Cent Fla br, 91; Ford Found Fel, 1965-1967; NYU-LFA Cook Travel Grant, 1974. *Mem:* Col Art Asn; Am Asn Mus; Fla Art Mus Dir Asn; Fla Asn Mus. *Res:* Italian Renaissance & Baroque theater; contemporary American art. *Specialty:* American 19th Century Art. *Interests:* Collecting; Reading; Travel; Acting. *Publ:* Auth, Italian Renaissance Festival Designs, Univ Wis Press, 73; Theater Designs in the Collection of Cooper-Hewitt Mus, Smithsonian, 86; Giulio Parigi's Stage Designs: Florence and The Early Baroque Spectacle, Garland, NY, 86; Cosimo Rosselli: Painter of the Sistine Chapel, Cornell Fine Arts Mus, Rollins Col, Winter Park, Fla, 2001; Theater Art of the Medici Univ Press of New England, 1980. *Mailing Add:* Cornell Fine Arts Mus Rollins Col 1000 Holt Ave Winter Park FL 32789-4499

BLUMENTHAL, FRITZ
PAINTER, PRINTMAKER
b Mainz, Ger, June 16, 13; US citizen. *Study:* Univ Wuerzburg, Frankfurt, Freiburg, Berne. *Work:* Metrop Mus Art & Mus Mod Art, NY; Nat Gallery Art & Nat Mus Am Art, Washington; Boston Mus Fine Arts; Victoria & Albert Mus, London; Stedelijk Mus, Amsterdam; St Louis Art Mus, Mo; and others. *Comn:* Prog cover designs, Gtr Middletown Arts Coun, NY State Coun Arts in collection of Mus Performing Arts at Lincoln Ctr, NY Pub Libr. *Exhib:* Solo exhibs, Albany Inst Hist & Art, Albany, NY, 52, Kenneth Taylor Gallery, Nantucket, Mass, 61 & 65, Gutenberg Mus, Mainz, Ger, 64, Kunstverein Ulm, Ger, 65; Nat Mus Am Art, Washington, 88; Marion Koogler McNay Art Inst, San Antonio, Tex, 88; The Monotype: Degas to Picasso, Mus Fine Arts, Boston, 90; De Bonnard A Baselitz, Biblio Nat, Paris, 92; and others. *Awards:* First Prize Painting, Nantucket Artists Asn. *Bibliog:* Dr Werner Spanner (auth), Fritz Blumenthal, Das Neue Mainz, 64 & Mainz, 83; La Liberte & Mogelon (coauths), The Art of Monoprint, Van Nostrand, 74; Dr D A W Koning (auth), article, De pharmacie en de Kunst, Vol IV, 76; and others. *Media:* Oil Casein; Monotypes. *Mailing Add:* 864 Silver Lake Scotchtown Rd Middletown NY 10941

BLUMRICH, STEPHEN
DESIGNER
b Gotha, Ger, June 9, 41; US citizen. *Study:* Kunstgewerbeschule Dept Fabric Design, BFA, 58. *Work:* Nat Collection Fine Arts; Opryland Hotel, Nashville, Tenn; White House Christmas Ornament Collection, 2001. *Comn:* S Cent Bell, Nashville, Tenn. *Exhib:* Ann Southern Tier Art Show, Corning Mus Glass, NY, 70-74; Lake Superior Int Craft Exhib, Tweed Art Mus, Duluth, Minn, 74; The New Fabric Surface, Renwick Gallery, 78; Surface Design Invitational, Purdue Univ, West Lafayette, Ind, 78; Games & Crafts, Philadelphia Art Alliance, 79; Show Biz, Fashion Inst Technol, NY, 80; Opening Exhib, Greenwood Gallery, 80. *Pos:* Ed, Surface Design J, 76-88; designer, Pea Ridge Purties, 84-2002. *Awards:* Craft/Art S, Thomson, Ga, 81; Golden Isles Art Festival, St Simons Island, Ga, 81. *Bibliog:* Dona Z Meilach (auth), The Great Batik Revival, Sphere Mag, 73; Mike O'Brien (auth), A special craftsman, Regist Guard, Eugene, Ore, 75. *Mem:* Surface Design Asn. *Media:* Fabrics, Quilts. *Mailing Add:* 323 Marks Ave Tullahoma TN 37388-6213

BLUNK, JOYCE ELAINE
ASSEMBLAGE ARTIST, SCULPTOR
b Moorland, Iowa, May 13, 39. *Study:* Univ Iowa, with Stuart Eddy, Hans Breeder & Byron Burford, BA, 63, MA, 70, MFA, 71. *Work:* Kebbel Villa, Oberpfalzer Kunstlerhaus, Schwandorf, Ger; Harvey Littleton Printmaking Studios, Spruce Pine, NC; Allan Stone pvt collection, NY; Univ Iowa Sch Art & Art Hist; W Carolina Univ Fine Art Mus, Cullowhee, NC. *Exhib:* group exhibs, Two Artist Invitational, Oberpfalzer Kunstlerhaus, Schwandorf, Ger, 90, Southeastern Juried Triennial, Fine Art Mus S, Mobile, Ala, 93, Exhib 280: Works Off Walls, Huntington Mus Art, WVa, 93, Artists in Residence, Chateau de la Napoule Found, France, 94, Nat Juried Exhib, Muse Gallery, Found Visual Arts, Philadelphia, Pa, 96, Nat Indoor & Outdoor Sculpture Show, Hoyt Inst Fine Arts, New Castle, Pa, 98, William King Regional Art Ctr, Abingdon, Va, 99 & Border Biennial, Mus York Co, Rock Hill, SC, 2000, Herndon Gallery, Antioch Col, Yellow Springs, Ohio, 2001, Tryon Ctr for Visual Art, Spirit Sq Galleries, Charlotte, NC, 2002, The Hunter Mus Am Art, Chattanooga, Tenn, 2002, Fayetteville Mus Art, NC, 2004, 88 Greenwich St Gallery, Nat Asn Women Artists, Ann Exhib, NY, 2004, Inaugural Exhib, Fine & Performing Arts Center, Western Carolina Univ, Cullowhee, NC, 2005, Goggle Works Center for the Arts, Reading, Pa, 2006; solo exhibs, Mint Mus Art, Charlotte, NC, 91, Kimura Gallery, Univ Alaska, Anchorage, 99, Black Mountain Ctr for the Arts, NC, 2002, The Cecilia Coker Bell Gallery, Coker Col, Hartsville, SC, 2002, Lipscomb Gallery, SC Gov's Sch for Arts & Humanities, Greenville, 2004, Artspace Gallery One, Raleigh, NC, 2004, Santa Fe Gallery, Santa Fe Col, Gainesville, Fla, 2005. *Pos:* exhib selection comt, Asheville Area Arts Coun, NC. *Teaching:* Artist in residence, W Carolina Univ, Cullowhee, NC, 97; artist-teacher visual art, Vt Col, Norwich Univ, Montpelier, Vt,

97-2000. *Awards:* Pollock-Krasner Found Grant, 91-92; NC Arts Coun & Nat Endowment Arts Residence Fel, La Napoule, France, 94; NC Arts Coun Visual Artist Fel, 96-97; Va Ctr for Creative Arts Fel, Stadt Künstlerhaus, Austria, 99; Fel Residency, Cill Rialaig Internat Artists' Retreat, Ballinskelligs, Ireland, 2003; Fel Residency, Nota Bene Loft Studio, Cadaqués, Spain, 2005. *Bibliog:* Tom Klobe (auth), The Third Int Shoebox Sculpture Exhib (catalog), Coun Cult Planning & Develop, 88; Mark Richard Leach (auth), Art Currents Six Material Redemptions (exhib catalog), Mint Mus Art, 91; Anne Forcinito & Jeff Petus (auths), NC Arts Coun Visual Artist Fel Traveling Exhib (catalog), Mint Mus Art, 97. *Mem:* Internat Sculpture Ctr; Nat Asn Women Artists. *Media:* Mixed Media. *Mailing Add:* 31 Samayoa Plc Asheville NC 28806

BOARDMAN, DEBORAH
PAINTER, CONCEPTUAL ARTIST
b Salem, Mass, 58. *Study:* Mt Holyoke Col, BA, 80; studied with Atelier Lucio Loubet, Paris, 81; Mass Col Art, BFA, 84; Tufts Univ, Sch Mus Fine Arts, MFA, 87. *Work:* Artist Book Collection, Mus Mod Art Libr, NY; Artist Book Collection, Mus Contemp Art, Chicago; Ryerson & Burnham Libr, Art Inst Chicago; Joan Flasch Artists' Book Collection, SAIC; Wing Collection, Newberry Libr, Chicago; Houghton Libr, Harvard Univ, Cambridge, Mass; Rare Books Collection, Waldo Libr, W Mich Univ; Rare Books Collection, Boston Public Libr; Chicago Cultural Ctr. *Exhib:* Solo exhibs: Good Luck (Lame Horse), Armstrong Gallery, Cornelle Col, Mt Vernon, Iowa, Stations of Mary, Gallery Eleven, Tufts Univ, Medford, Mass, 87, Mobius Performance Space, Boston, 88, Crane Gallery, Chicago, 89, Memento Mori, McAuley Gallery, Mt Mercy Col, Cedar Rapids, Iowa, 92 & Mutual Borders, Community United Methodist Church, Chicago, 94; NAME, The Enunciation (Or What the Oxen Said), Set Design, Waldorf Auditorium Theater, Chicago, 95; The Initiation, Set Design, Chicago, 95; Paper in Particular, Columbia Col, Mo, 96; Mary Mary, Quite Contrary, Women Made Gallery, Chicago, 96; Installation, Prairie Ave Gallery, Chicago, 97; Illumination, Ornamentation, Collaboration Decoration with Jeff Hillard, Prairie Ave Gallery, Chicago, 97; Domestic Taboo, Suburban Fine Arts Ctr, Highland Park, Ill, 98; Death, Dreams & Heraldry, Chicago Cult Ctr, 99; Fla Women Artists: The New Millenium, Taipai Fine Arts Mus, 1999; Out of Line: Drawings by Ill Artists, Chicago Cult Ctr; Picturing Death Project, McLean Co Arts Ctr, Bloomington, Ill, 2001; Deborah Boardman, Jan Cicero Gallery Project Space, Chicago, 2002; Remembrance, Evanston Art Ctr, Ill, 2003; Figures of Invention, The Work Space, NY, 2003; Deborah Boardman, Richard Rezac, Amy Vogel, Track House, Oak Park, Ill, 2004; New Work in Gilles, Werewolves & Other Dilemmas, Gescheidle Gallery, Chicago, 2005; 2nd Int Biennial for the Artist's Book, Bibliothecha Alexandrina, Egypt, 2006. *Pos:* Educ comt, NAME Gallery, Chicago, Ill, 91-93. *Teaching:* Vis painting, Univ Iowa, 88-89, asst prof 89-95; vis artist, Moorhead State Univ, Minn, 91; instr, School Art Inst Chicago, 97-; vis artist, Univ Southern Ind, 99. *Awards:* Ill Arts Coun Access Prog; Chicago Artists Int Prog Grant, City Chicago Dept Cult Affairs, 94, Regional Arts Projs Grant, 93; Visual Artists Fel, Ill Arts Coun, 2001. *Bibliog:* Eliot Nusbau (auth), Des Moines Register, 1/28/90; Elizabeth Condon (auth), The Mussell Secretes the Shell Which Shapes It, New Art Examiner, 9/90; Elisabeth Condon (auth), Communion, New Art Examiner, 3/94. *Media:* Painting, Artist Books, Installation. *Publ:* Memory & Influence (limited ed booklet); Mutual Borders (limited ed booklet), 94; Picturing Death (limited ed), 2000. *Mailing Add:* 1436 W Highland Ave Chicago IL 60660

BOARDMAN, SEYMOUR
PAINTER
b Brooklyn, NY, Dec 29, 21. *Study:* City Col New York, BSS, 42; Art Students League; Ecole Beaux Arts, Paris, France, Acad Grande Chaumiere, Paris, Atelier Fernand Leger, Paris, 46-52. *Work:* Whitney Mus Am Art, Guggenheim Mus & NY Univ; Walker Art Ctr, Minneapolis, Minn; Santa Barbara Mus Art; plus others. *Exhib:* Whitney Mus Am Art, 55, 61 & 67; Kunsthalle, Basel, Switz, 64; Albright-Knox Gallery, Buffalo, NY, 67; Andrew Dickson White Mus of Art, Cornell Univ, 71; one-man shows, Galerie Mai, Paris, 51, Martha Jackson Gallery, NY, 55 & 56 & Stephen Radich Gallery, NY, 60-61: & Dorsky Gallery, NY, 72; Anita Shapolsky Gallery, NY, 86; Anderson Gallery, Buffalo, NY, 94; plus others. *Collection Arranged:* Whitney Mus, Guggenheim Mus, Santa Barbara Mus Art, Calif, Walker ARt Ctr, Minn. *Teaching:* Instr painting & drawing, Wagner Col, Staten Island, NY, 57-58. *Awards:* Longview Found Award, 63; Guggenheim Fel, 72; Gottlieb Found Award, 79 & 83; Krasner-Pollock Found Award, 85, 91 & 98, 2001, 2003. *Bibliog:* Arts Digest, 4/55; Art News, 3/68; Arts, 1/80 & 3/92. *Media:* Acrylic, Oil. *Specialty:* Abstract Art. *Dealer:* Anita Shapolsky Gallery NY. *Mailing Add:* 234 W 27th St New York NY 10001

BOB, DADDY-O See Wade, Robert Schrope

BOBAK, BRUNO JOSEPH
PAINTER, PRINTMAKER
b Wawelowka, Poland, Dec 28, 23; Can citizen. *Study:* Art Gallery, Toronto, studied with A Lismer, D Medhurst, A Taylor, G Webber, 36, Cent Tech Sch, Ont, studied with C Goldhamer, R Ross, C Schaefer, E W Wood, dipl, 38-42, Cent Sch Art & Crafts, London, 44-45, City & Guilds Art Sch, London, 60. *Work:* Nat Gallery Can & Can Coun Art Bank, Ottawa, Ont; Oslo Kunstforening, Norway; S London Art Gallery, Eng; Seattle Art Gallery; Alberta Col Art, Calgary; Art Gallery, Greater Victoria, BC; Art Gallery, Hamilton, Ont; and many others. *Comn:* Murals, Expo, Montreal, 67, Univ NB & Dept Pub Works, Fredericton, 70. *Exhib:* One-man exhibs, City Art Gallery Leeds, 62, South London Art Gallery, 63, Oslo Kunstforening, Oslo & Stavanger Kunstforening, Stavanger, Norway, 63, Owens Art Gallery, Mt Allison Univ, Sackville, NB, 70-71; 1st Biennial Exhib, Mus Mod Art, Tokyo, 57; Brussels Int, Can Pavilion, Brussels, 58; 20th Biennial Int, Brooklyn Mus Art, 58; Contemp Can Art, Mex, 60; 19 Can Painters '62, Speed Mus, Louisville, 62; 4 Can Printmakers (traveling), Cent Wash State Col, 76; and others. *Pos:* Designer, concrete mural for facade, Vancouver Sch Art, 52-53; fine art coordinr & supevr, commissioner, sculpture & display, Atlantic artist for Expo, 67; resident artist, Univ New Brunswick. *Teaching:* Instr, head design, Vancouver Sch Art, BC, 47-57; dir, Space Art Ctr, Univ New Brunswick, Fredericton, NB, 62. *Awards:* First Prize Can Army Art Exhib, Nat Art Gallery Can, 44; Jessie Dow Prize, 71st Annual Spring, Exhib, Montreal Mus Fine Arts Montreal for Watercolor Eclipse, 54; C W Jefferys Award, Can Soc Graphic Art, Lugano, Switz, 55; K B Baker Memorial Purchase Award, Seatttle Art Mus, Washington, DC, 55; Monsanto Art Compt Prize, Montreal, 57; Royal Soc Can Govt, Overseas Fel, 55; First Prize, Exhib of Contemp Art, Vancouver Art Gallery, 60; Can Coun Sr Fel, 72; Silver Jubilee Medal, 78; Chosen for reproduction of Can 30-cent postage stamp, 82. *Bibliog:* R H Hubbard (auth), Development of Can Art, Nat Gallery, Ottawa, 63; J R Harper (auth), Painting in Canada, Univ Toronto Press, 66; S Pickins (auth), History of Canadian Society of Painters in Watercolour, Art Mag, winter, 70; S Raphael (auth), In Review-Montreal Art Scene, Art Mag, winter, 72; C Mungal (auth), Fredericton, Could You Live There?, Chatelaine, 77; J Morris (auth), 100 Years of Canadian Drawings, Toronto, 80. *Media:* Oil; Woodcuts. *Dealer:* Walter Klinkoff Gallery 1200 Ouest Rue Sherbrooke Montreal PQ H3A 1H9 Can. *Mailing Add:* c/o Walter Klinkoff Gallery 1200 Ouest Rue Sherbrooke Montreal PQ H3A 1H6 Canada

BOBICK, J BRUCE
EDUCATOR, PAINTER
b Clymer, Pa, Oct 25, 41. *Study:* Indiana Univ Pa, BS, 63, MS, 67; Univ Notre Dame, MFA, 68. *Work:* Mt Mercy Col, Cedar Rapids, Iowa; Western Ill Univ, Macomb; Springfield Art Mus, Mo; Ill State Mus, Springfield; Krannert Art Mus, Univ Ill, Champaign-Urbana. *Comn:* Stainless-steel kinetic sculptures, Carrollton Parks, Recreation & Cult Arts Dept, 88, Pinnacle Insurance Co, Carrollton, Ga, 89; wall-hung quilt, Omni Int Hotel, St Louis, Mo; two paintings for use as bedspread designs, All Star Sports & All Star Music; Disney World, Orlando, Fla, 92; oil painting, Ga Sports Hall Fame, Macon, Ga, 99. *Exhib:* Watercolor, USA Springfield Art Mus, Mo, 68,69,70,73, 75, 77, 89, 90 & 93; Nat Watercolor Soc: Oakland Art Mus, Calif, 70, Otis Arts Inst, Los Angeles, Calif, 73, Palm Springs Art Mus, 73, Calif State Univ, Northridge, Calif, 77, Laguna Beach Mus Art, Calif, 69, 71, 72, 79, Muckenthaler Cult Ctr, Fullerton, Calif, 2004, Brand Art Galleries, 2004; Nat Exhib Watercolor Soc of Ala, Birmingham Mus Art, 69-82; 164th Ann Am Watercolors, Prints & Drawings, Pa Acad Fine Arts, Philadelphia, 69; Nat Acad Design Galleries, NY, 70, 71; 17th Hunter Ann Exhib Paintings & Drawings, Hunter Mus Art, Chattanooga, Tenn, 78; Ga Mus Art, 89, Mus Art, Columbus, 91; Watercolor Now Fourth Biennial, Salt Lake City Art Ctr, Utah, 93-94; Albany Mus Art, 94; Watercolor Now Fifth Biennial, Knoxville Mus Art, Tenn, 95; From the Avant-Garde to the Present Day, Artists Union Exhib Gallery, St Petersburg, Russ, 96; Southern Quilts: A New View, Mus Am Quilters Soc, Paducah, KY, Huntsville Mus Art, Huntsville, AL, 90, 92. *Pos:* artist-in-residence High Mus of Art, Atlanta, Ga, 2000; Univ Pittsburgh, Semester-at-Sea, 2003; Natl Watercolor Society, Los Angeles, CA, 72, 73. *Teaching:* Assoc prof art, Western Ill Univ, 68-76; from assoc prof to prof & chmn dept art, WGa Col, 76-; vis prof painting, Univ Ga Studies Abroad, Cortona, Italy, 80; vis prof painting, Arrowmont Sch Arts & Crafts, Gatlinburg, Tenn, 84, 85, 86, 87, 88, 95 & 98, Guangxi Teachers Univ, Guilin, Peoples Repub China, 93; prof, chmn dept art State Univ of W Ga. *Awards:* Purchase Award, Ill State Mus, 71, Watercolor USA, 71 & 75; Ga Watercolor Soc Award, 82, 86, 91 & 93. *Bibliog:* Dorothy M Joiner (auth), Bruce Bobick: Images upon the subconscious, Art Papers, 1/85; Laura Stewart Dishman (auth), A patchwork of memory, imagination, Orlando Sentinel, 2/20/86; Carlotta M Eike (auth), Artifacts from imaginary culture explore archeological implications, Mus News, 11/88. *Mem:* Nat Watercolor Soc, Watercolor USA Honor Soc; Pittsburgh Watercolor Soc; Ga Watercolor Soc; Ala Watercolor Soc. *Media:* Watercolor. *Res:* Communication between artist and viewer. *Publ:* Auth, Images upon the subconscious, The Flying Needle, 5/86; Markings: Aerial Views of Sacred Landscapes (book review), Vol V, Visual Resources, 89; auth, Professional Practices Committeee Reexamines MFA Standards, CAA News, v.27, No.6, 11/2/2002. *Dealer:* Dorothy Moye & Associates, 866 E Ponce de Leon Ave Decatur GA 30030. *Mailing Add:* State Univ of W Georgia Dept of Art Carrollton GA 30118

BOBINS, NORMAN R
PATRON
Study: Univ Wis, BS, 64; Univ Chgo, MBA, 67. *Pos:* Sr vpres Am Nat Bank and Trust Co, 67-81; sr exec vpres, chieff lending officer Exchange Nat Bank Chicgo, 81-90; chmn, pres and chief exec officer LaSalle Nat Bank, Chicago, 90-; pres and chief exec officer LaSalle Bank Corp; sr exec vpres ABN AMRO Bank, NV, Netherlands; vchmn, Standard Federal Bank, NA, bd dirs; bd trustees Chicago Community Trust, Field Mus, Art Inst Chicago, Univ Chicago Hospitals; bd dirs Terra Found Art; exec bd Auditorium Theatre Council, Chicago; treas, bd dirs, Finanical Services Roundtable, Washington; chmn bd Chicagoland CofC, formerly; mem Bd Educ Chicgo, 94-. *Awards:* Human Rights Medallion, Am Jewish Comt, 92; Kreshet Rainbow Award, 97; Reach for Excellence Award, Midtown Educational Found, 98; Business Leadership Awad, DePaul Univ, 99; Jane Addams Hull House Medal, 2000; Chairman's Award, Boys & Girls Club, 2002; Lifetime Achievement Award, Asn Corp Growth, 2003; Richard J Daley Medal, 2005. *Mailing Add:* LaSalle Bank NA 135 S LaSalle St Fl3 Chicago IL 60603-4404

BOBROWICZ, YVONNE PACANOVSKY
INSTRUCTOR, WEAVER
b Maplewood, NJ, Feb 17, 28. *Study:* Cranbrook Acad Art; study with Anni Albers; with Paolo Soleri at Haystack Mountain. *Work:* Philadelphia Mus Art, 90. *Comn:* Woven wall, comn by Louis I Kahn, Kimball Mus, Ft Worth Tex, 72; woven wall hanging, Savings & Loan Bank, Pittsburgh, Pa, 77; Dupont Corp, Wilmington, Del.

Exhib: Walker Art Ctr, Minneapolis, Minn, 53; Mus Contemp Crafts, NY, 60; Philadelphia Mus Art, 63 & 300 yrs of Philadelphia Art, 76; Civic Ctr Mus Philadelphia, 67-73; Univ Pa Mus, Philadelphia, 75; Lousanne 14th Biennial of Tapestry, 89; group show, Tilburg Textile Mus, The Neth, 89; and others. *Teaching:* Lectr textiles & weaving, Drexel Univ, Philadelphia, 66-; instr weaving, Peters Valley, Leyton NY, summers 72 & 76. *Awards:* First Prize, Los Angeles Co Fair, 51; Grant for Excellence in Fiber Art, Leeway Found, 97. *Mem:* Am Craft Coun; World Craft Coun; Philadelphia Guild Handweavers. *Media:* Thread, fiber or metal. *Publ:* Contribr, Rugmaking, Golden Bks, 72; contribr, Hooked and Rya Rugs, Van Nostrand Reinhold, 74; contribr, Am Rugs and Carpets, William Morrow, 78. *Dealer:* Helen Drutt 1625 Spruce St Philadelphia PA 19103. *Mailing Add:* 2312 Spruce St Philadelphia PA 19103

BOCANEGRA, SUZANNE H
SCULPTOR
b Houston, Tex. *Study:* Univ Tex, Austin, BFA, 79; San Francisco Art Inst, MFA, 84. *Work:* Mills Col Art Gallery, Oakland, Calif. *Exhib:* Contemp Arts Mus, Houston, 82; solo exhibs, 3221 Gallery, Houston, 82, Christian A Johnson Mem Gallery, Middlebury Col, Vt, 88, Women's Studio Workshop, Rosendale, NY, 90, Victoria Munroe Gallery, NY, 90 & 92, SKEP, NY, 93, Calif Ctr Arts, Escondido, 93 & Queens Mus; 93; Summer Salon, Victoria Munroe Fine Art, NY, 92; Rope, Artists Space, NY, 92; Materials Revisions, Brattleboro Mus, Vt, 92; 93 New York 50, Socrates Sculpture Park, NY, 93. *Teaching:* Vis asst prof art, Middlebury Col, Vt, currently. *Awards:* Prix de Rome for Sculpture, 90; Mid-Atlantic Arts Coun Grant, 91; Marie Walsh Sharpe Arts Found Studio Grant, 93. *Bibliog:* Memory Holloway (auth), Suzanne Bocanegra/Sculpture Center, Arts Int, spring/summer 92; Marilou Blaine (auth), New life for old junk, Keene Sentinal, 9/1/92; Eleanor Heartney (auth), Suzanne Bocanegra, Art News, 10/92. *Mailing Add:* 66 Greene St New York NY 10012

BOCCIA, EDWARD EUGENE
PAINTER, WRITER
b Newark, NJ, June 22, 21. *Study:* Pratt Inst Art Sch, NY; Art Students League; Columbia Univ, BS & MA. *Work:* Univ Mass; St Louis Univ; State Hist Soc Mo; Mus Art, Ft Lauderdale, Fla; Nat Picture Gallery, Athens, Greece; Steinberg Gallery of Art, Washington Univ, St Louis. *Comn:* Stained glass, Clayton Inn, Mo; four wall paintings, First Nat Bank, St Louis; mural, Stations of the Cross & stained glass windows, Newman Chapel, Washington Univ, St Louis; religious drawings & 14 mural paintings, Temple Brith Sholom Kneseth Israel, St Louis; and others. *Exhib:* Gallery of the Masters, 90 & 92, St Louis, Mo, Am Gallery, 92, Pompeii Gallery, 95 & Fac Exhib, Steinberg Gallery, Wash Univ, St Louis, 98; Parkland Col Art Gallery, Champaign, Ill; Retrospective Exhib, St Louis Univ, 96; Fontbonne Col, 98; Borders Books, Phila, 99; Atelier A-E Gallery, New York City, 99; Mocra Gallery, St Louis Gallery, 99; Concordia Luth Ch Art Exhib, 2003; solo exhib, Sheldon Concert Hall, Bellweather Gallery, St Louis, 99, St Bonaventure Univ, NY, 2000, Monday Club, St Louis, 2003; McCaughen & Burr Gallery, Webster Groves, Mo, 2005; and others. *Teaching:* Dean, Columbus Art Sch, Ohio, 48-51; guest instr, Univ Sask, summer 60; guest instr, Webster Groves Col, summer 65 & Univ Minn, 86; prof emer fine arts, Washington Univ, St Louis, Mo, 1951-1986. *Awards:* Bronze Medal, Temple Israel, St Louis, 62; Knighted to Cavaliere, Pres Ital Repub, 79; Order of the Crown of King St Louis IX of France, St Louis Univ, 90. *Bibliog:* An Artist Who's Gone His Own Way, St Louis Post Dispatch, 85; Who's Who: Artist Edward Boccia, Dan's Papers Inc, Bridgehampton, NY, 92; Renaissance Man Edward Boccia, St Louis Post Dispatch, 96; Interview with the Artist, Webster-Kirkwod Times, 9/2005. *Mem:* Nat Soc Arts & Letters, St Louis Poetry Ctr; St Louis Poetry Center; St Louis Writers Guild. *Media:* Painter - Oil. *Publ:* Writers Challenge Voyages, 99; Missouri State Poetry Anthology, 99; Memories and Memoirs, Anthology of Missouri Poets, 2000; Flash Point, 2001; contbr, The Magic Fish, Pudding House Press, 2002; auth, Answering Neruda (poetry), Pudding House Press, 2006; auth, The Light of City and Sea (anthology), Suffolk Co Press, NY, 2006; auth, Long Island Sounds (anthology), N Sea Poetry Scene Press, NY, 2006. *Dealer:* McCaughen & Burr Webster Groves MO. *Mailing Add:* 600 Harper Ave Webster Groves MO 63119

BOCHNER, MEL
CONCEPTUAL ARTIST, ART WRITER
b Pittsburgh, Pa, 1940. *Study:* Carnegie Inst Technol, Pittsburgh, BFA(painting), 62. *Work:* Baltimore Mus Art; Mus Nat d'Art Mod, Paris, France; Whitney Mus Am Art, Mus Mod Art, Metrop Mus Art, NY; Brooklyn Mus; Art Inst Chicago. *Exhib:* One-man exhibs, Baltimore Mus Art, Md, 89, Butler Inst Am Art, Youngstown, Ohio, 91, Galerie Arnaud, Lefebvre, Paris, 94, Yale Univ Art Gallery, 95, Betsy Senior Gallery, NY, 95, Centro de Arte Helio Oiticica, Rio de Janeiro, Brazil, 99 & Sonnabend Gallery, NY, 2000; The Unique Print, Boston Mus Fine Arts, Mass, 90; American Photog & American Abstraction, Addison Gallery Am Art, Andover, Mass, 91; Immaterial/Objects, Whitney Mus Am Art, NY, 91; Marking the Decades: Prints 1960-1990, Baltimore Mus Art, Md, 92; Extended Relations, Andrea Rosen Gallery, NY, 94; Mapping: A Response to MOMA, Am Fine Art Co, NY, 95; Repicturing Abstraction: The Politics of Space, Anderson Gallery, Va Commonwealth Univ, Richmond, 95; Thinking Print: Books to Billboards 1980-95, 96, More Pieces for the Puzzle, 98, Mus Mod Art, NY; Robert & Jane Meyerhoff Collection: 1945-1995, Nat Gallery Art, Washington, DC, 96; New Art on Paper, Philadelphia Mus Art, 96; Serial Attitude, Addison Gallery Am Art, Andover, Mass, 97 & 98; Drawing is Another Kind of Language, Fogg Art Mus, Cambridge, Mass, 97. *Teaching:* Instr, Sch Visual Arts, NY, 65. *Awards:* Nat Endowment Arts, 74 & 82; Creative Arts Pub Serv Grant, 78; Award in Art, Am Acad & Inst Arts & Lett, 90; Artist Award, Col Art Assoc, 96. *Bibliog:* Jonathan Fineberg (auth), Art Since 1940 - Strategies of Being, Prentice Hall, NJ, 95; Paulette Roberts-Pullen (auth), Art in four acts, Style, 1/17/95; Roberta Smith (auth), Mel Bochner Constants and Variables 1966-96, NY Times, 12/96. *Publ:* Mental exercise: No 1 counting, Data, 2/72; Late Cezanne: A Symposium, Art in Am, 3-4/78; Renoir: A Symposium, Art in Am, 3/86; Statement on Abstraction, Tema Celeste, autumn 91

BOCK, WILLIAM SAUTS-NETAMUX'WE
ILLUSTRATOR, PAINTER
b Sellersville, Pa, Sept 18, 39. *Study:* Philadelphia Col of Art, BFA(illus), spec study with Robert Riggs; Lutheran Sem, Philadelphia, MA. *Work:* US State Dept. *Comn:* Watercolor series of Am cities, comn by Marriott Corp for reproduction in many cities, 3-dimensional art (Indian Mex) & murals, Marriott Camelback Inn, Phoenix, Ariz, 69-70; watercolor for Christmas card, Book of the Month Club, NY, 71 & 74; Olympic designs for Plexiglas etching, McDonalds, Willow Grove, Pa, 75. *Awards:* Honored by Exhib for Illustrations for Crusader King, Am Inst of Graphic Arts, New York, 74; Monthly Choice Award for Illustrations for Malcolm Yucca Seed, Philadelphia Children's Reading Round Table, 78. *Bibliog:* Mr & Mrs Philip Berman (interview), Berman Collection, Pub TV, Allentown, Pa, 69; B A Bergman (auth), The First Aristocrats, Sunday Bulletin, Philadelphia, 2/75; Gerry Wallerstein (auth), William Sauts-Netamux'we Bock, Wolf-Clan Chief of the Lenape, Bucks Co Panorama Mag, 1/76. *Mem:* Philadelphia Children's Reading Round Table. *Media:* Pen & Ink; Watercolor, Acrylic. *Publ:* Illusr, Wolf Hunt, Little Brown, 70; illusr & auth, Coloring Book of the First Americans, Lenape Indian Drawings, Middle Atlantic Press, 74; illusr, Tom Sawyer, Field Enterprizes, World Bk, 75; Of Whales & Wolves, Lothrop, Lee, 78; White Fang (film strip), Spoken Arts, 78. *Mailing Add:* 252 E Summit St Souderton PA 18964-1341

BODEM, DENNIS RICHARD
CONSULTANT
b Milwaukee, Wis, July 27, 37. *Study:* Wabash Col, BA, 59; Grad Sch, Univ Wis-Madison, 59-61. *Pos:* Asst archivist, State Hist Soc Wis, 61-64; chief resources div, Buffalo & Erie Co Hist Soc, NY, 64-66; state archivist, Div Mich Hist, Dept State, 66-72, cur, State Mus, 72-74; cur, Mann House, Concord, Mich, 74; dir, Jesse Besser Mus, 74-98; State Bd Very Spec Arts, Mich, 92-93; with Points North Rsch. *Mem:* Thunder Bay Arts Coun; Mich Coun Arts; Mich Mus Asn; Mich Asn Community Arts Agency; Am Records Mgt Asn; Soc Am Archivists. *Interests:* Representative works of outstanding US, Midwest and Michigan artists of the late 19th and 20th centuries for museum collection. *Publ:* Nine articles, three signed reviews and one booknote in professional journals; numerous articles and notes in newspaper. *Mailing Add:* 121 E White Alpena MI 49707

BODIN, KATE
EDUCATOR
Study: Boston Univ, BFA; Arts & learning, Endicott Col, Med. *Pos:* Dean of fac, Montserrat Col of Art, Beverly, Mass, 92-; Chairperson Gloucester Committee for Arts (mayoral appointment). *Mailing Add:* Montserrat Col Art Box 26 23 Essex St Beverly MA 01915

BODNAR, PETER
PAINTER, EDUCATOR
b Andrejova, Czech, Nov 27, 28; US citizen. *Study:* Flint Inst Arts, Mich, 41-44; Western Mich Univ, BS, 51; Mich State Univ, MA, 56. *Work:* Dallas Mus; Isaac Delgado Mus, New Orleans; Ft Worth Art Mus; Lakeview Ctr Arts, Peoria, Ill; State of Ill Ctr, Chicago. *Exhib:* One-man retrospectives, Isaac Delgado Mus, 66, Ill Art Coun Galleries, Chicago, 71, Newport Harbor Art Mus, Newport Beach, Calif, 74, Ill State Mus, Springfield, 77, Danforth Mus, Framingham, Mass, 93 & Aaron Galleries, Chicago, 96; Spirit of the Comics, Inst Contemp Art, Univ Pa, 69; one-man shows, Lakeview Ctr Arts, Peoria, 72 & Univ Ill, 82. *Pos:* Vis artist, Bradley Univ, spring 70, Univ Southern Calif, 74 & Univ NMex, 83; vis artist, Southern Methodist Univ, Dallas, 72 & 81, artist in residence, summer workshop, Taos, NMex, 72. *Teaching:* Asst prof art, State Univ NY, Col Plattsburgh, 56-58 & Univ Fla, 60-62; prof painting, Univ Ill, Urbana-Champaign, 62-92. *Awards:* Tamarind Lithography Workshop Inc Grant, 64; Univ Ill Fel, Ctr Advan Study, 67-68; Nat Endowment Arts Fel, 75-. *Bibliog:* Hiram Williams (auth), Notes for a Young Painter, Prentice-Hall, 65; Franz Schulze (auth), article, Art Int, summer 67; Peter Frank (auth), Peter Bodnar, Mauretania Inc, 92. *Media:* Oil, Acrylic. *Publ:* Contribr, Strung Out with Elgar on a Hill, 70; Portrait: Converse, 75. *Dealer:* Aaron Gallery Chicago. *Mailing Add:* 2504 E Perkins Rd Urbana IL 61801

BODNER, RITA R
PAINTER
b New York, NY. *Study:* Pratt Inst, 41-42; Newark Sch Fine & Indust Arts, 3 yr cert, 42-45; studied with John Grabach & Nicholas Reale. *Exhib:* NJ Watercolor Soc, Monmouth Mus, Lincroft, NJ, 84, 85 & 96; Painters & Sculptors Soc, Bergen Mus Arts & Sci, Ridgewood, NJ, 85; Members Exhib, NJ Ctr for Visual Arts, Summit, NJ, 89; Palm Beach Watercolor Soc, Cornell Mus, Boca Raton, Fla, 94; Garden State Watercolor Soc, Trenton City Mus, 95. *Teaching:* Workshops teacher watermedia & painting, Livingston Arts Asn, 94-95. *Awards:* Grumbacher Gold Medal, Essex Watercolor Club, 92; Catherine Lorillard Wolfe 1st Award in Watercolor, 95; Ada Cecere Mem Award, Nat Asn Women Artists, 96. *Mem:* Nat Mus Women Arts; Nat Asn Women Artists; Catherine Lorillard Wolfe Art Club; Soc Experimental Artists; Garden State Watercolor Soc. *Media:* Transparent, Acrylics. *Publ:* Numerous articles in Newark Star Ledger & Metro-West News Tribune. *Mailing Add:* 27 Shadowlawn Dr Livingston NJ 07039-3215

BODÓ, SÁNDOR
PAINTER, SCULPTOR
b Szamosszeg, Hungary, Feb 13, 1920; arrived in US, 1956; US in citizen 1963. *Study:* Col Fine & Appl Art, Budapest, Hungary; Brown Univ, BFA, 75; Sheffield Polytechnic Sch Art and Design, England; Royal Coll Art, London, M (in photog). *Work:* Tenn State Mus; First Tenn Bank, Nashville, Tenn; Pulaski Co Ct House, Little Rock, Ark; The Soc of the Cincinnati, Washington, DC; Vatican Mus, Rome; Hist Mus, Budapest; Musée de l'armée, Paris. *Comn:* The Founding Fathers of Nashville, First Tenn Bank, Tenn; portrait of Andrew Jackson, Royal Palace, Copenhagen, Denmark, 71; The History of Thoroughbred Horses Tennesse & Kentucky (mural), Green Pastures Farm, Brentwood, Tenn, 94. *Exhib:* Nat Housing Ctr, Washington, DC; Butler Inst Am Art, Youngstown, Ohio; Nat Acad Galleries, NY; Smithsonian Inst, Washington, DC; Brooks Mem Art Gallery, Memphis, Tenn; Citadel Mus, Charleston, SC; Parthenon, Nashville, Tenn; Budapest Hist Muzeum, Hungary, 90; Capitol Russel Rotunda, Washington, DC, 91. *Pos:* Bodo's Art Studio, Nashville, Tenn, 73-. *Awards:* Gold Medal Honor Sculpture, 63 & Gold Medal Honor Oil Painting, 66, Nat Arts Club, NY; 200 Bicentennial Medal; Award, Pro Cultura Hungarica, Budaphest, 90. *Mem:* Fel Am Artists Prof League; Nat Arts Club; Allied Artists Am; Am Medallic Sculpture Asn

BOEPPLE, WILLARD
SCULPTOR, EDUCATOR
b Oct 18, 45. *Study:* CCUNY, BFA, 69. *Work:* Met Mus Art, NY; Boston Mus Fine Arts; Storm King Art Ctr, Mountainville, NY; Nat Gallery of Kenya, Nairobi; Edmonton Art Gallery, Alberta, Can. *Comn:* Vermont State Coun on the Arts Goldstone Mem. *Exhib:* Mead Art Mus, Amherst Col, Mass, 88; Andre Emmerich Gallery, NY, 1991, 93; Francis Graham-Dixon Gallery, London, 94; Galerie du Tableau, Marseille, France, 95; Tricia Collins Grand Salon, NY, 97, 99; NY Studio Sch Gallery, NY, 99; Broadbent Gallery, London, 2001 & 2003; Andrew Mummery Gallery, London, 2002; Broadbent Gallery, NY, 2004; Salander O'Reilly, NY, 2004. *Pos:* Chmn, Triangle Artists Workshop, 93-2001. *Teaching:* prof sculpture, Boston Mus Sch, 76-85. *Bibliog:* Stephen Sandy (auth), The Sculpture of Willard Boepple, Acquavella Contemporary Art; Judith Barter (auth), Willard Boepple: Sculpture, Mead Art Mus, Amherst Col; Andrew Hudson (autho), Breaking Loose from Conventions, Willard Boepple: Sculpture 70-90. *Mem:* Century Asn. *Media:* Metal, Wood, Resin. *Dealer:* Salander O'Reilly Gallery 20 E 79 New York NY 10021; Boradbent Gallery25 Chepstow Cor London England W24XE

BOEVE, EDGAR GENE
EDUCATOR, PAINTER
b Marshalltown, Iowa, Sept 27, 29. *Study:* J Franklin Sch of Prof Arts, Inc, New York, cert; Calvin Col, Grand Rapids, Mich, AB; Univ Mich, Ann Arbor, MSD. *Work:* Calvin Theological Seminary Grand Rapids, Mich; Dordt Col, Sioux Center, Iowa; Catholic Info Ctr, Lansing, Mich. *Comn:* Sculpture, Painting, Pine Rest Hosp, Cutlerville, Mich, 74, 77 & 87; banners, Woodland Church, Grand Rapids, Mich, 75; mural, Bethany, Holland, Mich, 76; sculpture, Faith, Prayer, Tract League, 83; logo, North Hills Church, Troy, Mich, 83 & 90; PLP Corp, Grand Rapids, Mich, 89; Polamar Hosp, San Diego, Calif, 90; Hope Lutheran Church, Park Forest, Ill, 90. *Exhib:* Detroit Art Inst, Mich, 65; Kresge Art Ctr, East Lansing, Mich, 68; Kalamazoo Art Ctr, Mich, 72, Grand Rapids Art Mus, Mich, 75. *Teaching:* Prof art hist, Calvin Col, Grand Rapids, Mich, 58-91, chmn art dept, 65-91, emer prof, 91-. *Awards:* First Prize, 63 & 70 & Second Prize, 73 & 81, Christian Art Show, Peace Lutheran. *Mem:* Christians In the Visual Arts (pres, 79-83); Midwest Col Art Conf; Col Art Asn. *Media:* Oil, Acrylic. *Res:* Art educ, art hist. *Publ:* Auth, Childrens Art and the Christian Teacher, Nat Union Christian Sch, Concordia, Mo, 67, 2nd ed, 77; illusr, Youth Hymnal, Eerdmans, 68; illusr, The Touch of His Hand, World Home Bible, 76; illusr, The Gifted Church, Home Mission, Can Relig Conf, 77

BOGART, GEORGE A
PAINTER
b Duluth, Minn, Oct 30, 33. *Study:* Univ Minn, Duluth, BA; Univ Wash, MFA; also with Fletcher Martin, Philip Evergood & Dong Kingman. *Work:* Delgado Mus Art, New Orleans, La; Ill State Univ; Washburn Univ, Topeka, Kans; Okla State Collection; Univ Okla. *Exhib:* Dallas Mus Fine Arts, 64 & 65; Okla Art Ctr, 75 & 78; Gruenbaum Gallery, NY, 83; Univ Kanas, 84; Ark Art Ctr, Little Rock, 90; one-man shows, Univ Okla Mus Art, 93, Pittsburg State Univ, Kans, 96 & City Arts Mus, Okla City, 98; two-man show, Okla State Univ, 99; and others. *Teaching:* Instr, Univ Wash, formerly; prof art, Univ Tex, Austin & Pa State Univ, State College, formerly; prof art, Univ Okla, 70-98; prof art, Univ artist, Univ Calif, Berkeley, 78-79. *Awards:* Prize, Washburn Univ, 71 & Amarillo Art Mus, 75; Visions '80-'81, Midwest Art Asn. *Media:* Oil. *Publ:* Contribr, Southwestern Art; illusr, George Bogart drawings and paintings, 67. *Mailing Add:* Okla Univ Main Campus Dept Art Norman OK 73019

BOGART, MICHELE HELENE
HISTORIAN, CURATOR
b New York, NY, Oct 5, 52. *Study:* Art Students League; Smith Col, BA, 79; Univ Chicago, MA, 75, PhD, 79. *Exhib:* The Seelye Yrs, Smith Col Mus Art, Northampton, Mass, 74; Am Art Quest for Unity, Detroit Inst Art, Mich, 82-83; Fauns and Fountains, Parrish Art Mus, Southampton, NY, 85. *Pos:* Guest cur, Parrish Art Mus, 82-84; guest cur sculpture, Detroit Inst Art, Mich, 80-83. *Teaching:* Instr art, Am Sch, Chicago, Ill, 76-77; asst prof art hist, Univ Ga, Athens, 79-82; assoc prof, State Univ NY, Stony Brook, currently. *Awards:* Fel, Smithsonian Inst, 77-78; Joint Award, Res Found State Univ NY, 83; Winterthur Res Fel, Fel for Col Teachers & Independent Scholars, Nat Endowment Humanities, 94-95; Provost Fac Travel Grant, 85 & 87; Am Coun Learned Socs Grant-in-Aid, 87; Benno M Forman Fel, Winterthur Mus, 88; Nuala McGann Drescher Leave Fund Award, 88; Smithsonian Sr Postdoctoral Fel, 90. *Mem:* Col Art Asn; Am Studies Asn; Asn Am Art Historians (co-chair). *Res:* Nineteenth and twentieth century sculpture; architectural sculpture; reproductions and copies; illustration, photography, posters and commercial art. *Publ:* Auth, Photosculpture, Art Hist, winter 80; auth, On women and art, Ga Review, winter 80; auth, Development of a popular market for sculpture, J Am Cult, spring 81; auth, Four sculpture sketches for the New York Public Library, Bulletin Ga Mus, winter, 82; The Importance of Believing in Purity, Archives Am Art J, 84; Barking Architecture: the Sculpture of Coney Island, Smithsonian Studies Am Art, winter 88; Public Sculpture and the Civic Ideal in New York City 1890-1930, Univ Chicago Press, 89; Artistic Ideals and Commercial Practices: The Problem of Status for the American Illustrator, Prospects 15, 90; auth, Artists, Advertising, and the Borders of Art, Univ Chicago Press, 95. *Mailing Add:* Dept Art State Univ NY 100 Nicolls Rd Stony Brook NY 11794

BOGART, RICHARD JEROME
PAINTER
b Highland Park, Mich, Oct 30, 29. *Study:* Art Inst Chicago, dipl, 52; Univ Ill, 54; Black Mountain Col, NC, 56. *Work:* Brooklyn Mus; Yellowstone Art Ctr, Billings, Mont; Achenback Found, San Francisco; Mint Mus Art; Detroit Inst Art. *Exhib:* Conn Painting, Drawing & Sculpture Exhib, 78; Artist Showcase, Conn Comn on the Arts, 84; State of the Artists, Aldrich Mus, Ridgefield, Conn, 87; one-man shows, Poindexter Gallery, NY, 68-83, Meredith Long & Co, Houston, Tex, 77 & J P Natkin Gallery, 85, 86, 87 & 88; Douglas Drake Gallery, NY, 90-92; Gallerie 454, Birmingham, Mich, 93; The Artist As Native: Reinventing Regionalism, Babcock Galleries, NY, 93-94; Experiment in Art, Black Mountain Col, 2002-03; Museo Nacional Cento de Arte Reina Sofia, Madrid, Spain, 2002. *Awards:* Artist of yr, Art/Pl Gallery, Fairfield, Conn, 2000. *Bibliog:* Alan Gussow (auth), A sense of place--the artist & the American land, Sat Rev Press; Allan Gussow (auth), The Artist as Native: Reinventing Regionalism, Pomegranate Art Books, Calif; Robert Natkin (auth), Subject Matter and Abstraction--In Exile, Claridge Press St Albans; Artist & their spaces, Conn Mag, 10/87; other reviews in Art News, Arts, Art in Am & Time Mag. *Media:* Oil, Pastel. *Publ:* Auth, Richard Bogart: The Reflected Landscape (exhib catalog), 87; Richard Bogart: Latitutes (catalog), 93; No Other Shore (catalog), 99; Still Ponds (catalogue), 2001; Black Mountain Colege: Experiment in Art; ed, Vincent Katz. *Dealer:* Gallerie 454 15105 Kercheval Grosse Pointe MI 48230. *Mailing Add:* 378 Judd Rd Easton CT 06612

BOGDANOVIC, BOGOMIR
PAINTER
b Senje, Yugoslavia, Aug 20, 23. *Study:* Belgrade Univ, with Prof S Strala, Prof A Samojlov. *Work:* Over 3,000 in pvt collections; Mus Anchorage, Alaska; Presidential Palace, Indonesia; NY Times. *Exhib:* One-man shows, Scarborough Gallery, NY & Quadrangle Gallery, Dallas, 67-80; Pa Acad Fine Arts, Philadelphia; Nat Acad Fine Art, NY; Am Watercolor Soc, NY; Kennedy Galleries, NY; SW Gallery, Dallas, 90-98. *Pos:* Guest artist & demonstr for various art asns. *Awards:* Silver Medal, Am Watercolor Soc, 71; Gold Medal, Franklin Mint, 73; Audubon Artists Gold Medal, 97. *Bibliog:* Article, Am Artist Mag, 12/71. *Mem:* The Dolphin Fel-Am Watercolor Soc; Audubon Artists; Allied Artists Am; Knickerbocker Artist; hon mem Southwestern Watercolor Soc. *Media:* Oil, Pastel Watercolor. *Mailing Add:* c/o Southwest Gallery 4500 Sigma Rd Dallas TX 75244

BOGGS, FRANKLIN
MURALIST, SCULPTOR
b Warsaw, Ind, July 25, 14. *Study:* Ft Wayne Art Sch, Ind; Pa Acad Fine Arts. *Work:* Univ Wis, Madison; Tulane Univ, New Orleans, La; US War Dept, Washington, DC; Univ Wis, Milwaukee; Am Telephone and Telegraph, NJ; and others. *Comn:* Post office mural, Federal Works Agency, Washington, DC, 46; mural, New Mayo Clinic, Rochester, Minn, 53; mural, Crippled Children's Sch, Helsinki, Finland, 59; sculpture relief mem wall, Cumberland Gap, Tenn, US Dept Interior, 73; bronze relief wall, Beloit Corp, Wis, 81; and many others. *Exhib:* Pa Acad Fine Arts. *Pos:* Illusr, Tenn Valley Auth, 40-44. *Teaching:* Prof & artist in residence, Beloit Col, 45-82, chmn art dept, 55-78; lectr Am Indian Exhib, Finland & Sweden, 58-59. *Awards:* Gimbels Wis Exhib Prize, 52; Fulbright Res Grant to Finland, 58; Award of Merit for Precast Concrete Sculpture, 63. *Publ:* Army med paintings reproduced in art mags. *Mailing Add:* 2502 Shopiere Rd Beloit WI 53511

BOGGS, JEAN SUTHERLAND
MUSEUM DIRECTOR, ART HISTORIAN
b Negritos, Peru, June 11, 22; Can citizen. *Pos:* Dir, Nat Gallery Can, 66-76; dir, Philadelphia Mus Art, 79-82; chmn Sci Comt Degas Exhib, Nat Gallery Can, 84-88; sr adv, Andrew W Mellon Found, New York, 91-95. *Teaching:* Asst prof art, Skidmore Col, 48-49; asst prof art, Mt Holyoke Col, 49-52; assoc prof art, Univ Calif, 54-62; Steinberg prof hist art, Washington Univ, 64-66; prof fine arts, Harvard Univ, 76-79. *Awards:* Officer of the Order of Can; Lifetime Achievment Award, 99. *Mem:* Am Asn Mus; Asn Art Mus Dirs; fel Royal Soc Can; Col Art Asn (bd mem, 78-); and others. *Publ:* Auth, Drawings by Degas (exhib catalog), City Art Mus St Louis, 66; The building of a national gallery, Burlington Mag, 4/85; ed & coauth, Degas (exhib catalog), Nat Gallery Can, Ottawa & Metrop Mus Art, New York, 88; auth, Picasso and Things (exhib catalog), Cleveland Mus Art, Philadelphia Mus Art & Réunion des musées nationaux, Paris, 92; Degas as a Portraitist (exhib catalog), Degas Portraits, Kunsthaus Zurich, 94. *Mailing Add:* 4300 Blvd de Maisoneuve Apt 405 Montreal PQ K2P 2G2 Canada

BOGGS, MAYO MAC
SCULPTOR, EDUCATOR
b Ashland, Ky, Mar 22, 1942. *Study:* Univ Ky, with Mike Hall, BA(art); Univ NC, Chapel Hill, with Robert Howard, MFA(sculpture). *Work:* Gerald R Ford Libr; NC Govs Mansion; SC Govs Mansion; Huntington Galleries, WVa; NC Nat Bank, Charlotte; Jimmy Carter Libr. *Comn:* sculpture, comn by Ms Barbara Plott, Tryon,

NC, 89; sculpture, comn by Mr & Mrs Marshall Chapman, Spartanburg, SC, 90; large scale computer graphics (3' x 6'), office of Rick Harris Law Firm, Spartanburg, SC, 92; sculpture, comn by Lillian Jackson Braun, Tryon, NC, 94; sculpture, comn by Mr & Mrs Jack Kenan Four Sabot Farm, Landrum, NC, 94. *Exhib:* Spartanburg Co traveling exhib of twelve paintings, 91; Invitational Sculpture Exhib, Stone Hedge, Tryon, NC, 91; Invitational Group Exhib, Carolina Editions Gallery, Artista Vista, Columbia, SC, 91; Invitational exhib Art of the Upstate Gallery, Spartanburg/Greenville Airport, 91; Fourth Ann NCNB Art Exhib, Spartanburg, SC, 92; and others. *Teaching:* Tech asst, Univ Kentucky, 1968; fellowship, tchr basic and beginning sculpture, Univ NC, 1969-70; instr, Penland Sch Crafts, NC, 1973-75, vis scholar, 1976, summer faculty, 1977; asst dean, counselor, Ghost Ranch, Abiquiu, NMex, 1992; instr in art, Converse Col, Spartanburg, SC, 70-73, asst prof art, 1974-77, assoc prof, 1978-94, prof, 1994-, dept chair, 1997-. *Awards:* John W Oswald Res & Creativity Award, Univ Ky, 69; Kathryne Amelia Brown Fac Award, Converse Col, 72; Named Hon Artist of Spartanburg by proclamation of the Mayor of Spartanbug, 91; Best in Show Award, Fourth Ann NCNB Art Exhib, Spartanburg, SC, 92. *Mem:* Spartanburg Artists Guild; Am Asn Univ Profs; Tri-State Sculptors. *Media:* Steel Construction, Bronze Casts; Computer Graphics. *Mailing Add:* Converse College Art Dept 580 East Main St Spartanburg SC 29301

BOGHOSIAN, VARUJAN
SCULPTOR, EDUCATOR
b New Britain, Conn, June 26, 26. *Study:* Cent Conn Teacher's Col, New Britain, 46-48; Vesper George Sch Art, Boston, 48-50; Yale Univ Sch Art & Archit, BFA, 57, MFA, 59; Brown Univ, MA (hon), 65; Dartmouth Col, MA (hon), 69. *Hon Degrees:* Brown Univ, MA(hon), 59. *Work:* Mus Mod Art & Whitney Mus Am Art, NY; Albright-Knox Art Gallery, Buffalo, NY; Brooklyn Mus, NY; Boston Mus Fine Arts; Addison Gallery Am Art, Andover, Mass. *Exhib:* One-man shows, Stable Gallery, 63-66, Cordier & Ekstrom, NY, 69-88, Am Acad Rome, 86, Aldrich Mus Contemp Art, Ridgefield, Conn, 88, Claude Bernard Gallery, NY, 91, David Winton Bell Gallery, Brown Univ, 92 & Berry Hill Galleries, 97-99; Boîtes, Mus d'Art Mod de la ville de Paris & Maison de la Cult de Rennes, France, 76-77; Artists-in-Residence at Dartmouth, Hopkins Ctr, Dartmough Col, Hanover, NH, 88; Berry Hill, NY, 96; Alpha, Boston, 97; Irving Gallery, Palm Beach, 97; many others. *Pos:* sculptor-in-residence, Am Acad Rome, 66-67, 75; artist-in-residence, Dartmouth Col, Hanover, NH, 68; bd trustees, MacDowell Colony, Peterborough, NH, 82-, co-chmn bd trustees, 84-. *Teaching:* instr drawing & painting, Univ Fla, Gainesville, 58-59; asst prof advanced drawing, Cooper Union, NY, 59-64; instr, Pratt Inst, NY, 61; instr drawing, Yale Univ, 62-64; assoc prof art hist, Brown Univ, Providence, RI, 64-68; prof sculpture, Dartmouth Col, 68-96, George Frederick Jewett art prof, 82-96, prof emer, 96-. *Awards:* Fulbright Grant for Painting, Italy, 53; Nat Inst Arts & Lett Award, 72; Guggenheim Fel, 85; others. *Bibliog:* Dore Ashton (auth), article, Studio Int, 4/65; article, Time Mag, 2/9/70; article, Art Int, 3/81. *Mem:* Am Acad & Inst Arts & Lett; Nat Acad Design (assoc, 90, acad, 93). *Media:* Constructions, Collage. *Dealer:* Cordier & Ekstrom Inc 417 E 75th St New York NY 10021; Berry Hill New York NY. *Mailing Add:* Darmouth Col HB 6081 Visual Studies Off Hanover NH 03755

BOGOSIAN, ERIC
CONCEPTUAL ARTIST, WRITER
b Boston, Mass, Apr 24, 53. *Study:* Oberlin Col. *Exhib:* Matrix Theatre, Los Angeles; Portland Ctr Visual Arts, Ore; Inst Contemp Arts, London; Edinburg Festival, Scotland; Inst Contemp Arts, Boston; Drinking in America; Talk Radio, 88; Pounding Nails in the Floor with My Forehead, NY's Knitting Factory, 98 & Sex Drugs & Rock n Roll, 98; Griller, Goodman Theater, 98. *Awards:* Drama Desk Award & Obie Award, 86. *Mailing Add:* c/o Gerson Saines Mgmt 31 Rockland Ave Larchmont NY 10538

BOHAN, RUTH L
EDUCATOR, HISTORIAN
b Galesburg, Ill, Dec 27, 46. *Study:* Univ Ill, BA, 69; Univ Md, MA, 72, PhD, 80. *Pos:* Res assoc, Yale Univ Art Gallery, 79-80. *Teaching:* Prof art hist, Univ Mo, St Louis, 81-, chair, Dept Art & Art Hist, 95-98, 99-2003. *Awards:* Smithsonian Fel-Nat Collection Fine Arts, 75-76; Mellon Fel, Washington Univ, 80-81; J Paul Getty Fel, 85-86. *Mem:* Am Studies Asn; Col Art Asn; Mid-America Am Studies Asn; Modern Language Asn. *Res:* Early twentieth-century American modernism; Walt Whitman and the visual arts; material culture. *Publ:* Auth, The Societe Anonyme's Brooklyn Exhibition: Katherine Dreier and Modernism in America, UMI Res Press, 82; contrib ed, The Societe Anonyme and the Dreier Bequest at Yale University: A Catalogue Raisonne, Yale Univ Press, 84; American drawings and watercolors, 1900-1945, The St Louis Art Mus Bull, summer 89; Looking into Walt Whitman: American Art 1850-1920, Penn State Press, 2006. *Mailing Add:* Dept Art & Art History Univ Missouri 1 University Blvd Saint Louis MO 63121

BOHARY, JAMES
ARTIST
b Brooklyn, 40. *Work:* One-man shows include Hunter Mus, Chattanooga, Tenn, 1976; exhib in group shows at Johnson Mus Art Cornell Univ, Ithaca, NY, 1987, Philadelphia Mus Art Gallery, Pa, 1988, Neuberger Mus Art, Purchase, NY, 1998, Univ Art Mus State Univ of NY, Binghamton, NY, 2000, Kaoshiung Mus Fine Arts, Taiwan, 2001, Roberson Mus, Binghamton, NY, 2004, Nat Acad Design Mus, NY City, 2004, Valparaiso Univ Mus Art, Ind Univ Art Mus, Bloomington, others. *Exhib:* One-man shows incl Benson Gallery, Bridgehampton, NY, 1977, Landmark Gallery, New York City, 1980, Allan Stone Gallery, 1984, 1986, Joan Prats Gallery, 1985, 1987, 1989, 1993, 1996, John Guggenheim Gallery, 1986, Elizabeth Harris Gallery, New York City, 1994, 1998, 2001, James Baird Gallery, St John's NL Can, 2002, 2004, Elizabeth Harris Gallery, NY, 2005; exhib in group shows at New York Studio Sch, New York City, 1971, St Peter's Gallery, 1972, Brata Gallery, 1972, 1973, Leo Castelli Gallery, 1976, Rensselaer Polytechnic Inst, Troy, NY, 1980 Gruenebaum Gallery, New York City, 1982, Am Acad and Inst Arts and Letters, 1982, 1983, 1985, Galeria Joan Prats, Barcelona, Spain, 1984, 1986, Kouros Gallery, New York City, 1989, 1990, Benton Gallery, South Hampton, NY, 1992, Elizabeth Harris Gallery, New York City, 1993, 1995, 1999, J Johnson Gallery, Jacksonville Beach, Fla, 2002, James Baird Gallery, St John's NL, Can, 2003, Paintings from the collection, Nat Acad Design, 2004, Cosmos and Chaos - A Cultural Paradox, Roberson Mus, Binghamton, NY, 2004, Abstract Painters, Johnson Gallery, Jacksonville Beach, Fla, 2005; Rep in permanent collections Weatherspoon Art Ctr, Greensboro, NC, Tyler Art Ctr, Oswego, NY, State Univ, Austin, Texas, Oppenheimer and Co, Seattle, North Bay Art Ctr, Can, Chemical Bank, New York City, Greenville Art Ctr, SC. *Teaching:* adjunct lectr, Queens Col, 1990; vis artist, asst prof, Painting State Univ of NY, Purchase Col, Purchase, NY, 1998; vis artist, Vt Studio Ctr, 1998; vis artist, Nova Scotia Col of Art and Design, 1999; vis assoc prof, Dartmouth Col, 2003—2004. *Awards:* Grantee, Nat Endowment for Arts, 83; Am Acad Arts & Letters Award, 85; Certificate Merit, Nat Acad Design, NY, 93; Pollock-Krasner Found Grant, 99. *Mem:* Nat Acad Design (assoc, 92, acad, 94, Edwin Palmer Mem Prize 96, 2003). *Mailing Add:* c/o Elizabeth Harris Gallery 529 West 20th St New York NY 10011

BOHEN, BARBARA E
HISTORIAN, MUSEOLOGIST
b Bradford, Wiltshire, Eng, Apr 24, 41; US citizen. *Study:* Queens Col, City Univ NY, BA, 69; NY Univ Inst Fine Arts, MA (fine arts), 73, PhD(classical art), 79, Museum Mgmnt Inst, 82. *Work:* Kerameikos Mus, Athens, Greece; World Heritage Mus, Urbana, Ill. *Collection Arranged:* In Search of the Ancient Egyptians, 88, Kings Crusaders & Craftsmen, 89, Beyond the Himalayas, 90; and others. *Pos:* Dir, World Heritage Mus, Urbana, Ill, 81-2000; coauth & ed, Heritage (biann), Newsletter of the World, Heritage Mus, 81-2000; asst dir, Kerameikos Mus, Athens, Greece, 76-78; lectr, NYU, Washington Sq, 72-73. *Teaching:* Lectr art hist, Queens Col, City Univ NY, spring & summer, 73, Univ Ill, Urbana, fall 82; mus studies, Univ Ill, Urbana, 94-97. *Awards:* Fulbright Fel, Greek Archaeology (vases), 73; Danforth Fel, Greek vase painting studies, 74-76; Deutscheforschunggemeinschaft Fel, 79-81; Arnold O Beckman Research Award, Univ Illinois, 94; Chancellor's Academic Professional Excellence Award, 95. *Res:* Greek vase classification, Apulian vase studies, Egyptian mummies. *Interests:* Early Iron Age Archaeology. *Publ:* Auth, Origins of Greek Civilization, 75 & Greece, the Foundations of Greatness (audio visual progs), Reading Lab Inc, 87; Geometrischen Pyxiden, Walter de Gruyter, Berlin, 88; The Boeotian origin of an unusual geometric vase, J Paul Getty J, Vol 20, 92; Collaborative Investigation of the UI Egyptian Mummy, ACTA Cong Int Mummy Studies, 95; New Light on a Dark Age, Univ Mo, fall 96; Early Athenian Burial Monuments (monogr). *Mailing Add:* 2108 Georgetown Circle Champaign IL 68121

BOHLEN, NINA (CELESTINE EUSTIS BOHLEN)
PAINTER, DRAFTSMAN,PRINTS
b Boston, Mass, Mar 5, 31. *Study:* Radcliffe Col, drawing & painting with Hyman Bloom, BA, 53. *Work:* Fogg Mus Art; Boston Pub Libr; Brockton Mus. *Exhib:* Harvard Mus Comparative Zoology, 82; Van Buren Brazelton Cutling Gallery, 84; solo exhibs, Works on Paper, retrospective, Boston Pub Libr, 87 & Monotypes, retrospective, Pine Manor Col, 88 & 91; Drawings from Boston (with catalog), De Cordova Mus, Lincoln, Mass; Martin Sumers Gallery, NY, 91; Salute to Boston, Boston Pub Libr, 93; Women in Watercolor, 93, 99; Wendell Gallery Mus, Middlesex Community Col, 97; Kelly Gallery, 98, 99, 2000, 2001, 2002; others. *Teaching:* Pvt instr drawing & painting, 73-77, Newton Arts Ctr, 84-89, Pine Manor Col, 85-94; Tide's Institute & Mus of Art, 2003-2004. *Awards:* Am Acad Arts & Lett Award in Art, 77; Camargo Found, Cassis, France. *Bibliog:* Batoon Orphan-Illustrations, 81; Drawing from Boston, 87; Something about the Author, 90; Expose Mag, Harvard Univ, 2000; Drawing to See Goldstein & Fishman, 2004. *Media:* All. *Publ:* Illusr, Baboon Orphan, EP Dutton, 81. *Mailing Add:* 56 Fuller St Waltham MA 02154-5053

BOHLER, JOSEPH STEPHEN
PAINTER
b Great Falls, Mont, June 12, 38. *Study:* With Robert Lougheed, Wilson Hurley, John Pike, Robert Wood, Bill Reese & others; Art Instruction Sch, Minneapolis, Minn, 60. *Work:* Coca Cola Bottling Co, Kansas City, Mo; Johnson Co Bank, Kansas City, Kans; Phoenix Bank & Trust, Ariz; Smithsonian Inst, Washington, DC. *Exhib:* One-man show, C M Russell Mus, Great Falls, Mont, 72; Pastel Soc Am, NY, 80; Am Watercolor Soc, NY, 81; Allied Artists Am, Nat Arts Club, NY, 81-82; two-man show, CM Russell Mus, Great Falls, Mont, 94. *Pos:* Bd dir, Stuart Anderson Black Angus Enterprises, 80-81; pres, NW Rendevous Group. *Teaching:* Jade Fon Watercolor Workshops, Pacific Grove, Calif, 84-86 & Venice, Italy, 95. *Awards:* Arjomari/Arches/Rives Award, Am Watercolor Soc, 90. *Mem:* Rocky Mountain Nat Watermedia Soc; Allied Artists Am; Am Watercolor Soc; Nat Acad Western Art; Midwest Watercolor Soc. *Media:* Watercolor, Pastel. *Publ:* Peggy & Harold Samuels, Contemp Western Artists, 82; The Artistic Touch, 94. *Dealer:* Grapevine Gallery Box 132 Oklahoma City OK 73101. *Mailing Add:* Box 387 Monument CO 80132-8161

BOHNEN, BLYTHE
CONCEPTUAL ARTIST, PHOTOGRAPHER
b Evanston, Ill, July 26, 1940. *Study:* Smith Col, BA(art), 62; Boston Univ, BFA, 67; Hunter Col, MA(painting), 72. *Work:* Dallas Mus Fine Arts, Tex; McCrory Corp, Whitney Mus Am Art, Mus Mod Art, Metrop Mus Art, Brooklyn Mus Art, NY; Fogg Art Mus, Harvard Univ, Cambridge, Mass; Art Inst Chicago; Albright-Knox Art Gallery, Buffalo, NY; Guggenheim Mus, NY; Internat Ctr Photography, NY; and many others; Guggenhsim Mus, NY Univ; Internat Ctr Photography, NY Univ. *Comn:* Ceramic tile relief, wall mural (15' x 30'), Libr Blind, Record Storage Ctr, Trenton, NJ, 80-82. *Exhib:* Annual Survey of Am Painting (with catalog), Whitney Mus Am

Art, 71-72; Penthouse, Mus Mod Art, NY, 72, 91; Reflections 1971-72, Aldrich Mus Contemp Art, Conn, 71-72; Wadsworth Atheneum, Hartford, Conn, 75; Extraordinary Women, Mus Mod Art, NY, 77; Drawings of the 70's, Chicago Art Inst, 77; Permanent Collection of 20th Century Drawings, Metrop Mus Art; one-man exhibs, Int Cult Ctr (with catalog), Antwerp, Belg, 78, Galerie Camomille, Brussels, Belg, 78, Artline Gallery (with catalog), Hague, The Neth, 79, Contemp Art Ctr (with catalog), New Orleans, La, 80, PS 1, NY, 81, Light Gallery, NY, 84 & Galerie Mukai, Tokyo, Japan, 84; Self Portraits (with catalog), Gallery Plaza, Security Pac Nat Bank, Los Angeles, 85; Artists' Self-Portraits, Acad Arts, Honolulu, Hawaii, 85; New Portraiture, Light Gallery, NY, 86; First Person Singular, Self-Portrait Photog, 1840-1987 (with catalog), High Mus, Atlanta, Ga, 88; group exhib, San Jose Mus Art, San Jose, Calif, 98, Visions from America, Whitney Mus Art, New York City, 2002. *Collection Arranged:* Addison Gallery of Am Art, Phillips Academy, Andover, Mass; Aldrich Mus of Contemp Art, Ridgefield, Conn; Allen Art Mus, Oberlin Col, Oberlin, Ohio; Akron Art Mus, Akron, Ohio; Mus Art, Univ Mich, Ann Arbor; Art Mus, Princeton Univ; Ashville Art Mus, Ashville, NC; Baltimore Mus Art; Brooklyn Mus Art; Mus Fine Art, Boston; Art Mus, Univ Calif-Berkeley; Carnegie Mus Art, Pittsburgh; Ctr for Creative Photography, Univ Ariz, Tucson; Chase Manhattan Bank; Chrysler Mus, Norfolk, Va; Art Institute Chicago; Cincinnati Art Mus; Cleveland Mus Art; Dallas Mus Fine Art. *Teaching:* Lectr, Metrop Mus Art, 67-72; guest lectr mod mathematics & mod art, Metrop Mus Art, 78; FID; instr, Parsons Sch Design, 79-88. *Awards:* Artist-in-Residence Grant, 76 & Fel, 78, Nat Endowment Arts. *Bibliog:* Edward Lucie-Smith (auth), Art of the Seventies, 1980; Tom E Hinson (ed), Catalogue of Photography: The Cleveland Museum of Art, 1999; Willy Rotzler (auth), Constructive Concepts: The History of Constructive Art from Cubism to the Present, 1977; Ellen Handy (ed), Reflections in a Glass Eye, 1999; Victoria Thorson & Wendy Shore (eds), Great Drawings of all Times, 1981; Metrop Mus Art Bulletin, Old Masters-New Apprentices, 12/68. *Media:* Acrylic, Graphite, Silver, Gelatin Print. *Mailing Add:* 13 Orchard Hill Rd Norwalk CT 06851

BOHNERT, THOM (THOMAS) ROBERT
CERAMIST, EDUCATOR
b St Louis, Mo, Jan 3, 48. *Study:* Southern Ill Univ, Edwardsville, BA, 69; Cranbrook Acad Art, Bloomfield Hills, Mich, MFA, 71. *Work:* Flint Inst Art, Mich; Minneapolis Art Inst, Minn; Univ Iowa Mus, Iowa City; Cranbrook Acad Art, Bloomfield Hills, Mich; Boyman Mus, Rotterdam, Holland. *Exhib:* Young Americans/Clay Glass, Tucson Mus Art, Ariz, 78; Century Ceramics in the US 1878-1978, Everson Mus, Syracuse, NY, Renwick Gallery, Smithsonian Inst, Washington, DC & Cooper-Hewitt, NY, 79; one-person show, Exhibit A Gallery, Chicago, Ill, 79 & 81; A Response to Wedgewood, 2 Yr Traveling Exhib, Mus Philadelphia Civic Ctr, Pa, 80; Basket-Works, John M Kohler Arts Ctr, Sheboygan, Wis, 81; Painting and Sculpture Today. 1982, Indianapolis Mus Art, 82; Am Clay Artists: Philadelphia 83, Marian Locks Gallery East, 83; plus many others. *Teaching:* Instr ceramic & drawing, Southern Ill Univ, 71; instr ceramics & drawing, C S Mott Community Col, 71-; vis artist ceramics, Univ Mich, 77-78; prof art. *Awards:* Award, Detroit Inst Art, 76; Nat Endowment Arts Craftsmen Fel, 78-79; Creative Artists Grant, Mich Coun Arts, 83-84; John Simon Guggenheim Fel, 86-87. *Bibliog:* Helen Williams Drutt (auth), Contemporary Ceramics: A Response to Wedgewood, 81; Christopher Young (auth), Six Experiments in Sculpture: Thom Bohnert, Flint Inst Arts, 86; Gottfried Borrmann (auth), Ceramics of the world, Kunst & Handwerk, Dusseldorf, WGer, 84; Alice Westphal (auth), Putting Pottery in Perspective, Rockford Col, 90. *Media:* Ceramic, Metal. *Dealer:* Braunstein/Quay Gallery San Francisco; Loveed Fine Arts New York. *Mailing Add:* 6337 Flushing Rd Flushing MI 48433-2548

BOIGON, BRIAN JOSEPH
CONCEPTUAL ARTIST, WRITER
b Toronto, Ont, Aug 14, 55; Can citizen. *Study:* Ont Col Art, 73-76; Univ Toronto Sch Archit, BA, 76-80. *Work:* Art Gallery Ont, Toronto; Can Coun Art Bank, Ottawa, Ont. *Exhib:* Rauman und Installation, Wurttembergischer Kunstverein, Stuggart, WGer, 84; Mapping the Surface, Mendell Art Gallery, Saskatoon, Sask, 86; Logic Display, PS1, NY, 88; Speed Neutralization and the Spectacle of Sleep, 49th Parallel (with catalog), NY, 88. *Pos:* Ed, Impulse Mag, Toronto, 84-90. *Teaching:* Asst prof, Univ Toronto, Dept Fine Art & Archit, 86-90. *Bibliog:* Gordon Lebredt (auth), Staging Mondrian, C Mag, 84; Rick Rhodes (auth), Review, Art Forum, 88. *Media:* Mixed Media, Photography. *Publ:* Auth, Downtown, Impulse, 87; Kiss sugar good bye, Impulse Mag, 88; Victorian spacing and the international style, New Observations, 88; Inboard/Outboard, Fifth Collumn, 89; auth, Speed Reading Tokyo, P3 Mus, Tokyo, 90. *Dealer:* S L Simpson Gallery 515 Queen St W Toronto ON Canada M5V 2B4. *Mailing Add:* 299 Rushton Rd Toronto ON M6C 2X8 Canada

BOIS, YVE-ALAIN
EDUCATOR, CURATOR
b Constantine, Algeria, April 16, 52. *Study:* Baccalaureat Philosophie, Toulouse, 69; License de Lettres Modernes, Unive Paris, 73; PhD, Ecole des Hautes Etudes en Sci Sociales, 77. *Comn:* Co-curator De Stijl and French Archit in the 1920's, Institut Francais d'Architecture, 85, Piet Mondrian Retrospective, The Hague, Nat Gallery Art, Museum Modern Art, 95, L'Informe, mode d'emploi, Centre Georges Pompidou, 96, curator Matisse and Picasso: A Gentle Rivalry, Kimbell Art Mus, 99, Ellsworth Kelly: Early Drawings, Fogg Art Mus, High Mus, Arts Institute Chicago, Kunstmuseum, 99-2000. *Teaching:* Prof hist art, Johns Hopkins Univ, 89-91; Joseph Pulitzer Jr Prof, Modern Art Dept Fine Arts, Harvard Univ, 91; prof Sch Hist Studies, Inst for Adv Study, Princeton Univ, 2005-. *Mailing Add:* Inst for Advanced Study Princton U Einstein Dr Princeton NJ 08540

BOL, MARSHA C
MUSEUM DIRECTOR, HISTORIAN
b Shelbyville, Ind. *Study:* Univ NMex, MA (art hist) 80, PhD (art hist) 89. *Exhib:* Alcoa Found Hall of Native Americans, Carnegie Mus, 1998; Behind the Mask in Mexico, Mus of Int Folk Art, 1988. *Pos:* cur of edn, Maxwell Mus, Univ NMex, 82-84; cur of Latin Am Folk Art, Mus Internat Folk art, 84-90; cur of anthropology, Carnegie Mus Nat Hist, 90-98; dir, NMex Mus Fine arts, 2001-. *Teaching:* assoc prof mus studies, Univ Tex, San Antonio, 99-2001. *Res:* Native American Art History, specifically Plains Indian Womens' Arts. *Publ:* (auth) North, South, East West: American Indians and the National World, 98; (auth) Identity Recovered: Portrait of a Northern Arapaho Quillworker, 2001; (auth) Defining Lakota Tourtist Art, 1880-1915, 99; (auth) Collecting Symbolism Among the Arapaho, 96; (auth) Painting and Sculpture, The Spanish Borderlands, 93. *Mailing Add:* Mus Fine Arts PO Box 2087 Santa Fe NM 87504

BOLAS, GERALD DOUGLAS
MUSEUM DIRECTOR, EDUCATOR
b Los Angeles, Calif, Nov 1, 49. *Study:* Univ Calif, Santa Barbara, BA, 72, MA(art hist), 75; City Univ NY, PhD, 98. *Collection Arranged:* Gyorgy Kepes, 78, Richard Hunt: Three Places, 79, Old and Modern Master Drawings, 80, Greek Vases and Roman Glass, 80 & Arthur Osver: The University Years, 81, Washington Univ Gallery Art; Paris in Japan: The Japanese Encounter with European Painting, 87; Ketav: Flesh and Word in Israeli Art (auth, catalog), 96; and others. *Pos:* Asst to dir, Yale Univ Art Gallery, 75-77; dir, Washington Univ Gallery Art, 77-88, Portland Art Mus, Ore, 88-92, Ackland Art Mus, Univ NC, Chapel Hill, 94-2006. *Teaching:* Asst, Univ Calif, Santa Barbara, 73-74; adj asst prof, Washington Univ, 77-88; adj prof, Univ NC, Chapel Hill, 94-2006. *Awards:* NEH Mus Training Internship, Yale Univ Art Gallery, 75; Fel, Winterthur Mus & Nat Mus Am Art, Smithsonian Inst, 93. *Res:* Nineteenth century American art; history of art auctions, museums patronage and connoisseurship. *Publ:* Auth, Illustrated Checklist of the Washington University Collection, 81; American Responses to Western-Style Japanese Painting, In Paris in Japan: The Japanese Encounter with European Painting, Tokyo & St Louis, 87; numerous other articles and catalog forewords. *Mailing Add:* 508 Hawthorne LN Chapel Hill NC 27517-4904

BOLDING, GARY WILSON
PAINTER, CURATOR
b El Dorado, Ark, Nov 30, 52. *Study:* Hendrix Col, BA, 75; Brooklyn Col, with Philip Pearlstein, MFA, 89. *Work:* Chattahoochee Valley Art Mus, Lamar Dodd Art Ctr, La Grange, Ga; Duncan Gallery Art, De Land, Fla; Cornell Mus Art, Rollins Col, Winter Park, Fla; Polk Mus Art, Lakeland, Fla. *Exhib:* solo exhibs, Gallerie Michael Rasche, Freiburg, Ger, 99; Lorraine Ogilvie Gallery, Marlburg, Ger, 2002; Tatistcheff Gallery, NY, 2002; Bernice Steinbaum Gallery, Miami, Fla, 2003; Cornell Mus, Rollins Col, Fla, 2003; Polk Mus, Lakeland, Fla, 2006. *Collection Arranged:* Robert Fichter, Duncan Gallery Art, 91; The Ethical Object, Duncan Gallery Art, 91; Oscar Bluemmer: Watercolors & Gouaches, Duncan Gallery Art, 94; Worlds on Paper, Duncan Gallery Art, 94; Surrealist Sculpture with a Southern Gothic Twist, Duncan Gallery Art, 94. *Teaching:* Prof painting, Stetson Univ, De Land, Fla, 89-. *Awards:* Bank of Boston Award, 52nd Nat Soc 4 Arts, 90; Purchase Award, LaGrange Nat XVII, Chattahoochee Valley Art Mus, 92; Fla Individual Artist Fel, Fla Arts Coun, 94 & 2003. *Bibliog:* Joan Altabe (auth), Boldings work irreverent, well done, Sarasota Herald Tribune, 9/2/94; Cris Hassold (auth), Gary Bolding; Terror in the suburbs, Art Papers, 3-4/94, Roberta Favis (auth), Artists/Educators, Five in Florida, De Land Mus, 1/94. *Mem:* Col Art Asn. *Media:* Oil, Acrylic. *Dealer:* Arts on Douglas 123 Douglas St New Smyrna Beach FL 32168; Bernice Steinbaum Gallery Miami Fla. *Mailing Add:* 1105 S Beresford Rd Deland FL 32720-3521

BOLEN, JOHN E
ART DEALER, COLLECTOR
b Ft Gordon, Ga, Aug 27, 53. *Study:* Univ Calif, Los Angeles, AB, 75. *Collection Arranged:* Painting into Bronze: The Polychromed Bronze of Harry Jackson, Southwest Mus, Highland Park, Calif, 79; The Cowboy, San Diego Mus Art, 81. *Pos:* Co-dir, Bolen Gallery, Inc, Santa Monica & Los Angeles, Calif, 78-84, Bolen Publ, Playa del Rey, Calif, 79-84; co-owner, John & Lynne Bolen Fine Arts, Huntington Beach, Calif, 84-. *Teaching:* Lectr art collecting, privately, 76-78; pvt art marketing consult, 76-78. *Mem:* Art Dealers Asn Calif (bd dir, 80-83, vpres, 82-83). *Specialty:* Nineteenth and twentieth century American paintings, sculptures and original prints. *Publ:* Ed, Arthur Secunda, Monograph, 80, co-ed, Six Decades of American Prints, 1900-1960, 82, Grant Wood: Paintings, Drawings & Lithographs, 83 & The American Landscape: Current Visions, 83, Bolen Gallery, Inc. *Mailing Add:* PO Box 53394 Irvine CA 92619-3394

BOLEN, LYNNE N
ART DEALER, COLLECTOR
b San Diego, Calif, Feb 19, 54. *Study:* Univ Calif, Los Angeles, BS, 76, post grad, 76-78; Calif State Univ, Dominguez Hills, MBA, 98. *Pos:* Co-dir, Bolen Gallery, Inc, Santa Monica & Los Angeles, Calif, 78-84, Bolen Publ, Playa del Rey, Calif, 79-84; co-owner, John & Lynne Bolen Fine Arts, Huntington Beach, Calif, 84-. *Bibliog:* Critical reviews in Santa Monica Evening Outlook, 78-; var issues, Art Voices, 80-. *Mem:* Art Dealers Asn Calif (secy & mem bd dir, 82-83). *Specialty:* Nineteenth and twentieth century American paintings, sculptures and original prints. *Publ:* Co-ed, Six Decades of American Prints 1900-1960, 82, Grant Wood: Paintings, Drawings & Lithographs, 83, The American Landscape: Current Visions, 83, Bolen Gallery, Inc. *Mailing Add:* PO Box 53394 Irvine CA 92619-3394

BOLER, JOHN ALFRED
ART DEALER, COLLECTOR
b Minneapolis, Minn, Aug 26, 42. *Study:* Univ Minn, BA, 65; Univ Iowa, MA, 70. *Collection Arranged:* Guest Cur, Minnesota Voices, Minn Mus Am Art, 92-93. *Pos:* Dir & owner, Avanyu Gallery, Minneapolis, Minn, 82-87; pres & founder, Art Dealers Asn Twin Cities (Minneapolis & St Paul), 83-86; private dealer, John A Boler Indian and Western Art, Minneapolis, Minn, 87-; judge, Twin Cities Indian Market, 5/91; panelist, Dakota Arts Cong, 92; co-cur exhib, Minn Mus Am Art, 92-93. *Teaching:* Arts Law Conf, Walker Art Ctr, 85. *Awards:* Minn Gov's Award for Volunteerism in the Arts, 1991. *Mem:* Indian Arts Am (adv bd); Minn Am Indian Ctr Gallery; Minn Sate Arts Board (adv panelist). *Res:* Survey of Am Indian art of the Upper Midwest from prehistory to present. *Specialty:* Classic and contemp Am Indian and southwestern art. *Interests:* Contemp Am Indian and Southwestern art, 19th and 20th century French art, int folk art. *Publ:* Understanding American Indian Art, Parts I & II, Art Business News, 7 & 8/87; Anatomy of an Art Dealers' Association, Art Business News, 9/87; Indian Artists Are on Warpath, Art Business News, 9/88. *Mailing Add:* 4317 Third Ave S Minneapolis MN 55409

BOLGE, GEORGE S
MUSEUM DIRECTOR
b Trenton, NJ, 42. *Study:* State Univ NJ, Rutgers, BA & BS; Inst Fine Arts, NY Univ, MA; 87. *Hon Degrees:* Nova Univ, Ft Lauderdale, Fla, Honorary Dr of Humane Letts. *Collection Arranged:* The Dr & Mrs Meyer B Marks Cobra Art Collection; The Maurice Lipschult Collection of Constructed Reliefs; The Jean & David Colker Collection of Pre-Columbian Art; Eng Victorian Doulton Lambeth Stoneware from the Bernard J & Florence F Starkoff Bequest; Isadore & Kelly Friedmen Collection. *Pos:* Grad res asst & asst cur, Ancient Art Dept, Brooklyn Mus Art, NY; Fel, Nat Trust Hist Preserv; exec dir, Mus Art, Ft Lauderdale, Fla, 70-88, emer exec dir, 88-; Fine Arts Consult, 89-91; curatorial consult, Broward Co, Fla, 91-; exec dir, NJ Ctr Vis Arts, Summit, NJ, 91-94, Boca Raton Mus Art, Fla, 95-. *Bibliog:* Graphic Work of Renoir, Catalogue Raisonne compiled by Dr. Joseph Stella, Lund Humphries, Bedford & London, Eng, 1975. *Mem:* Am Asn Mus; Fla Asn Mus; Fla Art Mus Dirs Asn; Appraisers Asn Am; Pub Art & Design Committee; Broward Cult Coun. *Mailing Add:* c/o Boca Raton Mus Art Mizner Park 501 Plaza Real Boca Raton FL 33432

BOLGER, DOREEN
MUSEUM DIRECTOR, CURATOR
b Far Rockaway, NY, Jan 10, 49. *Study:* Bucknell Univ, BA, 71; Univ Del, Newark, MA, 73; Grad Ctr, City Univ NY, PHD, 83. *Collection Arranged:* J Alden Weir: An American Impressionist (auth, catalog), Metrop Mus Art, 83; William M Harnett, Metrop Mus Art, 92-93; American Impressionism and Realism, The Painting of Modern Life: 1885-1915 (coauth, catalog), Metrop Mus Art, 94-95. *Pos:* Cur, Metrop Mus Art, 89 & Amon Carter Mus, Ft Worth, Tex, 89-94; dir, Mus Art, RI Sch Design, 94-98 & Baltimore Mus Art, 98-; Assoc cur Am paintings and sculpture, Metrop Mus Art, 82-88; rsch assoc, then asst cur dept Am paintings and sculpture, Metrop Mus Art, 76-82; field rep, Mus Early Southern Decorative Arts, Winston-Salem, NC, 73; ann fund worker, Gordon Sch, East Providence, 96-; trustee, Williamstown Art Conservation Lab, Mass, 96-; reviewer gen operating support, Inst of Mus and Libr Svcs, 96, 97; mem educ and fel com, The John Nicholas Brown Ctr for the Study of Am Civilization, Brown Univ, 95-. *Teaching:* Adj prof, Brown Univ, 97. *Awards:* Chester Dale Fel, Metrop Mus Art, 74-76; Ailsa Mellon Bruce Vis Sr Fel, Nat Gallery Art, 90; Nat Endowment for Humanities Travel to Collections Grant, 92; Metrop Mus of Art Travel Grants, 78, 84, 88; City Univ New York Grad Ctr Fel, 73-74; Unidel Fel, Univ of Del, 72-73. *Mem:* Asn Art Mus Dirs; Phi Beta Kappa; Md Hist Soc (vis com), 96-; Providence Art Club. *Res:* Late 19th century American art. *Publ:* Auth, American Paintings in the Metropolitan Museum of Art: Volume III (a catalog of works by artists born between 1846 and 1864), Princeton Univ Press & Metrop Mus Art, 80; co-ed, Thomas Eakins and the Swimming Picture, Amon Carter Mus, Ft Worth, Tex, 96; auth, J Alden Weir: An American Impressionist, Univ of Del Press, 83; co-auth (H Barbara Weinberg and David Park Curry), American Impressionism and Realism: The Painting of Modern Life, 1885-1915, Metro Mus of Art, 94; auth, articles in jours including Antiques Mag, Am Art Jour, The Magazine Antiques,. *Mailing Add:* Baltimore Mus Art 10 Art Museum Dr Baltimore MD 21218-3898

BOLLIGER, THERESE
EDUCATOR, SCULPTOR
b Walde, Switz, Apr 28, 44; Swiss & Can citizen. *Study:* Sch Visual Arts, Berne, Switz, 60-61; Sch Visual Arts, Basle, Switz, 65-69. *Work:* Govt Ont, Hart House-Univ Toronto, Toronto Dom Bank, Can; Univ Western Ont, London, Ont; Mohawk Col, Hamilton, Ont; Govt Ontario; Hart House, Univ Toronto; Oakville Galleries, Oakville, Ontario; Univ Lethbridge, Lethbridge, Alberta; St Michael's Col, Univ Toronto. *Exhib:* Transference, Mercer Union, Toronto, 86; Word Perfect, Art Gallery Hamilton, Ont, 90; Nickle Mus, Calgary, Alta, 91-92; (K)ein Vergleich (with catalog), Southern Alta Art Gallery, Can, 91-92; Edmonton Art Gallery, Alta, 92; Stutter, Cold City Gallery, Toronto, 93; solo exhib, Dressing Hair and Wounds (with catalog), Kamloops Art Gallery, BC & Burnaby Art Gallery, BC, 93-94, Correspondences, Cold City Gallery, Toronto, 96, Blutbild/Wortbild, Moersbergerstrasse, Basel, Switz, 97 & Volatile Body/Volatile Language, Cold City Gallery, Toronto, 98; Snappy Title, YYZ, Toronto, 97; Cold City Artists, Cold City Gallery, Toronto, Cutting Edge (with catalog), ARCO, Madrid, Spain, 97 & 98, Exquisite Corpse in Lotusland, Presentation House Gallery, Vancouver, 97; Coming to One's Senses, Longdale Gallery, Toronto, 97; Common Ground, Harbourfront Gallery, Toronto, 98; The Word in Contemp Canadian Art, Mus Contemp Canadian Art, Toronto; Ellirris, Koffler Gallery, Toronto, Hartnett Gallery, Univ Rochester, NY; Mask and Metamorphosis, Art Gallery Hamilton, Ontario; Contemp Canadian Drawing Series, Gallery Stratford, Ontario. *Pos:* Toronto Art Coun Interdisciplinary Jury, 96; Acquisition Comt, Oakville Galleries, Ont, 91-93; Sabbatical, Basel, Switz, 97-98. *Teaching:* Instr drawing, Ont Col Art, Toronto, 82-89 & Univ Guelph, 82-84; prof sculpture, Erindale Col, Univ Toronto, 83-. *Awards:* Can Coun B, 86, 88. *Bibliog:* Dianne Bos, Ian Gray & Jane Perdue (auths), Artists Gardens at Harbourfront Centre 1990-1995, Harbourfront Centre, 96; Kym Preusse (auth), Volatile Body/Bolatile Language, Cold City Gallery, Toronto, 10/8-31/98; Carolyn Bell Farrell (auth), ellipsis, The Koffler Gallery, 1/7-2/21/99. *Mem:* Sculpture Garden, Toronto (bd dir, 89-92). *Publ:* Auth, Cutting Edge, ARCO, Cold City Galelry, Madrid, Spain, 2/97. *Dealer:* Cold City Gallery 686 Richmond St W Toronto M61 3C3. *Mailing Add:* 404 Markham St Toronto ON M6G 2K9 Canada

BOLOMEY, ROGER HENRY
SCULPTOR
b Torrington, Conn, Oct 19, 18; US & Swiss citizen. *Study:* Acad Bella Arte, Florence, Italy, 47; Univ Lausanne, 47-48; Calif Col Arts & Crafts, Oakland, 48-50. *Work:* Mus Mod Art, Whitney Mus Am Art, NY; Univ Calif Mus Art, Berkeley; San Francisco Mus Mod Art, Calif; Stadtische Kunst, Mannheim, Ger. *Comn:* Aluminum sculpture, Southridge Mall, Milwaukee, Wis, 70; two reliefs, Mutual of NY, Syracuse, 71; two bronze sculptures, S Mall Proj, Albany, 71; stainless steel sculpture, NY State Off Bldg, Hauppauge, 73. *Exhib:* Carnegie Inst Int, Pittsburgh, 64; Whitney Mus Am Art Sculpture Ann, 64; Quatriene Exposition Suisse Sculpture, Bienne, Switz, 66; Contemp Am Paintings & Sculpture, Univ Ill, Urbana, 67; American Sculpture, Univ Nebr, Lincoln, 70. *Collection Arranged:* Forgotten Dimension: A Survey of Small Sculpture in California Now Traveling Exhib, 82-84. *Teaching:* Assoc prof art, Herbert H Lehman Col, 68-75; prof & chmn dept art, Calif State Univ, Fresno, 75-83. *Awards:* First Prize & Purchase Award, Bundy Art Mus Sculpture Int, Waitsfield, Vt, 63; Sculpture Prize, San Francisco Art Inst 84th Ann, 65; Res Found Award, City Univ NY, 70. *Mem:* San Francisco Art Inst; Am Fedn Arts; hon fel Acad Fine Arts, The Hague, Netherlands. *Media:* Steel, Aluminum. *Mailing Add:* 6968 Sweatwater Ct Boulder CO 80301

BOLT, RON
ENVIRONMENTAL ARTIST, PAINTER
b Toronto, Ont, Oct 13, 38. *Study:* Northern Tech Sch (Gold Medalist), 55; Ryerson Polytech Sch, 57; Ont Art Col, 58. *Comn:* Stamp design, Can Post, 79; Newmarket Courthouse (mural), Govt Ont, 80; tapestry designs, Indo-Asian Tapestries Ltd, Toronto, 82; waterworks, Sheraton Hotels Int, Halifax, NS, 85; Govt Can, Can House, Sydney, Australia, 92. *Exhib:* Over 65 Can solo exhibs, 65-; Int Union Tourist & Cult Asn, Istanbul, 79; Canadian Printmakers (traveling, US & Mex), Bronx Mus, NY, 82; Int Biennial Print Exhib, Taipei, Repub China, 85 & 87; 39th NAm Print Exhib, Boston, 87; 3rd Biennial Exhib Prints, Wakayama, Japan, 89; Mexico (traveling, 6 pub galleries), Ont, 95-97; Le Mur Vivant Fine Art, London, Eng, 98; Pollock House, Glasgow, 98; Tate West, St Ives, Cornwall, Eng, 2000; Art Inst Shen Zhen, China 2000; Contemp Art Mus, Guang Zho, China; Liu Hai Su Art Mus, Shanghai, China, 2000; Albemarle Gallery, West End London, Eng, 2006; Three Rivers (Yukon) Traveling Across Can, 2004-; Le Mur Vivant, Fine Art London, 98; Pollock House, Glasgow, 98; Tate West, St Ives, Cornwall, Eng, 2000; Art Mus Shen Zhen, China, 2000; Contemp Art Mus, Guang Zho, China, 2000; Liu Hai Su Art Mus, Shanghai, China, 2000; Three Rivers Yukon Traveling Across China, 2004-. *Collection Arranged:* Queens Univ, 75; McMichael Canadian Collection, 76; Art Gallery Windsor, 77; Art Gallery Algoma, 84. *Pos:* Assoc, Royal Conservatory Music, Toronto; mem, Toronto City Hall Arts Advisory Brd, 1970; co-found, Art Mag; Trustee, Nat Portrait Gallery, Royal Ontario Mus, 2001. *Teaching:* Instr art, Northern Tech Sch, 71-74, Learning Resources Ctr, Toronto, 72-73 & Hibbs Cove Art & Music Ctr, Nfld, 72-73; guest speaker, juror & lectr, 80-. *Awards:* Purchase Award, Univ Guelph, Ont, 79; 125 medal, Govt Can, 92; Second Prize, Kochi Int Triennial Exhib, Japan, 90; Yukon 3 Rivers Journey, 2003; Queen's Jubilee Medal, 2003. *Bibliog:* High North, Beaver Mag, 79; St Ives, Portrait of an Art Colony, Tate Gallery, Eng, 94; Ron Bolt on Mexico, Mag Art, 96. *Mem:* Visual Arts Ont (dir, 75-81); hon life mem, Soc Can Artists; prof mem, Arts & Letters Club, Toronto; elected Royal Can Acad Art (exec coun, 86-92). *Media:* Oil, Acrylic; Printmaking. *Publ:* Contribr, Art Mag, 68-70; auth, Acrylics, Govt Ont Dept Cult & Recreation, 76; The Inner Ocean, Merritt Publ, 80; The Beat and the Still, North Eds Ltd, 90. *Dealer:* Loch Gallery 16 Hazelton Ave Toronto Ont M5R 2E2; Masters Gallery Ltd 815C 17th Ave SW Calgary AB T2T 0A1. *Mailing Add:* RR 1 Baltimore ON K0K 1C0 Canada

BOLTANSKI, CHRISTIAN
PAINTER, PHOTOGRAPHER
b Paris, Sept 6, 44. *Exhib:* Museu d'Arte Contemporani, Barcelona, 97; Espace du Grand Hornu, Mons, 97; solo exhibs, Villa delle Rose, Galleria d'Art Mod, Barcelona, 97, Kemper Mus Contemp Art Design, Kansas City, 98 & Mus d'Art Mod de la Ville de Paris, France, 98; Mus Contemp Art, Helsinki, 98; Arken Mus Mod Kunst, Copenhagen, 98; and others. *Awards:* Int Ctr for Photography Award, 97. *Mailing Add:* 146 Blvd Camelinat Malakoff 92240 France

BOLTON, RICHARD
SCULPTOR, PHOTOGRAPHER
b Omaha, Nebr, Mar 7, 56. *Study:* Art Acad Cincinnati, cert, 79; Cranbrook Acad Art, MFA (photog), 81; St John's Col, Annapolis, Md, MA, 85. *Exhib:* One-man shows, Wayne State Univ, Gallery 680, Detroit, Mich, 82, Photogallery, Detroit Pub Libr, 83, Sch Art Inst Chicago, Photog Gallery, 84, Fullerton Mus Ctr, Calif, 90, Calif Mus Photog, Calif, 90, List Visual Arts Ctr, Cambridge, Mass, 91, Capp St Proj, San Francisco, Calif, 92, Cranbrook Acad Art Mus, Bloomfield Hills, Mich, 92, Bellevue Art Mus, Seattle, Wash, 92 & Cambridge Arts Coun, Mass, 92; The Charade of Mastery, Whitney Mus Am Art, Downtown at Fed Reserve Plaza, NY, 90; Eye Gallery, San Francisco, Calif, 94; Univ Art Gallery, Univ Calif, Santa Barbara, 94;

Subject: Male Violence, Atlanta Col Art, Ga, 94; Documentation, 1987-1994, Red Eye Gallery, RI Sch Design, 94; Souvenir: Chronique d'Abidjan, Corcoran Gallery Art, Washington, 95-96. *Pos:* Dir pubs, Educators for Social Responsibility, Cambridge, Mass, 87-89; gen ed, Media & Society Ser, Univ Minn Press, 87-92; bd dir, Ctr Ecology & Soc Justice, Washington, DC, 92-95; assoc ed, Visual Sociology, 92-96; ser adv, Manchester Univ Press, 92-96; contrib ed, New Art Examiner, 92-; bd dir, Nat Campaign for Freedom of Expression, 93-96. *Teaching:* Instr, Lawrence Inst Technol, Sch Archit, 80-83; instr, Wayne State Univ, Dept Art & Art Hist, 83; asst prof cinema & photog, Southern Ill Univ, 83-86; instr, Visible Lang Workshop, Mass Inst Technol, 86-88, Visual Arts Prog, 89-91 374 chairperson, Dept Art Studio, Univ Calif, Santa Barbara, 91-93, assoc prof, 91-; vis artist, photog dept, Sch Mus Fine Arts, Boston, Mass, 91-92, artist in residence, 97. *Awards:* Capp St Found, San Francisco, 92; Production Grant, Andy Warhol Found, New York, 93; Lila Wallace Int Artists Grant, Arts Int/Inst Int Educ, New York, 94. *Bibliog:* Patricia Johnston (auth), An interview with Richard Bolton, Views, fall 90 & winter 91; New Art Examiner, summer 91; Diane Douglas (auth), Interview with Richard Bolton, NCECA J 12, 91-92. *Publ:* Ed, Studies in Photographic Criticism, Southern Ill Univ, 86; The Contest of Meaning: Critical Histories of Photography, MIT Press, Cambridge, 89; Culture Wars: Documents from the Recent Controversies in the Arts, New Press, New York, 92; auth, Beauty redefined, New Art Examiner, 11/93; Denial isn't just a river in Egypt, High Performance, fall 94

BOLTON, ROBIN JEAN
PAINTER, GRAPHIC ARTIST
b Americus, Ga, Sept 13, 43. *Study:* Univ Ga, BFA(graphic design), 65. *Work:* Liverpool NY Pub Libr; Cobb Co Bd Educ, Marietta, Ga; Liverpool United Methodist Church, NY; Bridgeport United Methodist Church, NY; Dewit Community Church, NY; Federation Hall, Talluhah Falls Sch, Ga; Georgia Com on Women, Labor Dept. *Comn:* 12 paintings, IBM Collection, Binghamton, NY, 81-85; 3' x 6' paintings, Cannon Corp, Rochester, NY, 84; two 4' x 5' paintings, CitiBank, Nat Landmark Bldg, Albany, NY, 84-85; Mobil Oil Corp, Rochester, NY, 84-85; 4' x 5' painting, comn by Lee Iacocca, New York, 87-88; painting, Ga Dept of Ed, 2001; designed label, Persimmon Creek Vineyard, Clayton, Ga; two 48″ x 60″ paintings, bd rm & CEO office, Farash Corp, Rochester, NY. *Exhib:* 100 Yrs-100 Works, Kirpatrick Art Ctr, Oklahoma City, Conguien Mus Art, Longview, Tex, Chatanooga Regional Hist Mus, Tenn, Fine Arts Mus South, Mobile, Ala, Islip Art Mus, NY, 89. *Pos:* Printer. *Teaching:* Com Art Supply, Syracuse, NY. *Awards:* First Prize, Cooperstown Nat Juried, Cooperstown NY Art Asn, 76; First Prize, Arena Nat, Binghamton, NY, 76; Henry Mallory Mem Award, Cooperstown Art Asn, 78. *Bibliog:* TV documentary, WCNY Public Television, Liverpool, New York, Syracuse, 1987; Gail Mountain (auth), Gloucester Daily Times, 92; Sharon Carson (auth), Boston Sunday Globe; Bev Leesman (auth), Syracuse New Times, 94. *Mem:* Nat Asn Women Artists, NY; Liverpool Arts & Crafts Guild, NY (lifetime hon mem). *Media:* Acrylic; Canvas. *Specialty:* fine arts and crafts. *Interests:* Reading, Cooking. *Dealer:* Nan Miller Gallery 3450 Winton Pl Rochester NY 14623

BOLTON-SMITH, ROBIN LEE
CURATOR, HISTORIAN
b Washington, DC, Oct 30, 41. *Study:* Smith Col, Northampton, Mass, BA, 63; Inst Fine Arts, NY Univ, MA, 75. *Collection Arranged:* Lilly Martin Spencer: The Joys of Sentiment (co-auth, catalog), Smithsonian Inst, 73; Portrait Miniatures in Private Collections, Smithsonian Inst, 76; Miniature Collection (auth, catalog), Cincinnati Mus, 85; Tokens of Affection: The Miniature in America, Met Mus, 90 & 91, Nat Mus Am Art, Smithsonian Inst, 91 & Art Inst Chicago, 91. *Pos:* Cur res asst, Nat Collection Fine Arts, Smithsonian Inst, 63-67, asst cur, 71-76, assoc cur, formerly; cur res asst, Metrop Mus Art, New York, 67-69; consult, 93-. *Res:* History of the American portrait miniature. *Publ:* Auth, Portrait Miniatures in Private Collections, Smithsonian Inst, 76; Five miniature collections, Col Art J, summer 79; Fraser's place in the evolution of miniature portrait, In: Charles Fraser of Charleston (exhib catalog), Gibbes Art Gallery, Charleston, SC, 83; Intro to Anson Dickinson, The Celebrated Miniature Painter 1779-1852 (exhib catalog), Conn Hist Soc, 83; The Miniature in America, Vol CXXXVIII, No 5, Antiques Mag, 11/90. *Mailing Add:* 3007 Que St NW Washington DC 20007-3081

BONANSINGA, KATE
CRITIC, CURATOR
b Lafayette, Ind, Aug 2, 62. *Study:* Univ Mich, Ann Arbor, BA, 83; Ind Univ E Asian Language Inst, 90; Univ Ill, Urbana-Champaign, MA, 91. *Collection Arranged:* Arts and Crafts Furnishings from Portland Collections, 95. *Pos:* Cur & dir, Hoffman Gallery, Ore Sch Arts & Crafts, 91-95; co-owner, BonaKeane Gallery, 95-98; visual arts critic, Willamette Week. *Teaching:* Asst prof art hist, Ore Col Art & Craft, 91-; instr fine arts, Univ Portland, 93-94, Nike Corp, 95-. *Mem:* Col Art Asn; Am Craft Asn; Soc Nam Goldsmiths. *Res:* Crafts; interiors; Contemporary ceramics. *Publ:* Auth of numerous reviews in Artweek, Reflex, Am Craft, Am Ceramics & Ceramics Monthly. *Mailing Add:* c/o Oregon Sch Arts & Crafts Hoffman Gallery 8245 SW Barnes Rd Portland OR 97225

BONAR, ALBERT J See Jalapeeno, Jimmy (Albert) J Bonar

BONILLA-MARTINEZ, NATASHA
DIRECTOR
b New York, NY, 57. *Study:* Vassar Col, BA, 81; San Diego State Univ, MA, 01. *Collection Arranged:* Co-curator, Spirit Capture: Native Americans and the Photog Image, Nat Mus of Am Indians, Smithsonian Inst, 01-02. *Pos:* Proprietor, cons, Cultura Works, San Marcos, Calif, 92-2000; dir visual arts and edu, Calif Ctr for the Arts, 2000-. *Teaching:* Instr, Univ San Diego, 99-2000. *Awards:* Gateways Rockefeller Fel, Guadalupe Cult Ctr, 1997-98. *Mem:* Am Asn Mus; Col Art Asn; Calif Mus Asn. *Publ:* Spirit Capture, Smitsonian Inst Press, 98. *Mailing Add:* Calif Center for Arts 340 N Escondido Blvd Escondido CA 92025

BONINO, FERNANDA
ART DEALER
b Torino, Italy, Jan 5, 27. *Pos:* Pres & dir, Galeria Bonino, Ltd, New York, 63-86, Buenos Aires, 74-81. *Mem:* Art Dealer Asn Am. *Specialty:* Contemporary paintings and sculptures; American; European; South American. *Mailing Add:* 48 Great Jones St New York NY 10012

BONNER, JONATHAN G
SCULPTOR
b Princeton, NJ, 47. *Study:* Philadelphia Col Art, BFA, 71; RI Sch Design, MFA, 73. *Work:* Am Craft Mus, NY; Ariz State Univ Art Mus, Tempe; Marshall Fields, Chicago; RI Sch Design Mus Art; Mus Fine Arts, Boston, Mass; and many pvt collections. *Comn:* Triple Inversion, Fidelity Investments, London, 95; At Rest, Harcourt Gen Corp Headquarters, Chestnut Hill, Mass, 95; Facing AS220 Bldg, Providence, RI, 99; Twin, Fidelity Mgmt, Smithfield, RI, 99; Metamorphosis, RI Col, Providence, 2000; Nashu Street Park, Boston, 99; many others. *Exhib:* Solo exhibs, Virginia Lynch Gallery, Tiverton, RI, 91, Hokin Kaufman Gallery, Chicago, Ill, 91, Peter Joseph Gallery, NY, 92 & 93, Newport Art Mus, RI, 93, Kavesh Gallery, Ketchum, Idaho, 94, Gallery Camino Real, Boca Raton, Fla, 94 & Peter Joseph Gallery, NY, 95, MA Ginsberg Gallery, Iowa City, 95 & 99, Wheeler Gallery, Providence, 98, many others; Masterworks, 91 & Masterworks Two (coauth, catalog), Peter Joseph Gallery, NY, 94; Am Works in Metal, Pritam & Eames, EHampton, NY, 90-92; Formed by Fire, Carnegie Mus Art, Pittsburgh, Pa, 93; Inaugural Exhib, Donald Becker Gallery, Miami Beach, Fla, 94, Joseph Gallery, NY, 91, 94 & 96. *Awards:* Nat Endowment Arts, 76 & 88; RI State Coun Arts Fel, 87 & 90; LEF Found Project Grant, 98; City of Providence Art Project Grant, 98. *Bibliog:* Bill Van Siclin (auth), Providence J, 5/28/93; Casa Vogue, 2/94; Jamie Epstein (auth), Metalsmith Mag, winter 94; Karen Chambers (auth), Metalsmith Mag, winter 96. *Mailing Add:* PO Box 6023 Providence RI 02940

BOODMAN, H CITRON
PAINTER, PRINTMAKER
b Pittsburgh, Pa, July 17, 27. *Study:* Carnegie-Mellon Univ, BFA, 48; DeCordova Mus, Lincoln, Mass with Donald Stoltenberg. *Work:* Free Libr Philadelphia, Pa; Univ Wyo; DeCordova Mus, Lincoln, Mass; Atlantic Richfield Oil Company, NY; IBM Corporate Collection; and others. *Comn:* 50 prints, Cambridge Art Asn, Mass, 68. *Exhib:* Minot Print & Drawing Nat Exhib, NDak, 74; Okla Nat Print Exhib, 74 & 76; 8th & 10th Nat Print Exhib, Silvermine Guild Artists, Conn, 74 & 76; DeCordova Mus, Lincoln, Mass, 75, 78, 79 & 80; one-person show, Cummings Art Ctr, Conn Col, New London, 76, Piper Gallery, Lexington, Mass,80, 82, 85 & 89; Mus Fine Arts, Boston, Mass, 76, In Celebration of Prints, Philadelphia Print Club Invitational, Pa, 80; Bird in the Hand Gallery, Sewickley, Pa, 84. *Pos:* Designer, Architectural Design Dept, Pittsburgh Plate Glass, Pa, 48-50; illustrative draftsman, State Dept, Washington, DC, 50-53. *Teaching:* Instr printmaking, pvt classes. *Awards:* First Prize, Corcoran Gallery, Washington, DC, 50; Purchase Prize, Strathmore Paper Company Award, Springfield, Mass, 76; Purchase Prize, 6th Ann Art Festival, NH, 76. *Bibliog:* C R Wasserman (auth), Ms Boodman Traces Stages of Printmakers' Art, Boston Globe, 72; Peter P Donker (auth), Helen Citron Boodman, collographs filled with imaginary architectural images, luscious in their subdued colorations, Worcester Telegram, 2/17/82. *Mem:* Cambridge Art Asn; Boston Visual Artists' Union; Women Exhibiting Boston; Boston Printmakers (pres, 82-83, treas, 83-85). *Media:* Crayon, Pastels; Ink. *Dealer:* The Garret Galleries 340 Huron Ave Cambridge MA 02138

BOOKATZ, SAMUEL
PAINTER, SCULPTOR
b Philadelphia, Pa, Oct 3, 10. *Study:* Cleveland Inst Art; Boston Mus Sch Art; Harvard Univ; Acad Grande Chaumiere & Colarossi, Paris; Am Acad Rome; also with Oskar Kokoschka Chaim Soutine & Ivan Mestrovic. *Work:* Corcoran Gallery Art, Phillips Gallery & Smithsonian Inst, Washington; Cleveland Mus Art, Ohio; Norfolk Mus Art & Sci, Va. *Comn:* Portraits of Pres & Mrs FD Roosevelt, 41; murals, comn by US Govt, US Naval Hosp, Norfolk, Va & San Diego, Calif, 42-45; murals, Govt Turn Key Housing for Aged, Prince George's Co, Md & Della Ratta Off Bldg, Bethesda, Md, 71; portrait, Gov David L Lawrence, Pa, 65; portrait of Joseph H Hirshhorn, Hirshhorn Mus & Sculpture Garden, Washington, DC, 78. *Exhib:* One-man shows, Cleveland Mus Art, 40 & Corcoran Gallery Art, 46, Corcoran Gallery Art, Washington, DC, 2/14/99 & 2/14/00, Hirshhorn Mus, Washington, DC; Pa Acad Fine Arts, Philadelphia, 52; Va Mus Art, Richmond, 55; Baltimore Mus Art, Md, 60. *Pos:* Govt artist & White House artist, 41-43. *Teaching:* Dir art, Samuel Bookatz Sch Art, Washington, 45-. *Awards:* William Page Award & Prix de Rome Award in the Arts, Boston Mus, 37; Inst Allende Fel, 54; Ford Found Grant, 62. *Bibliog:* Ruth Dancyger (auth), Samuel Bookatz-Cleveland Artist in the Nations Capitol, John Carroll Univ, 93. *Mem:* Disabled Am Vets Asn; Retired Officers Asn. *Media:* All Media. *Specialty:* Modern art. *Dealer:* Gene Rotberg Washington DC; Dick Kleinman Art Gallary 2210 Mayfield Rd Cleveland OH 44106. *Mailing Add:* 2700 Que St NW Washington DC 20007

BOOKER, CHAKAIA
SCULPTOR, PAINTER
b Newark, NJ. *Study:* Rutgers Univ, E Brunswick, NJ, BA, 76; City Col New York, MFA, 93; studied clay crafts with Deena Kolbert, New York, 79-81 & clay biz with Kent Kraus, 81-82. *Work:* Studio Mus Harlem, NY; Queens Mus Art, Flushing, NY; US Embassy, Dakar, Senegal; also pvt collections of Vera G List & Richard Bellamy; Snite Mus Art; Neuberger Mus Art. *Comn:* 3D tire sculpture, Neuberger Mus Art, Purchase, NY, 97; sculpture relief, Nat Aeronautics & Space Admin, dedicated Nat Mus Women, Washington, DC, 98; outdoor sculpture, Pub Art Fund, Metro Tech Ctr, Brooklyn, NY, 98; outdoor sculpture, Neuberger Mus Art, 98. *Exhib:* Solo exhibs,

Jamaica Arts Ctr, NY, 94, Queens Mus Art Bulova Corp Ctr, NY, 96; Int '94, Socrates Sculpture Park (exhib catalog), Long Island City, NY, 94-95; Outdoor Sculpture Party '95 DeCordova Mus & Sculpture Park, Lincoln, Mass, 95; The Listening Sky: An Inaugural Exhib of the Studio Mus in Harlem Sculpture Garden (with catalog), Studio Mus Harlem, NY, 95; Heat Up, Fukuyama Mus, Hiroshima, Japan, 96; 20th Century Am Sculpture at the White House, Washington, 96; Revalations, Neuberger Mus Art, Purchase, NY, 97; Postcards from Black Am: Contemp African Am Art, DeBeyerd Centre for Contemp Art, Breda, The Neth, 98, Frans Hals Mus, The Neth, 98; RUBBER, Robert Miller Gallery, NY, 98. *Pos:* Artist-in-residence, Studio Mus Harlem, 95-96; Designed/Produced Pottery for plays, Extenuating Circumstances, Division Street & Mass Appeal, 81. *Awards:* Connor Award, 90-92; Joan Mitchell Found Grant, 95. *Bibliog:* Michael Kimmelman (auth), Turning an alley into a showcase for sculpture, NY Times, 9/22/95; Holland Cotter (auth), Art in review, NY Times, 7/26/96; Sarah Schmerler (auth), Standing on ceremony, Time Out, Vol 49, 96. *Media:* Tires, Bones; Installationist, Mixed Media. *Publ:* A Guide of Sculpture Parks & Gardens, Publishing Ltd, 96. *Dealer:* Max Protetch Gallery 511 W 22nd New York NY 10011-1109; Anthony Archibald J 602 Tenth Ave New York NY 10036. *Mailing Add:* 608 E Ninth St No 2 New York NY 10009

BOONE, MARY
ART DEALER
b Pa, Oct 29, 51. *Collection Arranged:* New Work/New York, Los Angeles, Calif, 77; Painting 75/76/77, Sarah Lawrence Col, Bronxville, NY, 77; Painting, Hal Bromm Gallery, New York, 77. *Pos:* Asst dir, Bykert Gallery, formerly; owner, Mary Boone Gallery, 78-. *Specialty:* Contemp art. *Mailing Add:* 745 5th Ave New York NY 10151-0099

BOOTH, DOT
PAINTER, PRINTMAKER
b Chicago, Ill. *Study:* Univ Ala, Birmingham, 63-64; Univ South Fla, Tampa, 68-70. *Work:* Miss Mus Art, Jackson; Macon Mus Arts & Sci, Ga; City Miami, Fla; Columbus Mus, Ga; Pensacola Art Ctr, Fla. *Comn:* Orlando Exec Airport, Fla. *Exhib:* 40th & 43rd Ann Contemp Am Paintings, Soc Four Arts, Palm Beach, Fla, 69, 78, 81 & 87; Best of Fla, Pensacola Art Ctr, 70; Invitational, Mus Arts & Sci, Daytona Beach, Fla, 72; Selections from Permanent Collection, Miss Mus Art, Jackson, 78; Artists in Ga, High Mus Art, Atlanta, 78-79; Loch Haven Art Ctr Show, Orlando, Fla, 83. *Pos:* Scenic artist, EPCOT, 82. *Teaching:* Vis instr, Ringling Sch Art, 89. *Awards:* Philip Hulitar Award, 49th Ann Soc Four Arts, Palm Beach, Fla, 87; Purchase Award, Frontal Images, Jackson, Miss, 70; Best of Show, Gasparilla, Tampa, Fla, 78. *Bibliog:* Dot Booth--Hard Edge Realism, Orange Co Public TV, Fla, 73. *Media:* Oil, Acrylic; Serigraphy. *Mailing Add:* Booth Davis Studios 1939 Taylor Ave Winter Park FL 32792-3130

BOOTH, LAURENCE OGDEN
SCULPTOR, ARCHITECT
b Chicago, Ill, July 5, 36. *Study:* Stanford Univ, BA, 58; Mass Inst Technol, BArch, 60. *Work:* Art Inst Chicago. *Exhib:* Richard Gray Gallery, 76; Chicago 7 Architects, Walter Kelly Gallery & Richard Gray Gallery, 77; Frumkin Struve Gallery, Chicago, 80-81; New Chicago Architecture, Verone, Italy, 81; Harvard Grad Sch Design, 81; and many other group & one-man shows. *Pos:* Vis critic, Harvard Univ, 81-82; bd dir, Mus Contemp Art, Chicago. *Teaching:* Instr archit, Univ Ill, Chicago Circle, 69-71; vis prof, Univ Ill, 82. *Bibliog:* Amy Goldin (auth), Vitality vs greasy kid stuff, Art Gallery Mag, 72; article, Chicago Archit J, 81; article, New Chicago Archit, 81; and others. *Media:* Multimedia. *Publ:* Auth, Spiritual content of order, Arc Mag, 68; auth, Review of Stanley Tigerman sculpture, Art Scene Mag, 69. *Mailing Add:* 280 Arden Shore Dr Lake Bluff IL 60044-1331

BOOTH, MICHAEL GAYLE
PAINTER, SCULPTOR
b Soda Springs, Idaho, June 13, 51. *Study:* Boise State Univ, 74; Utah State Univ, BA, 78, MFA, 79. *Work:* Blue Mountain Community Col Grounds, Pendleton, Ore; State Capital Bldg Governors Chambers, Boise, Idaho; Large Monumental Sculpture, Freeway Junction, Pendleton, Ore; Quarterhorse Hall of Fame, Amarillo, Tex; Large Monumental Sculpture, CofC Visitors Ctr, Pendleton, Ore. *Comn:* Painting of Historic Boise, J R Simplot, Idaho, 88; Monumental Mural, Gold Beach Athletic Asn, Ore, 88; Series of Large Paintings, Park Ctr Sports Club, Boise, 89; Monumental Sculpture, Pendleton City, Ore, 93; Series/Collection of Sports Cars, US Sen Gordon Smith, Pendleton, Ore, 95; Hermiston Pub Libr, Ore, 98; Hermiston Ore Convention Ctr, 98; mural. *Exhib:* Ore Watercolor Soc, Ore Capital Bldg, Salem, 85; Watercolor USA, Mo, 86; Audubon Artists of Am, NY, 87; Nat Soc of Painters in Casein & Acrylic, NY, 88; The Cayuse Indians, Ore Trail Interpretive Ctr, Ore, 92. *Collection Arranged:* Regional Sculpture Masks, Alliance Varied Arts, 75; Nat Works on Paper, Coop Show with Utah State Univ, 76; Painting 78, Alliance Varied Arts, 78; Happy Canyon Western Art Invitational, 90-96. *Pos:* Dir, Alliance Varied Arts, 77-79; own, Artist Gallery & Frames, 83-88. *Teaching:* Art prof basic design & drawing, Utah State Univ, 79-80, drawing, design, appreciation, painting & sculpture, Blue Mountain Col, 88-, Eastern Ore Univ, 98-. *Awards:* First Place, Watercolor Div, Rock Springs Nat Art Exhib, 79; First Place, Artists Showcase, Utah State Univ, 80; Best of Show, Watercolor Soc Ore, 81. *Bibliog:* Mindy Carrel (auth), Gallery, Western Horseman, 5/92; Vicki Stavig (auth), One on one, Art of the West, 11-12/93; Diane Nodurft (auth), Balancing act equine images, 2-3/96. *Mem:* Audubon Artists Am; Watercolor Soc Ore; Nat Watercolor Soc; Nat Soc Painters in Casein & Acrylic. *Media:* Acrylic, Oil; Bronze, Concrete. *Publ:* Auth, Creating Dynamic Contrast Through the Properties of Color, Artwise Publs, 79; A Sketch of Pendleton, Artwise Publs, 93; Cayuse Indians, The Art of Michael Booth, Artwise Publs, 94; Watercolor Strategy, Artwise Publs, 95; The Paintings of Michael G Booth, The Reservation, Artwise Publs, 96. *Mailing Add:* 1335 Tutuilla Rd Pendleton OR 97801

BOOTH, ROBERT ALAN
SCULPTOR
b Mt Kisco, NY, 1952. *Study:* Art Inst Boston, 71-73; Mass Col Art, BFA, 76; Syracuse Univ, MFA, 78. *Work:* Equitable Life Assurance Soc, Syracuse Univ; Burchfield-Penney Art Ctr, Wright State Univ. *Comn:* Site sculpture, comn by Ted Stetler, Syracuse, NY, 77; sculpture, TRW Bearings Corp, Jamestown, NY, 81; site sculpture, Artpark, Lewiston, NY, 83; pub fountain restoration, Fredonia, NY, 91; Wright State Univ, 99. *Exhib:* 43 Western NY Exhibs, Albright-Knox Art Gallery, Buffalo, NY, 90; X Sightings, Anderson Gallery, Buffalo, NY; Working With Tradition: The Academic Artists, Birchfield Art Ctr, Buffalo, NY & NY State Mus, Albany, 93; 45 Western NY Exhib, Albright-Knox Art Gallery, Buffalo, NY 94; one-man show, Burchfield Penny Art Ctr, Buffalo, 95; New Work, Henri Gallery, Washington, 96; Chauataugua Ctr Visual Arts, NY, 97; Mass Col Art, Boston, 98; Wright State Univ, 99; Rosewood Art Gallery, 2003; Gallery 15, Rochester, NY, 2003; Buffalo Art Studio, NY, 2003; and others. *Pos:* Pres, Council Art Dept Chairs, State Univ NY, 93-96; Bd Mem, Mid-Am Col Art Asn, 97-2003. *Teaching:* Prof sculpture, State Univ NY Col, Fredonia, 78-2005, chmn, dept art, 88-96, distinguished tchg prof, 2005-. *Awards:* State Univ NY Fac Res Fel, 82 & 83; Scholarly Incentive Award, State Univ NY Col, 94; Artist Fel Grant, Chautauqua Funds for the Arts, NY, 95. *Mem:* Int Sculpture Ctr; Nat Sculpture Soc. *Media:* Mixed. *Mailing Add:* 3197 Rte 83 Fredonia NY 14063

BOOTH CABOT, M(ARY ANN)
PAINTER, PRINTMAKER
b Winston-Salem, NC, Sept 28, 42. *Study:* Univ Tenn, 66-67; Ga State Univ, 68-70. *Work:* Arthur Anderson & Co, Coca-Cola Inc, Kilpatrick & Cody Attorneys, Delta Airlines, Atlanta, Ga; Simon & Schuster Doubleday Publ, NY; Shamrock Hilton, Houston, Tex; Johnson & Johnson Inc, Mass; and others. *Comn:* Four art deco murals, Noelles Restaurant, Atlanta, Ga,; Delta Air Lines Crown Room, Hartsfield Int Airport, Atlanta, Ga; Park Seed Co, Greenwood, SC; Atlanta Flower Show. *Exhib:* Southern Watercolor Soc 4th Exhib (with catalog), Columbia Mus Arts & Sci, SC, 80; Southern Watercolor Soc 5th Exhib (with catalog), La Polytechnic Inst, Ruston, 81; 5th Int Exhib Botanical Art & Illus (with catalog), 83; Arnold Arboretum, Harvard Univ, Boston, Mass, 84; Southern Watercolor Soc 9th Exhib (with catalog), Miss Mus Art, Jackson, 85; Marie Selby Botanical Gardens, Sarasota, Fla, 85 & 94; State Botanical Garden, Athens, Ga, 88; Nat Flower Shows (Spring Exhibs), Philadelphia, Boston, Atlanta, Ann Arbor, Washington, DC, Syracuse, Mobile, Ala, & St Louis, Mo, 91-; and others. *Bibliog:* Inside Cobb Mag, spring 84; American Artists: an illustrated survey of leading contemporary Americans, Les Krantz (auth), 85; article, Southern Homes Mag, 84, 86 & 88; Female Artists in the United States 1900-1985: a Research and Resource Guide, Rutgers Univ Press, 86; Artists of Georgia, Vol I, 89 & Artists of the South II, 92, Mountain Productions Inc, Albuquerque; and others. *Mem:* Southern Watercolor Soc; Ga Watercolor Soc; Ky Watercolor Soc. *Media:* Watercolor. *Mailing Add:* c/o Lightwave Arts 3961 Loch Highland Pass Roswell GA 30075

BOOTHE, POWER
PAINTER, ADMINISTRATOR
b Mar 12, 45; US citizen. *Study:* Colo Col, BA, 67; Whitney Mus, Independent Study Prog, 67-68; Colo Col, Hon DA, 89. *Work:* Guggenheim Mus; Whitney Mus Am Art; NY Bank for Savings; Lehman Brothers; NJ State Mus; Stanford Univ Art Mus; and others. *Exhib:* Theodoron Award Show, 71, Art of this Decade, 74 & Recent Acquisitions, 75, Guggenheim Mus, NY; one-person exhibs, Power Booth, Paintings, 71-88, A M Sachs Gallery, 73, 74, 76, 77, 81, 82 & 85, Pvt Images, Los Angeles Co Mus Art, Calif, 77, Painting Show, PS1 Gallery, Brooklyn, NY, 77, Art & Dance, Inst Contemp Art, Boston, 82 & Hurlbutt Gallery, Greenwich, Conn, 88, Souyun Yi Gallery, 87 & 89, Harrison Gallery, 90, Time-Life Bldg, NY 90, Trenkmann Gallery, 91 & Robert Morrison Gallery, 92; Book-Objects by Contemp Artists, Albright-Knox Art Gallery, Buffalo, NY, 77; Between the Sexes, Md Art Place, NY, 94; The Persistence of Abstraction, Noyes Mus, Ocean Park, NJ, 94; Scratching the Surface, Stephen Haller Gallery, 94; New Paintings, Power Boothe, 95; Pioneers of Abstraction, Sidney Mishkin Gallery, 96. *Pos:* Co-dir, Mt Royal Grad Sch, Md Inst, Col Art, 95-98; ed, Am Abstract Artist J, 96-98; dir, Sch Art, Ohio Univ, 98-. *Teaching:* Instr painting, Sch Visual Arts, NY, 79-88; Princeton Univ, 89-95; Mt Royal Grad Sch, Md Inst, Col Art, 93-98; Sch Art, Ohio Univ, 1998-2001; dean, Hartford Art Sch, Univ Hartford, 2001-. *Awards:* Int Arts Grant, Nat Endowment Arts, 86 & 88; Guggenheim Fel Grant, 89; NY State Grant, 87 & 89; Pollock Krasner Found Grant, 89; NY State Arts Grant, 91; and many others. *Bibliog:* Gerard Haggerty (auth), Boothe at Haller, Art News, 94; Roberta Smith (auth), Power Boothe, NY Times, 95; Robert Edelman (auth), Power Boothe at Stephen Haller Gallery, 96. *Mem:* Am Abstract Artists. *Media:* Oil, Acrylic; Film, Performance. *Publ:* When the Fourth Soldier Falls, A Study of Pielo Della Francesca's Resurrection, issue, Reflex Horizons, 86; Abstraction and Meaning, Am Abstract Artists J, 98. *Mailing Add:* Hartford Art Sch Univ Hartford 200 Bloomfield Ave Hartford CT 06117-1599

BOOTZ, ANTOINE H
PHOTOGRAPHER
b Paris, France, Feb 27, 56. *Study:* Sciences-Politiques, Paris, 74-75; Sorbonne, Paris, 76-77; Univ St Charles, Marseille, France, 77-78. *Work:* Fonds Nat d'Art Contemporain, Paris; Galerie Baudoin Lebon, Paris. *Exhib:* Des Photographies dans le Paysage, Galerie de France, Paris, 81; Une Autre Photographie, Mus Andre Malraux, Creteil, France, 82; Saus Titre, Galerie Baudoin Lebon, Paris, 83-85; Saus Titre, Contemp Photog & Video from France, traveling US, 85-87. *Pos:* Freelance photogr for mags, 89-. *Awards:* Fel, Nat Endowment Arts, 86-87. *Mailing Add:* 123 W 20th St 2B New York NY 10011

BOPP, EMERY
PAINTER, EDUCATOR
b Corry, Pa, May 13, 24. *Study:* Pratt Inst Art Sch, NY; Yale Sch Painting & Design, with Josef Albers & William de Kooning, BFA; NY Univ; Rochester Inst Technol, MFA; Yale (graphic design prog), pioneer student under Alvin Eisenman, head & Alvin Lustig, 51. *Work:* Addison Gallery Am Art, Andover, Mass; Greenville Co Mus Art, SC; SC Arts Comn Collection; Hunter Gallery, Chattanooga, Tenn. *Exhib:* Bob Jones Univ, 62-64; Butler Inst Am Art Exhib, 66; Birmingham Mus Art, 66; Southeastern Exhib, Atlanta, Ga, 67; Greenville Co Mus Art, 68; plus others. *Pos:* Co-founder & chmn bd, Hampton III Gallery, Taylors, SC, 70-. *Teaching:* Chmn div art, Bob Jones Univ, 55-94, emer prof & chair, 94-. *Awards:* Purchase Award, Hunter Gallery Art, Chattanooga, Tenn, 65; Merit Award, Southeastern Exhib, Atlanta, 67; Purchase Award, Greenville Co Mus Art, 68. *Mem:* Southeastern Col Art Conf; Guild SC Artists; Col Art Asn Am; Cooperstown Art Asn, NY. *Mailing Add:* Div Art Bob Jones Univ Greenville SC 29614

BORA (BORAYER), VADIM MAKHARBEKOVICH
SCULPTOR, PAINTER
b Beslan, No Ossetia-Alania, Russia, Apr 9, 54. *Study:* Vladikavkaz Pedagogical Tech Col, Design & Drawing degree, 1969-73; Leningrad State Pedagogical Inst, Auditing, 1973-74; Leningrad Accad of Art, Auditing, 1973-74. *Work:* Spartanburg Co Mus of Art, Spartanburg, SC; Ministry of Culture Collection, Moscow, Russia; No Ossetia Mus of Art, Vladikavkaz, Russia; Anderson Arts Ctr, SC. *Comn:* Meditation - Terra Cotta, Bishop Chapel Retirement Ctr, St Louis, MO, 1996; Cat Walk, City of Asheville, NC, 1999; Animal Alley, Bronze, Buckhead Condominiums, Atlanta, Ga, 2000; Crucifix, synth Marble, St Mary's Episcopal Parish, Asheville, NC, 2000; The Wings of Freedom, Va Medical Ctr of WNC, NC, 2001; sculpture, On the Mend, Mission Hospitals, Asheville, NC, 2006. *Exhib:* Solo Exhibs incl: New & Different, The Artists Gallery, Wilmington, NC, 2004, Am Retrospective, Spartanburg Mus of Art, SC, 2005, In the Russian Tradition, Anderson Arts Ctr, 2006; group exhibs incl: The Artists, The Asheville Arts Coun, Asheville, NC, 2000, Sculpture Invitational, The Burke Country Arts Coun, Morganton, NC, 2001, 16 Patton, Asheville, NC, 2002, Int Florence, Biennale of Contemp Art, Florence, Italy, 2005; Ctr for Craft, Creativity & Design, Hendersonville, NC, 2006. *Teaching:* Art instr, Vladikavkaz Lycee of Art, Russia, 1988-90; instr, Singleton Arts Ctr, Flat Rock, NC, 1994-95; Principal, instr, Vadim Bora Studio-Gallery, Asheville, NC, 1998, Battery Park Sculpture Club, Asherville, NC, 2003, Spartanburg Mus Art, SC, 2004-05. *Mem:* Nat Sculpture Soc; Portrait Soc of Am; Mountain Sculptors; Tri-State Sculptors; Prof Artists Union of Russia. *Media:* Bronze, Terra Cotta, Oil, Canvas. *Specialty:* Portraiture, figurative, landscape, narrative. *Publ:* Arnold Wengrow, Artist Faces up to his works, Asheville Citizens, Times Gannet, 2004; Staff Publisher, Never at Rest, The Laurel of Asheville, Laurel Publ, 2004; Constance E Richards, Artists Retreat - Nuances of the Land, Pinnacle Living, Leisure Publ, 2005; Linda Conley, Vadim Bora, Spartanburg Herald Journal, 2005. *Mailing Add:* 30 1/2 Battery Park Ave Asheville NC 28801

BORAX, EDITH See Morrison, Edith Borax

BORCOMAN, JAMES
CURATOR
b Ontario, Can, Jan 17, 26. *Study:* Univ NB, BA; Univ BC, Vancouver; State Univ NY, Buffalo, MFA; hist photog with Beaumont Newhall & Nathan Lyons; LLD, Concordia Univ, Montreal, 96; Dr Fine Arts, Carleton Univ, Ottawa, 96. *Hon Degrees:* LLD, Concordia Univ, Montreal, 96; Dr Fine Arts, Carleton Univ, Ottawa, 96. *Work:* Nat Gallery Can, Ottawa. *Exhib:* Visual Arts Ottawa, 76. *Collection Arranged:* Goodridge Roberts Retrospective, 69, Four 19th Century Canadian Photographers, 70 & Photographs from the Collection, 75, Nat Gallery Can; The Photograph as Object Traveling Exhib (with catalog), 69; Nathan Lyons: Notations in Passing Traveling Exhib (with catalog), 72; Charles Negre (with catalog), Ottawa, 76; Brit Photographs from the Collection, 1844-1914, 76; Recent Acquisitions, 77; The Painter as Photogr: DO Hill, Charles Negre, Auguste Salzmann (with monograph), 78; The Magical Eye: Definitions of Photography, 80; Eugene Atget and his Precursors (with catalog), Ottawa, 82; Intimate Images (with catalog), Ottawa, 88; Karsh: The Art of the Portrait (with catalog), 89; The Cherished Image: The portrait in Photography, 89; Roger Mertin: O Tannenbaum, 91; Atget, Evans, Friedlander, 91; Magicians of Light (with catalog), 93; John Coplans, 94. *Pos:* Educ officer, Nat Gallery Can, 60-66, dir educ dept, 66-69, sr cur photographs, 67-94 & cur emer, 94. *Teaching:* Part time lectr hist photog & photog workshop, Univ Ottawa, Ont, 71-75; hon adj prof, Ariz State Univ, Tempe. *Awards:* Prize for Distinguished Achievement in Photog Hist, Photog Hist Soc of NY; Seal of City of Arles, France; Bronze Medal, Leipzig Bk Fair. *Bibliog:* Peter Bunnell (auth), The National Gallery photographic collection: An inquiry into the aesthetics of photography (series), Artscanada, 75. *Mem:* Soc Photog Educ. *Res:* Canadian art; history of photography 19th & 20th Century; European Art 14th-20th Century. *Collection:* National Gallery of Canada. *Publ:* Auth, Charles Negre, 1820-1880, 76, David Heath: A Dialogue with Solitude, 79, Eugene Atget, 1857-1927, 84 & Magicians of Light, 93, Nat Gallery Can; David Heath: A Dialogue with Solitude, 79 & Eugene Atget 1857-1927, 84, Nat Gallery Can; Karsh: The Art of the Portrait, Nat Gallery, 89. *Mailing Add:* Nat Gallery Can 380 Sussex Dr Ottawa ON K1N 9N4 Canada

BORDEAUX, JEAN LUC
ART HISTORIAN, CURATOR, ART EXPERT
b Laval, France, Feb 13, 37. *Study:* Univ Paris, Fac Sci, PCB, 59; Mus Nat d'Art Mod, Paris, study of museology with Jean Cassou, 58-60; Iowa State Univ, BS(journalism), 64; Ariz State Univ, MA(art hist), 66; Univ Calif, Los Angeles, PhD(art hist), 70. *Collection Arranged:* Baroque Paintings from the Getty Mus; Roman Portraits from the Getty Mus; Rodin from the Maryhill Collection, J Paul Getty Mus; The Rococo Age: French Masterpieces of the Eighteenth Century, High Mus, Atlanta; The First Painters of the King, New York, New Orleans & Columbus, Ohio; Unstretched Surfaces, Pompidou Ctr, Paris and LAICA, Los Angeles; Abstraction in Los Angeles, 1950-1980, Gribin Collection, CSUN and Univ Calif Irvine; The Fundamental Aspects of Modernism, Los Angeles & Albuquerque, NMex. *Pos:* Art critic & writer, Connaissance des Arts & Art Int, 73-86; asst cur paintings, J Paul Getty Mus, Malibu, Calif, 69-72; dir, Fine Arts Gallery, Calif State Univ, Northridge, 72-2005; guest cur, Calif Palace of the Legion of Honor, San Francisco, 75; chargé de mission, Mus du Louvre, France, 79-80; organized and cur numerous exhibs since 72; dir & head expert, Christie's France & Monaco Old Master Paintings & Drawings, 89-93. *Teaching:* Instr art hist, Univ Calif, Los Angeles, 69-72; dir fine arts gallery, Calif State Univ, Northridge, Calif, 72-81; prof art hist, Calif State Univ, Northridge, 69-, dir Mus Studies, 94-. *Awards:* Kress Fel, 70-71; Calif Arts Coun Exhib Grants, 74-75; J Paul Getty Trust Publ Award, 84; Found Paribas Publ Award, 84; Officier des Palmes Academiques, France, 86. *Mem:* Fr Soc Hist Art; Col Art Asn; Les Amis du Louvre; Los Angeles Coun Mus Art; Mus Contemp Art Los Angeles. *Res:* French painting from 17th to early 19th centuries; Twentieth Century Art Criticism; Italian Baroque art; Twentieth Century art; Mus Studies; Twentieth Century: The Age of the Collage. *Interests:* Contemporary art in New York and Los Angeles. *Publ:* Auth, articles, Burlington Mag, Am Art Rev, Art Int, Art in Am, Jour J Paul Getty Mus, Artibus et Historiae Gaz des Beaux Arts, Connaissance des Arts, and others; François Le Moyne and His Generation 1688-1737, (catalog raisonné), Arthena, 84-85. *Mailing Add:* 640 Kingman Ave Santa Monica CA 90402-1334

BORDES, ADRIENNE
PAINTER, INSTRUCTOR
b New York, NY. *Study:* NY Univ, with Philip Guston, BA, 57; Hunter Col, New York, with Tony Smith & Vincent Longo. *Exhib:* One-person shows, Capricorn Gallery, NY, 67 & 68 & Wilkes Col, Pa, 78; Six Artists, NY Univ, 68; Some New Beginnings, Brooklyn Mus, 68; Women in the Arts, Univ Wis, 72; Transitions, Wallace Gallery, State Univ NY, 79; Four Artists & A Writer, Fed Hall, NY, 82. *Teaching:* Adj instr painting, Hunter Col, New York, 78-80 & Adelphi Univ, 79-80; tenured asst prof hist archit & interior design, Fashion Inst Technol, 80-. *Awards:* Painting Grant, Millay Colony Arts, Austerlitz, NY, 75. *Bibliog:* Julia Ballerini (auth), Four Artists and a Writer, catalog, Fed Hall, NY, 82. *Mem:* Interior Design Educators Coun. *Media:* Acrylic. *Mailing Add:* 369 Seventh Ave New York NY 10001

BORETZ, NAOMI
PAINTER, EDUCATOR
b New York, NY. *Study:* Art Students League; Boston Mus Sch; Rutgers Univ, MA(art hist); City Univ New York, MA(fine arts). *Work:* Joslyn Art Mus, Omaha, Nebr; Solomon R Guggenheim Mus, Metrop Mus Art, Mus Mod Art & Whitney Mus Am Art, NY; Brit Mus London, Eng; Glasgow Mus, Scotland; Walker Art Ctr, Minneapolis, Minn; Fogg Art Mus; Harvard Univ, Cambridge, Mass; DeLand Art Mus, Fla; Yale Univ Art Gallery; Mus of Southwest, Midland, Tex; Asheville Art Mus, NC; and others. *Exhib:* Awards Exhib, Brooklyn Mus Art, 72; Middlesex Co Mus, NJ, 81; Condeso Lawler Gallery, NY, 87; Carnegie-Mellon Art Gallery, Pittsburgh, 89; Ulrich Mus Wichita State Univ, KS, 92; Noyes Mus, NJ, 94; Nelson-Atkins Art Mus, Mo, 94; Westbeth Gallery, 96; Mishkin Gallery, Baruch Col, 1997; Muhlenburg Col Art Gallery, 2002; and others. *Awards:* Va Ctr Creative Arts Fel, 86; Ossabaw Arts Found Fel, 75; Artist Fel, NJ State Coun Arts, 85-86; Tyrone Guthrie Art Ctr Fel, Ireland, 87; Writers-Artists Guild, Can, 88. *Bibliog:* Ian Woodcock (auth), article, Arts Mag, 7/72; interview, Brit Broadcasting Co Radio, 72-73; article, New York Times, 3/81; and others. *Mem:* Am Abstract Artists. *Media:* All Media. *Publ:* Auth, The reality underlying abstraction, In: Perception and Pictorial Representation, Praeger, 79; Watercolours with acetate, Leonardo, 78; and others

BORG, JOSEPH
PRINTMAKER
b New York, NY, Jan 26, 42. *Study:* Studied intaglio with Ruth Leaf; studied lithography with Dan Weldon; Nassau Community Col, AA, 80. *Work:* Mus Modern Art, Barcelona, Spain; Queensboro Col, NY; Tama Art Univ, Tokyo; World Bank, Washington, DC; Off of Lieutenant Gov, State Capital, Honolulu. *Exhib:* Int Print Show, Nat Libr Paris, France, 86; Int Prints, Mus de La Estaupa, Mex, 88; Print Int, Found de Collioure, France, 88; Mini Print Int, Mus Fine Arts, Boston, 89; solo exhib, Saigado Gallery, Akita City, Japan, 90; Mozart Exhib, Gallery Lincoln Ctr, NY, 91; Art Embassies Prog, US Dept State. *Pos:* Vpres, Rockville Ctr Arts Coun, 84-88; demonstr/lectr, various sch-art groups; master printer/tech adv, Ruth Leaf Print Studio, 88-. *Media:* Intaglio. *Mailing Add:* 159 Gordon Rd Valley Stream NY 11581

BORGATTA, ISABEL CASE
SCULPTOR, EDUCATOR
b Madison, Wis, Nov 21, 22. *Study:* Smith Col, 39-40; Yale Univ Sch Fine Arts, BFA, 44; Studio of Jose de Creeft, 44-45; Art Students League, 46. *Work:* Benton Mus, Univ Conn; Hudson River Mus, Col New Rochelle Mus; 4 pieces NYNEX Hqs, NY & Grand Hyatt Hotel, NY; Smith Col Mus; Okla Art Ctr; Chrysler Mus; Brooklyn Mus; Kranert Mus; Yeshiva Univ; City Univ Graduate Ctr: Hartford Athemeum: Donald Trump Buildings. *Comn:* Mem sculpture, New Rochelle, NY, 72; Grand Hyatt Hotel, NY; Zofital Spa, Rome; NYNEX, NY; Transnational Develop, NY; and others. *Exhib:* Pa Acad Fine Arts Ann, Philadelphia, 49-55; one-woman shows, Galerie St Etienne, 54 & 56 & Frank Rehn Gallery, 68, 71, 74 & 77; Hartford Atheneum, Nat Acad Ann Sculptors Guild, 71-88; Sid Deutsch Gallery, 84 & 87; Sweet Briar Col Mus, 86; Oklahoma Art Ctr, 87; Kyoto City Mus, Japan, 93. *Pos:* Deleg, Fedn Fine Arts, currently; exec bd, Sculptors Guild, currently. *Teaching:* Lectr sculpture, City Col New York, 60-71; assoc prof, Col New Rochelle, 73-78, prof, 78-. *Awards:* Yaddo Fel, 71, 72 & 73; Va Ctr Creative Arts Fel, 85, 86, 87, 88, 89, 90, 91 & 92; Sculpture

residency, Govt Greece, Delphi, 92, 93, Crete, 94, 95, 96; Ettl Grant, Nat Sculpture Soc, 95. *Bibliog:* Mark van Doren (auth), The sculptures of Isabel Case Borgatta, Galerie St Etienne, 54; William D Allen (auth), Borgatta's marbles, Arts Mag, 68; James R Mellow (auth), article in NY Times, 74; Virginia Watson-Jones (auth), American Women Sculptors, Oryx Press, 86; Isabel Case Borgatta: The Persistence of the Figure, Cincinnati Univ, 87; Shaping Space, Zelanski & Fisher, Hancourt Brace, 95, 2nd ed, 2006; Smith Voices, Smith College Press, 99; Mary Pat Fisher (auth), Women & Religion, Laurence King Publ, London, 2006; and many others. *Mem:* Women's Caucus Art; Artists Equity; Sculptors Guild (exec bd); Nat Sculpture Soc; The Century Asn. *Media:* Stone, Wood. *Res:* Continued research for publications, including Health Hazards for Artists. *Interests:* Environment, liberal politics. *Publ:* Auth, A Sculptor Changes, Women Artists Newsletter, 77; Casting landscapes in paper, Artists Mag, 86; The Persistence of the Figure, College Art Assoc, 87; The Figure Today, Women's Caucus for Art, 88; Profile of Isabel Case Borgatta, Nat Sculpture Soc, 2005; Series of Articles on Health Hazards for Artists, Pub Sculptors Guild Bulletins. *Mailing Add:* 463 West St Apt 1105 New York NY 10014-2010

BORGATTA, ROBERT EDWARD
PAINTER, SCULPTOR
b Havana, Cuba, Jan 11, 21; US citizen. *Study:* Nat Acad Design, 34-37; NY Univ, Sch Archit & Allied Arts, BFA, 40, Inst Fine Arts, 46-53; Yale Univ Sch Fine Arts, MFA, 42. *Work:* Norfolk Mus, Va; Ford Found. *Comn:* Mural & sculpture, Gutman Assocs, NY; stained glass design, Temple Emanu-el, Yonkers, NY, 60. *Exhib:* Audubon Artists Ann, 53-72; Whitney Mus Am Art Prizewinners Show, 54; Schettini Gallery, Milan, Italy, 57; Corcoran Gallery Art, 68; one-man shows, Babcock Galleries, 64 & 68 & Southern Vt Art Ctr, 77. *Teaching:* Prof painting & drawing, City Col New York, 47-80. *Awards:* Tiffany Fel, 42; Emily Lowe Found Award, 57; Newman Medal, Nat Soc Painters Casein, 69. *Bibliog:* American artists in Italian exhibit, Valligia Diplomatica, 10/57; An artist in his studio, House Beautiful, 3/60; John Canaday (auth), article, New York Times, 3/15/69. *Mem:* Audubon Artists; Am Watercolor Soc; Nat Soc Painters Casein. *Media:* Oil, Marble. *Dealer:* Babcock Galleries 20 East 67th St New York NY 10021. *Mailing Add:* 366 Broadway No 2B New York NY 10013-4803

BORGIA-ABERLE, NINA
CERAMIST, INSTRUCTOR, PUBLIC ARTIST
b New York, NY, 55. *Study:* Mass Col Art, Boston, 73-75; Syracuse Univ, NY, 75; State Univ New York, New Paltz, BFA, 79; Ohio State Univ, Columbus, MFA, 86. *Work:* Everson Mus Art; Metro Health, Kaiser Corp & Univ Hosp, Cleveland, Ohio; and others. *Comn:* Ceramic tile, Cent Ohio Psychiatric Hosp; ceramic tile, City Tucson, Ariz; Mural project, Stone Avenue Temple, 2001. *Exhib:* Solo exhibs, Columbus Cult Art Ctr, Ohio, 86, Licking Co Art Asn, Neward, 87, Sara Squeri Gallery, Cincinnati, 90, Swidler Gallery, Royal Oak, Mich & Leedy Voulkous Gallery, Kansas City, Mo, 91, Nancy Margolis Gallery, NY, 93 & Toni Birckhead Gallery, Cincinnati, Ohio, 93; Contemp Ohio Ceramics, Ohio Craft Mus, 94; State Univ NY, New Paltz, 95; Montgomery Col, Rockville, Md, 95; David Beitzel Gallery, NY, 96; Hand & Spirit Gallery, Scottsdale, Ariz, 96. *Teaching:* Instr ceramics, NY State Summer Sch Arts, Fredonia, 82, Ohio State Univ, 85-86; vis lectr drawing, Denison Univ, 87 & ceramics, Calif State Univ, Long Beach, 90; guest lectr, Ceramics Int Seminar, Calgary, Can, 91, Univ Ariz, 93, Denison Univ, Granville, Ohio, 94, Miami Univ, Oxford, Ohio, 94 & 96, Univ NMex, Las Cruces, 95 & Cleveland Inst Art, Ohio, 95; sculptor in residence at numerous Ohio schs; vis instr ceramics, Univ Ariz, Tucson, 94-95. *Awards:* Edith Fergus Gillmore Grant, 86; Nat Endowment Arts Individual Fel, 88 & 90; Ohio Arts Coun Individual Artist Fel, 89, 91 & 94. *Bibliog:* Exhibitions review, Am Ceramics, fall 91; 29th ceramic national, judgement call, Am Craft Mag, 10-11/93; Fiction, function, figuration, the 29th ceramic national, Ceramics Monthly Mag, 11/93. *Publ:* Auth, Ceramics and sculpture, Ceramics Art & Perception, No 23, 96. *Mailing Add:* 2929 W Via De Suenos Tucson AZ 85713

BORN, JAMES E
SCULPTOR
b Toledo, Ohio, Nov 16, 34. *Study:* Toledo Mus Sch, cert; Univ Toledo, BA, 59; Univ Iowa, Iowa City, MFA, 62. *Work:* Univ Iowa, Iowa City; Art Ctr Mus, Pine Bluff, Ark; Trans World Airlines, Los Angeles, Calif; Chartoff Productions, Santa Monica, Calif. *Exhib:* Sculpture & Ceramics, Butler Inst Am Art, Youngstown, Ohio, 68, 74, 75 & 77; One-man shows, Cent Mich Univ, 69, 77 & 84, Muskegon Community Col, 79 & Ferris State Univ, 85,. Gallery Abbott Kiney, Venice, Calif, 92, Mich Competition, Birmingham, Bloomfield Art Ctr, 92, Communication Trans World Airlines, LA Airport, Calif, San Diego Mus Art, 95, Mt Clemens Art Mus, Mich, 93-95, Saginaw Art Mus, 93-94; Mich Fine Arts Competition, Bloomfield Art Ctr, Birmingham, 92; Saginaw Mus, Mich, 93, 94, 95; Mt Clemens Art Ctr, Mich, 93, 94, 95; juried exhib, San Diego Mus Art, Calif, 95. *Teaching:* Asst prof sculpture, painting, design & drawing, Univ Calif, Humboldt, Arcata, 62-64 & Calif Western Univ, San Diego, 64-65; asst prof sculpture, design & painting, Univ Calif, Stanislaus, Turlock, 65-68; assoc prof sculpture, Cent Mich Univ, Mt Pleasant, 68-76, acting chmn, 72-74, prof sculpture, 76-. *Awards:* Sculpture Award, 92 & Laatsch Award-Sculpture, 93, Mich Competition, Saginaw Art Mus; Trustee Award, Mich Competition, Mt Clemens Art Ctr, 94. *Mem:* Col Art Asn; Mid-Am Art Asn. *Media:* Bronze

BORNSTEIN, ELI
PAINTER, SCULPTOR
b Milwaukee, Wis, Dec 28, 22; US & Can citizen. *Study:* Univ Wis, BS, 45 & MS, 54; Art Inst Chicago; Univ Chicago, 43; Acad Montmartre of Fernand Leger, Paris, 51; Acad Julian, Paris, 52, Univ Saskatchewan, D Litt, 90. *Work:* Walker Art Ctr, Minneapolis, Minn; Nat Gallery Can, Ottawa; Univ Calgary, Alta; Univ Sask & Mendel Art Gallery, Saskatoon; Ft Lauderdale Mus Art, Fla; Milwaukee Art Mus; Florsheim Collection, Chicago; Canadian Ctr Archit, Montreal; and others. *Comn:* Aluminum construction, Sask Teacher's Fedn, Saskatoon, 56; structurist relief, Univ Sask, Saskatoon, 58; structurist relief, Int Air Terminal, Winnipeg, 62; structurist construction, Wascana Ctr Authority, Regina, 83; hexaplane structurist relief, Synchrotron, Can Light Source Bldg, Univ Sask, 2003; Int Univ Bremen, Germany, 2006. *Exhib:* Retrospectives, Mendel Art Gallery, Saskatoon, 64, 82 & 96; Nat Gallery Can Biennial, Ottawa, 67; 2nd Int Biennial, Medellin, Colombia, 70; Can Cult Centre, Paris, France, 76; Glenbow-Alta Inst, Calgary, 76; York Univ Art Gallery, Toronto, 83; Fine Arts Gallery, Univ Wis, Milwaukee; Forum Art Gallery, NY, 2005, 2006; and others. *Pos:* Ed, The Structurist, 60-. *Teaching:* Instr drawing, painting & sculpture, Milwaukee Art Inst, 43-47; instr design, Univ Wis, 49; prof art, Univ Sask, 50-, head dept art, 63-71, prof emer, 90. *Awards:* Allied Arts Medal, Royal Archit Inst Can, 68; Hon mention, 2nd Int Biennial Exhib, Medellin, Colombia, 70; Gov Gen's Queen Elizabeth Silver Jubilee Medal, 77. *Bibliog:* Eli Bornstein: Selected Works/Oeuvres Choisies, 1957-1982, Mendel Art Gallery, 82; Eli Bornstein: Art Toward Nature, Jonneke Fritz-Jobse, Mendel Art Gallery, 96. *Media:* Constructed Relief. *Publ:* Auth of numerous articles and essays in The Structurist since 60-; In Directions in Art, Theory and Aesthetics, Faber & Faber, London, 68; Canadian Art Today, 69; Time as a Human Resource, Univ Calgary Press, 91; A Celebration of Canada's Arts 1930-1970, Scholar's Press, Toronto, 96. *Dealer:* Forum Art Gallery New York NY. *Mailing Add:* Box 378 RPO Univ Univ Sask Saskatoon SK S7N 4J8 Canada

BOROCHOFF, (IDA) SLOAN
PAINTER, PRINTMAKER
Study: High Mus Art, 39; Univ Ga, 39-40; Ga State Univ, 40; Chicago Sch Interior Decorating, dipl, 66; Atlanta Art Inst, 68. *Work:* Ga Inst Technol, Vet Admin & Lovett Sch, Atlanta; The Temple, Tucson, Ariz; Nat Acad Eng, Washington. *Comn:* Noah's Ark (print), Atlanta Jewish Welfare Fedn, 71; painting, Am Ort Campaign, Atlanta, 72. *Exhib:* One-woman shows, Ga Inst Technol Student Ctr & Lovett Sch Show, 71 & 75, Saginaw Art Mus, Mich, 98; Corcoran Mus, Washington; Rizzoli Gallery, NY; State of the Art, New Eng Fine Art Inst, Boston, Mass, 93; Col Notre Dame, Md, 93; In the Hosp Exhib, Med Col Ga, 94; Atlanta Archives, Atlanta Hist Ctr; Oral History, Nat Coun Jewish Women; Ga Sampler, Gwinnet Mus, Ga, 98-99. *Pos:* Vpres, Designs Unlimited Inc, Atlanta, 64-; pres, Sloan Borochoff Gallery; artist-auth, Atlanta Playhouse Theatre Ltd, 75-; artistic dir, Int Dogwood Festival Art Shows, Atlanta, 79-; producer/host weekly series Community TV, Atlanta Prime Cable. *Teaching:* Lectr, schs & workshops, 70-; dir, Int Jr Cult Exchange A. *Awards:* TV Caber Award, 84; Oscar d'Italia, Acad Ital Premio, 85; Invitation to White House Coffee, 89. *Mem:* Women in Film; Acad Cable Programming; Women's CofC; Int Platform Asn; Mat Mus Women. *Media:* Oil, Prints. *Publ:* Artist-Auth, Images of Women, WGTV & Atlanta Playhouse Theatre. *Mailing Add:* 3450 Old Plantation Rd NW Atlanta GA 30327

BOROFSKY, JON
PAINTER
b Boston, Mass, 42. *Study:* Carnegie Mellon Univ, BFA, 64; Ecole de Fontainbleau, summer 64; Yale Sch Art & Archit, MFA, 1942. *Exhib:* Autogeography, Whitney Mus Am Art, 75; one-man exhibs, Wadsworth Atheneum, 76, Mus Mod Art, NY, 78, Philadelphia Mus Art, 84, Corcoran Gallery Art, 86, Paula Cooper Gallery, NY, 95, FRAC Provence-Alpes-Cote d'Azur, France, 96 & Jonathan Borofsky: The GOD Project, Rose Art Mus, Brandeis Univ, Waltham, Mass, 97; Biennial Exhib, Whitney Mus Am Art, 79 & 81; New Dimensions in Drawing: 1950-1980, Aldrich Mus Contemp Art, 81; Murs, Musee Nat d'Art Mod, Paris, 81; Dynamix Traveling Exhib, Butler Inst Am Art, 82; New Works on Paper 2, Mus Mod Art, NY, 82; Recent Acquisitions from the Department of Drawings, Mus Mod Art, NY, 83; Entering the Eighties: Selections from the Permanent Collection of the Whitney Mus of Am Art, Whitney Mus Am Art, 83; Minimalism to Expressionism: Painting & Sculpture since 1965 from the Permanent Collection, Whitney Mus Am Art, 83; The Am Artist as Printmaker: 23rd Nat Print Exhib, Brooklyn Mus, 83; Currents, Inst Contemp Art, Boston, 83; An Int Survey of Recent Painting & Sculpture, Mus Mod Art, NY, 84; Video: Recent Acquisitions, Mus Mod Art, NY, 85; Figure as Subject: The Last Decade, Whitney Mus Am Art, 86; The Generic Figure, Corcoran Gallery Art, 86; Contemp Cutouts, Whitney Mus Am Art, 86 & 87; New Collections Group 1986, JB Speed Mus, 86; From the Collection of Sol LeWitt, Wadsworth Atheneum, 87; Avante-Garde in the Eighties, Los Angeles Co Mus Art, 87; Committed to Print, Mus Mod Art, NY, 88; New Art on Paper, Philadelphia Mus Art, 88; 20th Century Drawings from the Whitney Mus of Am Art, Whitney Mus Am Art, 88; Art in Place: Fifteen Yrs of Acquisitions, Whitney Mus Am Art, 89; Word as Image: American Art 1960-1990, Milwaukee Art Ctr, 90; The 1980's: A Selected View from the Permanent Collection, Whitney Mus Am Art, 91; Image and Likeness & Immaterial Objects, Whitney Mus Am Art, 91; De-Persona, Oakland Mus, 91; L'un et l'autre et vice et versa Espace Paul Ruquet, Bezier, France, 98; and many others. *Teaching:* Instr, Sch Visual Arts, NY, 69-77; instr, Calif Inst Arts, Los Angeles, 77-80. *Bibliog:* Phillip Smith, Jon Borofsky, Arts Mag, 3/78; John Russell (auth), Art: transformations of Jonathan Borofsky, New York Times, 10/24/80; Terri Friedman (auth), Terri Friedman meets with Jonathan Borofsky, Zing Mag, summer 97. *Mailing Add:* c/o Paula Cooper Gallery 534 W 21st St New York NY 10011

BOROWIEC, ANDREW
PHOTOGRAPHER, EDUCATOR
b New York, NY, Mar 27, 56. *Study:* Workshop with Garry Winogrand, Int Ctr Photog, NY, 79; Haverford Col, BA(Russian), Pa, 79; Yale Univ Sch Art, MFA(photog), New Haven, Conn, 82. *Work:* Canadian Ctr Archit, NY & Montreal; Cleveland Mus Art, Ohio; Chicago Art Inst, Ill; Houston Mus Fine Arts; Smithsonian Am Art Mus, Washington, DC. *Comn:* Photograph for Uncommon Places (exhib & bk commemorating the Bicentennial of the Constitution), Nat Trust Hist Preservation &

Soc Photog Ed, 87; photogs for hist archit in Canton, 1805-1940, Canton Art Inst, Ohio, 88-89. *Exhib:* One-man shows, Midtown Y Photo Gallery, NY, 94, OK Harris, NY, 97, Univ Arts, Philadelphia, Pa, 97, SRO Gallery, Tex Tech Univ, Lubbock, 99, Fla Int Univ, Miami, 99, Univ Notre Dame, S Bend, Ind, 99, Soc Contemp Hotog, Kansas City, Mo, 99 & others; Club House, United Nations, Geneva, Switz, 78; Le Poisson Banane, Arles, France, 81; Galerie Les Arcenaulx, Marseille, France, 82; Fraunces Tavern Mus, NY, 88; Xiamen Univ, Fuchane & Xian Fine Art Inst, Shaanxi, China, 92; Photospiva 93, Joplin, Mo, 93; Photowork 95, Poughkeepsie, NY, 95; Magic Silver Show, Cedar Falls, Iowa, 97; Photog and Industry, Cleveland Mus Art, Ohio, 98; Current Works 98, Soc Contemp Photog, Kansas City, Mo, 98. *Pos:* Asst dir workshops, Recontres Internationales de la Photographie, Arles, France, 79; staff photogr, Int Ctr Photog, NY, 79-80; fashion photogr, Lab Inst Merchandising, NY, 84; free-lance photog, Chronicle for Higer Educ, 87-93; dir, Sch Art, Univ Akron, Ohio, 90-95. *Teaching:* Instr, Parsons Sch Design, summer prog in photog, Paris, France, 80-82; guest lectr contemp Am photog, Universite d Aix-Marseille, France, 82; instr photog & art, Germantown Acad, Ft Wash, Pa, 82-83; New Sch Social Research, NY, 82-84; Parsons Sch Design, NY, 83-84; prof art, Mary Schiller Myers Sch Art, Univ Akron, Ohio, 84-; vis assoc prof art hist, Oberlin Col, Ohio, 90. *Awards:* Ohio Arts Coun Individual Artist Fel, 88, 98; John Simon Guggenheim Mem Found Fel, 98; Fel Award, Soc Contemp Photog, Kansas City, Mo, 98. *Publ:* Contrib, Blue Sky #10, Ore Ctr, Photog Arts, Portland, 94; The Photo Rev, 8/96; Double Take, Along the Ohio, Issue 9, 97; Green Mounains Rev, Vol XI, No 2, 98; Along the Ohio (monograph), Johns Hopkins Univ Press, Baltimore & London, 2000. *Dealer:* Lee Marks Fine Art 2208 E 350 N Shelbyville IN 46176. *Mailing Add:* c/o Univ Akron Sch Art 136 Folk Hall Akron OH 44325

BORSTEIN, ELENA
PAINTER, EDUCATOR
b Hartford, Conn, Feb 5, 46. *Study:* Skidmore Col, BS; Univ Pa, BFA & MFA. *Work:* Mus Mod Art; Mass Inst Technol; Everson Mus; Newark Mus; Phoenix Mus; and others. *Comn:* Ottawa Silica Corp, Ill; Whitco Chemical Co, NY. *Exhib:* Contemp Reflections, Aldrich Mus Art, Ridgefield, Conn, 74; 14 Am Artists, Corcoran Gallery/Aarhus Kunstmuseum Traveling Exhib, 77; Gifts of Drawing, Mus Mod Art, NY, 79; Everson Mus, 81; Skidmore Col, Saratoga Springs, NY, 82; Kathryn Markel Gallery, NY, 83; Andre Zarre Gallery, 90, 92, 93, 97 & 2000; JJ Brookings, San Francisco; and others. *Pos:* Art consult, Aarhus Kunstmuseum, Denmark, 74-75; vis artist, St Marys Col, Ind, Md Art Inst & Sch Visual Arts, 81. *Teaching:* Prof painting & photog, York Col, City Univ NY, 70-. *Awards:* Nat Endowment Arts Grant, 80; Creative Artists Pub Serv Prog Grant, 80; City Univ New York Res Award, 89, 91 & 93. *Bibliog:* David Shirey (auth), article, Arts Mag, 9/78; articles, Art Int, 1/80, NY Times, 3/16/80 & Art in Am, 12/2000. *Mem:* Col Art Asn (mem, Women's Caucus). *Mailing Add:* Fine Arts Dept York Col 9420 Guy Brewer Blvd Jamaica NY 11451

BOSMAN, RICHARD
PAINTER, PRINTMAKER
b Madras, India, 44. *Study:* Byam Shaw Sch Painting & Drawing, London, 64-69; NY Studio Sch, NY, 69-71; Skowhegan Sch Painting & Sculpture, Maine, 70. *Work:* Albright-Knox Art Gallery, Buffalo, NY; Australian Nat Gallery, Canberra; Brooklyn Mus, NY; Fogg Art Mus, Harvard Univ, Cambridge; Nat Mus Am Art, Washington, DC; Weatherspoon Art Gallery, Greensboro. *Exhib:* One-man exhibs, Galerie La Maquina Espanola, Madrid, 90, Galerie Biedermann, Munich, 91, Brooke Alexander, 91, 93 & 94, Galleria Toselli, Milan, 92, Fairfield Univ Gallery, Conn, 93, RI Sch Design Print Gallery, 93, Timmesh Gallery, Minneapolis, 93; Works on Paper, Curt Marrus Gallery, NY, 88; Sounding the Depths: 150 Yrs of Am Seascape, Am Fedn Arts, NY, 89; First Impressions, Walker Art Ctr, Traveling from Minneapolis to Baltimore, 89; Monoprints/Monotypes-Images by Twenty Contemp Artists, Univ Maine Mus Art, Orono, 89; Group show, Galeria La Maquina Espanola, Madrid, 89; Images of Death in Contemp Art, Patrick & Beatrice Haggerty Mus Art, Milwaukee, 90; Selected Paintings, Drawings and Sculpture, John Berggruen Gallery, San Francisco, 90 718. *Teaching:* Instr, NY Studio Sch, 72, Skowhegan Sch Painting & Sculpture, Maine, 82 & Sch Visual Arts, NY, 82-84; Teacher Skowhegan Sch Painting and Sculpture, Maine, 1982, Sch Visual Arts, New York City, 1983-1985, Univ Pa, Philadelphia, 1986, Temple Univ, Philadelphia, 1987, Columbia Univ, New York City, 1988-1990, Temple Univ, Philadelphia, 1991, RI Sch Design, Providence, 1992, State Univ of NY, Purchase, 1993, Fairfield Univ, 1993, Yale Univ, Norfolk, Conn, 1994-1998, Vassar Col, Poughkeepsie, NY, 1995-. *Awards:* Guggenheim fel, 1994. *Bibliog:* Jole de Sanna (auth), Milan: Richard Bosman, Toselli Gallery, Artforum, 12/86; Chavarri Ardujar (auth), La Pintura con sangre entra, Las Provincias, 7/87; Joy Hakanson Colby (auth), Richard Bosman, The Detroit News, 11/1/88. *Mem:* Nat Acad (assoc, 94, acad, 94). *Publ:* Coauth, Exit the Face, Mus Mod Art, NY, 82; illusr, Grasping at Emptiness, Kulchur Found, 85; The Captivity Narrative of Hannah Duston, Arion Press, San Francisco, 87; Nat Mus Am Art & Library of Congress, Washington, DC; Dannhoiser Found, Metrop Mus Art, Mus Mod Art, Whitney Mus Mod Arts Pub Libr, NY. *Mailing Add:* c/o Mark Moore Gallery Bergamot Station A1 2525 Mich Ave Santa Monica CA 90404

BOSTICK, WILLIAM ALLISON
PAINTER - WATERCOLOR, CALLIGRAPHER, DESIGNER, ILLUSTRATOR, PRINTMAKER
b Marengo, Ill, Feb 21, 13. *Study:* Carnegie Inst Technol, BS; Cranbrook Acad Art, with Zoltan Sepeshy & Maija Grotel; Detroit Soc Arts & Crafts, with John Foster; Wayne State Univ, MA(art hist). *Work:* Detroit Inst Arts, Cranbrook Acad Art Mus, Detroit Pub Libr, Wayne State Univ & Detroit Hist Mus; Evansville Mus Arts & Sci, Ind. *Comn:* 32 calligraphic panels on wood, 11 calligraphic lecterns & 1 large calligraphic quotation (with Christopher Bostick), Cath Cemeteries of Chicago for Resurrection Mausoleum, Justice, Ill, 71; 6 large acrylic paintings on architectural roots of Mich Nat Corp Hq Bldg, 90. *Exhib:* Exhib Mich Artists, Detroit Inst Arts, 36-63; Pepsi-Cola Exhib, 45; Scarab Club Gold Medal Exhib, 47-94; Mich Watercolor Soc, 48-94; one-man exhib, Arwin Galleries, 67 & 75 & Preston Burke Gallery, 96. *Pos:* Typographer, Detroit Typsetting Co, 35-36; graphic designer, Evans-Winter-Hebb, Detroit, 36-37; exec secy, Founders Soc, Detroit Inst Arts, 46-60, adminr & secy, 46-76; ed, Midwest Mus Quart, 59-60. *Teaching:* Instr drawing, Wayne State Univ, 46-47; instr calligraphy, Detroit Soc Arts & Crafts Art Sch, 61-63; instr hist of the book, Wayne State Univ Grad Sch, 62-67; instr calligraphy & art hist, Grosse Pointe War Mem & Edison Inst, 73-86 & Ctr Creative Studies, Detroit, 86-94; instr, Italic Handwriting in suburban Detoit, over 40 years, formerly. *Awards:* Scarab Gold Medal, Scarab Club Detroit, 62, 68 & 79; Knight, Order of Italy Solidarity; Chevalier, French Order of Arts & Lett. *Mem:* Scarab Club Detroit; Mich Watercolor Soc (cofounder); Soc Scribes, NY; Mich Asn Calligraphers; Soc Italic Handwriting. *Media:* Watercolor, Acrylic, Lithography. *Publ:* Illusr, Many a Watchful Night, 45; auth & illusr, England Under GI's Reign, 46; illusr, The Mysteries of Blair House, 48; auth, A Guide to the Guarding of Cultural Property, UNESCO, 77; auth & publ, A Manual on the Acquiring of a Beautiful and Legible Handwriting, 77, rev ed, 80 & Calligraphy for Kids, 91, La Stampa Calligrafica; Back to the Second Basic R-Ritin, 98. *Dealer:* Preston Burke Gallery 30448 Woodward Royal Oak MI 48073. *Mailing Add:* 23350 Old Orchard Tr Bingham Farms MI 48025

BOSZIN, ANDREW
PAINTER, SCULPTOR
b Pilis, Hungary, May 5, 23; Can & UK citizen. *Study:* House Creation, Independent Sch Art; Col Art. *Work:* Musee des Beaux Arts, Budapest, Hungary; Scottish Camp Asn, Edinburgh, Scotland; Sculptors Soc Can, Toronto; Pa State Univ, Fayette Campus, Uniontown; British Mus, London; and others. *Exhib:* Contemp Can Art, Ernst Mus, Budapest; one-man shows, Old Nat Gallery, Budapest, Hungary, 48, J B Aird Gallery, Toronto, 90, Medallist Show, Osoyoos, BC, 93, First Can Place, Exchange Tower, 94 & Vasarely Mus, Budapest, 96; Homage to Dante, Dante Mus, Verona, Italy, 86-88; Challenge & Tradition, Sculpture Soc Show, John B Aird Gallery, Toronto, 99; Brit Royal Acad Spring Show, London, 95. *Awards:* Grand Prix De Penture, Prix De Nat, 64; Honor Award, Spanish Medalist Asn, 68; Best Watercolor, Cosmopoliton Club, 81; Sculptors' Soc Can Medal Award, 85. *Bibliog:* Ian Ferguston (auth), Endre Boszin, Douglass Foulis, Edinburgh, 64; Tamas Tuz (auth), Endre Boszin, Kronika, Toronto, 79; Andrew Bozin (monogr), 92. *Mem:* Sculptors Soc Can (pres, 71-73, 79-83). *Media:* Cast Aluminum; Oil, Watercolor. *Publ:* Auth, A I Botar, Studio All, Toronto, Can, 92. *Mailing Add:* 39 Gilgorm Rd Toronto ON M5N 2M4 Canada

BOTERF, CHECK (CHESTER) ARTHUR
PAINTER, LECTURER
b Ft Scott, Kans, Apr 27, 34. *Study:* Univ Kans, BA, 59; Art Student League; Hunter Col, 63-64; Columbia Univ, MFA, 65. *Work:* Mus Mod Art, Chase Manhattan Bank, Columbia Univ, Fordham Univ, Rockefeller Univ & AT&T Corp, NY; Larry Aldrich Mus, Ridgefield, Conn; Des Moines Art Ctr, Iowa; Newark Mus, NJ; and others. *Exhib:* Solo exhibs, Tibor De Nagy Gallery, NY, 67, 68 & 70, Rice Univ, 74 & John Bernard Myers Gallery, NY, 71, 73 & 74; Indianapolis Mus Art, Inc, 68-69; Finch Col, 71; Recent Acquisitions, Mus Mod Art, NY, 71; Sewall Art Gallery, Houston, Tex, 86 & 88. *Teaching:* Lectr design & drawing, Hunter Col, 65-71; Brooklyn Mus Art Sch, 73; vis assoc prof fine arts, Rice Univ, Houston, 73-75, assoc prof art, 76-93, chmn art & art hist, 79-82, prof emer, currently. *Media:* Acrylic

BOTERO, FERNANDO
SCULPTOR
b Medellin, Colombia, 1932. *Study:* Acad San Fernando, Spain, 53; Prado Mus, Madrid, 54; Univ Florence, Italy, art hist with Roberto Longhi. *Work:* Mus d'Arte Mod del Vaticano, Rome; Birmingham Mus Art, Ala; Mus de Arte Mod, Bogota, Colombia; Mus Mod Art, Metrop Mus Art, Solomon R Guggenheim Mus, NY; Baltimore Mus Art, Md; Smithsonian Inst, Washington, DC; Ateneumin Taidemuseo, Helsinki, Finland; Museo de Bellas Artes, Caracas; Milwaukee Art Mus, Wis. *Exhib:* Solo shows include Dider Imbert Fine Art, Paris, 92, Traveling exhib, Avignon, 92-93, Marlborough Gallery, NY 93, Galeria Marlborough, Madrid, 94, Nac de Bellas Artes, Buenos Aires, 94, Fernando Botero, Museo d'Arte Moderna, Lugano, Switz, 97, Botero em Sao Paulo, 98, Museu de Arte de Sao Paulo, Brazil, 98 & Museo Nacional de Artes Visuales, Montevideo, Uruguay, 98, Abu Ghraib, Marlborough Gallery, NY, 2006; group shows include Gulf Caribbean Art Exhib, Mus Fine Arts, Houston, 56; Solomon R Guggenheim Mus, 58; Paintings from the Gres Gallery, Baltimore Mus Art, 59; Recent Acquisitions: Painting & Sculpture, Mus Mod Art, NY, 61; An Invitation to See: 125 Paintings from the Mus of Modern Art, Mus Mod Art, NY, 73; retrospectives, Traveling, Ger, 70, Mus Boymans-van Beuningen, Rotterdam, The Neth, 75, Traveling, Hirshhorn Mus & Sculpture Garden, 79, Traveling, Tokyo Art Gallery, Japan, 86, Helsinki City Art Mus, 94; Fall 1977: Contemp Collectors, Aldrich Mus Contemp Art, 77; Recent Development in Latin American Drawing, Art Inst Chicago, 87; The Ellen & Jerome Westeimer Collection, Okla Art Ctr, 87; Figures of Contemp Sculpture (1970-1990): Images of Man Traveling Exhib, Isetan Mus Art, Tokyo, Japan, 92; Latin American Artists of the 20th Century, Traveling Exhib, Estacion Plaza de Armas, Seville, Spain, 92-93; Lateinamerikanische Kunst Im 20 Jahrhundert, Mus Ludwig, Cologne, Ger, 92-93; Iv e01me Biennale de Sculpture Monte Carlo, Marisa del Re Gallery, NY, 93; Art Mus Americas, 96; Marlborough Gallery, 96; O'Hara Gallery, 97; Forma eta Figunazion: Blake-Parnell Bildumako Maisa-Lanak, Guggenheim Bilbao Mus, 98; Botero a Dinard, Palais des Arts de Dinard, 2002; Botero a Venezia: Sculture e dipinti, 2003; Palazzo Duccale, Venezia, Ital, 2003; Les Artistes des Animaux, Festival Int de Sculpture de Monet-Carlo, Monaco, 2002. *Bibliog:* Pierre Daix, Charles Virmaitre & Jean Cau (auths), Botero aux Champs-Elysees, fall 92; Edward J Sullivan (auth), Fernando Botero: Drawings &

Watercolors, Rizzoli, New York, 93; Miguel Canbajal (auth), Una Charla con Fernando Botero en nueva York, El Pais de los domingos, 11/15/98; and many others. *Publ:* Auth, Esta Noche Con Usted, Interview by Maria Elvira Salazar, Telemundo TV, USA, 7/27/88 & 9/24/88; Anna Marie Escallon, Botero New Works on Canvas, New York, Rizzoli, 97. *Mailing Add:* c/o Marlborough Gallery 40 W 57th St New York NY 10019

BOTT, H(ARVEY) J(OHN)
SCULPTOR, PAINTER
b Greeley, Colo, Dec 28, 33. *Study:* Art Ctr Sch Los Angeles; Inst Fine Arts, NY Univ; Art Students League; Kunstakademie-Dusseldorf & Bamberg, Ger, MBK, 55. *Work:* Rice Univ; New Orleans Mus Art; San Antonio Art Mus; Denver Art Mus; Bakersfield Art Mus, Calif; and many others. *Exhib:* Solo exhibs, San Jose, Calif, 77, Contemp Arts Ctr, New Orleans, La, 85, Ga Southern Univ, Statesboro, 89, Crocker Art Mus, Sacramento, Calif, 86, San Antonio Col, Tex, 95 & Sculpture Court, Houston Art League, Tex, 96; Contemp Arts Mus, Houston, Tex, 85; Texas Art Celebration, Houston, 89, Condeso-Lawler Gallery, NY, 90 & Galerie Muhlenbusch-Winklemann, Dusseldorf, Ger, 90-92; El Palomar, Houston, Tex, 94; Infinite Airport, Lamar Univ, Beaumont, Tex, 94; and many others. *Pos:* Artist-in-residence, Loft-on-Strand, Galveston, Tex, 69-78. *Teaching:* Glassell Sch Art, Mus Fine Arts, Houston, Tex, 92-. *Awards:* Plastik Reisestipeduim, Museen der Stadt Koln, Ger, 56; Premier Les Plus Sculpture, Prix de Paris, France, 65; and many others. *Bibliog:* Wendy Paris (auth), HJ Bott: Recent Systemic Structures, Sally Reynolds Fine Arts, Houston Chronicle, 8/27/94; Gathrine Anspon (auth), Minimalist, Geometric, Idiosyncratic, Pure: Harvey Bott, Public News, 12/97; Shaila Dewan (auth), DoV-ine Inspiration, Houston Press, 12/97. *Media:* All. *Publ:* Auth, ROBOTT Opera: A Time-warp Newscast, Univ St Thomas, Houston, 83. *Dealer:* Thom Andriola New Gallery 2639 Colquitt Houston TX 77098. *Mailing Add:* 4006 Barnes St Houston TX 77007-5706

BOTT, JOHN
PAINTER, CRITIC
b Gassaway, WVa, Sept 12, 36. *Study:* Troy State Univ, BS, 61; Univ NC, Chapel Hill, MFA, 69. *Work:* Witherspoon Gallery, Univ NC, Greensboro; NH Comn Arts, Concord; New Harmony Gallery Contemp Art, Ind; Bank NH, Concord; Chrystler Mus, Norfork, Va; Swope Gallery, Terre Haut, Ind; Springmills Inc, Lancaster, SC; Burlington Industs; Chrystler Mus, Norfolk, Va; Colby Sawyer Col; Bank of New Hampshire. *Comn:* Mural, Thoren Mus, Petersburg, Ind, 76-77; paintings, Highwood Building, Tewskbury, Mass. *Exhib:* Solo exhibs, Davidson Col, NC, 70 & Vanderbilt Univ, Nashville, 74; New Eng Contemp Artist, Ctr Arts, Nashua, NH, 87-88; New Harmony Gallery Contemp Art, Ind, 88; McGowan Fine Art, Concord, NH, 91; Kimball-Jenkins Mansion, Concord, NH, 97; Milbrook Gallery, Concord, NH, 99; Kimnall Union Academy, Plainfield, NH; and others. *Pos:* NH revs ed, Art New England, Boston, 84-86. *Teaching:* Prof painting, Greensboro Col, NC, 69-72 & Univ Evansville, Ind, 72-76; prof, Colby-Sawyer Col, New London, NH, 77-. *Awards:* Burlington Industs Award, Guilford Co Exhib, 71; Excellence Award, 30th Wabash Valley, 74 & Hoffman Award, 33rd Wabash Valley, 77, Sheldon Swope Gallery. *Bibliog:* Margo Clark (auth), New England contemporary art, Art New Eng, 12-1/88. *Media:* Watercolor, Acrylic. *Publ:* Paul Pollaro (exhib catalog), Phillips Exeter Sch & Lamont Gallery, 88. *Dealer:* New Harmony Gallery Contemp Art New Harmony IN; Gallery Mack Seattle Wash. *Mailing Add:* Colby-Sawyer Col Dept Art New London NH 03257

BOTT, MARGARET DEATS See Deats, Margaret (Margaret) Deats Bott

BOTTINI, DAVID WILLIAM
PAINTER, EDUCATOR
b Harrisburg, Pa, 61. *Study:* Mt St Mary's Univ, BA, 83; Savannah col Art & Design, MFA, 91. *Work:* Mt St Mary's Univ, Emmitsburg, Md; Fat Hat Films, Philadelphia, Pa; The Madeira Sch, McLean, Va; Farmers & Mechanics Bank, Waynesboro, Pa; The House on Cherry St, Bed & Breakfast Inn, Jacksonville, Fla. *Comn:* 3 panel paintings, Alexander Baer Asid, Bact, Md, 88; 2 paintings, lithograph prints, The Potomac Sch, McLean, Va, 96; 2 large paintings, The Madeira Sch, McLean, Va, 2004; large painting, John P Hunt, Philadelphia, Pa, 2004. *Exhib:* Wash Co Regional Exhib, Wash Co Mus, Hagerstown, Md, 82 & 84; Ann Nat Juried Exhib, Verizon Gallery, N Va Community College, Fairfax, Va, 2001; Ann Juried Nat Exhib, Arts Ctr, Shippensburg Univ, Shippensburg, Pa, 2003; group exhib, Artist Tree Exhib, Gallery Neptune, Bethesda, Mo, 2005; invitational, Int Salon of Small Works, New Arts Prog, Kutztown, Pa, 2006; invitational one-person, Featured Artist, Mary Condon Hodgson Gallery, Frederick Community College, Frederick, Md, 2006. *Pos:* Chair, Visual Art Dept, The Madiera Sch, McLean Va, 98-2003. *Teaching:* Instr, Art Studio, Episcopal High Sch, Jacksonville, Fla, 87-90, The Potomac Sch, McLean, Va, 92-97 & Susquehanna Univ, Selinsgrove, Pa, 2006-; interim instr, Studio, Sidwell Friend's Sch, Washington DC, 2005-2006. *Awards:* Master Teacher, Madiera Sch, 2001. *Bibliog:* Southern Accents Mag, 6/88; Madiera Today Mag, McLean, Va, Fall 2002; Hagerstown Herald Mail, 8/2006. *Mem:* Kids-in-Design, Prof Volunteer Orgn, 92-99; Nat Gallery Art Teacher Adv bd, 95-98; Wash Proj for the Arts, 2001-2002. *Media:* Acrylic. *Dealer:* Dabbert Gallery 76 S Palm Ave Sarasota Fla 34236; Foxhall Gallery Washington DC. *Mailing Add:* 2315 Edgewood Rd Harrisburg PA 17104

BOTTS, GREGORY
ARTIST
b Harrisburg, Pa, 52. *Work:* exhib in group shows at Mus Art RI Sch of Design, Providence, 1988. *Exhib:* One-man shows incl Earl McGrath Gallery, Los Angeles, 1987, Anne Plumb Gallery, New York City, 1989-94, Univ Arts Rosenwald-Wolf Gallery, Philadelphia, 1993, Ro Snell Gallery, Santa Barbara, Calif, 1993, Tony Shafrazi Gallery, New York City, 1993, CCS Gallery UCSB, Calif, 1997, others; exhib in group shows at Robin Lockett Gallery, Chicago, 1986, Richard Green Gallery, Los Angeles, 1990, NY Studio Sch Art Gallery, New York City, 1991, Cleveland Ctr Contemp Art, Ohio, 1994, Deutche Bank Lobby Gallery, NY, 1994, Baruch Col, 1995, Art Resources Transfer, New York City, 1998, Rotunda Gallery, Brooklyn, 1998, others. *Teaching:* Teacher var schs; lectr, NY Univ, NY Studio Sch, Brandeis Univ. *Awards:* Recipient award, Am Acad Arts and Letters; grantee Adolph and Esther Gottlieb grant. *Mem:* Nat Acad (assoc, 94, acad, 94). *Mailing Add:* 40 Ocean Pky Apt 1-L Brooklyn NY 11218

BOTWINICK, MICHAEL
MUSEUM DIRECTOR
b New York, NY, Nov 14, 43. *Study:* Rutgers Col, BA, 64; Columbia Univ, MA, 67. *Collection Arranged:* Coordr exhib, The Year 1200, Metrop Art Mus, NY, 69-70 & Masterpieces of 50 Centuries, 71. *Pos:* Asst cur, Medieval Art & the Cloisters, Metrop Mus Art, NY, 69, assoc cur, 70, asst cur in chief, 70-71; asst dir art, Philadelphia Mus Art, 71-74; dir, Newport Harbor Art Mus, 90-97, Univ Calif, Irvine, Calif, 97-98, Staten Island Inst Arts & Science, NY, 98; sr vpres, Knoedler-Monarco, 86-88; pres, Fine Art Group, 88-90; dir, Hudson River Mus, currently. *Teaching:* Instr, Columbia Univ, NY, 68-69 & City Univ NY, 69. *Awards:* Order of Leopold II, Belgian Govt, 80; Royal Order of Polar Star, Swedish Govt, 83. *Mem:* Am Asn Mus; Int Coun Mus; Col Art Asn; Asn Art Mus Dirs. *Mailing Add:* c/o Hudson River Museum 511 Warburton Ave Yonkers NY 10701

BOUCHARD, PAUL E
PAINTER
b Providence, RI, Sept 26, 1946. *Study:* Calif State Univ, Long Beach, BFA, 78. *Work:* Munic Collection, Beverly Hills, Calif; Art Mus, Calif State Univ, Long Beach; Coos Art Mus, Coos Bay, Ore; Vietnam Vet Mus Art, Dural, NSW, Australia; US State Dept, Washington; Nat Vietnam Vet Art Mus, Chicago. *Comn:* Paul Kasnits; C Lewis. *Exhib:* Artists You Should Know, Los Angeles Art Asn, Calif, 87; Healing the Wounds, Chapman Col, Orange, Calif, 88; Mixing It Up, Coos Art Mus, Ore, 88; one-man shows, Dreams of Ancient Answers, Franklin Furnace, NY, 89, Univ SDak, Vermillion, 91, Calif Brand Munic Gallery, Glendale, 92, Chabot Col, Hayward, Calif, Human Condition, Eastern Wash Univ, Cheney, 92, Vietnam Vets, Carriage House Art Ctr, Sydney, Australia, 92. *Awards:* Contribs to the Arts, Torrance, Calif, 85. *Bibliog:* Laurel Darrow (auth), Oh Say Can You See, Grants Pass Daily Courier 4/3/87; Russ Leadbrand (auth), Art Matters, Cambrian, 10/21/87; Keith Dilis (auth), Art, San Luis Obispo Telegram Tribune, 10/31/87. *Media:* Miscellaneous Media, Watercolor. *Dealer:* Los Angeles Co Mus Art Rental Gallery; Laguna Beach Mus Art Rental Gallery. *Mailing Add:* 166 Denton Rd Saratoga Springs NY 12866-9196

BOUCHER, TANIA KUNSKY
PAINTER, SCULPTOR
b Vilno, Russia, Feb 17, 1927; US citizen. *Study:* City Col New York, BS; Univ Pa, MS; Univ Del, BA; study with Tom Bostelle. *Work:* Delaware Theater Co, Wilmington, Del; W Chester Univ, Pa. *Exhib:* Univ Del, Newark, 92; Hotel Dupont Gallery, Wilmington, 92; Creative Visions, Lambertville, NJ, 92-93; Grand Opera House, Wilmington, Del, 93; Del Theater Co, Wilmington, 93; Aeolian Palace, Pocopson, Pa, 96; Chester Co Art Asn, Pa, 98; DeBottis Gallery, W Chester, 99 & 2000; W Chester Univ, 2002; Garrubo/Bazan, W Chester 2003; and others. *Pos:* Dir, Aeolian Palace Gallery, Pocopson, Pa, 75-85; ed, Aeolian Palace Press, 76-. *Teaching:* Art instr, Westtown Friends Sch, Pa, 64-69; art teacher, West Chester Adult Night Sch, 70-72. *Awards:* First Drawing Award, Chester Co Art Asn, 67; First Painting Award, Del Art Mus, 68; Judges Award, Old York Rd Art Guild, 69. *Bibliog:* Clint Collins (auth), biographical article, Delaware Today Mag, 9/81; Kerin Magill (auth), An exhibit of masks which reveal not conceal, Daily Local News, West Chester, Pa, 10/87; James G Blaine (auth), Boucher's mask's, The Kennett Paper, Pa 3/89; John Chambless (auth), Tania Boucher's World of faces, Daily Local News, West Chester, Pa, 10/96; and others. *Media:* Oil, Bronze, Prints. *Specialty:* Contemp painting & sculpture. *Publ:* Auth, Bostelle: Seated Self, 80; Bostelle Ninety Eight, 98. *Dealer:* Aeolian Palace Studio, Pocopson, Pa; Garrubo/Bazan Fine Art, W Chester, Pa. *Mailing Add:* Box 188 Mendenhall PA 19357

BOUCKAERT, HARM J G
ART DEALER
b Maastricht, Neth, June 7, 34; US citizen. *Study:* Neth Col Representation Abroad, BBA, 53. *Pos:* Owner, Harm Bouckaert Gallery Corp, 87. *Bibliog:* Articles, Venture Mag, 12/82 & Art Economist 5/31/82. *Specialty:* Contemp Am art. *Mailing Add:* Harm Bouckaert Gallery 100 Hudson St New York NY 10013

BOULDIN, MARSHALL JONES, III
PAINTER
b Dundee, Miss, Sept 6, 23. *Study:* Art Inst Chicago, 41-43; Belhaven Col, Jackson, Miss, Hon PhD Fine Arts, 72. *Work:* US House of Representatives, Wash; Fla State Capitol, Tallahassee; Sam J Ervin Mus, Morgantown, NC; Am Univ, Wash, DC; Mississippi State Capitol, Jackson. *Comn:* Portrait, children of Pres Richard Nixon, Republican Women, Wash, DC, 70; Sen Sam Ervin, NC Bar Assn, Charlotte, 74; Sen John Stennis, Miss State Univ Libr, Starkville, 77; Rep Claude Pepper, US House of Representatives, Wash, DC, 85. *Exhib:* One-man shows, Brooks Mus Art, Memphis, Tenn, 68, Lauren rodgers Mus, Laurel, Miss, 72, Fine Arts Mus of South, Mobile, Ala, 74, Mary Buie Mus Univ Miss, Oxford, 89, Miss Educ & Dev Ctr, Jackson, 89; Royal Soc British Artists, The Mall Galleries, London, Eng, 87, 88 & 89; Royal Soc of Portrait Painters, The Mall Galleries, London, Eng, 88, 89 & 90. *Bibliog:* Robert Thomas Jr (auth), His Portraits have Cachet in the South, The New York Times, 70; Jane Mortimer (auth), Protrait of a New Master, Miss Mag, 85; Stacy Doolittle (dir), Marshall Bouldin: A Delta Portrait (film), Miss Educ Television, 89. *Mem:* Nat Arts Club; Copley Soc Boston; Miss Inst Arts & Letters. *Media:* Oil. *Dealer:* Portraits Inc 985 Park Avenue New York NY 10028; Portrait Brokers of America 36B Church St Birmingham AL 35213. *Mailing Add:* 2500 Friars Point Rd Clarksdale MS 38614

BOURDEAU, ROBERT CHARLES
PHOTOGRAPHER
b Kingston, Ont, Nov 14, 31. *Study:* Univ Toronto; Queens Univ, Kingston, Ont. *Work:* Nat Gallery Can; Nat Film Board Can, Pub Arch Can, Ottawa; Smithsonian Inst; Mus d'art Contemp, Montreal. *Comn:* A photography study of bank archit, Parnassus Found, NY, 87. *Exhib:* Light 7, Hayden Gallery, 68; two-man exhib, New Eng Sch Photog, Cambridge, Mass, 75; Nat Gallery Can, 75; one-man exhib, Int Ctr Photog, NY, 80, Vancouver Art Gallery, 80, Art Gallery Ont, 81 & Aferimage Gallery, Dallas, 83. *Bibliog:* P Cousineau (auth), The Banff Purchase, John Wiley Publ, 79; monograph, Mintmark Press, 80. *Mem:* Royal Can Acad Arts. *Dealer:* Jane Corkin Gallery 179 John St Toronto M5T 1X4 Ont. *Mailing Add:* 1462 Chomley Crescent Ottawa ON K1G 0V1 Canada

BOURGEAULT, RONALD
APPRAISER
Pos: Antiques dealer, auctioneer, 70-; founder, principal, chief auctioneer, Northeast Auctions, Portsmouth, NH, 87-; owner, antiques shop, Salem, Mass, currently; Appraiser, Antiques Roadshow, WGBH-PBS, currently. *Teaching:* Lectr in field. *Awards:* Named one of Power Fifty Who Mattered Most, Art & Auction Mag, 2002. *Mem:* NH Antiques Dealers Asn; Nat Auctioneers Asn; Appraisers Asn Am. *Mailing Add:* Northeast Auctions 93 Pleasant St Portsmouth NH 03801

BOURGEOIS, DOUGLAS
PAINTER
b Gonzales, La, Aug 31, 51. *Study:* La State Univ, Baton Rouge, BFA, 74. *Work:* Southeastern Ctr for Contemp Art, Winston-Salem, NC; Nat Mus Am Art, Washington, DC; Virlane Found, New Orleans, La; Life Equitable, NY; Morris Mus Art, Augusta, Ga. *Exhib:* A New Quarter--Contemp New Orleans Artists, Lauren Rogers Libr & Mus Art, Laurel, Miss, 83; Gallery Review: New Orleans, Pensacola Mus Art, Pensacola, Fla, 86; Fine Arts Mus of the South, Mobile, Ala, 84; Boxes, Southeastern Ctr Contemp Art, Winston-Salem, NC, 85, Elvis, 87, SECCA 7 Eleven, 88; 1986 New Orleans Triennial, New Orleans Mus Art, La, 86; Visionary Imagists, Contemp Arts Ctr, New Orleans, La, 90; solo exhibs, Arthur Roger Gallery, New Orleans, La, 92, 93, 96 & 99; Grand Tradition: Permanent Collection in Context, Miss Mus Art, Jackson, Miss, 96; Body and Soul: Contemp Southern Figures, Columbus Mus Art, Ga, 97; The Ghost of Cornell, Contemp Art Ctr, New Orleans, La, 98; Spirit and Flesh, Art Mus WVa, Roanoke, 99. *Awards:* Visual Arts Fel; SECCA/RJR Indiv Arts Fel, Southeast 7, 87; La Div Arts Fel, 92. *Bibliog:* Roger Green (auth), Ten for the 90's, Art News, 90. *Media:* Oil. *Dealer:* Arthur Roger Gallery 136 Prince St New York NY 10012. *Mailing Add:* c/o Arthur Roger Gallery 432 Julia St New Orleans LA 70130

BOURGEOIS, LOUISE
SCULPTOR
b Paris, France, Dec 25, 1911; US Citizen. *Study:* Lycee Fenelon, Paris, Baccalaureate, 32; Sorbonne, 32-35; Ecole du Louvre, 36-37; Acad Beaux-Arts, 36-38; Acad Grande Chaumiere, 37-38; Atelier Fernand Leger, 38, Vaclav Vytlacil, 39-40; numerous hon degrees from US univs, 77-95. *Work:* Mus Mod Art, Whitney Mus Am Art, Metrop Mus Art, NY; NY Univ; Albright-Knox Art Gallery, Buffalo, NY; Denver Art Mus, Colo; Mus d'Art Mod, Paris; Storm King Art Ctr, Mountainville, NY. *Exhib:* Fine Prints for Mass Production, Brooklyn Mus, NY, 39; Arts for Victory: An Exhib of Painting, Sculpture & Graphic Arts, Metrop Mus Art, NY, 42; The Arts in Therapy, Mus Mod Art, 43; San Francisco Mus Art, 44 & 82; Mus Mod Art, NY, 44-45, 49, 51, 61-62, 67, 69, 74-76, 84-85 & 90-91; Whitney Mus Am Art, 45-93; Los Angeles Co Mus Art, 45; Pa Acad Fine Arts, 47; Brooklyn Mus, 48, 49, 77; Inst Contemp Art, Boston, 53; Walker Art Ctr, 54; Dallas Mus Contemp Art, 60; The New American Painting & Sculpture, The First Generation, Mus Mod Art, 69; OK Harris, NY, 78; Retrospective, Mus Mod Art, NY, 82-83 & 94-95; Soloman R Guggenheim Mus, NY, 92 & 93; solo exhibs, Galeria Karsten Greve, Milan, 94 & 96, Univ Art Mus, Univ Calif, Berkeley, 96, Gallery Paule Anglim, San Francisco, 96, Baumgartner Galleries, Washington, 96, Rupertinum, Salzburg, Austria, 96, Galerie Samuel Lallouz, Montreal, Can, 96 & Gallery Joseloff, Univ Hartford, 96; Tate Gallery, London, 95; Inside the Invisible, Inst Contemp Art, Boston, 96; The Material Imagination, Solomon R Guggenheim Mus, NY, 96; Passions Privées, Mus Mod Art, Paris, 96; Portrait of the Artists, Anthony d'Offay Gallery, London, 96; Montgomery Glasoe Fine Art, Minneapolis, 96; Robert Miller Gallery, 96; 25th Anniversary Show, Douglass Col, Rutgers Univ, 96; Signs of Life, Melbourne Int Biennial, Victoria, 99; Whitney Biennial, Whitney Mus Am Art, NY, 97. *Pos:* New Sch Soc Research, New York City, 1987. *Teaching:* Instr sculpture, Brooklyn Col, 63 & 68; instr sculpture, Pratt Inst, 64-65; field fac sculpture, Goddard Col, 71; instr, Cooper Union, NY, 78-79; Instr, Md Art Inst, Baltimore, 1984. *Awards:* Mayor's Award, New York Maison Francaise, New York Univ, 93; Art Prize, NORD/LB, 92; Biennial Award & Purchase Prize, Ueno Royal Mus, Tokyo & Hakone Open-Air Mus, Kanagawa-ken, Japan, 95; National Medal of Arts, 97; and others. *Bibliog:* Brigid Grauman (auth), Hoots for Mr Hoet's huge festival of art that's hot, Wall Street J, 7/14/92; Michael Kimmelman (auth), After many a summer, a sculptor comes of age, New York Times, sect 2, p 1, 27, 8/30/92, reprinted Int Herald Tribune, p16, 9/1/92; Keith Steward (auth), Psycho: Kunst Hall, Art forum, 9/92. *Mem:* Am Abstract Artists; Fel Am Acad Art & Sci, Boston; Am Acad & Inst Arts & Letts, NY; Distinguished Artist award for lifetime achievement 1989; Nat Acad (assoc, 90, acad, 94). *Media:* Mixed. *Publ:* Auth, Sculpture of the 80's (video), Business Arts Inc, 91. *Mailing Add:* Robert Miller Gallery 524 W 26th St Ground fl New York NY 10001-5541

BOURQUE, LOUISE
FILMMAKER
Study: Univ de Moncton, BA (comm), 1986; Concordia Univ, BFA (film produc), 1990; Sch Art Inst, Chicago, MFA (filmmaking), 1992. *Exhib:* Dir Films: The People in the House; 1994, Going Back Home, 2000; Self Portrait Post Mortem, 2002; The Bleeding Heart of It, 2005. *Teaching:* Film instr, Sch Mus Fine Arts, Boston. *Awards:* Whitney Biennial, Whitney Mus Art, NYC 2006. *Mailing Add:* 230 The Fenway Boston MA 02115

BOUTIS, TOM
PAINTER, PRINTMAKER
b New York, NY, Aug 25, 22. *Study:* Cooper Union, New York, BFA, 48; Skowhegan Sch Painting & Sculpture, summer 51; Cooper Union, hon BS. *Work:* Art Inst Chicago: CIBA-Geigy Collection, Ardsley, NY; Canton Art Inst, Ohio; Colby Col; Everson Mus, Syracuse, NY; Russell Sage Col, Albany NY; St Michaels Hosp, Newark, NJ; Atlanta Univ, New Orleans, La; Billard Univ, New Orleans, La. *Comn:* Drawings, NY Hilton Collection Am Art, 62. *Exhib:* One-man shows, Landmark Gallery, NY, 73, 75 & 77 Am Acad Arts & Letters, 88 & 89, Nat Acad, 91 & Greek Copnsulate, 94; Drawings Exhib, Uffizzi Mus, Florence, Italy, 57; Selected Painters of Soho, Lehigh Univ Mus, 74; CIBA-Geigy Collection, Summit Art Mus, NJ, 74; Gathering of the Avant Garde, Kenkeleba, NY, 88; and others. *Teaching:* Artist in residence painting, Summer Art Prog, Cooper Union, 69. *Awards:* Mark Rothko Found, 76; Nat Endowment for the Arts, 76; Adolphe Esther Gotleib Found Grant, 83; Am Acad Art Inst, 88-90; Rockefeller Found, Bellagio, Italy, 89. *Bibliog:* Sidney Delavante, (auth), Arts, 75; Peter Frank (auth), Art News, 77. *Mem:* Nat Acad. *Media:* Monoprints, Oils; Collage. *Mailing Add:* 162 E 82nd St New York NY 10028

BOVE, RICHARD
PAINTER, EDUCATOR
b Brooklyn, NY, Oct 21, 20. *Study:* Pratt Inst, BFA; Art Students League; Brera Acad, Milan, Italy. *Exhib:* Am Acad Design, NY; Philadelphia Mus Art; Corcoran Gallery Art, Wash, DC; Whitney Mus Art & Metrop Mus Art, NY; Brooklyn Mus. *Teaching:* Instr painting, Art Students League, 55-65; chmn dept painting, Pratt Inst, 70-74, prof painting, Grad Sch, 73-. *Awards:* Nat Acad Design Award; Louis Comfort Tiffany Found Award; Fulbright Fel, Italy. *Mem:* life mem Art Students League. *Media:* Concrete, Plastics. *Mailing Add:* 501 Atwood Ct Newtown PA 18940

BOWEN, CONSTANCE LEE
ART DEALER, CONSULTANT
b Ann Arbor, Mich, July 12, 52. *Study:* Northern Ill Univ, BA(art hist), 74; Univ Ill, MA(art hist), 78 & cert mus studies, 79; Ind Univ, MBA, 84. *Collection Arranged:* Henry Holmes Smith: Non-Camera Photographer (auth, catalog), Ind Univ Art Mus, 82; Dedication Exhibition: Selections from the Permanent Collection, 85 & Contemporary Virginia Woman Artists, 85, Sweet Briar Col Art Gallery; A Tribute to Alma Eikerman, Master Craftsman (auth, catalog), Ind Univ Art Mus, 85. *Pos:* Cur 19th & 20th century art, Ind Univ Art Mus, Bloomington, 79-83; dir, Sweet Briar Col Art Gallery, 84-86 & Francis Chapin estate collection, 90-96; assoc dir art, Josyln Art Mus, Omaha, Nebr, 86-87; pvt art dealer, Chicago, 88-; cur, Harold Haydon Estate Collection, 94-. *Teaching:* Dir, Arts Mgt Prog, Sweet Briar Col, Va, 84-86. *Mem:* Ill Arts Studies Found (pres, 93-). *Res:* 19th and 20th century European and American art. *Publ:* Auth, Henry Holmes Smith: Non Camera Photographer, Ind Univ Art Mus dedication exhib, 82; A Tribute to Alma Eikerman: Master Craftsman, 85, Ind Univ Art Mus, Bloomington

BOWEN, PAUL
SCULPTOR
b Wales, Britain, July 12, 51. *Study:* Chester Sch Art, 68-69; Newport Col Art, Wales, diploma, 69-72; Md Inst Col Art, Baltimore, MFA, 72-74. *Work:* Solomon R Guggenheim Mus, NY; Mus Fine Art, Boston; Welsh Arts Coun, Cardiff, Wales; Provincetown Art Asn & Mus, Mass; Walker Art Ctr; Fogg Art Mus, Cambridge, Mass. *Comn:* Shapeshifting, Uchidayoukou Corp, Tokyo. *Exhib:* one man shows, Mus Contemp Art, Ghent, Belgium, 89, Saidye Bronfman Ctr, Montreal, Can, 90, Cherry Stone Gallery, Wellfleet, Mass, 91, 93 & 98, Howard Yezerski Gallery, Boston, 93, 97-98, Provincetown Art Asn Mus, Mass, 96 & New Eng Sch Art, Boston, 98; Jaffe-Fried Gallery, Dartmouth Coll, Hanover, NH, 74-04; Cape Mus of Fine Art, Dennis, Mass, 74-04. *Collection Arranged:* Innovations in Contemp Sculpture, Aldrich Mus, Ridgefield, Conn, 88. *Pos:* Artist in residence, Dartmouth Coll, Hanover, NH, 05. *Teaching:* Truro Ctr Arts, Mass; Fine Arts Work Ctr, Provincetown, Mass. *Awards:* Welsh Arts Coun Award to Artists, 78; Fel, Mass Artists Found, 81 & New Eng Found Arts, Boston; Pollock-Krasner Found Grant, 87. *Bibliog:* Ann Wilson Lloyd (auth), Artifacts Reborn, Contemporanea, 10/89; BH Friedman (auth), Sculpture as Autobiography, Paul Bowen (exhib catalog), Provincetown Art Asn & Mus, 95; Sara London (auth), Paul Bowen: Beyond the Mythological 1986-1996 (exhib catalog), Provincetown Art Asn & Mus, 96; Jennifier Liese (auth), Paul Bowen: Sculptures 1974-2004 (catalog essay), Jaffee-Fried Gallery, Dartmouth Coll,. *Media:* Mixed. *Mailing Add:* 130 Dover Rd Williamsville VT 05362-9721

BOWEN-FORBES, JORGE C
PAINTER
b Georgetown, Guyana, May 16, 37. *Study:* Chelsea Sch Design, MFA, Eng, 72. *Work:* Nat Collection, Georgetown, Guyana; El Paso Mus Art, Tex; Kindercare Corp & Sellers Investment Corp, Montgomery, Ala; McCreary Cummings Fine Art Collection, Washington, Iowa; Leon Loards Gallery; Bomani Gallery, San Francisco. *Exhib:* Nat Sun Carnival, El Paso Mus, Tex, 74; Am Watercolor Soc, 74, 75, 77 & 84; Allied Artists of Am, Nat Acad, 75; African/Am Art of 80's, Mus African Arts, Buffalo, NY, 82; Nat Acad Design, NY; Frye Mus, El Paso, Tex; Wichita Centennial,

Kans; Newark Mus; 10 one-man exhibs worldwide. *Pos:* Art dir, Corbin Advt Agency, Bridgetown, Barbados; tech advisor, Ministry of Information & Culture, Barbados; Comml artist, Guyana Lithographic, Georgetown; nat juror Nat Arts Club, New York, 85, Nat Soc Painters in Casein and Acrylic. *Teaching:* Burrowes Sch Art, Guyana. *Awards:* Gold Medal of Honor, Allied Artists of Am, 75; High Winds Medal, Am Watercolor Soc; Gold Medal of Honor, Knickerbocker Artists, 78; Silver Medal of Honor, Allied Artists of NY, 78. *Mem:* Nat Watercolor Soc; Signature mem Am Watercolor Soc; Nat Soc Painters in Casein & Acrylics; Audobon Artists Am; Knickerbocker Artists. *Media:* Watercolor. *Publ:* Am Artist Mag, 85; Splash 2, Am Contemp Watercolors, 92; Creative Watercolors, Rockport, 96; Best of Watercolors, Rockport, 96; Best of Oil Painting, Rockport, 96; Best in Acrylic Painting; Am Poetry Ann. *Dealer:* Leon Loard Gallery 2781 Zelda Rd Montgomery Al 36106. *Mailing Add:* PO Box 1821 Oakland CA 94612

BOWER, GARY DAVID
PAINTER, DIRECTOR
b Dayton, Ohio, May 10, 40. *Study:* Ohio State Univ, BA(philos), 62 & MFA(painting), 65. *Work:* Whitney Mus Am Art, NY; Allen Art Mus, Oberlin, Ohio; Akron Art Inst; Dayton Art Inst; Walker Art Ctr, Minneapolis; Cincinnati Art Mus, Ohio; Cleve Art Mus; Richmond (Va) Mus of Art; Springfield (Mo) Art Mus. *Exhib:* Four Painters, Leo Castelli Warehouse Gallery, NY, 69; one-man shows, OK Harris Gallery, NY, 69 & 72, Univ Ky, 71, Akron Art Inst, 72 & Edward Thorp Gallery, NY, 84, Cleveland Ctr Contemp Art, 88, 69-93 abstracts, 93, Dayton (Ohio) Visual Arts Ctr, 94, Grosvenor Gallery, SUNY, Cobleskil, NY, 2000, Goreman Gallery, Hartwick Coll., Oneonta, NY, 2001; Whitney Mus Ann, 70. *Pos:* Dir, Ecole des Arts En France, 94-98. *Teaching:* Staff critic painting, Dept Educ, Whitney Mus Am Art, 68-74; lectr painting, State Univ NY, 85-87; assoc prof, Antioch Col, 88-94; vis prof, Ohio State Univ, Columbus, Ohio, 98-; adj prof SUNY, Cobleskill, NY, 2000-. *Awards:* James Broadus Award, Chicago Art Inst, 67; Achievement in Painting, Ohio State Fair, 70; Grant, Nat Endowment Arts, 82. *Bibliog:* Carter Ratcliff (auth), Gary Bower at the New Gallery, Art Am, 5-6/78; Robert Berlind (auth), Gary Bower at Max Protech, Art Am, 1/81; Michael Klein (auth), Gary Bower, Arts, 5/82; and others. *Media:* Oil & Acrylic on Canvas. *Dealer:* Linda Schwartz Gallery PO Box 120763 Covington KY 41012

BOWER, JOHN ARNOLD, JR
ARCHITECT, EDUCATOR
b Philadelphia, Pa, Apr 22, 30. *Study:* Student, Pa State Col, 49; Student, OH State Univ, 51; Univ Pa, BArch with hons, 53. *Comn:* Prin works incl Vance Hall, Wharton Grad Ctr (gold medal Am Inst of Architects Philadelphia chapter 1973, design citation 1968), Int House (gold medal Am Inst of Architects Philadelphia chapter 1967), Milles Sculpture Group (silver medal Am Inst of Archits Philadelphia chapter 1972), Gallery at Market E (cert excellence - urban design 1978), Soc Hill Townhouses (1st hon award Pa Soc Architts 1966), Princeton Forrestal Village (Merit award Pa Soc Archits 1987), Market St E Transp Mall Ctr, One Reading Ctr Off Tower, Baltimore Mus Art (restoration, additions), 1234 Market St Off Bldg, 1500 Walnut St Off Bldg, Marriott Philadelphia Conv Ctr Hotel. *Pos:* Draftsman John A. Bower, Senior Archit, Philadelphia, 50-51; designer Philadelphia Planning Comn, 53-54; sr designer, Vincent G. Kling Archits, Philadelphia, 54-61; partner, Bower & Fradley Archits, 61-78, Bower Lewis Thrower Archits, Philadelphia, 78-; mem design adv panel Dept Housing and Community Develop, Baltimore, 64-. *Teaching:* Prof archit, Univ Pa. *Awards:* Albert F Schenk traveling fel Univ Pa 54; fel, Fontainbleau Sch Fine Arts-Music, Paris, 54. *Mem:* Fel Am Inst of Archits (nat urban planning and design comt 74-75, nat comt on design 76-78); Nat Acad of Design (assoc, 75, acad, 94), Carpenter's Co, Hexagon Hon Soc, Tau Sigma Delta Clubs: Germantown Cricket. *Mailing Add:* Bower Lewis Thrower Archits 1216 Arch St Ste 9 Philadelphia PA 19107-2835

BOWERS, ANDREA
VIDEO AND INSTALLATION ARTIST
b Wilmington, OH, 65. *Study:* Bowling Green State Univ, BFA, 87; Calif Inst Arts, MFA, 92. *Exhib:* One-woman shows, Damaged Goods, Bliss, Pasadena, Calif, 94, Spanish Box, Santa Monica, Calif, 96, Spectacular Appearances, Santa Monica Mus Art, Calif, 98, Moving Equilibrium, Sara Meltzer Gallery, NY, 99, Intimate Strangers, 2000, Box with Dance of Its Own Making, Chouakri Brahms, Berlin, 2002, From Mouth to Ear, Goldman Tevis, Los Angeles, 2002, Virtual Arena, Sara Meltzer Gallery, NY, 2002, Magical Politics, Chouakri Brahms, Berlin, 2003, Nonviolent Civil Disobedience Training, Sara Meltzer Gallery, NY, 2004, Magazin 4 Voralberger Kunstverein, Austria, 2004, Mary Goldman Gallery, Los Angeles, 2004; group shows, Whitney Biennial Am Art, Whitney Mus Am Art, 2004, 100 Artist See God, Laguna Art Mus, San Francisco, 2003-04, Rendered, Sara Meltzer Gallery, NY, 2003, COLA 2003, Munic Art Gallery, Barnsdale Art PK, Los Angeles, 2003, Time-Share, Sara Meltzer Gallery, NY, 2002, Everybody Now, Bertha & Karl Leubsdorf Gallery, NY, 2001, Subject Plural, Contemp Arts Mus, Houston, 2001, Moving Pictures, Galerie Tommy Lund, Copenhagen, Denmark, 2000, Me Mine, Luckman Fine Arts Gallery, Calif, 99, Unfinished Hist, Walker Art Ctr, Minneapolis, 98-99, Dave's Not Here, Three Day Weekend, Los Angeles, 94. *Awards:* Regional Fel Visual Arts Sculpture, Western States Arts Fedn/Nat Endowment Arts, 95-96; Fel Visual Arts, City LA, 2003. *Mailing Add:* c/o Sara Meltzer Gallery 516 West 20th St New York NY 10011

BOWERS, CHERYL See Olsen Bergman, Ciel (Cheryl) Bowers

BOWES, BETTY MILLER
PAINTER, CONSULTANT
b Philadelphia, Pa. *Study:* Moore Col Art; Univ Pa; George W Elkins Europ Fel. *Work:* Philadelphia Mus Art, Pa Acad Fine Arts, Philadelphia; Reading Mus, Pa; Nat Acad Design, NY; Univ Southern Calif, Los Angeles. *Comn:* Maquette for tapestry, Sun Oil Co Inc, Radnor, Pa, 76 & comn by Mr & Mrs Harvey Stack, NY, 78. *Exhib:* Am Watercolor Soc, Nat Acad, NY, 58-79; Philadelphia Art Festival, Philadelphia Mus, 65; one-man shows, Reading Mus, Pa, 69 & Lehigh Mem Gallery, Bethlehem, 70; Nat Acad Ann, NY, 70-; Del Mus Ann, Wilmington Soc Fine Arts, 71; Pa Acad Fine Arts Ann, Philadelphia. *Pos:* Art consult, Sun Oil Co Inc, Radnor, 75-. *Awards:* Bronze Medal, 75 & 77, Silver Medal, 79 & Gold Medal of Honor, 85, Am Watercolor Soc. *Bibliog:* Norman Kent (auth), 100 Watercolor Techniques, 68, Wendon Blake (auth), Complete Guide to Acrylic Painting, 71 & Edward Betts (auth), Creative Landscape Painting, 78, Watson-Guptill. *Mem:* Am Watercolor Soc; Nat Acad Design (assoc, 75, acad, 94); Philadelphia Art Alliance; Philadelphia Watercolor Club; Audubon Artists. *Media:* Acrylic. *Dealer:* Newman & Saunders Gallieres Wayne PA. *Mailing Add:* 301 McClenaghan Mill Rd Wynnewood PA 19096-1012

BOWLER, JOSEPH, JR
PAINTER, ILLUSTRATOR
b Forest Hills, NY, Sept 4, 28. *Study:* Charles E Cooper Studios, New York; Art Students League. *Work:* Ann Exhib of Published Work for 1977, Soc Illusr 78. *Comn:* Portraits, Rose Kennedy, Rose Kennedy Wing, Albert Einstein Hosp, 71; Geri DeGaulle, Time cover; Julie & David Eisenhower, Saturday Evening Post cover; Family of Dr & Mrs Ellis Jones, GA, 90 - 05; Daughters of Mr & Mrs Hank Cram, SC 98 - 04. *Exhib:* Ann Exhib of Published Work for 1977, Soc Illusr, 78. *Pos:* judge, Portrait Soc of Am, self-portrait contest, 2006. *Teaching:* Instr painting, Parsons Sch Design, New York, 68-72; instr, MFA Independent Study Degree Prog, Syracuse Univ, 80-86. *Awards:* Artist of Yr, Artists' Guild New York, 67; Elected to the Illustr Hall of Fame, 92. *Bibliog:* Cory SerVaas (auth), Artist in the White House, Saturday Evening Post, summer 72; Joe Bowler--Artist Illustrator (film), & Arts the Thing Joe Bowler--Portraits (film), SCE-TV; Artist Joe Bowler, Southern Accents, winter 82. *Mem:* Soc Illusr. *Media:* Oil. *Specialty:* Joe Bowler Collection; The Red Piano Gallery, Hilton Head Island, SC. *Publ:* Portraits, The Artists Mag, 9/88; At My Easel, Thoughts of a Master Portraitist, Internat Artist, 12/2000. *Dealer:* Marilyn C Bowler Artist's Representation 9 Baynard Cove Rd Hilton Head Island SC 29928. *Mailing Add:* Nine Baynard Cove Rd Hilton Head Island SC 29928

BOWLES, MARIANNE VON RECKLINGHAUSEN See von Recklinghausen, Marianne Bowles

BOWLING, FRANK
PAINTER
b Bartica, Guyana, Feb 29, 36; US & Guyanese citizen. *Study:* Slade Sch Fine Art, Univ London; ARCA; Royal Col Art, London. *Work:* Contemp Art Soc, Tate Gallery, London; NJ State Mus, Trenton; Mus Mod Art, Whitney Mus & Metropolitan Mus, NY; Mus Fine Arts, Boston. *Exhib:* Whitney Ann, 69-72; Artist Immigrants to Am 1876-1976, Hirshhorn Mus, Washington, DC; solo exhibs, Whitney Mus Am Art, 71, Tibor de Nagy Gallery, NY, 75, 76, 79, 80 & 82, Serpentine Gallery, London, 86, Crawford Art Gallery, Cork, Ireland, 88, Royal West Eng Acad, Bristol, 89, Wilmer Jennings at Kenkeleba, NY, 91 & Nat Acad Sci, Washington DC, 93; Currier Gallery Art, Manchester, NH, 82; Art Ctr Hargate, St Pauls Sch, Concord, NH, 82; Heckscher Mus, Huntington, NY, 82; Kresge Art Ctr Gallery, Mich State Univ, 82. *Pos:* Independent freelance lectr. *Awards:* Guggenheim Fel, 67 & 73; Creative Artists Pub Serv Award, 75; Arts Coun Gt Brit Award, 77. *Mem:* Chelsea Arts Club, London, Eng. *Media:* Acrylic, Oil. *Dealer:* AFTU Bill Hodges Gallery 24 W 57th St New York NY 10019

BOWLING, GARY ROBERT
PAINTER
b Lamar, Mo, Feb 1, 48. *Study:* Mo Southern State Col, BS(art educ), 70, Univ Ark, Fayetteville, MFA, 74. *Work:* Sheldon Mem Art Gallery, Lincoln, Nebr; Mitchell Art Mus, Mt Vernon, Ill; Sioux City Art Ctr, Iowa; Johnson Co Community Col, Kans; Iowa State Univ, Ames; Univ Mo, Columbia; Univ Iowa, Iowa City. *Comn:* Paintings, Northwestern Life Insurance, Minneapolis, Minn, Iowa State Gateway Ctr, Ames, Norwest Bank, Hopkins, Minn, Fairview-Southdale Hosp, Minneapolis; McDonald's Hamb Univ, Chicago; N Lake Shore Hyatt, Chicago; Farm Bureau Hdq, Des Moines, Iowa. *Exhib:* Prairie Vistas, Joslyn Art Mus, Omaha, Nebr, 86; Contemp Landscape, Inst Creative Arts, Fairfield, Iowa, 87; Brunnier Art Mus, Ames, Iowa, 88; Mid Am Landscape, SW Minn, St Univ, Marshall, 89; New Masters, Huntington Mus Art, WVA, 92; Land of the Fragile Giants, Brunnier Art Mus, Ames, Iowa, 94; Midwestern Romanticism (with catalog), Ill Arts Coun, Lakeview Mus Art, Peoria & Beach Mus Art, Manhattan, Kans, 96-97. *Teaching:* Instr painting & drawing, Univ Ark, Fayetteville, 74; chmn art dept, Westmar Col, Le Mars, Iowa, 74-83. *Bibliog:* John Couper (auth), A sense of place, Joplin Mag, 86; C Butler et al (auths), Of Vapor & Denser Surfaces, (exhib catalog), Mitchell Mus, 87; Mark Stegmaier, Gary Bowling, Am Artist Mag, 88. *Mem:* Yaddo Fel. *Media:* Oil, Mixed Media. *Publ:* Auth, Land of the Fragiile Giants, Univ Iowa Press; Lela Gilbert, Lit by the Sun, Carpe Diem Books, 2001. *Dealer:* Groveland Gallery 25 Groveland Terr Minneapolis MN 55403; Olson-Larson Gallery 203 5th St W Des Moines IA 50265; Michael FitzSimmons Gallery 311 W Superior, Chicago Ill 60610. *Mailing Add:* PO Box 207 Lamar MO 64759

BOWLING, KATHERINE
PAINTER
b Washington, DC, 55. *Study:* Va Commonwealth Univ, BFA, 78. *Work:* Metrop Mus Art, NY; Orlando Mus Contemp Art, Fla; Phoenix Art Mus, Ariz; Brooklyn Mus Art, NY; Fisher Landau Center, Long Island City, NY. *Exhib:* Va Arts Biennial, Va Mus Fine Arts, 79; New Painting, Va Mus Fine Arts, 83; One-woman shows, Albright-Knox Mem Gallery, Buffalo, NY, 88, Blum Helman, Los Angeles, 90 & NY, 90, 92 & 94 & Orlando Mus Art, Fla, 94, Joseph Helman Gallery, NY, 96, 98, 01; Nocturnal Landscape, Whitney Mus Am Art, 89; group show, The Modern Landscape,

Queens Libr Gallery, Queensborough, NY, 96; Landscapes, David Floria Gallery, Woody Creek, Colo, 97; The Secret Garden, The Art Mus at Fla Int Univ, Miami, 97; Joseph Helman Gallery, NY, 98, 2000; Exurbia, Gallery Luisotti, Santa Monica, Calif, 2000; and others. *Awards:* Mid Atlantic Arts Found Fel, 88; NY State Found for the Arts Fel, 89; Grant, Nat Endowment Arts, 91. *Bibliog:* Grace Glueck (auth), Katherine Bowling, The New York Times, 4/98; Robert M Murdock (auth), Katherine Bowling, Review, 4/98; Mary Hrbacek (auth), Land to See (exhib catalog), Joseph Helman Gallery, 01

BOWLT, JOHN
ART HISTORIAN, EDUCATOR
b London, Eng, Dec 6, 43. *Study:* Univ Birmingham, Eng, BA, 65 & MA, 66; Moscow Univ, USSR, 66-68; Univ St Andrews, Scotland, PhD, 71. *Pos:* Dir, Inst of Modern Russian Cult, 79-. *Teaching:* Lectr Russian, Univ St Andrews, Scotland, 68-69; asst prof Russian, Univ Kans, Lawrence, 70-71; prof Russian art & lang, Univ Tex, Austin, 71-88; prof Russian art & lang, Univ Southern Calif, Los Angeles, Calif, 88-. *Awards:* Woodrow Wilson Nat Fel, 71; Fel Nat Humanities Inst, Yale Univ, 77-78; Fulbright-Hays Award to France, 81; Int Res & Exchanges Bd, 86, 88, 90, 96; Borehard Found to France, 95; Raubenheimer Outstanding Senior Faculty Award, Univ Southern Calif, 97. *Mem:* Am Asn Advan Slavic Studies. *Res:* Russian art and architecture of 18th, 19th and 20th centuries. *Mailing Add:* Dept Slavic Languages Univ Southern Calif Bldg THH 408 Mailcode 4353 Los Angeles CA 90081

BOWMAN, BRUCE
PAINTER, ART WRITER
b Dayton, Ohio, Nov 23, 38. *Study:* San Diego City Col, Calif, AA; Calif State Univ, Los Angeles, BA & MA; Univ Calif, Los Angeles. *Exhib:* Cypress Col, Calif, 77; Designs Recycled Gallery, Fullerton, Calif, 77; Pierce Col, Los Angeles, 78; Pepperdine Univ, Malibu, 78; Leopold-Gold Gallery, Santa Monica, 80-81. *Teaching:* Instr art, West Los Angeles Col, Culver City, 69-83, chmn art dept, 75-76, 83; instr art, Cypress Col, 76-77. *Media:* Oil. *Res:* Contemp art forms and techniques. *Interests:* Karate (black belt). *Publ:* Auth, articles in Arts & Activities Mag, Design Mag & Sch Arts Mag; Shaped Canvas, 76 & Toothpick Sculpture & Ice Cream Stick Art, 76, Sterling; Ideas: How to Get Them, R & E Publ, 85. *Dealer:* The Options Gallery 2665 Shell Beach Rd Shell Beach CA 93449. *Mailing Add:* 28322 Rey De Copas Malibu CA 90265

BOWMAN, GEORGE LEO
PAINTER
b Newburyport, Mass, Dec 25, 35. *Study:* Boston Sch Mus Fine Arts, 60; Tufts Univ, Medford, Mass, BS, 60. *Work:* Harvard Univ, Brookline, Mass; Va Mortgage Co, Norfolk; Honeywell Corp, Minn. *Exhib:* Adelson Gallery, 70-72, Copley Soc, 70-73, Boston, Mass; Grand Cent Gallery, NY, 73-76; Rockport Art Asn, Mass, 74-82; Joseph Kilbridge Gallery, Groton, Mass, 89. *Pos:* Asst art dir, DC Heath Publ Co, Boston, Mass, 63-67; illusr & designer, ASEC, Burlington, Mass, 78-92. *Teaching:* Instr design & drawing, Boston Sch Mus Fine Arts, 63-70. *Awards:* Nat Casein Show Painting Award, NY; Aldro Hibbard Painting Award, Rockport Art Asn, Mass; Copley Soc Painting Award, Boston, Mass. *Media:* Oil. *Publ:* New York Life Calender, 80-81. *Mailing Add:* 255 Percival Dr West Barnstable MA 02668-1222

BOWMAN, JEFF RAY
EDUCATOR, ADMINISTRATOR
b Oneida, Ky, Sept 5, 43. *Study:* Eastern Ky Univ, AB, 65; Ball State Univ, MA, 69, EdD(art, admin, coun psychol), 71; Yale Univ, 77. *Teaching:* Art instr, Jackson Co Sch Syst, McKee, Ky, 65-66; asst & doctoral fel, Dept Art & Teachers Col, Ball State Univ, 68-71; prog chmn art educ, Univ Houston, 71-74; guest lectr, Art & Pub Sch Groups, Tex & Miss, 73-75; prof art, Univ Southern Miss, 74-, chmn dept, 74-82. *Awards:* Nat Endowment for Humanities Award, 77. *Mem:* Nat Art Educ Asn; Ky Guild Artists & Craftsmen; Hattiesburg Civic Asn; Tex Art Educ Asn; Miss Alliance for Arts Educ. *Publ:* Coauth, Parochial Education Within the Diocese of Fort Wayne-South Bend, Ind, Phase I, Educ Serv Assocs, Muncie, 70; auth, Meeting the needs, Art Teacher, fall 74; auth, The spirit of the mountains, Southern Quart, 1/78; plus many others

BOWMAN, JERRY W
PAINTER
b Columbia City, Ind, Aug 3, 52. *Study:* Kalamazoo Col, BA, 74; Univ Mich, Ann Arbor; Kalamazoo Inst Arts. *Work:* Upjohn Co Corp Collection; Pharmacia Inc, Corp Collection; Springfield Art Mus, Mo; Pfizer Inc, Corp Collection; Bronson Mem Hospital Collection. *Comn:* painting, George Handley, Denver, Colo, 98; painting, Aaron Maule, Belfast, Ireland, 2000. *Exhib:* Watercolor West, Art & Cult Ctr, Brea, Calif, 92, 94, 96 & 97, 99; San Diego Watercolor Soc Int Exhib, Poway Ctr Performing Arts, Calif, 93; Watercolor USA, Springfield Art Mus, Mo, 93-94, 97, 2000-2001 & 2003; Rocky Mountain Nat, 93-94, 96, 98, 2000, 2003 & 2006; Northwest Watercolor Soc, Howard/Mandville Gallery, Kirkland, Wash, 94; Philadelphia Watercolor Club 95th Exhib, Pa, 95; Watercolor Now: Best of WC, Springfield Art Mus, 2003; Red River Watercolor Soc Ann, 2005; Adirondack OFAG Ann, 2006. *Awards:* 1st Prize, Kalamazoo Inst Arts, 99; Golden Palette Award, Rocky Mountain Nat, 2000; Major Cash Award, Watercolor USA, 2000 & 2003; many others. *Mem:* Kalamazoo Inst Art; Sig mem, Watercolor W & Rocky Mountain Nat Watermedia Soc; Watercolor USA. *Media:* Watercolor. *Publ:* Splash 5: Best of Watercolor, NLight, Cincinnati, OH, 98. *Mailing Add:* 83626 Waldron Lawton MI 49065

BOWMAN, JOHN
PAINTER
b Sayre, Pa, 53. *Study:* Rutgers Univ, BFA, 76. *Exhib:* Solo exhibs, Nine Gallery, NY, 83, White Columns & Virtual Garrison Gallery, New York, 84, Holly Solomon Gallery, NY, 85, 86, 87 & 89 & Jon Oulman Gallery, Minneapolis, Minn, 88; Petits Tableaux, Galerie Charles Cartwright, Paris, France, 86; Interiors, Proctor Art Ctr, Bard Col, Annandale-on-Hudson, 88; The Silent Baroque (with catalog), Galerie Thaddaeus Ropac, Salzburg, Austria, 89; Romance & Irony (traveling exhib), Mus Western Australia, Perth, Sydney, Australia, Auckland, NZ & Tampa, Fla, 90; Fernando Alcolea, Barcelona, Spain, 90. *Bibliog:* Richard Martin (auth), Fictions, Arts, 2/88; Eleanor Heartney (auth), Review: Fictions, Artnews, 2/88; Kim Levin (auth), Choices: Dwelling, Village Voice, 1/3/89. *Mailing Add:* Tibor Denagy Gallery 724 Fifth Ave New York NY 10019

BOWMAN, KEN
PAINTER
b Denver, Colo, Mar 28, 37. *Study:* Univ Colo; Art Inst Chicago, BFA, 63. *Work:* Utah Mus Fine Arts, Salt Lake City; Univ Art Mus, Berkeley, Calif; Denver Art Mus. *Exhib:* One-man exhibs, Tibor de Nagy Gallery, Inc, NY, 70-71, 73 & 79; Art on Paper, Weatherspoon Gallery, Univ NC, 71; 3rd Biennial Art, Medellin, Colombia, S Am, 72; Painting and Sculpture Today 1972, Indianapolis Mus Art, Ind, 72; 100 Artists 100 Yrs, Art Inst Chicago, 80. *Teaching:* Instr painting, Black Hawk Sch Art, Colo, summers. *Media:* Acrylic Polymer, Collage. *Mailing Add:* 3115 W 25th Ave Denver CO 80211-4611

BOWMAN, RUTH
ART HISTORIAN, EDUCATOR
b Denver, Colo, June 14, 23. *Study:* Bryn Mawr Col, AB, 44; NY Univ Inst Fine Arts, MA, 71; Rockefeller Found Sr Fel, Metrop Mus Art, 76. *Collection Arranged:* The New York Painter, A Century of Teaching: From Morse to Hofmann, Marlborough-Gerson Gallery, 67; A University Collects (tour with Am Fedn Arts), 65-68; Murals Without Walls, Newark Airport Murals of Arshile Gorky, Newark Mus, 78-79; Am Fedn Arts tour six mus, 79-80; Ruth Bowman & Harry Kahn 20th Century Am Self Portrait Collection (permanent), Nat Portrait Gallery, Washington, DC, 2006. *Pos:* Asst cur, Jewish Mus, 62-63; cur & dir, New York Univ Art Collection, Grey Art Gallery, 63-74; dir educ, Los Angeles Co Mus Art, 74-75; art commentator, KUSC/fm, Los Angeles, 79-84. *Teaching:* Adj asst prof art hist, Sch Continuing Educ, New York Univ, 65-70 & Sch Educ, 68-73; lectr art, Mus Mod Art, NY, 64-71, NY Univ, Washington Sq Col, 72-73 (Sunrise Semester-CBS); mus training, art hist courses, lectrs radio & TV, NY & Los Angeles; vis lectr, Univ Cal, Santa Barbara, spring 86. *Mem:* Am Asn Mus (vpres, 76-79); Am Fedn Arts (bd trustees); Col Art Asn; Asn Int des Critiques d'Art (AICA); Coun for the Arts. *Res:* 19th and 20th century American and European art and architecture. *Mailing Add:* 200 E 66th St Apt B2101 New York NY 10021

BOWRON, EDGAR PETERS
ADMINISTRATOR, HISTORIAN
b Birmingham, Ala, May 27, 43. *Study:* Colgate Univ, AB, 65; Inst Fine Arts, NY Univ, MA, 69, PhD, 79. *Exhib:* A Scholar Collects: Selections from the Anthony Morris Clark Bequest, Philadelphia Mus Art, 80-81; Pompeo Batoni (1708-87), Colnaghi, NY, 82; Pompeo Batoni and His British Patrons, The Iveagh Bequest, Kenwood, London, 82; Modern Art from the Pulitzer Collection: 50 Yrs of Connoisseurship, Fogg Art Mus, Cambridge & The St Louis Art Mus, 88; The Maurice Wertheim Collection and Other Impressionist and Post-Impressionist Paintings and Drawings from the Fogg Art Mus, Tokyo & Yamaguchi, 90; Art in Rome in the Eighteenth Century (ed, catalog), Houston & Philadelphia, 2000; Masterworks of 19th Century Ger Painting (ed, catalog), Mus Fine Arts, Leipzig & Houston, 2000. *Pos:* Educ lectr, Metrop Mus Art, 68-70; registr, Minneapolis Inst Arts, 70-73; cur Renaissance & baroque art, Walters Art Gallery, 73-78; cur Renaissance & baroque art & admin asst to dir, Nelson Gallery-Atkins Mus, Kansas City, Mo, 78-81; dir, NC Mus Art, 81-85; Elizabeth and John Moors Cabot dir & prof fine arts, Harvard Univ Art Mus, 85-90; Andrew W Mellon sr consult cur, Nat Gallery Art, Washington, DC, 91-92, sr cur paintings, 92-96; cur European art, The Audrey Jones Beck Mus Fine Arts, Houston, 96-. *Awards:* Nat Endowment Arts Fel, 75-76; Am Acad Rome Grant, 79-85; Robert H Smith Fel, Nat Gallery Art, 95. *Mem:* Asn Art Mus Dirs (trustee, 87-90); Mus Fine Arts, Boston (trustee, 88-90); Master Drawings Asn (bd dir, 87-). *Res:* European painting, 16th, 17th and 18th centuries. *Publ:* ed, The North Carolina Museum of Art: Introduction to the Collections, 83; Pompeo Batoni, A Complete Catalogue of His Works, Anthony M Clark (co-auth), 85; auth, European Paintings Before 1900 in the Fogg Art Mus, A Summary Illustrated Catalog, Cambridge, 90; Bernard Bellotto: The Fortress of Königstein, Wash, 93; contribr, Paintings of the Seventeenth and Eighteenth Centuries, Nat Gallery Art, Wash, 96; others. *Mailing Add:* Mus Fine Arts PO Box 6826 Houston TX 77265-6826

BOYD, JOHN DAVID
EDUCATOR, PRINTMAKER
b London, Ark, Jan 22, 39. *Study:* Calif State Univ, Long Beach, with Richard Swift, BA; Cranbrook Acad Art, with Lawrence Barker, MFA. *Work:* Tex Tech Univ; Ga State Univ; Univ NC, Chapel Hill; State Univ NY Col Potsdam; Springfield Art Mus, Mo. *Exhib:* Color Print USA, Tex Tech Univ, 94; Cimarron Nat Works on Paper, Okla State Univ, 95; States of Elvis Invitational, Knoxville, Tenn, 95-96; Nat Art Show at Dog Show, Wichita, Kans, 97; 35th NDak Print & Drawing Exhib, Grand Forks, 93; Watercolor, USA, Springfield Art Mus, Mo, 93; Delta Nat Sml Print Exhib, Five Art Gallery, Ark State Univ, Jonesboro, Ark, 96; Kans Triennial Traveling State Exhib, Melvane Art Mus & Salina Art Ctr, 98; Kansas Water Color Soc, 7 State Exhibs, Wichita Art Mus, Kans, 98; Art Show at the Dog Show, Century II Gallery & City

Arts Gallery, Wichita, Kans, 2000 & 2003; Baker Arts Ctr, 3rd Nat Art Exhib, Liberal, Kans, 2000; plus others; Taboo X, Southern Graphic Conf, Radisson Hotel, New Orleans, La & Carol Gallery, Tulane Univ, 2002; 104th Midwest Art Exhib, Birgir Sandzen Mem Gallery, Lindsborg, KS, 2002; one man show, Univ Kans, Lawrence, 2002; 32nd Juried Smokey Hill Art Competition, Hays Art Ctr, KS, 01. *Pos:* Cur, Lynwood Kreneck, Landmark Gallery, Tex-Technol Univ, Lubbock, Tex, 02. *Teaching:* Prof printmaking & drawing, Wichita State Univ, 72-. *Awards:* Mus Purchase, MOAK, Springfield Art Mus, Mo, 95. *Media:* Intaglio, Lithography. *Mailing Add:* 421 S Glenn Wichita KS 67213

BOYD, KAREN WHITE
EDUCATOR, FIBER ARTIST
b Akron, Ohio, Sept 8, 36. *Study:* Kent State Univ, BA(art educ), 58 & MA(studio art), 64; Tyler Sch Art, Temple Univ, MFA(weaving), 75. *Exhib:* Regional Craft Biennial, J B Speed Mus, Louisville, Ky, 70; Mid-States Craft Exhib, Evansville Mus, Ind, 73; Nat Fiber Design Show, Calif Polytech State Univ, San Luis Obispo, 75; 3rd Int Exhib Miniature Textiles, Brit Crafts Centre, London, 78. *Teaching:* Assoc prof weaving & textiles, Murray State Univ, 67-81, prof, 81-. *Awards:* Juror's Award, Ted Hallman, Nat Fiber Design Show, 75; Honorable Mention, Southeast 80 Craft Exhib, Tallahassee, Fla. *Mem:* Ky Guild Artists & Craftsmen; Handweaver's Guild Am; Asn British Craftsmen. *Dealer:* Am Art Inc Atlanta GA

BOYD, LAKIN
EDUCATOR, PRINTMAKER
b Athens, Ala, Aug 27, 46. *Study:* Univ Ala, BFA, 68 & MA, 70; Pratt Graphic Ctr, 70-71, intaglio with Michael Ponce de Leon. *Work:* Oscar Wells Mem Mus, Birmingham, Ala; Univ Ala, Tuscaloosa; Ala Arts Comn; Univ South; Pratt Graphic Ctr Print Collection, NY. *Exhib:* Nat Student Printmakers Travel Exhib, 68; 13th Dixie Ann, 72; one-man shows, Univ Ala & Judson Col, 73; 14th Ann Reece Regional, 74. *Teaching:* Asst prof graphics & art hist, Ala A&M Univ, Huntsville, 71-82. *Awards:* Purchase Award, Birmingham Art Asn, 67; Fulbright Grant to Belg & Neth, 75. *Mem:* Southeastern Col Art Conf; Am Asn Univ Prof; Nat Art Educ Asn; Am Crafts Coun; Ala Art Educ Asn. *Media:* Intaglio, Lithography. *Mailing Add:* 426 Eustis Ave SE Huntsville AL 35801-4110

BOYD, (DAVID) MICHAEL
PAINTER, GRAPHIC ARTIST
b Waterloo, Iowa, Nov 27, 1936. *Study:* With Philip Evergood, 57; Univ Northern Iowa, BA, 59. *Work:* Baltimore Mus Art; Albright-Knox Art Gallery, Buffalo, NY; Chrysler Mus Art, Norfolk, Va; Mint Mus Art, Charlotte, NC; Knoxville Mus Art, Knoxville, Tenn; Waterloo Mus Art, Iowa; Univ Ky Art Mus, Lexington; Robert Wood Johnson Univ Hosp, New Brunswick, NJ. *Comn:* Mural, EF MacDonald Co, Dayton, 82. *Exhib:* Recent Acquisitions, Albright-Knox Art Gallery, 81 & Baltimore Mus Art, 82; Ana Sklar Gallery, Miami, Fla, 84; Geometric Abstraction: Selections from a Decade, 1975-1985, Bronx Mus Art, NY, 85; JJ Brookings Gallery, San Jose, Calif, 87; one-man show, Davenport Mus Art, Iowa, Charles H MacNider Mus, Mason City, Iowa, Waterloo Munic Galleries, Iowa, 89, 90, Andre Zarre Gallery, NY, 90 & 94, Herbert F Johnson Mus Art, Ithaca, NY, Clinton, NY & Univ Ky Art Mus, Lexington, 91-92; one-man retrospective, Upstairs Gallery, Ithaca, NY, 95, Pardo Lattuada Gallery, NY, 2000; Galleria Le Bateleur, Rome, Italy, 2003; Coastline: Recent paintings, Artefact Pardo gallery, Milan, Italy, 03; Coastlines/Kustenlinie: Recent paintings, Artefact Pardo Gallery, Zurich, Switz, 2005. *Teaching:* Prof design, Cornell Univ, 68-96, emer prof, 96. *Awards:* Purchase Award, Everson Mus Art, 71; Yaddo Fel, 74; NY Found Arts, 88. *Bibliog:* Pat Sloan (auth), article, Arts Mag, 79; Lawrence Campbell (auth), Michael Boyd, Art in Am, 84. *Mem:* Am Asn Mus. *Media:* Acrylic on Canvas and Paper. *Dealer:* Artefact Pardo Gallery 119 E 31 St 1B New York NY; Alz Naviglio Pavese 52 20143 Milan Italy; Ramistrasse 25 Zurich 8001 Switzerland. *Mailing Add:* 78 Greene St New York NY 10012

BOYER, MARIETTA P
LIBRARIAN
b Vienna, Austria, July 26, 32; US citizen. *Study:* Wheaton Col, Norton, Mass, BA(art hist); Drexel Univ, Philadelphia, MLS. *Pos:* Photograph librn, Mus of Fine Arts, Boston, 56-61; asst, Slide Dept, Mus of Art, Philadelphia, 68-72; librn, Pa Acad of Fine Arts, 75-. *Mem:* Art Librn Soc NAm. *Mailing Add:* 242 Broughton Ln Villanova PA 19085-1914

BOYLAN, JOHN LEWIS
PAINTER, PRINTMAKER
b Cleveland, Ohio, Oct 8, 21. *Study:* Oberlin Col, 39-42; Cleveland Inst Art, 42; Univ NMex, BFA, 47; Art Students League, 47-50; study with Vaclav Vytlacil, Morris Kantor, Harry Sternberg, Will Barnet & Peter Piening. *Work:* Metrop Mus Art, NY; NY Pub Libr; Roswell Mus, NMex; Univ Pa Art Mus. *Exhib:* Soc Am Graphic Artists, 50 & 71; Royal Soc Painter-Etchers & Engravers, London, 54 & 56; solo exhib, Roswell Mus, 59 & 66; Japan Print Soc, Tokyo, 67. *Teaching:* Dir painting & design, Roswell Mus Art Sch, 50-51; instr painting & design, Inst Am Indian Art, Santa Fe, NMex, 66-, actg head fine arts, 74-75. *Awards:* Award of Merit, Am Asn State & Local Hist, 60. *Media:* Oil, Acrylic; Woodcut, Metal Plate Lithograph. *Mailing Add:* 250 E Alameda St No 519 Santa Fe NM 87501-2186

BOYLE, KEITH
PAINTER, EDUCATOR
b Defiance, Ohio, Feb 15, 1930. *Study:* Ringling Sch Art, Sarasota, Fla; Univ Iowa, BFA. *Work:* San Francisco Mus Art & Stanford Univ Mus, Calif; Mead Paper Corp, Atlanta, Ga; Nat Fine Arts Collection, Washington; Oakland Mus, Calif; Continental Bank, Chicago. *Exhib:* The Colorists, San Francisco Mus Art, 65; Drawings by 100 American Artists, Ann Arbor, Mich, 65; A Century of California Painting, 1870-1970, 70; Looking Westward, Joslyn Art Mus, Omaha, Nebr, 70; Retrospective Exhib of Paintings: 1965-1977, San Jose Mus Art, Calif, 78; Paintings: 1983-1984, Stanford Art Gallery; Schneider Mus, Ashland, Ore, 93. *Teaching:* Prof painting & drawing, Stanford Univ, 62-88, chmn grad studio prog, 83-88. *Awards:* Nat Endowment Arts Grant, 81-82; Philosophy East & West Mem Trust Grant, 86

BOYLE, (JAMES) NEIL
ILLUSTRATOR, PAINTER
b Granum, Alta, Can, Apr 5, 31. *Study:* Banff Sch Fine Art, 50; Art Ctr Col Design, BPA, 51-54; Chouinard Art Inst, 54-56. *Work:* US Air Force Hist Art Collection, Smithsonian Inst & Pentagon, Washington; NASA, Cape Canaveral, Fla; Sheriff's Permanent Collection, Los Angeles, Calif. *Comn:* Heritage Garden (mosaic), Mt Sinai Cemetery, Los Angeles, Calif, 80. *Exhib:* Solo exhibs, Vancouver Jockey Club, BC, 82 & Calgary Inn, Alta, 83; AICA Show, San Dimas, Calif, 85-96; Western Art in the Grand Tradition, Fallbrook, Calif, 86 & 88; SW Art in the Wine Country, Calistoga, Calif, 89-96; Autry Mus, Los Angeles, 95 & 96. *Teaching:* Instr painting & sculpture, Inst Art, Calif, 86-88. *Awards:* Gold Medal, Art Dirs Club Los Angeles, 63; Best in Show, Illustration West, 75 & Life Achievement Award, 85, Soc Illusrs Los Angeles; Signature mem, Oil Painters Am, Calif Art Club. *Bibliog:* Kay Kawolski (auth), Southwest Art, 80; John Manson (auth), Artist of the Rockies, 85; Vickie Stabik (auth), Art of the West, 88. *Mem:* Soc Illusrs Los Angeles (pres, 73, Air Force Chmn, 76); Am Indian Cowboy & Indian Artists; Calif Art Club. *Media:* Oil, Clay

BOYLE, RICHARD J
ART HISTORIAN, WRITER
b New York, NY, June 3, 32. *Study:* Adelphi Univ, BA; Oxford Univ, with Edgar Wind & John Pope-Hennessy; Art Student League, with Will Barnet. *Collection Arranged:* John Twachtman Retrospective, 66, Laser Light: A New Visual Art, 69, The Early Work of Paul Gauguin, 71 & Robert S Duncanson: A Centennial Exhibition, 72, Cincinnati Art Mus; Am Paintings from Newport, Wichita Art Mus, 69; Young Am Painters from PA Acad Fine Arts, 75; Milk & Eggs: The Am Revival of Tempera Painting, Brandywine River Mus, PA, 30, 50, 2002. *Pos:* Cur, Int Art Found, Newport, RI, summer 62; dir, Middletown Fine Arts Ctr, Ohio, 63-65; cur painting, Cincinnati Art Mus, 65-73; dir, Pa Acad Fine Arts, 73-83; art comn chmn, Redevelop Authority, Philadelphia, 75-83; consult, continuing educ prog, Philadelphia Col Art, 85-86; mem low illustration comt, New Britain Mus Am Art, 1999-. *Teaching:* Vis scholar, Moore Col Art, Philadelphia, 83-84; instr, Philadelphia Univ Arts, 84-87; adj prof art hist, Temple Univ, Philadelphia & Japan, 87-2005. *Awards:* Benjamin Franklin Fel, Royal Soc of Art, London, Eng; Literary Award for book (John H Twachtman), Athenaeum of Philadelphia, 76. *Mem:* Am Asn of Mus; Asn Historians Am Art. *Res:* Late nineteenth & twentieth century American art & culture, history of painting technique and technology. *Interests:* Research, Travel, Jogging, Reading. *Publ:* Contribr, French impressionists influence Am impressionists, Lowe Art Mus, Fla, 71; Auth, John Twachtman's Gloucester Years, Twachtman in Glouster: His Last Years, 1900-1902 (exhib catalog), IRA Spanierman Art, 87; auth, Lewis Henry Meakin: An American Landscape Painter Rediscovered, Cincinnati Art Galleries, 87; coauth, Sunlight & Shadow: Life & Art of Willard Metcalf, 88; auth, Technique, Technology and Gentility: The Style of American Impressionism, World Impressionism and Pleinairism, Chunichi Shimbun/Matsuzakaya Art Mus, Nagoya, Japan, 91; Connection with a Place: The Collection of the Brandywine River Museum (catalog), Chadds Ford, Pa, 91; Dow: American Sensei, Arthur Wesley Dows: His Art and His Influence, Ira Spanierman, Inc, 99; Max Kuehne: Artist & Craftsman, Hollis Taggart Galleries, 2001; Milk & Eggs: The American Revival of Tempera Painting, Brandywine River Mus and Univ Washington Press, 2002; Bob Kane: People & Places, Rizzoli Int Inc, 2002; From Hawthorne to Hofmann: Provincetown Vignettes, 1899-1945, Hollis Taggart Galleries, 2002. *Mailing Add:* Box 177 Salisbury CT 06068

BOYLEN, MICHAEL EDWARD
CRAFTSMAN, ART WRITER
b Stoughton, Wis, Dec 12, 35. *Study:* Yale Univ, with Josef Albers, AB, 58; Sch Am Craftsmen, pottery with Frans Wildenhain; Univ Wis, with Harvey K Littleton, MS, MFA; People's Republic China, 98. *Work:* Corning Mus Glass, NY; Cleveland Mus Art, Ohio; Mus Kunst & Gewerbe, Hamburg, Ger; Victoria & Albert Mus, London; Glasmuseum, Ebeltoft, Denmark. *Exhib:* New Am Glass, Dallas Mus Fine Arts, Tex, 67; Del Art Mus, Wilmington, 71 & 75; Fleming Mus, Univ Vt, Burlington, 75; Bergstrom Mus, Neenah, Wis, 76; Corning Mus Glass, NY; Mickelson Gallery, Washington, 78; and others. *Teaching:* Instr ceramics, Cleveland Inst Art, Ohio, 66; lectr design & ceramics, Lyndon State Col, Lyndonville, Vt, 67-76; prof art, Marlboro Col, Vt, 80-. *Awards:* LC Tiffany Found Grant, 65. *Bibliog:* Clemens Kalischer (auth), Glass--Michael Boylen, Vt Life Mag, 72; R&L Grover (auths), Contemporary Art Glass, Crown, 75; Paul Hollister (auth), Hollister on glass, Acquire, 12/76. *Mem:* Nat Coun Educ Ceramic Arts; Vt Coun Arts (pres, 74-76); Found Art Theory & Educ. *Media:* Clay; Glass. *Publ:* Auth, Studio glass in perspective, Studio Potter, 73 & In: 74 Crafts Annual, NY State Craftsmen, 74; Glass of Joel Phillip Myers, 10-11/80, Malcolm Wright (ceramics), 10-11/85 & Joel Phillip Myers at Holsten Galleries, 10-11/88, Am Craft; Frans Wildenhain: master of form, Studio Potter, 6/91; The ceramics of Asger Jorn, Studio Potter, 12/93; Frans Wildenhain: creative force & mentor, Nat Coun Educ Ceramic Arts J, 96. *Dealer:* Azuma Gallery 50 Walker St New York NY 10013. *Mailing Add:* Marlboro Col Dept Pottery Marlboro VT 05344

BOYNTON, JACK (JAMES) W
PAINTER, PRINTMAKER
b Ft Worth, Tex, Jan 12, 28. *Study:* Tex Christian Univ, BFA & MFA. *Work:* Mus Mod Art, Solomon R Guggenheim Mus & Whitney Mus, NY; Mus Fine Arts, Houston; Los Angeles Co Mus, Calif; and others. *Comn:* Go Freedom, 2nd Liberty Gala, Houston ACLU, Equal Justice, 6th Liberty Gala & Law and Order, 7th Liberty Gala, Tex;

Amarillo Art Ctr; Houston Festival 79, City of Houston; Time & Space Murals, Educ Wing, Dallas Mus Art. *Exhib:* Whitney Mus Am Art, 57-58, 67-68 & 80; Los Angeles Mus Art, 69; Collections of Mus of Southwest, Washington, DC, 78; Wood in Art, Mus Fine Arts, Houston, 79; one-man show, Univ Houston, Clear Lake City, Tex, 79; retrospective, Amarillo Art Ctr, 80; retrospective, Tex Christian Univ, 89; and others. *Teaching:* Instr, Univ NMex, summer 63; instr, Houston Mus Sch, 68-69; instr art, Mus Fine Arts, Houston, 68-69; instr art, Univ St Thomas, Houston, formerly; Univ St Thomas, Tex, 69-70. *Awards:* Tamarind Workshop Fel, 67. *Bibliog:* Douglas MacAgy (auth), James Boynton (monogr), Barone Gallery Inc, 59; Jerry Davies (auth), Retrospectrum Catalog, Amarillo Art Ctr, 80; Paul Rogers Harris (auth), Homecoming, Tex Christian Univ, 89. *Media:* Mixed. *Mailing Add:* 3723 Albans St Houston TX 77005-2001

BRACE, HILARY
PAINTER
b Seattle, Wash, Apr 24, 56. *Study:* Western Wash State Univ, BFA(painting), 83; Univ Calif, Santa Barbara, MFA(painting), 85. *Work:* Arco Res, Philadelphia, Pa; AT&T, Piscataway, NJ; Boise Art Mus, Idaho; ScutterKemper Insurance, Chicago, Ill; Western Washington Univ, Bellingham, Wash. *Exhib:* Solo exhibs, Bellingham Hardware Gallery, Wash, 83, Chrysalis Gallery, Fairhaven Col, Bellingham, Wash, 83, Tatistcheff Gallery, Santa Monica, 90, Sun Valley Ctr Arts & Humanities, Idaho, 93, Tatistcheff/Rogers Gallery, Santa Monica, 93 & 97 & Santa Barbara Contemp Arts Forum, Calif, 98, Craig Kovil Gallery, 2000 & 01, Craig Krull Gallery, Santa Monica, Calif, 2001 & 03, Edward Thorp Gallery, NY, 2002; Terrain: Observations of Nature, SOMA Gallery, San Diego, 95; group exhibs, Scissors, Paper, Stone: Nine Women Working, Santa Maria Mus Art Ctr, 95, Representing LA, Frye Art Mus, Wash & S Tex Inst of Art, Tex, 2000, Edward Thorp Gallery, NY, 2002 & 03; Land-Inspired Imagery, Anne Reed Gallery, Ketchum, Idaho, 96; Drawn Conclusions, Riverside Art Mus, 96; Romantic Landscape and Contemp Art, Armory Ctr Arts, Pasadena, Calif, 97; Landscapes of the Mind, Mt San Jacinto Community Col, Calif, 98; Small Images I, Ventura Col Main Gallery, Calif, 98; Elements, Los Angeles Munic Art Gallery & Barnsdall Art Park, Los Angeles, 98; The Great Drawing Show, Kohn Turner Gallery, Los Angeles, Calif. *Pos:* Mus adv comt, Univ Art Mus, Univ Calif, Santa Barbara, 84-85; exhib comt, Contemp Arts Forum, Santa Barbara, 91-96. *Teaching:* Teaching asst, Univ Calif, Santa Barbara, 83-85, lectr, 90. *Awards:* Purchase Award, Santa Barbara Co Arts Comn, 93; Fel, Nat Endowment Arts, 93; Grantee Pollock-Krasner Found, 97. *Bibliog:* New Romantics, Artweek, 9/97; Daydreams on Paper, Santa Barbara News Press, 7/17/98; Bracing Images, Los Angeles Times, 2/4/2000. *Media:* Pastel. *Dealer:* Craig Krull Gallery Santa Monica Calif

BRACH, PAUL HENRY
PAINTER
b New York, NY, Mar 13, 1924. *Study:* State Univ Iowa, BFA, 48, MFA, 50. *Work:* Los Angeles Co Mus of Art, Los Angeles; Phoenix Art Mus; Albuquerque Mus Fine Arts; Art Mus State Univ Iowa; Hechsher Mus, Huntington, NY. *Exhib:* Retrospective, Mulvane Art Ctr, Topeka, Kans; McAllen Int Mus, 94; Steinbaum Krauss Gallery, NY, 94, 96 & 97; Tucson Mus Art, 94 & 95; Guild Hall, East Hampton, NY, 95; one-man show, Steinbaum Krauss Gallery, NY, 96; Art Mus State Univ Iowa, 2002; and others. *Pos:* Fel, Tamarind Lithog Workshop, Los Angeles, 64, Albuquerque, NMex, 80 & 82; artist-in-residence, Am Fedn Arts, Albuquerque, 65. *Teaching:* Mem fac, Univ Mo, 50-51, New Sch Social Res, 52-55, New York Univ, 54-67 & 86-89, Parsons Sch Design, 56-67, Cooper Union, 60-62 & 79-82 & Cornell Univ, 65-67; chmn dept Visual Arts, Univ Calif, San Diego, 67-69; dean sch art, Calif Inst Art, 69-75; chmn div arts, Lincoln Ctr Campus, Fordham Univ, 75-79; Empire State Col, NY, 79-; Milton Avery Distinguished prof, Bard Col, 93. *Awards:* D Jerassi Grant, 89 & 91. *Bibliog:* Carol Kotrozo Donnel (auth), Art Int, 5-6/82; Susan Hellsten McGarry (auth), Southwest Art, 1/86; Vivien Raynor (auth), article, New York Times, 11/87, 7/90 & 11/90. *Mem:* Nat Acad Design. *Media:* Oil. *Publ:* Auth, John Mandel, Arts, 9/75; rev in Artforum, 10/76 & 12/78, Art in Am, 3-4/78, 1/79 & 1/84 & Art News, 1/79 & 12/85. *Dealer:* Arlene Bujese Gallery East Hampton NY. *Mailing Add:* PO Box 1201 Wainscott NY 11975-1201

BRADBURY-REID, ELLEN A
ADMINISTRATOR, EDUCATOR
b Louisville, Ky, Feb 26, 40. *Study:* Yale Univ; Univ Vienna, Austria, 60; Univ NMex, BA & MA, 66. *Collection Arranged:* African Oceanic Art, Am Indians, North and South; Am 20th Century, Regis Collection; Artifacts from Manhattan Project, Los Alamos. *Pos:* Res asst, Minneapolis Inst Art, 69-70, asst registr, 70-72, registr, 72-75 & cur primitive art, 75-79; dir, Mus Fine Arts, Mus NMex, 79, Santa Fe Festival Arts, 82; founder, Recursos Santa Fe, 84- & Royal Road Art Tours, 98. *Teaching:* Inst, Univ NMex, 67, Col Santa Fe, 96. *Mem:* Int Women's Forum; NMex Quincentennial Comn; Albequerque Mus Arts (adv bd); Founding Mem NMex Coalition for Hist Preservation. *Res:* American Indian Ghost Dance. *Publ:* Four-State Survey, the State of Regional Arts, ARTSPACE, Fall, 83; auth, Art Reviews, Albuquerque J, 85-86; co-ed, From the Faraway Nearby, A Biography of Georgia O'Keeffe, Addison-Wesley, 92; Auth, Native Arts and Crafts, (Southwest Indian Arts and Crafts Series), Salamander, 95; K. Villea & L Wagner (coauth), Contemporary Mexican Architecture and Design, Gibbs Smith, 2002. *Mailing Add:* 510 Alto St Santa Fe NM 87501-2517

BRADFORD, HOWARD
PRINTMAKER, PAINTER
b Toronto, Ont, July 14, 1919; US citizen. *Study:* Chouinard Art Inst, Los Angeles; Jepson Art Inst, Los Angeles; Calif Sch Fine Arts, San Francisco. *Work:* Philadelphia Mus Fine Arts; Boston Mus Fine Arts; Bibliotheque Nat France; Los Angeles Co Mus; NY Pub Libr. *Comn:* Print editions (100), Dallas Mus Fine Arts, 53, Hilton Hotel, NY, 64 & Asn Am Artists, NY, 67-69; Brentanos: Print Editions 1977-78. *Exhib:* Libr Cong Nat Print & Drawing Exhib, 51; Brooklyn Mus Print Ann, 52; Dallas Mus Fine Arts Nat Print Exhib, 53; 60 Am Printmakers, US Info Serv, Europe, 56; Carmel Art Asn, Calif, 72 & 76, 80-89 & 92-98. *Teaching:* Instr, Jerson Art Inst, Los Angeles, 49-51; guest instr, Univ Wis, 57 & Univ Salt Lake City, 59. *Awards:* Birds by Beach (serigraph), Libr Cong, 51 & Dallas Mus Fine Arts, 53; Guggenheim Fel Creative Printmaking, 60. *Bibliog:* Who's Who in America, 88-. *Mem:* Carmel Art Asn. *Media:* Silk Screen; Acrylic. *Publ:* Coauth (J Ross & C Romano), The Complete Printmaker, Free Press, NY, 72; coauth (C Zigorosser), Prints and Their Creators, Crown, 74. *Mailing Add:* 684 Alice St Monterey CA 93940

BRADFORD, MARK
PAINTER
b Los Angeles, Calif, 1961. *Study:* Calif Inst Arts, BFA, 1995, MFA, 1997. *Exhib:* Solo and two-person shows: Distribution, Deep River, LA, Calif, 1998, Floss, Walter McLean Gallery, San Francisco, 1998, European Wavy, Two Rivers Gallery, Pittsburgh, 1999, Color Theory, Luggage Store, San Francisco, 2000, I Don't Think You're Ready For This Jelly, Lombard-Freid Arts, NY, 2001, That Wasn't My Car You Saw, Finesilver Gallery, San Antonio, 2002, Patricia Faure Gallery, Santa Monica, Calif, 2002, Caught Up, Suzanne Vielmetter, LA Projects, 2002, Very Powerful Lords, Whitney Mus Am Art, NY, 2003, Bounce, REDCAT, LA, Calif, 2004, Grace and Measure, Sikkema Jenkins & Co, NY, 2005; Biennale Internazionale, Palazzo delgi Affari, Florence, Italy, 1999; Contemporary Art By African American Artists, The Art Mus of Princeton, NJ, 2000; Freestyle, Studio Mus in Harlem, NY, 2001, Black Belt, 2003; Ghetto Fabulous, Watts Tower Art Ctr, LA, 2002; Mixed Feelings, USC Fisher Gallery, LA, 2002; ARCO, Madrid, Spain, 2003; California Biennial, Orange County Mus Art, Newport Beach, 2004; inSite: Art Practices in the Public Domain, San Diego and Tijuana, 2005; Cut, Susanne Vielmetter LA Projects, 2005. *Awards:* Nancy Graves Found Grant. 2002; Joan Mitchell Found Grant, 2002; Louis Comfort Tiffany Found Grant, 2003; Bucksbaum Award, 2006. *Media:* All Media. *Mailing Add:* c/o Sikkema Jenkins & Co 530 West 22nd St New York NY 10011

BRADLEY, BETSY
MUSEUM DIRECTOR
Study: Millsaps Col, BA; Vanderbilt Univ, MA in Eng. *Pos:* Deputy dir, and community arts dir, Miss Arts Commission, exec dir, 1995-2001, Miss Mus Art, Jackson, 2001-; bd mem, Nat Assembly of State Arts Agencies; panelist, Nat Endowment for Arts; adv panel mem, Miss Sch Arts. *Awards:* Named one of Top 50 Bus Women, Miss Business J. *Mailing Add:* Miss Mus Art 201 E Pascagoula St Jackson MS 39201

BRADLEY, LAUREL E
EDUCATOR, GALLERY DIRECTOR
b Santa Monica, Calif, July 6, 52. *Study:* Univ Ore, Eugene, BA, 75; Inst Fine Arts, New York Univ, MA, 78, PhD, 86. *Collection Arranged:* Bruce Charlesworth (auth, catalog), 84, The Idea of Big, 85, Ingenious Fabrications: Recent Projects From the Fabric Workshop, 85, Roland Ginzel: A Retrospective (auth, catalog), 86 & Tragic and Timeless Today: Contemporary History Painting, 87, Gallery 400, Univ Ill, Chicago; Land Used: Environmental and Photography, Carleton Col Art Gallery, Minn, 98. *Pos:* Dir, Gallery 400, Univ Ill, Chicago, 83-87; dir exhibs & cur, Col Art Collection, Carleton Col, Minn, 96-. *Teaching:* Asst prof theory & criticism, Sch Art Inst, Chicago, 87-. *Mem:* Col Art Asn; Historians Brit Art; Am Asn Mus. *Res:* Trends in contemporary art and architecture; Victorian art and culture. *Publ:* From Eden to Empire: John Everett Millaiss' Cherry Ripe, 179-204, winter 91; Humor in Art: Occasional Papers Ser, Mus Beloit Col, Vol 1, 49-53, 91; Millais' Bubbles & the Problem of Artistic Advertising, Assoc Univ Presses, 96; Drawn into the Pre Raphaelite Circle: D G Rossetti's drawing of Elizabeth Siddali, Mus Studies, Art Inst Chicago, 92; The Englishmen of Pre-Raphaelite painting: A Critical Review, Collecting Pre-Raphaelites: The Anglo-American Enchantment, 97

BRADLEY, SLATER
PHOTOGRAPHER
b San Francisco, Ca, 75. *Study:* UCLA, BA, 1998. *Work:* Annandale-on-Hudson, NY, Ctr Curatorial Studies Mus, Bard Col, NY, 2003, Armory Photog Show, 2002, Here are the Young Men, Team Gallery, 2002, Universitatsstadt Kaiserslautern, Ger, 2002, Art + Pub, Geneva Switzerland, 2002, Arndt & Partner, Berlin, Ger, 2002, Video Cube, FIAS, Paris, 2001, Trompe Le Monde, Galerie Yvon Lambert, 2001, Home Town Hero, Refusalon, San Francisco, 2001, Spec Projects Series, PS1, NY, 2000, Charlatan, Team Gallery, New York City, 2000, Fried Liver Attack, 1999. *Exhib:* One-man shows incl, Taka Ishii Gallery, Tokyo, 2005, Matrix 216: Year of the Doppelganger, Univ Calif Berkeley Art Mus & Pacific Film Archive, 2005, Blum & Poe, Los Angeles, 2004, Stoned & Dethroned, Team Gallery, New York City, 2004, Annandale-on-Hudson, NY, Ctr Curatorial Studies Mus, Bard Col, NY, 2003, Armory Photog Show, 2002, Here are the Young Men, Team Gallery, 2002, Universitatsstadt Kaiserslautern, Ger, 2002, Art + Pub, Geneva Switz, 2002, Arndt & Partner, Berlin, Ger, 2002, Video Cube, FIAS, Paris, 2001, Trompe Le Monde, Galerie Yvon Lambert, 2001, Home Town Hero, Refusalon, San Francisco, 2001, Special Projects Series, PS1, NY, 2000, Charlatan, Team Gallery, New York City, 2000, Fried Liver Attack, 1999. *Mailing Add:* c/o Whitney Mus Am Art 945 Madison Ave at 75th St New York NY 10021

BRADLEY, WILLIAM STEVEN
MUSEUM DIRECTOR, CURATOR
b Salina, Kans, Aug 20, 49. *Study:* Univ Colo, BA, 71; Friedrich-Alexander Univ, 72; Northwestern Univ, MA, 74, PhD, 81. *Collection Arranged:* Gene Kloss: Six Decades of Printmaking, 84; Frank Reaugh: Scenes from the Texas Range, 84; Honky Tonk Visions, 86; Nine Texas Printmakers, 86; The Blue Star Exhibition: Contemporary Art

in San Antonio, 86; Lin Emery/Emery Clark, 89; Kazuo Kadonaga, 90; Richard Johnson/John Scott, 91; Contemporary Art from the K & B Corp Collection, 91; Elemore Morgan Photographs, 92; Edouard Duval Carrie: Migration of the Spirit, 2002. *Pos:* Cur art, Tex Tech Univ Mus, 83-85; chief cur, San Antonio Mus Art, 85-86; dir, Alexandria Mus Art, 87-92 & Davenport Mus Art, from 92. *Teaching:* Instr mod art, Wells Col, 79-81; lectr mod art, Cornell Univ, 80-81, Univ Tex, 86-87; tchr, Northwestern State Univ, La, 88-92. *Mem:* Col Art Asn; Am Asn Mus; Tex Art 150 (secy, 84-87); La Asn Mus (vpres, 88-89); Asn Art Mus Dirs. *Res:* Modern European art; contemporary American art. *Publ:* Auth, Gene Kloss: Six Decades of Prints, Tex Tech Univ, 84; Emil Nolde and German Expressionism, UMI Res Press, 86; Contemp Art in San Antonio, CASA, 86; contribr, Lynda Benglis/Keith Sonnier: A Decade of Sculpture, Alex Mus Art, 87; and others; Elemore Morgan, Jr, Where Land Meets Sky, U Southwest La, 99

BRADSHAW, DOVE
PAINTER, SCULPTOR
b New York, NY, Sept 24, 49. *Study:* Boston Mus Sch Fine Arts, BFA, 73. *Work:* Metrop Mus Art, Mus Mod Art & Whitney Mus Am Art, NY; Brooklyn Mus, NY; Philadelphia Mus Art; Ark Art Mus, Little Rock; Art Inst Chicago; Nat Gallery, Wash, DC; Break to Activate (wall piece), PS1, Inst Art & Urban Resources, NY, 77; Merce Cunningham Dance Co: Phrases & vieco: Deli Commedia, Coshmes, 84, Native Green, Arcade, 85, Points in Space, constumes & lighting, 86, Brit Broadcasting Co, 86, Carousel, costumes & Lighting, 87, Fabrications, decor & lighting, 87, Cargo X, decor & lighting, 89, The Paris Opera Ballet, 90, Trackers, 91, Philadelphia Ballet, Arcade; Dazzle Camouflage Set Design, Time and Space Theatre, NY, 83; Plain Air: Sandra Gering Gallery, 89, The Mattress Factory, Pittsburgh, Pa, 90 & P S 1 Mus, Long Island Ctr, NY, 91; Indeterminacy, 16 mm film, Mattress Factory Mus, 98; Mus Contemp Art, Los Angeles, Calif; Carnegie Mus Art, Pittsburgh, PA; Mattress Factory Mus, Pittsburgh, PA; Int Le Pompidon Ctr, Paris. *Exhib:* Drawings of the 80's (from the permanent collection), Mus Mod Art, 90; The Drawing Ctr, NY; Carnegie Int, Pittsburgh, Pa; Drawings of the '90's, Katonah Mus, NY; Rolywholover a Circus, Mus Contemp Art, Los Angeles, 93 & 98; Work from the Permanent Collection, Art Inst Chicago, 94; Guggenheim Mus, NY, 94; Menil Collection, Houston, Tex, 94; Mito Tower, Japan, 94; Philadelphia Mus, Pa, 95, 96, 99, 2000; Del Mus of Contemp Art, 2000; Rooseum Mus, Malmö, Sweden, 2000; Formformlessness: Dove Bradshaw, 1969-2003, Mishkin Gallery, NY, 03; and others. *Pos:* Artistic adv, Merce Cunningham Dance Co, 84-; Sandra Gering Gallery, NY, 89, 90, 93, 95 & 98; Barbara Krakon Gallery, Boston, 97; Linda Kirkland Gallery, NY, 98; Stalke Gallerie, Copenhagen, 96, 98, 2000, 2004; Stark Gallery, NY, 2001. *Teaching:* Sculpture, Sch Visual Arts, NY, 75-81. *Awards:* Sculpture, Nat Endowment Arts, 75; Pollock-Krasner Painting Award, 85. *Bibliog:* Gene Moore (auth), Windows at Tiffany's: The Art of Gene Moore, Harry N Abrams, 80; Judith Collishan Van Wagner (auth), Lines of Vision, Hudson Hills Press, New York, 89; Thomas McEvilley (auth), New York reviews, Art Forum, 1/90; The Odyssey of a Collector, Carnegie Mus Art, 96; T McEuilley (auth), Sculpture in the Age of Doubt, Allworth Press, New York, 2000. *Media:* All. *Specialty:* Fine Art. *Publ:* Fire Hose Postcard 1976-1992, Metrop Mus Art, NY; Indeterminary Contingency, Removal, Riverstone, Equivalents, Full, self produced, NY, 90-94; Plain Air, silver prints in portfolio, ed of 5, 91; Spent Bullets, Nils Borch Jensen, Copenhagen, 99. *Dealer:* Stalke Gallerie Veskerbrogade 14A Copenhagen. *Mailing Add:* 924 West End Ave New York NY 10025

BRADSHAW, ELLEN
PAINTER
b Rochester, NY. *Study:* Pratt Inst, Brooklyn, NY, BFA, 84. *Exhib:* Solo exhib, Bridge Cafe, NY, 95, Pace Univ, Schimmel Ctr for Arts, NY, 99, Pleiades Gallery, NY, 2000, Citibank Financial Ctr, NY, 2002, A Taste of Art, NY, 2003; group exhib, Lever House, NY, 98, Pleiades Gallery, NY, 99, Tribeca Fine Arts, NY, 2000, Butler Inst of Am Art, Youngstown, Ohio, 2001, Nat Arts Club, NY, 2002, Caesarea Gallery, Boca Raton, Fla, 2003, Pen & Brush, NY, 2003. *Awards:* William & Theresa Meyerowitz Mem Award, Audubon Artists Am 86th Annual, 2000; Sophia & Emmanuel Zimmer Award, Pen & Brush Reg non-mem Juried Show, 2001; Jane Peterson Mem Award, Salmagundi Club, Annual Combined Exhib, 2003. *Bibliog:* Bonnie Barney (auth), Perspectives, Yates Co Arts Coun, Vol 28, no 1, 2002; Thomas Lawrence (auth), Manhattan Arts International, 3-4/2000; Peggy Platonos (auth), Waterside Weekly, 8/98. *Mem:* Allied Artists Am Inc; Am Artists Prof League; Nat Asn Women Artists; NY Soc Women Artists; Pleiades Gallery Contemp Art, NY (pres, 2000-). *Media:* Miscellaneous Media. *Mailing Add:* 100 Beekman St Apt 25N New York NY 10038

BRADSHAW, GLENN RAYMOND
PAINTER, EDUCATOR
b Peoria, Ill, Mar 3, 22. *Study:* Ill State Univ, BS, 47; Univ Ill, MFA, 50. *Work:* Butler Inst Am Art, Youngstown, Ohio; Springfield Art Mus, Mo; Hollister, Inc, Libertyville, Ill; Landmark Systems Corp, Washington; San Diego Mus, Calif; and others. *Exhib:* 200 Yrs of Watercolor Painting in Am, Metrop Mus Art, NY, 66-67; Watermedia '70, Univ Colo, Boulder, 70; Watercolor USA Bicentennial, Springfield Mus Art, Mo, 76; Univ San Diego, 81; Univ Ill Fac Exhib, Nihon Univ, Tokyo, 83; Am Watercolor Soc invitational, Mus de la Acurela Mexicana, Mexico City, 89. *Pos:* juror, Wis exhib. *Teaching:* Prof art, Univ Ill, 52-86, emer prof, 86-; Master Classes, 6 Wks per year, Springmaid Watercolor Workshop, Myrtle Beach, SC, 86-. *Awards:* Barse Miller Mem Prize, 83; William A Paten Prize, Nat Acad Design, NY, 87; William P & Gertrude Schweitzer Prize, Nat Acad Design, NY, 93; Eileen Monaghan & Frederick Whitaker Prize, Nat Acad Design, NY, 96; Lifetime Achievement award Watercolor USA Hon Soc, 2000; Whitaker Prize, Nat Acad, 2001. *Bibliog:* Gerald F Brommer (auth), Understanding Transparent Watercolor, Davis Publ, 93; Christopher Schink (auth), Color and Light, Watson-Guptill, 95; Conceptual Caseins, Watercolor, Spring, 2002; Advice from Experts by Beth Patterson, Watercolors, Summer, 2004; Drawing on Words, by Lisa Wurster, Artist's Sketchbook, Feb, 2005. *Mem:* Am Watercolor Soc; Nat Watercolor Soc; Nat Soc Painters in Casein & Acrylic; Rocky Mountain Nat Watermedia Soc; Nat Acad (assoc, 87, acad, 94). *Media:* Casein, Collage. *Dealer:* Arline Fleischer Vienna VA. *Mailing Add:* PO Box 39 McNaughton WI 54543

BRADSHAW, LAURENCE JAMES
EDUCATOR, PAINTER
b St Paul, Kans, Sept 21, 1945. *Study:* Pittsburg State Univ, Kans, BFA, with Reed Schmickle, Bert Keeney, Alex Barde, Robert Blunk, Robert Russell, MA; Ohio Univ, MFA, with William Kortlander, Dana Loomis, Gary Pettigrew. *Hon Degrees:* Academia Italia, D. *Work:* Mercantile Libr, NY; Sioux City Art Ctr, Iowa; Joslyn Art Mus, Omaha; Sheldon Art Mus, Univ Nebr, Lincoln; Harmony House, Omaha, Nebr; Univ Nebr, Omaha; plus many others. *Comn:* Metrop Arts Coun, Omaha, 76; Omaha Symphony Assoc, 86; Reviewer of Manuscript, Collegiate Press Publ, Alta Loma, Ca, 96; Map Drawing, Univ Nebr Alumni Asn, Omaha, 97; Medal, Univ Nebr, Omaha, 98. *Exhib:* 38th Mother Load Nat, El Dorado Hills, Calif, 7th Celebration of the Arts, montpelier Cult Ctr, Laurel, Baltimore MD, 2004; 22nd Ann Nat, Alvin Community Col, Houston, Tex, Looking for Am, Nat Washington Gallery of Photog, Bethesda, MD, 2004; Invitational Int United Arab Emerites, 2005; and many others. *Collection Arranged:* 8th Annual All Media International, 2005; 7th Annual Faces International, 2006; 8th Annual Contemporary Art International, 2006; 8th Annual Collage and Mixed Media International, 2006; and over 100 others. *Pos:* Dir, Upstream People Gallery; Selected works; Omaha, Nebr, 98; dir,Univ Art Gallery, 74-76. *Teaching:* Instr life-drawing, painting & silkscreen, Akron Art Inst, Ohio, summer 73; prof drawing, design & painting, Univ Nebr at Omaha, 73-. *Awards:* Abby Award, Nebr Asn Advertisers, 2001; Honorable Mention, 2nd National Exhib, Georgetown, TX, 2004; Int Educator of the Year, 2004-2006, Eng; 100 Top Educators, England, 2005; plus over 60 nat & int art & teaching awards. *Mem:* Visual Artists and Galleries NYC; Vaga. *Media:* Mixed. *Res:* The Consequences of Combinin, The Right Then Left Brain Herrispheres, In Drawing, Univ Released, Time Grant Univ of Nebraska, Omaha, The River front Forum, Univ of Nebraska, Omaha,. *Specialty:* Hosting International Juried Exhib in all Media. *Interests:* Gardening, Reading, Travel. *Publ:* Illusr, Painting with Acrylics, Van Nostrand-Reinhold, 74; August Fires, Glover Davies, Abattoir Press, 78; Folk and Progressive Art, Ancient and New Values in Contemporary Art, Acad Italia, 84; New York Art Rev Am References Publ, Chicago, Ill, 88. *Dealer:* Upstream People Gallery; Internationals; Bemis Ctr Contemporary Art; Anderson O'Brien Fine Art Gallery. *Mailing Add:* Univ Nebr at Omaha Dept Art Omaha NE 68182

BRADSHAW, ROBERT GEORGE
PAINTER, EDUCATOR
b Trenton, NJ, Mar 13, 1915. *Study:* Princeton Univ, AB; Columbia Univ, MA. *Exhib:* NJ State Mus; Am Watercolor Soc; Boston Mus Fine Art; Cape Ann Soc Mod Art; NY World's Fair, 65; plus others. *Teaching:* Lectr art appreciation & hist; prof art, Douglass Col, Rutgers Univ, New Brunswick, 46-79, actg chmn dept art, 64-65, emer prof, 79-. *Awards:* Prize, NJ Watercolor Soc, 59 & Montclair Art Mus, NJ, 63. *Mem:* NJ Watercolor Soc; Hunterdon Co Art Ctr. *Media:* Watercolor, Acrylic

BRADY, CHARLES
PAINTER, SCULPTOR
b New York, NY, July 27, 26. *Study:* Art Student League, 48-51, with John Groth & Morris Kantor; with Marjorie Fitzgibbon, Ireland. *Work:* Seven works in Irish Arts Coun Collection, Dublin; Northern Ireland Arts Coun; NW Trust; Northern Bank Finance Corp; Bank of Ireland Collection; Art Students League. *Exhib:* Pa Acad Fine Arts, Philadelphia, 67; one-man show, Keys Gallery, Derry, Northern Ireland, 77; John Taylor Gallery, Dublin, 79, 81, 86, 88, 89 & 90; Delighted Eye, London, 80; Keys Gallery, Derry, Northern Ireland, 80; and others. *Teaching:* Artist-instr graphics, dept archit, Col Technol, Dublin, 70-71; lectr, Nat Col Art, Dublin, 75-83. *Awards:* P J Carroll Award, Living Art Exhib, Trinity Col, Dublin, 78; Appointment to the Institution of Honor for Creative Artists, Irish Arts Coun, Aosdána, 81; Landscape Prize, Oireachtas Exhib, 9/89. *Mem:* Life mem Art Student League; United Arts Club (hon chmn artist group, 71), Dublin; Figurative Image Group, Dublin (chmn, 85); L&P Financial Trustees of Ireland Ltd. *Media:* Oil; Lost-Wax into Bronze. *Dealer:* John Taylor 34 Kildare St Dublin 2 Ireland; Charles Cambell Gallery 647 Chestnut St San Francisco CA 94133. *Mailing Add:* One Royal Terr W Dun Leary Ireland

BRADY, LUTHER W
COLLECTOR, PATRON
b Rocky Mount, NC, 25. *Study:* George Wash Univ, Wash, AA, 44, AB, 1946, MD, 1948. *Hon Degrees:* DFA, Colgate Univ, 1988; DSc, Lehigh Univ, 1990; MD, Toyama Univ, 1996; Dr Honoris Causa, Heidelberg Univ, 1997; DFA, George Wash Univ, 2004. *Work:* Picker Gallery, Colgate Univ; Villanova Univ Gallery; Pa Acad Fine Arts; George Wash Univ. *Comn:* Joyce, comn by Sam Martin for George Wash Univ; Untitled, comn by Joe Mooney for George Wash Univ. *Pos:* Chmn, Friends Philadelphia Mus Art, 67-70; bd dir, Settlement Music Sch, Philadelphia, 75-; bd trustees, Philadelphia Mus Art, 75-; bd dir, Art Alliance Philadelphia, 78-80; bd dir, Santa Fe Opera, 79-; trustee, Curtis Inst Music, 90-; bd, Fleisher Art Mem, 1998-. *Teaching:* Prof & chmn, Hahnemann Univ, 59-; prof, Distinguished Univ, Sch Med Drexel Univ, 1998-. *Awards:* Distinguished Honoree Medal, Curtis Inst Music, 93; George Wash Univ Soc Medal, 95; James B Colgate Soc Medal, 95; Luther W Brady Curatorship of Japanses Art, Philadelphia Mus Art, 96. *Mem:* Int Arts-Med Asn; Asn of Artists Equity of Philadelphia; PAA (bd dir, 77-79); Found for Archit (bd dir, 82-87). *Media:* Collector paintings, sculptures. *Interests:* Abstract expressionists. *Collection:* American contemp art; Asian and Far Eastern porcelains and stone carvings; English sculpture; Works by John Walker, Jules Olitski, Sam Gillian, Oscar Bluemner, Fritz Scholder and others. *Publ:* Coauth, Principles and Practice of Radiation Oncology, Lippincott. *Mailing Add:* 230 N Broad St Philadelphia PA 19102-1121

BRADY, ROBERT D
SCULPTOR
b Reno, Nev, 46. *Study:* Calif Col Arts & Crafts, BFA, 69; Univ Calif, Davis, MFA, 75. *Work:* San Francisco Mus Mod Art; Oakland Mus; Crocker Mus, Sacramento, Calif; Stedelijik Mus, Amsterdam, Holland; Am Telegraph & Telephone, NY. *Exhib:* Calif Ceramics & Glass, Oakland Mus, 74; Modern Masks, Whitney Mus Am Art, 84; Best Picks, Oakland Mus, 86; Ten Yr Retrospective Traveling Exhib, Crocker Mus Art, Sacramento, 89; de-Persona, Oakland Mus, 91; solo exhibs, Braunstein/Quay Gallery, San Francisco, 91, 93, 95, 96, 98, 99, 2001-2003, NDak Mus Art, Grand Forks, 93, Horwitch, Lew Allen Gallery, Santa Fe, NMex, 94, 96, 98 & 2000, Calif State Univ, Sacramento, 94, Craft & Folk Art Mus, San Francisco, 95, Natalie & James Thompson Gallery, San Jose State Univ, Calif, 96 & John Elder Gallery, NY, 98 & 99; In Reverence of Wood, Univ Art Gallery, Calif State Univ, Haywood, 93; Human Nature/Human Form, Laguna Gloria Art Mus, Austin, Tex, 93; Made of Wood Traveling Show, Hewlett Packard, Palo Alto, Calif, 93-94; A Labor of Love, New Mus, NY, 96; Ceramic Sculpture from the East Bay, Calif State Univ, Hayward, 96; Prints from Wash Square Editions, San Jose State Univ Art Galleries, Calif, 97; Soc Arts Crafts, Boston, 97; Earth and Air, San Francisco Craft & Folk Art Mus, Calif, 97; The Mus of Arts and Sciences, Macon, GA, 99; Made in Calif: Art, Image and Identity, 1900-2000, Los Angeles Co Mus of Art, 2000. *Pos:* Prof art, Sacramento State Univ. *Bibliog:* Mary Webster (auth), The initiation, Artweek, 4/8/93; Lis Bensley (auth), City Focus, Santa Fe Hip and Hopping, Art News, 6/96; Michael Rush (auth), Robert Brady and Steven Whittlesey, Am Craft, 6-7/98. *Mem:* ENSECA. *Media:* Ceramic, Wood. *Publ:* Auth, Ceramic Sculpture (catalog). *Mailing Add:* c/o Braunstein Quay Gallery 430 Clementina St San Francisco CA 94103

BRAFF, PHYLLIS
CRITIC, CURATOR
b Boston, Mass. *Study:* Simmons Col, BS, BA; Columbia Univ, MA (art hist); Harvard Univ exten program. *Collection Arranged:* Images of George Washington, 76; Artists & East Hampton: A 100 Year Perspective (auth, catalog), Guild Hall Museum, 76; Falaise - historical collection house, 81; Thomas Moran: A Search for the Science (auth catalog), Guild Hall Museum, 80-81; The Surrealists & their Friends on Eastern LI at Mid Century (auth catalog), Guild Hall Museum, 96-97; Women Artists on Eastern LI, 98. *Pos:* cheif art curator & dir of mus collection, Nassau Co Div of Mus Services, 68-91; art critic, East Hampton Star, 69-85; art critic, New York Times (Long Island Section), 81-. *Awards:* NYSCA Grant, Artists on Long Island: A Hundred Year Perspective, 76; NY Coun for the Humanities, The Casble Theme in Am Archit, 84; NEA Grant, The Surrealists and their Friends on Eastern LI at Mid Century, 96. *Mem:* Am Soc for Hispanic Art Hist Studies (pres, 86-88); Int Asc of Art Critics (pres, USA section, 92-94, vpres, Int, 95-98). *Publ:* auth, Bibliography of 29th Century Art & Architecture, Worldwide Art Books, 68; auth, Bibliography of American Art & Architecture, Worldwide Art Books, 68. *Mailing Add:* 333 E 55th St New York NY 10022

BRAGAR, PHILIP FRANK
PAINTER, SCULPTOR
b New York, NY, May 10, 25. *Study:* Esmeralda Sch Painting & Sculpture, Mex City, with Raul Anguiano, Carlos Orozco Romero, Alfonso Ayala & Ignacio Aguirre, 54-59. *Work:* NY Pub Libr; Pasadena Art Mus, Calif; NJ State Mus, Trenton; Los Angeles Co Mus Art; Libr Cong, Wash, DC; Mus Mod Art, Mexico City; Jose Luis Cuevas Mus, Univ Mus Contemp Art, Mexico City; National Print Mus, Mexico City. *Exhib:* One-man shows, Galeria Antonio Souza, Mexico City, 68, Galeria Pecanins, 69 & 73, Lynn Kottler Gallery, NY, 81, Palace Fine Arts, Mexico City, 92, Mus Jose Luis Cuevas, Mexico City, 95 & Mus Univ Contemp Arte, Unam, Mex, 97; Nineteen Yrs of Woodcut Prints, 78, & Kafka by Bragar, 85, Galeria Pecanins, Mexico City; Biennial of Graphics, Mus Fine Arts, Mexico City, 79; Mus Mod Art, Mexico City, 87; Nat Print Mus, Mexico City, 90; Prehispanic Man/Contemp Man, Deleg Venustiano Carranza, Mexico City, 94; Paintings and Sculptures, Galeria Pecanins, Mexico City, 98; Metropolitan Univ, Mexico City, 2000. *Teaching:* Instr drawing, painting, design & printmaking & dir art dept, US Int Univ, Mexico City, 70-75. *Awards:* 1 yr grant paintings, Prehispanic Man/Contemp Man, Nat Fund for Cult & Art, 90; Grant, Nat System Creators Art, Mexico City, 93-96, 97-2000; Nat Fund Cult Art Us, The Human Beings, 2000-2001. *Bibliog:* Antonio Espinoza (auth), The Savage Expressionism of Philip F Bragar, El Nacional-Mexico City, 4/92; Lorna Scott Fox (reporter), Inseparable Man-Philip F Bragar, Poliester and Cotten-Mexico City, no 2, summer 92; Alfredo Rodriguez Ramirez (auth), Philip F Bragar, the alien, Novedades, Imágenes, Mexico City, 10/14/94, The City of Mexico Reflected in the painting of Philip F. Bragar (auth), Eduardo Alexandro Hernandez, Uel Universal, 01/14/2000. *Media:* Oil, Wood. *Publ:* Illusr poem, In: Armando Zarate's El Corazon Cae Fuera del Camino, 63; illusr, Dr Oswaldo Schon's Americans Under Mexican Law, 71. *Dealer:* Galeria Myra Nakatani Chihuahua, 97 Col Roma Mexico DF 06700. *Mailing Add:* Iztaccihuatl No 21 Col Hipodromo Condesa Mexico DF 06100 Mexico

BRAGG, E ANN BRAGG
PAINTER
b Liberty, NY, Mar 8, 35. *Study:* State Univ Col, Buffalo, NY, BS, 58; study with Edgar A Whitney, 75-80 & Paul Wood, 80-85. *Work:* American Bond Inc. *Exhib:* Am Standard Gallery, NY, 85; Firehouse Gallery, Nassau Community Col, 86; Women's Art Show, Purdue Univ, Ind, 86; Autotech Show, Long Island Coliseum, Nassau Co, 86; Nat Asn Women Artists, Tweed Mus Art, Univ Minn, 87; Nassau Mus Fine Arts, Roslyn, NY, 89; and others. *Pos:* Guest inst, Valley Stream High Sch & Celebration of Drawing, Workshop, Nassau Community Col; Judge & Demonstrator for Art Leagues, New York & Long Island. *Teaching:* Pvt lessons for problem children in elementary sch, 76-81; instr, abstract experiment watercolor, 5 Towns Mus & Art Found, 81-92; guest instr, drawing, Nassau Community Col, 86. *Awards:* Mario Cooper Award, Am Watercolor Soc, 81; Elizabeth Morse Genius Found Award, Nat Asn Women Artists, 88; Heckshire Mus Award, 90. *Bibliog:* Malcolm Preston (auth), Showing a bit of abstraction, News Day, 4/20/85; Helen A Harrison (auth), Heart of the matter figures as motif, 1/22/89 & From exuberant abstraction to detailed realism, 6/10/90, NY Times. *Mem:* Nat Asn Women Artists; Nat Art League. *Media:* All. *Mailing Add:* 2921 Cleveland Ave Oceanside NY 11572-1114

BRAIDEN, ROSE MARGARET J
PAINTER, ILLUSTRATOR
b Los Angeles, Calif, Nov 25, 23. *Study:* Mt St Mary's Col, Los Angeles, BFA; Calif Col Arts & Crafts, Oakland, MFA; Long Beach State, studied printmaking with Dick Swift; Univ Southern Calif; Univ Calif, Los Angeles. *Work:* Mt St Mary's Col, Libr & Gallery, Los Angeles. *Comn:* Stained glass windows, St Bernard's Church, Glendale; Design for wall mural, St Lawrence Church, 65; stained glass work, Roger Darricarrere Studios, 69; portraits, Univ Calif, Northridge, 76; bk illus, comn by Steve Pouliot, Banner & Assoc, 78; Egg Tempera portraits, comn by Dr Jeffrey Fried, 99; 20 Portraits Com by various people. *Exhib:* Etchings, Long Beach State Gallery, 68; Cody Gallery, Los Olivos, Calif; Paintings & Icons, Faulkner Gallery, Santa Barbara, Calif, 77; Founder Los Padres Water Colors, Soc- 1990; Cabrilla Art Ctr, 99-2003; Univ Calif Santa Barbara, 2003. *Pos:* Staff artist, Northern Trust Bank, 96-. *Teaching:* Prof art hist, Mt St Mary's Col, 68-70; prof, Santa Barbara City Col, 70- & Cate Sch, Carpinteria, 82-88. *Awards:* Local Hero Award, City Santa Barbara, 98. *Bibliog:* Ann Vail Van Horn (auth), Iconography & icons of the spirit, News & Rev, 78. *Mem:* Los Padre Watercolor Soc (founder). *Media:* Egg Tempera, Watercolor; Ink, Pencil. *Publ:* Illusr, Choices, 82; A Mother's Diary, 91. *Dealer:* Yellow Dog Graphics Santa Barbara CA; Cody Gallery Los Olivos. *Mailing Add:* 2929 Paseo Tranquillo Santa Barbara CA 93105

BRAIG, BETTY LOU
PAINTER, EDUCATOR
b Naylor, Mo, Apr 21, 31. *Study:* Phoenix Col, AA, 64; Ariz State Univ, BA, 70, MA, 73; int, nat & state seminars. *Work:* Tretyakov Gallery Art Sch, Moscow; Prague Acad Fine Art, Prague; Dean of Charles Univ, Prague; Frostburg State Univ, Frostburg, MA; Glendale Community Col, Ariz. *Comn:* Free Hanging Cross, Am Evangelical Lutheran Church, Phoenix, 72; Kieth Herring, Mural, City of Phoenix, 83; Heavenly Valley Resort, Lake Tahoe, Calif, 83; Gold Canyon Golf Resort, Ariz; 20 ft high cross, Mountain View Luthern Church, 2003; 18' x 10' mural, North Valley Medical Plaza, Paradise Valley, Ariz, 2002. *Exhib:* Nat Soc Painters Casein & Acrylic, NY, 80; Am Watercolor Soc Traveling Exhib, 80, 82 & 83; San Diego Int Watercolor Exhib, San Diego Art Mus, 82; Nat Energy Art Exhib, Denver, 82; Ariz Biennial, Tucson Mus Art, 82; Western Fedn Watercolor, Rocky Mountain Nat; Atrium Gallery, Ft Worth Mus Sci & Hist, Tex; one person exhib, Chandler Ctr for the Arts, Ariz. *Pos:* Phoenix Col, Ariz, Corrizo Sch Art, Ruiodoso, NMex; gallery dir, Phoenix Union High Sch Dist; Ambassador to Eastern Europe for Humanities (Delegation), 92. *Teaching:* Instr art, Phoenix Union High Sch Dist, 70-92, Ariz Artists Sch Art Teacher, Int Baccalaureate Examine, UK, elected art seminars, 98-; instr fine art, experimental painting & misc medias. *Awards:* Grumbacher Art Award, Ariz Watercolor Asn, 81; David Gayle Found Award, Western Fedn Watercolor, 82; Best of Show, Soc Experimental Artists, 94; Cutting Edge Award, 2006. *Mem:* Assoc mem Am Watercolor Soc; Ariz Watercolor Asn; Ariz Artist Guild; 22-30 Watercolorist Ariz; Int Soc Experimental Artists (signature); Western Fedn Watercolor Soc (signature); Mo Watercolor Asn. *Media:* Watercolor, Acrylic; Mixed. *Res:* SW wild flowers with medicinal properties. *Specialty:* Experimental water medias, mix of art disciplines. *Interests:* Global trends in art. *Publ:* Ariz Arts & Travel, Scottsdale Mag, 85; Southwest Art, Southwest Profile, 85; Creative Watercolor, 95, Best of Watercolor II, 97 & Best of Composition, Rockport Publ, 98; Watercolor Expressions, 2000; Watercolor Mag, 2001-03. *Dealer:* Braig Studio 5271 S Desert Willow Gold Canyon Ariz 85219; Visions Gallery St Marcos Way Chandler AZ 85224. *Mailing Add:* 5271 S Desert Willow Dr Gold Canyon AZ 85218

BRAITSTEIN, MARCEL
SCULPTOR, EDUCATOR
b Charleroi, Belg, July 11, 35; Can citizen. *Study:* École Beaux-Arts Montreal, dipl; Inst Allende, San Miguel Allende, Mex. *Work:* Montreal Mus Fine Arts, PQ; Art Gallery Ont, Toronto; Winnipeg Art Gallery, Man; Confederation Ctr, PEI; Can Coun Art Bank, Ottawa; Musée de Québec, Can. *Comn:* Monument, Right Hon A Meighen, Dept Pub Works, Can Govt, 69; wall sculpture & fireplace, Ministry of Social Affairs, Québec, 85; relief mural, Alcan House, Montreal, 89. *Exhib:* Spring Show, Montreal Mus Fine Arts, 61; Vermont USA, Bundy Art Gallery, 66; Panorama of Québec Sculpture, Mus Rodin, Paris, France, 70; First Int Biennial Small Sculpture, Budapest, Hungary, 71; Musée du Québec, 92. *Pos:* Dir, Dept Fine Arts, Univ Québec, Montreal, 86-91, retired. *Teaching:* Prof sculpture, Ecole Beaux-Arts Montreal, 65-69 & Univ Quebec, Montreal, 69-73 & 75-97; prof, Mt Allison Univ, 73-75. *Awards:* Sculpture Prizes, Quebec Govt, 59 & Montreal Mus Fine Arts, 61; Sculpture Prize, Montreal Mus Fine Arts, 61. *Bibliog:* E H Turner (auth), Sculpture in Canada, Can Art, 62; Jean Simard (auth), Marcel Braitstein, Sculpteur (monogr), Québec Sculptors Asn, 69; Yves Racicot (dir), Traces (video), Univ Que, Montreal, 91. *Mem:* Quebec Sculptors Asn (vpres, 69-71); Royal Can Acad Arts. *Media:* Welded Steel, Miscellaneous Media. *Publ:* Auth, Le temps, l'artiste et ses traces (essay) In: Ecrits et temoignages de 21 sculpteurs, Montreal, edition Fini-infini, 23-31, 93; Enfant traque, enfant cache (biography), Montreal, editions XYZ, 95; Les Mysteres de lile de Saber (novel), Granby, Que, Editions de la Paix, 10/98. *Mailing Add:* 3045 Montée Alstonvale Hudson PQ J0P 1H0 Canada

BRAKKE, P(ERRY) MICHAEL
PAINTER, EDUCATOR
b Douglas, Ariz, Apr 16, 43. *Study:* Univ Minn, BA, 66; Yale Univ Sch Art & Archit, BFA, 68, MFA, 68. *Work:* Solomon R Guggenheim Mus, NY; Joslyn Art Mus, Omaha; Mus Contemp Art, Chicago; Indianapolis Mus Art. *Exhib:* Solo exhib, Joslyn Art Mus, Omaha, 80 & High Mus Art, Atlanta, Ga, 87; Exxon Nat Exhib, Solomon R Guggenheim Mus, NY, 81; Art Inst Chicago, 81; Indianapolis Mus Art, 82 & 86; Mus Contemp Art, Chicago, 84; Bronx Mus Arts, NY, 87. *Teaching:* Prof painting, Oakland Univ, Rochester, 68-76, Univ Ill, Chicago Circle, 76-81 & Univ Tenn, Knoxville, 81-. *Awards:* Proj Completion Grant, 80 & Artists' Fel, 81, Ill Arts Coun; Nat Endowment Arts Fel, 85-86. *Bibliog:* Judith Russi Kirshner (auth), Michael Brakke, Artforum, summer 82; Paul Krainak (auth), Michael Brakke/sight specific, Atlanta Art Papers, 5-6/87; Patricia Phagan (auth), monogr, High Mus, 87. *Media:* Paint, Photographs. *Publ:* Co-ed, Artbook 2, 80 & auth, illusr, Anima Hostility, the Painting, Waiting, 80, NAME Gallery, Chicago & Nat Endowment Arts. *Mailing Add:* Univ Tenn-Dept Art Knoxville TN 37996

BRALEY, JEAN See Sargent, J McNeil

BRAMAN, NORMAN & IRMA
COLLECTOR
b West Chester, Pa, Aug 22, 32. *Study:* Temple Univ, BA, 55. *Pos:* With marketing and sales department Seagrams Distributors, New York City, 55-57; founder Keystone Stores, Philadelphia, 57-72; pres, Braman Enterprises, Miami, Fla, 72-; owner Philadelphia Eagles, 85-94; chmn, ARCONA, Miami, 85-87; bd dirs US Holocaust Memorial Council, Univ Miami Medical Sch, Am Israel Public Affairs Comt, Miami. *Awards:* Named one of Top 200 Collectors, ARTnews Mag, 2004, 2005, 2006. *Mem:* Greater Miami CofC. *Collection:* Modern and contemporary art, especially Am. *Mailing Add:* Braman Enterprises 2060 Biscayne Blvd Fl 2 Miami FL 33137-5024

BRAMHALL, KIB
PAINTER
b Morristown, NJ, June 12, 33. *Study:* Princeton Univ, AB(art & archeol), 55. *Work:* First Nat Bank of Boston, John Hancock Mutual Life Insurance Co & New England Life, Boston; Russell Reynolds Assoc, NY; Smart Fabrics, Ltd, Montreal. *Comn:* Painting for Cox Cancer Ctr, comn by Henry Guild, Boston, 75. *Exhib:* Seventeen one-man shows, NY, Boston, Santa Fe, Cincinnati, Palm Beach, New Haven, Martha's Vineyard, Cape Cod and Nantucket, 60-86; 24 New Eng Realists, Munson Gallery, Santa Fe, 78; 300 Yrs of Northeast Art, Copley Soc, Boston, 80; Am Realists, Coe Kerr Gallery, NY, 82, 83, 86 & 89; Craven Gallery, 97, 99. *Media:* Oil. *Dealer:* Bramhall & Dunn Vineyard Haven MA 02568; Luce House Gallery Tisbury MA; Craven Gallery W Tisbury Mass 02575. *Mailing Add:* RFD 900 Seven Gates Farm Vinyard Haven MA 02568

BRAMLETT, BETTY JANE
FINE ARTS ADMINISTRATOR, PAINTER, COLLAGE ARTIST
b Augusta, Ga. *Study:* Converse Col, Spartanburg, SC, BA; Univ NC, Chapel Hill; Columbia Univ, MA; Univ SC, Columbia, EdD, 83. *Work:* SC State Collections, Columbia; Spartanburg Arts Ctr Gallery, SC; Springs Mills Res & Develop Bldg, SC; C S Nat Bank Collection, Columbia, SC; Greenville City Hall Collection, SC. *Exhib:* 38th Ann Guild SC Artists, Juried Art Exhib, 88; 52nd Ann Exhib, Greenville Artists Guild, SC, 88; Joyce Dickinson Dowis Mem Art Exhib, Florence Mus Art, SC, 88; Invitational Women's Exhib, Roe Art Gallery, Furman Univ, Greenville, SC, 88; 16th Ann Shelby Art League Nat Show, Works on Paper, Rutgers Nat, 94; 30 Juried Shows, 95-2000; many exhib's up to 2005. *Pos:* Fine arts coordr, Spartanburg Co Sch Dist 7, 59-99, retired; arts comnr, SC Arts Comn, 77-80. *Teaching:* Instr art hist & art educ, Univ SC, Columbia, 69-73. *Awards:* SC Art Educator of the Yr, 88, Southeastern Supervisor of the Yr, 89; SC O'Neill Verner Award Art Educ, 89; Award of Merit, SC Watercolor Soc, 95-96. *Bibliog:* Jack Bass (auth), Porgy Comes Home, World Publ, 70; Seth Vining (ed), article, Tryon Daily Bulletin, NC, 70; Bramlett's Art Goes on Display, Spartanburg Herald-J, 70. *Mem:* Greenville Artists Guild; SC Watercolor Soc; SC Artists Guild (pres 77); So Watercolor Soc. *Media:* Watercolor, Acrylic, Collage. *Res:* A Comparison study of two methods for teaching art appreciation. *Interests:* Piano; beading. *Collection:* Many private collections. *Publ:* Auth, Glass on Glass, Sch Arts, 4/63; auth, Spartanburg's Adventure in Art, 4/67 & A Federal Program Can Be Successful, spring 73, SC State Dept; auth, Elementary Art Media, 73 & co-auth, Fine Arts Curricula, Spartanburg Co Sch Dist, 96. *Dealer:* Carolina Gallery Spartanburg SC; City Art Columbia SC

BRAMSON, PHYLLIS HALPERIN
PAINTER, EDUCATOR
b Madison, Wis, Feb 20, 41. *Study:* Yale Summer Art Sch, Norfolk, Conn, 62; Univ Ill, Urbana, BFA, 63; Univ Wis, Madison, MA(Vilas Fel), 64; Art Inst Chicago, MFA, 74. *Work:* Hirshhorn Mus; Mus Contemp Art, Chicago; Art Inst Chicago; Mus de Toulon, France; Corcoran Mus of Art. *Exhib:* Chicago & Vicinity Show, Art Inst Chicago, 74; Smithsonian Inst, Wash, DC, 76; Works on Paper, Art Inst Chicago, 78; solo exhibs, Dart Gallery, Chicago, 80, 83, 85, 88 & 92, Brody's Gallery, Wash, 87 & 93, Douglass Libr Gallery, Douglass Col, Rutgers Univ, New Brunswick, NJ, 91, G W Einstein Gallery, NY, 91, Printworks Gallery, Chicago, 92 & 97 & Phyllis Kind Gallery, Chicago, 94 & 96; Seattle Art Mus, 85; 43rd Biennial Exhib Contemp Am Painting, Corcoran Gallery Art, 93; 25 Yrs of Printing at Landfall Press, Art Inst Chicago, 96; Constructivists, Ctr Gallery, Ctr Creative Studies, Detroit, 96; Ft Wayne Mus, Ind, 2001; Carl Hammer Gallery, Chicago, 2002. *Pos:* Prof studio arts, Univ Ill, Chicago. *Teaching:* Instr drawing & painting, Columbia Col, Chicago, 72-82; vis artist, Univ Ill, 75, Univ Iowa, 79, Univ Chicago, 80, Art Inst Chicago, 81, Ind State Univ, 81, Univ Wis, 83 & Northwestern Univ, 83; assoc prof, Univ Ill, Chicago, 85-; vis artist & lectr, Univ Colo & Univ Nebr, 86 & Univ NMex, 90. *Awards:* Nat Endowment Arts Fel Grant, 76, 83 & 93; Sr Fulbright Scholar, Australia, 88; Guggenheim Fel, 93. *Bibliog:* John Russell (auth), article, New York Times, 3/12; Lisa Peters (auth), article, Arts Mag, 3/82; Cody Westerbeck (auth), Phyllis Bramson, Artforum, summer 86. *Mem:* Col Art Asn (bd dir, 89-92). *Media:* Oil, Mixed Media. *Dealer:* Printworks/Chicago 311 W Superior Suite 105 Chicago IL 60610. *Mailing Add:* 411 S Sangamon 4C Chicago IL 60607

BRANCH, WINSTON
PAINTER
b Castries, St Lucia, Mar 16, 47. *Study:* The Slade Sch Fine Art, BA, 70; British Sch at Rome, Univ Col London, 66-70; Prix de Rome, Itlay. *Work:* Berkeley Art Mus, Calif; British Mus, Victoria and Albert Mus, Contemp Art Soc, London; Schomburg Collection, NY; Kunsthaile, Hamburg, Ger; Neuer Berliner Kunstverein, Berlin, Ger. *Comn:* painting, Hewanorra Airport, St Lucia, 95; Cow Parade, Kansas City, Mo, 2001. *Exhib:* one-man shows, Hoshscule der Kunst, Berlin, 77, Jersey Art Coun, Bernie Gallery, Channel Isles, 87, Clink Wharf Gallery, London, 97 & Townsend Ctr for Humanities, Univ Calif Berkeley, 99; 23rd Bienal of Sao Paulo, Mus de Arte Moderno, Brazil, 96; Transforming the Crown: African, Asian and Caribbean Artists in Britain, 1966-1996, Studio Mus Harlem, NY, 97; Caribe: exclusion, fragmentacion y paraiso, Mus Extremeno e Iberoamericano de Arte Contemporaneo, Badajoz, Madrid, 98; 1st Bienal of Graphic Art of Latin Am, Buenos Aires, Arg, 2000. *Teaching:* artist-in-residence, Fisk univ, Nashville, Tenn, 73; asst adj prof, Univ Calif Berkeley, 98-99; assoc prof, Kansas State Univ, 2000-2001. *Awards:* John Simon Guggenheim Mem Fel Painting, 78; Purchase Award, 23rd Bienal Sao Paulo, Brazil, 96. *Mem:* Chelsea Art Club, London; Faculty Club, Univ Calif. *Media:* Acrylic. *Dealer:* Strecker-Nelson Gallery 332 Poyntz Ave Manhattan KS 66502

BRAND, MICHAEL
MUSEUM DIRECTOR
b Canberra, 1958. *Study:* Australian Nat Univ, Grad, 1979; Harvard Univ, MA, 1982, PhD, 1987. *Pos:* Founding head, Asian art Nat Gallery of Australia, 1988-96; asst dir, Queensland Art Gallery, Australia, 1996-2000; dir, Va Mus Fine Arts, Richmond, 2000-05; dir, J Paul Getty Mus, LA, Calif, 2006-. *Mailing Add:* Va Mus Fine Arts 200 N Blvd Richmond VA 23220-4007

BRANDENBERG, ALIKI LIACOURAS See Aliki, Liacouras Brandenberg

BRANDHORST, UDO
COLLECTOR
Pos: Founder Udo Brandhorst Mus, Brandhorst Art Mus, Munich; chmn Udo and Anette Brandhorst Found, Cologne, Ger. *Awards:* Named One of Top 200 Collectors, ARTnews magazine, 2004, 2005, 2006. *Collection:* Contemp art. *Mailing Add:* Brandhorst Mus Pinakothek der Moderne Barer Stra 40 Munich 80333 Germany

BRANDT, CAROLE
EDUCATOR
Study: Univ Ill, BS in Speech Educ, 59; Univ Ill, MA in Theatre Art, 62; Univ Iowa, Postgrad, 69; Southern Ill Univ, PhD in Directing and Dramatic Lit, 76. *Pos:* Mem nat comt Am Col Theatre Festival, Kennedy Ctr for Performing Arts, Wash, 78-89, 91-93; artistic dir, Cen Station Dinner, 82-83, Co ONSTAGE, Bloomington, 83-84; exec producer, bd dir Pa Centre Stage, 88-92; mem, Pa Adv, Coun for Arts in Educ, 90-92; dean, Meadows Sch of the Arts, Southern Methodist Univ, Dallas, 94-. *Teaching:* Teacher speech and drama, play dir, pub schs, Oak Lawn, Joliet, Maywood, Ill, 1959-65, 66-68; teaching asst, in speech Univ Ill, Urbana, 1961-62; teaching asst, in rhetoric, then instr educ play prod Univ Iowa, 1968-69; asst prof, theatre Ill State Univ, Normal, 1969-74; assoc prof, drama Ill Wesleyan Univ, Bloomington, 1975-82, dir, Sch Drama, 1977-82; prof, chrmn, dept theatre Univ Fla, Gainesville, 1984-88; Vis artist, prof, Idaho State Univ, Pocatello, 1984; prof, head dept, theatre arts, exec producer, artistic dir, Pa State Univ and Pa Centre Stage, Univ Park, 1988-94. *Awards:* AMOCO medal of excellence Am Col Theatre Festival, 81; Recipient Theatre Educator of Yr award Fla Assoc for Theatre Educ, 88; Kennedy Ctr medal, 89, 91, 93; Distinguished Alumni awrd Dept Theatre/So. Ill Univ, 96; Col Arts and Scis/S Ill Univ, 97. *Mem:* Fel Col Fel Am Theatre (former dean); Asn for Theatre in Higher Educ (found, bd gov 91-, pres 93-95); Nat Asn Sch Theatre (panelist, evaluator 87, 89-92, bd dir 91-); Soc for Stage Dir & Choreographers, Nat Theatre Conf (lifetime); Fla Theatre Conf (pres), Ill Theatre Asn. *Publ:* Co-auth: (video tape) Adjudication 1987; dir, Nat Evening of Scenes, Kennedy Ctr for Performing Arts, 1986, A Chorus Line, Hippodrome State Theatre, 1987. *Mailing Add:* So Meth Univ Meadows Sch Arts Off of the Dean PO Box 750356 Dallas TX 75275-0001

BRANDT, FREDERICK ROBERT
CURATOR
b Paterson, NJ. *Study:* Pa State Univ, BA, 60, MA, 63. *Collection Arranged:* Art Nouveau (contribr, catalog), 71; American Pewter (with catalog), 76; American Marine Painting (with catalog), 76; Allan D'Arcangelo, 79; David True: Paintings 1977-84 (catalog), 84; German Expressionist Art: The Ludwig & Rosy Fischer collection (with catalog), 87; Good Design Collection, Va Mus Fine Arts (with catalog); Harmony & Discord: American Landscape Painting Today (with catalog), 90; Design for Living: Post-War Furniture; Designed to Sell: Turn-of-Century Posters (with catalog), 1994; Celebrating Art Nouveau: The Kreuzer Collection, 2002. *Pos:* Interpretation asst, gallery div, Va Mus Fine Arts, 60-61; teaching asst, Pa State Univ, 61-63; asst prog dir, Va Mus Fine Arts, 63-77, assoc cur, 77-79, 20th century art, 83-96; cur, Sydney & Frances Lewis Collection, 72-; dir, The Sydney & Frances Lewis Found, 80-86; mem adv panel, Va Comn for Arts, 88-90; adv bd mem, Longwood Col Fine Arts, Farmville, Va, 90; bd ed adv, Studies in the Decorative Arts,

92; consult cur, 20th Century Design & Decorative Arts, Va Mus Fine Arts, 98-. *Awards:* Distinguished Alumni Award, Col Arts Pa State Univ, 89. *Mem:* Am Asn Mus. *Publ:* Auth various articles in antique periodicals, 71-92; The Sydney and Frances Lewis Decorative Arts Collection: Art Nouveau and Art Deco, ca 1895-1935, Collections Mag, 91; Designed to Sell: Turn-of-the-Century American Posters, 94; Made to Last a Century: The Roycroft Furniture Shop, Head, Heart & Hand: Elbert Hubbard and the Roycrofters, 94; Posters, Patrons and Publishers, The Mag Antiques, 11/94; Shattering the Southern Stereotype, 1998; Art & Deco, Possession Obsession: Andy Warhol and Collecting, 2002

BRANDT, KATHLEEN WEIL-GARRIS
EDUCATOR, ART HISTORIAN
b Cheam, Surrey, Eng. *Study:* Vassar Col, AB, 56; Univ Bonn, 57; Harvard Univ, AM, 58, PhD, 65. *Hon Degrees:* MA Oxford Univ. *Pos:* Ed-in-chief, Art Bull, 77-81; art historian-in-residence, Am Acad Rome, 75 & 81; consult Renaissance art, Vatican Mus, 87-. *Teaching:* Prof Renaissance art, NY Univ, 65-, Inst Fine Arts, 66-; Harvard Univ, 80-81. *Awards:* Lindback Found Award for Distinguished Teaching, 67; Research Prize, Alexander von Humboldt Found, 85; Officer, Order of Merit of The Italian Repub, 93. *Mem:* Col Art Asn; Renaissance Soc Am; Soc Archit Hist; NY Acad Sci. *Res:* painting, sculpture & architecture of the 15th and 16th centuries in Italy. *Publ:* Auth, The Santa Casa di Loreto, Garland Press, 77; coauth (with J D'Amico), The Renaissance Cardinal's Ideal Palace, Elefante Press, Rome, 82; auth, On Pedestals, Roemisches Jahrbuch fuer Kunstgeschicte, 84; Twenty-Five Questions About Michelangelo's Sistine Ceiling, Apollo, 87; Michelangelo's Pieta, Studies for Andre Chastel, 87; A marble in Manhattan: Ike Case for Michelangelo, Burlington Mag, 96. *Mailing Add:* 37 Washington Sq W No 16C New York NY 10011

BRANFMAN, STEVEN
CERAMIST, INSTR
b Los Angeles, Calif, Mar 5, 53. *Study:* Cortland State Univ, BA, 74, RI Sch Design, MAT, 75, studied with Gerald DiGusto, Norm Shulman, Jun Kaneko, John Jessiman. *Work:* Schein-Joseph Inst-Mus Ceramic Art, Alfred, NY; Canadian Clay and Glass Asn, Toronto; Concordia Col Art Mus, Ann Arbor, Mich; Fuller Mus of Art, Brockton, Mass; Weisman Art Mus, Minneapolis, Minn. *Comn:* Numerous pvt comns. *Exhib:* Artful Crafts, Fitchburg Art Mus, 89; Great Am Crafts, Starr Gallery, Mass, 90; Nat Invitational Exhib, Fisher Gallery, Farmington Valley, Conn, 92; Nat Invitational RaKu Exhib, Kreft Ctr Arts, Ann Arbor, Mich, 92, 94 & 95; Art by Choice, Art Complex Mus, Duxbury, Mass, 95; Solo show, Thayer Gallery, Braintree, Mass, 94 & 95; Steven Branfman & Students, 96; Six int recognized Raku Artists, Vt Clay Studio, Montpelier, 96; Dowd Fine Arts Ctr, State Univ NY, Cortland, 97; Escuela de Artesania, Mexico City, 98; NY in Raku, Currier Art Gallery, Manchester, NH, 98; Weisman Art Mus, Minneapolis, Minn, 2000; Guliford Handcrafts Ctr, Ct, 2003, 2005; NIT Inst Art, Natl Ceramics, Biennial, 2004; Lexington Arts & Crafts Soc, MA, 2004. *Pos:* Pres-dir, Potters Shop, Needham, Mass, 77-; mem, RI Sch Design Alumni Coun, 86; vpres & bd trustees, Studio Potter Organization, 90-. *Teaching:* Instr ceramics, Thayer Acad, Braintree, Mass, 78-; artist-in-residence ceramics, Lasell Jr Col, Newton, Mass, 85-88, Potters Sch, Needham, Mass; lectr, Osgood Lectr Series, Thayer Acad, 3/93 & Asn NE Prep Sch, 4/94. *Awards:* RI Sch Design Alumni Serv Award, 85; First-Prize Crafts, Concord Art Asn, 86. *Bibliog:* Potter Adds New Twists Using An Old Technique, Boston Sunday Globe, 9/10/95; Steven Branfman Leads Raku Weekend, Clay Times Mag, Jan/Feb 97; Raku At Amatlan, Ceramics Monthly, 1/2000. *Mem:* Am Crafts Coun; Mass Asn Crafts; Nat Coun Educ Ceramic Arts. *Media:* Clay-Raku Technique. *Publ:* Auth, Raku Basics, Pottery Making Illustrated, Supplement to Ceramics Mo, 1/94; contrib, Make it in Clay, Mayfleld Publ, 97; ed & contrib, Clay Times Mag; auth, Raku: a Practical Approach, Second Ed, Krause Publ, 2001; auth, Ireland Glass Technique, Ceramics Monthly, May 2002; auth, Potters Professional Handbook, Am Ceramic Soc, 2003. *Dealer:* Signature Galleries Boston MA; Baak Gallery Cambridge MA. *Mailing Add:* The Potters Shop 31 Thorpe Rd Needham MA 02494

BRANGOCCIO, MICHAEL DAVID
PAINTER, COLLAGE ARTIST
b Denver, Colo, July 18, 54. *Study:* Univ Northern Colo, BA, 77, MA, 80. *Work:* Arvada Ctr Art, Arvada, Colo; Nautilus Found, Tallahassee, Fla; IBM, Chicago, Ill; Southern Methodist Univ, Dallas, Tex; Hilton Hotel, Tokyo, Japan. *Comn:* Suite of collage on paper, Hilton Hotel, Shanghai, China, 88; acrylic on canvas, Infinity World Headquarters, Los Angeles, Calif, 89; 2 canvas murals, GKBI Towers, Indonesia, 95. *Exhib:* One-man shows include Nautilus Found, Tallahassee, Fla 92, 1/1 One Over One Gallery, Denver, 95, Olson-Larsen Gallery, Des Moines, 97, 99, 2001, 2002, 2004, William Havu Gallery, Denver, 99, 2001, Ruth Bachofner Gallery, Santa Monica, 99, 2004, Finer Things Gallery, Nashville, Tenn, 2001, Clarke Galleries, Stowe, Vt, 2004, Sardella Fine Arts, Aspen, 2005; Underwraps, Irvine Fine Arts Ctr, Calif, 88; Invitational, Claremont Grad Sch, Calif, 89; Iowa Artists, Des Moines Art Ctr, 94; National Artists Work on Paper, Riverside Art Mus, Calif, 96; Olson-Larsen Gallery, Des Moines, 96; Susan Street Gallery, Solana Beach, Calif, 97; The Des Moines Club, 98; Ruth Bachofner Gallery, 98, 2001, 2002, 2004; Antelope Valley Col, Lancaster, Calif, 98; Fine Things Gallery, 2002; Birds in Painting, Clarke Galleries, 2004. *Teaching:* Guest lectr, Octagon Ctr Arts, Ames, Iowa, 96, Legion Artss, Cedar Rapids, Iowa, 96, William Penn Univ, Oskaloosa, Iowa, 2005. *Bibliog:* Rick Deragon (auth), A synthesises of influences, Artweek, 7/89; Orville O Clark (auth), Michael Brangoccio, Chicago Tribune, 1/18; Mark Hinson (auth), Gallery brings back abstract expressionist, Tallahasee Democrat, 2/7/92. *Media:* Mixed Media on Canvas; Paper Collage. *Dealer:* William Havu Gallery 1040 Cherokee Denver Co 80204

BRANSBY, ERIC JAMES
MURALIST, EDUCATOR
b Auburn, NY, Oct 25, 1916. *Study:* Kansas City Art Inst, Mo, with Thomas Hart Benton & Fletcher Martin, cert(painting & printmaking); Colorado Springs Fine Arts Ctr & Colo Col, with Boardman Robinson & Jean Charlot, BA & MA(mural painting); Yale Univ, with Josef Albers & Carol Meeks, MFA(painting); Park Col, Kansas City, Mo, Hon Dr Fine Arts, 95; Univ Colo, DHL (Hon), 97. *Hon Degrees:* Park Col, Kansas City, Mo, DFA, 95; Univ Colo, LHD, 97. *Work:* Colorado Springs Fine Arts Ctr; Mo State Hist Soc Collection, Columbia; Brigham Young Univ Mus Art; Nelson Atkins Mus Art, Kansas City; Princeton Univ; Print Research Found, NY; Ga Mus Art, Athens, Ga. *Comn:* 8 panel mural, Loveland Mus, Colo, 88; fresco mural, Park Col Libr, Mo, 91; 12 panel mural, Kans State Univ, Manhattan, 86; 36 panel mural, Pioneer Mus, Colorado Springs, 94; 8 panel mural, Colorado Springs Airport, 95; fresco mural, Univ Ill, Urbana, 52; mixed media mural, Brigham Young Univ, Provo, Utah, 58; mixed media mural, Univ of Mo, Kansas City, 75; mixed media mural, St Paul Sch, Skokie, Ill; mixed media mural, Kans State Univ, Manhattan, Kans, 1988. *Exhib:* Housing & Urban Development Nat Community Art Competition; Joslyn Mus Biennial, Omaha, 72 & 78; Nat Ctr Fine Arts, Wash, 73-75; Smithsonian-Traveling Print, 79-80; West Surrey Col, Eng, 80; Nat Soc Mural Painters Centennial, NY Art Students League, 95; Ind State Univ, 97; Solo shows: Albrecht Kemper Mus, 1993, Colo Springs Fine Arts Center, 2002, Ga Mus Art, Univ Ga, 04,. *Teaching:* Asst instr, Yale Univ, 49-50; instr beginning drawing & design, Univ Ill, Urbana, 50-52; prof freehand drawing & design, Univ Mo, Kansas City, 65-84; prof emeritus advanced figure drawing, painting & printmaking Univ Mo, Kansas City. *Awards:* Edwin Austen Abbey Found, Fel (mural painting), 52; Kansas City Asn Trusts & Founds, 70; Veatch Award, Univ of MO, 77; Weldon Springs Grant, Univ MO, 80; Lifetime Achievement Award, Pres Benezet, Colo Col, 99; Pollock-Krasner Award, 2001-02. *Bibliog:* National Community Art Program, US Govt Printing Off (HUD), 73; Under the Influence, Students of Thomas Hart Benton, Albrech Kemper Mus, 73; From Roots to Soaring Visions (catalogue), Colo Springs Fine Arts Center, 2001; Eric J Bransby (auth), Figurative Connections, selected works, Ga State Mus Art, 2003. *Mem:* Nat Soc Mural Painters; and others. *Media:* Multimedia, Buon Fresco. *Res:* Design analysis of Piero della Francesca's mural cycle in the Church of San Francesco at Arezzo, Italy; development of lightweight portable fresco panels; design analysis of a byzantine mosaic mural cycle in the Kariye d'Jami church in Istanbul, Turkey. *Interests:* Renaissance & Mexican mural fresco techniques. *Publ:* The Buon Fresco Process (video), Univ Mo Video Network; Art-Do It, (A handbook for artists), Kendall/Hunt Publ. *Dealer:* Bransby Fine Arts 9080 Hwy 115 Colorado Springs CO 80926. *Mailing Add:* 9080 Hwy 115 Colorado Springs CO 80926

BRANSTETTER, GWENDOLYN H
PAINTER
b Beeville, Tex. *Study:* Tex Technol Univ, 49-50; private instruction with Minnie Miller Simpson, 57-61. *Work:* Nat Cowgirl Hall Fame & Western Heritage, Ft Worth, Tex; Refugio Co Hist Mus, Refugio, Tex; Com State Bank, Beeville, Tex; Woodsboro Indepent Sch Dist, Tex; First Nat Bank, Refugio, Tex; Dr Pepper Mus, Waco, Tex. *Comn:* oils, comn by James W Witherspoon, Hereford, Tex, 87; Landscape in oil, comn by Jame Armour, Dallas, Tex, 88; Western in oil, comn by William L Leach, Houston, Tex, 88; Western, comn by, Mr & Mrs Jimmy Craft, Refugio, Tex, 88; Texas Bluebonnets, comn by Watson, Waco, 88. *Exhib:* Int Cult Exchange, Tour Art Europe, Rome, Italy, 68; Western Heritage Art Show, Nat Cowgirl Hall Fame, Hereford, Tex, 77, 78 & 79; Texas Realism 1985, Tex Fine Arts Asn, Austin, Tex, 85; one-person Show, Refugio Co Mus, Refugio, Tex, 88; Invitational Western Art Show, Western Art Barn, San Antonio, Tex. *Teaching:* Instr oils for adults, Refugio Co Mus, 86-89, oil for children, 87-89. *Awards:* First Over-All in Show, Grumbacher, 58; First Over-All in Show, Winsor-Newton, 59; Selected to show from 1114, Tex Fine Arts Asn, 85; Nominated as honoree to be inducted into Nat Cowgirl Hall Fame, Hereford, Tex, 92. *Bibliog:* Adrian Shapiro (auth), Two Paths To Western Painting, Art Happenings Houston, summer 82; Joe Cavanaugh (auth), Branstetter Paintings, Refugio Co Press, 7/20/83; Mel McCombie (auth), Tex Realism, Austin Am-Statesman, 12/27/85; Carol M Highsmith and Ted Landphair (co-auth) Texas - A Photographic Tour, Random House, 98. *Media:* Oil, Watercolor. *Specialty:* Western, Wildlife, Landscape Art. *Interests:* Travel, Painting. *Publ:* Illustr, Gwendolyn H Branstetter, Louise S O'Connor (auth), Tales from the San'Tone River Bottom - A Cultural History, Vol 2, Historic Times, Wexford Pubs, Austin, Tex, 2001. *Dealer:* Cuero Art Gallery 608 Clinton Cuero TX 77954. *Mailing Add:* PO Box 143 1004 Douglas St Refugio TX 78377

BRANT, PETER M
PATRON
Pos: Chmn, chief exec officer, Brant Allen Industries, Inc; owner, Brant Publications (Interview Mag, Art in Am Mag); co-founder, Greenwich Polo Club, 1995-; Bd trustees, Solomon R Guggenheim Mus; Exec producer, (films) Basquiant, 1996, Pollock, 2000. *Mailing Add:* Brant Allen Industries Inc 80 Field Pt Rd Greenwich CT 06830

BRANTLEY, JAMES SHERMAN
PAINTER
b Philadelphia, Pa, Feb 1, 45. *Study:* Pa Acad Fine Arts; Philadelphia Col Art; Univ Pa. *Work:* Afro-Am Hist & Cult Mus; Am Mus at PAFA Chamber of Commerce of Del; Hampton Univ Mus; Fed Res Bank, Philadelphia, Pa. *Exhib:* Contemp Black Artists (with catalog), Whitney Mus Art, NY, 73; one-man shows, Sande Webster Gallery; Visions, Atmosphere Gallery, NY, 2000; New Acquisitions, Hampton Univ Mus, Va; From the Collection, Am Mus @ PAFA; Absence of Color, Philadelphia Mus of Art. *Awards:* Hallgarten Prize, Nat Acad Design; Louis Fine Purchase Award, Pa

Acad & Fancis Bergman Portrait Award. *Bibliog:* Internat Rev of African-Am Art, Vol 17, 2000; Wall St Jour, Mar 2000; Wilson Quarterly, Summer 2000; Painter's Progress, Gerard Brown (auth), Phila Weekly, 99. *Media:* Acrylic. *Publ:* ernat Rev of African-Am Art, Vol 15, 99; Ed Sozanski, Philadelphia Inquirer, 2/28/99; Brantley Exhib, Philadelphia Tribune, 1/6/99; African-Am Wishing Book, Running Press, 96. *Mailing Add:* 6915 Greenhill Rd Philadelphia PA 19151-2320

BRARDO, JOSÉ MANUEL
COLLECTOR
Pos: Co-owner Royal Savoy Resort, Funchal, Madeira, 88-; other enterprises including mining, media, wine. *Awards:* Named one of Top 200 Collectors, ARTnews Mag, 2004. *Collection:* Cntemporary art

BRASELMAN, LIN EMERY See Emery, Lin Emery Braselman

BRASETH, JOHN E
ART DEALER, CONSULTANT
b Seattle, Wash, May 23, 59. *Study:* Studied Northwest Art from 1930's to present. *Pos:* Dir & owner, Gordon Woodside-John Braseth Galleries. *Specialty:* Northwest masters: Morris Graves, William Ivey, Mark Tobey, Paul Horiuchi, Guy Anderson, Joseph Goldberg, Kenneth Callahan, Jacob Lawrence; plus others. *Mailing Add:* 2101 Ninth Ave Seattle WA 98121

BRATCHER, DALE
PAINTER
b Rockport, Ky, Jan 10, 32. *Study:* Univ Louisville, BCE, MCE. *Work:* Citizens Bank, Evansville, Ind; Evansville Mus Arts & Sci, Ind; Morehead State Univ, Ky; Coca Cola Co, Elizabethtown, Ky; Household Int Corp, Prospect Heights, Ill; Lucille Parker Markey Cancer Ctr, Lexington, KY; Lilly Interprise Coatings, Indianapolis, Ind; Doncaster Mus Art, Eng; Hillard & Lyons Ctr, Louisville, Ky; numerous pvt collections. *Comn:* Paintings, Lewisport Sch & Lewisport City Hall, Ky, 77; Pate House, Hancock Co, Ky, 77; 3 paintings, Hancock City, Ky; painting, Liberty Nat Bank & Trust, Louisville, Ky. *Exhib:* Watercolor USA, Springfield, Mo, 74, 83 & 88; Midwest Watercolor Soc Ann, 78-79 & 83; Rocky Mountain Nat Watermedia, Golden, Colo, 80-82; Nat Arts Club Open Watercolor Exhib, NY, 81-82; one-man shows, Grand Canyon Nat Park, Ariz, 81 & 83, Morehead State Univ, Ky, 83 & Doncaster Mus, South Yorkshire, Eng, 86 & 90; Headley-Whitley Mus Art, Lexington, Ky, 87; Evansville Mus Arts & Sci, Indiana, 91; Liberty Gallery, Louisville, Ky, 92. *Pos:* Artist. *Awards:* First Place, Art Works Show, Frankfort, KY, 81; Best of Show, Woman's Club Louisville, Ky, 82; Purchase Award, Reflections '83, Covington, Ky, 83. *Bibliog:* Articles, North Light, 3/83, Southwest Art, 9/84 & Am Artist, 3/85. *Mem:* Watercolor Soc Ala; Ky Watercolor Soc; Southern Watercolor Soc; Midwest Watercolor Soc; Ga Watercolor Soc. *Media:* Watercolor, Egg Tempera. *Dealer:* Owensboro Mus Fine Art 901 Frederica St Owensboro KY 42301; Indianapolis Mus Art 1200 W 38th St Indianapolis IN 46208. *Mailing Add:* 1529 Crosstimbers Dr Louisville KY 40245

BRATT, BYRON H
PRINTMAKER
b Everett, Wash, Dec 12, 52. *Study:* Western Wash Univ, BA(fine arts), 75. *Work:* Libr Cong, Wash, DC; Brooklyn Mus; Am Mus, Bath, England; New York Pub Libr; Addison Gallery Am Art, Phillips Acad, Andover, Mass. *Exhib:* Am Prints Today & 22nd Ann Print Exhib, Brooklyn Mus, NY; Am Color Print Soc, Philadelphia; 24th Nat Print Exhib, Smithsonian Inst, Wash, DC; RI Sch Design, Providence; Carnegie Inst, Pittsburgh; Int Print Co, Tokyo, Japan & Philadelphia. *Bibliog:* Andrew Stasik (auth), Am Prints & Print Marlow, 56-81, Print Rev, 82; Van Deventer (auth), Six Masters of Mezzotint, 87; Carol Wax (auth), The Mezzotint, Abrams, 90. *Media:* Mezzotint. *Mailing Add:* c/o Waterworks Gallery 315 Spring St PO Box 28 Friday Harbor WA 98250

BRATTON, CHRISTOPHER ALAN
SCULPTOR, VIDEO ARTIST
b Akron, Ohio, July 3, 59. *Study:* Birmingham - Southern Col, 77-79; Atlanta Col Art, BFA, 82; Whitney Mus Independent Study Prog, 84-86; Univ Wis, MFA, 94. *Exhib:* Counterterror: The North of Ireland, PBS/WNET, Channel 13 & Eng Film Festival, Boston, 90 & 92-93; Framing the Panthers in Black & White, Intercom, PBS/WNET Channel 13, 90 & 91; Video Viewpoints, Mus Mod Art, NY, 90; Wexner Ctr Contemp Art, Columbus, Ohio, 93; Small War: The United States in Puerto Rico, Ctr Cult Ruiz Belvis, Chicago, Ill, 95. *Pos:* Project dir Rise & Shine Productions, New York City video, comt on exhib's & events, instn-wide tech initiative, 97-98, chmn, dept of film, video, and new media Chicago, Ill, 2000-2001, dean of undergraduate studies, 2002-2004; pres, San Francisco Art Inst, Calif, 2004-; cur, Teaching TV, Artists' Space, NY, 90, vis artist Hallwalls, Buffalo, Educ Video Ctr, New York City, 91, RI Sch of Design, Providence, 92, Gallery 400, Univ Ill, Chicago, 94; coordr, producer Teaching TV, Deep Dish TV, 92; presenter Hunter Col Roundtable on Media and Culture, New York City, 92, The Ctr for 20th Century Studies, Univ Wis, Milwaukee, 92; grants panelist Nat Educ Asn Regional fel, Film in the Cities, Minneapolis, 93; panelist Guerilla TV, Ctr for New TV, New York City, 93. *Teaching:* Guest lectr, in video prod State Univ NY at Old Westbury, 86, Channel Four workshop, Derry Northern Ireland, 86, seminars New York Univ, panelist, NY Marxist Sch, Video, Educ & Culture, New York City, 89, Literacy on the Table seminar, Video and Literacy, Bronx, NY, Coun, on the Arts, 89, Columbus in Context, Union Theological Seminary, NY, Mediactive Conf Low Format Video & Media Educ, 90; guest lectr, Sch Visual Arts, 90, Sch the Art Inst, Chicago, Ill, 90; vis prof, ctr for modern cult & media Brown Univ, Providence, 91-92. *Awards:* Nat Endowment Arts, 82, 88 & 90; Recipient fel in sculpture, Nat Educ Asn, 88; grantee, Checkerboard Found, 89; NY State Coun on the Arts, 89, 91; Citation Nat Educ Film & Video Festival for Brooklyn, 89; Grand prize Int Youth Film & Video Festival, Warsaw for Brooklyn, 90; Bronze Apple for Walls and Bridges, 90; NY State Coun Arts Grant, 91; Artist's Residency fel, Wesner Ctr for Contemp Art, Columbus, Ohio, 93. *Publ:* Coauth (with Annie Goldson), Counterterror, Global Television, Mass Inst Technol Press, Boston, 88; Ed, cur: (videotape) Teaching TV, 91; dir, (videotapes), Counterterror The North of Ireland, 90, (Best Advocacy Work, The Atlanta Film and Video Festival 91, Silver Apple, Oakland, California National Educational Film and Video Festival, Finalist Athens,Ohio Festival) Framing the Panthers in Black and White (Am Film Fest Red Ribbon, New England Film and Video Fest Best Social Documentary, Australian Video Festival finalist, Hallwalls Festival of New Journalism, Buffalo, Jurors' award, Peoples Choice award The Global Africa Festival, Oakland, Calif, Special Jurors' award Black Maria Film and Video Fetival, East Orange, NJ, others), A Small War: The United States in Puerto Rico, 95. *Mailing Add:* San Francisco Art Inst 800 Chestnut St San Francisco CA 94113

BRAUCHLI, BYRON T
PHOTOGRAPHER, INSTRUCTOR
b Boulder, Colo, Feb 24, 60. *Study:* Univ Colo, BFA, 87; Univ Tex, Austin, MFA, 90. *Work:* Mus Fine Arts, Houston; Univ Austin, Tex. *Exhib:* Witcliff Gallery of Mexican & Southwestern Photog, Tex; Ctr for Creative Photog, Ariz; 5th Ann Gov's Exhib, Inst of Texan Cultures, San Antonio, 96, Encrucijadas, Galveston Fine Arts Ctr, Tex, 96; Recollecting, Harry Ransom Center, Univ Tex, 97, Festival of the Americans, Mus of Abilene, 97; Cult Refractions, Mus of Anthropology, Mex, 98; Fragamentos, Inst of Fine Art Univ Veracruz, Mexico, 99, Landscape and Modernity, 2000; Fresh Ink: Austin Print Workshops, Austin Mus Art, 99. *Pos:* coordr cult refractions project, US Mex Fund for Cult/Rockfeller Found, 96-97. *Teaching:* instr art photography, Austin Community Col, 94-. *Awards:* Juror Merit Award, New Am Talent, Austin Mus Art, 95; Expo 96 Award, 500x Gallery, 96; Fulbright Rsch/Lecture Scholar, Univ Veracruz, Mexico, 99-2000. *Bibliog:* Jeanne Claire Ryzin (auth) Culture Clashes, The Austin Am Statesman, 4/98; Rebecca Cohen (auth), Framing The Border, Austin Chronical, 5/98; Norberto Amador (auth), Refracciones Culturales, El Diario de Xalapa, Mexico, 99. *Mem:* Soc for Photographic Education; Tex Photography Soc. *Dealer:* Stephen L Clark Photography 1101 W 6th St AustinTX 78703. *Mailing Add:* PO Box 50539 Austin TX 78763-0539

BRAUDY, DOROTHY
PAINTER, PHOTOGRAPHER
b Los Angeles, Calif. *Study:* Univ, Ky, BA; NY Univ, MA(art educ); pvt study with Richard Pousette-Dart; Art Students' League, with Stamos, Kantor & Glasier; Columbia Univ Teachers Col. *Work:* Fed Reserve Bank, Richmond, Va; Mason Co Mus, Maysville, Ky; Rutgers Univ Mus, New Brunswick, NJ; Ellen Kim Murphy Gallery, 2000; Univ S Calif, 2006. *Comn:* Portrait comn by Richard Poirier, NY, 75; George Davis family, Calistoga, Calif, 79; John Irwin family, Baltimore, Md, 80; William Chamness family, Aberdeen, Ohio; Ira Brind family, Philadelphia, 85; Dorothy Lyman-Vincent Malle, Los Angeles, 86. *Exhib:* Viridian Gallery, NY, 77-78; One-person shows, B R Kornblatt Gallery, Baltimore, 79, Washington, 81, Goucher Col, 82, UPB Gallery, Berkeley, Calif, 84, Orlando Gallery, Los Angeles, 86 & 88, 871 Fine Arts, 93, USC Fisher Gallery, 94, Ellen Kim Murphy Gallery, 2000, Hamilton Galleries, 2006. *Teaching:* Prof art educ, Pratt Inst, New York, 71-77; prof art hist & drawing, Towson State Univ, Md, 78-79; prof visual arts, Goucher Col, Towson, Md, 79-83. *Bibliog:* Articles in Baltimore Sun, 9/81 & 9/83, Santa Monica Mirror, 10/2000; article in New Art Examiner, 10/81; Reviews in Los Angeles Times, 86, 88 & 94, ArtScene 12/88, Dreamworks, 88 & Art Week, 1/95; Women's Studies, 2003. *Media:* Oils, Watercolor, Photography. *Publ:* auth, Finishing the Hat, 2000; auth, Marking Time, 2006. *Dealer:* Hamilton Galleries. *Mailing Add:* 2008 N Oxford Ave Los Angeles CA 90027

BRAUER FERNS, CONNIE ANN
DESIGNER, GOLDSMITH
b Denver, Colo, May 4, 1949. *Study:* Colo State Univ, BFA, 71; Inst of Europ Studies, Vienna, Austria, 71; Rochester Inst of Technol, 72-73. *Exhib:* All-Colo Show, Denver Art Mus, 74; Flux, Fusion & Fireworks, Contemp Crafts Gallery, Portland, Ore, 80; Young Americans/Metal, NY, 81; Metalsmith 81, Univ Kans; Concepts Gallery, Carmel, 82; Hanson Gallery, Houston, 83; and others. *Teaching:* Instr jewelry, Metrop State Col, 83. *Awards:* Cash Award, Copper, Brass & Bronze Exhib, Univ Ariz, Tucson, 77; Cash Award, Colo Artist Craftsman Ann Show, 80; Cash Award, Inamori Jewelry Design Competition, 83. *Bibliog:* Fashion swirls into spring, 2/82, Fall fashion forecast, 8/83 & Fashion forecast, 8/83, Jewelers Circular Keystone. *Mem:* Am Craft Coun; Soc N Am Goldsmiths; and others. *Media:* Precious metals, Enamel. *Publ:* Contribr cover photograph, Small Sculptures Nat Catalogue, Cypress Col, 76. *Mailing Add:* 3875 Xavier St Denver CO 80212-2208

BRAUNSTEIN, MARK MATHEW
CURATOR, PHOTOGRAPHER
b New York, NY, Aug 6, 51. *Study:* Carnegie-Mellon Univ, 72; Pratt Inst, 73, MS, 78; State Univ NY, Binghamton, BA, 74. *Exhib:* Images 90, Images 94 & Images 2002, Mill Gallery; solo show, Conn Col, 91 & Mystic Nature Ctr, 92; Danforth Mus Art, Framingham, Ma, 2001; Hygienic Art Gallery, New London, Conn, 2002; Conn Col Arboretum, 2001-04. *Collection Arranged:* Wetmore Print Collection, Conn Col Website. *Pos:* Ed & researcher, Rosenthal Art Slides, Chicago, 78-80; asst ed, Art Index, 80-83; head, Slide & Photog Collection, RI Sch Design, Providence, 83-87; visual resources cur, Art Hist Dept, Conn Col, New London, 87-. *Teaching:* Photoshop workshops, Conn Col, 99-. *Awards:* Fac Develop Grants, RI Sch Design, 84-86; Cult & Animals Found Grant, 92; Art Libr Soc Travel Award, 95. *Bibliog:* Contemporary Authors, Vol 113, new revisions series, vol 50 & 105; I Witness Video (9 minutes),

NBC, 3/94; From There to Here, No Limits Commun, 2004. *Mem:* Visual Resources Asn; Col Art Asn. *Publ:* Auth, Vegetarianism in art (cover story), Vegetarian Times, 80; Rembrandt's Cologne Self-Portrait, Iris: Notes in the Hist of Art, 83; ed, Slide Buyers' Guide: International Directory of Slide Sources for Art & Architecture, Libr Unlimited, 86; full-page photo, Flora, Graphis, 129, 2002. *Mailing Add:* PO Box 456 Quaker Hill CT 06375-0456

BRAUNSTEIN, RUTH
ART DEALER
b Minneapolis, Minn. *Collection Arranged:* California Era, Update, Huntsville Art Mus, Ala; Richard Shaw: Illusionism in Clay (auth, catalog), 71-85. *Pos:* Dir, Braunstein/Quay Gallery, San Francisco, 61-. *Awards:* Woman of the Year, Art Table Inc, 96. *Bibliog:* David Jones (auth), 1971 early work (catalog), 71; Peter Voulkos (auth), Anagama works (catalog), 91; Robert Braty (auth), Sculpture, 96. *Mem:* San Francisco Art Dealers Asn (pres, 75-77, 95 & 96); Hadassah; Art Table Inc. *Specialty:* Contemporary art: sculpture, painting and drawing; ceramic sculpture, mostly American artists. *Mailing Add:* Braustein/Quay Gallery 430 Clementina San Francisco CA 94103

BRAUNSTEIN, TERRY (MALIKIN)
PHOTOGRAPHER, EDUCATOR
b Washington, DC, Sept 9, 1942. *Study:* l'Ecole des Beaux Arts, Aixen-en-Provence, France, 62; Univ Mich, Ann Arbor, BFA, 64; Md Inst Art, Baltimore, MFA, 68. *Work:* Mus Mod Art, NY; Victoria & Albert Mus, London, Eng; Long Beach Mus Art, Calif; Biblio Nat, Paris; Corcoran Gallery Art & Nat Mus Am Art, Washington; Getty Ctr, Los Angeles, Calif; Contemp Art Ctr, Moscow, Russia; Libr Congress, Washington, DC; and others. *Comn:* book and ser photographs Imagina Project, Universal Exposition, Seville, Spain, 92; Open Channels Video, Long Beach Mus Art, 92; pub art, Metro Blue Line Sta, Long Beach, 94; book Nat Mus Women in the Arts, 94; pub art, Dirty Windows (metro proj), Berlin, Ger, 96; serigraph, Moscow Studio, Russ, 96; Windows on Wilshire, Los Angeles Co Mus Art, 97; bronze and steel Navy Mem, City Long Beach, Calif, 2003; Porcelain enamel work Elevator Cabinet Improvement Project, City Hall, Long Beach, 2001; Bluff Erosion & Enhancement Project (with Craig Cree Stone), City of Long Beach, 2002. *Exhib:* Solo exhib, Almediterranea (catalog), Almeria, Spain, 90, Long Beach Mus Art, Calif, 91, Turner/Krull, Los Angeles, 92, Craig Krull, Los Angeles, 94, 95 & 97, Troyer Fitzpatrick Lassman, Washington, 94, Universidad de Salamanca, Spain, 96, Feria Int de Arte (ARCO 97), Madrid, Spain, 97, Centro de Exposiciones de Radaquilar, Almeria, Spain, 98 & Centro Andaluz de la Fotografia, Almeria, 2002; Photomontage/Photocollage: The Changing Picture 1920-1989, Jan Turner Gallery, Los Angeles, 89; Amb els Media, Contra els Media with (catalog), Sala Arcs Gallery, Barcelona, Spain, 90; Biennial I (with catalog), Calif Mus Photog, Riverside, 90; Primavera Fotografica (with catalog), Sala Arcs Gallery, Barcelona, Spain, 90; Virgin Territories, Long Beach Mus Art, 92; Imagina, Salas de Arenal, Universal Expos, Seville, Spain & traveling exhib (with catalog), 92 ; Photog Los Angeles Now, Los Angeles Co Mus Art, 95, LA Current: A Female Perspective, Armand Hammer Mus Art, Los Angeles, 95, Palazzo del Consoli, Gubbio, Italy, Viaggiatori, 98; Fractured Identity: Cut and Paste, Julie Saul Gallery, New York City, 94; Magic Realism: Violating Expectations, Univ Art Mus, Calif State Univ, Long Beach, 94; Redefining the Book: Eight Invited Artists, Braunstein/Quay Gallery, San Francisco, 94; Oltre la Grande Soglia (catalog), Centro Esposito della Rocca Paolina, Perugia and Milan, Italy, 94; Still Life, Still Here, Hunsaker/Schlesinger Gallery, Los Angeles, 96; LA Current: A Female Perspective, Armand Hammer Mus Art, Los Angeles, 96; Imagine (traveling exhib), Salas de Arenal, Universal Exposition, Seville Spain, 97; Via Ggiatori-Travelers, Palazzo dei Consoli, Gubbio, Italy & Los Angeles, 98; Imagina, Centro Andalus de la Fotografia, Almeria, 2000; Rooms With a View-Enter Laughing, Long Beach Mus Art, Calif, 2000-01. *Pos:* Vis artist, Smithsonian Inst, 78; guest cur Bookworks, Wash Project Arts, Washington, 80, artist bd mem, 80-84; artist mem, Advisory Comt Pub Art, Long Beach Percent-for- Art-Program, 90-94; design team, Street Facade Improvement Proj, Long Beach, 98. *Teaching:* Instr, Prince Georges Community Col, Largo, Md, 70-74; Northern Va Community Col, Annandale, 76-78; instr printmaking, Corcoran Sch Art, Washington, 78-79, assoc prof & coordr 3rd yr Fine Arts Prog, 79-86; guest artist, Chicago Art Inst, 84, Long Beach Mus Art, 88, Univ Mich, 89, Otis Art Inst, 91, Mills Col, 92 & San Francisco Art Inst, 93, Contemp Art Ctr, Moscow, 96; hon prof Corcoran Sch Art, 86; prof painting & mixed media, advanced students, Calif State Univ, 89; Pomona Col, Claremont, Calif, 89, Hampshire Col, Northampton, Mass, 90, Art Ctr Col Design, Pasadena, Calif, 91, Univ Complutense, Roqueta del Mar, Spain, 91; Otis Art Inst, Los Angeles, 95; Orange Coast Col, 98. *Awards:* Visual Artist fel, Nat Endowment for Arts, 85; Open Channels Video Grant, Long Beach Mus Art, 92; Nat Book Award, Nat Mus Women Arts, Washington, 94; Yaddo Artists Residency, Saratoga Springs, NY, 97, 99; Artists fel, Long Beach, Calif, 99; and others. *Bibliog:* Lewis (auth), Braunstein's fantasy montages, Wash Post, 10/18/86; Hunt (auth), Windows in Art, Los Angeles Times, 11/97; Gottleib (auth), Windows Turning Heads on Wilshire, Press Telegram, 10/97; Joselow (auth), Terry Braunstein, Envisioning Art for the People, 98; and others. *Media:* Photomontage, Artists Books. *Publ:* Auth, Windows, Vis Studies Workshop Press, 82; Theater or Life? (exhib catalog), Charlotte Salomon exhib, Judaic Mus, Washington, 83; Station identification, Kalliope Mag, 85; A Tale from the Fire, Nat Mus Women Arts, 95; Creating a Particular Horizon, Writing & the Artists Bk, Abracadabra, 96. *Dealer:* Craig Krull Gallery Bergamot Sta 2525 Michigan Ave Bldg B3 Santa Monica CA 90404. *Mailing Add:* 262 Belmont Ave Long Beach CA 90803

BRAUNTUCH, TROY
PAINTER, PRINTMAKER
b Jersey City, NJ, 54. *Study:* Calif Inst Arts, Valencia, BFA, 75. *Work:* Lannan Found, Los Angeles, Calif; Metrop Mus Art, Mus Mod Art, NY. *Exhib:* Solo exhibs, The Kitchen, NY, 79, Mary Boone Gallery, NY, 82, 83 & 85, Akira Ueda Gallery, Tokyo, Japan, 84, Kent Fine Art, NY, 88 & 90, The Living Room, Amsterdam, 89, Liliane & Michel Durand-Dessert, Paris, 90 & Gallerie Mai 36, Zurich, Switz, 97; New Talent/NY, Gallery Contemp Art, Cleveland, Ohio, 80; US Art Now, Konsthallen, Goteborg, Sweden, 81; Venice Biennale, Venice, Italy, 82; Nat Mus Art, Osaka, Japan, 83; Mus Mod Art, 84; Mus & Sculpture Garden, Washington, 84; Whitney Mus Am Art, NY, 89-90, Whitney Biennial, 2006

BRAVMANN, RENE A
ART HISTORIAN, EDUCATOR
b Marseilles, France, Dec 10, 39; US citizen. *Study:* Cleveland Mus Art, 57-61; Western Reserve Univ, BA, 61; Univ Wis, 61-63; Ind Univ, MA(fine arts), 65, PhD, 71. *Teaching:* Asst prof art hist, Univ Wash, Seattle, 68-72, assoc prof, 72-76, prof, 77-, chmn African studies, 69-75. *Awards:* Ford Found Fel, Am Coun Learned Socs, 66-68; Post-doctoral Res Grant, Soc Sci Res Coun, 72-73; Am Philos Soc Grant, 74. *Publ:* Auth, West African Sculpture, 70 & auth, Open Frontiers: The Dynamics of Art in Black Africa, 73, Univ Wash; auth, The diffusion of Ashanti political art, In: African Art & Leadership, 72; auth, Islam & Tribal Art in West Africa, Cambridge Univ, 74; auth, An urban way of death, African Arts, Vol 8, No 3. *Mailing Add:* Univ Wash Dept Art Hist Seattle WA 98195

BRAWLEY, ROBERT JULIUS
PAINTER, EDUCATOR
b Brainerd, Minn, Apr 24, 37. *Study:* Cent Wash Univ, 56-57; Frye Art Mus Sch, 58-61; San Francisco Art Inst, BFA, MFA, 64. *Work:* Art Inst Chicago; San Francisco Art Inst; Nelson-Atkins Mus Art, Kansas City, Mo; Hoyt Inst Fine Arts, Lancaster, Pa; Nat Mus Am Art, Washington, DC; and others. *Exhib:* San Francisco New Realism--Through the Photograph to Painting, San Francisco Mus Art, 71; Mid-Year Nat Exhib, Butler Inst Am Art, Ohio, 82 & 83; solo-exhibs, Capricorn Galleries, Bethesda, Md, 84 & Mongerson-Wunderlich, Chicago, Ill, 85; Mainstream Am, Butler Inst Am Art, Youngstown, Ohio, 87; Styles, Strands & Sequences, Deland Art Mus Fla, 91, Univ Fla, Gainesville, 91 & Tampa Mus Art, 92; The Besser Collection, Ark Art Ctr, Little Rock & Philbrook Mus Art, Tulsa, Okla, 93; Knickerbocker Ann 1994, Perry Gallery, Washington, DC, 94; Getting Real: 20th Century Am Realism, Southbend Regional Art Mus in 94, Nat Acad Arts & Letters Ann Purchase Exhib, NY, 94; Contemp Am Realist Drawings, Mus Chicago Art Inst, 2000. *Teaching:* Dir & instr drawing & painting, Acad Art Col, San Francisco, 69-71; assoc prof art hist & studio art, dir grad art studies & chmn art dept, Lone Mountain Col, 71-78; lectr, St Marys Col, Moraga, Calif, 81-; chmn art dept & prof studio art, Univ Kans, Lawrence, currently. *Awards:* Fulbright Fel, 66-67; Painting Awards, Mid-Year Painting Exhib, Butler Inst Am Art, 82 & 84 & Hoyt Nat Painting Show, Hoyt Inst Fine Arts, 82. *Bibliog:* Joann Lewis (auth), rev, Washington Post, 11/8/84; Margaret Hawkins (auth), rev, Chicago Sun-Times, 5/22/87; Ruth fine (auth),Contemporary American Realist Drawings, Artist of Chicago, 2000. *Media:* Alkyd; Graphite. *Dealer:* Jenkins-Johnson Galleries 464 Sutter St San Francisco CA 94108; Vander Griff Gallery 668 Canyon Rd Sante Fe NM 87501. *Mailing Add:* 1700 E 29th St Lawrence KS 66046-5489

BRECKENRIDGE, BRUCE M
CERAMIST, EDUCATOR
b Chicago, Ill, Oct 29, 29. *Study:* Wis State Col-Milwaukee, BS, 52; Cranbrook Acad Art, Bloomfield Hills, Mich, MFA, 53; Acad Grande Chaumier, Paris, 56. *Work:* Elvehjem Art Ctr, Univ Wis-Madison; Westum Mus, Racine, Wis. *Comn:* Two Ceramic Mural tiles, Apache Corp, Houston, Tex, 94. *Exhib:* Objects as Objects, Mus Contemp Crafts, NY, 68 & Coffee Tea and Other Cups, 71; Nat Ceramics Invitational Exhib, Nelson Gallery Atkins Mus, Kansas City, 69; Nat Ceramics Invitational, Scripps Col, 71; The Plastic Earth, John Michael Kohler Arts Ctr, Shebogan, Wis, 73. *Collection Arranged:* Richmond Art Ctr, Calif, 59-61; Mus Contemp Crafts, New York, 65-66. *Pos:* Asst dir, Richmond Art Ctr, Calif, 59-61; installation asst, Mus Mod Art, New York, 64-65; asst dir, Mus Contemp Crafts, New York, 65-66. *Teaching:* Instr ceramics, Brooklyn Mus Art Sch, 65-68; prof art-ceramics, Univ Wis-Madison, 68-. *Awards:* Residency, Vcross Found, Wyo. *Mem:* Nat Coun Educ Ceramic Arts. *Media:* Ceramics. *Publ:* Auth, New ceramic forms, 65, Wisconsin designer-craftsman, 69, Don Reitz exhibition, 70 & National invitational exhibition II, glass, 71, Craft Horizons. *Mailing Add:* 1715 Regent St Madison WI 53705-4117

BREDER, HANS DIETER
SCULPTOR, VIDEO ARTIST
b Herford, Ger, Oct 20, 35; US citizen. *Study:* Hochschule fuer Bildende Kunste, Hamburg, Ger, with Willem Grimm, asst to sculptor, George Rickey. *Work:* Cleveland Mus, Ohio; Joseph H Hirshhorn Collection, Washington, DC; Whitney Mus of Am Art, NY; Mus of Art, State Univ NY Col, Purchase; Mus of Art, Iowa City; Am Asn Advan Sci, Washington, DC; Prudential Ins Co NAm, Newark, NJ; Mus Mod Art, NY. *Comn:* Three outdoor sculptures, City of Hanover, Ger, 71. *Exhib:* Mus Contemp Art, Chicago, Ill, 68; Jewish Mus, 69, Exhibit Recent Acquisitions, Mus Mod Art, 84, Whitney Mus Am Art, NY, 87, 89 & 91; one-artist exhibs, Richard Feigen Gallery, Chicago, 67, 70, 72, NY, 67, 70, The Kitchen, Ctr Video & Music, NY, 75, Wolfgang Foerster Galerie, Munster, Ger, 79, 81, 82, 88 & 91, Schreiber/Cutler Inc, NY, 87, 88 & 89, Ruth Siegel Gallery, NY, 90; 2nd Videonale, Bonn, Ger, 86; 3rd Fukui Int Video Biennale, Japan, 89; Painting Beyond the Death of Painting, Kuznetzky Most Exhib Hall, Moscow, 89. *Pos:* Co-dir, Corroboree: Gallery of New Concepts, Univ Iowa, Iowa City, 77-. *Teaching:* Prof multimedia, Univ Iowa, Iowa City, 77-. *Bibliog:* Stephen Foster, Estera Milman (auths), The Media as Medium: Hans Breder's Berlin Work, Kans Quart, Vol 17, No 3, 85; Herman Rapaport (auth), Hans Breder and the Auras of Video, Art Criticism, Vol 4, No 1, 88; Donald Kuspit (auth), New York Reviews, Artforum, 5/89. *Publ:* Coauth, Speculum, Ctr for New Performing Arts, 73; coauth, Participatory Art and Body Sculpture with Mirrors, Leonardo: Art, Sci & Technol, 74. *Mailing Add:* 623 E College St Iowa City IA 52240-5122

BREDLOW, TOM
DESIGNER, BLACKSMITH
b Pontiac, Mich, 38. *Study:* Tex A&M Col, BA (math). *Comn:* Barrio-Historico (grilles, gates, doors, railings, downspouts), comn by H Kelley Rollings, Tucson, 70-; hand rails, comn by Harriet Hubbell, Hubbell House (SW Span Craftsmen), Santa Fe, NMex, 71; Peopleplay (public sculpture), Steven Nanini, Tucson, 80; historic preservation in stone, wood & leather & metals for Fred Harvey Co, Grand Canyon, 1983-1990; Reemployment of Harveycars (emblems & coach decoration), comn by Fred Harvey Transportation Co, Grand Canyon, 86-91; Iron, glass & wood entries, McCormick Residences, Houston & Santa Fe. *Exhib:* One-man show, Boyer Gallery, Tucson, 68 & 70; Ann Western Art Show, Mountain Oyster Club, Tucson, 72-82; Iron-Solid Wrought, Mus Southern Ill Univ, Mus Contemp Crafts, NY & Smithsonian Inst, Washington, DC, 76-77. *Collection Arranged:* Mouse doorbell, Mus and Art Gallery Collection, School of Art and Design, Southern Ill Univ; Dr Cyril Stanley Smith, MIT; Jim & Johanna Stephens, Tucson. *Pos:* Owner & sole craftsman, Bredlow's Blacksmith Shop, Tucson, 64-. *Teaching:* Guest lectr hist archaeol, Univ Ariz, speaker-demonstr, Ironworking Conv; guest lectr architectural embellishment, Col Architecture, Univ Ariz. *Awards:* Biennial Prize, Quinnell Biennial, Surrey, England, 76; Crown Sculptural and Decorative Ironwork citation, Meilach, 77. *Bibliog:* Ty Harrington (auth), Last Cathedral, Prentice-Hall, 79; R T Feller (auth), For Thy Great Glory, Community, 79. *Mem:* Hon artist Life Mem, Mountain Oyster Club, Tucson, 78-2004. *Media:* Metals, Wood. *Res:* Restoration work in wood, stone, metals. *Interests:* Japanese art, antique ironwork, antique furniture, folklore, folk art. *Publ:* Auth, Stagecoach, Frontier Times, summer 60; Anvils and coal smoke, Old West, winter 66. *Mailing Add:* 3524 N Olive Rd Tucson AZ 85719-1830

BREED, CHARLES AYARS
SCULPTOR, DESIGNER
b Paw Paw, Mich, Jan 31, 27. *Study:* Western Mich Univ, BS; Univ Wis, MA. *Work:* Midland Ctr Arts, Mich; Dow Chemical, Mich. *Comn:* Eternal Flame (Plexiglas), Temple Beth El, Spring Valley, NY, 66; Icon Screen (polyester), Hellenic Orthodox Church, Bloomfield Hills, Mich, 68; sculpture, Alden D Dow Ctr Arts, Midland, 82; sculpture, steelcase, Grand Rapids, Mich, 92; sculpture, Nat Endowment Arts, Washington, DC, 93; and others. *Exhib:* Craftsman USA 66, Mus Contemp Crafts, NY, 66, Plastic as Plastic Nat Invitational, 68; Made of Plastic Nat Invitational, Flint Inst Art, Mich, 68; Exhib 70, Columbus Art Gallery, Ohio, 70; First Biennial Int Small Sculpture Exhib, Budapest, Hungary, 71. *Pos:* Bd dir, Awareness Inc, Lansing, Mich, 62-64; bd dir, Midland Ctr Arts, 67-72. *Teaching:* Dir art, Nat Music Acad, 58-62; prof art & chmn dept, Delta Col, 62-83. *Awards:* Nat Merit Award, Mus Contemp Crafts, NY, 66; Outstanding Teacher Year, Bergstein Found, 67; Mich Coun Arts Artist Grant, 81; Delta Scholarly Achievement Award, 90; Beautification Award, City Midland, Mich, 92 & 93. *Bibliog:* Jack Brickhouse (auth), Everything is Double in Paw Paw, Paramount Films, 48; Curtis Bessinger (auth), Where does the design of a house begin, House Beautiful, 1/62; Rite of Spring--Detroit (videotape), PM Mag, 81-83. *Media:* Plastic. *Publ:* Auth, Plastic as a new art form, House Beautiful, 2/62; co-auth, Plastic-the visual arts in crafts, Crafts & Craftsmen, 67; auth, Unite equal opposites, Symposium, 80; Conceptual Art, Art in Am, 2/84. *Dealer:* Northwood Galleries 144 E Main Midland MI 48640. *Mailing Add:* Equiline Design 1320 W Main Midland MI 48640-2648

BREEN, HARRY FREDERICK, JR
PAINTER, SCULPTOR
b Chicago, Ill, Mar 4, 30. *Study:* Art Inst Chicago, with John Rogers Cox & Paul Wiegarht, BA, 53; Univ Ill, Urbana-Champaign, MA, 59. *Work:* Ill State Mus, Springfield; Butler Mus Am Art, Youngstown, Ohio; Krannert Art Mus, Champaign, Ill; Union League Club, Chicago; Lakeview Ctr Arts & Sci, Peoria, Ill. *Comn:* paintings & sculpture, Bishop's Chapel, St Mary's Cathedral Rectory, Peoria, Ill, 91; stained glass windows & sculpture, St Philomena's Church, Monticello, Ill, 92 & 94; mural, St Joseph's Cathedral, Mo, 95; mural, St Matthew Cath Church, Champaign, Ill, 97; sculpture & painting, High Sch St Thomas More, Champaign, Ill, 2000. *Exhib:* Mid-Yr Ann, Butler Mus Am Art, Youngstown, Ohio, 62, 63 & 65; Pa Acad Fine Art, 63 traveling in Europe, 64; Realism Revisited, Flint Art Inst, Mich, 66; 5th Biennial Relig Art, Cranbrook Acad, Detroit, Mich, 66; Ill Arts Coun Traveling Exhib, 67; Retrospective, Lakeview Ctr Arts & Sci, Peoria, Ill, 77; Univ Ill Painting Fac, Univ Tokyo & Nat Hist Mus Taipei, 81; and others. *Teaching:* Instr art, Pub Schs, Gary, Ind, 54-57 & Univ High Sch, Univ Ill, 57-79; prof art, Sch Art & Design, Univ Ill, Champaign, 59-85; vis prof art, Univ Wis, Madison, 68-69. *Awards:* Second Purchase Prize, Fourth Union League Exhib, Chicago, 61; Fourth Purchase Prize Oils, Mid-Yr Ann, Butler Mus Am Art, 63; Second Prize Sculpture, Ann Exhib, Hoosier Salon, Indianapolis, 63. *Media:* All; Clay. *Dealer:* Green Street Studio 24 E Green St Champaign Ill 61820. *Mailing Add:* 1107 W Church St Champaign IL 61820

BREER, ROBERT C
SCULPTOR, FILMMAKER
b Detroit, Mich, Sept 30, 26. *Study:* Stanford Univ, BA. *Work:* Mus Mod Art, NY; Mod Mus, Stockholm, Sweden; Anthology Film Archives, NY; Mod Art Mus, Krefeld, Ger; Centre Beaubourg, Paris, France. *Comn:* Design Pepsi Cola Pavilion, Expo '70, Japan; kinetic sculpture, IBM Plaza, Pittsburgh Arts Fete, 74; Mural, Film Forum, NY, 81. *Exhib:* The Machine as Seen at the End of the Mechanical Age, Mus Mod Art, NY, 68; Albright-Knox Art Gallery, Buffalo, NY, 71; solo exhibs, Mus Mod Art, NY, Albright-Knox Art Gallery, 76, Collective Living Cinema, NY, 77, Walker Art Ctr, 79 & Millenium, NY, 79; retrospective, Whitney Mus Am Art, NY, 77 & 80; Drawings for Animated Film, Drawing Ctr, NY, 78; Film as Film, Hayward Gallery, London, 79; NY Film Festival, 79; Whitney Biennial, 79, 81, 83, 85, British Art Coun traveling Exhib, 83; 1900-2000 Gallery, Paris, 90. *Pos:* Mem bd dir, Filmmakers Coop, NY, 67-72 & 75-88. *Teaching:* Prof kinetics, Cooper Union, 71-; instr, Hampshire Col, 74-79 & NY Univ, 77. *Awards:* Nat Endowment Arts Grant, 76; Am Film Inst Grant, 77; Guggenheim Found Fel, 78-79; Am Film Inst: Maya Deven Award 86. *Bibliog:* Adrienne Mancia & William Van Dyke (auth), Four artists as film makers, Art in Am, 1/67; Calvin Tompkins (auth), Onwards and upwards with the arts, New Yorker, 10/70; Lois Mendelson (auth), Robert Breer, UMI Res Press, 81; Robert Breer 5 & Dime Animator, Channel 4 England, 84; Jennifer Burford (auth), Robert Breer, Editions Paris Experimental, 99. *Mailing Add:* Cooper Union Cooper Sq New York NY 10003

BREIGER, ELAINE
PRINTMAKER, PAINTER
b Springfield, Mass. *Study:* Art Students League; Cooper Union. *Work:* Brooklyn Mus, NY; Libr Cong, Washington, DC; Honolulu Acad Art, Hawaii; Chase Manhattan Bank, NY; Mus Prints & Printmaking, Albany, NY. *Comn:* Print, Container Corp Am, 70. *Exhib:* Glaser Gallery, La Jolla, Calif; Contemp Gallery, Dallas; Martha Jackson Gallery, NY, 74; Pace Gallery, NY, 76; Source Gallery, San Francisco, Calif, 77; Silicon Gallery, Philadelphia, Pa, 99. *Pos:* Mgr, Printmaking Workshop, 68-70; chmn dept art, 92nd St YMCA, 72-76. *Teaching:* Instr techniques etching & intaglio printing, 92nd St YMHA, NY, 71-76; color etching, the combine print, Sch Visual Arts, NY, 77-. *Awards:* Creative Arts Pub Serv Fel, 74; Nat Endowment Arts Grant, 75. *Bibliog:* Una Johnson (auth), American Prints & Printmakers, Doubleday, 80. *Mem:* Visual Artists & Galleries Asn; Soc Am Graphic Artists; Boston Printmakers. *Media:* Etching; Acrylic, Oil

BREITENBACH, WILLIAM JOHN
SCULPTOR, EDUCATOR
b Milwaukee, Wis, Jan 21, 36. *Study:* Univ Wis, Milwaukee, BS, 62 & MS, 65; Stephen F Austin State Univ, MFA, 71. *Work:* Brentwood Col, NY; Del Mar Col, Corpus Christi, Tex; Stephen F Austin State Univ, Tex; Houston Baptist Univ, Tex; Sam Houston State Univ, Tex. *Comn:* Sculptural fountain, William Robert Murfin, Houston, 72; plywood wall sculpture, Performing Arts Ctr, Sam Houston State Univ, Huntsville, Tex, 76; Cent Tex Col, Killeen, 83. *Exhib:* Creative Collab, Rice Univ, Houston, 72; 9th Monroe Ann, Masur Mus Art, Monroe, La, 72; Southwest Graphics Invitational, Mex-Am Cult Exchange Inst, San Antonio, Tex, 72; Inst Visual Arts, Puebla, Mex, 81; Cult Activities Ctr, Temple, Tex, 84; and others. *Pos:* Chmn, Houston Area Art Curric Develop Comt, 82-86. *Teaching:* Supvr elem art, South Door Co Sch Dist 1, Brussels, Wis, 62-65; full prof art educ, design & drawing, Sam Houston State Univ, 65-. *Awards:* First Prize in sculpture, 5th Ann Exhib, Del Mar Col, 71; Merit Award for creative collab, Rice Univ, 71; Third Place Award, Assistance League Houston, 73. *Mem:* Tex Art Educ Asn; Nat Art Educ Asn. *Media:* Paper Mache, Fabricated Plywood; Ark. *Publ:* Auth, Art education and the modern age, Tex Trends in Art Educ, 68. *Dealer:* Umbrella Arts 2615 Old Houston Rd Huntsville TX 77340. *Mailing Add:* 2615 Old Houston Rd Sam Houston State Univ Huntsville TX 77341-6629

BREJCHA, VERNON LEE
GLASS BLOWER, CRAFTSMAN
b Ellsworth, Kans, Jan 30, 42. *Study:* Ft Hays State Univ, BA & MS; Univ Wis-Madison, MFA with Harvey K Littleton. *Work:* Corning Mus of Glass, NY; Mus of Contemp Crafts, NY; Kunstmuseum, Dusseldorf, Ger; Los Angeles Co Mus Art; Smithsonian Inst, Washington, DC. *Comn:* Chandelier Overland Park, Convention Ctr, Overland Park, Kans; Field Flow Wall Projects, KU Medical Ctr; Prairie Bounty De Bruce Grain Co KC, Mo; Sculpture, H & R Block World Center, Kanses City, MO. *Exhib:* Great Am Gallery, Atlanta, Ga, 86; Two-Man Glass Gallery, Bethesda, Md, 87; one-man, Marx Gallery, Chicago, Ill, 90, Hall Fame, Bonner Springs, Kans, 91, Vetro Marmo Arte, Columbus, Ohio, 95, Michael Kelly Gallery, San Antonio, 96, Wichita Ctr Arts, Kans, 97 & Soc Fine Arts, Chicago, 98, KL Fine Arts, Chicago, 99; Vessel Transformed, Pensacola Mus Art, Fla, 93; Graceland Col, Lamoni, Iowa, 93; Goblet Show, Porta Gallery, Chicago, 96; Glass Now 2002, Nat'l Liberty Mus, Philadelphia; One Man Leopald Gallery, Kansas City, MO, 2004. *Pos:* Prof Emer, 2003. *Teaching:* Asst prof glass, ceramics & sculpture, Tusculum Col, Greenville, Tenn, 72-76; asst prof design glass, Univ Kans, 77-81, assoc prof, 81-2002. *Awards:* First Place Purchase, Ceramics Northwest, CM Russell Mus, Great Falls, Mont, 70; Purchase Award, Tenn Bicentennial Art Exhib, State of Tenn, 76; Artist Fel, Nat Endowment Arts, 84; Kans Governor's Artist, 85. *Bibliog:* Polly Rothenberg (auth), The Complete Book of Creative Glass Art, Crown, 74; Elizabeth Campbell (auth), Kansas-Theme of glass artist Vernon Brejcha, Neues Glas, Dusseldorf, 82; Phyllis George (auth), Craft in America, Summit Group, 93; Paul Dorrell (auth) Living the Artists Life, Hilstead Pub, 2004. *Mem:* Am Crafts Coun; Nat Coun on Educ for the Ceramic Arts (glass panel chmn, 77); Glass Art Soc; Kans Artist-Craftsmen Asn. *Media:* blown glass. *Interests:* Photography, Figure Studies; Kans and NC Landscapes. *Publ:* Auth, Throw the Lid First, Ceramics Monthly, 70; contribr, The Complete Book of Creative Glass Art, Crown, 74; Crafts & Craftsmen of the Tennessee Mountains, Summit Press; auth, British hot glass, Glass Studio, 82; Craft in America, Summit Group, 93. *Dealer:* Glass Gallery 4720 Hampden Lane Bethesda MD 20814; Leopold Gallery 327 E 55th St Kansas City MO 64113. *Mailing Add:* 1111 East 1500 Rd Lawrence KS 66046

BREMER, MARLENE S
PAINTER, SCULPTOR
b Coburg, WGer; US citizen. *Study:* Fairleigh Dickinson Univ, NJ, BA, 79; William Paterson Univ, NJ, MA, 81; New York Univ, NY, cert(fine art appraisal), 89. *Work:* Pvt collections USA & Europe; Spritzwerke Herman Koch, Creidlitz, Ger; Treppen Zentrum Schaarschmidt GMBH, Hamburg, Ger; Bimar Int Asn, Allendale, NJ; Lotz Medizin technik GMBH, Munich, Ger. *Exhib:* Munic Gallery, Athens, Greece, 96; Catherine Lorillard Wolfe Art Club 106th Ann, New York City, 2002; The Art of Collecting, Morris Mus, Morristown, NJ, 2002 & 2003; Haworth Municipal Libr, NJ,

2004; Cynon Valley Mus, Aberdare, Wales, UK, 2004; BergenPac, Englewood, NJ, 2005; Maurice M Pine Pub Libr, Fairlawn, NJ, 2005; Gallery Merz, Sag Harbor, NY, 2005; Synagogue for the Arts, NY, 2006; Goggle Work Center Arts, Reading, Pa, 2006; Karpeles Libr Mus, Newburgh, NY, 2006; Port of Calls, Warwich, NY, 2006. *Pos:* Appraiser fine art, currently. *Teaching:* Instr sculpture, Ridgewood Community Sch, NJ, 84-85; adj prof art hist, Bergen Community Col, NJ, 85-88. *Awards:* Salute Award, Jacob Javits Bldg, NY, 88; Award Excellence, Old Church Cult Ctr, Demarst, NJ, 93; Beatrice G Epstein Mem, Nat Asn Women Artists, NY, 96; Award Excellence, Manhattan Arts Internat, NY, 2000; Hazel Witte Meml Award, NAWA 111th Ann Exhib, NY, 2000; Award, NY/Paris Competition, Inst Visual, Paris, France. *Bibliog:* Justin Lim (auth), Korean-Am Times, NJ, 93; Eileen Watkins (auth), Star Ledger, NJ, 95; Renee Phillips (auth), Manhattan Arts Int, NY, 96; 111th Exhib Catalog, NAWA: Atelier 14, New York, 2000; plus others. *Mem:* Nat Asn Women Artists, (asst hist, New York Chap, bd mem jury, exhibs comt); Artists Equity Asn; Salute to Women in the Arts, NJ; Painting Affiliate Art Ctr No NJ; City Without Walls, Newark, NJ; JSEA, Int Soc Experimental Artists, Chicago, Ill. *Media:* Mixed Media. *Mailing Add:* 440 Egan Pl Englewood NJ 07631

BREN, DONALD L
COLLECTOR
Study: Univ Wash, BA & MBA. *Collection:* Contemporary American art. *Mailing Add:* The Irvine Co 550 Newport Center Dr Newport Beach CA 92660

BRENDEL, BETTINA
PAINTER, LECTURER
b Luneburg, Ger; US citizen. *Study:* Hamburg, Ger, BA, 40; Kunstschule Schmilinsky, Hamburg, 41-42; Landes Hochschule Bildende Kuenste, Hamburg, 45-47, with Erich Hartmann; Univ Southern Calif, 55-58; New Sch Social Res, 68-69. *Work:* San Francisco Mus Art; Long Beach Mus Art; Mus fuer Konkrete Kunst, Ingolstadt, Ger; Max-Planck-Inst, Munich, Ger; and others. *Comn:* painting, Auditorium Werner-Heisenberg Inst, Munich, Ger. *Exhib:* Los Angeles Co Mus Ann, 55, 57, 59 & 61; Ester Robles Gallery, 1956-63; 58th Ann, San Francisco Mus Art, 66; On Mass and Energy, Santa Barbara Mus Art, 66; Women Artists, Santa Monica Col Art Gallery, Calif, 77; Los Angeles Artcore Gallery, 84; A Digital View, Art Store Gallery, Pasadena, 90; Digitals & Modules, Glendale, Calif, 90; Crossroads Sch, Santa Monica, Calif; retrospective (with catalog), Long Beach Mus Art, 98; solo exhib, Gallery 16-34, Santa Monica, Calif, 91, Particles & Waves, Bettina Brendel 1957-97, Long Beach Mus Art, 98, Symmetry & Sequences, David Lawrence Gallery, Beverly Hills, Calif, 2000; Downey Mus Art, Calif; computer art exhib, Gallery Wosimsky, Giessen, Ger, 2003, 2005. *Collection Arranged:* Grunwald Graphic Art Collection; Los Angeles Co Mus Art; Mus f Konkrete Kunst, Ingolstadt, Ger; Long Beach Mus Art, Calif; Hammer Mus, Los Angeles, Calif. *Pos:* Computer artist, Calif Mus Sci & Indust, Los Angeles, 88-92. *Teaching:* Instr, The Emergence of Mod Painting, Univ Calif, Los Angeles, 58-61, lectr art, Exten, spring 76; lectr, Thematic Option Prog, Univ Southern Calif, 80; lectr, symp Arte c Technologia, Gulbenkian Found, Paris, 85, Lisbon, Portugal, 87, Max Planck Inst Physics, Munich, Ger, 91, Loughborough Univ Technol, Eng, 96. *Awards:* Long Beach Mus Art, 60, 61; First Purchase Award, San Francisco Mus Art, 66; 2nd Prize, Palm Springs Art Mus, Calif, 99. *Bibliog:* Dr John Marburger (auth), Bettina Brendel, Paintings 70-82, 84; Bethany Price (auth), article, Long Beach Bus J, 3/98; William Wilson (auth), article, Los Angeles Times, 4/98; and others. *Mem:* Friends Graphic Arts, Univ Calif, Los Angeles; Univ Calif Los Angeles Art Coun; Am Physical Soc; Archives Am Art; Los Angeles Printmaking Soc; YLEM, Artists using Science & Technology, San Francisco. *Media:* Acrylic, Collage; Computer Art. *Res:* Theoretical physics and its relation to the arts. *Specialty:* Art & Science (physics). *Interests:* classical music; modern dance; poetry. *Collection:* Los Angeles County Mus Art; Hammer Mus; Long Beach Mus; Pvt Collection Travis Spitzer; Mus Concrete Art, Germany. *Publ:* Auth, The painter and the new physics, Art J, fall 71; The influence of atomic physics, Leonardo Mag, 73; Whenever in the World (poems), Stockton Press, 77; Atomic Patterns, YLEM Newsletter, Oakland Calif, 97, Symmetry. Art as Metaphor, 2000; Springer (auth), Experiments in Art and Technology, 2002. *Dealer:* David Lawrence Gallery 9507 Santa Monica Blvd Beverly Hills Calif 90210; Gallery Wosimsky Ger. *Mailing Add:* 1061 N Kenter Ave Los Angeles CA 90049

BRENER, ROLAND
SCULPTOR, EDUCATOR
b South Africa, 42. *Study:* St Martin's Sch Art, London, Eng. *Work:* Art Gallery, Greater Victoria; Art Gallery Ont, Toronto; Can Coun Art Bank & Nat Gallery Can, Ottawa; Kasmin Gallery, London, Eng; Mus d'Art Contemporain de Montreal; Radio City, Toronto; Nat Gallary of Canada; others. *Exhib:* Solo exhibs, Olga Korper Gallery, Toronto, 88, 90, 91 & 95, 97, 99, 2001, 2003, Monte Clark Gallery & Foto-Base Gallery & Project, Vancouver, BC, 93, Capital Z, Power Plant, Totonto, Ont, 94 & Macdonald Stewart Art Ctr, Guelph, Ont, 96, Portland Inst Contemp Art, Ore, 97, Spectra, NY, 2000, Deitch Projects, NY, 2000, NTT Inter-Comm Centre, Tokyo Opera City Tower, 2002; Devices, Josh Baer Gallery, NY, 91; Recent Acquisions, Vancouver Art Gallery, 94; Modern Metal, London Regional Art Gallery, Ont, 94; Fixing the Gaze, Olga Korper Gallery, Toronto, 94; In Habitable Places, Leonard & Bina Ellen Art Gallery, Concordia Univ, Montreal, 94. *Teaching:* Lectr, St Martin's Sch Art, London, Eng, 66-69; guest lectr, Univ Calif, Santa Barbara, 70-71; asst prof, Univ Iowa, 71-72; prof, Univ Victoria, 72-2000. *Bibliog:* Bruce Ferguson (auth), Nomad is an Island; Roland Brener, Vol 17, No 3, Vanguard, summer 88, 24-27; John Bentley Mays (auth), Engaging dialogues on art, 6/24/88, Caught between industry and art, 6/28/88, Globe & Mail, Toronto; Linda Genereux (auth), Fast Forward, Vol 6, No 4, winter 89; Philip Monk (auth), Recent Work by Roland Brener, C Mag, Issue 64, 11/99-2/2000. *Publ:* Roland Brener, (catalog) Art Gallery Greater Victoria, 1991; Claire Christie, Fixing the Gaze (catalog), 1994; Kristy Edmunds, Roland Brener: Discoveries in Digital Design (catalog), Portland Inst Contemp Art, 1997; other catalogs. *Mailing Add:* c/o Olga Korper Gallery 17 Morrow Ave Toronto ON M6R 2H9 Canada

BRESCHI, KAREN LEE
SCULPTOR
b Oakland, Calif, Oct 29, 41. *Study:* Calif Col Arts & Crafts, BFA, 63; Sacramento State Univ, 60-61; San Francisco State Univ, MA, 65; San Francisco Art Inst, 68-71; Calif Inst Integral Studies, San Francisco, PhD, 87. *Work:* Oakland Mus, Calif; Crocker Art Gallery, Sacramento; San Francisco Mus Art; Univ Art Mus (Berkeley); St Mary's Col Art Gallery (Moraga); Univ Ariz Art Mus. *Exhib:* Fac Show Sculpture, 73 & Ceramic Sculpture, 74, San Francisco Art Inst; solo shows, Braunstein/Quay Gallery, 73, 75, 78, 81 & 84; Clay, Whitney Mus, NY, 74; Exchange DFW/SFO, San Francisco Mus Art, 76; Illusionistic-Realism Defined in Contemp Ceramic Sculpture, Laguna Beach Mus, Calif, 77; The Great Am Foot, Mus Contemp Crafts, NY, 78; West Coast Sculptors, 78 & A Century of Clay, 79, Everson Mus; Clayworks, Univ Santa Barbara Mus, 79; A Century of Ceramics in the US 1878-1978, Renwick Gallery, Smithsonian Inst, 79-80; solo show, Braunstein/Quay Gallery, 81; and many others. *Teaching:* Instr sculpture, San Francisco Art Inst, 71-77; instr sculpture, San Francisco State Univ, 74-79; instr, Univ Calif, Davis, 80-81. *Awards:* First Place for Painted Flower, Oakland Art Mus, 62; Women's Archit League Award, Crocker Art Mus, 63; Award, Calif State Fair, 63. *Mem:* West/East Bag. *Media:* Clay, Mixed. *Mailing Add:* 4042 22nd St San Francisco CA 94114

BRESLAW, CATHY L
PAINTER, EDUCATOR
b Coral Gables, Fla, Nov 7, 51. *Study:* George Washington Univ, BA, 73; Howard Univ, Washington, DC, MSW, 78. *Work:* Maxwell Technologies, San Diego, Calif; Frontier Analytics, La Jolla, Calif; Che Bella, Phoenix Ariz; Ariz Fast Foods, Phoenix, Ariz; Saigon & Assocs, Los Altos, Calif. *Comn:* Series of 8 paintings, comn by Randall Moore, San Diego, 98. *Exhib:* Nat Watercolor Soc Travel Tour, Witchita Falls Mus & Art Ctr, Tex & Bade Mus, Berkeley, Calif, 97; Ann Nat Exhib (with catalog), Brea Civic & Cult Ctr Gallery, Los Angeles, 97; Nat Watercolor Soc, Downcy Mus Art, Calif, 97; Soc Layerists Multimedia, Bradford Col, Haverhill, Mass, 98; Nat Oil & Acrylic Soc, Columbia Col, Osage Beach, Mo, 98; Art in Flux, San Diego, Calif, 2000; Abstractions, Balboa Park, San Diego, Calif, 2000; plus others. *Teaching:* Instr painting & drawing, N Co Jr Community Col, 92-97; mixed media, Quail Gardens, Encinitas, 96-97; workshops in creativity, San Diego Watercolor Soc, 98-. *Awards:* Gold Medallion, Calif Watercolor Soc 29th Int Ann Open Exhib, Grumbacher, 97; Soc Experimental Artists Int Exhib Merit Award, Sarasota Art Ctr, 97. *Mem:* Sig mem Nat Watercolor Soc; Int Soc Multimedia Layerists; Int Soc Experimental Painters. *Media:* Acrylic, Mixed Media. *Interests:* Travel, Skiing, Golf, Reading. *Mailing Add:* PO Box 231122 Encinitas CA 92023

BRESLIN, NANCY
PHOTOGRAPHER
b Orange, NJ, Aug 18, 57. *Study:* Rutgers Univ, BA, 79; Univ Pittsburgh, MD, 83; Univ De, MFA, 00. *Exhib:* Int show, NJ Ctr for Visual Arts, Summit, 01, 02, 04, 05; Mem Exhib, De Ctr for Contemp Arts, Wilmington, 01, 02, 04; Life and Death in Paris, Mezzanine Gallery, Wilmington, 2001 & 02; Biggs Mus Am Art, Dover, Del, 03; A Pinhole Diary of Eating Out, Arlington Arts Ctr, Va, 2005; A Pinehold Diary of Eating Out, Saint Joseph's Univ, Phil, 2006. *Collection Arranged:* Arresting Images, Luther Brady Art Gallery, Washington, DC, 2003; Del Women's Conf Fine Arts Exhib, Newark, 05. *Teaching:* adj instr photog, Univ De, Newark, 01-. *Awards:* Artist Fel, De Div of Arts, 03. *Mem:* Soc for Photog Educ, sec mid-Atlantic board, 02-; De Ctr for Contemp Arts; Newark Arts Alliance, gallery commitee. *Media:* Pinhole Photography. *Publ:* auth, Deborah Turbeville, The Encyclopedia of Twentieth Century Photography, Lynne Warren (ed), Routledge, 2006. *Mailing Add:* 237 Cheltenham Rd Newark DE 19711

BRESLIN, WYNN
PAINTER, SCULPTOR
b Hackensack, NJ. *Study:* Syracuse Univ, 50; Ohio Wesleyan Univ, BFA, 54; Univ Del, MFA, 60. *Comn:* Sculpture, Immanuel Episcopal Church, Wilmington, DE, 62; painting, First Federal Bank, Newark, DE, 79. *Exhib:* Del Art Mus Regional Shows, 56-75; Benedictine Art Awards, Am Fedn Arts, 67; Woodmere Art Gallery, Philadelphia, 73-75; Philadelphia Art Alliance, 74; Catharine Lorillard Wolfe Art Club, Nat Arts Club, 74; Four State Regional show, Univ Del, 88; Chester Co Art Asn, 2002, 2003. *Pos:* owner studio, Del & Maine. *Teaching:* Art instr, Del Pub Schs, 54-63, Del Art Mus, 56-76 & Tatnall Sch, 64; instr adult pvt classes, 63-90; Artist-in-Educ Series, 81-94. *Awards:* First Prize Watercolor, Nat Orgn Women Art Exhib, Wilmington, 73; Ethel M Schnader Art Prize, Woodmere Art Gallery, Philadelphia, 74; First Prize Acrylic Painting, Univ Del, 88. *Bibliog:* From an artistic viewpoint, Univ News, Univ Del, 67. *Mem:* Nat League Am Pen Women (treas, Diamond State Br, 72-74); Wilmington Soc Fine Arts; Del Ctr Contemp Art; Chester Co Art Asn; The Boothbay Region Art Found. *Media:* Oil, Watercolor. *Specialty:* painting, watercolors, oils, acrylics. *Interests:* On-site travel painting. *Mailing Add:* 470 Terrapin Ln Newark DE 19711-2118

BRESTVANKEMPEN, CATEL PIETER
PAINTER
b Murray, UT, May 2, 58. *Work:* Leigh Yawkey Woodson Art Mus, Wausau, Wis; Bennington Ctr for the Arts, Bennington, Va; Springville Mus Art, Springville, Utah; World Ctr for Birds of Prey, Boise, Ind; Arizona-Sonora Desert Mus, Tucson, Ariz. *Exhib:* Christie's Wildlife Art Auction, Brit Mus, London, UK, 1995, 1998; Birds in

Art, Leigh Yawkey Woodson Art Mus, Wausau, Wis, 1996, 2001, 2002, 2005; Art of the Living World, Bonham's, Singapore, 1997; Taipei Eco Art Exhib, Nat Mus Hist, Taipei, Taiwan, 1999; one-man shows, Wildlife Experience Mus, Denver, Colo, 2003; Rose Wagner Art Ctr, Salt Lake City, Utah, 2005; Wilding Art Mus, Los Olivos, Calif, 2006; Western Visions, Nat Mus Wildlife Art, Jackson, Wyo, 2004-2006. *Awards:* Wildlife Medalion, Arts for the Parks, Nat Park Acad Arts, 1992; Award of Excellence, Art & the Animal, Soc Animal Artists, 1994, 1996,1997,2004; Most Honored Artist, 150 Yrs of Utah Art, Springfield Mus Art, 2002. *Bibliog:* Scott Bestul (auth), Natures Diversity, Inform Art, fall 1997; Janet Rae Brooks (auth), A Natural Obsession, Wildlife J, spring 2001; Darryl Whey (auth), Science, Art & Science Art, Birding, 2004. *Mem:* Soc Animal Artists. *Media:* Acrylic, Oil, Watercolor. *Publ:* Contribr, Natural Habitat, Spanierman Gallery, 1998; Illusr, Dinosaurs of Utah, Univ Utah, 1998; Contribr, Wildlife Art: 60 Comtemp Masters, Portfolio Press, 2001; Illusr, Biology of the Gila Monsters & Beaded Lizards, Univ Calif Press, 2005; Auth, Rigor Vitae: Life Unyielding, Eagle Mountain Publ, 2006. *Dealer:* Mill Pond Press 310 Center Ct Venice, FL. *Mailing Add:* PO Box 17647 Salt Lake City UT 84117-0647

BRETT, NANCY
ARTIST
b Jackson, Mich. *Study:* Univ Michigan, Independent Study, 67-68; Wayne State Univ, BFA, 69; Cranbrook Acad Art, MFA, 72. *Work:* Cranbrook Acad Art Mus, Bloomfield Hills, Mich; Herbert Johnson Mus Art, Cornell Univ, Ithaca, NY; Kidder Peabody, NY; Prudential, IBM, JP Morgan, Chemical Bank, NY; Library of Congress, Washington, DC. *Exhib:* Kindred Spirits, Hillwood Art Mus, CW Post, Long Island Univ, NY, 86; three-person show, Distant Vision: Contemp Landscape, Janice Charach Epstein Mus, West Bloomfield, Mich, 92; K&E Gallery, NY, 94; OIA Show, Police Bldg, 94; Pleasant Pebble, Workspace, NY, 95; one-woman shows, Painting Ctr, NY, 97, (auth, catalog) Cranbrook Acad Art Mus, Bloomfield Hills, Mich, 98, (auth, catalog) Hyde Collection Art Mus, Glens Falls, NY, 99; Gas Works Gallery, London, Eng, 97; Cornerhouse Gallery, Manchester, Eng, 97; Weatherspoon Art Gallery, Univ NC, Greensboro, 97; HAIR DO, Work Space, New York, NY, 97; Drawing in Present Tense, (auth, catalog) Parsons Sch Design, NY, 99; Williamsburg Art & Historical Ctr, Brooklyn, NY, 2000; Exit Art, Air Gallery, NY, 2002; Courthouse Gallery, Lk George Arts Project, 2002; IT Space, New York, NY, Art During Wartime, 2003; Ind State Univ, Terre Haute, Contemp Women Artists, 2005. *Teaching:* Vis artist, Sarah Lawrence Col, Bronxville, NY, 89 & 93, Skidmore Col, Saratoga Springs, NY, 93 & 97, Bennington Col, Vt, 93, State Univ NY, Purchase, 95, Yale Univ, 95 & State Univ, NY, Albany, 99; guest lectr, RI Sch Design, Providence, 93 & Sch Visual Arts, New York, 94 & 97; Parsons Sch Design, New York, 95-; Adj Prof, BFA Program,Parsons School Design, NY, 95-2002, MFA Prog, 98-2002; instr, Sarah Lawrence Col, Bronxville, NY, 2000-; vis artist, Columbia Col, Chicago, IL, 2001. *Awards:* Yaddo Art Fel & Residency, 83-88; Nat Endowment Arts, Visual Arts Fel, 91-; Pollock-Krasner Found Grant 2003-04; and others. *Bibliog:* Judy Collischan (auth), Something Other, catalog, 82; Helen Harrison (auth), Something beyond seeing, NY Times, 3/6/83; Judy Collischan (auth), Kindred Spirits, catalog essay, 86; Judy Collischan (auth), Nancy Brett, ARTS Mag, 91; Joy Hakanson Colby (auth), Artist paints a harsh view of the precarious world of childhood, Detroit News, 7/30/98; Keri Guten Cohen (auth), Painter casts an edgy eye on childhood, Detroit Free Press, 7/21/98; Debra Bricker Balkan (auth), Drawing in the Present Tense, 99. *Mem:* Artists Space; Col Art Asn. *Media:* Oil. *Publ:* Kathleen Monaghan (auth), A Loaded Brush, Hope Coll, Mus Art, Glens Falls, NY. *Mailing Add:* 457 Broome St New York NY 10013

BRETTELL, RICHARD ROBSON
EDUCATOR, CONSULTANT
b Rochester, NY, Jan 17, 49. *Study:* Yale Univ, BA, MA, PhD, 76. *Collection Arranged:* Four Directions in Modern Photography (auth, catalog), Yale Art Gallery, 73; The Drawings of Camille Pissarro (coauth, catalog), Ashmolean Mus, Oxford, England, 79; Camille Pissarro, Mus Fine Arts, Boston, 80-81; Paper and Light: The Calotype in France & Great Britain (coauth, catalog), Mus Fine Arts, Houston, 82-83; The Golden Age of Naples: Art & Civilization Under the Bourbons, 82, Mauristshuis: Dutch Painting of the Golden Age, 83-84, Degas in the Art Institute of Chicago (with Suzanne Folds, McCullagh, coauth catalog) 84 & The Art of the Edge: European Frames 1300-1900(coauth catalog), 86, Art Inst Chicago; Permanent Galleries, European Painting & Sculpture 1300-1900 (installation designer), Art Inst Chicago, 87-; The Art of Paul Gauguin, Nat Gallery Art, Washington, DC, Art Inst Chicago & Mus d'Orsay, Paris, 88-89; The Impressionist & the City, 91-92; Impression: Painting Quickly in France 1860-1890, Nat Gallery Art, London, Van Gogh Mus, Amsterdam, The Netherlands, Clark Inst, Williamstown, 2000-01. *Pos:* Cur, European Painting & Sculpture, Art Inst Chicago, 80-88; dir, Dallas Mus Art, Tex, 88-92; independent art historian & consult, 92-. *Teaching:* Asst prof hist art, Univ Tex, Austin, 75-80; vis prof, Yale Univ, 93 Harvard Univ, 95; prof, aesthet studies Univ Tex Dallas, 98-. *Awards:* Chevalier, Order of Arts & Letters, France. *Mem:* Col Art Asn; Soc Archit Hist. *Res:* French drawing, printmaking & painting, 1800-1914; American architecture of the 19th century; landscape painting; history of photography 1839-1900. *Publ:* Coauth, The Drawings of Camille Pissarro in the Ashmolean Mus (with Christopher Lloyd), Oxford Univ Press, 80; Painters & Peasants, Skira, 83; auth, An Impressionist Legacy: The Collection of Sara Lee Corporation, Abbeville Press, 86; French Paintings of the 19th Century: The Art Institute of Chicago, 3 vols, Abrams, New York/Art Inst Chicago, Ill, 87; and many other books, catalogs and articles. *Mailing Add:* 5522 Montrose Dr Dallas TX 75209-5610

BREUER, BRADFORD R
PATRON, MUSEUM DIRECTOR
Study: Austin Col. *Pos:* Dir, The Alamo, San Antonio, formerly; pres, San Antonio Mus Asn, formerly; mem adv bd, Ctr for Southwestern & Mexican Studies Austin Col; bd trustees, Amon Carter Mus, Ft Worth. *Mailing Add:* c/o Amon Carter Mus 3501 Camp Bowie Blvd Fort Worth TX 76107-2695

BREVERMAN, HARVEY
PAINTER, PRINTMAKER
b Pittsburgh, Pa, Jan 7, 34. *Study:* Carnegie-Mellon Univ, BFA; Ohio Univ, MFA. *Work:* Whitney Mus Am Art, NY; Albright-Knox Art Gallery, Buffalo; Baltimore Mus, Md; Jewish Mus, NY; Mus Mod Art, NY; Nat Portrait Gallery, Washington, DC; British Mus, London, Eng. *Comn:* Print ed, Asn Am Artists, 67; bronze ed, NY State Soc Pathologists, 73; print ed, Rochester Print Club, 80; print ed, Boston Pub Libr, 81; mural, Niagara Frontier Transportation Authority, Buffalo, 84. *Exhib:* one man shows Grand Rapids (Mich) Art Mus, 1977, FAR Gallery, NY, 1974 & 79, Gadatsy Gallery, Toronto, 1976, 78, 81, 84 & 87, Nardin Galleries, NY, 1980, Canton Art Inst, Ohio, 1987, Babcock Galleries, NY, 1990 & 91, Kalamazoo (Mich) Inst Arts, 1997, Butler Inst Am Art, 1997, Yeshiva Univ Mus, NY, 1997 & 2002, Gertrude Herbert Inst Art, Augusta, Ga, 2000 & Ind Univ Art Gallery, 2001; 35 Yrs in Retrospect, Butler Inst Am Art, Youngstown, Ohio, 71; Works on Paper: Recent Acquistions, Albright-Knox Art Gallery, Buffalo, 79; Minn Mus Art, 82 & 86; Mus Fine Arts, Houston, 88; Florian Mus, Carbonari, Romania, 99; Mus Civico Di Grafica, Brunico, Italy, 99; 12 Deutsche Int Print Biennale, Frechen, 1999; De Mini Gravura, Vitoria, Brazil, 2000; Quingdao Int Print Biennial, China, 2000; 4th Int Print Triennial, Lahti Art Mus, Finland, 2001; Zeichen Der Gegenwart, Vienna Art Ctr Gallery, Austria, 2002; 4th Egyptian Int Print Triennale, Cairo, 2003; 1er Concours Int d'Ex-libiris, Ankara, Turkey, 2003; Gracefield Arts Ctr, Dumfries, Scotland, 2004; Siuvkorn Univ Art & Culture Ctr, Bangkok, Thailand, 2004; Letkas, Greece, 2005; Mona Bismark Found, Paris, 2005; Inst Zacatecano Cultura, Guadalupe, Mex, 2005; US Embassy-Hollar Soc Gallery, Prague, Czech Republic, 2006; Tiposela Italiana Foundazione, Cornuda, Italy, 2006; Nat Inst Mus, Bitola, Republic of Macedonia, 2006. *Teaching:* Prof art, Univ Buffalo, 61-, SUNY Disting prof, 99-; artist-in-residence, State Acad Fine Arts, Amsterdam, Neth, 65-66; vis artist, Oxford Univ Ruskin Sch Fine Arts, Eng, summer 74 & 77; Pont Aven Sch Art, France, 95; Jagiellonian Univ, Poland, 97. *Awards:* Tiffany Found Grant, 62; Creative Artists Pub Serv Grant, 72; Nat Endowment Arts Fels, 74-75 & 80-81; award, Am Acad Arts & Letters, 1980 & 81; Va Ctr Creative Arts Fel, 93; Disting Tchg of Art award, Col Art Asn, 2002. *Bibliog:* Madeline Burnside (auth), New York Reviews: Harvey Breverman at the FAR Gallery, Art News, summer, 1979; Martin Heavisides (auth), Harvey Breverman at Gadatsy Gallery, Artsmagazine, Toronto, 3/1979; Gerrit Henry (auth), New York Review: Harvey Breverman at Nardin Galleries, Art News, 12/1980. *Mem:* Nat Acad Design (assoc, 92, acad, 94); Soc Am Graphic Artists; Audubon Artists, Inc. *Media:* Oil; Etching, Lithography. *Dealer:* Babcock Galleries 724 Fifth Ave New York NY; Wenniger Graphics Gallery 174 Newbury St Boston MA 02116. *Mailing Add:* 76 Smallwood Dr Buffalo NY 14226-4027

BREWER, PAUL
PAINTER
b Jan 24, 34. *Study:* La Co, BA, 1956; Famous Artist Sch, degree in advert design, 1959; Studied at Syracuse Univ & Am Art Acad, Chicago. *Work:* Potraits of: Jack Benny, Danny Kaye, Red Buttons, Danny Thomas, Don Murray, Phil Silvers, EG Marshall, David Susskind, Leonard Bernstein, Merv Griffin, Edward P Morgan, and others. *Exhib:* One man show, La Col, 1963, Chicago Sun-Times, Famous Artists Sch, Chicago Pub Libr, Chicago Press Club, and others. *Collection Arranged:* Union League Club, Chicago, Ill; Bell Telephone Co; Standard Rate & Data; Krantzen Studio; Commonwealth Edison; Ford Motor Co; Hartford Insurance Co; and others. *Teaching:* Instr painting, Art Ctr, Highland Park, Ill; Instr, Deerpath Art League, Lake Forest, Ill. *Awards:* Recipient award, Am Newspaper Guild, Artists Guild Chicago, Famous Artist Sch, Graphic Arts Coun, Hartford Illustration Award; Nat award. Louisville Rotogravure Asn; Awards of excellence in painting for In View exhib, 2004-; Graphic Arts Coun, Union League Club, Chicago 3, and others. *Mem:* La Alumni Asn, North Shore Art League; Chicago Soc Typographic Arts; Chicago Soc Communicating Arts (bd dirs); Deerpath Art League; Am Soc Portrait Artists; Famous Artists Sch Alumni Asn; Am Watercolor Soc (assoc); The Art Ctr; Artist Guild Chicago. *Media:* Portrait. *Specialty:* Fine Art; Portraits. *Interests:* Touring Art Galleries; photg; painting on location. *Publ:* Illusr, New in the City, Follett; illusr, Who Am I, McKnight; Illusr, Count a Lonely Cadence, Follett. *Dealer:* Carole Lynn Kuhrt. *Mailing Add:* 1160 S Green Bay Rd Lake Forest IL 60045

BREWSTER, ANDREA B
PHOTOGRAPHER, CONCEPTUAL ARTIST
b Boston, Mass, Aug 31, 62. *Study:* Pomona Col, BA(sculpture), 84; San Francisco Art Inst, MFA (other genres), 91; cert (web design), Ctr Electronic Arts, 2000. *Comn:* Market Street Art in Transit, San Francisco Art Comn, 93. *Exhib:* Corners, Artspace Annex, San Francisco, 91; Susan Watkins Award Winners, New Langton Arts, San Francisco, 92; New Directions, Bechtel Ctr, Stanford Univ, Palo Alto, 92; one-man show, Hayward State Univ, 92, Southern Exposure, San Francisco, 92 & The Lab, San Francisco, 93; Fairy Tales, San Francisco State, 93; Revolving Histories, San Francisco Camera Work, 94; San Francisco Arts Comn Gallery, 97; Berkeley Pub Libr, Calif, 98; Benicia Pub Libr, Calif, 98; Art Ctr, Benica, Calif, 99; Calif State Univ Chico, 2000. *Awards:* Susan Watkins Award, 91; William Davidowitz Fel, 92; Nat Endowment Arts Grant for Works on Paper, 93-94. *Bibliog:* Kenneth Baker (auth), Three women, San Francisco Chronicle, 91; David Bonetti (auth), Alternative transformations, San Francisco Examiner, 91; Reena Jana (auth), Transformations, Artweek, 93. *Media:* Photography, Text. *Mailing Add:* 698 56th St Oakland CA 94609

BREWSTER, MARGARET EMILIA
PAINTER
b Kaukauna, Wis, July 18, 32. *Study:* Univ Wis, Fox Valley, 1953. *Work:* Outagamie County Hist Mus, Wisconsin State Collection, Appleton, Wis. *Comn:* The Carnot Children, Mr & Mrs William Carnot, Kaukauna, Wis, 1970; The Vande Hey Children, comn Mr & Mrs Ron Vande Hey, Kaukauna, Wis, 1979; Hist Hotel Kaukauna, McCarty Curry Wydeven Peeters & Haak, Kaukauna, Wis, 1995; Outagamie County

Teachers Col, McCarty Curry Wydeven Peeters & Haak, Kaukauna, Wis, 1998; The Weyenberg Homestead, Weyenberg Family Mem, Kaukauna, Wis, 2004. *Exhib:* Celebrating Winter in the Twin Cities, Minn State Capital Rotunda, St. Paul, Minn, 1987; Cudahy Gallery for Wis Art, Milwaukee Art Mus, Milwaukee, Wis, 1991; The Hardy Gallery on Anderson Dock, Peninsula Art Center, Ephraim, Wis, 1995; Neville Mus 53rd Art Ann, William Bonfas Fine Arts Center, Escanaba, Mich, 1996; SE Art League Regional Show XII, Atrium Gallery, Indianapolis, Ind, 1997; Pike's Peak Watermedia IX, Colo Springs Art Center, Colo Springs, Colo, 1998; Vision 2000 Windy City Artists, ORT Tech Inst, Chicago, Ill, 2000; Northern Lights, White Bear Lake Art Center, White Bear, Minn, 2002. *Awards:* People's Choice, Waupaca Art Festival, 1996. *Mem:* NE Wis Arts Council; The Bay Area Watercolor Guild (publicity chair, 2002); Kaukauna Creative Arts Group (founder & coordr, 1991-); Nat Mus of Women in the Arts. *Media:* Watermedia, Oil. *Mailing Add:* 400 W Division St Kaukauna WI 54130

BREWSTER, MICHAEL
SCULPTOR, EDUCATOR
b Eugene, Ore, Aug 15, 46. *Study:* Pomona Col, Claremont, Calif, studied with John Mason, David Gray, BA, 68; Claremont Grad Sch, with David Gray & Mowry Baden, MFA, 70. *Work:* La Jolla Mus Contemp Art, Calif; Guggenheim Mus, NY; Fine Art Gallery, Univ Mass, Amherst; Mus RI Sch Design; Mus Contemp Art, Los Angeles; and others. *Comn:* Sonic installations for pvt parties in NY, 77, San Francisco, 78, Los Angeles, 80 & Hollywood, 84. *Exhib:* Newport Harbor Art Mus, 72 & 75; Artists Space, NY, 77 & 84; Ft Worth Mus Art, 77; Baxter Art Gallery, Calif, 77; Joslyn Mus Art, Nebr, 79; Galleria del Cavallino, Venice, Italy, 79; Whitney Mus Am Art, NY, 81; Los Angeles Co Mus Art, Calif, 81; Commune di Rimini, Italy, 82; Mus Contemp Art, Los Angeles, 85. *Teaching:* Instr sculpture, drawing & painting, Pomona Col, 71-73; asst prof, Dept Fine Arts, Claremont Grad Sch, 73-81, acting chmn dept, 75, 79, 83 & 87 & prof art, 81-. *Awards:* Nat Endowment Arts Fel, 76, 78, 84 & 90; Fel, Guggenheim Found, 88. *Bibliog:* Richard Armstrong (auth), review, Artforum, 11/79; Kay Larson (auth), reviews, New York Mag, 3/2/81 & 6/25/84; Suzanne Muchnic (auth), review, 8/25/81 & Robert Pincus (auth), review, 1/31/85, Los Angeles Times. *Mem:* Int Sculpture Ctr; Los Angeles Contemp Exhib; Am Asn Univ Prof. *Media:* Sound, Light. *Publ:* Auth, Inside, Outside, Down & Soliloquies, Baxter Art Gallery, 77; Michael Brewster, Galleria de Cavallino, Italy, 79; Happen-Stance, Herron Sch Art, 79; Touch and Go, Fine Arts Gallery, Calif State Univ, 85; Gone to Touch, Words & Spaces, Smith & Delio, Univ Press Am, 89. *Mailing Add:* 1165 Palms Blvd Venice CA 90291-9524

BREWSTER, RILEY
PAINTER
Exhib: Group exhibs including In the Spirit of Landscape V, Nielsen Gallery, Boston, 1999-2000, In the Spirit of Landscape VI, 2001, Nat Acad 181st Ann Exhib, 2006; solo exhib including Painting Ctr, NY, 1994, Jacob Lawrence Gallery, Wash, 2005. *Teaching:* asst prof painting and drawing, U Wash. *Mailing Add:* Sch Art Univ Wash Box 353440 Seattle WA 98195-3440

BRIANSKY, RITA PREZAMENT
PAINTER, INSTRUCTOR
b Grajewa, Poland, July 25, 25; Can citizen. *Study:* Montreal Mus Fine Arts, with Jacques de Tonnancour; also with Alexandre Bercovitch & Anne Savage, Montreal; Ecole Beaux-Arts Montreal; Art Students League, NY. *Work:* Mus Que; Nat Art Gallery, Ottawa, Ont; Montreal Mus Fine Arts, Que; Can Dept External Affairs, Ottawa, Ont; Dofasco, Hamilton, Ont; and others. *Exhib:* Second Int Biennial Exhib of Prints, Tokyo & Osaka, Japan, 60-61; Salon Int Femme Vichy, France, 60-61; UNICEF Int, UN, NY, 65; La Soc des Artistes Prof du Que, Edinburgh, Scotland & London, Eng; solo exhib, Accents Gallery, Ottowa, 88, 89 & 92, Galerie L'Art Francais, Montreal, 89-90, Galerie de Bellefeville, Montreal, 91, Emma Ciotti Gallery, Iroquois Falls, Ont, 92, Galerie Jean-Pierre Valentin, Montreal, 95 & 97, Cole St Luc Libr, Cote St Luc, Quebec, 97, Montreal Holocaust Mem Centre, 97 & Temple Emanuel, Montreal, 98, McGill Univ, Birks Bldg, Montreal, 1999-2001; group exhib, Canadian Artists Jerusalem 3000, Jerusalem, 96, Au Feminin, Chorxd'ouvres de la Collection du musee du Quebec, 97 & 98, Eradication de la pauvrete, Le Musee Marc-Auvele Fortin, Montreal, 97, Centre Cult Marie Fitzback, St George de Bauce, 98 & Pavillon desarts du palais Montealm, Quebec, 98, Gems & Gallery, Montreal, 2002. *Teaching:* Instr, Ctr for Creative Lifestyles, Montreal. *Awards:* Third Prize, 1st & 2nd Nat Exhib Prints, Burnaby, BC, 60 & 63; Purchase Award, Dawson Col, Montreal, 82; Purchase Award, Thomas More Inst, Montreal, 85. *Bibliog:* E Kilbourn (auth), 18 print-makers, Can Art, 61; Henriette Giordan (auth), Rita Briansky-Du vetement comme portrait, Printemps, 95; Corinne Bolla-Paquet (auth), Rita Briansky-Fragments de Pologne-du desastre, Vie Arts, autumn 96. *Media:* Oil, Pastel. *Publ:* Illusr, Rubaboo Reader, 68; Grandmother Came From Dworitz, Tundra Bks, Montreal, 69; Ten Etchings from Wm Shakespeare's Sonnets, 72; On Stage Please, McClelland & Stewart, Toronto, 77 & Holt, Rinehart & Winston, New York, 79; Le Nu dans l'art au Quebec, Marcel-Broquet Publ, 82; Le Paysage dans la Peinture au Quebec, Marcel Broquet, Publ, 84; Agenda D'Art 1997, Musée Du Quebec, 97; Can Collection of Nat Art Gleery of Can Ottawa, CD-rom, 98; Se Me Souviens, Coffret Commemoratif De La Chanson Québecoise, 98; The View from Here, Winnipeg Art Gallery, 2000; Holocaust Literature and Education, University Guelph, Ont, 2000. *Dealer:* Galeria Brigitte Des Roches 2110 Crescent St Montreal PQ H3G 2B8. *Mailing Add.* 2284 Regent Ave Montreal PQ H4A 2R1 Canada

BRICKNER, ALICE
PAINTER, PRINTMAKER
b New York, NY, 31. *Study:* Sarah Lawrence Col, with Kurt Roesch, Ezio Martinelli, Lux Feininger & Theodore Roszak, BA, 52; Pratt Graphic Art Ctr, with Seong Moy, Arnold Singer, Erich Monch & Ansei Uchima, 57. *Work:* Johnson & Johnson, Surgikos Collection; Pratt Graphic Art Ctr; Stuttgart Univ, Ger; plus pvt collections. *Exhib:* Solo exhibs, Donnell Libr Ctr, New York City, 1999, Howell Ctr, Beacon, NY, 1998; Chrysalis Gallery, Southampton, NY, 1998-2001; Sch House Gallery, Croton Falls, NY, 1997, 1999, 2000; Galye Wilson Gallery, Southampton, 1997; Scarborough Gallery, Chappaqua, NY, 1993, 1994, 1997. *Collection Arranged:* Works at PaintingsDirect.com, 2000-. *Mem:* New York Artists Equity Asn; Artist's Space. *Media:* Watercolor, Acryllics; Collage on Canvas

BRIDENSTINE, JAMES A
MUSEUM DIRECTOR, COLLECTOR
b Detroit, Mich, Nov 29, 45. *Study:* Col Holy Cross, AB, 67; George Washington Univ, MA, 75; Harvard Univ, Cert Mus Studies, 78. *Pos:* Assoc Cur, Detroit Inst Arts, 76-86; dir, Edsel & Eleanor Ford House, 86-90; exed dir, Kalamazoo Inst Arts, Mich, 90-. *Teaching:* Adj prof art hist, Western Mich Univ, 92-. *Mem:* Am Asn Mus; Col Art Asn; Midwest Mus Asn; Mich Mus Asn; Asn Art Mus Dirs. *Res:* American art history - 19th century contemporary art. *Mailing Add:* Kalamazoo Inst of Arts 314 S Park St Kalamazoo MI 49007-5100

BRIER, HELENE
PAINTER, PRINTMAKER
b Bronx, NY, May 16, 24. *Study:* Art Students League, 42-45; Nat Acad Design, with Robert Philipp, 45-47; New York Univ, with Don Eddy, BS (fine art), 74, Magna Cum Laude, New York Univ, Founders Day Award, 74. *Work:* Andrew Dickson White Mus Art, Cornell Univ, NY; Univ Notre Dame Art Gallery, Ind; NY Univ Art Collection; Housatonic Mus & Univ Bridgeport, Conn; Slater Mem Mus, Norwich, Conn; Nat Mus Women Arts Archive, Libr & Res Ctr, Washington. *Exhib:* Silvermine Ann, 70-80; Collection '83, Silvermine Ctr Arts, Richardson-Vicks Inc, Wilton, Conn, 83; solo exhibs, Silvermine Ctr Arts, 84 & 98 (with catalog), Slade Mem Mus, Norwich, 84, Mattatuck Mus, Waterbury, 84, Lyman Allyn Gus, New London, 85, Conn, Artist's Mus, NY, 91, Munson Gallery, 92, Art Gallery at Fairfield Univ, Conn, 98, Beach Series, Peter Miller Gallery, Woodbury, Conn, 2006; Variations on the Landscape, Silvermine Guild Libr, Curtis Pelham Gallery, New Caanan, Conn, 92; Seven Printmakers, Darien Libr, Conn, 92; Silvermine 70th Anniversary Jubilee, 92; Translations, Discovery Mus, Conn, 95; Silvermine Mem Spring Show, New Canaan, Conn, 96; Conn Acad Fine Arts, Hartford, 96; Westport Art Ctr Mems Show, 96; New Haven Paint & Clay Show, 96; Picture this Romantic Oils and Monotypes, Westport, Conn, 97; Natures Gift, Fairfield Univ, Conn, 98; Lockwood Matthew Mansion Mus, Norwalk, Conn, 98; Int Art Ctr of Kyoto, catalog monotype, Japan, 2002; Art of the Cure, New Britain Mus Am Art Catalog, Conn, 2001; Creative Arts Workshop, Monotype, New Haven, Conn, 2003; Moira Fitzsimmons Arons Art Gallery, Monotypes, Hamden, Conn, 2003; Left of the Bank Gallery, Old Greenwich, Conn, 2003; Interior Landscapes, PH Miller Studio & Gallery, Conn, 2004; Int Art Ctr Kyoto, Japan, 2004; Conn Treasures in their 80's, Univ Conn, Stamford, Conn, 2005. *Teaching:* Instr drawing & design, Univ Bridgeport, Conn, 75-79. *Awards:* First Prize, Lloyd Goodrich, 68; First Prize, Lawrence Alloway, 69; Silvermine Ann New Eng Exhib, Thomas Hess, 78. *Bibliog:* Eleanor Charles (auth), NY Times, 88; William Zimmer (auth), NY Times, 88 & 92; Tracey O'Shanghesay (auth), Republican-Am Newspaper, 4/1/2004; and others. *Mem:* Conn Acad Art; life mem Art Students League; New Haven Paint & Clay Club; Silvermine Ctr Arts. *Media:* Oil, Watercolor. *Publ:* Contribr, Mia Brech, Fair Press, 79; Eliz O'Neil, Fairfield Co Mag, 79; Martha Scott, Bridgeport Post, 79; 6 Days on the Shoreline (cover), New Haven Advocate Mag, 7/2-8/92; Betty Tyler, Minuteman (exhib catalog), Fairfield & Westport, Conn, 7/98; and others. *Dealer:* Nardin Fine Arts Somers NY; Silvermine Centre Arts New Canaan CT; PH Miller Studio & Gallery, Woodbury, CT; Left at the Bank Gallery, Old Greenwich, CT. *Mailing Add:* 58 Random Rd Fairfield CT 06825

BRIGGS, LAMAR A
PAINTER
b Lafayette, La, Nov 13, 35. *Study:* Univ Houston, 58; Art Ctr Los Angeles, 58; Colorado Inst Art, 60. *Work:* Chicago Art Inst, Ill; Mint Mus Art, Charlotte, NC; Mus Fine Arts, Houston; Denver Art Mus, Colo; Rutgers Univ Arch, NJ; Mus Modern Art, Budapest, Hungary. *Comn:* Pair of large canvases, Phoenician Hotel, Phoenix, Ariz, 88; large wall piece, Bd Room Miami Conv & Tourist Bur, Fla, 89; interior walls, 757 pvt plane, Geneva, Switz, 90. *Exhib:* Art for Pub Places, Saginaw Art Mus, Mich, 79; Large Scale Contemp Paintings, Mint Mus, 81; Acrylic on Paper, Amarillo Art Ctr, Tex, 82; Prints-USA 1982, Pratt Graphics Ctr, NY, 82 & Lockhaven Art Ctr, Orlando, Fla, 82; 50/50 Monotyped-Prints, Montgomery Col, Rockville, Md, 85; Then-Now-and-Then, Univ Houston Lavondale Annex, Tex, 85; Contemp Gallery Exhib, Mint Mus, Charlotte, 85; Small Wonders, Aspen Art Mus, Colo, 86; Intaglio Painting in the 1980's, Zimmerli Art Mus, New Brunswick, NJ, 90. *Pos:* Guest artist, Anderson Ranch Art Ctr, Snowmass, Colo, 90-94. *Awards:* Hall of Fame, Art Inst Colo, 2005. *Bibliog:* Avis Berman (auth), Lamar Briggs: Paintings & Works on Paper, 80; Una Johnson (auth), Lamar Briggs Monotypes, Moody Gallery, 82; Amei Wallach (auth), Lamar Briggs Monotypes, Books & Co, 81. *Media:* Monotype, Acrylic on Canvas. *Dealer:* Moody Gallery 2815 Colquitt Houston TX 77098. *Mailing Add:* 358 Seaspray Ave Palm Beach FL 33480

BRIGGS, PETER S
CURATOR, HISTORIAN
b Oak Park, Ill, Nov 6, 46. *Study:* Northern Ill Univ, BA, 72; Univ Ky, MA, 75; Univ NMex, PhD, 86. *Collection Arranged:* Landscape Art, Univ NMex Art Mus, 83; 100 Years of French Prints, Chronicles: Historical References in Contemp Clay & From 2 to 3 Dimensions: Richard Santiago's Sculpture & Drawings, 85; New Western Directions: Mark Klett & Rick Dingus, 86; 4x4: Sixteen Printmakers from the Four Corner States & The Brian Ransom Ceramic Ensemble, 87; Life & Land: The FSA Photographers in Utah, 1936-1941, Harrison Mus Art, 88; Human Components, Univ Ariz Mus Art, 92; Max Cole, 93; Day by Day: American Daily Life, 94; La Cadena

que No Se Corta, Traditional Arts Tucson's Mex Am Community, 96; Eminent Delights, Images of Time, Space and Matter, 96; Tucson Artists: 1970-1997, 97; Reasoned Excess, 17th Century European Prints, 98; The Order of Pictures, 2000; Rudolf Baranik, 2000; Lewis Alquist, 2000; Groundwork: Drawings by Jim Waid (auth, catalog), 2001; Robert Stackhouse, 2001; Ernest DeSoto, 2001-02; Bruce McGrew: A Retrospective (auth, catalog), 2002; Buring Images: Cage, Bennet, Chejnowski, 2002; Kolomon Sokol: The Human Spirit, 2003; Olivier Mosset; Recent Work, 2003; Natural Pursintis, 2003; Mario Morreno Zazueta, 2003; A Physical Art; The Intay Iro Prints of Andrew Rerish, 2003; Barte Billy, 2004; James G Davis, 2004; Jasper Johns, 2004 & 06; Labor and Leisure, 2005. *Pos:* Asst cur of collections, Maxwell Mus Anthrop, 76-78; registr, Univ NMex Art Mus, 79-82, cur collections, 82-84; dir & chief cur, Nora Eccles Harrison Mus Art, 84-89; chief cur, Tucson Mus Art, 89-90; cur collections, Univ Ariz Mus Art, 90-99, chief cur, 99-2004; Helen Devitt Jones Cur of Art, 2004-. *Teaching:* Instr, Univ Ky, 73-74, Univ NMex, 76-77 & 81; asst prof, Utah State Univ, 85-89; grad faculty, Tex Tech Univ, 2005-. *Awards:* Res Fel, Orgn Am States, 79; Tinker Found Res Grant, 80; Bainbridge Bunting Fel, 80-81; Nat Endowment Art research grant, 83-84; Nat Endowment Art Prof Fel, 83 & 92; Fac Res Grant, Utah State Univ, 88 & Univ Ariz, 94. *Mem:* Col Art Asn; Am Asn Mus. *Res:* Precolumbian art history especially lower Cent America; 20th Cent American & Latin American Art History; Social Art History; Village planning and architecture. *Publ:* Auth, La diversidad social de Panama Central: Los Restos Mortuorios del sitio de el Indio, Los Santos, Patrimonio Historico, Panama, 92; A Portion of Space, Larry Elsner Found, 92; Fatal Attractions: Central American Mortuary Arts and Social Organization in The Central Americans and Their Neighbors, Univ Colo, 93; Emigres: Ceramics in Cross-Cultural Perspective, NCECA, 94; The Order of Pictures, 2000; Groundwork; Drawings by Jim Waid, 2001; Bruce McGraw, A Retrospective, 2002; Concrete Art, 2003; Reasonable Probabilities; Collected Notes on Paintings of James G. Davis, 2004; ArtLies, 2005 & 06; and others. *Mailing Add:* 3410 40th ST Lubbock TX 79413

BRILL, GLENN
PAINTER, PRINTMAKER

b New York, NY, June 3, 49. *Study:* Moravian Col, BA, 70; Calif Col Arts & Crafts, Oakland, BFA(printing), 73; Tamarind Inst, Albuquerque, NMex, 76; Cranbrook Acad Art, MFA(printmaking), 79. *Work:* Brooklyn Mus, NY; Phoenix Art Mus, Ariz; San Jose Mus Art, Calif; Tamarind Inst, NMex; Stanford Univ, Calif. *Comn:* US News World Report 2400 Collection, Washington, DC, 85; painting, Hyatt Regency, Long Beach, Calif, 86; painting, IBM Corp, Boca Raton, Fla, 88; painting, AT&T Educ Ctr, Atlanta, Ga, 88; painting, Apple Computer, Cupertino, Calif, 90; Discovery Channel, Washington, DC, 92; PG & E, San Francisco, Calif, 92. *Exhib:* Solo exhib, San Jose Mus Art, Calif, 85; Between Painting & Sculpture, Palo Alto Cult Ctr, Calif; Paper Now, Cleveland Mus Art, Ohio, 86; Craft Today: Poetry of the Physical, Am Craft Mus, NY, 86; Aha Hana Lima, Honolulu Acad Art, Hawaii, 88; Fun & Games, Bruce Mus, Greenwich, Conn, 89; Beyond Words: The Book as a Metaphor for Art, Calif Craft Mus/San Francisco Craft Mus, 90; Pyramid Atlantic, A Decade of Paper, Montpelier Cult Ctr, Laurel, Md, 91; West Coast Monotypes, Sewell Art Gallery, Rice Univ, Houston, Tex, 91; James Renwick Alliance Auction, Renwick Gallery, Washington, DC, 92. *Pos:* Artist lectr acrylic paint educ prog, Binney & Smith, 92. *Teaching:* Instr, San Francisco State Univ, 83-90. *Awards:* Fel, Nat Endowment Arts, 84 & 86. *Bibliog:* Jessica Scarborough (auth), The seduction of pattern, Artweek Mag, 12/7/85; Victoria Geibel (auth), Beyond surface: paper objects, Metropolis Mag, 6/87; Cheryl White (auth), Glenn Brill/Allrich Gallery, Am Craft Mag, 6-7/89. *Media:* Painting, Printmaking. *Mailing Add:* 567 Forest St Oakland CA 94618

BRILLIANT, RICHARD
EDUCATOR, WRITER

b Boston, Mass, Nov 20, 29. *Study:* Yale Univ, BA, 51, MA, 56, PhD, 60; Harvard Univ, LLB, 54. *Comn:* The Fayum Portraits, Prog for Art on Film, NY, 88. *Exhib:* Jewish Portraits in Colonial & Federal Am, NY, 97; Likeness & Beyond, Portraits from Africa & the Other World, NY, 90; Group Dynamics, Exh Curator, New York Historical Soc, 2006. *Pos:* Ed-designate, Art Bull, 90-91, ed-in-chief, 91-94; dir, Ital Acad, Columbia Univ, 96-2000; consultant to pres & CEO, New York Historical Soc, 2004 & 2005; prof emeritus, Columbia Univ. *Teaching:* From asst prof to prof art hist, Univ Penn, 62-70; vis Mellon Prof fine arts, Univ Pittsburgh, 71; vis prof, Scuola Normale Superiore, Pisa, 74, 80 & 88, Princeton, 86; prof, Columbia Univ, 70-2004. *Awards:* Fulbright Grant, 57-59; Am Acad Rome, 60-62; Guggenheim Found Fel, 67-68; Nat Endowment Humanities Sr Fel, 72-73; Distinguished Senior Scholar, College Art Asn, Feb 2005. *Mem:* Col Art Asn; Ger Archaeol Inst; Am Acad Arts & Sciences. *Res:* Greek and Roman art and archaeology; theory and method in art history. *Interests:* Portraiture, Narrative, Historiography of Art History. *Publ:* Pompeii, AD 79: the Treasure of Rediscovery, Volair, 79; Portraiture, Reaktion & Harvard, 91; Commentaries on Roman Art, Pindar Press, 94; Facing the New World, Prestel, 97; My Laocoon, California, 2000; Group Dynamics, NY Hist Soc, 2006; and others. *Mailing Add:* 10 Wayside Ln Scarsdale NY 10583

BRINE, KEVIN R
PATRON

Study: Stern, MBA, 81. *Pos:* Partner, Sanford C Bernstein & Co; dir, Delphi Fin Group Inc; managing dir, Brine Mgt Inc; trustee, Whitney Mus Am Art, currently; bd dir, Joan & Sanford I Weill Med Col Cornell Univ; trustee, NY Univ. *Mailing Add:* c/o Whitney Mus Am Art 945 Madison Ave New York NY 10021

BRISTOW, WILLIAM ARTHUR
PAINTER, EDUCATOR

b San Antonio, Tex, Feb 1, 37. *Study:* Univ Tex, BFA, 58; Univ Fla, MFA, 60; also with Clinton Adams, Ernest Briggs & George Lockwood. *Work:* Dallas Mus Art; Houston Mus Fine Art; San Antonio Art League; WTex Mus, Lubbock; Longview Jr League, Tex. *Comn:* Migration (aluminum fountain sculpture), US Govt, HemisFair, San Antonio, 68; steel sculpture fountain, Turbine Support Co, San Antonio, 69; two tapestry murals, La Mansion Hotels, San Antonio, 80 & 81; tapestry mural & tapestry, Frost Nat Bank, San Antonio. *Exhib:* Southwest Print & Drawing Soc, Dallas Mus Fine Art, 60, Tex Ann, 60-63; Painting in the Southwest, Okla Art Ctr, Oklahoma City, 62; Artist of the Yr, San Antonio Art League, Witte Mus, 65; Nat Art Competition, Am Artist Mag, Circle Gallery, NY, 78; 14th Ann Prints & Drawings & 38th Ann Delta Competition, Ark Arts Ctr, Little Rock, 95; Film artist, Still Breathing, October Films, 98. *Collection Arranged:* Tex Commerce Bank, Houston; Sandia Corp, Albuquerque; Trammell Crow Co, Tulsa. *Teaching:* Instr painting & drawing, Univ Fla, Gainesville, 58-60; assoc prof painting & drawing, Trinity Univ, San Antonio, 60-79, prof, 79-99, chmn dept design & drawing, 65-78, prof emer, 99. *Awards:* Purchase Prize, Tex Ann, Houston Mus Fine Art, 62; First Prize Southwest Print & Drawing, Mrs Edwin B Hopkins Fund, Dallas Mus, 64; Mus STex Prize for Sculpture, Coca Cola Bottling Co, 66. *Bibliog:* An artist & teacher, born of the space & light of Texas, Chronicle Higher Ed, 12/2/87. *Mem:* Coppini Acad (hon life); San Antonio Watercolor Group (hon, life). *Media:* Acrylic, Oil. *Interests:* art as a socialization process. *Publ:* Auth, True Gesso--and other truths, Art & Academe, Visual Arts Press, Ltd, fall 88; The fresh glories of the Sistine Chapel, Houston Chronicle Mag, 4/30/89; Sublime vision: Color, light and the fourth dimension, Art & Academe, Visual Arts Press, Ltd, fall 89. *Mailing Add:* 344 Wildrose Ave San Antonio TX 78209-3817

BRITE, JANE FASSETT
CURATOR, DIRECTOR

b Chicago, Ill. *Study:* Marjorie Webster Col, BS, 57; Univ Wis, Milwaukee. *Work:* Fiber Revolution - Textile Mus, Washington, DC, 87; Exploration & Innovation, Textile Mus, Washington, DC, 90. *Collection Arranged:* Wisconsin Directions Three (auth, catalog), 84 & Wisconsin Directions Four (auth, catalog), 85; Schomer Lictner Retrospective (auth, catalog), 84; Emerging Imagist (auth, catalog), 85; Fiber R/Evolution, History of Fiber 50's-80's (auth, catalog), 86; The Force, Brian Richie & Dennis Nechtavel (performance/site installation cur), 87; Triangulation, Jill Sebastian, Debra Loewen, Jon Erickson, (performance/site installation cur); Women of Substance, Joyce Scott & Kay Lawal (performance/site installation cur); Diverse Works, Maryland Art Place (bd trustees); Curated & Cataloge: Rossbach- 40 years of exploration & Innovation in Fiber Sax Collection, 90; Toleto Mus, 97. *Pos:* Bd mem, Wis Arts, Madison, 82-85 & Art Reach, Milwaukee, 82-86; rev, Inst Mus Serv, Washington, DC, 83-84; ed bd, Acad Sci, Arts & Letts, 85-86; Art Reach, 82-85 & 88; bd trustees, Dance Circus, 86-. *Teaching:* Save & Sound, YMCA, Milwaukee, WI, 99-2003. *Mem:* Tempo-Prof Women (sem comn, 85-86); Wis Painters & Sculptors; Wis Designer Craftsmen; Tal-N-Art Consortium Inc (adv, 86). *Res:* Development of fiber arts of the last thirty years; history of Wisconsin art of the 30's & 40's. *Publ:* Coauth, The new directions-old pleasures in ceramic art, 85 & The evolution of art in Milwaukee, 86, Wis Acad Rev (Wis Acad Sci, Arts & Letts); auth, The Milwaukee J Gallery of Wisconsin Art, exhib catalogue. *Mailing Add:* 1610 N Prospect Ave No 1001 Milwaukee WI 53202-6702

BRITO, MARIA
SCULPTOR, PAINTER

b Havana, Cuba, Oct 10, 47; US citizen. *Study:* Fla Int Univ, Miami, BFA, 77, MS, 76; Univ Miami, Coral Gables, Fla, MFA, 79. *Work:* Olympic Sculpture Park, Seoul, Korea; Archer M Huntington Mus, Austin, Tex; Univ Fla, Tallahassee; Art in Public Places, Metro-Dade Ctr, Miami; Lowe Art Mus, Coral Gables, Fla. *Comn:* Sculpture, Seoul Olympic Organizing Comt, Seoul, Korea, 88. *Exhib:* The Decade Show, Studio Mus Harlem, New Mus Contemp Art & Mocha, Mus Contemp Hispanic Art, NY 90; Southern Exposures, High Mus Art, Atlanta, 91; Cuban Artists of the Twentieth Century, Mus Art, Ft Lauderdale, Fla, 93; Revelations/Revelaciones: Evanescene and Latino Art, Johnson Mus Art, Cornell Univ, Ithaca, NY, 93; Transcending the Borders of Memory, Norton Gallery Art, West Palm Beach, Fla, 94; and others. *Teaching:* adj prof, Barry Univ, Miami Shores, Fla. *Awards:* Visual Artists Fel, Nat Endowment Arts, 84 & 88; Pollock-Krasner Found Grant, 90; Virginia A Groot Found Grant, 94. *Bibliog:* Ricardo Pau-LLosa (auth), The Dreamt Objectivities of Maria Brito-Avellana, Dreamworks, Human Sci Press Inc, 86; Charlotte S Rubenstein (auth), American Women Sculptors, G K Hall & Co, 90; Lynette M F Bosch (auth), Maria Brito: Metonymy and metaphor, Latin Am Art Mag, 93; and others. *Mem:* Col Art Asn; Ctr Fine Arts; Ctr Contemp Art. *Media:* Mixed. *Mailing Add:* 8995 SW 75th St Miami FL 33173

BRITT, SAM GLENN
EDUCATOR, PAINTER

b Ruleville, Miss, Sept 26, 1940. *Study:* Memphis Acad Art, BFA; Univ Miss, MFA; Cape Cod Sch Painting, Provincetown, Mass, with Henry Hensche; Frudakais Acad Sculpture, Philadelphia, with Angelous Frudakais. *Work:* Union Bldg, Delta State Univ, Munic Art Gallery, Jackson, Miss; First Nat Bank, Cleveland, Miss. *Comn:* Drawing depicting the lifestyle of ancient Indians, Winterville Mounds Mus, Miss, 67; painting, Union Planters Nat Bank, Memphis, Tenn; painting, Mrs Pat Kerr, Memphis, Tenn. *Exhib:* One-man show, Gov's Mansion, Jackson, Miss; Bryant Galleries, Jackson, Miss & New Orleans, La, 83; Nat Bank Com, Memphis, Tenn, 83; Symphony Ball, Peabody Hotel, Memphis, Tenn, 83; 7 Am Impressionists, Gallery 3, Roanoke, Va, 85; and others. *Teaching:* Instr drawing & painting, Delta State Univ, 66-73, asst prof, 73-78, assoc prof art, 78-; pvt instr, Clarksdale, Miss, 73-; instr, Painting City Park, New Orleans, summer 85, Painting Workshops Unlimited, Jackson, Miss, 85 & 86 & Drawing Studio One, Gray, La, 85 & 86. *Awards:* Second Prize, Nat Painting Exhib, 64; Most Outstanding Work, Nat Small Painting Exhib, Hadley, 74; Best in Show, Crosstie Festival, 79. *Bibliog:* Ed Phillips (auth), Finding God's beauty in a simple world, Delta Scene Mag, 75; Featured on Miss Educ TV as a Miss Artist, spring 80. *Media:* Oil, Pastel. *Mailing Add:* 1105 University St Cleveland MS 38732-3665

BRITTON, DANIEL ROBERT
PRINTMAKER, EDUCATOR
b Colorado Springs, Colo, Apr 1, 49. *Study:* Univ Colo, BFA, 74, MFA, 76. *Work:* Corcoran Mus, Washington, DC; Portland Art Mus, Ore; Haggin Art Mus, Calif; Scottsdale Mus Contemp Art, Ariz; Tamarind Inst, NMex; Nelson Art Mus, Ariz; Bibliotecque Nat, Paris; Utah Mus Fine Arts, Salt Lake City; Lauren Rodgers Art Mus, Laurel, Miss; Huntsville Mus Fine Arts, Ala. *Comn:* McDonalds Corp, Chicago & Denver, 88. *Exhib:* Tenth Nat Print Competition, Univ Art Gallery, Minot, NDak, 81; DeKalb 81 Nat Print Competition, Swen Parsons Gallery, Ill, 81; Moravian Print Nat, Church Street Gallery, Bethlehem, Pa, 81; Am Drawing IV, Portsmouth Mus, 83; Haggin Art Mus, Stockton, Calif, 88; Albrecht Art Mus, St Joseph, Mo, 91; Bradley Univ Nat Print Exhib, Peoria, Ill, 91; NDak Nat Print & Drawing Competition, 92; 5th Int Biennial Graphic Arts, Novomesto, Slovenia, 98; 8th Int Print & Drawing Biennial, Taipei Art Mus, Repub China, 98; Monotypes, Fine Arts Gallery, Brigham Young Univ, Utah, 98; Am Printmaking, Moderna Galleria, Croatia, 99. *Teaching:* Vis prof lithography, Univ Utah, Salt Lake City, 91; prof art, printmaking, Ariz State Univ, 76-. *Awards:* Award of Merit, DeKalb Print Nat, 81; Stockton Nat Print Competition, Haggin Art Mus, Stockton, Calif, 88; Nat Honor Soc, Ariz State Univ, 91; Heitland Found Grant, Ger, 91; Artist fel Ariz Comn of the Arts, 98. *Bibliog:* Roberta Loach (auth), Printmakers, Visual Dialogue Mag, 79; Art in the Sun Belt, Art News, 80; Carol Kotrozo (auth), Drawing and Printmaking, Art Week, 81; Yingxue/Malone/Wampler, Contemp Am Painting, Jilin Fine Arts Pub, 99. *Mem:* Los Angeles Printmaking Soc; Southern Graphics Coun. *Media:* Lithography, Monotypes, Oil. *Publ:* Tamarind Technical Papers, 79 & 80. *Dealer:* G-Z Gallery Scottsdale AZ. *Mailing Add:* Sch Art Ariz State Univ Tempe AZ 85287

BROAD, ELI
COLLECTOR, PATRON
b New York, NY, June 6, 33. *Study:* Mich State Univ, BA(cum laude), 54. *Hon Degrees:* Southwestern Univ, LLD, 2000. *Pos:* Founding chmn & bd trustees, Mus Contemp Art, Los Angeles, Calif, 80-; nat trustee, Baltimore Mus Art, Md, 85-91; bd trustees, Arch of Am Art, Smithsonian Inst, Washington, DC, 85-; painting & sculpture comt, Whitney Mus, NY, 87-89; chmn adv bd, Art/89, Los Angeles, Calif, 89; founder, chmn, Kaufman and Broad Home Corp, Los Angeles, Calif, 93-; trustee, Mus Modern Art, NY, currently; CPA, 54-56; co-founder, chmn, pres, Chief Exec Officer, SunAmerica Inc (formerly Kaufman & Broad, Inc) Los Angeles, 57-2001. *Teaching:* asst prof, Detroit Inst Tech, 56. *Awards:* Founders Award, Occidental Col, 2000; Trustees Award, Calif Inst Arts, 2000; Chmns Award, Asia Soc Southern Calif, 2000; Named one of Top 200 Collectors, ARTnews Mag, 2004, 2005, 2006. *Mem:* Hillcrest Country Club; The Regency Country Club, LA. *Collection:* Museum quality works from approximately 1913 to present with a concentration on American art of the 70's, 80's & 90's; Contemporary Art. *Mailing Add:* Broad Foundation Ste 1200 10900 Wilshire Blvd Los Angeles CA 90024

BROCK, MARK L
ART DEALER, CONSULTANT
b Merritt Island, Fla, Jan 25, 66. *Study:* Boston Col, BS, 92. *Pos:* Consult, Brock & Co, currently. *Specialty:* American works of art, 1850-1950

BROCK, ROBERT W
SCULPTOR, EDUCATOR
b Tacoma, Ohio, June 27, 1936. *Study:* Sch Dayton Art Inst, 54-60, dipl, with Robert C Koepnick; Univ Dayton, BFA, 60; Ohio Univ, MFA, 62, with David Hostetler. *Work:* Dayton Art Inst; State Univ NY Col, Fredonia. *Comn:* Sculpture, Fillmore Suburban Hosp, 96. *Exhib:* Artists of Southern Ohio, Dayton Art Inst, 60 & 61; Ohio Sculpture & Ceramic Show, Butler Inst Am Art, Youngstown, 62; Western NY Show, Albright-Knox Art Gallery, Buffalo, 65-67, 69 & 75 & Outdoor Sculpture Exhib, 68; Unordinary Realities, Xerox Ctr, Rochester, 75. *Pos:* Mem adv comt, Burchfield Ctr, 70-84; chmn fine arts dept, State Univ Col, Buffalo, 70-73 & 81-85; pres, Patteran Artists Inc, Buffalo, 77-78; mem adv comt, Art in Subway, Buffalo, 81-85. *Teaching:* Prof sculpture, State Univ NY Col, Buffalo, 62-. *Mem:* Int Sculpture Ctr. *Media:* All Media. *Mailing Add:* 104 Fordham Dr Buffalo NY 14216

BROD, STANFORD
DESIGNER, EDUCATOR
b Cincinnati, Ohio, Sept 29, 32. *Study:* Col of Design, Archit, Art & Planning, Univ Cincinnati, BS(design), 55. *Work:* Nat Collection of Fine Arts, Washington, DC; Mus Mod Art, NY; Hebrew Union Col, Jewish Inst Relig Mus, Los Angeles; Contemp Art Ctr & Cincinnati Art Mus, Ohio. *Comn:* Urban Walls: Cincinnati (ten story bldg wall mural), Solway Gallery for Cincinnati Community, 72; Six Urban Banners, Contemp Art Ctr, 75, 520 Paolo, Brazil, US Pavilion. *Exhib:* Greetings, Mus Mod Art, NY, 66; Int Calligraphy Today; Urban Banner Designs Cincinnati Downtown Commercial Districts, 81; Tel Aviv Mus, 82; Int Art Exhib DRUPA, Dusseldorf, Ger, 82; traveling show, Calligraphia USA/USSR, Russia & USA, 90-92; and others. *Pos:* Designer, Rhoades Studio, Cincinnati, 55-62; designer, Lipson, Alport & Glass Inc, Cincinnati, 62-94, wood/brod design, 94-. *Teaching:* Exp typography, Art Acad Cincinnati, 60, 75, 91 illus, 91, 92, packaging design, 91, 92, 94, 96, 98, 2000, 2004 & corporate design, 92, 93, 95, 97, 99, 2001, 2003, 2005; adj prof graphic design, Col Design, Archit, Art & Planning, Univ Cincinnati, 62-. *Awards:* Communication Arts Award, Commun Arts J, 59, 64, 66 & 70; Typomundus 20/2 Int Award, 70; Int Typographic Composition Award, 70-72 & 75. *Publ:* Auth, Trademarks & Symbols of the World, 87; Letterheads 2; A Collection of Letterheads from Around the World, 89; Greeting Cards: A Collection from Around the World, 89; Expressive Typography, The Word As Image, 90; Fresh Ideas in Promotion 2, 96. *Mailing Add:* 3662 Grandin Rd Cincinnati OH 45226

BRODERICK, HERBERT REGINALD, III
EDUCATOR
b Bethesda, Md, July 16, 45. *Study:* Columbia Col, AB, 67; Columbia Univ, MA, 68, MPhil, 75, PhD, 78. *Teaching:* Instr art hist, Columbia Univ, 74-77, asst prof, 78; asst prof, Herbert H Lehman Col, City Univ NY, 78-84, assoc prof, 85-2001. *Awards:* Mrs Giles Whiting Found Fel, 74-75; Nat Endowment Humanities Fel, 81-82; PSC/City Univ NY Fac Res Awards, 81-82 & 88-89, 2004-05. *Mem:* Int Ctr Medieval Art; Int Soc Anglo Saxonists. *Res:* Iconography of the Old Testament in medieval art; Anglo-Saxon manuscript illumination. *Publ:* Auth, Some attitudes toward the frame in Anglo-Saxon manuscripts of the 10th and 11th centuries, Artibus & Historiae, Vol V, 82; Observations on the method of illustration in manuscript Junius II, Scriptorium, Vol XXXVII, 83; Observations on the creation cycle of the Sarajevo Haggadah, Zeitschrift, für Kunstgechichte, XLVII, 84; A Note on the Garments of Paradise, Byzantion, LV, 250-254, 85; Early Medieval Aspects of the American Renaissance, Medievalism in Am Culture, Vol I, Binghampton, pg 89-114, 87; and others. *Mailing Add:* 530 West End Ave New York NY 10024-3255

BRODERICK, JAMES ALLEN
ADMINISTRATOR, GRAPHIC ARTIST
b Chicago, Ill, 39. *Study:* St Ambrose Col, BA, 62; Univ Iowa, MA, 66. *Exhib:* SAMA-Open, 86, San Antonio Mus Art, 86; Recent Photog, Blue Collar Gallery, San Antonio, 86; Heat & Light, Univ Tex, San Antonio, 87; Close-Up, San Antonio Mus Art, 87; solo shows, Martin Rathburn Gallery, San Antonio, 93 & Inst Cult Pernano Norte Americano, Lima, Peru, 94; and others. *Teaching:* Asst Prof, Northwest Mo State Univ, Maryville, 66-76, dir art gallery, 67-76, chmn, Dept Art, 70-76; prof & chairperson, Dept Art, Tex Tech Univ, Lubbock, 76-83; prof, art, Univ Tex, San Antonio, 83-currently, dir, Div Visual Arts, 83-2002, chmn, Dept Art & Art Hist; prof Emer, 03. *Mem:* Tex Asn Schs Art (bd dir); Nat Coun Art Adminr (bd dir); Nat Asn Schs Art & Design (pres, 1999-2002, bd dir, 85-, fel); Col Art Asn. *Media:* Miscellaneous Media, Photography. *Mailing Add:* 1643 Ranch Rd 473 Boerne TX 78006

BRODEUR, CATHERINE R
PAINTER
b Los Angeles, Calif. *Study:* Art Students League, New York, with Daniel Greene, 75; Jack Callahan, Rockport, Mass, 77-79; John Howard Sanden, New York, 79-80. *Work:* Permanent Naval Art Collection, Sheet Metal Worker's Union, Washington; First Nat Bank Boston, Mass; Hamden Co Med Asn, Bay Bank Valley, Springfield, Mass; Bennington Ctr Arts, Vt. *Comn:* St Dominic (painting), Dominican Monastery, West Springfield, Mass, 85; The Last Supper (painting), St Alphonsus Col, Suffield, Conn, 87; portrait of Selectman, West Springfield Arts Coun, Mass, 88; series of 7 Saints, The Redemptorists Order, Washington, 91; St Gregory (paintings), St Gregory's Church, Indian Orchard, Mass, 99; Installation (portrait), Chicopee High Sch Libr, 2004. *Exhib:* Through Women's Eyes, Holyoke Mus, Mass, 88; Realists Today, Am Artists Mag, Denver, Colo, 89; Springfield Art League Invitational, Western New Eng Col, Mass, 89; The Realists, Mus Fine Art, Springfield, Mass, 90; 4 Women Artists, Wistariahurst Mus, Holyoke, Mass, 92; Ann VT Inst Natural Sci Exhib, Woodstock; The Nature Ctr Ann Exhib, Westport, Conn; Art of the Animal Kingdom Int Show, Bennington Ctr Arts, Vt; Western New Eng Col, Wilbraham, Mass, 97; Bay State Med, Springfield, Mass, 97; and others. *Teaching:* Instr gen art, Holyoke Home Info Ctr, 79-81; instr portraits, Wistariahurst Mus, 88-90. *Awards:* Margaret Fernald Dole Award, Hudson Valley Arts Asn, In Trust, 82, Merit Award, Springfield Art League Nat, 86; Wilkins Award, Academic Artists Assoc, Wilkins Art Consults, 90. *Bibliog:* Herb Rogoff (auth), Getting the Feel for People, Palette Talk No 66, 86; Angela Carbone (auth), Voices-Profile, Transcript Telegram, 1/14/89; Ruth Reininghaus (auth), The Salmagundian, spring 89. *Mem:* Hudson Valley Art Asn; Copley Soc Boston; Acad Artists Asn (vpres, 90-); Pastel Soc Am; North Shore Artists Asn. *Media:* Oil, Pastel. *Mailing Add:* 18 Saw Mill Park Southwick MA 01077-9355

BRODHEAD, QUITA
PAINTER, WRITER
b Wilmington, Del. *Study:* Pa Acad Fine Arts; Grande Chaumiere & Julienne's, Paris; with Arthur Carles & Alexander Archipenko; Fel Pa Acad Fine Arts. *Work:* Pa Acad Fine Arts, Philadelphia Mus Art, Woodmere Art Mus, Philadelphia, Pa; NJ State Mus, Trenton, NJ; Del Art Mus; Asheville Art Mus, NC; Butler Inst Am Art, Youngstown, Ohio. *Comn:* Mural, St Johns Episcopal Church, Bala Cynwyd, Pa, 30; mural, comn by E Ennalls Berl, Wilmington, Del, 33; crucifixion, St Anthony's Cath Church, Wilmington. *Exhib:* Pa Acad Fine Arts, Philadelphia; Philadelphia Art Alliance, Pa; one person exhibs, Thomas Jefferson Gallery, 81, Chez Barbier, Paris, 82, Am Col Gallery, Philadelphia, 83, Carspecken-Scott Gallery, Wilmington, Del, 92 & 93, Rosemont Col, Pa, 92, Cosmos Club, Washington, 93; one-man retrospective, Pa Acad Fine Arts; Prince St Gallery, NY, 96; Rosenfeld Gallery, Philadelphia, 98; Wayne Art Ctr, 99. *Pos:* Mem bd dir, Fel Acad Fine Arts, Pa, 30-50; Chmn exhib comt Nat Exhib Blind Artists. *Teaching:* Instr, Main Line Forum Arts. *Awards:* Gold Medal Award, 53 & Caroline Gibbons Grange Mem Award, 55, Fel Acad Fine Arts, Pa; Women's Caucus for Art, 2000. *Bibliog:* Edourdo Westerdahl (auth), The Painting of Quita Brodhead, El Dia, 61; Barbara Wolanin (auth), Quita Brodhead, Art Am, 92; Barbara Wolanin (auth), Quita Brodhead: capturing the vibes of the twentieth century, Woman's Art J. *Mem:* Artists Equity; Philadelphia Mus Art; Mus Mod Art, NY; Fel Pa Acad Fine Arts; Woodmere Art Mus; and others. *Media:* Oil, Acrylic. *Publ:* Auth, Remembering Arthur Carles, Arts Mag; narrator, Reflections of Arthur B Carles. *Dealer:* Hollis Taggart Gallery 78 E 73rd St New York NY

BRODIE, REGIS CONRAD
CERAMIST, PAINTER
b Pittsburgh, Pa, Nov 19, 42. *Study:* Ind Univ Pa, BSc (art educ) & MEd; Temple Univ, MFA. *Work:* World Ceramic Exposition Found, Icheon, Korea (outdoor installation); Escuela de Arte Francisco Alcatara (Nat Sch of Ceramics), Madrid, Spain; Museo de Ceramica, (Nat Ceramics Mus of Spain), Barcelona, Spain; Musee Nat de la Ceramique, (Nat Ceramics Mus of France), Sevres, France; Embassey of the United States of America, Cairro, Egypt,; Permanent Collections Nat, Ariz State Univ, Tempe, Ariz; Everson Mus of Art, Syracuse, NY: Delaware Art Mus, Wilmington, Delware, Tang Teaching Mus and Gallery, Skidmore Col, Saratoge Springs, NY; Southern Conn State Univ, New Haven, Conn, The Hyde Collection, Glens Falls NY, Long Beach Mus of Art, Long Beach, Calif. *Exhib:* Invitational Porcelain Exhib, Am Craft Mus, NY, 2000; The Int Exposition of Sculpture Objects & Functional Art (SOFA), Chicago, 2000, NY, 2001 & 2002; Am Masters, Sante Fe, NMex, 94-99; Inter-D2, Int Craft Exhib, McAllen, Tex; Interconnections, Univ Wales Inst, Cardiff, Wales, Eng. *Teaching:* Prof studio art, Skidmore Col, 69-, dir, Six summer art prog & AP summer art prog for high sch students, 72-. *Awards:* The Edwin M Moseley Fac Research Lectr, Skidmore Col, 88; The Ella Vandyke Tuthill Endowed Chair in Studio Art, Skidmore College (First Recipient 93-99); Vis Fel, Univ of Wales Inst, Ctr for Art and Design Ed, Cardiff, UK, May, 2001; 2004-2005 Residency Prog, Int Symposium on & construction of Outdoor Ceramic Sculpture, World Ceramic Exposition Found, Yeoju, Korea (One of Ten Ceramic Artistis Invited). *Bibliog:* Charlotte F. Speight & John Toki (auth), Make it in Clay: A Beginner's Guide to Ceramics, 2nd ed, Mayfield Publishing Company, 2001; Susan Peterson (auth), Working with Clay, 2nd ed, Prentice Hall, Laurence King Publ, London, Eng, 2002; Roberta Griffith (auth), Regis Brodie-A Vision Defined, Revista Ceramica, Nat Ceramics Mag of Spain, Madrid, Issue No 86, 2003. *Media:* Clay, Mixed Media. *Publ:* Auth, The Energy-Efficient Potter, Watson-Guptill Publ, 5/1982; auth, The Studio Potter, 6/97, Refiring a Second Chance (article), Vol 25, #2 Ceramics Monthly, 5/94, The Creative Process (article), 5 & 31-33; contribr auth (with Richard Zakin), Ceramics, Mastering the Craft (a section on multifiring with step-by-step photosand text), 238-241, Chitton Book Company, Radnor, Pa, 1990. *Dealer:* Loveed Fine Arts 575 Madison Ave Ste 1006 New York 10022. *Mailing Add:* 27 Wedgewood Dr Saratoga Springs NY 12866

BRODKIN, ED
PAINTER, CONCEPTUAL ARTIST
b New York, NY, Aug 21, 25. *Study:* Brooklyn Mus Art Sch, 51; Cooper Union, BFA, 75. *Exhib:* Solo shows, Pleiades Gallery, NY, 89, 91, 92, 94, 96, 97, 99, 2000, 02, 03, 05; group shows, New Yorkers in Barcelona, Cartoon Gallery, Spain, 91, NJ Ctr Visual Arts Int Juried Show, Summit, NJ, 97 & City Without Walls Gallery, Newark, NJ, 97, 98, 01; 48th Ann NE USA, Silvermine Gallery, New Canaan, Conn, 97, 2001 & 04; Galerie Roessler, Munich, Ger, 99, 2000; and others; Jersey City Mus Invitational, 02; Gwanguu - Biennal, Int Art Ctr, Gwangju, S Korea, 2003. *Pos:* Mem, Art & Design Adv Comn, Mercer Co Community Col, Trenton, NJ, 70-73; chmn, Pleiades Gallery, NY, 94-96, comt chmn, NY, 97-2003. *Teaching:* Instr fine & appl art, Mechanics Inst, NY, 61-62. *Awards:* Painting Award, Bergen Mus Art & Sci, 84; Award of Distinction, Rockport Publ, 97; Artist Showcase Award Winner, Manhattan Arts Int, 98, 99. *Bibliog:* Alexandra Shaw (critic), Manhattan Arts, 10/97; Sean Simon (critic), Artspeak, 10/97; Creative Inspirations, Rockport Publ, 12/97; and many others; Cornelia Seckel (critic), Art Times, 6/99; Gallery & Studio, 11/2003, 3/2005. *Mem:* NY Artists Equity Asn. *Media:* Various Paints, Varnishes, and non-retangular grounds. *Specialty:* Contemp Art. *Interests:* Chamber Music, Cosmology, books & essays. *Publ:* The Best of Acrylic Painting, 96 & Creative Inspirations, 97, Rockport Publ; Ed McCormack (auth), Gallery and Studio, 11/2000, 4/2002. *Dealer:* Pleiades Gallery 530 W 25th St New York NY 10001-5516. *Mailing Add:* 167 Garden Ave Paramus NJ 07652-1918

BRODSKY, ALEXANDER ILYA UTKIN
ARCHITECT, SCULPTOR
b Moscow, Russia 55. *Study:* Alexander Brodsky: Moscow Archit Inst, 78. *Work:* Mus Mod Art, NY; Hirshhorn Mus & Sculpture Garden, Washington, DC; Inst Contemp Art, Boston, Mass; Portland Art Mus, Ore; Bayly Art Mus, Univ Va. *Comn:* Interior, Atrium Restaurant, Moscow, USSR, 88; Pedestrian Bridge, Tacoma, Wash, 90; Monumental Sculpture in Courtyard, Europ Ceramics Work Ctr, Hertogenbosch, Neth, 91; lighting project 93-96, Yamagiwa Art Found, Tokyo, Japan, 92; Palazzo Nero, Wellington City Art Gallery, NZ, 92. *Exhib:* Paper Architecture: New Projects from the Soviet Union, List Visual Arts Ctr, Mass Inst Technol, Cambridge, Mass, 90; solo exhibs, Mus Art, Univ Ariz, Tucson, 92, Bayly Art Mus, Univ Va, Charlottesville, 93, Portland Ctr Visual Arts, Ore, 93 & Gallery 210, Univ Mo, St Louis, 94; group exhibs, SKVC Gallery, Ljubljana, Yugoslavia, 86, La Grande Halle de La Villette, Paris, France, 88, Deutsches Architektur mus, Frankfurt, Ger, 89, Found pour l'Archit, Brussels, Belgium, 90, Irving Galleries, Sydney, Australia, 91, Ewing Gallery, Univ Tenn, Knoxville, 92, The Rye Arts Ctr, NY, 93, de Saisset Mus, Santa Clara, Calif, 94, Wessel & Lieberman Books, Seattle, Wash, 95, Milwaukee Art Mus, Wis, 96, Govett-Brewster Art Gallery, New Plymouth, New Zealand, 2000. *Awards:* Second Prize, theater for Future Generations, OISTT Competition, Paris, 78; First Prize, Crystal Palace, Cent Glass Competition, Tokyo, 82; First Prize Archit, East Meets West in Design Competition, Jacob K Javits Conv Ctr, New York, 88. *Bibliog:* Lois Nesbitt (ed), Brodsky & Utkin, Princeton Archit Press, 91; Gregory Burke (ed), Palazzo Nero & Other Projects, Wellington City Art Gallery, NZ, 92; Constantin Boym (auth), New Russian Design, Rizzoli, 92. *Media:* Installation. *Mailing Add:* c/o Ronald Feldman Fine Arts 31 Mercer St New York NY 10013

BRODSKY, BEVERLY
PAINTER, ILLUSTRATOR
b Aug 16, 1941. *Study:* Brooklyn Col, BA, 1965; Painting with Ad Reinhardt; Color Theory with Burgoyne Diller. *Comn:* Phoenix Dance Theater (poster), Cubiculo Theater, New York, 1977; poster, Nat Endowment for the Arts, New York, 1980; poster, Long Wharf Theater, CT, 1980; New York City Opera (poster), Lincoln Center, New York, 1981; Jewish Book Month (poster), Jewish Welfare Commision, New York, 1982. *Exhib:* 18 New York, Galerie Bernhardt Steinmetz, Bonn, Germany, 1993; The Painting Center, New York, 1996; Broom Street Gallery, NY Artist's Equity, New York, 1997-1998; The Am Century Part II 1950-2000, The Whitney Mus, New York, 2000; Guild Hall, NY, 2000; Buying Time, Sotheby's, New York, 2001; solo exhib Art Basel, Miami, 2005; Three Voices, Flinn Gallery, Greenwich, Conn, 2005, Art Fair Verona, Italy, 2005, Barbara Paci Gallery, Pietra Santa, Italy, 2005. *Collection Arranged:* The Power of Drawing, Westbeth Gallery, 1997-1998. *Teaching:* adj prof drawing, Adelphi Univ, Long Island, NY, 1980-1985; field adv drawing, Vermont Grad Sch (Norwich Univ), 1987-1988; part time prof painting & color theory, Parsons Sch Design, New York, 1979-. *Awards:* Conn Comn Arts, 79; Nat Fine Arts Com Medal, 80; NY Found for Art Fel, 2000. *Bibliog:* A Change of Art, NY Mag, 90; Eighteen From New York, Juni Magazin fur Kuitur & Politik, 91. *Mem:* Hon mem, Poets House; Author's Guild; Mus of the Am Indian. *Media:* Oil, Egg, Tempera, Watercolor. *Publ:* auth, TheGolem, 76, Jonah, 77, Secret Places, 79, JB Lippincott; auth, The Story of Job, George Braziller, 86; auth, Buffalo, Marshall Cavandish, 2003. *Dealer:* Etra Fine Art 50 NE 40th St Miami FL 33137. *Mailing Add:* 55 Bethune St New York NY 10014

BRODSKY, EUGENE V
PAINTER
b New York, NY, 1946. *Study:* George Washington Univ, 63-64. *Work:* Metrop Mus Art, NY; Power Art Gallery, Sydney, Australia; Vassar Art Gallery, Poughkeepsie, NY; Picker Art Gallery, Colgate Univ, Hamilton, NY; Detroit Inst Art; Nat Gallery of Art, Washington, DC; Balitmore Mus of Art, MD; Yale Univ Art Gallery, New Haven, Conn; Mus Contemp Art, San Diego, Calif. *Exhib:* Imago Galleries, Palm Desert, Calif, 2004; Butler's Fine Art, East Hampton, NY, 2005; Gallery Camino Real, Boca Raton, Fla, 2005; Sears Peyton, NY, 2006. *Teaching:* teacher mixed media, Art Students League, 98-. *Awards:* Grant, Creative Artists Pub Svc, 75; John Simon Guggenheim Fel, 79 & 87; Nat Endowment Arts, 85; Drawing fel, NY Found Arts, 89. *Bibliog:* Alan G Artner (auth), Brodsky paintings save exhibition, Chicago Tribune, 82; Dore Ashton (auth), An art of process, Arts Mag, 85, 96; Phyllis Brams (auth), NY Times, 2000. *Media:* Mixed Media. *Dealer:* Sears-Peyton 210 Eleventh Ave New York NY 10001; Imago Galleries 45-450 Highway 74 Palm Desert CA 92260; Gallery Camino Real Gallery Center 608 Banyan Trail Boca Raton Fla 33431; Butlers Fine Art 50 Park Pl East Hampton NY 11937. *Mailing Add:* 121 Prince St Apt 4W New York NY 10012

BRODSKY, JUDITH KAPSTEIN
PRINTMAKER, EDUCATOR
b Providence, RI, July 14, 33. *Study:* Radcliffe Col, BA(art hist); Tyler Sch Art, Temple Univ, MFA. *Work:* Libr Cong, Washington, DC; Fogg Art Mus, Cambridge; NJ State Mus, Trenton; Princeton Univ, NJ; Newark Mus. *Comn:* The Magic Muse, traveling art environ (with Ilse Johnson, M K Johnson & Jane Teller), Asn Arts NJ State Mus, 72; Bicentennial Portfolio, Princeton, NJ, 75. *Exhib:* one-person shows, Brown Univ, 73, NY State Mus, 75, Douglas Col, 78 & Assoc Artists, Philadelphia, 79; many group shows, US & abroad. *Pos:* Assoc dir, Princeton Graphic Workshop, Inc, 66-68; owner, Castle Howard Press; nat pres, Women's Caucus Art, 76-78; assoc dean, Rutgers Univ, 81-82, assoc provost, 82-. *Teaching:* Lectr art hist, Tyler Sch Art, 66-71; asst prof printmaking, Beaver Col, 72-77, assoc prof, 77, actg chmn art dept, 77; assoc prof & chmn art dept, Rutgers Univ, 78-81. *Awards:* Purchase Prizes, NJ State Mus, 70 & 71 & Boston Printmakers, 71; Stella C Drabkin Mem Award, Am Color Print Soc, 77; and others. *Bibliog:* Miller & Swenson (auth), Lives and Works: Talks with Women Artists, Scarecrow Press, 81. *Mem:* Col Art Asn Am; Philadelphia Print Club; Calif Soc Printmakers; Boston Printmakers; Soc Am Graphic Artists; founding mem Coalition Women's Art Orgn. *Media:* Intaglio, Lithography. *Publ:* Auth, Some notes on women printmakers, Art J, summer 76; designed & publ, B J O Nordfeldt, Etchings, 77, Friends and Foes from A to Z, by Dorothea Greenbaum, 78 & Woman, A Portfolio, 78; auth, Rediscovering Women Printmakers: 1500-1850, Counterproof, spring 79; The Status of Women in Art, Feminist Collage, Columbia Teachers Col Press, 79. *Dealer:* Assoc Am Artists 20 W 57th St New York NY. *Mailing Add:* Visual Arts Mason Gross Sch Arts 33 Livingston Ave New Brunswick NJ 08901-1959

BRODSKY, STAN
PAINTER, EDUCATOR
b Brooklyn, NY, Mar 23, 25. *Study:* Univ Mo, BJour; Univ Iowa, with Jim Lechay & Byron Burford, MFA; Columbia Univ, EdD. *Work:* Baltimore Mus Art; Heckscher Mus, Huntington, NY; Dayton Art Inst, OH; Wm A Farnsworth Mus, Rockland, Maine; Parrish Mus, Southampton, NY; Lowe Art Mus, Miami, Fla; Telfair Mus Art, Savannah, Ga; Hyde Collection, Glen Falls, NY; Neuberger Mus, Purchase, NY; and others. *Comn:* Abstract Symbols (lobby mural), PRD Electronics, Syosset, NY, 70. *Exhib:* two-man show, June Kelly Gallery, 88, one-man show, 89, 91, 94, 99, 2003 & 2006; Centennial Open, Parrish Mus, Southampton, NY, 98; 173rd Ann, Nat Acad Mus, NY, 98; Retrospective 70's-90's (with catalog), Univ Bridgeport, Conn, 99; Labscapes, Coldspring Harbor Lab, NY, 2000; Long Island: Morning Noon and Night, Long Island Mus Art, Stonybrook, NY, 2001; group shows incl: Westport Art Ctr, About Paint, 2005, Gallery N, Abstraction Forty, Setauket, NY, 2005; two person show, Gallery Merz, Sag Harbor, NY, 2006; three person show, Gallery North, Setauket, NY, 2006. *Teaching:* Prof art, C W Post Ctr, Long Island Univ, 60-, prof

emer, 91-. *Awards:* Va Ctr Creative Arts, 85, 86 & 89; Yaddo Fel, Saratoga Springs, NY, 87, 96 & 2004; Trustees Award Scholarly, Creative Achievement, C W Post, Long Island, NY, Univ Brookville, Long Island, 91; and others. *Bibliog:* Ron Pisano (auth), Long Island Landscape Painting in the 20th Century, Little Brown & Co, 90; NY Review of Art, 4th ed, Krantz Pub Co, Chicago, 90; Dr J Collischan (auth), Transformations Into Color (catalog), Mus Retrospective, 91; Amei Wallach (auth), Seeing Through Seeing Beyond, Univ Bridgeport, 99; Marek Bartelik (auth), Synthesis: Redefining the Landscape. *Media:* Oil, Acrylic, Gouache. *Specialty:* Contemporary painting, sculpture, photography and wall hangings. *Interests:* Travel, music, literature, film. *Publ:* Illusr for poster, Enclosure VI, 2000 edition, Graphique de France, Boston, Mass, 88; Ionian Green IV, 500 Ed Color Q, Dayton, Ohio; Riding at Anchor, Waterline Bks, 94. *Dealer:* June Kelly Gallery 591 Broadway New York NY 10012. *Mailing Add:* 22 Sammis St Huntington NY 11743

BRODY, ARTHUR WILLIAM
PRINTMAKER, PAINTER
b New York, NY, Mar 2, 43. *Study:* Harvey Mudd Col, BS, 65; Claremont Grad Sch & Univ Ctr, MFA, 67. *Work:* Southern Ill Univ, Carbondale; St Lawrence Univ, Canton, NY; Ariz State Univ, Tempe; Hist & Fine Arts Mus, Anchorage, Alaska; Portland Mus, Ore; Kenai Bourough Sch District. *Comn:* Alaska State Courthouse, Fairbanks, Alaska; Hutchison Technology Center, Fairbanks, Alaska. *Exhib:* Print Club, 91; Harper Nat, 92; Print Club Albany, 92; Cimmeron Works on Paper, 93; Prints & the Paper, 95; Los Angeles Printmakers, 2003; and others. *Pos:* visualization res spec Arctic Region Supercomputing Ctr, Fairbanks, Alaska. *Teaching:* Instr printmaking, design, drawing, painting & art hist, beginning & advan; instr, Univ Alaska, 67-69; asst prof, Ripon Col, Wis, 70-75; from asst prof to assoc prof, 77-84, prof, 84-; printmaking & computer art, Univ Alaska; prof emeritus. *Awards:* Second Prize Printmaking, Harrisburg Nat, 92; Purchase Award, Cimmeron Works on Paper, 93; Prints & the Paper Award, 95; Los Angeles Printmakers, 2003. *Mem:* Los Angeles Printmakers; Pacific Arts Northwest. *Media:* Woodcut, Intaglio; Acrylic, Oil. *Res:* Virtual Reality user Interface; Landscape in virtual reality panoramic photography. *Specialty:* Alaskan Art. *Publ:* Auth, Communications & Intent, Communications--Tyrant or Liberator?, Ripon Col, 74; Painting the Landscape, Proceedings of Artic Sci Conf, 95. *Dealer:* The Alaskahouse Gallery 1003 Cushman St Fairbanks AK 99708. *Mailing Add:* PO Box 82533 Fairbanks AK 99708

BRODY, BLANCHE
PAINTER, PRINTMAKER
b Brooklyn, NY. *Study:* Hunter Col, 41-44; Boston Univ, BS, 49, MEd, 51; San Francisco Art Inst, with Richard Diebenkorn, 57-59. *Work:* Itel, San Francisco, Calif; El Dorado Press, Berkeley, Calif; Rene di Rosa, Bay Area Figuratives Mus. *Comn:* Logo, Anti-Defamation League Biennale Brit, 88. *Exhib:* San Francisco Women Artists, San Francisco Mus Art, Calif, 1957, 58, 1960, 1962, 1963, 1966 & 1967; Calif Painters Ann, Oakland Mus, 1958, 1962-64; Painted Flower Invitational, Oakland Mus, Calif, 59 & 64; Jack London Square, Oakland Mus, Calif, 59-67; Mid Yr Ann, Butler Inst Am Art, Youngstown, Ohio; West Coast Oil Painting Ann, Frye Art Mus, Seattle, Wash, 62, 63, 65 & 66; Natural & Supernatural, 64-66 & The Contemp Landscape, 68-69, San Francisco Art Inst, Calif. *Awards:* Second Prize, Oakland Mus, Jack London Square, 61; Ed Hill, El Paso, Tex, First Hon Mention, Biennale Int de Vichy, 64; First Prize, San Francisco Women Artists, 66-67; Hon Mention, Biennale Int del Deporter en las Bellas Artes, Barcelona, Spain, 67. *Bibliog:* James Normile (auth), The subject is children, Archit Dig, 11-12/73; Louis Chapin (auth), Looking west--to exuberance, Christian Sci Monitor, 10/25/78; Thomas Albright (auth), Art in the San Francisco Bay Area, 1945-1980. *Mem:* Artists Equity (mem bd 60-63); Valley Art Ctr. *Media:* Oil, Watercolor; Monotypes, Chalk. *Interests:* Psychology, Reading, Cooking, Travel. *Dealer:* Allan Stone Gallery 48 E 86th St New York NY 10028. *Mailing Add:* 19 Vista Del Orinda Orinda CA 94563

BRODY, CAROL Z
PAINTER, COLLAGE ARTIST
b Brooklyn, NY, July 5, 41. *Study:* Brooklyn Col, BA(cum laude), 62; Parsons Sch Design, 82-84. *Work:* Staten Island Borough Hall, NY; Snug Harbor Cult Ctr, Staten Island, NY; St Vincents Med Ctr, Staten Island, NY; Kidder-Peabody Offices, NY, Carmel, Calif & Mich; Metrop Savings Bank, Brooklyn, NY. *Comn:* Cover design (portrait), Women in History Month, Staten Island Borough Hall, 84; collage & watercolor painting, Smith Kline Beecham Pharmaceuticals Co, Parsippany, NJ, 91; cover design (invitation), Staten Island Inst Arts & Scis, 92. *Exhib:* Ann Nat Exhib, Knickerbocker Artists, Salmagundi Club, NY, 83 & 92; Layerists: Level to Level, Johnson-Humrickhouse Mus, Coshocton, Ohio, 90; one-woman show, Recent Watercolors, AT&T Corp Educ Ctr, Hopewell, NJ, 90 & Pen & Brush Club, NY, 92, 95, 01; Ga Watercolor Nat Exhib, Columbus Mus, 91; 167th Ann Exhib, Nat Acad Design, NY, 92; Soc Four Arts, Palm Beach, Fla, 97; Allied Artists of Am at Butler Inst of Am Art, Ohio, 01. *Teaching:* Instr watercolor, Art Lab, Snug Harbor, Staten Island, NY, 86-95; adj instr art educ, Col Staten Island City Univ, NY; instr watercolor, Armory Art Ctr, West Palm Beach, Fla, 97-98. *Awards:* Adriana Zahn Award, 90; First Place Solo Award, Pen & Brush Ann Mem, 90; Emil Carlson SCNY Award, Salmagundi Club, 96. *Mem:* Allied Artists; Catherine Lorillard Wolfe Art Club (vpres painting, 95); Salmagundi Club (jury awards, 89, admiss comt, 90-92); Soc Layerists Multi-Media; Pen & Brush (chmn watercolors, selection comt 90-96); Nat Watercolor Soc. *Media:* Watercolor, Acrylics. *Publ:* Illusr, Watercolor Mag, Am Artist Publ, 90; Layering, An Art of Time and Space, Soc Layerists Multi-Media, 91; The Best of Acrylic Painting, Rockport Publ, 96. *Mailing Add:* 801 Caraway Ct Wellington FL 33414

BRODY, DAVID
PAINTER, INSTRUCTOR
b New York, NY, Feb 16, 58. *Study:* Columbia Univ, 1975-79; Bennington Col, BA, 1979-81; Yale Univ, MFA, 1983. *Exhib:* Gun as Image, Mus of Fine Arts, Florida State Univ, Tallahassee, 1997; The Perception of Appearance, Frye Art Mus, Seattle, WA, 2002. *Collection Arranged:* Springfield Mus, Springfield, Ohio. *Teaching:* SACI, Florence, Italy, 1992-96; Asst prof, Univ of Wash, Seattle, WA, 1996-2000, assoc prof & chair painting & drawing, 2000-. *Awards:* Guggenheim, 1991; Fulbright, 1992; Elizabeth Found, 1994. *Bibliog:* Francine Koslow-Miller (auth), David Brody: Selected Paintings 1985-1994; Elisabeth Sussman (auth), David Brody: Selected Paintings 2001-2002. *Mem:* CAA. *Media:* Oil. *Dealer:* Gescheidle 118 N. Peoria Chicago Il 60607. *Mailing Add:* 1230 Madison Way Lynnwood WA 98037

BRODY, J(ACOB) J(EROME)
HISTORIAN, MUSEOLOGIST
b Brooklyn, NY, Apr 24, 29. *Study:* Brooklyn Mus Art Sch, with Gross & Ferren, 46-50; Art Students League, with Groth, 47; Cooper Union, cert, 50; Brooklyn Col, 50-52; Univ NMex, BA, 56, MA, 64 & PhD, 71. *Collection Arranged:* Early Masters of Modern Art, Isaac Delgado Mus Art, New Orleans, La, 59; Indigo, Mus Int Folk Art, Santa Fe, NMex, 61; Between Traditions (auth, catalog), Univ Iowa Mus, 76; Myth, Metaphor & Mimbreno Art, Maxwell Mus Anthrop, Univ NMex, Albuquerque, 77; The Chaco Phenomenon (auth, catalog), Maxwell Mus Anthrop 83-85; Mimbres Painted Pottery (auth, catalog), Am Fedn Arts 83-85; Mimbres Pottery, Roswell Mus Fine Arts, 83; Beauty From the Earth; Anasazi & Pueblo Indian Pottery (auth, catalog), from Collection of Univ Pa Mus, 90-93; A Bridge Across Cultures: Pueblo Painters in Santa Fe 1910-1932 (auth, catalog), Wheelwright Mus, 92; To Touch the Past: The Painted Pottery of the Mimbres People (auth, catalog), from collection of Weisman Mus Art, Univ Minn, 96; Better than the Picture of the Camera: Early Twenteith Century Pueblo Indian Painting, Univ Art Mus, NMex, 98. *Pos:* Cur art, Everhart Mus, 57-58; cur collection, Isaac Delgado Mus Art, 58-60 & Mus Int Folk Art, 61-62; dir & cur, Maxwell Mus Anthrop, NMex, 62-84; res cur, Sch Am Res 87-; res cur, Maxwell Mus Anthrop, NMex 88-; res assoc Lab Anthrop, Mus Indian Art & Cul, 90-. *Teaching:* Prof museology, Univ NMex, 63-, prof Am Indian art, 65- & emer status. *Awards:* Archaeol Soc NMex (honoree, 92); Conservation Award, Am Rock Art Res Asn, 98; Honoree, Native Am Art Studies Asn, 98; Disting Alumni Award, Col Fine Arts, 2000; Lifetime Contribution to the Humanities Award, NMex Endowment for the Humanities, 01. *Bibliog:* Joyce Szabo (auth), J J Brody, Archaeology, Art and Anthropology, Papers in Honor of J J Brody, Archaeol Soc NMex, 92. *Mem:* Soc Am Archaeol; Native Am Art Studies Asn; Am Rock Art Res Asn. *Res:* Native American art; Southwest Pueblo Indian prehistoric & historic arts, ethnic and modern art. *Publ:* Co-dir, Painted Earth, Program for Art on Film (film), Metrop Mus Art & Getty Found, 89; Auth, Anasazi and Pueblo Painting, USM Press & Sch Am Res, 91; Co-auth, To Touch the Past: The Painted Pottery of the Mimbres People, Hudson Hills Press, 96; auth, Pueblo Indian Painting: Tradition & Modernism in New Mexico 1900-1930, Sch Am Res Press, 97; A Day in the Life of a Mimbres Indian, Jaca Books, Milan, 98; Mimbres Painted Pottery, Revised Edition, Sch Am Res Press, 2004; Indian Paintings & White Patrons, UNM Press, 70; Between Traditions, U Iowa Mus, 76; Mimbres Painted Pottery, UNM Press, 77; The Anasazi, Jaca Books, Milan and Rozzoli, 90; co-auth, Mimbres Pottery: Ancient Art of the American Southwest, Hudson Hills Press, 83. *Mailing Add:* 15 Blue Crow Lane Sandia Park NM 87047

BRODY, MYRON ROY
SCULPTOR, PHOTOGRAPHER
b New York, NY. *Study:* Nat Inst Fine Arts, Mexico City; Philadelphia Col Art, BFA, 65; Grad Sch Fine Art, Univ Pa, MFA, 68; Ateneum, Helsinki, Finland, 68-69; Univ Va, 70-71; Harvard Univ, 75. *Work:* Univ of Arts; Princeton Univ Art Mus, NJ; Univ Va Art Mus, Charlottesville; Mus Nac Bellas Artes, Rio de Janeiro; US Dept of State; and others. *Comn:* Polished bronze, N Patrol Sta, Kansas City Police Dept, Mo, 77; polished bronze, Prudential Insurance Co Am, Plymouth, Minn; polished bronze, Technical Audit Ltd, Surrey, Eng. *Exhib:* Nelson Gallery-Atkins Mus, Kansas City, Mo; Allan Stone Gallery, NY; Wichita Art Mus, Kans; Kansas City Art Inst; Minneapolis Inst Arts; Dusseldorf Kunstakademie, Ger; Ark Art Ctr; and other group & one-person exhibs. *Pos:* EXPO 92, Seville, Spain; consultant US Information Agency. *Teaching:* Asst prof sculpture & design, Va Western Community Col, 69-76, chmn dept art, 69-72; adj prof ceramics, art educ & sculpture, Univ Va Sch Continuing Educ, 70-76; lectr sculpture, Hollins Col, Va, 75-76; chmn art dept & prof, Avila Col, Kansas City, Mo, 76-85; chmn art dept, Univ Ark, Fayetteville, 85-91, prof, 85-. *Awards:* Cert for Distinguished Serv, Mus Nacional de Belas Artes, Rio de Janeiro, 83; Fulbright-Hays Fels, Finland, 68, Eng, 73 & Ger, 91; Artists' Work Programmer, Irish Mus Mod Art, Dublin; and others. *Media:* Multimedia. *Publ:* Contribr, New Designs in Ceramics, 70; Decorative Art in Modern Interiors, 73-74; Visual Art & The End Usur: Who Uses Whom, Int Forum Design, Ulm, Ger, 90. *Mailing Add:* Univ Ark Main Campus Dept Art FNAR 116 Fayetteville AR 72701

BRODY, RUTH
PAINTER, GRAPHIC ARTIST
b New York, NY, Aug 11, 17. *Study:* Hunter Col, BA, 38; Columbia Univ, MA, 40. *Exhib:* 14th New Eng Ann, Silvermine Guild, Conn, 63; Graphics & Crafts Show, Hudson River Mus, Yonkers, NY, 70 & 71; Westchester-Putnam Art Teachers Exhib, Neuberger Mus, Purchase, NY, 77; Am Soc Contemp Artists Ann Exhib, 83-94; Mus Hudson Highlands, 83; Healing Legacies, Cannon Rotunda, Washington, 93; Mem Med Ctr Found, Las Cruces, NMex, 96; Fleming Mus, Burlington, Vt, 96; Glenbow Mus, Calgary, Alta, Can, 96. *Teaching:* Instr art, Secondary Schs, New York, 40-53; chmn art dept, Roosevelt High Sch, Yonkers, NY, 67-79. *Awards:* Second Prize, Bronx Coun Arts Paint Out, 75; Victor A Sachse Mem Award, Am Soc Contemp Artists; Nancy Ranson Mem Award, Am Soc Contemp Artists, 93. *Bibliog:* An artist is

inspired, Riverdale Press, NY, 11/6/80. *Mem:* New York Artists Equity Asn; Bronx Coun Arts; Am Soc Contemp Artists. *Media:* Watercolor, Pen & Ink; Intaglio, Monoprints. *Publ:* Auth, Using Artwork in the School Yearbook, Columbia Scholastic Press Asn Advisers Asn Bull, 71; Chance and Choice: An Art Game for the Creation of a Mural, Nat Art Educ Asn, 75. *Mailing Add:* 26 Point Terr Tariffville CT 06081-9641

BRODY-LEDERMAN, STEPHANIE
PAINTER, DRAWINGS
b New York, NY, 1939. *Study:* Univ Mich Sch Archit & Design, Ann Arbor, 59; Finch Col, BS (design), 61; C W Post Ctr, Long Island Univ, MA (studio art), 75. *Work:* Chase Manhattan Bank, Mus Mod Art, New York, NY; Newark Mus, NJ,; Prudential Insurance Co, NJ; Edward Albee Found, Montauk, NY; Insurance of NAm, NY; and others. *Comn:* Edition of 100 small artworks, Franklin Furnace, New York, NY, 83; poster, funded by Nat Endowment Arts Alternative Mus, NY. *Exhib:* Penthouse Aviary, Mus Mod Art, NY, 80; Butler Libr, Metrop Mus Art, NY, 85; NY Artists Bookworks, Mus Modern Art Libr, NY, 90; solo exhibs, Hebrew Home Aged, Riverdale, NY, 95, La State Univ, Shreveport, 95, Galerie Caroline Corre, Paris, 95, Marc Miller Gallery, East Hampton, NY, 96 & Williamsburg, Brooklyn, NY, 96, Heroes To Go, Arlene Bujese Gallery, East Hampton, NY, 97, Recent Work, 123 Watts Gallery, NY, 98, Edison Col, Fort Meyers, Fla, 2001, Iconic Imagery, Arlene Bujese Gallery, E Hampton, NY, Appetites, Cleary, Gottlieb, Steen & Hamilton Artists Prog, NYC, 2003, Role Call, Guild Hall Mus, E Hampton, NY, 2004, Pilot Light, OK Harris Fine Art, NYC, 2004; A Woman's Place, Mus Stonybrook, NY, 96; The L Word, 473 Broadway Gallery, NY, 96; Box, Fotouhi Cramer Gallery, NY, 96; Fields & Bulls, 123 Watts Gallery, NY, 96; Current under current: Working in Brooklyn, Brooklyn Mus, NY, 97; NY Drawers, Gasworks, London, Manchester, UK, 97; Art on Paper, Weatherspoon Gallery, Univ NC, Greensboro, NC, 97; The Next World: Text and/as Image/and/as Design and/as Meaning, Johanna Drucker (cur), Newberger Mus, Purchase, NY, 98; The Centennial Open, Parrish Art Mus, Southhampton, NY, 98; group shows, Material Cult, Univ Bridgeport, Conn, 2000, Text: Word and Image, Nassau Community Col, Garden City, NY, 2000, Here, There & Everywhere, Jean Deux Gallery, Brooklyn, 2000, Bookworks, Brooklyn Mus, 2000, City Arts Benefit, Matthew Marks Gallery, Brooklyn, 2000, Pierogi 2000/The Flat Files, Univ Arts, Philadelphia, Pa, 99, Animal, Limn Gallery, San Francisco, Ca, 99, Waxing Poetic, Montclair Art Mus, NJ, 99, ARTeur: Visual Codex, 450 Gallery, NYC, 2002, Insominia: Landscapes of the Night, Nat Mus Woman Arts, DC, 2003, 30 Years of Innovation, Ctr Book Arts, NYC, 2004, Diversity, Pratt Inst, Brooklyn, NY, 2005, Making Your Mark, Brooklyn Arts Coun, Brooklyn, NY, 2006. *Collection Arranged:* Edward Albee Foundation, Montaulk, NY, Am Womans Economic Development Corp, NYC, Archive of Concrete & Visual Poetry, Miami Beach, FL, Art Mus of Peale, Brampton, Ontario, Canada, ASCAP, New York, Barnes Hospital, St Louis, Brooklyn Mus Art, NYC, Center for the Arts, Vero Beach, FL, Fine Arts Mus Long Island, Hempstead, NY; Cumberland Health Facility, Brooklyn, NY; Doubleday Books, Garden City, NY; Erasmus Haus, Basel, Switz; Grafikhuset Futura, Stockholm, Sweden; Librairie Arcade, Osaka, Japan. *Awards:* Ariana Foundation for the Arts Grant, 1983; LINE Grant, NYS Coun on the Arts & NEA, 1984; Hassam & Speicher Purchase Award, Am Acad & Int Arts & Letters, NYC, 1988; Artists Grant, Artists Spece, NYC, 1989; E D Foundation Project Grant, 1991. *Bibliog:* Janis Edwards (auth), Extensions of the Book, Art Week, 8/10/85; Peter Stack (auth), Airport Shoe: One Show Fits All, San Francisco Chronicle, 12/87; Karin Lipson (auth), article, Newsday, 7/22/88. *Media:* Oil. *Publ:* Auth & illusr, Chocolate Cake, 79 & He Doesn't Walk Funny-He Wore Corrective Shoes, 79, pvt publ; Romantic couplet (the hustle) (portfolio), Paris Rev, 79; Spring Chicken, Artifacts at End of Decade, 81; The adventuress tries fantasy, Whitewalls, 83; Domestic Screams, 85. *Dealer:* OK Harris 383 W Broadway New York NY 10012. *Mailing Add:* 822 Madison Ave-Ste 4 New York NY 10021

BROEKE, JAN TEN See Ten

BROER, ROGER L
PRINTMAKER, PAINTER
b Omaha, Nebr, Nov 9, 45. *Study:* Eastern Mont Col, BA, 74; Cent Wash Univ, 74-75. *Work:* Mus Native Am Cult, Spokane, Wash; US Dept Interior, Browning, Mont; MSU, Billings; Univ SD; Evergreen Col. *Exhib:* Seventy group and thirty-five solo shows incl at Dept Interior, Washington, DC and Espace de Pierre Cardin, Paris. *Teaching:* Iowa State Arts Comn Workshop, 81; artist in schs, Arts Alaska Inc, 83-87; artist-in-residence, Wash State Arts Comn. *Awards:* Numerous awards in national shows, including the Red Cloud Show, Northern Plains Tribal Arts, 2000, Northwest Indian Arts, 2000. *Bibliog:* Jill Rowley (auth), Indian Country Today, 10/2000. *Mem:* Puget Sound Group Northwest Painters; Indian Arts & Crafts Asn. *Media:* Monotype; Mixed Media. *Publ:* Articles in various publications, including Contemp Western Artists and The Nebraskaland Mag. *Mailing Add:* PO Box 6412 Kent WA 98064

BROKER, KARIN
DRAFTSMAN, PRINTMAKER
b Pa, July 27, 50. *Study:* Univ Iowa, Iowa City, BFA, 72; Atelier 17, Paris, with Stanley Hayter, 73; Univ Wis, Madison, MFA, 80. *Work:* Cabo Frio Bienal Collection, Brazil; US Info Serv, Middle East; Brooklyn Mus Art, NY; Boston Mus Fine Arts, Mass; Smithsonian Instn; Nat Mus Am Art; plus others. *Comn:* Trophy (3-D drawing), InterFirst Bank & Houston Symphony, 83; RSVP, Bechtler Gallery, Charlotte, NC, 92. *Exhib:* One-person shows incl McClain Gallery, 03, Univ Denver, Colo, 95, Dakota Galleries, Houston, Tex, 95, Los Angeles on paper, Santa Monica, Calif, 95, Tex Myths and Realities, The Mus of Fine Arts, Houston, 95, Three Tex Artists of Yr in Russia (traveling) 96, London Original Print Fair, Royal Acad Art, London, 99, Gerhard Wurzer Gallery, Houston, 2000, plus many others. *Pos:* Pres, Southern Graphics Coun, 84-86; studio coordr, CAA Conf, Houston, Tex, 88. *Teaching:* Prof, Rice Univ, Houston, Tex, currently. *Awards:* Nat Endowment Arts Visual Artist Fel, 85 & 87; Dewar's Texas Do-ers, Tex, 89; Tex Art of Yr, Art League of Houston, 94. *Bibliog:* Carey Rote (auth), essay, Corpus Christi State Univ, 88; David Brauer (auth), essay, Rice Univ, 92; Susanna Sheffield (auth) BBK, Koln, Germany, 91; New Orleans Mus Art, La, 86; Alison de Lima Green (auth) Texas: 150 Works from the Museum of Fine Arts, 2000; Robin Montana Turner (auth) State of the Art Program Portfolios, Barrett Kendall pub, 99; plus many others. *Mem:* So Graphics Coun. *Media:* Drawing, Intaglio. *Publ:* Auth, Mad Artist-Printmaker (catalog), Tex Tech Univ, 83. *Dealer:* McClain Gallery, Houston. *Mailing Add:* 4916 Gibson St Houston TX 77007-5329

BROMMER, GERALD F
PAINTER, WRITER
b Berkeley, Calif, Jan 8, 27. *Study:* Concordia Teachers Col, BSc(educ), 48; Univ Nebr, MA, 55; Chouinard Art Inst; Otis Art Inst, Univ Southern Calif; Univ Calif, Los Angeles. *Hon Degrees:* Concordia Univ, Irvine, Calif, DLitt, 85. *Work:* Howard Ahmanson Collection, Los Angeles; Hughes Labs, Malibu; Pac Telesis, San Fransisco; State of Calif Collection, Sacramento; Utah State Univ; Owensboro Mus Fine Art, Ky; TRW, Sunnydale, Calif; Firestone Collection; Laguna Beach Mus Art; Univ Utah; Birmingham (Ala) Mus Art; Springfield Art Mus, Mo; Hickory Mus Art, NC. *Comn:* Series watercolors, Hilton Hotels, Las Vegas, Reno, Anaheim & San Francisco; Intercontinental Hotel, Los Angeles; Epcot Ctr, Orlando. *Exhib:* Am Watercolor Soc, NY, 69, 72 & 73; Nat Acad Design, NY, 71; Watercolor USA, Springfield, Mo, 73, 75 & 76; Nat Watercolor Soc, Los Angeles, 74, 75 & 77-; Royal Watercolor Soc, London, 75; Calif Art Club 2004-2006; plus over 160 one-man shows. *Pos:* Chief designer, Daystar Designs, Inc, 63-73; Artist-in-residence, Jonathan Club, Los Angeles, 98-. *Teaching:* Chmn dept art, Lutheran High Sch, Los Angeles, 55-74; instr, workshops, US & abroad, 75-2006. *Awards:* Landmark Purchase Award, Watercolor USA, 69; Crescent Cardboard Co Purchase Award, Nat Watercolor Soc, 72; Utah State Purchase Award, Watercolor West Invitational, 73. *Bibliog:* Splash 2, 10/93, Splash 3, 10/94, Creative Collage Techiques, 10/94, Splash 6, 10/98, North Light; The Best of Acrylic Painting, 96 & The Best of Watercolor Painting, 96, Quarry Bks, Rockport Publ; Landscape Inspirations, Rockport Pub, 97; Northlight: Watercolors in a Weekend, A David Charles Book, London, UK, 2000; Watercolor Expressions, Rockport Pub, 2001; Splash 7, The Power and Beauty of Light, 2002. *Mem:* Nat Watercolor Soc (treas, 63, vpres, 65-66, 80-81, pres, 67-68, 81-82); Nat Art Educ Asn; Watercolor USA Hon Soc; Nat Art Club, NY; Calif Art Club, Los Angeles; Int Soc Painters in Acrylic (hon pres). *Media:* Transparent Watercolor, Collage. *Interests:* art history. *Publ:* Auth, Exploring Transparent Watercolor, 93, The Art of Collage, 78, Discovering Art History, 81, 3rd ed, 93 & Exploring Drawing, 87, Davis; Watercolor and Collage Workshop, 86, Collage Techniques, 94, Watson-Guptill; Careers in Art, Davis, 99; Emotional Content: How to Create Paintings that Communicate, Int Artist, 2003. *Dealer:* Esther Wells Collection 1390 S Coast Hwy Laguna Beach CA 92652; New Masters Gallery PO Box 7009 Carmel CA 93921. *Mailing Add:* 11252 Valley Spring Lane Studio City CA 91602

BRONSON, A A (MICHAEL WAYNE TIMS)
POST-CONCEPTUAL ARTIST, WRITER
b Vancouver, BC, June 16, 46. *Work:* Art Gallery Ont, Toronto; San Francisco Mus Mod Art; Musee d'Art Contemporain, Montreal; Vancouver Art Gallery, Vancouver; Mus Mod Art, NY. *Comn:* Ursa Major and Taurus: Pavillion Fragments from the Starry Vault, Relief Mural, Toronto Stock Exchange, 83; Exterior Relief Sculpture, Ottawa Courthouse, 86. *Exhib:* Paris Biennale, Paris, 77; Venice Biennale, Can Pavilion, 80; Documenta 7 & 8, Kassel, Ger, 82 & 87; Int Survey Painting & Sculpture, Mus Mod Art, NY, 84; Artistic Collaboration in the Twentieth Century, Hirschhorn Mus, Washington, 84; solo shows, Art Gallery Ont, 85, Albright-Knox Art Gallery, 86, Wexner Ctr Visual Arts, Columbus, 93, San Francisco Mus Mod Art, Columbus, 93, San Francisco Mus Mod Art, 93, Stedelijk Mus, Amsterdam, 94, Nat Gallery Can, 95 & Mus Mod Art, NY, 96. *Pos:* Ed, File Mag, Toronto, 72-89. *Awards:* Toronto Arts Award, 89; Banoff Ctr Arts Nat Award, 93; Jean A Chalmers Award Visual Arts, 94. *Bibliog:* General Idea 1968-1984, Kunsthalle Basel, 84; Fin de Siecle, Wurttembergischer Kunstveren, Stuttgart, 92; Jean-Christophe Ammann (auth), Pharmacopia, Centre d'Art Santa Monica, Barcelona, 92. *Media:* Multi-media. *Publ:* Auth, Menage A Trois, Gen Idea, 78; co-ed, Performance by artists, Art Metropole, 79; auth, Getting Into the Spirits Cocktail Book, Gen Idea, 80; co-ed, Museums by artists, Art Metropole, 83. *Mailing Add:* c/o General Idea The Colonade 131 Bloor St W Apt 501 Toronto ON M5S 1R1 Canada

BRONSON, CLARK EVERICE
SCULPTOR
b Kamas, Utah, Mar 10, 39. *Study:* Art Instr Inst, 56-57; Univ Utah, 59. *Comn:* Hartford Stag (bronze), Hartford, Conn, 80; Chadwick Ram (bronze), Boone Crockett Buffalo Bill Hist Ctr, Cody, Wyo, 82. *Exhib:* Nat Acad Western Art, Nat Cowboy Hall Fame, 73, 74 & 75; Mzuri Safari Found Conf, Reno, Nev, 73 & 74; Mont Hist Soc, Helena, 78; C M Russell Art Show & Auction, Great Falls, Mont, 79-81; Nat Sculpture Soc, NY, 81. *Pos:* State of Utah Fish & Game Staff Artist, 60-63. *Awards:* First Prize, Nat Art Competition, Art Instr Inst, 57; Silver Medal (bronze sculpture), Nat Acad Western Art, 74, 75 & 77; Silver Medal (bronze sculpture), Nat Sclulpture Soc, 81. *Bibliog:* Don Jardine (auth), The continuing success of Clark Bronson, Illustrator, 71; Scott Dial (auth), Symbols of freedom, Southwest Art, 1/80; Richard P Christenson (auth), Bronson's love of life is forever frozen in bronze, Desert News, 9/81. *Mem:* Nat Acad Western Art; Nat Sculpture Soc; Soc Animal Artists; Wildlife Artists Int; Northwest Rendezvous Group. *Media:* Bronze sculpture and painting. *Publ:* Illusr, Nat Wildlife Mag, 63 & High Uintahs--Hi, 64, Album of North American Animals, 66, Album of North American Birds, 67 & Biography of a Grizzly, 69. *Mailing Add:* 1125 E Aspen Ridge Ln Provo UT 84604-6322

BROOKE, DAVID STOPFORD
MUSEUM DIRECTOR
b Walton-on-Thames, Eng, Sept 18, 31. *Study:* Harvard Univ, AB, 58, AM, 63. *Pos:* Asst cur, Fogg Art Mus, Cambridge, Mass, 60-61; asst to dir, Smith Col Mus, Northampton, 63-65; chief cur, Art Gallery Ont, Toronto, 65-68; dir, Currier Gallery Art, Manchester, NH, 68-77; dir, Clark Art Inst, 77-94. *Mem:* Asn Am Art Mus Dirs. *Res:* British painting of the eighteenth and nineteenth centuries. *Publ:* Coauth, James Tissot (catalog), Art Gallery Ont, 68; auth, Mortimer at Eastbourne and Kenwood, Burlington Mag, 68; James Tissot's amateur circus, Boston Mus Bulletin, 69; coauth, The Dunlaps of New Hampshire, Antiques, 70; auth, Raeburn's portrait of John Clerk of Eldin, Currier Gallery Bulletin, 71. *Mailing Add:* 767 N Hoosac Rd Williamstown MA 01267

BROOKE, PEGAN
PAINTER
b Orange, Calif, July 19, 50. *Study:* Univ Calif, San Diego, BA(literature), 72; Drake Univ, BFA(painting), 76; Univ Iowa, Iowa City, MA(painting), 77; Stanford Univ, MFA(painting), 80. *Work:* Guggenheim Mus; Univ Nebr Art Mus, Omaha; Iowa State Capitol Bldg, Des Moines; Bank Am Int Hq, San Francisco; San Francisco Mus Mod Art; and others. *Exhib:* Solo exhib, Scottsdale Ctr Arts, Ariz, 83, Saxon-Lee Gallery, Los Angeles, 89, Images Transformed, Oakland Mus, 92, Univ Calif Davis, 92, Joan Roebuck Gallery, Lafayette, Calif, 94 & 96, R B Stevenson Gallery, La Jolla, Calif, 96, 97, 99 & Winfield Gallery, Carmel, Calif, 98, Percival Galleries, Des Moines, 2000, Friesen Gallery, Sun Valley, Idaho, 2002, RB Steverson Gallery, San Diego, 2002, Anne Loucks Gallery, Glencoe,Ill, 2004, RB Stevenson Gallery, La Jolla, Calif, 2005; New Perspectives in Am Art, 83, Emerging Artists 1978-86, 88, Guggenhiem Mus; CA Directions in Painting, Alaska State Mus, 86; Survey of Calif Women Artists, Fresno Art Mus, 87; Landscape as Presence, San Jose Inst Contemp Art, 89; Joan Washburn Gallery, NY, 95. *Teaching:* Lectr, Univ Calif, Berkeley, 82, Davis, 83, Calif Col Art & Crafts, 83, Sonoma State Univ, 83 & prof art, San Francisco Art Inst, 84-; grad dir & full prof, San Francisco Art Inst. *Awards:* Marin Arts Coun Painting Grant, 92 & 98; Millary Colony Artist Residency, Austerlitz, NY, 2003; Artist Residencey, Pont Aven Sch Contemp Art, Pont Aven, France, 2005. *Bibliog:* Christine Tamblyn (auth), Pegan Brooke at Fuller Goldeen, Art News, 87; Mark Levy (auth), Pegan Brooke at Fuller Goldeen, Art in Am, 88; Suvan Geer (auth), Pegan Brooke, LA Times, 89; David Bonetti (auth), San Francisco Examiner, 92; Leah Ollman (auth), Art in America, 97; Robert Pincus (auth), San Diego Union-Tribune, 97, 99. *Mem:* Col Art Asn. *Media:* Oil. *Dealer:* R B Stevenson Gallery La Jolla CA; Winfield Gallery Carmel CA; Hemphill Fine Arts Washington, DC; FriesenGallery Seattle WA. *Mailing Add:* PO Box 857 Bolinas CA 94924

BROOKER, MOE ALBERT
EDUCATOR, PRINTMAKER
b Philadelphia, Pa, Sept 24, 40. *Study:* Pa Acad Fine Arts, cert, 63; Tyler Sch Fine Arts, BFA, 70, MFA, 72. *Work:* Cleveland Mus Art; Philadelphia Mus Art & Pa Acad Fine Arts, Philadelphia; Studio Mus Harlem, NY; Hampton Univ Mus, Va. *Comn:* Pub Libr Cleveland, 78; Karamu House, Cleveland, 80; 6 color lithograph, Philadelphia Mus Art, 93. *Exhib:* Recherche/Den Flexible, Charlottenborg Mus, Copenhagen, Denmark, 86; Choosing, Mus Sci & Indust, Chicago, 86; The May Show, Cleveland Mus Art, 86; Cult Perspectives, Gregrio De Matos Ctr Arts, Bahia, Brazil, 88; African-Am Abstraction in Printmaking, Calif Afro-Am Mus, Los Angeles, 89; 53rd Ann Mid-Year Exhib (auth catalog), Butler Inst Am Art, 89; Biennial 93, Del Art Mus, Wilmington, 93; The Unbroken Line 1897-1997, Pa Acad Fine Arts, 97. *Pos:* Chmn found dept, Parson Sch Design, 91-93. *Teaching:* Assoc prof painting, Cleveland Inst Art, 76-85; prof drawing & painting, Pa Acad Fine Arts, Philadelphia, 85-91; assoc prof, Moore Col Art & Design, Philadelphia, 95-. *Awards:* Artist Grant, Herewood Lester Cook Found, 81 & City of Philadelphia, 87; Cleveland Arts Fel, Women's Comn Cleveland, Ohio, 85; Pa Coun Arts Fel Painting, 89. *Media:* Oil on Canvas or Wooden Panel; Mixed Media. *Publ:* Auth, Six Perspectives 1984, Akron Art Mus, 84; Delighting the Eye, Cleveland Plain Dealer, 94; Moe Brooker, new directions, Philadelphia City Paper, 96; contribr, Seeing Jazz, Artist and Writers on Jazz, Smithsonian Inst, 97

BROOKINS, JACOB BODEN
SCULPTOR, CONSULTANT
b Princeton, Mo, Aug 28, 35. *Study:* Boise State Univ, AA(painting); Univ Ore, BS(ceramics), MFA(metalsmithing & sculpture); also with Max Nixon, Jan Zach, Robert James, James Hanson & Paul Buckner, Theo Rozack, David Hare, R Buckminster Fuller, Joseph Albers. *Work:* Northern Ariz Univ, Univ Ore; Barry Goldwater Int Airport, City of Phoenix, Ariz. *Comn:* Pvt Listed. *Exhib:* Ariz Comm Arts & Humanities Touring Exhib, 72-73; Southwestern Invitational, Yuma, Ariz, 72-73; Intermountain Crafts Exhib, Flagstaff, 73; Mus Northern Ariz, 77-79; Coconino Co Arts Ctr, 80-81; plus numerous exhibs at mus fine arts, univ galleries, col galleries, art ctrs & pvt commercial galleries. *Collection Arranged:* Nat Coun Educ Ceramic Arts Conf '72 Exhib, 72; Intermountain Crafts Exhib, Ariz Designer Craftsmen, Flagstaff, 73. *Pos:* Dir, Mus Northern Ariz Art Inst, 75-79; founder, dir, Cosnino Inst, 79-90; chmn, Coconino Co Arts Comn, 81-85; exec bd, Coconino Ctr Arts, 80-85. *Teaching:* Instr jewelry, Univ Ore, 67-68; assoc prof sculpture, Northern Ariz Univ, 69-75; instr ceramics, Yavapai Col, 79-80; volunteer instr applied crafts, US Peace Corps, Republic of Zaire & pvt. *Awards:* Nat Endowment Art, 77 & 78. *Mem:* Nat Coun Educ Ceramic Arts; Ariz Designer Craftsmen (mem bd dir, 70-75, state pres, 71-72); and others. *Media:* All media. *Interests:* sailing, trekking

BROOKNER, JACKIE
SCULPTOR, ENVIRONMENTAL ARTIST
b Providence, RI. *Study:* Wellesley Col, BA, 67; Harvard Univ, MA, 70; New York Studio Sch, 76-77. *Comn:* Grossenhain, Ger; Cinn, Ohio; Salway Park; Dreher Park, West Palm Beach, Fla; Roosevelt Community Center, San Jose, Calif. *Exhib:* Varieties of Sculptural Ideas, Max Hutchinson Gallery, NY, 84; traveling exhib, NY/Beijing, Shanghai Art Mus, Beijing Art Inst & Hong Kong Arts Festival, 87-88; Pamela Auchincloss Gallery, NY, 91; Exit Art, NY, 2006; solo exhibs, Diggs Gallery, Winston-Salem State Univ, NC, Hunter Mus Art, Chattanooga, Tenn, 95, Columbus Mus, Ga, 95, Univ N Tex Art Gallery, Denton, Nat Civil Rts Mus, Memphis, Tenn, 96, Crossing Borders, Krakow Poland, 94- & Native Tongues, Fundacio Joan Miro, Centre d'Estudio d'Art Contemporano, Barcelona, Spain, 97; and others. *Collection Arranged:* Dow Jones Collection; Becton Dickinson. *Pos:* Guest ed, Art J, Art & Ecology, summer 92. *Teaching:* Undergrad & grad, Parson Sch Design, NY, 77-; instr, Grad Sculpture Fac, Bard Col, 87; dean & instr, NY Studio Sch, 87; grad sculpture fac, Univ Pa, 94-2000; Harvard Univ, 2002. *Awards:* NY Found Arts Grant, 90 & 99; Nat Endowment Arts Grant, McKissick Mus, 94; Trust for Mutual Understanding, Gaia Inst, 97; others; Nat Endowment Arts Grant, 2002-03. *Bibliog:* Lauren de Boer (auth), Making Sense of Matter, Earthlight, fall 2000; Mara Scrupe (auth), Environment, Audience and Public Art in the New World (Order), Sculpture, 3/2000; Micke Bal (auth), Quoting Caravaggio, Univ Chicago Press, 99. *Mem:* Int Sculpture Asn; Col Art Asn. *Media:* Mixed Media, Ecological Art. *Publ:* Is Feminism An Issue for Students of the 80's and 90's?, Art J, Vol 50, No 2, summer 91; guest ed, On Art and Ecology, Art J, Vol 51, No 2, summer 92; M/E/A/N/I/N/G, Forum: On Creativity and Community, No 15, 5/94, Natural Reality/Artistic Positions Between Nature and Culture, Ludwig Forum fur Int Kunst, Aachen, Germany, 99; poetry, NY, winter, spring, 85-89, 99. *Mailing Add:* 131 Spring St New York NY 10012

BROOKS, BRUCE W
PAINTER, SCULPTOR
b New York, NY, July 10, 48. *Study:* Pratt Inst, BFA, 70, MFA, 75. *Work:* Queens Mus; SUNY, New Paltz; Best Products; Prudential. *Exhib:* Miss Mus Art, 81; one-man shows, OK Harris, NY, 81, 83 & 92; Brodway Windows, 95-96; Toby Fine Arts, 2001. *Teaching:* dir com photog prog, City Univ NY; prof, coord visual arts LaGuardia Community Col, CUNY. *Awards:* PSC, City Univ NY, 83, 85, 94 & 2002-03. *Mem:* USHA; Am Civil War Soc; Col Art Asn; ISHA; Friends of Bonsai. *Media:* Oil, Alkyd. *Mailing Add:* 108 Wyckoff St Brooklyn NY 11201-6307

BROOKS, DREX M
PHOTOGRAPHER, EDUCATOR
b Seattle, Wash, Dec 14, 52. *Study:* Ore State Univ, Corvallis, BFA(photog), 76; RI Sch Design, Providence, MFA(photog), 80. *Work:* Nat Mus Am Art, Smithsonian Inst; The Art Mus, Princeton Univ; RI Sch Design Mus Art; Bibliotheque Nationale, Paris; San Francisco Mus Modern Art; Amon Curter Mus; Mus of Fine Arts Utah. *Exhib:* Regional Photographers, Denver Art Mus, 87; Mountain West Biennial, Nora Eddes Harrison Mus, Logan, Utah, 89, 91; Sweet Medicine, Utah Mus Fine Arts, Salt Lake City, 92; Between Heaven & Home (with catalog), Nat Mus Am Art, Washington, DC, 92; Solo shows, Sweet Medicine, Utah Mus Fine Arts, Salt Lake City, 92, Reservations, Arvada Ctr Arts & Humanities, Colo, 2000, Am Perspectives: Photographs From the Polaroid Collection, Tokyo Metrop Mus Photog, 2000 & Drwx Brooks 25 Yrs, Salt Lake Art Ctr, 2001; Between Heaven and Home, Contemp Am Landscape Photographs, Nat Mus Am art, Smithsonian Inst, Washington, DC 1992. *Teaching:* Instr photog, Univ Colo, Denver, 83-88; prof photog & art, Weber State Univ, Ogden, Utah, 88-. *Awards:* Visual Artist Fel, Nat Endowments Arts, 88 & 92; Visual Artist Grant, Utah Arts Coun, 97; Hemingway Found Grant, 2000; Fr Ministry of Cult and Nat Endowment for the Arts, Residency Fel at LaNapoule Found, France, 93. *Bibliog:* Lucy R Lipparad (auth), The Lure of the Local: Senses of Place, 182-183, 97 & On the Beaten Track: Tourism, Art and Place, 126-127, 99, The New Press; Rebecca Solnit (auth), The Struggle of Dawning Intelligence: On Monuments and Native Americans, Harvard Design Mag, 54-56, fall 99. *Mem:* Soc Photog Educ. *Media:* Photography. *Publ:* contribr, Colorado: Visions of an American Landscape, Roberts Rhinehart Publ, 106, 91; Between Heaven and Home: Contemporary American Landscape Photographs, 13 & 42, 92; Sweet Medicine: Photographs of Indian Massacre Sites, Battlefields and Treaty Sites, Univ NMex Press, 95; RISD Views, Meridian Printing, 44, 96; Black and White Photography: An International Collection, Rockport Publ, 23 & 135, 2000. *Dealer:* Robischon Gallery 1740 Wazee Denver CO 80202. *Mailing Add:* 888 Bel Mar Dr Ogden UT 84403-1910

BROOKS, ELLEN
PHOTOGRAPHER
Study: Univ Wis, Madison; Univ Calif, Los Angeles, BA, 68, MA, 70, MFA, 71. *Work:* Mus Mod Art, NY; Nat Mus Am Art, Washington, DC; Nat Gallery Can, Ottawa; Musee d'Art Contemporain Montreal, Can; Albright-Knox Mus, Buffalo, NY. *Exhib:* Solo exhibs, Polaroid Project: Ellen Brooks, Vikky Alexander, Dorothy Goldeen Gallery, Santa Monica, Calif, 91, Wooster Gardens, NY, Vikky Alexander/Ellen Brooks, Ansel Adams Ctr, Friends Photog, San Francisco & Urbie et Orbie, Paris France, 92, Cleveland Ctr Contemp Art (traveling), Ezra & Cecile Zilkha Gallery-Wesleyan Univ, Middletown, Conn & Stux Gallery, NY, 93-94; Departures Photog 1923-1990 (traveling), Independent Curators Inc, 92; Between Home and Heaven, Nat Mus Am Art, Washington, DC, 92; Bennington Col, Vt, 92; Concept/Construct: Photoghraphy in Los Angeles Art 1960-1990, Laguna Art Mus, Calif, 93; Thomas Segal Gallery, Boston, Mass, 93. *Teaching:* Instr, San Francisco Art Inst, Calif, 73-82, Sch Visual Arts, New York, 85, Tisch Sch Arts, New York Univ, 84-92. *Awards:* Individual Fel, Nat Endowment Arts, 79 & 91; Phelan Award, Oakland, Calif, 72. *Bibliog:* Mary Ellen Haus (auth), Beyond Nature, Ellen Brooks, Tema Celeste, 1-2/89; Leslie Tonkonow (auth), Ellen Brooks, J Contemp Art, fall/winter 91; Carol Squires (auth), review, Artforum, 11/91. *Mailing Add:* 28 Hubert St New York NY 10013-2041

BROOKS, H(AROLD) ALLEN
HISTORIAN, LECTURER
b New Haven, Conn, Nov 6, 25. *Study:* Dartmouth Col, BA, 50; Yale Univ, MA, 55; Northwestern Univ, PhD, 57. *Hon Degrees:* Dalhousie Univ, DEng(hon causa), 84. *Teaching:* Prof, Univ Toronto, Ont, 58-86; vis prof, Dartmouth Col, 69; Mellon chair, Vassar Col, 70-71; vis prof, Archit Asn Sch Archit, London, 77-2004. *Awards:* Fels, Can Coun, 62, 75 & 78, Guggenheim, 73 & Victoria Univ, 83; Alice Davis Hitchcock Bk Award, Soc Archit Historians, 73; Asn Am Publ Scholar Bk Award, 97. *Mem:* Fel Soc Archit Historians (pres, 64-66, dir, 61-64, 67-70 & 71-74); Soc Archit Historians Gr Brit; Soc Study Archit Can; Int Comt Monuments & Sites; Frank Lloyd Wright Bldg Conservancy; Int Coun Mus (ICOM); Nat Trust Hist Preserv. *Res:* Frank Lloyd Wright & Le Corbusier. *Publ:* Auth, The Prairie School, Frank Lloyd Wright and His Midwest Contemporaries, Univ Toronto Press, 72; contribr & ed, Writing on Wright, Selected Comment on Frank Lloyd Wright, MIT Press, 81; auth, Frank Lloyd Wright and the Prairie School, Braziller, 83; ed & contribr, Le Corbusier, Princeton Univ Press, 87; auth, Le Corbusier's Formative Years, Univ Chicago Press, 97; contribr & ed, Prairie School Architecture, Univ of Toronto Press, 75; ed, The Le Curbusier Archive, 32 vols, Garland, 82-85. *Mailing Add:* 80 Lyme Road Apt 373 Hanover NH 03755

BROOKS, HARRY A
GALLERY DIRECTOR, ART DEALER
Study: Princeton Univ, BA, 35; Inst Fine Arts, New York Univ, 46-48. *Pos:* Vpres, Knoedler & Co, 46-68; pres, Wildenstein & Co, Inc, New York, NY, 68-. *Specialty:* Old and modern master paintings, drawings and sculpture by Henry Moore. *Mailing Add:* Wildenstein & Co 19 E 64th St New York NY 10021

BROOKS, JAN
SCULPTOR, LECTURER
b Quanah, Tex, Jan 28, 1950. *Study:* Columbia Col, Mo, AA, 70; Southern Ill Univ, Carbondale, BA, 72, MFA, 74. *Work:* Ark Art Ctr, Little Rock; Mint Mus Art, Charlotte; Nat Ornamental Metal Mus, Memphis; Southern Ill Univ Mus, Carbondale; Wustum Art Mus, Racine, Wis. *Comn:* Bronze & steel cross, St Barnabus Episcopal Church, Denton, Tex, 75; eight bronze panels, NC Dept Com-NC Arts Coun, Charlotte, 82; mixed metal interior reliefs, Aeronca Corp, Charlotte, 85. *Exhib:* The Goldsmith, Renwick Gallery, Smithsonian Inst, Washington, DC, 74; The Metalsmith, Phoenix Art Mus, 77; solo exhib, Southeastern Ctr Contemp Art, Winston-Salem, 80; Young Americans: Metal, Mus Contemp Crafts NY, 80; Toward a New Iron Age, Victoria & Albert Mus, London, Eng, 82; Am Metal Work, Kyoto Mus Traditional Indust, Japan, 83; USA-Portrait of the South, Palazzo Venezia, Rome, Italy, 84; Nine From NC, Nat Metal Mus, Memphis, Tenn. *Teaching:* Instr metal, Southern Ill Univ, Carbondale, 74-77; asst prof, Univ NC, Charlotte, 77-83. *Awards:* Designer-Craftsmen Award, NC Artists Exhib, NC Mus Art, 79; Merit Awards, 12th Competitive Exhib, Fayetteville Mus, 84 & Metal Sculpture Exhib, Millersville Univ, 84. *Bibliog:* Julie Hall (auth), Tradition and Change: The New American Craftsmen, E P Dutton, 76; Thelma R Newman (auth), The Container, Crown Publ, 76; Jane Kessler (auth), Jan Brooks Loyd, Art Papers, 80. *Mem:* Am Craft Coun (vpres, bd trustees, 86); Soc NAm Goldsmiths; Nat Campaign Freedom of Expression; Am Studies Asn. *Media:* Metal. *Publ:* Auth, Strategies for Interpretation (catalog), Cincinnati Arts Ctr. *Mailing Add:* 2120 Conejo Santa Fe NM 87505

BROOKS, JOHN H
MUSEUM DIRECTOR, EDUCATOR
b Cambridge, Mass, June 13, 35. *Study:* Princeton Univ, BA, 58; Columbia Univ, MA, 64. *Pos:* Staff lectr, Nat Gallery Art, Washington, DC, 64-68; assoc dir, Sterling & Francine Clark Art Inst, Williamstown, Mass, 68-. *Teaching:* Lectr Am art, Univ Md Col, 67-68 & North Adams State Col, Mass, 71-75. *Awards:* Grace May Tilton Prize in Fine Arts, 58. *Mem:* Am Asn Mus; Int Coun Mus. *Publ:* Active connections: paintings and other arts, Prism, Mus Art, Carnegie Inst, 80; Highlights of the Sterling and Francine Clark Art Institute, Williamstown, Mass, 81; Monet in Massachusetts (catalog), 85; Clark as a Collector (video), 88. *Mailing Add:* 43B Gale Rd Williamstown MA 01267-2806

BROOKS, WENDELL T
PRINTMAKER, EDUCATOR
b Aliceville, Ala, Sept 10, 39. *Study:* Ind Univ, BS(art educ), 62, MFA(printmaking; Martin Luther King Jr Fel, scholar, Southern Fel), 71; Woodstock Artist's Asn, scholar, summer 61; Pratt Graphic Art Asn, scholar, 62; Univ Md, 65-66; Howard Payne Col, 66-67. *Work:* Libr of Cong, Washington, DC; Nasson Col; Mount Union Col; Carleton Col; Bethel Col; plus others including pvt collections. *Exhib:* A Return to Humanism, Burpee Art Mus, Rockford, Ill, 71; Social Comment in Recent Art, Concordia Teachers Col, Seward, Nebr, 71; The Black Experience in Prints, Pratt Graphic Ctr, NY, 72; Black Artists of Am, NJ State Mus, Trenton, 72; Jew Jersey, 1972, 7th Ann Exhib, Trenton, 72; A Very Spec Invitational Show, McCarter Theatre, Princeton, NJ, 79; Black Artists/South, 79; plus many other group & one-man shows. *Teaching:* Instr printmaking, Ala A & M Univ, 67-68; asst prof printmaking & artist in residence, Nassan Col, 70; asst prof printmaking, Trenton State Col, 71-; lectr art at var art groups, cols & univs, 69-72. *Bibliog:* Article in Negro Heritage, 10/68; article in Chalkboard, 11/68; article in Christian Sci Monitor, 6/22/70; plus many other newspapers. *Mem:* Philadelphia Print Club. *Mailing Add:* 63 Florance Ave Apt 6 Ewing NJ 08618

BROOME, RICK (RICHARD) RAYMOND
PAINTER
b Pueblo, Colo, Oct 13, 46. *Study:* Northrop Univ, 67-71; Northrop Inst Tech, 68. *Work:* USAF Acad, Colorado Springs, Colo; Naval Air Mus, Pensacola, Fla; Air Force Mus, Dayton, Ohio; San Diego Art & Space Mus, Calif; Northrop Univ, Inglewood, Calif. *Comn:* T-33/Colo Rocky Mountains, 74, F-105/Vietnam, 75, B-1/USAF Acad, 79, F-15/USAF Acad, 81 & T-Birds/USAF Acad, 82, USAF Acad Cadets, Colorado Springs. *Exhib:* JOC Aviation Art Show, Craig Air Force Base, Selma, Ala, 76 & Scott Air Force Base, Ill, 77. *Awards:* Best Cover/Year, Rocky Mountain Collegiate Asn, 75. *Bibliog:* Will Robinson (dir), From Time to Time (film), KRDO TV, 80 & 81; Gary Olson (auth), Airplanes in art: Broome a master, Weekend, Colo Springs Sun, 3/7/80. *Media:* Acrylic. *Res:* Created 1450 plus historically accurate aviation originals involving complete detailed research. *Publ:* Illusr, 12 covers of Frontier Mag, Inflight Publ, 74-82; 3 covers of Talon Mag, USAF Acad, 75-82; 2 covers of Check Points Mag, USAF Acad, 80; 3 covers of Aerospace Historian, Univ Kans, 79-82. *Dealer:* Kemper Galleries 1624 N Academy Blvd Colorado Springs CO 80915. *Mailing Add:* 2809 Old Broadmoor Rd Colorado Springs CO 80906-3643

BROSEN, FREDERICK
PAINTER, PRINTMAKER
b New York, NY, Feb 1, 54. *Study:* City Col, NY, BA; Pratt Inst, MFA. *Work:* Metrop Mus Art, NY; New York Hist Soc; Rockefeller Found, NY; Hood Mus, Hanover, NJ; Mus City New York. *Comn:* Mural, John Hancock Co, Boston, 86; mural, Merrill Lynch, NY; mural, NYNEX, NY; mural, Mass Financial Serv, Boston. *Exhib:* New Talent Show, Brooklyn Mus, NY, 83; one-man show, Hopkins Ctr, Dartmoth, NH, 85, Schmidt-Bingham Gallery, NY, 94; Realism Today, Nat Acad Design, NY, 87; Painting Invitational, Am Acad & Inst Arts & Letters, NY, 90; Contemp Am Watercolors, Sewell Gallery, NY, 93. *Teaching:* Instr watercolor, Nat Acad Design, 93-94. *Awards:* Silver Medal, Royal Soc Arts & Letters, London, 76; Lucy B Moore Mem Award, Watercolor Soc, 88. *Bibliog:* Realism Today: American Drawings from Rita Rich Collection, 87; Henry Vazquez (auth), Recognizable Image, Bruce Mus, Conn, 85; Valerie R Rivers (auth), feature article on artist, Am Artist, 7/90. *Media:* Watercolor

BROSIUS, KAREN
MUSEUM DIRECTOR
Study: Butler Univ; Ecoles d'arts Americaines; Juilliard Sch Music; Hunter Col, City Univ of NY, MA summa cum laude,. *Pos:* Researcher, Res Found of City of NY, formerly; pub affairs officer, Pierpont Morgan Libr, formerly; sr philanthropic, arts, and commun exec Altria Group, Inc, New York City, formerly; dir Columbia Mus Art, SC, 2004-; bd dir, Arts & Bus Coun, ArtTable, currently. *Mem:* Am Asn Mus; Nat Endowment Arts. *Mailing Add:* Columbia Mus Art PO Box 2068 Columbia SC 29202

BROSK, JEFFREY
SCULPTOR
b New York, NY, Feb 15, 47. *Study:* Univ Pa, BA & BS, 70; Mass Inst Technol, MA(archit), 76. *Work:* Bank Am, San Francisco. *Comn:* IBM, Dallas, Tex. *Exhib:* Aldrich Mus Contemp Art; Hudson River Mus, Yonkers, NY, 78; solo exhibs, Max Hutchinson Gallery, NY, 83, Roanoke Mus Fine Arts, Va, 85, Fine Arts Ctr, Univ Mass, Amherst, 87, Stephen Rosenberg Gallery, NY, 88 & 90, Joan Robey Gallery, Denver, 91, Clark Univ, Worcester, Mass, 92 & Stephen Rosenberg Gallery, NY, 92; Construct Gallery, Chicago, 81; Galerie Alain Oudin, Paris, 81; Anne Reed Gallery, Ketchum Idaho, 90; Current Minimalists, Art Festival, Atlanta, Ga, 91; and many others. *Awards:* Grant, Pollock-Krasner Found, Inc. *Bibliog:* Hal Foster (auth), article, Artforum, 12/79; Michael Brenson (auth), Rev/Art, NY Times, 12/2/88; Stephen Westfall (auth), rev, Art Am, 4/89; Eleanor Heartney (auth), Rev, ARTnews, New York, 90; Mizue, Tokyo, Japan, 91. *Media:* All Media. *Dealer:* Stephen Rosenberg Gallery 115 Wooster St New York NY 10012. *Mailing Add:* 135 Spring St New York NY 10012-3858

BROSS, ALBERT L, JR
PAINTER
b Newark, NJ, June 29, 21. *Study:* Art Students League, with Messrs Dumond, Bridgeman & McNulty. *Work:* NJ State Mus, Trenton; AT&T, NY; Roebling Collection; Springville Mus Art, Utah; Hanover Park High Sch. *Exhib:* Nat Arts Club Print Show, NY, 72; Hudson Valley Art Asn Regional Show, White Plains, NY, 72; Acad Artists Asn, Springfield, Mass, 72; Springville Mus Art, 72. *Pos:* Consultant for Talens & Son, Langnickle Brush Co, formerly. *Teaching:* Retired teacher, 80. *Awards:* Award, Am Asn Univ Women, 72; Lt Melvin D Brewer Mem Award, 76; Gold Medallion Miniature Art Soc, New Jersey, 90. *Mem:* Life mem Art Students League; Hudson Valley Art Asn; Assoc Artists NJ; Hunterdon Co Art Ctr, NJ; Miniature Art Soc, NJ. *Media:* Oils, Watercolors, Pastels, Mixed Media. *Specialty:* Fine Arts. *Interests:* Cooking, Target Shooting, Gardening. *Publ:* The Four Seasons, published, 1993. *Dealer:* The Corywell Gallery 8 1/2 Coryell St Lambertville NJ; The Maritime Gallery at Mystic Seaport Mystic CT. *Mailing Add:* Village Rd New Vernon NJ 07976

BROTHERS, BARRY A
PAINTER, MURALIST
b Brooklyn, NY, Jan 18, 55. *Study:* Brooklyn Col, City Univ NY, BS(photog & art), 77, MFA(painting), 80. *Work:* Herbert F Johnson Mus Art, Cornell Univ, NY; Brooklyn Col Collection, NY; Am Broadcasting Co, Inc; Capital Cities/ABC Inc, NY. *Comn:* 7 paintings, 6 photographs for portfolio, US oil refineries, for Fortune Mag, NY, 81; six murals (two triptychs), Am Broadcasting Co Inc, Broadcast Opers Complex, NY, 85-86; mural, Capital Cities/ABC, Inc, Corp Hq, NY, 89. *Exhib:* New Realists, Adelphi Univ, Garden City, NY, 82; Brooklyn 83 & 85, Brooklyn Mus, 83 & 85; The Brooklyn Landscape, Ammo Artists Space, Brooklyn, 84; 12 Yr Retrospective, Brooklyn Mus, 84; 11th Ann Invitational, Henry Hicks Gallery, Brooklyn, 86; Printmaking at British Columbia, Mus Borough Brooklyn, NY, 87; In Search of the Am Experience, Mus Nat Arts Found, 89. *Pos:* Independent graphic/advertising artist, illusr & photogr, 74-; room screen, furniture design, computer software develop, 89-. *Awards:* DESI 9, Graphic Design, USA, 86; Landscape Painting Competition, Artists Mag, 87; In Search of the American

Experience, Mus Nat Arts Found, 89. *Bibliog:* American Artists--Survey of Leading Cont Am (essay), 85 & The New York Art Review (essay), 89, Krantz Co; Art Product News Mag (article), Grady Publ Co, 3/87 & 4/87; Contemporary Graphic Artists (essay) Gale Research Co, Publ, Vol 2, 87. *Media:* Oil, Acrylic. *Publ:* Contribr, Print Mag XXXVIII:2, (article), 3/84 & 4/84; Gran Bazaar Maf, (essay), Milan, Italy, 85; Graphic Design: USA, Kaye Publ, Corp, 8/86. *Mailing Add:* 1920 E 17th St Brooklyn NY 11229

BROTHERTON, NAOMI
PAINTER, INSTRUCTOR
b Galveston, Tex. *Study:* Baylor Univ, Waco, Tex, BA(fine arts); Art Students League, with Edgar A Whitney, Milford Zornes, Gerry Peirce, Robert E Wood, John Pike, Rex Brandt, John C Pellew & Charles Reid, Frank Francese, Rob Erdle, Don Getz, Ted Nutall. *Work:* S Ark Art Ctr, Eldorado; Baylor Univ Permanent Collection; Carlsbad Mus & Art Ctr, Carlsbad, NMex; Texas Instruments, Dallas; Republic Nat Bank, Dallas; and others. *Comn:* Purdy McGuire Engineers, Dallas, Tex, 99, and many others. *Exhib:* Southwestern Watercolor Soc, 64-88, 94 & 95, 2004; Am Watercolor Soc, NY, 67; Watercolor Okla, Oklahoma City, 75-76, 88, 90 & 91; Tex Watercolor Soc, San Antonio, 81 & 86, 2003; Western Fed Watercolor Soc, 89, 90, 93 & 2000; Art Focus XC, Dallas, 95, 96, 97; Southwestern Watercolor Soc Signature Show, Irving, Tex & Milan, Italy, 2001; Tex and Neighbors Exhib, 2003; Over 45 one-artist exhibs incl Tex Pub Libr, Palestine, 93, NE Tex Community Col, Mount Pleasant, 94. *Pos:* ptnr Artisan's Studio/Gallery. *Teaching:* Instr, Adult Watercolor Painting, 62-; instr, Artisan's Studio-Gallery, Dallas, 80-, Sul Ross State Univ, Tex, 80-81 & workshops across US & Bermuda sponsored by art orgns. *Awards:* Southwestern Watercolor Soc, 1987-1988, 2004; Nat Watercolor Okla, 1990; Western Fedn Watercolor Socs Award, 1993; Texas and Neighbors Exhib., Irving TX., 2003. *Bibliog:* Video tapes, Tree Painting in Watercolor, Night Scenes in Watercolor, 85 & Painting Flowers in Watercolor, 88; Am Artist Mag, article about Night Scenes, 3/91; Tex Watercolor Soc, 50 Yrs of Excellence, 99; plus others. *Mem:* Signature mem Okla Watercolor Asn; signature mem Tex Watercolor Soc; hon life mem Southwestern Watercolor Soc (pres, 67-68); signature mem Western Fedn Watercolor Soc. *Media:* Watercolor. *Res:* Watercolor Tech. to express times of day & kinds of weather. *Specialty:* Artisan's Studio/Gallery, Dallas TX. *Interests:* Watercolor instruction & exhib for 43yrs.; Florals with interest in TIMES OF DAY AND KINDS OF WEATHER, Painting landscapes. *Publ:* contribr, article, SW Art Mag, 11/96; The Best of Flower Painting, N Light Publ, 96; Encyclopedia of Watercolor Landscape Techniques, Quarto Publ, Gr Brit, 96; Art Focus XC, Watercolor Mag, spring 98; article, Watercolor Magie May, 11/2000, 2/2001 & 2/2003; coauth, Variations in Watercolor, North Light, 1981; Featured Articles about Night Scenes, Int Artist Mag, spring 2001

BROUDE, NORMA FREEDMAN
HISTORIAN, EDUCATOR
b New York, NY, May 1, 41. *Study:* Hunter Col, AB, 62; Columbia Univ, MA(Woodrow Wilson Found Fel), 64, PhD(Woodrow Wilson Dissertation Fel), 67. *Pos:* Mem of the Art Bulletin Editorial Advisory Comm, Col Art Asnof Am, 96-98. *Teaching:* Instr art hist, Conn Col, New London, 66-67; vis asst prof, Oberlin Col, Ohio, 69-70; asst prof art hist, Columbia Univ, NY, 72-73; vis asst prof, Vassar Col, Poughkeepsie, NY, 73-74; asst prof art hist, Am Univ, Washington, DC, 75-77, assoc prof art hist, 77-86, prof art hist, 86-. *Awards:* Nat Endowment Humanities Fel, 81-82; Mina Shaughnessy Scholar, 82; Bellagio Study & Conf Ctr Fel, Rockefeller Found, 91; Art Hist Recog Award, Women's Comm, Col Art Asn of Am, 2000. *Mem:* Col Art Asn Am; Women's Caucus Art. *Res:* Late 19th and early 20th century European painting. *Publ:* Auth, Degas and French Feminism Circa 1880, Art Bull, 88; auth & ed, World Impressionism: International Movement, 1860-1920, Harry N Abrams Inc, 90; auth, Impressionism, A Feminist Reading, 91, Georges Seurat, 92 & gen ed, The Rizzoli Art Series, 92 Rizzoli; co-ed (with Mary D Garrard), The Expanding Discourse; Feminism and Art History, Harper Collins, 92; The Power of Feminist Art: The American Movement of the 1970's, History and Impact, Abrams, 94; Gustave Caillalootte and the Fashioning of Identity in Impressconist Paris, Rutgers Univ Press, 2002; co-ed (with Mary D Garrard), Reclaiming Female Agency: Feminist Art History after Postmadernism, Univ of CA Press, 2005. *Mailing Add:* Dept Art American Univ 4400 Massachusetts Ave NW Washington DC 20016-8004

BROUDO, JOSEPH DAVID
EDUCATOR, PAINTER
b Baltimore, Md, Sept 11, 20. *Study:* Alfred Univ, BFA, 46; Boston Univ, MEd, 50. *Work:* Int Mus Ceramics, Faenza, Italy; Prieto Collection, Mills Col, Calif; Joan Mannheimer Collection; Mus Ceramic Art, Alfred Univ. *Comn:* mosaics, temples, Goversville, NY, Amsterdam, NY, Beverly, Mass. *Exhib:* Int Exhib, Ostend, Belg, 60; Ten Boston Area Craftsmen, NY World's Fair, 64-65. *Teaching:* Dept head & prof art, Endicott Col, 46-94, distinguished emer prof, 94-. *Awards:* Grand Prize, Int Exhib, Ostend, Belg, 60; Top Honors, Eastern States Expos & De Cordova Craftsmen Exhib; and others. *Mem:* Mass Asn Craftsmen (chmn, 55-56, dir, 72); Am Crafts Coun (exec coun, 71-72); Boston Soc Arts & Crafts (dir, 62-78); Cult Connection (dir, 87-90). *Media:* Acrylic, Oil; Watercolor. *Mailing Add:* Endicott College Dept Art 5 Gary Ave Beverly MA 01915

BROUN, ELIZABETH GIBSON
ADMINISTRATOR, HISTORIAN
b Kansas City, Mo, Dec 15, 46. *Study:* Univ Bordeaux, cert advanced study, 67; Univ Kans, BA, 68, MA, 69, PhD 76; Woodrow Wilson fel, 68-69; Ford Found fel, 70-72. *Collection Arranged:* Spencer Mus Art, Lawrence, Kans; Albert Pinkham Ryder, Nat Mus Am Art, Washington, DC, 89. *Pos:* Cur prints & drawings, Spencer Mus Art, Univ Kans, Lawrence, 77-83, actg dir, 82-83; assist dir, chief cur, Nat Mus Am Art, Smithsonian Inst, Washington, DC, 83-88, actg dir 88-89, dir, Smithsonian Am Art Mus (formerly Nat Mus Am Art, 89-. *Teaching:* Asst prof, Univ Kans, 78-83. *Mem:* Phi Beta Kappa. *Res:* History of American art and graphic arts. *Publ:* coauth Engravings of Marcantonio Raimondi, 81; coauth Benton's Bentons, 80; auth, Contents of Whistler's Art, Arts Mag, 87; auth, The Art of Lithography, Univ Houston, 87; auth, Benton, A Politician in Art, Smithsonian Studies in Am Art, spring 87; auth, Albert Pinkham Ryder, Smithsonian Press, 89. *Mailing Add:* PO Box 37012 Washington DC 20013-7012

BROWN, ALAN M, JR
DEALER, CONSULTANT
b New Rochelle, NY. *Study:* Syracuse Univ, BS, 69. *Collection Arranged:* Textiles of the Andes. *Pos:* Dir, Alan Brown Gallery, Hartsdale, NY, 72-2000; Owner, Alan Brown Gallery, Naples, FL. *Awards:* Arts Award, Westchester Arts Coun, 94. *Mem:* Coun Arts Westchester (trustee, formerly); Westchester Pub Art (bd dir, formerly); Pelham Art Ctr (art adv bd, currently). *Res:* Contemporary artists. *Specialty:* American Pop Art. *Interests:* Curating Public & Private Art Collections. *Collection:* Contemporary American art; folk art; Ancient Peruvian Textiles. *Dealer:* Alan Brown Gallery 901 7th St South Naples FL 34102. *Mailing Add:* 901 7th St S Naples FL 34102

BROWN, ALICE DALTON
PAINTER
b Danville, Pa, Apr 17, 39. *Study:* Acad Julian, Paris, 57; Cornell Univ, 58-60; Oberlin Col, Ohio, BA, 62. *Work:* Maier Mus Art, Lynchburg, Va; Springfield Mus Art, Mo; Tampa Mus Art, Fla; Met Mus Art, NY; Ashville Mus Art, NC. *Comn:* Painting, General Electric Co, 90; Am Home Products Corp, 94. *Exhib:* Collectors Choice, McNay Art Inst, San Antonio, Tex, 81, 89 & 90; one-woman shows, AM Sachs Gallery, NY, 82, 83 & 84, Katharina Rich Perlow Gallery, NY, 85; Fischbach Gallery, NY, 87, 89, 91, 93, 95, 98, 2000, 02, 04, 06; William Sawyer Gallery, San Francisco, 88; Springfield Art Mus, Mo, 99. *Awards:* Purchase Award, West Collection: Art & Law, 85. *Bibliog:* Camille Howard (auth), Light and Life, Springfield News-Leader, 10/99; Jia Difei (auth), Contemporary American Oil Painting, 99; enchanted Sanctuary: Alice Dalton Brown, Am Arts Quarterly, spring 2000; April Kingsley (auth), The Paintings of Alice Dalton Brown, 2002; poster reproductions pub by McGraw Pub. *Media:* Oil, Pastel. *Specialty:* Am Realist Art. *Publ:* J Bowyer Bell, Review, 96. *Dealer:* Fischbach Gallery 210 Eleventh Ave NY NY 10001. *Mailing Add:* 817 Central Ave #2 Peekskill NY 10566-2039

BROWN, ANITA
PAINTER
b Rosario, Arg, Aug 8, 16; US citizen. *Study:* Nat Acad Design, 34; Hunter Col, BA, 38. *Work:* Louise E Thorne Mem Art Gallery, Keene State Univ, NY; Roberson Ctr Arts & Sci, Binghamton, NY; Griffiths Art Ctr Gallery, St Lawrence Univ, Canton, NY; Butler Inst Am Art, Youngstown, Ohio. *Exhib:* New Talent, Country Art Gallery, Westbury, NY, 60; Group shows, Ligoa Duncan Gallery, NY, 64, Gallery 1199, NY, 78, Nat Acad Design, NY; Still Life Exhib, Japan Europe & Am, Storm King Art Ctr, Mountainville, NY, 67; Visions Past, Visions Present, Roberson Ctr Arts & Sci, Binghamton, NY, 80. *Awards:* Honorable Mention, Long Island Artists 13th Ann, Hofstra Col, 62; Molly Morpeth Canaday Mem Award, Nat Asn Women Artists, 75. *Mem:* Nat Asn Women Artists. *Media:* Oil, Woodcut, Etching. *Mailing Add:* 3 Fourth Rd Great Neck NY 11021-1505

BROWN, BETTY ANN
EDUCATOR, CRITIC
b Oklahoma City, Okla, June 6, 49. *Study:* Southern Methodist Univ, BFA, 71; Univ Tex, Austin, MA, 73; Univ NMex, Albuquerque, PhD, 77. *Collection Arranged:* Faces of Fiesta, San Diego State Univ, 82; Susan Kleinberg, Univ Southern Calif, Davidson Conf Ctr, 82; Sensuous Surfaces, Univ Southern Calif, 82; Generations, Conejo Valley Art Mus, 83; Caretas Mexicanas, Mexican mask exhib, Southwest Mus, 83; Space (Artists Spaces), Occidental Col, 86; Roland Reiss Retrospective, 91. *Pos:* Dir visual arts prog, Col Continuing Educ, Univ Southern Calif, Los Angeles, 81-; art critic for weekly newspaper, Reader, 81-83; auth, monthly series of previews on Los Angeles art exhibs, Artscene, 82-; auth, monthly column, Arts Mag, 82-; ed, Visions Mag, 86-87. *Teaching:* Asst prof art hist, Ill State Univ, 77-79; asst prof, Calif State Univ, Northridge, 79-81 & 86-; adj prof, Univ Southern Calif, 81-85; assoc prof art, Calif State Northridge, 88-. *Mem:* Art Table; Women's Caucus Art; Asn Latin Am Art (secy, 81-83); Inst Hispanic Media & Cult (bd dir, 82-83). *Res:* Contemporary Art, Ancient and contemporary arts of Latin America. *Publ:* Auth, numerous articles on Pre-Columbian art history and contemporary folk arts of Latin America; Exposures: Women and Their Art, 89; auth, numerous articles on contemp criticism. *Mailing Add:* Art Dept Cal St Univ Northridge 18111 Nordhoff St Northridge CA 91330-0001

BROWN, BRUCE ROBERT
PAINTER, SCULPTOR
b Philadelphia, Pa, July 25, 38. *Study:* Tyler Sch Art, Temple Univ, BFA(painting), 62, MFA(sculpture), 64. *Work:* Telfair Acad Arts & Sci, Savannah, Ga; Festival Arts Collection, Erie, Pa; WVa Arts & Humanities Coun; Gallery 5, Davao City, Philippines. *Comn:* Five Coins for Medal Arts Co, 71; Heroes of God, Rochester, NY, 72; Innauguration medallion for pres of Monroe Community Col, Rochester, NY, 72; Bronze relief, Dr Stabins Monroe Community Col bd trustees, 75; Acad achievement medallion for Monroe Community Col, 76; Bronze relief, pastor of church congregation in Rochester, NY, 77; Portrait of Cannionized St, Davao City, Philippines, 2002. *Exhib:* Nat Show, Pa Acad Fine Arts, Philadelphia, 62; Nat Show, Butler Inst Am Art, Youngstown, Ohio, 62-63; 21st Ann Int Exhib, Beaumont, Tex, 72; Bertrand Russel Peace Found Show, London, Eng, 72; Sunbird Gallery, Los Altos,

Calif, 87; Tyler Alumni Gallery, Temple Univ, Philadelphia, 87; Beaumont Nat Art Show, Beaumont Mus, Beaumont, Tex, 72; one-man show La State Univ, Baton Rouge, La, 73; plus others. *Pos:* sculpturer-in-residence St Gauden's Natural Hist Site, NH 69. *Teaching:* instr, adult painting prog, Dept Recreation, Philadelphia, 61-64; instr ceramics & art, Philadelphia Pub Sch, 65-66; instr art, West Liberty State Col, 67-68, head of sculpture dept; assoc prof art, Monroe Community Col, NY, 68-99; instr Philippines Rizal Col and Ford Acad of Fine Arts, DaVao City, 2001-03. *Awards:* Purchase Award, Arts & Humanities Coun WVa, 67; Purchase Award, Am Acad Arts & Lett, 68; Purchase Award, Erie Summer Festival Arts; Huntington 180 Exhib Award in Sculpture, Charleston, WVa, 68; Painting Award Appalachian Corridors, 68. *Bibliog:* Folio Mag Tyler Sch of Fine Art, Temple Univ, Philadelphia, Pa; Cabbages & Kings Mag, Monroe Community Col, Rochester, NY; Mindanao Times, Davao City, Philippines. *Mem:* Col Art Asn Am; Southern Sculptors Asn; Rochester Print Club; Artist's Equity Asn, NY. *Media:* Oil. *Res:* Inter-disciplinary art/math course, drawing the human figure. *Publ:* Auth, Robert Henkes, Sport in Art (guide for beginning illus); Artists USA; Printmaking USA

BROWN, CAROL A
PAINTER
b Rockville Centre, NY, July 15, 37. *Study:* Art Students League; Hnas Hoffman Sch, Cornell Univ, BFA, 57. *Work:* US Embassy, Athens, Greece; Drew Univ Mus, Madison, NJ; US Embassy, Ajbagat, Turkmenistan. *Exhib:* one-woman show, Roko Gallery, NY, Witkin Gallery, NY, Charles Lucien Gallery, NY & Rettig Y Martinez Gallery, Santa Fe, NMex. *Pos:* Guest artist/teacher drawing, Ray McSavaney Workshops, Utah. *Awards:* Nat Endowment Arts Fel. *Bibliog:* Lizbeth Marano (auth), Carol Brown at Witkin, Art in Am, 9/83; Lawrence Campbell (auth), Carol Brown at Witkin, Art in Am, 12/87; Eileen Myles (auth), Carol Brown at Charles Lucien, Art in Am, 10/90; John Brown (auth), Carol Brown. *Mem:* Col Art Asn; Artists Equity. *Media:* Oil, Colored Pencils, Mixed Media. *Publ:* Auth, Dean Brown-Photographs of the American Wilderness, Amphoto, 79; illusr, A God on Every Mountaintop, Scribner, 80; Canyon Sketchbook, Witkin Gallery, 87; Canyonlands, Travel & Leisure, 90

BROWN, CAROL K
PAINTER, SCULPTOR
b Memphis, Tenn. *Study:* Univ Miami, BFA, 78; Univ Colo, MFA, 81. *Work:* Denver Art Mus; Jacksonville Art Mus, Fla; Art Mus, Fla Int Univ, Miami; Miami Art Mus, Fla; Tampa Mus Art, Fla; and others. *Comn:* Sculpture, Fla Int Univ, Miami, Dade Co Art Pub Places, Miami, Fla, 87, Univ Fla, Gainesville, 88; Southeast Banking Corp, 89; and others; Progressive Insurance Co, 2006. *Exhib:* Denver Art Mus Invitational, 81; Art of Miami, Southeastern Ctr Contemp Art, Winston-Salem, NC, 85; Nat Endowment Arts-Fel Artists, Fla State Univ, Tallahassee, 85 & 86; The Hortt Exhib, Mus Art, Ft Lauderdale, Fla, 85, 86 & 87; solo exhibs, Bacardi Sculpture Plaze & Gallery, Miami, Fla, 88, Ctr Fine Arts, Sculpture Plaza, 87, Gloria Luria Gallery, Bay Harbor Island, Fla, 91, Nohra Haime Gallery, NY, 92, 94, 96, 2000, 01, Jacksonville Art Mus, 93, Jeff Baker Blau Gallery, Boca Raton, Fla, 93, Frederic Snitzer Gallery, 95 & Lehman Col, Bronx, NY, 96; Whitney Mus Am Art, 97; Nat Mus of Women in the Arts, Washington, DC, 2004; and others. *Teaching:* Instr, Miami-Dade Community Col, 86-87, New World Sch Arts, 91-. *Awards:* State Fla Fine Arts Fel, 83 & 92; Nat Endowment Arts Fels, 84 & 86; Southeastern Ctr Contemp Art Fel, 84. *Bibliog:* Janet Koplos, rev, Art in Am, 5/2001; Douglas F Maxwell (auth), rev, Carol K Brown at Nohra Haime Gallery, NY Arts, 2/2001; Michael Arog (auth), Art in America, 5/2004. *Media:* All Media; Acrylic. *Dealer:* Ambrosino Gallery 769 NE 125th St North Miami Fla 33161; Nohra Haime Gallery 41 E 57th St New York NY

BROWN, CECILY
ARTIST
b London. *Study:* B-Epsom Sch Art, Surrey, England, B-TEC Diploma in Art & Design, 1987; Morley Col, London, Attended Drawing & Printmaking classes, 1987-89; NY Studio Sch, 1992; Slade Sch Art, London, BA in Fine Arts, First Class Hon, 1993. *Work:* At Century's End: John P Morrissey Collection 90's Art, Mus Contemp Art, Fla, 1999; Directions, Hirshhorn Mus & Sculpture Garden, Washington, DC, 2002, Off, Murray Guy, NY; Off, Murray Guy, NY, 2003; Art, Whitney Mus Am Art, 2004. *Exhib:* Exhib incl Fete Worse Than Death, Laurent Delaye, London, 1994, Eagle Gallery, London, 1995, Taking Stock, NY, 1996, Deitch Projects, NY, 1997, Janice Guy Gallery, NY, 1997, Vertical Painting, PS 1 Contemp Art Ctr, NY, 1999, Pleasure Dome, Jessica Fredericks Gallery, NY, 1999, Facts & Fictions, Galleria in Arco Turin, Italy, 1999, Deitch Projects, NY, 2000, The Skin Game, Gagosian Gallery, Beverly Hills, Calif, 2000, Serenade, Victoria Miro Gallery, London, 2000, Gagosian Gallery, NY, 2000, Emotional Rescue: Contemp Art Project Collection, Ctr Contemp Art, Seattle, 2000, Days of Heaven, Contemp Fine Arts, Berlin, 2001. *Mailing Add:* c/o Gagosian Gallery 555 W 24th St New York NY 10011

BROWN, CHARLOTTE VESTAL
MUSEUM DIRECTOR, HISTORIAN
b Siler City, NC, June 3, 42. *Study:* Univ NC, Greensboro, BA(with honors), 64; Univ NC, Chapel Hill, PhD, 75. *Collection Arranged:* The New Narrative: Contemporary Fiber Art, 92; The Art of Building in North Carolina, 92; This is Not Tramp Art, 93; Bob Trotman: A Retrospective of Furniture and Sculpture, 94; A Multitude of Memories: The Work of Annie Hooper, 95; Textiles: Tradition and Innovation, Bedovin, Israeli, Palestinian, 96; Mark Hewitt Potter, 97; The Neugents: Close to Home, the Photographs of David Spear, 98; The Little Black Dress: From Sorrow to Seduction, 98. *Pos:* City of Raleigh, Hist Preservation, 81-82. *Teaching:* Asst prof, Duke Univ, 71-79; asst prof mod archit, NC State Univ, 89-90. *Mem:* Royal Oak Found; Am Asn Mus; NC Preservation/Hist Preservation Found; Vernacular Archit Forum. *Res:* Architectural history and theory, 19th and 20th century; American and English. *Publ:* Coauth, The Humanities, D C Heath, 89, 93 & 96; Architects and Builders in NC, Univ NC Press, 90. *Mailing Add:* NC State Univ Gallery Art & Design Box 7306 Univ Student Ctr Raleigh NC 27695-7306

BROWN, CHRISTOPHER
PAINTER
b Camp Lejeune, NC, 1951. *Study:* Univ Ill, Champaign-Urbana, BA, 72; Univ Calif, Davis, MFA, 76. *Work:* San Francisco Mus Mod Art, Univ Art Mus, Fine Arts Mus San Francisco & Security Pac Nat Bank, Calif; Chase Manhattan Bank, Metrop Mus, New York Pub Libr, Grey Art Gallery & New York Univ, NY; Gen Mills, Walker Art Ctr, Minneapolis, Minn; Sheldon Mem Art Gallery, Lincoln, Nebr; Mod Art Mus, Ft Worth, Tex. *Comn:* Painting, Fed Aviation Comn, Kansas City, Mo, 96. *Exhib:* solo exhibs, Campbell Thiebaud Gallery, San Francisco, 94 & 97, Mod Art Mus, Ft Worth, Tex (traveling), 95-96, Pasadena City Col Art Gallery, Calif, 97 & Edward Thorp Gallery, New York, 98, Friesen Gallery, Seattle, 2000, 2001, Byron Cohen Gallery, Kansas City, Missouri, 2001, John Berggruen Gallery, San Francisco, 2002; The Painted Room (traveling), Madison Art Ctr, Wis, 85-86; Chicago Int Art Exposition, Ill, 86 & 88; traveled to San Francisco Art Inst, Calif, 86; Newport Harbor Art Mus, Calif, 86 & 87; Contemp Arts Ctr, Cincinnati, Ohio, 87; Am Acad & Inst Arts & Letts, NY, 88; The Water Paintings, 1976-1987 (traveling), Univ Tex, Arlington, 88; Blum Helman, Los Angeles, Calif, 89; 10 Plus 10: Contemp Soviet & Am Painters, Mod Art Mus, Ft Worth, Tex, traveled to San Francisco Mus Mod Art, Milwaukee Art Ctr, Corcoran Gallery Art & Soviet Union, 90; Edward Thorp Gallery, NY, 92 & 95; Lyricism & Light, Palo Alto Cult Ctr, Calif, 94; Toward the Millennium: Contemp Paintings from Northern Calif, Monterey Mus Art, La Mirada, 97; Shasta Col Gallery, Redding, 99. *Teaching:* Prof art, Univ Calif Berkeley, 81-92. *Awards:* Fel, Nat Endowment Arts, 87; Award, Am Acad & Inst Arts & Letts, 88. *Bibliog:* John Yau (auth), Christopher Brown - New Paintings, 1990 (exhib catalog), Gallery Paule Anglim, 90; Jeff Kelley (auth), Christopher Brown - New Paintings-1994 (exhib catalog), Campbell-Thiebaud Gallery, 94; Michael Brenson (auth), History and Memory: Paintings by Christopher Brown, Mod Art Mus, Ft Worth, 95. *Dealer:* Campbell-Thiebaud Gallery San Francisco CA; Edward Thorp Gallery New York NY. *Mailing Add:* c/o John Berggruen Gallery 228 Grant Ave San Francisco CA 94108

BROWN, CONSTANCE GEORGE
GALLERY DIRECTOR, ART DEALER
Study: Perry Normal Sch, Boston, Dipl, 54, Northeastern Univ, 73-76. *Collection Arranged:* F Ladd, 76, F Brown, 77, Ingersoll & Bloch, 77, Dr A Noonan, 79 & G White & A Brown, 85, Seventeen Wendell Street. *Pos:* Chair & mem adv bd, Nat Ctr Afro-Am Art Mus, 80-; mem, Local Site Comt, Mass Art & Humanities, 85 & Art Planning Coun, Lena Park Develop Corp, Boston, Mass, 86; comt mem & chair, Archives of Am Art. *Mem:* Archives of Am Art. *Res:* Contemporary Black-American artists

BROWN, DANIEL
CRITIC, COLLECTOR
b Cincinnati, Ohio, Nov 4, 46. *Study:* Middlebury Col, AB, 68; Univ Mich, MA, 70. *Collection Arranged:* Constance McClure: A Retrospective & Rita Zimmerman: New Monoprints (guest cur), 86; New Art from Academe: An Overview, The Cent Exchange (guest cur), Kansas City, Mo, 88; Cincinnati Past & Present: The Golden Ages in the Visual Arts, Tangeman Fine Arts Gallery (guest co-cur), Univ Cincinnati, 88; Contemporary Landscape, KenCabCo (guest cur), 88; Figure It Out, Katz & Dawgs Gallery Inaugural Exhib (guest cur), Columbus, Ohio, 88; Lyrical Abstractions (guest cur), 89 & the Artist at Mid- Career: A Dialogue Between Cincinnati & Columbus (guest cur), 89-90,Katz & Dawgs Gallery, Columbus, Ohio; Arts Consortium, Cincinnati, Ohio; Interpretations of the Everyday Object, 91; Frescoes of Working People, 91; Landscape East and West, 91-92; Union Terminal, Cincinnati Multiculturalism: the Evolution and the Celebration Group Show, African-Am Mus, 91-92; Black Not White, in black and white, 92; Maple Knoll Retirement Community, 2001-. *Pos:* Art critic, Cincinnati Mag, 79-82, Dialogue Art J, Columbus, 83-, WCPO-TV, Cincinnati, 86- & Provincetown Arts, 88-, Cincinnati Herald, 92- & Everybody's News, 93-94; artist's model, Constance McClure, 84-, David Bumbeck, 84-85, Dan Boldman, 85-, Jerome Mussman, 85-, David DeVaul, 86 & Cole Carothers, 87-; art commentator, WKRC-TV, Cincinnati, 85; pres, Daniel Brown Inc, Independent Art Consultants; cur, KZF Gallery, Cincinnati, 87-94; regular guest columnist art issues, Cinncinnati Post, 91-; founding art ed & essayist, City Beat, 94-95; ed-in-chief, Antenna Arts Mag, 96-98; Cur KZF Gallery, 2004; Ed, www.Blvc Chip Review.com (poltics/arts), 2004; cur, Kidney Found Cincinnati, 2006-. *Teaching:* Guest lectr, Contemp Arts Ctr, Cincinnati, 84-86, Cincinnati Art Mus, 86 & Univ Cincinnati, 86 & 93-95; part-time lect printmaking, drawing & painting, Art Acad Cincinnati, currently; Meriamble Library fiction 2004; Univ Cinn Fiction 2004-2005, 06-. *Awards:* Winner, the Critics Purse, Dialogue Mag, 85. *Mem:* Contemp Arts Ctr, Cincinnati (trustee, 84-88); Enjoy the Arts, Cincinnati (trustee, 85-88, vpres, 86-88); Int Soc Art Critics, NY & Paris; Art Acad Cincinnati (trustee, 93-97); Visting nurses of Cinn (art ad), 2004. *Res:* Psychoanalytic and political implications of contemporary art. *Collection:* Contemporary prints, drawings and paintings of both national and regional artists. *Publ:* The Zen of Seeing (exhib catalog), Southern Ohio Mus & Cult Ctr, Portsmouth, 94; The Art of David Bumbeck (exhib catalog), Dartmouth Col, 95; Bukang Kim: A Retrospective (exhib catalog), Springfield Arts Ctr, Ohio, 96; Robert Knipschild (catalogue), Springfiled Arts Ctr; Beverly Erschell (catalogue article), Washington DC Gallery and Weston Gallery, Cincinnati; Contempary Neo-Pub, KZF, 2005. *Mailing Add:* 431 Collins Ave Cincinnati OH 45202

BROWN, DAVID ALAN
HISTORIAN, CURATOR
b Bellevue, Ohio, July 25, 42. *Study:* Harvard Col, BA(magna cum laude), 64; Cambridge Univ, Fulbright fel, 64-65; Yale Univ, MA, 67, PhD, 73. *Collection Arranged:* Berenson and the Connoisseurship of Italian Painting, 79, From Leonardo to Titian: Italian Renaissance Paintings from the Hermitage, 79, Raphael and America, 83 & Leonardo's Last Supper: Before and After, 84, Nat Gallery Art, Washington, DC. *Pos:* Cur Italian Renaissance painting, Nat Gallery Art, Washington, DC, currently. *Teaching:* Lectr art hist, Yale Univ, New Haven, Conn, 73-74 & Smithsonian Assoc Prog, Washington, DC, 75-. *Awards:* Finley Fel, Nat Gallery Art, 68-71; Fel Villa I Tatti, Harvard Ctr for Renaissance Studies, Florence, 69-70. *Mem:* Renaissance Soc Am; Col Art Asn. *Res:* Italian Renaissance painting; Leonardo Da Vinci; Correggio. *Publ:* Auth, articles on Leonardo Da Vinci and on Correggio, Mitteilungen des Kunst Historischen Inst, Florence, 71, Mus Studies, 72, Master Drawings, 74 & 75. *Mailing Add:* Nat Gallery Art Sixth & Constitution Sts Washington DC 20565

BROWN, DAVID LEE
SCULPTOR
Study: Cass Tech, 57; NC Sch Design, 60; Cranbrook Acad Art, 62. *Work:* John Hopkins Univ, Baltimore, Md; De Cordova Mus, Lincoln, Mass; Hirshhorn Mus & Sculpture Garden, Washington, DC; Milwaukee Art Ctr, Wis; Chase Manhattan Bank, NY. *Comn:* Sculptures, Reynolds Aluminium Corp, Richmond, Va, 76, Xerox Corp (monumental), Stamford, Conn, 78, Warner Lambert Co, Morris Plains, NJ, 81, Lincorp Corp, Dallas, Tex, 85 & Fla Nat Bank, Jacksonville, 86. *Teaching:* Instr sculpture, Cranbrook Acad Art, 60-61; prof design, Pratt Inst, NY, 72-. *Media:* Stainless Steel, All Media. *Dealer:* Grace Borgenicht Gallery 724 Fifth Ave New York NY 10019. *Mailing Add:* 621 Springs Fireplace Rd East Hampton NY 11937-1732

BROWN, DIANE
DEALER
b Cleveland, Ohio, Nov 23, 47. *Study:* Univ Wis, Madison, BA, 69; Univ Md, Col Park. *Pos:* Owner & dir, Diane Brown Gallery, Washington, DC, 76-82, Diane Brown Sculpture Space, Washington, DC, 79-83 & Diane Brown Gallery, New York, 83-92; dir, Art Adventures, NY, 93-99; cur, Corp Collection, Chancery Lane Capital, NY, 96-; priv art dealer, Diane Brown Fine Art, NY, 92-; pres & founder Rx Art Inc, NY, 2000-. *Teaching:* Instr, NY Univ, NY, 98-2001; lectr numerous univ & col in US & Can. *Mem:* ArtTable (prog comt mem, 89-91); Appraisers Asn Am, 98-. *Specialty:* Contemporary art with emphasis on sculpture. *Mailing Add:* 1 Astor Pl Apt 4K New York NY 10003

BROWN, EDITH RAE
SCULPTOR, MEDALIST
b Flushing, NY, Nov 9, 1942. *Study:* Art Students League; PietraSanta, Italy, studios and workshops of prof sculptors & painters. *Work:* Smithsonian Inst, Washington; Am Numismatic World Mus, Colorado Springs, Colo; Newark Mus, Newark, NJ; Nat Arts Club, NY. *Comn:* Comn by pvt collectors. *Exhib:* Chesterwood Mass, 89; Nat Arts Club, NY, 89-2003; Hecksher Mus, NY, 90; Fedn Int de'la Medille, Helsinki Art Mus, Finland, 90; Newark Mus, NJ, 91; Hungarian Nat Gallery, Budapest, 94; Patac Sztuki, Krakow, Poland, 95; Gallery Emanual, NY, 95; Gallerie Art Viva, Paris, 95-2003; Parsons Sch Design, Paris, 95; Lehman Col, UN 50th Ann, 96; L'Assemblee Nationale, Paris, 97; Festival Des Arts, Vayolles, France, 97; Salon D'Automne, Paris, 96-2003; Am Numismatic Soc Mus, Colorado Springs, 98; Beelden aan Zee Mus, The Hague, 98, Nat Asn Women Artists, 98; Nassau Mus Fine Arts, NY, 98; Biennale Int Citta di Firenza, 2000 & 2001; and others. *Pos:* Chmn sculpture exhibs; juror sculpture exhibs; lectr, demonstrate carving stone sculpture. *Teaching:* Stone carving. *Awards:* Salzman Award, Nat Arts Club, 95 & 96; Lelia Garin Sawyer Mem Award, Am Artists Prof League, 93, 95 & 96; Pietro Montana Mem Award, Hudson Valley Art Asn, 96. *Mem:* Pen & Brush Inc; Artists Equity, NY; Coun Am Artists Soc Inc (pres); Am Medallic Sculpture Asn (bd mem); Nat Asn Women Artists; and others. *Media:* Stone, Bronze. *Specialty:* Contemp Art. *Publ:* Auth, Artist expresses her need to create, Intermountain Jewish News, 6/11/85; Contemporary Sculpture, Chesterwood, 89. *Dealer:* Gallery Studio 55 Glen Cove Rd Greenvale NY 11548; Art Viva, Levallois-Perret, France. *Mailing Add:* 1494 Cedar Swamp Rd Brookville NY 11545

BROWN, GARY HUGH
PAINTER, EDUCATOR
b Evansville, Ind, Dec 19, 41. *Study:* DePauw Univ, Greencastle, Ind, BA, 63; Acad Belli de Arti, Rome & Florence, Italy, 63-64; Univ Wis-Madison, MFA, 66. *Work:* Elvehjem Art Ctr, Madison, Wis; Yale Univ, New Haven, Conn; Glenbow Art Mus, Alta, Can; Utah Mus Fine Arts, Salt Lake City; Tyler Mus Art, Tex; and others; 20th Century Fox; Int Mus Photography, George Eastman House; Mus Modern Art; plus many others. *Comn:* Ltd ed paper suite, Source Gallery, San Francisco, publ by Twinrocker, Ind, 76; mural, Osaka Univ, 85; tile courtyard & fountain, Sarah House, Santa Barbara, Calif, 94; Inst Cult Inquiry: 1997 AIDS Chronicle. *Exhib:* One-man shows, Fleischer-Anhalt Gallery, Los Angeles, Calif, 68, de Saisset Art Gallery, Univ Santa Clara & Santa Barbara Mus Art, 71-72, Comsky Gallery, Beverly Hills, Calif, 75, United Arts Club, Dublin, Ireland, 75, Source Gallery, San Francisco, 76 & 78, Art/Life Gallery, Santa Barbara, 82 & Ventura Col, 94, LifeLine, Villa Lila, Nijmegen, The Neth, 2000, plus others; Art-Space, Osaka-Tokyo, Japan, 85; Tokyo Munic Mus Art, 86; The Drawing 2000 Int Period Gallery, Omaha, Nebr; The Blake House Collection, Blake House, Kensington, Calif, 2000; plus many others. *Pos:* Artist-in-residence, Int Inst for Experimental Papermaking, Calif, 74, New Harmony, Ind, 76, Ateliershaus Worpswede, WGer, 82, Artist Union, Nishinomiaya, Univ Japan, 85 & Fez, Morocco, 93. *Teaching:* Prof painting & drawing, Univ Calif, Santa Barbara, 66-. *Awards:* Greenshields Found Grant for Europ Travel/Study, 63. *Mem:* Col Art Asn. *Media:* Drawing, Oil. *Interests:* Drawing, Painting, Papermaking, Art Jour. *Publ:* Illusr, Peter Whigham's The Blue Winged Bee, Anvil, 69; John Logan (auth), Poem in Progress, Dryad, 75; The Santa Cruz Mountain Poems, Morton Marcus (auth), Capra, 75, 2nd ed, 92; The Music of the Troubadors, Ross-Erikson, 79; Electroworks, George Eastman House & Chanticleer Press, 80; The Art of the Journal Princeton Architectural Press, to be released on June, 2005. *Dealer:* Svit Ozor Fine Arts Santa Barbara CA. *Mailing Add:* Art Dept Univ Calif Santa Barbara CA 93106

BROWN, GILLIAN
CONCEPTUAL ARTIST, PHOTOGRAPHER
Study: Brown Univ, Providence, RI, BA, 73; RI Sch Design, Providence, MAE, 77; Univ Calif, Los Angeles, MFA(photog), 80. *Work:* Addison Gallery Am Art, Andover, Mass; Art Mus, Princeton Univ; Bibliot Nat, Paris; Calif Mus Photog, Univ Calif, Riverside; Calif Inst Arts, Valencia. *Comn:* Permanent site works, Washington Proj Arts, 90. *Exhib:* Solo exhibs, Andover Gallery, Mass, 86, Gatehouse Gallery, Mt Vernon Col, 87, Constructions, Kathleen Ewing Gallery, Washington, 87, Notre Dame Col, Baltimore, Md, 90, Jones, Troyer, Fitzpatrick Gallery, Washington, 92 & Troyer, Fitzpatrick, Lassman Gallery, Washington, 96; Doubletake, Hans & Walter Bechtler Gallery, Charlotte, NC, 94; A View from Baltimore to Washington, Fine Arts Gallery, Univ Md, 94; Off the Mall, Corcoran Gallery Art, Washington, 94; Boston Now, Inst Contemp Art, Boston, 94; The Drawing Show, Bernard Toale Gallery, Boston, 95; Anxious Libraries, Photog Resource Ctr, Boston, 96; Constructed Photog, Addison Gallery Am Art, 97. *Awards:* Nat Endowment Art Fel, 90; Md State Arts Coun Grant, 92; Iowa State Arts Coun Grant, 93. *Bibliog:* Lenore D Miller (auth), Manipulated environments: photomontage into sculpture, Camerawork, spring/summer 94; Eric Renner (auth), Pinhole Photography, Focal Press, Boston, 95; Ferdinand Protzman (auth), It's the thought that counts, Wash Post, 3/2/96

BROWN, HILTON
PAINTER, EDUCATOR
b Momence, Ill, Sept 22, 38. *Study:* Goodman Theatre & Sch Drama, Art Inst Chicago, 56-58; Univ Chicago, 59; Skowhegan Sch Painting & Sculpture, Maine, summers 60 & 61; Sch of Art Inst Chicago, dipl fine arts(George T & Isabelle Brown foreign travel fel), 62, BFA, 63, MFA, 64; Univ Ill, Chicago, 62-63. *Work:* Baltimore Mus Art; Ball State Univ Art Collection; Macomb Community Col, Detroit; Goucher Col; Univ Md, College Park. *Comn:* Exterior wall paintings, City of Baltimore, 73-75; mural, T Johnson Sch, Baltimore, 79-80. *Exhib:* Chicago & Vicinity Show, Art Inst Chicago, 60; Nat Print Exhib, Brooklyn Mus, 64; Twelve Chicago Painters, Walker Art Ctr, Minneapolis, 65; 20th Mo Show, City Art Mus, St Louis, 66; Md Regional Exhib, Baltimore Mus Art, 75; Kornblatt Gallery, Baltimore, Md, 79; Leslie Lohman Gallery, NY, 80; Baltimore Mus Art, 86; Susan Isaacs Gallery, Wilmington, Del, 90; Akron Art Mus, Ohio; Spencer Mus Art, Univ Kans, Lawrence, 2002. *Collection Arranged:* The Art and Archives of Ralph Mayer, Art Technoligist, 94, Univ Del Gallery, Newark; Milk and Eggs - Am Tempera Paintings 1930-50, Brandywind River Mus, Chadds Ford, PA. *Pos:* Mem contemp art accessions comt, Baltimore Mus Art, 68-78; contrib ed, Am Artist Mag, 81-86. *Teaching:* Instr color, drawing & design, Sch of Art Inst Chicago, 62-65; asst prof drawing & compos, Sch Fine Arts, Washington Univ, 65-68; prof drawing, painting & printmaking, Goucher Col, 68-78, chmn art dept, 76-78; vis prof art hist, Winerthur Prog Conserv Art, Univ Del, 74-78, assoc dir, 78-80, prof art, art history and conservation, 78-, coordr, Ralph Mayer Ctr Artists Techniques, 84-88, Ralph & Bena Mayer prof, 84-88, Harriet T Baily prof art, art conserv, art hist, mus studies & women's studies, 92-; consult & lect, Ed Dept, Nat Gallery of Art, Wash, DC, 1990-. *Awards:* Renfrow Art Award, City Art Mus, St Louis, 65; Berney Award Painting, Baltimore Mus Art, 70. *Bibliog:* Franz Schultz (auth), Chicago Art Inst, 3/67; John Brod Peters (auth), Art views: Hilton Brown: New directions, St Louis Globe Democrat, 8/12/67; Lincoln F Johnson (auth), Retrospective shows Brown growth, The Sun, Baltimore, 2/24/77; Hilton Brown, the artist comes out, The Gay Paper, Baltimore, 9/80. *Mem:* Col Art Asn Am; Am Asn Univ Prof. *Media:* Acrylic, Pastel, Oil, Printmaking, Watercolor, Drawing, All Media. *Res:* History of the technology of Western European and Am art from 500 to the Present; history of gay and lesbian art, queer art. *Interests:* Gay, lesbian & queer art & artists; Anglo-Catholicism; gardening. *Publ:* Auth, Looking at paintings: Joseph Stella and John Storrs silverpoint drawings, 5/81, Looking at paintings: Paul Cadmus' playground, 1/82, History of watercolor, 3/83 & History of landscape painting, 2/84, Am Artist Mag; Auth, Art and Archives of Ralph Mayer, exhbition catalog, 94; Co-auth, exhibition catalog, Milk and Eggs, American Tempera Painting, 1930-50, 3/02. *Mailing Add:* 826 N Jefferson St Wilmington DE 19801

BROWN, JAMES
PAINTER, GRAPHIC ARTIST
b Brooklyn, NY. *Study:* Long Island Univ, BA, 54; Brooklyn Col, MS, 55; NY Univ & Yeshiva Univ. *Work:* Corpus Christi Mus, Tex; New York City Tech Col; York Col City Univ NY; Medgar Evers Col, Brooklyn, NY; Voluntariado del Museo de las Casa Reales, Casa de Bastidas, Santo Domingo, Dom Repub; House of Humour & Satire, Gabrova, Bulgaria. *Comn:* Portraits, New York City Pub Schs, 79; illus, Nat Asn Advan Colored People, NY, 80; illus, Revlon, USV Lab, 80; Black Winners (illus), comn by Melvin Douglas, 84; York Col, NY, 85; and others. *Exhib:* Minn Mus Art, Saint Paul, 79; Albrecht Art Mus, Saint Joseph, Mo, 80; Mus Philadelphia Civic Ctr, Pa, 80; Univ Mo, 80; Tulane Univ, La, 80; Queens Mus, NY, 84; Schenectady Mus, NY, 85; poster Shop Galerie, Martinique (WI), 86; Le Centre d'Arte, Haiti (WI), 88; Festival Arts, Port-au-Prince, Haiti, 89; US Pavillion, World's Fair, Seville, Spain, 92; Voluntariado del Museo de las Casas Reales, Santo Domingo, Dom Repub, 94; Sotheby's NY, 97. *Pos:* Supervisor art, New York Bd Educ, 74-83. *Teaching:* Critic, New Jersey State Col, 75; instr drawing, painting & printmaking, Intermediate Sch, New York, 76-78; guest artist, Corpus Christi Mus, 78; lectr bus of art, Col New Rochelle, NY, 79; panelist, Artists as Agents of Social Change: Five Views, Heckscher Mus, Huntington, NY, 86. *Awards:* Purchase Award & First Prize, C of C, Union, NJ,

79; Award, Greater Patterson Arts Coun NJ, 80; Best in Show, Festival on the Green, NJ, 81; and others. *Bibliog:* Georges Paul Hector (auth), Atelier de Reflexion: Conjonction ou itineraire a deux, Valcin II et James Brown, Le Nouvelliste, Port-au-Prince, Haiti, 11/11/89; Abril Peralta (auth), James Brown, Ventana: List in Diario, Santo Domingo, Dom Repub, 4/6/94; Rafael Median (auth), James Brown: Una Extraordinaria Exposition Individual en la Casa de Bastidas, Listin USA Mag Revista de Variodados, 3/2/94; and others. *Mem:* Coalition Black Artists (dir, 78-); Long Island Black Artists Asn (pres, 83-85). *Media:* Oil, Pastel; Carbon Pencil. *Publ:* Contribr, Interracial Books for Children, Coun on Interracial Bks for Children, New York, 79; illusr, Ten Little Niggers, St Albans Printing, New York, 81; Black Winners, Nat Asn Advan Colored People, 84. *Dealer:* Dorsey's Art Gallery 553 Rogers Ave Brooklyn NY 11225; Festival Arts Distributors Petionville Haiti. *Mailing Add:* 117-54 219th St Cambria Heights NY 11411

BROWN, JEFFREY ROGERS
DEALER, COLLECTOR
b Rockville Centre, NY, Feb 7, 40. *Study:* Dartmouth Col, AB, 61; Univ Pa, AM, 68; Univ Md. *Collection Arranged:* Jewish Art (collection of Mr & Mrs Jacob Schulman), 65; George Ortman, 71; Alfred Thompson Bricher (with catalog), 73; Leonard Baskin in Massachusetts, 74; Three American Purists: Mason, Miles, von Wiegand, 75; Peter Lyons Painting, 2003. *Pos:* Cur educ, Munson-Williams-Proctor Inst, Utica, NY, 64-67; cur collections, Indianapolis Mus Art, 69-73; dir, Mus Fine Arts, Springfield, Mass, 73-75; co-owner & dir, Brown-Corbin Fine Art. *Teaching:* Asst prof art, State Univ NY Cortland, 67-68. *Mem:* Private Art Dealers Asn; St Botolph Club. *Res:* American painting of 19th century; James Peale, Alfred Bricher & John Leslie Breck. *Publ:* Contribr, Recent Accessions--A Six Year Retrospective, Indianapolis, 72; auth, Alfred Thompson Bricher, Am Art Rev, Vol 1, 74 & Antiques, 76

BROWN, JONATHAN
HISTORIAN
b Springfield, Mass, July 15, 39. *Study:* Dartmouth Col, AB, 60; Princeton Univ, PhD, 64, Guggenheim Mem Fel, 81-82. *Pos:* Dir, Inst Fine Arts, New York Univ, 73-78; vis mem, Inst Advan Study, 78-79. *Teaching:* Asst prof art hist, Princeton Univ, 65-71, assoc prof, 71-73; from assoc prof to prof, Inst Fine Arts, NY Univ, 73-84, Carroll & Milton Petrie prof, 84-; Slade prof fine art, Oxford Univ, 81-82; Andrew W Mellon lectr fine arts, Nat Gallery Art, 94. *Awards:* Order of Isabel la Católica Award, 86; Medalla de Oro de Bellas Artes, Govt Spain, 86; Gran Cruz de Al Fonso X el Sabio, Gout, Spain, 96. *Mem:* Spanish Inst (bd dir, 87-96); Am Philos Soc; Real Acad de Bellas Artes de San Fernando (corresp mem); Am Acad Arts & Sci. *Res:* Spanish art 16th-19th centuries. *Publ:* Coauth, Velázquez, Painter and Courtier, 86; Spanish Paintings of the Fifteenth through Nineteenth Centuries, Nat Gallery Art, 90; The Golden Age of Painting in Spain, 91; Kings and Connoisseurs, 95; Picasso and the Spanish Tradition, 96. *Mailing Add:* 1 E 78th St New York NY 10021

BROWN, JULIA
DIRECTOR
b Washington, DC, Mar 9, 51. *Study:* Sir Lawrence Col, BA. *Pos:* Sr cur, Mus Contemp Art, Los Angeles, Calif, 81-86; dir, Des Moines Art Ctr, 86-91 & Skystone Found, 91-95; independent publ, 91-; cur spec exhibs, Guggenheim Mus, New York, 95-. *Awards:* Alfred Bar Award, distinguished publ, Col Art Asn, 92. *Mailing Add:* c/o Guggenheim Mus 575 Broadway New York NY 10012-4233

BROWN, JUNE GOTTLIEB
PAINTER, INSTRUCTOR
b Dunn, NC, June 21, 32. *Study:* With Leon Stacks, 64-70, Frederick Taubes, 73 & 75 & Robert F Calrow, 77 & 81. *Work:* DuPont & Co, Leland, NC; Dalton Collection, Charlotte, NC; Springs Mills, NY; United Carolina Bank, Southport, NC; Brunswick Co, Bolivia, NC; Fed Reserve Bank, Richmond, Va; J Arthur Dosher Memorial Hospital, Southport, NC; Fairley Jess & Isenberg, Southport, NC; Allegacy Fed Credit Union, Winston Salem, NC; pvt collection of Mr & Mrs Dennis Hatchell, Winston Salem, NC. *Exhib:* North Carolina Realism, Mint Mus, 74; Hoyt Nat Painting Show, Hoyt Inst Fine Arts, New Castle, Pa, 82; Allied Artists Am Ann Exhib, NY, 82, 86 & 2005; Nat Mid-Year Exhib, Butler Inst Am Art, 82 & 83; Salmagundi Club Open Competition, NY, 83; Henley Southeastern Spectrum, Galleries 214, Winston-Salem, NC, 83; Marinters Museum, Mystic, Conn, 89; Int Soc Marine Painters, 97-99; Dimensions, Winston Salem, NC, 2000; 20th Spring Fine Art Show, Wilmington, NC, 2002; Am Artists Professional League, NY, 2004-2005. *Teaching:* Instr art, Brunswick Community Col, 78-99. *Awards:* Emily Morse Mem Award, Salmagundi Club, 83; Traveling Show Award, Henley's Southeastern Spectrum, 83; Dorothy Watkeys Barberis Award, Catharine Lorillard Wolfe Show, 86:; First Place Moore Co Arts Coun, NC, 2000, second place acrylic, 2003 & 2004; Grumbacher Gold Medallion, 20th Spring Fine Art Show, Wilmington, NC, 2002; John Collins Mem Award, Am Artists Prof League, 2005. *Mem:* Am Artists Prof League & Am Soc of Marine Artists; Catherine Louillard & Wolfe Art Club; Assoc Artist od Winston Salem, NC; Assoc Artists, Southport, NC. *Media:* Acrylic, Oil. *Dealer:* City Art Works Gallery New Bern NC; Sunset River Gallery Calabash NC; Ricky Evans Gallery, Southport, NC. *Mailing Add:* 230 River Dr Southport NC 28461

BROWN, LARRY
PAINTER
b New Brunswick, NJ, June 1, 42. *Study:* Wash State Univ, Pullman, BA, 67; Univ Ariz, MFA, 70. *Work:* Walker Art Ctr; Indianapolis Mus Art; Minn Mus Am Art; Norton Mus Art, W Palm Beach, Fla; Newark Mus Art, NJ; Daum Mus Art, Sedalia, Mo; Portland Mus Art, Oreg. *Teaching:* Vis artist painting, Mont State Univ, Bozeman, 78, Iowa State Univ, Ames, 82, Ohio State Univ, Columbus, 83 & 86, NTex State Univ, 85, Rutgers Univ, 87, State Univ NY, Stonybrook, 87 & 91, NMex State Univ, 88, Ariz State Univ 88, Syracuse Univ, 88, Cooper Union, 91- & Sarah Lawrence Col, 97-2003-; adj prof, The Cooper Union, 91-. *Awards:* Nat Endowment Arts Fel, 79-80. *Bibliog:* Leslie Luebbers (auth), Mind & Matter/New American Abstraction (exhib catalog), 87; John Caldwell (auth), Ten Americans (exhib catalogue), Carnegie Mus Art, 88; Curt Barnes (auth), Constructed painting, Art J, 91; and others. *Mem:* Col Art Asn. *Media:* Oil. *Mailing Add:* 54 Franklin St Apt 4R New York NY 10013

BROWN, LAWRIE
PHOTOGRAPHER, EDUCATOR
b San Jose, Calif, Mar 11, 49. *Study:* San Jose State Univ, Calif, BA, 72; San Francisco State Univ, MA, 75. *Work:* Oakland Mus, Calif; San Francisco Mus Mod Art, Calif; Bibliotheque Nat, Cabinet Des Estampes, Paris, France; Ctr Creative Photography, Tucson; Stanford Univ Mus Art, Calif; Metropolitan Mus Art, New York, NY; Univ Louisville, KY; Univ Tex, Austin; and others. *Exhib:* Everson Mus Art, Syracuse, NY, 77; San Francisco Mus Mod Art, Calif, 78; Arco Ctr Visual Art, Los Angeles, 79; Il Diaframma-Canon, Milan, 82; Oakland Mus, Calif, 83; Boise Gallery Art, Idaho, 83; Hudson River Mus, Yonkers, NY, 84; Alternative Mus, NY, 84; Canon Photogallery, Amsterdam, 85; Friends Photog, Carmel, Calif, 85; Int Ctr for Photog, NY, 87; Houston Ctr for Photog, 87; Bank of Am, San Francisco; Univ Washington, Seattle, 2004; Barrett Art Ctr, NY, 2004; Mus Fine Arts, Fla State Univ, Talahassee, 2004; Monterey Mus Art, Calif, 2005; Univ Toledo Ctr Visual Arts, Ohio, 2005; Visual Arts Ctr NJ, Summit, 2006; Spiva Arts Ctr, Joplin, Mo, 2006. *Collection Arranged:* Sheldon Mem Art Gallery, Lincoln, Nebr, 2005; Who Is Imitating Whom? Photography & Photo-Realism in Art. *Teaching:* dir, Photog Dept, Cabrillo Col, Calif, 79-. *Awards:* Nat Endowment Photogrs Fel, 79; Polaroid Grants, 85, 86, 87 & 2005. *Bibliog:* Peter Hunt Thompson (auth), Untitled 6, Quarterly Friends Photog, 73; Hal Fischer (auth), Don Worth, Barbara Thompson, Lawrie Brown, Casey Williams, Art Week, 9/25/76; Leland Rice (auth), Contemporary California Photography, Camerawork Gallery, 78; ZOOM Int Mag, Milan, Italy, 2006. *Mem:* Soc Photog Educ; Friends Photog; San Francisco Mus Modern Art, Ctr for Photographic Arts, Carmel, Calif; SF Camera Work Gallery, Calif. *Media:* Photography. *Specialty:* Photography. *Collection:* Laundry Series, 24x36″ archival digital black & white photos. *Publ:* Auth, Legacy of Light, Knopf, 87; Darkroom Photog, San Francisco, 9-10/83 & 86; Exploring Color Photography, William Brown Pub, 89. *Dealer:* The Photographers Gallery Palo Alto CA; Scott Nichols San Francisco. *Mailing Add:* 2623 Willowbrook Ln No 114 Aptos CA 95003

BROWN, MARY RACHEL See Marais

BROWN, PAMELA WEDD
PAINTER, PRINTMAKER
b Cauderan, Gironde, France, Nov 21, 28; US citizen. *Study:* Academie Julian, Paris, 46-50; Ecole des Beaux Arts, Paris, 50; studied with Motoi Oi, Tokyo, 57-59 & Sarah Baker, 67-73. *Work:* Smithsonian Inst, Mus Am Hist, Washington, DC; Libr Cong, Print Div, Washington, DC; Nat Mus Women in Arts, Washington, DC; Christopher Newport Col, Hampton Roads, Va; Nat Inst Health (Cancer) Bethesda, Md. *Exhib:* Salon d'Automne, Musee de L'Art Moderne, Paris, 47; Ueno Mus, Tokyo, 59; Boston Arts Festival, Boston Common, Mass, 63; Grabados USA, Museo de Arte Moderno, Buenos Aires, 87; Int Prints 1, Int Monetary Fund, Washington, DC, 88; Winter Relief, Nat Mus Am Hist, Smithsonian Inst, 92; Solo exhib The Junior League of Washington, 82; The Art League, 83; The Washington Printmakers Gallery, 86, 89; Studio Gallery, 88, 91, 94, 97, 2000; Group Coast to Coast Artist Equity, 2001-2002; solo exhibs, Studio Gallery, Washington, 94 & Newman Gallery, Washington, 95, 2000; Studio Gallery, Washington, 97, 2000; India 2004. *Pos:* Artist in residence, The Art Barn, 86; exec dir, New Arts Ctr, (Washington Women's Arts Ctr), 87-88; pres, Washington Printmakers Gallery, 90-91. *Teaching:* Dir arts & crafts, Central YWCA, Toronto, Ont, Can, 50-51. *Awards:* Purchase Award, Junior League, 71; Equal Award, mems exhib, Art League, 80, 82, 85 & 86, 2000, 2001; Honorable Mention, Artists' Equity, 88 & 92. *Bibliog:* Daniel Barbiero (auth), The Generic Figure, Wash Art Reporter, 86; Francis Chenot (auth), Gravure a L'Americaine, Lanterne Bruxelles, 88; Charlotte Clark (auth), article, Eye Wash, 90; Janet Wilson (auth), Galleries, Washington Post, 91; Mary Betts Anderson (auth), Eye Wash, 92. *Mem:* The Art League; Wash Area Printmakers; Studio Gallery (co-pres, 92-93); Wash Proj Arts/Corcoran Artfile. *Media:* Monotypes, Painting, Drawing. *Dealer:* Studio Gallery 2108 R St NW Washington DC 20036. *Mailing Add:* 3500 Macomb St NW Washington DC 20016

BROWN, PEGGY ANN
PAINTER, INSTRUCTOR
b Ft Wayne, Ind, Mar 15, 34. *Study:* Marquette Univ, BS(jour); Ft Wayne Art Inst. *Work:* Ind Univ, Bloomington; Columbus Art Ctr, Ohio; Ricks Col, Rexburg, Idaho; Cooperstown NY Art Asn; Mus Art, Ft Wayne, Ind. *Comn:* Painting, Amoco Corp Int Hq, Chicago, Ill; painting, Marshall Town Bank, Ames, Iowa; painting, Ofc Controller of Currency, Chicago, Ill; painting, Standard Chartered Bank, Hong Kong; painting, Miami Herald, Fla. *Exhib:* Allied Artists Am, NY, 70-93; Nat Watercolor Soc, Los Angeles, 72-76, 79-85 & 93-94; Am Watercolor Soc, NY, 74, 76, 79 & 82; Nat Acad Design, 79 & 82; Watercolor USA, Springfield, Mo; Rocky Mountain Watermedia Nat, Golden, Colo; and others. *Pos:* Sem panelist & instr, currently. *Teaching:* Instr creative watercolor, Ind Univ, Ft Wayne, 74-82; instr workshops. *Awards:* Best of Show NWS Purchase, Nat Watercolor Soc, 93; Cash Award & Purchase Award, Watercolor USA, 94; Merit Award, Rocky Mountain Watermedia Nat, 94 & 2001. *Bibliog:* Gerald Brommer (auth), Collage Techniques; Nita Leland & Virginia Williams (coauths), Creative Collage Techniques, 94; The Best of Watercolor, Rockport Publ, 96. *Mem:* Nat Watercolor Soc; Allied Artists Am; Watercolor USA Honor Soc; Am Watercolor Soc (bd dir, 92); Rocky Mountain Watermedia Soc. *Media:* Transparent Watercolor, Drawings & Fiber Art. *Specialty:* Fine art. *Interests:*

Golf, camping and travel. *Collection:* Nat Accademy of Design, Indiana University, Fort Wayne Museum of Art. *Publ:* The Best of Watercolor II, Rockport Publ, 98. *Dealer:* Editions Limited Indianapolis IN; Cain Gallery Saugatuck MI & Oak Park IL; Prince Royal Gallery Alexandria Va. *Mailing Add:* 1541 N Claylick Rd Nashville IN 47448

BROWN, PETER C
SCULPTOR, PAINTER
b Port Chester, NY, Oct 10, 40. *Study:* Ohio Wesleyan Univ, BFA, 63; Cranbrook Acad of Art, MFA, 65. *Work:* Dannheiser Found, NY, The Prudential, NY, Brooklyn Union Gas Co, Brooklyn, NY; First Nat Bank Chicago, Ill; Sydney & Frances Lewis Found, Richmond, Va; Miami Univ Art Mus, Oxford, Ohio. *Exhib:* solo exhibs, 55 Mercer Gallery, NY, 80 & 82, Harm Bouckaert Gallery, NY, 82 & 84, Queens Mus, Flushing, NY, 82, M-13 Gallery, NY, 87 & 88, Winston Gallery, Wash, DC, 87; Approaches to Abstractions, Shanghai Exhib Ctr, Shanghai, China, 86; Dwellings, Althea Viatora Gallery, NY, 87; Vital Forces, Nature in Contemp Abstraction, Hecksher Mus, Huntington, NY, 91; Ten From Queens Mus, Paine Webber Gallery, NY, 92; Howard Scott Gallery, NY, 94 & 97; Grossman Gallery, Lafayette Col, Easton, Pa, 2003. *Teaching:* Asst prof fine art, Western Col, Oxford, Ohio, 65-70; instr painting, Philadelphia Art Mus, 71-72; prof fine art, LaGuardia Col, City Univ NY, 73-02. *Awards:* Creative Artists Pub Serv Prog Fel, NY State Coun Arts, 83-84; Fel, New York Found Arts, 85; Research Award, City Univ New York, 85, 88. *Bibliog:* Corinne Robins, rev, Sculpture, 3/89; Karin Lipson (auth), Nature in the abstract, around us and within, Newsday, 7/26/91; Helen Harrison (auth), The natural world and its mysteries, NY Times, 8/11/91. *Media:* Wood, Acrylics

BROWN, PETER THOMSON
PHOTOGRAPHER, EDUCATOR
b Northampton, Mass, June 5, 48. *Study:* Stanford Univ, BA, 71, MFA, 77. *Work:* Mus Fine Arts, Houston; Mus Mod Art NY; San Francisco Mus Mod Art; Stanford Univ Mus Art; Menil Collection, Houston. *Comn:* Rice Univ, 88-91. *Exhib:* Tony Cronin Mem Exhib, Mus Fine Arts, Houston, Tex, 79; Color from the Collection, Mus Fine Arts, Houston, 82; one-man shows, Art Alliance, Philadelphia, Pa, 82, Art Ctr, Waco, Tex, 83, Canon Gallery, Amsterdam, The Neth, 84, Alphaville Gallery, Piacenza, Italy, 84, Tyler Mus, Tex, 85 & Farrish Gallery, Rice Univ, 90; The Prehistoric in Contemp Art, NY State Mus, 89; The Mundy Collection, Mus Fine Arts, Houston, 91; The Pleasures and Terrors of Domestic Comfort, Mus Mod Art, NY, 91; Seeing the Forest Through the Trees, Contemp Art Mus, Houston, 92; Light Fantastic, Laguna Gloria Mus, Austin, 94; Recent Acquisitions, San Francisco Mus Mod Art, 94; and others. *Teaching:* Lectr photog, Stanford Univ, 76-77; prof photog, Rice Univ, 78-92; lectr, continuing ed(photog), Rice, 92-. *Awards:* Imogen Cunningham Award, 82; Fel, Nat Endowment Arts, 90; fel, Graham Found, 96; and others. *Bibliog:* April Rapier (auth), Amazing stories, Houston Ctr Photog Quart, winter 85; Lynn Herbert (auth), High plains/palin views, Cite, fall 90; Susan Chadwick (auth), Photography shows state of the art, Houston Post, 3/24/94. *Mem:* Col Art Asn; Soc Photog Educ; Houston Fotofest; Houston Ctr Photog. *Media:* Chromogenic Color Prints, Gleatin Silver Prints. *Publ:* Auth, Our town, Aperture, spring 92; The Pleasures and Terrors of Domestic Comfort, Mus Mod Art Press, 92; H A C Brummett, Lawyer, Life, 97; Great Plains, Doubletake, 98; On the Plains, WW Norton/Doubletake BK, 99. *Dealer:* Harris Gallery 1100 Bissonnet Houston TX 77006; Sandy Carson Gallery 1734 Wazee St Denver CO 80202. *Mailing Add:* 1113 Milford St Houston TX 77006

BROWN, PETEY
PAINTER
b W Orange, NJ. *Study:* Boston Univ Sch Fine and Applied Arts, BFA (painting), 75; Boston Univ Grad Sch Painting, 76. *Comn:* Hyatt Regency Hotel, Tampa, Fla, Four Seasons Hotel, Maui, Hawaii, Meridien at Coronado, San Diego, Hyatt Regency Hotel, Waikiki, Hawaii, Embassy Suites Hotel, Parsippany, NJ, Floridian Hotel, Vero Beach, Fla, Conrad Hotel, Uruguay. *Exhib:* One woman shows at Newton Arts Ctr, Massachusetts, 81, 84, Helen Shlein Gallery, Boston, 83, Patricia Heesy Gallery, NY City, 85, 86, David Brown Gallery, Provincetown, Massachusetts, David Brown Gallery, 87, Hunsaker/Schlesinger Gallery, Los Angeles, 89; group shows at Salem State Col, NH, 77, Cambridge Art Asn, Mass, 78, Fed Reserve Bank, Boston, 79, Danforth Mus, Framingham, Mass, 81, Helen Shlien Gallery, Boston, 82, Boston Visual Artists Union, 83, Provincetown Group Gallery Invitational, 84, Patricia Heesy Gallery, NY City, 85, 86, 87, Baltimore Mus Art, 86, Van Straaten Gallery, Chicago, 88, Hunsaker/Schlesinger Gallery, Los Angeles, 89, Gallery 99, Miami, 89, OIA Gallery, NY City, 90, Artists Space, 92, Gallery 148, NY City, 95, 96, New Art Ctr, 97, AIR Gallery, 2000, 2001, I-20 Gallery, 2003, Nat Acad Design Invitational, 2006. *Mailing Add:* 450 Broome St New York NY 10013

BROWN, ROBERT K
DEALER
b Springfield, Mass, May 22, 42. *Study:* Boston Univ, BS; Annenberg Sch Commun, Univ Pa, MCommun Arts. *Pos:* Dir & co-owner, Reinhold-Brown Gallery, New York, currently. *Mem:* Antiquarian Booksellers Asn Am; Int League Booksellers. *Specialty:* Rare posters relating to the early avant-garde including constructivism, functionalism, art nouveau-deco, Vienna secession; rare books on 20th century art and architecture. *Publ:* Contribr, Art Deco Minneapolis Inst, 70; ed, Art in Design in Vienna, 72; auth, Art Deco Internationale, Quick Fox, 77. *Mailing Add:* 120 E 86th St No 6B New York NY 10028-1062

BROWN, SARAH M
PAINTER, INSTRUCTOR
b Longview, Tex, Jan 30, 35. *Study:* Univ Chicago & Art Inst Chicago, BFA (with honors in figure drawing & figure paining), 1957; student, Tulane Univ, 1960, Odyssey Studio, Atlanta, 1978 & Watercolor Seminar, 1980. *Work:* former Pres Jimmy Carter; Sen Geraldine Ferraro; Reynolds Plantation; Great Waters, Eatonton, Ga; St Ives Country Club; Yoshima Ibashi, Asahi Inc, Tokyo; Portrait of Michael Feinstein, Calif State La; poster, Ducks Unlimited, Ga; mural, Road to War, AH Stephens Mem; portrait, Franklin D Roosevelt, Warm Springs Lodge. *Exhib:* One-woman shows, Longview (Tex) Art Asn, Pensacola Art Asn & Douglasville Cult Arts Ctr, 1995; Festival of the Masters, Lake Buena Vista, Fla; Knickerbocker Artists 31st Ann, NY; Catherine Lorillard Wolfe Art Club Exhibit; Nat Western Small Painting Exhib, Bosque Farms, NMex; Palm Beach Galleries, New Orleans; ABC Art and Frame Show, Atlanta, 1995; Safari Int Exhib, Galleria Mall, Atlanta, 1995; Callawolde Cult Arts Ctr, 2001; Delgado Mus No, La. *Pos:* dir art dept, Pensacola Adult Vocat Sch, 58-59; owner, Sarah Brown Studio-Gallery, New Orleans, 59-63, Atlanta, 63-89 & Roswell, Ga, 86-89; owner, Sarah Brown Studio-Gallery, Atlanta, 89-; founder, Sarah Brown Tours, 73-; The Little Brown Press, 76-. *Teaching:* ceramics, drawing & painting, Pensacola (Fla) Jr Col, 58; condr, seminars in field. *Awards:* Best of Show, 1st Place Nat Western Small Painting Exhib, 1982; 3rd Place show, 1st Place western category, Palm Beach Galleries; 1st place oils, NLAPW Ga State Competition. *Bibliog:* Articles in Veranda Mag, Ga. Wildlife Fedn Mag & Southeastern Wildlife Expo Dir. *Mem:* Nat League Am Pen Women; Nat Mus Women in the Arts (charter); Portrait Soc Am Inc; Atlanta Zool Soc; Ga Wildlife Fedn. *Media:* oil, watercolor. *Specialty:* Portraits, landscapes, florals & wildlife. *Interests:* Piano & golf. *Dealer:* Richard James Galleries Charleston SC; Keep It Art Sea Lincoln City Ore; Magnolia Gallery Greensboro Ga

BROWN, STEPHEN PAT
PAINTER, SCULPTOR
b Greeley, Colo, Aug 26, 50. *Study:* Colo State Univ, BFA, 72; Skowhegan Sch Painting & Sculpture, with Paul Georges, 72; Art Students League, with Gabriel Laderman; Brooklyn Col, with Philip Pearlstein, Allan D'Arcangelo, Lennart Anderson & Lois Dodd, MFA, 78. *Work:* Colo State Univ Gallery, Ft Collins; collections appear at Hosta Mus, New Bntain Mus of Am Art, The Speed Mus, The Albany Mus, Mattatuck Mus. *Exhib:* New Realism, Terrain Gallery, NY, 80; one-man show, Rosenberg Gallery, NY, 82; Hobart & William Smith Col, Geneva, NY, 82; Cortlandt Univ Gallery, NY, 82; Bodies and Souls, Artists Choice Mus, NY, 83; Contemp Am Still Life, One Penn Plaza, NY, 85; First Eight Years, Artists Choice Mus, 85; Life That Is Still, Sherry French Gallery, NY, 86; 161st Ann, Nat Acad Design, 86; Allan Stone Gallery, New York City, 87; Prince St Gallery, Rockefeller Gallery, State Univ of NY at Fredonia, 88; group show Allan Stone Gallery, 89. *Pos:* Studio asst, Alice Neel, NY, 74-75. *Teaching:* Guest artist studio art, La State Univ, 79; instr printmaking, Sch Art League, Brooklyn, NY, 79-80; guest lectr painting, Cortlandt Univ, NY, 82; artist-in-residence, Parsons Sch Design, 83, vis artist, 85, guest lectr, 86; Asst prof, Hartford Univ, 1988-. *Awards:* Charles Shaw Painting Scholar, Brooklyn Col, 78; Yaddo Residency, NY State Coun Arts, 79; Millay Residency, Edna St Vincent Millay, 80; recipient, Acad Award in Art, Am Acad of Arts and Letters, 94. *Bibliog:* Harold Lujar (auth), Stephen Brown, Arts Mag, 11/78; John Perrault (auth), New talent in NY, Soho Weekly News, 79; Michael Brenson (auth), Contemporary American still life, New York Times, 7/5/85; Judd Tully (auth), Still life feast, Art World, 85. *Mem:* Nat Acad. *Media:* Oil. *Mailing Add:* 47 Barnard Rd Granville MA 01034-9514

BROWN, SUSAN LT (HAVILAND SLIZYS)
PAINTER, SCULPTOR
b Upper Saddle River, NJ, May 30, 47. *Study:* Western Ky Univ, BA, 81; Univ Ariz, BFA, 82, MA, 84. *Work:* Balzekas Mus Lithuanian Cult, Chicago; NJ State Mus, Trenton; Los Angeles Co Mus Art; Roswell Mus Art, NMex; Lithuanian Ctr Contemp Art, Vilnius, Lithuania. *Comn:* Naples Italy (mural), Allstate Insurance Co, Burbank, Calif, 65; Children of the World (painting), Simi Valley Sch Dist, Calif, 72; Chipmunks in Spring (painting), UNICEF-UN, NY, 91; Christmas in the Park (art wreath), Tohono Chul Park, Tucson, Ariz, 94. *Exhib:* Curatoral Selection, Smithsonian Mus Mod & Contemp Art/Hirshhorn Mus Sculpt, Washington, 90, 2000, 2002, 2003; Art for Fine Causes, Tucson Mus Art, Ariz, 91; Daile 1991, Developmental Stages, Ciurlionis Art Gallery, Chicago, Ill, 91; The Death-Born in the USA, Lithuanian Mus Art, Lemont, Ill, 93; Daile 1993, Ciurlionis Art Gallery, Chicago, 93; Ind Univ Lithuanian Art, Ind Art Gallery, Gary, 93; Love-Meile Art Exhib, Ciurlionis Art Gallery, Chicago, 94; Lake Oswego Art Festival, Oreg, 2000; Lake Oswego Art Festival, Oreg, 2000, 2002. *Pos:* supt art, Clackamas Co, Oreg, 99-2000. *Awards:* Bagel Art Award, Lenders Bagel Nat Art Contest, 83; Visual Artists Fel, Nat Endowment Arts, 88; Art in Pub Places Award, Tucson Pub Comn, 89. *Bibliog:* Shannon Martindale (auth), Designing Women in Art, 89; Jay Rochlin (auth), Animaskures New Art Form, 89; Sheryl Borden (auth), Creative Living-Susan LT Brown, Plastic Art, 91-92. *Media:* Acrylic, Mixed Media; Wood, Clay. *Publ:* auth, Silly A to Z's of Arizona, 90; contribr, Arts & Crafts Catalyst Mag, Ind, Ann Porter, 90; Lithuanian Artists in North America, Galerijia, Al Kezys, 94; Encyclopedia Leidykla, Vilnius, Lithuania B Juodiene, 96-97; Beverly McFarland (auth), Calyx Jour, vol 21, 2003. *Dealer:* Aligimantas Kezys 4317 S Wisconsin Ave Stickney IL 60402

BROWNETT, THELMA DENYER
PAINTER, RESTORER
b Jacksonville, Fla, Oct 26, 1924. *Study:* Wesleyan Conserv, BFA(magna cum laude), 46, with Emile Holzhauer; Columbia Univ, 48, with Dr Edwin Ziegfield; Univ Ga, MFA, 52, with Lamar Dodd, James Johnson Sweeny & William Zorack. *Work:* Ga Mus Art, Athens; Gertrude Herbert Art Mus, Augusta, Ga; Atlanta Art Mus, Ga; Ringling Mus Art, Sarasota, Fla; also pvt collections in the US & abroad. *Comn:* Mural, Puppet Playhouse, Augusta, Ga, 51; hundreds of portraits, 56-; Reredos, St Peter's Church, Jacksonville, Fla, 58; Triptych, St Mark's Episcopal Church, Jacksonville, 63; mural, Off Bldg, San Jose Plaza, Jacksonville, 65. *Exhib:* High Mus Art, Atlanta; Ga Mus Art, Athens; Columbia Mus Art, SC; Beaumount Art Mus, Tex;

Bradenton Art Mus, Fla; Retrospective Exhib, Kent Campus, Fla Jr Col, Jacksonville, 84. *Pos:* Dir, Gertrude Herbert Art Inst, 51-55; art comnr, State of Ga, 54-57; chmn visual arts, Arts Festival Eleven, Jacksonville, 68-69; dir & owner, Art Unlimited 92, Jacksonville, 75-. *Teaching:* Chmn dept art, Augusta Col, 52-55 & Jacksonville Univ, 56-58; chmn dept art, Fla Jr Col, 65-70, prof art, 70-; restorer of paintings, pvt studio, 56-, Oxford Stained Glass Studio, 86-. *Mem:* Asn Ga Artists (pres, 53-55); Fedn Fla Artists (bd dir, 57-59); Jackson Coun Arts (mem bd dir, 69-); Fla Artist Group (secy-treas, 74-). *Media:* Oil Paints, Stained Glass. *Publ:* Auth, Painting, Student Handbook, 71, 75, 78 & 83; Painting, Studio Handbook, 78 & 83

BROWNING, COLLEEN
PAINTER
b Fermoy, Co Cork, Ireland; US citizen. *Study:* Slade Sch Art, London, Eng. *Work:* NY State Mus, Albany; Detroit Art Inst; Columbia Mus, SC; Milwaukee Art Ctr; St Louis Art Mus, Mo; and others. *Comn:* Olympic Editions 1976 (lithograph); Kent Bicentennial Portfolio (lithograph). *Exhib:* Five shows, Whitney Mus Am Art Contemp Ann, NY, 51-63; Art Inst Chicago, 54; solo exhibs, 7 at Kennedy Galleries, 68-69, Towson State Col, Md, 78 & Whichita Mus, 87; Cleveland Mus, Ohio, 75; Indianapolis Mus, Ind, 76; Butler Mus Am Art, 91; Nev Mus Art, 94; Southern Alleghenies Mus, Pa, 97; Thomas T Walsh Art Gallery, Fairfield Univ, Conn, 97-98; Rahr West Art Mus, Manitowoc, Wis, 97-98; Charles B Goddard Ctr Visual Arts, Okla, 97-98; Okla City Mus, 97-98. *Teaching:* Instr painting & drawing, City Col NY, 60-76; instr, Nat Acad Design, 79-81. *Awards:* Figure Composition Award, Stanford Univ, 56; Second Prize for oils, Butler Inst Am Art, 60 & 74; Adolph & Clara Obrig Prize, Nat Acad Design, 70; Art Medal Merit, Butler Art Inst, Ohio, 74. *Bibliog:* Jerry Tallmer (auth), NY Post, 76, 79 & 89; Greta Berman (auth), Arts Int, 8/84; Jim Auer (auth), article, Milwaukee J, 89. *Mem:* Academician Nat Acad Design (corresp secy, 72-73). *Media:* Oil. *Publ:* Illusr, Portrait of a Lady, Ltd Ed Club, 67; Every Man Heart Look Down, Crowell-Collier, 70; Downtown Is, McGraw-Hill, 72; Working Out a Painting, Watson-Guptill, 88; Can't Sit Still, Dutton Childrens Bks, 95. *Dealer:* Harmon Meek Gallery 601 Fifth Ave S Naples FL. *Mailing Add:* care of Kennedy Galleries 40 W 57th St New York NY 10019

BROWNING, DIXIE BURRUS
PAINTER, WRITER
b Elizabeth City, NC, Sept 9, 30. *Study:* Mary Washington Col; Richmond Prof Inst; and with Barclay Sheaks, Ray Prohaska & Ric Chin. *Work:* US Coast Guard Mus, New London, Conn; Statesville Mus Arts & Sci, NC; Duke Hosp Collection, Durham, NC; Wachovia Bank & Trust, Z Smith Reynolds Found, Winston-Salem. *Exhib:* Marine Exhib, James River Juried, Mariners Mus, Newport News, Va; Irene Leache Mem Biennial, Norfolk Mus Art, Va, 68; Regional Gallery Art, Boone, NC, 71 & 74; Manufacturers Hanover Trust Gallery, NY, 71; Southeastern Ctr for Contemp Art, Winston-Salem, 76. *Pos:* Founder & co-dir, Art Gallery Originals, Winston-Salem, 68-73; co-dir, Art V Gallery, Clemmons, NC, 74-75; pres, co-owner, Browning Artworks, Ltd, Frisco (Cape Hatteras) NC, 84-. *Teaching:* Teacher watercolor & acrylics, Arts & Crafts Asn Inc, Winston-Salem, 67-73; watercolor lectr & demonstr in schs & art orgns, NC, currently. *Awards:* Three First Prizes & one Second Prize, Southport Art Festival, 67, 68 & 71; Best in Show, Asn Artists NC, 71; Third Prize, Watercolor Soc NC, 76. *Bibliog:* Ola Mae Foushee (auth), North Carolina Artists, Univ NC; Anthony Swider (auth), Going to the Gallery, Winston-Salem & Forsyth Co Sch Syst, 69; Ward Nicholls (auth), Artists & Craftsmen in North Carolina, Wilks Art Guild, 74. *Mem:* Int Soc Artists; Assoc Artists Winston-Salem (vpres, 68-69); Watercolor Soc NC (co-organizer & pres, 72-73); Winston-Salem Arts Coun; Arts & Crafts Asn, Inc. *Media:* Watercolor, Chinese Ink. *Publ:* Illusr, North Carolina Parade, Univ NC, 66; contribr, Drawing & Painting the Natural Environment, Davis, 74; auth introd, Artists/USA 79-80, Found Advan Artists; auth film, Acrylics, The Contemporary Colors, Hunt Mfg Co. *Mailing Add:* 5316 Robinhood Rd Winston-Salem NC 27106

BROWNING, MARK DANIEL
PAINTER, SCULPTOR
b Miles City, Mont, Dec 26, 46. *Study:* Self taught. *Work:* Plains Art Mus, Moorhead, Minn & Fargo, ND; USDA/Human Nutrition Res Ctr & Univ NDak, Grand Forks, NDak; Custer Co Art Ctr, Miles City, Mont; Pillsbury Co/Corp Offs, Minneapolis. *Exhib:* Solo exhibs, Yellowstone Art Ctr, Billings, Mont, 81, Talley Gallery, Bemidji State Univ, Minn, 83, Plains Art Mus, Moorehead, Minn, 84 & Bismark Art Gallery, NDak, 92; 113th Am Watercolor Soc, Salmagundi Club, NY, 80; Watercolor USA, Springfield Art Mus, Mo, 82, 83 & 90; 10th Midwest Watercolor Soc, Neville Mus, Green Bay, Wis, 86; Collection of Mid-Am Artists, Art Ctr Minn, Wayzata, 87; and many others. *Pos:* Dir & bd dir, Custer Co Art Ctr, 76-79; pres, Mont Inst Arts, 76-78, bd dir, 76-81; studio artist & gallery owner, 79-; pres, Greater Grand Forks Arts & Humanities Asn, 86-88; exec dir, Custer Co Art Ctr, 95-; adv panel mem, Mont Cult & Aesthetic Trust, 96-; pres bd dir, Mont Art Gallery Dirs Asn, currently. *Awards:* Purchase Selection, Am Art, Pillsbury Co, 80; Honorable Mention, Midwest Watercolor Soc, Manitowoc, Wis, 80; Purchase Award, Midwestern Invitational, Plains Art Mus, 85. *Bibliog:* Sebby Wilson Jacobson (auth), Zaner gallery review, Times-Union, Rochester, NY, 85; Ron Netsky (auth), Art Agenda, Democrat & Chronicle, Rochester, NY, 85. *Mem:* Mont Arts Coun; signature mem Midwest Watercolor Soc; NDak Coun Arts; signature mem Nat Watercolor Soc. *Media:* Watercolor; Smooth Surface, Non-Traditional. *Publ:* Creative Watercolor, Rockport Publ

BRUBAKER, JACK
SCULPTOR, BLACKSMITH, DESIGNER, PAINTER
b Chicago, Ill, Aug 30, 44. *Study:* studied painting & drawing with Mary Brubaker, also at Art Inst Chicago, 64, Syracuse Univ, BFA, 66, Ind Univ, MFA, 68. *Work:* Joseph Hirshhorn Collection, Naples, Fla; Ind Univ Mus, Bloomington; and many others; Larry Hagman Collection; Douglas Cramer Collection; Ali McGraw Collection. *Comn:* Architectural works for pvt residences, pub bldgs, and churches. *Exhib:* Let There Be Light, Nat Ornamental Metal Mus, Memphis, Tenn, 84; Contemp Iron 87, traveling show, 87-89; solo exhib, Indianapolis Mus Art, Ind, 87, Jack Brubaker Sculpture, Judi Rotenburg Gallery, Boston, 89, Jack Brubaker Hand Forged Metals, Indianapolis Mus Art, 87; and many others in US & Europe; Sculpture, Bell Ross Gallery, 88; Toys, Metal Mus, 2000; Windvanes and Whirlygigs, Metal Mus, 2000; plus others. *Pos:* owner Jack Brubaker Designs. *Teaching:* teacher, advanced blacksmithing and design workshops for profls. *Awards:* Gold Trouser Button, Ctr for Metal Design, Aachen, WGer, 86. *Bibliog:* D Meilach (auth), Decorative and Sculptural Ironwork, Schiffer Pub, 2000; D Meilach (auth), The Contemporary Blacksmith, Schiffer Pub, 2000; D Meilach (auth), Direct Metal Sculpture, Schiffer Pub, 2000. *Mem:* Artist Blacksmith Asn Am (pres, 83-84); Brit Artist Blacksmith Asn. *Media:* Hot forged iron, bronze, copper, aluminum, paint. *Specialty:* Design history, sailing, boatbuilding. *Publ:* Dir, Forging Stone Cutting Tools (video), Artist Blacksmith Am, 81; and many others. *Mailing Add:* 5035 Earl Young Rd Bloomington IN 47408

BRUDER, HAROLD JACOB
PAINTER, EDUCATOR
b Bronx, NY, Aug 31, 30. *Study:* Cooper Union, cert, 51; New Sch Social Res; Pratt Graphic Art Ctr. *Work:* NJ State Mus, Trenton; Sheldon Mem Gallery, Lincoln, Nebr; Hirshhorn Mus, Washington, DC; Univ NMex Mus. *Exhib:* Corcoran Gallery Biennale, Washington, DC, 63; Modern Realism & Surrealism, Am Fedn Arts Traveling Show, 64, The Realist Revival, 72-73; 22 Realists, Whitney Mus Am Art, NY, 70; Aspects of the Figure, Cleveland Mus Art, 74; Am Family Portraits, Philadelphia Mus Art, 76; one-man shows, Armstrong Gallery, NY, 84 & 86 & Contemp Realist Gallery, San Francisco, 88; and others. *Pos:* Artist-in-residence, Aspen Sch Contemp Art, summer 67. *Teaching:* Assoc prof art, Kansas City Art Inst, 63-65; vis lectr, Pratt Inst, 65-66; prof emer art, Queens Col, 65-95, chmn art dept, 82-85. *Awards:* Purchase Prize, Am Acad Arts Letters, 78; PSC-BHE Fac Res Award, 76, 79, 84 & 88; Nat Endowment Arts Grant, 85-86. *Bibliog:* Ralph Pomeroy (auth), Harold Bruder and immediate family, Art & Artists, 10/68; Alan Gussow (interviewer), A sense of place, Saturday Rev Press, 72; Ralph Pomeroy (auth), Harold Bruder's Metaphors, Arts, 10/82. *Media:* Oil. *Publ:* Auth, Notes from the Prado, Art J, fall 72; Monumental Miniatures: The Drawings of Pierre Bonnard & Edward Vuillard, Drawing, 3-4/92; Breaking the ice: Emma Eames in search of the ideal, Opera Quart, winter 92; Romanized and romanticized: Mantegna's great Judith, Drawing, 9-10/92; Using linear rhythms for composition, Am Artist, 1/97. *Dealer:* Mitchell Algus Gallery 511 W 25th St 2nd Fl New York NY 10001

BRULC, LILLIAN G
PAINTER, SCULPTOR
b Joliet, Ill. *Study:* Art Inst Chicago, MFA(George D Brown Foreign Travel Fel), 64; Univ Chicago, MFA, 64; also with Franz Gorse, Austria. *Work:* Major works in permanent archit environ, smaller works in pvt collections. *Comn:* life-size bronze, mural, environ design, SVD Theologate, Chicago, 79-80; bronze relief, 83 & mural & mosaic, 86, Iron Range Interpretative Ctr, Chisholm, Minn; Holocaust Mem bronze & ceramic, Joliet Jewish Congregation Temple, Joliet, Ill, 89; bronze bas relief, Capitol Develop Bd, State of Ill, 92; series of 6 large murals, St Elizabeth Seton Church, Naperville, Ill, 2000; restoration ceiling murals, Daprato-Rigali Co, Chicago, 2004; and others. *Exhib:* Prints, Drawings & Watercolors 2nd Biennial by Ill Artists, Art Inst Chicago, 64; one-woman show, Drawings & Lithographs, Casa de Escultura, Panama City, 69; Murals for People (slide of Chicago works), Mus Contemp Art, Chicago, 71; 3rd Ann Celebration Women's Day, Erector Sq Gallery, New Haven, Conn, 88; Gallery Genesis, Chicago, 88, 89, 90, 91, 92 & 93; Univ Wis, Milwaukee, 94; Art Colony, Most Na Soci, Slovenia, 96; paintings, prints and drawings, Courtyard Gallery, CTU, Chicago, 2004. *Pos:* Artist-in-residence, Chicago Archdiocese Panama Mission, San Miguelito, 65-70, art adv & part-time resident, 73-79; artist-in-residence, Archdiocesan Latin Am Comt, Chicago, 71-72 & SVD Theologate, Chicago, 79-80; consult, Gallery Genesis, Chicago, 88; adv bd, Ill State Mus, Lockport, 95-97. *Teaching:* Asst instr lithography, Art Inst Chicago, 61-64; lectr theol & art, Divine Word Sem, Techny, Ill, 66-68; instr design, mat, portrait & drawing, Chicago Acad Fine Arts, 72-78. *Awards:* Merit Award, Slovenian Arts Coun, Univ Wis, Milwaukee, 94; Grant, Slovenian Arts Coun, Univ Wis, Milwaukee, 94; Resident, Artists' Colony, Slovenia, 96. *Bibliog:* Charlando (TV presentation), Univ Chicago WGN-9, 68; Edward Gobetz (auth), Lillian Brulc, Painter, Sculptor, Printmaker, Success Stories, SRCA; Mario Lewis Morgan (auth), Lillian Brulc Y Los Murales De San Miguelito, Panama City, Panama, 97; Darja Groznik (auth), interview, JANA, Ljubljana, Yugoslavia, 88. *Mem:* Environ & Art Comt, Archdiocese of Chicago; Chicago Women's Caucus for Art; Chicago Artists' Coalition. *Media:* Acrylic; Bronze. *Publ:* illusr, Thirsting For the Lord, Alba House, 76; auth, Visit with Franz Gorse in Carinthia, Austria, SRCA Publ, 78; illusr, Dream Visions, SRCA Publ; Old Testament Message (23 vols), Michael Glazier Inc; illusr, State Historical Soc. Murals, 94. *Dealer:* Studio L' Atelier. *Mailing Add:* L' Atelier 909 Summit Joliet IL 60435

BRUMER, MIRIAM
PAINTER
b New York, NY, Oct 7, 39. *Study:* Univ Miami, BA(art & Eng); Boston Univ, MFA(painting). *Work:* Chase Manhattan Bank, Citibank, NY; Boston Univ, Mass; Bell Labs, NJ; and many pvt collections; Payne Gallery Art, Moravian Col, Pa. *Comn:* Painting for office, NY Bank Savings, 73. *Exhib:* A Woman's Place: The Central Hall Gallery in the 1970's, Mus Stonybrook, NY, 96; A Woman's Place: Central Hall Gallery Artists in the 90's, Gallery North, Setauket, NY, 96; Found and funky, Hunterdon Art Ctr, Clinton, NJ, 97-98; one woman show The World Imagined, Payne Gallery Moravian Col, Bethlehem, Pa, 2001, Conant Hall, Princeton, 2002, Wooster Arts Space, NY, 2005; City Without Walls, NJ, 2000, 02; Obsession/Fixation,

Invitational, Ceres Gallery, NY, 2002; Nat Arts Club, NY, 2003; Skoto Gallery, NY, 2005. *Pos:* Writer & ed, Feminist Art J, NY, 72-74; educator, Queens Mus, 87-. *Teaching:* Asst prof studio art & art hist, NY Inst Technol, Old Westbury, 69-75; instr, Hunter Col, 76-81 & New York Univ, 83-; lectr studio art & art hist, Marymount Manhattan Col, New York, 83-; lectr art, The Looking Series, Queens Mus Art, 89-. *Awards:* Ludwig Vogelstein Found Grant, 76-77; Comt Visual Arts Grants, 79 & 80; Artist-in-Residence, NY Found Arts, 85; Artspeak, Will Grant, 87, 90. *Bibliog:* Kay Kenny (auth), Views by Women Artists, 82; Michele Kidwell (auth), Miriam Brumer, Arts Mag, (in prep); Diana Morris (auth), Eight, Women Artist News, 83; Michelle Kidwell (auth), Miriam Brumer, Arts Mag; Hedy O'Beil (auth), More than meets the eyes, Arts, 5/84; The Mojo of Masks, Dan Bischoff (auth), The Star Ledger, 8/2000; Sheila McKenna (auth), Miriam Brumer, Newsday, 9/5/2000; Myra Yellin Outwater (auth), Small Intimate Pieces Reveal Artist's Enormous Range, The Morning Call, 3/2001; Dan Bischoff (auth), Newark Show Uncovers 'Hidden Things', The Newark Star Ledger, 2/2002; Tony Sienzant (auth), Imagining Worlds Unseen, The Easton Times, 3/2001. *Media:* Acrylic, Assemblage. *Mailing Add:* 250 W 94th St New York NY 10025

BRUMER, SHULAMITH
SCULPTOR, INSTRUCTOR
b Russia, July 5, 24; US citizen. *Study:* Art Students League, with William Zorach; Columbia Univ, with Oronzio Malderelli. *Work:* Philbrook Art Ctr, Tulsa, Okla; Va Mus Fine Art, Richmond; State Univ NY, Plattsburgh; HAWA NAVA Collection, Zimmerli Mus, Rutgers Univ. *Exhib:* One-man show, Mus Fine Arts, Plattsburgh, NY; Philbrook Mus, Tulsa, Okla; Nat Acad Design, NY; Riverside Mus, NY; Va Mus Fine Arts; Bergen Mus, NJ. *Teaching:* Instr stone & wood carving, Sculpture Ctr Art Sch, 71-80. *Awards:* Knickerbocker Prizes, 57, 76 & 80; Gold Medal, Allied Artists, 86; Gold Medal, Knickerbocker Artists, 87; Silver Medal, Allied Artist, 96. *Mem:* Am Asn Contemp Artists; Nat Asn Women Artists; Audubon Artists; Allied Artists; Knickerbocker Artists. *Media:* Stone, Bronze. *Mailing Add:* 1 Union Square W New York NY 10003

BRUMFIELD, WILLIAM CRAFT
PHOTOGRAPHER
b Charlotte, NC, Jun 28, 44. *Study:* Tulane Univ, BA, 1966; Univ Calif, Berkeley, MA, 1968, PhD, 1973. *Work:* New Orleans Mus of Art, La; Nat Gallery of Art, Photographic Archives, Washington, DC; Libr of Congress, Prints and Photog's, Washington, DC; Arkhangelsk Mus of Art, Arkhangelsk, Russia; Nat Mus of Archit, Moscow, Russia. *Exhib:* Lost Russia: Duke Univ Mus of Art, Durham, NC, New Orleans Mus of Art, La, 1996-97, Univ of Mich Mus of Art, Ann Arbor, 1997-98; The Romanov Legacy, Memphis Brooks Mus of Art, Tenn, 1997-98; Orthodox Shrines of the North, Arkhangelsk Mus of Art, Arkhangelsk, Russia, 1999-2000; The Russian North, Nat Mus of Archit, Moscow, Russia, 2001. *Pos:* Cur, William C Brumfield Collection Univ Wash, Seattle, 2003 . *Teaching:* Asst prof, Harvard Univ, Cambridge, Mass, 1974-79; assoc prof, Univ Va, 1985-86; prof, Tulane Univ, New Orleans, La, 1981-. *Awards:* Notable book of the year award, NY Times Book Review, 1993; AAUP award, Illustration book category, 1996; Fel, Guggenheim Found, 2000. *Mem:* Russian Acad of Archit; Inst of Modern Russian Cult; Soc of Archit Historians; Soc of Historians of East European & Russian Art; Russian Acad of the Arts (hon mem 2006). *Res:* The history and photographic documentation of Russian Architecture. *Publ:* Auth, photogr, Gold in Azure, David Godine, 1983; auth, Origins of Modernism Russian Archit, Univ of Calif, 1991; auth, photogr, Hist of Russian Archit, Cambridge Univ Press, 1993; auth, photogr, Lost Russia, Duke Univ Press, 1995; auth, photogr, Landmarks of Russian Archit, Gordan & Breach, 1997; auth, photogr, Vologda Album, Tri Quadrata, 2005. *Mailing Add:* Tulane University 305 Newcomb Hall New Orleans LA 70118

BRUMLEY, TOM
MUSEUM DIRECTOR
Pos: Installation coordr, New Mus Contemp Art, New York City, dir oper. *Mailing Add:* New Mus Contemp Art 556 W 22nd St New York NY 10011

BRUMMEL, MARILYN REEDER
COLLAGE ARTIST, PRINTMAKER
b Syracuse, NY, Dec 29, 26. *Study:* Syracuse Univ, BFA, 48; also studied with Roberto De La Monica, 72 & Krishna Reddy, 78. *Work:* Newark Mus, NJ; Passaic Co Hist Soc, NJ; Govt Off Bldg (NJ State Coun Arts), Atlantic City; Nat Elec Rural Co-op Asn, Washington, DC; Pub Serv Elec & Gas Co, Bergen Co, NJ. *Comn:* Odyssey (30 prints), Art Ctr NJ, Tenafly, 76; Cryogenic Landscape (print), Arde Inc, Norwood, NJ, 83. *Exhib:* Womens Show Invitational, Everson Mus, Syracuse, NY, 74; Nat Arts Club Show, NY, 74; Silvermine Guild Artists, New Canaan, 75; 1st Biennial NJ Artists, Newark Mus, 77; Print Club Ann, Philadelphia, Pa, 78; Audubon Artists Ann, Acad Design, NY, 81; solo exhibs, Transformed Visions, Printmaking Coun NJ, 97 & Time and Space, Interchurch Ctr, NY, 98. *Awards:* Gold Medal Award, Catherine Lorrilard Wolfe Ann, 78; Director's Award, Bergen Community Mus, 89; Best Contemp Award, Kerygama Gallery, 90. *Bibliog:* David Speiegler (auth), Art Review, Bergen Record, 71 & 78; John Zeamon (auth), Art Review, Bergen Record, 89. *Mem:* Nat Asn Women Artist (chmn, mem extn), 92-93; Printmaking Coun NJ; Art Ctr Painting Affiliates (co-chmn); Computer Art Prints Asn. *Media:* Miscellaneous. *Dealer:* Prints Etcetera 1517 163rd St Whitestone NY 11357

BRUNDAGE, SUSAN LOUNSBURY
DEALER
b Orange, NJ, June 18, 49. *Study:* Smith Col, BA, 71. *Work:* Paine Webber Inc, NY. *Pos:* Treas, White Columns, New York, 78-; dir, Leo Castelli Gallery, New York, 97, Sperone Westwater Gallery, 99-2001. *Mem:* Art Table. *Specialty:* Contemporary American & European art. *Publ:* Ed, Jasper Johns-35 Years with Leo Castelli; Bruce Nauman-25 Years with Leo Castelli; James Rosenquist-30 Years with Leo Castelli; Technique, Collaboration & The Prince of Japser Johns, 96. *Mailing Add:* 448 W 23rd St Apt 3R New York NY 10011

BRUNET-WEINMANN, MONIQUE
CRITIC, CURATOR
b Toulon, France, Apr 30, 43; Can citizen. *Study:* Univ Paris X, with Pierre Francastel, Ecole des Hautes Etudes, Diplome d'Etudes Superieures en Lettres, 67; Univ Montreal, MA(hist art), 90. *Collection Arranged:* Louise Gadbois Retrospective, 1932-1982 (with catalog), 83, James Guitet, Propositions, X Positions (with catalog), 88 & Pastel Quebecois Comtemporain, 92, Univ UQAM Gallery, Montreal; Copigraphy: What Happened to the Women Pioneers?, ISEA, Galerie Arts Technologiques, Montreal, 95; Christian Tisari, 1977-1997, Désordre et des astres, Maison des arts de Laval & Des ordres et desastre, Maison de la Culture Côte-des-Neiges, 98; D'où Venons-nous? Que sommes-nous? Gù allons-nous?, Maison de la cult Frontenac, Maison des arts de Laval, 2000; Photos Géniques, Maison des arts de Laval, 2000; Mutations de Riopelle, MAC des laurendides, 03-04. *Pos:* Art critic, freelance, Vie des Arts, Montreal, Que, 74- & Contemporanea, Provincetown Arts, Parcours, 90-; cur, freelance, Univ Gallery, UQAM Montreal, 83- & Maison des arts de Laval, 95-; pres, CRITIQ, Complexe de Realisations Independant Transculturel et Interartiel du Que, 89-; Musee d'art contemp des laurentides, 2003-. *Teaching:* Lectr Fr Lit, McGill Univ, 71-73. *Awards:* Grand Prix Lit Conseil de la culture des Laurentides, 93-. *Bibliog:* Entrevue avec Monique Brunet, La Parole métèque, no 33, 10/99. *Res:* life and work of Jean Paul Riopelle. *Specialty:* Works, paintings & drawings, by Louise Gadbois & James Guitet. *Collection:* contemp Quebec art: Benoit, Canfieni, Jaque, L Gadbois. *Publ:* contribr, Fluid Exchanges: Artists & Critics in the Aids Crisis, Univ Toronto Press, 92; La Copigraphie et ses Connexions, Hull, Montcalm CRITIQ, 93; Esthetique des Arts Mediatiques I, Presses de l'Universite du Quebec, 95; Jean-Paul Riopelle, des Visions d'Amerique, Ed de l'Homme, Montreal, 97; Catalogue Raisonné Jean Paul Riopelle, vol I 1939-53, Hibou éd, 99; CDRom, Copigraphy: Elements for a Global History, Loplop ed, Montreal, 2000; Raisonné, vol II 1954-59, Acatos 'ed, Paris, 2004 & Montreal, 2005. *Mailing Add:* 229 Des Bois Rd Rosemere PQ J7A 1S4 Canada

BRUNI, STEPHEN THOMAS
MUSEUM DIRECTOR
b Philadelphia, Feb 3, 49. *Study:* George Wash Univ, BA, 1971. *Pos:* Curatorial asst, Del Art Mus, Wilmington, 1972-74, prog asst, 1974-77, admin asst, 1977-79, mgr support servs, 1979-82, asst dir admin, 1982-84, deputy dir admin, 1984-85, acting dir admim, 1985-86, exec dir, 1986-; Mem arts selection comt, Del State Arts Coun, 1985-86, State Division Librs., 1984-86; mem Gov's Arts Adv Comt, 1983-85; mem adv bd, Siena Hall and Seton Villa, Creative Artists Network; bd dir, Studio Group, Inc. *Mem:* Am Asn Mus, Asn Art Mus Dir, Bd Greater Wilmington Conv and Visitors Bur. *Mailing Add:* Delaware Art Mus 2301 Kentmere Pkwy Wilmington DE 19806

BRUNI, UMBERTO
PAINTER, GRAPHIC ARTIST
b Montreal, Que, Nov 24, 1914. *Study:* With Guido Nincheri, Montreal, 30-37; Ecole Beaux-Arts, Montreal, grad prof, 37. *Comn:* Bust of Brother Andre, St Joseph Shrine, Montreal, 39; religious scene at church (fresco), Montreal, 58; historical scene (oil), Rougier et Freres, Montreal, 59; Da Giovanni (mosaic mural), Montreal, 60; religious mosaic mural, Ste Elizabeth Church, Ville Emard, Que, 61; portrait of ex-Prime Minister Sauve, Quebec Parliament. *Exhib:* Solo exhibs, Figuratif a L'Abstrait, Mus Beaux-Arts, Montreal, 61 & Giotto Art Gallery, Rome, Italy, 62; Can Artist in Paris, Maison Que, France, 62; Art Coun Can, O'Keefe Ctr, Toronto, 62; Univ Quebec, 77-86; and many others. *Pos:* Cur, Univ Que, Montreal, 70-80, founder & dir, Gallery, 74-80. *Teaching:* Prof, Ecole Beaux-Arts, Montreal, 47-69; prof, Univ Que, Montreal, 70-80; Retired. *Awards:* Fel to Rome & Paris, Art Coun Can, 61-62; Research Fel to Rome & Paris, Que Govt, 72. *Mem:* Royal Can Acad Arts; Acad Gentium Pro Pace, Rome; Int Inst Conserv Hist & Artistic Works. *Media:* All. *Interests:* Didactical presentation of exhibitions. *Publ:* Auth, Signatures, Marcel Broquet Ed, 81. *Mailing Add:* 1325 Blvd D'Auteuil Laval PQ H7E 3J4 Canada

BRUNNER, JULIA See Castanis, Muriel (Julia Brunner)

BRUNO, ELLEN
FILMMAKER
b Providence, RI, Oct 23, 57. *Study:* Georgetown Univ, BA, 79; Stanford Univ, MA, 90. *Exhib:* San Francisco Int Film Festival; Sundance Film Festival; Charlotte Film Festival; New York Women's Film Festival; Vancouver Int Film Festival; Human Rights Film Festival, NY; Taiwan Int Film Festival, Taipei; Amnesty Int Film Festival, Amsterdam; Nat Educ Film Festival; Atlanta Film Festival; Santa Barbara Film Festival; Mountain Film, Telluride, Colo. *Awards:* Rockefeller Fel, 96; Guggenheim Fel, 98; Acad Motion Picture Arts & Sci Student Award. *Mem:* Pioneer Fund (bd mem, 98-); Film Arts Found. *Publ:* Film writer, Sacrifice, Samsara & Satya, A Prayer for The Enemy. *Mailing Add:* 3447 25th St San Francisco CA 94110

BRUNO, PHILLIP A
DIRECTOR, LECTURER
b Paris, France. *Study:* Columbia Col, BA(hist fine arts & archit); Inst Fine Arts, New York Univ. *Comn:* Restored 17th century house on Martha's Vineyard, Mass, 64. *Collection Arranged:* Ralph Rosenborg Retrospective, Washington, DC, 52; Jose Luis Cuevas, Paris, 55; Elmer Livingston Macrae, Nashville, 63; Tschang-yeul Kim, 79 & Enrico Donati, 80, FIAC, Grand Palais, Paris; Tschang-yeul Kim/Wolfgang Kubach & Anna Marie Wilmsen, 81; Dale Chihuly, Red Grooms, Claudio Bravo, Magdelina Abakanowicz, Bill Jackin, Manolo Valdes, Chakaia Booker, Fernando Botero. *Pos:* Weyhe Gallery, New York, 50-51; co-founder & assoc dir, Grace Borgenicht Gallery, 51-55; dir, World House Gallery, New York, 56-60; dir, Am Exhibs for La Napoule Found, New York & France; dir, Staempfli Gallery, New York, 60-89, co-dir, 81, assoc dir, Marlborough Gallery, New York, 89-; adv bd mem, Ossabaw Island Found, Savannah, Ga, 78-; art consult, First Am Nat Bank, Nashville, 80-81; assoc dir, Marborough Gallery, New York, 89-. *Teaching:* Guest lectr, Foreign Ministry Finland, Helsinki, 78 & Cornell Univ, 92. *Mem:* Hon life mem St Paul Art Ctr; hon mem Tenn Fine Arts Ctr Cheekwood, Nashville; Dukes Co Hist Soc, Edgartown, Mass; Munic Art Soc; Nat Trust Hist Preservation. *Specialty:* Contemporary. *Collection:* Mainly mid-twentieth century American watercolors and drawings, ranging from Marin to Kline, including Lachaise, Demuth, Tobey, Bravo, Lopez-Garcia, Wunderlich; Selections of the collection have been exhibited at the Palmer Art Mus, Penn State Univ, Hunverian Art Gallery, Glasgow, Scotland, Krannert Art Museum, Tennessee Fine Arts Center, Finch College Museum Art, Minn Mus, Vassar Art Col Gallery, Quqanheim Mus & The Phillips Collection. *Mailing Add:* 342 E 67th St No 11A New York NY 10021-6238

BRUNO, SANTO M
PAINTER
b June 29, 47. *Study:* Tyler Sch Art, Temple Univ, Philadelphia, Pa, BFA, 69, MFA, 71; studies with David Pease, Romas Viesulas & Steven Green. *Hon Degrees:* Atlanta Col Art, 80. *Work:* High Mus Art, Atlanta; Kilpatrick, Cody & Regenstein Collection; Stampe Nacional de Italia; Univ Osaka, Japan; Creiger Assocs, Boston. *Comn:* Five major painting-constructions, New Atlanta Hartsfield Int Airport, Ga, 80. *Exhib:* Solo shows, First Impressions of Atlanta, Image South Gallery, Atlanta, Ga, 72, Illusions of a Greek Spring, Gallerie Illien, 73, Crow Carter Presents Santo Bruno: A Five-year Select of Work, Crow-Carter & Assocs, 76, Recent Work, Javo Gallery, 77, A Selection of Work: 78-80, Atlanta Art Workers Coalition Gallery, 80; Mark Miller Gallery, EHampton, NY, 96; Flight Patterns, Forest Ave Consortium, Atlanta, 80; Artists and the Cyclorama Project, Colony Square, 82; Abstraction/Attraction, Newhouse Gallery, Staten Island, NY, 86; Bruce Lurie Gallery, NY, 87 & 88; Gotham Fine Arts, Ltd, 87; Dome Gallery, 88. *Pos:* Conserv contractor, Santo Bruno Fine Art, 83-; owner, Santo Bruno Fine Art, 91-. *Teaching:* Instr painting, Tyler Sch Art, Temple Univ, Rome, Italy, 70-71; instr painting & drawing, Atlanta Col Art, 71-78, head dept painting, 77-78. *Awards:* Nathan Margolis Mem Award, Temple Univ, 78; Exhib grant, NY State Council Arts, 91. *Bibliog:* Preview essay, Art Voices S, 1/78; Sherry Baker (auth), Interview with Santo Bruno, Off-Peachtree Mag, 2/78; Michael Fressola (auth), What's new at Newhouse, Staten Island Advan, 2/86. *Media:* Acrylic. *Interests:* Owns & maintains a personal collection of art work from the 16th century to modern art. *Dealer:* Marc Miller Gallery 3 Railroad Ave East Hampton NY 11937

BRUNO, VINCENT J
HISTORIAN, ADMINISTRATOR
b New York, NY, Feb 8, 26. *Study:* Bard Col, 46-48; Academie Julian, Paris, cert painting, 49; Kenyon Col, BA(philos art), 51; Columbia Univ, MA, 62, PhD, 69; Kenyon Col, DFA, 84. *Hon Degrees:* D, Kenyon Col, 84. *Teaching:* Instr art hist, Wellesley Col, 64-65; assoc prof, C W Post Col, Long Island Univ, 65-66; assoc prof, State Univ NY, Binghamton, 66-76, chairperson, 72-76; chmn dept art, Univ Tex, Arlington, 76-84, Ashbel Smith Chair prof, 84-93, dept art & art hist, prof emer, 94-. *Awards:* John Simon Guggenheim Mem Fel, 78-; Am Coun Learned Soc Grant-in-Aid, 80; Am Philos Soc Grant-in-Aid, 82; Nat Endowment Humanities, Fel, 86-87; Getty Found Grant, 89. *Bibliog:* Martin Robertson (auth), The classical palette: Review of Formand Color in Greek Printing, Times Lit Suppl, London 8/5/77; S R Roberts (auth), Review of form and color in Greek painting, Art Bulletin LXII, 80; A O Koloski Ostrow (auth), Review of Hellenistic painting techniques, Am J Archeol 91, 87. *Mem:* Col Art Asn Am; Archeol Inst Am; Am Inst Nautical Archeol; Am Sch Classical Studies, Athens; hon fel Am Acad Rome (mem, adv comt). *Res:* Conducted excavations at Cosa under auspices of American Academy in Rome and State Univ of New York at Binghamton, 68-72; ancient painting techniques. *Publ:* Contribr, Princeton Encyclopedia of Classical Sites, Int J Nautical Archaeol, In Memoriam Otto J Brendel; Hellenistic painting techniques: The evidence of the Delos fragments, Columbia Studies in the Classical Tradition, Vol XI, Leiden (monogr), 85; coauth, Cosa IV: The Houses; Memoirs of the American Academy in Rome, Vol XXXVIII, University Park, Pa, 93; Classical and post classical studies in memory of Frank Edward Brown (1908-1988), Studies Hist Art, Vol 43, 93; Functional and spatial analysis of wall painting: proceedings of the Fifth International Congress on ancient wall painting, Amsterdam Bulletin, 93. *Mailing Add:* 2554 Ocean Parkway Brooklyn NY 11235

BRUNSVOLD, CHICA
PAINTER
b Ypsilanti, Mich, 40. *Study:* Univ Mich, Sch Art, BS (design), 61, Sch Educ, cert, 62, MA (art), 62; studied with watermedia specialists Glen Bradshaw, Katherine Liu, Carole Barnes, Carlton Plummer, Cheng Khee Chee, Ralph Smith & others. *Work:* Birdlam; Waiting II; Bonding with Noah; Zooillogicals. *Exhib:* solo exhib, Art League Torpedo Factory Arts Ctr, Alexandria, Va, 96, Lombardi Cancer Ctr, Georgetown Univ Hosp, Washington, DC, 97, Children's Nat Med Ctr, 97, Burroughs-Chapin Art Mus, 97, Strathmore Hall Arts Center, Bethesda, Md, 97, Touchstone Gallery, Washington, DC, 98 & Ellen Noel Art Mus, 98, MSC Forseth Gallery, Tex A&M Univ, 99, The Artists Mus, Washington, 99, Children's Art Mus, San Angelo, Tex & Northwood Univ, Cedar Hill, Tex, 2000; Paine Art Ctr, Oshkosh, Wis, 2001; Art Station, Stone Mountain, Ga, 2001; Atrium Gallery, Fairfax INOVA Hospital, Fairfax, Va, 2002; Longwood Univ, Farmville, Va, 2003; Goodyear Cottage, Jekyll Island, Ga, 2003; This Century Gallery, Williamsburg, Va, 2003; Black Rock Arts Center, Germantown, Md, 2005; Visual Arts Center, NW Fla, Panama City, Fla, 2006; group exhib, Nat Watermedia, 1995-; and over 160 others. *Collection Arranged:* Arts in Embassies Program, Burma; The Art Station, Stone Mountain, Ga; Resurrection Med Ctr, Pediatric Wing, Chicago; Burroughs-Chapin Art Mus, Myrtle Beach, SC; Ellen Noel Art Mus, Odessa, Tex; Finnegan & Henderson, Atlanta; Longwood Univ, Farmville, Va; Paine Art Ctr, Oshkosh, Wis; Fairfax Inova Hosp, Va. *Pos:* Illusr gen, Cent Intelligence Agency, 62-67 & Ind Col Armed Forces, 67-68; First vpres, Potomac Valley Watercolorists, 91-93, pres, 93-95. *Teaching:* Instr water media painting at art clubs & organizations for past 30 years; instr workshop Stretching the Boundaries for Creative People, Ohio Watercolor Soc, 1997, 2002. *Awards:* Holbein Award, Tex Watercolor Soc, 97; Daler-Rowney Award, Taos Nat Exhib Am Watercolor IV, 98; Harrison Cady Award, Am Watercolor Soc Exhib, 99; Arts in Miss award, Grand Nat Exhib, 1995; Virginia Watercolor Soc, 2005; M. Graham & Company Award, Southern Watercolor Soc, 2006. *Bibliog:* Josef Woodard (auth), Notable works surface in watercolor exhibit (rev), Los Angeles Times, 5/2/96; Phaedra Greenwood (auth), Awards presented in national watercolor show (rev), Taos News, NMex, 10/9/97; Maureen Bloomfield (auth), Ones to Watch, Watercolor Magic (mag) Yearbook, 2001; It Ain't Over Till it's Over, Watercolor Magic mag., Creativity, 2001; Mary Beam (auth), Celebrating your Creative Self, Northlight Bks, 2001; Betsy Dillard Stroud (auth), Painting the Now, Watercolor Magic, 2006. *Mem:* Signature mem Nat Watercolor Soc; NW Watercolor Soc; signature mem Va Watercolor Soc; Ga Watercolor Soc; Miss Watercolor Soc (signature mem). *Media:* Acrylic, Watermedia. *Specialty:* Paintings. *Interests:* choir, tennis. *Collection:* Zooillogicals-bright whimsical paintings of birds and animals. *Publ:* Illusr, Birdlam, York Graphic Servs, 96; Illusr Waiting II, York Graphic Svcs, 99; The Doll & the Secret Garden II, The Finer Image, 2003; illusr, Confetti Mag, summer 2004; Night Blooms II, Exuberance, Who? & Eclipse, Old Town Editions, 2006. *Dealer:* The Art League 101 N Union St Alexandria Va; Broadway Gallery Fairfax Va. *Mailing Add:* 3510 Wentworth Dr Falls Church VA 22044

BRUNSWICK, CECILE R
PAINTER
b Antwerp, Belg, Jul 26, 30; US citizen. *Study:* Queens Col, BA, 52; Columbia Univ, MIA, 54; Art Students League, with Frank O'Cain, 92. *Work:* World Children's Art Mus of Okazaki, Japan; Canadian Mus of Civilization, Quebec; Pfizer Inc, NY; Sumitomo Marine & Fire Insurance Co, NY; Nat Westminster Bank, NY; Assilah Forum Found Mus, Morocco; Wills Eye Hosp, Pa; IBM, NY; Arthur Audersen, Va. *Exhib:* Paris-Washington Echange Artistique, Arts Etoiles, Paris, 93; Visual Perceptions, Nour Found, NY, 93; Relationships, Kavehaz Gallery, NY, 96; A Celebration of Possibilities, San Francisco, 99; Provence Paintings, Broome St Gallery, NY, 98 & Hidden Assets, 2000; Artsforum Gallery, NY, 2000; World Festival of Art, Slovenia, 01, Matthew Travis Gallery, Houston, Tex, 03; Paul Mellon Art Ctr, Choate, Wallingford, Conn, 2004; Artspace 129, Montclair, NJ, 2005; Mercedez-Benz, Manhattan Gallery, NY, 2005; Fraubliu su Gallery, NY, 2006; The Landmark Lobby Gallery, Tarrytown, NY, 2006; Karin Sanders Gallery, Sag Harbor, 2006; City Without Walls, Newark, NJ, 2006. *Awards:* Mus Prize, Hudson River Mus, 80; Third Prize, City of NY - Parks Dept, 90. *Bibliog:* Valerie Kellogg (auth), VOICE Art, 1/8/98; ABC Television, Business Now, BA-TV - Kathy Ryan, 6/4/2000; Antiques & the Arts Weekly, 11/19/04; Cecile Brunswick, Interior Design, 4/06. *Mem:* NY Artists Equity; Japan Soc; NY Artists Cir. *Media:* Oil, Watercolor, Pastels. *Interests:* Travel, Choral Singing. *Publ:* auth, New York Windows Calendar, Pomegranate Artbooks, 88; illus, Bologna Children's Book, Itabashi Mus, 94. *Dealer:* Franklin 54 Gallery 181 Christopher St New York NY 10014. *Mailing Add:* 127 W 96th St New York NY 10025-6482

BRUS, GUNTER
CONCEPTUAL ARTIST, PRINTMAKER
b Ardning, Austria, 38. *Study:* Sch Arts & Crafts, Graz, Austria; Acad Applied Arts, Vienna, Austria. *Work:* Mus Mod Art, NY; Libr Cong, Washington, DC; Tate Gallery, London, Eng; Albertina Mus, Vienna, Austria. *Exhib:* Dokumenta V, 72 & Dokumenta VII, 82, Kassel, Ger; Bodyworks, Mus Contemp Art, Chicago, Ill, 75. *Media:* All. *Mailing Add:* c/o Margarete Roeder Gallery & Editions 545 Broadway New York NY 10012

BRUSH, GLORIA (ELIZABETH) DEFILIPPS
PHOTOGRAPHER, EDUCATOR
b Chicago, Ill, Mar 29, 1947. *Study:* Sch Art Inst Chicago, BFA, 68, MFA, 72; and asst to Sonia Landy Sheridan. *Exhib:* Los Angeles Co Mus Art, 91; Minneapolis Inst Arts, 85, 86 & 96; Kohler Arts Ctr, 87 & 90; Ctr Photog, Woodstock, 88; Minn Mus Am Art, 82; solo exhibs, Real Art Ways, Hartford, 85, Print Club, Philadelphia, 85, Contemp Arts Ctr, New Orleans, 87, Plains Art Mus, Moorhead, Minn, 88, Clarence Kennedy Gallery, Cambridge, 88, The Light Factory, 91 & Blue Sky Gallery, Portland, 93, Sol Mednick Gallery, Univ Arts, Philadelphia, 99; Krannert Art Mus, Urbana-Champaign, Ill, 96; Santa Barbara Mus Art, 97; Sch Art Inst Chicago, 97, 2002; Siggraph Gallery, Los Angeles, 99, 2001, 2003; ASCI Digital 02, NY, 2002; Int D-Art 2002, Univ London, 2002. *Pos:* Arts policy adv, Charles K Blandin Found, 80-83; Arrowhead Regional Arts Coun, 81-83, bd mem, 96-; panel mem, Minn Artists Exhib Prog, 85-87. *Teaching:* Asst prof photog, Univ Minn, Duluth, 81-85, assoc prof & head, dept art, 85-89, prof & dept head, 89-2002, prof & actg dean, 96-97, prof &

photog area head, 2002-. *Awards:* Minn State Arts Bd Grant, 82 & 87; Nat Endowment Arts Photogr Fel, 83; Bush Found Artist Fel, 84; Film in the Cities/McKnight Photo Fel, 85, 90 & 97; Arts Midwest Photog Fel, 93; McKnight Arts & Humanities Rsch Award, 1992-1995. *Bibliog:* Holt Confer (auth), article, Polaroid Photo Educ, Vol 6, No 1, 89; Naomi Rosenblum (auth), A History of Women Photographers, 94; Gianni Romano (auth), article, Zoom Mag, 9/98; Innovation/Imagination: 50 Years of Polaroid Photography, 99. *Publ:* Auth, Photographing small scale objects: History, context & format, Leonardo, Vol XX, No 3, 87; Portfolio, Blue Sky No 7, Ore Ctr Photog Arts, 93. *Mailing Add:* 2909 Jefferson St Duluth MN 55812

BRUSH, LEIF
SOUND SCULPTOR, INSTRUCTOR
b Bridgeport, Ill, Mar 28, 32. *Study:* Art Inst Chicago, dipl(fel), 70, MFA(fel), 72. *Work:* Mills Col Libr; Inst Recherche Coord Acoustique & Musique Libr; Audio Arts Libr, London; Electroacustic de Bourges, France, 2002; and others. *Comn:* Minn Dept Trans/State Arts Bd, Milaca, 86. *Exhib:* Minneapolis Inst Arts, 77, 79, 86 & 89; Walker Art Ctr, Minneapolis, 79 & 80; Neuberger Mus, Purchase, NY, 81; Suono/Ambiente/Musica, Milan, Italy, 82; Minneapolis Col Art & Design, 82; Hudson River Mus, NY, 82; Mail Music, Monza, Italy, 83; Tweed Mus Art, 84; New Music Am, 80, 87; Yellow Springs Inst, Chester Sps, Pa, 87; The Aerial (cassette/CD), Nonsequitur, Issue 4, 92; Jukebox-in-the-sky (over deconstructed voting booth installation), Tweed Mus Art, Duluth, 94; Red Eye Theater, Minneapolis, 94; The Sound Symposium Lend Me Your Ears: Sound City Spaces, St John's, Nfld, Can, 94; Ear to the Ground (interactive, on-the-floor, sound installation), Nash Gallery, Minneapolis, 97; CD Zero, FACT, UK, 2000. *Pos:* Vis artist, Univ Victoria, 73, Univ Colo, 75, State Univ NY, Alfred, 76, Univ Md, Baltimore Co, 77, Wright State Univ, 78, Art Res Ctr, Kansas City, Univ NDak & ZBS Found, Fort Edward, NY, 79; res artist, Visual Studies Workshop, 84. *Teaching:* Instr audible constructs, Art Inst Chicago, 70-72; asst prof, Univ Iowa, Iowa City, 72-76; asst prof sculpture, Univ Minn, Duluth, 76-79, assoc prof, 79-87, prof art in tech, 87-2002; Terrain Instruments presentation & lect, Banff Centre Arts & Univ Calgary, 93. *Awards:* Fels, Jerome Found, 82 & Nat Endowment Arts, 73 & 83; Bush Found, 80; Minn Percent for the Arts, 86. *Bibliog:* David Moss (prod) Art You Can Hear, NPR, 86; New Music America, Am Pub Radio Network, 88; Soundviews: Sources, Nonsequitur, Santa Fe, 90; Sztuka Fabryka Radio, Belgium, 93 & 94; and others. *Media:* Multimedia. *Publ:* Contribr, Fifth Assembling, New York, 75; Soundings, Neuberger Mus, 81; Ear Mag, Vol IX, No 5, New York, 85; New Music America, Hartford, 84; Leonardo, Pergamon, Vol 17, 84 & Vol 23, Issue 20, 90; Musicworks, Toronto, 85; Experimental Musica Instruments, Vol VII, No 5, 92. *Mailing Add:* 2909 Jefferson Ct Duluth MN 55812

BRUSKIN, GRISHA
PAINTER, SCULPTOR
b Moscow, Russia, Oct 21, 45. *Study:* Art Inst Moscow, Russia, BA, 68. *Work:* Mus Mod Art, NY; Ludwig Mus, Cologne, Ger; Israel Mus, Jerusalem; State Pushkin Mus Fine Arts, Moscow; Art Inst Chicago. *Exhib:* Von der Revolution zur Perestroika, Kunst Mus Luzern, Switz, 83; Ich lebe Ichsehe, Kunst Mus Bern, 88; 100 Yrs of Russian Art 1889-1989, Barbican Art Gallery, London, 89; Chagall to Kitaj: The Jewish Experience in 20th Century Art, Barbican Art Gallery, London, 90; Ost-Kunst West-Kunst,Ludwig Forum Int Art, Aachen, 91; Von Malewitschbis Kabakov, Ludwig Mus, Cologne, Ger, 93; one-man show, State Pushkin Mus Fine Arts, Moscow, 93; Europa Europa, Kunst & Ausstellungshalle der Bundesrepublix, Bonn, Ger, 94. *Bibliog:* Suzanne Muchnie (auth), The unknown Soviet artist who won the West, Los Angeles Times Calendar, 7/31/88; Peter Selz (auth), Grisha Bruskin-The Unique Work, Cimaise No 220, 9-10/92; Jana Markova (dir), Grisha Bruskin in New York (film), 93. *Media:* Oil, Linen, Bronze, Steel. *Dealer:* Marlborough Gallery 40 W 57th St New York NY 10013. *Mailing Add:* 236 W 26th St No 705 New York NY 10001

BRUST, ROBERT GUSTAVE
PAINTER, WRITER
b Pittsburgh, Pa, Aug 14, 45. *Study:* Carnegie Mellon Univ, BA, 68; Conn Col, MA, 75; Pittsburgh Ctr Arts, 76-91. *Work:* Highmark Blue Cross Blue Shield, Pittsburgh, Pa; Monroeville Pub Libr, Pa; Hoyt Inst Fine Arts, New Castle, Pa; Washington & Jefferson Col, Washington, Pa. *Exhib:* Westmoreland Art Nat, Twin Lakes Park, Greensburg, Pa & Westmoreland Co Community Col, Youngwood, Pa, 90-91 & 93-95; Assoc Artists of Pittsburgh Ann, Carnegie Mus Art, 92; Three Regional Artists, Hoyt Inst Fine Arts, New Castle, Pa, 93; W&J Nat Painting Show, Olin Fine Arts Gallery, Washington & Jefferson Col, Pa, 92-97; Triennial, Southern Alleghenies Mus Art, Loretto, Pa, 96-97; Gallery Space, Monroeville Pub Libr, Pa, 84, 89, 93 & 97; Undercroft Gallery, Pittsburgh, Pa, 96; Pittsburgh Soc of Artists, Butler Inst Am Art, Salem, Ohio, 99; Southwestern Pa Regional, Southern Alleghenies Mus Art, Ligonier, Pa, 2000-2001. *Pos:* writer and ed, self employed, 67-01, Penn Art Asn, 78-01. *Teaching:* Instr painting, Penn Art Asn, Penn Hills, Pa, 82-83 & 87-90 & demonstr painting, 83-98; demonstr, E Suburban Artists League, Murrysville, Pa, 92 & 95. *Awards:* Best of Show, Penn Art Asn, 84, 85, 87, 89, 90, 93 & 95; Jurors Award, Pittsburgh Soc Artists, 90 & 97; Purchase Award, W&J Nat Painting Show, 94. *Bibliog:* Niles Campbell (auth), Photography influences perception of art, Pittsburgh Business Times, 7/88; Jane Crawford (auth), Painter brings nature's brilliance to light, Pittsburgh Post-Gazette, 8/88; Donald Miller (auth), Today at the arts festival, Pittsburgh Post-Gazette, 6/90. *Mem:* Penn Hills Arts Coun (bd mem, 88-2001 & vpres, 94-2001); Penn Art Asn (bd mem, 76-2001, pres 78-80); ESuburban Artists League (bd mem, 86-90); Pittsburgh Soc Artists (bd mem, 83-87); Assoc Artists Pittsburgh. *Media:* Acrylic. *Publ:* Coauth, Picture perception: An alternative view of reversible figures, Arts Educ Int J, 73; E&A, Penn Art Asn Newsletter, 78-2001; Interaction effects of picture & caption on humor ratings of cartoons, J of Social Psychology, 79; Humor & interpersonal attraction, J of Personality Assessment, 85; ed, Pittsburgh Soc Artists Newsletter, 87. *Dealer:* Pittsburgh Ctr for the Arts 6300 Fifth Ave Pittsburgh PA 15232; Studio Z Gallery 1415 E Carson St Pittsburgh PA 15203. *Mailing Add:* 836 Hamil Rd Verona PA 15147-2926

BRUZELIUS, CAROLINE ASTRID
DIRECTOR, HISTORIAN
b Stockholm, Apr 18, 49. *Study:* Wellesley Col, BA, 71; Yale Univ, MA, 73, MPhil, 74, PhD, 77. *Exhib:* Paesaggi Perduti Granet a Roma 1802-1822, Am Acad, Rome, 96. *Pos:* Dir, Am Acad Rome, Italy, 93-98. *Teaching:* Asst prof, Duke Univ, Durham, NC, 92, assoc prof, 86-89, chmn art dept, 89- & prof, 91-93, program, 99-. *Awards:* Fulbright Award, 85-88 & 93; Rome Prize, Am Acad Rome, 85-86; Guggenheim Found Fel, 97. *Mem:* Coll Art Asn. *Publ:* Auth, Longpont and the Architecture of the Cistercian Order in the Thirteenth Century, Analecta Cisterciensia, 79. *Mailing Add:* Dept Art & Art History Campus Box 90764 Duke Univ Durham NC 27708-0764

BRYAN, JACK L
PAINTER, SCULPTOR
b Lawton, Okla, Aug 30, 42. *Study:* Univ Okla, BFA, 65, post-grad work, 73-74; Tulsa Univ, MA(art hist, hons), 67. *Work:* Comanche Mem Hosp. *Comn:* Sculpture, YMCA, 88. *Exhib:* Arts Festival 1985, Carrier Found, Belle Mead, NJ; Songs of the Wichita Mountians, Kirkpatrick Gallery Okla Artists, 89; Wichita Landscapes (solo exhib), Wichita Falls Mus Art, Tex, 90; group exhib, Leslie Powell Gallery, Lawton, Okla, 91; Leslie Powell Landscape Show, 93; and others. *Pos:* Chmn, visual arts panel, Okla Arts Inst. *Teaching:* Chmn dept art, Cameron Univ, Lawton, Okla, 67-. *Awards:* Teacher of the Year, Lawton Arts & Humanities Coun, 84; Lawton Artist of the Year, 90. *Mem:* Nat Asn Sch Art & Design; Okla Summer Arts Inst; Leslie Powell Found. *Media:* Oil, Acrylic. *Publ:* Illusr, Meadowlark, 81, Cross Stitch, 82 & Southwest Pass, 83, Valentine Series, Hosanna Press, Chicago. *Mailing Add:* 10 NW 35th St Lawton OK 73505-6115

BRYAN, JOHN HENRY
PATRON
b West Point, Miss, 36. *Study:* Rhodes Col, Memphis, BA(Econ & Bus admin), 58. *Pos:* Joined Bryan Foods, 60; with Sara Lee Corp (formerly known as Consolidated Food Corp), Chicago, 60-; exec vpres to pres, Sara Lee Corp (formerly known as Consol Food Corp), 74, Chief Exec Officer, 75-2000, chmn bd, 76-2000, also bd dir's consult Sara Lee Corp, 2001-; bd dir, GM Corp, BP Amoco Corp, Bank One, Goldman Sachs Group, Inc; chmn bus adv coun, Chicago Urban League; bd gov's, Nat Women's Econ Alliance, Chicago; trustee, vchmn, exec comt, Univ Chicago, Rush-Presbyn.-St. Luke's Med Ctr; trustee Comt, Econ Develop; trustee, treas, Art Inst, Chicago; chmn, Catalyst, Chicago comt, Chicago Coun on Foreign Relations; memb trustee's coun, Nat Gallery Art, Wash; Pres com comt, on the arts & humanities; bd dir, Bus Comt for Arts; trustee, treas, Art Inst, Chicago, currently. *Awards:* Decorated Legion of Honor France, Order of Orange Nassau The Netherlands, Order of Lincoln medallion; named Man of Yr, Harvard Bus Sch Club Chicago, Exec Yr, Crain's Chicago Bus, 1992; named to Jr Achievement Chicago Bus Hall of Fame, 1992, Miss Hall of Fame; recipient Nat Humanitarian award, Nat Conference of Christians and Jews, William H Albers award, Food Marketing Inst. *Mem:* Bus Roundtable; Bus Coun; Grocery Manufacturers Asn (sr chmn bd, formerly). *Mailing Add:* Sara Lee Corp 3 1st Nat Plaza 70 W Madison St Ste 4500 Chicago IL 60602-4260

BRYAN, SUKEY
PAINTER
b Summit, NJ, Apr 4, 61. *Study:* Yale Univ, BA(fine arts), 83; Md Inst Col Art, MFA, 90. *Work:* Cathedral of the Incarnation, The Baltimore Mus Art, Baltimore; Piper & Marbury, Baltimore. *Exhib:* Next Generation, Addison Gallery Am Art, Andover, Mass, 93; solo exhibs, Galerie Francoise esf, Baltimore, Md, 94 & 2000 & C Grimaldis Gallery, Baltimore, Md, 95, 97 & 2000; Metamorphosis, Corcoran Gallery Art, Washington, 96; Juried Exhib, Lancaster Mus Art, Pa, 97; Elemental Forces, Univ Pac, Stockton, Calif, 98; Susan Cummins Gallery, Mill Valley, Calif, 98; Colo State Univ, Ft Collins, 99; Indianapolis Art Ctr, 99; Burroughs and Chapin Art Mus, SC, 2000; Wanatchee Valley Coll, Washington, 2000. *Pos:* Vis critic & lectr, Md Inst, Col Art, 95-97, Univ Md, Baltimore Co, 96 & Carroll Community Col, Md, 96, The Bently Sch, Berkeley, Calif, 2000. *Awards:* Individual Artist Award, Md Stat Arts Coun, 91; Nat Endowment Arts Visual Artists Fel, 93-94. *Bibliog:* Tony Merino (auth), Growth and atrophy: The empathetic landscape, Art Papers, Atlanta, 5/6/94; Mike Giuliano (auth), Land ho, Baltimore City Paper, 9/13/95; John Dorsey (auth), A refocused Sukey Bryan pours on talent, Baltimore Sun, 9/14/95; Mike Givliano (auth), Blow Up, Baltimore City Paper, 2/12/97; John Dorsey (auth), Dispassionate Paintings Show nature acting up, Baltimore Sun, 1/28/97. *Media:* Oil. *Publ:* Auth & illusr, Tidal Grass, pvt publ, 93. *Dealer:* C Grimaldis Gallery 523 N Charles St Baltimore Md 21201. *Mailing Add:* 921 Cottrell Way Stanford CA 94305

BRYANS, JOHN ARMOND
INSTRUCTOR, PAINTER
b Marion, Ohio. *Study:* Ringling Sch Art, Sarasota, Fla, 47-49; Burnsville Painting Classes, NC, 48-50; Jerry Farnsworth Studio, Sarasota, 50. *Work:* Columbus Mus, Ga; Abilene Mus & McMurray Col, Abilene, Tex; Muskingum Col, New Concord, Ohio; Appalachian State Univ, Boone, NC. *Comn:* Murals, Foundry Methodist Church, Washington, 72 & 78; mural, Coral Gables Methodist Church, Fla, 83; mural, US Embassy, Madrid, Spain, 94; mural, St Michael's Episcopal Church, Arlington, Va, 94; mural, Strathmore Hall Arts Ctr, Bethesda, Md, 00. *Exhib:* Ga Watercolor Nat, 85 & 92; Irene Leach Mem, Chrysler Mus, Norfolk, 88, 96 & 98; Watercolor USA,

Springfield Mus, 89, 95, 96, 98 & 99; Aqueous Nat, Louisville, KY, 92 & 00; Adirondacks Nat, Old Forge, NY, 92; Butler Inst Am Art, Youngstown, Ohio, 00; Nat Watercolor Soc, Calif, 00. *Pos:* Retired. *Teaching:* Instr drawing & painting, Hill's Art Sch, Arlington, Va, 1952-77; head dept art, McLean Arts Ctr, Va, 1965-73 & 1978-99; co-dir, Painting in the Mountains, Burnsville, NC, 1965-83; instr watercolor, Md Col Art & Design, Silver Spring, 1980-81. *Awards:* Awards, Va Watercolor Soc, 91-93, 95, 96, 98 & 00; Second Award, Baltimore Watercolor Soc, Mid Atlantic Regional, 92; Award, Nat Watercolor Soc, Calif, 00. *Bibliog:* Best of Watercolor 1 and 2, Rockport Press, Mass. *Mem:* Southern Watercolor Soc; Va Watercolor Soc; Ky Watercolor Soc; Ga Watercolor Soc; Baltimore Watercolor Soc. *Media:* Watercolor, Acrylic. *Dealer:* Art Scene, Inc, Bethesda, Md

BRYANT, DONALD
COLLECTOR
b Mount Vernon, Il, June 30, 42. *Study:* Denison Univ, Granville, OH, BA, 64; Washington Univ, St Louis, JD, 67; Chartered Life Underwriter, Chartered Fin Consultant. *Comn:* President Herbert Hoover Boys Club, St Louis, 87-; active Arts and Educ Council Greater St Louis, 83-, Dance St Louis, 88- Opera Theatre St Louis, 85-, Boy Scouts Am, 72-, St. Louis Art Mus, 90. *Pos:* Chmn, chief exec officer Donald L Bryant Assoc, St Louis, 68-75, Bryant Group, Inc, St. Louis, 75-. *Awards:* Named Outstanding Alumni, Sch of Law Washington Univ, 90; named one of Top 200 Collectors, ARTnews Mag, 2004. *Mem:* Million Dollar Round Table (life), The Int Forum, Asn Advanced Life Underwriters, St Louis Asn Life Underwriters, Estate Planning Council St Louis, Mo Bar Asn, Am Bar Asn, Bellerive Co Club (St Louis) (golf champ 76), Vintage Club (Indian Wells, Calif), Winged Foot (Mamaroneck, NY), Castle Pines (Castlerock, Calif), Meadowood (Napa Valley, Calif), Golf Club of Okla (Broken Arrow). *Collection:* Contemporary art. *Mailing Add:* Bryant Group Inc Ste 1200 701 Market St Saint Louis MO 63101-1884

BRYANT, LAURA MILITZER
WEAVER
b Detroit, Mich, Mar 3, 55. *Study:* Univ Mich Sch Art, BFA(summa cum laude), 78. *Work:* Xerox Corp, Rochester, NY; Seton Hall Univ Law School, NJ; Valparaiso Univ, Ind; City of St Petersburg; Mobil Oil Corp. *Comn:* Eli Lilly; Buffalo Lights, Foit-Albert Assoc; Sky Song, comn by Mr & Mrs D Bomberger, Indianapolis, Ind. *Exhib:* Albright-Knox Art Gallery, Buffalo, NY, 92; solo exhibs, Mod Art Gallery, Sarasota, Fla, 93, 94 & 95; Fiberart Int, 93, Pittsburgh Ctr Arts, Pa, 93; Crafts Nat, Pa State Univ, 93 & 95; Chataugua Fiber Int, Adams Art Gallery, Dunkirk, NY, 94; solo exhibs, Mod Art Gallery, Sarasota, Fla, 94 & 95 & Casements Cult Ctr, Ormond Beach, Fla, 96; Crafts Nat 30, Zoller Gallery, Penn State Univ, Pa, 96; Under Currents: Over View, Area Survey, Tampa Mus Art, Fla, 97; SE Fine Crafts Biennial II, Fla Gulf Coast Art Ctr, Bellair, 97; Spotlight 98, Arrowmont Sch Arts & Crafts, Gatlinburg, Tenn & Venice Art Ctr, Fla, 98; 45th Fla Craftsman Exhib, Art & Cult Ctr, Hollywood, 98; and many others. *Pos:* Own, Prism, currently. *Teaching:* Lectr fabric design & color, State Univ Col Buffalo, 87-89. *Awards:* Vern Stein Fine Art Award, Albright-Knox Art Gallery, 92; Fla Individual Artist Fel, 94-95; HGA Award of Distinction Spotlight 95, ACCSE, 95; Award of Merit, 45th Fla Craftsman Exhib, 98. *Mem:* Am Craft Coun; Fla Craftsman. *Media:* Fiber. *Dealer:* Modern Art Gallery 1665 10th St Sarasota FL 34236; Art Resources Gallery 494 Jackson St St Paul MN 55101

BRYANT, LINDA GOODE
ART DEALER, GALLERY DIRECTOR
b Columbus, Ohio, July 21, 49. *Study:* Spelman Col, BA, 72; City Univ New York, MA candidate. *Pos:* Dir, Just Above Midtown Gallery, NY, 74-86; dir educ, Studio Mus in Harlem, 74-75; panelist, NY State Coun on the Arts & DCA, 77-86; freelance artist. *Awards:* Grad Intern, Metrop Mus, 73, Rockefeller Fel, 73-74. *Bibliog:* Satterwhite (auth), Black Dealer/57th St, New York Post, 11/74; USA's Linda Bryant, African Woman, 76; Essence Woman, Essence Mag, 7/77. *Res:* American abstract art; theory on stylistic development in the 1970s termed contextures. *Specialty:* New and emerging artists working in contextualist vein; utilizing materials not heretofore used as primary in art object (smoke, hair, clothes, nylon mesh). *Publ:* Co-auth, Contextures (American Abstract Art 1945-1978), Just Above Midtown, 78. *Mailing Add:* 215 W 90th St New York NY 10024-1221

BRYANT, OLEN L
SCULPTOR, EDUCATOR
b Cookeville, Tenn, May 4, 27. *Study:* Murray State Col, BS; Cranbrook Acad Art, MFA; Inst Allende, San Miguel, Mex; Cleveland Inst Art; Art Students League. *Work:* Tenn Fine Arts Ctr Collection, Nashville; Hunter Gallery, Chattanooga, Tenn; Carroll Reece Mus, Johnson City, Tenn. *Comn:* Aura, St Phillips Episcopal Church, Franklin, Tenn, 87; The Actors, Tenn Performing Arts Ctr, Nashville, Tenn, 85; Sentinel, Austin Peay State Univ, Austin, 80 & Seeds, Libr, 87; Humanitarian Awards, Country Music Found, 86-89. *Exhib:* One-man shows, Tenn Fine Arts Ctr, 68 & 82, Hunter Gallery, 69, Evansville Mus, Ind, 70, Haas Gallery Bloomsburg, Pa, 71, Morehead Univ, 71 & Vanderbuilt Gallery, Nashville, 83. *Teaching:* Instr art, Shaker Heights Schs, Ohio, 58-61; instr art, Union Univ, 62-65; prof art, Austin Peay Univ, 66-91. *Mem:* Am Crafts Coun. *Media:* Wood, Clay. *Mailing Add:* 536 York St Clarksville TN 37040-2955

BRYANT, TAMARA THOMPSON See Thompson, Tamara

BRYCE, EILEEN ANN
PAINTER
b Tulsa, Okla, June 8, 53. *Study:* Inst European Studies, Vienna, Austria, 73; Southern Methodist Univ, BFA, 75; Univ Tulsa, MA, 78. *Work:* Chautauqua Art Mus, NY. *Exhib:* Chautauqua Nat Exhib of Am Art, Chautauqua Art Mus, NY, 81; Art Ann Two, Okla Art Ctr, Oklahoma City, 81; Tex Fine Arts Asn Nat Exhib, Laguna Gloria Mus, Austin, 82; Alexandria Mus Visual Arts, La, 82; First Ann, Provincetown Art Mus, Mass, 83; Nat Print & Drawing Exhib, Lee Hall Gallery, Clemson Univ, 83. *Awards:* Purchase Prize, Chautauqua Nat Exhib Am Art, New York, 80; Plaque of Distinction, Marietta Nat Exhib Am Art, 81; Painting Award, Alexandria Mus Vis Arts Invitational, 82. *Bibliog:* Articles, Art Voices, 9-10/81 & Tulsa Mag, 6/82; Arts Chronicle, Okla Educ TV Authority, 82. *Media:* Oils, Acrylic. *Dealer:* Leslie Levy Gallery 7141 Main St Scottsdale AZ 85251. *Mailing Add:* 1732 S College Tulsa OK 74104-6122

BRYCE, MARK ADAMS
PAINTER, PRINTMAKER
b San Francisco, Calif, July 4, 53. *Study:* Philadelphia Col Art, 69-71; Pa Acad Fine Arts, with Hobson Pitman, Morris Blockburn, Mayo Bryce & Arthur DeCosta, 70-74. *Exhib:* Nat Mid-Year Show, Butler Inst Am Art, 82; Allan Stone Gallery, NY, 88-89; Contemp Philadelphia Art, Philadelphia Mus Art, Pa, 90; Allan Stone Gallery, NY, 91; James Corcoran Gallery, Santa Monica, Calif, 92; John Berggruen Galley, San Francisco, 93; Contemp Landscapes & Recent Acquisitions of Sculpture, Larry Evans Gallery, San Francisco, 94; Mid-winter Exhib, Brian Grass Fine Art, San Francisco, 95; Brian Gross Fine Art, San Francisco, 95. *Teaching:* Instr drawing, Philadelphia Col Art, 80-82; lectr painting, Wilmington Soc Fine Arts, 83-84. *Awards:* Charles Smith Endowment Prize, Woodmere Open, 76; Award Merit, Reading Art Mus, 83; Outstanding Landscape Award & Award of Merit, Calif State Fair. *Bibliog:* David Fathergill Quinlan (auth), Raissonne (catalog), NJ, 85; John Driscoll & Arnold Skolnick (co-auth), The Artist and the American Landscape; Randall Barton (auth), Sacred Journey. *Media:* Oil, Pencil, Lithography. *Publ:* Am Artist, 90; color reproduction (oil), Guardian, 143, 95. *Dealer:* John Cacciola Gallery, 501 W 23rd St, NYC

BRYCELEA, CLIFFORD
PAINTER, ILLUSTRATOR
b Shiprock, NMex, Sept 26, 53. *Study:* Ft Lewis Col, Durango, Colo, study with Mick Reber & Stan Englehart, BA(art), 75. *Work:* Los Angeles Athletic Club, Calif; Transcoe Co, Houston, Tex; Norwest Bank & Jackson David Bottling Co, Durango, Colo; Albuquerque Federal Savings And Loan Asn, NMex; Burns Nat Bank & Tamarron Resort, Durango, Colo; and others. *Comn:* Mural, The Indian Ctr, Ft Lewis Col, Durango, Colo, 73; mural, Ft Lewis Admin, Durango, Colo, 74; mural, The Indian Ctr, Durango, Colo, 74; Dulce High Sch Gym, 83. *Exhib:* Gallup Ceremonial, Red Rock Park, NMex, 76-81; Am Inst Contemp Art Ann, San Dimas Exhib Hall, Calif, 80-82; Navajo Show, Mus Northern Ariz, Flagstaff, 80-82; Death Valley 49'ers Show, Mus Death Valley, Calif, 81; Indian Shows, Navajo Tribal Mus, Window Rock, Ariz, 82; Indian Market, Santa Fe, NMex, 80-96; IACA Markets, Denver & Mesa, Ariz, 87-96. *Awards:* Purchase Awards, NMex Watercolor Soc II, 76 & NMex State Fair, 77; Gold Medal Winner, Am Indian & Cowboy Asn Show, 81; 1st Place & Mem Award, Gallup Ceremonial Gallups NMex. *Bibliog:* Carey Vicanti (auth), Clifford Brycelea, Jicarilla Chirtain Newspaper, 6/81; Julie Pearson (auth), Southwest Art Mag, 6/92. *Mem:* Indian Arts & Crafts Asn. *Media:* Acrylic, Watercolor; Stonelitho, Photoprint. *Publ:* Contribr, Art Fever, Gallery West Inc, 81; illusr, Pieces of White Shell, 84; illusr-cover, Haunted Mesa, Bantam Books, 85; Southwest Art Mag, 92; Moon & Otter & Frog, Hyperion Books, 95. *Dealer:* Tohatin Gallery 145 W Ninth St Durango CO 81301; Tekakinitha Gallery Helen GA. *Mailing Add:* 1721 Montano St Santa Fe NM 87501-3389

BRYSON, LOUISE HENRY
PATRON
Study: Pomona Col, 93. *Pos:* Sr vpres, FX Networks, formerly; dir & chmn, KCET TV, LA, formerly; dir, SCalif Pub Radio, formerly; dir, Investment Co of Am, formerly; vchmn, J Paul Getty Trust, currently; exec, vpres, distribution & bus develop, Lifetime Television, currently; bd, councilors Annenberg Sch for Communications, Univ SCalif, currently. *Mailing Add:* Lifetime Television 309 W 49th St New York NY 10019

BRZOZOWSKI, RICHARD JOSEPH
PAINTER
b New Britain, Conn, Sept 9, 32. *Study:* Paier Art Sch, New Haven, Conn. *Work:* Grumbacher Collection, NY; Phoenix Mutual Inst, Hartford, Conn; Springfield Mus Art, Mass; CBT Bank, Hartford, Conn; Otis Elevator, Farmington, Conn. *Exhib:* Am Watercolor Soc, 94, 95, 96 & 05; Adirondacks Nat Exhib Am Watercolors, 96, 2002 & 04; Nat Acad Design, 92-96; Allied Artists, 2003-04; Copley Soc, Boston, Mass, 2000-01; Watercolor USA, 2001-02; and others. *Awards:* Paul Remmey Mem Award, Am Watercolor Soc, 95; Adolph & Clara Obrig Award, Nat Academy, 96; and others; Windsor & Newton Award, 2001; Sagendorph Memorial Award, Copley Soc, 2003; David Jeck-Key Award, 2003; John Young-Hunter Award, 2004; Old Forge Award, Adirondakc, 2005; Arches Watercolor Award, Casein Soc, 2004; John-Young-Hunter Mem Award, Allied Artists, 2004 & 05. *Mem:* Am Watercolor Soc (bd dir, 87-88, corresp secy, 2nd vpres); Conn Watercolor Soc (bd dir, 69-70); Nat Soc Painters Casein & Acrylics; Allied Artists Am; Copley Soc Boston. *Media:* Watercolor, Acrylic. *Publ:* Watercolor magic (article); Reproduction of painting included in Watercolor Expressions, The Best of Acrylic Paintings; Landscape Inspirations. *Mailing Add:* 13 Fox Rd Plainville CT 06062

BUBRISKI, KEVIN E
PHOTOGRAPHER
b North Adams, Mass, Nov 29, 54. *Study:* Bowdoin Col, BA, 75; Bennington Col, MFA, 97. *Work:* Ctr Creative Photog, Tucson, Ariz; Bibliot Nat, Paris; Mus Photographic Arts, San Diego; Boston Mus Fine Arts; Houston Mus Fine Arts; Mus Modern Art, NY; Metropolitan Mus Art, NY; Smithsonian Am Art Mus. *Exhib:* Mus Photog Art, San Diego, Calif, 90; In Tibet, traveling exhib, 91; Introductions, Robert

Koch Gallery, 91; Contemp Photo Journalism, ICP Uptown Gallery, NY, 91; Nat Arts Club, NY, 95; Freeman Ctr, Wesleyan Univ, Conn, 99; NY Hist Soc, New York City, 2002; Decordova Mus, Lincoln, Ma, 2002; Hallmark Mus, Turners Falls, Mass, 2006. *Pos:* Fine Art Photog. *Teaching:* Instr photog, Harvard Univ, summer 92, Bennington Col, 95-96, Williams Col, 99-2003; adj prof, Williams Col, 1999-2006. *Awards:* Nat Endowment Arts, 88; Fulbright Award, 89-90; Guggenheim Fel, 94-95; Asian Cult Coun Fel, 94-95; Hasselblad Masters Award, 2004. *Bibliog:* Double Take, 12/2001; Vince Aletti (auth), Village Voice, 8/15/2002; Ad Coleman (auth), Photography in NY, 1-2/2003; David Friend (auth), Watching the World Change-The Stories Behind the Images of 9/11. *Mem:* Explorers Club of NY. *Media:* Photog. *Specialty:* Photog. *Collection:* Documentary Photog. *Publ:* Auth, A Fine Art Book: Portrait of Nepal, Chronicle Books, fall 93; Power Places of Kathmandu, Inner Traditions, 95; Pilgrimage: Looking at Ground Zero, 2002; auth, Pilgrimage, Power House, 2002; Michael Rockfeller Photographs, New Guinea 1961, Harvard Univ Press, 2006. *Dealer:* Gallery Kayafas 450 Harrison Ave Boston MA 02118. *Mailing Add:* PO Box 559 Shaftsbury VT 05201

BUCH, GARY
PAINTER
b Harrisburg, Pa, Nov 5, 54. *Study:* Bloomsburg Univ, Pa, 72-76; Cent Wash Univ, Ellensburg, MFA(painting), 80; Skowhegan Sch Painting & Sculpture, 84. *Exhib:* 10th Ann Works on Paper Exhib, SW Tex State Univ, 79; Pacific NW Arts Festival, Bellevue Mus, Wash, 81; Maine Invitational, Bowdoin Col, Brunswick, Maine, 83; Inaugural Exhib, Barn Gallery, Ogunquit, Maine, 84; one-man shows, Hobe Sound Galleries, Portland, Maine, 84 & 87, Fla, 87 & Midtown Galleries, NY, 86; Maine Biennial, Portland Mus Art, 85. *Teaching:* Grad teaching asst painting & drawing, Cent Wash Univ, 78-80; vis artist, Salisbury Sch, Conn, 85-. *Awards:* Marguerite Zorach Scholar, Skowhegan Sch Painting & Sculpture, 84; Sports Renault Award, 85. *Bibliog:* Douglas C McGill (auth), Personal art, the Skowhegan experience, NY Times, 9/84; Edgar Allen Beam (auth), Gary Buch has made it, Maine Times, 3/86; Lorraine Karafel (auth), Gary Buch, Art News, 5/86. *Dealer:* Midtown Payson Galleries 745 Fifth Ave New York NY 10151. *Mailing Add:* 1085 Washington Ave Portland ME 04103-3629

BUCHANAN, BEVERLY
PAINTER, SCULPTOR
b Fuquay, NC, Oct 8, 40. *Study:* Bennett Col, Greensboro, NC, BS, 62; Columbia Univ, MS, 68, MPH, 69. *Work:* High Mus Art; Metrop Mus Art, NY; Tampa Mus Art, Fla; also many pvt collections. *Exhib:* Slivermine Guild Arts Ctr, 73; High Mus Art (two exhibs), 88; Albright Knox Gallery, 89; solo exhibs, Schering-Plough Hq Gallery, Madison, NJ, 92, Steinbaum Krauss Gallery, NY, 93 & 96, Gallery Contemp Art, Sacred Heart Univ, Fairfield, Conn, 96, Tubman African Am Mus, Macon, Ga, 96, Spirit Sq Ctr Arts Educ, Charlotte, NC, 96 & Beverly Buchanan, Art Mus Missoula, Mont, 97; retrospective (traveling), Montclair Mus Art, NJ, 94-96; Mus Mod Art, NY, 94; African-Am Women Artists, Sweet Briar Col, Va, 96; Bearing Witness (with catalog), Spelman Col Mus Fine Art, 96-99; Woman's Work, Columbus Mus, Ga, 96; Resonant Forms: Contemp African-Am Woman Sculptors, Smithsonian Inst, Anacostia Mus & Ctr African-Am Hist & Cult, Washington, DC, 98; House and Home: Private Spaces, Bernice Steinbaum Gallery, Miami, Fla, 2001. *Teaching:* Lectr & vis artist, var institutions, 90-96. *Awards:* Guggenheim Fel, 80; Pollock-Krasner Found Award, 94; Nat Endowment Arts Sculpture Fel, 94. *Bibliog:* Robert Morton (ed), American Images, The SBC Collection of Twentieth Century American Art, Harry N Abrams Inc, New York, 96; Henry Sayre (interviewer), Beverly Buchanan: Works in progress, In: A World of Art, Ore Pub Broadcasting, Annenberg/CPB Proj, 96; William Zimmer (auth), Sculptural installation of large intention, NY Times, 11/3/96. *Mailing Add:* c/o Bernice Steinbaum Gallery 3550 North Miami Ave Miami FL 33127

BUCHANAN, JOHN EDWARD, JR
MUSEUM DIRECTOR, ADMINISTRATOR
b Nashville, Tenn, July, 24, 1953. *Study:* BA English Lit & Art History, Uiv of the South, TN, 75; MA Art History with Specialization in the Area of: Japanese Influence of American Art & Architecture, Vandrbilt Univ, TN, 79; Oxford Univ, Oxford, England, 79. *Work:* Tenn State Mus, Nashville. *Exhib:* Imperial Tombs of China, 96; Splendors of Ancient Egypt, 98; Monet to Moore; The Millennium Gift of the Sara Lee Corp, 99; The Triumph of French Painting; 17th Century Paintings from the Mus of FRAME (French Regional and Am Mus Exchange), 2003; Hesse; a Princely Ger Collection, 2005. *Collection Arranged:* The Passion of Rodin: Sculpture from the B Gerald Cantor Collection, 88; Heirs to Impressionism: Andre and Berth Noufflard, 88-89; The World of Toulouse-Lautrec featuring The Guardsmark Collection (auth, catalog); Louis XV and Madame de Pompadour: A Love Affair with Style (auth, catalog); Odilon Redon: The Ian Woodner Collection (auth, catalog); Dale Chihuly; The George R. Stroemple Collection and Chihuly Over Venice, 97; Clement Greenburg; A Critic's Collection, 2000; Stroganoff; The Palace and Collections of a Russian Noble Family, 2000; Pais to Portland; Impressionist and Post-Impressionist Masters in Portland Collections, 2003. *Pos:* Coordr mus develop, Tenn State Mus, Nashville, 77-80; mus assessment prog coordr, Am Asn Mus, Washington, DC, 80-82; exec dir, Lakeview Mus Arts & Sci, Peoria, Ill, 82-86; dir, The Dixon Gallery & Gardens, Memphis, Tenn, 86-94; adv bd mem, WKNO (pub TV & radio), Children's Mus Memphis & Moss Lecture Series, Rhodes Col; exec dir, Portland Art Mus, Portland, Ore, 94-06; dir, Fine Arts Mus San Francisco, 2006-. *Awards:* Oxford Univ Fel, 79; Chevalier dans l'Ordre des Arts et des Lettres, French Govt, 90; Thomas W Briggs Community Serv Award, 90; Legion of Honor, awarded by the French Govt: Chevalier dans l'Ordre des Art et des Lettres, awarded by the French Govt: Int Citizen Award, Consular Corp of Oregon. *Bibliog:* Bailey, Mike Building and Empire of Art The Columbian July 24, 98; Boyer, Guy, Mille et une facons de Collectionner L'Oeil # 499, Sept, 98; McMillan Dan, Art Mus turns its eye to integrating North Wing, The Business Journal, 1/3/2003. *Mem:* Am Asn Mus; Asn Art Mus Dirs; Art Mus Asn; Presidental Appointee, Nat Mus Serv Bd, Inst of Mus and Libr Serv, Am Asn of Mus. *Interests:* 19th Century French Painting; Rodin; Jean Louis-Forain; 19th Russian Painting; 18 & 19th Century Decorative Arts; Gardens; English Silver, Early Cezanne. *Publ:* Auth, Resources for Small Museums and Historic Sites, Tenn State Mus, rev ed 79; Professional Concern Checklist, Am Asn Mus, 80; The new museum assessment program, Mus News, 7-8/80; An applicant's map to the museum assessment program, Hist News, 9/80; A reading map, Mus News, 11-12/81. *Mailing Add:* c/o de Young Golden Gate Park 50 Hagiwara Tea Garden Dr San Francisco CA 94118

BUCHANAN, NANCY
VIDEO ARTIST, CONCEPTUAL ARTIST
b Boston, Mass, Aug 30, 46. *Study:* Univ of Calif, Irvine, BA, 69, MFA, 71. *Work:* Mus Mod Art, NY; Mus Contemp Art, La Jolla, Calif; Mus Art, Long Beach, Calif; Allen Mem Art Mus, Oberlin, Ohio. *Exhib:* API Nat Video Fest, Am Film Inst, Los Angeles, 84 & 91; New Television, WNET, KCET, KGBH, NY, Los Angeles & Boston, 89 & 90; The 90's various PBS stations, NY, Calif & Chicago, 91; Committed Visions, Mus Mod Art, NY, 92; Art/Women/California 1950-2000: Paralells and Intersections, San Jose Mus Art, Calif, 02; City of Los Angeles, UCLA Hammer Mus, Westwood, Calif, 00; Zones of Disturbance, Steirischer Herbst, Graz, Austria, 97. *Teaching:* Asst Prof non-static art, Univ Wis, Madison, 82-84; fac, Sch of Film, Video, Calif Inst Arts, Valencia, 88-05. *Awards:* Individual Artist's Fel (video), Nat Endowment Arts, 83 & 89; Rockefeller fel, multimedia, 96; City of Los Angeles Indiv Artist's grant, 99. *Bibliog:* Nancy Grub (ed), Making Their Mark: Women Artists Move into the Mainstream, Abbeville Press, 89; Christine Tamblyn (dir) & Doug Hall & Sally Jo Fifer (eds), Significant Others, Illuminating Video, Aperture, 91; Linda Burnham & Steven Durland (eds), The Citizen Artist: 20 Years of Art in the Public Arena, The Critical Press, 98; Laura Cottingham, Not for Sale: Feminism and Art in the USA during the 1970s (videotape), Hawkeye Productions, 98. *Media:* Video; installation. *Mailing Add:* c/o Calif Inst Sch of Film Dept 24700 McBean Pkwy Valencia CA 91355

BUCHANAN, SIDNEY ARNOLD
EDUCATOR, SCULPTOR
b Superior, Wis, Sept 12, 32. *Study:* Univ Minn, Duluth, BA, 62; NMex Highlands Univ, Las Vegas, MA, 63. *Work:* Joslyn Art Mus, Omaha, Nebr; Springfield Art Mus, Mo; Jacksonville Art Mus, Fla; City Art Gallery, Manchester, Eng; Neuberger Mus, Purchase, NY. *Comn:* sculpture (26'), Omaha Int Airport, 86; sculpture new bldg Omaha, Enron Corp Am, 91; sculpture (46' high & 50 ton), Kutak Found Univ Nebr, Omaha, 92; 62' high sculpture, Pace Setter Corp, Omaha, Nebr, 94; 60' high sculpture, Wilkensin Mfg Co, 95. *Exhib:* Midwest Biennial, 64-70 & Nebr, 75, Joslyn Art Mus, Omaha, Nebr; Mid-Am Exhib, William Rockhill Nelson Gallery of Art, Atkins Mus Fine Arts, Kansas City, Mo, 65-66; Colo/Nebr Exchange Exhib, Omaha & Denver, 67; Report on the Sixties, Denver Art Mus, 69; Northwestern Biennial, SDak Mem Art Ctr, 72; one-man shows, Turner Park, Nebr, 80, Sheldon Mem Gallery, Univ Nebr, Lincoln, 86, Col St Mary, Omaha, 89-90 & Jackson Art Works, Onaha, 2000; Invitational Sculpture, SIll Univ, 96; Invitational Sculpture, SW Mo State Univ, 98; Sculpture of the 20th Centure, Neuberger Mus, Purchase, NY, 2002; Ctrl Park Sculpture Invitational, Omaha. *Collection Arranged:* Civic Art Center, Sioux Falls, SD; Joslyn Art Mus, Omaha, NE; Sheldon Art Gallery, Lincoln, NE; Tweed Gallery, Univ Minnesota, Duluth, MN; Bemidji State Coll, MN; Asheville. *Pos:* Vis sculptor, Manchester Col of Art & Design, Eng, 69-70; artist-in-residence, Southern Ill Univ, Edwardsville, 72, Bemidji State Col, Minn, 75 & Plattsburg State Univ, 78. *Teaching:* Prof sculpture, Univ Nebr, Omaha, 64-95. *Awards:* Purchase Awards, Midwest Biennial, Joslyn Art Mus, Omaha, Nebr, 64-66 & Western Wash State Col, 67; Nat Endowment for the Arts Grant, 75. *Bibliog:* Dr Judith Van Wagner (auth), Metal Paintings, Leonardo Mag, Spring 77 & Award Winning Sculpture, Margaret Harold Publ, 67; Dr Judith Collichan (auth), Welder sculpture of the 20th century, Neuberger Mus; Judy Van Wagner (auth), Leonardo May, Tornado Sculpture, 79. *Media:* Steel. *Specialty:* Sculpture. *Interests:* Classical Music. *Publ:* Award Winning Sculpture, Margaret Harold Publ, 67; Leonardo Magazine, Pub NY, London, Paris, Dr. Judy Van Wagner; Who's Who Nebraska Art, Merit Pub Co.; Sculpture Techniques, Form, Content, Arthur Williams Davis Pub, Worcester, MA, 90. *Dealer:* Jackwon Art Works Omaha NE. *Mailing Add:* 1202 S 62nd St Omaha NE 68106

BUCHER, FRANCOIS
HISTORIAN, EDUCATOR
b Lausanne, Switz, June 11, 27; US citizen. *Study:* Univ Bern, Switz, PhD, 55; Brown Univ, Hon MA, 61. *Pos:* Mem exec comt, Acad Spoleto, 65- & Int Ctr Medieval Art, 68-; pres, Nautilus Found, Lloyd, Fla, 87-; organizer int competitions, Urban Ecology, Sculptures & Archit Ave Arts, Ecopolis, 90-94, chmn, Ecopolis II, 95; co-dir, Archit Res Ctr, 93-; invitee, Interarch, Sofia, Bulgaria, 94. *Teaching:* From instr to asst prof art hist, Yale Univ, 54-60; assoc prof, Brown Univ, 60-63 & Princeton Univ, 63-70; prof, State Univ NY, Binghamton, 70-77, co-dir, Ctr Medieval & Early Renaissance Studies, 73-76; prof, Fla State Univ, Tallahassee, 78-96; co-dir, Archit Res Ctr, Lloyd, Fla, currently. *Awards:* Inst Advan Studies Fel, 62-63; Pres Nautilus Found, Lloyd, Fla; Getty Scholar, 89. *Mem:* Medieval Acad Am; Col Art Asn Am; Soc Archit Historians; fel Int Ctr Medieval Art. *Media:* History of Art, Writing. *Res:* Medieval architecture; contemporary art. *Collection:* Permanent collection World Art and Prints, Nautilus Foundation, 91-. *Publ:* Auth, Josef Albers, Despite Straight Lines, Yale Univ Press, 69, rev ed MIT Press, 77, The Pamplona Bibles, Yale Univ Press, 70; The Dresden sketch-book of vault projection, Acts 22nd Int Cong Art Hist, 71; Nature in the visual arts of the Middle Ages, Tenth Ann Conf Ctr Medieval & Early Renaissance Studies, State Univ NY Press, 78; Architector, Medieval Lodge-books, Abaris Press, 79; Ein Strahlendes Ende, Bertelsmann, Munich, 84. *Mailing Add:* Fla State Univ Dept Art Hist Tallahassee FL 32306

BUCHMAN, ARLES (ARLETTE) BUCHMAN
PAINTER, ASSEMBLAGE ARTIST
b Liverpool, England; US citizen. *Study:* Lycee Jules Ferry, Paris, France; Herne Bay Collegiate Sch, Eng; Silvermine Art Sch, Conn. *Work:* Randolph-Macon Col, NC; Guild Hall, Easthampton, NY. *Comn:* Mem portrait, Ardsley Sch, NY. *Exhib:* Parrish Art Mus, Southampton, NY; Monmouth Mus, NJ; Inst Mod Art, NY. *Pos:* Pres, Victor D'Amico Inst Art, 85-91. *Teaching:* Instr art, Mus Mod Art, 61-71; Victor D'Amico Inst Art, 63-96; Metrop Mus Art, 61-71. *Awards:* First Prize, Westchester Art Soc, 70; Best Abstract, Nat Asn Woman Art, 89. *Bibliog:* Brian O Doherty (auth), Art, wide variety display, NY Times, 62; Robert Blaisdell (auth), An Artist-Teacher, Video VDIA, 90. *Mem:* Nat Asn Women Artists; NY State Teachers Asn; Mamaroneck Artists Guild; Jimmy Ernst Alliance. *Media:* Multi-media. *Publ:* Coauth, Assemblage, Mus Mod Art, 70; contribr, Palate to Palate, Times Book, 78; Jardin des Modes, France, 82; You're Never Too Thin or Too Rich, Southampton, 88. *Dealer:* Media-Loft 50 Webster Ave New Rochelle NY 10801. *Mailing Add:* Eight Wildwood Cir Larchmont NY 10538-3427

BUCHMAN, JAMES WALLACE
SCULPTOR, EDUCATOR
b Memphis, Tenn, Dec 3, 48. *Study:* Dartmouth Col, BA; Skowhegan Sch Painting & Sculpture. *Work:* Mus Fine Arts, Springfield, Mass. *Comn:* 1980 Olympic Games, Lake Placid, NY; Gen Serv Admin, Pittsfield, Mass. *Exhib:* One-man shows, 75, Max Hutchinson Gallery, 79 & 83 & Haenah-Kent, NY, 91; Sculpture Invitational, Zabriskie Gallery, NY, 82; Rochester Polytechnic Inst, 87; Haenah-Kent, NY, 91, 92 & 94. *Teaching:* Marlboro Col, 80-82; asst prof, State Univ NY, Albany, 83-. *Awards:* Guggenheim Fel, 77; Nat Endowment Arts, 80. *Bibliog:* Ingeborg Hoesteret (auth), Buchman (Sculpture Now), Art Int, 6/15/75; Donald B Kuspit (auth), James Buchman at Sculpture Now, Art Am, 7-8/75; Alan Singer (auth), article, Arts Mag, 4/85

BUCHWALD, HOWARD
PAINTER
b New York, NY, 1943. *Study:* Cooper Union, New York, BFA, 64; Hunter Col, New York, MA, 72. *Work:* Whitney Mus Am Art; Butler Inst Am Art; Covington & Burling, Washington; Dow Jones; Prudential Insurance Co, Newark, NJ; and others. *Exhib:* Recent Acquisitions, Whitney Mus Am Art, 72; Biennial of Contemp Am Art, Whitney Mus Am Art, 73; Am Drawing, Whitney Mus Am Art, 73; one-man exhibs, Galerie Swart, Amsterdam, The Neth, 74, Nancy Hoffman Gallery, NY, 74-76, 78, 82-85, 87-89 & 94, Galeire Farideh Cadot, Paris, France, 76 & 78, Mary Boone Gallery, NY, 79 & 80, Frumkin Struve Gallery, Chicago, 82, Janet Steinberg Gallery, San Francisco, 86 & Tomasulo Gallery, Union Co Col, Cranford, NJ, 90, Nancy Hoffman Gallery, New York City, 98, 01; The Eighties, Am Ctr, Paris & Contemp Art Mus, Houston, 79; Collector's Show, Ark Arts Ctr, Little Rock, 92 & 94; Just Art, 110 Greene St, NY, 93; Series & Editions, Nancy Hoffman Gallery, NY, 94; News, Surprise & Nostalgia, Bertha & Karl Leubsdorf Art Gallery, Hunter Col, NY, 95; group exhibs, Ark Arts Ctr, Little Rock, 97-98, Nancy Hoffman Gallery, New York City, 98, 98-99, 99-00. *Collection Arranged:* Butler Inst Am Art, Youngstown, Ohio; Chase Manhattan Bank, NYC; Dow Jones; Goldman Sachs, NYC; Whitney Mus Am Art, NYC; Sonesta Hotels; Pacific Enterprises, LA. *Pos:* Chair, dept painting & sculpture, Columbia Univ, 88-89. *Teaching:* At Hofstra Univ, 69-71, Kingsborough Community Col, 72-74; prof, Pratt Inst, 72-, Princeton Univ, 75-82, 92-94 & Columbia Univ, 82-91; at Richmond Community Col, 73-74, Queens Col, 74-75, Barnard Col, 85-87 & State Univ NY, Stony Brook, 93-94. *Awards:* Guggenheim Fel, 74-75; Nat Endowment Arts, 81 & 89; Elizabeth Found Grant, 94; Pollock-Krasner Grant, 93-94; Adolph and Ester Gottlieb Found Grant, 99. *Mailing Add:* c/o Nancy Hoffman Gallery 429 W Broadway New York NY 10012

BUCK, JOHN
SCULPTOR
b Ames, Iowa, 46. *Study:* Kansas City Art Inst & Sch Design, BFA, 68; Sckowhegan Sch Sculpture and Painting, Maine, 71; Univ Calif, MFA, 72. *Work:* Albright-Knox Art Gallery; Art Inst, Chicago; Brooklyn Mus; Denver Mus; San Francisco Mus Mod Art; Seattle Art Mus; Mus Modern Art, NY; Denver Art Mus, Colo. *Comn:* The Loop (cast bronze), Ahmanson Com Develop, Chicago, Ill, 90; The Loop (sculpture), Ahmanson Commercial Develop, Chicago, 91; The Accompaniment (wood panel), 99, The Waltz (wood panel), Swedish Hosp, Seattle, Wash,99; The Hawk & the Dove (cast bronze), 99, Music in the Sky (cast bronze), Lewis & Clark Col, Portland, Oreg, 99; Sacramento 2002 (wood sculpture), Meridian Plz, Sacramento, Calif, 2003. *Exhib:* Mus Mod Art, NY, 72; one-man show, Carlo Lamagna Gallery, NY, 85, 86, 88, Contemp Arts Ctr, Honolulu, Hawaii, 87 & Fine Arts Mus San Francisco, John Buck: Woodblock Prints, 93 & touring US, Oakland Mus Calif, 99, Miami Univ Art Mus, Oxford, Ohio, 2000, Scottsdale Mus Contemp Art, Ariz, 2001, Contemp Mus, Honolulu, Hawaii, 2002 & others; Denver Art Mus, Denver, Colo, 79-80, touring US; Madison Art Ctr, Madison, Wis, 82-83; Brooklyn Mus, NY, 86-87, touring US; Mus Contemp Art, Chicago, Ill, 90; traveling exhib, Palm Springs Desert Mus, 94; Sculpture, 94; A Survey Exhib, Contemp Mus, Honolulu, 95; Holter Mus Art, Helena, Mont, 2002; Collection Highlights, San Jose Mus Art, Calif, 2002; Expanded Horizons (with catalog), Yellowstone Art Mus, 2003. *Pos:* vis artist, Univ Cin, Ohio, 76, Tandem Press, Univ Wis, Madison, 89 & Utah State Univ, Logan, 89. *Teaching:* Sculpture instr, Humboldt State Col, 73-75; asst prof, Mont State Univ, 76-90. *Awards:* Purchase Award, Fifth Ann Juried Art Exhibition, Univ Calif, Davis, 71; Individual Artist Grant, Nat Endowment Arts, 80; Awards Visual Arts, Nat Artists Award, 84. *Bibliog:* Bruce Guenther (auth), John Buck, John Berggruen Gallery, Carlo Lamagna Gallery, Zolla/Lieberman Gallery, Asher/Faure, Eve Mannes Gallery, 88; John Yau (auth), John Buck: Woodblock Prints, Fine Arts Museums of San Francisco, 93. *Media:* Wood, Bronze. *Publ:* John Buck, DC Moore Gallery, NY, 99; plus others. *Dealer:* Imago Galleries Palm Desert CA; Zolla/Lieberman Gallery Chicago IL; Greg Kucera Gallery Seattle WA; DC Moore Gallery NYC; Robischon Gallery Denver CO. *Mailing Add:* 11229 Cottonwood Rd Bozeman MT 59718

BUCK, PORGE
PRINTMAKER
b Washington, DC, Jan 31, 31. *Study:* Richmond Prof Inst, Col William & Mary, Va, 49-51; Ill Wesleyan Univ, BFA, 53. *Work:* NCNB Corp, Charlotte, NC; Maine Nat Bank, Augusta; Asheville Art Mus, Asheville, NC. *Exhib:* Pennell Printmakers Exhib, Libr Cong, Washington, DC, 56; Corcoran Gallery Art, Washington, DC, 57; Colburn Gallery, Kenyon Col, Gambier, Ohio, 83; Contemp Am Printmakers, The Print Club, Philadelphia, 83; Asheville Art Mus, NC, 85; Minneapolis Col Art & Design, Minneapolis, Minn, 88; Intermont Col, Bristol, 89; and others. *Pos:* Co-dir, Intaglio-Relief Soc, Asheville, NC, 78-; printer & dir, IRS Press Editioning, Black Mountain, NC, 92-. *Awards:* Purchase Award, Ark State Univ, 97; Purchase Award, Purdue Univ, 2000. *Mem:* Am Print Alliance; Southern Graphics Coun; Artists Equity Asn; Int Graphic Arts Found; Mid Am Print Coun. *Media:* Intaglio, Woodcut. *Mailing Add:* 309 Portman Villa Rd Black Mountain NC 28711

BUCK, ROBERT TREAT, JR
ART DEALER, GALLERY DIRECTOR
b Fall River, Mass, Feb 16, 39. *Study:* Williams Col, BA; New York Univ, with Dr Walter Friedlaender, MA. *Collection Arranged:* Sam Francis: Paintings 1947-1972 (with catalog), 72; Paintings by Auguste Herbin; Here and Now: 13 Young Americans; Modernist Painting; Pollock to the Present; Master Drawings from the Art Inst Chicago & Mus Mod Art; Homage to Albers; Max Bill, 74; Bradley Walker Tomlin: A Retrospective View, 75; Richard Diebenkorn: Paintings & Drawings 1943-1976, 76-77; Antoni Tapies: 33 Years of His Work, 77; Cleve Gray: Serial Paintings, 77; Sonia Delaunay: A Retrospective (with catalog), 80; Francois Modellet: Systems, 85; Beverly Pepper, 86; Tony Crabb, 86; Alfredo Jaan, The Face Next Time, 89; Leon Polk Smith, Selected Works 1943-92, 96; Ab Reinhardt Early Works, 99; Keith Sonnier, 99; Glisha Bruskin, Life is Everywhere, 99; Internat Sculpture Festival, Monte Carlo, 2000. *Pos:* Lectr-researcher, Toledo Mus Art, 64-65; asst cur & instr, Wash Univ, 65-67 & dir, Gallery of Art, 68-70; asst dir, Albright-Knox Art Gallery, Buffalo, 70-73, dir, 73-83; dir, Brooklyn Mus, 83-96; dir, Marlborough Gallery, NY, 97-. *Teaching:* adj assoc prof mus training, Univ Toledo, 65-66; adj assoc prof mus training & 19th & 20th century art, Wash Univ, 66-70; adj assoc prof mus training, State Univ NY Buffalo, 72-73. *Awards:* NY State Coun Arts Traveling Fel, summer 71; Nat Endowment Arts Fel Mus Professional, summer 75. *Mem:* Asn Art Mus Dir (trustee, secy, 73-96); Brooklyn Arts Coun (mem bd, 83-96); Arts Alliance, NY (mem bd, 84-96); Pratt Art Inst (mem bd, 84-92). *Res:* Nineteenth century French painting; art of the twentieth century

BUCKHARDT, TOM
ARTIST
b 1964. *Study:* State Univ NY, Purchase, BFA, 86; attended Skowhegan Sch Painting and Sculpture, Maine, 86. *Exhib:* Solo shows include Work on Paper, Hunterdon Mus Art, Clinton, NJ, 2005, FULL STOP, Caren Golden Fine Art, NY City, 2005-2006, Tibor de Nagy Gallery, NY City, 2006; group shows include PMW Gallery, Stamford, Conn, 91; Painting, Self-Evident: Abstraction, Spoleto Festival, Charleston, SC, 92; Salon, Art in General, NY City, 92; Fever, Exit Art, NY City, 92; Frankel Nathanson Gallery, Maplewood, NJ, 93; Point Now, Black and Greenberg Gallery, NY City, 95; Urban Tantra, Esso Gallery, NY City, 96; 25 Years of Visual Arts at Purchase, Neuberger Mus, NY, 96; Summer Salon, Frick Gallery, 97; Bernard Toale Gallery, Boston, 98; Summer Slam, Anna Kustera Gallery, NY City, 99; Works on Paper, Bridgewater, Lustberg and Bloomfield, NY City, 2000; Self-Made Men, DC Moore Gallery, NY City, 2001; totems, Tibor de Nagy Gallery, 2002; NY New Work Now! Currier Gallery Art, Manchester, NH, 2002-2003; In the Land of Nod, McDonough Mus Art, Youngstown, Ohio, 2004. *Awards:* Richard and hinda Rosenthal Found Award, Am Acad Arts and Letters, 2002; George Hitchcock Award, Nat Acad Arts, 2002; Best Emerging Artist Award, Int Asn Art Critics, 2003; Marie Walsh Sharpe Art Found Studio Grant, 92-93; NY Found for Arts Painting Grant, 96; Pollock-Krasner Found Grant, 97, 2005. *Mailing Add:* c/o Tibor de Nagy Gallery 724 Fifth Ave New York NY 10019

BUCKMAN, JAN K
WEAVER
b Minneapolis, Minn, Jan 24, 49. *Study:* Univ Wis, with Walter Nottingham; Univ Minn; St Olaf Col. *Work:* Minneapolis Inst Art; Charles A Wustum Mus Art, Racine, Wis; Erie Art Mus, Pa. *Exhib:* The Tactile Vessel, Am Craft Mus, NY, 90; The Am Hand: Fifty Yrs, Minn Mus Am Art, St Paul, 93; Out of the Vault, Wustum Mus Art, Racine, Wis, 93; Vessels as Sculptural Expression, Hand & Spirit Gallery, Scottsdale, Ariz, 94; Enhancing the Living Space, West Bend Art Mus, Wis, 96; Vestiges of the Vessel, Dennos Mus, Traverse City, Mich, 96; Contemp Int Baskets, Manchester, Eng, 99; Browngrotta Arts, Wilton, Conn, Synderman-Works Galleries, Philadelphia, 1999; Craft Alliance, St Louis, 2001. *Awards:* Wis State Arts Bd Fel, 89; Arts Midwest Fel, 91; NEA Fel, 94. *Bibliog:* Lou Cabeer (auth), Patterns of thought, Fiber Arts, 91. *Mem:* Am Craft Coun. *Media:* Basketry. *Publ:* Contribr, The Basketmakers Art, Lark Books, 86; The Tactile Vessel, Erie Art Mus, 89; Portfolio, Am Craft, 89. *Dealer:* Sybarys Royal Oak MI; Brown Grotta Wilton CT. *Mailing Add:* Two Hills Studio W8119 320th Ave Hager City WI 54014

BUCKNALL, MALCOLM RODERICK
PAINTER
b Twickenham, Eng; US citizen, 35. *Study:* Univ Viswa-Bharati, West Bengal, India, 54-55; Chelsea Art Sch, London, Intermediate Nat Dipl Design, 58; Univ Tex, Austin, BFA(hon), 61; Univ Wash, Seattle, MFA, 63. *Work:* Butler Inst of Am Art, Youngstown, Ohio; Okla City Art Mus; Univ of Va Art Mus, Charlottesville; Crescent Collection, Crescent Marketing Ctr & State of the Art Work Environment, Dallas, Tex. *Comn:* portrait of Dean Sharlot (oil), Law Sch Univ Tex, comd Law Sch Found.

Exhib: Graham Gallery, Houston, Tex, 85, 87 & 91; Third Coast Review, Aspen Art Mus, Colo, 87; Texas Dialogues: Blue Star Art Space, San Antonio, Tex, 91; Martin-Rathburn Gallery, San Antonio, 93, 94, 95 & 98; Familiar Faces, Okla City Art Mus, 93; Realism: With a Twist, Arlington Mus, Tex, 96; Southwest Biennial, NMex Mus Art, Santa Fe, 1974, 1976, 1978, 2003. *Pos:* art critic Amherst Jour Record, Mass, 63-65; gallery artist, Greenwich Village Art Ctr, NY, 63-65; gallery artist, Graham Gallery, Houston, Tex, 82-92; gallery artist, Martin Rathburn Gallery, San Antonio, Tex, 92-99; gallery artist, d Berman Gallery, Austin, Tex, 2000-. *Teaching:* Instr drawing & design, Univ Wash, Seattle, 61-63. *Awards:* Medal, Midyr Show, Butler Inst of Am Art, 72 & 76; Artist Fel, Nat Endowment Arts, 85-86; Nat Drawing Show, Del Mar Col, Corpus Christi, Tex, 95. *Bibliog:* Melissa Hirsch (auth), Malcolm Bucknall: Apprehension of Mystery, Dart Mag, spring 83; Greg Kot (auth), It's the Jesus and Nirvana Chain, Rolling Stone, 4/1/93; Wim Niehaus (auth), De Jesus - Liz Art, Oor, Amsterdam, Holland, 9/94. *Media:* Oil, Ink Drawing. *Dealer:* D Berman Gallery Austin TX; McMurtrey Gallery, Houston, Tex. *Mailing Add:* 4205 Shoal Creek Blvd Austin TX 78756-3518

BUCKNER, KAY LAMOREUX
PAINTER, DRAFTSMAN
b Seattle, Wash, Dec 26, 35. *Study:* Sch of Art, Univ Wash, BA(art), 58; Claremont Grad Sch, MFA(painting), 61, study with Roger Kuntz & Phil Dike. *Work:* Olympic Col, Bremerton, Wash; Ore State Univ, Corvallis; Ga-Pac Co, Portland, Ore; Emanuel Hosp, Portland, Ore; Wash State Dept Corrections; City of Seattle, Wash; Ga-Pac Co, Portland, Oreg. *Exhib:* Frye Art Mus, Seattle, 79; Oregon Mus Art, Eugene, 81; NMex Int, Clovis, 81; Nat Landscape Art Exhib, Springfield Art Mus, Ill, 82; Clark Gallery, Rockford, Ill, 82; Nat Women Art Exhib, Springfield Art Mus, Ill, 83; Jadite Galleries, NY, 88; Word Works, Seattle Ctr, 89; Contemp Works on Canvas, Md Fedn Art, Annapolis, 91; Her Hands, Albin Kuhn Gallery, Univ Md, Baltimore, 94; Salisbury State Univ, Md, 97; Whatcom Mus, Bellingham, Wash, 2000; Pa State Univ, Zoller Gallery, Univ Park, Pa, 2003; Rugs of the 21st Century, Textile Ctr, Minneapolis, Minn, 2004. *Teaching:* Adj asst prof, Univ Ore, 76-96. *Awards:* First Prize Painting, 18th Nat Greater Fall River Exhib, Mass, 76; First Prize, NMex Int Exhib, 81; Northwest Poets & Artists Calendar, Wash, 90; First Prize, TRugs of the 21st Century, Textile Center, Minneapolis, Minn, 2004. *Bibliog:* Dennis Wepman (auth), Kay Buckner's Luminous Vision, Manhattan Arts, 12/87; Miles Unger (auth), The Power of Metaphor, Manhattan Arts, June-July, 88; Jane Beatty (auth), Languages & Literature, McDougal, Littell & Co, 91. *Media:* Oil, Fibers. *Mailing Add:* 2332 Rockwood Ave Eugene OR 97405

BUCKNER, PAUL EUGENE
SCULPTOR, EDUCATOR
b Seattle, Wash, June 16, 33. *Study:* Univ Wash Sch Art, BA(sculpture), 59; Claremont Grad Sch, MFA(sculpture), 61, study with Albert Stewart; Fulbright grant, Slade Sch, Univ Col, London, 61-62. *Work:* Olympic Col, Bremerton, Wash; Salem Civic Ctr, Ore; Ore Mus Art, Eugene; First Nat Bank Ore, Portland; Multnoma Athletic Club, Portland, Ore. *Comn:* wood carvings, carved doors, Sacred Heart Gen Hospital, Eugene, Ore, 82-83; Entry Court Sculpture, Eastern Ore Correctional Inst, Pendleton, Ore, 88; wood carvings, Mount Angel Abbey, St Benedict, Ore, 85-86; two carved wood figure groups, Timberline Lodge, Ore, 90; copper/gold leaf wind vane & ceramic tile totem, South Seattle CC Duwamish Ctr, 2003-06; and others. *Exhib:* Northwest Artists, Seattle Art Mus, Wash, 64; solo exhib, Ore Mus Art, Eugene, 64, Jadite Galleries, NY, 88 & Frye Art Mus, Seattle, Wash, 93; Sculpture 67, Seattle Art Mus, Wash, 67; Mountain High III, Timberline Lodge, Ore, 81; Sculpture on the Green, Univ Portland, 82; retrospective, The Figure-Twenty-Five Yrs, Ore Mus Art, Eugene, 86; Contributing Artist: 1939-1989, Ore Hist Soc, Portland, Ore, 89; A Garden for Sculpture, Seattle Ctr, 92; Thirty-three Yrs of Sculpture with Paul Buckner, Chetwynd Stapylton, Gallery, Portland, 96. *Teaching:* Prof emer sculpture, Univ Ore, Eugene, 62-. *Awards:* Nat Sculpture Rev Prize, Nat Sculpture Soc, 77; Award of Distinction, Mainstreams 77, Marietta Col, Ohio, 77; Thomas F Herman Fac Achievement Award for Distinguished Teaching, Univ Ore, 95. *Bibliog:* Lorraine Widman (auth), Sculpture: A Studio Guide, Concepts, Methods, and Materials, Prentice Hall, Englewood Cliffs, NJ, 89; Mary Balcomb (auth), Paul Buckner: Sculptor, Am Artist, 6/80; Charlotte Graydon (auth), Nationally known sculptor takes crisp view of wood, The Oregonian, 9/10/84. *Media:* Wood Carving, Bronze Casting. *Mailing Add:* 2332 Rockwood Ave Eugene OR 97405

BUCKSBAUM, MELVA & RAYMOND LEARSY
COLLECTOR
Awards: Named one of top 200 collectors (with Raymond Learsy), ARTnews Mag, 2004; recipient Gertrude Vanderbilt Whitney Award for outstanding arts patronage & philanthropy, 2004. *Mem:* Whitney Mus Am Art (trustee 96-, vchmn 2004-), Tate Gallery (Int Committee). *Collection:* Contemporary art. *Mailing Add:* 646 Willoughby Way Aspen CO 81611

BUDNY, VIRGINIA
SCULPTOR, WRITER
b Maui, Hawaii, 44. *Study:* Vassar Col, with Concetta Scaravaglione, AB, 65; Columbia Univ, with Peter Agostini, 65-66; Univ NC, Greensboro, with Peter Agostini, MFA, 70; Inst Fine Arts, NY Univ, MA, 88; Metrop Mus Art, New York, cur studies cert, 92. *Work:* Smithsonian Inst; Vassar Col Art Gallery; Weatherspoon Art Gallery. *Exhib:* North Carolina Sculpture 79, Weatherspoon Art Gallery, Univ NC, Greensboro, 79; Am Porcelain Traveling Exhib, Renwick Gallery, 80-83; Illusion, Southeast Ctr Contemp Art, Winston-Salem, NC, 83; Contemp Trompe l'Oeil Painting and Sculpture, Boise Gallery Art & traveling, 83-85; Equitable Gallery, NY, 84; Alternative Mus, NY, 85; Brenda Kroos Gallery, Columbus, Ohio, 85; Desires, A Personal Gallery, Greensboro, 88; Sculptors Draw the Nude, Luise Ross Gallery, NY, 90. *Pos:* Res asst to Everett Fahy (chmn, Dept Europ paintings) Metrop Mus Art, NY, 93-; consult, The Lachaise Found, 03-. *Teaching:* Asst prof sculpture, Univ NC, Greensboro, 73-80; instr art hist, Continuing Educ, Cooper Union, NY Univ, 87-88; lectr art hist, Parsons Sch Design, 91-92, instr, 92; adj instr art dept, City Col NY, 97 & 2000; lectr, Parsons Sch Design & New Sch, 2004; lectr, IRP, New Sch, 2006. *Awards:* Yaddo Found Fel, 81; Am Philos Soc Grant, 84; June & Morgan Whitney Fel, Metrop Mus Art, 92-94; and others. *Bibliog:* William Zimmer (auth), rev, Arts Mag, 1/77; Jane D Scholl (auth), article, Smithsonian Mag, 2/81; Vivien Raynor (auth), rev, NY Times, 1/11/85. *Media:* Clay. *Res:* Leonardo da Vinci's creative process studied through his composition sketches. *Publ:* Auth, The poses of the child in the composition sketches by Leonardo da Vinci for The Madonna and Child With a Cat, Weatherspoon Gallery Asn Bull, 80; The sequence of Leonardo's sketches for The Virgin and Child with Saint Anne and Saint John the Baptist, Art Bull, 83; coauth (with Frank Dabell), Hard at Work 'di notte chome di dì': A close reading of Cosimo Rosselli's career with some new documents, in: Cosimo Rosselli: Painter of the Sistine Chapel, Cornell Fine Arts Mus, 2001; Benedetto da Maiano, Pulpit, Church of Santa Croce, Encyclopedia of Sculpture, 2004; Gaston Lachaise's American Venus, The Genesis and Evolution of Elevation, The American Art J, 2003-2004; Left Bank New York: Artist Off Washington Square, 1900-1950 (Exhib Catalog) La Maison Française NY Univ, 2006. *Mailing Add:* 324 E 81st Apt 6RW New York NY 10013

BUECHNER, THOMAS SCHARMAN
PAINTER, WRITER
b New York, NY, Sept 25, 26. *Study:* Princeton Univ, 44-45; Art Students League, 46-47; Ecole Beaux-Arts, Fontainebleau & Paris, France, 47-48; Levine-Shikler, 61-80. *Hon Degrees:* Elmira Col, LHD, 2001. *Work:* Bowdoin Col, Maine; Metrop Mus Art, Brooklyn Mus, Cornell Univ, NY; Nat Mus Am Art, Smithsonian Inst, Washington, DC. *Comn:* Portrait, Paul Sheaffer, Brooklyn Hosp, 65; portrait, Alice Tully, Lincoln Ctr; portrait, David Atwater, Grace Episcopal Church, 70; portrait, Joseph Hill, State Univ NY Downstate Med Ctr, 72; portrait, Alfred Gelhorn, Univ Pa; portrait, Robert Blum, Brooklyn Mus. *Exhib:* Artists of Am, Denver, Colo, 80-2000; AM Adler Fine Arts, NY, 82 & 84; Nat Acad Design; Metrop Mus Art, NY, 88; Weissenstein Regen, Ger, 89; OK Harris, NY; Arnold Gallery, Newport, 98; Melberg, Charlotte, NC, 2002. *Collection Arranged:* Vincent Van Gogh, Metrop Mus Art, New York, 49; Glass 1959, Corning Mus Glass, 59; Levine-Shikler (catalog), Brooklyn Mus, New York, 71; Artist Am, Denver, Colo, 80-98; Exactitude, Metrop Mus Art, 88. *Pos:* Dir, Corning Mus Glass, 50-60, pres, 71-; dir, Brooklyn Mus, 60-71; pres, Corning Glassworks Found, 71; Rockwell Mus, 76-; Market St Restoration Agency, 78-; pres, Steuben Glass, 72-86; illusr, Book World & Dubbings Electronics. *Teaching:* Head dept art, Corning Community Col, NY, 58-60; head painting & drawing, Heights Casino, Brooklyn, NY, 65-68; prof drawing arts & social change, Salzburg Sem Am Studies, 71, artist-in-residence, Haystack Mountain Sch, Maine; Pilchuck Glass Sch, Wash; landscapes & still life, Scottsdale Artist's Sch, Ariz, 87-2003; Bild Werk, Frauenau, Ger, 87-2003; Loveland Acad, Colo, 94-2003. *Awards:* Brooklyn Man of Year, Brooklyn Col, 63; Forsythia Award, Brooklyn Botanic Garden, 71; Gari Melcher's Gold Medal, Artist's Fel, 71; Bowdoin Col Award; Lifetime Achievement Awarad, Glass Art Soco, 2001. *Bibliog:* Article in Art News, 12/85; Am Artist, 6/80, 10/91, 94, 96 & 98; US Art, 7/88. *Mem:* Louis Comfort Tiffany Found (trustee, 71); fel Royal Soc Art; Century Club. *Media:* Oil, Watercolor. *Res:* American illustration, emphasis on cover artists; glass history with emphasis on art glass. *Publ:* Auth, Glass Vessels in Dutch Painting in the 17th Century, 52; auth, Norman Rockwell: Artist and Illustrator; Art of Ogdon Pleissner; Arts of David Levine; How I Paint, Harry N Abrams, 00. *Dealer:* West End Gallery Market St Corning NY; Melberg Charlotte NC; Principle Alexandria VA. *Mailing Add:* 1050B N RD Corning NY 14830

BUECKER, ROBERT
GALLERY DIRECTOR, PAINTER
b Pittsburgh, Pa, 35. *Study:* Pa State; Carnegie Tech. *Exhib:* Solo exhibs, Richard Feigen Gallery, NY, 63, 66 & 69 & Zolla/Lieberman Gallery, Chicago, 77; Other Ideas, Detroit Inst Arts, Mich, 69; Six Greek Crosses, 77 & Religious Work Retrospective, 79, Cathedral St John the Divine Mus Religious Art; and others. *Pos:* Owner, Buecker & Harpsichords, NY, 70-. *Bibliog:* Suzy Gablic (auth), article, Art News, 1/64; Michael Andre (auth), article, Village Voice, 8/11/75; Tom Johnson (auth), article, Village Voice, 3/25/81. *Res:* Contemporary New York art history. *Specialty:* Contemporary American art. *Mailing Add:* 465 W Broadway New York NY 10012-3147

BUEHLER, STUART M
JEWELER, PAINTER
b June 7, 45. *Study:* Humboldt State Univ, Arcata, Calif, 83. *Work:* Crocker Art Mus, Sacramento, Calif; Portland Art Mus; Smithsonian Inst; Oakland Mus. *Exhib:* Good as Gold: Alternative Materials in Am Jewelry, Smithsonian Inst, 81-83; California Crafts XIII, Crocker Art Mus, Sacramento, Calif, 83; First Impressions: Northwest Monoprints, Seattle Art Mus, 89; Of Magic, Power & Memory, Bellevue Art Mus, 92; The Edge of Childhood (with catalog), Heckscher Mus, Huntington, NY, 92; Jewels & Gems: Collecting California Jewelry, Oakland Mus, 94. *Awards:* Merit Award, Sculpture Exhibition, Am River Community Col, 65; Merit Award, Calif Crafts XI, Crocker Art Mus, 79. *Bibliog:* Lois Allan (auth), Finding the boneman, Artweek, 11/21/87; Sophie Dunn (auth), Marginality & Exile: The Work of Stuart Buehler, Metalsmith, summer 93. *Media:* Mixed Media. *Mailing Add:* 925 NW Flanders St Portland OR 97209-3123

BUGBEE-JACKSON, JOAN (MRS JOHN M JACKSON)
SCULPTOR, EDUCATOR
b Oakland, Calif, Dec 17, 41. *Study:* Univ Mont; Univ Calif, San Jose, BA & MA; Art Students League, with R B Hale; Sch of Fine Arts, Nat Acad Design; also with M Wildenhain, EvAngelos Frudakis, Joseph Kiselewski, Granville Carter & Adolph Block. *Work:* Cordova Pub Libr, Alaska. *Comn:* Alaska's Wildlife (bronze medal), 80; two sculpture murals, Alaska State Capital Bldg, Juneau, Alaska, 81; Gruening & Bartlett busts, Alaska State Capitol Bldg, Juneau, 82; plaque, Armin F Koernig, 85; two portraits, comn by Mr & Mrs Robert B Atwood, 85; Cordova Fisherman's Memorial Statue, 85; bronze relief, Alaska's Five Govenors, Loussac Libr, Anchorage, 86; Charles E Bunnell Bronze Statue, Univ Alaska, Fairbanks, 88; bronze, Sitka, Alexander Baranof Monument, Alaska, 89; bronze plaque plaque, Wally Noerenberg, Prince Wm Sound, Alaska, 89; Russian-Alaskan friendship plaques, Kayak, Is & Cordova, Alaska, Vladivostok & Petropavlovsk-Kamchatskiyi, Russia, 91. *Exhib:* One-woman show, Springvale, Maine, 70; Nat Sculpture Soc Ann, NY, 70-73; Allied Artists Am Ann, NY, 70-72; Nat Acad Design Ann, NY, 71 & 74; Joan Bugbee, Retrospective, NY, 72; Cordova Womanart Show, 86, 87, 88. *Teaching:* Instr design, De Anza Col, Cupertino, Calif, 67-68; instr pottery & glaze chem, Greenwich House Pottery, NY, 69-71; instr pottery, Prince William Sound Community Col, Cordova, 72-88. *Awards:* Helen Foster Barnet Prize, Nat Acad Design, 71; Daniel Chester French Prize, Nat Sculpture Soc, 72 & C Percival Dietsch Prize, 73; Allied Artist Am Award, 72; Citation, Alaska State Legislature, 81. *Bibliog:* Jim Seay (auth), A move for inspiration, Anchorage Daily News, 8/13/72; New Issues, Alaskan Medal Series, The Numismatist, 1/81; Ron Dalby (auth), Cordova's contemporary realist, Alaska Mag, 86; Rebecca Hom (auth), Cordova's Sculptor, Rualite Mag, 9/88. *Mem:* Fel Nat Sculpture Soc; Artists' Equity Asn. *Media:* Fired Stoneware Clay, Cast Bronze. *Publ:* Contribr, Nat Sculpture Review, winter 70-71, spring 71 & winter 81-82. *Mailing Add:* PO Box 374 Cordova AK 99574

BUI, PHONG
PAINTER
b Hue, Vietnam, 64; arrived in US, 80. *Study:* Philadelphia Col Art, BFA, 85; studied at NY Studio Sch Painting, 85-87. *Exhib:* Solo shows include Galleria ISA, Montecastellow, 94, Sussex County Community Col Gallery, NJ, 95, Homage to Meyer Schapiro: An Architectonic Installation, Holland Tunnel Art Projects, 2000, For Meyer and Lillian, Univ Arts, Phila, 2002, Hybrid Carnival for St Exupery #2 and #3, Sarah Bowen Gallery, 2005; group shows include Am Acad Arts and Letters, NY, 2005; Segments and Connections, Wooster Arts Space, NY, 2005; Continuous Mark: 40 Years of NY Studio Sch, 2005. *Teaching:* Lectr Parson Sch Design; teacher, Int Sch Art. *Awards:* Arcadia Traveling Fellowship; Hobenberg Traveling Fellowship; Charles Revson Found Grant; Pollock-Krasner Found Fellowship, 94. *Mailing Add:* c/o Sarah Bowen Gallery 210 N 6th St Brooklyn NY 11211

BUIST, KATHY
PAINTER
b Allendale, MI, Nov 12, 59. *Study:* Kendall Sch of Design, BFA, 1981; Vt Studio Ctr, 1993-1997; NY Academy of Art (cum laude), MFA, 1996; Va Ctr for the Creative Arts Fel, 1998. *Exhib:* Nabi Gallery, 98-2006; Holiday Show, Nabi Gallery, NY, 1999; Seasons, Elsa Mott Ives Gallery, NY, 2000; Landscapes Real & Imagined, Rye Arts Gallery, NY, 2001; Inaugural Show, Boston Art, Mass, 2002; Scott Freidrick Gallery, Allenhurst, NJ, 2003-2004; Frederick Gallery, 2003-06. *Pos:* Vis artist, Caldwell Community Col, 1998; Vis artist, Jersey Shore Arts Center, 2005. *Bibliog:* Phylis Branff (auth), NY Times, 97 & 98; L Mag, 2005; Expression of Nature, TriCity News, 2006. *Mem:* Jersey Shore Plein Art Painters; Nat Plein Air Painters; The Guild Shrewsbury. *Media:* Painter, Pastels. *Dealer:* Water St Gallery; Diana Ferrone Gallery. *Mailing Add:* 201 E 21st St Apt # 16E New York NY 10010

BUITRON, ROBERT C
PHOTOGRAPHER, VIDEO ARTIST
b E Chicago, Ind, Sept 21, 53. *Study:* Ariz State Univ, BFA, 80; Univ Ill, Chicago, MFA, 96. *Work:* Mexican Mus, San Francisco; New Orleans Mus Art; Bibliotheque Nationale, Paris, France; Ctr Creative Photog, Tucson; Consejo Mexicano de Fotografia, Mex. *Exhib:* Hecho En Latinoamerica II, Museo del Palacio de Bellas Artes, Mex, 81; Ten Photographers: Olympic Images, Mus Contemp Art, Los Angeles, 84; Chicago Art: Resistance & Affirmation, Wight Art Gallery, Univ Calif, Los Angeles, 90; Arizona Photographers, Ctr Creative Photog, Tucson, 90; Syncretism, The Art of the XXI Century, Alternative Mus, NY, 91; Turning The Map, Part two, Camerawork, London, Gt Brit, 92; From the West: Chicano Narrative Photog, Mex Mus, San Francisco, 95; Image and Identity, pARTs Photog Arts, Minneapolis, Minn, 2000; Cowboys, Indians, and The Big Picture, McMullen Mus Art, Boston, 2002; Only Skin Deep: Changing Visions of the Am Self, Int Ctr Photog, NY, 2003; 1984 Olympics Los Angeles to Present Work, Louis Carlos Bernal Gallery, Pima Coll, Tucson, Ariz; Post-Ironic Lull, Galaxy Gallery, Univ Mo, St Louis, 2005; Photography Midwest, Wis Union Galleries, Univ Wis, Madison, 2006. *Collection Arranged:* Chicanolandia, MARS Artspace (traveling exhib), 93; American Voices: Latino Photographers in the US, Foto Fest, Smithsonian Inst, 94; Picarte: Photography Beyond Representation, Heard Mus, 2003. *Pos:* Exec dir, MARS Artspace, Phoenix, 82-84; independent cur & writer, 89-. *Teaching:* Asst prof photography, Univ Minn, 98-2000; instr, Sch Art Inst Chicago, 2000-2002; instr, Col DuPage, 2000-. *Awards:* Visual Artist Fel, Nat Endowment Arts, 82; Artist Fel, Art Matters Found, 95; Photog Fel, Ill Arts Coun, 98. *Bibliog:* Richard Nilsen (auth), Calendar Captures Cultural Ironies, Arizona Republic, 1991; Holland Cotter, Loyal to Two Cultures: From Chicano Roots to a New Ambiguity, NY Times, 01. *Media:* Photography. *Publ:* Lucy Lippard (auth), Mixed Blessing, 1990; Gary D Keller, Contemporary Chicana & Chicano Art: Artist, Works, Culture & Education, Vol 1, 2002; Heather Fryer (auth), Cowboys, Indians, and The Big Picture, McMullen Mus Art, Boston, 2002; Coco Fusco & Brian Wallis (auth), Only Skin Deep, Int Ctr Photography, NYC, 2003; Catriona Rueda Esquibel, Aztec Princess Still at Large, 04. *Mailing Add:* 124 Division St Geneva IL 60134

BUITRON-OLIVER, DIANA
CURATOR
b Quito, Ecuador, Apr 17, 46; US citizen. *Study:* Smith Col, BA, 69; Inst of Fine Arts, New York Univ, MA, 72 & PhD, 76; Am Sch of Classical Studies, Athens, Greece, 72-73. *Pos:* Curatorial asst, Fogg Art Mus, Harvard Univ, 70-72; Andrew Mellon & Chester Dale Fel, Metrop Mus Art, New York, 73-75; cur Greek & Roman art, Walters Art Gallery, Baltimore, Md, 77-84; dir, Excavations in the Archaic Precinct, Kourion, Cyprus, 82-85; guest cur, Nat Gallery Art, Washington, DC. *Teaching:* Asst prof classics, John Hopkins Univ, 82-83; vis lectr, Smith Col, 87; prof lectr, Georgetown Univ, 88-94. *Mem:* Archaeol Inst Am; Am Asn Univ Women; Ger Archaeol Inst. *Res:* Greek art, specializing in Greek vase painting & Cypriot archaeology. *Publ:* Ed, New Perspectives in Early Greek Art, Washington, 91; The Odyssey and Ancient Art (catalog), Annandale-on-Hudson, 92; Excavations in the Archaic Precinct at the Sanctuary of Apollo at Kourion in Cyprus (in press); Auth, Attic Vase Painting in New England Collections, (Kerameus series), Douris (in press), 95. *Mailing Add:* 3401 Rolling Ct Chevy Chase MD 20815-4040

BUJESE, ARLENE
CURATOR, PRINTMAKER
b Hillsdale, NJ, May 8, 38. *Study:* Corcoran Sch Art, 64-70; Hood Col, Md, AB, 75, MA, 78. *Work:* Parrish Art Mus, Southampton, NY. *Exhib:* Four Graphic Artists, Parrish Art Mus, 70; Nat Exhib Prints & Drawings, Okla Art Ctr, 72; 11 Contemp Printmakers, Int Monetary Fund, Washington, 74; Printmakers of the Region, Guild Hall Mus, NY, 75; solo exhib, Arts Club Washington, 84; NJ National Print Exhib, Hunterdon Art Ctr. *Pos:* Dir & vpres, Phoenix II Gallery, Washington, 81-83; dir, Benton Gallery, Southampton, NY, 86-94; owner & dir, Arlene Bujese Gallery, East Hampton, NY, 94-2006; cur, Ossorio Foundation, Southampton, NY. *Teaching:* Instr design, Hood Col, Md, 81-84. *Awards:* First Prize for Graphics, Ann Student Exhib, Corcoran Sch, 69; Best in Any Media, Guild Hall Ann, 80; Exhib Comt Prize, Arts Club Washington, 82. *Media:* Etching. *Specialty:* Major contemporary American artists and the new generation of artists of Eastern Long Island. *Interests:* East End Hospice. *Publ:* Ed, 25 Artists: Hans Namuth and 24 Artists, Univ Publ Am, 82. *Mailing Add:* 40 Whooping Hollow Rd East Hampton NY 11937

BUJNOWSKI, JOEL A
PRINTMAKER, PAINTER
b Chicago, Ill, Dec 16, 49. *Study:* Western Ill Univ, BA, 72, MA, 74; Northern Ill Univ, MFA, 78. *Work:* State Ill Ctr Collection, Chicago, Ill; Lamar Dodd Art Ctr Collection, La Grange Col, Ill; Univ NDak Collection, Grand Forks; Univ Dallas Collection, Irving, Tex; Clemson Univ Collection, SC. *Exhib:* 11th Monroe Nat Art Exhib, Masur Mus Art, Monroe, La, 79; Wesleyan Int Exhib Prints & Drawings, traveling exhib, 80-81; 7th Univ Dallas Print Invitational, Tex & Gt Brit, 81-83; 79th & 80th Chicago & Vicinity Exhib, Art Inst Chicago, Ill, 81 & 84; New Am Graphics III, Mus in Europe, Africa & Asia, 83; 20th Ann All Media Exhib, Brea Civic Cult Ctr Gallery, Calif, 86; Int Biennial Print Exhib, Taipei Fine Arts Mus, Repub China, 87; solo exhib, Univ Ariz Mus Art, Tucson, 89; Third Biennial Exhib of Prints, Mus Mod Art, Wakayama, Japan, 89; 16th, 22nd, 23rd, 25th Bradley Nat Print & Drawing Exhib, Peoria, Ill, 77, 89, 91 & 95. *Teaching:* Asst prof printmaking & drawing, Univ Hawaii, Manoa, Honolulu, 86-87; dir, Harper Col Nat Print & Drawing; adj fac, currently; asst prof drawing & printmaking, Eastern Ill Univ, Charleston, Ill, currently. *Awards:* Award Excellence, Memphis State Univ, 85; Best of Show, Bradley Univ, 89; Arts Midwest & Nat Endowment Asn Regional, 90. *Bibliog:* Marcia Morse (auth), Fresh faces, new visions, Honolulu Sunday Star Bull, 9/14/86; Karl Moehl (auth), review, New Art Examiner, 90; Jerry Klein (auth), Peoria J Star, 90. *Dealer:* Chicago Ctr for Print 1509 Fullerton Chicago IL. *Mailing Add:* 11284 Lorenson Rd Montague MI 49437

BUKOVNIK, GARY
PAINTER, PRINTMAKER
b Cleveland, Ohio, Apr 10, 47. *Study:* Cleveland Inst Art, 66-68. *Work:* Mus Mod Art, Metrop Mus Art, NY; Boston Mus Fine Art; Brooklyn Mus; Art Inst Chicago; Mus Art, Carnegie Inst, Pittsburgh, Pa; Fine Arts Mus of San Francisco; Butler Inst of Am Art. *Comn:* watercolors, Peat, Marwick, Mitchell & Assocs, Atlanta, 86; watercolors, Bonaventure Hotel, Los Angeles, 86; watercolors, IBM, Atlanta, 86; image for poster, Metrop Opera, NY, 91; Watercolors, Comerica Bank, Costa Mesa & San Jose, 95. *Exhib:* Solo exhibs, Brooklyn Mus Art, NY, 84, Lisa Kurts Gallery, Memphis, 90, 91, 93, 98, 2002, Ansorena, Madrid, 91, de Saisset Mus, Santa Clara Univ, 91, Staempfli Gallery, 83, 84, 86, 87, 89 & 91, Garden Ctr Greater Cleveland, 92, Jakopic Gallery, Archit Mus, Ljubljuna, Slovenia, 94, Erickson & Elins Gallery, 96, 99, 2001, Memphis Botanic Garden, 97 & Southern Alleghenies Mus, 98, Neuhoff Gallery, 2000; Gene Baro Collects, Brooklyn Mus Art, 83; Bouquets to Art, MH de Young Mus, San Francisco, Calif, 90; Recent Acquisitions, Fine Arts Mus, San Francisco, 91; 20th Century Flower Painting, Ft Lauderdale Mus Art, 91; In the Garden, Bolinas Mus, 91; 50 Peintres en Hommage a Jean Lurcat, Abusson, France, 92; Space, Light & Form, Babcock Galleries, NY, 96; Butler Inst of Am Art, 2002; and others. *Awards:* George Bunker Award, Print Competition, Philadelphia Mus Art, 81; Award of Merit, Am Soc Mus Publ, 82 & San Francisco Arts Comn, 88; Vis Artist, Am Acad in Rome, 2003, 2005. *Bibliog:* Anna Novakov (auth), Speaking of flowers, Art Week, 87; Judith Gordon (auth), Dream Weaver, SF Mag, 4/90; Painter of Perfection, El Punto de las

Artes, Madrid, 1/18-24/91; and others. *Media:* Watercolor; Monotype, Lithograph. *Publ:* Flowers: Gary Bukovnik Watercolors & Monotypes, Harry N Abrams, 90; illusr, A Taste of San Francisco, Doubleday, 90; From a Breton Garden, Addison Wesley, 90. *Dealer:* Irving Galleries, 332 Worth Ave, Palm Beach, FL, 33480. *Mailing Add:* 1179 Howard St San Francisco CA 94103

BULKA, DOUGLAS
PAINTER, EDUCATOR
b 54. *Study:* Univ Mich, Ann Arbor, 73-75; Wayne State Univ, Detroit, Mich, BFA, 77, MFA, 86. *Work:* Detroit Inst Arts, Mich; Detroit Receiving Hosp, Mich; Northern Mich Univ Art Mus, Marquette; Wayne State Univ, Detroit, Mich. *Exhib:* Mich Artists 80/81, Univ Mich Mus Art, Ann Arbor, 81; Reactions to Mich, Muskegon Mus Art, 86; Isolate, Lemberg Gallery, Birmingham, Mich, 92, Curb Marks, 95; Mich Artists from the Permanent Collection, Detroit Inst Arts, 97; Drawn From Nature: Landscape Drawings & Watercolors from the Permanent Collection, Detroit Inst Arts, 97; Artists of the Midwest, Northern Mich Univ Mus, Marquette, 98. *Collection Arranged:* Ambient Luminosity, Detroit Artists Market, 97; The Print, Ann Arbor Art Ctr, 98. *Pos:* conservation program coord, Commn Art Pub Places, State of Mich, 90; bd dir & exhib com chair, Detrout Focus Gallery, Mich, 91-95; bd dir & exhib com chmn, Detroit Artists Market, Mich, 95-. *Teaching:* adj fac painting & drawing, Lawrence Tech Univ, Southfield, Mich, 81-82; adj fac painting & drawing, Wayne State Univ, Detroit, Mich, 84-87, 99-2000. *Awards:* Creative Artists Grant, Arts Found Mich and Mich Coun Arts & Cult Affairs, 92; Arts Midwest/NEA Regional Visual Artists Painting Fel, 96; Purchase Award Artworks Fund, 97; NEA & Arts Midwest, 97. *Mem:* Detroit Artists Market (exhib com 95-, bd dir exec com 99-2002, bldg com 99-2001); Detroit Inst of Arts (founder soc 2001). *Media:* Oil, Watercolor, Pastel. *Publ:* Joy Hakanson Colby (auth) There's Beauty in Freeways if You Ride with this Painter, The Detroit News, 9/7/95; Glen Mannisto (auth), Illuminating Visions, The Metro Times, 9/20/95; Marsha Miro (auth), Beauty in Unusual Places, The Detroit Free Press, 11/25/92. *Dealer:* Lemberg Gallery 23241 Woodward Ave Ferndale Mich 48220-1361. *Mailing Add:* 1438 Iroquois St Detroit MI 48214

BULKA, MICHAEL
CRITIC
Study: Va Commonwealth Univ, BFA in Sculpture, minor in Painting; Univ Ill, Chicago Circle, MFA in Studio Arts. *Exhib:* Critic contrib to P-Form, dialogue, C, Art in Am, World Art, New Art Examiner, New City ArtNet. *Mem:* Chicago Art Critics An. *Publ:* Critic contrib to P-Form, dialogue, C, Art in Am, World Art, New Art Examiner, New City ArtNet. *Mailing Add:* 1028 N Hermitage Ave #2F Chicago IL 60622

BULKIN SIEGEL, WILMA
PAINTER
b Philadelphia, Pa, Dec 2, 36. *Study:* New Sch, with Bruno Lucchesi, 1974-84; Nat Acad Design, NY, 1989-93; Art Inst Fort Lauderdale, with Barbara Dix, 1991; studied with Rownea Smith, 1991-94; MD, Women's Med Col Pa, 1962. *Work:* NY Presby Hsop, New York City; Hollywood Mem Regional Hosp, Fla; Sylvester Center Univ Miami, Fla; numerous private collections. *Comn:* Daniel D Cantor Ctr, Ft Lauderdale, Fla; painting, St Paul's Episcopal Ch, Paterson, NJ, 98; painting, Gold Found, New York City, 99-2000. *Exhib:* The Golden Yrs, Morani Gallery, Philadelphia, 96; Fla Int Univ, Miami, 97; Faces of AIDS Quilt, Mus Art, Ft Lauderdale, 97, Geneva, Switz, 98; Carnell Mus, Fla, 98; Shelter of the Home Within, Villanova Univ Art Gallery, Pa, 99; Marcella Geltman Gallery, Northern NJ, 1995; Bigger Than Life, Coral Springs Mus, Fla, 99, Young at Art Mus, Ft Lauderdale, Fla, 2001; solo exhibs Coral Springs (Fla) Mus, 1999, Survivors of AIDS (rotating exhib), 1999, State of Fla Pharmacy Conv, Naples, 1999, Hollywood (Fla) Memorial Regional Hosp, 1999, Art Explosion 2000, Jr League Ft Lauderdale, 2000, numerous others. *Pos:* rotating internship, Mt Sinai Hosp, NY, 1963, med resident, Temple Univ Hosp, 1964-65, hematology fel Mt Sinai Hosp, 1966, chemotherapy fel Mem Sloan-Kettering Hosp, 1967, asst prof medicine, emer oncology, Montefiore Med Ctr & Albert Einstein Col Medicine, Bronx, 1967-; med dir hospice Beth Abraham Hosp, Bronx, 1983-89; ret practice of medicine, 1990; speaker, Soc Art in Healthcare, Gainesville, Fla, 2002. *Teaching:* instr art in medicine, Univ Miami, 2000-. *Awards:* Dick Blick Award, Gold Coast Watercolor Soc, Fort Lauderdale, Fla, 94; First Prize, Am Physicians Art Asn Art Exhib, New Orleans, La, 1998, Orlando, 2000, Washington, 2002; Medial of Honor, Elizabeth Stanton Blake Memorial Award, NAWA, 99; Cecil Schapiro Mem Award, Nat Asoc Women Artists Exhib, New York City, NY, 2000; NAWA merit award for photog, Ann Norton Sculpture Gardens, West Palm Beach, 2001. *Bibliog:* The Golden Years, Channel 66, Philadelphia; The Faces of Aids, Milwaukee News, 97; The Fire of Life, Aids Resource Center Wis Benefit, 97; Art in Medicine, Am Asn Medical Coll; Enhancing Professionalism through Arts in Medicine, Assn Am Medical Col, 11/2000. *Mem:* Nat Asn Women Artists Inc (pres Fla chap, 2002-); 2+3 Artist Group Inc (pres 2000-2001); Fla Artrist Group Inc; Gold Coast Watercolor Soc (vpres 1997-1998, chmn community outreach 1998-1999); Ga Watercolor Soc; Catherine Lorillard Wolfe Asn (assoc); Int Arts-Medicine Asn; Am Physicians Art Asn; Soc Arts in Healing; Boca Raton Mus Art Artists Guild (juried exhibiting mem). *Media:* Watercolor. *Publ:* featured CNN-TV interview, 1998, other TV interviews. *Mailing Add:* 2504 Laguna Terrace Fort Lauderdale FL 33316

BULL, FRAN
PAINTER, EDUCATOR
b Orange, NJ, Sept 22, 38. *Study:* Bennington Col, Vt, BA, 60; Fashion Inst Technol, textile design, 62-63, NY Univ, MA, 80; pvt study/apprenticeship, malcolm Morley, New York, NY. *Work:* Baltimore Mus Art, Md; Brooklyn Mus Art, NY; Indianapolis Mus Art, Ind; NJ State Mus Art, Trenton; Speed Art Mus, Louisville, Ky. *Exhib:* The Am Photo Realist--an Anthology, Fisher Fine Art Gallery, London, Eng, 86; Pelican Variations, Seraphim Fine Arts, Tenafly, NJ, 87; Pulp Art: Investigations into Slurry, Katherine E Nash Gallery, Minneapolis, Minn, 98; City Without Walls, Newark, NJ 2000; Palettes of Summer, Walter Wickiser Gallery, New York, NY 2002; Brava Diva!, Karpeles Manuscript Mus, Charleston, SC, 2002; Night Passage, Printmaking Coun NJ, Somerville, NJ 2003; Ann Juried Member's Show, Woman Made Gallery, Chicago, Ill, 2005; Here Comes the Bride, Woman Made Gallery, Chicago, Ill, 2006; amoung others. *Teaching:* adj fac painting, New York Univ, New York, NY, 80-86; vis artist, Towson State, Md, 86-87; vis instr painting, Univ Wis, 88; vis artist, Univ W Bohemia, Plzen, Czec Republic, 2002-2003. *Awards:* AIGA Award; Cert of Merit, 7th Ann Feed the Baby, Feed the Soul, Competition, Hamilton, Ohio, 2000; Featured Artist, NJ State Coun on the Arts, Artist Gallery, 2002; Best in Show, Food Chain, Printmaking Coun NJ, 2002. *Bibliog:* Louis K Meisel (auth), Photo Realism, Harry Abrams, Inc, 80; David Bourdon (auth), Art: A painters aviary, Archit Digest, 81; Eileen Watkins (auth), Women paint women, Newark Star Ledger, 89; Douglas Anderson (auth), Barn dance, Vt Magazine, 10/2002; Gwen Donovan (auth), Local artists have broad scope, Star-Ledger, 9/22/2002; Marc Awodey (auth), There's something about Mary, Seven Days, 10/1/2003. *Mem:* Nat Asn Women Artists; Nat Mus Women in the Arts; Orgn Independent Artists. *Media:* Acrylic, Watercolor. *Collection:* Mus Mod Art, New York City; Nat Mus Wome in the Arts, Washington DC; The Brooklyn Mus, Brooklyn, NY; Baltimore Mus Art, Baltimore, Md; Indianapolis Mus, Indianapolis, Ind; John McEnroe Libr Collection, NY Studio Sch, New York, NY; Bo Alveryd, Malmo, Sweden; Yale Univ, New Haven, Conn; John Hopkins Univ, Balitimore, Md; Amherst College, Amherst, Mass; Johnson & Johnson, New Brunswick, NJ. *Publ:* Mordant Rhymes for Modern Times, Middletown Press, 90; Balm of My Dreams, 2003. *Dealer:* Morgan Gallery 472 Delaware Suite A Kansas City MO 64105; Sylvia White Gallery 560 Broadway Suite 206 New York City NY 10012. *Mailing Add:* PO Box 488 New Paltz NY 12561

BULL, HANK
CONCEPTUAL ARTIST, VIDEO ARTIST
Can citizen. *Study:* New Sch Art, Toronto, Can, 69. *Comn:* Mural, McMaster Univ, Hamilton, Ont, 72. *Exhib:* HP Show, A Space, Toronto, 76; Dokumenta 8, Kassel, 87. *Pos:* Pres & dir, Western Front, 73-88. *Awards:* B Award, Canada Coun, 80 & 87. *Publ:* HP in a Pickle, 74. *Mailing Add:* c/o Western Front 303 E 8th Ave Vancouver BC V5T 1S1 Canada

BULLARD, EDGAR JOHN, III
MUSEUM DIRECTOR
b Los Angeles, Calif, Sept 15, 42. *Study:* Univ Calif, Los Angeles, BA, 65, MA, 68; Nat Gallery Art, Samuel H Kress Found Fel, 67-68; Harvard Univ Inst Arts Admin, 71. *Hon Degrees:* Loyola U, New Orleans, LHD, 87. *Collection Arranged:* German Expressionist Watercolors in American Collections, 69, Mary Cassatt 1844-1926, 70 & John Sloan 1871-1951 (auth, catalog), 71, Nat Gallery Art, Washington, DC; Richard Clague 1821 1873, 74 & Zenga & Nanga: Paintings by Japanese Monks & Scholars, 76, New Orleans Mus Art; The Contemp South: Photog, US Info Agency, 77; The Wild West: Paintings and Sculpture by Frederic Remington and Charles M Russell, 79, Robert Gordy: Paintings and Sculpture 1960-80, 81 & Edward Weston and Clarence John Laughlin: An Introduction to the Third World of Photography (auth, catalog), 82, New Orleans Mus Art; Odd Nerdrum: The Drawings, New Orleans Mus Art, 94; Henry Casselli: Master of the American Watercolor, New Orleans Mus Art, 2000. *Pos:* Asst cur, J Paul Getty Mus, Malibu, Calif, 67, mus cur, Nat Gallery Art, 68-70, asst to dir, 70-71, cur spec projs, 71-73; dir, New Orleans Mus Art, 73-; trustee, Ga Mus Art, Univ Ga, 75-80, Knessel Hall Music Sch, Blue Hill, Maine, 1986-2002, La SPCA, 86-90, New Orleans Opera Asn, 1999-, Tulane Univ Col, 1999-2002, Amistad Rsch Ctr, Tulane Univ, 2001-, Haystack Mountain Sch Crafts, Deer Lake, Maine, 2003-, New Orleans Jazz Orchestra, 2004-. *Awards:* Louis Brandeis Humanitarian Award, 85; Mayor's Art Award, New Orleans, 93; Chevelier, Order Arts & Lett, France, 95; Order of the Republic of Egypt, 78. *Mem:* Am Asn Mus (trustee, 96-98); Col Art Asn Am; Nat Arts Club; Asn Art Mus Dir. *Res:* Late 19th & 20th century American and European art. *Publ:* Auth, Mary Cassatt: Oils and Pastels, Watson-Guptill, 72; A Panorama of American Painting (exhib catalog), 75; American paintings from the John J McDonough Collection, Antiques, 11/77; Two visions of the wild west: Frederic Remington & Charles M Russell, Southwest Art, 12/79; The Kinetic Sculpture of Lin Emery (exhib catalog), 82; auth, In Celebration of Light: Photographs from the Cheryl and James S Pierce Collection (exhib catalog). *Mailing Add:* New Orleans Mus Art PO Box 19123 New Orleans LA 70179

BULLOCK, JAMES BENBOW
SCULPTOR
b St Louis, Mo, 1929. *Study:* Wesleyan Univ, Middletown, Conn, BA, 50; San Francisco Art Inst, 67. *Work:* Chicago Athenaeum Sculpture Park; Whitman Col, Wash; Int Peace Arch Monument, Blaine, Wash; Grounds for Sculpture, Hamilton, NJ; Oakland Mus Calif. *Comn:* Chianti Sculpture Park, Sienna, Italy, 2001; Powder Coated Steel Spiral Auger, St Supery Winery, Napa Valley, Calif, 2005; Oakton Col, Des Plaines, Ill; Without Boundaries, Village of Schaumburg, Ill, 2005; Endless Stainless Steel Column, Oakland Mus, 2005. *Exhib:* Design Frontiers, Richmond Art Ctr, Calif, 85; Black & White, San Francisco Mus Mod Art, 85; Third Ann Sculpture Walk, Los Angeles Arts Coun, 89; Sixth Ann Henry Moore Exhib, Hakone Open Air Mus, Japan, 89; 5th Ann Int Festival des Art, Beaulieu-sur-Mer, France, 94; Europas Parkas Sculpture Park, Vilnius, Lithuania, 95; James A Michener Mus, Doylestown, Pa, 96; Color/Forms, City of Stamford, Conn, 2005; Kinetic Art, Shidoni Sculpture Garden, Santa Fe, NMex, 2005-06; On the Road to Silverado, St Supery Winery, Rutherford, Calif, 2005-06; Art Barrels 2005, Napa Valley Art Mus, Yountville, Calif, 2005-06; Sculpture 2006, Epperson Gallery, Crockett, Calif, 2006; Granger Art Gallery, Sonoma, Calif, 2006; Scultpures in the Olive Grave, Wolk Gallery, St Helena, Calif, 2006. *Pos:* Trustee, San Francisco Art Inst, 81-83; bd dir, Berkeley Art Ctr Mus,

Calif, 96. *Awards:* Ueno Royal Mus Purchase Award, Hakone Open Air Mus, 89; Second Prize, Festival des Art, Beaulieu-sur-Mer, France, 94; Europas Parkas Sculpture Park Purchase Award, 3rd Ann Int Sculpture Competition, Vilnius, Lithuania, 95. *Mem:* Int Sculpture Ctr. *Media:* Metal. *Mailing Add:* 12 Sandy Beach Rd Vallejo CA 94590

BUMBECK, DAVID
PRINTMAKER, EDUCATOR
b Framingham, Mass, May 15, 40. *Study:* RI Sch Design, BFA, 62; Syracuse Univ, with Robert Marx, MFA, 66. *Work:* NY Pub Libr; Metrop Mus Art, NY; Brooklyn Mus, NY; Wiggin Collection, Boston Pub Libr; Libr Congress, Washington, DC. *Exhib:* Boston Printmakers Nat Exhib, 67-86; Living Am Artists & the Figure, Mus Art, Pa State Univ, 74; 31st Nat Print Exhib, Brooklyn Mus, 78; Nat Print Exhib, Philadelphia Print Club, 79; Nat Exhib, Soc Am Graphic Artists, 79. *Pos:* Dir, Christian A Johnson Gallery, 73-85. *Teaching:* Instr painting & printmaking, Mass Col Art, Boston, 66-68; prof printmaking, Middlebury Col, 68-. *Awards:* David Berger Mem Award, Boston Printmakers Nat Exhib, 68; Purchase Award, Soc Am Graphic Artists Nat Exhib, NY, 79. *Mem:* Boston Printmakers (mem exec bd, 68-); Soc Am Graphic Artists; Nat Acad Design (assoc, 88, acad, 92). *Media:* Intaglio. *Dealer:* Mary Ryan Gallery 452 Columbus Ave New York NY 10024. *Mailing Add:* c/o Middlebury Col Ctr for Arts Rte 30 S Middlebury VT 05753

BUMGARDNER, JAMES ARLISS
PAINTER, EDUCATOR
b Winston-Salem, NC, 1935. *Study:* Univ NC; Salem Col, Winston-Salem; Richmond Prof Inst, BFA; prof emeritus; also with Hans Hofmann. *Work:* NC Mus Fine Arts, Raleigh; Va Mus Fine Arts; Philip Morris & Co, Richmond; Chrysler Mus, Norfolk, Va; Sidney & Frances Lewis, Richmond, Va; and others. *Exhib:* Art USA, NY, 59; Va Artist's Show, var times, 59-77; Art Across Am, NY, 65; Metarealities, Wash Proj Arts, 80; South Eastern Ctr Contemp Art Invitational, 81; Encuento Am Mus, Lima, Peru, 91; and others; Davidson Col, 1995; Univ Haifa, Israel, 1997. *Pos:* Guest set designer, Va Mus Theater, Waiting for Godot, 80. *Teaching:* Prof drawing & painting, Va Commonwealth Univ, 58-, prof emer, 96-. *Awards:* Five Special Awards Painting, NC Mus Art, 57-62; four Cert of Distinction, Va Mus Fine Art, 59-63 & 77; Purchase Prize, Southeastern Ctr for Contemp Arts, 77; and others. *Bibliog:* Metarealities rev, New Art Examiner, Vol 7, No 7, 4/80 & Gallery K rev, 9/85; Beyond refinement, Images & Issue, Vol 3, winter 80-81; and others. *Media:* Oil, Pastel. *Dealer:* Katryn Markel Fine Art 529 W 20th St NY NY 10011; Reynolds Gallery, 1514 W Main St, Richmond, Va 23220. *Mailing Add:* 435 Farmers Dell Ln Deltaville VA 23043

BUNN, DAVID
PHOTOGRAPHER
b Greensboro, NC, Apr 12, 50. *Study:* St Andrews Col, BA, 72; Univ Calif, Los Angeles, MFA, 84. *Work:* Newport Harbor Art Mus, Newport Beach, Calif; Long Beach Mus Art, Calif; Univ Nevada, Las Vegas. *Comn:* Los Angeles Central Libr. *Exhib:* One-man shows, Allied Arts Gallery, Las Vegas, 87, Sphere of Influence, Santa Monica Mus Art, 88 & 89, Deliberate Investigations, Los Angeles Co Mus Art, 89, Roy Boyd Gallery, Santa Monica, 90 & 92, Margins 6, Univ Calif, Santa Barbara Art Mus, 91 & Biennial III, Mapping Histories, Newport Harbor Art Mus, 91; 4-artists show, San Francisco Mus Mod Art, 89; Nat Mus Am Art, Smithsonian Inst, Washington, DC, 89; Open Channels, Long Beach Mus Art, 90; The Naming Of Colors, White Columns, NY, 93; Mapping, Univ Art Mus, Univ Tex, San Antonio, 94; Breda Art Festival, D Beyerd Mus, Breda, The Neth, 94; and others. *Teaching:* Assoc prof, Sch Fine Art, Univ Southern Calif, Los Angeles. *Awards:* Individual Artist Fels, Mass Artists Coun, 81, Long Beach Mus of Art Open Channels, 87, Nat Endowment Arts, 88 & 89. *Bibliog:* Kirby Gookin (auth), David Bunn at Brooke Alexander, Artforum, summer 98; Jan Tumlir (auth), Bueracratic Poetry, Art & Text, Art & Music Issue, 11/98; Roberta Smith (auth), In the eye of the collector, NY Times, 98. *Publ:* Digging Up South America (artist book), 90; Auth, A place for everything and everthing in its place, Discourse, fall 98

BUNN, KENNETH RODNEY
SCULPTOR
b Denver, Colorado, 1938. *Exhib:* Represented in collections of Nat Mus Wildlife Art, Wyoming, Denver Art Mus, John L Wehle Mus Sporting Art, Mumford, NY, Denver Zoological Gardens, Columbus Mus Art, Ohio, Leigh Yawkey Woodson Art Mus, Wausau, Wis, Thomas Gilcrease Mus, Tulsa, Okla, Janus Funds, Denver, Eiteljorg Mus Am Indian & Western Art, Indianapolis, Century Bank, Sante Fe, NMex. *Mem:* Nat Acad (assoc, 73, acad, 94); Artist Am; Soc Animal Artists; fel, Nat Sculpture Soc

BUNNELL, PETER CURTIS
EDUCATOR, CURATOR
b Poughkeepsie, NY, Oct 25, 37. *Study:* Rochester Inst Technol, BFA, 59; Ohio Univ, MFA, 61; Yale Univ, MA, 65. *Comn:* Masters of American Photography, US Postal Svc, 02. *Collection Arranged:* Photography as Printmaking, 68, Photography into Sculpture, 70, Clarence H White, 71, Mus Mod Art, New York; Princeton Univ Art Mus: Robert O Dougan Collection, 83 (auth catalogue); Minor White: The Eye That Shapes, 89 (auth catalogue); The Art of Pictorial Photography, 92; The Florence Gould Found Collection, 94; Ruth Bernhard: Photographs, 96; Photography at Princeton (ed, catalog), 98; Nineteenth-Century British Art, 99; M Jay Goodkind Collection of Photographs, 99; Edward Ranney Photographs, 2003 (auth catalogue). *Pos:* Cur photog, Mus Mod Art, NY, 66-72; cur photog, Art Mus, Princeton Univ, 72-2002, prof emer, 2002, dir, 73-78; actg dir, The Art Mus, 98-2000. *Teaching:* Vis lectr hist photog, Dartmouth Col, 68 & Inst Film/TV, NY Univ, 68-70; vis lectr hist photog, Yale Univ, 73; McAlpin prof hist, photo & modern art, Princeton Univ, 72-02, prof emer, 02. *Awards:* Guggenheim Mem Fel, 79; George Wittenborn Award, Art Libr Soc, 89; Hon Fel, Royal Photog Soc Gt Brit, 93. *Mem:* Soc Photog Educ (nat chmn, 73-77); Col Art Asn Am (bd dir, 75-79); Friends of Photog (bd trustees, 74-86, pres, 78-87, chmn, 87-92). *Media:* Photography. *Res:* History of photography with primary emphasis on the 20th century. *Publ:* Auth, Degrees of Guidance, 93; ed, The Florence Gould Foundation Collection of Nineteenth-Century French Photographs, 94; auth, Michael Kenna: A Twenty-Year Retrospective, 94; Thomas Joshua Cooper, 95; Ruth Bernhard: Photographs, 96; Siskind: The Bond and the Free, 97; Michiko Kon: Introduction, 97; Jerry N Uelsmann: Museum Studies, 99; Walter Chappell: Time Lived, 2000; Remembering Limelight, 2001; A Photographic Vision: Pictorial Photography, 1889-1923, 2003; La Photographie Pictorialiste, 2004; auth, Inside the Photograph, 2006. *Mailing Add:* Princeton Univ Dept Art & Archeol Princeton NJ 08544

BUNNEN, LUCINDA WEIL
PHOTOGRAPHER, COLLECTOR
b Katonah, NY, Jan 14, 30. *Study:* Atlanta Col Art, 70-71; also study with Michael Lesy, Minor White, Linda Connor, Duane Michaels & George Tice. *Work:* Mus Mod Art & Whitney Mus Am Art, NY; Pushkin Mus, Moscow; High Mus Art, Atlanta; R J Reynolds Industs, Winston-Salem, NC; Mus Fine Arts, Boston. *Comn:* 40 photographs, O'Hare Hyatt House, Chicago, 72; 40' mural & 5-screen slide show, High Mus Art, Atlanta, 74; film from slides, US Comn Civil Rights, Montgomery, 78; prints, Northside Hosp, Atlanta, 86; videos, High Mus Art, 88. *Exhib:* Portrait of Am, Smithsonian traveling exhib, 75-79; Movers and Shakers in Georgia, High Mus Art, Atlanta, 78; Atlantic Artists in Buenos Aires, Buenos Aires, Arg, 89; New Southern Photog: Between Myth and Reality, Aperture Found, NY, 91; The Rocker, Bernice Steinbaum Gallery, NY, 92; Out of Bounds, City Gallery East, Atlanta, Ga, 94; Exceptions; Artists' books and art books (touring), US Info Agency, Washington Project Arts, 94. *Collection Arranged:* Subjective Vision: The Lucinda Bunnen Collection of Photographs (with catalog), High Mus Art, Atlanta, 84. *Pos:* Bd dir, High Mus Art, 78-, Image Film & Video, 82-, Art Papers, 82-; Chair Hambidge Art Ctr, 98-02. *Awards:* Outstanding Leadership Award, Am Asn Univ Women, 75; Governor's Award Arts, Ga, 86; First Place, 2nd Ann Photog Contest, Atlanta Women's News, 90. *Bibliog:* profile, Lear's Mag, 5/90; Sarah Ferrell (auth), The Last Word, NY Times Bk Rev, 7/28/91; Picks & Pans, People Mag, 3/25/91. *Mem:* Friends of Photog; Int Ctr Photog; Eastman House; Visual Studies Workshop; and others. *Media:* Photography, Video. *Collection:* Contemporary photography, Outsider art, Coca Cola bottles, cows, heart rocks, knives, live dogs from New Mexico. *Publ:* Auth, Movers and Shakers in Georgia, Simon & Schuster, New York, 78; contribr, Family of Women, Ridge Press, 79; coatuth, Scoring in Heaven: Gravestones and Cemetary Art of the American Sunbelt States, Aperture, 91; Alaska: Trail Tales and Eccentric Detours, Icehouse Press, 92; The Rocker, Rizzoli, New York, 92. *Dealer:* Richard Eagan Fine Art, PO Box 190449, Miami Beach, Fl, 33119. *Mailing Add:* 3910 Randall Mill Rd NW Atlanta GA 30327-3102

BUNTS, FRANK
PAINTER, EDUCATOR
b Cleveland, Ohio, Mar 2, 32. *Study:* Yale Univ; Cleveland Inst Art; Case Western Reserve Univ, BA & MA. *Work:* Philadelphia Mus Art, Pa; Fine Arts Gallery, San Diego, Calif; Libr Cong, Washington; Corcoran Gallery Art, Washington; Cleveland Mus Art, Ohio; and others. *Exhib:* Cleveland Mus Art, Ohio; San Francisco Mus Art, Calif; Corcoran Gallery Art, Washington, DC; Indianapolis Mus Art, Ind; Mus Mod Art, Rijeka, Yugoslavia; San Diego Fine Arts Gallery, Calif; Nat Acad Sci, Washington, DC; Black & Herron Gallery, NY; Christie's, NY; Marion Deson Gallery, Chicago, Ill; Franz Bader Gallery, Washington, DC; Comara Gallery, Los Angeles, Calif; and others; Solo exhibs, Comara Gallery, Los Angeles, 1967, 68, St John's Coll, Annapolis, Md, 1972, Gallery 118, Mpls, 1974, Cath Univ Am, Washington, DC, 1978, Plum Gallery, Washington, DC, 1979, Flatiron Studio, New York City, 1987, Maryanne McCarthy Fine Art, New York City, 1988-89, Roberta Wood Gallery, Syracuse, NY, 1993, Effect/Cause Mail Project, 1993-95; others. *Collection Arranged:* Cleve Mus Art; Fine Arts Gallery, San Diego; Libr Congress; Corcoran Gallery Art, Washington, DC; Cooperstown Art Asn, NY; Chinese Artists Asn, Beijing. *Pos:* Full prof, Dir Grad Studio Prog, Univ Md. *Teaching:* Cleveland Inst Art, Ohio, 63-64; Ark State Univ, Jonesboro, Ark, 65-67; Univ Md, College Park, 67-77, dir, Grad Art Studio Prog, 71-77. *Awards:* Purchase Prize, Cleveland Mus Art, Ohio; and others. *Bibliog:* ICC Artist Database, CD Rom, Nippon Tel & Tel, Tokyo, Japan; The Catalog of American Drawings, Watercolors, Pastels and Collages, Corcoran Gallery Art Washington, DC; numerous articles in many newspapers; artwork in videos, The Man from UNCLE, 1966, Callanetics, MCA, 1986, Portrait of an Artist by Konrad Gylfson, 1986; music video, Always and Forever, Whistle, C C Prodns, 1990; documentary video, San Francisco Center for Visual Studios, 1990; film and edit, Breaking Some Eggs-A Wisconsin Breakfast, 2003. *Media:* Oil and Organic Resin on Canvas. *Mailing Add:* 15 W 24th St New York NY 10010

BUONAGURIO, EDGAR R
PAINTER, MURALIST
b Yonkers, NY, July 4, 46. *Study:* City Col New York, BA, 69; Teachers Col, Columbia Univ, MA, 72. *Work:* Joseph Hirshhorn Mus & Sculpture Garden, Washington, DC; Mint Mus Art, Charlotte, NC; Bronx Mus Arts, NY; Herbert F Johnson Mus Art, Cornell Univ; Everson Mus Art, Syracuse, NY. *Comn:* Fantail (mural), The Continental Group, Stamford, Conn, 80-81; Byzantine Dream, Continental Nat Bank, Ft Worth, 82; Labyrinth (mural), City Nat Bank, Baton Rouge, 83; Olympia & York, Inc, NY, 85; Develop Specialists, Inc, Chicago, Ill, 86. *Exhib:* Mint Mus Art, Charlotte, NC; Everson Mus Art, Syracuse, 83; Zolla-Lieberman Gallery, Chicago, Ill, 84; Gloria Luria Gallery, Bay Harbor Islands, Fla, 85; Jerald Melberg Gallery, Charlotte, NC, 85; Hadler/Rodriquez, Houston, Tex, 86; Oscarsson-Siegeltuch, NY, 87; and others. *Pos:* Critic, Arts Mag, New York, 77-80.

Teaching: Instr painting, Hudson River Mus, Yonkers, NY, 69-74; instr art & art hist, Riverdale Country Sch, Bronx, NY, 69-79; adj prof painting, Westchester Community Col, 72, Col New Rochelle, 74. *Awards:* Creative Artists Pub Serv Prog Fel Painting, 81-82. *Bibliog:* Ellen Lubell (auth), Edgar Buonagurio at Andre Zarre, Art in Am, 83; Phillip Verre (auth), Recent painting by Edgar Buonagurio, Arts Mag, 84; Grace Glueck (auth), Edgar Buonagurio, NY Times, 84. *Media:* Acrylic, Canvas. *Dealer:* Oscarsson-Siegeltuch Gallery 568 Broadway New York NY 10012; Zolla-Lieberman Gallery 356 W Huron Chicago IL 60610. *Mailing Add:* 1723 Holland Ave Bronx NY 10462

BUONAGURIO, TOBY LEE
SCULPTOR
b Bronx, NY, June 28, 47. *Study:* City Col New York, BA(fine arts), 69, MA(art educ), 71. *Work:* Heckscher Mus, Huntington, NY; Everson Mus Art, Syracuse, NY; Mint Mus Art, Charlotte, NC; Alternative Mus, NY. *Exhib:* Solo exhibs, Gallery Yues Arman, NY, 82, Everson Mus Art, Syracuse, NY, 82, Bronx Mus Arts, NY, 83, Contemp Arts Ctr, New Orleans, 83, Jerald Melberg Gallery, Charlotte, NC, 85 & Fine Arts Gallery, State Univ NY, Stony Brook, 86; Contemp self-portraits, Allan Frumkin Gallery, NY, 83; and others. *Teaching:* Prof and dir undergrad study, art dept, State Univ NY, Stony Brook, 76-. *Awards:* Creative Artists Pub Serv Fel for drawing, 80-81. *Bibliog:* April Kingsley (auth), Toby Buonagurio, Arts Mag, 80; Robert Lubar (auth), Toby Buonagurio, Arts Mag, 82; Thomas Piche (auth), Toby Buonagurio, Am Ceramics, 82; Ellen Lee Klein (auth), Toby Buonagurio: More optical bounce to the ounce, Arts Mag, 86; Ceramics Today: Toby Buonagurio USA (monogr), Editons Olizare, Geneva, Switz, 84; and others. *Mem:* Col Art Asn. *Media:* Ceramic, Mixed Media. *Publ:* Coauth, Ceramic directions: A contemporary overview, 83. *Mailing Add:* 1723 Holland Ave Bronx NY 10462-3926

BURCH, CLAIRE R
PAINTER, WRITER, FILMAKER
b New York, NY, Feb 19, 25. *Study:* Wash Sq Col, NY Univ, BA, 47. *Work:* Butler Inst Am Art, Youngstown, Ohio; Birmingham Mus, Ala; Brooklyn Mus, NY; Beth Israel Hosp, NY; North Shore Hosp; Guild Hall, Easthampton, NY; Columbus Mus, Ohio; pvt collection of James Bladwin, Paris, France, many others. *Comn:* Painting, Roche Image, 65. *Exhib:* One-man shows, Ruth White Gallery, NY, 63, Galerie L'Antipoete, Paris, France, 63, Southampton Col, 64-65 & Roko Gallery, 64; Westbeth Gallery, NY, 71 & 84; Berkeley Art Ctr, 81; Visual Art Prog, Broadcast on Bay Area Cable Stations KQED & Free Speech Channel, Boulder Colo; Artship Found, 2001; James Baldwin Mem Exhibit, Paris, 2001. *Awards:* Grants, City Berkeley, Berkeley Civic Arts, Alameda Arts Coun, Pulfin Found, San Francisco Found; Calif Arts Coun Award; Seva Found Award; San Francisco Found Award; Winfred Found Award; Alameda Arts Coun Award. *Mem:* NY Playwright's Cooperative. *Media:* Watercolor, Collage, Oil on Paper. *Publ:* Careers in Psychiatry, Macmillan; Notes of a Survivor, 72; illus, Shredded Millions, Alfonia, 82; Postscript to the Livermore Thousand, 83; James Baldwin (film), Entering Oakland (film), Thumbed a Ride to Heaven (film), Oracle Rising (film), Remembering the Summer of Love and Other Songs by Claire Burch (film), People's Park of Berkeley (film) & Homeless in the 90's (film); Solid Gold Illusion (art book & video), Regent Press, Oakland, 90; auth, Stranger in the Family, Bobbs Merrill, You be the Mother Follies, Norwood Editions, Homeless in the Nineties, Good by My Coney Island & Stranger on the Planet, Regent Press; and others. *Dealer:* Regent Press Gallery 6020A Adeline Oakland CA 94608. *Mailing Add:* 2747 Regent St Berkeley CA 94705

BURCHARD, PETER DUNCAN
WRITER, ILLUSTRATOR, PHOTOGRAPHER
b Washington, DC, Mar 21, 21. *Study:* Philadelphia Mus Sch Art, cert, 47. *Work:* Kerlin Collection. *Comn:* At least 100 book illus comn. *Exhib:* Anne Fuller Gallery, 78; David & Joyce Milne Libr Gallery, 2002. *Pos:* Freelance; adv panel, George Polk Awards, 85-. *Awards:* Guggenheim Fel, 66; Christopher Award, 73. *Mem:* Int PEN; Authors' Guild. *Media:* Black & White & Color Film. *Publ:* Illusr, Ocean Race, 78 & Chinwe, 79, G P Putnam's Sons; auth & illusr, Sea Change, Farrar Straus Giroux; Venturing: An Introduction to Sailing, Little Brown and Co; Charlotte Forten: A Black Teacher in the Civil War, Random House, 95; Lincoln and Slavery, Simon & Schuster, 99; and 80 books for major publ (one a major hist source for film Glory) & mus revs and profiles of mus dirs for "Connoisseur"; Frederick Douglass: For the Great Family of Man, Simon & Schuster, 2003

BURCHETT, DEBRA
ADMINISTRATOR, CURATOR
b Bremerhaven, Ger, Sept 26, 55; US citizen. *Study:* Univ Ky, Lexington, 74-75; Univ Calif, Irvine, with Craig Kauffman, Alexis Smith & Tony DeLap, BFA, 77, independent res under Melinda Wortz, BA, 78. *Collection Arranged:* Clothing Constructions, 79, Michelangelo Pistoletto, 79, Barry Le Va, New York Artist, Nat Endowment Arts Exhib, 80, Architectural Sculpture, Nat Endowment Arts Mus Prog, 80, Il Modo Italiano, Nat Endowment Arts Mus Prog, 83-84 & others, Los Angeles Inst Contemp Art. *Pos:* Gallery asst, Univ Calif, Irvine & Newport Harbor Art Mus, Newport Beach, Calif, 76-77; ed, Jour: Contemp Art Mag, 77-80; cur, Main & Entrance Galleries, Los Angeles Inst Contemp Art, 79-84; develop asst, Fine Arts Gallery, Mount St Mary's Col, 81 & Calif State Univ, Los Angeles, 83; dir, sales & admin, Gemini-G E L (graphics ed ltd), Los Angeles, 84-92 & The Litho Shop Inc/Sam Francis, Santa Monica, Calif, 92-; advert rep, Art Forum Mag. *Awards:* Nat Endowment Visual Arts Mus Prog Grant, 79; Critics Residency Grant, 79 & Artist Residency Grant, 80, Nat Endowment Arts; and others. *Bibliog:* Jennifer Seder (auth), Closet art, Los Angeles Times, 6/8/79; Germano Celant (auth), Culture, L'Europeo, Rome, Italy, 8/79; Melinda Wortz (auth), Clothing constructions, Art News, 9/79. *Mem:* Nat Asn Artists' Orgn (founding bd dir, 82-83); Graphics Arts Coun. *Publ:* Ed, Art and music, 70, issues 17-25, 77-80 & Another look at conceptualism, 79, J Southern Calif Art Mag; contribr, Visits: Kisch, Lere, Vogel & Scoops: Nordman, Irwin, Wheeler, 78 & ed spec issue, Art in Latin America (bilingual ed), 79, J Los Angeles Inst Contemp Art. *Mailing Add:* 1146 N Central Ave Apt 181 Glendale CA 91202

BURCHETT, KENNETH EUGENE
EDUCATOR, CONSULTANT
b Stockton, Mo April 26, 42. *Study:* Mo State Univ, BS, 66; Univ Tulsa, MA, 70; Univ NTex, PhD, 80. *Exhib:* 47th Ann Ten State, Moody Art Ctr, Shreveport, La, 70; 39th Ann Ten State, Springfield Art Mus, Mo, 70; 30th Okla Ann, Philbrook Mus, Tulsa, 70; Drawing Mid-USA 1, Spiva Art Ctr, Joplin, Mo, 76; Fine Arts Ann, Dallas Mus Fine Art, Tex, 78; Nat Painting, Pensacola Col, Fla, 80; Mid-Four Regional, Nelson-Atkins, Kansas City, Mo, 84; Group Invitational, Ark Arts Ctr, Little Rock, 87. *Pos:* educator, currently. *Teaching:* Prof & chmn art, Col of the Ozarks, Branson, Mo, 72-85; prof & chmn art, Univ Central Ark, Conway, 85-2000, prof 2000-. *Awards:* Alumni of the Year, UN Tex. *Mem:* Inter-Soc Color Coun; Col Art Asn Am; Nat Art Educ Asn; Am Asn Univ Prof. *Res:* Color Theory: Attributes of Color Harmony, Color Design and Color Applications. *Publ:* Auth, Art Vocabulary, Mental Measurements Yearbook, Gryphon, 78; Twelve Books on Color, 89 & Color Harmony Attributes, 91, Color Research & Application, Wiley & Sons; Faber Birren, Leonardo JISAST, Pergamon, 90; Color Education, Inter-Soc Color Coun News, 91; Artist and Audience and Living with Art, Studies in Art Edn, Jour of Issues and Res in Art Edn, NAEA, 93; auth, Color Harmony, Color Research and Application, Wiley and Sons, 2002; Bibliographical History of the study & use of color from aristotle to kandinslay, Mellen, 2005. *Mailing Add:* University of Central Arkansas Dept of Art McAlister Hall No 101 Conway AR 72032

BURCHFIELD, JERRY LEE
PHOTOGRAPHER, EDUCATOR, AUTHOR
b Chicago, Ill, July 28, 47. *Study:* Calif State Univ, Fullerton, BA(photo-commun), 71, MA(art), 77, MFA, 90. *Work:* Los Angeles Co Mus, Calif; St Louis Mus Art, Mo; Bibliot Nat, Paris; Minneapolis Inst Arts, Minn; Denver Art Mus; plus others. *Comn:* Pub bus installation, Newport Harbor Art Mus; mixed media installation, Orange Co Ctr Contemp Art, 91; mixed media installation, Calif Mus Photog, 92. *Exhib:* Studio Work, Los Angeles Co Mus Art, 82; Projections/Documentations, Calif Mus Photog, 92; Visions & Ecologies, Laguna Art Mus, 93; California Focus, Armand Hammer Mus, Univ Calif, Los Angeles, 95; Gun as Image, Mus Fine Art, Fla State Univ, 97; Photog, Orange Co Mus Art, 97; Out of Box, Orgn Co Mus Art, 99; Rear View Mirror, Calif Mus Photo, 2000; Am Perspective, Tokyo Metrop Mus Photo, 2000; Habitat, Laguna Art Mus, 2000; Primal Images, Calif Mus of Photog, Riverside, Calif; Secret Victorians, Mus of Photog Art, San Diego, Calif, 2003; Fahey Klein Gallery, Los Angeles, 2005. *Pos:* Asst dir, Newport Gallery, Newport Sch Photog, Calif, 73-75; dir/co-owner, BC Space, Photog Gallery, Laguna Beach, Calif, 73-87; dir photog gallery, Cypress Col Calif, 89-; cur, Minolta Gallery, Cypress, Calif, 95-98; contrib ed, No Mo Pomo Mag, 95-; co-founder, Laguna Wilderness Press, 2002; pres, The Legacy Project, non-profit org, 05. *Teaching:* Instr & lectr photog, Calif State Univ, Fullerton, 78-87; instr, Saddleback Col, Mission Viejo, Calif, 79- & Cypress Col, Cypress, Calif, 88-; instr, Orange Coast Col, 81-87. *Awards:* Photographer's Fel, Nat Endowment Arts, 81; Excellence Award, NISOD, 96; Numerous Purchase Awards; Outstanding Individual Artist, Orange Co Arts, 2001. *Bibliog:* Linda Bellon (auth), Jerry Burchfield: An interview, Obscura, fall 82; Jerry Burchfield, video by Longbeach Mus Art, 89; Habitat: Jerry Burchfield, Laguna Art Mus, 2000. *Mem:* Soc for Photog Educ; Found for Sustainability & Innovation. *Media:* Photography, Performance. *Specialty:* Photography. *Interests:* Nature. *Collection:* LA County Mus of Art, Oakland Mus of Art, Denver Art Mus,; Bibliotheque National, Paris; Kiyosato Mus of Photographic Art, Kyoto, Japan; Mus of Fine Art, Houston, Tx. *Publ:* illusr/contribr, Basic Darkroom Book, Plume, 77; contribr ed, articles in Darkroom Photog Mag, Vol 1, No 3 & 6, 79; auth & illusr, Darkroom Art, Amphoto, 80; auth, Photography in Focus, NTC Publ, 96; plus others; auth, In Transition, Great Park Conserv, 2003; Primal Images, Ctr for Am Places, 2004; cur & auth, Light as Substance, Cypress Col; ed & contribr, Edge of Air, Laguna Wilderness Press, 2005. *Dealer:* Scape Gallery, Corona Del Mar, CA; Fahey-Klein Gallery, LA; Joseph Bellows Gallery, La Jolla, CA. *Mailing Add:* 6 Meade Irvine CA 92620-2623

BURCKHARDT, YVONNE HELENE See Jacquette, Yvonne Helene

BURDEN, CHRIS
CONCEPTUAL ARTIST, SCULPTOR
b Boston, Mass, Apr 11, 46. *Study:* Pomona Col, BFA, 69; Univ Calif, Irvine, MFA, 71. *Work:* San Diego Mus Contemp Art, Calif; Mus Contemp Art, Los Angeles; Mus Mod Art, NY; Orange Co Art Mus, Newport Beach, Calif; Lannan Found, Los Angeles; Los Angeles Co Mus Art; Whitney Mus Am Art, NY; Mus Applied Arts, Vienna, Austria. *Exhib:* Documenta 6, Kassel, Ger, 77; The Mus as Site: Sixteen Projects, Los Angeles Co Mus Art, 81; Eight Artists: The Anxious Edge, Walker Art Ctr, Minneapolis, 82; A Recent Survey of Int Painting & Sculpture, Mus Mod Art, NY, 84; Modern Machines: Recent Kinetic Sculpture, Whitney Mus Am Art, 85; NO Contemp Am DADA, Henry Art Gallery, Univ Wash, Seattle, 85; one-man shows, Newport Harbor Art Mus (with catalog), Traveling Exhib, 88-89, Brooklyn Mus, NY, 91, Gagosian Gallery, 93 & 94, Galerie Anne de Villepoix, Paris, 94, Centre Georges Pompidou, Paris, 94, Centre d'Art Santa Monica (with catalog), Barcelona, Spain, 95, Mus Applied Arts (with catalog), Vienna, Austria, 96, The Reconstructive Gallery, Santa Ana, Calif, 97, Stockholm Konsthall, 99, Tate Gallery, London, 99, Gagosian Gallery, London, 2000, 03, The Arts Club of Chicago, 2001; Seven Obsessions: New Installation Work, White Chapel Art Gallery, London, 90; New Art for Newcastle, TSWA Four Cities Project, Eng, 90; New Works for New Spaces: Into the Nineties,

Wexner Ctr Visual Arts, Columbus, Ohio, 90-91; Dislocations, Mus Mod Art, 91-92; Chris Burdin, Lannan Found, 92; Helter Skelter, Mus Contemp Art, Los Angeles, 92; Whitney Biennial, Whitney Mus Am Art, NY, 93 & 97; Hors Limites, Centre Georges Pompidou, Paris, 94; Chris Burden, Lannan Found, 92; Helter Skelter, Mus Contemp Art, Los Angeles, 92; Fondation Cartier l'Art Contemporain, Paris, 99, 2001; The Am Century, 1950-2000, Whitney Mus Am Art, 2000; PS1 Contemp Art Ctr, Long Island, NY, 2001; un art populaire, Found Dartier por l'art Contmp, Paris, 2001; Art and War in the Times of the Media, Kunsthalle Wien, Vienna, 2003. *Teaching:* Asst to vis prof, Carpenter Ctr Visual Arts, Harvard Univ, Cambridge, Mass, 64; San Francisco Art Inst, 78; full prof, Univ Calif, Los Angeles, 78-; lectr, Small Skyscrapers, Los Angeles Forum for Archit and Urban Design Lect Series, Los Angeles Contemp Exhibs, 2003. *Awards:* New Talent Award, Los Angeles Co Mus, 73; Nat Endowment Arts Individual Artist Grant, 74, 76, 80 & 83; John Simon Guggenheim Fel, 78; Visual Artists Award, Flintridge Foundation, 97 & 98. *Bibliog:* Carl Loeffer, (editor) Performance Anthology: A Source Book for a Decade of California Performance Art, 79; Frances Morris (auth.) Chris Burden: When Robots Rule: The Two-Minute airplane Factory, 99. *Media:* Mixed Media. *Publ:* Auth, Chris Burden 1971-73, pvt publ, 73; Poem for LA (video), 75; Chris Burden 1974-77, pvt publ, 77; Full Financial Disclosure (video), 77; B-Car, The Story of Chris Burden's Bicycle Car, CHOKE Publ, 77. *Mailing Add:* c/o Gagosian Gallery 980 Madison Ave New York NY 10021

BURDOCK, HARRIET
HISTORIAN, PRINTMAKER
b Buffalo, NY. *Study:* Univ NMex, with Garo Antresian, BFA, 66; Kean Col, MA, 69; Pratt Graphics Ctr, New Sch Social Res, with Clare Romano & Federico Castellon. *Pos:* Lectr, NJ State Mus, Trenton, 67-68; asst, Art, Prints & Photog Div, NY Pub Libr, 80-. *Teaching:* Instr art hist, Bergen Co Col, Paramus, NJ, 78-79. *Mem:* Col Art Asn Am; Am Asn Mus; Int Coun Mus; Asn Hist Am Art; Print Club New York (founding comt, 92-). *Publ:* Auth, Notes from Russia, Graphic Arts Coun NY Newsletter, 77; auth, Woodcuts in China, Print Collector's Newsletter, 81. *Mailing Add:* c/o Art Prints & Photog Div NY Public Libr New York NY 10018

BURFORD, BYRON LESLIE
PAINTER, PRINTMAKER
b Jackson, Miss, July 12, 20. *Study:* Univ Iowa, BFA & MFA. *Work:* Worcester Art Mus, Mass; Walker Art Ctr, Minneapolis; Nelson-Atkins Gallery, Kansas City, Mo; Sheldon Art Mus, Lincoln, Nebr; High Mus Art, Atlanta, Ga. *Exhib:* Solo exhibs, Babcock Galleries, 66, 67, 69 & 75, Am Acad Arts Ann, NY, 66, 72, 79 & 96, Foxley/Leach Gallery, Washington, 87 & 92, Dartmouth Col, 92; Venice Biennale, Italy, 68; Bienal Arte Coltejer, Colombia, 70; Kunsthaus, Zurich, Switz, 72; and others. *Teaching:* Prof painting, Univ Iowa, 47-86, prof emer, 86; Univ Minn & Univ Mass, 67. *Awards:* Guggenheim Found Fel, 60 & 61; Ford Found Award, 61, 62 & 64; Nat Inst Arts & Lett Grants, 67, 72 & 75; Midwest Arts Nat Endowment Regional Fel, 88. *Media:* Acrylic, Alkyd, Prints. *Dealer:* Babcock Galleries. *Mailing Add:* 113 S Johnson St Iowa City IA 52240-5108

BURFORD, JAMES E
PAINTER, EDUCATOR
b Vancouver, Wash, July 25, 45. *Study:* Univ Oreg, BS, 71; Carnegie Mellon Univ, MFA, 78. *Work:* Portland Art Mus, Ore; Coos Art Mus, Coos Bay, Ore; Univ Art and Design, Helsinki, Finland; Superior Ct Pa Judges Chambers, Pittsburgh, Pa; Westinghouse Corp Collection, Pittsburgh, Pa. *Comn:* murals, Sheraton-Washington Hotel, DC, 84-85; dry ice pieces, Univ Ore, Eugene, 70; Corcoran Gallery of Art, Mentorship Program, Washington, DC, 2004-2005. *Exhib:* Grand Galleries Nat, Cascade Gallery, Seattle Ctr, Seattle, Wash, 72; 58th Ann NW Artists, Seattle Art Mus, Seattle, Wash, 72; Artists of Ore, Portland Art Mus, Portland, Ore, 72, Works on Paper, 74; One man show, Coos Art Mus, Coos Bay, Ore, 74; Seattle Arts Festival, Seattle Ctr, Seattle Art Mus, Seattle, Wash, 75; LaGrange Nat, Columbus Mus Art, Columbus, Ga, 78; Assoc Artists Pittsburgh, Carnegie Mus, 92, 97; Carnegie Mus, Pittsburgh, 72, 88, 89, 92 & 92; Fac Exhib, Corcoran Gallery Art, Washington, DC, 2004. *Pos:* dir, Gatehouse Gallery, Mt Vernon Col, Washington, DC, 78-99. *Teaching:* lectr color, Hirschhorn Mus, Washington, DC, 89, 90, 92; instr painting, Carnegie Mellon Univ, Pittsburgh, Pa, 76-78; assoc prof, Mt Vernon Col, Washington, DC, 78-99; adj instr, Univ Md, College Park, 99-01, Marymount Univ, Arlington, Va, 99-03, Art League Sch, Alexandria, 99-03; instr, Univ Md, 99-2001; adj instr, Corcoran Col of Art and Design Washington DC, 2001-. *Awards:* Purchase Award, Artists of Ore, Portland, 72; Jury Award, 68th Ann Carnegie Mus, US Steel, 78; Jury Award, Three Rivers Arts Festival Pittsburgh, Pa, 78; Arts and Humanities Grant, Mt Vernon Coll, Washington, DC, 81-83, 89; Fac Develop Grant, Mt Vernon Coll, Washington, DC, 86, 96, 97. *Mem:* Coll Art Asn. *Media:* Oil, Alky, Acrylic, Film, Color Pencil. *Specialty:* painting prints; drawing prints. *Interests:* painting, oil, alky, acrylic. *Publ:* John Wall (auth), Blair Art Museum Show, Patrong or Portland Art Mus, 72; George Johanson (auth), Ore Ann, The Oregonian Newspaper, 72; Nanc Unger (auth), The Teachers Show, Entertainment Gazette, 98. *Mailing Add:* 3222 1st Rd N Arlington VA 22201

BURFORD, WILLIAM E
DEALER, ADMINISTRATOR
b Lubbock, Tex, May 16, 36. *Study:* Tex Tech Univ, BA. *Pos:* Pres, Tex Art Gallery, Dallas, 76-; vchmn, Tex Comn on the Arts & Humanities, Austin, 76, chmn, 77-78; mem, Dallas City Art Comn, 77-. *Specialty:* Predominantly contemporary Western art with Americana, wildlife, landscapes, books and sculpture

BURG, PATRICIA JEAN
PAINTER, PRINTMAKER
b Windsor, Ont, Can, Jan 9, 34; US citizen. *Study:* Otis Art Inst, Los Angeles, MFA (cum laude), 66. *Work:* IBM Co, Los Angeles; Art in Embassies, White House Loan Collection; Standard Oil Co, NY. *Comn:* Oil paintings, Latham & Watkins, Los Angeles, 75 & 79, Allison Corp, Los Angeles, 75, Roberts Scott & Co, San Diego, 76 & Carson City Hall, Calif, 77. *Exhib:* Northwest Printmakers, Seattle Art Mus, Wash, 69; New Work-New Talent, Los Angeles Co Mus Art, Los Angeles, 74; Miriam Perlman Gallery, Chicago, 1990; Int Trienniel, Krakow, Poland, 1994; Laguna Art Mus, 2001; Contemp Prints, Nat Arts Club, NY, 2004; Belfast Print Workshop Gallery, Ireland, 2006; and others. *Pos:* Co-founder & dir, Triad Graphic Workshop, Los Angeles, 66-; co-owner, Art Source Gallery, Los Angeles, 75-. *Teaching:* Instr drawing, Otis Art Inst-Parsons, Los Angeles; instr drawing, Occidental Col, Eagle Rock, Calif; faculty, Woodbury Univ, Burbank, Calif. *Awards:* Purchase Awards, Mus Fine Arts, Boston, 68, Otis Art Inst, Los Angeles, 69, 10th Nat Calif Poly, Pomona, 1988; Merit Award, Western Books, 1986. *Bibliog:* Bentley Schaad (auth), The Realm of Contemporary Still Life, Reinhold Press, 65; Thelma R Newman (auth), Innovative Printmaking, Crown, 75; Constructions, Art Scene Mag, 3/90. *Mem:* Los Angeles Inst Contemp Art; Los Angeles Printmaking Soc (bd dir, 76-); Artists Econ Action. *Media:* Etching, Printing. *Specialty:* Modern art with emphasis on graphics and paintings. *Publ:* Contemporaries, LA Times, 5/98; 22 Printmakers, Sierra Vista Herald, summer 2003. *Dealer:* Tang Gallery 32 Main St Bisbee AR 85603. *Mailing Add:* 3666 Longridge Ave Sherman Oaks CA 91423-4918

BURGER, GARY C
MUSEUM DIRECTOR
b Greenville, SC, Nov 6, 43. *Study:* Williams Col, BA, 65; Williams Col, Clark Art Inst, MA, 76. *Pos:* Assoc dir, Mass Coun Arts & Humanties, 76-78; consult, New Eng Found Arts, 78-79; dir, The Berkshire Mus, 79-89, Williamstown Art Conserv Lab, 89-. *Mem:* New England Mus Asn (past pres); Nat Inst Conserv (trustee); Mass Arts Advocacy Comt; Asn Regional Conserv Ctrs (pres); Williams Col Mus AA vis comt. *Publ:* Auth, 100 American Drawings from the J D Hatch Collection, Heim Galleries, 76. *Mailing Add:* 324 Oblong Rd Williamstown MA 01267-3043

BURGER, W CARL
EDUCATOR, PAINTER
b Baden, Ger, Dec 27, 1925; US citizen. *Study:* NY Univ, BS, MA; Studies at Columbia Univ; Rutgers Univ; Parsons Sch Design, Art Students League, New Sch, NY. *Work:* Kean Univ, NJ; Bergen Mus; Chubb Asn; Newark Mus & State Mus, NJ; Exxon, NJ; Morris Mus; AT&T; Johnson & Johnson; Bristol Meyers; Schering Plough; Rutgers Univ Law Sch, Newark; British Airways, Newark Liberty Int Aiport; others; numerous int private collections. *Comn:* Space Mural, Lockheed Electronics, Woodbridge, NJ, 60. *Exhib:* Somerset Col, Tri-State Show, Somerville, NJ, 78; Watercolor Show, Holyoke Mus, Mass, 78; Newark Mus Triennial, 82; Am Drawing, Morris Mus, 85; Retrospecitve, NJ State Mus, 87; Co Col Morris, NJ, 2004; solo show, Noyes Mus, NJ; solo show, Newark Accad, NJ, 2006; and others. *Pos:* Set designer, Capemay Playhouse, 54-55 & Hillson's Theatre Stars, Binghamton, NY, 56. *Teaching:* Prof design & drawing, Kean Univ, Union, NJ, 60-93, prof emeritus, 93-. *Awards:* NJ State Coun Arts Grant, 81; Grimbacher Award Excellence in the Arts; Winsor Newton Award Excellence; Allied Artists Award, Nat Arts Club, NY, 2004; NY Central Award, Audubon Artists, 2005; Arts Bridge Award, Drawing, 2006; over 250 group show awards. *Bibliog:* Article in Art News, 9/83; featured numerous times on NJ Artists Series, NJ Pub TV, 86-. *Mem:* NJ Watercolor Soc; Hunterdon Art Ctr (trustee, 69-72); Audubon Artists (hon mem); Assoc Artists NJ (past pres, 80-83); Phi Delta Kappa; Am Legion. *Media:* Watercolor, Ink Drawings, Acrylic incorporated with Sand, Watercolors with Organic Plant Stains. *Publ:* review, Art News, 85; review, NY Times, 2002. *Dealer:* Frederick Gallery Allenhurst NJ; Danette Koke New York NY; Pedersen Gallery Springlake NJ; Coryell Gallery Lambertsville NJ. *Mailing Add:* 239 Beacon Hill Rd Califon NJ 07830

BURGESS, DAVID LOWRY
ENVIRONMENTAL ARTIST
b Philadelphia, Pa, Apr 27, 40. *Study:* Pa Acad Fine Arts, Philadelphia; Univ Pa; Inst Allende, San Miguel, Mex. *Work:* Lamont Libr, Harvard Univ, Cambridge, Mass; Mus Fine Arts, Boston; Smithsonian Collection, Washington; Archives, Boston Pub Libr; Pa Acad Fine Arts Mus, Philadelphia; Herning Mus, Herning, Denmark; De Cordova Mus, Lincoln, Mass; Archives of Lincoln Ctr, NY; MIT Archives, Cambridge, Mass. *Comn:* Common Light, City of Cambridge, Mass, 2000. *Exhib:* 25 Yr Retrospective, Mass Inst Technol List Visual Art Ctr; Earth, Air, Fire, Water, The Elements, Mus Fine Arts, Boston, 71; Master Drawings of the 19th & 20th Centuries, Mus Fine Arts, Boston, 72; Sky Arts Conference (co-ed catalog), Mass Inst Technol List Visual Art Ctr, 81, Linz, Austria, 82 & Munich, WGer, 83; De Cordova Mus, 85; Monocle, Hamburger Kunsthalle, 85; Pa Acad Fine Arts; Art Transition, Mass Inst Technol, Cambridge, 92; DLight, Univ Mass Gallery, Boston, 93; Pittsburgh Biennial, Pa, 94 & 95; Joseloff Mus, Hartford, Conn, 2000; and 150 other exhibs. *Pos:* Fel & sr consult, Ctr Advan Visual Studies, Mass Inst Technol, 71-; distinguished artist, ECHO, Univ Que, Montreal, 89. *Teaching:* Prof, Mass Col Art, Boston, 69-; dean, Col Fine Arts, Carnegie Mellon Univ, Pittsburgh, prof fine arts, currently; Koopman Distingquished chair visual arts, Hartford Sch Art. *Awards:* Rockefeller Found Grant, 84; Mass Coun Arts Proj Grant, 85; Nat Endowment Arts Individual Artist Grant, 86; Am Acad Arts & Letters, 1973; Nat Inst Art, 1973; Guggenheim Found, 1974; Kellogg Found, 2001-2002. *Bibliog:* articles, Boston Mag, 11/85 & Art in Am, 2/86; T Frick (auth), article, Sacred Theories of the Earth, 2/86. *Mem:* Arts Educ Am (adv bd, 78-); Nat Humanities Fac. *Publ:* Auth, Fragments, 69, Looking and Listening, 72 & Memory, Environment & Utopia, 75; and others. *Mailing Add:* 1375 Crodova Rd Pittsburgh PA 15206

BURGESS, JOSEPH JAMES, JR
PAINTER, EDUCATOR
b Albany, NY, July 13, 24. *Study:* Hamilton Col, BA, 47; Yale Univ, MA, 48; Pratt Inst, 52-54; Cranbrook Acad Art, MFA, 54. *Exhib:* Recent Drawings USA, Mus Mod Art, NY, 56; Drawing Nat, Calif Palace Legion Hon, San Francisco, 59; two-person show, Flint Inst Art, 56-65 DeWaters Art Ctr, Flint, Mich 64; Calif Design Ten Show,

Pasadena Art Mus, 68; First Ann City of Angels Int Exhib Photog, 74; Santa Fe Festival of Arts, 79; one-man exhib, Albany Inst Hist, Art, NY, 58 Ball State Teachers Col, 58, Historic Costume of the Orient, Sante Fe, NMex, 83. *Pos:* Designer & co-owner, Origins, retail & K/B Designs, wholesale, Carmel, Calif, 66-75 & The Gold Persimmon, retail & K/B Designs, wholesale, Santa Fe, NMex, currently; dir, Blair Galleries, Ltd, Santa Fe, NMex, 76-79. *Teaching:* Asst prof fine arts & head dept, St Lawrence Univ, Canton, NY, 54-55; art instr, chmn dept & dir, DeWaters Art Ctr, Flint Community Jr Col, 56-65; asst prof design, Ariz State Univ, Tempe, 65-66; asst prof art, NMex Highlands Univ, 82-83; instr drawing & design, Santa Fe Community Col, NMex, 86-90; workshops at Valdes Inc, Sante Fe NMex, 87-2000; lectr, Renesan Lectr Series: Art in Age of Transition, Col Santa Fe, 1-2/2000. *Media:* Mixed. *Specialty:* Painting, sculpture and graphics. *Publ:* Auth, Three Chinese Poems, Translations from Tang Dynasty poets, winter 61-62, Four Chinese poems, translations from T'ang poetry, fall 61 & Some thoughts on non-communication in the arts, spring 63, Mich Voices; auth, A random poem, translation from the T'ang Dynasty poet Wang Wei, 10/12/73, A shining legend, 9/10/74, Asia's first iron-clad warship, 5/19/75, Christian Sci Monitor; and many others. *Mailing Add:* 16 Caliente Rd Santa Fe NM 87505

BURGGRAF, RAY LOWELL
PAINTER, EDUCATOR
b Mt Gilead, Ohio, July 26, 38. *Study:* Ashland Col, BS, 61; Cleveland Inst Art, BFA, 68; Univ Calif, Berkeley, MA, 69, MFA, 70. *Work:* Mint Mus Art; Western Ill Univ; Montgomery Mus Fine Arts; Greenville Co Mus; Dekalb Col. *Comn:* Royal Caribbean Cruise Lines Inc, 85. *Exhib:* Artists of the Southeast & Texas, Isaac Delgado Mus Art, New Orleans, 71; The Great Buffalo Show, Cameron Univ Art Gallery, Lawton, Okla, 86; Ann Juried Exhib, Orlando Mus Art, Fla, 87; Four From Fla, Kennesaw State Col, Marietta, Ga, 90; Works on Paper, Nat Acad Sciences, Washington, DC, 90. *Teaching:* Asst prof painting & drawing, Fla State Univ, 70-. *Awards:* First Nat Bank Award, Mobile Art Patrons League, Ala, 71. *Mem:* Col Art Asn Am. *Media:* Acrylic. *Mailing Add:* 1507 Marion Ave Tallahassee FL 32303-5830

BURK, A DARLENE
DEALER, COLLECTOR
b Wheatland, Wyo, Dec 24, 29. *Study:* Calvin Goodman Sem, 76-80. *Pos:* Owner, Burk Gallery, currently. *Mem:* Rotary; Boulder City Arts Coun; Boulder City Chamber Commerce. *Specialty:* Western art, Indian culture, landscape and wildlife. *Collection:* Painting, Jeff Craven, Carol Harding; Clyde Ross Morgan. *Mailing Add:* 1305 Arizona St Boulder City NV 89005

BURKE, BILL
CERAMIST
Work: Xerox Corp, Rochester, NY; Perdue Univ, Art Galleries, Perdue, Ind; Univ N Dakota, Univ Art Galleries, Fargo, N Dakota. *Exhib:* Xerox Invitational, Xerox Hall, Rochester, NY, 73; Ceramics Invitational 74, Pratt Inst Art, New York, NY; John Michael Kohler Art Ctr, Sheboygan, Wis, invitational, 79; GLOVE Exhib Nat Invitational, travelling, Valencia Community Col, Fla, 83; Works Gallery, South Hampton, NY, 86; Regional Ceramics Invitational, Univ Miami, New Gallery, Coral Gables, Fla, 87; 1989 Ann Juried Exhib, Orlando Mus Art, Fla, 89. *Teaching:* Grad asst, State Univ Col- New Paltz, New York, NY, 73, grad teaching asst, 73 74, instr design, 74, assoc prof, Fla Int Univ, Miami, Fla, 74-94, prof, 94-. *Awards:* Fla Fine Arts Coun State Grant, 78-79 & 82; Merit Award, 30th Ann M Allen Hortt Exhib, Mus Art, Ft Lauderdale, Fla. *Mailing Add:* Dept Visual Arts Fla Int Univ Univ Park Campus Miami FL 33199

BURKE, DANIEL
MUSEUM DIRECTOR, EDUCATOR
Study: La Salle Univ, PhD. *Pos:* Vpres, acad affairs La Salle Univ, Philadelphia, pres, 69—77; founding dir, La Salle Univ Art Mus, 76—. *Teaching:* Teacher, Eng West Philadelphia Cath High Sch. *Mailing Add:* La Salle Univ Art Mus 1900 W Olney Ave Philadelphia PA 19141

BURKE, DANIEL V
PAINTER, EDUCATOR
b Erie, Pa, Apr 21, 42. *Study:* Columbus Col Art & Design, 60-62; Mercyhurst Col, BA(art), 69; Edinboro State Col, MEd(art), 72; MacDowell Colony, Peterborough, NH, 70 & 73. *Work:* Del Mar Col Art Gallery, Corpus Christi; Laguna Gloria Art Mus, Austin, Tex; Southern Utah State Col; IBM Corp, Austin; NC Nat Bank, Boone; and others. *Exhib:* Drawings USA, Minn Mus Art, St Paul, 75; One-Man Shows, Williams Col Mus Art, Mass, 81, Rike Ctr Gallery, Univ Dayton, Ohio, 83 & Gallery 937, Assoc Artists Pittsburgh, Pa, 96; Magahan & Penelecc Galleries, Allegheny Col, Pa, 84; Second Street Gallery, Charlottesville, VA, 92; 35th Nat Chautauqua Art Asn Show, NY, 92; Rosewood Arts Ctr Gallery, Kettering, Ohio, 93; Erie Art Mus, Pa, 93. *Teaching:* Prof art, Mercyhurst Col, 69-, dir dept art, 79-. *Awards:* Visual Arts Fel, Pa Coun Arts, 86 & 92; Director's Award, 35th Nat Show, 92; Joseph M Katz Mem Award, 84th Ann, Carnegie Mus Art, 94. *Mem:* Northwestern Pa Artists Asn (co-exec chmn, 75-); Assoc Artists Pittsburgh. *Media:* Acrylic

BURKE, JAMES DONALD
MUSEUM DIRECTOR, ADMINISTRATOR
b Salem, Ore, Feb 22, 39. *Study:* Brown Univ, AB, 62; Univ Pa, AM, 66; Fulbright-Hayes Fel, Holland, 68-69; Harvard Univ, PhD, 72. *Hon Degrees:* LHD, Maryville Univ, 97; DHL, Univ Mo, 98. *Collection Arranged:* Charles Meryon (auth, catalog), 74-75. *Pos:* Cur, Allen Art Mus, Oberlin Col, 71-72; cur drawings & prints, Art Gallery, Yale Univ, 72-78; asst dir, St Louis Art Mus, 78-80, dir, 80-99, dir emeritus, 99-. *Teaching:* Instr, Yale Univ, 72-78; scholar in residence, Univ Mo, 99-; E Desmond Lee scholar in residence, sr lectr art history & archaeology, Washington Univ, 2001. *Awards:* Nat Endowment Arts Mus Fel, 73. *Mem:* Am Asn Mus; Col Art Asn; Print Coun Am. *Res:* Sixteenth and seventeenth century Dutch and Flemish art; contemporary and modern art; American art; photography. *Publ:* Auth, Jan Both: Paintings, Drawings & Prints, 75. *Mailing Add:* Washington Univ Dept History & Archaeology Box 1189 Saint Louis MO 63110

BURKE, MARY GRIGGS
COLLECTOR
Study: Sarah Lawrence Col, BA; Columbia Univ, MA (clinical psychology); New Sch Social Res, postgrad. *Pos:* Pvt collector, Japanese art, St Paul, 66-; founder, pres, The Mary & Jackson Burke Found, New York City, 72-. *Awards:* Decorated Order of The Sacred Treasure (Japan); Second Level Gold and Silver Star (Japan); named one of top 200 collectors, ARTnews Mag, 2004. *Mem:* Freer Gallery Art, Smithsonian Inst (mem vis comt, currently); Metrop Mus Art; The Japan Soc, 59-77 (mem comt, currently); Japan House Gallery, (chmn, 69-75, 87-); William Beene fel NY Zoological Soc. *Collection:* Japanese Art. *Mailing Add:* Mary Livingston Griggs & Mary Griggs Burke Found 1400 Fifth St Ctr Saint Paul MN 55101

BURKE-FANNING, MADELEINE
PAINTER, INSTRUCTOR
b New Orleans, La, Feb 12, 41. *Study:* Davids Sch of Art, New Orleans, 76-78; Pensacola Junior Col, 82-88; workshops with Gerald Brommer & Don Andrews, 99. *Work:* Wise Choice Mus/Gallery, Sandestin, Fla; Kate Holms-Branton Gallery, Pensacola, Fla; Corner Copia, Orange Beach, Ala; Expressions Gallery, Pensacola, Fla; Artist Three, Perdido Key, Ala; Woodcock Gallery and Interiors, Pensacola, Fla; Stockamp Gallery, Pensacola, Fla: Michelle Ray Gallery, Pensacola, Fla. *Comn:* portrait, comn by Susan M Galens, United Way, Chattanooga, Tenn, 96; watercolor, St Johns Hospital, Harahan, La, 2000; portrait, comn by Earl P Burke Jr, Pel-Tex Oil Co, Houston, Tex, 2000; portrait, comn Daniel Gough, Pace, Fla, 2000; Portrait Comm by Cathy and Peter Butler, MD, 2004: Dr and Mrs Noel Pacheco, 2004-2005; Mr and Mrs Sims, Kurt and Tommi Stockamp MD, Pensacola, Fla; Mr and Mrs Michael Heller, Pensacola, Fla; Melba Harrell, Milton, Fla; Vernon and Angele Hargis, New Orleans, LA; Lauren E Glenn, Baton Rouge, LA. *Exhib:* Eclectic, World Trade Ctr, New Orleans, La, 96 & Pensacola Mus of Art, Fla, 97-98; Stages: Then and Now, Art and Design Mus, Fort Walton, Fla, 2000; one-woman show, Ducks Unlimited, Pensacola, Fla, 98 & 2000, Sam Houston Racetrack, Jockey Club, Houston, Tex, 2001; Go Figure 96! 97! and 98!, Cult Ctr Pensacola, Fla, 96-98; Art with an Edge, Artel Gallery, Pensacola, Fla, 99-2000; 26th Ann Transparent Watercolor Exhib, Visual Arts Center, Panama City, Fla, 2001; Northwest Fla, Stockamp Gallery, One Woman Show, Portraiture in Watercolor, 2005. *Pos:* presenter Watercolor Workshops, Desin Fla, Georgetown, Maine, New Orleans, La, Pensacola, Fla & Houston, Tex, 96-2000, 2004-2005; Bay St Louis, Miss, 2005. *Teaching:* instr watercolor, Pensacola Junior Col & City of Pensacola, Fla, 97-2000. *Awards:* Best in Show, International Trade Mart, 96; Best of Watercolor Distinction, Rockport Press, 97, 02; Collected Best of Watercolor, 2002, Distinction, Rock Port Press. *Bibliog:* Univ of West Florida (auth), Art and Healing, Univ of West Florida (TV), 97 & Go Figure 96! & 97! and 98!, 97; Donna Freckman (auth), Central Lights, Pensacola Today Mag, 98. *Mem:* Nat Mus Women in Arts; Am Soc Portrait Artists; Fla Watercolor Soc; Woodbine Figure Painters (secy, treas, 95 98); Bay Cliff Watercolor Soc (founder & pres, 96-2001); New Orleans Mus Art; La Watercolor Soc; Pensacola Mus Art; Northwest Fla Arts Coun; Eastern Shore Art Ctr and Mus. *Media:* Watercolor. *Interests:* Travel, photography, gardening, reading, horse back riding. *Publ:* contrib, Best of Watercolor, Painting Texture, Rockport Press, 97; contrib, Pensacola Today: Coastal Lights Art and Healing, Buschnell Publ, 98; contrib, The Insider, Sanpiper Publ, 2000; contrib, The Weekender, Pensacola News J, 2000; Collected Best of Watercolor, 2002, Rockport Press, Northlight Books. *Mailing Add:* Palm Cottage Studio 4160 Rommitch Ln Pensacola FL 32504

BURKETT, CHRISTOPHER G
PHOTOGRAPHER
b Corvallis, Ore, Aug 13, 51. *Study:* Self taught. *Work:* Mus Fine Arts, Boston; Portland Art Mus, Ore; Avon Libr, Ohio; Ctr Creative Photog, Tucson, Ariz; Univ Ky, Lexington. *Exhib:* Icons of the Sacred Earth, Inst Polytechnics, Tokyo, Japan, 90; one-man shows, Hult Ctr Performing Arts & Univ Ore, Eugene, 92; Am Landscapes, World Forestry Ctr, Portland, Ore, 93; The Tongass-Alaska's Magnificent Rainforest, Smithsonian Inst, Washington, DC, 95; A Photog Fair, West Foto, Sweden, 96; Photographs of Oregon, Off of Gov, Salem, Ore, 97; Light in the Forest, World Forestry Ctr, Portland, Ore, 99. *Awards:* Bernheim Found Fel, Univ Louisville & Bernheim Forest, 90-91. *Media:* Ilfochrome. *Publ:* Illusr, Northeastern Journey, Stinehour Press, 89; Robert Frost Seasons, Henry Holt Publ Co, 92; illusr & coauth, Camera and Darkroom, Camera & Darkroom Mag, 93; Fotografi-Sweden, Fotografi Mag, 97; View Camera, View Camera Mag, 97; and others. *Dealer:* Northwest by Northwest Gallery Cannon Beach OR; Photographic Image Gallery Portland OR

BURKHARDT, RONALD ROBERT
CONCEPTUAL ARTIST, PAINTER
b Jackson, MI, Jul 25. *Study:* Western Michigan Univ, BBA, 1970; Art Students League of New York, NY, 2003; National Academy of Fine Art, New York, NY, 2004. *Work:* Muhammad Ali Ctr & Mus, Louisville, KY; Gallery Asto, Los Angeles, CA; 7 Degrees Gallery, Laguna Beach, CA. *Comn:* Solar Hieroglyphs (acrylic on canvas 10' x 4') Phyllis George, NY & Los Angeles, 2005. *Exhib:* Rockefeller's Business Comt For The Arts, Forbes Gallery, New York, NY, 2002; Art Release Gallery / Trump Tower, NY, 2003; Banking on Art, Wells Fargo Bank, Laguna Beach, CA, 2003-2004; Watermill Mus Group Show, Watermill Mus, Watermill, NY, 2004; Paperworks (Judge: Art in Am Magazine, B. J. Spoke Gallery, Huntington, NY, 2005; Muhammad

Ali Quotations, Muhammad Ali Mus, Louisville, KY, 2005; Biennale Int Dell'Arte Contemporanea, Fortezza Da Basso, Florence, Italy, 2005; Magidson Fine Art, Sao Paolo, Brazil, 2005; One Fine Art Gallery, Chicago, 2005; Int Biennale Contemp Art, Klagen Furt, Austria, 2006. *Teaching:* guest prof, Western Mich Univ, 2006. *Awards:* Paperworks, B.J. Spoke Gallery, NY, Faye Hirsch, Juror, Sr Ed Art in Am Mag, 2005; Medici Medal for Mixed Media at Florence Biennale Contemp Art, 2005. *Bibliog:* John Capos (auth), Who's Here, Dan's Papers, Southampton, NY, 2004; Roberta Carasso (auth), Burkhardt Discovers There's Art in Taking Notes, Laguna News Post, 2005; Debbie Sklar (auth), The Art of Notetaking, Orange Co Register, LNN, 2005. *Mem:* Whitney Mus Am Art, New York, NY; MOMA, New York, NY; One Club, New York, NY; Laguna Art Mus, Laguna Beach, Calif. *Media:* Acrylic, Oil. *Interests:* Traveling; Writing; Karate; Motorcycling; Tennis. *Publ:* Auth, Is Creativity a Product of its Environment?, Adweek Magazine, NY, 80; auth, The return of the creative mind, Ad Age Mag. 80; auth, Keeping the Pasture Green, Adweek Magazine, NY, 1984; auth, Between the Lines, One.A Magazine, NY, 2004. *Dealer:* Scott Sichterman One Fine Art Gallery 209 W Huron Chicago Ill 60610. *Mailing Add:* 18 Peacock Path PO Box 1070 Quogue NY 11959

BURKHART, KATHE K
CONCEPTUAL ARTIST, WRITER
b Martinsburg, WVa, June 18, 58. *Study:* Cal Arts, BFA, 82, MFA, 84. *Work:* Flash Art Mus; Smak Mus, Ghent, Belg Collections; also pvt collections of Rogier & Hilde Matthys, Ghent, Belg, Ellen & Richard Sandor, NY, Andre Wilocx, Bruges, Belg, Carlo Pappruco, Turin, Italy & Robert Shiffler, Greenville, Ohio; Participant, INC 2003; Mitchell Algus Gallery, NY, 2003-2004. *Comn:* Banner, Los Angeles Contemp Exhib, 85; Mus Fine Art, Bruges, Belg, 97; Fuoi Uso, Italy, 95. *Exhib:* Selected Works from the Liz Taylor Series, Shoshana Wayne Gallery, Santa Monica, 92; Reframing Cartoons, Wexner Ctr, Columbus, Ohio, 92; From Media to Metaphor: About AIDS, Mus d'Art Contemp, Montreal, Que, 93; Rijksakad, Amsterdam, 94-96; Real Fake, Neuberger Mus, Purchase, NY, 95; Printemps/Etc, Groningen Mus, The Neth, 96; one-man shows, Serge Sorokko Gallery, NY, 97, Galerie DeLege Ruimte, Gent, Bel, 97, Mus V Schone Kunsten, Bruges, Belg, 97, 99, Shores Gallery, Amsterdam, 2000; and others; Bad Girls, UCLA Wight Mus, 94. *Pos:* Bookstore mgr, Los Angeles Contemp Exhibs, 82-85; freelance graphic designer for var clients, 85-; Prof, New York Univ, 2000-. *Teaching:* Vis artist painting, Mason Gross Sch Art, Rutgers Univ, New Brunswick, NJ, 91-92 & San Francisco Art Inst, 98; teacher Ohio State Univ, 94; teacher RISD, 99, New York Univ, 2000-. *Awards:* Arts Int Award, 93; Art Matters, 94; Funds for Fine Arts, Amsterdam, 98-2001. *Bibliog:* Helena Kontova (auth), Bad girl made good, Flashart, 10-11/90; Gianni Romano (ed), Velvet Revolution (exhib catalog), Galleria Arco, Turin, Italy, 93; Bad Girl Work 1983 - 2000, 2005 Hanus Press; Barbara Pollack, Art In America, 10/2004; Schambelan, Elizabeth Art Forum, 3/2005. *Mem:* Col Art Asn. *Media:* Image and Text. *Specialty:* Contemporary Art. *Interests:* Feminism, Literature, Politics, Psychology. *Publ:* Auth, From Under the 8 Ball, LINE, 85; The Torture Paintings, Culturcentrum, Bruges, Belgium, 97; The Double Standard Participant Press, 2005. *Dealer:* Andre Willocx Galerie de Lege Rumite Belgium; Mitchell Algus Gallery NYC 511 W 25th St NY NY 10011. *Mailing Add:* 47 S Fifth St Brooklyn NY 11211

BURKLE, RONALD W
PATRON
Pos: Pvt practice, 75-88; pres, Jurgensen's, Pasadena, Calif, 86-88; princ, Yucaipa Mgt Co, Claremont, 86-; chmn, Food 4 Less Supermarkets, La Habra, 89-; staff, Dominick's Finer Foods, Northlake, Ill, until 98; mem bd trustees, J Paul Getty Trust, 2001-; mem bd, exec comt, Campaign Against Youth Violence, currently; John F Kennedy Ctr for Performing Arts, Nat Urban League, Los Angeles Co Mus Art; co-chmn, Burkle Ctr for Int Relations, UCLA; mem educ adv bd RAND; founder, chmn bd trustees, Ralphs/Food4Less Found, The Fred Meyer, Inc, Found; bd mem, Children's Scholarship Fund, Carter Ctr, AIDS Project Los Angeles, currently; mem e-bd, Claremont Grad Univ; chmn bd, DARE Am; mem exec bd, for medical sci's, UCLA, currently. *Awards:* Named Humanitarian of Year, AFL-CIO; Man of Year, Los Angeles, Co Fedn Labor; recipient Whitney M Young Award. *Mailing Add:* 1200 Getty Ctr Dr Los Angeles CA 90049

BURKO, DIANE
PAINTER, EDUCATOR
b Brooklyn, NY, Sept 24, 45. *Study:* Skidmore Col, BS, 66; Univ Pa Grad Sch Fine Arts, MFA, 69. *Work:* Philadelphia Mus Art; DeCordova Mus, Lincoln, Mass; Reading Pub Mus; Am Tel & Tel; Wells Fargo Bank; Pa Acad Fine Arts; IBM, Tucson, Ariz; CIGNA Corp; Art Inst, Chicago, IL; Frerick Weisman Art Mus, Mineeapolis, MN. *Comn:* 1 percent RDA, Philadelphia Marriott, 95-96. *Exhib:* Whitney Mus Am Art, 81; Art Inst Chicago, 83; Tampa Mus Art, 86; Md Art Inst, 86; one-person shows, Hollins Col, 87, Marian Locks Gallery, 88, 90, 92 & 94, Nat Acad Sci, Washington, 91 & Moravian Col, 95-96; Perspectives - PA, Carnegie Mellon Univ, Pittsburgh, Pa, 88; Landscape: Work by Women Artists, Bryn Mawr Col, Pa, 94; Artist Made Objects, Locks Gallery, Philadelphia, 95; The River, Philadelphia Art Alliance, Pa, 98; A Sense of Place: Paintings by Diane Burko, Parthenon Mus, Nashville Tenn, 99; Volcano series, Locks Gallery, 2001, Pa; Earth, Water, Fire, Locks Gallery, PA, 2004; Paint/Pixel, Rider Univ Art Galler, NJ, 2005; Flow, Aidekman Art Center, Tufts Univ, MA, 2006; The Michener Mus, Pa, 2006; Diane Burko: Photographs, Locks Gallery, Pa, 2006. *Pos:* Pres & founder, Philadelphia Focuses on Women in Visual Arts, 73-75; Mayors Cult Adv Coun, 88-90; Art Comn Philadelphia, 92-96. *Teaching:* Prof drawing, painting & design, Philadelphia Community Col, 69-85, prof art, 73-, head art dept, 80-85; vis prof, Princeton Univ, 85. *Awards:* Pa Coun Arts Individual Artists Grant, 81 & 89; Nat Endowment Arts Visual Arts Fel, 85-86, 91-92; Bessie Berman Painting Grant, Leeway Found, 2000; Carter Ratcliff (auth) Volcano series, 01. *Bibliog:* Alexandria Anderson (auth), Burko-Locks, Art News, 91; Robert Rosenblum (auth), Luci ed Ombra di Bellagio - The Light & Shadow of Bellagio (exhib catalog), Locks Gallery, 94; David Bourdon (auth), Diane Borko, Land Survey: 1970-95 (exhib catalog), Moravian Col, 95. *Mem:* Col Art Asn Am (bd mem, 94-98); Women's Caucus Art (treas adv bd, 77-78 & 82-85); Philadelphia Volunteer Lawyers for Arts, (bd mem 86-89); Philadelphia Art Comn. *Media:* Oil, Acrylic. *Collection:* Colgate Univ, Picker Art Gallery, Hamilton, NY; De Cordova Mus, Lincoln, Mass; Hahnemann Hosp, Pa. *Dealer:* Locks 600 Wash Square S Ctr Philadelphia PA 19106. *Mailing Add:* 275 S 19th St Philadelphia PA 19103

BURKS, MYRNA R
PRINTMAKER, GALLERY DIRECTOR
b Chattanooga, Tenn, Oct 31, 43. *Study:* Ga State Univ, BFA, 71; Univ NMex, MA, 73, MFA, 76. *Work:* Hunter Art Mus, Chattanooga, Tenn; US Info Agency, var embassies; Univ NMex Fine Arts Mus, Albuquerque. *Exhib:* Third Hawaii Nat Print Exhib, Honolulu Acad Arts, 75; Northwest Int Small Format Print Exhib, Davidson Gallery, Seattle, Wash, 76; Women Artists '79: Paperworks, Art & Design Gallery, Univ Kans, Lawrence, 79; Selected Artists, Mulvane Art Ctr, Topeka, Kans, 79-80; Mo Works on Paper Traveling Exhib, 79-80; Texture in Prints, 81, Northwest Prints 82, Oregon Biennale, 85 & Western State Print Exhib, 85, Portland Art Mus; Northwest Print Coun Exhib, Galleri Norske Grafikere, Oslo, Norway, 85. *Collection Arranged:* Artists Choose Artists, Univ Mo-Kansas City, 79 & Missouri Artists: Works on Paper (auth, catalog), 80. *Pos:* Cur, Tamarind Inst, Univ NMex, 72-73, printer, 77; co-owner & printer, North Light Editions, Portland, Ore, 81-. *Teaching:* Instr art & dir gallery, Univ Mo-Kansas City, 78-80. *Awards:* Ford Found Res Fel, 76; Best of Show Award, Women Artists: Paperworks, 79. *Bibliog:* Donald Hoffman (auth), The history of the world traced through its scars, Kansas City Star, 9/79; Jan Schmitz (auth), The personal lure of Myrna Burks, Forum/Kansas City Artists' Coalition, 10/79; Leonard Koenig (auth), A portfolio of artwork, New Lett, Univ Mo-Kansas City, 79-80. *Mem:* Col Art Asn; Women's Caucus Art (adv bd Kansas City chap, 78-80); Kansas City Artist's Coalition (adv bd, 79-80). *Media:* Lithography, Mixed. *Publ:* Auth, Women artists, Forum/Kansas City Artists' Coalition, 12/79

BURLEIGH, KIMBERLY
PRINTMAKER, EDUCATOR
b Meadville, Pa, Apr 1, 55. *Study:* Ohio Univ, Athens, BFA, 77; Ind Univ, Bloomington, MFA, 80. *Comn:* Progressive Corp, Cleveland, Ohio; One person shows, Carnegie Mellon Univ, 2001, Fine Arts Work Ctr, Provincetown, Mass, 99. *Exhib:* One-person shows, Pittsburgh Plan for Art, Pa, 85 & Feature Gallery, Chicago, 86 & 87; John Michael Kohler Arts Ctr, Sheboygan, Wis, 92; Galerie 1900-2000, Paris, France, 94; Print Club, Philadelphia, Pa, 94; Galerie Toner in Sens en Bourgogne, France, 97 & 98; NY Digital Salon, Visual Arts Mus, NY, 98; Gallery N-Space at Siggraph, 2001; CEPA Gallery, Buffalo, 99. *Collection Arranged:* Progressive Corp, Cleveland, Ohio; Joan Flasch Artists Bk Collection, Art Inst Chicago; Bibliotheque Nat de France; Robert J Shiffler Collection & Archive; Galerie Toner in Sens en Bourgogne, France. *Pos:* Vis artist, Murray State Univ, Ky, 83. *Teaching:* Vis asst prof painting, Univ Utah, Salt Lake City, 81-82 & Ohio Univ, Athens, 86-89; asst prof, State Univ Tex, Nacagdoches, 82-83; assoc prof/grad prog dir fine art, Univ Cincinnati, 90-; prof, grad program dir fine art, Univ Cinn, 99-. *Awards:* Visual Artists Fel, Nat Endowment Arts, 87; Ohio Arts Coun Grant, 89 & 99; Artist Proj Grant, Ohio Arts Coun, 95, 97 & 99. *Bibliog:* David McCracken (auth), Words help tell the message in painting, Chicago Tribune, 9/25/87; Barbara Gallati (auth), New work, Arts Mag, 11/81. *Publ:* Cincinnati Portfolio II (lithograph), Mark Patsfall Graphics Inc, Cincinnati, Ohio, 93; Counterfeits I, self publ, Cincinnati, Ohio, 97; Device & Devices, self publ, Cincinnati, Ohio, 98; Reversions, self publ, Cincinnati, 2000. *Mailing Add:* c/o Univ Cincinnati Sch Art PO Box 210016 Cincinnati OH 45221

BURLESON, CHARLES TRENTMAN
PAINTER, EDUCATOR
b Charlotte, NC, June 15, 52. *Study:* Philadelphia Col Art, BFA, 74; RI Sch of Design, MFA, 76. *Work:* NC Arts Soc, Raleigh; Surry Col, Dobson, NC; Providence Jour Collection, RI; Mint Mus, Charlotte, NC; Queens Univ, Ont, Can. *Comn:* Outdoor mural, RI State Coun Arts, Providence, 77; A Case for Boxes (house box), RI Sch of Design Mus, 80, 2001. *Exhib:* One-man shows, Central Falls, NY, 80, Gallery Z, NY, 86 & Virginia Lynch Gallery, Tiverton, RI, 88; group shows, Alan Stone Gallery, NY, 80 & RI Sch of Design Mus Art, 90; Helander Gallery, NY, 90. *Collection Arranged:* Burelson Painting Prize Competition Exhib, 2003-04. *Pos:* Chief critic, EHP Prog, Rome, Italy, 85. *Teaching:* Prof illustr dept, RI Sch Design, 76-2005. *Awards:* Second Place Award, NC Arts Soc, 69; Purchase Award, Mint Mus Art, Charlotte, 74; Purchase Award, NC Mus Art, 75. *Bibliog:* Edward Sozanski (auth), Burleson's landscapes are striking, Providence J, 82; Edward Booth-Clibborn (auth), American Illustration, Abrams, 84; Drawings-Gallery Z, East Village Rev, 3-4/87; Chronos Mag, winter 2003. *Media:* Oil. *Specialty:* Am Art. *Publ:* Painting (cover piece), Where I'm Calling From Raymond Carver, Atlantic Monthly Press, 88. *Dealer:* Grand Central Gallery, Boston, MA; Erlich Gallery, Marblehead MA; Virginia Lynch, Tiverton, RI. *Mailing Add:* 7 Hayward Pl Rumford RI 02916

BURNETT, CALVIN
PAINTER, PRINTMAKER
b Cambridge, Mass, July 18, 1921. *Study:* Mass Col Art, BFA & BS; Sch Boston Mus Fine Arts; Boston Univ, MFA; studied with George Lockwood & Lawrence Kupferman. *Work:* Boston Mus Fine Arts, Mass; Oakland Mus, Calif; Fogg Art Mus, Harvard Univ; Wiggins Collection, Boston Pub Libr; Wellesley Col; plus others. *Comn:* Illus comn by DC Heath; illus, comn by Houghton Mifflin; illus, comn by Scott Foresman; illus, Boston Globe; illus, Atlantic Publishers. *Exhib:* San Francisco Mus Art; Mus Fine Art, Boston; Smithsonian Inst Traveling Exhib; Taller de

Graphico, Mex; Bazalel Nat, Israel; Brooklyn Mus. *Teaching:* Prof emer drawing & printmaking, Mass Col Art, 56-86. *Awards:* First Award Printmaking, Boston Printmakers, 59, 62 & 64; Leipzig Int Book Illus Exhib Award, Ger, 65; First Award Painting, Atlanta Univ Ann, 53, 61 & 68. *Bibliog:* M Holsen (auth), Introducing some Boston printmakers, The Connoisseur, London, 67; VE Atkinson (auth), Black Dimensions in Contemporary American Art, New Am Libr, 71; F van Almelo (auth), article, Tuesday Mag, 71. *Mem:* Boston Afro-Am Artists Asn; Northeastern Univ Afro-Am Master Artists in Residence Prog. *Media:* Oil; Mixed Drawing Media. *Publ:* Auth-designer, Objective Drawing Techniques, Van Nostrand Reinhold, 66; auth & illusr of children's bks; portfolios of fine prints, 68; impressions graphics workshop. *Dealer:* Sragow Gallery 73 Spring St New York NY 10012. *Mailing Add:* 87 Fisher St Medway MA 02053-2232

BURNETT, DAVID GRANT
HISTORIAN, CURATOR
b Lincoln, Eng, Oct 1, 40; Can citizen. *Study:* Birkbeck Col, Univ London, BA, 65; Courtauld Inst of Art, MA, 67, PhD, 73, under M Kitson. *Pos:* Cur contemp Can Art, Art Gallery Ont, Toronto, 80-84; dir Drabinsky Gallery, Toronto, 90-2000; chief cur, Art Vanst.com, 2000. *Teaching:* Lectr art hist, Univ Bristol, England, 67-70; assoc prof art hist, Carleton Univ, Ottawa, Ont, 70-80. *Res:* Contemporary Art. *Interests:* Flying, scale models. *Publ:* Guido Molinari: Quantificateur, 79; auth, Guido Molinari: Drawings, 80; auth, Alex Colville, 83; auth, Contemp Canadian Art, 83; auth, Harold Town, 86; auth, Jeremy Smith, 88; auth, Gershon Iskowitz, 82; auth, Masterpieces of Canadian Art, Nat Gallery Can, 90

BURNETT, PATRICIA HILL
PAINTER, SCULPTOR
b Brooklyn, NY. *Study:* Goucher Col, BA; Corcoran Mus Art Sch, Washington, DC; Soc Arts & Crafts; Inst Allende, Mex; Wayne State Univ; Truro Sch Art; also with John Carroll, Sarkis Sarkisian, Wallace Bassford, Walter Midener & Seong Moy. *Work:* Detroit Inst Arts, Ford Motor Co Collection, Detroit, Mich; Bloomfield Art Asn, Mich; Wayne State Univ; US Fed Judges, Washington, DC; Mich State Capital. *Comn:* Portrait, Indira Ghandi, Prime Minister, India; portrait, Margaret Thatcher, Prime Minister, Gt Brit; portrait, Corazon Aquino, Pres, Phillipines; portrait, Betty Ford (wife of Pres Gerald Ford); portrait, Violetta Chamorro, Pres Nicaragua; over 700 others. *Exhib:* Butler Mus Nat Art Show, Cleveland, Ohio, 72; Ms & Masters, Midland Ctr Arts, Midland, Mich, 75; Royal Acad Art, London, Eng; Forty-one one-woman shows. *Teaching:* Wayne State Univ, Oakland Community Col; Painting Techniques, Univ Mich Exten Courses & sculpture Techinques, Grosse Pointe War Mem, currently. *Awards:* Mich Women's Hall Of Fame, 89; Ten Most Distinguished Portrait Painters in America, 96; Distinguished Women, Am Fed Women Advert, 99. *Bibliog:* Christine Hinz (auth), Detroit artist: Feminist home-maker and painter, Daily News, Midland, Mich, 75. *Mem:* Mich Acad Arts; Detroit Soc Women Painters & Sculptors; Ibex Club (pres, 50-51); Sculptors Guild Birmingham; Portrait Club (US nat advisory bd, 77-). *Media:* Oil, Bronze, Clay. *Publ:* Contribr, Painting the Female Figure, Bassford, Watson-Guptill Founders Gallery, 73; auth, Have women artists been brushed aside?, Women in the Arts Mag, 75; The winds of change are blowing, Zonta Mag, Int, 75; Women today in Russia, Israel, India & Thailand, PHP Int Mag, Japan, 75; True Colors, Metrop Woman, 96. *Dealer:* Burnett Enterprises Inc

BURNS, JOSEPHINE
PAINTER
b Llandudno, North Wales, July 2, 17. *Study:* Cooper Union Art Sch, grad, 39, BFA, 76; Art Students League, 49 & 50. *Work:* C W Post Col Mus, Long Island Univ; Okla Mus Art, Oklahoma City; Bristol City Art Gallery, Whitworth Art Gallery, Manchester Univ, England. *Exhib:* Brooklyn & Long Island Artists, Brooklyn Mus, 58; one-woman shows, Alonzo Gallery, NY, 66 & Auld Alliance Gallery, Nashville, Tenn, 94; Community Gallery, Brooklyn Mus, 76, 77 & 80; Bergen Co Community Mus, 82; Mostyn Art Gallery, NWales, UK, 82 & 85-92; Salena Gallery, Long Island Univ, 84; Broekman Gallery, Chester, UK; Gallery Ynys Mon, Anglesey, North Wales, UK, 98; and others. *Pos:* Co-dir, Hicks Street Gallery, Brooklyn, 58-63; assoc dir, Brownstone Gallery, Brooklyn, 69-76. *Awards:* Resident Fel, MacDowell Colony, 60, 62, 64, 65 & 68; Resident Fel, Yaddo, Saratoga Springs, NY, 61. *Mem:* Artists Equity Asn, NY. *Media:* Oil, Pastel. *Publ:* Paintings 1982-1997, A Window on Two Worlds (catalog), 98. *Dealer:* Christine Holt Auld Alliance Gallery Westgate Ctr 6019 Highway 100 Nashville TN 37205. *Mailing Add:* 248 Garfield Pl Brooklyn NY 11215

BURNS, MARK A
CERAMIST
b Springfield, Ohio, Oct 5, 50. *Study:* Sch Dayton Art Inst, BFA, 72; Univ Wash, Seattle, MFA, 74. *Exhib:* Everson Mus Art, Syracuse, NY & Renwick Gallery, Smithsonian Inst, Washington, DC, 79; solo exhibs, Helen Drutt Gallery, Philadelphia, Pa, 75, 76, 82, 84 & 89, Happy Birthday Frank Furnets, Pa Acad Fine Arts, Philadelphia, Pa, 84, A Decade in Pennsylvania: 1975-1985, Soc Art & Craft, Verona, Pa, 86 & As Seen on TV, Univ Gallery, Calif State Univ, Chico, 86; Mus Philadelphia Civic Ctr, traveling, 80; Contemp Artists: An Expanding View (with catalogue), Wellesley Col Mus, Mass, Monmouth Mus Art, Lincroft, NJ & Squibb Gallery, Princeton, NJ, 86; Am Ceramics Now: 27th Ceramic Nat Exhibit, Everson Mus Art, 87; Perch Int Crafts, Triennial Twenty Americans: Am Figurative Ceramics, Art Gallery Western Australia, 89; Metamorphesis, Contemp Mus Ceramic Art, Shigaraki, Japan, 92. *Pos:* Asst prof, Philadelphia Col Art, Pa, 75-83, Tyler Sch Art, Temple Univ, Philadelphia, Pa, 81-82, Moore Col Art & Design, Philadelphia, Pa, 85 & Univ Nev Las Vagas, 91-92; vis prof, Univ Ariz, Tucson, 82-83 & RI Sch Design, Providence, 89-91; prof & head ceramics, Univ Nev, 92-. *Awards:* Nat Endowment Arts, 76 & 88. *Publ:* Coauth (with Louis DiBonis), Fifties Homestyle: Popular Ornament of the USA, Harper & Row, 88. *Dealer:* Helen Drutt Gallery 1721 Walnut St Philadelphia PA 19103. *Mailing Add:* Univ Nevada Las Vegas Art Dept HFA 122 B 4505 Maryland Parkway Las Vegas NV 89154

BURNS, MARSHA
PHOTOGRAPHER
b Seattle, Wash, Jan 11, 45. *Study:* Univ Wash, 63-65; Univ Mass, Amherst, 67-69. *Work:* Mus Mod Art, Metrop Mus Art, NY; Nat Mus Am Art, Smithsonian Inst, Libr Cong, Washington, DC; Ctr Creative Photog, Tucson, Ariz; Seattle Art Mus, City of Seattle Collection, Wash; Stedelijk Mus, Amsterdam; Dallas Mus Fine Art, Tex; San Francisco Mus Contemp Art, Fed Reserve Bank of San Francisco, Calif; Libr of Congress, Washington; and others. *Exhib:* Charles Cowles Gallery, NY, 92, 2001 & Portraits from Am, Susan Spiritus Gallery, Costa Mesa, Calif, 92; China 1989, One Path Three Vision, Ital, Seattle, Wash, 90; Western Women Photographers, Maveety Gallery, Portland, Ore, 90; Anniversary Show, Linda Farris Gallery, Seattle, Wash, 90; 1991 Nat Governors Asn Art Exhib, Wash State Convention & Trade Ctr, Seattle; People & Places, Northern Ill Univ Art Mus Gallery, Chicago, 91; SoHo at Duke, Five Artists from Charles Cowles Gallery, Duke Univ Mus Art, Durham, NC; To Collect the Art of Women: The Jane Reese Williams Collection of Photog, Mus NMex, Sante Fe, 92; Photographs: Jock Sturges, Plauto, Marsha Burns, Charles Cowles Gallery, NY, 92; group exhibs, Horse, The Male as Sexual Entity, Ron Judish Fine Arts, Denver, Colo, 2000, Am Persepectives: Photographs from the Polaroid Collection, Tokyo Metrop Mus of Photog, 2000-01. *Awards:* Photogr Fel, Nat Endowment Arts, 78; Awards in Visual Arts, Nat Mus Am Art, Southeastern Ctr Contemp Art, 81; photography fel, Nat Endowment for the Arts, 87-88. *Bibliog:* Gerard Malanga (ed), Scopophilia: The Love of Looking, Alfred Van de Mark Ed & Harper & Row, 85; Chris Bruce (auth, catalog) Cities, Henry Gallery Mus, Univ Wash, 87; articles, Korper, Polaroid Corp, 88; and others. *Dealer:* Charles Cowles Gallery 420 W Broadway New York NY 10012. *Mailing Add:* Charles Cowles Gallery 537 W 24th St New York NY 10011

BURNS, SHEILA
PAINTER, LECTURER
b Scotland; US citizen. *Study:* Detroit Soc Arts & Crafts; Wayne State Univ, BA. *Work:* Grand Rapids Mus, Mich; Wayne State Univ; Founders Soc Gallery Loan Collection, Detroit Inst Art; Hillberry Theatre, Wayne State Univ, Detroit. *Comn:* Grosse Prep Acad, Am Spoon Foods; Children's Hosp Mich. *Exhib:* Mich Biennial Exhib Painters & Printmakers, Grand Rapids Mus; Mich Acad Sci, Art & Lett & Mich Regional Exhib, Univ Mich; Blue Water Int Exhib, US & Can, 74 & 75; Eastern Mich Int, 75; plus many others. *Teaching:* Instr, secondary schs. *Awards:* Purchase Award, Mich Biennial Painters & Printmakers, Grand Rapids Mus; Watercolor Awards, Scarab Club Detroit. *Mem:* Am Asn Prof Artists. *Media:* Watercolor, Oil. *Publ:* Illusr, Detroit Free Press; illusr, Are Nursery Rhymes for Children? by Dr Edward Southern; Centennial Poster (ltd-ed), and other ltd-ed posters. *Dealer:* Galerie de Boicourt Birmingham MI 48011. *Mailing Add:* 23036 Ardmore Park Dr Saint Clair Shores MI 48081-2027

BURNS, STAN
PAINTER, SCULPTOR
b Suitersville, Pa. *Study:* Wayne State Univ, BA & MA; Detroit Soc Arts & Crafts, with Reginald Bennett, Sarkis; Pewabic Pottery with Mary Chase Stratton. *Work:* Wayne State Univ; Ford Motor Co; Founders Gallery Loan Collection, Detroit Art Inst. *Comn:* Numerous pvt comns & portrait comns. *Exhib:* Mich Acad Sci, Art & Lett & Mich Regional Exhib, Univ Mich; Mich Artists Exhib, Detroit Inst Art; Mich Watercolor Soc; Blue Water Int Exhib, 73 & 74; Eastern Mich Int, 75; solo-invitational, Bacardi Gallery, Miami; plus many one-man shows incl galleries in Dallas, Miami, Washington, DC, Detroit, Chicago & Kalamazoo. *Awards:* Board of Directors' Award, Scarab Gold Medal Show, Detroit; Blue Water Int Exhib, Port Huron Mus, Mich; Eastern Mich Int Exhib Award; Best of Show, Scarab Art Club; Gold Plaque, Detroit/Windsor Int Freedom Festival. *Mem:* Nat Asn Prof Artists; Scarab Club. *Mailing Add:* 23036 Ardmore Park Dr Saint Clair Shores MI 48081-2027

BURNSIDE, MADELEINE HILDING
CRITIC, MUSEUM DIRECTOR
b London, Eng, Oct 18, 48; US citizen. *Study:* Warwick Univ, Eng, BA, 70; Univ Calif, Santa Cruz, PhD (history of consciousness), 76. *Collection Arranged:* Universal Limited Art Editions: The First 10 Years (auth, catalog), Islip Art Mus, 83 & Guild Hall Mus, 84; Preparation & Proposition (auth, catalog), 84, The Living Carousel, 84, The Writing on the Wall (auth, catalog), 85 & Myths & Rituals for the 21st Century (auth, catalog), 86, Islip Art Mus. *Pos:* Ed assoc, Art News Mag, 73-79 & Arts Mag, 79-80; dir, Islip Art Mus, 80; exec dir, Mel Fisher Maritime Heritage Soc and Mus, Key West, Fla, 91-. *Teaching:* Asst art hist, Univ Calif, 72-73; adj prof art hist, Dowling Col, 83-. *Awards:* Fels, Harkness, 70, Ford Found, 73 & Helena Rubinstein, 75; Nat Endowment Arts, 80. *Res:* Contemporary art. *Publ:* Auth, Hard Line, Drawing as a Primary Medium, 84 & Luis Camnitzer, the Torture Series, 85, Islip Art Mus; coauth, Houston Conwill's St Matthew Passion, Alternative Mus, 86; coauth with Rosemarie Robotham, Spirits of the Passage, Simon & Schuster, 97. *Mailing Add:* Mel Fisher Maritime Heritage Soc and Mus 200 Greene St Key West FL 33040

BURPEE, JAMES STANLEY
PAINTER, INSTRUCTOR
b Oakland, Calif, Feb 12, 1938. *Study:* San Jose State Col, BA, 58; Calif Col Arts & Crafts, with James Weeks, MFA, 60. *Comn:* Painting, 13 x 4 ft, Dain Bosworth, Minneapolis, 92. *Exhib:* A Sense of Place: Artists & the Am Land, Sheldon Mem Art Gallery, Lincoln, Nebr, 73-74; one man shows, Col St Catherine, St Paul, Minn, 78, Nash Gallery, Univ Minn, 82 & 85, Artbanque Gallery, Minneapolis, 84, Katherine Nash Gallery, Univ Minn, 82 & 85, Flanders Contemp Art, Minneapolis, Minn, 93; Am Art; The Challenge of the Land, Pillsbury Co Sponsor, 81; two person show, Meetings & Archetypes: Minn Artists exhib prog, Minneapolis Inst Arts, 87 & Forum

Gallery, Minneapolis, Minn, 90; Environmental Show, MC Gallery, Minneapolis, 91; 22nd Anniversary Show, Flanders Contemp Art, Minneapolis, 94; and others. *Teaching:* From instr to asst prof & chmn, Art Dept, Midwestern Univ, Wichita Falls, Tex, 60-67; from asst prof to prof painting & drawing, Minneapolis Col of Art & Design, 67-; vis artist painting, Kansas City Art Inst, 74 & Calif Col of Arts & Crafts, 74 & 75; guest lectr, Calif Col Arts & Crafts, 79-80; lectr, Wash Univ, St Louis, 84; lectr, Tour for Milton Avery Show, Walker Art Ctr, Minn, 83. *Awards:* Fel Residency Found Karolyi, Venice, France, 89; Nat Endowment Arts Artist-in-residence, Volcanoes Nat Park, Hawaii, 73-74; Fel, MacDowell Colony, 76. *Media:* Acrylic. *Publ:* Illusr, Visual Studies by Frank Young, Prentice-Hall, 84. *Dealer:* Flanders Contemp Art 400 N First Ave, First Flr, Minneapolis, MN 55401; Bridge Square Gallery 16 Bridge Sq PO Box 341 Northfield MN 55057. *Mailing Add:* 3208 Aldrich Ave S Minneapolis MN 55408-3602

BURR, RUTH BASLER
PAINTER
b Chicago, Ill, Feb 12, 32. *Study:* Glendale Col; Pierce Col; UCLA; Laguna Beach Sch Art, Calif. *Work:* Calif Inst Technol, Pasadena; Univ Calif, Los Angeles Med Ctr, Westwood, Calif; Glendale Fed, Glendale, Calif; Transamerica Corp, Los Angeles. *Comn:* Over 100 murals, 53-70, over 100 portraits, 68-72, People in Los Angeles Co, Calif; 3 large oils of ships, Robinson Develop Co, Newport, Calif, 79; 75 paintings, Trans Am Corp, Los Angeles, Calif, 80-84. *Exhib:* Brand II, Brand, Glendale, Calif, 70; one woman show, Descanso Gardens, Hospitality Mus, La Canada, Calif, 70-92; Art Expo Cal Ann, Conf Ctr, Los Angeles, 87-92; featured artist, Los Angeles Co Fair, 92; Artist of Yr, Buena Park, Calif, 92; Phillips Gallery, Carmel, Calif. *Pos:* Co-chmn with Johnny Ray, Hear Found, Pasadena, Calif, 70-71; co-chmn, Art Under Oaks, Descanso Gardens Guild, 85-88. *Teaching:* Instr art, Los Angeles City Sch, 72-80; instr, Pasadena City Col, 75-80; instr, Brand Art Ctr, 80-86. *Awards:* Best of Year, 3 categories, Ebell Club, 82; First Place, Under Oaks, Descanso Gardens, 90. *Media:* Watercolor. *Mailing Add:* 27071 Glenar FF Ln San Juan Capistrano CA 92675

BURR, TOM
ARTIST
b New Haven, 63. *Work:* Update 92, 92-93, Tom Burr, 95-96, Stainless, 96-97, Parasite, 97-98, Slung Low, Kunstverein Braunschweig, 2000, Deliberate Living, Greene Naftali Gallery, NY, 2001, Deep Purple, Whitney Mus Am Art, 2002-03, Whitney Biennial Am. Art, 2004, It's All An Illusion, A Sculpture Project, Migros Mus fur Gegenwartskunst, Zurich, 2004, The Future Has a Silver Lining-Genealogies of Glamour, 2004. *Mailing Add:* c/o Galerie Almine Rech 127 Rue dv Chevaleret Paris 10013 France 75013

BURR, TRICIA
PAINTER
b Plainfield, NJ, Sept 15, 43. *Study:* Marshall Arisman Sch Visual Arts, 95; studied with Gerardo Ruiz, painting & engraving, 2004-05; studied with Anne Seelbach, Victor D'Amico Inst, NY & Keith Keller La Escuela, Mex; Belles Artes, San Miguel de Allendre, Mex; Mus Temporary Art, Tubingen Ger; Int Mus Col Mex. *Work:* Kulturhaus, Bremen, Ger; Cranbrook Art Mus, Bloomfield Hills, Mich; Mus of Contemp Art, Santiago, Chile; Contemp Art Ctr, New Orleans, LA; Yoshkar Ola Mus Fine Arts, Russia. *Exhib:* Bakers Dozen Int Col Exhib, Mex; Human Artefacts Exhib, Bremen, Ger; I Miss You Exhib, Acorn Gallery, Los Angeles, Calif; Human Pixel Project, Harvard Univ; Three Columns Gallery, Cambridge, Mass. *Pos:* Vpres, Savannah Col Art & Design, 86-92. *Teaching:* Pvt sessions in studio, currently. *Awards:* Painting Environ Scapes, 1999, Univ Ga, Painting Watercolor Underwater, 2000. *Mem:* Int Lomographic Soc; Int Orgn United Mail Artists (IOUMA), (pres at large); Int Breakfast Club (charter, bd dirs), 1986-. *Media:* Oils, Watercolors, Mixed Media & Acrylic. *Dealer:* Beacon Gallery 1606 Butler Ave Tybee Island GA 31328. *Mailing Add:* Pelican House 142 Pelican Dr Tybee Island GA 31328

BURRIS, BRUCE C
PAINTER, SCULPTOR
b Wilmington, Del, Dec 9, 55. *Study:* Nasson Col, Springvale, Maine, 77; San Francisco Art Inst, 87; Visual Art Access, 91. *Work:* Santa Cruz Co Mus Art, Santa Cruz, Calif; Nelson Art Gallery, Univ Calif, Davis; Daytona Mus Art & Sci, Ctr Graphic Arts Gallery, Fla; Macon Mus Arts & Sci, Ga. *Exhib:* Janet Fleisher Gallery, Philadelphia, Pa, 82; one-man shows, Braunstein Quay Gallery, San Francisco, 90 & 99, Anton Gallery, Washington, 90, Pavel Vavrys Gallery, Prague, Czech, 92, Urban Inst Contemp Art, Grand Rapids, Mich, 93, Braustein Quoy Gallery, San Francisco, Calif, 93, Nicolaysen Art Mus, Casper, Wyo, 94 & Mod Primitive Gallery, Atlanta, Ga, 94; Macon Mus Arts & Sci (with catalog), Ga, 96. *Pos:* dir, ARTREE, Lexington, Ky, 93-. *Teaching:* artist-in-residence, Artforce, Cincinatti, Ohio, 94 & The Writers Voice/YMCA, Lexington, Ky, 94; Workshops & Community Col, Installation, South Bend, Ind, 96; Community Arts Workshops, Macon Mus Arts & Sci, Ga, 96; prof, dir Minds Wide Open Art Ctr, 98-. *Awards:* Painting Fel, Vt Studio Colony, Johnson, 87, 88 & 89; Nat Endowment Arts Visual Arts Fel, Southern Arts Fedn, 94; Pollock Krasner Found Fel, 98. *Bibliog:* Chuck & Jan Rosenak (coauths), Mus Am Folk Art Encyclopedia of 20th Century American Folk Artists, 90; Michael S Bell (auth), The Burris flash, Visions Arts Quarterly, 9/91; David Minton (auth), Jed Clampett's unlucky cousins (dialog), Arts Midwest, 9-10/97; John Rapko (auth) Bruce Burris at Braunstein/Quay Gallery, Artweek, 3/2000; Mark Van Proyen (auth), San Francisco e-mail, Art Issues, 3/2000. *Mem:* Am Asn Mus; Nat Artists Equity. *Media:* Acrylic on Canvas, Painted Found Objects. *Dealer:* Braunstein/Quay Gallery 250 Sutter St San Francisco CA 94108

BURROUGHS, MARGARET T G
LECTURER, PAINTER
b St Rose, La, 17. *Study:* Chicago Normal Col, elem teacher's cert, 37; Chicago Teacher's Col, upper grade art cert, 39, summer study, 58; Art Inst Chicago, BA, 46, MA, 48; printmaking courses, 85-87; Inst Painting & Sculpture, Mexico City, sabbatical, 53; Columbia Univ, NY, adv grad sch, 59-60; Field Mus, Chicago, Nat Endowment Humanities grant, 68; Inst African Studies, Northwestern Univ, 68; Ill State Univ, 70; Lewis Univ, Lockport, Ill, LHD, 72; Art Inst Chicago, DFA, 87; N Cent Col Naperville, DFA, 88; Spellman Col, DFA, 98. *Hon Degrees:* Lewis Univ, Lockport, Ill, DHL, 1972; Sch Art Inst Chicago, DFA, 1987; North Central Col, Naperville, Ill, DFA, 1988; DePaul Univ, DHL, 1995; Univ Ill at Chicago, DFA, 2001; also Spellman Col, Atlanta, & Columbia Col, Chicago. *Work:* Atlanta Univ Art Collection; Howard Univ Art Collection; Ala A&M Univ Print Collection; Jackson State Col Art Collection, Miss; Johnson Publ Co. *Exhib:* S Side Community Ctr, 73; Highlights of the Atlanta Univ Collection, High Mus, Atlanta, Ga (traveling), 75; Two Centuries of Afro-Am Art, Los Angeles Co Mus (traveling), 76-77; Black Artists, W P A-Chicago-NY, Studio Mus, Harlem, 78; Two Centuries of Afro-Am Art, High Mus, Atlanta, Ga, 80; Ten Outstanding Afro-Am Artists, The White House, Washington, 80; one-woman retrospective, 40 Yrs of Art, Nicole Gallery, Chicago, 86; one-woman show, Prints, S Side Community Art Ctr, 87; Sapphire & Crystals, S Side Community Art Ctr, 87. *Pos:* Founder, Du Sable Mus African-Am Hist Inc, Chicago, dir, 61-85; comnr, Chicago Park Dist, 86-. *Teaching:* Substitute, Chicago Bd Educ, 40-45, elem 45-46; art & eng, Du Sable High Sch, Chicago, 46-69; asst prof, African & African-Am Art Hist, Art Inst Chicago, 68; prof African-Am Art & Cult, Elmhurst, Col, 68; prof African-Am Art, Barat Col, 69; prof humanities, Kennedy-King Col, Chicago, 69-79; lectr at numerous col & universities. *Awards:* Presidential Citation, Nat Conf Artists, White House, Washington, DC, 1980; Ida B Wells Celebrated Elders Award, Nat Coun Black Studies, St Louis, Mo, 1992; Benjamin C Mays Memorial Award,1994; Kepper of Flame Award, Delta Sigma Theta, 2000; Chicago African Am Hist Women Trailblazer Award, DuSable Univ, 2001; Lifetime Achievement Award, Chicago State Univ, 2001; Philanthropic Award, Genesis Housing Devel, 1999; Lifetime Achievement Award, African Am Arts, 2001; Mary Herrit Humanitarian Award, 2001; Award of Recognition, Asn Black Cult Centres, 2001. *Mem:* Nat Conf Negro Artists, Atlanta, Ga (founder); Art Inst Alumni Asn (bd dir). *Media:* Watercolor, Oil. *Publ:* Contribr, Critical Essays on Phyllis Wheatley, C K Hall & Co, 82; ed, Home, Broadside Press, 84; I, Child of the Promise, 84; Jazz Interlude (12 poems), 87; Poems, 87. *Mailing Add:* 3806 S Michigan Ave Chicago IL 60653

BURSHELL, SANDRA EVE
GRAPHIC ARTIST, PAINTER
b Philadelphia, Pa, Feb 13, 50. *Study:* Temple Univ, BA(art), 71; Tyler Sch Art, MEd, 75; Art Inst Chicago; studied with kobayashi, Handell, Hensche, Strand, Tarbet, Flattmann, Ozols. *Work:* World Trade Ctr, Ochsner Clinic, Mercy Baptist Med Ctr/Tenet Health Care, New Orleans, La; Hadassah Nat Hq, NY; Gates Prayer Synagogue, Metairie, La. *Exhib:* Degas Pastel Soc Biennial, World Trade Ctr, New Orleans, La, 88, 90, 94 & 96; Pastel Soc Am Ann Open Exhib, Nat Arts Club, NY, 92, 94, 95 & 96; Biennial Nat Show Pastel, Soc N Fla, Fort Walton Mus Art, 94 & 96; Southern Representational Painters Exhib, Isabel Anderson Comer Mus, Sylacauga, Ala, 96; By Herself, Hanson Gallery, New Orleans, La, 96. *Awards:* Finalist, Artist's Mag Portrait Painting Competition, 89; Strathmore Paper Co Award, Pastel Soc Am, 94; Nat Arts Club Award, Pastel Soc Am, 95. *Bibliog:* John Kemp (auth), Picturing What People Leave Behind, Am Artist's Mag, 95; John Kemp (auth), Picturing What People Leave Behind, Pastel Highlights Collector's Premiere Edition, 96. *Mem:* Int Asn Pastel Socs (secy, 95-); signature mem, Pastel Soc Am; Degas Pastel Soc (bd mem 92-); Am Artists Prof League; assoc, Allied Artists Am. *Media:* Pastel. *Publ:* Contribr, Showcase of American Pastel Artists (CD ROM), Visual Arts Multimedia Presentations, 95; Pastel Solutions, (Quarto) North Light Publ, 96; Pastel School, Reader's Dig, 96; Best of Pastel, Rockport Publ, 96

BURSON, NANCY
PHOTOGRAPHER, CONCEPTUAL ARTIST
b St Louis, Mo, Feb 24, 48. *Study:* Colo Women's Col, 66-68. *Work:* San Francisco Mus Mod Art; Libr Cong, Washington, 84-86; Whitney Mus; Victoria & Albert Mus, London; Metrop Mus Art. *Comn:* Big Brother, CBS News Special, NY, 83; updates of missing children, FBI, Washington, DC, 84-86; Mick & Keith, Rolling Stone Mag, NY, 86; Aged Marilyn Monroe, Good Morning Am, NY, 86; Beauty in the Future, NY Times Mag, 96. *Exhib:* Solo exhibs, Int Ctr Photog, NY, 85 & Jayne Baum Gallery, NY, 90, Clam Art Gallery, NYC, 2006; Identity, Palais de Tokyo, Paris, 85; Stills: Cinema & Video Transformed, Seattle Art Mus, 86; Photog of Invention: Am Pictures of the 80's, Nat Mus Am Art, Washington, Whitney Mus Am Art, 90, Elvis & Marilyn 2X Immortal ICA Boston traveling, 94-97, Photog after Photog, 95-96 & Identity & Alternity, Venice Biennale, Italy, 95; one-man retrospectives, Contemp Arts Mus, Houston, 92 & Recoutres Int Photographie, Arles, France, 96; Traveling Retrospectives: Seeing & Believing: The Art of Nancy Burson, Grey Art Gallery, NYC, Blaffer Gallery, Houston, Tex, Weatherspoon Mus, NC, Photo Espana, Madrid, 2002. *Teaching:* Vis artist photog, Kansas City Art Inst, Mo, 85; photog course, Tisch Sch Arts, NY Univ, 90-94; Vis artist, Harvard Univ, 97. *Awards:* Nat Endowment Arts Grant Photog, 91; Art Matters, 96; Nomination best mus show in NYC, Int Asn Art Critics, 2002. *Bibliog:* Elizabeth Hoyt-Atleins (auth), Art News Review, 5/90; Vince Aletti (auth), About Face: Redefining Normality with Nancy Burson, The Village Voice, 94, 4/21/92; A Defining Reality: The Photographs of Nancy Burson, Rebecca Busselle Aperture, 94. *Mem:* Col Art Asn. *Media:* Computer Generated Photography, Real Photography, Video. *Specialty:* Contemp photog. *Publ:* Photogr, Am Photogr, 85, Newsweek, 85, New York Post (cover), 85, Manipulator Mag, 85-86 & Smithsonian Mag; Composites, William Morrow, 86; Faces: Nancy Burson, publ by CAM, Houston, essay by Lynn Herbert, 92; FACES, Nancy Burson, Twin Palm Publ, 93. *Dealer:* Yossi Millo. *Mailing Add:* 548 Broadway New York NY 10012

BURT, DAN
PAINTER, INSTRUCTOR
b Owensboro, Ky, Aug 17, 30. *Study:* Ramon Froman Sch Art, Cloudcroft, NMex; Simon Michael Sch Art, Rockport, Tex; also with Harold Roney, Joy Carrington & William H Earle. *Work:* Tenneco Corp, Houston; Brownsville Art League Mus, Tex; Methodist Hosp, San Antonio; Arts Ctr at Old Forge, NY; South Ark Art Center, El Dorado, Ark; Ambulatory Care Ctr Sid Peterson Hosp, Kerrville, Tex. *Exhib:* Knickerbocker Artists, NY, 79, 84, 90-92; Allied Artists Am, 75 & 91-95, Nat Watercolor Soc, Brea, Calif, 87, 89 & 93-95, Audubon Artists, NY, 82, 89, 90, 92-95 & 98; Am Watercolor Soc, NY, 91 & 93-2006. *Pos:* Bd dir, Am Watercolor Soc NY, NY. *Teaching:* Oil & watercolor painting, Hill Country Arts Found, Ingram, Tex, 76-82 & 91-96; instr, for numerous watercolor soc throughout US, 91-. *Awards:* Gold Medal Honor Watermedia, Allied Artists Am 78th Ann Exhib, NY; Gold Medal Honor Watermedia, Knickerbocker Artists 42nd Ann Exhib, NY; Clara Stroud Mem Award, Am Watercolor Soc 126th Ann Exhib, NY; Silver Medal Hon, 52nd Ann Audobon Artists Exhib, NY, 94; Colorist's Award, 22nd Ann Rocky Mountain Nat Watermedia Exhib, Golden, Colo, 95; St Cuthbert's Paper Mill Award, Nat Watercolor Soc Exhib, Brea, Calif, 95; The Artist's Mag Award, 133rd Annual Am Watercolor Soc Int, NY, 2000; Best of Show Award, San Diego Watercolor Soc Int Exhib, San Diego, Calif, 97; Best of Show Award, 56th Ann Watercolor Soc Ala Exhib, Birmingham, Ala, 99; Ruth Rosenau Silver Medallion-Adirondacks, Nat Exhib Am Watercolors, Old Forge, NY, 2000; Nicolas Realie Memorial Award, 134th Am Watercolor Soc Int Exhib, NY, 2001; Best of Show Award, 26th Ann Midwest Watercolor Soc Exhib, Kankakee, Ill, 2002; CF Sahlin Medal, 137th Ann Am Watercolor Soc Int Exhib, NY, 2004; The Artist's Mag / Watercolor Magic Mag Award 138th Ann Am Watercolor Soc Int Exhib, New York, NY, 2005. *Bibliog:* Harry Reed (auth), article in Southwest Art, 3/78 & Art Voices S, 9-10-79; Mark Mitchell (auth), article in Am Artist Mag, 1/93; Betsy Stroud (auth), article in Southwest Art Mag, 11/93. *Mem:* Nat Watercolor Soc Calif; Allied Artists Am, NY; Audubon Artists; Am Watercolor Soc, NY; Watercolor West, Redlands, Calif; Transparent Watercolor Soc of Am. *Media:* Watercolor. *Publ:* Auth, article in Watercolor Magic Mag, 96; Paint Vibrant Watercolors with Pure, Clean Color, N Light Bks, 99; auth, article in Watercolor Magic Mag, 2003. *Dealer:* Port A Gallery 345 N Allister St Port Aransas Tex; Sandra Canavan Gallery 33 Scenic Loop Boerne Tex 78006. *Mailing Add:* 109 St Andrews Loop Kerrville TX 78028

BURT, DAVID SILL
SCULPTOR
b Evanston, Ill, Feb 20, 1917. *Study:* Harvard Univ, BA, 40. *Work:* Fine Art Ctr, Univ Wis, Milwaukee; US Art in Embassies Prog, Stamford Mus. *Comn:* Excelsior Hotel, Tulsa, 81; Bradley Int Airport, Hartford, Conn, 86; Philips Electronic Corp, Mahwah, NJ, 88; Chartwell Reinsurance Inc, Stamford, Conn, 90; Reliance Nat, NY, 96. *Exhib:* Pa Acad Fine Arts Exhib, 64; Northeast USA Exhib, 65, 67, 69, 70, 77, 80 & 81; 18 one-man exhibs, NY, Conn, RI, Colo, Tex & Ireland. *Pos:* Promotion writer, Archit Forum, Indust Design & Interiors. *Mem:* Sculptors League; Silvermine Guild Artists. *Media:* Hammered & Braised Sheet Metal. *Publ:* Auth, Detour to sculpture, Am Artist Mag. *Mailing Add:* 79 Hobson St Stamford CT 06902-8113

BURTT, LARICE ANNADEL ROSEMAN
PAINTER, SCULPTOR
b Philadelphia, PA, June 22, 28. *Study:* Boston Univ, with William A Smith, Dr Selma Burke. *Work:* Grand Canyon Nat Park Mus, North, Ark. *Comn:* Joan Krats, Noah, Lancaster, Pa, 88; Mr John Marcinek, Peaceable Kingdom, Calif, 90; Dr Bertram Brown, Give me your Tired, 95. *Exhib:* Stone Painting, Abington Art Ctr, Abington, PA, 76; Upstairs Gallery, 80-90; Arnot Art Mus, Elmira, NY, 87; Congressional Bldg, Washington, DC, 90-2000; Yale Univ, New Haven, CT, 95. *Pos:* demonstrator, workshops, Bucks Co Sch, 77-2002; art league, speaker, Doylestown AAW, Pa Craft Guild, 80-2000. *Teaching:* Demonstrations, CR Sch Syst, Neshanny, Central Buck, PA. *Awards:* hon mention, Woodmere Art Mus, 78; New Sculptor, Phillips Mill, 79; honorable mention, Doylestown Art League, 85. *Mem:* Artsbridge; Jane Michener Art Mus; Doylestown Art League (juried mem); Cult Arts Center, Bucks, Co; Pa Guilds of Craftsmen (juried mem). *Media:* Acrylics, GA Marble. *Interests:* Music, shows, tennis. *Publ:* Buck Co Courier Times, Art Sec, 77-90; Intelligencer, Art, 80-2000; Philadelphia Inquirer (bulletin), 1990; New Hope Gazette, Art, 2002. *Mailing Add:* 31 Beth Dr Richboro PA 18954-1901

BUSARD, ROBERTA ANN
PAINTER, SCULPTOR
b Muskegon, Mich, Apr 20, 52. *Study:* Study under Victor A S Robinson, 69; San Francisco Art Inst, 70-73; Silvermine Col Art, 71; Art Inst Boston, 71; Experimental Etching Studio Boston, 71 & 77; Laguna Beach Col Art & Design, 72; Eastern Mich Univ, 72; Mass Col Art BFA, 77; Wayne State Univ, MFA, 98. *Work:* US West Telecommunications, Denver; Diekmann & Assoc Ltd, Chicago; Sales, Goodloe & Golden, Atlanta; Anchorage Mus Hist & Art; Thomas M Morrisey/KATZ Television, Chicago. *Exhib:* 50th Nat Ann Midyear Painting Exhib, Butler Inst Am Art, 86; A World of Maps, Anchorage Mus Hist & Art, 94-95; Art in Embassies Prog, Am Embassy, Kuwait, 95-98; Selections NGO Forum, Elite Gallery, Moscow, 95; NGO Forum, Nat Mus Woman in the Arts, 96; and many others. *Pos:* Founding mem, exhib comt, bus comt, Vt Artists Collective, Burlington, 89-90; founding dir, The Kids Art Studio, S Burlington, 90-91; cur, The Black & White Project, Vt Women's Caucus for Art, 89-91; leader, No Limits for Women in the Arts, Ann Arbor, 91-92; exhib comt mem, Detroit Focus Gallery, 94-95; founder, Mich Woman's Caucus for Art, 94, pres, 94-95, co-pres, 96. *Teaching:* Int Sch Genoa, Italy, 76; Single Mothers' Project, Burlington, 90; The Kid's Art Studio, South Burlington, 90-91; guest lectr, Univ Mich, 92; Go Like the Wind Sch, Ann Arbor, 93-94; The Women's Art Project, Ann Arbor, 92-94; artist in residence, Summer Sch Sch Art Inst Chicago Ox-Bow, Saugatuck, Mich, 95. *Awards:* Jurors' Choice Mary Mellor Mem Fund Award for Painting Mixed Media & Drawing, San Francisco Women Artists Gallery, 94; Thomas C Rumble Graduate Fels, Wayne State Univ, 96-98; Jurors Choice Award, Paper Stars Nat Womens Exhib, San Francisco Women Artists, 94. *Bibliog:* Marika Christenson (auth), Busard-Thompson Show at Margolis Gallery, Arts & Entertainment, Co, 84; Nancy Booth Stringer (auth), Roberta Ann Busard: The art of poetic form, Art Light, J Mich, 12/92; John Carlos Cantu (auth), Busard's Paintings, Sculptures Worth Seeing at Arts Council Loft, Ann Arbor News, 3/95. *Mem:* Col Art Asn; Nat Womens Caucus Art; Chicago Artists Coalition; Nat Mus Women Arts; Int Sculpture Inst. *Media:* Miscellaneous Media. *Publ:* Contribr, New letters, Vol 59, No 4 (Etching Series, 71 & 77), Univ Mo Press, Kansas City, 93. *Mailing Add:* P O Box 130051 Ann Arbor MI 48113

BUSCH, RITA MARY
PAINTER, SCULPTOR
b Middletown, RI, July 14, 26. *Study:* Watercolor workshops: Robert Wood, 72, Charles Reid, 75 & Doug Walton, 85, Jane Burnham, 93 & Margaret M Martin, 94. *Work:* Fidelity Nat Bank, Oklahoma City; Presby Hosp Found, Oklahoma City; Consolidated Insurance Co, Tulsa, Okla; Country Club Publ, Oklahoma City; Weyerhauser Corp Hq. *Comn:* Watercolor paintings, Dorothea Land, Oklahoma City, 86; watercolor painting, Preston Nichols, Moore, Okla, 86; pastel portrait, Mrs Jack J Wells, Oklahoma City, 86; watercolor painting, (World Neighbors, Commemorative Piece), Mr & Mrs Douglas Ormseth, NY, 87; Watercolor painting, House of Hunan, Norman, Okla. *Exhib:* Okla Art Guild, North Park Mall, Oklahoma City, 84; Newport Art Festival, RI, 84, 86 & 94; Nat League Am Pen Women, Pirates Alley, Oklahoma City, 86; Okla Watercolor Traveling Exhib, 86; Narragansett Art Festival, RI, 94. *Pos:* Jr art coordr, State Fair Okla, 76-90. *Teaching:* Teacher, watercolor, St Lukes Sch Continuing Ed, Oklahoma City, 86, Geatches Art Sch, Oklahoma City, 86 & Arts Annex, Oklahoma City, 88-89; artist-in-residence, Skyview Elem Sch, Yukon, Okla, 90. *Awards:* Equal Merit Award, Okla Art Guild Juried Show, 84; First Place Watercolor & Oils, McAlester Art Fest, McAlester Art Guild, 81; First Place Pastel, Pen Women's Show, Nat League Am Penwomen, 86. *Mem:* Okla Art Guild (3rd vpres, 76-77, 2nd vpres Shows, 77-79, pres, 79-80); Okla Watercolor Asn; Nat League Am Pen Women, (pres, 90-92). *Media:* Watercolor, Pastels, Metal, Cast. *Dealer:* Margo K Shorney Shorney Gallery Fine Art 6616 N Olie Oklahoma City OK 73116. *Mailing Add:* 1220 N Glade Oklahoma City OK 73127-4158

BUSH, CHARLES ROBERT See Robb, Charles

BUSH, JILL LOBDILL
PAINTER
b Grand Island, Nebr, May 11, 42. *Study:* Tex Tech Univ, BA(adv art & design), 64. *Work:* Collection five paintings, First Fed Savings & Loan, Ft Smith, Ark; Holt Crock Clinic, Ft Smith, Ark, 80; Peace oil painting, Harris Methodist HEB Hosp, Ctr Women's Health, Bedford, Tex, 91. *Comn:* Dr OJ Wallenman Jr mem portrait, St Joseph Hosp Drs, Ft Worth, 79, Marion Day Mullins DAR portrait, Ft Worth Woman's Club, 80; Brig Gen Victor Carey, portrait, Darby's Rangers Mus, Ft Smith, Ark, 80; Coach Indian Jim Malone, portrait, Southern La State Univ, Hammond, 80; Dr Paul Parham mem portrait, TCU Libr Asn, Ft Worth, 87. *Exhib:* Knickerbocker 29th Ann, Nat Arts Club, NY, 79; Pastel Soc Am Exhib, Copley Mus, Boston, 79; 1st Ann Main St Tex Invitational, Ft Worth, 86; Pastel Soc Am Invitational, 3rd Salon Des Pastellists, Lille, France, 87; PSA Invitational Exhib, Ashland Area Gallery, Ky, 89; and others. *Teaching:* Instr figure drawing & oil painting, Ft Worth Art Mus Sch, 65-70; instr figure drawing & oil painting, Ft Worth Woman's Club, 73-76, instr oil, pastel & drawing, 74-79. *Awards:* Pastel Soc Am Award, San Marcus Nat, 79; Schwann Weber Award, Pastel Soc Am Eighth Ann, 80; First Place, Pastel Soc SW Ann, 85. *Bibliog:* Madlyn Ann Woolwich (auth), Pastel Interpretations, Northlight Bks, 92, Madlyn-Ann Woolwich (auth), Profiting from childrens portraits, Artists Mag, 10/95; Madlyn-Ann Woolwich (auth), The Art of Pastel Portraiture, Watson Guptill, 96. *Mem:* Pastel Soc Am; Pastel Soc SW. *Media:* Pastel, Oil. *Specialty:* Children's portraits. *Publ:* Contribr, Pastel Interpretations, Northlight Bks, 92-93; Still Life Techniques, Northlight Bks, 94; Art of Pastel Portraiture, Watson Guptill, 96. *Mailing Add:* 6440 Curzon Ft Worth TX 76116

BUSH, MARTIN H
MUSEUM DIRECTOR, HISTORIAN
b Amsterdam, NY, Jan 24, 30. *Study:* State Univ NY Albany, BA & MA, 58; Syracuse Univ, PhD, 66. *Collection Arranged:* Photo Realism: Rip-Off or Reality, 75; George Grosz, 75; Wayne Thiebaud, 75; Robert Goodnough, 75; Richard Pousette-Dart, 75; Duane Hanson, 76; W Eugene Smith, 77; Milton Avery, 78; Joan Miro, 78; Louise Nevelson, 78; Theodoros Stamos, 79; Kenneth Noland, 80; Figures of Contemporary Sculpture 1970-1990, 92; Kunst Haus Wien, Vienna, Austria, 94; and many others. *Pos:* Dir, E A Ulrich Mus Art, Wichita State Univ, 71-89, vpres acad resource develop, 74-89; pres, ACA Galleries, 89-93, Martin Bush Fine Arts Inc, 93-. *Teaching:* Instr, Syracuse Univ, 63-65, asst dean, 65-70. *Awards:* Wichitan of the Year, Wichita Sun, 76; Outstanding Educator, Kans Art Edu Asn, 79; Outdoor Sculpture collection named after Martin H Bush, Wuchita State Univ, 92. *Mem:* Am Asn Art Mus; Col Art Asn; Art Dealers Asn Am. *Res:* 20th century American art. *Publ:* Auth, Ben Shahn, Syracuse Univ, 68, & Dorris Cesar, 70; Duane Hanson, 76; Ernest Trova, 77; Robert Goodnough, Abbeville, 82; The Photographs of Gordon Parks, Ulrich Mus Art, 83; Philip Reisman: People are His Passion, Ulrich Mus Art, 86; and many articles, brochures and catalogs. *Mailing Add:* 117 77th St 7C New York NY 10021-1824

BUSHMAN, DAVID FRANKLIN
PAINTER, EDUCATOR
b Toledo, Ohio, Aug 2, 1945. *Study:* Univ Wis, MA, 68 & MFA, 69; also with Al Leslie, Jack Beal, James Rosenquist & Richard Artschager. *Work:* Johnson Wax Co, Racine, Wis; Wis State J, Madison; Univ Wis-Madison; C M Bruckner Collection, NY; Madison Art Ctr, Wis; and others. *Comn:* Mural, Mr & Mrs G Lauderdale, Ft

Lauderdale, Fla, 70; painting, H C Westerman, Brookfield Ctr, Conn, 73; portrait, Mr & Mrs S Crane, Chicago, 75; painting, Mr & Mrs James Stewart, Chicago, 75; painting, Racine Nat Bank, Wis, 80; and others. *Exhib:* Solo shows, Penn State Univ, State Col, 76, Gilman Galleries, Chicago, Ill, 78, Drawings by DF Bushman, Lakeview Mus Art, Peoria, Ill, 82; Realism Today, Evansville Mus Arts & Sci, Ind, 83; 14th Union League of Chicago Competition and Exhib, Artemesia Gallery & Union League Club, Chicago, 85; 1987 Nat Biennial, Sioux City Art Ctr, Iowa, 87; 72nd Hudson River Ann, Hudson River Mus, Yonkers, NY, 87; 1988 Mid America Biennial, Owensboro Mus Art, Ky, 88; Portland Art Mus, Ore, 83; and others. *Teaching:* Instr painting & drawing, Univ Wis-Madison, 67-69; asst prof painting & drawing, Univ Ill, Urbana-Champaign, 69-76, assoc prof, 76-; guest lectr, Louisville Art Ctr, Ky, 72; guest lectr, George Peabody Univ, 74, Univ Wis, 82. *Awards:* Cash Award, Nat Drawings, New York Univ, 69; Cash Award, Ill State Fair, 70; Award, Art Inst Chicago; and others. *Mem:* Col Art Asn; New Col Art Asn; Am Fedn Teachers. *Dealer:* Gilman Gallery 227 Ontario Chicago IL 60611. *Mailing Add:* Sch Art Design Univ Ill 408 E Peabody Rm 134 Champaign IL 61820

BUSHNELL, KENNETH WAYNE
PAINTER, EDUCATOR
b Los Angeles, Calif, Oct 16, 33. *Study:* Univ Calif, Los Angeles, BA(art), 56; Univ Hawaii, MFA(painting), 60. *Work:* Honolulu Acad Art, Hawaii State Found Cult & Arts; Bibliotheque Nationale, Paris; S Guggenheim Mus, NYC; Whitney Mus Am Art; MOMA, NY. *Comn:* Nieman Marcus (mural), 2001; steel sculpture Pearl Ridge Ctr, Hawaii, 84; two 23 ft wall reliefs, Kaiser Clinic Honolulu, 86; Kalakaua Ctr Proj, five wall reliefs 20 ft x 9 ft, Honolulu, 89; Painting on glass, 9 ft x 16 ft, Japan Travel Bureau, Honolulu, 89; Four Panels 6 ft x 17 ft mural project, First Hawaiian Bank, Main Branch, Honolulu; mural, Honolulu Airport, Inter Island Terminal, 2001. *Exhib:* Painting USA: The Figure, NY Mus Mod Art, 62; Baltimore Mus Art, 62; Drawings USA, St Paul Art Ctr, Minn, 63; 158th Ann Exhib, Pa Acad Fine Arts, Philadelphia, 63; NW Printmakers Ann, Seattle Mus & Portland Mus, 64; New Talent in the West, Salt Lake City Art Ctr, 68; Calif-Hawaii Exhib, San Diego Mus, 70; Int Print Biennial, Cracow, Poland, 74; Int Print Biennial, Honolulu Acad Art, 78-82; solo exhibs, Contemp Arts Ctr, Honolulu, Hawaii, 65 & 86, Honolulu Acad Art, 68 & 73, Sande Webster Gallery, Philadelphia, 81, 85, 88 & 92, Meissner Editions, Hamberg, 84, Maghi Betini Gallery, Amsterdam, 84 & Karen Fesel Gallery, Dusseldorf, WGer, 90, Contemp Art Ctr. *Pos:* Prof Emer Univ of Hawaii. *Teaching:* Prof art painting, Univ Hawaii, 61-81; prof art painting, C W Post Ctr, Long Island Univ, 78-79 & 83; chmn, Dept Art Univ Art Manoa, 91-. *Awards:* Purchase Award, Honolulu Acad Art, 68; First Award Painting, Calif-Hawaii Exhib, San Diego Mus, 74; Hawaii State Found Purchase Awards, 75, 81, 84, 86, 87, 2000, 06. *Mem:* Honolulu Printmaker's & Soc Am Graphic Artists; Am Abstract Artists. *Media:* Oil, Acrylic Polimer. *Collection:* Whitney Mus of Am Art, Monk, NY; S Guggenherim Mus; Fogg Mus, Havard Univ; Honolulu Academy of Arts, Hawaii State Foundation on Culture and the Arts; IBM Collection, New York City. *Dealer:* Fine Art Associates Ward Ctr Honolulu HI 96814; Karen Fesel Gallerie Dusseldorf Ger. *Mailing Add:* 2081 Keeaumoku St Honolulu HI 96822

BUSINO, ORLANDO FRANCIS
CARTOONIST
b Binghamton, NY, Oct 10, 26. *Study:* State Univ Iowa, BA, 52. *Pos:* Cartoonist, Sat Eve Post, McCall's, Ladies Home J, Sat Rev, Look, True, Argosy, Boys' Life, Family Circle & other US & foreign mags. *Awards:* Best Mag Cartoonist of Year, Nat Cartoonists Soc, 65, 67 & 68. *Mem:* Nat Cartoonists Soc; Mag Cartoonists Guild. *Mailing Add:* 12 Shadblow Hill Rd Ridgefield CT 06877-5221

BUSSABARGER, ROBERT FRANKLIN
SCULPTOR, PAINTER
b Corydon, Ind, Sept 17, 22. *Study:* Wittenberg Univ, with Ralston Thompson, AB, 44; Mich State Univ, with John de Martelli, Louis Raynor & Carl Schmidt, MA, 47; Ohio State Univ, with Paul Bogatay & Edgar Littlefield, 49-51. *Work:* Air India Collection, Bombay, India; Springfield Art Mus, Mo; Mo Hist Soc, Columbia; Columbia Art League & Archeol Mus, Univ Mo. *Comn:* 33 ft ceramic mural, Col Arts Sci, Univ Mo, Columbia, 91; 42 ft ceramic mural, Hanyang Univ, Ansan, Korea Libr, 95. *Exhib:* Sculptors Gallery, St Louis, Mo, 66; Acad Fine Arts, Calcutta, India, 69; Am Cult Ctr, Bombay, India, 69; solo exhibs, Chemould Art Gallery, Bombay, India, 78 & 84 & Urja Art Gallery, Baroda, India, India'a Artistry, The Unseen Revealed, MAA, 98, Ashby Hodge Gallery, Central Methodist Univ, Fayette MO, Sculpture & Painting Collection, 2004. *Collection Arranged:* Univ Mo Fine Arts Gallery, 55-59 & 63-67; Indian art exhib based on Bussabarger & Robins Collections, Univ Mo, Stephens Col, Westminster Col & Carleton Col. *Teaching:* Teacher art, Benton Harbor Jr & Sr High Sch, Mich, 48-49; asst prof art, Stephen F Austin State Univ, Nacogdoches, Tex, 51-53; prof art, Univ Mo-Columbia, 53-91, chmn dept, 70-73, prof emer art, 91-; vis prof, Hanyang Univ, Ansan, Korea, 95. *Awards:* Merit Award in Sculpture, 30th Springfield Ann, Mo, 60; Fulbright Fel India, 61-62; Hays Univ SAsia Ctr Fac Fel, 68-69; Univ Mo-Columbia Fac Alumni Award, 87. *Bibliog:* AB Pine (auth), Bussabarger & ceramic art, Mo Alumnus, 11/60; L Bhattacharia (auth), Robert Bussabarger, US Info Serv, 10/62; Bussabarger, Span Mag, Usis, India, 3/84; Bussabarger, Crafts Monthly, Seoul, Korea, 8/88. *Mem:* Mo Crafts Coun; Columbia Art League; Mid-Am Art Conf. *Media:* Clay; All Media. *Publ:* coauth & illusr, The Everyday Art of India, Dover, 68; coauth, The Makara, Archaeol, 1/70; Folk images of Sanjhi Devi, Atribus Asiae, 7/75; Mirrored Images, Splendors of Tamil Nadu, Marg, 80; Terrcotta Horses for Gods, Kings and Heroes, Art of Asia, Hong Kong, 9-10/2002. *Dealer:* Walnut Gallery Walnut St Springfield Mo. *Mailing Add:* 1914 Princeton Columbia MO 65203

BUSSCHE, WOLF VON DEM
PHOTOGRAPHER, PAINTER
b Ger; US citizen. *Study:* Columbia Col, studied art hist, 56-62; Columbia Univ Sch Painting & Sculpture, 59-62; Art Students League, 61-62; self-taught in photog. *Work:* San Francisco Mus Mod Art; Mus Mod Art, Int Ctr Photog, Metrop Mus, NY; George Eastman House, Rochester, NY; NY Pub Libr; Bancroft; and others. *Exhib:* Vision & Expression, George Eastman House, Rochester, NY, 69; Soc Encouragement Contemp Art Award Exhib, San Francisco Mus Mod Art, 80; Int Triennial Exhib Photog, Musee d'art et d'hist, Fribourg, Switz, 81; Metrop Mus, NY, 82; Pleasures & Terrors of Domestic Comfort, Moma, NY, 91; MNS of Phorographic Arts, San Diego, Calif, 2000; Mus de L'elysee, Lausanne, Switzland, 2002; numerous one-person exhibs. *Awards:* Who's Who in the West, 91. *Bibliog:* Carole Kismaric (auth), article, Camera, No 10, 71; Jerome Tarshis (auth), article, Art in Am, 1/81; Thomas Albright (auth), article, Art News, 4/82. *Media:* All. *Mailing Add:* 841 Contra Costa Ave Berkeley CA 94707

BUSTER, KENDALL J
INSTRUCTOR
Study: Corcoran Sch Art, Washington, DC, BFA, 81; Yale Univ, New Haven, Conn, MFA, 87. *Exhib:* Solo exhibs, Between Seduction and Reason, Rockville Arts Place, Md, 92, Portland State Univ, Ore, 94, Anderson Gallery, Richmond, Va, 96 & Baumgartner Galleries, Washington, DC, 96; Outdoor Sculpture Projects at Roosevelt Island, Sculpture Ctr, NY, 93; The Far Light, Univ Md, Baltimore Co, 94; The Return of the Cadaver Exquis, Corcoran Gallery Art, Washington, DC, 94; Baumgartner Galleries, Washington, DC, 95. *Teaching:* Instr, Corcoran Sch Art, Washington, DC, currently. *Awards:* Grant, Joan Mitchell Found, 96. *Mailing Add:* 500 17th St NW Washington DC 20006

BUSTO, ANA MARIE
PHOTOGRAPHER, SCULPTOR
b Bilbao, Spain, Jan 15, 52. *Study:* Barcelona, Spain, BA(journalism). *Exhib:* Counter-Representations, Brooklyn Mus, 85, Dream Machinations in Am, Minor Injury, Brooklyn, NY, 90; Race and Cult, City Col NY, 91; one-person shows, Entre Naturalezas, Forun, Tarragona, Spain, 92, Love Song, Rekalde, Bilbao, Spain, 94 & 2000, Working Shoes, Spais, Gerona, Spain & El Museo Del Barrio, NY, 96, Transportar, Museo de Arte Carrillo Gil, Mexico City, Mex, 97 & Night Flights, Metronom, Fundacio Privada d'Art Contemprani, Barcelona, Spain; Am Discover Spain 1, Spanish Inst, NY, 92; Fragments, Koldo Mitxelena, San Sebastian & Macba, Museu d'Art Contemporany, Barcelona, Spain, 96; Pierogi Files, Brooklyn Mus, NY, 98; Tal Como Nos Vemos, Circulo de Bellas Artes, Madrid, Spain, 99; and others; The Eyes Have It, Porter Troupe Gallery, San Diego, 2000; Women at Work, Southwester Col, Calif, 2001; Playa Giron, Valencia Bienal, Spain, 2001. *Awards:* NY Found Arts, 90; Nat Endowments Arts, 90; Spain Ministerio de Cultura, 97. *Publ:* Village Voice, New Observations, 85; NY Times, La Vanguardia, Spain, 89, El Pais, Spain, 90. *Mailing Add:* 107 Roebling Brooklyn NY 11211

BUSZKO, IRENE J
PAINTER
b Brooklyn, NY, Sept 22, 1947. *Study:* Pratt Inst, BFA, 69; Queens Col, MFA, 72. *Work:* Lehman Brothers Collection; Lloyd's Bank Int, NY; Chemical Bank & Citibank, Citicorp Ctr, NY; Mitsubishi Int, NY; Exxon, Tex. *Exhib:* group exhib, 157th Ann Exhib, Nat Acad Design, NY, 82; one-person exhib, Tatistcheff & Co, NY, 82, 85, 89, 94, 96 & 2001, Plandome Gallery, NY, 92, Queens Coun Arts, Woodhaven, NY, 94; Three Painters from NY, Bloomsbury Theater, London, Eng, 85; The Richmond Hill Series, Queens Mus, Flushing, NY, 86. *Pos:* Artist-in-residencies, Bear Mt Palisades Interstate Park, 77, Altos de Chavon, Dominican Republic, 83, Alfred Univ, NY, 83, Yosemite Nat Park, Calif, 93; Artist art colonies, Ossabaw Island Project, 79, Virginia Ctr for Arts, 83, Yaddo, 86-91, Blue Mountain Ctr, 2000, Millay Colony, 2003. *Teaching:* Instr painting, Nat Acad Design, 87-88. *Awards:* Creative Artist Pub Serv Grant, NY State Coun Arts, 76. *Media:* Oil on Canvas. *Publ:* Article, Am Artist Mag, 4/94. *Mailing Add:* 652 Broadway New York NY 10012

BUTCHKES, SYDNEY
PAINTER, SCULPTOR
b Covington, Ky, Oct 13, 22. *Study:* Cincinnati Art Acad, Ohio; Art Students League; New Sch Social Res, NY. *Work:* Metrop Mus; Brooklyn Mus, NY; Cincinnati Art Mus; Wadsworth Atheneum, Hartford, Conn; Nat Collection Fine Arts, Smithsonian Inst, Washington, DC; and others. *Comn:* Sculpture for lobby of Financial Progs Bldg, Denver, 69; hanging sculpture for bar of Ritz Carlton Hotel, Boston, 69; painting for lobby of Skidmore, Owings, Merrill, Chicago, 70; paintings, World Trade Ctr, NY & Continental Tel Co, Washington, DC. *Exhib:* Art for the Collector, San Francisco Mus Art, 65; Painting Without a Brush, Inst Contemp Art, Boston, 65; Painting Out from the Wall, Des Moines Art Ctr, Iowa, 67; Plastic as Plastic, Mus Contemp Crafts, NY, 69; Mus Acquisitions, Colorado Springs Art Ctr, 69; Art, Design and the Modern Corp, Nat Mus Am Art, Washington, DC, 85. *Awards:* Am Crafts Coun Hon Fel. *Mem:* Abstr Am Artists. *Media:* Acrylic Paint; Wood. *Mailing Add:* 340 E 57th St New York NY 10022-2951

BUTERA, VIRGINIA FABBRI
CURATOR, HISTORIAN
b Norristown, Pa, Nov 15, 51. *Study:* Trinity Col, Conn, BA, 73; Johns Hopkins Univ, MA(art hist), 75; City Univ NY, MPhil, 91, PhD program, ongoing. *Collection Arranged:* The Graphic Side of the Second Empire, Philadelphia Mus Art, 78; The Great American Fan Show (auth, catalog), Lerner-Heller Gallery, New York, 81; The Folding Image: Screens by Western Artists of the 19th and 20th Centuries (coauth, catalog), Nat Gallery Art, Washington, DC & Yale Univ Art Gallery, 84-85;

Contemporary Screens (auth, catalog), Contemp Arts Ctr, Cincinnati, Lowe Art Mus, Toledo Art Mus & City Gallery Contemp Art, Raleigh, 86-88. *Pos:* Fel, Nat Mus Am Art, Washington, DC, 76-77; asst, Dept Prints, Drawings & Photographs, Philadelphia Mus Art, 78-79, asst to dir, 79-81; co-chair & bd trustees, AIR Gallery, New York, 84-85; curatorial consult, Everything for Industry, Jersey City Mus, 88-89; bd trustees, NJ Ctr Visual Arts, 93-95. *Teaching:* Lectr art hist, Col St Elizabeth, Madison, NJ, 98-99. *Awards:* Smithsonian Mus Fel, 76-77; Nat Endowment Arts Grant, 78-79; First Prize, 50th Annual Frick Symposium, 90. *Mem:* Col Art Asn; Asn Am Mus. *Res:* European and American painting and sculpture, 1860 to the present. *Publ:* Auth, The fan as form and image in contemporary art, 81 & Investigating Jim Jacobs' sculpture and painting, 86, Arts Mag; Contemporary screens, Art Mus Asn Am, 86; Jim Jacobs: Screens, Mus of Art, Ft Lauderdale; co-auth, The Folding Image: Screens By Western Artists of the Nineteenth and Twentieth Centuries, New Haven: Yale Univ Art Gallery, 84. *Mailing Add:* 18 Fay Pl Summit NJ 07901

BUTLER, CHARLES THOMAS
MUSEUM DIRECTOR, CURATOR
b Pearisburg, Va, 51. *Study:* Univ Del, with William Inness Homer, BA(cum laude), 76; Univ NMex, with Beaumont Newhall & Tom Barrow, grad studies, 76-78. *Collection Arranged:* Recent Graphics from American Print Shops (auth, catalog), 86; Michael Eastman: Color Photographs (auth, catalog), 88; Gardens of Paradise: Oriental Prayer Rugs (textiles), 89; Enduring Impressions: Prints, 1960-1990 (graphics), 90; Dick Arentz: Outside the Mainstream (photographs; auth catalog), 91; Close to the Surface: The Expressionist Prints of Edvard Munch & Richard Bosman (graphics; auth catalog), 96; Body and Soul: Contemporary Southern Figures (painting & sculpture; auth, catalog), 97. *Pos:* Asst dir, Sioux City Art Ctr, Ind, 79-85; exec dir, Mitchell Mus, Mt Vernon, Ill, 85-88; dir, Huntington Mus Art, WVa, 88-94, exec dir, currently, Columbus Mus, GA, 94. *Awards:* Prof Year Award, Ga Asn Mus & Galleries, 1998. *Mem:* Midwest Mus Conf; Am Asn Mus; Southeastern Mus Conf (exec comt, 89-, vpres, 94-96, pres, 96-98); WVa Asn Mus (exec comt, 90-93); Mus Trustee Asn Adv Counc (chair, 1998-2003); Asn Art Mus Dirs. *Media:* Photography, Graphics, Contemporary Painting, Drawing. *Publ:* auth, New Talent, New York, Sioux City Art Ctr, 84; coauth, Edward McCullough: The Elegy Series, Mitchell Mus, 87; auth, Close to the Surface: Prints by Edvard Munch and Richard Rosman, Columbus Mus, 96; gen text ed, Heartland: Paintings by Bo Bartlett, 1978-2002, 2002; gen, Am Art in the Columbus Mus: Painting, Sculpture and Decorative Arts, 2003; gen text ed, Lines of Discovery, 250 Years Am Drawing in Columbus Mus, 2006. *Mailing Add:* 1251 Wynnton Rd Columbus GA 31906

BUTLER, EUGENIA P
CONCEPTUAL ARTIST
b Washington, DC. *Study:* Univ Calif Berkeley, with Robert Morris, James Melchert, H C Westerman, Eduardo Paolozzi & R B Kitaj, BA(art), 72. *Work:* Grunwald Coll, Armand Hammer Mus, Univ Calif, Los Angeles; NY Pub Libr, NY; Los Angeles Co Mus Art, Sackner Col, Fla. *Comn:* Public installation, Skhole Corp, Tokyo, Japan, 87, Lover's Bench for a New Millenium, 93, A Rube Goldberg Machine, 94, Univ art Mus, Calif State Univ, Long Beach. *Exhib:* The Kitchen Table, Art LA 93, Los Angeles, Calif, 93; The Office of 21st Century, Folk Art & Craft Mus, Los Angeles, Calif, 95; In the Pocket, Steirischer Hearbst Festival 96, Graz, Austria, 96; Drawn from LA, Pasadena Armory Ctr Arts, Calif, 96; Between Reality & Abstraction, Mus Fine Arts, St Petersburg, Fla, 96-97. *Teaching:* Lectr art, Southern Calif Inst Archit, 95-, Calif State Univ, Northridge, 96-; instr & adv, Art Ctr Col Design, 95-. *Bibliog:* Bonnie Clearwater (auth), Fantastic Furniture, Lannan Found, 87; J Lee Kaplan (auth), Reconfiguring Boundaries/Defining Spaces, Calif State Univ Long Beach, 94; Donna Stein (auth), Between Reality & Abstraction, Hillcrest Found, 95. *Mem:* Soc Col Pataphysics, Paris, France; Paul Pozzozza Mus, Dusseldorf, Ger. *Publ:* Contribr, The context of art/the art of context, Kunst & Mus J, 1-3/96; From the Center - Faculty Design Process at SCI-ARC, Monacelli Press, 96-97; ed, The Book of Lies, Vol One, SCI-Arc Pub Access Press, 96. *Mailing Add:* 672 S Ave 21 Studio 4 Los Angeles CA 90031-3706

BUTLER, GEORGE TYSSEN
PHOTOGRAPHER, FILMMAKER
b Chester, England. *Study:* Univ NC, BA (English), 1966; Hollins Col, Va, MA (English), 1967. *Exhib:* Films: Pumping Iron, 1977; Pumping Iron II: The Women, 1983; In the Blood, 1989; The Endurance: Shackleton's Legendary Antarctic Expedition, 2000; Schackleton's Antarctic Adventure, 2001; Going Upriver: The Long War of John Kerry, 2004; Roving Mars, 2006; Group exhib, Whitney Biennial, Whitney Mus Art, 2006. *Pos:* Writer, reporter, Newsweek Mag, NYC, 1969; freelance writer, photog, NH, 1970-75; pres, White Mt Films, NH & NY, 1975-. *Mem:* Fellow Royal Geographic Soc, London; Century Assn, NYC. *Interests:* Collecting antique photographs; farming; hunting; fishing; mountain climbing. *Publ:* Photog contribr (with Charles Gaines) Pumping Iron, 1974; auth, photog, Schwarzenegger-A Portrait, 1990; ed (with John F. Kerry), The New Soldier, 1971. *Mailing Add:* White Mountain Films PO Box 61 Holderness NH 03245-0061

BUTLER, HIRAM
ART DEALER
b Del Rio, Tex, 1951. *Study:* Univ Tex, Austin, BA, 76; Williams Col, Williamstown, Mass, MA(art hist). *Pos:* Asst cur iconography collection, Humanities Res Ctr, Univ Tex, Austin, 77; asst cur, Clark Art Inst, Williamstown, Mass, 78-79; intern, Nat Endowment Arts, Mus Mod Art, New York, 79-80; dir gallery, David Tunick Inc, New York, 80-81; dir, Delahunty Inc, Dallas, 81-84, Devin Borden Hiram Butler Gallery, Houston, Tex, 84-. *Publ:* Auth, The Cranfill Collection of Latin America, 76; contribr, Drawings, Design and Collage: Fifty Contemporary American Works on Paper from the Collection of Mr & Mrs Stephen D Paine, 79; auth, Downtown in the fifties, Horizon: Mag Arts, 6/81. *Mailing Add:* c/o Devin Borden Hiram Butler Gallery 4520 Blossom Houston TX 77007

BUTLER, JAMES D
PRINTMAKER, PAINTER
b Ft Dodge, Iowa, Aug 30, 1945. *Study:* Omaha Univ, Nebr, BS, 67; Univ Nebr, Lincoln, MFA, 70. *Work:* Brooklyn Mus, NY; Brit Mus, London, Eng; Tamarind Inst, Albuquerque, NMex; Libr of Cong, Washington, DC; Smithsonian Inst, Washington, DC. *Comn:* First Ill Print Comn, Ill Arts Coun, 73. *Exhib:* Corp Collections Show, Minn Mus of Art, St Paul, 72; Prints: Midwest Invitational, Walker Art Ctr, Minneapolis, 73; 19th Nat Print Exhib, Brooklyn Mus, 74; Mod Printmaking Exhib of Contemp Prints, Bevier Gallery, Rochester Inst of Technol, NY, 74; New Am Colorists, World Print Coun, San Francisco, 81; 30 Am Printmakers, Columbus, Ohio, 82; and others. *Teaching:* Asst prof, Southern Ill Univ, Edwardsville, 70-76; assoc prof, Ill State Univ, Normal, 76-81, prof, 81-. *Awards:* Robert Cooke Endowment Award, 1971 Mid-States Art Exhib, Evansville Mus of Arts & Sci, Ind, 71; First Place, Fine Art of Printmaking, Lexington, Ky, Nat Soc of Arts & Lett, 71; Nat Endowment Arts, 75-76 & 79. *Bibliog:* Clinton Adams & Susan Ellis (auths), Drawing Color Separations on Surfaced Mylar, Tamarind Tech Papers, 74; Experiments in affordable custom lithography, Print News, Vol 3, 2-3/81. *Mem:* Mid-Am Col Art Asn; Col Art Asn. *Media:* Lithography; Drawing, Oil. *Dealer:* Associated American Artists New York NY. *Mailing Add:* 102 Warner St Bloomington IL 61701-4227

BUTLER, JOSEPH THOMAS
CURATOR, WRITER
b Winchester, Va, Jan 25, 32. *Study:* Univ Md, BS, 54; Univ Ohio, MA, 55; Univ Del, MA(Winterthur Fel), 57. *Exhib:* Am Furniture from Westchester Collections: 1650-1880, Katonah Gallery, Katonah, NY, 86; The Am Eagle: An Enduring Symbol, Katonah Gallery, Katonah, NY, 89; Am Painted Furniture, Scarsdale Historical Soc, 90; Visions of Washington Irving, 91. *Collection Arranged:* Divided Loyalties, Philipsburg Manor, North Tarrytown, NY, 76-79 & Four Centuries of History, A Decade of Restoration. *Pos:* Cur & dir Collections, Hist Hudson Valley, Tarrytown, NY, 57-, emer, 93-; Am ed, The Connoisseur, 68-78; ed bd, Art & Antiques, 78-83; adj prof mus studies, Fashion Inst Tech, NY, 86-97; adj prof, Columbia Univ, Grad Sch Archit, 1976-1986. *Teaching:* Adj assoc prof archit, Columbia Univ, 71-81. *Mem:* Furniture Hist Soc; Victorian Soc in Am; Am Ceramic Circle; The Century Asn; SAH. *Res:* American decorative arts and architecture. *Publ:* Auth, American Antiques, 1800-1900, 65; Candleholders in America, 1650-1900, 67; coauth, The Arts in America, the 19th Century, 70; auth, Washington Irving's Sunnyside, 75; Van Cortlandt Manor, 78; Sleepy Hollow Restorations: A Cross Section of the Collection, 83; Field Guide to American Antique Furniture, 85; American Painted Furniture, 90. *Mailing Add:* 222 Martling Ave Tarrytown NY 10591-4756

BUTT, HARLAN W
SILVERSMITH, ENAMELIST
b Princeton, NJ, Mar 30, 50. *Study:* Tyler Sch Art, with Stanley Lechtzin, BFA, 72; Southern Ill Univ, with Brent Kington, MFA, 74. *Work:* Southern Ill Univ, Carbondale. *Comn:* University mace & jazz band commemorative, NTex State Univ, Denton; University mace, Southwest Adventist Col, Keene, Tex. *Exhib:* Solo exhibs, Wichita Art Assoc, Wichita, Kans, 88, Seika-do Gallery, Kyoto, Japan, 82 & 85, Nat Ornamental Metal Mus, Memphis, 83 & Contemp Crafts Gallery, Portland, Ore, 86; Int Exhibition Enameling Art, Ueno Royal Mus, Tokyo, 85; Enamels Int, Long Beach Mus Art, Calif, 85; Biennale, La Maison des Arts, Laval, Can, 86. *Collection Arranged:* Kyoto Metal: An Exhibition of Contemporary Japanese Metalwork (auth, catalog), 83-84. *Teaching:* Lectr metalworking, San Diego State Univ, Calif, 75-76; prof metalworking, Univ NTex, Denton, 76-. *Awards:* Merit Award, Int Exhib Enameling Art Comt, 85. *Mem:* Soc NAm Goldsmiths; Am Crafts Coun; NTex Enamel Guild; Enamel Guild West. *Media:* Metal. *Mailing Add:* 2375 Wood Hollow Rd Denton TX 76208

BUTTER, TOM
SCULPTOR, INSTRUCTOR
b Amityville, NY, Oct 19, 52. *Study:* Philadelphia Col Art, BFA, 75; Wash Univ, St Louis, Mo, MFA, 77. *Work:* Acad Fine Arts, Philadelphia; Metrop Mus Art, NY; Chase Manhattan Bank; Walker Art Ctr, Minneapolis; Indianapolis Mus Art, Ind; Albright-Knox Art Gallery, Buffalo, NY. *Exhib:* Transformation of the Minimal Style, Sculpture Ctr, NY, 84; solo exhibs, Curt Marcus Gallery, 86, 88, 91, 93 & 97, Nina Freundenheim Gallery, Buffalo, NY, 87 & 92, John Berggruen Gallery, San Francisco, 87-, Pence Gallery, Los Angeles, 88; Perspectives from Pennsylvania, Carnegie Mellon Univ Art Gallery, Pittsburgh, 87; Sculpture Inside Outside, Mus Fine Arts, Houston, Tex, 88-89; The 1980's A New Generation, Metrop Mus Art, NY, 88; Aronson Gallery, Parsons Sch of Design 99; and others. *Teaching:* adj, Parsons Sch Design; Assoc prof sculpture, RI Col of Design. 96-97; Corp Fac, Sculpture Prog, Parsons, Sch Design, 98-; cordr, Parsons Mus Fine Arts, currently. *Awards:* Nat Endowment Arts Grant, 80 & 82; NY Found Arts Grant, 87, 97; Silver Star Alumni award Univ of Arts, Philadelphia; Print Project, Univ Arts, Philadelphia, 95, Washington Univ, St Louis, 96. *Bibliog:* Wade Saunders (auth), Interview with ten sculptors, Art Am, 11/85; Michael Brenson (auth), rev, NY Times, 3/91; Nancy Princenthall (auth), rev, Art Am, 12/93; George Melrod (auth), rev, Sculpture Mag, 1-2/94. *Interests:* Bookeeping

BUTTERFIELD, DEBORAH KAY
SCULPTOR
b San Diego, Calif, May 7, 49. *Study:* San Diego State Col, Calif; Univ Calif, San Diego; Univ Calif, Davis, BA (with honors), 71, MFA, 73; Rocky Mountain Col, DFA (hon), Billings, Mont, 1997; Montana State Univ, DFA (hon) 1998. *Hon Degrees:* Rocky Mountain Col, Billings, Mont, Hon Dr Fine Arts, 97; Mont State Univ, Bozeman, Hon Dr Fine Arts, 98; Whitman Col, Walla Walla, Wa, Dr Fine Arts, 04. *Work:* Whitney Mus Am Art, Metrop Mus Art, NY; San Francisco Mus Contemp Art,

Calif; Israel Mus, Jeusalem; Walker Art Ctr, Minneapolis, Minn; Denver Art Mus, Denver, Colo; Smithsonian Am Art Mus, Washington, DC; US Embassy, Ottawa, Can. *Comn:* Copley Square, Boston, Mass; Portland Airport, Ore; Univ Calif Los Angeles, Franklin Murphy Sculp Garden; Denver Art Mus; Kans City (Mo) Zoo; White House, Washington, DC, 2000; Monte Carlo, Monaco, 2000; Smithsonian Inst, Washington, San Francisco Int Airport. *Exhib:* 2 Sculptors, Univ Mus Berkeley, Calif, 74; Whitney Biennial & The Decade in Review, Whitney Mus Am Art, NY, 79; 8 Sculptors, Albright-Knox Gallery, Buffalo, 79; Israel Mus, Jerusalem, 80; Arco Ctr Visual Art, 81; Walker Art Ctr, Minneapolis, 82; Dallas Mus Fine Arts, 82; Oakland, 83; Mile of Sculpture, Chicago, 85; Contemp Ar Ctr, Honolulu, 86; 20th Century Am Sculpture at the White House, Exhib VIII, 2000; others; one-woman show, Seattl Art Mus, Wash, 81, Walker Art Ctr, Minneapolis, Minn, 81, Dallas Mus Fine Arts, Tex, 82, Oakland Mus, Calif, 83, (auth, catalog), San Diego Mus Art, 96, Bellevue Art Mus, Wash, 2001, Holter Mus Art, Helena, Mont, 2002 & others. *Teaching:* asst prof, Mont State Univ, Bozeman, 79-83, adj prof, cons, 84-87; Asst prof sculpture, Univ Wis, Madison, 75-76. *Awards:* John Simon Guggenheim Mem Fel, 80; Individual Artist Fel, Nat Ednowment Arts, 80; Golden Plate Award, Am Acad Achievment, 93. *Bibliog:* Kenneth Baker (auth), Galleries: Butterfield horses, San Francisco Chronicle, 5/28/94; Robert Gordon (auth), Deborah Butterfield, Harry N Abrams. *Mem:* Nat Acad. *Media:* Natural Materials, Steel. *Publ:* Auth, Horses: The Art of Deborah Butterfield, Chronicle Bks, 92. *Dealer:* Edward Thorp Gallery 210 Eleventh Ave New York NY 10001; Zolla Lieberman Gallery 325 W Huron Chicago IL 60610. *Mailing Add:* 11229 Cottonwood Rd Bozeman MT 59718

BUTTERLY, KATHY
SCULPTOR
b Amityville, NY, 63. *Study:* Moore Col Art, Philadelphia, BFA, 86; Univ Calif, Davis, MFA, 90. *Exhib:* Solo shows include Moore Col Art, Philadelphia, 92, Clay Studio, 93, Franklin Parrasch Gallery, NY City, 94, 95, 96, 97, 98, 99, Bernard Toale Gallery, Boston, 2000, Tibor de Nagy Gallery, NY City, 2002, 2004, Shoshana Wayne Gallery, Santa Monica, Calif, 2003; group shows include Fourth Concorso Nazionale della Ceramica d'Arte: SAvona-Fortezza Primiar, Savona, Italy, 90; Contemp Ceramics, Bennington Coll Gallery, Vt, 92; Talentborse Handwerk, Munich, 94; Forms and Transformations of Clay, Queens Borough Public Library Gallery, Jamaica, NY, 97; Byron Cohen Gallery Contemp Art, Kansas City, Mo, 2000, 2002; 15th Anniversary Exhib, Franklin Parrasch Gallery, NY City, 2001; Kanazawa World Craft Forum, Japan, 2003; Very Familiar: Celebrating 50 Years of Collecting Decorative Arts, Carnegie Mus Art, Pittsburgh, 2004-2005. *Awards:* Anonymous Was a Woman Grant, 2002; Evelyn Shapiro Found Grant, 93; Empire State Crafts Alliance Grant, 95; NY Found for Arts Grant, 99. *Mailing Add:* c/o Tibor de Nagy Gallery 724 Fifth Ave New York NY 10019

BUTTI, LINDA
PAINTER, EDUCATOR
b Brooklyn, NY, Jan 15, 51. *Study:* Brooklyn Col, New York, with Philip Pearlstein & William T Williams, BA, 72, MFA(painting), 75. *Work:* Art Network, Staten Island, NY; Iona Col Permanent Collection of Art, New Rochelle, NY; Bell Atlantic, Atlanta, Ga; NBC Studios, NY; Staten Island Univ Hosp. *Comn:* Watercolor (mural, 4' x 5'), Catholic Telecommunication, NY, 88; wall mural, Network America; murals (two, 42" x 30"), Swanston Fine Arts Inc, Atlanta, Ga, 88. *Exhib:* Brooklyn '77 & Brooklyn '78, Brooklyn Mus, NY; solo exhibs, Newhouse Ctr Contemp Art, Snug Harbor Cult Ctr, NY, 85, New Visions, Princeton Univ, NJ, 89, St John's Univ, 93, SI Community Television Studios, 94 & Elaine Benson Gallery, 2000; Mem Exhib, Staten Island Mus, NY, 88; Contemp Spiritual Art Nat, Paul VI Inst Arts, Washington, 88; 51st Ann Artists Exhib, Guild Hall, Mus, Easthampton, NY, 89; Brenau Col Nat Exhib; Elaine Benson Gallery, 2000; New World Gallery, 2004; Mohawk Valley Art Ctr, 2006. *Collection Arranged:* Women in Art, Art Lab, Staten Island, NY, 2000. *Pos:* Assoc prof art, City Univ NY, 2001-. *Teaching:* Assoc prof, St Johns Univ, 81-, Iona-Seton Col, 84-88 & LaGuardia Community Col, 88-90, Molloy Col, 94-; lectr, Bronx Community Col, 83-85, Cult Pluralism, LaGuardia Community Col, 89 & Seurat & European Art, Staten Island Mus, Staten Island Inst Art, 91-98 & Molloy Col, 94; art prof, Art Lab Sch, Snug Harbor Cult Ctr, Staten Island, NY. *Awards:* NY State Coun Arts Grant, 91-98; NY Dept Cult Affairs Grant, 93. *Bibliog:* M Fressola (auth), Best of Both Worlds, SI Advance, 92; Marion Weesberg (auth), Dan's Papers, Honoring the Artist, 12/99; Diane Cable (auth), Columns, Profile of Artist Linda Butti, 10/99. *Mem:* Women in Arts Inc (pres, 2005-); Cath Artists Am (vpres, 94-); Col Art Asn. *Media:* Oil on Canvas, Mixed Media, digital art. *Specialty:* Digital artwork, New World Gallery, NY. *Interests:* Horticulture, Botan. *Collection:* Brenau Univ, NBC Studies, Mitsubishi Corp, St Vincent's Hosp. *Publ:* Auth, A few stars shine, NJ Star, 95. *Dealer:* Nancy Stein Gallery 340 W 57th St New York NY. *Mailing Add:* 65 Beverlyn Ave Staten Island NY 10301

BUTTS, H DANIEL, III
GALLERY DIRECTOR
b Pittsburgh, Pa, July 15, 39. *Study:* Yale Univ, BA, 60, BFA, 61; Pa State Univ, MA, 62. *Pos:* Dir, Arts & Crafts Ctr Pittsburgh, 65-68; dir, Mansfield Art Ctr, 68-. *Teaching:* Instr hist art, painting & drawing, Shady Side Acad, Pittsburgh, 62-65. *Mailing Add:* 699 Sloane Ave Mansfield OH 44903-1836

BUVOLI, LUCA
SCULPTOR
b Brescia, Italy, Jan 8, 63. *Study:* Acad Fine Arts, Venice, Italy, BFA, 85; State Univ NY, Albany, MA(fulbright scholar), 89; Sch Visual Arts, NY, MFA(studio art), 91. *Work:* The Mus of Modern Art, NY; The Norton Family Found, Los Angeles, Calif; Sonje Art Ctr, Seoul, Korea. *Comn:* The Big Wave Permanent art work for PS 253, Queens NY, Percent for the Art Program, Dept of Cult Affairs, NYC, Bd of Educ. *Exhib:* Selections, winter 94, The Drawing Ctr, NY, 94; one-man shows, John Weber Gallery, NY, 95, Santa Monica Mus Art, Calif, 96, Ariz State Univ Art Mus, 96, ACME, Santa Monica, Calif, 96; Johannesburg Biennale, South Africa, 97; Greater NY PS1 Contemp Art Ctr, Long Island City, 2000; solo shows incl John Weber Gallery, NY, 97, Cleveland Ctr for Contemp Art, Ohio, 99, MIT List Visual Arts Ctr, Cambridge, MA, 2000, Austin Mus of Art, Tex, 2000, Queens Mus of Art, NY, 2001, Philadelphia Mus of Art (Video Gallery), PA, 2001; Weatherspoon Art Mus, Greensboro, NC, 2003; Glassell Sch of Art, Mus of Fine Art, Houston Tex, 2003; Portland Inst for Contemp Art, Ore, 2002. *Teaching:* Asst prof artistic anat, Acad Fine Arts, Venice, Italy, 87-88; instr, Found Sculpture, Sch Visual Arts, NY, 98; instr experiments in drawing, RI Sch of Design, Providence, 98; instr sculpture, Sch of Visual Arts, NY, 2000-. *Awards:* Studio Prog Grant, Marie Walsh Sharpe Art Found, 95-96; Artist Fel, NY Found Arts, 97; Jerome Found Media Arts Prog Grant, 98; Film Production Grant, New York State Coun on the Arts, 99; Pollock Kranser Award, 2001; Peter Reed Foundation, Award, 2003. *Bibliog:* Carolyn G Anderson (auth), Ouverture: Luca Buvoli, Flash Art (Ital ed), 2-3/95; Gregory Volk (auth), Luca Buvoli at John Weber, Vol 86, No 1, 97-98, Art in Am, 1/98; Barry Schwabsky (auth), Drawing in Time: Reflections on Animation by Artists, Art on Paper, 3-4/2000; Barry Schwabsky (auth), The Accidental Superhero, World Art, summer 99; Gregory William (auth), Luca Buvoli, Frieze, 3-4/2000; Raphael Rubinstein (auth) Watching the Skies, Art in America, Nov 2004, pg, 152; Linda Yablonsky, Leaping Dialectics, In the Single Bound, NY Times, Arts & Leisure Section, Nov, 2, 2003, Pg, 24; Andrea Bellini, Luca Buvol, Learning to Fly, Flash Art Citalian Edition, Dec 2003- Jan 2004, pp 100-103. *Mem:* PS 122 Gallery (adv bd mem, 94-). *Publ:* Not-a-Superhero, It's time for Eternity (exhib catalog), Food House, Santa Monica, Calif, 94; Not-a-Superhero No 6 & No 7: The Origin of Not-a-Superhero (exhib catalog), AC Proj Room, New York, 95; Not-a-Superhero, I Presume (exhib catalog), Caffe Florian, Venice, Italy, 97; Inside and Outside Time, The Real Story (exhib catalog), Cleveland Ctr for Contemp Art, Ohio, 99; Flying - Practical Training for Beginners, (exhib catalog), MIT List Visual Arts Ctr, Cambridge, MA, 2000; Adaptng One's Senses to High Altitude Flying; Weatherspoon Art Mus, 2003; Luca Buvodi, Flying Preparatory Exericises, Exhib Catalog, Glassell School of Art, Mus of Fine Art, Houston, TX, 2003; Flying Practical Training for Internediate, (notes 97-2001) exhib catalog, 2002, Portland Inst of Contemporary Art, OR. *Dealer:* Autori Cambi, Rome; Devin Borden/Hiram Butler Gallery, Houston, Tex. *Mailing Add:* 32 Spring St No 8 New York NY 10012

BUXBAUM, ROBERT
SCULPTOR
b Brooklyn, NY, July 7, 39. *Study:* Work & study in the studio of Frederick J Kiesler, 62 & 64. *Work:* Chase Manhattan Bank, Union Carbide Corp & Xerox Corp, New York, NY; Owens-Corning Fibenglass Corp, Toledo, Ohio; Best Products Co, Richmond, Va. *Exhib:* Solo exhibs, Warren Benedek, 75, OK Harris, 77 & 55 Mercer, 82, NY; Abstraction: Alive & Well, Brainerd Hall, State Univ NY, Postdam, 75; Brookhaven Nat Lab, Brookhaven, NY, 79; Sculptural Works Incorporating Glass, NY Experimental Glass Workshop, NY, 80; Diversity, Univ RI, Kingston, 85. *Bibliog:* Shoichiro Higuchi (auth), Robert Buxbaum - Metaphysics of Transparency, IDEA, 87. *Mailing Add:* 119 Spring St New York NY 10012

BYARS, DONNA
SCULPTOR, COLLAGE ARTIST
b Rock Island, Ill. *Study:* Stephens Col, Columbia, Mo; Iowa State Univ, BA; Parsons Sch Design, NY. *Work:* Va Mus Fine Arts, Richmond; Bellevue Hosp Collection, NY; Pub Art Prog, Long Island Univ-C W Post; Santa Fe Mus; Chicago Art Inst. *Comn:* Site sculpture, Bard-Hudson Valley Studies, 78; site sculpture, New Wilderness Found, 78; site sculpture, Wave Hill, Bronx, NY, 79; Women & Wood, Katonah Mus, NY, 93. *Exhib:* Solo exhibs, 55 Mercer, 75, AIR Gallery, 77, 79, 84 & 87 & Hudson River Mus, 89; Aldrich Mus Contemp Art, Ridgefield, Conn, 75-76; Lunds Konsthall, Lunds, 81, & Kulturhurst, Stockholm, 82, Sweden; Schweinfurth Mus, Auburn, NY, 82; Va Mus Fine Art, 88; Hudson River Mus, 89; Max Hutchinson's Sculpture Fields, 88-96; In Three Dimensions: Women Sculptors of the 90s, Snug Harbor Cult Ctr, Staten Island, NY, 96. *Pos:* Dir, Parsons Gallery, Parsons Sch Design, New York, 84-86. *Teaching:* Instr drawing, Parsons Sch Design, 76-92; instr collage, New Sch for Social Res, New York, 77-. *Awards:* Artist-in-Residence Grant, Palisades Interstate Park, Am the Beautiful Fund, Washington, 76; Creative Artists Pub Serv Program Fel, 82. *Bibliog:* Gloria Orenstein (auth), The Reflowering of the Goddess, Pergamon Press; James J Kelly (auth), The Sculptural Idea, Arts Rev; Lucy Lippard (auth), Overlay: Ancient Images & Contemporary Art, Pantheon Bks. *Mem:* Women's Caucus Art, NY; Col Art Asn. *Mailing Add:* Five Woodworth Ave Yonkers NY 10701

BYERS, FLEUR
PAINTER, INSTRUCTOR
b Washington, DC. *Study:* Pomona Col, Claremont, Calif; Univ Pa, Corcoran Gallery Art, Washington, DC, 51; Pa Acad Fine Arts, 59; studies with Elliot O'Hara. *Work:* Salomon Brothers, NY; Polyclinic Hosp, Harrisburg, Pa; Bank America, Boston, Mass; McNees, Wallace & Nurick, Harrisburg, Pa; Shumaker & Williams Ins Co, Camp Hill, Pa. *Exhib:* 11th Biennial Northeast Regional Exhib, Susquehanna Art Soc, Selinsgrove, Pa, 96, 12th Biennial, 98, 13th Biennial, 2001, 14th Biennial, 2004; 26th Ann Juried Exhib, York Art Asn, Pa, 96; Greater Lafayette Mus Art, Ind, 96; Sheldon Swope Mus Art, Terre Haute, Ind, 96; juried traveling exhib, Nat Asn Women Artists, 96-98, 99, 2002, & 2003; Lancaster Mus Art, Pa, 95 & 2002, 2003, 2004; Saginaw Art Mus, Mich, 98; Purdue Univ Gallery, West Lafayette, Ind, 99; Midwest Mus Am Art, Elkart, Ind, 99; Laney Col, Oakland, Calif, 99; 8th Ann Nat Akron Soc of Artists Grand Exhib, Ohio, 98; Juried Exhib Doshi Gallery, Harrisburg, Pa, 98 & 99; Ann Juried Exhib York Art Asn, Pa, 98, 99, 2000, 2002, 2003, 2005; Ann Exhib Nat Asn Women Artists, NY, 99, 2002, 2003, 2005, 2006; 9th Ann Juried Art Exhib,

Elizabethtown Col, Pa, 99; Ann Juried Exhib, State Ms of Pa, Harrisburg, 99, 2003, 2005; Juried Exhib, Whitaker Ctr for Sci and the Arts, Harrisburg, 99, 2000, 2004, 2006; Ann Juried Exhib United Pastelists of Am, Clifton Arts Ctr, NJ, 00; Juried Exhib United Pastelists of Am, Edward Hopper House, Nyack, NY, 2001; solo shows incl Gallery at Walnut Pl, Harrisburg, 99, 2001, 2004, 2006, Pen and Brush Galleries, NY, 2000; Wyomissing Inst Fine Arts, Pa, 2001; York Art Asn, Pa, 2002; Pine Street Presbyterian Church, Harrisburg, Pa, 2003; Ann Exhib of Catharine Lorillard Wolfe Art Club, Nat Arts Club, Nat Arts Club, NY, Oct 2003, 2005; Doshi Gallery's Juried Exhib at Morrison Gallery, Penn State Univ, 2003-2004; Juried Exhib at Wayne Art Center, Wayne PA, 2003, 2004, 2005, 2006; Juried War Exhib, National Assoc of Women Artists Gallery NY, Feb 2004; Pen and Brush Galleries, NYC, 2005, 2006, York Art Assoc, PA, 2006, Studio Gallery 234, York, 2005, 2006. *Collection Arranged:* Arts for Peace & Justice Exhib, Strawberry Sq, Harrisburg, Pa, 90, 91, 92, 93, 94, 95, 96, 97, 98 & 99, 2000-2005; Adventures in Creativity, Strawberry Sq, Harrisburg, Pa, 00; Salomon Bros, NY; Charles Dear, Interior Design, NY; Polyclinic Hosp, Harrisburg; Dauphin Deposit Bank, Harrisburg. *Pos:* curator, Arts for Peace and Justice Exhibs Harrisburg, 90-2006. *Teaching:* Instr oil painting, Mechanicsburg Art Ctr, Pa, 90; instr all mediums, Home Studio, New Cumberland, Pa, 93-00; instr drawing & pastels, Lower Paxton Twp, Harrisburg, Pa, 94, 95, 96, 97 & 98, Boscov's Campus of Courses, Camp Hill, Pa, 94; Bald Eagle Art League, Williamport, Pa, 12/94 & 6/98; York Art Asn, York, Pa, 1999-2005; instr painting & drawing various art ctrs. *Awards:* Honorable Mention, Ann Pastel Exhib, Pen & Brush, NY, 2/97; Catherine Lorillard Walfe Art Club Cash Award, 101st Ann Exhib, Nat Arts Club, NY, 10/97; Second Prize, Juried Realism Exhib, Doshi Gallery, Harrisburg, Pa, 1/98; William Meyerowitz Meml Award, 109th Ann Exhibition Nat Asn Women Artists, NY, 98; Honorable Mention Graphics, Susquehanna Art Soc 12th Biennial Exhib, Selinsgrove, Pa, 98; Bronze Plaque for a pastel of exceptional merit Pastel Soc Am, York Art Asn 28th Ann Juried Exhibit, York, Pa, 98; Solo Show Award, Pen and Brush, NY, 99; 2nd Prize for Pastels, 29th Ann Juried Exhibit York Art Asn, 99; HK Holbein Award, Oil Pastel Asn, Nyack, NY, 99; 1st Prize Graphics, York Art Asn Winter Exhibit, 99; Mister Art.com Award, Oil Pastel Asn, Edward Hopper Art Ctr, Nyack, NY, 2000; Bald Eagle Art League 2nd Prize in Pastels, 30th Ann Juried Exhibit, York Art Asn, 2000; 1st Prize Graphics Winter Exhibit, York Art Asn, 2000; Honorable Mention in Pastels, York Art Asn, 2000; 2nd Prize Susquehanna Art Soc, 13th Biennial Juried Exhib, Pa, 2001; Art Times Award, 105th Ann Exhib, CL Wolfe Art Club, NY, 2001, Charlotte Dunwiddle Memorial Award, 106th Ann Exhib, 2002; Merit Award United Pastelists Am, Nyack, NY, 2001; First Prize/Pastels, 32nd Ann Juried Exhib, York Art Asn, Pa, 2002; 1st Prize, Pastels, Mechanicsburg Art Ctr, PA, April, 2003; Atlantic Papers Award, 62nd Annual Juried Exhib of Audubon Artists in NY, Oct 2004; 3rd Prize, Mechanicsburg Art Ctr, PA, Sept, 2004; Award of Excellence, Regional Juried Exhib, 2005; 2d Pl Award, Healing Hearts Exhib, Performing Arts Ctr, Pa State Univ, York, 2005; 1st Award, Pen and Brush Galleries, NYC, 2006; 3d Prize for Pastels, Art Assoc Harrisburg, 2006; 2d Prize, 35th Ann Juried Art Exhib, Arnold Art Gallery, Lebanon Valley Coll, Annville, PA, 2006. *Bibliog:* Pastel Drawings, Patriot-News, Harrisburg, Pa, 12/19/97, Local Artist is part of exhibit in NY, 9/26/97; Traveling Art, Daily Rocket-Miner, Rock Springs Wyoming, 6/30/98; The Best of Drawing & Sketching, Rockport Publ, 98; Patricia Seligman (auth), How to Paint Trees, Flowers & Foliage; Linda Barr (auth), Artist Brings Skills to Mechanicsburg, 99; Zachary Lewis (auth) Arts for Peace, Patriot-News, 00; Ruth Summer (auth), Fleur Byers, Oil Pastel Artist, The Pastel Jour, 3-4/2002; USA Showcase, Fleur Byers, Pastel Artist Int, 9-10/2002; March Meeting, Franklin County Art Alliance, Chambersburg Pa, March, 2000; Fleur Byers and Maureen Buckholz to Exhib, Berks Arts, Reading PA, April-May, 2001; Three Artists Show at YAA, The York Dispatch, York Pa, 1/31/2002; Exhib features Area Artists, Community Courier, York Pa, 2/13/2002; Endless Options, Intelligencer Journal, Lancaster PA, 6/14/2003; Best of Pennsylvania Artists, 2006. *Mem:* Nat Asn of Women Artist; Catharine Lorillard Wolf Art Club; Nat League of Am Pen Women; Oil Pastel Asn Int; Susquehanna Art Mus; Lancaster Art Mus; Art Asn of Harrisburg; York Art Asn; Art Ctr of Mechanicsburg; YorkArts; Pen & Brush Inc. *Media:* Oil Pastel, Charcoal, Graphite, Colored Pencil, etching. *Res:* Study combinations of various mediums; Study effects of light and weather. *Specialty:* Fine Art; Impressionist city and country scenes. *Interests:* Soc Concerns, poetry, literature, music, hiking, swimming. *Publ:* Coauth, Committee Sponsors Harrisburg Exhib,West Shore Shopper, Camp Hill, Pa, 7/29/98; Arts for Peace, Justice Exh to Open with Reception Today, Patriot-News, Harrisburg, Pa, 7/31/98; Art, Poetry, & Prose Featured at Exhib, Harrisburg Times, Harrisburg, Pa, 8/7/98; Art for Peace and Justice, Sentinel, Carlisle, Pa; Exhib of Fleur Byers, Art Work, Harrisburg City Calendar, Harrisburg, PA, April, 99; Inst of the Art-Multmedia Works, Patriot-News, Harrisburg PA, 4/20/2001; Pine Street Church-Painting by Fleur Byers, Patriot, News, Harrisburg, PA, 3/21/2003. *Dealer:* Gallery at Walnut Place 413 Walnut St Harrisburg PA; Studio Gallery 234 300 S Pershing Ave York PA 17403

BYNUM, E (ESTHER PEARL) ANDERSON
CURATOR, PRINTMAKER
b Henderson, Tex, Dec 19, 22. *Study:* Dallas Mus Fine Arts, 52; NTex State Univ, BA, 65; Univ Md, MA, 72, advan grad specialist cert, 73; also lithography with Tadeusz Lapinski. *Work:* US Civil Serv Bldg, Washington, DC; Montgomery Co Contemp Print Collection & Montgomery Co Pub Schs, Md. *Exhib:* NY Int Art Show, 70; Baltimore Mus, 73-74; Jersey City Mus, NJ, 74; 26th Ann Exhib, McNay Art Inst, San Antonio, 75 & 32nd Ann, 81, Tex Watercolor Soc; Lowe Art Mus, Univ Miami, Fla, 75. *Pos:* Cur, Four Oaks Gallery, Henderson, Tex, 80-. *Teaching:* Instr art, Montgomery Co Pub Schs, Rockville, Md, 65-75, elem art coordr, 75-79; artist in educ, Longview Pub Sch, Tex Art Coun, 84-86. *Bibliog:* Articles in Henderson Daily News & Longview, Tex Arts Coun. *Mem:* Tex Watercolor Soc; Am Craft Coun; Graphics Soc. *Media:* Watercolor, Lithographs. *Publ:* Contribr, monthly visual arts article, Henderson Daily Newspaper. *Dealer:* Four Oaks Gallery 709 Hwy 43 Henderson TX 75652. *Mailing Add:* 711 Highway 43 Henderson TX 75652

BYRD, JERRY
PAINTER
b Fullerton, Calif, Mar 6, 47. *Study:* Univ Calif, Irvine, BFA, 70, MFA, 72. *Work:* Mus Contemp Art, Melbourne, Australia; Crocker Art Mus, Sacramento, Calif; Newport Harbor Art Mus, Newport Beach, Calif; Laguna Beach Mus Art, Calif. *Comn:* Paintings on canvas, AT&T, San Francisco, 77, IBM, San Jose, 82, Carol Beadel, Santa Barbara, 84 & Peabody Hotel, Orlando, Fla, 86. *Exhib:* The First Decade, Fine Arts Gallery, Univ Calif, Irvine, 75; Painting and Sculpture Today, Indianapolis Mus Art, 76; Current Concerns, 76 & New Directions in Southern California Art, 78, Los Angeles Inst Contemp Art; Geometric Abstraction, Inst Art, Boston, 81; Calif Contemp Artists, Laguna Beach Mus Art, Calif, 84. *Awards:* Fine Arts Patrons Award, Univ Calif, Irvine, 69; Nat Endowment Arts Fel, 74. *Bibliog:* Robert Hutchinson (auth), Scale and modern comfort, Archit Digest, 79; Clark Poling (auth), Geometric Abstraction: A New Generation, Boston Inst Contemp Art, 81; Suvan Geer (auth), Emphasis on formalism, Art Week, 84. *Media:* Oil, Acrylic. *Publ:* Illusr, College Algebra (auth, Louis Leithold), MacMillan Publ Co, Inc, New York, NY, 80. *Dealer:* Ivory-Kimpton 55 Grant Ave San Francisco CA 94108. *Mailing Add:* 1137 Palms Blvd Venice CA 90291-3524

BYRD, ROBERT JOHN
ILLUSTRATOR, INSTRUCTOR
b Atlantic City, NJ, Jan 11, 42. *Study:* Philadelphia Mus Col Art, BFA(graphic arts), 66. *Work:* Free Libr Philadelphia; Philadelphia Col Art. *Exhib:* Soc Illusr, NY, 71-77; Graphis Press, Zurich, Switz, 74-77; Philadelphia Art Alliance, 74; Bologna Worlds Children's Book Fair, Italy, 75; Design & Illustration: USA, Teheran, Iran, 78; Graphis Poster & Ann, Zurich, 78-79. *Teaching:* Portfolio sem illusr, Philadelphia Col Art, 76-77; adj instr illus, Moore Col Art, Philadelphia, 77-. *Awards:* Citation Merit, Soc Illusr, 76; Jr Lit Award for The Gondolier of Venice, 76 & The Detective of London, 78. *Bibliog:* Diana Klemin (auth), The portfolio of Robert Byrd, Am Artist, 71; Linda Munich & Marty Jacobs (producers), For Your Information, WKBS TV, 78. *Mem:* Philadelphia Children's Reading Round Table; Illusr Guild (Graphic Arts Guild). *Publ:* Illusr, Rebecca Hatpin, 73, Pinch Penny Mouse, 74, The Gondolier of Venice, 76 & The Detective of London, 78, Windmill Bks

BYRN, BRIAN DOUGLAS
CURATOR, ASSEMBLAGE ARTIST
b Corydon, Ind, Mar 25, 58. *Study:* Butler Univ; Ind Univ, Bloomington; Univ Louisville; Ind Univ Southeast, BA(fine art), 81; Ind Univ, South Bend, MS(educ), 96. *Work:* Midwest Mus Am Art, Elkhart, Ind; Ft Wayne Mus Art, Ind; Floyd Co Mus, Ind Univ Southeast Collection, New Albany, Ind; South Bend Regional Mus Art, Ind. *Exhib:* Myths, Domestic Tragedies & Other Psycho-Sexual Sub-Urban Adventures, Zephyr Gallery, Louisville, Ky, 91; A Journey Through Alternate Reality, Ind Univ Southeast Art Gallery, New Albany, Ind, 91; Regional Artists Biennial, Ft Wayne Mus Art, Ind, 92; Forces: Seldom Seen/Never Heard, Southwestern Mich Col, Dowagiac, Mich, 93; Drawing in Four Parts, Goshen Col Art Gallery, 97. *Collection Arranged:* Milt Hinton: Images of Jazz, 85; The Lillian Florsheim Collection of Geometric Abstract, 86; Extremes: Three Regional Views, 91; Indian Summer: A Trilogy Highlighting Native Americans, 93; American Traditions: 19th Century Works of Americana, 93. *Pos:* Cur exhib & educ, Midwest Mus Am Art, Elkhart, Ind, 81-. *Teaching:* Adj lectr art, Ind Univ, South Bend, 88-89; asst prof, Goshen Col, 93-97. *Awards:* Indianapolis Mus Art Award of Merit, 70th Ann Ind Artists Show, 85; JG Blank Ctr Art Best of Show, 4th Ann Area Artists Exhib, 90; Ft Wayne Mus Art Award Excellence, Regional Artists Bienniel, 92. *Bibliog:* Erik Novak (mgr ed), Midwestern odyssey, Arts Ind, 91; Diane Heilenmann (critic), A journey through alternate reality, Courier J, 1/91, Jeanne Derbeck (critic), Lightning field inspiration, South Bend Tribune, 2/21/93. *Mem:* Am Asn Mus; Asn Ind Mus. *Media:* Paper. *Publ:* Co-auth, Nature: Forms and Forces, Loyola Press, 85; Variations on a Theme: World's Fairs of the 80s, Loyola Press, 87; illusr, Rainforests of the World, ABC-CLIO, Inc, Santa Barbara, 94; illusr, Belize Mag, 94 & 96

BYRNE, CHARLES JOSEPH
DESIGNER
b Louisville, Ky, Oct 15, 43. *Study:* Univ Louisville, BS; Wayne State Univ. *Comn:* Various Exhib Designs, Detroit Inst of Arts, 73-80; Contemp Arts Ctr, Cincinnati, 81-84; Univ Calif, Berkeley. *Exhib:* Buckminster Fuller Portfolio, Gettler Paul Gallery, 81, NY Art Dir Club Ann Exhib, 82, 83 & 84; Archit Photog Exhib, CAGE Gallery, 82, Local Color Photog Exhib, Tangeman Fine Arts Gallery, Univ Cincinnati, 82, Advert Club Cincinnati Ann Exhib, 81-84, Cincinnati Art Dir Club Ann Exhib, 79-84, Poster, Brodie Gallery, Univ Cincinnati, 82 & 83, Color and Contract, Photog Exhib, Carl Solway Gallery, Cincinnati, 84; Cult Posters Exhib, Univ Louisville, 82, Posters, Portland Mus, Louisville, Ky, 84. *Pos:* Cur, Dept of Fine Arts, Univ Louisville, Ky, 63-66, asst univ designer, 66-70; chief designer graphics & signage, Smith, Hinchman & Grylls Assoc, Inc, Detroit, 70-76; owner, Colophon Design Studio, Cincinnati & Colophon, San Francisco, 78-84, Chuck Byrne Design, Oakland, Calif, 85-; contrib ed, Print Mag, 88-. *Teaching:* Instr, Interior Designers Guild, San Diego, 77-78; instr, Cincinnati Acad Art, 80, Acad Art Col, San Francisco, 92-93; adj fac, Univ Cincinnati, 81-84; assoc prof design, Calif Col Arts & Crafts, 88-91; fac, San Jose State Univ. *Awards:* Commun Arts Mag Award, 74, 81 & 85; Commun Graphics Award, Am Inst of Graphic Arts, 74, 75 & 82-85; Awards, Art Dirs Club Cincinnati, 79-83. *Bibliog:* Print Magazine Casebook 8, Environ Graphics, 90; Carol Stevens (auth), Chuck Byrne, Print Mag, Sept/Oct, 90; Gatta, Lange, Lyons (auths), Foundations of Graphic Design, Davis Publ Inc, Worcester, Mass, 90. *Mem:* Am Inst Graphic Arts. *Media:* Print Graphics. *Publ:* Coauth, Computer Graphics, Mich Soc Archit Bull, 4/75; Downtown vs Suburban Shopping Centers: a Clear Case of Identity, Detroit Free Press Mag, 2/76; numerous articles for Print Magazine, 86-. *Mailing Add:* 5528 Lawton Ave Oakland CA 94601

BYRNES, JAMES BERNARD
ART HISTORIAN, MUSEUM DIRECTOR
b New York, NY, Feb 19, 17. *Study:* Nat Acad Design, New York, 36-38; Am Artists Sch, New York, 38-40; Art Students League, 41-42; Univ Perugia; Istituto Meschini, Rome, 51-52. *Exhib:* Man Ray, Paris & Los Angeles (catalog); Track 16, Robert Berman Galleries; Degas and New Orleans (catalog essay), New Orleans Mus Art, 1999. *Collection Arranged:* Edgar Degas, His Family & Friends in New Orleans (auth, catalog), 65; Odyssey of an Art Collector--The Collection of Mr & Mrs Frederick S Stafford, Paris (auth, catalog), 66; Arts of Ancient & Modern Latin America (auth, catalog), 68; Rothko (auth, catalog), 74; Artist as Collector--Ethnic Art (auth, catalog), 75. *Pos:* Cur mod & contemp art, Los Angeles Co Mus, 46-54; dir, Colorado Springs Fine Arts Ctr, 54-56; assoc dir, NC Mus Art, 56-58, dir, 58-60; dir, New Orleans Mus Art, 61-72; dir, Newport Harbor Art Mus, Newport Beach, Calif, 72-75; consult fine arts, 1978-; symposium, Modern Art in Los Angeles in the Late Forties, Getty Res Inst, 2003. *Teaching:* Vis prof hist 20th century art, Univ Southern Calif, 50, Univ Fla, Gainesville, 60-61. *Awards:* Knight in the Order of Leopold II, Belg Govt, 72; Hon Title, Dir emer, New Orleans Mus Art, 89; Man of Yr for Art, Isaac Delgado Fellows Award, New Orleans Mus Art, 1999. *Mem:* Sr mem Appraisers Soc Am; Appraisers Asn Am; Am Asn Mus; Int Coun Mus; hon life mem Am Inst Designers; and others. *Res:* Nineteenth and twentieth century art; Edgar Degas; pre-Columbian and African art. *Mailing Add:* James B Byrnes & Assoc 7820 Mulholland Dr Los Angeles CA 90046

BYRON, CHARLES ANTHONY
DEALER
b Istanbul, Turkey, Dec 15, 1920. *Study:* Ecole Libre Sci Polit, Paris, France; Univ Paris; Harvard Univ; BA, LLB & MA. *Pos:* Dir, Byron Gallery, NY. *Specialty:* Modern paintings. *Mailing Add:* 25 E 83rd St No 7E New York NY 10028-0421

BYRON, MICHAEL
PAINTER
b Providence, RI, 1954. *Study:* Kansas City Art Inst, BFA, 76; NS Col Art & Design, MFA, 81. *Exhib:* Mus Mod Art, NY, 83; Boymans-Van Beuningen, Rotterdam, The Neth, 86; solo exhibs, Aldrich Mus Contemp Art, 87, Mus Boymans-Van Bueningen, Rotterdam, 91, Galerie Barbara Farber, Amsterdam, 91, Elga Wimmer Gallery, Broadway, NY, 93, Galerie Philippe Gravier, Paris, France, 93 & Anders Tornberg Gallery, Lund, Swed, 94; Whitney Biennial, Whitney Mus Am Art, NY, 89; Maryland Inst Art, Baltimore, 91; Selections from the Permanent Collection, Phoenix Art Mus, Ariz, 92; Recent Donations & Acquisitions, Whitney Mus, NY, 92. *Teaching:* Vis artist, RI Sch Design, 85, NS Col Art & Design, Halifax, 85 & 92 & Hochsch voor Kunsten (grad level), Arnhem, Neth, 91-92; guest lectr, Sch Visual Arts, New York, 88 & Hochsch Hertenbosch voor Kunst, Den Bosch, Neth, 91; asst prof, Washington Univ, St Louis, Mo, 94-. *Bibliog:* Anna Tilroe (auth), Volkskrant, Een Kolossale Bruine Mandarijn, 11/1/91; Wouter Welling (auth), Het Poetische Theater van Michael Byron, Kunstbeeld, 91; Jurriaan Benchop (auth), Interview with Michael Byron, Metropolis M, 91. *Dealer:* Baron-Boisante 50 W 57th St New York NY 10019. *Mailing Add:* 329 Belt Ave #301B St Louis MO 63112-4512

BYRUM, DONALD ROY
EDUCATOR, PRINTMAKER
b Hertford, NC, June 19, 42. *Study:* RI Sch Design, BFA, 67; Univ Mich, MFA, 69; spec studies in lithography with John Maggio, 79. *Work:* Minn Mus Art, St Paul; Chrysler Mus Art, Norfolk, Va; BYK Gulden Lomberg Chemische Fabrik GMBH, Konstanz, WGer; Am Embassy, Madrid, Spain; Yale Univ Art Gallery. *Comn:* Etching & aquatints, comn by Dryden Gallery, NY. *Exhib:* Minn Printmakers, Minn Arts Coun, 69-70; Talent Six, Minn Mus Art, St Paul, 73; Contemp Master Prints, Winthrop Col Gallery, 76; Eastern US Print Exhib, Spirit Sq Art Ctr, NC, 79-81; Southeastern Ctr Contemp Art, Winston-Salem, NC, 80; Don Byrum-Reflections Portfolio Traveling Exhib, 81-82; Mint Mus Art, 81; New Am Graphics US State Dept Tour, 82-83; Southern Printmakers, Southern Graphics Coun, 84, 88 & 90. *Pos:* Dir & cur, Lincoln Art Gallery, Mankato State Univ, 69-74; chmn dept visual arts, Univ NC, Charlotte, 82-92; dir, Rowe Art Gallery, Univ NC, Charlotte, 83-85. *Teaching:* Asst prof printmaking, Mankato State Univ, 69-74; asst prof, 74-80, assoc prof, Univ NC, Charlotte, 80-. *Awards:* Purchase Awards, Minn Printmakers, Minn Arts Coun, 70 & NC Artists, Asheville Mus, 77; Fayetteville Mus Art Award, 79; Purchase Award, Eastern US Print Exhib, Fac Res Grant Computer Graphics, 89 & 92 & Res Leave, Computer Graphics, fall 92; Outstanding Computer Curric Award, 89. *Mem:* Nat Coun Art Adminrs; State Bd, NC Art Ed Asn; Southeastern Col Art Asn (conf comm); Conf Comt, Southeastern Col Art Conf; Col Art Asn Am; NC Art Ed Asn (State bd). *Media:* Etching & Lithography. *Dealer:* Hodges Taylor Gallery 227 N Tryon St Charlotte NC 28202. *Mailing Add:* 7801 Steele Creek Rd Charlotte NC 28217-3007

C

CABLE, MAXINE ROTH
SCULPTOR
b Philadelphia, Pa. *Study:* Tyler Sch Fine Art, Temple Univ, AA; Corcoran Sch Art, George Washington Univ, AB; Am Univ, with Hans Hofmann. *Work:* Allied Chem Corp Gallery, NY; Nat Acad Sci, Washington, DC; George Washington Univ. *Comn:* Environ sculpture, Allied Chem Corp, 69-70; sculpture, Wolf Trap Farm Performing Arts, Va, 73. *Exhib:* Area Exhibs, Corcoran Gallery Art, 55-67; Artists Equity Traveling Exhib, Columbia Mus, SC, 73-74; one-woman shows, Adams Morgan Gallery, Washington, DC, 64, Hodson Gallery, Hood Col, Frederick, Md, 69, Gallery Ten, Washington, DC, 75, 76, 79 & 83 & Art Dept, Cath Univ Am, 83. *Pos:* Dir, Glen Echo Graphics Workshop, Md, 75. *Teaching:* Consult art, Montgomery Co, Md, 57-65 & Head Start Prog, Washington, DC, 70. *Awards:* Sculpture Award, David Smith, Corcoran Gallery Art, 55; First Prize in Painting, Smithsonian Inst, 67. *Bibliog:* Washington Artists Today, Artists Equity Asn, 67; Art for Public Places, Dept Housing & Urban Develop, 73. *Media:* Mixed, Natural and Man-Made. *Mailing Add:* 7000 Buxton Terr Bethesda MD 20817-4404

CABOT, HUGH
PAINTER
b Boston, Mass, Mar 22, 1930. *Study:* Vesper George Sch Fine Arts; Boston Mus Fine Arts Sch; Col of Americas, Mexico City; Asmolean, Oxford Univ, Cambridge, England. *Work:* Univ Ariz, Tucson; Harwood Found Art, Taos, NMex; Tucson Med Ctr; Washburn Univ, Topeka, Kans; Starmont Vail Med Ctr, Topeka, Kans; Chandler Ctr Arts, Chandler, Ariz; Booth Mus Western Art, Cartersville, Ga. *Comn:* Great American Rodeo Cowboy (lifesize figure), Las Vegas Hilton Hotel, 85. *Exhib:* Korea, Mitsubichi Gallery, Tokyo, Japan, 58 & Tokyo Press Club; La Marine Americaine, Mus de la Marine, Paris, 63; Oper Palette, every maj city in free world incl Nat Gallery Art. *Pos:* official combat artist, Korean War. *Awards:* First, Second & Third Awards, Tex Tri State, 69; Artist of Year, Scottsdale, Ariz, 78. *Bibliog:* Jim Newton (auth), Those Cabots, Phoenix Gazette, 74; Meet Hugh Cabot, Ariz Living, 75; Danny Medina (auth), Hugh Cabot, Ariz Art Talk, 82; David M Brown (auth), Tubac Artist---Hugh Cabot, Greyhawk Mag, 85; Allen Scott (auth), Cabots cowboy, Tucson Lifestyle, 86; Hugh Cabot, Kathy Engle editor Green valley News, 03. *Mem:* Salmagundi Club. *Media:* Oil, Watercolor, Charcoal, Pastel. *Publ:* Auth-illusr, Korea one, Globe Publ, 1954. *Dealer:* Olivia Cabot, Hugh Cabot Gallery, # 10 Calle Iglesia, Tubac, Ariz, 85646. *Mailing Add:* PO Box 1478 Tubac AZ 85646

CADDELL, FOSTER
PAINTER, INSTRUCTOR
b Pawtucket, RI, Aug 2, 21. *Study:* RI Sch Design; pvt study with Peter Helck, Robert Brackman & Guy Wiggins. *Work:* Lyman Allyn Mus, New London, Conn; Senate Gallery Washington, DC; Brown Univ Military Libr, Providence, RI. *Comn:* Off portraits of Sen Thomas J Dodd, Washington & Judge LP Moore, US Circuit Ct Appeals, Second Dist, NY, Sen Christopher J Dodd, Washington, (only Artist to paint Offical Protraits of Father and Son US Senators, Both Hanging in Washington); portrait of Dr George S Avery, Brooklyn Botanical Gardens, NY; portrait of Carl Cuttler, Mystic Seaport Mus, Conn; relig paintings for many denominations incl Church of Eng; portraits of many bus & civic leaders. *Exhib:* Am Artists Prof League Grand Nat Exhib, 70-92; Am Watercolor Soc Ann, Nat Acad Galleries, 71; Slater Mus, Norwich Acad, 71-80; Nat Arts Club, NY, 73-80; Pastel Soc of Am, 85-2004; Conn Pastel Soc, 85-2005; one-man show, Providence Art Club, 48 & 63, Slater Mem Mus, Norwich Free Acad, 76 & Heritage Plantations, Sandwich, Mass, 85; Soc Rep Pastellistes De France & Inst Exhib, Lille, France, 87; Acad Fine Arts, Beijing, China, 97. *Pos:* Lithograph artist, Providence Lithograph Co, 39-51; artist with Far East Air Force, 43-46. *Teaching:* Instr, Foster Caddell's Art Sch, currently. *Awards:* Best Show, Conn Pastel Soc, 89 and awards 90, 94, 98, 99, & 2001-2003, 2004, 2005; Grumbacher Award, Pastel Soc Am, 91 & 2005, Master Panelist, 97 & elected to Hall of Fame, 98; Allied Artist Award, Pastel Soc Am, 94; Conn Soc of Portrait Artist Lifetime Achievement Award, 2005; and many others. *Bibliog:* David Lewis (ed), Landscape Painting Techniques, Watson-Guptill, 84; Madlyn Woolwich (ed), Pastel Interpretations, Northlight, 93; Madelyn Woolwich (ed), The Art of Pastel Portraiture, Watson-Guptill, 96. *Mem:* Am Portrait Soc; Am Artists Prof League; Acad Artists Am; Salmagundi Club; Pastel Soc Am; Lyme Art Asn (Elected Life Member); and others. *Media:* Oil, Pastel. *Interests:* Collecting Antique Arms. *Publ:* Illusr, series sports bks, Little, Brown & Co; auth & illusr, Keys to Successful Landscape Painting, 76, Keys to Successful Color & Keys to Painting Better Portraits, 82, Pitman & Sons, London & Watson-Guptill; Foster Caddell's Keys to Successful Landscape Painting, Northlight, 93; The Best of Pastels II, 98; The Best of Sketching & Drawing, Rockport Publ, 98; contrib to work on websites; Pastel Jour, 2000; Pastel Artist Internat, 2002. *Dealer:* Court Yard Gallery, 12 Water St Mystic Ct 06355. *Mailing Add:* Northlight 47 Pendleton Hill Rd Voluntown CT 06384

CADE, WALTER, III
PAINTER, COLLAGE ARTIST
b New York, NY, Jan 17, 36. *Study:* Inst Mod Art, NY. *Work:* City of Miami Beach, Fla; Va Beach Art Mus; Rockefeller Found; Bruce Mus; Fine Arts Mus of the South; Nat Mus Am Art Smithsonian Inst. *Exhib:* Art Ann, 69-70, Contemp Black Artists in Am, 71, Whitney Mus Am Art, NY; Corcoran Gallery, Washington, 72; one-man shows, Ocean Co Col, 77, Jackson State Univ, 80 & Olin Mus Art, Bates Col, Maine, 93; Miss Mus Art, Jackson, 81; Tampa Mus, Fla, 82; Tuscon Mus Art, Ariz, 83; Two-person show, Lewiston-Auburn Col, Maine, 93; group shows, New Eng Fine Arts Inst, Mass, 93 & Lewiston-Auburn Col, Maine, 94. *Awards:* First Prize, Fine Arts Mus South, Mobile, Ala, 82; Best in Show, Bruce Mus, Greenwich, Conn, 84 & 94. *Bibliog:* Article in The Florida Arts Gazette, 5/80; article in The Christian Sci Monitor, 7/93; article in Maine Sunday Telegram, 9/93. *Media:* Acrylic, Collage. *Dealer:* Sanda Webster Gallery 2018 Locust St Philadelphia PA 19103. *Mailing Add:* 172-03 119th Ave Jamaica NY 11434

CADIEUX, MICHAEL EUGENE
EDUCATOR, PAINTER
b Missoula, Mont, June 15, 40. *Study:* Univ Mont, BA & MA. *Work:* Univ Mont Fine Arts Collection, Missoula; Yuma Fine Arts Asn, Ariz. *Exhib:* Spokane-Pac NW Ann, Cheney Cowles Mus, 66; SW Yuma Fine Arts, 66-68; Ariz Ann, Phoenix Art Mus, 67; Tucson Art Mus Ann, Ariz, 68; Mid-Am, Nelson-Atkins Mus, Kansas City, Mo, 72, 30 Miles, 75; Mid-Am, St Louis Art Mus, 72; Davidson Nat Drawing, Davidson Col Galleries, 75. *Collection Arranged:* Univ Wis Ctr Syst, 67; Univ Md, 67; Western Asn

Art Mus Traveling Exhib, 69; fac shows, Spiva Art Ctr, Memphis Acad, 75-78; Mo Art Coun-Mid Am Arts Alliance Shows. *Pos:* Reviewer art publ, SE Asia in Rev, 76-. *Teaching:* Instr painting & drawing, Ariz Western Col, Yuma, 66-69; assoc prof art hist, Kansas City Art Inst, Mo, 69-. *Awards:* Third Place, 2nd Southwestern, Yuma Fine Arts, 67; Grant Study in India, US Off Educ, 71. *Bibliog:* Donald Hoffman (auth), Here's Art all in a row, Kansas City Star, 72 & Michael Cadieux, Kansas City Star, 77. *Media:* Painting Collage. *Res:* Cross-cultural art history. *Publ:* Auth, The mural tradition in Indian painting, SE Asia in Rev, 77. *Mailing Add:* Dept Art Hist Kansas City Art Institute 4415 Warwick Kansas City MO 64111

CADILLAC, LOUISE ROMAN
PAINTER, INSTRUCTOR
b Central City, Pa. *Study:* Univ Northern Colo, BA, 54, MA, 64; with Sylvia Glass, Calif, Gene Matthews, Colo & Chen Chi, NY. *Work:* Denver Public Libr Western Hist Div; Jefferson Sch Credit Union, Lakewood, Colo; Jewish Community Ctr, Denver; Leroy Springs & Co, Myrtle Beach, SC. *Exhib:* Metrop Exhib, Denver Art Mus, 60; Rocky Mountain Nat Watermedia, Foothills Art Ctr, Golden, Colo, 74-91; Nat Watercolor Soc, Palm Springs Mus Fine Art, Calif, 82-93; solo exhib, Univ Northern Colo, 84; Nat Acad Design, NY, 86 & 88; Am Watercolor Soc, NY, 92-94. *Pos:* Juror, Painting Competitions, Critic & Group Sessions. *Teaching:* Instr sec & elem art, Jefferson Co Pub Sch, Lakewood, Colo, 57-67, adaptive art specialist, 74-83; instr, Watermedia Workshops; Dillman's Sand Lake, Wis; Acapulco with Flying Colors Workshops; Leech Studio, Sarasota, Fla; Ed Day Gallery Workshops, Ont, Can; Italy and Greece with Flying Colors Workshop. *Awards:* Rocky Mountain Nat Watermedia Top Award, Foothills Art Ctr, 91; Gold Medal of Honor, Am Watercolor Soc, 92; Leila Gardin Sawyer Award, Nat Acad Design, New York, 86 & 88. *Bibliog:* Watercolors for Grades 4, 5 & 6 (film), KRMA TV, Denver Pub Sch, 75. *Mem:* Nat Watercolor Soc; Rocky Mountain Nat Watermedia Soc; Am Watercolor Soc; Soc Experimental Artists. *Media:* Watermedia, Mixed Media. *Publ:* Artists Mag, 92; Splash I & II & IV, 92, 93 & 95; Judging Watermedia Competitions and Your Workshop Dollars, Watercolor, spring 96 & Loosen Up, fall 96; Art Clinic, Professional art instructors evaluate your work, Artist's Mag, 3/99. *Dealer:* Edward Day Gallery Kingston Ont K7L 2Z4 Canada. *Mailing Add:* 880 S Dudley St Lakewood CO 80226

CADY, DENNIS VERN
CONSERVATOR, PAINTER
b Portland, Ore, Nov 10, 44. *Study:* Portland State Univ; Brooklyn Mus Art Sch, (Max Beckman Mem Grant), Painting & drawing with Rubin Tam, 69-71; Pratt Inst Graphic Ctr; Empire State Col, BS, plus independent study of tech aspects of paper restoration; Margo Fieden Galleries, New York, apprenticeship in restoration and preserv of works on paper, 74-77. *Work:* Franklin Furnace, NY; NY Publ Libr, South Street Seaport Mus; South Street Seaport Mus, NY; Univ Toronto, Can. *Comn:* Poster, 72, costumes for dance (with Frank Garcia), 74, costumes, 77, Phillis Lamhut Dance Co; poster, Emery Hermans Dance Theatre, 75, sets & props, Murray Louis Dance Co, 76. *Exhib:* One-man shows, Brownstone Gallery, Brooklyn, NY, 91, Mapletree Gallery, Pauling, NY, 94, Gallery at Hunter Mountain, NY, 94; Regional Art Ann, Schenectady Mus Art, 92; Kelmscott Gallery, Cold Springs, NY, 93; Catskill Watercolors, Gallery at Hunter Mountain, NY, 93; Millbrook Gallery, NY, 94; Greene Co Arts Coun Landscape Show, Chatham, NY, 94. *Pos:* Freelance restorer, New York, 77-. *Awards:* Nat Scholastics Award, New York, 62; America the Beautiful Fund Grant, 91. *Bibliog:* The Print Collector's News Letter, XV, 4, 9/84 & 10/84; Dennis Cady (auth), Amy Winter, Nature Imitates Art, Brownstone Gallery, Brooklyn, NY, 91. *Media:* Oil, Watercolor. *Publ:* Auth, Block Prints by Dennis Cady, Hillside Ctr, Portland, Ore, 71; Wall Street Blue Prints by Dennis Cady, Baun Printshop, New York, 84. *Dealer:* Art Adv Serv Inc New York NY; Art Planning Consult New York NY. *Mailing Add:* 57 Courtney Ave Newburgh NY 12550-6303

CADY, SAMUEL LINCOLN
PAINTER, INSTRUCTOR
b Boothbay Harbor, Maine, July 21, 43. *Study:* Univ NH, Durham, BA, 65; Ind Univ, Bloomington, MFA, 67. *Work:* Addison Gallery Am Art, Andover, Mass; Prudential Insurance Co, Newark; Pac Securities Int Bank, Los Angeles, Calif; Gen Elec, Fairfield, Conn; Peabody Essex Mus, Salem, Mass; Butler Inst, Youngstown, Ohio; Orlando Mus of Art, FL; Farnsworth Art Mus, Rockland, Maine; Portland Art Mus, Portland, Maine. *Comn:* NH State Percent for Art Prog, Laconia Vocational Tech. *Exhib:* Whitney Biennial (with catalog), Whitney Mus Am Art, NY, 75; solo exhibs, Holly Solomon Gallery, NY, 76, 78-80, 83 & 84, Hampshire Col, Amherst, Mass, 78, Capricorn Gallery, Bethesda, Md, 79, Castelli-Goodman-Solomon Gallery, E Hampton, NY, 82 & Fujii Gallery (with catalog), Tokyo, 84 & 88, Round Top Ctr Arts, Damariscotta, Maine, 94, Howard Yeserski Gallery, Boston, 90, 94 & 96 & Mary Ryan Gallery, NY, 94, 98 & 2004, Barbara Gillman Gallery, Miami Beach, Fla, 95, Yezerski Gallery, 2000, 2002, Caldbeck Gallery, 2001, 2003 & 2005 Portland Mus of Art, Maine, Mapping Maine, Portland Mus of Art, Biennial, 1998, 2003 & 2005, Univ Maine Mus Art, Bangor, 2006; Retrospective Exhib, 1966-1986, Addison Gallery Am Art (with catalog), 87; Gwenda Jay Gallery, Chicago, 89; Mainstream Am: The Collection of Philip Desind, Ohio, 87 & Masters of The Masters, Sch Vis Arts Fac, Butler Inst, Youngstown, Ohio, 98; On the edge: 40 yrs of Maine Painting, Maine Coast Artists Gallery, Rockport, 92; Islands, Caldbeck Gallery, Rockland, Maine, 97 & 99; Work of the 90's. *Teaching:* Instr drawing, painting & printmaking, Univ NH, Durham, 68-69; instr grad workshop, Sch Visual Arts, NY, 84-. *Bibliog:* Ken Greenleaf (auth), Cady, A native son, forges images into icons, Maine Sunday Telegram, 8/94; Cate McQuaid (auth), Angels come down to earth, Boston Globe, (9/26/96); Ken Johnson (auth), rev, NY Times, (5/8/98); Cate McQuade (auth), rev, Boston Globe, (9/14/2000, 9/20/2002); Edgar Allen Beem (auth), Back home in friendship, Down East Mag, (9/2002); Grace Glueck (auth), NY Times, (11/12/2004); Harpers Mag, reproductive edition, (1/2005); Edward Gomez (auth), Art & Antiques, (2/2005); Cynthia Nadelman (auth), Art News, (3/2005). *Media:* Oil on Canvas, Silkscreen. *Interests:* Boating, hiking. *Publ:* Contrib, Inner/Urban, First St Forum, St Louis, Mo, 81; Time Out: Sport and Leisure in America Today, Tampa Mus, Fla, 83; Fujii Gallery (with catalog), Tokyo, Japan, 84 & 88; Addison Gallery Am Art Retrospective (with catalog) Andover, Mass, 87. *Dealer:* Howard Yezerski Gallery 14 Newbury St Boston MA 02116; Mary Ryan Gallery 525 W 26th St New York NY 10001; Caldbeck Gallery Rockland 12 Elm St Maine 04841. *Mailing Add:* Box 208 Friendship ME 04547

CAFFERY, DEBBIE FLEMING
PHOTOGRAPHER
b Mar 6, 48. *Study:* San Francisco Art Inst, BFA, 75. *Work:* Mus Mod Art, NY; Metrop Mus Art, NY; Mus Photog Arts, San Diego, Calif; George Eastman House, Rochester, NY; Smithsonian Inst. *Exhib:* Mus Photog Arts, San Diego, 89; Carry Me Home, Nat Mus Am Hist, Smithsonian Inst, 90; O'Coracao Da Cienca, Centros Estudo Photographie, Coimbra, Port, 91; Visages, Paysages et Autves Rivages, Centre Art Contemporain, Brussels, Belg, 92; Photo Essays from the South, Ctr Creative Photog, Tucson, Ariz, 92; The South by its Photographers, Burmingham Mus Art, 96. *Pos:* Frelance Photogr & teacher. *Awards:* Governor's Art Award, La, 89; Lou Stouman Prize Photog, San Diego Mus Photog Arts, 96-97. *Bibliog:* Debbie Fleming Caffery, Carry Me Home, Smithsonian Press, 90. *Publ:* Double take, Ctr Photog, Duke Univ, 96. *Dealer:* Howard Greenberg Gallery 120 Wooster New York NY. *Mailing Add:* 105 Washington St Breaux Bridge LA 70517

CAHANA, ALICE LOK
PAINTER
b Budapest, Hungary, Feb 7, 29; US citizen. *Study:* Talpiot Teachers Col, Tel Aviv, 49-51; independent studies, Boras, Sweden, 51-56; Univ Houston, Tex, 61-66; Rice Univ, with prof Joe Tate, Dadi Virz, Bob Camblin & Basilous Poulos, 69-77. *Work:* US Holocaust Mem Mus, Washington; Sarvar-Auschwitz (diptych), Yad Vashem, Jerusalem, 95. *Comn:* The Wollstein Family, 2005. *Exhib:* From Ashes to the Rainbow--A Tribute to Raoul Wallenberg, Skirball, Los Angeles, 87; Rotunda US Cong, 87; Pa Acad Fine Art, 88; Sacred Text, B'nai Brith Klutznic Nat Jewish Mus, Washington, 95; Remembering not to forget, Holocaust Mus, Houston, 96. *Awards:* To Everything there is a Season (mono print), presented to Pres Carter, Pres Sadat & Prime Minister Begin, to hon Israel-Egypt peace treaty, 79; recognized by Pres Clinton, nat gathering Holocaust survivors, 95. *Bibliog:* Triumph of the Spirit (video), EDAR, PBS, Baltimore, 95; Pres Clinton tribute & art presentation, CBS, Yad Vashem, Jerusalem, 95; Steven Spielberg (dir), The last Days (film), 98-99. *Media:* Acrylic, Mixed Media. *Mailing Add:* 9002 Ferris Houston TX 77096

CAHILL, JAMES FRANCIS
HISTORIAN, EDUCATOR
b Ft Bragg, Calif, Aug 13, 26. *Study:* Univ Calif, Berkeley, BA, 50; Univ Mich, with Max Loehr, MA(Louise Wallace Hackney Scholar, 50-52), 53, PhD(Fulbright Scholar, 54-55), 58. *Collection Arranged:* Guest-dir, The Art of Southern Sung China (with catalog), Asia House Gallery, New York, 62, Fantastics and Eccentrics in Chinese Painting (with catalog), 67 & Scholar-Painters of Japan: The Nanga School (with catalog), 72. *Pos:* Cur Chinese art, Freer Gallery Art, Washington, DC, 58-65. *Teaching:* Prof hist art, Univ Calif, Berkeley, 65-96. *Awards:* Louise Wallace Hackney Scholar, 50-52; Fulbright Scholar, 54-55; Guggenheim Fel, 72-73; Charles Eliot Norton Prof Poetry, Harvard Univ, 78-79. *Mem:* Col Art Asn Am. *Res:* Chinese and Japanese painting; Chinese bronzes. *Publ:* Auth, Chinese Painting, Skira, Geneva, Switz, 60; coauth, The Freer Chinese Bronzes, 67; auth, Hills Beyond a River: Chinese Painting of the Yuan Dynasty, 76; Parting at the Shore, Chinese Painting of the Early & Middle Ming Dynasty, 78. *Mailing Add:* 1515 Josephine St Berkeley CA 94703

CAI, GUO-QIANG
CONCEPTUAL ARTIST, SCULPTOR
b Fujian Quanzhan, China, Dec 8, 57. *Study:* Shanghai Drama Inst, BA (stage design), 85; Univ Tsukuda, 89-91. *Work:* Guggenheim Mus; Kroller-Muller Mus, Holland; Contemp Art Mus, Tokyo, Japan; Cartier Foundacion pour l'art Contemporian, Paris, France; Mod Mus Stockholm, Sweden; Mus Modern Art, NY; Fonds Nat d'Art Contemp & Mus du Contemp, Lyon, France; Ludwig Found; Riiksmuseum, Kröller-Müller, Arnheim, The Neth. *Comn:* True Collection (gun powder drawings), SMAK Mus van Hedendaags Kunst Gent, Belg, 96; Percent for Art Proj, Bronx Criminal Court, NY, 98, Pub Sculpture/Installation, New York City, 2000; Permanent Installation (outdoor), Naoshima Contemp Art Mus, Japan, 98; Crystal Tower (sculpture), Nat Gallery Australia, 2000; Onestone pub sculpture/installation, City of New York, 2000. *Exhib:* Project to Extend the Great Wall of China by 10,000 meters, Gobi Desert, Jiayuguan City, China, 93; Hugo Boss Prize 1996, Solomon Guggenheim Mus, NY, 96; Future Past Present, 47th Venice Biennial, Italy, 97; Flying Dragon in the Heavens, La Mus, Denmark, 97; Cult Melting Bath: Projects for 20th Century, Queens Mus Art, NY, 97; Inside Out: New Chinese Art, San Francisco Mus Modern Art, Calif, 98; I Am the Y2K Bug, Kunsthalle Wien, Vienna, Austria, 99; Open End (with catalog), Mus Modern Art, NY, 2000; Biennale of Sydney 2000, Art Gallery New S Wales, Australia, 2000; one-man show, 69th Regent Armory, NY, 2000, Contemp Art Gallery, Vancouver, Can, 2001, Musee d'art Contemporain Lyon, France, 2001, Shanghai Art Mus, China, 2002, Hakone Open Air Mus, Japan, 2002, Mus Modern Art, NY, 2002, Galleria Civica di Arte Contempoanea Trento, Italy, 2002 & Tate Modern, London, Eng, 2003; 2000 Bienniel Exhibition (with catalog), Whitney Mus Am Art, NY, 2000; Outbound, Houston Contemp Arts Mus, Tex, 2000; Form Follows Fiction (with catalog), Castello di Rivoli Museo d'Arte Contemporanea, Turin, Italy, 2001; The Power of Art - The 2nd, Prefectural Mus Art, Hyogo, Japan, 2002; Royal Acad Art, London, 2002; Ce Qui Arrive (with catalog),

Fondation Cartier pour l'art contemporain, Paris, 2002. *Awards:* Oribe Award, Japan, 97; Venice Biennial Int Award, 99; Alpert Award, CalArts, 2001. *Bibliog:* Dawei Fei (auth), Cai Guo-Qiang, 2000; Marek Bartelik (auth), Cai Guo-Quing - Shanghai Art Museum, Art Forum, 2002; Dana Friis-Hansen & others (auth) Cai Guo-Qiang, Phaidon Press Ltd, 2002. *Media:* Installation Art. *Mailing Add:* 46 Great Jones St Apt 5 New York NY 10012-1162

CAIN, DAVID PAUL
PAINTER, INSTRUCTOR
b Indianapolis, Ind, Oct 14, 28. *Study:* Univ NMex, Albuquerque, 48-49; Earlham Col, Richmond, Ind, BA, 50; Madison Art Sch, Conn, 79. *Work:* Old Jailhouse Found, Austin, Tex; Int Ctr Photog, NY. *Exhib:* US Army Art Show, European Command, Munich, Ger, 52; one-man shows, Earlham Col, Ind, Aiden House, Mass, Yale U, Conn, and others. *Teaching:* Teacher art & photog, Grove Sch, Madison, Conn, 70-74; teacher art, Lincoln High Sch, San Jose, Costa Rica, 75; photog. teachr, Guilford Art Sch, Conn, 76-77; instr oil painting, Meridian Art Gallery, Conn, 78- & Hamden Arts Comn, Conn, 78-. *Mem:* Brownstone Group, Meriden, Conn; Guilford Art League, Conn; Madison Art Soc, Conn (pres, 81-); Mt Carmel Art Asn. *Media:* All. *Dealer:* Fischer Gallery Boston St Guilford Conn 06437. *Mailing Add:* PO Box 5421 Hamden CT 06518

CAIN, JOSEPH ALEXANDER
PAINTER, EDUCATOR
b Henderson, Tenn, May 27, 20. *Study:* Univ Calif, Berkeley, BA, 47, MA, 48. *Work:* Butler Inst Am Art, Youngstown, Ohio; Nat Watercolor Soc Collection; Witte Mus, San Antonio, Tex; Univ Utah Permanent Collection; Laguna Gloria Mus, Austin, Tex. *Comn:* Oil mural, CofC, Corpus Christi, Tex, 59; mosaic mural, comn by Freeman Martin, Spohn Hosp, 62; mosaic murals, comn by Joe Williams, Buccaneer Bowl, 65. *Exhib:* Philadelphia Watercolor Club Exhib, Pa Acad Fine Arts, 65; Butler Inst Am Art Mid-Year Ann, 65; Southwestern Watercolor Soc Regional Show, Dallas, 69; Nat Watercolor Soc Ann, Los Angeles, 69; Watercolor USA, Springfield Art Mus, Mo, 73; Am Painters in Paris, 75; Nat Acad of Design, NY, 77-78. *Pos:* Critic, Art News and Reviews, Corpus Christi Caller-Times, 56-74. *Teaching:* Prof art, Del Mar Col, 50-82, chmn dept, 66-82. *Awards:* Juror's Award of Merit, Pa Festival Art, Pa State Univ, 79; Best in Show, 7th Ann Div Show, Corpus Christi Art Ctr; Top Award, 68th Ann Nat Show, Tex Fine Arts Asn. *Mem:* Fel Royal Soc Arts; Nat Watercolor Soc; Tex Fine Arts Asn (third vpres, 77-78); Tex Watercolor Soc (third vpres, 71-72); Nat Soc Painters Acrylics & Casein; Tex Fine Arts Asn (regional dir, 70). *Media:* Acrylic, Watercolor. *Publ:* Auth, The Ten, Art Voices-South, 3/78. *Mailing Add:* 402 Troy Dr Corpus Christi TX 78412-2716

CAISERMAN-ROTH, GHITTA
PAINTER, PRINTMAKER
b Montreal, Que, Mar 2, 23. *Study:* Parsons Sch Design, BA; Art Students League; Ecole Beaux-Arts, with Albert Dumouchel & Jennifer Dickson. *Work:* Montreal Mus Fine Arts; Vancouver Art Gallery, BC; Confederation Art Gallery, Charlottetown, PEI; London Pub Libr & Art Mus, Ont; Beaverbrook Art Gallery, Fredericton, NB; and others. *Comn:* Hommage a Dumouchel, Univ Que Press, 72; and others. *Exhib:* Expo '67, 67; Joint Int Exhib, Soc Can Etcher-Painters & Engravers & Can Soc Graphic Arts, 70; group show, Can Embassy, DC, 70; one-person show, Waddington Galleries, Montreal, 70; Dominion Gallery, Montreal, Can. *Teaching:* Instr art, Concordia Univ, 60, Queen's Univ, 63 & Saidye Bronfman Ctr, Montreal, 70; John Abbott Col, 88. *Awards:* Can Govt Centennial Medal, 67; Fel Eplor, Can Coun, 88; and others; Gov Gen Painting Award, 2000. *Mem:* Can Soc Painter Etchers; Can Soc Graphic Art; Royal Can Acad Art; Can Coun; Graphia 3710 Inc. *Media:* Acrylic; Mixed, Graphics. *Publ:* Auth, Ghitta Caiserman-Roth (paintings & drawings), 88; Insights, Discoveries, Surprizes (with Rhoda Cohen), McGill Queens Press, 93. *Dealer:* Galerie J P Borduas Montreal; Galerie Jean Claude Bergeron

CAIVANO, ERNESTO
ARTIST
b Madrid, Spain, 72. *Study:* The Cooper Union, BFA, 99; Columbia Univ, MFA, 2001. *Exhib:* Exhibs incl Group, Intercontinental Gallery, Montreal, Can, 1999, Part 01, Wallach Gallery, New York City, 2000, Thesis Exhib, Columbia Univ, New York City, 2001, Medium, Roy Neiman Gallery, New York City, 2001, Miami Ambassador, Fredric Snitzer Gallery, Miami, Fla, 2002, Shallow Interiors, Rivington Arms Gallery, New York City, 2002, Amenities, Gershwin Hotel, New York City, 2002, My Sources Say Yes, Guild & Greyshkul, New York City, 2003, Terrarium, Bronx River Art Ctr, NY, 2003, Druid Wood as a Superconductor, Space 101, Brooklyn, 2003, Game Over, Grimm/Rosenfeld, Munich, 2003, New Topography, Geoffrey Young Gallery, Great Barrington, Mass, 2003; Group Show, Grant/Selwyn Fine Art, Los Angeles, 2003, St Valentine's Day Massacre, 85 Chambers, New York City, 2003, Placemaker Gallery, Miami, 2004, PS1 Contemp Art Ctr, Long Island, 2004, Whitney Biennial, Whitney Mus Am Art, 2004 Summer Drawing Exhib, David Zwirner Gallery, New York City, 2004; one-man shows incl Arboreal, 31 Grand Inc, Brooklyn, 2003, Mating Grounds, Richard Heller Gallery, Los Angeles, 2004. *Awards:* Recipient Joan Sovern award, 2000, 2001; Hayward prize, Am Austrian Found, 2001 & 2002; Salzburg Kunstakademie Fel, 2002. *Mailing Add:* 48 Eldridge St #6E New York NY 10002

CAJERO, MICHAEL RAY
ENVIRONMENTAL ARTIST, SCULPTOR
b Tucson, Ariz, May 26, 47. *Study:* Univ Ariz, BFA(studio art), 69; Kent State, MFA(drawing, painting & art hist), 76. *Exhib:* Alumni exhib, Mus Art, Univ Ariz, Tucson, 85; solo exhib, Shemer Art Ctr, Scottsdale, Ariz, 89; The Death Cart, Roswell Mus Art, NMex & Central Arts Collective, Tucson, Ariz, 90; Human Components - Light Altars, Mus Art, Univ Ariz, Tucson, 92; The Painted Bride, A Triangular Rotation, Philadelphia, 93. *Teaching:* Part-time instr drawing & design, Community Servs Campus, Pima Community Col, Tucson, Ariz, 77-94; instr drawing & sculpting, Tucson Mus Art Sch, Ariz, 84-; adj prof drawing & design, Pima Community Col, 99-. *Awards:* Nat Endowment Arts Visual Arts Fel, 93-94; Artist in Residence Fel, Tucson Partnership Inc, 93; Pima Arts Coun Visual Arts Fel, Tucson, 94; New Genre fel, Tucson. *Bibliog:* Wesley A Rusnell (auth), Invitational Exhib, Roswell Mus Art, 90. *Media:* Installation, Environments. *Mailing Add:* 408 N Fremont Tucson AZ 85719

CAJORI, CHARLES F
PAINTER
b Palo Alto, Calif, Mar 9, 1921. *Study:* Colorado Springs Fine Arts Ctr; Cleveland Art Sch; Columbia Univ; Skowhegan Sch Painting & Sculpture. *Work:* Corcoran Gallery Art; Mitchner Collection, Univ Tex, Austin; Walker Art Ctr, Minneapolis; Whitney Mus Am Art, NY; Metrop Mus, NY; Hirshhorn Mus, Washington. *Exhib:* Decade of Am Drawings, Whitney Mus Am Art, 65; Solo exhibs, Landmark Gallery, 75 & 81, Ingber Gallery, 76, NY, Gross McCleaf Gallery, Philadelphia, 83 & 85, Am Univ, Washington, 88 & NY Studio Sch, NY, 88, 2000, Cent Conn State Univ, 92, Dartmouth Col, 96, Wright State Univ, Dayton, Ohio, 2004, Lohin-Geduld Gallery, New York City, 2004, David Findlay Gallery, New York City, 2005; Loeb Ctr, NY Univ, 70 & Artists Choice Mus, NY, 83 & 84; Conn Painters, Wadsworth Atheneum; Conn Artists, Bruce Mus, Greenwich; Conn Now, New Britain Mus. *Teaching:* Instr drawing & painting, Cooper Union Art Sch, 56-65; instr drawing & painting, NY Studio Sch, 64-; emer prof, Queens Col, Flushing, NY, 86-. *Awards:* Nat Endowment Arts, 81; Benjamin Altman Figure Prize, Nat Acad Design, New York, 83, 87 & 94; Guggenheim Fel, 2001. *Bibliog:* Interview in Transfer, fall-winter 89/90; Andrew Forge (auth), About Cajori's Paintings, CCSU Exhibition Catalogue, 92; Martica Sawin (auth), exhib catalog, NY Studio Sch, 2000. *Mem:* Col Art Asn Am; Nat Acad Design (assoc, 82, acad, 87). *Media:* Oil. *Dealer:* David Findlay Jr Gallery 41 E 57th St NY NY 10022; Lohin Geduld Gallery 531 W 25th St NY NY 10001. *Mailing Add:* 2338 Litchfield Rd Watertown CT 06795

CALABRO, JOANNA SONDRA
PAINTER, SCULPTOR
b Waterbury, Conn. *Study:* Paier Col Art, 65-66; Rice Univ, 77; studied with Bruno Lucchesi, Italy, 82. *Work:* US Embassies, Braitislava, Slovakia; Ambassador Theodore E Russell pvt collection. *Comn:* Sculpture, comn by Graham Doorland, Airborne Express, Seattle, Wash, 84. *Exhib:* Juried exhib, Champions Art Show, Houston, Tex, 74 & Art League Houston, 74, 76 & 77; one-woman show, Wilmington Col, Ohio, 83 & Rockport Art Asn, Mass, 89-92; Salmagundi Art Club Nat Show, NY, 84; N Am Sculpture Exhib, Golden, Colo, 85. *Pos:* Juror, numerous art shows in Conn, Tex, Ohio & Mass, 70-98; bd selectman, Rockport Art Coun, 94. *Teaching:* Instr sculpture & painting, Five Star Gallery, Houston, Tex, 74-76. *Awards:* First Place Award, Am Pen & Brush Women, 75; Martha Moore Award, Rockport Art Asn, 89 & Excellence in Any Medium, 98. *Bibliog:* Kit Van Cleave (auth), Winning a Struggle, SW Art, 78. *Mem:* Am Artist Prof League; Rockport Art Asn; Am Medallic Sculpture Asn; Copley Soc; Guild Boston Artists. *Media:* Oil; Clay, Metal. *Publ:* Contrib, Goddesses for Every Season, Element Books, 95; Best of Oil Painting, Rockport Publ, 96; Portrait Inspirations, Quarry Books, 97; Arts Pleides N, Pleiades Publ, 97; A Gallery of Marine Art, Rockport Publ, 98. *Dealer:* Fine Arts Rockport Gallery 49-B Main St Rockport MA 01966

CALABRO, RICHARD PAUL
SCULPTOR, PAINTER
b Yonkers, NY, June 27, 1937. *Study:* Univ Ga, BLA, 62; Sch Visual Arts, New York, 66; Pa State Univ, MFA, 68. *Work:* Pa State Univ Mus, State College, Pa; Univ Mass, Amherst; Mus Mod Art, NY; Venice Video Libr, Italy. *Exhib:* Information, Mus Mod Art, NY, 70; solo exhibs, Henri Gallery, Washington, DC, 70, Max Hutchinson Gallery, NY, NY, 72 & Shippee Gallery, NY, 85 & 86; Categorizing (solo exhib), Moore Col Art, Philadelphia, Pa, 75; Lenore Gray Gallery, Providence, RI, 88. *Teaching:* Prof sculpture, Univ RI, 68-. *Awards:* Fulbright Fel, 68; Nat Endowment Arts Grant, 77; RI State Arts Coun Grant, 79 & 88. *Dealer:* Shippee Gallery 41 E 57th St New York NY. *Mailing Add:* 119 Boon St Narragansett RI 02882

CALAMAR, GLORIA
PAINTER
b New York, NY, Sept 7, 21. *Study:* Otis Art Inst, Los Angeles, 39-43; Art Students League, scholar, 43-45, State Univ NY, New Paltz, BA(art hist), 69-70. *Work:* Nat Mus Am Art, Washington; Santa Barbara Mus, Calif; Mt St Mary Col; Art Students League. *Exhib:* Solo exhibs, Mus d' Art Moderne dela Ville de Paris, France, 67, Univ Calif, Berkeley, 69, Georgetown Univ, 74, Alkamal Gallery, Jerusalem, Israel, 81 & Beaux Arts Ctr, Tunis, Tunisia, 81; Los Angeles Mus Art, 54; Bertrand Russel Centenary Invitational, London, 72-73; Drawings & Watercolors of India, Swastika Gallery, Jaisalmer India, 84; Victorian Houses, Humboldts Finest Gallery, Eureka, Calif, 88; Lighthouses, Starr King Gallery, Unitarian Church, San Francisco, Calif, 88; Santa Barbara Faulkner Gallery, 92, 93 & 94. *Teaching:* Instr studio courses & art hist, Orange Co Community Col, 63-68 & Santa Barbara City Col, 75-79; art hist, Mt St Mary Col, New York, 68-69; instr drawing, Univ Calif, Santa Barbara, 79. *Awards:* Nat Endowment Arts Grant, 80-81; Residency Grant, Dorland Mountain Art Colony, Temecular, Calif, 83; Award, Santa Barbara Visual Artists League, 92-96. *Bibliog:* A gift is indicated, Trumpeteer Mag, 49; Gloria Calamar has affinity for her subject, Am Artist Mag, 4/69. *Mem:* life mem, Woodstock Art Asn; life mem, Art Students League NY; charter mem, Artists' Equity Asn, NY. *Media:* Watercolor, Oil. *Publ:* Auth, The Adventuress a Remarkable Travel Experience, Independent News Alliance, 69; Palette Talk, Grumbacker, Publ, #28; Kalavita: A Little Town Where a Clock Never Moves; Tar Pits Park Landmark Proposal, Santa Barbara Co Hist Landmark Adv Comn. *Mailing Add:* Studio 12 227 W de la Guerre Santa Barbara CA 93101

CALDERON, EDUARDO T
PHOTOGRAPHER
b Arequipa, Peru, Aug 19, 49; US citizen. *Study:* Univ Wash, BA, 72. *Work:* Bibliot Nat de France, Paris; Mus, Carnavalet, Paris; Whatcom Mus, Bellingham, Wash; Seattle Arts Comn; King Co Arts Comn, Seattle, Wash; Seattle Mus, Seattle, WA; Microsoft Coll, Redmond, VA. *Comn:* Portraits of Jazz Musicians, Port of Seattle, 92; Poetry & Photog in the Buses, Seattle Metrotransit, 96; 4 Culture, Seattle, WA: Brightwater H2O treatment plant, 2004. *Exhib:* One-man shows, Burk Mus, Seattle, 82, Whatcom Mus, Bellingham Wash, 82, Eastern Wash Univ Art Gallery, 87, Port Angeles Fine Arts Ctr, Wash, 92, Kirkland Arts Ctr, 92-93, Sea-First Gallery, Seattle, 93, Esther Claypool Gallery, Wash, 2000, 02, William Traver Gallery, Wash, 93, 95 & 98; Seattle Art Mus, 79 & 96; Western Front, Vancouver, BC, 84; Fisher Gallery, Los Angeles, 84; group exhibs, Sun Valley Ctr for the Arts, Idaho, 2000, Genisis Loci, Mahlum Archit, Wash, 2002; solo exhib, Photog Ctr, NW Seattle, WA, 2004. *Pos:* Artist-in-residence photog, Wash Arts Comn, 86-88. *Awards:* Artist Fel, Nat Endowment Arts, 93; Travel Grant, Arts Intl, 93; Govs Writer Award, Wash State, 94; Artist Trust fel, Seattle, 98; Artist Trust Gap Grant, Artist Trust of Wash, 2001. *Bibliog:* Regina Hackett (auth), Seattle Post Intellegencer, 87, 93, 2001 & 2002; Kirby Olson (auth), Surrealism in Peru, Reflex, 88; Jake Seniuk (auth), People & places, On Center, 92. *Mem:* Artist Trust. *Media:* Black & White Photography. *Publ:* illusr, Spirit & Ancestor, Univ Wash, 87; contribr, Artists a la napoule, Editions du cygne, 93; coauth, Jackson Street after hours, Sasquatch, 93; Zyzzyva, summer 96; Photo Metro, spring 96; A Millenium Reflection, Univ Wash Press, 99. *Dealer:* Esther Claypool Gallery, Seattle

CALDWELL, ELEANOR
JEWELER, EDUCATOR
b Kansas City, Mo, May 1, 27. *Study:* Southwest Mo State Univ, Springfield, BS in Educ, 48; Columbia Univ, MA, 53, EdD, 59. *Work:* Colo Women's Col, Denver; Ft Hays Kans State Col, Hays; Denver Pub Schs; Northern Ill Univ, DeKalb; Sheldon Mem Art Gallery, Lincoln, Nebr. *Comn:* Presidential medallion, Northern Ill Univ, 70; 3 graphic images, private col, 2002. *Exhib:* Am Jewelry, Smithsonian Inst Traveling Exhib, 55-57; Handweaving II, Smithsonian Inst Traveling Exhib, Denver Art Mus, 58-59; Own Your Own Exhib, Denver Art Mus, Colo, 61-63 & 65-67; Jewelry & Precious Metalsmiths, Wichita Art Asn, 72; Toys Designed by Artists, Ark Art Ctr, Little Rock, 75 & 78; Am Metalwork 1976, Sheldon Mem Art Gallery, Lincoln, 76; The Metalsmith Int Exhib, Phoenix Art Mus, Ariz, 77; Metalsmith Int, Univ Kans, Lawrence, 81; Soc N Am Goldsmiths' Int, Cranbrook Acad Art, 87; Wichita Nat Decorative Arts, Wichita, 88; Contemp Jewelry Invitational, NY, 89; and many others; D'Art, Mus Art, Tucson, Ariz, 1998, 2002, 2004. *Pos:* Bd Trusteee, Tucson Mus Art, 96-; fine arts bd, Univ Ariz, Tucson, 1999-. *Teaching:* Assoc prof jewelry & graphics, Ft Hays Kans State Univ, 54-57 & 64-67; assoc prof jewelry & graphics, Edinboro State Col, Pa, 60-62; prof jewelry & metals, Northern Ill Univ, 67-83, prof emer, 83-; prof jewelry & metals, Arrowmont Sch of Crafts, Univ Tenn, Gatlinburg, 74-77 & 82-88. *Awards:* Jewelry Award, 12th Nat Decorative Arts, Cent States Craftsmen's Guild, 57; Purchase Award, 5th Ann Own Your Own Exhib, Denver Pub Schs, 61; Res Grant, Nothern Ill Univ Grad Sch, 68-82. *Bibliog:* Meg Torbert (ed), American Jewelry, Design Quart, Walker Art Ctr, 59 & 61; Lois E Franke (auth), Handwrought Jewelry, McKnight & McKnight, 62; Jon Nelson (auth), American Metalwork 1976 (slide set), Sheldon Mem Art Gallery, Lincoln, 76; Slide Bank, Phoenix Arts Comm, Ariz, 90. *Mem:* Soc of NAm Goldsmiths; Am Crafts Coun; Mus Art Tucson; Nat Mus Women in the Arts (charter mem). *Media:* Jewelry and related objects in gold and silver; graphic and collage images. *Interests:* contemp glass, paintings & prints by Am Indian artists. *Dealer:* Sanders Galleries 6420 N Campbell Tucson AZ 85718. *Mailing Add:* 7900 N LaCanada Dr Apt 2225 Tuscon AZ 85718

CALDWELL, MARTHA BELLE
EDUCATOR, HISTORIAN
b Chapel Hill, NC, Dec 12, 31. *Study:* Cornell Univ, BA; Univ Miss, MA; Ind Univ, MA & PhD. *Pos:* Mem exec bd, Am Comt Irish Studies, 81-83. *Teaching:* Instr art hist, Westhampton Col, Univ Richmond, 60-63 & Rice Univ, 66-68; from asst prof to prof art hist, James Madison Univ, 68-. *Awards:* Award of Distinction, Southeastern Col Art Conf, 88. *Mem:* Southeastern Col Art Conf (pres, 84-87); Col Art Asn; Soc of Archit Historians; Am Comt Irish Studies; Am Inst of Archaeol. *Res:* Nineteenth and twentieth century art and architecture. *Publ:* Auth, Alfred Charles Bossom: Specialist in Bank Design, Alfred Charles Bossom's American Architecture 1903-1926, Dennis Sharp (ed), London, 84

CALDWELL, SUSAN HAVENS
HISTORIAN, EDUCATOR
b Clinton, Okla, June 9, 38. *Study:* Washburn Univ, Topeka, Kans, BA, 61; Cornell Univ, Ithaca, NY, PhD, 74. *Teaching:* Asst prof art hist, Boise State Univ, 74-76; asst prof, Univ Okla, 76-81, assoc prof, 81-. *Awards:* Regents Award for Superior Teaching, Univ Okla, 85; Superior Teaching, Col Fine Arts, Univ Okla, 86 & 96, Outstanding Fac Award, 98; Okla Gov Art & Educ Award, 94. *Mem:* Col Art Asn Am; Midwest Art Hist Soc; Int Ctr Medieval Art; Am Soc Hispanic Art Hist Studies. *Res:* Medieval, specifically Spanish Romanesque; portal development, liturgical relationships to sculpture; contemporary criticism; medieval art patronage by women. *Publ:* Reading Medieval Art Objects: Relationships Between Art and Liturgy in the Middle Ages, In: Songs of Glory: Medieval Art from 900-1500, 85; Urraca of Zamora and San Isidoro in Leon: Fulfillment of a Legacy, Woman's Art J, 86; And They Sang A New Song: Twenty-Four Musical Elders at Santiago de Compostela, video, 88; Meret Oppenheim: The Fur-Lined Tea Corp, Saucer, and Spoon, Contemp Masterworks, Chicago & London, 91; Queen Sancha's Persuasion (mongr), Ctr Medieval & Renaissance Studies, 2000

CALHOUN, LARRY DARRYL
PAINTER, CERAMIST
b Revere, Mo, Oct 9, 37. *Study:* Iowa Wesleyan, BA(art); Univ Iowa, MA(ceramics). *Work:* Bowling Green State Univ, Ohio; Barnes Hosp, St Louis, MO; Emerson Elec, St Louis, MO; Kane Co Courthouse, Ill. *Comn:* Outdoor sculpture, Ill Arts Coun for Decatur, Ill, 78. *Exhib:* Ann Crafts Exhib, Butler Mus Art, Youngstown, Ohio; Designer Craftsman Biennial, Columbus Mus Art, Ohio; Ann Crafts Exhib, J B Speed Mus, Louisville, Ky & Evansville Mus Art, Ind; Invitational, Akron Art Inst, Ohio; Marietta Crafts Regional, Ohio; Realism Today: Mitchell Mus Regional Exhib, Marion, Ill, Evansville Art Mus, Ind, Western, Ill Univ, Sch Med, Springfield. *Pos:* Owner, Village Arts, 76-; Ill craftsman-in-residence, Ill Arts Coun, Decatur, 77-78. *Teaching:* Instr art, Westmar Col, Le Mars, Iowa, 61-63; asst prof art, Millikin Univ, Decatur, Ill, 63-70; assoc prof ceramics, Akron Univ, 70-76; assoc prof & chmn dept art, MacMurray Col, Jacksonville, Ill, 79-2000, prof emeritus, 2000-. *Awards:* Prize, Ball State Univ Small Sculpture & Drawing Exhib. *Mem:* Woodrow Wilson Fel, 60-61. *Media:* Oil, Pastel. *Specialty:* regional abstracts. *Dealer:* Gallery 33, 536 Burns Ln, Springfield, Ill, 62702; Village Arts, 320 S Diamond, Jacksonville, Ill, 62650. *Mailing Add:* 320 S Diamond Jacksonville IL 62650-2451

CALIFF, MARILYN ISKIWITZ
PAINTER, COLLAGE ARTIST
b Memphis, Tenn, Apr 27, 32. *Study:* Memphis Col Art, BFA, 70; Univ Memphis, MFA, 88. *Work:* Memphis Brooks Mus Art, Overton Park; Leo Bearman, Sr Collection, Memphis, Tenn; Boyle Investments, Memphis, Tenn; Nathan Walberg Collection, Miami, Fla; The Pie Lady Corp Collection, Memphis, Tenn. *Comn:* Glass mosaic murals (with Barbara Shankman), Memphis Hebrew Acad, 62, Baron Hirsch Synagogue, 64 & Memphis Jewish Community Ctr, 68. *Exhib:* one-woman exhibs, Earth Art Gallery, West Palm Beach, Fla, 89, Univ Northern Ala, Florence, 91 & Oak Ridge Cult Arts Ctr, Tenn, 91, Stamp Francisco, Rubber Stamp Art Gallery, San Francisco, Calif, 95 & Salem Col, Winston-Salem, NC, 97; First Int Fe-Mail Artistamps Exhib, Rubber Stamp Art Gallery, San Francisco, Calif, 97; Nat League Am Penwomen Biennale, Univ Tampa, Lee Scarfone Gallery, Fla, 98; Morocca Cafe, 99; Germantown Pub Libr, 2000; Wimbleton Sportsplex, 2001; Germantown Performing Arts Ctr, 2001; Tenn Art Mus, Nashville. *Teaching:* adj prof, SW Tenn Com Col, 2002-06. *Awards:* First in Oils, 13th Mid-South Exhib, Brooks League, 68; Three Purchase Prizes, First Tenn Artists & Craftsman Show, 72; First Place Acrylics, Tenn State Art Competition, Nat League Am Penwomen, 89, First Place Mixed Media, 91, First Place Photog, 95; Purchase Prize, All Tenn Artist, Tenn State Mus, 01; Arts in Park Photography Prize, Memphis, Tenn. *Bibliog:* Fine Arts Trader, 6/94; USA Weekend, 8/25-27/95; Memphis Mag, Vol XXI, No 11, 2/97. *Mem:* Penwomen; Nat Mus Women Arts; Nature Conservancy; Hadassah Artist Link (pres, 2004-05). *Media:* All Media. *Publ:* Auth, Your First Quilt, 72; The Pillow Book, 73; Travelin' with Marilyn, Newsletter, pvt publ, 96. *Dealer:* Paul Edelstein Gallery, Memphis. *Mailing Add:* 5305 Denwood Ave Memphis TN 38120

CALKINS, ROBERT G
HISTORIAN, EDUCATOR
b Oakland, Calif, Dec 29, 32. *Study:* Princeton Univ, BA, 55, Harvard Univ, MA, 62, PhD, 67. *Teaching:* Prof hist art, Cornell Univ, 66-. *Awards:* Grant, Am Coun Learned Soc, 73 & APS, 80. *Mem:* Int Ctr Medieval Art (mem bd adv, 71-, dir & vpres, 80-81, pres, 81-); Col Art Asn; Medieval Acad Am. *Publ:* Auth, Distribution of labor: The illuminators of the hours of Catherine of Cleves, Transactions Am Philos Soc, 79; Monuments of Medieval Art, Dutton, 79; Illuminated Books of the Middle Ages, Cornell Univ Press, 83 & 85, Programs of Medieval Illumination, Helen Foresman Spencer Mus Art, 84; Medieval Architectute in Western Europe from AD 300 to 1500, Oxford Univ Press, 98. *Mailing Add:* Dept Hist Art Cornell Univ 35 Goldwin Smith Hall Ithaca NY 14853

CALLAHAN, AILEEN LOUGHLIN CALLAHAN
PAINTER, MURALIST
b Dayton, Ohio. *Study:* Boston Univ, BFA, 68, MFA, 70; Skowhegan Sch Painting & Sculpture, Summer Grants, 68 & 69; Escuela Nac de Pintura y Escultura, Mex city, Fel study with David Alfaro Siquieros & Juan O'Gorman, 70-72. *Work:* Hotel Camino Real, Mexico City; Boston Univ; Clinic Collection, City of Boston; McMullen Mus Art, Boston Col. *Comn:* Interior wall, Skowhegan Sch Painting & Sculpture, Maine, 69; interior mural (2 walls), Inst Contemp Art, Boston, 75; exterior wall, San Felipe Church, Albuquerque, NMex, 79. *Exhib:* Nat Competition Exhib, Pindar Gallery, NY, 89; Nat Affiliate Members Exhib, Soho 20 Gallery, NY, 90; Small Works Nat Exhib, Amos Eno Gallery & NY, 90 & 91; Invitational Exhib, Pratt Manhattan Gallery, 91; Invitational Exhib, Am Acad Arts & Letts, NY, 94; Drietzer Gallery, Brandeis Univ, 97; McMullen Mus, Boston Col, 99; Hofstra Univ, NY, 01; New Bedford Art Mus, MA, 2005; and others. *Teaching:* Lectr fine arts, Boston Col, 79-, Regis Col, Weston, Mass, 79-98 & Lesley Col, Cambridge, Mass, 88-91, Univ Mass, Boston, 91-. *Awards:* Lincoln Fel to Mexico, Mexican Gov, 70-72; Blanche E Coleman Award, Coleman Trust, 84; Jurors Award, Small Works, Amos Eno Gallery, 90. *Bibliog:* P Fernandez Marquez (auth), Aileen Loughlin Callahan, El Nac, 7/23/72; Theresa Gawlas (auth), Regis Professor collaborates with poet on book, Wayland-Weston Town Crier, 10/1/87; Joyce Cohen (auth), Corporal places: paintings by Aileen Callahan, Art New Eng, 6/94. *Mem:* Women's Caucus for Art. *Media:* Oil, Fresco. *Publ:* Auth, A painter's language: the color of wind, Regis Today Mag, 87; The Face of Art Once Removed, Regis Today Mag, 92; Dante's Heads: The Plume & The Pallette, 01; Eye to Eye: Leviathan, 03. *Mailing Add:* 69 Harvey St No 12 Cambridge MA 02140

CALLARI, EMILY DOLORES
PAINTER, RESTORER
b New York, NY. *Study:* Sch Indust Arts, New York, 37; Art Students League, 45-69; Bryant Youth & Adult Ctr, Queens, 50; Wash Irving Evening Trade, 53; Wall St Art Asn, 64-68; studied with Brackman, Olinsky, Green. *Work:* Portrait, Venice Art Ctr, Fla; two religious paintings, pvt collection of Bishop Nevins, Diocese of Venice, Fla. *Comn:* life size madonna, comn by J Chorbajian, Church Bd, Holy Martyrs Armenian Church, Bayside, NY, 58; portrait of late dist Judge James Gordon, comn by Mrs J Gordon, Louisville, Ky, 90; portraits of family, owners of Duke Garden Ctr, Venice, Fla, 75-99; portrait of Chloe Embree, Jacaranda, Venice, Fla, 96; various portraits mems of Blumenstaad family, Chicago, 98. *Exhib:* Knickerbocker Artists, Nat Acad Exhibs, NY, 59; Wall St Art Asn, NY, 64-68; Travel Award Exhib, Wall St Art Asn, London, Amsterdam, Paris & Bourse, 68-69; one-person retrospective, Caldwell Trust, Venice, Fla, 96; Italian Heritage Fest, Venice Art Ctr, Fla, 98; Women's Support & Enrichment Ctr, Venice, Fla, 98. *Collection Arranged:* Portrait painting in the permanent collection of Venice Art Ctr, FL. *Pos:* Art adv, Hollywood Jewelry Co, New York City, 47-60; secy, Salmagundi Art Club, New York, 70-73; Artists Fel, New York, 70-73. *Teaching:* Portraiture, Venice Recreation, Sarasota Co, 74-80; Venice Art Ctr, 74-96. *Awards:* First Prize, Nat NY State Pavilion, 68; First Prize, Wall St Art, New York, 68; First Prize, Venice Art Ctr, Fla, 90; First awrds and travel awards for portrait paints, London, Paris, Amsterdam. *Bibliog:* Various articles, Venice Gondolier, 73-96; The Weekly, 96. *Mem:* Life mem, Art Students League; Catherine Lorillard Wolfe Art Club; fac mem, Venice Art Ctr; Sarasota Co Coun Arts; Nat Mus of Women in the Arts. *Media:* Oil, Pastel, Portraits. *Publ:* Illus, ad copy, Women's Wear, 50. *Dealer:* Final Touch Frame Gallery Venice FL. *Mailing Add:* 606 Home Park Rd Venice FL 34292-2827

CALLE, PAUL
PAINTER, WRITER
b New York, NY, Mar 3, 28. *Study:* Pratt Inst. *Work:* Thomas Gilcrease Inst Am Hist & Art, Tulsa, Okla; Nat Cowboy Hall Fame & Western Heritage Ctr, Oklahoma City; Nat Air & Space Mus, Washington; NASA Fine Art Collection; US Dept Interior; and others. *Comn:* NASA, Cape Kennedy, Jet Propulsion Lab, Star City, Moscow, USSR, 68-75; Basic History of Iron & Steel, Basic Indust, 68-70; Nat Park Serv, Mesa Verde, Yosemite, Cape Hatterus, 70-74; Classics in Surgery, Schering Co, 71-73; and others. *Exhib:* 1st & 2nd Convocation Western Art, Dallas, Tex; NASA Eyewitness to Space, Nat Gallery Art, Washington, 70; NASA Apollo-Soyuz, Moscow, 75; 25 Yr Retrospective, Thomas Gilcrease Mus, 92; Prix de West Invitational, 92-2007; and others. *Awards:* Mill Pond Press Award, Northwest Rendezvous, 79 & 80; Silver Medal Drawing, Nat Acad Western Art, 92; Nona Jean Hulsey Award, Prix de West Invitational, 95; and others. *Mem:* Soc Illusr; Northwest Rendezvous Group. *Media:* Oil, Pencil. *Publ:* Auth & illusr, The Pencil, Watson & Guptill, 75; Paul Calle An Artist's Journey, Mill Pond Press. *Mailing Add:* 149 Little Hill Dr Stamford CT 06905-2322

CALLIS, JO ANN
PHOTOGRAPHER
b Cincinnati, Ohio. *Study:* Univ Calif, Los Angeles, BA(art), 74; MFA(photog), 77. *Work:* Biblio Nat, Paris, France; Carnegie Inst, Pittsburgh, Pa; Corcoran Gallery Art, Washington; Mus Mod Art, NY; San Francisco Mus Mod Art; Getty Mus, Los Angeles, Calif; Nat Mus of Modern Art, Tokyo. *Exhib:* Oakland Mus, 77, 83 & 91; Milwaukee Art Ctr, 79; Fogg Art Mus, 80; Whitney Mus Am Art, 81 & 86; Contemp Arts Mus, Houston, 81; Los Angeles Co Mus Art, 82 & 87 (with catalog); San Francisco Mus Mod Art, 83 & 84; Mus Contemp Art, Los Angeles, 84; solo exhibs, Mus Contemp Art, Los Angeles (with catalog), 85, Dorothy Goldeen Gallery, Santa Monica, 92, G Gibson Gallery, Seattle, 93, Laurence Miller Gallery, NY, 93, Cleveland Mus Art, Ohio, 94 & Craig Krull Gallery, Santa Monica, 94, 95, 99 & 2001; Cranbrook Acad Art Mus (with catalog), 88; High Mus Art (traveling, with catalog), 89; Mus Mod Art, NY, 89 & 91; Denver Art Mus, 91; (Basically) Black & White, Riverside Art Mus, Calif, 92; Patterns of Influence, Ctr Creative Photog, Univ Ariz, Tucson, 92; Clay Out of Context, Univ Art Gallery, San Diego State Univ, 93; Am Made-The New Still Life (with catalog), Isetan Mus Art, Tokyo, 93; group exhibs, Armory Ctr for the Arts, Calif, 2000, Ctr for Creative Pgotog, Univ of Ariz, 2000, USC Fisher Gallery, Los Angeles, 2000. *Pos:* Workshop, San Francisco Art Inst, 78, Friends Photog & Ansel Adams Ctr Photog, San Francisco, 80, 86 & 90; juror, Friends Photog, Ferguson Grant & Ansel Adams Ctr Photog, San Francisco, 87; panelist, Bush Artist Fel Preliminary, St Paul, Minn, 90. *Teaching:* Instr photog, Calif State Univ, Fullerton, 77-78, Univ Calif, Los Angeles, 77-, Calif Inst Arts, Valencia, 76-. *Awards:* Awards in the Visual Arts, 89; Guggenheim Fel, 90; Photogr Fel, Nat Endowment Arts, 91; City of Los Angeles Cult Affairs Grant, 2001. *Bibliog:* Susan Kandel (auth), Enigmatic fabrications, Los Angeles Times, 6/11/92; Lita Barrie, On the scene: Los Angeles, Artspace, 9-10/92; JoAnn Callis: A fascination with transformation, Cal Arts Current, Vol 5, No 3, 5/93. *Mailing Add:* c/o Craig Krull Gallery Bergamot Sta 2525 Michigan Ave Bldg B3 Santa Monica CA 90404

CALLUORI HOLCOMBE, ANNA
CERAMIST
b Newark, NJ, Sept 15, 52. *Study:* Montclair State Univ, NJ, BA, 70; La State Univ, MFA, 74. *Exhib:* Solo exhib, Wash Univ, St Louis, 81 & Mem Art Gallery, Rochester, NY, 91 & Archie Bray Found Gallery, Helena, Mont, 91; 51st Int Ceramic Art Competition, Int Mus Ceramics, Faenza, Italy, 98; The Still Life Transfigured, Clay Place, Pittsburgh, Pa, 2000; Albert Kemper Mus, St Joseph, MO, 2002; Mulvane Art Mus, Topeka, Kans, 2002; Birger Sandzea Gallery, Lindsburg, Kans, 2002; Solo, ATR Vallauris Gallery, France, 2003; Int Acad of Caramils mems Exhib; World Ceramils Exposition, Icheon & Korea, 2004; First Int Triennial of Silicats Arts, Kecskenet, Hungary, 2005. *Collection Arranged:* Ceramics Invitational, 80, Functional Ceramics with a Decorative Approach, 81 & Retrospective: Fred Brian, 84, Ill Wesleyan Univ, Bloomington; National Council Education Ceramic Arts Show (auth, catalog), traveling, 83-86 & 91; New Approaches to Figurative Art & Retrospective: Jack Wolsky, 86, Tower Fine Arts Gallery, Brockport, NY; Off the Pedestal, On the Walls, Village Gate Art Ctr, Rochester, NY; Int Mus Ceramics, Faenza, Italy; Jingdezen Ceramic Inst, China; Keramikmuseum, Westerwald, Germany. *Pos:* Dir, Tower Fine Arts Gallery, State Univ NY, Brockport, 84-94; head, art dept, Kansas State Univ, Manhattan, 94-2000; juror, Am Ceramic Soc Centennial Nat Juried Exhib, 96 & Int Cone Box Exhib, Orton, Found, 98. *Teaching:* Asst prof art, Ill Wesleyan Univ, Bloomington, 79-84; assoc prof art & gallery dir, State Univ NY, Brockport, 84-94; assoc prof art, Kans State Univ, 94-, prof, 98-. *Awards:* Int Ceramics Award, Sidney Meyer Found, Australia; Gold Medal, 46th Int Exhib Ceramics, Italy, 89; Sidney Meyer Found Int Ceramics Award, Shepperton Art Gallery, Australia, 97. *Bibliog:* Richard Zakin (auth), Ceramics, Mastering the Craft, Chilton Bk Co, 90; richard Zakin (auth), Electric Kiln Ceramics (3rd ed), Chilton, 94; Craft & Art of Clay, Susan Peterson (4th ed), Richard Zakin (auth), Hand-Formed Ceramics: Creating From and Surface, Chilton Bk Co, 96; Best of Pottery, Rockport Publ, 96. *Mem:* fel Nat Coun Educ Ceramics Arts (pres-elect 92-94, dir exhibs, 83-86 & 89-91, pres, 92-94, past pres, 96-98); Empire State Crafts Alliance, NY; Am Crafts Coun; Col Art Asn (prof practice comt 2000-03); Nat Coun Art Admin (bd mem, 98-); Elected Mem of Int Acad of Art, 2002; Col Art Asoc, Int Committee, 2005; Prof Proctices Comm 2001-2005. *Media:* Ceramics. *Res:* Ceramic Sculpture. *Publ:* Auth, Master of fine Arts and careers, Nat Coun Art Adminrs Ceramics Art J, 80; Still life vignettes, 11/93 & Faenza: group study at the National Institute, 5/97, Ceramics Monthly; About My Work, Chinese Potters Newsletter, 2000; Building a Better Box, Pottery Making Illust, Vol 2, 99. A residencey in Vallauris, Ceramics Tech, (No.18), 2004. Give and Take: using Slip Tech, Pottery making Illust, 2004. *Dealer:* Strecker-Nelson Gallery Manhattan KS; Oxford Gallery Rochester NY. *Mailing Add:* 1502 N 10th St Manhattan KS 66502

CALMAN, W(ENDY) L
PRINTMAKER, PHOTOGRAPHER
b New York, NY, Feb 23, 47. *Study:* Univ Pittsburgh, BA(art hist), 69; Tyler Sch Art, Temple Univ, MEd, 70, MFA(printmaking), 72. *Work:* Honolulu Acad Arts; Ark Art Ctr, Little Rock; Del Mar Col; Int Ctr Photog, George Eastman House, NY; House of Humor and Satire, Gabravo, Bulgaria. *Exhib:* Photog Unlimited, Fogg Art Mus, Harvard Univ, 74; Uniquely Photog, Honolulu Acad Arts, 79; 16th Joslyn Biennial, Joslyn Art Mus, 80; Photofusion, Pratt Manhattan Ctr Gallery, NY, 81; Sights Unseen, AIR Gallery, NY, 82; Works on Paper, Am Haus, Hamburg, Ger, 87; Group Invitational, Aula Acad Fine Arts, Warsaw, Poland, 92; 2nd Bharat Bhavan Int Biennal Prints, Bhopal, India, 95. *Teaching:* Instr drawing & printmaking, Univ Tenn, Knoxville, 72-76; assoc prof printmaking, Ind Univ, Bloomington, 76-. *Awards:* Best Graphic Award, 16th Joslyn Biennial, Joslyn Mus Art, 80; Master Arts Fel, Ind Arts Coun, 85. *Bibliog:* K Wise (auth), Photographer's Choice, Addison House Found, 75; Thelma Newman (auth), Innovative Printmaking, Crown Publ, 77; Virginia Watson-Jones (auth), Contemporary American Sculptors, Oryx Press, 86. *Mem:* Col Art Asn; World Print Coun; Philadelphia Print Club. *Media:* All. *Mailing Add:* 500 S Hawthorne Dr Bloomington IN 47401

CAMARATA, MARTIN L
ARTIST, EDUCATOR
b Rochester, NY, June 10, 34. *Study:* NY State Univ, Buffalo, BA, 56; NY Univ, MA, 57. *Work:* Mus Belles Artes, Caracas, Venezuela; Univ of the Pac; Mus Palace of Legion Fine Arts, San Francisco. *Exhib:* Twenty-Second Painting Ann, Butler Inst Am Art, 57; Boston Printmakers Ann, 62-66; Philadelphia Print Club Ann, 65 & 66; Print-Drawing Ann, Pa Acad Fine Arts, 65, 66 & 68; Potsdam Ann Print-Drawing, NY, 74; one-man shows, McKissick Mus, Univ SC & Ore State Mus Fine Arts, Eugene, Ore. *Teaching:* Prof drawing & printmaking, Calif State Univ, Stanislaus, 64-. *Awards:* First Prize Print, William J Keller Award, 56; Best of Show, Calif State Fair Art Exhib, 65; Fulbright Fel, Rome, Italy, 58-59. *Bibliog:* T Albright (auth), rev in San Francisco Chronicle, 72 & 75. *Publ:* Auth, Lithography at Collectors Press, Artists Proof Mag, 72. *Mailing Add:* Art Dept Calif State Univ 801 W Monte Vista Ave Turlock CA 95382

CAMBER, DIANE WOOLFE
MUSEUM DIRECTOR, CURATOR
b Miami Beach, Fla. *Study:* Barnard Col, Columbia Univ, BA(art hist); Boston State Col, MEd(visual arts); Mass Col Art. *Collection Arranged:* Chaim Gross: Sculpture & Drawings (auth, catalog), 82; Charmion von Wiegand: Her Art & Life (auth, catalog), 82; Origins of Modern Design in Art Nouveau & Art Deco (auth, catalog), 82; Frank Lloyd Wright: Decorative Objects, Prints, Drawings, Fla Projects (auth, catalog), 84; Mid Century Design: Decorative Arts 1940-1960 (auth, catalog), 85; French Art, Sackner Arch Visual & Concrete Poetry (auth, catalog), 87; Seventy Years of Miami Architecture (auth, catalog), 88; Richard Wagner's Bayreuth Festival Performance of the Ring Cycle Art, Costume & Scenery 1876-1988, 89; A Collection in the Making: Architectural Arts, 90; Carlos Alfonzo: New Work (with catalog), 90; Highlights of the John & Johanna Bass Collection (with catalog), 90; Art Deco Toys, 91; Humberto Calzada (with catalog), 91; The Normandie: Floating Art Deco Palace, 93; Legacy of a Tsarina: Master Paintings from Pavlovsk, 95. *Pos:* Mus lectr, Albright-Knox Mus, Buffalo, 62-64 & Mus Fine Arts, Boston, 68-69; mus educator, De Cordova & Dana Mus, Lincoln, 67-68; assoc dir, Miami Design Preserv League, 78-80; actg dir, Bass Mus Art, 80-82, exec dir, 82-; adv coun, Mus Trustee Asn; bd dir, Chaim Gross Found. *Teaching:* Art specialist, La Pub Sch, 70-77; instr hist furniture design, Ft Lauderdale Art Inst, 78-79. *Awards:* Chevalier de L'Ordre des Arts des Lettres. *Bibliog:* Vicki Sanders (auth), Basking in Bass glory, 1/84, Richard Capen (auth), Salute to South Florida's best, 12/84, & Diane Camber, Profile, Miami Herald; Linda

Ferber (auth), The curators word Barnard's art historians, Barnard Alumnae Mag, fall 91; The Achiever: Turning Vision into Reality at the Bass Museum, (profile), Miami Today, 96. *Mem:* Fla Art Mus Dirs Asn (vpres, 84-86, pres, 86-); Asn Art Mus Dirs; Am Asn Art Mus Dirs; Artable; Mus Trustee Asn. *Mailing Add:* Bass Mus Art 2121 Park Ave Miami Beach FL 33139

CAMERON, BROOKE BULOVSKY
EDUCATOR, PRINTMAKER
b Madison, Wis. *Study:* Univ Wis, Madison, BS(art educ; honors); Univ Minn summer art hist tour of Europe with Prof Lorenz Eitner; Univ Iowa, with Mauricio Lasansky, MA(printmaking); NY Univ, viscosity printing workshop with Krishna Reddy, 82-83; Pratt Manhattan Graphics Ctr, litho & photo litho with James Martin & Ryo Watanabe; studied with Vito Giacalone, China & Japan, 84. *Work:* Emory Univ, Atlanta, Ga; Univ Ga Mus Art; Springfield Art Mus, Mo; Ringling Mus, Sarasota, Fla; Rockford Col Dept Art Collection; Univ Wis, Madison, Wis; Stephens Col, Columbia, Mo; Indianapolis Mus Art, Ind; Ga Mus Art & Univ Ga, Athens; Portland Art Mus, Ore; United Telephone, Kansas City; Tri-con Indust(s), Matto City Japan. *Comn:* Miss Willie, ed prints, Lakeside Studios, Mich, 77. *Exhib:* "Americas 2000: Works on Paper", Minot, ND, 94; 16th Ann Quad State Juried Exhib, Quincy Art Ctr, Ill, 96; For the Visual Arts 4th Anniversary 5 State Regional Show, Juanita Hammons Hall Performing Arts, Springfield, Mo, 96; two person exhib, Western Ill State Univ, Macomb, 96; Int Print Exhib, Portland Mus Art, Ore, 97; 49th Ann Nat Juried Print Exhib, Hunterdon Mus Art, Clinton, NJ, 2005; 30th Bradley Int Print & Drawing Exhib, Peoria, Ill, 2005; Ann Boston Printmaker's Exhib, Boston Univ, 2005. *Collection Arranged:* Heart of Am Nat Printmaking Exhib, Univ Mo. *Teaching:* Instr art & art hist, Tex Christian Univ, Ft Worth, 66-67; from instr to prof fine arts, Univ Mo, 67-, chmn dept art, 79-82. *Awards:* Printmaking Award, Crown Ctr Exhib Halls, Kansas City, Mo, 74; Univ Mo Res Coun Grant for Contemp Chinese Painting, 94; Purchase Award, Lynward Mem Purchase Prize, 44th Nat Hunterdon Mus Art, Hunterdon, NJ. *Bibliog:* many reviews in newspapers. *Mem:* Col Art Asn; Women's Caucus Art; Kansas City Print Coalition; Southern Graphics Coun. *Media:* Intaglio, Photo-intaglio. *Specialty:* prints. *Interests:* travel. *Publ:* Contribr, Managing the Academic Department 17-18, Am Coun Educ & MacMillian Publ Co, 83; Greater Midwest Int, (catalogue), Central Mo State Univ, Warrensburg, 2005; Boston Printmakers, N Am Print Biennial (catalogue), Boston Univ, 2005; 30th Bradley Int Print & Drawing Exhib (catalogue), Peoria, Ill, 2005. *Dealer:* Lakeside Studios 150 S Lakeshore Rd Lakeside MI 49116; Paint Box Gallery Sister Bay WI. *Mailing Add:* 923 College Park Columbia MO 65203

CAMERON, DUNCAN F
MUSEUM DIRECTOR
b Toronto, Ont, Feb 1, 30. *Pos:* Sr adminr, Royal Ont Mus, Univ Toronto, 56-62; pres & chmn bd, Janus Mus Consult Ltd, Toronto, 62-71; nat dir, Can Conf Arts, Toronto, 68-71; dir, Brooklyn Mus, NY, 71-73; pres, P S Ross & Co, Mgt Consult, Toronto, 75-77; dir & chief exec officer, Glenbow-Alta Inst, Calgary, 77-88; dir emer, Glenbow-Alberta Inst, Calgary, 88-89; independent consult & teaching worldwide, 89-. *Teaching:* Occasional lectr museology, Royal Ont Mus, Univ Toronto, 71-76; adj prof art criticism, Univ Western Ont, London, 76-77; vis teaching fel mus studies, Massey Univ, NZ, 95. *Awards:* Samuel H Kress Found Res Grant, 74; Merit Award, Can Mus Asn, 85; Chai Award, Calgary Jewish Community Coun & Can Jewish Cong, 86. *Mem:* Fel, Can Mus Asn; Can Asn Mus Dirs; Can Art Mus Dirs Orgn; Int Coun Mus; Commonwealth Asn Mus (past pres); fel Glenbow Alta Inst; fel United Kingdom Mus Asn. *Publ:* Auth, The Arts in Canada 1975: A Viewpoint, Can Coun, 75; Gold for the Gods: A Review, Gazette, Quart Can Mus Asn, winter 77; An Introduction to the Cultural Property Export and Import Act, Dept Secy State, Govt Can, 77; and others. *Mailing Add:* 3438 Six St SW Calgary AB T2S 2M4 Canada

CAMERON, ELSA S
CURATOR, CONSULTANT
b San Francisco, Calif, Nov 19, 39. *Study:* San Francisco State Univ, BA, 61, MA, 65. *Collection Arranged:* Native American Ceramics: Contemporary Pueblo Works, 73, Works of Benemeno Serrano, 74, Food Show, 76, Foot Show, 76 & 86, Downtown Ctr & Downtown Dog Show, 78, M H de Young Mem Mus, San Francisco, Calif; The Right Foot 80, Lights, Chairs, Tools, S Fairport; French Marionettes; Treasures of the Yellow River: Xian China, Guam Int Airport; Architecturally Integrated Public Art for GTAA/Toronto Pearson Int Airport, 99-2006; Mexican Folk Art, 99; Magic Lanterns, 2000; Historic Aviation Collection, Malton Gallery, Cincinnati, OH, 2001-2006; History fo Canadian Aviation, 2005; History of Toronto, 2006. *Pos:* pres, Community Arts Int, 76-; cur in charge, Fine Arts Mus San Francisco; dir, Fine Arts Mus Sch & Mobile Outreach Prog, 76-82; founding dir & chief cur, San Francisco Int Airport Mus, 83-99; art mgr & consulting cur, Greater Toronto Airports Authority, Toronto, Can, 99-2006; art consultant, Design Ave: Chen Du City Project, China, 2005-2006. *Teaching:* prof mus studies, Univ Art Mus, Berkeley, Calif, 81-82; Asst prof art, Univ Southern Calif, 82-83; public art & mus studies prof, Univ Southern Calif, Los Angeles, Calif, 95-96. *Awards:* Nat Endowment for the Arts Grant to Mus Prof & Res Grant; LIFF Found Exhib Grant; Ford Found Grant Special Mus Proj. *Mem:* Am Asn Mus; Int Coun Mus; Profl Art Consultants. *Res:* Museum education and community arts. *Specialty:* Pueblo ceramics & Native American art forms. *Publ:* Contribr, Museum as educator, Univ Calif, Berkeley, 78; assorted mus publs. *Mailing Add:* Community Arts International 15 Douglass St San Francisco CA 94114

CAMERON, ERIC
PAINTER, EDUCATOR
b Leicester, Eng, Apr 18, 35. *Study:* Kings Col, Univ Durham, Newcastle, Eng, BA, 57, study with Lawrence Gowing, Victor Pasmore & Richard Hamilton; Courtauld Inst, Univ London, Acad Dipl(hist art), 59. *Work:* Art Gallery Ont, Toronto; Nat Gallery Can, Ottawa, Ont; Mus Art Contemp Montréal; Glenbow Mus Calgary; Vancouver Art Gallery, BC; Montreal Mus Fine Arts. *Exhib:* Woods II, Nat Gallery Can, 71 & Woods I, Art Gallery Ont, 71; Videoscape, Art Gallery Ont, 74; Int Video Exhib, Aarhus, Denmark, 76; Paintings in Mixed Exhib, Art Gallery NS, Halifax, 77; Newspaper Paintings & Lawn, Anna Leonowens Gallery, Halifax, NS, 77; Keeping Marlene Out of the Picture--and Lawn, Vancouver Art Gallery, BC, 78; Divine Comedy, Nat Gallery Can, 90; Exposer/Cacher, Mus Art Contemp Montreal, 93; Eng Roots, Tate St Ives, Leeds City Art Gallery, 98; Voici, Palais des Beaux-Arts de Bruxelles, 2000; L'Oeuvre Programme, Musee d'Art Contemporair, Bordeaux, 2005. *Pos:* Dir grad prog, NS Col Art & Design, Halifax, 76-87; dept art, Univ Calgary, head, 87-97. *Teaching:* Lectr art & art hist, Univ Leeds, Eng, 59-69; assoc prof painting & video, Univ Guelph, Ont, 69-76. *Awards:* Governor generals Award in Visual and Media Arts, 2004; Gershon Iskowitz Prize, 94. *Mem:* Univs Art Asn Can (Ont rep, 72-73, secy-treas, 73-76 & 76, vpres, 76-79); fel Royal Soc Arts; Royal Can Acad. *Media:* Oil, Acrylic. *Publ:* Auth, Mac Adams: The Mysteries, 76, Dan Graham: Appearing in Public, 76, Art as Art and the Oxford Dictionary, Vanguard, 77 & Bill Beckley's Lies, 77, Artforum; Bent Ayis Approach, Nickle Arts Mus, Calgary, 84; Divine Comedy, Nat Gallery Can, 90. *Mailing Add:* Dept Art 2500 Univ Dr NW Calgary AB T2N 1N4 Canada

CAMFIELD, WILLIAM ARNETT
HISTORIAN
b San Angelo, Tex, Oct 29, 34. *Study:* Princeton Univ, AB, 57; Yale Univ, MA, 61, PhD, 64. *Teaching:* From asst prof to assoc prof mod Am & mod Europ art, Univ St Thomas, Houston, Tex, 64-69; from assoc prof to prof, Rice Univ, Houston, Tex, 69- & Joseph & Joanna Nazro Mullen prof, 80. *Awards:* Am Philos Soc Grant, 65; Am Coun Learned Socs Grant-in-Aid, 68, Fel, 73-74; Nat Endowment Humanities Fel, 81; Guggenheim Fel, 88; and others. *Bibliog:* F Will-Levaillant (auth), Picabia et la machine: symbole et abstraction, Rev l'Art, Paris, No 4, 69; Douglas David (auth), Big Dada, Newsweek, 9/70; Christopher Green (auth), Francis Picabia, his art, life and times, Burlington Mag, 11/81; David Hopkins (auth), Max Ernst: Dada and the dawn of surrealism, Burlington Mag, 7/93. *Mem:* Col Art Asn; founding mem Asn l'Etude Dada Surrealisme; co-founder Tex Conf Art Historians. *Res:* Emphasis on Dada in Paris and art in France from about 1910 to 1925. *Publ:* Francis Picabia, Guggenheim Mus, 70; Francis Picabia, Princeton Press, 79; Tabu Duda, Kunsthalle Bern, 83; Marcel Duchamp Fountain, Menil Collection, 89; Max Ernst, Prestel Verlag, 93; The Paintings of Frank Freed, Mus Fine Arts, Houston, 93; and others. *Mailing Add:* Dept Art & Art Hist Rice Univ 6100 Min St Mail Stop 21 Houston TX 77005-1892

CAMHI, MORRIE
PHOTOGRAPHER, EDUCATOR
b New York, NY, Aug 16, 28. *Study:* Univ Calif, Los Angeles, BA, 56. *Work:* San Francisco Mus Mod Art; Ctr Creative Photog, Tucson; Oakland Mus; Israel Mus, Jerusalem; Magnes Mus, Berkeley. *Exhib:* Haiku, Camerawork, Christchurch, NZ, 76; Petaluma, San Francisco Art Inst, 77; Espejo, Ctr Contemp Photog, Chicago, 78, Oakland Mus, 78 & Ctr Creative Photog, Tucson, 83; Humanism, Consejo Fotografia, Mexico City, 79; Jews of Greece, Magnes Mus, Berkeley, 80; AD: Vantage, San Francisco Mus Mod Art, 83 & 85. *Pos:* Assoc ed, Photoshow Mag, 79-81; Periscope Mag, 96-. *Teaching:* Mem fac photog, San Francisco City Col, 69-88; instr sem, Friends Photog & Univ Calif, Photoforum (New Zealand). *Awards:* Grants, Nat Endowment Arts, 77, Columbia Found, 78 & Magnes Mus, 80. *Bibliog:* Milton Meltzer (auth), Eye of Conscience, Follett Press, 74; Don Owens (auth), articles, Picture Mag, 78 & 80; features, Photo Metro. *Mem:* Soc Photog Educ. *Media:* Black & white photography. *Res:* Nature of medium; marketplace; international overview. *Publ:* Auth, Eye of Conscience, Follet, 74; Morrie Camhi, monograph, MIN Books, 87; The Prison Experience, Tuttle Press, 89; Faces & Facets. The Jews of Greece, Caratzas Publ, 95; contribr, Lenswork Quarterly. *Dealer:* Cityscape Gallery 97 E Colorado St Pasadena CA 91105; MIN Gallery 402 Masa Ebisu Tokyo 150 Japan. *Mailing Add:* 95 Marshall Ave Petaluma CA 94952

CAMP, DONALD EUGENE
PHOTOGRAPHER
b Meadeville, Pa, July 28, 40. *Study:* Tyler Sch Art, BFA, 87, MFA, 89. *Work:* Mus Am Art, Philadelphia; Philadelphia Mus Art; Pa Convention Ctr, Philadelphia; Arco Corp, Philadelphia; Blue Cross Blue Shield, Philadelphia. *Comn:* Smithsonian Inst; Bklyn Mus. *Exhib:* Philadelphia Selection, Alternative Mus, NY, 91; Art Now, Philadelphia Mus Art, 91; Dust Shared Hearts, Noyes Mus, Brigantine, NJ, 92 & Swarthmore Col, Pa, 95; Mich State Univ Mus Art. *Pos:* Staff photogr, Philadelphia Evening & Sunday Bull, 72-81. *Teaching:* Asst prof photog, Tyler Sch Art, 89-91; sr lectr pub image, Univ of the Arts, 95; vis asst art, Ursinus Coll, 00-01. *Awards:* Guggenheim Fel, John Simon Guggenheim, 95; Nat Endowment Arts Fel, 95; Pew Fel, 95. *Mem:* Soc Photog Educators (nat bd dir, 90-94); The Print Ctr. *Media:* Photography, Works on Paper. *Mailing Add:* c/o Gallery 339 339 S 21st St Philadelphia PA 19103

CAMPBELL, DAVID PAUL
PAINTER, INSTRUCTOR
b Takoma Park, Md, 36. *Study:* Art Students League, 57-58 & 61. *Work:* Mus Fine Arts, Boston; Metrop Mus Art, NY; Art Inst Chicago; Boston Pub Libr; Pierce Atwood (corp collection) Portland, Maine. *Comn:* Painting, Gillette Co, Boston, 80. *Exhib:* A Sense of Place, Univ Nebr & Joslyn Mus, 73; Brockton Art Mus Triennial, Mass, 80; Perspectives on Contemp Am Realism, Pa Acad Fine Arts, 82 & Art Inst Chicago, 83; San Francisco Mus Mod Art, 85; Contemp Drawings from Boston Collections, Mus Fine Arts, Boston, 86-87; Boston Ann Drawing Show, 87, 88 & 91; The Pursuit of Excellence, Hubbard Mus, Ruidoso Downs, NMex, 91; Nat Acad Ann Show, Nat Acad NY, 94, 96 & 2006; Bergen Mus, Paramus, NJ, 95; Biennial, Portland Mus of Art, Portland, Maine, 98 & 05. *Teaching:* Instr life drawings, Montserrat Col, Beverly,

Mass, 89; instr watercolor, NE Sch Art, Boston, 90, Jewish Community Ctr, Newton, Mass, 90-; instr watercolor & drawing, Mus Fine Arts, Boston,1992-2001, Maine Col Art, Portland, 2001-. *Awards:* Purchase Award, Watercolor USA, Hallmark Inc, 74; Grant, Adolph & Esther Gottlieb Found, 87, Pollock-Krasner Found, 90 & 96; Appreciation Award, City Somerville, Mass, 93. *Bibliog:* Peter Merchant, John Pennington & Wendy Mason (dirs), David Campbell, Words and Watercolors (videotape), Somerville Educ TV, 84; Frank H Goodyear Jr (auth), Perspectives on Contemporary American Realism, Pa Acad Fine Arts, 82; Alvin Martin (auth), American Realism, San Francisco Mus Mod Art & Henry N Abrams, 85. *Mem:* Nat Writers Union; Graphic Artists Guild. *Media:* Oil, Drawing. *Publ:* Looking at trees, The Sun Mag, 11/92; poem, Beloit Poetry J, fall 95; Windows of the Soul (anthology), 95; 5 poems, Struggle Mag, 2003; 4 poems, Sensations Mag, fall 03. *Dealer:* Frost Gully Gallery PO Box 202 Freeport Maine 04032. *Mailing Add:* 37 Stone Dr Cape Elizabeth ME 04107

CAMPBELL, GRAHAM B
PAINTER
b Kent, Eng, 46. *Study:* Chesterfield Art Col, Eng, 61-65; Birmingham Art Col, studied with John Walker, 66-69; Yale Sch Art, MFA, 78. *Work:* Walker Art Gallery, Liverpool Art Mus, Eng; Touchstone Gallery, NY; Ikon Gallery, Birmingham, Eng; Midland Art Ctr, Eng; NY Studio Sch Gallery. *Exhib:* Art of the State, Rose Art Mus, 82; Four, Rose Art Mus, 82; CDS Gallery, NY, 84, 85, 86, 87, 89, 91, 92, 94 & 95; Recent Acquisitions, Rose Art Mus, 85; Emerging Artists, EF Hutton Collection, NY, 87. *Teaching:* Instr, Brandeis Univ, currently. *Awards:* Mazer Grant, Brandeis Univ, Mass, 82 & 85; Louis Comfort Tiffany Found Award in Painting, Tiffany Found, 86; Grant, John Simon Guggenheim Mem Found, 96. *Bibliog:* Grace Glueck (auth), Graham Campbell, New York Times, 9/20/85; M Poirier (auth), Graham Campbell, New York reviews, ArtNews, 11/85; Theodore F Wolff (auth), Further exposure, Christian Science Monitor, 7/7/86. *Mailing Add:* Art Dept Brandeis Univ PO Box 9110 Waltham MA 02454-9110

CAMPBELL, NANCY B
PRINTMAKER
b Syracuse, NY, May 28, 52. *Study:* Syracuse Univ, BFA, 74; Univ Mich, MFA, 76. *Work:* Philadelphia Mus Art, Pa; Libr Cong, Washington; Worcester Art Mus, Mass; Mt Holyoke Col Art Mus, South Hadley, Mass; Syracuse Univ Art Collection, NY. *Exhib:* Collaboration in Print, Stewart & Stewart Prints: 1980-90, Detroit Inst Arts, Mich, 91 & Kalamazoo Inst Arts, Mich, 91; Southern Graphics Coun Traveling Exhib, Ohio Univ, Athens, Univ Ga, Athens, Adams State Col, Alamos, Colo, 98, 99; Janet Turner Nat Print, Calif State Univ, Chico, 99; Nat Printmaking 2000, Col NJ, Ewing; Pacific States Nat Exhib, Univ Hawaii, 2000; many others; Bangain US, Flusso Gallery, NY, 2004; NAZU Int Biennale, NAZU, Japan, 2004. *Pos:* Chairperson art dept, Mt Holyoke Col, South Hadley, Mass, 92, 95, 2003, 2005. *Teaching:* Asst prof studio art, Oberlin Col, Ohio, 79-80 & Univ Hartford, Conn, 80-81; assoc prof studio art, Mt Holyoke Col, South Hadley, Mass, 81-, dir printmaking workshop, 98-; Prof of Art, Mount Holyoke Col, 1981-present. *Awards:* Patron Award, Ralph E Cades Family Found, 63rd Int Exhib Print Club, Philadelphia, 87; Juror's Commendation, Boston Printmakers 43rd Am Print Exhib, 91; Award, Springfield Art League 72nd Ann Exhib, 91. *Bibliog:* Richard Field & Ruth Fine (auth), A Graphic Muse: Prints by Contemporary American Women, Hudson Hills Press, 87; Ellen Sharp, Collaboration in Print: Stewart & Stewart Prints: 1980-1990, Mich Coun Arts, 91; Gloria Russell (auth), Mediums Come Together at Art Exhibition, Sunday Republican, Springfield, Mass, 92. *Media:* Screenprinting, Lithography. *Collection:* Phila Mus of Art, Phila, PA; The Library of Congress, Wash, DC; Worcester Art Museum, Worcester, MA; Syracuse Univ of Art Collections, Syracuse, NY; Illinois State Univ, Normal, IL; Mount Holyoke Col Art Mus, S Hadley, MA; Lamar Univ, Beaumont, TX; Haggin Mus, Stockton, CA; Amoco Products, Denver, CO; Michigan Bell Tel; Nova Scotia Col of Art & Design, Halifax, Nova Scotia, CA; Tenn Technological Univ; Univ of Conn, Storrs, CT; Univ of Dallas, Irving, TX; Univ of Hartford, W Hartford, CT; Univ of Mass, amherst, MA; Univ of Mass, Boston, MA; Univ of NH, Durham, NH; Univ of RI, Kingston, RI; Univ of VT, Burlington, Vt. *Dealer:* Alice Simsar Fine Art 1103 Baldwin Ave Ann Arbor MI 48107. *Mailing Add:* 369 Middle St Amherst MA 01002

CAMPBELL, NAOMI
PAINTER, PUB ARTIST
Study: Art Students League, NY. *Work:* Arts for Transit (div MTA), NYC; NY Pub Libr, NYC; Art Students League NYC; ASPCA, NYC; Swift Corp, NYC. *Comn:* City of NY Permanent Subway Art, Arts for Transit, 2005; City of Irving Permanent Art, Tex, Irving Arts Center: Human Servs Bldg Entrance, 2006; painted scroll (4'x15'), Maimonides Hosp, Cancer Treatment Center, NYC, 2006. *Exhib:* Butler Mus Am Art, 2001; Exhib of Int Art of the Fan (traveling exhib to Seoul, Korea), Tokyo Metrop Mus Art, Japan, 2003; Along the Way MTA Arts for Transit 20 yr Retrospective Exhib, Paine Webber UBS Gallery, NYC, 2005; The League Then & Now, Gallery Salute to the 130th Anniversary of the Art Students League NY, 2005. *Pos:* Selection Comt, Arts for Transit, NY; Judge, various art orgns & cols in NYC including Salmagundi Center Am Art & Lehman Col Art Dept. *Awards:* Dianne Bernhard Silver Medal Award; Dr Clifford Wheeler Wells Pastel Award; Audubon Artists of Am Gold Medal of Hon, 2004; Pastel Journal Award, Pastel Soc Am Ann Exhib, 2006. *Bibliog:* Hon Mention, Portrait Div, Artist Mag, 2002; Vera Haler (auth), 100 Years of the Subway, Newday NY.com (video interview with artist), NY, 10/2004; Celia McGee (auth), Sunday Now, Carving Out a Niche, Daily News NYC, 10/30/2005. *Mem:* Allied Artists of Am; Salmagundi Club; Pastel Soc Am (signature mem); Nat Watercolor Soc (signature mem); Am Soc Portrait Artists (signature mem); Audubon Artists Am; Catherine Lorillard Wolfe Art Club. *Media:* Painting, Sculpture. *Publ:* Looking Beyond, A Constant Process, Int Artists Publ, 2004; auth, The Source of Life, Watercolor Magic Mag, 8/2005; The Portraits of Life, Pastel J Mag, 12/2006; Pure Color: The Best of Pastel, North Light, 2006. *Mailing Add:* 177 7th Ave Apt 3L Brooklyn NY 11215

CAMPBELL, REBECCA
ARTIST, INSTRUCTOR
b Salt Lake City, Utah, 1971. *Study:* Pacific Northwest Col Art, Portland, Ore, FRA, 1994; Vt Studio Ctr, resident, 1998; Univ Calif, Los Angeles, MFA, 2001. *Exhib:* Solo shows include Dreaming in Vertigo, Gallery 8, Portland, Ore, 1992, Domestics, Crossroad, Portland, 1993, Consent, Blue Boutique, Salt Lake City, 1997, Pink, Cordell Taylor Gallery, Salt Lake City, 1998, sky garden, Art Barn, Salt Lake City Arts Council, 1999, Boy Crazy, Atrium Gallery, Salt Lake City Library, 1999, Thin Skin, LA Louver, 2002, 2005; Sex and Death, Boyde Gallery, Portland, 1992, Regeneration, 1993; Scarcity and Excess, Portland Art Mus North, 1993; Out of the Closet, Salt Lake Art Ctr, 1999; Women's Work, Union Gallery, Univ Utah, 1999; LA Louver, 2003, 2004, 2005. *Pos:* Input colorist, Dark Horse Comics, Mikwaukie, Ore, 1994; chair adv bd, Zoos, Arts and Parks Fun, Tier II Cultural/Botanical Orgns, 1997; cur educ, Salt Lake Art Ctr, Utah, 1997-99; project coordr, Youth Educ, Dept Cultural Affairs, Los Angeles, 1997. *Teaching:* High sch art instr, Int Learning Program, Ore, 1995-96; art specialist, Salt Lake City Sch Dist; teaching asst/Artsbridge fellow, Univ Calif Los Angeles, Artsbridge emer scholar mentor, 2001; visual arts specialist/curriculum author, Teh Accelerated Sch, Los Angeles, 2000; vis prof, Calif State Univ, Fullerton, 2002. *Awards:* Werner Hirsch Drawing Award; Feitelson Arts Found Award. *Mailing Add:* c/o LA Louver 45 North Venice Blvd Venice CA 90291

CAMPBELL, RICHARD HORTON
PAINTER, PRINTMAKER
b Marinette, Wis, Jan 11, 21. *Study:* Cleveland Sch Art; Art Ctr Sch, Los Angeles; Univ Calif, Los Angeles. *Work:* Theater Guild Am, NY; Hilton Hotel, Denver. *Exhib:* Los Angeles Co Mus, Calif; Denver Mus; Frye Mus, Seattle, Wash; Oakland Art Mus, Calif; De Young Mus, San Francisco. *Pos:* Dir, Los Angeles Art Asn. *Awards:* Second Prize, Los Angeles All-City Exhib, 51; First Prize, Cleveland May Show, 54; First Prize, 7th Festival of Arts, Los Angeles, 58. *Mem:* Nat Watercolor Soc; Los Angeles Art Asn; fel Int Inst Arts & Lett. *Media:* Oil, Acrylic. *Mailing Add:* 643 Baylor St Pacific Palisades CA 90272

CAMPBELL, WILLIAM HENRY
PAINTER - ACRYLIC & WATERCOLOR
b Philadelphia, Pa, Sept 14, 15. *Study:* La France Art Inst, 28-30; Fleisher Art Mem, 30-33; Univ Pa, 33-34; Philadelphia Col Art, with Earl Horter, Franklin Watkins & Alexey Brodovitch, dipl, 37. *Work:* Univ Del, Newark; Berman Mus, Collegeville, Pa; Nat Mus Am Art, Washington; Duke Univ Art Mus, NC; Bryn Athyn Col, Pa; McCann Sch Art, Petersburg, Pa; Woodmere Art Mus, Philadelphia, Pa; and others. *Comn:* Portraits, Univ Del; art, Container Corp of Am; Saturday Evening Post. *Exhib:* Pa Acad Fine Arts, Philadelphia, 35; Art Inst Chicago, 45; Philadelphia Art Alliance, 48 & 56; Philadelphia Mus Art, 62; Artist's Equity Asn, Civic Ctr, Philadelphia, 68, 71, 75 & 78; Am Col, Bryn Mawr, 87-94; The Ideal Made Real, Berman Mus (with catalog), Collegeville, Pa, 96; Paths to Abstract Art, Woodmere Art Mus, with catalog, Philadelphia, 98; Raab Gallery, Philadelphia, 1/00. *Collection Arranged:* Antonio Martino Retrospective, Woodmere Art Mus, 82; 8 Abstract Artists, Am Col, Bryn Mawr, 93; Water Color as a Creative Medium, Plastic Club, Philadelphia, 93; Artists of Imagination, Am Col, 95. *Pos:* Art dir, Pa Railroad, Philadelphia, 53-58. *Teaching:* Instr illus, Moore Col Art, Philadelphia, 50-52; instr water media, Philadelphia Col Art, 63-65; painting instr, Philadelphia Sketch Club, 63-65. *Awards:* Philadelphia Sketch Club Medal, 95; Gold Medal, Plastic Club, 96, 02; Award, Acrylic Soc Nat Arts Club, 84 & 85. *Bibliog:* Art, Design & the Modern Corp, Nat Mus Am Art, 85; The Ideal Made Real, Berman Mus, Collegeville, PA, 96; Paths to Abstract Art, Woodmere Art Mus, 98; and others. *Mem:* Life mem Philadelphia Sketch Club; life mem Philadelphia Watercolor Club; The Plastic Club. *Media:* Acrylic on paper and canvas, realistic and abstract. *Mailing Add:* 552 N 23rd St Philadelphia PA 19130

CAMPELLO, FLORENCIO LENNOX
CRITIC, PAINTER WATERCOLOR
b Guantanamo, Us Naval Base, Cuba, Sept 6, 56. *Study:* Univ Wash Sch Art, BS(art), 81; Naval Postgrad Sch, Monterey Calif, MS, 87. *Work:* McManus Mus, Scotland, Brusque Mus, Brazil, San Bernardino Co Art Mus, Calif, Musee des Duncan, France, Frick Mus, Ohio, Meadows Mus Art, Shreveport, La, Hunter Mus, Tenn. *Exhib:* one-man shows, The Hub Gallery, 79, Arts Northwest Gallery, Wash, 81, Galeria Sevillana, Spain, 84, Warehouse Gallery, Scotland, 92, Chevrier's Presidio Gallery, Calif, 93-94, Fraser Gallery, Wash, DC, 96-99, 2001, 49 West, Md, 97, Eklektikos Gallery, Wash, DC, 2000, represented by, Fraser Gallery; exhib incl, Sacramento Fine Arts Ctr, Calif, Rock Springs Art Ctr, Wyo. *Pos:* Art critic, Dimensions Mag, Norfolk, Va, 94-99, Greater Reston Arts Center, Reston, Va, 97, Gallery West, Alexandria, Va, 97, Pitch Mag, City Beat, Manassas J; Adv, DC Arts & Humanities Commission, Wash, 99-2001; guest cur, Athenaeum, Alexandria, Va, 2001; assoc dealer Sothebys.com; cur From Here and From There: A Survey of Contemp Cuban Art Frazer Gallery, Bethesda, Md, 2003; info warfare adv, KSI, Arlington, Va, 97-, Visions Mag for the Visual Arts, Va Beach, 95-2000, Crier Media, Alexandria, 99-. *Awards:* Decorated Meritorious Service medal US Navy, Navy Commendation Medal (4), Navy Achievement Medal (2); recipient second prize, Bellgrade Art Festival, 97 & 98. *Mem:* Art Dealers Asn of Greater Wash. *Mailing Add:* c/o Crier Media Group Inc 112 S Patrick St Alexandria VA 22314-3027

CAMPER, FRED
EDUCATOR
b Chicago, Il, 47. *Study:* Mass Inst of Tech, BS in Physics, 71; NYU, Dept Cinema Studies. *Pos:* Lab technician, for a co specializing in environ measurements of radioactivity. *Teaching:* teacher, film-making, and film history Sch Art Inst Chicago, 76-82; teacher asst, NYU, 72, instr, 73; teacher, Am Melodrama, 2000; Lectr on art, photog, and film for coll and univ in NY, NJ and Ill; lecturer in the field; teacher,

reading course in art issues Univ Ill at Urbana-Champaign; co-founder, member a film by, 2003-. *Awards:* Recipient Lisagor award, 99, Film Preservation Honor, Anthology Film Archives, 2001, Best DVD award, Cinemarati, Exceptional Achievement in Criticism award, 2004. *Mem:* Nat Writers Union, Int Asn of Arts Critics, Chicago Art Critics Asn (co-found, mem). *Publ:* Freelance writer, publisher (film articles for a variety of periodicals, catalogues and books), 1968—, writer on film Chicago Reader, 1976, 1986—, writer on art, 1989—, writer (of reviews of art and photg exhib and interviews with artists), 1993—. *Mailing Add:* PO Box A3866 Chicago IL 60690-3866

CAMPOS-PONS, MARIA MAGDALENA
PHOTOGRAPHER, VIDEO ARTIST
b Matanzas, Cuba, 59. *Study:* Nat Sch Art, Havana, Cuba, 80; Higher Inst Art, ISA (painting), Havanna, Cuba, 85; Mass Col Art, 88. *Work:* Mus Nat Ctr African Am Artists, Boston, Mass; Mus Fine Arts, Boston, Mass; Mus Contemp Art, Tokyo, Japan; Nat Mus Fine Arts, Havana, Cuba; plus many other pvt & pub collections. *Comn:* Wall Installation, Hosp Provincial de Pinar del Rio, Cuban Fund Fine Arts, Cuba, 87; Space for Love, Embassy Hotel, Room 44, London, Ont, Can, 90. *Exhib:* No Man is an Island, Young Cuban Art, Porin Taidemuseo, Finland & Plaffy Palace, Vienna, Austria, 90; Cuba OK, Stadische Kunsthalle, Dusseldorf, Ger, 90; Ethos, York Quay Gallery, Harbor Front, Toronto, Can, 92; Our View of Struggle, Gallery 44, Ctr Contemp Photogr, Toronto, Can, 92; Blood Sweat N' Tears, MU Gallery, Boston, Mass, 92; The Year of the White Bear, Walker Ctr Arts, Minneapolis, Minn, 92; Ways to See: New Art from Massachusetts, Inst Contemp Art, Boston, 92; El Corazon Sangrante/The Bleeding Heart, Fundacion Mus de Bellas Artes, Caracas, Venequela, 93; 4 Artists Edition, Space, Boston, Mass, 93; Memos for the Next Millennium, Boston Ctr Arts & Space, Boston, Mass, 93; Seventh Triennial Exhib, Fuller Mus Art, Brockton, Mass, 93; Transcending the Bordes of Memory, Norton Gallery & Sch Art, W Palm Beach, Fla, 94; Fotofest, Int Festival Photogr, George R Brown Convention Ctr, Houston, Tex, 94; Rejoining the Spiritual: The Land in Latin Am Art, Md Inst Col Art, Baltimore, 94; Human/Nature, New Mus Contemp Art, NY, 95; Cuba, la Isla Posible, Ctr de Cult Contemporania, Barcelona, Spain, 95; my magic pours secret libations, Mus Fine Arts, Fla State Univ, Tallahassee, 96; Latin-Am Women Artists 1915-1995, Denver Art Mus, Nat Mus Women Arts, Wash, DC, 96; Witness, Leonard & Bina Ellen Art Gallery, Montreal, Que, Edmonton Art Gallery, Alberta, Dunlop Art Gallery, Regina, Saskatchewan, Can & Southeast Mus Photogr, Daytona Beach, Fla, 96; Latin Am Artists, DNA Gallery, Provincetown, Mass, 96; Skin, M M Campos-Pons & Sandy Slone, Craiger/Dane Gallery, Boston, Mass, 96; Caribbean Visions: Contemp Painting and Sculpture, Wadsworth Atheneum, Hartford, Conn, 97; The Portrait as Object/The Figure as Ground, Howard Yezerski Gallery, Boston, Mass, 97; The Constructed Photograph, Addison Gallery Am Art, Philips Acad, Andover, Mass, 97; Trade Routes, Johannesburg Biennale, S Africa, 97; Invasion, Saaremaa Biennale, Kuressaare, Estonia, 97; Am Voices, Latino Photogrs in the US, Smithsonian Inst, Wash, DC, 97; The Caribean Vision, Smithsonian Inst, Washington, DC, 98; Exile, Nat Gallery Can, Ottawa, 98; Ackland Art Mus, Univ NC, Chappel Hill, 2000; solo exhibs, MIT List Visual Arts Ctr, 99-, Howard Yezerski Gallery, Boston, 00, 02, Nat Gallery Can, Ottawa, 00, Cleveland Art Mus, 01, Schneider Gallery, Chicago, 01, Mus Contemp Art, Sapporo, Japan, 01, Tkasmatsu City Mus Art, Japan, 01, El Museo del Barrio, New York City, 01, Gallery Pack Milan, 02, Henie Onstad Kunstsenter, Oslo, Norway, 02, Echigo-Tsumari Art Triennial, Japan, 03; group exhibs, Gallery Naga, Mass, 99, South Shore Art Ctr, Cohasset, Mass, 99, Liverpool Biennial Contemp Art, 99, DC Moore Gallery, New York City, 2000, The Art Gallery, Paul Creative Arts Ctr, Univ NH, 2000, Tokyo Metrop Mus Photog, Japan, 00, Davis Mus and Cult Ctr, Wellesley Col, Mass, 2000, Apex Art Curatorial Ctr, New York City, 2000, El Museo del Barrio, New York City, 01, Mus Contemp Art, Baltimore, 01. *Collection Arranged:* Ctr for Devel Vis Arts, Havana, Cuba; Mus Contemporary Art, Tokyo; Mus Fine Arts, Boston; Mus Nat Ctr of African Am Artists, Boston; Nat Gallery Can, Ottawa; Nat Mus Fine Arts, Havana, Cuba; Vancouver Art Gallery; Polaroid Collection, Boston; Norton Mus, West Palm Beach, Fla; MacArthur Found, Chicago. *Pos:* co-coord, Aesthetic and Fine Art Seminar, Revolution and Culture Mag, 89-90; jury, Provincial Competition of Fine Arts, Santa Clara, Cuba, 89, 5th Edition of Eduardo Abela Fine Art Competitioin, Havanna, 90, Provincial Competion of Regino E Boti, Guantanamo, Cuba, 90, Provincial Competition of Fine Arts, Matanzas, Cuba, 90, Sch of Mus of Fine Arts Annual Student Exhib and Dana Pond Painting Awards, Boston, 92 & Nat Exhib WAC Transforming Tradition, Boston, 96; curatorial project, Articule Gallery, Montreal, Can, 91 & Inst of Contemp Art, Boston, 92; asst curator, The Space Gallery, 92; prof, Sch of MFA, Boston, 98-2000. *Teaching:* asst prof, Boston Univ; prof aesthetic and painting, Higher Inst of Art, Havanna, Cuba, 86-89; vis prof, 3d Installation, RI, 94, Mass Col of Art, Boston, 95 & 96 & Sch of Mus of Fine Arts, Boston, 97. *Awards:* Regional Fel, New Eng Found Arts, Mass, 93-94; Art Reach 95 Award, Nat Congress Art & Design, Salt Lake City, Utah, 95; Ella Jackson Artist & Scholars Fund, Truro Ctr Arts, Castle Hill, Mass, 96; Biennial Competition, Louis Comfort Tiffany Found, 97; Polariod Artist Support Program, Boston, 2000. *Bibliog:* Grace Consoli (auth), Meanwhile the Girls were Playing, Arts Media, 99; Temin Christine (auth), A Delicate Spin on a Life in Cuba, Boston Globe, 11/17/99; David Wildman (auth), Technology Doesn't over Whelm the Art, Boston Globe, 10/10/99. *Publ:* Auth, Aperture No 141, New York, fall 95; Beacon Press, Summer 98. *Dealer:* Schneider Gallery. *Mailing Add:* c/o Schneider Gallery Inc 230 W Superior Chicago IL 60610

CANDAU, EUGENIE
LIBRARIAN
b San Francisco, Calif, Jan 26, 38. *Study:* Fat City Sch Finds Art, MFA, 73; San Francisco State Univ, BA, 74; Univ Calif, Berkeley, MLS, 78. *Collection Arranged:* Kaethe Kollwitz, San Francisco Mus Art, 70; Hand Bookbinding Today, An International Art (traveling exhib), San Francisco Mus Mod Art, 78. *Pos:* Librn, Fine Arts Libr, San Francisco Mus Mod Art, 68-. *Mem:* Col Art Asn; Art Libr Soc NAm (exec bd, 90-91); Pac Ctr Bk Arts (exec bd, 83-86); Berkeley Civic Arts Comn, 83-90; Berkeley Art Ctr (exec bd, 90- & pres, 95-97). *Interests:* Arts of the book; modern & contemporary art. *Publ:* Bibliographies for San Francisco Mus Mod Art publ: Edward Ruscha, Philip Guston, Sigmar Polke, and others, 70-; auth, articles and reviews in Fine Print and Art Week, 76-; Hand Bookbinding Today, An International Art (exhib catalog), 78; contribr, P Selz, In: Art in Our Times, Abrams, 81; and others. *Mailing Add:* 2108 Derby St Berkeley CA 94705

CANDIOTI, BEATRIZ A
PAINTER
Study: Col Nac, with Ramos Mejia, AA, 50; Univ Louisville, BA, 80, Univ KY, 86-90. *Work:* Nat Mus Am Art, Smithsonian Inst, Washington, DC; Floyd Co Art Mus, New Albany, Ind; Galerie Triangle, Washington, DC. *Exhib:* One-woman show, Galerie Triangle, Washington, DC, 83; James Hunt Baker Galleries, NY, 83; Kentucky Tradition in Am Landscape Painting 1800 to the Present, Owensboro Mus Fine Art, Ky, 83; Capital Art from Kentucky, Lazenby Assoc, Washington, DC, 85; Kentucky Art Exhib, J B Speed Art Mus, Louisville, 86. *Awards:* First prize, Art Asn Harrisburg, Pa, 84; Catherine Lorillard Wolfe Award, 85; Kentucky Artist Award, Ky Gen Assembly, 90. *Mem:* Nat Asn Women Artists. *Mailing Add:* 1110 NE 184th St Miami FL 33179-4614

CANIER, CAREN
PAINTER, EDUCATOR
b New York City, NY, Mar 25, 53. *Study:* Cornell Univ, BFA, 1974; Boston Univ, MFA, 1976. *Work:* Herbert F Johnson Mus of Art, Ithaca, NY; Art Mus, SUNY, Albany; Am Acad, Rome, Italy; Chemical Bank (Corp Collection), NY; Am Hess (Corp Collection), NY; AT&T (Corp Collection), Chicago. *Exhib:* Solo exhib, Robert Schoelkopf Gallery, 85 & 91; Solo exhib, (invitational), Bowery Gallery, NY, 2001; Solo exhib (traveling), Boston Univ Sherman Art Gallery, Mass, 2002; Les Fables de LaFontaine (traveling), Cent pour l'Art et la Cult, Inst Am Univ, 2002-2003; Allegories Imagined Landscapes, Concord Art Asn, Concord Mass, 2003; Between Perception & Invention, Sharon Arts Ctr, Petersburgh, NH, 2005. *Teaching:* Prof art, Rensselaer Polytechnic Inst, 1978-. *Awards:* Rome Prize, Am Acad in Rome, 1977-78; Artist Fel, NY Found Arts, 85 & 90; Ingram Merrill Found Grant, 1986; Pollock Krasner Found Grant, 1990. *Bibliog:* Ken Johnson (auth), CarenCanier, Arts Mag, 1985; Katherine French (auth), Caren Canier, Boston Univ, 2002; Jeanne Duval (auth), Between Perception & Invention, Sharon Arts Ctr, 2005; Koren Christofides (auth), Fables of LaFontaine, Univ Wash Press, 2006. *Mem:* Col Arts Asn of Am; Soc of Fels, Am Acad in Rome. *Media:* 2D Mixed Media, Oil, Matte Acrylic

CANNIFF, BRYAN GREGORY
DESIGNER, DIRECTOR
b Minneapolis, Minn, Dec 26, 48. *Study:* Minneapolis Col Art & Design, BFA, 71. *Collection Arranged:* Designer, The Life of Florence Ziegfeld (and 40 other maj shows), New York City Mus, 75 & Bicentennial Exhib, South St Seaport Mus, 76. *Pos:* Art dir, New York City Mus, 72-75; designer, South St Seaport Mus, NY, 75-76 & Mus Mod Art, NY, 76-79; art dir, Saturday Rev Mag Corp, NY, 79-80, Panorama Mag, 81 & Boating Mag, 81-83; creative dir, Popular Mechanics Mag, 83-. *Awards:* NY Art Dirs Club Awards, 80, 84 & 87; Creativity Awards, 82-98; Desi Awards, 82-98. *Mem:* Visual Club; Soc Illusr; Am Inst Graphic Arts; Soc Pub Designers; NY Art Dir Club. *Mailing Add:* 281 W 11th St New York NY 10014

CANNING, SUSAN M
HISTORIAN, CRITIC
Study: Calif State Univ, BA, 70; Pa State Univ, MA(art hist, Fulbright Fel), 73; PhD(art hist), 80. *Collection Arranged:* Henry Van de Velde (auth, catalog), Konniklijk Mus & Kroller Muller, 88; The Order of Things (auth, catalog), Trinity Col, Hartford, 93; Myself: Your/other (auth, catalog), Castle Gallery, 93, Mediums the Message (auth, catalog), 95 & Alternative Measurer (auth, catalog), 98. *Teaching:* Asst prof art hist, Univ NC, 79-86; assoc prof art hist, Oberlin Col, Ohio, 88 & Col New Rochelle, NY, 89-. *Awards:* Fulbright Res Fel, Belgium, 86; Scholar in Residence, NY Univ, 95. *Mem:* Col Art Asn; Asn Historians 19th Century Art; NY Univ Assoc; Nat Asn Arts Admin; Visual Resource Asn. *Res:* 19th century Belgian art, especially James Ensor, Henry Van de Velde and Les Vingt. *Publ:* Auth, Henry Van de Velde, Painhryst Drawings, Royal Mus Antwerp, 88; Le Cercle des XX, Tzwern-Aisinber, 89; The Order of Anarchy, Col Art Asn, 94; Le foule et le boulevard: James Ensor the sheer politics of everyday life, Peter Lang Publ, 97; Visionary politics: the social subject of James Ensor, Barbicon, London, 97. *Mailing Add:* Art Dept SAS Col New Rochelle 29 Castle Place New Rochelle NY 10805

CANNULI, RICHARD GERALD
PAINTER, GALLERY DIRECTOR
b Philadelphia, Pa, Feb 2, 47. *Study:* Villanova Univ, BFA, 73; Art Students League, 75; Pratt Inst, MFA, 79. *Comn:* Paintings, St Nicholas Tolentine Church, Bronx, 77-79, Assumption-St Paul Parish, Mechanicville, NY, 78 & St Augustine Prep Chapel, Richland, NJ, 80-81; Dedication Cross, Connelly Ctr, Villanova Univ, 80; Design the Chapel, Biscayne Col, Fla, 81. *Exhib:* Expressions, Earth Art, Mus Philadelphia Civic Ctr, 79; Creative Dimensions, Carrier Found, Bellmead, NJ, 79; Liturgical Art, Pavilion Gallery, Mt Holly, NJ, 81; Watercolors of Europe, Palace of Arts Gallery, Minsk & Byelorussia House Artist Creations Gallery, Riga, Latvia, 91-92; New Watercolors, E China Normal Univ Art Gallery, Shanghai, China, 92 & 95; A Survey of Work 1968-1995: Paintings, Fabric and Sculpture, Villanova Univ Art Gallery, Pa, 95; Art and Religion, Balch Inst Ethnic Studies, Philadelphia, Pa, 97; Connections: Religion and Art (traveling exhib), Asn Uniting Religion & Art, 98; A Brushed with God: Contemp Religious Icons, Lawrence Gallery, Rosemont Col, Pa, 98; Behold the Wood of the Cross: The Crucivix in Art and Worship, Galleria

Inter-Cult Ctr, Georgetown Univ, Washington, DC, 99. *Teaching:* Instr studio art & hist, Msgr Bonner High Sch, Drexel Hill, Pa, 73-78; asst prof studio art, Villanova Univ, 7996, dir, Art Gallery, 79-, chmn, Dept Art & Art Hist, 90-, assoc prof, 96-. *Media:* Oil, Fabric. *Mailing Add:* Studio Art/Theater Dept Villanova Univ 800 Lancaster Ave Villanova PA 19085

CANO, MARGARITA
PAINTER
b Havana, Cuba, Feb 27, 32. *Study:* Univ Havana, PhD, 56, MLibSc, 62; studies in art hist & mus conserv with Helmut Ruheman from Nat Gallery, London, Eng. *Exhib:* South Fla Arts Ctr, Miami Beach, 94; Cult Res Ctr, Miami, 98; Dade Co Cult Resource Ctr, Miami, 2003; Coral Gables Libr, Fla, 2003; Books and Books Art Gallery, Coral Gables, Fla, 2005. *Collection Arranged:* Cintas Fellows, Paintings by Cuban Artists (auth, catalog), Miami-Dade Pub Libr, Fla, 77; The Romance of an Era, Colonial Art in Cuba, Main Libr, 80; The Miami Generation, Cuban Mus, Miami, 83; Art of the Bound Book, 85 & Some of Our Favorite Things, 86, Main Libr; Cintas Fellows Revisited, Main Libr, 88. *Pos:* Registr, Julio Lobo Found, Napoleonic Art Mus, 57-58; art librn, Miami-Dade Pub Libr, 63-93; bd dir, Cuban Mus, Miami & Cintas Found, NY, Miami Book Fair Int & Bass Mus, Miami Beach, 97; panelist, National Endowment for the Arts, Washington, DC, 97. *Teaching:* Instr contemp Latin Am art, South Campus, Miami-Dade Community Col, 77, instr hist Latin Am art, 82. *Awards:* Cintas Found Fel, 75-76. *Mem:* Art Libr Soc NAm; Am Libr Asn. *Media:* Encaustic, Mixed-Media. *Res:* Contemporary Latin American art. *Publ:* Auth, How to Bridge the Art Gap, Art Libr Soc NAm, 76; Dictionary of Latin American Artists (bibliog), Cintas Found, 76. *Mailing Add:* 501 SW 24th Ave Miami FL 33135

CANO, PABLO D
SCULPTOR, EDUCATOR
b Havana, Cuba, Mar 11, 61; US citizen. *Study:* Miami-Dade Community Col, Wolfson Scholar, AA, 80; Md Art Inst, BFA, 82; Queens Col, MA (Cintas fel), 86. *Work:* Miami-Dade Pub Libr & Miami-Dade Community Col, Miami; Cintas Found, NY. *Exhib:* Carnival of Critters, Main Libr Gallery, Miami, 81; The Miami Generation (with catalog), Cuban Mus Arts & Cult, Miami 83 & traveling nationally, 83-85; Celebration The Holiday Tradition, Mus Art, Ft Lauderdale, Fl, 88; and many others in the US, Colombia & France. *Teaching:* Instr advan drawing, New World Sch Arts, 88; prof humanities, Miami Dade Community Col, Med Ctr Campus, 92. *Bibliog:* Helen Kohen (auth), Bright days for art in South Florida, Art News, 12/80; Giulio V Blanc (auth), Pablo Cano, Noticias de Arte, 9/81; and others in Miami Herald, Miami News, El Herald & Diario Las Americas, 80-81. *Media:* Miscellaneous. *Publ:* Illusr, The Thorns are Green My Friend, Ediciones Universal, 88; El Niño de Guano, Poemario Angel Gaztelu. *Dealer:* Pablo Cano Portrait Art Studio; Gomez Gallery Baltimore MD. *Mailing Add:* 501 SW 24th Ave Miami FL 33135-2933

CANRIGHT, SARAH ANNE
PAINTER
b Chicago Ill, Aug 20, 41. *Study:* Art Inst Chicago, BFA. *Work:* Kresge Found, NY; Art Inst Chicago; Nat Collection Fine Art, Washington, DC; Chase Manhattan Bank, London; AT&T Corp, Richmond, Va; and others. *Exhib:* Whitney Biennial, NY, 74; Phyllis Kind Gallery, Chicago, 74-79; Franklin Furnace, NY, 79-81; Pam Adler Gallery, NY, 79-81 & 83-84; Walker Art Ctr, Minneapolis, 81; Artemesia Gallery, Chicago, 86; Marvin Seline Gallery, Austin, Tex, 87; and others. *Teaching:* Instr, Princeton Univ, 78-; instr, Skowhegan Sch Painting & Sculpture, 80; sr lectr, Univ Tex, Austin, 82-. *Awards:* Armstrong Award, Art Inst Chicago, 71; Nat Endowment Arts Fel Grant, 75 & 78-85; Creative Artists Pub Serv Prog Grant, 77. *Bibliog:* Robert Storr (auth), article, Arts Mag 9/81 & Art in Am, 2/85; Douglas Cameron, (auth), article, Art News, 5/85; Mel McCombie (auth), article, Art News, 5/87. *Mem:* Am Abstract Artists. *Media:* Oil. *Dealer:* Pam Adler Gallery 37 W 57th St New York NY 10019. *Mailing Add:* 161 Mulberry St New York NY 10013

CANTINE, DAVID
PAINTER
b Jackson, Mich, June 7, 39. *Study:* Univ Iowa, BA, 62, MA, 64. *Work:* Mazur Mus, Monroe, La; Alta Art Found; Edmonton Art Gallery. *Exhib:* One-man shows, Univ Saskatchewan, Univ Alberta & Northern State Univ, 66, 67 & 69, Mazur Mus, 72 & Kraushaar Galleries, NY, 77, 82, 88, 02 & 04, Vanderleelie Gallery, Edmonton, 94, 97,2000, 02 & 04, Cristopher Cuits Gallery, Toronto, 2000 & 04. *Pos:* Prof Artist, currently. *Teaching:* Prof art, Univ AB, 65-96. *Media:* Oil, Acrylic Polymer. *Res:* Color as structure. *Dealer:* Kraushaar Galleries 724 Fifth Ave New York NY; Vanderleelie Gallery Edmonton AB Canada; Christopher Cutts Gallery, 21 Morrow Ave, Toronto, Ont, Can; Aaron Galleries, Chicago. *Mailing Add:* 99 St Georges Crescent Edmonton AB T5N 3M7 Canada

CANTINI, VIRGIL D
EDUCATOR, ENAMELIST, SCULPTOR
b Italy, Feb 28, 20. *Study:* Carnegie Inst Technol, BFA, 46; Univ Pittsburgh, MA, 48; Duquesne Univ, Hon DFA, 81. *Work:* Wichita Mus Art, Kans; Carnegie Mus Art, Pittsburgh, Pa; Westmoreland Co Mus Art, Greensburg, Pa; Hillman Libr, Univ Pittsburgh; Point Park Col. *Comn:* Three sculptures & two tapestries, Hillman Libr, 69 & Nat Sci Bldg, 74, Univ Pittsburgh; Joy of Life (fountain sculpture), Urban Redevelop Authority, Pittsburgh, 69; Skyscape (enamel mural), Oliver Tyrone Co, Pittsburgh, 71; enamel murals, Univ Pittsburgh, 75 & 77. *Exhib:* Assoc Artists Pittsburgh, 45-70; Pittsburgh Int, Carnegie Mus Art, 61,64 & 67; one-man shows, Westmoreland Co Mus Art, 62 & Pittsburgh Plan Arts, 62, 67, 72, 75 & 78; Enamels 50-80, Brookfield Craft Ctr Gallery, Conn, 81. *Pos:* Vpres, Pittsburgh Coun for Arts, 68-70; Pres, Asn Artists Pittsburgh. *Teaching:* Prof art & chmn dept studio arts, Univ Pittsburgh, 52-99. *Awards:* Guggenheim Fel, 58; Pope Paul VI Bishop's Medal, 64; Davinci Medal-Ital Sons & Daughters Am, Cult Heritage Found, 68. *Bibliog:* Dorothy Sterling (auth), article, Am Artist, 52; Helen Knox (auth), article, Pitt Mag, 64; Lloyd Davis (auth), article, Appalachian, 67. *Mem:* Assoc Artists Pittsburgh (pres, 62-64); Arts & Crafts Ctr (vpres, 55-57); Pittsburgh Plan Arts; Col Art Asn Am; Am Crafts Coun. *Media:* Enamel. *Mailing Add:* 205 S Craig St Pittsburgh PA 15213

CANTONE, VIC
CARTOONIST, LECTURER
b New York, NY, Aug 7, 33. *Study:* Sch Art & Design, New York, grad, 52; Art Inst Schs, Inc, Minneapolis, grad, 78; Nassau Col, Garden City, NY, AA(cum laude), 78; Hofstra Univ, with Prof John Wildeman, Hempstead, NY, BA, 79; post-grad, 85-; Fulbright Scholar, Japan, 87. *Work:* Mus Cartoon Art, Ohio State Univ; US Presidential Librs (Johnson, Ford & Reagan); Geo-Graphics: Political Cartoons and the Environment, Hofstra Univ Mus, 90; Smithsonian Inst. *Exhib:* Int Pavillion Humor, Montreal, Can; Smithsonian Inst. *Collection Arranged:* Political Cartoons/Caricatures, Int Salon Cartoons, Montreal, 76-89; Best Editorial Cartoons of the Year, 75-2004; Reins of Power, Mus Cartoon Art, Boca Raton, Fla, 79; Geo-Graphics: Political Cartoonists on the Environment, 90 & The Reagan Presidency, 93, Hofstra Mus; No Laughing Matter: Political Cartoonists on the Environment, Smithsonian Inst, 91-96. *Pos:* Newsroom, cartoonist, Newsday, Melville, NY, 54-59; political cartoonist, caricaturist, NY Daily News, 59-91; ed art, Newsweek, 74-82; political cartoonist & caricaturist, King Features/North Am Syndicate, 91-; Wall Street Journal Report (nat tv), 82-83; cur & dir, Geo Graphics, Political Cartoons & The Environment, Hofstra Mus, 90; courtroom artist, Cablevision News 12, 91-2001; No Laughing Matter: Political Cartoonists on the Environment, Smithsonian Inst, 92-96; ed & pub mag, 74-79, editl cartoons Travel Weekly Mag, 73-91, others; editorial cartoonist, The Brooklyn Papers, 95-2002. *Teaching:* Lectr, Nassau Col, 77, Hofstra Univ, 79 & 86, NY Press Club, 80, 86 & 98, Asn Am Ed Cartoonists, 83, 84 & 86 & John Jay Col Criminal Justice, 85 & 98, Queens Col, 96, 97, & 98. *Awards:* George Washington Honor Medal, Freedoms Found, 78; Golden Press Award, 79; Hon Legion Award, NY, Police Dept, 94 & 96; The Reuben Award, Deadline Club, NY, 2003; Nat Cartoonist Soc. *Bibliog:* Cover story, Vic Cantone, Editorial Cartoonist, Illusr Mag, 79; Reach Out, Cable & Satellite, 5/83; Faces & Places, NY Daily News, 85. *Mem:* Soc Prof Journalists; Asn Am Ed Cartoonists. *Media:* Print, Video. *Res:* Acquired Knowledge of Nonverbal Communication Theory. *Publ:* Auth & illusr, Topo the Mouse, T S Denison & Co, 69; The Sea Circus, Chicago Tribune, 70; newspaper articles; first amendment themes, Ed & Publ Mag, 74-79. *Dealer:* Rothco Cartoons Syndicate 1463 44 St Brooklyn NY 11219; King Features/North Am Syndicate 235 E 45 St New York NY 10017; artistmarket.com Syndicate 35336 Spring Hill Farmington Hills Mich 48331-2044

CANTOR, FREDRICH
PAINTER, PHOTOGRAPHER
b New York, NY, July 8, 44. *Study:* Pratt Inst, 62-64, 66 & 67; San Francisco Art Inst, 66; Cooper Union, 69; studied with Philip Pearlstein. *Work:* Pa State Mus; New Orleans Mus Art, La; Sheldon Mem Art Gallery, Univ Nebr, Lincoln; Univ Mass Mus Art, Amherst; Bibliot Nat & Mus Carnavalet, Paris, France; Musee Nicéphore Niépce, Chalon S/Saone, France. *Exhib:* One-man shows, Robert Schoelkopf Gallery, NY, 76, Sheldon Mem Art Gallery, Univ Nebr, Lincoln, 79, Galeria Diaframma, Milan, Italy, 80, Galerie Delpire, Paris, France, 80 & 82, La Galerie Le Trepied, Geneva, Switz, 81, Marcuse Pfeifer Gallery, NY, 81 & Musee Nicephore Niepce, Chalon, S/Saone, France, 85; Galerie Philippe Fregnac, Paris, 83; Am Ctr, Paris, 84; Spazi Contemp Art, Housatonic, Mass, 94; Nicholas Davies & Co, NY, 95; and others. *Teaching:* Special instr photographic printing, St Martin's Sch Art, London, Eng, 71; adj lectr photog, Brooklyn Col, NY, 74-76; instr photog & drawing, Sch Visual Arts, NY, 75-76, Parsons Sch Design, New York, 77-78. *Awards:* Fel, Yaddo, 78; Fel, Va Ctr Creative Arts, 79, 80 & 84; Fel, McDowell Colony, 80; Fel Grant, NY State Found Arts, photog, 87. *Bibliog:* Hilton Kramer (auth), Fredrich Cantor, New York Times, 3/27/76 & 5/17/81; Janet Malcolm (auth), Fredrich Cantor, The New Yorker, 5/29/76; Carole Naggar (auth), Fredrich Cantor-Dictionnaire des Photographes, Editions Seuil, Paris, 83. *Media:* Silver Gelatin & Kodalith Prints; All. *Publ:* Auth, Rome: Vol 1, 77 & Paris: 1982, 82, pvt publ; illusr, Soul Survivors, Ticknor & Fields, 83. *Mailing Add:* 338 W 11th St New York NY 10014

CANTOR, MIRA
PAINTER, DRAFTSMAN
b New York, NY, May 16, 44. *Study:* State Univ NY, Buffalo, BFA, 66; Univ Ill, Champaign-Urbana, MFA, 69. *Work:* Mus Fine Arts, Boston; Boston Pub Libr; Honolulu Acad Arts, Hawaii; State Found, Honolulu; Rose Art Mus; Brandeis Univ, Waltham, Mass. *Comn:* Portraits comn by Negroponte Family, Brookline, Mass, 78; portraits comn by Baumann Family, Dusseldorf, Ger, 79; portrait comn by Renate Bohmer, Essen, Ger, 79; portrait comn by Dieter Schroder, Dusseldorf, Ger, 79. *Exhib:* One-person show, Galerie Lohrl, Ger, 78, De Cordova Mus, 86, Tokyo Am Ctr, Japan, 87 & Northeastern Univ, 88, 90; Boston Invitational '78, Brockton Art Ctr, Mass, 78; Three Dimensional Possibilities, Rose Art Mus, Waltham, Mass, 79; Centerbeach, Ctr Advan Visual Studies, Mass Inst Technol, 79 & 80; Fitchburg Art Mus, 92; Am Ctr, Egypt, 95, Genovese Sullivan Gallery, Boston, 99, 2002, 2005. *Collection Arranged:* Rose Art Mus, Brandeis Univ. *Pos:* Consult, Massport, 81-82; coordr visual arts, Northeastern Univ, 85-87; consult, Urban Arts, Boston, 89-90. *Teaching:* Instr painting & drawing, Univ Hawaii, Honolulu, 70-71; instr drawing, Mass Inst Technol, 78-80; instr, Northeastern Univ, Boston, 83-87, asst prof, 88-91, assoc prof, 91-2004, prof, 2004-. *Awards:* Artist-in-residence Award, Univ Hawaii, 82; Res & Develop Fund, Northeastern Univ, 89; Fac Exchange, Univ Alexandria, 91; Fulbright Scholar, 94. *Bibliog:* Robert Taylor (auth), Show Yields Fresh Perspectives, 4/84, Christine Temin (auth), Mira Cantor: Drawings that Dance, 5/88, Running Freeze 4/90, Boston Globe; Nancy Stapen (auth), New England Portraitists in 80's

Keep Faces Fresh, 1/89, Artist Wasteland Embodies Life-and-Death Questions, 5/90, Boston Herald; Mira Cantor (article), Arts and Sciences Chronical, Northeastern Univ Col of Arts and Sciences, 3/90. *Mem:* Col Art Asn. *Media:* Multi-Media, Drawing, Painting. *Dealer:* Genovese Sullivan Gallery Boston. *Mailing Add:* 99 Dunster Rd Apt 2 Jamaica Plain MA 02130-2733

CANTOR, RUSTY
PAINTER, SCULPTOR
b New York, NY, Aug 6, 27. *Study:* Art Students League, NY. *Work:* Nat Mus Women Art; Art in Embassies Prog, Washington; Inst Am Indian Art Mus, Santa Fe, NMex. *Exhib:* San Francisco Arts Comn Gallery, 87; Am Embassy, New Delhi, India, 90-92; Calif Poly State Univ, 92; Grand Palais, Paris, France, 93; NAWA Lever House, NY, 95; ISE Art Found, NY, 96; Gallery Everarts, Paris, France, 97; group exhibs Claudia Chapline Gallery, Stinson Beach, Calif 90, Blackhawk Gallery, Danville, Calif, 94, Lynnhouse Gallery, East Bay Bronze, Antioch, Calif, 95, ISE Art Foun, SoHo, NY, 96, Christensen Heller Gallery, Oakland, Calif, 97, ACCI Gallery, Berkeley, Calif, 99, Interiors, Artisans Gallery, Mill Valley, Calif, 2000, many others; solo exhibs, Compass Gallery, Glasgow, Scotland, 70, Inst Am Indian Art Mus, Santa Fe, NMex, 84, Gallery 92, Half Moon Bay, Calif, 91, Sub-ver-sive Spirituality, Bade Mus, Berkeley, Calif, 92, Addison St Window Gallery, Berkeley, Calif, 93, SOMAR, San Francisco, Calif, 97, The Atrium @ 600 Townsend, San Francisco, 99, 940 Gallery, Berkeley, Calif, 04, Atrium Gallery, San Francisco, Calif, 05. *Pos:* bd dir, Nat Women's Caucus Art, 90-93, vpres Pacific region, 99 & 2000; exec comt mem, Northern Calif Coun Nat Mus Women Artists, 91-92. *Teaching:* Nut's & Bolts, self-management for women artists, 92-. *Awards:* Ada Cecere Award, Nat Asn Women Artists. *Bibliog:* Article in Calif Art Review, Am Reference Publ Corp, 89. *Mem:* Northern Calif Womens Caucus Art (pres, 89-92, 99 & 2000); Northern Calif Coun Nat Mus Women Artists; Nat Asn Women Artists; Pacific Rim Sculpture Group. *Media:* Acrylic, Glass, Bronze. *Interests:* Writing, reading and environment. *Publ:* The Feisty Woman's Plan Ahead Guide, WCA Handbook, Science of Mind, 96

CANTRELL, JIM
PAINTER
b Sulpher, Okla, Nov 23, 35. *Study:* Univ Nebr, Lincoln, BFA, 58; Pa State Univ, 59; Univ Northern Colo, Greeley, MA, 65. *Work:* Sheldon Mem Art Gallery, Lincoln, Nebr; Albrecht-Kemper Mus Art, St Joseph, Mo; Owensboro Mus Fine Art, Ky; Austin Peay State Univ, Tenn; Miss Mus Art, Jackson; JB Speed Art Mus, Louisville, Ky; and others. *Comn:* Canvas murals of the 12 Apostles and Holy Family, St Joseph Proto Cathedral, Bardstown, Ky, 85; 3 oil paintings, Abbey of Gethsemani, Trappist, Ky, 89; 7 oils (portraits of Abbots), St Meinrad Monastery, Ind; 10 oils, Heavenhill Bourbon Heritage Ctr, Bardstown, Ky, 2004; portrait, Univ Evansville, Ind, 2005. *Exhib:* One-man shows, Sheldon Mem Art Gallery, 70, Hunter Mus of Art, Chattanooga, Tenn, 73, Distelheim Galleries, Chicago, 75 & JB Speed Art Mus, 85; Butler Inst Am Art, Youngstown, Ohio, 90, 2000; Albrecht-Kemper Mus Art, St Joseph, Mo, 91; Evansville Mus Arts & Sci, Ind, 92; Southeastern Ctr Contemp Art, Winston, Salem, NC, 94; Mus Nebr Art, Kearney, 95; The Millennium Painter, Owensboro Mus Fine Art, Ky, 2001. *Pos:* Resident artist, Berea Col, 70-71; independent studio artist, Bardstown, Ky, 71-. *Teaching:* Guest instr art, Univ Northern Colo, summer, 66; assoc prof art, John F Kennedy Col, 66-70; vis artist, Austin Peay State Univ, Tenn, 88. *Awards:* Al Smith Fel, 92; Southern Arts Fedn Fel, 94; Alumni Award for creative achievement, Univ of No Colo, 2000. *Bibliog:* Jim Cantrell, Am Artist Mag, 7/87; Allen Gussow (auth), The Artist as Native, Pomegranate Publ, 93; Henry Adams (auth), Jim Cantrell, 94. *Mem:* Ky Guild Artists & Craftsmen (bd trustees, 73-75 & 78-79); Louisville Visual Arts Asn; Chamber of Commerce. *Media:* Oil, Watercolor. *Publ:* Auth, Cut decoration, 75 & Studio management, 85, Ceramics Mo; Kentucky Reflected: a study in Character and Setting, JB Speed Mus, 5/85; The Fragmented Image, Nat Acad Sci, Washington, 91; New American Paintings III, Open Studio Press, 95. *Mailing Add:* c/o Bardstown Art Gallery 214 W Stephen Foster Ave Bardstown KY 40004

CANTWELL, WILLIAM RICHARD
PAINTER, PRINTMAKER
b Philadelphia, Pa, July 24, 1947. *Study:* Trinity Col, Conn, BA, 69; Sch Visual Arts, studied drawing & illustration with Jack Potter, 77-84; Pratt Inst & Manhattan Graphics Ctr, studied etching with David Finkbeiner, 85-86. *Comn:* Public Relations Booklet, Consolidated Edison, NY, 77; Citibank Bldg & New York Skyline (drawings), Citibank, NY, 78; portrait series, Fairbanks Rehabilitation Asn, Alaska, 85. *Exhib:* Key West Art Festival, Fla, 86, 87, 88; Westport Art Festival, Conn, 86, 87, 88; Mystic Art Festival, Conn, 86, 87, 88; Gracie Sq Art Festival, NY, 86-88; Miami Beach Festival Arts, 87, 88; Maitland, Fla Art Fest, 87-88; Gasparilla Art Festival, Tampa, 89; Beaux Arts Festival, Coral Gables, 88-89; Wickford Art Festival, RI, 89-90; Coconut Grove Arts Festival, Fla, 92, 93 & 94; Cherry Creek Arts Festival, Denver, Colo, 92, 93 & 94; Festival of the Masters, Disney World, Fla, 92, 93 & 94; Winter Park Arts Festival, Fla, 95; and others. *Teaching:* Art therapist & painting instr, The Grove Sch, Madison, Conn, 69-70; instr graphics & photog, The Reece Sch, NY, 70-77. *Awards:* First Place, graphics, Washington Square Outdoor Exhib, New York, 79 & 85 & Key West Old Island Days Art Festival, 86; Philip Isenberg Award, Salmagundi Club, New York, 81; Rowland A Dufton Award for best of Watercolor show, 88; Second Third Place, watercolor, Washington Square Art Exhib, 88. *Media:* Watercolor, Etching, Serigraphy. *Publ:* Illusr, Around the system: We don't just work here, Consolidated Edison, New York, 77; Celebrity choice, Playbill Mag, New York, 83; Circling Manhattan, Dramalogue, Hollywood Co, New York, 83; Portraits, Fairbanks Rehabilitation Asn, Alaska, 85. *Mailing Add:* 201 W 92nd St No 4B New York NY 10025-7400

CAO, GILDA
PHOTOGRAPHER, PAINTER
b Cienfuegos, Cuba, Dec 17, 56; US Citizen. *Study:* Abroad Studies Eng, Univ of London, BFA, 86; NY Univ, Tisch Sch Arts, 88; Parsons Sch of Design, currently attending. *Work:* Gerald W Moore, Banker, Miami, Fla; Gunther Weiss, Art Collector; Paul Steiner; Douglas Oliver, Philanthropist, NY. *Exhib:* Tribeca Art Loft, New York City, 98; Fleet Bank, Empire State Bldg, NY, 99; Salon Di Pierro Martin, Ger, 2000. *Pos:* Cur, Zepol, Cuban Fine Art, 92; art posing, Pratt Sch of Design, 97-2004; poet, auth, Free lance assignments, currently. *Teaching:* instr, yoga, self mastery, pvt sessions, currently. *Bibliog:* Jewish Voice, NYC, 2006. *Media:* Photography, Poet. *Collection:* Silver gelatin modern heroine, a multifaced mobile image with alternate point of view

CAPA, CORNELL
PHOTOGRAPHER, MUSEUM DIRECTOR
b Budapest, Hungary, Apr 10, 1918. *Study:* Madach Imre Gymnasium, Budapest, 28-36. *Exhib:* Margin of Life, Ctr of Inter-Am Relations, NY, 74; Johnson Mus, Cornell Univ, Ithaca, NY, 75. *Pos:* Staff & contrib photogr, Life Mag, NY, 46-67; mem photogr, Magnum Photos, NY & Paris, 54-; guest dir, The Concerned Photogr, Riverside Mus, NY, 66, The Concerns of Roman Vishniac, Jewish Mus, NY, 73, Behind the Great Wall: China, Metrop Mus Art, NY, 72 & The Concerned Photogr Two, Israel Mus, Jerusalem, 73; exec comn, Overseas Press Club NY, 67-70 & 69-73; ed, The Concerned Photogr One & Two, Grossman/Viking, 69-72; exec dir, Int Ctr Photog, 74-94, founding dir emer, 94-. *Teaching:* Lectr photog, New York Univ, 68-72 & Int Ctr Photog, 74-. *Awards:* Honor Roll, Am Soc Mag Photogr, 75; Joseph A Sprague Mem Award, Nat Press Photogr Asn, 76; New York Mayor's Award of Honor, 78. *Bibliog:* Feature prof, Who Am I?, NBC Television, Channel 4, 71; Center of Concern, CBS Television, 77; Richard Whelan (auth), Cornell Capa's lighthouse of photography, Artnews, 4/79. *Mem:* Magnum Photogs (pres, 57-60); Overseas Press Club New York; Am Soc Mag Photogr. *Publ:* Coauth (with Maya Pines), Retarded Children Can Be Helped, Channel Press, 57; coauth (with Matthew Huxley), Farewell to Eden, Harper & Row, 64; coauth (with J M Stycos), Margin of Life, 73 & ed, International Center of Photography Library of Photographers (first six titles), 74, Grossman Publ. *Dealer:* Magnum Photog Inc 261 Park Ave South New York NY 10036

CAPES, RICHARD EDWARD
GRAPHIC ARTIST, INSTRUCTOR
b Atlanta, Ga, Nov 6, 42. *Study:* Univ Ga, Athens, BS, 65, MA, 69; Univ Ga, Cortona, Italy, 70. *Work:* Barnwell Mem Garden Art Ctr, Shreveport, La. *Comn:* 200 Years (painting), Collectors Wall Gallery, Sarasota, Fla, 76; illus, Southside Sch, Sarasota, Fla, 83; graphic symbol of Venice, Fla, Chamber Commerce, 92; painting, City Sarasota, Fla, 94; Arthur Andersen LLP, Sarasota, Fla, 2000. *Exhib:* Two Southern Draughtsmen, Addison Gallery Am Art, 72; Brooks Mem Art Gallery, 72; 32nd Ann Exhib, Jacksonville Art Mus, Fla, 81; 36th Ann Exhib, Lee Scarfone Gallery, Univ Tampa, Fla, 86; two person show, Creative Edge, Bradenton, Fla, 92; 43rd Ann Fla Artists Group Inc Show, Sarasota, Fla, 92. *Teaching:* Asst prof art educ, Univ Southern Miss, 71-73; asst prof art, Morehead State Univ, 73-74. *Awards:* Southeast Bank Award, 80 & Hamel Mem Award, 81, Fla Artist Group Inc; First Prize, Arvida State Fla, 83; First Place Art, United First Fed Savings & Loan, Fla, 86. *Bibliog:* Wayne Mayhail II (auth), Gulfcoast People, Gulf Coast Publ, 89; Ralph Montgomery (ed-auth), article, Bus Magiziner, 89. *Mem:* Manatee Art League; Sarasota Visual Arts Ctr; Fla Artist Group Inc; Anna Maria Island Art League; Fla Watercolor Soc; and others. *Media:* Ink, Watercolor. *Publ:* Illusr, Sarasota Scene - Historical, 4/90; illusr, cover, Bus Magazine Yearbook, 90; cover, SARASOTA: A Sentimental Journey, Libr Cong, 91; auth & illusr, Richard Capes Drawings Capture Siesta Key, Libr Cong, 92. *Dealer:* Art for the World Gallery Sarasota Fla; Islan Gallery West Holems Beach FL. *Mailing Add:* 2116 Florinda St Sarasota FL 33581

CAPLAN, CONSTANCE ROSE
COLLECTOR
b Philadelphia, Pa, Dec 28, 35. *Study:* Goucher Col, BA, 57; Johns Hopkins Univ, MA, 78. *Pos:* pres, The Time Group, Baltimore, 86-; Managing dir, Caswell J Caplan Charitable Trusts, Baltimore, 87-; Trustee, off, pres-elect, Baltimore Mus Art, 87-; bd dir, Preserv Md, 89-, Wash & Baltimore Regional Asn, 91-, Downtown Partnership Baltimore Inc, 91-; overseer Baltimore Sch for Arts, 90-; mem libr adv coun, Milton S. Eisenhower Libr, The Johns Hopkins Univ, 93-; pres, Mt Vernon Cult Dist; bd dir, Baltimore Community Found; trustee Dia Ctr Arts, NY; chmn, Community Arts Partners Task Force, Baltimore. *Awards:* Named one of Md's Top 100 Women, The Daily Record, 99; Top 200 Collectors, ARTnews Mag, 2004; Recipient Baltimore City Mayor's Award, Mount Vernon Sq. *Interests:* Cooking, gardening, archaeology & hiking. *Collection:* Contemporary art. *Publ:* Editor: Bawlamer, 1971. *Mailing Add:* Time Group 701 Cathedral St Baltimore MD 21201

CAPLAN CIARROCCHI, SANDRA
PAINTER, INSTRUCTOR
b Winnipeg, Man, 36. *Study:* Univ Man, BFA, 57; Boston Univ, MFA, 60; Yale Univ, 60-61. *Work:* Winnipeg Art Gallery; J A MacAulay Collection, Toronto; Boston Mutual Life Insurance; Bellevue Hosp, NY; Connor Clark Inc, Toronto. *Exhib:* one-person exhibs, Winnipeg Art Gallery, 74, Cast Iron Gallery, NY, 94 & Brooklyn Botanic Garden, 97, Westbeth Gallery, NY, 2003, Paintingsdirect.com, 2005; Maine Coast Artists Exhibs, 74-77; Watercolor, Contemp View, Fairleigh Dickinson Univ, 81; Views by Women Artists, Fordham Univ, 82, Gallery 53, Cooperstown, NY, Still Life-Landscape; Atlantic Gallery, 86; First Street Gallery, 89; Artists Equity Show, 97, 98. *Teaching:* Instr art, Mus Mod Art, NY, 65-71, Village Community Sch, NY, 71-79, Lenox Sch, NY, 79-89, & Nat Acad Design 89-, Town Sch, NY, 89-2001,. *Awards:*

Can Coun Award, 61-62; Woodstock Art Asn Award Watercolor, 83; 3rd Prize Painting, Cooperstown Art Asn Nat Competition. *Bibliog:* John Graham (auth), article, Winnipeg Free Press, 74; John Perrault (auth), article, Soho Weekly News, 76; article, Artspeak, 1/86; David Daniel (auth), In the Galleries Art & Antiques, 4/89. *Mem:* Artists Equity Asn. *Media:* Oil, Pastel, Watercolor. *Interests:* still life with landscape views. *Publ:* Illusr, Fair Game--Hunter's Cookbook (Great American Cooking Schools), Irena Chalmers Cookbooks Inc, 83. *Mailing Add:* 463 W St Apt D 1004 New York NY 10014-2010

CAPOBIANCO, DOMENICK
PAINTER, SCULPTOR
b St Louis, Mo, Dec, 22, 28. *Study:* Washington Univ, St Louis, Mo, BFA, 58; Skowhegan Sch Painting & Sculpture, 58 & 59. *Work:* Univ Dallas, Tex; Newark Public Libr, NJ; Mus Mod Art, Skopje, Acad Beaux-Arts, Ljubljana, Yugoslavia; Graphische Sammlung Albertina, Vienna, Austria; Mus Contemp Art, Fredrickstad, Norway; Nat Mus Krakow, Poland; Weatherspoon Mus, Univ NC, Greensboro; Mus Petit Format, Couvin, Belgium; Musee du Petit Format, Couvin, Belgium; Mus for Internat Contemp Graphic Art, Fredrikstad, Norway; Nat Mus of History, Taipei, Taiwan; Nat Mus of Krakow, Poland; Weatherspoon Mus, Univ of NC at Greensboro; Kharkiv Mus, Ukraine; and others. *Comn:* Stage Sets: Experimental Death Unit #1, LeRoy Jones, St Marks Theatre, 64, Forensic & The Navigators, Sam Sheppard, Theatre Genesis, 67, Willy the Germ, Murray Mednick, Theatre Genesis, 68 & The Hunter, Murray Mednick, Theatre Genesis, 68. *Exhib:* Solo exhibs, Univ North Carolina, 67, Sky Piece over Soho, 74, Sky Piece over MOMA, 76, 55 Mercer Gallery, 79, 80, 82, 84, 85 & 86, Am Ctr, Belgrade, Yugoslavia, 82-83, Condeso/Lawler Gallery, NY, 81, Rutgers Univ, NJ, 81, 77, 73, 74, Verita Gallery, Tokyo, 90, Al Galerie Gerlinde Walz, Stuttgart, 93 & Glaskasten, Leonberg, Stuttgart, 96, plus others; Brooklyn Mus Print Exhib, NY, 76; Brooklyn Mus, NY, 78; Gallery artists, Condeso/Lawler Gallery, NY, 83; Gathering of Avant-Garde, Lower East Side 1948-70, NY, 85; Himmelsschreiber: Diemensionen eines fluchtigen mediums, Kassel, 86; Maubeuge-Sculpt 87/III, France, 87; Of Paper, Pigment & Glass, Castle Gallery, Col New Rochelle, 87; Al Gallery, Stuttgart, Ger, 93; Y2K Int Ex & Symposium of Prints, Taipei Fine Arts Mus, Taiwan, 2000; plus many others. *Teaching:* Instr painting, Washington Univ, St Louis, Mo, 57-58; lectr, Art Dept, Univ NC, Greensboro, 67; prof, Art Dept, Rutgers Univ, 67-. *Awards:* Creative Artists Pub Serv Prog Grant, 76; 2 Purchase Awards, Int Exhib Graphic Art, Ljubljana, Yugoslavia, 77; Guggenheim Fel Grant, 84-85; Internat Triennial of Graphic Art award, Bitola, Macedonia, 97. *Bibliog:* Allen Tannenbaum (auth), Soho Weekly News, 10/74; Tiffany Bell (auth), Arts Mag, 5/79; Peter Wallach (dir), film interview; A Life in Art/F Conway, 86; Joe Pollack (auth), article, St Louis Post-Dispatch, 8/31/86; and others. *Media:* Oil, Canvas; Mixed Media. *Dealer:* Studio 13 133 Eldridge St New York NY 10002; Galerie Al Edenhallstr.19 70597 Stuttgart Ger. *Mailing Add:* 133 Eldridge St New York NY 10002-3710

CAPONI, ANTHONY
SCULPTOR, EDUCATOR
b Pretare, Italy, May 7, 21. *Study:* Univ Flore, Italy; Cleveland Sch Art; Walker Art Ctr, Minn; Univ Minn, BS & MEd. *Work:* Minneapolis Inst Art; St Cloud State Col; Minn Mus Am Art, Caponi Art Park and Learning Ctr. *Comn:* Wax models for all bronze motifs, Eisenhower Libr, Abilene, Tex, 60; The Granite Trio, (32 tons carved granite sculpture), St Cloud Mall, Minn, 73; Copper Christ, (24 ft hammered copper sculpture), Edina, Minn, 78; Boulders on Boulders, (3 ton carved limestone sculpture), Minneapolis, Minn, 82; Pompeii, (17 panel bronze sculpture, 150 ft length), Caponi Art Park, Eagan, Minn, 88. *Exhib:* Walker Art Ctr, Minneapolis, 47-58; St Paul Gallery Art, 47-58; Iowa State Teachers Col, 58; Minneapolis Art Inst Ann; solo-show, Minnesota Mus Art, Rochester Art Ctr & Tweed Gallery, Duluth, Minn, 72; Minnesota Artists Look Back 1948-1988, Minn Mus Art & Salone del Palazzo Communale, Modena, Italy, 88-89; retrospective, Macalester Col, St Paul, Minn, 91. *Pos:* founder and artistic dir Caponi Art Park and Learning Ctr. *Teaching:* Prof art & chmn dept, Macalester Col, 1949-1991. *Awards:* Two Purchase Prizes, Minn Inst Art, 47-48; Ford Found Grant, 64; Italian Heritage Award, City of St Paul, 91. *Bibliog:* Moira Harris (auth), Monumental Minnesota: A Guide to Outdoor Sculpture; Public Art in Minnesota, Forecast Pub Artworks; various articles in St Paul Pioneer Press, ThisWeek Newspaper, Minneapolis Star Tribune & Eagan Sun Current. *Media:* Stone. *Publ:* Auth, Boulders & Pebbles of Poetry & Prose, Independence Press, 72; Auth, Voice from the Mountains, Ruminator Press, 2002. *Mailing Add:* 1215 Diffley Rd Eagan MN 55123-1415

CAPONIGRO, PAUL
PHOTOGRAPHER
b Boston, Mass, Dec 7, 32. *Study:* With Benjamin Chin & Minor White. *Work:* Comfort Gallery, Haverford Col, Pa; Int Ctr Photog, NY; Portable Works Collection, Phoenix, Ariz; Mus voor Fotografie, Antwerpen, Belig. *Exhib:* Solo exhibs, Mus Mod Art, NY, 68 & 69, San Francisco Mus Art, 70, Art Inst Chicago, 72, Albright-Knox Art Gallery, Buffalo, 76, High Mus Art, Atlanta, 79, Simon Lewinsky Gallery, San Francisco, 80, Univ Wis-Lacrosse Fine Arts Gallery, 80, Images, Cincinnati, 81, Marlborough Gallery, NY, 81, Photog Gallery, Philadelphia, 81 & Worcester Art Mus, Mass, 81; Looking at Photographs, Mus Mod Art, NY, 73; Am Masters, Smithsonian Inst, 74; Photog in Am, Whitney Mus Am Art, 74; 14 Am Photographers, Baltimore Mus Art & traveling, 75; The Land: Twentieth Century Landscape Photogs, Victoria & Albert Mus, London, Eng, 76; 100 Master Photographers, Mus Mod Art, NY, 76; Mirrors and Windows: Am Photog Since 1960, Mus Mod Art, NY & traveling, 78-80; Am Photog of the '70's, Art Inst Chicago, 79; Discovering Am 1959-70, Art Inst Chicago, 79; American Landscape, Mus Mod Art, 81; A Century of Am Landscape Photog, High Mus Art, Atlanta, 81; Seattle Art Mus, 83; Nat Mus Am Art, Smithsonian Inst, Washington, 84; Mus Mod Art, NY, 85; Photog and Light, Los Angeles Co Mus Art traveling exhib, 87; Decade by Decade-20th Century American Photog, Ctr Creative Photog, Tucson, Ariz, 89; Photographs from the Permanent Collection: A Sesquicentennial Celebration (with catalog), Haverford Comfort Gallery, Haverford Col, Pa, 90; The Beauty of Essence retrospective, Vision Gallery, Calif, 90; Megaliths, Cymbeline, NY Shakespeare Festival, 90; Photo Lore, Hartnell Col, Salinas, Calif, 90; Inlaid Silver: Polaroid Images from the 1960's, Ctr Photog Art, Carmel, Calif, 96; Meditations in Light, Farmsworth Art Mus, Rockland, Maine, 96 & Mus NW Art, La Conner, Wash, 99; Ancient Sentinels, Schmidt-Bingham Gallery, NY, 98; Megaliths, Markosian Libr Gallery, Salt Lake Community Col, 98; Photographs from the Permanent Collection: People and Places, DeCordova Mus & Sculpture Park, Lincoln, Mass, 98; Measure of Nature: Landscape Photographs from the Permanent Collection, Art Inst Chicago, 98; Courtesy of the Artist, Princeton Univ Art Mus, 98. *Pos:* Consult photo res dept, Polaroid Corp, Cambridge, 60-70; workshops at numerous places, 70-74; in residence, Maine Photog Workshop, 79-81. *Teaching:* Instr creative photography, NY Univ, 67-71; instr photography, Yale Univ, 71-86; lectr at numerous universities & art schs throughout the US. *Awards:* Guggenheim Fel, 66 & 75; Nat Endowment Arts Photog Fel, 71 & 74 & Grants, 75 & 82; Art Dirs Club NY Award, 74. *Bibliog:* Hal Fischer (auth), Sensual luminosity and misplaced beauty, Artweek, Vol II, No 24, 13, 7/5/80; Owen Edwards (auth), The gravity of Stone, Am Photogr, Vol 7, No 2, 13-14, 8/81; Margaret Lake (auth), Paul Caponigo (article), ARTnews, 9/98. *Mem:* Founder Am Heliographers Asn. *Publ:* Megaliths, Little Brown & Co, 86; Graphis No 252, Tribute to Polaroid, 11-12/87; Seasons, Little Brown & Co, 88; Photography: Art & Technique, Focal Press, 89; Writing with Light (photo essay), Parabola Mag, fall 91. *Dealer:* Andrew Smith Gallery 76 E San Francisco Santa Fe NM 87501. *Mailing Add:* 20 Prior Ln Cushing ME 04563-3111

CAPORAEL, SUZANNE
PAINTER
b New York, NY, Aug 5, 49. *Study:* Otis Art Inst, Los Angeles Co, BFA, 77, MFA, 79. *Work:* Los Angeles Co Mus Art, Los Angeles; San Francisco Mus Mod Art; Art Inst Chicago, Ill; High Mus Art, Atlanta; JB Speed Art Mus, Louisville; Carnegie Inst, Pittsburgh; Nat Mus of Women in Arts, Washington; Los Angeles Ms of Contemp Art, Los Angeles Co Mus of Art; plus others. *Exhib:* Suzanne Caporael, Newport Harbor Art Mus, Newport, 84 & Santa Barbara Mus Art, Calif, 86; Summer 1985, Mus Contemp Art, Los Angeles, 85; Avant Garde In The Eighties, Los Angeles Co Art Mus, Los Angeles, 87; Presswork, Nat Mus Women in the Arts, Washington, DC, 91; Individual Realities, Sezon Mus Art, Amagasaki, Japan, 91; solo shows incl The Elements of Pigment, Kohn Turner Gallery, Los Angeles, 98, Richard Gray Gallery, Chicago, 98, The Lemberg Gallery, Birmingham, Mich, 98, Suzanne Caporael, Karen McCready Gallery, NY, 2000, Melt New Paintings, Kohn Turner Gallery, Los Angeles, 2000, plus others. *Teaching:* Univ Calif, Santa Barbara & San Francisco Art Inst. *Awards:* Nat Endowment Arts, 86. *Bibliog:* Kenneth Baker (auth) Abstracts with a hint of nature, San Francisco Chronicle, 4/16/94 Suzanne Caporael at the Wirtz gallery, 5/26/92, Galleries, 5/27/87; Monroe Hodder (auth) Inner natures, Visions, summer 95; Kim Levin (auth), Suzanne Caporael, Village Voice, 5/97; Nancy Doll (auth), Suzanne Caporael (catalog) Kohn Turner Gallery, Los Angeles, Richard Gray Gallery, Chicago, 96; Howard Fox (auth) Avant-gard in the eighties, (catalog) Los Angeles Co Mus of Art, 87, California viewpoints - Suzanne Caporael, Santa Barbara Mus of Art, 86; plus others. *Media:* Oil on Canvas. *Specialty:* Modern & Contemporary Masters. *Mailing Add:* c/o Richard Gray Gallery Suite 2503 875 N Michigan Chicago IL 60611

CAPORALE-GREENE, WENDE
PAINTER, INSTRUCTOR
b Bronx, NY, Dec 13, 56. *Study:* Paier Col of Art / Albertus Magnus Col, BFA, 83; Art Students League; Nat Acad of Design; NY Acad, with Ken Davies & Rudolph Zallinger; Private workshops with Daniel Greene, Nelson Shanks, Burton Silverman, Richard Whitney, Thomas Fogarty, Mary Beth Mackenzie & Frank Mason. *Work:* Phillips Med Systems, Inc, Shelton Conn. *Comn:* illus assignments, Readers Digest, Macmillan Publ, Harper & Row, Xerox & Tennis Mag; portraits, John & Caroline Walker, NY, 98, Diana & Will Fiske, Conn, 99, Cornelia Guest, 2004, Laurie & Eric Widing, 2005, Virginia & Jim Collins, Va, 2006. *Exhib:* Pastel Soc of Am Exhibs, NYC, 1983-2005; Allied Artists Am Nat Exhib, NYC; Hammond Mus, N Salem, NY; Hermitage Mus, Norfolk, Va; The One Show, Children's Bk Illus, Master Eagle Gallery, NYC; Soc Illusr Mus Ilus, NY; Monmouth Co Mus, Monmouth, NJ; Nat Art Competition / Am Artist Mag at Grand Central Gallery, NY; Contemp Master Pastelists, Galerie Luminous, Taichung, Taiwan. *Pos:* lectr/demonstr, for Nat Orgn including the Portrait Soc Am, Pastel Soc Am. *Teaching:* instr, pastel painting, Northern Westchester Ctr for the Arts, NY, 1993-2005; instr painting, Katonah Art Ctr, NY, 2005-; pvt workshops, Kimberly, Wis, Hilton Head, SC, Scottsdale, Ariz, Santa Fe, NMex & Asheville, NC, 2004-. *Awards:* Honor Award, Conn Pastel Soc, 1993; Howard Chandler Christy Award for portrait or figure, Pastel Soc Am, NY, 95; Am Artist Prof League for Realistic Pastel, Pastel Soc of Am, 2000; Canson, Inc Award, Pastel Soc Am, NY, 2004; MH Hurlimann Armstrong Award, Pastel Soc of Am, 2005. *Bibliog:* Madlyn Ann Woolwich, The Art of Pastel Portraiture, Watson-Guptill, 95; Feature Article, Pastel Artist Int, 9/99; Madlyn Ann Woolwich (auth), Pastel Interpretations, N Light Publs, 2003; Featured Artist, Pastel J, 11/03-12/03; Ginia Bellafante (auth), Formal Portraits Dress Down, NY Times, 2005; Maureen Bloomfield (auth), Pure Color, The Best of Pastel, N Light Publs, 2005. *Mem:* Pastel Soc of Am (master pastelist); NY Portrait Soc of Am. *Media:* Oil, Pastel. *Publ:* auth, The pastel page, Am Artist Mag, 4/99; auth, Painting Children's Portraits in Pastel, Int Artist Mag, 2001; auth, Words from the wise; the art of the portrait, Int Artist Mag, 4/2006-5/2006. *Dealer:* Portaits Inc New York NY; Portraits S Raleigh NC; ThePortraitSource Flat Rock NC. *Mailing Add:* 742 Titicus Rd PO Box 438 North Salem NY 10560

CAPORASO, PAT M
ART DEALER
b Englewood, NJ, Nov 27, 52. *Study:* Pratt Inst, Brooklyn, NY, BFA, 70-74. *Pos:* Dir, Castelli Galleries, New York, NY, 77-91; pvt dealer & consult, currently. *Mem:* Fine Art Print Dealers Asn; Art Dealers Asn of Am. *Media:* Painting & Drawing. *Specialty:* Contemporary art, late 1950s to the present; modern art; Jasper Johns: Roy Lichtenstein; Robert Rauschenberg: Ellsworth Kelly; Bruce Nauman; Andy Warhol; Cy Twombly; Frank Stella; Ed Ruscha. *Publ:* Print Collector's Newslett, NY Times

CAPPELLAZZO, AMY
APPRAISER, WRITER
Study: Fine Arts, BA, NY Univ; Urban Design and City Planning, Pratt Inst, MA, New York City; Dir Rubell Family Collection & Found, Miami; inte co-head, post-war and contemp art dept Christie's, New York City. *Pos:* Bd dir, Los Angeles Contemp Exhibs; lectr in field. *Mailing Add:* Christie's/NY 20 Rockefeller Plz New York NY 10020

CAPPS, KENNETH P
SCULPTOR
b Kansas City, Mo, April 10, 39. *Study:* Univ Calif, San Diego, BA, 73, MFA, 75. *Work:* Storm King Art Ctr, Mountainville, NY; Sculpture Park Alfred Schmela, Düsseldorf, Ger; Oakland Mus, Calif; San Diego Mus Contemp Art, La Jolla, Calif; Fed Res Bank, Los Angeles, Calif; Mus of Modern Art, NY; plus others. *Comn:* Konoids, outdoor sculpture, San Diego Unified Port Dist, Calif, 85; sculpture, Garden Grove, Calif, 87. *Exhib:* Sculpture in the Fields, Storm King Art Ctr, Mountainville, NY, 73; Pub Sculpture Urban Environ, Oakland Mus, Calif, 74; The Minimal Tradition, Aldrich Mus, Ridgefield, Conn, 79; Sculpture in Calif 1975-80, San Diego Mus, Calif, 80; Constructed Metal, Univ Calif Santa Barbara, 84; A San Diego Exhib, San Diego Mus Contemp Art, La Jolla, Calif, 85 & Sculpture Arenas, Mandeville Gallery, Univ Calif, La Jolla, 87; Metered Atmosphere, Brandstater Gallery, Loma Linda Univ, Calif, 87; Metophor of Function, San Diego State Univ, Calif, 90; Send and Receive Comm Sound Work, Hyde Gallery, Grossmont Col, El Cajon, Calif, 99; Sharjah Arts Mus, Sharjah United Arab Emirates, 2000; New Additions Outdoors, Grounds for Sculpture, Hamilton, NJ, 2003; Solo shows incl Kenneth Capps Sound Sculpture, 1984-92, Calif Ctr for Art Mus, Escondido, Calif, 97, Quint Contemp Art, La Jolla, Calif Sculpture and Drawings, 98; Pub Projects, Calif Ctr for the Arts, Escondida, Calif, 2001-2002; ArtExchange, San Francisco, Calif, 2003; "Backyard" Carlsbad Sculptor, Garden 2004-2005; plus others. *Awards:* Fel, drawing, 83, sculpture, 87, Nat Endowment Arts, 86; Pollock-Krasner Found, 86; Engelhard Found, Boston, Mass, 88. *Bibliog:* Tara Collins (auth), Kenneth Capps, Arts Mag, 9/76; David Lewinson (auth), Forty-two Emerging Artists, San Diego Mus Contemp Art, 85; Francis Colpitt (auth), Art in Am, 5/87; Robert Pincus (auth), On the cutting edge with steel, San Diego Union, 87; Robert & Andrea Perine (auths), San Diego Artist, Artra Publ Inc, 88, Dona Z Meilach (auth) The Contemporary Blacksmith, Schiffer Pub, Ltd, 2000; Dona Z Meilach (auth), Direct Metal Sculpture, Schiffer Pub, Ltd, 2001. *Media:* Steel/Mixed. *Specialty:* Contemporary Art. *Dealer:* Quint Contemporary Art La Jolla CA; Fran Preisman Fine Art - artnet.com. *Mailing Add:* 1175 Hoover St Carlsbad CA 92008

CARBONE, DAVID
PAINTER, CRITIC
b New York, NY, Nov 29, 50. *Study:* Skowhegan Sch Painting & Sculpture, with Laderman, Noland, Diao, Marden, Blaustein, Morley, Beal, 70; Sch Mus Fine Arts, Tufts Univ, with Feininger, Cox, Schwartz & Rubenstein, BFA, 71; Brooklyn Col(fel), with Holty, Holtzman, Bontecou, Stone, Ernst, Pearlstein, Russell & Groell, MFA, 74. *Exhib:* one-person shows, Zoe Gallery, Boston, David Brown Gallery, Provincetown, 86, Mass, Contemp Realist Gallery, San Francisco, 93 & Art Mus, Univ Wis, Milwaukee, 95; Landscape Painting, 1960-1990, Spoleto Festival, Gibbes Mus & Bayly Mus, 90; New Am Figure Painting, Contemp Realist Gallery & Clemson Univ, 92; Shooting Gallery, 2001; B Rubstein & His Legacy, SMFA, Boston, 2002; Courtland Jessup Gallery, 2003; Drawins Conclusions, Paintings, NY Art Gallery, 2004; The Body & its Dangers, The Painting Ctr NY, 2005. *Teaching:* Instr painting, Brooklyn Col, 74-75; lectr art hist, Boston Mus Sch, 75- & instr grad sem, 76-81; vis artist painting & art hist, Knox Col, 83; vis artist painting, Montserrat Art Sch, 85; vis assoc prof, Pratt Inst, 87, Stanford Univ, 90 & Parsons Sch Design, 91; assoc prof, State Univ New York, Albany, 93-. *Awards:* Ingram-Merrill Award, 85; Charlene Engelhard Award, 86. *Bibliog:* John Hollander (auth), The Italian Tradition in American Art in Landscape Painting 1960-1990, 90; Thomas Bolt (auth), New American Figure Painting (catalog), 92; The Nude in Contemporary Art, Aldrich Mus Contemp Art, 99; and others. *Mem:* Col Art Asn; Inst Asn Art Critics. *Media:* Oil. *Publ:* The Field Beyond Chassy, Antaeus, 80; Francis Bacon, 9/90, Carlo Maria Mariani, 1/91, Susana Jacobson, 3/91, Eugene Leroy, 4/91 & Jim Nutt, 12/91, Art Antiques; Alfred Russell, Modern Painters, fall 91 & Art Antiques, 92; The Subject Matter in View, Mod Painters, autumn 97; and others; The Return of the Mad Mahatma, Mod Painters, winter, 2001; Edwin Dickinson: A Transcendental Vision, Mod Painters, Autumn, 2003. *Dealer:* Hackett-Freedman Gallery 250 Sutters 4th Fl San Francisco CA 94108. *Mailing Add:* 330 Broome St New York NY 10002

CARBONI, STEFANO
CURATOR
Work: Auth: Glass From Islamic Lands: The al-Sabah Collection, 2001; co-auth (with David Whitehouse): Glass of the Sultans: Twelve Centuries of Islamic Masterworks, 2001; Co-cur (with Linda Komaroff) (exhibs) The Legacy of Genghis Khan: Courtly Art and Culture in Western Asia, 1256-1353 (Alfred H Barr Junior Award for exhib catalogue, Col Art Assoc, 2004). *Pos:* Assoc cur, dept Islamic Art Metrop Mus Art, New York City. *Mailing Add:* Met Mus Art 1000 Fifth Ave New York NY 10028-0198

CARD, ROYDEN
PAINTER, PRINTMAKER
b Cardston, Alta, Aug 2, 52; US citizen. *Study:* Brigham Young Univ, BFA, 76, MFA, 79. *Work:* Springville Mus Art, Utah; Mus Fine Arts, Salt Lake City; Latter Day St Church Mus Hist & Art, Salt Lake City; Smithsonian Inst Libr, Washington, DC; Ill St Univ. *Exhib:* two-person, Woodworks, Ariz St Univ, Tempe, 89, Canyons, Courtyard Gallery, Salt Lake City, Utah, 89; N Mountain Invitational, Kimball Art Ctr, Park City, Utah, 92; View of Nine, Salt Lake Arts Ctr, 95; Nat Soc of Painters in Casein & Acrylic Expos, NY, 96; 19th Ann Open Expos, Salmagundi Club, NY, 96; Atrium Gallery & Finch Lane Gallery, Salt Lake City, Utah, 98; Parkside Nat Small Print Exhib, Univ Wis, Knosha, 98. *Teaching:* Instr printmaking, Brigham Young Univ, 80-96, Univ Utah, 90-; instr painting & drawing, Utah Valley Community Col, Orem, Utah, 92. *Awards:* Best in Landscape, St George Regional, St George Mus Art, Utah, 2000; Elsie Ject-Key Mem Award, Nat Soc Painters Casein & Acrylic Ann, Salmagundi Club, NY, 2000. *Mem:* Nat Soc Painters in Casein & Acrylic. *Media:* Relief, Acrylic. *Publ:* Illusr, Dialogue, A Journal of Mormon Thought, Dialogue Found, Vol 18, No 1, 85; 00449544xxxL Morgans Utah, Red Butte Press, Univ Utah Marriott Libr, Salt Lake City, Utah, 87; Vern Swanson, Robert Olpin, Utah Art Peregrine/Smith Press, Layton, Utah. *Dealer:* Annex Galleries 604 College Ave Santa Rosa CA 95404; Sego Gallery 637 E 500 S Salt Lake City UT 84102

CARDILLO, RIMER ANGEL
PRINTMAKER, SCULPTOR
b Montevideo, Uruguay, Aug 17, 44. *Study:* Nat Sch Fine Arts, Uruguay, MFA, 68; Weissenssee Sch Art & Archit, Berlin, Ger, 70; Leipzig Sch Graphic Art, Leipzig, Ger, 71. *Work:* Prints Cabinet of Berlin, EGer; Chicago Art Inst, Ill; Mus Mod Art, NY; Cabinet Des Estampes, Bibliotheque Nationale, de Paris, France; Allen Mem Art Mus, Oberlin Col, Ohio. *Comn:* Charruas y Montes Criollos, Installation, Museo Fernando Garcia, Montevideo, Urugay, 91; Camera Sixtine, street light boxes, First Biennial of Mercosur, Porto Alegre, Brazil, 97; Nandu, Installation Islip Art Mus, Long Island, 98; Suite of prints, Galeria Sur, Montevideo, Uruguay, 98; Suite of bronze sculptures, Ulla & Greger Olsson Art Collection, Belgium, 99. *Exhib:* Int Biennial Graphic Art, Sakaide, Japan, 88; Europe and the Third World, Messepalast, Vienna, Austria, 88; Ceremony of Memory, Ctr Contemp Art, Santa Fe, NMex, 89; Arte dell Uruguay nel Novecento, Inst Italo-Latin Am, Roma, Italy, 89; La Tierra: Visiones de Am Latina, Mus Contemp Hispanic Arts, NY, Mus de Bellas Artes, Caracus, Venezuela, 90; Echoes of the Spirit, Atlanta Col Art Gallery, 90; solo exhibs, Rimer Cardillo: Works on Paper (with catalog), Galeria Sur, Uruguay, 92, Espinillo, Nat Mus Anthrop, Montevideo, 94, Pachamazon, Calvin Morris Gallery, NY, 96, Rimer Cardillo: Recent Work, Calvin Morris Gallery, NY, 98 & Araucaria (with catalog), Bronx Mus Art, 98; Rejoining the Spiritual: The Land in Contemp Latin Am Art, Md Inst Col Art, Baltimore, 94; Twenty-fifth Anniv Exhib, Artists Talk Back: Reaffirming Spirituality, Part III, El Museo del Barrio, NY; In the Making: The First Ten Yrs of the Permanent Collection, Islip Art Mus, NY, 96; Landscapes: An Exhib of Sculpture, The Wash Sculptors Group & Art Mus Am, Org Am States, Washington, DC, 97; First Mercusol Biennial, Porto Alegre, Brazil, 97; Araucaria, Rimer Cardillo, Ten Yrs Journey, Bronx Mus Arts, NY, 98; Biennial Venice Italy, 2001, Uruguayan Pavillion, Int Biennial Graphic Arts, Ljubljana, Yugoslavia, 2005. *Pos:* Artist-in-residence, Southern Ill Univ, 79-81; Bd dir, NY Found Arts, 93-96; panel mem, N State Coun Arts, 94-95; bd adv, Intar Gallery, N, 91-96 & Gallery Montevideo, 98-. *Teaching:* Prof painting, Nat Circle Fine Arts, 72-74; prof graphics, State Univ NY, Purchase, 88-90; instr graphics, Printmaking Workshop, NY, 88-; part time prof, State Univ NY, Col Purchase, 88-94; prof, State Univ NY, Col New Paltz, 94-. *Awards:* Fel, Adolf and Esther Gottleib Found, 88; Spec Proj Fel, NY State Coun Arts, 89; Fel, Pollock Krasner Found, 90; Guggenheim Fel, 97. *Bibliog.* Victor Zamudio-Taylor (auth), Ceremony of Memory (contemp commentary), Sante Fe Ctr Contemp Arts, 88; Susana Torruella Leval (auth), Identity and Change, The Latin American Challenge, Hispanic Art Tour III, 88-89; Sullivan Edward (ed), Latin Am Art in the Twentieth Century, Phaidon Press, 96; Grady T Turner (auth), Rimer Cardillo at Cavin-Morris, Art in Am, 10/96; Joe Vojko, Rimer Cardillo at Calvin-Morris, Rev 1, No 1, 4/96; Lucy R Lippard (auth), Travel & Hierarchy in the Work of Rimer Cardillo, Bienal Venice, Italy, 2001. *Mem:* Fodo Del Sol Gallery, Washington, DC. *Media:* All Media. *Dealer:* Cavin Morris Gallery 560 Broadway 4th Fl NY; Greger Olsson Gallery Clos de Differdance 14 B-1410 Waterloo Belgium. *Mailing Add:* 208 W 105th St Apt 1 New York NY 10025-3983

CARDINAL, MARCELIN
PAINTER, COLLAGE ARTIST
b Gravelbourg, Sask, Can, Apr 26, 20. *Study:* Self-taught. *Work:* Quebec Mus, Que; Mus Fine Arts of New Mex, Santa Fe; Hirshhorn Mus, Wash; Mus d'Art Mod, Dunkerque, France; Mus d'Art Contemporain, Montreal; Smithsonian Inst. *Comn:* Mural, Metro St Michel, Montreal, CTCUM, 86; L'Art Dans la Rue/paintings on billboards, Benson & Hedges, Montreal, 77; paintings on billboards, Montreal Olympics, 76. *Exhib:* Guggenheim Mus, NY, 54 & 58; Albright-Knox Art Gallery, Buffalo, NY, 60; Galerie Denyse Delrue, Montreal, 62; 5th Int Art Fair, Basel, Switz, 74; Galerie Gilles Corbeil, Montreal, 73, 74 & 75; Mus du Quebec, 76; Mus d'Art Mod, Dunkerque, France, 77; Mus d'Art Contemporain, Montreal, 77 & 78; Don Stewart Gallery, Toronto, 82; Galerie Daniel Beauschene, Montreal, 85; Galerie Frederic Palardy, Montreal, 90; plus others. *Awards:* Creation et Recherche, Minister Cult Affairs, Quebec, 72, 73, 75 & 78. *Bibliog:* Christian Allegre (auth), article, Vie des Arts, 72; Profile: Marcelin Cardinal, Art Mag, 3/79; Germain Lefebvre (auth), Marcelin Cardinal, Temps, Espace Et Continuite--Vie Des Arts, 82. *Mem:* Soc Prof Artists Quebec (vpres, 72-73); hon mem Conseil de la Peinture Du Quebec. *Media:* Acrylic, Collage Artist. *Mailing Add:* 4897 Queen Mary Rd Apt 15 Montreal PQ H3W 1X1 Canada

CARDOSO, ANTHONY
PAINTER, SCULPTOR
b Tampa, Fla, Sept 13, 30. *Study:* Univ Tampa, BS(art); Art Inst Minn, BFA; Univ SFla, MA; Elysion Col, PhD. *Work:* Minn Mus Art, St Paul; Suncoast Credit Union Bldg, Tampa, Fla; Ringling Mus Archives Sarasota, Fla; and others. *Comn:* Sports Authority, Tampa Stadium Off, 71; sports theme paintings, Leto High Sch & Pierce High Sch, Tampa, 71; two murals, Sun Coast Credit Union Bldg, Tampa, Fla, 75; Immigrant Statue, Tampa, Fla, 93. *Exhib:* Drawings USA, Minn Mus Art, St Paul, 71; Rotunda Gallery, London, Eng, 72; Brussells Int, Belg, 73; Ringling Mus Archives, Sarasota, Fla, 78; Accademia Ital Exhib, Terma, Italy, 80-85; Centro Studi E Ricerche Della Nazioni, Italy, 86; and many others. *Collection Arranged:* Sculpture, Remingtons (6), J. E. Fraser (1); etchings, Rembrandt, Monet, Whistler, Picasso, Goya, Dali, others; prints, Norman Rockwell, Lasey Rivers, others. *Pos:* Supt art, Hillsborough City Schs, 85-89, studio dir, 89-94, gallery dir, 91-94, 2003, art supervisor, 1985-91, pvt instr, 2003. *Teaching:* Instr Jefferson High, A P Leto High. *Awards:* Gold Medal Award & Victory Statue; Palma D'Oro D'Europa, Accademia D'Europa, 89; Merit Award, Hillsborough Co, Fla State Fair, 94, 95 & 96; and others. *Bibliog:* Bertrand Sorlot (auth), article in La Rev Mod, 71; articles, Tampa Tribune, 75-92 & Acad Italia, 80-86. *Mem:* Fla Arts Coun; Ringling Art Mus Archives; Fla League Arts; Acad Italia, Italy; Tampa Art Coun. *Media:* Oil, Acrylic. *Res:* Fdns of rt ed & fine arts (Ph.D). *Specialty:* Fine arts. *Interests:* sculpture collection. *Collection:* Western art paintings & sculpture, prints & etchings. *Publ:* Contribr, La Rev Mod, 71 & 72; Acad Italia, 80-86; Tampa Tribune, 83-92; St Petersburg Times, 92; Gazeta Newspaper, Tampa, 2003; Auth, The Philosophical Foundations of Art Education. *Dealer:* Art Studio I & Gallery 3208 Nassau St Tampa FL 33607; El Prado Art Gallery 4318 El Prado Blvd Tampa FL 33629. *Mailing Add:* 3208 Nassau St Tampa FL 33607

CARDUCCI, JUDITH
PAINTER
b Norwood, Mass, Feb 25, 35. *Study:* Quinnippiac Col, Conn, Hist Art, with CA Brodeur, 60; Myers Sch Art, Univ of Akron, Ohio. *Work:* Univ Maine, Mus Art, Bangor, Maine; Hosp Special Surgery, NY; City Hall Coun Chamber, Hudson, Ohio; Cleveland State Univ, Ohio; State Teachers Retirement Syst & Educ Asn Bldgs, Columbus, Ohio. *Comn:* Many portrait comn's. *Exhib:* Pastels Only, Ann Nat Shows, Nat Arts Club, NY, 96, 97, 99, 2000-2005; Cincinnati Art Club, Ann Nat Shows, View Point, Ohio, 96, 98, 2001-; Am Artists Prof League, Salmagundi Club, NY, 97; La Fond Galleries, Ann Nat Show, La Fond Gallery, Pittsburgh, Pa, 98 & 99; Degas Pastel Soc, Biennial Shows, Int Trade Ctr, New Orleans, La, 98 & 2000; Catharine Lorilard Wolfe Ann Nat Show, Nat Arts Club, NY, 98 & 2000; Lexington Art Club, Ann Show, The Nude, Lexington, Ky, 2001. *Pos:* Bd & fac, Portrait Soc Am, 2006-. *Teaching:* Instr, Cuyahoga Valley Art Ctr, Ohio, 98-; fac mem, Portrait Soc Am, 99-; Workshops, eu plein air & portraiture, Southern France, 2006; workshops in pastel & portraiture by invitation. *Awards:* Best of Show, Portrait Soc Am, Wash, DC, 98; Best of Show, La Fond Galleries Nat Annual Show, Pittsburg, Pa, 98; Best of Show, The Nude, Lexington Art Club, 2001. *Bibliog:* Betsy Hosegood (auth), Paint! Portrait & Figure, Roto Vision (Watson-Guptill), 2000; DC Selor (auth), Judith B Carducci, The Pastel J, 8/04; M Stephen Doherty (auth), Drawing on Life, Am Artists Mag, 02. *Mem:* Portrait Soc Am (founding mem, 99-); Pastel Soc Am (chmn, Critique Comt, 2004-); Degas Pastel Soc (juried mem, currently); Am Artists Prof League; Salmagundi Club (juried mem, currently); Cincinnati Art Club (juried mem). *Media:* Pastel, Charcoal, Conte Crayon, Ink, Graphite. *Publ:* auth, Dare to See Fleshtones, Artists Mag, 98; auth, Drawing, The Foundation for Portraitrure, Portrait Soc Am, 2001; contribr, Best of Portrait Painting, North Light Books, 98; contribr, How Did you Paint That? 100 Ways to Paint People & Figures, Int Artists, 2004. *Dealer:* Church Gallery Gauger Rd Bath Ohio. *Mailing Add:* 197 Sunset Dr Hudson OH 44236

CARDUCCI, VINCENT
CRITIC, CONCEPTUAL ARTIST
b Detroit, Mich, June 30, 53. *Study:* Mich State Univ, BFA, 75; New Sch for Social Rsch, MA, 02. *Work:* Blue Cross/Blue Shield, Mich; Lasalle Bank, Mich; Franklin Furnace Arch Inc, NY; Gilbert & Lila Silverman Found, Mich. *Exhib:* Urbanology: Artists View Urban Experience, Ctr for Creative Studies, Detroit, 89; Text/Image, Detroit Artists Market, 92; The Detroit Show, Ctr Galleries, 94. *Pos:* Regional ed (Mich), New Art Examiner, Chicago, Ill, 84-96; contribr, Art Forum, New York, 89-92; ed, Detroit Focus Quart, 93-98; contrib ed, New Art Examiner, Chicago, 96-2002; contrib writer, Metro Times, Detroit, 2002-. *Teaching:* Instr lib arts, College for Creative Studies, Detroit, 2006. *Bibliog:* Gerhard H Magnus (auth), Vincent A Carducci at Creative Arts Gallery, New Art Examiner, 86; Joy Hakanson Colby (auth), The Art of the Real, Detroit News, 92; Dennis Alan Nawrocki (auth), Art in Detroit Public Places, Wayne State Univ Press, 99. *Res:* Esthetic and social issues in contemporary art. *Publ:* Regional reflections: Mainstream modernism reflected through local loyalty, New Art Examiner, 95; Peter William's Black Humor, New Art Examiner, 01; Lynne Avadenka: The Work of Art in the Wake of Sept 11, Metrotimes, 02; Chromatic Interactions: Alison McMaugh, Art & Australia, 02; Tom Otterness: Public Sculpture and the Civic Ideal for the Post Modern Age, Sculpture, 2005. *Mailing Add:* 1305 E Fifth St Royal Oak MI 48067

CAREY, ELLEN
PHOTOGRAPHER
b New York, NY, June 18, 52. *Study:* Art Students League, NY, 70; Kansas City Art Inst, BFA, 76; State Univ NY, Buffalo, MFA, 78. *Work:* Albright-Knox Art Gallery; Fogg Mus; Mus Fine Art, Houston; Patrick Lannan Found, Palm Beach, Fla; Chase Manhattan Bank, NY; Lightworks, Syracuse, NY; Dannheiser Found, NY; Picker Art Gallery, Colgate Univ, Hamilton, NY; Brooklyn Mus, NY; Whitney Mus Am Art, NY; and others. *Comn:* 7 Light Boxes, Madison Sq Garden, Exec Hq, NY, 90-93; Highland Hosp, Rochester, NY; Wadsworth Atheneum; Saint Francis Hosp, Hartford, Conn. *Exhib:* In Western NY (with catalog), Albright-Knox Art Gallery, 77; Contemp Photog, Fogg Art Mus, Harvard Univ, 80; The Markers (with catalog), San Francisco Mus Mod Art, 81; Some Contemp Portraits, Contemp Arts Mus, Houston, 82; Painting, Pattern, Photograph, Addison Gallery Am Art, Phillips Acad, Andover, Mass, 82; Figures: Forms and Expressions (with catalog), Albright-Knox Gallery, 82; Contemp Self-Portraiture in Photog, Hayden Art Gallery, Mass Inst Technol, 83; Hallwalls Ten Yrs (with catalog), Albright-Knox Gallery, 84; Self-Portrait/Photog 1840-1985 (with catalog), Nat Portrait Gallery, London, Eng, 86; Recent Acquisitions, Brooklyn Mus Art, 86; one-person exhibs, Art City, NY, 86, Simon Cerigo, NY, 87, Int Ctr Photog, NY, 87, John Good Gallery, NY, 89, Schneider-Bluhm-Loeb Gallery, Chicago, 90, Nat Acad Sci, Wash, DC, 92 & Gallery 954, Chicago, 94, Cleveland Ctr for Contemp Art, 97, Lougheborough Univ Sch Art & Design, Leicestershire, Eng, 99; First Person Singular: Self-Portrait in Photog, 1840-1988 (with catalog), High Mus, Atlanta, 88; Appropriation and Syntax: Uses of Photog in Contemp Art, Brooklyn Mus, 88; The Photog of Invention: Am Pictures of the 1980's, Nat Mus Am Art, Smithsonian Inst, Washington, DC, Mus Contemp Art, Chicago & Walker Art Ctr, Minneapolis, 89; David C Ruttenberg Collection (with catalog), Art Inst, Chicago, 91; Colt 4 (with catalog), Wadworth Atheneum, 92; Life Lessons, Art Inst Chicago, 94; The Instant Image, Park Ave Atrium, NY, 94; The Abstract Urge, Ansel Adams Ctr Photog, San Francisco, 94; The Camera I, Self Portraits from the Audrey & Sydney Irmas Collection (with catalog), Los Angeles Co Mus Art, 94; Beyond the Camera, Large-Scale Manipulated Photographs, Artspace, New Haven, Conn, 94; Making Pictures, Caldwell Col, NJ, 94; Issues and Identities: Recent Acquisitions in Contemp Photog, Art Inst Chicago, 94; Abstract Photographs, Baltimore Mus Art, 95; Eye of the Beholder: The Avon Collection, Int Center for Photog, NY, 97; Photog's Multiple Roles, The Mus of Contemp Photog, Chicago, 99; and others. *Pos:* Cur, Vrej Baghoomian, Gallery, NY. *Teaching:* Asst, State Univ NY Buffalo, 76-78, instr, 77, 78; vis artist, instr, Int Ctr Photog, NY, 81-83; vis artist, RI Sch Design, Providence, 83; vis artist, Columbia Col, Chicago, Ill, 90; asst prof photog, Hartford Art Sch, Univ Hartford, Conn, 85-. *Awards:* Coffin Grant, Univ Hartford, Conn, 81, 90 & 91; Nat Endowment Arts Grant, 84; Polaroid 20 x 24, Polariod Corp, Boston, Mass & NY, 84-98; Conn Comn on the Arts Grant, 98; Te Found Grant, 99. *Bibliog:* Vince Aletti (auth), Voice Choice, Village Voice, 11/26/96; William Zimmer (auth), A family album with no pictures, The NY Times, 12/10/2000; Barbara Pollack (auth), National reviews, Artnews, 1/01; Lyle Rexer (auth), Ellen Carey at Real Art Ways, Art in Am, 6/01. *Dealer:* Jayne H Baum 26 Grove St Apt 4C New York NY 10014. *Mailing Add:* c/o Jayne H Baum Gallery 26 Grove St Apt 4C New York NY 10014

CARIOLA, ROBERT J
PAINTER, SCULPTOR
b Brooklyn, NY, Mar 24, 27. *Study:* Pratt Inst Art Sch; Pratt Graphic Ctr. *Work:* Fordham Univ; De Pauw Univ; La Salle Col; Hofstra Col; Topeka Pub Libr, Kans; N Merrick Pub Lib & Long Beach Mus, Islip Libr, NY; St Brendans Church, NY. *Comn:* Murals, Walker Mem Baptist Church, Bronx, NY, 75; two chapel murals, Mt St Mary Cemetery, Queens, NY, 77; four chapel murals, paintings, St John's Mausoleum, Queens, NY, 73-74; mural painting, St Johns Luthern Church, Merrick, NY, 92; Indian monument sculpture, Merrick, NY, 93; metal murals, etched glass windows & doors, 2 Large Mosaics, St Raymonds, Bronx, NY; four foot bronze statue, Mother Teresa, Outdoor Grotto, Our Lady of Lourdes Church, 2004, Masapequa Pk, NY, 2004. *Exhib:* Boston Mus Printmakers Exhib, 62; Corcoran Gallery Art, Washington, DC, 63; Pa Acad Fine Arts, Philadelphia, 63; Vatican Pavilion, NY World's Fair, 64; Nat Acad Design, NY, 70; one-man show, Long Beach Mus, Long Beach, NY, 85. *Collection Arranged:* Vatican Pavilion, 1964; Temple Emanuel, 1997; Our Lady of Lourdes Church, 2004-2006. *Pos:* Art consult, Cath Youth Orgn, Rockville Centre, NY, 67-; art coordr, St John's Cloister, Queens, NY, 72-74. *Teaching:* Instr art, La Salle Acad, Oakdale, NY, 63-65, Catholic Youth Orgn Summer Wkshop & Huntington Twp Art League, 71 & Nat Art League, Douglaston, NY, 94-2006-. *Awards:* Grantee, Tiffany Found, 64 & 66; Grumbacher Cash Award, Silvermine Guild Artists, New Canaan, Conn, 76; Grantee, NY State Coun Arts, 92; and others. *Bibliog:* A V LesMez (auth), Cariola, Long Island Rev Mag, 64; Balt Carlson (auth), Vatican Pavilion gets Long Island exhibit, New York Times, 8/27/64; Jeanne Paris (auth), Cariola's works on exhibit at Merrick Gallery, Long Island Press, 5/28/67. *Mem:* Prof Artists Guild (pres, 69-70); hon mem Cath Fine Arts Soc. *Media:* Acrylic; Metal, Mosaics. *Res:* Ancient art & old masters tech. *Specialty:* Fine art painting & sculpture. *Interests:* Classical Music, opera, photog. *Collection:* Fordham Univ, Hofstra Collection; High Schs Murals; Jacqueline Kennedy Onnasis, Dina Merrill (actress), collection of Wooster. *Publ:* Illusr, Writers's Ann, 58; Sign Mag, 71; contribr, Liturgical Arts Mag, 71-72; Equine Images, fall 91. *Dealer:* Landing Gallery Woodbury NY; Soundview Gallery Port Jefferson NY. *Mailing Add:* 1844 Gormley Ave Merrick NY 11566

CARL, JOAN
SCULPTOR, PAINTER
b Cleveland, Ohio, Mar 20, 26. *Study:* Cleveland Sch Art; Chicago Art Inst; Mills Col; with Dong Kingman; Bordman Robinson; Carl Morris; apprenticeship, Albert Wein; New Sch Art, with Arnold Mesches & Ted Gilien. *Work:* NC Mus Art, Raleigh; Int Cult Ctr for Youth, Jerusalem, Israel; The Temple Mus, Cleveland, Ohio; Thomas Bros Maps, Irvine Calif; Judah Magnes Mus, Berkeley; NE Ohio Mus, Cleveland, Ohio; also pvt collections. *Comn:* Bronze Family Group, CPC, Brea, CA; aluminum pillars, Zinkal Ltd, Tel Aviv, Israel; GFRC Relief, Mountian View, Brea, Calif; Bronze Relief, CHP, Sacramento, Calif; Marble Wall Relief, Temple Bat Yahm, Newport Beach, Calif. *Exhib:* Chai (graphics), Nat & Int Traveling Show, 74-75; Brand Libr Gallery, Glendale, Calif, 83; Feldhyme Libr Gallery, San Bernardino, Calif, 87; Milkin Gallery, Los Angeles, Calif, 88; Burbank Art Ctr, Calif, 90; Courtwright Gallery, Los Angeles, Calif, 94; Decker Studio Gallery, North Hollywood, Calif, 96; North Hollywood Gallery, 97; Gallery 825, North Hollywood, 98. *Pos:* Fac, Valley Ctr

of Arts, Los Angeles, 59-64 & Univ Judaism, 90-94; lectr Title III Prog, San Bernardino, Inyo & Mono Co, Calif, 67-69. *Teaching:* Instr, Univ Judaism, 84-88, 94-95. *Awards:* Honorable Mention, Nat Orange Show, San Bernardino, 58 & Calif State Fair, Sacramento, 70 & 72; Design Award, Ceramic Tile Inst, 75. *Bibliog:* Will H Tagress (auth), Valley sculptor believes in reflecting world around her, The News, 74. *Mem:* Founding mem Calif Confederation Arts; Artist Equity Asn, Inc (past pres); Los Angeles Art Asn (pres, 94-97). *Media:* Multimedia. *Collection:* Works in all sizes and materials: Bronze, marble, hardwood, etc. Also watercolors and drawings. *Publ:* Illusr, A World of Questions and Things, 50; Discovery Unlimited, A Guide to Raising a Creative Child, 81; The Canrelvalis of Eusebius Asch, 99. *Mailing Add:* 4808 Mary Ellen Ave Sherman Oaks CA 91423

CARLBERG, NORMAN KENNETH
SCULPTOR, PHOTOGRAPHER
b Roseau, Minn, Nov 6, 28. *Study:* Brainerd Jr Col, Minn, 47-49; Minneapolis Sch Art, 50; Univ Ill, Urbana, 53-54; Yale Univ, BFA, 58, MFA, 61. *Hon Degrees:* Md Inst Col Art, Baltimore, PhD. *Work:* Addison Gallery Am Art, Phillips Acad, Andover, Mass; Whitney Mus Am Art, NY; Schenectady Mus, NY; Pa Acad Fine Arts, Philadelphia; Hirshhorn Mus, Washington, DC; Guggenheim Mus, NY. *Comn:* Modular screen, Baltimore City Hosp, 65; four modular sculptures, Baltimore City Schs, Northern Parkway Jr High, 70-73 & for PS 39, 73-75; modular column, Harry Seidler, Trade Group Complex, Canberra, Australia, 73-75 & Black Widow (steel modular), 75-; Winter Wind, Painted Steel 26' x 26', Riverside Ctr, Brisbane, Australia; Uno Y Dos, Steel 12' x 12' x 10', Milford Mills, Baltimore, Md. *Exhib:* Recent Sculpture USA, Mus Mod Art, NY, 59; Structured Sculpture, Galerie Chalette, NY, 60; one-man shows, Cath Univ, Santiago, Chile, 60 & Baltimore Mus Art, 68; Whitney Ann, Whitney Mus Am Art, 62. *Teaching:* Instr sculpture, Cath Univ, Santiago, 60-61; sculptor in residence, Rinehart Sch Sculpture, Md Inst Col Art, Baltimore, 61-97. *Awards:* Fulbright Teaching Grant, Santiago, Chile, 60, Purchase Award, Ford Found, 62; Mus Prize, Baltimore Mus Art, 66. *Bibliog:* Josef Albers (auth), The Yale School-Structured Sculpture, Art in Am, 61; George Rickey (auth), Constructivism, George Braziller, 67; Peter Blake (auth), Architecture for the New World, the work of Harry Seidler, Wittenborn & Co, 73. *Media:* All Media. *Mailing Add:* 4450 Roland Springs Dr Baltimore MD 21210

CARLHIAN, JEAN PAUL
ARCHITECT
b Paris, Nov 7, 19; arrived in US 1948; naturalized 1954. *Study:* Univ Paris, Bachelier es Lettres, 36; Harvard Univ, M (city planning), 47; Ecole des Beaux Arts, architecte diplome par le goubernement, 48. *Comn:* Principal works include Christian A Johnson Memorial Bldg, Middlebury Col, Mather House, Quincy House, Leverett House, Harvard, Baker Hall and McCollum Ctr of Harvard Bus Sch, Col Ctr, Vassar Coll, The Quadrangle, Brown Univ, Mus Nat Heritage, Univ Vt Billings Ctr, Nat Mus African Art, Sackler Mus, S. Dillon Ripley Ctr, GE Co, Management Developement Inst, Cornell Univ, The Andover Cos, Smith Col, Ctr for African, Near Eastern, and Asian Cultures at Smithsonian Inst. *Pos:* Designer Harrison and Abramoitz, NY City, 49, Coolidge, Shepley, Bulfinch adn Abbott, Boston, 50-57; assoc Shepley, Bulfinch, Richardson and Abbott, 58-62, partner, 63-72, vpres, dir, 72-89, consulting principal, 89-; mem. Royal Commission on Teaching of Architecture, 63-64, Back Bay Architectural Commission, Boston, 66-79, Landmarks Commission, Boston, 69-76; bd dirs Boston Architectural Ctr, 78-80, Western European Architectural Found, 90-92, adv 93-. *Teaching:* Instr, asst prof Grad Sch Design, Harvard Univ, 48-55; vis critic Yale Univ, 58-61, 63-64, RI Sch Design, 62-63, 77 Rice Univ, 65, Harvard Univ, 78, 81; artist-in-residence Am Acad Rome, 75. *Awards:* Nat Endowment Arts Design fellow, 76-77, 78-79; Wheelwright fellow, Harvard Univ, 47; named Chevalier de l'Ordre des artes et des lettres. *Mem:* Fel, AIA (chmn comt aesthetics, 68, chmn comt on design 69, AIA Firm Award, 73, Edward C Kemper Award, 89); Royal Soc Arts; mem, Nat Acad Design (assoc, 81, acad, 94); Acad d'Architecture; Boston Soc Architects; Soc Architectural History; Smithsonian Inst. *Publ:* contributes to Encyclopaedia Britannica, Dictionary of Am Biography, and articles to professional journals. *Mailing Add:* Shepley Bulfinch Richardson & Abbott 40 Broad St Ste 600 Boston MA 02109-4305

CARLILE, JANET (HILDEBRAND)
PAINTER, EDUCATOR
b Denver, Colo. *Study:* Cooper-Union, BFA, 66; Pratt Inst, MFA, 72. *Work:* Brooklyn Mus, NY; Brooklyn Col Print Collection, NY; Printmaking Workshop Print Collection, NY; Library of Congress Collection; Neuberger Mus, Purchase, NY; Hirshorn Collection, Washington, DC; Hirshorn Collection, Smithsonian; Metrop Mus Print Collection; Dutchess Co Community Col. *Comn:* Sneffel's Range (drawing), NY Health & Hosp Corp, 84; ed of prints, Woodstock Sch Art, NY, 84; poster, Ouray Alpine Holiday, Ouray, Colo, 93. *Exhib:* Soc Am Graphic Artists Show; Assoc Am Artists Gallery, NY, 71-84; 50 Yrs Am Printmaking, 74 & Am Landscape Paintings, 76, Brooklyn Mus, NY; solo exhib, Blue Mountain Gallery, NY, 80; Alpine Artists Show, Ouray Colo Arts Asn, 84; Woodstock Artists, Woodstock Artists Asn, NY, 82. *Pos:* Adv, Printmaking Workshop, 68-86 & Woodstock Sch Art, 80-86; asst dir, Brooklyn Mus Art Sch, 73; pres, Ouray Arts Asn, 92 & 93; head BFA prog, Brooklyn Col, 94. *Teaching:* Instr printmaking, Sch Visual Arts, 70-72 & Brooklyn Mus Art Sch, 71-80; prof, dir printmaking, Brooklyn Col, NY, 71-94. *Awards:* Hirshhorn Purchase Award, Soc Am Graphic Artists, 72; Creative Artists Pub Serv Drawing & Printmaking Award, 80; Creative Incentive Grant, City Univ New York, 93, 98, 99, 2000; Pollack/Knasner Grant, 2002-03; Nomintaed Am Acad Arts & Letters. *Bibliog:* Kaplan (auth), American landscape painting, Am Artist Mag, 84. *Media:* Watercolor; Oil; Prints (etching). *Res:* 2-D Media. *Interests:* skiing, hiking, yoga. *Collection:* Smithsonian, Hirshorn Collection; Brooklyn Mus; Mus at Purchase Women's Mus. *Dealer:* Carlile Fine Arts; Red Mountain Gallery. *Mailing Add:* PO Box 1004 Ouray CO 81427

CARLIN, ELECTRA MARSHALL
DEALER
b Ft Worth, Tex. *Study:* George Washington Univ, BA. *Pos:* Dir, Carlin Galleries, formerly. *Mem:* Ft Worth Art Asn; Dallas Mus Art Asn. *Specialty:* American artists and craftsmen; Eskimo prints and carvings. *Mailing Add:* 2401 Warner Rd Ft Worth TX 76110-1756

CARLSON, CYNTHIA J
PAINTER, EDUCATOR
b Chicago, Ill, Apr 15, 42. *Study:* Chicago Art Inst, BFA; Pratt Inst, MFA. *Work:* Va Mus Fine Art, Richmond; Guggenheim Mus, NY; Philadelphia Mus of Art; Metrop Mus Art, NY; Allem Mem Art Mus, Oberlin, Ohio. *Comn:* Mendik Co Inc, Eleven Penn Plaza, NY, 84; mural, Md State Arts Coun, Baltimore-Washington Int Airport, 85; Los Angeles Metro Rail System, 92; Percent for Art Comn, Criminal Justice Ctr, Philadelphia, Pa, 95. *Exhib:* Artpark, 77; one-woman exhibs, Allen Mem Art Mus, Oberlin, Ohio, 80; Lowe Art Mus, Coral Gables, Fla, 82; Milwaukee Art Mus, Wis, 82; Albright-Knox Art Gallery, Buffalo, NY, 85; Queens Mus, Flushing Meadow, NY, 90. *Teaching:* Assoc prof art, Philadelphia Col Art, 67-81, prof, 81-86; prof, Queens Col, City Univ NY, 86-. *Awards:* Nat Endowment Arts Grant, 75, 78, 80, 87; PSC-CUNY Res Award, 88, 90. *Bibliog:* Patricia Stewart (auth), High decoration in low relief, Art in Am, 2/80; April Kingsley (auth), Cynthia Carlson: The subversive intent of the decorative impulse, Arts Mag, 3/80; Regan Upshaw (auth), Cynthia Carlson: Memento Mori, Art in Am, 7/86. *Mem:* Col Art Asn (bd dir). *Media:* Acrylic, Oil. *Mailing Add:* 139 W 19th St New York NY 10011

CARLSON, GEORGE ARTHUR
SCULPTOR, PAINTER
b Elmhurst, Ill, July 3, 1940. *Study:* Am Acad Art; Chicago Art Inst; Univ Ariz. *Work:* Amon Carter Exhib Hall, Ft Worth, Tex; Indianapolis Mus Fine Arts, Eiteljorg Mus Am Indian & Western Art; Outdoor Mus Art, Englewood, Colo; Genesee Mus, Rochester, NY; also pvt collections of Harrison Eiteljorg, Senator Barry Goldwater, Mr & Mrs John Marion, Edward Bass, Art Nicholas, Lois Rice, Fritz Scholder, Arnold Schwarzenegger, Bill Cosby, Robert Mehi, Dr Bane Travis, Dr David M Smith & Dr N Jill Warren; Western & Wildlife Mus, Jackson Hole, Wyo. *Comn:* Monument of prospector, Washington Park, Denver, 77; portrait bust, comn by Bill Cosby, 79 & Bill Harrah, 81; Navajo John (bronze sculpture), Foreign Diplomat Coun, Washington, 81; Paul Robeson, comn by Bill Cosby. *Exhib:* Nat Acad Western Art, Okla, 74-80; retrospective, Indianapolis Mus Fine Arts, Ind, 79-80; one man shows, Smithsonian Inst, Nat Hist Mus, Washington, 82, The Tarahumara, Indianapolis Mus Art, Stremmel Galleries, Reno, Nev, 82 O'Grady Galleries, Chicago, Ill, 83 & Gerald Peters Gallery, Santa Fe, NMex, 77, 85 & 88; Artist Am Show, Denver, 81-98; Nat Sculpture Soc, NY, 81-; Artists of Am show, Denver, Colo, 81-98; Kyoto World Expos Hist Cities, Traveling Show, 87; Ky Derby Mus, Lexington, 88; Spirit of the West, West One Bank tour of Utah, Idaho & Washington, 91; Hakone Open-Air Mus, Tokyo, 91; High Plains Heritage Mus, Spearfish, SDAk, 91-92; Denver Seven, Nat Cowboy Hall Fame, Okla City, 92; Western Rendezvous Show, Park city, Utah, 95; Prix de West, Nat Cowboy Hall Fame, Okla City, 95-98; Leading the West, Munson Gallery, Santa Fe, NMex, 98; Western Invitational, Autry Western Heritage Mus, Los Angeles, 98; Coors Invitational, Denver, Colo, 98; The Governor's Invitational, Denver, Colo, 98. *Awards:* Gold Medals, 74, 78, 80 & 85, Prix de West, Best of Show, 75, Silver Medals, 76 & 81, Nat Acad Western Art. *Bibliog:* Gene Autry (auth), George Carlson, Dignity in Art, Western Heritage Mus, 93; Donald Martin Reynolds (auth), Masters of Americas Sculpture, Abbeville Press, Gilcrease Mus Rendezvous, Tulsa, Okla, 94; Donald J Hagerty (auth), Leading the West: One Hundred Contemporary Painters and Sculptors, Northland Publ, 97. *Mem:* Nat Acad Western Art; Nat Sculpture Soc. *Media:* Bronze; Mixed. *Publ:* Auth, The Tarahumara, pvt publ, 77. *Dealer:* Nedra Matteuccis Fenn Galleries 1075 Paseo de Peralta Santa Fe NM 87501; Montgomery Gallery 353 Sutter St San Francisco CA 94108. *Mailing Add:* c/o Nedra Matteucci's Fenn Galleries 1075 Paseo de Peralta Santa Fe NM 87501

CARLSON, JANE C
PAINTER
b Boston, Mass, Sept 1, 28. *Study:* Art Students League; Mass Col Art; study with Charles Kinghan & Robert Davis. *Exhib:* Allied Artists Am, 69-83; Am Artists Prof League, 70-83; Am Watercolor Soc, Nat Acad Design, NY, 71-83; Audubon Artists, 73-83; Art for the Parks, Nat Exhib, 87; Nat Acad of Design, NY; Nat Arts Club, NY; NY World Trade Ctr; Knickerbocker Artists Nat Exhbn; Grand Central Galleries, NY; Lever House, NY; Frye Mus, Seattle; Muckenthaler Cult Ctr, Calif; Ctrl Wyoming Mus of Fine Arts. *Teaching:* Watercolor demonstrations; watercolor & oil workshops. *Awards:* Robert Simmons Award, 71, Maynard Landa Memorial Award, 77, Windsor Newton Award, 81, Muriel Alvord Award, 82, Hudson Valley Art Asn; Twin Brooks Award, 77, William McKillap Prize, 79, Gold Medal, 82 & 97, Best in Show (Gold Medal), 85, Award for Excellence (Gold Medal), 87, Members Award with Solo Show, 91, Gold for Oil, 93, Award for Watercolor, 95, Kent Art Asn; High Winds Medal, 83 & 85, American Watercolor Society; James Holton Award, 72, Knickerbocker Artists; Robert Simmons Award, 78, Catherine Lorellard Wolf; Open Show Award, 80, Salmagundi Club; Jules Bauer Award, 81, New Rochelle Art Asn; Guilia Palermo Award, 82, Audubon Artists of America; Dassler Award, 85, Adirondacks National; Award for Excellence, 87, Arts for the Parks National Show (100 paintings for National Tour). *Mem:* Am Watercolor Soc (bd dir, 1977); Am Artists Prof League; Audubon Artists; Allied Artists Am; Hudson Valley Art Asn; Knickerbocker Artists. *Media:* Oil, Watercolor. *Publ:* Am Artists Mag Watercolor Pg. *Dealer:* The Art Studio Pondfield Rd Bronxville NY 10708; The Edgartown Gallery Martha's Vinyard Mass; Paradise Gallery Boca Grande Fla. *Mailing Add:* Candlewood Isle PO Box 364 New Fairfield CT 06812

CARLSON, MARY
SCULPTOR
b Stevens Point, Wis, Mar 21, 51. *Study:* Sch Visual Arts, BFA, 73. *Work:* Chase Manhattan Bank, NY. *Exhib:* Solo exhibs, Curt Marcus Gallery, NY, 86, Michael Klein Inc, NY, 87, Max Protetch Gallery, NY, 92, Holly Solomon Gallery, NY, 94 & Bill Maynes Gallery, NY, 96, 97 & 99; Identia E Alterita, Venice Biennale, Italy, 95; Shirts & Skins, Contemp Mus, Honolulu, 96; Body Language, Fla State Univ, 96; and others. *Awards:* Guggenheim Found, 93. *Bibliog:* William Zimmer (auth), Everyday Expectations With a Twist, NY Times, 12/23/90; Gretchen Faust (auth), New York in Review, Arts Mag, 2/91; Holland Cotter (auth), Art in Review, NY Times, 4/10/92. *Mailing Add:* 167 N Ninth St Brooklyn NY 11211-2009

CARLSON, ROBERT MICHAEL
GLASS BLOWER, PAINTER
b Brooklyn, NY, Nov 19, 52. *Study:* City Col NY, 70-73; Pilchuck Sch, 81-82. *Work:* Corning Mus Glass, NY; Glasmuseum, Frauenau, Ger; Glasmuseum, Ebeltoft, Denmark; Los Angeles Co Mus Art; Toledo Mus Art; Indianapolis Mus Art; Tampa Mus Art. *Exhib:* Design Visions-Int Directions, Art Gallery West Australia, Perth, 92; Clearly Art/Pilchuck Connection, Whatcom Co Mus, Bellingham, Wash, 92; Interglas Symposium Exhib, Crystalex, Novy Bor, Czech, 91; The Frozen Moment, Bellvue Art Mus, Wash, 91; Glass Inventions/Silica Dreams, Mus Craft & Folk Art, San Francisco, 89; Masters of Contemp Glass: Selections from the Glick Collection, Indianapolis Mus Art, 97; Telling Compelling Tales: Narration in Contemp Glass, Holter Mus, Helena, Mont, 98; Clearly Inspired, Contemp Glass and Its Origins, Tampa Mus Art, 99; Contemp Craft from the Saxe Collection, Fine Arts Mus San Francisco, 04; Int Glass Invitational, Habatat Galleries, Boca Raton, Fla, 2004. *Teaching:* Vis artist, glass art, Calif Col Arts & Crafts, Oakland, 89; fac, glass art, Pilchuk Sch, Stanwood, Wash, 89-90 & 92; fac, Penland Sch Crafts, NC, 94 & Bild-Werk Art Acad, Frauenau, Ger, 96. *Awards:* Award of Merit, Ariz Bienniel, Tucson Mus Art, 86; Jurois Award, 5th Ann Capitol Invitational, The Glass Gallery, 86; Nat Endowment Arts, Fel, 90; John Hauberg fel, Pilchuch Sch, Stanwood, Wash, 2000; Hon Lifetime Membership award, Glass Art Soc, 2004. *Bibliog:* Dick Weiss (auth), Robert Carlson, Class Work Mag, 90; Bonnie Miller (auth), Chronical Books, 91; Ron Glowen (auth), The Symbolism of Alchemy, Am Craft, 94. *Mem:* Glass Art Soc (bd dir 92-, vpres, 93); Glass Art Society (pres, 94-96); Am Crafts Coun. *Media:* Multimedia. *Mailing Add:* PO Box 11590 Bainbridge Island WA 98110

CARLSTROM, LUCINDA
PAINTER, PRINTMAKER
b Jamestown, NY, Sept 8, 50. *Study:* Ringling Sch Art, Sarasota, Fla, 68-70; Atlanta Col Art, Ga, BFA, 74; Inst Allende, San Miguel, Mex, 73. *Work:* Contemp Hotel, Walt Disney World, Lake Buena Vista, Fla; DeKalb Jr Col, McClatchey, Cody Rodgers & Regenstein, Atlanta, Ga; Barnett Banks, Barnett Holding Co, Jacksonville, Fla; Eldorado Hosp, Tucson. *Exhib:* Walt Disney World, Lake Buena Vista, Fla, 74-79; New Orleans Mus Art, 75; US Info Agency Traveling Exhib, 76-78; High Mus Art Gallery, Atlanta, Ga, 79-. *Awards:* Best Graphics, Space Coast Arts Festival, Cocoa Beach, Fla, 75; Best Watercolor, Southeastern Arts & Crafts Festival, Macon, Ga, 76; Second Award, Art Festival Atlanta, 79. *Mem:* Artists Equity Asn; Univ Mich Artists Guild; Ga Watercolor Soc. *Media:* Watercolor; Etching. *Mailing Add:* 1075 Standard Dr NE Atlanta GA 30319-3357

CARMEAN, E A, JR
HISTORIAN, CURATOR
b Springfield, Ill, Jan 25, 45. *Study:* MacMurray Col, BA(hist art), hon PhD, 81; Univ Ill, with Allen Weller. *Collection Arranged:* The Collages of Robert Motherwell (with catalog); Friedel Dzubas (with catalog); Modernist Art 1960-1970 (with catalog); Morris Louis: Major Themes & Variations (with catalog); The Subjects of the Artist (with catalog); Mondrian: The Diamond Compositions (with catalog); Morton G Neumann Collection (with catalog); Picasso: The Saltimbanques (with catalog); Kadinsky: The Improvisations. *Pos:* Cur 20th century art, Mus Fine Arts, Houston, 71-74; cur 20th century art, Nat Gallery Art, 74-84; dir, Ft Worth Art Mus, Tex, 84-91, Memphis Brooks Mus Art, 92-. *Teaching:* Lectr art hist, Univ Ill, Urbana, 67-69; vis prof 20th century art, Rice Univ, 73-74; vis prof 20th century art, George Washington Univ, 75-76. *Awards:* Guggenheim Found Fel, 78-79. *Mem:* Col Art Asn; Am Asn Mus. *Res:* Picasso & cubism; abstract expressionism; modern sculpture. *Publ:* Auth, Braque the papier colles, 82; David Smith, 82; Je suis le cahier:The sketchbooks of Picasso, 87; Nancy Graves, 87; Helen Frankenthaler - A painting retrospective, 89. *Mailing Add:* 954 Harbor View Dr Memphis TN 38103-8838

CARMICHAEL, DONALD RAY
PAINTER
b Elnora, Ind, Dec 26, 22. *Study:* Herron Art Inst, BFA, 51; Univ Tenn, Knoxville, MFA, 75; also with John Taylor & David Freidenthal, New York & Edwin Fulwider, Ford Times & Garo Antreasian, NMex. *Work:* Tenn State Mus, Nashville; Jackson-Madison Co Pub Libr, Tenn; Casey Jones Railroad Mus, Jackson, Tenn; Tarble Arts Ctr, Charleston, Ill; Bristol Art Ctr, Tenn; and others. *Comn:* Life size statue, Carl Smith Agency, Jackson, 67; official seal (engraving), Jackson State Community Col, 67; five panel mural, History of Jackson, McDonalds, Inc, 68. *Exhib:* Three-man show, Lynn Kottler Galleries, NY, 71; 23rd Grand Prix Int, Deauville, France & Palace Fine Arts, Rome, Italy, 72; Watercolor USA, Springfield Art Mus, 74-75; Southeastern Collection of Contemp Art, Mich Artrain Tour, 74; and others. *Collection Arranged:* Lawrence Calcagno Retrospective, 82-83; Walter Sorge Retrospective, 83-84; Watercolor III, Fourth and Fifth Biennial, 83-85; Med Illustr, CIBA Collection, Frank Netter, Md, 84. *Pos:* Pres, Jackson Art Asn, 65-67; pres, Jackson Arts Coun, 68-70; chmn visual arts adv panel, Tenn Arts Comn, 72-75, field rep, 75-78; dir, Tarble Arts Ctr, Eastern Ill Univ, Charleston, 78-85, emer dir, 85-; bd mem, Cent Ill Arts Consortium, 78-84; mem rev comt, Art in Archit, Capital Develop Bd, Ill, 79-82; dir exhib, Venice Art Ctr, FL, 87-, pres 93-94. *Teaching:* Instr painting, Shelbyville Art League, Ind, 51-55; instr art appreciation, Union Univ, Tenn, 64-66, instr drawing, painting & composition, 66-74; grad asst, Univ Tenn, Knoxville, 74-75; instr evening classes, Dyersburg State Community Col, Tenn, 76-77; instr art theory, Eastern Ill Univ, Charleston, 80-84; instr watercolor, Venice Art Ctr, Fla, 87. *Awards:* Purchase Award, Enjay Chem Nat, 66; Tennessee Painting Today Purchase Award, Tenn Arts Comn, 67; Tennessee Watercolor Soc Purchase Award, 75. *Bibliog:* William T Alderson (auth), Tennessee lives, Historical Rec Asn, 71; article, La Rev Mod, 72; Mary Ann Beckwith (auth), Creative Watercolor & Techniques, 96. *Mem:* Fla Suncoast Watercolor Soc; Tenn Watercolorist (dir & mem chmn, 71-73); Southern Watercolor Soc; co-founder Tenn Watercolor Soc (pres, 74); Fla Artist Group Inc (dir, 97, vpres, 99, pres, 2001-03). *Media:* Watercolor, Oil. *Publ:* Contribr, Edward Betts, auth, Creative Seascape Painting, 81; Jerry McLish (auth), Marine Art - A Collection of Fine Art, 98. *Dealer:* Venice Art Ctr Venice FL 34285. *Mailing Add:* 860 Stewart St Englewood FL 34223-2844

CARNWATH, SQUEAK
PAINTER
b Abington, Pa, May 24, 47. *Study:* Goddard Col, 69-70; Calif Col Arts & Crafts, MFA, 77. *Work:* Oakland Mus; San Francisco Mus Mod Art. *Exhib:* group exhibs, Professor's Choice, Pomona Col, Claremont, Calif, 92, Contemp Uses of Wax & Encaustic, Palo Alto Cult Ctr, Calif, 92, New Additions 1991-1992, Alice Simsar Gallery, Ann Arbor, Mich, 92, Fine Arts Presses, City Hall, Civic Ctr, San Francisco, Calif, 92, Art Contact, Central Exhib Hall, St Petersburg, Russia, 92, Am Art Today: Heads Only, Art Mus Fla, Int Univ, Miami, 94, Here & Now: Bay Area Masterworks from the di Rosa Collections, Oakland Mus, Calif, 94; solo exhibs, Ledis Flam Gallery, NY 93 & 94, OK Harris/David Klein Gallery, Birmingham, Mich, 94, Chrysler Mus, Norfolk, Va, traveling, 94, David Beitzel Gallery, NY, 96 & 98, Cohen Berkowitz Gallery, Kansas City, Mo, 97, Squeak Carnwath, Seeing in the Dark, Calif Mus Art, Luther Burbank Ctr Arts, Santa Rosa, Calif, 98 & Undraped Human Being, John Berggruen Gallery, San Francisco, Calif, 98. *Teaching:* Teaching asst ceramics, Calif Col Arts & Crafts, Oakland, 71, 76, guest artist, 77-78, 79, 82, shopmaster ceramics, 80-82; instr, Ohlone Col, Fremont, Calif, Calif Col Arts & Crafts, Oakland, 78; vis artist, Univ Calif, Berkeley, 82-83; prof art, Univ Calif, Davis, 83-, grad adv, 85-88, 90-92; vis prof & assoc dean, Sch Fine Arts, Calif Col Arts & Crafts, 93-94; prof in residence, Dept Art Practice, Univ Calif, Berkeley, 98. *Awards:* Guggenheim Fel, 94; Artist-in-Residence, Alma B C Shapiro Residency for a Woman Painter, Yaddo, Sarasota Springs, NY, 96; Hometown Heroes, Oakland Artists Who Have Made a Difference, Office of the Mayor, Oakland, Calif, 96. *Bibliog:* S Winn (auth), Ramps & ghosts, Artnews, 11/80; S Boettger (auth), From the sunnyside, Art in Am, 1/83 & Impolite figure, Artforum, 10/83. *Media:* Oil. *Dealer:* David Beilzec Gallery New York NY. *Mailing Add:* 229 Harrison St Oakland CA 94607

CARO, ANTHONY
SCULPTOR
b New Malden, Eng, 24. *Study:* Christ Col, Cambridge(eng), 42-44; Regent St Polytechnic Inst, London, 46; Royal Acad Sch, London, 47-52. *Exhib:* Galerie Altair Palma, 2002; Galerie Besson London, 2002; La Pedrera Barcelona, 2002; Galeria Metta Madrid 2002; Mitchell-Innes & Nash NY 2002-2005; Frederik Meijer Sculpture Park Grand Rapids, 2003; Meadows Mus Dallas, 2003; Hubert Gallery NY, 2003; Artemis Greenberg van Doren, NY 2003; Soeul Mus of Art 2004; Galerie Daniel Templon Paris, 2005; Mitchell-Innes & Nash, NY, 2005; Marc Selwyn Fine Art/Daniel Weinberg Gallery, Los Angeles, Calif, 2005; Portland Art Mus, Portland, Ore, 2006; Ivan Centre Julio Gonzalez, Valencia, Spain, 2006; Joyerias Grassy, Madrid, Spain, 2006. *Pos:* Coun mem, Royal College of Art, 81-83; coun mem, Slade Sch Art, 1982-1992; Trustee Tate Gallery, 82-89, Fritzwilliam Mus, 84-, International Sculpture Ctr, 98; Senior Academician Royal Academy of Art, 2004. *Teaching:* instr, St Martin's Sch Art, London, 51-83; instr, Bennington Coll, Vt, 63-65. *Awards:* Sculpture Prize, First Biennale des Jeune Artistes, Paris, 59; Knighthood, Queens Birthday, Honours, 87; Henry Moore Grand Prize, Japan, 1991; Chevalier des Arts et Lettres, 1996; Lifetime Achievement Award, Int Sculpture Ctr, 1997; Order of Merit, 2000; Cristobal Gabarron Found Award, 2004; Julio Gonzalez Award, 2005. *Bibliog:* Dieter Blume Catalogue Raisonnee Vol's I-XIII 1942-2000; Richard Whelan Anthony Caro, 74; Ian Barker (ed) The Judgement 99, Giovanni Carandente Anthony Caro and Twentieth-Century Sculpture 99; Ian Barker Anthony Caro: Quest for the New Sculpture, 2004; Julius Bryant Anthony Caro: A Life in Sculpture 2004, Paul Moorhouse (ed) Anthony Caro 2005, Paul Moorhouse Interpreting Anthony Caro, 2005. *Mem:* Accademia delle Belle Arte di Brera, Milan, Italy (hon mem, 1992); Royal Inst British Architects, London (hon fel, 1997); Royay Soc British Sculptures (hon fel, 1997); Glasgow Sch Art, Scotland (hon fel, 1998); Bretton Hall Col, Univ Leeds Eng (hon fel, 1998); Univ Arts, London (hon fel, 2004). *Collection:* Represented in over 150 Public Collections Worldwide as well as 100's of Private Collections. *Dealer:* Annely Juda Fine Art London; Mitchell-Innes & Nash NY. *Mailing Add:* 111 Frognal Hampstead London NW3 6XR United Kingdom

CARONE, NICOLAS
ARTIST
b NY City, NY, Jun 4, 17. *Study:* student, Nat Acad. *Work:* incl Group Exhibs, Mus of Modern Art (Rome), The Whitney, Metrop Mus of Art, The Hirshhorn, The Balitimore Mus of Art. *Exhib:* Solo Exhibs, Frumkin Gallery, Stable Gallery, Staempfli Gallery; group exhibs, Brussels World's Fair, The Venice Biennale, The Tate Gallery, The Geitain Group (Japan), The Hirshhorn. *Pos:* Found mem NY Studio Sch. *Teaching:* teacher, painting Yale Univ, Columbia Univ, Brandeis Univ, Cornell Univ, Cooper Union, Sch of Visual Arts, Skowhegan Sch. *Awards:* Named Nat Acad, 2001; recipient The Rome Prize; Am Acad of Arts and Letters, Childe Hassam Grant. *Mem:* Nat Acad

CAROOMPAS, CAROLE J
PAINTER, INSTRUCTOR
b Oregon City, Ore. *Study:* Calif State Univ, Fullerton, BA, 68; Univ Southern Calif, MFA, 71. *Work:* Los Angeles Co Mus Art; New Mus, NY; Nora Eccles Harrison Mus of Art, Utah State Univ, Logan; Berkeley Mus; Orange Co Mus; Santa Barbara Mus; and others. *Exhib:* Los Angeles - New Work, Mus Mod Art, NY, 76 & Maps, 77; Art about Art, Whitney Mus Art, NY, 78; Michael & Dorothy Blankfort Collection, Los Angeles Co Mus Art, 82; Corcoran Biennial, Corcoran Gallery Art, Washington, DC, 93; Around the Dinner Party, Armand Hammer Mus, Calif, 95-96; Some Grids, Los Angeles Co Mus Art, 96; Patterns of Excess, Beaver Col, Pa, 96; Cirrus Gallery, Los Angeles, 96; solo show, Mark Moore Gallery, Santa Monica, Calif, 97, 99, 2000; Otis Gallery, Otis Col Art & Design, Los Angeles, 97; San Jose Mus of Art, 02-; Western Project, 2003; Western Project (solo show), 2004. *Pos:* Professor, Otis Col Art Design. *Teaching:* Fac mem painting, Otis Col Art Design, 81-. *Awards:* Adolph Y Esther Gottlieb Grant, 93 & 2005; Grant, City of Los Angeles, 2000; Grant, Calif Community, 2005; Grant, Peter S. Reed Found, 2006. *Bibliog:* Terry Myers (auth), Reviews, New Art Examiner, 10/94; Amelia Jones (auth), Reviews, Art Forum, 11/94; Michael Duncan (auth), LA rising, Art in Am, 12/94 & Essay, 11/98; Christopher Knight (auth), LA Times, 97, 98,99,2000; David Pagel (auth), Art Issues, 98; Michael Duncan, Art in America Article Essay, 98; and others. *Media:* Acrylic. *Specialty:* Contemporary Art. *Publ:* Auth, Dreams of the lady of the castle perilous & portfolio: the songs she sang to herself, Paris Review, 81; The Weavers Dream - A Lullabye, Whitewalls, 81; La Lucha (the Struggle) Record Album with Chas Smith & Tim Biskup, self-publ, 89; Intro - & Another Fairy Tale, Lace, 89; Before & After Frankenstein: The Woman who knew too much, Sue Spaid Gallery, 92. *Dealer:* Western Project/ 3830 Main Street, Culver City, CA, 90232. *Mailing Add:* 1250 Long Beach Ave #118 Los Angeles CA 90021-2339

CARP, RICHARD M
ADMINISTRATOR, EDUCATOR
b Madison, Wis, June 10, 49. *Study:* Stanford Univ, BA, 71; Pacific Sch Relig, MA, 77; Grad Theological Union, PhD, 81. *Pos:* Dir grad prog, Calif Col Arts & Crafts, 86-87; vpres acad affairs, Kansas City Art Inst, 89-91; chair, Northern Ill Univ, DeKalb, 91-. *Teaching:* Assoc prof interdisciplinary, Calif Col Arts & Crafts, 82-88; prof, Art Inst Southern Calif, 88-89; spec proj image bank teaching world religions, Nat Endowment Humanities, 88-92; prof & sr grad fac interdisciplinary, Northern Ill Univ, DeKalb, 91-; spec proj co-dir, Nat Endowment Humanities, Univ Hawaii, 93. *Mem:* Am Acad Relig; Asn Integrative Studies; Col Art Asn; Soc Values Higher Educ; Am Asn Univ Women. *Res:* Art; material culture; religion and the construction of perception. *Publ:* Contribr, Tracing Common Themes: Comparative Courses in the Study of Religion, Scholars Press, 93; contribr & ed, Saber es Poder/Interventions: Urban Revisions: Current Projects for the Public Realm-Museum of Cont Art LA, ADOBE-LA, 94; auth, Lost in the desert: Mark C Taylor, disfiguring art, architecture, religion, Art J, spring 94; auth, Perception & Material Culture: Historical & Cross-Cultural Perspectives, Historical Reflections/Reflexions Historiques, fall, 97; contribr, Beyond Schultz: Absence Face to Face, Wish I Were: Felt Patways of the Self, Magna Publ, 98. *Mailing Add:* Northern Ill Univ Sch Art De Kalb IL 60115

CARPENTER, DENNIS (BONES) WILKINSON
PHOTOGRAPHER, EDUCATOR
b Meridian, Miss, June 7, 47. *Study:* Univ Ky, BArch, 72; Univ Fla, MFA, 79. *Work:* Jacksonville Art Mus, Fla; Polaroid Corp, Clarence Kennedy Gallery, Cambridge, Mass; Polaroid Int, Amsterdam, Neth; St Petersburg Mus Fine Art, Fla; Univ Fla, Gainesville. *Exhib:* Graphics Invitational, Mint Mus, 80; solo exhib, Univ Denver, 82, Light Factory, Charlotte, NC, 83, Webster Univ, St Louis, 83 & Photogenesis Gallery, Albuquerque, 83, Photographers Choose Photographers, Name Gallery, Chicago, 83. *Pos:* 606-257-9000, Home: 606-254-5146. *Teaching:* Assoc prof photog, Univ Ky, Lexington, 73-; grad teaching asst, Univ Fla, Gainesville, 77-79; dir photog, Penland Sch Crafts, NC, 83. *Awards:* Best of Show, The Landscape, Crealde Sch Art, 81 & Each Image Unique, Catskill Ctr Photog, 81; Nat Endowment Arts Fel, 83. *Mem:* Soc Photog Educ; Col Art Asn; Friends Photog. *Media:* Mixed. *Mailing Add:* Univ Ky Col Fine Arts/Art Dept 207 Fine Arts Bldg Lexington KY 40506-0022

CARPENTER, EARL L
PAINTER
b Long Beach, Calif, Nov 13, 31. *Study:* Chouinard Art Sch, 1 yr; Art Ctr Col Design, 4 yrs. *Work:* Mus Northern Ariz, Flagstaff; also in pvt collections of Olaf Weighorst, Sen Barry Goldwater, John Colton & Will Auther. *Exhib:* Retrospective, Wyo State Arch & Hist Dept, 74; Grand Canyon Art, Northern Ariz Univ, Flagstaff, 78; Artist of the Rockies 10th Anniversary Exhib, Pueblo, Colo, 83; Nat Park Acad Art, Wyo, 87; Gov's Invitational, Cheyenne, Wyo; Northern Ariz Univ, Flagstaff, 98; Grand Canyon Asn Art, Kolb Studio, 2000. *Pos:* Tech illusr, Advert Art (Agency), 60-65; profl artist, currently. *Teaching:* pvt instr. *Awards:* Stacey Scholar, 67 & 69; Arts for the Parks. *Mem:* Grand Canyon Art Asn; Grand Canyon Trust; Phoenix Art Mus. *Media:* Oil, Gouache. *Specialty:* Southwestern Art. *Interests:* Photography. *Publ:* Illusr, paintings in Ariz Highways Mag, Phoenix, 73, 74 & 87; article, Southwest Art Mag, 1/81 & US Mag, 9/88; Art of the West, 4-5/90, 11-12/92 & 11-12/97; The Majesty of the Grand Canyon, First Glance Bks, 98; Art Talk 98, Scottsdale, Ariz, 98; askart.com. *Dealer:* Windrush Gallery Sedona AR; Stewart Galleries Palm Springs CA. *Mailing Add:* PO Box 25906 Munds Park AZ 86017-5906

CARPENTER, GEORGE ROBERT
PAINTER
b Boston, Mass, Dec 13, 28. *Work:* Peabody Mus, Salem, Mass; Farnsworth Mus, Rockland, Maine; Nat Gallery, Ottawa, Ontario, Can; Galerie Simoes, EDE, Holland; Monterey Mus, Monterey, Calif. *Exhib:* Down Erst Gallery, Wash, DC, 1971; Dogg & Cighards Gallery, Boston, 1975; Morency Freres Montreal, 1980; Ruth Carolson Gallery, Mendocino, Calif, 1983; Rockport Art Asn, Mass; Anchorage Fine Arts, Anchorage Mus, AK. *Awards:* Am Watercolor Soc, 1968; Purchase award, Watercolor USA, 1975; Rockport Art Asn, Winter Group Show, 1998. *Mem:* Watercolor USA Honor Soc; Cockport Art Asn; Ogunquit Art Asn; North Shore Art Asn; Salmagundi club. *Media:* Watercolor. *Mailing Add:* Box 1812 Ogunquit ME 03907

CARPENTER, JOSEPH ALLAN
GRAPHIC ARTIST, CARTOONIST
b Providence, RI, Feb 8, 21. *Study:* RI Sch Design, BFA, 47. *Work:* Rehoboth Antiquarian Soc Mus, Mass. *Comn:* Portraits of retirees, Allied Signal Co, E Providence, RI, 65-78. *Exhib:* One-man shows, Attleboro Mus, Mass, 79 & Providence Art Club; Bard Co Showcase, NY. *Pos:* Ad mgr, Mason Can Co, 56-60; art dir, Fram Co Bendix, 60; creative dir, Automotive Div, Allied Signal, 84. *Media:* Watercolor. *Publ:* Auth & illusr, Only Golfers Know The Feeling, Mobray Co, 83 & 84, Bob Adams Inc, 91. *Mailing Add:* 72 Elm St Rehoboth MA 02769

CARPENTER, LINDA BUCK
SCULPTOR, ASSEMBLAGE ARTIST
b Los Angeles, Calif, July 22, 52. *Study:* Immaculate Heart Col, Los Angeles, 71-72; Calif State Univ, Sacramento, BA, 80, MA, 87. *Work:* Sculpture Grebitus and Son Jewelers. *Comn:* Art in Pub Places Prog, Sacramento Co, 89. *Exhib:* Northern Calif Artists Competition, Open Ring Gallery, Sacramento, 81; Americans in Glass, traveling nationally and internationally, 84-86; Artists Working in Glass, Richard L Nelson Gallery, Davis, Calif, 84; Int Exhib Glass Craft, Kanazawa, Japan, 88 & 90; Sacramento Capital Club, Calif, 96. *Bibliog:* Karen Wilson (dir), Glass Artists, Arts Alive Program, KVIE-TV, Pub Broadcasting, 83; Suzanne Foley (auth), The measure of success, Am Craft, 84; Ellen Schlesinger (auth), Glass as texture, line, color, Sacramento Bee, 1/27/85; Victoria Dalkey (auth), Elegant Expressionism, Sacramento Bee, 5/31/87. *Media:* Flat Glass

CARR, CAROLYN K
CURATOR, HISTORIAN
b Providence, RI. *Study:* Smith Col, BA; Oberlin Col, MA; Case-Western Reserve Univ, PhD. *Collection Arranged:* Ohio: A Photographic Portrait (auth, catalog), 80, The Image in American Painting and Sculpture 1950-1980 (auth, catalog), 82, Akron Art Mus, Ohio; Gaston Lachaise: Portrait Sculpture (auth, catalog), Nat Portrait Gallery, Wash, DC, 85; Then and Now: American Portraits of the Past Century (auth, catalog), Nat Portrait Gallery, 88; American Art at the 1893 World's Columbian Exhib (auth, catalog), Nat Portrait Gallery, 93; Rebels: Painters & Poets of the 1950s, 99; Hans Namuth: Portrait, 99; A Brush with History: Paintings from the Nat Portrait Gallery, 2001; Retratos: 2000 Years of Latin American Portraits, 2004. *Pos:* Art critic, Akron Beacon J, Ohio, 68-74; chief cur, Akron Art Mus, Ohio, 78-83; deputy dir & chief curator, Nat Portrait Gallery, Washington, DC, 84-. *Teaching:* Instr art hist, Kent State Univ, 63-65. *Mem:* Col Art Asn; Am Asn Mus. *Res:* Post 1945 American art; late nineteenth century American art; photography. *Specialty:* 18th, 19th, & 20th Century Portraiture. *Mailing Add:* 4943 Hillbrook Lane NW Washington DC 20016

CARRERO, JAIME
PAINTER, EDUCATOR
b Mayaguez, PR, June 16, 31. *Study:* Polytechnic Inst, Columbia Univ, BA(art hist); Pratt Inst, MS. *Work:* Ponce Mus, PR; Mus Inst PR Art & Univ PR, San Juan; Inter-Am Univ Collection, San German. *Comn:* Illus for bk, Cuentos Puertorriquenos, 73. *Exhib:* Univ PR, San Juan, 60 & 65; Inst Cult PR, San Juan, 62; Acad Fine Arts, Calcutta, India, 65; Ateneo Puertorriqueno, San Juan, 66; Ponce Mus, 86; Springfield Mus, Mass, 90. *Teaching:* Prof painting, drawing & art hist, Inter-Am Univ, 57-; prof art hist, Rum, Mayaguez, PR, 74-75. *Bibliog:* Josemilio Gonzalez (auth), Jaime Carrero, Pintor, El Mundo, 60; Drawings by Jaime Carrero, El Corno Emplumado, Mex, Nos 26, 28 & 30, 64-66; Drawings: The San Juan Star. *Media:* Acrylic, Watercolor. *Mailing Add:* Urb Sado Corazon Anasco PR 00610

CARRICO, ANITA
LIBRARIAN
b Bronx, New York, June 30, 38. *Study:* State Univ NY, Buffalo, BA(art history), 74, MLS, 79. *Pos:* Asst Librn, Albright-Knox Art Gallery, Buffalo, NY 79-81; librn, Baltimore Mus Art, Md, 81-89; head librn, Philadelphia Mus Art, Pa, 89-94 & Univ Archit Libr, Md, 94-. *Mem:* Art Libr Soc NAM (secy 89-91); Asn Archit Sch Libr; Wash Art Libr Resources Comt (co-chmn, 96-). *Mailing Add:* c/o Univ Md Archit Libr College Park MD 20742

CARRINO, DAVID
PAINTER
b New York, NY, 1959. *Study:* New Sch Social Res, 78; Sch Visual Arts, New York, BFA, 81. *Exhib:* Solo exhibs, Scott Hanson Gallery, NY, 88 & Tony Shafrazi Gallery, NY, 89 & 91, Schoolhouse Ctr, Provincetown, 98, 99, 2000; Am Art Today: Surface Tension, Art Mus, Fla Int Univ, Miami, 92; Rena Branston, San Francisco, 92; Wooster Gardens, NY, 92; Tony Shafrazi Gallery, NY, 93; Schoolhouse Ctr, Provincetown, 2000; New Editions, Pace Editions, New York City, 97. *Bibliog:* Joshua Decter (auth), New York reviews, Flash Art, 3-4/90; Collins & Milazzo (auths), Outside America: Going Into the 90's (exhib catalog), Fay Gold Gallery, Atlanta, 91; Ken Johnson (auth), Vogue Arts, Vogue, 8/91; The New Yorker, 10/14/91; Stephen Westfall (auth), American Art Today: Surface Tension (essay), Art Mus, Fla Int Univ, Miami, 92; Brook Adams (auth), New Humanist Photography, Print Collectors Newsletter, May-June 96; Two by Two for AIDS and Art, Dallas Mus of Art, AMFAR auction catalogue; 5th International Biennial Print Exhibit, People's Republic of China, exhibition catalogue, 91; and others. *Mailing Add:* 233 W 13th St Apt 1 New York NY 10011-7713

CARROLL, JAMES F L
PAINTER, SCULPTOR
b Postville, Iowa, Sept 4, 34. *Study:* Colo State Col, BA, 56, MA, 62; Univ Colo, Boulder, MFA, 66; also studied with Richard Ellinger, Sir Robin Phillipson, Joan Brown, Roland Reiss. *Work:* Kutztown Univ, Kutztown, Pa; St Mary's Col Md; Muhlenberg Col, Allentown, Pa; Pa State Univ, Berks Campus, Reading, Pa; Reading Pub Mus, Pa; and others. *Exhib:* One-man exhibs, 112 Workshop, NY, 77, Lehman Col Gallery, City Univ NY, 77, Artists Open Studio, Kutztown, Pa, 85, 89, 92 & 96, Martin Art Gallery, Muhlenberg Col, Allentown, Pa, 97, Open Studio, Kutztown, Pa, 2000; Summer Gallery Outdoor Sculpture Show, Pa State Univ, 88-91; 2nd Exhib, Sculpture Garden, Maria Feliz Gallery, Jim Thorpe, Pa, 90; Masterpieces, Martin Art Gallery Exhib, Muhlenberg Col, Allentown, Pa, 98; Maria Feliz Gallery, Jim Thorpe, Pa, 2000; MCS Gallery, Easton, Pa, 2000; Cedar Crest Col, Art Gallery, Paper Forms, Allentown, 2000; Reading Area Community Col, Works on Paper, Reading, 2002; Reading Area Community Col, Works on Paper, Reading, 2002; Tempkins & Cressman Galleries, Cedar Crest Col, 2005; Rosefsky Gallery, Binghamton Univ, NY, 2004. *Pos:* Dir & pres, New Arts Prog, Kutztown, Pa, 74-; nominator, Award in Visual Arts, AVA, 90-91 & Nat Found for Advancement in Arts, NFAA, 92-97; juror, Gallery 33, Hershey, Pa, 91; panel mem, Pa Coun on the Arts, 90-92. *Teaching:* Prof fine arts, Kutztown Univ, Kutztown, Pa, 66-99; adj fac, Muhlenberg Col, Allentown, PA, 91 & Cedar Crest Col, Allentown, 99-2001; lectr, Yale Univ, 82, Pratt, Bklyn, 86, Lehigh Univ, Bethlehem, Pa, 88, Slade Sch Art, London, 92, WITF-FM PBS Radio, Harrisburg, Pa, Phoeniz Gallery, NYC, 2002, SUNY, 2004, Cedar Crest Col. Allentown, Pa, 2005; instr, Alvernia Col, Reading, 2003; instr, La Guardia Community Col, NY, 2004 & 05. *Awards:* Exceptional Acad Serv Cert, Commonwealth of Pa, 78; Nat Sculpture Show, Touring Exhib, Statesboro, Ga, 79; Visual Arts Grant, Nat Endowment Arts, 80; Visual Arts Award, Kutztown Univ, 82, 85, & 88; Pollock-Krasner Grant, 2004. *Bibliog:* Tim Higgins (auth), Carroll's NAP brings mtns, 8/5/86, Geoff Gehman (auth), Nature plays host to 43, Morning Call Newspaper, 8/26/90; Marilyn J Fox (auth), A solo new arts exhib, Eagle/Times Newspaper, 8/2/92; Tim Higgins (auth), James Carroll drawing convey his cerebral concepts of space, 8/30/97. *Mem:* Am Asn Mus; Int Sculpture Ctr; Lehigh Valley Arts Coun (bd mem, 89-92); Col Art Asn. *Media:* Paint. *Publ:* Contribr, 11th, 10th, Critical & 8th Assembling, Assembling Press, 78-81; In and Out of New York, Hunter Yoder, 80; auth, 71 Small Works on Paper, 65-81, & In and Out of Kutztown, 82, James Carroll; Essay, Paul Harryn (catalogue), Lehigh Univ, 91; Foreword essay, Julius Tobias (catalogue), 92. *Mailing Add:* 173 W Main St Kutztown PA 19530

CARSON, G B
CONSULTANT, ART DEALER
b Helena, Mont, Feb, 28, 50. *Study:* Univ Calif, Berkeley, BA(art hist), 77. *Collection Arranged:* Le Desert de Retz: An 18th Century French Folly Garden, Calif Palace Legion Hon, San Francisco, 91; Nathan Oliveira Figure Studies, Schneider Mus Art, So Oregon Univ, Ashland, 2002. *Mem:* Graphic Arts Coun, Fine Arts Mus, San Francisco; Asn Study of Dada & Surrealism. *Specialty:* California art of the 1960's. *Mailing Add:* PO Box 8502 Berkeley CA 94707

CARSON, JOANNE
EDUCATOR
Study: Univ Ill, BA; Univ Chicago, MFA. *Work:* Options, Mus Contemp Art, Chicago, 1985, Whitney Biennial, Whitney Mus Am Art, New York City, 1985, Frederick Weisman Collection, Fleming Mus, Burlington Vt, 2001, Brooklyn Mus, 2002. *Exhib:* One-woman shows incl, Plus Ultra Gallery, Brooklyn, 2001, Sylvia Schmidt Gallery, 1994, Ruth Siegel Gallery, New York City, 1990; exhib in group shows at Spring Exhib, Am Acad of Arts and Letters, 2002, New Works on Wood, Frederick Weisman Collection. *Pos:* Prof & chairperson, art dept Univ at Albany, State Univ of NY. *Awards:* Recipient Purchase Prize Sculpture, Am Acad of Arts and Letters, 2002; Rome Prize Fel Painting, Am Acad Rome, Artists Fel, Nat Endowment Arts. *Mailing Add:* Univ at Albany State Univ of NY Art Dept 1400 Wash Ave FA Albany NY 12222

CARSON, SOL KENT
PAINTER, PRINTMAKER, SCULPTOR, ADMINISTRATOR
b Philadelphia, Pa, Jun 7, 17. *Study:* Temple Univ, BFA, 40-44; Minerva Univ, Italy, PhD, 58-60; Phi Delta Kappa. *Work:* Philadelphia Mus Art, Pa; Philadelphia Libr, Pa; Millerville Univ, Pa; Temple Univ, Medical Sch, Philadelphia, Pa. *Comn:* Stone Study Mother Katherine, Convent, Cornwells Heights, Pa; Bronze Bust, Dean Cadd Thomas, Philadelphia, Pa; Paul Bunyon Mural Panel, Am Lumber Corp, Philadelphia, Pa; many portraits. *Exhib:* One man exhib, Wis State Univ, Wis, 67; Int League for Peace & Freedom, Philadelphia, 67; 100 distinguished painters, Philadelphia Fidelity, Pa, 67; Int Exhib, Civil Ctr Mus, Philadelphia, Pa, 68; Carson, Prints, Los Gatos Chambers, Calif, 94. *Pos:* dir, dept visual educ, Temple Univ, Philadelphia, Pa, 44-47; consult, mus, Univ Pa Mus, 45-46. *Teaching:* instr, drawing & painting, Philadelphia Bd of Educ, Adult Div; asst prof, Temple Univ, Tyler Sch, 40-45; prof, drawing & painting, Wis State Univ, 64-66. *Awards:* Fel, Established printmaking dept, Tyler Philadelphia, Temple Univ, 40-46. *Mem:* Nat Educ Asn; Am Asn Univ Prof; Pa State col & Univ Asn; Artist Equity & Asn Pa State Col & Univ, Retired Fac. *Media:* Acrylic, Oil. *Publ:* auth, To my son, my wife, to myself, Nat Libr of Poetry, Harbinger House, 95. *Mailing Add:* 447 Alberto Way C128 Los Gatos CA 95032

CARSWELL, JOHN
MUSEUM DIRECTOR, PAINTER
b London, Eng, Nov 16, 31. *Study:* Wimbledon Sch Art, Surrey Eng, 46-48; Royal Col Art, London, ARCA, 48-51. *Work:* Arts Coun Gt Brit. *Exhib:* One man shows, Hanover Gallery, London, 56 & Fischbach Gallery, NY, 66. *Collection Arranged:* Islamic Binding & Bookmaking (auth, catalog), 81-82; Blue & White: Chinese Porcelain & Its Impact on the Western World, (auth, catalog), 85; The Mosaics of Jordan (with catalog), 92. *Pos:* Cur, Oriental Inst Mus, Univ Chicago, 78-85, dir, David & Alfred Smart Gallery, 85-87; dir, Sotheby's Asian Islamic Dept 88-. *Teaching:* Prof fine art, Am Univ Beirut, Lebanon, 56-76. *Bibliog:* G Hovrari (auth), Arab Seafaring (new ed), Princeton Univ Press, 95. *Mem:* Oriental Ceramic Soc (coun mem); Royal Soc Asian Affairs (vpres). *Media:* Oil, Paper. *Res:* Islamic art and architecture; Far eastern ceramics; cross-cultural contacts in Asian Art. *Publ:* Auth, Coptic Tattoo Designs, Am Univ Beirut, 58; New Julfa: Armenian Churches & Other Buildings, Oxford Univ Press, 68; coauth, Kutahya Tiles and Pottery in Armenian Cathedral of St James, Jerusalem, Oxford Univ Press, 72; Chinese Ceramics in Sadbeok Hanim Museum, Istanbul, 95. *Mailing Add:* Islamic Dept 34-35 New Bond St London W1A 2AA England United Kingdom

CARSWELL, RODNEY
PAINTER, EDUCATOR
b Carmel, Calif, Dec 15, 46. *Study:* Univ NMex, BFA, 68; Univ Colo, MFA, 72. *Work:* Univ NMex, Albuquerque; Univ Colo, Boulder; Ill State Mus, Springfield; Evansville Mus Art, Ind; Art Inst Chicago; Prudential, NY. *Exhib:* Chicago & Vicinity Show, Art Inst Chicago, 73, New Horizons in Art, Chicago, 73; Chosen Object, Joslyn Mus, Omaha, Nebr, 77; Surfaces: Two Decades of Chicago Painting, Seventies & Eighties, Terra Mus Am Art, Chicago, 87; Good Painting, Art Gallery, State Ill Bldg, Chicago, 88; Am Acad Arts & Letts, NY, 91; Renaissance Soc, Chicago (catalog), 93; Feigen Inc, Chicago, 95; and others. *Teaching:* Assoc prof painting & drawing, Univ Ill, Chicago, formerly, prof, currently. *Awards:* Nat Endowment Arts Fel, 91; LC Tiffany Fel, 93; Guggenheim fel, 89; and others. *Bibliog:* William Wilson (auth), Rodney Carswell, Los Angeles Times, 3/13/87; Dennis Adrian (auth), Two Decades of Painting in Chicago, Beneath the Surfaces, Art Examiner, 12/87; Buzz Spector (auth), Rodney Carswell (exhib catalog), Art Mus, Univ Okla, 88. *Media:* Oil, Wax. *Dealer:* Feigen Inc 742 N Wells Chicago IL 60610

CARTER, (CHARLES) BRUCE
PRINTMAKER, EDUCATOR
b North Adams, Mass, May 15, 30. *Study:* Albright Art Sch, Buffalo, NY, dipl, 51; State Univ NY Buffalo, BS, 52; Pa State Univ, Univ Park, MEd & DEd, 58. *Work:* Nat Hist Mus, Univ Oslo, Norway; Philadelphia Mus Art; State Art Mus, Raleigh, NC; Amarillo Art Ctr, Tex. *Comn:* Painted mural, Narvik City Coun, Norway, 62 & mosaic mural, 63; mosaic mural, Kiruna, Sweden, 62; painted mural, Nat Mus, Gettysburg, Pa; mosaic mural, Nordsland Banken, Leknes, Norway, 68. *Exhib:* Soc Am Graphic Artists, NY, 71; 2nd Triennial Int Exhib Contemp Xylography, Nat Mus Xylography, Carpi, Italy, 72; Hokkaido Print Asn Int Exhib, Sapporo, Japan, 72; 3rd Int Print Biennial Exhib, Art Mus, Epinal, France, 75; Return to the Crucible, The Pentagon, DC, 76; Wounded Knee: An Am Tragedy, Amarillo Art Ctr, Tex, 76; 6th Nat Print Exhib, Los Angeles, 78; Nat Hist Mus, Univ Oslo, Norway, 80; The Warsaw Woodcuts, Ghetto Fighters Mus, Israel, 81. *Pos:* Art consult, Poetry on the Buses, Pittsburgh, 76-. *Teaching:* Prof printmaking-drawing, Carnegie Mellon Univ, Pittsburgh, 63-93; retired. *Awards:* Purchase Prizes, Nat Mus Xylography, Carpi, Italy, 72 & Univ Wis-Madison, 75. *Mem:* Col Art Asn; Philadelphia Print Club; Artists' Equity Asn. *Media:* Woodcut, Lithography. *Publ:* Coauth, Wounded Knee: An American Tragedy (film), WQED-TV, 72. *Mailing Add:* 343 Sperryville Rd Glenfield NY 13343

CARTER, CAROL
PAINTER
b Sumter, SC, 1955. *Study:* Principia Col, Elsah, Ill, BA, 77; Washington Univ, St Louis, Mo, MFA, 84. *Work:* Arjomari, Arches, Rives Paper, Inc; Blue Cross/Blue Shield, St Louis, Mo; Citicorp, Maui, Hawaii; Renaissance Ctr Club, Detroit, Mich; Suwa Art Mus, Japan; and others. *Comn:* Edison Brothers, St Louis, Mo; Renaisance Ctr, Detroit, Mich. *Exhib:* One-woman shows, Elliot Smith Gallery, St Louis, Mo, 90, Diane Nelson Gallery, Laguna, Calif, 90, Ethical Soc, St Louis, Mo, 92, Galleria Blagas, Detroit, Mich, 93, R Duane Reed Gallery, St Louis, Mo, 94 & 96 & Stein-Bartlow Gallery, Chicago, Ill, 94; Artists and The Am Yard, Wustum Art Mus, Racine, Wis, 91; Watercolor USA, Springfield Art Mus, Mo, 93; Watercolor, Strecker Gallery, Manhattan, Kans, 93; Boats, Elliot Smith Gallery, St Louis, Mo, 93; H2O Color Invitational, Univ Wis, Whitewater, Wis, 93; St Louis Art, Cedar Rapids Art Mus, Iowa, 98; Belgade, Ctr Contemp Art, St Louis, Mo; Fla Skies, Maryville Univ, 2000; and many others. *Pos:* Gallery owner & operator, Rockport, Mass & St Louis, Mo, 76-79; asst, B Z Wagman Gallery, St Louis, 85-86. *Teaching:* Teaching assistantship, Wash Univ, St Louis, 83-84; watercolor instr, Fine Arts Inst, Wash Univ, 85-, drawing instr, Sch Archit, 89-91, Principia Col, 91; vis artist, Metrop Honors Art, St Louis, 88 & 90, Univ of Denver, 89. *Awards:* Award, Five State Watercolor, Wichita Art Mus, Kans, 89; Purchase Award, Watercolor USA, Springfield Art Mus, Mo, 91; M-AAA/Nat Endowment Arts Fel Award in Painting & Works on Paper, 94; Art Award, Nat Asn Women Bus Owners, 98. *Bibliog:* J P Wolf (auth), Introspective Reflections, Am Artist Mag, 10/89; Paul Harris (auth), Ideas are the Work of These Six Area Artists, St Louis Post-Dispatch, 6/91; Carol Shepley (auth), Appropriate Art: Group Show is all about Boats, St Louis Post Dispatch, 8/93; Carol Shepley (auth), Work by Gallery Artists, St Louis Post Dispatch, 5/94. *Mem:* Art St Louis. *Media:* Acrylic, Watercolor. *Dealer:* Peter Bartlow 44 E Superior Chicago IL 60611. *Mailing Add:* 4450 Laclede Ave Saint Louis MO 63108

CARTER, CURTIS LLOYD
MUSEUM DIRECTOR, EDUCATOR
b Moulton, Iowa, Oct 10, 35. *Study:* Taylor Univ, Upland, Ind, 60; Spec student, Harvard Univ, 61 & Brandeis Univ, 66; Boston Univ, PhD, 71. *Collection Arranged:* Jan Fabre: Passage, 98; A Passion for Porcelain: Three Centuries of Meissen Floral Painting, 98; Joseph Friebert at Ninety, 98; In the Lion's Den: The Bible Images of Marc Chagall, 98; Feng Mengbo: Video Games, 98. *Pos:* Chmn, Comt Fine Arts,

Marquette Univ, 76-84; dir, Haggerty Mus Art, Marquette Univ, 84-; pres, Dance Perspectives Found Inc, 87-98. *Teaching:* Asst prof aesthet & philos, Marquette Univ, 7684, prof, 84-; instr, Les Aspin Ctr Govt, Wash, DC, 96-. *Awards:* Wis Dance Coun Award, 92. *Mem:* Wis Alliance Arts Educ (co-chmn, 74-79); ARTREACH Milwaukee Inc (founding pres & bd mem 75-81, mem, currently); Nat Endowment Arts & Humanities (panelist & referee, 84-); Dance Perspectives Found (vpres 78-87, pres 87-). *Res:* Cultural identity of works of art; curatorial frameworks for understanding art in culturally diverse societies; improvisation in the arts; arts and technology; dance aesthetics; contemporary visual arts. *Publ:* Ed & contribr, Franta (exhib catalog), 92; Contemporary Folk Art (exhib catalog), 93; The Art of Design 2 (exhib catalog), 93; Wisconsin Artists: A Celebration of Jewish Presence (catalog), 94. *Mailing Add:* Marquette Univ Haggerty Mus Art 13th Clybourn Milwaukee WI 53233

CARTER, DAVID GILES
HISTORIAN, MUSEOLOGIST
b Nashua, NH, Nov 2, 21. *Study:* Princeton Univ, with CR Morey & AM Friend, AB, 44; Harvard Univ Grad Sch Arts & Sci, with P Sachs, CR Post, C Kuhn & others, MA, 49; Inst Fine Arts, New York Univ, 51, with W Cook, E Panofsky & G Schoenberger. *Collection Arranged:* Turner in America (with Wilbur D Peat), 56; The Young Rembrandt and His Times, 58; The GHA Clowes Collection, 59; Dynamic Symmetry, 61; El Greco to Goya (with Curtis Coley), 63; The Weldon Collection, 64; Masterpieces from Montreal, 66; The Painter and the New World, 67; Rembrandt and His Pupils, 69; Jan Menses, 76; and others. *Pos:* Curatorial asst, Metrop Mus Art, New York, 50-54; cur paintings & prints, John Herron Art Mus, 55-59; dir, Mus Art, RI Sch Design, 59-64 & Montreal Mus Fine Arts, 64-76; self employed consult; mem adv comt, Mt Holyoke Col Art Mus Art, 76-; trustee, Eli Whitney Mus, Hamden, Conn, 78- & New Haven Colony Hist Soc, 90-97; trustee, New Haven Colony Hist Soc, 90-97, pres, 97-2000, bd mem, 2000-. *Teaching:* Lectr, Ind Univ, Bloomington, 58-59. *Awards:* Gold Medal of Ital Cult, Ital Ministry Foreign Affairs, 63. *Mem:* ICOM; Mediaeval Acad; Grolier Club; Royal Soc Arts; plus others. *Res:* Northern Renaissance; secondary interest in Mannerist and Northern Baroque painting. *Publ:* Auth, Rencontre avec Valentin, l'Oeil, 70; The Winnipeg flagellation and the master of the View of St Gudule, Miscellanea in Memoriam Paul Coremans (1908-1965), Bull de l'Institut royal du Patrimoine artistique, xv, 75; Spanish itinerary, 5/76 & Northern Baroque and the Italian connexion, 5/76, Apollo; Montreal mus des beaux-arts, Art Gallery, 4-5/76; and others. *Mailing Add:* 100 Edgehill Rd New Haven CT 06511-1320

CARTER, DEAN
SCULPTOR, EDUCATOR
b Henderson, NC, Apr 24, 22. *Study:* Corcoran Sch Art; Am Univ, BA; Ogunquit Sch Painting & Sculpture; Indiana Univ, MFA; Ossip Zadkine Sch Art, Paris, France. *Work:* Cranbrook Acad Art, Mich; Charlotte Plaza, NC; Wash & Lee Univ; Wichita Art Asn Galleries, Kans; Harrisonburg Community Hosp, Va; Mus of Southern Decorative Arts, Winston-Salem, NC. *Comn:* welded bronze screen, Roanoke Mem Hosp, Va, 70; three piece bronze group, St Joseph's Preparatory Sch, Philadelphia, 70; welded bronze relief, First Colony Ins Co, Lynchburg, Va; bronze portrait, Stuart Cassell, Va Polytech Inst, 77; bronze sculptures, Ikenoue Christ Church, 3-15-8, Iguchi, Mitaka-shi, Tokyo, 95; plus others. *Exhib:* Pa Acad Fine Arts, Philadelphia, 54; Cini Found, Venice, Italy, 64; Smithsonian Circulating Exhib, 69-71; one-man show, Artists' Mart, Washington, 70; Contemp Gallery Art Ann Sculpture Show, Winston-Salem, 71. *Pos:* Mem art adv bd, Va Highlands Community Col, Abigdon, 69-71 & Mountain Empire Community Col, Wise, 71-75; consult, US Fine Arts Surv, 72. *Teaching:* Founder art dept, Va Polytech Inst & State Univ, 63-; artist in residence, USA Studies Abroad, Cortona, Italy. *Awards:* Sculpture Comn, Va/Md Sch Veterinary Med, 91; Allied Artist Award for Sculpture, 92; Odk G Burk Johnston Award for Outstanding Teacher-Adminr, 92; plus others. *Bibliog:* Ted Kliman (dir), A World of Sculpture (film), Va Polytech Inst & State Univ, 62; WM White, Jr (auth), Sculpturing by Dean Carter, Maelstrom, 66; WC Burleson (auth), On campus--Dean Carter, Context, summer 69. *Mem:* Soc Wash Artists; Southern Sculptors Asn (vpres, 66-68); Am Crafts Coun (state rep, 65); Col Art Asn Am; Am Fedn Art; plus others; Southeastern Col Art Conf (pres, 77). *Media:* Bronze, Wood. *Dealer:* Art Pannonia LLC Blacksburg Va 24060; Miller 11 Main Blacksburg Va 24060. *Mailing Add:* 1011 Highland Cir Blacksburg VA 24060

CARTER, FREDERICK TIMMINS
PAINTER, ILLUSTRATOR
b Galveston, Tex, Sept 22, 25. *Study:* Franklin Sch Prof Art, New York, grad with hons, 45-48. *Comn:* Paintings, El Paso Natural Gas Co, Tex, Ford Motor Co, Dearborn, Mich. *Exhib:* Tex Ann Paintings Exhib, Dallas, Houston & San Antonio Mus; Audubon Artists Nat Exhib, Nat Acad Galleries, NY; Sun Carnival Nat Exhib, El Paso Mus Fine Art; Nat Soc Painters in Casein, NY. *Media:* Acrylic. *Publ:* Illusr, Frank Mangan's Bordertown, El Paso, & Bordertown Revisited; Ford Times Mag; Fort Bliss History; auth & illusr, Frederic Carter's Depot. *Dealer:* Frederick Carter Studio 5744 Beaumont El Paso TX 79912. *Mailing Add:* 5744 Beaumont Pl El Paso TX 79912-5341

CARTER, GARY
PAINTER, SCULPTOR
b Hutchinson, Kans, Mar 12, 39. *Study:* Art Ctr Col Design, BFA, 71. *Work:* Nat Cowboy Hall Fame, Oklahoma City; C M Russell Mus, Great Falls, Mont; Mont Hist Soc, Helena; Gould Inc, Chicago; Cowboy Artists Am Mus, Kerrville, Tex; Wrigley Collection, Chicago, Ill. *Comn:* Mont Centennial Painting Comn (1889-1989), Pepsi-Cola Corp; mural, 1st Security Bank of West Yellowstone; mural, Big Sky Ski Resort; Phillip Anshutz Corp; Cutthroat Communs. *Exhib:* Cowboy Artists of Am Ann, Phoenix Art Mus, 82-2003; Western Heritage, Shamrock Hilton, Houston, 84; Buffalo Bill Art Show, Cody, Wyo, 86; Cowboy Artists of Am miniature show Ann, Kerrville, Tex, 90-96 & retrospective, 96; Wildlife of the Am West Art Mus, Jackson, Wyo, 88, 89 & 90; Booth Western Art Mus, Cartersville, Ga; Int Mus Horse, Lexington, Ky, 92; Eiteljorg Mus Am Indian & Western Art, Indianapolis, 95; Southwest Mag Traveling Show, 96. *Teaching:* Taught Art Seminar, C Mus, Kerrville, Tex, 86; head group workshop, Cowboy Artists Am Mus, 82, 83, 85, 88, 91, 93, 95. *Awards:* Artist of the West 1990, San Dimos Festival of Western Arts; Gold Medal Award, Cowboy Artist Am Exhib, Phoenix Art Mus, 90 & 97; Award Excellence, Western Heritage Invitational Art Show, 96. *Bibliog:* Dale Burk (auth), A Brush with the West; Chase Reynolds, Old Masters of the West. *Mem:* Cowboy Artists Am (pres, 85-86). *Media:* Oil. *Publ:* Auth, Western Horseman, 9/88; auth & illusr, Horse & Rider, 7/87; auth, Art of the West Mag, 4-5/88, feature article & cover, 11-12/93; Southwest Art Mag, 3/89; Big Sky J, winter 94-95. *Dealer:* GCWAPC Inc 12075 Marina Loop West Yellowstone MT 59758; Carter Western Art PO Box 338 West Yellowstone MT 59758. *Mailing Add:* PO Box 338 West Yellowstone MT 59758

CARTER, HARRIET (ESTELLE) MANORE
PAINTER
b Grand Bend, Ont, Mar 22, 29. *Study:* Dundas Valley Sch Fine Arts, Ont. *Work:* Sarnia Pub Libr & Art Mus, Ont; Art Gallery Brant, Brantford, Ont; Can Coun Art Bank; Hart House, Univ Toronto; Can Soc Painters Watercolour Diamond Jubilee Collection presented to her Majesty Queen Elizabeth II for the Royal Collection of Drawings and Watercolours at Windsor Castle; and many other pvt collections both in Can & US. *Comn:* Cloud Flowers (show), comn by Univ BC. *Exhib:* Traveling Exhib, 70-83 & Fifty Yrs, 75, Can Soc Painters Watercolour; On View Traveling Exhib, Ont, 76-77; Can Watercolour Soc Japan & Can Exhib, 76-77; Ont Soc Artists Ann Exhib, Oakville Centennial Gallery, 77; Cloud Flowers Traveling Exhib, 81-82; solo exhib, Nancy Poole's Studio, Toronto, 72-83. *Pos:* Commercial designer, Dominion Glass Co, Wallaceburg, Ont, 49-52. *Teaching:* art classes, secondary adult night sch. *Awards:* Hon Award, Can Soc Painters Watercolour, 69; Ont Soc Artists 100th Ann Exhib Awards, 72; Purchase Award, London Pub Art Gallery & Mus, 72; Royal Can Merit Award, Energy Mint Coin Design, 81. *Bibliog:* Tom Thompson Memorial Gallery Museum of Fine Art Show, Art Mag, 71; Kay Kritzwiser (auth), Four exhibits mind stretching style, Toronto Globe & Mail, 72; Lenore Crawford (auth), Manore Carter art gets message across, London Free Press, 73. *Mem:* Can Soc Painters Watercolour; Ont Soc Artists; Royal Can Acad Arts. *Media:* Watercolor. *Interests:* Antiques, collecting. *Collection:* The royal Colleciton of Drawings and Watercolours, Windsor Castle; Can Coun Art Bank; London Reg Art Gallery. *Dealer:* Nancy Pooles Gallery 16 Hazelton Ave Toronto ON M5R 2E2. *Mailing Add:* 78 MacLennan Ave Hamilton ON L8V 1X6 Canada

CARTER, JERRY WILLIAMS
VIDEO ARTIST, MOSAIC ARTIST
b Wichita, Kans, Apr 19, 41. *Study:* Univ Md, BA, 68; Chicago Art Inst, 69; Acad Fine Arts Finland, 70; Centro Int Studi L'Insegnamento Mosaico, cert, 70; L'Ecole Nat Superieur Beaux Arts Paris, with Gustave Singier, 71; Acad Belli Arti Ravenna, with Pomadoro, 72; Univ Studi Bologna, cert, with Bovini, 71; Nat Inst Design Finland, 73; Antioch Univ, Columbia Visual Arts Ctr, MFA, 81; Ctr Creative Imaging, Camden, Maine, 93, Beta Test Site: Day Star Digital, 92-94. *Work:* The Phillips Collection, Washington; Pinacoteca Comunale Ravenna, Italy; Kunstgewerbemuseum der Stadt Köln, Cologne, Ger; Nat Mus Am Art, Washington, DC. *Comn:* Descent of the Holy Spirit (venetian glass mosaic), Church Holy Spirit, Forrestville, Md, 78; Cascade (ceramic & venetian glass mosaic sculpture), Vista Int Hotel, Washington, 83; mosaic monumnet, UNESCO, Ravenna, Italy, 83; Second Genesis, American Peace/Ecology Monument (cast concrete relief & glass mosaic monument), comn by High Patronage of the Pres of Italy & European Parliament, Ravenna, Italy, 88; Flight of Fantasy (plastic & glass relief-mosaics), Montgomery Co Sch, Bethesda, Md, 86; Human Rights Monument (cast concrete monolith & glass mosaic), comn by City of Moscow, Russ, 92. *Exhib:* Solo exhib, Layering in Stone & Glass, Am Asn Advan Sci, Washington, DC, 87; M'ysuri, Georgian Cult Center, Moscow, USSR, 90; Galeria Esplanade (Metsovaara), Helsinki, Finland, 90; Amerika Hauser (USIS), Cologne, Munich, Ger, 90; retrospective, Natcher Ctr, Bethesda, Md, 96; and many others. *Pos:* Art dir, ABC-TV, Washington, DC, 66-68; artist-in-residence, Iittala Nuutijärvi Glass Factory, Finland, 89-; forensic art consult, 84-. *Awards:* Fulbright Ital, 84; Medallion of Ravenna, presented by Mayor, Ravenna, Italy, 84; 100 Most Significant, Corning Glass Int Rev, 86; invited participant, Global Forum, Supreme Soviet & Soviet Acad Sci, Moscow, USSR, 90; invited guest-partic, Solidarnosc 10th Anniversary, Gadansk, Poland, 90; Mac Users Group Digital Art Competition, New York, 96. *Bibliog:* L Krantz (auth), American Artists, 85; Jennifer Gibson (auth), Reflections in stone and glass, an American reinterprets the art of mosaics, In: The World and I, 10/87; Igor Ignatiev (auth), The creative process and creations of Jerry Carter, Echo of the Planet, Tass, Moscow, USSR, 10/88; C Frazier Smith (auth), Monumental mosaic, Baltimore Sun Mag, 11/88; I Wiman (auth), Expecting the unexpected: Some ancient roots to current perceptions of nature, Ambio, Royal Swedish Acad Sci Publ, Stockholm, Sweden, XIX, No 24, 90; TA Yasui (auth), Jerry Carter and the international mural mission, Wash Post, 4/16/90; E Egoreva (auth), Artist Jerry Carter, Decorative Arts USSR, Moscow, USSR, 7/90; G Nicola (auth), Jerry W Carter-Glass Mosaic, Neues Glass, Freschen, Ger, 2/91; ML Trechovich (auth), Artist in the City, Moscow, 88; G. Bovini (auth), Ravenna Art and History, 91. *Mem:* Int Asn Contemp Mosaicists, Ravenna, Italy (founding mem); MARS Gallery Asn, Moscow, Russ. *Media:* Glass, Digital Imaging. *Publ:* Auth, Mosaic: Medium for the Times, Presso il centro stampa del comune di Ravenna, Italy, 80, Parco Della Pace Ravenna, Longo Ed, 90. *Dealer:* JW Carter & Assoc 10502 Bucknell Dr Silver Spring MD 20902. *Mailing Add:* 10602 Bucknell Dr Silver Spring MD 20902-4254

CARTER, MARY
PAINTER, PRINTMAKER
b Hartsdale, NY. *Study:* Art Students League, with Reginald Marsh, Robert Beverly Hale & E Dickenson, 51-55; Hunter Col, 67, Sch Visual Arts, 68; Parsons Sch, 81. *Exhib:* Audubon Artists Ann, 54 & Nat Acad Design, NY, 56, 57 & 72; Hartford Atheneum Show, Conn, 56; Pa Acad Fine Arts, 57; Philadelphia Sketch Club, 58; Ball State Art Gallery, 58 & 63; Nat Competition, Springfield Art Mus, Mo, 66; Ann Drawings & Sculpture Show, Del Mar Col, Corpus Christi, Tex, 67; Hudson Guild Invitational, NY, 75- & solo show, 85-; visual dialogues show, office of C Virginia Fields, Borough Pres Manhattan, 2005. *Mem:* Art Students League. *Media:* Oil, Tempera. *Mailing Add:* 253 W 16th St New York NY 10011

CARTER, NANETTE CAROLYN
PAINTER, PRINTMAKER
b Columbus, Ohio, Jan 30, 1954. *Study:* L'Accademia di Belle Arti, Italy, 75; Oberlin Col, Ohio, BA, 76; Pratt Inst Art, New York, MFA, 78. *Work:* Newark Mus, NJ; Herbert Johnson Mus Art, Cornell Univ, Ithaca, NY; Studio Mus, Harlem, NY; Libr Cong, Washington, DC; and many others. *Comn:* Mural, Dwight Englewood Sch, NJ, 80; color poster for concert, Jazzmobile, Avery Fisher Hall, NY, 85; color poster exhib, Black Women in the Arts 1990, Montclair State Col, NJ; Poster, Snug Harbor Hills ASSN, 2005. *Exhib:* Solo shows at GRN 'Namdi Gallery, NY, 2006; group shows include Biennial Print Exhib, Brooklyn Mus, NY, 81; Bennington Col, Vt, 91; Hillwood Art Mus, Brookville, NY, 92; Nat Mus Women Arts, Washington, DC, 92; Univ Mass Amherst, 93; Del Art Mus, 93; RI Sch Design Mus; Parrish Art Mus, Southampton; Yale Gallery Art, Conn; Philadelphia Mus Art. *Teaching:* Instr printmaking and drawing, Dwight Englewood Sch, Englewood, NJ, 78-87; prof, City Col NY, 92; Prof Pratt Inst Art, Brooklyn, NY, 2001. *Awards:* Nat Endowment Arts Grant, 81; New York Found Arts, 90; Pollock-Krasner Found Inc Grant, 94; and others. *Bibliog:* Phyllis Braff (auth), rev, New York Times, 12/1/91; Richard Leslie (auth), The New Art Examiner, Chicago; Ann Gibson (auth), A Century of African American Art: The Paul R Jones Coll, 2004. *Mem:* Col Art Asn. *Media:* Oils, Monoprints. *Publ:* Illusr (cover), Midnight Birds, Mary Helen Washington (auth), Japan, 82; Bearing Witness, Rizzoli Int Publ Inc, NY; auth, The Chemistry of Color (catalog), Pennsylvania Academy of the Fine Arts, 2005. *Dealer:* June Kelly Gallery New York NY; GR N'Namti Gallery, Detroit, MI; Sante Webster Gallery, Philadelphia, PA. *Mailing Add:* 788 Riverside Dr New York NY 10032

CARTER, SAM JOHN
PAINTER, SCULPTOR
b Des Moines, Iowa, Mar 20, 43; Can citizen. *Study:* Calif State Univ, Long Beach, BA, 65, MA, 82; Univ Toronto, BL Arch, 70; Ikenobo, Ikebana, Kyoto, Japan, 82. *Work:* Ont Sci Ctr & Ont Place, Toronto; Nat Gallery, Ottawa; Expo 86 & Artists Gallery, Vancouver. *Comn:* Flower Totoms, Govt Can, Vancouver, BC, 80; Vancouver Sea Flowers, Jonathan's Seafood, BC, 81; China Lion, Wons, Vancouver, BC, 82; Vancouver-Papal Visit, Pageant & Chair of Catholic Church, BC, 84; Parade, Theme Pageant, Expo 86, Vancouver, 86. *Exhib:* Summer Numbers, A Space, Toronto, 70; Ont Col Art Gallery, Toronto, 71; Spoleto Festival, Italy, 71; World Wildlife Event, United Nations Conf, Stockholm, Sweden, 71; Art-Subterranean, Mus Mod Art, Mexico City, 80; Kado-Flower Way, Contemp Fine Arts Gallery, Tokyo, Japan, 85. *Pos:* Sr designer, Ont Sci Ctr, 65-71; Chmn, found div, Emily Carr Col Art & Design, 73-86. *Teaching:* Instr cult probe, Ont Col Art, 70-71. *Bibliog:* Yamashita (auth), Gardens of the world project, Ikenodo J, Kyoto, 83-84; Rule (auth), Art in season, Western Living, Vancouver, 85; De Vecchi (auth), Fantasy as partner, Vogue Decoration, Paris, 4/86. *Mem:* Ikenobo Ikebana Soc; Craftsman's Asn BC; Vancouver Community Arts Coun; Circle Craft Cooperative. *Publ:* Auth, Celebration of Paper, Arts Coun, 80; Some Roads to Here, Can Soc For Educ through Art, 80; Art and the City, Peregrine, 80; Kado-World Garden, Ikenobo J, 83. *Dealer:* Dianne Farris Gallery BC Canada. *Mailing Add:* Emily Carr Col Art & Design 1399 Johnston St Vancouver BC V6H 3R9 Canada

CARTER, YVONNE PICKERING
PAINTER, EDUCATOR
b Washington, DC, Feb 6, 39. *Study:* Traphagen Sch, cert, 59; Howard Univ, AB, 62, MFA, 68. *Work:* NC Mus, Raleigh; Federal Reserve Bank, Richmond, Va; Gibbes Gallery, Charleston, SC; Miami-Dade Co Libr, Fla; Montgomery Co Print Collection, Md; Artery Orgn, Md. *Exhib:* Gathered Visions: Selected Works by African-Am Women Artists; Performance Art: Maverick Street Litany, Dock St Theatre, Charleston, SC, 92; Book As Art VI, Nat Mus Women in the Arts, Washington, 94; Beyond Africa: Cult Influences in Am Art, Greensboro Cult Ctr, NC, 94; Gathering Medicine: Coast to Coast: Nat Women Artists of Color, Art in General, NY, 94; Fondo Del Sol Visual Art Ctr, Washington, 95; Nathan Cummings Found, NY, 96; My Magic Pours Secret Libations, Fla State Univ Mus Fine Arts, Tallahassee, 96; and others. *Pos:* Dept chair, Mass Media, Visual & Performing Arts Dept. *Teaching:* Prof design & painting, Univ District of Columbia, Washington, 71-. *Awards:* DC Comn Arts & Humanities Visual Arts Award, 81, 82 & 94; Fac Res Grant, 84. *Bibliog:* Curtia James (auth), Review of Gathered Visions, Art Papers, 91; Beth Joselow (auth), The Book As Art VI, Washington Rev, 4-5/94; Gumbo Ya Ya: Antholoy of Contemporary African-American Women Artists, Mid March Press, 95. *Mem:* Washington Women's Art Ctr; Women's Caucus Art; Col Art Asn. *Media:* Watercolor, Constructions. *Mailing Add:* 526 24th St NE Washington DC 20002

CARTMELL, HELEN
PAINTER, DESIGNER
b Bridgeport, Conn, Jan 6, 23. *Study:* Detroit Soc Arts & Crafts, scholar, 41; LaNapoule Art Found, France, 85 & 87; Fel France, 87; Wayne State Univ; Vt Studio Ctr, 91; also with Jack Beal, Sondra Freckelton & Milt Kobayashi. *Work:* Wayne State Univ Collection; Chrysler Corp, Detroit; Int Nickel Co, NY; Ford Motor World Hq; Avon Corp; Ossabaw Island Project, Ga; Port Huron Mus Art; Russ Consulate, Soviet Repub; and many others. *Exhib:* One-person shows, Ashley-Chris Gallery, Mich, 94, Flint Inst Arts, Mich, 98, Ambleside Gallery, Mich, 98, Kettering Univ, Mich, 2000, Univ Liggett Sch, Mich, 2004; Ecole Du Fois, La Cerqueux, France, 89; Drawing Exhib, South Bend, Ind, 90; Port Huron Art Mus, Mich, 93; Ashley/Chris Gallery, Grosse Point, Mich, 94; Port Huron Art Mus; Ambleside Gallery, Grosse Pointe, Mich, 98; Kettering Univ, Flint, Mich, 2000. *Pos:* Educ media art dir, Ctr Instrnl Technol, Wayne State Univ, Detroit, Mich, 67-85. *Teaching:* Media Spec, Wayne State Univ, Detroit, Mich. *Awards:* Purchase Award First Place for Best Oil, Port Huron Art Mus, 93 & Hon Mention, 93; Silver Medal, Scarab Club, Detroit, Mich, 68 & 97; Juror's Award (Best of Show), Birmingham Annual Exhib, Mich; and many others. *Bibliog:* William Tall (auth), article, Detroit Free Press, 75; M Meilgaard (auth), The Eccentric, Birmingham, Mich, 87; K Michele Moran (Arts & Entertainment ed), O & G Newspapers, 98 & 2004; Christopher R Young (contrib writer arts), Flint Jour, 2000. *Mem:* Detroit Soc Women Painters. *Media:* Oil, Conti Pencil; Pen & Ink, Graphite. *Dealer:* Ambelside Gallery 528 S Elm St Greensboro NC 27406. *Mailing Add:* 21700 Winshall Rd Saint Clair Shores MI 48081-2776

CARTWRIGHT, CONSTANCE B & CARROLL L
COLLECTORS
Mem: Mus Mod Art (drawing comt). *Collection:* Late 19th and 20th century drawings; Chinese blue and white porcelain; French antique furniture. *Mailing Add:* 435 E 52nd St New York NY 10022

CARTWRIGHT, DERRICK
MUSEUM DIRECTOR
b San Francisco, Calif, 1962. *Study:* Univ Calif, Berkeley, BA; UCLA, MA, 1988; Univ Mich, PhD in Art Hist, 1994. *Work:* Jose Clemente Orozco in the US, 1927-1934; Ambassadors of Progress: American Women Photographers in Paris, 1900-1901; Luis Gispert: Loud Image. *Pos:* dir, Musée d'Art Américain, Giverny, France, 1998-2000; Hood Mus Art, Dartmouth Col, 2000-04; SDMA, 2004-. *Teaching:* Prof art hist, Univ San Diego, 1993-98; San Diego Mus Art, 2004-. *Mem:* Asn Art Mus Dirs; Baleda Park Cult Partnership (vpres). *Mailing Add:* San Diego Mus Art PO Box 122107 San Diego CA 92112-2107

CARTWRIGHT, ROY R
CERAMIST
Study: Mt San Antonio Col, Walnut, Calif, 55-56, 57-58; Univ Southern Calif, Los Angeles, 56-57; Calif Col Arts & Crafts, Oakland, BFA(ceramics), 61; Rochester Inst Technol, NY, MFA(ceramics), 63. *Work:* Cincinnati Bell System; Univ Fla, Miami; Cleveland Mus Art; Johnson Collection Am Crafts; Everson Mus, Syracuse, NY. *Exhib:* Solo shows, Art Asn Harrisburg, Pa, 89, Contemp Art Ctr, Cincinnati, Ohio, 89, Swindler Gallery, Royal Oak, Mich, 91 & Carnegie Art Ctr, Covington, Ky, 92, Miami Univ Mus Art, Ohio, 97-98 & Ohio Univ, 98; Carnegie Art Ctr, Covington, Ky, 90; Dawson Gallery, Rochester, NY, 90; Northeast Mo State Univ, Kirksville, Miss, 91; Design Smith Gallery, Cincinnati, Ohio, 98. *Teaching:* Cleveland Art Inst, 63-64; Univ Ill, 64-65; Univ Cincinnati, 65-; lects, talks & panel discussions, var cols & univs, 76-91. *Awards:* Research Equip Award, Univ Res Coun, 90; Visual Artist Fel, Nat Endowment Arts, 90; Individual Artist Grant, Ohio Arts Coun, 91 & 94. *Bibliog:* Rev, Panorama, 10/89; rev, City Beat, Cincinnati, 2/12-18/98; rev, Dialogue, 11-12/89 & 5-6/98; and others. *Mem:* Delta Phi Delta. *Mailing Add:* 8164 Kemperidge Ct Cincinnati OH 45249

CARULLA, RAMON
PAINTER, PRINTMAKER
b Havana, Cuba, Dec 7, 1936; US citizen. *Study:* Self taught. *Work:* Detroit Inst Art, Mich; Mus Tamayo, Mexico; Mus Fine Art, Montreal, Can; Mus Latin Am Art, Washington, DC; Bass Mus, Miami Beach, Fla; CBS Internat Corp Collection, NY; Cincinnati Art Mus; Contemp Mus Art, Panama City, Panama; New Sch of Social Research, NY; Japan Print Asn Collection, Tokyo; Boca Raton Art Mus, Fla; Cuban Mus Art & Culture, Miami, Fla; Taiwan Mus Art; and numerous others. *Comn:* Eastern Nat Bank, Coral Gables, Fla. *Exhib:* Paper as a Medium, Fla Int Univ & Smithsonian Inst, 79-80; one-man shows, VI Graphic Biennial, San Juan, PR & Malcolm Brown Gallery, 85, Le Grand le Jeunne Auhordi-Grand Palais, Paris, France, 88, Cuban Collection Fine Art, The Dreamer Series, Miami, 98 & Breaking Barriers, Mus Art, Ft Lauderdale, Fla, 98, Ramon Carulla People and Places, Corbino Galleries, Longboat Key, Fla, 2000; 20 Yrs After, Bacardi Gallery, Miami, 87; Carbunar '99', The Int Small Engraving Salon, Florean Mus, Rumania, 99, Carbunar 2000, 2000; Contemp Art Auction, Durban Segnini Gallery, Coral Gables, Fla, 2000; I Bienal Argentina de Grafica Latinoamericana, Museo Nacional del Grabado, Buenos Aires, 2001; Latin-Am Masters of Today & Tomorrow, Artspace, Virginia Miller Gallery, Coral Gables, Fla, 2001; and others. *Collection Arranged:* Florean Mus, Maramures, Romania. *Teaching:* Guest lectr, Cranbrook Acad Art, Bloomfield Hills, Mich, Wayne State Univ, Detroit, 83 & Cleveland State Univ, Ohio, 85; private art instr. *Awards:* Silvia Daro Dawidowicz Award, Metrop Mus & Arts Ctr, Coral Gables, Fla, 82; First Prize, Sixth Biennial of Latin Am Graphic Art, San Juan, PR, 83; Hon Men, IX Biennial of Ibero-American Art, Palacio de Bellas Artes, Mex, 94; Fel, Cintas Found, Inst Int Educ, 73-74, 79-80. *Bibliog:* R Pau Llosa (auth), The origins of Cuban art, Miami Herald, 10/81; Ramon Carulla and the Latin American Expression, Vanidades Mag, 10/82; Armando Alverez Bravo (auth), El mundo alucinante de Ramon Carulla, El Nuevo Herald, 10/91. *Mem:* Miami Art Mus, Miami, Fla. *Media:* Oil on Canvas & Paper, Mixed Media, Printmaking. *Publ:* (Carulla) Schweyer-Galdo Editions, 85. *Dealer:* Naomi Silva Gallery, Atlanta, GA; Sonnet Galleries, Sarasota, FL; Gora Gallery, Montreal, Canada. *Mailing Add:* 4735 NW 184th Terr Miami FL 33055-2936

CARVALHO, JOSELY
PRINTMAKER, PAINTER
b Sao Paulo, Brazil, Sept 21, 42. *Study:* Printmaking with Marcelo Grassman & Darel, 61-63, Woodcut with Shiko Munakata, 65, Sch Archit, Washington Univ, St Louis, Mo, BA, 67. *Work:* Casa de las Americas, Havana, Cuba; Mus Mod Art, NY; Bronx Mus Art, NY; Mus de Bellas Artes, Caracas, Venezuela; Brooklyn Mus, NY. *Comn:* Spectacolor Board-Times Square, Pub Art Fund, NY, 88. *Exhib:* Committed to Print, Mus Mod Art, NY, 88; Diary of Images: It's Still Time to Mourn, Hillwood Mus, Brookville, NY, 91; Diario De Imagens: Dia Mater, Museu De Arte De Sao Paulo (MASP), Sao Paulo, Brazil, 92; Mus Contemp Art, San Paolo, Brazil, 94; Olin Gallery, Kenyon Col, Ohio, 95; North Gallery, Miami-Dade Community Col, Fla, 96. *Teaching:* vis prof, Sch Archit, Nat Univ Mex, 71-73; vis prof silkscreen, State Univ NY, Purchase, 88; artist-in-residence, Franklin & Marshall Col, Lancaster, Pa, 88; vis artist painting, State Univ NY, Purchase, 92. *Awards:* Nat Endowment Arts Fel, 75-76 & 95-96; NY State Coun Arts, 78-82; NY Found Arts Fel, 84, 85. *Bibliog:* Arlene Raven (auth), Rape, Ohio State Univ, 85; Lucy Lippard (auth), Following the Dots, Connecting Project/Conexus, 87; Deborah Wye (auth), Committed to Print, Mus Mod Art, 88. *Mem:* Heresies Collective; Women Caucus Art. *Media:* Multi Media. *Publ:* Mothers, Mags & Movie Stars, Heresies Collective, 85 & Story of Elza; auth, The Meal, 86; coauth, with Conexus, Connection Project, 87; illusr, We Hold Our Ground, Ikon, 88; illusr (cover), Abortion and Woman's Choice, Northeastern Univ Press, 90. *Dealer:* Terne Gallery 38 E 57th St 6th Floor New York NY 10022. *Mailing Add:* 216 E 18th St New York NY 10003

CASADEI, GIOVANNI
PAINTER
b Rome, Italy, Mar 13, 56; US citizen. *Study:* Scuola-Libera-Del-Nudo, Rome, Italy, 78-83; Pa Acad Fine Arts, Philadelphia, cert, 88-92. *Exhib:* Recent Paintings, Philadelphia Mus Art, 94; Still Life and Landscape, Mulligan-Shanoski Gallery, San Francisco, 96; Paintings of Landscapes & Interiors, Design Art Gallery, Drexell Univ, Pa, 96; Italian Journey, Hahn Gallery, Philadelphia, 97; recent paintings, Carspecken-Scott Gallery, Wilmington, Del, 97; The Unbroken Line, Philadelphia, 97. *Teaching:* Instr landscape painting, Manayunk Art Ctr, Philadelphia, 97- & Main Line Art Ctr, Haverford, Pa, 97-. *Awards:* Henry Scheidt Travel Scholarship, Ann Student Show Pa Acad Fine Arts, 91 & Philadelphia Mayor's Award, 92; Elizabeth-Greenshields Found Grant, Montreal, Can, 98. *Bibliog:* Judith West (auth), Portfolio-Giovanni Casadei, Seven Arts Mag, Vol 4, No 4, 4/96. *Media:* Oil. *Dealer:* Hahn Gallery 8439 Germantown Ave Philadelphia Pa 19118. *Mailing Add:* 1326 Moore St Philadelphia PA 19148-1500

CASANOVA, ALDO JOHN
SCULPTOR, EDUCATOR
b San Francisco, Calif, Feb 28, 1929. *Study:* San Francisco State Univ, BA, 50, MA, 51; Ohio State Univ, PhD, 57. *Work:* Whitney Mus, & Nat Acad Design NY; San Francisco Mus Art; Sculpture Garden, Palm Springs Mus, Calif; Sculpture Garden, Univ Calif Franklin Murphy Sculpture Garden; Joseph Hirshhorn Private Collection; Genesis, acquisition Rancho Santa Ana (Calif) Botanic Garden. *Comn:* Skidmore, Owings & Merrill, Archit, San Francisco, 66; Atlantic-Richfield Co, Los Angeles, 69; Washington Mutual Savings Bank, Seattle, 69; Calif Inst Technol, Pasadena, 74; Univ Judaism, Los Angeles, 81; and many others. *Exhib:* Pa Acad Ann, Philadelphia, 62-67; Art Dealers Asn Am, Parke-Bernet Gallery, NY, 64; solo exhibs, Esther Robles Gallery, Los Angeles, 67, Santa Barbara Mus, 67 & Calif Inst Technol, 72; New Vein, Smithsonian Inst, SAm travel tour, 68-70; New Acquisitons, Whitney Mus Am Art, NY, 70; New Acquisitions Show, Nat Acad, 92; Masterworks of Am Sculpture, Fleischer Mus, Scottsdale, Ariz, 99; In Memoriam, Sept 11, Nat Sculpture Soc, NY, 2002; Aldo Casanova Retrospective, Williamson Galleries, Claremont Cols, Claremont, Calif, 2002. *Pos:* Juror, Am Acad New York, 64 & 74; sculptor in res, Am Acad, Rome, 75. *Teaching:* Asst prof sculpture, Antioch Col, 56-58; asst prof, Temple Univ, 61-64, assoc prof, 68-70; prof, Scripps Col, 66-, chmn art dept, 71-73, prof emeritus; summer fac, Skowhegan Sch Painting & Sculpture, Maine, 74, head summer fac, 75; vis prof, State Univ NY, Albany, 80-81. *Awards:* Acad in Rome Fel, 58-61; Louis Comfort Tiffany Award, 69; Speyer Sculpture Prize, Nat Acad Design, 94; Tallix Prize, Nat Sculpture Soc, 94, Morris Prize, 96. *Bibliog:* Anthony Padovano (auth), The Process of Sculpture, Doubleday & Co, 81; Jonathan Block & Jerry Leisure (auth), Understanding Three Dimensions, Prentice-Hall, 87. *Mem:* FAAR, NY; Nat Acad Design (assoc, 92, acad, 93); Nat Sculpture Soc NY (mem exec com). *Media:* Bronze, Casting; Carving, Stone or Wood. *Dealer:* Carl Schlosberg Fine Arts 15447 Valley Vista Blvd Sherman Oaks CA 91403. *Mailing Add:* 230 Armstrong Dr Claremont CA 91711-1772

CASAS, FERNANDO R
PAINTER, DRAFTSMAN
b Cochabamba, Bolivia, Mar 25, 46. *Study:* Colo Col, BA; Rice Univ, MA, PhD; pvt training with Raul Prada. *Work:* Nat Mus Art, La Paz, Bolivia; Pinacoteca Nac, Cochabamba, Bolivia; Art of the Americas Collection (B Duncan), NY; Mus Fine Arts, Houston. *Comn:* Five paintings about Society, Baker World Trade, Houston, 80; mural, Hermman Hosp, Houston, 90. *Exhib:* One-man shows, Harriet Griffin Gallery, NY, 76 & Mus Nacional De Arte, La Paz, Bolivia, 88; Toni Jones Gallery, Houston, 79 & 80; Heritage Gallery, Los Angeles, 79; Duveen Gallery, Houston, 79; Galeria Emusa, Bolivia, 86; Blue Mt Gallery, NY, 89. *Awards:* First Nat Award Painting & First Nat Award Drawing, Concurso Nac de Artes Plasticas, Bolivia, 72 & 73. *Bibliog:* Itsuo Sakane (auth), The Asahi Shimbun, Japan, 8/83, 5/84 & others; Flocon (auth), Curvilinear Perspective, Univ Calif Press, 87; Pintura Boliviana del siglo XX, BHN Bolivia, 89. *Media:* Oil; Mixed. *Publ:* Auth, Flat sphere perspective, Vol 16, No 1, 83 & Polar perspective: A graphical system for creating two dimensional images representing a world of four dimensions, Vol 17, No 3, 84, Leonardo; and others. *Dealer:* Beowulf Fine Arts Ltd 12620 I-45 N Suite 218 Houston TX 77060 Tel: 713-872-1342

CASAS, MELESIO (MEL)
PAINTER, EDUCATOR
b El Paso, Tex, Nov 24, 29. *Study:* Univ Tex, El Paso, BA, 56; Univ of the Americas, Mex, MFA, 58. *Work:* Nat Mus Am Art, Smithsonian Inst; pvt collections incl Jim & Ann Harithas, NY, Robert Wilson, Houston, Tex, Joe Nicholson, San Antonio, Tex & Todd Spites, Santa Fe, NMex, June A Nickles, Austin; Smithsonian Nat Mus Am Art. *Exhib:* Artists of the Southeast & Tex, Biennial Painting & Sculpture, 71; Tex Painting & Sculptures: 20th Century, 72; Mex-Am Art Symp, Trinity Univ, 73; 12 Tex Artists, Contemp Art Mus, Houston, 74; 1975 Biennial Contemp Am Art, Whitney Mus Art, 75; Dale Gas--Chicano Art of Tex, Contemp Arts Mus, Houston, 77; Showdown, Alternative Mus, NY, 83; Chicano Expression, INTAR, NY, 86; Ft Worth Art Festival, Tex, 86; one-man show, Laguna Gloria Mus, Austin, Tex. *Pos:* Book reviewer, Choice Mag, Am Libr Asn, 54-; panels, San Antonio Art Coun & Nat Endowment Arts, 86. *Teaching:* Prof art, design & painting, San Antonio Col, Tex, 61-90; retired. *Awards:* Purchase Prize, 59 & Cash Award, 64, El Paso Art Mus; Cash Award, San Antonio Art League, 66 & Ft Worth Art Festival, 86. *Bibliog:* Jacinto Quiarte (auth), The Art of Mexican Americans, Univ Tex, 73; article, Art News, 12/77; Mimi Crossley (auth), Dale Gas at the Contemporary Art Museum, Art in Am, 1-2/78. *Mem:* Founding mem Con Safo Painters; Fine Arts Comn, San Antonio, Tex. *Media:* Acrylic. *Mailing Add:* 40 SilverHorn Dr San Antonio TX 78216

CASDIN-SILVER, HARIET
ARTIST
b Worcester, Mass, Feb 10, 25. *Study:* Columbia Univ, 1946-48; Univ Vt, AB, 1946. *Exhib:* The 3rd Int Distinguished Artists Exhib, Joseloff Gallery, Hartford, Conn, 98; The Nude In Contemp Art, Aldrich Mus, Ridgefield, Conn, 99; The Time of Our Lives, New Mus of Contemp Art, NY, 99. *Pos:* Artist in Residence, Holography Lab Inst of Physics, Kiev, Ukraine, 89; Artist in Residence, Univ Ghent, Belgium 92; fel, Ctr Advan Visual Studies MIT, 76-85. *Teaching:* Vis Lectr, Royal Col of Art, London, 92; Asst Prof, Brown Univ, Providence, RI, 74-78; Prof, Grad & Continuing Educ, Mass Col Art, 99. *Awards:* Rockefeller Found Fel, 1978-82; Shearwater Found Award, 1987, 01. *Publ:* auth, Miles Unger, She Adapts a Science of Ilusion to her Art, NY Times, 01; Christine Temin, Visions of Light, The Boston Globe, 98. *Dealer:* Arthur Dion at Gallery NAGA, 67 Newbury St, Boston, Mass, 02116. *Mailing Add:* 99 Pond Ave D403 Brookline MA 02445

CASEBERE, JAMES E
PHOTOGRAPHER, SCULPTOR
b Lansing, Mich, Sept 17, 53. *Study:* Mich State Univ, 71-72; Minneapolis Col Art & Design, BFA, 76; Whitney Mus Independent Study Program, 77; Calif Inst Arts, MFA, 79. *Work:* Neuberger Mus, Purchase, NY; Walker Art Ctr, Minneapolis, Minn; Victoria Albert Mus, London; Tampa Mus, Fla; Mus Mod Art, NY; Mus Fine Art, Boston. *Comn:* Minn Hist Ctr, St Paul, 91. *Exhib:* Fabricated to be Photographed, San Francisco Mus Mod Art, Albright-Knox Gallery, Buffalo, NY, Newport Harbor Art Mus, Newport Beach, Calif & Univ NMex, Albuquerque, 79-80; Sculpture on the Wall, Aldrich Mus Am Art, 86; Photog Fictions, Whitney Mus Am Art, 86; Arrangements for the Camera: A View of Contemp Photog, Baltimore Mus Art, Md, 87; Suburban Life: Plotting the Am Dream, Whitney Mus Am Art, 89; Pleasures and Terrors of Domestic Comfort, Mus Mod Art, NY, 91; More Than One Photog, Mus Mod Art, NY, 92; solo-exhibs, Addison Gallery of Am Art, Phillips Acad, Andover, Mass, 2000, Lisson Gallery, London, 2000, Bernier Eliades, Athens, Greece, 2001, Goldman Fine Art, Boston, 2001, Gallerie Tanit, Munich, 2001, Inst of Contemp Arts, Phila, 2001 & Sean Kelly Gallery, New York City, 2001; Photog & Art: Interactions Since 1946, Los Angeles Co Mus Art; and others; Architecture as Metaphor, Mus of Modern Art, New York City, 97; Selections from the Permanent Collection, Whitney Mus of Am Art, 97; Within These Walls, Kettle's Yard, Cambridge, Eng, 97; Elsewhere, Carnegie Mus of Art, Pitts, 97; The Luminous Image, Alternative Mus, New York City, 97; PhotoImage: Printmaking 60s to 90s, Mus of Fine Arts, Boston, 98; Where: Allegories of Site in Contemp Art, Whitney Mus of Am Art, Stamford, Conn, 98; Insties: Interior Space in Contemp Art, Whitney Mus of Am Art, Stamford, Conn, 2000; Supermodel, Mass Mus of Contemp Art, NorthAdams, 2000; Inside Out: Reality of Fiction?, Sean Delly Gallery, New York City, 2000; Making Pictures: Contemp Am Photog, Asheville Art Mus, NC, 2000; Staged and Manipulated: Photog Fictions from St Louis Collections, St Louis Art Mus, Mo, 2000; Open Ends: Architecture Hot and Cold, Sets and Situations, Mus of Modern Art, New York City, 2000; Flash Back, Barbara Farber/La Serre, Trets, France, 2000; Art on Paper 2000, Weatherspoon Art Gallery, 2000; Photo-Synthesis: Recent Develop in Contemp Photog, Dela Ctr for Contemp Arts, 2001. *Teaching:* Asst prof photog, Rockland Community Col, 85-88; vis artist, Calif Inst Arts, 84, Boston Mus Sch, 89, RI Design, 91, Cooper Union, 94, Sch Visual Arts, 94-95, Harvard Univ, 96 & Yale Univ, 97. *Awards:* Visual Artist Fels, 82, 86 & 90, Nat Endowment Arts; Visual Artist Sponsored Proj Grant, NY State Coun Arts, 82; Fel, New York Found Arts, 85, 89 & 94; Guggenheim Fel, 95. *Bibliog:* Art: James Casebere, W, 5/2001; William L Hamilton (auth), An artis's novel take on history: he lets the walls talk, NY Times, 5//28/2001; Deborah Everett (auth), James Casebere, NYArts, 6/6/2001. *Publ:* Auth, In the 2nd Half of the 20th Century, CEPA Gallery, Buffalo, 82. *Mailing Add:* 303 E Eighth St Apt 2F New York NY 10009-5211

CASELL, JOACHIM See Casellas, Joachim

CASELLAS, JOACHIM
PAINTER
b Gerona Prov, Spain, Aug 1, 27; US citizen. *Study:* Col Sacred Heart, Gerona, Spain, BA, 48; Inst Escolar. *Work:* Mus Provincial & Tossa Mus, Gerona, Spain; paintings The Whistle House, Wash. *Comn:* White House, Washington, DC. *Exhib:* Salon de Octobre, Galleria Leytana, Barcelona, Spain, 50; Brazil Biennial, Brazil, 51; Paris

Group, Paris, France, 52; Art Who? Ocean Springs, Miss, 88; Casell Gallery, New Orleans, La, 88; Artist Showroom, New Orleans, La, 88. *Pos:* Pres Cafiu Gallery. *Teaching:* lectr art, pastel technique. *Awards:* Merit Award, Ocean Springs Art Asn, 88; First Place, Fall Festival, Biloxi Art, 88. *Bibliog:* Sota La Boira, Diputacio de Gerona, Mus D'Art. *Mem:* Ocean Springs Art Asn. *Media:* Pastel, Miscellaneous Media. *Interests:* Ancient history, plants. *Dealer:* Capell Gallery 818 Royal St New Orleans LA 70116. *Mailing Add:* Casell Galleries 818 Royal St New Orleans LA 70116

CASEY, JOHN THAYER
PAINTER, SCULPTOR
b New London, Conn, June 27, 31. *Study:* Univ Ore, BA (Ina McClung Scholar, 57-58); Calif Col of Arts & Crafts, MFA with Nathan Oliveira & Harry Krell. *Work:* Univ Ore, Eugene; State of Ore, Salem, Monmouth & Pendleton; Coos Art Mus, Ore. *Exhib:* 68th Western Ann, Denver Art Mus, 62; 22nd Spokane Ann, Cheney Cowles Mus, Wash, 70, 72, 74 & 76; 32nd Ann NW Watercolor Exhib, Seattle Art Mus Pavilion, Wash, 71; Watercolor West, Brea, Calif, 96 & Riverside, 97; All-Ore Art Ann, Salem, 98, 2001 & 2002; Expressions West, Coos Art Mus, 2000 & 2002; Expressions West, 2005; Watercolor West, Brea, Calif, 2006. *Teaching:* Assoc prof drawing, painting & design, Western Ore Univ, Monmouth, 65-88, emer prof. *Awards:* Grad Teaching Scholar, Calif Col Arts & Crafts, 61-62. *Bibliog:* Lorraine B Widman (auth), Sculpture: A Studio Guide to Concepts, Methods & Materials, Prentice-Hall, 90-; A Duca & L Loscutoff (coauths), The Best Acrylic Painting, Rockport Publ, 96 & Creative Inspiration, 97. *Media:* Acrylic, Watercolor; All Media. *Mailing Add:* 1870 NW Alder St McMinnville OR 97128

CASEY, KIM L
PAINTER, EDUCATOR
b Dexster, Maine, Apr 18, 64. *Study:* Plymouth State Col, BS (art educ), 82; Brooklyn Col, MFA, 97. *Work:* So Ho Soda Corp, NY. *Exhib:* Graduate Show, Brooklyn Col, NY, 97; Currier Mus, Manchester, 97; Weber Nat, Weber State Univ, Ogden, Utah, 2000; 20th Century Fairwell, Central Mich Univ, 2000; Plymouth State Univ, NH, 2000; Invitational, Shelburne Farms Mus, Vt, 2000; Franco Am Ctr, 2003; Frnaklin Pierce Col, 2003. *Collection Arranged:* Soho Soda, Bklyn Col. *Teaching:* prof studio art, Plymouth State, NH, 97-2000, Notre Dame Col, NH, 98-99 & Univ NH, 99-2000. *Awards:* NH State Coun on Arts Fel; prof artists grant, state of NH. *Mem:* Cause Women in Arts; NH Art Asn; Col Art Asn. *Media:* Oli. *Publ:* contribr, Artists, The Daily Chautaugua, 97, New York Gallery Guide, 98, Landscape Artists, Boston Globe, 99 & 2000, art sect, Manchester Union Leader, 2003. *Dealer:* NH Art Asn State St Portsmouth NH 03801; The Barn Gallery Ogunquit ME; New Hampshire Art Asn Portsmouth NH. *Mailing Add:* 244 Locust St Dover NH 03820

CASEY, TIM (TIMOTHY) WILLIAM
PAINTER
b Lawton, Okla, July 19, 47. *Study:* Art Acad Cincinnati, 65-68; RI Sch Design, BFA, 70, MFA, 72. *Work:* Chase Manhattan Bank, NY. *Comn:* Painting, Vera List for Jewish Mus, NY, 86. *Exhib:* Solo show, Gabrielle Bryers, NY, 85-86 & Tomoko Liguori, NY, 88; A Radical Plurality, William Paterson Col, Wayne, NJ 86; Artists Space, NY, 90-91. *Teaching:* Instr drawing, RI Sch Design, 73-74; instr drawing & painting, State Univ NY at Purchase, Exten Sch, 86-89; artist in residence, Studio in a Sch, PS 11, 89-. *Awards:* Studio Program, PS 1, The Clocktower, 86. *Bibliog:* John Russell (auth), Review, NY Times, 85; Grace Glueck (auth), Review, New York Times, 85; Stephen Westfall (auth), Review, Art in Am, 88. *Media:* Oil, Watercolor. *Mailing Add:* 99 Commercial St Brooklyn NY 11222

CASH, SARAH
MUSEUM DIRECTOR, CURATOR
b New Haven, Conn, Oct 26, 58. *Study:* Smith Col, BA, 80; Williams Col(art hist), MA, 86; Mus Mgt Inst, Berkeley, cert, 96. *Collection Arranged:* Ominous Hush: The Thunderstorm Paintings of M J Heade (auth, catalog), Amon Carter Mus, 94; Thomas Cole's Paintings of Eden, Amon Carter Mus, 95; Thomas Eakins and the Swimming Picture (auth, catalog), Amon Carter Mus, 96-97; The Gilded Cage: Views of American Women 1872-1921, Corcoran Gallery of Art, 2002. *Pos:* Sr res assoc Am paintings, Nat Gallery Art, 86-89; asst cur, Amon Carter Mus, Fort Worth, Tex, 90-95; dir, Maier Mus Art, Randolph-Macon Woman's Col, 95-98; Bechhoefer cur am art, Corcoran Gallery Art, Washington, DC, 98-. *Teaching:* Adj fac mus studies, Randolph-Macon Woman's Col, Va, 96-98. *Mem:* Am Asn Mus, Washington; Col Art Asn Am, NY. *Publ:* Coauth, American Naive Paintings in the National Gallery of Art (catalog), 91; auth, Martin Johnson Heade's paintings of Manchester, Mass, Am Art J/Kennedy Galleries, 96. *Mailing Add:* 412 S Taylor St Arlington VA 22204

CASH, SARAH See Cash, Sarah

CASIDA, KATI
PRINTMAKER, SCULPTOR
b Viroqua, Wis, Mar 28, 31. *Study:* Univ Wis-Madison, BS(art educ), 53; New Sch Social Res, with Antonio Frasconi, New York, 55. *Work:* Syntex Corp, Palo Alto & City Percent Art Prog, Brea, Calif; Ore Art Comn, Salem; Int Paper Co, NY. *Comn:* Sculpture (steel), Spectrum Ctr, Criswell Co, Dallas, 83; sculpture (aluminum & steel), Lurie Co, San Francisco, 85; sculpture (wood & trees) Viroqua City Park, Wis, 87; sculpture (aluminum), Oakland City Ctr, Calif; plus many other comn sculptures. *Exhib:* Oakland Mus, 94; Contract Design Ctr, San Francisco, 94; '94 Sculpture, Syntex Corp, Palo Alto, Calif, 94; '94 handmade papers sculpures, Magnolia Edits, Oakland, Calif, 94; sculpture, San Francisco, Calif, 2000; Oakland Mus, Calif, 2002; solo exhib, Gallery 555, Solvorn, Norway, 2004; Steel Gallery, 2005; New Nordic Designs, Nordic 5 Arts, San Francisco, 2006. *Pos:* Sculpturer, currently. *Teaching:* Instr art & art hist, Upsala Col, East Orange, NJ, 55-56. *Awards:* Am Asn Univ Women, La Crosse, Wis, 50; Open Proposals, City of Oakland, 91. *Bibliog:* Radio, Jonsok sculpture, Nat Norweg Broadcasting Co, 6/85; Andrea Workman (auth), Casida-modern sculptor, Viking Mag, Minneapolis, Minn, 12/85. *Mem:* Int Sculpture Ctr; Calif Soc Printmakers; Nat Women's Art Caucus; The Nat Mus of Women in the Arts, Wash, DC; Pacific Rim Sculptures Group; Am Scandinavian Found, Sons of Norway & Am Indian Mus. *Media:* Woodcut, Metal, Aluminum, Copper & Handmade papers. *Specialty:* outdoor sculptures. *Interests:* dance; traveling. *Collection:* Many private collections. *Publ:* Coauth, Jonsok sculpture, Viking Mag, Minneapolis, Minn, 12/85; Sculpture for Missing Persons, Hellenic J, San Francisco, 3/92. *Mailing Add:* c/o Studio 1570 La Vereda Rd Berkeley CA 94708

CASLIN, JEAN
ARTS ADMINISTRATOR
b Washington, DC. *Study:* Boston Univ, BA(art hist, Eng lit), 74; Stanford Univ, MA(art hist), 77. *Pos:* Exec dir, Houston Ctr Photog, 88-. *Teaching:* Lectr photog hist, Boston Col, 85-88; lectr, Univ Houston, 89-90. *Mem:* Soc Photog Educ. *Mailing Add:* c/o Houston Ctr for Photography 1441 W Alabama Houston TX 77006

CASS, BILL
PAINTER
b Chicago, Ill, 1954. *Study:* Univ Ill, Champaign-Urbana, BFA, 77; Art Inst Chicago, MFA, 81. *Work:* Krannert Art Mus, Champaign, Ill; Madison Art Ctr, Wis; Prudential Insurance, Arthur Anderson & Co, Container Corp & Chicago Pub Libr; Philip Morris Co Inc, NY; plus many others. *Exhib:* One-man exhibs, Mariane Deson Gallery, Chicago, 87, Trinity Christain Col, Palos Heights, Ill, 87, G W Einstein, NY, 88, Roy Boyd Gallery, Chicago, 89, 92 & 95, Rockford Col, Ill, 93, Augen Galleries, Portland, Ore, 94 & Peoria Art Guild, Ill, 98; From America's Studio: Drawing New Conclusions (with catalog), Betty Rymer Gallery, Sch Art Inst Chicago, 92; Nat Drawing Invitational, Ark Art Ctr, Little Rock, 92; Landscape, Univ Wis, Whitewater, 96; Second Sight-Show of Chicago Printmaking, 1945-present, Block Gallery, Northwestern Univ, 96; Magical Realism, Gallery NW, NW Ind Univ, Gary, 97; The Art of Painting CHICAGO, Trinity Christian Col, Palos Heights, Ill, 98; and many others. *Teaching:* Vis artist, Art Inst Chicago, 82-; lectr full time, Northwestern Univ, currently. *Awards:* Ill Arts Coun Fel Grants, 84, 85 & 88; Regional Visual Arts Fel, Arts Midwest/Nat Endowment Arts, 87. *Bibliog:* Numerous articles in Artweek, New Art Examiner, Chicago Sun-Times, Art News and other publ. *Dealer:* Marianne Deson Gallery 340 W Huron Chicago IL 60610; Roy Boyd Gallery 739 N Wells Chicago IL 60610 Tel: 312-642-1606. *Mailing Add:* 355 Marengo Rd Harvard IL 60033

CASSARA, FRANK
PAINTER, PRINTMAKER
b Partinico, Sicily; US citizen. *Study:* Colorado Springs Sch Fine Arts, Colo; Univ Mich, MS(design); also spec study, Atelier 17, Paris, France. *Work:* Libr Cong, Washington, DC; Bibliot Nat, Paris, France; Stedelijk Mus, Amsterdam, Neth; Detroit Inst Arts; Free Libr Philadelphia; Nat Mus Am Art, Smithsonian, Washington, DC; Owen Ill, Toledo, Ohio; and others. *Comn:* Mural, US Post Off, East Detroit, 39; mural, Donald Thompson Sch, Highland Park, Mich, 39; mural, US Post Off, Sandusky, Mich, 40; mural, Water Conditioning Plant, Lansing, Mich, 41; mural, Palio, Ann Arbor, Mich, 96. *Exhib:* Seventh Int Exhib Lithography & Wood Engr, Art Inst Chicago, 39; 1st Exhib Am Printmakers, Gallerie Nees Morphes, Athens, Greece, 65; 22nd Nat Exhib Prints, Libr Cong, 71; Atelier 17: A Retrospective, Elvehjem Art Ctr, Madison, Wis, 77; Toledo Mus Art, Ohio, 82; Mus Art, Univ Mich, Ann Arbor, Mich, 86; DeWaters Art Ctr, Flint, Mich, 90; Birmingham Bloomfield Art Center (BBAC), Birmingham, Mich, 2006; and others. *Teaching:* Instr drawing, Detroit Soc Arts & Crafts, 46-47; prof printmaking, Univ Mich, 47-83, emer prof art, currently. *Awards:* Over 50 awards in nat & regional exhibs; Rackham Res Grants, Univ Mich, 61, 68, 74 & 75. *Bibliog:* Kresge Art Mus Bulletin, Vol VII, 92, Mich State Univ. *Mem:* Nat Acad Art. *Media:* Oil; All. *Publ:* Contribr, Artists' Proof, A Collectors Edition, 71. *Mailing Add:* 1122 Pomona Rd Ann Arbor MI 48103

CASSELL, BEVERLY
PAINTER
b Montgomery, Ala, 36. *Study:* Univ Ga, Athens, MFA(art & philos), 60, study with Lamar Dodd & Howard Thomas; NY Univ, NY, 63. *Work:* Disney Studios, Burbank, Calif; Ga Mus, Athens; Taiwan Mus Art, Taichung; US Embassy, Manila, Philippines; Univ House, Univ Calif, Santa Cruz. *Exhib:* Taiwan Mus, Taichung, Taiwan, 89; Los Angeles Co Mus Art, 92; Nagasaki Mus Art, Japan, 92, 93 & 94-96; Judson Gallery, New York City, 99; Modern Art Gallery, Los Angeles, Calif, 99; NOHO Art Gallery, North Hollywood, Calif, 2000. *Pos:* Founder & dir, Artist Conf Network, Int, 83-; regional arts coun, City of Los Angeles, Calif, 98, adv coun, 99. *Teaching:* Univ Colo, Denver, 67-69; Univ Calif Santa Cruz, 72-80; UCLA Exten, 86-89; Getty Mus Art Educ Ser, Los Angeles, 92. *Awards:* Los Angeles Cult Affairs Coun Grant for Los Angeles Inner City Youth Water Sculpture Proj. *Bibliog:* Article, Calif Art Review, 89; 4th International Contemp Art Fair Catalog, Art Los Angeles, 89. *Mem:* Artist Conf Network Int (dir). *Media:* Oil, Gouache. *Publ:* Leaven, NY, 80; Design Int, 89; Calif Art Rev, 89; Quarry West, rev ed 94

CASSELL, ROBERT E, JR
PHOTOGRAPHY
b Jackson, Tenn. *Study:* Vanderbilt Univ, BE, 1964; Univ Tenn, MS, 1966; Univ Mass, Arts Mgt, 2006. *Exhib:* Members Gallery, Arts Depot, Abingdon, Va, 2005; Selected Work, Va Int Col, Bristol, Va, 2006; Juried Photog Show, Va Highlands Festival, Abingdon, Va, 2006. *Pos:* Arts admin, Depot Artists Asn, Abingdon, Va, 2001-. *Mem:* Pro Art Asn, Wise, Va (pres, vpres, secy, 1993-); Va Highlands (bd dir, 2003-); Va for the Arts (2004-); Southwest Va Artisans Center (steering comt, 2005-). *Mailing Add:* 2100 Louita Ave Kingsport TN 37660

CASSELLI, HENRY CALVIN, JR
PAINTER
b New Orleans, La, Oct 25, 46. *Study:* Student, John McCrady School Fine and Applied Arts, 1967. *Work:* Libr Congress; New Orleans Mus; Hunter Mus, Tenn; Greenville Mus, SC; Albany Mus, Ga; Am Tel & Tel, NY; The White House, Nat Portrait Gallery, Washington, DC. *Comn:* La State Univ, Baton Rouge, 78; WC Bradley, Columbus, Ga; portrait of Pres R Reagan, Nat Portrait Gallery, Smithsonian Inst & The White House. *Exhib:* Solo exhibs, Lauren Rogers Mus, 72 & Greenville Co Mus, SC, 80; Smithsonian Traveling Drawing Exhib, 72-75; Hunter Mus, Tenn, 81; Am Watercolor Soc, NY, 71-86; and others. *Awards:* High Winds Medals, 76, 77, 79 & 88, Silver Medal, 86 & Gold Medal, 87, Am Watercolor Soc. *Bibliog:* Doreen Mangan (auth), Henry Casselli, Am Arts; Susan Meyer (auth), 20 Figure Painters, Watson-Guptill, 79; article, Southern Accent Mag, 81; Betty Harvey (auth), Henry Casselli, Art West Digest, 85; John Kemp (auth), Henry Casselli, Am Artist. *Mem:* High Winds medal 1976, 77, 79, 88, Silver medal 1986, Gold medal 1987; Am Watercolor Soc (vpres, 79-80); nat juror 1979; Nat Acad Design, NY (assoc, 88, acad, 94). *Media:* Watercolor, Pastels. *Publ:* Contribr, The Natural Way to Paint, Davis, 78; Using Color, Dobie, Watson-Guptill, 86. *Dealer:* Tex Art Gallery, Dallas; Mongerson-Wunderlich, Chicago, IL. *Mailing Add:* 4015 N Labarre Rd Metairie LA 70002-1820

CASSIDY, MARGARET CAROL (MRS JOHN MANSHIP)
SCULPTOR
b Whitinsville, Mass. *Study:* Framingham State Col, BS, 44; Univ Mass, Amherst, MS, 49; Smith Col; Rosary Col Grad Sch Fine Arts, Florence, Italy, MA, 54. *Work:* Britain Mus Am Art, Conn; NY Univ Bobst Libr, NY; Holy Cross Col Dinand Libr, Worcester, Mass; Framingham & Bridgewater State Col Librs, Mass; Vatican Collections, Rome; and others. *Comn:* Madonna & St Joseph (sculpture), Holy Spirit Church, Kyoto, Japan, 61; Cardinal Newman, 63, Newman Ctr, Amherst, Mass, St Jude, 81; Risen Christ, St Anthony's Maronite Church, Springfield, 71 & St Mary's Church, Uxbridge, Mass, 75; stained glass, New Britain Mus of Am Art; L L Winship Medal for the Boston Globe; Three Medals, Newman Ctr, Univ Mass. *Exhib:* Nat Acad Design Ann, NY, 66 & 79; three-man show, New Britain Mus, Conn, 71; Burr Artists, Metrop Mus Art, NY, 76. *Teaching:* Asst prof art, Bridgewater State Col, 64; artist-in-residence, Univ Southern Ill, Edwardsville, 76 & Castleton S Col, Vt. *Awards:* Campidoglio D'oro, Burckhardt Acad, Rome, 78; Richard Reechia Award; NShore Pres Award. *Bibliog:* Articles in Madmoiselle, 53, Boston Globe, 79 & Dict Am Sculptors, 84. *Mem:* Salmagundi Club; Catharine Lorillard Wolfe Art Club; Pen & Brush Club; Burr Artists; Rockport Art Asn. *Media:* Bronze. *Res:* Card catalog of all American artists. *Mailing Add:* 175 Federal St Fl 16 Boston MA 02110-2257

CASSIDY, VICTOR MONOD
EDITOR, WRITER, CRITIC
b Madison, Wis, Nov 30, 40. *Study:* Columbia Univ, BA(english), 62; Univ Wis, MA(econs), 66. *Pos:* Tech. ed, Sargent & Lundy, Chicago, 1974-80; sr ed, Specifying Eng Cahners Inc., Des Plaines, Ill, 1980-84; ed, Modern Metals Mag Delta Comms, Chicago, 1984-95; prin, Market Advantage, 1995-97; managing ed, Software Strategies mag Putman Pub Co, Chicago, 1997-. *Awards:* Nat Endowment of the Humanities res grantee, 72-73; recipient awards Ill Arts Coun, 88 & 90; Graham Found, 90. *Mem:* Chicago Art Critics Assoc

CASSILL, HERBERT CARROLL
PRINTMAKER, EDUCATOR
b Percival, Iowa, Dec 24, 28. *Study:* State Univ Iowa, BFA, 48, MFA, 50, with Mauricio Lasansky. *Work:* Mus Mod Art, NY; Cleveland Mus Art; Brooklyn Mus; Libr Cong, Washington, DC; Oakland Art Mus, Calif. *Exhib:* Libr Cong, 52, 54 & 60; six shows, Philadelphia Print Club, 53-60; Int Exhib Graphic Arts (shown in Europe), Mus Mod Art, 54, Modern Art in the USA (shown in Europe), 55; Soc of Am Graphic Artists Overseas Exhib, US State Dept, 60. *Pos:* Head dept printmaking, Cleveland Inst Art, 57-91. *Teaching:* Instr printmaking, State Univ Iowa, 53-57, emer prof. *Awards:* Tiffany Found Fel Printmaking, 53; Purchase Prize, Philadelphia Print Club, 56; First Prize, Print Show, State Univ NY, Potsdam, 61. *Media:* Intaglio, Wood. *Dealer:* William Busta. *Mailing Add:* 3084 Coleridge Rd Cleveland OH 44118

CASSULLO, JOANNE LEONHARDT
PATRON
b Glen Cove, NY, Dec 2, 55. *Study:* Roanoke Col, Salem, Va, BA(eng, elementary educ & fine arts) 78; So Methodist Univ, MFA, 82. *Pos:* Dir, counseling & educ, PCI Inc, Ft Worth, Tex, 78-80; vpres, bd dir, Phoenix House Found, Inc, New York City, 82-; gallery asst, Washburn Gallery Inc, New York City, 83-86; trustee, Whitney Mus Am Art, New York City, 85-; pres, Dorothea L Leonhardt Found, New York City, 88-. *Teaching:* Cert teacher, elementary educ, Va, formerly. *Awards:* Helen Rubinstein Fel in Mus Studies. *Mem:* RxArt, Children's Advocacy Ctr of Manhattan; Housing Enterprises for Less Privileged (HELP USA). *Publ:* Contribr, articles and jour's. *Mailing Add:* c/o Whiteny Mus Am Art 945 Madison Ave New York NY 10021

CASTAGNO, JOHN EDWARD
ART DEALER, PAINTER
b Philadelphia, Pa, July 19, 30. *Study:* Univ Arts, Philadelphia, 50; Pa Acad Fine Arts, 60-61; Barnes Found, Pa, 63-64. *Work:* Butler Inst Am Art, Ohio; Tweed Mus, Duluth, Minn; Los Angeles Co Mus, Calif; Lakeview Mus Arts & Sci, Peoria, Ill; Birmingham Mus Art, Ala. *Comn:* Philadelphia Poster, United Van Lines/Quaker Storage, Pa, 76. *Exhib:* one-man exhib, Pa Acad Fine Arts, Philadelphia, 71, Lakeview Mus Arts & Sci, Peoria, Ill, 72, Cedar Rapids Mus Art, Iowa, 72 & Tweed Mus, Duluth, Minn, 72. *Collection Arranged:* Europahaus, Vienna, Austria, 72; Mus NMex, 73; Art Alliance, Philadelphia, 76; Tweed Mus, Duluth, Minn, 76; Newman Galleries, Philadelphia, 76. *Pos:* Artists' Signatures Identification expert. *Teaching:* Artist in residence, Villanova Univ, Pa, 73. *Awards:* 1st Prize Painting, Del Co Arts Festival, 69; 1st Prize Sculpture, Upper Merion Cult Ctr, Pa, 72. *Bibliog:* Victoria Donohoe (auth), article, Philadelphia Inquirer, 3/7/71; article in Cedar Rapids Gazette, 4/23/72; The Flag in the Art of Our Country, Am Heritage BK, 76. *Mem:* Pa Acad Fine Arts Alumni. *Media:* Mixed Media. *Res:* Abstract Artists of the World. *Specialty:* 19th & 20th century Am/European paintings. *Publ:* Auth, Artists As Illustrators, 89, American Artists Signatures & Monograms 1800-1989, 90 & European Artists Signatures & Monograms 1800-1990, 90, Old Masters' Signatures & Monograms 1400-born 1800, 96 & Latin American Artists Signatures & Monograms, Colonial Era - 1996, 97, Scarecrow Press; Auth, Artists' Monograms and Indiscernible Signatures 1800-1991, Scarecrow Press, 91. *Mailing Add:* 1142 Synder Ave Philadelphia PA 19148-5522

CASTANIS, MURIEL (JULIA BRUNNER)
SCULPTOR
b New York, NY, Sept 27, 26. *Study:* Self-taught. *Work:* New Sch Social Res, NY; Martin Margulies Collection, Coral Gables, Fla; Gordon Hanes Collection, Winston-Salem, NC; Norton Gallery Art, West Palm Beach, Fla; Sydney & Frances Lewis Found, Richmond, Va; and others. *Comn:* Montgomery Co, Md, 90; IBM, Atlanta, Ga 90; Flatbush Subway, Crossing the Threshold, Steinbaum Gallery, New York City, 99; Harmon Meek Gallery, Naples, Fla, 2001; OK Harris, NY Gallery, 2001. *Exhib:* Solo exhibs, OK Harris Works of Art, NY, 80, 83, 85, 87, 89, 93 & 97, City Univ NY Grad Ctr, NY, 84, Carpenter Ctr Visual Arts, Harvard Univ, Cambridge, Mass, 85, Tweed Courthouse, NY, 85, Trout Gallery, Dickinson Gallery, Carlisle, Pa, 86 & Broadway Windows, NY Univ, NY, 87 & Harmon Meek Gallery, 99; The Classic Tradition in Recent Painting and Sculpture, Aldrich Mus Contemp Art, Ridgefield, Conn, 85; Contemp Sculpture from Fla Collections, Univ Gallery, Univ Fla, Gainesville, 87; Classical Concerns, Twining Gallery, NY, 87-88; Frontiers in Fiber: The Americans, int traveling exhib, NDak Mus Art, Grand Forks, NDak, 88-90; Architectural Art: Affirming the Design Relationship, traveling exhib, Am Craft Mus, NY, 88-90; Grace Hokin Gallery, Palm Beach, Fla, 91; Crossing the Threshold (traveling), Steinbaum Krauss Gallery, 98. *Teaching:* Instr advan sculpture, Cooper Union, NY, 78-79; lectr, Col NJ, 98, Univ Kans, 98. *Awards:* Tiffany Found Sculpture Grant, 77; Award for Outstanding Design, Show Bus, 77; Award of Distinction, Va Mus Fine Art, 79. *Bibliog:* Grace Glueck (auth), article, New York Times, 8/7/81; Peter Carlson (auth), Design: American Craft Museum, Art News, 5/88; Carl Little (auth), Collaboration: art & architecture, Art New Eng, 5/88; and others. *Media:* Cloth. *Publ:* Contribr, Speak out the arts & Behind every art, Village Voice, 3/70; Her story, Know Inc, 73; Women in the Year 2000, Arbor Press, 74; Are you a closet collector, Heresies Collective, winter 78. *Dealer:* O K Harris Gallery 383 W Broadway New York NY 10012. *Mailing Add:* 444 Sixth Ave New York NY 10011

CASTILE, RAND
MUSEUM DIRECTOR
b NC, July 15, 38. *Study:* Drew Univ, BA; Urasenke Tea Ceremony Hq, Kyoto, Japan; also study with Grand Master Sen Soshitsu, XV, diplomae, Drew Univ, LHD, 94. *Collection Arranged:* Four exhibs per yr, Japan House Gallery, 71-86. *Pos:* Lectr, Japanese art & tea ceremony, US & Japanese Univs & mus; dir, Japan House Gallery, Japan Soc Inc, NY, 70-85; consult-panelist, Nat Endowment Arts, 75; consult, Nat Endowment Humanities, 75-; bd adv, Japan Study Ctr, Columbia Univ; dir emer, The Avery Brundage Collection, Asian Art Mus San Francisco, 85-94; mem, Maine Arts Comn, 97. *Awards:* Fulbright Scholar, 66-67; Mayor's Award of Honor for Arts & Culture, New York, 82. *Mem:* Asn Art Mus Dir Emer; Metrop Mus Art (vis comt); Am Asn Mus; US-Japan Educ & Cult Conf; US Can Cult Coun; Century Asn. *Publ:* Auth, numerous articles in Art News, Geijutsu Shincho, Bijutsu Techo, Orientations, J of Nat Tokyo Nat Mus & Print Collector's Newslett, 63-; The Way of Tea, 72; Ikeda & Ida: Two Japanese Printmakers, 74; Japanese Art Now: Tadaaki Kuwayama & Rikuro Okamoto. *Mailing Add:* 120 SW Peacock Blvd # 203 Port St Lucie FL 34898

CASTILLO, MARIO ENRIQUE
PAINTER, MURALIST, EDUCATOR
b Rio Bravo, Coah, Mex, Sept 19, 45. *Study:* Ill Inst Design, cert, 64; Sch Art Inst Chicago, BFA, 69; Sch Fine Arts, Univ Southern Calif Los Angeles, post grad studies, 69-70; Calif Inst Arts, Valencia, MFA, 72, post grad studies, 73-74; Pasadena City Col, 77; Calif State Univ Los Angeles, 80; East Los Angeles City Col, 81 & 82 & Univ Calif Dominguez Hills, 87 & 88; Nat Univ, Inglewood, Calif, 89. *Work:* Nat Mus Am Art, Washington, DC; San Francisco Mus Art; Denver Art Mus; Albuquerque Mus, NMex; Portland Art Mus, Ore. *Comn:* Metafisica (mural), 68 & Wall of Brotherhood (mural), 69, City of Chicago, Ill; mural (painting), El Mercado Co, Los Angeles, 82; four paintings, Latino Inst, Chicago, 91; two murals, Mex Am Fine Arts, Chicago, 92. *Exhib:* Sacred Images-New Visions, Riverside Art Mus, Calif, 89; solo exhibs, Inst Hispanic Cult Studies, Santa Monica, Calif, Orlando Gallery, Sherman, Okla, 89, Sangre De Cristo Arts Ctr, Pueblo, Colo, 91 & Prospectus Art Gallery, Chicago, 91-92; Day of the Dead, Mex Fine Arts Mus, Chicago, Ill, 90; Cara (traveling show), Fresno Art Mus, 91, Tucson Mus Art, 91 & Smithsonian Inst Nat Mus Am Art, 92. *Pos:* Artist/designer, Lukas & Assocs, 65-66; artist, City of Chicago, Bd of Educ, 67-68; artist/designer, El Mercado Co, Los Angeles, 81-83. *Teaching:* Art instr design, Santa Monica City Col, summer 73; asst prof fine arts, Univ Ill, Champaign-Urbana, 73-76; art instr design, Immaculate Heart Col, Los Angeles, 79-80; painting instr fine arts, Exceptional Childrens Found, Los Angeles, 85-86; art instr fine arts, Plaza de La Raza, Los Angeles, summer 89; full time fac mem, Dept Art & Design, Columbia Col, Chicago, 90-. *Awards:* First Place Painting, 74, First Place Drawing, 75 & First Place Photog, 75, Hispanic Art Exhib, Mus Sci & Indust, Chicago. *Bibliog:* Sebastian Rotella (auth), Ancient art inspires a modern man, LA Times, 12/8/89; Lyman Pitman (auth), Hands, feet, eyes, lead viewers to artist's mind, Chieftain, Pueblo, Colo, 4/28/91; Olga Herrera (auth), Castillo exhibit opens

innovative local gallery, Lawndale News, Chicago, 10/24/91. *Media:* Acrylic, Mixed Media. *Res:* Mesoamerican art; Mexican murals. *Interests:* Archeology and music. *Collection:* Collector of prints & works on paper. *Publ:* Contribr, Pictures For Writing, Bantam Books, 69; Mural Manual, Beacon Press, 75; Towards's A People's Art-The Contemporary Mural Movement, Dutton & Co, 77; Canto Al Pueblo Anthology, Penca Books, San Antonio, 78; Community Murals: The People's Art, Assoc University Presses, Cranbury, NJ, 82. *Dealer:* Prospectos Gallery Chicago Ill; LA LLorona Gallery Chicago Ill. *Mailing Add:* 10101 S Ave M Chicago IL 60617

CASTLE, WENDELL KEITH
SCULPTOR
b Emporia, Kans, Nov 6, 32. *Study:* Univ Kans, BFA & MFA; various hon degrees. *Hon Degrees:* MD Inst of Art, DFA, 79; St John Fisher Col, LHD, 87; State Univ NY, DFA, 97. *Work:* Mus Fine Arts, Boston; Nordenfieldske Kunstindustrimus, Norway; Philadelphia Mus Art; Metrop Mus Art, Am Craft Mus, NY; Renwick Gallery, Smithsonian Inst; and others. *Comn:* Clock sculpture, Pillar Bryton Partners, Orlando, Fla; commemorative piano, Steinway & Sons, Long Island, NY; outdoor clock sculpture, Hammerson Can, Inc, Toronto; art furniture, Cincinnati Art Mus; clock sculpture, Maccabees Mutual Life Insurance Co, Southfield, Mich. *Exhib:* Art & Relig, Vatican, Rome, 78; Masterpieces of Time, Taft Mus, Cincinnati, Ohio, 85 & Renwick Gallery, Nat Mus Am Art, Smithsonian Inst, Washington, 85-86; Mus Fine Arts, Boston, 88; Furniture of Wendell Castle, Detroit Inst Arts, 89, Delaware Art Mus, 90, Va Mus Fine Arts, 90; solo exhibs, Morgan Gallery, Kansas City, Mo, 94 & 97, Peter Joseph Gallery, NY, 94, 95 & 96, Anne Reed Gallery, 95 & 96, Savannah Col Art & Design, 96, Leo Kaplan Modern, NY, 97 & 99, Indigo Galleries, Fla, 98 & R Duane Reed Gallery, St Louis, 98, Riley Hawk Galleries, Seattle, 2000 & 2001 & Habatat Gallery, Boca Raton, Fla, 2001; The White House Collection of Am Crafts, George Walter Vincent Smith Art Mus, Mass, 96; The White House Collection of Am Crafts, Mint Mus, Charlotte, NC, 99 & Decorative Arts Mus, Little Rock, Ark, 99; SOFA, Seventh Regiment Armory, NY, 98, 99, 2000 & 2001; Recent Acquisitions, Metrop Mus of Art, New York City, 99 & Recent Acquisitions: Selected Additions to the Modern Design Collection, 99. *Pos:* hon trustee, Renwick Art Gallery, Smithsonian Inst, 90; bd mgrs, Mem Art Gallery, Rochester, 86-92; Bd dir, Nat Mus Am Art & Rochester Mem Art Gallery, NY, 92. *Teaching:* Instr drawing, Univ Kans, 60-61; assoc prof furniture design, Rochester Inst Technol, 62-70; prof sculpture, Wendell Castle Workshop, 80-88; artist-in-residence, Rochester Inst Technol, 84-. *Awards:* Nat Endowment Arts Grants, 73, 75, 76 & 88; Gold Medal Award, Am Craft Coun, 97; Lifetime Achievement Award, Arts & Cultural Coun for Greater Rochester, 98; Masters of Medium Award, James Renwick Alliance, 99; Award of Distinction, Furniture Soc, 2001; and many others. *Bibliog:* Tod Riggio (auth), Carpenter, Castle, Frid, Krenov and Maloof Honored, Woodshop News, 6/2001; Designer's Whimsical Works Blur Line Between Furniture and Sculpture, The PlainsDealer, 6/2001; Gregory Kuharic (auth), Gregory Kuharic to speak about twentieth century crafts, Antiques & The Arts Weekly, 5/29/2001. *Mem:* Am Craftsman Coun; NY State Coun Arts; Am Craft Coun (trustee, 86-); Nat Mus Am Art Comn (comn alumni group, 2000); Arts & Cult Coun for Greater Rochester (arts award comt, 97); Am Craft Mus (hon mem dir's forum, 91). *Media:* Wood. *Publ:* coauth, The Wendell Castle Book of Wood Lamination, Van Nostrand Reinhold, 80; The Fine Art of the Furniture Maker, Mem Art Gallery, 81; Furniture by Wendell Castle, Giovannini/Taragin/Cooke, Hudson Hills Press, 89. *Dealer:* Gerald Peters Gallery 1011 Paseo de peralta Santa Fe Nm 87501; Habata Gallery 608 Banyan Trail Boca Raton FL 33431; Leo Kaplan Modern Fuller Building 41 E 57th St NY 10022; Morgan Gallery 114 SW Blvd St Louis MO 64108. *Mailing Add:* 80 Oakwood Ln Scottsville NY 14546

CASTORO, ROSEMARIE
SCULPTOR
b Brooklyn, NY, Mar 1, 39. *Study:* Mus Mod Art, New York, scholar, 54-55; Pratt Inst, BFA(cum laude), 57-63. *Work:* Berkeley Mus, San Francisco; Woodward Found, Washington, DC; Chase Manhattan Bank; Mus Mod Art, NY; Newark Mus, NJ; Boca Raton Mus, Fla; Bank of America World Hdqrs, San Francisco, Calif; Goldman & Sachs; Lindtas/World-Wide; Merrill Lynch, NY; Univ of Mass, Amherst; Wadsworth Atheneum, Conn; Allen Art Mus, Oberlin, Ohio. *Comn:* Procession of Strokes, NY State Coun Arts, 72; Hexatryst, Gen Serv Admin, Topeka, Kans, 79; 24 Flashers, Art Park, Lewiston, NY, 79; Etherial Concrete Flasher, Athena Found, Long Island City, NY, 86; Talk to Each Other, Woodstock, Saurgerties, NY, 94; Trapazoid, Creative Time, Battery Park City, NY. *Exhib:* Solo shows, Hal Bromm Gallery, NY, 79, 80, 83, 87, 92 & 97, Julian Pretto Co, NY, 78 & 79, Am Ctr, Paris, 83, Eaton-Shoen Gallery, San Francisco, 84 & 86, Newark Mus, 91, Stellar Graphics, Paris, France, 93 & Arnaud Lefebvre, Paris, France, 93, 95, 96, 97, 98 & 99, Eaton Fine Arts, West Palm Beach, Fla, 00-01, Tibor de Nagy Gallery, 71, 72, 73, 75, 76, 78, 80, 81, 83, 85, 89; Highlights of the 70-71 Art Seasons, Aldridge Mus Contemp Art, Conn, 71; Acquisitions, Mus Mod Art, NY, 85-86; Five Artists, Otis Art Inst, Los Angeles, Calif, 76; Painting & Sculpture Today, Indianapolis Mus Art, IN, 80; Hirshhorn Mus, Washington, DC, 81; Sculptors Working, Jan Baum Gallery, Los Angeles, Calif, 90; PS #1, lONG island City, NY, 2004. *Teaching:* Hunter Col, NY, 72, Calif State Univ, Fresno, 73, Philadelphia Col Art, 74, Mt Berry Col Art, Ga, 74, Syracuse Univ, NY, 75, Univ Colo, Boulder, 77, Stockton State Col, NJ, 83 & Boston Mus Sch, 85; tchr sculpture Am Univ, Corciano, Italy, 00-. *Awards:* Fel Guggenheim, 71; NY State Coun Arts Grant, 72 & 74; Nat Endowment Arts Grant, 75 & 85; Tiffany Found, 77; Pollack-Krasner Grant, 89-90 & 97-98. *Bibliog:* Carter Ratcliff (auth), article, Art Int, 5/75, Art in America, 79; Lucy Lippard (auth), article, Artforum, 7/75; Madeline Deschamps & Carl Andre (auths), Barbara Rose (catalog), Arnaud Lefebvre, 93; Gordon McConnell (auth), article, Colorado Daily. *Media:* All. *Specialty:* Contemp Art. *Publ:* Auth, Artists transgress all boundaries, Art News, 1/72; ed, Art in the mind, 70 & Conceptual Art, 72; Tracks, 75; autobiog essay, Meaning No 10, 91. *Dealer:* Hal Bromm Gallery 90 W Broadway New York NY 10007; Arnaud Lefebure 30 rue Nazarine 75006 Paris France. *Mailing Add:* 151 Spring St New York NY 10012

CASTRILLO, REBECCA
PRINTMAKER, PAINTER
b Santurce, PR, Jan 18, 54. *Study:* Art Students League, 71-73; Univ PR, Rio Piedras, BFA (1 year interchange prog Univ Piso, Italy, 73), 75; Pratt Inst, Brooklyn, MFA, with Clare Romano, Walter Ragalsky, George Mackneil & Claudio Júarez, 78; studied printmaking with Robert Blackburn, 79. *Work:* Asoc Artes Graficas Panamericanas, Venezuela; Museo Del Barrio-Bronx, NY; Lincoln Hosp, Printmaking Workshop Collections, NY; Saloon de la Sociedad de Bellas Artes, Rueil De Mal Maison, France, Pratt Inst, NY. *Comn:* El Rostro De La Bailarina, Carton De Venezuela, 86. *Exhib:* Printmaking Workshop Traveling Exhib, USA, 85; Biennal of Latin Am Graphics, Mocha Mus Contemp Arts, NY, 86; Saloon Vardol en el Centro Cult de Orval, Saloon Mus, Orval, France, 90; Biennal of Latin Am Graphics, Mus Arsenal De La Marina, Inst PR Arts, San Juan, PR, 94; IX Biennal Ibeoamericana of Graphics, Palacio De Bellas Artes, Mexico City, 94. *Teaching:* Prof fine arts, Art Student League, San Juan, PR, 80-94, Univ Interamericana PR, 86-94 & Eckerd Col, St Petersburg, Fla, 88. *Awards:* First Prize in Painting, Certamen Ateneo Puertorriqueño, San Juan, PR, 75; First Prize, Mobil Oil Corp, 84; Merit of Professional Growth Award, Inst Cult PR, 94; and others. *Mem:* Nat Asn Women Artists, NY; Assoc Mujeres Artistas De PR (vpres, 83-94); Women Caucus for Arts, NY. *Media:* All Media. *Mailing Add:* 1012 Calle Puerto Principe URB Las Americas Rio Piedras PR 00921

CASTRUCCI, ANDREW
PAINTER, SCULPTOR
b West Hoboken, NJ, Sept 14, 61. *Study:* Sch Visual Arts, BFA, 83. *Work:* Mus Modern Art, NY; Whitney Mus Am Art, NY; Stedelijk Mus Modern Art, Amsterdam, Holland; Mus Zu Berlin, Ger; Centre Georges Pompidou, Paris, France. *Comn:* mural, 99 Park Ave Office Bldg, Sammy Ofer, NY, 96; mural, World Trade Ctr, Allesandra Grassi, Milan, Italy, 97; mural, Water Surface, Galerie Christian Schneeberger, St Galen, Switzerland, 98; mural, Fish Hook Falls Asleep, Andrea Stillacci, Milan, Italy, 99; mural, Skyline, Bullet Space, NY, 2000. *Exhib:* If You Lived Here, Dia Art Found, NY, 89; In Transit, New Mus, NY, 93; The Realm of the Coin, Queens Mus, NY, 93; Fever, Traveling Exhib, Wexner Ctr, Columbus, Ohio, 94; In Memory of., Mus Modern Art, NY, 94; Urban Encounters, New Mus, NY, 98; The End, Ind Vision Contemp Art, NY, 2000; Le Case D'arte de Pasquale Leccese, New York City (a) Self-Portrait, Milan, Italy; Life of the City, Mus Modern Art, NY, 02; The River Speaks, Generous Miracles (catalog), 99; Tower I, II, Sch of Visual Arts, 02-03; Blood, Rubber, Fixative, Tribes Gallery (with catalog), 03. *Collection Arranged:* Ave D - DADA, Bullet Space, 90; Your House is Mine, Bullet Space (catalog), 91; A Continuation of Something Else, Bullet Space (catalog), 97; Confusion, Sch visual Arts, 99; Zeor Infinite/Finite, Sch Visual Arts, 2000. *Pos:* co-dir, A&P Gallery, NY, 84-86; dir, Bullet Space Printshop, NY, 88-98; mem, cur, Bullet: An Urban Artists collaborative, NY, 85-2003. *Teaching:* teacher fine arts dept, drawing, Sch Visual Arts, 85-86; teacher hosp audiences, drawing, painting, sculpture, Hosp Audience, 98-2003; teacher graphic design, artists books, Sch Visual Arts, 98-2003; teacher painting & drawing, CW Post Col, Long Island Univ, 01-03; teacher, Experimental TV, Conn, 2000; teacher, Art Matters, 88-89; teacher, North Star Found, 84. *Awards:* Award, Andy Warhol Found, 92; Grant, Artists Colony, Macdowell/Yadoo, 94-95. *Bibliog:* Art in America, 2/2000; Art Forum, 10/91; The River Speaks (catalog), 99; Your House is Mine, 88-92. *Mem:* Bullet Space: An Urban Artists Collaborative. *Media:* Acrylic, Oil; Metal, Wood, Printmaking. *Res:* Painting, sculpture, prints, artists books, drawings. *Publ:* Newsweek, 1/25/93; Time Out NY, 8/28/97; NY Times, 8/14/98. *Dealer:* Bullet Space Alexandra Rojas 292 E 3rd St New York NY 10009-8963; Generous Miracles Gallery 524 W 20th St New York NY 10011. *Mailing Add:* 292 E 3rd St New York NY 10009-8963

CASWELL, HELEN RAYBURN
PAINTER, WRITER
b Long Beach, Calif, Mar 16, 23. *Study:* Univ Ore Sch Fine Arts. *Comn:* mural, Villa Sienna, Redwood City, Calif, 99; mural, St Ignatius Ch, San Francisco, 2000; stain glass window, Meth Ch, Sebastopol, Calif, 98. *Exhib:* De Young Mus Show, Soc Western Artists, 61; one-man shows, Northwest Mo State Col, 66 & Rosicrucian Mus, San Jose, 70; Montalvo Cult Ctr, Saratoga, 68. *Awards:* James D Phelan Award for Narrative Poetry, 58; San Francisco Browning Soc Award, 66; Roberts Writings Award, 90. *Media:* Oil, Printmaking. *Publ:* Auth, Growing in Faith Library, Abingdon, 89; Jesus for Little People, Broadman-Holman, 94; A Little Book of Friendship, Thomas Nelson, 95; A Little Book of Prayers, Thomas Nelson, 95; The Parables of Jusus, Abingdon, 98; illusr St Francis Celebrate Christmas, Loyola Press, 99. *Dealer:* Ballantyne & Douglas Bend Oreg. *Mailing Add:* 13207 Dupont Rd Sebastopol CA 95472-9787

CASWELL, JIM (JAMES) DANIEL CASWELL-DAVIS
SCULPTOR, CERAMIST
b St Boniface, Man, Nov 9, 48. *Study:* Calif State Univ, Northridge, with Peter Plagens, Walt Gabrielson, Karen Carson & Howard Tollefson, 66-71. *Comn:* Vases, Manufacture Nat de Sevres, Sevres, France, 86. *Exhib:* Scripps Ann, Lang Art Gallery, Claremont, Calif, 82; Pacific Currents, San Jose Mus Art, 82; Art and/or Craft, Kanazawa, Japan, 82; Clay for Walls, Renwick Gallery, 83; On and Off the Wall, Oakland Mus, 83; Triennale de la Porcelaine, Nyon, Switz, 86; 27th Ceramic Nat Exhib, Everson Mus, Syracuse, NY, 87; Am Ceramics Now, Am Craft Mus, NY, 87; East-West Contemp Ceramics, Olympic Invitational, Seoul, Korea, 88. *Awards:* Nat Endowment Arts Fel, 83; Fel, Centre Nat des Arts Plastiques, 85 & 86. *Media:* Ceramic. *Dealer:* Jane Corkin Gallery 179 John St Suite 302 Toronto ON Canada. *Mailing Add:* 2208 Cloverfield Blvd Santa Monica CA 90405

CASWELL-LINHARES, SALLY
PAINTER, PRINTMAKER
b Brockton, Mass, Nov 1, 41. *Study:* Studied with George Lockwood, 61-62; Mass Col Art, Boston, BFA, 65; RI Col, Providence, MAT, 77; Univ Mass, Dartmouth, MFA (Distinguished Thesis), 90. *Work:* US Naval War Col Mus, Newport; Slide Libr, RI Sch Design, Providence; Slide Libr, Copley Soc Boston; Antique Automobiles: Reflections, Sweet-T, Sleek 31 (Watercolor Triptych), Autozone Corp, off Chief Exec Officer & Pres, Memphis, Tenn, 2002. *Comn:* Portrait & landscape paintings, comn by many pvt collectors, 62-; New England Watercolors, NEICO Microwave Co, Hopkinton, Mass, 81; The Four Seasons (watercolor paintings), Blue Cross of Boston, Framingham, Mass, 85; Spinakers Sailing Past Prudence Island (watercolor diptych), Citizens Bank, Pawtuxet, RI, 85; and others. *Exhib:* Pittsburgh Nat Aqua Media, Pittsburgh Ctr Arts, 83; Int Energy Art Show, Foothills Art Ctr, Golden, Colo, 83; Riggs Gallery, San Diego, Calif, 84-85; Japan-Am Exchange, Japan Watercolor Soc, Tokyo, 86; Faculty Exhib, Woods-Gerry Gallery, RI Sch Design, Providence, 87-94; Art Northeast USA, Silvermine Galleries, New Canaan, Conn, 88; All New Eng Exhib, Duxbury Art Complex Mus, Mass, 89, 97; Emerging Artists, Univ Mass, Dartmouth, 90; Cornwall Gallery Invitational, Jamaica Plains, Mass, 92; Hera Gallery Invitational, 92; Then & Now, Mass Col Art Tower Gallery, Boston, 93; Embracing Diversity, Attleboro Mus, Mass, 98; Reveal and Conceal, 19 on Paper, Newport Art Mus, RI, 2002-2003; solo shows: Providence Art Club, Dodge House gallery, 97, 00, 02, 05; and others; Ann Nat Exhib, Chautauqua Center Visual Arts, Chautauqua, NY, 2006. *Pos:* Bd mem, Pawtucket Arts Coun, 86-88 & Nat Mus Women Arts, RI, 97-98; dir art gallery, Community Col RI, Warwick, 95-99. *Teaching:* Instr watercolor & design, RI Sch Design, 86-94; adj asst prof drawing, life drawing, 2-D design, color, watercolor, acrylic painting, Community Col, RI, 87-; instr spec studies, watercolor painting, Chautaugua Inst, NY, 96-; pvt instr for watercolor painting and art historical tour of Florence, Siena, and Tuscany, 2000. *Awards:* First Prize, RI Watercolor Soc, 89; Minna Walker - Smith Award, New Haven Paint & Clay Club, New England & NY, 80; Joseph Boland Watercolor Award, Bristol Art Mus, 83; Finalist, Art for Preserving Our Nat Resources, Am Artist Mag, 90; Providence Art Club Award, 96; First Prize & Best of Show, Fall River Art Asn Ann Regional Exhib, 96; First Prize, Cape Cod Art Asn Open Jurried Exhib, 97. *Bibliog:* Arturo Vivante (auth), Review, Boston Rev Arts, 6/72; Bill Van Siclen (auth), Sensing emotion in city & sea, Providence J, 3/88; Robert C Fisher (auth), A little greatness, Am Artist Mag, 8/90. *Mem:* Wickford Art Asn; Copley Artist, Copley Soc Boston; Providence Art Club; RI Watercolor Soc; 19 on Paper. *Media:* Acrylic, Oil, Watercolor; All Media, Lithography. *Publ:* Illusr, The Watchman, Identity Press, Cambridge, 71; The Trident: Centennial Edition, Yearbook of US Naval War College, 84; An Anniversary Collection 1984-1988; Winning Poems from the Pawtucket Arts Council Annual Poetry Competition, RI State Coun Arts, 88; Spiritual energy, Innerview Mag, summer 89; and others. *Dealer:* Gallery at Caterpillar Hill, Sedgwick, ME; Sally Caswell Fine Art, www.caswellart.com. *Mailing Add:* 611 Warren Ave Swansea MA 02777

CATCHI
PAINTER, PRINTMAKER
b Philadelphia, Pa, Aug 27, 20. *Study:* Briarcliff Jr Col, 37; Commercial Illus Studios, 38-39; also with Leon Kroll, Harry Sternberg & Hans Hofman & with Angelo Savelli, Positano, Italy; Acad Int Medicea Bella Arte Firenze, Italy, hon degree, 83. *Work:* Rosenberg Found, Hofstra Univ, Hempstead, NY, Jane Voorhees Zimmerli Art Mus Rutgers, State Univ NJ. *Exhib:* One-person shows, Rayburn Hall, Washington, DC, 68 & 76, Gallerie Arte Spenetti, Florence, Gallery Coin d'Arte, Genoa, Wichita Fall Mus, Tex, 86, Longview Art Mus, Tex, 87 & City of Florence, Italy, 89. *Pos:* Artist-in-residence, Friends Acad, Locust Valley, NY, 84, Vt Studio Ctr, Johnson, Vt, 2002, 03. *Awards:* Goldie Paley Award, Nat Asn Women Artists, 77; Winston Mem Prize, 80; First Prize, Riverside Mus, NY; Dr Maury Leibouvitz Art Award, 86; Emily Lowe Award, 89. *Bibliog:* Nan Ickeringill (auth), Art & at home with Catchi, New York Times, 68; Doris Herzig (auth), She has painted since she was 12, Newsday, 68; Molly Sinclair (auth), Oil brush & canvas, Atlanta Constitution, 69. *Mem:* Nat Asn Women Artists (pres, 81-85); Audubon Artists; Int Platform Asn; New York Soc of Women Artists (pres, 84-86); Artists Equity, New York (bd, 86-90). *Media:* Oil, Watercolor, Stone, Cast Metals. *Publ:* Illusr (cover), La Revue Art Moderne Mag, France, 7/75 & 6/78; doc book, Int Sculpture Symp, Tex, 76. *Mailing Add:* 2 Gristmill Ln Manhasset NY 11030

CATE, PHILLIP DENNIS
HISTORIAN, DIRECTOR
b Washington, DC, Oct 19, 44. *Study:* Rutgers Univ, BA(art hist), 67; Ariz State Univ, MA(art hist), 70. *Collection Arranged:* Meryon's Paris/Piranesi's Rome (with catalog), 71; The Ruckus World of Red Grooms (with catalog), 73; Japonisme: Japanese Influence on French Art, 1854-1910 (with catalog), 75; The Color Revolution, color lithography in France 1890-1900 (with catalog), 78; Circa 1800: The Beginning of Modern Printmaking, 1775-1835 (catalog), 80; Theophile Alexander Steinlen, 1859-1923 (auth, catalog), 82; The Circle of Toulouse-Lautrec (auth, catalog), 85; Matsukata Collection of Ukiyo-e Prints from Tokyo National Mus (auth, catalog), 88; Eiffel Tower: A Tour de Force (auth, catalog), 89; Pissarro to Picasso Color Etching in France, 92; The Spirit of Monmartec Cabarets Humor and the Advant-garde 1875-1905 (auth catalog), 96. *Pos:* Asst to dir, Pa Acad Fine Art, 67-68; dir, Jane Voorhees Zimmerli Art Mus, Rutgers Univ, 70-; Supervision of Curatorial and Acad Activities, 2003-present. *Mem:* Print Coun Am; Asn Art Mus Dirs; Col Art Asn; Grolier Club. *Res:* 19th century French Art & Soc. *Publ:* Ed & essayist, The Graphic Arts & French Soc, 1871-1914, Rutgers Press, NB, 88; essayist, L'Estampe Originale: Artistic Printmaking in France 1893-1895, Van Gogh Mus, Amsterdam, 91; From Pissarro to Picasso; Color Etching in France, Bibliotheque Nationale, Paris, 92; The Spirit of Martwartu Cabarets, Humor and the Avant-garde 1875-1905, 96; Breaking the Mold; Sculpture in Paris from Dauimer to Rodin, 2005

CATLETT, ELIZABETH
SCULPTOR, GRAPHIC ARTIST, PRINTMAKER
b Washington, DC, Apr 15, 19; Mexican citizen, US citizen. *Study:* Howard Univ, Wash, DC, BS(art), 36; State Univ, Iowa, MFA, 40; Art Inst, Chicago; Art Students League, NY; privately with Ossip Zadkine, NY, 44-. *Hon Degrees:* Morgan State Univ, Baltimore, Md, DHL (hon); Tulane Univ, New Orleans, LA, DHL (hon); Howard Univ, Washington, DC, DHL (hon); Maryland Col of Art, Dr Fine Arts (hon); Pratt Inst, Dr Fine Arts (hon); Spelman Col, Atlanta, GA, Dr Fine Arts (hon); Parsons Sch of Design, New York, Dr Fine Arts (hon); Cornell Col, Iowa, Dr Fine Arts (hon). *Work:* Modern Art Mus, Metrop Mus Art, Whitney Mus Am Art, NY; New Orleans Mus Art, La; Nat Mus Am Art, Washington, DC; Mod Art Mus, Mex; Baltimore Mus Art; High Mus, Atlanta, Ga; San Francisco Mus Art; William and Camille Cosby pvt collection; Rev Douglass Moore pvt collection. *Comn:* Life-size figures (2 bronzes), comn by Secy of Educ, Mexico, 81; marble carving, Fla A & M Univ, 89; bronze relief, Atlanta City Hall, Ga, 90; marble carving, Colgate, 92; wood carving, Legler Branch Pub Libr, Chicago, Ill; bronze Louis Armstrong Monument, New Orleans, La, 73; bronze, Monument to Ralph Ellison, comn by Riverside Park Fund, NY; bronze monument, Sojourner, comn by Sacramento Metrop Art Comn, Calif, 98. *Exhib:* One-woman shows, Modern Art Mus, Mex, 70, Studio Mus Harlem, NY, 71-72, Saxon Summer Place, Dresden, 73 & New Orleans Mus Art, La, 83; Miss Mus Art, Jackson, 90; Montgomery Mus Art, Ala, 91; Polk Mus Art, Lakeland, Fla, 91-92; June Kelly Gallery, NY, 93; print retrospective, Hampton Univ Mus, Va, 93; 50 Yr Sculpture Retrospective, Neuberger Mus, NY, 98; Blaffer Gallery, Houston, Tex, 98; Baltimore Mus Art, 99; Afro-Am Mus of Art, Los Angeles, Calif, 99; Spelman Col, Atlanta, GA, 99. *Teaching:* Head dept art, Dillard Univ, New Orleans, La, 40-42; head dept & prof sculpture, Nat Sch Fine Arts, Nat Univ, Mex, 58-73. *Awards:* Brit Coun Grant, 71; Alumni Award, Howard Univ, Washington, DC, 79; Nat Award, Women's Caucus Art, 81; Award, Nat Sculpture Conference, Works by Women, Cincinnati, Ohio, 87; Amistad Arts Award, New Orleans, 90; Art Award, Nat Coun 100 Black Women, NY, 91; Civil Rights Award, Delta Sigma Theta, 94; Creative Spirit Award, Pratt Inst, 95; Distinguished Alumni Award, Univ of Iowa, 96. *Bibliog:* Juan Mora (dir), Elizabeth Catlett (film), Contemp Crafts, Los Angeles, Calif, 78; Samella Lewis (auth), The Art of Elizabeth Catlett, Handcraft Studios, 84; Stephanie S Oliver (auth), Elizabeth Catlett, Essence Mag, 85; Elizabeth Catlett Sculpture, Neuberger Mus of Art, Purchase, NY, 98; Melanie Herzog (auth), Elizabeth Catlett, an American Artist in Mexico, Univ of Wash Press, 2000. *Mem:* Hon life mem Women's Caucus Arts; Salon de La Plastica Mexicana; Nat Acad. *Media:* Wood & Stone Carving, Bronze. *Publ:* The Negro Artist in Am, Am. Contemp Art, 1-2/44; A Tribute to the Negro People, Am. Contemp Art, 46; The Negro Artist & Am Art, Freedom Ways, spring 61; The Role of the Black Artist, Black Scholar, 6/75; Responding to Cultural Hunger, Reimaging Am: The Arts of Social Change, New Soc Pub, 90. *Dealer:* Ellen Sragow Gallery 73 Spring St New York NY 10012; June Kelly Gallery 591 Broadway New York NY

CATON, DAVID
PAINTER
b Pasadena, Calif, Sept 13, 55. *Study:* Univ Houston, BFA, 79; Yale Univ, MFA, 81. *Work:* Tex Commerce, Houston, Tex; Tex A&M Univ, Houston. *Exhib:* Wilhelm Gallery, Scottsdale, Ariz, 87 & 88; Bill Ross Gallery, Memphis, Tenn, 88; Bienville Gallery, New Orleans, 88; Harris Gallery, Houston, 90 & 95; Harris Gallery, Houston, 98, 99, 00, 01, 02; A Sense of Place, Williams Tower, Houston, 2001. *Awards:* Visual Arts Fel Painting, Nat Endowment Arts, 85 & 87. *Dealer:* Harris Gallery 1100 Bissonnet Houston TX 77005

CATTAN, EMILIA
PAINTER, PRINTMAKER
b Mexico City. *Study:* Escuela Nal Bellas Artes 80; Draw-Paint E Elizondo, 95; Art Claustro De Sar Juana, Art 88; Univ Ibero Americana, Lit, 90. *Work:* Galeria Centro Deportivo Isdaelita, Mexico, DF; Mus Techologico Chapultepec, Mexico, DE; Banco Mercantil, Mexico, DF; Alianza Francesa, Mexico, DF; Inst Mex Northamericano De Relacidnes Exteridres, Mexico, DF. *Comn:* Cruz-Roja Mex Sieche Mex DF, 86; Les Artistes DUXX, Paris, 93; Pro Mo-Arte, 95; Directorio Re Las Artes Plasticas, Mexico, DF, 94. *Publ:* Les Artistes Del XX Siècle, Arts Est Images De Monde, Paris; Directorid De Las Artes Plasticas, Mexico, DF. *Mailing Add:* Reforma 2233 Mexico DF 11020 Mexico

CATTANEO, (JACQUELYN A) KAMMERER
PAINTER, INSTRUCTOR
b Gallup, NMex, June 1, 44. *Study:* Tex Women's Univ, Denton, 62-64; studied with Frederick Taubes, 72-73, Sergei Bongart, 78, Bettina Steinke, 85, Ben Konis, 76-77, Daniel Greene, 84, Everett Raymond Kinstler, 85, Albert Handell, 96, 97 & 98. *Work:* Gallup Pub Libr Permanent Collection, NMex; NMex State Capitol, Gov & Mrs Bruce King Collection & Lt Gov & Mrs Casey Luna; Blessed Katharine Drexel (portrait), Sacred Heart Cathederal; Rehoboth McKinley Christian Hosp. *Comn:* Portrait of Calvin C Hall, Univ NMex; portraits, Sunwest Bank, First State Bank, City of Gallup & El Rancho Hist Hotel, Gallup, NMex; Sisters Blessed Sacrement, Bensalem, Pa; Blessed Mother Teresa of Calcutta, Sacred Heart Cathedral, 2004. *Exhib:* Catharine Lorillard Wolfe Art Club, NY, 84-94; Best & the Brightest Invitational, O'Briens Art Emporium, Scottsdale, 86; Ann Exhib, Pastel Soc W Coast, Sacramento, Calif, 89-94; Asn pour Du Prom Du Patrimone Artistique Francias, Paris, France, 91; Ann Exhib, Pastel Soc West Coast, Sacramento, Calif, 89-94; Int Nexus, 92 Fine Art Exhib, Trammell Crow Pavilian, Dallas, Tex; Women Reflect, Carlsbad Mus Fine Arts, Carlsbad, NMex, 92; one-woman show, Carol's Art & Antiques, Liverpool, NY, 97. *Pos:* Vchmn, Gallup Area Arts Coun & Coop Gallery, 70-88; judge fine arts, Inter-tribal Ceremonial Gallup, NMex, 80, 84 & 92; comt mem, Gallup NMex Multi-Cultural Ctr, 87-88; mem, Soviet Union Deleg to Leningrad, Moscow,

Russ & Kiev, Ukraine, 90; mem, US Women Artists Middle East Deleg Exchange Prog, Jerusalem, Ibillin, Tel Aviv, Isreal, Cairo & Egypt & Italy, 92; mem, US Women Artists Deleg to Rio de Janeiro, Igaccu Falls, Manaus & Amazon Village, Brazil, 94; US Women Artist Deleg Spain, Greece, Turkey, 96. *Teaching:* Instr art for children, Studio Corner, Gallup, NMex, 65-78 & pvt instr, 97-; instr portraiture, Carizo Lodge, Ruidoso, NMex, 78, San Juan Col, Farmington & Univ NMex, Gallup, 85-86, The Maritimes, ThunderBay, Konoca, Ont, 2000. *Awards:* Pastel Soc Am, 2004; Second Place Pastel, Catherine Larillar Wolfe Art Club, New York City, 2005; Merit Award, Pastel Soc. West Coast's Signature Mem, 2006. *Bibliog:* Herbert Lieberman (auth), A Guide to Contemporary Art, 81. *Mem:* Oil Painters Am; Allied Artists Am; Salmagundi Club, NY; Pastel Soc of the West Coast (signature mem); Am Portrait Soc (signature mem); Pastel Society of Am, Signature Mem. *Media:* Oil, Pastel. *Publ:* Contribr, Southwest Art, Pastel Society of West Coast Profile, 11/87; Artists of New Mexico Volumn III, Mountain Productions, Albuquerque, NMex, 90; Northlight, Northlight Book Club, Vol 23, No 162, 10/91; NMex Art Buyers Guide (cover & insert), 98; Momentum NCEA Mag (cover & ed); Int Artist Mag, 2005. *Dealer:* Jordan Artworks 11050 Summerlin Square Dr Ft Meyers Beach Fla 33931; Cogswell Gallery, Vail CO; Grimshaw Fine Art, The Variant Gallery, Taos. NM. *Mailing Add:* c/o Studio Corner 210 E Green Gallup NM 87301

CATTELAN, MAURIZIO
ARTIST
b Padua, Italy, 60. *Work:* Projects 65, Mus Modern Art, NY, 98; Centre Pompidou, Musée National d'Art Moderne, Paris, 2000; Over the Edges, Stedelijk Mus voor Acutuele Kunst, 2000; Felix, Mus Contemp Art, Chicago, 2002; Dreams & Conflicts: Dictatorship of the Viewer, La Biennale di Venezia, Venice, 2003; Whitney Biennial Exhib, Whitney Mus Am Art, 2004. *Exhib:* 49th Venice Biennale, La Biennale Di Venezia, Venice, 2001; Irony, Fundación Joan Miró, Barcelona, 2001; HOLLYWOOD IS A VERB, Gagosian Gallery, London, 2002; Dreams & Conflicts: Dictatorship of the Viewer, La Biennale di Venezia, Venice, 2003; Bodily Space: New Obsessions in Figurative Sculpture, Albright-Knox Art Gallery, Buffalo, NY, 2004; The Big Nothing, Inst Contemp Art, Philadelphia, 2004; None of the above, Swiss Inst, NY, 2004. *Mailing Add:* c/o Marian Goodman Gallery 24 West 57th St New York NY 10019

CATTERALL, JOHN EDWARD
PAINTER, EDUCATOR
b Sheridan, Wyo, Jan 12, 40. *Study:* Univ Wyo, BA, 66; Wash State Univ, MFA, 68. *Work:* Brooklyn Mus, NY; Detroit Inst Arts, Mich; Cranbrook Acad Art; Univ Colo, Boulder; Tex Tech Univ. *Comn:* Triptych, Barnett Winston Co, Jacksonville, Fla, 78; diptych, R J Reynolds Corp, Winston-Salem, NC, 80; IBM Corp, Boca Raton, Fla, 86; Apache Corp, 95. *Exhib:* New Am Graphics, Elvehjem Art Ctr, Madison, Wis, 75; Int Print Biennial, Ministry Cult & Art, Kracow, Poland, 76; Int Print Exhib, Cranbrook Acad Art, 80; solo exhib, Yellowstone Art Ctr, Billings, Mont, 80; Recent Acquisitions, Brooklyn Mus, 81; Western Skies--Western Eyes, Colo Inst Arts, Denver, 82; Int Print Invitational, Korean Print Soc, Seoul, 83. *Pos:* Bd dir, Artspace Mag, 86; adv bd, Ucross Found, 93-. *Teaching:* Asst prof painting & printmaking, Univ SFla, 71-75; prof & dir, Mont State Univ, 75-82; prof & dept head, NMex State Univ, 82-88; chmn & prof, Art Dept, Univ Fla, 88-. *Awards:* Purchase Awards, Boston Printmakers Exhib, 70 & Potsdam Prints, State Univ NY, 75; Best of Show, Printmaking Exhib, Univ Colo, 75. *Bibliog:* Coke Van Deren (auth), The Painter & The Photographer, 72. *Mem:* Northwest Print Coun, Portland, Ore (bd mem, 80-82); World Print Coun; Col Art Asn; Nat Coun Arts Admin. *Media:* Acrylic, Oil. *Dealer:* Art Sources Jacksonville Fla; Adair Margo Gallery El Paso TX. *Mailing Add:* Univ Nev Las Vegas Dept Art 4505 Maryland Pkwy Las Vegas NV 89154

CAUDURO, RAFAEL
PAINTER, MURALIST
b Mexico City, Mex, Apr 18, 50. *Study:* Univ Iberoamericana, indust design, 68-72. *Work:* Mus Mod Art, Cuevas Mus, Alfa Cult Ctr, Mex; Contemp Art Mus (MARCO), Monterrey, Mex. *Comn:* Postage stamp, Dept Communs, Mexico City, 85; Communications (mural), Dept Communs, Mex, Vancouver, Brit Columbia, Can, 86; London Underground (mural), Paris Metro (mural), City Coun, Mexico City, 89; History Travels in the Caboose (mural), Ministry Commun & Transport, Mexico City, 93. *Exhib:* Images for the Children, Children's Mus Manhattan, 90; The Blessing of Spring, Casa de la Cultura Mex-Japan, Mexico City, 91; one-man shows, Colegio Bachilleres, Mex, 92, Flint Inst Art, Mich, 93, La Poética Tiempo, Kennesaw State Col Gallery Art, Atlanta, Ga, 93, Inst Cult Mex, NY, 94, Inst Tecnológico y Estudios Superiores Monterrey, Mex, 95, Gráficas y Dibujo, Mus Nac Estampa, Mex, 95 & De Angeles Calvarios y Calaveras, Mus Palacio Bellas Artes, Sala Nac, Mex, 95; Drawings and Prints, Museo Nacional Estampa, Mexico City, 95; De Angeles, Calvarios y Calaveras, Palace Fine Arts, Nat Hall, Mexico City, 95; and many others. *Bibliog:* Jorge A Manrique (auth), Cauduro: cual realismo, La Jornada, 4/91; Donald Kuspit, Rafael Cauduro (exhib catalogue), Mex Cult Inst, NY, 94; Alfonso Ruiz Soto, Ilusionismo critico (catalogue), Palace Fine Arts Show, 95. *Media:* Oil, Acrylic. *Publ:* Coauth, Rafael Cauduro, MoArt Mus, Mex, 91; Elena Poniatowska, Cauduro, Leon's City Mus, 92; Donald Kuspit, Rafael Cauduro, Mex Cult Inst New York, 94. *Dealer:* Louis Newman Galleries 322 N Beverly Dr Beverly Hills CA 90210. *Mailing Add:* c/o Saturno 12 Jardines de Cuernavaca 62360 Cuernavaca Morelos 62360 Mexico

CAVA, PAUL
ART DEALER, PAINTER
b Brooklyn, NY, May 15, 49. *Study:* New Sch Social Res, 65; Richmond Col, NY, BA, 72; Rochester Inst Technol, MFA, 75. *Work:* Free Libr Philadelphia, Pa; Biblioteque Nationale, Paris, France; Houston Mus Fine Arts. *Exhib:* Drawings from the Collection of Milt Brutten & Helen Herrich, Ben Shahn Gallery, Wm Paterson Col, Wayne, NJ, 81; Still Modern After All These Yrs, Chrysler Mus, Norfolk, Va, 82; Photocollage, Contemp Arts Mus, Houston, Tex, 82; Contemp Philadelphia Photogrs, Pa Acad Fine Arts, 84; Art Extreme, Philadelphia, Pa, 85; Twining Gallery, NY, 88; Jessica Berwind Gallery, Philadelphia, 89; Tradition and the Unpredictable (with catalog), Mus Fine Arts, Houston, 94. *Pos:* Pvt dealer 19th & 20th century photog, 75-79; Owner & dir, Paul Cava Gallery, 79-94. *Awards:* Artist Fel, Pa Coun Arts, 81. *Media:* All Media. *Specialty:* Contemporary art

CAVAGLIERI, GIORGIO
ARCHITECT
b Venice, Italy, Aug 1, 1911; arrived in US 1939; naturalized 1943. *Study:* Superior Sch Engineering, Milan, Italy, D (archit engineering), 32, student special city planning, 34. *Comn:* principal works in US include Fenton Hall reconstruction, Fredonia Col, Astor Library restoration and conversion to NY Public Theatre, NY Shakespeare Festival, Jefferson Market Courthouse restoration and conversion to NY Public Library, Branch Library, Riverdale, NY, NY Public Library main bldg, Periodical Dept, Public Sch 32, SI, Kip's Bay branch library; Principal works in Milan, prior to World War II; assoc architect Pension Bldg/Nat Mus Bldg Arts, Washington; architect-in-charge Rosary Hall, US Military Acad Mus; Eldridge St. Synagogue restoration, NY City, Chapel of the Good Shepherd reconstruction, Roosevelt Island, NY. *Pos:* Apprenticeship R Candela, NY office, JO Chertkof, Baltimore office, Benjamin Franklin 34-39; proprietor Giorgio Cavaglieri firm, NY City, 46-; trustee Nat Inst Architectural Educ, chairman bd trustees, 57-60. *Teaching:* Adj prof Sch Architectuer Pratt Inst, 56-69. *Awards:* Decorated Bronze Star; Gold Medal Honor Architecture, Archtl League NY, 56; Bard Award, spec citation City Club NY, 68; Illuminated scroll Municipal Art Soc NY, 66; Clients Award, NY State Asn Architects, 64; Sidney L Strauss Memorial, NY Soc Architects, 77; Award for Excellence in Design NY City Art Commission, 92; Design Award for Preservation, Gen Serv Administration, 92; Lucy Moses Award, NY Landmark Conservancy, 2002; Bronze Medal, Fine Art Federation NY, 2002. *Mem:* Fel, Am Inst Architects (pres NY chapter 70-71, House Improvement Award, 61, Honor Award, 68, Distinguished Architecture Award, 85, Presdl citation 1990, Medal of Honor NY chapter, 90); mem. Municipal Art Soc NY (pres 63-65, 4th Ann Preservation Award 92); Archtl League NY (vpres 61-63); Am Soc Interior Designers (vpres 84-85, 87-88, medal 85); Fine Arts Federation NY (pres 70-72, 74-76, 2000-01, Centennial Yr honoree 95); NY Council Arts and Government NY City; Victorian Soc (Outstanding in Preservation Award, 86); Nat Acad (assoc 70, acad, 84)

CAVALIERE, BARBARA
CRITIC, HISTORIAN
b New York, NY. *Study:* State Univ NY Stony Brook, BA, 75; Queens Col, City Univ New York. *Pos:* Contrib ed, Arts Mag, New York, formerly; contribr, Acad Am Encycl, 21 vols, Arete Publ Co Inc, Princeton, NJ, 78-80, Contemp Artists, St Martin's Press; prod ed, Metrop Mus, currently. *Awards:* Helena Rubenstein Fel, Whitney Mus Am Art, 75; Art Critic's Fel, Nat Endowment Arts, 80. *Mem:* Int Asn Art Critics (chmn, mem comt, 81-84, treas 84-90); Found Community Artists, NY; Nat Writer's Union. *Res:* 19th and 20th century art, especially abstract expressionism and contemporary art of 1940's to present. *Publ:* Auth, Theodoros Stamos in perspective, 12/77, The making of ometa, 10/80, Vir heroicus sublimis: Building the idea complex, 1/81 & Possibilities II, 9/81, Arts Mag; Notes on Mark Rothko & Early abstract expressionism: The 1940's, Flash Art, 1-2/79. *Mailing Add:* Metropolitan Mus Art Editorial Dept 1000 Fifth Ave New York NY 10028

CAVAT, IRMA
PAINTER, EDUCATOR
b New York, NY. *Study:* New Sch Social Res; Archipenko Art Sch; Acad Grande Chaumiere, Paris; also with Ozenfant, Paris & Hans Hofmann; William de Kooning Studio. *Work:* Mus Modern Art; Flint Mus; Art Inst Detroit; Delgado Mus. *Comn:* wall of portraits, Fac Club, Univ Calif, Santa Barbara, 68; mural, pvt hotel, Athens, Greece, 70; wall piece, Los Angeles, Calif, 70; Santa Barbara Mall & Ventura Mall, Calif, 76. *Exhib:* Festival of Two Worlds, Spoleto, Italy, 58-59; Ten Americans, Palazzo Venezia, Rome, 60; solo exhibs, Santa Barbara Mus, Calif & Phoenix Mus, Ariz, 66-67; Kennedy Galleries, 82 & 84; Feingarten Gallery, Los Angeles, 86; Preston Burke, Detroit, 87; Arts and Letters, Santa Barbara, 2000; H Pollack Fine Arts, Summerland, Calif, 2002. *Teaching:* Prof painting & drawing, Univ Calif, Santa Barbara, 64-. *Awards:* Yaddo Fel, Trask Found, 50; Fulbright Fels, 56-58; Creative Arts Inst Award, Univ Calif, 70; Humanities Award, Univ Calif, 88. *Media:* Oil, Mixed Media. *Mailing Add:* 802 Carosam Rd Santa Barbara CA 93109

CAVE, LEONARD EDWARD
SCULPTOR, EDUCATOR
b Columbia, SC, Oct 22, 1944. *Study:* Furman Univ, BA; Univ Md, College Park, with Kenneth Campbell, MA. *Work:* Herbert F Johnson Mus Art, Cornell Univ, Ithaca, NY; George Meany Ctr for Labor Studies, Silver Spring, Md; Columbia Mus of Art, SC; Nations Bank. *Comn:* Official Seal, Dept of State, Washington, DC; Ascendancy, Oliver Carr Co, Washington DC, 87. *Exhib:* Solo show, Brody's Gallery, Washington, DC, 89, 91 & 93 & Ctr Creative Studies, Detroit, Mich, 91; Outdoor Sculpture, Kouros Gallery, NY & Ridgefield, Conn, 93-94; marble sculpture, Virginia Miller Galleries, Coral Gables, Fla, 94. *Teaching:* Asst prof art, Georgetown Univ, 70-77. *Awards:* Chaim Gross Sculptor's Exhib First Prize, Nat Young Sculptors Guild, 69; Alaska State Arts Coun Grant. *Bibliog:* William Bradley (auth), Art, Magic Impulse & Control, Prentice-Hall, 73; Dona Z Meilach (auth), Woodworking, The New Wave, Crown Publ Inc, 81. *Mem:* Sculptors Guild; Washington Sculptors Group (pres, 83-86). *Media:* Stone; Wood. *Dealer:* Annie Gawlak 1750 Lamont NW Washington DC 20010; Artspace/Virginia Miller Galleries 169 Madeira Ave Coral Gables FL 33134. *Mailing Add:* care of Palm Avenue Gallery 45 South Palm Ave Sarasota FL 34236

CAWLEY, JOAN MAE
ART DEALER, PUBLISHER
b McKeesport, Pa. *Study:* Okla State Univ, BA, 48; Univ Okla, teaching cert, 52; Univ Mich, MA, 57. *Pos:* Docent prog chmn, Wichita Art Mus, 63-68; pres, Wichita Art Mus, 68-69. *Mem:* Scottsdale Gallery Asn. *Specialty:* Art of the southwestern United States; posterprints; Publ of posters and prints, 1 location in Scottsdale, Ariz, 1 location in Tempe, Ariz. *Mailing Add:* Joan Cawley Gallery Ltd 7135 E Main St Scottsdale AZ 85251

CAWOOD, GARY KENNETH
PHOTOGRAPHER - GELATIN SILVER
b Chattanooga, Tenn, Jan 17, 47. *Study:* Auburn Univ, BArchit, 70; E Tenn State Univ, MFA, 76. *Work:* Baltimore Mus Art, Md; Nat Mus Am Art; Libr Cong; New Orleans Mus Art; Corcoran Gallery Art, Washington. *Exhib:* Solo exhibs, Hass Gallery, Bloomsburg Univ, Pa, 2000, Stevenson Union Gallery, So Ore Univ, Ashland, 2000, Gallery A4, Southern Ill Univ, 2001, Historic Ark Mus, Little Rock, 2002, A4 Gallery, Boston College of Art, Mass, 2002, New Harmony Gallery Contemp Art, Ind, 2002, Aquinas College, 2004, Gallery 1401, Univ of Arts, Philadelphia, 2005; two-person exhibs, Ascherman Gallery, Cleveland, Ohio, 82 & Project Art Ctr, Cambridge, Mass, 82, New Acumony Gallery, Indiana, 02; Recent Acquisitions, Corcoran Gallery Art, Washington; Current Works, Soc Contemp Photog, Kansas City, 87-89; Obstacles (auth, catalog), traveling exhib; Photog in the Minimalist Era, Iowa State Univ, Ames; Three Photographs, Munson-Williams Proctor Inst, Utica, NY, 98; invitational exhib Art and Science, York Arts, York, Pa, 2000, Brooks Perspective, Memphis Brooks Mus, 2001, Cazenovia College, Cazenovia, NY, 2006; plus many others. *Pos:* head photog area, Dept Art, Univ Ark, Little Rock, Ark. *Teaching:* Adj prof photog, Univ Del, 75-76; assoc prof, La Tech Univ, 76-85; assoc prof, Univ Ark, Little Rock, 85-96, prof, 96-; fac, Sch Photog Studies, Prague, Czech Repub, 95-98. *Awards:* Visual Artist Fel Grant, Nat Endowment Arts, 82; Visual Artist Fel Grant, Arkansas Arts Coun, 90; Visual Artist Fel Grant, Mid-Am Arts Alliance, 96. *Bibliog:* Mark Power (auth), The Spiritual Landscape, Photo Rev, winter, 89; John Cunnally (auth), Take Only Pictures, Leave Only Footprints, No 12, 9/90; John Dorsey (auth), Photos Show Us What We Miss If We Can't See - Or Don't, Maryland Life, Baltimore Sun; Michal Janta (auth), U(S) Porny Realisimns Garyho Cawooda, Cesky Tydenik, 8/5/96; Roy Proctor (auth), Cawoods' still pictures will put your mind in motion, Richmond Times Dispatch, Va, 11/11/99; Pam Dillon (auth), The everyday and odd shown in new light, Dayton Dailey News, Ohio, 1/16/2000; Edawrd J Sozanski (auth), Life After Dark, Philadelphia Inquirer, 2/8/05. *Mem:* Phi Kappa Phi; Soc for Photog Edu. *Media:* Photog. *Interests:* Furniture design. *Publ:* Contribr, Southern Eye, Southern Mind: A Photographic Inquiry, Memphis Acad Arts, 81; American Infra Red Survey, Photo Survey Press, 82; Century of Vision, SW Louisiana Univ Mus Art; Scenes Unseen, White Rose Press; The Watchmans Room (monograph), Whatelseitis, 02. *Dealer:* Gallery 26 Little Rock Ark. *Mailing Add:* Dept Art Univ Ark Little Rock AR 72204

CAZORT, MIMI
CURATOR, HISTORIAN
b Little Rock, Ark. *Study:* Washington Univ, St Louis, Mo, BFA, 53; Univ Mich, Ann Arbor, MA, 61, PhD, 70. *Pos:* Cur prints & drawings, Nat Gallery Can, Ottawa, 67-97; mem, Int Adv Comt, Keepers Pub Graphic Collections. *Teaching:* Adj prof art hist, Carleton Univ, Ottawa, 77-. *Awards:* Osler Fel, Hist Med, 88. *Mem:* Print Coun Am. *Res:* European drawings, concentration in North Italian, late eighteenth century; anatomical illustration, 1400-1900. *Publ:* Coauth (with Catherine Johnston), Bolognese Drawings in North American Collections, Ottawa, 80; auth, Bella Pittura: The Art of the Gandolfi, Ottawa, 94; The Ingenious Machine of Nature: Four Centuries of Art and Anatomy, Ottawa, 96. *Mailing Add:* 91 Concord N Ottawa ON K1S 0Y7 Canada

CECIL, CHARLES HARKLESS
PAINTER
b Kansas City, Mo, May 12, 45. *Study:* Haverford Col, Pa, BA(with honors), 67; Yale Univ Grad Sch, 67-69; with RH Ives Gammell, Boston, Mass, 69-71 & Richard F Lack, Minneapolis, Minn, 72-73. *Work:* Haverford Col Libr, Pa; West Bend Gallery Fine Arts, Wis; House, Children's Hosp, Philadelphia, Pa; Am Philos Soc, Philadelphia, Pa; Thomas Jefferson Univ, Philadelphia, Pa. *Comn:* Portrait, Dr Gilbert White, past pres, Haverford Col, 72; portraits comn by Count & Countess Carl Klingspor, (Sweden), 88; portrait, Henry S Cecil MD, President Emer, Children's Seashore House, Children's Hosp, Philadelphia, Pa, 90; portrait, Jonathan Evans Rhoads, MD, past pres, Am Philos Soc, Philadelphia, Pa, 92; portrait, Francis E Rosato, MD, Samuel D Gross prof surgery & chmn Dept Surgery, Thomas Jefferson Univ, Philadelphia, Pa. *Exhib:* Twin City Art Exhib, Minneapolis, Minn, 75; 154th & 155th Ann, Nat Acad Design, NY, 79 & 80; one-man show, Univ Club Chicago, Ill, 80; Boston Painters of the Light, Dallas, Tex, 84; Am Realism Abroad, Colby Col, Waterville, Maine, Butler Inst Am Art, Youngstown, Ohio & Wichita Art Mus, Kans, 90; 10th Anniversary Exhib, Charles H Cecil Studios, London, 2001; Florence and Beyond, Cohasset, Mass, 2003. *Teaching:* Dir, Charles H Cecil Studios, Borgo San Frediano, Florence, Italy, currently; instr, Brit Inst, Florence, Italy, currently; co-dir, Studio Cecil-Graves, Florence, Italy, formerly; instr, Villa Schifanoia Grad Sch Fine Arts, Florence, Italy, formerly. *Awards:* Julius T Hallgarten First Prize for Oil Painting, 79, Benjamin Altman Second Prize Landscape, 80, Nat Acad Design; Grant for Painting, John F & Ann Lee Stacey Found, 80; three ann grants, Elizabeth Greenshields Found, Montreal; RHI Gammell Found Grant, 86-2001. *Media:* Oil. *Publ:* Coauth, Realism in Revolution, The Art of the Boston Sch, 86. *Mailing Add:* Borgo Sun Frediano 68 Florence 50124 Italy

CECULA, MAREK
SCULPTOR
b Poland, Apr 23, 44. *Study:* prof develop through various apprenticeships, Poland, Israel, Brazil, 68-74. *Work:* Smithsonian Nat Mus Art, Washington, DC; Los Angeles Co Mus Art, Calif; Mus Fine Art, Boston, Mass; Cooper Hewitt Mus, NY; Mus Hertkruithuis, S'Hertegenbosch, The Neth; Carnegie Mus of Art, Pittsburgh, Pa; Mus of Fine Arts, Boston, Mass. *Comn:* Art Project 79, Yeroca Art Ctr, Brazil, 97. *Exhib:* Functional Glamor, Mus Het Kruithius, S'Hercogenbosch, The Neth, 87; Contemp Porcelain, Hudson River Mus, Yonkers, NY, 90; 29th Ceramic Nat, Everson Mus Art, Syracuse, NY, 93; More Then One, Am Craft Mus, NY, 93; 96 Ceramic Competition, San Angelo Mus Fine Art, Tex, 96; Hygiene, Ctr for Contemp Art, Warsaw, Poland, 99; Defining Moments of Contemp Ceramics, Los Angeles Co Mus Art, Calif, 99; Ceramic Nat 2000, Everson Mus Art, Syracuse, NY, 2000; solo exhibs, Galeri Ram, Oslo, Norway, 2000; Interface, Garth Clark Gallery, NY, 2002; Am Craft Mus, NY, 2001; Univ Art Gallery, Sonoma State Univ, Rohert Park, Calif, 2002; Dolphin, Kansas City, Mo, 2002; John Michael Kohler Arts Ctr, Sheboygan, Wis, 2003. *Collection Arranged:* Scatology Series, Garth Clark Gallery, 94; Hygiene, Modernism San Francisco, 97; Hygiene-Marek Cecula, Ctr for Contemp Art, 99. *Teaching:* Dept coord ceramics Parsons Sch Design, NY, 84-. *Awards:* Fel Award, NY Found for the Arts, 95; Fel Award, Luis Comfort Tiffany Found, 99; Residency Grant, European Ceramic Work Ctr, 99; Grand Arts, Project Grant, Kansas City, Mo, 2001. *Bibliog:* Lydia Tugendraych (auth), Vision of Sensual Sterility, Ceramic Art and Perception, 94; John Perreault (auth), Marek Cecula Fundamental Desire, Am Ceramic, 95; Jozef Mrorzek (auth), Marek Cecula, Centrum Sztokchspolczesney, 99. *Media:* Clay. *Publ:* auth, Marek Cecula Fundamental Desires, Am Ceramics, Jun 95, Hygiene, Kerqmik Mag, Mar 97, Marek Cucula at Garth Clark, Art in Am., Dec 97, Marek Cucula at Modernism, World Sculpture News, Nov 98, Material & Attitude Marek Cecula Violations, Ceramic Art & Perception, 2000. *Dealer:* Garth Clark Gallery 24 W 57th St New York NY 10019. *Mailing Add:* 107 Sullivan St New York NY 10012

CEDERQUIST, JOHN
FURNITURE MAKER, SCULPTOR
b Altadena, Calif, Aug 7, 46. *Study:* Calif State Univ, Long Beach, BA, 69, MA, 71. *Work:* Renwick Gallery, Smithsonian Inst & MCI Corp World Hq, Washington, DC; Am Craft Mus, NY; Oakland Mus, Calif; Art Inst Chicago; Craft & Folkart Mus, Los Angeles. *Exhib:* Solo exhibs, Parnham House, Dorset, Eng, 78, Laguna Beach Mus Art, Calif, 83, Craft & Folk Art Mus (with catalog), Los Angeles, Calif, 83, Franklin Parrasch Gallery (catalog publ), NY, 91, 93, 95 & 97; Material Evidence: Master Craftsmen Explore Colorcore, Renwick Gallery, Smithsonian Inst, 84; New Am Furniture: The Second Generation of Studio Furnituremakers (traveling, with catalog), Mus Fine Arts, Boston, 89-90; Circa 1990, Franklin Parrasch Gallery, 90; The Endowed Chair (with catalog), 92; California Dreaming, Franklin Parrasch Gallery, NY, 92; Material Vision: Image & Object (with catalog), Tarble Arts Ctr, Eastern Ill Univ, 93; Transcending Boundaries, 53rd St YWCA, NY, 93. *Teaching:* Instr art, Saddleback Community Col, 76-. *Awards:* Nat Endowment Arts Fel, 75, 77 & 86. *Bibliog:* Franklin Parrasch (auth), John Cederquist, Franklin Parrasch Gallery, New York, 91, Karen Sandra Smith (auth), The Art of Illusion, Art of Calif, 11/92, Arthur C Danto, (auth), Master of illusion, House and Garden Mag, 12/96. *Mailing Add:* 34971 Calle Fortuna Capistrano Beach CA 92624

CEGLIA, VINCENT
PAINTER
b Braintree, Mass, Mar 11, 23. *Study:* Brooklyn Mus Sch of Art; Pratt Inst. *Work:* Pa State Univ; Educ Testing Serv, Princeton, NJ; Am Can Co, Princeton, NJ; Sun Oil Co, Philadelphia; Am Int Insurance Co, Milan, Italy; Am Embassy, Oslo, Norway. *Comn:* Wall mural, Town of Legro, Lake Orta, Italy. *Exhib:* Philadelphia Mus Art, 71; Philadelphia Art Alliance, 71 & 75; Butler Inst of Am Art, Youngstown, Ohio, 72; Am Watercolor Soc, 75, 77 & 86; 154th Ann Exhib, Nat Acad Design, NY, 79 & 85; Colletiva Arti Figurative, Rome, Italy, 81; retrospective exhib (1950-1985), Trenton City Mus & Mercer Col, 86; James A Michener Art Mus, 89-90 & 2002; solo exhibs, Woodmere Art Mus, Philadelphia, 91, 2000 & Galleria d'Arte Liberty, Angerra, Lake Maggiore, Italy, 2000; Trenton City Mus, NJ, 2000; Philips Mill Ann Fall Exhib, Solebury, Pa, 2002; and others. *Teaching:* Asst prof visual arts, Trenton Jr Col, 60-68; assoc prof visual arts, Mercer Co Community Col, West Windsor, NJ, 68-86 & prof eme, currently; dir, painting wkshps in Gargonza, Tuscany, summers 75-78 & Lake Maggiore, 79-86, Italy. *Awards:* First Patron Prize, Phillips Mill Juried Exhib, 68, 70, 75, 76, 83, 87 & 96; Dana Prize, 79, Zimmerman Prize, 81 & Best of Show, 83, Philadelphia Watercolor Club Exhib; Schweitzer Prize, Nat Acad Design, 94. *Bibliog:* Watercolor 92, Am Artist Mag, 92; The Watercolor World's 1994 Winners, The Artist, 94. *Mem:* Am Watercolor Soc; Philadelphia Watercolor Soc (Crest Medal, 97 & 98); Salmagundi Club, NY; Philadelphia Sketch Club; and others. *Media:* Watercolor, Acrylic. *Publ:* Illusr, Vaughn Associates Architects, Vaughn Assoc, 69; auth & illusr, Watercolor page, Am Artist Mag, 77 & 92; and others. *Dealer:* Coryell Gallery 9 1/2 Coryell St Lambertville NJ. *Mailing Add:* 34 Swan St Lambertville NJ 08530

CELANT, GERMANO
CURATOR
Study: Genoa Univ, Genoa, Italy, PhD(hist mod art). *Collection Arranged:* Mapplethorpe vs Rodin, Kunsthalle Dusseldorf, Ger, 92; Robert Mapplethorpe, Louisianne Mus, Denmark, 92; Louise Nevelson, Palazzo Esposizioni, Rome, 93; Keith Haring, Rivoli, Turin, Italy, 93 & Mass Inst Tech, Boston, 94; Rebecca Horn (with Nancy Spector), Solomon R Guggenheim Mus, New York, 93; Osmosis: Haim Steinbach & Ettorre Spalletti (with Nancy Spector), Solomon R Guggenheim Mus, New York, 93; The Italian Metamorphosis, 1943-1968, Solomon R Guggenheim Mus, New York, 94 & traveling to Milan & Wolfsburg; Claes Oldenburg, Nat Gallery Art, Washington, DC, 95 & traveling to Los Angeles, New York, Bonn & London; Jim

Dine, Guggenheim Mus, New York, 99; Museo corres Venice, 99; Giorgio Arwapei, Guggenheim Mus, New York, 2000; plus numerous others. *Pos:* Sr cur, contemp art, Solomon R Guggenheim Mus, NY, 89-; contrib ed, Artforum & Interview. *Publ:* Mario Merz, Electra, Milan-New York, 89; Ugo Mulas, Motta, Rizzoli Int, Milan-New York, 89; Fausto Melotti, Electra, Milan-Venice, 90; Remo Salvadori, Fabbri, Milan, 91; Ettore Spalletti, IVAM, Valencia, 92; Jannis Kounellis, Fabbri, Milan, 92; Robert Mapplethorpe, Electa, Milan, 9; Claes Oldenburg/Coosje van Bruggen, Milan, Skira, 99; Mariko Mori: Dream Temple, Milan, Fondazione Prada, 99; Walter De Maria, 1999 Milano 2000, Milan, Fondazione Prada, 99; Marc Quinn, Milan, Fondazione Prada, 2000; Giorgio Armani, New York, 2000; plus others. *Mailing Add:* c/o Solomon R Guggenheim Mus 575 Broadway New York NY 10012

CELENTANO, FRANCIS MICHAEL
PAINTER, EDUCATOR
b New York, NY, May 25, 28. *Study:* NY Univ Inst Fine Arts, MA, 57; Acad Fine Arts, Rome, Italy, Fulbright Fel, 57-58. *Work:* Mus Mod Art, NY; Albright-Knox Art Gallery, Buffalo; Fed Reserve Bank, San Francisco; Seattle Art Mus, Wash; Rose Art Gallery, Brandeis Univ, Waltham, Mass. *Comn:* Painting, Hwy Bldg, Wash State Hwy Dept, 70; mural, Port of Seattle, Seattle-Tacoma Airport, 71; mural, Seattle City Light, 74; mural, Lincoln Mutual Savings Bank, Seattle, 79. *Exhib:* The Responsive Eye, Mus Mod Art, NY, 65; Kinetic & Optical Art Today, 65 & Plus by Minus: Today's Half Century, 68, Albright-Knox Art Gallery; Whitney Ann, Whitney Mus Am Art, 67; Pacific Cities, Auckland City Art Gallery, New Zealand, 71; 1st Western States Bienniel Exhib, Nat Gallery Fine Arts, Washington, DC, 79; retrospective, Portland Ctr Visual Arts, Ore, 86. *Teaching:* Prof art, Univ Wash, 66-97; prof emer, Univ Wash, 97-. *Awards:* Int Artist's Sem Award, Fairleigh Dickinson Univ, 65; Nat Endow Arts Fel, 90; Western States Arts Fedn. *Bibliog:* Kingsbury (auth), Art, Francis Celentano, 1/70, Seattle Mag, 1/70; Kangas (auth), Francis Celentano, transcendence & negation, exhib catalog, 81; catalog, Francis Celentano, Selected Paintings, 1954-995, Safeco Exhib Catalogue, Seattle, 3/2-4/20, 1995. *Media:* Acrylic on Plastic, Acrylic on Canvas. *Dealer:* Laura Russo Gallery, Portland, Ore; Bryan Ohno Gallery, Seattle. *Mailing Add:* 1399 NE 106th St Seattle WA 98125-7538

CELIS, PEREZ
PAINTER, SCULPTOR
b Buenos Aires, Argentina, Jan 15, 39. *Study:* Fine Arts Sch, Art Master, 64; Orden del Sol, Peru, Comendador, 85. *Work:* Mus Modern Art, NY; Museo de Arte Moderno, Buenos Aires; Mus Contemp Latin & Am Art, Washington; Museo de Bellas Artes, Caracas, Venezuala; Museo de la Universidad de Rio Piedras, Puerto Rico. *Comn:* Mural Ezeyza Airport, 74, Buenos Aires Airport, 79, Argentinian Airlines, Paris, 82, Government; sculpture, government, Rosario, 88; Mercedes Bens, Japan; Mitsui, Tokyo. *Exhib:* V Bienal of Art, Museo Bellas Artes, Tokyo, Japan, 66; Biennal of Jeunes Artists, Museo Gran Palais, Paris, 71; Perez Celis, Museo de Bellas Artes, Caracas, 79, Nat Ctr Arts, Ottawa, Canada, 86; Perez Celis Antes y Ahora, Centro Cult, Buenos Aires, 85; Contemp Abstract, Kiserlet Mus, Budapest, 85; Perez Celis, Galeria de Art Moderno, San Jose, Costa Rica, 88; Mira Show, 7 USA Mus, 88. *Teaching:* Instr, Abstract Art, Parson Sch-Altos de Chovon, 80; lectr, Abstract Art, Mus Visual Arts, Detroit, Mus Contemp Art, Washington, Ann Arbor Univ, Art Col, Mich & Ctr Visual Arts, Ottawa, Can. *Awards:* III Award, Salon Nacional, 70; Alba Award, Salon Nacional, Museo Edwardo Sivori, 72; Prix du Jury, Contemp Art, Grand Prixde Monaco, 80. *Bibliog:* Gaston Dielh (auth), Perez Celis, Goglianone Publ, 83; F Ted Castle-Peter Frank (coauths), Perez Celis, Shapolvsky Publ, 88; IBM (auth), Perez Celis, Adin visual-video, 90. *Media:* Oil, Mixed Media. *Mailing Add:* c/o Anita Shapolsky Galleries 152 E 65th St New York NY 10021

CELLI, PAUL
PAINTER, EDUCATOR
b Boston, Mass, May 8, 35. *Study:* Mass Col Art, BFA, 60; RI Sch Design, MFA, 62. *Work:* Bank of Boston. *Exhib:* Providence Art Festival, RI, 61-69; New Eng Contemp Artists Asn, Boston, 63; Berkshire Mus, Pittsfield, Mass, 66; one-man shows, Bennett Col, Millbrook, NY, 67, Carpenter Ctr, Harvard Univ, 76, Mass Col Art, 2001. *Teaching:* Prof 4D theory, Mass Col Art, 70-. *Bibliog:* Horn (auth), Contemporary Graphic Artists, Vol 1, 85. *Media:* Oil, Acrylic. *Publ:* Auth, Ink Comics, Number 3: An Art Comic Book, Nat Distribution. *Mailing Add:* PO Box 391 Needham MA 02474

CELMINS, VIJA
PAINTER
b Riga, Latvia, Oct 25, 1939. *Study:* John Herron Inst, Indpls, BFA, 62, Univ Calif, Los Angeles, MFA, 65. *Work:* Art Inst of Chicago; Baltimore Mus of Art; Carnegie Inst Mus of Art, Pittsburgh; Met Mus Art, NY; Whitney Mus Am Art, NY; San Francisco Mus of Modern Art; Nat Gallery of Art, Washington; and many others. *Exhib:* Retrospective, Whitney Mus Am Art, NY, 93; Sheldon Mem Art Gallery & Sculpture Garden, Univ Nebr, Lincoln; Whitney Biennial, Whitney Mus Am Art, NY, 97, 99-2000; one-person shows, McKee Gallery, NY, 96, Inst of Contemp Art, London, 96-97, Museo Nacional de Arte Reina Sofia, Madrid, 96-97, Kunstmuseum Winterthur, Switz, 96-97, Mus fur Moderne Kunst, Frankfurt, Ger, 96-97, Anthony d'Offay Gallery, London, 99, Cirrus Gallery, Los Angeles, 2000-2001, McKee Gallery, NY, 2001, Mus of Contemp Art, Basel, Switz, 2001; Fondation Cartier pour l'art contemporain, Paris, 97-98; Mus of Fine Arts, Boston, 98; Whitechapel Art Gallery, London, 98, 2001; Aspen Art Mus, Colo, 99; Exhbn Ctr of Centro Cult de Belem, Portugal, 98; La Fundacio Joan Miro, Barcelona, Spain, 98; Montreal Mus of Fine Arts, Can, 99-2000; The Hirshhorn Mus and Sculpture Garden, Smithsonian Instn, Washington, 99-2000; James Cohan Gallery, NY, 2000; San Francisco Mus of Modern Art, 2000-2001; Pori Art Mus, Finland, 2001-; and many others. *Teaching:* Univ Calif, Irvine; Calif Inst of the Arts, Valencia, 76-77; Cooper Union, New York, 84; Yale Grad Sch, 87. *Awards:* MacArthur Found Fel, 97; Coutts Contemp Art Found Award, 2000-2001. *Bibliog:* Dennis Cooper (auth), rev, Artforum, 2/89; Gerard Haggery (auth), article, Art Am Mag, 3/89; Rev, Art Am Mag, 93; Dave Hickey (auth), Vija Celmins, Artforum, Dec 99; Keith Patrick (auth), Formal Dress, Contemp Visual Arts, issue 26, 2000; Karl Erickson & Andrew Falkowski (auth), Style Representation, New Art Examiner, Mar 2000; Vija Celmins, Art on Paper, Nov-Dec 2000; Toba Khedoori/Vija Celmins, Mus fur Gegenwartkunst, Apr 3, 2001. *Mem:* Nat Acad. *Publ:* Contemporary Women Artists, Laurie Collier Hillstrom and Kevin Hillstrom (ed), St. James Press, 99; Examining Pictures: Exhibiting Paintings, Cornerhouse Pubs, Manchester, UK, 99; Art at Work: 40 Years of the Chase Manhattan Collection, New York, 2000; Painting as a Language: Material, Technique, Form and Content, Jean Robertson and Craig McDaniel, Harcourt Col Pub, New York, 2000; Treasure from the Art Institute of Chicago, Hudson Hills Press, New York, 2000; Celebrating Modern Art: Highlights of the Anderson Collection, San Francisco Mus of Modern Art, Mondadori Printing, Italy, 2000. *Mailing Add:* McKee Gallery 745 Fifth Ave New York NY 10151

CEMBALEST, ROBIN
EDITOR
Study: Yale Univ, BA. *Pos:* Ed Asst, Art Forum; staff, Forward Newspaper; exec ed, ARTnews Mag, NYC, 88-94, 99-; contrib writer, New York Times, Wall Street Journal. *Awards:* Recipient, National Headliner Award, Siluruians Award for Arts/Cultural Reporting. *Mailing Add:* ARTnews Magazine 48 W 38th St New York NY 10018-0042

CENCI, SILVANA
SCULPTOR
b Florence, Italy, Aug 4, 26. *Study:* Manzoni Inst, Italy; Acad Fine Art, Italy, 49; Acad Grand Chaumiere, Paris, 49-50. *Work:* Uffizi Gallery Mod Art & Numero Gallery, Florence, Italy; Bundy Art Mus, Waitsfield, Vt; Metrop Boston Transit Authority; Merchants Bank, Manchester, NH; and others. *Comn:* Monumental sculpture, Pavilion Archit, New Haven, Conn, 61; two lions explosively formed, Graham Jr Col, Boston, 63; baptistry doors, Carter & Woodruff Archit, Keene, NH, 65; fountains, Western Front Restaurant, Cambridge, Mass, 67 & Sasha Montagu, Brookline, 69. *Exhib:* New Eng Art Today, Northeastern Univ, 62; Bristol Art Mus, RI, 67; New Eng Sculptors Asn, Boston City Hall, 69 & Contemp Art-Italian Heritage, 75; ten-year retrospective, Bristol Art Mus, 77; and others. *Pos:* Artist-in-residence, City of Boston, 71-73. *Teaching:* Instr art, Brookline Art Ctr, 66-69. *Awards:* Gold Hammer Award, Medea, Italy, 58; First Honorable Mention, Design in Transit, Inst Contemp Art, 71; Blanche Coleman Award, 74; World Culture Prize, Salsomaggiore Terme, Italy. *Bibliog:* Al Kaliman (auth), Odyssey Implosion/Explosion, WBZ-TV, 64; John A Hughes (auth), Explosion in Northwood, NH Profiles, 64; Richard Hadley (auth), The state we are in, Channel 11 TV, NJ, 75. *Mem:* NH Art Asn; Artists Equity Asn. *Mailing Add:* 42 Legrow Rd Gray ME 04039-9538

CENSOR, THERESE
SCULPTOR
b Antwerp, Belgium; US citizen. *Study:* Mus Mod Art, New York; New Sch Social Studies; Art Life Studio, New York. *Work:* Smithsonian Inst, Washington, DC; Mus Art, La Jolla, Calif; Bergman Collection, Israel Mus, Jerusalem; Butler Inst, Youngstown, Ohio. *Exhib:* Small Sculpture from USA, Int Arts Prog; US Comt Int Asn of Art, Helsinki, Finland; Princeton Univ, NJ; New Eng Shows, Silvermine Guild of Artists, New Canaan, Conn. *Mem:* Audubon Artists; Nat Asn Women Artists; NY Soc Women Artists; Artists Equity of NY; Hudson River Contemp Artists. *Media:* Welded Metal, Stone. *Mailing Add:* 525 E 86 St New York NY 10028-7512

CERNUSCHI, ALBERTO C
DEALER, CRITIC
Study: Univ Milan, Univ Lausanne, Kensington Univ, Calif, PhD. *Pos:* Founder, Cernuschi & Caravan de France Galleries, Paris, France, Tokyo & New York; trustee, Cernuschi Mus, Paris. *Teaching:* Lectr mod art, Ecole du Louvre, Mus Cernuschi. *Mem:* Appraisers Asn Am; Art Hist Asn. *Specialty:* Modern art. *Publ:* Constructive Manifesto; Theory of Autodeism; Life and Voyages of Century; A Tale of Two Centuries Etc; contribr, McMillan's Dictionary Art. *Mailing Add:* 500 E 83rd St New York NY 10028-7208

CERVENKA, BARBARA
EDUCATOR, PAINTER
b Cleveland, Sept 28, 39. *Study:* Siena Heights Col, Studio Angelico, Adrian, Mich, 57-64, BA, 64; Wayne State Univ, Detroit, 67-69; Univ Mich, Ann Arbor, 69-71, MFA, 71. *Work:* Alumni Mem Mus & Univ Mich, Ann Arbor; Eastern Mich Univ, Ypsilanti; Jesse Besser Mus, Alpina, Mich; Clarke Col, Dubuque, Iowa; Dennos Mus, Traverse City, Mich; and others. *Exhib:* Watercolor USA, Springfield, Mo, 69, 73 & 75; Mid-Mich Show, Midland, 71; Am Watercolor Soc Show, NY, 73; Mich Watercolor Soc Show, 89, 90, 91 & 97; Toledo Area Artists Show, Ohio; Exus and Orixas-Opening Doors to Brazil, Art Exchg Gallery and Mus, Detroit. *Collection Arranged:* Cuadros of Pamplovia Atta: Textile Pictures by Women of Peru - traveling exhib, 89-96; O Pelourinho Popular Art from the Historic Heart of Brazil - traveling exhib; Ayacucho - Tradition and Crisis in Peruvian Popular Art - traveling exhib, 98-. *Teaching:* Instr drawing & watercolor, Siena Heights Col, 71-78; adminr, Adrian Dominican Sisters, Mich, 78-82; asst dean, Univ Mich Sch Art, 84-94; assoc prof art dept, Siena Heights Univ, Adrian, Mich, chair, 97-2000. *Awards:* First Prize, Toledo Area Artists Show, 73; First Award, Detroit Inst Arts, Mich Watercolor Soc, 97; Award, Mich Watercolor Exhib, 2000. *Mem:* Mich Watercolor Soc; Col Art Asn; Watercolor USA Hon Soc. *Media:* Watercolor. *Res:* Popular Art of Central and South America, especially of Peru and Brazil; Co-director of con-vida popular Arts of Am. *Mailing Add:* 307 Maple Ridge Ann Arbor MI 48103

CETIN, ANTON
PAINTER, PRINTMAKER
b Bojana, Croatia; Sept 18, 1936; Can citizen. *Study:* Sch Applied Arts, dipl, 59; Acad Fine Arts, Masters dipl, 64. *Work:* Ontario Collection, Toronto, Can; Univ Mich, Dearborn; Princeton Univ; Salon XX, Bogota, Colombia; Oberhausmuseum, Passau, Germany; and others. *Exhib:* One-man shows, Atelier E Noel, Paris, France, 1968, Isetan Gallery, Tokyo, Japan, 74, Galerie Le Creuset, Brussels, Belgium, 74, Art Gallery Hamilton, Can, 78, Heritage Gallery, Los Angeles, 79, Galeria Juan Martin, Mex, 79, Salon XX, Bogota, Columbia, 81, Mannheimer Abendakademie, Ger, 81 & Gilman Galleries, Chicago, 83; Mus del Chopo, Mex, 93; Salas Nac de Cultura, Palais de Glace, Buenos Aires, 94; Mus Mcpl de Arte J C Castagnino, Mar del Plata, Argetina, 95; Mus & Gallery Ctr (with catalog), Zagreb, Croatia, 96; Mus Bjelovar, Croatia, 97; City Mus, Varazdin, Croatia, 98; Art Gallery, Split, Croatia, 98; Gallery Fine Arts & Waldinger Gallery, Osijek, Croatia, 2000, Hermann Hesse Mus, Calw, Ger, 2000, Mercedes Zentrum, Stuttgart, Ger, 2000-2001, Gallery Anton Cetín, Cazma, Croatia, 2001, State Archives in Rijeka & Gallery Kortil, Rijeka, Croatia, 2002, Multicultural Art Gallery, Halifax, Can, 2003, Mus Mimara (with monograph), Zagreb, Croatia, 2004 & 05, CsI, Vienna, Austria, 2004-05 & Mus Vukovar, Croatia, 2005; and many others. *Awards:* Artist of the Year, Toronto, Can, 86; The Order of Croatian Danica (Morning Star), highest honor in the field of Cult in Croatia, 95; The Order of Croatian Interlace, highest honor in the field of development and high repute of Croatia, 95; Mare Nostrum Croaticum, for outstanding contribution to culture and historic values, 2001. *Bibliog:* Stuart Reid, Rudolf Wesner, Josip Depolo (auths), shows at City Mus (catalog), Varazdin & Art Galllery (catalog), Split, Croatia, 98; Art Gallery and Waldinger Gallery (catalog), Osijek, Croatia, 2000; Celins Life and Work, MIL Media, Zagreb, Croatia, 2002-05; Branka Hlevnjak (auth), Celin, Life and Work, Zagreb, Croatia, 2004; and others. *Media:* Oil, Acrylic; Etching, Aquatint, Lithography; Pastel. *Mailing Add:* 916-5 Greystone Walk Dr Toronto ON M1K 5J5 Canada

CHABOT, AURORE (MARTHA)
SCULPTOR
b Nashua, NH, July 30, 49. *Study:* Pratt Inst, BFA, 71; Univ Colo, Boulder, MFA, 81. *Work:* Taipei Fine Arts Mus; Tucson Mus Art; Pushkin Mus, Moscow; Mus Decorative Arts, Riga, Latvia; Mint Mus. *Comn:* Tile mural, Univ Ariz Marley Bldg, 97; tile mural, Skyharbor Airport, Phoenix, 2001; Tile Mural, Vortex of Time & Space, Sky Harbor Internat'l Airport, Phoenix, AZ, 2002. *Exhib:* Solo exhibs, Mary H Dana Women Artist Series, Mabel Douglass Libr, Douglass Col/Rutgers Univ, 90, Univ of Ariz Art Mus, 90, Univ Nebr, Lincoln Gallery Art, Dept Art & Art Hist, 94, Manchester Craftsmen Guild, Pittsburgh, Pa, 94; Featured Artist Sandy Carson Gal, Sofa, Chicago, 97; Substance: Materials, Process and Vision in Clay, Tex Woman's Univ, Denton, 98; San Angelo Mus Fine Arts, Tex, 99; Paper Pots II & III, John Elder Gallery, New York City, 99 & 2001; The World Community of Ceramists, The Herndon Gallery, Antioch Col, 99; Freewheeling, Five Ceramic Masters from the Univ Colo, Dairy Ctr for Arts, Boulder, 2000; Clay Out West, Laramic Community Col, Cheyenne, Wy, 2000; Clay Odyssey Civic Ctr, Helena, MT; Ceramics Cult Connections, State Mus, Suny, Plattsburgh; Clay on the Wall, Gallery 128, New York City, 2001; Clay West, 2003, Inter Mountain Invitational, Nora Eccles Harrison Mus of Art UT State Univ, Logan UT; Clay, Making Connections Ceramic Triennial Roswell Mus & Art Ctr, Roswell, NMex, 2003; Glaze Storm Artists, Univ of Indianapolis, IN, Tile; Matter and Motif, Baltimore Clayworks, Baltimore, MD, 2004. *Awards:* Artist-in-Residence Award, Va Ctr Creative Arts, 94; Individual Artist Fel Grant, Western Arts Fedn, 95 & Tucson Pima Arts Coun, 97; Small Res Grant, Univ Ariz, Tucson, 96; Univ of Ariz, Col of Fine Arts Incentive Grant, 2001; Sabbatical Leave Award, Univ AZ, 2002; Fel of the Council Award, Nat Council on Educ for the Ceramic Arts, 2005. *Bibliog:* Joyce Tognini (auth), A Soviet Reunion, 6-7, 2-3/92; Richard Zakin (auth), Electric Kiln Ceramics (cover Jacket), 93; Charlotte Speight (auth), Hands in Clay, Photog Portfolio, 4th edit, 99; The Craft and Art of Clay, by Susan Peterson, 99; Ceramics Ways of Creation by Richard Zakin, 99; Making Ceramic Sculpture by Raul Acero, 2000; Contemporary Ceramics by Susan Peterson, 2000; Ceramic Mastering the Craft by Richard Zakin, 2001; Allan Chasanoff Ceramic Collection Catalogue, Mint Mus, 2000; Di Morgenthal & SJE Tourtilloh, Ceramics Art and Perception Cellular Synchronicity, Issue 48, 2002; 21st Century Ceramics (catalog), The Penland Book of Ceramic; Master Classes in ceramic techniques, 2003; 21st C. Ceramics in the US & Canada.Review by Robert Silberman pp45-85; Electric Kiln Ceramic, 3rd ed, 2004, Richard Zakin (auth), American Craft, Mag, April/May, 2004; The Sculpture Reference by Arthur Williams, Tile Making & Installing, by Angelica Pozo, 2005. *Mem:* Col Art Asn; Am Craft Coun; Nat Coun Educ Ceramic Arts (dir at large, bd dir, 99-2001, juror emerging artists, 2000-01); Nat Council of Educ for the Ceramic Arts (pub dir, Nat bd dir, 2001-04). *Media:* Ceramics, Mixed. *Publ:* Auth, articles, Nat Coun Educ Ceramic Arts J, 84, 85, 87, 89, 91-92, 92-93 & 95; Editor, NCECA Journals, 2001, & 2003. *Dealer:* Sandi Carson Gallery. *Mailing Add:* 823 S Second Ave Tucson AZ 85701

CHADWICK, WHITNEY
CRITIC, HISTORIAN
b Niagara Falls, NY. *Study:* Middlebury Col, BA, 65; Pa State Univ, MA, 68, PhD, 75. *Hon Degrees:* Dr Honoris Causa, Univ Gothenburg, Sweden, 2003. *Teaching:* Assoc prof art hist, Mass Inst Technol, Cambridge, Mass, 72-78; prof art hist, San Francisco State Univ, 78-; vis prof, Art Hist, Williams Col, 2003. *Awards:* Fel, Mary Ingraham Bunting Inst, 92; Vis Res Scholar, Univ Ulster, Belfast, 2002; Clark Fel, Sterling and Francis Clark Art Inst, 2002. *Mem:* Col Art Asn. *Res:* Surrealism; contemporary art; feminism. *Publ:* Woman, Art and Soc, Thames and Hudson, 90; coed (with Isabella de Courtivron), Significant Others: Creativity & Intimate Partnership, Thames & Hudson, 93; auth, Leonora Carrington: La Realidad de la imaginacion, Ediciones ERA, Mexico City, 94; Mirror Images: Women, Surrealism and Self Representation, MIT, 98; The Art of Romaine Brooks, Univ Calif, 2000; coed (with Tirza Latimer), The Modern Woman Revisited: Paris Between the Wars, Rutgers Univ Press, 2003. *Mailing Add:* 871 DeHaro St San Francisco CA 94107-2705

CHAET, BERNARD ROBERT
PAINTER, EDUCATOR
b Boston, Mass, Mar 7, 24. *Study:* Boston Mus Sch, with Karl Zerbe, 42-45; Tufts Univ, BS, 49; Md Inst, Col Art, Hon Dr Fine Arts, 85. *Hon Degrees:* Doc Fine Arts, Maryland Inst Art, 85. *Work:* Fogg Art Mus, Harvard Univ; Univ Calif Art Gallery, Los Angeles; Brooklyn Mus, NY; Addison Gallery Am Art, Andover, Mass; RI Sch Design Mus, Providence; and others. *Exhib:* Univ Ill Biennial Am Painting, 51, 53 & 60; Golden Yrs of Am Drawing 1900-56, Brooklyn Mus, 56; Recent Drawings USA, Mus Mod Art, NY, 56; Corcoran Biennial Am Painting, Washington, DC, 62; Pa Acad Fine Arts Ann, Philadelphia, 62; and 37 one-man exhibs. *Collection Arranged:* Baltimore Mus Art, Baltimore, MD; Metropolitan Mus Art, New York, NY; Am Art Mus, Washington, DC; Smithsonian Am Art Mus. *Awards:* Grant, Nat Found Humanities Arts, 66-67; Hassam & Speicher Fund Purchase Award, Am Acad & Inst Arts & Lett, 81; Distinguished Teaching Art Award, Col Art Asn, 86; Benjamin Altman Prize, Edwin Palmer Mem Prize, Henry Ward Ranger Purchase Prize, Nat Acad Design, 97, 99, 2001, 2003. *Bibliog:* Margaret Mathews (auth), article, Am Artist, 9/82; Janice C Oresman (auth), article, Arts Mag, 11/82. *Mem:* Nat Acad Design (assoc, 92, acad, 94). *Media:* Oil, watercolor, drawing. *Publ:* Auth preface, 20th Century Drawing (catalog), Yale Art Gallery, 55; Artists at Work, Webb, 61; The Art of Drawing, Holt, 71, 77, & 83; An Artist's Notebook: Techniques and Materials, Holt, 79. *Dealer:* Alpha Gallery 121 Newbury St Boston MA 02116; David Findlay Jr, New York, NY. *Mailing Add:* 141 Cold Spring St New Haven CT 06511

CHAFETZ, SIDNEY
PRINTMAKER, EDUCATOR
b Providence, RI, Mar 27, 1922. *Study:* RI Sch Design, BFA, 47; Acad Julian, Paris, 47-48; L'Ecole Am Beaux Arts, Fontainebleau, 47; with Fernand Leger, Paris, 48 & SW Hayter, Atelier 17, 50-51. *Work:* Libr Cong, Washington; Morgan Libr, NY; Dahlem-Staalische Mus; Philadelphia Mus Art; British Mus; Mus Art, NY. *Comn:* Dedication etching, Ohio State Univ Col Law, 64; Hawthorne Keepsake, Ohio State Univ, 64; Robert Lowell Poster, Int Poetry Forum, Pittsburgh, Pa, 67; F Scott Fitzgerald Keepsake, Fitzgerald Newsletter, Ohio State Univ, 68; Poor Richards Almanacks Original Woodblock Portrait, Imprint Soc, Barre, Mass, 70; Ozick Epodes, Logan Elm Press, Ohio State Univ. *Exhib:* Ten Yrs of Am Prints, 1947-57, Brooklyn Mus, NY, 57; Young Am Printmakers, Mus Mod Art, NY, 58-59; 1st Biennial Int Gravure Sur Bois, Banska Bystrica, Czech, 70; 2nd Triennial Int Graphica Contemp, Capri, Italy, 72; 30-Yr Retrospective, Antioch Col & throughout Ohio, 78-79; Satire & Homage, Chafetz Graphics, 88; Perpetrators, exhib of original prints circulating in US & Europe, 92-. *Teaching:* Emer prof art, Ohio State Univ, 48-82, prof emer, 82-; vis prof art, Univ Ariz, spring 65, Univ Wis-Madison, summer 67 & Univ Denver, summer 71 & 79; Fulbright Sr lectr, Univ Belgrade, Yugoslavia, 80. *Awards:* Fulbright Fel, 50-51; Governors Award, Ohio, 91; Outstanding Printmaker, Mid Am Print Coun, 98. *Mem:* Soc Am Graphic Artists; Am Color Print Soc; Am Asn Univ Prof; Nat Acad Design (assoc, 81, acad, 91). *Media:* Woodcut, Intaglio. *Publ:* Auth, Chafetz Graphics: Satire and Homage, The Ohio State Univ Pres, 88. *Dealer:* Susan Teller Gallery 568 Broadway New York NY 10012. *Mailing Add:* Ohio State Univ Dept Art Columbus OH 43210

CHAGOYA, ENRIQUE
PRINTMAKER
b Mexico City, Mex, 53. *Study:* San Francisco Art Inst, BFA, 84; Univ Calif, Berkeley, MA, 86, MFA, 87. *Work:* San Francisco Mus Mod Art, Fine Arts Mus San Francisco & Mexican Mus, San Francisco, Calif; Centro Cultural/Arte Contemporaneo, Mexico City, Mex; Mex Mus, San Francisco; Whitney Mus of Am Art, NY; Nat Mus of Am Art, Smithsonian Inst, Washington, DC. *Exhib:* Two-person exhib, San Jose State Univ, Calif, 89, Mex Mus, San Francisco, 93, Wash State, Pullman, 94, Fisher Gallery, Los Angeles, 95-96 & Zolla/Liberman Gallery Inc, Chicago, 99, Track 16 Gallery, Santa Monica, Calif, 2000, 01; Muertos de Gusto Day of the Dead: Memory & Ritual, Mex Fine Arts Ctr Mus, Chicago, Ill, 93; Art Is, Art Mus Santa Cruz Co, Calif, 94; solo shows, Galeria de la Raza, San Francisco, Calif, 96, Smith-Anderson Gallery, Palo Alto, Calif, 96, Stanford Univ, 97, Univ Colo, Boulder, 97, David Beitzel Gallery, NY, 97, Gallery Paule Anglim, San Francisco, 97 & 2000, San Marco Gallery, Dominican Col, San Rafael, Calif, 98, George Adams Gallery, New York City, 2000, Track 16 Gallery, Santa Monica, Calif, 2000, Nev Mus of Art, Reno, 2000, Forum for Contemp Art, St Louis, 2001, Univ of Tex, El Paso, 2001 & Lisa Sette Gallery, Scottsdale, Ariz, 2001; Mex Mus, San Francisco, 97; Art From Around the Bay, San Francisco Mus Mod Art, Calif, 98; Mouse: An Am Icon, Alt Mus, NY, 98; Images of Resilience, Nat Steinbeck Ctr, Salinas, Calif, 99; Homage to the San Francisco Art Inst, Hackett Freedman Gallery, San Francisco, 99; Other Narratives, Contemp Arts Mus, Houston, 99; Dia de los Muertos, Museo del Barrio, New York City, 99; Valle de la Luna: Works be Mexican, Latino and Chicano Artists, Sonoma Valley Mus of Art, Calif, 2000; Looking towards the future, SFMOMA Rental Gallery, San Francisco, 2000; Tempus Fugit: Time Flies, Nelson-Atkins Mus of Art, Kansas City, Mo, 2000; Open Ends, Mus of Modern Art, New York City, 2000; Comic Relief, Rena Bransten Gallery, San Francisco, 2001; and many others. *Teaching:* Mem faculty to assoc prof printmaking, Stanford Univ, Calif. *Awards:* Eisner Prize, Univ Calif, Berkeley, 86; Western States Arts Fedn Regional Fel, Santa Fe, NMex, 92; Nat Endowment Arts, 93; Biennial Competition, Louis Comfort Tiffany Found, 97; Am Acad Arts & Letters, 97. *Bibliog:* John Rapko (auth), Enrique Chagoya at gallery Paule Anglim, ArtWeek, 12/2000; David Bonette (auth), Chagoya's wondrous clash of cultures, San Francisco Examiner, 10/27/2000; Jack Fisher (auth), Artist's work crosses the ages as well as

cultures, San Jose Mercury News, 10/15/2000. *Publ:* Illusr, Mr Sugar Came to Town, Children's Book Press, 89; auth, Friendly Cannibals, Artspace Bks, 97; coauth, Codes Espangliensis: From Columbus to the Border Partol, City Lights Press, 2000. *Dealer:* Gallery Paule Anglim 14 Geary St San Francisco CA. *Mailing Add:* 59 Arroyo Wa San Francisco CA 94127-1805

CHAIKLIN, AMY
PAINTER
b Newark, NJ, Oct 4, 55. *Study:* New York Studio Sch, Paris, France, studied with Elaine de Kooning, 76; Wash Univ, Sch Fine Arts, BFA, 77. *Work:* Mus Mod Art, Libr, NY; Franklin Furnace Arch, NY; Visual Studies Workshop Arch, Rochester, NY; Art Circolo, E V, Munich, Ger; Sergei Diaghilev Art Ctr, Marble Palace, St Petersburg, Russ. *Comn:* Eyes on You (mural), Fashion Moda, Bronx, NY, 83; Media Girls (mural), Eyes and Ears Found, San Francisco, Calif, 84; Girl with Pet Rat (mural), Limbo Gallery, NY, 84; Berlin Beauties (mural), comn by Maria Makkaroni, Berlin, Ger, 84. *Exhib:* Purgatory & Paradise, Metrop Mus Art Libr, NY, 86; solo exhibs, New Paintings, Galerie Schrill, Berlin, Ger, 90, Sergei Diaghilev Art Ctr, Marble Palace, St Petersburg, Russia, 92, Hamburg Messe, Hamburg, 93 & Galerie im Saalbau (with catalog) Berlin, Ger, 95; Fine Arts Mus Long Island, Hempstead, NY, 91; Erotische Kunst, Galerie Schwarz, Griefswald, 93 & 10 Jahre Druckhof Schwarz, 94; Nature Morte, NY Studio Sch Gallery, 93; Art Multiple, Dusseldorf, 94; Erotik Mit Dem Weiblichen Auge, Galerie Art of Fee, Hamburg, Ger, 95; Am Art, Galierie Mainz, Berlin, Ger, 96; Sex Sells, Galerie Boudoir, Berlin, Ger, 96; Gallery Onetwentyeight Invitational, NY, 98. *Awards:* Artist-in-Residence, Cite Int des Arts, Wash Univ, 88; Artist-in-Residence, Stiftung Starke, Berlin, Ger, 92-94; Artist Fel, Women Studio Workshop, Rosendale, NY, 98. *Bibliog:* Tina Fleisher (auth), Radio SFBIII, Red Zeitpunkle, Berlin, 9/8/95; Katrin Betting Muller (auth), TIP, Kunst Notizen, 104, 9/21/95; Aber aha Klein (auth), MT Lokal Anzeiger Kreuzberg, Galerie Mainz, Berlin, 2/7/96. *Media:* Oil, Watercolor

CHALIF, RONNIE
SCULPTOR
b New York, NY. *Study:* Parsons Sch Design, 53; NY Univ, BS(art ed), 54. *Work:* Guild Hall Mus, East Hampton, NY; Zimmerli Art Mus, New Brunswick, NJ; World Trade Ctr, NY; Continental Tel Co, Washington; Gen Elec Int Hq, Fairfield, Conn. *Comn:* Cadillac Fairview (lobby sculpture), comm by Barbara Tamerin, Dallas, Tex, 80. *Exhib:* One-man shows, Guild Hall Mus, East Hampton, NY, 68, Fed Courthouse, NY, 84-85, Jacob J Javits Federal Bldg, NY, 86, Marymount Manhattan, Col, NY, 86, Benton Gallery, Southampton, 87-89 & Arlene Bujese Gallery, E Hampton, 96; New Directions in Sculpture, Heckscher Mus, Huntington, NY, 77; On the Leading Edge, GE Inaugural Exhib, Fairfield Conn, 83; US Home Headquarters, Houston, Tex, 1990. *Teaching:* Sculpture, 74-89. *Awards:* Award in Sculpture & Painting, Guild Hall Mus, 68 & 83; B G Epstein Award, Nat Asn Women Artists, 91, Freelander Mem Award, 92. *Bibliog:* Rose C S Slivka (auth), From the studio, East Hampton Star, 3/11/93, 7/25/96 & 7/30/98, 4/8/99; Aspects of Abstraction, July 27, 1997; Sheridan Sansegundo (auth), At the Galleries, 7/30/98 & 9/8/99; Rose Sliuka (auth), From the Studio, 9/23/99; Robert Long (auth) One Foot Over the Line, 10/07/2004; Ronnie Chalif at Gayle Wilson Marion (auth) Marion Wolberg Weiss. *Mem:* NY Soc Women Artists; Nat Asn Women Artists; Artist Craftsmen NY (bd mem, formerly); Women in the Arts Found; Women Caucus for Art; Pres, Neuropathy Asn. *Media:* Stone. *Specialty:* Contemporary Long Island Artists of East End. *Interests:* Opera, Medical Research. *Publ:* auth, Excersizing with Neuropathy. *Dealer:* Arlene Bujese Gallery Newton Lane East Hampton NY 11937. *Mailing Add:* PO Box 20 Water Mill NY 11976

CHALKE, JOHN
CERAMIST, SCULPTOR
b Gloucestershire, Eng, Sept 28, 40; Can citizen. *Study:* Bath Acad Art, Wiltshire, Eng, teacher's cert art educ, 62. *Work:* Victoria & Albert Mus; Massey Found; Alta Art Found; Can Coun Art Bank; Ceramics Monthly Collection; Burlington Art Ctr Collection; Mus Civilization, Ottawa, Can. *Exhib:* Int Exhib Ceramics, Victoria & Albert Mus, London, Eng, 72; First & Second Int Ceramic Exhib Taipei, Taiwan, 85 & 92; Second World Teriennial Exhib, Yugoslavia, 87; Nat Biennial Ceramics Trois Rivieres, Que, 88-; over 270 nat & int ceramics exhibs. *Pos:* Solo juror, 20th Fletcher Challenge Ceramics Award, NZ, 96, Sydney Meyer Int Ceramics Award, Australia, 2000. *Teaching:* Instr ceramics, var art schs in Southern Eng, 64-68; instr visual fundamentals, Univ Alta, Edmonton, 71-76; instr, Univ Calgary, Alta, 76-83; instr, Alta Col Art, Calgary, Alta, 86-92; independent studio artist, currently. *Awards:* Can Coun Grants, 72, 78, 82, 84, 93 & 97; Alta Cult Grant, 83, 88, 92 & 99; Award in Fine Craft (first recipient), Gov Gen Can, 2000. *Bibliog:* Hildegard Storr-Britz (auth), Contemporary International Ceramics, 78; Charlotte Speight (auth), Images in Clay Sculpture, 83; Robin Hopper (auth), The Ceramic Spectrum, 84; and thirty three other bks on ceramics. *Mem:* Acad Italia; Int Acad Ceramics; Alta Crafts Coun; Alta Potter's Asn. *Media:* Clay. *Res:* Original glaze research using cryolite. *Specialty:* Fine Art. *Interests:* Ceramic archaeology, early western North American history & western Canadian wildlife. *Publ:* Contribr, numerous photographs & articles, Ceramics Monthly Mag, 3/75-3/02 & 9/04; Ceramic Review, UK, 9/94, 7/95, 7/97 & 3/06; Ceramics: Art & Perception, 90-99; Studio Potter Magazine, 12/95 & 6/06. *Dealer:* Paul Kuhn Fine Arts Calgary Alb Can; Jonathon Bancroft-Snell Gallery London Ont Can. *Mailing Add:* 429 12th St NW Calgary AB T2N 1Y9 Canada

CHALLIS, RICHARD BRACEBRIDGE
DEALER, LECTURER
b London, Eng, Aug 12, 20; US Citizen. *Study:* King's Col Sch, London, 34-37; Chelsea Col, 38-39. *Collection Arranged:* Roger Kuntz Retrospective, Laguna Beach Mus Art, Calif, 77; Moderator, The Ruth Stoever Fleming Collection, Newport Beach, 85; Publ, Newport-Mesa Unified Sch Dist. *Pos:* Founder & dir, Challis Galleries, 50-82; art dir, Los Angeles Home Show, 65-67; consult, Esther Wells Collection, 1983-. *Teaching:* Lectr, Marketing of Fine Art, Orange Co Dept Educ & Univ Calif Irvine. *Mem:* Laguna Beach Festival Arts; Art Inst S Calif; life mem Laguna Art Mus, Orange Co Mus Art. *Media:* Contemporary Paintings & Sculpture. *Specialty:* 20th century paintings and sculpture. *Mailing Add:* 1390 S Coast Hwy Laguna Beach CA 92651

CHALMERS, KIM
EDUCATOR, ADMINISTRATOR
b New York, NY. *Study:* Univ Southwestern La, BFA, 71; Fla State Univ, MFA, 73. *Comn:* mosaic, Western Ky Univ. *Exhib:* one-man show, Nothing Up My Sleeve, Univ North Fla, Jacksonville, 74, Endless Maze and Sarcophagal Robes, Francis Marion Col, SC, 78, Simple Explanations, Florence Mus, SC, 86, My Blue Haven, Univ Western Carolina, Cullowhee, NC, 88, 2000, Museo Int de Electrografia, Cuenca, Spain, 92, Guild of Instruction, Daito Bunka Univ, Higashimatsuyama, Japan, 95, Sailors Garden, Downtown Glass Gallery, Hartsville, SC, 97, Labyrinth, Ivan Wilson Fine Arts Center, Bowling Green, Ky, 2000, They Seemed as Giants, Centennial Art Ctr, Tenn, 2002, Quamgmire, Lindsey Wilson Collection, Ky, 2003, Hazmat Janice Mason Art Mus, Cadiz, Ky, 2004, Selection, Tenn Tech, 2004; Faculty Art Exhibition, Western Ky Univ, Bowling Green, 2000; Ownesboro Art Giuld 35th Juried Competition, Ky, 2000; Firstar Juried Competition, Bowling Green, Ky, 2000; New Works, Houchens Gallery, Bowling Green, 2002; Kinderkite, Franklin, Ky, 2002; They Seem as Giants, Centennial Art Ctr, Nashville, Tenn, 2002; Ky Nat Juried Competition, Murray, 2003; and others. *Pos:* founder & dir, Art Dept Gallery, 73-80, New Gallery, 80-83, Bell Art Gallery, 83-91 & Downtown Glass Gallery, 96-98. *Teaching:* prof, Coker Col, 73-99, dept chmn, 85-99; prof, head dept art, Western Ky Univ, 99-. *Awards:* Fulbright Fel, 80; Coker Prof Devel Grant, London, Eng, & Paris, 88; Southeast Arts Fedn Regional Fel, Nat Endowment Arts, 94; Fac Devel Grant, Studio Sabbatical, 95; Al Smith Individual Fel, Ky Arts Coun, 2006. *Mem:* CAA; SECAC. *Media:* Painting, all media

CHAMBEAUX, JANE
PAINTER, SCULPTOR
b France, July 31, 43; Fr & US citizen. *Study:* Univ Montpellier, France, MA, 62; Alger Algeria Art Hist & Conservateur, MA, 64; M, Beaux Arts Conservateus. *Work:* Vatican, Roma, Italy; Sorbonne, Paris, France; Mus de Beaux Arts d'UNET, Bordeaux, France; S Miami Art Ctr & City Hall; Elysee Pres Palace, Paris, France; Sapporo Mus; Sorbonne-Sapporo Beer Mus. *Comn:* Paintings, Miami Metrop Mus, 86-87; paintings, Luxembourg Mus, Paris, France, 89; paintings, Sorbonne, Paris, 90-93; paintings comn by Presidency, Paris, 91; paintings, Mus d'UNET, Bordeaux, 93-94 & 98. *Exhib:* Jane Chambeaux, Miami Metrop Mus, 86-87 & Found Napoleon, Paris, 95; Les Three Amen'ques a Paris, Mus du Luxembourg, Paris, 89; Beam of Light, Paris City Hall, 90-91; L'aura de Createurs, Chapelle de la Sorbonne, Paris, 90-92; Les 3 Ameriques a Paris. *Collection Arranged:* Grand Prix & Biennial of Miami, 88, 90 & 92; Grand Prix of South Miami (with catalog), 89, 91 & 93; Grand Prix of Japan, 97; Grand Prix of Sapporo, 97; Grand Prix Mondial, UNET, France, 98; Sapporo Beer, Biennial of Sapporo. *Pos:* Art critic, Inst Int Miami, 90-98; cur, Int Art Plus, 87-98; ed, Elite de Beaux Arts, Inst Int, 90-97; dir/conservateur, Musee de Beaux Arts, France. *Teaching:* dir Internat Art Inst of Miami. *Awards:* Many awards from various cities in France, Japan & SFla, 87-97. *Bibliog:* Exhibit for Revolution (catalog), 89, Chapelle de la Sorbonne, 90 & Flamboyance, 91, Minister Cult, France. *Mem:* Int Art Plus-France (pres, 86-98); Int Art Connection-France (pres, 87-98); Art Connection Plus-France (pres, 87-98). *Media:* Sand; Plastic. *Res:* influence of melatonin hormone in the creation of famous artists' creations. *Collection:* Vatican-Louvre Min of Culture, Elysee Palace, City Hall of Paris, Luxembourg Mus, Sorbonne Mus, others. *Publ:* Coauth, catalogs, Musee de Beaux Arts d'UNET, 86-98; ed, Art Passion, 98; auth articles to various mags in field. *Dealer:* Art Inst of Miami

CHAMBERLAIN, ANN
PHOTOGRAPHER
Study: Smith Col, Mass, BA, 73; San Francisco State, MA(creative arts), 81, MFA(concept design), 87; Fulbright Scholar, Univ Am, Puebla, Mex, 87-88. *Work:* Calif Supreme Court Foyer, 98-99; Pleasanton Val Vista Park, Calif, 2000-01; Ocean Ave Art Master Plan, San Francisco, 01. *Comn:* San Francisco Pub Libr (in collab with Ann Hamilton) & San Francisco Arts Comn, Gen Garage; bus shelters, Nat Endowment Arts Interarts. *Exhib:* 50 Yrs of Photog; Fulbright 50th Anniversary, Calif State Univ, Long Beach, 96; Stain, Gallery 16, San Francisco, 96; Collaborations: Genetic Fingerprint, San Francisco Art Inst, 96; Vital Signs, San Francisco Arts Comn Gallery, 97; When Borders Migrate, San Francisco Art Comn Gallery, 98; Osaka Global Cult Show, Japan, 2000; Hospital GCC, Paris, 01. *Teaching:* Artist in schools, Col Arts & Crafts, San Francisco, 79-81; coordr Artists in Schs Prog Exploratorium, 82-88; photogr-in-residence, Alaska State Coun Arts, Huslia, 84; artist-in-residence, visual studies workshop, 88; prog dir, Headlands Ctr Arts, 89-93; vis lectr, San Francisco State Univ, 90-91, 96 & 97, Calif Col Arts & Crafts, 92, 94 & 97, San Francisco Art Inst, 93-96 & 98 & Mills Col, 96-99; fac San Francisco Arts Inst, 99-01. *Awards:* Col Arts & Crafts Artist in Community Grant for Garden Proj, 94-95; Visual Arts Fel Photog, Nat Endowment Arts, 94-95; Creative Work Fund for garden design, Univ Calif, San Francisco, Mt Zion Cancer Ctr, 95-97. *Dealer:* Gallery 16 1616 16th St San Francisco CA 94103. *Mailing Add:* 250 30th St San Francisco CA 94117

CHAMBERLAIN, CHARLES
CERAMIST, EDUCATOR
b Brockton, Mass. *Study:* Mass Col Art, BFA; Col Ceramics, Alfred Univ, MFA. *Work:* Smithsonian Inst, Washington, DC; Mass Col Art, Boston; Col Ceramics, Alfred Univ, NY. *Comn:* 14 Stations of the Cross, St Paul's Episcopal Ch, Greenville, NC. *Exhib:* Artist, Craftsmen, Inst Art, Jacksonville, Fla, 73; one-man retrospective,

NC Mus Art, Raleigh, 73; 27th Ceramics Nat, Everson Mus, Syracuse, NY, 74; Craft Multiples, Smithsonian Inst, Washington, DC, 75; North Carolina Clay, Raleigh, 92. *Teaching:* Instr ceramics, Worcester Art Ctr, Mass, 65 & Univ NH, 66-67; prof ceramics, East Carolina Univ, Greenville, NC, 67-2003, chmn design dept, 82-85, prof art; retired. *Awards:* Best in Show, Mass Asn Craftsmen, 65; Merit Award, Emerging Craftsmen of New Eng, 65; Hon Mention, Piedmont Craftsmen Ann, 71. *Mem:* Piedmont Craftsmen; Am Crafts Coun; Nat Coun Educ Ceramic Art. *Media:* Clay, Mixed Media. *Mailing Add:* 2307 E Third St Greenville NC 27858-1606

CHAMBERLAIN, DAVID (ALLEN)
SCULPTOR, PAINTER
b Canton, Ohio, Aug 11, 49. *Study:* Princeton Univ, with Joe Brown & James Seawright, BA(archit design), 71, Teaching Art Inst; Colo Col, 72; Univ Pa, with Robert Engman & Neil Welliver, MFA(sculpture), 77. *Work:* Nat Mus Am Art, Washington; Delaware Mus Art, Wilmington; Detroit Inst Art, Mich; British Art Mus, London, Eng; Asian Art Mus, San Francisco; and many others. *Comn:* Cantata, Horne Libr, Babson Col, Wellesley, Mass, 81; TORUS, Stratus Computer Inc, Marlboro, Mass, 86; A Une Passante, M C Wallace Libr, Wheaton Col, Norton, Mass, 91; Ballette, Southworth Libr, Canton Col, NY, 91; Eroica, Morgridge Auditorium, Univ Wis, Madison, 92. *Exhib:* Pucker/Safrai Gallery, Boston, Mass, 79-97; solo exhibs, Everson Mus Art, Syracuse, NY, 83, 85, Lyme Acad Fine Arts, Old Lyme, Conn, 85 & 86, Gibson Gallery, SUNY at Potsdam, NY, 87, Pucker/Safrai Gallery, Boston, Mass, 81, 84 & 88 & MacLaren/Markowitz Gallery, Boulder, Colo, 91; solo retrospectives, The Art Complex Mus, Duxbury, Mass, 88, McKissick Mus Art, Columbia, SC, 90 & Muskegon Mus Art, Mich, 96; Renjeau Gallery, Concord, Mass, 89-98; Aspen Grove Galleries, Aspen, Colo; Muse A Muse Gallery, Tokyo; and many others. *Pos:* Fel/panelist, Conf World Affairs, Boulder, Colo, 89-98; vis artist collabr, US Indochina Arts Proj, Repub Vietnam, 95; vis artist, Johannesberg, South Africa, 97. *Teaching:* Co-dir & artist-in-residence, Arts Col House Prog, Univ Pa, 75-77; assoc prof, Univ SC, Columbia, 90-91; adj prof, Rivier Col, Nashua, Ntl, 91-94. *Awards:* Red Ribbon Award, Am Film Festival, 82; SC Arts Comn Individual Artist Grant, 91; KBK Found Grant, 91. *Bibliog:* Search for Perfection (film), FIS/Pucker Safrai, 82; Melodic Form: The Sculpture of David Chamberlain, David Godine, 90; David Chamberlain: Artistry in Motion (film), SC-ETV/PBS, 92. *Mem:* New Eng Sculptors Asn; Col Art Asn. *Media:* Bronze, Oil Monotypes. *Publ:* Haven't We Met (album), 91, Released (album), Cahoots Quartet, 93. *Mailing Add:* c/o Pucker-Safrai Gallery 171 Newbury St Boston MA 02116

CHAMBERLAIN, JOHN ANGUS
SCULPTOR
b Rochester, Ind, Apr 16, 1927. *Study:* Art Inst Chicago, 51-52; Univ Ill; Black Mountain Col, 55-56. *Work:* Los Angeles Co Mus Art; Guggenheim Mus, Mus Mod Art, Whitney Mus Am Art, NY; Dallas Mus Fine Arts; Albright-Knox Art Gallery; and many others. *Comn:* Detroit Deliquescence (sculpture), US Gen Serv Admin for Fed Plaza, 79; Coloured gates of Louisville: the inevitable return of the indefatigable Dr Fahey (wall relief), Ky Ctr Performing Arts, 88; Der Turm Von Clytie (sculpture), Friedrichstadt Passegen Atrium, Berlin, Ger, 94. *Exhib:* Guggenheim Mus, 74; Whitney Mus Am Art, 69, 80 & 90; Va Mus Fine Arts, Richmond; Mus Mod Art, NY; Corcoran Gallery Art, Washington, 71; Smithsonian Inst, Washington, 75; Metrop Mus Art, 78; Philadelphia Mus Art, Pa; Albright-Knox Art Gallery, Buffalo, NY; Butler Inst Am Art, 83; Mus Contemp Art, Chicago, 90; Pace Wildenstein, 94-96 & 98; Beat Cult & the New Am: 1950-1965, Whitney Mus Am Art, 96; Solomon R Guggenheim Mus, 96 & 98; retrospective, Mus of Contemp Art, Los Angeles, 86, Staatlich Kunsthalle Baden-Baden, Ger & Staatliche Kunstsammlungen Dresden, Ger, 91; John Chamberlain: Sculpture 1988 2001, Waddington Galleries, London, 2002; Pace Wildenstein, NY City, 98, 2004; Dan Flavin & John Chamberlain: Sculptures, Gagosian Gallery Madison, NY City, 2003; Crossroads of Am Sculpture, Indianapolis Mus Art, 2000, Lenore and Burton Gold Collection of 20th-Century Art, High Mus Art, Atlanta, 2001, Art Downtown NY Painting and Sculpture, Wall St Rising, 2002, Design is not Art, AAM Aspen Art Mus, Colo, 2005, Bilderwechsel III - Amerikanische Malerei, Mus Frieder Burda, Baden-Baden, Ger, 2006. *Pos:* Artist-in-Residence, Skowhegan Sch Painting & Sculpture, Maine, 85; art dept, Am Acad & Inst Arts & Letts. *Teaching:* Master-in-residence, Santa Fe Inst Art, NMex, 94. *Awards:* Creative Arts Awards, Brandeis Univ, 84; Lifetime Achievement Awards, Brandeis Univ, 84, Int Sculpture Ctr, Washington, DC, 93 & Nat Arts Club, NY, 96; Skowhegan Medal, Skowhegan Sch Painting & Sculpture, Maine, 93; Artists Award, Nat Arts Club, 97; Distinction in Sculpture Honor, SculptureCenter, NY, 99. *Bibliog:* Duncan Smith (auth), In the Heart of the Tinman: An Essay on John Chamberlain, Art Forum, Jan 84; William Wilson (auth), The Galleries: La Cienega Area, Los Angeles Times, Mar 15, 85; Douglas C McGill (auth), Art People, NY Times, Aug 1, 86; David Lee (auth), article The Times of London, London, 4/24/87; Edward S Sozanski (auth), Work of four prominent sculptors, The Philadelphia Enquirer, 3/17/88; Jack Flam (auth), Making the gallery rounds, Wall St Journal, 3/22/89; Peter Clothier, Living with Art, Artnews, 5/90; and many others. *Mem:* Int Sculpture Ctr; Pub Art Fund Inc; Artists Rights Soc; Am Acad and Inst Arts and Letters. *Publ:* Conversations With Myself, Pace Ed. *Mailing Add:* c/o Pace Gallery 32 E 57th St New York NY 10022

CHAMBERLIN, SCOTT
SCULPTOR, CERAMIST
b Orange, Calif, Oct 14, 48. *Study:* Calif State Univ, San Francisco, BA(art), 73; NY State Col Ceramics, Alfred Univ, MFA(ceramic art), 76. *Work:* Dordrecht Mus, Holland; Ceramic Collections, Alfred Univ, NY; Denver Art Mus, Colo; Everson Mus, Syracuse, NY; Het Kruithuis Mus, Holland. *Exhib:* Clayworks Invitational, Carmel Col Art Gallery, Oxford, Eng, 78; North California Clay Routes: Sculpture Now, San Francisco Mus Mod Art, 79; solo exhibs, Dordrecht Mus Art, 80 & Exposorium Vriej Universiteit, Amsterdam, The Neth, 81; New Works in Clay, Hadler-Rodriguez Gallery, NY, 83; California Art 1984, Laguna Beach Mus Art, Calif, 84; San Francisco Art Acad, 85; Craft Today: Poetry of the Physical, Am Craft Mus, NY & Denver Art Mus, 86; Ceramics Now: 27th Nat Exhib, Everson Mus Art, Syracuse, NY, 87; A Different Garden: Dorothy Weiss Gallery, San Francisco, 87; Arvada Ctr Arts & Humanities, Denver, Colo, 88. *Teaching:* Lectr ceramics, Camberwell Sch Art, London, Eng, 76, 78 & 83; asst prof fine art ceramics, Univ Colo, Boulder, 85-. *Awards:* Soc Encouragement Art Award, San Francisco Mus Mod Art, 79; Artist Fel, Colo Coun Arts & Humanities, 86; Nat Endowment Arts Individual Artists Fel Grant, 86 & 90. *Bibliog:* C R Grant (auth), Keramishce objecten van Scoitch, Mus News, Holland, 80; Joanne Burstein (auth), Review of tall sculptural pots, Images & Issues Mag, 81; Wendy Dubin (auth), rev, Am Ceramics, 6/84; M F Parges (auth), review, Am Ceramics, winter 87. *Media:* Clay; Terra Cotta. *Publ:* Auth, Source & stimulus, Ceramic Rev Mag, London, Eng, 79. *Dealer:* Dorothy Weiss Gallery 254 Sutter St San Francisco CA 94108; Rule Contemp & Modern Denver CO

CHAMBERS, BRUCE WILLIAM
HISTORIAN, CONSULTANT
b Cincinnati, Ohio, June 22, 41. *Study:* Yale Univ, BA, 63; Univ Rochester, MA, 70; Univ Pa, PhD, 74. *Pos:* Asst dir curatorial serv, Mem Art Gallery, Univ Rochester, 76-, actg dir, 79-80; dir, Univ Iowa Mus Art, 80-81; assoc, Berry-Hill Galleries, NY, 82-; dean grad studies, Fashion Inst Technol, 94-2000. *Teaching:* Asst prof art hist, Emory Univ, Atlanta, 70-76; adj prof, Univ Rochester, NY, 76-80. *Mem:* Col Art Asn; NY State Coun Arts. *Res:* Nineteenth and twentieth century American art and iconography. *Publ:* Auth, Pythagorean puzzle of Patrick Lyon, Art Bull, 6/76; Thomas Cole and the ruined tower, Currier Gallery Bull, 11/83; Robert Henri's Street Scene with Snow, Yale Art Gallery Bull, winter 86; Old Money: American Trompe l'Deil Images of Currency, Berry-Hill, 88; Willard L Metcliff: A Partial History of the Renaissance; Spanierman Gallery, 03. *Mailing Add:* 191 Glen Pkwy Hamden CT 06517-1512

CHAMBERS, KAREN
CRITIC, CURATOR
b Madison, Ind, Sept 28, 48. *Study:* Wittenberg Univ, 66-70, BFA, 70; Case-Western Reserve Univ, study with Wolfgang Stechow, 73; Univ Cincinnati, MA, 78. *Pos:* Cur asst, Dayton Art Inst, Ohio, 70-73; asst registr, Cincinnati Art Mus, 75; asst cur, Contemp Arts Ctr, Cincinnati, 75-77; asst dir, Sperone Westwater Fischer, New York, 77-79; asst dir, Droll/Kolbert, New York, 79-80; dir, Susan Caldwell, 81; ed, New Work, 83-86. *Mem:* Col Art Asn; Am Asn Mus; Glass Art Soc; Int Asn Art Critics; Asn Independent Historians Art. *Res:* Glass arts. *Specialty:* Contemporary. *Publ:* Auth, Fragments, Tangeman Ctr Fine Arts Gallery, Univ Cincinnati, 83; Chihuly: Color Glass & form, Kodausha Int Ltd, 86; Trompe l'Oeil at Home, Rizzoli Int, 91; Glass from Ancient Craft to Contemporary Art 1962-1992 & Beyond, Morris Mus, 92; Tell Me a Story: Narrative Art in Clay and Glass, Taft Mus, 93

CHAMBERS, PARK A, JR
EDUCATOR, PHOTOGRAPHER
b Wheeling, WVa, Oct 29, 42. *Study:* Kent State Univ, BFA, 68, MFA, 70. *Work:* The Chicago-Tokyo Bank & Shatkin Trading Company, Chicago, Ill; Johnson & Johnson, Elmhurst, Ill; Kent State Univ, Ohio. *Comn:* Wrist Sculpture, comn by Fred Gordon, Skokie, Ill, 73; Installation/Performance, Focus on the Arts, Highland Park, Ill, 75; Body Sculpture, Friedman Leather Fashions, NY, 79-80; Baby Sculpture, SSF Inc, Chicago, Ill, 75-88. *Exhib:* 51st Ann, Cleveland Mus Art, Ohio, 69; 22nd Ann, Butler Inst Am Art, Youngstown, Ohio, 70; Form in Fiber, Deson-Zaks Gallery, Chicago, Ill, 72; Sculpture in New Media, Ill State Mus, Springfield, 73; Fiber Forms, Cincinnati Art Mus, Ohio, 78; Fiber as Art, Metrop Mus, Manila, Philippines, 80; Art for AIDS, Vopol Gallery, San Francisco, Calif, 86; Figure & Place, Artemisia Gallery, Chicago, Ill, 88; Private/Pub, Betty Rymer Gallery, 92. *Collection Arranged:* Extensions & Spirit & Image: Art of Vodoo, SAIC Gallery, 86 & 87; SAIC, Idaho State Univ, Pocatello, 87. *Pos:* Juror, Univ Chicago, Ill, 72; lectr, Mus Contemp Art, 72; artist-in-residence, Highland Park High Sch, Ill, 74-75; vis artist, Ctr Creative Studies, Detroit, Mich & Univ Ariz, Tucson, Ariz, 88. *Teaching:* Instr metal & fiber, Kent State Univ, Ohio, 68-69; instr fiber, Akron Art Inst, Ohio, 69-70; prof fiber & material studies, Chicago, Ill, 70-. *Awards:* Experiment Materials, Brunswick Corporation, Chicago, Ill, 69; Individual Grant, Nat Endowment Arts, 76; Ill Arts Coun, Independent Artist Grant, 98. *Bibliog:* Robert Glauber (auth), Skyline, Chicago, 72; E Chung & A Sandoval (coauth), The New Plastics, Vis Arts Ctr Alaska, 82; D Consentino (auth), Spirit & Image, Vol 21, No 1, African Arts, 87. *Media:* Photo Images, Embellishment. *Publ:* Contribr, Decorative Art in Modern Interiors, Studio Vista Limited, London, 71; Techniques of Rya Knotting, Van Nostrand Reinhold Co, 71; Soft Sculpture, Crown Publishers, 74; How to Create Your Own Designs, Doubleday & Co, 75; Hardcore Crafts, Ballantine Books, 76. *Mailing Add:* 2416 W Addison Chicago IL 60618

CHAMBERS, TIMOTHY JEROME
PAINTER
Study: Cape Sch Art, with Henry Hensche & Cedric B Egeli, Provincetown, Mass, 82-93; Atelier Lack, with Richard Lack, Minneapolis, 83-84; private apprenticeship with Cedric B Egeli, Annapolis, Md, 84-86 & 90; Am Acad Art, with Irving Shapiro & Mr Parks, 86; NY Acad Art (full scholar), New York, 87; studied with Sebastian Capella, 88. *Work:* Portrait Brokers Am Portrait Gallery, Birmingham, Ala & Atlanta; Portrait Inst, NY; Lyzon Gallery, Nashville. *Exhib:* Pastel Soc Am, NY, 92, 94 & 95; Portrait Inst, NY, 96. *Teaching:* Instr art, Lake Ridge, Va, 94-. *Awards:* Ann Juried Show Finalist, Pastel Soc Am, New York, 92, 94 & 95; Outstanding Achievement Award, Nat Portrait Sem, 93; Nat Portrait Competition Finalist, Portrait Inst & Am Artist Mag, 96. *Media:* Pastel, Oil

CHAMBERS, WILLIAM MCWILLIE
PAINTER, ART DEALER
b Baton Rouge, La, Aug 6, 51. *Study:* La Tech Univ, Ruston, 69-71; Kansas City Art Inst, Mo, BFA, 73; New York Studio Sch, with Leland Bell, 73-74. *Exhib:* One-man shows, Bowery Gallery, NY, 93, Peter Madero Gallery, NY, 94 & Tricia Collins-Grand Salon, NY, 95 & 97, Barbara Levy Gallery, Fire Island, NY, 98, Fischbach Gallery, NY, 2002. *Pos:* VPres, Grace Borgenicht Gallery, NY, 74-95 & co-cur, Fifty Years of Canadian Landscape Painting, 86; dir, DC Moore Gallery, NY, 95-96; pvt dealer 96-. *Bibliog:* Articles in Art in Am, 3/95 & NY Times, 3/97. *Media:* Oil, Watercolor, Woodcut. *Specialty:* 20th century American, & European Art/Milton Avery, Max Beckmann, Jean Arp, Wolf Kahr. *Publ:* Ed of numerous exhib catalogues, 74-; Jose de Rivera-Constructions, Taller Ediciones, Madrid, 80. *Dealer:* Studio visits by appointment. *Mailing Add:* 319 E 50th St New York NY 10022

CHAMBERS, WILLIAM THOMAS
PAINTER
b Chicago, Feb 12, 40. *Study:* Am Acad Art, dipl, 62; Northeastern Ill Univ, BA, 73. *Work:* Northwestern Univ, Evanston, Ill; Ill State Capitol, Springfield; Kennedy Ctr & Comsa Corp, Washington; Carol Jones Contemp Art Collection, Chicago. *Comn:* Painting, comn by arnold Weber, Northwestern Univ, Evanston, Ill, 90; painting, comn by Gov James R Thompson, Springfield, Ill, 92; painting, Carol Jones Gallery, Chicago, 93; painting, comn by Melvin Laird, Comstat Corp, Washington, 95; painting, comn by Martin Fienstein, Washington Opera Co, 96. *Awards:* Award, Portrait Inst Ann Competition, 83; Best Show, Oil Painters Am Ann Midwest Show, 95; Award, Oil Painters Am Ann Nat Competition, 96. *Mem:* Oil Painters Am. *Media:* Oil, Pastel. *Mailing Add:* 1607 S Harvard Ave Arlington Heights IL 60005

CHAN, LO-YI CHEUNG YUEN
ARCHITECT
b Canton, China, Dec 1, 1932; arrived in US 1942; naturalized 1954. *Study:* Dartmouth Col, BA, 1954; Harvard Univ, MA (archit), 1959, postgrad (Appleton fellow), 1960. *Hon Degrees:* Dartmouth Col, DArts, 2004. *Exhib:* Exhibitions at Mus Modern Art, Whitney Mus Am Art, Columbia Univ, Nat Acad Design, Boston Archit Ctr. *Pos:* Assoc IM Pei & Partners, NY City, 1960-65; architect 1965-2002; panelist Am Arbitration Asn, 1972-80; bd dirs Parks Council, NY City, 1971-85, pres, 1974; bd dirs Berkshire Taconic Community Found, 2000-; trustee Community Serv Soc, NY City, 1977-86, Henry St Settlement, 1980-99, Colby-Sawyer Col, 2003; mem NY City Art Commission, 1992-97, Berksire Sc, 1992-. *Teaching:* Adj asst prof architecture Columbia Univ, 1963-67; vis critic Col Architecture, Cornell Univ, 1965-68, Harvard Univ, 1976, 70, 80, Mass Inst Tech, 1977, Lingnan Found, 1986-, chair 1990-. *Awards:* Nat Endowment for Arts Design fellowship 75-76

CHANDLER, ANGELYN SANDERS
MUSEUM DIRECTOR
b Atlanta, Ga. *Study:* Emery Univ, BA, 57. *Pos:* Exec dir, Atlanta Int Mus Art Design, 93-. *Mailing Add:* c/o Atlanta Int Mus Art & Design 285 Peachtree Ctr Ave Atlanta GA 30303

CHANDLER, ELISABETH GORDON
SCULPTOR, INSTRUCTOR
b St Louis, Mo, June 10, 13. *Study:* Pvt study with Edmondo Quattrocchi; Art Students League; Grad, Lenox School, 1931. *Hon Degrees:* St Joseph's Col, Conn, LHD, 2001. *Work:* Bronze, Columbia Univ Sch Law; Tonkin Gulf Memorial, (bronze relief), Aircraft Carrier USS Forrestal; Princeton Univ; John Jay, First Chief Justice, (bronze), Pace Univ Sch Law; and many others. *Comn:* Albert A Michelson (bust), Hall of Fame for Great Americans, NY Univ; Adlai E Stevenson (bust), Princeton Univ; Chief Justices Harlan Fiske Stone & Charles Evans Hughes (busts), Columbia Univ; Queen Anne (statue), Queen Anne's Co Courthouse Sq, Centerville, Md, 77; St Frances Cabrini & Don Bosco, St Patrick's Cathedral, NY; and others. *Exhib:* Mattatuck Mus, Waterbury Conn, 49; Nat Acad Design Ann, NY, 50-83; Nat Sculpture Soc Ann, 53-83; Allied Artists Am, NY, 61-82; Smithsonian Inst, Wash, 63; Paul Mellon Art Ctr, Wallingford, Conn; Old State House, Hartford, Conn; Kindred Spirits, Laci de Gerenday & Elisabeth Gordon Chandler, Chauncey Stillman Gallery, 2006; and others. *Pos:* Trustee, Brookgreen Gardens, 89-97; founder & trustee, Lyme Acad Fine Arts, Old Lime, Conn, 76-, chair sculpture dept. *Teaching:* Prof sculpture, Lyme Acad Fine Arts, Old Lime, Conn. *Awards:* Thomas R Proctor Prize, Dessie Greer Prize, Nat Acad Design, 60, 79, 85; Gold Medal, Am Artists Prof League, 60, 69, 73 & 75; Silver Medal Citation, Nat Sculpture Soc, 92; named Citizen of Yr, Town of Old Lyme, Conn, 1985; Pietro Montana Mem prize Hudson Valley Art Asn, 1995; Citation, State of Conn, 1995.; Governors Arts award Conn Comn on the Arts, 2000; Gari Melchers award Artist's Fel, 2002. *Mem:* Fel Nat Sculpture Soc (rec secy, 73-76); fel Am Artists Prof League (dir, 71-73); Nat Acad Design (assoc, 73, acad, 79); Nat Sculpture Rev; Fel: Int Inst Arts and Letters, Am Artists Prof League, Nat Sculpture Soc (coun 1976-85, Tallix Foundry award 1979, John Spring Found award 1986, John Cavanaugh Mem prize 1991, Silver medal, citation 1992, Herbert Adams Mem medal for serv to Am sculpture); Conn Communs for the Arts (Governors medal 2000); Am Prof Artists League, Coun Am Artists Soc, Lyme Art Asn (pres, 1973-75); Nat Arts Club, Fed Int de la Medaille. *Media:* Bronze. *Mailing Add:* 2 Mill Pond Ln Old Lyme CT 06371

CHANDLER, MICHAEL ROBERT
PAINTER
b Denver, Colo, June 27, 50. *Study:* Univ Colo, BFA, 72. *Exhib:* Anniottanta, Galleria Comunale d'Art Moderna, Bologna, Italy, 85; Mus Art, Providence, RI, 85; Art--Made in the USA, Stadtische Mus, Regensberg, Ger, 88; Eco Art 92, Mus de Arte Mod do Rio de Janeiro, Brazil, 92; Slow Art: Painting in NY Now, PSI, NY, 92; Am Acad Exhib Painting & Sculpture, Am Acad Arts & Lett, NY. *Bibliog:* Michael Kimmelman (auth), article, NY Times, 1/10/92; Alfred Corn (auth), article, Art News, 4/92; Francesco Bonami (auth), article, Flash Art, 5-6/92. *Media:* Oil on Canvas. *Dealer:* Galerie Paal Boaderstrassi 84 P-80469 Munchen; In Khan Gallery 415 W Broadway New York NY 10012. *Mailing Add:* 83 Canal St New York NY 10002

CHANG, JASON
PAINTER
b Taiwan, 40; US Citizen. *Study:* Col New Rochelle, MA (arts). *Work:* Asia Bank, NY; Pastel Mus, Suzhow, China; N Am Pastel Artists Gallery; Golden Eagle Inst; Taipei Cultural Ctr. *Comn:* portrait, Pres Windstar Construction Co, 2003; portraits, pvt comn by Dr. Cheng, 2004. *Exhib:* solo show, Master Pastelist Jason Chang, 99 Art Ctr, Taipei, Taiwan; Allied Artists Am, Butler Inst Am Art. *Collection Arranged:* Contemp Master Pastelists Exhib, Pastel Soc Am, Taiwan, 94 & 2006. *Pos:* pres, N Am Pastel Artists Asn, 97-; vpres, Golden Eagle Inst. *Teaching:* instr, Nat Taiwan Acad Fine Art, formerly; instr, Col New Rochelle, formerly; instr, Pastel Soc Am, Sch Past & Nat Arts Club, currently. *Awards:* Am Artists Prof League Award, 2000 & 01; Pastel Soc Am, Annual Exhib Award & Master Pastelist; Award, 72nd Am Artists Prof League, 2000; Silver Medal, Audubon Artists, 2005. *Mem:* Allied Artists Am; Pastel Soc Am; N Am Pastel Artists Asn; Audubon Artists Inc. *Media:* Pastels, Oil. *Publ:* Contributor to many art publications including International Pastel Magazine, Pastel Society of America of the Butler Institute of American Art & il Pastello Conteporaneo in Europe (Europastello). *Mailing Add:* 151-56 21st Ave Flushing NY 11357

CHANNING, SUSAN ROSE
ADMINISTRATOR, PHOTOGRAPHER
b Englewood, NJ, Aug 16, 43. *Study:* Pa State Univ, BA(fine arts) & BA(gen arts & sci), 65; George Washington Univ, MFA, 67. *Work:* Polaroid Corp. *Exhib:* Cleveland Mus Art; Eighteenth Ann Corcoran Gallery of Art Area Show, Washington, 67; Camera Movements, Moore Col Art Gallery, Philadelphia, 83. *Collection Arranged:* Design in Transit, State Subway Station Competition, Inst Contemp Art, Boston, 71; Points of View, Recent Work by Area Photographers (auth, catalog), Inst Contemp Art, Boston, 72; Art of the State, Recipients & Finalists in Painting, Printmaking & Drawing, Rose Art Mus, Brandeis Univ, Waltham, Mass, 77 & 79; Photography Fellowship Recipients, Mass Inst of Technol Creative Photog Gallery, Cambridge, Mass, 78; Uncensored: An Exhibition of Previously Censored Work from the Midwest, 87; In Their Own Space, 88; Interaction: New Video Installations, 89; Urban Evidence, Contemporary Artists Reveal Cleveland, Cleveland Ctr Contemp Art & Cleveland Mus Art, 96. *Pos:* Performing arts prog coordr & art instr, Wadsworth Atheneum, Hartford, Conn, 68-70; dir urban action prog & spec proj, Inst Contemp Art, Boston, 70-72; asst dir, Mass Coun Arts & Humanities, Boston, 72-73; dir artists fel prog, Artists Found Inc, Boston, 73-82; consult, WGBH New TV Workshop, Boston, 78-79, and others, 86-96; dir, Prints in Progress, Philadelphia, 83-85; dir, Spaces Gallery, Cleveland, Ohio, 86-; panelist, Nat Endowment Arts & Photog Fel; on-site evaluator, Visual Artists Orgn advan prog. *Teaching:* Instr photog & serigraphy, Wadsworth Atheneum, Hartford, Conn, 68-70. *Mem:* Ohio Arts Coun; Visual Arts & Crafts (adv panel); Percent for Art (core comt mem). *Publ:* Ed, Cleveland: New Possibilities, Civic Re-Vision, Buster Simpson-West Sixth Streetscape (exhib catalog), Spaces, 88; Creating in Crisis: Making Art in the Age of AIDS (exhib catalog), Spaces, 94; Radical Ink (exhib catalog), Spaces, 95. *Mailing Add:* 3069 Scarborough Rd Cleveland OH 44118-4064

CHAO, BRUCE
SCULPTOR
b Boston, Mass, Nov 17, 48. *Study:* Wayne State Univ, Detroit, Mich; RI Sch Design, Providence, BFA, 73, MFA, 75; Univ Wis, Madison. *Work:* Corning Mus Glass, NY. *Exhib:* Solo exhibs, An Invisible Barrier, 77, Angels, 78 & 89, O K Harris Gallery, NY, Suspended, PS1 Auditorium, NY, 79, Joslyn Art Mus, Omaha, Nebr, 81 & RI Col, Providence, 93; Washington Proj Arts, 80; Glas 86, Leerdam, The Neth; Glass: Another View, Univ Hawaii, 87; Glassworks, Renwick Gallery, Smithsonian Inst, Washington, 90; Glass Installations, Am Craft Mus, NY, 93. *Teaching:* Asst prof, RI Sch Design, Providence, 82-88, assoc prof, 88-92, prof art, glass dept head, 94-. *Awards:* Finalist Award, sculpture, Mass Artists Fel Prog, 91; RI Sch Design Res Grant, 94; US/Japan Creative Artist Fel, Nat Endowment Arts, 96; NEA Artist Fel Grant, 76, 81, 90. *Bibliog:* Carol Doran-Khewhok (auth), Glass: Another View, New Work, summer 87; Helmut Ricke (auth), Again - Glass and the Fine Arts, Neus Glas, 10-12/86; Donald Kuspit (auth), Bruce Chao's Arc From Purity to the Uncanny, Glass Mag, 93; and others. *Mem:* Glass Art Soc. *Mailing Add:* Rhode Island Sch Design 2 College St Providence RI 02903

CHAPELLIN, HELENA See Wilson, Helena Chapellin Wilson

CHAPIN, DEBORAH JANE
PAINTER, INSTRUCTOR
b Fort Collins, Colo, Jan 15, 54. *Study:* Univ Va, BS, 76; USDA, cert, 90-93; Nat Acad Design, with Raymond Kinstler, 99, with Sam Adoquei, 2002. *Work:* Fed Reserve Bank, Richmond, Va; John Nuveen Co, NY; Pardoe Properties, Washington, DC; Schultz Inc, St Louis, Mo. *Comn:* Wetlands and Wildlife 2007 calendar, DNR restoration projects & Chesapeake Bay Wetlands (fundraising prog). *Exhib:* Artist Am Exhib, Colo Hist Mus, Denver, 88, 90; ASMA Marine Exhib, Md Hist Mus, Baltimore, 89; ASMA Marine Exhib, RJ Schaffer Mus, Mystic, Conn, 92; one-woman show, Meridian Int Ctr, Washington, DC, 92, 97, Nat Arts Club, New York City, 98 & 2003; Salon des Independants, Grand Palais, Paris, France, 93, 94; Salon Socite Nationale des Beaux Arts, Louvre, Paris, France, 99, 2000 & 2001; Ketterer 17-20th Century Marine Art Exhib, Hamburg, Ger, 2000; Arts for the Parts Top 100, Jackson Hole, Wyo, 2004-05; SEWE, Charleston, SC, 2005-06; Natural World Observed, Nat

Arts Club, NY, 2005; Natural World Observed, Winter Park Colo, 2006. *Teaching:* instr painting, NAPPAP, 97-2006. *Awards:* President's Award, Chesapeake Bay Found, 90. *Bibliog:* Edward Archibald (auth), Dictionary of Sea Painters, London, 89; Gerlinde de Beer (auth), Allgemeines Kunstlerlexikon, 97; The Artists Blue Book, 2000-06. *Mem:* Nat Arts Club; Artists Fel; Calif Arts Club; Nat Acad Prof Plein Air Painters (founder, 99); Societe Nat des Beaux Arts. *Media:* Oil on Linen. *Specialty:* plein air painting, wildlife and nature art. *Interests:* Conservation Programs, wildlife & nature walks & safaris. *Collection:* Casa Genota, Historic Home of Eugene O'Neille, Sea Island, Ga. *Publ:* contribr Chesapeake Bay Mag, 5/1983, 5/90; Marine Art, Am Art Mag, 6/88; US Art, Adams Pub, 12/90; auth, Recording the Sea & Surf, Am Artist Mag, 10/95 & Capturing Life & Movement in Plein Air, New Horizon Studios, 11/2000; Gerlinde de Beer (auth), Ludolf Backhysen, 2001. *Mailing Add:* NHStudios 7034 Woodstream Terrace Lanham Seabrook MD 20706

CHAPLIN, GEORGE EDWIN
PAINTER, EDUCATOR
b Kew Gardens, NY, Aug 30, 31. *Study:* Yale Univ Sch Art, with Josef Albers, BFA & MFA. *Work:* Yale Univ Gallery; Trinity Col, Conn; World Bank, Washington, DC; Mattatuck Mus, Conn; Bayer Corp, Tarrytown, NY. *Exhib:* Carpenter Ctr, Harvard Univ, 74; Dept of State, Washington, DC, 76-80; New Britain Mus, Conn, 77; Conn 78 Invitational, Carlson Art Gallery, Univ Bridgeport; Mattatuck Mus, Waterbury, Conn, 78; Slater Mem Mus, Norwich, Conn, 81; Munson Gallery, New Haven, Conn, 91; Corbino Gallery, Longboat Key, Fla, 98; Desiree Snyder Gallery, 2004. *Collection Arranged:* Trinity College, Hartford, CT; Mattatuck Mus, Wallingford, CT. *Pos:* adj prof Fine Arts, Trinity College, Hartford, CT. *Teaching:* Head dept painting, Silvermine Col Art, 65-71; dir studio prog, Trinity Col, Hartford, Conn, 72-91, prof fine arts, 78-88, Charles S Nutt prof emer fine arts. *Awards:* David G Lyon Award, 31st New England Ann, Conn, 81; 1st Prize, 1st Faber Birren Color Award Exhib, Stamford Art Asn, Conn, 81. *Bibliog:* Bernard Chaet Holt (auth), The Art of Drawing, Rinehart and Winston, Inc; Paul Zelanski (auth), Color, Prentice Hall, Inc, Fourth & Fifth Ed. *Media:* Oil, Pastel. *Dealer:* Swanson Reed Contemporary Louisville Ky; Greene Contemporary Sarasota Fla. *Mailing Add:* 91 Elm St Apt 218A Manchester CT 06040

CHAPLINE, CLAUDIA BEECHUM
PAINTER, ART DEALER, ASSEMBLAGE ARTIST
b Oak Park, Ill, May 23, 30. *Study:* Corcoran Sch Art, 48-53; George Wash Univ, Wash, AB, 53; Conn Col Sch Dance, 54 & 56; Wash Univ, St Louis, Mo, MA, 56; Univ Mo, 56-57; Phi Beta Kappa. *Work:* Univ Calif, Los Angeles; Downey Mus Art, Calif; Fine Arts Mus, San Francisco; Norcal, San Francisco; Morris Graves Mus, Eureka, Calif. *Comn:* performance proj, City Santa Monica, Calif, 81; Subway, Nuremburg, Ger, 94; sculpture, Hotel Radisson, Antigua, Guatemala. *Exhib:* Galerie Christa Riedel, Frankenthal, Ger, 2000; Marin Civic Ctr, San Rafael, Calif, 2000; War Meml Mus, Seoul, Korea, 2001; Olema Valley Ranches Today, Claudia Chapline Gallery, 2002; Exchg Exhib, Somarts, Axis Mundi, San Francisco & Paris, 2002; Calif State Univ Dominvez Hills, 2005; Rosicrucian Egyptian Mus, San Jose, Calif, 2005. *Collection Arranged:* Performance Series 74-80, Inst Dance & Experimental Art, Introductions, 85-86; San Francisco Civic Arts Festival, 88 & 89; Calif Arts Coun, Artists-in-Residence, 82 & Art in Pub Bldg, 84-90. *Pos:* Founder dir, Inst Design & Experimental Art, Calif, 74-87; coordr, Artists in Social Inst, Calif Arts Coun, Sacramento, 82-84; mgr, Art in Pub Bldgs, Calif Arts Coun, 84-90; owner, Claudia Chapline Gallery, Stinson Beach, Calif, 87-; dev dir, Bolinas Mus, 90; pub Art Consult, City of Berkeley, Calif, 2002-05. *Teaching:* Instr dance, Wash Univ, 53-56; instr, Univ Mo, 56-67; asst prof, Univ Calif, Los Angeles, 60-67 & Calif State Univ, Northridge, 61-64. *Awards:* Artist Res, Norcal, San Francisco, 99, Stinson Bench, Bolinas Community Fund, 2000 & DeYoung Mus Arts, San Francisco, 2000; Marin Arts Coun Community Arts Grant, 2001; Zellerbach Family Fund, 2002. *Bibliog:* Pacific Sun, 10/28/98; San Francisco Chronicle, Evening News Mag, 99; Niche Mag, winter 2003; Craft of No Calif, 2003; J Rigler (auth, video), Conversation with Instersting Characters, 99. *Mem:* San Francisco Art Dealers Asn; Art Table; Pub Art Works of Marin; Col Art Asn; Women's Caucus for Art. *Media:* Acrylic, Assemblage, Installation. *Specialty:* Contemporary art of Northern California. *Collection:* Fred Blackman, Italo Scanga, Harold Schwarm. *Publ:* Auth, Tension-Line, High Performance, 78; ed numerous articles in Artists News, 81; Egret, 96; Calle Aldama, 96; Artists Dialogue, 97-98. *Mailing Add:* PO Box 1117 Stinson Beach CA 94970

CHAPMAN, GARY HOWARD
PAINTER
b Xenia, Ohio, July 25, 1961. *Study:* Berea Col, Ky, BA(art), BS(indust art), 84; Cranbook Acad Art, Mich, MFA(painting), 86. *Work:* Birmingham Mus Art; Huntsville Mus Art, Ala; Montgomery Mus Art & Ala State Coun Arts, Montgomery, Ala; Mobile Mus Art, Ala; the Ogden Mus Art, New Orleans, La; The Meridian Mus Art, Miss. *Comn:* oil painting, Hoar Construction Co, Birmingham, Ala. *Pos:* CAA mentor, 2003. *Teaching:* Prof painting & drawing, Univ Ala, Birmingham, 1990-; instr painting, Arrowmont Sch Arts & Crafts, Gatlinburg, 1998, 2000, 2002. *Awards:* Painting Fel, Ala State Coun Arts, 1994, 2002 & Nat Endowment Arts/Southern Arts Fedn, 1996; Red Clay Survey Purchase Award, Huntsville Mus Art, Ala, 1998; Purchase Award, Meridian Mus, 2000. *Mem:* Southeastern Cols Art Conf; CAA Col Art Asn. *Media:* Oils. *Publ:* Contribr, New American Paintings, book 3, 16 & 52, Open Studio Press. *Mailing Add:* 1425 16th Ave S Birmingham AL 35205

CHAPMAN, H PERRY
EDUCATOR
Study: Swathmore Col, BA; Princeton Univ, PhD. *Pos:* Assoc chmn, prof, Dept Art Hist Univ Del. *Awards:* Fel Woodrow Wilson Ctr, 90-91, Nat Endowment for Humanities, 93-94, Guggenheim Mem Found, 2004. *Bibliog:* Co-curator (exhibiton) Jan Steen: Painter and Storyteller, National Gallery Art & Rijks museum, Amsterdam, 96—97; author: Rembrandt's Self-Portraits: A Study in Seventeenth-Centuty Identity, 1990; editor: Univ Del. Art Bulletin, 2000—04. *Mailing Add:* Univ Del Dept Art Hist Office 323 OCL 318 Old College Newark DE 19716-2516

CHAPMAN, ROBERT GORDON
JEWELER, PAINTER
b Los Angeles, Calif, 26, 41. *Study:* Ventura Col; San Jose Univ, with Fred Spratt & J Richard Sorby, BA(painting), with David Hatch, John Leary & Dr Robert Coleman, MA(jewelry design), Pupil Serv Credential(career coun in visual arts). *Work:* Metal Arts Guild, San Francisco; San Jose State Univ Gallery; San Jose Art League. *Comn:* Moon Pendant (commemorating first lunar landing), 68; Ring, comn by David San Jose, 69; plus pendants, rings, pins & body adornment comn by various individuals. *Exhib:* Art '65, Univ Santa Clara; Calif Expos of the Arts, 66-69; Crafts 10, 67; Western US Traveling Exhib, 68; Triton Mus, Santa Clara, Calif, 69; Eastside Fac Show, 81. *Pos:* Dir, Group 21 Gallery, Los Gatos, Calif, 72-73; mem art educ screening comt, San Jose State Univ, 73-; bd dir, San Jose Art League, formerly. *Teaching:* Instr art & chmn dept, Piedmont Hills High Sch, San Jose, 64-74; instr jewelry & metalsmithing, West Valley Col, Saratoga, Calif, 66-; coun visual arts, Santa Teresa High Sch, San Jose, 74-. *Awards:* Ellen Brucker Jewelry Award, 69; Achiever of the Year in Art, Nat Pen Women Asn, 69; San Jose Regional Art Second Award, 75. *Mem:* Metal Arts Guild San Francisco; Calif Art Educators Asn. *Media:* Aqueous, Silver, Gold. *Publ:* Auth, An Analysis of Photomicrography as a Design Source for Lost-Model Jewelry, 69. *Mailing Add:* 6060 Loma Prieta Dr San Jose CA 95123

CHAPMAN, WALTER HOWARD
PAINTER, ILLUSTRATOR
b Toledo, Ohio, Dec 7, 1912. *Study:* Cleveland Inst Art; John Huntington Polytech, Cleveland; Art Students League; study portraiture with Rolf Stoll, Cleveland and figure painting with Jon Corbino, NY. *Work:* Toledo Fedn Art Collection, Toledo Mus Art; Zanesville Art Mus, Ohio; Springfield Mus Art, Mo; Univ Toledo; Toledo Trust Co, Ohio; Erma Bombeck Collection; others. *Comn:* Five portraits, Law & Sci Bldgs, Univ Toledo, 70 & 77; Bicentennial painting, Waterville Chamber of Commerce, Ohio, 76; three portraits, First Fed Bank, Toledo, 77; Portrait: Bishop Donovan, Holy Rosary Cathedral, Toledo Ohio, 90; portrait, Univ Toledo, 90; portrait Barney Quilter, Speaker of House, 1999; others. *Exhib:* Watercolor USA, Springfield Mus Art, Mo, 72; Zanesville Mus Art, 73 & Ella Sharp Mus, Jackson, Mich, 74; Springfield Art Ctr, Ohio, 74; Mid-Yr Ann, Butler Mus Art, Youngstown, Ohio, 75; One-man show, Sun City Mus Art, Ariz, 87; retrospectives, Toledo Mus Art, 88 & Zanesville Art Ctr, 88; Anne S K Brown Military Collection, Brown Univ, Providence, RI, 95; Allied Artists of America Retrospective Show, Butler Mus Art, Youngstown, Ohio, 2001; Painters of Cape Ann, Canton Mus Art, 2001. *Pos:* Illusr, NY, 39-42; combat artist, US Army, 43-45; creative dir, Phillipps Assoc, Toledo, 46-80; owner, Chapman Art Gallery, Sylvania, 70-2005. *Teaching:* Instr illus, Toledo Mus Sch Design, 55-89; instr portrait & figure, Toledo Artists Club 55-64, instr watercolor landscape-Lourdes Col, Sylvania Ohio, 89-2000, Toledo Mus, 2002-2004. *Awards:* Bronze Medal, 45; First Award, Summer Show, Salmagundi Club, New York, 72; Grumbacher Gold Medal, 88; Outstanding Contrib to the Arts, Toledo Arts Commn, 88; Award Distinction, Ohio Watercolor Soc, 92; 2 Roulet Gold Medals, Toledo Fedn Arts, 1990-91, Best of Portrait Show, 2001. *Bibliog:* Murray Kalis (auth), article in Art Rev, 68; Article in Toledo Blade Mag, 88. *Mem:* Allied Artists Am; Salmagundi Club; Toledo Fedn Art Soc (pres, 54-56); Ohio Watercolor Soc (bd mem, 77); NW Ohio Watercolor Soc (pres, 71-72); Watercolor USA (honor soc, 86); Toledo Artist Club. *Media:* Watercolor, Oil. *Specialty:* Watercolor, Oil painting. *Interests:* Raising money for different things; Lathrope House, Part of the Underground Railroad-donated to Auction Procicedes for saving & restoring this house; Sept 11-2003 Prints made of World Trade Ctr Disaster, Sales donated to AM Red Cross over $8000 to date. *Collection:* Jennison Wright Company, Taledo Trust, Toledo Federation of Art collection. *Publ:* Contribr (cartoons), Stars & Stripes & Railsplitte, US Army newspapers, 45; illusr, Battle of Germany, Viking Press, 46; contribr ed cartoons, Toledo Monitor, 65; contribr, Prize Winning Art, Allied Publ, 66; contribr (cover art), Exhibit Mag, 67. *Dealer:* Chapman Art Gallery 5151 S Main St Sylvania OH 43560. *Mailing Add:* 6001 Gregory Dr Sylvania OH 43560

CHAPPELL, BERKLEY WARNER
PAINTER, PRINTMAKER
b Pueblo, Colo, Mar 21, 34. *Study:* Univ Colo, BFA, 56, MFA, 58; studied with Mark Rothko, Jimmy Ernst, Cari Morris. *Work:* San Francisco Mus Art; Henry Gallery, Univ Wash, Seattle; Tacoma Mus Art, Wash; Univ BC, Vancouver; Salishan Lodge, Gleneden Beach, Ore. *Exhib:* Young West Coast Artists, Pasadena, Calif, 59; Abstract Expressionism Today, San Francisco, 60 & Landscape Painting Today, 61; Am Printmaking Today, Ger, Greece, France, 69; Grand Gallerie, Seattle, 75; San Francisco Mus Art; Hunterdon Mus NJ; Pasadena Mus Art; Portland Mus Art; and others. *Collection Arranged:* Portland Mus Art, Portland, OR. *Teaching:* Asst painting, Univ Colo, 56-58; instr to asst prof painting, Univ Puget Sound, Tacoma, 58-63; asst prof to prof painting & printmaking, Ore State Univ, Corvallis, 63-97; ret, 1997. *Awards:* Purchase Awards, San Francisco Art Inst, 61 & Henry Gallery, Univ Wash, 64 & 69; Oregon State Univ Found; Grayco Found, Portland, OR; Grants, finish the unprinted editions of the late Wendell H. Black, printmaker and mentor, Univ Colo. *Media:* Oil, Engraving. *Mailing Add:* 2230 NW 29th St Corvallis OR 97330-1244

CHAPPELL, MILES LINWOOD
HISTORIAN, EDUCATOR
b Norfolk, Va, June 6, 39. *Study:* Col William & Mary, BS, 60; Univ NC, Chapel Hill, with Philipp Fehl, Frances Huemer & Joseph Sloane, PhD(art hist), 71. *Collection Arranged:* Rubens in Prints (auth, catalog), Col William & Mary, 77; Arthur Strauss and the German Expressionists (auth, catalog), Col William & Mary, 78; Disegni dei Toscani a Roma 1580-1620 (coauth, catalog), Uffizi Gallery, Florence, 79; Drawings from the Herman Collection (auth, catalog), Muscarelle Mus Art, Col William & Mary, 83; Cristofano Allori (auth, catalog), Pitti Gallery, Florence, 84; Age of Caravaggio (catalog), New York, 84; Il Seicento Fiorentino (contribr, catalog), Florence, 86; Disegni di Lodovico Cigoli (auth, catalog), Uffizi Gallery, 92; Cigoli tra manierismo e barocco (intro, catalog), Pitti Gallery, 92; Fine Art of Drawing, Muscarelle Mus Art, Col William & Mary, Va, 93 & Drawn on the Spot: Landscape Drawings, 16C-20C, 95; Tuscan Drawings, New York, 2000. *Pos:* Assoc ed, Studies in Iconography, 76-81, ed, 81-82; art adv bd, Interlochen Ctr Arts, 90-; art historian and critic. *Teaching:* Assoc fel, Harvard Univ Ctr Italian Renaissance, Florence, 90; prof art hist, Col William & Mary, 71-, chancellor prof, 86-. *Awards:* Nat Endowment Humanities Fel, 83; Res Grants, Nat Endowment Humanities, Sammuel Kress Found & Am Philosophical Soc. *Mem:* Col Art Asn Am; Southeastern Col Art Conf (mem bd dir, 78-84); Renaissance Soc Am; Kunsthistorisches Inst, Florence. *Res:* Renaissance and Baroque art; old master drawings; British and Colonial American painting. *Publ:* Auth, Cristofano Allori's depictions of St Francis, Burlington Mag, 71; Cigoli, Galileo and Invidia, 75 & John Smibert's Italian sojourn, 82, Art Bulletin; Missing paintings by Cigoli, Paragone, 82; Identification of S Coccapani drawing collection mark, Master Drawings, 83; Fuseli: Antique and Nightmare, Burlington Mag, 86; Drawings by Cigoli, Master Drawings, 89. *Mailing Add:* Dept of Art & Art Hist Col William & Mary Williamsburg VA 23185

CHAPPELLE, JERRY LEON
CERAMIST, SCULPTOR
b Fredericktown, Mo, Nov 14, 39. *Study:* Murray State Univ, BS; Univ Minn, MFA. *Work:* High Mus Art, Atlanta, Ga; Greenville Co Mus Art, SC; Ga Coun Arts; La Sch Visual Impaired, Baton Rouge, La; Pres Carter Ctr, Atlanta, Ga. *Comn:* Ceramic mural, Sally Julius Mem, Miller Libr, La Plume, Pa, 80 & Kelly Airforce Base, San Antonio, Tex, 85; ceramic & stucco mural, St Gregory's Episcopal Church, Athens, Ga, 81; mural, Mohasco Entrance, High Point, NC, 86; ceramic mural, Mus Arts & Sci, Macon, Ga, 90; ceramic mural, Veterans Admin Hospital, Dallas, Tex, 98. *Exhib:* Fun and Fantasy, Xerox Corp Gallery, Rochester, NY, 73; Regional Invitational, Gallery Contemp Art, Winston-Salem, NC, 75; Hopkins Gallery Art, Ohio State Univ, Columbus, 80; Greenville Co Mus Art, SC, 81; Carrol Reece Mus, Johnson City, Tenn, 88; Ceramic Mural Cohen's of Atlanta, 2005. *Pos:* Dir, Scorpio Rising Workshops, 70-77; vis artist, Ohio State Univ, 80; co-owner Happy Valley Pottery, Inc, 70-; co-owner, chappelle Gallery, 1999-. *Teaching:* Instr ceramics, Univ Minn, 69-70; asst prof ceramics, Univ Ga, 70-76. *Awards:* Two First Prizes, Atlanta Arts Comt, 75; Second Prize, Covington Arts Exhib, Covington Art Ctr, 74; Artist Initiated Grant, Ga Endowment Arts, 89. *Bibliog:* Larry Smith (auth), Ceramic Art (film), Univ Ga, 74; Evolution of the Artist Craftsman in Georgia, Highlight of Contemporary Ceramics (film), Ga NEA-TV, 74; HGTV, The Good Life, 2001. *Mem:* Am Crafts Coun; Piedmont Craftsmen Inc. *Media:* Clay, Glass. *Dealer:* Sandler Hudson Gallery 1009 A Marietta St NW Atlanta Ga 30318. *Mailing Add:* 1210 Carson Graves Rd Watkinsville GA 30677

CHARKOW-HOLLANDER, NATALIE
SCULPTOR
b Philadelphia. *Study:* Taylor Sch Fine Arts. *Work:* Nice Caves & Their Inhabitants, 97; Birth of the Milky Way, 2002. *Exhib:* Solo show Reliefs in Stone, Lohin Geduld Gallery, 2004. *Teaching:* Founder, prof, sculpture dept, Philadelphia Col Art (now Univ Arts); prof Yale Univ, Boston Univ, Queens Col, City Univ NY, Univ Pa. *Mem:* Nat Acad (acad, 2003)

CHARLES, DURANT See Rizzie, Dan

CHARLES, LARRY
PAINTER, LECTURER
b South Bend, Ind, Mar 17, 51. *Study:* Ind Univ; Ariz State Univ; Scottsdale Artists' Sch. *Exhib:* The Art of Illusion, Woodson Art Mus, Wausau, Wis, 2003; Trompe L'Oeil Style, Phoenix Art Mus, Phoenix, Ariz, 2003. *Teaching:* instr liberal arts, Univ So Calif, Los Angeles, 86-87. *Mem:* Trompe L'Oeil Soc Artists (co-founder 2001-). *Media:* Acrylic, Oil. *Publ:* Auth, International Artist, 2002. *Dealer:* Eleanor Ettinger Gallery 119 Spring St New York NY 10012. *Mailing Add:* 14926 N 86th Ln Peoria AZ 85381

CHARLES, MICHAEL RAY
ARTIST
b Lafayette, La, 67. *Study:* McNeese State Univ, BA, Lake Charles, La, 85; Univ Houston, MFA, 93. *Exhib:* Solo shows including Barnes-Blackman Galleries, Houston, 91; Tony Shafrazi Gallery, NY City, 94, Now is the Time, 95, Bamboozled, 2000; Michael Ray Charles, Albright Knox Gallery, Buffalo, 97; Group shows including Houston Int Festival: The Case for Art, Lawndale Art and Performance Ctr, Houston, 92, Tex Contemporary: Acquisitions of the 90s, Mus Fine Arts, Houston, 93, Looking Forward Looking Black, Balt Mus Art, 2002. *Teaching:* painting workshop instr, Mus Fine Arts, Houston, drawing instr, sculpture workshop instr; Drawing workshop instr, Blaffer Gallery, Univ Houston, intermediate painting instr; art instr, 5th Ward Enrichment Prog, Houston, Mental Retardation Authority, Houston; lectr to prof studio art and painting, Univ Tex, Austin, 93-. *Mailing Add:* Univ Tex Austin Fine Arts 1 Univ Sta D1400 Austin TX 78712-0340

STANLEY, CHARLES J See Pittore, Carlo

CHARLESWORTH, SARAH E
PHOTOGRAPHER, CONCEPTUAL ARTIST
b East Orange, NJ, Mar 29, 1947. *Study:* Barnard Col, BA, 69. *Work:* Baruch Col, Int Ctr Photog, Mus Mod Art, NY Pub Libr & Whitney Mus Am Art, NY; Los Angeles Co Mus Art & Mus Contemp Art, Los Angeles, Calif; High Mus Art, Atlanta, Ga; Nat Mus Am Art, Smithsonian Inst, Washington, DC; Victoria & Albert Mus, London; Birmingham Mus Art, Ala; Cleveland Mus Art; Internat Ctr Photog, NY; Israel Mus, Jerusalem; Mus Contemp Art, San Diego; Mus Fine Art, Boston; Princeton Univ Mus, NJ; Vancouver Art Gallery, BC, Can; Rose Art Mus, Waltham, Mass; Berkely Art Mus, Univ of Calif; NY Pub Libr, NY; and many more. *Exhib:* Solo exhibs, Jay Gorney Mod Art, NY, 89-91, S L Simpson Gallery, Toronto, Can, 86 & 90, Galerie Xavier Hufkens, Brussels, Belg, 91, Paley Wright Gallery, London, Eng, 91, The Queens Mus Art, Queens, NY, 92, Mus Contemp Art, San Diego, Calif, 97 & Nat Mus Women Arts, Washington, DC, 98, Fay Gold Gallery, Atlanta, 98, Margo Leavin Gallery, Los Angeles, 2000, Gorney Bravin & Lee, NY, 2000; The Photog of Invention: Am Pictures of the 1980's, Nat Mus Am Art, Smithsonian Inst, Washington, DC, 89; Image World: Art and Media Cult, Whitney Mus Am Art, NY, 89; Figuring the Body, Mus Fine Arts, Boston, Mass, 90; Motion & Document-Sequence & Time: Eadward Muybridge & Contemp Am Photog (traveling show/catalog), Nat Mus Am Art, Smithsonian Inst, Washington, DC, 91; Victoria & Albert Mus, London; Quotations: The Second History of Art (catalog), Aldrich Mus Contemp Art, Ridgefield, Conn, 92; solo exhibs, Queens Mus Art, NY, 92, Galerie Carola Mosch, Berlin, Ger, 92, Rena Bransten Gallery, San Francisco, Calif, 92, Jay Gorney Mod Art, NY, 93, Galerie Rizzo, Paris, France, 93 & S L Simpson Gallery, Toronto, Can, 93, Margo Leavin Gallery, Los Angeles, Calif, 2000, Gorney Bravin + Lee, NY, 2000, 02, & 03; From NY: Recent Thinking in Contemp Photog, Donna Beam Fine Art Gallery, Univ Nev, Las Vegas, 93; Commodity Image, Int Ctr Photog, NY & Inst Contemp Art, Boston, Mass, 93; Image Makers, Nassau Co Mus Art, Roslyn Harbor, NY, 93; Am Art Today: Heads Only, Art Mus, Fla Int Univ, Miami, 94; From the Collection: Photog, Sculpture, Painting, Whitney Mus Am Art, NY, 94; Rudiments dun Musee Possible I, Ctr Contemp Art, Geneve, Switz, 94; Transmitting Truth: Reformulating News Media Information, Sch of Art Inst Chicago, Ill, 94; The Am Century: Art & Cult 1950-2000 (cat), Whitney Mus Am Art, NY, 99; Double Vision, Nexus Contemp Art Ctr, Atlanta, 99; Photog Now, Contemp Arts Ctr, New Orleans, 2000; The One Chosen, De Saisset Mus, Calif, 2000, Brauer Mus, Ind, 2000; La Collection Yvon Lambert, Avignon, France, 2000; Photo-Synthesis, Gallery Camino Real, Boca Raton, Fla, 2001; and many others; group exhibs, The Whitney Mus of Am Art, NY, 99, Women's Mus, Wash DC, Feminism and Art, 2002. *Pos:* Vis artist-lectr, Soc Photog Ed, 83; Artists Talk on Art, 83; guest lectr, Sch Visual Arts, 83; Int Ctr Photog, 83; vis artist-critic, RISD, Providence, RI, 83 & 84. *Teaching:* Instr photog, NY Univ, 83-85; Rutgers Univ, New Brunswick, NJ, 83; vis lectr, Boston Univ, 86; Dept Fine Arts, NY Univ, 86; Tyler Col, Temple Univ, Philadelphia, Pa, 87; vis artist & lectr at numerous universities & museums; instr masters program in photog and related media, Sch Visual Arts, NY, 92-, academic advisor, 96-; instr, RI Sch Design, Providence, 2000. *Awards:* Creative Artists Pub Serv Fel, 77; Nat Endowment Arts Fel, 76, 80 & 83; John Simon Guggenheim Fel, 95. *Bibliog:* Maria Campitelli (auth), Sarah Charlesworth, Juliet, 2-3/92; Elizabeth Hess (auth), Materialized Girls, Village Voice, 4/20/93; Gianni Romano (auth), Sarah Charlesworth, Zoom, 11-12/93; Dave Hickey (auth), A Matter of Time: On Flatness, Magic, Illusion & Morality, Parket, issue 40/41, summer 94; Susan Fisher-Sterling (auth), Sarah Charlesworth, exhib cat, Site, Santa Fe, 97; Frank Green (auth), Master Juggler: The Restless Experiments of Sarah Charlesworth, Cleveland Free Press, 98; Ann Barclay-Morgan (auth), Sarah Charlesworth - A Retrospective, Camera Austria Internat, 98; Christine Temin (auth), Photo Synthesis: in a 20 year retrospective at the Rose Art Museum, Sarah Charlesworth transforms the medium and the message of photography, The Boston Globe, 5/7/99; Vince Aletti (auth), Voice Choice: Photo: Sarah Charlesworth, The Village Voice, 1/25/2000; Jerry Saltz (auth), The I-Don't-Get-It-Aesthetic, The Village Voice, 1/25/2000; Marth Schwendener (auth), Art Reviews: Sarah Charlesworth at Gorney Bravin + Lee, Time Out New York, 2000; David Pagel (auth), Sarah Charlesworth - Magical Forms, Los Angeles Times, 1/28/2000; Michael Cohen (auth), Review: Sarah Charlesworth at Gorney Bravin + Lee, Flash Art, May-June, 2000; Laurence A Marschall (auth), Book in Brief: The Story of P (illustr), The Sciences, Jan-Feb, 2001. *Publ:* Contribr, Art in Am, 79 & Artforum, 82; auth, Glossolalia, Bomb Mag, spring 83; A Lovers Tale, Wedge Press, 84; auth, Laurie Simmons, ART Press, 95; auth, Questions of Feminism: 25 Responses, October, Winter 95; auth, La Differenza Tra I Sessi Nell'Arte, Terna Celeste, 94. *Dealer:* Gorney Bravin & Lee 534 W 26th St New York NY 10001. *Mailing Add:* c/o Jay Gorney Modern Art 534 W 26th St New York NY 10001

CHARLOT, MARTIN DAY
PAINTER, MURALIST
b Athens, Ga, Mar 6, 44. *Study:* Apprenticeship with Jean Charlot & Ansel Adams. *Work:* Bishop Mus, Honolulu; State Found Cult & Arts, Honolulu; The Queen Emma Found, 91; Metrop Mus Art, NY; City of Honolulu. *Comn:* King Kamehameha IV and Queen Emma (6' x 7' mural), Queen Emma Found, 91; Hawaii at Peace, Fruits of our Labor (6' x 27' mural), New Honolulu Police Hq, 93; Beyond Words (4' x 14' mural), Children's Dental Ctr, Inglewood, Calif, 96; Science, Nature & Technology (7' x 15' mural), Ventura Co Discovery Ctr, Thousand Oaks, Calif, 98; (mural) The Children's Dental Center, 99; Legal Offices Steve Thomas, Wilshire Blvd, Santa Monica, 2001; and many others. *Exhib:* One-man shows, De Mena Gallery, NY, 67, Hawaii State Libr, Honolulu, 72, Volcano Art Ctr, 76, Contemp Arts Ctr, Hawaii, 79, Fed Bldg, 80, Kauai Libr, 80, Ala Moana Center, Honolulu, 83 & Hawaii Loa Col, 84; East West Ctr, 86; State Found Cult & Arts Retrospective, 87; An Am Palette, a Dance Celebration of Am Art & Mus, Principia Col, Ill, 89; Brockman Gallery, Los Angeles, 89; Louis Stern Fine Arts, Los Angeles. *Pos:* Illusr, Collins Assoc, NY, 69; art dir,

Bravura Films, Mountain View, Calif, 70; contribr, Ha'ilono Mele, 79-80; illusr, Honolulu Advertiser Progress Edition, 82. *Teaching:* Lectr art & film, Univ Hawaii, 62-; lectr filmmaking, St John's Univ, Minn, 69; teacher cinema, Honolulu Acad Arts, 70; artist-in-schs, Doe Sch Syst, Hawaii, 75; lectr, Fresno Calif Univ, 83 & Honolulu Acad Arts. *Awards:* Fel in Perpetuity, Metrop Mus Art, NY, 79; Akamai Business Award, Kaneohe Bus Group, 83. *Bibliog:* On paper gallery, Commun for Peace, Aqua Planet Inc, Japan, 89; Les Krantz (auth), Calif Art Rev, 89; Made in Paradise (film), 95; Harry N Abrams Inc (auth), Art of the State Hawaii, 99; and others. *Mem:* Hawaii Film Bd (perpetual mem); Pac Film Inst; mem Screen Actors Guild; Film Makers Coop, NY; Hawaii Orgn Arts (founder, 92); NAACP (hon chmn); Waiahole-Waikane Community Asn (founding steering com mem, art dir); First Hawaii Int Film Festival (founding bd dir, art dir). *Media:* Oil, Acrylic. *Publ:* Illusr, How to Make Your Own Hawaiian Musical Instrument, Bess Press, Inc, 88; cover, White Bread, Hawaii Rev, Univ Hawaii, 89; J Am Planning Asn, Hunter Col, NY, 90; contribr, Kalapana Will Be Forever, film, 90; illusr, Design Stock Certificate, Blue Rider Entertainment Inc, 97; auth & illusr, Surfaces, WW Norton & Co, New York, 96; Art of the State Hawaii, Harry N. Abrams, Inc, 99; Contemporary Chicana and Chicano Art, Bilingual Press, 2002, Arizona State Univ,; The Crucifixion in American Art, McFarland & Co, Inc, North Carolina and London, 2003. *Mailing Add:* 123 C N Maple St Burbank CA 91505

CHARNEY, MELVIN
SCULPTOR, ARCHITECT
b Montreal, Que, Aug 28, 35. *Study:* Sch Art & Design, Montreal Mus Fine Arts; McGill Univ, BA(archit), 58; Yale Univ, MA(archit), 59. *Work:* Nat Gallery Can, Ottawa, Ont; Art Gallery Ont, Toronto; Fonds Nat d'Art Contemporain, Paris; Mus Contemp Art, Chicago, Ill; Musee d' art contemporain de Montreal. *Comn:* Installation, XXI Olympic Comt, Montreal, Que, 76; Mus d'Art Contemporain, 79, de Montreal; Installation Mus Contemp Art, Chicago, 82; Sculpture; Canadian Tribute to Human Rights, Ottawa, 86; Environmental Sculpture; City of Montreal, 90; Canadian Centre for Archit, Garden and Sculpture, 1991, Montreal; Sculpture and place des Moulins, City of Sherbrooke, 2004. *Exhib:* Acad der Kunsye, Ger, 1982, Mus nationale des beaux-arts du Que, 1985, Melvin Charney: Canadian Pavilion, Venice Biennale of Art, Italy, 1986; Nat Mus Contemp Art, Seoul, 90; Retrospective, Can Centre Archit, Montreal, 91-92; Centre Cultura Contemporania, Barcelona, 94; Mus Nat d'art Mod, Paris, 94; Powerplant Gallery, Toronto, 1995; Israel Mus, Jerusalem, 1996; Can Pavilion, Venice Biennale of Archit, 2000; Musee d' art contemporain in de Monreal, 79 & 2002; Canadian Mus of Contemp Photog, Ottawa, 2003; and others. *Pos:* Founding Board of Directors, Coseils des arts et lettres du Quebec. *Teaching:* Prof archit, Univ Montreal, 64-95. *Awards:* Berliner Kunstlerprogramme Award, Deutscher Akademischer Austauschdienst, 82; Prix du Quebec Paul-Emile-Borduas, 96; Order of Quebec, 2004; Comdr, Order Arts & Letters, France, 2006. *Bibliog:* Alexander Tzonis (auth), Melvin Charney 1970-1979, Cultural Affairs, Que, 79; Allesandra Latour (auth), Parables & Other Allegories-The Work of Melvin Charney 1975-1990, CCA/MITPress, 91; Jean-François Chevrier (auth), Melvin Charney-Parcours-About Reinvention, FRAC Basse-Normandie, France, 98; Pierre Landry (auth), Melvin Charney, Musee d art contemporary de Montreal, 2003. *Mem:* Canadian Artists Representation; Royal Canadian Acad; Royal Archit Inst of Can. *Media:* Photography, painting, drawing, welded steel and aluminum sculpture. *Publ:* Auth, Memo Series, Artform, 71; Pour une définition de l'architecture au Que, U d M Presses, 72; Art as Urban Activism, Archit Design, London, 77; Signs of recognition, ciphers of deception, Parachute, 84; The Gardens of Transient and Intractable Cities, Art et Jardins, Musée d'art contemporain de Montréal, 2000; Tracking Images: Un Dictionnaire. Canadian Center for Architecture, 2000. *Dealer:* Frederieke Taylor Gallery, 535 West 22nd Street, 6th Fl New York, NY 10011; Nicholas Metivier Gallery, 451 King Street West, Toronto, ON M5VIK4, Canada. *Mailing Add:* 3620 Marlowe Ave Montreal PQ H4A 3L7 Canada

CHASE, ALLAN (SEAMANS)
SCULPTOR, MURALIST
Study: Univ Ga, BFA. *Comn:* Brass on steel, Sherwood Theatre, Gainesville, Ga, 66 & Oxford Chem Co, Atlanta, 67; welded steel, Woodward Acad, College Park, Atlanta, 68; 17 steel & polyester murals, Fla, 71-75. *Exhib:* 5th Biennial Nat Relig Art Exhib, Bloomfield, Mich, 66; Southeastern Ann Exhib, Atlanta, 66 & 68; Piedmont Park Arts Festival, Atlanta, 66-72; Mus Arts & Sci, Macon, Ga, 67; C & S Bank, Atlanta, 75. *Pos:* Designer, Gi-Gi's Restaurants, Fla & Rochester, NY, 65-. *Teaching:* Instr, DeKalb Community Col, 80-81. *Media:* Steel, Other Metals; Relief Painting on Hardboard. *Dealer:* Art Gallery 1200 Foster St NW Atlanta GA 30318. *Mailing Add:* 3779 Vermont Rd NE Atlanta GA 30319-1208

CHASE, DORIS (TOTTEN)
VIDEO ARTIST, SCULPTOR
b Seattle, Wash, Apr 29, 23. *Study:* Univ Wash; also with Mark Tobey. *Work:* Mus Mod Art, Kobe, Japan; Art Inst Chicago; Nat Collection Fine Arts & Smithsonian Inst, Washington; Mus Fine Arts, Boston; Mus Mod Art & NY Univ, NY; and others. *Comn:* Steel & Bronze, Wash State Arts Comn, 70; Wash State Conv Ctr; Kerry Park, Seattle; Nat Endowment Arts; Seattle Ctr Found, 99. *Exhib:* One-man shows, Western Mus Asn Circulating Exhib, 70-72 & Henry Gallery, Univ Wash, Seattle, 71, 78 & 98; Metrop Mus Art, NY, 74; Calif Palace Legion Hon, 78; Mus Mod Art, NY, 78, 81 & 93; Georges Pompidou Ctr, Paris, 82-85, AIR Gallery, NY, 83; 911-Media Arts Ctr, 89, 92 & 94; DC/TV '90, NY; Woodside/Braseth Gallery, Seattle, Wash, 90 & 93; Seattle Art Mus, 92 & 94; Mus NW Art, La Conner, Wash, 94; Am Inst Architects, 95; New Acquisitions, Mus Northwest Art, La Corner, Friesen Fine Arts, Seattle, WA, 2003. *Awards:* Nat Endowment Arts Fel, 76; NY State Coun Arts Grant, 80; Govs Art Award, State Wash, 92; Retirement Res Found Grant, 93; Seattle Arts Comn Grant, 95; Col Art Asn Tribute, Seattle Art Mus, 2004. *Bibliog:* Articles in Newsweek, 7/3/78, NY Times, 3/18/81 & Videography, 9/81, Sightlines, spring, 86 & Seattle Times; Robin Schanzenbach (dir), Doris Chase: Portrait of the Artist (documentary film), Pub Broadcasting Serv, 85; Dr Patricia Failing (auth), Doris Chase: Artist in Motion (book & video), Univ Wash Press, 92; Cynthia Goodman (auth), Digital visions, Sculpture Mag, 97, 99; KCTS, Doris Chase - Circle at the Center (video), 99. *Mem:* Women/Artist/Filmmakers (pres, 78); Asn Independent Video & Filmmakers; NY Film Coun (bd mem); 911-Media Arts (bd mem). *Publ:* dir, Doris Chase Dance Series, 70-79, Concept Series, 80-85, By Herself, 95-90, the Chelsea, 93; Sophi, 89; By Herself (series), 90; The Chelsea, 93; auth, "By Herself" series discussion guide, 95. *Dealer:* Terra Nova Films, Whitney Mus New York NY, MoMA. *Mailing Add:* 900 University St Seattle WA 98101

CHASE, JACK S(PAULDING)
SCULPTOR
b Burlington, Vt, Mar 4, 41. *Study:* US Military Acad, BS, 63; Univ Vt, Burlington, MS, 72. *Work:* Cathedral Church St Paul, Burlington, Vt; Champlain Valley Union High Sch, Hinesburg, Vt; Smithsonian Mus (Nat Zoological Park) & Am Cancer Soc, Washington. *Comn:* Bronze tree, Heckler & Koch, Arlington, Va, 81; steel mobile, Nat Zoological Park, 90; bronze mem trophy, Lake Champlain Yacht Club, Shelburne, Vt, 83; bronze tree, comn by Bishop Harvey Butterfield, South Burlington, Vt, 83; Welded Mem Sculpture, US Army For Sci & Technol Ctr, Charlottesville, Va. *Exhib:* Nat Vietnam Mem Design Winners, Am Inst Archit, Washington, 81; Nat Defense Univ, Washington, 86; US Army Intelligence Agency, Washington, 88; US Army War Col, Carlisle, Pa, 90; Fisher Galleries, Washington, 96 & 98. *Pos:* Owner, Birch Pond Sculpture, Jericho, Vt, 82-. *Awards:* Most Popular Sculpture Award, Exhib Vt Artists, Norwich Univ, 80 & 82; Phillippe Citation Distinguished Pub Serv Art, Gen Elect Found, 82; and others; Best of Show, WestFest, Westfield, Mass, 99. *Bibliog:* Donna Carpenter (auth), Yankee Artist, Monogram, Gen Elect Co, 83; Anne Brown (auth), Witness Trees, High Roads Folio, 85; Catherine Orr (auth), A man for all seasons: Jack Chase, Lookout Mag, 86. *Mem:* Vt Crafts Coun. *Media:* Welded Metal, Computer Design in Stainless Steel. *Mailing Add:* 42 Snipe Island Rd Jericho VT 05465

CHASE, JEANNE NORMAN
PAINTER, PRINTMAKER
b Spokane, Wash, Feb 15, 29. *Study:* Calif State Univ, BFA, 59. *Work:* LaGrange Col, Ga; Chattahoochie Mus Art, Ga; Kyoto Internat Wood Soc, Japan; Portland Mus of Art, Ore; Spencer Mus Art, Univ of Kans. *Exhib:* Manhattan Graphic Soc, NY, 99; Print exhib, Veliko Art Gallery, Bulgaria, 2000; Women Contemp Artists Exhib, Selby Gallery, 2001; Exh Van Horn Art Ctr, Tex, 2003; Venice Art Ctr, Fla, 2003; Fine Arts Collectors Exhib, Sarasota, Fl, 2004; Nat Pen Women Exhib, Tampa Univ, Fla. *Collection Arranged:* Spencer Mus Art, Kans; Muban Found, Chonqing, China; Pres Jimmy and Rosalyn Carter, Plains, Ga. *Pos:* Lectr, Women in the Arts. *Teaching:* Instr, figure drawing & painting & chmn fine arts, Ringling Sch Art, Fla, 79-93 & workshops, Wild Acres, NC, 84-87. *Awards:* First Prize, Southeastern Art Exhib, 76; Merit Awards, Longboat Art Ctr Nat & Daytona Mus Art, 79. *Bibliog:* Alicia Caldwell (auth), Activist artist prepares series, Bradenton-Herald, Fla, 12/29/85; Joan Altabe (auth), A Creative Force, Sarasota Herald Tribune, 96; Thirza Jacocks (auth), Hello Sincerity, 96 & Studio Work of Jean Norman Chase, 98, Pelican Press. *Mem:* Artists Equity; Women's Caucus Arts; Fla Artists Group; Nat League Pen Women; Womens Contemporary Artists. *Media:* Pencil, Oil, Printmaking. *Publ:* Auth, Drawing in another dimension, Design Mag, 76; Artists and Their Cats, Midmarch Press, 90; New American Paintings, Open Studios Press, 96. *Dealer:* Mickelson Gallery 707 G St NW Wash DC 20001; 1817 Ingram Ave Sarasota FL 34232; Esposito Gallery, Alpine, Tex. *Mailing Add:* 1817 Ingram Ave Sarasota FL 34232

CHASE, LOUISA L
PAINTER
b Panama City, Panama, Mar 18, 51; US citizen. *Study:* Syracuse Univ, BFA, 73; Yale Univ Sch Art, MFA, 75. *Work:* New York Pub Libr, Mus Mod Art, Metrop Mus Art & Whitney Mus Am Art, NY; Morton Neumann Family Collection, Chicago, Ill; Newsweek, NY; Corcoran Gallery Art, Libr Cong, Washington, DC; Albright-Knox Art Gallery, Buffalo, NY. *Comn:* Silkscreen print, Lincoln Ctr, New York, 81. *Exhib:* Whitney Biennial, Whitney Mus Am Art, NY, 81; Am Landscape, Whitney Mus, Fairfield Co, Conn, 81; New Visions, Aldrich Mus, Ridgefield, Conn, 81; one-person exhibs, Robert Miller Gallery, NY, 81, 82, 84 & 86, Harcus-Krakow Gallery, Boston & Galerie Inge Baker, Cologne, 83, Mira Goddard Gallery, Toronto, 84 & 89, Paul Cava Gallery, Philadelphia, 84, Margo Levin Gallery, Los Angeles, 85, Texas Gallery, Houston, 87 & Brooke Alexander, NY, 89; Block Prints, Whitney Mus Am Art, 82; Am Artist as Printmaker: 23rd National Print Exhib, Brooklyn Mus, 83; Prints from Blocks: Gauguin to Now, Mus Mod Art, NY, 83; Currents, Inst Contemp Art, Boston, 84; An Int Survey of Recent Painting & Sculpture, Mus Mod Art, NY, 84; Drawing Acquisitions: 1981-1985, Whitney Mus Am Art, 85; Selections from the Frederick R Weisman Collection (traveling), 87; The New Generation, The 80's, Am Painters & Sculptors, Metrop Mus Art, NY, 88; Making Their Mark, Women Artists Move into the Mainstream, 1979-85 (traveling), 89; Landscapes, Brooke Alexander, 89. *Teaching:* Instr painting, RI Sch Design, Providence, 75-79, Sch Visual Arts, New York, 80-82. *Awards:* Nat Endowment Arts, 78-79 & 82-83; Creative Artists Pub Serv Prog, 79-80. *Bibliog:* Margaret Moorman (auth), Louisa Chase, Brooke Alexander, Artnews, summer 89; Richard Kalina (auth), Louisa Chase, Arts Mag, 5/89; Michael Brenson (auth), Works from nature, Louisa Chase, NY Times, 2/17/89. *Media:* Oil. *Dealer:* Brooke Alexander 59 Wooster St New York NY 10012. *Mailing Add:* 6 Varick St New York NY 10013

CHASE, W(ILLIAM) THOMAS
CONSERVATOR
b Boston, Mass, May 31, 40. *Study:* Oberlin Col, Ohio, BA, 62; NY Univ, MA, 67, conserv cert, 67; Brit Coun Course on conserv of antiquities, 69. *Pos:* Wadsworth Atheneum, Hartford, Conn, 62 & 63; conservator to Nemrud Dagh Excavations, Adiyaman Villayet, Turkey, 64; Chester Dale Fel in Conserv Dept, Metrop Mus Art, New York, 66; asst conservator, Freer Tech Lab, 66-68, head conserv, 68-97; adv to John D Rockefeller 3rd Fund for Thai Bronze Treatment Proj, 73-75; head, Chase Art Serv, 97-. *Mem:* Fel Int Inst Conserv Hist & Artistic Works; hon fel Am Inst Conserv (pres, 2003-2005); Washington Conserv Guild (vchmn, 68-69, pres, 70). *Res:* Technical studies of Oriental art, particularly ancient Chinese bronzes and belt-hooks, mirrors and other objects; corrosion study and analysis. *Publ:* Coauth (with Gettens & Clarke), Two early chinese weapons with meteoritic iron blades, Freer Occasional Papers, 71; auth, Bronze Disease and Its Treatment, Dept Fine Arts, Thailand, 75; co-ed, Corrosion and Metal Artifacts, Nat Bur Stand, 77; co-auth (with U Franklin), Early Chinese Black Mirrors and Pattern-Etched Weapons Ars Orientalis XI; coauth, Islamic metalwork, Freer Gallery, 85. *Mailing Add:* 4621 Norwood Dr Chevy Chase MD 20815

CHASE-BIEN, GAIL
PAINTER & PASTEL
b Lowell, Mass, May 16, 46. *Study:* Calif Col of Art, BFA (with High Distinction), 1978; Calif Col of Art, MFA (with High Distinction), 1980. *Work:* di Rosa Mus, Sonoma, Calif; Sonoma Art Mus, Sonoma, Calif; Hughes Corp, Los Angeles, Calif; Shearson Lehman Corp, NY; Mustard's Restaurant, Napa Valley, Yountville, Calif. *Comn:* Art Work Int, Sultan of Brunei, Beverly Hills Hotel, Los Angeles, Calif; Carneros Alambic, Remy Martin Winery, Napa, Calif. *Exhib:* Ann 111th Exhib, San Francisco, Art Inst, San Francisco, Calif, 1992; California Landscape, Hewlett Packard Corp, San Mateo, Calif, 1994; California Grandeur and Genre Exhib, Bedford Gallery, Walnut Creek, Calif, 1996; Calif Col of Arts & Crafts, Alumni Exhib, CCAC Gallery, San Francisco, Calif, 1999; Gail Chase-Bien, I Wolk Gallery, St. Helena, Calif, 2003, 2006; Parallel Convergence, Napa Valley Mus, Yountville, Calif, 2004. *Pos:* Foun River Sch, Middle Sch for the Arts, Napa, Calif, 1995; Dir Fine Arts, River Sch, Napa, Calif, 2004; Bd, Napa Col Performing Arts Center, Napa, Calif, 2006; Bd Mem, Napa Arts Coun, Napa, Calif, 2006. *Teaching:* Instr painting, Col of the Redwoods, Fort Brag, Calif, 1983-1986; Visual artist, Napa Arts Coun, Napa, Calif, 2003-2004. *Awards:* Curator's Choice, Terra Infirma, Napa Valley Mus, 2004. *Bibliog:* Robert Taylor (auth), Brockton Mus Exhib, Boston Globe, 1989; Terri Cohen (auth), Gail Chase-Bien, Artweek Mag, 1992; Leonard Shlain (auth), The Paintings of Gail Chase-Bien, Parallel Convergence Catalog, 2004. *Mem:* Napa Arts Coun (bd mem, 2006); Napa Col Performing Arts (bd mem, 2006). *Media:* Oil. *Publ:* Coauth, Gail Chase-Bien, Napa Valley Mus, 2004. *Mailing Add:* 1086 La Londe Ln Napa CA 94558

CHASE-RIBOUD, BARBARA
SCULPTOR, WRITER
b US, June 26, 39. *Study:* Temple Univ, BFA, PhD; Yale Univ, MFA; Mulhouse Col, PhD; Univ Conn, PhD. *Work:* Mus Mod Art, NY; Newark Mus, NJ; Beaubourg Mus, Paris; NY State Off Bldg; Metrop Mus Art, NY; Nat Collections, France; Foley Sq Off Bldg, NY; and others. *Comn:* Fountain, Kiron Arts & Communications, Paris, 92; multi-colored bronze sculpture, Lannan Found, Los Angeles; bronze & silk sculpture, Metrop Mus, NY; Gen Serv, Washington. *Exhib:* One-man shows, Mass Inst Technol, Boston, 70, Berkeley Univ Mus, 73, Detroit Art Inst, 73, Indianapolis Art Mus, 73, Mus Mod Art, Paris, 74, Kunstmuseum, Dusseldorf, 74, Kunstmuseum, Baden-Baden, 79, Mussee Reatu, Artes, 80, Bronx Mus, NY, 81 & Passadena Col Mus, Los Angeles, 90; Kiron Arts & Communications, Paris, 94; Equitable Life Gallery, 96; Mus NC, 97; Mus Mod Art, Ft Worth, 97; Smithsonian Inst, 98. *Pos:* Lectr, US State Dept, Tunisia, Senegal, Mali, Ghana, Ivory Coast, and others, currently. *Awards:* John Hay Whitney Fel; Carl Sandberg Prize, Best Am Poet, 88; Knighthood in Arts & letters, French Govt, 96. *Bibliog:* American Women Sculptors, Rubinstien, 91; Abrahms Jenson (auth), The Sculpture of Barbara Chase-Riboual, Munro Women Artists, 97. *Mem:* Century Asn, NY; PEN; Am Ctr NY. *Media:* Multicolored Bronze, Silk. *Publ:* Auth, Sally Hemings--A Novel, (French, Ger, Ital, Spanish & Swed transl), Viking, 79; Valide--A Novel(French, Ger, Ital transl), William Morrow, New York, 86; Portrait of a Nude Woman as Cleopatra, 88 & Echo of Lions, 89, William Morrow; The President's Daughter, Crown, NY, 94; Egypt's Nights, Felin, Paris, 94. *Mailing Add:* c/o Pegalston Fine Arts 407 Central Park W Suite 6C New York NY 10025

CHATMAS, JOHN T
PAINTER, SCULPTOR
b Marlin, Tex, Nov 1, 45. *Study:* Univ Tex, Austin, BFA, 68; Pratt Inst, MFA, 70. *Work:* Univ Tex, Austin; Baylor Univ, Waco, Tex; Bank Paribas, Dallas. *Exhib:* Artists Biennial, New Orleans Mus Art, 73; Southwest Tarrant Co Ann, Ft Worth Art Mus, 77; Made in Tex, Univ Tex, Austin, 79; NTex Invitational, NTex State Univ, 79; Small Works, 80 Wash Sq E Galleries, NY Univ, 80; New Am Talent, Laguna Gloria Art Mus, Austin, 86; solo exhibs incl: Baylor Univ, 92, New Am Talent, Austin Mus Art, 95, City Images, Divaldo Archa, Prague, Czech Repub, 96, Visions Int Competition, Art Ctr Waco, 2002. *Teaching:* Instr art & art hist, McLennan Community Col, 70-. *Awards:* First Place Award, Art Ctr Waco, 1977; Fac Develop Leave Grant, McLennan Community Col, 85; Visual Artists Fel, Art Matters Inc, New York, 90; Merit Award, Contemp Art Ctr Ft Worth, Tex, 97. *Bibliog:* Gordon McConnell (auth), The paintings of John Chatmas, Cult Activities Ctr, Temple, Tex, 10/83; Janet Kutner (auth), Mystery Cloaks Intriguing Show, Dallas Morning News, 10/14/91; Susie Kalil (auth), Texas Ranges: Houston From Boogeymen to the End Result of Constructivist Theory, Art News, 12/82; Paul Rogers Harris (auth), John Chatmas: Paintings, The Art Center, Waco, Tex, 2/17/1979, 3/11/1979. *Media:* Acrylic, Oil, Miscellaneous Media. *Mailing Add:* 1315 N 34th St Waco TX 76710

CHATTERJEE, JAY (JAYANTA)
ADMINISTRATOR, EDUCATOR
b Calcutta, India, Mar 19, 36: US citizen. *Study:* Indian Inst Technol, BArch(hons), 58; Univ NC, MRP, 62; Harvard Univ, MArch, 65. *Pos:* Dean, Col Design, Archit, Art & Planning, Univ Cincinnati, 82-. *Awards:* Thomas Jefferson Award, AIA; Disting Svc Award, ACSP. *Mem:* Am Planning Asn; Asn Collegiate Schs of Planning (pres, 83-85); ICFAD; NASAD; Contemp Arts Ctr; AIA (assoc). *Publ:* Contribr, Managing University Team in Partnership Planning, Sage, 82; Schools and the Private Sector in Partnership, Rutgers, 84. *Mailing Add:* 20 Rawson Woods Cir Cincinnati OH 45220-1331

CHATTERLEY, MARK D
SCULPTOR
b Highland Park, Mich, Aug 22, 57. *Study:* Mich State Univ, BFA, 79, MFA, 81. *Work:* Holocaust Mus, St Petersburg, Fla; NC State Univ Visual Art, Raleigh; Jinro, Seoul, Korea; James Wallace Art Trust, Auckland, NZ; Kresge Art Mus, Mich State Univ, East Lansing. *Comn:* Three sculptures, Wharton Ctr Performing Arts, East Lansing; installation, Governor's Mansion, Lansing, Mich. *Exhib:* Lansing Art Gallery, Mich, 88 & 98; Kendall Col Art & Design, Grand Rapids, 88; Clay USA, Radford Univ, Va, 89; Univ Cincinnati, Ohio, 90; Kresge Art Mus, Mich State Univ, East Lansing, 91; Sculpture Exhib, Pa State Univ, 91; Egner Fine Arts Ctr Gallery, Univ Findlay, Ohio, 92; Adrian Col Art Gallery, Mich, 93; Raynor: Master and His Circle, Muskegon Mus Art, 94; Sixteenth Mich Artist's Competition, Art Ctr Battle Creek, Mich, 94; Life Imitating Art of Art Imitating Life?, Mackerel Sky Gallery, East Lansing, Mich, 95; Cincinnati Art Mus Spec Exhib, 96; Ester Prangley Rice Gallery, Western Md Col, 97; The Spirit of Clay, Art Works Gallery, Norfolk, Va, 97; The Artfull Home, Ann Arbor Art Ctr, Mich, 97; Mythic Fire, Edenside Gallery, Louisville, Ky, 97; Sculpture Michigan, Frederick Meijer Gardens, Grand Rapids, Mich, 98. *Awards:* Festival of the Masters First Place for Sculpture, Walt Disney World, Fla, 93; Mich Potter's Asn First Place Ceramics '95, Habatat-Shaw Gallery, Pontiac, Mich, 95; Fletcher Challenge Ceramics Award of Merit, Auckland, NZ, 98. *Mailing Add:* 231 Turner Rd Williamston MI 48895

CHAVEZ, JOSEPH ARNOLD
SCULPTOR, INSTRUCTOR
b Belen, NMex, Dec 25, 39. *Study:* Univ Albuquerque, BS(art educ), 63; Univ NMex, MA(art educ), 67, MA(art), 71; Univ Cincinnati, 74. *Work:* Slide Libr Collection, Univ Southern Ala; plus numerous works in pvt collections across the nation. *Exhib:* One-man shows, Jonson Gallery, Univ NMex, 71 & 76; NMex Arts & Crafts Fair Ann, Albuquerque; Southwest Arts & Crafts Fair Ann; Southwest Crafts Biennial, Santa Fe Folk Art Mus, 74; State Fair Dallas, Tex, 75; Gallery A, Taos, NMex; Aldridge Gallery, Albuquerque; Hispanic Market, San Francisco Nat Mus, 90; Denver Art Show, 90. *Teaching:* Art, Lincoln Jr High, Albuquerque, 63-70; supvr student teachers art educ, Univ NMex, 70-71; teacher art, Sandia High Sch, Albuquerque, 71-; instr art, Univ Albuquerque, summer 70; supvr student teachers art educ, Univ Cincinnati, 74; artist in residence, Pueblo, Colo, 90. *Awards:* Sculpture, Festival in the Pines, Flagstaff, Ariz, 90; Second Place, Pottery & Sculpture Expos, Rio Grande Art & Crafts Fair, 74; Spec Merit, State Fair Tex, 75; Fourth Place, NMex State Fair Sculpture Exhib, 83. *Bibliog:* Dr Jacinto Quirarte (auth), Mexican-American Artists, Univ Tex, 73; The Man Who Fell to Earth, London Film Co, 75; Joseph Chavez (auth, videotape), The Art of Carving Stone. *Mem:* Designers & Craftsmen NMex (pres, 73); Art Advocacy. *Media:* Stone, Wood. *Publ:* Auth, Critique on art, Col St Joseph News, 64; auth, Space filled & fulfilled, Southwest Art, 4/82. *Dealer:* Gallery A Taos NM; Aldridge Gallery Albuquerque NM. *Mailing Add:* 4618 Sorrel Ln SW Albuquerque NM 87105-6388

CHAVOOSHIAN, MARGE
PAINTER, EDUCATOR
b New York, NY, Jan 8, 25. *Study:* Art Students League, New York, 41-45; study with Reginald Marsh, 41 & Mario Cooper, 77. *Work:* NJ State Mus, Trenton; Morris Mus, Morristown; Rutgers Univ, New Brunswick, NJ; Mercer Co Cult & Heritage Comn; Johnson & Johnson, New Brunswick, NJ; Mus at San Larre, Venice, Italy; Zimmerli Mus, Rutgers Univ, New Brunswick, NJ; and others. *Comn:* Holiday design (reproduction), Multiple Sclerosis Soc, Trenton Chap, 73 & Nat Dist, 74; historic bldg series (30 paintings), NJ State Coun Arts, 80; holiday poster, Port Authority NY & NJ, 81; painting (reproduction), Armenian Sisters Acad, Philadelphia, Pa, 81. *Exhib:* Solo exhibs, Rider Univ, 74, 2000, NJ State Mus, 81 & Trenton City Mus, 84 & 88, Arts Club of Washington, DC, 91, Louise Melrose Gallery, Frenchtown, NJ, 2002; Group shows, Frye Mus, Seattle, Wash, 83; Owensboro Mus Fine Art, Ky, 83; Allied Artists Am Nat Exhib, Salmagundi Club, NY, 83; 200 Yrs of Am Drawings, Morris Mus, NJ, 84; Catherine Lorillard Wolfe Nat Exhib, Nat Arts Club, NY, 85; Nat Asn Women Artists, Jacob Javitz Fed Bldg, NY, 86; Philadelphia Watercolor Club 70th Ann Exhibit, Port Hist Mus, 88, Ursinus Col, 94 & 96; Nat Watercolor Soc, 98; Lancaster Art Mus, PA, Newark Mus, NJ, Noyes Mus, NJ, Phillip-Muriel Berman Mus, PA, Woodmere Mus, PA; Philadelphia Watercolor Soc, Noyes Mus Art, Oceanville, NJ, 2002; and many others. *Pos:* illustrator, John David Mens Store, NY, 43-44; artist, Fawcett Publs, 45-46; artist on campus, Pa State Univ, 46-48; Consult art, Title 1 Prog, teacher-student workshop, Trenton Pub Sch, NJ, 66-73; artist-at-large, NJ Chap Nat Orgn, Alliance Art Educ, 79-81; corresp secy, Trenton Artist Workshop Asn, 86-. *Teaching:* Studio instr painting & drawing, Princeton Art Asn, NJ, 77-79; asst prof watercolor, Mercer Co Col, West Windsor, NJ, 85-91; Watercolor Workshops, Chalfonte Hotel, Cape May, NJ, 88-2006, Hilton Leech Studios Workshops, 98-99, Art Ctr, Sarsota, Fla, 2001-2003. *Awards:* Silver Medallion, Garden State Watercolor Soc, Grumbacher, 81; Bermel Award Traditional Watercolor, Monmouth Mus, NJ Watercolor Soc, 84; Gold Medallion, Am Artists Prof League, 90, Title of Fel, 91 & Best in Show, 91; Bronze Medal, Catherine L Wolfe Art Club, NY, 2000 & 2004; Ken

McCann Mem Award, Garden State Watercolor Soc 35th Ann Open, 2005; Thomas Moran Award for Watercolor, Salmagundi Nat Show, NY, 2006. *Bibliog:* William D Gorman (auth), Marge Chavooshian paints the cities, Artform Mag, NJ, 11/81; Nancy Alderman (auth), Woman of the month, Woman's Newspaper, Princeton, 9/84; Pat Van Gelder (auth), The Watercolor page, Am Artist, 10/88. *Mem:* Catherine Lorillard Wolfe Art Club; Philadelphia Watercolor Soc; Nat Asn Women Artists; Allied Artists Am; Nat Watercolor Soc (signature mem); Am Artists Prof League (nat and NJ chpts); NJ Watercolor Soc, Garden State Watercolor Soc; Am Watercolor Soc (signature mem). *Media:* Watercolor, Pen & Ink. *Interests:* Piano, gardening, travel, plein air painting. *Collection:* Public: Zimmerli Mus, Rutgers Univ, NJ, NJ State Mus, Trenton Rider Univ, NJ, Art Mus, Venice, Italy; PSE&G, Johnson & Johnson, Schering Plough Corp, Arts Club of Wash, Mercer County Culture & Heritage Comm, Bristol Myers Squibb. *Publ:* Auth, Travel tips from the pros, 3/85, Quick tips, 7/85 & The watercolor page, 10/88, Am Artist Mag; Best in Watercolor, 95, Places in Watercolor, 96 & Landscape Inspirations, 97, Rockport Publ; The Best of Sketching and Drawing, Rockport Pubs, 99; The Artistic Touch 3, Creative Art Press, 99; Trenton Artist Workshop Asn, 25 Years, 2004; Phillips Mill 75th Anniversary Retrospective Exhibit, Phillip Mill Community Asn, 2005. *Dealer:* Coryell Gallery Lambertville NJ; Lawrence Gallery Lawrenceville NJ; Bordentown Gallery Bordentown NJ. *Mailing Add:* 222 Morningside Dr Trenton NJ 08618

CHEANG, SHU LEA
FILMMAKER
Exhib: Color Schemes, Whitney Mus Am Art, NY, 90; Those Fluttering Objects of Desire, Whitney Mus Am Art Biennial Exhib, NY, 93; Fresh Kill, Berlin Int Film Festival, 94 & Whitney Mus Am Art Biennial, NY, 95; Bowling Alley, Walker Art Ctr, Minneapolis, 95; Elephant Cage Butterfly Locker, Atopic Site Exhib, World Wide Web, Tokyo, 96; Buy One Get One, NTT/ICC Biennial Exhib, World Wide Web, Tokyo, 97. *Awards:* Moving Images Installation & Interactive Media Fel, Rockefeller Found. *Dealer:* Woo Art 133 W 19th St 3rd Floor New York NY 10011. *Mailing Add:* 355 Bowery New York NY 10003

CHECEFSKY, BRUCE E
PHOTOGRAPHER
b Peckville, Pa, Apr 14, 57. *Study:* Keystone Col, AA, 77; Kutztown Univ, BS, 80; Cranbrook Acad Art, MFA, 82. *Work:* Mus Mod Art, Saitama, Japan; Mus Mod Art, Lodz, Poland. *Comn:* Photograms, Cleveland Pub Libr, Ohio, 96. *Exhib:* One-man shows, Ctr Contemp Art (with catalog), Warsaw, Poland, 91, McDonough Mus Art, Youngstown, Ohio, 96 & Cleveland Ctr Contemp Art (with catalog), 96; 20/20 Vision, Cranbrook Acad Mus, Bloomfield Hills, Mich, 94; Language of Place (with catalog), Mus Mod Art, Saitama, Japan, 95. *Mailing Add:* 2240 Professor Ave Cleveland OH 44113

CHEE, CHENG-KHEE (JINYI XU)
PAINTER, EDUCATOR
b Fujian, China, Jan 14, 34; US citizen. *Study:* Nanyang Univ, Singapore, BA, 60; Univ Minn, Minneapolis, MA, 64; studied watercolor painting with Dong Kingman & Edgar Whitney. *Work:* Univ Minn & 3-M Co, St Paul; Tweed Mus Art, Duluth, Minn; Purdue Univ, Calumet, Ind; China Acad Fine Arts, Hangzhou, China; Fujian Prov Art Mus, China. *Comn:* Lakeshore Surf (painting) 88, Winter Lake View (painting), 95, Lake Superior Paper Industs, Duluth, Minn. *Exhib:* Minn Mus Art, St Paul, 76; Am Watercolor Soc Ann, 75, 78, 79, 81, 91, 94, 95 & 98, 01, 03; Rocky Mountain Nat Watermedia Exhib, Foothills Art Ctr, Golden, Colo, 76, 78, 80, 84 & 90-93; Allied Artists Am Ann, Nat Art Club, NY, 80, 82 & 91-96, 97, 99, 2000, 01, 03; Nat Watercolor Soc Ann, 83-85 & 92, 02, 03, Adirondacks Nat Exhib Am Watercolors, 82, 83, 86, 89, 91, 92 & 95, 98, 97, 98, 2000, 02, 03, 04; Singapore Nat Art Mus, 97; Bloomington Art Ctr, 2003. *Pos:* Sr librn, Univ Minn, Duluth, 65-78. *Teaching:* Instr, Univ Minn, Duluth, 78-80, asst prof, 81-88, assoc prof, 88-. *Awards:* Gold Medal, Allied Artists Am 67th Ann, 80; Gold Medal, Knickerbocker Artists Ann, 90 & 93; Silver Medal, Am Watercolor Soc Ann, 91; and others. *Bibliog:* Marcia Brown (auth), The Eastern Mountain Walks on Water, Cheng-Khee Chee China Exhib (catalog), 87; Hugh E Bishop (auth), Chee Pursuing Excellence, Lake Superior Mag, 5/95; Lok Tok (auth), Master Watercolorist Cheng-Khee Chee, Cheng-Khee Chee Southeast Asia Exhib (catalog), 97. *Mem:* Am Watercolor Soc; Transparent Watercolor Soc Am; Nat Watercolor Soc; Allied Artists Am; Watercolor USA Honor Soc. *Media:* Watercolor, Chinese Brush Painting. *Publ:* Contribr, Learn Watercolor the Edgar Whitney Way, 94; Splash 3: Ideas and Inspirations, 94; The Best of Watercolor, Rockport Pub, 95; Splash 4: The Splendor of Light, 96; Splash 5: The Glory of Color; The Watercolor World of Cheng-Khee Chee; Old Turtle Illustrations, 91; Noel Illustrations, 2005. *Dealer:* Chee Studio 1508 Vermilion Rd Duluth MN 55812. *Mailing Add:* 1508 Vermilion Rd Duluth MN 55812-1526

CHEEK, RONALD EDWARD
PAINTER, INSTRUCTOR
b Greenville, SC, Dec 6, 42. *Study:* Ringling Sch Art & Design, BFA, 71; Art Students League, with Frank Mason, Theodoros Stamos & Charles Alston; New Sch Social Research, with Joseph Floch. *Work:* Columbia Mus Art & SC State Mus, Columbia; Augusta Mus, Ga; The Citadel Mus, Charleston, SC; Albany Mus Art, Ga; Jasper Rand Art Mus, Westfield, Mass; Lakeland Mus Art, Fla; Sioux Indian Mus, US Dept Interior, Rapid City, SDak. *Comn:* Plant Remedies: Medicine of the American Indians, Blair-Murrah Exhibs, 91; Anniston Mus Art, Ala, 96; Cox Arboretum, Dayton, Ohio, 96; Bartlesville Art Mus, Okla, 97; Clark Co Heritage Mus, Las Vegas, Nev, 97; Charlotte Mus of History, NC, 2002. *Exhib:* one-man shows, Jasper Rand Art Mus, Westfield, Mass, 79, Old Hyde Park Art Ctr, Tampa, Fla, 81, Cayuga Mus Hist Art, Auburn, NY, 81, Citadel Mus, Charleston, SC, 81, Sioux Indian Mus, Rapid City, SDak, 82, Manatee Community Col, Bradenton, Fla, 83, Univ SFla, Sarasota, 85; Venice Art Ctr, Fla, 90; Anderson Co Art Ctr, SC, 91; Longwood Gardens, Kenneth Sq, Pa, 92; Cartwright Ctr, Univ Wis, Lacrosse, 93; Nat Hist Ore Trail Intrepretive Ctr, US Bur Land Mgt, Baker City, Ore; Jefferson Patterson Park and Mus, Prince Frederick, Md, 98; Lewis and Clark Interpretive Ctr, Great Falls, Mont, 99. *Teaching:* Art instr figure & drawing, Manatee Art League, Bradenton, Fla, 78-80; art instr all media & drawing, Manatee Area Vocational-Technical Ctr, 78-; art instr portrait & drawing, Sarasota Co Vocational-Technical Ctr, 78-90; art instr pastel painting & drawing, Sarasota Visual Ctr Art, 91-; instr all media & drawing, Manatee Community Col, 96-, Pickens Co Mus Art & Hist, 96- & Manatee Art League, 96-. *Awards:* Golden Jubilee Award, Sarasota Art Asn, 76; First Place, Paul Dorfmuller Mem Pastel Compitition, 82; First Place, Pickens Co Mus Art Invitational, 88. *Bibliog:* Drawings by Ronald Cheek, Sioux Indian Mus & US Dept Interior, 82; Forty works at forty, Sarasota Herald Tribune, 83; South Carolina Art Collection, Columbia Mus Art, 86; Biographical Ency of American Painters, Sculptors, and Engravers of the US - Colonial to 2002. *Mem:* Old Hyde Park Art Ctr, Tampa, Fla; Art Ctr, St Petersburg, Fla; Venice Art Ctr, Fla. *Media:* Pastel. *Mailing Add:* 617 E Main St Easley SC 29640

CHEMECHE, GEORGE
PAINTER, SCULPTOR
b Baghdad, Iraq, May 11, 34; US citizen. *Study:* Avni Sch Fine Arts, Tel Aviv, 56-59; Ecole des Beaux Arts, Paris, 60-63. *Work:* Guggenheim Mus, NY; Denver Art Mus; Fogg Mus, Boston; San Francisco Mus Mod Art; Herbert F Johnson Mus Art, Cornell Univ, Ithaca, NY; and others. *Awards:* Am-Israel Cult Found Award, 60. *Bibliog:* Jean Pierre Vandigaum (auth), Interview with the artist, Art Press, Paris, 77; John Perreault (auth), article, in: Soho News, 77; Ruth Bass (auth), article, in: Art News, 81. *Media:* Oil, Pastel, Metal. *Mailing Add:* 222 W 23rd St No 422 New York NY 10011-2311

CHEN, ANNA CHAIHUE
PAINTER
b Taiwan. *Study:* Art Inst Philadelphia, AS, 1973. *Work:* Daytona Beach Mus of Arts & Sci, Daytona Beach, Fla; Polk Mus of Arts, Lakeland, Fla; Walt Disney World, Co, Orlando, Fla; Orlando Int Airport, Orlando, Fla; Kissimmee Ct House, Kissimmee, Fla. *Comn:* (watercolor), comn by Patrick Knipe, 1996; (watercolor), comn by Noreen Schumann, Naples, Fla, 2001; (watercolor), comn by Chalotte Houser, Merritt Island, Fla, 2002; (watercolor), comn by Ether Van Kessel, DeBary, 2002; (watercolor), comn by Marrianne Dowling, DeBary, Fla, 2002. *Exhib:* Fla Watercolor Soc Am Exhib, Mus of Fine Arts, St Petersburg, Fla, 1991-1996; Collectors Exhib, Daytona Beach Mus of Arts, Daytona Beach, Fla, 1993; FWS Ann Exhib, Deland Mus of Art, Deland, Fla, 1994; The Artis Mag Competition, Cincinnati Art Club, Cincinnati, Ohio, 1997; AWS Ann Int Exhib, Galleries of the Salmagundi Club, NY, 2004-2006. *Awards:* Best of Show, Mt Dora Art Festival, Mt Dora Art Ctr, 1993-1995; Arts Mag Competition, Arts Mag, 1997; Best of Show, Sausalito Art Festival, Sausalito Art Festival LLc, 2005; Edgar Whitney Mem Award, Am Watercolor Soc Exhib, Salmagundi Art Club, NYC, 2006. *Bibliog:* Marilyn Watman-Feldman (auth), Winter Spring Watercolor Painter, Winter Park Outlook, 1990; Dianne Copelon (auth), Heritage Flavors Chens Work, Orlando Sentinel, 1995; Jennifer Modenessi (auth), Spotlight, Contra Costa Sunday Times, 2005. *Mem:* Am Watercolor Soc (signature mem); Nat Watercolor Soc (signature mem); Fla Watercolor Soc (signature mem); Int Artist Soc (signature mem). *Media:* Watercolor. *Publ:* Contribr, Tropical Joy Artists of Taiwan, Artists Mag Point Fine Arts Inc, 1994; contribr, Best of Watercolor Painting Texture, Rockport Publs Inc, 1997; Best of Watercolor Painting Composition, Rockport Publs Inc, 1997. *Mailing Add:* 9604 Velevetleaf Cir San Ramon CA 94582

CHEN, HILO
PAINTER
b Taiwan, Repub of China, Oct 15, 42; US citizen. *Study:* Chong Yen Col, BS(archit). *Work:* Guggenheim Mus; Byer Mus, Evanston, Ill. *Exhib:* Wadsworth Atheneum, Hartford, Conn, 74; Indianapolis Mus of Art, 74; Pa State Mus of Art, 74; Baltimore Mus of Art, 75; Lafayette Natural Hist Mus & Planetarium, La, 75; Edwin Ulrich Mus, Wichita State Univ, Kans, 76. *Collection Arranged:* New-Photo Realism, Wadsworth Atheneum, 74. *Bibliog:* Robert Hughes (auth), An omniverous & literal dependence, Arts, 6/74; Andrea Mikotajuk (auth), American realists at LKM, Arts, 1/75; Dorothy Belden (auth), Realism exaggerated in Ulrich Art Exhibition, Wichita Eagle, 3/76. *Media:* Oil on Canvas, Watercolor on Paper. *Dealer:* Louis K Meisel 141 Prince St New York NY 10012. *Mailing Add:* c/o Lois K Meisel Gallery 141 Prince St New York NY 10012

CHENEY, LIANA DE GIROLAMI
HISTORIAN, CURATOR
b Milan, Italy, 1942; US citizen. *Study:* Univ Miami, BA, 68, MA(art hist), 70; Worcester Art Ctr, Mass, studied ceramics, 70; Wellesley Col, Mass, 71, post-grad study, Renaissance art; Boston Univ, PhD(Renaissance, Mannerism & Baroque art), 78. *Collection Arranged:* Karl May, 80, Thomas Nast, Illustrator, 84 & J Beuys, 84, Univ Lowell; Whistler, 84, Lawrence Kupferman, 85, Samuel P Howes, 86 & Photographs of Cambodia, 87, Whistler House Mus, Lowell; and many other exhibitions at Univ Mass Lowell and Whistler House Mus Art, Lowell. *Pos:* Consult, Nat Endowment Humanities Art Hist Grants, 80-; cur, Whistler House Mus, Lowell, 84-. *Teaching:* Instr art hist, Boston Col, 73-74; from instr to prof art hist, Univ Mass-Lowell, 74, chairperson art dept, 83-97; chair, Cult Studies Dept, 2000-. *Awards:* Samuel H Kress Found Grants, 73, 73 & 74; Nat Endowment Humanities Grants, 77-78, 79-82, 89 & 92; Mass Coun Arts & Humanities Grant, 85-86; Am Learned Soc, 90; Teaching Award, Univ Mass, Lowell, 2002. *Mem:* Col Art Asn Am; Renaissance Soc Am; Emblematic Soc; Victorian Soc Am; Save Venice Inc; PreRaphaelite Soc. *Res:* Italian art history; Pre-Raphaelite painters. *Publ:* Coauth (with P Marks), The Whistler Papers, 86 & The Whistler Notes, Lowell, 88; ed,

Vanitas and Vanities: Symbols in the Arts, Edwin Mellen Press, 92; Pre-Raphaelitism, Edwin Mellen Press, 92; Botticelli's Neoplatonic Images, Scripta Humanitatis, 93; Self-Portraits of Women Artists, Scolar Press, 97; Essays on Women Artists, 2 vols, 2002; Vasari's Homes, 2006; Vasari's Teachers, 2006. *Mailing Add:* 112 Charles St Boston MA 02114

CHENG, CARL FK
ENVIRONMENTAL ARTIST, SCULPTOR
b San Francisco, Calif, Feb 8, 42. *Study:* Univ Hawaii, 63; Univ Calif Los Angeles, Dickson Art Ctr, BA, 63, MA, 67; Folkwang Arts Sch, Essen, Ger, 64-65. *Work:* Fred Weisman Collection, Pepperdine Col, Malibu, Calif; Exploratorium, San Francisco; George Eastman House, Eastman Kodak, Rochester, NY; David Bermant Collection, Santa Barbara; many other pvt collections. *Comn:* Marine Station, Metro Rail, Metrop Transit Authority, Los Angeles, 95; Tilted Landscape, Tempe Arts Comn, Ariz, 95; community island pond, Pier 11, Percent for Arts Proj, NY, 97-98; Everglades Trespass, Library Project, Broward Co, Fla, 2000; Santa Monica Art Tool, Calif, 88; Santa Monica Libr, Calif, 2005. *Exhib:* Water Projects, ASG Gallary, Nagoya, Japan, 88; Impression of an Invisible Sculp, List Visual Arts, Mass Inst Tech, Cambridge, 88; 66 Percent Water, Capp St Projs, AUT, San Francisco, 89; 40 Yrs of Assemblage, Wight Gallery, Univ Calif Los Angeles, 89; solo exhib, Survey, 25 years of John Doe Co, Contemp Art Forum, Santa Barbara, Calif, 91, Quality of Light, Int Exhib, Cornwall Eng, Newlyn Art Gallery, Penzance, 97 & Installation, Santa Monica Art Mus, Bergamont Ctr, Calif, 98; Artec Bianale, Nagoya, Japan, 93; 5th Bienal of Havana, Cuba, 94; Investigations, Munic Art Gallery, Los Angeles, 96; Turbulent Landscapes Exploratorium (3 yr traveling exhib), San Francisco, Calif, 96; COLA: Individual Artist Grant Exhib, Munic Art Gallery, Barnsdall Park, Los Angeles, 97; Organic Lab Mus, Santa Monica Mus Art, Calif, 98; and others; Nature Observed, installation, Sculpture Ctr, NY, 2000. *Teaching:* Instr, Otis Art Inst, Claremont Grad Sch art dept & Dickson Art Ctr, Univ Calif, Los Angeles. *Awards:* Visual Arts Grant, Nat Endowment Arts, 82 & 86; Getty Visual Arts Grant, Getty Mus, 90; Los Angeles Cult Arts Grant, 90, 96 & 97; Flintridge Found Grant, 2004. *Bibliog:* JS Willette (auth), Profile of artist vision, Art Quart, fall 93; Peter Frank (auth), Art pick of the week (review of investigations show), LA Weekly, 6/96; W Wilson (auth), Investigations Show review, LA Times Calendar, 6/4/96; and others; Mark Johnston (auth), Contemporary Art in Southern California, Craftsman House, 99; Shifting Perceptions, Pacific Asia Mus, Pasadena, Calif, 2000; Carl Cheng, Works Mag No. & R. Whitaker, Editor. *Mem:* Mus Contemp Art, Los Angeles; Sculpture Inc. *Media:* Installations, Public Art. *Interests:* Cooking. *Publ:* Web Links; Carl Cheng on Google. *Dealer:* John Doe Co Santa Monica CA. *Mailing Add:* 1518 17th St Santa Monica CA 90404

CHENG, EMILY
PAINTER
b New York, NY, July 28, 53. *Study:* Rhode Island Sch Design, BFA, 75, New York Studio Sch of Painting, Drawing & Sculpture. *Hon Degrees:* fellow, Nat Endowment, 82-83, Yaddo, 95, NY Found, 96. *Exhib:* One-man shows Hanart TZ Gallery, 96, Bravin Post Lee, New York City, 97, Metrop Mus Manila, Philippines, 97, Schmidt/Dean Gallery, Phila, 98, Byron Cohen Gallery, Kansas City, Mo, 2001, Plum Blossoms, NY, 2004, Ayala Mus, Makati, Manila, Philippines, 2006; group exhib, Hanart 20th Anniversary Exhib, Hong Kong Art Ctr, HK The Ann, Nat Acad Arts, NY, 2004, Microcosm Brewery Projects Space, Los Angeles, Calif, Magical Gardens, Kidspace at MASS MoCA, North Adams, Mass, 2005. *Teaching:* instr, Sch Visual Arts, RI Sch Design, currently. *Awards:* Nat Endow Arts Fel, 82-83. *Bibliog:* Yeon-Shim Chung (auth), Emily Cheng Unity of East and West, The Art Mag Wolgan Missol, 7/2000; Abstracting the Meaning, The NY Times, 9/24/2000; Jonathan Goodman (auth), Ornament as Knowledge, Ornament as Desire, Yishu, winter, 2003; Impy Pilapil (auth), Rekindling Wonder, Philippine Star, 7/3/2004; Chris Moylan (auth), Emily Cheng and Lois Conner, Arts Asia Pacific, fall, 2004. *Mem:* Coll Art Asn. *Media:* Oil. *Dealer:* Winston Wachter Fine Art NY; Plum Blossom Gallery NY; Schmidt Dean Gallery Philadelpha PA. *Mailing Add:* 439 Lafayette St New York NY 10003-7007

CHENG, FU-DING
FILMMAKER, PAINTER
b Palo Alto, Calif, Feb 5, 43. *Study:* Sch Archit, Univ Southern Calif; Alliance Francaise, Paris; Univ Calif, Berkeley, BArch. *Exhib:* New Am Filmmakers, Whitney Mus Am Art, NY, 70; Yale Film Festival, 72; Belg Int Film Festival, 73; Asian-Am Film Festival, NY, 86 & 92; Tokyo Int Film Festival, 87; Houston Int Film Festival, 90; Art retrospective Magic Realism and Beyond, Available Light Gallery, Los Angeles, 98; film retrospective Zen-Tales for the Urban Explorer, UCLA/Armand Hammer Mus, Los Angeles, 2000. *Teaching:* Instr art, Univ Calif, Los Angeles, 76-82, Shamk Apprentice Galley, 97-. *Awards:* Independent grant, Film Proj, Am Film Inst, 77; First Place, Foothill Nat Film Festival, Foothill Col; Gold Prize, Houston Int Festival, 90. *Bibliog:* Zen-tales for the Urban Explorer (video), LA Weekly, 2000; Urban Mystic (videolage), Brave New Artists of Video, LA Times. *Mem:* Independent Feature Project, West. *Media:* Film video; Watercolor, Acrylic. *Publ:* Auth, Los Angeles Times Calendar, Brave New Artists Video, 87; auth, Video Lace, Urban Mystic, 87; illusr (children's book), Dream-House, Hampton Rds Publ, 2000. *Dealer:* Cinergy Entertainment Santa Monica CA. *Mailing Add:* 209 Seventh Ave Venice CA 90291

CHEPP, MARK
MUSEUM DIRECTOR, ADMINISTRATOR
b Milwaukee, Wis. *Study:* Univ Wis, Milwaukee. *Collection Arranged:* Howard Schroedter Retrospective Exhib, 87; Robert Von Neumann: Works On Paper, 1930-1970, (auth, catalog) 89; African Art From the Richard Hunt collection, 89; The Quentin and Emmy Lou Schenk Collection of Ehtiopiana, 90; Ethel Cook: The Young'n With A Wild Brush, 91; Imaging Faith: Greek And Russian Icons, 1500-1900, 91; The Columbian Encounter, 92; An Unexpected Orthodoxy: The Paintings of Lorenzo Scott (auth, catalog), 93; Conversations: The Paintings of Frances Hynes (auth, catalog), 93. *Pos:* Cur, Univ Wis, Milwaukee Art Mus, 74-91; dir, Springfield Mus Art, 91-. *Mem:* Am Asn Mus; Ohio Mus Asn; Asn Midwest Mus. *Publ:* Auth, Remains To Be Seen (exhib catalogue) John Michael Kohler Arts Ctr, Sheboygan, 83; Howard Schroedter (exhib catalogue) Univ Wis, Milwaukee, 87. *Mailing Add:* 107 Cliff Park Rd Springfield OH 45501

CHER-KILLIGAN, BEATRICE MICHELLE
PAINTER, PRINTMAKER
b Buenos Aires, Argentina; US citizen. *Study:* L'Alliance Francaise, Paris, France, 73; Miami Dade Community Col, Fla, AA, 93; Fla Int Univ, BFA, (magna cum laude), 95; Univ Miami, MFA, (cum laude), 97. *Work:* Art in Public Places, Fla Int Univ N Campus & Miami Pub Libr; Thompson Tech, Armenia Mus Mod Art, Paris; Armenian Embassy, Buenos Aires, Arg; United Airlines, Corp Latin Am Div, Coral Gables, Fla; and others; Cornell Mus, Fla. *Comn:* Mural, comn by Charles Aznavour, Paris, 88; mural, Nourhan Fringian Found, Paris, 90; mural, comn by Jean Paul Robin, Miami, 96. *Exhib:* L'a Rentree Artistique a'st Germaine, Galery Hautefeuille, Paris, 88-92; Les Artistes Independants Grand Palais des Champs Elysees, Paris, 90-92; Gallery Artist, Galerie Nesle, Paris, 89-92; Juried Exhib, Art Mus Fla, Miami, 93; 42nd Ann All Fla Exhib, Boca Mus, Boca Raton, 93; Living Traces, Sala St Martin Mod Art Mus, Buenos Aires, Arg, 98; Art Miami, Fla, 99, 2000 & 01. *Pos:* Dir, Gables Art Gallery, Miami, Fla, 78-82; vice chmn, City Coral Gables Cult Affairs Bd, 95-97; mem rep, Coral Gables Adv Cult Bd, 96-98. *Teaching:* Adj prof, Arts & Philos Dept, Miami-Dade Community Col, Kendall Campus & Visual Arts Dept, New World Sch Arts, Miami; instr Univ Phoenix, Ft Lauderdale, Fla; instr Barry Univ, Miami, Fla; prof, head animation, illust dept, Am Int Univ, currently. *Awards:* Best Mix Media, Univ Miami Alumni, 95; Pearls Award in Color, Pearls Art Supply, 95; Place St Michel Award, Hotel St Michael, 95. *Bibliog:* Christina Elizadle (dir), A Pleno-Beatriz Cher Painter, BCC Multimedia Cablevision; Margarita Delgado (dir), Beatriz Cher-Artist Painter, WLRN TV Channel 17; Carol Damian (auth), Beatriz Cher Collector of Memories, Fall 98; Carol Damian (auth) Art Miami, 2000. *Mem:* Salon Des Independants Oficial. *Media:* All Media. *Collection:* N Fringian Foundation & Armenian Museum of Modern Art, Paris, France; Art in Public Places, Tallahasee, Fla; Lucent, Holland; Florida International University, Miami Fla; Miura Museum of Contemporary Art, Tokyo, Japan. *Publ:* Article, Interior visions, Beatrice Cher's passion, Art Speak, 90; article, Beatrice Cher's adagio in Paris, France, Aim Mag, 90; auth, Artist Profile (No 2), Liam Univ, 92; auth, Astur Profile, Joan Miller, 96. *Mailing Add:* 525 Coral Way Coral Gables FL 33134-4925

CHERMAYEFF, IVAN
DESIGNER, PAINTER
b London, Eng, June 6, 32; US citizen. *Study:* Harvard Univ, 50-52; Inst Design, Ill Inst Technol, four Moholy-Nagy scholar, 52-54; Yale Univ Sch Design, BFA(Mohawk Paper Co Fel), 55. *Hon Degrees:* Portland Sch Art LLD, 81; Corcoran Sch Art, D Fine Arts, 91; Univ Arts, Philadelphia, D fine Arts, 91. *Work:* Addison Gallery; Mus Modern Art, NY. *Exhib:* Industry Sculpture Show, Butler Inst Am Art, Youngstown, Ohio, 71; Venice Biennale, 72; Va Mus Art, Richmond, 74; Jacksonville Art Mus, 75; Addison Gallery, Andover, Mass; Corcoran Mus Art, Washington, 95; Visual Arts Mus, NY, 95. *Pos:* Trustee & comt mem painting & sculpture, film, design, Mus Mod Art, NY, 65-85; vpres, Yale Arts Asn, 68-76; mem comt arts & archit, Yale Univ Coun, 71-; mem comt Visual & Environmental Studies, Harvard Univ Bd Overseers, 72-80; vpres, Am Inst Graphic Art; bd trustees, New Sch Social Res, 1986-2002; bd overseers, Parsons Sch Design, 1986-2002. *Teaching:* Instr design, Brooklyn Col, 56-57 & Sch Visual Arts, 59-65; Andrew Carnegie prof design, Cooper Union; Joyce C Hall distinguished prof, Kansas City Art Inst; vis prof, Univ Calif, Los Angeles, 98. *Awards:* Yale Arts Medal, 85; Hon Doctorate Fine Arts, Corcoran Mus Art, Washington & Univ Arts, Philadelphia, 91; RDI Hon, Roy Soc Arts, Conn, 92; Soc of Illustrators, gold medal, 2002. *Bibliog:* Douglas Davis (auth), article, Newsweek Mag, 71 & 200 American leaders, Time Mag, 74. *Mem:* Am Inst Graphic Arts (vpres, pres & bd dir, 60-); Int Design Conf Aspen (vpres & co-chmn bd dir, 67 & 90); Indust Designers Soc Am; Alliance Graphique Int; Benjamin Franklin fel Royal Soc Arts. *Publ:* Auth, Observations on American Architecture, Viking, 72; First Shapes, Firstwords, Abrams, 92. *Dealer:* Ricco/Maresca Gallery New York NY. *Mailing Add:* 140 E 81st St New York NY 10028

CHERNICK, MYREL
MULTIMEDIA ARTIST
Study: RI Sch Design, 70-72; Rutgers Univ, BA, 74; Art Inst Chicago, MFA, 76. *Work:* On the Couch; Mommy Mommy; On the Table; From the Inside/Out; The Women in His Life; Dangling Participles; and others. *Exhib:* Washington Sq Windows, Grey Art Gallery, NY, 90; Collage: New Applications, Lehman Col Art Gallery, Bronx, NY, 91; Dirt and Domesticity: The Construction of the Feminine, (with catalog) Whitney Mus Am Art, NY, 92; Under Contract, Randolph St Gallery, Chicago, Ill, 93; Living with Cobwebs, Video Pool Studio, Winnepeg, Can, 95; Projects, (with catalog), Islip Art Mus, NY, 96; Giftland VI, Printed Matter, NY, 97; Generations, AIR Gallery, NY, 97; Big Art in Small Places, Judson Mem Church, NY, 97 & El Bohio Cult Ctr (video), NY, 98; Relics and Remembrance, The Bristol Art Mus, Bristol, RI, 98; Mothers Mother Other Lover, Hanes Art Ctr, Univ NC, Chapel Hill, 98; Motherlode, Mills Pond House Gallery, St James, NY, 99; Now We're Thirteen, Synagogue for the Arts, NY, 99; Generations II, AIR Gallery, NY, 2000; Review/New, Synagogue for the Arts, NY, 2000; The Judson House Project, NY, 2000. *Collection Arranged:* New Work, New York/Outside New York, (catalog), New Mus, 84; In Three Dimensions: Women Sculptors of the 90's, (catalog), Snug Harbor Cult Ctr, 95. *Teaching:* instr 4-D design, Pratt Inst Found, 2001. *Awards:* Creative

Artists Pub Serv Prog Fel, 80; Nat Endowment Arts Visual Artist Fel, 89-90 & 95; US/Can Creative Artist Residency, Nat Endowment Arts, 95. *Bibliog:* David McKracken (auth), Under Contract, The Chicago Tribune, 2/12/93; Cliff Eyland (auth), Transition and Trajectory: The Art of Myrel Chernick, 97; Myrel Chernick (auth), Curating Winnipeg/NY, Poolside, Video Pool Mag, 98; Michelle Grabner (auth), Test Family: Children in Contemporary Art, New Art Examiner, Oct 99; Mother Reader, Moyra Davey (ed), Spring 2001 (text by the artist). *Mem:* Col Art Asn. *Publ:* In Three Dimenstions: Women Sculptors of the '90s, Catalogue of Women Sculptors, The Snug Harbor Cult Ctr, 95; Cathy Valenza (auth) essay, Projects, Islip Art Mus, 96; Cliff Eyland (auth), essay, Living with Cobwebs, 99. *Mailing Add:* 7 Mercer St Apt 4R New York NY 10013

CHERNOW, ANN
PAINTER, PRINTMAKER
b New York, NY, Feb 1, 36. *Study:* Syracuse Univ, 53-55; NY Univ, BS, 57, MA, 69; with Irving Sandler, Jules Olitski, Hale Woodruff & Howard Conant. *Work:* Yale Univ Art Gallery; Zimmerli Mus Rutgers Univ; Portland Mus, Ore; Nat Mus Women Arts, Washington, DC; Reading Pub Mus, Pa; Davison Art Ctr, Wesleyan Univ, Conn; Metroploitan Mus Art, NY; Brooklyn Mus, Mus of the City of New York; and others. *Comn:* Artist of the year, United Way, Tri-towns, Conn, 85; Friends of Music 91, Year of Mozart Celebration; Soc Am Graphic Artists; The Art of Persuasion (poster), Nat Arts Club, NY Soc of Etchers, 2006. *Exhib:* Solo shows, Munic Mus, St Paul, France, 96, Westchester Comm Col, NY, 97, Janer Gallery, NY, 98, Stamford Mus & Nature Ctr, Conn, 98, Kincannon Fine Arts, Tex, 99, Siena Col, Mich, 99, Queens Col, NY, 99 & Uptown Gallery, NY, 99; Stonemetal Press, Tex, 96; Broadway Gallery, Troy, NY, 97; Assoc Artists Southport, NC, 97; Institut Franco-Americain, Rennes, France, 97; Harwick Mus, Oneonta, NY, 97; World Fine Art Gallery, NY, 98; Boston Ctr Arts, 98; Gallery 551, San Francisco, Calif, 98; Housatonic Mus Art, Conn, 98; Stamford Mus & Nature Ctr, Conn, 98; Graphicarts Ctr, Conn, 98; Uptown Gallery, NY, 98; Silvermine Guild, 2005; Uptown Gallery, 2006. *Teaching:* Instr studio work, Mus Mod Art, NY, 66-70; instr painting & drawing, Silvermine Col & Silvermine Guild, 68-80; instr art hist, Univ Conn, 69; prof emer, Norwalk Community-Tech Col, 82-; printmaking, Univ Ind, 1999; Nat Acad, NY, 2000. *Awards:* Audubon Artists Award for Etching, 97; Eisner Found Award, NY, 98; Lifetime Honors, Silvermine Guild, Conn, 2005. *Bibliog:* Ann Chernow's Work at Yale, Conn Post, 2/98; feature article & cover mag, Fairfield Co Times, 3/98; Gifted Choices of a Guest Curator in Stamford, NY Times, 4/19/98; Herbert Lust (auth catalog), 9/92; Article in NY Times, 99 & Westport Mag, 2/2000; Catalog Raisonee of Prints, 1968-2005, Amity Art Foundation, CT. *Mem:* Silvermine Guild Art; Print Club Philadelphia; Soc Am Graphic Artists, NY; Nat Drawing Asn; Am Print Alliance; Albany Print Club; Calif Soc Printmakers; Los Angeles Printmakers; Nat Acad. *Media:* Oil; Miscellaneous Media; Printmaking. *Publ:* Auth, Reuben Nakian, sculptor, 69, Palette Mag, Conn Art Asn; art ed & contribr, Communitas, New Eng, 79, contribr, The NY quart, Greens Mag & Art Life, 94. *Dealer:* Dorothy Rogers Fine Art Santa Fe NM; Uptown Gallery 1194 Madison Ave New York NY 10128; Albert Merola Gallery Provincetown MA. *Mailing Add:* 2 Gorham Ave Westport CT 06880

CHESHIRE, CRAIG GIFFORD
PAINTER, EDUCATOR
b Portland, Ore, Dec 31, 36. *Study:* Univ Ore, BA, 58, with David McCosh, MFA, 61; also with Francis Chapin. *Work:* Mus Art, Eugene, Ore; Univ Ore; Eastern Ore Col. *Exhib:* Northwest Artists Ann, Seattle; Artists of Ore Ann, 58-75; Northwest Painters, Smithsonian Inst Traveling Exhib, 59; Mus Art, Eugene, 61-74; Gallery West, Portland, 72; Visions & Perceptions Gallery, Eugene, 80; Littman Gallery, Portland State Univ, 87 & 94. *Teaching:* Assoc prof drawing & painting, Portland State Univ, 63-81, prof, 78-92, emer prof, 92-. *Awards:* Ina McClung Award in Painting, 61 & Ore Develop Fel, 62, Univ Ore; Purchase Award, Mus Art, Eugene & Ore Arts Comn, 74. *Mem:* Portland Art Mus; Am Asn Univ Prof. *Media:* Oil, Watercolor. *Publ:* Ed, David McCosh (monogr), Mus Art, Univ Ore, 85; Sketchbooks of David McCosh, Mus Art, Univ Ore, 94. *Mailing Add:* 3540 SW 108th Ave Beaverton OR 97005

CHESLEY, JACQUELINE
PAINTER, MOSAIC ARTIST
b New York City, Jan 4, 36. *Study:* Workshop with Wolf Kahn, 1975; Vermont Studio Sch (scholarship) - 1995. *Work:* Newark Mus, Newark, NJ; Morristown Mus, NN; D I Dupont Nemours, Del; Horsham Hospital, Ambler, Pa; Monmouth Col, Long Branch, NJ. *Comn:* Ballentine Mansion, Newark, Mus, Newark, NJ, 1990. *Teaching:* pastel workshops, Pastel Soc, Somerset Art Asn, Princeton Art Asn. *Mem:* Pastel Soc of Am. *Media:* All Media, Pastel. *Publ:* coauth, American Artist, 1983 & 1989; contrib, Oil Pastel, Watson Guptil, 1990; contrib, New Jersey, Harry Abrams, 1999; contrib, Creative Composition & Design, N Light Books, 2003. *Dealer:* Walker Kornbluth Gallery 7-21 Fairlawn Ave Fairlawn NJ. *Mailing Add:* 95 Clark Ave Ocean Grove NJ 07756

CHESLEY, PAUL ALEXANDER
PHOTOGRAPHER
b Red Wing, Minn, Sept 10, 56. *Study:* Ariz State Univ; Univ Minn; Colo Mountain Col. *Work:* Bell Mus of Natural Hist, Minn; Honolulu Acad, Hawaii. *Exhib:* One-man shows, Ecuador, Colorado Springs Fine Arts Ctr, 74 & Gargoyle Gallery, Colo, 75; Nature, Nishi Ginza Galleries, Tokyo, Japan, 75; Indians of the Andes, Birmingham Mus Art, Ala & Sci Mus Minn, 75; retrospective, James Ford Bell Mus Natural Hist, Minn, 75; Nature, Honolulu Acad Art, Hawaii, 76. *Awards:* Photo Design Stock Award. *Bibliog:* Julia Scully (auth), Four photographers, Mod Photog, 7/77; Constance Brown (auth), It's always hot springs time in the Rockies, Smithsonian, 11/77 & Woman Alive, Quest, 11/77; and others. *Media:* Color Photography. *Publ:* Along the Continental Divide, Nat Geographic Bk; Compass Guide to Colorado; Compass Guide to Hawaii; Thirteen Day in the Life, Book Projs; Compass Guide to Minnesota, Bangkok Thailand Book, Passage to Vietnam Book Proj. *Mailing Add:* Box 94 Aspen CO 81612

CHESLEY, STEPHEN C
PAINTER, PRINTMAKER
b Schenectady, NY, Nov 19, 52. *Study:* Va Commonwealth Univ, BS, 75; Clemson Univ, SC, MA, 80. *Work:* Columbia Mus Art, SC; SC State Art Collection; Erskine Col, SC; Savannah Col Art & Design, Ga; Fed Reserve Bank, Charlottte, NC. *Exhib:* Emerging Artist, Columbia Mus Art, SC, 81; Orlando Mus Art Juried Exhib, Fla, 88; SC Contemp Images, Owensboro, Ky, 91; Montgomery Mus Fine Art Biennial Exhib, Ala, 94; Lure of Low Country, Gibbs Mus Art, Charleston, SC, 94; Nat Endowment Arts Exhib, SE Ctr Contemp Art, Winston-Salem, NC, 96. *Collection Arranged:* Southern Range, Converse Col, 95. *Awards:* Southeastern Ctr Contemp Art Fel, Nat Endowment Arts, 96. *Bibliog:* Dr William V Eiland (auth), To capture the feel of night, US Art, May-June 90; Jane Kessler (auth), Chiaroscuro - Cont Study of Night and Dark, Montgomery Mus Fine Arts, Sept-Oct 94; Kristina Montiuidas Kutus (auth), In the Dingy, Gibbs Mus Art, Feb-May 94. *Media:* Oil, Pastel. *Dealer:* Irene Morrah Ingold Art Broker 206 Overbrook Greenville SC 29607. *Mailing Add:* 3324 Prentice Ave Columbia SC 29205

CHESNEY, LEE R, JR
PAINTER, PRINTMAKER
b Washington, DC, June 1, 20. *Study:* Univ Colo, BFA, 46; Univ Iowa, MFA, 48; Univ Michoacan, Morelia, Mex; also with James Boyle, James Lechay & Mauricio Lasansky. *Work:* Rosenwald Collection, Nat Gallery, Art, Washington, DC; Mus Mod Art, NY; Tate Gallery Art, London; Bibliot Nat, Paris; Nat Gallery Art, Stockholm, Sweden. *Comn:* Honolulu Print Soc, 75 & 83; Honolulu Acad Art, 77; Univ Hawaii Centennial Comn, 82; Wycross Press Comn, 84. *Exhib:* Six Artists in Paris, Am Cult Ctr, Paris, 64; Epinal Print Biennial, France, 70-71; Cite Int des Arts, Paris, France, 79; Contemp Arts Ctr, Honolulu, 80; 10 yr retrospective, Fisher Gallery, Univ of Southern Calif, 68; BMIC Galerie, Paris, 81; Salon de Mai, Paris, 82; Honolulu Acad of Art, 85; Portland State Univ Gallery, 88; Univ Fla Gallery, 89; Amon Carter Mus, Ft Worth Tex, 90; Worcester Art Mus, Mass, 91; Mona Bismark Fedn, Paris, France, 91; Spectrum of Innovation, Nelson-Atkins Mus, Kansas City, Mo, 90; Williams/ Lamb Gallery, Long Beach, 90-92; Davis Dominquez Gallery, (solo) Tucson Ar, 99; Parsons Sch of Art & Design in Paris, France, 98, solo; Hawaii Satate Mus of Art Inauqural Exhib 2002; Hawaii State Mus of Art 2005. *Pos:* Adv bd, Los Angeles Printmaking Soc, 67-. *Teaching:* Univ Ill, 50-67; assoc dean fine arts, Univ Southern Calif, 67-72; fac mem, Univ Hawaii, 72-84; Louis D Beaumont vis distinguished prof, Wash Univ, 79; Lacoste Sch France, 89; UCLA, 89-90. *Awards:* 56-57 Sr Fulbright Research AW Award Am Acad in Rome, 64; Vera List Purchase Award, Soc Am Graphic Artists, 65; Univ Hawaii/Ford Found Fac Enrichment Award, Paris, 78-80; Fond Gardilanne-Moffat Studio Award, Cite Intern des Arts, Paris, 78-83. *Bibliog:* Wayne Miyamoto (auth), Lee Chesney--25 years of printmaking. *Mem:* Soc Am Graphic Artists; Col Art Asn Am; Los Angeles Printmaking Soc (adv bd, 67-); Hawaii Artists League; Honolulu Printmaking Soc; NW Prints Coun; Southern Graphics Conf. *Media:* Oil; Acrylic, Etching, Encgraving. *Specialty:* Painting; Prints, and Sculpture. *Publ:* Contribr, Printmaking today, Col Art J, Vol XIX, No 2; A brief glance at Ukiyo-e and Hanga, Japan Print Quart, winter 67; Teaching in art grad progs, J Educ Perspectives, fall 77. *Dealer:* Davis Dominquez Gallery 154 East 6th Tucson, AZ, 85705; Tobey C Moss Gallery 7321 Beverly Blvd Los Angeles CA 90036. *Mailing Add:* 14601 Whitfield Ave Pacific Palisades CA 90272-2645

CHESNEY, LEE ROY, III
PRINTMAKER, EDUCATOR
b San Antonio, Tex, July 5, 45. *Study:* Univ Ill, with Dennis Rowan, Eugene Telez, BFA; Univ Calif, Los Angeles, with Ray Brown; Ind Univ, with Rudy Pozzatti, Marvin Lowe, MFA. *Work:* Honolulu Acad Arts; San Diego State Univ Mus; State Univ NY Potsdam; Dickinson State Col Mus, NDak; Graphic Chem & Ink Co Collection, Chicago. *Exhib:* Libr Cong, Nat Collection Fine Arts, Smithsonian, Washington, DC, 69 & 73; 1st Int Pratt Graphics, Bath, Eng, 73-74; Int Print Biennials, Epinal, France, 75 & 77; Boston Printmakers, 82; Prints USA, 82; Pratt Graphics, NY, 82; and others. *Pos:* Prog dir art dept, Univ Tex, 78-81, grad adv, 81-88. *Teaching:* Assoc instr printmaking, Ind Univ, Bloomington, 69-72; instr design & prints, Univ Tex, Austin, 72-75, asst prof printmaking, 75-78, assoc prof art, 78-, assoc chair art and art history, currently. *Awards:* Graphic Chem & Ink Purchase Award, Soc Am Graphic Artists, 73; Honolulu Acad Arts Purchase Award, 73; Prints from Am Univs Purchase Award, US Info Agency, 74. *Mem:* Col Art Asn Am; The Southern Graphics Coun; Soc Am Graphic Artists, NY. *Media:* Intaglio, Mixed Media. *Mailing Add:* Univ Tex at Austin Fine Arts 1 University Station D1400 Austin TX 78712-0340

CHEVINS, CHRISTOPHER M
PAINTER, DRAFTSMAN
b New York, NY, May 31, 51. *Study:* Yale Univ, BA, 73; Rutgers Univ, with Leon Golub, MFA, 81 (Teaching Fel). *Work:* Jane Voorhees Zimmerli Mus, Rutgers Univ, New Brunswick, NJ; Continental Insurance Co, Piscataway, NJ. *Exhib:* New Galleries of Lower East Side, Artists Space, NY, 84; Fusion, Paulo Salvador, NY, 84 & 85; Smart Art, Harvard Univ, Sert Gallery, Cambridge, Mass, 85; New Art NY, Lidewij Edelkoort, Paris, France, 85; Urban Mythologies, Fine Arts Ctr, Univ RI, Kingston, 86; 12 Emerging Artists, Hudson River Mus, 87-88. *Teaching:* Instr painting, Mason Gross Sch of Arts, 81-82. *Bibliog:* Joseph Masheck (auth), Smart Art, Willis, Locker & Owens, 84. *Mem:* Found Community Artists. *Media:* Oil on Canvas. *Mailing Add:* 10 Beach St Third Flr New York NY 10013-2425

CHIA, SANDRO
PAINTER
b Florence, Italy, 46. *Exhib:* 10th Biennial de Paris, Mus Mod Art, Paris, 77; Recent Acquisitions: Drawings, 81 & An Int Survey of Recent Painting & Sculpture, 84, Mus Mod Art, NY; Figures: Forms & Expressions, Albright-Knox Art Gallery, CEPA Gallery & Hallwalls, Buffalo, 81; Aspects of Ital Art Now, 82, Recent European Painting, 83 & Fifty Yrs of Collecting: An Anniversary Selection; Painting Since World War II, 87-88, Solomon R Guggenheim Mus, NY; 60'80 attitudes/concepts/images, 82 & Trustee's Choice, 83, Aldrich Mus Contemp Art, Ridgefield, Conn; New Art, Tate Gallery, London, 83; via NY, Mus Contemp Art, Montreal, 84; The Human Condition, Biennial III, San Francisco Mus Mod Art, 84; solo exhibs, The Mezzanine Gallery, Metrop Mus Art, NY, 84, Recent Works, Galerie Thaddaeus Ropac, Paris, 93, Studio d'Arte Raffaelli, Paintings & Works on Paper, Kohn Abrams Gallery, Los Angeles, 93, Grand Salon, NY, 94, Recent Paintings, Waddington Galleries, London, 94, Galleria d'Arte Mod, Rome, 95 & Siney Janis Gallery, 96, Sandro Chia, Galerie Enrico Navarra, Paris, 2001, Archeol Mus of Florence, Miti E Leggende, 2002; Six in Bronze, Brooklyn Mus, NY & Newport Harbor Art Mus, Newport Beach, Calif, 84-85; States of War, Seattle Art Mus, 85; New Art of Italy, Joslyn Art Mus, Omaha, Nebr, traveling, 85-86; Philadelphia Collects Art Since 1940, Philadelphia Mus Art, Pa, 86; Selections from the Frederick R Weisman Collection, Pa Acad Fine Arts, Philadelphia, 87; The Reemergent Figure, Storm King Art Ctr, Mountainville, NY, 87; Int Art Show for the End of World Hunger, Minnesota Mus Art, St Paul, traveling, 87-88; Utopia-Arte Ital 1950-1993 (with catalog), Salzburger Festspiele, 93; Drawing the Line Against Aids (with catalog), Biennale di Venezia & AmFar Int, Venice, 93; Works on Paper & Sculpture, Waddington Galleries, London, 93; Salama-Caro Gallery, 94; Nat Mus Contemp Art, Seoul, Korea, 95; Thinking Print: Books to Billboards, 1980-95, Mus Mod Art, NY, 96; Mus of Modern Art, NY, 2000. *Bibliog:* Deidre Stein (auth), Sandro Chia, Grand Salon, ARTnews, spring 94; Nancy Princethal (auth), Sandro Chia at 65 Thompson Street, Art in Am, 10/94; Matt Diehl (auth), Sandro Chia, Artnews, 10/94; and many others

CHIAN-CHIU, CHOW
PAINTER, HISTORIAN
b Canton, China, Dec 23, 1910. *Work:* Tsing Hwa Univ, Peking; Hopkins Ctr Art Galleries, Dartmouth Col, NH; Cernuschi Mus, Paris; Lawrence Univ, Canton, NY; Hist Mus, Washington, DC. *Exhib:* Yugoslavia traveling exhib, Kansas State Univ, Univ Calif, Berkeley, Stanford Univ, Calif, Univ Pittsburgh, Pa, Univ Rochester, NY & others; Art Mus Seattle, Wash; Dartmouth Col, Hanover, NH; and others. *Teaching:* Pres, Int Studio Chinese Art, 52-67; instr Chinese art, Grove Art Sch, Miami Art Ctr, Fla, 68-70; pres, Chow Studio, 70-94. *Awards:* Respect Award, Inst Chinese Cult, New York, 70; Gold Medal & Jin Ding Award, Cent Gov Republic China, 80; Oscar Award, D'Italia, 85. *Bibliog:* Walter Foster (auth), Chinese Art, film, Wilbur T Blume, 62. *Mem:* Chinese Artist Asn, Nanking; Chinese Artist Asn, Hong Kong; hon mem Miami Artist Asn. *Media:* Watercolor. *Publ:* Coauth, Easy Way to do Chinese Painting, 61; coauth, Chinese Painting No 2, 72; auth, The Biographies of Chinese Painting New School Founder in History, Libr Cong, 75; A Comprehensive Guide of Chinese Painting, 80; Chinese Painting, Poetry, Calligraphy, 90; Portflio Chinese Paintings, 90. *Mailing Add:* 2740 Le Jeune Rd Coral Gables FL 33134

CHIANESE, CAROL BURNARD

CHIANESE, CAROL BURNARD
PAINTER
b Susquehanna, PA, Feb 01, 42. *Study:* Bloomsburg Univ, BS Bus, 1963; Meredith Col, Credit Hours, 1977-1978; Art Study, Giverny, France, Cert, 2005. *Work:* IBM Corp, Poughkeepsie, NY; SAS Inst, Cary, NC; Morehead Planetarium, Chapel Hill, NC; Carolina Power & Light, Raleigh, NC; Wachovia Bank & Trust, Raleigh, NC. *Comn:* Branch Bank & Trust Co, Raleigh, NC, 1997; Carolina Power & Light, Raleigh, NC, 1998; Elon Col, Elon, NC, 2000; SAS Inst, Cary, NC, 2001; Raleigh Red Wolf Sculpture, City of Raleigh Arts Comn, Raleigh, NC, 2001. *Exhib:* A Colorist Vision, Kinston Coun of Arts, Kinston, NC, 1986; Twelve Women Artists, Fayetteville Mus Art, Fayetteville, NC, 1991; Landscape Impressions, Wilkes Art Gallery, N Wilkesboro, NC, 1994; Shades of Pastel, Lauren Mus Art, Laurel, Miss, 2000; Celebrating 25 Years, Fayetteville Mus Art, Fayetteville, NC, 2004; For Pastels Only, Pastel Soc of Am 33rd Ann, NYC, 2005; Three in Giverny, Artspace Upfront Gallery, Raleigh, NC, 2006. *Awards:* Allied Artists Award, Pastel Soc Am, Allied Artists of Am 28th ann, 2000; Jim Lynch Award, Pastel Soc of Am 29th ann, Jim Lynch Co, 2001; Strathmore Award, Pastel Soc of Am 30th ann, Strathmore Artist Papers Co, 2002. *Bibliog:* Valerie Rivers (auth), Small Art Groups, Am Artist Mag, 1988; Raleigh Red Wolf Ramble, City of Raleigh Arts Comn, 2002; Blue Greenberg (auth), 3 Impressionist Artists, Durham Herald Sun, 2006. *Mem:* Pastel Soc Am (Master pastelist); Pastel Soc West Coast (Signature mem); Pastel Soc Southeast; Artspace Artists Asn (Juried mem); Capital Art League (Charter mem). *Media:* Oils, Pastels. *Publ:* Contribr, Small Art Groups, Am Artist Mag, 1988; contribr, Artists of the Carolinas, Mountain Productions, 1990; contribr, Raleigh Red Wolf Ramble, City of Raleigh Arts Comn, 2002; contribr, 3 Impressionist Artists, Durham Herald Sun, 2006. *Dealer:* Artspace Inc 201 E Davie St Raleigh NC 27601. *Mailing Add:* 4900 N Hills Dr Raleigh NC 27612-4006

CHIARENZA, CARL
PHOTOGRAPHER, HISTORIAN
b Rochester, NY, Sept 5, 35. *Study:* Rochester Inst Technol, AAS, 55, BFA, 57; Boston Univ, MS, 59, AM, 64; Danforth Found Teacher Grant, 66-68; Harvard Univ, PhD, 73. *Work:* Los Angeles Co Mus Art; Nat Mus Am Art, Washington, DC; Philadelphia Mus Art; Mus Mod Art & Int Ctr Photog, NY; Art Inst Chicago, Contemp Photog & Exchange Nat Bank, Chicago; Minneapolis Inst Arts; Mus Fine Arts, Boston & Houston; Int Mus Photog, George Eastman House, Rochester; Ctr Creative Photog, Tucson; Fogg Art Mus, Cambridge; and others. *Exhib:* One-person shows, SE Mus Photog, 95-96, Rochester Int Technol, 96, Witkin Gallery, NY, 96, Castellani Art Mus, 97, Hobart & William Smith Col, 97, High Mus Art, Atlanta, 97 & Univ Iowa Mus Art, 97-98, Stephen Cohen Gallery, Los Angeles, Calif, 99, Robert Klein Gallery, Boston, Mass, 99, Spectrum Gallery, Rochester, NY, 99, Troyer Gallery, Washington, DC, 99, Alan Klotz/Photocollect, New York City, 2000 & Spectrum Gallery, 2002, Spectrum Gallery, 2002, Hartnett Gallery, Rochester, NY, 2003, Photog Gallery, Univ RI, 2003,-2004, Carl Solway Gallery, Cincinnati, Ohio, 2004-2005, Center for Photog Arts, Carmel, Calif, 2005; Garden of Civilization, Ansel Adams Gallery, 96; Everson Biennial, Everson Mus Art, Syracuse, NY, 96; La Photographie au present: L'annee 1996 dans les collections de la Bibliotheque Nationale de France, 97; Bibliotheque Nationale, Paris, Faculty Show, Hartnett Gallery, 97; The Jude Peterson Collection, Fitchburg Art Mus, 98; Heliography: The Retrospective, Hugo de Pagano Gallery, NY, 98; Years Ending in Nine, Photographs from 1889-1989, Mus Fine Arts, Houston, Tex, 98; The Hotchkiss Sch, Lakeville, Conn, 98; Works on Paper: Digital Printmaking at Singer Editions, Robert Klein Gallery, Boston, 98; On the Nature of Landscape, Mt Holyoke Col Art Mus, 98; Sun Valley Ctr Arts, 98; Princeton Univ Art Mus, 98-99; Ctr Creative Photog, Tucson, 99, 2001; Yale Univ Art Gallery, 99; The Fitchburg Art Mus, 2000; Harvard Univ Art Mus, 2000; Visual Arts Gallery, Adirondack Community Col, Queensbury, NY, 2000, 2001; Mill Art Ctr & Gallery, Honeoya Falls, NY, 2000; Nazareth Col Arts Ctr, 2000; DeCordova Mus and Sculpture Park, Lincoln, Ma, 2000-01; Boise Art Mus, 2001; Fitchburg Art Mus, 2001; Davison Art Ctr, Wesleyan Univ, 2001; Kiyosato Mus Photog Arts, Japan, 2001; Spectrum Gallery, Rochester, 2001; Amon Carter Mus, Ft Worth, 2002; The Rosenwald-Wolf Gallery, Univ Arts, Philadelphia, 2002; Dunedin Fine Art Ctr, Fla, 2002; Visual Studies Workshop Gallery, 2002; The Troyer Gallery, Washington, DC, 2002; Nazareth Col Arts Center, Foyer Gallery, Rochester, NY, 2004; Fitchburg Art Mus, 2004-2005, Mass. *Pos:* Ed, Contemp Photogr, Boston, 66-69; co-founder, Imageworks Ctr & Sch, Cambridge, Mass, 71-73; chmn, Dept Art Hist, Boston Univ, 76-81; vis comt, Harvard Univ Art Mus, 95, chair, Photogr Collections Comt, 95-; bd trustees, Visual Studies Workshop, 80-2000. *Teaching:* Prof art hist, Boston Univ, 63-86; vis prof photog hist & theory, Visual Studies Workshop, Rochester, NY, 73-74; Harnish vis artist, Smith Col, 83-84; Fanny Knapp Allen prof art hist, Univ Rochester, 86-98 & artist-in-residence, 98-; vis prof, Cornell Univ, 91-92. *Awards:* Mass Arts & Humanities Foun Fel, 75-76; Nat Endowment Arts Fel, 77-78 & 90-91; Arts Coun Artist Award, Greater Rochester, 96; and others. *Bibliog:* AD Coleman (auth), Carl Chiarenza: Pushing the Envelope (exhib catalog), High Mus, 11/97; Stephen Prokopoff (auth, exhib catalog), Landscapes of the Imagination, Univ Ia Mus Art, 1/98; AD Coleman (auth), Tears and Pressures, Photo Review, 15-19, winter 98. *Mem:* Soc Photog Educ (bd dir, 68-73); Photog Resource Ctr (bd trustees, 77-); Friends of Photog (adv trustee, 79-83). *Media:* Black and White Photography. *Res:* Twentieth century American photography. *Publ:* coauth, Heinecken, Friends Photog, 80; auth, Eye & Mind: The seriousness of wit, Kenneth Josephson, Mus Contemp Art, Chicago, 83; Gary Winogrand (essay), Image, vol 34, no 3-4, 91 & vol 35, no 1-2, 92; Chiarenza: Landscapes of the Mind, David R Godine, Boston, 88; Evocations, Nazraeli Press, Tucson, 2002; The Peace Warriors of 2003, Nazraeli Press, Tucson, Ariz, 2005. *Dealer:* Stephen Cohen Gallery 7358 Beverly Blvd Los Angeles CA 90036; Robert Klein Gallery 38 Newbury St Boston Ma 02116. *Mailing Add:* 5 Edgemere Dr Rochester NY 14618

CHIARLONE, ROSEMARIE
CONCEPTUAL ARTIST
b Philadelphia, Pa, June 12, 51. *Study:* Pa Acad Fine Arts, 1969-1971; Fla Int Univ, BFA, 1972-1974; Fla Int Univ, MA, 1977-1979; Visual Arts Fel, Fla Dept State, Fla, 1982, 2000; Pollock Krasner Found Grant, NY, Found, NY, 1985; Fla Enhancement Grant, Miami-Dade Dept Cult Affairs, 2004. *Work:* Nat Mus Women in the Arts, Washington, DC; Art in Public Places, Miami, Fla; Art in Public Places, Tampa, Fla; Arthur & Matta Jaffe Collection of Bks & Aesthetic Objects, Boca Raton, Fla; Fla Int Univ, Miami, Fla. *Comn:* Carolina Monaco (2 paintings), Royal Carribean Cruise Lines, Miami, Fla, 1985; Assemblage for Princess, Miami City Ballet, Miami Beach, Fla, 1987. *Exhib:* 10th Anniversary Exhib, Ctr Book & Paper Arts, Chicago, Ill, 2004; Matter & Spirit, Wells Book Ctr Wells Col, Aurora, NY, 2004; For Everyone & No One, Mus of Contemp Art, N Miami, Fla, 2005; Lifestyle, Space Lab, Spaccs Gallery, Cleveland, Ohio, 2005; Journey, Noyes Mus Art, Oceanville, NJ, 2006; Book as Art, Nat Mus Women in Art, Washington, DC, 2006. *Bibliog:* Fred B Adelson (auth), Narrative Images Alluring World, NY Times, 2000; Christopher Healy (auth), Book It Art Gallery or Libr, Cleveland Scene, 2003; Helen Frederick (auth), Collaboration as a Medium, Pyramid Atlantic, 2005. *Mem:* Nat Mus of Women Arts; Pa Acad Arts; Mus Contemp Art; Noyes Mus Art; Fontaneda Soc. *Publ:* Auth, Rosemarie Chiarlone, Boxes & Books, Art Papers, 1994; auth, In Three Shows: Mus Looks Beyond Region, NY Times, 2002; auth, Book It Art Gallery or Library, Cleveland Scene, 2003; auth, Dissent: Political Voices, 2005. *Mailing Add:* 200 E San Marino Dr Miami Beach FL 33139

CHICAGO, JUDY
PAINTER, SCULPTOR
b Chicago, Ill, July 20, 39. *Study:* Univ Calif, Los Angeles, BA, 62, MA, 64;. *Hon Degrees:* Russell Sage Col, DFA, 92; Smith Col, Northampton, Mass, DFA, 00; Lehigh Univ, Bethlehem, Pa, LHD, 00; Duke Univ, Durham, NC, DFA, 02. *Work:* Brooklyn Mus; San Francisco Mus Mod Art; Oakland Mus Art; Butler Inst Am Art, Youngstown, Ohio; Pa Acad Fine Arts, Philadelphia; Los Angeles Co Mus Art; and numerous others. *Exhib:* The Dinner Party, San Francisco Mus Mod Art, 79, Traveling throughout US, Can, Scotland, Eng, Ger & Australia; one-person exhibs, ACA Galleries, NY, 84, 85 & 86, Marilyn Butler Fine Art, Santa Fe, NMex, & Scottsdale, Ariz, 85, Lyons Matrix Gallery, Austin Tex, 94, Flanders Gallery, Minneapolis, 96,

Cline LewAllen Gallery, Santa Fe, 96 & Galerie Simonne Stern, New Orleans, 96; Holocaust Project: From Darkness Into Light (traveling exhib, auth catalog), Spertus Mus, Judaica & 6 venues in US, 93; Sources and Collaborations (traveling exhib), Austin Mus Art, Tex & three other locations, 94; In a Different Light, Univ Art Mus, Univ Calif, Berkeley, 95; Division of Labor: Women's Work in Contemp Art, Mus Contemp Art, Los Angeles, 95; Sniper's Nest: Art That Has Lived with Lucy R Lippard (traveling), Ctr Curatorial Studies Mus, Bard Col, 95; Sexual Politics: Judy Chicago's Dinner Party & Feminist Art History, Armand Hammer Mus, Univ Calif, Los Angeles, 96; Hanart TZ Gallery, Taiper, Taiwan, 97; Trials and Tributes, New Orleans Mus Art, La, 2001; Voices from the Song of Songs, Fitzwilliam Mus, Cambridge, Eng, 2001; Resolutions: A Stitch in Time, Am Craft Mus, NY, 2000 & Skirball Cult Ctr, Los Angeles, Calif, 2001. *Pos:* co-founder, Feminist Art Prog, Calif Inst Arts, Valencia, 71-73. *Teaching:* founder, instr, Feminist Studio Workshop, 73-74; asst prof, Calif State Univ, 69-71; vis prof, Ind Univ Bloomington, 97, artist-in-residence, 99; artist-in-residence, Col of St Catherine, St Paul, Minn, 75; vis prof, artist-in-residence, Duke Univ, Durham, NC, 00, Univ NC, Chapel Hill, 00; prof-in-residence, Western Ky Univ, Bowling Green, 01. *Awards:* Nat Endowment Arts, 77; Streisand Found Grant, 92; Serv to Field Award, Spertus Mus Judaice, 94; Getty Grant Prog, 97; proclamation, City of Albuquerque, 96. *Bibliog:* Guy Cross (auth), An Interview with Judy Chicago, The Mag, Santa Fe, 9/96; Susan Fernandez (auth), Judy Chicago: artist and woman, St Petersburg Times, 10/6/96; Paula Harper (auth), The Chicago Resolutions, Art in Am, 6/2000; and others. *Mem:* Women's Caucus Art. *Media:* Mixed Media. *Publ:* Auth, Birth Project, Doubleday/Anchor, 79; Judy Chicago: The Dinner Party, Athenaum, Ger, 87; The Dinner Party, Viking/Penguin, 96 Beyond the Flower: The Autobiography of a Feminist, 96; Through the Flower: My Strugle as a Woman Artist, Yuan-Liou Publ Co Ltd, Taiwan, 97; coauth, Women and Art, 99. *Dealer:* Lew Allen Contemporary 129 W Palace Ave Santa Fe NM 87501. *Mailing Add:* PO Box 1327 Belen NM 87002

CHICHURA, DIANE B
ADMINISTRATOR, ART DEALER
b Queens, NY. *Study:* Pratt Inst, BS, 54; Columbia Univ, MA, 57; Fordham Univ, PhD, 80. *Pos:* Dist dir, Related Arts, West Hempstead Pub Schs, 68-98; co-owner, Isis Gallery, Ltd, Searingtown, NY, 82-; consult, NY State Educ Dept. *Teaching:* W Hempstead Pub Schs, Fordham Univ Grad Sch, 77-79. *Mem:* Int Soc Educ Art; US Soc Educ Art; Nat Art Educ Asn; NY State Art Teachers Asn (prog chmn, 70, 74 & 82); Long Island Art Teachers Asn. *Publ:* Co-auth, Super Sculpture: Using Science, Technology and Natural Phenomena in Sculpture, Van Nostrand Reinhold, 74; contribr, Cognition and the Visual Art Experience, In: Tapestry: The Interrelationships of the Arts in Reading & Language Development, Collegium Book Publ, Elmsford, 79; coauth, Cognitive Model for Visual Arts Experience & Interactive Development of a Cognitive Curriculum for Visual Arts Experience-Based on the Dynamic Process of Equilibrium, Fordham Univ, 80. *Mailing Add:* 47 Dogwood Rd Searingtown NY 11507

CHIHULY, DALE (PATRICK)
SCULPTOR, GLASS ARTIST
b Tacoma, Wash, Sept 20, 1941. *Study:* Univ Wash, Seattle, BA, 65; Univ Wis, Madison, MS, 67; RI Sch Design, Providence, MFA, 68. *Hon Degrees:* RI Sch Design, Hon Dr Art, 86; Univ Puget Sound, Tacoma, Wash, Hon Dr Art, 86; Calif Col Arts & Crafts, Oakland, Hon Dr Art, 88; Pratt Inst, Hon D, 95; Gonzaga U, Spokane, Wash, Hon D, 96; Brandeis U, DHL, 2000; Univ Hartford, Conn, Hon DFA, 2001. *Work:* Am Craft Mus, Cooper-Hewitt Mus, Metrop Mus Art, Mus Mod Art & Whitney Mus Am Art, NY; Contemp Arts Ctr Hawaii & Honolulu Acad Arts, Hawaii; Seattle Art Mus; Wadsworth Atheneum, Hartford, Conn; San Francisco Mus Mod Art, Calif; Los Angeles Co Mus Art, Calif; Nat Mus Am Hist & Renwick Gallery, Nat Mus Am Art, Smithsonian Inst, Washington, DC; numerous others. *Comn:* Victoria and Albert Mus, London, Eng; Atlantis, Paradise Island, Bahamas; Bellagio, Las Vegas, Nev; Naples Mus Art, Fla; Benaroya Hall, Wash. *Exhib:* Habitat Gallery, Detroit, 80-83; Charles Cowles Gallery, NY, 81-83; Betsy Rosenfield Gallery, Chicago, 81-83; World Glass Now, Hokkaido Mus Mod Art, Sapporo, Japan, 82; The Wisconsin Movement-Glass in Form, Priebe Art Gallery, Univ Wis, Oshkosh, 82; The Descendents, NDak Mus Art, Grand Forks, 83; 11th Ann Nat Invitational Contemp Am Glass, Columbus Col Art & Design, Ohio, 83; Mus Arts & Crafts, Hamburg, 92; Alaska Baskets, Skagway City Mus, Alaska, 98; Montana Macchia, Holter Mus Art, Helena, Mont, 98, Paris Gibson Sq Mus Art, Great Falls, Mont, 98, Hockaday Ctr Arts, Kalispell, Mont, 98 & Custer Co Art Ctr, Miles City, Mont, 98; Mus Tower David, Jerusalem, Israel, 99; Chihuly: Glass Master, Hsinchu Municipal Cult Ctr, Taiwan, 99; Installations, Hiroshima city Mus Contemp Art, Contemp Art Ctr Va, Va Beach & Mint Mus Craft & Design, Charlotte, NC, 99; Masterworks in Glass, Nat Gallery Australia, Canberra, 99; Installations, Knoxville Mus Art & Ark Arts Ctr, Little Rock, 2000; A Transparent Legacy, Seattle Art Mus, Washington, 2006; Niijima Float Installation, Tacoma Art Mus, Washington, 2006; Material Matters, LA County Art Mus, Calif, 2006; one-man show, Oklahoma City Mus Art, Okla, 2002, Phoenix Art Mus, Ariz, 2002, Ft Wayne Mus Art, Ind, 2002, Monterey Mus Art, Calif, 2002, Wash State Hist Mus, Tacoma, 2002, Tyler Mus Art, Tex, 2002 & Mus Centre Vapriikki, Tampere, Finaland, 2002, Frederick R Weisman Mus Art, Pepperdine Univ, Malibu, Calif, 2004, Fairchild Tropical Botanic Garden, Coral Gables, Fla, 2004, Colorado Springs Fine Arts Ctr, 2005, Royal Botanic Gardens, Kew, Surrey, UK, 2006, Marlborough Gallery, NY, 2006, Franklin Park Conservatory, Columbus, Ohio, 2006, R Duane Reed Gallery, St Louis, Mo, 2006; numerous others. *Teaching:* instr cereramics, RI Sch Design, 69-75, head dept sculpture and prog glass, 76-80; educ coordr & co-founder, Pilchuck Glass Ctr, Stanwood, Wash, 71-; affil prof, Univ Wash, 94-95. *Awards:* Distinguished Artists Gold Medal Award, Univ Arts, Philadelphia, 2000; Lifetime Achievement Arts Award, Corp Coun Arts/Artsfund, 2001; Gold Medal Award, Nat Arts Club, NY, 2002. *Bibliog:* Liz Seymour (auth), Man of glass, Attaché, 11/1998; Sarah Greenburg (auth), Glass act: Dale Chihuly in Seattle, London and Jerusalem, Art Newspaper, 5/1999; John Russell Taylor (auth), Sculpting with light, London Times, 06/27/2001. *Mem:* Seattle Int Film Festival (bd adv, 93); Seattle Art Fair (adv comt, 93); Pilchuck Artistic Adv Comt, 93-94; Northwest Aids Found (assoc bd mem, 94). *Media:* Blown Glass. *Publ:* Auth, Dale Chihuly: Chihuly in the ligth of Jerusalem 2000, Ariel, Israel Rev Arts and Letters, 55-57, 99; Chihuly Jerusalem 2000, 2000, Chihuly Projects, 2002 & Chihuly Gardens & Glass, 2002, Portland Press. *Mailing Add:* Chihuly Studio 1111 NW 50th St Seattle WA 98107-5120

CHILD, ABIGAIL
FILMMAKER, VIDEO ARTIST
Study: Radcliffe Col, Harvard Univ, BA magna cum laude, 68; Yale Univ Sch Arts, MFA(graphics/photog/film) with honors, 70; studies Peabody Mus, Harvard Univ, Univ NMex, Anasazi Originis with Dr Irene Williams, 66, Harvard Univ, Chiapas Project, Mexico with Dr Evon Vogt, 67, Sch Visual Arts, New York, NY, 69 & Univ Film Study Workshop, Hampshire Col, Opitcal Printing Workshop, 75. *Work:* Mus Modern Art, NY; Donnell Pub Libr, NY; Mass Col Art, Brookline; Miami Dade Co Pub Libr, Fla; Univ Calif, Berkeley; Pompidou Centre, Paris; Arsenal, Berlin; Harvard Univ Film Archive; Chicago Public Libr; Art Inst Chicago; San Francisco Univ, Calif; and many others. *Comn:* Cake & Steak, Oberhausen, 2004; The Future Is Behind You, film, LEF, 2004; On The Downlow, film, MTV, 2005; Mirror World, film, Radoliffe Inst, 2006. *Exhib:* Whitney Biennial, Whitney Mus Am Art, NY, 97; Nelson Atkins Mus, Kansas City, 98; Va Community Ctr Art, Sweet Briar, 98; Rocky Mountain Film Ctr, Boulder, 98; Women and Society, Col Univ, 99; Fin de Siecle, NY & France, 99; Surface Noise, NY Film Festival, 2000; Dark Dark, NY Film Festival, 2001; Featured Soloist, Providence Women's Film Fesitval, 2001; Cake & Steak, New Wave Festival Premiere, Brooklyn Acad Music, 2002; Artists Presentation, Carnegie Melon Univ, 2002; Conversations at the Edge, Chicago Art Inst, 2003; Subtalk, Lincoln Ctr, NY Video Festival, 2003; The Future is Behind You, NY Film Festival, 2004; Narrative & Film, Interval Conference, Buffalo, NY, 2005; Thinking Hands, Beijing New Art Projects Space, 2006; Mirror World, Bollywood Series, Pacific Film Archive, 2006; and many others. *Teaching:* Asst prof Mass Col Art, 85; adj prof, Sch Visual Arts, NY, 89-90; assoc prof humanities & arts, Hampshire Col, 90-91; prof, Sarah Lawrence Col, 91-99; sr fac, ch, film-animation Sch Mus Fine Arts, Boston, 99-. *Awards:* Nat Endowment arts Interarts Grant, 90; Fulbright Fel, 92-93; John Simon Guggenheim Film Fel, 95-96; LEF Found Fel, 2003-2005; Radcliffe Inst Grant, 2005-2006. *Bibliog:* Kevin Thomas (auth), Screening room, LA Times, 10/16/97; Manola Darghis (auth), rev, LA Weekly, 10/18/97; Jeffrey Skoller (auth), Home sweet home, after image, 11-12/98; Scott MacDonald (auth), A Critical Cinima, Univ Calif Press, Vol 4, 2003; Tom Gunning (auth/foreword), This is Called Moving: A Critical Poetics of Film, Univ Ala Press, 2004; Karen Schiff (auth), Fragment Fiesta!: Abigal Child Agassiz House, Radcliffe Inst, in: Big Red & Shiny, No 42, 5/2006; and many others. *Mem:* NY Filmmakers Coop, 80-; Canyon Film Coop, 84-; London Filmmakers Coop, 86-; Light Cone, Paris, 86-; NY CINE Women, 98-; IFP, 2006-. *Media:* Experimental Film & Video. *Publ:* Auth, Climate/Plus, Coincidence Press, San Francisco, 86; A Motive for Mayem, Potes & Poets Press, Conn, 89; Resurgent: An Anthology of Women's Writing, Southern Ill Press, 92; Mob, O Press, Calif, 94; Scatter Matrix, Roof Bk, NY, 96; Artificial Memory, 1+2, Belladonna Press, Brooklyn, NY, 2001; This is Called Moving: A Critical Poetics of Film, Univ Ala Press, 2005; and many others. *Mailing Add:* 303 E Eighth St New York NY 10009

CHILDERS, MALCOLM GRAEME
PHOTOGRAPHER, PRINTMAKER
b Riverside, Calif, Feb 19, 45. *Study:* Humboldt State Univ, Arcata, Calif, BA, 69; Fullerton State Univ, Calif, MA, 72. *Work:* Springfield Art Mus, Mo; Tenn State Mus, Nashville; Meadows Mus Art, Shreveport, La; Brooks Mem Art Gallery, Memphis, Tenn; Standard Oil Co-Ind; MdGraw Hill; Merck Corp. *Exhib:* Appalachian Corridors Biennial Art Exhib 4, Charleston, SC 75; Bradley Print Show, Peoria, Ill, 75-76; La Grange Nat Competition II, Ga, 75-76 & 86; Tenn Bicentennial Exhib, Nashville, Tenn, 76; and others. *Teaching:* Instr printmaking, Loma Linda Univ, Calif, 72-74; asst prof drawing, painting & printmaking, Southern Col, Collegedale, Tenn, 74-86; Instr Cleveland State Col, Tenn, 84; Instr Printmaking Univ of Tenn, Chattanooga, 85; Mesa State Col, Grand Juction, Colo, 2006. *Awards:* Purchase Awards, La Grange Nat II, La Grange Art Mus, 75, Mid-South Biennial, Brooks Mem Art Gallery, 75 & Tenn Bicentennial, State of Tenn, 76. *Media:* All media. *Publ:* Roadsongs: A Journey Into The life and Mindscapes of An American Artist, The Real Earth, Wind River Press, 2001. *Dealer:* Real Earth Art Productions. *Mailing Add:* 2910 Kell Rd Signal Mountain TN 37377-1033

CHILDS, CATHERINE O See Catchi

CHILDS, DAVID
ARCHITECT, PATRON
Study: Yale Sch Art and Architectre, grad. *Comn:* Principle works include Washington Mall Master Plan and Constitution Gardens, Metro Ctr, US News and World Report Hq, Four Seasons, Park Hyatt and Regent Hotels, Bertelsman Tower at Time Square, AOL Time Warner Hq at Columbus Cir, expansion of Dulles Int Airport main terminal, Washington, DC, US Embassy, Ottawa, Can, T-3 Terminal, Changi Int Airport, Singapore, The Freedom Tower at the World Trade Ctr Site, Worldwide Plaza, NY Mercantile Exchange, JFK Int Arrivals Bldg, Bear Sterns Hq, Riverside So, Stuyvesant Sch Bridge. *Pos:* Sr designer, Pennsylvania Ave Comn, 1968-71; with, Skidmore, Owings & Merrill, 1971-84, consulting design ptnr, 1984-; chmn, Nat Capital Planning Comn, 1975-81, Comn Fina Arts, 2002-; bd dir, Am Acad in Rome, Munic Art Soc, Nat Bldg Mus; trustee, Mus Modern Art. *Mailing Add:* Skidmore Owings & Merrill 24 Fl 14 Wall St New York NY 10005

CHILDS, ELIZABETH CATHARINE
HISTORIAN, EDUCATOR
b Denver, Colo, July 5, 54. *Study:* Wake Forest Univ, BA, 76; Columbia Univ, MA, 80, PhD, 89. *Pos:* Lectr & prog asst Educ Dept, Metrop Mus Art, NY, 76-81; mus lectr, Mus Mod Art, NY, 79; res assoc, Solomon R Guggenheim Mus, 87-91. *Teaching:* Lectr & asst prof mod art hist, State Univ NY, Purchase, 87-92; asst prof, Washington Univ, 92-98, assoc prof, 98-. *Awards:* Gould Fel, Princeton Univ, 92-93; Univ Fel, NEH, 96-97; CASVA Sr fel, Nat Gallery Art, 97. *Mem:* Col Art Asn; Midwest Art Hist Soc; Asn Historians Nineteenth Century Art. *Res:* Exoticism in modern art (especially Gauguin); political caricature; art and censorship; photography. *Publ:* ed, Suspended License: Censorship & the Visual Arts, Univ Washington Press, 97; contribr auth, Degas to Picasso: the Artist and the Camera, Dallas Mus Art with Yale, 99; contribr auth, Vincent Van Gogh and the Painters of the Petit Boulevard, Rizzoli, 2000; contribr auth, Gauguin: Tahiti, Boston Mus of Fine Arts, Musee d'Orsay, 2003. *Mailing Add:* Washington Univ Dept Art History & Arch Campus Box 1189 1 Brookings Dr Saint Louis MO 63130-4899

CHILTON, FRED
PAINTER
b Las Cruces, NMex, June 14, 44. *Study:* Ctr for Creative Studies, Detroit, Mich, 63-66. *Work:* One-man shows Branigan Cult Ctr, 83, Adobe Patio Gallery, 87, Studio W Gallery, 92, Glenn Cutter Gallery, 99, 2000; juried shows NM W/C Soc, 99, 2000. *Comn:* Mural, Lady of Guadalupe Cath Church, Tortugas, NMex, 85; vicariate banners, comm by Cath Diocese of Las Cruces, NMex, 85; book cover, illustrated history of Las Cruces, Linda Harris (auth); poster, NMex Wine & Vine Soc, 96; commemorative poster, 5th Ann Las Cruces Mariachi Conf, 98; commemorative poster, Internat Mariachi Conf, 98, 99, 2000. *Exhib:* 50th Ann Mid-Year, Butler Inst Am Art, Youngstown, Ohio, 86; Watermedia 86, Mont Watercolor Soc; Close to the Border, NMex State Univ, Las Cruces, 86; Rio Bravo Watercolor Exhib, El Paso Mus Art, 87; 121st Ann Exhib Am Watercolor Soc, 88; El Paso Art Asn Ann Exhib, Sierra Med Ctr, 92; Am Watercolor Soc, 94; and others. *Teaching:* Carrizo Lodge, Riudoso, NMex, Rio Grande Artes Workshops. *Awards:* Bronze Medal Color Photog, Scarab Club of Detroit, 78; Grumbacher Gold Medal, Salamagundi Club, 82; Huthsteiner Purchase Award, 88; Silver Medal, El Paso Mus Art, 88; Best of Show, NMex Watercolor Soc, 92, 93, 94; Best of Show, Sierra-Providence Annual Exhib, El Paso Internat Mus, 2000; 2d Pl Figure, 3d Pl Figure, 4th Pl Figure, Hon Mention, Watercolor Mag Ann Competition, 2006. *Mem:* El Paso Art Asn; NMex Watercolor Soc; signature mem Am Watercolor Soc. *Media:* Watercolor, Oil. *Publ:* Contemp Western Artists, Southwest Art Publ, 82; NMex Mag, 5/93; Watercolor magic, Artists Mag, 4/95; The Artist's Mag, 2001-04; La Ventana Mag, 2005; Watercolor Magic Mag, 2006. *Dealer:* Patio Gallery Las Cruces NMex; William Bonney Gallery Mesilla NMex. *Mailing Add:* PO Box 8436 Las Cruces NM 88006

CHIMES, THOMAS JAMES
PAINTER
b Philadelphia, Pa, Apr 20, 1921. *Study:* Art Students League. *Work:* Philadelphia Mus Art; Mus Mod Art, NY; Ringling Mus Art, Sarasota, Fla; Wadsworth Atheneum, Hartford, Conn; Aldrich Mus, Ridgefield, Conn. *Exhib:* Recent Acquistions, Mus Mod Art, NY, 62; retrospectives, Jacksonville Mus, Fla, 68 & Ringling Mus, 69; Biennial, Whitney Mus Am Art, NY, 75; Pa Acad Fine Arts, Philadelphia, 75; Philadelphia/Houston Exchange, Inst Contemp Art, Philadelphia, 77, 91 & 94; Locks Gallery, Philadelphia, 83, 88, 90, 92, 95, 97, 99, 2001, 03; Carnegie Mellon, Pittsburgh, 88; Onassis Ctr, NY, 94 & 95; 2000 Biennial, Del Art Mus, Wilmington, 2000; Royal Hibernian Acad, Dublin, Ireland, 2001; Conceptual Realism, Rosenwald-Wolf Gallery, Univ of the Arts, Philadelphia, Pa, 2000. *Awards:* Residency, Pa Coun Arts, 79; Fel, Nat Endowment Arts, 87. *Bibliog:* S Martin & S Berg (auths), Tom Chimes, Moore Col, 86; Livingston (auth), Thomas Chimes, Locks Art Publ, 92; P Murphy & I Barsky (auths), Conversation Pieces, Univ Pa, 94. *Media:* Oil. *Publ:* Illusr, Cymbalum Mundi, Des Periers/Knapp, Bookman Assocs, 65; Antonin Artraud, Man of Vision, Knapp, David Lewis, 69. *Dealer:* Locks Gallery. *Mailing Add:* c/o Locks Gallery 600 Washington Sq S Philadelphia PA 19106

CHIN, MEL
SCULPTOR
b Houston, Tex, 51. *Study:* Peabody Col, Nashville, Tenn, BA, 75. *Work:* Birmingham Mus Art, Ala; Harold Wash Libr, Chicago, Ill; Menil Found, Houston, Tex; Mus Fine Arts, Houston, Tex; Prudential Service Corp, Newark, NJ. *Comn:* Ecliptic Fence, Houston, Tex, 86; Conditions for Memory, Central Park, NY, 89. *Exhib:* The Manila Palm, Contemp Art Mus, Houston, 78; Fire, Contemp Arts Mus, Houston,79; solo exhibs, Frumkin/Adams Gallery, 88, Hirshhorn Mus & Sculpture Garden, Washington, 89 Walker Art Ctr, 90, Menil Collection, Houston, 91, Storefront for Art & Archit, NY, 91, Fabric Workshop & Swathmore Col, Philadelphia, 92 & Colo State Univ, Ft Collins, 95; Out of This World, Contemp Arts Mus, Houston, 94; Landscape As Metaphor (with catalog), Denver Art Mus, Colo & Columbus Mus, Ohio, 94; Equal Rights & Justice (with catalog), High Mus, Atlanta, 94; Refuse/Refuse, Honolulu Acad Arts, 94; Old Glory: The Am Flag in Contemp Art, Cleveland Ctr Contemp Art, 94; group show, Robert McClain & Co, Houston, 94; Sculpting with the Environment/A Natural Dialogue, Pratt Inst, NY, 94; Black Male (with catalog), Whitney Mus Am Art, 94; Murder, Bergamot Sta Arts Ctr, Santa Monica, Calif, 95; Grounded, ART/OMI, 95; Texas Myths & Realities, Mus Fine Arts, Houston, 95; KNOWMAD, Frederieke Taylor Gallery, NY City, 2000, Render, Frederieke Taylor Gallery, NY City, 2003, Do Not Ask Me, Sta Mus, Houston, 2006. *Pos:* Vis artist & lectr at numerous mus & univs, 89-94; Lamar Dodd hon chair fine arts, Univ Ga, Athens, 94-97; consult prof, Stanford Univ, Calif, 98; sculpture prof, Cooper Union, NY City, 99. *Awards:* Nat Endowment Arts Grant, 88, 90 & 91; Creative Capital Grant, 2001; Penny McCall Found Award, 91; Cal Arts Alpert Award Visual Arts, 95; Joan Mitchell Found award, 97, Nancy Graves Found award, 2004. *Bibliog:* William Zimmer (auth), Everything I say is art is art, she said, NY Times, 5/1/94; Mary Voelz Chandler (auth), Off the wall art, Rocky Mountain News, 5/15/94; Tracey C Hummer (auth), dialogue, Rev, 11-12/94. *Mailing Add:* c/o Frederieke Taylor Gallery 535 W 22nd St 6th Fl New York NY 10011

CHIN, RIC
LECTURER, PAINTER, CALLIGRAPHER
b Hong Kong, July 16, 35; US & UK citizen. *Study:* State Univ NY, BA; Art Students League; Sch Chinese Brushwork, New York; also with Barse Miller, Cheng Dai-Chien & Wang Chi-Yuan; Normal Univ Taiwan, MFA. *Work:* Nat Palace Mus, Taiwan; Penang Mus, Malaysia; Manhattan Savings Bank, Eastchester, NY; Houston's Ethan Allen Gallery, Greensboro, NC; Wantagh Sch Syst, NY; and pvt collections. *Exhib:* Am Artists Prof League Grand Nat, Lever House, NY, 71-75; Nat Palace Mus Ann, Taiwan, 74; one-man shows, Winston-Salem Hyatt House, NC, 74 & Ctr Asian Studies, St John's Univ, NY, 75; United Va Bank; and others. *Pos:* Dir, Bertrick Assoc Artists Inc, Seaford, NY, 65-74. *Teaching:* Lectr Chinese cult & art, Long Island Univ, 70-71; instr Chinese brushwork, var workshops, Southeastern US & Nat Art League, Douglaston, NY; nat painting & cooking lectr tour in 78 cities & on 34 TV shows, 77-78. *Mem:* Salmagundi Club (mem bd dir, 74 & 75); Am Artists Prof League; Sumi-E Soc Am; Nat Art League; Art League Nassau Co; Va Beach Arts Ctr; Chinese Calligraphy Asn, NY. *Media:* Watercolor, Water-Ink. *Res:* Rice paper with controlled texture. *Mailing Add:* PO Box 444 Pleasant Garden NC 27313

CHING-BOR, PAUL
PAINTER
b China, 63. *Exhib:* solo exhibs, Butler of Am Art, 2000, Spanierman Gallery, 2002; Parrish Art Mus; Springfield Art Mus; Allentown Riverside Art Mus; Sangre De Cristo Art & Conf Ctr; numerous group exhibs. *Collection Arranged:* Pvt and Corp Art Collections. *Awards:* Gold Medal of Hon, 97 & 2000; Silver Medal of Hon, Allied Am, 98. *Dealer:* Spanierman Gallery NY City; Eckert Fine Art Naples Fla. *Mailing Add:* 76 Clarke Ave Jersey City NJ 07304

CHINN, YUEN YUEY
PAINTER, PRINTMAKER
b Kwantung, China, Dec 24, 1922; US citizen. *Study:* Columbia Univ, Brevoort Eickmeyer fel, 52-53, BFA, 53, study with Shahan, Heliker & Mangravite, 53-54, MFA, 54; Atelier 17, Paris with W Hayter, 58-59. *Work:* Nat Collection Fine Arts; Wadsworth Atheneum Mus; Fogg Art Mus; Nat Mus, Stockholm. *Comn:* Mural, comn by Mrs Joanna Gunderson, 71. *Exhib:* Young Am Printmakers, Mus Mod Art, NY, 53-54; one-man exhibs, Beno Gallery, Zurich, 56, Galerie Numaga, La Chaux-de-Fonds, 57, Franz Bader Gallery, Washington, DC, 57 & 71, Galerie Karl Flinker, Paris, 64 & 73, Galerie Rene Andrieu, Toulouse, 65, Bryon Gallery, NY, 65 & 66, Club 44, La Chaux-de-Fonds, 67 & Brooklyn Col, 77; Corcoran Gallery Art, Washington, DC, 56; Fulbright Painters, Whitney Mus Am Art, Santa Barbara Mus Art, Smithsonian Inst & Springfield Art Mus, traveling, 58-59; Abstrakt Landskap, Nat Mus, Stockholm, 60; Salone de Mai, Musee Nat d'Art Mod, Paris, 61; Galerie Gervis, Paris, 67; Mi-Chou Gallery, NY, 70; Galerie Karl Flinker, 62 & 78; and many others. *Teaching:* Adj teacher, Brooklyn Col, 75-. *Awards:* Fulbright Fel, 54-55; John Hay Whitney Fel, 56-57. *Bibliog:* Otto Hahn (auth), Review Art in Paris, Art Int, 5/64; Studio Int, 263, 5/64; Cimaise, 9/64. *Media:* Oil, Gouache. *Dealer:* Galerie Karl Flinker 25 Rue de Tournon Paris France

CHINNI, PETER ANTHONY
SCULPTOR, PAINTER
b Mount Kisco, NY, Mar 21, 28. *Study:* Art Students League; Acad Belle Arti, Rome, Italy; also with Roberto Melli, Rome & Felice Casorati, Turin; Manhattanville Col, NY. *Work:* Whitney Mus Am Art, NY; Mass Inst Tech; New Orleans Mus Fine Art, La; Nat Gallery Art, Smithsonian Inst, Washington, DC; Rockefeller Collection. *Comn:* Stainless steel sculpture, City of Columbia, Mo, 78; stainless steel sculpture, City of NY, 84; wood sculpture, St Patrick's Church, Yorktown Heights, NY, 84. *Exhib:* Whitney Mus Am Art Ann, 64-65; Biennale Roma, 69; Gallery Mod Art, Rome, 70; Beeckestijn Mus, Velsen, The Neth, 76; Ixelle Mus, Brussels, Belgium, 76; Denver Art Mus, 92; Audubon Ann, NY, 95. *Awards:* Award Comn for Columbia, Mo Outdoor Steel Sculpture, 79; Gold Medal for Sculpture, Audubon Ann, 95. *Bibliog:* Anton Henze (auth) Der Plastiker Peter Chinni, Germany; Maria Torrente Foti (auth) Le Mostre, Homo Nuova Scienza, Milan, Italy; Douglas MacCash (auth) Arts & Entertainment, the Times Mag, New Orleans. *Mem:* Artist's Equity, NY; Int Sculpture Ctr, Washington, DC. *Media:* Bronze, Stainless Steel; Oil, Acrylic. *Specialty:* Abstraction and Realism in Painting and Sculpture. *Dealer:* Galerie Lafitte 533 St Louis MO; Galerie Lafitte New Orleans LA 70130

CHIROUSSOT-CHAMBEAUX, JANE
CURATOR, CRITIC
b France, July 7, 43. *Study:* Ecole de Beaux Arts, Alger, Master, 64 & conservateur, Paris, 84; Mus de Beaux Arts, Directeur, 90. *Hon Degrees:* Master Beaux Arts Conservateur. *Comn:* Queen of England; King of Spain; Vatican, Elysee Palace; Sappor Beer, CNN, Luxembourg Mus. *Exhib:* Grand Prix & Bienials, France, USA, Japan. *Collection Arranged:* Les 3 Ameriqus, Mus du Luxembourg, 89; L' Aura de Createous, Chapeue de la Sorbonne, 90 & 91; Grand Prix de Paris, Found Napoleon, 92; Biennale d' Aquitaine, Mus de Beaux Arts, 93; Salon d' Automne, Mus de Beaux Arts, 95 & 96; Biennale Grand Prix, Japan, 95-99; Biennial Grand Prix, USA, 1995-2000. *Pos:* Pres, IAP, IAC, Inst IC & AM, 87-96; cur, Mus de Beaux Arts, 90-96, Mus de Sapporo, Japan, 97-. *Teaching:* teacher Inst d'Art Contemp Paris. *Awards:* Meda1, Mayor Miami, 92; Grand Cordon, Encouragement Pub, 95 & Inst Art Cult, 96; various medals in art field; City of Paris Silver Medal, 02; Governor Gold Medal, 02. *Media:* Sand, metallic oxyds. *Interests:* Organ, piano, guitar, painting, sculpture. *Dealer:* Music des Beaux Arts d'Unet. *Mailing Add:* 310 Glenridge Key Biscayne FL 33149

CHMUTIN, KONSTANTIN G
PAINTER, PRINTMAKER
b Leningrad, USSR. *Study:* Archit Fac, Leningrad Higher Sch Civil Eng, 70. *Work:* NY Pub Libr, Dept Prints & Drawings; Herbert F Johnson Mus Art, Cornell Univ, Ithaca, NY; Victoria & Albert Mus, London; Hist Dipl Collection, Ashmolean Mus, Oxford, Eng; Krakow Nat Mus, Poland. *Comn:* Exlibris, Bristol City Mus, Eng, 91; Presentation Print, Print Club, Rochester, NY, 95; Presentation Print, Soc Am Graphic Artists, NY, 99; Presentation print, Hyde Court Tennis Club, Dorset, England, 2002. *Exhib:* Royal Acad Summer Exhib, Royal Acad Fine Arts, London, 91-93, 95-96, 2000, 2001, 2002; Food in Printmaking, NY Pub Libr, 94; Maestri Incisoridisan Pietroburgo, Erizzo Mus, Verona, Italy, 94; Nordgrafia, Gotland Art Mus, Sweden, 96; 150 Trondheim Art Soc Anniversary Exhib, Trondheim Mus Art, Norway, 96; Mezzotint-Art of Darkness, New Orleans Mus Art, La, 96; Int Print Exhib, Portland Art Mus, Ore, 97; Prints of the World, 12th Nat Cult Fest, Kagawa, Japan, 97; Triennial Cracow-Nuremberg '98, Nuremberg, Ger, 98; 15 Nat Biennial Exhib, Los Angeles Printmaking Soc, 99; 2 Engraving Biennial of Ile-de-France, Versailles, France, 99; Cracow Int Print Triennial Exhib, Mus Arte Moderna, Rio de Janeiro, 99; Intergrafia '2000, Triennial, World Award Winners Gallery, Katowice, Poland, 2000; Small Engraving Exhib, 2nd Int, City Mus, Cremona, Italy, 2001; Int Print Biennial of Latin Am & the Caribbean, San Juan, PR, 2001; Cancer Research UK's Art for Life, Christie's Exhib, London. *Teaching:* lectr & demonstrator of mezzotint technique, Glasgow Print Studio, Scotland, 92; instr printmaking, Univ Miami, 93, Community Col Miami, 93; instr printmaking, Print Club Rochester, 96; instr printmaking, Conn Graphic Art Ctr, 97; instr printmaking, Rochester Institute Technology, 2002. *Awards:* Hon Medal, 7th Biennial of Small Forms of Graphics, State Art Gallery, Lodz, Poland, 91; First Prize, 1 Small Print Competition, Arts Coun, Limerick, Ireland, 95; Thomas Moran Award, Spring Auction Exhib, Salmagundi Club, NY, 97; A I Friedman Merchandise Award 67 Soc Am Graphic Artists Nat Mems Exhib, 99; 3Purchase Awards Grunwald Ctr Graphic Arts/Armand Hammer Mus, 15 Nat Biennial/Los Angeles Printmaking Soc, 99; Four Winds Inc Purchase Award Soc Am Graphic Artists 68 Ann Nat Mems Exhib, 2000. *Bibliog:* Chris Waddington (auth), Mezzotints at NOMA, Laginappe Paper, 96; Nicole Rivard (auth), Mezzotint, The Hour, 97; Michael Petrenko (auth), The Glass Bead Game, Encyl Contemp Ex-Libris, Vol XXVII, AM da Mota Miranda, Portugal, 2000; George Bumgardner (auth), Complex Psychology Adds to Chmutin's Mezzotints, Ithaca Journal, 96. *Mem:* St Petersburg Artists Asn, Russ; Royal Soc Painter-Printmaker, London; Soc Am Graphic Artists, NY. *Media:* Mezzotint; Pastel. *Publ:* Contribr, Mezzotint History & Techique, Abrams Thames & Hudson, 90; The Best of Printmaking-International Collection, Rockport Publ, 97

CHO, Y(EOU) J(UI)
PAINTER
b Taiwan, China, Nov 3, 50; US citizen. *Study:* Nat Taiwan Normal Univ, BFA, 73; State Univ NY, Albany, MA, 77. *Work:* Hong Kong Fine Art Mus; pvt collections of Martin Margulies, Coconut Grove, Fla & Max Palevesky, Los Angeles; Taipei Fine Art Mus; Taiwan Mus Art, Taichung; Miss Mus Art, Jackson. *Exhib:* Solo exhibs, O K Harris Works Art, NY, 86, 88, 90, 93, 97 & 2002, Hong Kong Inst Prom Chinese Cult, 88, Frank Bernarducci Gallery, 89, Kiong Gallery, Atlanta, 94, Asia Art Ctr (auth, catalog), Taipei, Taiwan, 95, Gallery 456, New York City, 99 & OK Harris Works of Art, New York City, 2002; NY Observed, Frank Bernarducci Gallery, NY, 89; Chinese Am Arts Coun, NY, 89; Contemp Drawing Exhib, Cheng Piin Gallery, Taipei, Taiwan, 90; Dual Cultures, Nassau Co Mus Art, Roslyn, NY; Norton Ctr for Arts, Centre Col, Danville, Ky, 95; The World Bank, Washington, DC, 95; Cherng Pun Gallery, Taipei, Taiwan, 95; Alternative Mus, NYC, 95-96; Asia Art Ctr, Taipei, Taiwan, 96 & 2002; New World Art Ctr, New York City, 96; Heritage Arts Int Auction, Taipei, 97; Kao Hsiung Mus Fine Arts, Taiwan, 97; Raritan Valley Community Col Gallery, Somerville, NJ, 97; Taiwan Int Art Fair, Taipei, 98 & 2000; Nat History Mus, Taipei, 2000; 15th Asian Int Art Exhib, Taipei, 2000; OK Harris Works of Art, New York City, 2000; Dimensions Art Ctr, Taipei, 2001; Hammond Mus, North Salem, NY, 2001; New Realist Painting in Taiwan Since 1970s, Asia Art Ctr, Taipei, Taiwan, 2002; Below the Canal after 9/11, Asia Art Ctr, NY, 2003; Everything OK at OK Harris, Brevard Mus Art & Sciences, Melbourne, Fla, 2003-2004; Mountain Jade Show, Natural History Mus, Taipei, Taiwan, 2004; Asian Fusion Gallery, Asian Cult Ctr, NY. *Pos:* Vis artist, Nat Changhua Univ, Taiwan, 95, Chinese Univ, Hong Kong, 96 & Taitung Teachers Col, Taiwan, 2000. *Teaching:* Nat Changhua Univ, Taiwan. *Awards:* First Prize, Prov Mus Taiwan, 73; Nat Endowment Cult & Art, Changhua Univ, Taiwan, 95. *Bibliog:* and others; Mun-Lee Lin (auth), Mind and Spirit: Women's Art in Taiwan, Taipai Fine Art Mus, Taiwan, 98; Huang K-Nan (auth), Wall, Nat History Mus, Taiwan, 2000; The 15th Asian Int Art Exhib, China Times, Tainan, Taiwan, 2000. *Media:* Acrylic, Oil; Watercolor. *Publ:* Auth, Family Ties, Krasdale Foods Gallery, White Plains, NY, 93; Visions in Between, Taipei Gallery, New York, 93; Between East & West: Transformations of Chinese Art in the Late 20th Century, Discovery Mus, Bridgeport, 94; A Womans Views: Equality, Development & Peace, World Bank Staff Art Soc, Washington, 95; Artist-Taiwan Art, Tsai-C Ni, Artist Mag, Taiwan, 95; and others. *Dealer:* O K Harris Gallery 383 W Broadway New York NY 10012. *Mailing Add:* 20 Greene St Apt 4A New York NY 10013-2503

CHODKOWSKI, HENRY, JR
PAINTER, EDUCATOR
b Hartford, Conn, Mar 30, 1937. *Study:* Univ Hartford, BFA, 61; Yale Univ, MFA, 63. *Work:* Nat Gallery Greece, Athens; Phillips Collection, Nat Collection Fine Arts, Washington, DC; Philadelphia Mus; DeCordova Mus, Mass. *Exhib:* One-man shows, JB Speed Art Mus, 68, 72 & 78, Duke Univ Mus, 72, Middendorf Gallery, Washington, DC, 75, Allan Stone Gallery, NY, 79 & The Hellenic-Am Union, Athens, 85 & 91, Miami Univ Art Mus, Oxford, Ohio, 1999, Univ Ky Art Mus, Lexington, 1999-2000, Dishman Art Gallery, Lamar Univ, Beaumont, Tex, 2000; Gallery Contemp Art, Winston-Salem, NC, 74; Hassam & Speicher Exhib, Am Acad & Inst Arts & Letters, NY, 82; Twenty-one American Artists on Paper, Warsaw Acad Fine Arts, Warsaw, Poland, 88. *Teaching:* Prof advan & grad painting, Univ Louisville, 73-. *Awards:* Polaroid Corp Grant, 68; Award for Excellence in Teaching & Scholarship, Univ Louisville, 78; Al Smith Fel, Ky Arts Coun, 89-90; Richard Florsheim Art Fund grant, 1988. *Bibliog:* Jay Kloner (auth), The precisionist paintings of Henry Chodkowski, 10/75 & Henry Chodkowski, 3/79, Arts Mag; Mary Machas (auth), Taosim and the Minoan Labyrinth, The Athenian, 5/85. *Media:* Acrylic, Miscellaneous Media. *Dealer:* Heike Pickett Gallery 110 Morgan St, Versailles, KY, 40383; B Deemer Gallery, 2650 Frankfort Ave., Louisville, KY, 40206. *Mailing Add:* 2015 Baringer Ave Louisville KY 40204-1401

CHONG, ALBERT VALENTINE
PHOTOGRAPHER, EDUCATOR
b Kingston, Jamaica, Nov 20, 58. *Study:* Sch Visual Arts, NY, BFA, 81; Univ Calif, San Diego, MFA, 91. *Work:* Baltimore Mus Art; Tampa Mus Art; Schomberg Ctr Res Black Cult, NY; Mus Nat Ctr African Am Artist, Boston; Bronx Mus Arts. *Comn:* Absolut Chong for Abolut Expressions (campaign mission), Absolut Spirits Company. *Exhib:* Constructed Images, Studio Mus Harlem, NY, 89; Am Pictures of 1980's, Nat Mus Am Art, Washington, 89; Convergence, Photo Resource Ctr, Boston, 90; Decade Show, New Mus Art, NY, 90; Interrogating Identity, Grey Art Gallery, NY, 91; Pleasures & Terrors Domestic, Mus Modern Art, NY, 91; Ancestral Dialogues, Ansel Adams Ctr Photog, San Francisco, 94; 5th Havana Biennial, Wifredo Lam Ctr, Cuba, 94; one-man show, Projections, Throckmorton Fine Arts, New York City, 2001, Family Love: Photographs by Albert Chong, Zora Neale Hurston Nat Mus of Fine Arts, Eatonville, Fla, 2002, Nurturing Spirits: Photographs by Albert Chong, African Am Mus, Philadelphia, 2003, others; group exhibs, Mundos Creados: Ijans Amerikanse Fotografie, 2002 Photo Festival at Fries Mus, Leeuwarden The Neth, 2002, Un/familiar Territory, San Jose Mus of Art, 2003, others; Venice Biennial, Venice, Italy, 2001; Ritter Art Gallery, Fla, 2001; Committed to the Image, Black Photographers Contemp Brooklyn Mus of Art, 2001. *Teaching:* Instr photog, Sch Visual Arts, 85-88; vis scholar art/photog, Mira Costa Col, 89-91; asst prof art/photog, Univ Colo, 91-; assoc prof, RI Sch Design, 96. *Awards:* Regional (WESTAF), Los Angeles Conv Ctr, Nat Endowment Arts, 91; Nat Endowment Arts Fel, 92; CoVisions Award, Colo Coun Arts, 93; Guggenheim Fel, 98; Pollock/Krasner Grant, Pollock Krasner Found, 98; WESTAF Award, 2001. *Mem:* Soc Photog Educators. *Media:* Mixed. *Dealer:* Chelsea Galleria Miami FL; Skoto Gallery NY

CHONG, PING
DIRECTOR, VIDEO ARTIST, CHOREOGRAPHER, VIS ARTIST
b Oct 2, 46. *Study:* Pratt Inst, 64-66, Sch Visual Arts, 67-69. *Hon Degrees:* Cornish Col, DFA, 98; Kent State Univ, DHL, 2004. *Work:* Site-specific installations, Mass Inst Technol, Albert & Vera List Visual Arts Ctr, Cambridge, 85 & Three Rivers Arts Festival, Pittsburgh, 88. *Comn:* In the Absence of Memory (light installation), New England Found Arts, 89; Tempus Fugit, Haggerty Mus Art, Marquette Univ, Milwaukee, Wis, 90; A Facility for the Containment and Channeling of Undesirable Elements, Artists Space, NY, 92. *Exhib:* Haggerty Mus Art, Milwaukee, Wis; Lafayette Col Gallery, Easton, Pa; Austin Ctr Arts, Hartford, Conn; Artists Space, NY; Testimonial, Transculture, Venice Biennala, Italy, 95. *Pos:* Founder & dir, Ping Chong & Co. *Awards:* Five Nat Endowment Arts Fel, USA; Bronze Star Award, Sacramento Int Film & Video Festival, Calif, 89; Silver Award, Dance on Camera Festival, 93; sustained achievement, Obie Award, 77 & 2000; Bessie Award, 92 & 99. *Media:* Theatre. *Publ:* Dir, Education of the Girl Child (video), 73; co-dir, Paris, KCTA-TV, 82 & Turtle Dreams, WGBH-TV, (videos), 87; dir, A M/A M--The Articulated Man (film), 82; Plage Concrete (video) WGBH TV Ser, 88; script auth, Kindness, 88; script author, Nuit Blanchz, 88; script auth, Snow Captain, 89; I Will Not be Sad in this World, WNYE TV, 93; script auth, Gaijin, 95; script auth, Truth & Beauty, 2001; script auth, The East-West Quartet, 2005. *Mailing Add:* 47 Great Jones St New York NY 10012

CHOO, CHUNGHI
SILVERSMITH, FIBER ARTIST, EDUCATOR
b Inchon, Korea, May 23, 38; US citizen. *Study:* Cranbrook Acad Art, Bloomfield Hills, Mich, MFA, 65. *Work:* Metrop Mus Art, Mus Mod Art, Am Craft Mus, Cooper Hewitt Mus, NY; Musee des Arts Decoratifs, Paris, France; Art Inst Chicago; Victoria & Albert Mus, London, Eng; Mus fur Kunsthandwerk, Frankfurt, Ger; Detroit Inst Art, Detroit, Mich; Mus Fine Arts, Houston, Tex; Long House Res, East Hampton, NY; plus others. *Exhib:* Young Americans 1969, Mus Contemp Crafts, NY; one-woman show, Jack Lenor Larsen Show Rm, NY, 71; Fabric Vibrations, Eastern & Western Europe, Near & Far East & Pac Islands sponsored by Smithsonian Inst, 72-75; N Am Goldsmith, Renwick Gallery, Washington, DC & traveling, 74-77; Forms in Metal: 275 yrs of Metalsmithing in Am, Mus Contemp Crafts, NY & traveling, 75-76; Dyers Art, Mus Contemp Crafts, NY, 76; Int Fiberworks, Cleveland Mus Art, Ohio, 77; For the Table Top, Am Craft Mus, NY and traveling, 80-82; Craft Today: Poetry of Physical, Am Craft Mus, NY and traveling, 86-88; Craft Today USA, Europ traveling exhib, Am Craft Mus & US Information Agency, 89-92; Seoul Int Metal Artists Exhib, Seoul Arts Ctr, Korea, 99; Defining Craft, Am Craft Mus, NY, 2000; Women Designers in the USA 1900-2000; Diversity and Difference, Bard Grad Ctr, NY, 2000; plus others. *Teaching:* Prof jewelry & metalsmithing, Sch of Art & Art Hist, Univ Iowa, 68-, F Wendell Miller Disting Prof art, head of jewelry and metal arts program. *Awards:* Nat Endowment Art Grant, 81; AMOCO Excellence in Teaching Award, 87; Regents Award for Faculty Excellence, 93; plus others. *Bibliog:* Jack Lenor Larsen (auth), Dyer's Art, Reinhold; Katherine Pearson (auth), American Crafts; Robert Rorex (auth), Chunghi Choo, works in Metal & Silk, 10/82; Robert Rorex (auth) Metalsmith, Winter/91, American Craft, Univ Iowa metal artists, Oct/Nov 94. *Mem:* Soc Am Silversmiths. *Publ:* Photog, American Crafts, Stewart Tabori and Chang, Art in the World, 3rd dit., Holt Rinehart; Modern Design in the Metropolitan Museum of Art 1890-1990, Harry N Abrams; Art in Context, 4th edit., Harcourt Brace Jovanovich. *Mailing Add:* 2 Glenview Knolls NE Iowa City IA 52240

CHOW LEUNG, CHEN-YING
PAINTER, CALLIGRAPHER
b Canton, China, Mar 20, 21. *Study:* Art Teacher Training Col, China. *Work:* Hopkins Ctr Art Galleries, Dartmouth, NH; Mus Cernuschi, Paris, St Lawrence Univ, Canton, NY; Fla Int Univ, Miami; Hong Kong Univ; Conn Col, New London. *Exhib:* Dartmouth Col, Hanover, NH, Art Mus Seattle, Wash, Kans State Univ, Manhattan, Stanford Univ, Calif & Univ Pittsburgh, Pa; and widely in China, Japan, UK, Hong Kong, Yugoslavia, Can, Australia, New Zealand. *Teaching:* Prof, Int Studio Chinese Art, 52-67; instr Chinese art, Grove Art Sch, Miami Art Ctr, Fla, 69-70; pres & prof, Chow Studio, 69-94. *Awards:* Gold Medal & Jin Ding Award, Cent Gov Republic China, 80; Oscar Award d'Italia, 85. *Bibliog:* Foster (auth), Chinese Art (film), Wilbur T Blume, 62. *Mem:* Chinese Artist Asn, Hong Kong; hon mem Miami Artist Asn; hon chmn Canton Artist Asn, China. *Media:* Watercolor. *Publ:* Coauth, Easy Way to do Chinese Painting, 61; coauth, Chinese Painting No 2, 72; A Comprehensive Guide of Chinese Painting, 80; Chinese Painting, Poetry, Calligraphy, 90; Portfolio of Chinese Paintings, 90. *Mailing Add:* 2740 Le Jeune Rd Miami FL 33134

CHRIST-JANER, ARLAND F
PAINTER, PRINTMAKER
b Garland, Nebr, Jan 27, 22. *Study:* Carleton Col, BA, 43, LLD, 67; Yale, BD, 49; Univ Chicago, JD, 52; Coe Col, hon LLD, 61; Monmouth Col, hon LHD, 67; Carleton Col, LLD, 67; Colo Col, hon LLD, 71. *Hon Degrees:* Curry Col, hon LHD, 72; Cornell Col, hon LHD, 99. *Work:* Am Repub Ins Co, Des Moines, Iowa; Bankers Trust Co, NY; Hershey Foods Corp, Pa; Montclair Art Mus, NJ; Motion Picture Asn Am, NY; Indianhead Mills, NY; and others. *Exhib:* Nat Print Competition, Auburn Univ, Ala; Nat Print & Drawing Exhib, NMex Univ; Columbia Art League, Mo, 76; one-man shows, Carleton Col, 80, Columbia Col, 81; plus others. *Pos:* Pres, Cornell Col, Boston Univ, New Col & Stephens Col, formerly; pres, Ringling Sch Art & Design, Sarasota, Fla, 84-96, emer pres, 96-; dir, Independent Col Univ Fla, Fla Independent Col Fund; trustee, New Col Found, Marie Selby Botanical Gardens; assoc, Independent Col Art & Design; vpres, Nat Asn Sch Art & Design, 93-96; adv bd, Sun Bank/Gulf Coast; interim dir, Ringling Mus Art & Ringling Mus Art, Sarasota, Fla, 2000. *Mem:* Am Acad Arts & Scis; Nat Asn Sch Art & Design (future's comt, 2 yrs). *Media:* Graphic. *Mailing Add:* Ringling Sch Art & Design 2700 N Tamiami Trail Sarasota FL 34234

CHRISTENBERRY, WILLIAM
PAINTER, SCULPTOR, PHOTOGRAPHER
b Tuscaloosa, Ala, Nov 5, 36. *Study:* Univ Ala, Tuscaloosa, BFA, 58, MA(painting), 59; Kansas City Art Inst, Hon DFA, 83. *Work:* Corcoran Gallery Art, Libr Cong & Nat Mus Am Art, Washington; Mus Mod Art, Whitney Mus Am Art, NY; San Francisco Mus Mod Art; Baltimore Mus Art, Md; Philadelphia Mus Art, Pa; Pace McGill Exhibit, New York City, 2001, Creager Mus, 2001, Univ Cincinnati Galleries, 2001. *Comn:* Southern Wall, US Gen Serv Admin, Washington, DC, 78; Cola Wall, Arnold and Porter, Washington, DC, 83; Of Time & Place: Walker Evans & William Christenberry, Amon Carter Mus, Ft Worth, Tex & Friends of Photography; Potomac Wall, Phillip Morris Corp, 89. *Exhib:* Washington: 20 Yrs, Baltimore Mus Art, 70; New Sculpture: Baltimore-Washington-Richmond, Corcoran Gallery Art, 70; Eastern Central Regional Drawing Exhib, Philadelphia Mus Art, 70; Wilderness, Corcoran Gallery Art, Washington, DC, 71; Artists at Work, Baltimore Mus Art, 72; one-man exhibs, Corcoran Gallery Art, 73, Baltimore Mus Art, 73, Corcoran Gallery Art (with catalog), 77, Philadelphia Mus Art, 91, Southside Gallery, Oxford, 94, Nancy Drysdale Gallery, Washington, 94 & Pace McGill Gallery, NY, 95; Fourteen Am Photogrs, Baltimore Mus Art, 75; The Presence of Walker Evans (with catalog), Inst Contemp Art, Boston, 78; Washington Art on Paper: 1962-1978 (drawing), Corcoran Gallery Art, 79; Am Photog of the '70s, Art Inst Chicago, 79; Southern Fictions, Contemp Arts Mus, Houston, 83; A Second Talent: Painters & Sculptors Who Are Also Photographers, Aldrich Mus Contemp Art, 85; Recent Acquisitions, Mus Mod Art, NY, 88; Looking South: A Different Dixie, Birmingham Mus Art, 89; Morgan Gallery, Kansas City, Mo, 93; Debut, Kemper Mus Contemp Art & Design, Kansas City, Mo, 94; Worlds in a Box, White Chapel Art Gallery, London & Sheffield, Eng, Edinburgh, Scotland & Norwich, 94; Duchamps Leg, Walker Art Ctr, 94; Am Studies, Art Forum Praterinsel, Munich, Ger, 94; plus many others. *Pos:* Vis artist painting, Yale Univ Summer Sch Art & Music, 91 & 93; self-employed artist, currently. *Teaching:* Instr art, Univ Ala, Tuscaloosa, 59-61; from asst prof to assoc prof art, Memphis State Univ, 62-68; assoc prof art, Corcoran Sch Art, Washington, DC, 68-74, prof, 74-; vis artist painting, Yale Univ Summer Sch Art & Music, 91 & 93. *Awards:* Individual Artists Fel, Nat Endowment Arts, 76; John Simon Guggenheim Mem Fel, 84; Art Matters Grant, New York, 94. *Publ:* William Christenberry Southern Photographs, Aperture Inc, 83. *Mailing Add:* 2739 Macomb St NW Washington DC 20008

CHRISTENSEN, BETTY (ELIZABETH)
ILLUSTRATOR, PAINTER
b Collingdale, Pa. *Study:* Philadelphia Col Art, cert; Art Students League; Nat Acad, with Jack Pellew, Am Watercolor Soc. *Work:* Mattatuck Mus, Waterbury, Conn; Hoffman Fuel, Danbury, Conn. *Exhib:* Am Watercolor Soc Ann, Nat Acad, NY, 57-59, 61-63, 66, 69 & 78; 200 Yrs: Watercolor Painting in Am, Metrop Mus Art, NY, 66; Invitational, 81 & Conn Classic Arts, 82, Mus Art, Sci & Indust, Bridgeport, Conn; Putman Arts Coun, Mahopac, NY, 81 & 85; Allied Artists Ann, Nat Arts Club, NY, 85; Conn Watercolor Soc Ann, New Haven, 85; Sheffield Art League Spring Show, Mass, 85 & 86; Catherine Lorillard Wolfe Art Club, NY; Art on the Mountain, Wilmington, Vt; Solo shows, Brooks libr, Brattleboro, Vt. *Awards:* Best-in-Show, Bethel Art League, 91; Ridgewood Award, Kent Art Asn, 95; Grumbacker Gold Medal, Richter Art Asn, 95. *Mem:* Am Watercolor Soc; Allied Artists Am; Conn Watercolor Soc; Kent Art Asn; Conn Classic Arts. *Media:* Watercolor,Oil. *Publ:* Illusr, A Few Thoughts on Trout, Simon & Schuster, 86. *Mailing Add:* 25 West St Newtown CT 06470

CHRISTENSEN, DAN
PAINTER
b Cozad, Nebr, 1942. *Study:* Kansas City Art Inst, BFA, 64. *Work:* Metrop Mus Art, Mus Mod Art, NY; Hirshhorn Mus, Washington, DC; St Louis Art Mus, Mo; Denver Mus Art; Guggenheim Mus, NY; Ludwig Collection, Wallraf-Richartz Mus, Cologne, Ger; Whitney Mus Am Art, NY; Ft Lauderdale Mus Fine Art, Fla; Portland Mus Art, Oreg. *Exhib:* Corcoran Biennial, Washington, DC, 69; Guggenheim Mus, NY, 69; Color & Field 1890-1970, Albright-Knox Gallery, Buffalo, NY, 70; The Structure of Color, Whitney Mus, NY, 71; Douglas Drake Gallery, Kansas City, Kans, 81, 87, 88, 91 & 94; Miro in Am, Mus Fine Arts, Houston, Tex, 82; 46th Ann Nat Midyear Show, Butler Inst Am Art, Youngstown, Ohio, 82; Philip Johnson: Selected Gifts, Mus Mod Art, NY, 85; Important Works on paper, Meredith Long & Co, Houston, Tex; Salander-O'Reilly Galleries, NY, 90 & 91; one-man shows, Ivory-Kimpton Gallery, San Francisco, 82, Salander-O'Reilly Galleries Inc, NY, 82, 83, 84 & 87, Lincoln Ctr Gallery, NY, 83 & 84 & Edwin A Ulrich Mus Art, Wichita State Univ, 84; Vered Gallery, East Hampton, NY, 90; Salander-O'Reilly Gallery, Beverly Hills, Calif, 91; ACA Galleries, NY; Eva Colton Gallery, Chicago, 93; Galleryism, Seoul, Korea, 94; Salander-O'Reilly Gallery, NY, 99, 2000; Dorothy Blau Gallery, Miami, 2001. *Teaching:* Instr, Sch Visual arts, 78-82. *Awards:* Grant, Nat Endowment Arts, 68; Fel, Guggenheim Found, 69; Theodoran Award, 69; Grant, Gottlieb Found, 85; Grant, Pollock-Krasner-Gravite, 92. *Bibliog:* Grace Glueck (auth), Like a beginning, Art in Am, 5-6/69; Emily Wasserman (auth), New York, Artforum, 9/69; Valentin Tatransky (auth), New Work in New York, Mus Mag, 7-8/81; Donald Hoffman (auth), Masterly technique distilled, Kansas City Star, 5/23/82; Hearne Pardee (auth), Dan Christensen, Art News, 1/19/95; Karen Wilkin (auth), At the Galleries, Partisan Rev, Fall 99; Eleanor Heartney (auth), Dan Christensen and Ronnie Landfield at Salander-O'Reilly, Art in Am, 2/2001. *Publ:* Fine Young Artists Theodoron Awards, Guggenheim Mus, 69; Kenworth Moffett (auth), Dan Christensen: Galleryism Catalog, Seoul, Korea, 94. *Mailing Add:* 188 Neck Path East Hampton NY 11937

CHRISTENSEN, DON B
PAINTER, COLLECTOR
b Gothenberg, Nebr, Mar 10, 48. *Study:* Univ Nebr, 68; Kansas City Art Inst, 69-70. *Exhib:* Flaming Youth, 75 Warren St Gallery, NY, 75; solo exhib, Douglas Drake Gallery, NY, 92; Douglas Drake Gallery, 92 & 93; Plants, Animals & Small Abstractions, Margulies Taplin Gallery, Miami, Fla, 95; Personal Abstraction, Art in General, NY, 97; Intimate Universe, James Howe Fine Arts Gallery, Kean Univ, Union, NJ, 97; NY2K, Livestock Gallery, NY, 99; Om Show, Dorsky Gallery, NY, 99; Winter Paper, Catherine Moore Gallery, NY, 2000. *Awards:* Fel in Painting, Nat Endowment Art, 91; Fel, New York Found Arts, 96; New York Arts Alliance Stipend, 2000. *Media:* Oil. *Mailing Add:* 81 Warren St New York NY 10007

CHRISTENSEN, LARRY R
PAINTER, INSTRUCTOR
b Manti, Utah, Jan 18, 36. *Study:* Utah Tech Col, cert, 2 yrs. *Work:* Salt Lake Co Fine Arts Collection; Utah Arts Coun, Salt Lake City; Salt Lake City Chamber Com, Vet Admin & Am Express, Salt Lake City; First Interstate Bank, Salt Lake City; Fairview Mus of Art, Fairview, Utah, 2000; Sanpete Co Commisision, Mantl, Utah, 2001. *Comn:* Idaho Telephone Dir Cover, 61, portrait of pres, 62, Mountain Bell; Eccles Art Ctr, 2003. *Exhib:* Springville Mus Art Nat, Utah, 69-93; Univ Utah Mus Fine Art, 76-79; Watercolor West Transparent Watercolor, Calif, 80-84; Western Fedn Southwestern Watercolor Socs, NMex, 84, Tex, 93; Southam Gallery, 88-95; Dixie Col Invitational, St George, Utah, 91-95; and others. *Pos:* Art dir, Mountain Bell, 71-79; instr, Christensen Watercolor Workshop, Salt Lake City, 75, 76, 79, 80 & 93; Div Continuing Educ, Univ Utah, 75, Photo Blue Workshop, 77-. *Teaching:* Kimball Art Ctr, Park City, Utah, 92. *Awards:* Silver 2nd Award, Utah State Expos, 70; First Place, Cody Country Art 70 & 81; Cash Award, Salt Lakes Art Coun, 81. *Mem:* Assoc mem Am Watercolor Soc; Utah Watercolor Soc; assoc mem Watercolor Soc Calif. *Media:* Watercolor, Pencil. *Publ:* Contribr, Art West, 72. *Dealer:* Southam Gallery 50 E Broadway Salt Lake City UT 84111. *Mailing Add:* 3534 Dover Hill Dr Salt Lake City UT 84121-5527

CHRISTENSEN, NEIL C
PAINTER
b Imperial, Nebr, Oct 28, 47. *Study:* Univ Nebr, Lincoln, BFA, 78, MFA, 84. *Work:* Peru State Col, Nebr; Mus Nebr Art, Kearney; Sioux City Art Ctr, Iowa. *Exhib:* 18th Joslyn Biennial, Joslyn Art Mus, Omaha, Nebr, 84; People on Paper, Sheldon Mem Art Gallery, Lincoln, Nebr, 86; 37th Spiva Art Ctr, Joplin, Mo, 87; Ceremonial Gardens, Haydon Gallery, Lincoln, Nebr, 90; Rall Gallery, Doane Col, Crete, Nebr; Celebrations & Ceremonies, Haydon Gallery, 91; Solo exhib, Sioux City Art Ctr, Iowa, Mus Nebr Art, Kearney. *Awards:* Vreeland Award, Univ Nebr, 84; Cash Award, 18th Joslyn Biennial, Joslyn Art Mus, 84; Purchase Award, 1987 Biennial, Sioux City Art Ctr, 87; Purchase Award, T J Majors Exhib, Peru State Col, Nebr. *Bibliog:* Am Szabat (auth), Christensen still lifes reveal reverence, Lincoln J, 1/18/90; Kyle MacMillian (auth), Minimalism an influence on painter's still life work, Omaha World Herald, 7/31/91; Kathryn Cates Moore, Artist keeping strict hours now, Lincoln J-Star, 9/15/91. *Media:* Oil on Panel. *Dealer:* Haydon Gallery Hardy Bldg Suite A 335 N 8th St Lincoln, NE 68508. *Mailing Add:* 3709 Holmes Park Rd Lincoln NE 68506-4645

CHRISTENSEN, SHARLENE
PAINTER, INSTRUCTOR
b Fountain Green, Utah, Aug 24, 39. *Work:* Equitable Life & Casualty Utah Collection; Salt Lake Visitor Ctr, Salt Lake City; Salt Lake Co Fine Arts Collection, 87; Salt Lake CofC; W C Swanson Family Foun, Ogden, Utah, 2000; Fairview Mus of Art, Fairview, Utah, 2000. *Comn:* Salt Lake Visitor & Convention Center, Salt Lake City, Utah. *Exhib:* Springville Mus Art, Utah, 69-93; Eccles Art Ctr, Ogden, Utah, 75,

79, 88 & 2003; Audubon Artists 38th Ann, NY, 80; Utah Watercolor Soc, 75-95; Watercolor West, Riverside, Calif, 80; San Diego Int Watercolor Exhib, 81; Kimball Art Ctr, Park City, Utah, 84, 89 & 92; Southam Gallery, 88-99; Am Watercolor Soc, NY; and many others. *Pos:* Artists-in-schs prog, Nat Found Arts & Utah Inst Fine Arts, 73-74. *Teaching:* Instr watercolor, Salt Lake Art Ctr, 72-84; Christensen Workshops, 75-, Summer Arts Inst, Kimball Art Ctr, Park City, Utah, 92; instr watercolor, subjects in nature, Kimball Art Ctr, 88; A Way of Seeing through Watercolor, 92. *Awards:* Award of Excellence, Utah Watercolor Soc, 78; Equitable Life & Casualty Utah Collection Purchase Award, 85; Jurors Choice Award, Loge Gallery, 85. *Bibliog:* Ann Poore (auth), article in Salt Lake Tribune, 3/88; George Dibble (auth), Art Scene, Salt Lake Tribune, 5/88. *Mem:* Am & Utah Watercolor Soc; assoc mem Am Watercolor Soc. *Media:* Transparent Watercolor. *Publ:* Contribr, Art West, 72; Dict Utah Artists; Robert Olpin, 80; Women Artists of Utah, Springville Mus of Art, 80. *Dealer:* Southam Gallery 50 E Broadway Salt Lake City Utah 84111. *Mailing Add:* 3534 Dover Hill Dr Salt Lake City UT 84121

CHRISTENSEN, VAL ALAN
PRINTMAKER, GALLERY DIRECTOR
b Valentine, Nebr, Jan 26, 46. *Study:* Univ Nebr-Lincoln, with Thomas P Coleman, BFA, 68; Wichita State Univ, MFA, 70; Cambridge Univ, Eng. *Work:* Sioux City Art Ctr, Iowa; Sheldon Mem Art Gallery, Lincoln, Nebr; Kearney State Col, Nebr; Hastings Col, Nebr; Springfield Art Mus, MO. *Exhib:* Thirty-fifth Nat Graphic Arts & Drawing Exhib, Wichita Art Asn, Kans, 71; 29th Nat Print Exhib, Silvermine Guild of Artists, New Canaan, Conn, 72; 3rd Ann Nat Print Exhib, Ga State Univ, Atlanta, 72; 43rd Ann Art Exhib, Springfield Art Mus, Mo, 73; Nebraska 75, Joslyn Art Mus, Omaha, 75; one-person show, Sheldon Mem Art Gallery, Lincoln, 76. *Collection Arranged:* John and Pam Finley Collection of African Art; Marianne Keown Collection; Vivian Olson Collection. *Pos:* Artist-in-sch, Grand Island Cent Cath, 75-79; panel mem, Community Arts Prog, Nebr Arts Coun, Omaha, 77-79; dir, Spiva Atr Ctr, 79-93; assoc prof of art, Mo Southern State Univ, Joplin, 79-. *Teaching:* Asst prof printmaking, Univ Nebr-Lincoln, 71-72; instr printmaking/drawing, Hastings Col, Nebr, 72-75; asst prof art, Mo Southern St Univ, 79-2002; assoc prof, 2002-. *Awards:* Vreeland Award, Univ Nebr-Lincoln Found, 67; Purchase Awards, 40th Ann Art Exhib, Springfield Art Mus, Mo, 70 & 33rd Ann Fall Show, Sioux City Art Ctr, 71. *Mem:* Mid-Am Col Art Asn; Col Art Asn. *Media:* Intaglio prints. *Interests:* African Art. *Mailing Add:* 426 N Pearl Ave Joplin MO 64801-2463

CHRISTIANSEN, DIANE
PAINTER, CARTOONIST
b Grinnel, Iowa, Oct 27, 58. *Study:* Grinnel Col, Iowa, BA(antrhop), 81; Loyola Univ, Chicago, MSW, 90; Art Inst Chicago, MFA(painting), 90. *Work:* South Bend Art Ctr, Ind. *Exhib:* Solo exhibs, Artemisia Gallery, Chicago, 85 & 91, Race St Gallery, Grand Rapids, 86, Ill Cent Gallery, Peoria, 88, World Tattoo Gallery, Chicago, 90, Chicago Cult Ctr, 92, Lorenzo Rodriguez Gallery, Chicago, Ill, 93 & Second St Gallery, Charlottesville, Va, Gigantic Women, Miniature Work, Gallery II, Chicago, 90; Itinerary, MWMWM Gallery, Chicago, 91; group show, Lannon Cole Gallery, Chicago, 91, Narratives of Loss, Univ Wis, Milwaukee, 93 & Three Paintings, Edinboro Univ, Pa, 94. *Awards:* Purchase Prize, Michiana Regional Show, South Bend, Ind, 86; Full Merit Scholarship, Art Inst Chicago, 88; Visual Arts Fel Award, Arts Midwest, Nat Endowment Arts Regional, 92. *Bibliog:* Susan Alexis Collins, Diane Christiansen, Walter Andersons, New Art Examiner, 12/91. *Media:* Oil on plaster. *Publ:* Chicago Tribune, 4/93 & 4/94. *Mailing Add:* 2022 W Crystal St Chicago IL 60622-3129

CHRISTIANSON, LINDA ANN
CERAMIST, SCULPTOR
b Rice Lake, Wis, July 19, 52. *Study:* Hamline Univ, BA, 74; Banff Ctr Sch Fine Arts, Residency, 75-77. *Work:* Glenboe Mus, Calgary, Alta; Minn Hist Soc, St Paul; Ariz State Univ, Tempe; Parks Can, Ottawa, Ont; Frederick R Weisman Mus, Minneapolis, Minn. *Exhib:* The Am Hand: 50 Yrs of Crafts, Minn Mus Am Art, St Paul, 92; Ice Fishing Houses of the Great North, Minn Mus Am Art, St Paul, 92; Auckland Mus, NZ, 95; Bridge IV, Soc Contemp Crafts, Pittsburgh, Pa, 96; Independent Makers: Ten Ceramic Artists, Ohio State Univ, 96; Ceramics Ann, Scripps Col, Claremont, Calif, 96; Pottery, Gallery Shun, Tokyo, 96; one person exhibs, Linda Christianson, Pottery for Use and Pleasure, Laumeier Sculpture Park, St Louis, Mo, 97 & Linda Christianson, Manchester Craftsmen's Guild, Pittsburgh, Pa, 99. *Collection Arranged:* Shimpo Am. *Teaching:* Lectr ceramics, Syracuse Univ, New York, 97, Konsthantverks Ting, 98, Ransater, Sweden, La State Univ, Baton Rouge, New York State Univ, New Paltz & Women's Studio Workshop, Rosendale, NY, 99. *Awards:* McKnight Found Fel, 90, 96 & 97; Nat Endowment Arts Fel, 93; Minn State Arts Bd Fel, 99. *Bibliog:* Jack Troy (auth), Woodfired Stoneware & Porcelain, Chilton Bks, 94; Karen Wood (auth), Tableware in Clay, Crowood Press, 99; Daniel Rhodes (auth), Clay & Glazes for the Potter, Krause Publ, 2000. *Mem:* Nat Coun Educ Ceramic Arts. *Media:* Clay, Mixed Media. *Mailing Add:* 35703 Vibo Trail Lindstrom MN 55045

CHRISTIE, ROBERT DUNCAN
PAINTER
b Saskatoon, Sask, April 8, 46. *Study:* Univ Sask, BA, 67, hon degree(fine arts), 68, BEd, 70. *Work:* Mendel Art Gallery, Saskatoon, Sask; Edmonton Art Gallery; Norman Mackenzie Art Gallery, Sask Arts Bd, Regina; Can Coun Art Bank, Ottawa. *Exhib:* Canada X Ten, Edmonton Art Gallery, 74; Abstraction West, Nat Gallery Can, 76; solo exhibs, Edmonton Art Gallery, 78, Norman Mackenzie Art Gallery, Regina, Sask, 81 & Mendel Art Gallery, Saskatoon, 82. *Pos:* Gallery supvr, Univ Sask, Saskatoon, 73-82. *Teaching:* Lectr art, Univ Sask, Saskatoon, 83. *Bibliog:* Liz Wylie (auth), article, Artmag, Vol 12, No 50, 80; Nancy Tousley (auth), article, Calgary Herald, 82. *Media:* Acrylic on Canvas. *Dealer:* Can Art Galleries Calgary AB; Waddington & Shiell Galleries Ltd Toronto ON. *Mailing Add:* 725-13th St E Saskatoon SK S7N 0M1 Canada

CHRISTISON, MURIEL B
EDUCATOR, MUSEUM DIRECTOR, HISTORIAN
b Minneapolis, Minn. *Study:* Univ Minn, BA & MA; Univ Paris Inst Art & Archaeol, dipl (art hist); Univ Brussels, dipl (art hist). *Exhib:* The Impressionist & Post-Impressionists, 51, Goya, 53, Masterpieces of Chinese Art, 55, Les Fetes Galantes, 55, Masterpieces of Am Silver, 60 & Sport & the Horse, 60, Va Mus Fine Arts, Richmond; Art of India & Southeast Asia, 63 & For Your Home, 66 & 70, Univ Ill; plus many others. *Pos:* Cur researcher, Minneapolis Inst Arts, 36-42, head educ dept, 44-47; assoc dir, Va Mus Fine Arts, Richmond, 48-61; consult, Ark Art Ctr, 61; assoc dir & oper dir, Krannert Art Mus, Univ Ill, Champaign-Urbana, 62-71, dir, 71 & 75-82, dir emer, 82-; coun mem, Am Asn Mus, 72-82, sr examiner, 82-; interim dir, Muscarelle Mus, William & Mary Col, Williamsburg, Va, 84-85 & 93-94; evaluator, Univ Tex, Austin, 78, Wash Univ, St Louis, 80, Ohio Arts Coun, 84 & SC Arts Comn, 86. *Teaching:* Instr art in civilization & Am art, Univ Minn, Minneapolis, 45-47; dir grad prog art mus studies, Univ Ill, 72-82; vis prof art, Col William & Mary, 83-98. *Awards:* Carnegie Scholar, Inst Int Educ, 36; CRB Fel, Belg-Am Educ Found, 38; Distinguished Serv, Midwest Mus Conf, 82. *Mem:* Asn Art Mus Dirs; Am Asn Mus; Soc Preserv Va Antiquities; Soc Archit Hist (Va chap). *Publ:* The artmobile, an experiment in education, Art J, 55; Le Museobus de Virginia Museum of Fine Arts, Mus, Unesco, 55; 25th anniversary in Virginia, 60 & The design game, 71; Professional Practices in University Art Museums, 80; plus many exhib catalogues & other mus publ, auth of about 75 mus titles. *Mailing Add:* 5700 Williamsburg Landing Dr Apt 125 Williamsburg VA 23185-3779

CHRISTMAN, REID AUGUST
PAINTER
b Brooklyn, NY, Oct 28, 48. *Study:* Nat Acad Fine Art, NYC, scholarship with Daniel Green, 1971; Art Students League, New York, 1972; Scholarship studies with Robert Brackman & Everett R Kintsler. *Work:* Elliott Mus, Stuart, Fla. *Comn:* many pvt comn. *Exhib:* ASMA Contemp Am Marine Art, Vero Beach Mus Art, Fla, 2004; Save the Bay, Invitational Exhib, Gallery on Merchants Square, Williamsburg, Va, 2004-2005. *Awards:* Leonard Kestenbaum, Ann, Allied Artist Am, 1993; Leon Stacks Mem, 81st Ann, Allied Artist Am, 1994; M Grumbacher Gold Medallion, Grand Nat, Am Artists Prof League, 1994. *Bibliog:* Contrib, Vero Beach Magazine, Moulton Publ, 2005. *Mem:* Allied Artists of Am; Am Artists Prof League; Am Soc Marine Artists. *Media:* Acrylic, Oil, Pastel. *Interests:* Marine art, landscapes & still life. *Publ:* Contrib, Best of Oil Painting, Rockport Publ, 1996. *Dealer:* Admiralty Gallery 3315 Ocean Dr Vero Beach FL 32963-1959. *Mailing Add:* 165 23rd Ave Vero Beach FL 32962

CHRISTO & JEANNE-CLAUDE
ENVIRONMENTAL ARTISTS
b Gabrovo, Bulgaria, June 13, 35; immigrated to New York, NY, 64; Jeanne-Claude: b France, June 13, 35; immigrated to New York, NY, 64. *Study:* Christo: Fine Arts Acad, Sofia, 52-56, Jeanne-Claude: Univ Tunis, BA, 52. *Hon Degrees:* 11 times Doctors Honoris Causa. *Work:* The Whitney Mus Am Art, NY; Centre National d'Art et de Culture Georges Pompidou & Musee d'Art Moderne de la Ville, Paris; The Tate Gallery & Victoria and Albert Mus, London; The Hara Mus Contemp Art & The Seibu Mus, Tokyo; Nat Galerie, Berlin; Walker Art Ctr, Minneapolis; Albright-Knox Mus, Buffalo; Kaiser Wilhelm Mus, Krefeld, WGer; Rijks Mus, Kroller-Muller, Otterloo, Neth; Stedelijk Mus, Amsterdam, Neth; Boymans van Beumingen Mus, Rotterdam, Neth; Fogg Mus, Cambridge, Mass; Corcoran Gallery Art, Washington DC; Galleria degli Uffizi, Florence; Mus of Modern Art, NY; Nat Gallery, Washington, DC; many others. *Exhib:* Iron Curtain-Wall of Oil Barrels, blocking the Rue Visconti, Paris, 62; Wrapped Fountain & Wrapped Medieval Tower, Spoleto, 68; Wrapped Kunsthalle, Berne, Switz, 68; 5,6000 Cubic Meter Package, Documenta 4, Kassel, Air Package 280 ft high, 68; Wrapped Mus Contemp Art, Chicago, 69; Wrapped Coast, Little Bay, One Million Sq Ft, Sydney, Australia, 69; Wrapped Vittorio Emanuele, Piaza Duomo & Wrapped Leonardo de Vinci Monument, Piazza Scala, Milan, 70; Valley Curtain, Grand Hogback, rifle Colo, 1970-72; The Wall, Wrapped Roman Wall & Wrapped Ocean Front, Newport, RI, 74; Running Fence, Sonoma and Marin Counties, Calif, 70-72; Wrapped Walk Ways, Loose park, Kansas City, MO, 77-78; Surrounded Islands, Biscayne Bay, Greater Miami, Fla, 80-83; The Pont Neuf Wrapped, Paris,75-85; The Umbrellas, Japan & USA, 84-91; Wrapped Reichstag, Berlin, 71-95; Wrapped Trees, found Beyeler and Berower Park, Riehen-Basel, Switz, 97-98; The Wall, 13,000 Oil Barrels, Gasometer, Oberhausen, Ger, 99; The Gates, Cent Park, New York City, 2005. *Bibliog:* Werner Spies (auth), Christo: Surrounded Islands, Biscayne Bay, Greater Miami, Florida, 1980-1983, Dumont Buchverlag, Cologne, WGer, 84; Dominique Laporte (auth), Christo, Art Press/Flammarion, Paris, 85; Burt Chernow (auth), Christo and Jeanne Claude (biog), St Martin's Press, NY, 2002; Films: Christo and Jeanne-Claude, Wrapped Trees, Gebrüder Hissen, EstWest, 98; Christo and Jeanne-Claude, On the Way to Over the River, Gebrüder Hissen, EstWest, 2005; Christo and Jean-Claude: The Gates, 1979-2005, Albert & David Maysles, 2006; and many others

CHRISTOPHERSON, HOWARD MARTIN
PHOTOGRAPHER, ART DEALER
b Duluth, Minn, Sept 26, 55. *Study:* Self taught. *Work:* Arthur Andersen Company, St Paul, Minn; AT&T Minneapolis, Minn; Minn Hist Soc; Univ Minn Art Mus; First Bank, Minneapolis, Minn; Dahl and Assoc, St Paul, Minn; Heritage Insurance Company, Sheboygan, Wis; Schnieder USA, Plymouth, Minn; Lessors Inc, Egan, Minn; Medtronic Inc. *Exhib:* Minnesota Collects, Minn History Center, St Paul, 94; Art on the Plains, Plains Art Mus, Fargo, NDak, 98; The Nest, Minn State Fair, 98; Return to the Satiric Dancer, Fed Reserve Bank Gallery, Boston, Mass, 99; Figural

Works in all Media, Watkins Gallery, Winona State Univ, 2000; one-man shows, Icebox Gallery, 90, 91, 92, 97, 99. *Pos:* dir & owner, Icebox Gallery, Minneapolis, Minn, 88-. *Awards:* grant, Forecast Pub Artspace Productions, 82; Que Award for Art-A-Whirl, Mayor of Minn; grant, Union Depot Place, St Paul; Second Place for photog, Minnesota State Fair, St Paul, 95

CHRYSSA
SCULPTOR
b Athens, Greece, 33; US citizen. *Study:* Acad Grande Chaumiere, Paris, 53-54; Calif Sch Fine Art, 54-55. *Work:* Mus Mod Art, NY, Whitney Mus Am Art, Guggenheim Mus, Metrop Mus, NY; Albright-Knox Art Gallery, Buffalo, NY; Walker Art Ctr, Minneapolis; Corcoran Gallery of Art, Washington; Art Inst Chicago; Philadelphia Mus of Art; and others, including European museums. *Comn:* Skimore, Owings & Merill, Chicago. *Exhib:* One-man shows, Solomon R Guggenheim Mus, 61, Mus Mod Art, NY, 63, Pace Gallery, 66 & 67, Harvard Univ, 68, Galerie Rive Droite, Paris, 69 & Whitney Mus Am Art, NY, 72, Albright Knox Mus, NY, 83, Mus Cycledic Art, Athens; Whitney Mus Am Art, NY, 72; Musee de l'Art Moderne de la Ville de Paris, France, 79; Kunsthaus, Zurich, 79; Urban Icons (with catalog), Albright-Knox Art Gallery, Buffalo, NY, 82-83; Leo Castelli, NY, 88, 91, 96. *Bibliog:* Lucy R Lippard (auth), Pop Art, Praeger, 66; Gregory Battcock (ed), Minimal Art: A Critical Anthology, Dutton, 68; Diane Waldman (auth), Chryssa: Selected Works 1955-1957, Pace Gallery, 68; Sam Hunter (auth), Chryssa, Verlag Gerd Hatje, Stuttgart, WGer, 74; Pierre Restany (auth), Chryssa, Harry Abrams, New York, 77; Itanos (auth.) Chryssa Cinema Oasis, 96 (book); Donald Kuspit (auth) Chryssa, Cycladic Books, Itanos, 97. *Publ:* Chryssa, Cityscapes Thames and Hudson, N.Y., 90. *Dealer:* Irving Gallery 332 Worth Ave Palm Beach FL; Leo Castelli Gallery 59 E 79th St New York NY 10021-0258

CHU, JULIA NEE
PAINTER
b Shanghai, China, Dec 10, 40 US citizen. *Study:* Univ Calif Los Angeles, BA, 78, MFA, 81. *Work:* MCA Music Corp, Nashville, Tenn; Hong Kong Mus, Sumitomo Co, Osaka, Japan; Landmark Tower, Yokohama, Japan; Calif Mart, Los Angeles; Four Seasons Hotel, Hong Kong; and others. *Comn:* Central Plaza, Hong Kong; paintings (14' x 16'), GKBI Tower, Jakarta, Indonesia, 95; painting (9' x 12'), New Island Printing Ltd, Hong Kong, 96; paintings (12' x 10'), Grand Hyatt, Hong Kong; MGM Studios, Calif. *Exhib:* Solo exhibs, Taipei Fine Arts Mus, Taiwan, 89, Tokyu Bunkamura Art Ctr (catalog), Tokyo, 95 & Hong Kong Univ Sci & Technol Art Gallery (catalog), 96; Sydney Univ, Australia, 92; Macau Mus Invitation Show, 92; Composite Expression (catalog), Chinese Cult Found, San Francisco, 95; Now a Dream of East, New Asian Invitational (catalog), Kirin Plaza, Osaka & Japan Forum, Tokyo, 95; In Search of Identity, Invitational Calif Chinese Artists, Chinese Cult & Info Ctr, Taipei Gallery, NY, 96; and others. *Teaching:* Grad, Teaching fel, Univ Calif, Los Angeles, 80-81. *Awards:* Ford Found Grant, 80. *Bibliog:* Amano Taro (auth), A Challenge to Modernism: Julia Nee Chu (exhib catalog), Yokohama Mus Art, 95; Belinda Chang (auth), In search of identity, World J, World Daily, Monterey Park, Calif, 8/18/96; Holland Cotter (auth), 7 artists on the trails of cultural identity, NY Times, 8/23/96. *Mem:* Asian Am Art Ctr, NY; Art Action, Hong Kong. *Media:* Acrylic, Oil. *Dealer:* Annex Gallery 453 6th Ave San Diego CA 92101; EDL Assocs 3221-B Cains Hills Pl Atlanta GA 30305; Sin Sin Fine Art G/F No1 Prince's Terr Mid-Levels Hong King; Fresh Paint Arts 9355 Culver Blvd Ste B Culver City CA; Jim Robischon Gallery 1740 Wazee St Denver CO; Daniel Fine Arts 3337 Laguna Canyon Rd Ste D LaGuna Beach, CA. *Mailing Add:* 1520 17th St Santa Monica CA 90404

CHUNG, Y DAVID
PAINTER, PRINTMAKER
b Bonn, Ger, Feb 21, 59. *Study:* Univ Va, 76-79; Corcoran Sch Art, BFA, 88. *Work:* Mus Fine Arts, Boston. *Comn:* Mural, New York City Dept Cult Affairs, 93; pub monument, SPARC, Koreatown, Los Angeles, Calif, 94; mural, Rosslyn Metro Station, WMATA Comn, 97; Md State Hwy Admin, 99. *Awards:* Nat Endowment Arts Fel, 93; Giverny Fel, Lila Wallace Reader's Dig Fund, 95; Artist Award, Korean Am Alliance, 98; ArtsLink Collab Project Award, 98, 99. *Mem:* Afro-Asian Relations Coun (treas, 88-91); Wash Proj Arts (bd dir, 88-94); Hist Soc Wash; Asian Am Arts & Media (bd dir, 90). *Dealer:* Gallery K Washington DC

CHUNN, NANCY
PAINTER
Study: Calif Inst Arts, Valencia, BFA, 69. *Work:* City of Chicago; Ms Found of Women, New York City; Mus of Contemp Art, Chicago; NY Times, New York City; Progressive Corp, Cleve; Prudential Insurance Co Am, Newark, NJ. *Comn:* Painting, Uptown Branch Libr, City Chicago, 93-95; IS 125, Queens, NY (painting), New York City, in progress, since 95. *Exhib:* Minn Mus Am Art, 86; Mint Mus Art, 87; solo exhibs, Concord Gallery, NY, 84, Hewlett Gallery, Carnegie Mellon Col Fine Art, Pittsburgh, 86, Mus Contemp Art, Chicago (with catalog), 87, Feature Gallery, Chicago, 87 & Ronald Feldman Fine Arts, NY, 87, 89, 92 & 96, Inst Contemp Art, Portland, Maine, 97, Corcoran Mus Art, Washington, DC, 98, Addison/Ripley Fine Art, Washington, DC, 98, Olin Art Gallery, Gambier, Ohio, 2000 & Univ Ark at Little Rock, Little Rock, Ark, 2001; Transformations of Text: Visual Arts and the Written Word, Helen Day Art Ctr, Stowe, Vt, 98; Summer Exhib 98, Ronald Feldman Fine Arts, 98; Baroque Bash: A Fan Fantasy, The John and Mable Ringling Mus of Art, Sarasota, Fla, 98; Marcel Sitcoske Gallery, San Francisco, 99; SMIRK: Women, Art and Humor, Firehouse Art Gallery, Garden City, NY, 2001; group exhib, Presidential Suite, Nassau Co Mus of Fine Arts, Roslyn Harbor, NY, 2003; group exhib, Off the Press, Southeast Mus of Photog, Daytona Beach Community, Daytona Beach, Fla, 2003; Art on Paper, Weatherspoon Art Gallery, Greensboro, NC, 97; Strike! Printmakers as Social Critics, Lewis & Clark Col, Portland, Ore, 2001. *Teaching:* Painting Dept, Sch Visual Arts, currently. *Awards:* Fel Painting, Nat Endowment Arts, 85 & 95. *Bibliog:* Nacy Brooke Mandel (auth), All the news that's fit to stamp, Rubberstampmaddness, 3-4/99; Deborah Frizzell (auth), Bawdy burlesque, raucous ribaldry, NY Arts 6, 4/2001; Szanto Andras (auth), A business built on the hard-to-sell, New York Times, 10/6/2002. *Publ:* Front Pages, 98; Valerie Stivers (auth), Wherefore art now?, Time Out, 11/16/2000. *Dealer:* Ronald Feldman Fine Arts 31 Mercer St New York NY 10013. *Mailing Add:* 182 Grand St Apt 4W New York NY 10013

CHURCH, MAUDE
PAINTER, ASSEMBLAGE ARTIST
b Berkeley, Calif, June 15, 49. *Study:* Calif Col Arts & Crafts, Oakland, BFA, 72; Byam Shaw Col Art, London, Eng, MA, 73. *Comn:* Red & Yellow (mural), Calif Sch Prof Psychology, San Francisco, Calif, 74; Curved Space (mural), comn by J V Ferrero Jr, Palos Verdes, Calif, 76; Oasis (triptych), comn by Pamela & Joe Bonino, Palm Springs, Calif, 84. *Exhib:* Retrospective, Riverside Art Mus, Calif; Starburst: Maude Church, Bank Am World Hq, San Francisco; Exchange Exhib: San Francisco-Berlin, Amerikahaus Gallery, Berlin, Ger; California Artists, 81, Oakland Mus, Calif; 3rd Ann Women's Nat, Triangle Gallery, Washington, DC; Marine Art, Coos Art Mus, Coos Bay, Oregon. *Pos:* Pres, North Calif Artists Equity Asn, 78-79; adv bd dir, Bay Area Lawyers Arts, 78-79; nat bd dir, Women's Caucus for Art, 89-92; art dir, Mindscape, Novato, Calif, 94-96; sr artist, Sega-Soft, Redwood City, Calif, 96. *Teaching:* Adj fac, Calif Sch Prof Psychology, Alameda, 74-93; assoc prof art, Lone Mountain Col, San Francisco, Calif, 75-76. *Awards:* Fine Art Merit Award, San Francisco Arts Festival, 77; Outstanding Young Woman of the Year, 79; Sculpture Award, small sculpture exhib, Medocino Art Ctr, Calif, 90. *Bibliog:* Arthur Bloomfield (auth), City's art in the right place, San Francisco Examiner, 9/28/78; Sylvie Roder (auth), Tight formats, Artweek, 10/15/83; Kim Anno (auth), A propensity for animals, Bay Area Reporter, 9/12/85. *Mem:* Women's Caucus Art; Artists Equity Asn (pres, 78-79); Pro Arts, Oakland, Calif. *Media:* Acrylic, Assemblage Artist. *Publ:* Album cover, Holly Near, Watch Out, 84; Two posters, The Nature Co, 87; art dir, The Adventures of Peter Rabbit (CD-Rom), Mindscape, 95. *Mailing Add:* 1175 Glen Ave Berkeley CA 94708

CHURCHILL, DIANE
PAINTER
b Bronxville, NY, Jan 8, 41. *Study:* Wellesley Col, BA(art hist); Brooklyn Mus Art Sch; Hunter Col, MA (painting). *Work:* Chase Manhattan Bank Collection, NY; Reliance Group Inc, Mass; Jay Hambridge Art Found, Rabun Gap, Ga; Weehawken Twp; Grolier Publ; Wellesley Col Collections; Robert Yaeger Health Ctr, Pomona, NY. *Comn:* Lori Adler, NY. *Exhib:* Soho 20 Gallery, 76, 78 & 80; solo exhib, Gallery 107, Brooklyn Hopper House, Nyack, Cal Tech, San Luis Obispo, Calif; William Carlos Williams Ctr, Rutherford, NJ; St Peter's Artcorp Ctr, NY; Gallery 93, Nyack, NY, 98; Rockland Ctr for the Arts, 2000; Tweed Gallery, NJ, 87; Soho 20 Gallery, NY. *Pos:* Artist catalyst, Brigade-In-Action, NY, 68-73; publ & ed, Fourth St, 71-73; field rep, Visual Arts Dept, NY State Coun Arts, NY, 76-77. *Teaching:* Teacher art, Hudson Sch, Hoboken, NJ, 79-88 & Fieldston Lower Sch, 87-. *Awards:* Yaddo, 68; NJ State Coun Arts Fel, 79-80 & 85-86; Karoly Found, Vence, France, 88; Fondaçion Valparaiso, Spain, summer 2001. *Bibliog:* Carlotta Swardon (auth), Artist makes masks to reveal, not conceal, NY Times, 2/17/91; Beth Kissinger (auth), Unmasked, Jersey J, 5/22/91; Nancy Capiocco (auth), Windows to the Soul, Rockland J News, 10/30/92. *Mem:* NY Wellesley Artists Group. *Media:* Acrylics. *Interests:* Imagery connected to women, color. *Mailing Add:* 88 Clinton Ave South Nyack NY 10960-4617

CHUSID, EVETTE
PAINTER
b Newark, NJ. *Study:* Newark Sch Fine & Indust Art; Traphagen Sch Fashion, studied with Virginia Cobb, Nicholas Reale, Catherine Chiang Liu & Fran Larsen, 80-90's. *Exhib:* Solo exhib, NJCVA Mus, Summit, NJ, 87, Lever House, NY, 91; Bergen Mus, Bergen Co, NJ, 89; Mennen Corp, NJ, 90; Bellmead Corp, NJ, 90-94; Monmouth Mus, NJ, 94. *Awards:* Best Show, Essex Watercolor Club, 96. *Mem:* Audubon Artists, NY; Nat Asn Women Artists (bd, 92-94); NJ Ctr Visual Arts; Essex Watercolor Club, NJ. *Media:* Watercolor, Acrylic. *Publ:* Articles, Newark Star-Ledger, 80, 90 & 93. *Mailing Add:* 24 Hutton Ave No 14 West Orange NJ 07052-4849

CHUTJIAN, SETA LEONIE See Injeyan, Seta L

CHWAST, SEYMOUR
GRAPHIC ARTIST, ILLUSTRATOR
b New York, NY, Aug 18, 31. *Study:* Cooper Union; Parsons Sch Design, Hon PhD, 92. *Work:* Mus Mod Art, NY; Cooper-Hewitt Mus, Smithsonian Inst; Libr Congress; Israel Mus; Whitney Mus, NY. *Exhib:* Musee Des Arts Decoratif, The Louvre, Paris, France, 71 & 73; A Century of Am Illus, Brooklyn Mus, 73; one-man shows, Cooper Union, NY, 86; Jack Gallery, NY, 87; Lustrare Gallery, NY, 91; Bradley Gallery, Milwaukee, 92; GGG Gallery, Tokyo, 92; Recruit Gallery, Osaka, 92; Michael Kisslinger Gallery, NY, 94; Suntory Mus, Osaka, Japan, 97; SVA Gallery, NY, 97; Nagoya Design Ctr, Nagoya, 99. *Pos:* Publ & art dir, The Push Pin Graphic Bi-Monthly Mag, 56-80; dir, Push Pin Studios, NY, 75-82; partner, Pushpin Lubalin Peckolick, Inc, 82-86; pres & dir, Pushpin Group Inc, 82. *Teaching:* Instr design & illus, Cooper Union, 75-81. *Awards:* St Gauden's Medal, Cooper Union; Several medals, NY Art Dir Club; Art Dir Club Hall of Fame, 83; Am Inst Graphic Arts Medal, 85. *Bibliog:* T Nishio (auth), Seymour Chwast, Shinkosha Publ, Tokyo, 74; Mann Mit Nase (man with nose): Seymour Chwast, Frankfurter Allgemeine Zeitung, 81; Seymour Chwast, GGG Bks, 97. *Mem:* Am Inst of Graphic Arts; Art Dir Club of NY; Graphic Artists Guild; Alliance Graphique Internationale. *Publ:* Illusr, Harry's Bath, Bantam Press, 89; The Alphabet Parade, Harcourt Brace, 91; The 10 Circus Rings, Harcourt Brace, 92; Mr Morlin and the Turtle, Greenwillow, 96; Traffic Jam, Houghton Mifflin, 99

CIANCIO, JUNE (KIRKPATRICK)
PAINTER, INSTRUCTOR
b Wilkinsburg, Pa, June 26, 20. *Study:* Carnegie-Mellon Univ, BFA, 42; Columbia Teachers Col; Hans Hoffman Sch; Art Students League, with Will Barnet. *Work:* Parrish Art Mus, Southampton, NY; Nassau Community Col, Garden City, NY; Citibank New York. *Exhib:* One-person shows, Parrish Art Mus, 74, Long Beach Mus, NY & Barns, E and W Sister Show with Grace Alexander, 2003; 27th Ann, Nat Soc Painters Casein & Acrylic, NY, 80; 85th Ann, Catherine Lorillard Wolfe Art Club, NY, 81; Elaine Benson Gallery, Bridgehampton, NY, 93; Photogrs E, Sag Harbor, NY, 95; Plaine Aire Paintings Watermill Mus, 2006. *Teaching:* Instr watercolor, Parrish Art Mus, Southampton, NY, 76-79. *Awards:* Paul Pazinas Award, Allied Artists Am, 83; Medal Honor, Nat Soc Painters Casein & Acrylic, 94; Award of Excellence, Southampton Artists. *Mem:* Guild Hall; assoc mem Audubon Artists; Nat Soc Painters Casein & Acrylic; Southampton Artists. *Media:* Acrylic, Watercolor, Monoprints, Photog. *Collection:* pvt collections. *Mailing Add:* 13 W Argonne Rd Hampton Bays NY 11946

CIANFONI, EMILIO F
CONSERVATOR, PAINTER
b Rome, Italy, Oct 9, 46; US citizen. *Study:* Drawing, painting & restoration with Giustino Caporali, 58-63, Manieri Art Inst, 60-63, Acad di Belle Arti, 64-66; conserv of paintings at Inst Centrale del Restauro, 66-67, Rome; Art Students League, New York, 70-72; Baldwin Sch (glazes chemistry), New York, 73. *Comn:* Paintings, Lowenbrau Co, Munich, Bavaria, Ger, 67; painting & sculpture, comn by Pacifici Family, Rome, Italy, 67; mural, Church Hosp Comples, Vilalba, Italy, 69; Bicentennial Coins Competition, Metrop Mus Art, NY, 74. *Exhib:* Galeria Modigliani, 63, 20th Century Competition, City Bldg, 64 & Mus Mod Art, 65, Rome; New Talent (2 shows), Betty Parsons Gallery, NY, 74; Primitive & Contemp Art, Tucson, Ariz, Betty Parsons Gallery, 75; UN Group Am Exhib, NY, Truman Gallery, 77. *Pos:* Design painter-conservator, Gucci Shops, Rome & NY, 68-70; sr craftsman, Alva Reproductions, NY, 70-72; restorer, Metrop Mus of Art, NY, 72-74; chief conservator, Vizcaya Mus & Gardens, 75-. *Awards:* First Prize, 20th Anniversary of Italian Partisans Competition, Rome, 64; Second Prize, Ciac Poetry & Arts Competition, Rome, 66. *Mem:* Am Inst Conserv Hist & Artistic Work; Int Inst Conserv Hist & Artistic Work; Asn Preserv Technol. *Media:* Mixed. *Dealer:* Truman Gallery 38 E 57th St New York NY 10022

CIARDIELLO, JOSEPH G
ILLUSTRATOR
b Staten Island, NY, July 22, 1953. *Study:* Parsons Sch Design, with Maurice Sendak & Jim Spanfeller, BFA, 75. *Work:* Soc of Illusrs, NY, (permanent collection). *Exhib:* Soc Illusrs Ann Exhib, NY, 1974-; Soc Publ Designers, NY, 79 & 86; Art Dirs Ann, Art Dirs Club, NY, 80 & 87; Graphic Art & Illustration, Quebec City, Can, 85; The Illustrator & The Environment, Soc of Illusrs, NY, 90; Sci/Fi & Fantasy, Soc Illusrs, 92; Eye on Am: Editorial Illustration in the 90s, Norman Rockwell Mus, 99; One Man Show, Soc Illustrators, 99; Illustrating the Sea, Mystic Seaport, 2004. *Teaching:* Guest lectr illus, Fashion Inst Technol, Parsons Sch Design & Montclair State Col, 80- & Moore Col Art; adj prof illus, Montclair State Col, Upper Montclair, 81; co-instr illus, Parsons Sch Design, 87; Syracuse Univ MFA Prog, summer 2000. *Awards:* Silver Award, Soc Publ Designers, 79; Silver Medal, Soc of Illusrs, 92, 99, 2006; Steven Dohanos Award, 2006. *Bibliog:* Tom Goss (auth), Mini-portfolio Joe Ciardiello, Print Mag, 84; Marion Muller (auth), Drawing pens & drumsticks, Upper & Lower Case, 84; Scott Gutterman (auth), article, How Mag, 1-2/87; article, Idea Mag, Japan, No 208, 88 & No 219, 90, Warren Burger (auth), Communication Art, 94. *Mem:* Graphic Artists Guild; Soc Illustrators. *Media:* Pen & Ink, Watercolor. *Interests:* Jazz/blues music (plays drums). *Publ:* Illusr, Around the World in 80 Days, 88; Moby Dick, 89, 20,000 Leagues Under the Sea, 90, Dr Jekyll & Mr Hyde, 91, Reader's Digest; Art for Survival, Graphis Press, 92; The Savage Mirror: Contemporary Caricature, Watson Guftill, 92; Like Jazz, Spanfeller Press, 92; The Illustrated Portraits, Rolling Stone Press, 2000; The Illustrator in America, publ 2000; The Blues, Harper Collins, 2003; Illus Now, Taschen, 2005; and others. *Mailing Add:* 35 Little York Mt Pleasant Milford NJ 08848

CIARROCCHI, RAY
PAINTER, EDUCATOR
b Chicago, Ill. *Study:* Chicago Acad Fine Arts; Wash Univ, BFA, with Fred Conway; Boston Univ, MFA. *Work:* Ciba-Geigy Collection, Ardsley, NY; Citibank, NY; Owens-Corning Glass Found; Brooklyn Mus; The Hosp Corp of Am. *Exhib:* One-man shows, Tibor De Nagy Gallery, 71, 72, 74, 76, 78, 80, 83 & 85, Fischbach Gallery, 86 & 89, landscapes 78-91, Marsh Gallery, Modlin Fine Arts Ctr, Univ Richmond, Va, Katharina Rich Perlow Gallery, 93 & 96; Ray Ciarrocchi-Latitudes of Light, A Traveling Exhib in Italy, Aug-Sept, 2004; Am Watercolors, 1800 to the Present, Brooklyn Mus, NY, 76; Works on Paper from the Ciba-Geigy Collection, Neuberger Mus, Purchase, NY, 77; The Face of the Land, Southern Alleghenies Mus Art, Loretto, Pa, 88; Painterly Realism, traveling exhib, Houston, Tex; and others. *Teaching:* Instr painting & drawing, Parsons Sch Design, New York, 66-71; adj prof, Sch Arts, Columbia Univ, 69-71 & 76- & Baruch Col, City Univ New York, 76-94; vis artist, Md Inst Col Art, 71-72; instr, Brooklyn Col, 72-76. *Awards:* Fulbright Grant to Italy, 63-64; Tiffany Grant, 67; Ingraham Merrill Found Grant, 77 & 82-83. *Bibliog:* Richard Waller (auth), Ray Ciarrochi - Landscapes 1978-91; Julia Ayres (auth), Monotype: Painterly Printmaking, 91; Nina Mallory (auth), Ray Ciarrochi: Italian Landscapes, 96. *Media:* Oil, Mixed Media. *Dealer:* Katharina Rich Perlow Gallery 41 E 57th St 13th Fl New York NY 10022. *Mailing Add:* 55 Bethune St Apt D 1004 New York NY 10014-2010

CICANSKY, VICTOR
SCULPTOR
b Regina, Sask, Feb 12, 35. *Study:* Univ Sask, Saskatoon, BEd, 64; Univ Sask, Regina, BA, 67; Univ Calif, Davis, MFA, 70, with Bob Arneson & Roy DeForrest. *Work:* Sask Govt Arts Bd; Can Coun Art Bank; Sacramento State Col; Mus of Mod Art, Tokyo, Japan; Mus of Mod Art, Montreal; Mus Fine Arts, Montreal; The Glenbow Mus, Calgary; and many others. *Comn:* The Grain Bin (group scultpure), Sask Olympics Art Comt, Montreal, 76; The Old Working Class (sculpture), Saskatoon, 77 & The New Working Class (sculpture), 81, Sask Govt; Regina-My World (sculpture), Co-op Life Insurance Co Bldg, Regina, Sask, 79; The Garden Fence (mural), Can Broadcasting Corp, 83-84; Founders Awards (sculpture), Sask Writer's Guild, 84; Heritage Seeds (sculpture), Sask Govt, 85. *Exhib:* Contemp Ceramics, Mus of Fine Arts, Kyoto, Japan, 71; Int Ceramics, Victoria & Albert Mus, London, Eng, 72; Trajectories 73, Musee de Art Moderne de Ville de Paris, France, 73; Espace 5, Montreal, Que, 74; Fired Clay Show, Greater Victoria Art Gallery, Victoria, BC, 75; NY Clay, Monique Knowlton Gallery, NY, 75; one-man show, MacKenzie Gallery, Regina, Glenbow Mus, Waterloo Art Gallery & Mendel Art Gallery, 83, Susan Whitney Gallery, 84, Woltjen/Udell Gallery, Edmonton, 85 & Grunwald Gallery, Toronto, 85; and many others. *Teaching:* From assoc prof art to prof, Univ Regina, Sask, 70-85. *Awards:* Can Coun grants/travel & work, 68, 69, 71, 74 & 83; Kingsley Ann Award/Sculpture, Sacramento, 69; Royal Albert Award, Ceramic Sculpture, Toronto, 71. *Bibliog:* Personal bests, Can Art, fall 85; Christopher Hume (auth), Voluptuous clay veggies set off titters at the Grunwald's, Toronto Star, 10/11/85; Karen Wilken (auth), Sculpture, Can Encyl, 85. *Media:* Clay. *Publ:* Contribr to Arts Mag, Fall 70, Mus of Mod Art J, Amsterdam, 4/71, Arts Can, 5/73; Art & Artists, 8/73, Time, 4/73 & ArtsCan, 230/231; Hand & Eye, Glorious Mud (television series), CBC Television, 2/16/84. *Mailing Add:* c/o Mira Godard Gallery 22 Hazelton Ave Toronto ON M5R 2E2 Canada

CICCONE, AMY NAVRATIL
LIBRARIAN
b Mich, Sept 19, 50. *Study:* Wayne State Univ, 72, BA(art hist); Univ Mich, 73, AMLS, specializing in art librarianship. *Collection Arranged:* Hidden treasures, The Chrysler Mus, 85-86; Samuel Johnson (auth), Univ Southern Calif, 88. *Pos:* Librn, Norton Simon Mus, Pasadena, Calif, 74-81; ed, Art Librs Soc of NAm Directory of Members, 75-77; chief librn, Chrysler Mus, Jean Outland Chrysler Libr, Norfolk, Va, 81-88; Archit & Fine Arts Libr, Univ Southern Calif; head librn, Archit & Fine Arts Libr, Univ Southern Calif, Los Angeles, 88-97; bibliographer art & archit, Univ Southern Calif, Los Angeles, 97-; Actg asst univ librn pub serv, Univ Southern Calif, Los Angeles, 93-95; Assoc Coord. collection deveolp, 2004-. *Mem:* Art Libr Soc NAm (mem chmn, 75-77, mem coordr, 79, facilities standards comt, 86); Dec Arts Roundtable (coord, 91-93); Strategic Planning Task Force (chmn, 94-96, conference co-chair, 2001). *Res:* Art Mystery fiction. *Interests:* Decorative Arts, Medieval Art/Architecture. *Publ:* Contribr, Art Libr Soc NAm Newsletter, 75-77; Art Documentation, 83-88; contrib ed, Art Reference Serv Quart, 90-98; mysteries for Art libraries, column, Arlis/na update, 1999-. *Mailing Add:* 12718 Westminster Ave Los Angeles CA 90066

CICERO, CARMEN LOUIS
PAINTER
b Newark, NJ, Aug14, 26. *Study:* Newark State Col, NJ, BS, 51; Hunter Col, NY, 53; Montclair State Univ, MFA, 91. *Work:* Guggenheim Mus, NY; Mus Mod Art, NY; Whitney Mus, NY; Metropolitan Mus Art, NY; Nat Mus Am Art, Washington, many others; Fogg Art Mus, Harvard; Hirshorn Mus, Washington, DC; Mint Mus, NC; Montclair Art Mus; and others. *Exhib:* 6 Whitney Mus Anns, 55-66; (26) one-man shows, incl Peridot Gallery; Premiere Bienale de Paris, France; Graham Gallery, NY; June Kelly Gallery, NY; Karen Johnson Gallery, San Francisco. *Teaching:* Mem fac, Sarah Lawrence Col, 59-68; retired prof, Montclair State Col, 60-02. *Awards:* Guggenheim Found Fel, 57 & 63; Purchase Prize, Ford Found, 65. *Bibliog:* Charles Le Clair (auth), The Art of Watercolor, Prentis-Hall & Color in Contemporary Painting, Watson-Guptil; William Gerdts (auth), Painting & Sculpture in NJ, Nostrand Co. *Mem:* Mem Graham Gallery New York City; Nat Acad (assoc, 91, acad, 93). *Media:* Oil, Acrylic. *Dealer:* June Kelly Gallery 591 Broadway New York NY 10012

CIEZADLO, JANINA A
CRITIC, EDUCATOR
Study: Ind Univ, Bloomington, MFA in Printmaking; Ind Univ, Bloomington, MA in Comparative Lit. *Teaching:* adj prof, dept liberal educ Columbia Col; adj asst prof, dept art and design Univ Ill at Chicago. *Mem:* Chicago Art Critics Asn. *Publ:* Published (reviews, scholarly monographs, articles, poetry, exhib work), art critic Chicago Reader, Afterimage, Journal of Media Arts and Cultural Criticism. *Mailing Add:* 7200 W Oak 4NE River Forest IL 60305

CIFOLELLI, ALBERTA
PAINTER, PRINTMAKER
b Erie, Pa, Aug 19, 31. *Study:* Cleveland Inst Art, dipl(painting), 53; Kent State Univ, BS(art educ), 55; Fairfield Univ, MA, 75 (commun). *Comn:* Mitsubishi Capital, Rockefeller Ctr. *Exhib:* one-woman shows, Noho Gallery, 82, Kaber Gallery, NY, 83, Sacred Heart Univ, 98, Reece Galleries, NY & Housatonic Mus Art, Bridgeport, Conn, 2000; A State of Artists, Invitational, Aldrich Mus Contemp Art, Ridgefield, Conn; The Natural Image Invitational, Stamford Mus, Conn, 88; Harmon-Meek Gallery, Naples, Fla, 89; 400 Yrs of Women Artists Touring Exhib, Nat Mus Women, Washington, DC; The Conn Biennial, Bruce Mus; 50 Yr Retrospective, Stamford Mus, 99; and others. *Collection Arranged:* Nat Mus Women Arts; Reagan Libr, Semi Valley, Calif; Housatonic Mus Art, Bridgeport, Conn; Francis Lehman Loeb Art Ctr, Vassar Col; United Nations, NY; United Nations, NY. *Pos:* chair-woman, Art Dept

Laurel Sch, Shakerhts, 65-69; Vpres, Westport Weston Arts Coun, Conn, 78-79; artists-in-residence, Djerassi Found, 86; chairwoman, Inst Visual Artists, 88-89; juror undergrad achievement, State Univ NY, Stony Brook, 2000; cur, Special Exhib About Paint, Westport Arts Ctr, 2005; Cur About Paint, 2005 Westport Art Ctr. *Teaching:* Instr painting & life drawing, Cleveland Inst Art, 67-70; prof life drawing & design, Sacred Heart Univ, 79-; prof, Grad Sch Painting, Col New Rochelle; invited guest instr, Fairfield Schs. *Awards:* Doris Kreindler Mem Award, Nat Soc Painters in Casein & Acrylic, 74; four grants, Conn Comn Arts; Residency to live and work at Djerassi Found, Woodside, Calif, Summer 86; 100 Outstanding Women in Conn, UN Woman's Conf, 2000; Artist of Yr Award, Art Place, Southport, Conn, 2000; Artist of Yr Award, Art Place, Southport, Conn, 01; Alberta Cifolelli: Housatonic Mus Art, 02; Dir's Choice, Silvermine Galleries, New Canaan, Conn, 03. *Bibliog:* Deborah Frizzell (auth), Alberta Cifolelli, 98; Donald Kuspit (auth), Biophiliac Paintings, Nature All the Way, 98; William Zimmer (auth), Flowers and More, NY Times, 99; Jaquiline Moss (auth), Alberta Cifolelli, Arts Mag, 4/1982; Mark Daniel Cohen (auth), Brightening of the Spirit - Art of Alberta Cifolelli, 02. *Mem:* Visual Artist & Gallery Asn; Westport Arts Ctr (vis arts chmn, 76-); trustee Silvermine Guild Artists (bd dir, 78-83); Women's Caucus for Art, NY Chap; Artists Fel, NY; Artists Fel Inc; NY Artists Equity Archives Am Art. *Media:* Oil, Pastel, Printmaking. *Specialty:* White Gallery, Lakeville, Conn, 2004-2006. *Dealer:* PMW Stamford Conn; Silvermine Galleries New Canaan Conn; White Gallery Lakeville Conn; The White Gallery, Lakeville, Conn. *Mailing Add:* 8 Plover Lane Westport CT 06880

CIKOVSKY, NICOLAI, JR
CURATOR, HISTORIAN
b New York, NY, Feb 11, 33. *Study:* Harvard Col, AB; Harvard Univ, AM & PhD. *Collection Arranged:* Sanford Robinson Gifford, Univ Tex Art Mus, 70-71; The White Marmorean Flock; Nineteenth Century American Women Neoclassical Sculptors, Vassar Col Art Gallery, 72; William Merritt Chase: Summers at Shinecock (catalog), 87; Raphaelle Peale Still Lifes (catalog), 88; Paintings, Manoogian Collection, 89, Whistler, 95, Winslow Homer (auth, catalog), 95. *Pos:* Dir, Vassar Col Art Gallery, 71-74; sr cur, Am & Brit Painting Nat Gallery Art, Washington, DC, 83. *Teaching:* Assoc prof art, Vassar Col, 71-74; prof art, Univ NMex, 74-83. *Awards:* Guggenheim Fel, 78-79; Kress Sr Fel, Ctr Advan Study in Visual Arts, Nat Gallery Art, 82-83. *Res:* Nineteenth & twentieth century American painting and sculpture. *Publ:* ed, Samuel FB Morse's Lectures on the Affinity of Painting with the Other Fine Arts, 83; coauth, George Inness, 85; Winslow Homer, 90; Winslow Homer Watercolors, 91; George Inness, 93. *Mailing Add:* Nat Gallery Art 4th St & Constitution Ave Washington DC 20565

CIMBALO, ROBERT W
PAINTER, PRINTMAKER
b Utica, NY. *Study:* Pratt Inst, Brooklyn; Syracuse Univ; Socita Di Dante Alighari, Belle Arte & Univ Studi Roma, Rome. *Work:* Kirkland Art Ctr, Clinton, NY; Munson-Williams-Proctor Inst, Utica, NY; Syracuse Univ; State Univ NY Col Cortland; Pratt Inst. *Comn:* Portrait of Past Pres, Utica Col, NY. *Exhib:* Dante's Inferno Traveling Exhib to various cols and univs; many works incl in public & pvt exhibs. *Teaching:* Assoc prof art hist & studio art, Utica Col, Syracuse Univ, 78-. *Awards:* Targo D'oro Premio D'italia, 86. *Media:* Oil. *Publ:* Illusr, East Utica, Munson Williams Proctor Inst, fall 71; Frank, Catherine and Vito, Black Locust Press, 79; September 11, 2001 Victory Poster. *Mailing Add:* 1602 Harrison Ave Utica NY 13501

CINTRON, JOSEPH M
PAINTER, EDUCATOR
b Ponce, PR, Aug 4, 21. *Study:* Univ Dayton, BA, 43; Ohio State Univ, 51; Cleveland Inst Art, dipl, 54; with Robert Brackman, Madison, Conn, 62; Art Students League, with Sidney Dickinson, David Leffel, Howard Sanden, Gustav Rehberger & Harvey Dinnerstein. *Work:* Univ Hospitals Cleveland; La Fortaleza, San Juan, Puerto Rico; Case Western Reserve Univ, Cleveland; The Cleveland Clinic, Ohio; Cleveland Play House; and others. *Comn:* Portrait, Eric Fromm, Case Western Reserve Univ, Cleveland, Ohio, 69; Portrait, Gov Luis a Ferre, La Fortaleza, San Juan, PR, 74; Portrait Dr Dudley Allen, Univ Hospitals, Cleveland, 80; Portrait Bishop Gregory Rozman, Klagenfurt, Austria, 85; Portrait Jack Anderson, Washington, DC, 96; and others. *Exhib:* Canton Art Inst Regional, 65-69; Cleveland Mus Art Regional, 69; Nat, Butler Inst Am Art, 70; Sch of Fine Arts, Willoughby, Ohio, 72; Int Platform Asn, Washington, DC, 81-98; Northern Ohio Invitational, 83; Kuban Galleries, Cleveland, 84; and others. *Teaching:* Prof painting & drawing, Cleveland Inst Art, 56-, Cooper Sch Art, 63-82, Sch Fine Arts, Willoughby, Ohio, 82-96. *Awards:* Painting Award, Cuyahoga Valley Art Ctr, 67 & 68; First Place, 81 & 94, Popular Award, 83, Second Place, 84, Merit Award, 86, 94 & 97, Int Platform Asn; and others. *Bibliog:* Marie Kirkwood (auth), Cintron Trademark is Realism, Sun Press, Cleveland, 8/5/71; Gloria Borras (auth), Pintar Rostros es Captar Almas, Puerto Rico Ilustrado, San Juan, 3/30/75. *Mem:* Int Platform Asn; Art Students League, NY. *Media:* Oil, Pastels. *Dealer:* The Bonfoey Galleries Cleveland Ohio. *Mailing Add:* Cleveland Inst Art 11141 E Blvd Cleveland OH 44106

CIPRIANO, MICHAEL R
PAINTER, EDUCATOR
b Waterbury, Conn, 1942. *Study:* Cent Conn State Col, BS, 67, MS, 69; Univ Conn, 70; Columbia Univ, MA, 75, EdD, 77. *Work:* Col New Rochelle, NY; Richard Judd Collection, Cent Conn State Univ, New Britain; Howell Cheney Vocational Inst, Manchester, Conn; Manchester Community Col, Manchester, Conn; Wheaton Col, Norton, Mass; Mus Am Art, New Britain, Conn; William Benton Mus, Univ Conn, Storrs; Housatonic Mus, Bridgeport, Conn; Arguments for Abstraction, Atelier Lizio, Naples, Fla, 2003, Eastern Conn State Univ (with catalog), 1994. *Comn:* Large painting canvas, 84 & installation six large mural paintings, Conn Comn on the Arts, Manchester, 84. *Exhib:* Wadsworth Atheneum, Hartford, Conn, 82; Works on Paper, Cartwright Hall Gallery, Bradford, Eng, 84; Hewlett-Woodmere Gallery, NY, 85; Atria Gallery, Hartford, 86; Watson Gallery, Norton, Mass, 89; Bushnell Gallery, Conn Artists Showcase & Conn Coun Arts, Hartford, 89; Chen Gallery, Central Conn State Univ, 1998 & 2004; SUNY Westchester, 1999; Maxwell Fine Arts, 2002, 03, 04 & 05; solo exhibs, Artworks Gallery, Hartford, Conn, 95, Farmington Art Guild, Conn, 93 & Akus Gallery Eastern Conn State Univ, 94, Col New Rochelle, NY, 96. *Pos:* Bd dir, New Brit Arts Comt, 80- & Artworks Gallery, Hartford, 81-83; Univ Arts Coun, New York, 82; Fine Arts, Cent Conn State Univ, 88; bd mem, Conn Acad Fine Arts, 95-; consult acquisitions comt, New Brit Mus Am Art, 96-, acquistion and loan comt, 2001-; Art Space, Ctr Visual & Performing Arts, 96-; Media & the Arts, Conn Bus & Indust Asn. *Teaching:* Prof fine arts, Cent Conn State Univ, 73-86, chmn dept art, 86-96; Charter Oak State Col, 95-; vis artist, Farming Sch Dist, 95; prof emer, Col New Rochelle, 96-. *Awards:* Best in Show, 84 & Gen Elec Prize, Conn Watercolor Soc; Purchase Award, Conn Comn on the Arts, 84. *Bibliog:* Bernard Hanson (auth), Museum of American Art, New Britain, Saltbox Gallery & West Hartford-Michael Cipriano, Art in New England, 81; William Zimmer (auth), Diverse show opens gallery, 11/25/84 & Charlotte Libov (auth), Public art thrives with State support, 4/27/86, New York Times; New abstracts display strength, Emotion in Manchester Exhib, Hartford Courant, 10/89. *Mem:* Nat Arts Admin Asn; Artists Equity Asn; Arts Space, Ctr Visual & Performing Arts; Conn Art Asn; Conn Watercolor Soc. *Media:* Acrylic, Mixed Media. *Specialty:* Contemp Art. *Publ:* Auth, Artist, an unused resource, Sch Arts, 72; Arts: Frills or fundamentals, CAEA, 77. *Dealer:* Maxwell Fine Arts, Peekskill, NY. *Mailing Add:* 76 Pendleton New Britain CT 06053

CIRICLIO, S(USAN) E (FAY)
PHOTOGRAPHER, EDUCATOR
b New York, NY, Nov 27, 46. *Study:* Phoenix Col, Ariz, AA, 69; Calif Col Arts & Crafts, BFA, 72; Mills Col, Oakland, Calif, MFA, 74. *Work:* San Francisco Mus Mod Art; Oakland Mus, Calif; Barnsdall Collection, Los Angeles; Siebu Mus, Tokoyo; Kiyosato Mus Photog Art, Yamanashi, Japan. *Comn:* Eyes & Ears Found, 79. *Exhib:* New Photog, MH deYoung, San Francisco, 74; SF/LA/NY, San Francisco Art Inst, 77; Billboard Show, San Francisco Mus Mod Art, 79; Calif Women in Photog, Axiom Ctr for the Arts, Cheltenham, Eng, 87; Young Californians, Siebu Mus, Tokoyo, 89; Forecast, Mus of NMex, Sante Fe, 94; An Artist and His Circle, Kiyosato Mus, Yamanashi Japan, 98. *Pos:* acad vpres, Calif Col of Arts & Crafts, 86-87, 89-92, dept chair photog, 99-. *Teaching:* instr photog, Chabot Col, Hayward, Calif & San Francisco Art Inst, 73-86; prof photog, Calif Col Arts & Crafts, 77-. *Awards:* Photog Fel, National Endowment, 79. *Bibliog:* Thomas Garver (auth), New Photography, MH deYoung Mus, 74; Robert Heinecken (auth), West Coast Revision, SF Camerawork Quart, 85; Van Deren Coke (auth) Forecast, Mus of NMex, 94. *Mem:* Col Art Asoc; Society for Photog Educ; San Francisco Mus of Mod Art; SF Cameraworks (bd mem, 83-86); Oakland Mus. *Media:* Photog. *Interests:* History, Gardening. *Collection:* San Francisco Mus of Modern Art; Oakland Mus; Mills Col. *Mailing Add:* 2095 Arrowhead Drive Oakland CA 94611

CISCLE, GEORGE
CURATOR
b Baltimore, Md, Sept 15, 47. *Study:* Loyola Col, BA, 69; Univ NC, MEd, 72; studied under Isamu Noguchi. *Collection Arranged:* Keith Martin Retrospective, 87; Kindred Spirits, 88; Outcry: Artists Answer AIDS (ed, catalog), 90; Photo Manifesto, 91; Catfish Dreamin', 92; Ignisfat, 96; 15 Year Survey of Baltimore Art, 96; Joyce J Scott Kickin it with the Old Masters, Baltimore Mus Art, 2000; Everlasting by Ann Fessler, 2003. *Pos:* Dir, George Ciscle Gallery, 85-89; dir & founder, The Contemp, Baltimore, Md, 89-96; cur in residence, Md Inst Art, 97. *Teaching:* Instr fine arts, Cardinal Gibbons High Sch, Baltimore, 69-72, State Col Pub Sch, 74-76; teacher-coordr, Baltimore Co Pub Sch, 76-85. *Mem:* Am Asn Mus. *Publ:* Contribr, Mining the Museum, The New Press, 94; Eyewinkers, Tumbleturds and Candle Bugs: The Art of Elizabeth Talford Scott, Md Inst, 98. *Mailing Add:* 201 Edgevale Rd Baltimore MD 21210

CISNEROS, GUSTAVO ALFREDO & PATRICIA PHELPS
COLLECTOR
b Caracas, Venezuela, Jun 1, 45. *Study:* Babson Col, Wellesley, Mass, BBA, 68. *Pos:* Pres, Chief Exec Officer, Organización Diego Cisneros, Venezuela, 68-, Galerías Preciados, Spain, Spalding-Evenflo; chmn bd, All Am Bottling Co, Coral Gables, Fla; int adv comt, Chase Manhattan Bank, 81-; int adv coun, Pan-Am World Airways, 83; founding mem, worldwide adv bd, Beatrice Foods Corp, 84-. *Awards:* Decorated Order of El Libertador, Order Andrés Bello, Order Francisco de Miranda, Order Cruz de las Fuerzas Armadas de Cooperación, Order Mérito al Trabajo (Venezuela), Order of Isabel La Católica (Spain); named one of top 200 collectors, ARTnews Mag, 2004. *Bibliog:* Auth: (biography) Pioneer, 2005. *Mem:* Knights of Malta. *Collection:* Latin American, European & American Modern & Contemporary Art; Latin American landscape from 17th & 21st Century; Amazonian Ethnographic objects. *Mailing Add:* Apartado 60039 Chacao Caracas Venezuela

CISNEROS, JOSE B
ILLUSTRATOR, PAINTER
b Villa Ocampo, Durango, Mex, Apr 18, 10; US citizen. *Study:* Self-taught. *Work:* Palace Govs, Santa Fe; El Paso Mus Art; Hidalga Co Hist Mus, Edinburg, Tex; Univ Tex Libr, El Paso; Farm & Ranch Mus, Las Cruces, NMex; Pres George Bush pvt collection; and many others. *Comn:* Hidalgo Co Hist Mus, Edinburg, Tex, 83-95. *Exhib:* Witte Mus, San Antonio, 69; Panhandle Plains Mus, Canyon, Tex, 69; Gilcrease Art Ctr, Tulsa, Okla, 71; Exposicion de Dibujos de Jose Cisneros, El Inst Mexicano Norte-Americano de Relaciones Culturales, Mexico City, 73; Cavalry Mus,

El Paso, 81; Riders across the Centuries, Univ Tex Libr, El Paso, 83; Branigan Cult Ctr, Las Cruces, NMex, 91. *Awards:* Ralph Emerson Twitchell Award, Hist Soc NMex, 94; Owen Wister Award, Western Writers Am, 97; Designated Living Legend, Westerners Int, 98. *Bibliog:* Jeff Dykes (auth), Fifty Great Western Illustrators, Northland Press, 75; Peggy & Harold Samuels (auth), Artists of the American West, Doubleday, 76; John O West (auth), Jose Cisneros: An Artist's Journey, Tex Western Press, 93. *Mem:* Nat Asn Arts & Letters. *Media:* Pen & Ink, Colored Pencils. *Publ:* Illusr, Across Aboriginal America, Tex Inst Letters, 47; Journey of Fray Marcos de Niza, Southern Methodist Univ Press, 49; The Spanish Heritage of the Southwest, Tex Western Press, 52; auth & illusr, Riders Across the Centuries, Tex Western Press, 84; illusr, Borderlands: The Heritage of the Lower Rio Grande through the Art of Jose Cisneros, Hidalgo Co Hist Mus, 98. *Mailing Add:* 3703 Hueco Ave El Paso TX 79903-2809

CITRON, HARVEY LEWIS
SCULPTOR
b New York, NY, June 26, 42. *Study:* Pratt Inst, Brooklyn, BFA, 65, Academia di Belli Arti, Rome, Italy, 68. *Comn:* St John Baptist, Archdiocese of Philadelphia, Pa, 76. *Exhib:* Contemp Am Realism Since 1960, traveling exhib in US & Europe, 81-83; Neo-objective Sculpture, Dart Gallery, Chicago, 82; Artists Choice: First 8 Yrs, Artists Choice Gallery, NY, 85; Works on Paper, Tianjin Acad Fine Arts, Tianjun, China, 85; Group Sculpture/Painting, Union Club, NY, 89; Works on Paper, Drawing Univ Arts, Phildelphia, 89; group exhib, Artists Notebook Preliminary Study, Univ Arts, Phildelphia, 91, Painting Sculpture Grad Sch Figurative Art, NY Acad Art, 92, 18 Sculptors, Philadelphia Art Alliance, Philadelphia, 92. *Teaching:* Adj assoc prof sculpture, Univ Arts, 81-89; assoc prof sculpture, NY Acad Art, 87-89. *Bibliog:* Hilton Kramer (auth), Five gallery realist show, New York Times, 80; F H Goodyear Jr (auth), Contemporary American Realism Since 1960, New York Graphic Soc, 81; A G Artner (auth), Dart displays contemporary view of human form, Chicago Tribune, 82. *Media:* Bronze, Clay. *Mailing Add:* 57 Warren St No 7 New York NY 10007-1018

CIVALE, BIAGIO A
PRINTMAKER, PAINTER
b Rome, Italy, Aug 11, 35. *Study:* Acad Grande Chaumiere, Paris, 53-55; Fine Arts Acad, Rome, dipl(art educ), 58; NY Univ, 83-90; State Univ NY, Purchase, 84. *Work:* Gabinetto Naz Stampe, Rome; Mod Sacred Art Gallery, Montecatini Mus, Florence, Italy; Argenton-Sur-Creuse Mus, France; Mus Espanol Arte Contemp Madrid, Spain; Mod Mus, Stockholm; Sforza Castel Pub Collection of Prints, Milan, Italy. *Comn:* Large Panels for Ital Air Force Club, Cagliari, Italy, 58; Large Panels for NATO Ctr, Chateauroux, France, 62; Crucifixion for Sacrestia, Scarperia Church, Florence, Italy, 74; New Testament & Christmas Panels, Dicomano Church, Florence, Italy, 75. *Exhib:* 42 yr retrospective, Yonkers Educ & Cult Ctr, NY, 92; 40 yr retrospective, Palazzo Ranghiasci, Gubbio, 90; San Ban Kan Ginza Gallery, Tokyo, Japan, 92; Zhejang Acad Fine Arts, Hangzhou, Peoples Republic of China, 92; Silpakorn Univ, Bangkok, Thailand, 93; Nat Taiwan Art Inst, 95; Karmer Mus, Kulturforum, Kempen, Ger, 97; Sarah Lawrence Col, Bronxville, NY, 98; Upper View, Peekskill, NY, 2002; The Coffey Gallery, Kingston, NY, 2002; Molloy Col Art Gallery, Rockville Centre, NY, 2004; GR Art Gallery, Mamaroneck, NY, 2004. *Pos:* Art critic, 50-90, cur, 74-2005. *Teaching:* Instr art educ, Roosevelt High Sch, Yonkers, NY, 79 & 80. *Awards:* Third place, Sea Heritage Marine Art, Southport, NY, 88. *Bibliog:* Luigi Servolini (auth), Incisori D'Italia, EIA, Milano, 74; Biagio Civale, Woodcuts and Linocuts, 1950-1990, Edition Heliodor, Westbury, NY, 90; New American Paintings, Open Studios Press, 94. *Media:* Oils, Etchings, Woodcuts, Tempura. *Dealer:* Castillon Fine Arts 159 Madison Ave New York NY 10016. *Mailing Add:* 311 Lee Ave Yonkers NY 10705

CIVITELLO, JOHN PATRICK
PAINTER
b Paterson, NJ, Aug 17, 39. *Study:* William Paterson Col, BA, 61; NY Univ, MA, 62. *Work:* Nat Mus Am Art, Smithsonian Inst, Washington; Monterey Peninsula Mus Art, Calif; 3M Co, St Paul, Minn; NBC-TV, NY; Lloyd's Bank, Calif; Comput Sci Corp, Los Angeles. *Exhib:* 30th Biennial Am Art, Corcoran Gallery Art, Washington, 67; What's Happening in Soho, Univ Md Art Gallery, 71; one-man show, Art Club Chicago, 74; Am Acad Arts & Lett Ann, 76; Drawing Today in NY, Sewall Art Gallery, Houston, Tex & Dayton Art Inst, Ohio; and others. *Pos:* Art project dir, Great Falls Historic District, Paterson, NJ, 78. *Awards:* Prix-de-Rome, Italy, 68-70; Creative Artists Pub Serv Grant, Cult Coun Found, 72; Childe Hassam Purchase Award, Am Acad Arts & Lett, 76. *Bibliog:* E Bilardello (auth), Pittori Americani a Roma, Margutta-Periodico d'Arte Contemporanea, Rome, 70; article, Arts Mag, 7/75. *Mem:* Am Acad Rome Alumni Asn; Found for Community Artists, NY. *Media:* Acrylic. *Publ:* Lenswork Quart, 5/95. *Mailing Add:* 3239 N Arrowhead Ave San Bernardino CA 92405

CIVITICO, BRUNO
PAINTER, EDUCATOR
b Dignano D'Istria, Italy, Sept, 1, 42; US citizen. *Study:* Rutgers Univ, 60; Pratt Inst, BFA, 66; Ind Univ, MFA, 68. *Work:* Bayly Mus, Univ Va, Charlottesville; Boston Pub Libr; Chemical Bank & Claude Bernard Galleries, NY, NY. *Comn:* Silkscreen poster, NH Comn Arts, Theater by the Sea, Portsmouth, NH, 80; mural, Clemson U. SC, 2000. *Exhib:* Brooklyn Col Faculty Past & Present, Davis & Long & Schoelkopf Gallery, NY, 77; Realism and Metaphor, USF Art Galleries, Tampa, Fla, 80; Narrative Painting, Alan Frumkin, NY, 81; Cleveland Mus Ann, Ohio, 83; one-man shows, Robert Schoelkopf Gallery, NY, 72, 74, 77, 80 & 84, Manchester Inst Art & Sci, NH, 87 & Contemp Realist Gallery, San Francisco, 90 & 92; and others. *Pos:* cur, Landscape Pty, 60-90, Gibbes & Bayly Mus, 92, Univ SC, 2000. *Teaching:* Instr, Pratt Inst, 69; lectr, Brooklyn Col, 71, Princeton Univ, 72, Boston Univ, 79, Sch Art, Yale Univ, 82, Wash Univ, St Louis, 85 & NY Acad Art, 91; asst prof, Univ NH, 73-79; vis artist, Tyler Sch Art, Philadelphia, 80-81 & Cleveland Inst Art, 82-83; adj asst prof painting, Queens Col, NY, 83-85; vis prof, Parsons, NY, NY, 91. *Awards:* Fel, Guggenheim Found, 79; Nat Endowment Arts Fel, 81; Fel, Ingram Merill Found, 89; and others. *Bibliog:* Edward Lucie-Smith (auth), American Art Now, William & Morrow, 85; Charles Jencks (auth), Post Modernism, Rizzoli, 87; John L Ward (auth), American Realist Painting 1945-1980, UMI Res Press, 89. *Media:* Oil. *Publ:* Auth, An analysis of recent landscape and narrative paintings by Gabriel Laderman, Am Artist, 86. *Dealer:* Horchetl/Friedman Gallery San Francisco. *Mailing Add:* 2 Wragg Sq Charleston SC 29403-6209

CLANCY, PATRICK
PHOTOGRAPHER, CONCEPTUAL ARTIST
b Hornell, NY, Oct 19, 41. *Study:* Pratt Inst, BS, 64; Yale Univ, BFA, 64 & MFA(painting), 67. *Work:* Hallmark Collection. *Comn:* Photog mural, NMex Arts Div, Youth Diagnostic & Develop Ctr, Albuquerque, 86. *Exhib:* Spaces, Mus Mod Art, NY, 69 & 70; Works for New Spaces, Walker Art Ctr, Minneapolis, 71; solo shows, Diverse Works, Houston, 86, Houston Ctr Photog, 86, Visual Studies Workshop, Rochester, NY, 92 & Inst Studies Arts, Ariz State Univ, 93; A Chaos of Delight, Del Ctr Contemp Arts, 96. *Teaching:* Lectr & res assoc, Pulsa Sem, Yale Univ, 67-72; vis artist, Calif Inst Arts, 71 & 72; asst prof hist of cinema & environ art, Colgate Univ, NY, 74-80; vis artist photog, film hist & sculpture, Univ NMex, 80-85; vis artist filmmaking, film hist & theory, San Francisco Inst, 84; prof & chair, Photog & New Media Dept, Kansas City Art Inst, 86-. *Awards:* Video Fel, Nat Endowment Arts, 88; Mid Am Arts Alliance/Nat Endowment Arts Photog Fel, 93; Visual Artists Fel Photog, Nat Endowment Arts, 95. *Bibliog:* Scott MacDonald (auth), Patrick Clancy's photoscrolls, Afterimage, 5/81; Edward Bryant (auth), The recent photoscrolls of Patrick Clancy, Artspace, spring 86. *Mem:* Soc Contemp Photog; Friends of Art, Nelson-Atkins Mus Art, Kansas City, Mo. *Media:* Photography, Assemblage. *Publ:* Auth, Video as attitude (brochure essay), Mus Fine Arts, Santa Fe & Univ NMex, 83; Text and photo interventions, In: Cinematograph: A Journal of Film and Media Art, San Francisco Cinemathque, 88; Telefigures and cyberspace, In: Re-Thinking Technologies, Univ Minn Press, 93; The imaging effect, In: The Simulated Presence, Inst Studies Arts, Ariz State Univ, 94. *Dealer:* Stephen Cohen Gallery 7358 Beverly Blvd Los Angeles CA 90036. *Mailing Add:* 6 E 62nd Terr Kansas City MO 64113

CLAPSADDLE, JERRY
PAINTER, DESIGNER
b Hastings, Nebr, Dec 12, 41. *Study:* Drake Univ, Des Moines, Iowa, BFA, 64; Ind Univ, MFA, 66. *Work:* Chase Manhattan Bank, NY & Wilmington, Del; Student Loan Mktg Asn, Washington, DC; Washington Post; Hyatt Regency, Baltimore & Crystal City, Va; Swiss Bank Corp, World Trade Ctr, NY. *Comn:* Mural, Artery Orgn, 82; mural wall & sidewalks, Bethesda Gateway Bldg, 86; print ed, Washington Area Lawyers for the Arts, 86; Stuart St Paving, Ballston Metrop Ctr, Arlington, Va, 90. *Exhib:* Pattern Painting, PS1, NY, 77; Max Protetch Gallery, 77 & Protetch-McIntosh Gallery, 77 & 79, Washington, DC; Maryland Biennial, Baltimore Mus Art, 78; The Emerging Generation, Washington Proj for the Arts, 79; McIntosh-Drysdale Gallery, Washington, 81 & 87; Am Inst Architects, Washington, 86 & 89; and many others. *Pos:* Exhib organizer, Fine Arts Ctr, Univ RI, Kingston, 71-74; dir, Fine Arts Ctr Gallery, State Univ NY, Oneonta, 74-76. *Teaching:* From instr to asst prof studio art & printmaking, Univ RI, Kingston, 67-74; asst prof painting, Univ Md, College Park, 76-80; assoc prof, Studio, George Mason Univ, Fairfax, Va, 81-. *Awards:* Artists' Fel, 80 & Art in Pub Places Grant, 84, Nat Endowment Arts; Works in Progress Grant, Md State Arts Coun, 82. *Bibliog:* Paul Richard (auth), A decade's painted daydreams, 8/30/80 & Ben Forgey (auth), Jerry Clapsaddle at Montpelier, 4/11/83, Washington Post; Maeve Bee (ed), New faces-new images, Ocular, fall 80. *Mem:* Col Art Asn; Washington Proj Arts. *Media:* Acrylic, Brick. *Publ:* Designer of exhib catalogs, Linda Benglis: Physical & Psychological Moments in Time, 75, Michelle Stuart, 75, State Univ NY & Maurice Prendergast: Art of Impulse & Color, 76 & From Delacroix to Cezanne: French Watercolor Landscapes of the 19th Century, 77 & The Public as Patron, 79, Univ Md. *Dealer:* B R Kornblatt 406 7th St NW Washington DC 20004. *Mailing Add:* 2215 Marthas Rd Alexandria VA 22307-1827

CLARK, CAROL
ART HISTORIAN, CURATOR
b New York, NY, July 21, 47. *Study:* Univ Mich, AB(with distinction), 69, MA, 71; Cleveland Mus Art, Kress Found Fel, 72-75; Case Western Reserve Univ, PhD, 81; Amherst Col, AM (hon), 92. *Pos:* Cur paintings, Amon Carter Mus Western Art, Ft Worth, Tex, 77-84; exec fel, Prendergast Proj, Williams Col Mus Art, 84-87. *Teaching:* Instr art hist & mus studies, Tex Christian Univ, Ft Worth, 75-77; lectr art hist, Williams Col, 85-87; assoc prof fine arts & Am studies, Amherst Col, 87-92, prof, 92-. *Awards:* William R Kenan, Jr Professorship, 2000-2004. *Mem:* Col Art Asn; Am Studies Asn; Western Hist Asn. *Res:* American 19th & early 20th century painting. *Publ:* Auth, Thomas Moran's Watercolors of the American West, Univ Tex Press, 80; A Romantic Painter in the American West, Alfred Jacob Miller: Artist on the Oregon Trail, 82; Charles Deas, Am Frontier Life, 86; coauth, Maurice Brazil Prendergast & Charles Prendergast, Catalogue Raisonne, 90; The Robert Lehman Collection, Vol VIII: American Drawings and Watercolors, Metrop Mus Art, 92. *Mailing Add:* Amherst Col Fine Arts Dept Amherst MA 01002

CLARK, CLAUDE
INSTRUCTOR, PAINTER
b Rockingham, Ga, Nov 11, 1915. *Study:* Philadelphia Mus Sch Art, dipl; Barnes Found, painting Fel, 42-44; Sacramento State Col, BA; Univ Calif, Berkeley, MA. *Work:* Pa Mus, Philadelphia; Atlanta Univ, Ga; Oakland Mus, Calif; Fisk Univ, Tenn; Nat Collection Art, Smithsonian Inst, Washington; Hampton Univ, Va; Am Mus,

Wilberforce, Ohio; Young Meml Mus; Philadelphia Mus Art; plus others. *Comn:* Freedom Morning (canvas interpretation), Philadelphia Orchestra Asn, 44. *Exhib:* Negro Artist Comes of Age, Brooklyn Mus, 45; Black American Artists 1750-1950 traveling exhib, Los Angeles Co Mus, 76-; Black Artists-South, 79; Hidden Heritage: Afro-American traveling exhib, 85-; Choosing: Afro-Am Art, 1925-1985, Masters Art Exhib, Salvador-Bahia, Brazil, 88; Introspective: Contemp Art by Americans & Brazillians of African Descent, Los Angeles, 89; Traveling 50 yr retrospective of paintings, 90; solo exhibs, Early Yrs 38-54, Bomani Gallery, San Francisco, 95, Apex Mus, Atlanta, Ga, 96, Thelma Harris Gallery, Oakland, Calif, 97, Foothill Col, Oakland, Calif, 97; A Visual Heritage 1945 to 1980: Bay Area African-American Artist, Triton Mus, Santa Clara, Calif, 97; Salute to President, Harvey-Hampton Univ, Hampton, Va, 98. *Pos:* Artist, Fed Art Proj, Philadelphia, 39-42. *Teaching:* Assoc prof art, Talladega Col, Ala, 48-55; instr art, Alameda Co Schs, Calif, 59-68 & Merritt Col, 68-81. *Awards:* Carnegie Found Grants Res, Painting & Ceramic Res, 49-50 & 51. *Bibliog:* David Driskell (auth), Retrospective Exhib, Fisk Univ, 72; Halima Taha (auth), Collecting African American Art, Crown Pubs, 98; African American Dance in History and Art, Nat Afro-Am Mus and Cultural Ctr, Wilberforce, Ohio, 99; Guide to Black Artists, Detroit, 97. *Mem:* Am Soc Composers Authors & Publ; Nat Coun Arts; Am Asn Univ Prof. *Media:* Oil. *Publ:* Auth, A Black Art Perspective, 70. *Dealer:* Thelma Harris Gallery Oak Calif; Stella Jones Gallery New Orleans La. *Mailing Add:* 788 Santa Ray Ave Oakland CA 94610

CLARK, EDWARD
PAINTER
b New Orleans, La, May 6, 1926. *Study:* Art Inst Chicago, 46-51; Acad de la Grande Chaumiere, Paris, France, 52. *Work:* Aldrich Mus Contemp Art, Ridgefield, Conn; Centio des Arts Mod, Guadalajara, Mex; Mus Solidarity, Titograd, Yugoslavia; La State Univ, Baton Rouge. *Exhib:* Salon D'Automme, 52 & Salon des Realites Nouvelles, 55 & 85, Mus d'Art Mod, Paris; Prix d'Othn Friese, Mus des Arts Decoratifs, Paris, 55; The Brata Groupe, Mus Mod Tokyo, Japan, 60; Biennial, Whitney Mus, NY, 73; Bicentennial Banners, Hirshhorn Mus, Washington, DC, 76; Icarus Odyssey, Centro de Arte Moderno, Guadalajara, Mex, 79; retrospective, Studio Mus of Harlem, NY, 80; Realities Nouvelles, 1984, Grand Palais, Paris, 84. *Awards:* Creative Artists Pub Serv Award, New York, 59; Nat Endowment Arts Grant Painting, 72 & 81. *Bibliog:* Article, Edward Clark, pushbroom in action, Art Int, 70; Corrine Robbins (auth), Pluralist Era in American Art, Harper & Row, 83; article, Edward Clark, statement, Issue Mag, 85. *Mem:* Asn des Anciens de la Cite Internationale des Arts, Paris. *Media:* All. *Dealer:* Larry Randall 82-30 138th St Kew Gardens NY 11435; Julia Hotton 202 E 76th St New York NY 10021. *Mailing Add:* 4 W 22nd St New York NY 10010-5802

CLARK, EMERY ANN
PAINTER, ENVIRONMENTAL ARTIST
b New Orleans, La, Sept 12, 1950. *Study:* Newcomb Col, BFA, 72; Sch Fine Arts, Boston Univ, 69; Skowhegan Sch Painting & Sculpture, 71; Tulane Univ, MFA, 81. *Work:* New Orleans Mus Art & Virlane Found, New Orleans, La; IBM, Washington, DC; Chase Manhattan Bank, Miami, Fla; Hunter Mus Art, Chatanooga, Tenn. *Comn:* NOMA Nile (29' 6" 45 mile color environmental installation), New Orleans Mus Art, La, 77; Art by the Yard (1000' x 5' painted canvas), Art Coun New Orleans, La, 82 & Barbara Gillman Gallery, Miami, Fla, 83; Sea Wall (environmental installation 40 x 41), Touro Med Off Bldg, New Orleans, La, 83; New Orleans Intl Airport & Arts Council with NO Art Installation, 89-92; Ochsner Clinic Fdtn, Healing Arts Prog, 2003-2005. *Exhib:* Artists' Biennial, New Orleans Mus Art, La, 75 & 77; La Major Works, La World Expos, New Orleans, 84; The Art of New Orleans, Southeastern Ctr Contemp Art, Winston-Salem, NC, 84; Landscape, Cityscape, Seascape, Contemp Arts Ctr, New Orleans, La & NY Acad Art, NY, 86; Barbara Frederick Gallery, Washington, DC, 86; Fishbach Gallery, NY, 86; Tampa Triennial, Tampa Mus Art, Fla, 88; 50th Ann Nat Exhib Contemp Am Paintings, Soc Four Arts, Palm Beach, Fla, 88; one-person show, Lowery Sims (with catalog), Alexandria Mus Art, Univ Art Mus, Univ La in Lafayette, Southern La, Univ La, State Univ, 98-99. *Teaching:* Vis artist, New Orleans Ctr Creative Arts, 74-76; instr, Tulane Univ, 79-81. *Awards:* Thomas J Watson Traveling Fel, 72; 1st Prize, 50th Ann Nat Exhib Contemp Am Painting; Spec Guest, Aspen Inst Humanistic Studies, Aspen Co, 74. *Bibliog:* John Kemp (auth), An Artist's Sense of Place, Am Artist, Vol 52, 62-65, 6/88; Lowery Sims (auth), catalog, Alexandria Mus, 89. *Mem:* Contemp Arts Ctr New Orleans (bd mem, 76-89, co-chmn Arts Comt, 77, Arts Comt, 78-81 & 86-88, chmn Arts Comt, 80-81, vpres, 78 & 82-84); Women's Caucus Arts; Col Art Asn; Nat Asn Artists Orgn; New Orleans Ctr Creative Arts Community (Liaison bd, 80-89, pres, 84-85). *Media:* Painting, Environmental Art. *Publ:* Univ Art Mus Catalog, Bomb Mag, New York, No XXII, 46-47, fall 90. *Mailing Add:* 2407 Lakeshore Dr Mandeville LA 70448-5737

CLARK, GARTH REGINALD
DEALER, HISTORIAN
b Pretoria, Republic SAfrica, May 15, 47. *Study:* Royal Col Art, London with Lord Queensberry & Edwardo Paolozzi, MA, 76. *Exhib:* Hans Coper: A Retrospective, Gardiner Mus, Toronto, Can, 85. *Collection Arranged:* A Century of Ceramics in the US Traveling Exhib (auth, catalog), 79; The Contemporary American Potter Traveling Exhib (auth, catalog), Smithsonian Inst, 80; Michael Carden: A Portrait, NCECA Conference, 81; Ceramic Echoes: Historical References in Contemporary Ceramic Art (auth, catalog), Nelson Atkins Mus, 83. *Pos:* Dir, Inst Ceramic History, Los Angeles, 79-81. *Teaching:* Art historian ceramics, Univ Calif, Los Angeles, 78. *Awards:* Morton Professor, Ohio Univ, 81; Eleventh Wittenborn Mem Award for Art Book of the Year, 89; Fel, Royal Col Art, 96. *Mem:* Decorative Art Soc; Inst Ceramic History; Art Libr Soc NAm. *Publ:* Auth, Ceramic echoes, Contemp Art Soc, 83; co-auth, American Potters Today, Victoria & Albert Mus, London, 86; auth, American Ceramics: 1876 to the Present, 87, The Eccentric Teapot, 89, The Mad Potter of Biloxi: The Life and Art of George E Ohr, 89 & The Book of Cups, 90, Abbeville Press; co-auth, American Ceramics in The Everson Museum, Rizzoli, 88; The Potters Art: A Complete History of British Pottery, Phaidon, 95. *Mailing Add:* c/o Garth Clark Gallery 24 W 57th St Suite 305 New York NY 10019-3918

CLARK, JON FREDERIC
EDUCATOR, GLASS BLOWER
b Waterloo, Wis, Aug 13, 47. *Study:* Univ Wis, BSc; Royal Col Art, London, MFA. *Work:* Royal Col Art, London, Eng; Archie Bray Found, Helena, Mont; Portnoy Ltd, NY; Hadler Galleries, NY; Lannan Found, Palm Beach, Fla. *Exhib:* New Am Glass, Focus WVa, Huntington, 76; Contemp Art Glass, Lever House, NY, 76; Art of Craft, The Am View, Ill State Univ, Normal, 76; Nat Glass III, Univ Wis, Madison, 76; Nat Craft Exhib, Del Mus Art, Wilmington, 76; Philadelphia Craft Show, Philadelphia Mus Art, 77. *Collection Arranged:* Cup Show, Fritz Driesbach, 76 & Eisch Retrospective, Littleton Collection, 77, Tyler Sch Art, Temple Univ, Philadelphia. *Teaching:* Glass technician, Calif Col Arts & Crafts, Oakland, 73; assoc prof, Tyler Sch Art, 73-82. *Bibliog:* Judith Stein (auth), Exhibition Review, Vol 3 (1) & Richard Avidon (auth), Exhibition Review, Vol 4 (1), Glass Art Mag. *Mem:* Am Crafts Coun; Glass Art Soc; Nat Coun on Educ for Ceramic Arts. *Media:* Glass, Polyester. *Mailing Add:* 7703 Union Ave Elkins Park PA 19027-2621

CLARK, KATHRYN J
CONCEPTUAL ARTIST, PHOTOGRAPHER
b Kendrick, Idaho, Feb 7, 50. *Study:* Univ Calif, Santa Barbara, MFA; Univ Kans, BGS. *Exhib:* Palimpsests, New Mus, NY, 89; Mindfull Affection, Artemicia Gallery, Chicago, 90; View (auth catalog), Hirshhorn Mus, Washington, DC 91; Home Land (auth catalog), Contemp Arts Forum, Santa Barbara, 92; AB Ecedarium, Taylor Libr Vassar Col, Poughkeepsie, 92. *Pos:* Mem bd dir, Contemp Arts Forum, Santa Barbara, Calif, 86-88; exec dir, Summer Solstice Celebration, Santa Barbara, Calif, 88-89; mem bd dir, Body Positive, NY, 92-. *Teaching:* Lectr, photog, Univ Calif, Santa Barbara, 86-90, book arts, 90-91. *Awards:* Purchase Prize, Santa Barbara Mus Art, 86; Individual Artist Award, Santa Barbara Co Arts Asn, 89; Artist Fel, Nat Endowment Arts, 92. *Bibliog:* J Wood (auth), Kathryn Clark Village Voice, 10/9/90; E Heartney, Kathryn Clark, Art News, 11/90; J P Borum, Kathryn Clark, Art Forum, 1/91. *Mem:* Col Art Asn. *Media:* Photography. *Specialty:* 20th Century, Contemporary, American & European art. *Dealer:* Richard Eagan Fine Art PO Box 939 New York NY 10024-0540

CLARK, LYNDA K
MUSEUM DIRECTOR, EDUCATOR
b Miami, Fla. *Study:* Fla Atlantic Univ, BFA, 69; Calif State Univ, Long Beach, MA, 86. *Exhib:* Maurice Le Grand Le Seuer Sullins (catalog), 87-88, Robert Lostutter, 89, New Work, John Balsley, 90, Native Am Workers of Clay: 2500 BC-1500 AD, 92; Point of Contact: Western Artists/Japanese Artisans (colored woodblock prints), (catalog), 93; The Ness Collection: Northern Plains Tribal Art, 94; To Make a Proud Appearance, Native Am Dance & Ceremonial Clothing, 94; Signe Stuart: Retrospective (catalog), 95, Native Sons: Harvey Dunn & Oscar Howe, 97; Robert J Aldera: Retrospective, 99; Corporals, Cooks & Cowboys: African Americans in the Black Hills, 2000; Sacred Duty & Warrios and Weapons of the Northern Plains (catalog), 2000. *Pos:* Asst cur, Long Beach Mus Art, Calif, 83-86; cur, Ill State Mus, Springfield, 86-88; dir, Niu Art Mus, Dekalb, Ill, 89-93, SDak Art Mus, Brookings, 93-98; exec dir, Journey Mus, Rapid City, SDak, 98-; ind curator, 2000-; gov appointee, SD Arts Coun, 2003. *Teaching:* Art hist & studio art, Spokane Falls Community Col, 80-83; Art Hist (contemp Am Art, 50-present), Sangamon State Univ, Springfield, Ill, 88; Mus studies, Northern Ill Univ, 90-93. *Awards:* Fel Nat Endowment Arts, 86; Fel Kellogg Found, 86. *Mem:* Am Asn Mus; Soc Am Mosiac Artists. *Res:* Comtemporary American artists; 20th century folk and outsider art; traditional and contemporary Native American art. *Publ:* Maurice LeGrand Leseuer Sullins: Paintings, Ill State Mus, 87; Outside USA: Out of This World, Maurice Sullins, Kunstforum Int, Cologne, Ger, 3-4/91; Sacred Duty: Warriors and Weapons of the Northern Plains, 2000. *Mailing Add:* PO Box 9028 Rapid City SD 57709

CLARK, MARIE
SCULPTOR
b Philadelphia, Pa. *Study:* Univ Pa, BA; Tyler Sch Art; Philadelphia Mus Sch Art; study with I Sankowsky, G Utesche, Arlene Love & Joe Greenberg. *Comn:* Alabaster abstract, comn by F Wallace, Bordentown, NJ, 74; wood abstract, comn by J Thomas, Haddenfield, NJ, 75; wood abstract, comn by O Ryan, Philadelphia, Pa, 83; epoxy torso, comn by J Montague, 84. *Exhib:* Six Sculptors from 3 states to complement mod sculpture from the Guggenheim, Allentown Mus, 85; Touch to See, Kemerer Art Mus, Bethlehem, Pa, 85; Statton Art Festival, Vt, 85-93; Gov's Exhib of Paintings & Sculpture, Vt, 87; Sculpture to Touch (traveling), Children's Mus, Martin Luther King Mus, Washington & and Loyda Col Art Gallery, Baltimore, Md, 87; solo exhibs, Southern Vt Art Ctr, 85, Beside Myself Gallery, Vt, 86 & 90, Third St Gallery, Philadelphia, Pa, 88; and others. *Awards:* Woodmere Art Mus Sculpture Award, 78; 2nd Best in Show, Norwich Univ, 83; Best Sculpture, Southern Vt Art Ctr, 88. *Mem:* Philadelphia Acad Fine Arts; Vt Coun Arts; Philadelphia Art Alliance; Womens Caucus for Arts. *Media:* Wood, Stone, Bronze, Epoxy. *Publ:* Festival of the Arts, Southern Vt Art Center, 85; Contribr, Sculpture to touch, Gwendolyn Cafritz Grant, Washington, 3/4/87; Around & About (J), Bill Reed, Vt, 7/25/90. *Dealer:* Ward Nasse Gallery NY

CLARK, MARK A
CURATOR
b Dayton, Ohio, Jan 20, 31. *Study:* Oxford Study Group, Oxford Univ, Eng, 94. *Collection Arranged:* The Lipton Collection of Antique Tea Silver, 58; Glass from Area Collections, 66; The Folger Collection of Antique Silver Coffee Pots, 67; Paul Storr Silver in American Collections (with catalog), 72; Vermeil Collection (catalog),

White House, Washington, 72; A Tricentennial Celebration: Norfolk, 1682-1982 (catalog), 82; American Silver--A Survey of the Chrysler Museum Collection, 82; English Silver from the Chrysler Museum Collection, 83; When the New Century Arrived: Art of 1900, 85; Art Pottery and Beyond: American Ceramics from the Chrysler Museum Collection, 86; Treasures for the Table, Silver from the Chrysler Museum (catalog), Norfolk, Va, 89; Proud Possessions: A Community Collects (exhib catalog), Chrysler Mus, Norfolk, Va, 92; Southern Pottery from the Chrysler Museum, 94; Benjamin Wade Owen III: Potter, Chrysler Mus, 95; Art Pottery from the Collection of the Chrysler Museum of Art, 96-97; The Art of the Silversmith: Silver from the Permanent Collection of the Chrysler Museum of Art, 97; Treasures for the Community: The Chrysler Collects, 1989-1996, 97. *Pos:* cur dec arts, Chrysler Mus, Norfolk, Va, 76-. *Mem:* Decorative Arts Soc

CLARK, MICHAEL
MUSEUM DIRECTOR
Study: Corcoran Sch Art, BA. *Work:* Clark in Context: Day of the Revolutionary, Mus Contemp Art, 2003; rep in permanent collections, Nat Gallery Art, DC. *Exhib:* exhib incl, Clark & Hogan: Paintings & Collab, Barry Gallery, 2002-03. *Pos:* Founder & co-dir Mus Contemp Art, Wash, 91-. *Mailing Add:* Mus Contemp Art 1054 31st St Washington DC 20007

CLARK, MICHAEL VINSON
PAINTER, PRINTMAKER
b Tex, Nov 20, 46. *Work:* Corcoran Gallery Art, Nat Collection Fine Art, Nat Gallery Art & Phillips Collection, Washington, DC; Everson Mus, Syracuse, NY. *Exhib:* One-man shows, Mus STex, Corpus Christi, 78 & Harry Lunn Gallery, DC, 79; The Art of Organic Form, Smithsonian Inst, Washington, DC, 68; New Painting: Structure, Corcoran Gallery, 68; Nat Drawing Soc Show, Philadelphia Mus Art, Pa, 70; Ten Washington Artists 1950-1970, Edmonton Art Gallery, Can, 70; Washington Art: Twenty Yrs, Baltimore Mus of Art, 70; 75th Anniversary, Cooper-Hewitt Mus, NY, 77; Critics Choice 1977, Lowe Mus, Syracuse Univ, Syracuse, NY, 77; Dimock Gallery, George Washington Univ, DC, 79; Images of the 70's, Nine Washington Artists, Corcoran Gallery Art, DC, 80. *Awards:* Purchase Award, Nat Drawing Soc, Philadelphia Mus, 70; Purchase Award, 35th Corcoran Biennial Contemp Painting, 77. *Bibliog:* James Harithas (auth), Michael Clark, Everson Mus Art, 73. *Publ:* Illusr, The Art of Organic Form, Smithsonian Inst, 68. *Mailing Add:* 220 E 60th St Suite 6H New York NY 10022-1406

CLARK, ROBERT CHARLES
PAINTER, LECTURER
b Minneapolis, Minn, Aug 31, 20. *Study:* Minneapolis Sch Art; Walker Gallery Art Sch, Minneapolis. *Work:* Los Angeles Co Mus Hist, Sci & Art, Los Angeles; Norton B Simon Inc, Hunt's Foods & Industs Found, Los Angeles; Glendale Fed Collection of Calif Art. *Comn:* The Resurrection (mural), Forest Lawn Mem Park, Glendale, 65. *Exhib:* Artists of Los Angeles & Vicinity, Los Angeles Co Mus Art, 55-58; Illusion & Reality, Santa Barbara Mus Art, Calif, 56; one-man shows, Calif Palace of Legion of Honor, San Francisco, 56 & Rosicrucian Egyptian Mus, San Jose, 73; Charles & Emma Frye Mus, Seattle, Wash, 57-58. *Pos:* Background artist, Natural Hist Dept, Los Angeles Co Mus, 54-62. *Awards:* Artists of Los Angeles & Vicinity Award, Los Angeles Co Mus Art, 55; Purchase Award, Palos Verdes Estates Art Gallery, 56. *Bibliog:* Janice Lovoos (auth), The tempera paintings of Robert Clark, Am Artist, 12/69; William F Taylor (auth & producer), Robert Clark: An American Realist (film), 74; Elizabeth Rigby (auth), Robert Clark: A perfectionist's medium, Southwest Art, 1/79. *Media:* Tempera, Watercolor. *Mailing Add:* c/o Zantman Art Galleries PO Box 5818 Carmel CA 93921

CLARK, ROBERTA CARTER
PAINTER, ILLUSTRATOR
b St Louis, Mo, May 2, 24. *Study:* Purdue Univ; Ctr Creative Studies, Detroit, 48-51; Art Ctr Sch, Los Angeles, 53-54; Art Students League, with Hirsch, 59; also studied with John Terelak, Don Stone & Charles Reid. *Work:* Brookdale Col, Lincroft, NJ; Rutgers Univ, New Brunswick, NJ; Monmouth Med Ctr, Long Branch, NJ; Wash & Lee Univ, Lexington, Va; Seton Hall Univ, South Orange, NJ; and others. *Exhib:* Soc Western Artists, De Young Mus, San Francisco, 54; Midwest Watercolor Soc, 83-92; Am Watercolor Soc, 85, 87, 89 & 92; Nat Acad Exhib, NY, 90; Adirondacks Nat Exhib Am Watercolors, 90, 91 & 92; and others. *Teaching:* Instr workshops, Calif, St Louis, Hilton Head, Rockport, Mass, Vt & Pocono Pines, Pa. *Awards:* Silver Medals, NJ Watercolor Soc Ann, 78, 81 & 85 & Grumbacher Inc, 82, 85, 87 & 88; Cent NY Watercolor Soc Award, Adirondacks Nat Exhib Am Watercolors, 90, Harold Coopersmith Award, 91 & Paul Mowrey Mem Award, 92; Garden State Watercolor Soc Award, 91; and othrs. *Mem:* NJ Watercolor Soc (secy, 76-78, pres, 79-82); Rockport Art Asn; Master Transparent Watercolor Soc Am; Am Watercolor Soc; Garden State Watercolor Soc. *Media:* All Media. *Publ:* Illusr, The Littles, thirteen bk ser, Scholastic Inc, 70-2004; auth & illusr, How to Paint Living Portraits, North Light, 90; Painting Children's Portraits, North Light, 93. *Dealer:* Anchor & Palette Gallery Bay Head NJ. *Mailing Add:* 47B Cheshire Sq Little Silver NJ 07739-1433

CLARK, TIMOTHY JOHN
PAINTER, EDUCATOR
b Santa Ana, Calif, June 30, 51. *Study:* Art Ctr Col Design, with Paul Marciel Souza & Harry Carmean, 69-70; Chouinard Art Inst, with Donald W Graham & Harold M Kramer, CFA, 72; Calif Inst Arts, BFA, 74; Calif State Univ, Fullerton, with Victor Joachim Smith, 75; Calif State Univ, Long Beach, with Joyce Wahl Treiman, MA, 78. *Work:* Nat Portrait Gallery/Smithsonian; Sherman Found; Millard Sheets Collection; El Paso Mus Fine Art; Mus Mission San Juan Capistrano; Farnsworth Art Mus, Rockland, Maine. *Comn:* various portrait commns; Hammer Galleries, 2004-2005; Rose Galleries, Realism Now, 2004; Ctr for Maine Contemp Art, 2005; Topkapi Mus, Istanbul, 2002. *Exhib:* Ann Exhib, Nat Acad Design, NY, 80, 98 & 2000; solo exhibs, Mus Mission San Juan Capistrano, 96-97, Bowers Art Mus, Santa Ana, Calif, 2000 & Parker Ranch Art Mus, Kamuela, Hawaii, 2000; Grand Cent Art Galleries, NY, 93; Artists of Am, Colo History Mus, Denver, 2000; Worcester Art Mus, Mass, 98. *Teaching:* Prof drawing & painting, Orange Coast Col, Costa Mesa, Calif, 74-79 & Coastline Col, Fountain Valley, Calif, 76-; instr drawing, Saddleback Col, Mission Viejo, Calif, 76-77; instr watercolor, Univ Hawaii, 82, Worcester Art Mus, Mass, 94- & Art Students League, New York, 95-; National Academy School, 2004-. *Awards:* First Place, San Diego Int Watercolor Exhib, 77; Nominated for Emmy, Focus on Watercolor, PBS-TV, 89; Excellence in Educ NISOD Award, Univ Tex, Austin, 97; William A Paton Award, The Nat Acad, NY, 2000; The President's Award, Nat Arts Club, Exhibiting Members Show, 2003; The Slazman Award, Nat Arts Club Exhibiting Members Show, 2004. *Bibliog:* Brad Bonhall (auth), His Art and Soul, Los Angeles Times, 3/27/2000; Daniel Chang (auth), The Art of Being Prepared, Orange Co Register, Calif, 3/18/2000; Virginia Wright (auth), Painting by Painting Room by Room, The Times Record, Brunswick, Maine, 5/11/2000; Richard Chang (auth), In the Eye of the Artist, Orange Co Register, 9/10/2002. *Mem:* Nat Arts Club, NY; Artist's Fel, NY. *Media:* Watercolor, Oil. *Publ:* Contribr, Learning from the Pros, Watson-Guptill, 85; Tips on analyzing your subject, Am Artist Mag, 87; Focus on Watercolor, Watson-Guptill 87; Learning from the Best, Watercolor Mag, fall 96; Winslow Homer's Watercolor Techniques, Watercolor Mag, fall 98; Art Review, The Art Times, Aug. 2004. *Dealer:* Hammer Galleries, 33 W. 57th St. New York, NY. *Mailing Add:* PO Box 2728 Capistrano Beach CA 92624

CLARK, VICKY A
CURATOR, HISTORIAN
b Atlanta, Ga. *Study:* Univ Calif, Los Angeles, BA, 72; Univ Calif, Davis, MA, 74; Univ Mich (teaching fel, 75-77), PhD, 79. *Collection Arranged:* Lothar Baumgarten, Jeff Wall, Meg Webster, Barbara Bloom, Carnegie Mus Art. *Pos:* Cur educ, Carnegie Mus Art, Pittsburgh, 81-89, assoc cur contemp art, 89-94; cur, Pittsburgh Ctr Arts, 96-. *Teaching:* Instr, Univ Toledo & Toledo Mus Art, 79; asst prof, Univ RI, 80 & Skidmore Col, Saratoga Springs, NY, 80-81; adj prof, Chatham Col, 87-, Univ Pittsburgh, 91-, Carnegie-Mellon Univ, 96-. *Mem:* Col Art Asn. *Res:* Contemporary art. *Publ:* Richard Serra in Pittsburgh, Carnegie Mag, Vol LVIII, No 4 8/86; On the Meaning of Art at the End of the Century in Carnegie International, Carnegie Mus Art, 88; Auth & Ed, International Encounter: The Carnegie International & Contemporary Art, 1896-1996, Carnegie Mus Art, 96; auth, Recycling Art History (exhib, catalog), Pittsburgh Ctr Arts, 98; auth, Women in Mus, The New Art Examiner, 95. *Mailing Add:* Pittsburgh Ctr Arts 6300 5th Ave Pittsburgh PA 15232

CLARK, VICKY JO
PAINTER
b Lamesa, Tex, Sept 14, 37. *Study:* Abilene Christian Univ Tex, 56-59, studied with Ben Konis, Albert Handell, Daniel Greene. *Work:* Abilene Christian Univ, Tex; Seminole High Sch, Tex; First Int Bank, Houston, Tex; Plaines Nat Bank, Lubbock, Tex; Post Nat Bank, Tex. *Comn:* Mural, Primary Cafeteria, Seminole Pub Sch, Tex, 91; Ten paintings of children, Southwest Meml Hosp, Houston. *Exhib:* Salmagundi Club, NY, 88, 89, 90, 91 & 92; Catharine Lorillord Wolfe, Nat Arts Club, NY, 88, 89 & 90; Maryland Pastel Soc, Johns Hopkins Sch Med, Baltimore, 89 & 91; Pastel Soc SW, Dallas, Tex, 90; Pastel Soc NMex, 96. *Teaching:* Workshops pastel, Tex & NMex. *Awards:* First Place, Southeastern Pastel Soc, 89; Purchase Award, A&A Guffuni, Pastel Soc Am, 89; Pastel Soc Am Plaque, Salmagundi, 89; Merit Awards in Chicago, 89, Dallas, 90 & Seattle, 91. *Mem:* Pastel Soc Am; Catherine Lorillard Wolfe; Pastel Soc Southwest. *Media:* Pastel. *Interests:* painting children & western landscapes. *Publ:* Auth, The best of Pastel & Floral Inspriations, Rockport Publ, Inc; The Best of Pastel 2, Rockport Pub, Inc, Cover Story, The Pastel Jour, Oct/Nov 99; articles and paintings The Pastel Jour, Oct/Nov 2000; cover and article, Pastel Arstist Int, 1-2/2001; cover, Feist Phonebook, High Plains, 2003-2004, High Panhandle, 2003-2004; cover, Daniel Smith Catalogue, 2005-2006. *Dealer:* Diaz Fine Art Gallery 674 Vine St PO Box 813 Bufallo Gap Tex 79508. *Mailing Add:* 607 SW Avenue 1 Seminole TX 79360

CLARK, WILLIAM W
HISTORIAN
b Tampa, Fla, Jan 17, 40. *Study:* Pa State Univ, BA(with hons); Columbia Univ, MA & PhD. *Pos:* Ed, Gesta, 88-91; prof art, Queens Col, City Univ New York, 67-. *Teaching:* Prof medieval archit, Queens Col & Grad Ctr, City Univ NY, Flushing, 67-. *Awards:* Grants, Nat Endowment Arts, Am Coun Learned Soc & J Paul Getty Trust. *Mem:* Col Art Asn; Societe Francaise d'Archeologie; Int Ctr for Medieval Art; Centre des Recherches d'Archeologie Medievale; Medieval Acad Am. *Res:* Twelfth-century early Gothic architecture and sculpture in France and England. *Publ:* Auth, Spatial innovations in the chevet of Saint-Germain-des-Pres, J Soc Archit Historians, no 38, 79; Laon Cathedral: Architecture, Harvey Miller Publ, London, vol 1, 83 & vol 2, 87; The first flying buttresses: A new reconstruction of the nave of Notre-Dame de Paris, Art Bull, no 66, 84; Suger's church at Saint-Denis: The state of research, In: Abbot Suger and Saint-Denis, 86; Medieval Architecture, Medieval Learning, Yale Univ Press, New Haven, 92. *Mailing Add:* Dept Art Queens Col Flushing NY 11367

CLARK-LANGAGER, SARAH ANN
GALLERY DIRECTOR, CURATOR
b Lynchburg, Va, May 14, 43. *Study:* Randolph-Macon Woman's Col, Lynchburg, Va, BA(art hist), 65; Univ Wash, Seattle, MA(art hist), 70; City Univ New York, Grad Ctr, PhD(art hist), 88. *Collection Arranged:* Northwest Traditions (auth, catalog), Seattle Art Mus, 78; Sighted/Sited at Western: Drawings for Sculpture, Western Gallery, Western Wash Univ, 90; Northwest Native Am & First Peoples Art, Western Gallery,

93; Chairs: Embodied Objects (catalog), Western Gallery, 93; Stars & Stripes: 20th Century Prints & Drawings, Western Gallery, 94; Photographs from America, 96; Focus on WWU Collections: The Last Five Decades (catalog), Western Gallery, 99; Northwest Artists' Books (coauth), Western Gallery; Decades of Giving: Virginia Wright and Sculpure at Western (auth), Western Gallery, 99; Western Tableaux: 100 Years (coauth), Western Gallery, 99; Surface Tension, Western Gallery, 2003; A Sofa and., Northwestern Artists & 20th Century Designer Furniture, 2003; Noguchi & Dance, Western Gallery, UWV, 2005; The Alan & Vera Leese Collection, Gift of Mariah Boylan, Western Gallery, 2006. *Pos:* Assoc cur, modern art, Seattle Art Mus, 75-79; cur, 20th century art, Munson-Williams Proctor Inst, Utica, NY, 81-86; gallery dir, Univ NTex, Denton, 86-88; gallery dir & cur of Outdoor Sculpture Collection, Western Gallery, Western Wash Univ, Bellingham, 88-. *Teaching:* Assoc, Educ Dept, Yale Univ Art Gallery, 65-67; assoc, Educ Dept, art history, Albright-Knox Art Gallery, Buffalo, 67-68; assoc, Educ Dept, art hist, Seattle Art Mus, Wash, 71-75; asst prof, art hist, Univ N Tex, Denton, 86-88; adj prof, Western Wash Univ, 88-. *Awards:* Outstanding Achievement Award (fund raising), Western Foundation, Western Washington Univ, 99; Faculty Recognition Award, Board of Trustee, Western Washington Univ, 2003; and many others. *Mem:* Wash Art Consortium, (vpres, 89-90, pres, 90-92); Am Asn Mus. *Publ:* intro auth, Metalcraft, Western Gallery, 98; Faculty Review/Preview: 98-99, Western Wash Univ, 99; Perspective on Excellence: A Century of Teaching and Learning at Western Washington Univ, 2000; Sculpture in Place: A Campus as Site, Marquand Books/Western Wash Univ, 2002; Susan Bennerstrom, Univ Wash Press, 2000; Isamu Noguchi; Beyond Red Square In Isamu Noguchi and Skyviewing Sculpture. Japan Week 2004. *Mailing Add:* 2970 N Shore Rd Bellingham WA 98226

CLARKE, ANN
PAINTER, EDUCATOR
b Norwich, Eng, Aug 27, 44; Can citizen. *Study:* Slade Sch Fine Art, Univ Col, London, dipl fine art & design. *Work:* Can Coun Art Bank; Westburne Collection, Montreal; Hill Trust Fund Collection, Calgary, Alta; Prov Courthouse Collection, Edmonton, Can; Queensland Art Gallery, Brisbane, Australia. *Exhib:* Abstraction West: Emma Lake and After, Nat Gallery, Ottawa, Ont & Mendel Art Gallery, Saskatoon, Sask, 76; Mus d'Art Contemp, Montreal, Que, 76; one-person shows, Edmonton Art Gallery, 77, Southern Alta Art Gallery, 79 & Gallery One, Toronto, 86, Gallery One, Toronto, Ont, 99 & 2000, 30 Yr Survey, The Thunder Bay Art Gallery, Ont, 2000; Seven Prairie Artists, Art Gallery of Ont, 79; Threshold of Colour, Edmonton Art Gallery, 82; Ultima Thule, Definately Superior Gallery, Thunder Bay, Ont, 95; Inner Landscapes-16xOne, Gallery One, Toronto, Ont, 96; The Tweed Contemp Artists' Series, the Tweed Gallery, Duluth, Minn, 98; Faculty Show, Thunderbay Art Gallery, Ont, 2004; solo, Paths of Desire, Prairie Art Gallery, Grandeprairie, Alta, 2004, Triptych, Verb Gallery, Kingston, Ont, 2006, Random Courses, Swamp Ward Project, Kingston, Ont, 2006. *Pos:* Art coodr, Royal Ont Mus, Toronto, 85-86; artistic dir, Kingston Artists Asn Int, 88-90. *Teaching:* Asst prof art, NS Col Art & Design, Halifax, 75-76; lectr art, Univ Alta, Edmonton, 76-84 & Red Deer Col, 79-80, Grant McEwan Col, 80-84; lect art, Univ Guelph, Ont, 85-91; lectr art, Queen's Univ, Kingston, Ont, 88-91; prof, Visual Arts, Lakehead Univ, Thunder Bay, Ont, 92-. *Awards:* Can Coun Art Bank Award, 73 & 76; Govt Alta Cult Award, 74; Can Coun Art Award, 78-79; Can Council Senior Award, 1999; Ont Arts Council Senior Award, 2003. *Bibliog:* Article, Ken Carpenter (auth), Ann Clarke, Art Mag, 6/81; David Burnett & Marilyn Schiff (auths), Contemporary Canadian Art, 83; Karen Wilkin (auth), Ann Clarke, Vie des Arts, 86. *Media:* All Media. *Dealer:* Gallery One Toronto Ont; Roomz Thunderbay Ont. *Mailing Add:* 294 Pearl St Thunderbay ON P7B 1E6 Canada

CLARKE, BUD (WARREN) F
DESIGNER, PAINTER
b Windsor, Vt, Jan 10, 41. *Study:* Art Students League, 59-63; Sch Visual Arts, with Milton Glazer. *Pos:* Art dir, McCalls Corp, 68-70; art dir, McGraw Hill Inc, NY, 70-81; founder, Bud Clarke & Assocs, 81-84; pres, Clarke/Thompson Design, 84-. *Teaching:* Instr mag design, 77-, instr media commun, 78-, Sch Visual Arts, NY. *Awards:* Cert of Merit, Art Dir Mag; Soc Publ Designers; Jesse H Neal Award, Am Bus Press, 80 & 82. *Bibliog:* Roy Paul Nelson (auth), Publication Design, William C Brown, 78. *Mem:* Soc Publ Designers; McGraw Hill Art Dirs Club (pres, 74-78). *Media:* Magazines, Printed Material, Watercolor, Mixed Medium. *Mailing Add:* 65 Pokonoie Rd Ulster Park NY 12487-5080

CLARKE, JOHN CLEM
PAINTER
b Bend, Ore, June 6, 37. *Study:* Ore State Univ; Mexico City Col; Univ Ore, BFA, 60. *Work:* Whitney Mus Am Art, NY; Dallas Mus Art, Tex; Va Mus Fine Arts; Metrop Mus Art & Mus Mod Art, NY; Baltimore Mus Fine Arts, Md. *Exhib:* Bi-Ann, Whitney Mus, 67-73; Realism in Am, touring USA; Mus Mod Art, NY; Aspects of Realism, touring Can, 76-78; Illusion and Reality, touring Australia, 77-78; Art About Art, Whitney Mus, NY, 78; Contemp Am Realism Since 1960, Pa Acad Fine Arts, Philadelphia, 81; The Ponderosa Collection, Butler Inst Am Art, Youngstown, Ohio, 83. *Media:* Oil on Canvas. *Mailing Add:* c/o Louis K Meisel Gallery 141 Prince St New York NY 10012

CLARKE, JOHN R
HISTORIAN, CRITIC
b Pittsburgh, Pa, Jan 25, 45. *Study:* Georgetown Univ, AB, 67; Yale Univ, MA, 69, PhD, 73. *Teaching:* Asst prof hist art, Yale Univ, 75-80; asst prof, Univ Tex, Austin, 80-82, assoc prof, 82-87, prof, 88. *Awards:* NEH grants, 95, 99; Guggenheim grant, 2002. *Mem:* Col Art Asn Am (vpres, 96-98, pres 98-2000); Archaeol Inst Am; Int Asn Study Ancient Mosaics; Am Coun Learned Soc (bd dir, currently). *Res:* Humor in Ancient Roman Visual Culture, 100 BC-AD250. *Publ:* Auth, Roman Black & White Fiigural Mosaics, NY Univ Press, 79; The Houses of Roman Italy, 100 BC-AD 250: Ritual, Space and Decoration, Univ Calif Press, 91; Looking at Lovemaking: Constructions of Sexuality in Roman Art, 100 BC-AD 250, Univ Calif Press, 98; Roman Sex, 100BC-AD250, Abrams, 2003; Art in Lives of Ordinary Romans: Visual Representation & Non-elite Viewers in Italy, 100 BC-AD 315, Univ Calif Press, 2003. *Mailing Add:* Univ Tex Dept Art & Art Hist Austin TX 78712

CLARKE, KEVIN
PHOTOGRAPHER, CONCEPTUAL ARTIST
b New York, NY, Mar 20, 53. *Study:* Cooper Union, BFA, 76; studied sculpture under Chris Wilmarth, Hans Haacke, Dore Ashton & Reuben Kadish. *Work:* Brooklyn Mus, NY; San Antonio Mus Art, Tex; Mus Wiesbadan & Fluxeum, Wiesbaden, Ger; Nat Gallerie, Berlin; Int Ctr Photog, NY; Smithsonian Inst; Cold Spring Harbor Lab. *Comn:* 7 murals for atrium, B-W Bank, Stuttgart, Ger; Portrait James D Watson, Cold Spring Harbor Lab, NY; Portrait Jacques Lowe, NY Acad Sci. *Exhib:* The Red Couch, Int Ctr Photog, NY, 84, Summer Rencontres, Ampitheater Arles, France, 84 & Tampa Mus Art, Fla, 90; Kaufhauswelt (Dept Store World), Frankfurter Kunstverein, Ger, 80; Blood, Schirn Kunsthalle, Frankfurt, Ger, 2003; Photo Espagne, 2002; Hecksher Mus Art, NY, 2003. *Bibliog:* Encounters with the Portrait, catalog Ralf Christofori, 2002; The End of the Art World. Vernal Passage, by Robert C. Morgan, Allworth Press, NY, 1999. *Interests:* genetics. *Collection:* William N Copley, Ann and James Harithas, DG Bank, others. *Publ:* Coauth, Kunstund Medien, Materialien Zur Documenta 6, Documenta, 1977; auth, Kaufhauswelt, Schirmer & Mosel, Muarch, 1980; The Red Couch, a Portrait of America, Harper & Row, 1984; Kevin Clarke Portraits, NY Kunsthalle; coauth, Gene Worlds, Bundeskunsthalle, Bonn, 1998; Kevin Clarke, by Alan Jones, Tema Celeste, 1999; Blood, Prestel Publs, 2001; Dust to DNA, Ars Genetica, Inc, 2002. *Dealer:* Galerie Michael Sturm, Stuttgart, Ger; Galleria de Arte Pilar Parra, Madrid, Spain. *Mailing Add:* 407 Greenwich St New York NY 10013

CLARO, PAUL
SCULPTOR
b Edison, NJ, Jan 14, 54. *Study:* Rutgers Univ, BA, New Brunswick, NJ, 70; Art Student League, NY, 78. *Comn:* Sculpture, Musical Masterpiece, comn by Don Henley, Los Angeles, 90; monument, Music Hall of Fame, Calif, 95; sculpture, Song in Sculpture, comn by Dominique Francisco, Calif, 2001. *Pos:* Owner, Musical Gallery, Santa Monica, Calif, 90-. *Teaching:* Instr, art & sculpture, NYU, 79-88; Instr, pvt sessions, 90-. *Awards:* First Place Award, Sculpture & Painting Exhib, Calif Art Gallery, 2000; Silver Medal, Nat Sculpture Soc, 2001, 2003 & 2005. *Bibliog:* Don Johns (auth), Bringing Music out in Sculpture, Boboo Publ, 91; Erin MacGeorge (auth), Muscial Sculptures, Tunes Publ, 94. *Mem:* Nat Sculpture Soc; Am Art Asn (secy, 2000-); Calif Art & Sculpture Soc. *Media:* Clay & Metal. *Interests:* Musicians of the 80's & 90's; Sailing. *Dealer:* Muscial Gallery 1111 Santa Monica Blvd Santa Monica Calif 94440. *Mailing Add:* 8 Newton St Belchertown MA 01007-9669

CLAYBERGER, SAMUEL ROBERT
PAINTER, EDUCATOR
b Kulpmont, Pa, Mar 26, 26. *Study:* Chouinard Art Inst, Los Angeles; Jepson Art Inst; study with Don Graham, Rico Lebrun & Richard Haines. *Work:* Pasadena Art Mus, Calif. *Exhib:* One-man shows, Pasadena Art Mus, 60, Laguna Beach Mus Art, Calif, 67, Era Marguerite Gallery, San Marino, 91, Prufrock Gallery, Pasadena, 2000, Heritage Gallery, La, 93 & 98,Art Acad, La, 01, Chouinard Found Sch Art, South Pasadena, 2003-2005, Unitarian Universalist Church, St Monica 99 & 2005; Group shows, Calif, Longbeach Mus Art, 65-66, La Jolla Mus Art 69-70, Oceanside Mus Art, 2001 Calif Watercolor Soc. *Pos:* Designer-colorist, UPA Pictures Inc, Burbank, 53-58 & Jay Ward Prod Inc, Los Angeles, 59-64. *Teaching:* Instr design, Chouinard Art Inst, 60; instr design & painting, Otis Art Inst of Los Angeles Co, 63-69, asst prof drawing & painting, 69-79; instr drawing, Otis Parsons, 79-91; instr figure painting, landscape, Chouinard Found Art, South Pasadena, 2003-2006. *Awards:* Nat Watercolor Soc, 56, 58, 60 & 69; Los Angeles All-City Exhib, Home Savings & Loan, 62. *Bibliog:* Joseph Mugnaini & Janice Loroos (auths), Drawing: A Search for Form, Reinhold, 65; George De Groat (auth), Sam Clayberger eyes the human condition, Star News, Pasadena, 70; Paul J Karlstrom (interviewer), taped interview archives, Am Art, Smithsonian Inst, 81; Joseph Mugnaini, Expressive Drawing, Davis Publ, 88; Gerald W Brommer (auth), The Art of Sketching, Clinker Press, ltd ed portfolio, 2000. *Media:* Acrylic, Watercolor. *Publ:* The Erotic Drawings of Sam Clayberger, Clinker Press, ltd ed portfolio, 2000. *Mailing Add:* 486 Mavis Dr Los Angeles CA 90065-5054

CLAYSON, S HOLLIS
ART HISTORIAN
b Itasca, Ill. *Study:* Wellesley Col, BA, 68; Univ Calif, Los Angeles, MA, 75, with T J Clark, PhD, 84. *Teaching:* Asst prof art hist, Wichita State Univ, 78-82; Asst prof Northwestern Univ, Evanston, Ill, 82-90, assoc prof & chair, 91-2001, Charles Deering McCormick prof teaching excellence, 93-96, prof, 2001; Koldyke outstanding teaching prof, 2004. *Awards:* Col Art Asn Teaching Award, 90; Am Coun Learned Soc Fel, 90-91; Sr Fel, Northwestern Univ Humanities Ctr, 94-95; Clark fel, 2003; Getty Res Inst Fel. *Mem:* Col Art Asn; Midwest Victorian Studies Asn; Midwest Art Hist Soc; Asn Art Historians, Eng. *Res:* Social iconography of later 19th century French art. *Publ:* Auth, catalog for The Second Exhibition, 1876, A Failed Attempt, The New Painting, Impressionism 1874-1886, The Fine Arts Mus, San Francisco & The Nat Art Gallery Art, Washington, DC, pp 145-159, 86, Painted Love: Prsotitution in French Art of the Impressionist Era, 91, (co-edited) Understanding Paintings: Themes in Art Explored and Explained, 2000, Paris in Despair: Art and Everday Life Under Siege, 1870-71; Painted Love: Prostitution in French Art of the Impressionist Era, Yale Univ Press, 91; essay: The Sexual Politics of Impressionist Illegibility, Dealing with Iegas: Representations of Women and the Politics of Vision, Richard Kendall & Griselda Pollock (eds), London, 92; others. *Mailing Add:* Northwestern Univ 2439 Ridgeway Ave Evanston IL 60201

CLAYTON, CHRISTIAN
PAINTER
b Denver, Colo, 1967. *Study:* Art Ctr Col of Design, BFA, 1989-91. *Exhib:* Clayton Brothers solo shows: Green Pastures, La Luz de Jesus Gallery, Calif, 2001, Candy Lackey, Roq La Rue Gallery, Seattle, 2002, Six Foot Eleven, La Luz de Jesus Gallery, 2003, Art Statements, Art Basel, Miami, Fla, 2004, I Come From Here, Mackey Gallery, Houston, Tex, 2004, Wishy Washy, Bellwether Gallery, NY, 2006, The Armory Show, 2006, Madison Mus Contemporary Art, Wis, 2006, Alyce de Roulet Williamson Gallery, Calif, 2006; Clayton Brothers group shows: Tribute to La Luz de Jesus Gallery, Track 16 Gallery, Santa Monica, 1998, Collaborations, New Image Art Gallery, calif, 2000, School Girls, Fish Tank Gallery, Brooklyn, 2001, Decipher, Eighth Floor Gallery, NY, 2002, Burning Brush, Six Space Gallery, Calif, 2002, The Burbs, DFN Gallery, NY, 2003, Assembly, Front Room Gallery, Brooklyn, 2003, Qee Show, OX-OP Gallery/Toy 2R Company, Tokyo, 2004, Tree Trimmings, Track 16 Gallery, 2004, Stranger Town, Dinte Fine Art, NY, 2005, Move 13, Clementine Gallery, NY, 2005, Visual Language, Mackey Gallery, Houston, Tex, 2005, Drawn to Expression, Alyce de Roulet Williamson Gallery, Calif, 2006; solo shows: 17 Souls, La Luz de Jesus Gallery, Calif, 1995, Out of Order, 14996, Loved to Give, 1998, I am Little, 2000; group shows: The Narrative Image, Ozone Art Gallery, SoHo, NY, 1996, The Young and the Restless, Bucheon Gallery, San Francisco Gallery, Calif, 1998, Move 2, New Image Art Gallery, 1998, California Artists, Ann Nathan Gallery, Chicago, 1998, The Portrait Show, New Image Art Gallery, 2001. *Pos:* Mem, The Clayton Brothers. *Teaching:* Tchr experimental media, Art Ctr Col of Design, Pasadena, Calif, 1995-. *Media:* Miscellaneous Media. *Mailing Add:* The Clayton Brothers PO Box 622 Verdugo City CA 91046

CLAYTON, ROBERT
PAINTER
b Dayton, Ohio, 1963. *Study:* Colo Inst Art, 1981-83; Art Ctr Col of Design, BFA, 1986-89. *Exhib:* Clayton Brothers solo shows: Green Pastures, La Luz de Jesus Gallery, Calif, 2001, Candy Lackey, Roq La Rue Gallery, Seattle, 2002, Six Foot Eleven, La Luz de Jesus Gallery, 2003, Art Statements, Art Basel, Miami, Fla, 2004, I Come From Here, Mackey Gallery, Houston, Tex, 2004, Wishy Washy, Bellwether Gallery, NY, 2006, The Armory Show, 2006, Madison Mus Contemporary Art, Wis, 2006Alyce de Roulet Williamson Gallery, Pasadena, Calif, 2006; Clayton Brothers group shows: Tribute to La Luz de Jesus Gallery, Track 16, Santa Monica, 1998, Collaborations, New Image Art Gallery, Calif, 2000, School Girls, Fish Tank Gallery, Brooklyn, 2001, Decipher, Eighth Floor Gallery, NY, 2002, Burning Brush, Six Space Gallery, Calif, 2002, the Burbs, DFN Gallery, NY, 2003, Assembly, Front Room Gallery, Brooklyn, 2003, Qee Show, OX-OP Gallery/Toy2R Company, Tokyo, 2004, Tree Trimmings, Track 16 Gallery, 2004, Stranger Town, Dinter Fine Art, NY, 2005; solo shows: 75 Pints, La Luz de Jesus Gallery, 1994, Lucky 13, 1995, No Rhyme or Reason, 1997, 14 Gold Teeth, 1999; group shows: Antagonist, Pacific Design Ctr, Calif, 1995, California Artists, Ann Nathan Gallery, Chicago, 1998, Move 2, New Image Art Gallery, 1998, The Portrait Show, 2001. *Pos:* Mem, The Clayton Brothers. *Teaching:* Tchr experimental media, Art Ctr Col of Design, Pasadena, Calif, 1996-. *Media:* Miscellaneous Media. *Mailing Add:* The Clayton Brothers PO Box 622 Verdugo City CA 91046

CLEARY, B J B See Cleary, Barbara B

CLEARY, BARBARA B
PAINTER, INSTRUCTOR
b Durant, Okla, Aug, 10, 35. *Study:* Univ Okla, BS, 58; Univ Central Okla, MA, 63; also studied with John Pike, Edgar Whitney & M Douglas Walton. *Work:* Muchnic Gallery, Atchinson, Kans; Winfield Art Ctr, Kans, City of Salina, Kans, City of Newton, Kans, Main Hurdman, Kans. *Exhib.* Kansas Watercolor Soc 5-State, Wichita Art Mus, 85, 86, & 88; Art Ann V,Cult Arts Ctr, Tulsa, Okla, 86; Southern Watercolor, Okla Art Ctr, Okla City, 87-88; National Watercolor Oklahoma, Okla Art Ctr, Oklahoma City, 88-89; 115th Am Watercolor Soc, Nat Gallery, NY. *Teaching:* Ft Scott Community Col. *Awards:* Past Pres Award, Fall Nat, Bakersfield, Calif, 85; Patron Award, Kans Watercolor Soc 4-State, 85; Patron Arts Award, Southern Watercolor Soc, 87. *Mem:* Kans Watercolor Soc (bd dir, 78-79, 84-85 & 86-87); Images II, Fine Arts (chmn, 88-90). *Media:* Watercolor; oil. *Publ:* Contribr, The Best of Kansas Arts and Crafts, State of Kans, 88. *Dealer:* Richard Hamilton 17201 E 40 Hwy Independence MO 64055

CLEARY, MANON CATHERINE
EDUCATOR
b St. Louis, Nov 14, 42. *Study:* Attended, Univ Valencia, Spain; Attended, Cocoran Sch Art; Wash Univ, St Louis, BFA, 64; Temple Univ, MFA, 68; Pi Beta Phi. *Work:* One woman shows incl Mus Modern Art Gulbenkian Found, Lisbon, Portugal, 1985; group exhib incl Art Inst Chicago, Huntsville (Ala) Mus, 1987, Boca Raton (Fla) Mus Art, 1987, Holter Mus, Helena, Mont, 1996, Alternate Mus, New York City, 1996, Kasteyev Mus, Almaty, Kazakstan, 1996, Nat Mus Women in the Arts, Wash, 2000. *Teaching:* Instr, fine arts State Univ NY, Oswego, 68-70; instr to assoc prof, DC Teachers Col, Wash, 70-78; from assoc prof to prof art Univ DC, 78—2004, acting chmn dept, 85-86, 90-91; assoc dean, Col Liberal & Fine Arts, 92-94, acting coordr, art prog, 94—2000. *Awards:* Recipient Fac Res award, Univ DC, 84, 89; Mayor's 14th annual Award for excellence in an artistic discipline, 98; individual artist grantee DC Commission on the Arts, 2000-01. *Mem:* Mem Col Art Assoc

CLEARY, SHIRLEY CLEARY COOPER
PAINTER, WRITER
b St Louis, Mo, Nov 14, 42. *Study:* Washington Univ, St Louis, BFA, 64; Tyler Sch Art, Temple Univ, MFA, 68; The Corcoran Mus Sch, 69-71. *Work:* Fedn Flyfishers Int Mus, W Yellowstone, Mont; Washington State Art Pub Places Collections; Herning Hojskole, Denmark; Nat Parks Found, Hokonui Heritage Center & Mus, Gore, NZ. *Comn:* Portrait of Gov Swinden, Sen Melcher, Sen Baucus, Cong Williams (medallion), comn by Mont Democratic Party, Helena, 85-90; Limited prints, Mont ambassadors, comn by State of Mont, Helena, 86; Poster, Mont Water Quality Month, comn by State of Mont, 91; Poster, 100 Years Fish Technology Ctr (USTD), 92; Patron Paintings, Mont State Trout Unlimited. *Exhib:* C M Russell Mus, Great Falls, Mont, 83, 86-98 & 99-2000; Western Wildlife Gallery, San Francisco, Calif, 88; Arts for the Parks (US Tour), 89, 94, 97, 98 & 2002; Women Artists of the West, Calif, 90 & 92; Maryland Waterfowl Festival, 93, 94, 95 & 96; Women Artists & the West, Tucson Mus Art, 94 & 95; Am Mus Fly Fishing, Manchester, Vt, 97; 1st Place, Casper Artist Guild Int Miniature Exhib, 2004; Grand Prize, Rocky Mountain Art Show, 2005. *Pos:* Bd mem, Mont Arts Coun, 73-82; guest artist, Herning Hojskole, Denmark, fall 81; artist-in-residence, Rivermeadow, Jackson Hole, 89-94 & 97. *Awards:* Best of Show, 3rd Ann Miniature Exhib, El Dorado Gallery, Colo, 84; First Place Acrylic & Gouache Painting, Bosque Art Gallery, NMex, 84 & 85; First Place, Ore Trout Stamp, 90; First Place, Asn NW Steelheaders Stamp, 92; Nat Trout Unltd Conservation Comms Award, 99; Artist of the Year, Nat Trout Unltd, 2001. *Bibliog:* Ann Geracimos (auth), Shirley Cleary-artist of the West, Am Artist Mag, 4/81; Vivian A Paladin (auth), Shirley Cleary-eclectic artist in the West, Art West, 7/81; Judy Hughes (auth), Feeling the Splash of the Water, The Angling Art of Shirley Cleary, Wild Life Art News, 9/92; The Fine Art of Flyfishing, US Art, 7/94. *Media:* Gouache, Oil. *Publ:* Illusr, covers, Mont Outdoors, 81-86, 92 & Flyfisher's Mag Int Fedn Flyfishermen, 86; La Forza Opaca della Tempera, Disegnare & Dipingere, 11/87; illusr, Fly Fishing Quarterly; Fly Fisherman Mag. *Dealer:* Horizon Fine Art 165 N Center St Jackson WY 83001; Wild Wings Inc S Hwy 61 Lake City MN 55041-0451; Ponderosa 944 Springhill Hamilton MT 59840. *Mailing Add:* 1804 Beltview Dr Helena MT 59601

CLEAVER, RICHARD BRUCE
SCULPTOR
b Camden, NJ. *Study:* Md Inst Col Art, BFA(magna cum laude), 77; Univ, Wis, MA, 80. *Work:* Erie Art Mus, Pa; Sallie May Loan Corp, Washington; St Paul Companies, Minn; Del Art Mus, Wilmington; Corcoran Gallery Art, Washington, DC. *Exhib:* Art Sites, Corcoran Gallery Art, Washington, DC, 96; Contemp Am Ceramics, Loveland Mus, Colo, 97; All the World's a Stage: Mixed Media Dioramas by Tom Duncan & Richard Cleaver, Noyes Mus, Oceanville, NJ, 98; Del Art Mus Biennial, Wilmington, 98; Family Ties, Peabody Essex Mus, Salem, Mass, 2003. *Awards:* Ind Artist Grant, Md State Arts Coun, 92, 95, 99, 2003; Crafts Fel, NEA, 94. *Bibliog:* Joe Vajtko (auth), Icons for Iconoclasts: Recent works by Richard Cleaver, Joel H Springer & Christian Vergane (rev), 21-26, 12/15/96; Barry Schwabsky (auth), Schwabsky: Critic, 14-15, Washington Rev, Critics' Residency Prog, 4/5-97; Hidden Stories in the Work of Richard Cleaver, Sch Arts, 1/98. *Mailing Add:* 201 Edgevale Rd Baltimore MD 21210

CLEMENT, KATHLEEN
PAINTER, GRAPHIC ARTIST
b Ord, Nebr, May 28, 28. *Study:* Univ Nebr, BA, 50; with Frank Gonzalez, 67-69; Univ Am, with Toby Joysmith, 77-79; Mus Studies, Paris, 80. *Work:* Mus Mod Art, Isidro Fabela Cult Ctr & Inst North Am Cult Relations, Mexico; House of Humour & Satire, Gabravo, Bulgaria, 88. *Comn:* Paintings comn by, Co Minera Autlan, Elias Mussali & Jacobo Margolis; Rudolf Mosny; Embotelladora De Sinaloa. *Exhib:* Solo exhib, Rossi Gallery, Morristown, NJ, 83, Mus Puebla, Mex, 91, Mus Fine Arts, Toluca, Mex, 92, San Miguel De Allende, GTO; Latin Am Art, Ger, Austria, 88; Biennal-Humour & Satire, Gabravo, Bulgaria, 89; Rafael Matos Gallery, Mex, 90; 2n Bienal, Mus de Monterrey; Museo de Historia Natural, Med DF, 2000, Gurp de Los 100, Mexico, DF; Mus of the City, Leon, Queretaro, Mex, 99; and others; Pablo Goebel Fine Arts 2003, Mexico, DF. *Awards:* Prize in Graphics, Nebr Reg Compt, 48; Delta Phi Delta; Purchase Prize, Bienal, Gabrovo, Bulgaria, 88. *Bibliog:* Jorge J Crespo de la Serna (auth), article, Novedades, 3/30/76; Berta Taracena (auth), article, Tiempo, 5/24/82; Gloria Bucco (auth), article, Vail Daily, 4/485; Unicorno Blanco, Mex, 90; John Maxim www.herald.com International Edition The Miami Herald Sept 7, 2003, www.mexiconews.com.mx. *Mem:* SOMART; Foro de Arte Contemporanio. *Media:* Acrylic, Pen & Ink. *Dealer:* Sibley 111 E 7th St #55 New York NY 10009; Pablo Goebel Fine Arts. *Mailing Add:* Tulipan 359 Col El Toro Contreras Mexico 10610 DF Mexico

CLEMENT, SHIRLEY
PAINTER
b New York, NY July 7, 22. *Study:* Ringling Sch Art, two yrs; Amagansett Art Sch, Sarasota, Fla, two yrs. *Work:* Univ Fla, Gainesville; Davenport Munic Gallery, Iowa; Henry Ward Ranger Fund, NY. *Exhib:* Am Watercolor Soc, Nat Acad, NY, 50-; Watercolor Show, Phoenix Mus, 68; Winterpark Sidewalk Art Festival, Fla, 71; Disneys Festival of the Masters, Lake Buena Vista, Fla, 74; Nat Acad Show, NY & High Mus, 74; Allied Artists, Nat Arts Club, NY, 74. *Awards:* Salmagundi Award, Am Watercolor Soc, 69; William A Paton Award, Nat Acad Design, 74; Verda Karen McCracken Young Award, Am Watercolor Soc, 77. *Mem:* Am Watercolor Soc; Fla Artist Group; Fla Watercolor Soc; Sarasota Art Asn; Manatee Art League. *Media:* Watercolor, Acrylic. *Publ:* Auth, article on The watercolor page, Am Artist, 4/48. *Mailing Add:* PO Box 5771 Sarasota FL 34277-5771

CLEMENTE, FRANCESCO
PAINTER
b Naples, Italy, Mar 23, 1952. *Study:* Univ Rome, 1970. *Work:* Whitney Mus Am Art & Mus Mod Art, NY; Philadelphia Mus Art; Guggenheim Mus, Bilbao; Saatchi Collection, London; Stedelijk Mus, Amsterdam; Guggenheim Mus, Bilbao, Italy; Art & Project, Sloopdort, The Netherlands; Kunstsmus, Basel, Switzerland. *Exhib:* l'Identite Ital: Arten Ital depuis 1959, 81 & Magicians of the Earth, 89, Mus Mod Art, Paris; Homo Sapiens: the many images, 82 & Trustee's Choice, Aldrich Mus Contemp

Art, Ridgefield, Conn, 83; New Work on Paper 2: Borofsky, Clemente, Merz, Penck, Penone, 82, An Int Survey of Recent Painting & Sculpture, 84, India & the Contemp Artist, 85, For 25 Yrs: Crown Point Press, 88 & Allegories of Modernism: Contemp Drawing (with catalog), 92, Mus Mod Art, NY; solo exhibs, James Corcoran Gallery, Los Angeles, Calif, 83, Francesco Clemente Prints 1981-1985, Mezzanine Gallery & Metrop Mus Art, NY, 85, The Departure of the Argonaut, Mus Mod Art, NY, 86, The Argentario Paintings, Art Inst Chicago, Ill, 87, The Graphic Work, Milwaukee Art Mus, traveling, 88, Three Worlds, Philadelphia Mus Art, Pa, traveling, 90-91 & Gallery Bruno Bischofberger, Zurich, 96, Indianapolis Mus Art, 98, Solomon R Guggenheim Mus, NY, 99, Galleria Civica di Arte Contemporanea, Trento, Italy, 2001, Museo Archeologico Nazionale, Ital, 2002, Gagosian Gallery, London, 2002, The Hardwood Mus of Art, Univ of NMex, Taos, 2002; Recent European Painting, Solomon R Guggenheim Mus, NY, 83; The Human Condition, Biennial III, San Francisco Mus Mod Art, Calif, 84; Images & Impressions, Walker Art Ctr, Minneapolis, Minn, traveling, 84-85; States of War, Seattle Art Mus, 85; New Art of Italy, Joslyn Art Mus, Omaha, Nebr, traveling, 85-86; Philadelphia Collects Art Since 1940, 86 & New Art on Paper, 88, Philadelphia Mus Art; Avante-garde in the eighties, Los Angeles Co Mus, Calif, 87; Int Exhib to End World Hunger, Minnesota Mus Art, St Paul, traveling, 87-88; The World of Art Today, Milwaukee Art Mus, Wis, 88; Contemp Watercolors: Europe & Am, Univ NTex Art Gallery, Denton, 94; The Ossuary, Luhring Augustine, NY, 94; Pacifico Yokohama Exhib Hall, Tokyo, 94; A New York Time: Selected Drawing of the Eighties (with catalog), Bruce Mus, Greenwich, 95; Muse? Transforming the Image of Women in Contemp Art, Galerie Thaddeus Ropac, Paris, 95; Whitney Biennial, Whitney Mus Am Art, NY, 97; Art Inst Chgo, 87-01; Phila Mus Art, 90-01; Centre Georges Pompidou, Musée national de l'art moderne, Paris, 94-02; Solomon R Guggenheim Mus, NYC, 99-02; Museo Archeologico Nazionale di Napoli, 2002-03. *Bibliog:* Ann-Sargent Wooster (auth), Francesco Clemente, Du, Mag of Cult, 1/94; Carol Kimo (auth), Francesco Clemente, Gagosian, ARTnews, 4/94; Judith Trepp (auth), Francesco Clemente, Bruno Bischofberger, ARTnews, 5/94; numerous others in art mags & newspapers; Francesco Clemente Three Worlds, Phila.,1989. *Publ:* Auth, William Burroughs: The Creative Observer, Flash Art, vol XXXVI, no 172, 94. *Dealer:* Gagosian Gallery 980 Madison Ave New York NY 10021. *Mailing Add:* 684 Broadway New York NY 10012

CLEMENTE, JOANN P
PAINTER
Study: Univ S Fla; Univ Tampa, Fla; NY Sch Interior Design, 83; Barbizon Sch, Forest Hills, NY, 84. *Work:* Restoration of Religious Statues, St Columbkille Church, Ft Myers, Fla. *Comn:* Painting, World Reknown Scuba Diver, Bruno Cherubini, Rome, Italy, 97; painting, rep to President Clinton, Washington, DC, 98. *Pos:* Interior designer, sales, Nebr Furniture & Belmont Furniture, Tampa, Fla, 70's; designer, motifs, self employed, Ft Myers, Fla, currently; painter, fine arts, self employed, Ft Myers, Fla, currently. *Media:* Acrylic, Oil, Watercolor, Designer. *Mailing Add:* 11110 Caravel Cir Fort Myers FL 33908-3980

CLEMENTS, ROBERT DONALD
SCULPTOR, EDUCATOR
b Pittsburgh, Pa, Dec 24, 37. *Study:* Carnegie-Mellon Univ, BFA(painting), 59; Pa State Univ, MA(art), 62, PhD(art educ), 64. *Work:* Nat Mus Am Arts, Smithsonian Inst, Washington; Jacksonville Mus Arts; AT&T; Chase Manhattan Bank; Coca Cola USA. *Comn:* Sculpture, Fifty Yuppies, Arts festival Atlanta, 87; Indian Creek MARTA Sta, Atlanta; sculpture, SE Atlanta Park & Recreation Ctr; folk art plazas, Corp Olympic Development, Atlanta; sculpture, Musical Gambol, Los Altos, Calif. *Exhib:* One-man show, Totems to Southerners & the South, Hunter Mus Art, Montgomery Mus & Asheville Mus; Nat Sculpture, 80; South Exhib, Palazzo Venezia, Rome, 84; Atlanta in France, Sorbonne, Paris & Toulouse, 85. *Pos:* Art consult, Arts & Humanities Prog, US Off Educ, 68-69. *Teaching:* Asst prof art, Ball State Univ, 64-68; assoc prof art, Univ Ga, 69-81, prof art, 81-94, emer prof, 94-. *Awards:* Energy Art Award, 82; Univ Affil Fel, Ga VAP, 86-; Ga Endowment Arts, Artist Grant, 87; Meigs Teaching Award, 93. *Bibliog:* Cynthia Bickley Green (auth), Robert Clements, Art Papers, Vol 10, No 5, 86; Joy Lee (auth), Wood sculpture, Arts/Crafts, spring 80; Charlotte von Glasersfeld (auth), article, Art Papers, 11/83; Barbara Mackenzie (auth), Old & new blend in Clements' sculpture, Atlanta Constitution, 7/22/86. *Mem:* Nat Art Educ Asn; Ga Art Educ Asn; Southern Asn Sculptors; Int Sculpture Ctr. *Media:* Metal. *Publ:* Auth, The inductive method of teaching visual art criticism, J Aesthetic Educ, 7/79; Modern architecture's debt to creative education, Gifted Child Quart, summer 81; Metaphor in Art Education, Art Educ, 9/82; The inductive method of teaching visual art criticism, J Aesthetic Educ, 7/79; coauth (with Claire Clements), Art and Mainstreaming, Art Instruction for Exceptional Children in Regular Classrooms, Charles C Thomas, 84; Emphasis Art: A Qualitative Art Program for Elementary & Middle School, Addison Wesley Longman, 92, 96 & 2000. *Mailing Add:* 155 Bar H Ct Athens GA 30605

CLERK, PIERRE
PAINTER, SCULPTOR
b Atlanta, Ga, Apr 26, 28. *Study:* Loyola Col; McGill Univ; Montreal Sch Art & Design; Acad Julian, Paris; Acad Grande Chaumiere, Paris. *Work:* Mus Mod Art, Guggenheim Mus, Whitney Mus Am Art & Brooklyn Mus, NY; Nat Gallery Can, Ottawa, Ont; Mus Contemp Art, Montreal. *Comn:* City Walls, NY; Com Bank of Kansas City; First Wis Develop Corp, Milwaukee; sculpture, City Toledo, 83; Continental Bank of Ill, Chicago; and others. *Exhib:* Venice Biennale, Italy, 56-58; Carnegie Int, Pittsburgh, 58; ROSC Int, Dublin, Ireland, 71; one-man exhibs, Everson Mus Art, Syracuse, NY, 77, Waterside Plaza, Monumental Outdoor Sculpture, NY, 77-78, Iran-Am Ctr, Tehran, Iran, 78 & Metrop Mus, Manila, Philippines, 78; Can Cul Ctr, Paris, 80; and others. *Pos:* Artist-in-residence fel, Tamarind Inst Albuquerque, NMex. *Awards:* US State Dept Lectr & Travel Grant, 77-78; Pollack/Krasner Grant, 90; Elizabeth Found Grant, 93; and others

CLEVELAND, ROBERT EARL
ADMINISTRATOR, EDUCATOR
b Union, Miss, June 8, 36. *Study:* Miss Col, BA; Univ Miss, MFA; Univ Tenn, EdD. *Work:* Univ Miss Fine Arts Ctr, University, Miss; Miss College, Clinton, Miss; Carson-Newman College, Jefferson City, Tenn. *Comn:* Redwood sculpture, Carson-Newman Col, 76; redwood sculpture, First Nat Bank, 85; wood & fibre glass resin sculpture, First People's Bank, 85. *Exhib:* Second Nat Print & Drawing Exhib, Dulin Gallery Art, Knoxville, Tenn, 67; Tenn Watercolor Exhib, Cheekwood Mus, Nashville, 75; Quinlan Ann Art Exhib, Gainesville, Ga, 76; Carroll Reece Mus, Johnson City, Tenn, 77; Owensboro Mus Fine Arts, Ky, 79; Somerhill Gallery, Durham, NC, 80; Goldsboro Ann Art Exhib, NC, 85; Sacred Arts Seven Exhib, Wheaton, Ill, 85; Whiting Gallery, Fairhope, Ala, 86; 50-yr retrospective, Toledo Mus Art, 88. *Pos:* Artist-illusr, Ling-Temco-Vought Inc, Dallas, Tex, 61-62; retired, 95; Art Restorer. *Teaching:* Instr art, Univ Miss, Oxford, 63-64; prof art & chmn dept, Carson-Newman Col, Jefferson City, 64-95. *Awards:* First Prize Painting, Morristown Art Competition, Tenn, 66 & Macon Ann Arts Exhib, Macon Arts Coun, 73; First Prize Drawing, Oak Ridge Relig Art Exhib, Oak Ridge Art Ctr, Tenn, 76; Second Prize, Centennial Photography Exhib, Knoxville, Tenn, 85. *Mem:* Nat Asn Schs Art; Nat Coun Art Adminrs; Southeastern Col Art Conf; Tenn Watercolor Soc. *Media:* Watercolor, Drawing. *Res:* Arts administration in higher education and art and law issues. *Publ:* Auth, Art and the Law, 77 & auth, The Art Department Chairperson: An Ambiguous Role, 78, Nat Coun Art Adminrs; The law: Public aid and the private sector, 78 & Art administration in pursuit of efficacy, 83, Fac Studies; Structured Models for Managing Conflict, Fac Studies, Secac Review 85; An Overview of Professional Opportunities in Art, Secac Review, 87; Evaluating Student Art: More Than Just Grading, Secac Review, 88; auth, Jefferson City: 200 Years in Pictures, Tenn Vallery Publ, Knoxville, Tenn, 2003; auth, Reflections of Faith in an Artistic Journey, Mossy Creek Publ, 2004. *Mailing Add:* 143 E Old Andrew Johnson Hwy Jefferson City TN 37760

CLIFF, DENIS ANTONY
PAINTER, INSTUCTOR
b Victoria, BC, Aug 8, 42. *Study:* Univ Victoria, BEd, 65; New Sch Art, 66-67. *Work:* Nat Gallery Can, Art Bank Gallery, Ottawa; Charlottetown Confederation Ctr Arts, PEI; Univ Sask, Saskatoon; Art Gallery of Northumberland, Cobourg, Ont. *Comn:* Murals, Ostler Sch Nursing, Toronto, 70, Simcoe Bd Educ, Ont, 71, Eaton Ctr, Toronto, 78 & Fisher-Price, Toronto, 79; Parkdale Focus Mural, Toronto, 92. *Exhib:* New Blood, Rodman Hall Art Ctr, St Catherines, Ont, 73; Can Invitational, Can Consulate, Chicago, 77; Artists Coop Toronto at Nexus, Philadelphia, 78; Explorations, Thames Art Ctr, Chatham, Ont, 80; Toronto Exchange, Mem Univ, St Johns, Nfld, 81; Retrospective Contor Gallery, Toronto, Can, 2000. *Pos:* Dir, Artist's Co-op, Toronto, 77-82; pres, Arts Sake Inc, 78-80; vpres, Workscene Co-op Gallery, 88-89; prog coordr Sir Sanford Fleming Col, 99-. *Teaching:* Artist-in-residence, Canador Col, North Bay, Ont, 72-74 & Arts Sake, Toronto, 77-79; vis prof, York Univ, Toronto, 79-82; asst prof, Univ Victoria, 82-84; instr, Toronto Sch Art, 85-, steering comt mem, 91-; Sir Sandford Fleming Col Diploma Program, 2000. *Awards:* Best Painting, 70 & Best in Show, 71, City Toronto Ann; Can Coun Grant, 79; Ontario Arts Coun Award, 88. *Bibliog:* Sandra Shaul (auth), Altered egos: An exhibition of drawings by Denis Cliff, 77; Diane Pugen (auth), article, 78, Art Mag; Margie Kelk (auth), Denis Cliff: Drawings, 92; Martha Perkins (auth), Cliff changes the way people view paintings, 2006. *Mem:* Royal Can Acad Art. *Media:* Acrylic on Canvas, Drawing on Paper Collage. *Interests:* Film; Food; Reading. *Dealer:* Contor Galleries 51 Yonge St Toronto Ont Can. *Mailing Add:* 207A Cowan Ave Toronto ON M6K 2N7 Canada

CLIFT, WILLIAM BROOKS
PHOTOGRAPHER
b Boston, Mass, Jan 5, 44. *Study:* Workshop Paul Caponigro, 59. *Work:* Metrop Mus Art, Mus Mod Art, NY; Art Inst Chicago; Mus Fine Arts, Boston; Nat Gallery, Canberra, Australia; Fogg Art Mus, Yale Univ; Mus Fine Arts, Santa Fe; Libr Congress, Washington, DC; Nat Mus Am Art. *Comn:* Photographs, Old City Hall, Boston, Mass Coun Arts, 70, American Co Courthouses, Joseph Seagrams & Sons, NY, 75-76, American Images, Am Tel & Tel, NY, 78 & Hudson River, Readers Digest Asn, 85-88. *Exhib:* Solo exhibs, Old City Hall, Boston, Worcester Art Mus, Mass, 71, Landscapes, Mus Fine Art, Santa Fe, 79, Phoenix Art Mus, 81, Chicago Art Inst, 87 & Amon Carter Mus, Ft Worth, Tex, 87; Court House, 77, Mirrors and Windows, 78 & Am Landscapes, 81, Mus Mod Art, NY; Counterparts, Metrop Mus Art, NY, 82; Landmarks Reviewed, Pensacola Mus Art, Fla, 83; one man shows, Boston Atheneum, Mass, Eclipse Gallery, Boulder, Colo, 83, Bank Santa Fe, NMex & Susan Harder Gallery, NY, 84; Western Spaces, Burden Gallery, NY, 85; retrospective, Equitable Gallery, NY, 93. *Awards:* Fels, Nat Endowment Arts, 72 & 79 & Guggenheim Found, 74 & 80. *Bibliog:* Erla Zwingle (auth), Romancing the stones, Am Photogr, 6/87. *Mem:* Charter mem Asn Heliographers; NMex Coun Photog. *Publ:* Coauth, American Images, McGraw-Hill, 79; contribr, American Photographers in the National Parks, Viking, 81; Counterparts-Form and Emotions in Photographs, Metrop Mus Art, 82; Landmarks Reviewed, Pensacola Mus Art, 83; Photographic Viewpoints, Boston Mus Fine Arts, 85; auth, Certain Places, William Clift Eds, 87; A Hudson Landscape, William Clift Eds, 93. *Mailing Add:* PO Box 6035 Santa Fe NM 87502

CLIFTON, MICHELLE GAMM
SCULPTOR, FILMMAKER
b Los Angeles, Calif, July 11, 44. *Study:* Yale Univ, summer scholar, 65; Univ Ill, Urbana, with Lee Chesney, BFA, 66; Pa State Univ, with Carol Summers, MFA, 68. *Work:* Mus City New York; Los Angeles Co Mus Art; Meany Ctr for Labor Studies, Silver Spring, Md; State Univ NY Col, Potsdam; US Info Agency, Washington, DC. *Comn:* Soft NY Times, comn by Carey Peck, A O Sulzberger at NY Times, 76; Bathroom Faucet (3-D billboard), Pasco Hernando Community Col, Brookville, Fla,

79. *Exhib:* Libr Cong, Washington, DC, 69; Fun & Fantasy, Xerox Ctr, Rochester, NY, 73; Renwick Gallery, Smithsonian Inst, Washington, DC, 74-75; Dayton Art Inst, Ohio, 77; two-person show, Cordy Gallery, NY, 77; Whimsy, Taft Mus & Cincinnati Inst of Fine Arts, 78; one-person shows, Great Am Foot Show, Mus Contemp Crafts, NY, 78 & US Military Acad, West Point, 81; Mus Art, Carnegie Inst, Pittsburgh, 79; and others. *Pos:* Art dir, Hardtimes Movie Co, Garrison, 72-; art dir & vpres, Hudson River Film Co, Garrison, 77-; art dir & production mgr, Henry Hudson's River: A Biography (film), 79. *Teaching:* Asst drawing & printmaking, Pa State Univ, 66-68. *Awards:* Hon Mention as Art Dir, Emmy Winner Christina's World, 77; Cine Golden Eagle Award, 79; Grand Award, Houston Int Film Festival, 79. *Bibliog:* Steven Lindstedt (auth), Soft Sculpture, Family Creative Workshop, 76; Erica Brown (auth), Bunking in a barnyard, New York Times, 12/25/77; Carol Sama (auth), Michelle Gamm Clifton lives in a material world, Houston Home & Garden, 5/77. *Mem:* Am Crafts Coun; Nat Acad TV Arts & Sci. *Media:* Fabric, Stuffing. *Publ:* Illusr series, Gerald Ford's America, San Francisco Pub TV, 75; auth & illusr cover, New York City couch, Art Now Gallery Guide, summer 77. *Mailing Add:* South Mountain Pass Garrison NY 10524

CLINE, CLINTON C
PRINTMAKER, EDUCATOR
b Granite City, Ill, Oct 21, 34. *Study:* E Los Angeles Col, AA, 62; Calif State Univ, Long Beach, BA, 65, MA, 68. *Work:* Univ Tex, Irving; Univ SDak; Downey Art Mus, Calif; Palm Springs Mus, Calif; Drake Univ, Des Moines, Iowa. *Exhib:* 15th Joslyn Biennial, Joslyn Art Mus, Omaha, Nebr, 78; 21st Nat Exhib, Okla Art Ctr, Oklahoma City, 79; Univ Tex Nat, Irving, 79; traveling group, Collagraph Problem Solving, 88-90; 16th Harper Col Nat, 92; 36th Ann, Unterdon Art Ctr, 92. *Collection Arranged:* 1975 Governor's Awards for the Arts and Humanities, 75; In Their Own Image, Southern Conn State Col, 76. *Teaching:* Lithography, Univ Colo, Boulder, 69-, full prof, currently. *Awards:* Purchase Awards, Los Angeles Printmaking Soc, 79 & Vermillion Nat Print & Drawing, 79. *Bibliog:* Leonard Edmundson (auth), Etching, Van Nostrand Reinhold, 73; Eldon L Cunningham (auth), biog, A Primary Form of Expression. *Media:* Lithography, Intaglio. *Publ:* Publisher, First National Colorado Print and Drawing, 74; Border to Border print publ, Univ SDak, Univ Colo, Univ Neb, Univ Minn; Int Juried, Univ SDak; First Nat Printmaking Slides & Video Exchange, E C Cunningham. *Dealer:* One Over One Denver CO. *Mailing Add:* 10909 Patterson Ct Denver CO 80234-3945

CLINTON, PAUL ARTHUR
PRINTMAKER, INSTRUCTOR
b Salem, Ore. *Study:* Ore State Univ, BA, 68; Tamarind Lithography Workshop, master printer, 70; Univ SFla, MFA, 77. *Work:* Mus Mod Art, NY; Brooklyn Mus; Pasadena Art Mus, Calif; Tex Technol Univ, Lubbock; Gruenwald Graphics Art Found, Univ Calif, Los Angeles. *Comn:* Sculpture, City of Tacoma, 84. *Exhib:* Univ Wis, Madison, 75; Univ Dallas, Irving, 75; State Capitol Mus, Olympia, Wash, 78; Brooklyn Mus, 79; Okla Art Ctr, Oklahoma City, 81; Wash Painting & Sculpture, 83; and others. *Collection Arranged:* Collaboration, Prints by Major American Artists, Tacoma Art Mus, 81. *Pos:* Master printer, Tamarind Lithography Workshop, Los Angeles, 69-70; master printer, Gemini, Los Angeles, 70; master printer, Cirrus Ed, Los Angeles, 70-71; master printer, Graphicstudio, Univ SFla, Tampa, 71-76; proprietor, Arch Press. *Teaching:* Asst prof, Univ SFla, Tampa, 71-76; instr, Pierce Col, Tacoma, Washington, 77-. *Awards:* Printers Fel & Ford Found, 69. *Mem:* NW Print Coun; World Print Coun. *Media:* Lithography, Intaglio. *Publ:* Contribr, Printmaking: History and Process, Holt, Rinehart, Winston, 78; contribr, Graphic Studio, National Gallery of Art, Prestel. *Mailing Add:* 1702 Adams St Steilacoom WA 98388

CLOSE, CHUCK
PAINTER
b Monroe, Wash, July 5, 40. *Study:* Everett Jr Col, Wash, 58-60; Yale Summer Sch Music & Art, Norfolk, Conn, 61; Univ Wash Sch Art, Seattle, BA, 62; Yale Univ Sch Art & Archit, New Haven, Conn, BFA, 63, MFA, 64; Acad Fine Arts, Vienna, Austria, Fulbright grant, 64-65. *Hon Degrees:* Hon DFA, Mass Inst Art, Boston, 92; LHD, Skidmore Col, Saratoga Springs, NY, 93; Hon DFA, Colby Col, Maine, 94; Hon DFA, Univ Mass, Amherst, 95; Hon DFA, Yale Univ, 96; Hon doctorate RI Sch Design, 97; Hon DFA, Md Inst Col of Art, Baltimore, 98; Hon DFA, Corcoran Sch of Art, Washington, 99; Hon DFA, Bard Col, 99; and many others. *Work:* Mus Mod Art, Whitney Mus Am Art, Metrop Mus Art & Solomon Guggenheim, NY; Walker Art Ctr, Minneapolis; Neue Gallerie, Aachen, Ger; Art Gallery Ont, Toronto; Albright-Knox Art Gallery, Buffalo; Nat Gallery Art, Washington, DC; and many others. *Exhib:* One-man shows, Butler Inst Am Art, Youngstown, Ohio, 89, Art Inst Chicago, 89-90 & 96, Aldrich Mus Contemp Art, Ridgefield, Conn, 89-90, Va Mus Fine Arts, Richmond, 93, Mus Mod Art, NY, 93 & (traveling), 98, Pace Wildenstein MacGill, NY, 96, Archives Am Art Smithsonian Inst, NY, 96-97 & Mus of Modern Art, NY, 98, (traveling) 98-99; group shows include Whitney Biennial Exhib, Whitney Mus Am Art, NY; 22 Realists, Whitney Mus Am Art, 70, Baltimore Mus Art, Md, 76, Wadsworth Atheneum Mus (with catalog), Hartford, Conn, 77-78, Contemp Arts Mus (with catalog) Houston, 85; Retrospective, Walker Art Ctr, Minneapolis, traveling, 80-81; Narcissism: Artists Reflect Themselves, Calif Ctr Arts Mus, Escondido, 96; Attention to Detail (Realism in All Forms), Louis K Meisel Gallery, NY, 96; A Decade of Giving: The Apollo Society, Toledo Mus Art, 96; Portraits, James Graham & Sons, NY, 96; Some Recent Acquisitions, Mus Mod Art, NY, 96-97; Painting into Photog/Photog into Painting, Mus Contemp Art, Miami, 96-97; Hirshhorn Mus & Sculpture Garden, Smithsonian Inst, Washington, DC; traveling exhib originating in Mus of Modern Art, New York City, 1998-99; Photographs by Chuck Close, Worcester Mus of Art, 1999, 2000; Chuck Close Prints: Process and Collaboration, Met Mus of Art, 2004. *Teaching:* Instr art, Univ Mass Sch Art, Amherst, 65-67; Sch Visual Arts, NY, 67-71; New York Univ, 70-73. *Awards:* Infinity Award, Int Ctr Photog, 90; Acad-Inst Awards in Art, Am Acad & Inst Arts & Lett, 91 & elected to Acad, 92; New York State Governor's Arts Award, 97; Artist Advocate Award, Alliance of NY State Arts Orgns, 99; Nat Medal of Arts, Washington, 2000; and many others. *Bibliog:* Barbara Harshman (auth), An interview with Chuck Close, 6/78, Kim Levin (auth), Chuck Close: Decoding the image, 6/78 & Lisa Lyons (auth), Close portraits, 80, Arts Mag; HH Annason (auth), History of Modern Art: Painting, Sculpture, Architecture, 3rd ed, New York, Harry N Abrams Inc, 86; Robert Storr & Lisa Lyons (coauth), Chuck Close, Rizzoli Int Publ, New York, 87; and many others. *Mem:* Am Acad Rome, NY (bd trustees); Am Acad Arts & Letts, NY (bd dir); Hospital Audiences Inc, NY; Am Acad Arts & Scis; Nat Acad (assoc, 90, acad, 92). *Media:* All Media. *Dealer:* Pace Wildenstein 32 E 57th St New York NY 10022. *Mailing Add:* c/o Pace Wildenstein 32 E 57th St New York NY 10022

CLOSE, FRANK
STAINED GLASS ARTIST, SCULPTOR
b Dec 28, 47. *Study:* Univ Ky, BA, 71; stained glass with Casey Lewis & Peter Mollica, Berkeley, Calif, 75; glass design with Kenneth van Roenn, Univ Ky, 76 & Ludwig Schaffrath, Berkeley, Calif, 77; glass painting with Albinas Elskus, Washington, DC, 78; hot glass with Fred Mercer, Louisville Sch Art, Ky. *Comn:* cntry piece, Oliver Wendell Holmes Libr, Phillips Acad, Andover, Mass, 89; lead & glass piece (5' x 5'), Costain Group, Lexington, Ky, 90; two works, (73" x 94" each), Office Ctr, Short Hills, NJ, 90; Totem MCMXCI, IBM Data Ctr, Rochester, NY, 91; Suspended Construction, Minn Percent Arts, Alexandria, 92. *Exhib:* Wood & Glass, 86 & Crafts Invitational, 87, Southeastern Ctr for Contemp Art, Winston-Salem, NC; Glass Invitational, Ind Univ Southeast, New Albany, 86; Glasswork, Ky Art & Craft Gallery, Louisville, 87; group shows, Triangle Gallery, Lexington, Ky, 88 & John Davis Gallery, NY, 88; 2e Salon Int du Vitrail 1989, Chartres, France. *Pos:* Cur, Waller Gallery exhibs, Lexington, Ky, 79-82; Henry Faulkner, Opera House Gallery, Lexington, Ky, 82; lectr, many univ & mus. *Teaching:* Instr, Univ Ky, Lexington, 70-83. *Bibliog:* Contemporary glass (catalog), Louisville Art Gallery, 86; New Work in New York, New Work, winter-spring 86; Glasswork (catalog), Ky Art & Craft Found Gallery, 87. *Mailing Add:* 255 W 23rd St New York NY 10011-2312

CLOSE, MARY
PAINTER, PASTELIST
b Morristown, NJ, Nov 30 51. *Study:* Col of New Rochelle, BFA, 1973; Parson's Sch of Design, 1979; Int Ctr of Photog (Pat Blue), 1999. *Collection Arranged:* Wit, Whimpsy & Humor, Castle Gallery, New Rochelle, 1997. *Pos:* Illusr, Kukasiewicz Design & Freelance, 1976-1986. *Awards:* Adriana Brina Award, Pastel Soc of Am, 1991; Beatrice Vare Award, Pastel Soc of Am, 1995; Pastel J Award, Pastel Soc of Am, 2000. *Bibliog:* Tom Nicholas & John Terelak (auths), Best of Oil Painting, Rockport Publs, 1996; Karen Frankel (auth), Mary Close's Significant Still Lifes, Am Artist Mag, 1997; Best of Drawing & Sketching, Rockport Publs, 1998. *Mem:* Pastel Soc of Am. *Media:* Acrylic, Oil. *Publ:* Illusr, A Book of Cut Flowers, William Morrow & Co, 1983. *Dealer:* New Arts Gallery (Tony Carretta) 513 Maple St Litchfield CT 06759. *Mailing Add:* PO Box 1496 Lakeville CT 06039

CLOSE, TIMOTHY
MUSEUM DIRECTOR
Pos: exec dir, Boise Art Mus, Boise, Idaho, currently; Exec dir, Albany Mus Art, Ga, formerly. *Mailing Add:* Boise Art Mus 670 S Julia Davis Dr Boise ID 83702

CLOTHIER, PETER DEAN
WRITER, CRITIC
b Newcastle-on-Tyne, Eng, Aug 1, 36; US citizen. *Study:* Cambridge Univ, Eng, BA & MA; Univ Iowa, PhD. *Work:* Los Angeles Co Mus Art; Univ Southern Calif. *Pos:* Dean Col, Otis Art Inst, 76-79, actg dir, 77-79, dean, Col Fine & Commun Arts, Loyola-Marymount Univ, 81-85. *Teaching:* Asst prof comparative lit, Univ Southern Calif, Los Angeles, 68-76. *Awards:* Dart Award for Acad Innovation, Univ Southern Calif, 72; Art Critics Fel Grant, Nat Endowment for Arts, 76-77; Rockefeller Found Humanities Fel, 80. *Bibliog:* Joseph E Young (auth), Re-evaluating the tradition of the book, Art News, 75; Peter Plagens (auth), Chiaroscuro by Peter Clothier, Art in Am, 86; Rebecca Solnit (auth), Dirty-Down by Peter Clothier, Artweek, 87. *Publ:* Auth, Otto Natzler, Am Ceramics, 91; Christos Umbrella Fantasy, Art News, 92; Richard Koshalek, MOCA's Maverick, Art News, 92; David Hockney, Abbeville Modern Masters, Abbeville Press, 94; While I am not Afraid, High Mountain Press, 97. *Mailing Add:* 2341 Ronda Vista Dr Los Angeles CA 90027

CLOUDMAN, RUTH HOWARD
CURATOR
b Oklahoma City, Okla, June 11, 48. *Study:* Washington Univ, St Louis, BA, 70; Bryn Mawr Col, Pa, MA, 73. *Pos:* Asst cur, Joslyn Art Mus, Omaha, Nebr, 73-75, chief cur, 75-78; guest cur, Sheldon Gallery, Univ Nebr, Lincoln, 78-79; assoc, Newhouse Galleries, New York, 80-84; sr cur, Portland Art Mus, 84-90; chief cur, Mary & Barry Bingham, sr cur Europ & Am Art, J B Speed Art Mus, Louisville, 90-. *Mem:* Col Art Asn; Am Asn Mus. *Res:* Early 20th century modernism; contemporary art. *Publ:* Preston Dickinson, 1889-1930 (exhib catalog), Sheldon Mem Art Gallery, Univ Nebr, 79-80; Perspectives 4: Cindy Sherman (exhib catalog), Portland Art Mus, 86; Frederick Bridgman, The Funeral of a Mummy, Am Art Rev, summer 92; In Pursuit of Excellence: The Wendell and Dorothy Cherry Collection (exhib catalog), J B Speed Art Mus, 94. *Mailing Add:* J B Speed Art Mus 2035 S Third St Louisville KY 40208

CLOUGH, CHARLES SIDNEY
PAINTER
b Buffalo, NY, Feb 2, 51. *Study:* Pratt Inst, Brooklyn, NY, 69-70; Ontario Col Art, Can, 71-72. *Work:* Albright-Knox Art Gallery, Buffalo, NY; Everson Mus, Syracuse, NY; Brooklyn Mus, NY; Dayton Art Inst, Ohio; Indianapolis Mus Art; Von Lintel Gallery, NY, 2002; Newport Art Mus, 2003; and others. *Comn:* Mural, Niagra Frontier

Transportation Authority, 84; video, Music Television Network, 85; Sony Corp, 92. *Exhib:* Solo exhib, Brooklyn Mus, NY, 85 & 94, Galeria Peccolo, Livorno, Italy, 86, Am Fine Arts Co, NY, 87, Nina Freuden heim Gallery, Buffalo, NY, 88, Scott Hanson Gallery, NY, 90, Burchfield Ctr, State Col NY, 91, Barbara Gillman Gallery, Miami, 91, State Univ NY at Potsdam, 91, Castellani Art Mus, Niagara Falls, NY, 92, Grand Salon, NY, 93, 94 & 99, Galerie Liesbeth Lips, The Neth, 94 & 2000. *Pos:* Co-Founder, Hallwalls Inc, Buffalo, NY, 74, pres bd dir, 77-79. *Teaching:* teacher, Columbia Univ, NY, 2001. *Awards:* Painting Fel, Nat Endowment Arts, 82 & 89; Graphic Artists' Fel, Creative Artists Pub Serv Prog, 83. *Bibliog:* Carter Ratcliff (auth), Playful redemption, paintings by Charles Clough (catalog essay), State Univ NY, Potsdam, 91; Elizabeth Licata (auth), Charles Clough's dreampix, Art in Am, 7/92; Charles A Riley II (auth), Uncanny likeness-recent paintings by Charles Clough (catalog essay), Grand Salon, 94; Nancy Whipple Grinnell (auth), Newport Folio, Newport Art Mus, 2003. *Media:* Mixed. *Mailing Add:* 124 Thompson St New York NY 10012

CLUTZ, WILLIAM
PAINTER
b Gettysburg, Pa, Mar 19, 33. *Study:* Mercersburg Acad, 47-51; Univ Iowa, 51-55; Art Student's League, NY, 57. *Work:* Mus Mod Art & Chase Manhattan Bank, NY; Joseph H Hirshhorn Collection, Washington, DC; Fogg Art Mus, Cambridge, Mass; Metrop Mus Art, NY; plus many others. *Comn:* Salomon Bros, NY; 3rd Nat Bank, Dayton, Ohio; Minn Mutual Life Insurance, St Paul; Mobil Corp; and others. *Exhib:* Pa Acad Fine Arts Ann, Philadelphia, 64-66; one-man shows, Condon Riley Gallery, NY, 59, David Herbert Gallery, NY, 62, Bertha Schaefer Gallery, 63, 64, 66 & 69 & Graham Gallery, 72, Triangle Gallery, San Francisco, Calif, 67, Brooke Alexander Gallery, NY, 73, NY Stick Exchange, 2002; Alonzo Gallery, 77- 79; Tatistchaff & Co, NY, 81, 82 & 84; John C Stoller Co, Minneapolis, 83; Nicholas Davis Gallery, NY, 97; Katharina Rich Perlow Gallery, NY, 99, 2000, 01, 02 & 05. *Teaching:* Instr, Parsons Sch Design, New York, 69-95. *Bibliog:* Of Time and Place: American Figurative Art from the Corcoran Gallery, Smithsonian, Inst, 81; Janice C. Oresman (auth), William Clutz, ARTS Mag, 11/84; Gerrit Henry (auth), Art in America, 2/98. *Mem:* Nat Acad. *Publ:* auth, Five Decades of NY Streets, 2002; auth, Pictorial Overview, 2004. *Mailing Add:* Katharina Rich Perlow Gallery 41 E 57 St New York NY 10022

CLYMER, ALBERT ANDERSON
PAINTER
b Memphis, Tenn, Feb 16, 42. *Study:* Tex A&M Univ, with Joseph Donaldson, Napa Col with Frank Altamura. *Work:* White House, Washington; Newport Mus Mod Art, Calif; Oakland Mus Mod Art, Calif; Berkeley Mus Mod Art, Calif; San Francisco Mus Mod Art, Calif; Levi Straus, San Francisco, Nut Tree, Calif. *Comn:* Ten paintings for Army Recruiting, US Army Reserve, Mountain View, Calif, 77; 30 paintings for Episcopal Homes Found, Santa Rosa, Calif, 77; 20 Abstract Indian Forms, Shorebirds, Tiburor, Calif, 87. *Exhib:* Dallas Mus Fine Arts, Tex, 65; Depot Gallery, Yountville, Calif, 90; Shore Birds, Tiburon, Calif, 90; Mesa Gallery, San Francisco, 90; Blue Heron Gallery, Yountville, Calif, 94; Mondavi Winery, Oakville, Calif, 94; plus 224 one-man shows. *Pos:* Bd dir, Depot Gallery, Yountville, Calif, Blue Heron Gallery, Yountville, Calif, 93. *Teaching:* Instr, Experimental acrylic tech on paper & masonite, Blue Heron Gallery, 94. *Awards:* First Prize in Mod Oil, Vintage 76 Int, 68 & Santa Rosa Statewide Ann, 71 & 72. *Bibliog:* Stephens (auth), Albert Anderson Clymer, La Rev Mod, Paris, 66 & 74; Paul Gillette (auth), The Single Man's Indispensable Guide Handbook, Playboy Press, 73; Artist of Northern California, Mountain Publ, 89. *Mem:* Berkeley Arts Crafts Coop. *Media:* Acrylic on Masonite, Paper. *Publ:* Illusr, Oakland Redevelopment Agency's Annual Report, Abby Press, 66; Bodega Bay, Nut Tree, 75; (catalog), Works by Albert Anderson Clymer, Arlene Lind Gallery, 78. *Dealer:* Naked Horse Gallery 4151 N Marshall Way Suite B Scottsdale AZ 85251; Shore Birds On The Boardwalk Tiburon CA 94920. *Mailing Add:* c/o Naked Horse Gallery 4151 N Marshall Way Suite B Scottsdale AZ 85251

COATES, ANN S
CURATOR, PHOTOGRAPHER
b Louisville, Ky. *Study:* Univ Louisville, BA, 63, MA, 69; New York Sch Interior Design, Cert, 65; Arrowmont Sch Arts Crafts, Tenn. *Work:* Brown-Forman Distillers Corp; James G Brown Regional Cancer Ctr; Actors' Theatre Louisville; Kentucky Fried Chicken, Brown & Williamson. *Exhib:* China Triptych, Speed Mus, Louisville, Ky; Paper 90, Headley-Whitney Mus, Lexington, Ky; Southeast 81 Craft Competition, Lemoyne Art Found, Tallahassee; Thread and Fiber, Alexandria Mus, La; Handmade Paper Nat Invitational, Liberty Gallery, Louisville; Paradigms of Perserverence, Louisville Visual Art Asn; and others. *Collection Arranged:* Edward Weston 1958-1968, 68; Kentucky Threads, Louisville Art Gallery. *Pos:* Cur slides, Univ Louisville, 69-. *Teaching:* Instr mod art, Univ Louisville, 69-; lectr, Univ Ky, Lexington & Louisville Craftsmen's Guild. *Awards:* Bronze Medal, Great Quilts of America, Good Housekeeping, 78; Ky Found for Women Grant. *Bibliog:* Sarah Lansdell (auth), Paper works show uncovers artist's passion for the medium, The Courier, 7/20/80; Karen Hisle (auth), Ann Coates mixes work with pleasure, Scripps-Howard Press, 7/9/80; Fiber Arts Design Book, Hasting House, 80. *Mem:* Col Art Asn; Art Libr Soc NAm; Soc Archit Historians. *Media:* Fiber. *Res:* Paper Conservation; preservation; women artists. *Publ:* The Female Image in the Nineteenth Century (film), Univ Louisville, Women's Studies Ctr, 78. *Mailing Add:* 1819 Woodbourne Ave Louisville KY 40205-2147

COATES, ROSS ALEXANDER
HISTORIAN, PAINTER
b Hamilton, Ont, Nov 1, 32. *Study:* Univ Mich; Art Inst Chicago, BFA; NY Univ, MA & PhD. *Work:* Finch Col; Univ Calif, Berkeley; Univ Alta; State Univ NY, Stonybrook; NY Univ; and others. *Exhib:* Whatcom Mus, Bellingham, 83; Space Gallery, Los Angeles, 84; Northwestern Artists Workshop, Portland Ore, 85; Art Gallery Hamilton, Ont, Can, 88; one-man shows, Thirteen Whirlwinds (installation), Gallery II, Wash State Univ, Pullman, WA, 90, Northview Gallery, Portland Community Coll, Ore, 90, Fisher Gallery, Cornish Sch Art, Seattle, 91, & UOP Gallery, McCaffrey Ctr, Univ Pacific, Stockton, Calif, 92, Getting From One Place, Fine Arts Ctr, Port Angeles, Wash, 91, Dreamtime, Pritchard Gallery, Univ Idaho, Moscow, 92; Some Assembly Required, Bumbershoot, Seattle, Wash, 89; Sun Valley Ctr Arts, Idaho, 91; Storie Naturali, Artists' Books, Genoa, Italy, 91; Come to Your Senses, collaborative pieces with Marilyn Lysohir, Bellevue Art Mus, Wash, 91; Dreams and Shields, Salt Lake Art Ctr, Utah, 92; Inter, Kunsthalle, Holstebro, Denmark, 92; Installation with Marilyn Lysohir: Secrets of an Ancient Heart, SPF Rodovre, Denmark, 94; Installation: Hunting, Salt Lake Art Ctr, 94. *Teaching:* Art tutor, Canon Lawrence Col, Uganda, EAfrica, 68-70; prof dept fine arts, Wash State Univ, 77-. *Awards:* Idaho Arts Comn Artists Grant, 90 & 94. *Media:* Oil. *Res:* Non-Western art, particularly Africa; occult and how it relates to contemporary art. *Publ:* Ed, Some Thoughts on the Problems of Artists in Contemporary Africa, J African Studies, Univ Calif, LosAngeles, 78; Gard Okello in Six Artists, African Arts, Univ Calif, Los Angeles, 79; Gods Among Us: American Indian Masks, State Univ San Diego, 90. *Mailing Add:* Wash State Univ Dept Fine Arts Pullman WA 99164-7450

COBB, HENRY N
ARCHITECT
b Boston, Mass, April 8, 1926. *Study:* Harvard Col, BA, 47; Harvard Grad Sch Design, M (archit), 49. *Hon Degrees:* Bowdoin Col, DFA, 85; Swiss Federal Inst Technology, doctor honoris causa in technical sci, 90. *Pos:* Architect Hugh Stubbins, 49-50, Webb & Knapp, Inc, 50-55; founding partner IM Pei & Assocs, 55-66; partner IM Pei & Partners, 66-89; partner Pei Cobb Freed & Partners, 89-; trustee Chicago Inst Archit and Urbanism, 82-85, 89-94, Brearley Sch, 75-80; trustee Am Acad in Rome, 72-90, emeritus, 90-; pres Harvard Grad Sch Design Asn, 69-71; mem adv council Cooper Union Sch Art and Archit, 67-71; adv council Princeton Univ Sch Archit, 85-; chair design arts program overview panel Nat Endowment for the Arts, 84-88. *Teaching:* William Henry Bishop vis prof, Yale Univ Sch Archit, 73, 78, Charlotte Sheperd Davenport vis prof, 75; architect in residence, Am Acad in Rome, 92; studio prof and chair dept archit, Harvard Univ Grad Sch Design, 80-85, adj prof archit and urban design, 85-88, vis lectr, 88-. *Awards:* Poses Creative Arts Award: Medal for Architecture, Brandeis Univ, 81; Lifetime Achievement Award, NY Soc Architects, 92; Topaz Medallion for Excellence in Architectural Educ, Asn Collegiate Sch Architecture & Am Inst Architects, 95. *Mem:* Fel, Am Inst Architects (chair comt design, 71; Medal of Honor, 82) and Am Acad Arts and Sci; Am Acad Arts and Letters (Arnold W Brunner Prize architecture, 77); Nat Acad (assoc, 83, acad, 90); Soc Architectural Historians (dir 81-84); Architectural League NY (exec comt 68-71, 75-80, 88-). *Mailing Add:* Pei Cobb Freed & Partners 88 Pine St New York NY 10005

COBB, JAMES
PAINTER
b La Mesa, Calif, 51. *Study:* Self taught. *Work:* San Antonio Mus Art, Tex; Huntington Mus, Austin, Tex; Butler Collection, Dallas, Tex. *Comn:* Mural, Centro de La Correspondensia, Tepoztlan, Morelos, Mex, 85; limited edition poster, Hal Bromm Gallery, NY, 88; Streetfare J Bus Posters Proj, San Francisco, Calif, 89. *Exhib:* Solo exhibs, Blue Collar Gallery, Tex, 87, Read Stremmel Gallery, 89, Adams-Middleton Gallery, Dallas, Tex, 90, Jansen-Perez Gallery, San Antonio, Tex, 91, Los Angeles, Calif, 92 & 94, Robinson Galleries, Houston, Tex, 93, Lanning Gallery, Houston, Tex, 95 & Theater De Lieve Vrouw Gallery, Amersfoort, The Neth, 95; Conventional Forms/ Insidious Visions, Glasell Sch Art, Mus Fine Art, Houston, 93; Bob Wilson Collection, Meadows Gallery, Mus E Tex, 94; Personal Stories, Rockport Ctr Arts, Tex, 94; Phantoms, Freaks & the Fantastic, Diverse Works, Houston, 94. *Awards:* Residency, London Studio Proj, Eng, 94; Visual Arts Fel, 96; Art Matters Inc, NY, 96. *Bibliog:* Visions Mag, Vol II, No 2, San Antonio; Express News, San Antonio, 7/3/94; Voices of Art, San Antonio, 8/94. *Mailing Add:* 217 E Rische St San Antonio TX 78204

COBB, RUTH
PAINTER
b Boston, Mass, 1914. *Study:* Mass Col Art, BFA, 93. *Work:* Boston Mus Fine Arts; Va Mus Fine Arts, Richmond; Butler Inst Am Art, Youngstown, Ohio; Munson-Williams-Proctor Inst, Utica, NY; Brandeis Univ, Waltham, Mass. *Exhib:* Am Watercolor Exhib, Metrop Mus Art, NY, 52; 22nd Biennial Int Watercolor Exhib, Brooklyn Mus, NY, 63; Am Watercolor Soc Ann, 68-77 & 80-83; Watercolor USA, Springfield Art Mus, Miss, 69; 35 Yrs in Retrospect, Butler Inst Am Art, 71; 45th Ann, Butler Inst Am Art, 81; and others; Women's Studies Research Ctr, Brandeis Univ, 2003. *Awards:* Purchase Award, Nat Acad Design, 68; Emily Lowe Award, 74 & Emily Goldsmith Award, 75, Am Watercolor Soc; Adolph Obrig Award, Nat Acad Design, 82. *Bibliog:* Article & reproductions in Am Artist Mag, 4/79; Artist at Work, Channel 5 TV, Boston, 81; and others. *Mem:* New Eng Watercolor Soc; American Watercolor Soc; Allied Artists Am; Nat Acad Design (assoc, 75, acad, 94). *Media:* Watercolor, Acrylic. *Publ:* Incl in, Watercolor Bold & Free, Watson Guptill, 80; Incl in, Best of Watercolor, Rockport Publisher, 1995; Incl in, Painting with the White of Your Paper, North Light Bks, 1994; Incl in, Splash No 1 Best Contemporary Watercolors, North Light Bks, 1991; Incl in, 100 Watercolor Techniques, Watson Guptill. *Mailing Add:* 125 A Seminary Ave #333 Newton MA 02466

COBB, VIRGINIA HORTON
PAINTER, LECTURER
b Oklahoma City, Okla, Nov 23, 33. *Study:* William Schimmel, Ariz, 1966; Community Col, Denver, 1967; Edgar Whitney, NY City, 1966; Univ Colo, 1967; Chen Chi, NY City, 1974. *Work:* Foothills Art Ctr, Golden, Colo; Nat Acad of Design, NY; NMex Watercolor Soc, Albuquerque; St Lawrence Univ, Canton, NY. *Exhib:* Am

Watercolor Soc, Nat Acad Galleries, NY, 73-85; Butler Inst Am Art, Youngstown, Ohio, 75; Nat Acad Design, NY, 78-85; San Bernadino Co Mus, 78; Nat Watercolor Invitational, 81; one-person exhib, Stuhr Mus, Grand Island, Nebr, 82; and others. *Teaching:* Lectr & demonstr, Emphasis-KRDO Channel 13, Colorado Springs, Colo, 77; instr, Crafton Hills Col Master Seminars, Yucaipa, Calif, 77, 78 & 81; instr, Univ Alaska, Anchorage, 81; lectr & demonstr, Pub Broadcasting Serv, KAKM, Anchorage, 81; Master Class/Santa Fe Painting Workshops/Friedman Cobb Studios, 1989-; guest lectr, Watermedia 2000; Houston; lectr, Station KRDO-TV, 1977, Francis Marion Col, Florence, 1981, Station KAKM, Anchorage, 1981. *Awards:* Walter Biggs Mem Award, Nat Acad Design, 78 & 81; High Winds Medal, 81; Silver Medal Honor, Am Watercolor Soc, 83; Adolph & Clara Obrig Prize, 85; Am Artist Achievement award, 1994. *Bibliog:* Southwest Art Mag, 11/79; Todays Art Mag, 3/79; Houston Home & Garden, 2/80. *Mem:* Nat Acad Design (assoc, 78, acad, 94); Dolphin fel Am Watercolor Soc; Watercolor USA Honor Soc; Rocky Mountain Watermedia Asn. *Media:* Mixed Watermedia; Graphics. *Publ:* Contribr, Am Artist Mag, 1/79

COBURN, BETTE LEE
PAINTER
b Chicago, Ill, July 31, 22. *Study:* Grinwell Col, Iowa; Chicago Art Inst; Univ NC. *Work:* Fed Reserve Bank, Charlotte, NC; SC Arts Comn, State Art Col, Columbia; Greenville Co Mus Arts, SC; Univ SC, Columbia; Univ Ga, Athens. *Comn:* Painting, comn by Pres, Ivey's, Greenville, SC, 62; city seal, Greenville City Bd, SC, 65; painting, First Fed Bank, Henderson, NC, 68; State Governer's Comt, Columbia, SC 69; Astro Theatre's I & II, Greenville, SC, 73. *Exhib:* Atlanta High Mus Art, Ga, 69; Nat USA Travelling Exhib Oils, London Pub Art Mus, Ontario, 70; 23rd Grand Prix Int, Deuville Expo Mus, France, 72; retrospective, SC State Mus, Columbia, 88; Greenville Co Art Mus, SC, 88; Florence Mus Art, SC, 89; Invitational Exhib, State Mus Art, Columbia, SC, 89; Art's Symposium 2nd Exhib, Greenville Co Mus, SC, 89. *Teaching:* Instr painting, Greenville Co Art Mus Sch, 65-83. *Awards:* Selected for Artworks, McCormick Arts Coun, 92; Selected 10,000 Plus Exhib, Sch Art Inst Chicago, 94; Selected Invitational Exhib, SC Governor's Sch Arts, 94. *Bibliog:* Rene Borel (auth), Le Semaines International de La Femme, 69; Jack A Morris (auth), 39 Contemporary Artists of SC, 70; Elizabeth Montgomery (auth), Poet without words, Greenville Woman Mag, 5/87. *Mem:* Greenville Mus Art Sch (chmn, educ comt, 61-62); Greenville Artists Guild (pres, 65); Nat Asn Women Artists (mem comt, 70); SC State Arts Comn (selection comt, 74 & 75); SC State Artists Guild (pres, 81). *Media:* Oils & Acrylics; Mixed Media. *Dealer:* Hampton III Gallery 10 Gallery Ctr Taylors SC 29687. *Mailing Add:* 436 Henderson Rd Greenville SC 29607

COBURN, RALPH (M H)
PAINTER
b Minneapolis, Minn, Aug 10, 23. *Study:* Mirski Art Sch, with Esther Geller, Carl Nelson, Barbara Swan & John Wilson, 46-49; Mass Inst Technol, 47; Acad Julian, 50. *Work:* Stedlijk Mus, Amsterdam; Mus Mod Art, Caracas, Venezuela; Brockton Art Mus, Mass; Chase Manhattan Bank, NY; Smithsonian Inst. *Exhib:* Mass Inst Technol, 54 & 76; Mirsks Gallery, 55; Alpha Gallery, 69 & 80; West End Gallery, Gloucester, Mass, 96; Alpha Gallery, 96. *Media:* Oil, Acrylic; Pen and Ink, Watercolor. *Dealer:* Alpha Gallery 14 Newbury St Boston MA 02116. *Mailing Add:* 1269 Washington St Gloucester MA 01930-1051

COCCHIARELLI, MARIA GIOVANNA
PAINTER, MURALIST
b Brooklyn, NY, Apr 10, 56. *Study:* Syracuse Univ, NY, BA (art hist), 1978; Queens Col, CUNY, MS (art ed), 1985, MFA, 2004. *Hon Degrees:* Queens Col, BFA, 85. *Work:* Sprint Contemp Art Col, Overland Park, Kan; Hallmark Contemp Art Col, Kansas City, Mo; Manelst Mus, Oslo, Norway; Wyo State Mus, Cheyenne; Omaha Children's Mus, Nebr. *Comn:* Interior Tile Installation, Sites for the students publ art, Bronx, NY, 1991-92; 6 interior banners, World, NYC School Construc Auth, Bronx, NY, 1992-93; mural, Struggle, Socrates Sculture Park, Long Island City, NY, 1993; art garden, Art of Envi, Wyo Alliance Arts Ed, Laramie, 1996; art garden, Art of Envi, Gem Theater Jazz Mus, Kansas City Mo, 1999. *Exhib:* Metamorphosis of a Butterfly, Penn State Zolar Gal & Travel, Pa, 1991; Visual Aids: Positive Action, Clock Tower Mus, New York City, 1991; Self-Images of Wyo Artists, Wyo Arts Council, (traveled thru stat), 1994; Woman The Artist's View, Bennington Ctr for Arts, Vt, 1995; Reinventing the Emblem, Yale, Univ Art Gal, New Haven, Conn, 1995; Wyo Artists, Nicolaysen Art Mus, Casper, 1996; H2O Works on Paper, Manêlyst Mus, Oslo, Norway, 1999; Leedy Volkos Invitational, Kansas City, Mo,1999. *Collection Arranged:* Freeing The Angel From The Stone (sculpture) (auth, catalog), Attilio Piccirilli, 2005; Sicilian Journey (photograpahs) (auth, catalog), Janine Coyne, 2006; Identity Theft (auth, catalog), Antonio Petracca, 2006; Painting Up the Town (auth, catalog), Ital Am Mus, 2006. *Pos:* ed cur, Unv Wyo Art Mus, 1993-96; prog dir, Grand Arts, Kansas City, Mo, 1997-98; cur collec, Italian Am Mus, New York City, 2004-. *Teaching:* instr, watercolor & art hist, Kansas City Art Inst, 1998-2000 (summer); muralist mural painting, Mo Arts Coun Statewide, 1999-2000; adj prof art visual, Kean Univ, Union, NJ, 2004-05. *Awards:* Emerging Artist Award, Ollantay Gal, Asn Queens Artists, 1984; Fellowship Award, Vt Studio Colony Artists, 1988; Best in Show, Culture Without Borders, Affil Group, 1998. *Bibliog:* Tom FinKelpearl, Michele Cohen (auth), Art for Learning, Municipal Art Soc, 1994; Liliane Francuz (auth), Self Images of Wyo Artists, Wyo Arts Coun, 1995; Lesley K. Baier (ed), Reinventing the Emblem, Yale Univ Press, 1995. *Mem:* Am Asn Mus. *Media:* Oil, Acrylic, Watercolor, All Print Media. *Res:* Contemp Ital Am Artists in the market place. *Interests:* Developing a new mus in Southern Colo called Mus Friends. *Dealer:* Jane St. Lifer 140 Riverside Blvd New York NY 10069. *Mailing Add:* 184-36 Avon Rd Jamaica NY 11432

COCHRAN, DOROTHY PARCELLS
PRINTMAKER, GALLERY DIRECTOR
b Teaneck, NJ, Aug 4, 44. *Study:* Montclair Univ, BA, 66, MA, 70; Sch Arts, Columbia Univ, MFA, 84; studied with Bob Blackburn, Anthonmy Harrison, Roberto DeLamonica, John Ross & Jane Wilson. *Work:* Zimmerli Mus, Rutgers Univ; Ga Mus Fine Arts; Mus Mod Art Libr, NY; New York Pub Libr; Bristol-Myers-Squibb, Princeton, NJ. *Comn:* Design Harmony, principla, Gail Lindsey, Wake Forest, NC. *Exhib:* 37th Boston Printmakers Nat, Rose Art Mus, Brandeis Univ, 85; Selections, Artists Space, NY, 86; NJ Arts Ann: Printmaking & Photog, NJ State Mus, Trenton, 89; Editions: The 1st 5 years-An Artist Book Collaboration, Newark Mus, 94; The Guardians, The Ctr Gallery, Demarest, NJ, 94; A View of One's Own, Jane Voohees, Zimmerli Mus, New Brunswick, NJ, 94. *Pos:* Dir/cur, The Galleries at the Interchurch Ctr, NY, 86-. *Teaching:* Asst prof printmaking, Columbia Univ, NY, 83-84 & City Univ NY, 85-86; vis artist, Southwest Crafts Ctr, San Antonio, Tex, 94; printmaking chr, Old Church Cult Ctr, School of Art, NJ, 88-. *Awards:* Fel, NJ State Coun Arts in Printmaking & Mixed Media, 82 & 85; Jane Turner Mem Award, Nat Asn Women Artists Ann, 92 & Esther Gayner Mem Award, 94. *Bibliog:* Kay Larson (auth), Selections from the artist file, Artist Space, 9/85; William Zimmer (auth), High spirits in Montclair, New York Times, 1/19/86; Dan Cameron (auth), The old back & forth, Arts Mag, 2/86. *Mem:* Col Art Asn; Nat Asn Women Artists. *Media:* Printmaking, Drawing. *Specialty:* contemporary art. *Mailing Add:* The Interchurch Center 475 Riverside Dr New York NY 10115

COCKER, BARBARA JOAN
PAINTER, GALLERY DIRECTOR
b Uxbridge, Mass, Oct 16, 23. *Study:* Becker Col, 43; Mt St Mary Col, 45; NY Sch Interior Design, 68. *Work:* Central Jersey Bank & Trust, Rumson, NJ; Midlantic Bank, Edison, NJ; President's House, Monmouth Col, West Long Branch, NJ; Riverview Hospital, Red Bank, NJ; First Union Bank, NJ; Frist Union Bank, Rumson, NJ. *Comn:* Ocean paintings, comn by Judge William Kirkpatrick, Rumson, NJ, 69; ship painting, comn by William Crawford, Singer Island, Fla, 70; ocean paintings, comn by Dr J Putnam Brodsky, Rumson, NJ, 70; sea marsh painting, comn by Daniel Riley, Greenwich, Conn, 92; mural sea painting, comm by Nancie B Taylor, Montecito, Calif. *Exhib:* Catharine L Wolfe Club, Nat Acad, NY, 70; solo exhibs, Guild Creative Artists, NJ, 76, 94 & 95, Nantucket Art Asn, 88, 91 & 95, Monmouth Co Libr, NJ, 91, 95 & 99, Art Alliance, Red BAnk, NJ, 92, Captiva Island Civic Ctr, Fla, 94, 97, Pen & Brush Club, NY 96, Sun Trust Bank, Fla, 97, PNC Bank, NJ, 97; Monmouth Beach Cult Ctr, NJ, 2000, 01 & 03. *Pos:* Pres, owner & dir, Paintings of the Sea Gallery, Nantucket, Mass, 75-98. *Teaching:* Pvt instr sea painting. *Awards:* Woman of the Year, Zonta Int, 83; Spec Award, Pen & Brush Club, NY, 84; Blue Ribbon, Monmouth Arts Gallery, NJ, 92 & 94; Best in Show, Mammouth, Arts, NJ, 95, 01 & 03. *Bibliog:* Capturing the surf, Art & Antiques, 89; Nino Marini (ed), Profile of the sea, Captiva Chronicle, 92; Stella Farwell (auth), Sea creativity, Captiva Current, 94. *Mem:* Coast Guard Arts Program. *Media:* Acrylic on Canvas. *Res:* sea poetry. *Specialty:* painting of the sea. *Interests:* sea. *Publ:* Prayer for Nantucket, 96; The Sea Around Me (feature article), Becker Col Alumnis Magazine, Warcester, Ma, 71 & 05. *Mailing Add:* 3 Rumson Rd Rumson NJ 07760

COCKRILL, SHERNA
PAINTER, INSTRUCTOR
b Chicago, Ill. *Study:* Univ Ark, BA & MA; Malden Bridge Sch Art, 67 & 68; also study with R V Goetz, 65-69; with Albert Handell, 80-81. *Work:* Smithsonian Inst Archives Am Art, Washington, DC; Ozark Art Ctr, Springdale; Nat Mus Women Arts, Washington, DC; Mid-Am Mus, Hot Springs, Ark. *Comn:* Many portrait comn. *Exhib:* Greater New Orleans Nat Exhib, 73; Tex Fine Arts Asn Ann, Austin, 73-74; Governor's Distinguished Artists Exhib, 76; Five State, Univ Ark, 79-83; Art Expo '83, Dallas; Laguna Gloria Mus Austin, Tex Fiesta Exhib, 84, 86; Sequoya Exhib (Univ Ark), 80-86; Easton Rooms, Rye, E Sussex, Eng, 87; Romney Bay Gallery, Kent, Eng, 87; Gov Collection, Ark, 95; Ark Artists Registry Invitational, 96; Faberge Competitive Exhib, 96; one-woman show, Arts Ctr Ozarks, Ark, 97, Walton Arts Ctr, Ark, 98 & Sager Creek Arts Ctr, Siloan Springs, Ark, 2000; Eighteenth & Nineteenth Nat Womens juried exhib, League Am Penwomen at the Walton Art Center, 2001-2002; WRMC Found Permanent collection (2 paintings), 8/2002; Central Arkansas Library System, Arts Ctr Ozarks, 7/2002; 12 th Annual Fall Regional exhib, 2005, Salon Int,San Antonio, Tex, 5/2006; and others. *Teaching:* Instr oil painting, Ozarks Arts Ctr, 72-75; also pvt classes. *Awards:* Grand Prize, Arkansas State Festival Art, 73; First Prize in Art, Little Rock Ten State Arts Fair, State of Ark, 73; Top Award Ark Festival Art, 73 & 74 & Top Award Ark Festival & Art Invitational, 75; 5 State Competitive Award for Sequoia, Univ Ark, 86; 2d Prize, Greater New Orleans Nat. *Mem:* Ozark Artists & Craftsmen (bd dir, 75-). *Media:* Oil, Acrylic. *Specialty:* The New Realism; Rivermarket and Boswell. *Publ:* Auth, Women artists in mid-USA, Feminist Art J, Brooklyn, 74-75. *Dealer:* Boswell Gallery 5606 R St Little Rock AR 72701; Selby Pictures Ltd, London; Rivermarket Art Space, Little Rock, AR; Rocky Creek Gallery Fayetteville AR; Greg Thompson, Fine Arts, Little Rock, AR. *Mailing Add:* 1295 Wood Creek Apt 8 Fayetteville AR 72701

CODDING, MITCHELL ALLAN
MUSEUM DIRECTOR, ADMINISTRATOR
b Bartlesville, Okla, Sept 20, 54. *Study:* Univ Okla, BA in Spanish, 1954; Univ Ky, PhD in Spanish, 2000. *Teaching:* visiting asst prof, Univ Calif, Riverside, 1983-83. *Awards:* Edward Larocque Tinker fel The Hispanic Soc Am, 1982, John Carter Brown Libr. fel Brown Univ, 1982. *Publ:* Co-author: Maps, Charts, Globes: Five Centruies of Exploration, 1992, co-editor: Coastal Charts of the Americas and West Africa from the Sch of Luis Teixeira, circa 1585, 1993, Facsimiles from an Illuminated Hebrew Bible of the Fifteenth Century at The Hispanic Society of Am, 1993, Defining the Americas: Accounts and Images of Latin Am from the European Encounter through Independence, 1997. *Mailing Add:* Hispanic Soc Am 613 W 155th St New York NY 10032-7501

CODE, AUDREY
PAINTER
b Pittsburgh, Pa, Oct 6, 37. *Study:* Carnegie Mellon Univ, with Balcomb Greene, BFA, 59, MFA, 61; Provincetown Workshop, Mass, 61. *Work:* Aldrich Mus Contemp Art, Ridgefield, Conn; Chautauqua Art Mus, NY; Fulton Co Arts Coun, Gloversville, NY. *Comn:* Murals, St John's Church, 62 & Sr Citizens Ctr, 75, Pittsburgh, Pa; mural, Cyclerama, Los Angeles, 70. *Exhib:* Contemp Reflections, Aldrich Mus, Ridgefield, Conn, 78; Arte Fiera, Bologna, Italy, 78; PS1, NY, 78; solo show, Frank Marino Gallery, NY, 79, PSI, NY, 86; West End Gallery, Portland, Maine, 88, Los Angeles Nicola Gallery, Los Angeles, Calif, 88, Celebrity Ctr, NY, 88; Herbert F Johnson Mus, Ithaca, NY, 81; Alchemy, Hankook Gallery, NY, 83; More Than Meets the Eye, NY, 85; PSI Mus, 86; Group Shows, Andre Zarre, NY, 86, 88, 90 & 93 Rabbett Gallery, New Brunswick, NJ, 89; Blondie's Gallery, NY, 93-94. *Teaching:* Vis artist, San Francisco Art Inst, 79; lectr, Stuyvesant Group, New York, 80-94; Westchester Community Col, 88. *Awards:* Creative Artists Pub Serv Fel, NY State Coun Arts, 81. *Bibliog:* Corinne Robbins (auth), Audrey Code's drawings, F Marino, 79; Diana Morris (auth), Eight, Women Artists News, 83; Alchemy, Artspeak, 83; Sherry Miller (auth), West End Gallery, Oct 88. *Mem:* Women Arts; Women's Caucus Art. *Media:* Acrylic, Graphite. *Publ:* Illusr, Life Forms of the 70's, Independent Press, 75; auth & illusr, Eggplants and Other Murders, Chrome Press, 82; auth, Alchemy, Chrome Press, 83. *Dealer:* Blondie's New York NY. *Mailing Add:* 70 Grand St New York NY 10013-2264

CODELL, JULIE FRANCIA
HISTORIAN, ADMINISTRATOR
b Chicago, Ill, Sept 19, 45. *Study:* Vassar Col, AB, 67; Univ Mich, MA(English), 68; Ind Univ, MA(art hist), 75, cert(renaissance studies), 77, PhD(comparative lit & arts), 78. *Collection Arranged:* Montana Women Artists and the Environment (auth, catalog), Missoula Mus Arts, 82; Photographs of Edward S Curtis, Custer City Art Ctr, Miles City, Mont, 88; Scene/Seen out the window, retrospective exhib of Gennie DeWeese, Missoula Mus Art, 96. *Pos:* Chair, Art Dept, Univ Mont, 88-90; dir, Sch Art, Ariz State Univ, Tempe, 91-2001, prof art history and English, 2001-; ed, J pre-Raphaelite Studies, 91-94, book rev ed, 95-. *Teaching:* Instr, Western Ill Univ, 68-71; asst prof art hist & criticism, Univ Mont, Missoula, 79-83, head slide libr, Dept Art, 79-90, assoc prof, 83-89, prof, 89-90; prof, Ariz State Univ, 91-. *Awards:* NEH Fel, 1993, 2003; Huntington Fel, 2004; Getty Fel, 2006. *Bibliog:* D McNamer (auth), Julie Codell, art historian, Missoulian, 80; Carol Woodruff (auth), From Renaissance to Robocop, Visions, 88; Trudy Thompson Rice (auth), Women in the Arts, Ariz State, 94. *Mem:* Col Art Asn; Research Soc Victorian Periodicals (vpres); Interdisciplinary Nineteenth-Century Studies; Asn Asian Studies; Victorian Interdisciplinary Studies Western US (secy). *Res:* Film, India under the Raj, colonial Photog, Victorian art. *Publ:* Ed, Encounters in the Victorian Press, Palgrave Macmillan, 2004; Gentlemen Connoisseurs & Capitalism, Cultured Identities & The Aesthetics of Britishness, Manchester United Press, 2004; ed, Genre, Gender, Race & World Cinema, Blackwell's, 2006; Excursive Discursive in Gandhi's Autobiography, Life Writing & Victorian Culture, Ashgate, 2006; Imperial Masculinity Mimicry & the New Women, Arts & the British Empire, Manchester United Press, 2006. *Mailing Add:* c/o Sch Art Ariz State Univ Tempe AZ 85827-1505

COE, ANNE ELIZABETH
PAINTER
b Henderson, Nev. *Study:* Ariz State Univ, BA, 70, MFA, 80; Univ PR, 78. *Work:* Centro Arte Mod Guadalajara, Mex; NDak Mus Art, Grand Forks; Scottsdale Ctr Arts, Ariz; Smithsonian Inst; Eiteljorg Mus, Indianapolis; Columbus Mus Art, Ga. *Comn:* McDonald's Corp, Ill; Mural & set design, Warner Brothers, Tempe, Ariz, 76. *Exhib:* Tucson Mus Art Biennial, 82; Whatever Happened to the Avant Garde, Ctr Contemp Art, Santa Ana, Calif, 83; Segal Gallery, NY, 85; Am Art Now, Columbus, Ga, 85; Women of the American West, Bruce Mus, Greenwich, Conn, 85; Art From the Drivers Seat traveling exhib, 93-96; 4th Ann New Art of the West, Eiteljorg Mus, Indianapolis, 94; Art & the Law traveling exhib, 94. *Pos:* Arts producer, KAET-TV, Phoenix, Ariz, 77-80; artist-in-residence, Ariz Comn Arts, 81-83. *Teaching:* Drawing & life drawing, Ariz State Univ, 76-78; painting, Scottsdale Artists Sch, Ariz, 96. *Bibliog:* Robert Ewing (auth), Esthetic badness, Artweek, 82; Jesse Mullins (auth), Razing Ariz, Art Today, 9/88; Kiana Dicker (auth), Anne Coe, Southwest Art, 6/92. *Media:* Acrylic on Canvas. *Dealer:* Horwitch Newman Gallery Scottsdale AZ; Anne Reed Gallery Ketchum ID. *Mailing Add:* 5776 E Forest St Apache Junction AZ 85219-9506

COE, HENRY
PAINTER
b Baltimore, Md, Oct 23, 46. *Study:* Roanoke Col, Salem, Va, BA, 69; Md Inst Col Art, MFA, 72. *Work:* Kanagawa Mus Mod Art, Japan; Acad Arts, Easton, Md; L'Association des Amis de La Grande Vigne, Dinan, France. *Comn:* Mural, Baltimore City Sch System, Md, 78; M D Anderson Cancer Ctr, Houston, Tex, 93. *Exhib:* Maryland Art Place, Baltimore, Md, 88; Horizons, Maryland Landscapes, Md State Arts Coun & Md Hist Soc; An Outside View, Univ Md, Univ Col, College Park; Musee du Chateau de Bochefort-En-Terre, Brittainy, France, 94; Hoffberger Gallery, Balt Hebrew Congregation, Md, 98. *Pos:* artist-in-residence, Rochffort-Enterre, France, 94. *Teaching:* art instr, Chesapeake Col, Md, 73-74. *Awards:* Edward Maxwell Award, Md Biennial Exhib, Baltimore Mus Art, 80; Md State Arts Coun Grant, 92; Artist Residency, Les Amis de La Grande Vigne, Dinan, France, 98. *Bibliog:* Joanne Dudziak, (auth), Heart Works, Baltimore Mag, 12/88; Sarah Tanguy (auth), A Brush with Maryland, Mid-Atlantic Country, 3/94; Sally Faulkner (auth), The Dissappearing Landscape, Am Artist, 9/94. *Media:* Oil. *Dealer:* C Grimaldis Gallery 523 N Charles St Baltimore Md 21201; Marybell Galleries 740 N Franklin St Chicago Ill 60610; Harris Gallery 1100 Bissonnet Houston Tex 27005. *Mailing Add:* 3300 Gibbons Ave Baltimore MD 21214-2658

COE, RALPH TRACY
CONSULTANT, HISTORIAN
b Cleveland, Ohio, Aug 25, 29. *Study:* Oberlin Col, BA, 53; Yale Univ, MA, 57. *Collection Arranged:* Many exhibs at Nelson Gallery, 59-79; Sacred Circles: 2000 Years of American Indian Art, Arts Coun Great Britian, 76; Lost & Found Tradition Native American Art 1965-1985, traveling exhib, Am Fedn Arts, 86-. *Pos:* Asst cur, Nat Gallery Art, 57-59; cur paintings & sculpture, Nelson Gallery Art, Kansas City, Mo, 59-82, asst dir, 65-77, dir, 77-82; freelance cur, 82-. *Teaching:* Lectr, Univ Kans, 70-82, Univ NMex, 91. *Mem:* Asn Art Mus Dirs (trustee, 79-82, pres 81-82); Am Asn Mus; Am Fedn Arts (trustee, 77-82); Col Art Asn Am; Soc Archit Historians; Southwest Asn on Indian Affairs (trustee, 84-). *Res:* French 19th century painting; modern art; ethnology. *Publ:* Auth, Impressionist and post-impressionist paintings in Washington, Burlington Mag, 59; co-ed, American Architecture and Other Writings, Harvard Univ, 61; auth, Pissarro's Jardin des Mathurins, Nelson Gallery Art & Atkins Mus Bulletin, 63; Sacred Circles: Two Thousand Years of North American Indian Art (catalog), 76; Dale Eldred: Sculpture into Environment, Regents Press of Kans, 78; Lost and Found Traditions: Native American Art 1965-1985 (catalog), 86. *Mailing Add:* 1701 Agua Fria Santa Fe NM 87501

COE, SUE
PAINTER
b Tamworth, Staffordshire, Eng, 51. *Study:* Royal Col Art, London, Eng, 70-73. *Work:* Metrop Mus Art, Mus Mod Art & NY Pub Libr, NY; Nat Mus Am Art, Smithsonian Inst, Washington; Whitney Mus Am Art, NY; Brooklyn Mus Art, NY; Nat Mus Women in the Arts, Washington; Libr Congress, Washington; San Francisco Mus Mod Art; plus others. *Exhib:* Biennale, San Francisco Mus Mod Art, 84; Art Inst Chicago, 86; The New Avant-Garde, Los Angeles Co Mus Art, 87; Committed to Print, Mus Mod Art, NY, 88; Advocacy in Art, Aldrich Mus Contemp Art, 91; solo shows, Brody's Gallery, Wash, 94, Jonson Gallery, Univ NMex, 94, Visual Arts Gallery, Univ Ala, 95, Mesa Col Gallery, San Diego, 95, Bread & Roses, NY, 95, Galerie St Etienne, NY, 96 & Salt Lake Art Ctr, 96, The Tragedy of War, Galerie St Etienne, NY, 2000; Concept in Form, Artists' Sketchbooks & Maquettes, Palo Alto Cult Ctr, Calif, 95; Art & the Law (traveling), West Publ, 95; In the Light of Goya, Univ Art Mus, Berkeley, 95; Working in the 90s, Col Mainland Art Gallery, Texas City, Tex, 96; A Critical Reality: Sue Coe and Paul Marcus, ACA Galleries, NY, 97; Art on the Edge: The Werner and Elaine Danheiser Collection, Mus Mod Art, NY, 97; Taboo: Repression and Revolt in Modern Art, Galerie St Etienne, NY, 98; One-woman shows incl Sue Coe: Recent Works, Visual Arts Gallery, Univ Ala, 95, Mesa Col Gallery, San Diego, 95, Sweatshops 1995: Works by Sue Coe, Bread and Roses, NY, 95, Sue Coe's Ship of Fools, Galerie St Etienne, NY, 96, Sue Coe: We All Fall Down, Salt Lake Art Ctr, Utah, 96, Heel of the Boot: Prints by Sue Coe, Ariz State Univ Art Mus, Tempe, Univ Ill, others, 97-99T; Open Ends, The Mus of Modern Art, NY, 2000. *Pos:* Illusr, Time Mag, New York Times. *Awards:* Outstanding Nat Activist Award, The Culture and Animals Found; Nat Academician, 1994. *Bibliog:* Susan Gill (auth), Sue Coe's inferno, Artnews, 10/87; Peter Schjeldahl (auth), My Coe Dependency, Village Voice, 5/8/96. *Mem:* Nat Acad (assoc, 93, acad, 94). *Media:* Graphite, Gouache, Watercolor, Printmaking. *Specialty:* German and Austrian Expressionism, Am & European self-taught Art, Grandma Moses. *Publ:* Auth, X (The Life & Times of Malcolm X), 86; Liverpool's Children, New Yorker, 12/13/93; Scenes from an AIDS ward, Village Voice, 2/22/94; The Sweatshop, 1994, 11/7/94, Keeping Vigil, 1/9/95, New Yorker; Dead Meat, (auth) Four Walls Eight Windows, 96 (Genesis Award 91); Pit's Letter (auth), Four Walls Eight Windows, 2000; AIDS Prevention Mural computer work (auth), RedHot Orgn, 98; Political Illustration of the Late Twentieth Century, 2001; How to Commit Suicide in South Africa, 83; auth, Paintings and Drawings, 85; Police State (exhib catalog), 87; Bully: Master of the Global Merry-Go-Round, 2004; Sheep of Fools.a song cycle for 5 voices, 2005. *Dealer:* Galerie St Etienne 24 W 57th St New York NY. *Mailing Add:* Galerie St Etienne 24 W 57th St New York NY 10019

COFFEY, DOUGLAS ROBERT
PAINTER, EDUCATOR
b Cleveland Heights, Ohio, Dec 27, 37. *Study:* Cleveland Inst Art, dipl, 59; Univ Denver, BFA, 61; Western Reserve Univ, MA, 65. *Work:* Xerox Corp, NY; Kodak Corp, Rochester, NY; Cleveland Mus Art. *Exhib:* Butler Inst Am Art Exhib, Youngstown, Ohio, 63; Rochester Fingerlakes Exhib, 71; 13th Ann Rochester Festival of Relig Art, 71; 16th Nat Print Exhib, Hunterdon Art Ctr, 72; one-man show, Mem Art Gallery, 75. *Teaching:* From assoc prof fine arts to prof, Rochester Inst Technol, 67-82; prof fine arts, Sch Art & Design, Sch Am Crafts, 82-. *Awards:* Sullivan Award for Painting, Fingerlakes Exhib, 70; First Award, 13th Ann Festival of Relig Art, 71; Painting Award, Mem Art Gallery, 75. *Media:* Polymer, Oil. *Dealer:* Jo Sibley 9 Union St Nantucket MA 02554

COFFEY, JOHN WILLIAM, II
CURATOR, MUSEUM DIRECTOR
b Raleigh, NC, Mar 12, 54. *Study:* Univ NC, Chapel Hill, BA, 76; Williams Col, MA(hist art), 78. *Collection Arranged:* Four artists: Biederman, Maddrell, Ross, Saganic (auth, catalog), 81, Maine Artists Invitationals, 82-84, Alex Katz: Small Works, 85 & Yvonne Jacquette: Tokyo Nightviews (auth, catalog), 86, Bowdoin Col Mus Art; Twilight of Arcadia: American Landscape Painters in Rome, 1830-1880 (auth, catalog), 87, Lucy Sallick: In the Vicinity of the Self (auth, catalog), 87 & New England Now: Contemp Art from Six States (coauth, catalog), 87, Bowdoin Col Mus Art; Referees: Dotty Attie, Christopher Hewat, John O'Reilly (auth, catalog), 90 & Making Faces: Self-Portraits by Alex Katz (auth catalog), 90, NC Mus Art; Finding the Forgotten: Landscape Paintings by John Beerman (auth, catalog), 91 & Moshe Kupferman: Between Oblivion and Remembrance (auth, catalog), 91, Louis Remy Mignot: A Southern Painter Abroad (coauth, catalog), 96. Sign and Gesture: Contemporary Abstract Art from the Haskell Collection, NC Mus Art (auth, catalog),

99, Color, Myth & Music: Stanton Macdonald-Wright and Synchromism (contribr, catalog), 2001. *Pos:* Asst to dir, Williams Col Mus Art, 78-79, actg dir, 79-80; cur, Bowdoin Col Mus Art, 80-88; mem adv comt, Maine State Comn Arts & Humanities, 82-85, Maine Coast Artists Gallery, 86 & Baxter Gallery, Portland Sch Art, 86-88; cur, Am & Mod Art, 88-; visual arts panel, NC Arts Coun, 90-91; dir, visual arts, Israel-NC Cult Exchange, 94-97; bd mem, NC Global Ctr, 98-2000; chief cur, 94-2005, dep dir art, 2001-, NC Mus Art. *Teaching:* Instr art hist, Williams Col, 79-80; adj instr, Art Hist, Ohio, 2001; adj instr, Univ NC, Chapel Hill, 2004-. *Mem:* Maine Festival Arts (vpres, 82-83, pres, 83-84). *Res:* American and Modern Art. *Publ:* Christine Woelfle (sculptor), Baxter Gallery, Portland Sch Arts, 87; auth, Vantage on High essay, In: Yvonne Jacquette (exhib catalog), DC Moore Gallery, 96; Louis Remy Mignot, Antiques, 11/96; contribr, North Carolina Museum of Art Handbook of the Collections, 98; Moshe Kupferman: Work Diary (exhib catalog), Tel Aviv Mus Art, 98; contribr, In Pursuit of Refinement: Charlestonians Abroad, 1740-1860 (catalog), Gibbes Mus Art, 99. *Mailing Add:* NC Mus Arts 4630 Mail Svc Ctr Raleigh NC 27699-4630

COFFEY, SUSANNA JEAN
PAINTER
b New London, Conn. *Study:* Univ Conn, Storrs, BFA, 77; Yale Sch Art, MFA, 82. *Work:* Art Inst Chicago, Catherine T & John D MacArthur Found, Vanderberg Foods, Chicago, Ill; Mariam Coffin Canaday Libr, Bryn Mawr Col; Minneapolis Mus Art; Northwestern Univ. *Exhib:* Solo exhibs, Sazama Gallery, Chicago, 91 & 92, Gallery Three Zero, NY, 94, The Alpha Gallery, Boston, 95, Lyons Wier & Ginsberg Gallery, Chicago, 96, Tibor de Nagy, NY, 97 & 99, Galeria Alejandro Sales, 98 & Dartmouth Col, Hanover, NH, 98, Marguerite Oestreicher Fine Art, New Orleans, La, 2000, Alpha Gallery, Boston, Mass, 2000, Tibor de Nagy Gallery, NY, 2001, Weatherspoon Art Gallery, Univ NC, 2001; Statewide Survey, Rockford Art Mus, Ill, 95; Inside Out (with catalog), Aldrich Mus Contemp Art, 95; Image & Eye, NY Studio Sch, 95; 47th Ann Am Acad Purchase Exhib, 95; Evanston Art Ctr, Ill, 96; group exhibs, Artists to Artists, the Marie Walsh Sharpe Art Found Exhib, Ace Gallery, NY, 2002, Painting: a Passionate Response, the Painting Ctr, NY, 2002. *Pos:* vis critic, Royal Col Art, London, 1995, Vt Studio Ctr, 1994; panel mem, Harvard Ctr for Religious Studies, 2001. *Teaching:* Teaching asst, Yale Univ, 1982; prof, painting Sch of the Art Inst of Chicago, 1982-, Oxbow, Mich, 1985-; Vis artist, var schs, 1983-; adj assoc prof, Univ Ill, 1983; Artist in resident, Dartmouth Col, 98. *Awards:* Louis Comfort Tiffany Found Award, 93; Acad Award, Am Acad Arts & Lett, 94; Acad award in art Am Acad of Arts and Letters, 1995; Guggenheim Fel, 96; named to Nat Acad, 2001. *Bibliog:* Eileen Myles (auth), Rev, Art in Am, 7/94; Vivien Raynor (auth), Rev, NY Times, 6/11/95; Charles Hagan (auth), Rev, NY Times, 7/14/95. *Mem:* Nat Acad of Design. *Mailing Add:* Sch of Art Inst of Chicago 37 S Wabash Ave Chicago IL 60603-3002

COFFIN, ANNE GAGNEBIN
PATRON
Study: Smith Col, BA. *Pos:* feature writer Look Mag, New York City, 61-71; Cur, exhib organizer, Am Art: The Last 4 Decades, London, 77; NY rep, newsletter ed, Villa I Tatti, Harvard Univ Ctr for Italian Renaissance Studies, Florence, 84-92; dir, Int Print Ctr, New York City, 2000-; Brit-Am Arts Asn, 95-; co-chmn, Contemp Arts Coun, Mus Modern Art, New York City, currently. *Mem:* NY Landmarks Conservancy, New York City, (bd dir, 81-); Chamber Music Soc Lincoln Ctr, New York City (bd dir, 84-); Century Asn. *Mailing Add:* 20 E 9th St 3AB New York NY 10003

COFFIN, J DOUGLAS
SCULPTOR, PAINTER
b Lawrence, Kans, Aug 6, 46. *Study:* Kans Univ, BFA, 71; Cranbrook Acad Art, MFA, 75. *Work:* Nat Mus Am Indian, Smithsonian Inst, NY; Inst Am Indian Arts Mus, Mus Indian Arts Cult, Wheelwright Mus Am Indian, Santa Fe; US Embassy, Malawi, Africa. *Comn:* Sun Shield, Inn Anasazi, Santa Fe, 92; African Spirit Totem, Madhvani Group, Nairobi, Kenya, 93; Medicine Wheel Totem, Haskell Indian Nations Univ, Lawrence, Kans, 94; Kansas Totem #1, City of Lawrence, Kans, 95; Mountain Spirit Totem, Markham Winery, Napa, Calif, 95. *Exhib:* Celebrations (inaugeral exhib), Nat Mus Am Indians, Smithsonian Inst, NY, 94-95; Ceremony: From the Inside Out, Inst Am Indian Arts Mus, Santa Fe, NMex, 96; 20th Century Am Sculpture at the White House, Washington, DC, 97-98; Many Moons (with video catalog), Wheelwright Mus, Santa Fe. *Bibliog:* Michelle Wolford (auth), Southwest Artists, Am Net TV, 94; Linda Barskey (auth), Art of Doug Coffin, E Net TV, 98. *Media:* Steel. *Mailing Add:* c/o Waxlander Gallery 622 Canyon Rd Santa Fe NM 87501

COGAN, JOHN D(ENNIS)
PAINTER
b Wichita Falls, Tex, Feb 24, 53. *Study:* Tex A&M Univ, BS, 75; Rice Univ, MA, 78, PhD, 81. *Work:* San Juan Col & Citizens Bank, Farmington, NMex. *Comn:* acrylic painting, Afternoon at Echo Amphitheater, San Juan Col, 97; triptych acrylic, The gentle Light of Evening, Bernalillo Co Courthouse, 2000. *Exhib:* Arts for the Parks Top 100, Nat Park Acad Arts, Jackson, Wyo, 92, 94, 95, 96; solo invitational, Henderson Fine Arts Bldg, San Juan Col, Farmington, NMex, 94. *Awards:* Landscape Merit Award, Arts for Parks, Nat Park Acad Arts, 94; Arts for Parks Collectors Award, Nat Park Acad Arts, 95. *Bibliog:* Netta Pfeifer (auth), John Cogan, Southwest Art Mag, 10/89; Vicki Stavig (auth), Isn't it grand, Art West Mag, 3/90; Shirley Behrens (auth), A Spiritual Peace, Art West Mag, 9/95. *Media:* Acrylic. *Publ:* Auth & illusr, Landscape painting pitfalls, Artists Mag, 9/93; Capitalize on the versatility of acrylic, Art Materials Today Mag, 9/94; The varied faces of acrylics, Artists Mag, 7/95. *Dealer:* Chris and Joyice Gere El Prado Galleries Tlaquepaque Village PO Box 1849 Sedona AZ 86339; Bill & Debbie Bunch Galleries W 260 N Cache Jackson WY 83001; Lee Youngman Galleries 1316 Lincoln Ave Callistaga CA 94515; Artifacts GAllery 302 E Main Farmington NM 87401. *Mailing Add:* 5102 Lee Ln Farmington NM 87402

COGGER, CASSIA ZAMECKI
PAINTER
Study: Univ Colo, Boulder, degree in art hist and studio arts; Art Students' League, NY. *Exhib:* Solo shows at Nemick and Thompson Gallery, 2002; group shows include Nat Acad Mus, NY, 2006. *Pos:* Vpres Art Students' League, NY, 2006. *Mailing Add:* c/o Art Students League 215 W 57th St New York NY 10019

COGSWELL, DOROTHY MCINTOSH
EDUCATOR, PAINTER
b Plymouth, Mass, Nov 13, 09. *Study:* Yale Univ, BFA & MFA. *Work:* Springfield Mus Fine Arts, Mass; Wisteriahurst, Holyoke Mus, Mass; Newport Art Asn; Mt Holyoke Col; Gordon Libr, Worcester Polytechnic Inst. *Comn:* Mural, Libr, 44, mural, Buckland Hall, 61 & mural & relief, Torrey Hall, 63, Mt Holyoke Col. *Exhib:* New Haven Paint & Clay Club, 29-; NY Watercolor Soc, 32-; Am Watercolor Soc, 33-; Conn Acad, 37; NY World's Fair, 39; restrospective, Mt Holyoke Art Mus, 74; and others. *Pos:* Dir collections, Mt Holyoke Col, 70-74. *Teaching:* Prof art hist, Mt Holyoke Col, 39-74, emer prof, 74-. *Awards:* First Prize in Watercolor, Eastern States Exhib, 41; Fulbright lectr, Nat Art Sch, Sydney, Australia, 57-58; Purchase Prize, Holyoke Bicentennial, 76. *Mem:* Manatee Art League (vpres, 81-83); Mt Holyoke Friends Art (chmn, 47-60); Mount Holyoke Art Adv, 83-. *Media:* Watercolor, Acrylic. *Publ:* Auth, A visitor's impressions of Australian art, Soc Artists, Sydney, 58; Mount Holyoke College art collection, Col Art J, 72

COGSWELL, MARGARET PRICE
INSTRUCTOR
b Evanston, Ill, Sept 15, 25. *Study:* Wellesley Col, BA, 47; Pratt Inst; Art Inst Chicago; Columbia Univ; Art Students League, Georgetown Univ, MA, 89. *Collection Arranged:* Communication Through Art, 64; The American Poster (ed, catalog), 68; American Exhib, 34th & 35th Venice Biennales, 68 & 70; Explorations, 70; The Audio-Visual Mag, 72; George Catlin's American Indians, 74; Images of an Era: The American Poster (with catalog), 75. *Pos:* Head dept publ & assoc foreign exhib, Am Fedn Arts, 55-66; ed, The Am Artists Series, 59-63; chmn, 50 Bks of the Yr, Am Inst Graphic Arts, 64; dep chief, Off Prog Support, 66-80, Nat Collection Fine Arts, Smithsonian Inst, 66-, mem, Women's Coun, 77-81, vchmn, 79, deputy cur of educ, 81-84, coord spec academic progs, 84-. *Teaching:* Smithsonian Inst, 70. *Awards:* Gold Medal for Printmaking, Am Artist Mag, 53. *Mem:* Am Asn Mus; Col Art Asn. *Publ:* Ed, The Ideal Theater: Eight Concepts, 63; co-ed, The Cultural Resources of Boston, 64; ed, Sao Paulo 9, 67; Images of an Era: The American Poster 1945-75, 76; National Survey of Assembility in Museums, 89. *Mailing Add:* 2929 Connecticut Ave NW Washington DC 20008-1435

COHAN, JAMES
GALLERY DIRECTOR
Study: Wash Univ, St Louis, BA; New Mus, New York City, Intern. *Pos:* With John Weber Gallery; dir, Paula Cooper Gallery; sr dir, Anthony d'Offay Gallery, 91-99; owner, dir, James Cohan Gallery, New York City, 2000-. *Mailing Add:* James Cohan Gallery 533 W 26th St New York NY 10001

COHAN, ZARA R
GALLERY DIRECTOR, EDUCATOR
b Elizabeth, NJ, Aug 11, 28. *Study:* Newark State Col, Union, NJ, MA (fine arts), 68-70; Kunsthistoriches Inst, Florence, Italy, with Dr U Middledorf, 71; Creative Arts Div, NY Univ, 72-74. *Collection Arranged:* Recent Acquisitions (auth, catalog), 80; 81 More, Tony Smith, 81; Faculty Drawing: New Attitudes (auth, catalog), 83; Retrospective: John Button an American Painter (coauth, catalog), 84 & Let's Look at Pictures: 19th Century Museum Views (auth, catalog), 84; Cur Nancy DryFoos Sculpture and Print collection, Kean Univ Gallery, Union, NJ. *Pos:* Admin, Mus Mod Art, New York, 56-64; educ supv, NJ State Mus, Trenton, 66-68; dir, James Howe Gallery, Union, NJ, 70-91; chairperson, Small Mus Comt, Mid Atlantic Asn Mus, 81; treas, vpres & pres, Mus Coun NJ, 77-79, bd trustees, 85-86 & 87-91; secy bd dir & trustee, Elizabeth Develop Co, 80-. *Teaching:* Asst prof mus training & art educ, Kean Univ, NJ, formerly. *Awards:* Award of Recognition, NJ Hist Comn, 89. *Mem:* Am Asn Mus

COHELEACH, GUY JOSEPH
PAINTER, SCULPTOR
b New York, NY. *Study:* Cooper Union, with Don Eckelberry, grad; Col William & Mary, Hon Dr Arts, 75. *Hon Degrees:* Col of William & Mary, Hon Dr Arts, 75. *Work:* Nat Wildlife Gallery, Washington; Nat Audubon Soc; Am Mus Natural Hist; Beware, presented to Pres of US. *Comn:* American Eagle, US Govt, presented to VPres Agnew, 71; Elephant, African Safari Club, Washington, for Pres of US, 72; Leopard & Elephant, World Wildlife Fund, 72; and others. *Exhib:* Houston Mus Natural Hist, Tex, 94; Cleveland Mus Natural Hist, Ohio, 94-95; Blauvelt Mus, Oradell, NJ, 95; Newark Mus, 96; Carnegie-Mellon, Pittsburgh, 96-97; Newark Mus, NJ, 96; John J Audubon Mus, KY, 97; Rory Tory Peterson Inst, NJ, 97, 2002; Haly Libr Mus, Tex, 97-98; Fort Worth Zoo, Tennison Gallery, Tex, 98; Blauvelt Mus, NJ, 98; Neville Pub Mus, Wis, 99; Michelson Mus, Tex, 99; Burpee Mus, Ill, 99-2000; West Valley Art Mus, Ariz, 2000-01; Courthouse Cult Arts Ctr, Fla, 2002; The Wildlife Experience Mus, Colo, 2003; R W Norton Art Gallery, La, 2003; Vero Beach Mus Art, Vero Beach, Fla, 2004-2005; Ward Mus of Wildfowl Art, Salisbury, Md, 2005; Hiram Blaurelt Mus, Oradell, NJ, 2005; Oshkosh Pub Mus, Oshkosh, Wis, 2006-2007. *Awards:* Guy Coheleach, Prints Mag, 79 & Mich Outdoors, 79; Master Artist, Leigh Yawkee Art Mus, Wis, 83; 8 Awards of Excellance, from SAA. *Bibliog:* Roger Caras (auth), Quest: An Artist & His Prey; Terry Weiland (auth), Coheleach, Briarpatch Press, 88; Terry Weiland (auth), Guy Coheleachs Animal Art, DDR Publ, 94. *Mem:* Soc Animal Artists (vpres); Explorer's Club; African Safari Club; Adventurer's Club.

Media: Oil, Tempera. *Interests:* First occidental artist to exhibit in post-WWII Peking. *Publ:* Illusr, Nat Wildlife Mag, 67-; Readers Digest, 67-; Int Wildlife Mag, 71-; auth, The Big Cats-The Paintings of Guy Coheleach, Harry Abrams, 82; Wildlife Art News, 84 & 93; auth/illustr, The African Lion as Man-Eater, Panther Press, 2003. *Dealer:* K & K Wildlife Art. *Mailing Add:* c/o Pandion Art PO Box 96 Bernardsville NJ 07924

COHEN, ADELE
SCULPTOR, PAINTER
b Buffalo, NY. *Study:* Art Inst Buffalo; Albright Sch Buffalo; Parsons Sch Art, NY. *Work:* Burchfield Ctr, Western NY Forum Am Art, State Univ NY, Buffalo; Newark Mus, NJ; Univ Mass, Amherst; Skirball Mus, Los Angeles, Calif; Albright Knox Art Gallery, Buffalo, NY. *Comn:* Fando & Lis stage sets, NY State Theatre, Buffalo Fine Arts Acad & Workshop Repertory Theatre, 67; Gorge Legend Arbor (sculpture), Art Park & Co, Lewiston, NY, 78; Chesterwood (sculpture), Nat Trust Hist Preserv, Stockbridge, Mass, 83, 86 & 90; sculpture, Sti-Co Ind, Orchard Park, NY. *Exhib:* Burchfield Ctr, Western NY Forum Am Art, State Univ NY, Buffalo; Albright-Knox Art Gallery, Buffalo; Art Across Am Inst Contemp Art, Boston; Foreign Inst Group Exhib, Dortmund, WGer; Kanazawa Art Exhib Exchange Show, Japan; State Univ NY, Buffalo; 98th Ann Exhib, Nat Asn Women Artists; New World Art Ctr, NY; Sylvia White Gallery, New York City & Santa Monica, Calif; David Anderson Gallery, Buffalo, NY; StiCo Indust, Orchard Park, NY. *Teaching:* Instr drawing, State Univ NY, Buffalo, 74-75. *Awards:* Buffalo Courier Express Award, 32nd Western NY Exhib, Albright-Knox Art Gallery, 69; Janet E Turner Prize, 88th Ann Exhib Nat Asn Women Artists, 77, Mem Award, 98, New York City Award, 98 & Ann Award, 99; Yaddo Fel (sculpture & drawing) Saratoga, NY, 88. *Bibliog:* Jane Marinsky (auth), Adele Cohen: Tracing Her Inner Image, 77; Elaine Hancock Jones (auth), Adele Cohen: Gorge Legend Arbor, In Process, 78; Ethel Moore (auth), The Inner Image: Adele Cohen 1960-80, 80. *Mem:* Nat Asn Women Artists. *Media:* Oil, Pastel. *Publ:* Auth The Wayward Muse, Albright Knox (catalog), Buffalo, NY, 87; Transforming Images, Poetry/Rare Books Collection, Univ Buffalo, NY, 89. *Dealer:* Art Communications International (CD Rom); Sylvia White Contemporary Artist Services 2022 B Broadway Santa Monica CA 90404

COHEN, ALAN BARRY
PHOTOGRAPHER, EDUCATOR
b Harrisburg, Pa, Aug 28, 43. *Study:* NC State Univ, BS, 66; Ill Inst Technol/Inst Design, MS(photog), 72. *Work:* Art Inst Chicago, Ill; High Mus Art, Atlanta, Ga; Baltimore Mus Art, Md; Nat Mus Am Art, Washington, DC; Metrop Mus Art, NY. *Exhib:* The Picture in the Picture, Galerie Neumann, Dusseldorf, Ger, 93; Visions of a Nation: Photographs by Mex & Am Photog, Smart Mus Art, Chicago, 94; Now (death camps), Friedrich-Ebert-Stiftung: Landesburo Thuringen, Erfurt, Ger, 95; 50 Yrs-Liberation from Auschwitz-Birkenau, Literaturhaus, Frankfurt, Ger, 95; Indelible Traces, Chic Cult Ctr, 96; The Holocaust: Voices, Portraits, Places, Gallery 312, Chic, 97; All Chic: An Electronic Exhib: U-Turn E-Zine Issue #2, 98; Works from the Gallery, Carol Ehlers Gallery, Chic, 98; Opening the Shutter: 150 Yrs of Photog, Kresge Art Mus, Mich State Univ, E Lansing, Mich, 98; Narrative & Abstraction in 20th Century Photog: Works by W Eugene Smith & Alan Cohen, Block Mus, 98; Not on any Map, Betty Rymar Gallery, Sch Art Inst Chic, 99; Block Mus Art, Northwestern Univ, Evanston, Ill, 2001. *Pos:* Bd dir, New Art Examiner, 90-92; reviewer, Nat Endowment Humanities, 80-85. *Teaching:* Instr photog, Ill Inst Tech, Chicago, 72-74; vis artist photo hist/photog, Columbia Col, Chicago, Ill, 76-86; adj assoc prof, Art Inst, Chicago, Ill, 86; vis artist photog & photo hist, DePaul Univ, Chicago, Ill, 92. *Awards:* Grant & Fel Nat Endowment Arts & Nat Endowment Humanities, 78. *Bibliog:* Alan Artner (auth), Photographic Memory, Chic Tribune (vol #7, p13), 5/18/97 & Cohen's Death Camp Photographs (vol #5, p7), 3/28/96; Michael Weinstein (auth), The Holocaust: Voices, Portraits, Places, New Art Exam (reproduction, p98), 12/97; W E Smith & Alan Cohen (photog), 20th Century Photography of Print World (reproduction, pp39), 98; Mark Towner (auth), Three Decades of Midwestern Photography: 1960-1990, Davenport Mus Art, 92; Sander Gilman (lect & pub), Contemporary Photography Sees History: The Work of Alan Cohen, 2001. *Publ:* Coauth, From Pictorialism to Precisionism, A B Bookman, 84; JNO Cook: Radically recycled cameras, Mass Inst Tech, 90; interview (text) with Cook; The Black Trans-Atlantic Experience: The Photographs of Stephen Marc (interview), Univ Ill Press, 92; Midwestern Photography: 1960-1990 (includes statement), Davenport Mus Art, 92; An as Yet Untitled Mono, Univ Chicago; On European Ground, 2001. *Dealer:* Eleanor Barefoot Gallery, New York. *Mailing Add:* 4001 N Ravenswood Ave Ste 605 Chicago IL 60613-2425

COHEN, ARTHUR MORRIS
PAINTER, GRAPHIC ARTIST
b New York, NY, Jan 2, 28. *Study:* Cooper Union, 48-50, Art Students League with Edwin Dickinson, 50 & 60. *Work:* Metrop Mus Art, NY; Brooklyn Mus; Hirshhorn Mus, Washington; New York Hist Soc; Boston Mus Fine Art. *Exhib:* Solo exhibs, Munson Gallery, Chatham, Mass, 85, 88 & 89, Kornbluth Gallery, Fair Lawn, NJ, 86, E End Gallery, Provincetown, Mass, 86 & 87, Phoenix Gallery; Salute to the Great Bridge, NY Hist Soc, 83; Urban Graphics, NY, 83; Hudson Guild Gallery, NY, 84; Jewish Community Ctr, Bayonne, NJ, 84; Assoc Am Artists Inc, NY, 84; Provincetown Art Asn, 85 & 86; Kornbluth Gallery, Fair Lawn, NJ, 88; and others. *Teaching:* Instr painting, Sch Agean, 87. *Awards:* Guggenheim Fel; Pollock-Krasner Fel; Gottlieb Fel. *Bibliog:* Gerrit Henry (auth), Art Am, 4/83; Carl Little (auth), Arts Mag, 6/83; Vivian Raynor (auth), NY Times, 4/27/86 & 5/8/88; and others. *Mem:* Provincetown Art Asn; Nat Acad Design, NY. *Media:* Oil. *Publ:* Cover, House of Light, 90. *Dealer:* East End Gallery Provincetown, MA; Swansborough Gallery, Wellfleet, MA. *Mailing Add:* 55 Tiemann Pl New York NY 10027

COHEN, BRUCE JOEL
PAINTER
b Santa Monica, Calif, Dec 26, 53. *Study:* Univ Calif, Santa Barbara, BA, 75. *Work:* Guggenheim Mus; San Diego Mus Art; Pacific Telesis Group, San Francisco; Atlantic Richfield Co, Calif; Philip Morris Inc, NY. *Exhib:* New Perspective in Am Art, Guggenheim Mus, 83; Images of Am Pop Cult Today, La Fouret Mus, Tokyo, 89; Frederick Weisman Found, Palm Springs Desert Mus, 84. *Bibliog:* William Wilson (auth), The galleries, Los Angeles Times, 1/83; Ronnie Cohen (auth), Bruce Cohen, Art Forum, 12/87; Cathy Curtis (auth), Los Angeles Times, 3/89. *Media:* Oil on Canvas. *Mailing Add:* 2502 21st St Santa Monica CA 90405

COHEN, CHARLES E
HISTORIAN, EDUCATOR
b New York, NY, July 11, 42. *Study:* Columbia Univ, AB, 63; Princeton Univ, MFA, 65; Harvard Univ, PhD, 71. *Pos:* cur drawings, Pordenone 500th Anniversary, 84. *Teaching:* Tutor Harvard Univ, Cambridge, Mass, 67-68; head teaching fel, 69-70; asst prof art Univ Chicago, 70-75; assoc prof, 75-80; chmn art dept, 85-89; Resident Master Pierce Hall, prof art, Mary L Block, 80-; chmn comt visual arts. *Awards:* Delmas Found Fel, 80; Guggenheim Found Fel, 83-84; Nat Endowment Humanities Univ Fel, 89-90. *Mem:* Col Art Asn Am; Midwest Art Hist Soc; Renaissance Soc Am. *Res:* Venetian & North Italian painting and drawing in the Renaissance. *Publ:* Auth, I disegni di Pomponio Amalteo, GEAP, 75; Pordenone's Cremona Passion Scenes & German Art, Arte Lomberda, 76; The Drawings of Giovanni Antonio da Pordenone, La Nuova Italia, 80; Pordenone not Giorgione, Burlington Mag, 80; The Art of Giovanni de Pordenone, Cambridge, 96. *Mailing Add:* Univ Chicago Art History Dept 5540 S Greenwood Ave Chicago IL 60637

COHEN, CORA
PAINTER
b New York, NY, Oct 19, 43. *Study:* Bennington Col, with Paul Feeley, David Smith & Tony Caro, BA, 64, MA, 72. *Work:* Chase Manhattan Bank, NY; RCM Capital Management, San Francisco, Calif; NY Pub Libr, NY; Swed State Art Coun, Yale Univ, New Haven, Conn. *Exhib:* Sandra Gering Gallery, NY, 92; Painting Self-Evident: Evolutions in Abstraction, Piccolo Spoleto Festival, Charleston, SC, 92; An Esemplastic Shift, 92 & The Fetish of Knowledge, 92, A/C Proj Room, NY; Contemp Surfaces, Pamela Auchincloss Gallery, NY, 92; Libidinal Painting, White Columns, NY, 93; 30th Anniversary Exhib, Leo Castelli Gallery, NY, 93; Inaugural Show, The Painting Ctr, NY, 93; Heterogeneity, Abstraction & Virtual Space, Out of the Blue Gallery, Edinburgh, Scotland, 94; Mirage, Penine Hart Gallery, NY, 94; solo exhibs, Everson Mus, Syracuse, NY, 74; Max Hutchinson Gallery, NY 79,80, 84; Wolff Gallery, 88; Holly Solomon Gallery, 90; David Beitzel Gallery, NY, 94 Joslyn Art Mus, Omaha, Nebr, 96, Hering Raum Bonn, Ger, 97, 98 & 99, Rena Bransten Gallery, San Francisco, Calif, 97, Belvedere Strabe 149a, Koln, 99, Bentley Gallery, Scottsdale Ariz, 2005, Abaton Garage, Jersey City, NJ, 2005; New Arts Program, Kutztown PA, 93, Jason McCoy Gallery, 93; Paintings & Altered X-Rays (with catalog), Gallerie Mariann Ahnlund, Umea, Sweden, 96 & Sarah Moody Gallery Art, 96; Stalke Out of Space, Copenhagen, 98; Art on Paper, Weatherspoon Art Gallery, Greensboro, 98; Coalition for the Homeless Benefit & Auction, NY, 98; Barbara Davis Gallery, Houston, Tex; Galerie Mariann Ahnlund, Stockholm Art Fair, 98; A Sustaining Passion, The Tsagaris/Hilberry Collection, Cedar Rapids Mus Art, Iowa & Dubuque Mus Art, Iowa, 98; Benefit Photog Auction, CEPA Gallery, NY, 98; Bentley Gallery, Scoattsdale, Ariz, 99, 2002,2005; McCoy, KC, 2000; MCoy, Chelsea, NY, 2001; Emory & Henry Col, Emory, Va, 2003; Jason McCoy Gallery, NY, 2004. *Pos:* asst prof art, Univ NC, Greensboro, 98-2003. *Teaching:* Vis artist painting, Art Inst Chicago, 83, 85, 91, 92 & 97, Univ Chicago, 84, Art Inst Chicago, 85, Boston Mus Sch Fine Arts, 85, 94; lectr, NY Studio Sch, 89 & Tyler Sch Art, 90; adj fac, NY Univ, 90-97; vis prof, Sch Art Inst Chicago, 93; vis artist, New Arts Prog, Kutztown, Pa, 93, Vt Studio Ctr, 90, 97, 99, 2006. *Awards:* NY Found Arts, 89; Pollock/Krasner Award, 97; Kohler Fund Award, Univ NC, 99; The National Endowment for the Arts, 87; Adolph & Esther Gottlieb Found Award, 2006. *Bibliog:* Anders Bjorkman (auth), Vasterbottens-Kuriren, The Earth Reddens and Bursts, Umea, Sweden, 96; Eleanor Heartney (auth), Art in Am, 6/98; Raphael Rubenstein (auth), Not a Mirage, Art in Am, 12/2002. *Mem:* Col Art Asn. *Dealer:* Jason McCoy 41 E 57th St NY. *Mailing Add:* 287 Broadway New York NY 10007

COHEN, DAVID
CRITIC, GALLERY DIRECTOR, EDITOR
b London, Apr 20, 1963. *Study:* Univ Sussex, Eng, BA, 1985; Courtauld Inst Art, London, MA, 1987. *Pos:* gallery dir, NY Studio Sch Drawing, Painting and Sculpture, 2001-; critic, art, & contrib ed, The New York Sun, currently; ed, publ, artentical.com, currently. *Teaching:* vis prof, Western Carolina Univ, NC, 2004-2005. *Mem:* Internat Asn Art Critics. *Publ:* Auth, Henry Moore in the Bagatelle Gardens, Paris, Lund Humphries, 93; coauth, Un siécle de sculpture anglaise, Galerie nationale Jeu de Paume, 96; coauth, Lucian Freud: Etchings in the Collection of Paine Webber, Yale Ctr British Art, 99; ed, Artcritical.com, 2000-; auth, Jock McFadyen: A book about a painter, Lund Humphries, 2001; coauth, Henry Moore: Sculpting the 20th Century, Yale, 2001; auth, Alex Katz Collages (exhib catalog), Colby College Mus Art, 2005. *Mailing Add:* NY Studio Sch 8 W 8th St New York NY 10011

COHEN, ELAINE LUSTIG
PAINTER, DESIGNER
b Jersey City, NJ, Mar 6, 1927. *Study:* Sophie Newcomb Col, Tulane Univ, 45-46; Univ Southern Calif, BFA, 48. *Work:* Mus Mod Art, NY; Am Tel & Tel; Chase Manhattan Bank; Newark Mus; Atlantic Richfield, Calif. *Comn:* Graphic designs for Am Fedn Arts, Philip Johnson (architect), Lincoln Ctr, Fed Aviation Agency & Meridian Bks. *Exhib:* One-person exhibs, Janus Gallery, Los Angeles, 82 & 85, Gloria

Luria Gallery, Bay Harbour Islands, Miami, Fla, 82, Carson Sapiro Gallery, Denver, Colo, 82, Exit Art, NY, 85, Cooper Hewitt Nat Design Mus, NY, 95 & Julie Saul Gallery, NY, 95; An Affair of the Heart: Artist's Valentines, Albright Knox Art Gallery, Buffalo, 85; Reconstructivism Space 504, NY, 95; Out of Wood, Rachel Adler Gallery, NY, 95; Am Typography in the 1960's, GGG Gallery, Tokyo, 96; The Avant-Garde Letterhead, Cooper Hewitt Mus, 96; Magie der Zahl, Staatgalerie, Stuttgart, Ger; Eye of the Beholder, Photographs from the Avon Collection, Int Ctr Photog Midtown, 97; The Re-Associated Image, Flanders Contemp Art, Minneapolis, 98; Women Designers in the USA 1900-2000, The Bard Grad Ctr, Bard Col, NY, 2000; Mondial Echo's, Mondriaan Harris Amersfort, The Neth, 2000. *Pos:* Designer (with Alvin Lustig), until 48-56; freelance designer, 56-69; mem adv comt art & archit, Yale Univ Sch Design, 57-62; freelance painter, currently. *Mailing Add:* 160 E 70th St New York NY 10021

COHEN, FRANK
COLLECTOR
b Cheshire, Eng, 44. *Pos:* Founder, Glyn Webb Home Improvement Stores; mem judging panel, Turner Prize, Tate Mus, Britain, 2003. *Awards:* Named one of top 200 collectors, ARTnews mag, 2004. *Collection:* Achievements include art collection that is largest outside of London, over 1,000 pieces; includes work by Edward Burra, Damien Hirst, Eduardo Paolozzi; Contemporary Art. *Mailing Add:* The Frank Cohen Collection 3 Grafton Pl London 1 United Kingdom 5

COHEN, GEORGE MICHAEL
EDUCATOR
b Brookline, Mass, Sept 24, 31. *Study:* Harvard Univ, AB, 55, AM, 58; Boston Univ, PhD, 62. *Teaching:* Prof, Hofstra Univ, 70-. *Bibliog:* A History of American Art; Essential American Art. *Mem:* Appraisers Asn Am. *Publ:* Auth, The bird symbolism of Morris Graves, Col Art J, 58; The paintings of Charles Sheeler, 59 & The lithographs of Thomas Hart Benton, 62, Am Artist; The sculpture of John B Flannagan, Artvoices, 65; The art of George Catlin, Art & Antiques, 81. *Mailing Add:* 80 Wintercress Ln East Northport NY 11731

COHEN, HAROLD
ARTIST-THEORIST, EDUCATOR
b London, Eng, May 1, 28. *Study:* Univ London, Diploma(fine arts), 51. *Work:* Tate Gallery, London; Stedelijk Mus, Amsterdam, Holland; Victoria & Albert Mus, London; Los Angeles Co Mus Art, Calif; Walker Art Ctr, Minneapolis, Minn. *Comn:* Wall hanging, Milan Triennale, 63; tapestry, Brit Petroleum Co, 65. *Exhib:* Documenta, Kassel, WGer, 64 & 77; 33rd Venice Biennale, 66; one-man shows, Mus d'Art Contemporain, Montreal, Que, 67, Victoria & Albert Mus, 68 & Stedelijk Mus, 77; Three Behaviors for the Partitioning of Space, Los Angeles Co Mus Art, 72; Retrospective, Scottish Arts Coun Gallery, Edinburgh, 76; Harold Cohen: Drawing, San Francisco Mus Mod Art, 79; Computers & the Visual Arts: The Research & Drawings of Harold Cohen, Sierra Nevada Mus Art, 79; and others. *Pos:* Vis scholar, Artificial Intelligence Lab, Stanford Univ, 73-75. *Teaching:* Instr art, Univ Col London, 61-65; prof art, Univ Calif, San Diego, 68-, chmn visual arts dept, 68-69, dir, Ctr Art/Sci Study, 74-, emer prof, currently. *Awards:* Harkness Fel of Commonwealth Fund, 59-61; Purchase Award, Gulbenkian Found, 61; Nat Endowment Arts Workshop Grant, 76. *Publ:* Auth, The making of a tapestry, 67, Apropos work in progress, 68 & On purpose, 74, Studio Int; The material of symbols, First Ann Symposium on Symbols & Symbol Processing, Univ Nev, 76; What is an Image?, Int Joint Conf Artificial Intelligence, Tokyo, Japan, 79. *Mailing Add:* Univ Calif San Diego 9500 Gillman Dr Circa-0037 La Jolla CA 92093-0327

COHEN, HAROLD LARRY
DESIGNER, EDUCATOR
b Brooklyn, NY, May 24, 25. *Study:* Pratt Inst Art Sch, Brooklyn; Northwestern Univ; Inst Design, BA. *Pos:* Dir, Inst Behav Res, Silver Spring, Md, formerly; dean sch archit & environ design, State Univ NY, Buffalo, formerly, prof, currently. *Teaching:* Prof design, chmn dept & dir design res & develop, Southern Ill Univ, Carbondale, formerly. *Awards:* Five Good Design Awards, with Davis Pratt; Mus Mod Art Awards, 49-53. *Mailing Add:* 600 Main St Buffalo NY 14202-3030

COHEN, JEAN
PAINTER
b New York, NY, Aug 1, 1927. *Study:* Pratt Inst, Brooklyn, 44-45; Cooper Union Art Sch, New York, 46-49; Skowhegan Sch Painting & Sculpture, Maine, summer 50. *Work:* Ciba-Geigy Corp, Ardsley, NY; Hampton Inst Mus, Va; Bocour Color Collection, Garnersville, NY; Colby Col Mus, Waterville, Maine; Wright State Univ Mus. *Exhib:* Contemp Artists, Riverside Mus, NY, 63; Pa Acad Regional, Philadelphia, 64; Visual R&D, Univ Tex Art Mus, Austin, 73; Contemp Am Painting, Randolph-Macon Col, 74; West Bronx Art League, Bronx Mus, 75. *Pos:* Consult, West Bronx Art League, 69-75; founder, Landmark Gallery, NY; cur, Magic Circle Exhib, Bronx Mus Arts, 77. *Teaching:* Instr painting & design, Cooper Union, spring & summers, 51-63; lectr painting, Philadelphia Col Art, 62-69; lectr painting, Queens Col Art Dept, 72-75; Jersey City State Col, Philadelphia Col Art, 81-86 & La State Univ, spring 90. *Awards:* Landscape Painting Prize, Skowhegan Sch Painting, 50; Creative Artists Pub Serv Grant, 80; Adolph Gottlieb Grant, 84. *Mem:* Artists Equity; Am Abstract Artists. *Media:* Oil, Compressed Charcoal. *Dealer:* Cape Split Place Addison ME 04606. *Mailing Add:* 60 Westminster Dr Shirley NY 11967

COHEN, JEAN R
CERAMIST, COLLECTOR
b Colorado Springs, Colo, Apr 13, 35. *Study:* Penland Sch Crafts; Maples Mills Sch Crafts; Arrowmont Sch Crafts; Visual Arts Ctr; also, study with Richard La Fean, Jane Peiser, Elsa Rady, Ralph Baccera, David Leach, Don Pilcher, Rudi Staffel, Catherine Hiersoux & Sally Silberberg. *Work:* Towson State Univ Gallery, Baltimore; Vessels Aesthetic, Taft Col, Calif. *Exhib:* Md Craft Coun Biennial Exhib, Maryland, 81 & 83; Contemp Crafts Exhib, Del Art Mus, Del, 82; Lloyd Herman Selects, Arlington Arts Ctr, Va, 82; Am Hand Inc, Washington, DC & NY, 83 & 84; Everson Mus Art, NY, 84; Crafts Nat, Buffalo State Col, NY, 85; Am Ceramic Nat, Calif, 86. *Teaching:* Teacher, Potters Guild Baltimore, Md, 77-82; workshop instr, Washington Kiln Club, 84 & Santa Barbara State Col, 86. *Awards:* Purchase Award, Vessels Aesthetic, 83. *Mem:* Clayworks of Baltimore, Md; Potters Guild of Baltimore, Md; Am Craft Coun. *Publ:* Ceramics Monthly, 4/86. *Mailing Add:* 6104 Eastcliff Dr Baltimore MD 21209-3514

COHEN, JEM ALAN
FILMMAKER, VIDEO ARTIST
b Kabul, Afghanistan, Aug 28, 62; US citizen. *Study:* Wesleyan Univ, BA (with hon), 84. *Work:* Whitney Mus Art, NY; Mus Modern Art, NY; Screen Gallery at Federation Square, Melbourne, Australia; Donnell Media Ctr, NY; Walker Art Ctr, Minn. *Comn:* video Buried in Light, High Mus Art, Atlanta, 94; film/video Amber City, Ondavideo, Pisa, Italy, 99; film/video Blood Orange Sky, Officine, Catania, Sicily, Italy, 2000; Waterfront Diary, Rotterdam Int Film Festival, Neth, 2001; Chain X Three, Australian Ctr for the Moving Image. *Exhib:* Locarno Int Film Festival, Switz, 99; Berlin Int Film Festival, Ger, 2004; Whitney Biennial, Whitney Mus Art, NY, 2000; Premieres, Mus of Modern Art, NY, 2005. *Awards:* Fel Rockefeller Found, 95; Creative Capital Found Grant, 2000; Guggenheim Fel, 2001; Independent Spirit Award, Feb, 2005. *Bibliog:* Mike Plante (auth), Glass Is a liquid: Interview with Jem Cohen, Cinemad Mag #2, 99; Luc Sante (auth), A Captivating Wit, NY Times, 7/16/200; Rhys Graham (auth), Just Hold Still, Semses of Cinema, 10/2000; Michael Almereyda (auth), Eyes wide Open, Artforum, 3/2005. *Media:* film: 16mm, super 8; video: DV. *Publ:* contribr, Two Times Intro, Raygun Press, 98, Patti Smith/Complete, Doubleday, 99; auth, Instrument (booklet essay), Dischord, 99; Catalog Essay: Cinematexas, 2004. *Dealer:* Video Data Bank Chicago IL

COHEN, JOAN LEBOLD
HISTORIAN, PHOTOGRAPHER
b Highland Park, Ill, Aug 19, 32. *Study:* Smith Col, BA, 54. *Work:* Smith Col Mus Art; Harvard Law Sch; Atlantic Richfield Corp Collection; NYNEX; Paul, Weiss, Rifkind, Wharton & Garrison, NY, Hong Kong, Beijing; Embassy of United States of America, Phnom Phen, Cambodia. *Exhib:* Shadows of Mt Huang, Univ Art Gallery, Berkeley, Calif, Austin, Tex & Princeton, NJ, 81; Alisan Fine Arts, Hong Kong, 87 & 89; Smith Col Alumnae House, 90, 94, 98 & 2004; Kendall Gallery, Wellfleet, Mass, 91; Soho Photo Gallery, NY, 94-2005; Castle Hill Gallery, Truro, Mass, 2001, 02; Photo NY, 2004. *Collection Arranged:* Painting the Chinese Dream, 82 & The New Generation of Chinese Art, 90, Northhampton, Mass; New York, The City and It's People, Bejing, 85; Artists from China, Bronxville, NY, 87; Between East & West, Bridgeport, Conn, 94-95; CCIC, Hong Kong, 86. *Pos:* Guest cur, Smith Col Mus Art, 82 & 90, Brooklyn Mus, NY, 83, Worker's Cult Palace, Beijing, 85, Sarah Lawrence Col Art Gallery, 87, Discovery Mus, Bridgeport, Conn, 94; Registrar, Corcaran Gallery of Art, Washington DC, 2005-2006. *Teaching:* Lectr, Dept Pub Educ, Mus Fine Arts, Boston, 65-71; lectr Asian art & film, China, Japan & India, Sch of Mus Fine Arts, Tufts Univ, Boston, 68-90. *Awards:* Two awards for bk, China Today & Her Ancient Treasures, 74 & 75; Smith Col Medal, 90. *Mem:* Fairbank Ctr E Asian Studies, Harvard Univ; Modern China Seminar of Columbia Univ. *Media:* Photography. *Interests:* Contemp Chines art. *Publ:* Buddha, Seymour Lawrence Delacore, NY, 1969; co-auth, China Today and her Ancient Treasures, Abrams, NY, 1974, 2nd ed, 80, 3rd ed, 86; Anchor, Monuments of the God Kings, Abrams, NY, 1975; The New Chinese Painting, 1949-1986, Abrams, NY, 1987. *Dealer:* Photo Researchers 60 E 56th New York NY 10522. *Mailing Add:* 1095 Park Ave New York NY 10128-1154

COHEN, JONATHAN JACOB
DESIGNER, CRAFTSMAN
b Boston, Mass, Aug 13, 55. *Study:* Cornell Univ, studied with Dennis Ichiyama, BA, 78. *Comn:* Jones, Grey & Bailey Law Offices, Bellevue, Wash, 85; Pacific Denkmann Co, Seattle, Wash, 87; Whitten residence, comn by Mr & Mrs G Whitten, Bellevue, Wash, 88; living & dining room, comn by Mr & Mrs R Levien, Weston, Conn, 91. *Exhib:* Embellishment Upon Function, Henry Art Gallery, Seattle, Wash, 80; Nat Invitational, Am Crafts Gallery, Cleveland, Ohio, 84, 85 & 86; Furniture That Keeps Secrets, 84 & Nat Invitational, 87 & 88, NW Gallery of Fine Woodworking, Seattle, Wash; Wood Invitational, Signature Gallery, Boston, Mass, 85; one-man exhib, Dark Dancers, NW Gallery of Fine Woodworking, 89, Rain Forest Show, 92 & one tree, 93. *Teaching:* Vis prof furniture design, Univ Wash, 87-2000. *Awards:* (2) First Place Awards, Special Crafts Exhib, Bellevue Art Mus, Wash, 81; Artist's Trust Gap Grant, 93. *Bibliog:* A V Chastain Chapman (auth), Fine Furniture Making, Am Craft, 12-84; Sharon O'Boyle (auth), Tomorrows Antiques, Wash Mag, 3-85; J Queener Shaw (auth), Enchanted Woods, Pacific NW Mag, 5-87. *Mem:* Am Crafts; Furniture Soc. *Publ:* Ed corresp for Fine Woodworking Mag, 83-. *Dealer:* Entree Hbre Gallery Manhattan NY

COHEN, LEWIS CARROLL
SCULPTOR, EDUCATOR
b Minneapolis, Minn, Apr 19, 36. *Study:* Student, Univ Minn, 53; Postgrad, Ecole des Arts Decoratif, Paris, 63; Diploma with hons, Mus Sch, Boston, 62; Claremont (Calif) Col, MFA, 76. *Comn:* Exhib sculpture in solo exhibs Four Oaks Gallery, Pasadena, Calif, 1985, Twentieth Century Gallery, Williamsburg, 1988, Martin Sumers Gallery, New York City, 1990, Muscarelle Mus of Art, Williamsburg, 1993; commissioned works incl Portrait of Henry Mudd, Harvey Mudd Col, sculpture of Reverand James Blair, Tercentenary of Col of William and Mary, 1993. *Pos:* Interim dir, Laguna Beach Sch Art, 1980. *Teaching:* Inst, Boston Univ, 1964-67; lectr, Calif State Univ, Long Beach, 1970-87; inst, Laguna Beach (Calif) Col Art, 1973-85; asst prof, Scripps Col,

Claremont, 1974-75; assoc prof, then prof Col of William and Mary, Williamsburg, Va, 1987-. *Awards:* Recipient Prix de Rome Am Acad in Rome, 1967-70; named Nat Acad, 1992. *Mem:* Nat Acad Design (assoc, 90, acad, 92). *Mailing Add:* Coll of William and Mary Dept of Fine Arts Williamsburg VA 23185

COHEN, LYNNE G
PHOTOGRAPHER, EDUCATOR
b Racine, Wis, July 3, 44. *Study:* Slade Sch Art, London, 64-65; Univ Wis, Madison, BS(art), 67; Univ Mich, 68, Eastern Mich Univ, MA(art), 69. *Work:* Int Mus Photog, George Eastman House, Rochester, NY; Mus Mod Ville Paris; Nat Gallery Can, Ottawa; Victoria & Albert Mus, London; Metrop Mus Art, NY. *Comn:* Centre d'Art Contemporain de Guerigny, France, 91; Wexner Ctr Arts, Columbus, Ohio, 96; Univ Valencia, 98. *Exhib:* Solo Exhibs, Int Ctr Photog, NY, 78, Mus Gestaltung Zurich, Switz, 89, FRAC Limousin, 92, PPOW, NY, 92 & 96, Robert Klein Gallery, Boston, 95, Karsten Schubert Gallery, London, 96, Galerie des Archives, Paris, 96, PPOW, NY, 96, Kirkland Fine Arts Ctr, Millikin Univ, Ill, 98 & Mus voor Fotografie, Antwerp, 98; Victoria & Albert Mus, London, 89; Double Mixte, Galerie Nat Jeu Paume, Paris, 95; Passions Privees, Mus d'Art Mod Paris, 96; Wexner Ctr Arts, Columbus, Ohio, 97; and others. *Collection Arranged:* Art Inst Chicago, Ill; Kinsthaus, Zurich, Switzerland; Met Mus Art, MYC; Musee d'Art Moderne de la Ville Paris, France; Nat Gallery Can. *Teaching:* Lectr photog art, Eastern Mich Univ, Ypsilanti, 68-73; from lectr to prof visual art, dept visual arts, Univ Ottawa, 74-; vis artist & prof, Sch Art Inst Chicago, 84 & 92; Ecole des Beaux-Arts de Bordeaux, 94 & 96; Nova Scotia Col Art & Design, 96. *Awards:* Logan Award, Art Inst Chicago, 67; Sr Arts Grant, Ont Arts Coun, 85; Sr Arts Grant, Can Coun, 86, 89 & 95. *Bibliog:* Marc Freidus (auth), Typologies, Nine Contemporary Photographers, Newport Harbor Art Mus (exhib catalog & bk); Jean-Pierre Criqui (auth), Double Mixte, Galerie Nat du Jeu de Paume (exhib catalog & bk), Paris, 95; Mark Robbins and Sarah Rogers (auths), Evidence: Photography and Site (group exhib catalog & bk), 96. *Media:* Art, Photography. *Publ:* Contribr, Creative Cameria, 4/78; Occupied Territory, Aperture, NY, 88; Contact Sheet, 89 & 96; Lost and Found, FRAC-Limousin, 92. *Dealer:* PPOW 476 Broome St New York NY 10013; Galerie Rodolphe Janssen 35 rue de Livourne 1050 Bruxelles

COHEN, MICHAEL S
CERAMIST, PHOTOGRAPHER
b Boston, Mass, Mar 7, 36. *Study:* Mass Col of Art, BFA, 57; Cranbrook Acad of Art, Bloomfield Hills, Mich, 61; Haystack Mountain Sch Crafts, Deer Isle, Maine, 61. *Work:* Mus of Mod Art, NY; Mus Contemp Crafts, NY; Johnson Collection Contemp Crafts, Wis; Everson Mus, Syracuse, NY; Addison Gallery, Andover, Mass. *Exhib:* Syracuse Int, Everson Mus, 62, 64 & 66; Am Studio Pottery, Victoria & Albert Mus, London, Eng, 63; 10th Int Exhib of Ceramic Art, Smithsonian Inst, Washington, DC, 65; one-man shows, Soc of Arts & Crafts, Lexington, Mass, 74 & Gallimaufry, Croton-on-Hudson, NY, 76; Objects USA, Mus Contemp Crafts, NY, 70; Crafts 1970, Boston City Hall, Mass; Potter's Wheel, DeCordova Mus, Lincoln, Mass, 76; and others. *Awards:* Nat Endowment Arts grant, 74; Master Craftsman grant, Nat Endowment Arts, 75; 2nd Int Symposium, Tenn, 75. *Bibliog:* Peter Sabin (auth), Studio Production, Studio Potter, 76. *Mem:* Am Crafts Coun; Mass Asn of Craftsmen; Asparagus Valley Potters Guild (pres, 75-89). *Media:* Stoneware. *Interests:* Tile production. *Publ:* Smithsonian Archives of American Art, 8/2001. *Mailing Add:* 107 Amherst Rd Pelham MA 01002

COHEN, MILDRED THALER
ART DEALER, GALLERY DIRECTOR
b New York, NY, 21. *Study:* Hunter Col, New York, BA, 42; Pratt Inst Libr Sch, Brooklyn, NY, BLS, 43. *Collection Arranged:* Women Students of William Merritt Chase, 73; Ethel Paxson, 76; Nell Choate Jones, 79; Frederic Taubes, 81; Three Generations of Wiggins: Carleton, Guy C, Guy A, 81; Robert Hallowell, 83; Anne Blodgett, 85, 88, 92 & 95; Eliot Clark, 88; Samuel Rothbort, 89; Rachel Hartley, 91; Frank Kleinholz, 92; Anthony Springer, 96; Joseph Margulies, 97; Allen Blagden, 98; Hildegarde Hamilton, 99; Samuel Brecher, 99, 2003; James Bowman Consor, 2000, 04. *Pos:* Librn, Mus French Art, French Inst, New York, 43-45; dir, The Marbella Gallery, Inc, New York, 71-. *Mem:* Appraisers Asn Am Inc. *Specialty:* Nineteenth and early twentieth century American Paintings. *Publ:* Auth, Tonalism, an American Interpretation of the Landscape, 93; auth, Robert Hallowell, an artist Rediscovered, 83 & Eliot Clark, artist, scholar, world traveler, 90. *Mailing Add:* 28 E 72nd St New York NY 10021

COHEN, REINA JOYCE
GRAPHIC ARTIST, PRINTMAKER
b New York, NY, Mar 28, 31. *Study:* Cooper Union, NY, 51; The New School, 66. *Work:* Nassau Co Med Ctr, Hempstead, NY; Vitelco, St Thomas, US VI; St Laurence Univ, Canton, NY. *Comn:* Monoprints, Winrock Inn, Albuquerque, NMex, 90; Ltd Ed Collector Plates, Braford Exchange, Eng, 99. *Exhib:* Firehouse Gallery, Nassau Comm Col, Hempstead, NY, 81; Space Group Korea, Seoul, 82 & 84. *Awards:* First Prize, Freeport Arts Coun, 79; Award of Excellence, Independent Art Soc, 84 & 90; Grant, Mid Atlantic Arts Found, Baltimore, Md, 91. *Mem:* Nat Asn Women Artists; Independent Art Soc. *Media:* Miscellaneous Media, Etching. *Publ:* Floral Prints, Manor Art Ent Ltd, 93-94. *Dealer:* Art Rep Inc 279 Woodmere St Islip Terrace NY 11752; Printworks 251-27 Gaskell Rd Little Neck NY 11363. *Mailing Add:* 29 Farmstead Ln Glen Head NY 11545-2601

COHEN, RONNY
CRITIC, DEALER
b New York, NY, Apr 19, 50. *Study:* Finch Col, BA, 72; Inst Fine Arts, MA, 74, PhD, 79. *Collection Arranged:* Energism, PS 1 Critical Perspectives, 82; New Spiritual Abstraction of the 1980's Nohra Haime Gallery, NY, 84; Alan Shields: A Survey of His Prints, Cleveland Ctr Contemp Art, 86; Nature In Art, Contemp Art at 1 Penn Plaza, NY; Meticulous Realist Drawing, Squibb Gallary, Princeton, NJ, 89; An Artist's Christmas, Midtown Payson Galleries, NY, 90; Watercolor Across the Ages, Bristol-Myers Squibb, Princeton, NJ, 91; Margo Hoff: Canvas Collages, Sidney Miskin Gallery, Baruch Col, NY, 94. *Pos:* Ed, The Art Dealer's Newsletter, 83-85; NY columnist, The Art Newspaper, 95-97. *Teaching:* Cooper Univ, 89; Col Staten Island, City Col NY, 91-94; Grad Sch Figurative Art, NY Acad Art, 94; instr grad sch fig art, NY Acad Art, 94, 96, 97, RI Sch Design, Providence, 96; ICP Workshops, NY, 96-2000. *Awards:* Danforth Found Fel, 72-79; Fulbright-Hays Fel, US & Italian Govt, 76-77. *Bibliog:* Art, The New Yorker, 12/31/90; Publ Weekly, 1/10/94; Art Librn J, summer 94. *Mem:* NY Artists Equity Asn; Inst Fine Arts Alumni Asn; Int Asn Art Critics. *Publ:* Auth, Energism: An attitude, 9/80 & Alexandra Exter's designs for the theater, 9/81, Artforum; Drawing the meticulous realist way, 3/4/82; New abstraction V, PCN, 4/5/87; Minimal Prints, PCN, 6/90; Tschang Yeul Kim, Hudson Hills, 93; over 400 articles & revs; auth, Shirley Smith Catalogue, Kans State Univ, 2000. *Mailing Add:* PO Box 20241 New York NY 10021-0064

COHEN, SOREL
CONCEPTUAL ARTIST, PHOTOGRAPHER
b Montreal, Que. *Study:* Concordia Univ, Montreal, BFA, 74, MFA, 79. *Work:* Nat Gallery Can, Ottawa, Ont; Bibliot Nat, Paris; Mus d'Art Contemporain, Montreal Mus Fine Arts; Winnipeg Art Gallery, Manitoba. *Exhib:* An Extended and Continuous Metaphor, PS 1, NY, 83; Productions and the Axis of Sexuality, Walter Philips Gallery, Banff, 84; Visual Facts, Third Eye Ctr, Glasgow, 85; Doppleganger/Cover, Galerie Aorta, Amsterdam, 85; et les ateliers de femmes, Mus d'Art Contemporain, Montreal, 86; Songs of Experience, Nat Gallery of Can, 86; Figures, Cambridge Darkroom, 87. *Pos:* Bd mem, Galerie Optica, 80-88. *Awards:* Bourse du Quebec, Ministere des Affairs Culture, 83; Arts Grant B, Can Coun, 85; Duke & Duchess Award in Photogr, Can Coun, 88. *Bibliog:* R Graham & G Godmer (auths), monogr essays, Mus d'Art Contemporain, 86; Therese St Gelais, rev, Parachute, 86-87; Bob Wilkie (auth), Telling pictures, revealing histories, Afterimage, Vol 17, No 9, 4/90. *Dealer:* Wynick Tuck Gallery 80 Spadina Ave Toronto Ont M5V 2J3 Canada; Samuel LaLourre Gallery Montreal Can. *Mailing Add:* 631 Lansdowne Ave Montreal PQ H3Y 2V7 Canada

COHEN, STEVEN A
COLLECTOR
Study: Univ Pa Wharton Sch, BS (econ). *Pos:* Trader, Gruntal & Co, 78—92; chmn, founder, Strategic Air Command Capital Adv, 92—. *Awards:* Named one of top 200 collectors, ARTnews Mag, 2004; Ranked by Forbes one of the World's Richest People. *Mem:* Michael J Fox Found (bd mem, currently); Steven & Alexandra Cohen Found (co-founder, currently); painting & sculpture comt Mus Modern Art. *Collection:* Impressionism, Modern & Contemporary Art. *Mailing Add:* SAC Capital Adv 72 Cummings Pt Rd Stamford CT 06902

COHN, BARBARA G See Bisgyer, Barbara G (Cohn)

COHN, FREDERICK DONALD
DEALER, APPRAISER
b Monroe, Mich, May 3, 31. *Study:* Univ Wis, BA, 54; Detroit Col Law, LLB, 57. *Pos:* Art dealer, Images Gallery, Toledo, Ohio, currently. *Mem:* Appraisers Asn Am; Toledo Mus Art, Pres Coun. *Specialty:* Nineteenth and twentieth century American painting, print and sculpture. *Mailing Add:* 4343 W Bancroft St Apt 4F Toledo OH 43615-3958

COHN, MARJORIE B
CURATOR, HISTORIAN
b New York, NY, Jan 10, 39. *Study:* Mt Holyoke Col, BA, 60; Radcliffe Col, AM, 61. *Hon Degrees:* Mt Holyoke Col, DFA, 96. *Collection Arranged:* Albrecht Durer, 1471-1528 (auth, catalogue), Mt Holyoke Col, 71; Wash & Gouache, Watercolor at Harvard, Fogg Art Mus, Harvard Univ, 77; Ingres Collection (auth, handbook), 81 & Gray Collection of Engravings (auth, handbook), 86, Fogg Art Mus; A Noble Collection: the Spencer Albums of Old Master Prints (auth, handbook), Fogg Art Mus, 92; Touchstone: 200 Years of Artists' Lithographs, Fogg Art Mus, 98. *Pos:* Conservator works of art on paper, Fogg Art Mus, Harvard Univ, 62-89, curator prints, 89-, actg dir, 90-91; mem bd examr (paper), Am Inst for Conserv, 76-78, mem nominating comt, 77 & ed jour. *Teaching:* Guest lectr print hist, Boston Univ, 73; vis lectr print hist, Wellesley Col, 73; vis asst prof print hist, Brown Univ, 75; sr lectr fine arts, Harvard Univ, 77-. *Mem:* Fel Int Inst for Conserv; fel Am Inst for Conserv; fel Am Acad Arts Sci. *Res:* History, materials & techniques of traditional graphic arts. *Publ:* Contribr, A Note on Media and Methods, Tiepolo, A Bicentenary Exhibition, Fogg Art Mus, 70; Wash & Gouache: A Study of the Development of the Materials of Watercolor, Fogg Art Mus, 81; contribr, Pursuit of Perfection: Works by J A D Ingres, J B Speed Mus, 83; Francis Gallery Gray and Art Collecting for America, Harvard Univ Art Mus, 86; A Noble Collection: The Spencer Albums of Old Master Prints, Harvard Univ Art Mus, 91. *Mailing Add:* Harvard Univ Art Mus Print Dept-Mongan Ctr 32 Quincy St Cambridge MA 02138

COHN, RICHARD A
DEALER
b New York, NY, Feb 20, 24. *Study:* Univ Wis. *Pos:* Pres, Richard A Cohn Ltd, New York, 65-; partner, Kimmel/Cohn Photography Arts, New York, 74-. *Specialty:* Twentieth century German Expressionism. *Mailing Add:* Richard A Cohn Ltd One W 64th St New York NY 10023

COIT, M B
PAINTER, SCULPTOR
b New London, Conn. *Study:* Univ Conn, BFA, 68. *Comn:* Triptych, Mitsui Manufacturers Bank, Los Angeles, Calif, 83. *Exhib:* Images, Bowers Mus, Santa Ana, Calif, 87; LA Art, Gallery Q, Tokyo, Japan, 87; Designations, Los Angeles Co Mus Art, Calif, 87; one-man show, Branslater Gallery, Riverside, Calif, 89; Artist's Book,

Anchorage Mus, Alaska, 90; traveling exhib, Southern Calif Decade 1980-89; Contemp Artists, Univ Calif, Los Angeles, 90. *Bibliog:* Suzanne Muchnic (auth), Galleries downtown, LA Times, 11/2/84; Melinda Wortz (auth), article, Loma Linda Univ, 89; Roger Churches (auth), M B Coit: lucid lights, Loma Linda Univ, 89. *Media:* Acrylic, Oil; Plastic

COKE, VAN DEREN
PHOTOGRAPHER, HISTORIAN
b Lexington, Ky, July 4, 21. *Study:* Univ Ky, BA; Ind Univ, MFA; Harvard Univ; Acad Art Co, San Francisco, LHD, 86. *Work:* Mus Mod Art, NY; Int Mus Photog, Rochester, NY; Nat Gallery Can, Ottawa, Ont; San Francisco Mus Mod Art; Sheldon Mem Art Gallery, Lincoln, Nebr. *Exhib:* Witkin Gallery, NY, 74; Oakland Mus, 75; Galerie die Brucke, Vienna, 75; Schoelkopf Gallery, NY, 76; Art Mus, Univ NMex, 82; Albuquerque Mus, NMex & Phoenix Art Mus, Ariz, 86. *Pos:* Dir, Univ NMex Art Mus, 62-67 & 72-79; dir, George Eastman House, 70-72; dir dept photog, San Francisco Mus Mod Art, 79-; bd dir, Mus Fine Arts, Santa Fe, NMex, 85-, Univ NMex Art Mus, 90- & Georgia O'Keeffe Mus, Santa Fe, NMex, 96-. *Teaching:* Asst prof photog & art hist, Univ Fla, 58-61; assoc prof, Ariz State Univ, 61-62, adj prof, 83-88, distinguished prof, 88-92; prof, Univ NMex, 62-70 & 72-79, chmn dept art, 62-70; lectr, St Martin's Sch Art, London, 71; prof art hist, Univ Rochester, 71-72; vis prof, Univ Calif, Berkeley, 73; distinguished vis prof, Univ Calif, Davis, 74. *Awards:* Sr Fulbright Fel, NZ, 89; Distinguished Int Career in Photog Award, 92; Int Achievement in Photog Award, Repub of San Marino, 92. *Bibliog:* Robert Routh (auth), An interview with Van Deren Coke, Peterson's Photo Mag, 4/11/76; Janzita Rover (auth), No party line: a conversation with Van Deren Coke, Exposure, Vol 20, 82; Liz Lufkin (auth), Van Deren Coke: Pied piper of the avant garde, Am Photogr, 6/85. *Mem:* Col Art Asn Am (bd dir, 72-76); Int Folk Art Found (bd dir, 68-76); Guadalupe Found (bd dir, 76-79); Soc Photog Educ (bd dir, 67-70). *Res:* The use of photographs by artists; twentieth century American painters; contemporary photographers; Mexican Figural Ceramic Folk Art. *Publ:* Avant-Garde Photography in Germany, 1919-1939, 81; Auth, Val Telberg, 83; Secular and Sacred, Photographs of Mexico, 92; Forecast: Shifts in Direction, 94; Robert C May: Photography, Univ Ky Art Mus, Lexington, 95. *Mailing Add:* c/o Mission Gallery 138 E Kit Carson Rd Taos NM 87571

COKENDOLPHER, EUNICE LORAINE
PAINTER, INSTRUCTOR
b Sonora, Tex, April 17, 31. *Study:* Tex Womans Univ, 48-50; studied with Don Stone, Edgar Whitney, Zoltan Szabo, George Cherepov, Bud Biggs, Naomi Brotherton & Howard Wexler, 75-89. *Work:* Southern Guild Artists & Craftsmen, Bowling Green, Ky; Baptist Med Ctr Found, Oklahoma City. *Comn:* Noah and the Ark, First United Methodist Church, Burkburnett, Tex, 81. *Exhib:* Tex Fine Arts Citation Exhib, Laguna Gloria Mus, Austin, Tex, 80; Aqueous 79', Ky Watercolor Soc, 79; The Best of Southwest Watercolor Soc, Brookhaven Col, Dallas, 81 & 84; Southern Watercolor Soc Seventh Ann, Asheville Art Mus, NC, 83; Ga Watercolor Soc Fifth Nat Exhib, Valdosta State Col Fine Arts Bldg, 84. *Teaching:* former instr watercolor, Wishing Well Studio, Burkburnett, Tex, 84. *Awards:* Award Merit, Aqueous 79, Ky Watercolor Soc Nat Exhib, 79; Mary Jo Weale Award, Southern Watercolor Soc Nat Exhib, 83; Second Place, Best of Southwest Watercolor Soc, 84. *Mem:* Southwestern Watercolor Soc; Tex Watercolor Soc. *Media:* Watercolor, Oil. *Mailing Add:* 1200 Clover Dr Burkburnett TX 76354

COKER, CARL DAVID
PAINTER, EDUCATOR
b Greensboro, NC, Feb 8, 1928. *Study:* Art Students League with Robert Beverly Hale; Univ NC; Univ NMex with Randall Davey, Raymond Jonson, Richard Diebenkorn & Enrique Montenegro, BFA & MA; Ill State Univ, DTA. *Work:* Philbrook Mus, Tulsa; Univ Okla Mus, Norman; Jonson Gallery, Univ NMex, Albuquerque; Mus of NMex, Santa Fe; El Paso Mus Art, Tex; Internat Mus Art, El Paso Tex; US Embassy, Lima, Peru. *Comn:* Welded steel altarpiece, Holloman Air Force Hosp Chapel, USAF, 67; painting, Farmers & Merchants Bank, Tulsa, 75; fiberglass painting, 76 & welded steel sculpture, 77, Hicks Park, City of Tulsa; stainless steel sculpture (36' high) Gerald Hines Int, Redman Plaza, Tulsa OK, 83. *Exhib:* Tex Ann, Dallas Mus of Fine Arts, 60; Ill Print & Drawing Show, Art Inst Chicago, 63; Nat Drawing Show, Bucknell Univ, 65; Five NMex Artists, Pronaf Mus, Juarez, Mex, 65; NMex Sculptors, 66 & NMex Painters, 67, Mus of NMex, Santa Fe; Instituto Cult Peruano Norte Americano, 79; Galeria Forum, Lima, Peru, 80; Arte Sin Limetes, 4 cities in Mex & US. *Teaching:* Instr painting, ETex State Univ, Commerce, 56-61; asst prof painting-sculpture, NMex State Univ, Las Cruces, 64-68; prof painting, Univ Tulsa, 68-87, retired, 89; guest artist, Escuela Nacional de Bellas Artes, Lima, Peru, 79-80, Claremont Col, Calif, 84. *Awards:* Fulbright Teaching/Res Grant, Lima, Peru, 79-80; Gold Medal, Painting, El Paso Mus, 88; Best of Show, El Paso Ann, 92; Best of Show, Internat Mus Art, El Pasi, Tex, 2000. *Mem:* Taos Art Assoc; Asociacion Peruana de Artistas Plasticas. *Media:* Acrylic, Wood Sculpture. *Mailing Add:* 2250 Rosedale Las Cruces NM 88005

COLANGELO, CARMON
ADMINISTRATOR, PRINTMAKER
b Toronto, Can, Oct 29, 57. *Study:* Univ Windsor, BFA, 81; La State Univ, MFA, 83. *Work:* Fogg Art Mus, Harvard Univ; Butler Mus Am Art, Steubonville, Ohio; Nelson-Atkins Mus Art, Kansas City, Mo; Univ Minn, Minneapolis; Clemson Univ, SC; Natl Mus Am Art, Washington, DC; Whitney Mus Art, NY; Exhib prints in shows US-Korea Int, 89; Boston Printmakers 42nd, 90; silvermine Int, 92, New World Contemp Prints, Balt, 93. *Exhib:* Colorprint USA, Lubbock Fine Arts Ctr, Tex, 94; solo exhib, Philadelphia Print Club, 95; Minn Nat Print Biennial, Katherine E Nash Gallery, 96; A Thought Intercepted, Calif Mus Art, Santa Rosa, 97; Litografia Contemporanea, Museo Nacional, Buenos Aires, 97; Drawn To Stone, Kennedy Mus Art, Athens, Ohio, 98; Slovenia Print Biennial, Slovenia Graphic Art, Novomesto, 98; Allographies, Univ Mus, Indiana, Pa, 98; Blasted Impulses and Beautiful Impossibilities, Univ Deleware, Newark, Del, 2000; Re-Tracings, Univ Chapel Hill, NC, 2001; Fountains of Age, Sandler-Hudson Personal Gallery, Atlanta, Ga, 2002; Da, Da, Da, Hope St Gallery, Liverpool Contemp Biennial, Eng, 2002; Phantasmogoria, Scuola Int di Grafica, Venice, Italy, 2003; Laura Mesaros Gallery, WVa Univ, WVa, 2004; Phantasmogoria, Museo de Pueblos, Guanajuato, Mex, 2004. *Pos:* Chmn div art, WVa Univ, 93-97; dir, Sch Art, Univ Ga, Athens, 97-; Instr Louisiana State Univ, Baton Rouge; 84; asst prof art W VA Univ, Morgantown, 84-88; assoc prof, 88; dir grad studies in art, 89; assoc chair div art, 93; dir & distinguished res prof Lamar Dodd Sch Art, Athens, GA, art prof. *Teaching:* Prof printmaking, WVa Univ, 84-97 & Univ Ga, 97-. *Awards:* Judith Lieber Award, Soc Am Graphic Arts, 93; Governors Award, WVa Juried Exhib, Arts & Humanities, 95; Applebaum/Charbonnel, Minn Nat, Charbonnel Inks, 96; Senior Research Grant Fine Arts, Univ GA, 98; Distinguished Research Prof, Univ GA, 2003; Deem Distinguished Lectr, WVa, Univ, WV, 2004. *Bibliog:* E C Cunningham (auth), Printmaking: A Primary Form of Expression, Colo Press, 92; Paul Krainak (auth), Appalachian high, Art Examiner, 97; Lynn Allen & Phyllis McGibbon, Best of Printmaking, Rockport Pupl, 97; Cong Zhiyuan, The Window Overseas, Chinese Printmaking, Vol 12, 98; Joel Ginson (AUTH), Carmon Chameleon, Georgia Magazine, June 2003; Michael Slaven (auth), Phantasmogoria, Art Papers, 2004. *Mem:* Col Art Asn; Southern Graphics Coun (bd mem, 95-96); Contemp Art Ctr, Atlanta, GA; Ga Mus Art; Natl Col Art Administrators; Southern Graphics Council (bd mem, 95-97). *Publ:* Contribr, Remote Simulations, Contemp Impressions, 95. *Dealer:* Sandler-Hudson Gallery, Atlanta, GA. *Mailing Add:* Univ of GA Lamar Dodd Sch Art 100 B Visual Arts Athens GA 30602

COLANTUONO, ANTHONY
HISTORIAN
b Somerville, NJ, May 5, 58. *Study:* Rutgers Univ, BA, 80; Johns Hopkins Univ, MA, 82, PhD, 87. *Teaching:* Vis asst prog art hist, Wake Forest Univ, 88-89; asst prof, Vanderbilt Univ, 89-90; asst prof southern baroque art, Univ Md, College Park, 90-96, assoc prof 16th & 17th Century Italian, French & Spanish Art, 97-, assoc chair Art Hist & Archaeology. *Mem:* Col Art Asn; Renaissance Soc Am. *Res:* Theory and interpretation of Italian renaissance through the 17th century and Italian and French baroque art. *Interests:* 15th-17th Century European art, literature & music; theories of art, poetics, rhetoric, general cultural history, mythography, emblem literature & general iconology. *Publ:* auth, Dies Alcyoniae: The Invention of Bellini's Feast of the Gods, Art Bull, 73, 237-256, 91; auth, Interpréter Poussin: Métaphore, similarité et maniera magnifica, in: Nicolas Poussin (Acts of the International Colloquium, Paris 1994), II, 649-665, 96; auth, Guido Reni's Abduction of Helen: The Politics and Rhetoric of Painting in Seventeenth-Century Europe, Cambridge Univ Press, 97; The Mute Diplomat: Theorizing the Role of Images in 17th Century Political Negotiations, in: The Diplomacy of Art, Nuova Alfa, 2000; auth, Poussin's Osservazioni sopra la pittura: Notes or aphorisms, Studi Secenteschi, 41, 2000

COLAO, RUDOLPH
PAINTER
b Peekskill, NY, Dec 26, 27. *Study:* Art Students League, with Frank V Dumond, Edwin Dickinson & Frank Mason, 49-52. *Work:* Springville Mus, Utah. *Exhib:* Ann Exhib, Hudson Valley Art Asn, White Plains, NY, 83; Allied Artists Am, NY, 84; Nat Acad Design, NY, 84; Western Heritage Fair, Houston, Tex, 84-85; Summer Exhib, Rockport Art Asn, Mass, 88. *Teaching:* Instr drawing & painting, Art Students League, NY, 84-87; instr oil painting, Scottsdale Artists Sch, 87-88. *Awards:* Silver Medal, 81 & Gold Medal, 85, Rockport Art Asn; John Young Hunter Award, Allied Artists Am, 84. *Bibliog:* Herbert E Abrams (auth), The Teaching of Frank Dumond, Am Artist, 74; Jill Warren (auth), Rudolph Colao, Southwest Art, 82; Charles Movalli (auth), A Conversation with Rudy Colao, Am Artist, 84. *Mem:* Allied Artists NY; Knickerbocker Artists; Rockport Art Asn; Hudson Valley Art Asn. *Media:* Oil, Watercolor. *Mailing Add:* 2 South St Rockport MA 01966

COLARUSSO, CORRINE CAMILLE
PAINTER, INSTRUCTOR
b Boston, Mass, Mar 22, 52. *Study:* Yale Summer Sch Art & Music, 72; Univ Mass, BFA, 73; Tyler Sch Art, Temple Univ, Philadelphia, MFA, 75. *Exhib:* Corcoran Gallery Art, Washington, DC, 75; Inst Contemp Art, Recife, Brazil, 76; O'Kane Gallery, Univ Houston, Tex, 77; 30 Women Artists, Peachtree Ctr, Atlanta, Ga, 78; one-person show, Oglethorpe Univ, Atlanta, 78; Personal Statements: Drawing, Southeastern Ctr Contemp Art, Winston-Salem, NC, 79; Atlanta Women's Invitational, Agnes Scott Col, 79. *Teaching:* Asst drawing, Univ Mass, Amherst, 72-73; grad teaching asst, Tyler Sch Art, 74-75; fac mem found design & drawing, Atlanta Col Art, 75-, dept head found studio, currently. *Awards:* MacDowell Colony Fel, 77 & 79; Fulbright-Hayes Res Grant, India /Nepal, 78. *Mailing Add:* 1683 Johnson Rd NE Atlanta GA 30306-3148

COLBY, BILL
PRINTMAKER, PAINTER
b Beloit, Kans, Jan 8, 27. *Study:* Univ Denver, BA, 50; Univ Ill, Champaign, MA, 54. *Work:* Libr Cong, Pennell Print Collection, Washington, DC; Seattle Art Mus; Wichita Art Mus, Kans; Portland Art Mus, Ore; Tacoma Art Mus, Wash; Nat Art Acad, Hangzhou, China. *Comn:* Painting, Kilworth Chapel, Univ Puget Sound, Tacoma, Wash, 67; prints, Weyerhauser Corp, Tacoma, 82; prints, NW Print Coun, Portland, Ore, 93 & 97; prints, Everett Event Ctr, Wash, 2005. *Exhib:* State Capitol Mus, Olympia, Wash, 74, 76, 78, 80 & 91; solo exhib, Kittredge Gallery, Tacoma, 79, 87, 89, 95, 02; Art Alliance Gallery, Philadelphia, 79; Bellevue Art Mus, Wash, 79, 83 & 85; retrospective, Tacoma Art Mus, 86; Univ Hawaii, Hilo, 93; Sandpiper Gallery, Tacoma, 93, 95, 98, 00, 03, 04, 06; and others. *Teaching:* Prof printmaking, Univ

Puget Sound, Tacoma, Wash, 56-89, dir Kittredge Gallery, Univ Puget Sound, 58-65 & 83-89. *Awards:* Arts award, Pierce Co, Wash, 02. *Mem:* Am Color Print Soc, Philadelphia; Puget Sound Sumi; Tacoma Arts & Crafts Asn; NW Printmakers. *Media:* Woodcut, Etching; Acrylic, Watercolor. *Publ:* Portrait of an Artist, Pierce Co Mag, 2/82; Jet Dreams: Art of NW 50's, Univ Wash Press, Seattle, 95

COLBY, JOY HAKANSON
CRITIC
b Detroit, Mich. *Study:* Detroit Soc Arts & Crafts; Wayne State Univ, BFA; Hon Dr Fine Arts, Ctr Creative Studies, 98. *Pos:* Art critic, Detroit News, 50-. *Awards:* Art Achievement Award, 83, Wayne State Univ; Detroit Press Club Award Arts Writing, 84; Award for Achievment, Ctr for Creative Studies, 89. *Mem:* Mich Coun Arts (adv, 72-79); Detroit Coun Arts; New Detroit Inc Arts Comt; Bloomfield Hills Arts Coun. *Publ:* Auth, Art & A City, 56; Arts and Crafts in Detroit, Detroit Inst Arts, 76. *Mailing Add:* Detroit News 615 W Lafayette Detroit MI 48231

COLBY, VICTOR E
SCULPTOR, EDUCATOR
b Frankfort, Ind, Jan 5, 17. *Study:* Corcoran Sch Art; Ind Univ, AB, 48; Cornell Univ, MFA, 50. *Work:* Ithaca Col Mus; Munson-Williams-Proctor Inst, Utica, NY; St Lawrence Univ, Canton, NY; State Univ NY Col Cortland; Roberson Mus, Binghamton, NY. *Comn:* Wall sculpture, Wilson Nuclear Physics Lab, Cornell Univ, 68. *Exhib:* One-man shows, Hewitt Gallery, 58, The Contemporaries, 66 & Hartley Gallery, 74. *Teaching:* Prof sculpture, Cornell Univ, 50-82; retired. *Media:* Wood. *Mailing Add:* 642 Peru S Lansing Rd Groton NY 13073-9733

COLE, BRUCE
HISTORIAN, EDUCATOR
b Cleveland, Ohio, Aug 2, 38. *Study:* Western Reserve Univ, BA, 62; Oberlin Col, MA, 64; Bryn Mawr Col, PhD, 69. *Teaching:* Asst prof art hist, Univ Rochester, NY, 69-73; assoc prof art hist, Ind Univ, Bloomington, 73-77, prof, 77-88, distinguished prof, 88-. *Awards:* Fel, Nat Endowment Humanities, 72-73, Guggenheim, 75-76 & Am Coun Learned Soc, 79-80. *Mem:* Acad Senese degli Intronati; Nat Coun on Humanities. *Res:* Art of Renaissance Italy. *Publ:* Auth, Masaccio and the Art of Early Renaissance Florence, 80 & Sienese Painting in the Age of the Renaissance, 85, Ind Univ Press; coauth, Art of the Western World, Simon & Schuster, 89; Piero della Francesca, Harper Collins, 91; Giotto: The Scrovegni Chapel, Braziller, 93; Studies in the History of Italian Art: 1250-1550, Pindar, 96. *Mailing Add:* Dept Fine Arts Bloomington IN 47401

COLE, DONALD
PAINTER
b New York, NY, Oct 31, 30. *Study:* Bucknell Univ, BS(civil eng); Univ Iowa, MFA. *Work:* Worcester Art Mus, Mass; Portland Art Mus, Oreg. *Exhib:* One-man exhibs, Frank Marino Gallery, 81 & 82, State Univ NY, Plattsburgh, 86, Kidi Gallery, Japan, 92, Toyama Ginko, Japan, 92, Ishikawa Denki, Japan, 92 & Gallery 17, Kanazawa, 93, Nancy Hoffman Gallery, New York City, 73, 75, 78; Foster/White Gallery, Seattle, Wash, 2001; Jeffrey Moose Gallery, 2001; Gallery 070 Vashon, WA, 2004. *Teaching:* Parsons Sch Design, NY, 77-94 & Fashion Inst Technol, 83-94. *Awards:* Creative Artists Pub Serv Grant/Painting, NY State Coun Arts, 75; Nat Endowment Arts Artists Fel Grant, 78. *Bibliog:* Caril Dreyfuss McHugh (auth), Donald Cole, Arts Mag, 5/81; Ellen Lubell (auth), article in Arts Mag, 73, 75 & 78; Robert Berner (auth), Donald Cole, Arts Mag, 4/82. *Media:* Acrylic. *Dealer:* Gallery 070, 17633 Vashon Hwy, Vashon WA, 98070. *Mailing Add:* 25718 Wax Orchard Rd SW Vashon WA 98070

COLE, GRACE V
PAINTER, DRAFTSMAN
b Chicago, Ill. *Study:* École Albert du Fois with Ted Seth Jacobs, Vihiers, France; Lill St Studio, Chicago; Prairie State Col, Chicago Heights, Ill; Art Inst Chicago; Univ Chicago; pvt apprenticeships in painting, drawing & sculpture. *Work:* Bristol Meyers Gallery, Evansville, Ind; Ill Col & Trinity Episcopal Church, Jacksonville, Ill; Sigma Alpha Epsilon, Univ Tenn, Knoxville; Coe Col, Cedar Rapids, Iowa. *Comn:* 4 portraits, Scharfman Orgn, NY, 87; 1 portrait, Rockford Col, Ill, 88; 2 portraits, Episcopal Diocese of Chicago, Ill, 88; 10 portraits, Medinah Country Club, Ill, 88-90; 3 portraits, Bank of Louisville, Ind, 89-90; The MacArthur Found, Chicago, Ill, 2003. *Exhib:* Fine Art Bldg Gallery, Ill, 99-2005; Chicago Athenaeum Mus, Ill, 2000-03; Col of Lake Co, Ill, 2001; Arts Club of Chicago, Ill, 98-2005; Cahoon Mus of Am Art, 2001-06; Arts Club of Wash, DC, 2000; Univ of West Fla, 2000; Univ of Ill, Chicago, 2000; Anne Loucke Gallery, 2001-05. *Teaching:* Instr drawing & painting, Cole Studio, Chicago, 80-; instr painting, Prarie State Col, Chicago Heights, 84-95; instr painting & portraits, Suburban Fine Art Ctr, Highland Park, Ill, 90-93; instr drawing & painting, Old Town Triangle Asn, Chicago, 91-. *Awards:* Golden Apple Award, Prairie State Col, Chicago Heights, Ill, 94. *Bibliog:* Karl Moehl (auth), Illinois artist, New Art Examiner, 9/86; Chicago Tribune, 8/16/91 & 3/20/92; Star Publ, Chicago Heights, 3/19/92. *Mem:* Ill Arts Alliance, Chicago; Ill Comt for the Nat Mus of Women in the Arts, Washington, DC, (pres, 2002-03); The Arts Club, Chicago. *Media:* Oil; Drawing Materials. *Dealer:* Portraits Inc 985 Park Ave NY NY 10028; Anne Louchs Gallery, Glencoe, Ill; Fine Arts Bldg Gallery; Ellen Posture, Highland Park, Ill, Agt. *Mailing Add:* 4900 Marine Dr #311 Chicago IL 60640-7827

COLE, HAROLD DAVID
HISTORIAN, EDUCATOR
b Tulsa, Okla, Feb 28, 40. *Study:* Univ Tulsa, BA, MA(art criticism), with Alexander Hogue & Harry A Broadd; Ohio State Univ, MA(art hist), PhD, with Franklin Ludden. *Work:* Art Gallery, Univ Tulsa, Okla; Art Gallery, Baldwin-Wallace Col, Berea, Ohio; Art Gallery, Cumberland Col, Williamsburg, Ky; Art Gallery, Nicholls State Univ, Thibodaux, La. *Exhib:* 32nd Ann Springfield Ann Ten-State Exhib, Springfield Art Mus, Mo, 62; 12th Ann Own Your Own Exhib, Denver Art Mus, Colo, 68; 51st Ann May Show, Cleveland Mus Art, Ohio, 69; one-man shows, Cumberland Col, 70 & 72 & Nicholls State Univ, 71. *Collection Arranged:* Kenneth R Weedman Exhib (auth, catalog), 73. *Pos:* Mem visual art panel, Ohio Arts Coun, 77-79. *Teaching:* Prof art hist, Baldwin-Wallace Col, 66-, Malicky chair humanities, 94-. *Awards:* Special Jury Mention, Cleveland Mus Art May Show, 69; Strosacker Award for Excellence in Teaching, 77; Bechberger Award for Excellence in Counselling, 95. *Mem:* Col Art Asn; Midwest Art Hist Asn; Int Ctr Medieval Art; Monument Historique. *Res:* Thirteenth century French sculpture and architecture; 19th century French painting. *Publ:* Auth, Kenneth R Weedman Sculpture Exhibition, Crafts Horizons, 72; coauth, Grant Reynard: His Life & Work, Baldwin-Wallace Col, 75. *Mailing Add:* Baldwin Wallace Col Dept Art Berea OH 44017

COLE, HERBERT MILTON
HISTORIAN, PHOTOGRAPHER
b Newton, Mass, Apr 15, 35. *Study:* Williams Col, BA, 57; Columbia Univ, MA, 64, Columbia Univ, PhD, 68. *Collection Arranged:* African Arts of Transformation (auth, catalog), Univ Calif, Santa Barbara, 70; The Arts of Ghana (auth, catalog), Mus Cult Hist, Univ Calif, Los Angeles, 75-77; Igbo Arts: Community & Cosmos (coauth, catalog), Los Angeles, 84; Icons: Ideals & Power in the Arts of Africa (auth), Natural Mus African Art, Smithsonian Inst; Deceptive Realities: Authenticity & Quality in African Art, Univ Art Mus, Univ Calif, Santa Barbara; I Am Not Myself: The Art of African Masquerade, UCLA, 85. *Pos:* Consult ed, African Arts, Univ Calif, Los Angeles, 70-. *Teaching:* Prof African art hist, Univ Calif, Santa Barbara, 68-. *Awards:* Ford Found Foreign Area Fel, 66-67; Nat Edownment Humanities Younger Humanist Fel, 72-73; Rockefeller Sr Fel, Smithsonian Inst, 87-88. *Mem:* Col Art Asn; Arts Coun African Studies Asn. *Media:* Photography. *Res:* Arts of tropical Africa. *Publ:* Ed, African Art and Leadership, Univ Wis-Madison, 73; auth, The Arts of Ghana, Univ Calif, Los Angeles, 77; Mbari: Art and Life Among the Owerri Igbo, Ind Univ Press, 80; plus many others. *Mailing Add:* 3874 Crescent Dr Santa Barbara CA 93110-1225

COLE, JEAN (DAHL)
PAINTER
b Greeley, Colo, Jan 30, 47. *Study:* Univ Calif, Berkeley, BA(design), 68; studied with Charles Reid, Irving Shapiro, Frederic Wong, Zolton Szabo & Steve Quiller. *Work:* Leanin' Tree Mus Western Art, Boulder, Colo; Sisters Charity Health Care Systems; Clayton G Mammel Collection; Thomas Cousins Collection; Donald & Susan Sturm Collection; Philip Anchutz Collection; Storage Technology, Inc, Invesco. *Exhib:* Six on Paper, Metro State Col, Denver, Colo, 94; Watercolor West, Brea Cult Ctr, Colo, 94; Rocky Mountain Nat, Watermedia Exhib, Foothills Art Ctr, Golden, Colo, 94, 96, 98. 99 & 2002; one-man show, Arvada Ctr for the Arts & Humanities, Republic Plaza Botanica Spectaculum, Univ Northern Colo, 2000; Colo Watercolor Soc State Watermedia Exhib, Colo Hist Mus, Denver, 94, 95, 96, 98 & 99; Am Watercolor Soc, 94, 97 & 99; Watermedia VIII, Univ Colo, Colorado Springs, 96; Contemp Watermedia Invitational, Univ Southern Colo, 97; Watermedia IX, Colorado Springs Fine Art Ctr, 98; Colo Wyo Biennial, OneWest Art Ctr, Ft Collins, 98; NW Watercolor Soc Ann Open Exhib, Wash State Conv & Trade Ctr, Seattle, 98. *Pos:* Demonstrations & workshops for various art groups. *Awards:* Award for Excellence, Colo Watercolor Soc State Exhib, 97 & Pres Award, 98, 99; Merchandise Award, NW Watercolor Soc Ann Open, 98; Reed Memorial Award, Calif Watercolor Asn Watercolor Competition, 98; Best of Show, Rocky Mountain Nat, 98. *Mem:* Signature mem Nat Watercolor Soc; signature mem Colo Watercolor Soc (treas, 90-91, pres, 92); signature mem Am Watercolor Soc,; signature mem Rocky Mt Nat Watermedia Soc. *Media:* Transparent Watercolor. *Publ:* Contribr, Artist's Mag, 11/92; Spotlight, Rocky Mountain News, 12/9, 11/94 & 4/2000; Light and Shadow, 97 & Best of Watercolor 2, 97, Basic Flower Painting, Northlight, Watercolor Magic, 95-98, Rockport Publ; The Scene, Denver Post, 8/29/98. *Dealer:* Hayden Hays Gallery Colo Springs Colo 80901. *Mailing Add:* 3800 E 4th St Denver CO 80206-4558

COLE, JULIE KRAMER
PAINTER
b Springfield, Ohio, June 9, 42. *Study:* Colo State Univ, Ft Collins, 60-62; Colo Inst Art, Denver, grad, 63. *Work:* San Dimas City Hall, Calif; Home St Bank, Loveland, Colo. *Exhib:* Am Royal Western Art Show, Kansas City, 84 & 85; Governor's Western Art Show, North Platte, Nebr, 84-88; Am Indian and Cowboy Asn Show, San Dimas, Calif, 88-91; Minneapolis Western & Wildlife Show, Minn, 89, 90 & 92; Classic Am Western Art Show, Beverly Hills, Calif, 90 & 91. *Pos:* Freelance fashion illusr, 63-80; illusr, Leanin' Tree Publ Co, 84-, Antrock, 90, Johnson Creative Arts, 90 & Bradford Exchange, 92; prof western artist, Cole Fine Art Inc, 86-. *Awards:* Festival Choice, 88; Silver Medal, 89; Gold Medal, Am Indian & Cowboy Asn Show, 90; Hall of Fame, Colo Inst Art, 92. *Media:* Pastel, Gouache. *Publ:* Auth, Western Horseman, 4/89; US Art, 4/91, 3/93, 7/93, 8/93, & 3/94; Bradford Exchange, 7/93 & 11/94; Collectors Mart Mag, 7/93. *Mailing Add:* c/o The Art Co 2926 E Broadway Blvd Tucson AZ 85716-5312

COLE, MAX
PAINTER
b Hodgeman Co, Kans, Feb 14, 37. *Study:* Univ Ariz, Tucson, MFA, 64. *Work:* La Jolla Mus Contemp Art; Dallas Mus; Utah Mus; Los Angeles Co Mus; Tel Aviv Mus; Metrop Mus; and others. *Exhib:* Whitney Mus Am Art Biannual, 75; New Abstract Painting, Los Angeles Co Mus, 76; 35th Biannual, Corcoran Gallery Art, 77; one-person exhibs, Sidney Janis Gallery, NY, 77 & 79, Los Angeles Louver Gallery, 79, 80 & 83, Miami-Dade Col, 82, Cologne Art Fair, Ger, 90, Kiyo Higashi Gallery, Los Angeles, 91, 93, 94 & 95, Kunstraum, Kassel, Ger, 91 & Mus Folkwang, Essen, Ger, 92; Zabriskie Gallery, NY, 87; Galerie Helene Grubair, Miami, 88; Haines

Gallery, San Francisco, 88, 91 & 96; Stark Gallery, NY, 96; Galerie Schlegl, Zurich, 96; and others. *Teaching:* Asst prof painting, Pasadena City Col, Calif, 67-79; adj assoc prof, Columbia Univ, New York, 85-91. *Awards:* Nat Endowment Arts Fel, 83; Pollock-Krasner Fel, 86; Res Fel, Indo-US Subcommission, 88; and others. *Mailing Add:* 195 E Third St New York NY 10009

COLE, WILLIE
SCULPTOR
b Somerville, NJ, 55. *Study:* Boston Univ Sch Fine Arts, 74-75; Sch Visual Arts, New York, BFA, 76; Art Students League, New York, 76-79. *Work:* Nat Gallery Art, Washington, DC; Whitney Mus Am Art & Mus Mod Art, NY; Yale Univ Art Gallery, New Haven, Conn; Mus Contemp Art, Chicago. *Comn:* Gateway to Knowledge, Pub Div Sch Facilities, City of NY, 96; African Headrest, Dept Cult Affairs, City of Chicago, 96. *Exhib:* One-person exhibs, St Louis Art Mus, 92, The Contemp at Baltimore Mus Indust, 94, Ctr Res Contemp Art, Univ Tex, Arlington & Univ Arts, Philadelphia, 95, Mus Mod Art, NY & Birmingham Mus Am Art, Ala, 98, Morris Mus, Morristown, NJ, 99, Game Show: Installations and Sculptures, Bronx Mus of the Arts, NY 2001, Willie Cole: Before and After, Alexander and Bonin, NY, 2002; Promising Suspects (with catalog), Aldrich Mus Contemp Art, Ridgefield, Conn, 94; Archeological Urban Dada (with catalog), Whitney Mus Am Art, Champion, 95; Resonance, Roland Gibson Gallery, State Univ NY, Col Potsdam, 95; Subversive Domesticity (with catalog), Edwin A Ulrich Mus Art, Wichita State Univ, 96; Thinking Print: Books to Billboards 1980-95, Mus Mod Art, NY, 96; Sculpture from NJ, NJ Ctr Visual Arts, Summit, 96; Performance Anxiety (with catalog), Mus Contemp Art, Chicago & Mus Contemp Art, San Diego, 98; Biennial Exhib Pub Art (with catalog), Neuberger Mus Art, Purchase, NY, 97; NJ Arts Ann, Newark Mus, 97; Biennial at Ben Shaw Galleries: Lines of Direction, William Patterson Univ, Wayne, NJ, 98; Alternative Measures (with catalog), Castle Gallery, Col New Rochelle, NY, 98; group exhibs, Everything and Anything, Wave Hill, NY, 2001, The Cult of Violence, Univ Gallery, Fine Arts Ctr, Univ Mass and Bowdoin Coll Mus of Art, Mass, 2002, Shadows and Silhouettes: the Dangerous Faces of Willie Cole and Juan Logan, Memphis Coll of Art, Tenn, 2002. *Awards:* Penny McCall Found Grant, 91; Louis Comfort Tiffany Found Grant, 95; Joan Mitchell Found Award, 96; and others. *Bibliog:* Grace Glueck (auth), New concepts in printmaking 2, NY Times, 37, 7/10/98; Carol Diehl (auth), Willie Cole, Art News 97, No 1, 134, 1/98; Dan Bischoff (auth), Steam iron works make scorch in art world, Sunday Star-Ledger, Sect 4, 1, 1/17/99. *Mailing Add:* c/o Alexander & Bonin 132 Tenth Ave New York NY 10011

COLEMAN, A(LLAN) D(OUGLASS)
CRITIC, LECTURER
b New York, NY, Dec 19, 1943. *Study:* Hunter Col, Bronx, NY, BA, 64; San Francisco State Col, MA, 67; New York Univ. *Collection Arranged:* Silver Sensibilities, Snug Harbor Cultural Ctr, Staten Island, NY, 80 & Catskill Ctr Photog, 82; The Erotic in Photography: Contemporary Trends, Cameravision, Los Angeles, 82; Tisch Sch Arts, New York Univ, 85; Testimonies: Photography and Social Issues, Houston Fotofest, 90. *Pos:* Photog columnist, Latent Image, Village Voice, 68-73; photog critic, New York Times, 70-74; contrib ed, Camera 35, 75-82, Lens' on Campus, 83-87; vpres, Photog Media Inst, Inc, 77-; founder/organizer, Conf on Photog Criticism, 77-; bd dir, Photog Resource Ctr, 78-82; critic-in-residence, Int Ctr Photog, NY, 79; founding ed, Views: A New Eng J Photog, 79-81; mem bd advisors, Ctr Photog Woodstock, 82-93 & Los Angeles Ctr Photog Studies, 82-; photog critic, New York Observer, 88-97; columnist, Camera & Darkroom, 89-95, European Photog, WGer, Photo Metro, 89- & Photography in New York, Juliet Art Mag, Italy, 93-. *Teaching:* Mem fac photog criticism, New Sch Social Res, New York, 70-71, 79-81, vis lectr, Col Art, Md Inst, 71-73, Instr photog, Dept Film/TV, New York Univ, 78-82, asst prof, Dept Photog, 83-93. *Awards:* Hasselblad Found Grant, Sweden, 91; Fulbright Scholar, Sweden, 94; Writing on Photography Infinity Award, Int Ctr Photog, 95. *Bibliog:* Video interview, Video Databank, Sch Art Inst Chicago, 77; Craig Morey & Ted Hedgpeth (auths), interview, San Francisco Camerawork Newslett, 10/82; Video interview, Md Inst Col Art, 83. *Mem:* Int Asn Art Critics (exec vpres & chmn, mem comt, 87-93); Authors Guild; PEN Am Ctr; Int Soc Gen Semantics; Nat Writers Union; Am Soc Journalists & Authors. *Res:* Hist of photography, examining the impact of the invention of the lens on Western culture between 1500 to present. *Publ:* Coauth, The Photography A-V Program Directory, PMI Inc, 80; Looking at Photographs: Animals Chronicle, 95; Tarnished Silver: After the Photo Boom, 96; auth, Dept of Field: Essays on Photography, Mass Media and Lens Culture, Univ NMex Press, 98; The Digital Evolution, Nazrael Press, 98. *Mailing Add:* 465 Van Duzer St Staten Island NY 10304

COLEMAN, CONSTANCE DEPLER
PAINTER
b Macomb, Ill, Sept 9, 26. *Study:* Dominican Col, San Raphael, Calif, 45-47; Calif Sch Fine Arts, San Francisco, with Mark Rothko & David Parks, 47-49; Cincinnati Art Acad, Ohio, with Paul Chitlaw, 63-65. *Comn:* All work commissioned by private clients. *Exhib:* James Huntbarker Gallery, Palm Beach, 79; Wondrous Wildlife, Int Wildlife Juried Show, Cincinnati, Ohio, 83; A B Crosson Jr Gallery, Cincinnati, Ohio, 84; Portraits for Commission, McIntosh-Drysdale Gallery (with Gifford Myers & Bruce Sharp), Washington, DC, 86; Albion Gallery, Santa Barbara, Calif, 87; Durenberger Friends, San Juan Capistrano, 92; Waterhouse Gallery, Santa Barbara, Calif, 98-; Portraits by Artists, Beverly Hills, 98; Sarah Davenport Gallery, London, 98; Zantman Galleries, Carmel, Palm Desert, 98; William Secord Gallery, NY, 98; Carmel Art Asn, 98. *Pos:* Designer & illusr, paper products, greeting cards & wall paper, portraying animals in human situations, 49-70; "Member of the Family" gift products, 88. *Teaching:* Dir, teacher & founder, Primary Art Dept, Cincinnati Country Day Sch, Ohio, 62-68. *Bibliog:* Marcia Smith (auth), They pant for arf art, Dallas Times Herald, 5/14/84; article, Pet Portraits, Epcot Mag, Disney Cable-TV, 84; feature articles in numerous mag & newspapers incl USA Today, Los Angeles Times & Prints Mag. *Mem:* mem, Comm Art Pub Places, Carmel, Calif. *Media:* Oil, Silverpoint. *Publ:* Illusr, Joy in a Wooly Coat, H J Kramer, Inc, 89. *Dealer:* Portraits Inc 985 Park Ave New York NY 10028; Carmel Art Asn Carmel CA. *Mailing Add:* 415 Milton St Cincinnati OH 45202-0927

COLEMAN, DONNA LESLIE
PAINTER, INSTRUCTOR
b Philadelphia, Pa, Nov 16, 54. *Study:* RI Sch Design, BFA(honors), 77; Brooklyn Col, MFA, 82. *Exhib:* One-woman show, Arlington Arts Ctr, Va, 92, Gallery K, Washington, DC, 96, 00 & New Horizons Gallery, Children's Hosp, Washington, DC, 96; Options 93, Washington Proj for Arts, 93; Fashion Happening, Gallery K, Washington, DC, 98; Mather Gallery, Case Western Reserve Univ, 02; Meditated Nature, HereHere Gallery, Cleveland, Ohio, 2003; Featured Artist, Dead Horse Gallery, Cleveland, Ohio, 2003; Go Figure, Sandusky, Ohio, 2004; Vanishing Borders: Contemp Environmental Art, Herndon Gallery, Antioch Col, Yellow Springs, OH, 2006. *Pos:* Dir, Dreamcatcher Summer Arts Camp, Washington, DC, 97-. *Teaching:* Art teacher, Rye Country Day Sch, NY, 86-89, Browne Acad, Alexandria, Va, 89-98, Fillmore Arts Ctr, Washington, DC, 91-, Sidwell Friends Sch, 97-; vis ast prof of Art, Oberlin Col, 2002-; art teacher, Firelands Asn Vis Arts, 2001-. *Awards:* Grants-in-Aid, DC Comn Arts, Washington, DC, 92, 95 & 98; Fel Award, Art Matters, NY, 92 & 95; Ohio Arts Council, Indiv Artist Fel Award, 2002. *Media:* Oil on Canvas. *Res:* narrative paintings. *Mailing Add:* 22 King St Oberlin OH 44074

COLEMAN, FLOYD WILLIS
EDUCATOR, PAINTER
b Sawyerville, Ala, Jan 13, 39. *Study:* Ala State Univ, with Hayward L Oubre, BA, 60; Univ Wis, with Robert Burkert, MS, 62; Univ Ga, with Edmund B Feldman, PhD, 75. *Work:* Oakland Mus, Calif; High Mus Art, Emory Univ, Spelman Col, Atlanta Univ, Atlanta, Ga. *Exhib:* Am Drawing Ann, Norfolk Mus Arts & Sci, Va, 62; 18th Southeastern Ann, High Mus Art, Atlanta, Ga, 63; 30 Contemp Black Artists, Minneapolis Inst Arts, Minn, 68; Spiral: Afro-Am Art of the Seventies, Mus Nat Ctr Afro-Am Artists, Boston, 80; Recent Works on Paper, Last Stop Gallery, Richmond, Va, 88. *Teaching:* Asst prof, Clark Col, Atlanta, Ga, 65-71; assoc prof, Southern Ill Univ, Edwardsville, 76-80, prof, 81-83; prof & chair, Jackson State Univ, 83-87; prof & chair, Howard Univ, 87-. *Awards:* Fels, Ford Found, 68-70, Esso Found, 71 & Nat Endowment Humanities, 76-77. *Mem:* Col Art Asn Am; Nat Conf Artists (co-chmn, 70-71). *Media:* Mixed-Media on Paper. *Res:* African continuities in Afro-American art; Mexican influences on Mayan architecture; the art of Felrath Hines & the Spiral group; Black artists of the South. *Publ:* Auth, African influences on Black American art, 76 & Toward an aesthetic toughness in Afro-American art, 78, Black Art Quart; Popular images in Afro-American art, J Soc Ethnic & Special Studies, 80; coauth, Black Design: Systems, Elements, Applications, 84, Prentice-Hall. *Mailing Add:* 13014 Daley St Silver Spring MD 20906-5104

COLEMAN, GAYLE
LECTURER, CONSERVATOR
b Allentown, Pa, Mar 15, 54. *Study:* Lehigh Univ, Bethlehem, Pa, BA; Art Restoration Tech Inst, cert & apprenticeship; Nova Law Sch. *Pos:* Art conservator, Lehigh Univ, Bethlehem, Pa, 76-; freelance art restorer, Pa; partner, Coleman Art Gallery, Allentown, 76-; lectr var cols & univ. *Mem:* Am Inst for Conserv of Hist & Artistic Work; Asn for Preservation Technol; Am Bar Asn. *Res:* Microchemical analysis of art work; moral rights & art conservation. *Mailing Add:* 17216 Hampton Blvd Boca Raton FL 33496

COLEMAN, JUDY
PHOTOGRAPHER
b New York, NY. *Study:* Cornell Univ, BA, 66; Univ Calif, Los Angeles, MFA, 83. *Work:* Los Angeles Co Mus Art, Los Angeles; Bibliotheque Nationale, Paris; Art Inst Chicago; San Francisco Mus Art; Minneapolis Mus Art. *Exhib:* Celebrating Two Decades in Photog, Grunwald Ctr Graphic Arts, Frederick S Wight Art Gallery, Univ Calif, Los Angeles, 1985; Judy Coleman, G Ray Hawkins Gallery, Los Angeles, 1987; Judy Coleman & Vladimir Zidlicky, Robert Koch Gallery, San Francisco, 1988; Judy Coleman, Fay Gold Gallery, Atlanta, 1988; Judy Coleman, Laguna Mus Art, Laguna Beach, Calif, 1989; The Photog of Invention: Am Pictures of the 1980s, Nat Mus Am Art, Smithsonian Instn, Washington, & Walker Art Center, Minneapolis, 1989; Art 21 90, Basel, Switz, 1990; Judy Coleman: Photo Exhibition, Parco Gallery, Tokyo, 1990; Judy Coleman: New Work, G Ray Hawkins Gallery, Santa Monica, Calif, 1993; Nude, Spiral Hall, Tokyo & Atrium Gallery, Fukuoka, Japan, 1993-94; Painting Perspectives, Jerrold Burchman Contemp Art, Santa Barbara, Calif, 1994; Judy Coleman Retrospective, Ctr Photogr Arts, Carmel, Calif, 1996; Ten Yrs: Photog Exhibit, Ctr Photog Art, Carmel, 1999; African Nights/African Dreams, G Ray Hawkins Gallery, Los Angeles, 1999-2000; Body Work: Photographs of Nudes, Minneapolis Inst Arts, 2001. *Teaching:* Instr, Univ Calif, Los Angeles, 84-86. *Awards:* Nat Endowment Arts, Fel, 84-85 & 88-89. *Bibliog:* Judy Coleman, Twin Palms Publs, Altadena, Calif, 1989; Laguna Art Mus Exhib Catalog, 1989; The Nude and Contemporary Photography, H20 Co Ltd, Tokyo, 1994; Seven Seas Mag, Tokyo, 1999; Arts Mag of Minneapolis Inst Arts, June 2000; numerous articles and catalogs. *Media:* Gelatin Silver Prints, Oil Paint. *Dealer:* G Ray Hawkins Gallery, 300 N Crescent Heights Blvd Los Angeles Calif 90048. *Mailing Add:* 116 Quarterdeck Mall Marina Del Rey CA 90292

COLEMAN, LORING W
ARTIST
b Boston, Apr 1918. *Study:* Middlesex Sch, Grad; Scott Carbee Sch of Art, Grad, Boston. *Work:* exhib in group shows, High Art Mus, Milton Col, Mus of Fine Arts, Rep in permanent collections, Mus of Fine Arts, Parrisch Art Mus. *Exhib:* Exhibs incl Retrospective, Concord Art Assoc, Francesca Anderson Fine Art, St Botolph Club,

Central Place Galleries, Shore Galleries, exhib in group shows, Am Watercolor Soc, Knickerbocker Artists, Munson Gallery, Milton Col, Addison Gallery of Am Art, Represented in permanent collections, Salmagundi Club, Butler Inst of Am Art, Canton Art Inst, Concord Pub Libr. *Pos:* rep, Francesca Anderson Find Art, Lexington, Mass. *Teaching:* Prof, painting, sculpture Middlesex Sch. *Awards:* Salmagundi Club, Lifetime Achievement Award; recipient Strathmore Paper Co Award; Elizabeth K Ellis Artists Fel Award. *Mem:* Nat Acad (assoc, 91, acad, 94). *Mailing Add:* c/o Francesca Anderson Fine Art 56 Adams St Lexington MA 02420

COLEMAN, M L (MICHAEL LEE)
PAINTER, INSTRUCTOR
b Livingston, Mont, May 11, 41. *Study:* Univ Wyo, BS, 63; with James Disney, Loveland, Colo, 69 & 75, Hall Diteman, Billings, Mont, 77 & Wilson Hurley, Albuquerque, NMex, 85. *Work:* Northern Natural Gas, Omaha, Nebr; Iowa Beef Producers; Home Nat Banks, Arkansas City, Kansas City & Scottsdale, Ariz; JW Holmes & Assoc, Scottsdale, Ariz; Webtrend Graphics, Vista, Calif. *Exhib:* Mus Native Am Cult Art Show & Auction, Spokane, Wash, 80 & 81; Sun Valley Western Art Auction & Exhib, Idaho, 80 & 81; Stockmen's Found Art Show & Auction, Calgary & Edmonton, Alta, 81; Art of the West, Ger Mus, Munich, 81. *Teaching:* Instr workshops, Sedona, Ariz. *Awards:* Best of Show, Stockmen's Found Art Show and Auction, Calgary, Alta, 81. *Bibliog:* Kathe McGehee (auth), M L Coleman's dramatic landscapes, Art West Mag, Vol III, No 6; Dale Burk (auth), A Brush with the West, Mountain Press, 80; Peggy & Harold Samuels (auths), Contemporary Western Artists, SW Art Publ, 82. *Media:* Oil. *Dealer:* Sheri D Coleman 650 Sunset Pass Rd Sedona AZ 86351. *Mailing Add:* Sunset Pass Studios 200 Sunset Pass Rd Sedona AZ 86351-9519

COLEMAN, MICHAEL B
PAINTER
b Provo, Utah, June 25, 46. *Study:* Brigham Young Univ. *Work:* Buffalo Bill Hist Mus, Cody, Wyo; Kennedy Gallery, NY; J N Bartfield Galleries, NY; Legacy Galleries, Jackson, Wyo. *Comn:* Boone & Crockett Club; Alaska Prof Hunters Asn. *Exhib:* Springville Mus Nat; Nat Acad Western Art, Nat Cowboy Hall of Fame, Oklahoma City; Buffalo Bill Hist Ctr; Charlie Russell Mus; Kennedy Galleries; Wunderlich Gallery; Gerold Peters Gallery, Santa Fe, NMex; Artists Am, Denver; J N Bartfield Gallery, NY. *Bibliog:* Diane Cochrane (auth), Romantic Western landscapes, Am Artist, 1/75; Susan Myers (auth), Twenty American Landscape Painters; Romantic Western painter, SW Art Mag, 2/77; and others. *Media:* Oil. *Dealer:* J N Bartfield Galleries 30 W 57th St New York NY 10019. *Mailing Add:* 2822 Rolling Knolls Dr Provo UT 84604-4832

COLEN, DAN
ARTIST
b Leonia, NJ, 79. *Study:* RI Sch Design, BFA (painting), 2001. *Work:* Secrets & Cymbals, Smoke & Scissors (My Friend Dash's Wall in the Future), 2004-2006; Untitled (going, going, go.), 2005; Holy War, 2006; The Awesome Power of Nature, 2006; Rama Lama Ding Dong, 2006; Untitled (Vete al Diablo), 2006. *Exhib:* solo exhibs, Seven Days Always Seemed Like A Bit of An Exaggeration, Rivington Arms, NY, 2003; Potty Mouth, Potty War, Pot Roast, Pot is a Reality Kick, Gagosian Gallery, NY, 2006; Secrets & Cymbals, Smoke & Scissors (My Friend Dash's Wall in the Future), Peres Projects, Los Angeles, 2006; group exhibs, First Show, Rivington Arms, NY, 2002; Art Works for Hard Money, Gavin Brown's Enterprise, 2003; Galerie du Jour, Paris; The Armory Show with Peres Projects, NY, 2005; Bridge Freezes Before Road, Barbara Gladstone Gallery, 2005; Interstate, Nicole Klagsbrun Gallery, NY, 2005; Whitney Biennial, Day for Night, Whitney Mus Am Art, NY, 2006; Infinate Painting with Villa Manin-Centre for Contemp Art, Passariano, Codroipo, Ital, 2006; Axis of Praxis, Midway Contemp Art, Minneapolis, Minn, 2006; USA Today, Royal Accad Arts, London, 2006; Fantastic Politics, Nat Mus Art, Architecture & Design, Oslo, Norway, 2006. *Media:* Mixed Media. *Mailing Add:* c/o Rivington Arms 102 Rivington st New York NY 10002

COLES, THELMA
EDUCATOR
b Portsmouth, Va, Aug 18, 52. *Study:* San Diego State Univ. *Exhib:* San Antonio Mus Art, Tex, 89; Mus Art, Univ Tex, El Paso, 89; Univ Southern Ill, Carbondale, 89; Yuma Art Ctr, 90. *Teaching:* Assoc prof art, Univ Tex, Austin, 78. *Awards:* Nat Endowment Arts, 77, 80, 84 & 86. *Publ:* Auth, The Art of Tenuous Affils, Matchsmith, Vol 6, No 3, summer 86. *Mailing Add:* Art Dept Univ Tex Art 3 338 Austin TX 78712

COLESCOTT, ROBERT H
PAINTER, EDUCATOR
b Oakland, Calif, Aug 26, 25. *Study:* Univ Calif, Berkeley, BA, 49 & MA, 52; with Fernard Leger, Paris, France, 49-50; San Francisco Art Inst, hon DFA, 94. *Hon Degrees:* Md Inst, Col of Art, DFA; San Francisco Art Inst, DFA, 94. *Work:* Metrop Mus Art, Whitney Mus & Mus Mod Art, NY; Seattle Art Mus, Wash; San Francisco Mus Mod Art; Boston Mus Fine Art, Mass; Corcoran Gallery Art, Washington, DC; and others. *Exhib:* Art About Art, 78 & Biennial 83 & 84, Whitney Mus, NY; solo exhibs, Phyllis Kind Gallery, NY & Chicago, 87, 89, 90, 91, 94, 98 & 2000, Recent Paintings, Greg Kucera Gallery, Seattle, Wash & Univ Tex, El Paso, 89, Arthur Roger Gallery, New Orleans, 90, New Work, Howard Yezerski Gallery, Boston, 90 & 98, Linda Cathcart Gallery, Los Angeles, Calif, 90 & 93, Recent Work, Univ Colo Mus, Boulder, 91, N'Namdi Gallery, Chicago, 99 & 2000; Black USA, Overholland Mus, Amsterdam, 90; The Art Advocacy, Aldrich Mus Art, Ridgefield, Conn, 91; Black Male, Whitney Mus, NY, 93; A Portrait of Our Times: An Introduction to the Logan Collection, San Francisco Mus Mod Art, Calif, 98-99; retrospective, (traveling) Walker Art Ctr, Mpls, Queens Mus of Art, Queens, NY, Univ of Ariz Mus, Tucson, Portland Art Mus, Oreg, Univ of Calif, Berkeley Art Mus, Sheldon Mem Art Gallery & Sculpture Garden, Univ of Nebr, SITE, Sante Fe, 1998-2000; Looking Forward, Looking Black, Mus of Elaine L Jacob Gallery, Wayne State Univ, Mich, 99; Refining the Imagination: Tradition, Collecting and the Vassar Educ, Frances Lehman Loeb Art Ctr, Bassar Col, Poughkeepsie, NY, 99; Strength and Diversity: A Celebration of African-Am Artists, Carpenter Ctr, Harvard Univ, Mass, 2000; Self Made Men, DC Moore Gallery, 2001; Humor and Rage, Pundacio Caixa Catalunya, 2001. *Pos:* Artist-in-residence, Am Res Ctr, Egypt, 64-65; mem artists adv bd, New Mus of Contemp Art, 85-88; panelist, NEA Award Grants in Painting, Washington, DC, 82. *Teaching:* Assoc prof drawing & art educ, Portland State Univ, Ore, 57-66; assoc prof painting, Am Univ, Cairo, 66-67; prof art, Calif State Col, Stanislaus, 70-74, Univ Ariz, 88-89; lectr, Univ Calif, Berkeley, 74-79; instr, San Francisco Art Inst, 79-85; vis artist, Univ Ariz, Tucson, 83- & prof art, 85-90, regents prof art, 90-98, emer prof, 98-; lectr, numerous mus, workshops and univs, 74-. *Awards:* Nat Endowment Arts Grant for Creative Painting, 76, 80 & 83; Guggenheim Found Fel, 85; Celebration of Influential Artists of Our Time Honor, Artfair/Seattle, 97; Artist/Teacher of the Year Award, Nat Coun of Arts Adminrs, 93; Fel, John Simon Guggenheim Found, 85; Robert Colescott Day Honor, Houston, 89; Grant, Mary Walsh Sharpe Found, 91. *Bibliog:* Davis Alam (auth), History Reawakened and Revisited by Artist, Colo Daily, 1/22/91; Brooks Adams (auth), Robert Colescott at Phyllis Kind, Art in Am, 7/91; Fay Hirsch (auth), Ecole de Paris is Burning, Arts Mag, 9/91. *Mem:* Nat Acad. *Media:* Mixed. *Publ:* Auth, The Reimaging of America, New Society Publishers, 90

COLESCOTT, WARRINGTON W
PRINTMAKER, PAINTER
b Oakland, Calif, Mar 7, 21. *Study:* Univ Calif, Berkeley, BA & MA; Acad Grande Chaumiere, Paris; Slade Sch Art, Univ Col, London. *Work:* Metrop Mus Art, Mus Mod Art, NY; Brooklyn Mus, NY; Art Inst Chicago; Nat Collection Art, Smithsonian Inst, Washington; Milwaukee Art Mus, Wis; Whitney Mus Am Art; Chasen Mus Art, Madison, Wis. *Comn:* Milwaukee Art Mus Print Forum, 96, 2001; Albany NY Print Club, 96; Color print USA, 98; NY Print Club, 2002. *Exhib:* Biennial Int, Ljubljana, Yugoslavia, 81, 83, 85 & 87; one-man shows, Tampa Mus Art, 87, Perimeter Gallery, Chicago, 88, 91, 93, 95, 98, 2002 & 40 Yrs of Printmaking, Elvehjem Mus, Univ Wis, 88; Warrington Colescott Retrospective, Univ SDak Galleries, 92; Art Galleries, State Univ NY, Albany, 95; Milwaukee Art Mus, 96, 2001 & 06; Int Print Triennial Crakow, Poland, 97; Integrafia 200, Poland; Macau Int Prints, 2000; 10th Int Print Biennial, Varna, Bulgaria, 99; Millenium Grafica, Yokohama & Taipei, 2000. *Pos:* Co-dir, Mantegna Press, Hollandale, Wis. *Teaching:* Prof art, Univ Wis, Madison, 49-86, Leo Steppart chair prof, 79-84, prof emer, dept art, 86-; Richard Koopman Distinguished chair visual arts, Hartford Art Sch, Conn, 94-95. *Awards:* Guggenheim Fel, 65; Nat Endowment Arts Artists Fel, 76, 79, 83-84 & 93-94; Fulbright Fel, 57-58; Emer printmaker, Southern Graphics Coun, 1991; Major award, Int Print Triennial Krakow, 1997. *Bibliog:* EC Cunningham (auth), Printmaking, Univ Colo Press, 91; Tim Porges (auth), New Art Examiner, 5/95; Pat Gilmour (auth), Warrington Colescott, Milwaukee Art Mus, 96; and others. *Mem:* Fel Wis Acad Sci, Arts & Lett; Mid Am Print Counc; Am Print Alliance; Nat Acad Design (assoc, 91, acad, 92). *Media:* Etching; Painting on Paper. *Publ:* Illusr, Death in Venice, Aquarius Press, 71; illusr (covers), 30 Years of Printmaking, Brooklyn Mus, 76 & Art News Mag, 3/77; illusr, Since Man Began to Eat Himself, Perishable Press, Mt Horeb, Wis, 85; Improvisations, Dieu Donne Press, NY, 92; interview & comnd print, Contemp Impressions, vol 10 no 1, Spring 2002; co-auth (with Arthur Howe), Progressive Printmakers: Wisconsin Prtists and the Print Renaissance, Univ Wis Press, 1999. *Dealer:* Peltz Gallery 1119 E Knapp St Milwaukee WI 53202; Perimeter Gallery 210 W Superior St Chicago IL 60610; Grace Chosy Gallery Madison Wis. *Mailing Add:* 8788 County Rd A Hollandale WI 53544-9423

COLETTE, S
CONCEPTUAL ARTIST, SCULPTOR
b Borain-Tunis, Tunisia, Oct 8, 53; US citizen. *Study:* Self taught. *Work:* Ludwig Mus, Cologne, Ger; Brooklyn Mus, NY; Mus Contemp Art & Newport Harbor Mus, Los Angeles; Gugenheim Mus, NY; Aldrich Mus, Conn; Weatherspoon Art Mus, NC. *Exhib:* Norton Mus, Fla, 74; Camille (installation & sculpture), Mus Mod Art, NY & Paris Biennale, 77; Out of the House, The Last Stitch (installation), Whitney Mus Am Art, NY, 78; Mus Contemp Art, Houston, 81; one-woman retrospective, 10-years of work, Kunstverein-Munster, Ger, 81, Ludwig Mus, Cologne, Ger, 86; Mus Mod Art, Vienna, 81; Mus Mod Contemp Art, NY, 90; one-woman shows, Rempire Gallery & Dorsky Gallery, NY, Galerie Bodenshatz, Basel, 91, House of Olympia, 95, Eugenia Cucalon Gallery, NY, 96, Le Salon de la Refusee, Girshwin Hotel Gallery, NY, 97 & Carol Johnssen Gallery, Munich, Ger, 97; The Nude Photograph (traveling exhib), Ludwig Mus, Cologne, Munich, Hamburg & Berlin, 91; Fla Int Univ Art Mus, Miami, 93; Model Home Exhib, Mus Contemp Art & Mus Contemp Crafts, Lausanne, Switz, 95; Newport Harbor Mus, Los Angeles, 95; Intersection/the social and the personal, Mus Contemp Art, Los Angeles, 95 & 96; Constructed Photographs, Ludwig Mus, Cologne, 95; Art/Fashion, Guggenheim Mus, NY, 97; Sex Industry, Stux Gallery, NY, 97; Modular Composite, Cent Fine Arts Gallery, NY, 98; and others. *Teaching:* Instr painting, NY Univ, 83; guest prof sculpture, Yale Univ, Conn, 87; guest prof multi media, Inst Chicago, 87, Banff Ctr, Can, 85-87, Univ NC, 92. *Awards:* Creative Artists Pub Svc Prog Grant, 76; Mixed Media Grant, Nat Endowment Arts, 77 & Sculpture Grant, 86; Ger Acad Exchange Service Grant, Berlin, 84. *Bibliog:* Charlie Khearn (dir), short film, 95; Paul Shinkell (dir), Colette the Artist (doc), 93; Colette - New Paintings & Works (monogr), Kammerer, 85. *Media:* Mixed Media. *Mailing Add:* House of Olympia 213 Pearl St New York NY 10038

COLINA, ARMANDO G
GALLERY DIRECTOR, EDITOR
b Veracruz, Mex, Mar 30, 35. *Study:* Univ Mex, BA. *Exhib:* Zoologia Fantastica Homenaje A Jorge Luis Borges, Inst Artes Graficas De Oaxaca, Mex, 12/3/99-3/9/2000, Casa De Am, Madrid, Spain, 5/5-6/4/2000, Centro Cult Circulo De Arte, Barcelona, Spain, 7/26-9/11/2000; La Vitalidad De Un Artista, Kunstforeningen, Copenhague, Denmark, 11/27/99-2/27/2000, Helsinki City Art Mus, Finland, 3/31-5/28/2000; Homenaje Al Lapiz, Mus Jose Luis Cuevas, Mex, 12/9/99-3/9/2000; Sol Y Vida Mexican Modern Art: 1900-1950, Nat Gallery of Can, 2/24-5/17/2000; Francisco Toledo, Whitechapel Art Gallery, Londres, 4/14-6/7/2000, Mus Nat De Arte Reina Sofia, Madrid, Spain, 6/20-6/28/2000. *Collection Arranged:* Francisco Zuniga: Ten Years of Graphic Work, Montreal, New York & Wash, 84; Itinerant exhib 17 mus throughout world, 85-94; Carlos Merida: An Hommage, Museo de Arte Moderno, Guatemala; Imagen de Mex: Frankfurt Kunsthalle, Vienna & Dallas, Tex, 87; Art in Latin Am: London, Stockholm & Madrid, 87-88; Remedios Varo, Madrid & Monterrey, Mex, 88-89; Francisco Toledo, Homage to Jorge Luis Borges, Fantastic Zoology; Frida Kahlo, Japan & Australia, 89-90; Un panorama del Arte Mex, Inst Cult Mex, Washington, 90; Mex Masters, CDS Gallery, NY, 90; V Triennale Klein-plastik, Fellbach, Ger & Wilhelm Lehmbruck Mus, Duisburg, Ger, 92; Nat Homage to Carlos Merida, Fine Arts Palace Mus, Mus de Monterrey, Mex, 92-93; Voces de Ultramar, Las Palmas de Gran Canaria & Madrid, 92; The World of Frida Kahlo, Schirn Kunsthalle, Frankfurt, Ger, Mus Fine Arts, Houston, Tex, Hague, Holland, 93; V Trienale of Small Scale Sculpture, Fellbach, Ger & Wilhelm Lembruck Mus, Duisburg, Ger, 93; Bilder un Visionen, Mexikanische Kunst zwichen Avantgarde und Aktualltat, Mus Wurth, Kunzelsau, Santiago de Compostela, Spain & Dusseldorf, Kunsthalle, Ger, 95-96; Siqueiros/Pollack Pollack/Siqueiros, Dusseldorf, Kunsthalle, Ger, 95. *Pos:* Art consult, currently; owner, Arvil Art Gallery, currently; trustee, Mus Monterrey, NL, Mex; Museo Arte Contemporaneo, Oaxaca, Mex; art advisor & appraiser to Secretaria de Hacienda y Credito Pub, Mex; greeting card oper consult, Unicef, 92-93; mem, Visual Arts Comt, INBA, Mex. *Awards:* Europalia Mexico, 93. *Mem:* Asn Mex Comerciantes Arte & Anticuarios (pres, 96). *Specialty:* Contemporary Latin American & Mexican art. *Publ:* Arte Precolombino de Mex, 88; The World of Frida Kahlo, 93; Homenaje Nacional a Carlos Merida, 93; Siqueiros, El lugar de la utopia, 94; Imagenes y Visiones, arte mexicano entre la vanguardia y la actualidad, 96. *Mailing Add:* c/o Galeria Arvil SA Cerrada de Hamburgo No 9 Mexico 6 DF Mexico

COLKER, EDWARD
PAINTER, GRAPHIC ARTIST
b Philadelphia, Pa, Jan 5, 27. *Study:* Philadelphia Col Art, grad; NY Univ, BS & MA; spec study with E&J Desjobert, Paris. *Work:* Mus Art, Philadelphia; Univ Ariz, Tucson; NY Pub Libr Print Collection; Mus Mod Art, NY; NY Univ; and others. *Comn:* Lithography ed, Print Club, Philadelphia, 66, Int Graphic Art Soc, NY, 66 & 69 & Ill Arts Coun, 73; Edition for Print Club of NY, 2004. *Exhib:* Philadelphia Mus Art, 67; Am Art Today, Pa Acad Fine Arts, 68; solo exhibs, Kenyon Gallery, Chicago, 75, Neuberger Mus, Purchase, NY, 85-86 & Univ Ill, Chicago, 86; Nat Collection Fine Arts, Washington, DC, 77; Works on Paper, Yugoslavia, 82; Univ of Arts, 86; State Univ NY, Albany, 90; Cooper Union, 93; Univ Ariz, 98-99; Bates Col Mus Art, Lewiston, Maine, 98-99; Neuberger Mus Art, State Univ NY, Purchase, 98-99; Poets House, NY, 2003. *Collection Arranged:* FMC Collection, 20th Century Mus Art, 74-75. *Pos:* consult, Works on Paper, US Int Commun Agency, 82; Natl Endowment for the Arts, 80, 88. *Teaching:* Assoc prof fine arts, Univ Pa Grad Sch Fine Arts, 68-70; prof & dir, Sch Art & Design, Univ Ill, Chicago Circle, 72-78, res prof art, 77-80; dean, visual arts, State Univ NY, Purchase, 80-85; chmn dept art, Cornell Univ, 85-86; provost, Univ Arts, 86-91, Cooper Union, 91-95 & Pratt Inst, 95-98, 2003. *Awards:* Guggenheim Fel, 61; Univ Ill Res Bd, 77; Graham Found, 77; R Florsheim Art Fund, 97. *Bibliog:* Zigrosser (auth), The Appeal of Prints (appreciation), 70; introd essay In: New York Landscape, 81; Five Decades in Print, 98. *Mem:* Col Art Asn Am; Caxton Club; Ctr for Bk Arts; Grolier Club. *Publ:* Contribr, The Fall (lithos), 77; From South Dakota (lithos), 78; Aesthetique du Rale (lithos), 78; Selections, Essay on Nature, Emerson, Sky at Ashland, Anania (lithos), 85; All Souls (lithos), Norris, 93; Sutzkever, Beneath the Trees, 2004. *Mailing Add:* 512 Millwood Rd New York NY 10549

COLLADO, LISA
COLLAGE ARTIST, ASSEMBLAGE ARTIST
b Washington, DC, June 24, 44. *Study:* Radcliffe Col, 62-63; Art Students League, with Edward Giobbi, Leo Manso & Xavier Gonzales 78-80; Empire State Col, State Univ NY, BA, 85; NY Univ, MA, 93. *Work:* Adirondack Community Col, Queensbury, NY; Everson Mus Art, Syracuse, NY; Wash Co Mus Fine Arts, Hagerstown, Mass; New Eng Community of Contemp Artists, Brooklyn, Conn; Casa Argentina en Tierra Santa, Jerusalem. *Comn:* Hist placque, Egyptian Tourist Off, NY, 86; biog in collage, F Aley Allen, NY, 86; Ode to Black (portrait), Hist Month, 99; glass sculpture, comn by Nasser Al Nassir, NY, 89; Art Gallery, Saratoga County Coun of Art, Saratoga Springs, NY. *Exhib:* Diana Fever, The Emerging Collector, NY, 90; Women Artists Series, Rutgers Univ, NJ, 96; World Youth Summit-Peace Agenda, St Ulrich bei Steyr, Austria, 96; Galerie pro arte Kasper, Morges, Switz, 96 & 2004; Global Art Project, Tucson, Ariz, 98, 2002 & 2006; Alchemy, Nabisco Brands Gallery, East Hanover, NJ, 2000; Blue, City Without Walls Gallery, Newark, NJ, 2001; Cathedral Center for the Arts, Phoenix, Ariz, 2005; Karpetes Manuscript Mus, 2006. *Pos:* Lectr, Nat Asn Women Artists traveling Painting Exhib; organizer, Nat Asn Women Artists; cur, Collage Insights, NY, 2003. *Awards:* Hontense Fern Mem Award, 2000; Florence B Anderson Mem Award, 1996 & 2003; Prix due Pub, section Art Brut, Singulier et Insolite, 2004. *Bibliog:* Cynthia Maris Dantzic (auth), Design Dimensions: An Introduction to the Visual Surface, Prentice-Hall, 89; Cynthia Maris Dantzic (auth), 100 NY Painters, Schiffer, 2006. *Mem:* Nat Asn Women Artists; Nat Collage Soc; Lower Adriondack Regional Art Coun. *Media:* Acrylic, Mixed Media, Collage. *Specialty:* Collage. *Interests:* Classical music, reading, helping women artists in their careers. *Collection:* Estate of Willen de Kooning, NY; June Kelly, NY; Jahia Halim, Cairo, Egypt. *Publ:* Coauth article on Nasser Ovissi, Editorial La Gran Enciclopedia Vasca, 88. *Mailing Add:* 28 King Street Warrensburg NY 12885

COLLENS, DAVID R
DIRECTOR, CURATOR
Study: Franklin Pierce Col, BA (Am lit), 69; studies in print making, New York, 71-72; studies in art hist, New Sch Social Res, New York, 72-73. *Collection Arranged:* David Smith, 76; Alexander Liberman, 77; Anthony Caro, 81; Mark di Suvero, 25 Years of Sculpture and Drawings, 85; The Reemergent Figure - Seven Sculptors, Storm King Art Ctr, 87; William Tucker: The American Decade 78-88, 88; Alexander Calder: Five Grand Stabiles, 88; Wandering Into Memory: Sculpture by Anne and Patrick Poirier, 89; Complex Visions: Sculpture and Drawings by Alice Aycock, 90; Enclosures and Encounters: Architectural Aspects of Recent Sculpture, 91; Ursula von Rydingsvard: Sculpture, 92; Siah Armajani: Recent Work, 93; Mia Westerlund Roosen: Sculpture and Drawings, 94; Mark di Suvero, 95, 96; The Fields of David Smith, 97-99 (auth, catalog, 96); Andy Goldsworthy, Storm King Art Ctr, 2000; Grand Institutions: Calder's Monumental Sculptures, 2001-2003, (auth, catalog, 03); Chakaia Booker, Storm King Art Ctr, 2004; Richard Bellamy & Mark di Suvero, 2005-2006, (auth, catalog, 06). *Pos:* dir, chief cur Storm King Art Ctr, Mountainville, NY, 74-, bd trustees, 74-; adjudicator, Winston-Salem Univ Sculpture Garden Contest, NC, 83; mem arts adv comt, Metrop Transportation Authority, New York, 85-94. *Mem:* AAM. *Publ:* contribr, Sculpture at Storm King, 80, A Landscape for Modern Sculpture: Storm King Art Ctr, 85; co-auth, Mark di Suvero at Storm King Art Ctr, Abrams, 96; contribr, The Fields of David Smith, 99, Earth, Sky and Sculpture, Storm King Art Ctr, 2000; contribr, Calder, Storm King Art Ctr, 2003; contribr, Richard Bellamy & Mark di Suervo, Storm King Art Ctr, 2006. *Mailing Add:* Storm King Art Ctr Old Pleasant Hill Rd PO Box 280 Mountainville NY 10953-0280

COLLERY, PAULA
PAINTER
b Glen Cove, NY, Dec 15, 54. *Study:* Tyler Sch Art, Temple Univ, Philadelphia, BFA(painting & photog), 79. *Exhib:* Solo exhibs, Gracie Mansion Gallery, 83 & Germans Van Eck Gallery, 85, NY, Gallery Six to Six, 87; Hats Off, New Mus, NY, 83; Totem Show, NY, 84; Chill Out, Kenkeleba Gallery, NY, 84; Bernice Steinbaum Gallery, NY, 84; Harm Bouchaert Gallery, NY, 85; Edinburgh Festival, Scotland, 85; Group nude show, Gallery Six to Six, NY, 90; Starving Artist Cookbook, Dooley Le Cappellaine Gallery, NY, 92; group exhibs, Maxfish, NY, 95, Hayday, E Village artist from the 80's, Life Cafe, NY, 98, Starving Artist Cookbook, video series, Anthology Film Archives, NY, 2001, Reaction, EXITART, NY, 2002. *Awards:* Art Fel Residency Va Ctr Arts, 88, Cummington, 85; MacDowell Colony Residency, 84, 85; Konstepedemin Residency, Gothenberg, Sweden, 2000. *Bibliog:* David Herhkovits (auth), Art in Alphabetland, Art News, 9/83; Ted Castle (auth), article, Art Monthly, London, 83; Vivien Raynor (auth), article, New York Times, 2/84; George Dellea (auth), Starving Artists, New York Times, Style Sect, 5/1992. *Mem:* AAM. *Media:* Oil. *Mailing Add:* 100 St Mark's Pl No 3 New York NY 10009

COLLIER, ANNA
PHOTOGRAPHER
b Los Angeles, 1970. *Study:* Calif Inst Arts, Valencia, Calif, BFA, 93; Univ Calif, LA, MFA, 2001. *Exhib:* Solo shows include One to One, Three Day Weekend, Los Angeles, 95, Inst Visual Arts, Univ Wis, 98, MARCH FOXX, West Gallery, Los Angeles, 2001, 2002, Jack Hanley Gallery, San Francisco, 2004; group shows include LACE video screening of LA video artists, 93; Summer Group Show, Three Day Weekend, LA, 94, Thanks! 94, Dave's Not Here, 95; Art Dogs, George's, Calif, 2000; Summer Group Show,Goldman Tevis, 2000; I Want More, Temple Bar Gallery, Dublin, Ireland, 2001; New Wight Art Gallery, UCLA, 2001; MARC FOXX, 2001, 2002, 2003; A Show That Will Show That a Show Is Not Only a Show, The Project, 2002; Bay Area Now III, Yerba Buena Ctr Arts, San Francisco, Calif, 2002; Portraiture, Karyn Lovegrove Gallery, Calif, 2003; Makeshift World, Stephen Wirtz Gallery, San Francisco, Calif, 2003; 17 Reasons, Jack Henley Gallery, 2003; Nicole Klagsbrun Gallery, NY, 2004; Whitney Biennial: Day for Night, Whitney Mus Am Art, 2006; represented in collections of San Francisco Mus Modern Art, Mus Contemp Art San Diego, La Jolla, Calif, LA County Mus Art. *Teaching:* Vis faculty Art Ctr, Pasadena, Calif, 2002-2003, Calif Col Arts, San Francisco, 2002-, new genres dept San Francisco Art Inst, Calif, 2003. *Mailing Add:* c/o MARC FOXX Gallery 6150 Wilshire Blvd Los Angeles CA 90048

COLLINGS, BETTY
SCULPTOR, WRITER
b Wanganui, NZ, Jan 15, 34. *Study:* Ohio State Univ, BFA, 71, MFA, 74. *Work:* Israel Mus. *Exhib:* Solo shows, Urdang Gallery, 79, 80, 83, 89 & 90, Antioch Univ, 82, Grad Ctr, City Univ NY, 83 & Ukraine Union Artists, Kiev, 92, Castleton Col, 94; Carnegie Gallery, Ky, 2004; TAO III, Ohio Wesleyan Univ, 89; The Figure's Edge, Akron Univ, 92; Art League Invitational, Ft Hayes, 92; Celebrating Our Own, Arlington, 93; Castleton Col, 94 & 97; TAO VI, 97; Seeing Abstractly, Va Cult Arts Comn, 97; Action Replay: Post Object Art, Artspace & Govett Brewster Gallery, NZ, 98; Convergence VI, Providence, RI, 98; Carnegie Art Center, 2003-06; Contemp Art & The Matlenatical Instinet, Tweed Mus 2004. *Collection Arranged:* Contemp Collection of Ohio State Univ, 75-80. *Pos:* Dir, Ohio State Univ, Gallery Fine Arts, 74-80, ed acquisitions, 76-78; consult, Oberlin Col, 81-82; invited cur, Wright State Univ, 81, Va Commonwealth Univ, 82, Bard Col, 82 & Cleveland Ctr Contemp Art 85; Int exhib consult, Ohio Arts Coun, China, 88; cur, Ohio-Shaaanxi Exchange, 90-91, Kiev-US exchange, 92-93; cur & prog dir, Artists Org, 97; dir, Artists On Art, 2002-. *Awards:* Distinguished Service Award, Art League, 80; Sculpture Fel, 81-82 &

Critism Fel, 83-84, Ohio Arts Coun; Eight Misc Awards for Sculpture, 76-90; Distinguished Serv Award, Ohio Dept Nat Resources, 98. *Bibliog:* Roberta Smith (auth), article, NY Times, 12/22/89; V Watson Jones (auth), American Women Sculptors, Oryx Press, 90; N & J Heller (auths), An Ency of 20th Century American Women Artists, Garland, 93. *Mem:* Int Asn Art Critics; Artists' Orgn (pres, 85-87, dir prog, 87-). *Media:* Plastic, Clay, Bronze. *Interests:* science, gardening. *Publ:* Auth, Sculptural Views on Perceptual Ambiguity: Thomas Macaulay 1968-1986 (catalog), Dayton Art Inst, 86; Shaanxi-Ohio (posterlogue), The Artists Orgn, 90; Akio Hizume's Democracy Steps for Cedar Falls, TAO posterlogue, 97. *Mailing Add:* 1991 Hillside Dr Upper Arlington OH 43221

COLLINS, DAN (DANIEL) MCCLELLAN
PAINTER
b Los Angeles, Calif, Aug 20, 54. *Study:* Ark State Univ, 76; Santa Monica Col, AA, 79; Art Center Col Design, Los Angeles, BFA, 83. *Comn:* Franklin & Argyle, Hollywood C of C, 86. *Exhib:* Mus Sci & Indust, Ontario, Calif, 83; Hollywood-Inside & Out, Los Angeles Munic Art Gallery, 86; Small Works, Jose Drudis-Biada Gallery, Los Angeles, 87; group exhib, Mus Neon Art, Los Angeles, 88. *Pos:* Dir-cur, Goski Gallery, Los Angeles, 84-86. *Media:* Wood, Oil. *Mailing Add:* c/o Lisa Sette Gallery 4142 N Marshall Way Scottsdale AZ 85251

COLLINS, HARVEY ARNOLD
MURALIST, EDUCATOR
b High Springs, Fla, Aug 22, 27. *Study:* Univ Fla, with Fletcher Martin, BFA, 51; MFA, 52; LHD, 82. *Comn:* All Faiths Mural, St; 75 Year History of Olivet Col (mural), Bourbonnais, Ill, 82; mural, Nazarene Publ House, Kansas City, Mo, 83; Weakley Mem Mural, Bradley Pub Libr, Ill. *Pos:* Chmn dept art, Olivet Nazarene Univ, Bourbonnais, Ill, 71-91. *Teaching:* Instr painting, drawing & ceramics, Largo Jr High Sch, Fla, 58-71; prof painting & art hist, Olivet Univ, Bourbonnais, Ill, 71-91; art instr, Santa Fe Community Col, Gainesville, Fla. *Bibliog:* 75th Anniversary Mural (exhib catalog), Nazarene Publ House, Kansas City, Mo, 1/84. *Mem:* Mid-Am Col Art Asn; Nat Coun Art Adminr; Nat Art Educ Asn. *Media:* Acrylics, Oils

COLLINS, HOWARD F
HISTORIAN
b Buffalo, NY, Oct 28, 22. *Study:* Albright Art Sch, Buffalo, with Charles Burchfield, Ralston Crawford & Isaac Soyer, dipl, 43; State Univ NY Col, Buffalo, BS, 47; Columbia Univ, MA, 54; Univ Pittsburgh, with William S Heckscher & Charles Seymour Jr, PhD, 70. *Teaching:* Assoc prof art hist, Kutztown State Col, 60-65; from assoc prof to prof, WVa Univ, 65-72, chmn div art, 69-71; prof, Univ Nebr, Lincoln, 72-. *Mem:* Col Art Asn Am; Mid-Am Col Art Asn; Renaissance Soc Am; assoc Int Inst Conservation; Asn Historians Am Art. *Res:* Fifteenth century Venetian painting. *Publ:* Major narrative paintings by Jacopo Bellini, Art Bull, 9/82; The Cyclopean Vision of Jacopo Bellini, Pantheon, 82; Time, space and Gentile Bellini's Miracle of the Cross at Ponte S Lorenzo, Gazette Beaux Arts, 12/82; Pictorial space in Donatello's relief panels on the high altar of the santo in Padua, Arte Veneta, XLII, 87; The Decagonal Temples of Jacopo Bellini, Paragone, 9/90. *Mailing Add:* 1930 C St Lincoln NE 68502-1649

COLLINS, JIM
SCULPTOR, COLLAGE ARTIST
b Huntington, WVa, Sept 12, 34. *Study:* Marshall Univ, AB, 57; Univ Mich, Ann Arbor, MPH, 61; Ohio Univ, MFA, 66. *Work:* Tenn Aquarium, Chattanooga; City of Chattanooga; Milwaukee Art Ctr, Wis; Tenn State Mus, Tenn; River Gallery Sculpture Garden, Chattanooga, Tenn. *Comn:* Volumes (stainless steel fountain), Bicentennila Libr, Chattahooga, 2001; The Community (stainless steel), Sheriff's Bldg, Rockland Co, NY, 2002; Football Watcher, Stainless Steel and Powder-coat, Mattoon HS, Mattoon, Ill, 2003; Limerick Herd, 32 Silhouettes of life-sized animals, powder-coat aluminum, four sites along dual carriageways in Co Limerick, Ireland, 2004; Three Cows, powder-coated aluminum, Art Dist, Chatanooga, Tenn, 2004. *Exhib:* Art of Tennessee, A survey of Visual Arts Through Time and in Every Region of the State, First Ctr of Vis Arts, Nashville, TN, 2003; Watchers, Ten Sculptures by Invitation, Kilkenny Arts Festival, Kilkenny, Ireland; 4th Ann NC Outdoor Sculpture Exhibition, Greensboro, NC, 2006; solo shows, Appalachian Center for Crafts, Smithville, Tenn, 2006; Univ Tenn, Chattanooga, 2006. *Teaching:* Prof art, Univ Tenn, Chattanooga, 66-83. *Awards:* Spirit of South Award, Univ Mobile, Ala, 2000; Broyhill Purchase Award, 15th Annual Sculpture Celebration, Lenoir, NC, 2000; cash award, Art with a Southern Drawl, Univ of Mobile, 2001 & 16th Ann Sculpture Celabration, 2001; purchase award, The Best of Tenn, Tenn State Mus, 2001; distinguished artist award, presented by Mayor Bob Corker, Chatanooga, TN, 2004. *Bibliog:* A Catalogue of the American Collection, Hunter Mus Art, 85; Jim Collins Art: 1963-2003, Two Hands Art Publishing, NC, 2003; Art of Tenn, Frist Center for the Visual Arts, Nashville, Tenn, 2003. *Mem:* Southern Asn Sculptors (pres, 70-71); Int Sculpture Ctr. *Media:* Metals, Mixed Media, Collage. *Publ:* Auth introd, A Handbook to British Landscape Painters, 70; auth, Women Artists in America, 18th Century to the Present, 75 & Women Artists in America II, 76. *Mailing Add:* 201 N Palisades Dr Signal Mountain TN 37377

COLLINS, KATHLEEN
EDUCATOR
b Chicago. *Study:* Stanford Univ, BA(psychology), minor in fine arts, MFA(photog). *Work:* Art Inst Chicago; Cleveland Art Mus; Centro Cultural/Arte Contemp, Mexico City, Mex; Chrysler Mus, Norfolk, Va. *Pos:* chmn, applied photog dept, Sch Photog Arts & Sci, Rochester Inst Tech; coordr, summer workshops; dean, Sch Art & Design, NY State Col ceramics; pres, Kansas City Art Inst, 1996-. *Teaching:* prof, Alfred Univ. *Mailing Add:* Kansas City Art Inst Office of President 4415 Warwick Blvd Kansas City MO 64111-1874

COLLINS, LARRY RICHARD
PAINTER, PHOTOGRAPHER
b Spokane, Wash, July 15, 45. *Study:* Univ Okla, BFA, 67, Ind Univ, studied with James McGarrell, Mass Col Art, MFA, 80, La Napoule Art Found, studied with Jack Beal. *Work:* Sheldon Mem Art Gallery, Univ Neb, Lincoln; Worcester Art Mus, Worcester, MA; Mus Art Univ Okla, Norman; Boston Pub Libr, Mass; Berg Collection, NY Pub Libr, NY. *Comn:* Paintings, Tiffany & Co, NY. *Exhib:* Eight State Exhibition of Southwest Am Art, Okla Art Ctr, Okla, 62-66; Realistic Directions, Zoller Gallery, Pa State Univ, 83 & Recent Acquisitions, Sheldon Mem Art Gallery, Lincoln, Nebr, 83; one-man shows, Mabee-Gerrer Mus Art, Shawnee, Okla, 84 & NY Pub Libr, 87; Am Artist Mag: 50th Anniversary Exhib (traveling) 87; Emerging Artists, Provincetown Art Asn & Mus, Mass, 96; Newbury Col, Brookline, Mass, 2000; Ann Exhib, Nat Acad Design, NY, 82, 86. *Collection Arranged:* David Davis Collection, Kennedy to Kent State, vintage photos, Worcester Art Mus, Mass. *Pos:* Gallery Dir, Schoolhouse Ctr & Design, Mass, 98-2003; dir, Larry Collins Fine Art, Provincetown, MA, 2004-. *Teaching:* Prof anat, Mass Col Art, Boston, 79-82 & 85-95; instr drawing, Univ NH, Durham, 86-88; prof, Montserrat Col Art, Beverly, Mass, 94-95. *Awards:* Bronze Star, combat art, US Army, Republic Vietnam, 1968; Travel Fel, Creative Arts Studies Found, 84; Individual Arts Fel, NH State Coun Arts, 88; Artists Opportunity Grant, NH State Coun Arts, 90. *Bibliog:* Laurie Hurwitz (auth), Profiles: Larry R Collins, Am Artist, 6/87; Norman A Geske (auth), The American Painting Collection of the Sheldon Memorial Art Gallery, Univ of Nebr, 88; Dan Frambach, Larry Collins: Every Shadow is a Proof of Life, Provincetown Arts, 2003/04. *Mem:* Provincetown Art Asn. *Media:* Oil. *Specialty:* Vintage photos. *Publ:* Illusr, Old Love Story (with Allen Ginsberg), Lospecchio Press, New York, 86; The Hopper House at Truro (with Lawrence Ferlinghetti), Lospecchio Press, 96; auth, Painting in Boston: 1950-2000; auth, Provincetown Arts, 2003-05; illusr, TOW, Eileen Myles (auth), Lospecchio Press, New York, NY, 2005. *Dealer:* Larry Collins Fine Art, 145 #2 494 Commercial St Provincetown MA 02657. *Mailing Add:* PO Box 2 Provincetown MA 02657

COLLINS, PAT LOWERY
PAINTER, ILLUSTRATOR
b Los Angeles, Calif. *Study:* Univ Calif, Los Angeles, 49-50; Univ Southern Calif, BA, 53; studied with Donald Stoltenberg, Sydney Hurwitz & King Coffin, DeCordovia Mus, 59-60; Brandeis, with Mitchel Siporin, 68. *Work:* Artsbank State of NH, Concord; Hitachi Corp, Tokyo, Japan; Hitachi Corp & First NH Bank, Manchester; Pandick Press Bldg, Boston, Mass. *Comn:* Protrait of Eileen, comn by Surette Family, Hamilton, Mass, 84; protrait of Annie, comn by Elbroch Family, Peterborough, NH, 89; poster, Childrens Librns of NH, Manchester, 93; portrait of Michaela, comn by Murphy Family, Beverly Farms, Mass, 94 & portrait of Desi, 95. *Exhib:* New Eng Exhib Painting & Sculpture, New Canaan, Conn, 78 & 04; 5th & 6th Arts Biennial, NH Inst Art, Manchester, 87 & 89; Large Art Summer Open 2, Sharon Arts Ctr, NH, 93; FEMINA: A Celebration of Woman, New Eng Col Gallery, Henniker, NH, 98; New Art New Eng, Newport, NH, 97; Tell Me a Story, MPG Gallery, Boston, 2000; 9th Ann Essex art Ctr, Lawrence, Mass, 02. *Teaching:* Vis artist & instr life drawing, Worcester Art Mus, 98-; Instr, Worcester Mus Art. *Awards:* E F Hutton Award, 5th NH Arts Biennial, 87; Best of Show, Arts North Mag, 96. *Bibliog:* Stacy Milbouer (auth), Talent exceeds bounds, Nashua Telegraph, 9/27/87; D Quincy Whitney (auth), Children's author awarded as novelist, Boston Globe, 11/17/91; Gail Mountain (auth), Shaping up, Gloucester Times, 1/23/97. *Mem:* Soc Children's Bk Writers & Illusrs; Auths Guild; Concord Art Asn; North Shore Artists Asn. *Media:* Oil, Pastel. *Specialty:* Contemporary Art. *Interests:* Singing with Chamber Chorus. *Publ:* Illusr, Shadow Boy, Orchard Bks, 91; auth, I am an Artist, Millbrook Press, 92; illusr, Remember The Red Shouldered Hawk, Putnam & Sons, 94; Dreams of Glory, Atheneum, 95; A purr-fect mystery, In: Storyworks, Scholastic, 10/95. *Dealer:* MPG 228 Newbury St Boston MA 02116; Boston Corporate Art Art 3 Manchester NH. *Mailing Add:* 3 Wauketa Rd Gloucester MA 01930-1423

COLLINS, PAUL
PAINTER
b Muskegon, Mich, Dec 11, 37. *Study:* Self-taught. *Work:* Gerald R Ford Mus, Grand Rapids, Mich; off pres, Jerusalem; Amway Japan Ltd, Tokyo; Puskin Mus, Moscow, USSR; Palace de la Presidence du Senegal, Dakar, Senegal, Africa. *Comn:* Special Olympics (series of 14 portraits), Joseph P Kennedy Found, 79; Martin Luther King Non-Violent Peace Prize Medal (sculpture), comn by Corretta Scott King, 80; Challenger VII Logo (sculpture & logo), & First US Women Astronaut (commemorative plaque), NASA, 82; America at Work (series of 24 portraits), Amway Corp, 83; American Portrait of Japan (15 painting series), Amway Japan Ltd, Tokyo, 95. *Exhib:* Ill State Mus, Springfield; Mus Sci & Indust, Chicago & Los Angeles; Sioux Indian Mus, SDak; Studio Mus, Harlem, NY; Smithsonian Mus, Washington, DC; Am Cult Ctr, Paris, London, Nairobi, Kenya, Lagos, Nigeria, Dakar, Senegal & Madrid, Spain; White House, Washington, DC; Palais Des Congress, Paris; Collegium Artisticum, Sarajevo; Meguro Gajoen Mus, Tokyo; Mus Performing Arts, NY. *Awards:* Mead Book Award, New York, 72; Am Artists Top Twenty Figure Painters in US, 80; Golden Centaur, Accademia Italia, del Artie delle Lavoro, Italy, 82. *Bibliog:* Save the Children, Paramount Pictures; Paul Collins in Israel, Israeli Films Inc; Paul Collins Voices of Israel, CBS Sunday Morning Show. *Media:* Dry Oil, Own Media. *Publ:* Black Portrait of an African Journey, Eerdmans Publ, 71; Other Voices-A Native American Tableau, NAEC Publ, 74; Gerald R Ford-A Man in Perspective, Eerdmans Publ, 76; Great Beautiful Black Women, Johnson Publ, 78; 20 Figure Painters & How They Work, Watson-Guptill Publ, 79. *Dealer:* Collins Fine Art Amway Grand Plaza Hotel 220 Lyon NW Grand Rapids MI 49503. *Mailing Add:* 615 Kent Hills Dr Grand Rapids MI 49505

COLLINSON, JANICE
PAINTER, GALLERY DIRECTOR
b Newark, NJ, June 27, 48. *Study:* Westminster Col, 66-68; Georgian Court Col, BA, 70; studied painting with James Leslie, Jr, Art Alliance, 98-99. *Work:* Hist Allaire Village, Allaire State Park, Wall, NJ; Med Ctr Ocean Found, Brielle, NJ; Spring Lake Community Theatre, NJ; White Lilac Inn, Spring Lake, NJ. *Comn:* archtl renderings of homes, Diane Turton Realtors, NJ, 80-; design commemorative postmarks, Hist Allaire Village, Wall, NJ, 82-2000; archtl rendering of Kidsbridge, Chetkin Gallery, Red Bank, NJ, 99; bldg renderings Law Offices of Norman Hobbie, Toms River, NJ, 2000. *Exhib:* Ann Miniature Show, Paper Mill Playhouse, Millburn, NJ, 95; invitational shows Sr Christina Geis Gallery, Lakewood, NJ, 90, Gallery at Medford Leas, NJ, 99, Peck Sch Gallery, Morristown, NJ, 2000. *Pos:* arranger exhbns Evergreen Gallery, Spring Lake, NJ, 87-. *Teaching:* art tchr K-12, Borough of Point Pleasant, NJ Schs, 70-74; watercolor tchr, Sea Girt Lighthouse, Sea Girt, NJ, 90-. *Bibliog:* Three Artists, Garden State Home & Garden, 92; Spring Show: Favored Season, The Coast Star, 94. *Mem:* Manasquan River Group of Artists (co-pres, 84-86, prog chair 91-2000). *Media:* Watercolor, Ink. *Publ:* illus Cooks and Artists of the Jersey Shore, Hoffman Press, 80; illus Cuisine and Art, Hoffman Press, 89. *Dealer:* Evergreen Gallery 308 Morris Ave Spring Lake NJ, 07762. *Mailing Add:* 2421 Beech St Manasquan NJ 08736

COLLISCHAN VAN WAGNER, JUDY K
CRITIC, CURATOR
b Red Wing, Minn, Oct 19, 40. *Study:* Hamlinc Univ, BA, 62; Nat Univ Mex, 63; Ohio Univ, MFA, 64; Univ Iowa, PhD, 72. *Collection Arranged:* Monumental Drawings by Sculptors: Serra, Westerlund, Nonas, Jensen, Fishman, Nozkowski and others, 82, Paintings from the Mind's Eye, 83, Seymour Lipton, 84-85, Michelle Stuart, 85 & Walter Murch, 86, Hillwood Art Gallery, Long Island Univ, C W Post Campus, Greenvale, NY, 82; Lines of Vision: Drawings by Contemporary Women, 89; End Papers (19th & 20th century drawings), Paper Spaces, 97, Biennial for Public Art, 97, 99 & 2001, Glass Houses, 98, Clay Bodies, 99, Comtemporary Classicism, 2000 & Welded, Sculptre of the Century, 2000, Neuberger Mus Art, SUNY. *Pos:* Admin Dir, The Printmaking Workshop, 95-96, Dir, Hillwood Art Mus, Long Island Univ, C W Post Campus, Greenvale, NY, 82-94; critic, Arts Mag, 84-; co-chmn, New York State Coun Arts, Visual Art Panel, 87-90; assoc dir curatorial affairs, Neuberger Mus Art, SUNY, Purchase, 96-2000. *Teaching:* Instr, Kansa Sate Univ, 64-66; instr, Univ No Iowa, 70-71; asst prof, Univ Omaha Nebr, 72-75; assoc prof contemp art, State Univ NY, Plattsburgh, 75-83; adj prof contemp art, Long Island Univ, C W Post Campus, Greenvale, NY, 82-. *Awards:* Kress Found Res Grant, 70; Award, State Univ NY, 81. *Mem:* AICA. *Res:* Contemporary art, particular art by women and minorities. *Interests:* fine arts. *Publ:* Auth, Women Shaping Art, Praeger, 84; Lines of Vision: Drawings by Contemporary Women, Hudson Hills, 89; Welded Sculpture of the Twentieth Century, Hudson Hills Press, Inc, New York, 2000. *Mailing Add:* 248 E 7th St Apt 11-12 New York NY 10009

COLLYER, ROBIN
SCULPTOR, PHOTOGRAPHER
b London, Eng, Mar 7, 49; Can citizen. *Study:* Ont Col Art, Toronto, 67-68. *Work:* Nat Gallery Can & Can Coun Art Bank, Ottawa; Art Gallery Ont, Toronto; Mus d'Art Contemporain, Montreal; Can Cult Ctr, Paris, France. *Exhib:* Carmen Lamanna Gallery, Toronto, Ont, 71, 72, 74, 76, 78, 79, 81 & 83, Mt Allison Univ, 76 & Etherington Art Ctr, 82; Nat Gallery Can, Ottawa, 73; Kunsthalle, Basel, Switz, 78; Seven Toronto Artists, Artists' Space, NY, 80; Frankfurter Kunstverin, Frankfurt; Akademie der Kunste, Berlin; traveling retrospective, Can & US, 82 & 84; Ctr Int d'Art Contemporain, Montreal, 85. *Pos:* Bd dir, Trinity Square Video, 79-82. *Teaching:* Instr, Ont Col Art, Toronto, 75; NS Col Art, Halifax, 77. *Awards:* Can Coun Grants, 69-71, 73, 74 & 76-69; Can Coun Sr Arts Grant, 80. *Bibliog:* David Burett & Marilyn Schiff (auths), Contemporary Candian Art, Hurtig Publ, Edmonton, 83. *Mem:* Can Coun Adv Art Panel; Trinity Square Video. *Media:* Mixed Media; Photography, Video. *Publ:* Contribr, Impulse, summer 80; co-prod & co-dir, The Girl Can't Fly It (film), A Space & Broadcast Serv, Toronto, 80; Darn These Hands (film), A Space & Rogers Cable TV, Toronto, 80; co-prod, Sculpture of Here and Now (film), Toronto. *Dealer:* Susan Hobbs Toronto ON. *Mailing Add:* 57 Pemberton Ave Willowdale ON M2M 1Y2 Canada

COLMAN, VIRGINIA O'CONNELL
SCULPTOR, GRAPHIC ARTIST
b Manhasset, Long Island, NY. *Study:* Columbia Univ, BS(art), 47; Teachers Col, Columbia Univ, MA(art), 68; sculpture with Minoru Niizuma, 74-80; watercolor with Edgar A Whitney & George Post. *Work:* Ambulatory Monitoring Inc, Ardsley, NY; sculpture (carved stone), Leonia Libr, NJ, 98. *Exhib:* Silvermine Guild Artists, New Canaan, Conn, 75; Newark Mus, NJ, 77 & 79; Trenton City Mus, Trenton, NJ, 90; Patterson Mus, 91 & 94; Interchurch Ctr, NY, 92, 93 & 94; Ringwood Manor Barn Gallery, NJ, 93; Nabisco Gallery, East Hanover, NJ, 93; and many more. *Pos:* Art ed & staff artist, Collier's Encyl, 49-52; art dir, Girl Scouts USA, NY, 52-56; promotion art dir, Macfadden Publ, NY, 56. *Teaching:* Instr stone carving, Sculpture Ctr, NY, summer 80 & 90. *Awards:* Silver Medal, Audubon Artists Ann, 79; Ida Becker Award, Catharine Lorillard Wolfe Art Club, NY, 86 & 88; Anna Hyatt Huntington Award, Snug Harbor Cult Ctr, Catharine Lorillard Wolfe Art Club, NY, 91. *Bibliog:* Winnie Bonelli (auth), Union City Dispatch, 8/73; Eileen Watkins (auth), Newark Star-Ledger, 6/87, 10/88, 4/21/91 & 10/18/92. *Mem:* Sculptors Asn NJ (corresp secy, 74-78, rec secy, 88-92); Stone Sculpture Soc NY (corresp secy, 78-80, treas, 80-85); Catharine Lorillard Wolfe Art Club, NY (bd mem, 89-91 & 92). *Media:* Marble, Limestone. *Mailing Add:* 2452 Laurelwood Dr Apt C Clearwater FL 33763-1500

COLMER, ROY DAVID
PHOTOGRAPHER
b London, Eng; US citizen. *Study:* Hochschule fur Bildender Kunste, Hamburg, Ger, 60-65; New Sch/Parsons with George Tice, 78 & Lisette Model, 82. *Work:* Mus Mod Art, Mus City New York & Chase Manhattan Bank, New York, NY; Brooklyn Mus, NY; Mus d'Ixelles, Brussels, Belg; NY Pub Libr; Jack S Blanton Mus Art; Univ Tex, Austin; and others. *Exhib:* Recent Acquisitions, Mus Mod Art, NY, 87; Selected Photographs, Brooklyn Mus, NY, 89; Mean Streets: Am Photographs From the Collection, 1940's-1980's, Mus Mod Art, NY, 91; Open Mind: The LeWitt Collection, Wadsworth Atheneum, Hartford, Conn, 91; Queens Mus Art, Bulova Corp Ctr, NY, 93; one-man show, Okla Harris Works Art, NY, 2000; Red, Mitchell Algus Gallery, NY, 1999; Für Hanne, Galerie Ascan Crone, Hamburg, Ger, 2001; Life of the City, Mus Modern Art, NY, 2002; Mitchell Algus Gallery, NY, 04; Jack S Blanton Mus Art, Univ Tex, Austin, 04; Recent Aquisitions: New York Street Photography From the 1960's and 1970's, NY Pub Libr, 2006; America/Americsa, Jack S Blanton Mus of Art, Univ Tex, Austin, 2006; High Times/Hard Times (traveling exhib), 2006. *Teaching:* Asst prof painting, Univ Iowa, 70-71; vis lectr, Univ Cincinnati, Ohio, 71; instr photog, New Sch/Parsons, NY, 87-95. *Awards:* Guggenheim Fel, 88; Found Contemp Performance Arts Inc, 90. *Publ:* Contrib, Copy Art, Horseguard Lane Pro, 78; auth, Roy Colmer/Photographs, pvt publ, 87; contrib, The Human Presence, Yale Sch Art, 89; Doors NYC, 2001; Trucks NYC, 2001; Movie Houses, 2003; Headlines, 2003. *Dealer:* Mitchell Algus Gallery, 511 W 25th St, 2d fl, New York, 10001. *Mailing Add:* 1642 E Carson St Long Beach CA 90807

COLNURN, MARTHA
FILMMAKER, ANIMATOR
Study: Md Inst Col Art, Baltimore, BA, 94; Royal Accad Art, Holland, MA, 2002. *Comn:* Spiders In Love: An Arachnogasmic Musical, 2000, Skelehellavision, 2001, Cats Amore, 2002, Groscher Lansangriff: Big Bug Attack, 2002, Secrets of Mexuality, 2003, A Little Dutch Thrill, 2004, Cosmetic Emergency, 2005 and many others. *Exhib:* solo shows, INSE(X)CTS Major Art Fair, Amsterdam, Neth, 2002, Frankfurter Kunstverein, Young & Upcoming, Frankfurt, Ger, 2003, WINDOW gallery, Walter Van Beirendonk Fashion shop, Antwerp, Belg, 2003; group shows, Courthouse Gallery, Anthology Film Archive, NY, 2000, Las Palmas, Transmision: Emerging Artists living around the North Sea, Rotterdam, Neth, 2001, Outline Gallery, Haunted House of Art, Amsterdam, Neth, 2002, Diana Stigter Gallery, Amsterdam, 2003, Site Specific, Deiska, Amsterdam, 2003, Luggage Nanjing Art Inst Gallery, Nanjing, China, 2004, Vixens, Diana Stigter Gallery, Amsterdam, 2004, Liste Art Fair, Diana Stigter Gallery, Basel, Switz, 2004, Sideshow Gallery, Williamsburg, NY, Whitney Biennial: Day for Night, Whitney Mus Am Art, NY, 2006 and others; film screenings, LA Film Festival, Egyptian Theatre, Calif, 2004, Utah Arts Festival, 2004, Super 8 Special 2004, Basel, Switz, 2004, Rotterdam Int Film Festival, Neth, 2005, DUTCH OPEN, Amsterdam, 2005, Brampton Indie Arts Festival, Calif, 2005 and many others. *Pos:* vis artist, Norway, 2003, MIT, Mass, 2005 & Sch Mus Fine Arts, Boston, 2005. *Teaching:* vis prof animation, San Francisco Art Inst, 2001; Basics of Subversive & Traditional Animation, Rotterdam, Neth, 2002; vis tutor, Dutch Art Inst, Enschede, Neth, 2003; lectr, animation workshop, Nanjing Art Inst, China, 2004; vis artist & prof, Calif Inst Arts, 2004. *Awards:* Best Animated Film, NY Underground Film Festival, 99 & 2003; Sarah Lawrence Col Film Award, 2002; and many others. *Mailing Add:* c/o Stux Gallery 530 W 25th St New York NY 10001

COLOMBINI, SUSAN MURPHY See Murphy, Susan Avis Murphy Colombini

COLOMBO, CHARLES
PAINTER
b Wilmington, Del, Nov 3, 27. *Study:* Pa Acad Fine Arts, Philadelphia; Art Students League with Charles DeFeo; privately with Frank E Schoonover. *Work:* Pvt collections throughout US & abroad including The Vatican, Rome, Italy, Prince Ranier, Monaco, former Vpres & Mrs Walter Mondale & Senator Joseph R Biden, Jr. *Comn:* Hagley Powder Mills, comn by State of Del for Pres J F Kennedy, 62. *Exhib:* Am Watercolor Soc, 66-81; Nat Arts Club, NY, 66-75; Charles & Emma Frye Mus, Seattle, 75; Colonnade Des Artes Gallery; Lake Buena Vista, Disneyworld, Fla. *Awards:* Watercolor Award, Pa Acad Fine Arts, 49; Scholar Award, Pa Acad Fine Arts; Watercolor Award, Del Art Mus, Wilmington, 56. *Bibliog:* Frederick Kramer (auth), Brandywine Tradition Artists, Great Am Ed, New York, 71; Nancy Mohr (auth), Charles Colombo, A part of the Brandywine tradition, Delaware Today, Wilmington, 71; article, Art News, 5/83. *Mem:* Am Watercolor Soc; Rehoboth Art League. *Dealer:* Gallery At Greenville Wilmington DE; Maxwell Gallery San Francisco CA. *Mailing Add:* 1410 Delaware Ave Apt B1 Wilmington DE 19801-3203

COLP, NORMAN B
PHOTOGRAPHER, CURATOR
b Bronx, NY, Sept 3, 44. *Study:* Queens Col, Flushing, NY, BA(art), 67; Pratt Inst, Brooklyn, NY, 67; Parsons Sch Design, NY, 71. *Work:* Corcoran Gallery Art, Smithsonian Archive Am Art & Smithsonian Inst, Washington; Univ Calif, Berkeley Art Mus; Victoria & Albert Mus, Nat Art Libr, London, Eng; Wadsworth Atheneum, Hartford, Conn; Whitney Mus Am Art; and others. *Comn:* Porcelain enamel signs, Creative Sta/MTA, NY, 91; zoetrope-B/W photo images with John Billingham, Nat Shopping Ctrs, Hamden, Conn, 91. *Exhib:* After the Fact: Select from LeWitt Collect, Wadsworth Atheneum, Hartford, 96; Small Wonders, CEPA, Buffalo, 97; Role Model, Hugo de Pagano, NY, 98; The Tiny Cinema, Red Mills, Claverack, NY, 2001; FotoFest, Houston, 2002 & 06; Art in Embassies Program, US Dept State, Havana, Cuba & Lima, Peru, 2003; Fine Print Auction, Foto Fest Int, Houston, 2004; Collage, Univ Calif, Berkeley Art Mus, 2004; Daumenhimp The Flipbook Show, Kunstalle, Dusseldorf, Ger, 2005, Foto Mus, Antwerp, Belg, 2006. *Collection Arranged:* Stories Your Mother Never Told You, White Plains Publ Libr, 82; Less is More, Pratt

Graphics Ctr, 82; One Cubic Foot, Metrop Mus Art, 83; From the Beginning, Pratt Graphics Ctr, 84; The Impractical-Practical, White Plains Pub Libr, 84. *Pos:* Assoc cur, Alternative Mus, NY, 79-80; cur exhibs, Ctr Book Arts, NY, 80-83 & exhib coord, 83. *Teaching:* Instr, book art, Sch of Visual Arts, NY, 82-86 & Pratt Graphics Ctr, NY, 83-84. *Awards:* Workshop in Residence, Mus Holography, 85, Fieldcrest Cannon Inc, 91; Creative Stations, MTA, 91; The Merchant and Ivory Found, 2002; Foto Fest Award, 2002. *Bibliog:* Don Williams (reporter), News 4 New York, WNBC-TV, 6/3/92; Cathy Courtney (auth), Private Views & Other Containers, estamp/London, 6/92; Melissa Bank (auth), The Girls' Guide to Hunting and Fishing, 99, 2000. *Media:* Sequential Images, Framed & Accordion Books. *Specialty:* Contemp photography & Painting. *Publ:* Auth, The Thrice Told Tale, 77, pvt publ; An Old Saw, 82, A Primer on Art Criticism, 83, Crazy Hair, 83 & Freud's Recipe, 83, Hand & Mind Books. *Dealer:* Marsha Ralls The Ralls Collection 1516 31st St NW Washington DC 20007. *Mailing Add:* 180 West End Ave 3R New York NY 10023

COLPACCI, VIORICA
SCULPTOR
b Romania, US citizen. *Study:* Inst Fine & Decorative Arts, Bucharest, Romania, MFA; NY Univ, MA. *Work:* Galati Mus, Romania; Romania-State Collections; Marrieta Col, Ohio. *Comn:* Mural, al fresco, Sch #24, Bucharest, Romania, 70. *Exhib:* First Int Exhib, Ertfurt Mus Art, Ger, 74; 16th Int Art Competition, Perugia Mus Art, Italy, 74; 32nd Int Competition Ceramics, Frenza, Italy, 74; Craft Nat, Marietta Col, Ohio, 80; Jubilee 50, Nat, League NH, Manchester, 81; group exhib, Bergen Mus, Paramus, NJ, 83; Galex 18 Int, Gallesburg Pub Art Ctr, Ill, 84; 2nd Int Shoebox Sculpture Exhib, Univ Hawaii Art Gallery, 85. *Awards:* Charles Murphy Award, Nat Asn Women Artists, 83. *Bibliog:* Karen Rychlewski (auth), Marrieta Craft Nat, Ceramics Monthly, 81; Sharon Webster (auth), The Greatest Show - V Colpacci, VanGuard Press, Vt, 8/85. *Mem:* Nat Asn Women Artists; Sculptor Guild. *Media:* Bronze & Welded Steel

COLPITT, FRANCES
HISTORIAN, CRITIC
b Tulsa, Okla, Dec 19, 52. *Study:* Univ Tulsa, BFA, 74, MA, 77; Univ Southern Calif, PhD, 82. *Collection Arranged:* Finish Fetish: LA's Cool School, Univ Southern Calif, 91; Knowledge: Aspects of Conceptual Art, Univ Calif, Santa Barbara, 92; In Plain Sight (abstract painting in Los Angeles), Blue Star Art Space, San Antonio, 94; Chromaform: Color in Sculpture, Univ Tex, San Antonio, 98; Neo-Rococo, Univ Tex, San Antonio, 2000; Glow: Aspects of Light in Contemporary America Art, Univ Tex, San Antonio, 2002. *Pos:* Corresponding ed, Art Am, currently. *Teaching:* Vis lectr & vis asst prof art hist, Univ Calif, Santa Barbara, 82-88; vis asst prof, Cornell Univ, 85-86, Univ Southern Calif, 88-90; asst prof, Univ Tex, San Antonio, 90-94, assoc prof, 94-; dept chair art & art history, Univ Tex, 2002-. *Mem:* Int Asn Art Critics; Col Art Asn. *Res:* Contemporary abstract painting and sculpture; theories of 20th century criticism; minimal and conceptual art. *Publ:* The Shape of Painting in the 1960s, Col Art J, 91; Going against the grain: Report from Texas, Art Am, 95; Between Two Worlds, Art Am, 98; Space City Takes Off, Art Am, 2000; ed, Abstract Art in the Late Twentieth Century, Cambridge Univ Press, 2002. *Mailing Add:* Dept Art & Art History Univ Texas San Antonio TX 78285-0642

COLQUHOUN, PETER LLOYD
PAINTER, INSTRUCTOR
b New York, NY, Dec 1, 55. *Study:* Pratt Inst, BFA, 89; Brooklyn Mus Art Sch, with Francis Cunningham; Art Students League, with Robert B Hale. *Work:* Bank of NY; Southeast Mo State Univ Mus; Fine Arts Mus Long Island. *Comn:* portrait, Giussepe Manzari, Rome, Italy, 85; portrait, Henry Barnett, NY, 97, 98; Lower Manhattan (cityscape), Zweig/Glaser Advs, NY, 98. *Exhib:* Roerich Mus, NY, 87; Audubon Artists, NY, 93-2000; Fine Arts Mus Long Island, Hempstead, NY, 93; Nat Acad Design, 97, 2000. *Pos:* artist in residence, Helene Wurlitzer Found, Taos, NMex, 2001, Rochefort en terre, Md Inst Col Art, 2002. *Teaching:* teacher painting, NY Acad, 80-83, Ctr del Arte Verrochio, Siena, Italy, 84-85. *Awards:* Internship, Peggy Guggenheim Mus, Venice, 84; Grant, Adolf & Esther Gottlieb Found, 93 & 2001; Pollack-Krasner Found Grant, 2002. *Bibliog:* Shyka Cohen (auth), catalog entry, Ice Gallery, 96; Tracy O'Shaughnessy (auth), Exhibit Is the Art of Evocative, Waterbury Republican Am, 99; Familiar Views of Downtown, Tribeca Tribune, 99. *Mem:* NY Artist Equity Asn (bd dir, 98-, columnist Artist's Proof 98-); Audubon Artists; Fedn Mod Painters & Sculptors; Orgn Independent Artists. *Media:* Oil. *Specialty:* American and German artists (2Dd & 3D). *Dealer:* Galorie Von Stechow Frankfurt Am Main. *Mailing Add:* 105 Duane St Studio Apt 4C New York NY 10007

COLSON, GREG J
SCULPTURE, CONCEPTUAL ARTIST
b Seattle, Wash, 56. *Study:* Calif State Univ, Bakersfield, BFA, 78; Claremont Grad Sch, Calif, MFA, 80. *Work:* Mus Mod Art, NY; Hirshhorn Mus, Washington, DC; Panza Collection, Lugano, Switz; Tsaritsino Mus Contemp Art, Moscow, Russ; Mus Contemp Art, Los Angeles. *Exhib:* One-man shows, Lannan Mus, Lake Worth, Fla, 88, Sperone Westwater, NY, 90, 91, 94, 2001, Konrad Fischer Gallery, Dusseldorf, Ger, 91, Kunsthalle Lophem, Brugges, Belg, 94, Krannert Art Mus, Champaign, Ill, 96, 1000 Eventi, Milan, Italy, 98, Galleria Cardi, Milan, Italy, 2001, 2003, Griffin Contemp, Venice, Calif, 98, 99, 2001, 2004-2005, Gian Enzo Sperone, Rome, 92, 99, Baldwin Gallery, Aspen, Colo, 2002, 2006; Laboratory, Russian Mus, Leningrad, 90; Mapping, Mus Mod Art, NY, 94; 100 Yrs of Calif Art, Orange Co Mus Art, Newport Beach, Calif, 97; Panza Collection, Mus Contemp Art, Los Angeles, Calif, 2000; da Warhol al 2000, Palazzo Cavour, Regione Piemonte, Turin, Italy, 2000; Arte Americana: Ultimo Decennio, Museo d'Arte della Ravenna, Italy, 2000; Colson, Pardo, Murakami, Tower, Mars Gallery, Tokyo, 92; Amerika-Europa: Sammlung Rosenkranz, Von der Heydt Mus, Wuppertal, Ger, 2002. *Bibliog:* Pontus Hulten and Peter Wegner (auth's), Greg Colson, Wale and Star Press, 1999; Robert Evren (auth), Greg Colson, Galleria Cardi, Milan, 2001; Genevieve Devitt (auth), Greg Colson: The Architecture of Distraction, Griffin, Santa Monica, Calif, 2006. *Media:* Wood, Metal, Paint. *Dealer:* Sperone Westwater 415 W 13th St New York NY 10014; Galleria Cardi Piazza S Erasmo 3 Milan Italy I-20121; Baldwin Gallery 209 S Galena St Aspen CO 81611; Griffin Contemporary 55 N Venice Blvd Venice CA 90291; Gian Enzo Sperone Via di Pallacorda 15 Rome Italy 00186. *Mailing Add:* 751 Palms Blvd Venice CA 90291

COLTON, JUDITH
EDUCATOR, HISTORIAN
b New York, NY, Mar 21, 43. *Study:* Smith Col, Northampton, Mass, BA, 63; Inst Fine Arts, New York Univ, MA, 65, PhD, 74. *Teaching:* Art hist, Bennington Col, 71-72; instr art hist, Queens Col, City Univ New York, 72-73; asst prof art hist, Yale Univ, 73-78, assoc prof, 78-. *Awards:* James L Clifford Prize, Am Soc 18th Century Studies, 78; Ingram Merrill Found, 79-80; Fel, Am Coun Learned Socs, 82-83. *Mem:* Col Art Asn Am; Am Soc 18th Century Studies; Garden Hist Soc. *Res:* 17th and 18th century art in Italy, France and England; concentrating on the history of painting sculpture and garden design. *Publ:* Contribr, Architectura, 74; Eighteenth-Century Studies, 76; auth, The Parnasse Francois: Titon du Tillet and the Origins of the Monument to Genius, Yale Univ Press, 79; contribr, Studies on Voltaire and The Eighteenth century, 80; Art the Ape of Nature: Studies in Honor of H W Janson, 81

COLVILLE, ALEXANDER
PAINTER, PRINTMAKER
b Toronto, Ont, Aug 24, 1920. *Work:* Nat Gallery Can; Mus Mod Art, NY; Wallraf-Richarts Mus, Cologne, Ger; Ctr Nat Art Contemporain, Paris; Boymans-Van Beuningen Mus, Rotterdam; and others. *Exhib:* Fischer Fine Art, London, 77; Art Gallery Ont, Toronto; Staatliche Kunsthalle, Berlin; Ludwig Mus, Cologne, 83; Teien Mus, Tokyo, 85; Montreal Mus Fine Arts, 94. *Awards:* Companion Award, Order of Can, 82. *Bibliog:* David Burnett (auth), Colville, McClelland & Stewart, Toronto, 83; Philip Frye (auth), Alex Colville, Montreal Mus Fine Arts, 94. *Dealer:* Ann Kitz 470 Francklyn St Halifax NS B3H IA9. *Mailing Add:* PO Box 550 Wolfville NS B0P 1X0 Canada

COLWAY, JAMES R
PAINTER
b Oneida, NY, Nov 12, 20. *Study:* Syracuse Univ Sch Art, 45-48, Univ Col, 46-48. *Work:* US Embassy Prog (17 paintings shown), Washington; Butler Inst Am Art, Youngstown, Ohio; Lyman Allyn Mus, Univ Conn, New London; Munson-Williams Proctor Inst, Utica, NY; Slater Mem Mus, Norwich, Conn; and others. *Comn:* 41 painting reproductions, comn by Aaron Ashley & Hedgerow House. *Exhib:* Grumbacher Show, Grand Cent Art Gallery, NY, 64; one-man shows, Chase Gallery, NY, 69, St Lawrence Univ, 70, Grand Haven Art Ctr, Mich, 70 & 75 & Arvest Galleries, Boston, 76; Munson-Williams-Proctor Inst, Utica, NY; Schweinfurth Mus, Auburn, NY. *Pos:* Sr vpres & dir, Oneida Ltd, retired; pres, Colway Assocs, currently. *Bibliog:* Show rev, Art News, 5/69; Grumbacher's Palette Talk, 78. *Mem:* Am Artists Prof League; Cent NY Watercolor Soc; Artists Equity Asn. *Media:* Water Media, Oil. *Mailing Add:* 101 The Vineyard Oneida NY 13421

COLWELL, JUDITH KOGOD
CERAMIST
b New York, NY, Dec 16, 49. *Study:* George Washington Univ, BA, 71; Corcoran Sch Art; Inst Allende, Mex. *Comn:* AARP, Washington DC; Freddie Mac, McLean, Va; Xerox Corp, Washington, DC. *Exhib:* Washington Craft show, Smithsonian Mus, Washington, DC, 88-95; Designs for Dining, Smithsonian Mus, Washington, DC, 89; Studio Ceramics Invitational, Berea Col, Ky, 90; Common Ground-Diverse expressions in clay, Sawtooth Ctr For Visual Art, Winston Salem, NC, 91; Women's Visions Invitational, Montgomery Col, Rockville, Md, 92; The Wichita Nat, Kans, 93; Mid-Atlantic Craft Exhib, Towson, Md, 94; Kutani Int Exhib Decorative Ceramics, Japan, 97. *Awards:* Individual Artists Award in Crafts, Md State Arts Coun, 90 & 92; Finalist, Mid-Atlantic/NEA Regional Visual Arts Fel, 91 & 93. *Bibliog:* Nine Washington, DC area potters, Studio Potter Mag, Vol 9, No 1, 12/80; Connie Stapleton (auth), At Home with Commissions, Washington Mus Arts, 5-6/88; Pat Ross (auth), Formal Country, Viking, 89. *Mem:* Am Craft Coun; Torpedo Factory Artists Asn, Alexandria, Va. *Media:* Clay. *Publ:* Auth, Portfolio: Washington Craft show, Sales Surprises, Ceramics Monthly, 88

COMINI, ALESSANDRA
HISTORIAN, WRITER, EDUCATOR
b Winona, Minn, Nov 24, 34. *Study:* Barnard Col, with Julius Held, BA, 56; Univ Calif, Berkeley, with Herschel Chipp, MA, 62; Columbia Univ, PhD, 69. *Teaching:* Asst prof art hist, Columbia Univ, 69-74; vis prof, Yale Univ, 73; prof, Southern Methodist Univ,74-83, univ distinguished prof, 83-2005. *Awards:* Grand Medal Hon for serv to Austrian Repub, 90; Lifetime Achievement Award, Womens Caucus Art, 95; United Methodist Scholar Teacher Award, 96. *Mem:* Am Soc Composers, Auth & Publ; Tex Inst Letters; Col Art Asn. *Res:* Foreign artists in Rome 1750-1914; Gothic revival and German romanticism; the visual Brahms, the visual Schoenberg, Berg, Webern, Mozart, R Strauss, Bruckner & Mahler; Alma Mahler and her Vienna; women artists; Scandinavian artists. *Publ:* The Changing Image of Beethoven: A Study in Myth-Making, Rizzoli Int Publ, 87; Käthe Kollwitz, Yale Univ Press, 92; Egon Schiele, Abrams, 94; Violetta & Her Sisters, Faber & Faber, 94; auth, In Passionate Pursuit: A Memoir, George Braziller Publ, NY, 2004; and others. *Mailing Add:* 2900 McFarlin Dallas TX 75205

CONAL, ROBBIE
PAINTER
b New York, NY, 1941. *Study:* Stanford Univ, MFA, 78. *Exhib:* Col Notre Dame Art Gallery, Belmont, Calif, 80; San Francisco Mus Mod Art, San Francisco, Calif, 81; UGA Fine Arts Gallery, Athens, Ga, 82; Gallery 500X, Dallas, Tex, 84; Cleveland Ctr Contemp Art Galleria, Ohio, 88; poster projects, False Profit, Los Angeles, NY, Washington, Houston, 88, Sex, Drugs & Rock & Roll, Los Angeles, NY, Chicago, San Francisco, Oakland, Berkeley, Washington, DC, 89 & Plan Ahead, Los Angeles, NY, New Orleans, San Francisco, Oakland, Berkeley, Washington, DC; The Armory Ctr for the Arts, Pasadena, Calif, 90. *Mailing Add:* c/o Robert Berman Gallery Bergamot Sta 2525 Michigan Ave C2 Santa Monica CA 90404

CONANT, JAN ROYCE
REPRESENTATIONAL PAINTER
b Boston, Mass, Sept 14, 30. *Study:* Boston Mus Sch Fine Arts, 48-51; Cincinnati Art Acad, 51-53. *Work:* Wyndham Rose Hall Hotel, Montego Bay, Jamaica, West Indies; Smith-Worthington Saddlery Co, Hartford, Conn; Chukka-Cove Farm, Ltd, St Ann, Jamaica, West Indies. *Comn:* 4 Paintings, Contract Art, Centerbrook, Conn; more than 360 commissioned paintings in pvt collections; painting & logo, Source Inc, Branford, Conn. *Exhib:* Solo exhibs, Conn Bank & Trust Co, Hartford, 71, Jamaica by Jan, Runaway Bay Hotel, West Indies, 80, Chester Art Gallery, 87 & Lyman Allyn Mus, New London, Conn, 89, Jamaica Mutual Life, Kingston, 97, Lyme Acad Fine Arts, 98-2003, Pet Connection, Lyme Art Asn, 99-2006; Catherine Lorillard Wolfe Art Club, NY, 86 & 89; Am Soc Equine Art, Lexington, Ky, 87, 90 & 95; W Graham Arader Gallery, NY, 93. *Mem:* Artists Equity Asn; Am Soc Equine Art; Lyme Acad Fine Arts; Conn Comn Arts; East Lyme Art Asn; Lyme Art Asn (dir, curently). *Media:* Oil, Watercolor. *Specialty:* Equestrain sports; Animal Portraits; Nature. *Interests:* Animal behavior. *Publ:* Children of Light, Ithaca Pres, 2005; Dowsing for Animals Well-being, 2005-2006. *Dealer:* Stonefield Farm Studio LLC. *Mailing Add:* Stonefield Farm Three Bridges Rd East Haddam CT 06423

CONAWAY, GERALD
SCULPTOR, PAINTER
b Manson, Wash, Feb 15, 33. *Study:* Everett Jr Col, Wash, ABA; Univ Wash, Seattle, with George Tsutakawa & Everett Dupen, BA (art educ), MFA (sculpture). *Work:* Anchorage Fine Arts Mus, Alaska; Alaska Methodist Univ, Anchorage; Nat Gallery Art. *Comn:* William H Seward (marble monument), Mutual Ins Co, NY & Anchorage Centennial, Anchorage, 67; concrete wall sculptures, Raymond Lawson, AIA, 73; aluminum sculptures, Gen Serv Admin Fed Bldg, Fairbanks, Alaska, 79 & Pub Safety Bldg, Fairbanks, Alaska, 81; Benny Benson Mem (aluminum), Anchorage, 83. *Exhib:* All Alaska, Anchorage, 65-70; Western Regional Craft Show, Portland, 67; Sculpture Northwest, Seattle, 68. *Pos:* Sign writer & artist, Univ Wash, 54-65; graphic artist, Boeing Airplane Co, 57. *Teaching:* Instr art, Northshore Sch Dist, Wash, 57-65; from assoc prof to prof art, Alaska Methodist Univ, 65-76. *Awards:* Sculpture Award, All Alaska, 65-70; Jewelry Award, Western Regional Craft Show, 67. *Mem:* Nat Art Educ Asn. *Media:* Wood, Stone. *Dealer:* Francine Seders Gallery 6701 Greenwood Ave N Seattle WA 98103. *Mailing Add.* 2457 Cottonwood St Anchorage AK 99508-3931

CONAWAY, JAMES D
PAINTER, EDUCATOR
b Granite City, Ill, Oct 9, 32. *Study:* Southern Ill Univ, Carbondale, Ill, BA; Univ Iowa, Iowa City, MA, MFA. *Work:* Am Embassy Collection; Waterloo Munic Art Gallery, Iowa; Davenport Munic Art Gallery, Iowa; Sloan Kettering Cancer Inst, NY; Frederick Weisman Mus, Minneapolis, Minn. *Comn:* Painting, Texaco Oil Co, Houston, 81; CoBank, Minneapolis, 2006. *Exhib:* Art for the Embassies, Smithsonian Inst, Washington, DC, 67; Midwestern Ann Competition, Joslyn Art Mus, Omaha, 73; Mid Yr Biennial, Butler Inst Am Art, Youngstown, Ohio, 74; Manisphere, Winnepeg Art Ctr, 74; Marietta Int Painting Exhib, Ohio, 76; Wiseman Art Mus, Minneapolis; New Am Painting Number II, Exhib in Print, Open Studio Press. *Teaching:* Asst prof, Univ Wis, Stevens Point; prof painting & drawing, Anoka Ramsey Col, Minneapolis; prof painting, Hamline Univ, St Paul. *Awards:* Purchase Award, Davenport Munic Art Gallery, 63, Waterloo Munic Art Galleries, 65; Donors Prize, Walker Art Ctr Biennial, 66. *Bibliog:* By the time he got to Phoenix, Arizona Arts & Lifestyle, Spring; James Conaway (auth), Minneapolis-Santa Fe connection, Southwest Profiles, 5/83; Worn wood helps to define the landscape, Minneapolis Star Tribune, 4/97. *Mem:* Mid-Am Col Art Asn (treas, 77-78); Artist Equity; Traffic Zone Co-Operative, 1995-. *Media:* Oil on canvas, Oil on old wood. *Specialty:* Representational paintings & drawings from Am artists. *Interests:* Int travel. *Publ:* New Am Paintings, 1997. *Dealer:* Groveland Gallery 25 Groveland Terr Minneapolis MN 55403; Grace Chosy Gallery 1825 Monroe St Madison WI 53703; Artsource LA 11901 Santa Monica Blvd #555 Los Angeles 90025; Lydon Fine Art 309 W Superior St Chicago IL 60610. *Mailing Add:* 2758 Benjamin St Minneapolis MN 55418

CONCANNON, GEORGE ROBERT
PAINTER
b Berkeley, Calif. *Study:* Stanford Univ, BA; Harvard Univ, MA; Can Col. *Exhib:* Gulbenkian Nat Mus, Lisbon, Port. *Teaching:* Univ Calif, Berkeley. *Mem:* World Affairs Coun; Urban Land Inst; Am Indust Coun. *Media:* Oil on Canvas, Expressionistic Realism. *Dealer:* Woollahra Gallery Sydney Australia; Wind-Borne Gallery Darien CT. *Mailing Add:* 2995 Woodside Rd Woodside CA 94062

CONDESO, ORLANDO
PRINTMAKER
b Lima, Peru, Dec 31, 47. *Study:* Visual Arts, Lima; Pratt Graphics Ctr, NY. *Work:* Nat Mus Hist, Repub China; Harlem Art Collection, NY; Orgn Am States, Washington, DC; Braniff Int, Lima; Cult Peruvian NAm Inst, Lima. *Exhib:* Second Biennial of Latin Am Prints, San Juan, PR, 72; 2nd Int Print Exhib, Mus Mod Art, Sao Paulo, Brazil, 72; 18th Nat Print Exhib, Brooklyn Mus, NY, 72; Young Artists 1973, Int Play Group Inc, NY, 73; Calif Palace Legion Honor, San Francisco, 73; Nat Mus Hist, Repub China, 73; 2nd Miami Graphics Biennial, Fla, 75; one-man shows, Pensacola Art Ctr, Fla, 77, Ivone Briceno Gallery, Lima, Peru, 78, Usdan Gallery, Bennington, Vt, 79, Nobe Gallery, NY, 79, Forum Gallery, Lima, Peru, 81 & 85, Wilson Arts Ctr, Rochester, NY, 82 & Pancho Fierro Gallery, Lima, Peru, 91; NJCVA Fac Exhib, Schering-Plough Corp, Madison, NJ, 89; Printers of The Vinalhaven Press, Fogg Gallery, Vinalhaven, Maine, 89; Earth Works JJCVA, Summit, NJ, 91. *Pos:* Co-owner, Condeso-Lawler Gallery, currently. *Teaching:* Photog tech printmaking, Lower East Side Printshop, NY, 82-84; etching instr, Cooper Union, NY, 83; etching instr, NJ Ctr Visual Arts, Summit, 89-90. *Awards:* First Prize, 5th Nat Print Competition, USA Embassy, Lima, 70; Award, 5th Ann Exhib, Pratt Graphics Ctr, 72; Purchase Award, 2nd Miami Graphics Biennial, 75. *Media:* Acrylic, Silkscreen. *Publ:* Art News, 3/71; Printshop Calendar, New York, 75; Escandalar Mag No 7, New York, 79; Art Gallery Scene, Jan Issue, 83. *Mailing Add:* 217 E 22nd New York NY 10010

CONDON, BRODY KIEL
GRAPHIC ARTIST
b Nayarit, Mex, 1974. *Study:* Univ Fla, BFA, 97; Skowhegan Sch Painting & Sculpture, 2001; Univ Calif San Diego, MFA, 2002. *Exhib:* One-man shows, Staring Contest, Sushi Visual Art, San Diego, 2000, Half Life, Marcuse Gallery, San Diego, 2001, Chinatown, C-Level, Los Angeles, 2002, Adam Killer, Electronic Orphanage, Los Angeles, 2002, EndGames, The Kitchen, NY, 2003, Untitled War, Machine, Los Angeles, 2004, Children of the Apocalypse, Mus Hef Domain, Neth, 2006, Worship, Virgil de Voldere Gallery, NY, 2006; group shows at Flauma: Series for Non-Archit, Space Untitled, NY, 2001, Glitch, Oslo Art Acad, Norway, 2001, New Fangle, Herbst Exhib Hall, San Francisco, 2002, Provocations, Next Art Festival, Orlando, Fla, 2003, While You Were Playing, Flux Factory, NY, 2003, Digital Media, Am Mus Moving Image, NY, 2003, Electrofringe, New Castle, New South Wales, 2003, Whitney Biennial, Whitney Mus Am Art, 2004. *Teaching:* Vis prof, Central Nationalities Univ, Beijing, 2002, ICAM, Univ Calif, San Diego, 2003; adj prof, studio arts Univ Calif Irvine, 2004-. *Awards:* Geraldine R Dodge Found Fel; Col Art Asn, 2001; Future of the Present Grant, Franklin Furnace, 2002; Interpolis NV Grant, 2005; Creative Capital Grant, 2006

CONDREN, STEPHEN F
PAINTER
b Chicago, Ill, Sept 4, 1951. *Study:* Sch Art Inst Chicago, BFA, 80; Northern Ill Univ, MSA, 96. *Work:* Chicago Hist Soc, Ill; Cuneo Mus & Gardens, Libertyville, Ill; Harris Bank, Libertyville, Ill; Village of Libertyville, David Adler Mus, Ill; David Adler Cult Ctr, Ill. *Comn:* Pen & Ink Wash, John F Cuneo, Grayslake, Ill, 85; oil painting, Kenneth Eichelburger, Libertyville, Ill, 85; watercolor painting, Mr Webber, Grayslake, Ill, 86; oil painting, Alier Jorgenson, Libertyville, Ill, 2004; oil painting, Rotary Club Chicago, Ill, 2004. *Exhib:* Landscapes, David Adler Cult Ctr, Libertyville, Ill, 94; Lake Forest Art Show, Lake Forest Gallery, Ill, 95, Open Show, Studio, Libertyville, Ill, 95; Lake Co Vistas, Galerie Brang & heinrich, Stuttgart, Ger, 2000; Current Works, Union League Club, Chicago, Ill, 2004. *Teaching:* instr, Chicago Sch Art & Design, 73-75; instr, Col Lake Co, 85-; instr, Chicago Pub Sch, 2003-. *Awards:* First Place, USS Midway Frequent Winds, NY, 76. *Mem:* Arts Club Chicago; Univ Club Chicago; Union League Club Chicago; Int Vis Ctr (bd mem, currently); Rotary One, Chicago (bd mem, currently). *Media:* Acrylic, Oil, Watercolor, Educator, Illustrator, Instructor. *Dealer:* Marty Lazer 329 W 18th St Suite 306 Chicago Il 60616. *Mailing Add:* Condren Galleries Fine Arts Bldg 410 S Michigan Ave Ste 400 Chicago IL 60605

CONE, MICHELE C
CRITIC, HISTORIAN, CURATOR
b Paris, France, May 21, 32; US citizen. *Study:* Studied at Inst d'Art et d'Archeol, Sorbonne, 67-68; Bryn Mawr Col, BA; NY Univ, PhD, 88. *Pos:* vpres mem & bd mem, Asn Int des Critiques d'Art, 97-. *Teaching:* fac, Sch Visual Arts, NY, 80-. *Awards:* Chevalier daus l'ordre des Arts en Lettres, 79. *Mem:* Art Table; Col Art Asn; AICA. *Res:* Art and Visual Propaganda in the 20th Century. *Interests:* Contemp art; music; 1940's art and design; asian art. *Publ:* auth, The Roots and Routes of Art in the 20 Century, Horizon Press, 1975; auth, Artists under Vichy: A Case of Prejudice and Persecution, Princeton Univ Press, 92; contribr, The Art of the Everyday, NY Univ Press, 97; The Jew in the Text, Thames & Hudson, 96; Fascist Visions in France and Italy 1890-1945, Princeton, 97; auth, French Modernisms: Perspectives on Art Before, During and After Vichy, Cambridge, 2001. *Mailing Add:* 260 W Broadway New York NY 10013

CONELLI, MARIA ANN
ADMINISTRATOR, EDUCATOR, HISTORIAN
b Brooklyn, NY, Nov 1, 57. *Study:* Brooklyn Col, BA, 80; NY Univ, MA, 83; Columbia Univ, MPhil; Columbia Univ, PhD, 92. *Pos:* Chair, Parsons/Smithsonian Inst, New York City and Washington, 92-2001; dean, Fashion Inst Tech, New York City, 2001-. *Teaching:* Educator, Metrop Mus of Art, New York City, 81-84; instr, Parsons Sch of Design, 83-2001. *Awards:* J Paul Getty Postdoctoral fel, 1997; Pub Works Challenge grantee, Nat Endowment for the Arts, Wash, 2002-03. *Mem:* Fel: Am Acad in Rome (fel 1987-88); Col Art Assoc. *Publ:* Contr articles to prof jour; co-edit: Newsletter Decorative Art Soc, 1995—; books. *Mailing Add:* Dean Sch Grad Studies E315 27th St & 7th Ave New York NY 10001

CONESA, MIGUEL A
PAINTER, ILLUSTRATOR
b Ponce, PR, Sept 29, 52. *Study:* Jose Azaustre Acad, Ponce, PR, 67-68; Escuela Artes Plasticas, San Juan, PR, 72; Augusta Col, Ga, 75-77. *Work:* Carnegie Libr, Ex-Libris Collection, San Juan, PR; Libr Univ Rio Piedras, PR; Ponce Art Mus, Luis A Ferre Found, PR; McDuffie Co Mus, Thomson, Ga; and over 300 works in pvt collections in

the US, PR, Latin Am & Europe. *Comn:* Homenaje a la Grandeza del Paisaje Puertorriqueno, assemblage-mixed media mural, Image Makers Corp, 84-88. *Exhib:* South Eastern Artist, High Mus, Atlanta, Ga, 76; Retrospective, Ponce Art Mus, PR, 80; 14 Yr Retrospective, Col Tech, Ponce, PR, 84; Inter-Am Univ, Ponce, 85; Col Abogados de PR, Santurce, 88; Second Expo Arte Ponceno, Col Tech, Ponce, PR; 7 works submitted to Sotheby's Latin Am auction, NY, 88; Catholic Univ, Law Sch, Ponce, 93; and others. *Pos:* Post card designer, Graficas Nativas, Domingo Cabrera, Rio Piedras, PR, 71-72; illusr, Korsevish Advert Agency, Atlanta, Ga, 77-78; illusr, TASC Fed Govt, Ft Gordon, Ga, 81-83; creative dir, MC Studio Mod Design, Hato Rey, PR, currently; vpres, Avant Garde Productions, Ponce, PR, 84-85; pres, Graphitec, currently; pres & art instr, Taller Galeria San Jose, Ponce, PR, currently; adv, Stewart Inc, Simplicity Plan, Ponce, PR Gr, 94-96; Legado Historico, San Juan, 96-97. *Teaching:* Gertrude Herbert Inst Art, Augusta, Ga, 76-77; Centro Tabaiba-Playa Ponce, PR, 84-85; Academia Christo Rey, Ponce, 85; Prof Sch Photog, Ponce, PR, 88. *Awards:* Best Show Scholar Award, Luis Ferre Found, 70-71; Best Show, Ga Depot Art Festial, McDuffie, 75; Bailies' Award, Augusta Col, Bailies' Studio, Augusta, 75. *Bibliog:* Antonio Molina (auth), History of Painting in Puerto Rico, Gran Enciclopedia de PR, vol 8, 73; Fay Rice (auth), Profile on Miguel Conesa, Art Voices South, 5-6/81. *Mem:* Int Platform Asn, Cleveland; Ponce Art Mus, Ponce, PR; Image Makers Corp, Ponce, PR. *Media:* All. *Publ:* Auth, Museo de Arte de Ponce, Odicea Cultural, La Fuente Informativa, 3/86; El Digital, Western Digital Caribe, Ponce, PR, 88-89. *Dealer:* Euro-Am Consult Mems Group Inc Jean Daniel Etchevers Mutis 255 Ponce de Leon Ave Hato Rey PR 00919; Art International Karl Berdejoo Insignares 1060 Ashford Condado PR 00907

CONFORTE, RENEE See McKee, Renee Conforte

CONFORTI, MICHAEL PETER
HISTORIAN, MUSEUM DIRECTOR
b Bradford, Mass, Apr 3, 45. *Study:* Trinity Col, Conn, BA, 68; Harvard Univ, MA, 73, PhD, 77. *Pos:* Cataloguer, Sotheby & Co, London & NY, 68-71; cur sculpture & decorative arts, Fine Arts Mus, San Francisco, 77-80; chief cur & Bell Mem cir, Minneapolis Inst Arts, 80-94; dir, Sterling & Francine Clark Art Inst, Williamstown, Mass, 94-. *Teaching:* Adj prof art hist, Univ Minn, 86-94 & Williams Col, 95-. *Awards:* Fel Art Hist, Am Acad Rome, 75-77; Charles Montgomery Award, Robert Smith Award, 87; Getty Guest Scholar, CASVA, 88. *Mem:* Am Asn Mus; Decorative Arts Soc; Am Ceramics Circle; Silver Soc; English Ceramic Circle; Soc Archit Historians; and others. *Res:* Sculpture and decorative arts, 17th to 20th centuries; museum history and history of collecting. *Publ:* Auth, Deaccessioning in American Museums: Some Thoughts for England, Apollo, 8/89; Expanding the Canon of Art Collecting in Museums, Mus News, 9-10/89; History, Value and the 1900s Art Museum, J Mus Mgmt & Curatorship, 9/93; Museums Past and Museums Present: Some Thoughts on Institutional Survival, J Mus Mgmt & Curatorship, 12/95; The Idealist Enterprise and the Applied Arts, in A Grand Design (exhib catalog), Baltimore et al, 97; and others. *Mailing Add:* c/o Sterling & Francine Clark Art Mus 225 South St Williamstown MA 01267

CONGER, WILLIAM
PAINTER, EDUCATOR
b Dixon, Ill, May 29, 37. *Study:* Art Inst Chicago, 56-57; Univ NMex, with Elaine deKooning, BFA, 61; Univ Chicago, MFA, 66. *Work:* Mus Contemp Art, Chicago; Art Inst Chicago; Ill State Mus, Springfield; Jonson Mus, Albuquerque; Portland Mus, Wash; Rockford Art Mus, Univ Club Chicago; Davis Mus, Wellesley College, Union League, Chicago. *Comn:* Painting for IBM Corp, 86; City of Chicago Painting & Glass Windows, 2002; McCormick Place, Chicago, 2006. *Exhib:* Chicago & Vicinity, Art Inst Chicago, 63, 71, 73, 78, 80-81 & 84-85; one-man shows, Krannert Ctr Performing Arts, Urbana, Ill, 76, Zaks Gallery, Chicago, 78, 80 & 83, Boyd Gallery, Chicago, 85, 87, 90, 92, 94, 97-2002, 2004; Janus Gallery, Santa Fe, 92 & Jonson Mus, Albuquerque, NMex, 98; Walters Gallery, Tulsa OK, 2001; Tadu Contemp, Santa Fe, NMex, 2003, 2005; Visions-Painting & Sculpture of Distinguished Alumni 1945 to present, Art Inst Chicago Sch Gallery, 76; Chicago Abstractionists, Grae Gallery, St Louis, Mo, 87; Printmaking in Chicago 1935-95, Blook Gallery, Northwestern Univ, 96, 2005; Art in Chicago 1945-1995, Mus Contemp Art, Chicago, 96-97; Albuquerque '50s, Univ Mus, Albuquerque, 90; Ill State Mus, 2005; Metcap, Chicago, 2006. *Pos:* Mem bd dir, Oxbow, Saugatuk, Mich, 83-86; adv bd, Renaissance Soc, 88-2002. *Teaching:* Prof art, DePaul Univ, Chicago, 71-85, chmn dept, 71-77 & 80-85; vis artist, Univ Southern Ill, 84, Sch of Art Inst Chicago, 85, Univ Iowa, 96; prof & chmn dept art theory & practice, NWestern Univ, Evanston, Ill, 84-98; Northwestern Univ, 98-2006, prof emer, 2006. *Awards:* Bartels Prize, 71 & Cluseman Prize, 73, Art Inst Chicago; Ill Acad Fine Arts Award Nominee, Chicago, 92. *Bibliog:* Art in Am, 11/85; M Gedo (auth), The meaning of artistic form & the promise of the psychoanalytic method, Vol 2, No 3, Art Criticism, 86; Carol Volk (auth), Art & Antiques, 4/92; S Taylor, auth, Art in Am, 7/97; G Holg (auth), William Conger, Art News, 1/95; Art News, 12/2000. *Mem:* Arts Club Chicago; Sons of The Am Revolution. *Media:* Oil. *Res:* Manet & Perspective, other art hist & practice topics. *Specialty:* Contemp Art. *Interests:* US Hist, Science, Philosophy. *Collection:* Mod & Contemp Art, mainly Chicago; Native Am; Rare books & Hist Doc. *Publ:* Looking & dreaming in New York & Chicago, No 1, Chicago/Art/Write, 85 & Abstract painting: Fact, fiction, paradox, No 2, & Art Limits, No 4, 87; Drawing, No 13, WhiteWalls, 86; The Journal of Eugene Delacroix, Psychoanalytic Studies of Biog, Int Univs Press Inc, 87; contribr, Gedo, Looking at Fine Art from The Inside Out, 94; The MFA Filling the Gap between Seeing & Saying, Alumni Exhib Catolog, Northwestern Univ, 2001. *Dealer:* Roy Boyd Gallery 739 N Wells St Chicago IL 60610; Printworks Gallery, Chicago, Ill. *Mailing Add:* 3500 N Lake Shore Dr Apt 15A Chicago IL 60657

CONKLIN, ERIC
ARTIST
b Baltimore, Md, Apr 20, 50. *Work:* Historic Ark Mus, Little Rock; The Sherlock Holmes Mus, London; Leigh Yawkey Woodson Art Mus, Wausau, WI. *Exhib:* Works by Contemp Md Artists, The Govt House, Annapolis, Md, 2000; Phoenix Art Mus, 2003; Leigh Yawkey Woodson Art Mus, Wausau, Wis, 2003; The Art of Illusion, Teopel Oeil Soc of Artists, Philabrook Mus of Art, Tulsa, Okla, 2004; Smith Kramer Mus Toor, 2004-2007. *Pos:* research historian, Trompe l'Oeil Soc Artists, 2001-. *Teaching:* Mus Lectures & Demonstr, Phoenix Art Mus, Phoenix, Ariz; Philbrook Art Mus, Tulsa, Okla; Woodson Art Mus, Wausau, Wis. *Awards:* Exhib III, Works by Contemp Md Artists, 1st Lady Glendening, 2000; Best of Show, York Art Asn, 2001; Annie Award, 2003; Cult Arts Found of Awwe Arundel Co, Visual Arts, Md. *Mem:* Trompe l'Oeil Soc Artists (founding mem, rsch historian, 2001-); Md Hall Sch Arts; Delaplaine Visual Arts Ctr; York (Pa) Art Asn; Md Fedn Art; Allied Artists Am. *Media:* Hand mixed Oil on Panel. *Res:* Dutch perspective boxes, American & European trompe l'oeil painting; Anamorphic Cylindees and Cowicalmirror Images. *Specialty:* Trompe l'Oeil. *Publ:* Ed, Best of the West: New Mexico, Southwest Art, 2002; Birds in Art, Woodson Art Mus; Edgaetown Art Gallery orignal paintings, 2004. *Dealer:* Cynthia McBride McBride Gallery 215 Main St Annapolis MD 21401; Eleanor Ettinger Gallery, NYC; Edgartown ARt Gallery, Edgartown, MA. *Mailing Add:* 3895 Greenmeadow Ln Davidsonville MD 21035

CONKLIN, JO-ANN
MUSEUM DIRECTOR, CURATOR
b Great Barrington, Mass, Dec 22, 52. *Study:* Md Inst Col of Art, BA, 79; Univ Iowa, MA (art hist), 88. *Collection Arranged:* Landscape: James Casebere, Univ Iowa Mus Art, 91, Pajama: An Arists Coterie at Play, 94, Inscape: Odd Nerdrum, 95 & Rudolf Koppitz: Viennese Master of the Camera (auth, catalog), 96; Map of Temper, Map of Tenderness: Annette Messager (auth, catalog), Brown Univ, 97 & False Witness: Joan Fontaebera and Kahuf Selesnick, 2000. *Pos:* registr, Univ Iowa Mus Art, 86-96 & cur of graphic arts, 86-96; dir, David Winton Bell Gallery, Brown Univ, 96-. *Publ:* auth & ed, Art by Women: The Louis Noun Collection, Univ Iowa Mus Art, 90 & Photographs from the Collection of Carlton Willer, 93; ed, Crafting the Media: Patrons & Certisums in Theme, Brown Univ, 99. *Mailing Add:* 69 Hillside Ave Providence RI 02906

CONLEY, ZEB BRISTOL, JR
COLLECTOR, GALLERY DIRECTOR
b Andrews, NC, Feb 12, 36. *Study:* Mars Hill Col, 55-57; Col William & Mary, 57-61; NMex Highlands Univ, 63. *Collection Arranged:* Alfred Murang Retrospective, Mus of the Southwest, Midland, Tex, 85. *Pos:* Dir, Jamison Galleries, Santa Fe, 73-98, bd mem, 74-98, pres, 81-98; guest cur, Mus of the Southwest, Midland, Tex, 85. *Specialty:* Traditional Southwestern art, specializing in Taos and Santa Fe masters. *Mailing Add:* PO Box 1900 Andrews NC 28901

CONLON, JAMES EDWARD
SCULPTOR, HISTORIAN
b Cincinnati, Ohio, Dec 9, 35. *Study:* Ohio State Univ, BS(art educ), 59, MA(fine arts), 62. *Work:* Fine Arts Mus South Mobile; Fine Arts Mus York, Ala; Symbiotic Series, Mobile Arts Coun; Moses, Springhill Ave Temple, Mobile, Ala. *Comn:* sculptural relief, Mobile, Ala Airport; Three Angels (wall relief), Seventh Day Adventist Church, St Elmo, Ala, 82; Gateway, Cathedral Sq, Mobile Arts Coun & Mainstreet Mobile, Ala, 93; At Play (life-size tableau) Univ S Ala Women's & Children's Hosp, 96. *Exhib:* Southern Asn Sculptors Traveling Exhib, Smithsonian Inst; Competition 75, Mobile, Ala, 75; two-person show, Fine Arts Mus South-Mobile, 77; Montgomery Mus Art, 78-79; Ala Sculptors Invitational, 80. *Teaching:* Instr, Ind Univ, Bloomington, 62-65; from asst prof to assoc prof, Univ S Ala, Mobile, 65-73, prof, 74-97, prof emer art & art hist, 98-. *Awards:* Award to Develop the Ethnic Am Art Slide Libr, Samuel H Kress Found, 72-75; Award to Produce a Reference Index of Afro-Am Art, Am Revolution Bicentennial Comn, 73; Univ Res Grant, 76-77. *Mem:* Ala Alliance Arts Educ; Mobile Watercolor and Graphic Arts Soc (pres, 2003). *Media:* Woods, Limestone, Cast & Laminated Plastics. *Res:* An investigation of stylistic development in Afro-American, Mexican American and Native American art from 1800 to the present; adaptation of the industrial process of cultured marble to the production of hollow-cast figurative forms 1983-1986. *Interests:* figurative & organic forms in sculpture. *Publ:* Coauth, An Afro-American slide project, Col Art Asn J, winter 70. *Dealer:* Gallery 54 54 Upham St Mobile AL 36607. *Mailing Add:* 1613 Sugar Creek Dr W Mobile AL 36695-2938

CONLON, WILLIAM
PAINTER, PRINTMAKER
b Albany, NY, 41. *Study:* Sch Visual Arts, 60-63; Sch Art & Archit, Yale Univ, BFA & MFA, 65-67. *Work:* Dallas Mus Fine Arts, Dallas, Tex; Grand Rapids Art Mus, Mich; Albright-Knox Art Gallery, Buffalo, NY; Brooklyn Mus; Lincoln Ctr Performing Arts. *Comn:* List Art Posters, Lincoln Ctr Performing Arts, NY; Saatchi & Saatchi, Los Angeles,. *Exhib:* Whitney Mus Am Art, 72; solo exhibs, Andre Emmerich Gallery, NY, 77, 80, 81, 85-87 & Carnegie Inst Mus Art, Pittsburgh, 81; Hunter Col MFA Faculty Artists: 1981-1993, Hunter Col Art Gallery, NY, 93; Hunter Col (invitational), NY, 94; Color-Sign & System & Sensibility, Stark Gallery, NY, 95; Vesti-Daine Gallery, Scottsdale, Ariz, 96; Nat Acad, NY, 06. *Teaching:* Summer sch art fac, Yale Norfolk Sch Music & Art, Conn, 68; instr art, grad sch admis comt & undergrad student adv, Yale Univ Sch Art & Archit, New Haven, Conn, 67-70; instr art, curric comt & grad admis comt, Hunter Col, NY, 70-71; adj prof art, grad adv, grad admis comt & lectr, Univ Calif, Irvine, 71-74; guest adj, Brooklyn Col, NY, fall 74; fac app, gallery comt, art criticism, Sarah Lawrence Col, Bronxville, NY, 75-79; prof studio art & dir studio arts prog, Fordham Univ, Col Lincoln Ctr, NY, 79-92 (tenured, 86), chair

div art, 93- & prof, theatre & visual arts, currently. *Awards:* Nat Endowment Arts, 77, 89 & 90. *Bibliog:* Gene Baro (auth), William Conlen Paintings 1969-1981 (catalog, exhib), Mus Art Carnegie Inst, Pittsburgh, Pa, 10/81-1/3/82; Robert Murdock (auth), the Gray Cycle-William Conlon (exhib, catalog), Andre Emmerich Gallery, NY, 85. *Mem:* Nat Coun Art Admins. *Mailing Add:* 461 Broome St New York NY 10013

CONN, DAVID EDWARD
PRINTMAKER
b Jersey City, NJ, Apr 10, 41. *Study:* Newark Sch Fine Arts, NJ; Md Inst Col Art, Baltimore, BFA, with Peter Milton, 67; Univ Okla, Norman, MFA, 70. *Work:* Ark Art Ctr, Little Rock; Ft Worth Art Mus, Tex; Modern Mus Art, Campinas Sao Paulo, Brazil. *Exhib:* 20th Exhib Southwestern Prints & Drawings, Dallas Mus Art, 75; Joslyn Art Mus, 78; 1984 int Art Competition, Los Angeles; Texas Visons, Mus Art Am Southwest, Houston, 86; 4th Int Exhib, Lodz, Poland; Int Prints II, John Szoke Graphics Gallery, NY, 88. *Pos:* Chmn dept art & art hist, Tex Christian Univ, 90-94. *Teaching:* Prof art-printmaking, Tex Christian Univ, 69-. *Awards:* Ford Fel, Painting, 66-67; Purchase Award, Ark Print, Drawing & Crafts, Ark Art Ctr, 71; Individual Fel Printmaking, Drawing & Artists Bks, Nat Endowment Arts, 84. *Bibliog:* American Printmakers 74--Graphics Group, Arcadia, Calif, 74. *Media:* Intaglio, Waterless Lithography. *Mailing Add:* 1024 Shaw Ft Worth TX 76110

CONN, LAURENCE
CURATOR, PAINTER
b Chicago, Ill, 45. *Study:* Univ Ill, Chicago, 63-64; Chicago Acad Fine Arts, BFA, 64-68. *Work:* Jones, Day, Reavis & Pogue & First Nat Bank, Chicago; Billy Graham Ctr Mus, Wheaton, Ill; Burroughs Corp, NY; Ingersol Rand Corp, Rockford, Ill; Shea Archit, Minneapolis. *Exhib:* Wisconsin Directions II, Milwaukee Art Ctr, 78; System & Structure, UW Wis Green Bay, 83, Priebe Art Ctr, Oshkosh, 83,Burpee Art Mus, Rockford, Ill, 83, Ukranian Inst Mod Art, Chicago, 84; Contemp Spiritual Art, Washington DC, 88; Sacred Arts, Billy Graham Mus, Wheaton, Ill, 90; Univ NMex, Albuquerque, 90. *Pos:* Cur, Franklin Sq Gallery, currently, Ancient Echoes Collection, Richard J Daley Col Gallery & Space 900. *Media:* Acrylic, Graphite. *Dealer:* Deson Saunders Gallery Chicago IL; Anderson & Anderson Gallery, Minneapolis MN

CONNEEN, JANE W
PRINTMAKER, BOOK ARTIST
b Montclair, NJ, April 19, 21. *Study:* With George Parker, Emily Hatch, Sally Kugelmeyer & David Sander; Lehigh Univ. *Work:* Hunt Inst Botanical Doc, Pittsburgh, Pa; Mus City New York; Skillman Libr, Lafayette Col, Easton, Pa. *Comn:* Drawings, Allentown Art Mus, Pa, 75 & Pa Chamber Commerce, Harrisburg, 76. *Exhib:* Solo exhib, Lehigh Univ & Kemerer Mus, Bethlehem, Pa, 85 & Skillman Libr, Lafayette Col, Easton, Pa, 95; Philadelphia Print Club, 82; Royal Soc Miniature Painters, London, 83; 20-yr Retrospective Exhib, Lehigh Univ, 90; Book Arts 93, Can Bookbinders & Book Artists' Guild. *Pos:* miniature book pub. *Awards:* Best in Show & First in Graphics, Am Nat Miniature Show, Laramie, Wyo, 80; First in Graphics, Miniature Painters, Sculptors & Gravers Washington, DC, 83, Miniature Art Soc Fla, 84 & Miniature Art Soc NJ, 85; Distinguished Book award from The Miniature Book Soc, 90; Norman Forgue Award, Miniature Book Soc, 2001. *Bibliog:* Louis Bondy (auth), Miniature Books, Sheppard Press, London, 81; Lillian Wachtel (auth), Miniature Herb Books, The Herb Quarterly; David P Richards (auth), How to Discover Your Own Painting Style, North Light Books; Christina Feliciano (auth), Making Books by Hand, Quarry books, Rockport Publishers, Inc. *Mem:* Miniature Painters, Sculptors & Gravers Soc, Washington, DC; fel Int Guild Miniature Artisans; Printmaking Coun NJ; Miniature Book Soc. *Media:* Hand-Colored Etchings; Limited Edition Miniature Books, Gouache Landscapes, Wood Engraving. *Publ:* Auth & illusr, The Winding Roads of Ireland, 90; The Language of Herbs I, II, & III (miniature bks), 91; Staithes; The Story of a Yorkshire Fishing Village (miniature bk); Covered Bridges of Bucks County, Pennsylvania, 96; Wildflowers of Wickham Park, Florida, 96; Violets, 93; Dixie Cups, 95; Strawberries, Their History & Uses, 95; Santas, 97; Angels, 98; The Star Spangled Banner, 2000; Assisi, 2000; Ireland: A Gallery of Small Gouache Paintings, 2002; Achill Island, 2003. *Dealer:* The Snow Goose Gallery, Main St, Bethlehem, PA, 18018. *Mailing Add:* 127 Hengestone Waynesville NC 28789

CONNEEN, MARI M
PAINTER
b Allentown, Pa, Dec 21, 46. *Study:* Self taught. *Work:* Lowe Art Mus, Miami, Fla; Pensacola Visual Arts Mus, Fla; Loch Haven Art Ctr, Orlando, Fla; Walt Disney World, Orlando, Fla; Hunt Botanical Inst, Pittsburgh, Pa; Brevard Mus Art & Science, Melbourne, Fla; Orlando Mus Art, Fla; IBM Corp, NC; Southern Progress, Birmingham, Ala. *Comn:* Two large watercolors of sea life, Song of Norway Cruise Line, Miami, Fla, 87. *Exhib:* Allied Artists of Am 85th Watercolor Exhib, Nat Arts Club, NY, 84; Adirondacks Nat Exhib, Old Forge Art Ctr, 84-99; Miss Watercolor Exhib, Mus Art Jackson, 87 & 93; Okla Watercolor Exhib, Okla Art Ctr, 87, 88, 92 & 93; Boca Raton Mus, 90; Nat Watercolor Soc, 93 & 94. *Awards:* Best of Show, Winter Park Art Festival & Coconut Grove Art Festival, 83; Experts Choice, Artist Soc Int, 84; Nat Watercolor Soc, 93. *Bibliog:* Article on Camelias, Southern Accents Mag, 12/91; Orlando Mag, 3/94; Fla Today Newspaper; Watercolor Magic, 2003; Space Coast Living, 2003. *Mem:* Nat Mus Women in Arts; Am Artist Prof League; Guild Natural Sci Illusr; Southern Watercolor Soc; Nat Watercolor Soc; Fla Watercolor Soc; Watercolor USA Honor Soc. *Media:* Watercolor; Lithography. *Interests:* Environmental Issues. *Publ:* Auth, Watercolor '86, Am Artists, 86; Best of Flower Paintings, 96; Painting Texture, Rockport Press, 97; Best of Watercolor, 97; Best of Flower Painting II, 99. *Dealer:* J Lawrence Gallery 535 W Eau Gallie Blvd Melbourne Fla; Grand Cent Art Galleries Inc 24 W 57th Ave New York NY 10019. *Mailing Add:* 457 Crystal Tree Dr Waynesville NC 28785

CONNELLY, CHUCK
PAINTER
b Pittsburgh, Pa, 1955. *Study:* Tyler Sch Art, Philadelphia, Pa, BFA, 77. *Work:* Metrop Mus Art, NY; Brooklyn Mus Art, NY; Portland Art Mus, Ore; J B Speed Mus, Louisville, KY; Tucson Mus Art, Ariz. *Exhib:* New Narrative Painting, Museo Tamayo, Mexico City, Mex, 84; solo exhib, Northern Ill Univ Art Gallery, Chicago, 84-85; Aldrich Mus Contemp Art, Ridgefield, Conn, 84 & 86; Painting & Sculpture Today, Indianapolis Mus Art, Ind, 86; Nassau Co Mus Art, Roslyn, NY, 91; Big Ideas, Tucson Mus Art, Tucson, Ariz, 92; Transport, Maier Mus Art, Lynchberg, Va, 94; The Figure: Another Side of Modernism, Song Harnor Cult Ctr, Staten Island, NT, 2000; A Gift of Vision, Tucson Mus Art, Ariz, 95. *Awards:* Gottlieb Found Grant, 99. *Bibliog:* Eleanor Heartney (auth), Chuck Connelly at Lennon, Weinberg, Art in America, 5/92; Ronny Cohen (auth), Chuck Connelly, Artforum, 2/93; Judith Page (auth), Chuck Connelly, ArtPapers, 3/95. *Media:* Oil. *Dealer:* Lennon Weinberg Inc 560 Broadway Suite 308 New York NY 10012-3945

CONNELLY, JOAN BRETON
HISTORIAN, EDUCATOR
Study: Princeton, BA, 76; Bryn Mawr Col, MA, 79, PhD, 84. *Teaching:* Assoc prof fine arts, classical art & archit, NY Univ, currently; dir, NYU Yeronisos Island Excavations, Cyprus. *Awards:* Honorary Citizenship, Peyia Municipality, Republic of Cyprus; Lillian Vernon Chair for Teaching Excellence, NYU; Appointed to the US Cultural Property Advisory Comt by Pres George W. Bush, 2003; John D. and Catherine T. MacArthur Foundation Fellowship, 97; Visiting Fellowships All Souls College, Magdalen College and New College, Oxford; Phi Beta Kappa Visiting Fellowship; NYU Presidential (Mellon) Fellowship; NYU Golden Dozen Teaching Award; Metrop Mus Art Classical Fellowship and Norbert Schimmel Fellowship. *Mem:* Soc Preservation Greek Heritage, Trustee; Soc Anitquaries London; Royal Geographical Soc; Explorers Club; Soc Women Geographers; Archaeological Inst Am; Cyprus American Archaeological Research Inst (former trustee); Oxford Philological Soc; Pilgrims of the United States. *Interests:* Greek sculpture and vase painting, Greek myth and religion, Cypriot archaeology, the Hellenistic East. *Mailing Add:* 110 Bleecker St Apt 22F New York NY 10012-2101

CONNER, ANN
PRINTMAKER, PAINTER
b Wilmington, NC, Aug 11, 48. *Study:* Salem Col, NC, BFA, 70; Salem-Hofstra Summer Prog, Asolo, Italy, 70; Univ NC, Chapel Hill, MACT, 72, MFA, 75. *Work:* Fogg Art Mus, Harvard Univ, Cambridge, Mass; Mus Fine Arts, Boston; Libr Cong, Washington; NY Pub Libr, NY; List Visual Arts Ctr, Mass Inst Technol; and others. *Comn:* Cinnamon, Philip Morris USA, Charlotte, NC. *Exhib:* Independante Exhib of Prints, Kanagawa Prefectural Gallery, Yokohama, Japan, 84-95; 69th Int Competition Prints, Print Club, Philadelphia, 94; Releif Prints, Winthrop Univ Galleries, Rock Hill, SC, 94, After Appalachia, WVa Univ, Morgantown, 95; In Relief, Contemp Am Relief Prints, Lincoln, Nebr, 98; solo exhibs, Gray Gallery, Greenville, NC, 98, Flatbed Press, Austin, Tex, 98; Int Print Ctr, NY, 2002-2006. *Teaching:* Prof painting, Univ NC, Wilmington, 72-. *Awards:* NC Governor's Bus Award Ed, 91; Summer Initiative Award, Univ NC, Wilmington, 93; Cahill Award, 93; UNCW Fac Res Award, 04. *Bibliog:* Susan Tallman (auth), Utopia/Dystopia, Print Club, Philadelphia, 92; Appalachian High Resisting Mis-Representation, New Art Examiner, 97; The Best in Printmaking, Rockport, Publ, 97; Working Proof, Art on Paper, 99, 2000, 02. *Mem:* Southern Graphics Coun; Los Angeles Printmaking Soc; Print Club, Pa; Print Consortium; Col Art Asn Am. *Media:* Woodcut and Acrylics. *Publ:* New York Art Review, Les Krantz, 88; Modern Graphics, Art of the 80's, Libr Cong, 89; Printworld Directory of Contemp Prints, 85-86, 88-89 & 93; Print News, Prints from Blocks, 85; The Complete Manual of Relief Printmaking, Kindersley, 88. *Dealer:* Flatbed Press 2832 E Martin Luther King Blvd Austin Tx 78702; Somerhill Gallery 3 Eastgate Chapel Hill NC 27514. *Mailing Add:* 329 Stradleigh Rd Wilmington NC 28403

CONNER, BRUCE
GRAPHIC ARTIST, COLLAGE ARTIST, FILMMAKER
b McPherson, Kans, Nov 18, 1933. *Study:* Wichita Univ; Univ Nebr, BFA; Brooklyn Mus Art Sch; Univ Colo. *Hon Degrees:* San Francisco Art Inst, Hon DFA, 86. *Work:* Guggenheim Mus, Whitney Mus Am Art, Mus Mod Art, NY; Art Inst Chicago; Los Angeles Co Art Mus, Norton Simon Mus, Los Angeles; Rose Art Mus, Brandeis Univ, Waltham Addison Gallery, Andover, Mass; San Francisco Mus Mod Art, Calif. *Comn:* Poster, NY Film Festival, Am Fedn Arts, 65; San Francisco Dancers Workshop Poster, 67. *Exhib:* The Art of Assemblage, Mus Mod Art, NY, 60; Whitney Biennial, Whitney Mus Am Art, 82 & 97; Retrospective, Inst Contemp Art, Univ Pa, 67 & de Young Mem Mus, San Francisco, 74; Am Sculpture of the Sixties, Los Angeles Co Art Mus, 67; Belly-Button Art of the Seventies, Newport Harbor Art Gallery, 72; Tyler Mus Art, Tex, 74; Smith-Andersen Gallery, Palo Alto, Calif, 74, 84 & 86; MH DeYoung Mem Mus, 75; one-person show, Northpoint Gallery, San Francisco, Calif, 81, Smith Andersen Gallery, Palo Alto, Calif, 84 & 86, Michael Kohn Gallery, Santa Monica, Calif, 90, Smith Andersen Editions, Palo Alto, 96, Kohn Turner Gallery, Los Angeles, 97 & Witchita Art Mus, Kans, 97; Beat Cult and the New Am 1950-1965, Whitney Mus, NY, 95 & MH DeYoung Mem Mus, San Francisco, 96; Solo Exhibs, Curt Marcus Gallery, New York City, 92, 95, 97, 98, 2000, Kohn Turner Gallery, Los Angeles, 99-, Susan Inglett Gallery, New York City, 95, 2000, Gallery Paule Angum, San Francisco, 93, 96, 2000, 2000BC: The Bruce Conner Story Part II, Walker Art Center, Minneapolis, 99, Mod Art Mus, Fort Worth, Tex, 2000, MH De Young Memorial Mus, San Francisco, 2000, Mus Contemp Art, Los Angeles, 2000. *Pos:* Pres & founder, Rat Bastard Protective Asn, San Francisco, 58-61; dir, bd dir, Canyon Cinema Coop, San Francisco, 69-72 & 85. *Teaching:* Instr film making, Calif Col Arts & Crafts, 65-66; undergrad sem, Wasted Time, San Francisco Art Inst, 66-67. *Awards:* Nat Endowment Arts, 84; Mus Contemp Art Grant, 84; Calif Tamarack Found Grant,

85; Ford Found Fel Grant, 64, Am Film Inst Film Making Grant, 74, Guggenheim Fel Painting, 75. *Bibliog:* Carl Belz (auth), 3 films by Bruce Conner, Film Cult Mag, spring 67; Anthony Reveaux (auth), Bruce Conner (films), Film in the Cities, 81. *Media:* Ink on Paper, Engraving Collage. *Publ:* Coauth, Bruce Conner/Mike McClure, Averhahn Press, 67, The Adventures of a Novel in Four Chapters, 91; auth, The Dennis Hopper One-Man Show, Crown Point Press, Vols I-III, 71-73. *Dealer:* Gallery paule Angum 14 Geary San Francisco CA 94108; Kohn Turner Gallery 454 N Robertson Blvd Los Angeles CA 90048. *Mailing Add:* c/o Smith Andersen Editions 440 Pepper Ave Palo Alto CA 94306

CONNER, LOIS
PHOTOGRAPHER
b Long Island, NY, Feb 12, 51. *Study:* Pratt Inst, BFA, 75; Yale Univ, MFA, 81. *Work:* Mus Mod Art & Metrop Mus Art, NY; Smithsonian Inst, Nat Mus Art, Washington, DC; Victoria & Albert Mus, London, Eng; Nat Gallery Victoria, Melbourne, Australia. *Comn:* Wave Hill, Botanical Gardens, NY, 90; The Cuyahoga River, Gund Found, Cleveland, Ohio, 91. *Exhib:* Photographs from the Collection, Victoria & Albert Mus, London, Eng, 87; Photographs of China, Canton Art Mus, China, 88; China, Cleveland Mus Art, Ohio, 88; Landscapes, Bombay Ctr Photog, Bombay, India, 90; In the Shadow of the Wall (auth, catalog), Taiwan Mus Art, Taichung, Rep China, 92; Between Heaven & Home, Smithsonian Inst, Washington, DC, 92; Mus Mod Art, NY, 92. *Teaching:* Adj prof photog, Fordham Univ, New York, & Cooper Union, New York, 91; asst prof photog, Yale Univ, New Haven, Conn, 91-. *Awards:* Fel, Nat Endowment Arts, 83; Guggenheim Fel, 84; Fel, NY State Coun Arts, 79. *Bibliog:* Dang Ho Liu (auth), In the Shadow of the Wall, Taiwan Mus Art, 92. *Dealer:* Laurence Miller Gallery 138 Spring St New York NY 10012. *Mailing Add:* 36 Gramercy Park E No 4-E New York NY 10003

CONNIFF, GREGORY
PHOTOGRAPHER, WRITER
b Jersey City, NJ, May 3, 44. *Study:* Columbia Univ, BA, 66; Univ Va Law Sch, LLB, 69; with William Weege (printmaker), 71-72. *Work:* Mus Mod Art, NY; Ctr Creative Photogr, Tucson, Ariz; Mus Fine Arts, Boston, Mass; San Francisco Mus Mod Art; Corcoran Gallery Art, Washington; Art Inst Chgo. *Comn:* Nat Rd Proj, John Hopkins Univ Press; Urban Gardens, George Gund Found. *Exhib:* Solo exhibs, Corcoran Gallery Art, 79, Toledo Mus Art, 83, Akron Art Mus, Ohio, 86, Mus Contemp Photogr, Chicago, 86, Cleveland Mus Art, 2002, Ludwig Mus, Budapest, 2002; Fogg Art Mus, 80; A Century of Landscape, High Mus Art (catalog), 81; The Lens in the Garden, Hudson River Mus, Yonkers, NY, 84; Two Days in Louisiana, Milwaukee Art Mus, Wis, 89; Between Home and Heaven, Nat Mus Am Art, Washington, 92; Crossing the Frontier (catalog), San Francisco Mus Mod Art, 96, 2001; Camera and Ink; Judy Pfaff and Gregory Conniff; Milwaukee Mus of Art, 2004. *Pos:* Consult ed (landscape), Johns Hopkins Univ Press. *Awards:* Nat Endowment Arts Photog Fel, 80-81, 92-93; Wis Arts Bd Visual Arts Fel, 78, 84 & 90; John Simon Guggenheim Mem Fel, 89-90. *Bibliog:* Jane Livingston (auth), Gregory Conniff, Corcoran Gallery Art, 79; David Tannous (auth), Gregory Conniff, Art Am, summer 80; Kent Williams (auth), In His Own Image, Isthmus, 11/24/89. *Media:* Photography. *Publ:* Auth & illusr, Common Ground: Vol 1 of an American Field Guide, Yale Univ Press, 85; Between Home & Heaven: Contemporary American Landscape Photography, Univ NMex Press, 92; What is Landscape?, Univ Tex Press, 95. *Mailing Add:* 1426 Rutledge St Madison WI 53703-3835

CONNOLLY, JEROME PATRICK
PAINTER, MURALIST
b Minneapolis, Minn, Jan 14, 31. *Study:* Univ Minn, BS (art educ); also with Francis Lee Jaques. *Work:* Diorama backgrounds & murals in 36 mus, incl Carnegie Mus, Pittsburgh, James Ford Bell Mus, Minneapolis, George C Page Mus, Los Angeles, Smithsonian Mus Nat Hist, Taipei Zoo Educ Bldg, Taiwan, Transp Mus & many others. *Exhib:* Sportsman's Gallery of Art & Bks, NY; Crossroads of Sport, NY; Abercrombie & Fitch, NY & San Francisco; Petersen Gallery, Los Angeles; one-man show, Abercrombie & Fitch, NY, 72; and others. *Pos:* Staff artist, Ill State Mus, Springfield, 58-60, Natural Sci Youth Found, Westport, Conn, 60-65; free lance artist, 65-. *Awards:* First place, Wildlife Art Show, East Stroudsberg Univ, 93. *Mem:* Susquehanna Valley Art Soc. *Media:* Oil, Acrylic. *Interests:* fishing & ballooning. *Publ:* Illusr, Adelbert the Penguin, 69; The Deer Family, 69; Aise-ce-bon: a Raccoon, 71; Saga of a Whitetail, 81; 15 children's books & contribr, Audubon Mag, Nat Wildlife, Hartford Life Insurance Co calendar & Pa Game News. *Mailing Add:* 804 Sunbury Rd Shamokin Dam PA 17876

CONNOR, LINDA STEVENS
PHOTOGRAPHER, INSTRUCTOR
b New York, NY, Nov 18, 44. *Study:* RI Sch Design, BFA, with Harry Calahan; Inst Design, Ill Inst Technol, MS, with Aaron Siskind. *Work:* Boston Mus Fine Arts, Mass; Art Inst Chicago; Int Mus Photog, George Eastman House, Rochester, NY; Mus Mod Art, NY; San Francisco Mus Mod Art, Calif. *Exhib:* One-person shows, Visual Studies Gallery, Rochester, NY, 76, Ctr Photog Studies, 76 & de Young Mem Mus, San Francisco, 77, Art Inst Chicago, Ill, 88, Spiral Journey Mus Contemp Photog Chicago, Ill, 89, Gail Gibson Gallery, Seattle, Wash, 98 & Glenn Horowitz Bookseller, East Hampton, NY, 98; Vision Gallery, Boston, 81; Light Gallery, NY, 81; Corcoran Gallery Art, Washington, DC, 82; Calif Mus Photog, Riverside, 83; San Francisco Mus Mod Art, 92; Measure of Nature: Landscape Photographs from the Permanent Collection, Art Inst Chicago, 98; What Art Is Art For?, Oakland Mus, Calif, 99. *Teaching:* Prof, San Francisco Art Inst, 69. *Awards:* Nat Endowment Arts Grant, 76, 88; Guggenheim Fel, 79; Peer Award, Friends of Photog, 86; Charles Pratt Mem Award in Photog, 88; Flintridge Found Grant Award, 2002. *Mem:* Soc for Photographic Educ; Photo Alliance. *Media:* Photography. *Publ:* Contribr, Calif Mus Photog Bul, Vol 2, No 2; Marks in Place, Univ NMex Press, 87; Spiral Journey, Contemp Mus Photog, Chicago, 90; Women in Photog, Abrams, 90; Lumanance, Ctr Photog Arts, Calif, 95; Earth & Sky, Lodima, Pa, 2006. *Dealer:* Haines Gallery 49 Geary St San Francisco Calif 94108; Yancey Richardson 535 W 22nd St New York NY 10011. *Mailing Add:* 87 Rutherford San Anselmo CA 94960

CONNOR, MAUREEN
SCULPTOR, EDUCATOR
b Baltimore, Md. *Study:* Pratt Inst, NY, MFA, 73. *Work:* Irish Mus Mod Art; The Avon Corp, NY; Zentrum Fur Kunst Und Medientechnologie, Karlsruhe, Ger. *Exhib:* Aldrich Mus Contemp Art, Ridgefield, Conn, 93 & 94; Nat Mus Art, Seoul, Korea, 93; Whitney Mus Am Art Biennial, 93; solo exhibs, Alternative Mus, NY, 94-95, Baxter Gallery, Maine Col Art, Portland, 95, PPOW, NY, 95, William F Brush Gallery, St Lawrence Univ, Canton, NY, 96, Galerie Sima, Nuremburg, Ger, 96, Mus of Modern Art, NY, 96, Kunstraum Munich, Ger, 97 & Inst Contemp Art, Philadelphia, 97, Curt Marcus Gallery, 98, Museo de Arte Modern, Buenos Aires,Argentina, Queens Mus of Art, Corona Park, NY, 2000, Curatorial Studies, Riverdale, NY, 2006; The Telematic Room, Neue Gesellschaft fur Bildende Kunst, Berlin, Ger, 96; The Visible & the Invisible, Inst Int Visual Arts, Univ Col, London, 96; Feed and Greed, Mus Angewande Kunst, Vienna, Austria, 96; Dress for Millenium Eve, Fabric Workshop, Philadelphia, 96; Mus Mod Art, Screening Video Viewpoints, 96; City Canibal, 98; Memorable Histories & Historic Memories, Bowdoin Col, Mus Art, 98; Queens Artists: Highlights of the 20th Century, Queens Mus Art, NY, 98; Xmas, Kent Gallery, NY, 99; A room with a view, Sixth@Prince, Fine Art, 99; Salome, Castle Gallery, New Rochelle, NY, 99; Size Matters, Gate Gates et al, Brooklyn, NY, 99; The End, Exit Art/The Third World, NY, 2000; Representing: A Show of Identities, The Parish Art Mus, Southampton, NY, 2000; Likeness of Being: Contemp Self Portraits, DC Moore Gallery, 2000; All You Need is Love, Laznia Ctr for Contemp Art, Gdansk, Poland, 2000; Do You Have Time?, Liebman Magnan Gallery, NY, 2001. *Teaching:* numerous lectures at art schs & universities, 76-2001; guest prof, Akad Bildenden Kunst, Munchen, Ger, 95-96; prof sculpture & installation, Queens Col, City Univ NY, 90-. *Awards:* Guggenheim Fel, 95; Nat Endowment Arts Fel, 95; NYFA Individual Artists Fel, 99; NYSCA Finishing Funds Award for "Growing Older" at QMA, 2000; NYSCA Media Project Grant, Queens Mus of Art, 2000; Harvestworks Digital Media Arts Artist-in-Residence, 2000. *Bibliog:* Martha Schwendener (auth), Maureen Connor, Love at First Site, Time Out, 2/5-12/98; Mira Schwirtz (auth), Maureen Connor, Curt Marcus Gallery, Flash Art, 5/98-6/98; Laura Frost & Tim Griffin (auth), She saw/He saw, Two Views of Maureen Connor, 6/98-7/98; Amelia Jones (auth), Performing Bodies, Calif Univ Press, 98; Ken Johnson (auth), Review: Seductions and Games: Recent Video Installations by Maureen Connor, The NY Times, 1/19/2001; Sarah Valdez (auth), Rules of the Game: Maureen Connor Makes Socially Conscious Art with a Twist, Time Out NY, 1/18-25, 2001. *Mailing Add:* 10 Leonard St New York NY 10013-2929

CONRAD, JOHN W
EDUCATOR, CERAMIST
b Cresson, Pa, Aug 3, 35. *Study:* Indiana Univ Pa, BS; Carnegie-Mellon Univ, Pittsburgh, MFA(ceramics); Univ Pittsburgh, PhD. *Work:* Mesa Col, San Diego, Calif; CW Wang, 98; Nona Powers, 2000. *Exhib:* Tiffany Invitational, NY, 65; one-man show, Sculpture Gallery, San Diego, Calif, 76; Small Sculptures: Nat Cypress Fine Arts Gallery, Cypress, Calif, 76; Ceramics Design 76, Sculpture Gallery, San Diego, 76; Soup Tureens--1976, Campbell Mus, Camden, NJ, 76; Faith Nightingale Gallery, 93; Signature Gallery, Group Show, 95 & 98; Art Scene Gallery, 96; Gallery Alexander, Group Show, 96, 97 & 98; Tea for Two, Grove Gallery, UCSD, 98. *Pos:* Officer & Allied Craftsmen San Diego, 85-. *Teaching:* Part time instr, Carnegie Mellon Univ, 60-63; prof ceramics & chmn dept, Mesa Col, San Diego, 1966-2000, Mesa Col Fac Exhibs, Ceramic Artists San Diego, 1975-2000, Allied Craftsmen, 76-, Group Ceramics Exhibs, Seattle, 80, NCECA Conf, San Diego, 93, Faith Gallery, 93, Signature Gallery, 95 & Art Scene Gallery, 96. *Awards:* Distinguished Alumni, Indiana Univ Pa, 93; Teaching Excellence Award, Nat Inst for Staff and Organizational Development, Univ Tex at Austin, 93. *Mem:* Col Art Asn; Nat Coun Educ Ceramic Arts; Ceramic Artists San Diego; Allied Craftsmen San Diego. *Media:* Porcelain. *Publ:* Auth, Ceramic Formulas: The Complete Compendium, MacMillan, 73; Contemporary Ceramic Techniques, Prentice-Hall, 77; Contemporary Ceramic Formulas, MacMillan, 80; Ceramic Windchimes, 85, Advance Ceramic Manual, 88 & Cone Six Ceramics, 99; Studio Ceramic Dict, 90; Ceramic Extruder for the Studio Potter, Falcon Publ, 2000

CONRAD, NANCY R
PAINTER
b Houston, Tex, Jan 29, 40. *Study:* Houston Mus Fine Arts; Randolph Macon Woman's Col, BA; Glassell Sch, HMFA. *Work:* El Paso Mus Fine Arts, Tex; Continental Oil Co Collection & Dresser Indust Collection, Houston; Aviation Am Bldg, Love Field, Dallas; Allied Bank Group; Chase Banks, Corpus Christi, Midland, New Braunfels, Arlington, Tex. *Comn:* Allied Bank Systems, First City Banks, 84-85; Stauffer Hotel, Trammel Crow Properties, Austin, Tex, 86; Astrodome Sheraton, 89. *Exhib:* Sun Carnival Exhib, El Paso Mus Fine Arts, 73-75; Tex Painting & Sculpture, Dallas Mus Fine Arts; 52nd Ann Nat Exhib, Shreveport, La, 74; Nat Women's Yr Exhib, 79; Women & Their Work, touring show, 80-81; Staged & Stages, Blaffer Gallery, Univ Houston, 85; Tex Visions, 86; Summer Group Show, Gallery 3, 2002, Art Crawl, 2002; Harris Gallery, 2005; Artists of Tex, Harris Gallery, 2004. *Teaching:* Pvt instr. *Awards:* Foley Award, Foley's of Houston, 70; First Place Jurors Choice, Assistance League of Houston, 73; Purchase Award, El Paso Mus Art, 73. *Bibliog:* Articles in Southwest Art Mag, Art Mag, Art Voices South, & Artweek Newspaper; San Francisco, Texas Artist, Vol II. *Mem:* Mus Fine Arts Houston; Oil Painters Am. *Media:* Oil, Drawing, Digital Imagry. *Interests:* Montana & Texas landscapes in oil,

pastel, and archival photography. *Collection:* Randolph Macon Woman's College; El Paso Museum. *Publ:* illusr, Little Flower, Child Welfare League, 2000. *Dealer:* Harris Gallery 1100 Bissonet Houston TX 77005; harrisgalleryhouston.com. *Mailing Add:* 2230 Mimosa Dr Apt A Houston TX 77019-5626

CONRAD, PAUL FRANCIS
CARTOONIST, SCULPTOR
b Cedar Rapids, Iowa, June 27, 24. *Study:* Univ Iowa, BA, 50. *Work:* Huntington Libr, San Marino, Calif; Libr Cong, Washington, DC; Sch Communications, Syracuse Univ; Univ Wichita; Univ Mo. *Exhib:* Bronze sculptures & cartoons, Los Angeles Co Mus Art, 79; Brand Libr Gallery, 85; Guggenheim Gallery, Chapman Col, 90; Bakersfield Col Art Gallery, 90; Downey Mus Art, 91; Fullerton Mus Ctr, 93; Palos Verdes Art Ctr, 94; Huntington Mus, 95. *Pos:* Ed cartoonist, Denver Post, 50-64, Los Angeles Times, 64-93; cartoonist, Los Angeles Times Syndicate; lectr, Cooke-Daniels Lectr Tours, Denver Art Mus, 64. *Awards:* Sigma Delta Chi Award, 63, 69, 71, 81, 82, 87 & 97; Pulitzer Prize Ed Cartooning, 64, 71 & 84; Robert F Kennedy Award, 85, 90, 92 & 93; Fel, Soc Prof Journalists; Hugh Hefner First Amendment Award, Print Journalism, 90; and many others. *Media:* Pen, Ink; Bronze. *Publ:* Coauth (with Malcolm Boyd), When in the Course of Human Events, Sheed and Ward, 73; auth, The King and Us, Clymer Publ, 74; Pro and Conrad, Neff-Kane/Presido Press, 79; Drawn and Quartered, Harry N Abrams, 85; Con artist, Los Angeles Times, 93

CONSAGRA, PIER
PAINTER, SCULPTOR
b Rome, Italy, 54. *Study:* RI Sch Design, Brown Univ, BA. *Work:* US Trust, NY; Steven Paine, Boston, Mass; Progress Corp, Mayfield, Ohio; Jerry Speyer, NY; New Mus Contemp Art. *Exhib:* Solo exhibs, Fluid Geometry, Conn Col, New Haven, 90 & Barbara Toll Mus, NY, 93; Vertical Slice, Cummings Gallery, New London, Conn, 92; Barbara Toll Fine Arts, NY, 93; Holly Solomon Galleries, SoHo, 98. *Teaching:* Adj asst prof sculpture, Columbia Univ, 93-. *Awards:* NY Found for Arts Fel, 87; Nat Endowment Arts Fel, 89. *Bibliog:* Michael Benson (auth), article, NY Times, 6/1/90. *Media:* Miscellaneous Media. *Publ:* Contribr (cover), Sportsman of the Year Orel Hershiser, Sports Illus, 88. *Dealer:* Barbara Toll Fine Arts 146 Greene St New NY 10012. *Mailing Add:* 542 Broadway New York NY 10012

CONSEY, KEVIN E
MUSEUM DIRECTOR, ADMINISTRATOR
b New York, NY, Jan 15, 52. *Study:* Hofstra Univ, BA, 74; Univ Va, Charlottesville, 75; Univ Mich, Ann Arbor, MA(mus practice art hist), 77; Kellogg Sch of Mich, Northeastern Univ, MBA, 99. *Collection Arranged:* African Art (auth, catalog), Art Mus, Univ Mich, 76 & 77; Real, Really Real, Super Real, 81. *Pos:* Dir, San Antonio Mus Art, 80-83 & Newport Harbor Art Mus, 83-89, dir & Chief Exec Officer, Mus Contemp Art, Chicago, 89-98; dir, Univ Calif Berkeley Art Mus, 99-05. *Teaching:* Instr art hist, Univ Toledo, 75-76; asst prof & dir, Emily Lowe Gallery, Hofstra Univ, 77-80; vis prof, Univ Tex, San Antonio, 81-83. *Mem:* Asn Art Mus Dirs; Col Art Asn; Visual Arts Panel, Tex Comn Arts; Int Coun Mus. *Res:* Twentieth century European and American art. *Publ:* Coauth, Pompeii as Style, In: Pompeii as Source and Inspiration, Univ Mich, 77; ed, Art for the People--New Deal Murals on Long Island, Hofstra Univ, 78; Off the Wall--Environments and Installations, San Antonio Mus Art, 81. *Mailing Add:* 78 San Mateo Rd Berkeley CA 94707-2016

CONSTANTINE, GREG JOHN
PAINTER, EDUCATOR
b Windsor, Ont, Can, Feb 14, 38. *Study:* Andrews Univ, Mich, BA; Mich State Univ with Angelo Ippolito, MFA, Univ Calif, Los Angeles. *Work:* Grand Rapids Art Mus, Mich. *Exhib:* Ark Nat, 69; Chicago & Vicinity, Chicago Art Inst, 71; Mich Artists, Detroit, 71; Philbrook Art Ctr, Tulsa, Okla, 75; LaGrange Nat, Ga, 75. *Teaching:* Chmn dept painting & art hist & prof art, Andrews Univ, 63-. *Awards:* W & B Clusman Prize, Chicago Vicinity Show, Chicago Art Inst, 71. *Bibliog:* J Heriksen (auth), Artist, Insight Mag, 70; O Young (auth), Editor, Focus Mag, 75. *Mem:* Mus Contemp Art, Chicago; Col Art Asn; Mid-Am Art Asn. *Media:* Acrylic; Photography. *Publ:* Auth, article, Spectrum Mag, 75. *Mailing Add:* 9648 Painter School Road Berrien Center MI 49102

CONSTANTINI, EDUARDO
COLLECTOR
Pos: Founder & pres, Consult, Buenos Aires, currently; founder, MALBA (Museo de Arte Latinoamericano de Buenos Aires), Argentina, 2001—. *Awards:* Named one of top 200 collectors, ARTnews Mag, 2004. *Collection:* 20th Century Latin American Art. *Mailing Add:* Malba Coleccion Constantini Avda Figueroa Alcorta 3415 Buenos Aires C1425CLA Argentina

CONTE, JEANNE LARNER
PHOTOGRAPHER, ENAMELIST
b Dallas, Tex, May 25, 28. *Study:* Lindenwood Col, St Charles, Mo, 46-47; Univ Ala, Tuscaloosa, 47-49; Ohio Domenican, Columbus, 65-66; Ohio State Univ Continuing Educ, 88 & 89. *Work:* Art Communication Int. *Comn:* photos & text/brochure, comn by pvt individual, Upper Arlington, Ohio, 89; 22 color photos for book Columbus: City of Discovery, Windsor Publ, 91; Ohio Garden Slide Presentation, Dawes Arboretum, 91. *Exhib:* ACI On-Line Gallery Exhib, 96; Ohio Artists & Craftmen's Invitational, Massilon Mus, 76; Invitational Exhib, Aaron Faber Gallery, NY, 79; State of the Art '93 New Eng Art Expo, Boston, 93. *Pos:* photojournalist. *Awards:* Blue Ribbon, Wagnalls Mem, 8/6/77. *Bibliog:* Jacqueline Hall (auth), Art Show Critique, Columbus Dispatch, 72. *Mem:* Homer Hon Soc Int Poets. *Interests:* Cultures of World, especially Middle East. *Publ:* auth with photographs, German Village, 94, 2d edit, 98; Holy Sands of Jordan, World & I, 96; contribr & photog, Seeking Harmony, World & I Mag, 98, Tapestry of Horrors, SRS Mandarin, 2000, Miracles on Way to Malula, The Word, 2000 & A Rapt Remembering, The Luthrson, 2000; auth with photographs, Advent Anticipation, 2000; auth with photographs, Wonder of Christmas, 2002; auth with photographs, Covered Bridges of Ohio, 2003; auth with photographs, World & I, 2003; calendar with photographs, Country Living, 2003

CONTINI, ANITA
ADMINISTRATOR, CURATOR
b Cleveland, Ohio, Jan 16, 44. *Study:* Cleveland Music Settlement, scholar, 60; Elizabeth Seton Col, Yonkers, NY, AAS, 64; Hofstra Univ, Long Island, NY, BA, 66. *Collection Arranged:* Ruckus Manhattan by Red Grooms (auth, catalog), 75-76, Ruckus Manhattan, 81 & Art on the Beach (auth, catalog), 82, Creative Time Inc. *Pos:* Exec dir & pres, Creative Time Inc, New York, 73-86; pres & bd mem, Athena Found Inc, New York, 78-; vpres & dir, World Finan Ctr Arts & Events Prog, 86-. *Awards:* Certs Merit, Ruckus Manhattan, 76 & Masstransiscope, 81, Munic Art Soc. *Bibliog:* Grace Glueck (auth), New home, new look for Ruckus Manhattan, New York Times, 12/18/81; Carrie Rickey (auth), Taking care of artists' business, Village Voice, 1/5/82; Damon Wright (auth), Art and commerce, New York Times, 4/17/94. *Mem:* Arts & Bus Coun New York

CONTINOS, ANNA
PAINTER, DESIGNER
b New York, NY. *Study:* Hunter Col, BA. *Work:* Gov Christine T Whitman; Am Fuji Seal Inc, NJ; IE DuPont De Nemours & Co, Wilmington, Del; Bell Labs - Holmdel, Piscataway, NJ; Ctr for Health Affairs, Princeton, NJ; also many pvt collections in the US, Can, Taiwan, S Africa, Spain, Eng, Ireland, PR & Japan. *Exhib:* Solo shows, Art Spirit Gallery, Clinton, NJ, 82, Zeta Gallery, Shrewsbury, NJ, 85 & New Brunswick Cult Ctr, NJ, 85 & Short Hills Art Gallery, NJ, 88; Trenton City Mus Invitational, NJ, 84; NJ Watercolor Soc Montclair Mus & Monmouth Mus, 84-92; Nat Asn Women Artists Traveling Painting Exhib (7 locations), 91-92; 73rd Ann Philadelphia Watercolor Club, Noyes Mus, Oceanville, NJ, 92. *Awards:* Award for Excellence, Somerset Art Asn Ann, 80; Best Show, Princeton Art Asn Ann, Princeton Microfilm Corp, 83; Forbes Award, NJ Watercolor Soc Ann, Forbes Mag, 90. *Mem:* NJ Watercolor Soc; Catherine Lorillard Wolfe Art Club; Nat Asn Women Artists. *Media:* Watercolor. *Dealer:* Short Hills Art Gallery, NJ. *Mailing Add:* 315 Willowbrook Dr North Brunswick NJ 08902-1245

CONVERSE, ELIZABETH
PAINTER, WRITER
b Springfield, Ill, Jan 17, 46. *Study:* Lake Forest Col, BA, 67; Performance Group/Drama, 70-72; Sarah Lawrence Writing Ctr, 90-92; Pasadena City Col, 96; Pacific Oaks Col, teaching degree, MA, 99. *Work:* Provincetown Art Mus, Provincetown, Mass; Pasadena Hist Mus; Sierra Madre Art Comn; Pasadena Cent Libr. *Comn:* Harvest Ball, pvt comn, Darien, Conn, 88; murals & paintings, Susan Chen, Zonshine Develop, Los Angeles, 92; Calif Living Histories, City of Los Angeles; Mayor Riordan; Lightbringer Gallery. *Exhib:* Provincetown Art Mus, Conn; Sound/Shore Gallery, Port Chester, NY, 86-88; Gallarie Bonheur, Greenwich, Conn, 87; Lozano Restaurant, 94; Pasadena Armory, 95; and others. *Pos:* Writer, dir & actor, Alexyz Partnership, 78-83; vpres & creative dir, Productions Syst, Inc, 82-89. *Teaching:* S Bay Contemp Art Mus, 92, Monrovia Unified Sch Dist, La Canada Unified Sch Dist, Pasadena Unified Sch Dist, Pacific Oaks Col. *Awards:* Nat Endowment Arts Grant, 77. *Media:* All Media. *Publ:* Articles in Pasadena Weekly, Visions Mag, The Muses, Art Week & LA Reader. *Mailing Add:* 851 Woodland Dr Sierra Madre CA 91024

COOK, JOSEPH STEWART
PAINTER
b Glendale, Calif, Aug 5, 35. *Study:* Art Ctr Sch Design (scholar), Los Angeles, 53; Otis Art Inst (scholar), Los Angeles, 53-54; Chouinard Art Inst, Los Angeles, 55-58. *Work:* Springfield Mus, Mo; Home Savings & Loan, Los Angeles; Joslyn Art Mus. *Exhib:* One-man shows, RJ Dibbs Gallery, Pacific Palisades, Calif, 55, Marian Gallery, Mt St Mary's Col, Los Angeles, 61, WAA Wilshire Gallery, Los Angeles, 62, Paideia Gallery, Los Angeles, 64; Oakland Art Mus, 65; Calif Palace Legion Hon, 66; San Francisco Mus Mod Art, 66; Joslyn Art Mus, 67; Va Mus Fine Arts; Palm Springs Desert Mus, Calif, 79, 82 & 94; Chateau Tours Mus, France, 86; Brand Libr Gallery, Glendale, Calif, 87; Northern Ariz Univ Gallery, Flagstaff, 89. *Pos:* Asst art coordr, City Los Angeles, 59-61. *Awards:* James Phelan Biannual Award, Calif Palace Legion, Hon, 65; Watercolor USA Purchase Award, 73; Second Place, Watercolor W Ann, 77. *Mem:* Watercolor USA; Pacific Palisades Art Asn (pres, 60); Westwood Art Asn (pres, 61-62); Nat Watercolor Soc (pres, 76). *Media:* Watercolor, Oils. *Mailing Add:* 25195 Stewart Pl Carmel CA 93923

COOK, KATHLEEN L
PAINTER
b Amarillo, Tex, Mar 19, 49. *Study:* Amarillo Col, AA (sci), 69; Tex Tech Univ, BFA, 73; studied with Daniel Greene, 79; studied with Albert Handell, 82. *Work:* San Antonio Art League; San Marcos Telephone Co, Tex. *Comn:* 200 portrait comns in various cities, Tex, 82-92, 2005. *Exhib:* Images, McAllen Int Mus, Tex, 86; solo exhibs, About Light, Mus SW, Midland, Tex, 87, Green House Gallery, San Antonio, Tex, 92 & Ellen Noel Art Mus, Odessa, Tex, 95; Plains Hist Mus, Canyon, Tex, 89-91; Animals In Art, La State Univ Sch Vet Med, 98; Degas Pastel Soc Biennial Exhib, New Orleans, La, 2000. *Pos:* Illusr, art dir, Hemphill-Wells, Lubbock, Tex, 70-80; bd dir, Hill Country Arts Found, Ingram, Tex, 83-85. *Teaching:* Instr pastel-figure/still-life, Hill Country Arts Found, Ingram, Tex, 82-2002; invitational one-week workshops pastel, Dallas, Houston, McAllen, Midland, Amarillo & Lubbock, Tex. *Awards:* Best of Show, Pastel Soc W Coast, 89 & Pastel Soc NMex, 97,

Grand Prize, Pastel Artist Int Mag Competition, 2000; Best of Show, Pastel Soc of SW, 2000. *Bibliog:* Survey of contemporary art of the figure, Am Artist Mag, 2/85; Susan Embry (auth), Kathleen Cook, SW Art Mag, 8/89. *Mem:* Pastel Soc Am; Knickerbocker Artists. *Media:* Pastel, Oil. *Collection:* Portrait/Figure, Landscape, Still-life, animals, Contemp Realism. *Publ:* Coauth, Looking around the color wheel, Am Artist Mag, 92; Auth, Exploring the How and Why of Painting Pastel, Artist Internat Mag, 2000. *Dealer:* Riverbend Fine Art Marble Falls TX. *Mailing Add:* 1303 Vesper Lu Kerrville TX 78028

COOK, LIA
TAPESTRY ARTIST, EDUCATOR
b Ventura, Calif, 1942. *Study:* Univ Calif, Berkeley, BA, 65, MA, 73. *Work:* Am Craft Mus, NY; Galerie de la Tapisserie et d'Art Textile, Beauvais, France; Mus Mod Art, Metrop Mus Art, NY. *Comn:* Embarcadero Ctr, San Francisco, 74; City Hall, Fairfield, Calif, 76; Art in Archit Prog, US Gen Serv Admn, Richmond, Calif, 76; Rensselaer Polytechnic Inst, 79; Mercantile Bank, Tex, 86. *Exhib:* Solo exhibs, Renwick Gallery, Nat Mus Am Art, 80, San Jose Mus Art, Calif, 80, Nat Mus Am Art, Smithsonian inst, 96, R Duane Reed Gallery, St Louis, 98, Perimeter Gallery, Chicago, 99, Miami Univ Art Mus, 00, Nancy Margolis Gallery, 01, Arlene LewAllen Gallery, Santa Fe, NMex, 02; The Art Fabric: Mainstream, San Francisco Mus Mod Art, traveling, 81-84; Celebration 25, 81 & The Pattern Show, 82, Am Craft Mus, NY; Jacquard Textiles, Cooper-Hewitt Mus, NY, 82; Fiber Directions, Brunnier Gallery and Mus, Iowa State Univ, 82; retrospective, Galerie Nat de la Tapisserie et d'Art Textile, Beauvais, France, 83; Mus Fine Arts, Boston, 02; Dean Lesher Regional Ctr for the Arts, Walnut Creek, Calif, 02; Am Textile History Mus, Lowell, Mass, 03; and many others. *Collection Arranged:* Racine Art Mus, Wis; Cleveland Mus Art; Mus Bellerive, Zurich; Am Craft Mus; Metrop Mus Art; Milwukee Art Mus; Mus Art, RI Sch Design; Nat Mus Am Art, Smithsonian Inst; Mus Mod Art; Oakland Mus, Calif. *Pos:* artist-in-residence, Fondazione Arte della Seta Lisio, Florence, Italy, 90, Jacquard Project, Muller-Zell, Ger, 91, Philadelphia Col Textiles & Scis, 95. *Teaching:* Prof art, Calif Col Arts & Crafts, Oakland, 76-. *Awards:* Fels, Nat Endowment Arts, 74-75, 77-78, 86, 92-93, 94; Special Proj Grant, Nat Endowment Arts, 81; Calif Arts Coun Artist Fel Grant, 90; fel, Am Craft Coun, 97; Flintridge Found Fel, 00. *Bibliog:* Barbaralee Diamonstein (auth), Handmade in America: Conversation with Fourteen Craftsmasters, Harry M Abrams, New York, 84; Maureen Conner (auth), The tapestries of Lia Cook, Arts Mag, 2/85; Nancy A Corwin (auth), Lia Cook, Monograph from Nat Acad Sci Exhib, 90; Jon Carver (auth), Lia Cook, THE Mag, 10/2002. *Media:* Rayon. *Publ:* Auth, Ed Rossbach as Educator: A Personal View, Ed Rossbach: 40 Years of Exploration and Innovation in Fiber Art, Textile Mus, Lark Bks, Washington, DC, 90. *Dealer:* Perimeter Gallery Chicago IL; Arlene LewAllen Gallery Santa Fe NM. *Mailing Add:* 2127 Bonar St Berkeley CA 94702

COOK, MICHAEL DAVID
PAINTER, VIDEO ARTIST
b Ramey, PR, July 16, 53. *Study:* Fla State Univ, BFA, 75; Univ Dallas, MA, 76; Univ Okla, MFA, 78. *Work:* Mus Contemp Art, San Diego; Sandra Conn & Assoc, Chicago; World Book Corp, Chicago; Polaroid Corp, NY. *Exhib:* 77th Ann Exhib by Artists of Chicago & Vicinity, Art Inst Chicago, 78; New Dimensions--Time, Mus Contemp Art, Chicago, 80; Working Drawings, Hunter Gallery, NY, 81; War Games, Kitchen, NY, 82; solo exhibs, NAME Gallery, Chicago, 82, Grayson Gallery, Chicago, 83, Wenger Gallery, La Jolla, Calif, 84, Janet Steinberg Gallery, San Francisco, Calif, 86, Recent & Past Work, Art Mus, Univ NMex, Albuquerque, 89, Animal-Vegetable or Mineral?, Mus Fine Arts, Santa Fe, 90 & Charity, Shidoni Contemp,Tesuque, NMex, 90; The End of the World, New Mus Contemp Art, NY, 83-84; System and Structure, Allen Priebe Art Gallery (traveling), 83-84; Myth & Magic, Wenger Gallery, Los Angeles, 87; Social Space, Janet Steinberg Gallery, San Francisco, 88; 20 X 40, Jayne Baum Gallery, NY, 89; Playing with Fire, Ctr Contemp Arts, Santa Fe, 90-91. *Teaching:* Vis artist painting & drawing, Video Univ Ill, Champaign-Urbana, 78-80; asst prof, Univ Ill, Chicago, 80-83; vis lectr, Univ Calif, Berkeley, 83-85, Univ Calif, Davis, 85; Spec vis fac, San Francisco Art Inst, 85; asst prof painting & drawing, Univ NMex, Albuquerque, currently. *Awards:* Ford Found Fac Res Grants, 78 & 79; Ill Arts Coun Fel, 82; Nat Endowment Individual Artists Fel, 84-85; Teacher of Year Award, Univ NMex, 89-90. *Bibliog:* Janet Kutner (auth), Graf-feet-i, glitter and crab claws, Artnews, 79; Pat Tomson (auth), article, New Art Examiner, 82; Lynn Gumpert (auth), The End of the World (catalogue), New Museum, New York, 83; Kenneth Baker (auth), Filtering Apocalypse through illusions, San Francisco Chronicle, 5/13/86; Ina Russell (auth), Signs of the global village, Artweek, 2/6/88. *Publ:* Auth, Radiation Remains the Same, Phono Record, Grayson Gallery, 83. *Mailing Add:* 2709 NE Morris St Albuquerque NM 87112-1666

COOK, R SCOTT & SOUSSAN A E
ART DEALER, CRITIC
Study: NY Univ, MA, 75. *Specialty:* 20th Century European paintings, sculpture & drawings; Latin American art. *Publ:* Auth, Space Shots, Art Am, 82; Bruce Conner, Artforum, 82; Andre Masson, Arnold Herstand, 84; The Brothers Duchamp, Arnold Herstand, 86; Rene Magritte, Arnold Herstand, 86. *Mailing Add:* 1063 Madison Ave New York NY 10028-0223

COOK, RICHARD L
ADMINISTRATOR, SCULPTOR
b Big Spring, Tex, Oct 30, 34. *Study:* Univ NMex, BA(art), 67, MA(sculpture), 68; studied with Charles Mattox, Van Derem Coke & John Pearson. *Work:* Mus Fine Arts, Univ NMex, Albuquerque; New Orleans Mus Art, La; Masur Mus Art, Monroe, La; Fine Arts Gallery, Nicholls State Univ, Thibodaux, La; La Bi-Centennial Arts Ctr Collection, Baton Rouge, La. *Exhib:* Southern Asn Sculpture Nat Traveling Exhib, Southern States & DC, 69-70; Masur Ann, Masur Mus Art, Monroe, La, 69, 70 & 72; 8-State Exhib, Okla Art Ctr, 70; Mobile Nat, Mobile Art Ctr, Ala, 72; New Orleans Biannual, New Orleans Mus, La, 73; Sculpture-NMex, Mus Fine Arts, Santa Fe, 75. *Collection Arranged:* New Mexico Collects the 20th Century (auth, catalog), 85; Selections '90-Minority Artists of New Mexico (auth, catalog), 90. *Pos:* Pres, Southern Asn Sculptors, 71-72; deputy dir, NMex Arts, 80 & 81; pres, Nat Coun Art Admin, 89 & 90. *Teaching:* Assoc prof sculpture, Nicholls State Univ, 68-74; prof, Col Santa Fe, NMex, 84-; vis scholar art, Eastern Washington Univ, 93. *Awards:* First Award, 7th Monroe Ann, Mazur Mus, 70; Second Award, Southern Asn Sculptors, Ga Southern Col, 70; Purchase Award, La Bicentennial Exhib, La Art Comn, 73. *Mem:* Nat Mus Neon Art; Col Art Asn Am; Nat Coun Art Adminr (bd dir, 88, pres, 89-90). *Media:* Mixed Media. *Publ:* Auth, On kinetic art with electric light, 72 & Kinetic art-the luminetic system with no sound, 75, Leonardo Peraiagon Press; ed, The Sculpture Quarterly, Southern Asn Sculptures, 72-74; auth, Art in the schools, Albuquerque J, 85; coauth, Selections-90 minority artists of New Mexico, Arts Advocate, Vol 4, No 6, 90. *Mailing Add:* Dept Art Col Santa Fe 1600 St Michael's Dr Santa Fe NM 87505-7634

COOK, ROBERT HOWARD
SCULPTOR, MEDALIST
b Boston, Mass, Apr 8, 21. *Study:* Demetrios Sch, 38-42; Beaux Arts, Paris, under Marcel Gaumont, 45. *Work:* Whitney Mus Am Art, NY; Pa Acad Fine Arts, Philadelphia; Va Mus Fine Arts, Richmond; Hirshhorn Collection, Washington, DC; State Univ NY, Oneida. *Comn:* Lifeline, Sun Co, Radnor, Pa, 78; Off the Water, Sun-Co, 79; Emerging, Saudi Arabia, 81; Camel, Saudi Arabia, 82; Stretch, Saudi Arabia, 82; Giant, Woodlands, Tex. *Exhib:* One-man shows, Inst Contemp Art, Boston, 51, Birmingham Mus Fine Arts, Ala, 67, Mint Mus Art, Charlotte, NC, 68, Va Mus Fine Art, Richmond, 68 & Schenectady Mus Art, NY, 77; Pa Acad Fine Arts; Whitney Ann; Nat Acad Design; Boston Art Festival; Univ Ill; Biennale Venezia, Italy, 51; and other group & one-man shows. *Awards:* Second Prize, Prix de Rome, Am Acad Rome, 42; Cash Award & Best-of-Show, Nat Acad Arts & Lett, 48; Tiffany Award, Tiffany Found, 48. *Bibliog:* Tracy O'Kates & Arnold Eagle (auth), World of Robert Cook (27-minute doc), Beechtree Productions, 77; work of Robert Cook (10 min film), CBS Sunday Morning with Charles Kuralt, 6/30/91. *Mem:* Sculptors Guild; Nat Sculpture Soc. *Media:* Bronze, Wood. *Publ:* Auth, Family Album in Bronze (photographs by Franco Romagnoli), 76, Twelve commissions, 78, In motion, 80, Circles & Cycles, 97, Jasillo. *Dealer:* Henry Cook 79 St Rose St Jamaica Plain Boston MA 02130. *Mailing Add:* Piazza Borghese 91 Rome 00186 Italy

COOK, SILAS BALDWIN
DIRECTOR
b Exeter, NH, Oct 10, 61. *Study:* Wesleyan Univ, BFA, 87. *Exhib:* Curator, Performing Judaism, Douglas F Cooley Mem Art Gallery, 2002; Curator, A Selection of Print from the Collection of William and Nell Givler, Douglas F Cooley Mem Gallery, 2001; Curator, Raymond Saunders: Paintings and Drawings, Douglas F Cooley Mem Art Gallery, 2001; Curator, Differences Preserved: Reconstructed Tombs from the Liao and Song Dynasties, Douglas F Cooley Mem Art Gallery, 2000; Curator, William Kentridge Films and Prints, 1989-99, Douglas F Cooley Mem Art Gallery, 1999. *Pos:* Art Dir/Cur, DF Conley Mem Art Gallery, Reed Col, Portland, Ore, 89-. *Mailing Add:* Reed Coll Douglas F Cooley Art Gallery 3202 SE Woodstock Blvd Portland OR 97202-8199

COOK, STEPHEN D
PRINTMAKER, DRAFTSMAN
b Jackson, Miss, Sept 10, 51. *Study:* Miss Col, BA, 73; Univ Miss, MFA, 75; Royal Col Art, London, cert, 76. *Work:* Victoria & Albert Mus, London; Southern Graphics Coun Print Arch, Oxford, Miss; Miss Sch Supply Co, Jackson; Meridian Mus Art; Mississippi Mus Art. *Exhib:* One-man shows, Janet Redmont Gallery, Millsaps Col, 87 & Miss Art Asn Gallery, Jackson 77 & Meridian Mus Art, 79, Samuel Marshall Gore Gallery, Miss Col, 1999; Mid-South Biennial, Brooks Mem, Memphis, 74; Comparisons & Contrasts, Soviet Union Tour, 79-81; Southeast Mo State Univ Nat Print Invitational Exhib, 81; Southern Graphics Council Member Touring Exhib, 86-88; Art Around Miss, Meridian Mus Art, 2006. *Pos:* guest lectr, Ioan Andrescu Visual Arts Acad, Cluj, Romania, 95. *Teaching:* Chmn dept printmaking, Miss Mus Art Sch, 77-78; instr printmaking & drawing, Univ Miss, Oxford, 78; instr, Hinds Junior Col, Raymond, 80, Miss Col, Clinton, 83-90, asst prof, 90-2003, assoc prof, 2003-; adj instr, Jackson Pub Schs, 82. *Awards:* Bellamann Mem Found Ann Award, 75; ITT Corp Int Fel, London, 75-76; Award of Merit, Miss Artists Competitive, 78. *Mem:* Southern Graphics Coun (vpres, 86-88, pres, 88-90). *Media:* Etching, Wood Engraving; Charcoal, Pastel. *Interests:* folk music. *Publ:* Contribr, J Royal Col Art, 76; Interchange, ITT Fel Publ, 87; Perspective, Miss Mus Art, 92; Faithworks Mag, 2000. *Mailing Add:* 3924 Oakridge Dr Jackson MS 39216

COOK-CONTRERAS, SHELLEY
CONCEPTUAL ARTIST, SCULPTOR
b Omaha, Nebr. *Study:* Univ Ga, BFA (drawing and painting, E R Durough Scholar, Ga Artists Purchase Award), 82; San Francisco Art Inst, MFA, 90; Phi Kappa Phi. *Work:* Univ Ga, Atlanta. *Comn:* Social Structures, Inst for Studies in the Arts, Tempe, Ariz. *Exhib:* San Francisco Festival, de Fabriek, Eindhoven, The Neth, 92; Operation Amorfus, Ridehuisets, Venner, Aarhus, Denmark, 92; one-woman shows, Artist's TV Access, Tempe Ariz, 93, Inst Studies Arts, Tempe, Ariz, 94, Inst Nat Bellas Artes, Mexico City, Mex, 96 & Ice House Complex, 2001; Cleveland Performance Festival, Publ Sites, Ohio, 94; Instituto Nat de Belles Artes, Mexico City, Mex, 94 & 96; Blasthaus Gallery, San Francisco, Calif, 96; Oakland Mus Art, Calif, 99; Mus Modern Art, San Francisco, Calif, 2000; Works Gallery, San Jose, Calif, 2001. *Pos:* Prod coordr, The Well of Patience, Shatki Prod, 88; freelance ed, camera person, 89-; video educ mgr, Bay Area Video Coalition, 90-92; cameraperson, Tolsa, 96; panelist, New

Genre Artists Fel Selection, Calif Arts Coun, 2001. *Teaching:* Instr video & installation art, San Francisco Art Inst, 89-90; private instr movement, 92-; instr performance art, Deep Creek Sch, Telluride, Colo, 94; guest artist, instr, Acad San Carlos, 94 & Inst Nat Bellas Artes, Mexico City, 96; instr spatial arts, Sch Art and Design, San Jose State Univ, Calif, 99-. *Awards:* Honor Award, Marin Co Film and Video Festival, 90; Residency & Res Grant, Inst Studies Arts, 93; Individual Artist's Fel, Nat Endowment Arts, 93 & Calif Arts Coun, 96; Res Grant, Calif State Univ, 2001. *Media:* Installation, Performance Sculpture. *Res:* Painting and architectural design; performance art; installation sculpture; human movement, dynamics, body therapy; movement re-education. *Mailing Add:* 3030 Ingalls St San Francisco CA 94124

COOKE, JODY HELEN
PAINTER, EDUCATOR
b Wind River, Wyo, Oct 25, 22. *Study:* Univ Calif, Berkeley, BA(fine arts); Univ Minn, MA; Calif Col Arts & Crafts, Calif State Univ, Hayward; Univ Ore, PhD with June King McFee, Gordon Kensler & Vincent Lanier, Calif State Univ, advert study. *Work:* Calif State Univ, Hayward; Alaska State Mus, Juneau; Anchorage Hist Fine Arts Mus; Laussac Libr, Anchorage, Alaska. *Exhib:* Three-man show, Allied Arts Gallery, Sacramento, 67; All Alaska Exhib, Alaska Hist & Fine Arts Mus, 76 & 77; Contemp Arts of Alaska, Smithsonian Inst, Washington, DC, 78; one-man show, Anchorage Hist & Fine Arts Mus, 79; On and of Paper, Alaska, 81 & traveling exhib, 83-84; Civic Ctr Gallery, Fairbanks, Alaska; Stonington Gallery, Anchorage Hist & Fine Arts Mus, 85. *Teaching:* Head art dept, Col Siskiyous, 64-67; asst prof art & educ, Univ Iowa, 69-70 & Ore State Univ, 70-73; lectr art educ, Calif State Univ, Sacramento, 73-74; assoc prof & dir exhib, Univ Alaska, 74-88, chmn art dept, 76-78, prof art, 86-88. *Awards:* Merit Award, Auburn Arts Festival, Calif, 66; Purchase Awards, All Alaska Competition, 77 & Alaska State Bank, 81. *Bibliog:* Reid Hastie (auth), Encounter With Art, 61; J K McFee & R Degge (auths), Art Culture & Environment: A catalyst for teaching. *Mem:* Visual Arts Ctr Alaska; Anchorage Adv Arts Comn; Alaska Artists Guild; Anchorage Mus Asn. *Media:* Oil, Acrylic. *Collection:* Drawings, prints, paintings and pottery of contemporary artists

COOKE, JUDY
PAINTER
b Bay City, Mich, July 8, 40. *Study:* Boston Mus Sch Fine Arts, Hons dipl, 63; Tufts Univ, Medford, Mass, BFA, 65; Reed Col, Portland, Ore, MAT, 70. *Work:* Boston Mus Sch of Fine Arts; Portland Art Mus, Ore; Ranier Bank & Pac Northwest Bell, Seattle; Itell Corp, San Francisco; Bank Am, San Francisco; Hewlett Packard Co, Portland, Ore. *Comn:* Hewlett Packard Co, Portland, Ore; Spieker Properties, Lake Oswego, Ore, 2000. *Exhib:* Prospect: Northwest 72, Seattle Art Mus Pavilion, 72; Northwest Ann, Seattle Art Mus, 73 & 74; Aesthetics of Graffiti, San Francisco Mus Mod Art, 78; Blackfish Gallery 6th Anniversary Exhib, Portland, Ore; Expo 86, Vancouver, BC; Elizabeth Leach Gallery, Portland, Ore, 87, 91, 93, 95, 97 & 2001; Esther Saks Gallery, Chicago, Ill, 90; solo show, Fassbender Gallery, Chicago, Ill, 96. *Pos:* Founding mem, Blackfish Gallery, 79-84. *Teaching:* Assoc prof, Pac NW Col Art, Portland, Ore, 86-. *Awards:* Purchase Award, Portland Art Mus, 73; Painting Award, Seattle Art Mus Pavilion, 73; Boston Mus traveling fel, 65 & 74; Visual Artist Fel Painting, Nat Endowment Arts, 89; Bonnie Bronson Fel, Portland, Ore, 93; Edvard Munch Residency, Oslo, Norway, 96. *Bibliog:* Bruce Guenther (auth), Fifty Northwest Artists, Chronicle Bks; Lucy Lippard (auth), Northwest passage, Art in Am, 7-8/76; Lois Allen (auth), Contemporary Art in the Northwest Craftsman House, Gordon & Beach Publ Int, 95. *Media:* Oil Paint, Mixed Media

COOKE, SAMUEL TUCKER
PAINTER, EDUCATOR
b Gainesville, Fla, Dec 4, 41. *Study:* Stetson Univ, with Fred Messersmith, BA; Univ Ga, with Lamar Dodd & Howard Thomas, MFA. *Work:* Asheville Art Mus, NC; Mint Mus Art, Charlotte, NC; Univ Ga Collection; Hunter Gallery Art, Chattanooga, Tenn; Davidson Col, NC. *Exhib:* Nat Drawing & Small Sculpture Exhib, Ball State Univ, 72-74; Davidson Col Nat Print & Drawing Exhib, 74-75; Gallery Contemp Art Realist, Winston-Salem, NC, 74-75; Southeastern Drawing Invitational, Mint Mus, Charlotte, 79; one-man shows, New Morning Gallery, Asheville, 78, Somerhill Gallery, Durham, 79 & 81 & Asheville Art Mus, 80. *Teaching:* Chmn dept art, Univ NC, Asheville, 68-79. *Awards:* 3rd Davidson Nat Drawing & Print Award, Knight Publ Co, 74; 39th Southeastern Painting & Drawing Award, Wachovia Bank NC, 74; Mint Mus Award for Realism in North Carolina, NC Arts Coun, 74. *Dealer:* New Morning Gallery 3 1/2 Kitchen Pl Asheville NC 28803; Somerhill Gallery 5504 Chapel Hill Blvd Durham NC 27707. *Mailing Add:* 65 Kenilworth Rd Asheville NC 28803-2542

COOPER, MARK F
SCULPTOR, COLLAGE ARTIST
b Evensville, Ind, Oct 5, 50. *Study:* Ind Univ, BS, 72; Tufts Univ, MFA, 80. *Work:* Corcoran Mus, Washington DC; Fogg Art Mus, Cambridge Mass; Duxbury Art Mus Complex, Duxbury, Mass; Fuller Mus, Brockton, Mass; Children's Mus for the Arts, NY; Capital Children's Mus, Washington, DC. *Comn:* collage sculpture, Cambridge Hosp, Mass, Praecis Pharmaceutical, Walthem, Mass & Bates Sch, Salem, Mass, 2000; bronze sculpture, Driscoll Sch, Brookline, Mass, 2000; Anderson Consult, Boston. *Exhib:* 50 Yrs of Collecting, City Mus Paris, France, 98; Artists as Teachers, Mc Mullen Mus, Chestnut Hill, Mass, 99; one-man show, Duxbury Art Mus, Duxbury, Mass, 99, Nao Project Gallery, Boston, 2002; Collaborative, Boston Mus Fine Arts, 99, 2002, 2003; Getting Along, Peabody Essex Mus, Salem, Mass, Whitney Mus of Am Art at Philip Morris, NY & Newhouse Ctr for Contemp Art at Snug Harbor Cult Ctr, Staten Island, 2000; Open Circle, Davis Mus, Wellesley, Mass, 2000. *Pos:* bd mem, Int Child Art Found, Washington DC, 98- & Creativity in 21st Century, 99-; steering comt, Open Soc Inst, NY, 2000-. *Teaching:* asst prof ceramics, Boston Col, 78-; instr fine arts, Sch of Boston Mus Fine Arts, 78-. *Awards:* Vision Grant, Boston Fund, 98; Grant, Mass Cult Coun, 99; Commun Fel, Open Soc, 99-2000. *Bibliog:* Molly Hochkeppel (auth), Gardens Become Galleries, The Patriot Ledger, 5/23/2000; Work of Art, The Evening Star, Salem, Mass, 6/22/2000; Judith Montminy (auth), Art Museum Dusts Off Its Treasures, Boston Globe, 10/3/99; Diane C Lore, Getting Along at Snug Harbor, Staten Island, 12/7/99. *Mem:* Int Sculpture Asn. *Media:* Mixed Media. *Res:* Visual Language-how meaning begins with context. *Dealer:* 511 Gallery New York NY. *Mailing Add:* 52 St James Ave Somerville MA 02144

COOPER, PAULA
DEALER
b Mass, Mar 14, 38. *Study:* Pierce Col, Athens, Greece; Sorbonne, Paris; Goucher Col, Baltimore, Md; Inst Fine Arts, NY Univ, Art Students League, 59-60. *Hon Degrees:* RI Sch Design, DFA (hon), 95. *Pos:* Asst, World House Galleries, NY, 59-61; pvt dealer, NY, 62-63; Paula Johnson Gallery, NY, 64-65; dir, Park Place Gallery, 65-67; owner/dir Paula Cooper Gallery, 68-. *Awards:* ArtTable Award for Distinguished Svc to the Visual Arts, 2001; hon, NY Studio Sch, 2001. *Mem:* Art Dealers Asn Am (bd dir, 82-86, 88-90, vpres, 97-2000). *Specialty:* Contemp art. *Mailing Add:* 534 W 21st St New York NY 10011

COOPER, RHONDA H
GALLERY DIRECTOR, CURATOR
b New York, NY, Nov 5, 50. *Study:* Hunter Col, BA, 71; Univ Hawaii, Honolulu, MA, 72; Cornell Univ, 74-75. *Collection Arranged:* The Asian Collection (auth, catalog), Dayton Art Inst, 79; World of Japanese Theater (auth, catalog), Queens Mus, 83; Carl Andre Sculpture (ed, catalog), 84, Toby Buonagurio Selected Works (auth, catalog), 86, Eight Urban Painters, 86 & Permutation and Evolution: Edgar Buonagurio 1974-1988 (auth, catalog), 88, State Univ NY, Stony Brook; Robert Kushner: Silent Operas (auth, catalog), 89; Kit-Yin Snyder: Enrico IV (auth, catalog), 90; City Views (ed, catalog), 92; Wood (ed, catalog), 93; Paper Works (ed, catalog), 94; Maura Sheehan: Dora: Big Girls Don't Cry (coauth, catalog), 94; Eighteen Suffolk Artists (ed, catalog), 95; Pat Hammerman (auth, catalog), 95; Long Island Artists: Focus on Materials (ed, catalog), 98; Loren Madsen:Six Million Monkeys (ed catalog), 1999; 15 Asian American Artists (co-cur, ed catalog), 2001. *Pos:* Cur Asian art, Dayton Art Inst, 76-79; cur exhibs, Queens Mus, NY, 82-83; dir, Univ Art Gallery, State Univ NY, Stony Brook, 83-. *Teaching:* Instr Asian art, Univ Bridgeport, Conn, 74-76 & Art Inst Boston, 80-81; adj lectr Asian art & arts mgt, State Univ NY, Stony Brook, 84-. *Mem:* Am Asn Mus. *Publ:* Auth, Orthodoxy & Eccentricity in 17th Century China, Dayton Art Inst, 78; Zeng Shanqing, Hsiung Shih Art Monthly, 9/91; co-auth, Masterpieces of Chinese Art, Todtri, 97; The paintings of Yang Yanping, catalog essay, Goedhuis Contemp, 1999. *Mailing Add:* University Art Gallery SUNY Stony Brook NY 11794-5425

COOPER, RON
SCULPTOR
b New York, NY, July 24, 43. *Study:* Happy Valley Sch, Ojai, Calif, Chouinard Art Inst, Los Angeles. *Work:* Chicago Art Inst; Kaiser Wilhelm Mus, Krefeld, West Ger; Stedelijk Mus, Amsterdam, Neth; Whitney Mus Am Art, Solomon R Guggenheim Mus, NY. *Comn:* Floating Volume Atmosphere (sculpture), Libr Cong Dept Copyright & Artist, 68; sculpture, Frederick Weisman Found, Los Angeles, Calif, 88; bronze sculpture, Pac Enterprises Corp, 90; The Big Picture (bronze sculpture), IBM/Maguire Thomas Partners, Santa Monica, Calif, 90-91; Whirlpool in Labyrinth, 91-99. *Exhib:* Whitney Ann Painting, 69; Theodoran Awards, Guggenheim Mus, 71; Documenta V, Kassel, WGer, 72; State of California Painting, Brigham Young Univ Gallery, Utah, 73; Light, Lang Art Gallery, Scripps Col, Calif, 74; California Light, Cedars Sinai Med Ctr, Los Angeles, 77; Attitudes: Photog in the 70's, Santa Barbara Mus Art, 79; one-man exhib, La Jolla Mus Art, 73, Rosamund Felsen Gallery, Los Angeles, 79, 80 & 81, Peppers Art Gallery, Univ Redlands, Calif, 81, Advance Art Gallery, Rinconada, NMex, 83; Gallery 454, Los Angeles, Calif, 87 & 88; Gallerie Sena West, Santa Fe, NMex, 88 & 89; solo exhibs, Sena Gallery West, Santa Fe, NMex, 88, Pac Enterprise Comn, Los Angeles, Calif, 89, Maguire Thomas Comn, Santa Monica, Calif, 90, Sena Gallleries, Santa Fe, NMex, 91; Minimal, Cirrus Gallery, Los Angeles, 91; Collectors Gallery Ranchos De Taos, 2000; Charlotte Jackson Gallery, Santa Fe, 2001. *Pos:* Bd dir, Los Angeles Inst Contemp Art, 81-. *Awards:* Los Angeles Co Mus Art Purchase Award, 68; Nat Endowment Arts Award, 70 & 80; Theodoran Purchase Award, Guggenheim Mus, 71. *Bibliog:* Jane Livingston (auth), Two generations in LA, Art Am, Vol 57:95, 1/69; Colin Gardner (auth), Ron Cooper, Artforum, 12/85; Peter Clothier (auth), Ron Cooper at Ovsey, Art Am, 1/86. *Mem:* Artist Equity Asn (bd dir, 80-81). *Dealer:* Broschofsky Gallery 411 6th St Ketchum ID 83340

COOPER, SUSAN
SCULPTOR, PAINTER
b Los Angeles, Calif, Apr 25, 47. *Study:* Univ Calif, Berkeley, BA, 68, MA, 70; Calif State Univ, Northridge. *Work:* Denver Art Mus, Colo; Kaiser Permanente, Colo; Westin Hotel, Cancuun, Mex; City & Co Denver; Denver Pub Libr; Denver Parks & Recreation Dept. *Comn:* Sculpture, Denver Parks & Recreation, 91; painting, Kaiser Permanente, 92; sculpture, Denver Pub Libr, 93; relief murals, City & Co Buildings, 93; Kaiser Permanente, Lafayette, Colo, 2004. *Exhib:* Centennial Exhib, San Francisco Mus Mod Art, Calif, 71; Four Corners Biennial, Phoenix Mus Art, Ariz, 73; solo exhib, Roswell Mus, NMex, 73, Inkfish Gallery, Denver, Colo, 83, 85, 88 & 90; Colo Ann, 76 & 80 Recent Acquisitions, 83 & Mayor's Awards, 88, Denver Art Mus, Colo; retrospective, Jonson Gallery, Univ NMex, Albuquerque, 80; Nat Mus Women in Arts, Significant Colo Women Artists of 20th Century, 88; Henri Gallery, 89; Galeria Expositum, Mexico City, 92. *Pos:* Dir, Rocky Mountain Women's Inst, Denver, Colo, 77-80, pres, 83-84. *Teaching:* Instr drawing, Community Col of Denver,

Red Rocks, Colo, 77; instr, painting & drawing, Metrop State Col, 87-; instr, Univ Colo, Denver, 89-90. *Awards:* Guest Residency, Yaddo, Saratoga Springs, NY, 73; First Prize, Poster Competition, Colo Lawyers for the Arts, 86; Colo Visions Proj Grant, Colo Coun Arts, 94 & 95. *Bibliog:* Lindy Lyman Moore (auth), Susan Cooper, winter 78-79 & Katharine Smith-Warren (auth), Susan Cooper, fall 84, Artspace Mag; Irene Clurman (auth), Pastels at Inkfish, Rocky Mountain News, 1/18/83; Howard Rissoti (auth), Susan Cooper at Henri, Art Forum, 2/90; Jennifer Heath (auth), The Art is at Home, Rocky Mountain News, 1/8/88; Mary Chandler (auth) Rocky Mt News, 10/05. *Mem:* Ctr for Idea Art, Denver (bd mem); Pirate, Contemp Art Oasis; Mizel Cult Arts Ctr. *Media:* Wood, Steel. *Dealer:* Inkfish Gallery 1810 Market St Denver CO 80202; Henri Gallery 1500 21st St NW Washington DC 20036. *Mailing Add:* 1 Winwood Dr Englewood CO 80110-6023

COOPER, THEODORE A
DEALER
b Cleveland, Ohio, Feb 20, 43. *Study:* Muskingum Col, BA, 65; Ind Univ, 67. *Pos:* Asst dir, IFA Galleries, 68-70; dir, Studio Gallery, 70-71; pres & dir, Adams Davidson Galleries, Inc, 71-; mem art adv panel, Internal Revenue Serv. *Teaching:* Teaching asst introd art, Ind Univ, 65-67; instr, George Washington Univ, 95-. *Mem:* Sr mem Am Soc Appraisers; Wash Art Dealers Asn (pres, 81-87, 91-93); Art Dealers Asn Am. *Specialty:* 19th and early 20th Century American Masters. *Publ:* Marble and Bronze: 100 Years of American Sculpture 1840-1940, Garamond Pridemark Press, 84; The Artist as Explorer: Luminist Visions of 19th Century America, Mus Press, Washington, DC, 86; Intimate and Visionary: 200 Years of American Master Drawings, 1790-1990, Weadon Publ, 90. *Mailing Add:* 2727 29th St NW Washington DC 20001

COOPER, WAYNE
PAINTER, SCULPTOR
b Depew, Okla, May 7, 42. *Study:* Valparaiso Univ; Famous Artist Sch; Gary Artist League, Cowboy Artists Am, Kerrville, Tex; American Atelier, NY. *Work:* Okla Heritage Mus, Okla City; Paint Horse Gallery, Breckenridge, Colo; Joe Wade Gallery, Santa Fe; Concetta D Gallery, Albuquerque; Heritage Gallery, Scotsdale, Ariz; Tribes Gallery, Norman, Okla; Black Hawk Gallery, Saratoga, Wyo; Gilcrease Mus Inst Am Hist & Art, Tulsa, Okla. *Comn:* Christ Descending (oil), Endtime Tabernacle, Tulsa, Okla, 69; Painting of Christ, Church of God, Depew, Okla, 74; lithograph ed, Am Express Co, NY; four large paintings (oil), Will Rogers Mus, Claremone, Okla; fourteen hist paintings, Okla State Capitol. *Exhib:* Country Beautiful, Minn, 68; Nat Show, Tyler, Tex, 69; Ft Wayne Mus, 75; Valparaiso Univ, 75; Gilcrease Mus, Tulsa; one-man shows, Will Rogers Mus, Claremont, Okla, Ky Univ & Circle Galleries. *Awards:* Best of Show, Twas Bay Show, Gilcrease Mus, Tulsa, 76 & America Beautiful Miniature, Nat Small Painting Show, Albuquerque, 91; First Place for Oils, Southern Shores, Gary, Ind, 70; First Place for Watercolor, Ft Wayne Mus, 75. *Mem:* Ind Artists & Craftsmen; Cowboy Hall of Fame; Cowboy Artists of Am. *Media:* Oil, Bronze. *Interests:* Western, Indian and Landscapes. *Mailing Add:* 126 W 1025 S Kouts IN 46347

COOPERSMITH, GEORGIA A
MUSEUM DIRECTOR
b Phillipsburg, NJ, May 19, 50. *Study:* Syracuse Univ, 68-70, MFA, 77, PhD, 92; Rochester Univ Technol, BFA, 73. *Collection Arranged:* Expressionist Impulses in Recent American Art, 84; Variations on a Theme-Figurative Art, 85; The North Country Landscape, 86; Howardena Pindell Paintings & Drawings, 92-95; Shattering the Southern Stereotype: Jack Berl, Nell Blaine, Dorothy Gillespie, Sally Urnn, Cy Twumbly, 98. *Pos:* Asst cur, Mem Art Gallery, Rochester, 79-81; dir, Roland Gibson Gallery, Potsdam, NY, 81-91,; Ctr Visual Arts, Farmville, Va, currently. *Teaching:* Instr mus studies & gallery practices, State Univ & Col Arts & Science, Potsdam, 81-91, Longwood Col, 95. *Mem:* Am Asn Mus; Northeast Mus Conf; Col Art Asn; Piedmont Coun for the Humanities. *Publ:* Auth, Paintings & Photographs, Moholy-Nagy, Mem Art Gallery, 78; Drawings & Watercolor, Mem Art Gallery, 79; Sculpture from the Johnson Atelier, Brainerd Art Gallery, 82; The Twentieth Anniversary Exhibition of the Vogel Collection, 82. *Mailing Add:* Longwood Ctr Visual Arts Longwood Col 129 N Main St Farmville VA 23901

COOVER, CHRISTOPHER R
APPRAISER
Pos: Asst, bookseller, Albert J Phiebig, formerly; cataloger, rare book dept, Sotheby's, formerly; head, rare book dept, Strand Bookstore, New York City, formerly; sr cataloger, books & manuscripts dept, Christie's, New York City, 80-85, sr specialist, manuscripts, vpres, 85-; appraiser, Antiques Roadshow, WGBH-PBS, currently. *Teaching:* lectr, on rare manuscripts, currently. *Awards:* Recipient Res Grant, Bibliog Soc Am, 86. *Mem:* Manuscript Soc (trustee, 89, pres, formerly). *Publ:* Ed, New Grove Dictionary Music. *Mailing Add:* Christie's 20 Rockefeller Plaza New York NY 10020

COOVER, DORIS GWENDOLYN
PAINTER, PRINTMAKER
b Beaverdam, Wis, Aug 8, 1917. *Study:* Woodbury Univ, 37; studied with Fred Mitchum, Dallas Mus Arts. *Work:* Int Sci Technol Mag, NY; Scoville Manufacturing Co, Danbury, Conn. *Exhib:* 34th Ann Autumn Exhib, Delgado Mus, New Orleans, 58; Dallas Mus Art, 59; Mus Fine Arts Houston, 59; Showcase Plus & 60, Neuberger Mus, Purchase, NY, 60; solo exhibs, Briarcliff Col, NY, 69, Silvermine Guild Artists, Conn, 70, Katonah Gallery, NY, 71, Am Can Corp, Greenwich, Conn, 71, Village Gallery, Croton, NY, 74, Kirby Ctr, Cameron Park, Calif, 85-89 & Va Barrett Gallery, Chappaqua, NY, 92-95; Whitney Mus & Guggenheim Mus, NY; Carnegie Inst, Pittsburgh, Pa; Art Inst Chicago; Boston Mus Art; Parsons Sch Design; and 46 other int & regional exhibs. *Teaching:* Painting for Enjoyment, Chappaqua Sch System, NY, 67-74. *Awards:* Best of Show, Friday House, 85; Best of Show, 85, First & Second Prize, 90 & Hon Mentions, 94-95, Motherlode Art Show, Placerville, Calif; W Colo Watercolor Show Hobbin Award, 98. *Bibliog:* Marian Kisch (auth), Silk screens, Patent Trader Newspaper, NY, 68; Les Krantz (auth), 1990 Calif Art Review, Am References Inc, 90; Betsy Peses (auth), Designs for nature with dash of emotion, Mountain Democrat Newspaper, Calif, 92. *Mem:* Westchester Art Soc. *Media:* Oil, Watercolor; Silk Screen. *Publ:* Illusr, cover design, Int Sci Technol Mag; Best of Watercolor-Painting Color & Best of Drawing and Sketching, Rockport Publ. *Dealer:* Virginia Barrett Gallery 11 Memorial Dr Chappaqua NY 10514. *Mailing Add:* 3008 Twin Oaks Rd Cameron Park CA 95682

COPE, LOUISE TODD
COLLAGE ARTIST
b Ventnor, NJ, June 17, 30. *Study:* Syracuse Univ, BA (fine arts), MLA & MA; Independent Textile Res, Guatemala, Scandinavia, Nepal, Bhutan & Thailand. *Work:* Australian Crafts Coun; NC Mus Art, Raleigh; Del Art Mus, Wilmington; Kutztown State Col Collection, Pa; Helen Drutt Collection; Pfannebecker Collection. *Exhib:* Invisible Artist, Philadelphia Mus Art, 73-74; Women's Work, Am Art, Civic Ctr Mus, Philadelphia Nat Exhib, 74; 2nd & 3rd Int Miniature Exhib; Thread Poem Traveling Show, Australia, 78; NC Mus Hist, 83; collab with Marcia Plevin Dance Co, Two Survivors, NC Mus Art, 83; Silkworks, Gayle Willson Gallery, Southampton, NY, 84; Arvada Ctr Arts, Colo, 85-86; Wearable Art: A National Experience, Springfield, Ill, 85; Columbia Mus Art, 88-89. *Teaching:* Instr fibers, Haystack Sch Crafts, 69-89; chmn dept textiles, Moore Col Art, 70-74; teacher textiles, Penland Sch Crafts, NC, summers 70-72 & 81-86; tutor textiles, Wincester Sch Art, Eng, summer 73; teacher fibers, var workshops in US, Eng & Can; asst fac, Starking Sch Ministry, Berkeley, 96-, Sophia Ctr, Oakland, 96-. *Awards:* NC Mus Art Purchase Award, 71; Del Art Mus Purchase Award, 70; NC Mus Art Award, 83. *Mem:* World Crafts Coun; Am Crafts Coun. *Media:* Fiber. *Publ:* Auth, Thread Poems, 76 & Sleeves, A treasury of ideas, techniques & patterns, 88, Coat of Arms Press. *Mailing Add:* 1683 Scenic Ave Berkeley CA 94709

COPENHAVER-FELLOWS, DEBORAH LYNNE FELLOWS
SCULPTOR, PAINTER
b Spokane, Wash, Jan 2, 48. *Study:* Holy Names Col, Fort Wright, BA (fine art), 70. *Work:* Bronze Stage Coach, Pro Rodeo Hall Fame, Colorado Springs, 81; Monumental Statue, Hecla Mining Co, Coeurdalena, Idaho, 91; Life Size Bronze Scout, Boy Scouts Am, Diamond Lake, Wash, 92; Frank Irwin Mem, Univ Tex, Austin, 86; BUSI Bronze Sculpture, Remington Park, Oklahoma City, 90. *Comn:* Vietman War Mem, Mont State, Missoula; Inland Pacific Vietnam War Mem, Spokane, Wash; Bing Crosby Mem, Gonzaga Univ, Spokane, Wash; Benny Binion Mem, Las Vegas; Korean War Mem, Wash State, Olympia; Lady of the Sea, Anacortes, Wash. *Exhib:* Buffalo Bill Art Show, Whitney Mus, Cody, Wyo, 92. *Awards:* Best of Show Sculpture, Mus Native Am Cult, 85. *Bibliog:* Southwest Art Mag, 85. *Media:* Bronze; Oil. *Dealer:* BigHorn Gallery Copy WY; Alterman Morris Dallas TX. *Mailing Add:* PO BOX 805 Sonoita AZ 85637-0805

COPPEDGE, ARTHUR L
PAINTER, EDUCATOR
b Brooklyn, NY, Apr 21, 38. *Study:* Brooklyn Mus Art Sch, with David Levine & Isaac Soyer; Art Students League; Pratt Graphic Ctr. *Work:* Brooklyn Mus, NY; Studio Mus Harlem, NY; First Edition Inc; Chase Manhattan Bank NAm. *Comn:* Mural painting, Servo-Mation Corp, NY, 67; paintings & drawings, US Dept of Interior, DC, 75-76; paintings, Am the Beautiful, NY, 77. *Exhib:* Smithsonian Inst, DC; Ann Awards, Am Acad Arts & Letts, NY; Nat Gallery Jamaica, US Embassy, Jamaica, 83; Mus Contemp Art, San Francisco; one-man exhib, Schenectady Mus, NY, 88; Edward Hopper House, Nyack, NY, 90; Christie's, NY, 90. *Pos:* Bd mem, Found for Community of Artists, dir exhib dept, New Muse Mus, 76-78; consult, African-Am Caribbean Cult Ctr, Brooklyn, NY; bd mem, NY State Coun Human, currently; exec vpres bd mem, Artists Equity and Artists Welfare Fund, NY. *Teaching:* Instr portraiture, painting & drawing, Brooklyn Mus, 73-78; instr painting & drawing, Ethical Cult Soc, 76-; guest lectr, New Sch Social Res, Cornell Univ & Studio Mus, Harlem, Nat Acad Art Sch, 94-95; instr drawing, Jamaica Sch Art, Jamaica, West Indies. *Awards:* Jerome Straka Award, Nat Arts Club, 77. *Bibliog:* Painting My World (film, 26 min). *Mem:* Art Students League; Allied Artists; Brooklyn Arts & Cult Asn (consult, 78, bd mem re-grant prog, 81-82); Brooklyn Consortium Artists & Arts Inc. *Media:* Oil, Watercolor. *Publ:* Contribr, Attica Book; illusr, Intimate Portrait of Martin Buber, Viking Press; Essence Mag; auth, Found for Community of Artists; contribr, Cult Post, Nat Endowment Arts, Artspeak; cover illus, Blood on the Forge, Double Day, 92-93. *Dealer:* Brooklyn Consortium for Artists & the Arts 135 Eastern Parkway Brooklyn NY 11238. *Mailing Add:* 451 Mac Donough St Brooklyn NY 11233

COPT, LOUIS J
PAINTER
b Emporia, Kans, Jan 29, 49. *Study:* Emoria State Univ, BA, 71; Art Students League (New York), 85; Univ Kans - Landscape Class, 86. *Comn:* Grand Canyon (oil), Kans Geological Survey, Lawrence, Kans, 91; watercolor landscape, City of Lawrence, Kans, 91; Grand Canyon (oil), Mike Hayden (Asst Secy Interior), Washington, DC, 92. *Exhib:* Mid-4, Nelson-Atkins Mus, Kansas City, Mo, 87; Kans Watercolor Soc, Wichita Art Mus, 87-92; Kansas 9 - Kansas 8, Mulvane Art Mus, Topeka, 89-90. *Pos:* Pres, Lawrence Arts Comn, 85-86; bd mem, Asn Community Arts Kans, 91-; Kans Watercolor Soc, 85-93. *Awards:* Purchase Awards, Kans Watercolor Soc, 86, 89-90; Purchase Awards, Corporte Woods, 89-90; Am Artist Award, 5th Nat Midwest Pastel Soc, 90. *Bibliog:* Richard LeComte (auth), Artist scours landscape, Lawrence J World, 90; Jan Witkowski (auth), Craft art-survival, Topeka Capital J, 92; Louis Copt (auth), Winter watercolors, The Artist's Mag, 92. *Mem:* Kans Watercolor Soc; Assoc Arts

Agencies of Kans; Lawrence Arts Comn (pres 85-86); Lawrence Art Guild (pres 84-85); Midwest Pastel Soc. *Media:* Oil, Watercolor. *Publ:* Auth, Finding color in the winter landscape, The Artists Mag, 92; illus, Battle for the prairie, Earthwatch, 92. *Dealer:* Kyle Garcia 2900 F Oakley Brookwood Ctr Topeka Kans 66614. *Mailing Add:* 1935 E 850 Rd Lecompton KS 66050-4062

CORAOR, JOHN E
MUSEUM DIRECTOR, ADMINISTRATOR
b Woodbury, NJ, Nov 30, 55. *Study:* Syracuse Univ, BFA, 77; Pa State Univ, MA, 81, PhD, 85. *Pos:* Managing ed, Museologist Quart, 80-83; exec dir, Tempe Arts Ctr, Ariz, 85-88; dir, Hecksher Mus Art, Huntington, NY, 88-. *Teaching:* Asst educ, HF Johnson Mus Art, Ithaca, NJ, 77-79; instr, Pa State Univ, State College, 81-85. *Awards:* Northeast Mus Conf Fel, 80; Mayoral Proclamation in Recognition of Outstanding Service, City of Tempe, 88. *Mem:* Am Asn Mus; Mid-Atlantic Asn Mus (actg ed, 82-83, chmn publs comt, 72-94); Mus Asn Ariz (rep to exec bd, 87-88); Suffolk Co Cult Affairs Adv Bd, 90-; NY State Asn Mus; and others. *Publ:* Auth, Documentation, evaluation & dissemination: Museologist, 82; The perforative viewer: some pedagogical reflections from a phenomenological perspective, Pa State, 84; Fifty years of the museologist, Museologist, 85. *Mailing Add:* 7 Newbury Pl Huntington NY 11743-3240

CORBIN, GEORGE ALLEN
HISTORIAN, WRITER
b Detroit, Mich, Oct 23, 41. *Study:* Oakland Univ, Rochester, Mich, BA(art hist), 63; Bucknell Univ, Lewisburg, Pa, MA, 68; Columbia Univ, MA(art hist), 71, PhD(primitive & pre-Columbian art), 76. *Teaching:* From asst to assoc prof & chair art, Lehman Col, New York, 69-. *Mem:* Col Art Asn. *Res:* Art of the South Pacific Islands, particularly Melanesia and Polynesia; African, North American Indian and pre-Columbian art. *Publ:* Auth, The art of the Baining: New Britain, Exploring the Visual Art of Oceania, Univ Press Hawaii, 79. *Mailing Add:* Dept Art City Univ NY Lehman Col 250 Bedford Park W Bronx NY 10468

CORBINO, MARCIA NORCROSS
CRITIC, WRITER
b Tulsa, Okla. *Study:* Duke Univ, BA, 49; Art Students League, 50. *Collection Arranged:* Multiple Visions: A History of Art in Sarasota, Selby Gallery, Ringling Sch Art and Design, 2000; Quintessential Contemporary: Art from Private Collections on Longboat Key, Longboat Key Ctr for Arts, 2/04. *Pos:* Writer & photogr, Sarasota Jour, 74-77; critic, Sarasota Herald Tribune, 77-82; consult, Corbino Galleries, 85-2003 & Speakers Bur Fla Humanities Coun, 96; critic, Longboat Observer, 96-2001. *Teaching:* instr, The Edn Ctr, Longboat Key, 96; instr Inst Creative Writing, Adult & Community Educ, 2003-06. *Awards:* Nat Endowment Arts Critic fel, 80. *Bibliog:* Su Byron (auth), Artistic Licence: A Sarasota Wordsmith Lives Her Passion, Sarasota Downtown and Beyond, 4/2002. *Mem:* Int Asn Art Critics. *Res:* Contemporary American and Latin American art. *Collection:* The Circus, Art Ctr Sarasota, 1/2005. *Publ:* Helen Sawyer: Memories of a Morning Star, 95; Gail Symon Hicks: The Painted Garden, 96; contrib, Dorothy Gillespie, 98; Travels in the Labyrinth: Mexican Art in the Pollak Collection, Univ Pa Press, 2001; A History of Visual Art in Sarasota, Univ Press Fla, 3/2003; photograph of Evan Hunter, A Mystery Writers' Colony, Sarasota Mag, 2/05; Jon Corbino and The Pleasures of the Bathing Beach: A Slice of Life in America, 1939, Nassau County Hist Soc Journal, 04; Literary Lions, Sarasota Mag, 11/04; A Fine Madness: True Tales from the Days when Sarasota was an Artists' Colony, Sarasota Mag, 11/03; Lillian Burns, West Coast Woman, Sarasota, Fla, 2/01; Steir's waterfalls make a splendid exhibition, The Longboat Observer, Longboat Key, Gla, 2/10/00; catalog, Julio Antonio: Images and Commentaries, Panama Mus Art, 7/99. *Mailing Add:* 1111 N Gulfstream Ave No 6B Sarasota FL 34236

CORDY-COLLINS, ALANA (KATHLEEN)
CURATOR, EDUCATOR
b Los Angeles, Calif, June 5, 44. *Study:* Univ Calif, Los Angeles, BA (art hist), 70, MA (archeol), 72, PhD (archeol), 76. *Pos:* Mem chmn, Archeol Inst Am, San Diego Chap, 77-78, pres, 79-81; cur, Latin Am Collections, San Diego Mus Man, 79-. *Teaching:* Instr archeol, Univ Calif, Los Angeles 72-74; instr art & archeol, Univ Calif, San Diego 74-79 & San Diego Mesa Col, Calif, 75-80; assoc prof anthrop, Univ San Diego, 80-. *Awards:* Altman Art Award, Univ Calif, Los Angeles, 72. *Res:* Iconographic study of Chavin & Peru art; shamanic art; function of art in culture. *Publ:* Ed, Pre-Columbian Art History, Selected Readings, Vol 2, 82; auth, The Cerro Sechin massacre: Did it happen?, Mus of Man Ethic Technotes, No 18, 83; Ancient Andean art as explained by Andean ethnohistory: An historical review, 83 & coauth (with D D McClelland), Upstreaming along the Peruvian north coast, 83, Brit Archeol Reports; Mega-Ninos, Spondylos Shells, and the Chimor-Calangone Connection, J New World Archaeol, Inst of Archeol, Univ Calif, Los Angeles (in press). *Mailing Add:* Mus of Man Balboa Park 1350 El Prado San Diego CA 92101

CORKERY, TIM (TIMOTHY) JAMES
PAINTER, EDUCATOR
b Washington, DC, Oct 30, 31. *Study:* Univ Chicago Univ Col, 55-59; Art Inst Chicago, BFA, 60; Inst Allende Univ Guanajuato, Mex, MFA, 64. *Work:* Baltimore Mus Art; Idaho First Nat Bank, Boise; Alcoa Aluminum Co, Pittsburgh; Johnson & Johnson Inc, Newark, NJ. *Comn:* Mural for pub housing, Dept of Housing & Community Develop, Baltimore, 73; indoor mural for Univ Baltimore, Mayor's Adv Comt for Art & Cult, 79; indoor mural for Arts Tower, Baltimore, 80. *Exhib:* Eighteenth Area Exhib, Corcoran Gallery Art, Washington, DC, 67; one-man shows, Royal Marks Gallery, NY, 69 & 70, Jefferson Place Gallery, Wash, DC, 71 & Max Hutchinson Gallery, NY, 73 & 74; Univ Md, Baltimore Co, 75; Univ Ore Mus Art, 78. *Collection Arranged:* Seventeenth Area Exhib (cataloged), Corcoran Gallery Art, Washington, DC, 65; Washington 20 Years (cataloged), Baltimore Mus Art, 70; Mem Gallery, Albright-Knox Gallery, 70 & 75; New Washington Painting (cataloged), Hayden Gallery, Mass Inst Technol, 71; Washington Art, Richmond Mus Exten, 71; Artists Making Art, Baltimore Mus Art, 72; Synergy-Artists One Plus One Equals Three (cataloged), Thorpe Intermedia Gallery, Sparkill, NY, 82. *Teaching:* Instr fine arts & painting, Corcoran Sch Art, Washington, DC, 65-67; instr painting, Md Inst Col Art, Baltimore, 67-77; vis artist painting, Univ Ore, Eugene, 77-78, Sch Art, Inst Chicago, 78 & RI Col, Providence, 89-95. *Awards:* Purchase Awards, Baltimore Mus 70 & Macht Found, 70; Munic Art Soc Award, 72. *Bibliog:* Sidra Stich (auth), Five Washington artists, Art Int Mag, 12/71; Carter Ratcliff (auth), article, Art Spectrum Mag, 2/75; Ellen Lubell (auth), article, Arts Mag, 2/75. *Mem:* Col Art Asn Am. *Media:* Oil on Canvas. *Mailing Add:* 3 Theresa Ct Providence RI 02909

CORMACK, MALCOLM
CURATOR, HISTORIAN
b Birmingham, Eng, Dec 6, 35. *Study:* Courtauld Inst Art Univ London, BA, 59; Cambridge Univ, Eng, MA, 65. *Pos:* Asst keeper, City Birmingham Mus & Art Gallery, Eng, 59-62; from asst keeper to keeper, Fitzwilliam Mus, Cambridge, 62-76; cur paintings, Yale Ctr Brit Art, 76-91; Paul Mellon cur, Va Mus Fine Arts, 91-. *Teaching:* Instr art hist, Cambridge Univ, 62-76; instr, Yale Univ, 76-. *Mem:* Walpole Soc. *Mailing Add:* 515 Wild Life Tr Richmond VA 23233-6427

CORMIER, ROBERT JOHN
PAINTER, LECTURER
b Boston, Mass, May 26, 32. *Study:* R H Ives Gammell Studios, cert. *Work:* Maryhill Mus, Goldborough, Wash; Superior Courthouse, Cambridge, Mass; Univ Sch, Shaker Heights, Ohio; Salem Courthouse, Mass; Suffolk Co Courthouse, Boston, Mass. *Comn:* Portraits for St Michael's Church, Charleston SC; John Hancock Mutual Life Insurance Co, 81; Mass Appellate Court, Boston, 83; Mass Supreme Judicial Court, Boston, 90; Boston Col Law Sch, Newton MA, 90; 1st & 2nd Uninesralist, Unitarian Church, Boston, 92. *Exhib:* New Eng Artists Contemp Ann, 54-69; Guild of Boston Artists, 60-90; Boston Arts Festival, 62; Coun Am Artists Socs, NY, 66; Springfield Mus, Mass, 79. *Pos:* Mem, City Art Comn, Boston, 82-, Chmn, 90-95; bd mem, Brown Fund, Boston, 89-; designator, Henderson Found, 89-. *Teaching:* Instr drawing & painting, Vesper George Sch Art, 69-83; instr, studio & artasns. *Awards:* Gold Medal of Honor, Coun Am Artists Socs, 65; Greenshields Found Award, 70; Award Distinction, Guild Boston Artists, 93. *Mem:* Guild Boston Artists (secy, bd gov, 70-81 pres, 82-94); Copley Soc Boston (vpres, 70-77); Portraits, Inc. *Media:* Oil, Pastel. *Mailing Add:* 30 Ipswich St Boston MA 02215-2237

CORN, WANDA M
HISTORIAN, EDUCATOR
b New Haven, Conn, Nov 13, 40. *Study:* Washington Square Col, New York Univ, BA, 63; Inst Fine Arts, New York Univ, MA, 65, PhD, 74. *Collection Arranged:* The Color of Mood: American Tonalism, 1880-1910, (auth, catalog), 72; The Art of Andrew Wyeth (auth, catalog), 73; American Art: An Exhibition from the Collection of Mr & Mrs John D Rockefeller 3rd, 76; Grant Wood: The Regionalist Vision (auth, catalog), 83-84. *Pos:* Vis cur, Fine Arts Mus, San Francisco, 72, 73, 76 & 84 & Minneapolis Inst Arts, 82-84; comnr, Nat Mus Am Art, Smithsonian, 88-95; acting dir, Stanford Mus, 89-91; dir, Stanford Humanities Ctr, 92-95; Smithsonian coun, 2001; art adv com, Terra Found, 99-, bd dir, 2002; bd trustees, Wyeth Found for Am Art, 2002. *Teaching:* Lectr Am art, Univ Calif, Berkeley, 70 & 76; from asst prof mod Europ & Am art to assoc prof, Mills Col, 70-80; assoc prof Am art hist, Stanford Univ, 81-88, prof, 89-, chmn, 89-91, 99-00 & assoc chair, 95-97; named Robert and Ruth Halperin prof, art history, 2000. *Awards:* Smithsonian Fel, Nat Mus Am Art, 78-79; fel, Woodrow Wilson Int Ctr Scholars, 79-80; fel, Stanford Humanities Ctr, 82-83; Am Coun Learned Soc Awards, 82 & 86; Regents Fel, Smithsonian Inst, 87; Charles C Eldredge Prize for Distinguished Scholarship in Am Art, 2000; Phi Beta Kappa Undergraduate Teaching Award, 2002; Radcliffe Inst Fel, Harvard Univ, 2003, 2004. *Mem:* Col Art Asn (bd dir, 70-73 & 80-84); Women's Caucus Art (adv bd, 80-84); Am Studies Asn (nat coun, 86-89). *Res:* American art from the Civil War to the present. *Publ:* Auth, Coming of Age: Historical Scholarship in American Art, Art Bul, LXX, pp 188-207, 6/88; auth, The Great American Thing: Modern Art and National Identity, 1915-1935, Univ of Calif Press, 99. *Mailing Add:* Stanford Univ Dept Art and Art History Stanford CA 94305-2018

CORNELL, DAVID E
CERAMIST, SCULPTOR
b Kalispell, Mont, Feb 24, 39. *Study:* Mont State Univ, BS (art); Archie Bray Found, with Kenneth Ferguson & David Shaner; Corcoran Sch Art, with Teuro Hara & Richard LaFean; Alfred Univ, MFA (ceramics), with Bob Turner, Val Cushing & Daniel Rhodes. *Work:* Greenville Art Mus, SC; Charles M Russell Gallery, Great Falls, Mont; Libby Dam, Treaty Tower, Vis Ctr, Libby, Mont; Archie Bray Found, Helena, Mont; Mont State Univ, Bozeman. *Comn:* Ceramic fountain fixtures, Mont State Univ Libr, 64; Treaty Panel (sculpture), US Army Corps 18 Engineers & Mont Hist Soc, 75. *Exhib:* Tenth Int Exhib Ceramic Art, Smithsonian Inst, Washington, DC, 66; Norfolk Mus Art, Va, 66; Harriman Gallery, Orange Co Community Col, Middletown, NY, 69; Handblown Glass Exhib, Corning Glass Ctr, NY, 69; Mint Mus Art, NC, 70; Appalachian Corridors: Exhib 2, Charleston, Wva, 70; NW Crafts Show, Henry Gallery, Seattle, Wash, 71; Cheney Cowles Mem Mus, Spokane, Wash, 73; Mont State Hist Soc Exhib, Poindexter Gallery, Helena, 75. *Pos:* Artist-in-residence, Penland Sch of Crafts, 69-70; dir, Archie Bray Found, 70-77; owner-mgr, Pear Blossom Pottery, Talent, Ore; pres, Clayfolk, Inc, 78-79. *Awards:* First Prize, Univ Exhib, Mont State Univ, 64; Jury Award, 11th Biennial NW Ceramics, Ore Ceramics Studio, 65; Best of Show, 11th Ann Own Your Own, Southern Colo State Col, 74. *Bibliog:* Mary Lou O'Neil (auth), Archie Bray Found, Mountain Lines, Mountain Bell

Tel & Tel, 11/70; David Depew (auth), Archie Bray Found, Ceramics Mo, 5/72; Jerry Metcalf (auth), Today at the Bray, Mont Arts, Mont Inst Arts, 76. *Mem:* Helena Arts Coun (vpres, 73); Mont Art Gallery Dir Asn (secy, 75-76); Nat Coun Educ in Ceramic Arts; Am Crafts Coun; Glass Art Soc. *Media:* Ceramic. *Mailing Add:* 2316 S Pacific Hwy Talent OR 97540-9633

CORNELL, HENRY
PATRON
Study: Grinnell Col, BA, 76; NY Law Sch, JD, 81. *Pos:* Assoc, Davis Polk & Wardwell, New York City, 81-84, Goldman Sachs & Co, New York City, 84-94, partner, managing dir, 94-. *Mem:* Asian Art Mus, San Francisco (trustee, currently); Whitney Mus Am Art. *Mailing Add:* Whitney Mus Am Art 945 Madison Ave New York NY 10021

CORNELL, THOMAS BROWNE
SCULPTOR
b Cleveland, Ohio, Mar 1, 37. *Study:* Amherst Col, Mass, BA, 59; Yale Univ, 59-60. *Work:* Mus Mod Art, NY; Princeton Univ Libr; Lessing J Rosenwald Collection, Nat Collection Fine Arts, Washington, DC; Cleveland Mus Art, Ohio; Harvard Univ, Cambridge, Mass; Bibliotheque Nationale, Paris; Bowdoin Col, ME; Grunewald Collection, Univ Calif, Los Angeles; Nat Mus Am Art, Washington, DC; NY Public Libr; Bienecke Libr Archive, Yale Univ, Conn; and others. *Comn:* Mural, 64 & portrait, 79, Bowdoin Col, Brunswick, Maine; bronze plaques, Maine State Comn on Arts & Humanities, 68; Dionysus (bronze plaque), J Walter Thompson Inc, NY, 70; portrait, Va Engineering Found, 81; mural, John Hancock Mutual Life Insurance Co, Boston Mass, 86. *Exhib:* Contemp Painters & Sculptors as Printmakers, Mus Mod Art, NY, 66; Living Am Artists & the Figure, Pa State Univ, 74; 30 Yrs of Am Printmaking, Brooklyn Mus, NY, 76; one-man shows, A M Sachs Gallery, NY, 79 & 81 & G W Einstein Co, NY, 86 & 89-97; Santa Barbara Mus Art, Calif, 80; Utopian Visions, Contemp Art Coun, Mus Mod Art, NY, 87 & 88; Am Painting After the Death of Painting, Kuznetsky Most, Moscow USSR, 89; Bowdoin Col Mus Art, 90; Nat Acad Design, NY, 91, 93 & 96-2006; Anniversary Exhib, Portland Mus Art, 93; Maine Printmakers 1980-2005, Portland Mus Art & Ctr Maine Contemp Art, 2006; Gross McCleaf Gallery, Philadelphia, 2006. *Collection Arranged:* Thomas Cornell Drawings & Prints, 71, & Paintings--the Birth of Nature, 90, Bowdoin Col; and others. *Teaching:* Instr art, Univ Calif, Santa Barbara, 60-62; lectr visual arts prog, Princeton Univ, NJ, 69-71; prof present art & chmn art dept, Bowdoin Col, 63-82, Richard E Steele prof art, currently. *Awards:* Fulbright Grant, 66; Ford Found Grant, 70; Pollock-Krasner Found Grants, 93; and others. *Bibliog:* Charles Jencks (auth), Post-Modernism: The New Classicism in Art & Architecture, Rizzoli, Publ, 87; Carl Little (auth), Paintings of Maine, 90; Edgar Allen Beam (auth), Maine Art Now, 90; Carl Little (auth), More Paintings of Maine, 2006; David Becker (auth), The Imprint of Place, Printmaking 1800-2005, 2006. *Mem:* Col Art Asn; Union of Maine Visual Artists; Nat Acad Design (assoc, 83, acad, 94). *Media:* Oil, Pastel; Etching, Monotype. *Publ:* Illusr, The Monkey, pvt publ, 59; The Defense of Gracchus Babeuf, Gehenna Press, 64, Univ Mass, 67 & Schocken Press, 71; illusr & ed, Frederick Douglas, 64, illusr & ed, William Lloyd Garrison, 64 & illusr, Composed for Dying, 64, Tragos Press; illusr, Voiceprints, Romulus Eds, 89; Ethan Frome, Ascensius Press, 2001

CORR, JAMES D
PAINTER, COLLEGE EDUCATOR
b Missoula, Mont, Feb 13, 31. *Study:* Western Mont Col, BS (art); Univ Mont, ME (art); also with Peter Volkous & Walter Hook. *Work:* Western Gallery & Co High Sch, Dillon, Mont; Univ Collection, Missoula; Copper City Mus, Anaconda, Mont; Beaverhead Chamber Mus Dillon, Mont. *Comn:* Pioneer Fed Bldg, Lewes & Clark Diurama Beaurhead Co Mus. *Exhib:* Electra, Helena, Copper Camp Festival, Butte, Mont; Mondak, Sidney, Mont. *Collection Arranged:* Seidensticker Wildlife Collection. *Teaching:* Emer prof, Western Mont Col, 70-. *Awards:* Mary Baker Emerick Art Chair; UM Western Distinguished Alumni. *Mem:* Mont Watercolor Soc. *Media:* Multimedia. *Mailing Add:* 515 South Dakota Dillon MT 59725

CORREA, FLORA HORST
PAINTER
b Seattle, Wash, Feb 16, 08. *Study:* Univ Wash, BA (art); also with Kenneth Callahan, Sergei Bongart, Richard Yip, Raymond Brose, Mark Tobey & Rex Brandt. *Work:* Craftsman Press, Seattle; Pac First Fed Savings & Loan Asn, Seattle; Rainier Bank, Seattle; Krusteaz Centennial Mills Collection, Oberto, Trident Seafoods; Univ Ore. *Comn:* painting, Bellevue's Sister City, Yao, Japan. *Exhib:* Puget Sound Area Exhib, Frye Art Mus, 64-65, 67-68 & 75; Northwest Watercolor Ann, Seattle, 64-67 & 72-75; Univ Ore Invitationals, 67 & 71-72; Watercolor Exhib, Seattle Pac Col, 75; Grand Galleria Exhib, 75; Nat Biennial Exhib, Nat League Am Penwomen, 86 & 91. *Pos:* past chmn daytime art lect program Seattle Art Mus; former pres, Women Painters of Wash. *Awards:* Excellence in Art Award, Older Womens League, 73-80; First & Second in Watercolor, 79 & 81, First & Second in Oils, 70 & 81, Penwomen's Wash State Biennial. *Bibliog:* Linda Plumb (auth), Flora Correa's distinctive collage art, View Northwest, 5/75. *Mem:* Northwest Watercolor Soc (secy, 67); Women Painters of Wash (pres, 69-70); Nat League Am Penwomen (vpres, Artist Div, Seattle Br, 74-77); Olympic Art Asn, Seattle (pres, 74-77). *Media:* Watercolor, Oil, Collage. *Mailing Add:* 919 109th Ave NE Bellevue WA 98004

CORRIS, MICHAEL
CONCEPTUAL ARTIST, WRITER
b Brooklyn, NY, Aug 14, 48. *Study:* Brooklyn Col, BA, 70; Md Inst Col Art, MFA, 72; Visual Artist fel, Nat Endowment Arts, 74; Artist Book Grant, NY State Coun Arts, 87; Univ Col London, Phd (hist), 96. *Work:* Mus Mod Art, NY; Victoria & Albert Mus, London; Univ Maine Mus Art, Orono, Maine; Mus Contemp Art, Geneva, Switz; Tate Gallery, London. *Exhib:* Documenta V, Friedrichianum, Kassel, Ger, 72; Art Press, Victoria & Albert Mus, London, 76; Art and Language, Nat Gallery Art, Melbourne, Australia, 76; Drawing Now, Mus Mod Art, NY, 76; Committed to Print, Mus Mod Art, NY, 88; Souls Le Soleil, Villa Arson, Nice, France, 88; 1968, Le Consortium, Dijon, France, 92; The Magic of Numbers, Staatsgalerie, Stuttgart, Ger, 97. *Pos:* Corresp, Art Forum Int, NY, 91-95; adv, Arts Coun Eng, 93-95; ed adv, Art & Text, Sydney, NSW, 94-. *Teaching:* Sr lectr art theory, Oxford Brookes Univ, 90-96; vis lect art, Goldsmiths' Col, London, 91-, Slade Sch At, London, 93-; Reader, art theory & hist, Oxford Brookes Univ, 96-. *Awards:* Mary E Lopresti Award, ARLIS Southeast, 87. *Bibliog:* Jan Avgikos (auth), Absence As Presence, New Works Univ Maine Mus Art, 88; Charles Harrison (auth), Essays on Art & Language, Basil Blackwell, 91; Thomas Dreher (auth), Konzeptuelle Kunst in Amerika und England Zwischen 63 & 76, Frankfurt: Lang, 92. *Mem:* Asn Art Historians, Gt Brit; Col Art Asn. *Media:* Offset Lithography, Computer Aided Design; Digital Commun Networks. *Res:* Modernist art in the US 1930-1965; politics and theory in international art since 1965, contemporary video, film and artist organizations, information and exchange groups. *Publ:* Auth, As if the Pillars of Society, 87 & My Frankenstein, 91, Clarte Press; contribr, Art Has No History, Verso Press, 94; Art and Ideas: Postmodernism, Phaidon Press (in prep); Inside a New York Art Gang: Selected Documents of Art & Language in New York, in Artists Think: The Late Works of Ian Burn, Sydney: Power Publ, 96; We Have Submerged Victoriously, Art & Language, Barcelona Fondacion Tapies, 99. *Mailing Add:* Oxford Brookes Univ Sch Art Publ & Music Oxford 0X3 OBP United Kingdom

CORSO, SAMUEL (JOSEPH)
STAINED GLASS ARTIST, PAINTER
b Monroe, La, Jan 11, 53. *Study:* La State Univ, Baton Rouge, BFA, 75, MFA, 77; studied mosaics, sumi-e & bronze sculpture with Paul A Dufour, 77, 78 & 79. *Work:* River Oaks Sq Arts & Crafts Ctr, Alexandria, La; Louisville Arts Club, Ky; Signal Corp, La Jolla, Calif; Duravent Corp, Redwood, Calif; Premier Bancorp, Baton Rouge, La. *Comn:* Mosaic & stained glass, St Francis Cabrini Hosp, Alexandria, La, 88; mosaic mural, Sisters Charity Incarnate Word, Houston, Tex, 90; stained glass, Soc of Jesus Retirement Home, New Orleans, 90; bronze sculpture, Emmy Lou Biedenharn Found, Monroe, La, 90; stained glass, Jesus Good Shepherd Cath Church, Monroe, La, 94-97. *Exhib:* Mint Mus Art, Charlotte, NC, 78 & 80; Missoula Mus Art, Mont, 88; Materials, Hard & Soft, Denton, Tex, 88; La Festival Arts, Masur Mus Art, Monroe, 89; Tex & Neighbors Exhib, 90; Southeastern Juried Competition, Fine Arts Mus South, Mobile, Ala, 90; and others. *Pos:* Bd dir, Baton Rouge Gallery, currently. *Teaching:* Instr, Arrowmont Sch Arts & Crafts, Gatlinburg, Tenn, 78, 83 & 88; asst prof drawing & design, La State Univ, Baton Rouge, 81, instr, 83-91. *Awards:* Hon Mention, Am Crafts Coun Southeast, 86; 2nd Place, Terrebonne Hist & Cult Soc, 88; La Div Arts Fel, 82. *Bibliog:* Albert Lewis (auth), Stained glass goes to college, Glass Mag, Vol V, No 4, 78; Lisa Corbin (auth), A painter's viewpoint, Prof Stained Glass, 5/91; Robert Kehlmann (auth), Neus Glass. *Mem:* La State Arts Coun; Am Crafts Coun. *Media:* European & Domestic Glass; Watercolor, Oil Pastel. *Publ:* Contribr, Robert Jenson's & Patricia Conway's Ornamentalism, Clarkson N Potter, 81; auth, New glass review No 4, Corning Mus, 82; Spectrum, Glass Mag, 12/82; contribr, Experiments in Water, 88 & How to Make an Oil Painting, 90, Watson/Guptil Press. *Dealer:* Worldwide Art Resources & Design Inc 257 E Main St Harbor Springs MI; Creative Resources: Art & Imaging Gallery Inc 162 N Woodward Ave Birmingham MI. *Mailing Add:* 615 Steele Blvd Baton Rouge LA 70806

CORTESE, DON F
PRINTMAKER, INSTRUCTOR
b Chicago, Ill, Dec 30, 34. *Study:* Art Inst Chicago, BFA; Syracuse Univ, MFA. *Work:* Libr Cong, Washington; Art Inst Chicago; Boston Pub Libr; Houghton Libr, Harvard Univ; Uffizi Gallery, Florence, Italy. *Comn:* Intaglio Print, Impressions Workshop, Boston, Mass, 71; etching on experimental paper, Boise Cascade, 80; 60th Int Paper Conf, Ottawa, Can, 85; 25th Anniversary Syracuse Pulp & Paper Found, 85; 120th Anniversary King & King Architects, Handmade paper & print, Syracuse, NY, 88. *Exhib:* Int Print Competition, Seattle Art Mus, Wash, 71; Artists of Cent NY, Munson-Williams-Proctor Inst Mus, Utica, NY, 76; Breaking the Bindings-Am Book Art Now, Eivehjem Mus, Univ Wis, 83; Self-Portraits, Am Artists, Uffizi Gallery, Florence, Italy, 83; Int Exhib Hand Papermaking & Artists Books, AldenBiesen Castle, Belg, 94; paper/print/pulp, Frans Masereel Int Graphic Ctr, Belg, 95; Multiple Affinities: CEPA Gallery, Buffalo, NY, 96; 50th Anniversary Boston Printmakers, Bakalar Gallery, Boston, 97. *Collection Arranged:* New England Land Grant Universities Workshop, 81; Exhib of Visiting Printmakers, Herter Gallery, Univ Mass, 82; Botany of Papermaking Invitational, Mo Botanical Garden Libr, St Louis, 81; Italian J/Solo, Schweinfurth Art Ctr, Auburn, NY, 92. *Teaching:* Prof hand papermaking & book arts printmaking, Sch Art, Syracuse Univ, NY, 65-; chmn dept studio arts, Syracuse Univ, 93-96. *Awards:* Ford Found Grant, Hand Papermaking, Print & Book, 80; Empire State Crafts Alliance Grant, NY, 89; NY State Artists Proj Grant, 94. *Bibliog:* E C Cunningham (auth), Printmaking-A Primary Form of Expression, Univ Press Colo, 92; The Best of Printmaking-An International Collection, Rockport Publ, 97. *Mem:* Col Art Asn; Boston Printmakers. *Mailing Add:* 8062 Cazenovia Rd Manlius NY 13104

CORTINES, RAMON C
PATRON
Pos: Superintendent of schs, San Francisco; chancellor New York Pub Sch System, 1993-95; exec dir, Pew Network for Standards Based Reform, Stanford Univ; mem bd trustees, Brown Univ, J Paul Getty Trust, Scholastic Inc, Spec Olympics Inc, San Francisco Symphony, Pub Policy & Higher Educ; mem adv bd, Teachers Support Netowork. *Mailing Add:* J Paul Getty Trust 1200 Getty Dr Los Angeles CA 90049

CORTOR, ELDZIER
PAINTER, PRINTMAKER
b Richmond, Va, Jan 10, 16. *Study:* Art Inst Chicago, 36 & 41; Inst Design, Ill Inst Technol, 42-43; Columbia Univ, New York, 47. *Work:* Nat Gallery Am Art, Washington, DC; Mus Mod Art & Am Fedn Art, NY; Mus Fine Arts, Boston; Art Inst Chicago; Schomburg Ctr, NY Public Libr, 98. *Comn:* Painting, comn by Julius Rosenwald Fel, Chicago, 45-47; painting, comn by John Simon Guggenheim Fel, NY, 49-50. *Exhib:* Free Within Ourselves, Nat Mus Am Art, Wash, DC, 94; African-Am Art-20th Century II, Rosenfeld Gallery, NY, 95; Art in Chicago, 1945-1995, Mus Contemp Art, Chicago, 96-97; Michael Rosenfeld Gallery, New York City, 2000, 01, 02 & 03; Ken Keleba Gallery, New York City, 2000; Indiana Univ Art Mus, 2006. *Teaching:* Instr, Ctr Art, Port au Prince, Haiti, 49-51 & Pratt Inst, Brooklyn, NY, 72-74. *Awards:* Bertha A Florsheim Award, Am Artists, 45 & William H Bartels Award, Chicago Artists, 46, Art Inst Chicago; Hon Mention, Painting USA, Carnegie Inst, Pittsburgh, 47. *Bibliog:* Elso Honig Fine (auth), The Afro-American Artist, NY; Romare Bearden & Harry Henderson (auths), A History of African-American Artists, Pantheon, 93; Sharon F Patton (auth), African American Art, Oxford Univ Press, NY, 98; Romare Bearden & Harry Henderson (auths), A History of African-American Artists, Pantheon, 93. *Mem:* Artist Fel, Inc; Soc Am Graphic Artists. *Media:* Oil. *Dealer:* Michael Rosehfeld Gallery; Kenkeleba Gallery. *Mailing Add:* 35 Montgomery St New York NY 10002

CORWIN, SOPHIA M
PRINTMAKER, PAINTER
b New York, NY. *Study:* Nat Acad Sch Fine Arts; Art Students League; Hoffman Sch; Archipenko Sch; Phillips Gallery Art Sch, Washington, with Karl Knaths, scholar, 45; NY Univ, BA & MA(creative arts). *Work:* Middlesex Univ Hosp, New Brunswick, NJ. *Exhib:* One-woman shows, Capricorn Gallery, Creative Art Gallery, NY, Colony Gallery, O Street Gallery, Washington & Hansen Gallery, 89-90, NoHo Gallery, 89-96 & Visual Art Wooster Street, NY; Baltimore Mus Art; Silvermine Guild Arts Ctr; Corcoran Gallery Art; Bergen Mus & Middlesex Gen Hosp, NJ; Aegis Gallery; Union Col; Albright Knox Art Gallery, 95-96; and many other group shows. *Awards:* Nat Sculpture Competition Award, US Dept Housing & Urban Develop; Painting Award, Nat Asn Women Artists, 85; Honorarium for Sculpture, Queens Mus Art. *Mem:* Nat Asn Women Artists; Am Soc Contemp Artists; Women's Caucus on Art; Sculptors League. *Media:* Steel, Marble, Oil, Acrylic. *Publ:* Auth, article, Women's Studies Arts, Sculptors League, 78; article, Nat Community Arts Prog Forhud, 78; article, Women Artists, 78. *Dealer:* Bill Ratner 2386 Silver Ridge Rd Los Angeles CA 90039

COSTA, EDUARDO
CONCEPTUAL ARTIST, PAINTER
b Buenos Aires, Argentina. *Study:* Univ Buenos Aires, MA; studied Eng & Am Lit with Jorge L Borges. *Work:* Costume Inst, Metrop Mus Art, NY; New York Univ Libr; Columbia Univ Libr; Yale Univ Libr. *Exhib:* Fashion and Surrealism, Fashion Inst Tech, NY, 87 & Victoria & Albert Mus, London, Eng, 88; Latin-Am Spirit, Bronx Mus Arts, NY, 88-89; The Art Mall, New Mus, NY, 92; Talking Paintings, IBEU, Rio de Janeiro, Brazil, 94; Elga Wimmer Gallery, NY, 95. *Teaching:* Guest artist & lectr, Cooper Union, 84-88. *Bibliog:* Jeff Weinstein (auth), All fashion involves ideas, Village Voice, 10/5/82; Deborah Drier (auth), Obession, Art in Am, 2/88; Berta Sichel (auth), chilinelron/Costa, Art Nexus, 10/92; Gilberto de Abreu (auth), Obra de Arte Tambem é Gente, O Globo, RJ, Brazil, 3/28/94. *Media:* Mixed Media; Acrylic Paint. *Publ:* Auth, The Shower Curtain, Even, Village Voice, 12/22/87; Tunga, Pellegrino, Art in Am, 7/94; Oiticica, Clark and Pape, Art News, 12/94; Tellez, Art in Am, 11/96. *Dealer:* Elga Wimmer Gallery 560 Broadway New York NY 10012

COSTAN, CHRIS
PAINTER, COLLAGE ARTIST
b Chicago, Ill, Sept 18, 50. *Study:* Univ Ill, Chicago, BA, 73, Santa Reparata Print Workshop, Florence, Italy, 74, Univ Wis, Madison, MA/MFA, 75. *Work:* Mus Mod Art; Brooklyn Mus, NY; Nelson-Atkins Mus Art, Kansas City, Mo; Art Inst Chicago; Newark Mus, NJ. *Exhib:* New Work, NY (exhib catalog), Seattle Art Mus, & Spencer Mus Art, 88; Committed to Print, Mus Mod Art, NY, 88; Print Selections from the Permanent Collection, Brooklyn Mus, NY, 90; Return of the Cadavre Equis (exhib catalog), Corcoran Gallery Art, Drawing Ctr, 93-94; The Atmosphere, Art, Native Wisdom & Science, Univ Gallery, Albany, NY, 93; Xenographic Nomadic Wall, XLV Venice Biennale, 93; Drop Dead Painting, 103 Reade St, NY, 94; Internal External (auth, catalog), Goldstrum Gallery, 95; FAO Gallery, NY, 96; solo show, Cheryl Pelavin Fine Art, 03. *Awards:* Nat Endowment Arts, 89-90; Gottlieb Found, 95; NY Found Arts, 99. *Bibliog:* Ronny Cohen (auth), New York reviews, Art Forum, 5/89; Kay Larson (auth), Art/Kay Larson, New York Mag, 3/9/92 Daniel Grant (auth), Art in brief, Berkshire Eagle, 7/21/94; Cover Mag, Joel Silverstein, 98; Tribeca Trib, Jennifer Dalton, 98. *Media:* Acrylic. *Publ:* Auth, Art by Chance (exhib catalog), Nelson-Atkins Mus Art, 89; Intaglio Printmaking in the 1980's (exhib catalog), 90; Presswork: The Art of Women Printmakers (exhib catalog), 91; IInternal External, Richard Martin, 95. *Dealer:* Cheryl Pelavin Fine Art, 13 Jay St New York NY 10007. *Mailing Add:* 303 Park Ave S No 515 New York NY 10010

COSTANZA, JOHN JOSEPH
SCULPTOR, CERAMIST
b New York, NY, June 24, 24. *Study:* Tyler Sch Fine Arts, Temple Univ, BFA, 49; Univ Pa, cert, 43. *Work:* Philadelphia Col Performing Arts; Harcum Jr Col, Bryn Mawr, Pa. *Comn:* Ceramic murals, University City High Sch, Philadelphia Sch District, Pa; Paragon Industry, West Orange, NJ, Ampacet Corp, Mt Vernon, NY; Monsanto Corp, Montvale, NJ; Rauch, Duban & Venturi, Architects & Shubert Theatre, Philadelphia. *Exhib:* Nat Ceramic Competition, Everson Mus Art, Syracuse, NY, 58, 60, 62 & 64; NY World's Fair Invitational, 64-65; Smithsonian Drawing Nat, Washington, & traveling, 64-67; Painting, Drawing & Sculpture Invitational, Univ Del, Newark, 66-68; Philadelphia Regional Art Show, Philadelphia Mus Art, 67; Ceramics Invitational, Philadelphia Civic Ctr Mus, 67, 70 & 73; Ceramics Invitational, Mus Contemp Crafts, NY, 68, 75 & 77. *Pos:* Designer, Potters of Wall St, New York, 50-51. *Teaching:* Art, Devereux Sch, Devon, Pa, 51-53 & Sayre Jr High Sch, Philadelphia, 53-57; teacher ceramics, West Chester High Sch, Pa, 57-63; prof ceramics, Moore Col Art, Philadelphia, 63-73. *Awards:* Purchase Award, Univ Del Art Show, 65; Purchase Prize, Temple Univ Alumni Show, 68; First Prize, Sculpture, William Penn Mem Mus, Harrisburg, Pa, 71. *Bibliog:* Jack Bookbinder (dir), Black History, The Making of a Mural (film), Philadelphia Sch District, 75; Dr Burton Wasserman (auth), Exploring the Visual Art, Davis Publ, 76; Louis G Redstone (auth), Public Art-New Directions, McGraw Hill, 80. *Mem:* Artists Equity Asn; Am Craftsman Coun. *Media:* Clay. *Publ:* Ed, Gerry Williams's Nine Philadelphia Potters, Daniel Clark Found, 73. *Dealer:* Carol Schwartz Art Gallery Chestnut Hill & Bethlehem Pike Philadelphia PA 19118. *Mailing Add:* 737 Polo Rd Bryn Mawr PA 19010-3825

COSTELLO, CYNTHIA ANN
PAINTER, GRAPHIC ARTIST
b St Paul, Minn, Jan 26, 1952. *Study:* Knox Col, BA(art), 74; Brooklyn Col (Charles A Shan Mem Scholar), MFA, 80; Fashion Inst Technol, ASS (textile design), 82. *Work:* Tower Productions, NY; Blue Cross Blue Shield Office, Philadelphia, Pa; Russell Reynolds Assoc; Pan Am Bldg, NY; Dewey Ballantine, Inc, NY. *Exhib:* 30 New York City Painters, Houghton House Gallery, Hobart & William Smith Cols, Geneva, NY, 82; Soho in the South, Archie Wolfe & Assoc, Memphis, Tenn, 83; Great Swamp XXV, Somerset Co Environ Educ Ctr, Basking Ridge, NJ & Nabisco Brands Inc Gallery, East Hanover, NJ, 85; Summerscape II, Gross McCleaf Gallery, Philadelphia, 86; Montauk Club, Brooklyn, NY 88; one-woman show, Prince Street Gallery, 83, 86, 89 & 94. *Pos:* Textile designer, Waverly Fabrics, 81-83; textile designer, Covington Fabrics, 84; textile designer & stylist, Anju Woodridge, New York, 85-89; textile wallcovering stylist, Schumacher & Co, 89-91; creative dir, New York Graphic Soc, 92-94. *Teaching:* Cur asst art hist, Brooklyn Col, NY, 78-80, asst instr painting, 80; instr drawing, Brooklyn Skills Exchange, NY, 79. *Awards:* Scholar, Skowhegan Sch Drawing & Sculpture, Maine, 80; Residency, Va Ctr Arts, Sweet Briar, 86. *Bibliog:* Paintings reproduced for contemporary interiors, Mod Living Mag, Japan, 83; Breda Joy (auth), Painting the Irish landscape, The Kerryman, Ireland, 84; articles, New York Art Review & Art & Antiques, 94. *Mem:* Graphics Artists Guild; Women's Art Registry, Minneapolis, Minn. *Media:* Oil, Pastel. *Dealer:* Gross McCleaf Gallery 1713 Walnut St Philadelphia PA 19103

COSTIGAN, CONSTANCE FRANCES
PAINTER, EDUCATOR
b NJ, July 3, 35. *Study:* Boston Mus Sch Fine Arts; Simmons Col, BA; Am Univ, MA; Univ Va; Univ Calif, Berkeley. *Work:* Phillips Collection, Washington; Hirshhorn Mus, Washington; Univ Iowa Mus; Dimock Gallery, George Wash Univ; also pvt collections in US, Eng, Can, Europe & India. *Exhib:* 19th Area Exhib, Corcoran Gallery Art, 74; solo show, Phillips Collection, Washington, 77, Barbara Fiedler Gallery, Washington, 79 & 82; 25 Washington Artists, Realism & Representation, Foundry Gallery, Washington, 80; Del Mus Art, Wilmington, 80; Surface/Structure: Fiber Innovations, Arlington Arts Ctr, Va, 82; 10 Yrs, A Retrospective, Northern Va Community Col, 83; Franz Bader Gallery, Washington, 85 & 90; Hampshire Col Gallery, Amherst, Mass, 96; Soho 20 Gallery, NY, 97; Corkran Gallery, Rehoboth Art League, Del, 98; From The States, Nat Mus Women Arts, Washington, DC, 98; Visual Arts Gallery, Habitat Center, New Delhi, India, 2003; Lavinia Ctr, Milton, Del, 2003; Hodson Gallery, Hood Col, Frederick, Md, 2005. *Collection Arranged:* Elements of Art: Line (auth, catalog), Arlington Arts Ctr, Va, 80; Hirshhorn Mus & Sculpture Garden; Phillips Collection; Dimock Gallery, George Washington Univ, Washington, DC; Univ Iowa Mus, Iowa City; private col US, Can, Gt Brit, Europe, India. *Pos:* Exhib designer, Smithsonian Inst, 57-59, mus serv, 61-70. *Teaching:* Instr studio art & crafts, Arlington Co Pub Sch, 70-76; instr drawing, design & painting, Smithsonian Inst, Washington, 70-76; prof, George Wash Univ, 1976-2002, emerita prof fine arts, 2003-; distinguished vis prof, Am Univ in Cairo, Egypt, 80-81; vis prof, drawing, Haystack, Mt Sch Crafts, Deer Isle, Me, 90. *Awards:* Grant Award, Lester Hereward Cooke Found, Washington, 78; GSAS Facilitating Fund, George Wash Univ, Washington, 90; and many others. *Bibliog:* Lenore Miller (auth), Constance Costigan, Phillips Collection, Washington, 77; Jean Lawlor Cohen (auth), Constance Costigan: Spirit Fields: Paintings and Pastels, Franz Bader Gallery, Washington, 90. *Mem:* Am Crafts Coun; Fel Royal Soc Arts; Fel MacDowell Colony; Fel Ossabow Island Project; Col Art Asn. *Media:* all medias. *Publ:* Elements of Art: Line, Arlington Arts Ctr, Arlington, Va, 80. *Dealer:* Philadelphia Mus Art Art Works Gallery. *Mailing Add:* 210 NE Market St Lewes DE 19958

COTE, ALAN
PAINTER
b Windham, Conn, 37. *Study:* Sch Mus Fine Arts, Boston, MA, 60. *Work:* Solomon R Guggenhim Mus, Mus Mod Art, Whitney Mus Am Art, Paine Webber Group Inc, NY; J Patrick Lannan Found, Palm Beach, Fla; Suermondt Mus, Collection Ludwig, Aachen, Ger; Rutgers Mus of Art, New Brunswick, NJ; Mus of Fine Arts, Phoenix; Mus of Contemp Art, Miami. *Exhib:* Biennial, Corcoran Gallery Art, Washington, DC, 75; American Drawing in Black and White, Brooklyn Mus, NY, 80; Three Am Painters, Axiom Gallery, Melbourne, Australia, 81; Recent Aquisitions: Paintings and Sculpture, Mus Mod Art, NY, 83; Big Abstract Drawings, Pratt Inst Gallery, NY, 86; Mark d'Montbello Fine Art Gallery, NY, 97; Recent Paintings, Marist Col (illustr catalog), NY, 2002. *Teaching:* Prof Emer, art-painting, Bard Col, Hudson, NY, 70-2003; retired. *Awards:* Fel, Mus Fine Arts, Boston, 61-64; Guggenheim Award, 84; Painting Award, Nat Endowment Arts, 89. *Media:* Acrylic, Oil. *Mailing Add:* PO Box 1298 Port Ewen NY 12466

COTHREN, MICHAEL WATT
EDUCATOR
b Nashville, Ark, Apr 9, 51. *Study:* Vanderbilt Univ, BA, 73; Columbia Univ, MA, 74, PhD, 80. *Pos:* Consult cur medieval stained glass, Glencairn Mus, Bryn Athyn, Pa. *Teaching:* Prof art hist, Swarthmore Col, 78-. *Mem:* Int Ctr Medieval Art; Medieval Acad Am; Soc Francaise d'Archeologie; Corpus Vitrearum USA. *Res:* Gothic art and architecture, especially stained glass. *Publ:* Auth, The Iconography of Theophilus Windows in the First Half of the Thirteenth Century, Speculum 59, 84; The Choir Windows of Agnieres (Somme) and a Regional Style of Gothic Glass Painting, J Glass Studies 28, 86; The Twelfth-Century Crusading Window of the Abbey of Saint- Denis: Praeteritorum enim Recordatio Futurorum est Exhibitio, with Elizabeth A R Brown, Journal of the Warburg and Courtauld Institutes 49, 86; The Seven Sleepers and the Seven Kneelers: Prolegomena to a Study of the 'Belles Verrieres of Rouen Cathedral, Gesta 25, 86. *Mailing Add:* Swarthmore Col Dept Art Swarthmore PA 19081

COTSEN, LLOYD E
PATRON
b Feb 25, 1929. *Study:* grad, Princeton Univ, 1950; Harvard Univ, MBA, 1957. *Pos:* With Neutrogena Corp (formerly Natone), 57-95, pres, Neutrogena Corp, 67-95, Chief Executive Officer, 82-95, chmn, 91-95; pres, Costen Mgt Corp, Los Angeles, 94-; mem bd trustees, J Paul Getty Trust, 2002-. *Collection:* Worldwide Folk Art. *Mailing Add:* J Paul Getty Trust 1200 Getty Ctr Dr Los Angeles CA 90049

COTTER, HOLLAND
CRITIC, HISTORIAN
Study: Harvard Col, AB, 70; Columbia Univ, M Phil, 92. *Pos:* Ed, NY Arts J, 76-80; contrib ed, Art in America; ed assoc, Art News; art critic, New York Times, currently. *Mem:* Int Asn Art Critics. *Publ:* NY Times; Art in America; Art News; Arts Mag; Flash Art. *Mailing Add:* 91 Payson Ave Apt 6E New York NY 10034

COTTER, JAMES EDWARD
SCULPTOR, DESIGNER
b Corning, Iowa, Mar 13, 44. *Study:* Wayne State Col, BFA, 67; Univ Colo, 68; Univ Wyo, MA, 69. *Work:* Nat Broadcasting Corp, NY; Wayne State Col, Wayne, Nebr; Blount Found, Montgomery, Ala; McDonald's Corp, Oak Brook, Ill; Mr & Mrs Gerald Ford, Vail, Colo. *Exhib:* Midwest Biennial, Joslyn Art Mus, Omaha, Nebr, 64; Denver Art Mus, Denver, Colo, 69, 79 & 86; Artists Working in Metal, Sheldon Mus, Lincoln, Nebr, 76; Nat Ornamental Metal Mus, Memphis, Tenn, 79; Copper 2, Mus Art, Tucson, Ariz, 80; solo exhib, Nat Ornamental Metal Mus, Memphis, Tenn, 80; The Great Am Cowboy, traveling exhib, Libr Cong, 83-84. *Pos:* Mem, Design Rev Bd Comt, Town of Vail, Colo, 74; mem adv bd, Colo Mountain Col, Vail, Colo, 74-80; adminr, Summer Vail Workshops Symp, Vail, Colo, 75-76. *Teaching:* Instr metalsmithing, Colo Mountain Col, Vail, Colo, 71-76; instr jewelry, Pendland Sch, Pendland, NC, 78. *Bibliog:* Murray Bovin (auth), Jewelry Making, 67; Lee & Jay Newman, Electroplating & Electroforming, Crown Publ. *Mem:* Soc N Am Goldsmiths Conf. *Media:* Metal & Stone; Mixed Media. *Dealer:* J Cotter Gallery 234 Wall St Vail Co 81657. *Mailing Add:* PO Box 385 234 E Wall St Vail CO 81657

COTTINGHAM, LAURA JOSEPHINE
CRITIC, WRITER
b Alexandria, Ky, Feb 4, 59. *Study:* Univ Chicago, BS, 81; Whitney Mus Independent Study Program. *Pos:* Managing ed, Art & Auction, 86-89; contrib ed, Contemporanea, Venice, Italy, currently; adv bd NY, Balcon, Madrid, Spain, currently. *Res:* Contemporary art, Feminism. *Publ:* Auth, The Feminist De-Mystique, Flash Art, 89; Why Second Wave Feminism Failed, Silent Baroque, 89; Thoughts Are Things: What is a Woman?, Contemporanea, 90; The Prison House of Language, Contemporanea, 90; Critical Poetics, Contemporanea, 90. *Mailing Add:* 172 E Fourth St No 8H New York NY 10009-7312

COTTINGHAM, ROBERT
PAINTER, PRINTMAKER
b Brooklyn, NY, Sept 26, 35. *Study:* Pratt Inst, New York, 59-63, AA, 62. *Work:* Guggenheim Mus Art, Whitney Mus Am Art, Metrop Mus Art, Mus Mod Art, NY; Art Inst Chicago; Philadelphia Mus Art; Baltimore Mus Art, Md; Birmingham Mus Art, Ala; Butler Inst Am Art, Youngstown, Ohio; Fogg Art Mus, Harvard Univ, Cambridge, Mass; Honolulu Acad Arts, Hawaii; Hunter Mus Art, Chattanooga, Tenn; Libr Cong, Washington; Milwaukee Art Mus, Wis; St Louis Art Mus, Mo; Tate Gallery, London, Eng; Utah Mus Fine Arts, Univ Utah, Salt Lake City; Va Mus Fine Arts. *Comn:* Permanent Public Installation of 12 enamel panels depicting American Railroad Imagery, Union Station, Hartford, Conn. *Exhib:* Recent Acquistions, Whitney Mus Am Art & Hirshhorn Mus & Sculpture Garden, 77; one-man exhibs, Brenda Kroos Gallery, Cleveland, Ohio, 92, Butler Inst Am Art, Youngstown, Ohio, 92, Rahr-West Art Mus, Maritowoc, Wis, 90, Lyman Allyn Art Mus, New London, Conn, 91, Harcourts Contemp, San Francisco, Calif, 91, Nat Mus Am Art, Smithsonian Inst, Washington, DC, 98-99, Still Lifes, Forum Gallery, NY, 2000, Robert Cottingham: paintings, gouaches, drawings, prints Cline Fine Art, Sante Fe, NMex, 00; Takada Gallery, San Francisco, 94; Triton Mus, Santa Clara, Calif, 94; Struve Gallery, Chicago, 94; Robert Cottingham, An Am Alphabet, Montgomery Mus Fine Art, Ala, 96; Realism Knows No Bounds, Van de Griff Gallery, Santa Fe, NMex, 98; It's Still Life, Forum Gallery, NY, 98; Collector's Show, Art Art Ctr, Little Rock, 98; Twentieth Century Am Drawings, Ark Art Cen, 99; Nat Acad Design, NY, 99; A Century Am Dream, The Chunichi Shimbun, Naka-ku Nagoya, Japan, 00; Nat Acad Design: 176th Ann Exhib, New York City, 01; Carol Craven Gallery, West Tisbury, Mass, 02. *Collection Arranged:* Abilene Cristian Univ, Tex; Ackland Art Mus, Univ NC, Chapel Hill; Amarillo Mus Art, Tex; Ark Arts Cen, Little Rock; Art Inst Chicago, Ill; Baltimore Mus Art, Md; Birmingham, Mus Art, Ala; Cleveland Mus Art, Ohio; Del Art Mus, Wilmington; Denver Art Mus, Colo; Long Beach Mus Art, Calif; Milwaukee Mus Art, Wis; Mus Am Art, Smithsonian Inst, Washington, DC; RI Sch Design, Providence; St Louis Art Mus, Mo; Tampa Mus Art, Fla; Univ Iowa Mus Art, Iowa City; Univ Ky Art Mus, Lexington; Univ Mich Mus Art, Ann Arbor; Utah Mus Fine Arts, Univ Utah, Salt Lake City; others. *Pos:* Art dir, Young & Rubicam Advertising, New York, 59-64 & Los Angeles, 64-68. *Teaching:* instr, Art Ctr Col Design, Los Angeles, 69-70, Nat Acad Design, 91; artist-in-residence, Wesleyan Univ, Middletown, Conn, 87-92, Nat Acad Design, New York, 91, Marie Walsh Sharpe Art Found, Colorado Spring, Colo, 94. *Awards:* Nat Endowment Arts Grant, 74-75; Walter Gropius Fel, Huntington Mus Art, WVa, 92; MacDowll Colony Residency, 93-94; Chubb Life Am Fel, 94. *Bibliog:* Roberta Smith (auth), Hudson Valley Conversations, NY Times, 7/18/97; JoAnn Lewis (auth), Man of letters: Robert Cottingham turned America's signs into symbols, Washington Post, 10/24/98; Ann Landi (auth), Who hails from Hopper, ARTnews, 4/98. *Mem:* Nat Acad Design (assoc, 90, acad, 94). *Media:* Acrylic, Oil, All Media. *Dealer:* Forum Gallery 745 5th Ave New York NY 10151. *Mailing Add:* PO Box 604 Newtown CT 06470-0604

COTTONE-KOLTHOFF, CAROL
PAINTER, ILLUSTRATOR
b San Pedro, Calif, May 24, 54. *Study:* Calif State Univ, Long Beach, BFA, 77, MFA, 80; Loyola Marymount Univ, Los Angeles, educ credential, 80. *Comn:* Tunnels (mural), Marymount Col, Palos Verdes, Calif, 80; Aviary-Hummingbirds, San Diego Zoo, 93. *Exhib:* Juried Exhib, Butler Inst Am Art, Youngstown, Ohio, 81; Nat Women's Caucus for the Arts, Nat World Exhib, New Orleans, 85; Twelve and Under Invitational, Golden West Col, Huntington Beach, Calif, 90; Wildlife 92, San Bernardino Mus, Calif, 92; 6th Ann Animals in Art, State Univ, Baton Rouge, 93; Calif State Expos, Del Mar, 93; and others. *Teaching:* Lectr art-draw/paint, Calif State Univ, Long Beach, 81-83; instr art-draw/paint, Monterey Penninsula Col, 87-89; instr art-design, Southwestern Col, Chula Vista, 91-. *Awards:* Award, Western Fedn Watercolors Soc Exhib, 90; First Place Show Award, City of Brea, Calif, 91; Del Mar Award, City of Del Mar, Calif, 93. *Bibliog:* Carol Katchen (auth), The natural beauty of birds, Artist's Mag, 10/94. *Publ:* Contribr, Splash III, North Light Publ, 94. *Mailing Add:* 5085 Argonne Ct San Diego CA 92117

COUCH, URBAN
CONSULTANT, EDUCATOR
b Minneapolis, Minn, Apr 27, 27. *Study:* Minneapolis Sch Art, BFA, 51; Skowhegan Sch Painting & Sculpture, 51; Cranbrook Acad Art, MFA, 59; Kyoto, Japan, 64-66. *Work:* Minneapolis Inst Arts; Walker Art Ctr, Minneapolis; Sioux City Art Ctr, Iowa; Cranbrook Mus, Bloomfield Hills, Mich; Hirshorn Collection, Washington; plus 188 others. *Exhib:* Walker Art Ctr, 59; Neville Mus Invitational, Green Bay, Wis, 67; Art in the Embassies, US State Dept, Sophia, Bulgaria & Canberra, Australia, 68-71; Minneapolis Inst Arts, 68; Difference of a Decade, Lee Nordness Galleries, NY, 69; 60 Yr Visual Resume, Morgantown Art Ctr, WVa, 98; plus 72 others. *Pos:* Cur, S Pac Art Collection, WWII, graphic designer, USN, Calif, 45; design consult, Control Data Corp, 60-62; pres, Minneapolis Col Art & Design, 62; consult-examiner prog, Comn on Cols & Univs, Chicago, 62-63; consult & examiner, NASAD Asn, 63-, chmn div art, 71-81; dir, galleries & art collections, WVa Univ, 81-92, chmn div art, 87-89; founder, pres, Couch Concepts: Learning Concepts for Tomorrow's Tomorrow, 88-. *Teaching:* Instr art, Minneapolis Col Art & Design, 55-70, chmn found prog, 59-62, actg dir, 63, asst to dir, 63-64, actg chmn fine arts div, 65-66, chmn painting dept, 68-71; instr advan painting, Walker Art Ctr, 57-61; instr art, Kingswood Sch, Bloomfield Hills, Mich & Bloomfield Hills Art Ctr, 58-59; grad workshop, Univ Minn, 59-61; instr advan painting, Minnetonka Art Ctr, Minneapolis, 59-61; artist in residence, Minn Jr Cols, summers 67-69; instr grad painting, Calif Col Arts & Crafts, summer 70; prof emer painting, WVa Univ, 71-92; emer prof, Honors Prog, Univ WVa, 92-, ed coordr, 92-. *Media:* All Media. *Mailing Add:* 1160 Charles Ave Morgantown WV 26505

COUGHLIN, JACK
PRINTMAKER, SCULPTOR
b Greenwich, Conn, Feb 19, 32. *Study:* Art Students League; RI Sch Design, BFA, 54, MS, 61. *Work:* Metrop Mus Art & Mus Mod Art, NY; Norfolk Mus Arts & Sci, Va; Staedelsches Kunst Inst, Frankfort, Ger; Nat Collection Fine Arts, Washington; Mus Mod Art, NY. *Comn:* Ed original prints, Asn Am Artists, 62-79, Int Graphic Arts Soc, 66 & 68, Silvermine Guild Artists, New Canaan, Conn, 67, Graphic Studio, Dublin, Ireland, 71 & Franklin Mint, Pa, 77, Springfield Mus, 83; ongoing drawings for The New Republic. *Exhib:* Nat Inst Arts & Lett, 1970; Soc Am Graphic Arts, NY, 1971-92; Nat Acad Design Ann Exhib, 1974-96; 4th Int Graphic Biennial, WGer, 1976; 3rd Norwegian Int Print Biennale, Norway, 1976; Fifth Int Print Exhib, Barcelona, Spain, 1985, 1988. *Pos:* Academican, Nat Acad Design, 72-96. *Teaching:* Prof drawing & printmaking, Univ Mass, Amherst, 60-94, emer prof, 94-. *Awards:* Nat Exhib Award for etching, Soc Am Graphic Artists, 77 & 81; Nat Exhib Awards for drawing & printing, Nat Acad Design, 80, 82 & 83; NDak Am Drawing Biennial, 90. *Bibliog:* Robin Skelton (auth), Imagination of Jack Coughlin, 70, Jack Coughlin: Irish portraits, 72 & Jack Coughlin: A Perspective View, 80, Malahat Rev, Univ Victoria, BC; article, Am Artist Mag, 6/86. *Mem:* Nat Acad Design (assoc, 72, acad, 90); Soc Am Graphic Artists; Boston Printmakers. *Media:* Watercolor, Etching, Relief Sculpture. *Interests:* Playing blues harmonica. *Publ:* Illusr, Mnemosyne Lay in Dust, 66 & Synge-Petrarch, 71, Dolmen Press, Dublin, Ireland; Grotesques, 20 Etchings by Jack Coughlin, Aquarius Press, 70; 13 Irish Writers, Etchings, Godine Press, 73; Impressions of Bohemia, Pac Rim Galleries, 86; Auth A Brush with the Blues. *Dealer:* Golden Cod Galleries E Commercial St Wellfleet MA 02667; Michaelson Gallery S Pleasant St Amherst MA 01002. *Mailing Add:* N Leverett Rd Montague MA 01351

COULTER, LANE
SILVERSMITH, HISTORIAN
b Chelsea, Mass, Jan 16, 44. *Study:* Univ Ill, BFA, 69; Univ Okla, MFA, 74. *Work:* Wustum Mus, Racine, Wis; Absolut Corp, New York City. *Comn:* MACE, Tex A&M Univ, College Station, 90; Absolut, Absolut Vodka, New York City, 90; Chalice, St Marks Church, Norman, Okla, 84. *Exhib:* Absolut Southwest, Mus Am Folk Art, New York City, 90; Double Vision 3, Wustum Mus, Racine, Wis, 95; Contemproary Am Pewter, Nat Ornamental Metal Mus, Memphis, Tenn, 95; NMex Jewelers, Millicent Rogers Mus, Taos, NMex, 98; Souvenir NY, Aaron Faber Gallery, New York City, 92; Silver New Forms III, Fortunoff Corp, New York City, 92. *Collection Arranged:* Am Indian Jewelry, Nat Ornamental Metal Mus, 94; Hojalateria, Mus Internat Folk Art, 91. *Pos:* co-founder Summer Vail Metal Symposium, Colo, 75-85. *Teaching:* instr, Tex A&M, 69-72; assoc prof jewelry design, Univ Okla, Norman, 72-83; vis prof jewelry, Univ Tex, Austin, 86, Ariz State Univ, 87; prof metal work, Inst Am Indian Art, Santa Fe, NMex, 89-2001. *Awards:* Southwest Book award, Border-Regional Librs, 1990. *Mem:* Soc North Am Goldsmiths; Antique Tribal Art Dealers Asn. *Media:* Metal, Silver, Pewter. *Res:* Navajo Saddle Blankets; New Mexican Furniture, 19th Century; New Mesican tinwork. *Publ:* auth, Metalwork of Ann Orr, Ga Mus Art, 94; coauth, American Indian Jewelry, Dict World Art, 96; auth, American expressions, Am Craft, 97; auth, New Mexican Tinwork, Antiques Mag, 99; ed, Navajo Saddle Blankets, 2002. *Dealer:* Jett Gallery Old Santa Fe Mail Sante Fe NMex 87501. *Mailing Add:* 2120 Conejo Santa Fe NM 87505

COUPER, CHARLES ALEXANDER
PAINTER, INSTRUCTOR
b Portsmouth, NH, Feb 19, 24. *Study:* Vesper George Sch Art, Boston, cert; Cape Sch Art, Provincetown, Mass, with Henry Hensche; Ernest Lee Major Studio, Boston. *Work:* Greenshields Mus, Montreal; Attleboro Mus, Mass; Heritage Mus, Provincetown, Mass; Biblioteca Publica Collection San Migual de Allende, Mexico; Smithsonian Inst; Cape Mus of Fine Art, MA. *Comn:* Pastel portrait, Judge Phillip, Wolaver QC, NS, Can, 80. *Exhib:* One-man shows, Cape Cod Art Asn, 73, Soratoga Gallery-Bridgetown, NS, 92 & Guild Boston Artists, 73, STFX Univ Art Gallery, Antigonish, Nova Scotia, 2004; Allied Artists Am, NY, 74; Grande Prix Int, Cannes, France, 74; Deauville Int, France, 75. *Pos:* Mem, Provincetown Art Comn, Mass, 78-79. *Teaching:* Instr life drawing & painting, Vesper George Sch Art, 55-; instr, Swain Sch Design, New Bedford, Mass, 65-68. *Awards:* Award of Distinction, Pastel Soc Can, 92 & First Jury Award, 94; Gloria Layton Mem Award, Allied Artists Am, NY; First Jury Award for Still Life, Pastel Soc Can, British Columbia, 2000; plus others. *Bibliog:* Critical rev in La Rev Mod, Paris, 69; The Best of Canadian Pastels, Art Instruction Assocs, Sarasota, Fla; Robin Metcalife (auth of text) Art and Craft of Nova Scotia. *Mem:* Pastel Soc Can; Artist de Peintre de La Cote d'Azur; Visual Arts NS. *Media:* Oil, Pastel. *Specialty:* Couper Studios, Bear River Nova Scotia, Vis Arts Gallery. *Interests:* Architecture, Gardening, Carpentry. *Publ:* contributor to many Canadian art publications. *Dealer:* Flight of Fancy Gallery Bear River NS. *Mailing Add:* 735 Riverview Rd 7 Bear River NS B0S 1B0 Canada

COUPER, JAMES M
PAINTER, EDUCATOR
b Atlanta, Ga, Nov 21, 37. *Study:* Atlanta Art Inst; Ga State Univ; Fla State Univ. *Work:* Ga Dept Natural Resources; and others; John & Mable Ringling Mus, Sarasota, Fla; Miami Met Mus & Art Ctr, Coral Gables, Fla; Mus of Art, Ft Lauderdale, Fla; Art in Pub Bldgs, State of Fla; Art in Pub Places, Miami Dade Co, Fla; The Blount Collection, Montgomery, Ala; many others; Frost Art Mus, Miami, Fla. *Comn:* Mural, 20th Century Fox, 68. *Exhib:* Fla Int Univ, Miami, Fla, 93; Barbara Gillman Gallery, Miami, 93; Bellaire Art Ctr, Fla, 94; Ormond Beach Mem Mus, Fla, 96; Metro Dade Cult Resource Ctr, 96; plus many others. *Collection Arranged:* Art of the Asian Mountains, 69; The Artist & The Sea, 69; Art of Italy, 69; Up & Out, 69-70. *Pos:* Asst to dir, Miami Art Ctr, 67-70; art mus founder, dir, Fla Int Univ, 77-80. *Teaching:* Instr painting, Miami-Dade Jr Col, 64-68; instr painting, Miami Art Ctr, 65-72; from instr to prof painting, Fla Int Univ, 72-, chmn art dept, 77-78, MFA prog founder, dir, 98-2000. *Awards:* Fla Individual Artist Grant, 83 & 90; Yaddo Fel, 87; Hambidge Ctr Fel, 90, 91, 94 & 2001. *Bibliog:* Reviews, Art News, 87, Miami Herald, 86-2003 & St Petersburg Times, 96. *Media:* Oil. *Res:* continuing use of landscape imagery in paintings concerned with ecological concerns, specifically the preservation of wilderness. *Specialty:* Contemp Art. *Interests:* Traveling. *Dealer:* Barbara Gilman Gallery 3814 NE Miami Ct. Miami FL; Center for the Earth Gallery 3204 N Davidson St Charlotte NC; Micahel Murphy Gllery 2722 McDill Ave Tampa FL; Allyn Gallup Contemporary Art 556 Pineapple Ave Sarasota FL. *Mailing Add:* 7845 SW 118th St Miami FL 33156

COUPON, WILLIAM
PHOTOGRAPHER, FILMMAKER
b New York, NY, Dec 3, 52. *Study:* Syracuse Univ, BS(television), 74. *Work:* Chase Bank Collection, NY. *Exhib:* The Indigenous People, US Senate Rotunda, 94; Ethnographic Pictures, Gerald Peters Gallery, Santa Fe, NMex, 95; Social Studies Sixteen: Turkish Kurds, FotoFest '96, Houston, 96; Yakut Gallery, Moscow, 96. *Pos:* portrait photogr, Issey Miyake, Japan, 88-96. *Media:* Photography. *Dealer:* Fahey-Klein Gallery Los Angeles CA; Baudoin Lebon Gallery Paris France

COURTNEY, SUZAN
PAINTER, PRINTMAKER
b Mobile, Ala, Sept 6, 47. *Study:* Tulane Univ, 68-69; Kingston-Upon-Hull Col Art, Hull, Eng, dipl art & design, 73; Whitney Mus Independent Study Prog, 74-75; Yale Univ Sch Art, MFA, 77. *Work:* Insurance Co N Am, Ericson Gallery & Davis, Markel and Edwards, NY; Gasperi Gallery, New Orleans; Fine Arts Mus of the South, Mobile, Ala. *Exhib:* Solo exhibs, Univ S Fla, 77, Fine Arts Mus, Mobile, Ala, 87, Gasperi Gallery, New Orleans, La, 89 & Galerie Gordon Pym & Fils, Paris, 92; Two Decades of Abstraction, traveling nationally, 79; Five New York City Artists, Ericson Gallery, NY, 81; Invitational Exhib, Bristol Art Mus, Eng, 81; Perspectives South, 82 & Invitational, 84, Ericson Gallery, NY; Urban Spirit, City Without Walls, Newark, NJ, 85; New Urban Artists, Int Monetary Fund, Washington, DC, 85-86; Folk-Funk Show, Gasperi Gallery, New Orleans, La; Small Works, Parsons Sch Design, 89; Europa - Am, 360 E-Venti, NY - Rome, Pino Molica Gallery, 92; Miauhaus, NY, 92; Dieu Donne Papermill Inc Group Show; Ala Impact-Contemp Artists with Ala Ties, Mobile & Huntsville, Ala, 95; St Kolumba Exhib, Rapid Transit Gallery, Savannah Col Art & Design, 98. *Pos:* Visiting artist, Princeton Univ, Rutgers Univ & Spring Hill Col, 84-86, Reading Univ & Slade Sch Art, London, Eng, 86. *Teaching:* Instr painting & drawing, RI Sch Design, Providence, 79-83 & Univ South Fla, Tampa, currently; adj prof painting & drawing, Southampton Col, NY, 83-84; adj prof color theory, Rutgers Univ, NJ, 85-92; adj prof drawing, Parsons Sch Design, 87-92. *Awards:* Skowhegan Sch Painting Fel; Susan Whedon Prize Painting, Yale Sch Art, 75; Edward Albee Studio Award, Montauk, NY, 80. *Media:* Oil on Canvas. *Publ:* New York Art Review, 88. *Dealer:* Gasperi Gallery New Orleans LA. *Mailing Add:* 530 Canal St No 3W New York NY 10013

COURTRIGHT, ROBERT
COLLAGE ARTIST, PAINTER
b Sumter, SC, Oct 20, 26. *Study:* St John's Col, Annapolis, Md; New Sch Social Res, NY, 47-48; Art Students League, 48-52. *Work:* Musee de l'Art Moderne & de l'Art Contemporain, Nice, France Collection de l'Etat, Paris, France; Metrop Mus Art, NY; Nichido Mus, Casama, Japan; San Francisco Mus Mod Art, Calif; Aldrich Mus Contemp Art, Ridgefield, Conn. *Exhib:* Smithsonian Inst, Washington, DC, 56; Mus Mod Art, NY, 57; Carnegie Int, Carnegie Inst, Pittsburgh, Pa, 59; Festival Int de la Peinture, Cagnes-sur-Mer, France, 76; Am & Europe, A Century Mod Masters from Thyssen-Bornemisza Collection, traveled in Australia & NZ, 79-81; C Grimaldis Gallery, Baltimore, 95, Kouros Gallery, NY, 95 & 97, Knocke, LeZout, 96, Galerie Bernard Cats, Brussels, 96 & 97, Galerie Jean Jacques Dutko, 96. *Bibliog:* Calvin Tompkins (auth), Robert Courtright, Andrew Crispo Gallery, NY, 79; Ralph Pomeroy (auth), Light and substance: The collages of Robert Courtright, Arts Mag, 12/79; Jeffrey Robinson (auth), Robert Courtright: Collage-Masks, Andrew Crispo Gallery, NY, 81. *Media:* Papier Mache, Acrylic. *Mailing Add:* 80 Varick St New York NY 10013

COUTURIER, MARION B
DEALER, COLLECTOR
Study: Univ Lausanne, Switz, cert de Francais et Langues; Univ Dijon; Columbia Univ. *Pos:* Owner, Couturier Galerie, 61-; art dir consult, 1986-. *Teaching:* Instr, Broadies, art history extension courses. *Specialty:* Consultant, major private, museums & corporate collections, impressionists, post impressionists & contemporary art, pre-Columbian African tribal art sculpture & graphics. *Interests:* Work with major private and museum collections, selecting works from the modern to the contemporary. *Collection:* Contemporary artists in all media; Latin American artists for merit and variety of their work; Cuban art all media & photgraphy in Calif branch; Int exhibs (Korda Exhib, Bition: Victoria & Albert Mus, London. *Mailing Add:* Couturier Gallery 166 N La Brea Los Angeles CA 90036

COVE, ROSEMARY
SCULPTOR, PAINTER
b New York, NY, Jan 11, 36. *Study:* Parsons Sch Design. *Work:* Weatherspoon, NC; NY Times; Tallix Inc; CIBA Geigy, NY; Conti Commodities. *Exhib:* Ingber Gallery, 73-90, Thompsen Gallery, 90; Lincoln Ctr, 92; Graham Modern, 92; Gremillion Gallery, 94-2000; Rivington Gallery, 98-2000; Gremillion Gallery, 2000-05; Rivington Gallery, 2000-05; Ann Norton Sculpture Garden, 2006; Artists' Museum of NY City, 2006. *Awards:* Nat Endowment Residency Grant, 84; NY State Coun Arts Grant, 86; Ford Found Award. *Bibliog:* Allen Ellingswieg (auth), Rosemary Cove, 75 & Natalie Edgar (auth), Rosemary Cove, 78, Arts Mag; Dorothy Beskind (auth), Rosemary Cove (film), 77; Ed McCormack (auth), Art Speak. *Mem:* Women in Arts; Artists Equity; Am Medalists Soc. *Media:* Terra-Cotta, Corten Steel; Oil, Ink. *Mailing Add:* 71 Waller Ave White Plains NY 10605

COVEY, ROSEMARY FEIT
PRINTMAKER, ILLUSTRATOR
b Johannesburg, SAfrica, July 17, 54. *Study:* Studied printmaking under Barry Moser, 68-72; Cornell Univ (archit), 74; Maryland Inst Col Art (printmaking), 76. *Work:* Print Collection of Georgetown Univ, 27 prints, Washington; Cocoran Mus Art, Washington; Nat Mus Am Hist, Washington; NY Pub Libr, 16 prints; and many others. *Comn:* Seven cover illustrations, Wash Post/Book World, Washington, 80-90; 90th Anniversary Print, Int Fedn Metalworkers, Zurich, Switz, 83; seventeen illustrations, World & I Mag, Washington, 86-87; two wood-engravings prints, Gen Elec Astro-Space, Princeton, NJ, 91-92. *Exhib:* one-woman exhib, Jane Haslem Gallery, Washington, 92, Interlochen Ctr Arts, Mich, 92, Martin Sumers Graphics, 95, Georgia Southern Univ, Statesboro, Time Gallery, Chicago, 95, Saginaw Valley State Univ Art Gallery, Univ Ctr, Mich, 97, Butler Inst Am Art, Youngstown, Ohio, 97; Los Angeles 12th Nat Print Exhib, Frederick S Wright Gallery, Univ Calif, Los Angeles, 93; Women Printmakers: 18th Century to Present, Nat Mus Women Arts, Washington, 94; Am Self Portraits in Prints, Jane Haslem Gallery, traveling, 95; Calvin Col Art Mus, Grand Rapids, Mich, 95; Indiana Art Mus, Bloomington, 95; Print Club Albany's 19th Nat Print Exhib, Schenectady Mus, NY, 95; William Floyd Gallery, NY, 2003; Grand Central Art Center, Univ California, Fullerton, 2005. *Pos:* Permanent studio, Torpedo Fac Art Ctr, Alexandria, Va, 82-; artist in res, Grand Central Art Ctr, Santa Ana, CA, 2004. *Awards:* National Printmaking Grant, Alpha Delta Kappa Found, 92; Rockefeller Found Fel, Bellagio, Italy, 98. *Bibliog:* Marriott Michel (auth), Art reflects

conflict, Wash Post, 85; Rosemary Covey's graphic response to emotions, Am Artists Mag, 86; Eric L Mackenzie (auth), Rosemary Feit Covey: The Prints 1970-1990, Eric L Mackenzie, 90. *Mem:* Torpedo Fac Artists Asn (pres Target Gallery, 93-94); Soc of Graphic Artists. *Media:* Wood Engraving. *Publ:* Shadows & Goatbones, Scop Publ, 92; Stark Naked on a Cold Irish Morning, Scop Publ, 92; Peking Street Peddlers, Bird & Bull Press, 94; Hearsay, Strange Tales from the Middle Kingdom, William Morrow Inc, New York, 98; Beauty and the Serpent: Thirteen Tales of Unnatural Animals, Simon and Schuster, 2001. *Mailing Add:* 118 N Patrick St Alexandria VA 22314

COVI, DARIO A
HISTORIAN
b Livingston, Ill, Dec 26, 20. *Study:* Eastern Ill State Teachers Col, BEd, 43; State Univ Iowa, MA, 48, with William S Heckscher; NY Univ, with Richard Offner, PhD, 58. *Hon Degrees:* Eastern Ill Univ, LHD, 2003. *Pos:* Mem exec comt, Ky Arts Comn, 65-70. *Teaching:* From instr to prof art hist, Univ Louisville, 56-70; prof, Duke Univ, 70-75; Hite prof, Univ Louisville, 75-91, prof emer, 91-. *Awards:* Am Coun Learned Socs Fel, 64; Fulbright-Hays Fel, 68-69; Gladys Krieble Delmas Found Grant, 79. *Mem:* Col Art Asn Am; Southeastern Col Art Conf; Renaissance Soc Am; Midwest Art Hist Soc; Ital Art Soc; Leonardo Da Vinci Soc. *Res:* Italian Renaissance art. *Publ:* Auth, Prints from the Allen R Hite Art Institute Collection (exhib catalog), 63; contribr, McGraw-Hill Dict Art, Art Bull, Burlington Mag, Renaissance Quart & other nat art publ; auth, The Inscription in Fifteenth Century Florentine Painting; contribr, The Dictionary Art, Encyclopedia of Sculpture; Andrea del Verrocchio Life and Work, Leo S Olschki Editore, Florence, 2005. *Mailing Add:* Hite Art Inst Univ Louisville Louisville KY 40292

COVINGTON, HARRISON WALL
PAINTER, SCULPTOR
b Plant City, Fla, Apr 12, 24. *Study:* Univ Fla, 42-43; Hiram Col, 43; Univ Fla, BFA(hons), 49, MFA, 53. *Work:* Herron Mus Art, Indianapolis, Ind; Everson Mus Art, Syracuse, NY; John & Mable Ringling Mus Art, Sarasota, Fla; Jacksonville Mus Art, Fla; Nat Gallery Art, Washington. *Comn:* sculpture bas relief, Fla Fed Savings & Loan, 74; portraits of pres, 70, 76 & 84, sculpture bas relief, Univ South Fla, 75; Sculptured Figures, Int Shrine Hq, 80; Bronze Figure, Barnstormer, Tampa Int Airportm 2005; Bronze Figure, Firefighter Hillsborough Co, Fla, 2005. *Exhib:* Mus Director's Choice, throughout Southeastern US, 56-59; Painting USA: The Figure, Mus Mod Art, NY, 62; NY World's Fair, 64; Fla 17, Pan-Am Union, Washington, 68; Graphic Studio USF, Brooklyn Mus, 78; Tampa Mus Art, 87. *Teaching:* Instr art, Univ Fla, 49-61; prof art, Univ S Fla, 61-82, chmn visual arts prog, 61-67, dean, Div Fine Arts, 67-72, dean, Col Fine Arts, 77-82, prof emer, 82- & dean emer, 82-. *Awards:* Sloan Found Grant, 47; Guggenheim Fel, 64. *Bibliog:* Gene Baro (auth), Graphic Studio USF: An Experiment in Art and Education (exhib catalog), Brooklyn Mus, 78. *Media:* Acrylic, Plastic, Bronze. *Mailing Add:* 11809 Vera Ave Tampa FL 33618

COWAN, AILEEN HOOPER
SCULPTOR, PAINTER
b Windsor, Ont, June 11, 26. *Study:* Univ Toronto, BA; Queen's Univ, Kingston, Ont; Univ Toronto. *Work:* Univ Western Ont; Robert McLaughlin Gallery, Oshawa, Can. *Comn:* J Gush, Toronto; Govt of Ont. *Exhib:* Agnes Etherington Gallery, Queen's Univ, Kingston, Ont, 74; Merton Gallery, Toronto, 79; McDowell Gallery, Toronto, 80; Sculptors Soc BC, Robson Sq Media Ctr, Vancouver, 80; J Aird Gallery, Toronto, 89 & 90; retrospective, Stock Exchange Tower, Toronto, 94; President's Exhib, SSC Gallery, 2003. *Collection Arranged:* Arranged & curated permanent coll of Sculptor's Soc of Can, (traveling exhib), 81. *Pos:* Cur, permanent collection, Sculptor's Soc Can; Pres and Life Mem, Sculptor's Soc of Can, formerly. *Teaching:* Univ Toronto, Ont, formerly. *Awards:* Augusts Kopmanis Mem Award, 80. *Bibliog:* Article, Athens News, Greece, 7/72; article, Art Mag, Toronto, Vol 5, No 15, 73. *Mem:* Sculptors Soc Can; Soc of Painters in Watercolors. *Media:* Bronze, Acrylic. *Res:* Polyesters. *Specialty:* Canadian Art. *Interests:* Sculpture & Painting. *Collection:* RS McLaughlin Gallery, Oshawa. *Publ:* Earth and You, Vol XVI, 87. *Dealer:* Gallery Helena 277 Strathallan Wood, Toronto ON Canada, M5N1T7. *Mailing Add:* c/o Gallery Helena 277 Strathallan Wood Toronto ON M5N 1T7 Canada

COWAN, RALPH WOLFE
PAINTER
b Pheobus, Va, Dec 16, 31. *Study:* Art Students League, New York, 51. *Work:* Carter Presidential Ctr, Atlanta, Ga; Portsmouth Mus, Va; Royal Palace Monaco; Graceland, Memphis, Tenn. *Comn:* Palace Collection, comn by King Fahd, Saudi Arabia, 84; 3 portraits, comn by King Hassan II, Morocco, 84; 18 portraits, comn by HM Sultan Hassanal Bolkiah, Brunei, 85; 2 portraits, comn by Pres Augusto Pinochet, Chile; 4 portraits, comn by Pres Sheik Zayed, United Arab Emirates. *Exhib:* One-man retrospective, Portsmouth Mus, Va, 84; Ft Lauderdale Mus Art, Fla. *Awards:* Portsmouth Notable, Portsmouth Hall of Fame, Va, 87; Best in Show, Norton Mus Art, Norton Artist Guild, 88. *Bibliog:* Doug Stewart (auth), Making Faces is a Hard Days Fight, Smithsonian Mag 11-5-88; Linda Marx (auth), Painter Fights Back, People Mag, 9/4/89. *Mem:* Art Students League; Portrait Inst; Am Portrait Soc; Am Soc Artists. *Media:* Oil. *Publ:* Auth, A Personal Vision, self published, 88. *Mailing Add:* 243 29th St West Palm Beach FL 22407-5207

COWART, JACK
MUSEUM DIRECTOR, CURATOR
b Ft Riley, Kans, Feb 7, 45. *Study:* Va Military Inst, BA, 67; Johns Hopkins Univ, PhD (art hist), 72. *Collection Arranged:* Henri Matisse: The Early Years in Nice, 1916-1930 (coauth, catalog), Nat Gallery Art, Washington, DC, 86-87; Georgia O'Keeffe, 1887-1986, Nat Gallery Art, Washington, DC, 87-88; Matisse in Morocco: The Paintings and Drawings, 1912-1913 (coauth, catalog), Nat Gallery Art, Washington, DC, 90-91; ROCI--Rauschenberg Overseas Culture Interchange, Nat Gallery Art, Washington, DC, 91; Ellsworth Kelly--The Years in France: 1948-1954 (coauth, catalog), Nat Gallery Art & Galerie Nal du Jeu de Paume, 92. *Pos:* Asst cur paintings, Wadsworth Atheneum, Hartford, Conn, 72-74; cur 19th & 20th Century Art, St Louis Art Mus, St Louis, Mo, 74-83; head & cur, Dept Twentieth-Century Art, Nat Gallery Art, Washington, DC, 83-92; deputy dir & chief cur, Corcoran Gallery Art, Washington, DC, 92-. *Res:* Post-war American & European painting & sculpture. *Publ:* Coauth, Henri Matisse Paper Cut-Outs (exhib catalog), St Louis Art Mus & Detroit Inst Arts, 77; auth, Roy Lichtenstein, 1970-1980, Hudson Hills Press Inc, 81. *Mailing Add:* c/o Corcoran Gallery Art 500 17th St NW Washington DC 20006

COWIN, JACK LEE
PRINTMAKER, PAINTER
b Indianapolis, Ind, July 29, 47. *Study:* Herron Sch Art, Ind Univ, BFA, 69; Univ Ill, MFA, 71. *Work:* Chicago Art Inst, Ill; Okaido Mus, Japan; Ind Mus Art, Indianapolis,; Cleveland Mus Art, Ohio; Brooklyn Mus Art, NY. *Exhib:* Canadian Prints, Can Exhib Ctr, Tokyo, 85; Am Prints in Paris, Gallerie Chislaine Huosenot, France, 92; The Angling Art of Jack Cowin, Atlanta, Ga, 95; Landfall Press - 25 yrs Printmaking, Milwaukee Mus Art, Wis, 96; Basel Print Show, Switz, 97 & 98. *Teaching:* Prof printmaking, Univ Regina, Sask, Can, 71-. *Awards:* 20 American Printmakers, Soc Am Graphic Artists, 79; Purchase Award, Ind 500 Arts Festival, 79. *Bibliog:* Andy Oko (auth), Country Pleasures, Fifth House Press, 84. *Media:* Drawing, Etching. *Dealer:* The New Van Streaten Gallery 316 W Superior St Chicago IL. *Mailing Add:* 2029 Elphinstone St Regina SK S4T 3N5 Canada

COWLES, CHARLES
ART DEALER, COLLECTOR
b Santa Monica, Calif, Feb 7, 41. *Study:* Stanford Univ, 63. *Pos:* Pres & publ, Artforum Mag, 65-79; cur mod art, Seattle Art Mus, 75-79; art dealer, Charles Cowles Gallery, 80-; bd trustee, New York Studio Sch, 85-; trustee, Wolfsonian, Fla Int Univ, Miami Beach, 95-; hon trustee, Laumeier Park, St Louis, 96-. *Bibliog:* Laura de Coppett & Alan Jones (coauths), The Art Dealers, Potter. *Mem:* Art Dealers Asn Am. *Specialty:* Modern and contemporary art. *Collection:* Contemporary art, Japanese folk art & photography. *Mailing Add:* Charles Cowles Gallery 537 W 24th St New York NY 10012

COWLEY, EDWARD P
PAINTER, EDUCATOR
b Buffalo, NY, May 29, 25. *Study:* Albright Art Sch; Buffalo State Col, BS, 48; Columbia Univ, MA, 49; Nat Col Art, Dublin, Ireland, Ford Found Fel, 55. *Work:* Albany Inst Hist & Art, NY; Schenectady Mus, NY; Smith Col, Northhampton, Mass; Colgate Univ, Hamilton, NY; Berkshire Mus, Pittsfield, Mass. *Comn:* The Minerva Window (stained glass), The Sunya Alumni Asn, 94. *Teaching:* Prof art & chmn dept, State Univ NY, Albany, 56-75, prof art, 76-88. *Awards:* State Univ NY Res Grant, 66 & 74. *Media:* Pastels, Stained Glass. *Collection:* Altamont NY Stained Glass Panel Collection of Marijo Doucherty. *Mailing Add:* PO Box 198 Altamont NY 12009

COX, ERNEST LEE
SCULPTOR, EDUCATOR
b Wilmington, NC, June 1, 37. *Study:* Col of William & Mary, BA(fine arts); Cranbrook Acad of Art, Bloomfield Hills, Mich, MFA(sculpture); Mich State Univ, Oakland. *Work:* St Petersburg Pub Libr, Fla; Eckerd Col, St Petersburg; Univ S Fla, Tampa; 1st Nat Bank of Atlanta, Ga; 1st Nat Bank of Tampa, Fla. *Comn:* Steel sculptures, 64, Fed Deposit Ins Corp, Washington, DC, 65 & Gulf Life Ins Co, Jacksonville, 67. *Exhib:* The 17th Va Artists Exhib, Va Mus Fine Arts, Richmond, 58; 24th Ann NC Artists Exhib, NC Mus Fine Arts, Raleigh, 61; 20th-22nd Southeastern Ann Exhibs, High Mus Art, Atlanta, Ga, 65-67; Fla 17, Pan Am Union, Washington, DC, 68; 15 Fla Artists Sculpture Exhib, Gallery Contemp Art, Winston-Salem, NC, 70; solo exhibs, Jacksonville Mus of Art, Fla, 73 Fla Art Fellows Exhib, Mus Fine Arts, St Per; 15 Fla Artists Sculpture Exhib, Gallery Contemp Art, Winston-Salem, NC, 70; one-man show, Jacksonville Mus Art, 73; Fla Art Fellows Art Exhib, Mus Fine Arts, St Pertersburg, Fla, 82 & Fla Art Fel Exhib, Norton Gallery Art, Palm Beach, 89. *Teaching:* From instr to prof sculpture, Univ S Fla, Tampa, 62-, chmn art dept, 71-73, prof emer, 94-. *Awards:* Second Prize, Fla Sculptors 7th Ann Exhib, 63; First Prize, Fla State Fair Fine Arts Exhib, 65; Purchase Prize, Southeastern Sculpture Exhib, Atlanta Chamber of Commerce, 69; Fla Art Fel, 82 & 89. *Media:* Welded, Forged Steel. *Mailing Add:* 7309 Bozman Neavitt Rd Bozman MD 21612

COX, MARION AVERAL
PAINTER, INSTRUCTOR
b Washingtonville, Ohio. *Study:* With H Gauguin, W Goodrich, H Radio, B I Payne, C Wallace, J M Jehu, N Bel Geddes, Max Reinhardt (Ger), and many others. *Exhib:* Sixty Text Books, Am Inst Graphic Arts, Grand Cent Palace, 44 & 54; 13th Ann Ohio Artists & Craftsmen, Massillon Mus, 48; 14th New Yrs Show, Butler Art Inst, 49; Am Painting Today, Metrop Mus Art. *Pos:* Art dir, Universal Studios, Universal City, Calif, 28-30; tech illusr, My Own Studio & Gallery, Salem, Ohio, 38-52; architect, Translux Construct, 50-; auth, Readex Book Exchange, Cave Creek, Ariz, 68-; dir, ART-o-Technic Inst, currently. *Teaching:* Teacher art theory & practice, Art-O-Technix Inst, Carefree, Ariz, 75-. *Mem:* Am Asn Advan Sci. *Media:* Mixed. *Publ:* Illusr, E T Smith (auth), Exploring Biology, 38

COX, PAT
ASSEMBLAGE ARTIST, SCULPTOR
b Pasadena, Calif. *Study:* Mills Col, Oakland, Calif BA, 43, MA, 44; studied with Hans Burkhardt, 66, Charles Garabedian, 68, Gordon Wagner, 80. *Work:* Fresno Art Mus, Calif; Walker Art Collection, Garnett, Kans; Univ Calif, Los Angeles, Med Art Asn; Aerie Sculpture Gardens, Palm Desert, Calif. *Exhib:* Rental Gallery Exhib, Los

Angeles Co Mus Art, Calif, 78; Int Contemp Art Fair, Los Angeles Conv Ctr, Calif, 86-88 & 92; Art Auction 88, Newport Harbor Art Mus, Calif, 88; Gatherings, S Ore State Col, Ashland, 96; Holter Mus Art, Helena, Mont, 97; Edge, Image, Information, The Collage Aesthetic at the End of the 20th Century, ARTernatives, San Luis Obispo, Calif, 98; Alchemy, Nabisco Gallery, E Hanover, NJ, 2000; Nat Smallworks, Bloomingdale Mus, ILL; Cult Legacies, Pasadena Mus of Hist, Calif, 2002; Fire in the Heart, Schneider Mus of Art, Ashland, Ore, 2003. *Collection Arranged:* Francis de Erdely & San Pedro Artists Part I & II, Beckstrand Gallery, Palos Verdes Art Ctr, 85, Barbara Spring: Wood Sculptor (auth, catalog) 87 & Visions/Inner Voices, 88. *Pos:* mem bd trustees, Los Angeles Art Asn, Calif, 72-77; juror, Nat Watercolor Soc, Los Angeles, Calif, 81-82; chmn exhib comt, Palos Verdes Art Ctr, Rancho Palos Verdes, Calif, 82-86. *Awards:* Purchase Award, Angels Gate Cult Ctr, 83; Pasadena Soc Artists First Award, Downey Mus Art, 90; First Award, Palos Verdes Art Ctr, 98. *Bibliog:* Ruth Askey (auth), Mixed messages, Artweek, 87; Gerald Brommer (auth), Collage, the Dynamic Medium, Watson Guptill, 94; Bridging time and space (essays on layered art), Markowitz Publ, 98. *Mem:* Pasadena Soc Artists (juror, 73, 81); Nat Watercolor Soc (1st vpres, 80, 4th vpres, 84); Soc Layerists Multi Media; Nat Mus Women Arts. *Media:* Assemblage; Mixed Media. *Mailing Add:* 3421 La Selva Pl Palos Verdes Estates CA 90274

COX, PETER
ARTIST
b New York, NY, 42. *Study:* Phoenix Sch of Design, Grad; Parsons Sch, Grad. *Work:* exhib in group shows, Amot Mus, 1993; Rep in permanent collections, Arnot Mus, Redding Mus. *Exhib:* Exhib incl, Carolyn Hill Gallery, 1989-91, Joseph Keiffer Inc, 1992, Louis Newman Galleries, 1993, CFM Galleries, 1994, Gallery Dai, 1996, M B Modem, 1998; exhib in group shows, Artists of Am, 1981-92, John Pence Gallery, 1991-92, In Collaboration Gallery, 1992, Allan Stone Gallery, 1995-96, Nat Arts Club, 1997, M B Modem, 1997, Survey of the Am Figure in Painting, 1820-Present Babcock Galleries, 2000, Represented in permanent collections, Ark Art Ctr, Nat Acad of Design. *Pos:* Vpres, Nat Arts Club, 86-97; mem, Nat Acad of Design Mus Sch, 2002—; rep, Caravaggio Studios Inc. *Teaching:* instr, Arts Students League, 84-; NY Acad of Art, 94—2000. *Awards:* Cert of Merit, Nat Acad of Design, 88; Gold Medal, Nat Arts Club, 88 & 97; Gary Melchers Award, Artist Fel, 998. *Mem:* Nat Acad. *Mailing Add:* c/o Caravaggio Studios Inc 315 W 39th Suite #506 New York NY 10018

COX, RICHARD WILLIAM
HISTORIAN, WRITER
b Los Angeles, Calif, July 13, 42. *Study:* Univ Calif, Los Angeles, BA(hist), 64, MA(hist), 66; Univ Wis, Madison, MA(art hist), 70, PhD(art hist), 73. *Teaching:* Instr Am art, Univ Wis, River Falls, 71-74; from asst prof to prof Am art & hist prints, La State Univ, 74-. *Awards:* Solon Buck Award for Best Article, Minn Hist, 75; Nat Endowment Humanities Fel, 75. *Bibliog:* Matthew Baigell (auth), The American Scene: American Painting of the 1930s, Praeger, 74; James Dennis (auth), Grant Wood, A Study in Art & Culture, Viking, 75. *Mem:* Col Art Asn; Art Educ Asn; La Hist Soc. *Res:* American painting and graphic arts in 1900-1945 period; contemporary art. *Publ:* Art Young: Cartoonist from the middle border, Wis Mag Hist, 77; Caroline Durieux: The lithographs of the 1930's and 1940's La State Univ Press, 77; Adolf Dehn--jazz age satirist, Arch Am Art J, 78; Southern works on paper, 1900-1950, Southern Arts Fedn, 80; coauth (with Clinton Adams), Adolf Dehn, Catalogue Raisonne of the Lithographs, Minn Hist Soc Press, 87; (with Carlton Overland), Warrington Colescott, Forty Years of Printmaking, A Retrospective, Elvehjem Mus Art, Univ Wis, 89. *Mailing Add:* La State Univ Sch Art 123 Art Bldg Baton Rouge LA 70803

COYLE, TERENCE
PAINTER
b Williamstown, Mass, Sept 7, 25. *Study:* Columbia Univ, 46-48; Hunter Col, 50; Art Students League, 64-70. *Work:* Mus City of NY; Fordham Univ, Lincoln Ctr, NY; Billy Rose Collection, NY Libr Performing Arts; NY State Mus, Albany; Chubb & Son Inc, NY; Butler Mus Am Art. *Exhib:* Am Artists Prof League, Lever Brothers Bldg, NY, 76; Nat Arts Club, Nat Arts Gallery, NY, 81; Last Days of the Helen Hayes Theatre, Sharon Creative Arts Found, Conn, 83; Places Please, Astor Gallery, Lincoln Ctr, NY, 84; Curtain Call at the Helen Hayes, Fordham Univ, Lincoln Ctr, NY, 86; Lincoln Ctr Gallery; Berkshire Mus, Pittsfield, Mass, 05; Russian Embassy to UN, 05; Butler Mus Am Art, 06. *Collection Arranged:* Retrospective at 80, Selected Works 1955-2005, Nat Arts Club, 2005. *Teaching:* Instr oil painting, Art Students League, 74-; lectr artistic anatomy, Nat Acad Design, Sch Fine Arts, New York, 79-; instr figure portrait painting, Scottsdale Artists Sch, Ariz, ann workshop, 85; instr drawing workshop, Nat Arts Club. *Awards:* Award for graphic design, Communications Art Exhib, Am Inst Graphic Design, 79; Silver Medal, Nat Art League, 83. *Bibliog:* Artist chronicle's theatre demise, Lakeville J, Conn, 9/1/83; Richard Nielson (auth), The skin's game art/rev, Ariz Republic, 2/14/87; article, Hazelton Standard, 3/20/89. *Mem:* Life mem, Art Students League; Am Artists Prof League; Artist's Equity; Nat Art League; Nat Arts Club, NYC. *Media:* Oil, Watercolor. *Publ:* Coauth, Anatomy Lessons From the Great Masters, Watson-Guptill, 77; Albinus on Anatomy, Watson-Guptill/Dover, 79 & 88; auth, Master Class in Figure Drawing, Watson-Guptill, 85; (video) The Painters Mind, 96. *Dealer:* Jo-an Fine Art Gallery 247 E 77th St New York NY 10021. *Mailing Add:* T Coyle c/o Jo An PO Box 6020 New York NY 10150

COYNE, JOHN MICHAEL
PAINTER, EDUCATOR
b St Stephen, NB, 50. *Study:* Mt Allison Univ, BFA, 75; Univ Regina, MFA, 77. *Work:* Art Gallery NS, Halifax; Husky Oil, Calgary; Placer Dome, Inc, Toronto; Midland Doherty, Xerox Canada, Abitibi Price, Toronto; Air Canada, Toshiba Canada; Bank of NS, Toronto; Govt, Nfld & Labrador; Mt Allison Univ; Sir Wilfred Grenfell Col; and others. *Exhib:* Art Gallery NS, Halifax, 80; Acadia Univ Art Gallery, Wolfville, NS, 83; Edmonton Art Gallery, Alberta, 84; St Mary's Univ, Halifax, 84; Mira Godard Gallery, Toronto, 86; Grenfell Col, Corner Brook, Nfld, 87 & 89; Gallery 78, Fredericton, NB, 88; Mem Univ Art Gallery, 90; Emma Butler Gallery, St John's, Nfld, 90; Arts & Cult Ctr, Corner Brook, Nfld, 97; Franklyn Gallery, Corner Brook, Nfld, 2003. *Teaching:* Asst prof, Acadia Univ, Wolfville, NS, 77-84, assoc prof & head art dept 83-86; founding head dept visual arts Mem Univ, Grenfell Col, Corner Brook, Nfld, 86-92, prof, 91-, head div arts, 99-. *Awards:* Grant, Greenshield's Found, Montreal, 76. *Bibliog:* C MacLaughlin (auth), Atlantic lines, Heritage Can Mag, 2/79; Dr Helen J Dow (auth), Michael Coyne: A Retrospective, Acadia Univ Art Gallery, 83; Arts Atlantic Winter 85, 87 & 91; Colleen O'Neill (auth), Michael Coyne, Sir Wilfred Grenfell Col Art Gallery, 90. *Mem:* Col Art Asn. *Media:* Acrylic, Digital Imaging. *Mailing Add:* Dept Visual Art Mem Univ Sir Wilfred Grenfell Col Corner Brook NL A2H 6P9 Canada

COYNE, PETAH E
SCULPTOR, PHOTOGRAPHER
b Oklahoma City, Okla, Sept 30, 53. *Study:* Art Academy Cincinnati, Grad, 77; Kent State Univ. *Hon Degrees:* Cincinnati Art Acad DArt (hon), 2001. *Work:* The Brooklyn Mus, Whitney Mus Am Art, Mus Mod Art, NY; San Diego Mus Contemp Art, La Jolla, Calif; The Speed Mus, Louisville, KY; Contemp Mus, Honolulu, Hawaii; Mus. Modern Art, NY; Phoenix Art Mus; Detroit Inst. of Art; and others. *Exhib:* Grand Lobby Installation, Brooklyn Mus, NY, 89; Art Contemporain Vision 90, Centre Int d'Art Contemporaine, Montreal, CN, 90; Coyne-Hurtman Collaboration, Neuberger Mus, Purchase, NY, 92; Petah Coyne Sculpture, Contemp Mus, Honolulu, Hawaii, Cleveland Ctr Contemp Art, Ohio, Ctr Contemp Art Santa Fe, NMex, 92-93; Millennium Messages, Smithsonian Traveling Exhib, organized by Heckscher Mus Art, Huntington, Long Island, NY, 99, Contemp Mus, Baltimore, 2000, Mus of Modern Art (Glen Dimplex Artist's award), Dublin, 2000; solo exhibs, Corcoran Gallery Art, Wash, High Mus Art, Atlanta, Ga, Laurence Miller Gallery, NY, 96-97 & Fairy Tales, Galerie Lelong, NY, 98, 2001, Butler Gallery, Kilkenny Castle, Ireland, 99, Byron Cohen Gallery, Kansas City, Mo, 99, 2001, Julie Saul Gallery, NY, 2001, First Ctr for Contemp Art, Tenn, 2001; group exhibs, Detroit Inst of Arts, Mich, 2001, Galerie Lelong, NY, 2002, Memphis Col of Art, Tenn, 2003. *Teaching:* Grad fac painting/sculpture, Sch Visual Arts, 90-94. *Awards:* Guggenheim Mem Foun, Guggenheim Found, 89; Nat Endowment Arts Fel Sculpture, 90; Sirus Proj, art-in-residence, Cobh, Co Cork, Ireland, 2000; Hon Doctorate, Cincinnati Art Acad, Ohio, 2001. *Bibliog:* Lasse Antonsen (auth), Installation by Petah Coyne, Massachusetts Contemp, 91; David Rubin (auth), Petah Coyne, Cleveland Ctr Contemp Art, 92; Tony Carlson (auth), Beauty and the Beast (film), 92. *Mem:* Skowhegan Sch Painting & Sculpture, NY (bd gov, 88-94); Orgn Independent Artist (bd dir, 88-92); Sculpture Ctr, NY (bd dir, 90-93). *Dealer:* Galerie Le Long, 526 W 26th St, New York NY, 10001. *Mailing Add:* 477 Broome St New York NY 10013

COZAD, RACHAEL BLACKBURN
MUSEUM DIRECTOR
b Berkeley, Calif, 1964. *Study:* Texas Christian Univ, BA; Calif State Univ, Los Angeles, MA. *Collection Arranged:* St. Benedict's Abbey, Atchison, Kans, 2005-. *Pos:* exhibs mgr & registrar, Calif Center for the Arts, San Diego, 93-94; Iris and B Gerald Cantor Found, Los Angeles, Calif, cur exhibs 94-97, exec dir & chief cur, 98-2001; dir, Kemper Mus Contemp Art, Kansas City, MO, 2001—; juror, Va Beach 50th Ann Boardwalk Art Show & Festival, Va, 2005. *Mem:* ArtTable (prog comt, 96-98, advocacy comt, 98-2000, ch southern calif chap, 2000); Am Asn Mus; Mus Assessment Prog; Peer Rev Panel, US Gen Serv Admin, Art in Architecture Prog, 2002-. *Publ:* El Dia de los Muertos: The Life of the Dead in Mexican Folk Art, 87; Rodin: A Magnificent Obsession, 2001; Frederick J. Brown: Jazz, Blues & Other Icons, 2002; Wayne Thiebaud: Fifty Years of Painting, 2003; The Kemper Mus of Contemp Art: The First Ten Years, 2004. *Mailing Add:* Kemper Mus Contemp Art 4420 Warwick Blvd Kansas City MO 64111-1821

CRABLE, JAMES HARBOUR
MULTI-MEDIA ARTIST, INSTRUCTOR
b Bronx, NY, Aug 30, 39. *Study:* State Univ NY, Buffalo, BS, 62; Rochester Inst Technol, NY, MFA, 66; Chelsea Sch Art, London, Eng, HDA, 70. *Work:* Adolph Coors Co; Bell South Corp; AT&T Collection, Washington; Equitable Life Assurance Soc Am; State Univ NY Art Collection, Albany; IBM Collection; Chrysler Mus, Norfolk, Va; Everson Mus, Syracuse, NY; Duke Univ, Durham, NC; Art Mus Western Va, Roanoke. *Exhib:* one-man shows, Va Mus Fine Arts, Richmond, 76, Southeastern Ctr Contemp Art, Winston-Salem, 78, Gallery K, Washington, 79 & 82, Monterey Penninsula Mus Art, Monterey, Calif, 89, Interform Gallery, Osaka, Japan, 89, Fresno Metrop Mus Art, Calif, 90, Photo Forum, Pittsburgh, Pa, 91 & Camera Obscura, Denver, Colo, 93; Continuum VII, Dulin Gallery Art, Knoxville, 82; Over the Blue Ridge, Roanoke Fine Art Invitational, Va, 87; Collage: Four Directions, San Jose Mus Art, Calif, 88; group shows, Roanoke Mus Art, Va, 91, NY Art Expo, Jacob Javits Ctr, New York City, 92, Chrysler Mus, Norfolk, Va, 93, Art Dealers Exhib, NY, 94 & Sawtooth Gallery, Winston-Salem, NC, 94; JJ Brookings Gallery, San Francisco, 95; Art Mus Western Va, Roanoke, 96; Austin Mus, Tex, 97; Md Fedn Art, Annapolis, 97; Peninsula Fine Arts Ctr, Newport News, Va, 98; Mobile Mus Art, Ala, 99; Hite Art Inst, Univ Louisville, 2000; Target Gallery, Torpedo Factory Art Ctr, Alexandria, Va, 2002; Touchstone Gallery, Washington, DC, 2003; Mus West, Palo Alto, Calif, 2004; AIPAD, The Photog Show, NY, 2005. *Teaching:* Assoc prof art survey, drawing & art educ, State Univ Col Brockport, NY, 66-69; lectr found studies, Croydon Col Art, Surrey, Eng, 70-71; prof drawing & art survey, James Madison Univ, Harrisonburg, Va, 73-. *Awards:* Fel, Nat Endowment Arts Southeastern Fel, 79; Va prize invisual arts, presented by Gov Gerald Baliles, 87; Guild Award, Peninsula Fine Arts Ctr Exhib, Newport News, Va, 92; Shenandoah Valley Artist of Yr, Shenandoah Valley Ann Visual Arts Awards, 93; and many others. *Mem:* Col Art Asn Am; Va Art Educ Asn. *Media:* Photo-collage. *Mailing Add:* 261 Green St Harrisonburg VA 22802-2046

CRAFT, DAVID RALPH
PAINTER, PHOTOGRAPHER
b Elberton, Ga, July 31, 45. *Study:* ETenn State Univ, BS, 67. *Work:* Appalachian State Univ; Blount Inc, Montgomery, Ala; Tenn Arts Comn, Nashville; Hunter Mus Art; Tenn Valley Authority. *Exhib:* Landscape & Genre Painting Tennessee, 1810-1985, traveling exhib; Art USA: The South, New Orleans Mus, 75-77; 11th Ann Nat Drawing & Small Sculpture Competition, Del Mar Col Art Ctr, 77; Am Drawings I, II & IV, Portsmouth Arts Ctr, 78 & 82; More Than Land and Sky: Art from Appalachia, Nat Mus Am Art, Washington & touring, 82-84; Carroll Reece Mus, Johnson City, Tenn, 93. *Teaching:* Instr, Hunter Mus Art, 75-84; teacher photog Girls Prep Sch, 84-. *Awards:* Purchase Awards, Dulin Gallery Nat, 76, Mt Holyoke Nat, 76 & Lauren Rogers Regional, 79. *Media:* Acrylic, Oil. *Dealer:* Margaret Townsend Gallery 406 High St Chattanooga TN 37403. *Mailing Add:* 2926 Nurick Dr Chattanooga TN 37415

CRAFT, DOUGLAS D
PAINTER, EDUCATOR
b Greene, NY. *Study:* Univ Iowa; Univ Chicago; Art Inst Chicago, BFA; Syracuse Univ; Univ NMex, MA in Painting. *Work:* Mus Mod Art & Whitney Mus Am Art, NY; Art Inst Chicago; Univ NMex, Albuquerque; Newark Mus, NJ; Smithsonion Inst, Washington, DC; Warner Lambert World Hq, Morris Plains, NJ; Butler Inst Am Art, Youngstown, Ohio; many others. *Comn:* Paintings, comn by Mr & Mrs Daniel Weinstein for Edward Weinstein Ctr Performing Arts, Nat Col Educ, Evanston, Ill, 72. *Exhib:* One-man shows, Royal Col Art, London, 64, Traverse Festival Gallery, Edinburgh, 65, Mus Art, Carnegie Inst, Pittsburgh, Pa, 68 & Jersey City Mus, 78, 55 Mercer Gallery, NY, 80, Col Ctr Art Gallery, New Rochelle, NY, 90, Bratton Gallery, Inc, NY, 90, Rosefsky Studio Art Gallery, State Univ NY, Binghamton, 93, Retrospective (with exhib & catalog), Butler Inst Am Art, Youngstown, Ohio, 93, Del Art Ctr Gallery, Narrowsburg, NY, 96, Del Art Ctr Gallery, Narrowburg, NY, 2002; De Ctr Art Gallery, Narrowburg, NY, 2004; Butler Inst of Am Art, Youngstown, NY, 2005 and others; Rose Fried Gallery, NY, 68; Three Person Show, Studio K, Long Island City, NY, 85; Montclair Art Mus, Montclair, NJ, 84; Contemp Syntax, Rutgers Univ, NJ, 87; Collage at NAME, NAME Gallery, Chicago, 88; Retrospective (exhib & catalog), Works on Paper (1974-1995), Makee Gallery, Mo, Gray Gallery, Ill & Keokuk Gallery, Ia, 97; Station Gallery, Katonah, NY, 93; Del Arts Ctr Gallery, Narrowsburg, NY, 95; Schick Art Gallery, Skidmore Col, Saratoga, NY, 95; Paul McCarron Gallery, NY, 96. *Collection Arranged:* Art Institute Chicago; Mus Modern Art, NYC; Whitney Mus Am Art, NYC; Newark Mus, NJ; Jersey City Mus, NJ; Butler Institute Am Art, Youngstown, Ohio; Smithsonian Institution, Washington, DC; Memorial Art Gallery, Univ Rochester, NY; Univ Ky, Lexington. *Pos:* Vis artist in residence, Univ Ky, 64; Am artist in residence, Royal Col Art, London, Eng, 64-65; vis artist-critic, Sunderland Col Art, Eng, 65 & Gloucestershire Col Art, Cheltenham, Eng, 65; cur, Fourteen Women Artists, Castle Gallery, New Rochelle, 82 & cur of Paper, Pigment & Glass, Castle Gallery, New Rochelle, 87. *Teaching:* Assoc prof painting, Art Inst Chicago, 55-66 & Carnegie Inst Technol, 66-69; vis artist, Cooper Union, 69-71 & Sch Visual Arts, New York, summer 88; prof painting, Col New Rochelle, 71-91; vis lectr, artist, Skidmore Col, Saratoga Springs, NY, 93. *Awards:* Harry Allison Logan Mem Award, Chautauqua Inst, NY, 63; Logan Bronze Medal & Prize, Art Inst Chicago, 66; Jury Award/Distinction in Painting, Mus Art, Carnegie Inst Int, 68. *Bibliog:* Max Wykes-Joyce (auth), Douglas Craft, Arts Rev, London, 64; Cordelia Oliver (auth), Exhibitions at Edinburgh, Guardian, 65; D L Shirey (auth), Douglas Craft Show in Jersey City, NY Times, 78; Vivien Raynor (auth), A magnetic group of 8 in Jersey City, NY Times, 80; Vivien Raynor (auth), Show of collages opens new exhibit hall in New Rochelle, New York Times, 88. *Media:* Acrylic, Oil. *Dealer:* Paul McCarron Fine Arts & Prints New York NY; River Gallery Narrowsburg NY; Paul Zoubok, Collages, NY, NY. *Mailing Add:* PO Box 245 Jeffersonville NY 12748

CRAFT, LIZ
ARTIST
b LA, 70. *Study:* Otis Parsons, BA, 1994; UCLA, MFA, 1997. *Work:* It's All An Illusion, Migros Mus fur Gegenwartskunst, Zurich, 2004, Whitney Biennial, Whitney Mus Am Art, 2004, Seeing Other People, 2004. *Exhib:* One-woman shows incl, Richard Telles Fine Art, Los Angeles, 1998, Centrum fur Gegenwartskunst Oberosterreich, Linz, Austria, 2001, Galerie Nathalie Obadia, Paris, 2001, Pub Art Fund, NY, 2002, A Real Mother For Ya, Sadie Coles HQ, London, 2002, Marianne Boesky Gallery, 2003; exhib in group shows at Happy Trails, Col Creative Studies, Univ Santa Barbara, 1999, Hot Spots, Weatherspoon Gallery, Univ NC, 1999, Good Luck for You, Transmission Gallery, Edinburgh, 2000, Calif Dreamin', Gallery Art, Carlsen Ctr, Johnson Co Community Col, Kansas City, 2000, Young & Dumb, ACME, Los Angeles, 2001, Play it as it Lays, The London Inst Gallery, 2002, Wheeling - Krad Kult Tour! Motorcycles in Art, Frankfurt Am Main, Ger, 2002, 3-D, Friedrich Petzel Gallery, 2003, The Thought That Counts, Sister, Los Angeles, 2003. *Mailing Add:* c/o Marianne Boeksy Gallery 535 W 22nd St New York NY 10011

CRAIG, JAMES HICKLIN
CONSULTANT
b Chester, SC, Jul 23, 37. *Study:* Univ SC, 56; Cincinnati Col Conservatory Music, 59; Juilliard Sch Music, 60; Paris, 60. *Pos:* Cur, decorative arts NC Dept Archives & Hist, Raleigh, 62-64; principal, James Craig Fine & Decorative Arts, 65-69; pres, Craig & Tarlton, Inc, Raleigh, 69-85; fine arts consult, Independence, Va, 85-; consult, to NC Gov's Mansion bd, acquisitions comt, currently. *Mem:* Sparta Mus Project, Raleigh Chamber Music Soc, New York City Chamber Opera Theater (bd dir, currently); Mint Mus Art, Charlotte, (trustee 2000-). *Interests:* Gardening. *Collection:* American Art & Antiques, violins & related meaterial. *Publ:* Auth, The Arts & Crafts in NC 1699-1840, 65 (listed by Montgomery as part of 100 best in field). *Mailing Add:* James Craig Fine Arts PO Box 397 Independence VA 24348-0397

CRAIG, SUSAN V
LIBRARIAN
b Newton, Kans, Nov 11, 48. *Study:* Univ Kans, BA, 70; Emporia State Univ, MLS, 71. *Pos:* Indexer, Art Index, H W Wilson Co, New York, 71-74; art hist & classics librn, Univ Calif, Berkeley, 75-81; art librn, Univ Kans, 81-. *Teaching:* Instr art bibliog, Univ Calif, Berkeley, 81. *Mem:* Art Libr Soc NAm (secy 75-77, chmn, 86). *Publ:* auth, Survey of Current Practices in Art & Architecture Libraries, Jour Libr Admin, Vol 39, No 1, 2003, 91-107; auth, Biographical Dictionary of Kansas Artists Active before 1945, web publ. *Mailing Add:* 1717 Indiana St Lawrence KS 66044-4049

CRAMER, DOUGLAS S
COLLECTOR, PATRON
b Louisville, Ky. *Study:* Northwestern Univ, 49-50; Sorbonne, Paris, 51; Univ Cincinnati, BA, 53; Columbia Univ, MFA, 54; Beta Theta Pi. *Pos:* Production asst, Radio City Music Hall, New York City, 50-51; with, script dept Metro-Goldwyn-Mayer, 52; managing dir, Cincinnati Playhouse, 53-54; instr, Carnegie Inst Tech, 55-56; TV supv, Procter & Gamble, 56-59; broadcast supv, Ogilvy, Benson & Mather, 59-62; vpres, prog develop, ABC, 62-66, 20th Century-Fox-TV, LA, 66-68; exec vpres, in charge prod Paramount TV, 68-71; ind prod, pres, Douglas S Cramer Co, 71-; exec vpres, Aaron Spelling Prod, 76-87, vchmn, 88-90, bd trustess, 83-96; pres, Mus Contemp Art, Los Angeles, 90-93, 1st vchmn, 93-96; trustee, Int Coun Mus Modern Art, New York City, 93-; pres, bd trustees, Douglas S Cramer Found, 93--; trustee, MOMA NY, 93-. *Awards:* Named one of Top 200 Collectors, ARTnews Mag, 2004. *Bibliog:* Grace Glueck (auth), Artful LA, NY Times Mag, 11/23/86; Peter Clothier (auth), Douglas Cramer: Passionate Perfectionist, Art News, 2/87; Bob Colacello (auth), At Home on the Ranch, Vanity Fair, 4/88. *Mem:* Mus Contemp Art, Los Angeles; Ctr Theater Group (bd dir, 85-90); Int Coun Mus Mod Art (chmn painting & sculpture comt, 96); Am Ballet Theater (Nat bd dir, 88-93); Univ Club New York City. *Collection:* Approximately 600 works of contemporary American art from 1960 to the present; Contemporary art, especially 60's & 80's. *Publ:* Executive prodr.: Star Trek, 1968-69, Bridget Loves Bernie, CBS-TV, 1972-73, QB VII, 1973-74, Dawn: Portrait of a Teenage Runaway, NBC-TV, 1976, Danielle Steel's Fine Things, 1990, Kalediscope, 1990, Changes, 1991, Daddy, 1991, Palomino, 1990-91, Secrets, 1991, Heart Beat, 1992, Star, 1993, Message to Nam, 1993, Vanished, 1995, Family Album, 1994, Perfect Stranger, 1994, No Greater Love, 1995, Mixed Blessings, 1995, Zoya, 1995, Family of Cops I & II, CBS-TV, 1995-96, The Ring, 1996, Remembrance, 1996, Full Circle, NBC-TV, 1996, Family of Cops III, 1999; co-exec. prodr.: Love Boat, ABC, 1977-86, Vegas, ABC, 1978-81, Wonder Woman, ABC, 1975-77, CBS, 1977-78, Dynasty, 1981-89, Hotel, 1983-87, Trade Winds, 1993; prodr.: (feature film) Sleeping Together, 1995; author: (plays) Call of Duty, 1953, Love Is A Smoke, 1957, Whose Baby Are You, 1963, Last Great Dish, 1994, Lust For Murder, 1995. *Mailing Add:* PO Box 713 Lakeville CT 06039-0713

CRAMER, RICHARD CHARLES
PAINTER, EDUCATOR
b Appleton, Wis, Aug 14, 32. *Study:* Layton Sch Art, BFA; Univ Wis-Milwaukee, BS, Univ Wis-Madison, MS, 61, MFA, 62. *Work:* Pa Acad Fine Arts; Everhart Mus, Scranton, Pa; Everson Mus, Syracuse, NY; Univ Wis; Philadelphia Mus; plus others. *Comn:* Mosaic mural, Temple Univ, Student/Fac Ctr, 81. *Exhib:* Drawings Biennial, Norfolk Mus Art, 65; Drawings, Smithsonian Inst traveling exhib, 65; one-man shows, Gloria Cortella Gallery, NY, 77-78, Barbara Fiedler Gallery, Washington, DC, 77 & Pa Acad Fine Arts, Philadelphia, 78; Chromatic Structure, Philadelphia Col Art, 80; Geometric-Abstractions, Inst Contemp Art, Boston, 81; Am Abstraction, Mieisel Gallery, NY, 85. *Teaching:* Prof painting & drawing, Tyler Sch Art, Temple Univ, 66-. *Awards:* Prizes, Milwaukee Art Inst, 54, Syracuse Allied Artists, 64 & Munson-Williams-Proctor Inst, Utica, NY, 65; and others. *Media:* Acrylic, Oil. *Publ:* Reconstructivist painting, Artspace, 3-4/90; Drawing in the 80's, White Walls, spring 86

CRANDALL, JERRY C
PAINTER, HISTORIAN
b La Junta, Colo, Apr 1, 35. *Study:* Woodbury Col, Los Angeles, Calif, 60. *Work:* Favell Mus, Klamath Falls, Ore; Koshare Indian Mus, La Junta, Colo; Bianchi Mus, Temecula, Calif. *Comn:* Robert Conrad as Pasquinelle in Centennial, comn by Robert Conrad, Malibu, Calif, 78; Wild Bill Hickok, Petersen Publ Co, Beverly Hills, Calif, 75; Custer's Last Stand, comn by Dr Larry Frost, Monroe, Mich; Luftwaffe aircraft for pvt Ariz collector; Aces of the Word Aircraft for pvt Tex collector. *Exhib:* Rotary Club Amarillo, 84-86; Tulsa Gilcrease Mus Art, 84-; Western Art in the Grand Traditon, 86-; Champlin Mus Art Show, 90 & 91; Air Aces Symp, 92 & 94; and others. *Pos:* Historical tech adv, Universal Studios film Centennial, 78, Columbia Pictures film The Mountain Men, 79 & Arts & Entertainment hist series The Real West; speaker, Professional Motivation in the Arts, Univ Calif, Riverside, 80-81, Forum Am Soc Aviation Artists, 90. *Awards:* Gold & Silver Medals, Western Artists Am Ann Exhib & Sale, 81. *Bibliog:* Phylllis Barton (auth), Creative credibility, Southwest Art, 10/80; Historical authenticity in art, Man at Arms, 11/83; Air Classics, 3/92, 12/92, 11/93 & 11/94. *Mem:* Little Big Horn Asn; Am Fighter Aces; Tailhook; Am Soc Aviation Artistsn; Los Angeles Soc Illusr. *Media:* Oil, Acrylic. *Publ:* Illusr, Marsielles, Star of Africa, 69 & Battle of Britain, 70, JWC Publ; Guns of the Gunfighters (cover), Petersen Publ Co, 75; General Custer and the Battle of the Little Big Horn, Garry Owen Press, 76; Aviation a History through Art, p-51, (cover); auth & illus, J626 pictorial (cover), Marseille (cover), Me109F,6,K (cover), J67 (cover), Eagles of the Luftwaffe, Fighter Aces of the Luftwaffe (cover); and others. *Dealer:* Eagle Editions Ltd PO Box 580 Hamilton MT 59840. *Mailing Add:* 752 Bobcat Ln Hamilton MT 59840-9355

CRANDALL, JUDITH ANN
GALLERY DIRECTOR, WRITER
b Milwaukee, Wis, Aug 20, 48. *Study:* El Camino Jr Col, Univ Ariz. *Comn:* Cowgirls: Early Images & Collectibles, Schiffer Publ. *Collection Arranged:* Eleventh Ann Membership Show for Women Artists of the American West, 83; Phoenix Forum Am Soc Aviation Artists, 88; coordr, Aviation Art Exhib, Champlin Mus, Mesa, Ariz, 90 & 91; Air Aces Symp, Mesa, Ariz & Atlanta, Ga, 92 & 93, Albuquerque, 95. *Pos:* Staff writer, Southwest Art Mag, Houston, 74-; dir, Saddleback Western Art Gallery, Calif, 78-80; owner, Eagle Ed, Hamilton, Mont, currently; ed, Aerobrush, Am Soc Aviation Artists, 99-90; guest ed, Great Am Aviation Artists, Challenge Publ, Calif. *Publ:* Auth, The Custer centennial, 76, Retrospective view of the year, 80 & Women artists of the American West, 82 & over 40 artists biography profiles, Southwest Art Mag; Little Chief, Air Classics Mag, 88; The artist's wife, AeroArt Mag, 88; auth, Cowgirls Early Images and Collectibles; contribr, various aviation art publ. *Mailing Add:* 752 Bobcat Ln Hamilton MT 59840-9355

CRANE, ARNOLD H
PHOTOGRAPHER
b Chicago, Ill, July 17, 32. *Study:* Col Law, DePaul Univ, Ill, JD, 55. *Work:* Metrop Mus Art & Mus Mod Art, NY; Art Inst Chicago, Ill; Kunsthaus, Zurich, Switz; Biblioteck Nat, Cabinet des Estampes, Paris, France. *Exhib:* Portraits of Photographers, Corcoran Gallery, Washington, DC, 74, Wellesley Col, Mass, 75, Kansas City Mus Art, 77, Univ Miami, Lowe Art Mus, Coral Gables, Fla, 79 & Univ Ill, Krannert Art Mus, 85; Selections Ruttenberg Collection, Art Inst Chicago, 92; Landscape of the Body, Mus Contemp Art, Chicago, 93. *Teaching:* adj prof, Univ Miami, 84. *Awards:* Photobuch Prize, Eastman Kodak Ger, 96; Internat New Photo Award, White House News Photos, 01. *Mem:* Am Soc Media Photogr; White House News Photog Asn. *Dealer:* Galerie AmDom Burkhart Arnold Cologne Germany; Arlene Lewallen Gallery Sante Fe NM. *Mailing Add:* 680 N Lake Shore Dr Apt 1202 Chicago IL 60611

CRANE, BARBARA BACHMANN
PHOTOGRAPHER, EDUCATOR
b Chicago, Ill, Mar 19, 28. *Study:* Mills Col, with Alfred Neumeyer, 45-48; NY Univ, BA(art hist), 50; Inst of Design, Ill Inst Technol, with Aaron Siskind, MS(photog), 66. *Work:* Libr Cong, Washington; High Mus Art, Atlanta; Art Inst Chicago; Mus Mod Art, NY; Bibliot Nat, Paris; Nat Mus Am Art, Smithsonian, Washington; Mus Contemp Photography Columbia Col, Chicago; Ctr Creative Photography, Tucson. *Comn:* 26 photomurals, Baxter Travenol Labs, Deerfield, Ill, 75; Chicago Epic (photomural), Chicago Bank Commerce, Standard Oil Bldg, Chicago. *Exhib:* One-woman shows, Friends of Photog, Carmel, Calif, 69 & 75, Tweed Mus Art, Univ Minn, Duluth, 86, Spertus Mus Judaica, 92-93, Prague House Photog, Czech Repub, 93, Galerie Suzel Berna, Paris, 94, Gallery 954, Chicago, 94 & Mills Col Art Gallery, Oakland, Calif, 97; San Francisco Mus Mod Art (with catalog), 85; Montreal Mus Fine Arts, Que (with catalog) & traveling, 94; When Aaron Met Harry, Mus Contemp Photog, Chicago, Ill, 96; Art in Chicago: 1945-1995, Mus Contemp Art, Chicago, 96-97; Midwest Photographers Project: Illinois Photography in the 1990's, Mus Contemp Photog, 96-97; Body in the Lens, Montreal Mus Fine Arts, Que, 97. *Collection Arranged:* Art Inst of Chicago, Bibliotheque Nationale, Paris, Center for Creative Photography, Univ Ariz, Internat Mus Photography, George Eastman House, Rochester, New York, John D & Catherine T MacArthur Foundation, The Nat Mus Mod Art, Kyoto, Japan, Library of Congress, Washington, DC. *Pos:* Mem, educ adv bd, Polaroid Corp, 85; Visual arts panel, MacDowell Colony, 89-90. *Teaching:* Prof photog, Sch Art Inst Chicago, 67-93, emer prof, 93-; vis prof photog, Philadelphia Col of Art, 77, Sch Mus Fine Arts, Boston, 79 & Cornell Univ, Ithaca, NY, 83, Bezalel Acad Art & Design, Jerusalem, Israel, 87, Bezalel. *Awards:* Nat Endowment Arts Grant, 74 & 88; Guggenheim Found Fel in Photog, 79; Polaroid Corp Assistance Grant, 79-94; Ill Arts Coun Grant, 85 & 2001; Young Women's Christian Asn Outstanding Achievement Award, Art, 87; Artist of the Year, Union League Club of Chicago, 2006. *Bibliog:* Mary Sherman (auth), rev, Chicago Sun Times, 3/25/88; Alice Thorson (auth), rev, Wash Times, 2/9/89; JoAnn Lewis (auth), rev, Wash Post, 2/11/89; Bernard Welt (auth), rev, New Art Examiner, 4/89. *Mem:* Soc Photog Educ (mem bd, 72-76); Friends of Photog (trustee, 75-81). *Media:* Various Photographic Processes. *Publ:* Auth, Flora Photographica, Thames & Hudson, 92; contribr, A History of Women Photographers, Abbeville Press, New York, 94; Bystander: A History of Street Photography, Bulfinch Press, 94; The Body: Photographs of the Human Form, Chronicle Bks, 94; Exhibiting Photography: Twenty Years at the Center for Creative Photography, Univ Ariz, 96; Barbara Crane: 1948-1980; Barbara Crane: Urban Anomalies; Barbara Crane: Chicago Loop; Barbara Crane: The Evolution of a Vision. *Dealer:* Stephen Daiter Gallery Chicago; Flatfile Gallery Chicago IL. *Mailing Add:* 1017 W Jackson Blvd #1A Chicago IL 60607

CRANE, BONNIE LOYD
ART DEALER, GALLERY DIRECTOR
b Minneapolis, Minn, Aug 24, 30. *Study:* Sweet Briar Col, Va, BA (cum laude), 50; Bryn Mawr Col, Pa, MA, 72; studied with Hobson Pittman. *Collection Arranged:* Blanche Ames, Artist & Activist (auth, catalog), Brockton Art Mus, 82; Crane Collection: Special Exhibitions, Boston Sch, 85-86; Bruce Crane, Am Tonalist, 10-11/86; Tonalism, 10 & 11/87; Inspiration Cape Ann, summer 88; Gentle Art of Still Life, 89; Theresa Bernstein Centennial Exhib, 90; Interiors, 92; Russian Light I & II (auth, catalog), 95 & 96; Nikolai Timkov, 99; Three Boston Artists, 2003; Arthur Wesley Dow; Theresa Bernstein and Wm Meyerowitz, 05; Play Ball, Art of Baseball, 05; New England Sunlight, 2006; Theresa Bernstein, 2006; Little Picture Show: 1987-2006. *Pos:* Cur & dir educ, Brockton Art Mus, Brockton, Mass, 81-82; cur, Clark Gallery, Lincoln Station, Mass, 81-85; owner, Crane Collection, Boston, Mass, 85-, Wellesley, 96-2005 & Cape Ann 2005-. *Teaching:* Lectr Am painting, Mus Fine Arts Sch, Houston, Tex, 75-76 & Rice Univ, 76; studio teacher drawing & painting, Cairo Am Col, Egypt, 78-79. *Mem:* Archives Am Art; Nat Acad Design; Artcetera (bd mem); Handel & Haydn Soc (bd mem); Friends of Art, Sweet Briar Col (bd mem, 92); St Botolph Cub (co-chair art com, 2002-03); Cape Ann CofC; North Shore Women in Bus. *Specialty:* American painting of the 19th & early 20th centuries, especially Hudson River School, New England landscapes & the Boston School, also traditional contemporary artist. *Publ:* Auth, Artist & activist Blanche Ames, Brockton Art Mus & Smith Alumnae Quart, 82; The Gentle Art of Stilllife; Russian Light. *Mailing Add:* c/o Crane Collection Cape Ann 11 Central St Manchester-by-the-Sea MA 01944

CRANE, DAVID FRANKLIN
CERAMIST, EDUCATOR
b Hamilton, Ohio, Aug 16, 53. *Study:* Northern Ariz Univ, Flagstaff, BFA, 76, Ill State Univ, Normal, Ill, MFA, 78. *Work:* IBM Corp, Charlotte, NC; Souran Bank, Roanoke, Va; Fred Marer Collection, Los Angeles, Calif; Neville Pub Mus, Green Bay, Wis; Ill State Univ, Normal; Southern Progress Corp. *Exhib:* Marrietta Col Crafts Nat, Grover Herman Fine Arts Ctr, Ohio, 78; Clay and Fiber: Fifteen View Points, Charles Wustain Mus, Racine, Wis, 78; Young Americans Clay/Glass, Mus Contemp Crafts, NY, 78; Biennial Exhib Crafts, Mint Mus Art, Charlotte, NC, 79; 36th Ann Nat Ceramics Invitational, Lang Art Gallery, Scripps Col, Claremont, Calif, 80; Earthenware USA, Hand & Spirit Gallery, Scottsdale, Ariz, 81; Southeast Seven 9, Southeastern Ctr Contemp Art, Winston-Salem, NC, 86; Clay Az Art, Crafts Mus, Helsinki, Finland, 87; Running Ridge Gallery, 89; Uncommon Vessels, Fla Gulf Coast Art Ctr, 90. *Pos:* Artist-in-Residence, Ford Found, Univ Ga, Athens, 78-79; dir, Armory Art Gallery, Va Tech, 89. *Teaching:* Visiting instr, art-ceramics, Univ Ga, Athens, 79-80; instr, ceramics, Callanwolde Fine Arts Ctr, Atlanta, Ga, 79-80; assoc prof art-ceramics, Va Tech, Blacksburg, Va, 80-. *Awards:* Award of Excellence, Radford Univ, 84; Secca-Seven Art Fel, RJ Reynolds Corp, 86; Va Mus Fel, 89. *Bibliog:* Mark Erikson (auth), Sophisticated Clay, Va Gazette, 84; Patricia Mattews (auth), David Crane, Am Ceramics, 5/88. *Mem:* Nat Coun Educ Ceramic Arts. *Publ:* Contrib, Low-Fire: Other ways to work in clay, Davis, 80; Images of Clay Sculpture, Harper & Row, 83. *Dealer:* Schneider Gallery 230 Superior St Chicago IL. *Mailing Add:* 1449 Lusters Gate Rd Blacksburg VA 24060

CRANE, JEAN
PAINTER
b Battle Creek, Mich, July 25, 33. *Study:* Syracuse Univ, BFA, 55. *Work:* Wustum Art Mus, Racine, Wis; Madison Art Ctr, Wis; The Kemper Collection; Northwest Mutual Life Collection; Miller Brewery Collection. *Exhib:* Watercolor USA, Kohler Art Ctr; Wisconsin Biennale; Am Watercolor Soc, NY; Paine Art Ctr, Wis; Layering: An Art of Time and Space, Albuquerque Mus Art, 85; and others. *Teaching:* pvt teacher. *Awards:* First Place, Wustum Art Mus, 89; Emily Lowe Award, Am Watercolor Soc, New York, 81. *Bibliog:* Review, New Art Examiner, Chicago, 3/81. *Mem:* Wis Watercolor Soc; Wis Painters & Sculptors. *Media:* Watercolor. *Dealer:* Katie Gingrass Gallery 241 N Broadway Milwaukee WI 53202; Leslie Levy Gallery 7135 Main St Scottsdale AZ 85251. *Mailing Add:* N64 W5691 Columbia Rd Cedarburg WI 53012

CRANE, JIM (JAMES) G
PAINTER, CARTOONIST
b Hartshorne, Okla, May 21, 27. *Study:* Albion Col, BA; State Univ Iowa, MA; Mich State Univ, MFA. *Work:* Walker Art Ctr, Minn; Joslyn Mus, Omaha; Wis State Univ, River Falls; St Cloud State Col, Minn; Centro Colombo Amercano, Cali, Colombia. *Exhib:* 28th Biennial, Corcoran Gallery Art; 149th Ann, Pa Acad Fine Arts, Philadelphia; Mich Artists, Detroit Art Inst; Painting of the Yr, Smithsonian Inst, Ringling Mus, Sarasota; Centro Colombo Americano, Cali, Colombia; Walker Art Ctr, Minneapolis; Arts in Embassies Prog, Lima, Peru & Katmandu, Nepal. *Teaching:* Chair & prof, Univ Wis, River Fall, 58-62; Prof art, Eckerd Col, 63-94, artist-in-residence, 88-94, emer prof, 94-. *Awards:* Award Tampa Mus, Fla, 82; Robert A Straub Distinguished Teacher Award, Eckerd Col, 87; Friends Arts Art Educator Award, Pinellas, Art Coun, 95. *Media:* Acrylic Collage, Acrylic Painting. *Publ:* Auth, Great Teaching Machine, 66 & Parables, 71, John Knox; Inside Out, 67; illusr, A Funny Thing Happened on the Way to Heaven, 69; illusr, Kalabashee and His Sisters, 2002; ed, Aspects J, Acad Sr Professionals Eckerd Col, 96; plus others. *Mailing Add:* 11000 9th St E Saint Petersburg FL 33706-1112

CRANE, MICHAEL PATRICK
MUSEUM DIRECTOR, CURATOR
b St Louis, Mo, Dec 24, 48. *Study:* Art Inst Chicago, MFA(design & commun), 76. *Work:* Jean Brown Arch, Tyringham Inst, Mass; Arch Sohm, Markgroningen, WGer; Mus Contemp Art, Univ Sao Paulo, Brazil; Mod Mus, Stockholm, Sweden. *Exhib:* 03-23-03, Nat Gallery Can, Ottawa, Ont, 77; Open Ring Gallery, Sacramento, 79; Berry Col, Mt Berry, Ga, 79 & 80; Union Gallery, San Jose, 80; La Mamelle, San Francisco, 81; and others. *Pos:* Original mem & co-dir, Name Gallery, Chicago, 73-74; ed, Running Dog Press, San Jose, 74-; adminr, All the Chicago Fog Performance Gallery, Chicago, 75-76; res fel, Inst Advan Studies in Contemp Art, San Diego, Calif, 77-78; gallery dir, Calif State Univ, Sacramento, 78-79; gallery dir, San Jose State Univ, 79-83; gallery & mus dir, Arvada Ctr Arts & Humanities, Colo, 83-86; gallery dir, Univ Colo, 86-94; sr cur, Bellevue Art Mus, 95-97; partner, SAY Terrazzo Designs, 97-. *Teaching:* Vis artist, Univ Chicago & Calif State Univ, Sacramento, 77; vis artist, San Diego State Univ, 78; lectr, Calif State Univ, Sacramento, 78-79 & San Jose State Univ, 79-83; vis artist, Sch Art Inst, Chicago, 79; vis artist, Ariz State Univ, 79; asst prof, Univ Colo, 86-94. *Publ:* Contribr, Anti-Object Art, Northwestern Univ Press, 74; auth, Fill in This Space, 75 & Landscapes I'd Love to Perform/Do, 76, Running Dog Press; ed, Correspondence Art, Contemp Arts Press, 83. *Mailing Add:* 7720 Missy Ct St Louis MO 63123

CRANSTON, MEG
SCULPTOR
b Baldwin, NY, Sept 25, 60. *Study:* Kenyon Col, BA, 82; Calif Inst Arts, MFA, 86. *Work:* Mus Modern Art, NY Pub Libr. *Comn:* Sculpture, Los Angeles Metrop Transit Authority, Norwalk, 94. *Exhib:* One-man show, Santa Monica Mus Art, 88 & Carnegie Mus Art, Pittsburgh, 93; Facts and Rumors, Witte de Withe Ctr Contemp Art, Rotterdam, The Neth, 92; Songs of Innocence, Songs of Experience, Whitney Mus at Equitable Ctr, NY, 92; Helter Skelter, Mus Contemp Art, Los Angeles, 92; Open 93 Emergency, Aperto: 93 LaBiennale di Venezia, Venice, Italy, 93; Jenseits von Eden, Mus Schloss Moslgkav, Munich, Ger, 94. *Pos:* Ed, J: A Contemp Art Mag, 86-88; reviews ed, Art Coast, 88-89. *Teaching:* Fac art/criticism, Otis Art Inst, Los Angeles, 87-97; lectr art, Univ Calif, Los Angeles, 93-97. *Awards:* Penny McCall Found Grant, 92; John Simon Guggenheim Mem Found Fel, 94. *Bibliog:* David Pagel (auth), Christmas on earth: Meg Cranston's objects and installations, ARTSMag, summer 91; Christine Schneider (auth), Was wirklich zahlt, ELLE Mag, 1/94; Christine Schneider (auth), Jane's Balloon, East of Eden, Mus Schloss Mosigkav, 94. *Media:* All Media. *Dealer:* 1301 Gallery 1301 Franklin St Santa Monica CA 90404

CRARY, JONATHAN KNIGHT
ART HISTORIAN
b New Haven, Conn. *Study:* San Francisco Art Inst, BFA, 73; Columbia Univ, BA, 75, MA, 78, PhD, 87. *Pos:* Found ed, Zone, 85. *Teaching:* Vis lectr, Univ Calif, San Diego, 83 & 85; asst prof, Columbia Univ, 87. *Awards:* Mellon Fel in Humanities, 87-89; J P Getty Fel Art Hist & Humanities, 90-91; Guggenheim Fel, 91. *Res:* Contemporary art and culture. *Publ:* Auth, Passage from virgin to bride, 77 & Real estate opportunities, 78, Arts Mag; Delirious operations, 78, Artforum; Eclipse of the Spectacle, Art After Modernism, 84; Techniques of the Observer, MIT Press, 90. *Mailing Add:* 310 W 106th St New York NY 10025-3429

CRAVEN, DAVID JAMES
PAINTER, COLLAGE ARTIST
b London, Ont, Dec 18, 1946. *Study:* Univ Western Ont, BA, 69; Ont Col Art, 71-73. *Work:* Nat Gallery Can, Ottawa, Ont; Art Gallery Ont, Toronto; Vancouver Art Gallery; Montreal Mus Fine Art; Winnipeg Art Gallery. *Exhib:* One-man shows, Musée d'Art Contemporain, Montreal, Que, 78 & Vancouver Art Gallery, BC, 78; Paris Biennale, Musée d'Art Moderne de la Ville de Paris, 80; Material Matters, Clocktower, NY & Norton Mus, Palm Beach, Fla, 80; Canada in Birmingham, Ikon Gallery, Birmingham, Eng, 81; Psychodrama, Philadelphia Art Alliance, Pa, 85. *Bibliog:* Peter White (auth), David Craven: Recent Work, Southern Alta Art Gallery, 78; Sandra Shavl (auth), David Graven: The Signification of Collage, Parachute Mag, 79; Stephen Westfall, David Craven, Art in Am, 84. *Media:* Acrylic on Board. *Dealer:* Sable-Castelli Gallery 33 Hazelton Ave Toronto ON M5R 2E3 Canada. *Mailing Add:* 329 W 21st St New York NY 10011-3025

CRAVEN, WAYNE
ART HISTORIAN, WRITER
b Pontiac, Ill, Dec 7, 30. *Study:* John Herron Art Sch, Indianapolis, Ind; Ind Univ, BA, 55, MA, 57; Columbia Univ, PhD, 63. *Collection Arranged:* Co-cur, Exhib Celebrating the Creative American (sculpture sect), White House, Washington, DC, 65; guest cur, 200 Years of American Sculpture, Whitney Mus Am Art, New York, 76. *Pos:* Mem bd ed, The Am Art J, New York, 74-, Smithsonian Am Art Mus, Washington DC, Peale Family Papers, Yale Univ, New Haven; mem adv bd, Daniel Chester French Papers, Nat Trust, Washington, DC, 75-. *Teaching:* Instr art hist, Wheaton Col, Norton, Mass, 58-60; H F du Pont Winterthur prof art hist, Univ Del, Newark, 60-98, emeritus. *Mem:* Col Art Asn; Victorian Soc in Am (mem adv comt, 72); NSS; AAS. *Res:* Eighteenth and nineteenth century American painting and sculpture. *Publ:* Auth, Sculpture in America, Univ Delaware Press, 84 & Colonial American Portraiture, Cambridge Univ Press, 86; American Art: History and Culture, McGraw-Hill, 2002; plus many journal articles on Am art. *Mailing Add:* Art Hist Dept Univ Del 318 Old College Newark DE 19716

CRAWFORD, BILL (WILBUR) OGDEN
ILLUSTRATOR, ADMINISTRATOR
b Northfield, NJ, Oct 5, 41. *Study:* Hussian Sch Art, AST, 65. *Hon Degrees:* Rocky Mt Col Art Design, BFA. *Work:* Philadelphia Mus Art; Smithsonian Inst, Washington, DC; Am Bank. *Comn:* Paper sculpture and Poster for Exhib to Benefit the Philadelphia Aids Task Force, 90 & 92. *Exhib:* Bakers Art, Mus Contemp Crafts, NY; Christmas Exhib, Smithsonian Inst; Illustration, Philadelphia Art Alliance & Soc Illusr, NY; Design, Art Dir Show, NY; Int Design Exhib, Brussels, Belg, Japan & France; NY Art Dirs Ann. *Pos:* Pres, Artist Guild Del Valley; pres, Int Coun Design Schs, 93; art dir ann poster, Big Brothers Big Sisters, Phila chpt, 94-; adv bd, Upper Darby Sch System, 98-. *Teaching:* Instr advert design, Hussian Sch Art, 65-88, asst dir design, 74-88, vpres dir educ, 81-88 & asst dir bus art, 83-88; lectr & consult, graphic design & illus; lectr paper sculptures, Art Careers Portfolio Develop. *Awards:* Gold Award, Philadelphia Art Dirs Ann, 90; Gold & Silver Award, Int 3D Illus exhib, 90 & 92; Gold & Best of Show Award, Philadelphia Artists Guild, 91; Outstanding Career Achievement, Pa Asn Pvt Sch Admin Hall of Fame, 93. *Bibliog:* Raymond Ballinger (auth), Design with Paper, Van Nostrand Reinhold, 82. *Mem:* Philadelphia Watercolor Club; Artist Guild Del Valley (pres, 74-75, exec off, 76-90); Art Dir Club Philadelphia; Int Coun Design Sch. *Media:* Paper Sculpture, Calagraphs, Watercolor, Mixed Media. *Publ:* Contribr, Cookies and Breads--The Bakers Art, Van Nostrand Reinhold, 67; Illusr 20, Hastings House, 78; illusr, The Collector, 86; illusr, Vol I & Vol III, Rockport, 91-93. *Mailing Add:* 90 Bethel Rd Glen Mills PA 19342-1514

CRAWFORD, CATHERINE BETTY
PAINTER
b Ingersoll, Ont, Feb 5, 10. *Study:* Univ Toronto, BA; summer study with Eliot O'Hara & at Doon Sch & Queen's Univ; also study with Gordon Payne, E H Varley & Carl Schaeffer; painting groups in England, Ireland & Philippines. *Work:* London Art Gallery, Ont; Arch Can Painter-Etchers, Hamilton, Ont; Woodstock Art Gallery, Ont. *Exhib:* Western Art League Shows, London, Ont & Soc of Can Painter-Etchers, var yrs; one-man shows, London, Burlington & Woodstock, 48-67 & London, 73; Brantford, 73; retrospective show, Ingersoll, 86; Seven Painters, Woodstock Gallery, 89; Public Art Gallery, 89. *Awards:* Purchase Award, London Women's Comt at Gallery, 53; First Prize for Watercolor, Western Fair, London, 64, Woodstock Gallery, 74; Govt Grant Purchase Award, Ingersall Theatre Performing Arts, 92. *Media:* Watercolor. *Mailing Add:* One Duke Ln Ingersoll ON N5C 2L1 Canada

CRAWFORD, RACHEL See Imlah, Rachel Crawford

CRAWFORD, RAINIE
PAINTER
b East Lyme, Conn. *Study:* Studied with Robert Brackman, Nancy Reilly & William Schultz. *Exhib:* Hudson Valley Art Asn; Pastel Soc Am; Salmagundi Club; Allied Artists Am; Academic Artists Asn; Catherine Lorillard Wolfe Art Club; Numerous Nat Exhibs. *Awards:* George Inness Jr, Mem Award; Joseph V Giffuni Mem Award; Mary Lou Fitzgerald Mem Award. *Mem:* Signature mem & Master Pastelist, Pastel Soc Am; Fel artist mem, Am Artists Prof League; Allied Artists Am; Acad Artists Asn; Conn Pastel Soc. *Media:* Pastels. *Publ:* illustr, Best of Pastel II, Rockport Publishers. *Mailing Add:* 21 Mountainview Ave New Milford CT 06776

CRAWFORD, THOM COONEY
PAINTER, SCULPTOR
b Boston, Mass, Sept 23, 44. *Study:* Provincetown Workshop, 63 & 64; Spring Hill Col, Mobile, Ala, BS, 66-62; Syracuse Univ, MFA, 66-67; RI Sch Design, 69. *Work:* Univ Pa; Everson Mus; Prudential Insurance Co; Rockford Art Mus, Ill; Amoco Products. *Comn:* Interior & Exterior (painting & sculpture), Prickly Mt Architectural Project, Warren, Vt, 67; Exterior (painting & sculpture), Bundy Art Mus, Waitesfield, Vt, 69; Mem stone sculpture, Allassio, Italy, 90. *Exhib:* One-man exhibs, M-13 Howard Scott Gallery, NY, 91 & 96, Nama Gallery, Tel-Aviv Israel, 94, Albright Col Ctr Arts, Reading, Pa, 94, Trinity Church & Art Initiatives, NY, 95, St Peter's Church, NY, 96 & Allentown Art Mus, 96; Post Modernism Metaphors, Alternative Mus, NY, 81; New Visions, Aldrich Mus Contemp Art, Ridgefield, Conn, 81; NY Visions, Janus Gallery, Los Angeles, 83; Queens Mus, 83; PS 1, Proj Rm, NY, 83; Monique Knowlton Gallery, NY, 84; M-13 Gallery, NY, 86; Basel Art Fair, Switz, 87; Sculpture Maquette, Hakone Open Air Mus, Japan, 94. *Teaching:* Asst prof sculpture, LaFayette Col, 90-95, Parsons Sch Design, New York, 95-. *Awards:* Creative Artists Pub Serv Prog Fel, 82-83; Nat Endowment Arts Fel, 85. *Bibliog:* Virginia Wiegand (auth), The Philadelphia Inquirer, 9/25/94; Barbara MacAdams (auth), Art News, 12/94; Holland Cotter (auth), NY Times, 8/95; and others. *Media:* Bronze, Mixed Media. *Publ:* Auth & illusr, Raising of the Heart, Limited Ed, Queen City Eds, 72; auth, Alpha Omega (print portfolio), Graphico Uno, 88. *Dealer:* M-13 Howard Scott Gallery 72 Greene St New York NY 10012. *Mailing Add:* 2899 W Lake Rd Skaneateles NY 13152-9432

CREAN, HUGH R
ADMINISTRATOR, LECTURER
b Tralee, Ireland. *Study:* Nat Univ Ireland, BA, 73; Univ Calif, Davis, MA, 76; Grad Ctr, City Univ New York, PhD, 90. *Pos:* Chmn & founder, Restoration Dept, FIT, New York, 87-; lectr, Educ Dept, Metrop Mus Art, New York, 78-. *Publ:* Auth, European furniture to 1840, 95, Art conservation, 96, Encylopedia Americana. *Mailing Add:* 401 Manhattan Ave New York NY 10026-2024

CREECH, FRANKLIN UNDERWOOD
SCULPTOR, GRAPHIC ARTIST
b Smithfield, NC, Oct 14, 41. *Study:* Univ NC, Chapel Hill, summers 63 & 64; Duke Univ, BA, 64; Fla State Univ, MS, 66; Det Danske Selskab, Holbaek, Denmark, printing with Hugo Arne Bock. *Work:* Duke Univ Art Mus; NC Nat Bank; Appalachian State Univ; Rauch Indust; Mint Mus, Charlotte, NC. *Exhib:* 1971 Crafts Exhib, Gallery Contemp Art, Winston-Salem, NC, 71; 8th Int Grand Prix du Cote d'Azur, Cannes, France, 72; 1972 Regional Painting Exhib, Lauren Rogers Mus Art, Laurel, Miss, 72; dedication of the Storyteller, Gastonia, NC, 78; solo exhib, Goldsboro Arts Ctr, 80; and others. *Pos:* Chmn, Johnston Community Col, 80-. *Teaching:* Instr pottery, design & graphics, Gaston Col, Dallas, NC, 66-, chmn dept, 69-77; vis instr, Duke Univ, spring, 81; instr, Atlantic Christian Col, 81; chmn commercial art dept, Johnston Tech Col, currently. *Awards:* Purchase Award, Piedmont Drawing & Graphic Show; First Place, Appalachian Nat Drawing Competition, 77; Second Place, First Sofa Exchange, 77. *Bibliog:* Artist in the 33rd North Carolina Artists exhibition, La Rev Mod, 10/71; feature in Profiles, Art Voices of the South, 78 & NC State Mag, 12/79. *Mem:* Am Crafts Coun; World Crafts Coun; Nat Art Educ Asn. *Media:* Multi-Media. *Publ:* The development of art departments in the community college, Art Teacher Mag, 1/76. *Mailing Add:* 36 Autumn Dr Four Oaks NC 27524-9300

CREECY, HERBERT LEE
PAINTER, SCULPTOR
b Norfolk, Va, Aug 14, 39. *Study:* Atlanta Col Art, 64; Stanley W Hayter-Atelier 17, Paris, France, 64-65. *Work:* Whitney Mus Am Art, NY; High Mus Art, Atlanta, Ga; Akron Mus Art, Ohio; Indianapolis Mus Art, Ind; Norton Gallery Art, West Palm Beach, Fla; and others; pvt collections include AT&T, Chicago, McDonald Corp, Oak Brook, Ill, Fed Res Bank, Richmond, Va, IBM, Raleigh, NC, Chase Manhattan Bank,

NY, Cannon chapel, Emory Univ, Atlanta, GA, Indianapolis Mus of Art, Ind, many others. *Exhib:* Herb Creecy: Recent Work, High Mus Art, Atlanta, Ga; 35th Biennial Exhib Am Painting, Corcoran Gallery Art, Washington, 77; Abstraction, Southeastern Ctr Contemp Art, 85; Painting & Things, Nexus Contemp Art Ctr, 88; Painting: 70's - 80's, Lamar Dodd Art Ctr, 88. *Teaching:* Lectr, Univ Ga; Studies Abroad Program, Cortona, Italy; vis lectr, Univ Tenn, Knoxville. *Awards:* Governor's Grant, Ga Coun Arts. *Media:* Acrylic, Oil; Miscellaneous. *Publ:* Artforum Int, summer 88; Southern Homes, 5-6/89; Southern Accent, 1-2/90; Veranda, summer 90; Pegasus, 9-10/99. *Mailing Add:* 55 25th St NW Atlanta GA 30309-2008

CREEVY, BILL
PAINTER, WRITER
b New Orleans, La, June 24, 1942. *Study:* La State Univ, New Orleans, BA(hist), 65, Baton Rouge, MFA, 68; Brooklyn Mus Art Sch, 69 (Max Beckmann Scholar). *Comn:* Paintings of New York, Munic Asst Corp, NY, 81. *Exhib:* 161st Ann Exhib, Nat Acad Art, NY, 85; Am Artist Mag Golden Anniversary Nat Art Competition, San Francisco, St Louis & NY, 87; Int Exhib, Pastels Only, Soc Pastelistes de France, Lille, France, 87; 38th Art of NE USA, Silvermine Guild Arts Ctr, New Canaan, Conn, 87; 16th Ann Open Exhib, Pastel Soc Am, NY, 88. *Pos:* Art dir, Brooklyn Pub Libr, New York, 69-; asst dir, First Street Gallery, New York, 76-. *Teaching:* Asst graphics & drawing, La State Univ, 66-68; instr painting, Brooklyn Mus Art Sch, 69. *Awards:* J Klimberger Mem Award for Still Life, Pastel Soc Am, 87, Nat Arts Club Award for Excellence, 88, Uschi Grueterich award, 2000, Shirley Epstein award, 2002; C R Gibson Award for Mixed Media, Silvermine Guild Arts Ctr, 87; Art Masters award, Am Artist Mag, 97. *Bibliog:* Golden Anniversary winners, Am Artist, 87; Eileen Myles (auth), Bill Creevy at First Street, Art in Am, 88. *Mem:* Pastel Soc Am; Degas Pastel Soc. *Media:* Pastel, All. *Publ:* Auth, What Counts is What's Underneath: Pastel techniques by Bill Creevy, Artist's Mag, 3/88, rev ed; The Pastel Book, Bill Creevy, 91 & The Oil Painting Book, 93, Watson Guptill. *Dealer:* Cole Pratt Gallery 3800 Magazine St New Orleans LA. *Mailing Add:* 6 Greene St New York NY 10013

CRESPIN, LESLIE A
PAINTER, ASSEMBLAGE ARTIST
b Cleveland, Ohio, Sept 30, 47. *Study:* Univ Capetown, 68-69; Hiram Col, 69-70; also apprenticed under Ray Vinella. *Work:* Harwood Found Mus Art, Taos, NMex; Carlsbad Fine Arts Mus, NMex; Monsanto Int, NY, St Louis; Midland Savings & Loans, Denver; Johnson-Humrick House Mus, Ohio; Maytag, NY & Santa Fe. *Comn:* 4-Monsanto Int, NY & St Louis, 88, 89 & 90; Rolm Corp Div of IBM Corp, Dallas; Santa Fe Contract Design, Odessa, Tex; Am Express, 98. *Exhib:* Western Reserve Exhibition, Cleveland Mus Art; Roanoke Fine Arts Mus; Beachwood Mus, Ohio, 85; Russian Icon Exhib, Fechin Inst, Taos, 86; Recent Paintings, Harwood Found, Mus Taos Art, 87 & 89; N Miami Mus Ctr Contemp Arts, Miami, Fla, 89; Johnson-Humrick House Mus, Ohio, 90; Carson Co Square House Mus, Tex, 90-91; Ctr Arts Southwest, Santa Fe, NMex, 90; Miniatures, Albuquerque Mus, 93-98; Hungers, Goddard Ctr Visual Arts, Okla, 93; 3rd General Show, Taos, 94; Upper Edge Gallery, Aspen, Colo, 94; Lumina Gallery, 98; and others; Lumina Gallery, 2000. *Teaching:* Instr design, Taos Sch Fine Art, NMex, 77. *Awards:* Masterfield Award, North Coast Collage Soc, 85 & 87; Best of Show, The Spectral Pallette of Taos Art, Taos Art Asn, 88; Best of Show Abstract, Taos, NMex, 98. *Bibliog:* Peggy Ridgeway (auth), Creating art from the emotion, Art Gallery, 83; V Forman (auth) Energized at Tracy Felix, Artspace, Springs Mag CO, 85; American Artists: An Illustrated Survey of American Contemporaries, The Krantz Co, 85; S Parlo (auth) Lights Up On Taos, Southwest Profile Mag, NMex. *Mem:* Fechin Inst; Albuquerque United Artists; North Coast Collage Soc; Soc Layerists Multi-Media. *Media:* Mixed media. *Interests:* Rare books, travel. *Dealer:* Lumina Gallery 239 Morada Lane Taos NM; V Richards Greenwich CT. *Mailing Add:* 414 Camino De La Placita No 9 Taos NM 87571

CRESPO, MICHAEL LOWE
WRITER, PAINTER
b New Orleans, La, Jan 3, 47. *Study:* La State Univ, BA; Queens Col, MFA. *Work:* New Orleans Aquarium, Mclhenny Collection La State Univ, City Nat Bank Collection, Baton Rouge, La; Taco Bell Corp, San Diego, Calif; Entergy Corp, Little Rock, Ark. *Exhib:* Simms Fine Art, New Orleans, La; Mesur Mus, Monroe, La; McMurtrey Gallery, Houston, Tex; Transco Energy Tower Gallery, Houston, Tex; Kurts Bingham Gallery, Memphis, Tenn; Artists' Choice Mus, NY; Contemp Art Ctr, New Orleans, La. *Pos:* Dir, Sch Art, La State Univ. *Teaching:* Instr painting, Univ Southwestern La, 71; prof, La State Univ, 71-; vis artist painting, Purdue Univ, 74. *Awards:* La Div Arts Artist Fel; Southern Arts Fed Fel, Nat Endowment Arts. *Media:* Oil on Canvas, Watercolor. *Publ:* Auth, Watercolor Day by Day, Watson-Guptill, New York, 87; Experiments in Watercolor, Watson-Guptill, New York, 88; How to Make An Oil Painting, Watson-Guptill, New York, 90; Watercolor Class, Watson-Guptill, New York, 94. *Mailing Add:* 535 Cornell Ave Baton Rouge LA 70808-4613

CRESS, GEORGE AYERS
PAINTER, EDUCATOR
b Anniston, Ala, Apr 7, 21. *Study:* Emory Univ; Univ Ga, BFA, MFA. *Work:* Tenn Fine Arts Ctr; High Mus, Atlanta, Ga; Ford Motor Co; Birmingham Mus, Ala; Mint Mus, Charlotte, NC; plus many others. *Exhib:* Pa Acad Fine Arts; Springfield Watercolor Ann; one-man shows, Grand Cent Moderns, NY, Addison Gallery Am Art 20 Yr & 50 Yr Retrospective, Hunter Gallery & var southeastern mus; Nat Mus Am Art, Washington, DC; Bampton Arts Centre, Oxon, Eng; and others. *Pos:* Pres SE Col Art Conf, 56, 66 & 83; chmn, Tenn Col Arts Coun, 66-68. *Teaching:* Instr art, Judson Col, Marion, Ala, 45-46, Mary Baldwin Col, Staunton, Va, 46-47, Univ Md, 47-48, Univ Ga, 49, 65 & 69, Univ Tenn, 49-51, Ont Dept Educ, 63 & Univ SC, 67; Guerry prof art, painter-in-residence, Univ Tenn, Chattanooga, 51-84, Guerry prof art emer, 84-. *Awards:* Southeastern Ann, Birmingham Mus Ann & Atlanta Arts Festival; Gov's Award in the Arts, Tenn, 90; Gov's Artist of Excellence Award, Ga, 90. *Mem:* Southeastern Col Conf (pres, 56, 66 & 83). *Media:* Oil, Watercolor. *Mailing Add:* 414 E View Dr Chattanooga TN 37404

CRETARA, DOMENIC ANTHONY
PAINTER, EDUCATOR
b Chelsea, Mass, Mar 29, 46. *Study:* Boston Univ Sch Fine Arts, BFA(magna cum laude), 68, MFA, 70, Tanglewood Inst, summer 68. *Work:* Metrop Mus Art; Duxbury Art Complex, Mass; McBall Corp, Chicago, Ill; Triton Mus Art, Santa Clara; Univ Del; Riverside Art Mus, Calif; Wiggins Print and Drawing Coll, Boston Pub Libr. *Comn:* mural, comn by Joel Schumacher, 92; portrait, comn by Dr Sylvia Maxson, Long Beach, Calif, 2000; Schomburg Gal, Santa Monica, Calif, 2002. *Exhib:* one-man shows, Segal Gallery, NY, 84, 85, Koplin Gallery, Los Angeles, 86, Victor McNeil Gallery, NY, 88, Koslow Gallery, Los Angeles, 90, John Thomas Gallery, Los Angeles, 91, 93, Alon Gallery, Boston, 91, 93, Brenda Taylor Gallery, NY, 95, 96, Martin Zambito Gallery, Seattle, 98, Frye Art Mus, Seattle, 2001, Schomburg Gallery, Santa Monica, 2002; West Art and the Law, Traveling, Kresge Art Mus, Mich, 95-96; retrospective, Las Vegas Art Mus, 98; Frye Art Mus, Seattle, 2001; Koplin Gallery, Los Angeles, 2000, 02; Carnegie Art Mus, Oxnard, Calif, 2003; Mid Tenn State Univ, Murfreesboro, 2004. *Teaching:* Instr painting & design, DeCordova Mus Art, Lincoln, Mass, 71-74; chmn dept fine arts & prof painting & drawing, Art Inst Boston, 73-86; prof painting, Calif State Univ at Long Beach, 86-. *Awards:* Fulbright Hays Grant, Florence, Italy, 74; Camargo Found Grant Artist-in-Residence, Cassis, France, 78-79; Boston Padua Sister Cities Grant, 84; Distinguished Scholarly & Creative Achievement Award, CSULB, 94 & Distinguished Fac Teaching Award, 98; Outstanding Prof Yr, Calif State Univ, Long Beach, 2003. *Bibliog:* Articles, Arts Mag, 12/84, Artweek, Los Angeles, 4/87, 4/90, 8/02, Los Angeles Times, 4/87 & 4/90, Am Artists, 12/92, Oil Highlights: Figures, 1/96 & Am Arts Quart, Fall 98, Fall 2000; A Course in Figure Drawing, Artist's Mag, 6/90; Article, Am Artist Mag, 12/92, Art Scene, 4/02. *Mem:* Col Art Asn; Seattle Acad Fine Arts (bd adv). *Media:* Oil, Charcoal. *Publ:* Contribr, Figure Drawing, 76, The Art of Responsive Drawing, rev ed, 77 & Painting: Perceptual and Technical Fundamentals, 79, Prentice Hall; One Hundred American and European Drawings, Prentice Hall, 82; auth, A course in life drawing, Artist's Mag, 6/90; auth, Planning a Well Structured Portrait, Am Artist, 96; contbribr painting reproductions, in: Contemporary American Oil Painting, Jilin Fine Arts Publ House, 99 & Sex: Portraits of Passion, Watson Guptill, 99. *Dealer:* Schomburg Gallery Santa Monica, Calif. *Mailing Add:* Dept Art Calif State Univ 1250 Bellflower Blvd Long Beach CA 90840

CREWDSON, GREGORY
PHOTOGRAPHER
b Sept 26, 62. *Study:* State Univ NY, Purchase, BA, 85; Yale Sch Art, Yale Univ, MFA, 88. *Work:* Brooklyn Mus Art, NY; Metrop Mus Art, Mus Mod Art & Whitney Mus Art, NY; Los Angeles Co Mus Art; Mus Fine Arts, Boston; John D & Catherine T MacArthur Found, Chicago; Solomon R Guggenheim Mus, NY; San Francisco Mus Modern Art. *Exhib:* Solo exhibs, Houston Ctr Photog, 92, Ruth Bloom Gallery, Los Angeles, 92, 95, Feigen Gallery, Chicago, 93, 94, Palm Beach Community Col Mus Art, Palm Beach, Fla, 94, Luhring Augustine, NY, 95, 97, Jay Jopling/White Cube, London, 95, Galleri Charlotte Lund, Stockholm, 95, Galerie des Carmes, La Fleche, 95, Ginza Artspace, Shiseido Co, Tokyo, 96, 99, Cleveland Ctr for Contemp Art, 97, Marc Foxx Gallery, Los Angeles, 98, Galleri Charlotte Lund, Stockholm, 98, Emily Tsingou Gallery, London, 99; John Michael Kohler Art Ctr, Sheboygan, Wis, 99, Emily Carr Inst Art Design, Vancouver, 00, Luhring Augustine Gallery, NY, 00, 02, SITE, Santa Fe, 01, Gagosian Gallery, Beverly Hills, 02, Aspen Art Mus, 02; Recent Photography Acquisitions: Selections from the Permanent Collection, Whitney Mus Am Art, 94; Home Sweet Home and Other Fables, St Louis Art Mus, 94; Perfect World, Univ Buffalo Art Gallery, NY, 96; Show and Tell, Lauren Wittells Gallery, NY, 96; Digital Gardens, Power Plant, Toronto, Ont, 96; Nature/Cult and the Postmodern Sublime, Bard Ctr for Curatorial Studies, 96; Prospect 96, Frankfurter Kunstverin, Frankfurt, Ger, 96; Gothic, Inst Contemp Art, Boston, 97; The Set Up, Barbara Farber Galerie, Amsterdam, 97; Telling Tales, Art Gallery New S Wales, Sydney, Australia, 98; Affinities with Architecture, Belk Gallery, W Carolina Univ, Cullowhee, NC, Carroll Reece Mus, E Tenn State Univ, Johnson City & Anderson Gallery Sch Arts, Va Commonwealth Univ, Richmond, 99; Under/Exposed, Varldens Storsta Fotoutstallning, Stockholm Tunnelbana, Sweden, 99; Musee des Beaux Arts de Montreal, 2000; Art at MoMA since 1980, 2000; Mus Art, Atlanta, 2000; Eleni Koroneou Gallery, Athens, 2000; The City Gallery of Prague, 2001; Univ Auckland Art Gallery, New Zealand, 2001; Worcester Art Mus, Mass, 2002; Samsung Mus Modern Art, 2002; Paine Webber Art Gallery, New York City, 2002; Mus Contemp Art, Tokyo, 2003; Mass Mus Contemp Art, North Adams, 2003-. *Teaching:* Instr, State Univ NY, Purchase, 88-93, Sarah Lawrence Col, Bronxville, NY, 90, Cooper Union, NY, 90-93, Sch Visual Arts, NY, 93, Vassar Col, Poughkeepsie, NY, 93 & Yale Univ, 93-. *Awards:* Visual Arts Fel, Nat Endowment for the Arts, 92. *Bibliog:* Hilarie M Sheets (auth), Gregory Crewdson: the burbs and the bees, Artnews, 10/94; Alan Artner (auth), Photography exhibit exposes Plot against suburban sprawl, Chicago Tribune, 10/7/94; Simon Grant (auth), Close encounters, Ikon Gallery, Art Monthly, 10/94. *Dealer:* Luhring Augustine Gallery 531 W 24th St New York NY 10011. *Mailing Add:* 247 16th St Brooklyn NY 11215

CRILE, SUSAN
PAINTER
b Cleveland, Ohio, 1942. *Study:* Bennington Col, BA, 65; Hunter Col, 71-72. *Work:* Metrop Mus Art, NY; Phillips Collection, Hirshhorn Mus, Washington, DC; Brooklyn Mus, NY; Albright-Knox Art Gallery, Buffalo, NY; Cleveland Mus Art, Ohio. *Exhib:* Works on Paper, Va Mus Fine Arts, Richmond, 75; Whitney Ann Exhib Am Paintings,

Whitney Mus Am Art, NY; Geometric Abstraction: A New Generation, Inst Contemp Art, Boston, 81; IBM Gallery & Neilsen Gallery, NY, 89; Nat Gallery Art, Washington, DC, 90; Detroit Inst Art, Mich, 91; Nat Mus Women Arts, Washington, DC, 91; group exhibs, Andre Emmench Gallery, NY, 92, Bard Col, 92 & Denver Mus, 93, Hunter Col Fac Exhib, Times Square Gallery, NY, 2000, Small Works, Nina Freudenheim Gallery, Buffalo, 2000, Friendships in Arcadia: Writer and Artists at Yaddo in the 90s, Art In General, NY, The Hyde Collection, Glen Falls, NY, 2000, When This You See Remember Me, Prints by Contemp Women Artists from the Collection, Univ Ariz Mus Art, Tempe, 2001, 177th Ann Exhib, Nat Acad Design, NY, 2002, Shark's Ink, 1976-2001, a 25 Yr Retrospective, Gallery of Contemp Art, Univ of Colo Springs, 2002; solo exhibs, Grad Sch Design, Harvard Univ, Cambridge, Mass, 94, James Graham & Sons, NY, 95, Herbert R Johnson Musart, Cornell Univ, Ithaca, NY, Middlebury Art Mus, Middlebury Col, Vt, 95, Nat Coun Cult, Arts & Letts, Kuwait City, Kuwait, 95, James & Graham & Sons, NY, 98, James Graham & Sons, NY, 2001; Hot Art: The Fires of War, Univ Ariz Mus Art, Tucson, 2003; Am Acad Arts & Letters, NY, 99; Hyde Mus, Glen Falls, NY, 2000. *Pos:* Vis critic, Univ Pa, Philadelphia, 80. *Teaching:* Yadelo, Saratoga Springs, 70, 71, 73, 76 & 99; McDowell Colony, Peterboro, NH, 72; Instr painting, Princeton Univ, 74-76, Sch Visual Arts, NY, 76-82 & Sarah Lawrence Col, 76-78 & Barnard Col, 83-86; prof, Hunter Col, 82-. *Awards:* Ingram Merrill Found Grant, 72; Fel Nat Endowment Arts, 82, 89-90; Residence painting, Am Acad in Rome, 90. *Bibliog:* Jeremy Strick (auth), St Louis Art Mus Publ, 4/94; Elizabeth Frank (auth), Art News, 10/94; Celia McGee (auth), New York Times, 4/24/94; Susan Cheever (auth), Friendships in Arcadia: Writers and Artists in Yaddo in the 90's, The Corporation of Yaddo, 2000. *Mem:* New York Univ Inst of Humanities (print making); Yaddo (bd dir, 91-). *Media:* Oil, Pastel. *Publ:* Ralph Humphrey: Voices (catalog), Ralph Humphrey, The Late Paintings on Paper, Hunter Col City Univ NY, 91. *Dealer:* James Graham & Sons New York NY. *Mailing Add:* 168 W 86th St New York NY 10024

CRILLEY, JOSEPH JAMES
PAINTER
b Philadelphia, Pa, 20. *Study:* Philadelphia Col Art, 39; Fleisher Mem Graphic Sketch Club; Temple Univ, Pa, 60; student of Peter de Rothermel & Albert Gold. *Work:* Margaree Salmon Mus; Nova Scotia, Can; James A Michener Art Mus, Doylestown, Pa; Philadelphia Sketch Club; The Kiski Sch, Saltsburg, Pa. *Exhib:* Nat Acad of Design, NY; MD Hist Soc, Baltimore; Bianco Gallery, Buckingham, Pa; Coryell Gallery, Lambertville, NJ; and many others; solo exhib, Crest Gallery, Holicong, Pa, Artfull Eye Gallery, Lambertville, NJ, Pennswood Village, Newtown, Pa, 2000, Gratz Gallery, New Hope, Pa, 2001, others. *Teaching:* Art instr, Hope-Solebury High Sch, New Hope, Pa, 55-61. *Awards:* Award of Excellence, Mystic Int Conn, 91; Lee M Loeb Mem Award; Am Artists Prof League Award. *Mem:* Audubon Artists; Salmagundi Club; Philadelphia Sketch Club; The Kiski Sch, Saltsburg, Pa; and others. *Media:* Oil. *Specialty:* Boats, people, buildings, street scenes. *Mailing Add:* 3781 Aquetong Rd Carversville PA 18913

CRIMMINS, JERRY (GERALD) GARFIELD
PAINTER, SCULPTOR
b Minneapolis, Minn, Feb 9, 40. *Study:* Minneapolis Col Art, BFA, 65; Pratt Inst, MFA, 67. *Work:* Pratt Inst, Brooklyn, NY; Southern Ill Univ, Carbondale; Philadelphia Mus Art; Minneapolis Inst Arts; Rotterdamse Kunstichting, Neth. *Exhib:* The Artists' Book, Univ Calif, San Diego at La Jolla, 77; Words & Images, Philadelphia Col Art, 79; Southern Alleghenies Mus, Pa; one-man shows, Hansen Fuller Goldeen Gallery, San Francisco, Calif, 80, Touchstone Gallery, NY, 80, DC Armory, Washington, 81, Rodger LaPelle Galleries, Philadelphia, Pa, 82, Moore Col Art & Design, 86; Imaginary Lands, Rotterdam Arts Found, The Neth, 83; Return of the Narrative, Palm Springs Desert Mus, Calif, 84; group exhibs, Fleisher Mus, Palm Springs Desert Mus, Tyler Sch Art, Southern Alleghenies Mus; Snyderman Gallery, Philadelphia, Pa, 96; Alliance Francaise, NY, 2000; many others. *Collection Arranged:* Philadelphia Mus Art; Minneapolis Mus Art; Rotterdamse Mus Art; Southern Ill Univ; Pratt Inst; Philadelphia Free Libr; many pvt collections. *Teaching:* Instr, Tyler Sch Art, Philadelphia, 67-68; prof basic arts & sculpture, Moore Col Art & Design, Philadelphia, 68-2003. *Awards:* Purchase Award, So Ill Univ, 72 & Philadelphia Mus Art, 80; Men of Achievement Award, Cambridge, Eng, 81 & 82; Nat Endowment Arts Grant, 83; Pollock-Krasner Found Grant, Pa Coun Arts, 90. *Bibliog:* John Russel (auth), article, New York Times, 4/21/80; T Albright (auth), article, San Francisco Chronicle, 84; articles, Ariz Daily Star, 98, Miami Herald, 98, Kirkus Revs, 98 & Publ Weekly, 98. *Mem:* Marine Corps Asn; US Seagoing Marina Asn. *Media:* All Media. *Specialty:* fine art, paintings, sculpture, etc. *Publ:* Auth & illusr, Thicker than Blood, Cold Chair Press, 76; The Song of the Fair Haired, pvt publ, 77; Visitors Guide to La Republique de Reves, Synapse Art Press, 80; The Secret History of La Republique de Reves, Reverian Govt, 83; The Republic of Dreams: Areverie, W W Norton & Co, New York, London, 98; French rights Editions du Seuil, German ed, Droemer-Knurde Die Republic der träume. *Dealer:* Jeffery Fuller Fine Arts Limted 730-32 Carpenter Philadelphia PA 19119. *Mailing Add:* 153 Roberts Ave Glenside PA 19038

CRIMP, DOUGLAS
CRITIC, EDUCATOR
b Coeur d'Alene, Idaho. *Study:* Tulane Univ, BA(art hist), 68; City Univ New York, MPhil, 83, PhD, 94. *Pos:* Curatorial staff, Solomon R Guggenheim Mus, 68-71; ed assoc, Art News, 71-76; guest cur, Visual Arts Gallery, New York, 72 & Artists Space, New York, 77; managing ed, October, 77-83, exec ed, 83-86, ed, 86-90; series ed, October Bks, MIT Press, 88-90. *Teaching:* Instr art hist, Sch Visual Arts, New York, 70-76; vis instr, Dept Art Hist, NS Col Art & Design, Halifax, 82, Visual Arts Prog, Princeton Univ, 86, Mason Gross Sch Arts, Rutgers Univ, 88 & Cooper Union, New York, 88, Calif Inst Arts, Valencia, spring 89 & 90, Sarah Lawrence Col, 90-91; prof visual & cult studies, Univ Rochester, 92-. *Awards:* Art Critics Fel, Nat Endowment Arts, 73 & 84; Frank Jewett Mather Award, for distinction in art criticism, Col Art Asn, 88; On the Museum's Ruins Grant, Getty Publ, 92. *Mem:* Int Asn Art Critics; Col Art Asn. *Publ:* Auth, The Boys in my Bedroom, Art in Am, 2/90; Art acts up: A graphic response to AIDS, Out/look, summer 90; On the Museum's Ruins, Mass Inst Techol Press, 1993; Melancholia and Moralism, MIT Press, 2002. *Mailing Add:* 139 Fulton St New York NY 10038

CRISP-ELLERT, JOANN
PAINTER, WRITER
b Syracuse, NY, 24. *Study:* Syracuse Univ, BFA, 46; Am Univ, Wash, DC, MFA, 62, PhD, 72; Yale Univ (Andrew Mellon Fel), with Esteban Vicente, Vincent Scully & Sam Hunter, 73; dipl (3rd level), Sorbonne, Paris; studied at Royal Col Art. *Work:* Syracuse Univ, NY; Lockheed Corp, Atlanta; George Mason Univ, Fairfax, Va; Am Univ, Washington, DC; George Meany Gallery & Ctr Labor Studies, Silver Spring, Md; Pres's Collection, Am Univ; Krauz Collection, St Augustine, Fla; Casa Monica Collection, St Augustine; Peggy Bailey Collecion, St Augustine. *Comn:* Landscape mural, Amerika Haus, Heidelberg, Ger, 65; cityscape mural, Dura Corp, Washington, DC, 80; garden mural, comn by M Berkowitz, Washington, DC, 96; abstr wall mural, comn by Maxine Taylor, Baltimore, Md, 97; floral mural, Am Asn Univ Women, St Augustine, Fla, 98. *Exhib:* Stonehouse Revisited, Cosmos Club, Wash, DC, 82; Toys in the Tower, Hist Savage Mill, Md, 89; Breakfast at Tiffany's, Gallery 10 Ltd, Wash, DC, 93; Passport to St Augustine, Watkins Collection, Am Univ, Wash, DC, 95; St Augustine Fenestration Ser, Arts Club, Wash, DC, 96; Scenographics of Paris, George Meany Gallery & Ctr Labor Studies, Silver Spring, Md, 98; St Augustine Art Asn, From Giotto to Joann, 2004. *Pos:* Asst art cur, Colonial Williamsburg Restoration, Va, 46-49; art specialist, Arlington Co, Va, 65-90; mus art specialist, Hirshhorn Mus, 72-73; pres, Artists Equity, Washington, DC, 81-83; secy & vpres, Art Galleries St Augustine, 95-96; cult chmn, Am Asn Univ Women, 97-99; bd dir, Old St Augustine Village Mus; pres's coun, Hagler Col, St Augustine. *Teaching:* asst prof art hist, Univ Md, Ruislip London, Eng, 52-55; prof art educ, Univ Va, Fairfax, 1970-1974; prof art educ, George Mason Univ, Fairfax. *Awards:* Amerika Haus Gold Medal, Heidelberg, Ger, 65; Best of Show, Am Fedn Women's Club, 80; Art Barn Best of Show, Washington, DC, 82. *Bibliog:* Michael Welzenbach (auth), Royal visions, Wash Post, 4/30/85; J W Mahoney (auth), Le Rivage, Wash Art, 10/9/87; Terry Parmelee (auth), Scenes of Paris: JoAnn Crisp-Ellert, KOAN, 5/98. *Mem:* Womens Caucus Art; Textile Arts Guild, St Augustine (secy, 97-99); St Augustine Art Asn; Col Art Asn; Film Soc St Augustine; Hibiscus Garden Club; GFW Club. *Media:* Acrylic, Oil, Watercolor. *Res:* Bloomsbury Group. *Interests:* Writing & Poetry. *Collection:* Medieval & Renaissance Art, Gothic Architecture. *Publ:* Auth, The Bauhaus & Black Mt College, Penn State Press, 72; Henry Klumb in Puerto Rico-Arch at the Service of Society, J AIA, 7/72; Hercules, Talleyrand Press, 86; Pablos Search, 97 & Pablo in Paris, 98, Townet Press; Pablo in 3099 Qui St 19 Palace Gate, Mulkey Press, 2004. *Dealer:* Dr RB Ellert 48 Sevilla St St Augustine Fla 32084. *Mailing Add:* Anderson Cottage 48 Sevilla St Saint Augustine FL 32084

CRISPO, DICK
PAINTER, PRINTMAKER
b Brooklyn, NY, Jan 13, 45. *Study:* Ariz Sch Art; Carmel Art Inst; Monterey Peninsula Col; Hartnell Col; St Sophia Divinity Sch; also with Victor DiGesu, Sam Colburn, Jan Hannah, Alexander Napote, Kay Rodgers & others. *Work:* Libr Cong, Washington, DC; Bibliot Nat, Paris, France; Inst Nac de Bellas Artes, Mexico City, Mex; Mus Western Art, Tokyo, Japan; Nat Libr Ireland, Dublin; plus others. *Comn:* Ecology (mural), Monterey High Sch, Calif, 72; Ecology, Robert Louis Stevenson Sch, Pebble Beach, Calif, 72; Spirit of Youth, Carmel Youth Ctr, Calif, 73; History of the Migrant Worker (mural), Opportunity Indust Ctr, Salinas, Calif, 74; Twelve Master Teachers of the World (mural), Church of Antioch, Pacific Grove, Calif, 75. *Exhib:* Calif State Fair, Sacramento, 64; Small Painting Biennial, Purdue Univ, 68; Univ Calif, Berkeley, 72; Pan-Am Graphics, Mexico City, 72; Western Graphics, Tokyo, 73; and others. *Pos:* Chmn, Fine Arts Div, Monterey Co Fair, 72-74; co-founder, Mus on Wheels, Monterey, 74-; exhib dir, Pacific Grove Art Ctr, 74-; art counr, Monterey Co Probation Dept, 75-; Am cult specialist to Latin Am for USIS. *Teaching:* Instr arts & Crafts, York Sch, Monterey, 71-73; instr folk & ethnic arts, Monterey Peninsula Col, 74-75; instr folk & ethnic arts & art hist, St Sophia Divinity Sch, Pacific Grove, 75-; vis lectr, Univ Calif, Santa Cruz, Interdisciplinary Studies Dept, Porter, Col. *Awards:* All Calif Watercolor Competition Third Prize, Pacific Grove, 67; San Juan Bautista Invitational Second Prize, Calif, 68; Gold Medal, Acad Italy, 79; plus others. *Bibliog:* Pat Griffith (auth), An artist with a sense of humor, Carmel Valley Outlook, Carmel, Calif, 72; Robert Miskimon (auth), Social Consciousness of Art, Pine Cone, Carmel, 73. *Mem:* Artists Equity; Carmel Art Asn; Pacific Grove Art Ctr; Pac Art Asn (chmn); Art Workers United. *Media:* All. *Res:* Eclectic study of world folk art. *Collection:* Folk and eccentric art from over 40 countries. *Publ:* Auth, Contemporary Print Making Renaissance in Japan, 69; dir, Dick Crispo Maker of Images, Frasconi-Selzer Films. *Dealer:* Bronstein & Sigg Gallery. *Mailing Add:* PO Box 1952 Carmel CA 93921

CRISS, CHERYL LYNN
PAINTER
b San Diego, CA, Dec 16, 1947. *Study:* The Design Inst, San Diego-1987-89; Private studies. *Exhib:* Am Watercolor Soc Int, New York City, 1990-92, 1997-98, 2000; Museum Juried Exhib, San Diego Mus of Art, Calif, 1996 & 98. *Pos:* bd mem, San Diego Mus of Art (Artists Guild), 1992-96; vpres, San Diego Watercolor Soc, 1992-94; pres, West Coast Watercolor Soc, 2006. *Awards:* Edgar Whitney, AWS Int, 1998 & 2000; High Winds Medal, AWS Int, 2006. *Mem:* signature mem, Am Watercolor Soc; signature mem, Watercolor West; pres & signature mem, West Coast Watercolor Soc; past vpres, San Diego Watercolor Soc; US Coast Guard Artist. *Media:* Watercolor. *Publ:* auth & illus, Getting the Size Right, The Artist's Magazine,

1994; auth & illus, Water Color Magic-Featured Artist, 1998; auth & illus, The Quality of Light, North Light Books, 2004; auth & Illus, Textures of Life, The Artist's Magazine, 2004; auth & illus, Dry Spell, The Artist's Mag, 2005. *Dealer:* Neora Matteucci Fine Art 555 Canyon Road Santa Fe NMex. *Mailing Add:* 9574 Paseo Mountril San Diego CA 92129

CRIST, WILLIAM GARY
VISUAL ARTIST, EDUCATOR
b Pocatello, Idaho, Jan 17, 37. *Study:* Univ Wash, Seattle, BA (art educ), 66; Cranbrook Acad Art, Detroit, MFA (sculpture), 71; study with Michael Hall, Julius Schmidt, Joseph Beuys, Nam June Paik & Klaus Rinke; Staatliche Kunstakademie, Dusseldorf, WGer, 81 & 83. *Work:* Cameron Univ, Lawton, Okla; Univ Mo, Kansas City; Gen Serv Admin, Washington. *Exhib:* Noho Gallery, NY, 79 & 80; Staatliche Kunstakademie, Dusseldorf, W Ger, 81; XVth Ann Int Electronic Music Festival, 85; Randolph Street Gallery, Chicago, 86; Oppression/Expression, Contemp Arts Ctr, New Orleans, 86; Pleiades Gallery, 10th Ann Juried, NY, 92. *Teaching:* Asst prof art, Wesleyan Col, Macon, Ga, 71-72; instr art, Cameron Univ, Lawton, Okla, 72-74; asst prof art, Univ Mo, Kansas City, 74-81, assoc prof art, 81-88, chair, dept art & art hist, 85-89, prof art, 88-; dir 2 and 3D computer graphics, Univ Mo Video Network, 89-. *Awards:* Interdisciplinary Arts Fel Prog, Rockefeller Found & Nat Endowment Arts, 86; Southwestern Bell Telephone Found, 92. *Media:* Mixed Media, Electronics. *Res:* Computer multimedia art; synthesis of various technologies into visual art; visual and audio relationships of space and time, art on the internet. *Publ:* Auth, article, High Performance Mag, Issue 32; Coherent light and Electronics as Creative Mediums, Okla State Arts Comn, 73; interview with Joseph Beuys, 82 & interview with Nam June Paik, Forum Mag, 5/86; auth, Underground art in Poland, Col Art Asn, Toronto. *Mailing Add:* Univ Mo Dept Art & Art Hist Kansas City MO 64110

CRISWELL, WARREN
PAINTER, PRINTMAKER
b Sept 19, 36. *Study:* Self-taught. *Work:* The Ark Arts Ctr, Little Rock; McKissich Mus, Univ SC, Columbia, SC; Univ Ark Little Rock; Hendrix Coll, Conway, Ark; Ctrl Ark Lib Sys, Little Rock. *Exhib:* One-man shows, Ulysses at Circe's: Drawings of W Criswell, Capitol Arts Ctr, Taipei, Taiwan, 1993, Works of Warren Criswell, Wichita Ctr Arts, Wichita, Kans, 2000, Warren Criswell: Perceptions & Conceptions, Historic Ark Mus, 2001 & Warren Criswell: Shadows, Ark Arts Ctr, Little Rock, 2003; Body & Soul: Contemp Southern Figures, Columbus Mus, Columbus, Ga, 1997, Mobile Mus Art, Mobile, Ala, 1997, Miss Mus Art, Jackson, Miss, 1998 & Cummer Mus Art, Jacksonville, Fla, 1998; About Face (with catalog), Ark Arts Ctr, Little Rock, 2001. *Awards:* Residency award, Mid-Am Arts Alliance, 1994; Fel grant, Mid-Am Arts Alliance & NEA, 1996; Individual Artist fellowship grant for painting, Ark Arts Coun, 2003. *Bibliog:* Gwen Diehn (auth), Simple Printmaking, Lark Books, New York, 2000; Werner Trieschemann (auth), A lighter Shade of Criswell, Ark Democrat Gazette, 7/15/2001; Peter Frank (auth), Warren Criswell: Shadows, 2003. *Dealer:* Helen Scott Cantrell Gallery 8206 Cantrell Rd Little Rock AR 72227; Carolyn Taylor Taylor's Contemporary Fine Arts Inc 204 Exchange Hot Springs AR 71901. *Mailing Add:* 7700 Rolling Manor Dr Benton AR 72015

CRITE, ALLAN ROHAN
PAINTER, ILLUSTRATOR
b Plainfield, NJ, Mar 20, 10. *Study:* Boston Mus Sch Fine Arts, 29-36, Painter's Workshop, Fogg Art Mus, 40's, Harvard Univ, AB, 68, Suffolk Univ, Hon Doc Humanities, 78, Emmanuel Col, Hon Doc FA, 83, Mass Col Art, Hon Doc FA, 88, Gen Theological Sem Episc Church, Hon Doc Div, 94. *Work:* Boston Pub Libr, Mass; Nat Ctr Afro-Am Artists, Mass; Mus Am Art, Washington, DC; Libr Boston Athenaeum, Mass; Mus Mod Art, NY; and many others. *Comn:* Insignia, USS Wilson, Navy; mural, Grace Church, Martha's Vineyard, Mass; Stations (Cross), Holy Cross Church, Morrisville, Vt; mural, St Augustine's Church, NY; banners & altar pieces, St Stephen's Episcopal Church, Mass. *Exhib:* Fogg Mus Art, Harvard Univ, 30 & 95; WPA exhib, Mus Mod Art, 36; Boston Mus Fine Arts, 78; Mus Nat Ctr Afro-Am Artists, 78, 85, 88 & 94; Afro-Am Hist & Cult Mus, Philadelphia, 79, 94; Allan Rohan Crite: A Retrospective, Mus Nat Ctr Afro-Am Art, 90; Against the Odds, Harlem Renaissance Artists, Newark Mus, NJ, 93; Alone in a Crowd, Black Printmakers - 30's & 40's, Equitable, NY, 93; Free Within Ourselves, Mus Am Art, Smithsonian, 94; Revelation, Nat Black Arts Festival, ITC, Atlanta, Ga, 94; and many others. *Pos:* Artist-historian, Semitic Mus, Harvard Univ; eng, draftsman/illustr Tech Equip, Naval Shipyard, Boston, 40-70; muralist, Rambusch Decorating Co, 49-50; libr, Grossman Libr, Harvard Univ, 74-89. *Teaching:* Lectr Christian art, Oberlin Col, 58; lectr drawing, Regis Col, 58; instr drawing, Roxbury Community Col, 77-78; lectr, Eye of the Beholder, Isabell Stewart Gardner Mus, 94; vis lectr art & liturgical art at many schs & cols nationally. *Awards:* 350th Ann Harvard Univ, Medal, Harvard Univ, Mass, 86; Men of Vision Award, Mus African-Am Hist, Mass, 92; Stain Glass Window, Christ Church, Bronxville, NY, 94; Cert Appreciation Life Contributions to Visual Art, St Bartholomew's Episcopal Church, 94; and many others. *Mem:* Community Fel, Mass Inst Technol, Mass. *Media:* Watercolor, Lithography. *Res:* American Peoples of Color, Afro-Asian, Afro-American; Cultural Heritage of US. *Publ:* Auth, Three Spirituals from Earth to Heaven, Harvard Univ Press, 48; Rediscovery of Cultural Heritage of US (paper), Libr Boston Athenaeum, 68; illusr, Book of Revelation, Limited Ed Book Club, NY, 94; The Lord's Prayer, an interpretation, The Seabury Press, Inc, 54; Blacks Who Died for Jesus, a history book by Mark Hyman, Winston-Derek Publ Inc, 83. *Dealer:* J Cox & Assocs PO Box 2414 Boston MA 02208. *Mailing Add:* 410 Columbus Ave Boston MA 02116-5910

CRIVELLI, ELAINE
ENVIRONMENTAL ARTIST, SCULPTOR
b Philadelphia, Pa, Dec 4, 50. *Study:* Westchester Univ, BFA, 78; Univ Del, with Joe Moss, MFA, 82. *Comn:* Sculpture installations, Univ NC, Chapel Hill, 82 & Gotham Design, Dobbs Ferry, NY, 88; Movement Int Theater, 87; Please Touch Mus, Philadelphia, Pa, 90. *Exhib:* Artists by Themselves, Sushi Gallery, San Diego, Calif, 87; Altered Sites, Fairmount Park, Philadelphia, 88; Playable Art, Moore Col Art, Philadelphia, 89; Shadow Play, Please Touch Mus, Philadelphia, 90; Bergen Gallery, Savannah, Ga, 91; Common Wealth, Univ Mus, Ind Univ Pa, 95; Small Computers in the Arts, Silicon Gallery, Philadelphia, 96; Photog: Contemp Prospects, Hist Yellow Springs Inst, Chester Springs, Pa, 96. *Pos:* Gallery dir, Painted Bride Art Ctr, Philadelphia, 84-87; vis artist, Wimbledon Sch Art, Eng, Kingston Univ, Kingston-upon-Thames, Eng, Ruskin Sch Fine Arts, Oxford, Eng & Studies Abroad Prog, Univ Ga, Cartona, Italy, 93. *Teaching:* Lectr 3-D design, Philadelphia Col Art, 83-; prof design & drawing, Philadelphia Col Textiles & Sci, 87-; prof, Chestnut Hill Col, Pa, 87-89 Savannah, Ga, 89-93 & Am Sch London, 93-95. *Awards:* Fel, Univ Del, 80. *Bibliog:* Ronnie H Cohen (auth), Artpark, Artforum, 82; Deborah Curtis (auth), Introduction to Visual Literacy, Prentice Hall, 86; Edward J Sozanski (auth), On galleries, Philadelphia Inquirer, 2/26/87; Beth Wilcox (auth), Creating Art at Artpark, Sculpture Mag, 89. *Mem:* Sculptors Int; Col Art Asn. *Media:* Mixed Media. *Mailing Add:* 413 E Front St Media PA 19063-3522

CRON, MARIE-MICHELE
CURATOR, CRITIC
b North Africa, Apr 14, 61; Can citizen. *Study:* Lycee Cezanne Aix-en Provence, France, BACC, 79; UQAM, Que, Can, BACC(art hist), 84 & MA(art hist), 98. *Exhib:* Circonvolutions (auth, catalog), Museo Carrillo Gil, Mex, 94; Artifice, Centre Saidye Bronfman, Montreal, 96 & 98. *Pos:* Art critic, Le Devoir, Montreal, 94-95; independent cur, Video Exhib in Can & Mex, 94-98. *Res:* Video art in the seventies. *Publ:* Auth, Voces Sensibles/Voix Sensibles, 97, Opera; House/Boat-Vivan Sundaram, Oboro, 96; C Guilbert, S Murphy, M Grov: Video-Roman Rendezvous, Du Cinema Quebecois, 97

CRONIN, ROBERT (LAWRENCE)
PAINTER
b Lexington, Mass, Aug 10, 36. *Study:* RI Sch Design, BFA, 59; Cornell Univ, MFA, 62. *Work:* Boston Mus Fine Arts; Brooklyn Mus; Nat Air & Space Mus, Washington, DC; Mus Art, Carnegie Inst, Pittsburgh, Pa; Nat Acad Mus, NY. *Comn:* On Speculation (sculpture), Lippincott Co, 82-; RS Reynolds Mem Award, 82. *Exhib:* Inst Contemp Art, Boston, 71; Gimpel Fils, London, 82; Gimpel & Weitzenhoffer Ltd, NY, 82, 84, 87 & 89; Gimpel-Hanover & Andre Emmerich Galerien, Zurich, 83; Klonaridis Gallery, Toronto, 84 & 86; Gallery Hiro, Tokyo, Japan, 89; Yoh Art Gallery, Osaka, Japan, 89; The Tin Yrs, A Survey of the 1980's, Fitchburg Art Mus, Mass, 90, Dillon Gallery, NY, 96 & 99; Kouros Gallery, NY, 2004. *Pos:* Self employed artist. *Teaching:* Instr painting, Bennington Col, 66-68; instr art, Brown Univ, 68-71; instr art, Sch Worcester Art Mus, 71-80. *Awards:* Mass Arts & Humanities Grant, 75; Mass Artists Found Grant, 79; Adolf & Esther Gottlieb Found Individual Support Grant, 91. *Bibliog:* Hilton Kramer (auth), New Talent, NY Times, 6/17/73; Hilton Kramer (auth), article, NY Times, 9/21/74; Max Wykes-Joyce (auth), Robert Cronin, Gimpel Fils, London Arts Rev, 4/9/82. *Mem:* Nat Acad Design. *Media:* Oil on canvas. *Dealer:* Dillon Gallery 555 W 25th St NY NY 10001; Lascano Gallery 297 Main St Great Barrington Mass 01230. *Mailing Add:* PO Box 74 Falls Village CT 06031

CROOKS, W SPENCER
PAINTER, LECTURER
b Ireland, July 26, 17; US citizen. *Study:* RI Sch Design, cert, Shrivenham Am Univ, Eng, cert; summer sem with Edgar Whitney; RCA Scholar (scenic design), Berkshire Music Ctr, Roger Williams Col, Hon DFA, 86. *Work:* RI Sch Design Fine Art Mus; Boston Symphony Hall, Mass; Pawtucket Boys Club, RI; Mayor's Office, City Hall, Providence, RI. *Comn:* Watercolor, covers for RI Providence J, 61-65; watercolor, Old Colony Banks, RI, 71-73; watercolor, Indust Leasing Corp, Indust Nat Bank, Providence, RI, 72; Irish Cult Exchange Comn RI, 82. *Exhib:* Watercolor USA, Springfield, Mo, 64; Am Watercolor Soc Ann, Nat Acad Art Gallery, 67, 72 & 75; Springfield Mus Fine Arts, 75; one-man show, Rockport Art Asn, 75 & Trinity Col, Dublin, Ireland, 82; Ireland's Nat Art Gallery, Dublin, 84. *Pos:* Creative artist, Hallady, Inc, Providence, RI, 52-58 & Hassenfeld Inc, Central Falls, 59-60; art dir, Cardono Inc, Pawtucket, 60-61; demonstr, watercolor, Grumbacher's Palette Talk, 75. *Teaching:* Instr Watercolor, Brown Univ Exten Sch, 68-74, Cranston East High Sch (adult educ), 65-68 & URI-NARR-Bay Campus, 90-; teacher graphic art, RI Col, 72- & instr watercolor, 74-75. *Awards:* Travel Award, Washington Sq Show, New York, Forbes Mag, 67; James G Geddes Mem Award, Rockport Art Asn, 71; RI Heritage Hall Fame, 86. *Mem:* Providence Watercolor Club, Rockport Art Asn, Mass; Cape Cod Art Asn, Barnstable, Mass; Philadelphia Watercolor Club; Am Watercolor Soc; RI Heritage Hall Fame (bd dir, 87). *Media:* Watercolor; Pen, Ink. *Publ:* Illusr, Providence J Mag Sect, 61-65; ed, DeCordova Mus Gallery (catalog), 62; RI Sch Design Alumni Bull, 75; illusr, Palette Talk, Grumbacher Artist Material, NY, 75; Yankee Mag, Dublin, NH, 82. *Dealer:* Bert Gallery Omni Biltmore Hotel Kennedy Plaza Providence RI 02903. *Mailing Add:* Crooks & Corona 12 Soprano Cir Cranston RI 02920-4229

CROPPER, M ELIZABETH
HISTORIAN, LECTURER
b Dewsbury, Yorkshire, Eng, Aug 11, 44. *Study:* Newnham Col, Univ Cambridge, BA(hon), 67; Bryn Mawr Col, PhD, 72. *Teaching:* Prof art hist, Temple Univ, 73-; prof, Johns Hopkins Univ, 85-; Andrew W Mellon prof, Nat Gallery Art, 94-96, dean CASVA, 2001; Dean CASVA, Nat Gallery of Art; Dir Villa Spelman, 85-01. *Awards:*

Arthur Kingsley Porter Prize, 76; fel, Villa I Tatti, Harvard Univ & Leopold Schepp Found, 78-79; Samuel H Kress Fel, 84-85. *Mem:* Col Art Asn; Renaissance Soc Am; vis mem Inst Advanced Study, Princeton; Fel Am Acad Arts & Scis; Philadelphia Mus Art (painting comt). *Res:* Italian Renaissance and Baroque art. *Publ:* Auth, On beautiful women, 76 & Poussin and Leonardo, Art Bulletin, 80; The Ideal of Painting, Princeton Univ Press, 84; Pietro Testa 1612-50 (exhib catalog), Philadelphia Mus Art, 88; coauth (with Charles Dempsey), Nicolas Poussin: Friendship and the Love of Painting, Princeton Univ Press, 96. *Mailing Add:* 1336 31st St NW Washington DC 20007

CROSBY, RANICE W
MEDICAL ILLUSTRATOR, EDUCATOR
b Regina, Sask, Can, Apr 26, 15. *Study:* Conn Col, AB; Johns Hopkins Med Sch, under Max Broedel; also under Robert Brackman; Johns Hopkins Univ, MLA. *Pos:* Illusr for N J Eastman, Johns Hopkins Hosp, currently. *Teaching:* Assoc prof & dir emer, dept art as appl to med, Johns Hopkins Med Sch, 44-. *Awards:* Asn Med Illusr: Fel, Lifetime Achievement Award; William P Didusch Award, Am Urological Asn. *Mem:* Asn Med Illusr; Am Asn Univ Prof. *Publ:* Illustrator for medical textbooks and journals; Max Brôdel: The Man Who Put Art into Medicine, Springer/Verlag. *Mailing Add:* 3926 Cloverhill Rd Baltimore MD 21218-1707

CROSMAN, CHRISTOPHER BYRON
MUSEUM DIRECTOR, WRITER
b Chicago, Ill, June 25, 46. *Study:* Washington & Lee Univ, BA, 68; Oberlin Col, 70-72. *Collection Arranged:* Painterly Panels: Jonathan Santlofer & Arlene Slavin; James Brooks: 25 Years of Work, 63-88; An Eye For Adornment; Shared Visions: American Landscapes; Voyages of the Modern Imagination; By Land and Sea: Selected Works from the Collection of Andrew & Betsy Wyeth; and others. *Pos:* Cur educ, Albright-Knox Art Gallery, 80-84; peer rev panel, NY State Coun Arts, 82-84; dir, Heckscher Mus, 84-88 & Farnsworth Libr & Art Mus, 88-; field revs (reader), Inst Mus Servs, 85-86 & 92-93; chmn, Maine Arts Comn, 95-; reviewer, Am Asn Mus & Mapi, 96. *Teaching:* Instr art hist, Empire State Col, Buffalo, NY, 79-81. *Mem:* Am Asn Mus, Maine League Hist Soc and Mus, Rotary. *Publ:* Exhib catalogs & video interviews with artists; Co-auth: From Mus, Libraries and Galleries: Artists on Tape, 1984; contribr articles to prof jours.; co-prod, video documentaries, 1974-84; cur exhib. *Mailing Add:* Farnsworth Art Mus 16 Mus St Rockland ME 04841-0466

CROSS, YVONNE
SCULPTOR, PAINTER
Study: Acad di Belli Arti, Florence, Italy, MFA, 1978; various additional studies throughout Italy, France & US, 1970-94. *Exhib:* Solo-exhibs, Gallery Juarez, Los Angeles, 82, Gallery Juarez, Palm Desert, 83, 44 Wilshire Gallery, Beverly Hills, 84-88, Pacific Design Ctr, Calif, 86 & Cross Art Gallery, Beverly Hills, 94-97, others; IV Bienal de Escultura, Portugal, 91; Touchables, Ga Tech Univ Gallery, Atlanta, 92; 1st Ann Art in Park Show, West Hollywood, Calif, 93; 20 Yrs Retrospect 1974-1994, Cross Art Gallery Exhib, Beverly Hills, Calif, 95; Les Oubliees d'Avignon, France, 1993. *Collection Arranged:* Embassy Collections, US Dept State, Washington, DC; Materials Res Collection, Pa State Univ, State College, Pa; Cedars-Sinai Med Ctr, LA, Calif; Nat Found for Prevention of Cancer, Denver, Colo; St James Episcopal Sch, LA, Calif. *Media:* Sculpture - All Media, Painting - Oil. *Interests:* Music composition and composing, antiques. *Mailing Add:* PO Box 752 Beverly Hills CA 90209-5752

CROSSGROVE, ROGER LYNN
PRINTMAKER, EDUCATOR
b Farnam, Nebr, Nov 17, 21. *Study:* Kearney State Col; Univ Nebr, BFA; Univ Ill, MFA; Univ Michoacan, Mex. *Work:* Butler Inst Am Art, Youngstown, Ohio; Montclair Art Mus, NJ; Des Moines Art Ctr, Iowa; New Britain Mus Am Art; Inst Mex-Norteamericano Relac Cult, Mexico City. *Exhib:* Whitney Mus Am Art, NY, 56; Pa Acad Fine Arts, Philadelphia, 64; Audubon Artists, NY, 68; Conn Watercolor Soc, Wadsworth Atheneum, Hartford, Conn, 70; Monotypes, Pratt Graphics Ctr, NY, 72; New Am Monotypes, SITES, 78; William Benton Mus Art, Storrs, Conn, 91. *Pos:* Contribr & ed, Artists Proof, 67-68. *Teaching:* Prof art & assoc chmn dept graphic arts, Pratt Inst, 52-68; prof art, Univ Conn, 68-88, prof emer, 88. *Awards:* Emily Lowe Award, 51; Gold Medal, Nat Arts Club, 67; Am Watercolor Soc Award, 64 & 67. *Bibliog:* Henry N Rasmusen (auth), Printmaking with Monotype, Chilton, 60; Joann Moser (auth), Singular Impressions: The Monotype in America, Smithsonian Inst Press, Washington, 97; Phil Braham (auth), Exposed/Naked Men, Thunder's Mouth Press, 2000; David Leddick (auth), Male Nude Now, Univers, 2001. *Mem:* Conn Acad Fine Arts; Conn Watercolor Soc; Artworks Gallery, Hartford, Conn. *Media:* Monotype, Photography. *Res:* Monotype in Am. *Collection:* Mex graphic art, Taller de Grafica popular, Alfredo Zalce and Jean Charlot. *Publ:* Contribr, Paperbound Books in Print, 63. *Mailing Add:* 362 Gurleyville Rd Storrs CT 06268

CROTTO, PAUL
PAINTER, SCULPTOR
b New York, NY, Oct 24, 22. *Study:* Art Students League; Beaux-Arts, Florence, Italy; also with Fernand Leger, Paris. *Work:* Villeneuve-sur-Lot Mus, France; Mus Art Int, San Francisco; Galerie Grave, Munich, Ger. *Comn:* Portraits, LE Kaplan, NY & Robert Aries, Paris. *Exhib:* Mostra Artisti Am, Florence, 51; Mostra Int, Bordighera, Italy, 53; Am Painters in France, Galerie Craven, Paris, 53; Salon Automne, Paris, 56; Salon Comparaisons, Mus Mod Art, Paris, 68. *Awards:* Prix Int de Peinture, Villeneuve-sur-Lot, 63. *Bibliog:* T Ehrenmark (auth), American Artist in Sweden, Dagens Nyheter, 63; A Blasco Ibanez (auth), American artist in Paris, Los Angeles Herald Examiner, 68; Betty Werther (auth), Art, Time-Life, Paris, 69. *Mem:* Soc Coop Entre Aide Artistes. *Media:* Oil; All. *Mailing Add:* 19 Rue Cauchois Paris F-75018 France

CROUCH, NED PHILBRICK
SCULPTOR, CURATOR
b Nashville, Tenn, Mar 14, 48. *Study:* Austin Peay State Univ, Clarksville, Tenn, BS(art), 72; Cranbrook Acad Art, Bloomfield Hills, Mich, MFA(sculpture), 74. *Work:* Tenn Fine Arts Comn, Nashville; Cheekwood Fine Arts Ctr, Nashville; Ark Arts Ctr, Little Rock; Montgomery Bell Acad, Nashville; Austin Peay State Univ, Clarksville. *Exhib:* Mich II, Flint Inst Arts, Flint, Mich, 74; Mid-South Biennial, Brooks Mem Art Gallery, Memphis, Tenn, 75; Artists Biennial, New Orleans Mus Art, 75; Nat Sculpture USA, Huntsville Mus Art, Ala, 75; 18th Ann Delta Exhib, Ark Arts Ctr, Little Rock, 75; Tenn Bicentennial, Brooks Mem Art Gallery, Memphis, 76; Invitational, Southeastern Ctr Contemp Art, Winston-Salem, NC, 77. *Pos:* Guest cur, Am Folk-Exhib of 20th Century Quilts, Drawings & Sculpture, Vanderbilt Univ, Nashville, 76-; consult spec proj, Cheekwood Fine Arts Ctr, Nashville, 77-. *Teaching:* Instr sculpture, Austin Peay State Univ, Clarksville, 74-75. *Awards:* Hon Mention, Delta Exhib & Purchase Award, Toys by Artists, 75, Ark Arts Ctr, Little Rock; Purchase Award, Tenn Bicentennial, Tenn Fine Arts Comn, 76. *Mem:* Col Art Asn Am; Midwest Regional Conservation Guild. *Media:* Welded Steel, Wood. *Mailing Add:* 114 E Glenwood Dr Clarksville TN 37040-3553

CROUSE, MICHAEL GLENN
EDUCATOR, PRINTMAKER
b Grand Rapids, Mich, June 20, 49. *Study:* Kendall Sch Design, Grand Rapids, dipl, 70; Atlanta Col Art, BFA, 77; Univ Mich, Ann Arbor, MFA, 79. *Work:* Ga Dept Educ, Atlanta; Huntsville Mus Art. *Exhib:* Serial Imagery, Huntsville Mus Art, Ala, 82; Southeastern Graphics Int, Mint Mus Art, 82; Wesleyan Second Int Exhib Prints & Drawings, Macon Mus Arts & Sci, Ga, 82; Ninth Int Miniature Print Competition, Pratt Graphics Ctr, NY, 83; Second Int Miniature Print Exhib, Space Group Seoul, SKorea, 83; Red Clay V, Huntsville Mus Art, Ala, 83. *Teaching:* Instr art, Ill Col, 79-80; asst prof printmaking, Univ Ala, Huntsville, 80-. *Awards:* Charles Brand Machinery, Pratt Graphics Ctr Int Miniature Print Competition, 79; Purchase Award, LaGrange Nat VI, LaGrange Col, 81 & 24th NDak Print & Drawing Show, Univ NDak, 81. *Mem:* Col Art Asn; Southeastern Col Art Conf. *Media:* Mixed Media. *Dealer:* Absteins Gallery Art & Framing 1139 Spring St Atlanta GA 30309. *Mailing Add:* 133 Oakcrest Rd Huntsville AL 35811-9057

CROVELLO, WILLIAM
SCULPTOR
b NY City, 1929. *Study:* Studied at RI Sch Design, Art Students' League, Columbia Univ. *Work:* Cube Curved, Time Life Bldg, NY; Sense, Pier 86, NY; Pleiade and Argo, Park Ave Plaza, NY; Katana, Pepsi Co Sculpture Park, Purchase, NY. *Exhib:* Palazzo Vecchio, Florence, Italy; Passedoit Gallery; AM Sachs Gallery; Jack Gallery; Condeso/Lawler Gallery; Carnegie Int; Tokyo Mus; Hermitage Mus; Malmo Kunsthalle, Sweden; NC Mus; Babcock Galleries; represented in permanent collections of Ghent Mus Art, Belgium, Malmo Kunstall, Sweden, NC Mus Art, Raleigh, Sangre de Christo Mus Art, Pueblo, Colorado, Univ Houston, Tex, Wadsworth Athenaeum

CROWLEY, CHARLES A
CRAFTSMAN
b Baltimore, Md, Oct 8, 58. *Study:* Mass Col Art, Boston, studied welding techniques, 83; Boston Univ, BFA(metalsmithing), 84. *Exhib:* Sculptural Objects, Wetsman Collection, Birmingham, Miss, 92; Celebration of Excellence, Soc Arts & Crafts, Boston, 93; Vessels Invitational, Iowa State Univ, 93; Metals Invitational 1994, Univ Akron, Ohio, 94; Don Brecker Gallery, Miami Beach, Fla, 94. *Teaching:* Instr metalsmithing, Brookline Ctr Adult Educ, 88-89; Lexington Ctr Arts & Crafts, 88-92; continuing educ instr metals, Mass Col Art, 89-92. *Awards:* Fel, Mass Coun Arts, 86; First Prize, Fortunoff Sterling Silver Design Competition, NY, 90; Fel, Nat Endowment Arts. *Media:* Metal. *Dealer:* Jan Wetsman Brimingham MI. *Mailing Add:* 6 Eveleth Rd Gloucester MA 01930

CROWN, KEITH ALLEN
PAINTER
b Keokuk, Iowa, May 27, 1918. *Study:* Art Inst Chicago, 36-40, 45-46, BFA, 46. *Work:* Phillips Collection, Washington, DC; Springfield Mus, Mo; Univ Tex Art Mus, Austin; Crain Collection, Laguna Beach, Calif; Brown Univ Libr Military Collection. *Exhib:* California Artists, Witte Mus, San Antonio, Tex, 65; Painting as Painting, Univ Tex Art Mus, Austin, 68; Lyric View, Lang Gallery, Scripps Col, 74; Looking at a Strange Land, Mus Fine Arts, Santa Fe, NMex, 77; one-man shows, Drawings from World War II, AIC, 1944, MH de Young Mus, San Francisco, Calif, 1947, Pasadena Mus Art, Calif, 1953, Drawings from World War II, Los Angeles Co Mus, Calif, 1953Long Beach Mus Art, Calif, 1966, Ariz State Univ Mus Art, Tempe, 78, Univ Utah Mus Art, Salt Lake City, 78, Va Polytech Inst & State Univ & Univ Ariz Mus Art, Tucson; Retrospectives, Los Angeles Municipal Art Gallery, 87; Palos Verdes Art Ctr, Calif, 88; Fine Arts Gallery, Riley Mus, Kans State Univ, Manhattan, 89; Columbia Col Retrospective, 2000; William Woods Univ, Fulton, Mo, 2001; New Directions Gallery, Taos, NMex, 2001; Gene Crain Collection, Laguna Art Mus, 2002. *Teaching:* Prof painting & drawing, Univ Southern Calif, 46-83, prof emer, 83-; prof painting, Univ Ill, 70-71 & 77-78 & Univ NC, 79. *Awards:* Purchase Awards, Nat Watercolor Soc, 60, 63 & 71; Purchase Award, Watercolor USA, Springfield Mus, Mo, 1974; Distinguished Lifetime Achievement Award Watercolor USA Honor Soc, 2003. *Bibliog:* Article, Am Artist Mag, Fall 78; Sheldon Reich (auth), Keith Crown Watercolors, Univ Mo Press, 86. *Mem:* Artists Equity Asn (LA bd dir, 49-50); Nat Watercolor Soc (vpres, 58, pres, 59); Watercolor USA Honor Soc. *Media:* Watercolor, Oil. *Publ:* Contribr, Content of Watercolor, Van Nostrand Reinhold; Master Class in Watercolor, 75, Mastering Color and Design in Watercolor, 80 & Watercolor Bold and Free, 81, Watson-Guptill; Cover, Watercolor of the Huntington Libr, San Marino, Calif for Am Libr Mag bicentennial issue, 76. *Dealer:* Gallery A Taos NMex 87571. *Mailing Add:* 819 Edgewood Ave Columbia MO 65203

CROWN, ROBERTA LILA
PAINTER, CONCEPTUAL ARTIST
b New York, NY. *Study:* Queens Col, MA, 70. *Exhib:* Best Ann, Queens Mus, Flushing, NY, 89; solo exhib, Queens Col Art Ctr, Flushing, NY, 89; A Salute to Women, Nat Mus Women Arts, Washington, DC, 91; Schering Plough Gallery, 95; Chubb Gallery, 97; Solo exhib, Uniproperty Gallery, NY, 98; Canajoharie Mus NY, 2000; Jamison-Carnegie Heritage Hall Mus, Ala, 2001; Cornell Medical Gallery, NY, 2002; Citicorp Gallery, NY, 2003; Pace Univ, NY, 2003; Queen Col Art Ctr, Flushing, NY, 2005; Broome Street Gallery, NY, 2005. *Pos:* Exec coordr, Women Arts Found Inc, 80-2002. *Teaching:* Fine arts, Corlears JHS, 56 & 69-95. *Awards:* Mary K Karasick Mem Award, 91 & Leila Sawyer Mem Award, 92, Nat Asn Women Artists. *Mem:* Women in the Arts Found, Inc (exec coordr, 80-); Women's Caucus Art; Artists Equity; Nat Women's Asn Women Artists. *Media:* Oil on Canvas, Acrylic on Canvas. *Interests:* Travel. *Publ:* Contribr, Triangle Annual, Triangle, 87; IBM Nachrichton-Excellence, IBM, 89. *Mailing Add:* 1175 York Ave New York NY 10021

CROZIER, RICHARD LEWIS
PAINTER, EDUCATOR
b Honolulu, Hawaii, Dec 28, 44. *Study:* Univ Wash, Seattle, BFA (painting), 68; Univ Calif, Davis, with Wayne Thiebaud, MFA (painting) 74. *Work:* J B Speed Mus, Louisville, Ky; Am Embassy, Zaire; Greenville Art Mus, NC. *Comn:* Paintings Juvenile Court Bldg, Charlottesville-Albemarle Comt Arts, Va, 80-81; Cover, Am Libr Asn J, Chicago, 75; painting, Brown-Forman Corp, Louisville, 91. *Exhib:* Maier Mus, Lynchberg, Va, Mt Holyoke Mus, South Hadley, Mass; Arts Club of Wash, DC, 2004; Pence Gallery, Davis, Calif, 2005. *Teaching:* Prof studio art, Univ Va, 74-. *Awards:* Purchase Award, Southeastern Ctr Contemp Art, 77. *Bibliog:* John Arthur (auth), Spirit of Place, Bulfinch, 89; R Crozier & Thomas Bolt (coauths), Inventing the Landscape, Watson Guptill, 89; Green Woods and Crystal Waters, John Arthur (auth), Philbrook Mus of Art, Tulsa, Okla, 99; Kelly and Rasmussen (auths), The Virginia Landscape, Howell Press, 2000; Marianne Doezema (auth), Changing Prospects, Cornell Univ Press, 2002. *Media:* Oil. *Dealer:* Reynolds Gallery 1514 West Main St Richmond VA 23220. *Mailing Add:* 624 Preston Pl Charlottesville VA 22903

CRUM, DAVID
PAINTER
b Peoria, Ill, Dec 6, 38. *Study:* Independently with John Chamberlain. *Work:* Long Beach Mus, Calif; Baruch Col Gallery, NY; Mills Col Art Mus, Calif. *Exhib:* Newport Beach Mus, Calif, 66; Paintings on Paper, Glassboro Col Gallery, NJ, 72; Recent Acquisitions, Aldrich Mus, Ridgefield, Conn, 74; New Directions in Contemp Art, Santa Barbara, Calif, 82; Bank Am World Hq, San Francisco. *Teaching:* Vis assoc prof painting, La State Univ, 84. *Bibliog:* Peter Frank (auth), article, Soho Weekly News, 76; Sam Hunter (auth), New Directions in Contemporary Art, Princeton, NJ, 81; Judith Stern (producer), Fresh air, Nat Pub Radio, 81. *Mem:* Nat Arts Club. *Media:* Acrylic. *Dealer:* Frederich Spratt San Jose CA. *Mailing Add:* 5327 Fairfax Ave Oakland CA 94601

CRUM, KATHERINE B
MUSEUM DIRECTOR, EDUCATOR
b Palo Alto, Calif, Dec 10, 41. *Study:* Stanford Univ, BA, 62, MA, 64; Hunter Col, NY, MA (art hist), 74; Columbia Univ, PhD (art hist), 84. *Collection Arranged:* Richards Ruben & Michael Goldberg, 84, George Mayocole, Lynn Mayocole & Bill Taggart, 84, Color Abstraction in the 1980's, 85, Figurative Art of the New York School, 85, Women Artists of the Surrealist Movement, 86, Bradley Walker Tomlin, 89, Baruch Col Gallery, City Univ New York & Clyde Connell, Mills Col Art Gallery, 92; Ron Nagle: A Survey Exhibition, 93; Wally Hedrick on Love and Art, 93; Luis Cruz Pizaseta: Dislocations, 94; No Two Alike!, The Ceramic Art of George E Ohr, 2000; plus others. *Pos:* Dealer & owner, Nicholas Wilder Gallery, Los Angeles, 64-69; cur exhibs, Inst Res Hist, New York, 80-83; dir, Baruch Col Gallery, City Univ New York, 83-89 & Mills Col Art Mus, Oakland, Calif, 91-. *Teaching:* Adj asst prof art hist, Baruch Col, City Univ New York, 74-89. *Mem:* Col Art Asn; Am Asn Mus. *Res:* 20th century art; 13th & 14th century Italian painting. *Publ:* Ed, Places of Origin, Inst Res Hist, 80; contribr, Western Civilization, Houghton Mifflin, 81; auth, The Cudner-Hyatt House, Scarsdale Hist Soc, 82; Figural Art of the New York School, Baruch Col, 85. *Mailing Add:* c/o Mills Col Art Gallery 5000 MacArthur Blvd Oakland CA 94613

CRUMP, WALTER MOORE, JR
PRINTMAKER, PAINTER
b Winston-Salem, NC, Mar 18, 41. *Study:* Gilford Col, NC, 61-64; Harvard Univ Exten, 64-66; Boston Univ, BFA, 70. *Work:* DeCordova Mus, Lincoln, Mass; Philadelphia Mus Art; Nat Mus Am Art, Smithsonian Inst; Libr Congress Print Collection; NC Mus Art, Raleigh; NY Pub Libr; Citicorp World HQ; RJ Reynolds World HQ. *Exhib:* Davidson Nat Drawing & Print Exhib, NC, 73; Color Print USA, Tex Tech Univ, Lubbock, 75; Artists Under 36, DeCordova Mus, 76; Int Miniature Print Exhib, Pratt Graphics Ctr, NY, 77; Boston Printmakers Nat Exhib, Mus Fine Arts, Boston, 75-88 & DeCordova Mus, 77 & 79; Korean Exchange Print Exhib, Seoul, 78; Silvermine Nat Print Exhib, New Canaan, Conn, 78, 80 & 83; one-man shows, Plum Gallery, Washington, DC, 80, 82 & 88; Tacer Gallery Tort, Spain, 85; Wauz Gallery, 86 & 87. *Teaching:* Chmn art dept & instr printmaking, Commonwealth Sch, Boston, 72-; lectr & slide presentations, DeCordova Mus, 78 & Nat Collection of Fine Arts, Washington, DC, 79. *Awards:* Purchase Prize & First Prize, Dulin Nat Print & Drawing Competition, Knoxville, Tenn, 78 & 79; A P Hanks Mem Purchase Prize, Print Club Int Biennial, Philadelphia, 79; Purchase Prize, Boston Printmakers Exhib, 76-79. *Mem:* Boston Visual Artists Union; Boston Printmakers. *Media:* Intaglio; Oil. *Mailing Add:* 516 E Second St Boston MA 02127-1463

CRUMPLER, DEWEY
PAINTER, MURALIST
Study: San Francisco Art Inst, BFA; San Francisco State Univ, MA; Mills Col, MFA. *Work:* Western Addition Cult Ctr; San Francisco Mus Mod Art; Calif Hist Soc; Joseph Lee Recreation Ctr. *Exhib:* Corcoran Gallery Art, Washington; Univ Hawaii; San Jose Mus Art; Galerie Resche, Paris. *Pos:* Adv bd, San Francisco Art Comn Gallery. *Teaching:* Calif Col Arts & Crafts, San Francisco State Univ, Stanford Univ & Univ Calif, Berkeley; assoc prof painting & drawing, San Francisco Art Inst, 90-; lectured at numerous cols & universities throughout the US. *Awards:* Outstanding Achievement Award, Nat Artists' Conf; Eureka Fel Award Painting, 93; Nat Endowment Arts Award, 95. *Dealer:* Porter Troupe Gallery 301 Spruce St San Diego CA 92103. *Mailing Add:* 1095 Siler Pl Berkeley CA 94705-1536

CRYSTAL, BORIS
PAINTER
b Poland, Dec 25, 31; US citizen. *Study:* Plocer's Sch Fine Arts, 62-63; Acad Fine Arts, Israel, 63-64. *Work:* Israel Mus, Tel-Aviv; Journalist House Art Gallery, Tel-Aviv; Herzl Inst, NY; Nicholas Roerich Mus, NY; Mus Mod Art, NY; and numerous other mus. *Exhib:* Journalist House Art Gallery, Tel-Aviv, 66; Herzl Inst Art Gallery, NY, 68; Nicholas Roerich Mus, NY, 70; Mus Mod Art, NY, 72; Lerner Art Gallery, NY, 75; La Galerie Mouffe, Paris, France, 77; and numerous others. *Collection Arranged:* Herzl Int Exhib USA, 65; Human Relations Coun in Coop with Art League USA, 68; Int Group Exhib of Paintings, Sculpture & Graphics, New Haven, Conn, 71. *Awards:* Int Award, Crown Art Gallery, 71; Vallombreuse Prize, Biarritz, France, 76; Gold Medal, Acad Italia, 80. *Bibliog:* Max Founry (auth), article, Art News, 69. *Mem:* Artists Equity Asn; Art League NY. *Media:* Oil, Watercolor. *Dealer:* Ella Lerner 241 E 76th St New York NY 10021

CUCULLU, SANTIAGO
PAINTER
b Buenos Aires, Argentina, 69. *Study:* Hartford Art Sch, BFA, 92; Minneapoplis Col Art & Design, MFA, 99. *Work:* Mus Contemp Art, NY, 2003, Works on Paper, Blum & Poe Gallery, Los Angeles, 2003, How Latitudes Become Forms, Walker Art Ctr, Minneapolis, 2004, Whitney Biennial, Whitney Mus Am Art, 2004, Mori Art Mus, Tokyo, 2004, Hammer Mus, Los Angeles, 2004. *Exhib:* One-man shows, Boom Gallery, Minneapolis, 99, Art Houston, Barbara Davis Gallery, Houston, 2002, Wiyya To Hell Owwa That, Julia Friedman Gallery, Chicago, 2003, Art Basel Miami: Art Statements, Barbara Davis Gallery, Houston, 2003, Arco: Madrid Project Room, Julia Friedman Gallery, Chicago, 2004, Works on Paper, Blum & Poe Gallery, Los Angeles, 2003, How Latitudes Become Forms, Walker Art Ctr, Minneapolis, 2004, Delectable Reason of Sleeps, Perry Rubenstein Gallery, NY, 2005; group shows, Esacio de Pensamiento, Bueno Aires, Argentina, 95, Dumb & Evil, Calhoun Sq Gallery, Minneapolis, 98, Push, Pull Pop, 99, XL, Weinstein Gallery, Minneapolis, 2000, 13 From Minneapolis, Minneapolis, 2002, Fresh-The Altoids Collection, 2003, Fiction: Truth in Photography and Painting, Timothy Taylor Gallery, London, 2004, How Would You Light Heaven, Carlier I Gebauer, Berlin, 2004, How Latitudes Become Forms: Art in a Global Age, Contemporary Art Mus, Houston, 2004, Wanderlust, Julia Friedman Gallery, NY, 2005, Sticks and Stones, Perry Rubenstein Gallery, NY, 2005, Singapore Biennale, 2006, Archipeinture, Camden Arts Centre, London, 2006. *Awards:* Jerome Emerging Artist Fel, Minneapolis Coll Art & Design, 2000. *Mailing Add:* c/o Perry Rubenstein Gallery 527 West 23rd St New York NY 10011

CUEVAS, JOSE LUIS
DRAFTSMAN
b Mexico City, Mex, Feb 26, 34. *Study:* Sch Painting & Sculpture (La Esmeralda, Inst Nac Bellas Artes), Mexico City. *Work:* Mus Mod Art & Solomon R Guggenheim Mus, NY; Brooklyn Mus, NY; Mus of Albi & Lyons, France; Metrop Mus Art, NY. *Exhib:* Biennial Venize, Italy, 72; Palais Beaux Arts, Brussels, Belg, 74; Warsaw Gallery, Poland, 75; Ludwig Mus, Cologne, Ger, 78; Mus Mod Art, Mexico City, 79; World Print Awards, San Francisco Mus Art, 83; Frederick S Wight Art Gallery of UCLA, 84; Mus Mod Art, Mexico City, 85; Musee d'Art Moderne de Liege, Belgium, 86; Alvar Alto Mus, Helsinki, Finland, 86; Pinacoteque Nationale Musee Alexandre Soutzos, Athens, Greece, 87; Orangerie Palais Auersperg, Vienna, Austria, 87. *Teaching:* Resident artist, Philadelphia Mus Sch Art, 57; lectr art, San Jose State Col, 70, Fullerton Col, 75 & Wash State Univ, 75. *Awards:* First Int Prize for Drawing, V Biennial of Sao Paulo, Brazil, 59; First Int Award, Mostra Bianco e Nero, 62; Award Excellence, 29th Ann Exhib, Art Dir Club, Philadelphia, 83. *Bibliog:* Carlos Fuentes (auth), Los mundos de Jose Luis Cuevas, Misrachi Gallery, Mexico City, 70; Daisy Ascher (auth), Revelando a Jose Luis Cuevas, Madero, Mex, 79; J B Ponce (auth), Jose Luis Cuevas: Genio O Farsante?, Ed Signos, 83; J M Tasende (auth), Tasende Gallery - 1982, La Jolla, Calif, 82. *Publ:* Illusr, Crime by Cuevas, Lublin Ed, 68; Homage to Quevedo, 69 & Cuevas Comedies, 71, Collectors Press; Roberto Sanesi, Jose Luis Cuevas, Centro Arte/Zarathustra, Milano, Italy, 78; J M Tasende, Jose Luis Cuevas Letters, 82, Peter Selz, Intolerance, 83 & J M Tasende, Twenty five years with Jose Luis Cuevas, La Jolla, Calif, 92, Tasende Gallery; Carlos Fuentes, The Buried Mirror, Houghton Mifflin, NY, 92. *Mailing Add:* c/o Tasende Gallery 820 Prospect St La Jolla CA 92037

CULBERTSON, JANET LYNN (MRS DOUGLAS KAFTEN)
PAINTER, ENVIRONMENTAL ARTIST
b Greensburg, Pa, Mar 15, 32. *Study:* Carnegie Inst Technol, BFA, 53; Art Students League, 54; NY Univ, MA, 63; Pratt Graphic Arts Inst, 64-65. *Work:* Nat Mus Women Arts, Washington, DC; State Mus Harrisburg, Pa; St Petersburg Mus Art, Fla; Heckscher Mus, Huntington, NY; Stone Quarry Hill Art Park, Cazenovia, NY; and others. *Exhib:* One-woman shows, Lerner-Heller Gallery, NY, 71-73 & 75- 77, Benson Gallery, Bridgehampton, NY, 78, 81, 83, & 89, Nardin Gallery, NY, 81, Stone Quarry

Hill Art Park, Cazenovia, NY, 96, Suffolk Col, Riverhead, NY, 96, Atelier A/E, NY, 97, Univ Alaska, Anchorage, 97 & Nat Acad Sci, Washington, DC, 98, Huntington Arts Coun Gallery, NY, 2002, Earth First, Univ of Nebr, Omaha, 2002, Cambridge Arts Ctr, Mass, 2003; Guild Hall Mus Invitational, E Hampton, NY, 89; Islip Mus, NY, 90 & 92; C W Post Hillwood Mus, Brookville, NY, 90 & 94; Acme Art Co, Columbus, Ohio, 91; Babcock Traveling Exhib, 93-94; Anita Shapkolsky Gallery, NY, 95; Listening to the Earth, Hamilton Univ, Clinton, NY, 95; Rediscovering the Landscape of the Americas (traveling exhib), Gerald Peters Gallery, NMex, 96-98; Women Realists, Ringling Sch Art & Design, Sarasota, Fla, 97; Univ Bridgeport, Conn, 99; What on Earth (8 works), Earth 2000, Univ of Miami, Fla, 2002, 20 Industrial Park Works, Wave Hill, Bronx, NY, 98; Toxic Landscapes traveling exhib, Puffin Found, 2002; National Mus of Women in the Arts, Wahington, DC, 2004; Cent Col, Ohio, 2005; Antioch Col, Ohio, 2005; Seton Hill Univ, Gettysburg, Pa, 2006. *Teaching:* Instr art, Pace Col, 64-68; adj prof, Pratt Art Inst, 73-74 & Southampton Col, NY, 76 11/9/80 & 5/20/90. *Awards:* Creative Artists Pub Serv Award, Graphics, NY, 89; First Prize & Mus Grant, Hillwood Art Mus, New York, 94; Purchase Award, Hoyt Mus, 95; Purchase Award, Nassau Co Mus, NY, 97; New York East End Arts Coun Grant, 2002-03; Ludwig Vogelstein Grant, 2003. *Bibliog:* Jenni Schlossman (auth), Political Landscapes, Women's Art J, 93; and others, Rose Silvka, East Hampton Star, 5/26/94; Helen A Harrison (auth), NY Times, 3/96; Phyllis Braff (auth), NY Times, 89, 93, 95, 2000. *Mem:* Womens Caucus Art; Artists Equity; Greenpeace; Sierra Club; Earthwatch; Art Alliance of East Hampton. *Media:* Acrylic, Oil, Mixed media. *Interests:* Birds, Music. *Collection:* National Mus of Women in the Arts, Washington, DC; Foog Museum, MA; St. Petersburg Mus, FL; Telfair Mus, GA; Nat Acad Sciences, Washington, DC. *Publ:* Auth, articles in Feminism and Ecology, 81; article in Women Artists Newsletter; article in Terra Nova, 4/89; article, in Gallerie, Vol 8, 90. *Mailing Add:* 46 Hilo Dr PO Box 455 Shelter Island Heights NY 11965

CULBRETH, CARL R
SCULPTOR
b Mineola, NY, Dec 2, 52. *Study:* Nassau Community Col, AA (studio art), 73; Univ Vt, BS (art educ), 75; Univ Del, MFA (ceramic sculpture), 79. *Work:* Syracuse Univ; Roberson Ctr Arts & Sci, Binghamton, NY. *Exhib:* Ten Artists Under 30, Fine Arts Mus Long Island, Hempstead, NY, 81; Wards Island Sculpture Site, NY, 81; Brooklyn Mus, NY, 81; East Coast Clay, Sculpture Ctr, NY, 82; The Figure: New Form, New Function, Arrowmont Sch Gallery, Gatlinburg, Tenn, 83; Ancient Inspirations, Contemp Interpretations, NY State Mus, Albany, 83; Three Dimentions, Univ Tex, El Paso. *Pos:* Resident ceramist & gallery dir, Clayworks Studio Workshop, New York, 79-80; dept head, Terra Cotta, MJM Studios, Hoboken, NJ, 85-. *Teaching:* Adj assoc prof art, Long Island Univ, 80-85; coordr ceramics prog, Parsons Sch Design, 80-84. *Bibliog:* Donna Harkavay (auth), article, Am Ceramics, 8/82; Martin Ries (auth), article, Re-Dact, 11/83. *Mem:* Am Crafts Coun; Nat Coun Educ Ceramic Arts; Col Art Asn. *Media:* Clay. *Mailing Add:* 189 Upper Mountain Ave Montclair NJ 07042-1905

CULLIGAN, JENINE ELIZABETH
CURATOR, ADMIN
b Lexington, Ky, Dec 15, 59. *Study:* Univ Kentucky, Lexington, KY, BA, 84; Case Western Reserve Univ, Cleveland, OH, MA, 87. *Collection Arranged:* Toulouse-Lautrec to Picasso-Master Prints from Watercolor, Switzerland, 95; Edward L Edwan Sr, From the Prism's Edge, 96; The Face of Justice: Portraits of John Marshall, 2001; A Grand Term: Over Here, Over There, Prints from Daywood Coll, 2002; Through American Eyes: Two Hundred Yrs of Am Art, 2003; Winslow Anderson Coll Haitian Art, 2004; Never Done: Works By Women Artists from the Puzzudo Miller Collection, 2006. *Pos:* Asst Educ Coordr, Univ Kentucky Art Mus, Lexingon, KY, 87-88; Assoc Cur, Delaware Art Mus, Wilmington, DE, 88-96; Sr Cur, Huntington Mus Art, Huntington, WV, 99-. *Awards:* Anne Worthington Callahan Award, Univ Ky, 84; Stone Fel, Case Western Reserve Univ, 85; AAM Cur Travel Stipend Award, AAM, 90. *Mem:* Am Asn Mus; Col Art Asn; Asn Art Mus Cur. *Res:* Generalist; America Art late 19th Century-Contemporary. *Publ:* Ed, John O'Kulick: Transformations in Perspective, Deleware Art Mus, 91; ed, Robert Stackhouse, Deleware Art Mus, 91; co-auth, Edward L Looper: From the Prism's Edge, Deleware Art Mus, 96; co-auth, Fifty years of Collecting Huntington Mus Art, 2001; co-auth, Through American Eyes, Huntington Mus Art, 2003. *Mailing Add:* Huntington Museum of Art 2033 McCoy Rd Huntington WV 25701-4999

CULLING, RICHARD EDWARD
PAINTER, COLLAGE ARTIST
b Detroit, Mich, Dec 5, 51. *Study:* Wayne State Univ, BFA, 74, Univ Mich Sch Art, MFA, 88. *Work:* Univ Mich Permanent Collection, Ann Arbor. *Exhib:* 11th Mich Biennial, Kresge Art Mus, E Lansing, 88; Figuring It Out, Calvin Col, Grand Rapids, Mich, 88; What's New in Art, Galesburg Civic Ctr, Ill, 88; Animal Art, United Auto Workers, Gen Motors Resource Bldg, Auburn Hills, Mich, 88; Two Person, Univ Mich, Flint, 88; A Matter of Painting, Detroit Focus, Mich, 88. *Teaching:* Instr painting, Univ Mich, 86-88; instr painting, Paint Creek Ctr Arts, 88. *Awards:* Artist Grant, Mich Coun Arts, 84; Guggenheim Award, 85; Res Fel Award, Univ Mich, 87. *Bibliog:* Marsho Miro (auth), 2 Artists find there's no place like home, Detroit Free Press, 1/16/83. *Mem:* Col Art Asn. *Media:* Oil. *Dealer:* Mary C Wright 568 N Woodward Birmingham Mich 48154. *Mailing Add:* 38798 Kingsbury Livonia MI 48154

CULVER, MARGARET VICTORIA
DIRECTOR, ARTIST
b Liverpool, Eng, Aug 31, 48. *Study:* Manchester Metropolitan Univ, BSc (graphic design), 1969. *Work:* Real Tart Gallery, New Plymouth, New Zealand; Hill Country Arts Found, Ingram, TX; Turchin Arts Ctr, Boone, NC; Public Gallery, Monmouth Medical Ctr, Long Branch, NJ; Monmouth Cty Clerks Offices, Freehold, NJ. *Comn:* Taunton School, Gail Jordan, Prin, Howell, NJ, 1992. *Exhib:* New Comers Exhib, City Without Walls, Newark, NJ, 1998; Botanical Awards, La Quinta Cult Ctr, Albuquerque, NMex, 2002; Focus on Sculpture, Grounds for Sculpture, Hamilton, NJ, 2005; 20th Ann Juried Show, Ocean Cty Artists Guild, Island Heights, NJ, 2006; 8th Int Collage Exchange, Real Tart Gallery, New Plymouth, New Zealand, 2006. *Collection Arranged:* The Art of Healing, NJ Ctr for Healing Arts, 2000; The Flower Show, Cork Gallery, Lincoln Ctr, 2002; 43rd Anniversary Exhibit, Guild at Monmouth Mus, 2003; Guild of Creative Art Exhibition Modern, Agriculture Bldg, 2005; Guild of Creative Art Bi-Monthly Exhibit, Monmouth Cty Clerk's Offices, 2006; 25th Congressional Art Competition, 12th Dist High School Awards, 2006. *Pos:* Exec dir, Guild of Creative Art, 2000-. *Awards:* Botanical Awards, Gallery Print, Wis, 2002; Art Alliance, Jean Townsend 18th Ann Juried Show, Art Alliance of Monmouth Cty, 2003; Judge's Award, Members Juried Show, Art Soc Monmouth Cty, 2005. *Bibliog:* Mitchell Seidel (auth), Some Assembly Required, Star Ledger, 4/1999; Anita Stratos (auth), Many Emotions Conveyed Through Art, Greater Media Newspapers, 6/2003; Shannon Mullen (auth), Releasing Memories, Asbury Park Press, 11/2005. *Mem:* Guild of Creative Art (dir 2000-); Art Alliance of Monmouth Cty (bd mem 1996-2000); Freehold Art Soc; Art Soc of Monmouth Cty; Shore Inst for the Contemporary Arts. *Media:* Collage Artist. *Dealer:* The Guild of Creative Art Rt 35 Shrewsbury NJ. *Mailing Add:* 39 Forrest Hill Dr Howell NJ 07731

CULVER, MICHAEL L
PAINTER, CURATOR
b Louisville, Ky, Sept 10, 47. *Study:* Univ Louisville, BA(sculpture), 72, MA(painting), 77 & PhD(art hist), 86. *Work:* Ogunquit Mus Am Art, Maine; Owensboro Mus Fine Art, Ky; Univ Louisville, Brown & Williams Tobacco Co & Humana Corp, Louisville, Ky; Kennebunk Savs Bank, Maine; RI Sch Design Mus Art. *Comn:* Poster & program cover, Louisville Ballet, 83. *Exhib:* Nat Arts Club Gallery, NY, 87; solo-exhibs, Headley-Whitney Mus, Lexington, Ky & Owensboro Mus Fine Arts, Ky, 88; Nat Show, Viridian Gallery, NY, 88; US State Dept Art In Embassies Prog, Indonesia, 92-; Ctr for Maine Contemp Art, Rockport, 2002; Unity Col Art Gallery, Maine, 2004. *Collection Arranged:* Painting & Drawing, 1985-2005; Dozier Bell Exhib, 91; Walt Kuhn: American Master, 92; The Art of Jack Levine, Ogunquit Mus Am Art, Maine, 92; Will Barnet: Works of six Decades (auth, catalog), 94; The Art of George Tooker, 96; Hughie Lee-Smith: A Retrospective, 97; Charles H Woodbury & His Students, 98; Painted Air: American Impressionism, 2000; Landscapes by Wolf Kahn, 2002; The Art of Janet Fish, 2004; The Figure in Am, 2006. *Pos:* Pres, Ky Art Educ Asn, 79; cur, Ogunquit Mus, Am Art, 83-, assoc dir, 95-2001, exec dir, curator, 2001-; chair, Maine Art Mus Trail Orgn, 2003. *Teaching:* Instr human Am studies, Univ Louisville, Ky, 81-82. *Awards:* Fulbright-Hayes Grant, 77; Grad Proj Award, Univ Louisville, 80, 82; Grad Dean's Fel, Univ Louisville, 81-83. *Media:* Acrylic. *Res:* Twentieth century American art. *Publ:* Auth, Examination of illustrations for pound's a draft of XVI Cantos, Paideuma J, Univ Maine, 83; Realistic art of Henry Strater (exhib catalog), Washington & Lee Univ, 86; Henry Strater an American original (exhib catalog), Owensboro Mus Fine Arts, 88; Charles H Woodbury and his Students, Am Art Review, 98; History of the Ogunquit Museum of American Art, Am Art Rev, 2000; exhib catalog, Landscapes by Wolf Kahn, 2002. *Dealer:* Mathias Fine Arts Trevett ME 04571; Swanson Reed Galleries 1377 Bardstown Rd Louisville KY 40204. *Mailing Add:* Shore Rd PO Box 815 Ogunquit ME 03907

CULVER, VICKY See Culver, Margaret Victoria

CUMMENS, LINDA TALABA See Talaba, L (Linda) Talaba Cummens

CUMMING, GLEN EDWARD
GALLERY DIRECTOR
b Calgary, Alta, Can, July 2, 36. *Study:* Alberta Col Art, 4 yr dipl. *Exhib:* Chris Dikeakos: Sites and Place Names, 98; Monument: William Eakin, 98; The Word in Contemp Canadian Art, 98. *Collection Arranged:* Images; Photo Works from the Mocca Collection, 2000. *Pos:* Cur, Regina Pub Libr Art Gallery, Sask, 67-69; dir, Kitchener-Waterloo Art Gallery, Kitchener, Ont, 69-72; dir, Robert McLaughlin Gallery, Oshawa, Ont, 72-73; dir, Art Gallery Hamilton, Ont, 73-89; dir, 49th Parallel Gallery, Contemp Can Art, 89-92; dir, Art Gallery North York, Ont, 93-95; dir, Mus Contemp Canadian Art, Toronto Ontario, 95-2000; dir, Art Gallery Windsor, Ontario, 2001-04. *Awards:* Queen Elizabeth Prize, 60; Alberta Visual Arts Bd Scholar, 60-62. *Mem:* Int Asn Art Critics; Int Couns Mus; Asn Art Mus Dirs (emeritus mem). *Specialty:* Canadian and International Art. *Publ:* Auth, Contemporary Art of Senegal, 79; Viewpoint: 29 by 9, 81; El Dorado, Gold from Ancient Colombia, 82; Living Imprssions, Contemp Can Graphics, 89; Walter Bachinski: Approaching Classicism, 91. *Mailing Add:* 3943 Riverside Dr East Windsor ON N8Y 1B1 Canada

CUMMING, ROBERT H
ARTIST, PHOTOGRAPHER
b Worcester, Mass, Oct 7, 43. *Study:* Mass Col Art, Boston, BA, 65; Univ Ill, Champaign, MFA, 67. *Work:* Mus Fine Arts, Houston; Mus Mod Art, NY. *Comn:* Outdoor sculpture, Walker Art Ctr, Minneapolis, Minn, 70; Nation's Capitol Documentation, Corcoran Gallery, Washington, DC. *Exhib:* Art by Telephone, Mus Contemp Art, Chicago, 69; 9 Artists-9 Spaces, Walker Art Ctr, Minneapolis, Minn, 70; 24 Young Los Angeles Artists, Los Angeles Co Mus, 71; Narrative Art, Palais des Beaux Arts, Brussels, Belg, 75; Whitney Biennial, NY, 77 & 81; Paris Biennale, Mus d'Art Mod, France, 77; Mirrors and Windows, Mus Mod Art, NY; and others. *Teaching:* Instr painting & drawing, Univ Wis, Milwaukee, 67-70; lectr photog,Univ Calif, Los Angeles, 74-. *Awards:* Frank Logan Prize, Chicago Art Inst, 69; Nat Endowment Arts Awards, 72, 74 & 83; Guggenheim Fel, 80. *Bibliog:* M Jochimsen (auth), Story Art, Mag Kunst, Mainz, Ger, 2/74; C Hagen (auth), Robert Cumming's

Subject-Object, Artforum, summer 83. *Media:* Multimedia. *Publ:* Auth, Picture Fictions, Anaheim, Calif, 71; The Weight of Franchise Meat, Anaheim, Calif, 71; A Training in the Arts, Toronto, Can, 73; A Discourse on Domestic Disorder, Irvine, Calif, 75; Equilibrium and the Rotary Disc, Meriden, Conn, 80. *Dealer:* The Print Club Ctr Prints & Photographs 1614 Latimer St Philadelphia PA 19103. *Mailing Add:* 342 Haydenville Rd Whately MA 01093

CUMMINGS, DAVID WILLIAM
PAINTER
b Okmulgee, Okla, July 15, 37. *Study:* Kansas City Art Inst, Mo, BFA, 63; Univ Nebr, Lincoln, MFA, 67. *Work:* Whitney Mus Am Art, NY; Los Angeles Co Mus Art, Calif; Phoenix Art Mus, Ariz; Mus Contemp Art, Antwerp, Belg; Aldrich Mus Contemp Art, Ridgefield, Conn; and others. *Exhib:* Lyrical Abstraction, Philadelphia Mus Art, Pa, 70 & Whitney Mus Am Art, 71; 20th Century Am Artists, Corcoran Gallery Art, Washington, DC, 71; Contemp Reflections, Aldrich Mus Contemp Art, 71-72; one-man shows, Allan Stone Gallery, NY, 74-77 & 82, Gallery Alexandra Monett, Bruxelles, Belg, 75, 77, 79 & 82, Ericson Gallery, NY, 80 & Shahin Requicha Gallery, Rochester, NY, 83, Gallery Jupiter, Little Silver, NJ, 87; AMB Galleries, Hoboken, 89; Cabrillo Col, Aptos, Calif, 91; Rabbet Gallery, New Brunswick, NY, 96; and others. *Pos:* Vis artist, Ohio State Univ, Columbus, 74, Univ Iowa, Iowa City, 76, Univ NDak, Grand Forks, 81, SUNY, Purchase, 84, Cabrilllo Col, Aptos, Calif, 91 & Ariz Western Univ, Yuma; coordr painting symposium, Colo Mountain Col, Vail, 76-78. *Teaching:* Instr, State Univ NY, 67-71; assoc prof, City Univ NY, 71-89; prof, St Peters Col, Jersey City, NJ, 85-2003, adj fac, Parsons Sch Design, NY. *Awards:* John Lehmann Award, St Louis Mus Art, Mo, 65; Woods Found Fel, Univ Nebr, 66-67; Painting Fels, NJ State Coun of the Arts, 85 & 91. *Bibliog:* Jacques Meuris (auth), David Cummings Plus Minus Zero, 11/79; Theodore F Wolff (auth), The Colorist's Art, The Christian Sci Monitor, 9/10/80; Susan Dodge Peters (auth), A master of color, Rochester City News, 4/28/83. *Media:* Oil, Pastel. *Dealer:* Rabbet Gallery 120 Georges Rd New Brunswick NJ 08901. *Mailing Add:* 106-108 Hopkins Ave Jersey City NJ 07306

CUMMINGS, MARY T
ADMINISTRATOR, CONSULTANT
b Minneapolis, Minn, May 22, 51. *Study:* Univ Minn, BA(art hist), 73; Univ Mich, MA(art hist), 76; Ind Univ, MA(arts admin), 81. *Pos:* Lectr, Minneapolis Inst Arts, 77-78; asst to dir, Tweed Mus, Duluth, Minn, 78-79; dir, Missoula Mus Arts, Mont, 81-89; assoc dir, Minn Mus Art, St Paul, 89-. *Teaching:* Instr art hist, Macalester Col, St Paul, 77-78 & Univ Minn, Duluth, 78-79; vis prof art hist, Univ Mont, Missoula, 88-. *Mem:* Am Asn Mus; Women Mus Dir & Admin Caucus; Mont Art Gallery Dir Asn (pres, 83-86); Asn for Asian Studies. *Res:* Impact of museums on small communities; approaching art and visual images for the layman; nature of museums; Asian art (various topics). *Publ:* Auth, The Lives of the Buddha in the Art and Literature of Asia, Univ Mich, 85; Asian Di-Visions: A Contrast Between China and Japan (exhib catalog), 82 & The Primal Plastic Pool: Contemporary Art of the West (exhib catalog), 85, Missoula Mus; The artist and the museum: Some mutual expectations, The Crafts Report, 86; On learning to look and the function of museums, Mus Studies J, 88. *Mailing Add:* 137 E Curtice Saint Paul MN 55107-3271

CUNINGHAM, ELIZABETH BAYARD (MRS E W R TEMPLETON)
ART DEALER
b New York, NY. *Study:* Bronxville Sch, NY; Vassar Col, Poughkeepsie, NY; Finch Col, NY, BA; Hunter Col, New York, MA(art hist). *Pos:* Exec secy, Olana Preserv Inc, New York, 65-66; dir publicity, Comt to Rescue Italian Art, New York, 66-67; asst to pres, Nat Trust for Hist Preserv, 68-70; asst dir, Reese Palley Art Gallery, New York, 70-72; pres, Cuningham Ward Inc, 72-78; Betty Cuningham Gallery, 78-82; Hirsch & Adler Modern, New York, 82-. *Mem:* Drawing Soc Inc (exec comt, 70-80); Art Dealers Asn, 79-81. *Specialty:* Contemporary painting. *Mailing Add:* 16 Studio Arcade Bronxville NY 10708

CUNNICK, GLORIA HELEN
PAINTER
b New York, NY. *Study:* Art Students League; New York Univ; Long Island Univ, CW Post, BFA, 87. *Work:* Fine Arts Mus Long Island, Hempsted, NY; Rutgers Univ, Zimmerli Art Mus; Pall Corp; Islip Mus, NY. *Comn:* Touched by Light, Unitarian Church. *Exhib:* Tex Nat 95, Nacogdoches, Tex, 95; Islip Mus, NY, 96; BJ Spoke Gallery, Huntington, NY, 96; Nat Asn Women Artists, Athens Cult Ctr, Greece, 96; and others. *Awards:* Winner, Fine Arts Mus, Long Island, NY, 93; Silver Award, Nassau Co Mus, 94; First Place Award, Nassau Co Arts Coun, 94; Best in Show Award, Great Neck Libr, 96; Award of Excellence, BJ Spoke Gallery, Nassau, 99. *Bibliog:* Betty Ommerman (auth), Artist Math Equals Award, NewsDay, 1/26/92; Phyllis Braff (auth), Juried exhibition winners, NY Times, 94; Arlyne Boltson (auth), Membership plus three, Northport J, 96. *Mem:* Nat Asn Women Artists; Long Island Network Women Artists; Manhasset Art Asn Inc; Artist Network Great Neck; and others. *Media:* Acrylic, Encaustics. *Publ:* Biographical Encylclopedia American Painters, Sculptors & Engravers of US, Colonial - 2002. *Mailing Add:* Three Orchard Farm Rd Port Washington NY 11050

CUNNINGHAM, BEN
SCULPTOR, JEWELER
b Laguna Beach, Calif, June 23, 61. *Study:* Ind Univ, Pa, BS, 85, MA, 91; RI Sch Design, MFA, 93. *Work:* Charles A Wustum Mus Fine Arts, Racine, Wis. *Comn:* Calafornia Brooch, Renwick Gallery, Smithsonian Mus Art, Washington DC. *Exhib:* Charles A Wustum Mus Fine Arts, Racine, Wis, 93, 94, 98, 99 & 2000; 83rd Exhibition of the Associated Artists of Pittsburgh, Carnegie Mus Fine Art, 94; Fla National-X, Fla State Univ Mus Fine Arts, Tallahassee, 95 & 2000; Art of the State: Pennsylvania, State Mus Pa, Harrisburg, 98 & 2000; SVA 2000, Palmer Mus Art, Univ Park, Pa, 2000; Drawing the Lines, Univ of Central Eng, Inst Art & Design, Birmingham, Eng, 2000; In Our Own Backyard, Lancaster Mus Art, Pa, 2000. *Pos:* installation technician, Sol Koffler Gallery & Woods Gerry Gallery, Providence, RI, 91-93; glass asst, Kathleen Mulcahy & Ron Desmett, Oakdale, Pa, 93-95; sculptor & jewler, BC Designs, Indiana, Pa, 89-; designer & producer, Riverside Design Group, Pittsburgh, Pa, 85-. *Awards:* Art Matters, New York, 96; Painted Bride Award, Philadelphia, Pa, 96; PCA Fel Visual Arts-Sculpture, Mid Atlantic Arts Found, Baltimore, 99. *Bibliog:* Frank Lewis (auth), Observations, Metalsmith, Vol 16, 96 & Exhibition in Print, Vol 16, 97; Kathleen Brown (auth), Moving Metal, Metalsmith, Vol 19, 99. *Mem:* Col Art Asn; Soc Nam Goldsmiths; ACC; Soc Sculptors; Soc Arts & Crafts. *Mailing Add:* 760 Josephine Ave Indiana PA 15701

CUNNINGHAM, E C (ELDON) LLOYD
PRINTMAKER, EDUCATOR
b Colby, Kans, Mar 2, 56. *Study:* Wichita State Univ, Kans, BFA, 79; Univ Colo, Boulder, MFA, 82. *Work:* Kaiser Med Found, US Univ Colo, Univ Dallas, Univ S Dakota; Quest Corp, Denver, Emprise Bank, Wichita. *Exhib:* Colorprint USA, Nat Invitational Exhib, Tex Tech Univ, Lubbock, 98; Midwest Select, South Bend Regional Mus Art, Ind, 94; solo exhib, Clayton Staples Gallery, Wichita State Univ, Kans, 95; Twenty Twenty Vision, Arvada Ctr Arts & Humanities, Colo, 96; MAPC Board of Directors Print Exhib, Floyd Co Mus, New Albany, Ind, 96; Midlands Invitational 2000, Joslyn Art Mus, Omaha, NE; Invitational Print Exhibition State Univ NY, Brockport, 2000; The Sixteenth Nat Print Invitational, Univ Dallas, Irving, Tex, 99; Mapping Destinetions Laredo, Tex, 2004; Walking on Water Int Invititional State Univ of NY, Brockport, 2004. *Pos:* Master printer, Master Eds Ltd, Englewood, Colo, 82-84. *Teaching:* Prof printmaking, Metrop State Col, Denver, 83-. *Awards:* Best Show, Works on Paper, Reuben Saunders Gallery, 80; Communs 1988 Best Show, 1999 Broadway Gallery, 88; Takach Corporation Award, 3rd Biennial Print Exhibn, Bus in the Arts Ctr Manitou Springs, Colo, 2000; Eagan Award for Excellence In Art, Wichita State Univ, 2001. *Bibliog:* Bloomsbury Rev, Vol 12, No 8, 12/92; Choice Current Revs Acad Librs, Vol 30, No 4, 12/92; Los Angeles Print Soc J, spring 93. *Mem:* Col Art Asn; Nat Asn Schs Art Design; Southern Graphics Coun; Mid Am Print Coun (pres, 94-). *Media:* All Media. *Publ:* Auth, National Printmaking Slide/Video Exchange, Metrop State Col, 90; Printmaking A Primary Form of Expression, Univ Press Colo, 92; Higher Education Logic for Print Making, EC Cunningham Pub, 2000; Times They Are a Changin, article Graphic Impressions J, 2001; Book Introduction for Lynwood Kreneck, Printmaking, Texas Tech Univ Press, 2003. *Mailing Add:* Campus Box 59 PO Box 173362 Denver CO 80217-3362

CUNNINGHAM, FRANCIS
PAINTER, INSTRUCTOR
b New York, NY, Jan 18, 31. *Study:* Art Students League, with Edwin Dickinson & Robert Beverly Hale. *Work:* Berkshire Mus, Pittsfield, Mass; Royal Theatre, Copenhagen; Security Pac Nat Bank, San Francisco; General Foods, Minneapolis; EP Dutton, NY; and other. *Exhib:* One-man shows, Hirsch & Adler Galleries, NY, 68, 70 & 75, Berkshire Mus, Pittsfield, Mass, 69, Distelheim Galleries, Chicago, 70 Mickelson Gallery, Washington, 71, Danish Consulate, NY, 87, Marsh Gallery, Univ Richmond, Va, 89, Gallerihusex, Copenhagen, Denmark, 95, Pro Persola Gallery, Stockholm, 98, Hudson River Gallery, Dobbs Ferry, NY, 2000 & Laurel Tracey Gallery, Red Bank, NJ, 2000, 01 & 02; two-man exhib, Forum Gallery, 79; Franciscan Provience, NY, 83; New Brooklyn Sch, NY, 82; Tel Aviv Mus, Isreal, 99; Laurel Tracey Gallery, 2000, 2002, 2003, 2004; Fedn of Modern Painters, New York City, 2001, Art Students League of NY, 2001; Galerie Susanne Ho/Jriis, Copenhagen, Denmark, 2002; exhib in group shows at Nat Acad Design, numerous others. *Pos:* Co-found & dir, NY Acad Sch Art, 80-85; co-found & dir, New Brooklyn Sch Life Drawing, Painting & Sculpture, Inc, 80-83. *Teaching:* Instr painting & drawing, Brooklyn Mus Art Sch, 62-80, Art Students League, NY, 80-83, 2003, New Brooklyn Sch, 80-85 & NY Acad Art, 83-85. *Awards:* Berkshire Art Asn Purchase Award, Berkshire Mus, 68; Louis Comfort Tiffany Found Grant, 73; Audubon Artists Awards, 73, 77, 80, 85, 93; Giula Palermo Award, 98; named Nat Academician, Nat Acad of Design, 1994; fel, Bogliasco Found, 1997; Recipient of the Benjamin West Clinediust Medal for Exceptioal Artistic Merit, Artists Fel, 2004. *Mem:* Nat Acad Design (assoc, 92, acad, 94); Art Students League; Audubon Artists; Fel, Bogliasco Found, 97. *Media:* Oil, Pencil. *Publ:* Coauth, Polykleitos' Diadoumenos: Measurement & animation, Art Quart, summer 62; illusr, Fundamentals of Roentgenology, 64. *Dealer:* Laurel Tracey Gallery 10 White St Red Bank NJ 07701. *Mailing Add:* 789 West End Ave No 11D New York NY 10025-5469

CUNNINGHAM, J
SCULPTOR
b Greenwich, Conn, Sept 18, 40. *Study:* Kenyon Col, BA, 62; Yale Sch Art & Archit, BFA, 63, MFA, 65. *Work:* Many pvt collections. *Exhib:* Many one-man shows. *Teaching:* Prof art, Davidson chair, Skidmore Col, Saratoga Springs, 67-. *Awards:* Fel in Sculpture, Univ Pa, 66. *Publ:* Techniques of pyramid-building in Egypt, Nature, 3/3/88. *Mailing Add:* 35 Loughberry Rd Saratoga Springs NY 12866

CUNNINGHAM, MERCE
CONCEPTUAL ARTIST
b Centralia, Wash. *Study:* Cornish Sch Col Art; Univ Ill, LHD, 72; Wesleyan Univ, Hon Dr Arts, 95. *Exhib:* Walker Art Ctr, Minneapolis, Minn, 98; Fundacio Antoni Tapies, Barcelona, Spain, 99; Serpentine Gallery, London, 99; Castello di Rivoli, Turin, Italy, 99; Whitney Mus Am Art, NY, 99. *Teaching:* Dance, Merce Cunningham Dance Studio, 53-. *Awards:* Award of Honor for Arts & Culture, Mayor of NY, 83; Kennedy Ctr Honors, Washington, DC, 85; Nat Medal Arts, Pres George Bush,

Washington, DC, 90; Praemium Imperiale award for theatre/film, Japan Art Asn, 2005. *Bibliog:* Elliot Caplan (auth), Cage/Cunningham, Cunningham Dance Found, 90 & Beach Birds for Camera, 93; David Vaughan (auth), Merce Cunningham 50 Years, Aperture, 97. *Media:* Human body. *Mailing Add:* Cunningham Dance Found 55 Bethune St New York NY 10014

CUNNINGHAM, SUE
PAINTER, ILLUSTRATOR
b Newton, Ill, Oct 19, 32. *Study:* Southern Ill Univ, Carbondale; Millikin Univ, Decatur, Ill; study with Irving Shapiro, Zoltan Szabo & Maxine Masterfield. *Work:* Mead Johnson & Co; US Coast Guard; Quaker Oats Co, Danville, Ill; Bristol Myers Corp, Evansville, Ind; Hillside Acad, Hillside, Ill. *Comn:* Eight watercolor paintings, VA Kibler & Assoc, Architects, Newton, Ill, 81 & 85; eleven watercolor paintings, Comfort Inn, Vandalia, Ill, 85. *Exhib:* Mid-Am Biennial, Owensboro Mus Fine Art, Ky, 82 & 86; Nat Watercolor Soc Travel Show, 84; Ky Watercolor Soc Aqueous, 84; Adirondacks Nat Exhib Am Watercolors, 84 & 92; Am Watercolor Soc, 85; La Watercolor Soc, New Orleans, 85; Nat Arts Club Watercolor Open, NY, 86; Allied Artists Am, NY, 86; Nat Watercolor Okla, Okla Art Ctr, 86 & 87; Watercolor USA, Springfield, Mo Mus Art, 87; Gov Exec Mansion, Ill, 87. *Pos:* Regional Rep, Nat Watercolor Soc, 87-91; Official Coast Guard Artist. *Teaching:* Art marketing seminars; instr, watercolor workshops. *Awards:* First Place Watercolor, Ill State Fair Prof Art Exhib, 84; Award of Excellence, St Louis Art Affair, West Port Plaza & West Co Art Asn, 85; Juror's Award, Realism Today, Evansville Ind Mus Art, 89; St Louis Artists Guild, 86 & 87; Watercolor Ill Biennial, 85, 87 & 90. *Bibliog:* William Michael (auth), Self-portrait makes "watercolor page", Herald & Rev, Decatur, Ill, 9/18/86. *Mem:* Signature Mem, Nat Watercolor Soc; Assoc Am Watercolor Soc; Assoc Ky Watercolor Soc. *Media:* Watercolor. *Publ:* auth & illusr, Watercolor page, Am Artist Mag, 9/86. *Mailing Add:* 112 Manchester Dr Decatur IL 62526

CUNO, JAMES
MUSEUM DIRECTOR
b St. Louis, Apr 6, 51. *Study:* Willamette Univ, BA in Hist, 1973; Univ Ore, MA in art Hist, 1978; Harvard Univ, MA in Fine Arts, 1980; Harvard Univ, PhD in Fine Arts, 1985. *Pos:* Asst cur, prints Fogg Art Mus, Harvard Univ, Cambridge, Mass, 1980-83; asst prof, dept art Vassar Col, Poughkeepsie, NY, 1983-86; dir, Grunwald Ctr for Graphic Arts, UCLA, 1986-89; dir, Hood Mus Art, Dartmouth Col, Hanover, NH, 1989-91; dir, Univ Art Mus Harvard Univ, Cambridge, Mass, 1991-2003; dir, Courtauld Inst of Art, London, 2003-2004; pres, Eloise W Martin dir Art Inst of Chicago, 2004-; Trustee Wadsworth Atheneum; panelist Nat Endowment of the Humanities, Nat Educ Assoc; mem pub grant adv comt, Getty Grant Prog, 1991-96; mem vis comt, J Paul Getty Mus. *Mem:* Asn Art Mus Dir (trustee, pres). *Publ:* Auth, ed exhib catalogues (with others) Foirades/Fizzles: Echo and Allusion in the Art of Jasper Johns, 1987, Politics and Polemics: French Caricature and the Revolution, 1789-1799, 1988, Scenes and Sequences: Recent Monotypes by Eric Fischl, 1990, Jonathan Borofsky: Prints and Multiples, 1982-91, 1991, The Popularization of Images: Visual Culture Under the July Monarchy, 1994; contribr articles to prof jour. *Mailing Add:* Art Inst of Chicago 111 S Michigan Ave Chicago IL 60603-6110

CUPPAIDGE, VIRGINIA
PAINTER, EDUCATOR
b Brisbane, Queensland, Australia, Aug, 14, 43; US & Australian citizen. *Study:* Orban Art Sch, Sydney, Australia, 62; Mary White Sch Fine Art, Sydney, Australia, MFA, 65. *Work:* Neuberger Mus, State Univ NY, Purchase; Art Gallery NSW, Australia; Chase Manhattan Bank, NY; Whitney Commun, NY; Kingsborough Commun Col, Brooklyn, NY. *Comn:* Mural, Brisbane Grammar Sch, Queensland, Australia, 84; Australia Consulate, NY. *Exhib:* Solo exhib, Gallery A, Sydney, Australia, 74-82, Susan Caldwell Gallery, NY, 75, Penrith Regional Gallery, NSW, 83, Stephen Rosenberg, NY, 86-89, 93 & 95, Bloomfield Galleries, Sydney, Australia, 85-87; Robin Gibson Gallery Sydney, 94 & 98; World Bank, Washington, 96; Can Heritage Touring Exhib, 98; Stella Downer Fine Art, Sydney, Australia, 2006; plus many other solo exhibs. *Teaching:* Vis artist painting, Univ Calif, Berkeley, 75 & Santa Barbara, 84; guest lectr, Pratt Inst, Brooklyn & Lehman Col, Bronx, 77-82; assoc prof, Lehman Col Art, 92-98 & Col Mt St Vincent, Bronx; assoc prof art, CUNY. *Awards:* CAPS Award, NY, 75; Macdowell Colony Fel Peterborough, NH, 75; Guggenheim Fel, 76. *Bibliog:* Art in Am, 90; Australian Weekend Mag, 92; The Australian, 94. *Mem:* Col Art Asn; NY Found Arts; Women's Caucus Art NY; Art Table NY; Creative Coalition. *Media:* Oil. *Interests:* Art & jazz. *Dealer:* Rosenberg & Kaufman Fine Art 115 Wooster St New York NY 10012. *Mailing Add:* 235 E 87th St #7G New York NY 10128-3225

CURLEY, DONALD HOUSTON
PAINTER, LECTURER
b Halifax, NS, Apr 4, 40. *Study:* Nova Scotia Col Art & Design, 58; Art Students League, New York, 59-61 & 66-68; Royal Acad, London, 69-70; study with Dean Cornwell & Frank Reilly, New York, Daniel E Greene, 1992-98. *Work:* Art Gallery NS & NS Art Bank, Halifax, NS; Mus Natural Sci, Ottawa; Royal Can Mint. *Comn:* Cover, painting, World Wildlife Annual Publication, 82; cover, painting, The Art of Survival, 88; cover, Art Impessions, 91; gold coin design, The Royal Can Mint, Ottawa, 96; four silver coin designs, Royal Can Mint. *Exhib:* Leigh Yawkey Woodson Art Mus, Wausau, Wis, 96; Witte Mus, San Antonio, Tex, 96; Carnegie Mus Natural Hist, Pittsburgh, Pa, 96; Neville Pub Mus, Green Bay, Wis, 97; Del Mus Natural Hist, Wilmington, 97; Friends of the Wild, Can Nat Tour on Behalf of Endangered Spaces, World Wildlife Fund, 90; Birds In Peril, Buckingham Gallery, Toronto, 94; Galerie De Bellefeuille, Montreal, Que, Can, 94; Shot Tower Gallery, Columbus, Ohio, 97; Algonquin Mus, Ont, Can, 97 & 98; Walt Disney World, Fla, 98. *Pos:* Dir, W Vancouver Acad Fine Art, 64-66. *Teaching:* Lectr art hist, Dalhousie Univ, Halifax, NS, 73. *Awards:* Hon Fel, Int Biog Asn, Cambridge, Eng; Queen Elizabeth II Golden Jubilee Commemorative Medal for World Fine Art Master, Halifax, Can, 2002; Internat Artist Grand Prize Award, Internat Mag, 6/2002. *Bibliog:* David M Lank (auth), The Wilderness Art of Donald Curley, Arts Atlantic, 83; Alexandra Thompson (auth), The Art of Don Curley, Art Impressions, 8/91; Yvonne Sheppard (auth), Donald Curley: Coming Full Circle. *Mem:* Visual Arts NS; NS Art Gallery; Can Soc Endangered Birds; Soc Animal Artists; Int Biog Asn, Cambridge, Eng. *Media:* Oil. *Collection:* The Gallery of Nova Scotia,-Nova Scotia Art Bank, The Royal Bank of Canada,- National Mus of Natural Sciences, Ottwa,-; Royal Canadian Mint, Bell Canada, World Bank, Washington,- The Claridge of Collection Montreal; Maritime Tel & Tel, Nova Scotia, The Bank of Australia, Ducks Unlimited, Canada, McCains Food, New Brunswick, Toronto Dominion Bank, Bombardier, Quebec, Crownex, Toronto. *Publ:* Auth, Chris Bacon & Don Curley Pushing Their Limits In Costa Rica, Art Impressions, 7/92; Extremadura, Spain, Birds of Wild, 12/94; Eleven Canadians selected for art & the animal exhibition, Art Impressions, 6/95; Becoming Part of the Scene, Art Impressions, 1/96; Reaffirming his Vision of the Wilderness, Mag Art, 6/96; Greenhouse Gallery of Fine Art, San Antonio, Tex; Island at the Edge, Publisher, Douglas & McLntyre; The Art of Survival, Publisher, Canadian Wildlife Associates; Atlas of Breeding Birds of the Maritime Provinces, publisher, Nimbus Publishing Limited; Wildlife Art, pub, Rockport Pub, Inc. *Mailing Add:* Box 530 101 Queen St Chester NS B0J 1J0 Canada

CURMANO, BILLY X
CONCEPTUAL ARTIST, SCULPTOR
b 1949; US citizen. *Study:* Univ Wis, Milwaukee, BFA, 73, MS, 77; Art Students League, 82. *Work:* Franklin Furnace Arch, NY; Temple Univ, Philadelphia; Milwaukee Art Mus, Wis; Munic Mus, Ourense, Spain; Mus Mod Art, NY; and others. *Comn:* video, Franklin Furnace Archive, 99; mural, Ranch Community Svc, 99; sculpture & mural, Fosston Schs, 85; mural, Rogers Elem Sch, 84; video, Canadian Pub Television, 80. *Exhib:* Orange Co 16th Ann, Brea Civic Cult Ctr, Calif, 82; 10th Small Works, NY Univ, 86; Oppresion/Expression, The Contemp, New Orleans, 86; The Drought, Minneapolis Inst Arts, 88; Fax & Sound Art, Artpool, Budapest, Hungary, 92; History of Disappearence, The Contemporary, Gateshead, Eng; and others. *Teaching:* Vis artist experimental art res, intermedia art, Univ NC, Chapel Hill, 95 & Ill State Univ, Normal, 96; drawing, Winona State Univ, Minn, 98. *Awards:* Mayor's proclamation: Billy X Curmano Day, St Louis, Mo, 92; Mayor's proclamation: Billy X Curmano Day, New Orleans, La, 97; McKnight Found Interdisciplinary Art Fel, 97. *Bibliog:* Reggie McLeod (auth), River rapping, Chicago Tribune, 8/1/88; Tom Strini (auth), Doing The Mississippi, Stroke By Stroke, Milwaukee J Sentinel, 10/12/97; Mary Beth (auth), Adventures with Billy, LA WEEKLY, 2/12/99. *Mem:* Col Art Asn. *Media:* Mixed. *Publ:* Contribr, Libres D'Artista--Artists Books, Metronom, 81; Mail Art Book, Japan Artists Union, 82; High performance, Astro Artz, 81-83; Swimmin', Part II: The Drought, Minneapolis Inst Arts, 88; Art Journal, Col Art Asn, New York, 92 & 2006. *Dealer:* Art Works USA Rushford MN 55971. *Mailing Add:* 28401 Hartwood Dr Rushford MN 55971

CURNOW, KATHY
EDUCATOR
Study: Pa State Univ, BA(art hist), 76; Ind Univ, Bloomington, MA(art hist), 80, PhD(art hist & African studies), 83. *Pos:* Exec asst, Am Found Negro Affairs, Nat Educ & Res Fund, Philadelphia, Pa, 88-89. *Teaching:* Adj asst prof, Dept Hist Art, Univ Pa, Philadelphia, 89-91; vis asst prof, Cleveland State Univ, Ohio, 90-91, asst prof, 91-94, assoc prof, 95-; vis Fulbright assoc prof, Art Dept, Univ Benin, Nigeria, 97-98. *Awards:* Nigerian Nat Learning Materials Award, 87; Nat Endowment Humanities Collaborative Grant, 93-98; Fulbright Award, 97-98. *Mem:* Arts Coun African Studies Asn (mem bd, 93-97, secy/treas, 95-97); African Studies Asn; Col Art Asn; Delta Studies Asn; Midwest Art Historians Asn. *Publ:* Auth, Nigerian Museums, Museum News, No 67, 46-47, 1/88; Alien or Accepted: African Perspectives on the Western "Other" in 15th and 16th Century Art, Soc Visual Anthropology Rev, No 6, 38-44, 1/90; Oberlin's Sierra Leonean Saltcellar: Documenting a Bicultural Dialogue, Allen Mem Art Mus Bulletin, No 44, 12-23, 2/91; Prestige and the gentleman: Benin's ideal man, Art J, No 56, 75-81, 2/97; The Art of Fasting: Benin's Ague Festival, African Arts, No 30, 4/97; and others. *Mailing Add:* Cleveland State Univ 111AB Cleveland OH 44115

CURRAN, DARRYL JOSEPH
PHOTOGRAPHER, PRINTMAKER
b Santa Barbara, Calif, Oct 19, 35. *Study:* Ventura Col, AA, 58; Univ Calif, Los Angeles, BA, 60 & MA, 64. *Work:* Mus Mod Art, NY; Nat Gallery Can, Ottawa; Int Mus Photog, George Eastman House, Rochester, NY; Royal Photog Soc, Bath, Eng. *Exhib:* Vision & Expression, George Eastman House, 68; Photog into Sculpture, Mus Mod Art, NY, 70; Photog into Art, Brit Arts Comn, 73; one-man shows, Focus Gallery, San Francisco, Calif, 74, Midway Studios, Univ Chicago, 75, Art Space, Los Angeles, 78 & Chaffey Col, 82; Traveling group show, Empowered Images, US Info Agency Collections, Los Angeles Co Mus Art. *Collection Arranged:* Graphic/Photographic (auth, catalogue), Art Gallery, Calif State Univ, Fullerton, 71; 24 From LA (auth, catalogue), San Francisco Mus Mod Art, 73; Photo Visionaries, Floating Wall Gallery, Santa Ana, Calif, 76; Los Angeles Perspectives, Secession Gallery, Victoria, BC, 76. *Pos:* Bd dir, Los Angeles Ctr for Photog Studies, 1973-77, pres, 1980-84, juror & chmn, Los Angeles Olympic Organizing Comt Photog Comn Proj for 1984 Olympic Games. *Teaching:* Prof creative photog, Calif State Univ, Fullerton, 1967-2001; vis artist photog, Sch of Art Inst Chicago, spring 1975. *Awards:* First Place in Photog, 76 Calif Art Expo, Calif State Fair, 76; Nat Endowment Arts Photogrs Fel, 80; Calif Mus Photog Award, Career Achievement, 86; Hon Educator, Soc Photog Educ, 96. *Bibliog:* Robert Stuart (auth), Light & Substance, Univ NMex, Coke/Barrow, 74; Lewis/Alger (auth), Darryl Curran Photographs 1967-1981 (exhib catalog), Chaffey Col, 82; Judy Freeman (auth), The Photographic: Two Points of View (exhib, catalog), Calif State

Univ, Fullerton. *Mem:* Soc Photog Educ (bd dir, 1975-1979); Nat Coun Art Administr (1995-1999). *Media:* Photographic & Digital Media. *Publ:* Contribr, Revolution in a Box, Univ Calif, Riverside, contribr, Untitled 11, Emerging Los Angeles Photographers, Friends of Photog, Carmel, Calif; Object, Illusion, Reality, Calif State Univ, Fullerton, 79; LA Issue, Los Angeles Ctr Photog Studies, 79. *Dealer:* G Ray Hawkins, Los Angeles; Wm Marten Gallery, Rochester. *Mailing Add:* 10537 Dunleer Dr Los Angeles CA 90064

CURRAN, DOUGLAS EDWARD
PHOTOGRAPHER, WRITER
b Seaforth, Ont, Aug 7, 52. *Study:* Ryerson Polytech Inst, Toronto, BAA, 77; Banff Sch Fine Arts, Alta, scholar, 79. *Work:* Nat Film Bd Can, Ottawa; Alta Art Found, Edmonton; Walter Phillips Gallery, Banff Ctr, Alta; Olden Camera Gallery, NY; Edmonton Art Gallery; Winnipeg Art Gallery, Man. *Comn:* Alberta 1980, PhotoProject, Alta 57th Comn, Edmonton, 80; Metis Settlements of Alberta, Fedn Metis, Edmonton, 81; Structured Paradise: The National Park Experience, Banff Ctr, Parks Can & Whyte Mus, Alta, 85. *Exhib:* Recent Acquisitions, Nat Film Bd Can, Ottawa, 79; Seven, Walter Phillips Gallery, Banff, Alta, 81; Folk Concepts of Outer Space, Edmonton Art Gallery, 81 & traveling, 81-83; Primary Colour, Harbourfront, Toronto, 82; Document, Nat Film Bd Can, Ottawa, 83; Nat Touring Exhib, Edmonton Art Gallery, 85. *Teaching:* Sessional instr photog, Univ Alta, Edmonton, 83-84. *Awards:* Grants, Can Coun, 77 & 78; Alta Writers Guild Non Fiction Award, 85. *Bibliog:* Doug Clark & L Wedman (auth), Keepsake, Artswest Publ, 82; Metisism: A Cultural Identity, Fedn Metis Settlements, 82; Contemporary Photographs, Nat Film Bd Can, Hurtig Publ, 84. *Publ:* Auth & photogr, In Advance of the Landing: Folk Concepts of Outer Space, Abbeville Press, 86. *Mailing Add:* 2046 Curling Rd North Vancouver BC V7P 1X4 Canada

CURRERI-ERMATINGER, DYANA M
DIRECTOR, CURATOR
b New York, NY, May 26, 52. *Study:* Calif State Univ, Sacramento, BA (fine art), 77, MA (fine art & technol), 79; Kellogg Found Fel arts educ, 84; Univ Calif, Berkeley, cert art admin, 86, J Paul Getty Found/Mus Mgmt Inst, 2000. *Collection Arranged:* Crocker Art Mus, Sacramento, Calif, 83-84; Hands to Work Hearts to God: Shaker Crafts from Western Collections, City of Palo Alto Cult Ctr, 87; Bay Area Sculpture: Metal, Stone & Wood, City of Palo Cult Ctr, 88; Accomodating Change: An Architectural Solution to Affordable Housing, Calif Col Arts & Crafts Archit Sch, 90; From Plastic Form to Printers Plate: 16 Sculptor/Printmakers traveling exhib (auth, catalog), Calif Col Arts & Crafts, 92; Hybridization: Contemporary California Crafts (1975-present), Nine Decades of Northern California Crafts (coauth, catalog), Calif Col Arts & Crafts, 94, Silver Tears (an installation by Dennis Oppenheim), Calif Col Arts & Crafts, 95; Judy Dater (a selected survey), Calif Col Arts & Crafts, 96; Elwood Collection, WSA Mus of Art, 99-2000. *Pos:* Asst cur, Crocker Art Mus, Sacramento, 83-84; cur, City Palo Alto, 84-89; dir exhib & pub prog, Oliver Art Ctr, Calif Col Arts & Crafts, 89-; dir Washington State Univ Mus Art, 98-2000; exec dir, chief cur Fresno Art Mus, 2001 . *Teaching:* Lectr art practice, Consumnes River Col, Sacramento, 82; assoc prof art admin & mgt, Calif Col Arts & Crafts, 89-97; prof Honors Col, Washington State Univ, 99-2000. *Bibliog:* Sara Frankel (auth), Home is Where his Heart is, San Francisco Examiner, 9/12/90; Charles Talley (auth), Social Fiber, Art Week, 8/20/92; Mary Hull Webster (auth), Dater at CCAC, Artweek, Aug 96. *Mem:* ArtTable Northern Calif (chair, 94-96); Western Mus Asn; Am Asn Mus; Non-Profit Gallery Asn Bay Area (pres, 85-87); ArtTable Inc NY (bd mem/secy 96-98); Washington Art Consortium. *Res:* Northern Calif Art and Craft 1950, Northwest art 1930, Am Art 1900, Shaker Craft and Design. *Interests:* Modern and contemporary Am Art, fine craft, design and architecture. *Publ:* Coauth, Image/Object/Place: Photography and Installation, Calif Col Arts & Crafts, 91; auth, Corollaries of Apprehension: West Coast Painting, Calif Col Arts & Crafts, 92; Linda Fleming/Dennis Leon: Sculpture, Calif Col Arts & Crafts, 93. *Mailing Add:* c/o Fresno Art Mus 2233 N First St Fresno CA 93703

CURRIE, BRUCE
PAINTER, PRINTMAKER
b Sac City, Iowa, Nov 27, 11. *Study:* Art Students' League of New York, 31-32. *Work:* Nat Acad Design, NY; State Univ NY, Albany; Butler Inst Am Art, Youngstown, Ohio; Colorado Springs Fine Arts Ctr; Kalamazoo Inst Arts, Mich. *Exhib:* Whitney Mus Am Art, 57; Am Acad & Inst Arts & Letts, 60 & 77; Albany Inst Hist & Art, 65, 68, 70, 75 & 76; Munson, Williams Proctor Inst, Utica, NY, 68, 69, 72 & 73 & Nat Acad Design, 69-92; Colorado Springs Fine Arts Ctr, Colo, 71; one-man show, Windham Fine Arts, Windham, NY, 2004; plus many others. *Teaching:* Artist-in-residence, Syracuse Univ, 79. *Awards:* Am Watercolor Soc Awards, 58, 68, 75, 81, 85 & 97; Medal Hon, Audubon Artists, 62, 82, 98 & 2000, other awards, 63, 68, 70, 71, 76, 79, 82, 87, 89 & 90; Benjamin Altman Figure Prize, Nat Acad Design, 79. *Mem:* Nat Acad Design (assoc, 68, acad, 70); Am Watercolor Soc; Audubon Artists; Woodstock Artists Asn. *Media:* Oil, Acrylic, Woodcuts. *Dealer:* Fletcher Gallery 40 Mill Hill Rd Woodstock NY 12498. *Mailing Add:* 72 Boggs Hill Woodstock NY 12498

CURRIE, STEVE
SCULPTOR
b Flint, Mich, Sept 1, 54. *Study:* Univ Mich, BFA, 77; Yale Univ, MFA, 84. *Work:* Metrop Mus Art, NY; Walker Art Ctr, Minneapolis, Minn; Albright-Knox Art Gallery, Buffalo; Des Moines Art Ctr, Iowa; Brooklyn Mus, NY; Weatherspoon Art Gallery, Univ of NC, Greensboro, NC; Modern Art Mus of Ft Worth, Tex; Orange Co Mus of Art Newport Beach, Calif. *Exhib:* The 1980's: A New Generation of Am Painters & Sculptors, Metrop Mus Art, NY, 88; Innovations in Sculpture, Aldrich Mus Contemp Art, Ridgefield, Conn, 88; Height, Width, Length: Contemp Sculpture from the Weatherspoon Collection, Weatherspoon Art Gallery, Univ NC, Greensboro; Am Narrative Paintng & Sculputure: The 1980's, Nassau Co Mus Art, Roslyn Harbour, NY, 91; Fabricated Nature, Boise Art Mus, Idaho, 94; solo exhibs, Weatherspoon Art Gallery, Greensboro, NC, 95, Miami-Dade Community Col (with catalog), Miami, Fla, 95, Slusser Gallery, Univ Mich, Ann Arbor, Mich, 96; Energy Inside- Bucksbaum Ctr for the Arts, Grinnell Univ Grinnell Iowa, 2001; Knockout Fairground 80 Wash Sq E Galleries NY Univ NY, 2002; solo exhib, Elizabeth Harris Gallery, NY, 2006. *Awards:* Igor Found Grant, 86; Nat Endowment Arts Award for Sculpture, 88; NY Found Arts Award for Sculpture, 90 & 97. *Bibliog:* George Melrod (auth), Steve Currie, Art in Am, 5/94; Patricia C Phillips (auth), Steve Currie, Artforum, 4/94. *Media:* All Media. *Dealer:* Revolution Gallery 23257 Woodward Ave Ferndale MI 48220. *Mailing Add:* 106 Franklin St Brooklyn NY 11222

CURRIN, JOHN
ARTIST
b Boulder, Colo. *Study:* Carnegie Mellon Univ, BFA, 84; Yale Univ, MFA, 86. *Exhib:* One man shows include Regen Projects, LA, 96, 99, 01, 02,02, 04; Kerlin Gallery, Dublin, 2000; Mus Contemporary Art Chgo, 2000, 03; Sadie Coles HG, London, 2000, 03; Mus Contemporary Art, San Diego, 2000, 04; Victor Miro Gallery, London, 2001; Centre Pompidou Musée Nat d'Arte Moderne, Paris, 2002; Mus Fine Arts, Boston, 2003; Milw Art Mus, 2003; Whitney Mus Am Art, 2003, 04; Museo de Arte Moderne de la Ciudad de Buenos Aires, 2005; Inst Contemporary Art, Boston, 2005; Fondos Regionales de Arte Comtemporaneo Ile-de-France y Poitou-Carentes, 2005; Andrea Rosen Gallery, 92, 94, 95, 97, 2003; group exhib include Wide Walls, Stedelijk Mus, Amsterdam & Inst Contemporary Art, London, 95; Narcissism: Artists Reflect Themselves, Calif Center for Arts, Escondido, 96; Projects 60, Mus Modern Art, NY, 97; Heart, Body, Mind, Soul: Am Art inthe 1990s, Whitney Mus Am Art, 97; Tate Gallery Selects: Am Realitites--Views From Abroad, 97; Pop Surrealism, Aldrich Mus Contemporary Art, Conn, 98; Young Americans 2: New Am Art, Saatchi Gallery, London, 98; Carpenter Centre for Visual Arts, Harvard Univ, 99; Examining Pictures: exhibiting paintings, Whitechapel Art Gallery, London, 99. *Mailing Add:* c/o Regen Projects 629 N Almont Dr Los Angeles CA 90069

CURRY, KEVIN LEE
CURATOR, DIRECTOR
b Louisville, Ky, Feb 2, 57. *Study:* Centre Col Ky, BA, 79; Univ N Tex, 86. *Work:* Univ NTex, Denton. *Comn:* installation, Cliff & Jody Cohen, Atlanta, Ga, 86; Installation, Murray Camp, Austin, Tex, 90. *Exhib:* 2nd Big Name Invitational, 500 Exposition Gallery, Dallas, 79; Accountrements of Power, DW Gallery, Dallas, 86; Learning to Live with our Mistakes, Univ Tex-Dallas, Richardson, 86; Life in Airports, 2633 Commerce, Dallas, 87; Installed, 2633 Commerce, Dallas, 88; Kevin Curry, Jeff Elrod, Paul Meinel, 2633 Commerce, Dallas, 88; Critics Choice, D-Art Visual Art Ctr, Dallas, 88; Two of Everything, NRH Gallery, Ft Worth, Tex, 98. *Collection Arranged:* Distinctive Vision I-IV, 7-8/87, 8/88, 7/89, Distinctive Vision V, 9/89, Pivotal Signals, 7/90, Counter Signals, 8/90, Contemp Tex Art; Stars Over Texas, James Pace, Hills Snyder, Frank Tolbert, 3/90; Trance Medial: Mysticism and Technology in Contemporary Texas Art, 3/91; Substance and Subversion: New Political Art, 9/91; Joe Allen and Drew Deleo, 9/91; Small Works and Installations, 6/92; Individual Ideologies, 93; Ken Havis Retrospective, 93; Binary Ground: Contemporary Landscape & Enviromental Art by Texas Artists, 94; The Figure Reconsidered, 95; New Texas Talent, 95. *Pos:* Gallery mgr, Foster Goldstrom, Dallas, Tex, 83-86; co-dir, Distinctive Vision Dallas & Austin, Tex, 87-91; dir, Univ NTex, Denton, 88-89; co-dir, Curry/Camp Exhibs, Dallas & San Antonio, 91-92; dir, Dallas Artists Res & Exhib, Tex, 91-92; Kevin Curry Exhibs, Arlington, Tex, 92-; co-dir NRH Gallery, Ft Worth, Tex, 97-99. *Teaching:* Grad fel, Drawing I & II, 86-88. *Bibliog:* Charles Dee Mitchell (auth), Staying Power, Dallas Observer, 7/90; Janet Kutner (auth), DARE selects Kevin Curry as first director, Dallas Morning News, 4/91; Shannon Dawson (auth), The Right Direction, Dallas Observer, 4/91. *Mem:* Kimbell Art Mus. *Specialty:* Contemporary Texas art. *Mailing Add:* 2514 White Oak Ln Arlington TX 76012-4849

CURTIS, DOLLY POWERS
SCULPTOR, WEAVER
b Bronx, NY, April 25, 42. *Study:* Pa State Univ, BS, 60-63; NY Univ, MA, 63-65; Brookfield Craft Ctr, Conn, 73-86. *Work:* Southern Conn State Univ; Choate Sch Art Dept; Marymount Col; Gov Residence, State Conn; Smithsonian Inst Archives Am Art. *Comn:* Knotted sculpture, Landplan Partnership, Southport, Conn, 77; numerous comns for private residences, northeast US, 77-; woven wall, Richard Bergmann Architects, New Canaan, Conn, 80; weavings, Naperville Corp Ctr, Ill, 82; woven hanging, Coopers & Lebrand CPA, Hartford, Conn, 83; and others. *Exhib:* Solo exhibs, Woven Folds--Fabric Drawing in Space, Pindar Gallery, NY, 80, 81 & 82 & Woven Environmental Sculpture, Wesleyan Univ, Conn, 82; Art in Craft Media Traveling Exhib, 81-83; Pa State Univ Mus Art, 82; Fiber: The Artist's View, C W Post Ctr, Long Island Univ, 83; The Newport Art Mus, RI, 85; Mus Art, Sci & Industry, Conn, 85; and others. *Pos:* Owner, Archit Textiles, Easton, Conn, 73-; Independent TV producer, 86-. *Teaching:* Instr weaving, Brookfield Craft Ctr, Conn, 77, Haystack Mt Sch, Deer Isle, Maine, 77. *Awards:* State Conn Grant, 76; Outstanding Achievement Design, Women in Design Int, 83; Best in Fiber, Soc Conn Craftsmen, 85; Outstanding Service in Leadership Award, Pa State Col Educ, 86. *Bibliog:* Patricia Hubbell (auth), Her weavings soar thru space & Kossia Orloff (auth), Reforming fabric, Women Artists News, fall 82; Martha B Scott (auth), article, Art Voices, 1-2/81; Donna Clemson (auth), Weaving Magician, The Penn Stater, 82; article on videotape, Dolly Curtis--Fiber artist, Crafts Report, 5/86. *Mem:* Artists Equity Asn; Am Crafts Coun; Women's Caucus Art; Surface Design Asn; Artist-Craftsmen New York. *Media:* Fiber, Textiles. *Publ:* Auth, State Grant: A two Way Street, Shuttle, Spindle, Dyepot, fall 77; contribr, Architectural Ornament, Van

Nostrand Reinhold, 82; Designing for Weaving, Hastings House Publ, 82; Fiberarts Design II, Lark Publ, 83; Women Working Home, Rodale Press, 83. *Dealer:* Silvermine Galleries New Canaan Conn; Judy Birke Corp Consult New Haven CT. *Mailing Add:* 35 Flat Rock Rd Easton CT 06612-1703

CURTIS, ROBERT D
SCULPTOR
b Susanville, Calif, Mar 28, 48. *Study:* Univ Ariz, BFA (sculpture), 70; Ariz State Univ, MFA (sculpture & design), 72. *Exhib:* Wis Directions 2, Milwaukee Art Mus, 78; Anita J Welch Mem Nat Competition & Sculpture Exhib, Scottsdale Ctr Arts, Ariz, 79; Wis Sculpture, Wustum Mus Fine Arts, Racine, 79; two-person exhib, Arts Club Chicago, Ill, 82; one-person exhib, Kit Basquin Gallery, Milwaukee, 82; Int Art Expo, Navy Pier, Chicago, 82 & 83. *Pos:* Consult restoration & installation of large scale sculpture, Bradley Family Found, Milwaukee, Wis, 78-; consult restoration & installation of large scale sculpture, Milwaukee Art Mus, 79. *Teaching:* Instr design & sculpture, Univ Wis, Milwaukee, 72-73; instr drawing, 3-D design, sculpture, Mt Mary Col, 75-. *Awards:* Shapes of 77 Stainless Steel Sculpture Competition, Vollrath Co, Wis, 77; Grant-in-Aid, Wis Arts Bd, 78; First in Sculpture Competition, City Madison, 83. *Bibliog:* Judith M Kaiser (auth), New Dimensions in Wisconsin Art: Robert Curtis, Exclusively Yours, The Patten Co, 80; Karen Thorsen-Collins (auth), Opening exhibition: Kit Basquin Gallery, New Art Examiner, 12/81. *Mem:* Int Sculpture Ctr; Col Art Asn; Wis Painters & Sculpture Inc (pres, 76-78). *Media:* Steel, Stone. *Mailing Add:* 4109 Edgevale Ct Chevy Chase MD 20815-5909

CURTIS, VERNA P
CURATOR
Study: Univ Calif, Berkeley, BA, 67; Ariz State Univ, Tempe, 70-72; Univ Wis, Milwaukee, MA(art hist), 74. *Collection Arranged:* Walker Evans from the Collection of Arnold H Crane, 81, Lewis W Hine: Child Labor Photographs (auth, catalog), 82, Art in the Streets: 19th Century French Posters, 83, Atget's Paris, 84, Toulouse-Lautrec Prints from the Permanent Collection, 86 & La Tauromaquia: Goya, Picasso and the Bullfight, 86, Milwaukee Art Mus, Wis. *Pos:* Cur asst, Art Hist Galleries, Univ Wis-Milwaukee, 74; asst cur, Milwaukee Art Mus, 74-76, assoc cur, collections & exhibs, 77-80, assoc cur, prints, drawings & photographs, 81-85, cur, 86-. *Teaching:* Inst print connoisseurship, Univ Wis-Milwaukee, 79, instr photog hist, 84; instr print hist, Milwaukee Art Mus, 83. *Awards:* Nat Endowment Arts Grants, 82 & 84; Govt of Spain Grant, 86; Getty Trust Grant, 86. *Mem:* Print Coun Am. *Publ:* Auth, The Photograph and the Grid, 84 & Nic Nicosia's Realities, 85, Milwukee Art Mus; Warrington Colescott, Perimeter Gallery, Chicago, 85. *Mailing Add:* 4109 Edgevale Ct Chevy Chase MD 20815-5909

CUSACK, MARGARET WEAVER
ILLUSTRATOR
b Chicago, Ill, Aug 1, 45. *Study:* Pratt Inst, BFA (cum laude), 68. *Comn:* Hanging & poster, Am Express Co, NY, 84; hanging, Culinary Inst Am, Hyde Park, NY; hanging, Seagram's Bldg, NY; hanging, Yale New Haven Hosp, Conn; hanging, Bishop Mugavero Ctr Geriatric Care, Brooklyn, NY, 94. *Exhib:* 20th Century Images of George Washington, Fraunces Tavern Mus, NY, 82; The Christmas Carol Sampler, Art Dir Club, NY, 83; NY Soc of Illustrators Exhib to Japan (traveling), Tokyo, Japan, 84; Looking at Earth, Smithsonian Nat Air & Space Mus, Washington, DC, 86; Fine Contemp Illustrators, E Tenn State Univ, 89; The Art Quilt, Atrium Gallery, NY, 91; Fiber Stars, Yeiser Art Ctr, Poducah, Ky, 91; Celebrating the Stitch, Newton Art Ctr, Mass, 92; Fiber Arts, Garrison Art Ctr, NY, 92. *Teaching:* Lectr dimensional illus, The Art Quilt & Fabric Col. *Awards:* Soc of Illusr Award, 74, 81, 82, 84 & 85; Art Ann Award, Communication Arts Mag, 76 & 81; Alumni Achievement Award, Pratt Inst, 88. *Bibliog:* Art Product News, 10/89; Step by Step Graphics Mag, 7/92; Needle Arts Mag, 9/94. *Mem:* Graphic Arts Guild; Am Crafts Coun; Children's Book Illusr Group; Brooklyn Commun Arts Prof; Art Quilt Network, NY. *Media:* Fabric Collage, Soft Sculpture. *Publ:* The Christmas Carol Sampler, Harcourt Brace Jovanovich, 83; Contemporary Pictorial Quilts, Gibbs Smith Pub, 93; Fabric Sculpture, Rockport Pub, 94; Fabric and Needlework Illustration, Graphic-Star, 94. *Mailing Add:* 124 Hoyt St Brooklyn NY 11217-2215

CUSHNER, STEVEN J
PAINTER
b Cleveland, Ohio May 4, 54. *Study:* RI Sch Design, BFA, 76; Univ Md, MFA, 80. *Work:* Corcoran Gallery Art & Washington Post Corp, Washington DC. *Exhib:* Solo exhibs, Baumgartner Gallery, Washington, 91, 1708 Gallery, Richmond, Va, 93, Hemphill Fine Arts, Washington, 93, 96, 98, 02, Reynolds Gallery, Richmond, Va, 99, William Busta Gallery, Cleveland, Ohio, 01, The Art Gallery, Univ Md, College Park, 02, Pente Fine Arts, Washington, 96,; A New Nature, Emerson Gallery, McLean, Va, 94; 3 Washington Artists, City Gallery, Raleigh, NC, 94; Repicturing Abstraction, 1708 Gallery, Richmond, Va, 95; Reynolds Gallery, Richmond, Va, 95; Chance and Necessity, Md Art Place, Baltimore, 98; Monoprints, Goya Girl Press, Baltimore, 98; 505 Gallery, Washington, DC, 99. *Collection Arranged:* Ruesch Int, Washington, DC; Corcoran Gallery Art, Washington, DC; Hirshhorn Mus and Scultpure Garden, Washington, DC; Washington Post Corp. *Teaching:* adj prof, Corcoran Sch Art, 87-; adj prof, Vt Col, Montpelier, 95-. *Awards:* Nat Endowment Arts, 93; Vis Artist Fel, DC Comn on the Arts, 98. *Dealer:* Hemphill Fine Arts 1027 33rd St NW Washington DC 20007. *Mailing Add:* 1339 Franklin St NE Washington DC 20017

CUSICK, NANCY TAYLOR
COLLAGE ARTIST, ASSSEMBLAGE ARTIST
b Washington, DC. *Study:* Am Univ, BA, 59, MA, 61, with Gates, Calfee, D'Artista and Summerford; Corcoran Art Sch, 68; Univ Calif, 71, with Lindgren, 71. *Work:* Mus Fine Arts, Pangborn Corp, Hagerstown, Md; Am Univ, Libr Cong, Nat Mus Women in Arts, Corcoran Gallery Art, Washington; US Embassy, Madagascar; Turkish-Am Assoc, Ankara & Izmir, Turkey; Helenic-Am Union, Athens, Greece; Mus de Arte Moderno, Buenos Aires, Arg. *Exhib:* Wash Artists Ann, Smithsonian Inst, 60-69; Area Exhib, Corcoran Gallery Art, 67; Southeastern Museums Tour, Corcoran Gallery Art, 73; solo exhibs, Antalya Mus Painting & Sculpture, Turkey, 90, Univ Calif, Los Angeles, 90, Gallery 10 Ltd, Washington, 90, Goldman Art Gallery, Rockville, Md, 91, Gallery 10 Ltd, 93, Cork Gallery, Lincoln Ctr, NY, 94, Nat Mus Women in Arts, Washington, 94; China World Trade Ctr, Beijing, China, 95; Elite Gallery, Moscow, Russia, 95; US Info Agency, Washington, 96; Nat Mus Women in Arts, Washington, 96; Gallery 10 Ltd, Washington, 96. *Pos:* Exec dir, Wash Women's Arts Ctr, DC, 79-80; contrib ed, Women Artists News, New York, 80-; Wash coordr, Int Festival Women Artists, UN Mid-Decade Conf Women, Copenhagen, Denmark, 80; proj dir, Focus Int-Am Women in Art, UN Decade Conf, Nairobi, Kenya, 85; pres, Gallery 10 Ltd, 91-92; arts caucus rep, Nat Women's Conf Comt, 91-92. *Teaching:* Instr painting & art hist, Dunbarton Col Holy Cross, 66-72; instr art, Prince George's Col, 72-77; lectr & workshop dir, Dokuz Eylul Univ, Izmir, Turkey, 89, Hacettepe Univ, Ankara, Turkey, 89, Bilkent Univ, Ankara, Turkey, 89. *Awards:* First Prize Painting, Soc Wash Artists, 66; Best Show, Hagerstown Mus, 67; Award of Excellence, Women's Caucus for Art, 96. *Bibliog:* David Barrows (auth), Nancy Cusick, The In Tower, 5/93; Mary D Garrard & Norma Broudee (auths), The Power of Feminist Art, 94; Diane Beal (auth), Artists in Beijing: Focus on Women, Koan, 11/95; Global Focus: Women in Art & Culture: Women in the arts, Nat Mus of Women in Arts, Winter/95; Cynthia Redecker (auth), Washington, Moscow artists stage a different kind of summit, Moscow Times, 9/95; Terry Parmelee (auth), Press patter, Washington Print Club, winter/96; Success on a Global Scale: Women artists Exhibit in China, Women in Arts, Nat Mus Women in the Arts, spring/96; Eleanor Kennelly (auth), Exhibit of Global Works of small art on view in museum's great hall, Wash Times, 5/12/96. *Mem:* Artists Equity Asn; Col Art Asn; Coalition Women's Art Orgn; Women's Caucus Art; Soc Wash Artists. *Media:* Mixed Media, Oil. *Mailing Add:* Gallery 10 1519 Connecticut Ave NW Washington DC 20036

CUSWORTH, CHRISTYL
PAINTER, CONSERVATOR
b Neptune, NJ, Mar 14, 63. *Study:* Col of NJ, BA, 1986; Univ of New Orleans, 1994; NY Univ, 2001. *Work:* ceramic tile mosaic, The Crusifix; ceramic tile mosaic, Columbus; oil on canvas, Star Night Over Lambertville; oil on canvas, Morning Tower; wood & steel, Nailed Cross. *Comn:* pvt, Murals (5), La Childrens Mus, La, 1994. *Exhib:* Art for Arts Sake, Contemp Arts Ctr, New Orleans, 1992; A Group of Women Artist, Ellarslie Mus, Trenton, NJ, 1996; 24th Ann Juried Art Exhib, Lambertville Hist Soc at Coryell Gallery, Lambertville, NJ, 2004. *Collection Arranged:* Julian Schnabel (Sculpture), Pace Gallery, NYC, 1990; Sartain Collection, Moore Col, 1997; The Philadelphia Ten, Moore Col, 1998; Ron Gorshov, 2005. *Pos:* Owner (conservator), Christyl Cusworth Paintings Conservator LLC, 1995-; Owner, Antietam (fine art bronze casting foundry), 1988-1991; Salah Hudson Conserv, 1991-1995. *Awards:* Joyce & Jermy Award, 24th Ann Coryell Gallery, 2004. *Bibliog:* Bibi Dietz (auth), Vanishing Paintings, Hunterdon Co Democrat, 2004. *Mem:* AIC (Prof assoc, 2002). *Media:* Oil, Mixed. *Specialty:* Painting. *Dealer:* Peoples Store, 28 N Union St Lambertville NJ 08530. *Mailing Add:* 54 S Main Lambertville NJ 08530

CUTFORTH, ROGER
CONCEPTUAL ARTIST, PAINTER
b Lincolnshire, Eng, 1944. *Study:* Nottingham Col Art, Eng, 62-63; Ravensbourne Col Art, Eng, 63-66. *Work:* Walraf-Richartz Mus, Cologne, Ger; Metrop Mus Art, NY; Mus Abteiberg, Monchengladbeck, Ger; Mus Mod Art, NY. *Exhib:* Mus Mod Art, NY, 70 & 80; Int Cult Ctr Mus, Antwerp, Belg, 75; Contemp Art Mus, Zagreb, Yugoslavia, 76; Vienna Int Biennale, Austria, 81; Sydney Biennale, Australia, 81; Trouble in Paradise, A & M Artworks, NY, 82; Randolf Macon Women's Col, Lynchburg, Va, 83; Contemp Triptychs, Edith C Blum Art Inst, Bard Col, Annandale-on-Hudson, NY, 84; Houston Ctr Photog, Tex, 86; solo exhib, Bauer House, Univ Tex, Austin, 88; Dos Amigos Gallery, Terlingua, Tex, 88 & 90; Work From The Seventies, Hall Bromm Gallery, NY, 90; San Angelo Mus Fine Arts, Tex, 91; Slapshot, Boston Mus Modern Art, 00. *Teaching:* Instr intro photog, New York Univ, 84. *Awards:* Visual Artists Fel, Nat Endowment Arts, 84. *Bibliog:* Valentin Tatransky (auth), article, Arts Mag, 78; Loredana Parmesani (auth), article, Segno, 79; Jean Fisher (auth), article, Aspects, 81; Grace Glueck (auth), The triptych lives on in modern variations, NY Times, 7/1/84. *Media:* Color Photographs; Watercolor. *Publ:* Auth, The Empire State Building, private publ, 69; The Visual Book, private publ, 70; Cleopatra's Needle/Eiffel Tower/Empire State Building, private publ, 71. *Dealer:* Hal Bromm Gallery 90 W Broadway New York NY 10007. *Mailing Add:* HC 65 Box 276D Alpine TX 79830-9801

CUTLER, AMY
PAINTER, SCULPTOR
b Poughkeepsie, NY, 74. *Study:* Staatliche Hochschule fur Bildende Kunste, Ger, 94-95; Cooper Union Sch Art, NY, 97; Skowhegan Sch Painting & Sculpture, 99. *Work:* Art for Parks, Brooklyn Mus, 1999, Rural Crossing, 195 Bedford Av, NY, 1999, Artists in the Marketplace, Bronx Mus, 2000, Terrors and Wonders: Monsters in Contemp Art, De Cordova Mus & Sculpture Park, Lincoln, Mass, 2001, Stranger Than You, New Langton Arts, San Francisco, 2001, Works on Paper, The Weatherspoon Art Mus, Greensboro, NC, 2002; Open House: Working in Brooklyn, Brooklyn Mus Art, 2004, Whitney Biennial, Whitney Mus Am Art, 2004, The Drawn Page, Aldrich Mus Contemp Art, Ridgefield, Conn, 2004, About Painting, Tang Mus, Saratoga Springs, NY, 2004. *Exhib:* Exhib incl, 80 Wash Sq East Galleries, NY, 98, Summer Voices, Miller Block Gallery, Boston, 99, Miller Block Gallery, Boston, 2000, Dialogues: Amy Cutler/David Rathman, Walker Art Ctr, Minneapolis, 2002, Inst Contemp Art, Philadelphia, 2002, Once Upon A Time, Kohler Art Ctr, Sheboygan, Wis, 2003, Kemper Mus of Contemp Art, Kansas City, Mo, 2004; group shows at Small Works, Rendered, Sara Meltzer Gallery, NY, 2003. *Awards:* Roma Hort Mann Found Grant, 99. *Mailing Add:* c/o Whitney Mus Am Art 945 Madison Ave New York NY 10021

CUTLER, BESS
ART DEALER
b Salem, Mass, Dec 13, 49. *Study:* Brandeis Univ, BA, 71; Sch Mus Fine Arts, Tufts Univ, MFA, 76. *Pos:* Partner, Cutler-Stavandis Gallery, Boston, 78-82; owner & dir, Bess Cutler Gallery, New York, 83-. *Specialty:* Contemporary artists. *Mailing Add:* PO Box 99 Sebec ME 04481-0099

CUTLER, ETHEL ROSE
PAINTER, DESIGNER, EDUCATOR
b New York, NY. *Study:* Hunter Col, BA, 36; Columbia Univ, MA, 37; Sch Prof Arts, cert advert & interior design; NY Univ, 60-70; Univ Mo; Inst Design, Ill Inst Technol; Am Artist Sch; New Sch Social Res, with Yasuo Kuniyoshi & Alexei Brodovitch; Walden Univ, Inst Advan Studies, PhD, 79, Fashion Inst Technol (computer graphic), Nat Acad Design (painting). *Work:* Permanent collections of NY Univ, Gray Art Gallery Study Ctr, Jewish Mus & Mus City New York; Artist Equity Inc, New York City. *Exhib:* New York City Ctr Gallery; Young Am Artist Group, NY; Lynn Kottler Galleries, NY; Artist Equity Exhib, NY; East Galleries, NY Univ; Broome St Gallery, New York City; and others. *Pos:* Design consult, artist & designer, 50. *Teaching:* Instr fine arts, Women's Col, Univ NC, Greensboro, 43-47; instr interior design & 2 to 3 dimensional design, Adelphi Col, 47-50; asst prof interior design & related arts, Univ Mo-Columbia, 50-55; asst prof surface design, RI Sch Design, 55-59. *Awards:* Award for Boats, New York City Ctr Gallery, 59; Award for Brothers, Macy's Gallery; Grant, Metrop Mus Art, NY, 68 & Walden Univ. *Mem:* Col Art Asn Am; Artists Equity Asn; Women in Design; Am Soc Interior Designers; Art Dir Club; Metropolitan Mus Art. *Media:* All. *Res:* Techniques of William Morris and the arts and crafts movement of the Beaux Arts, the Bauhaus and other influences of the 19th century; the garden as an aesthetic experience, its influence on selected artists. *Mailing Add:* 230 E 88th St New York NY 10128

CUTLER, JUDY A GOFFMAN
MUSEUM DIRECTOR
b New Haven, Conn, Feb 7, 42. *Study:* Univ Pa, BA, 63; Univ Pa, MA, 64. *Collection Arranged:* Norman Rockwell (toured Japan), Isetan Mus, 92; Maxfield Parrish Retrospective (toured Asia & USA), 95; Norman Rockwell & Sat Evening Post (toured France), 94; Great Am Illstr, (toured Japan), 95. *Pos:* Gallery Dir, Am Illustrators Gallery, NYC, 85-; Gallery Dir, Judy Goffman Fine Art, Pa & NY, 69-85; Art Dealer, Blue Bell, Pa, 65-69. *Bibliog:* Ann Berman, An illustration Mus Debuts, Archit Digest, 99; Bill Van Siclen, Fine-Tuning The Picture, Providence Jour, 2000. *Mem:* Nat Arts Club; AAM; AFA; New England Mus Asn; Mus Store Asn; Soc Illustrators. *Specialty:* American illustration in the country. *Interests:* Illustration Art. *Collection:* American Imaginist Collection. *Publ:* Maxfield Parrish, 93, Maxfield Parrish: A Retrospective, 95; Parrish & Poetry: A Gift of Art and Words, Pomegranate Art Books, 95; Maxfield Parrish: A Treasury of Art, Thunder Bay Press, 2001; Maxfield Parrish and the American Imagist 2004. *Mailing Add:* Nat Mus Am Illus Vernon Ct 492 Bellevue Ave Newport RI 02840

CUTLER, LAURENCE S
MUSEUM DIRECTOR
b New Haven, Conn, Aug 27, 1940. *Study:* Univ Pa, BA, 62; Harvard, March, 66, MAUD, 67. *Work:* Chase Manhattan Bank Caribbean Hqrs; US Emb Staff Housing; Sugarloaf/USA Ski Area; Fire/Police Hqrs, Westford, Mass; pub housing project, Boston; Bally's Park Place Casino/Hotel; Reconstructed Biafra, Nigeria. *Collection Arranged:* Cur, Rockwell: The Great American Storyteller, toured Miss & Va, 1986; cur, Norman Rockwell Illustrator, toured Italy, Palazzo Expo, 1990; cur, Norman Rockwell (auth, catalog), toured Japan, Isetan Mus, 1992; cur, Great American Illustrators, Fukishima, (coauth, catalog), 1993; cur, Maxfield Parrish: A Retrospective (coauth, catalog), toured Asia & US, 1995. *Pos:* co-founder, Ecodesign Int, Inc, 66, reacquired, 80; group dir, NAm, GGT/USA Adv, 88-91; founder, ARTShows and Products, 94; adv dir, Am Illustrators Gallery, NY, 84-; founder (with Judy Goffman Cutler), Nat Mus Am Illustration & Am Civilization Found, 98-. *Teaching:* teaching fel, Harvard, 65-71, asst prof, 65-71; asst prof, MIt, 69-74. *Awards:* Fulbright-Hayes grant; Harvard Univ Milton Fund grants & scholarship; grant, NEA; design awards, AIA; Alpha Rho Chi gold medal, Harvard Univ; honorific title Oniyasha Igwe of Okigwe, Igbo Tribe, Nigeria. *Bibliog:* Ann Berman (auth), Illustration museum Debuts, Archtl Digest, 12/99; Lita Solis-Cohen (auth), National Mus of American Illustration, Maine Antiques Digest, 11/99; Bill Van Siclen (auth), Fine Tuning the Picture, Providence Jour, 9/21/2000. *Mem:* Nat Arts Club; Harvard Club; Am Asn Mus; AFA, New Eng Mus Asn; Royal Inst Brit Archs. *Res:* collaborative efforts of Edith Wharton & Maxfield Parrish. *Specialty:* illus art from Golden Age Am Illus. *Interests:* Art, Architecture, Urban Design, Poetry and Music. *Collection:* American Imagist Collection; The Preeminart American Illustration Collection in the Nation. *Publ:* Coauth, Industrialized Building Systems, MIT Press, 71; coauth, Recycling Cities for People, Van Nostrand Reinheld, 75; coauth, Housing Systems for Designers & Developers, 95; coauth, Maxfield Parrish and the American Imagists, 2004; coauth, Maxfield Parrish: A Retrospective, 95. *Mailing Add:* Nat Mus Am Illus Vernon Ct 492 Bellevue Ave Newport RI 02840

CUTLER, RONNIE
PAINTER
b New York City. *Study:* Columbia Univ Art Sch, 57; Brooklyn Mus Art, Art Sch, 58; Art Students League, 59-60. *Work:* Art Students League Collections, NY; Commerce Bank, Memphis, Tenn; Nat Mus of Women in the Arts, Washington; plus pub and pvt collections. *Exhib:* Artists of Manhattan, Whitney Mus, NY, 54; 54th Ann Competition, Delgado Mus, New Orleans, La, 55; 5th Ann Competition, Berkshire Mus, Pittsfield, Mass, 56; Alumni Show, Brooklyn Mus, NY, 56 & 58; Casein Soc, Riverside Mus, NY, 57; Audubon Artists, Nat Acad Design, NY, 58 & 84; one-woman shows, Bodley Gallery, NY, 79, Ronrich Gallery, NY, 89, 90 & 91; Providencetown Art Mus, Mass, 93; Salmagundi Club exhib, Am Watercolor Soc, NY, 99, 2000; Monique Goldstorm Gallery, NY, 2002; International Works on Paper, Watercolor, 2003; William Whipple Mus and Gallery SW State Univ Minn, 2005. *Awards:* Alumni Purchase Award, Art Students League, 60; Best of Show, Southern Berkshire Community Arts Coun, 79 & 80; Silvermine Guild Artists, New Canaan, Conn; First Prize in Oil, Painters & Sculptors Soc, NY; First Prize in Oil, Sheffield Art Asn, Mass, 86, 87 & 88; Frederix/Tara Award, Audabon Artists, 58th Ann Yr, 2000; First prize Oil Works on Canvas, Pen and Brush, NYC, 2003. *Bibliog:* An Illustrated Survey of the City's Mus, Galleries and Leading Artists, New York Art Rev. *Mem:* Art Students' Leauge (life); Salmagundi Club, NY; Am Watercolor Soc; Pen & Brush. *Media:* Oil, Watercolor. *Dealer:* Monique Goldstrom Gallery NYC. *Mailing Add:* 175 W 12th St Apt 11J New York NY 10011-8206

CUTLER-SHAW, JOYCE
CONCEPTUAL ARTIST, SCULPTOR
b Detroit, Mich. *Study:* New York Univ, BA, 53; Columbia Univ, 53-54; Univ Calif, San Diego, MFA, 72. *Work:* Spec Collections Artists Bks, Mus Mod Art, NY; Teylers Mus Haarlem, Neth; Getty Ctr Libr, Artists Books, Los Angeles, Calif; Johnson Mus, Cornell Univ; Albertina Mus, Vienna, Austria; Wellcome Inst, London, Eng. *Comn:* Namewall for Los Angeles Int Airport, Los Angeles Bd Airport Commissioners, Calif, 74; Charity Namewall for New Orleans Charity Hospital, New Orleans Downtown Development District, La, 80; Balboa Park Activity Ctr & Artist Mem Design Team, City of San Diego, 96-99; 2 metal street corner sculptures, Stone Crest Village Sculptures, Irvine Co, San Diego, Calif, 98-99; The Sycamore Leaf Canopy, The Railing of Wild River Grasses, The Sycamore Leaf Cascasde, 3 works for Mission Valley Branch Library, San Diego, 99-2002. *Exhib:* Three Directions, Newport Harbor Art Mus, Calif, 76; Am Narrative Art, Contemp Art Mus, Houston, Tex, 77; Un Espace Parle, Galerie Gaetan, Geneva, Switz, 78; Other Child Book, Palace of Cult and Sci, Warsaw, Poland, 79; Arteder 82, Balboa, Spain, 82; Nat Acad Sci, Washington, 86; Teylers Mus, Haarlem, The Neth, 90; Artist's Bks, Nat Mus Women in the Arts, Washington, 92; Calligraphia USA/USSR, Int Typeface Corp, Traveling Minsk, etc, USSR & USA, 90-93; Insite 94, Vet Admin Med Ctr, San Diego, 94; Hosp Gen, Tijuana, Mex, 94; Sci & Artists Book, Smithsonian Inst, Washington, 95-96; The New Anatomists, Wellcome Inst, 99; Festchrift für Konrad Oberhuber, Nordico Mus der Stadt, Linz, Austria, 00; Libr Quartet, Four conCurrent exhibs; UC San Diego Coastal Libr, Athena, in Music & Art, Libr, two Pub Libr, 2003; Chiayi Cultural Center, Taiwan, 2005. *Collection Arranged:* Albertina Graphic Mus, Vienna; Getty Ctr Libr; Mus Modern Art, NYC; Teyler's Mus, Haarlem, The Netherlands; Tate Gallery Libr, London; Univ of CA SanDiego (Joyce Cutler-Shaw Archive) Library of Congress, Yale Univ Library SP Collections. *Pos:* Dir, Art & Artists: Video/Audio Archive, 74-80; TV interviewer/project dir, Art & Artists, KPBS-TV, San Diego, Calif, 79-80; chairwoman, Pub Art Adv Coun, San Diego, Calif, 78; adv coun, San Diego City Architect, 90-92; vis scholar (artist & residency), Sch Med, Univ Calif, San Diego, 92-; artist in res, Chiayi Co, Taiwan, 2005. *Teaching:* Vis arts fac contemp art, Palomar Col, San Marcos, Calif, 74-78; vis fac contemp art, San Diego State Univ, Calif, 78-80 & Univ Calif, Irvine, 79-80; vis fac contemp art, Fine Art Drawing Sch of Medicine, Univ Calif, 97-. *Awards:* Nat Endowment Arts Media Grant, Video Portrait, 81-82; Nat Endowment Arts Grant, 85-87; Purchase Prize, Alphabet of Bones Poster, Purchase Prize, State Univ NY, 91; Design Award, Am Inst Architects San Diego, Canopy, Mis Valley Libr, 02. *Bibliog:* M Vogel (auth), Die Dame und der Vogel, Vaterland Luzern, Switz, 10/4/79; Moira Roth (auth), catalog essay, Johnson Mus, 86; catalogue essay, Johnson Mus, Cornell Univ, 86; Joyce Cutler Shaw (auth) Leonardo, MIT, Journal, 94; Bettyann Kevles (auth), Naked to the Bone, Rutgers Univ Press, NJ, 97; Library Quartet; Joyce Cutler Shaw (ex Catalogue) Athenaeum Music and Art Library, 2003. *Mem:* Col Art Asn; Woman's Caucus Arts; Landmark Art Projects (founding mem, secy, 78-84 & pres, 85- 92); San Diego Coun Design Prof. *Media:* Multi-Media, Drawing; All Media. *Publ:* Alphabet of Bones, Kretschmer & Grossman, Frankfurt, W Ger 87; Three Cages, Ctr for Book Arts, New York, 92; The Anatomy Lesson: The Body, Technology and Empathy, In: Leonardo, Vol 27, No 1, 29-38, 94; Being Energy and Light, Semiotica Mouton de Bruyter, Berlin, NY, 95-115, 2001; The Anatomy Lesson; Univ The Fasciculus Medicinie, Rubin Price Publisher CT, 2004 (limited Ed of 50). *Mailing Add:* 7969 Engineer Rd Ste 211 San Diego CA 92111

CUTRONE, RONNIE BLAISE
PAINTER
b New York, July 10, 48. *Study:* Sch Visual Arts, 70. *Work:* Mus Mod Art, NY; T'Venster Mus Arts Coun, Rotterdam, Holland; Patrick Lannen Collection, Fla; Morton Neumann Family Collection, Kalamazoo, Mich; Eli Broad Found, Santa Monica, Calif. *Exhib:* One-man show, Venster Arts Coun, Rotterdam, The Neth, 83, Venice Biennale, Italy, 84, Lorenzelli Arte, 95 & 2003; From the Streets, Greenville Co Mus, NC, 83; Impressionism to New Wave, High Mus Art, Springfield, Ill, 86; Sacred Images in Secular Art, Whitney Mus, NY, 86; Comic Iconoclasm, ICA, London, Eng, 87; Avant Garde in the 80's, Los Angeles Co Mus, Calif, 87. *Bibliog:* Robert Becker (auth), article, Interview Mag, 82; Jeanne Silverthorne (auth), article, Art Forum, 83; Tommaso Trini (auth), article, Flash Art, 84. *Media:* Acrylic, Watercolor; Silkscreen. *Specialty:* Pop Art - A Continuing History, Marco Livingstone. *Collection:* Cover - Pop Art, Lucy Lippard. *Publ:* Auth, Ronnie Cutrone Watercolors, Salvatore Ala Gallery, 84; Ronnie Cutrone, Tony Shafrazi Gallery, 85; New Used and Improved Art for the 80's, Abbeyville, 87. *Dealer:* Matteo Lorenzilli Milano Italy. *Mailing Add:* 274 Lake Drive Lake Peekskill NY 10537-1105

CUTTLER, CHARLES DAVID
HISTORIAN, LECTURER
b Cleveland, Ohio, Apr 8, 1913. *Study:* Ohio State Univ, BFA & MA; Inst Art & Archeol, Paris, France; Univ Bruxelles; Inst Fine Arts, NY Univ, PhD. *Exhib:* Cleveland May Show, Ohio, 35-36; Philadelphia Watercolor Ann, Pa, 37. *Pos:* Guest lectr, Sem Europ Art & Civilisation Belg, Ghent, summer, 69, Tokyo, 79, Brussels, 88. *Teaching:* Asst instr art hist, Ohio State Univ, 35-37; from instr to asst prof art hist, Mich State Univ, 47-57; from assoc prof to prof, Univ Iowa, 57-83, res prof, 65-75, emer, 83-. *Awards:* CRB Fel, Brussels, 53-54; Fulbright-Hays Sr Fel, Brussels, 65-66; Assoc mem, Royal Belgian Acad, 87. *Mem:* Col Art Asn Am; founding pres Midwest Art Hist Soc; Renaissance Soc Am; Medieval Acad Am; Int Ctr Medieval Art; Hist Netherland Art (hon life). *Res:* Netherlandish and German art of the 14th to 16th centuries; art of Hieronymus Bosch. *Publ:* Lisbon Temptation of St Anthony by Jerome Bosch, 57; Northern painting, from Pucelle to Bruegel, XIVth, XVth & XVIth Centuries, 68, 73 & 91; Auth, Further Grunewald Sources, Zeitschrf Kstgesch, 87; Errata in Netherlandish art: Jan Mostaert's New World Landscape, Simiolus, 89; Exotics in Post-Medieval Art: Giraffes and Centaurs, Artibus et Historiae, 91. *Mailing Add:* 1691 Ridge Rd Iowa City IA 52245-1628

CYPHERS, PEGGY K
PAINTER, PRINTMAKER
b Baltimore, MD, April 19, 54. *Study:* Maryland Inst Col Art; Towson Univ, BFA, 77; Pratt Inst, MFA, 79. *Work:* Saks Fifth Ave Hq, Cincinnati, Ohio; Libr Congress, Smithsonian Inst, Washington; Aldrich Mus, Conn; Nat Mus Women Arts, Washington; Weatherspoon Mus, Greensboro, NC; Johnson & Johnson, NJ; Anchorage Mus, Alaska. *Exhib:* Recent Acquisitions, Aldrich Mus, Conn, 86; solo exhibs, EM Donahue Gallery, NY, 88, 90, 91, 93, 96 & 98, Galerie Asback, Copenhagen, Denmark; Prints from Solo Impressions, Nat Mus Women Arts, Washington, 96; Cheryl Haines Gallery, San Francisco, 96; Proposition Gallery, 2003; Art Resources Transfer, 2003. *Pos:* Auth, NY in Review (monthly article) Arts Mag, 88-90; Art Reviews, Tema Celeste, 2005, Mag, Milan, Italy. *Teaching:* Instr, painting & drawing, Parsons Sch Design, 88, Pratt Inst, 89-98, New York Univ, 90-95 & Univ NC, Greensboro, 95; adj assoc prof of painting, Pratt Inst, 89-05, coord painting & drawing, 02-03, dir Pratt in Tuscany, 02, 03; vis artist-in-residence, Univ NC, fall 96. *Awards:* Yaddo Artist-in-residence, 94; Va Ctr Creative Arts, 95; Fac Develop Fund, Pratt Inst, 96; Award in Painting, Nat Endowment for the Arts; Elizabeth Found for the Arts Award, 98. *Bibliog:* Jed Perl (auth), Peggy Cyphers, Gallery Going: Four Seasons in the Art World, Harcourt Brace Jovanovich, 231-233, 91; Ellen Handy (auth), Peggy Cyphers, Art Mag, 2/92; Ronny Cohen (auth), Peggy Cyphers, Artforum, 7/96; Eleanor Heartney (auth), Peggy Cyphers, Art in Am, 1/99. *Mem:* Col Art Asn. *Media:* Acrylic, Sand. *Specialty:* Contemporary painting and installation. *Publ:* Ed, Progress (mag), New Observations, 58. *Dealer:* Donahue Sosinski Art New York. *Mailing Add:* 315 Broadway New York NY 10007

CYRUS, JAMAL
ARTIST
b Houston. *Study:* Univ Houston, BFA (digital media & photog), 2004. *Exhib:* Univ Mus, S Tex Univ; Station Mus Contemp Art, Houston; Lawndale Art Ctr, Houston; Arthouse, Austin, Tex; Whitney Biennal, 2006. *Pos:* instr, art prog, Project Row Houses, Houston, Tex; instr, Shade Tree Project Fashion Club; mem, Otabenga Jones & Assoc

CZACH, MARIE
HISTORIAN, CURATOR
b Chicago, Ill. *Study:* Sch Art Inst Chicago, BAE, 67; Columbia Univ, New York, MA, 68; Univ Ill at Urbana-Champaign, PhD, 85. *Pos:* Res assoc, George Eastman House, Rochester, NY, 68-70; asst cur photog, Art Inst Chicago, Ill, 70-72; dir, Mus Gallery, Western Ill Univ, Macomb, 74-78 & Sioux City Art Ctr, Iowa, 85; South Suburban Col, South Holland, Ill. *Teaching:* Dir studies, hist & criticism of photog & contemp art, Columbia Col, Chicago, 72-74. *Mem:* Col Art Asn; Nat Coun Resource Develop; Nat Soc Fund Raising Exec; Develop Coun Chic. *Res:* Nineteenth-century art criticism; contemporary American art; history of photography; Semiotics. *Publ:* Auth, A Directory of Early Illinois Photographers, Western Ill Univ, 77; History of Photography Visual Resources (articles), Afterimage. *Mailing Add:* 25862 Carey Plaza Wauconda IL 60084

CZARNIECKI, M J, III
MUSEUM DIRECTOR, CONSULTANT
b San Francisco, Calif, May 28, 48. *Study:* Xaverius Col, Antwerp, Belg, dipl, 67; Wabash Col, Ind, BA, 71; Art Inst Chicago, 71-72; Columbia Col, Chicago, 73; Middlebury Col, Vt, 78; Salzburg Seminars, Austria, 89. *Work:* Magnolium, 82. *Collection Arranged:* Masters of Twentieth Century Photography (co-cur), Ringling Mus, 76; Before It's Too Late: The Photography of Edward S Curtis (cur, catalog), Miss Mus Art, 78; Southern Realism (dir), Miss Mus Art/Southern Arts Fedn, 78-81; Dance Image: A Tribute to Serge Diaghilev (dir), Miss Mus Art, 79; Russian Stage Designs: Scenic Innovation, 1900-1930 (dir), Miss Mus Art, 82; Paul Manship: Changing Taste in America (dir, Catalog), Minn Mus Art, 85-88; A Lighter Shade of Pale: Photographic Influences in Other Media, Minn Mus Art, 89; Cuba-USA: The First Generation, Fondo del Sol Visual Arts Ctr with Minn Mus Art, 92; Shared Visions, Minn Mus Art, 93; A Bridge of Light (photog of John Varnier), Minn Mus Am Art, 93; Colo/Wyo Biennial 94, One W Art Ctr, 94; Diversity Art Works, 95; Shadow Catcher (ES Curtiss), 99-; Hennepin Govt Ctr, Visualizing the Blues, 1998-2000. *Pos:* Dir, Miss Mus Art, 76-83 & Minn Mus Art, 83-93; consult, Nat Endowment Arts & Inst Mus Services, 78-96; cur-in-residence, US Info Agency, Sofia, Bulgaria, 82; bd dir, Intermedia Arts, Minn, 85-91, Pub Art, St Paul, 88-, Concourse Arts, 89-94; visual arts chair, Minn/Cuba Proj, 85-; chair, Minn Archit Designer Selection Bd, 90-99; principal & chief exec officer, S/RI Cult Planners, Minn, 92-; pres, Inst Photog Studies, 93-98; bd trustees Coll Visual Arts, 97-, Franconia Sculpture Park, 96-, Am Mus Asmar Art, 2000-. *Teaching:* Instr photog, Wabash Col, Ind, 70-71; lectr hist photog, Art Inst Chicago, 72-74; dir educ, Ringling Mus Art, 74-76; lectr MBA arts prog, State Univ NY, Binghamton, 83-88, 90-94; lectr, Arts Admin, Metrop State Univ, Minn, 87. *Awards:* Am Field Serv Scholar, 66-67; Raymond Fund Grantee, 73; Hon Award Am Inst Archit, St Paul Chap, 87; McKnight Found Fel, 89; Fel, Salzburg Seminars, 89. *Mem:* Miss Inst Arts & Letts (founding dir, 79-83); Am Asn Mus (mem chair, 87-90); Int Coun Mus; Assoc Art Mus Dir (89-94); Nat Ctr Nonprofit Bds; Minn Coun Nonprofits. *Media:* Photography, Conceptual Art. *Publ:* Through the Sky in the Lake (photogs), Milkweed Editions, 90. *Mailing Add:* 123 Farrington Saint Paul MN 55102-2101

CZARNOPYS, THOMAS J
SCULPTOR
b Grand Rapids, Mich, Dec 17, 57. *Study:* Sch Art Inst, BFA (art educ), 82. *Work:* Mus Contemp Art, Chicago; Wexner Ctr Arts, Columbus, Ohio; Milwaukee Art Mus, Wis; Grand Rapids Art Mus, Mich. *Exhib:* Solo exhibs, Grand Rapids Mus, Mich, 87, Contemp Arts Ctr, Cincinnati, Ohio, 88, Mus Contemp Art, Chicago, 88 & 89, Va Mus Fine Arts, Richmond, 89, Zolla/Lieberman Gallery, Chicago, 95, Mark Moore Gallery, Santa Monica, Calif, 95-96 & Ill Art Gallery, 96-97; The Nature of Sculpture, Jacksonville Art Mus, Fla, 91; About Landscape, Wexner Ctr Arts, Columbus, Ohio, 91; Zolla/Lieberman Gallery, Inc, Chicago, 94, 95, 96 & 97; Wink Wink, Space Gallery, Chicago, 95; Szinhaz Galeria, Hungary, 95; Art in Chicago: 1945-1995, Mus Contemp Art, Chicago, Ill, 96; Paper Thin, Stephen Wirtz Gallery, San Francisco, Calif, 98; and others. *Teaching:* Vis artist, Sch Art Inst Chicago, 88 & Mich State Univ, East Lansing, 90. *Awards:* Nat Endowment Arts Fel Grant, 90; Ill Arts Coun Grant, 90. *Bibliog:* Lynne Warren (auth), Options 35: Tom Czarnopys, Mus Contemp Art, 88; Kathryn Hixson (auth), Latitudes: Focus on Chicago, Aspen Art Mus, 88; Sarah Rogers-Lafferty (auth), About Landscape, Wexner Ctr Arts, 91. *Media:* Mixed, Bronze. *Mailing Add:* c/o Zolla/Lieberman 325 W Huron Chicago IL 60610

CZESTOCHOWSKI, JOSEPH STEPHEN
MUSEUM DIRECTOR
b Brooklyn, NY, Aug 8, 50. *Study:* Univ Ill, Champaign-Urbana, BA, 71, MA, 73; Jagiellonian Univ, Cracow, Poland, dipl, 71. *Collection Arranged:* Marvin D Cone--Retrospective, Cedar Rapids Mus Art, 80; Atelier 17--New Directions, Cedar Rapids Mus Art, 81; Mauricio Lasansky, Cedar Rapids Mus Art, 82; Maurice Lasansky Collection-Selected Works, Cedar Rapids Art Asn, 86-87; James Swann-A Catalog Raisonne Chicago Soc Etchers, Prairie Print Makers, Woodcut Soc, Cedar Rapids Art Asn, Iowa, 89; Grant Wood & Marvin Cone Collection, Cedar Rapids Mus Art, 90; Mervin D Cone: Art As Self Portrait, Cedar Rapids Mus, 90; Grant Wood: Prints & Drawings, Cedar Rapids Art Asn, 91; Masterpieces from Museu de Arte de Sao Paulo, Brazil, 97; Butler Inst Anthen Exhib, 03. *Pos:* Student asst, Krannert Art Mus, Univ Ill, 72; art ed, Perspectives Inc, Wash, DC, 72-75; cur collections, Brooks Mem Art Gallery, Memphis, Tenn, 73-75; exec dir, Cedar Rapids Mus Art, 78-95; dir, Decker Gallery, Md Inst, Col Art, 75-78, Dixon Gallery & Gardens, Memphis, Tenn, 95-98; cur, Int Arts, Torch Press, 88. *Awards:* Fel Comt Relig & Art in Am, 76; Smithsonian Inst Foreign Currency Prog Res Award, 76-; Nat Endowment Arts, 1A Arts Coun, 78-; First Nancy Hanks Mem Award, Am Asn Mus, 85; Nat Endowment Arts Mus Fel, 86. *Bibliog:* Iowa's Young Successes, Des Moines Register, 8/7/83; Museum interview, Cedar Rapids Gazette, Iowa, 10/11/85; Building on a legacy, Horizon Mag, 3/86; Rev, Des Moines Regist, 12/3/89; Interview, The Iowan, fall 90. *Mem:* Am Asn Mus (sr examiner, Accreditation Comn); Am Asn Art Mus Dirs (mem, Future Directions Comt); Col Art Asn; Int Coun Mus; Am Coun Arts; and others. *Res:* Nineteenth & early twentieth century American paintings, drawings and prints; contemporary American painters and printmakers; Polish art. *Publ:* Dixon Gallery & Gardens Permanent Collections Catalog, 96; Robert Rosenblum, Modern Masters, 2000; Anne Pingeot, Degas Sculptures, 2002; Apollo Degas, 6/2002; Georgia O'Keeffe: Visions of the Subline, 05. *Mailing Add:* c/o International Arts Torch Press 319 Goodwyn Memphis TN 38111

CZIMBALMOS, SZABO KALMAN
PAINTER, EDUCATOR
b Esztergom, Hungary, 1914. *Study:* Royal Hungarian Acad Fine Arts, Budapest, grad, 36; also with J Haranghy & E Domanowsky, Vienna, Prague, Munich, Paris, London & Rome. *Work:* Nat Gallery Budapest; City Mus Esztergom, Hungary; Staten Island Mus, NY; Staten Island Community Col. *Comn:* Murals 32 churches US; Hungarian Govt & pvt owners. *Exhib:* Pulitzer Art Gallery, NY; Int Inst, Detroit; Univ Del, 80; Staten Island Mus; Le Salon, Paris; one-man shows & group exhibs in Hungary, Ger, France & Monaco. *Pos:* Owner, Czimbalmos Art Studio, Esztergom, 37-38, studio, Reichenbach, Ger, 45-49 & Staten Island, NY, 50-; art dir & partner, Hungarian Doll & Handcraft Factory, Reichenbach, formerly; art dir, Hungarian Relief, New York, 50; dir, Czimbalmos Pvt Art Sch, 55-. *Awards:* Hungarian Art Award, Budapest, 34; Staten Island Mus Prize, 62, 64, 67 & 71; St Stephan Gold Medal, Pannonia Exhib, 71; City Award, Ezstergom, Hungary, 85. *Mem:* Bavaryan Fine Art Soc; Staten Island Mus Art (vpres art sect, 61-62, pres, 63-64, exec bd, 63-75); Pannonia World Orgn Hungarian Artists (chmn bd dir, 67-). *Media:* All

CZUMA, STANISLAW J
HISTORIAN, CURATOR
b Warsaw, Poland, Oct 26, 35; US citizen. *Study:* Jagiellonian Univ, BA & MA; Paderewski Found Scholar studies in India, 58-60; Nat Defense Foreign Lang Fel studies in India, 65-67; Banares Hindu Univ, with Vasudeva S Agrawala; Univ Calcutta, with S K Saraswati; Sorbonne, with Louis Renou; Univ Mich, with Walter Spink, PhD, 68. *Collection Arranged:* Cambodian Art, Asia Soc Gallery, New York

(with catalog), 69; Permanent Indian Gallery, Brooklyn Mus; Indian Art from the George P Bickford Collection, Cleveland Mus (with catalog), 75; Kushan Sculpture, Cleveland Mus, Asia Soc Gallery, Seattle Mus (with catalog), 85-86. *Pos:* Ford Found curatorial trainee, Cleveland Mus, 68-69; cur Oriental art, Brooklyn Mus, 69-72; cur Indian & Southeast Asian Art, Cleveland Mus, 72-. *Teaching:* Res asst Oriental art, Univ Mich, Ann Arbor, 62-64; adj prof, Case Western Reserve Univ, 72-2001. *Mem:* Asn Asian Studies. *Res:* Art of India and early southeast Asia, especially Kushan, Gupta & Early Medieval India, SE Asia with the focus on Cambodia, Himalayan Art. *Publ:* Auth, Gupta style bronze Buddha, 2/70, A masterpiece of early Cambodian sculpture, 4/74, Mathura sculpture in the Cleveland Mus Collection, 3/77 & Mon-Dvaravati Buddha, 9/80, The School of Kashmiri Ivories, 10/88, Bulletin Cleveland Mus; coauth, Masterworks of Asian Art, Cleveland Mus Art Catalog, 98; Ivory Sculpture, Art & Architecture of Ancient Kashmir, Marg Publ, Bombay, 89; The Kailasanatha Temple at Ellora, Makaranda, 90; Some Tibetan and Tibet Realted Acquisitions of the Cleveland Mus of Art, Oriental Art, 92-93; Masterworks of Asian Art, The Cleveland Mus of Art, (Catalogue), Cleveland Mus Art, Cleveland, OH, 98. *Mailing Add:* Cleveland Mus Art Asian Art Dept 11150 East Blvd Cleveland OH 44106

D

DABBERT, PATRICIA ANN
CERAMIST, SCULPTOR
b Albuquerque, NMex, Feb 22, 43. *Study:* Univ Hawaii, 62; Univ NMex, Albuquerque, BFA, 65; Ind Univ, Bloomington, MA, 67. *Work:* Bowling Green State Univ, Ohio; Owens-Ill Corp, Toledo, Ohio; State Savings Bank, Columbus, Ohio; 1st of Am Bank, Michigan City, Ind; JG Blank Ctr Arts, Michigan City. *Comn:* wall sculpture, Porter, Wright, Morris, Arthur, Miami, Fla, 88; wall sculpture, comn by Mr/Mrs L Hoodwin, Michigan City, 90; Holiday at the White House (Christmas ornament), comn by Hillary R Clinton, Washington DC, 93; wall sculpture, comn by Mr/Mrs G Abraham, Burr Ridge, Ill, 94; wall sculpture, comn by Mr/Mrs R Hull, Sarasota, Fla, 97. *Exhib:* Lakefront Festival Arts, Milwaukee Art Ctr, 93; Boca Raton Mus Art, Fla, 95; Las Olas Mus Arts Festival, Mus Art, Ft Lauderdale, Fla, 96; Beaux Arts Festival Art, Lowe Art Mus, Coral Gables, Fla, 96; Gasparilla Art Festival, Tampa Art Mus, Fla, 97; Flint Art Fair, Flint Inst Arts, Mich, 97. *Pos:* juror art show, Chesterton Arts & Crafts Fair, Ind, 88 & Prom Mgt Asn, Michigan City, 76. *Teaching:* instr art appreciation, Purdue North Cent, Westville, Ind, 68-73; instr advan art, Elston Sr High Sch, Michigan City, 73-84. *Bibliog:* Berk (auth), What to Do with 3 Tons of Clay, News Dispatch, 83; Grosswiller (auth), Area Artists Show New Paintings & Clay Works, Dunebeat, 83; Brewster (auth), Festival News, Crosby Gardens Art Festival Program, 87. *Mem:* Mich Guild Artists & Artisans; Artists & Craftsmen Porter Co; Sarasota Co Arts Coun; Fla Craftsmen. *Media:* Porcelain, Clay. *Publ:* contribr, Guild 3 Source Book of American Craft Artists, 87 & Guild 4 Source Book of American Craft Artists, 88, Guild Publ; contribr, Columbus Arts Festival Brochure & Poster, Greater Columbus Arts Coun, 91; auth, Sunshine Artist, Sunshine Artist Mag, 95; contribr (with S Peterson), The Craft & Art of Clay, 98. *Dealer:* Dabbert Gallery 76 S Palm Ave Sarasota Fl 34241. *Mailing Add:* 4819 Hoyer Dr Sarasota FL 34241

DABLOW, DEAN CLINT
PHOTOGRAPHER, EDUCATOR
b Superior, Wis, Aug 26, 46. *Study:* Univ Wis, Stevens Point, BS(educ), 69; Univ Iowa, MA, 72, MFA, 74. *Work:* New Orleans Mus Art, La; Kansas City Art Inst, Mo; Mus Art, Univ Okla; Corcoran Gallery, Washington; Baltimore Mus Art. *Exhib:* Photog in Louisiana 1900-1980, New Orleans Mus Art, 80; Louisiana Major Works, La World's Fair, 84; traveling exhib, A Century of Vision: La Photog 1884-1984; LaGrange Nat XI, Ga, 86; Southeastern Juried exhib, Mobile Mus Art, Ala, 96; Red Clay Survey, Huntsville, Ala, 2005. *Collection Arranged:* The rain are fallin: Photographs from the Farm Security Admin in Louisiana 1935-1943 (traveling exhib), 95. *Teaching:* Prof art, La Tech Univ, Ruston, 76-, photo program coord, currently. *Awards:* Artist Fel Grant Color Photog, La Arts Coun, 82; Purchase Award, 16th Ann Prints, Drawings & Crafts, Ark Art Ctr, 83 & LaGrange Nat XI, Ga, 86; Southern Arts Fedn/Nat Endowment Arts, Regional Photog, Fel, 87. *Bibliog:* Natalie Canavor (auth), Popular Photography, 4/83; Turner Browne & Elaine Partnow (ed), Photographic Artists & Innovators, MacMillan, NY, 83. *Mem:* Soc Photographic Educ. *Media:* Archival Ink Jet Digital Photographs. *Publ:* Contribr, Creative Camera International Yearbook, Coo Press, London, 77; New Photographics/78 (cover), Cent Wash State Col, 78; Camera, CJ Bucher Ltd, Lucerne, Switz, 9/81; The rain are fallin: A Search for the People and Places Photographed by the Farm Security Administration in Louisiana, 1935-1943, Scrub Jay Press, Tollhouse, Calif, 2001. *Mailing Add:* La Tech Univ Ruston LA 71272

DACEY, PAUL
PAINTER
b Toledo, Ohio, Jul 16, 60. *Study:* Lacoste Summer Arts Prog, France, 1982; Artists Environ Found, 1982; Ellen Battell Stoeckel Fel, Yale Univ 83; Cleveland Inst Art, BFA, 1984. *Work:* Toledo Mus of Art, Ohio; Progressive, Mayfield Village, Ohio; Dechert, Price & Rhoads, NY; Cleary, Gottlieb, Steen & Hamilton, NY; Novell, San Jose, Calif. *Comn:* Worlds without End, Nokia, Dallas, Tex, 1999; Room of 18, US Embassy, Ottawa, Can, 1999; WWE, Credit Suisse First Boston, London, Eng, 1999-2000; Grus, US Embassy, Kampala, Uganda, 2000; The Fall of Man, Mr & Mrs Banta, NY, 2002. *Exhib:* Winter Show, Cleveland Ctr Contemp Art, Cleveland, Ohio, 1984; Small Works, NY Univ, NY, 1996, 1998; The Form of the Formless, 2002, Ten Yrs, Kunstverein Grafschaft Bentheim, Neuenhaus, Ger, 2003; Toledo Area Artists, Toledo Mus of Art, Ohio, 2004; 39th Juried Exhib, Parrish Art Mus, Southampton, NY, 2005. *Bibliog:* Rebekaa Scott (auth), Art of the Disc, The Toledo Blade, 1/3/1999; Heidi Mocklinghoff (auth), Stamp on the Wall, Munstersche Zeitung, 5/6/2002; Von Thomas Kern (auth), Of Cosmos, Game & Chaos, Graftchafter Nachreich Ten, 5/7/2002. *Media:* Acrylic on plastic discs. *Dealer:* Maxwell Davidson Gallery 724 5th Ave 4th floor NY NY 10019. *Mailing Add:* 35-21 80th St Apt 23 Jackson Heights NY 11372

D'AGOSTINO , CLAUDIO A
SCULPTOR
b Toronto, Canada, Apr 9, 63. *Study:* study under Laura Peterson, 91-95, Domenico Mazzone 95-98. *Work:* US Marine Corps Command Mus, San Diego; The White House, Washington, DC; Spreckels Organ, Balboa Park, San Diego, 2004. *Comn:* Pres and Mrs Clinton Flower Sculpture, Nat Italian American Found, Washington, DC, 94; Drill Instructor Sculpture, MCRD Mus Historical Soc, San Diego, 2002; Lt Dan Daly, MCRD Command Mus, San Diego, 2003; Consul Gen Clin Robertson, Can, 2004; Congressman John R Lewis Ga, Washington, DC, 2006. *Exhib:* San Diego Sculpture Guild, San Diego Sculpture Mus, 97; Holiday Gala & Art Fair, San Diego Mus Art, 96; Art Walk San Diego, 96. *Pos:* Instr, Claudio D'Agostino Studio, San Diego, 2005-. *Teaching:* Sculpture, Portraiture, D'agostino Studio, 2004-. *Awards:* 1st Place, Ceramics Expo, City of San Diego, 95; Commanding Gen, Marines of MCRD, WRR, Medal and Award, 97. *Bibliog:* Nat Sculpture Soc NY issue newspaper, 5-6/2003; NIAF Wash DC news mag, 5/2003. *Mem:* Nat Sculpture Soc, NY; Cova San Diego; San Diego Sculpture Guild; San Diego Commn Arts & Culture. *Media:* Bronze, Miscellaneous Media. *Interests:* Human and life study; Portraiture, bas-relief to monumental; Bronze and others. *Publ:* Cpl Anthony D Pike, Sculpted in History, The Chevron MCRD, 02; Nat Sculpture Soc, 03; Nat Sculpture Soc, 2004-2005. *Mailing Add:* PO Box 632992 San Diego CA 92163

D'AGOSTINO, PETER
VIDEO ARTIST, EDUCATOR
b New York, NY, July 29, 45. *Study:* Acad Fine Arts, Italy, 65; Sch Visual Arts, New York, BFA, 68; San Francisco State Univ, MA, 75. *Work:* Artists Mus, Lodz, Poland; Long Beach Mus Art, Calif; Palais des Beaux-Arts, Charleroi, Belg; Nat Gallery Can, Ottawa; Mus Mod Art, NY. *Comn:* Performances: Angel Island, San Francisco Mus Mod Art, 77; Alpha Week of Int Performances, Mus Mod Art, Bologna, Italy, 77; San Francisco BART, San Francisco Mus Mod Art, 78; DC Metro, Washington Proj for Art, 79; Teletapes, TV Lab, WNET, NY, 81; STRING Cycles, Inst Contemp Art, Boston. *Exhib:* Time/Space/Sound: 1970's, San Francisco Mus Mod Art, 80; solo exhibs, Peter d'Agostino Interaction & Intervention, 78-99, Art Space, Auckland, NZ, 93, Banff Ctr Arts, Can, 94, Weatherspoon Gallery, Univ NC, 95, Univ Art Mus, Berkeley, 95, Cult Space, Brasilia, Brazil, 97, Lehman Col Art Gallery, NY, 99; Whitney Mus Am Art Biennial, 81; Philadelphia Mus Art, 87; Construction in Process, Kino Mus, Lodz, Poland, 90; Tele-Visions: Channels for Changing TV, Long Beach Mus Art, 91; Montage 93: Int Festival of Image, Rochester, NY, 93; Angles of Incidence: Video Reflections of MultiMedia Artworks, Banff Centre Arts, 93; New Light: The Electronic Cinema, Nat Gallery Art, Washington, DC, 95; Info Art, Kwangju Biennale, Korea, 95; Expo Arte, Guadalajara 97, VI Int Contemp Art Festival, Mex, 97; New Video, Sch Visual Arts, Rio de Janeiro, Brazil, 97; Images for the Millennium, Long Island Ctr Photog, NY, 98. *Pos:* Dir, Temple/London, 88; artist in residence, Television Laboratory WNET/Thirteen. *Teaching:* Instr art, Lone Mountain Col, 73-76 & San Francisco Art Inst, 76-77, San Francisco; asst prof art & art hist, Wright State Univ, Dayton, Ohio, 77-80; vis prof art, Univ NC, Chapel Hill, 82; prof commun, Temple Univ, 82-; fel, Ctr Advan Visual Studies, Mass Inst Technol, 83-85; vis artist, Am Acad Rome, 86; prof film and media arts and dir New-Tech Lab, Temple Univ, Philadelphia, 82-. *Awards:* Nat Endowment Arts Awards, 74, 77, 79, 85 & 89; Fulbright Fel, Brazil, 96-97; Rockefeller Found, Bellagio Ctr Fel, Lake Como, Italy, 97. *Bibliog:* Hal Fischer (auth), Cinematic Structures, Afterimage, summer 78; Paula Marincola (auth), Peter D'Agostino, review, Artforum, 11/87; David Tafler, (auth), The Circular Text: Interactive Video, Reception and Viewer Participation, Journal of Film and Video, summer 88. *Mem:* Col Art Asn Am; Int Network Arts. *Media:* Video, Film Photography. *Publ:* Ed, Transmission, Tanam Press, 85; Essays, Alumination, 90; contribr, Illuminating Video, Aperture, NY, 91; co-ed, Transmission Toward a Post-Television Culture, Sage Publ, 94; contribr, Theories & Documents of Contemporary Art, Univ Calif Press, 96. *Dealer:* Electronic Arts Intermix 536 Broadway New York NY 10012. *Mailing Add:* 523 Shoemaker Rd Elkins Park PA 19027

DAHILL, THOMAS HENRY, JR
PAINTER, EDUCATOR
b Cambridge, Mass, June 22, 25. *Study:* Tufts Col, BS, 49; Harvard Univ, summer 53; Sch Mus Fine Arts, Boston, dipl, 53, cert, 54; Skowhegan Sch Painting & Sculpture; Am Acad in Rome, Fel, 55-57; Max Beckmann Gesellschaft, Murnau, Ger, resident, 56; Emerson Col, AM, 67. *Work:* Fogg Mus, Lenin Libr, Moscow. *Comn:* Film strip, life of George Washington Carver, 61; portrait, Dr Richard D Pierce, 74; drawing series on Madagascar, 83 & Bali, 85; Life Cycle (mural), First & Second Church Boston, 98; portrait, James & Susan Jackson, Brookline, Mass, 95; portrait, Haig der Muderosian, Emerson Col, 95; murals, Dock, 2005 & Village, 2006, Middlesex Canal Mus, Billerica, Mass. *Exhib:* Boston Art Festival, 55, 56 & 63; Archit League, NY, 58; Int Bienale Relig Art, Salzburg, Austria, 58-59; Emerson Col, 64 & 67; Drawings of NAfrica exhib through Mus Fine Arts Boston to galleries of New Eng prep schs, 67-69; St Botolph Club, 90; The Incredible Ditch (auth, catalog), Widener Libr, Harvard Univ, 98; Tufts Univ, 99; Middlesex Canal Mus, Billerica, 2005. *Teaching:* Lectr gen art hist & contemp use of art in churches; instr hist art, Tufts Univ, 54-55 & 60-65; instr dept drawing, Sch Mus Fine Arts, Boston, 58-71; prof fine arts & chmn dept, Emerson Col, 67-95, summer sch abroad, Europe, Africa & Asia, 67-82, prof

emer, 95-; guest, Minister of Cult, Moscow, USSR, summer, 74. *Awards:* Abbey Mem Fel to Am Acad in Rome, 55-57. *Mem:* MacDowell Colonists; Boston Ctr Arts; Soc Fel Am Acad in Rome; Medici Soc. *Media:* Acrylic on Canvas; Pen & Watercolor. *Publ:* Contribr, Seaburg, Dahill Publ, 97; illusr, Cambridge on the Charles, 01; Linda Yeaton Poetry, Magic House, illusto, 2004. *Mailing Add:* 223 Broadway Arlington MA 02474

DAHL, STEPHEN M
PHOTOGRAPHER
b Frederic, Wis, Sept 13, 53. *Study:* Univ Wis, Eau Claire, BA, 71-75; Univ Wis, Madison, MA (social work), 78-79; Minneapolis Col Art & Design, Minn, 84-85; Film in the Cities, St Paul, Minn, 84-87; Visual Studies Workshop, Rochester, NY, 85. *Work:* St Paul Co, Minn; Damark Int, Minneapolis, Minn; Minn Hist Soc, St Paul. *Exhib:* Heartland: Regionalist Vision of the Am Farm, Univ Art Mus, Univ Minn, 90; Black & White Photographs from My Goodhue Co Farm Family Documentary, 93; Farm Life, Opsis, NY, 93; solo show, Minn Governors Residence, St Paul, Minn, 93 & Univ Northern Iowa, Cedar Falls, 94; Katherine Nash Gallery, Univ Minn, 95; Face Value in Pursuit of the Person, Minn State Col Art & Design, 98; Working: The Photogs of Stephen Dahl, Parts Photog Arts, Minn, 99; Minnesota 2000 Documentary Project Exhib, Minn Hist Soc, St Paul, 2000. *Pos:* Social worker, Waushara Co Dept Social Servs, Wautoma, Wis, 75-78 & Hopkins Sch Dist, Minn, 79-. *Teaching:* Artist-in-residence, Minn State Arts Bd, St Paul, Minn. *Awards:* Minn State Arts Bd Photog Fel, St Paul, Minn, 92 & 96; McKnight Fel, 93; Minn Hist Soc, 98; Jerome Found Travel & Study Grant, St Paul, 2000. *Publ:* working: Photographs of Working People by Stephen Dahl, Parts Photo Arts, 99; Minnesota in Our Time: A Photographic Portrait 12 Photographers Document the Turn of the Century, Minn Hist Soc Press, 2000

DAHLSTROM, NANCY GAIL
PRINTMAKER, PAINTER
b Buffalo, NY, Nov 29, 48. *Study:* State Univ NY, Buffalo, BFA, 70; Ohio Univ, MFA, 73. *Work:* Roanoke City Civic Ctr & Hollins Col, Roanoke, Va; Fed Reserve Bank Gallery & First & Merchants Bank, Richmond, Va; US Govt, 10 Foreign Embassies. *Exhib:* Solo exhib, Yard Quilts, Roanoke Mus Fine Art, 77; Papermaking & Paper Using, Southeast Ctr Contemp Art, Winston-Salem, NC, 79-80; 4 With Paper, traveling in Va, 79-80; Atelier Nord Etchers, Gallery F15, Jeløya Island, Norway, 82; Paperworks, Va Mus, Richmond & traveling, 82-84; Albright-Knox Gallery, Buffalo, NY, 85; Atelier Nord: 20 Yrs (with catalog), Galleri Aktuell Kunst, Oslo, 85; Contemp Sculpture by Virginia Artists, Portsmouth Mus, Va, 85. *Teaching:* Assoc prof art, printmaking & drawing, Hollins Col, Roanoke, Va, 73-. *Awards:* 2nd Place Printmaking, Allentown Exhib, Buffalo, NY, 72; 1st Prize Printmaking, Roanoke Mus Fine Art, Va, 75; Cabell Fel, One Year Travel & Art in Paris, Greece, Norway, 87-88. *Bibliog:* Heller (auth), Printmaking Slide Set, Crystal Publ, Aspen, Colo, 83; Annie Cheatham & Mary Clare Powell (auths), This Way Day Break Comes, New Soc Publ, 86. *Mem:* Col Art Asn. *Publ:* Illusr, article, in: Hand Papermaking Manual, Roanoke Valley Arts Coun, 79

DAIGNEAULT, GILLES
CURATOR, CRITIC
b Montreal, Que, Apr 20, 43. *Study:* Univ D'Aix-Marseille, Doctorate es lettres, 70. *Collection Arranged:* L'art au Quebec Depuis Pellan, Musee Quebec, 88; F Sullivan & D Moore, Musee de Rimooski, 89; Montreal 1942-1992, Galerie de L'ugam, 92; Art Actuel-Presences Quebecoises, Chateau Biron, France, 92. *Pos:* Art critic, Soc Radio-Can, 78-89 & LeDevoir, Montreal, 82-88. *Mem:* Asn Int des Critiques D'Art (depuis, 80). *Publ:* coauth, La Gravure au Quebec 1940-1980, Heritage, Montreal, 81; auth, L'Art au Quebec Depuis Pellan, Musee du Que, 88; coauth, Art Actuel-Presences Quebecoises, Paris, 92; coauth, Montreal 1942-1992, L'Anarchie Resplendissante de la Peinture, Univ du Que, 92. *Mailing Add:* 4596 Christophe Colomb Montreal PQ H2J 3G6 Canada

DAILEY, CHUCK (CHARLES) ANDREW
MUSEOLOGIST, PAINTER
b Golden, Colo, May 25, 35. *Study:* Univ Colo, BA(art), 61; study in Western Europe, 62-63. *Work:* Mus NMex Permanent Collection, Santa Fe; Vincent Price Collection, Hollywood, Calif; US Dept Interior, BIA Collection, Washington, DC. *Exhib:* Fiesta Biennial, 64 & 65 & Southwest Biennial, 68, Mus NMex; NMex State Fair, Albuquerque, 68; one-man show, Gallery 5, Santa Fe, 64; J F Kennedy Performing Art Ctr, Washington, DC, 73. *Collection Arranged:* New Mexican Santero, 70-71 & World of Folk Costume, 71-72, Mus Int Folk Art, Spanish Endure (Spanish hist in Southwest), Palace of Governors, Mus NMex; Indian Arts & Crafts, J F Kennedy Ctr Performing Arts, Washington, DC, 73; One with the Earth traveling exhib, US & Can, 76-89; Mus Am Southwest, Canova, Italy, 94; 35th Anniversary Exhib, Inst Am Indian Arts Mus, 97. *Pos:* Mus preparator, Univ Colo Mus, Boulder, 59-61; exhibs tech, Mus Northern Ariz, Flagstaff, 62-63; cur-in-charge exhib div, Mus NMex, 64-71; mus workshop presentations, NMex, Alaska, Okla, Ariz & Wash & Smithsonian Inst. *Teaching:* Mus training dir, Inst Am Indian Arts, Santa Fe, 89. *Bibliog:* Catherine Wenzell (auth), Artists of Santa Fe, privately publ, 68. *Mem:* NMex Asn Mus; Am Indian Mus Asn; Am Asn Mus; Midwest Mus Asn; Far West Mus Asn; Nat Mus Am Indian. *Media:* Acrylic. *Publ:* Auth, Creating a Crowd, NMex Asn Mus, 72; Bringing a Unique Perspective to Museum Work, Mus News, 5-6/77; A Selection of contemporary art by Native Americans from the Museum of the Institute of American Indian Arts, Ohio Univ Press, 81; Major Influences in the Development of 20th Century Native American art, 82 & Many ways of seeing: The anniversary of the Institute of American Indian Arts, 83, Inst Am Indian Arts Press; Institute of American Indian Arts Mus Training, IAIA Printing, 2000. *Mailing Add:* 39 Apache Ridge Rd Santa Fe NM 87505-8906

DAILEY, DAN (DANIEL) OWEN
SCULPTOR, EDUCATOR
b Philadelphia, Pa, Feb 4, 47. *Study:* Philadelphia Col Art, BFA(glass), 69; RI Sch Design, MFA(glass), 72. *Work:* Corning Mus Glass, Metrop Mus Art, NY; Smithsonian Mus, Washington, DC; Nat Gallery Victoria, Melbourne, Australia; High Mus Art, Atlanta, Ga; Philadelphia Mus Art; Los Angeles Co Mus Art; Boston Mus Fine Arts; and others. *Comn:* Orbit cast glass relief (mural), Rainbow Room Rockefeller Ctr, 87; cast glass relief (mural), Marietta Mem Hosp, Ohio, 88; Exuberance cast glass relief (mural), Vail Transportation Ctr, Colo; Sea Grass in Wind (12' x 16' cast glass mural), Northern Essex Co Courthouse, 91; cast glass mural, Los Angeles Co Mus, 93; Glass Mural, 92nd St Y, NY, 98; Vase, The Mayo Clinic, Rochester, MN, 2001; Byzantine Sconces, Restaurant Daniel, NY, 2002; Chandelier, The Providence Performing Arts Ctr, RI, 2004. *Exhib:* One-man shows, Mass Inst Technol Gallery, 75 & 77, Theo Portnoy Gallery, NY, 77 & 79-82, Habatat Galleries, Detroit, Mich, 81, 83, 89 & 90, Heller Gallery, NY, 85, Betsy Rosenfield Gallery, Chicago, Ill, 86, 88 & 90, Habatat Galleries, Boca Raton, Fla, 87-2005, Rosenwald/Wolf Gallery, Philadelphia Col Art, Renwick Gallery, Smithsonian Inst, Washington, DC, 87, Kurland/Summers Gallery, Los Angeles, 88 & 90 & Kaplan Gallery, NY, 90-2005; 1990 Economic Summit of Industrialized Nations, Rice Univ, Houston; Los Angeles Co Mus Art, 94; Kestner Mus, Ger, 94; Musee des Arts, Decoratifs Paris, 94; Toledo Mus Art, 94; and others. *Pos:* Guest designer, Fabrica Venini, Murano, Venice, Italy, 72-73; designer & freelance artist, Cristallerie Daum, Paris & Nancy, France, 75- & Steuben Glass, NY, 82-; Nat bd adv, Univ Arts, Philadelphia, Pa, 89-, Renwick Gallery, Smithsonian Inst, Washington, DC; owner, Dan Dailey Inc Studio, Kensington, NH, 77-; bd dir, Glass Art Ctr, Bradford Col, Mass; bd Governors, Mus of Art & Design, NY, 2000. *Teaching:* Teaching fel glass, RI Sch Design, Providence, 70-72; assoc prof glass, Mass Col Art, Boston, 73-89, chmn three-dimensional fine arts dept, 74-79, dir glass prog, 73-89, prof, 89-; res fel sculpture & glass, Mass Inst Technol, Ctr for Adv Visual Studies, 75-80; fac mem, Pilshuck Glass Sch, Stanwood, Wash, 74-; Haystack Mountain Sch Crafts, Deer Isle, Maine, 76-, trustee, 83-92. *Awards:* Fulbright-Hays Grant as Designer, Fabrica Venini, Murano, Italy, 72-73; Nat Endowment for the Arts Fel, 79; Masters Fel, Creative Glass Ctr Am, 89; The President's Distinguished Artist Award, The Univ of the Arts, Philadelphia, PA, 2001. *Bibliog:* Marsha Miro (auth), Two approaches to glass: one sophisticated the other sophomoric, Detroit Free Press, 6/90; Jane Holtz Kay (auth), Architects expand use of glass art, NY Times, 7/90; Dan Dailey: Simple Complexities in Drawing & Glass 1972-1987 (catalog), Rosenwald Wolf Gallery & Renwick Gallery; Dan Daily and Linda Mac Neil: Art in Glass and Metal, Printed on the occasion of the Exhib at The Art Center at Hargate, St Paul School, 99; Dan Daily and Linda MacNeil: Art in Glass and Metal, Printed on the occasion of the Exhib at The Art Center at Hargate, St Paul's School, 99; Yelle, Richard Wilfred, International Glass Art, Schiffer Publishing, 2003. *Mem:* Life Mem Glass Art Soc Am (bd dir, pres, chmn bd, 80, 81-82); fel Am Craft Coun; NY Experimental Glass Workshop (bd dir, 1978-88); Mus of Arts and Design. *Media:* Glass, Metal. *Dealer:* Leo Kaplan Modern 965 Madison Ave New York NY 10021. *Mailing Add:* 2 North Rd Kensington NH 03833

DAILEY, MICHAEL DENNIS
PAINTER, EDUCATOR
b Des Moines, Iowa, Aug 2, 38. *Study:* Univ Iowa, BA & MFA. *Work:* Smithsonian Inst, Washington, DC; Munic Gallery Mod Art, Dublin, Ireland; Seattle Art Mus, Wash; Mercyhurst Col, Erie, Pa; Mus of Mod Art, NY. *Exhib:* Art Across Am, San Francisco Mus Art, 65; Ultimate Concerns Drawing Exhib, Ohio Univ, Athens, 65; one-man shows, Tacoma Art Mus, Wash, 66 & 75, Mus of Northwest Art, Conner, Wash, 2002, Fountain Gallery, Portland, 71, 73, 77, 81 & 84, Francine Seders Gallery, Seattle, 71, 74, 76, 78, 84, 87, 90, 94, 96, 97, 2000, 2003, 2004, William Sawyer Gallery, San Francisco, 72, 74, 76 & 82 & Laura Russo Gallery, Portland, 89, 93, 95, 98, 2000, 2003; Drawings USA, St Paul Art Ctr, Minn, 66 & 68; 73rd Western Ann, Denver Art Mus, Colo, 71; Art of the Pacific Northwest, Smithsonian Inst, 74; Am Acad & Inst Arts & Lett, NY, 86. *Teaching:* Prof drawing & painting, Univ Wash, 63-98, prof emeritus, 98-. *Awards:* Purchase Award, Mercyhurst Nat Graphics Exhib, Erie, Pa, 65; First Place Award Painting, Wash State Ann Art Exhib, 67; Northwest Watercolor Soc Award, 30th Ann Northwest Watercolor Exhib, Seattle Art Mus, 70. *Media:* Acrylic, Oil. *Dealer:* Francine Seders Gallery 6701 Greenwood Ave N Seattle WA 98103; Laura Russo Gallery 805 NW 21st Ave Portland OR 97209. *Mailing Add:* 5805 17th Ave NE Seattle WA 98105-2511

DAILEY, VICTORIA KEILUS
WRITER, ART DEALER
b Los Angeles, Calif, Jan 21, 48. *Study:* Univ Calif, Los Angeles, BA, 70. *Collection Arranged:* Chemical Printing: The Invention of Lithography (auth, catalog), 80; The Poltroon Press: 10th Anniversary Retrospective (auth, catalog), 80; Joby Baker: Prints, Drawings Monotypes (auth, catalog), 80; Auguste Lepere Wood engravings (auth, catalog), 81; Terry De Lapp: Recent Still Life Paintings, 81. *Mem:* Printing Historical Soc; Bibliographical Soc Am; Graphic Arts Coun; Antiquarian Booksellers Asn Am (bd govs, 80-); Groiler Club, NY. *Specialty:* 19th century prints and drawings, mainly French and English; art and illustrated books. *Publ:* Ed, Frijoles Canyon Pictographs, Pegacycle Press, 81; Henri Riviere, Peregrine Smith, 83. *Mailing Add:* 8216 Melrose Ave Los Angeles CA 90048

DAILY-BIRNBAUM, ELAINE
PAINTER
b Wichita, KS, Jan 02, 43. *Study:* St Joseph's Col, BS, 1984; Special study with Glenn Bradshaw, 2000-2002. *Work:* Univ of Wis Hosp & Clinics, Madison, Wis; Wis Dept of Transportation, Green Bay, Wis; Powell & Goldstein LLP. *Exhib:* San Diego Watercolor Soc Int Edhib, 1998-1999, 2001-2003; Three-Women exhib, Women in

Abstraction, Center for Visual Arts, Wausau, Wis, 2000; Am Watercolor Soc Int Exhib, 2002-2003, 2006; Nat Watercolor Soc Int Exhib, 2002, 2005; Rocky Mountain Nat Watermedia Exhib, 2005-2006. *Awards:* Gold Medal Award, Calif Watercolor Soc Nat Exhib, 2004; Best Show Award, Rocky Mountain Nat Watermedia Exhib, 2005; Silver Medal Award, Am Watercolor Soc Int Exhib, 2006. *Mem:* San Diego Watercolor Soc (signature mem 2001); Nat Watercolor Soc (signature mem 2002); Am Watercolor Soc (signature mem 2006). *Media:* Acrylic, Oil, Miscellaneous Media, Watercolor. *Mailing Add:* 5887 Woodsedge Rd Madison WI 53711

DALE, RON G
CERAMIST, SCULPTOR
b Spruce Pine, NC, Jan 26, 49. *Study:* Penland Sch, 71, 74 & 78; Goddard Col, Plainfield, Vt, BA, 77; La State Univ, Baton Rouge, MFA, 79. *Work:* John Michael Kohler Arts Ctr, Sheboygan, Wis; Asher-Faure Gallery, Los Angeles; Lockerbie Manufacturing Inc, Los Angeles. *Exhib:* Westwood Clay National, Downey Mus, Calif, 81; Betty Asher's Cups, Triton Mus, Santa Clara, Calif, 82; Still Lifes, Asheville Art Mus, NC, 83; solo exhib, Southeastern Ctr Contemp Art, Winston-Salem, NC, 83; Lagrange National, Lamar Dodd Art Ctr, Ga, 84; National Furniture Invitational, Am Crafts Coun, Tupelo Arts Ctr, Miss, 85. *Teaching:* Asst prof ceramics, Univ Miss, Oxford, 80-; vis instr ceramics, Penland Sch, NC, summer 85. *Bibliog:* Bova (auth), Ron Dale: Emerging talent, Nat Coun Educ Ceramic Arts J, 8/83; article, Ron Dale, Ceramics Monthly, 3/84; article, Paint on clay, Am Craft. *Mem:* Nat Coun Educ Ceramic Arts; Craftsmen's Guild Miss. *Media:* Clay, Wood. *Publ:* Auth, George E Ohr: Mad Biloxi Potter, Univ Miss, 83; George Ohr exhibition, Nat Coun Educ Ceramic Arts J, 83. *Dealer:* Martha Schneider Gallery 2055 Green Bay Rd Highland Pk IL 60035; Mario Villa Gallery 3988 Magazine St New Orleans LA 70115. *Mailing Add:* 42 County Rd 411 Oxford MS 38655

DALE, WILLIAM SCOTT ABELL
HISTORIAN, EDUCATOR
b Toronto, Ont, Sept 18, 21. *Study:* Univ Toronto, BA & MA; Harvard Univ, PhD. *Collection Arranged:* Philip Aziz: Hidden Icons (exhib catalog), London Regional Art & Hist Mus, Ont, 96. *Pos:* Res cur, Nat Gallery Can, Ottawa, Ont, 51-57; cur, Art Gallery Toronto, 57-59; dir, Vancouver Art Gallery, BC, 59-61; asst dir, Nat Gallery Can, 61-66, dep dir, 66-67; chmn, visual arts dept, Univ Western Ont, 67-75, 85-87. *Teaching:* Prof art hist, Univ Western Ont, 67-87, Prof emer, 87-. *Mem:* Col Art Asn Am; Medieval Acad Am; Royal Soc Arts; Int Ctr Medieval Art. *Res:* Romanesque ivories; sculpture of Chartres West; Exeter Cathedral; ancient & medieval perspective. *Publ:* Contribr, Arts in Canada, 58; Oxford Companion to Art, 70; The British Museum Yearbook, 76; Latens Deitas: The Holy Sacrament Altarpiece of Dieric Bouts, Vol XI, No 1-2, Revue d'Art Canadienne/Can Art Rev, 84; Donatellos Chellini Madonna: Speculum Sine Macula, Vol CXLI, No 397, Apollo, 3/95. *Mailing Add:* 1517 Gloucester Rd London ON N6G 2S5 Canada

D'ALESSIO, HILDA TERRY See Terry, Hilda

D'ALESSIO, NATALIE MARINO
PAINTER
b Elizabeth, NJ. *Study:* NY Univ, BA, 71; New Sch Social Res, 74; Summit Art Ctr, cert, 81; NJ Ctr Visual Arts; study with Philip Sherrod, Street Painters, NY; Accademia Bedriancense, Calvatone, Italy, Master Acad Art, 82. *Work:* Essex Co Div Aging, Orange, NJ; US Tang Soo Do Moo Duk Kwan Fedn Inc Mus, Springfield, NJ; Div Cult Affairs Essex Co, Newark, NJ; Soo Bahk Do Asn Hist Mus, Seoul, Korea. *Exhib:* Nabisco Brands Inc Invitational, NJ, 85; Florence Art Gallery, Dallas, Tex, 86; Rosalyn Sailor Fine Arts, Philadelphia, PA & Margate, NJ, 90, 91 & 92; Tom Winers' Art Insights, NY; Marino Galleries, NJ; and others. *Pos:* Cur & dir, Corridor Case Exhib, Summit Art Ctr Mus, NJ, 79-81, dir, art forum, 80-86. *Teaching:* Instr advan painting, Union Col Cont Educ, Cranford, NJ, 81-82 & Riker Hill Art Park, Livingston, NJ, 83-86; instr art, Union Bd Educ, Union Co, NJ, 84-86. *Awards:* Gold Medal, European Banner Arts, Calvatone, Italy, 84; Ludwig Vogelstein Found Grant, 85-86; Union Co Art Grant NJ State Coun Arts, 89; Best of Pastel, Pastel Soc Am, 96. *Bibliog:* R DuBois (auth), D'Alessio brings feeling to the 2-Dimensional canvas, Art Voices South, 3-4/79; Rochelle Holt (auth), D'Alessio on cities and nudes, Art Workers News, 4/79; E Forman Singer (auth), rev, World Press, 81. *Mem:* Artists Equity; Women's Caucus Art; Riker Hill Art Asn, Livingston, NJ (steering comt, 84-86, secy, 85-86). *Media:* Pastel, Oil. *Publ:* Contribr, Masters Published in Gold, Nat Res Study Ctr, Calvatone, Italy, 83; illusr, Valhalla 6 Lifespan, Merging Media

DALEY, CATHY
PAINTER
b Toronto, Ont. *Study:* Ont Col Art, 73-75; Arts Sake Inc, 78-80. *Work:* Can Coun Art Bank, Ottawa, Ont; MacDonald Stewart Art Ctr, Guelph, Ont; Art Gallery Peterborough, Ont. *Exhib:* (K)ein Vergleich, Southern Alberta Art Gallery, Lethbridge, Alta, 91; solo shows, Prince George Art Gallery, BC, 92, Art Gallery York Univ, North York, Ont, 94, Paul Petro Contemp Art, Toronto, 98 & Art Gallery of Kelowna, BC, 98; Identity, Main Access, Winnipeg, 92; Nat Drawing Show, Open Space, Victoria, BC, 94; Trames De Memoire (with catalog), Centre D'Expression, St Hyacinthe, Que, 96; Between Body & Soul, Leonard & Bina Ellen Gallery, Concordia Univ, Montreal, Que. *Teaching:* Instr Drawing, Univ Toronto, 88-89; instr drawing & painting, Ont Col Art, 88-. *Awards:* Arts Grant B, Can Coun, 93, 95 & 96; Sr Grant, Ont Arts Coun, 93 & 94. *Bibliog:* Roni Feinstein (auth), Art in Am, 2/96; Renee Baert (auth), Trames de Memoire (exhib catalog), 98; Nancy Tousley (auth), Calgary Herald, 3/99. *Mem:* Visual Arts Ont. *Publ:* Contribr, Borderlines, 89; Impulse, 90; Fireweed, 94; illusr, Kay Darling, Coach House Press, 94. *Dealer:* Paul Petro Contemp Art 265A Queen St W Toronto ON M5V 174. *Mailing Add:* 130 Berkeley St Toronto ON M5A 2W9 Canada

DALEY, WILLIAM P
CERAMIST
b Hastings-on-Hudson, NY, Mar 7, 25. *Study:* Mass Col Art, BS; Columbia Univ Teachers Col, MA. *Hon Degrees:* The Univ of the Arts, DFA, 94; Maine Col of Art, DFA, 93. *Work:* Philadelphia Mus Art; St Louis Mus, Mo; Everson Mus Art, Syracuse; Los Angeles Co Mus; Victoria & Albert Mus, London; and others; Met Mus of Art, NY; Newark Mus of Art, NJ; Mont Mus of Art, Charlotte, NC. *Comn:* Ceramic screen abacus, comn by Int Bus Machines Corp, Seattle World's Fair, 61; ceramic & copper modular wall, SAfrican Airlines, NY, 70; ceramic wall, Fairfield Maxwell Corp, NY, 72; ceramic screen (10ft x 20ft), Ritz Theatre, Philadelphia, 78; Baptismal font, St Pauls, Elkon Park, Pa, 89. *Exhib:* Philadelphia: Three Centuries of Am Art, Philadelphia Mus Art, 76; A Century of Ceramics in the United States, Everson Mus, Syracuse; Am Ceramics Now, Everson Mus, 88; Craft Today USA, Mus des Art Decoratifs, Paris, France, 89; Hartland Gallery, Philadelphia, Pa, 90. *Pos:* Mem adv bd clay studio, Philadelphia & Haystack Sch Crafts, 90. *Teaching:* Prof ceramics & design, Philadelphia Col Art, 57-, chmn crafts dept, 66-69, prof emer; guest prof ceramics, Univ NMex, 72; Disting prof emeritus, Univ of the Arts, Philadelphia, 90. *Awards:* Distinguished Achievement Arts Award, Mass Col Art, 80; First Distinguished Univ Prof, Univ Arts, Philadelphia Col Arts & Design, 89; Distinguished Teaching of Art Award, Col Art Asn of Am, 91. *Bibliog:* Garth Clark (auth), American Potters - the work of twenty modern masters, Keramik der Welt, Gottfried Borman, 81; Peter Dormer, article in The New Ceramics, 86; article in Am Ceramics, 8/2/90. *Mem:* Hon life mem, Nat Coun Educ Ceramic Arts. *Media:* Clay. *Publ:* Auth, Notes on sources: A presentation, Nat Coun Educ Ceramic Arts J, Vol 1, No 1, 80; On drawing, Am Ceramics, Vol 1, No 1, 82; The geometry of residence, Nat Coun Educ Ceramic Arts J, Vol 4, 83. *Dealer:* Drutt Gallery 2220 Rittenhouse St Philadelphia, PA, 19103. *Mailing Add:* 307 Ashbourne Rd Elkins Park PA 19027

DALGLISH, JAMIE
PAINTER, VIDEO ARTIST
b Bryn Mawr, Pa, May 7, 47. *Study:* Art Acad Cincinnati (scholar), 70; RI Sch Design, BFA, 74; Nat Ctr Experiments TV, San Francisco, Calif, 74. *Work:* Chase Manhattan Bank, NY; Sydney & Francis Lewis Wing, Va Mus, Richmond; Polaroid Corp, Cambridge; Armand Hammer pvt collection. *Comn:* Painting, comn by Mr & Mrs Stephen Abramson, NY, 82. *Exhib:* Eight from NY, State Univ Stony Brook, NY, 80; solo exhib, Port Washington Pub Libr, NY, 80, Braathen-Gallozzi Gallery, NY, 80, Barbara Braathen Gallery, NY, 81-82 & 85-89, Serra di Felice Gallery, NY, 83, Sarah Rentschler Gallery, NY, 85, OK Harris Works Art, NY, 91-93 & Hugo de Pagano Gallery, NY, 97; Signs, Semiotics, Behavior (video), Mus Art, RI Sch Design, Providence, 82; Video-USA, Centre d'Art Contemporain, Geneva, Switz, 84; King Lear's High Theatre of Sovereign Immunity-Come (T) Here (video), Limelight, NY, 86; Drawing Exhib, Long Island Univ, Brookly, NY, 86; Art Against AIDS (with catalog), NY, 87; Real Paint, Procter Art Ctr, Bard Col, NY, 88; Abstraction and Reality, Montogomery Ctr, NJ, 92; Young Guns: East Coast Artists, Nev Inst Contemp Art, Las Vegas, 94; Int Artists Established in New York City, Mus de la Ciudad, Madrid, Spain, 97; Hypertexture, Florence Lynch Gallery, NY, 2003; Vice Versa, MATCH Artspace, NY, 2005. *Awards:* Polaroid Corp Grant, 89; Pollock-Krasner Found Grant Award, 2006-07. *Bibliog:* Frederick Ted Castle (auth), Jamie Dalglish, Art Mag, 6/91; Lilly Wei (auth), Review of Exhibitions: Jamie Dalgish at OK Harris, Art Am, 5/94; Walter Robinson (auth), Review, Artnet Mag, 10/96; Jerome Davis (auth), Talking Heads, Vintage Mag Series, 86. *Mem:* ASCAP. *Media:* All. *Publ:* Contrib, photos, Mademoiselle, 9/92. *Dealer:* O K Harris Gallery 383 W Broadway New York NY 10012. *Mailing Add:* 325 North End Ave # 8R New York NY 10282

DALGLISH, MEREDITH RENNELS
SCULPTOR, EDUCATOR
b Bryn Mawr, Pa, Apr 15, 41. *Study:* Goddard Col, Plainfield, Vt, BA, 65; Claremont Grad Sch, Claremont, Calif, MFA, 83. *Work:* Gallery Contemporanea, Jacksonville, Fla; Deland Mus Art, Fla; Albertson-Peterson Gallery, Orlando, Fla; Stetson Univ, Deland, Fla; Hilton Hotel, Atlanta, Ga; Orlando Fla Mus Art, IBM Corp, Miami, Fla, Ramada Inn, Beverly Hills, Calif, Sheraton, Scottsdale, Ariz, Omni Int, Miami, Fla, San Francisco Mus Art, and others. *Comn:* Mementoes in In-Laws (film), Los Angeles, Calif, 80; sculptures, Sheraton, Scottsdale, Ariz; sculptures, comn by Ralp Rudin, Los Angeles, Calif, 84, & Bill Bailey, Beverly Hills, Calif, 85; wall sculptures, Design Continuum, Atlanta, Ga, 90. *Exhib:* Westwood Ceramics Invitational, Downey Mus, Calif, 82; Ceramics Nat Invitational, Scripps Col, Claremont, Calif, 84; Dimensions, Los Angeles Co Mus Art, Calif, 85; Sculpture Carved & Forged, Tampa Mus, Fla, 87; 100 Yr Nat Asn Women Artists Celebration, Jacob Javits Ctr, NY, 89; Spotlight '89, Univ Fla, Gainesville, 89; one-woman shows, MIEL Ctr, Miami, 94, 1st Union Bank, Ft Lauderdale, Fla, 95; Earth Day Celebration, St Thomas Univ, Miami, 95, 96 & 97; Take Back the Earth, Temporary Art Installation, Sao Paulo, Brazil, 97 & 2001; Int Ceramics Festival, Sãn Paulo, Brazil. *Collection Arranged:* Frances Lewis Collection, Richmond, Va; IMP Corp, Miami, Fl; Hilton Hotel, Atlanta, Ga; Ramada Inn, Beverly Hills, Ca; Sheraton-Scottsdale, Az; San Francisco Mus of Art; LA Co Mus, Los Angeles. *Pos:* Co-dir, Venice Ceramics Gallery, Calif, 77-78; dir, Ibis Fine Arts Gallary, Pasadena, Calif, 84-85; dir/cur, Ormond Mem Art Mus, Ormond Beach, Fla, 86-87; mem adv bd, Volusia Co Arts Comn, Daytona, 90-91; founder & dir, Inst Women & Creativity, 92. *Teaching:* Assoc prof, ceramics, Rio Hondo Col, Whittier, Calif, 84; prof, ceramics, Daytona Beach Community Col, Fla, 87-88; art specialist, art appreciation, Volusia Co Schs, Deland, Fla, 89-90; prof, Miami-Dade Community Col, Fla, 90-92, Fla Int Univ, Miami, 93-; artist-in-residence, Proj Leap, Palm Beach Co, 96- & Univ Miami, 96; artist-in-educ, State Fla, 97-2001; instr, workshops for women artists, San Paulo, Brazil, 97 & 99; vis artist, guest artist & lectr in the field throughout the US and abroad; arts-in-medicine, Univ Miami, 96 & 2001. *Awards:* Artistic Merit, Ruth Chenven, NY, 89; Artist-in-Education Award, State of Fla, 97-99; Project Leap Award, Palm Beach Co, Fla, 97-99. *Bibliog:* Judy Chicago (auth), The Dinner Party, Anchor Doubleday, 79; Mac McCloud (auth), Trends in clay, Artweek,

8/82; J Demetrakas (dir), Right Out of History: The Making of the Dinner Party (film). *Mem:* Nat Asn Women Artists, NY; Women's Caucus Arts; Nat Soc Multi-Layerists; Nat Coun Educ Ceramic Arts; Col Art Asn. *Media:* Mixed-media. *Res:* Women and their creativity. *Publ:* Contribr, Old Market Craftsmen Cookbook, Ree Schonlau, 82; auth, Ron Fondaw (catalog), Ormond Mus, 87; Art in America, Letters, 7/92; Mus of Arts & Sciences, Daytona, Fla; How to View Art Booklet for Middle & High School Age. *Dealer:* Albertson-Peterson Gallery 329 Park Ave S Winter Park FL 32789

DALLAS, DOROTHY B
PAINTER, PRINTMAKER
b New York, NY. *Study:* Watercolor study with Ed Whitney, 78-80; Pratt Inst, Brooklyn, NY, BFA, 79, MFA, 81. *Work:* Bergen Co Freeholders, Courthouse, Hackensack, NJ. *Exhib:* Landscapes by Member Artists, Katonah Mus Art, NY, 88; 100 Yrs/100 Works Centennial Traveling Exhib, Islip Mus & others, 89; Hudson River Regional Watercolor Exhib, Woodstock Art Asn, NY, 89; NJ Watercolor Soc 50th Ann Exhib, Montclair Mus, NJ, 89; Am Watercolor Soc 129th Int Exhib, NY, 96; 175th Ann Exhib, Nat Acad Design, 2000. *Pos:* Guest cur, watercolor exhib, Art Ctr N NJ, New Milford, 76; judge, Teen Arts Prog, NJ State Dept Educ, Ramapo Col, 88-90. *Awards:* Grumbacher Medallion, Nat Asn Women Artists 99th Ann, Colo, 88; First Prize, Hudson River Regional Watercolor Exhib, Woodstock Art Asn/Ulster Co Art Asn, 89; Gold Medal for Watermedia, Catharine Lorillard Wolfe Art Club, 102nd Ann, 98. *Bibliog:* Best of Watercolor, 95, Best of Watercolor II, 97 & Abstracts in Watercolor, 96, Rockport Publ. *Mem:* Art Ctr Watercolor Affiliates (founder, 78, secy, 78-86, pres, 86-90); NJ Watercolor Soc (prospectus chmn, 81-, nominating chairperson, 96-); Catharine Lorillard Wolfe Art Club, Inc (bd dir, 82-88, pres, 89-92); Nat Asn Women Artists (bd dir, 85-89); Katonah Mus Artists Asn; Baltimore Watercolor Soc. *Media:* Watercolor, Collage. *Mailing Add:* 378 Eastwood Ct Englewood NJ 07631

DALLMANN, DANIEL FORBES
PAINTER, PRINTMAKER
b St Paul, Minn, Mar 21, 42. *Study:* St Cloud Univ, BS, 65; Univ Iowa, MA, 68, MFA, 69. *Work:* Nat Collection Fine Arts, DC; Art Inst Chicago; Yale Univ Art Mus, New Haven, Conn; Chemical Bank, NY; J B Speed Art Mus, Louisville, Ky; and others. *Exhib:* Contemp Self Portraits, Allan Frumkin Gallery, NY, 82; New Vistas: Contemp Am Landscape, Hudson River Mus, NY & Tucson Mus Art, Ariz, 84; Conjuring Reality: The Paintings and Drawings of Daniel Dallman and Paul Wiesenfeld, J B Speed Mus Art, Louisville, Ky, 84; Am Realism: Twentieth Century Drawings & Watercolors, San Francisco Mus Mod Art, 85; Realism Today, Nat Acad Design, NY, 88; The Landscape Observed, Md Inst, Baltimore, 90; Solo exhib, Etchings, Lithographs & Drawings, Davidson Gallery, 93, New Paintings,Tatistcheff & Co, NY, 93, Paintings, Davidson Gallery, Seattle, 94, Paintings & Drawings, Payne Gallery, Moravian Col, Bethleham, Pa, 97, Kendall Gallery, Miami-Dade Comm Col, Fla, 97, Little Sleepers and Other Small Works, Dartmouth Col, Hanover, NH, 98 & Dancers and Dreamers, Creighton Univ, Omaha, Nebr, 98; 20th century Figurative Paintings, Forum Gallery, NY, 94. *Teaching:* Prof drawing & printmaking, Tyler Sch Art, 69-. *Awards:* Visual Arts Fel, Pa Coun Arts, 87. *Media:* Oil; All Media. *Dealer:* Claire Oliver Fine Arts Philadelphia PA. *Mailing Add:* 713 Mount Vernon St Lansdale PA 19446-3405

D'ALMEIDA, GEORGE
PAINTER
b Paris, France, June 30, 34; US citizen. *Exhib:* Rolly-Michaux Gallery, NY, 79, 81, 83 & 86 & Boston, 80, 82 & 86; Galleria Rotta, Genoa, 77, 80, 89 & 93; one-man exhib, Venice Biennial, 88; Galleria La Bussola, Turin, 89; and others. *Media:* Acrylic, Watercolor. *Dealer:* Galleria Rotta Via XX Settembre 181r Genoa; Rolly Michaux Gallery Boston MA. *Mailing Add:* Casina di Selvole 53017 Radda in Chianti Siena Italy

DAL POGGETTO, SANDRA HOPE
PAINTER
b Sonoma, Calif, Nov 2, 51. *Study:* Univ Calif, Davis, with Manuel Weri, Wayne Thiebaud, Robert Arneson, BA(hon), 75; San Francisco State Univ, with Robert Bechtle, MA(painting & drawing), 82. *Work:* South Bay Contemp Mus Art, Torrance, Calif. *Exhib:* Nature Morte (panelist), South Bay Contemp Mus Art, Torrance, Calif, 92; Gender/Geography: New Works by Montana Women Artists, Holter Mus Art, Helena, 95; Artists Who Teach (with catalog), Paris Gibson Mus Art, Great Falls, Mont, 95; SDP: An Exhib of Paintings, Augusta State Univ, Ga, 96; Mostra '96: Painting & Sculpture, Mus Italo Americano, San Francisco, 96. *Teaching:* Instr painting & drawing, Napa Valley Col, Calif, 85-86; instr life drawing, Archie Bray Found Ceramic Arts, Helena, Mont, 94-95; instr drawing, Mont State Univ, Bozeman, 95-96. *Awards:* Fel Painting, Helene Wurlitzer Found, NMex, 96; Artist-in-residence, Holter Mus Art, Helena Nat Forest, Mont, 96; Pouch Cove Found resident, Newfoundland, 2000. *Bibliog:* Will Torphy (auth), article, Artweek, 1/85; Kate Regan (auth), Shimmering Rays & a Troubled lyricism, San Francisco Chronicle, 2/85; Jerome Tarshis (auth), Jerome's unknowns, San Francisco Focus, 7/85. *Media:* Oil, Egg Tempera. *Publ:* Auth, Duccio in the eye of the hunt (essay), Gray's Sporting J, 10/96; In the eye of the elk (essay), The Structurist, 12/96. *Dealer:* Ed Russell Graystone Gallery 250 Sutter St San Francisco CA 94108. *Mailing Add:* 430 Monroe Ave Helena MT 59601

DALY, NORMAN
PAINTER, SCULPTOR
b Pittsburgh, Pa, Aug 9, 1911. *Study:* Univ Colo, BFA; Ohio State Univ, MA; grad study, Paris; Inst Fine Arts, NY Univ. *Work:* Rochester Mem Art Gallery, NY; Herbert F Johnson Mus Art, Ithaca, NY; Everson Mus Art, Syracuse; Univ Wash, Seattle; St Paul Mus Art, Minn; Wooster Col & Oberlin Col, Ohio; Munson-Williams-Proctor Inst, Utica, NY; Ithaca Col, NY. *Comn:* Stained glass windows, Mt Savior Monastery, Pine City, NY; bas-relief, Meditation Rm, Student Union, NY State Univ, Cortland. *Exhib:* One-man shows, Akron Art Mus, 72; Indianapolis Art Mus, 73; Romisch-Germanisches Mus, Cologne & City Hist Mus, Boctium, Ger, 74; Inst Contemp Art, Univ Pa & Tyler Sch Art, Temple Univ, 80 & 81, Philadelphia; Roberson Art Ctr, 82; Rotterdam Coun Arts Touring Exhib, The Neth, 83; Rochester Mem Art Gallery, NY; State Univ NY, Albany; Johnson Mus Art, Cornell Univ, 2004. *Pos:* Playwright, currently. *Teaching:* Prof art, Cornell Univ, 42-. *Awards:* Yaddo Fel, 71 & 76; Nat Endowment Arts Fel, 74; Cornell Distinguished Teaching Award, 81; First Staged Reading of drama, Still-Walkers, Cornell, 88. *Bibliog:* Charles Michener (auth), The fabulous Llhuroscians, Newsweek, 2/28/72; Kenneth Evett (auth), Llhuros, New Repub, 1/12/72; David Galloway (auth), The Civilization of Llhuros, Cleveland, 9/72. *Media:* Mixed-Media. *Res:* kinetic identification in pictorial analysis. *Publ:* Illusr, Epoch, 71; contribr, Abrazas Press, 72; auth, The Civilization of Llhuros, 72; Llhuros-Eine Entdeckte Kiltur-1974; Leonardo, Pergamon Press, Oxford, Eng, Vol 3, 91. *Mailing Add:* 110 N Quarry St Ithaca NY 14850

DALY, STEPHEN JEFFREY
SCULPTOR, DRAFTSMAN
b Governors Island, NY, July 4, 42. *Study:* San Jose State Univ, Calif, BA, 64; Cranbrook Acad Art, Mich, MFA(sculpture), 67. *Work:* Oakland Art Mus, Calif; Tex A&M Univ; Am Acad Rome, Italy; McNey Mus, San Antonio, Tex; Blanton Mus Art, Univ Tex, Austin; Polytechnic Univ, Valencia, Spain. *Comn:* Codema 2000, Commd Steel Sculpture, Havana, Cuba, 2000; monumental wall work, Matthews & Branscom B Law Firm, San Antonio, Tex, 2000. *Exhib:* 85th San Francisco Art Inst Ann, MH de Young Mem Mus, Calif, 65; Objects USA, Smithsonian Mus, Washington, 69; The Metal Experience, Oakland Art Mus, Calif, 71; one-man shows, Am Acad, Rome, 75, Triton Mus, Santa Clara, Calif, 77, William Campbell Contemp Art, Ft Worth, Tex, 87, 89-91, 93, 2002 & 2004, and McNay Art Mus (catalog), San Antonio, Tex, 88; group shows, Texas Currents, San Antonio Art Inst, 86 & New Sites-New Work, San Jose Inst Contemp Art, 86, The Blue Star Exhib, Blue Star Space, San Antonio, Tex, 86, Third Coast Review, Aspen Art Mus, Colo, 87, Another Reality (catalog), Hooks-Epstein Galleries Inc, Houston, Tex, 89 & A Century of Sculpture in Tex (catalog), Archer M Huntington Art Gallery, Univ Tex, Austin, 89; Hooks-Epstein Galleries, Houston, Tex, 91 & 93; The Figure, Grounds for Sculpture, Hamilton, NJ, 94-95; Pier Walk 97, Navy Pier, Chicago, 97; drawing, Ravel Fine Arts, Austin, Tex, 2000; Made in Texas, Waco Art Center, Waco Tex; Grounds for Sculpture, ISC Bd, Hamilton, NJ 2001; Mutamentum, Int Group Traveling Show, Italy, Ger & USA, 2001-2003; WM Havu Gallery, Denver, Colo, 2002 & 2005; F.A.T., Univ Gallery, Fresno State Univ, Calif, 2006; and many others. *Pos:* Art & archit Panel, Tex Comn Arts, Austin, 80-82; coordr, 4th Tex Sculpture Symp, 81-83; bd trustees, Int Sculpture Ctr, Hamilton, NJ, 97-2000; consult, Overland Partners, San Antonio, Tex, 2003-2004. *Teaching:* Univ Minn, Minneapolis, 67-69, Humboldt State Univ, 69-79, Univ Tex, San Antonio, 79-81, Univ Tex, Austin, 81-. *Awards:* Prix de Rome, Am Acad Rome, Italy, 75; Louis Comfort Tiffany Award Sculpture, 77; Centennial Fel Fine Arts, Univ Tex, Austin, 83-84 & 88-91; Milam Centennial Fel, Univ Tex, 90-91; FRA Rsch Grant, Univ Tex, 95, 2001. *Bibliog:* Howard Smagula (auth), Texas Currents (catalog), San Antonio Art Inst, 85; Annette Carlozzi (auth), Third coast rev: a look at Tex art, Aspen Art Mus, Colo, 88; Susie Kalil (auth), Stephen Daly, McNey Mus (exhib catalog), 88; Marina Pastor (auth), The Art of Giant Fighting, Polytechnic Univ Press, Valencia, Spain, 2001. *Mem:* Fel Am Acad Rome, NY; Int Sculpture Ctr, Washington. *Media:* Metals, Cast. *Publ:* Retrospective Catalogue, Polytechnic Univ, Valencia, Spain. *Dealer:* Wm Campbell Contemporary Art 49355 Byers Ft Worth TX 76107. *Mailing Add:* Dept Art Univ Tex Mail Code D 1300 Austin TX 78712-1285

D'AMATO, JANET POTTER
ILLUSTRATOR, CRAFTSMAN
b Rochester, NY. *Study:* Pratt Inst; Harriet FeBland Workshop; Sarah Lawrence. *Comn:* Recreate church in miniature, 02. *Exhib:* Art Dir Club, NY, 89. *Awards:* Merit Award, Dimensional Illusr Inc, 89. *Bibliog:* Anne Commire (auth), Something About the Author, Gale Publ, 75; Carmel Marchionni (auth), Lifestyles, Westchester Gannett Publ, 75 & 77; D Russo (auth), article, Westchester Spotlight; The Village Voice, April 2004. *Media:* Acrylic, Collage, Wood Assemblage. *Res:* Primitive and folk art and crafts, American Indian and African. *Interests:* Miniatures, quillwork and various other crafts. *Publ:* Auth & illusr, Gifts to Make for Love or Money, Golden, 73; Colonial Crafts for You to Make, Messner, 75; Quillwork, Craft of Paper Filigree, 75 & Italian Crafts, 77, Evans; Native American Craft Inspirations (book), Evans, 92; How Do We Recycle Plastic (book), Greenwillow Press, 92; illusr, Ecology Basics, Prentice Hall, 86; and others. *Mailing Add:* 32 Bayberry St Bronxville NY 10708

DAMAZ, PAUL F
WRITER, ARCHITECT
b Portugal, Nov 8, 17; US citizen. *Study:* Ecole Speciale Archit, Paris, France, BA(arch); Inst Urbanisme, Sorbonne, Paris, MA(town planning). *Pos:* coun mem, Arts Acquisition Comt, State Univ NY Stony Brook, 70; dir, Fine Arts Fedn NY, 72-75. *Teaching:* Design critic archit, Columbia Univ, 52-53. *Awards:* Arnold Brunner fel, Archit League NY, 58. *Bibliog:* Anne Le Crenier (auth), Names, Archit & Eng News, 67. *Mem:* Am Inst Archits; Am Inst Planners; Ordre Architectes, France; Archit League NY; Munic Arts Soc. *Res:* Integration of art in modern architecture; art in public spaces. *Collection:* Contemporary art, mostly North and Latin American. *Publ:* Auth, Art in European Architecture, 56 & Art in Latin American Architecture, 62, Van Nostrand Reinhold. *Mailing Add:* 218 Old Stone Hwy East Hampton NY 11937

DAMIANOVIC, MAIA
CRITIC, CURATOR
b Ely, Eng, May 23, 59. *Study:* Ecole des Beaux Arts & Ecole du Louvre, Paris, France, studio prog, 78-80; Univ Paris, The Sorbonne, art & archit, 79-80; Univ Toronto, Ont, BFA, 83. *Collection Arranged:* Prommissory Notes, Artifact Gallery, Tel Aviv, Israel, 94; Border Crossings, Corine Maman Mus & Rehouot Mus, Israel, 95; Transformal, Vienna Secession, Austria, 96; Dissin the Real, Lombard-Freid, NY & Krinzinger, Vienna, Austria, 98. *Pos:* Contrib ed, Tema Celeste Arte Contemporanea, 95-. *Bibliog:* Carol Kino (auth & critic), Time Out, New York, 2/98; Marcus Metzringer (auth & critic), Der Standard, Vienna, 6/98; Johanna Hofleitner (auth & critic), Die Presse, Vienna, 6/98. *Publ:* Auth, On the Point of a Dilemma, Art Press, 97; Scandals of Want, Miyagi Mus, Japan, 97; Painting Outside of Confines, Tema Celeste Arte Contemporanea, 97; Giving Unreality to a Strong Sense of Reality, Mus Mod Art, Vienna, 97; Terminal Souvenirs, Nordic Inst Contemp Art, 98

D'AMICO, LARRY
PAINTER, PRINTMAKER
b Ossining, NY, 1951. *Study:* Sch Visual Arts, New York, 69-70; Silvermine Col Art, Conn, 70-71; San Francisco Art Inst, 71-72; State Univ NY, Purchase, BA, 77. *Work:* US State Dept, Washington, DC; Kaiser Found, Chase Manhattan Bank, NY; Pace Univ, Brooklyn. *Exhib:* Plein-Air: A Tradition Honored, Castle Gallery, New Rochelle, NY, 88; solo exhib, Helio Gallery, NY, 89 & Scarborough Gallery, Chappaqua, NY, 89; Am Landscape, Broden Gallery, Madison, NY, 89; Hudson River Contemp, Hudson River Gallery, Ossining, NY, 89. *Bibliog:* Vivian Raynor (auth), Plein air tradition, New York Times, 6/88; Ina Pasch (auth), As landscapes vary, so do artists styles, Wis State J, 11/89. *Media:* Oil, Pastel; Print

DANA, URIEL
PAINTER, SCULPTOR
b Chicago, Ill, Nov 12, 54. *Study:* Col Marin, Kentfield, Calif, 81-83; study with Gage Taylor, 83-85. *Work:* Jamaica Nat Gallery Art, Kingston; US Embassy, Georgetown, Guyana; Hyatt Regency Hotel, Kauai, Hawaii; Gen Motors; Dow Jones Sustainability Index, 2000; STMicroelectronics Inc, 2000; Patagonia, 2000; Novozymes Biotech, 2001; numerous other corp collections. *Comn:* paintings, Out on a Limb (miniseries), 85; murals, Casa Madrona Hotel, Sausalito, Calif, 93. *Exhib:* 100 Views of the Sun, San Francisco Arts Comn, Southern Exposure Gallery, 1985; Awards of Honor, San Francisco Arts Comn, 1985; US State Dept Tour, 1987; Art Awards 88, Bellevue, Wash, 1988; The Mythic Image, Rosicrucian Egyptian Mus, San Jose, Calif, 1993; Seaside Art Gallery, Nags Head, NC, 1996; Alien X-Mass, Anon Salon, San Francisco, 1996; SMARTS Gallery, San Francisco, 2002. *Collection Arranged:* Crystal Energy, Col Marin, Kentfield, Calif, 83. *Pos:* Gallery asst, Col Marin Art Gallery, 81-83. *Teaching:* Lectr, US State Dept Tour, Arts Am Prog, Jamaica & Guyana, 87. *Bibliog:* Gage Taylor (auth), Interview with Uriel Dana, Art Am, 98. *Media:* Oil; Cast Metal. *Publ:* monthly column, Living on the Edge, Patrons of Sirius Art Newsletter, 1997

DANBY, KEN
PAINTER, PRINTMAKER
b Sault Ste Marie, Ont, 1940. *Study:* Ont Col Art, Toronto, 58-60. *Hon Degrees:* Algoma Univ Col & Laurentian Univ, Hon Dr Fine Arts. *Work:* Indianapolis Mus Fine Art, Ind; Mus Mod Art, NY; Montreal Mus Art, PQ; Art Inst Chicago; Univ Calif Art Gallery, Berkeley. *Comn:* Designer Series III Can Olympic Coins 1976 Olympics, Montreal; Orgn Serigraph, The Royal Can Acad Arts, 83; Commemorative Medal Winter Olympics, Calgary Barclay's Bank, 86; Orgn watercolour Ltd Ed Prints, Deloitte & Touche, 93; Kodak Canada Inc, Calgary Stampede's Trail, 2000. *Exhib:* Living Am Artists & the Figure, Pa State Univ, 74; Aspects of Realism, Rothman's Touring Can Exhib, 76-78; Champions of Am Sport, The Nat Portrait Gallery, Washington, Chicago, Los Angeles & NY, 81; The Sporting Life, Gallery Stratford, Stratford, ON, 99; Art Miami, Miami, Fla; solo exhibs, Canadian Contemp Printmakers, Bronx Mus Fine Arts, NY, 82, Am's Cup Gallery, Newport, RI, 83, Galerie Mihalis, Montreal, Que, 83, A Celebration of Amateur Sport, Queens Park, Toronto, Can, 85, Halton Hills Cult Ctr, Georgetown, Ont, 86, 25 Yr Retrospective, MacDonald Stewart Art Ctr, Guelph, Ont, 87, Gallery Moos, NY, 89, Graphic Retrospective, Harris Gallery Fine Art, Ottawa, Ont, 90, Drawing & Watercolours, Art Gallery Algoma, Sault Ste Marie, Ont 97, Our Hockey Legends, June to December, Bruce Co Mus, Southampton, Ont 97, Ken Danby: New Paintings, Joseph D Carrier Art Gallery, Toronto, Can, 98 & The Sporting Life, Gallery Stratford, Ont, 99, Macdonald Stewart Art Ctr, Guelph, ON, 2002, Bernaducci Meisel Gallery, NY, 2005. *Pos:* Bd dir, Can Coun, 85-91; bd trustees, Nat Gallery Can, 91-95. *Awards:* Queen's Can Silver Jubilee Medal, 77; The 125th Anniversary Commemorative Medal of Can, 92; Award Merit, City Sault Ste, 95, Order of Ontario, 2001 & Order of Can, 2001; Queen's Golden Jubilee Medal, 2002. *Bibliog:* Joan Murray (auth), Home Truths: A Celebration of Family Life by Canada's Best Loved Painters, Key Porter Books Ltd, Toronto, Can, 97; Michael Burtch (dir), Ken Danby Retrospective Drawings and Watercolours, Art Gallery of Algoma, Sault Ste, Marie, Ont, 97; Brian Vallee (producer/dir), Ken Danby: Behind the Mask, Life & Times Television, 98. *Mem:* Royal Can Acad Arts; Drawing Soc Can. *Media:* Egg Tempera, Watercolor; Serigraphy, Silkscreen. *Dealer:* Mill Studios Corp RR4 Guelph Ontario Can N1H 6J1; Gallery Moos Ltd 622 Richmond St Toronto Ontario Can M5V 1Y9; Bernaducci Meisel Gallery 37 W 57th St New York NY 10019-3411; Masters Gallery 815C- 17th Ave SW Calgary AB T2T 0A1 Canada. *Mailing Add:* RR No 4 Guelph ON N1H 6J1 Canada

DANCE, ROBERT BARTLETT
PAINTER, PRINTMAKER
b Tokyo, Japan, May 31, 34; US citizen. *Study:* Philadelphia Col Art, with Henry C Pitz & W Emerton Heitland. *Work:* NC Mus Fine Art, Raleigh; R J Reynolds Indust, Winston-Salem, NC; Hanes Dye & Finishing, Winston-Salem; Miss Mus Art, Jackson; Wachovia Bank & Trust, Winston-Salem. *Exhib:* Mystic Int, Conn, 86; Arts for the Parks, Smithsonian Inst, Washington, DC, 87; Artist's Sketchbooks, Southeastern Ctr Contemp Art, 88; one-man retrospective, Southeastern Ctr Contemp Art, 91; Mystic 100, Conn, 92. *Awards:* First Place, NC Watercolor Soc, 73, 74 & 77, Assoc Artists Winston-Salem, 72, 73 & 74; Smithsonian Inst, Washington, DC, 87. *Bibliog:* Susan E Meyer (auth), 40 Watercolorists and How They Work, Watson-Guptill, 76 & Sir Isaac Pitman & Sons Ltd, Great Brit, 76; Wendon Blake (auth), The Alkyd Painting Book, Watson-Guptill. *Mem:* NC Watercolor Soc; Assoc Artists Winston-Salem. *Media:* Watercolor, Alkyd, Woodcut. *Publ:* Illusr, Things Invisible to See, Advocate Publ Group, 79; The Medium is the Message, Am Artist, 79; Yankee Mag, 9/80; Printing Atmospheric Effects, Am Artist, 85; Artist Mag, London, Eng, 1-2/88; plus others. *Dealer:* Southeastern Ctr for Contemp Art 750 Marguerite Dr Winston-Salem NC 27106; Mystic Seaport Gallery Mystic CT. *Mailing Add:* 1803 Cambridge Dr Kinston NC 28504-2005

D'ANDREA, JEANNE
EDITOR, DESIGNER
b Chicago, Ill, Dec 9, 25. *Study:* Art Inst Chicago; Colo Col, with Rico Lebrun; Univ Chicago, with Joshua Taylor, Ulrich Middledorf & Carlos Castillo, PhB & MA. *Collection Arranged:* Gericault, Los Angeles Co Mus Art, 71; Women Artists: 1550-1950, 76; Treasures of Mexico, 78; and others. *Pos:* Designer sets, costumes, Turnau Opera Co, NY & Arlington Opera Theatre, Arlington, Va, 59-72; head dept educ, Ringling Mus Art, Sarasota, Fla, 60-62; coordr exhibs & publ, Los Angeles Co Mus Art, 69-81, ed & design consult, 81-. *Mem:* Col Art Asn Am. *Mailing Add:* 751 Avenida Pequena Santa Barbara CA 93111

DANE, WILLIAM JERALD
LIBRARIAN
b Concord, NH, May 8, 25. *Study:* Drexel Inst Technol, MLS; NY Univ Inst Fine Arts; Sorbonne, Paris, France; Attingham Park Summer Sch, Eng; Palladio Studies, Vicenza, Italy, 80; Victorian Soc Summer Sch, London, 81, Philadelphia, 83, Glasgow, 91, Budapest, 98, studied art & archit, Cent Ger, 96, Prague, 2000, Amsterdam, 2002, Slovenia, 2005. *Collection Arranged:* Fine Print Collection, Newark Pub Libr; 150 Years of Graphic Art in New Jersey; Silkscreen, A Survey Show of Serigraphs & Screenprints for the NJ State Coun on Arts; Prints by Joseph Pennell; Posters & Prints form Puerto Rico, 195; Hidden Treasures: Japanese Art, 91; Glorious World Bk Illus, 92; Printmaking Workshop of Robert Blackburn, 94; Salute to SAGA, 94; Lorenzo Homar's Graphics, 94; Lasting Impressions: Greater Newark's Jewish Legacy, 95; Japanese Art in the 20th century, 96; A Potpourri of Pop Art: Prints, Posters & Pop-Ups, 97; Over There, 1917-1918: A Victory Salute to the USA in Posters, 98; 20th Century American Illustrations, 98; Nostalgic & Unforgettable Travel Posters from the 20th Century, 99; Women Printmakers, 2000; New, Non-Objective and Abstract Prints, 2000; A Graphic Sanctuary for Animals, Birds and a Few Fish-A Zoo on Paper, 2000; Shopping Bags Go Worlwide-Fabulous Bag Designs as an International Portable Art, 2000; The USA and World War II, 60 Years After; Sculptures As Printmakers, 2003; The Arts of Etching & Engraving to Honor Whistler, 2003; Hollywood Nostalgia: Great Stars in Movie Stills; Garbo, Hepburn & Brad Pitt, Too!, 2003; Celebration of the Vitality and Joys of Multiculturalism: A Century of Print Collecting, 2004; Architectural Books, Posters & Prints from the Pre-Digital Era, 2004; The Essence of Illustration Then & Now from Shaped Poetry to Peter Rabbit, 2004; Visual Recollections of The Music Scene: Clara Schumann to Ray Charles, 2005; 7th Gala Exhib, Shopping Bags! Infinite Sign Solutions for an Everyday Product; A Salute to Two Great 20th Centure Artists: Picasso & Lichtenstein in Prints, Posters, and Notable Books, 2005; John Cotton Dana: Innovative Libr Mus Founder 50th Anniversary of His Birth in 1856, 2006. *Pos:* Supvr art & music libr, Newark Pub Libr, 67-90; supvr spec collections, Newark Pub Libr, 91-. *Teaching:* moderator, Rutgers Univ, Newark, 95-2004. *Awards:* Distinguished Service Award, Art Libr Soc NAM, 98; Libr Service Award, NJ Libr Asn, 98; Lifetime Achievement Award, NY Chap, Victorian Soc in Am, 2002; Soc Am Graphic Artists Award, 2003. *Mem:* Victorian Soc Am (nat bd mem, 74-80, chmn NY chap, 72-74); Victorian Soc (co-chmn educ comm, 90); Grolier Club, NY; Art Libr Soc NAm (treas, 86-88); ARLIS; NJ State Coun Arts (Essex Co block grant juror, 88-93); Council for the Ctr Innovative Print, Rutgers Univ, 2003-; Adv Bd Mem Printmaking Council NJ, 2000-. *Publ:* Auth, Picture Collection Subject Headings, 69; contribr, Arts in America: A Bibliography, Smithsonian Inst Press, 79; auth, Networking and the Art Library, Drexel Libr Quart, fall 83; John Cotton Dana: A Contemporary Appraisal of his Contributions & Lasting Influence on the Library & Museum Worlds, 90; The History of Fine Printing in Newark, 88. *Mailing Add:* Five Washington St Newark NJ 07101

DANHAUSEN, ELDON
SCULPTOR, EDUCATOR
Study: Art Inst Chicago, James Nelson Raymond Foreign Traveling Fel, BFA, 47. *Work:* Hackley Art Gallery, Muskegon, Mich; Civic Ctr, New Orleans, La; Standard Club Chicago; Roosevelt Univ, Chicago. *Comn:* Sculpture, Int Minerals & Chem Corp, Skokie, Ill, 60; sculpture, Home Mutual Appleton, Wis, 63; sculpture, WOC TV, Davenport, Iowa, 64; sculpture, Civic Ctr, New Orleans, 67; sculpture, 150 N Wacker Dr Bldg, Chicago, 71. *Exhib:* Downtown Gallery, NY; Chicago Ann Show, Art Inst Chicago, 45-60; Rivinia Festival Art Exhib, 57, 59 & 60; Am Business & the Arts, San Francisco Mus Art, 61; Sculpture 70, Art Inst Chicago, 70. *Teaching:* Prof emer, Art Inst Chicago, currently. *Awards:* Linde Co Prize, Chicago Ann Show, Art Inst Chicago, 60; Citation for Art in Architecture, Am Inst Archit Iowa Chap, 63. *Bibliog:*

Meilach & Kowal (auth), Sculpture Casting, Crown; Meilach (auth), Contemporary Stone Sculpture, Crown; Meilach (auth), Creative Carving, Reilly & Lee. *Publ:* Auth, Art in the market place, sculptor's viewpoint, Chicago Mkt Scene, 3/70; contribr, Contemporary Stone Sculpture, Crown. *Mailing Add:* 1418 N LaSalle Dr Chicago IL 60610-1304

DANI
SCULPTOR, PAINTER
b Los Angeles, Calif, Mar 11, 33. *Study:* Pasadena City Col, 51; Laguna Beach Sch Art, 80; Orange Coast Col, 90; Calif State, Long Beach, 90. *Hon Degrees:* inducted in Orange Coast Col Hall of Fame. *Work:* 36 orginal bronze sculptures & enumerable paintings, etchings, & serigraphs. *Comn:* Magic Doves, comn by Brenda Payne & Bob Brown, Sacramento, Calif, 80. *Exhib:* Traditional Artsits Exhib, San Bernardino Co Mus, Redlands, Calif, 77; Ann Invitational, Nat Acad Design, NY, 78; Hudson Valley Art Asn, Westchester Ctr, White Plains, NY, 78; Ann Exhib, Salmagundi Club, NY, 80; Fallbrook Invitational, 96; Art-A-Fair Festival, Calif, 98; Featured sculpture, Gallerie Gabrie, 00; Calif Art Club 90th and 92nd & 94th Gold Medal exhib, Hist Mus, 00, 02; Millard Sheets Gallery Sculpture Show, 02; one woman show, Simic New Renaissance Gallery, 02 & 03; Am Artists Prof League, 76 Grand Nat Exhib, 2004; Catharine Lorillard Wolfe Art Club, 108th Exhib, 2004. *Collection Arranged:* RW Norton Found; Favell Mus; Carnegie Arts Ctr Mus. *Pos:* designer, catalogs and flyers, Amineo Int; co-chair Orange Co Artists Showcase, 2000. *Teaching:* art instr, Costa Mesa Dept Recreation, 70-79; Newport Mesa Unified Sch Dist, Hard of Hearing Prog; Costa Mesa art league; instructural guide, Ramona High Sch and San Vicente Valley Club (pres). *Awards:* Mrs John Newington Award, Hudson Valley Art Asn, 81; First Place Sculpture Award, Catharine Lorillard Wolfe Mem Show, NY, 95; Art Fest Award for Sculpture, Am Artist Prof League, NY, 95; HA Fadhi Sculpture Award Am Artists Profl League Show, 98; First Place Sculpture Award, Artist Eye Show, Calif, 2000; Leila Gardin Sawyer Mem Award, Am Artists Prof League, 02. *Bibliog:* Richard Buffum (auth), Dream woman exists, Los Angeles Times, 80; Noel Goldblatt (auth), People of the century, Presidential Villa, 82; Julia Carroll Myer (auth), Artists in the 1990's, Manhattan Arts, 91. *Mem:* Am Artists Prof League; Catherine Lorillard Wolfe Nat Arts Club; Hudson Valley Arts Asn; Orange Co Fine Arts, Inc; Rembrandt mem, Acad Fine Arts Found; sculptor mem, CAC; Art Inst San Diego. *Media:* Bronze. *Publ:* Akim Exhib & Auction, Sotherbys, NY, 96. *Dealer:* Simic New Renaissance Galleries 1205 Prospect St La Jolla CA 92037; Galerie Gabrie 597 Green St Pasadena CA 91101. *Mailing Add:* 15619 Indian Head Ct Ramona CA 92065

DANIEL, KENDRA CLIVER KRIENKE
DEALER, PAINTER, COLLECTOR
b Plainfield, NJ. *Study:* Drew Univ, with Lee Hall & Peter Chapin, BA; Nat Acad Design, with Philip Isenberg, watercolor with Nicholas Reale. *Work:* Drew Univ Collection, Madison, NJ; Douglass Col Collection, New Brunswick, NJ; US Steel. *Comn:* Portrait of retiring dean, Douglass Col, 70; portrait--US Steel, Coun Tennant, Summit, NJ, 70; Christmas card design, Spaulding for Children, Westfield, NJ, 72; drawing of AT&T Bldg, AT&T Int Hq, Basking Ridge, NJ, 78; and others. *Exhib:* Group sh ,w, AT&T Hq Gallery, Basking Ridge, 79. *Collection Arranged:* 19th Century American Paintings, 82; American Paintings, Nabisco Gallery, 84; Fifty Years of 19th Century American Painting, Schering-Plough, 86; Childhood Enchantments, Mus Cartoon Art, 89; Children's Illustrators, Johnson & Johnson Gallery, 90; Art for Children, Hotel Wales, NY. *Pos:* Free lance portrait artist, 70-75; art dealer, framer & designer, Whistler's Daughter Gallery, 74-; art dealer, Whistler Gallery, 84-90 & Kendra Krienke Fine Art, 90-2005. *Awards:* Purchase Award, Drew Univ, 68; Selection Award for Christmas Card, Spaulding for Children, 72. *Bibliog:* The seven hottest collectibles, Metrop Home Mag, 4/91; Works of wonder, Country Living, 3/93; and many others. *Mem:* Soc Illusrs, 91-. *Media:* Watercolor, Mixed Media. *Specialty:* Original Art By Illustrators For Children and Fantasy, 1880- 1950, including Arthur Rackham, Kay Nielsen, Jessie Willcox Smith, Fanny Young Cory, Harold Gaze, Ludwig Bemelmans, among others. *Interests:* jazz, animals rights and resucue; reading, collecting art & antiques. *Collection:* folk art, original vintage art for children, Yves Saint Laurent couture jewlry, antique toys, vintage christmas. *Publ:* Contribr, Art Lovers Cookbook, 75; American Illustrator Art, Random House, 91; Arpi Ermouyan, Famous American Illustrators, Soc Illusr, 98; Myth, Magic and Mystery, 96; ten full color exhib catalogs. *Mailing Add:* 140 Ashley Pl Park Ridge NJ 07656

DANIELS, ASTAR CHARLOTTE LOUISE DANIELS
STAINED GLASS ARTIST, PAINTER
b Fostoria, Ohio, Nov 27, 20. *Study:* Toledo Mus Sch of Design, 50-52; pvt study with colorist, Emerson Burkhart, Columbus, Ohio, 52-54; Thomas Moore Col, 71-73; Univ Cincinnati, Ohio, AA(summa cum laude), 77; Ohio Univ, Athens, 84-85. *Work:* Gallery of Findlay Col, Ohio; Gallery of Anne T Case Sch, Akron, Ohio; Gallery of Brown Univ, Providence, RI; Gallery of Defiance Col, Ohio; Ohio Youth Bldg, Columbus, Ohio; Gallery Gen Hos, Cincinnati, Ohio. *Comn:* Bapistry mural, comn by Mr & Mrs W J Poorman, Forest, Ohio, 53; choir loft mural, Buckland Congregational Christian Church, Ohio, 54; hereford mural, comn by Mr Jason Miller, Forest, Ohio, 57; outside mural, comn by Mr & Mrs Joseph Newhard, Carey, Ohio, 58. *Exhib:* Toledo Area Artists' Exhib, Toledo Art Mus, Ohio, 52-55; Columbus Art League Exhib, Columbus Art Mus, Ohio, 53; First Duo-Sister Show Gallery 8, Toledo Art Mus, Ohio, 55; Schaff Gallery, Cincinnati, Ohio, 96. *Pos:* Dir art, Ohio State Fair, Columbus, 55-57 & Sr Girl Scout Round-Up, Button Bay, Vt, 62. *Teaching:* Private lessons in Forest & Cincinnati, Ohio, 50-66; dir/instr art, Defiance Col, Ohio, 56-57; instr art/drama, Methodist summer camp, Sabina, Ohio, 60-64; instr art/drama, Fairview Arts Ctr, Cincinnati, 77-78; instr art, Acad Proj Succeed, Losantiville Sch, Cincinnati, 96. *Awards:* Scouters Award, 57; Cert of Achievement, Charlotte R Schmidlapp Found, 77. *Bibliog:* Emma Fundaburk & Thomas Davenport (coauths), Art in Public Places in the United States, Bowling Green Univ Popular Press, 75. *Mem:* Citizen Diplomat Soc for Positive Future (visit to USSR 1986); Soc for Universal Human (founding mem); Nat Mus of Women in the Arts (founding mem). *Media:* Leaded Stained Glass; Oil. *Interests:* World travel, mentoring young women, meta physical phenomena, healing arts. *Collection:* Works by Hal Lotterman, Raphael Gleitzman, Evelyn E Wentz, Emerson C Burkhart, Alan Melis, David Fisher, Irene Satala, Elisabeth Haley. *Publ:* Auth & illusr, Aiming in His Direction, Capozzolo, 71; illusr, Women's Spirit Bonding, Pilgrim Press, 83. *Mailing Add:* 101 Solway Court Cary NC 27511

DANIELS, DAVID ROBERT
PAINTER, EDUCATOR
b Albion, Mich, Apr 26, 48. *Study:* Cent Mich Univ, MA, 70; special study with Jack Beal & Sondra Freckelton, 92-94 & Janet Fish, 95. *Work:* Nat Inst Health, Bethesda, Md; Quadrangle Corp, Washington; Mich Educ Asn, East Lansing; East Jordan Hist Soc, Mich; Home Nat Bank, Arkansas City, Kans. *Comn:* Watercolor 28" x 60", Nat Inst Health, Bethesda, Md, 89; Quadrangle Watercolor, Quadrangle Corp, Washington, 90. *Exhib:* Montpelier/Invitational, Laurel, Md, 92; Rock Creek Gallery/Invitational, Washington, 93. *Pos:* Dir educ, A Salon, Washington, 92-96; instr, Coupeville Arts Ctr, 97. *Teaching:* Instr watercolor, Smithsonian Inst, 83-96, Northern Va Community Col, 84-96 & Haystack Mountain Workshops, 86-94. *Awards:* Best of Show, Capitol Hill Art League, 89; Best of Show, Washington Watercolor Asn, 89 & 96. *Bibliog:* Mood in watercolor, Am Artist Mag, 91; Al Avery (dir), Dave Daniels Watercolorist, Montgomery TV, 94; The color blue, Am Artist Mag, spring 95. *Mem:* Washington Watercolor Asn; Southern Watercolor Soc; Artist Equity; Capitol Hill Art League; Rockville Art Place. *Media:* Watercolor. *Publ:* Contribr, Mood in watercolor, Am Artist Mag, 91; Dave Daniels Watercolorist, Penn State Press, 94; illusr, Pathways/Cover Design, Lou DeSalba, 94; Contribr, The color blue, Am Artist Mag, 95; auth, Flowers in Watercolor, Rockport Publ. *Mailing Add:* 8012 Piney Branch Rd Silver Spring MD 20910-5244

DANIELS, MARTHA K
SCULPTOR
b Brooklyn, NY, Sept 21, 43. *Study:* Cooper Union, NY, 61-64; studied with John Hovannes, 62-64 & Dorothy Dehner, 62-64; Metrop State Col, Denver, Colo, BA (fine arts), 75. *Work:* Denver Art Mus, Dept Contemp Art, Colo; Kirkland Mus, Denver, Colo; Taco Bell Corp Art Collection, San Francisco, Calif; City & Co Denver, Colo; Playboy Art Collection, Chgo. *Comn:* Murals, Co Coun Arts, Trinidad, Colo, 89; Sculpture, Modern Archit, Denver, Colo, 90; Sculpture Installation, Kaiser Permanent, Aurora Colo, 95; Tile Collection, US Dept Interior, El Paso, Tex, 96; Tile Mural, Colo Dept Transp, Denver, 2004. *Exhib:* Solo exhib, Diana & Actaeon, Artyard, Denver, Colo, 94, Grotto, Denver Art Mus, Colo, 2000; Wash Art 78, Annual Exhib, Int Art Dealers Assn, Wash, DC, 78; Mino Ceramics Exhib, Mino, Japan, 90; Egypt of the Mind, Denver Art Mus, Colo, 98; Kirkland Mus, Colo Art, Denver, 98; Website exhib, Int Mus Ceramics, Faenza, Italy, 2003-04; Colo Art, Denver Hist Mus, Colo, 2004; Denver Art Mus, Scene, Colo; Decade of Influence, Denver Mus Contemp Art, 2006. *Teaching:* Tchr, Art Student's League, Denver. *Awards:* Fel Award, Colo Coun on Arts, 89 & 01; Fel, Rocky Mountain Women's Inst, Denver, Colo, 95; Artists Grant, Denver Art Mus, Colo, 99. *Bibliog:* Dr Donald Kuspit (auth), The Myths in Depths (monograph), Denver Art Mus, 2000; Joshua Hassel (auth), Grotto, KBDI Channel 12 (video), Denver, Colo, 2001; Elizabeth Schlosser (auth), Colo Clay Artists, Lee Ballentine, 2005. *Mem:* Pirate Artist's Gallery (dir, 85-89); Spark Gallery (mem, 81); Fel Rocky Mountain Women's Inst; Art Student's League. *Media:* Clay, Bronze, Concrete. *Interests:* Historic preservation; Design and Ceramics, Collecting ceramics, mexicana, regional art. *Publ:* contribr, auth, Ceramics Monthly Mag, 4/03; plus numerous articles. *Dealer:* Robert Nichols Contemporary Clay 419 Canyon Rd Santa Fe NM 87501; William Havu Gallery 1040 Cherokee St Denver Colo 80204

DANIELSON, PHYLLIS I See Gillie, Phyllis I Danielson

DANK, LEONARD D
ILLUSTRATOR, CONSULTANT
b Birmingham, Ala, Dec 21, 29. *Study:* Cornell Univ, BA, 52; Sch Med Illus, Mass Gen Hosp, Boston, cert, 55; Art Students League; Jules Laurents Studio, NY. *Work:* McGraw-Hill Publ Co, NY; Stravon Educ Press Inc, NY; H S Stuttman Co Inc, Conn; Proj-in-Health, NJ; Doubleday & Co Inc, NY; PW Communications, NJ; Contemp Orthopaedics, Calif. *Comn:* The Brain in Hypertension Parts I & II (animated films), Merck, Sharp & Dohme, 78; Drug Induced Movement Disorders (animated film), Dupont Pharmaceuticals, 83; health & fitness posters, Esquire Mag, 85-88. *Exhib:* Art of Medicine Exhib, Soc of Illustr, 86. *Pos:* Staff artist, Plastic Surgery Clin, Manhattan Eye & Ear Hosp, New York, 55-57 & Eye Bank for Sight Restoration, New York, 57-59; owner, Leonard Dank Studio, New York, 59-61; owner, Medical Illus Co, New York & Cutchogue, NY, 61-; consult med illusr, St Luke's-Roosevelt Hosp Ctr, New York, 61-83, Contemp Orthopaedics Publ, 81-83; consult med illusr, Harper & Row, Publ, NY, 82-, PW Commun Inc, NJ, 82-86, Esquire Mag Health & Fitness Clinic, NY, 85-88 & Whittle-Time Commun Inc, 88-94. *Awards:* First Prize Motion Picture, Am Col Surgery, 59 & 62; Better Teller Award, Asn Indust Advertisers, 73; Outstanding Children's Sci Book Award, Nat Sci Teachers Asn, 82; Cert Merit, Soc of Illus, 86. *Mem:* Asn Med Illusr; Guild Natural Sci Illusr. *Media:* Multi. *Publ:* Coauth, Clinical Obstetrics & Gynecology, 73-76, Gynecologic Operations, 78, Harper & Row; illusr, The Male His Body, His Sex, Anchor Press/Doubleday, 79; Dr Fishbein's Illustrated Medical Encyclopedia, 79 & Every Woman's Health 80, 82, & 85, Doubleday & Co; Electromagnetic Spectrum 79, Jupiter 81 & Space Colony 82, Elsver-Nelson; Principles of Human Anatomy, 83, 86, 90, 92 & 95, 99, Principles of Anatomy & Physiology, 84, 87, 90, 92 & 96, 2000, Introduction to Human Body, 88, 90 & 92, 95, 97, Harper Collins. *Mailing Add:* Medical Illustrators Co PO Box 944 Cutchogue NY 11935

DANLY, SUSAN
CURATOR, HISTORIAN
b Chicago, Ill, July 27, 48. *Study:* Univ Wis, Madison, BA, 71; Brown Univ, MA, 77, PhD, 83. *Collection Arranged:* The Railroad in the American Landscape (with catalog), 81; Shadow Catchers: Photographs of Native Americans from the Huntington Collections (with catalog), 85; Prints & Drawings American West, 85; The Modern Poster: American Graphic Design in the 1890's, 85; Early Pasadena Artists, 86; Light, Air, and Color, 90; Telling Tales, 91; Language as Object: Emily Dickinson and Contemporary Art, 97. *Pos:* Asst cur Am art, The Huntington Libr, 84-86, assoc cur, 86-; cur, Pa Acad Fine Arts, 88-93, Mead Art Mus, 93-. *Teaching:* Vis fac am art, Univ Calif, Los Angeles, 85, Univ Pa, 90. *Awards:* Huntington Libr Fel, 90; Wintethur Fel, 93. *Mem:* Col Art Asn; Am Studies Asn. *Res:* 19th Century American Art with speciality in history of photography. *Publ:* Auth, Edward Weston in Los Angeles, Huntington Libr, 86; The Railroad in American Art, Mass Inst Technol Press, 87; Facing the Past, Pa Acad Fine Arts, 92; Eakins and the Photograph, Smithsonian Inst Press, 94. *Mailing Add:* Mead Art Mus Amherst Col Amherst MA 01002

DANOFF, I MICHAEL
MUSEUM DIRECTOR, WRITER
b Chicago, Ill, Oct 22, 40. *Study:* Univ Mich, BA, 62; Univ NC, Chapel Hill, MA, 64; Syracuse Univ, PhD, 70. *Collection Arranged:* Art in Our Time, travelling exhib, 80; Image in American Painting & Sculpture: 1950-1980 (co-auth, catalog), Akron Art Mus, 81; Cindy Sherman, Inc, 83; Robert Mangold, 84; Jeff Koons (auth, catalog), 88; Gerhard Richter: Painting (co-auth, catalog), Mus Contemp Art, Chicago, 88; Peter Halley: Paintings,89-92; Andy Warhol: Print Portfolios, 93; Contemplation: Five Installations, 96, Des Moines Art Ctr, Iowa. *Pos:* Cur collections, Dickinson Col, 70-73; cur, Michener Collection, Univ Tex, 73-74; cur collections & exhibs, Milwaukee Art Ctr, 74-80; assoc dir chief cur, Milwaukee Art Mus, 74-80; dir, Akron Art Mus, 80-84, Mus Contemp Art, Chicago, 84-88, San Jose Mus Art, 88-91 & Des Moines Art Ctr, 91-97; dir art prog, Neuberger & Berman. *Teaching:* Asst prof 19th & 20th Century & contemp art, Dickson Col, 70-73, Univ Tex, Austin, 73 & Univ Wis-Milwaukee, 75-80; adj prof, Univ Wis, Milwaukee, 78, Univ Akron, Ohio, 84, Univ Ill, Chicago, 88; lectr, San Jose State Univ, Calif, 90. *Awards:* Nat Endowment Arts Mus Prof Fel, 73. *Bibliog:* Rev, NY Times, 10/2/77; Helen Cullinan (auth), Italianate-Palazzo-Post Office, Art News, 9/81; Hilton Kramer (auth), An audacious inaugural, NY Times, 9/20/81; cover story, Arts & Books section, San Jose Mercury News, 11/20/88. *Mem:* Col Art Asn Am, 67-; Am Asn Mus, 74-; Asn Art Mus Dir, 80-98; Ill Arts Alliance (trustee, 86-88); Creative Time (trustee 2000-); Vera Lint. *Res:* Contemporary art history & criticism. *Publ:* Auth, Gallery Guides to Collections, Milwaukee Art Ctr, 74-75; Mary Nohl: sophisticated naive, Midwest Art, 75; Europe in the Seventies, Art in Am, 1/78; Paintings That Make Your Retinas Dance, Art News, 11/81; Art and Commodities, Affinities and Intuitions: The Gerald S Elliott Collection of Contemporary Art, The Art Institute of Chicago/Thomas & Hudson, Chicago/New York, 90. *Mailing Add:* Neuberger Berman LLC 605 3rd Ave New York NY 10158

DANTO, ARTHUR COLEMAN
CRITIC
b Ann Arbor, Mich, Jan 1, 24. *Study:* Wayne State Univ, BA, 48; Columbia Univ, MA, 49; Univ Paris, Postgrad, 50; Columbia Univ, PhD, 52. *Hon Degrees:* Sch Visual Arts, Hon Dr, 95, Pa Accad Fine Arts, Hon Dr, 96, Conn Col, Hon Dr, 97, Wayne State Univ, Hon Dr, 99, Ctr Creative Studies, Col Art & Design, Detriot, Hon Dr, 2001, Mass Col Art, Hon Dr, 2002, Columbia Univ, Dlitt, 2004. *Pos:* editor J Philosophy, 65-, pres, 87-; art critic The Nation, 84-; contrib ed ARTFORUM; consult ed for various other publications. *Teaching:* Instr Unive Colorado, Colo, 50-51; mem fac, Columbia Univ, 52-, Johnsonian prof, philosophy, 75-92, chmn dept, 79-87, co-dir, Ctr for Study of Human Rights, 78-92; prof emer, 92; lectr, Andrew W Mellon Fine Arts, 95. *Awards:* fel Fulbright Found, 49; Am Coun Learned Socs, 61, 70; Guggenheim Found, 69, 82; prof, Arts and Scis; Am Philosophical Asn (vpres 69, pres 83); Fulbright distinguished prof Yugoslavia, 76; Recipient prize for distinguished criticism Mfr-Hanover/Art World, 85; George S Polk award for criticism, 85; Am Soc Aesthetics (vpres 87, pres 89); Nat Book Critics Circle prize for criticism, 90; ICP Infinity prize for writing in photog, 93; Prix Philosophie, 2003; Icelandic Literary Prize, Non-fiction, 2005. *Mem:* Fel Am Asn for the Advancement of Sci; Am Soc Aesthetics (vpres 87, pres, 89); Col Art Asn (Frank Jewett Mather prize for criticism); Am Philosophical Asn (vpres 69, pres 83). *Publ:* auth: Nietzsche as Philosopher, 1965; Analytical Philosophy of Hist., 1965; Analytical Philosophy of Knowledge, 1968, What Philosophy Is, 1968; Mysticism and Morality, 1972; Analytical Philosophy of Action, 1973; Jean-Paul Sartre, 1975; The Transfiguration of the Commonplace, 1981 (Lionel Trilling Book prize 1982); Narration and Knowledge, 1985; The Philosophical Disenfranchisement of Art, 1986; The State of the Art, 1987; Connections to the World, 1989; Encounters and Reflections: Art in the Hist. Present, 1990 (National Book Critics Circle Prize for Criticism, 1990),; Beyond the Brillo Box: Art in the Post Hist. Period, 1992; Mark Tansey: Visions and Revisions, 1992; Robert Mapplethorpe, 1992; Embodied Meanings: Critical Essays and Aesthetic Meditations, 1994; Playing with the Edge: The Photographic Achievement of Robert Mapplethorpe, After the End of Art: Contemporary Art and the Pale of Hist., 1997 (Eugene Kayden prize 1997); The Body/Body Problem, 1999; Philosophizing Art, 1999; The Madonna of the Future, 2000; The Abuse of Beauty: Aesthetics and the Concept of Art, 2003; Unnatural Wonders: Essays in the Gap Between Art and Life, 2004. *Mailing Add:* 420 Riverside Dr New York NY 10025-7773

DANTZIC, CYNTHIA MARIS
EDUCATOR, PAINTER
b Brooklyn, NY, Jan 4, 33. *Study:* Bard Col, 50-52; Yale Univ, with Josef Albers & Jose de Rivera, BFA, 55; Pratt Inst, MFA, 63. *Work:* Brooklyn Mus; Adirondack Mus, NY; Adelphi Univ Gallery; Rose Art Mus, Waltham, Mass; Univ Mass Gallery, Amherst; Edson Tool Bldg, Belleville, NJ; many private collections; Bard Col. *Comn:* Modular paintings, NY Soc Gen Semantics, 68 & Springbok Ed, Kansas City, Kans, 74; stained glass windows, Church Resurrection, Lakeland, Fla, 75; portrait Mary Susan Miller, Berkeley Inst, Brooklyn, 79; Above and Beyond (ed photog collages), Brooklyn Art & Cult Asn, 83; calligraphic parchment, Charles Ives, Berkshire Inst for Theology & Arts, 2004. *Exhib:* Solo exhibs, East Hampton Gallery, NY, 66, Resnick Gallery, Long Island Univ, 83 & St John's Univ, NY, 95, Crosby Studio Gallery, New York City, 2005; group exhibs, The Wit of It, Delgado Mus, New Orleans, 72; Affect-Effect, La Jolla Mus Art, 79; Interior-Exterior, 80 & 100 New Acquisitions, 81, Brooklyn Mus; Common Ground: NY Abstract, Galerie Arts Visuels, Que, 82; Donnell Libr, 95-; Blue Mountain Gallery, 95-2006. *Collection Arranged:* Art Festival for NAACP Legal Defense (auth, catalog), Brooklyn Mus, 63; Jia-Xuan Zhang, Chinese calligraphy and photography, Long Island Univ, 98. *Pos:* Panelist, Regrant Panel NY Arts Funding, Brooklyn Arts & Cult Asn, 85-96; Consult/Analyst, NGDA, Online Database, Cooper Union, New York City, 99-2000. *Teaching:* Asst prof art, Brooklyn Ctr, Long Island Univ, 65-70, assoc prof, 70-75, prof, 75-, dir dept, 77-79, chmn, 80-86; adj assoc prof, Cooper Union, 92-99, adj prof, 99-2002. *Awards:* Stipend Award Animation, Brooklyn Art & Cult Asn, 82; Newton Award for Excellence in Teaching, 88; Trustee Award for Scholarly Achievement, Long Island Univ, 90; Trustee Lifetime Award for Achievement in Art and Art Educ, 2000. *Bibliog:* Talk of the town, New Yorker, 5/28/66; Marie Avona (auth), Cynthia Dantzic, Multi-media Artist, Pratt Reports, 6/79; Herbert Keppler (auth), Expand Your View: Cynthia Dantzic's Photo collages, Mod Photog, 1/84; The Gang's All Here, photo-collage, Popular Photog, 2000; Venice, with an old Nikon, a 50 mm Lens and a Daily Diary, article & 7 photos, Popular Photography, 2001. *Mem:* Col Art Asn; Am Asn Univ Prof; Founds Art & Teacher Educ; Soc Scribes (bd governors); Park Slope Civic Coun (trustee). *Media:* Pencil, Photography, calligraphy. *Interests:* Americana and Tribal Art, Piano, Non-Western Calligraphies. *Publ:* Auth, An invitation to the butterfly ball, NY Times Book Rev, 5/76; illusr, Biography, Confrontation, Long Island Univ, 79; auth & illusr, Design Dimensions: An Introduction to the Visual Surface, 90; auth & illusr, Prentice-Hall Drawing Dimensions: A Comprehensive Introduction, 99; auth & illusr, Antique Pocket Mirrors, Pictorial & Advertising Miniatures, Schiffer, 2002; auth, 100 New York Painters, Schiffer, 2006. *Mailing Add:* 910 President St Brooklyn NY 11215

DANZIGER, FRED FRANK
PAINTER
b Pittsburgh, Pa, Feb 24, 46. *Study:* Pa Acad Fine Arts, cert, 70. *Hon Degrees:* Mary Butler Painting Prize, 00. *Work:* Philadelphia Mus Art; Pa Acad Fine Arts, Philadelphia; Ashville Mus Art, NC; Wichita Art Mus, Kans; Woodmere Art Mus, Philadelphia. *Comn:* Mural on medical history, Med Col Pa, 95. *Exhib:* Art & the Law, Minn Mus Art, Minneapolis, 79; Recent Acquisitions, Noyes Mus, Oceanville, NJ, 86; Fel Ann, Pa Acad Fine Arts, Philadelphia, 88; Fel Ann, Michener Mus, Doylestown, Pa, 90; Recent Acquisitions, Woodmere Art Mus, Philadelphia, Pa, 92; Statewide Ann, State Mus Pa, Harrisburg, 92; Mainly Maine, Sherry French Gallery, New York, NY, 2006. *Teaching:* Instr painting & art hist, Art Inst Philadelphia, 73-; instr portrait painting, Pa Acad Fine Arts, 98-. *Awards:* Tiffany Grant, Nat Competition, Tiffany Found, 73; Alexander Prize, Painting Ann, Cheltenham Art Ctr, 89; Coyne Prize, Woodmere Painting Ann, Woodmere Mus, 92. *Bibliog:* Nicholas Roukes (auth), Acrylics Bold & New, Watson-Guptil, 87; Anna B Francis (auth), The Road to Recognition, Am Artist Mag, 91; Edward Sozanski (auth), On Art's Healing Edge, Philadelphia Inquirer, 91. *Mem:* Fel Pa Acad Fine Arts (treas, 80-84). *Media:* Acrylic, Oil. *Publ:* Auth, The Alone Ranger & Other Paintings, pvt publ, 79; What does big art have against nature, Philadelphia Inquirer, 91. *Dealer:* Rodger PaPelle Galleries 122 N Third St Philadelphia PA 19106; Sherry French Gallery 601 W 26th St New York NY 10001. *Mailing Add:* 22 Hunter Rd Coatesville PA 19320-4314

DANZIGER, JOAN
SCULPTOR
b New York, NY, June 17, 34. *Study:* Cornell Univ, BFA, 54; Art Students League, 54-55; Acad Fine Arts, Rome, cert art, 56-58. *Work:* Nat Mus Am Art, Smithsonian Inst, Nat Mus Womens Art, Am Univ, Capitol Children's Mus, Discovery Channel, George Washington Univ, Washington, DC; Jacksonville Mus Arts & Sci, Fla; NJ State Mus, Trenton; New Orleans Mus Art, La; Susquehenna Art Mus, Pa; Artery Corp, Md, Discovery Channel, NY, Lab Sch, Washington, DC, Am Univ, George Washington Univ, Univ Md, Susquehenna Art Mus, Pa. *Comn:* Suspended sculpture, Md Fine Arts Comn & Frostburg State Col, Md, 75; two sculptures, AFL-CIO Labor Studies Ctr, Silver Springs, Md, 76; three sculptures, Convention Ctr, Washington, DC, 85; five sculptures, comn by George Taylor, Dist Ct, Md, 90; bronze sculpture, Grounds for Sculpture, Hamilton, NJ, 2000-2001; Discovery Channel, Md; Fish Out of Water, City of Baltimore; Party Animals, DC Commission of the Arts. *Exhib:* one-man shows, Jacksonville Mus Art & Sci, 79, Fendrick Gallery, Wash, 79, Terry Dintenfass Gallery, NY, 80, Joy Horwich Gallery, Chicago, 82, NJ State Mus, Trenton, 82, Benjamin Mangel Gallery, Philadelphia, 84, La World Expos, New Orleans, 84, Textile Mus, Wash, 85, Nat Mus Women Arts, 87, San Antonio Art Ctr, 87; Joy Horwich Gallery, Chicago, 82; La World Exposition, New Orleans, 84; Osuna Gallery, Wash, DC, 90; Stamford Mus, Ct, 96; Grounds for Sculpture, NJ, 99; Cork Gallery, London, Eng, 2002. *Pos:* Visual arts panelist, DC Comn Arts & Humanities, 74-80; pres, Wash Sculptors Group, 94-99. *Teaching:* Visual arts panelist, DC Community Arts & Humanities, 74-79 & 84-85; artist-in-residence, AFL-CIO Labor Studies Ctr, 75; vis artist & lectr, Smithsonian Inst, 80-82; sculpture panelist, NJ State Coun Arts, 82. *Awards:* Nat Endowment Arts Grant, 75; Int des Arts, Paris, Grant, 86. *Bibliog:* Constance Dodge (auth), Fantasy Sculpture, Albany News, NY, 78; Cynthia Nadelman (auth), article, Art News, 80; Maryse Pailla (auth), Profile, Art Voices, 81; Joanna Shaw Eagle (auth), American women in sculpture, Harpers Bazaar, 81; Michael

Welzenbach (auth), The Magical Menagerie, Washington Post, 84; Virginia Watson-Jones (auth), Contemporary American Women Sculptors, 86. *Mem:* Washington Sculptors Group; Int Sculpture Ctr; Soc Art Imagination; Sculpture Guild. *Media:* Mixed-Media Sculpture. *Mailing Add:* 2909 Brandywine St NW Washington DC 20008

DAOU, ANNABEL
CONCEPTUAL ARTIST, DRAFTSMAN
b Beirut, Lebanon. *Study:* Barnard Col; Columbia Univ. *Exhib:* one man shows, Slipping, Conduit Gallery, Dallas, 2001, Striptease, Elizabeth Found for the Arts, NY, 2002, The Last Painting Show, Conduit Gallery Dallas, 2004, Ideas about the Thing & the Thing Itself, Gallery Joe, Philadelphia, 2005; New Space, Conduit Gallery, Dallas, Tex, 2002; A Three Week Show, Gallery Joe, Philadelphia, Pa, 2003; NADA, Josee Bienvenu Gallery, Miami, Fla, 2005; Series, Gallery Joe, Philadelphia, Pa, 2006; America, Josee Bienvenu Gallery, New York City, 2006. *Collection Arranged:* Sarah Ann & Werner H Kramarsky, NY; Howard Rachofsky, Dallas; US Trust, Dallas; Goldman Sachs, London; Museo Nacional de Bellas Artes, Havana. *Pos:* Cur, Aporia, Elizabeth Found Gallery, 2006. *Bibliog:* Roberta Fallon (auth) Artblog, 2006; David Markus (auth), Brooklyn Rail, 2006; Elizabeth Kley Time Out, NY, 2006. *Dealer:* Josee Bienvenu Gallery New York City NY; Gallery Joe Philadelphia PA. *Mailing Add:* 1 W 85th St 7A New York NY 10024

DAPHNIS, NASSOS
PAINTER, SCULPTOR
b Krokeai, Greece, July 23, 1914; US citizen. *Study:* Art Students League, New York, 46-49; Acad Frochot, Paris, 50-51; Inst Statale D'Arte, Florence, Italy, 51-52. *Work:* Mus Mod Art, NY; Whitney Mus, NY; Guggenheim Mus, NY; Albright-Knox Gallery, Buffalo, NY; Pittsburgh Mus Art, Pa. *Comn:* Wall mural, City Walls Inc, NY, 69 & 71; construction process, Arlen Realty, NY, 71; Jewish Mus, Miami, Fla; Bas Mus; Corcoran Gallery, DC; Univ of Miami, Fla. *Exhib:* One-man exhibs, Mint Mus, Charlotte, NC, 49, Leo Castelli Gallery, NY, 59, Albright-Knox Mus, Buffalo, NY, 69, Everson Mus, 69 & Andre Zarre Gallery, NY, 74 & 76; Corcoran Gallery Biennial, 59, 63 & 69; Ann Exhib Painting, Whitney Mus Am Art, 59, 61, 64, 65 & 67; Purist Painting, 61 & Geometric Abstraction in Am, 62, Walker Art Ctr; Am Abstract Expressionists & Imagists, Guggenheim Mus, 61; Ann Exhib Sculpture & Drawing, Whitney Mus Am Art, 62; Highlights of the 68-69 Season, Aldrich Mus, 69; one-man retrospective, works since 1951, Albright-Knox Mus, Buffalo & Everson Mus, Syracuse, NY, 69; Pittsburgh Int, Carnegie Inst, 70; Birmingham Festival Art, Birmingham Mus Art, 76; Provincetown Painters 1890s-1970s, Everson Mus Art, 77; Color & Forum, Boca Raton Mus, Fla & Butler Art Inst, Youngstown, Ohio, 93; and many others. *Awards:* Nat Found Arts & Humanities Award, 66; Nat Endowment Arts Grant, 71; Guggenheim Mem Found Fel, 77; Pollack-Krausner Found, 86. *Bibliog:* Denys Chevalier, Hydromorphics, Col Allendy, Paris, 50; John Gruen (auth), Biomorphic Paintings, Kouro's Gallery, 85; Robert M Murdock (auth), Thirty Years with Leo Castelli, Castelli Gallery, 90. *Mem:* Am Abstract Artists. *Media:* Oil, Enamel. *Dealer:* Anita Shapolsky Gallery 152 E 65th St New York NY 10021; 362 W Broadway New York NY 10013. *Mailing Add:* 362 W Broadway New York NY 10013

DARLING, SHARON SANDLING
MUSEUM DIRECTOR, HISTORIAN
b Mitchell, SDak, Feb 28, 43. *Study:* NC State Univ, BA; Duke Univ, MAT; Winterthur Summer Inst, Am Dec Arts; Northwestern Univ, MBA. *Exhib:* Chicago Metalsmiths; Chicago Ceramics and Glass; Chicago Furniture; Haymartket!1886; Motorola: A Journey Through Time & Technology. *Pos:* Cur dec arts, Chicago Hist Soc, 75-86; dir, Motorola Mus, 86-2005; dir, Motorola Innovation Ctr, 2006. *Awards:* Charles F Montgomery Prize, Decorative Arts Soc, 85. *Res:* Decorative arts of Chicago and the Midwest; industrial arts. *Interests:* Architectural terra cotta, Gardening. *Publ:* Chicago Metalsmiths, (with Gail Farr Casterline) 77; Chicago Ceramics and Glass, 80; Chicago Furniture, 84; TECO: Art Pottery of the Prairie School, 89; Common Clay, 03. *Mailing Add:* 4N227 Burr Rd Saint Charles IL 60175

DARR, ALAN PHIPPS
CURATOR, HISTORIAN
b Kankakee, Ill, Sept 30, 48. *Study:* Northwestern Univ, BA, 70, Inst Fine Arts, NY Univ, MA, 75, PhD(art hist), 80; Metrop Mus Art, cert mus training, 76; Univ Calif, Berkeley, mus mgt, 80; Harvard Univ, Ctr Italian Renaissance Studies, Villa I Tatti, Florence, postdoctoral fel, 88-89; Ctr Advan Study Visual Arts, Nat Gallery Art, Washington, Paul Mellon Vis Sr Fel, 94. *Pos:* Grad intern, Metrop Mus Art, NY, 76; asst cur, Detroit Inst Arts, 78-80, assoc cur, 80-81, cur in charge European sculpture & decorative arts, 81-96, Walter B Ford II Family cur Europ sculpture & decorative arts, 97-. *Teaching:* Instr, NY Univ, 76; adj prof, Wayne State Univ, Detroit, 82-. *Awards:* Fel, Nat Endowment Humanities & Rush H Kress Found, 88-89; Florence J Gould fel, 90; Bronze medal, Accademia del Discgno, Florence, 86; Paul Mellon Vis Sr fel, CASVA, Washington, 94; award, Samuel Basil Trust Scholarship, Royal Collection Studies Program, Eng, 2002. *Mem:* Col Art Asn; Renaissance Soc Am; ICOM; AAM; Am Ceramic Cir; Italian Art Soc; and others. *Res:* Italian Renaissance and Baroque sculpture and decorative arts; Pietro Torrigiani and Italian Art in Renaissance England. *Publ:* The Romantics to Rodin: Nineteenth Century French Sculpture from North American Collections (coauth, catalog), 80; The Influence of Paris: European and American Sculpture 1830-1930 (coauth, catalog), 81-82; Italian Renaissance Sculpture in the Time of Donatello (auth, catalog), 85; Donatello e i Suoi: Scultura fiorentina del primo Rinascimento (auth, catalog), 86; Coauth, Francesco da Sangallo, Burlington Mag, 12/87; Donatello Studien (co-ed & coauth, catalog), 89; Verrocchio and Late Quattrocento Italian Sculpture (co-ed & coauth, catalog), 92; contribr, Kunst des Cinquecento in der Toskana, Kunsthistorisches Institut, Florence, 92; auth, The Figure Revisited (catalog), Int Ceramics Seminar, 94; Woven Splendor: Five Centuries of European Tapestry in the Detroit Institute of Arts (coauth, catalog), 96; The Dodge Collection: Eighteenth-Century French and English Art in the Detroit Institute of Arts (organizer & coauth, catalog), 96; auth, The Medici, Michelangelo and the Art of Late Renaissance Florence (catalog), Art Inst Chicago, Detroit Inst Arts, 2002; auth, Italian Sculpture in the Detroit Inst Art (catalog), 2 vols, 2002; auth, A Pair of Large Bronze Deities in Detroit, New Research and an Attribution to Danese Cattaneo (catalog), Nat Gallery Art, Ctr for Advanced Study in Vis Arts, Washington, DC *Mailing Add:* c/o Detroit Inst Arts 5200 Woodward Ave Detroit MI 48202

DARRIAU, JEAN-PAUL
EDUCATOR, SCULPTOR
b New York, NY, Nov 24, 29. *Study:* Pratt Inst, 47-48; Brooklyn Col, BA, 51; Univ Minn, MFA, 54. *Work:* Hirshhorn Mus & Sculpture Garden; Ind Univ Fine Arts Mus; Colorado Springs Art Ctr; Minneapolis Inst Art; Albert List Collection; Interracial Movement/Entrance to City, City of Bloomington, Ind. *Comn:* Man and Woman (aluminum), Jersey City State Col, 69; Adam and Eve I (bronze), 68, Adam and Eve II (bronze), 73 & four portrait busts, 76, Ind Univ Campus; Red, Blond, Black and Olive (limestone), City Bloomington, Ind, 80. *Exhib:* One-man show, Grippi Gallery, NY, 62; Sculptors Guild, NY, 70-72; FAR Gallery, NY, 72-73; Privileges and Silences, Ind Univ, Bloomington, 82 & Univ Chicago, 83; Sch Fine Arts, Ind Univ, 84; Mussavi Arts Ctr, NY, 85. *Teaching:* Instr, State Col, Arkadelphia, Ark, 53, Oberlin Col, 54 & Colo Col, 57-61; instr, Ind Univ, Bloomington, 61-, head sculpture dept, 61-72. *Awards:* Fulbright Grant, 55-57 & 66-67; res grants, Colo Col, 59 & Ind Univ. *Mem:* Col Art Asn; CAA Gay/Lesbian Caucus (bd mem). *Publ:* Contribr, Visions and Voice of the New Midwest, James A Rock & Co, 78; self-publ catalogs, 83 & 88. *Mailing Add:* 324 N Jefferson St Bloomington IN 47408-4158

DARROW, PAUL GARDNER
PAINTER, EDUCATOR
b Pasadena, Calif. *Study:* Colorado Springs Fine Art Ctr; Claremont Grad Sch & Univ Ctr. *Work:* Pasadena Art Mus, Calif; Times-Mirror Collection, Los Angeles; US Navy, Washington; Lytton Savings & Loan Collection, Los Angeles; Long Beach Mus Art, Calif. *Comn:* Murals, Air France, Los Angeles, 61, Balboa Yacht Club, 63 & Newport Bank, Calif, 71; Wells Fargo Bank, Costa Mesa, Calif, 78. *Exhib:* Corcoran Gallery, 54; Smithsonian Inst, 55; Oakland Art Mus, Calif, 64; solo exhibs, Newport Harbor, 72 & Gallerie Forma, El Salvador, 75; retrospective, Scripps Col, 73 & (with catalog) Lang Gallery, 92; Southern California 100, Laguna Beach Mus Art, 77; California Photographers, Claremont Galleries, 78. *Teaching:* Prof emer art & chmn dept, Scripps Col, 60-92, emer prof, 92-; prof emer art, Claremont Grad Sch, 70-92, emer prof, 92-; Cal Tech, 70-74. *Awards:* Purchase Award, Pasadena Art Mus, 58; Res Grant, Ford Found, 69; Nat Endowment Humanities Grant, 73. *Bibliog:* Bently Schaad (auth), The Realm of Contemporary Still Life Painting, 62 & Edmondson (auth), Printmaking, 72, Van Nostrand Reinhold. *Mem:* Calif Watercolor Soc; founding mem Los Angeles Printmaking Soc. *Media:* Collage, Mixed Media. *Specialty:* Contemp. *Publ:* Illusr, Aldous Huxley, Paris Rev, 62; Psychological Perspectives, C G Jung JG Jung Inst, 70; illusr, The Academic Bestiary, Wm Morrow, 74; auth, A Retrospective (catalog), Lake Gallery, Scripps Col, 92; auth, A Decade of Mixed Media & collage (catalog), Huntington Beach Art Ctr, 2001. *Dealer:* Peter Blake Gallery 326 N Coast Hwy Laguna CA 92651. *Mailing Add:* 690 Cuprien Way Laguna Beach CA 92651

DARTON, CHRISTOPHER
PAINTER
b New York, NY, Dec 9, 45. *Study:* New York Inst Technol, BFA, 69; Pratt Inst Grad Sch, MFA, 71. *Exhib:* Daniel Weinberg, San Francisco, Calif, 79; Mary Boone Gallery, 80. *Media:* Acrylic Paint. *Publ:* Auth, Matter as subject, Arts Mag, 11/77. *Mailing Add:* 9 E 16th St 4th Fl New York NY 10003-3189

DAS, RATINDRA
PAINTER, INSTRUCTOR
b India. *Study:* Univ of Calcutta, BA; Univ Toronto, MA; Am Acad Art (studied with Irving Shapiro); Workshops with Robert E Wood, Frank Webb, Serge Hollerbach. *Work:* Miller Art Mus, Sturgeon Bay, Wis; DuPage Co Courthouse, Winfield, Ill; Kane Co Courthouse, Geneva, Ill; Amoco Corp, Chicago, Ill. *Exhib:* Transparent Watercolor Soc, Elmhurst Art Mus, Elmhurst, Ill, 2004; Places & Faces, Gray Gallery Quincy, Univ, Quincy, Ill, 2005; Paintings from Around, Bloomingdale Art Mus, Bloomingdale, Ill, 2005; Transparent Watercolor, Kankakee Co Mus, Kankakee, Ill, 2005; Am Watercolor Soc Ann, Salmagundi Club, NY, 2005-2006; Images of Mexico, Efren Gonzalez Gallery, Ajijic, Mex, 2006. *Teaching:* Instr, Independent Teaching Workshops (throughout country & Mex). *Awards:* Louis Kaep Award, Am Watercolor Soc, 2004; Fred Albrecht Award, Am Watercolor Soc, 2005; Paul Schwartz Mem Award, Am Watercolor Soc, 2006. *Mem:* Am Watercolor Soc (signature mem); Nat Watercolor Soc, (signature mem); Watercolor West, (signature mem); Transparent Watercolor Soc Am, (master status, signature mem); Ariz Watercolor Asn (signature mem). *Media:* Watercolor. *Publ:* Contribr, Strengthen your Paintings by Dynamic Composition (B), Northlight Publ, 1994; contribr, Best of Watercolor (B), Rockport Publ, 1997; contribr, The Artistic Touch 3 (B), Creative Art Press, 1999; auth, The Artists Mag (Art), F E W Publ, 2001; auth, Watercolor Magic (Art), F E W Publ, 2005. *Mailing Add:* 1938 Berkshire Wheaton IL 60187

DASENBROCK, DORIS (NANCY) VOSS
DESIGNER, PAINTER
b Horicon, Wis, Nov 6, 39. *Study:* Wis State Univ, Oshkosh, BS, 62; Fla State Univ, Tallahassee, MFA, 67; Univ Md, College Park, BS, 89. *Work:* Fla State Univ Fine Arts Collection, Tallahassee; Mus Art, Ft Wayne, Ind; US House Rep, Washington, DC. *Comn:* Contemp design, St Matthew's Episcopal Church, St Petersburg, 69; altar,

Bowie, Md, 70, stained glass designs, 79, All Saints Lutheran Church, Bowie, Md. *Exhib:* Am Acad Arts & Lett, NY, 69 & 70; West Bend Galley Fine Art, Wis, 76; St Paul Mus Art, Minn, 77; Tweed Mus Art, Duluth, Minn, 77; South Alleghenies Mus, Loretto, Pa, 78; Mus Tex Tech Univ, Lubbock, 78; Fed Bldg, Washington, DC, 79. *Collection Arranged:* Artists Today Traveling Exhib, Prince George's Col, Marlboro Gallery, 79; Photography 79, Capital Ctr Gallery, 79. *Pos:* Exhib specialist, Capital Park Planning Comn, Riverdale, Md, 78-79; designer & illusr, Sterling Inst, Washington, DC, 79; media designer & coordr, Am Genetics Corp, Bethesda, Md, 79-; dir advert, GTCO Corp, Rockville, Md, 85-87, advert & mktg consult, 87-. *Teaching:* Instr, Montgomery Col, Takoma Park, Md, 69-70; instr, Bowie State Col, Md, 75-76, George Mason Univ, Fairfac, Va, 78-79. *Awards:* Childe Hassom Purchase Award, Am Acad Arts & Lett, 69; Art Purchase Award, Benedictine Corp, 76; Award Excellence, Simpson Paper Co, 80. *Bibliog:* Brian Abbott (auth), Artist profile, Bowie Blade, Md, 6/3/76. *Mem:* Washington Women's Art Ctr; Women's Caucus Art; Artists Equity Asn; Md Fedn Art; Southern Watercolor Soc. *Media:* Watercolor, Oil; Pen & Ink. *Publ:* Illusr, Probing the physical world: Excursions, Fla State Univ, Tallahassee, 67; Air Conditioning - Refrigeration and Heating, Nat Radio Inst, Washington, DC, 73; Householder's Appliance Repair Course, McGraw-Hill, 74; Job Assessment and Career Development Guide, Sterling Inst, 79; Photography, McGraw-Hill, CEC, 88. *Dealer:* Jansson Art Gallery Rte 6A Barnstable MA 02637. *Mailing Add:* 1407 Pennington Ln Bowie MD 20716-1829

DASH, ROBERT
PAINTER
b New York, NY, June 8, 34. *Work:* Brooklyn Mus, NY; Hirshhorn Mus, Washington; Pittsburgh Mus Art; Joslyn Art Mus, Omaha, Nebr; Philadelphia Mus Art; Parrish Mus, Southhampton, NY; Heckscher Mus, Huntington, NY; Guggenheim Mus; Boston Mus Fine Arts; Guildham (Easthampton) Yale Univ; MIT; The Nelson Gallery, Kansas City, KS. *Comn:* Centennial, Cheseborough-Pond's Inc. *Exhib:* Landscapes by Five Americans, Festival of Two Worlds, Mus Mod Art Traveling exhib, 66; The New Realism, Hirschl & Adler Galleries, NY, 81; New Acquisitions, Hirshhorn Mus, 83; Earthly Pleasures, Fort Wayne Mus, 88; Darkness, Guild Hall, East Hampton, 91; Irreverence, Int Monetary Fund, Washington, 94; ACA Galleries, 2001; Berrie Art Ctr, 2003. *Pos:* Writer, bi-weekly column, East Hampton Star. *Teaching:* Adj prof advan painting, spring 70, 75, 77 & 81 & Master Wkshp, 85 & 94, Southampton Col; vis prof, State Univ NY, Stony Brook, 88. *Awards:* New York Times, 10 Best Garden Books, 2001. *Bibliog:* An artist's garden, House & Garden, 87; Erica Lennard (auth), Madison Cox, 93; Peter Beales (auth), Visions of Roses, 96. *Mem:* Madoo Conservancy (founder & pres); Nature Conservancy (trustee); Peconic Land Trust (adv); Garden Conservancy Am (founder); NY Cult Soc. *Media:* Oils, Pastels. *Publ:* Notes from Madoo, Houghton-Mifflin, 2000. *Dealer:* Patricia Hamilton. *Mailing Add:* 618 Sagg Main St PO Box 362 Sagaponack NY 11962

DASKALOFF, GYORGY
PAINTER
b Sofia, Bulgaria, May 15, 23; US citizen. *Study:* Acad Fine Arts, Sofia, grad. *Work:* Metrop Mus Art, NY; Nat Mus, Sofia; Royal Libr, Brussels, Belg; Butler Inst Am Art, Youngstown, Ohio. *Comn:* Mural, comn by ARA, Ann Arbor, Mich; portrait of Judge Theodor Levin, Detroit Bar Asn, 71; An American Family (mural), comn by Amos Cahan, NY, 73. *Exhib:* Bulgarian Art in Berlin, 58, Moscow, 59 & Prague, 59; Int Biennial Graphic Arts, Ljubliana, 59; Int Exhib Graphics, Leipzig, 60; Comparisons, Paris, 65-67. *Awards:* First Prize for Graphics, Bulgaria, 54 & 59. *Bibliog:* Pierre Rouve (auth), article, Arts Rev, London, 6/3/61; L L Sosset (auth), article, Les Beaux Arts, Brussels, 5/6/65; Pierre Lubecker (auth), article, Politiken, Copenhagen, 5/25/67. *Media:* Oil. *Mailing Add:* 14 Cooper Ln East Hampton NY 11937-2220

DASS, DEAN ALLEN
PRINTMAKER, PAINTER
b Hampton, Iowa, Nov 16, 1955. *Study:* Univ Northern Iowa, Cedar Falls, BA, 78; Tyler Sch Art, Temple Univ, MFA, 80. *Work:* Va Mus Fine Arts; Kans State Univ; Univ Nebr; Univ Dallas; Brooklyn Mus Art; Philadelphia Mus Art; Walker Art Ctr, Minneapolis, Minn; Alderman Libr, Univ Va. *Exhib:* Nat Print Exhib, 81 & Artist as Printmaker, 83, Brooklyn Mus, NY; New Acquisitions, Walker Art Gallery, Minneapolis, 86; solo exhibs, Dolan Maxwell Gallery, Philadelphia, 86 & 89, Projects & Portfolios, Brooklyn Mus, 89, Danville Mus, Va, 90 & Schmidt/Dean Gallery, Philadelphia, 91 & 96, Galleria Harmonia, Jyvaskyla, Finland, 97 & 2001, Univ Wyo Art Mus, 98, Schmidt Dean Gallery, Philadelphia, 96, 99 & 2001, 3A Gallery, San Francisco, Calif, 2000, Les Yeux Du Monde, Charlottesville, Va, 2001 & Univ Akron, 2003; Bradford Biennial, Eng, 89; Graphic Triennial, Alvar Aalto Mus, Finland, 90; 1708 Gallery, Richmond, Va, 90; Int Print Biennial, Maastricht, The Neth, 93; Univ Ala, Tuscaloosa, 95; Creativa Graphica, Alvar Aalto Mus, Finland. *Teaching:* Instr printmaking & drawing, Kutztown Univ, 83-84; asst prof, Univ Va, Charlottesville, 85-90, assoc prof, 91-, prof, 98-. *Awards:* Purchase Award, Charlotte Printmakers Soc, NC, 83; Artist's Fel, Pa Coun Arts, 85; Va Prize in Printmaking, Va Comn Arts, 88. *Bibliog:* Jukka Yli-Lassila (auth), Rakkaus, Joka Kypsyy, Keskisuomalainen, 6/1/97; Elina Puranen (auth), Uusien Ulottuvuuksien Loytoretki, Keskisuomalainen, 3/9/98; Martin Lammon (auth), Arts & Letters, fall 99; Faye Hirsch (auth), Art on Paper, 3-4/2000; Eliz Sutton (auth), 64 Mag, 4/2001. *Media:* Oil, Print. *Publ:* Auth, Mineral Light, Journey to the Self, New Literary Hist, 95; Ed, The Land of Wandering. *Dealer:* Schmidt Dean Gallery Philadelphia PA. *Mailing Add:* Univ Va 990 Allendale Dr Charlottesville VA 22901-9228

DATER, JUDY
PHOTOGRAPHER, WRITER
b Hollywood, Calif, June 21, 41. *Study:* Univ Calif, Los Angeles, 59-62; San Francisco State Univ, BA, 63, MA, 66. *Work:* Addison Gallery Am Art, Phillips Acad, Andover, Mass; Fed Reserve Bank, San Francisco & Mus Mod Art, San Francisco; Int Ctr Photog, Metrop Mus Art & Mus Mod Art, NY; Boston Mus Fine Arts, Mass; Libr Congress, Washington, DC; and many others; Fogg Art Mus, Harvard Univ, Cambridge, Mass; Int Ctr Photog, NY. *Exhib:* One-person exhibs, Oakland Mus, Calif, 74, San Francisco Mus Mod Art, Calif, 84, Matsuya Dept Store, Ginza, Tokyo, Japan, 92, Int Ctr Photog, NY, 94, Galeries Arlesiennes, 25th Recontres Int de la Photog d'Arles, France, 94, Calif Col Arts & Crafts, Oakland, 96 & Judy Dater Photographs, Fotogaleria del Treato General San Martin, Buenos Aires, Argentina; Photogs of Women, 72 & Mirrors & Windows (with book), Mus Mod Art, NY, traveling, 78, Photog in Am (with book), 74 & Suburban Home Life: Tracking the Am Dream (with catalog), Whitney Mus Am Art, NY, 89; Pvt Realities: Recent Am Photog (with book), Boston Mus Fine Arts, 74; Women in Photog: An Historical Survey (with book), traveling, 75, Faces Photographed (with catalog), From the Permanent Collection, 84 & Photog in California 1945-1980 (with book), traveling, San Francisco Mus Mod Art, 84; Photo Facts & Opinions (with book), Addison Gallery Am Art, Andover, Mass, 81; Subjective Vision (with catalog), The Lucinda W Bunnen Collection of Photogs, 83 & First Person Singular: Self-Portrait Photog 1840-1987 (with catalog), High Mus, Atlanta, Ga, 88; The Art of California, Selections from the Steinman Collection, 84 & Picturing California (with book), Oakland Mus, Calif, 89; Self as Subject, Honolulu Acad Art, Hawaii, 85; Reclaiming Paradise (with catalog), Tweed Mus Art, Duluth, Minn, traveling, 87; Meaning at the Crossroads: The Portrait in Photog (with catalog), Bowdoin Col Mus Art, Brunswick, Maine, 94; Cycles (traveling show), Los Angeles Co Munic Hall, 94-95; Choices, Smith Anderson Galleries, Palo Alto, Calif, 96; A History of Women Photographers, Akron Art Mus, Ohio, 97; Collection, Int Ctr Photog, NY, 97. *Collection Arranged:* Imogen Cunningham: A Portrait Traveling Exhib, (auth, catalog), New York Graphic Soc, 79. *Pos:* Freelance artist/photogr, self-employed, currently. *Teaching:* Instr, Univ Calif, San Francisco, 66-74, San Francisco Art Inst, 74-78, 92 & 94, Int Ctr Photog, New York, 87-90, San Jose City Col, 96- & Univ Calif, Berkeley, 96-; guest instr, Kansas City Art Inst, 85; lectr & workshop leader throughout the US, Europe & Japan. *Awards:* Nat Endowment Arts Fel, 76 & 88; J S Guggenheim Mem Found fel, 78; Indiv Artists Grant, Marin Arts Coun, 87. *Bibliog:* Image, George Eastman House, Int Mus Photog & Film, vol 37, nos 1 & 2, 94; History of Photoprahy, Kinsey Inst & Erotic Photog, vol 18, no 1, Spring 94; American Photo, vol V, no 4, 7-8/94; plus many others. *Mem:* San Francisco Camerawork; Soc Photog Educ. *Publ:* Auth, Imogen Cunningham: A Portrait, New York Graphic Soc, Boston, Mass, 79; coauth, Judy Dater: Twenty Years, Univ Ariz Press, 86; Body & Soul: Ten American Women, Hill & Co, Boston, Mass, 88; Cycles, Kodansha, Tokyo, Japan, 92; Cycles, Curatorial Assistance, Inc, Pasadena, Calif, 94; plus many others. *Dealer:* Smith Anderson Ed 440 Pepper St Palo Alto CA 94306. *Mailing Add:* 2430 5th St No J Berkeley CA 94710

DAUB, MATTHEW FORREST
PAINTER, GRAPHIC ARTIST
b New York, NY, Aug 29, 1951. *Study:* Southern Ill Univ, Carbondale, BA, 81, MFA, 84. *Work:* Metrop Mus Art & Mus City, NY; Evansville Mus Arts & Sci, Ind; Mitchell Mus, Mt Vernon, Ill; Sheldon Swope Art Mus, Terre Haute, Ind. *Exhib:* Solo exhibs, Evansville Mus Arts & Sci, Ind, 83, Sherry French Gallery, NY, 84, 86, 88, 91 & 93, Jan Cicero Gallery, Chicago, Ill, 87, 89, Evansville Mus Arts & Sci, Ind, 94, Owensboro Mus Fine Art, Ky, 95, Sheldon Swope Art Mus, Terre Haute, Ind, 95, Headley Whitney Mus, Lexington, Ky, 95 & Louisville Art Asn, Ky, 95; Exactitude: New Acquisitions, Met Mus Art, NY, 87-89; Trains & Planes: The Influence of Locomotion in Am Painting, Nat Acad Scis, Washington, 89 & 90; Art and the Law, 92, 95, 96; Am Acad Arts & Lett Invitational (painting & sculpture), NY, 96; MB Mod Gallery, NY, 99; Demuth Mus, Lancaster, Pa, 2000; Reading Pub Mus, Pa, 2001; Sheltered, Lafaette Col, Easton, Pa, 2005; Imaging Industry: Pa Coal & Steel, Lebanon Valley Col, Annville, Pa, 2006; Visions of the Susquehanna, Lancaster Mus Art, 2006. *Teaching:* Prof fine arts, Kutztown Univ Pa, 87-. *Awards:* Purchase Awards, 35th & 36th Ann Mid-States Art Exhib, Evansville Mus, 82 & 83; Ill Arts Coun Fel, 86; Pollock-Krasner Fel, 92. *Bibliog:* Dan Wood (auth), The Craft of Drawing, Harcourt Brace Javonovich; Gerrit Henry (auth), Signs of the Times (catalog essay), American Watercolors, Engagement Calendar, Metrop Mus Art, 91; David Dewey (auth), The Watercolor Book. *Media:* Watercolor, Conte Crayon. *Publ:* Auth, The watercolor page, Am Artist, 82; Carolyn Plochmann: A Charmed Vision, Evansville Mus Arts & Sci, 90; Carolyn Plochman, Am Artist, 90. *Mailing Add:* 237 Dreibelbis Station Rd Lenhartsville PA 19534

DAUGHERTY, MICHAEL F
EDUCATOR, SCULPTOR
b Seattle, Wash, Sept 30, 42. *Study:* Univ Wash, Seattle, 60-62; Univ Barcelona, Spain, 64-65; Univ Wash, Seattle, BA(sculpture), 69; Univ Tenn, Knoxville, MFA(sculpture), 71. *Comn:* Outdoor fountains, comn by Walter H Stevens, Knoxville, 70, Genevieve Stoughton, Oak Ridge, 71, Alvin Rotenberg, Baton Rouge, 73, Janice Sachse, Baton Rouge, 74 & Derwood Facundus, Baton Rouge, 76. *Exhib:* 16th Joslyn Biennial, Joslyn Art Mus, Omaha, Nebr, 80; Nat Drawing and Sculpture Exhib, Del Mar Art Gallery, Corpus Christi, Tex, 81; Nat Sculpture Exhib, Westwood Ctr Arts, Los Angeles, Calif, 81; Biennial Five State Exhib, Fine Arts Gallery, Port Arthur, Tex, 81; Art for Arts Sake, Contemp Arts Ctr, New Orleans, La, 81; and many others. *Teaching:* Asst, Univ Tenn, 69-71; instr, Art Ctr, Oak Ridge, Tenn, 70; assoc prof sculpture, La State Univ, 71-. *Awards:* Purchase Award, Tenn Sculpture 1970, Tenn Arts Comn, 71; Purchase Award, 7th Ann Mobile Art Exhib, Mobile, Ala, 72; Second Place Award, Biennial Five State Exhib, Port Arthur, Tex. *Mem:* Southern Asn Sculptors; Col Art Asn; Int Sculpture Ctr; Southeastern Col Art Asn. *Dealer:* Adelle M Taylor Gallery 3317 McKinney Ave Dallas TX 75204. *Mailing Add:* 5246 N Chalet Ct Baton Rouge LA 70808-4843

DAUTREUIL, LINDA TRAPPEY
PAINTER
b New Iberia, La, Mar 16, 48. *Study:* Univ La, Lafayette, BA, 69, BFA, 84. *Work:* Univ Art Mus, Lafayette, La; Ochsner Found Collection, New Orleans Mus Art. *Exhib:* Louisiana Open, Masur Mus Art, Monroe, La, 94; Artists Alliance, Lafayette, La, 95; Artists Ann, Slidell Cult Art Ctr, Slidell, La, 98; Project Harmony, Contemp Arts Ctr, New Orleans, 98; Laredo Nat, Laredo Ctr for Arts, Laredo, Tex, 99; Living in Louisiana, Alexandria Mus Art, 99; La Women's Caucus Invitational, St Tammany Art Asn, Covington, La, 2000. *Pos:* asst to dir, Univ Art Mus, Lafayette, La, 90-92, cur of educ, 93-94. *Awards:* First Place Mixed Media, Laredo Center for Arts, 99; Best of Show, St Tammany Art Asn, 97; First Place Painting, South Cobb Arts Alliance, 98. *Bibliog:* Douglas Maccash (auth), Landscapes and Surreal Paintings, Times Picayune, 5/2000; Judith Bonner (auth), New Orleans Art Rev, 6/2000; Brian Flafaye (auth), Times of Acadiana, 9/2000. *Mem:* St Tammany Art Asn; Contemp Art Ctr; Baton Rouge Gallery; La Arts Partnership. *Media:* Acrylic. *Dealer:* Brunner Gallery 522 N New Hampshire St Covington LA 70433; Lowe Gallery 75 Bennett St Atlanta GA 30309. *Mailing Add:* 251 S Jahncke Ave Covington LA 70433

DAVENNY, WARD L
PRINTMAKER, PAINTER
b Hartford, Conn, July 27, 51. *Study:* San Francisco Art Inst, Calif, BFA (printmaking), 77; Yale Univ, New Haven, Conn, MFA (printmaking & painting), 82; studied with Gabor Peterdi, Michael Mazur, William Bailey, Bernard Chaet & Lester Johnson. *Work:* Fogg Mus, Cambridge, Mass; Minneapolis Inst Arts, Minn; Honolulu Acad of Arts, Hawaii; Newark Pub Libr Print Collection, NJ; Boston Pub Libr, Wiggins Collection, Boston, Mass; Coll Charleston, SC; Brit Mus London; McNay Art Inst, San Antonio, Tex; Hawaii State Found for Arts; and others. *Comn:* Print Ed, Contemp Mus, Honolulu, Hawaii, 91. *Exhib:* Solo exhibs, Mary Ryan Gallery, NY, 89, 93, 95, 98 & 2001, Contemp Mus, Honolulu, 91, Trout Gallery, Dickinson Col, Carlisle, Pa, 93 & Univ Long Island, Southampton, 96, Collective Visions 1967-1997, Honolulu Acad of Arts, 97; Prints & Paper, San Diego Art Inst, 93; Gettysburg Col, Schmucker Hall, Pa, 94; Printwork '94, Art Inst Poughkeepsie, NY, 94; Changing Nature, Susquehanna Art Mus, Harrisburg, Pa, 99; Filling the Sky, Halsey Gallery, Coll Charleston, SC, 2000; and others. *Pos:* chmn dept Art & Art Hist, Dickinson Coll, 99-. *Teaching:* asst prof studio art, Univ Conn, Storrs, 88 & Univ Hawaii, Honolulu, 88-92; asst prof painting, drawing & printmaking, Dickinson Coll, Carlisle Pa, 92-94, assoc prof, 94-. *Awards:* Nat Endowment Arts Fel, 85 & 93; Univ Conn Res Found Grant, 87; Univ Hawaii Res Coun Grant, 89; Dickinson Coll Res Devel Grant, 93; Pa Coun for Arts Fel Grant, 96; Dickinson Coll Summer Scholar Award, 99, 2001. *Media:* Drawing, Lithography, Intaglio

DAVENPORT, BILL
SCULPTOR
b Greenfield, Mass, 1962. *Study:* RI Sch Design, BFA(sculpture), 86; Univ Mass, MFA(sculpture), 90. *Work:* Miss Liberty on the Bayou (installation), Buffalo Bayou Artpark, Houston, Tex, 92; Leopard and Dubuffet Rocks (installation), Houston Art League Sculpture Court, Houston, Tex, 93. *Exhib:* Solo exhib, Viewing Room, Houston, Tex, 94, Inman Gallery, Houston, Tex, 94, 95, 97 & 99, Cristinerose Gallery, NY, 97, Art with Cats, Good/Bad Art Collective, Denton, Tex, 97, Sala Diaz, San Antonio, Tex, 98 & Angstrom Gallery, Dallas, Tex, 99; The Home Show (with catalog), Univ Tex Art Gallery, San Antonio, 95; Continental Discourse: Art of Mexico and the United States Today (with catalog), San Antonio Mus Art, Tex, 95; New Work III, Barry Whistler Gallery, Dallas, Tex, 95; Chateau Marmot Int Art Fair, Los Angeles, Calif, 95; Tex Art Celebration, Cullen Ctr, Houston, Tex, 96; Los Angeles Nat Art Exhib, Spanish Kitchen Gallery, 96; Buttered Side Up: 3 Houston Abstractionists, Arlington Mus Art, Tex, 96; Five Year Anniversary Exhib, Inman Gallery, Houston, Tex, 96; The Big Show, Lawndale Art & Performance Ctr, Houston, Tex, 96; The Red Hot End of Summer Show, Barry Whistler Gallery, Dallas, Tex, 96; The Incredible Shrinking Art Show, Small Projs Gallery, Univ Houston, Tex, 96; Buttered Side Up, Hallwalls Contemp Arts Ctr, Buffalo, NY, 96 & Koffler Gallery, Toronto, Ont, Can, 96; Disiptoey, Strategies For Abstraction, Angstrom Gallery, Dallas, Tex, 97; Women's Work, Arlington Mus Art, Tex, 97; Equal Pay: A Labor Exchange, Revolution Summer Art Space, Houston, Tex, 97; New Work: Gallery Artists, Inman Gallery, Houston, Tex, 97 & 98; Thread, Cristinerose Gallery, NY, 97; Material World: Artists and their Materials, Austin Mus Art, Tex, 98; Extremely Shorts, Aurora Picture Show, Houston, Tex, 98; Blunt Object, Smart Mus Art, Univ Chicago, Ill, 98; Unravelled, City Gallery at Chastain, Atlanta, Ga, 98; Nirvana, British Coun Window Gallery, Prague, Czech Repub, 98; The Texas Show, ABC No Rio, NY, 98; Artistic Centers: Houston-Galveston, Galveston Arts Ctr, Tex, 98; Hot Spots, Weatherspoon Art Gallery, Univ NC, Greensboro, 99; Threshold, Kohler Arts Ctr, Sheboygan, Wis, 99; By Design, Contemp Art Collective, Las Vegas, Nev, 99. *Awards:* Core Fel, Glassell Sch Art, Mus Fine Arts, Houston, Tex, 90-92; Individual Artist Grant, Cult Arts Coun Houston & Harris Co, 96; Louis Comfort Tiffany Grant, 97. *Bibliog:* Stephanie Cash (auth), Artworld: Awards, Art Am, 4/98; Jan Estep (auth), Blunt object, New Art Examiner, 12/98-1/99; Alan G Artner (auth), Blunt object works embrace popular culture, Chicago Tribune, 10/2/98. *Mailing Add:* c/o Barry Whistler Gallery 2909B Canton St Dallas TX 75226

DAVENPORT, RAY
PAINTER, PRINTMAKER
b Rockville Centre, NY, May 5, 26. *Study:* Pratt Inst, cert(advert design), 48; Univ SC, Columbia, 80. *Work:* SC Permanent Collection, Columbia; Ronald Reagan Libr; Stone Container Corp, Chicago, Ill; SC Nat Bank, Sumter & Columbia; Chernoff/Silver & Assocs, Columbia, SC. *Comn:* Oil painting, First Fed Savings & Loan, Sumter, SC, 75; oil painting, Black River Elec Coop, 89. *Exhib:* 14th Hunter Ann, Hunter Mus Art, 74; SC Watercolor Soc First Ann, Columbia Mus Art, SC, 78; Am Artists First Nat Art Competition, Circle Galleries, Soho, NY, 78; Allied Artists Am 70th & 72nd Ann, Nat Arts Club, NY, 83 & 85; Capricorn Galleries, Bethesda, Md, 90; JF Kennedy Ctr Performing Arts, Washington, DC, 91; and others. *Teaching:* Central Carolina Technical College, Oil Painting Instr, 66-73. *Awards:* Atto Newer Award, Allied Artists Am 70th Ann, 83 & Gloria Benson Stacks Award, 72nd Ann, 85; Merit Award, Modern Maturity National Seasoned Eye Competition, 90; Best in Show, Milton Baline Award, 41st Mystic Art Festival, 98. *Mem:* Nat Soc Painters Casein & Acrylic; Allied Artists Am; Guild SC Artists (secy & treas, 77-78, pres, 88-89); mem with excellence, SC Watercolor Soc. *Media:* Acrylic, Oil, Lithography. *Dealer:* City Art Gallery Columbia SC; The Spencer Art Galleries, Charleston, SC. *Mailing Add:* 274 Keels Rd Sumter SC 29154

DAVENPORT, REBECCA READ
PAINTER, LECTURER
b Alexandria, Va, June 29, 43. *Study:* Pratt Inst, Brooklyn, NY, BFA(with honors), 66-70; Univ NC, Greensboro, MFA, 70-73. *Work:* Baltimore Mus Art, Md; Corcoran Gallery Art, Washington, DC; Chrysler Mus, Norfolk, Va; Federal Reserve Bank, Richmond, Va. *Exhib:* Selected 20th Century Nudes, Harold Reed Gallery, NY, 78; Mus d'Art Mod de la Villes de Paris, France, 78; Taft Menagerie, Taft Mus, Cincinnati, Ohio, 80; Images of the 70's, Corcoran Gallery Art, Washington, DC, 80; Inside Out, Newport Harbor Art Mus, Newport Beach, Calif, 81; Real, Really Real, Super Real, San Antonio Mus, Tex, 81; Contemp Am Realism Since 60, Pa Acad Fine Art, Philadelphia, Pa, 81. *Awards:* Cert of Distinction, Va Mus, Richmond, 73; Third Gold Palette, IV Festival IX de la Peinture, Cagnes Sur Mir, France, 77; Artist Fel, Nat Endowment Arts, 79. *Bibliog:* Theodore F Wolff (auth), Solving the mystery of the missing subject, Christian Sci Monitor, 10/1/80; Aubyn Kendall (ed), Real, Really Real, Super Real, San Antonio Mus Asn, 81; Frank H Goodyear (auth), Contemporary American Realism Since 1960, New York Graphic Soc, 81. *Media:* Oil. *Dealer:* Osuna Gallery 406 Seventh St NW Washington DC; Aberbach Fine Arts 988 Madison Ave New York NY. *Mailing Add:* 82 Dolphin Point Dr Beaufort SC 29902-1715

DAVES, PHILLIP EDWARD
PAINTER, SCULPTOR
b Elk City, Okla, June 27, 33. *Study:* Okla State Univ, BS, 55; Kansas City Art Inst, 68; Univ Tex, Dallas, BA(cum laude), 78. *Work:* Kans Mus Hist, Topeka; Columbia Green Col, Hudson, NY. *Exhib:* 38th Midyear Show, Butler Inst Am Art, 74; Santa Fe Festival Arts, NMex, 81; West/82 Art & the Law, St Paul, Minn, 82; Allied Artist of Am, NY, 90, 92 & 96. *Awards:* First Place, Franklin Mint Design Competition, 73; Best of Show, Phillips Petroleum Art Ann V, 84; Gold Medal Honor (oil), Allied Artists Am, 90. *Bibliog:* Gregory M Zeigler (auth), Art in Santa Fe, Lakeshore Press, 87. *Media:* Oil. *Dealer:* Cline Fine Arts 526 Canyon Rd Santa Fe NM 87501; El Presido Gallery 7000 E Tanque Verde Tucson AZ 85715

DAVID, CYRIL FRANK
DRAWINGS, PAINTER
b London, Eng, July 13, 20; US citizen. *Work:* Metrop Mus Art, New York, NY; Nat Mus Am Art, Washington, DC; Ark Art Ctr, Little Rock. *Exhib:* Art of Drawing, Staempfli Gallery, NY, 80, 84-89; Members Selections, Corcoran Gallery Art, Washington, DC, 80; one-man shows, Staempfli Gallery, NY, 86, Ark Art Ctr, 84 & 93 & Mus Art, Ft Lauderdale, Fla, 96. *Awards:* Nat Endowment Arts Fel, 80; Best Miniature Work, Guild Hall Mus, 82; Creative Artists Pub Serv Fel, NY State Coun Arts, 83. *Media:* Graphite. *Mailing Add:* PO Box 100 Sag Harbor NY 11963

DAVID, IVO
PAINTER, WRITER
b St Leucio del Sannio, Italy, Nov 22, 34; US citizen. *Study:* Lyceum, cert, 52; Inst Fine Arts, 56; Int Acad Fine Arts Paestrum, Italy, 88; Acad Fine Arts & Lit Micenei, Italy, 89; Peastum Acad Fine Arts; Acad Fine Arts and Liters Micenel; Senator of Acad Fine Arts and Literature of Micenel, IT-. *Work:* Museo Storico Royal Palace, Caserta, Italy; White House; Lupoli Nikko Art Collection Air Force Inc, Roma, Italy; Pa Fed Bank, Newark, NJ. *Comn:* Triborough Bridge, Seton Hall Univ, Ctr Ital Cult, South Orange, NJ, 67; Tompkins Park, H Rohback Art Col Inc, NY, 75; mural, Fed & V Visceglia Corp, Newark, NJ, 75; mural, Union Ctr Realty Corp, NJ, 81; Protest Against the Wars, Union Ctr Realty Corp, NJ, 93; and others. *Exhib:* Centenary Unification Italy, Royal Palace Gallery Mus, Caserta, Italy, 57; solo exhibs, Crcspi Art Gallery, NY, 64, Les Salon des Nations a Paris, 84, Garden State Art Ctr, Holmdel, NJ, 91 & Pen & Brush Art Gallery, NY, 91; State of the Art 1993, New Eng Fine Arts Inst, Boston, 93; Les Malamut Art Gallery, NJ, 93; Fountain Ponte's Reception, NJ, 95; NY Univ, NY, 97; Musee Des Beaux Arts, D'Unet, France, 98; Inst Int D'Arts Plastiques, Boedeaux, France, 98; Biennale Int Arte Contemp, Florence, Italy, 2003, 2005. *Pos:* Planning designer, Candeub, Fleissig & Assocs, Newark, NJ, 63-65; chief art designer, Archit Fed Bus Ctr, Newark, NJ, 65-73; art consult, Williams & London, Newark, NJ, 73-75; art dir, Follia, NY, 86-94 & Ponte Mag, NJ, 92-. *Teaching:* Instr art & design, Gen Serv Admin, Air Force, Caserta, Italy, 58-61; western art, Ctr Ital Cult, Seton Hall Univ, 62-65; painting, Holy Face Monastery Ital Cult, 65-68. *Awards:* Cert Merit Award, New Art Fusionism '56, Biog Inst, Cambridge, Eng; Gold Medal & Award Cert, Acad Miceney, Italy, 92; Gold Plate Award, Acad Int Fine Arts, Micenei, Italy, 97. *Bibliog:* Gizzi, Rossi & Tanelli (auths), the Davids fusionism, NY Mag, 83; Mario Fratti (auth), The manifest of fusionism of David, Follia Mag, 89; R Beltrame (auth), David & Dante, Reportage Art, Italy, 92; Ivo David; An Italian-American Painter in America, La Follia Di NY, 89 Ed. *Mem:* Fed Art Asn NJ; Clifton NJ Art Asn; Academie des Lettre et des Arts du Perigord, Bordeaux, France; Acad Fine Arts & Sci Paestum, Italy; Acad Arts, Letters & Sci, Italy; and others. *Media:* Oil, Mixed Media. *Res:* How men can be free through Art. *Publ:* Auth, Manifest of Fusionism '56, Libr Cong, Washington, DC, 89; Salvador Dali my teacher, Reportage, Italy, 92; Analysis & critique, S Scutella's Orchidea D Ponte, ItAm, USA, 92; The Fusionism of Ivo David A Search for Freedom in Art-Edition of Ponte Italo-Americano, NY

DAVID-WEILL, MICHEL ALEXANDRE & HELENE
COLLECTOR
b France, Nov 23, 32. *Study:* Inst Scis Politiques, 53. *Pos:* Partner, Lazard Freres & Co, 61-65, partner, Lazard Freres & Cie, 65-, sr partner, 75-, Lazard Freres & Co, New York City, 77-95, chmn, Lazard Freres & Co LLC, 95-; vchmn, Groupe Danone, 70; bd dir, Eurazeo, 72-, pres, 2003; trustee, Metrop Mus Art, NY, 85-; bd dir, Publicis Groupe SA, 90; bd gov, Soc NY Hosp, currently. *Awards:* Named one of Top 200 Collectors, ARTnews Mag, 2004. *Mem:* Acad des Beaux-Arts; Academie des Beaux-Arts; Clubs: Brook, New York City, Knickerbocker, New York City. *Collection:* 17th to 19th century French painting; contemporary art. *Mailing Add:* Lazard Freres & Co LLC 30 Rockefeller Plaza 59th fl New York NY 10112

DAVIDEK, STEFAN
PAINTER, PRINTMAKER
b Flint, Mich, May 15, 24. *Study:* Flint Inst Arts, with Jaroslav Brozik; Art Students League, with Morris Kantor; Cranbrook Acad, with Fred Mitchell. *Work:* Detroit Inst Arts, Mich; Flint Inst Arts, Mich; Muskegon Community Col & Hackley Art Mus, Mich; Albion Col; McClaren Hosp, Flint, Mich; Women's League, Univ Mich; Prince Corp, Holland, Mich; Genesee Co Courthouse Murals, Flint, Mich. *Comn:* interior murals, Zehnders, Frankenmuth, Mich, 80 & 81; chapel wall, MaClaren Hosp, Flint, Mich; ceiling decoration, St Paul, Flint, Mich; Chancel mural, St Lorenz, Frankenmuth, Mich; ceiling decoration, Sunset Mem Chapel, Flint, Mich; mosaics, St Luke's, Flint, Mich; St Roberts, Flushing, Mich; Carol Church II; Pierson Childrens Mus, Sloan Mus, Flint, Mich; Genesse County Courthouse; any many others. *Exhib:* Flint Ann, 46-90; Butler Midyear Show, 59; Pa Acad Fine Art 9; Buckham Art Space, Flint, Mich; Alma Col Print Ann, 89-94; Mich Directions, Flint Area Artists; Flint Inst of Arts. *Pos:* Artist, Printmaker, Decorative Consultant. *Teaching:* Instr Arts, Haystack Mtn Crafts, Summer Art Programs. *Awards:* Founder's Prize, 61 & Lou R Maxon Prize, Detroit Inst Art; Purchase Award, Alma Print Show, Mich, 91; Purchase Award, Alma Print Show, 93-95; Purchase Award, Flint Inst Arts. *Media:* Oil, Watercolor, Serigraphy, Silkscreen. *Specialty:* DeGraff Fine Art, Saugatuck, MI. *Dealer:* DeGraff Fine Art Inc 403 Water St & Main PO Box 1025 Saugatuck Mich 49453. *Mailing Add:* 5391 W Coldwater Rd Flint MI 48504-1025

DAVIDOVICH, JAIME
PAINTER, VIDEO ARTIST
b Buenos Aires, Arg, Sept 27, 36; US citizen. *Study:* Nat Col, Buenos Aires, Arg, 54-58; Univ Uruguay, 59-61; Sch Visual Arts, New York, 63. *Work:* Mus Mod Art, Buenos Aires, Arg; Mus Belas Artes, Rio de Janiero, Brazil; Dayton Art Inst, Ohio; Everson Mus Art, Syracuse, NY; Akron Art Inst, Akron, Ohio. *Comn:* Carroll Wall Proj, John Carroll Univ, Cleveland, Ohio, 71. *Exhib:* One-man show, Retrospective 1962-1972, Drake Univ, Des Moines, Iowa, 71, Am Mus of Moving Image, 90, Mus Modern Art, Buenos Aires, 99, Lehman Col, NY, 2000; Exp in Art & Technol Show, Lake Erie Col, Ohio, 71; Five Artists, New Gallery, Cleveland, Ohio, 72; Arte de Sistemas, Mus Mod Art, Buenos Aires & Mus Fine Arts, Santiago, Chile, 72; Akron Art Inst, Ohio, 72-73; Whitney Mus Am Art, NY, 76; Long Beach Mus Art, Los Angeles, 81; Ctr Media Arts, Paris, France, 82; Video & Television Festival, Maastrich, The Neth, 82; TV on TV, Tex Tech Univ, 84; Exit Art, NY, 86; Lecagy/Legado, The Old State House, Hartford, Conn; Zocalo 1975-98, Mus of Modern Art, Buenos Aires, 98; Painting in Real Time, Lehman Col Art Gallery, NY, 99; The End: An 18 yr History of Exit Art, Exit Art, NY, 00. *Pos:* Rep to US, DiTella Found Art Ctr, Buenos Aires, Arg, 65; founder & mem bd dir, New Orgn Visual Arts, Cleveland, Ohio, 72-73; pres, Artists Television Network, 77-83; bd dir, Artists Television Proj, Univ Iowa, 87; res fel, Sch Art & Art Hist, Univ Iowa, 87. *Teaching:* Prof painting, Sch Visual Arts, Bahia Blanca, Arg, 61-62. *Awards:* Grand Prize, Adhesive Tape Proj, Dayton Art Inst, Dayton, Ohio, 74; Creative Artists Pub Serv Prog grants, NY State Coun Arts, 75 & 82; Visual Arts Fels, Nat Endowment Arts, 78, 84 & 90; Video 81, San Francisco Video Festival, 81; Artist-in-Residence, World Trade Ctr, NY, 2001; Grantee, NEA Visual Art Fel, 84, 90. *Bibliog:* Ellen Stern (auth), The inner tube, New York Mag, 4/17/78; TV finds its place among fine art, Plain Dealer, 5/29/80; Video artists still seek a showplace for their work, New York Times, 6-19-83; 16 Autumn, Real Life Mag, 86; and others. *Mailing Add:* 67 E 11st Apt 219 New York NY 10003

DAVIDOW, JOAN CARLIN
DIRECTOR, CURATOR
b New York, NY, July 27, 40. *Study:* Jacksonville Univ, BA, 62; Univ Fla, MFA, 81. *Exhib:* Dallas Mus Art, 89; Tex Meets New York - Facing the Millennium, The Song Remains the Same, 96; Moving Pictures, 2005. *Collection Arranged:* Spanish Remnants: Border Real & Imagined, 92; Digital Dramas: Computer-Generated Photography & Video, 95; Texas Meets New York: Facing the Millenium, The Song Remains the Same, 96; Space: Architecture + Installation, 97; A Cool Show: abstract paintings, 98. *Pos:* Art critic, KERA Pub Radio N Tex, 84-91; actg asst cur contemp art, Dallas Mus Art, 89-91; dir, Arlington Mus Art, 91-2000, Dallas Ctr for Contemporary Art, 2001-; juror, Mitchell A Wilder Pub Design Awards Competition, Tex Asn Mus, 89, 97, 42d Ann Invitiational, 2002, Longview Mus Fine Arts, Tex, 2002, Mayfaire-by-the-Lake, Polk Mus Art, Lakeland, Fla, 2004; panel, Art & Design Program, DART, Victory Light Rail Sta, Design Site-Specific Com, 2000, Artist Selection, Waterworks, Dallas Cultural Affairs, Pub Works, Dallas, 2004. *Awards:* KATIE Award finalist, Best Specialty Reporting, Dallas Press Club, 85; Review Panelist, Tex Comn Arts, 92-93. *Bibliog:* Sheila Taylor Wells (auth), Joan of art, Ft Worth Star-Telegram, 96; Catherine Cuellar (auth), High profile, Dallas Morning News, 98; Michael Ennis (auth), Joan of art, Tex Monthly, 98; Michael Ennis (auth), National Spotlight: Unlikely Upstart, Art News, 2000; Steve Carter (auth), The Radar Art, Dallas Modern Luxury, 2006. *Mem:* Tex Fine Arts Asn (bd mem, 87-97); Dallas Artists Res & Exhib (found bd, 89-91); Emergency Artists Survival League (found bd, 92-96); Art Table. *Res:* Texas contemporary art. *Publ:* Auth, Texas Figurative Drawings (exhib catalog), 89, Celia Alvarez Munoz: Abriendo Tierra Breaking Ground (exhib catalog), 90 & Harry Geffert: Bronze Allegories (exhib catalog), 90, Dallas Mus Art; Texas Realism, with a Twist: Paintings & Drawings (exhib catalog), 95 & Women's Work: Themes Associated with the Women's Realm (exhib catalog), 97, Arlington Mus Art. *Mailing Add:* Dallas Contemporary 2801 Swiss Ave Dallas TX 75204

DAVIDSON, ABRAHAM A
ART HISTORIAN, PHOTOGRAPHER
b Dorchester, Mass, June 27, 1935. *Study:* Harvard Univ, AB(cum laude), 57; Hebrew Teachers Col, Boston, BJed, 60; Boston Univ, MA(art hist), 60; Columbia Univ, PhD(art hist), 65. *Work:* Cigna Corp; Bank Leumi; Pub Libr Newark, NJ; Villanova Univ; Lehigh Univ; Sheldon Mem Art Gallery, Univ Nebr; Phila Free Libr, Philadelphia, PA. *Exhib:* One-man shows, Paley Libr, Temple Univ, 72 & 81, Painted Bride Art Gallery, Philadelphia, 74, Burlington Co Community, Gloucester Co Col, NJ, 79 & 93 & Villanova Univ, 82, Cafe Gallery, 1521, Philadelphia, 97. *Teaching:* Vis lectr, Univ Iowa, 63; instr art hist, Wayne State Univ, 64-65; asst prof, Oakland Univ, 65-68; from asst prof to prof art history, Tyler Sch Art, Temple Univ, 68-; Prof Art Hist, Temple Univ. *Awards:* Group 17 Prize for Photog, Detroit Inst Arts, 69; Travel Grant, Nat Endowment Humanities, 85. *Bibliog:* Burt Wasserman (auth), People and places come to life in collection of photographs, NJ Courier Post, 11/10/79; Burt Wasserman (auth), Abraham Davidson, New Art Examiner, 4/83; Victoria Donohoe (auth), A photographer takes a scholarly approach, Philadelphia Inquirer, 2/27/87; Helene Ryesky (auth), A Traveler's Eye, Art Matters, 12/2000. *Mem:* Col Art Asn. *Res:* History of 19th and 20th century American painting and sculpture. *Publ:* Auth, The Eccentrics & Other American Visionary Painters, Dutton, 78; Early American Modernist Painting 1910-1935, Harper & Row, 81, rev ed 86; Ben Solowey, A Monograph (monogr), Optique Gallery Press, 88; The armory show and early modernism in America, Am Art in 20th Century, Painting & Sculpture, 1913-1993, 93; Ralph Albert Blakelock, Penn State Press, 96; The Paintings of EM Saniga, Rutledge Press, 2001. *Mailing Add:* 1810 Rittenhouse Sq Apt 701 Philadelphia PA 19103

DAVIDSON, DAVID ISAAC
PAINTER
b Chicago, Ill, Nov, 22, 25. *Study:* Sch Art Inst Chicago, BAE, 48; Ind State, MS, 49; Am Army Univ, Bamburg, Germany, 45-46. *Work:* Ill State Mus, Springfield; Ellis Island, US Justice Dept Immigration, NY; Cole Taylor Bank, Chicago; State of Ill Gallery, Chicago. *Comn:* Portrait Mayor Richard J Daley, Daley Col, Chicago, Ill, 77; State Capitol Mural Finalist, State Ill, Springfield, 89. *Exhib:* 54th Ann Chicago Show, Art Inst Chicago, Ill, 50; Artists for Peace, Peace Mus, Chicago, Ill, 83; Ill State Capital Murals, Ill State Mus, Springfield, Ill, 89; One man show, Renner Gallery Blackburn Univ, Carlinsville, Ill, 90, Artemnisia Gallery, Chicago, Ill, 84, Dog House, Joy Horwitz Gallery, Chicago, Ill, 90; Images Am Immigration, Nationwide Touring Exhib, NY, Los Angeles, 91-93; Art & Law, Nationwide Touring Exhib, Chicago, Reno, Pittsburg, 95-96; retrospective, Harper Col, 2006. *Teaching:* Instr adv, painting & drawing, Chicago Pub Sch, Chicago, Ill, 50-85; lectr, portrait artist, Chicago Conv & Tourism Bur, Chicago, Ill, 77-83; instr, portrait, life drawing, Evanston Art Ctr, Evanston, Ill, 87-89; guest lectr, Harper Col, 2006. *Awards:* Ill Art Fel, Fel Competition, State Ill, 85; State Capitol Mural Finalist, Murals, Ill State Mus, 89; Purchase Prize, Images of Am Immigration, Dept Justice, 91. *Bibliog:* Harold Haydon (auth), Artist for Peace, Chicago Sun Times, 5/13/83; Michael Bopesteel (auth), David Davidson Exhib, Evanston Review Peioneer Press, 10/3/85; Lee Krantz (ed), Chicago Art Review, Am References Inc, 89, 90, 91. *Mem:* Sch of Art Inst Chicago Alumni Asn. *Media:* Oil painting, Acrylic, Instructor, Educator. *Dealer:* PLG Fine Art 5640 Taylor Rd Naples FL 34109. *Mailing Add:* 1 The Court of Harborside Apt Northbrook IL 60062

DAVIDSON, HERBERT LAURENCE
PAINTER, PRINTMAKER
b Green Bay, Wis, Sept 6, 30. *Study:* Art Inst Chicago, Anna Raymond Foreign Traveling Fel, 56. *Work:* Kemper Ins Co; Playboy Mag; Pullman Bank of Chicago; Rahr West Mus, Manitowoc, Wis; Walter Heller Corp, Chicago; Signode Corp, Glenview, Ill. *Exhib:* Butler Inst Am Art, Youngstown, Ohio, 65; Alta Col of Art, Calgary, 76; Mendel Art Gallery, Saskatchewan, Can, 77; Chicago Cult Ctr, 79; Syracuse Univ, Lubin Hall, 80; Sao Paolo Mus, Brazil; and others. *Bibliog:* Article, Am Artist Mag, 7/80. *Mem:* The Arts Club Chicago. *Media:* Oil; Lithography. *Dealer:* Wadle Galleries 128 W Palace Santa Fe NM. *Mailing Add:* 413 E Illinois Ave Morris IL 60450-2219

DAVIDSON, IAN J
COLLECTOR, PATRON
b Toronto, Ont, July 21, 25. *Study:* Univ BC, BA;. *Pos:* Dir, Vancouver Art Gallery, 70-74; mem adv art comt, Can Coun, 75-; dir, Community Arts Coun, Vancouver. *Teaching:* Archit at Univ Toronto, Univ BC, Carleton Univ & Bezalel Acad, Jerusalem, Israel. *Awards:* Awards in archit in every major design award prog. *Mem:* Asn Royal Can Acad Art; fel Royal Archit Inst Can. *Interests:* Commissioning original works by major artists in the non-objective and conceptual fields. *Mailing Add:* 405-1600 Howe St Vancouver BC V6Z 2L9 Canada

DAVIDSON, JEAN
PAINTER
b New York, NY. *Study:* Study with Moses Sawyer, 53; New Sch Social Res, with Peggy Bacon, 54; also with DeHirsh Margules, 54-59. *Work:* Corcoran Gallery, Washington; Greenville Co Mus Art, SC; Elvehjem Mus Art, Madison, Wis; Metrop Mus Art, NY; Indianapolis Mus Art, Ind, 95. *Exhib:* Artists by Artists, Capricorn

Gallery, NY, 67; NY Studio Sch Drawing Benefit, 72; 300 Artists to the Support of the NY Studio Sch, Xavier Fourcade Gallery, NY, 76; Unknown Universes, Pace Univ, NY, 79; Chelsea Artweek 1980, Cult Found, NY, 80; Albright-Knox Members Gallery, Buffalo, NY, 81; Gathering of the Avant Garde 1948-1970, Kenkeleba Gallery, NY, 85; Robert Ferst Ctr Arts, Westbrook Gallery, Ga Tech Univ, Atlanta, Ga, 97. *Awards:* Esther & Adolph Gottlieb Found Grant, 80; Archives Am Art, 96. *Bibliog:* Gordon Brown (auth), revs, Arts Mag, 76; Will Grant (auth), The past is always present, Artspeak, 84; Lawrence Campbell, Special Feature: Painting of Kaldis by Je. *Media:* Oil

DAVIDSON, MAXWELL, III
DEALER
b New York, NY, Feb 8, 39. *Study:* Williams Col, BA(art hist), 61. *Pos:* Owner, Maxwell Davidson Gallery, 76-. *Mem:* Art Dealers Asn Am. *Specialty:* 19th & 20th century masters and contemporary painters. *Mailing Add:* Maxwell Davidson Gallery 724 Fifth Ave 4th Fl New York NY 10019

DAVIDSON, NANCY
SCULPTOR, PHOTOGRAPHER
b Chicago, Ill. *Study:* Univ Ill, Chicago Circle, BA, 72; Art Inst Chicago, MFA, 75. *Comn:* Wall installations, City Chicago, 80, AT&T, 81 & IBM, 85. *Exhib:* Abstract Art in Chicago, Mus Contemp Art, Chicago, 76; Ten Painters, Walker Art Ctr, 77; 100 Yrs 100 Artists, Art Inst Chicago, 79; New Dimensions Surface, Mus Contemp Art, Chicago, 79; Works on Paper, Albright-Knox Gallery, 80; Berkshire Mus, Mass, 83; Empty Dress, Neuberger Mus, 93; Bad Girls, Univ Calif, Los Angeles, 94; Nova Sin Gallery, 98; Dorsky Gallery, 98. *Teaching:* Asst prof, Univ Ill, Champaign, 77-79, Williams Col, Mass, 80-84 & State Univ NY, Purchase, 84-. *Awards:* Fel, Nat Endowment Arts, 78, Yaddo Found, 80 & Mass Coun Arts, 81 & 84; Pres Award State Univ Purchase, 94; Anonymous Was a Woman Found Award, 97; Pollock-Krasnergrantee, 2001; Creative Capital Award, 2005. *Mem:* Col Art Asn. *Publ:* Ed, NAME Book I: Artists Statements on Art, Name Gallery, 77; Clothing as Subject, Artjournal, 95; Carnivaleyes, Nova Sin Gallery, 98. *Dealer:* Shoshana Wayne Gallery Santa Monica CA; Miller Gallery, New York City, NY. *Mailing Add:* 137 Duane St NW New York NY 10013

DAVIES, HARRY CLAYTON
PAINTER, PHOTOGRAPHER
b Wilmington, Del, Mar 3, 40. *Study:* Columbia Univ, BS, 66, MA, 69; Adelphi Univ, MA, 80. *Work:* Adelphi Univ, Garden City, NY; Wash Co Mus Fine Art, Hagerstown, Md; Fine Arts Mus Long Island, NY; Sci Mus of Long Island; Islip Art Mus, NY. *Exhib:* Fine Arts Mus Long Island, Hempstead, 81; 2nd Invitational Show, Long Island Univ, Greenvale, 82; Eight by Ten, Wash Co Mus Fine Arts, Hagerstown, Md, 86; Heckscher Mus, Huntington, NY, 90, Manhattan Ctr Gallery, NY 96; Giordano Gallery, Dowling Col, Oakdale, NY, 97; Islip Art Mus, East Islip, NY, 99; Adelphi Univ, Garden City, NY, 2004; Boothbay Region Art Found, 2006. *Teaching:* Prof painting, drawing, & theory, chmn dept art, Adelphi Univ, 81-2004, prof emer, 2004. *Bibliog:* Long Island Looks Ahead (interview), WSNL Channel 67, Smithtown, NY, 6/82. *Mem:* William Morris Soc, London, UK; Charles Rennie Mackintosh Soc, Glasgon, Scotland; Boothbay Region Art Found, Boothbay, Maine. *Media:* Photog. *Res:* Megalithic monuments of Britain & Ireland. *Specialty:* Painting, Photog. *Mailing Add:* PO Box 355 Boothbay ME 04537

DAVIES, HAYDN LLEWELLYN
SCULPTOR, PAINTER
b Rhymney, Wales, Nov 11, 21; Can citizen. *Study:* Ont Col Art, AOCA, 47; Univ Western Ont, 65; Univ Toronto, 74. *Work:* Mus d'Arte Mod, Venice, Italy; Ctr Arts, Vero Beach, Fla; Galleria Nazionale d'Arte Mod e Contemporanea, Rome, Italy; Mus Royaux des Beaux-Arts de Belgique Art Mod, Brussels, Belg; Nat Mus Wales, Cardiff; Victoria & Albert Mus, London, Eng; Art Mus SE Tex, Beaumont; Gov Ontario, Toronto; Art Mus of Boca Raton, Fla. *Comn:* Homage (laminated cedar), Lambton Col Arts & Technol, Sarnia, Ont, 74; Space Composition for Rebecca (fabricated aluminum), Burlington Art Ctr, Ont, 78; Space Composition Red (fabricated aluminum), Govt Ont, Windsor, 78; Space Composition (fabricated aluminum), Trinity Sq, Bell Can, 84; Composition with Five Elements (fabricated welded steel), Gulf Can Ltd, Toronto, 80; Honda of Canada Mfg Inc, Alliston, Ont, 86 & 87. *Exhib:* Contemp Sculpture at the Guild, Can Acad Arts, 80; Bridges Exhib, Pratt Inst, NY, 83; Ontario Art on View, Ont House, Paris, 82/84; Community Sculpture'85, 9 sculpture exhib, Cambridge, Ont, 85; Royal Can Acad Arts, Toronto, 87; solo exhibs, Planar Constructions, 87-89: Burlington Cult Ctr, Ont, 89, Stratford Art Gallery, Ont, 89, Ctr for Arts, Vero Beach, Fla, 90, Anita Shapolsky Gallery, NY, 91; Art Mus SE Texas, Beaumont, 92 & Asheville Art Mus, NC, 93; and others. *Teaching:* Artist-in-residence, Indian River Community Col, 82-83 & Ctr Arts, Vero Beach, Fla, 86; guest lectr, Sculpture Univ Toronto, 74 & Lambton Col Art & Technol, 75. *Awards:* Sculptor's Soc Can Award, On View, 76; Grants, Can Arts Coun, 78 & 80, Ont Arts Coun, 80, 81, 82 & 89 & Can Dept of External Affairs, 90. *Bibliog:* Nick Roukes (auth), Masters of Wood Sculpture, Watson-Guptill Publs, New York, 80; Jeanne Parkin (auth), Art in Architecture, Visual Arts, Ont, 82; Fern Bayer (auth), The Ontario Collection, Fitzhenry & Whiteside, Toronto, 84; Arthur Williams (auth), Sculpture/Technique, Form, Content, Davis Publications, Worcester, Mass, 89; Bryce Kanbara (auth), Haydn Llewellyn Davies, Planar Constructions (exhib catlogue), 91. *Mem:* Royal Can Acad Arts. *Media:* Wood, Steel. *Dealer:* Anita Shapolsky 99 Spring St New York NY 10012. *Mailing Add:* 10 Rose Park Crescent Toronto ON M4T 1P9 Canada

DAVIES, HUGH MARLAIS
HISTORIAN, MUSEUM DIRECTOR
b Grahamstown, S Africa, Feb 12, 48; Brit citizen. *Study:* Princeton Univ, AB, 70, MFA, 72, PhD, 76. *Collection Arranged:* Artist & Fabricator (auth, catalog), 75, Richard Fleischner (auth, catalog), 77, Stephen Antonakos (auth, catalog), 78, Sam Gilliam (auth, catalog), 78, Al Souza (auth, catalog), 79, John Walker (auth, catalog), 79, George Trakas (auth, catalog), 80, Prints of Barnett Newman (auth, catalog), 83, Martin Puryear (coauth, catalog), 84; at Univ Gallery, Univ Mass, Amherst; Sitings: Alice Aycock, Richard Fleischner, Mary Miss & George Trakas (auth, catalog), La Jolla Mus Contemp Art, 86; Richard Long (auth, catalog), La Jolla Mus Contemp Art, 89. *Pos:* Asst dir, Monumenta Int Sculpture Exhib, Newport, RI, 74; dir, Univ Gallery, Univ Mass, Amherst, 75-83, Mus Contemp Art San Diego, 83-; panel mem fed adv comt int exhibs, 90-94; co-cur Whitney Mus Am Art Biennial, 00. *Teaching:* Vis asst prof, Amherst Col, Mass, 80-83. *Awards:* Nat Endowment Arts Fel, 81-82 & 95. *Mem:* Asn Art Mus Dirs (bd trustees 94-01, pres 97-98); Col Art Asn; Art Mus Asn Am; Friends Art & Preservation in Embassies (profl adv com 98-). *Res:* 20th century American and European painting, sculpture, photography, design and architecture. *Publ:* Coauth (with Horton Davies), Sacred Art in a Secular Century, Liturgical Press; The Prints of Barnett Newman, Barnett Newman Found, 83; coauth, Francis Bacon, Abbeville, 86; auth, 25 Years of Installation Art, Mus Contemp Art, San Diego, winter 97; Francis Bacon the Papal Portraits of 1953, 01; and others. *Mailing Add:* c/o Mus Contemp Art San Diego 700 Prospect St La Jolla CA 92037-4228

DAVIES, KENNETH SOUTHWORTH
PAINTER, INSTRUCTOR
b New Bedford, Mass, Dec 20, 25. *Study:* Mass Sch Art, Boston; Yale Sch Fine Arts, BFA, 50. *Hon Degrees:* New Eng Sch Law, Boston, DFA. *Work:* Wadsworth Atheneum, Hartford, Conn; New Britain Mus Am Art, Conn; Detroit Inst Arts; Springfield Mus Fine Arts, Mass; Univ Nebr, Lincoln. *Comn:* US Postage Stamp commemorative for pharmacy, US Postal Serv, 72, chemistry, 76; Metrop Opera, 83. *Exhib:* Am Symbolic Realism, London, Eng, 50; Carnegie Inst Int, 52; Whitney Mus Am Art Ann, 52; Univ Ill Ann, 52; 25 yr retrospective exhib, New Britain Mus Am Art, 71; Retrospective at 80, Washington Co Mus Fine Arts, 2005-2006; New Bedford Whaling Mus, 2006. *Teaching:* Sr Portfolio, Paier Col Art, Hamden, Conn, 53-81, vis prof & dean emer, 81-91. *Awards:* Louis Comfort Tiffany scholar, 50; Purchase Award, Berkshire Mus, Pittsfield & Springfield Mus, Mass, 50; Hon DFA. *Mem:* Conn Acad Fine Arts (coun mem, 70, pres, 74-76). *Media:* Oil. *Specialty:* Realistic Painting & Sculpture. *Publ:* Auth, Painting Sharp Focus Still Lifes, 75 & Ken Davies-Artist at Work, 78, Watson-Guptill. *Dealer:* Cavalier Galleries, Greenwich, Conn. *Mailing Add:* PO Box 526 Madison CT 06443

DAVILA, MARITZA
PRINTMAKER
b Santurce, PR, Apr 18, 52. *Study:* Univ PR, BA, 74; Pratt Graphics Ctr, with Andrew Stasick & Margot Lovejoy, 74, Pratt Inst, MFA, 77. *Work:* Nat Library of Paris, France; Mus of the Univ of Puerto Rico; Maine Printmaking Workshop at Vinalhaven, Maine; Ateneo Puertorriqueno, San Juan; Taller Galeria Fort, Cadaques, Spain; Univ of Cincinnati, Mid-America Print Council; Southern Graphics Council Archives, Univ of Miss; Mus of Art, Warsaw, Poland; Museo del Barrio, New York City, NY; Southern Graphics Council, Archives, Univ of Miss; Nat Library of Congress, Washington, DC. *Comn:* Reimpression of Thomas Hogarth plate, comn by AG Burkhart, Memphis, 85, 88 & 92; Book Art, comn by Mr & Mrs Reissman. *Exhib:* Solo: Art Ctr, Ark State Univ, 2000; Taproots Sch of the Arts, St Louis, Mo, 2001; Two Artists: Joysmith Gallery, Memphis, Tenn, 2003; Montreal Int Miniature Print Biennial, Can, 2002; Side by Side, Memphis Brooks Mus of Art, 2002; Mid Am Print Council, Juried Mem Exhib, Denver Int'l Airport, 2002; First Contact Invitational Nontoxic Exhib, Gracefield Art Ctr, Dumfries, Scotland, 2002; Solar Plate Revolution Portfolio, Southern Graphics Council, Gallery at First and Second Church Unitarian Universalist, Boston; Whitney Art Works, Greenport, NY, and others, locations, 2003; Delta Nat Small Prints Exhib, Bradbury Gallery, Ark State Univ, Jonesboro, Ark, 2003; Memphis Col of Arts Faculty Exhib, Memphis Tenn; SC Stare Mus, Thresholds, Expressions of Art and Spiritual Life, Columbia, SC, 2003-2004. *Pos:* Dir, Atabeira Press; mgr, Printmaking Workshop. *Teaching:* Instr art, Am Mus Natural Hist, NY, 79-81; artist-in-residence, Bd Educ, NY, 80; Prof of fine Arts, Memphis Col of Art, Tenn, 1982-; 2002-2003 bd mem, Latino Memphis, Inc. *Awards:* Purchase Award, Moravian Col, Bethlehem, Pa, 84; Award Printmaking, Ateneo Puertorriqueno, 85; Printmaking Medal Hon, Nat Asn Women Artists, 87; Prix de Dessin et Gravure Salon Int du Val d' Or a la Salle des Fetes d'Orval, France Asn Plastica Latina, 1996; Juror's Special Mention Pressed and Pulled VI Georgia Col & State Univ, Milledgeville, 1997; Faculty Enrichment Award, Memphis Col of Art, 1996, 1998, 2000, 2003-2004. *Bibliog:* Reuben Abruna (dir), Myths and Creations (film), New York Univ, 80; Davila to Conduct Workshop, Art Show at DSU Art Center, Bolival Commercial, Miss, 11/91; Fredric Koeppel Rev, Miss Coun Arts Fac Show, Commercial Appeal, 91. *Mem:* Los Angeles Printmaking Soc; Southern Graphic Coun; Mid Am Print Coun, 1998-; Memphis Childrens Adv Ctr, Visual Arts, comt for the Heart Auction. *Media:* Print Making. *Interests:* Music & Literature. *Publ:* Mario Alegre Barrios (auth), Etreel mito y la memoria, Por Dentro, SJPR El Nuevo Dia, 96; Art & Letters: Jour of Contem Culture, Maritza Davila, Featured Artist, Georgia Col & State Univ, Milledgeville, Georgia, Issue One Spring 1999, p 80 (cover art and eight works in color); Henkes, Robert, Latin Am Women Artists of the United State: The Works of 33 Twentieth-Century Women, 12/1998 McFarland & Co Inc, Publ. *Dealer:* Albers Fine Arts Gallery 1027 Yates Rd Suite 101 Memphis TN 38119; Galeria Botello Hato Rey Puerto Rico. *Mailing Add:* 3233 N Waynoka Circle Memphis TN 38111-3610

DAVIS, BEN H
PHOTOGRAPHER, PAINTER
b Syracuse, NY, June 5, 47. *Study:* Stetson Univ, Fla, ABA; Univ Fla, BS(commun); Fla State Univ, MFA. *Work:* Ctr Creative Photog, Univ Ariz, Tucson; Mus Mod Art, NY; Ctr Advan Visual Studies, Mass Inst Technol, Cambridge; Lomholt Formular Archive, Falling, Denmark; Int Mus Photog, George Eastman House, Rochester, NY. *Exhib:* Mass Inst Technol, 81; Other Cinema, Syracuse Univ, 84; Ars Electronica, Stadt Mus, Linz, Austria, 86; Biennale Venice Int Art Exhib, 86; Boston Computer Mus, 87; Fla State Univ, 94; Hemphill Fine Arts, 2000; and others. *Pos:* Illusr, Fla State Archives & Mus, 74-75; dir, Senoj, Inc, Atlanta, Ga, 76-; dir, Visual Computing, MIT, 86-91; res assoc, Mass Inst Technol Ctr Educ Computing, 91-95; prog mgr commun, Getty Info Inst, 96-2000, RazorFish, Inc, 2000. *Teaching:* Instr video & drawing, Atlanta Col Art, 75-86, chmn, Dept Electronic Imagery, 76-86; Mass Inst Technol, 83-84; Mass Inst Techol Visual Arts Prog, 86-90. *Awards:* Fel, Nat Endowment Arts, Alternative Spaces, 77-78; Fel, Ctr Advan Visual Studies, 83-84. *Bibliog:* Infra-thin multimedia, Visual Resources Mag, 6/91; Digital Museums, Aperture Mag, summer, 94; The culture machine, Sci Am, 8/96. *Mem:* IMAGE Film & Video, Atlanta, Ga; Int Interactive Communications Soc, Atlanta, Ga. *Media:* Photo Electronic Media, Paint. *Publ:* Auth, Role of the artist, Community TV Rev, 4/81; Sky Disc: Implications, Ctr Adv Visual Studies, Mass Inst Technol, 84; The age of computer art, Atlanta Art Papers, 1-2/86

DAVIS, BRAD (BRADLEY) DARIUS
PAINTER
b Duluth, Minn, Apr 24, 42. *Study:* St Olaf Col, 61; Univ Chicago, 62; Art Inst Chicago, 63; Univ Minn, BA, 66; Hunter Col, 70. *Work:* Neue Galerie, Sammlung Ludwig, Aachen, WGer; Walker Art Ctr, Minneapolis; Whitney Mus Am Art, Mus Mod Art, NY; Saarland Mus, Saarbracken, WGer; and others. *Exhib:* Biennial, 64 & two-person show, 66, Walker Art Ctr, Minneapolis; Ann Exhib, 72 & Am Drawings '63-'73, 73, Whitney Mus Am Art; solo exhibs, Holly Solomon Gallery, NY, 75, 79, 81 & 83; The New Bestiary: Animal Imagery in Contemp Art, Inst Contemp Art, Va Mus, Richmond, 81; Friends of Corcoran Gallery 20th Anniversary Exhib, Corcoran Gallery Art, 81; New Work in Black and White, 81 & A Penthouse Aviary, 81, Art Lending Serv, Mus Mod Art, NY; Decoration and Representation, Alta Col Art Gallery, Can, 82; New Decorative Works from the Collection of Norma & William Roth, Loch Haven Art Ctr, Orlando & Jacksonville Art Mus, Fla, 83; New Decorative Art, Berkshire Mus, Pittsfield, Mass, 83; Back to the USA Traveling Exhib, Kunstmus, Lucerne, Switz, Rheinische Landesmus, Bonn & Kunstverein, Stuttgart, Ger, 83-84; and many others; Landscape/Cityscape, Art Gallery, State Univ NY Potsdam, 78; Pattern & Decoration, Sewall Art Gallery, Rice Univ, 78; Green Magic, Rutgers Univ Gallery, 79; Dekor, Kunstverein, Mannheim, Ger, 80; Am Drawings, Venice Biennale, Italy, 80; and many others. *Awards:* First Prize & Spec Jury Award, Minneapolis Inst Art Biennial, 65; Second Prize & Purchase Prize, Walker Art Ctr, 66. *Bibliog:* Alexandra Anderson (auth), Clay gardens, Portfolio, 3-4/82; Klaus Ahrens (auth), Schreie und Flustern, Stern Mag, Hamburg, Ger, 5/83; Klaus Honnef, New York Aktuelle, Kunstforum Int, 5/83. *Media:* Mixed

DAVIS, CHARLES BURDIS, III
ART DEALER, COLLECTOR
b Raleigh, NC, Apr 4, 45. *Study:* Univ NC, BA, 70. *Exhib:* African Art from New Orleans Collections, 89; Wild Spirits, Strong Medicine, 89; Voruba, Nine Centuries of African Art and Thought, 90; Icons, Ideals and Power in the Art of Africa, 90. *Pos:* Prin, Davis Gallery, New Orleans, currently; vis arts comt, Loyola Univ, 89-. *Awards:* Beaux Arts Award, Contemp Arts Ctr, 88. *Mem:* New Orleans Contemp Arts Ctr (adv bd, 84, 85, 86 & 90); Wyes Art Auction, New Orleans (adv bd, 83-86). *Specialty:* African art. *Collection:* African and contemporary art and photography. *Publ:* Auth, The Animal Motif in Bamana Art, Davis Gallery, 81

DAVIS, CHRISTINE
PHOTOGRAPHER
b Vancouver, BC, 62. *Study:* York Univ, Toronto, BFA, 84. *Work:* Bibliot Nat Paris; Bruce Peel Spec Collection, Edmonton, AB; Can Mus Contemp Photog, Ottawa; Mus Beaux-Arts, Montreal; Nat Libr Can, Ottawa. *Comn:* Women's Law Asn Ont, Law Soc Upper Can, Osgoode Hall, Toronto, 2000. *Exhib:* Collectif Generation, Livres d'Artistes, Victoria & Albert Mus, 90; The Body-Le Corps (exhib catalog), Kunsthalle Bielefeld, Ger, 94; Fixing the Gaze (exhib catalog), Olga Korper Gallery, Toronto, 94, Contours, 97, New Photog, 2002; Press/Enter (exhib catalog), The Power Plant, Toronto, 95; Perspective '95 (exhib catalog), Art Gallery Ont, Toronto, 95; Rekalde Sala Expos, Bilbao, Spain, 96; solo exhibs, Macdonald Stewart Art Ctr (exhib catalog), Guelph, Ont, 93, Olga Korper Gallery, Toronto, 95, 98, 2000, Galeria Palma Dotze, Viafranca, Spain, 96 & Galeria Helga de Alvear, Madrid, 96, 99, Power Plant, Toronto, 2000, Mus des Beaux-Arts de Montreal, 2003. *Pos:* Ed collective mem, Border/lines, 84-88. *Bibliog:* News (auth), The Sibylline eye: North American women photographers, Flash Art, 1-2/91; Chantal Pontbriand (auth), De la violence et du language, Parachute, No 71, 93; Deirdre Hanna, Poetic perspective opens AGO doors to new talent, NOW, Toronto, 11/30/95. *Mem:* Founding mem, Pub Access Collective (ed, 86-); YYZ Artist's Outlet (bd dir, 89-). *Publ:* Coauth (with Nicole Brossard), Typhon Dru, Collectif Generation, Paris, 90; auth, Hyperbole, Texts, No 6, fall 91; Artists' Project, C Mag, No 33, spring 92; Work in progress, Nuevas Visiones/Nuevas Pasiones, Santander, 1999; 20thc Lexicon, ed Christine Davis & Ken Allen, PUBLIC, 19/20, 2000. *Mailing Add:* c/o Olga Korper 17 Morrow Ave Toronto ON M6R 2H9 Canada

DAVIS, D JACK
EDUCATOR, ADMINISTRATOR
b Canton, Tex, May 17, 38. *Study:* Baylor Univ, BA, 59, MA, 61; Univ Minn, PhD, 66, studies with Reid Hastie, Paul Torrance & Malcolm Myers. *Pos:* Assoc dir & dir evaluation, Aesthetic Educ Prog, Arts in Gen Educ Proj, Cemrel Inc, St Louis, Mo, 69-71; dir grad progs, Univ NTex, Denton, 71-75 & chair art dept, 76-83; ed, Studies in Art Educ, Nat Art Educ Asn, 75-77; dean, Sch Visual Arts, 93-2004; dir, N Tex Inst for Educators on Visual Arts, 2004. *Teaching:* Instr art, Wayland Col, Plainview, Tex, 61-63; prof, Tex Tech Univ, 65-69; prof, vprovost & assoc vpres acad affairs, Univ NTex, Denton, 83-93; prof, Univ N Tex, Denton, Tex, 1993. *Awards:* Distinguished Fel, 89 & Lowenfeld Award, 90, Nat Art Educ Asn; Tex Art Educator Year, 91; Art Educator of the Yr, 2005. *Mem:* Life mem Nat Art Educ Asn (chmn higher educ div, 73-75); Tex Art Educ Asn (pres, 87-89). *Res:* Res trends in art educ. *Publ:* Ed, Behavioral Emphasis in Art Education, Nat Art Educ Asn, 75; The visual arts: A classroom myth or an accountable program?, Nat Asn Sec Sch Principals Bulletin, 11/79; auth, Research on Teacher Education, Teacher Education in Visual Arts, Macmillan, 90; An Experiment in School/Museum//University Collaboration, Metrop Univs, 94; coauth, Professional Conferences for Art Educators: A Pilgrimage to Excellence, 97; coauth, Doctorate Study in art educ at Univ of N Tex, 2001. *Mailing Add:* 2007 Locksley Ln Denton TX 76201

DAVIS, DARWIN R
MUSEUM DIRECTOR, ADMINISTRATOR
b Goodrich, Mich, Sept 5, 43. *Study:* Mich State Univ, BA, 65, MA, 68. *Pos:* Dir, Saginaw Art Mus, 72-74 & Art Ctr Battle Creek, 74-80; exec dir, Krasl Art Ctr, 81-. *Mem:* Am Asn Mus; Mich Mus Asn (vpres, 75-77, pres, 77-79, treas, 81-82). *Mailing Add:* 707 Lake Blvd Saint Joseph MI 49085

DAVIS, DOUGLAS MATTHEW
ARTIST, CRITIC
b Washington, DC, Apr 11, 33. *Study:* Abbott Art Sch, Washington, DC: Am Univ, BA, 56; Rutgers Univ, NJ, MA, 58. *Work:* Metrop Mus Art & Solomon R Guggenheim Mus, NY; Ludwig Mus, Cologne, Ger; Dahlem Mus, WBerlin; Venice Biennale Archive, Ital; Hirshhorn Mus & Sculpture Garden, Washington, DC; Walker Art Ctr, Minneapolis, Minn; Wadsworth Atheneum, Hartford, Conn; Polaroid Internat Collection, Boston; The World's First Collaborative Sentence, Lehman Col, NY; Whitney Mus Am Art, NY. *Comn:* Metabody, comn by George Watermen, III; Three Silent and Secret Actors, comn by Eugene M Schwartz. *Exhib:* Retrospective, Everson Mus, Syracuse, 72; San Francisco Mus Art, 75; Projected Video, Whitney Mus Am Art, NY & San Paulo Biennale, 75; Documenta 6, Kassel, WGer, 77; Arbeiten, Works 1970-1977, Berlin 1977-78; Neuer Berline Kunstverein (with catalog), 78 & Neue Galerie, Aachen, WGer, 78; Centre Georges Pompidou, Paris, 81; Whitney Mus Am Art, 81; Mus Sztuki (with catalog), Lodz, Poland, 82; Guggenheim Mus, NY, 88; solo exhibs, Solomon R Guggenheim Mus (with catalog), NY, 88, Contemp Arts Ctr, Cincinnati, Ohio, 88, Col Art Asn, Little Rock, Ark, 89, Kunstverein Cologne, Ger, 89, Centro de Arte y Communicacion, Harrod's en Arte, Buenos Aires, 91, Redness: A New Room, Ronald Feldman Fine Arts, NY, 92, Charter Oak Cult Ctr, 93; Kunstverein, Cologne, 89; Menage A Trois, Satallite TV Performance, 89; Ronald Feldman Fine Arts, NY, 91 & 92; Lehman Col Art Gallery, 94; Galerie St Gewais, Geneva, 94; Mus Sztuki, Poland, 95; Metrop Mus, NY; Whitney Mus Am Art, NY; Blast Art Benefit, X-Art Found, New York City, 96; Withdrawing, Ronald Feldman Fine Arts, NY, 96. *Collection Arranged:* Wallraf-Richartz Mus, Cologne; Finch Col Mus, NY; De Saisset Art Gallery, Calif; Everson Mus Art, NY; Panza di Biuma, Milan; Eugene M Schwartz, NY; Aalene St Gewais, Geneva; George Waterman 3, M/C; Egidio Marzona, Udine; Kunstudt Medien, Karlsrule; Gary Welz, NY; Scott Weinkle, NY & Miami, Fla; Whitney Mus AM Art, NY; Metropolitan Mus, NY; Ray Nashen, Tex. *Pos:* Critic/sr writer archit & photog, Newsweek, 69-88; dir, Int Network Arts, 79-; visual arts policy panel, Nat Endowment Arts, 80-83; advisor archit & design, Art in Embassies Prog, US Dept State, 86-88; consult in media, Rockfeller Found; lectr, USC, Los Angeles, 92, Tretyakov Gallery, Moscow, 93, Inst Contemp Art, Moscow, 93 & Sch of Art Inst Chicago, 94; dir, Vis Arts in Digital Agre, Turst ofr Mutual Understanding, NY, 99-2005. *Teaching:* Vis artist, Corcoran Sch Art, 70 & 71, State Univ NY, Buffalo, 73; art critic in residence, NY Univ, 75; regents lectr, Univ Calif, San Diego, 76; instr advanced video & performance, Int Network Arts, State Univ NY Purchase, Philadelphia Col Art, 76-, Columbia Univ, Univ Calif, Los Angeles; vis prof, Artcener Col, Pasadena, 88-90; vis prof art & design, Univ Calif, Los Angeles, 90-91; vis prof, Moscow State Univ; adj prof, Lehman Col, City Univ NY; adj prof fine arts, Univ of Southern Calif, Los Angeles, 92-93; Bard College, Annandale-on-Hudson, NY; St Petersburg Univ, Russia; Russian Inst Humanities, Moscow. *Awards:* Nat Endowment Arts Grants, 70 & 75; NY State Coun Arts Grant for Creative Work in Mixed Media, 70; Chairman's Grant, Nat Endowment Arts, 81 & Nat Pub Radio, 83; McDowell Colony Fel, 85; Graham Found, 87 & 88; Gifford Found, 87 & 88; Intermedia Arts, Boston, 88; Trust for Mutual Understanding, 89 & 91; Rockefeller Found Grant, 90; Fulbright Scholar, 94-95; many others. *Bibliog:* Irving Sandler (auth), Questions NY-Moscow, San Francisco Mus Mod Art, 76; Robert Atkins (auth), The art world & I go on line, Art In Am, 12/95; many others; Donald Kuspit (auth), Douglas Davis, Guggenheim Mus Cataloghue, 86. *Mem:* Fulbright Asn. *Media:* Videotape, Printmaking. *Publ:* auth, Fragments for a New Art of the 70's, Pape-Ruddy Art Asocs, Los Angeles, 75; co-ed, The New Television, Mass Inst Technol Press, 76; auth, Artculture: Essays on the Post-Modern, Harper & Row, 77; Photography as Fine Art, 83; The Museum Transformed, 90; The Five Myths of TV Power, 93; many others. *Dealer:* Ronald Feldman Fine Arts 31 Mercer St New York NY 10013. *Mailing Add:* 80 Wooster St New York NY 10012

DAVIS, ELLEN N
HISTORIAN
b Hackensack, NJ, July 20, 37. *Study:* Inst Fine Arts, NY Univ, with Peter H Von Blanckenhagen, PhD, 73. *Teaching:* Assoc prof ancient art hist, Queens Col, City Univ New York, 66-. *Awards:* Art Award, Coun Grad Studies. *Mem:* Archaeol Inst Am; New York Soc (pres, 80-83); New York Bronze Age Colloq. *Res:* Aegean metalworking, painting and connections with Egypt. *Publ:* Auth, The Vapheio cups: one Minoan & one Mycenean?, Art Bulletin LVI, 74; The icongraphy off the Thera Ship Fresco, In: Greek Art and Icongraphy, Univ Wis Press, 83; Youth and age in the Thera Frescoes, Am J Archaeol, 86; The Cycladic Style of the Thera Frescoes, Thera and the Aegean World, 90. *Mailing Add:* 225 E 76th St Apt 6 New York NY 10021-2141

DAVIS, JACK R
PAINTER, EDUCATOR
Study: Cent State Univ, Okla, BA; Univ Okla, MFA(painting & printmaking). *Work:* State of Okla Collection & Traveling Exhib; Okla Univ Col Nursing; Christ the King Church; Okla State Health Asn; and many others. *Exhib:* Kans State Univ Exhib to Grad Midwestern Univs, 69; one-man shows, Painting Prints & Vacuum Forms, Contemp Arts Found, Oklahoma City, 70, Graphic Retrospective, Emporia, Kans, 70 & Ten-O-One Gallery, Oklahoma City, 81-82; 31st Ann Exhib Okla Artists, Philbrook Art Ctr, Tulsa, 71; State of Okla Art Collection Exhib, Okla Art Ctr, 82; Okla Oil Men's Asn, 81; Chumming's Gallery, Edmond, Okla, 82; two-man exhib, Kirkpatrick Mus, 86. *Teaching:* Instr art, Okla Arts & Sci Found, 67-70; prof art, Oklahoma City Univ, 69-; instr art, state supported art classes for all fifth graders in Oklahoma City Pub Sch Syst, 71-72; instr, Okla Art Ctr, currently. *Awards:* Graphics Awards, 30th & 31st Ann Exhib Okla Artists, Tulsa, 70-71 & 57th Ann Tulsa Regional Exhib, 71. *Media:* Mixed. *Mailing Add:* 1213 NW 38th St Oklahoma City OK 73118-5425

DAVIS, JAMES GRANBERRY
PAINTER
b Springfield, Mo, 31. *Study:* Wichita State Univ, Kansas, Mo, BFA, 54, MFA, 60. *Work:* Metrop Mus Art, NY; Nat Mus Am Art, Washington, DC; Univ Ariz Mus Art, Tucson; Ariz State Univ Mus Art, Tempe; Mulvane Art Ctr, Kans. *Comn:* Large painting, Container Corp Am, NY, 65. *Exhib:* Arizona's Finest, Tempe Art Ctr, 82; 38th Corcoran Biennial, Washington, DC, 83; Solo exhibs, Germans Van Eck Gallery, NY, 84, Basil Art Fair, Switz, 85, Hans Redmann Gallery, Berlin, WGer, 86, 88 & 89, Marilyn Fine Arts, Santa Fe, NMex, 87, Shoshana Wayne Gallery, Santa Monica, Calif, 87, Etherton Gallery, Tucson, Ariz, 87 & Andrea Ross Gallery, Santa Monica, Calif, 89; Modern Am Printmaking, Am-Haus, Ger, 85; The Neo-Figure, Riva Yares Gallery, Scottsdale, 85; Artists Who Teach, Nat Mus Art, Washington, DC, 87; 25 Yr Retrospective, Tucson Mus Art, 88; Evidence, San Antonio Mus Art, Tex, 89; The Hunger Project, Scottsdale Ctr Arts, 89. *Teaching:* Assoc prof, Wichita State Univ, Kans, 59-62; instr painting & printmaking, Univ Mo, Columbia, 67-69; asst prof painting, Univ Ariz, Tucson, 79-70, assoc prof, 70-. *Awards:* Purchase Award, Kans Artists Ann, 62, Topeka Art Ctr, 66, Eastern Mich Univ, 68 & Tucson Art Ctr, 74. *Bibliog:* Anita Winegate (auth), James G Davis, Artspace, 1/79; Barbara Cortright (auth), Interview with James G Davis, Phoenix Mag, 1/80; Carol Cratoza (auth), James G Davis, Art Voices S, 3/80. *Media:* Oil; Lithography, Monotype. *Mailing Add:* Linda Vista Ranch PO Box 160 Oracle AZ 85623

DAVIS, JAMES ROBERT
CARTOONIST
b Marion, Ind, July 28, 45. *Study:* Ball State Univ. *Hon Degrees:* Ball State Univ, LHD; Purdue Univ, DFA. *Pos:* Artist, Groves & Assoc Advert, Muncie, Ind, 68-69; asst to cartoonist, Tumbleweeds (comic strip), 69-78; adv bd, Calif Mus Cartoon Art, 85-; pres & Chief Exec Officer, Paws Inc - Garfield Corp, 78-. *Awards:* Emmy Awards for Writing Best Animated Special, 85 & CBS Prime Time Specials; Distinguished Alumni Award, Am Asn State Col & Univ, 85; Segar Award for All Round Excellence, 85 & Best Humor Strip Cartoonist, 86, Nat Cartoonist Soc. *Mem:* Nat Cartoonists Soc; Newspaper Comics Coun. *Publ:* Auth, Garfield Mix & Match Storybook, 82 & Garfield the Knight in Shining Armor, 82, Random House; Garfield Takes the Cake, 82, The Garfield Treasury, 82 & Garfield Weighs In, 82, Ballantine. *Mailing Add:* c/o Paws Inc 5440 E County Rd 450 N Albany IN 47320

DAVIS, JAMES WESLEY
PAINTER, WRITER
b Los Angeles, Calif, Oct 9, 40. *Study:* Calif Col Arts & Crafts, BA(educ) & BFA; Univ Colo, MA & MFA(Inst Arts & Humanities Fel), 67. *Work:* Minn Mus Art; Ill State Mus; Alberta Col Art; Mulvane Art Mus; Laguna Gloria Mus; and others. *Exhib:* Mid-Am 4, St Louis Art Mus & Nelson/Atkins Mus, 72; Smithsonian Inst Traveling Show, 73-74; Calgary Int Biennial, Alta Col Art Gallery, 74; Mid-Year Ann, Butler Inst Am Art, 74 & 75; 19th Mid-South Biennial, Brooks Mem Gallery, 75; Irwin Collection, Kvannert Mus, 80; Watercolor USA, Springfield Mus, 85; 6th Alabama Works on Paper, Int Auburn Art Assoc, 85; Am Watercolors, Chateau de Tours, France, 87. *Pos:* Assoc Dean, College Creative Art & prof, art dept, San Francisco State Univ, 89-. *Teaching:* Instr painting & art hist, Univ Ark, 67-69; prof painting & drawing, Western Ill Univ, 69-81; vis prof, Univ Colo, 82; head art dept, ETex State Univ, 80-83; chmn art dept, Ind State Univ, 88-89; dir, Inter-Arts Ctr, San Francisco State Univ, 89-. *Awards:* Sworovski Int Award, Sworovski of Belg, 67; James D Phelan Award, 73. *Bibliog:* S W Semaj (auth), Memories, Structure, Vol 2, No 3; Alfred Frankenstein (auth), Visual, surreal acrobatics, San Francisco Chronicle, 1/74; Sylvia Brown (auth), Editorial highlights, City Mag, 2/16/74. *Mem:* Col Art Asn Am. *Media:* Acrylic, Watercolor. *Publ:* Auth, Self-actualized sculpture, Sculpture Int, Vol 3, No 2; Unified drawing by means of hybrids and grids, Leonardo, Vol 5, No 1; Some perceptual considerations on Vermeer and op art, Studies in the 20th Century, 73; Revival in the slumbering cornfield, Art J, fall 74; On mounds, Studio Int, 4/74. *Mailing Add:* 1541 Union St Alameda CA 94501

DAVIS, JERROLD
PAINTER
b Chico, Calif, Nov 2, 26. *Study:* Univ Calif, Berkeley, BA, 53, MA. *Work:* Carnegie Inst Int, Pittsburgh; Santa Barbara Mus Art, Calif; Los Angeles Mus Art; San Francisco Mus Art; Oakland Mus Art; and others. *Exhib:* One-man shows, Calif Palace of Legion of Honor, 60-64, Flint Art Inst, 64, Newport Harbor Art Mus, Newport Beach, Calif, 73 & retrospective, Richmond Art Ctr, Calif, 80; Especially for Children, Los Angeles Co Mus, 65; Univ Ariz, 67; Lytton Ctr, Los Angeles, 67 & 68; A Sense of Place, 74; and others. *Teaching:* Instr, Univ Calif, summer 67. *Awards:* Guggenheim Fel, 58-59; Am Fedn Arts-Ford Found artist in residence grant, Flint, Mich, 64; Prizes, Calif Palace Legion Honor, 60 & 62; and others. *Mailing Add:* 66 Twain Ave Berkeley CA 94708-1735

DAVIS, KEITH F
CURATOR, HISTORIAN
b Middletown, Conn, June 29, 52. *Study:* Drew Univ, 70-72; Southern Ill Univ, BS(cinema & photog), 72-74; Univ NMex, MA(art hist), 79. *Collection Arranged:* Hallmark Photog Collection (Hallmark Cards Inc), from which m any exhibs and publs have been produced. *Pos:* Intern, Int Mus Photog, Eastman House, Rochester, NY, 78-79; cur, Fine Art Collections, Hallmark Cards Inc, Kansas City, Mo, 79-; vis rsch prof art history, Univ Mo, Kansas City, 1995-. *Awards:* Beaumont Newhall History of Photography Award, Univ NMex, 77; Nat Endowment Humanities Fel, 86-87. *Mem:* Soc Photographic Educ (bd dir, 84-87). *Res:* History of 19th and 20th century photography. *Publ:* contribr, auth, Photography in Nineteenth Century Am, Abrams, 91; An American Century of Photography: From Dry-Plate to Digital, 2d edit, Hallmark/Abrams, 99; contrib auth, Taken by Design: Photography at the Institute of Design, 1937-1971, Art Inst Chicago/Univ Chicago, 2002; American Horizons: The Photographs Art Sinabaugh, Hudson Hills, 04; contribr auth, Art Fredrick Sommer: Photography, Drawing, Collage, Yale Univ Press, 05. *Mailing Add:* Hallmark Cards Inc 2501 McGee Kansas City MO 64108

DAVIS, KIMBERLY BROOKE
GALLERY DIRECTOR, ART DEALER
b Los Angeles, Calif, Nov, 25, 53. *Study:* Pratt Inst, BFA, 74. *Pos:* Admin asst, Inst Art & Urban Res, 75; admin asst, Guggenheim Mus, 76; assoc dir, Judith Selkowitz Fine Arts, 76-79; dir, Bernard Jacobson Gallery, Los Angeles, 79-84 & New York & Los Angeles, 83; dir, LA Louver Gallery, Venice, Calif, 85-. *Mem:* Fels Contemporary Art, Dir Circle, Moca, LA. *Specialty:* Painting and sculpture by leading American and European contemporary artists, fine art prints. *Mailing Add:* LA Louver Gallery 55 N Venice Blvd Venice CA 90291

DAVIS, L CLARICE
BOOK DEALER, ART LIBRARIAN
b Akron, Ohio. *Study:* Univ Akron, BA(fine arts), 55; Univ Calif, Los Angeles, MLS, 61, MA(art hist), 68. *Pos:* Chief librn, Los Angeles Co Mus Art, 63-68; owner & mgr, Davis Art Book Store & Gallery, Los Angeles, 71-79, partner, Davis & Schorr Art Books, 79-91, L Clarice Davis, Fine & Applied Art Books, 91-; actg unit head, Art Libr, Univ Calif, Los Angeles, 73-75; art reference librn, Beverly Hills Pub Libr, 88-94. *Teaching:* Asst prof mod art hist, Calif State Univ, Northridge, 61-63 & 68-69; lectr, Otis Art Inst, Los Angeles, 69-70. *Mem:* Art Libr Soc NAm; Antiquarian Booksellers Asn Am. *Specialty:* Out of print art books and exhibition catalogues. *Publ:* Contribr bibliog catalog, R B Kitaj, 65 & Peter Voulkos, Sculpture, 65, Los Angeles Co Mus Art; contribr introd, Pornography in Fine Art From Ancient Times, Los Angeles Elysium, 69; auth, Annuals of auction sales, Art Libr Soc NAm Newsletter, 12/76. *Mailing Add:* 6131 Atoll Ave Van Nuys CA 91401

DAVIS, LISA CORINNE
PAINTER, EDUCATOR
b Baltimore, Md, 58. *Study:* Cornell Univ, Ithaca, NY, 76-78; Pratt Inst, Brooklyn, NY, Haskell Travel Fel, 79, BFA(painting, hons), 80; Hunter Col, NY, MFA(painting), 83; apprenticeships with painters Jennifer Bartlett, 79-82, Jack Tworkov, 82 & Elizabeth Murray, 81-82. *Work:* Mus Mod Art, NY; J Paul Getty Mus; Nat Mus Women Arts, Washington; Victoria & Albert Mus, London; Art Inst Chicago. *Exhib:* Solo exhibs, Second St Gallery, Charlottesville, Va, 94, Munic Gallery, Atlanta, 94, Halsey Gallery, Sch Arts, Col Charleston, SC, 94, Dell Pryor Galleries, Detroit, 94, Proj Rm, Bronx Coun Arts, 97-98, ALJIRA, Ctr Contemp Art, Newark, NJ, 97-98, June Kelly Gallery, NY, 98, 00, Lehman Col Art Gallery, 01, New Work, June Kelly Gallery, NY, 2002; Allegory and Identity, Visceglia Art Ctr, Caldwell Col, NJ, 96; Dell Pryor Galleries, Detroit, 96; Artist in the Marketplace Benefit Exhib, Bronx Mus Arts, NY, 96; The Sense of Touch, Ceres Gallery, NY, 97; Waxing Poetic: Encaustic Art in America, Monclair Mus Art, NJ, 99; Book Art 12: Artist's Books from teh Library and Research Center, Nat Mus Women in Arts, Washington, DC, 2000; Paper Remix, Gallery Dieu Donne, Papermill, NY, 2001; Cultural Collaging, Univ RI, 2002. *Teaching:* Artist-in-residence & instr art, Studio in a Sch, 90-92; instr art, Lehman Col, 91-92; adj fac drawing & 3-D design, Foundation Dept, Parsons Sch Design, 92, acad adv, 92-93, coordr design studio, 93 & Col Coun, 94-; instr drawing, Outreach Prog, Cooper Union Sch Art & Archit, 93-94; lectr, Moore Col Art, Philadelphia, 94, Col Charleston, SC, 94 & Art in Gen, NY, 95; instr drawing, Yale Univ, 95, prof, 97-; vis artist & lectr, Norfolk Summer Prog, 96; asst prof, Sch Art, Yale Univ, 1998-2004; asst prof, Hunter Col, 2004. *Awards:* Mid Atlantic Arts Found Regional Fel, 92; Fac Develop Grant, Parsons Sch Design, 93; Visual Artist Fel, Nat Endowment Arts, 95-96 & NY Found for Arts; Biennial Artists Award, Louis Comfort Tiffany Found, 2001; Yaddo Residency, 2002. *Bibliog:* Nicholas Drake (auth), "Transparent Brown" requires some thought, Post & Courier, 11/94; Abby Goodnough (auth), Personal responses to a page of history, NY Times, 6/96; Ken Johnson (auth), review, NY Times, 6/98. *Mem:* Art in Gen. *Publ:* Illusr, The Red Coat, Flockophobic Press, New York, 90; Birthmark (Simon Perchik, auth), Flockophobic Press, New York, 92. *Mailing Add:* 323 W 39th St Studio 1002 New York NY 10018

DAVIS, MEREDITH J
GRAPHIC ARTIST, EDUCATOR
b Pittsburgh, Pa, May 15, 48. *Study:* Pa State Univ, BS, 70, Med, 74; Cranbrook Acad Art, with Katherine & Michael McCoy, MFA, 75. *Work:* Mead Libr Ideas, Dayton, Ohio; Am Inst Graphic Arts, NY. *Exhib:* Am Inst Graphic Arts, NY, 75, 82-83, 85 & 88; Mead Ann Report Competition, NY, 80; Soc Typographic Arts, Women in Design, Chicago, 81 & 88; NY Art Dir Club, 81 & 83; NY Type Dir Club, 82-85; 88; Am Asn Mus, 84 & 87; Ryder Gallery, Chicago, 85; Cranbrook: The New Discourse (with catalog), 94. *Pos:* Cur educ, Hunter Mus Art, 75-76; partner, Communication Design Inc, Richmond, Va, 79-89. *Teaching:* prof communication arts & design, Va Commonwealth Univ, 76- 89; prof graphic design, NC State Univ, dir grad prog, currently; Dir, PhD in Design. *Awards:* Excellence in Ann Report Design, Mead Libr Ideas, 81; Excellence Visual Communication, Designers Choice, Indust Design Mag, 82 & Creativity 13, NY Art Dir, 83; Gold Medalist, Wash AA Dirs, 85; Silver & Gold Medalist, Case Cover Competition, Washington, 85; Choice Award, Asn Col & Research Libr, 99; AIGA 2005 Nat Medal & Fel. *Bibliog:* Annual reports: Business as usual?, Art Direction Mag, 81. *Mem:* Am Inst Graphic Arts (bd dir, 95-98); Graphic Design Educ Asn (pres, 86-88 & 92-94, vpres, 90-92, bd dir, 94-96); Am Ctr Design (bd dir, 90-96, pres, 96-2000, chmn bd, 98-2000). *Publ:* Contribr, The role of education in research, Design J, 83; coauth, Design as a Catalyst for Learning, Asn Supv & Curric Develop, 98; Design-Based Education, Arts Educ Policy Rev, 98; Design in Education, Int Interior Design Asn, 98; Design and Social Responsibility, Jack Williamson (ed), 98; Design In Context: An Introduction to Graphic Design Theory, Thames & Hudson, 2007; and others. *Mailing Add:* NC State Univ Box 7701 Raleigh NC 27695

DAVIS, PHILIP CHARLES
PHOTOGRAPHER, WRITER
b Spokane, Wash, Oct 15, 21. *Study:* Albright Art Sch, Buffalo, NY, cert. *Work:* Mus Art Inst Chicago; Int Mus Photog, Rochester, NY; Detroit Art Inst; Mus Mod Art, NY. *Comn:* Outdoor exhib photos, Univ Mich Sesquicentennial Comt, 66. *Exhib:* One-man show photographs, Kalamazoo Art Ctr, Mich, 62; The University, Univ Mich, Ann Arbor, 66; three-man show photographs, 831 Gallery, Birmingham, Mich, 71; Group Invitational, Kresge Art Ctr, Mich State Univ, 72 & 79; Midwest Invitational, Walker Art Ctr, Minneapolis, Minn, 73-74; The Art of the Photogravure, Colo Photog Arts Ctr, Denver, 79. *Teaching:* From instr to prof art, Univ Mich, Ann Arbor, 48-. *Awards:* Gold Medal, 59, Silver Medal, 60 & Bravo Gold Medal, 61, Art Dirs Club Detroit. *Bibliog:* Irving Desfor (auth), Camera Angles, Assoc Press Newsfeatures, 72. *Mem:* Soc Photog Educ. *Publ:* Auth & illusr, The university, 67, Take Photography Step by Step, 70, Photography, 72, revised 79 & The Dexter Portfolio (50 set ed), 72. *Dealer:* The Halstead Gallery 560 N Woodward Birmingham MI 48011. *Mailing Add:* 7373 Webster Church Rd Whitmore Lake MI 48189-9628

DAVIS, ROBERT
PAINTER
b New York, NY. *Study:* Parsons Sch Design, cert, 55; Cranbrook Acad Art, Mich, 57; study with Ezio Martinelli. *Exhib:* one-man shows, Mus Northern Ariz, Flagstaff, 80, Francine Seders Gallery, Seattle, 85, 89 & Columbia Tower Club Gallery, Seattle, 91; Mich Focus Exhib Detroit Inst Arts & Flint Inst Arts, 75; Mich Artists Exhib, Univ Mich, Ann Arbor, 76; Gorden Woodside / John Breseth Gallery, 82, 83, Seattle; Still Lifes, Francine Seders Gallery, Seattle, 86; 44th Pac Northwest Prof Arts Exhib, Bellevue Art Mus, Wash, 90; McConnell Gallery, San Luis Obispo, Calif, 03. *Media:* Acrylic, Gouache-Vinyl. *Mailing Add:* 7205 Nudoso Rd Atascadero CA 93422-7009

DAVIS, RONALD
PAINTER, PRINTMAKER
b Santa Monica, Calif, June 29, 37. *Study:* Univ Wyo, 55-56; San Francisco Art Inst, 60-64. *Work:* Los Angeles Co Mus; Mus Mod Art, NY; Tate Gallery, London; Albright-Knox Art Gallery, Buffalo; San Francisco Mus Art. *Exhib:* A News Aesthetic, Washington Gallery Mod Art, DC, 67; Documenta 4, Kassel, Ger, 67; Whitney Mus Am Art Ann, NY, 67; Color, Univ Calif, Los Angeles Art Galleries, 69; Venice Biennial, Italy, 72; Four Contemp Painters, Cleveland Mus Art, 78; solo shows, Blum Helman Gallery, NY, 79, 81, 84 & 88, Asher/Faure, Los Angeles, 82-84, Trumps, Los Angeles, 85, NY Acad Scis, 86, Sedong Art Ctr, Ariz, 87, Blum Helman Los Angeles & Santa Monica, Calif, 87, 89 & 91, DEL Fine Arts, NMex, 92 & Jaquelin Loyd Contemp, 98; Prints from Tyler Graphics, 85; Walker Art Ctr, Minneapolis, Minn; Digital Visions: Computers and Art, Everson Art Mus, Syracuse, NY, 87-89; NMex Sculpture, Stables Gallery, Taos, 91; Seven Painters, Nicholas Alexander Gallery, NY, 95. *Teaching:* Instr, Univ Calif, 67. *Awards:* Nat Endowment Arts, 68. *Bibliog:* M Fried (auth), Ronald Davis: Surface and illusion, Artforum, 4/67; R Hughes (auth), Ron Davis at Kasmin, Studio Int, 176, 12/68; B Rose (auth), American painting, Vol 2, 70. *Media:* Cel-Vinyl, Acrylic, Canvas; Computer Graphics. *Collection:* Contemporary art. *Mailing Add:* PO Box 293 Arroyo Hondo NM 87513

DAVIS, STEPHEN A
PAINTER
b Ft Worth, Tex, Apr 24, 45. *Study:* Claremont Grad Sch, MFA, 71. *Work:* San Francisco Mus Art; Oakland Mus; Univ Art Mus, Berkeley, Calif; Addison Gallery Am Art, Andover, Mass; Mus Contemp Art, Los Angeles, Calif; El Paso Mus Art, Tex. *Exhib:* Solo exhibs, Hansen-Fuller Gallery, San Francisco, Calif, 72, 74 & 76, Hudson River Mus, Yonkers, NY, 79-80, Malinda Wyatt Gallery, New York, 85, Gallery Paule Anglim, San Francisco, Calif, 87, Jernigan Wicker Gallery, San Francisco, 92 & 95 & Mattress Factory, Pittsburgh, Pa, 90; Am Abstraction at the Addison, Addison Gallery Am Art, Andover, Mass, 91; Christiane Chassay, Montreal, 96; The Nave Mus, Victoria, Tex, 97; Harlingen Mus, Tex, 97; McAllen Mus, Tex, 97; and others. *Pos:* Cur & Four Berkeley Artist, Hansen-Fuller Gallery, 70; Lansdowne Lect, Univ Victoria, Can, 91. *Teaching:* Lectr, Univ Santa Clara, Calif, 75-77, Univ Calif, Santa Barbara, 78, Sarah Lawrence Col, New York, 79-80, State Univ NY, Purchase, New York, 82; artist-in-residence, Wright State Univ, Dayton, Ohio, 77 & Hunter Col, 95-96; asst prof, Hunter Col, New York, 86-93; vis assoc prof, Stanford Univ, Calif, 94-95, Hunter Col, New York, 95-; vis prof, Claremont Grad Sch, Calif, 2001, The Frank Mohr Inst, Groningen, Holland, 2001. *Awards:* Gottlieb Found Award, 93-94; Joan Mitchell Found Grant, 95 & 96; Nat Endowment Arts, 75-76, 78-79 & 87-88. *Publ:* Stephen Davis (auth), Paintings, Washington Project for the Arts, (catalog), 86; Stephen Davis (auth), Jacob and His Twelve Sons, Addison Gallery Am Art, (catalog), 90; Stephen Davis (auth), 70's, 80's, 90's, Jernigan Wicker Fine Arts (catalog), 92. *Mailing Add:* 70 Thomas St New York NY 10013-3820

DAVIS, THELMA ELLEN
PAINTER
b Las Animas, Colo, Sept 1, 25. *Exhib:* Catherine Lorillard Wolfe Art Club, NY, 82; one-woman show, Rosicrucian Mus, San Jose, Calif, 83; Pastel Soc Am Ann, Nat Arts Club, 90; Pastel Soc West Coast Ann, Sacramento Fine Art Ctr, Sacramento, Calif, 92; Soc Western Artists Ann, Hall Flowers, San Francisco, 92; Pastel Soc Am Nat Arts Club, 95-97. *Awards:* Klimberger Mem Award, Pastel Soc Am, 93; Barnard Award, Pastel Soc West Coast, 94; Sanford Corp Award, Pastel Soc Am, 95. *Mem:* Pastel Soc Am; Pastel Soc West Coast; Soc Western Artists; Gold Country Artists. *Media:* Pastel, Oil. *Mailing Add:* 6666 Acorn Hill Placerville CA 95667

DAVISON, BILL
EDUCATOR, PRINTMAKER
b Burlington, Vt, Sept 23, 41. *Study:* Albion Col, BA, 63; Univ Mich, MFA, 66. *Work:* Libr Cong, Washington, DC; Dartmouth Col, Hanover, NH; Mus Mod Art, NY; Yale Univ, New Haven, Conn; Wesleyan Univ, Middletown, Conn; and many others. *Exhib:* Boston Printmakers 20th Ann Nat Exhib, Boston Mus Fine Arts, 68; one person exhibs, The Univ Gallery, Univ S Calif, Los Angeles, 77, Fla Ctr Arts, Univ S Fla, Tampa, 77, Davison Art Ctr, Wesleyan Univ, Middletown, Conn, 78, Kathryn Markel Gallery, NY, 78, Roy Boyd Gallery, Chicago, 79, Colby-Sawyer Col, New London, NH, 83 & Albany Acad Gallery, Albany, NY, 85; Nat Print Exhib, 77 & Thirty Yrs of Am Printmaking, 77, Brooklyn Mus, NY; High Tech/High Touch: Computer Graphics in Printmaking, Pratt Manhattan Gallery, NY, 87; Int Exhib Prints, Print Club, Philadelphia, 88; Post Industrial Expression, Sordoni Gallery, Wilkes Col, Wilkes-Barre, Pa, 88; Univ Dallas Nat Print Invitational, Tex, 89; Light Aberrations: A National Exhib of Photographs & Prints, Univ Tex, San Antonio, 90; Int Symposium Electronic Art, Croningen, The Neth, 90; Exhib Electronic Art, Art Centre, Punkaharju, Finland, 91; Dakotas Int: Works on Paper, Univ S Dak, Vermillion, 91; 10th Int Conference on Computer Graphics (SIGGRAPH), Chicago, 92. *Teaching:* Assoc prof, Univ Vt, Burlington, 68-81, prof, 90-. *Awards:* Indiv Grant, Vt Coun Arts, 70-71 & 78-79; Artist's Fel, Nat Endowment Arts, 74-75; Vis Artist's Fel, Brandywine Workshop Offset Inst, Philadelphia, 88; MacDowell Colony Fel, Peterborough, NH, 89; Award of Distinction, PRIX ARS Electronica 90, Linz, Austria, 90. *Bibliog:* A Class Portrait, Arts Mag, 10/81; Print News, 12/81; New Images, Ocular, winter 82; Sculptors find new ways with wood, NY Times, 12/2/84; Bill Davison: New screenprints - John Cage: New etchings, Art New Eng, 6/90. *Publ:* Art & Technology (catalog), Lehigh Univ, Bethlehem Univ, Pa, 83; The Ways of Wood (catalog), Org of Independent Artists, Inc, New York, 84; Visual Proceedings - SIGGRAPH 1992 (catalog), Chicago, 92. *Mailing Add:* c/o Dept Art 304 Williams Hall Univ Vermont Burlington VT 05405

DAVISON, LYNN
PAINTER, PRINTMAKER
b St Albans, Vt, Aug 7, 43. *Study:* Studied at Ringling Sch Art, Sarasota, Fla, 63-65, Univ South Fla, Tampa, 67. *Work:* Southern Alleghenies Mus Art, Lorretto, Pa; Ringling Mus Art, Sarasota; Polk Mus Art, Lakeland, Fla; Vero Beach (Fla) Ctr Arts; Van Wezel Performing Arts Hall, Sarasota. *Exhib:* Is Baroque Alive, Ringling Mus, Sarasota, 92, 95, 97, 2000; Boca Raton (Fla) Mus, 92, 93, 97, 98; Southern Fedn/NEA Fellowship, Atlanta Col Art Gallery, 92; Orlando (Fla) Mus, 92; Nat Competition, Alternative Mus, NY, 96; Ga Rev Anniversary, Ga Mus, Athens, 97; Dramatic Realism-New Baroque, Southern Alleghenies Mus 97; Butler Inst Nat, Butler Inst, Youngstown, Ohio, 97; All Fla Invitational, Boca Raton Mus, 2001. *Teaching:* adj instr figure painting, Riwgling Sch Art, 2001-. *Awards:* Fel, Fla Arts Coun, 88-89, 94-95, 99-2000, Southern art Fedn /NEA, 92, Vt Studio Ctr, 99. *Bibliog:* Joanne Milani (auth), Lynn Davison, Tampa Tribune, 97, 2000; Donald Miller (auth),The New Baroque, Pittsburgh Post Gazette, 97; Annette Hattan (auth), Georgia Review review, Georgia Review, 97. *Media:* Oil, Paint. *Dealer:* Mira Mar Gallery 1284 N Palm Ave Sarasota FL 34236; Trinity Gallery 315 E Paces Ferry Rd Atlanta GA 20305; Wood St Gallery 1239 N Wood St Chicago IL 60622. *Mailing Add:* 5015 14th Ave SW Naples FL 34116

DAVISON, NANCY R
PRINTMAKER
Study: Smith Col with Leonard Baskin, BA, 66; Univ Mich, MA, 73; Univ Mich, PhD, 80. *Work:* DeCordova Mus & Sculpture Park, Lincoln, Mass; Mus Art, Univ Mich, Ann Arbor; Print Dept, Boston Publ Libr, Mass; Avesta Industrisdad, Sweden; IBM, Pittsburgh, Pa. *Comn:* Auction 91-The Nubble, PBS Channel 10 WCBB, Portland, Maine; numerous house portraits for pvt collections. *Exhib:* Archit in Contemp Printmaking, Boston Archit Ctr, Am Inst Archit, Washington, DC & Univ NH, Durham, 94-95; Maine Printmaking 1995, Round Top Ctr Arts, Damariscotta, Maine, 95; Int Grafiks, Avesta Konst, Sweden, 97; Illustrator's Downeast, Brick Store Mus, Kennebunk, Maine, 97; solo exhib, Aichi Shukutoku Univ, Nagoya, Japan, 98; City Views: Works on paper from permanent collections, De Cordova Mus & Sculpture Park, Lincoln, Mass, 98. *Collection Arranged:* American Sheet Music

Illustration (auth, catalog), Mus Art, Univ Mich, 73. *Pos:* keeper of prints asst, Boston Publ Libr, Mass, 67-70; consult & print cataloger, William L Clements Libr, Ann Arbor, Mich, 72-73; owner & operator, BlueStocking Studio, York Beach, Maine, 85-. *Awards:* Pittsburgh Print Group Ann Purchase Award, Westinghouse Electric Corp, 82; Purchase Award, 36th Ann Boston Printmakers Exhib, 84; Boston Printmakers Award, Duxbury Art Complex, 90. *Mem:* Boston Printmakers; Oqunquit Art Asn (pres, 88-); Print Consortium; Oqunquit Arts Collaborative (founder & pres, 97-). *Media:* Etching, linocut. *Res:* 19th century historical prints. *Specialty:* Works on art on paper. *Publ:* Contribr, The grand triumphal quick-step, Prints in & of America to 1850, Univ Press Va, 70; A Jackson in cartoons, American Printmaking Before 1876, Libr Cong, 75; Bickham's musical entertainer, 18th Century Prints in Colonial America, Colonial Williamsburg Found, 79; auth, E W Clay: American Political Caricaturist of the Jacksonian Era, Univ Microfilms, 80; E W Clay & the American Political Caricature Business, Prints & Printmakers of New York State, Univ Syracuse, 86. *Mailing Add:* PO Box 1257 York Beach ME 03910

DAVIS PRICE, DORIS C
PAINTER, PRINTMAKER
b Millsboro, Del, 29. *Study:* Temple Univ, 47-50; Empire State Col (SUNY), Old Westbury, BS(Painting & Writing), 74. *Work:* Del State Univ, Dover; York Col (CUNY), Queens, NY; Medgar Evans Col (CUNY), Brooklyn, NY; Nanticoke Indian Mus, Millsboro, Del; Apex Mus, Atlanta, Ga; and others. *Exhib:* Solo exhibs, Am Int Col, Springfield, Mass, 80, Fordham Univ, NY, 84, Carvel State Orrico Bldg, Wilmington, 95 & 99, Del State Univ, Dover, 96, Del Tech & Community Col, 2000; New Prints, North East, Print Club, Philadelphia, Pa, 85; OPA 3rd Int Exhib, Pen & Brush Gallery, NY, 86; Ann Juried Exhib, Knickerbocker Artists, NY, 86; NYNEX Corp, White Plains, NY, 92; Readers Digest, Pleasantville, NY, 92. *Pos:* Treas, Roosevelt Island Artists' Asn, 83-84; mem adv bd, Del State Univ, Dover, 99 & 2000. *Awards:* Hon Mention, Anthropology in Art, Queens Col (CUNY), 87 & 90; Special Merit Award, Artdex Int, 94; Third Place Award, Tri-State Exhib, Art Inst Gallery, Salisbury, Md; First Place Award in portraiture, Dover Art League, 2000. *Bibliog:* Mel Tapley (auth), Painters Price & Coppedge pick flowers, NY Amsterdam News, 3/8/87 & Spiral Gallery presents two unique artists, 10/10/87; Julie Stump (auth), Texture of the Spirit, News J, Wilmington, Del, 3/1/95; Kay Parsons (auth), Painting loving challenge for Millsboro Artist, Sussex Countian, Georgetown, Del, 2/28/95. *Mem:* Jamaica Arts Ctr Co-op; Knickerbocker Artists; Rehoboth Art League; Millsboro Art League; Dover Art League. *Media:* Acrylic, Pastel; Etching. *Collection:* Library of Congress, Mac Author Award Winner Robert Blackburn print collection. *Publ:* Illusr, Madonna on cloud nine, Response, United Methodist Church, 85; The Best of Acrylic Painting, Rockport Publ, 96. *Dealer:* Savacou Gallery 240 E 13th St New York NY 10003. *Mailing Add:* 30295 Mt Joy Rd Millsboro DE 19966

DAVY, WOODS
SCULPTOR
b Washington, DC, Oct 6, 49. *Study:* Univ NC, Chapel Hill BFA(Morehead Scholar), 72; Univ Ill, Champaign/Urbana, MFA, 75. *Work:* Palm Springs Desert Mus, Calif; Orange Co Mus Art, Calif; Fed Reserve Bank, San Francisco; Long Beach Mus Art, Calif State Univ, Long Beach; Los Angeles Co Mus Art, Armand Hammer Mus Art, Los Angeles. *Comn:* IBM, Gaithersburg, Md, 90; Sterling Drug Co, Collegeville, Pa, 92; Xerox Corp, NY, 93; Prudential Real Estate, Calif, 98; Cedars Sinai Hosp, Los Angeles, 98. *Exhib:* Solo exhibs, Security Pacific Bank Plaza, Los Angeles, 80 & McIntosh/Drysdale Gallery, Houston, 84-86; Sculpture 1975, nat traveling exhib, 75; Six Los Angeles Sculptors, Fed Reserve Bd, Washington, DC, 80; New Art of Downtown Los Angeles, nat traveling exhib, 82-84; The Forgotten Dimension, nat traveling exhib, 82; New Pub Art, Otis Art Inst, Los Angeles, 84; Monuments To, Univ Art Mus, Long Beach, Calif, 85; Arco Sculpture Garden, Am Film Inst, Los Angeles, 86; New Sculpture, Works Gallery, Long Beach, Calif; Pier Walk, Chicago, 97; Imago Gallery, Palm Desert, Calif, 98. *Pos:* Bd dir, Los Angeles Contemp Exhibs, 84-85; arts adv coun, Cedars Sinai Hosp, Los Angeles, 84-98. *Bibliog:* William Wilson (auth), How real is the downtown phenomenon? Los Angeles Times, 9/20/81; Carol Everingham (auth), Critic's choice, Houston Post, 5/3/85; JoAnn Lewis (auth), Woods Davy's sculptures, Washington Post, 2/8/86. *Media:* Steel and Stone in combination. *Dealer:* Jan Abrams Fine Art New York NY. *Mailing Add:* 562 San Juan Ave Venice CA 90291

DAWDY, DORIS OSTRANDER
WRITER, HISTORIAN
b Minn. *Study:* MacPhail Sch Music, Minneapolis; Los Angeles City Col. *Bibliog:* Contemporary Authors; Lois Swan Jones (auth), Art Research and Resources/A Guide to Finding Art Information. *Mem:* San Francisco Hist Soc; The Mus Soc, San Francisco; Nat Mus Women Arts. *Res:* American Indian paintings, arts and crafts, and other furnishings; Artists of the American West born prior to 1900; Asian American Artists born before 1910. *Publ:* Auth, Annoted Bibliography of American Indian Painting, Heye Found, 68; Artists of the American West, Swallow, 74 & 80, Vol II, 81 & Vol III, 85 & 87, Ohio Univ Press; The Wyant Diary: An Artist with the Wheeler Survey in Arizona 1873, Ariz and the West, Univ Ariz Press, 80; George Montague Wheeler: The Man and the Myth, Ohio Univ Press/Swallow Press, 93. *Mailing Add:* 3055 23rd Ave San Francisco CA 94132

DAWLEY, JOSEPH WILLIAM
PAINTER
b Nashville, Ark, June 19, 36. *Study:* With Raymond Froman, 58-61; Southern Methodist Univ, BFA, 59; Dallas Mus Fine Arts, 60; Art Students League, 61. *Work:* Mus Arts & Crafts, Columbus, Ga; Davenport Mus Art, Iowa; Southern Methodist Univ, Dallas, Tex; Notre Dame Univ; The Mayo Clinic. *Comn:* Official portrait, Mother Elizabeth Ann Seton, comn by St Patricks Cathedral, 75. *Exhib:* Allied Artists Show, NY, 69 & 70; Acad Artists Show, Springfield, Mass, 69 & 70; Hudson Valley Art Show, White Plains, NY, 69 & 70; Am Artists Prof League, NY, 69-71; Salmagundi Club Show, NY, 70 & 72. *Pos:* Creator comic strip, Chief, 64-67; owner, Joseph Dawley Gallery, 77-87. *Teaching:* Instr, DuCret Sch of Arts, Plainfield, NJ. *Awards:* Figure or Portrait Anonymous Award, Acad Artists, 69; William Collins Award, Hudson Valley Art Asn, 69; Jane Peterson Portrait Award, Allied Artists, New York, 70. *Bibliog:* Susan Stock (auth), A stricken painter tries a new style and finds new success, New York Times, 8/2/92; Dowling & Hollister (auth), The rebirth of an artist, Life Mag, 6/93; Smith & Plimpton (auth), Chronicles of courage (chapter), Random House, 93. *Mem:* Allied Artists Asn; Hudson Valley Art Asn; Am Artists Prof League; Acad Artists. *Media:* Oil. *Specialty:* Original Fine Art including drawings, etchings, 3-dimensional works. *Publ:* Auth, Character Studies in Oil, 72, The Painters' Problem Book, 73, Painting Western Characters, 75 & Painters' Problem Book II, 78, Watson-Guptill; auth, Seeing & Painting the Colors of Nature, Watson-Guptill, 87. *Dealer:* The Artful Deposit Inc 201 Farnsworth Ave Bordentown NJ 08505; Gallery LaFone Georgetown Washington DC

DAWSON, DOUG
PAINTER, INSTRUCTOR
b Oak Park, Ill, Aug 23, 44. *Study:* Macalester Col, St Paul, Minn, BS, 66, Drake Univ, Des Moines, Iowa, 69. *Comn:* World Relief, Mali-West Africa, Guaranty Bank, Queen Anne Inn & Littleton Med Clinic, Colo. *Exhib:* Allied Artist Exhib, NY, 82 & 91; Palais Rameau in Lille, Paris, France, 87; Pastel Soc SW, Tex, 95-; Audubon Artists, NY, 95 & 2000; Pastel Soc Am, NY, 93-2004. *Collection Arranged:* Blue Cross/Blue Shield Collection, Denver, Colo; US Senate Off, Washington; Coutts Mus Art, El Dorado, Kans.; Ferrett Exploration Collection- Gibson, Dunn, Gulf cher Law Firm. *Pos:* Founding bd mem, Denver Art Students League, 87-; consult, Summer Inst Linguistics, SAm, 88-. *Teaching:* Instr painting, drawing, anat, Colo Inst Art, Denver, 78-99; instr, Denver Art Students League, 86-; instr, pastels, Museo del Quijote, Guanajuato, Mexico, 90; Acad Art-Suriname, S America. *Awards:* Master Pastelist, Pastel Soc Am, NY; Goldsmith Award, Am Watercolor Soc, NY; Silver Medal Excellence, Audubon Artists, NY; P Scty Southwest: Tex; Roe Award, Mc Stayaward; Int assoc Pastel Soc; Best of show, Calif; Master Circle Award, Int Asn Pastel Soc, 2005. *Bibliog:* Artists Mag, 4/86 & 9/87; Focus Mag, Santa Fe, 89, 92 & 98; Am Artist Mag, 10/96. *Mem:* Am Watercolor Soc; Pastel Soc Am; Pastel Soc SW; Pastel Soc Ore; Pastel Soc No Fla. *Media:* Pastel, Oil. *Publ:* Capturing Light & Color with Pastel, North Light, 8/91. *Dealer:* Ventana Fine Art 400 Canyon Rd Santa Fe NM 87501; Telluride Art Gallery, Telluride, Colo; Pinon Gallery, Denver, Co.; Corpus Christ Art, Connection Gallery, TX; Total Arts Gallery Taos NMex. *Mailing Add:* 8622 W 44th Pl Wheat Ridge CO 80033

DAWSON, JESSICA
CRITIC
Pos: Writer, Wash City Paper; art critic, galleries column Wash Post; art critic, Wash Post.com, 2001-; Freelance art critic. *Mailing Add:* Wash Post 1150 15th St Washington DC 20071

DAWSON, JOHN ALLAN
PAINTER, SCULPTOR
b Joliet, Ill, Sept 12, 46. *Study:* Northern Ill Univ, BFA, 69; Univ NMex; Ariz State Univ, MFA, 74. *Work:* Ulrich Mus Art; Phoenix Art Mus, Ariz; Ark Art Ctr, Little Rock; Okla Art Ctr, Oklahoma City. *Exhib:* Segal Gallery, NY; Ariz Invitational 75, Phoenix Art Mus, 75; one-man shows, Ark Art Ctr, Little Rock, 79, Okla Art Ctr, Oklahoma City, 79, Springfield Mus Art, Mo, 80 & Sheldon Mem Collection, Univ Nebr, Lincoln, 80; Wedding Series, Elaine Horwitch Gallery, Scottsdale, Ariz, 82; James Ratliff Gallery, 99; over 50 one man shows. *Pos:* Artist-in-residence, Mesa Pub Schs, Ariz Comn Art, 74. *Awards:* Purchase Award, Del Mar Col, 73 & El Paso Mus Art, 75. *Bibliog:* C D Kotrozo (auth), article, Art Voices South, 5/79; A Johns (auth), The wedding series, Ariz Arts & Lifestyle, winter 82; Claude Marks (ed), World Artists, 80-90. *Media:* Oil; Bronze. *Mailing Add:* 10246 E Brown Rd Mesa AZ 85207

DAWSON, ROBERT E
SCULPTOR
b Sacramento, Calif, 50. *Work:* Centro Cult de la Raz, San Diego, Calif. *Exhib:* In Tifada: Birth of a Nation, Spectacolor Lightboard, NY, 90; Chicano Art: Resistance and affirmation 1965-1985, Wight Art Gallery, Univ Calif Los Angeles, 90; La Fronter/The Border, 93; solo exhib, Boehm Gallery, 94. *Teaching:* Asst prof, Calif State Univ, San Marcos, 91-. *Awards:* Nat Endowment Arts, Fel, 86-88. *Mailing Add:* c/o Visual & Performing Arts Prog Col Arts & Sci Calif State Univ San Marcos CA 92096-0001

DAWSON, ROBERT H
PHOTOGRAPHER
b Sacramento, Calif, 50. *Study:* Univ Calif, Santa Cruz, BA, 72; San Francisco State Univ, MA, 79. *Work:* Mus Mod Art, NY; Libr Cong, Washington, DC; San Francisco Mus Mod Art, Calif. *Exhib:* Great Central Valley Traveling Exhib, Calif Acad Sci, 86. *Pos:* Pres, treas & bd dir, Soc Photog Educ Western Reg Bd, 82-87; affil artist, Headlands Ctr Arts, Marin Co; vpres bd dir, San Francisco Camera Work, 86-91. *Teaching:* Instr photog, Bay Area col & univ, 81-; lect & workshops, throughout US; chmn, Photog Dept, City Col San Francisco, 91-93. *Awards:* Visual Arts Fel, Nat Endowment Arts, 88 & Art Matters Inc; James D Phelan Award, San Francisco Found; Photographer's Work Grant, Maine Photog Workshops; and others. *Publ:* Contribr, The Pyramid Lake Project, 89; A River Too Far: The Past and Future of the Arid West, 91; Arid Waters: Photographs From the Water in the West Project, 92; Farewell, Promised Land Project, 92. *Mailing Add:* c/o San Franicsco Art Commission Gallery 401 Van Ness Ave San Francisco CA 94102

DAY, BURNIS CALVIN
PAINTER, INSTRUCTOR
b Hepzibah, WVa. *Study:* Ctr Creative Studies-Col Art & Design; Famous Artists Sch, 68; AAS, Oakland Comm Col Art, 69. *Work:* Washington County Mus Fine Arts, Md; Univ Utah, Mus Fine Arts; Univ Mont, Mus Fine Arts; Mus Northern Ariz, Flagstaff; Mus of City of New York; and others. *Comn:* Painting, Tom Davis Agency, Detroit & Cleveland, Ohio, 70; Detroit Bus & Civic League, 78; mural of 4 sporting events, Detroit Recreation Dept, 78; painting & portrait, Detroit Bus & Civic League, 74. *Exhib:* Original Paintings by Mich Artists, Detroit Inst Arts, Mich, 76; 9th Ann Nat Small Painting Exhib, NMex Art League, Albuquerque, 79; 4th Ann Nat Am Show, Laramie Art Guild, Wyo, 79; Cult Exchange Trends, Gallery Tanner, Los Angeles, Calif, 84; Int Platform Asn, Mayflower Hotel, Washington, 89; State of the Art, 93, NE Art EXPO, New Eng Fine Art Inst, Boston, Mass. *Pos:* Art assoc, Cal Summers' House of Art, Detroit, Mich, 71-77; art dir, Urban Screen Process, Detroit, Mich, 72-73; freelance artist, 77-. *Teaching:* Instr life drawing, Pittman's Gallery Inc, Detroit, Mich, 73-74; painting, Detroit Recreation Dept, Mich, 85; mixed media, Wayne Co Community Col, Detroit, Mich, 85-98; art instr drawing & painting, UAW-Chrysler Nat Training Ctr, Detroit, Mich, 92-95-98; summer art instr mixed media, St Scholastica Summer Day Camp, Detroit, 94-98. *Awards:* 1st & 2nd Place, US Tank Automotive, 77; Cert of Recognition, US Zone Comt, 77; Semi-Finalist, United Auto Workers 50th Anniversary Poster, 86. *Bibliog:* George B Eichorn (auth), Recreation center new sports mural, Detroit News, 4/78; Lora Frankel (auth), National Young Audiences Week, YAMD Newsletter, Winter 79; Marie Teasley (auth), Burnis Day in DIA Collect, Michigan Chronicle, 12/87. *Media:* Acrylic, Oil. *Publ:* Auth, A Description of Neogeometric/Burnis C Day, private publ, 85; Article, Art, artists & my paintings, Projected Int/Burnis C Day, 89; The work book, Scott & Daughters Publishing, 90; Am Artist, Survey of Leading Contemps, American References, 89. *Dealer:* 21st Century Video PO Box 0255 Detroit MI 48231-0255

DAY, GARY LEWIS
PRINTMAKER, PAINTER
b Great Falls, Mont, Sept 29, 50. *Study:* Mont State Univ, BA, 75; Fla State Univ, MFA, 76. *Work:* Ariz State Univ, Tempe; Trenton State Col, NJ; Sheldon Mem Gallery, Lincoln, Nebr; Joslyn Art Mus, Omaha, Nebr. *Exhib:* one person show, Sheldon Mem Gallery, Lincoln, Nebr, 84, William Jewell Col, Kansas City, Mo, 88; Thirty Yrs of Am Printmaking, Brooklyn Mus, NY, 76; 62nd Ann Int Competition, Print Club, Philadelphia, Pa, 86; Nat drawing 87, Trenton State Col, NJ; Midlands Invitationals, Joslyn Art Mus, Omaha, Nebr, 90. *Collection Arranged:* Drawing Invitational (auth, catalog), Univ Nebr, Omaha, 79. *Teaching:* Instr art, Metrop Tech Community Col, Omaha, 77-79; vis lectr lithography, Creighton Univ, Omaha, 79; assoc prof drawing, Univ Nebr, Omaha, 79-. *Awards:* Purchase Award, Appalachian Nat Drawing Competition, 79; Res Fel, Univ Nebr, 85; Purchase Award, Nat Drawing Exhib, Trenton State Col, 87; Visual Artists Fel Grant, Nat Endowment Arts, 87-88. *Bibliog:* The Picture Show, Nebr Educ TV doc, 85. *Media:* Intaglio, Lithography. *Publ:* Contribr, Colleagues: An Inter-Media Anthology of Artists, Pittore Euforico, 79; Another Normal Conception, Univ Ill, 80; An American Portfolio, Univ Ariz, 81. *Mailing Add:* 3033 S 107th St Omaha NE 68124-2435

DAY, HOLLIDAY T
CURATOR, CRITIC
b Nashville, Tenn, Dec 25, 36. *Study:* Wellesley Col, Mass, BA, 57; Univ Chicago, MA, 79. *Collection Arranged:* Siah Armajani, 80; Martin Puryear, 80; George Sugarman retrospective (auth, catalog), 81; Jennifer Bartlett, 82; Joyce Kozloff, 82; Elyn Zimmerman, 85; New Art of Italy (auth, catalog), 85; Art of the Fantastic: Latin Am 1920-1987, 87; Power: Its Myths & Mores in American Art 1961-1991 (auth, catalog), 91; Forefront: 23 exhibs; Poetry of Form: Richard Tuttle, 92; Felrath Hines, 95; Francesco Clemente: Indian Watercolors, 97; Kiki Smith, 99; Crossroads of American Sculpture: David Smith, Geo Rickey, John Chamberlain, Robert Indiana, William Wiley & Bruce Nauman (auth, catalog), Indpls Mus Art, 2000. *Pos:* Writer, New Art Examiner, Chicago, 76-79, contrib ed, 79; cur Am art, Joslyn Art Mus, Omaha, Nebr, 80-85; cur contemp art, Indpls Mus Art, 85-99 & sr cur contemp art, 99-2000. *Awards:* Wellesley Scholar, 56; Nat Endowment for the Arts critic's travel grant, 78-79; Am Mus Asn Merit Award, 81. *Bibliog:* Today's Art, The Indianapolis Register, Sec B, 2/97, 113. *Res:* Surfaces of David Smith's sculpture. *Publ:* History of Sculpture in the Midwest, Encyclopedia of the Midwest, Ohio State Univ, 2003; Biomimicry: The Art of Imitating Life, Nat Coun Educ for the Ceramic Arts, 2005. *Mailing Add:* 1207 Golden Hill Dr Indianapolis IN 46208

DAY, JANET S
ADMINISTRATOR
Pos: Sr vpres, Robert Morris Col, Ill; pres, Art Inst Ill, 98-. *Mailing Add:* Art Inst Atlanta 6600 Peachtree Dunwoody Rd 100 Embassy Row Atlanta GA 30328

DEADERICK, JOSEPH
PAINTER, EDUCATOR
b Memphis, Tenn, Jan 17, 30. *Study:* Univ Ga, BFA, 52; Cranbrook Acad Art, MFA, 54; Ind Univ, 58-59. *Work:* Kalamazoo Col, Mich; numerous pvt collections. *Comn:* Ceramic tile mural, Univ Wyo, Laramie, 68; faceted glass window, Lutheran Campus Ctr, Laramie, 68. *Exhib:* Sixth Midwest Biennial, Joslyn Art Mus, Omaha, Nebr, 60; Brooklyn Mus Biennial Print Show, 64; Drawing USA Traveling Show, St Paul, Minn, 66-68; one-man show, Colorado Springs Fine Arts Ctr, 67; Fedn Rocky Mountain States Traveling Show, 66-72; 20 yr retrospective, Univ Wyo Art Mus, 78. *Teaching:* Instr design, Ind Univ, Bloomington, 56-59; prof art, Univ Wyo, Laramie, 59-93, prof emer, 93-. *Awards:* First Place Award Design, Franklin Mint, 72; Nat Award Excellence in Design, Printing Indust Am Graphic Arts Competition, 72. *Media:* Multimedia. *Publ:* The Stage: A Series of Poetic Drawings by Joseph Deaderick, Univ Wyo, 78. *Mailing Add:* 24 Camino Costadino Santa Fe NM 87505-9140

DEAL, JOE
PHOTOGRAPHER, EDUCATOR
b Topeka, Kans, Aug 12, 47. *Study:* Kansas City Art Inst, BFA, 70; Univ NMex, MA, 74, MFA, 78, study with Van Deren Coke. *Work:* Mus Mod Art, NY; Mus Fine Arts, Houston; Int Mus Photog at George Eastman House, Rochester, NY; Ctr Creative Photog, Tucson; Oakland Mus; Mus Contemp Art, Los Angeles, J Paul Getty Trust. *Comn:* Photogs const mus, Mus Contemp Art, Los Angeles, 84-86; site photogs New Mus, J Paul Getty Trust, 84-97. *Exhib:* New Topographics: Photographs of a Man-Altered Landscape, Int Mus Photog at George Eastman House, Rochester, Princeton Univ & Otis Art Gallery, Los Angeles, 75-76; Contemp Am Photographs, Mus Fine Arts, Houston, 77; Am Images: Photog 1945-1980, Barbican Art Gallery, London, 85; Joe Deal: Men and Women, St Louis Art Mus, 91; Joe Deal: Southern California Photographs, 1976-1986, (exhib catalog), Los Angeles Munic Art Gallery, 92; Making Architecture, J Paul Getty Mus, Los Angeles, 97. *Pos:* Mem overview panel, Visual Arts Prog, Nat Endowment for the Arts, 91-92, chair, 92; bd dir, Col Art Asn. *Teaching:* Lectr photog, San Francisco Art Inst, summer, 76; prof art, Univ Calif, Riverside, 76-89; dean, Washington Univ, Sch Fine Art, St Louis, 89-. *Awards:* Nat Endowment Arts Photogr Fel, 77 & 80; Guggenheim Fel, 83. *Bibliog:* Carter Ratcliff (auth), Route 66 revisited: The new landscape photography, Art in Am, 1-2/76; Joe Deal: New Topographics, Northlight Five, Ariz State Univ, 77; Estelle Jussim & Elizabeth Lindquist-Cock (auths), Landscape as Photograph, Yale Univ, 85. *Mem:* Col Art Asn. *Mailing Add:* 93 Congdon St Providence RI 02906

DE AMARAL, OLGA
TAPESTRY ARTIST
b Bogota, Columbia, 1932. *Study:* Colegio Mayor De Cundinamarca, Bogota, Columbia, 51-52; Cranbrook Acad Art, Bloomfield Hills, Mich, 54-55. *Work:* Mus Mod Art, Metrop Mus Art, NY; Art Inst Chicago; Mus d'Art Mod de la Ville de Paris, France; Nat Mus Mod Art, Kyoto, Japan. *Comn:* Tapestry, Peachtree Plaza Hotel, Atlanta, Ga, 76; tapestry, Embarcadero Ctr, San Francisco, Calif, 79; tapestry, Miami Int Airport, Fla, 82; tapestry, Nations Bank Plaza, Atlanta, Ga, 93; tapestry, Judicial Scribeners Asn, Tokyo, Japan, 98. *Exhib:* 42nd Venice Biennial, Italy, 86; Cuatro Tiempos (with catalog), Mus de Arte Mod de Bogota, Columbia, 93; Latin Am Women Artists 1915-1995 Traveling Exhib (with catalog), Milwaukee Art Mus, Phoenix Art Mus, Denver Art Mus, Nat Mus Women Arts, Washington, DC & Ctr Fine Arts, Miami, 95-96; Nine Stelae & Other Landscapes Traveling Exhib (with catalog), Fresno Art Mus, Art Mus Americas, Wash, DC & Cleveland Inst Art, Ohio, 96-97; Restrospective 1965-1996 (with catalog), Mus de la Tapisserie Contemporaine, Angers, France, 97. *Awards:* Guggenheim Fel, 73. *Media:* Fiber. *Dealer:* Bellas Artes 653 Canyon Rd Santa Fe NM 87501. *Mailing Add:* PO Box 8010 Santa Fe NM 87504

DEAN, JAMES
PAINTER, CURATOR
b Fall River, Mass, Oct 14, 31. *Study:* Swain Sch Design, New Bedford, Mass. *Work:* Nat Aeronaut & Space Admin, Dept Interior & Smithsonian Inst, Washington, DC; MBNA Collection. *Comn:* Contemp Christmas stamps, US Postal Serv, 85 & 87. *Exhib:* Smithsonian Inst Traveling Exhib, 72-73; Corcoran Gallery Art, Washington, DC, 74; 107th Ann, Am Watercolor Soc, NY, 74; Washington Area Art, US Info Agency Worldwide Tour, 75-76; Nat Air & Space Mus, Washington, DC, 81-83; Foster Harmon Galleries Am Art, Sarasota, Fla, 83-90; Eyewitness to Apollo II, Nat Air & Space Mus, Washington, DC, 89; Artrain-Artistry in Space, 99-2002. *Collection Arranged:* Eyewitness to Space, Nat Gallery Art, Washington, DC, 65; The Artist and Space, Nat Gallery Art, Washington, DC, 69; Inaugural Exhibit, Nat Air & Space Mus, Washington, DC, 76; Apollo II-25th Anniversary, Nat Air & Space Mus, Washington, DC, 94. *Pos:* Dir fine arts prog, Nat Aeronaut & Space Admin, 61-74; cur art, Nat Air & Space Mus, 74-80. *Awards:* Cert Merit, Nat Acad Design, NY, Award of Excellence, Com Arts Mag, 76 & 77; Citation of Excellence, Am Inst Graphic Arts, 76-77. *Bibliog:* R J Williams (auth), James Dean painter of the past, Southern Living Mag, 6/73; Alice Laurich (auth), James Dean, Focus Mag, 9-10/75; Jack Perlmutter (auth), Duality of James Dean, Art Voices South, 7-8/79. *Mem:* Hereward Lester Cooke Found (bd trustees, 73-); Torpedo Factory Artists Asn (pres, 83-84). *Media:* Watercolor. *Publ:* Coauth, Eyewitness to Space, Abrams, 72, Artrain Catalog, 99; auth, Artist and space, Interdisciplinary Sci Rev; illusr, Liftoff, Grove, 88; auth, Paul Calle-An Artist's Journey, Millpond Press, 93; Splash 3, North Light, 94. *Dealer:* Torpedo Factory Art Center 105 N Union St Alexandria, VA. *Mailing Add:* 4804 King Richard Dr Annandale VA 22003

DEAN, KEVIN LEE
GALLERY DIRECTOR, EDUCATOR
b Evanston, Ill, Mar 19, 50. *Study:* Western Ill Univ, BA(art & art educ), 72, MA(studio art), 76, grad art his prog, 76-77. *Pos:* Exec dir, Galesburg Art Ctr, Ill, 77-79; arts ed, Longboat Observer, Longboat Key, Fla, 80-96; dir, Selby Gallery, Ringling Sch Art & Design, Sarasota, Fla, 94-. *Teaching:* Dist specialist art, Spoon River Dist, Fairview, Ill, 73-76; adj instr art & art hist, Carl Sandburg Col, Galesburg, Ill, 77-78; instr, Ringling Sch Art & Design, Sarasota, Fla, 85-. *Mem:* Am Asn Mus; Southeastern Mus Conf; Fla Art Mus Dir Asn. *Publ:* Auth, Syd Solomon (exhib catalog), Ringling Mus, Sarasota, Fla, 90; coauth, Painting in the 80's (video script), Bus Arts Inc, 91; auth, Arlene Erdich & the Attraction of Opposites, A Erdich, 92; intro to David Budd (exhib catalog), 96 & The Third Eye (exhib catalog), 96, Ringling Sch, Sarrasota, Fla, 96. *Mailing Add:* 901 Indian Beach Dr Sarasota FL 34234

DEAN, NAT
PAINTER, EDUCATOR
b Redwood City, Calif, 56. *Study:* Calif Inst Arts, 71-76; Cooper Union Advancement Sci Art, 75; San Francisco Art Inst, BFA, 77; Capricornus Sch Bookbinding & Restoration, 77-81, & other studies. *Comn:* "Box-Book", Jean Brown Archive, Tyringham, Mass, 82; ornament, White House, Washington, DC, 99-2000. *Exhib:*

Ruth Bachofner Gallery, Santa Monica, Calif, 90; Orange Co Ctr Contemp Art, Santa Ana, Calif, 90; Memorial/Remembrance, Ctr Gallery, Wolfson Campus, Miami-Dade Community Col, Fla, 91; Book as Art, Boca Raton Mus Art, Fla, 91; Gods, Devils & Clowns, Los Angeles Contemp Exhibs, Calif, 91; San Francisco/Science Fiction: SF/SF, San Francisco & NY, 1983; A Tribute to AIDS, Sarasota, Fla, 1994. *Collection Arranged:* Fukuoka Cult Ctr, Japan; San Francisco Mus Mod Art; Aratex ARA Art Prog, Calif; San Jose State Univ, Union Gallery, Calif; & many others. *Pos:* Owner/designer, Ruta Zinc/Fine Arts, San Francisco & Los Angeles, Calif, 78-90; dir/owner, Artist Tools & Resources Survival, Calif & Fla,78-, Calif & NMex, 96-; dir, career planning & placement & coop educ & internships, Inst Arts, Valencia, Calif, 86-89; dir, Ctr Career Servs, Ringling Sch Art & Design, Sarasota, Fla, 89-92; columnist, Art Maker Mag, 2001; designer/producer one-of-a-kind fashions, Ruta Zinc Handmade, Santa Fe, NMex, 2001-; expert witness various legal cases, Calif, NMex, NY, 1978-. *Teaching:* Instr artist survival skills & bus art, Col New Rochelle, 80, Sch Visual Arts, 81, San Francisco Art Inst, 81 & 82, State Univ NY, Potsdam, 82, Calif Col Arts & Crafts, 84-87 & Calif Inst Art, 88 & 89; guest lectr, Humbolt State Univ, 87 & 90, Calif Col Arts & Crafts, 88-93, Chapman Col, Orange, Calif, 89, Pac Northwest Col Art, Portland, Ore, 89, San Diego State Univ, Calif, 89 & Univ SFla, Tampa, 91; sem presenter, Los Angeles Convention Ctr, 88-93; guest lectr & artist, Calif Inst Arts, Valencia, 88-93; guest lectr & consult, Savannah Col Art & Design, 88 & 89; adj fac & lectr, Ringling Sch Art & Design, Sarasota, Fla, 89-92; project dir, A Dialogue Among Peers lectr series, 1996-04. *Awards:* Wash State Arts Comn Artist Resource Bank, 88; Fla Arts Coun Vis Artists Roster, 90-93; Ringling Sch Art & Design Prof Develop Grant, Sarasota, Fla, 90; and others. *Bibliog:* Revs, LA Times, Calif, 87 & 90; revs, LA Weekly, Calif, 88; interview, La Bete Mag, Miami, Fla, 92; and others. *Mem:* Col Art Asn; Women's Caucus Arts; Nat Asn Artist Orgns; Nat Artists Equity Asn; Am Coun Arts; and others. *Media:* Acrylic; Mixed Media, Fiber, Wood Panels. *Specialty:* Fine Arts. *Publ:* Contribr, Whitewalls: a magazine of writings by artists (visual piece), Whitewalls, 83; Visions (column), Ringling Sch Art & Design, 89-92; For the Working Artist, 89; The Visual Artist's Business & Legal Guide, Prentice Hall, 95; and many others. *Mailing Add:* 110 Sierra Azul Santa Fe NM 87507-0188

DE ANDINO, JEAN-PIERRE M
DEALER, COLLECTOR
b San Juan, PR, June 11, 46. *Study:* George Washington Univ; Univ NC. *Mem:* Am Soc Appraisers (accredited sr appraiser); Appraisers Assoc Am (cert sr appraiser). *Specialty:* Nineteenth and twentieth century masters and contemporary art. *Collection:* Unique images on paper. *Mailing Add:* De Andino Fine Arts 2450 Virginia Ave NW Washington DC 20037

DEANGELIS, JOSEPH ROCCO
SCULPTOR, PAINTER
b Providence, RI, Apr 22, 38. *Study:* RI Sch Design, BFA, 66; Syracuse Univ, NY, MFA, 68. *Work:* Art Gallery London, Ont; Art Gallery of Windsor, Ont, Can; Omer's Collection, Toronto, Ont; Univ Windsor, Ont, Can. *Comn:* Wood Sculpture of America's Symposium, City North Vancouver, British Columbia, 77; Fibreglass Wall Relief Sculpture, Ont Provincial bldg, Windsor, Ont, 78; Painted Wall Mural, Ciocaro Club, Windsor, Ont, 84-85; SIte Specific Concrete Sculpture, Chelton Corp, City of Toronto, Toronto, Can, 88; concrete and granite sculpture fountain, Rinterzo, Windsor Sculpture Garden, Ont, 97; painted relief sculpture, First Unitarian Church Olinda, Ruthven, Ont, 97; interactive sculpture, Snake Rattle and Roll, Child's Place, Windsor, Waterfront, Ont, 97; slate, granite and terrazzo sculpture fountain, Odette Sculpture Park, Windsor, Ont, 97; 13 foot bronze sculpture, 5th Ann Int Sculpture Symposium, Chanchun, China, 2001. *Exhib:* Ontario Now, traveling, 76; Spectrum Canada, Montreal Olympics, 76; London Art Gallery, Ont, 77; Canadian Place, Toronto, Ont, 77; Agnes Etherington Gallery, Kingston, Ont, 81; Visual Rhythms, Toronto Sculpture Garden, Ont, 84; New Canadian Sculpture, The Windsor Symposium, Art Gallery Windsor, 85; solo exhib, Sculpture, Chatham Cult Ctr, Ont, 86, Intentions of Colour, Ten Horses and an Inch Worm, Art Gallery Windsor, Ont, 96; 24 Canadians in New York City, Amos Enos Gallery, NY, 86; The Great White North, Staten Island Inst Scis, 88; Skulptur x 7, USA, Invitational Sculpture Exhib, Kulturforum-Meschengladbach, Ger, 91; Art For Cystic Fibrosis, Fogolar Club, Windsor, 96; RI Sch Design, 8th Ann Int Juried Exhib Woods Gerry Gallery, Providence, RI and the Boston Design Center, Mass, 96; Work From Italy, Galleria 3 Via Dei Albizi, Florence, 97; Art for All, Art Gallery Windsor, Ont, 97; Canadian Portraits, Artcite Gallery, Windsor, Ont, 97; Work/Site:15 Yrs at the Toronto Sculpture Garden, Art Gallery Ont, Toronto, Can, 97 (publication); Eye of Experience, BCE Place, Toronto, Can, 98; Duty Free, Exchange Exhib, Detroit Contemp Gallery, Mich, 99; New mems 2002 Part One, The Sculpture Soc Can, Can Sculpture of Can, Can Sculpture Ctr, Exchange Tower, Toronto, Can, 2002. *Teaching:* Lectr, Univ Mich, Ann Arbor, 68-69; assoc prof, Visual Art Dept, Univ Windsor, Ont, 77-; lectr, Sch Visual Arts, Univ Windsor, Ont, Can; prof emeritus, 70-. *Awards:* Sculpture Award, Art Gallery London, 75; Ont Arts Coun Grants, 77 & 84; 35th Ann Southwestern Ont Exhibs, Art Gallery Windsor, Can; 32nd Ann Western Ont Exhib, London Art Gallery, London, Ont, Can; 5th Ann Brant Open Jury Exhibitor's Art Gallery Bratford, Ont, Can. *Bibliog:* Ann Rosenberg (auth), Wood sculpture of the Americas, Capilano Review, No 12, 77; Arthur Perry (auth), Vancouver: Wood sculpture of the Americas, Art Mag, 10-11/77; David Quintner (auth), Angelic sculptural work suspends tactile senses, Windsor Star, 3/81. *Mem:* Visual Art Ont; Sculptors Soc Can; Mich Watercolor Soc Art Cite. *Media:* Miscellaneous Media. *Publ:* The Windsor Exhib, 5 Canadian Sculptors, Art Gallery of Windsor, Ont, 1985; Sculpture/Toronto An Illustrated Guide to Toronto's Historic and Contemporary Sculpture with area maps by June Ardiel, photos by Aleg Capon, 1990; Drawing/Collage, The Windsor Review J Arts, Univ Windsor, spring 97; Odette Sculpture Garden, Dept of Parks and Recereation, Windsor, Ont, 2002. *Mailing Add:* 1690 Front Rd La Salle PQ N9J 2B6 Canada

DE ARMOND, DALE B
PRINTMAKER, ILLUSTRATOR
b Bismark, NDak. *Study:* Study with Dannie Pierce, Carol Summers & Jules Heller. *Work:* Alaska State Mus; Anchorage Hist & Fine Arts Mus, Alaska Methodist Univ, Anchorage. *Exhib:* Charles & Emma Frye Art Mus, Seattle, Wash, 70; Alaska State Mus, Juneau, 75; Anchorage Hist & Fine Arts Mus, 77; Mus of Sci, Boston, 78. *Awards:* Purchase Award, Alaska Centennial, 67; First Prize Woodblock, All-Alaska Show, Exxon Corp, 75. *Bibliog:* Pat McCullough (auth), Alaskan Artist, Alaska J Hist & Art, 76; article, Am Artist, 4/82. *Media:* Woodblock, Wood Engraving. *Publ:* Auth, Juneau A Book of Woodcuts, 73, Raven, 75 & Dale De Armond, A First Book of Prints, 79, Northwest Publ; Berry Woman's Children, Greenwillow Bks, 85. *Dealer:* Rie Munoz Gallery 210 Ferry Way Juneau AK 99801. *Mailing Add:* 120 Katlian St Sitka AK 99835

DEARMOND, MEGAN
SCULPTOR
b Kansas City, Mo. *Study:* Univ Kans, BFA (sculpture & art history), 95; Univ Ariz, MFA, 99. *Exhib:* Biennial, Tucson Mus Art, Ariz, 97; Ignition, Mus Contemp Art, Tucson, Ariz, 98; Another Arizona, Ariz State Art Mus, Tempe, 98. *Pos:* tech specialist, Oakland Mus Calif, 2000-. *Teaching:* instr, Univ Ariz, Tucson, 98, 99. *Awards:* Fel, Tucson Pimar Arts Coun, 2000; Fel, Ariz Comn Arts, 2000; Grad Dean's Fel, Univ Ariz, 2000. *Bibliog:* Richard Nilson (auth), The jury is in, Ariz Repub, 3/98; Linda J. Barkman (auth), Emerging artists, Phoenix Home and Garden, 3/2000. *Media:* Metal

DEATS, MARGARET (MARGARET) DEATS BOTT
ART DEALER, WRITER
b Houston, Tex, May 27, 42. *Study:* Univ Houston; Univ St Thomas, Houston; Glassell Sch Art, Houston. *Collection Arranged:* Gulf Coast Invitational Sculpture Exhib, 76; Houston Festival Sculpture Invitational, 79; Lovett Inn, Houston, 89; HJ Bott's D-O-V 20th Anniversary exhib, 92. *Pos:* Fine Arts writer, Galveston Daily News, 71-75; owner-pres, Loft-on-Strand Gallery, 71-78; pvt dealer, 78-; bd mem, Artlies Mag, 93-96. *Bibliog:* Gay McFarland (auth), Living on The Strand, Sculptor & Wife Preserve Old Building, Houston Post, 5/73; Dancie Perugini (auth), Loft-on-Strand, Houston Town & Country Mag, 4/76. *Mem:* Galveston Co Cult Arts Coun (bd mem, 73-74). *Specialty:* Contemporary paintings, sculpture, conceptual art and process installations. *Publ:* Carol Gerhardt Photos, FOTOFEST 90 (catalog); The Abstract Expression: Houston Artists Martonette Borromeo & Jennie Couch, Mus & Art Mag, 1/93; Diverseworks celebrates ten years of exhibitions & performances, Mus & Arts Mag, 6/93; Luis Jiménez, ArtLies, 6-9/96; Paul Suttman, ArtLies, 10/12/96. *Mailing Add:* 4006 Barnes St Houston TX 77007

DEBARRY, CHRISTINA
PAINTER
b Lviv, Ukraine. *Study:* Newark Sch Fine Arts; NY Univ, BF (arts & art educ); Art Student League, NY. *Exhib:* Pastel Soc Am, ann exhib, 90-2004; Europastel Exhib Italy, Russia; X'ian Acad Fine Art, China; Du Pastel Exhib, France; Luminous Gallery, Taiwan; Salmagundi Club, non-mem exhib, 99-2003; Catherine Lorillard Wolfe Art Club, 2002. *Teaching:* instr, pastel painting in var workshops and demonstations, currently; instr, traveling workshops: China, Tex, Mich, Minn, NC, SC, Philadelphia, NY & NJ, as well as outside US; Can, Bermuda, France and Mex, formerly. *Awards:* Dianne B Bernhard Gold Medal Award, Allied Artists Am, Nat Arts Club, NYC; Gold Medal Pastel Award, Art Spirit Found, Audubon Artists, NYC; HB Holbein Award, Pastel Soc Am; Honoree, Art du Pastel en France, 2006. *Mem:* Pastel Soc Am (pres emer, 98-2001); Allied Artists Am (vpres, currently); Catharine Lorillard Wolfe Art Club; AAPL (fellow); Audubon Artists. *Media:* Pastels & Oils. *Interests:* Still Life, florals, animal portraits, landscapes. *Publ:* illustr, Best of Pastels, I & II, Floral Inspirations, Rockport Publ; auth, Basic Landscape, Stroking the Fires of Autumn, Joys of Summer, Artist's Mag; auth, Best of Floral Painting, North Light Books; auth, Contemporary Master Pastelists, Galerie Luminous, 94; illstr, Great Am ART WORKS, cover illus on box pastels. *Mailing Add:* 10 Harvale Dr Florham Park NJ 07932

DEBEERS, SUE
PHOTOGRAPHER
b Tarrytown, NY, Aug 9, 73. *Study:* Parson Sch Design, NY, BFA, 95; Columbia Univ, MFA, 98. *Work:* Working in Brooklyn, Brooklyn Mus, 2004; Whitney Biennial, Whitney Mus Am Art, 2004. *Exhib:* One-woman shows incl Heidi 2, Deitch Projs, NY, 2000, Photog/proj room: Ghost Stories Mag, Sandroni Rey, Los Angeles, 2001, Photog, Kunstlerhaus Bethanian, Berlin, 2002, Hans & Grete, Kunst Werke, Berlin, 2003, The Dark Hearts, Sandroni Rey at Statements, Basel, Miami, 2004; group shows at Imaginary Beings, Exit Art, NY, 95, Terra Bomba, 96, 26 Positions, Miriam & Ira D Wallach Gallery, NY, 97, Scope 3, Artist's Space, NY, 98, The Searchers, 99, Death Race, Threadwaxing Space, NY, 2000, Fresh: The Altoids Curiously Strong Collection, Int Monster League, Derek Eller Gallery, NY, 2003, SCREAM, Anton Kern Gallery, NY, 2004; SCREAM, Anton Kern Gallery, NY, 2004. *Pos:* Artist-in-residence Wexner Ctr, Ohio, 99. *Awards:* Franklin Furnace Fund for Performance Art, 98-99; Joan Sovern Award Excellence in Sculpture, 99; Philip Morris Emerging Artist Prize, AM Acad Berlin, 2001. *Mailing Add:* c/o Whitney Mus Am Art 945 Madison Ave New York NY 10021

DEBELLEVUE, LUCKY
SCULPTOR
b Lafayette, La, 57. *Study:* Univ Soutwestern La, BFA, 1983; Univ New Orleans, MFA, 1987. *Work:* Mus Contemp Art, Chicago, 1999, Dalamas Mus, Falun, Sweden, 1986, Brooklyn Mus Art, 1997, Mus D'hondt-Dhaenens, Deurl, Belgium, 2000. *Exhib:* Solo exhib at, Feature Gallery, 1997, Realismus Studio, Berlin, 1997; group

exhib at, Contemp Arts Ctr, New Orleans, 1986, Four Walls, Brooklyn, 1992, Artists Space, New York City, 1992, The Drawing Ctr, New York City, 1993, Universidad de Buenos Aires, 1995, Gasworks, London, 1997, Cornerhouse, Manchester, Eng, 1997, D'Amelio Terras Gallery, New York City, 1998, Galerie Emmanuel Perrotin, Paris, France, 1998, Stephen Friedman Gallery, London, 1999, Grand Arts, Kansas City, 1999, The Neth Gallery Art, Rotterdam, 1999, Galeria d'Arte Moderna, Bologna, Italy, 2002, Wexner Galleries, Columbus, Ohio, 2004; others. *Awards:* Joseph H Hazen Rome Prize Fel in Visual Arts, Am Acad in Rome, 2004-05. *Mem:* Col Art Asn. *Mailing Add:* Feature Inc 530 W 25th St New York NY 10001

DE BLASI, ANTHONY ARMANDO
PAINTER, EDUCATOR
b Alcamo, Sicily, Italy, Jan 1, 33; US citizen. *Study:* Art Students League, with Sidney Dickenson, Univ RI, BA; Ind Univ, Bloomington, with William Bailey, James McGarrell, Henry Hope & Albert Elsen, MFA. *Work:* Ulrich Mus of Art, Wichita, Kans; Detroit Art Inst; Ind Univ, Bloomington; Best Products Co Inc, Richmond, Va; Greenfield Energy Corp, Los Angeles, Calif. *Exhib:* Midyear Show Contemp Am Art, Butler Inst, Youngstown, Ohio, 67; Mus Mod Art (Penthouse), NY, 68; one-man shows, Spectrum Gallery, NY, 68, 69, 71 & 73, Detroit Art Inst, 72, Razor Gallery, NY, 75 & 77 & Louis K Meisel Gallery, NY, 85, 87, 88, 89, 91, 93 & 95, Fine Arts Gallery, SUNY, Oneonta, NY, 98; Hokin Kaufman Gallery, Chicago, Ill, 88; group shows, Hokin Gallery, Bay Harbor Islands, Fla, 90, Jaffe Baker Blau Gallery, Boca Raton, Fla, 95, Dorothy Blau Gallery, Bay Harbor Island, Fla, 97; invitational, Abstract Image Makers, Bradley Univ, Peoria, Ill, 2001; and others. *Teaching:* Chmn & instr, Washington & Jefferson Col, 63-66; prof painting & drawing, Mich State Univ, 66-86; instr, Sch Visual Arts, 88-90. *Awards:* Louis Comfort Tiffany Found Grant, 66-67; Founders Purchase Prize, Detroit Art Inst, 70; Individual Artist Grant, Mich Coun Arts, 83; NY Found for the Arts Fel in painting, 2006. *Bibliog:* Emily Wasserman (auth), rev, In: Artforum, 4/68; Atirnomis (auth), rev, In: Arts Mag, 12-1/70; Gene Baro (auth), The 33rd Corcoran Biennial (catalog), 73; and others. *Mem:* Art Students League. *Media:* Acrylic. *Mailing Add:* 376 Broome St 3 Flr New York NY 10013

DEBONNE, JEANNETTE
PAINTER, PRINTMAKER
b Los Angeles, Calif, Dec 2, 37. *Study:* Univ Calif, Los Angeles, studied with William Brice, John Paul Jones & Jan Stussy, BA, 59. *Work:* Mich State Univ, Lansing; Mitsubishi Corp, Cambridge, Mass; Pepsi Cola Corp, Seattle; Xerox Corp, Honolulu; Mercedes Benz N Am, Chicago, Ill; and others. *Comn:* Oil painting, Bixby Development Corp, Los Angeles, 86; oil painting, Morris Bergreen Coll, Greenwich, Conn, 91; oil painting, Church of St Paul in the Desert, Palm Springs, Calif, 95; Mich State Univ, Lansing, Mich. *Exhib:* Mus Art Auction, Palm Springs Desert Mus, Calif, 95; Blue Mountain Small Works Invitational, Blue Mountain Gallery, NY, 95; solo exhib, Valerie Miller Fine Art, Palm Desert, Calif, 95 & 97, Miranda Galleries, Laguna Beach, Calif, 98, Reflections from the Roof of the World, Learsi Gallery, Palm Desert, Calif, 2000; Mystic Quest, Santuario de Guadalupe, Santa Fe, NMex, 96; Myths and Miracles, Miranda Gallery, Laguna Beach, Calif, 96; St Paul's Cathedral, San Diego, Calif, 97; Palm Desert Gallery, Calif, 98; Galerie Hyna, Munich, Ger, 98. *Teaching:* Instr drawing, Village Ctr for Arts, Palm Springs, Calif, 88-90. *Awards:* East African Wildlife Soc First Prize in Painting, Whaletail Int, Nairobi, Kenya, 91. *Bibliog:* Douglas Deaver (auth), Jeannette DeBonne: Paintings, Fact Publ, 94; Judith Gross (auth), Painter finds her rhythm, The Desert Sun, 7/2/95. *Media:* Oil. *Mailing Add:* 653 Commercial Rd Suite 3 Palm Springs CA 92262

DE BOSCHNEK, CHRIS (CHRISTIAN) CHARLES
PAINTER, PRINTMAKER
b Cannes, France, Apr 24, 47; US citizen. *Study:* Cleveland Art Inst; Akron Univ. *Work:* Weiskoff, Silver & Co, NY; Newark Mus, NJ; Kelly, Drye & Warren, Stamford, Conn; US Steel Co, Pittsburgh, Pa; Sherman & Sterling, NY. *Exhib:* One-man shows, Akron Art Inst, Ohio, 71, Kathryn Markel Gallery, NY, 82, Queens Mus, NY, 88 & Elizabeth McDonald Gallery, NY, 88; Tibor de Nagy Gallery, NY, 73; OK Harris Gallery, NY, 79; Lerner Heller Gallery, NY, 82; Edith C Blum Art Ctr, Annandale on Hudson, 84; Hallwalls, Buffalo, NY, 85; Richard Green Gallery, NY, 86; and others. *Awards:* Yaddo Fel, 80. *Publ:* Articles in Cover Mag, spring 80 & winter 81, Arts Mag, 3/82, 9/86 & 2/88 & Artnews Mag, 4/82. *Mailing Add:* 90 S Fourth St Brooklyn NY 11211-5505

DE BRETTEVILLE, SHEILA LEVRANT
DESIGNER, EDUCATOR
b Brooklyn, NY, Nov 4, 40. *Study:* Barnard Col, Columbia Univ, BA(art hist); Yale Sch Art & Archit, MFA(graphic design). *Hon Degrees:* Calif Col Arts & Crafts, hon doctorate, 91; Moore Col Art, hon doctorate, 95. *Work:* Victoria & Albert Mus, London; Design Collection, Mus Mod Art, NY; Pub Libr, Los Angeles & NY. *Comn:* 40 under 40 show, Archit League, NY, 65; spec issue design, Art Soc Wis, 70; Frederick Weisman Found Art, 85; Pub Art Proj: Biddy Mason: Time & Place, Los Angeles, 90; Path of Stars, New Haven, 94. *Exhib:* Communications Graphics, Am Inst Graphics Art, 72; 5e Biennale des Arts Graphiques, Brno Czech, 72; Color, Am Inst Graphic Arts, Whitney Mus, 74; Poster from the Vietnam Yrs, NY, 75; At Home, Long Beach Mus Art, 84; Let's Play House, Bernice Steinbaum Gallery, 86; Cooper Hewitt Mus Design Biennial, 2000. *Pos:* Typographer, Yale Univ Press, New Haven, Conn, 65-68; designer, Olivetti, Milan, Italy, 68-69; designer, Calif Inst Arts, 69-74; co-founder & pres, Woman's Bldg Community Gallery, 73-; juror, Nat Endowment Arts-Civil Serv Comn, 75; co-founder, ed & designer, Chrysalis Mag, 77-; design dir, Los Angeles Times, 78-81; chmn, Dept of Commun, Design & Illus, Otis Art Inst of Parsons Sch of Design, Los Angeles, 81-. *Teaching:* Dir inst & graphic design dept, Calif Inst Arts, 70-74; chmn, dept commun design, Otis/Parsons Univ; lectr at var cols & univs; dir grad studies graphic design, Yale Univ Sch Art. *Awards:* Grand Award Excellence, Soc Publ Designers, 71; Communication Graphics Awards, 72 & five Gold Medals, Calif 2 Exhib, Am Inst Graphic Arts; IBM Fel, Int Design Conf, Aspen, 74; Gold Medal Award, Nat Design Legend, 2005. *Bibliog:* Gilles de Bure (auth), Right on Sheila, Creations Recherches Esthetiques Europeenes, 73; articles, Commun Arts, 6/83 & Eye, 93; Steven Harris, Deborah Bank (ed), Architecture of the Every Day, Princeton Archit Press, 97. *Mem:* Am Inst Graphic Arts; Internat Alliance Theatrical Stage Employees; Col Art Asn. *Media:* Steel, Brass, Concrete and stone. *Publ:* Ed, Calif Inst Arts: Prologue to a community, Vol 7 No 2 & A reexamination of some aspects of the design arts from the perspective of the women designer, Arts Soc, 74; auth, A reevaluation of design, Icographic 6, 73; Habitability, In: Proc of the Calif Chap Am Inst Archit, 74; Feminist Design, Space & Soc, 6/83; Lure of the Local, 98. *Mailing Add:* 146 Deepwood Dr Hamden CT 06517-3452

DEBROSKY, CHRISTINE A
PAINTER
b Kingston, NY, Dec 10, 51. *Study:* Albert Handell, pastel workshops, 80; Woodstock Sch Art (Art Students League), 90; Wolf Kahn workshop, 93. *Work:* Key Corp Collection, Albany, NY; Standard & Poor's, NY; Renssalaer Polytechnic Inst, Troy, NY; Pfizer Chemical Corp; McGraw Hill Inc, NY. *Comn:* Residence mural project, Anderson Sch, Staatsburg, NY, 82; pastel landscape/diptych, Key Corp/Greenhut Galleries, Albany, NY, 92; Kingston Hosp, NY. *Exhib:* Pastel Soc Am, Harmon/Meek Gallery & Gallery on Venetian Bay, Naples, Fla, 92; Pastel Soc Am Ann, Nat Arts Club, NY, 93, 94, 99 & 2002; Pastel Soc West Coast Int, Roseville, Calif, 98, 2000, 2001 & 2003; Europastel, Italy & St Petersburg; Southern Vt Arts Ctr, 2002 & 2005; Soc Am Impressionists, 2006. *Teaching:* Pastel instr, Woodstock Sch Art, 98-; aquamedia instr, Barnett Art Ctr, 98-; instr, Led painting workshops, Tuscany & Venice, Italy, Burgundy, France, 2000-. *Awards:* Scott Award/landscape, Barbara & Gary Scott, Pastel Soc Am Ann, 9/91; Pastel Soc award, W Coast, 98, 2001 & 2003; distinguished pastellist award, Pastel Soc, W Coast, 2003. *Bibliog:* Landscape Inspirations, Rockport Publ, 91; Raymond J Steiner (auth), Christine Debrosky at the Woodstock Artists Asn, Art Times, 5/94; Janet Cassidy (auth), Combining Watercolor and Pastel for Exciting Results, Pastel Jour, 1-2/2002. *Mem:* Degas Pastel Soc; Woodstock Artists Asn; signature mem Pastel Soc Am; Pastel Soc West Coast; L'Ant du Pastel, France & USA, 2006. *Media:* Pastel, Oil. *Dealer:* Fouontainside Fine Art Wilmington NC; The Crane Collection Cape Ann MA; Walker Korngluth Fairlawn NJ; Windham Fine Arts Windham, NY. *Mailing Add:* 141 Mountain View Ave Tillson NY 12486

DE CAMPOS, NUNO
PAINTER, INSTRUCTOR
b Porto, Portugal, Nov 20, 69; Portuguese citizen. *Study:* Univ Porto, Portugal, licensiatura, 94; Sch Mus Fine Arts, Tufts Univ, Boston, MFA, 99. *Exhib:* Solo shows at Clifford Smith Gallery, Boston, 1999, 2001, 2003, LFL Gallery, NY, 2003; Collection of Arthur Goldberg, Danforth Mus, Framingham, Mass, 2000; Art Cetera, Mills Gallery, Boston Ctr for Arts, 2000; Realistic Means, The Drawing Ctr, NY, 2002; She's Come Undone, Artemis, Greenberg Van Doren Gallery, NY, 2004; Private Lives, Westby Gallery, Rowan Univ, NJ, 2004; Extended Painting, Prague Biennale, 2005; The Outwin Boochever Portrait Competition Exhib, Nat Portrait Gallery, Washington, DC, 2006. *Collection Arranged:* Fogg Art Mus, Harvard Univ. *Teaching:* lectr painting, Mass Col Art, Boston, 2000; instr painting, Art in NE Summer Workshop, Bennington Col, Vt, 2000; instr painting & drawing, Sch Mus Fine Arts, Boston, 2001. *Awards:* Calouste Culbenkian Found Scholar, 96-99; Marie Walsh Sharpe Art Found Award, 2000; Grant, Mass Cult Coun, 2000; NY Found Arts, Artists Fellow Painting, 2006. *Bibliog:* Francine Koslow Miller (auth), Talentos para Onoyo Milenio, Elle Mag, Portugal, 1/2000, Art Forum, 2/2000, Harper's Mag, 1/2001. *Mem:* Inst Contemp Art; Col Art Asn. *Dealer:* Clifford Smith Gallery 450 Harrison Ave Fl 3 Boston MA 02130. *Mailing Add:* c/o NY Found for Arts 14th Floor 155 Avenues of the Americas New York NY 10013-1507

DECAPRIO, ALICE
PAINTER, PHOTOGRAPHER
b Marshall, Mich, Feb 10, 19. *Study:* Mich State Univ, AB; Northwestern Univ, MA;. *Work:* Ocean Co Col, NJ; US Navy; RCA Corp Hq, NY; Chatham Savings & Loan; Ringling Mus, Sarasota, Fla. *Comn:* Drawings, Ringling Mus, Sarasota, Fla, 78 & 80; US Navy-NY Harbor Oper Sail activities, 76-77; Navy Women at Work, USS Vulcan, 79; brochure, Albaz Corp, Riyadh, Saudi Arabia, 81; and others. *Exhib:* One-person shows, Nat Arts Club, 77, S Vt Art Ctr, 77 & Sarasota Centennial Comt, Fla, 86; AT&T Corp Hq, NJ, 80; Plymouth Harbor, Women's Res Ctr (photog), Sarasota, 91; Unity Gallery, Sarasota, 96. *Teaching:* Instr watercolor, Madison-Chatham Adult Sch, 68-76, instr outdoor sketching, 70-81, Creative Learning Workshop, Rockport, Mass, 77-82; instr sketching, Hilton Leech Studio Workshops & Traveling Two-Arts Workshops, 85-90; workshops, France & Portugal, 93-98. *Awards:* Naval Art Coop & Liaison Comt Bronze Medal for Achievement in Watercolor, Salmagundi Club, 78; Best in Show, Visual Arts Ctr, Sarasota, Fla, 97; Best in Show, Longboat Key Art Ctr, 98. *Mem:* Fla Watercolor Soc; NJ Watercolor Soc; Nat League Am Pen Women; Women's Caucus for Art. *Media:* Watercolor; Photography. *Dealer:* Art Uptown 1367 Main St Sarasota FL 34236. *Mailing Add:* 3963 Country View Dr Sarasota FL 34233

DECARAVA, ROY RUDOLPH
PHOTOGRAPHER, EDUCATOR
b New York, NY, Dec 9, 19. *Study:* Cooper Union Art Sch, 38-40; RI Sch Design, Hon PhD, 85; Md Inst Col Art, Hon PhD(art), 86. *Work:* Metrop Mus Art, Mus Mod Art, NY; Mus Fine Arts, Houston; Ctr Creative Photog. *Comn:* The Nation's Capitol in Photographs, Corcoran Gallery Art, 76; American Images, Am Tel & Tel, NY, 78. *Exhib:* Always the Young Strangers, Mus Mod Art, NY, 53; The Family of Man, Mus

Mod Art, NY, 53; The Photographers Eye, Mus Mod Art, NY, 64; Photog in the Fine Arts, Metrop Mus Art, NY, 64; Thru Black Eyes, Studio Mus Harlem, 69; Photog in Am, Whitney Mus Am Art, 74; solo exhibs, Mus Fine Arts, Houston, 75, Clarence Kennedy Gallery, Boston, 82 & Ziikha Gallery, Wesleyan Univ; Mirrors & Windows, Mus Mod Art, NY, 78; Silver Sensibilities, Newhouse Gallery, Staten Island, 80; The Sound I Saw, Studio Mus Harlem, 83. *Teaching:* Dir photog, Kamoinge Workshop, New York, 63-66; adj instr, Cooper Union Art Sch, 69-72; prof, Hunter Col, 75-; app distinguished prof, Art, 88. *Awards:* Guggenheim Fel Photog, 52-53; Outstanding Achievements in Photography, Int Black Photogr, 79; Spec Citation Photojournalism, Am Soc Mag Photogr, 83. *Bibliog:* A D Coleman (auth), Roy DeCarava, Popular Photog, 70; Elton Fax (auth), Seventeen Black Artists, Dodd, Mead Co, 73; Pat Leighton (auth), Roy DeCarava, Photograph, Vol 1, No 3, 77. *Mem:* Friends Photog (mem bd trustees, 82-); Photo Resource Ctr. *Publ:* Coauth (with Langston Hughes), The Sweet Flypaper of Life, Simon & Schuster, 55, republ, Howard Univ Press. *Dealer:* Witkin Gallery 415 W Broadway New York NY 10012. *Mailing Add:* The DeCarava Arch 81 Halsey St Brooklyn NY 11216-1902

DE CASTRO, LORRAINE
SCULPTOR, CERAMIST
b Rio Piedras, PR, July 19, 46. *Study:* Univ PR, BA, 72, studied welding with John Balossi, 77; New York Univ, grad studies, 82-84. *Work:* Museo de Arte de Ponce, PR. *Exhib:* Clay and Fire: Seven Ceramists, Inst Cult, San Juan, 86; Growing Beyond, Women Artists from PR, Orgn Am States, Washington, DC, Mus del Barrio, NY & Caribe Gallery, PR, 87-88; Ceramics From PR, EuroAm Gallery, Caracas, Venezuela, 90; Women Artists: Protagonists of the 80's, Museo delas Casas Reales, Dominican Republic, Mus Contemp Art, San Juan, PR, 90; Weaving Images, Normandie Gallery, San Juan, PR, 91, 25 Anniversary: Art League of San Juan, PR, 92; and others. *Teaching:* Prof ceramics, Art Students League of San Juan, 80-; prof, Univ PR, 89-. *Bibliog:* Charlotte Speight (auth), Images in Clay Sculpture, 83. *Mem:* Mujeres Artistas de PR, Inc; Sculptors Asn PR. *Media:* Clay. *Dealer:* Botello Gallery Cristo St Old San Juan PR 00936. *Mailing Add:* G-16 Granada St Vistamar Marina Carolina PR 00983

DE CHAMPLAIN, VERA CHOPAK
PAINTER, PRINTMAKER
b Ger; US citizen. *Study:* Art Students League; spec studies with Edwin Dickinson. *Work:* Butler Inst Am Art, Youngstown, Ohio; Slater Mus, Norwich, Conn; Ga Mus Art, Athens; Evansville Mus Art & Sci, Ind; Smithsonian Inst Arch Am Art, Washington; NY Univ. *Comn:* Portrait, Liederkranz Found, NY, 79 & 91; pvt portraits & landscapes comns. *Exhib:* Metrop Mus Art, NY, 79; B Altman Gallery, NY, 82; Consulate Gen, Fed Republic of Ger, 86; Traveling exhib, 88-89; Broome St Gallery, Soho, NY, 91-93; Avery Fisher Hall, Cork Gallery, 94; Cornell Univ Med Libr, NY, 95, 96 & 98. *Teaching:* Art dir & instr oil painting, Emanu-El Ctr, New York, 68-. *Awards:* Twilight & Onteora Club Award, Haines Falls, NY, 65; US Investor Award, 69; First Prize-World Award, Acad Ital, Parma, 85, 87. *Bibliog:* Samuel M La Corte (auth), Creative images, Clifton Leader, 70. *Mem:* Fel Royal Soc Arts; Artists Equity Asn New York; Kappa Pi; Nat Soc Arts & Lett (art chmn Empire State, 69-); Art Students League; and others. *Media:* Oil, Watercolor; All. *Publ:* Auth, article, ArtSpeak, 3/86; article, Marketletter from Rosenthal & Co, 3/24/86. *Mailing Add:* 1801 E 26th St Brooklyn NY 11229-2437

DECHAR, PETER
PAINTER
b New York, NY, Apr 19, 42. *Work:* Mus Mod Art & Whitney Mus Am Art, NY; Larry Aldrich Mus, Conn; Walker Art Ctr, Chicago; Fiberglass Tower Art Collection. *Exhib:* Highlights from the 1967 Season, Larry Aldrich Mus, Conn, 67; Contemp Painting & Sculpture, Krannert Art Mus, 67; Whitney Mus Am Art Ann, NY, 67 & 69; one-man shows, Cordier & Ekstrom Gallery, NY, 67, 69 & 75; Twentieth Century Art from the Rockefeller Collection, Mus Mod Art, NY, 69. *Media:* Oil. *Mailing Add:* 455 Carroll St Brooklyn NY 11215

DECIL, STELLA (DEL) W
PAINTER, INSTRUCTOR
b Indianapolis, Ind, Apr 26, 21. *Study:* Indianapolis Acad Com Art, 38-39; John Heron Art Inst, 39-40. *Work:* Pueblo Grande Mus, Trevor Browne High Sch, Phoenix; The Velerans Admin Medical Ctr, Prescott, Ariz; Detroit Inst Arts, Mich; Banks of Rio Grande, Las Cruces, NMex; Mayo Ctr for Womens Health, Scottsdale, Ariz; Bank Vt, Great Western Bank & Trust, Phoenix; Columbia Med Ctr, Phoenix; Bench Friedlander, Cleve. *Exhib:* Phoenix Art Mus, Four Corners Biennial; 49th Ann Hoosier Salon, Firebird Festival, Scottsdale, Ariz; Ann FACET Woman Art Nat, Taos, NMex; Past, Present, Future Southwest Contemp, Yavapai Col; In Celebration of Women, Mayo Center, Scottsdale, Ariz; Images of Faith, Artistic Images Gallery, Prescott, Ariz, 2005. *Collection Arranged:* Mature Eye, Prescott Fine Arts Asn, 96-00. *Pos:* pres, Scottsdale Artists League, 73-74, Ariz Watercolor Asn, 80; art dir, Frank R Jeleff Co, Wash DC, 50, Wm H Block Co, Indianapolis, Ind, 52-62, Diamonds, Phoenix, Ariz, 62-66; curator, Mature Eye, Prescott Fine Arts Asn, 96-2001. *Teaching:* instr painting & drawing, Phoenix Art Mus, 76-78, Phoenix Parks & Recreation Dept, 80's, Workshops Art Groups, Ariz, NMex, 80's through 2005. *Awards:* Celebrate the Desert, City of Mesa, Ariz, 85; Advertising Woman of the Year, Indianapolis Ad Club, 58; 1st Mixed Media, Yavapai Co Women in the Arts, 88; 1st Mixed, Southwestern Contemp, 89; 2nd Oil, Yavapai Women in the Arts, 90; 1st Watercolor, 2nd Oil, Prescott Fine Arts Asn, 2002. *Bibliog:* Phoenix Republic, Indianapolis News & Star, Ariz Living, Phoenix Mag. *Mem:* Northern Ariz Watercolor Soc; Ariz Artists Guild; Ariz Watercolor Asn (pres, 80-81). *Media:* Oil, Watercolor. *Publ:* contribr, PV Artist Del Decil, Prescott Courier, 97, Decil Collection on Display, Sonoran News, 97 & Arizona Senior World Art Profile, Ariz Senior World, 4/2000. *Mailing Add:* 9460 East Towago Dr Prescott Valley AZ 86314-7140

DECKERT, CLINTON A
PAINTER
b Chicopee, Mass, May 17, 59. *Study:* self taught. *Work:* Univ Conn, Storrs; Naugatuck Valley Community Col, Conn; Greater Hartford Art Coun, Conn; Northend Sr Ctr, Hartford, Conn; New Britain Rock Cats Baseball Stadium, Conn. *Comn:* Cow Parade, Hartford Mag, Conn, 2003; Wall mural, Univ Conn, West Hartford, 2004. *Exhib:* I Dream & I was Dreaming, Artworks Gallery, Hartford, Conn, 1997; Surrealist and the Poet, Univ New Haven, Conn, 2000; Gala, Wadsworth Atheneum, Hartford, Conn, 2000; Brave Destiny Int, Williamsburg Art & Hist Ctr, Brooklyn, NY, 2003; Surreal Mindscapes, Stevens Gallery, Univ Conn, Storrs, Conn, 2004; New Britain, Mus Am Art, Juried Show, Conn, 2004; Warner Theatre Atrium Gallery, Torrington, Conn, 2004; Pump House Gallery, Hartford, Conn, 2004; Winter Blues, Artworks Gallery, Hartford, Conn, 2005; Polonaise Gallery, Woodstock, Vt, 2005; Lotus Fine Art & Design, Woodstock, NY, 2005; White Heat, White Space Gallery, New Haven, Conn, 2006; Oil Drum Art Exhib, New England Carousel Mus, Bristol, Conn, 2006; Heartbeat, Aldrich Contemp Art Mus, Ridgefield, Conn, 2006. *Pos:* Pres, Artworks Gallery, Hartford Conn, 97-99, pres, 91-92; pres, In home Art Serv, Southington, Conn, 95-2000. *Teaching:* lect, Conn Art Educ Asn Fall Conference, Farmington Marriott, 2004; lect, Manchester Art League & Cheshire Art League, 2005; lect, Manchester Art Asn, 2006. *Awards:* Individual Artist Fel Grant, Grater Hartford Arts Coun, 99 & 2002; Peoples Choice Award, Artwell Gallery; Best in Oils, Southinghton Arts Asn, 2003; Bank N Award, Southington Arts Asn, 2004; Aesthetic First Prize, Oil Drum Art, Artspace, Hartford, Conn, 2005. *Bibliog:* Steve Starger (auth), Clinton Deckert at Art Works, Art N Eng, 1997; Pat Seremet (auth), Art Works Works, Java - Hartford Courant, 2002; Will Steigerwald (auth), The Walls have Eyes and Ears, Art Is Mag, 2005; Pamela Morello (auth), Painter's award winning work balances art and function, Southington Citizen, 2005; Nancy L Rodgers (auth), Altered Awareness, Art Is Mag, 2005; Feature, Cloning the drama, Southington's inventive exhibition, Kool-Record Journal, 2006. *Mem:* Artworks GAllery, Hartford, Conn (pres, 91-92, 97-99, vpres, 93-96, prog chmn 2000-03, mem chmn 2004); New Britain Mus Am Art, Conn; Wadsworth Atheneum, Hartford, Conn; Real Arts Way, Hartford, Conn. *Media:* Oil on Canvas, Acrylic. *Dealer:* J Whitney Gallery 405 Queen St Southington Conn 06489; White Space Gallery 1020 Chapel St 2nd Floor New Haven Conn 06510; Lotus Fine Art & Design Inc 33 Rock City Rd Woodstock NY 12498; Polonaise Gallery 15 Central St Woodstock Vt 05091. *Mailing Add:* 55 Blossom Way Southington CT 06489-1878

DE CREEFT, LORRIE J See Goulet, Lorrie

DECTER, BETTY EVA
PAINTER, SCULPTOR, WRITER
b Birmingham, Ala, 1927. *Study:* Self taught & Otis Art Inst. *Comn:* Painting, comn by Mr & Mrs Norman, Pauma Valley, Calif, 86; portrait, Carolyn Tapp, 95-96. *Exhib:* Solo exhibs, Crocker Bank, Beverly Hills, Calif, 80, Roger Morrison Gallery, Los Angeles, Calif, 85, Bonwit Tellers, Beverly Hills, Calif, 86, Ivey's Dept Store, Gainesville, Fla, 86, Brand Libr Art Gallery, Glendale, Calif, 88, Riverside Co Mus, 89 & San Francis Gallery, Crossroads Sch Arts & Scis, Santa Monica, 92; Artists Equity Bienale Exhib, Brand Libr Art Gallery, Glendale, Calif, 87; Loyola Law Sch, SCalif Women's Caucus Art, 88; 16th Ann Multi Media Juried Art Show, Creative Arts Ctr Gallery, Burbank, Calif, 91; Laguna Mus Art, 97; Finegood Art Gallery, Woodland Hills, Calif, 98; The Grove, Pacific Grove, Calif, 99. *Teaching:* instr painting & collage, workshops; instr, workshops in studio, teaching collage and monotypes, currently. *Awards:* Cash Award, Assocs Brand Libr Award, Creative Arts Ctr Gallery, Burbank, Calif, 91; Bronze Award, Calif Discovery, 94. *Bibliog:* Women's Caucus Art, Feisty Women (video), 2/89; Mary Alice Cline (auth), Colors & Cultures Weigh in at a Ton of Kimonos, Press Enterprise, 4/16/89; Rita Townsend & Ann Perkins (coauths), Bitter Fruit, Hunter Publ Co, 92; and others. *Mem:* Women's Caucus Art; Artists Equity; NY Artists Equity; Monotypes on Etching Press. *Media:* Acrylic, Mixed Media on Canvas. *Interests:* Founder: Carpal Tunnel, Publishing Co, 2005. *Publ:* Contribr, Contemporary Women Artists Calendar & Datebook, Cedco Publs, 92, 93 & 94; Mutiny and Mainstream, Midmarch Press, 92; Contribr, Luz bilingual mag, 93. *Mailing Add:* 5412 W Washington Blvd Los Angeles CA 90016

DE CUNTO, JOHN GIOVANNI See Giovanni

DE DONATO, LOUIS
PAINTER, INSTRUCTOR
b New York, NY, Aug 29, 34. *Study:* Art Students League, with Frank Reilly, 55-61. *Work:* Abe Sharp Found, Maine; Navy Art Combat & Laison, Washington. *Exhib:* Allied Artists Am Ann Exhib, Nat Arts Club, NY, 81 & 93; Soc Animal Artists Exhib, Acad Natural Sci, Philadelphia, 82 & Topeka, Kans, 83; Am Artists Prof League, NY, 93; SSA Exhib, Bennington, 94; Salmagundi Club, Ann Exhib, 94. *Teaching:* Instr life drawing & painting, Salmagundi Club, New York, 72-. *Awards:* Isabel Steinschneider Mem Award, Hudson Valley Art Asn, 95; Don Donaldson Award, Salmagundi Club 95 & Antonio Cirino Award, 96; Jane Impastato Award, Salmagundi Club, 94; Pres Award, Am Artists Prof League, Grand Nat Exhib, 96. *Mem:* Salmagundi Club (bd dir, 70-90); Allied Artists Am; Soc Animal Artists (bd dir, 76-86); Am Artists Prof League; Hudson Valley Artists Asn; and others. *Media:* Oil. *Publ:* Illusr, Nat Inst Art & Design, Northwest Sch, 64. *Dealer:* Husberg Fine Arts Gallery Scottsdale AZ; Gregory Gallery Darien CT. *Mailing Add:* 400 E 77th St Apt 105 New York NY 10021-2303

DEEM, GEORGE
PAINTER
b Vincennes, Ind, Aug 18, 32. *Study:* Sch Art Inst Chicago, BFA, 58, with Paul Wieghardt & Boris Margo. *Work:* Indianapolis Mus Art, Ind; Stiftung Ludwig, Aachen, Ger; Evansville Mus Arts & Sci, Ind; Mus Mod Art, San Francisco; Russian State Mus, St Petersburg, Russia. *Comn:* Painting, Nutter, McClennen & Fish, Boston,

88; painting, Paul, Weiss, Rifkind, Wharton & Garrison, NY, 90; MGM Mirage Resorts, Las Vegas, Nev, 98. *Exhib:* one-man show, Indianapolis Mus Art, 74-75, Witte Mem Mus, San Antonio, Tex, 75, Evansville Mus Arts & Sci, Ind, 79 & 93, Harn Mus Art, Univ Fla, 93, Polk Mus Art, Lakeland, Fla, 94, Ind State Mus, 94 & Wichita Ctr Arts, Kans, 94, Pavel Zoubok, Inc, NY, 02, Nancy Hoffman Gallery, NY, 00, Collaboration George Deem and Peter Angelo Simon, Evansville Mus Arts & Sci, Ind, 01, Pavel Zoubok, 2004, New Britain Mus Am Art, Conn, 2005; Whitney Mus Am Art, NY, 78; Wilhelm-Lehmbruck Mus, Duisburg, WGer, 78; Pa Acad Fine Arts, Philadelphia, 81; Allentown Art Mus, Pa; Ft Wayne Mus Art, Ind, 84; Chicago Int Art Expo, 85-86; Nassau Co Mus Art, NY, 94, 2000. *Pos:* Artist-in-residence, Evansville Mus Arts & Sci, 79; secy exec comt, MacDowell Colony Fels 82-86; vis artist, Ill State Univ, Normal, 82; vis artist, Branson Sch, Calif, 95. *Teaching:* Instr, Sch Visual Arts, NY, 65-66; instr painting, Leicester Polytech, Eng, 66-67 & Univ Pa, Philadelphia, 67-68. *Bibliog:* video profile, Evansville Mus Art, Ind, 93; Art School, Thames & Hudson Ltd, London, 93 & NY, 2005 (rev ed); Reagan Upshaw (auth), George Deem at Nancy Hoffman, Art Am Mag, 7/2000; Edward Leffingwell (auth), George Deem at Pavel Zonbok, Art Am Mag, 7/2002. *Media:* Oil on Canvas; Mixed. *Publ:* Auth, AANABABCAC, Sun & Moon, fall 79; A Painting For Babies, Benzene, fall 81; Extra Genre, White Walls, summer 81; Actual Size, Benzene, fall-winter 83-84; Drawing, White Walls, spring 86; auth, How to Paint a Vermeer, A Painter's History of Art, Thames & Hudson, New York & London, 2004. *Dealer:* Pavel Zoubok, Inc, 533 W 23rd St, New York, NY 10011. *Mailing Add:* 10 W 18th St New York NY 10011-4617

DE FAZIO, JOHN
SCULPTOR
b Reading, Pa, Jan 23, 59. *Study:* Philadelphia Col Art, BFA, 81; San Francisco Art Inst, MFA, 84. *Work:* MTV Network, NY; Honolulu Art Mus, Hawaii; Banff Arts Ctr, Can; Shigeraki Mus, Japan; Kohler Art Ctr, Sheboygan, Wis; Wexner Art Ctr, Columbus, Ohio; The Mint Mus, Charlotte, NC; The Univ Art Mus, Berkeley, Calif; Am Craft Mus, NY. *Comn:* Designer, MTV Conf Rm, Time Sq, NY, 95; designer, Am Craft Mus Visionaries Award, 2000. *Exhib:* One man shows, Fun Gallery West, San Francisco, Calif, 85, B-Side Gallery, NY, 86, Ohio State Univ, Gallery Fine Arts, Columbus, 87, La Luz De Jesus Gallery, Los Angeles, Calif, 88 & Garth Clark Gallery, NY, 92; NCECA Exhib, Contemp Crafts Gallery, Portland, Ore, 88 & Philadelphia Col Art, Pa, 92; Against Nature, Los Angeles Contemp Exhibs, Calif, 89; Serious Fun Festival, Lincoln Ctr, NY, 90; Post Pop and Beyond, Bess Cutler Gallery, Los Angeles, Calif, 91; Off the Wall, Am Craft Mus, NY, 92; 12 San Angelo Ceramic National, San Angelo Mus, Tex, 98; Subversive Souvenirs, Contemp Arts Collective, Las Vegas, 98; Scripps Ann, Calif, 99; Paradise 8, Exit Art, NY, 99; and others; Luster, Henry Urbach Gallery, NY, 99; The Clay Studio, Phila, 2000; The Figure, Dolphin Gallery, Kansas City, 2000; Superobjects, Lost Vegas Gallery, Los Vegas, 2000; Allan Chasnoff Collection, The Min Mus, Charlotte, NC, 2000; World Ceramic Exposition, Korea, 2001; Chelsea Rising, Contemp Arts Ctr, New Orleans, 2001; Confrontational Clay, Am Craft Mus, NY, 2001; Blondies and Brownies, Aktionsforum Praterinsel, Munich, Ger, 2001. *Teaching:* Ohio State Univ, Columbus, 87; Univ Nev, Las Vegas, 98; artist in residence, Mont State Univ, Bozeman, 89, Marymount Manhattan Col, NY, 2001; vis prof San Francisco Art Inst, 2005-. *Awards:* Change Inc, Visual Arts Grant, 90; Empire State Craft Allience, Artist Grant, 91; NY Found Arts Fel, 91; Nat Endowment Arts, 86; Art Matters Incorp, Visual Artists Fel, 86, 87, 89. *Bibliog:* Gretchen Atkins (auth), Tulip vases at Garth Clark Gallery, Ceramics: Art & Perception, No 26, 96; Ezra Shales (auth), An unprudish moment, Am Ceramics, 4/99; Ken Johnson (auth), Confrontational Clay, NY Times, 3/5/2001. *Media:* Clay, Mixed Media. *Publ:* Illus, Stardum Stories by Dave Hickey, Art by John DeFazio, Artspace Books, 99; David Rubin (ed), Chelsea Rising, catalog, CAC, New Orleans, 2001; Allen Chasno ff Collection Catalogue, Mary F Douglas, The Min Mus, Charlotte, NC, 2001. *Mailing Add:* San Francisco Art Inst 800 Chestnut St San Francisco CA 94107

DEFAZIO, TERESA GALLIGAN
PAINTER, GALLERY DIRECTOR
b Philadelphia, Pa, May 5, 41. *Study:* Moore Col Art, with Paulette VanRoekins, Dolya Goutman, Ranulph Bye & Leonard Nelson, BFA, 63; Acad Fine Arts, with Louis Sloan, Seymour Remenick & Glen Rudderow, 89-90. *Work:* Rosemont Collection, Radnor Twp Sch Dist, Wayne, Pa. *Exhib:* Ann Exhib Small Oils, Philadelphia Sketch Club, 91 & 92; Ann Juried Exhib, The Plastic Club, Philadelphia, 91 & 92. *Collection Arranged:* Northern Images (Inuit & NW Coast Nat Am Art), Rehoboth Art League, Del, 98; Invitational Masters Exhib, Salisbury State Univ, Md, 99. *Pos:* Mgr, Newman Galleries, Bryn Mawr, Pa, 74-77; dir, Newman Galleries, Philadelphia & Bryn Mawr, 85-90; mgr, Art Space Gallery, Gladwyne, Pa, 90-95, regional coordr, currently. *Mem:* Fel Pa Acad Fine Arts; Philadelphia Art Dealers Asn (secy 87-89); Moore Col Art Alumnae Asn; Rehoboth Art League; Sussex Arts Coun. *Media:* Oil. *Publ:* Coauth & ed, Moore Col Art Alumnae J, 70s; Kenneth R Nunamaker, 1890-1957, 84, Joe Brown-A Retrospective Exhibition, 87, John Folinsbee-Following His Own Course, Newman Galleries, 90

DE FOREST, ROY DEAN
PAINTER, SCULPTOR
b North Platte, Nebr, Feb 11, 30. *Study:* Yakima Jr Col, 48-50; Calif Sch Fine Arts, 50-52; San Francisco State Col, BA, 53, MA, 58. *Work:* San Francisco Mus Art; Art Inst Chicago; Joslyn Art Mus, Omaha, Nebr; Philadelphia Mus Art; Whitney Mus Am Art, NY; plus others. *Exhib:* Ann Watercolor, Drawing and Print Exhib, San Francisco Mus Art, 57; Winter Invitational, Calif Palace Legion of Honor, San Francisco, 62, 63 & 64; 67th Am Exhib (with catalog), Art Inst Chicago, Ill, 64; Imagadventure, Walker Art Ctr, Minneapolis, 65; solo exhibs, Inst Contemp Art, Boston, 77 & 78, Marilyn Butler Gallery, Santa Fe, NMex, 89, Frumkin/Adams Gallery, NY, 90 & 93, Fuller Gross Gallery, San Francisco, 89 & 90, Stanford Mus Art, Calif, 90, John Beggruen Gallery, San Francisco, 92 & George Adams Gallery, 97, Rpay DeForest & Gaylen Hanson: Paris Gibson Square Mus, Mont, Yellowstone Art Mus, Mont, Mus of Northwest Art, Wash, Shneider Mus of Art, Ore, Plains Art Mus, NDak, 98-2001, George Adams Gallery, NY, 2002; Am Drawings 1963-1971 (with catalog), Whitney Mus Am Art, NY, 73; 1973 Biennial Exhib Contemp Am Art (with catalog), Whitney Mus Am Art, NY, 73; Extraordinary Realities, Whitney Mus Am Art, 73; retrospective (with catalog), San Francisco Mus Mod Art, 74, travelled to Ft Worth Art Ctr, Tex, Utah Mus Fine Arts, Salt Lake City & Whitney Mus Am Art, NY, 74-75; Painting and Sculpture in California: The Modern Era (with catalog), San Francisco Mus Art, 76; Huntsville Mus Art, Ala, 77; Decade in Review: Selections from the Seventies, Whitney Mus Am Art, NY, 79; Am Drawings in Black and White: 1970-80, Brooklyn Mus, NY, 80; The Figurative Tradition and the Whitney Mus Am Art (with catalog), Whitney Mus Am Art, NY, 80; Twentieth Century Art: Highlights of the Permanent Collection, Whitney Mus Am Art, NY, 81; 100 New Acquisitions, Prints, Drawings and Photographs, Brooklyn Mus, NY, 81; Drawings by Painters, Boston Mus Fine Arts, Mass, 82; A Private Vision: Contemp Art from the Graham Gund Collection (with catalog), Boston Mus Fine Arts, Mass, 82; Large Scale Drawings, Frumkin/Adams Gallery, NY, 92; 40th Anniversary Exhib: Selections from the Richard Brown Baker Collection (with catalog), Frumkin/Adams Gallery, NY, 92; Masters of Mischief II, Frumkin/Adams Gallery, NY, 94; X-Sightings, Anderson Gallery, Buffalo, NY, 94; A Singular Visoin: Prints from Landfall Press, Mus Mod Art, NY, 97; Frogs and Dogs: Roy De Forest and David Gilhooly, Ariz State Univ, Tempe, 2000; The Lighter Side of Bay Area Figuration, Kemper Mus Contemp Art, Kansas City, Mo & San Jose Mus Art, 2000; Mobilia Gallery, Cambridge, Mass, 2001-02; and many others. *Pos:* Dir, Larsen Gallery, Yakima Jr Col, 58-60. *Teaching:* Instr, Calif Col Arts & Craft, Oakland, 64-65; from asst prof to assoc prof, Univ Calif, Davis, 65-82, prof, 85-. *Awards:* Nealie Sullivan Award, San Francisco Art Asn, 64; Purchase Prize, La Jolla Art Mus, 65; Nat Endowment Arts Grant, 72. *Bibliog:* Thomas Albright (auth), Wildest of funk art, San Francisco Chronicle, 2/6/69; Charles Johnson (auth), The new symbolism, Sacramento Bee, 4/13/69; Grace Glueck (auth), Of beasts and humans: Some contemporary views, NY Times, 11/14/82; Helen L Kohen (auth), An affair with the land, Miami Herald, 1/17/86. *Mem:* San Francisco Art Asn. *Dealer:* George Adams Gallery 41 W 57th St New York NY 10019. *Mailing Add:* PO Box 47 Port Costa CA 94569

DE GALBERT, ANTOINE
ART FOUNDATION ADMIN
b 55. *Study:* political sci. *Pos:* Corp mgt positions; owner Galerie Antoine de Galbert, Grenoble, France, formerly; founder & pres la maison rouge-found, antoine de galbert, Paris, 2004-. *Awards:* Named one of Top 200 Collectors, ARTnews magazine, 2004, 2006. *Collection:* Contemporary and primative art. *Mailing Add:* la maison rouge 10 blvd de la bastille Paris 75012 France

DEGENEVIEVE, BARBARA
PHOTOGRAPHER, EDUCATOR
b Wilkes-Barre, Pa, May 21, 47. *Study:* Wilkes Col, Wilkes-Barre, Pa, BFA, 69; Southern Conn State Col, New Haven, MS(art educ), 73; Univ NMex, Albuquerque, studied with Betty Hahn, Sandi Fellman, Van Deren Coke and Beaumont Newhall, MFA(photog, teaching asst), 80. *Work:* Univ NMex Fine Arts Mus, Albuquerque; Seattle Mus Art; State of Ill Art Acquistion Collection, Chicago & Ellensburg; Calif Inst Arts, Valencia; Tokyo Metrop Mus Photog. *Exhib:* Personal/Political: Sexuality Self Defined, Gallery 2 & Photog: Inventions & Innovations, Art Inst Chicago, 90; Parents, Mus Contemp Art, Dayton, Ohio, 92; solo exhibs, Etherton/Stern Gallery, Tucson, Ariz, 92, Univ Colo, Denver, 93, Eye Gallery, San Francisco, 94 & Gallery 954, Chicago, 95; Flesh Fetish, Fragment: A Romance, Film in the Cities, Minneapolis, Minn, 93; What She Wants Traveling Exhib, United Kingdom, 93-95; Mirror Mirror, San Jose Inst Contemp Art, 94; Art About Life: Contemp Am Cult, Ind Univ Fine Arts Gallery, Bloomington, 95; Monitors: Reviewing Cult Expression, Art Inst Chicago, 95; Ill Photog in the 90's, Mus Contemp Photog, Chicago, 96; Art in Chicago, 1945-1995, Mus Contemp Art, Chicago, 96; Pink, Jean Albano Gallery, Chicago, 97; Discomfort: Contemp Women Photogrs, Santa Barbara Contemp Arts Forum, Calif, 97; Who Do You Think You Are, Tom Blackman Fine Arts, Chicago, 98; The Grotesqueness of Desire, Inside ART, Chicago, 99. *Collection Arranged:* Women in the Southwest (auth, catalog), 78 & 79; Intimate Statements, 79; Work by Women, 81; Altered States (auth, catalog), 82; Articulated Disparities: Renegotiating Masculinity, Gallery 1, San Jose State Univ, 91; Reimaging Masculinity, Works Gallery, San Jose, Calif, 91; No More Heroes: Unveiling Masculinity (auth, catalog), San Francisco Camerawork Gallery, 91. *Pos:* Cur, Reimaging Masculinity, Works Gallery, San Jose, Calif, 91; bd dir & exhib comt, San Francisco Camerawork Gallery, 90-94; chairperson, Dept Photog, Sch Art Inst Chicago, 95-; bd dir, Edelman Workshops, Chicago, 97-. *Teaching:* Asst prof, Univ Ill, Champaign, 80-89, chairperson photog, 83- 89; vis artist, Sch Art Inst Chicago, 85-86 & prof, 94-; assoc prof, Calif State Univ, San Jose, 89-94, prof, 94-; vis artist, San Francisco Art Inst, 90-93. *Awards:* Ill Arts Coun Artists Fel, 87; Visual Artists Fel, Nat Endowment Arts, 88; Art Matters Found Fel, 96. *Bibliog:* PhotoVision, Barcelona, Spain, No 23, 93; On Arts Edge: Barbara DeGenevieve at odds with the NEA: Chicago Tribune, 8/18/94; Sex, Fear & the NEA: An Interview with Barbara DeGenevieve F Newsmag, 10/94. *Mem:* Soc Photog Educ. *Media:* Photography, Video. *Publ:* Ed, No More Heroes, SF Camerawork Quart, summer/fall 91; Masculinity & its Discontents, San Francisco Camerwork Quarterly, summer/fall, 91; Letting Us Look: Scandolous Genders, San Francisco Camerawork Magazine, fall 94; My Mother's Body, Herotica 4, 96. *Dealer:* Vernon Ezell Gallery 954 954 W Washington Chicago IL 60607. *Mailing Add:* Sch Art Inst Chicago Photog Dept 280 S Columbus Dr Chicago IL 60603

DEGETTE, ANDREA M
FILMAKER, DIRECTOR
b Denver, Colo, Sept 6, 62. *Study:* Univ Colo, Boulder, 80-82; Tisch Sch Art, NY Univ, BFA, 84; Duke Univ, 98-. *Work:* Duke Univ Med Ctr; Ctr Doc Studies, Durham, NC; Mint Mus Art. *Comn:* For the Sense of It, Fayetteville & Cumberland Co Arts Comn, NC, 95; Art of Community (video), Chapel Hill Pub Arts Comn, 97; NC Dir Artists, NC Arts Coun, Raleigh, 97; Wanted X-Cheerleaders, comn by Kim Irwin, Raleigh, 97; Video in the Classroom, State of NC, 98. *Exhib:* A Better Heaven, Bug Theatre, Denver, Colo, 96; Sisters from Apex, Midnight Express Theatre, Santa Monica, Calif, 97 & Mint Mus Art, Charlotte, NC, 97-98. *Pos:* Video artist in creative arts for various pub schs, 87-; video facilitator & producer, Cary Youth Proj, Page Walker Art Ctr, NC, 96-98; Adj prof, Piedmont Community Col, NC, 95-97. *Awards:* Best Dramatic Short Film, NC Film & Video Festival, 96; Emerging Artist Grant, 96; NC Arts Coun Fel, 97. *Mem:* Women Make Movies; NC Media Arts Alliance. *Publ:* Dir & filmmaker, films & videos, viewed Univ NC & NC Pub TV, 95-98. *Mailing Add:* 407 W King St Hillsborough NC 27278

DEGIULIO, LUCAS
ARTIST
b Dearborn, Mich, 77. *Study:* Minneapolis Col Art & Design, BFA (mixed media), 2000. *Exhib:* Midway Contemp Art, Minneapolis, 2003; 6th Ann Monster Drawing Rally, Southern Exposure, San Francisco, 2006; Day for Night, Whitney Biennial, 2006; New Langton Arts, San Francisco, 2006. *Mailing Add:* Southern Exposure 2901 Mission St San Francisco CA 94110

DEGN, KATHERINE KAPLAN
ART DEALER
b New York, NY. *Study:* Haverford Col, Pa, BA, 86. *Pos:* Dir, Kraushaar Galleries, NY, 91-. *Specialty:* Twentieth century & Contemporary American art. *Publ:* Coauth, Kraushaar Galleries catalogs. *Mailing Add:* c/o Kraushaar Galleries 724 Fifth Ave New York NY 10019

DE GOGORZA, PATRICIA (GAHAGAN)
SCULPTOR, PRINTMAKER
b Detroit, Mich, Mar 17, 36. *Study:* Smith Col, BA, 58; S W Hayter's Atelier 17, Paris, France, 58-60; Goddard Col, Plainfield, Vt, MA, 75. *Work:* Collection Ville de Paris (Louvre), France; Victoria & Albert Mus, London, Eng; Boston Mus Fine Arts; Provincetown Art Asn Mus, Mass; Bard Col, Annandale-on-Hudson, NY. *Comn:* Tobias & the Angel (granite), Kerson, at Worcester, Vt, 87; Sun/Moon Cycle (granite), Johnson State Col, Vt, 89; Riverbirds (large marble sculpture), Marble St Sculpture Park, W Rutland, 91; Pegasus (marble), 92, Merman & Dolphin (marble), 93, Mermaid (marble), 93, Burlington, Vt Bike Path; Tree of Life (wood polychrome), Pavilion Bldg, Montpelier, Vt, 95; cell/drum fountain, Guatamalan Green Marble, J Thompson, Morristown, VT; Alcyone (marble), T. Coates Rodney Co, NY. *Exhib:* Five Sculptors, Putney Sch, Vt, 93; Stone Sculpture Group, No Bias Gallery, North Bennington, Vt, Wood Art Gallery, Montpelier, Vt & Castleton State Col, Vt, 93 & 97; Southern Vt Art Ctr, Manchester, 93-97; Helen Day Art Ctr, Stowe, Vt, 94-97, 98-2004; West Branch Sculpture Garden, Stowe, Vt, 94-98; Manifest Poetry, Stone Sculpture Exhib, Northfield, Vt, 98; Vt Arts Coun Sculpture Garden, Montpelier, Vt, 2005-2007; solo exhib, Julian Scott Gallery, Johnston State Col, Vt, 2005, Ox Bow Gallery, 2005. *Pos:* Bd mem, Printmaking Workshop, NY, 70-74, Vt Coun Arts, 89-92 & Carving Studio, WRutland, Va, 90-94. *Teaching:* Bard Col, Annandale on Hudson, NY, 66-71; Goddard Col, Planfield, Vt, 73-81; Univ Vt, Burlington, 81; Vt Col, Montpelier, 88-93; vis artist, Carving Studio, W Rutland, Vt, 88-03; instr, Vt Clay Studio, 94-97; sculpture dept, Johnson State Col, 96; instr sculpture workshop, Akaroa, New Zealand, 99, 03, 04 & 05; instr, VSC, 2001-,02 & 03; Johnson St MFA Prog, Vt, 2006. *Awards:* First Prize Sculpture, Norwich Ann, Vt, 78 & 86; First Prize, All Vt Juried Show, Bundy Mus, Waitsfield, Vt, 82. *Bibliog:* V Watson-Jones (auth), Contemporary Women Sculptors, Oryx Press, Phoenix, Ariz, 85; Jason Kornick (auth), Creating a Life of Art, 3-5, Vt Maturity. *Mem:* Soc Am Graphic Artists; Provincetown Art Asn; Vt Women's Caucus Art; Vt Coun Arts; found Art Resource Asn. *Media:* Wood, Stone; Color Etching, Copper. *Interests:* Violinist, Vermont Philharmonic, Montpelier Chamber Orchestra. *Dealer:* Clarke Gallery Stowe VT. *Mailing Add:* 1580 Dog Pond Rd East Calais VT 05650

DE GROAT, DIANE
ILLUSTRATOR, DESIGNER, WRITER
b Newton, NJ, May 24, 47. *Study:* Pratt Inst, 65-69, BFA. *Comn:* Children's Book Council. *Exhib:* Soc Illusr Ann Nat Exhib, NY, 72 & 75; Insides, 74 & Ann Bk Show, 77, Am Inst Graphic Arts, NY; Poster USA/74, Art Dir Club, 74 & 85; Master Eagle Gallery, NY, 81, 83-85; Southeast Ohio Arts Ctr, 90; Kimberly Gallery, NY, 90; Michelson Gallery, Amherst, Mass, 96-; Original Art, Soc Illustrators, 2000. *Collection Arranged:* DeGrummond Collection. *Pos:* Designer & art dir, Holt, Rinehart & Winston, NY, 69-72. *Awards:* Ark Diamond Primary Award, 98-99; NC Childrens Book Award, 98. *Mem:* Soc Children's Bk Writers; Author's Guild. *Media:* Watercolor, digital. *Publ:* Little Rabbit's Loose Tooth, Crown, 75; Dr Ruth Talks to Kids, Macmillan, 93; auth/illusr, Roses are Pink, Your Feet Really Stink, 97 & Trick or Treat, Smell My Feet, Harper Collins, 98; and 100 other titles. *Dealer:* Michelson Gallery Northampton Mass. *Mailing Add:* 134 Flat Hills Rd Amherst MA 01002

DE GUATEMALA, JOYCE BUSH VOURVOULIAS
SCULPTOR
b Mexico City, Mex, Feb 25, 1938; Guatemalan citizen. *Study:* Univ Mex, 58; Univ Wis, 59; Silpakorn Univ, 60-62. *Work:* Fed Reserve Bank Pa, Philadelphia; Mus Mod Art Mex City, Chapultepec/Mexico City, Mex; Orgn Am States & Mus Mod Art Latin Am, Washington; Nat Mus Hist & Fine Arts, Escuela Nac De Bellas Artes & Guatemalan Chamber Indust, Guatemala City; Open Air Sculpture Symposium & the World Invitational Open Air Sculpture Exhib commemorating the 24th Summer Olympic Games, Olympic Park, Seoul, Korea. *Comn:* Nat Fine Arts Sch of Guatemala, Guatemala City, 75; OAS & Mus Mod Art Latin Am, Washington, 77; Exmibal-El Estor, Exmibal, Guatemala, 77; Kensington Town House Project, Redevelopment Authority of Philadelphia, Pa, 81; Elkins Park Free Lib, Pa, 85. *Exhib:* Guggenheim Mus/Olympiad of Art, Seoul, Korea, 88; solo exhibs, Medicine Wheel, 90, Marian Locks Gallery, Philadelphia, 91, 14 Sculpturs Gallery, Soho, NY, 92, Estela Shapiro Gallery, Mexico City, Mex, 92, Philadelphia Mus Art, Pa, 92 & Barbara Gillman Gallery, Miami Beach, 94 & 97; Gallery Artists, Estela Shapiro Gallery, Mexico City, Mex, 92; Books as Art, Barbara Gillman Gallery, Miami Beach, Fla & New World Sch Arts, Miami, Fla, 93; Metro-Dade Art in Pub Places, Brickell Ave, Miami, Fla, 93; Three Latin Am Artists, Barbara Gillman Gallery, 94; Centro Nac Expos, Madrid, 97; Contemp Artists Mus, Americano, Madrid, Spain, 97; State Mus Pa, 98. *Pos:* Vpres, Asociacion Tikal, 68-73; dir, Fine Art Comt, Patronato de Bellas Artes, 72-75; bd dir, Brandy Wine Work Shop, Philadelphia, Pa. *Awards:* Hon Mention for Sculpture Certamen Permanente Centro Americano, Guatemala; Miguel Gracia Granados Medal, Guatemala City, Guatemala, 76; VLI Corp Fel, Djerrasi Found Artist-in-Residence Grant, Woodside, Calif, 85 & 94. *Bibliog:* Deborah Victoria Curtis (auth), Visual Literacy, 85; Virginia, Watson-Jones (auth), Contemporary American Women Sculptors, Oryx Press, 86; Gallery Hyundai (ed), Olympic Sculpture Park Guide, Seoul Olympic Organizing Comt, 88; Ante Glibota (ed), Olympiad Art Catalogue, Seoul Olympic Organizing Comt, 88. *Mem:* Roy Soc Brit Sculptors, London; Asn Tikal; Int Sculpture Ctr, Washington, DC. *Media:* Stainless Steel, Wood. *Dealer:* Barbara Gillman Gallery The Sterling Bldg 939 Lincoln Rd, Miami Beach, FL 33139. *Mailing Add:* 320 Fairview Rd Glenmoore PA 19343

DE GUZMAN, EVELYN LOPEZ
PAINTER, PRINTMAKER
b New York, NY, June 14, 47. *Study:* City Univ New York, BA, 70; Hunter Col, Grad Sch, MA, 74; Pratt Inst; Parsons Sch Design. *Work:* Museo del Barrio & Bronx Mus, NY; Citibank Corp, NY; Museo de Ponce, PR; Mus Contemp Hispanic Art, NY; US Am Art Collection. *Exhib:* Puerto Rican Artists, Bronx Mus, NY, 81; Mus Contemp Hispanic Art, NY, 84 & 85; Project Am, Villa Taverna (traveling worldwide), NY, Washington, DC; Latin Roots, Nat Coun La Raza, Washington, DC, 90; Journeys, Martin Luther King Libr, Washington, DC, 92; Origin of Am States, Washington, DC. *Teaching:* Instr, high sch & elem syst. *Bibliog:* Grace Glueck (auth), Art: Puerto Rican show in the Bronx, New York Times, 1/26/79; Elaine Wechsler (auth), Space: The inside, the outside, Artspeak, 11/81; Juan Bujan (auth), La Geometria Dinamica de Evelyn Lopez de Guzman, La Voz, 12/3/81. *Mem:* Women Arts; Women's Caucus Art; Asn Artist Run Galleries; Brooklyn Arts Cult Asn Inc. *Media:* Acrylic, Paste; Mixed Media. *Publ:* Contribr, New York Art Yearbook, Noyes Art Books, 75-; Puerto Rico: Its people, its artists, Lightsource, 77. *Dealer:* Noho Gallery 168 Mercer St New York NY 10012; MOCHA 584 Broadway New York NY 10012. *Mailing Add:* Two Hamilton Ct Sterling VA 20165-5625

DEGUZMAN, NICOLE
DIRECTOR
b Sioux City, Iowa, Dec 16, 77. *Study:* U Calif, Santa Barbara, BA, 03. *Work:* UCSB Women's Ctr Art Gallery, Santa Barbara; UCSB Univ Art Mus. *Collection Arranged:* Women Expanding their Borders, multi-media, 02; Three Women, solo-exhib, 02; The Power of Women, multi-media. *Mem:* Univ Calif Art Historians Club, pres, 02-. *Publ:* Charlotte Bocheler, Sensual Women, Santa Barbara News Press, 01. *Mailing Add:* Univ Calif Women's Center Art Gallery Bldg 434 Santa Barbara CA 93106

DE HEUSCH, LUCIO
PAINTER
b Sherbrooke, Que, 1946. *Study:* Univ Que Montreal & Ecole des Beaux-Arts Montreal, Que, 66-69. *Work:* Muse d'Art Contemporain, Mus des Beaux-Arts de Montreal, Univ Que, Montreal, PQ; Mus de Que; Calif Col Arts & Crafts; Can Coun Art Bank; Ministry of External Affairs, Ottawa, Ont. *Exhib:* Solo exhibs, Musee d'Art Contemporain, Montreal, Que, 75, Galerie Graff, Montreal, Que, 85, 88, 91 & 92, Olga Korper Gallery, Toronto, Ont, 85, 87, 92 & 96, Ayot-de Heusch, Galerie Champlain, Universite Bishop, Lennoxville, Que, 87, Recent Paintings, Olga Korper Gallery, Toronto, 90, Art 23 '92, Basel, Switz, 92 & Centre D'Exposition des Governeurs, Sorel, Que, 93; Art 16, Bale, Switz, 85; L'Art Pense, Galerie d'Art de l'Univ de Sherbrooke, Quebec, 85 & traveling throughout Canada; Ouevres Charnieres, Galerie Graff, Montreal, 86; Graff: 20 Ans d'Affiches, Place des Arts, Montreal, 86; Parti Pris Plenture, Galerie UQAM, Montreal, Que, 93, Leslleux Incertains, 95 & Ayot-L'esplegie, Hommage, 96. *Awards:* Research Grant, Can Arts Coun, 74, 75 & 77; Ministry of Cult Affairs, Que Govt, 75 & 77; Materials Assts Grants, Can Arts Coun, 81 & 84; Accessibilite Grant, 85, Bourse du Que, 85, Que Govt. *Bibliog:* Articles, La Presse, Montreal, 84, PEI, 85; articles, Le Devoir, Montreal, 10/5/85, 1/24/86 & 1/25/86; John Bentley May (auth), article, Globe & Mail, 12/17/87. *Mailing Add:* c/o Olga Korper Gallery 17 Morros Ave Toronto ON M6R 2H9 Canada

DE KANSKY, IGOR
PAINTER, SCULPTOR
b Nice, France, May 19, 26. *Study:* Ecole Nationale des Arts Appliques, dipl, 45; Ecole des Beaux Arts, Univ Paris, 46; Academie de la Grand Chaumiere, with Othon Friez, 46. *Comn:* bas relief wood, Orthopaedic Hosp, Los Angeles, 82; bas relief wood, Claremont McKenna Col, Calif, 84; City of Pasadena, 97; painting and wood carved doors, Shrine for Virgin of Guadalupe, Pasadena, 2000-01; several large paintings, Private Collector, San Diego, Calif, 2003. *Exhib:* Calif Design Show,

Pasadena Art Mus, 62, 65 & 68; Otis Art Inst, Los Angeles, 65; Valley House Gallery, Dallas, 67; one-man show, Woodbury Univ, Burbank, Calif, 89; retrospective, Woodbury Univ, 91. *Pos:* Guest Speaker, Plato Soc, Univ Calif Los Angeles, 96. *Awards:* Purchase Award, Calif Design Show, Oakland Art Mus, 62; Award of Merit, Am Craftsman Coun, 62. *Bibliog:* Beverly E Johnson (auth), An ancient expression in modern dress, Los Angeles Times, 62; American designer craftsmen, NY Times, 62; Architectural Digest, 64-83. *Media:* Lacquer; Wood, Watercolor. *Specialty:* Painting, sculpture. *Interests:* Drawings. *Dealer:* Artitude Gallery, Paris, France. *Mailing Add:* 481 N Sunnyside Ave Sierra Madre CA 91024

DE KERGOMMEAUX, DUNCAN
PAINTER, EDUCATOR
b Premier, BC, July 15, 27. *Study:* Banff Sch Fine Art; Inst Allende, Mex; Hans Hofmann Sch Fine Art. *Work:* Nat Gallery Can; London Regional Art Gallery; Art Gallery Ont; Study Collection, Carleton Univ, Ottawa, Ont; and others. *Comn:* Exterior wall mural, Vanier Post Off, Dept Pub Works, Can, 70; Man Centennial Caravan, Dept Secy State & Man Govt, 70; shaped banners, Schoeler, Heaton Archit, Univ Ottawa, 71; mall environment, Schoeler, Heaton Archit, Garneau Sch, Orleans, Ont, 71; and others. *Exhib:* 3rd & 6th Biennials Can Art, Nat Gallery Can, Can Painting, Albright Knox Gallery, 66; DeKergommeaux-DeNiverville Touring Exhib, Nat Gallery Can, 67-68; Loranger Gallery, Toronto, 80 & 81; Take Two Touring Exhib, 80-84; An Art of Ordered Sensations, London Regional Art Gallery, 86; Process, Structure, Meaning (with catalog), London Regional Art Gallery, 95; Vanishing Icons, St John's, New Foundland, 2002; and others. *Pos:* Dir, Can Pavilion Art Gallery, Expo 67, Montreal, 66-67; chmn dept visual arts, Univ Western Ontario, 81-84, emer prof, 93-. *Teaching:* Prof drawing & painting, Univ Western Ont, 80-; vis prof drawing & painting, Banff Sch Fine Arts, summer 74-75; vis prof, NS Col Art, summer 80. *Awards:* Monsanto Can Art Competition, 57; Purchase Award, Minneapolis Biennial, Boutels, 58; Art Wall Competition, Benson & Hedges, 71. *Bibliog:* Groves (auth), DeKergommeaux at the Blue Barn, Can Art, 63; M Teitlebaum (auth), An Art of Ordered Sensations (exhib catalog), 86; Jose Barrio-Gray (auth), Process, Structure, Meaning (exhib catalogue). *Mem:* Royal Can Acad Arts. *Media:* Oil. *Dealer:* Thielsen Galleries, London, Ontario

DE LA CRUZ, CARLOS
COLLECTOR
b Havana, Cuba. *Study:* Univ Pa, BS, 1962, MBA (finance), 63; Univ Miami Sch Law, Fla, JD, 72. *Pos:* Car dealership exec, formerly; chmn, Eagle Brands, Coca-cola Bottlers, Puerto Rico, Trinidad and Tobago, currently. *Awards:* Alexis de Tocqueville Award for outstanding philanthropy, United Way, 97; Nat Community Serv Award, Simon Weisenthal Ctr, 98; Named one of top 200 art collectors, ARTnews Mag, 2004. *Collection:* Contemporary Art, especially Latin American. *Mailing Add:* 5 Harbor Pl Miami FL 33149-1715

DELACRUZ, JERRY J
PAINTER, COLLAGE ARTIST
b Denver, Colo, Dec 21, 48. *Study:* Rocky Mountain Col Art & Design AA, 72. *Work:* Denver Art Mus; Univ Colo, Boulder; Kinder Morgan, Wells Fargo Banks, Deloitte & Touche, Denver. *Comn:* exterior tile mural, Denver Zoo, 75; oil on canvas, Denver Public Schs, 77; painting, Theatre Under Glass Lobby, Denver, 79; acrylic on canvas, Travelers Insurance, 88; acrylic on canvas, Keeney Design, Denver, 90. *Exhib:* Expresiones Hispanas, Mexican Cult Inst, San Antonio, 88; Expresiones Hispanas, Triton Mus Art, Santa Clara, Calif, 89; Latino/Latina Art, San Jose Ctr for Latino Arts, Calif, 94; De La Cruz REM Revisited, Sangre de Cristo Art Ctr, Pueblo, Colo, 95; Fifth Ann Benefit Exhibit, El Museo de las Americas, Denver, 99; Colorado 2000, Colorado Springs Fine Arts Ctr, 2000; American Drawing Biennial, Muscarelle Mus Art, Williamsburg, VA, 2000; Arte y Muerte, La Casa de Gobierno de Tiaxcala, Mexico City, Mex, 2000; Kinder, Morgan, Denver; Wells Fargo Banks, Denver; Deloitte & Touche, Denver. *Pos:* bd dir, Colo Hispanic Arts Coun, Denver, 72-74; pres, bd dir, chmn, Art Barn Inc, Denver, 83-84; bd dir, Art Student League of Denver, Colo, 87-. *Teaching:* instr drawing & painting, Rocky Mountain Col Art & Design, Denver, 72-74; instr figure drawing, drawing technique, Colo Inst Art, Denver, 83-84; instr advan painting, Art Students League, Denver, 87-. *Bibliog:* Shirley Gonzales (auth), DeLaCruz: Displays Range, New Haven Register, 83; Betsy Howard (auth), DeLaCruz: He Mixes Styles, Denver Mag, 87; Mary Chandler Voetz (auth), DeLaCruz: Never Say Never, Rocky Mountain News, 88. *Media:* Oils, Acrylics, Collage. *Dealer:* Young Fine Art Ltd 1415 Logan St Denver CO 80203. *Mailing Add:* 3001 Lawrence St Denver CO 80205

DE LA CRUZ, ROSA
COLLECTOR
Exhib: THAT PLACE, Moore Space, 2002. *Pos:* Co-founder, Moore Space, Fla, 2001; cur (exhib) THAT PLACE, Moore Space, 2002. *Awards:* Named one of top 200 collectors, ARTnews Mag, 2004; recipient Alexis de Tocqueville Award for outstanding philanthropy, United Way, 97; Simon Weisenthal Ctr Nat Community Serv Award, 98. *Mem:* Mus Contemp Art N Miami, Fla; Miami Art Mus (aquisition comt, currently); Mus Contemp Art Chicago (exhib comt, currently). *Collection:* Contemporary Art, especially Latin American. *Mailing Add:* 5 Harbor Pl Miami FL 33149

D'ELAINE
PAINTER, LECTURER
b Puyallup, Wash, Mar 19, 32. *Study:* Cent Wash State Univ, BA, 54; Univ Wash, MFA, 58; Univ London, research of sea hist. *Work:* Nova Scotia Art Mus, Can, 62; Prince/Princess Eleski, Russia; Int Foreign Govt, Japan, Sweden & Ger; Vancouver BC Mus, Can; Whatcom Mus, Bellingham, Wash; Microsoft Corp Collection; World Bank Exhib, Washington, DC, 2004; and numerous others. *Comn:* sea books illus, comn by Dept Navy for USS Bremerton submarine; Rosicrucian Order, New Zealand; Thunderbird, US Navy, Officer's Ward Room, USS Bremerton, 84. *Exhib:* Seattle Art Mus, 59, 62, 65 & 73; Pac Arts Ctr Hauberg Gallery, Seattle, Wash, 92; Northwest Ann Exhib, Bellevue Art Mus, Wash, 92; State of the Art '93, New Eng Fine Arts Inst Nat Exhib Am Contemp Art, Boston, 93; Biennial Art Exhib Wash State Chapter Nat League Am Pen Women, Frye Art Mus, Seattle, 93; one-man shows, Edmonds Art Mus, Wash, 94, Karshner Mus, Puyallup, Wash, 94, Ilwaco Heritage Mus, Wash, 94, Northlight Gallery, Everett, Wash, 95, Myths of the Americas, Karshner Mus, Puyallup, Wash, 95, Tides of Ages, Art Ctr Gallery, Seattle Pac Univ, Wash, 95, Newark Gallery, Seattle, Wash, 95 & Contemp Northwest Artists Gallery, Maryhill Mus, Goldendale, Wash, 96; Five Indian Myth paintings, Cent Wash Univ Conv Ctr, Ellensburg, 94; Of the Nature of Water Exhib, Corvallis Art Ctr, Ore, 95; United Nartions Headquarters, NY, 2004; Seas of Antiquity, Odyssey Maritime Discovery Ctr, Waterway Gallery, Seattle, 2005-; over 500 others. *Teaching:* art educator, Seattle, WA 54-78; Instr drawing & painting, Mus Hist & Indust, 54-56, Edmonds Adult Classes, 57-62 & Seattle Pub Schs, 60-70; lect, various univs, community cols & asns, 58-95; art consult, Wash state area, 78-. *Awards:* Exhib Award, Nat League Am Pen Women Biennial, Wash State Chap, Frye Art Mus, Seattle, 93; 1st Place Award, Women Painters Wash Exhib, Ilwaco Heritage Mus, 93; Cert of Award, 14th Ann Northwest Int Art Competition, Whatcom Mus Hist & Art, 94; Selected for Artist Resource Bank, Oregon Arts Commision, OR 2002-. *Bibliog:* Feature stories in Seattle Times, Seattle Post Intelligencer & Nat Art Mag; Prince George Citizen, British Columbia, Can, San Jose, Calif News Repartor. *Mem:* Kappa Pi; Nat Artist Equity Asn; Nat Mus Women Artists; Women Painters Wash; Am Coun Arts; Nat Pen Women. *Media:* Acrylic, Oil. *Dealer:* Pisces Studio 16122 72nd Ave W Edmonds WA 98020. *Mailing Add:* 16122 72nd Ave W Edmonds WA 98026-4517

DE LAMA, ALBERTO
PAINTER, PRINTMAKER
b Havana, Cuba. *Study:* Am Acad Art, Chicago, with William Mosby & Joseph Vanden Broucke. *Work:* Pullman Bank, Chicago; Talman Home Fed Savings Art Collection, Chicago; Jim Walter Corp, Tampa, Fla; Delta Airlines, Atlanta, Ga; Galeria Vanidades, Miami, Fla; & others. *Comn:* Corp Portraits, Celotex Corp. *Exhib:* Galeria Sans Souci, Caracas, 73 & 76; Wildlife Gallery, Minocqua, Wis, 73-79; Talisman Gallery, 76; one-man shows, Tamiami Hall, Miami, LeBlanc Wildlife Gallery, Minocqua, Wis, Talisman Gallery, Bartlesville, Okla, Galeria Sans Souci, Caracas, Univ Club Tampa, Galeria Vanidades, Miami, Tampa Yacht Club; and others. *Pos:* Pres, Graphic Direction Inc, Tampa Fla. *Teaching:* Instr painting & drawing, Am Acad Art, 69-74. *Awards:* Diamond Awards 70 & 71 & Gold Medal, 72-75, Palette & Chisel Acad Fine Arts; Third Prize, Munic Art League, Chicago, 74; First Prize Harriet Bitterly Mem Award, Chicago, Ill, 76. *Bibliog:* Armando Alvarez Bravo (auth), La Manera de de Lama, El Nuevo Herald, 8/96; Maria Elena Saavedra (auth), Expone Alberto de Lama, Diario de las Americas, 8/96; Esther Hammer (auth) Artist painting impressions of Tampa, The Tampa Tribune, Tampa, Fla. *Media:* Oil; Etchings. *Res:* Canvas Stretching; Granted Canvas Stretching Patent, 76. *Specialty:* Mr de Lama's works. *Publ:* Auth, Tercer Aniversario Puente Mariel, Cayo Hueso, 80-83. *Dealer:* Graphic Direction Inc. *Mailing Add:* c/o Graphic Direction Inc 3005 W Horatio St Tampa FL 33609

DELANEY, JANET CLARE
PHOTOGRAPHER
b Los Angeles, Calif, Aug 26, 52. *Study:* San Francisco State Univ, BA, 75; San Francisco Art Inst, MFA, 81. *Work:* Harry Ransom Humanities Res Ctr, Univ Tex, Austin; Mus de la Photographie a Charleroi, Belgium; Bancroft Libr, Univ Calif Berkeley. *Exhib:* Solo exhibs, NS Col Art & Design, 81, Form Follows Finance, Camerawork Gallery, San Francisco, 81, Nicaragua: A Grandmother's Story, Rutgers Univ, NJ, 87, Col Bakersfield, Calif, 87, Univ Pac, Stockton, Calif, 88, Santa Clara Univ, 93 & Univ Colo, Boulder, 96; Stories of the City, Ctr Arts, San Francisco, Calif, 92; Nicaragua: A Grandmother's Story, Santa Clara Univ, Calif, 93; Ctr Visual Arts, Oakland, Calif, 95; Calif Works, Exhib Hall, Sacramento, Calif, 96; Women Artists Ser, Rutgers Univ, 96; Home Fires, Univ Colo, Boulder, 96 & Blue Sky Gallery, Portland, Ore, 99; New Photog, SF Mus Mod Art Artists Gallery, 2000; Works on Paper, La State Univ, Baton Rouge, 2000; Discoveries, Fotofest, Houston, Tex, 2001; Prosaic Beauty, Flatfile, Chicago, 2001; and others. *Pos:* Co-owner, Duck Soup Color Darkroom, 79-91; bd dir, San Francisco Camerawork Gallery, 82-84; Freelance photogr, 85-97. *Teaching:* Instr color photog, Col San Mateo, 80-91; instr photojournalism, Santa Clara Univ, 86-95; instr color, Univ Calif, Berkeley, 83, 88-98; instr, The View Camera, San Francisco Art Inst, 91, 94 & 97; instr, Calif State Univ, Hayward, 98-99. *Awards:* James D Phelen Award in Photog, 79; Photog Survey Grant, 79 & Photog Fels, 82 & 86, Nat Endowment Arts; Award of Excellence, Calif Works Exhib, 96; Ruttenbery Finalist, Friends of Photog, 96. *Publ:* Contribr, Fiction International, Central American Writings, San Diego Univ Press, 86; San Francisco Observed, Chronicle Books, 86; Valiant Women in War and Exile, City Lights Books, 87; Good Neighbors: Affordable Family Housing, Jones, Petus, Pyatok, 96; illus, Frog Face, Henry Holy Co, 98. *Mailing Add:* 2110 Byron St Berkeley CA 94702

DELANEY, ROBERTA
PRINTMAKER
b Jamaica, NY. *Study:* State Univ NY, BS (art educ), 59; Tufts Univ & Sch Mus Fine Arts, MFA, 84. *Work:* Houghton Libr, Harvard Univ, Cambridge, Mass; Mus Fine Arts, Boston; Boston Pub Libr; Libr Cong, Nat Gallery Libr, Washington DC. *Exhib:* Turning the Page, Honolulu Art Ctr, 97; Artist Books from the Boston Printmakers, Traveling Exhib, 99; Transactions and Transformations, Northeastern Univ, Boston, 99. *Teaching:* assoc prof studio printmaking, drawing, Wheaton Col, Norton, Mass, 79-92. *Awards:* Award Works on Paper, Mass Cult Coun, 2000. *Mailing Add:* 46 Pleasant St Sherborn MA 01770

DELAP, TONY
SCULPTOR, PAINTER
b Oakland, Calif, Nov 4, 27. *Study:* Menlo Jr Col, Calif; Calif Col Arts & Crafts, Oakland; Claremont Grad Sch, Calif. *Work:* Mus Mod Art, Whitney Mus Am Art & Guggenheim Mus, NY; Walker Art Inst, Minneapolis; San Francisco Mus Art; Tate Gallery, London, Eng; Los Angeles Co Mus Art; and others. *Comn:* Sculpture-fountain complex, CCH Bldg, San Rafael, Calif, 70; City of Inglewood, Calif; City of Santa Monica, 91; Los Angeles Airport. *Exhib:* Whitney Mus Am Art, 64; Chicago Art Inst, 64; Mus Mod Art, NY, 64, 65 & 67; solo exhibs, Robert Elkon Gallery, 65-84, Newport Harbor, 77, Casat Gallery, La Jolla, 77, Calif State Col, Chico, 79, Janus Gallery, Venice, Calif, 79, Beatrix Wilhelm, Stuttgart, Ger, 92, Gudrun Spielvogel, Munich, Ger, 93, Mark Moore Gallery, Santa Monica, 94, 95 & 96, The House of the Magician: An Installation of Reconstructed Works 1967-1979, Calif State Univ, Fullerton, 94 & Modernism, San Francisco, 96; Contemp Am Sculpture, Whitney Mus Am Art, 66; Am Sculpture of the Sixties, Los Angeles Co Mus Art, 67; Calif Painting and Sculpture: The Modern Era, San Francisco Mus Art, 76; Corcoran Biennial, 78; Art for the Pub, Dayton Art Inst, 88; Finish Fetish, Fisher Gallery, Univ Southern Calif, 91; Shape: Forming the Los Angeles Look, Calif State Univ, Fullerton, 95; Generations: The Lineage of Influence in Bay Area, Richmond Art Ctr, 96; Focus IV: Orange Co Artists, John Wayne Airport, 97; Selected Painting & Work on Paper: Modernism, San Francisco, 98. *Teaching:* Lectr fine arts, Univ Calif, Davis, 63-64; prof fine arts, Univ Calif, Irvine, 65-91. *Awards:* First Prize Sculpture, Los Angeles Dept Airports, 76; Award for Painting, Nat Endowment Arts, 83; IDM Corp Competition Sculpture Comn Award, 85. *Bibliog:* Alan Solomon (auth), Tony DeLap: The Last Five Years, Univ Calif, Irvine, 68; Gene Cooper (auth), DeLap, The Edge as Form and Metaphor, 77; Tony Delap, The House of the Magician, Calif State, Fullerton, 94. *Dealer:* Mark Moore Gallery Santa Monica CA; Modernism San Francisco CA. *Mailing Add:* 225 Jasmine St Corona Del Mar CA 92625

DE LARIOS, DORA
SCULPTOR
b Los Angeles, Calif, Oct 13, 33. *Study:* Univ Southern Calif, BFA, 57. *Work:* Oakland Art Mus, Calif; Craft & Folk Art Mus, Los Angeles; Security Pacific Bank Collection. *Comn:* Ceramic mural (8ft x 40ft), Compton Co Libr, Calif, 73; cement mural (8ft x 10ft), Security First Nat Bank, 76; ceramic mural (8ft x 16ft), Norwood Co Libr, Calif, 77; ceramic mural (5ft X 20ft) & 2 ceramic panels (3ft X 6ft), Makaha Inn Resort, Oahu, Hawaii, 79; Friendship Patterns (6ft X 26ft cement mural), Cent Park Develop, Nagoya, Japan, 79; porcelain mural (7ft X 40ft), Hilton Hotel, Anaheim, Calif, 84; porcelain mural with lacquered & patina wood sects (5'6ft X 15'6ft), Huntley Hotel, Santa Monica, Calif, 85; and many others. *Exhib:* Am Crafts at the White House, Renwick Gallery, Smithsonian Inst, Washington, DC, 77 & Contemp Craft Mus, NY, 77; Craft & Folk Art Mus, Los Angeles, 77; Kohler Art Ctr, Wis, 77; Everson Mus, Syracuse, NY, 77; Indianapolis Mus Art, Ind, 78; Southern Alleghenies Mus Art, St Francis Col, Loretto, Pa 82; Western Regional Conf, Logan, Utah, 82; one-woman retrospective, Wooster Col, Ohio, 83; Los Angeles Munic Art Gallery, Barnsdall, Calif, 84. *Teaching:* Vis instr ceramics, Univ Southern Calif, Los Angeles, 58, & Univ Calif, Los Angeles, 79. *Awards:* Purchase Award for Ceramic Sculpture, Calif State Fair, 61; Certificate of Honor, Women in Design Int. *Bibliog:* Elain Levin (auth), Dora De Larios, Ceramic Monthly, Vol XXVI, No 8, 10/78; Lorelei McDevitt (auth), Art & artisan-public spaces, Designer West, Vol XXVIII, No 1, 11/80; article, Dora De Larios, Ceramica, Madrid, Spain, Vol V, No 17, 83; Lorelei McDevitt (auth), Art & artisans-the evolving mask of Dora De Larios, Designers West, Vol XXXI, No 10, 8/84; Monika Guttman (auth), An artist who needs her Space-Dora De Larios, Santa Monica Evening Outlook Newspaper, 8/85. *Media:* Clay, Wood, Cememt. *Mailing Add:* 3914 Huron Ave Culver City CA 90232-3804

DE LA TORRE, DAVID JOSEPH
MUSEUM DIRECTOR
b Santa Barbara, Calif, June 14, 48. *Study:* Univ San Francisco, BA, 70. *Collection Arranged:* Rockefeller Collection of Mexican Folk Art (proj dir), Mex Mus, 86; FRIDA, 87; Diego Rivera, 88; Passion with Reason: The Mex Sch, HAA, 96; The Art of Antonio Wartorell, 2000. *Pos:* Curatorial asst, Fine Arts Mus San Francisco, 77-81; develop dir, Triton Mus Art, 81-84; exec dir, Mex Mus, 84; panelist, Nat Endowment Arts, 84-89 & 92; consult, Hawaii State Found Cult & Arts, 91-; assoc dir, Honolulu Acad Arts, 91-. *Mem:* Am Fed Arts; Am Asn Mus; Western Mus Asn. *Publ:* Contribr, The Art of Rupert Garcia, Mex Mus Chronicle Books, 86; Nelson A Rockefeller Collection of Mexican Folk Art, Mex Mus Chronicle Books, 85; The Marvelous/The Real: Carmen, Lomas, Garza, 87. *Mailing Add:* Honolulu Acad Arts 900 S Beretania St Honolulu HI 96814

DELAURO, JOSEPH NICOLA
SCULPTOR, EDUCATOR
b New Haven, Conn, Mar 10, 1916. *Study:* Yale Univ, BFA (Alice Kimball Fel, Tiffany Fel & Elizabeth Pardee Scholar), 41; Univ Iowa, MFA, 47; also in Italy, 53, 62, 66 & 71. *Work:* In private collections of Dr D Corradini, Quito, Ecuador, Dr B Clemente, Akron, Ohio, Rev Ralph Kowalski, Detroit & Bishop Ernest Primeau, Manchester, NH. *Comn:* Mankato stone sculpture, St Columba Cathedral, Youngstown, Ohio, 59; glass & plastic mural, Windsor Bd Educ, Ont, 64; bronze sculpture, Hiram Walker & Sons, Ltd, Ont, 67; bronze sculpture, Detroit Pub Libr, Mich, 67; bronze sculpture, Jewish Community Centre, Windsor, Ont, 70. *Exhib:* Walker Gallery, Minneapolis, 47; Mich Regional Exhib, Detroit, 48; Ecclestical Art Guild, Detroit, 50; Fine Arts Dept Fac Exhib, Art Gallery Windsor, Ont, 70-72; Biannale de Fiorino, Florence, Italy, 71. *Teaching:* Prof sculpture & drawing, Marygrove Col, Detroit, 47-59; prof, Univ Windsor, formerly. *Mem:* Fel Royal Soc Arts; Nat Sculpture Soc; Col Art Asn Am; Mid Am Col Art Asn; Univ Art Asn Can. *Media:* Bronze, Marble. *Mailing Add:* 41110 Fox Run Apt T16 Novi MI 48377-4823

DE LA VEGA, ANTONIO
PAINTER, DESIGNER
b El Paso, Tex, July 13, 27. *Study:* NY Univ; Art Students League; also study in Mex, Spain, France, Italy & Port. *Comn:* Lt Gen James Gavin (portrait), Gavin Hall, Hq 82nd AB Div, Ft Bragg, NC, 92. *Exhib:* Pintores Nuevos, Galeria Ciga, Buenos Aires, Arg, 60; Antonio de la Vega, Galeria Fuentes, Mexico City, Mex, 61; Spanish Impressions, Galeria Gran Via, Madrid, Spain, 62; Portugal Viejo, Galeria Sesimbra, Lisbon, 66; de la Vega, Galeria Botto, Rome, Italy, 68; Rockland Col, 88; Bronx Mus Art, 89. *Pos:* Art dir & designer, Cushing & Nevell, Inc, New York, 51-62 & Persons Advertising Inc, New York, 63-74; free-lance art dir, designer & illusr advert, 74-76; sr art dir, Stogel Co, New York, 76-88. *Teaching:* Individual advan painting tech instr. *Mem:* Nat Asn Portrait Painters; Am Artists Prof League; Am Inst Graphic Arts; Artists Guild New York (vpres, 64-65); Southwest Art Found. *Media:* Oil, Acrylic. *Mailing Add:* 702 Henderson Dr Jacksonville NC 28540-4476

DE LA VERRIERE, J J
GOLDSMITH, SCULPTOR
b Paris, France, Mar 8, 32; US citizen. *Study:* Ecole Nat Art Decoratifs, BA, Paris, France, 49; Escuela de Artes Suntuarias, Barcelona, Spain, 51; London Cent Col, Eng, 57; Pratt Inst, with Prof Albert, MFA, 75; Hunter Col, MA(art hist), 79. *Work:* Cooper Mus, NY; Nat Mus Design; Contemp Crafts Mus; Metrop Mus, NY; Mus Mod Art, NY. *Comn:* Monstrance, Eglise du Gesu, Montreal, 59; Masonic Jewelry, 68, Ritual pieces, 70 & commemoration medals, 75, var Masonic Lodges, Ritual Pieces, NY, Hermes NY, Arman, Venet. *Exhib:* Solo exhibs, Pellicone Gallery, Southampton, NY, 82, Retrospective, Goldberg Gallery, NY, 85 & Pompidou Mus, Paris, 85; Caroline Corre Gallery, Paris, 83; Small Works, NY Univ, 83-85; B Fendrick Gallery, Washington, DC, 83; Alan Stone Gallery, NY, 88. *Teaching:* Instr enameling, Haystack Sch Art, 68; asst prof sculpture & electroforming, Pratt Inst, 72-75. *Awards:* First Prize Jewelry, Greenwich Village Outdoor Show, 61-80 & New York Craftsmen, 63, 68-82. *Bibliog:* Ancient Metallurgy in Art, 70; Berber Jewelry in Morocco, 89 & The Hand, 90. *Mem:* NY Craftsmen; Am Crafts Coun; Am Goldsmith Asn. *Media:* Gold, Silver, Precious and Semi-Precious Stones; Rare Woods, Ivory. *Publ:* Auth, Electroforming for Jewelry & Sculpture, 70. *Mailing Add:* 99 MacDougall St No 18 New York NY 10012-5031

DE LA VERRIERE, JEAN-JACQUES See De La Verriere, J J

DEL CHIARO, MARIO A
HISTORIAN
b San Francisco, Calif, Apr 22, 25. *Study:* Univ Calif, Berkeley, BA, 50, MA, 51, PhD, 56. *Pos:* Chmn art hist, Univ Calif, Berkley, 69-70, 79-80. *Teaching:* Assoc prof, Univ Calif, 62-66, prof, 66-93, emer prof, 94. *Awards:* Metrop Mus Art Fel, 53-54; Prix de Rome, Am Acad Rome, 58-60; Nat Endowment for the Humanities Fel, 77; Order of Merit of the Ital Repub, Cavaliere Officale. *Mem:* Archeol Inst Am, Studi Etruschi ed Italici, Florence; Archeol Inst, Berlin; Archeol Inst (Ger), Rome; Europ Acad Sci & Art, Salzburg. *Media:* Archeology. *Res:* Ancient art; archeology. *Publ:* The Genucilia Group, Berkeley, 57; auth, Etruscan Red-Figured Vase-Painting at Caere, Berkeley, 74; The Etruscan Funnel Group, Florence,74; Classical Art at the Santa Barbara Mus Art: Sculpture, 84; Studies in Honor of DA Amyx, 86. *Mailing Add:* c/o Univ Calif Dept Art Hist Santa Barbara CA 93106

DELEHANTY, SUZANNE
MUSEUM DIRECTOR
b Worcester, Mass, July 18, 44. *Study:* Skidmore Col, BA(art hist) 65; Univ Pa, grad study (art hist), 66-68. *Collection Arranged:* Nancy Graves: Sculpture & Drawing 1970-72, 72; Agnes Martin (with catalog), 73; Six Visions (with catalog), 73; Robert Morris/Projects, 74; Cy Twombly: Paintings, Drawings, Constructions 1951-1974 (with catalog), 75; Video Art (with catalog), 75; George Segal: Environments (with catalog), 76; Pieces & Performances, 76; Improbable Furniture (with catalog), 77; Paul Thek/Processions (auth, catalog), 77; Dwellings, 78; On Sculpture/Christo, di Suvero, Irwin & Segal, 79; Richard Artschwager/Themes: The Transformation of Illusion and Reality (auth, catalog), 79; On Soundings (auth, catalog), 81; Roni Horn/Space Buttresses, 86; The Window in Twentieth-Century Art (with catalog), 86; David von Schlegell/Recent Work, 89; Fred Sandback/Sculpture (with catalog), 89. *Pos:* Curatorial asst, Inst Contemp Art, Univ Pa, 68-71, dir, 71-78; dir, Neuberger Mus, State Univ NY, Purchase, 78-88; dir, Contemp Arts Mus, Houston, 89-94 & Miami Art Mus, Fla, 95-. *Awards:* Outstanding Young Women Am, 80. *Mem:* Asn Art Mus Dir; Urban League of Greater Miami. *Mailing Add:* Miami Art Mus 101 W Flagler St Miami FL 33130

DELGYER, LESLIE
ENVIRONMENTAL ARTIST, PAINTER
b Plainfield, NJ, Sept 11, 46. *Study:* duCret School of the Arts with Dudley V duCret & Marjorie Van Emburgh, 68. *Work:* Series of 5 Endangered Animals, World Wildlife Int Stamp Prog, Leigh Yawkey Woodson Art Mus, Wausaw, Wis; Hunterdon Med Ctr, Flemington, NJ; Ronald Reagan Presidential Mus, Calif; Hiram Blauvelt Art Mus, Oradell, NJ; W Valley Art Mus, Surprise, Ala. *Comn:* Conserv stamp collection: New Zealand Tuatara, 90, African Mountain Zebra, 90, Egyptian Caracal, 91, Asian Goitered Gazelle, 92 & Russian Siberian Tiger, 93, World Wildlife Fund Int. *Exhib:* Cleveland Mus Natural Hist, Ohio, 99; Burpee Mus Natural Hist, Rockford, Ill, 99; Utah Mus Natural Hist, Salt Lake City, Utah, 2000; Norton Art Mus, Shreveport, La, 2000; North Mus Natural Hist and Sci, Lancaster, Pa, 2000; Nat Geographic Soc, Wash, DC, 02; Utah Mus Natural History, Salt Lake City, 03; The Canton Mus of Art, Ohio, 02; One person show, Blauvelt Art Mus, Oradel, NJ, 03; West Valley Art Mus, Surprise, Ariz, 04; Univ of Nebr State Mus, Lincoln, Nebr, 05; Ariz-Sonora Desert Mus, Tucson, Ariz, 06; Muscarelle Mus Art, Col of William & Mary, Williamsburg,

Va, 2006; Neville Pub Mus, Green Bay, Wis, 2006. *Pos:* Bd Trustees, duCret Sch, 85 & vpres bd trustees, 87; hist & paliamentarian, Soc Animal Artists, 87, asst secy exec bd, 89 & secy, 94, pres, 2004. *Awards:* Cert Spec Cong Recognition, 2000; US House Reps Citation, 2000; State NJ Senate and Gen Assembly Citation, 2000. *Bibliog:* Joni Kinslow (auth), Spotlight on art: Leslie Delgyer artist, Pleasure Hunt Mag, 7-8/83; NJ State of the Arts Broadcast (film), WNJN, WNYC & WHMM, 5-6/90. *Mem:* Pastel Soc Am, Nat Arts Club, NY; Soc Animal Artists; duCret Sch; Nat Mus Women Arts, Wash; Salmagundi Club, NY. *Media:* Pastel. *Publ:* 30th Annual Exhibition and National Museum Tour Society of Animal Artists, US Art Mag, 11/90; The Best of Pastels 2-Collected by the Pastel Society of America & Wildlife Art, Rockport Publ, 98-99. *Mailing Add:* 168 Westervelt Ave North Plainfield NJ 07060

DE LISIO, MICHAEL
SCULPTOR
b New York, NY. *Work:* Joseph H Hirshhorn Mus, Washington, DC; Minneapolis Inst Arts; Wichita Mus, Kans; Christ Church Col, Oxford Univ; Smith Col Mus Art, Mass; Mus City of New York; Addison Gallery Am Art, Andover, Mass; and others. *Exhib:* One-man shows, Minneapolis Inst Arts, 71 & Brooke Alexander Gallery, NY, 78; Addison Gallery Am Art, Andover, Mass, 73; Princeton Univ Libr, 73; Smith Col Mus Art, Northampton, Mass, 74; Zabriskie Gallery, NY, 86; McMullen Mus; Princeton Univ Libr; Boston Col, Mass; and others. *Bibliog:* Robert Phelps (auth), article, Life Mag, 1/29/71; Martha Saxton (auth), article, Connoisseur, 9/85; Helicon Nine, J Women's Arts & Lett, 88. *Media:* Terra Cotta, Bronze. *Publ:* Sanford Schwartz (auth), The Art Presence Stoney Conley Interview, Boston Col, 98. *Mailing Add:* 32 E 64th St New York NY 10021

DELISLE, THOMAS CHARLES
FILMMAKER, PHOTOGRAPHER
b Ind, Sept 3, 73. *Study:* Ind Univ, BA 98. *Work:* Mus Mod Art, NY; Titzer Mus, Scipro, Ind; Hans Der Kulter Der Welt, Berlin, Ger. *Comn:* photog portriat, comn by Trace Mayer, NY; sculpture, comn by Sydney King, Louisville, Ky. *Exhib:* Structures, Carnegie Ctr, Newport, Ky, 98; Road Trip, New Vision Gallery, Louisville, Ky, 99; Themas, Am Mus Inc, Washington DC, 2000. *Pos:* asst dir, Mary Andersen Ctr for Arts, 96-99. *Teaching:* instr photog, Artopia-Louisville Visual Art Asn, 99-2000 & Zachary Taylor Elem, 2000. *Awards:* Ky Arts Coun Award, Ky Arts Coun, 2000. *Mem:* Artswatch, Louisville; EyeConomy Inc. *Publ:* contrib, Vision Infinity, Gunthar Media, 98. *Dealer:* Galerie Hentz 913 E Market St Louisville KY 40204. *Mailing Add:* 7424 Kensington Rd Lanesville IN 47136

DELL, ROBERT CHRISTOPHER
ENVIRONMENTAL ARTIST, EDUCATOR
b Nyack, NY, Feb 22, 50. *Study:* NY State Univ Col, Oneonta, BS(educ), 72; NY State Univ Col, New Paltz, MFA(sculpture), 75. *Exhib:* Solo exhibs, Vorpal Gallery, Chicago, 78, NY, 81 & 88, San Francisco, 85, New Acquisitions Gallery, Syracuse, NY, 83, Blue Hill Cult Ctr, Pearl River, NY, 87 & 98, Am Cult Ctr, Reykjavik, Iceland, 88, Mid-Hudson Arts & Sci Ctr, Poughkeepsie, NY, 92, installation, Grotto & Castle Geyser Groups, Yellowstone Nat Park, 96, Akuregri Art Mus, Iceland, 99, Geysir, Haukadaker, Iceland, 99 & Reykjavid Munic Art Mus, 2001; Albert Neikan Sch of Engineering, The Cooper Union, New York City, 2004; 14 Sculptors Gallery, NY, 85 & 94; MIT Mus, Mass Inst Technol, Cambridge, Ma, 90-91; geothermal sculpture installation, Perlan, Reykjavik, Iceland, 91-; Lehigh Univ, Bethlehem, Pa, 91-92; Galleri Ofeigur, Reykjavik, Iceland, 93-94; Mass Inst Technol Mus, Ctr Advan Visual Studies, Cambridge, 94; installation, Tish Gallery, Tufts Univ, Medford, Mass, 95; installation, Carpenter Ctr Visual Arts, Harvard Univ, 95; Old Faithful, Grotto & Castle Geyser Groups, Yellowstone Nat Park, 96; Kresge Oval, Mass Inst Technol, Cambridge, Mass, 97; NJ City Univ, NJ, 98; Nassau Community Col, Garden City, NY, 99. *Pos:* Mem, Archit and Community Appearance, Bd of Review, Town of Orangetown, 79-, vice chairman, 87-; master scenic artist, One Life to Live, Am Broadcasting Co, NY, 88; res fel, Ctr for Advan Visual Studies, Mass Inst Technol, Cambridge, 93-95, res affil, 95-96; Research Fel, The Cooper Union Research Found, New York City, 2004-; Artist in Residence, The Cooper Union (sch of Engineering) 2004. *Teaching:* Guest speaker, Cooper Union Sch Art, Mass Inst Technol, Harvard Univ, State Univ NY & Nassau Community Col; vis artist, Akureyri Sch Visual Art, Iceland; Adj Prof, The Cooper Union, New York City, 2003-; Adj Prof Westchester Community Col, Valhalla, NY, 2003-2004. *Awards:* Fulbright Res Grant, 88; Coun Arts Grant, Mass Inst Technol, 97; Am-Scandinavian Found Fel, 99. *Bibliog:* review, D. Dominick Lombardi (auth),99 & Helen Harrison (auth), 99, New York Times; The Sculpture Mag review by D. Dominich Lomhard; 2001; Iceland Review, article by Jenita McCormack, Iceland, 2001. *Media:* Geothermal Sculpture, Mixed Media. *Publ:* contribr, Leonardo, MIT Press, vol 33, no 3,. *Dealer:* Galleri Ofeigur Skolavordustigur 5 Reykjauik Iceland. *Mailing Add:* 421 Washington St Tappan NY 10983

DELLA-VOLPE, RALPH EUGENE
PAINTER, EDUCATOR
b NJ, May 10, 23. *Study:* Nat Acad Design; Art Students League. *Work:* Chase Manhattan Bank Collection, NY; Treas Bldg, Washington, DC; Slater Mus, Norwich, Conn; Pennell Collection, Libr of Cong, Washington, DC; Wichita Art Asn, Kans. *Exhib:* Pa Acad Fine Arts, Philadelphia, 52; Babcock Galleries, NY, 60-63; Butler Inst Am Art, Ohio, 63; Final, Nat Inst Arts & Lett, NY, 63 & 64; Columbia Mus, SC, 76; Seattle Art Mus, Wash; Berkshire Mus, Pittsfield, Mass; Grand Cent Galleries, NY. *Teaching:* Prof drawing & painting & artist in residence, Bennett Col, 49-77; prof drawing & painting, Marist Col, Poughkeepsie, 77-79. *Awards:* Libr of Cong Purchase Award, 52; Berkshire Mus Drawing Prize, 54; MacDowell Fel, MacDowell Art Colony, 63; Finalist, Nat Inst Arts & Letters, 1964. *Media:* Oil. *Dealer:* Abby M Taylor Fine Art Greenwich CT; Vincent Vallarino Fine Art New York NY. *Mailing Add:* 241 South Road Millbrook NY 12545

DEL LA VEGA, VEGA GABRIELA
PAINTER, ILLUSTRATOR
b Mexico, Oct 19, 46. *Study:* Art Student League, 86-90; Acad San Carlos, 88-90; with Alton Tobey, NY, 90-95; Hon degrees from Centro de estudios univ Londres 80-96 & Jamar arte y literatura 85-96. *Work:* Encuentro de escritoras y pintoras, Ateneo, Madrid, Espana; Conclave de signos, Inst Politecnio Nat Mexico DF; La daza interna, Mus Franz Mayer Mexico DF; Elogio de una sospechosa, Mus de Arte Mod, Mexico DF; Inmediaciones de Van Gogh, Mus Rufino Tamayo, Mexico DF. *Comn:* Latin Am Art Show, Thorton Donnovan Sch, New Rochelle, NY, 93; Batalla de Otumba, Inst Mexiquense Cultura, Edo, Mexico, 93; Ezra Pound, Jomar arte literatura, Mexico DF; Crees saberlo todo, Bibliog Mexicana, Mexico DF 96; Si te labra prision mi fantasia, Bibliog Mexicana, Mexico DF, 96. *Exhib:* Desnudisima, Estud Churubusco, Mexico, 91 & 92; Ocho Mujeren Enel Arte, Foro Cult Delegacion Magadalena Contreras, Mex DF, 93; Chili Pepper Fiesta, Brooklyn Botanic Garden, NY, 94; De amor y desvarios, Casa del Lago, Chapultepec, Mexico DF, 94; Seven Mexican Artists, Broome St Gallery New York 94, 95 & 96. *Teaching:* Instr Mex Lit & Art, Lart Lycco Jean Jacques Rousseau, Paris 75-77; instr, Art Univ Nat Autonoma, Mexico DF, 80-84; instr, Centro de estudios Univ, Londres, 84-86. *Awards:* premio Nac Cuento, Tampico Tamaulipas, 85; Premio de acuarela, Casa de la acuarela, Mexico DF, 91 & 92. *Bibliog:* Jose Luis Cuevas (auth), Rene Char, Revista Siempre, 90; Francisco Del Rio (auth), Pintores, Directorio de las artes plasticas, 93-95; Sergio Loyo (auth), Sirenas, Periodico 1990, 95. *Mem:* Students League; Artist's Equity; Amigos de los parques Mexico y Espana (pres, 92-96); Jomar aite y Literatura (du, 85-96); Centro de estudios Univ Londres (dir, 80-96). *Media:* Oil, acrylic. *Publ:* Illusr, Inmediaciones de Van Gogh de Rene Char, 84 & Elagio de una sospechosa de Kene Char, Lince Ed, 89; La muerta de Krishna de Sitakant Mahapatra, 93 & De amor y desvaris de Patricia Vidal, 94, Jomar arte y literatura; Si te labra prision mi fantasia de Guadalupe Elizalde, Bibliofilia Mex, 96. *Dealer:* Norma Clavel M Citlaltepetl 45-302 Col Hipodroma Mexico DF Mexico 06100. *Mailing Add:* Col Hip Condesa Av parque Mexico 55 PH Mexico DF 06170 Mexico

DELLER, HARRIS
ADMINISTRATOR, CERAMIST
b Brooklyn, NY, Jan 28, 47. *Study:* Calif State Univ, Northridge, BA, 71; Cranbrook Acad Art, Mich, MFA, 73. *Work:* Ill State Mus, Springfield; Shigarnki Mus, Japan; Cranbrook Mus Mich; Everson Mus, Syracuse, NY; Am Craft Mus, NY. *Exhib:* Am Porcelain, Renwick Gallery, Smithsonian Inst, 80; solo exhibs, Int Commun Agency, Seoul, S Korea, Heroe and Icons, Mod Art Mus Ft Worth, 88, Brevard Mus Art, Fla, 98; The Service of Tea, Cooper-Hewett Mus, NY, 84; Am Clay Artist, Port of Hist Mus, Philadelphia, 85; Poetry of the Physical, Am Craft Mus, NY, 86; Crafts Today, Musee des Beau Arts, Paris; Altered States, Ctr for Visual Arts, Denver, 96; Davis Collection, Ariz State Univ, 99; Scripps Col Ceramics Ann, 2000. *Teaching:* Vis instr Ceramics, Sch of Art Inst Chicago, 73; instr, Ga Southern Col, Statesboro, 73-75; prof ceramics, Southern Ill Univ, Carbondale, 76-, dir, Sch Art & Design, currently. *Awards:* Fulbright Hays Fel, Coun Int Exchange of Scholars, 81; Artist Fel, Ill Arts Coun, 86, 87, 89 & 99; Artist Fel, Arts Midwest, 90. *Bibliog:* Pat Degner (auth), Deller's Witty, Unpretentious Ceramics, St Louis Post Dispatch, 12/7/84; Nancy Gardner (auth), Harris Deller, American Ceramics, vol 6, no 4, summer 88; Harris Deller, Ceramics Monthly, vol 36, no 6, 88; Yih Wen Kuo (auth), Ceramic Art Mag, Harris Dellen, 94; R Zakin (auth), Ceramics, Ways of Creation, 99; The Best of Pottery 1 & 2, Rockport Publ, 96 & 99. *Mem:* Nat Asn Schs Art & Des; Nat Coun Educ in Ceramics Arts (publ chair, 94). *Media:* Porcelain. *Publ:* Is glaze dead?, The Studio Potter, Vol 24, 12/95. *Mailing Add:* Southern Ill Univ Sch Art Carbondale IL 62901

DELLIS, ARLENE B
MUSEOLOGIST, CRAFTSMAN
b Brooklyn, NY, Apr 12, 27. *Study:* Antioch Col; Univ NC, Greensboro, BA. *Pos:* Head lending serv, Brooklyn Mus, NY, 49-55; head traveling exhibs & registr, Solomon R Guggenheim Mus, NY, 55-63; registr, Gallery Mod Art, NY, 64; registr, Marlborough-Gerson Gallery, NY, 64-67; exhib coordr, Inst of Contemp Art, Boston, 67-68; registr, ed-designer & dir traveling exhibs, Bernard Danenberg Galleries, NY, 69-72; asst to dir, La Boetie Gallery, NY, 72-77; assoc dir, Helios Gallery, NY, 78-79; fine leather designer craftsman, 76-79; registr, Lowe Art Mus, Univ Miami, Coral Gables, Fla, 79-82; exhib mgr & sr registr, Ctr for Fine Arts, Miami, Fla, 82-95, retired. *Publ:* Ed, Max Weber Drawings, 72; Kurt Seligman: His Graphic Work, 73; ed & designer, Hans Bellmer: Graphic Work, 74; auth, Kurt Seligman Graphics, Mus Fine Arts, Springfield, Mass, 74. *Mailing Add:* 14 Stoner Ave Apt 3J Great Neck NY 11021

DELLOSSO, GABRIELA
PAINTER
Study: Nat Acad Fine Arts, NY, 99-2001; Art Students League, NY, 93-2001; Sch Visual Arts, NY, BA, 89-92. *Exhib:* Two-person show, Sundance Gallery, Bridge Hamton, NY, 98; Juried 86th Ann Exhib, Allied Artists of Am, Nat Arts Club, NY, 99; Red Dot Exhib, Art Students League, NY, 2000; Sarah's Circle Benefit Show & Auction for Homeless Women, Swedish Am Mus Ctr, Chicago, Ill, 2001; Cork Gallery Exhib, Lincoln Ctr, NY, 2002; Nat Midyear Show 67th Ann Juried Exhib, Butler Inst Am Art, Youngstown, Ohio, 2003; Allied Artists of Am, An Invitational Touring Mus Exhib, 2003-05. *Collection Arranged:* Permanent Collections, Salmagundi Club Mus, NY; Saturday Evening Post Soc; Pvt and Gallery Collections. *Teaching:* teachers aid, Nat Acad Fine Arts, NY, 99-2001; teachers aid, Arts Students League, NY, 97-99, 93-94. *Awards:* Honorable Mention Award, Best Art of 2002, Artists Mag; Best in Show, Pen & Brush, Inc, NY, 2002; Isabel Steinschneider Mem Award, 2002. *Mem:* Catherine Lorillard Wolfe Art Club, NY (bd mem, vpres, painting chmn, currently); Allied Artists of Am, NY (bd mem, news ed, 99-); Salmagundi Club,

NY (juror, 2001-02); Art Soc of Old Greenwich, Conn (juror, 2001-02). *Media:* Oil, Acrylic. *Publ:* Article The Artists Mag, Dream Studio Art Competition, 95; article The Artists Mag, Annual Art Competition, 98; article Gallery & Studio Mag, Painting Review, 2002. *Dealer:* Simon & Schuster; Harper & Collins; American Girl Magazine; Random House; Willowisp Press. *Mailing Add:* 441 Albany Ct West New York NJ 07093

DELONEY, JACK CLOUSE
PAINTER, ILLUSTRATOR
b Enterprise, Ala, Nov 2, 40. *Study:* Auburn Univ, BFA, 64. *Work:* First Nat Bank, Montgomery, Ala; First Ala Bank, Birmingham; Coca Cola Co, Montgomery, Ala; Pope & Quint Co, Mobile, Ala; Fla Gas Corp, Winter Park, Fla. *Exhib:* Seventh Juried Art Exhib, Mobile Art Mus, 72; Mainstreams 73 & 76; Hudson Valley 46th Nat, 74; WTex Watercolor Asn Nat, 75; Rocky Mountain Nat Watermedia, Colo, 76; Okla Nat Watercolor Exhib, Okla Mus Art, 76; and group and one-man shows. *Pos:* Book designer, Methodist Publ House, Nashville, Tenn, 64-65; illusr & painter, Ft Rucker, Ala. *Awards:* Purchase Award, People's Bank & Trust, Tupelo, 72; Best Landscape, NJ Miniature Art Soc, 73; Purchase Award, Bluff Park Show, Birmingham, Ala, 77. *Mem:* Ala Watercolor Soc; La Watercolor Soc; Southern Watercolor Soc; assoc mem Am Watercolor Soc; assoc mem Allied Artists of Am. *Publ:* article, North Light, 4/78. *Mailing Add:* 101 Rebecca Ln Ozark AL 36360-7620

DELONG, DAVID G
EDUCATOR, CURATOR
Study: Univ Kans, BA; Univ Pa, with Louis I Kahn, MA(archit), 63; Columbia Univ, PhD(archit hist), 76. *Collection Arranged:* Design in America: The Cranbrook Vision 1925-1950; Bruce Goff: Toward Absolute Architecture; Louis I Kahn: In the Realm of Architecture; Frank Lloyd Wright: Designs for an American Landscape. *Teaching:* Prof archit & city & regional planning, Grad Sch Fine Arts, Univ Pa, currently. *Awards:* Fulbright Fel, 67-68; Vis Scholar, Getty Ctr Hist Art & Humanities, 89; Guggenheim fel, 97. *Mem:* Frank Lloyd Wright Bldg Conserv (bd dir); Philadelphia Hist Preserv Corp (bd dir); Nat Coun Preserv Educ (bd dir); Preserv Alliance Greater Philadelphia (dir); Soc Archit Historians (dir). *Publ:* Ed, Working with Mr Wright: What it Was Like; Wright in Hollywood: Visions of a New Architecture; American Architecture: Innovation and Tradition. *Mailing Add:* Dept Archit Sch Fine Arts Univ Pa 207 Meyerson Hall Philadelphia PA 19104

DE LORY, PETER
PHOTOGRAPHER, INSTRUCTOR
b Cape Cod, Mass, Oct 2, 48. *Study:* San Francisco Art Inst, BFA(photog), 71; Univ Colo, MFA(photog), 74. *Work:* Minneapolis Inst Art; William Hayes Fogg Art Mus, Harvard Univ, Cambridge, Mass; Mass Inst Technol, Cambridge; Nat Gallery Can, Ottawa, Ont; Addison Gallery Am Art, Andover, Mass; Nat Mus Am Art, Smithsonian Inst, Washington; Seattle Mus Art; San Francisco Mus Mod Art; Princeton Univ, NJ; Univ Washington Medical Center, Seattle; The Brookings Inst, Washington, DC, The Brainerd Found, Seattle, The Art Inst Chicago, Ill Seattle Mus Art, Washington; Brookings Institute, Washington, DC. *Comn:* Wash State Art Comn (3' X 20' color mural), S Kitsup High Sch, Port Orchard, 85; Seattle Water Dept, 96; Sound Transit, Photographer in Residence, Seattle, 2000, 2001, 2002; Wenatchee mural project, Confluence, collaberation (with Kay Kirkpatrick), 2000; Seattle Arts Commission, Photographer in Residence, Seattle Public Utilities, Washington, 99. *Exhib:* One-man show, Addison Gallery Am Art, 74; Carl Siembab Gallery Photog, Boston, Mass, 76; Sheldon Mus Art, Lincoln, Nebr, 77; The West: Real & Ideal, Univ Colo, 77; Univ Oreg, Eugene, 82; Southern Alta Art Gallery, Can, 83; Gallery Interform, Usaka, Japan, 86; Scheinder Mus Art, Ashland, Ore, 87; Santa Monica Col, Calif, 88; Blue Sky Gallery, Portland, Ore, 96; Whitman Col, Walla Walla, Wash, 2000; City Works, Bank Am Gallery, Seattle, 2001; Lisa Harris Gallery, Seattle, 2003. *Pos:* Dir photog dept, Sun Valley Ctr Arts & Humanities, 75-79. *Teaching:* Instr photog, Ctr Eye Sch, Aspen, 69-71; asst photog, Minor White Workshop, Hotchkiss, Conn, 72-73; instr advan photog, Sun Valley Ctr Arts & Humanities, Idaho, 74-78; instr, Sch Art Inst Chicago, 80 & 84, Univ Wash, Seattle, 82, Portland Sch Art, Maine, 83, State Univ Calif, San Jose, 86-90 & San Francisco Art Inst, 91; Univ NMex, Albuquerque, 95. *Awards:* Western States Art Found Fel, Boise Art Gallery, 76-77; Nat Endowment Arts Photogr Fel, 79; Artist Fel, Calif Art Coun, 90; and others. *Bibliog:* Alex Sweetman (auth), Peter deLory Photographs, An Afterimage, Visual Studies Workshop, Rochester, NY, 11/76. *Mem:* Soc Photog Educ. *Media:* Black & white photography. *Publ:* Contribr, Aperture, Inc, 73; Creative Camera, English, 12/73; Auth, The Wild and the Innocent, Calif Mus Photog, Riverside, 87; Railwork: Rebirth of Commuter Rail, Sound Transit, Seattle. *Mailing Add:* 619 Western Ave No 19 Seattle WA 98104

DELOYHT-ARENDT, MARY ARENDT
PAINTER
b Independence, Mo, Mar 10, 27. *Study:* Christian Col, AA, 46; Univ Mo, BFA, 49. *Work:* Empire Machinery; Valley Nat Bank; Mayo Clinic, Scott, Ariz; Giant Indust, First Interstate. *Comn:* Watercolors Ariz Mountains, IBM, 81-82; Michael R Ellis Inc, Phoenix, Ariz, 88; Ariz Biltmore, Phoenix, 91; Merriott's Camelback Inn, Scottsdale, 92; Mayo Clin, Scott, Ariz; pvt collections. *Exhib:* Western Fedn Watercolor Soc, Houston, Tex, 79; Southwest Watercolor Soc, Dallas, Tex & 79, Ardmore, Okla, 80; solo shows, SR Brenner Gallery, Carmel, Calif; Artists of the West Invitational, Ariz Bank, Phoenix, 85-90; Nat Watercolor Soc, Brea, Calif, 85-87; Plein Air Painters of Am, Avalon, Calif, 87, 2000; and others. *Collection Arranged:* US Embassy Switzerland, Mayo Clinic, Scottsdale, Ariz. *Awards:* Best of Show, Ariz Watercolor Asn, 80 & 81; Grumbacher Silver & Gold Medallion, Ariz Watercolor Soc, 84; Best of Show, Desert Plein Air, Palm Springs, 2000; Award of Excellence, Desert Plein Air, 2001-2002. *Bibliog:* In Plein View, Phoenix Mag, 92; Fresh aer, Plein air, Watercolor Magie, 97; On Location Primer, Watercolor Magie, 98; Advice From Experts, Watercolor (Am Artist Mag), 99; The Plein Air Magazine, 1/2005; Arizona Republic, 2003. *Mem:* Ariz Artis Guild (pres, 76-78, bd dir); Royal mem Ariz Watercolor Asn (bd dir); 22X30 Prof Watercolor Critique Group; signature mem Nat Watercolor Soc; Am Acad Women Painters; signature mem Plein Air Painters of Am. *Media:* Watercolor, Oil. *Specialty:* Plein air paintings in watercolor. *Interests:* bible study, singing. *Publ:* Portal Posters, Calif; Splash 5; Best of Flower Painting; Keys to Painting Houses and Fruit; Splash of The Language of Landscape, publ Int Artist Mag. *Dealer:* S R Brennen, Scottsdale Ariz; Gallery A Taos NM; Courtyard Gallery New Buffalo Mich; Gold Nugget Gallery Wichenburg Ariz; Millyard Gallery Uppermill Eng. *Mailing Add:* 2617 N 58th St Scottsdale AZ 85257

DE LUCA, JOSEPH VICTOR
EDUCATOR, PAINTER
b Niagara Falls, NY, Mar 1, 35. *Study:* Bowling Green State Univ, BS, 57 & MA, 58; Mich State Univ, Clifton McChesney & Angelo Ippolito, MFA, 65. *Work:* Toledo Mus Art, Ohio; Univ Omaha, Nebr; Grand Rapids Mus, Mich; Ford Motor Company, World Headquarters, Dearborn, Mich; Bowling Green State Univ, Ohio; Western Mich Univ, Kalamazoo; Arts Coun of Greater Kalamazoo Epic Center, Mich; Mich State Univ; Krasl Art Ctr, St Joseph, Mich; and others; Dennis Mus Ctr, Traverse City, Mo; and others. *Comn:* Cyma & Silver Square (oils & aluminum on canvas), Renaissance Ctr, Detroit, Mich, 76; Pierre Marquet Hotel, Minneapolis, Minn, 89; Northwestern Nat Life Insurance Co, Minneapolis, Minn, 89. *Exhib:* two-person exhib, Gallery Artemus, Ghent, Belg, 81, Northwestern Mich Col, Dennos Mus Ctr, Traverse City, 94; Solo exhib, State Univ NY, Binghamton, 96; Traverse Area Arts Coun, 99; Art Below Zero, Tranverse Arts Coun, Dennos Mus Center, Transverse City, Mich, 2000; Just Touch It, 2000; Fontana Summer Festival, Kalamazoo, 2000; Participated Gallery, NorthPort, Mich, 2000 & 2001; solo exhib, Gallery 544, Transverse City, New World Order, 2002; Hatties of Suttons Bay, Mich, 2003; Little Cities Gallery, Kalamazoo, Mich, 2005; Mott Community Col, Flint, Mich, 2005; Art Reach Gallery Mich, Mt Pleasant, 2006; Bella Galleria, Old Mission, Mich, 2006; Northwest Regional, Dennis Mus Ctr, Northwestern Mich Col, Traverse City, 2006; and others. *Collection Arranged:* Works by George Ortman (auth, catalog), 69; Works by Angelo Ippolito (auth, catalog), 70; Works by Harry Brorby (auth, catalog), 71; Works by Clifton McChesney (auth, catalog), 72; Works by Graduates & Undergraduates, Bowling Green, Western Mich Univ, 73. *Pos:* Gallery dir (part time), Gallery Two, Western Mich Univ, Kalamazoo, 67-71; Danforth Assoc, Nat Invitational Educators Asn, 76-84. *Teaching:* Instr art, Findlay High Sch, Ohio, 58-62; instr drawing, painting & art educ, Central Mich Univ, Mount Pleasant, 62-66; prof drawing & painting, Western Mich Univ, Kalamazoo, 66-96; Art Workshop, Arezzo, Italy, 2006. *Awards:* Director's Choice Award, Kalamazoo Art Inst, 88; NW Regional Exhib 2nd Prize, Northwestern Mich Col, Dennos Mus Ctr, 96; Purchase Award, Krasl Art Ctr, 83; All Mich Regional, Muskegon Mus Art, Mich, 91. *Bibliog:* Amy Sult (auth), Last picture show, Kalamazoo Gazette, 96; Paul Samra (auth), On the Town Arts Mag, W Mich, 96; Artwatch, Transverse Mag, Transverse City, Mich, 96; Arts Borealis, Arts Mag, Transverse City, Mich, 96, 99, & 2002; Nancy Sundstrom Arts Ed, Transverse City Record Eagle, 2002; Christopher Young (auth), Flint J, 2004, Grayce Scholt (auth), 2006. *Mem:* Arch Am Art, Smithsonian Inst; Kalamazoo Inst Arts; Traverse Area Arts Coun; Dennos Mus Center, Mich. *Media:* Mixed. *Interests:* Contemporary Art. *Dealer:* Bella Galleria Old Mission Mi; Belstone Gallery Traverse City Mich. *Mailing Add:* 6369 Secor Rd Traverse City MI 49684

DE LUISE, ALEXANDRA
CURATOR, LIBRARIAN
b New York, NY. *Study:* New York Univ, BA(art hist), 77; Rutgers Univ, MA(art hist), 80, MLS, 81. *Pos:* Asst librn serials, Frick Art Reference Libr, NY, 81-83; acquisitions librn, Can Ctr Arch, Montreal, 83-90; librn, European Sculpture & Decorative Arts Dept, Metrop Mus Art, NY, 90-91; art librn & cur, Queens Col Art Ctr, City Univ NY, 91-2000; coordr, instr, Queens Col, City Univ NY, 2000-. *Mem:* Art Libr Soc NAm (NY chap, vchmn, 94, chmn, 95); Libr Asn City Univ NY; Asn Col & Res Libr (NY chap); Am Libr Asn. *Res:* Art serials and their history; electronic content retrieval, art databases; art methodology. *Interests:* Italian art between the two world wars; Dutch prints and drawings. *Publ:* auth, A bibliography of current art journals in Eastern Europe & Soviet Union, summer 82; auth, Architecture school publications, spring 87, & New design journals, fall 92; auth, Art Documentation; Le Arti and intervention in the arts, RACAR, 92; auth, Ploos van Amstel, Christian Josi & the collection d'imitations, Quarendo, summer 95; auth, Journals of the century in the visual arts, The Serials Librarian, Vol 39, No 4, 2001; auth, Art Documentation: Full Text of Not? All Illustrations or Not?, fall 2003; auth, chap in: Guide to the Literature of Art History 2, Max Marmor & Alex Ross (eds), Am Libr Asn, Chicago, 2005. *Mailing Add:* Queens College Benjamin S Rosenthal Library 65-30 Kissena Blvd Flushing NY 11367

DELVALLE, EDUARDO See Gomez, Mirta & Eduardo Delvalle

DEMANCHE, MICHEL S
PAINTER, PHOTOGRAPHER
b Ft Worth, Tex, Aug 16, 1953. *Study:* Univ Tex, Arlington, BFA, 75; North Tex State Univ, MFA, 80. *Work:* Wise Co Heritage Mus, Decatur, Tex; North Tex State Univ Collection, Denton; Grant Arnold Collection, State Univ Oswego, NY; Art Inst & Gallery Salisbury. *Comn:* Frito Lay Corp; Robert Crill. *Exhib:* Showdown, Alternative Mus, NY, 83; Visions of Childhood, Whitney Mus Am Art, NY, 84; Introductions, Judy Yoven Gallery, Houston, Tex, 88; Holiday Pictures, Frito Lay, Dallas, Tex, 88; Texas Women Artist, Nat Mus Women Art, Washington, 88; Artscape 90, Mount Royal Sch Art, Baltimore, MD, 90. *Pos:* Asst prof art, Univ Md, Eastern Shore; pres, Art Inst & Gallery Salisbury, 95-96; dir, Salisbury Alternative Space Gallery. *Awards:* Second Place Multi-Media, Art Quest, 86; Governor's Citation Award & Individual

Artist Grant: Photography, 93. *Bibliog:* Dr Mark Thistlewaite (auth), Michel Demanche, Artspace, spring 84; Wade Wilson (auth), Captain Midnight vs the forces of evil, Dallas Arts Rev, No 20, 86; Gary McKay (auth), New Wave of Texas Artist, Ultra, 3/88. *Mem:* Wash Proj Arts; Col Art Asn; Women in Photogr. *Media:* Mixed Media. *Dealer:* Finer Side Galleries 205 W Main St Salisbury MD 21853; Wade Wilson Gallery Chicago, IL. *Mailing Add:* c/o William Campbell Contemp Art 4935 Byers Ave Ft Worth TX 76107

DE MARIA, WALTER
SCULPTOR
b Albany, Calif, Oct 1, 35; US citizen. *Study:* Univ Calif, Berkeley, BA(hist) & MA(art), 53-59. *Work:* Mus Mod Art, Whitney Mus Am Art, NY; Basel Kunstmuseum, Basel, Switz; Mus Boymans-van Beuingen, Rotterdam. *Comn:* NY Earth Romm (earth, peat & bark), Dia Art Found, NY, 77. *Exhib:* Sculpture of the 60's, Los Angeles Co Mus, 67; Whitney Mus Am Art Sculpture Ann, 68; Information, Mus Mod Art, NY, 70; one-man exhibs, Dia Art Found, NY, 79 & 80, Kunsthaus Zurich, 92; Akron Art Mus, 92; Va Mus Fine Arts, Richmond, 92; Transform, Kunstalle Basel, Switz, 92; Minimalist Works on Paper, Susan Sheehan Gallery, NY, 93; Some kind of fact, Some Kind of fiction, Sperone Westwater, 94; Dia Ctr for the Arts, NY, 97; Museo d'Arte Contemporanea Roma, 2003. *Awards:* Guggenheim Fel, 69-70; Mather Sculpture Prize, 72nd Ann Exhib, Art Inst Chicago, 76; Inauguration of sculpture on the occasion of the Bicentennial, Bur Nat Assembly, Paris, 91. *Bibliog:* Jeffery Deitch (auth), Artificial Nature, Deste Found Contemp Art, Greece, 90; Kikuko Amagasaki (auth), Pharmakon 90, Akira Ikeda, Tokyo, 90; Robert Rosenblum (auth), Towards a definition of new art, New Art, NY, 91. *Media:* Earth. *Publ:* Contribr, Hard core (land film ed 100), 69. *Dealer:* Gagosian Gallery 980 Madison Ave New York NY 10021. *Mailing Add:* c/o Gagosian Gallery 980 Madison Ave New York NY 10021

DEMARTIS, JAMES J
PAINTER
b Corona, NY, Mar 30, 26. *Study:* Acad Fine Arts, Florence, Italy, 50-54. *Work:* Pvt collections in Europe & US. *Exhib:* One-man shows, Ward Eggleston Gallery, Ruko Gallery, Marcaleo Gallery, Artemis East Gallery & Hicks St Gallery. *Awards:* Emily Lowe Award Painting, 61. *Mem:* Artists Equity. *Dealer:* Brownstone Gallery 76 Seventh Ave Brooklyn NY 11217. *Mailing Add:* 329 E Main St North Adams MA 01247-4427

DEMATTIES, NICK
PAINTER
b Honolulu, Hawaii, Oct 19, 39. *Study:* Calif State Univ, Long Beach, BA, 64; Inst Design, Chicago, with Misch Kohn, MS, 67. *Work:* Los Angeles Co Mus Art; Brooklyn Mus Art; Cabinet Estampes, Bibliot Nat Paris; Libr Cong; San Francisco Mus Mod Art. *Comn:* Swengle-Robbins, 87. *Exhib:* Bentley Gallery, Scottsdale, Ariz, 94; Wenninger Gallery, Rockport, Mass, 94; Montreal Int, Que, 94; Nat Painting Exhib, Albuquerque, NMex, 94; Washington & Jefferson Nat Painting Show, Washington, Pa, 94; and others. *Pos:* Founder & dir, Pac Northwest Graphics Workshop, 70-75. *Teaching:* Instr, San Diego State Col, 67-69; asst prof, Mt St Mary's Col, Calif, 69-70; vis prof, Univ Ore, 72; Asst Prof, Albion Col, Mich, 73-74; asst prof, Ariz State Univ, Tempe, 74-76, assoc prof, from 77, then prof, currently prof emeritus. *Awards:* First Place & Cash Award, Biennial, Fuller Art Ctr, Los Alamos, NMex, 91; Purchase Award, 5th Ann McNeese Nut, Lake Charles, La, 92; Cash Award, W & J Nat Painting Show, Washington, Pa, 94. *Bibliog:* Articles, Phoenix Gasette, 2/8/90, Artspace, winter 84 & 85 & Scottsdale Progress, 4/4/86; Articles, Art Voices S, 11-12/79 & 9-10/81 & Portfolio Mag, 7-8/81; and others. *Media:* Acrylic, Oil. *Dealer:* Bentley Gallery 4161 N Marshall Way Scottsdale AZ 85251. *Mailing Add:* Sch Art Herberger College Fine Arts Ariz State Univ PO Box 871505 Tempe AZ 85287-1505

DEMETRION, JAMES THOMAS
MUSEUM DIRECTOR
b Middletown, Ohio, July 10, 30. *Study:* Miami Univ, BS(educ), 52, Simpson Col, Hon DFA, 84, UCLA, Univ Vienna. *Collection Arranged:* Egon Schiele & The Human Form, 71; Paul Klee, 73; 25 Yrs Am Painting 1948-1973, 73; European Art: The Postwar Years 1945-1955, 78; Giorgio Morandi: Retrospective, 81; Francis Bacon, 89; Jean Dubuffet, 43-63, 93; Stanley Spencer: An English Vision, 97; Clyfford Still, 2001. *Pos:* Cur, Pasadena Art Mus, Calif, 64-66, dir, 66-69; dir, Des Moines Art Ctr, Iowa, 69-84; mem mus adv panel, Nat Endowment Arts, 73-76; mem int adv comt, Stuart Found, La Jolla, 81-90; dir, Hirshhorn Mus & Sculpture Garden-Smithsonian Inst, 84-. *Mem:* Asn Art Mus Dir (treas, 76-77, 1st vpres, 78-79, pres, 79-80). *Mailing Add:* Hirshhorn Mus & Sculpture Garden Independence Ave & Eighth SW Washington DC 20560

DE MILLE, LESLIE BENJAMIN
PAINTER, SCULPTOR
b Hamilton, Ont, Apr 24, 27; US citizen. *Study:* Art Students League, NY. *Work:* Portraits, two US Pres; Death Valley 49ers Collection; Navy Art Mus, Washington, DC; Five past Pres, Whittier Col Collection, Calif; Ronald Reagan Libr, Simi, Calif. *Comn:* Portrait, Ronald Reagan, Calif, 67; portrait, Richard M Nixon, Washington, DC; paintings, US Sixth Fleet, Mediterranean (naval combat artist), 72 & Pearl Harbor, Hawaii painting, 73; bronze sculpture, Pres Reagan & Gorbachev, Reagan Libr, White House, 88; bronze monument, Hillside, Sedona, Ariz, 91. *Exhib:* Death Valley 49ers Exhib, Calif, 69-84; Grand Nat Ann Exhib, Am Artists Prof League, NY, 71-; one-man show, Hamilton Place, Ont, Can, 91; and others. *Teaching:* Organizer, dir & instr, sem for art orgn in US, 66-; instr, Nat Portrait Seminar, 81; fac instr, Scottsdale Artists Sch, Ariz, currently; workshop tour, Hawaii, 92, 95. *Awards:* Best Show, 71 & Gold Medals, 76, 79 & 80, Am Artists Prof League, NY; Best Show, Death Valley 49ers Inc, 80; and others. *Bibliog:* Portraits in Pastel (series of half-hour programs), Pub Broadcasting System, 81-; Feature article, SW Art Mag, 9/81; feature article, Am Artists Mag, 6/85; feature article, Art of The West Mag, 5-6/94. *Mem:* Fel Am Inst Fine Arts; fel Am Artists Prof League; Coun Traditional Artists Soc (pres, formerly); Death Valley 49ers Inc (pres, formerly); Pastel Soc Am; Salmagundi Club; Pastel Soc W Coast. *Media:* Oil, Pastel. *Publ:* How to Draw Cats and Kittens, Walter Foster, 79; Portraits in Pastel, PBS Pub, 81; Painting with Pastels, Foster Art Libr Ser, 84. *Mailing Add:* 155 Creek Rock Rd Sedona AZ 86351-7379

DEMING, DAVID LAWSON
SCULPTOR, EDUCATOR
b Cleveland, Ohio, May 26, 43. *Study:* Cleveland Inst Art, with William McVey & John Clague, BFA; Cranbrook Acad Art, with Julius Schmidt, MFA. *Work:* Ft Worth Nat Bank, Tex; San Antonio Mus & Pub Libr Austin, Tex; Longview Mus Art, Tex; First City Ctr, Austin, Tex; Ark Art Ctr; Columbus Mus Art. *Comn:* Bronze Bust Winthrop Rockefeller for Winrock Int; Barbara Jordan Award Medalion; Harold Russell Award Medalion; Bobbit Bust, Rebecca Johnson, Libr Cong. *Exhib:* One-man exhib, Adams-Middleton Gallery, Dallas; Kouros Gallery Group Shows, NY; Int Chicago Art Expos, Navy Pier. *Pos:* Chmn, Dept Art & Art Hist, Col Fine Arts, Univ Tex, 92 & dean, 96-98; pres, Cleveleand Inst Art, 98. *Teaching:* Instr sculpture, Sch Fine & Appl Arts, Boston Univ, 67-68; instr sculpture & drawing design, Univ Tex, El Paso, 70-72; prof sculpture & drawing, Univ Tex, Austin, 72-. *Awards:* Am Inst Archit Award of Honor. *Mem:* Tex Sculpture Asn; Int Sculpture Asn. *Media:* Steel, Bronze. *Mailing Add:* Cleveland Inst Art 11141 E Blvd Cleveland OH 44106-1700

DEMISSIE, YEMANE I
FILMMAKER
Study: L'Inst Catholique, Paris, France, diploma (French lang and lit), 85; Moorehead State Univ, Minn, BA (French), 86 & BS (mass commun), 86; UCLA, MFA (film directing & production), 92. *Exhib:* DC Int Film Festival, Kennedy Ctr, 97; London Film Festival, Nat Film Theatre, Eng, 97; House Cult, Berlin, 98; Mus Fine Arts, Boston, 98; Ger Nat Film Mus, Frankfurt, 98; Am Film Inst Film Festival, Los Angeles, Calif; Int Film Festival, Rotterdam, The Neth; Contemp African Diaspora Film Festival, NY. *Pos:* Writer, dir, producer, Treacherous Crossings, 86-; dir aquisitions, Producer Servs Group Inc, 87-92; first asst dir, Big Bang Lies, 90, Where Beans Grow, 91, That's What Women Want, 92, Genesis Pure, 94; asst dir, co-ed, res, Imperfect Journey, 94; line producer, Through the Door of No Return, 97; continuity writer, SDI Media USA, 97-; line producer, first asst dir, My Soul to Keep, 2001. *Awards:* John Simon Guggenheim Mem Found Fel, 98; Indep Film & Filmmaker Grant, Am Film Inst,; Production Grant, Montecinemaveritá Found; Film Fund, Göteborg Film Festival; Artists Fel, Calif Arts Coun; Nat Resources Fel. *Publ:* dir, Tumult, 97; auth, Gilding on the goblet, Part I, 5/2000, Part II, 9/2000, Ras Hailu's choice, 12/2000, The treasure in the Cellar, 1/2001, Educating Hiruy, 3/2001 & Goum-Goum-Shah!, 5/2001, Seleda.com. *Mailing Add:* PMB 1405 264 S LaCienga Blvd Beverly Hills CA 90211

DE MONTE, CLAUDIA
SCULPTOR, CUR
b Astoria, NY, Aug 25, 47. *Study:* Col Notre Dame, Md, BA; Cath Univ Am, MFA. *Hon Degrees:* Col Santa Fe, LHD, 2004. *Work:* Indianapolis Mus Art, Ind; New Orleans Mus; Del Mus; Ft Lauderdale Mus; Brooklyn Mus; Tucson Mus; Flint Institute Art. *Comn:* Brooklyn Pub Libr, NY, 90; Sch Construct Authority, NY, 93; NMex Arts Coun, Socorr, NMex, 97; New York City Percent for Art, Queens Supreme Ct, NY, 98; Univ Northern Iowa, 2003; NM Rt 66, Santa Rosa. *Exhib:* one person shows, Corcoran Mus Art, Washington, DC, 76, Miss Mus Art, Jackson, 80, Ft Worth Art Mus, Tex, 80, Marion Locks Gallery, Philadelphia, 80 & Gracie Mansion Gallery, NY, 84, 85, 88 & 89; NY Now, Gothenberg Mus, Sweden; Biennial Paper Art, Dupen Mus, Ger; Retrospective, Chokladfabriven, Malino Swede, 98; Liesbeth Lips Gallery, Rottendam, The Neth, 99; Flint Inst Art, Mich, 2000; Tucson Mus, Ariz, 2001; Mus Southwest, Midland, Tex, 2002; Contemp Art Ctr, New Orleans, La, 2005; Kunsthatle, Tallin, Estonia, 2004; Univ Md Art Gallery, 2006. *Pos:* Prof Art Dept, Univ Md, 72-2005, prof emerita, 2005-. *Teaching:* Prof, Univ Md, Col Park, 72-2005, prof emerita, 2005-. *Awards:* Fel in Sculpture, NY Found; Agnes Gund Grant, Anchorage Found Tex; Cantor Family Found. *Bibliog:* G Henry (auth), Claudia De Monte, Art Am, 9/84; article, Claudia De Monte, New York Times, 9/27/85. *Mem:* EuroAm Women Coun; Art Table; NY Women's Forum. *Media:* Wood; Bronze. *Res:* Global homes art; Outsider art. *Interests:* int travel; women's issues. *Publ:* auth, Women of the World: A Global Collection, 2000. *Dealer:* Jean Albano Gallery Chicago Ill; Barbara Gillman Gallery Miami Fla; June Lekky Gallery NY; Cole Pratt Gallery Los Angeles CA. *Mailing Add:* 96 Grand St New York NY 10013

DE MONTEBELLO, PHILIPPE LANNES
ADMINISTRATOR, MUSEUM DIRECTOR
b Paris, France, May 16, 36; nat US, 55. *Study:* Harvard Col, BA (magna cum laude), 58; New York Univ Inst Fine Arts, BA, 63, MA 76. *Hon Degrees:* Lafayette Col, LFA, 1979; Dartmouth Col, LLD, 2004; Bard Col, DHL, 1981; Iona Col, DFA, 1982. *Collection Arranged:* Greek Art of the Aegean Islands, 11/79; Clyfford Still, 11/79; Horses of San Marco, 2/80; Seventeenth Century French Painting, 6/82; Cimabue, 1/82; Vatican, 1/83; Manet, 9/83; Liechtenstein: the Princely Collections, 10/85, Van Gogh in Saint-Remy and Auvers, 11/86, Zurbaran, 9/87, Degas, 10/88, Canaletto, 11/89, Velazquez, 10/89, From Poussin to Matisse: The Russian Taste for French Painting, 5/90. *Pos:* Asst cur to assoc cur Europ paintings, Metrop Mus Art, NY, 63-69, vice dir curatorial & educ affairs, 74-77, actg dir mus, 77-78, dir, 78-, chief exec officer, 99-; dir, Mus Fine Arts, Houston, Tex, 69-74; bd trustees, Inst Fine Arts, NY Univ; mem ed bd Int Jour Mus Mgt and Curatorship; mem adv coun depts art and

archeology, Columbia Univ. *Teaching:* Lectr, Curatorial Studies, NY Univ Inst Fine Arts. *Awards:* Woodrow Wilson Fel, NY Inst Fine Arts, 61-62; Gallatin Medal & Fel, NY Univ, 81; decorated chevalier Legion d' Honneur, France, Encomienda de Numero de la Orden Isabel la Catholica, Spain, officer Ordre de Leopold, Belgium, Knight Comdr, Pontifical Order St Gregory the Great, comdr Order Arts and Letters, 01; Gold Medal Nat Inst Soc Sci, 89, Spanish Inst, 92; Rebekah Kohut award Nat Coun Jewish Women, 93; Living Landmark award NY Landmarks Conservancy, 01; Mayoral proclamation, 02; Nat Medal of Arts, 03. *Mem:* Asn Mus Art Dirs (mem art com); Mus Coun New York City; Am Fedn Arts (trustee exec com); Am Asn Mus. *Publ:* Auth, Peter Paul Rubens, McGraw, 68; contribr, Metrop Mus Art Bull & others. *Mailing Add:* Metrop Mus Art 1000 Fifth Ave at 82nd St New York NY 10028-0113

DE MOURA SOBRAL, LUIS
HISTORIAN, CRITIC
b Viseu, Port, June 24, 43; Can citizen. *Study:* Univ Louvain, Belg, MA(art hist), 73, PhD, 76. *Collection Arranged:* Le surrealisme portugais (auth, catalog), Galerie UQAM, Montreal, 83; Pintura Estrangeira dos seculos XVI, XVII e XVIII da Coleccao Nogueira da Silva (auth, catalog), Nogueira da Silva Mus Minho Univ, Braga, 95-96; Bento Coelho (1620-1708), e a Cultura do seu Tempo (auth, catalog), Inst Portugues do Patrimonio Arquitectonico, Lisbon, 98. *Pos:* Cur, Montreal Mus Fine Arts, 71-75; ed, Racar, 83-89. *Teaching:* Asst prof, Univ Montreal, 76-81, assoc prof, 81-87, chair, 87-95, prof 87-. *Mem:* Am Soc Hispanic Art Hist Studies; elected mem Nat Acad Fine Arts, Portugal. *Res:* Baroque painting; Portuguese baroque painting; Iberoamerican colonial art; surrealism. *Publ:* Critical study, Luis Nunes Tinoco, Elogio da Pintura, Galeria de Pintura do D Luis, 91; Vilallonga Les lieux du reve, Cloister of dreams, Ed Broquet, Montreal, 93; Pintura e poesia na epoca barroca, Lisbon, Ed Estampa, 94; Do Sentido das Imagens, Lisbon, Estampa, 96; Pintura Portuguesa do Seculo, XVII, Historias, Lenda, Narritivas, Lisbon Museo Nacional de Arte Antiga, 2004. *Mailing Add:* Dept Hist Art Univ Montreal PO Box 6128 Centreville Montreal PQ H3C 3J7 Canada

DEMPSEY, BRUCE HARVEY
MUSEUM DIRECTOR
b Camden, NJ, July 4, 41. *Study:* Fla State Univ, BA, MFA; study exten sch, Florence, Italy; Mozarabic manuscripts with Gulnar Bosch. *Collection Arranged:* Photons-Phonons (elec sculpture), 71; Lewis Comfort Tiffany, 72; Realizations and Figurizations, 72; Karl Zerbe Mem Exhib, 73; Photo Phantisists, 73; Colors (photog exhib), 74; Talent USA, 76; Elizabethan Portraiture, Nat Portrait Gallery, London, 76; New Realism, 77; New Floridians No 1, 77; The Florida Connection: Jim Rosenquist & Robert Rauschenberg, 77; Helen Frankenthaler, 77; New Floridians No 2, 78 & No 3, 79; The Flowing Word: Chinese Calligraphy, 79; Contemporary Stained Glass, 79; Duane Hanson, 80; Currents: A New Mannerism, 81; Joseph Raffael: Recent Works, 82; Calligraphy, Ming Dynasty, 82; Arakawa: Graphic Works, 82; Master Craftsmen, 83; Empress Dowager Forbidden City, 83; Masami Teraoka, 83; Ramses II: Pharaoh & His Time, 87. *Pos:* Dir art gallery, Fla State Univ, 68-74; dir, Jacksonville Art Mus, 75-. *Teaching:* Instr fundamental art & art hist, Fla State Univ, 66-74. *Awards:* Fla Arts Recognition Award, State of Fla, 86-87. *Mem:* Am Asn Mus. *Publ:* Auth, Lewis C Tiffany-Beauty in Many Mediums, 72. *Mailing Add:* 2415 Mandarin River Ln Jacksonville FL 32223-1358

DEMSKY, HILDA GREEN
PAINTER
b Kingston, Pa, Jul 2, 36. *Study:* Carnegie Mellon Univ, BFA, 58; Hunter Col, MA, 63. *Comn:* Mural, Lobby walls, H Thomas Slater Ctr, White Plains, NY, 91. *Exhib:* Galeria Nacional, San Jose, Costa Rica; Gov's Mansion, Harrisburg, Pa; Fidelity Investments Corp Gallery, Boston, Mass; Mount Sinai Hosp, NY; Thomas H Slater Ctr, White Plains, NY; Westmoreland Mus Am Art, Greensburg, Pa; Hammond Mus, Salem, NY; Meridian Int Ctr, Wash, DC; Mona Ena Gallery, Mykonos, Greece; Sophia Wanamaker Gallery, Costa Rica; The Arts Ctr, Saratoga Springs, NY; The Rye Arts Ctr, NY; Pen & Brush Gallery, NY; Pleides Gallery, NY; Fordham Univ Gallery, Lincoln Ctr, NY. *Teaching:* Art teacher, New York City Bd Educ, 59-72, White Plains (NY) City Sch Dist, 72-; prof, clinical field supv Manhattanville Col, Purchase, NY, 2001-02. *Awards:* Arts fel painting, Coun for Basic Educ, Italy, 92; Fulbright Fel to Netherlands, Natl Endowment Arts, 92; Environ Art, Found on the Sound, Read, Puffin Found, 99; NY Found for Arts, SOS Awards & NY St Coun for Arts, 99, 2000 & 2005; Saltonstall Found for the Arts, 2005; Henry Faurest Mem Fel at Mary Anderson Ctr for Arts, IN, 2006. *Bibliog:* Roberta Hershenson (auth), Turning Beach Dross into Works of Art, NY Times, 9/4/94; William Zimmer (auth), Recognizing Self Portraits by Americans, NY Times, 2/8/98; Eleanor Heartney (auth), Take Me to the Water (Mus catalog), 2005. *Mem:* Fulbright Asn, Nat Arts Task Force; Univ Coun Art Educ (bd mem, 2002-2003); Nat Asn of Astronomical Artists; Pleiades Gallery (bd mem, 2004); Pen & Brush Gallery (bd mem, 2005); Mamaroneck Artists Guild, Artists Circle of NY City. *Media:* Oil, Acrylic, Watercolor. *Res:* Contemp women artists; Chinese women artists. *Interests:* Women artists, travel, tennis. *Collection:* Nat Gallery Costa Rica. *Dealer:* Jordana Alford 917 Commonwealth Ave Newton Mass 02459. *Mailing Add:* 24 Orsini Dr Larchmont NY 10538-1642

DE MUSÉE, MORAN
SCULPTOR
b Bryn Mawr, Pa, Sept 28, 50. *Study:* studied El Camino Col, Redondo Beach, Calif, Calif State Univ, Long Beach, Acad Di Belle Arti, Italy. *Work:* Il Passaggio Moresco, Fundacion Valparaiso, Rio Aguas, Spain, 95. *Comn:* Sculpture, City of Santa Monica, 86. *Exhib:* Sculpture, Calif State Univ, San Bernardino, 88; Artist Do Opera, Brand Gallery, Glendale, Calif, 2001; Klaudid Marr Gallery, Sante Fe, N Mex, 2004. *Awards:* Fel, Fundacion Valparaiso, 95. *Bibliog:* Douglas Ditonto, Le Graveur (film), 75. *Publ:* You Call This Art, Los Angeles Mag, 89; Los Angeles: Realm of Possibility, Windsor Pub, 91. *Mailing Add:* PO Box 2422 Toluca Lake CA 91610

DENES, AGNES
ENVIRONMENTAL ARTIST, CONCEPTUAL ARTIST
b Budapest, Hungary; US citizen. *Study:* City Univ New York; New Sch Social Res, New York; Columbia Univ; Ripon Col, hon DFA, 94. *Hon Degrees:* Ripon Col, Wis, PhD (hon) (fine arts), 94. *Work:* Metrop Mus Art, Mus Mod Art, Whitney Mus Am Art, NY; Nat Mus Fine Arts, Washington; Moderna Museet, Stockholm, Sweden; John D & Catherine T McArthur Found, Chicago; Philadelphia Mus; Corcoran Gallery of Art; Smithsonian Inst, Washington; Israel Mus, Jerusalem; Wexner Ctr for the Arts, Columbus, Ohio; Honolulu Acad of Arts, Hawaii; and many others. *Comn:* Circle of Megaliths with Sun Dial, Int Ctr Preserv Wild Animals, Ohio, 90-95; Introspection I Evolution (mural), comn by Harold Wash Libr Ctr, City Chicago Pub Art Prog, 90-91; Hot/Cold Earthship with Heartbeat (45 ft wooden barge), Mus Contemp Art, Helsinki, 92; Tree Mountain-A Living Time Capsule, Pinsio gravel pits (400 yr proj), Ylojarvi, Finland, 92-96; A Forest for Australia (6000 trees planted), Melbourne, 98; Poetry Walk - Reflections: Pools of Thought (with time capsule), 2000; The Irish Hunger Memorial, Battery Park, NY, 2000; Nienwe Hollandse Waterlinie, Holland, 2000; The Golden Tree, Göteborg Internationella Konstbiennal, Sweden, 2001. *Exhib:* Minn Mus Art Traveling Show, St Paul, Kolnishcer Kuntsverein, Cologne, Ger, 87; Mus Contemp Art, Helsinki, Mus Tampere, Finland, 92; Epand La Defense, Paris, France, 93; Staatsgalerie, Suttgart, Ger, 97; Am Acad in Rome, 98; Museu d'Art Contemporani, Barcelona, 2000; Venice Biennale, Italy, 2001. *Teaching:* Instr fine arts, Sch Visual Arts, NY, 74-79; instr, Skowhegan Sch Painting & Sculpture, Maine, 79 San Francisco Art Inst, Calif, 76, Univ Genoa, Sch Archit, Italy, 86; guest lectr in numerous universities, museums & art centers in the US & Eur; speaker, Global Forum Environ & Develop Human Survival, The Kremlin, Moscow, USSR, 90, Unced 92, Global Forum Parlimentary Earth Summit, Rio de Janeiro, Brazil, 92 & Global Forum Gen Assembly, Kyoto, Japan, 93; vis critic, Sch Archit, Univ Pa, Philadelphia, 91. *Awards:* Hassam & Speicher Fund Purchase Award, Am Acad Art & Letts, 85; Eugene McDermott Achievement Award Mass Inst Technol, 90; Fel, Carnegie Mellon Univ, 93; Rome Prize, Am Acad Rome, 97-98; Watson Award, Carnegie Mellon Univ, 99; Nat Endowment Fel (4); NYSCA Grants (4); DAAD Fel, Berlin; Studio for Creative Inquiry Fel; Ctr for Advanced Visual Studies, MIT Fel; Courant Inst at NYU Fel, 96-. *Bibliog:* J Hartz (ed), Agnes Denes A Monograph, Herbert F Johnson Mus Art, Cornell Univ, 92; Adachiara Zevi (auth), The Visual Philosophy of Agnes Denes, L'Architettura, Rome, Italy, 10/98; Ricardo Barreto (auth), Sculptural Conceptualism: A New Reading of the Work of Agnes Denes, Washington, DC, No 4, 99; Krystyna Wasserman (auth), Book as Art XI - Inside the Artist's Book, Women in the Arts, 99; Beryl Smith (auth), Lives and Works: Talks with Women Artists, vol 2, 99; Barbara Nemitz (auth), Trans Plant: Living Vegetation in Contemporary Art, 2000; Grissim, Graham & Carpenter (auths), Nothing, 2001. *Media:* All Media. *Publ:* Auth, Sculptures of the Mind, Univ Akron Press, 76; Paradox & Essence, Tau/Ma Publ, Rome, Italy, 77; Isometric Systems in Isotropic Space: Map Projections, 79; Book of Dust: The Beginning and the End of Time and Thereafter, 86, Visual Studies Workshop; Notes on Eco-Logic: Environmental Art Work, visual Philos & Global Perspective, Leonardo, 93; Artistic vision & molecular genetics, Art J, spring 96; The Serial Attitude (catalogue), Wexner Ctr for the Arts, Ohio Univ, 98; Light on the New Millennium - Wind From Extreme Orient (catalogue), Met Art Mus, Pusan, Korea, 98; Afterimages: Drawing Through Process (catalogue), Mus of Contemp Art & MIT Press, 99; Force Fields Phases of the Kinetic (catalogue), Museu d'Art Contemporari de Barcelona, Spain, 2000; Art & Mathematics 2000 (catalogue), The Cooper Union for the Advancement of Sci & Art, 2000; Kinds of Drawing (catalogue), Herter Art Gallery, Univ of Mass, 2001. *Mailing Add:* 595 Broadway New York NY 10012

DE NIKE, MICHAEL NICHOLAS
SCULPTOR, WRITER
b Regina, Sask, Sept 14, 23; US citizen. *Study:* Nat Acad Fine Arts; also with Jean de Marco & Carl Schmitz. *Work:* Dernick Resources, Houston, Tex. *Comn:* Albert Payson Terhune Mem, Collie Fanciers Am, Paramus, NJ, 71; Medallion, Int Chef's Asn, NY, 72; Stations of the Cross, Christ Church, Pompton Lakes, NJ, 75; Bicentennial Mural, Twp Wayne, NJ, 75; Young St Francis (bronze), St David's in Kinnelon, NJ; and others. *Exhib:* Nat Acad Design, NY, 64; Audubon Artists, 65; Knickerbocker Artists, 65; Nat Sculpture Soc Ann, 66; Am Artists Prof League, 74; and others. *Pos:* Dir & founder, Am Carving Sch, Wayne, NJ, 74-90. *Teaching:* Instr woodcarving, Fair Lawn Adult Educ, 68-74; adj fac, Essex Co Col, Newark, NJ, 74-75; Am Woodcarving Sch, 74-89; Passaic Co Col, 76-80. *Awards:* Dr Ralph Weiler Award, Nat Acad Design, 64; Herald-News Award, Passaic-Clifton, NJ, 69; Allied Artists Am Award, 75. *Mem:* Am Artist Prof League; Nat Sculpture Soc; Knickerbocker Artists. *Media:* Wood, Stone. *Mailing Add:* Whiskey Creek II 92 Thunder Rd Brevard NC 28712

DENKER, SUSAN A
HISTORIAN, CRITIC
b New York, NY, Apr 2, 48. *Study:* Harvard Univ, BA, 66; Wellesley Col, MA, 79; Brown Univ, ABD, 82. *Teaching:* Lectr art hist, Tufts Univ, 76-; studio fac & chmn art hist, Sch of Mus Fine Arts, Boston, 80-. *Awards:* Res Grant, French Govt, 69; Fel, Samuel Kress Found, 77-78; Russell T Smith Award, Boston Mus Sch, 92. *Mem:* Col Art Asn. *Res:* Modern European art, 1880 to present; American art, 1940 to present; Mondrian's relationship to European and American avant-garde art; women film directors. *Publ:* Coauth, Europe in Torment: 1450-1550, 74 & French Watercolors & Drawings: 1800-1910, 75, RI Sch Design Mus Art; auth, Sandi Slone: A Retrospective Exhib 1972-1981, Watson Gallery, 81; De Stijl: 1917-1931, Visions of Utopia, Art J, fall 82. *Mailing Add:* Apt 7 361 Harvard St Cambridge MA 02138

DENMAN, PATRICIA (PAT DENMAN) PRICE
PAINTER
b Paterson, NJ, 32. *Study:* Van Emburgh Sch Art, 50-51; study with Maxwell Stewart Simpson, 60-64, Nicholas Reale, 73-76. *Work:* Hershey Chocolate Corp, Pa; AT&T, Bedminster, NJ; NJ Bell, Somerville, NJ; US Trust Co, NY; Chubb Corp, Bridgewater, NJ. *Exhib:* Grand Nat Exhib, Salmagundi Club, NY, 83 & Am Watercolor Soc, 87-91; Audubon Artists, 87-89; Nat Arts Club, 87-89; Nat Acad Design, 88, 90 & 92; Allied Artist Am, 89; Butler Inst Am Art, 2001; and others. *Pos:* Dir, trustee & instr, Somerset Art Asn, Inc, Far Hills, NJ, 71-74; Juror of Selection Awards. *Teaching:* Watercolor Workshops, Somerset Art Asn, Inc. *Awards:* Mary S Litt Medal, Am Watercolor Soc, 87; Adolph & Clara Obrig Prize, Nat Acad Design, 90; Merwin Altfeld Award, Nat Watercolor Soc, 91. *Bibliog:* Jim Kosvanek (auth), Transparent Watercolor Wheel. *Mem:* Am Watercolor Soc (asst corresp secy, 90-2001); NJ Watercolor Soc (vpres, 86-89 & pres, 90-92); Audubon Artists; Nat Asn Women Artists; Nat Watercolor Soc. *Media:* Watercolor. *Publ:* American Artist, Watercolor Page, 9/92. *Dealer:* Gallery Nine Main St Chatham NJ; Left Bank Gallery Wellfleet Cape Cod MA. *Mailing Add:* 29 Beechwood Rd Basking Ridge NJ 07920

DENNETT, LISSY W
SCULPTOR
b Vienna, Austria, May 3, 26; US citizen. *Study:* Brooklyn Col, BA, 48; Haber Sch Sculpture. *Exhib:* Nassau Co Mus Art, 92; Firehouse Gallery, 93; Guild Hall Mus, 94; Plandome Gallery, 95; Nat Asoc Women Artists, 96; Neshe Alpan Gallery, Roslyn. *Pos:* Pres, Sculptors Inc, Port Washington, NY, 86-90, pres 90-; pres, Artists Network of Great Neck, 90-95. *Teaching:* Instr sculpture, Great Neck Adult Educ, 88-. *Awards:* Sculpture award, Chelsea Ctr Nassau Co Off Cult Develop, 90; Artist Network Award for Sculpture, Nassau Co Mus, 92; Sculpture Award, Great Neck Libr, 94; Artist of Distinction, Great Neck Center Visual & Performing Arts, 2005; Outstanding Teacher & Fac Mem, Great Neck Adult Educ Center, 2006. *Mem:* Artists Network Great Neck; Nat Asn Women Artists (Centennial Comt); Visual Arts Alliance Long Island (rec secy, 88-96). *Media:* Stone, Clay. *Dealer:* Neshe Alpan Gallery Huntington NY. *Mailing Add:* 10 Canterbury Rd No 1C Great Neck NY 11021

DENNIS, DON W
PAINTER, INSTRUCTOR
b Reading, Pa, Jan 21, 23. *Study:* Kutztown State Col, Pa, BS(art educ), 51; Pratt Inst, Brooklyn, NY, 51-52; with Edgar A Whitney 65-68; also with Barse Miller, 69-70 & 72. *Work:* Miami Univ, Oxford, Ohio; First Nat Bank of Cincinnati, Madeira, Ohio; Reading Mus, Pa; Utstein Kloster, Norway; Bell Telephone; General Electric; Provident Bank, Cincinnati. *Comn:* 12 paintings (offshore oil rigs), Phillips Petroleum, Stavanger, Norway, 79. *Exhib:* One-man shows, Reading Mus & Art Gallery, Pa, 68 & Wyannie Malone Mus, Hopetown, Bahamas, 85 & 86; Am Watercolor Soc Ann, Nat Acad, NY; Cincinnati Art Mus Invitational, Ohio, 77; All-Ohio Watercolor Show, Massillon Mus, Ohio, 78; Ohio Watercolor Soc Ann, Ohio, 79, 80, 81, 82, 83, 84, 85 & 86; Group show - Kulturhus, Grimstad, Norway, 87. *Pos:* Art dir, Gibson Greetings, Cincinnati, 68-73; conductor watercolor workshops, Maine, Martha's Vineyard, Bahamas & Norway, 73-88; self-employed artist-teacher, 73-. *Teaching:* Guest instr, Miami Univ, Oxford, Ohio, Wine Country Workshops, Napa Valley, Calif, 87-88. *Awards:* Emily Lowe Mem Award, 80, Walser Greathouse Medal, 82, Am Watercolor Soc; M Grumbacher Bronze Medallion, Ohio Watercolor Soc, 81; and others. *Bibliog:* The Watercolor Page, Am Artist, 8/82. *Mem:* Am Watercolor Soc (Midwest vpres, 76-77); Cincinnati Art Club (pres, 71-73); life mem Ohio Watercolor Soc (trustee, 80-85); Cincinnati MacDowell Soc; assoc Nat Acad Design. *Media:* Watercolor. *Publ:* Contribr, Master Color & Design in Watercolor, Watson-Guptill Publ; Exploring Color, Light Publ; Making Color Sing

DENNIS, DONNA FRANCES
SCULPTOR, PRINTMAKER
b Springfield, Ohio, Oct 16, 42. *Study:* Carleton Col, BA, 64; Col Art Study Abroad, Paris, 65; Art Students League, with Stephen Greene, 66. *Work:* Walker Art Ctr, Minneapolis, Minn; Brooklyn Mus, NY; Chase Manhattan Bank; Neuberger Mus, Purchase, NY; Indianapolis Mus Art, Ind; and others. *Comn:* Entrance maze, Musical Theater Lab, Kennedy Ctr, Washington, DC, 77; Mad River Tunnel (outdoor sculpture), Dayton City, Ohio, 81; Moccasin Creek Cabins (outdoor sculpture), Aberdeen, SDak, 83; Steel Fence & ceramic medallions, PS 234, NY, 88; North Plaza, Klapper Hall, Queens Col, City Univ New York, 95; fence, Wonderland Sta, MBTA, Boston, 95; fence, IS 5, Queens, 96; fence, Am Airlines Terminal, JFK Airport, NY, 98, Terminal One, 2002. *Exhib:* One-Woman shows incl Holly Solmon Gallery, NY, 76,80,83,98: Contemp Arts Ctr, Cin, 79; Neuberger Mus of Suny Purchase, 85, Univ Gallery: Univ Gallery, Univ Mass, Amherst, 85, Brooklyn Mus, 87: Indianapolis, Mus Art, 91-98, Sculpture Ctr, New York City, 93; Dayton Art Inst, 2003; 5 Myles, Brooklyn, NY, 2005; Group Exhib Venice Biennale, Italy, 82, 84; Whitney Mus, NY, 79, 81,Tate Gallery, London, 83, Hirshhorn Mus, Washington, 79, 84, Biennial of Pub Art, Neuberger Mus, 97, Asheville (NC) Mus Art, 98, Palazzo Ducale, Genoa, Italy, 2004. *Teaching:* Instr Skowhegan Sch Art, Maine, 82, Sch Visual Arts, NY, 83-89 & Princeton Univ, NJ, 84 & State Univ NY, Purchase, 84-88; assoc prof, State Univ NY, Purchase, 90-96, prof, 96-. *Awards:* NY State Creative Artist Pub Serv Grant, 75 & 82; Nat Endowment Arts Grant, 77, 80, 86 & 94; Community Service Award for Excellence in Urban Design, Parks Coun NY, 89; Distinguished Achievement Award, Carleton Col and Carleton Alumni Asn, 89; Bessie Award for Set Design for Quintland, 92; NY Found Arts Fel, 85 & 92; Pollock Krasner Grant 2005. *Bibliog:* George Melrod (auth), Reviews: Donna Dennis at the sculpture center, Art in Am, 10/93; Roberta Smith (auth), 42nd St puts on heavy make-up and smiles a summer smile, The New York Times, 7/29/94; Nancy G Heller (auth), Why Painting is Like a Pizza: A Guide to Understanding and Enjoying Modern Art, Prince Univ Press, 2002; Deborah Everett (auth), Donna Dennis Home Away from Home, Sculpture, 06/2006. *Mem:* NY Found Arts (bd govs, 88-91). *Media:* Mixed Media, Installation. *Collection:* Brooklyn Mus; Walker Art Center; Microsoft Art Collection; Indianapolis Mus; Neuberger Mus; Ludwig Forum for Internationale Kunst Aachen Germany; Martin Z Margulies Collection. *Publ:* Illusr, Hotels, Z Press, 74; auth, The presence of the past, Domus Mag, 10/80; coauth (with K Elmslie), 26 Bars, Z Press, 87. *Mailing Add:* 131 Duane St New York NY 10013

DENNISON, KEITH ELKINS
CONSULTANT, CURATOR
b Oakland, Calif, Sept 20, 39. *Study:* San Francisco State Univ, BA; grad studies, Dr Ernest Mundt; spec training, MH DeYoung Mem Mus, San Francisco. *Collection Arranged:* Horizons, A Century of California Landscape Painting; La Pendule Francaise, A Selected Survey of French Clocks 1750-1900; Ecclesiastical Arts 13th Through 17th Centuries. *Pos:* Asst cur educ, M H DeYoung Mem Mus, 68-70; visual arts adv, Calif Arts Comn, Sacramento, 70-71; dir, Haggin Mus, Stockton, Calif, 71-86; fine arts consult, 86-. *Teaching:* Instr museology, Univ of the Pac, 74-. *Publ:* Auth, Horizons, a century of California landscape painting, 70. *Mailing Add:* 3631 Portsmouth Cir N Stockton CA 95209

DENNISON, LISA
MUSEUM DIRECTOR
b NJ, May 13, 1953. *Study:* Wellesley Col, BA, 75; Brown Univ, MA in Art Hist, 78. *Pos:* intern, Solomon R. Guggenheim Mus, NYC, 73, asst cur, 81-89, assoc cur, 90-91, collections cur, 91-94, cur of collections exhibs, 94-96, chief cur, 96-, dep dir, 96-05, dir, 2005-. *Teaching:* instr, Sch Visual Arts, NY, 83-84. *Mem:* ArtTable, NY; Société Kandinsky; bd dir, Byrd Hoffman Found, NY; Int Adv Bd, Louis T Bloudin Found; Creative Arts Adv Bd, Brown Univ. *Mailing Add:* Solomon R Guggenheim Mus 1071 5th Ave New York NY 10128-0112

DENSON, G ROGER
CRITIC, WRITER
b Buffalo, NY, Feb 2, 56. *Study:* New York State Univ, Buffalo, BA(arts & humanities), 78, with Paul Sharits & Hollis Frampton. *Pos:* Cur Performance, video, 78-80 & exhibs dir, 80-82, Hallwalls, Buffalo, NY. *Teaching:* prof Criticism Homosocial and Homoerotic Art, Grad Studies, Sch Visual Arts, New York City, 2006. *Mem:* Gallery Asn NY State (bd dir, 81-87); Alternative Mus (bd dir, 87-91). *Res:* Cultural studies and the critical analyses of the languages and values of criticism, cross-cultural relations, gender and authority politics, and the development of a nomadic criticism. *Publ:* coauth, Interview with Renée Green, Flash Art, 10/91; Maura Sheehan, Routing out cultural ghosts, Art In Am, 4/94; Capacity: History, The World and The Self, Gordon & Breach Publ, 96; Watercourse Way: The Paintings of Pat Steir, Art In Am, 11/99; Philip of Naples and the Evacative Geometry of History, Parkett No 26, 90. *Mailing Add:* 131 W 15th St Suite 23 New York NY 10011

DENTE, ROBERT
SCULPTOR, PAINTER
Study: Paier Sch Art, New Haven, Conn, 68-69; Hartford Art Sch, Univ Hartford, Conn, Bd Regents Scholar, Better Homes & Gardens Scholar, Hartford Art Sch Scholar, Standard Builders Corp Scholar, 69-73, BFA(magna cum laude), 73; Hartford Grad Ctr, Conn, 80-82; Barbieri Ctr Rome, Italy, 83. *Exhib:* Solo exhibs, Casa Cultura, San Luis Potosi, Mex, 92, Canal Art Gallery, Univ Veracruz, Mex, 92, New Britain Mus Am Art, Conn, 93, Paesaggio Gallery, Canton, Conn, 94 & 96 & Julie Heller Gallery, Provincetown, Mass, 95; Monotype Today 11, 100 Pearl Gallery, Hartford, Conn, 93; New Worlds, Mattatuck Mus, Waterbury, Conn, 93; Work in Progress, Cent Conn State Univ, New Britain, 93; Gallery Artists, Paesaggio Gallery, Canton, Conn, 94-95; Kid-On-A-Stick, Real Art Ways, Hartford, Conn, 97; one-man show, Bachelieri-Candonsky Gallery, Kent, Conn, 98. *Pos:* Cur asst & exhib preparator, Wadsworth Atheneum, Hartford, Conn, 71-75. *Teaching:* lectr art hist & studio arts, Manchester Community Col, Conn, 75-77; adj fac painting, drawing & computer graphic design, Hartford Art Sch, Univ Hartford, Conn, 75-; graphic designer & programmer, Hartford Grad Ctr, Conn, 80-83; instr art, New Eng Monotype Workshop, Bennington Col, Vt, 87; fac art hist, drawing & watercolor, Lago de Grada, Italy, 89. *Awards:* Nat Endowment Arts Fel, 95-96; Weir Farm Heritage Trust Visiting Artist, 96-97. *Dealer:* Bachelieri-Cardonsky Gallery Main St Kent CT 06757. *Mailing Add:* 56 Auburn Rd West Hartford CT 06119-1303

DENTLER, ANN LILLIAN
PAINTER
b Pittsburgh, Pa. *Study:* Pa State Univ, 1974, 2002; McNeese Univ, 1986, 2000. *Exhib:* one-woman shows incl: Calcasieu Marine Bank, Lake Charles, La, 1997, Hibernia Bank, 1998, Wise Estate, Sulphur, La, 1999, McNeese Univ, 1999, 2000-2002; group exhib's incl: McNeese State Univ, Frazer Libr, Lake Charles, La 1985-, Am Art Gallery, 1994-99, Agora Gallery, Soho, New York City, 1996, Abercrombie Gallery, McNeese Univ, Lake Charles, La, 2000 & 2001. *Pos:* found, pres, secy, Asn La Artists Inc, Lake Charles, La, 1984-; workshop leader, Bus of Art, 2004-. *Teaching:* instr, continuing educ portraiture McNeese Univ, Lake Charles, 1995-. *Awards:* Best of Show award, Calcasieu Mus, Calcasieu Nat Arts Festival, 1986; Outstanding Artist Year award, Gateway Found, 1987. *Mem:* Assoc La Artists (found, 1984, pres, 1984, 85, 86, 2003-, secy 1990, workshop instr 1986-99, 2000-); Nat Mus Women in Arts; Arts Net. *Media:* Oil, Acrylic, Watercolor. *Mailing Add:* Annie's Artworks 2223 W Sale Rd Lake Charles LA 70605-2323

DENTON, PATRY
PAINTER, INSTRUCTOR
b Scottsbluff, Nebr, July 20, 43. *Study:* Art Students Tour, Europe, 60; Univ Kans, 61; Univ Denver, cert painting, 62; studied with Alex Powers, Don Andrews, Mary Todd Beam & others. *Work:* Wind River Collection; Mus Tex Tech Univ; Hospital Building & Equipment, St Louis, Mo; United Banks Colo, Denver; Synergen, Inc, Boulder; and

many in pvt collections. *Exhib:* solo shows, W Nebr Art Ctr, 75, 81 & 90 & Foothills Art Ctr, 74 & 78; Am Watercolor Soc 125th & traveling show, NY, 92-93; Western Fed Watercolor Soc, 92 & 93, Nat'l Realism 93 & 94, Parkersburg, WV; Nat Watercolor Soc, 92; Nat Realism, Parkersburg, WVa, 93 & 94; and many other group & one-man shows. *Collection Arranged:* West Tex Mus Art, Lubbock, Tex,; Parkersberg Art Center, Va; Synergenics, Inc, Boulder, Colo; Coors, Golden, Colo; and others. *Pos:* Designer, Blaine Lindquists Glimmering Touch Specialty Clothing. *Teaching:* Instr workshop & GI Sketch Club, Aurora, Nebr; instr, Arapahoe Community Col, 94, 95 & 99. *Awards:* Brown Williamson Award, Ga Watercolor Soc, 88; Ruth Roseneau Silver Medallion, Adirondack Nat Watercolor, 91; Georgia Nat Watercolor, 88 & 92; Helen Corrubia Mem Award-Graphics, Okla Art Workshop 11th Nat, 94. *Bibliog:* B Hosicowa (auth), Art of Pat Denton, Empire Mag, Denver Post, 11/12/72; Susan Thurston (auth), Leafprints, Today's Art, 5/84. *Mem:* Foothills Art Ctr; Southwestern Watercolor Soc; Colo Watercolor Soc; signature mem Nat Watercolor Soc; Signature mem Georgia Watercolor Soc. *Media:* Watercolor, Miscellaneous Media. *Publ:* The Artists Mag, 3/88 & 3/92; Am Artist, 3/93; Best Colored Pencil II, 94; Creative Watercolor, 95. *Dealer:* Vern Stein Fine Art Buffalo NY; Robinson's Gallery Wichita Falls TX. *Mailing Add:* 2948 Pierson Way Lakewood CO 80215

DENZLER, NANCY J
SCULPTOR, PAINTER
b Newport, Ark, Apr 17, 36. *Study:* Dayton Art Inst, studied with Anthony Paterson, Dwayne Hatchet & Seymore Drumelvitch, 68; State Univ NY, Buffalo, BFA(magna cum laude), 76, MFA, 78. *Work:* Orchid Park Pub Libr, NY; Kensington High Sch, Buffalo, NY; Lewisburg Pub Libr, Ohio; NW Urgent Care Facility, Tucson, Ariz, 2006. *Comn:* luminarias, Del Pueblo Public Art Commn, Tucson, Ariz. *Exhib:* Mems exhib, Albright-Knox Mus, Buffalo, NY, 76; Creative Artists Prog (CAPS) State Mus, NY State Mus, Albany, 81; Portrait Sculpture, Contemp Points of View, State Univ NY, Bethune Gallery, Buffalo, 83; 25 Regional Artists, Montserrat Col Art, Beverly Mass, 84; solo exhibs, Patterson Art Gallery, Westfield, NY, 84 & Barn Gallery, Danvers, Mass, 94; Recent Members, Copley Soc Boston, 96; Am Plains Artist Kwahadi Kiva Indian Mus, Amarillo, Tex, 2005; Am Acad Equine Art, Lexington,Ky, 2006. *Pos:* Artist-in-residence, Kensington High Sch, 78-79; judge, Marblehead Festival Arts, 81; lectrs & demonstr, NY Coun Arts, 82. *Teaching:* Instr, figure & found drawing, State Univ NY, Buffalo, 76-79. *Awards:* Best of show, 4th Ann Open Invitational, Assoc Art Orgn Western NY, 76; CAPS Fel, NY State Coun Arts Creative Artists Prog, 79; 20th Ann Arts for the Parks Top 100, Jackson Hole, Wyo, 2006. *Bibliog:* Benjamine Kline (auth), Oil keeps her on her toes, Dayton Daily News, 10/18/68; Paul Chimers (auth), Everything she touches turns to art, The Amherst Bee, 9/6/78; Donna Furlong (auth), A versatile artistry, Lynn Daily Evening Item, 11/17/80. *Mem:* Copley Soc Boston; Boston Visual Arts Union; Asn Art Orgn Western NY; founding mem, Artists Comt & Gallery NY; Marana Arts Council; Oil Painters Am; Tucson Pima Co Arts Council. *Dealer:* Hawthorne Fine Art 105 Essex St Salem Mass 01970. *Mailing Add:* 9685 N Linda Vista Place Tuscon AZ 85742

DE PALMA, BRETT
PAINTER, SCULPTOR
b Lexington, Ky, June 19, 1949. *Study:* Peabody Col, Nashville, TN, BA, 70; Boston Sch Mus Fine Arts, BFA, 72; Tufts Univ, Medford, Mass, MFA, 73. *Work:* Kunsthalle, Malmo, Sweden; Tenn State Mus, Nashville; Smithsonian Health & Hosp Orgn, NY. *Comn:* Paintings, Metro/Nashville, Tenn, 86. *Exhib:* One-person exhibs, Emilio Bazzoli Gallery, Modena, Italy, 82 & 83, Anders Tornberg Gallery, Lund, Sweden, 88, Fawbush Gallery, NY, 88 & 89; Phillipe Brit Gallery, NY, 89, Colleen Greco, NY, 90, Tenn State Mus, Nashville, 90 & Jacob Karpio, San Juan, Costa Rica, 90; Documenta 7, Kassel, WGer, 82; Correspondences, NY Art Now, Laforet Mus, Harajuku, Tokyo, Japan, 85; Contemp Am Collage, 1960-85, Univ Mass, Amherst, 87; Recent Acquisitions, Kunsthalle, Malmo, Sweden, 88; Robert Thompson Gallery, Minneapolis, Minn, 90; Indiana Univ, Bloomington, Ind, 90; Echo Press, Ft Wayne Mus, Ind, 90; Tenn Art Comn, Nashville, 90; Montebello Mansion, Nyack, NY, 90. *Teaching:* Vis fel painting, Princeton Univ, NJ, 89-90; lectr, painting, Sch Visual Arts, NY, 89-90. *Awards:* Nat Endowment Arts Grant, 87. *Bibliog:* Edward Lucie-Smith (auth), American Art Now, William R Morrow, New York, 85; Mario Diacono (auth), Social Icons, private publ, Boston, Mass, 85; Donald Kuspit (auth), review, Artforum, summer 88. *Media:* Oil, Acrylic, Assemblage, Mixed Media. *Mailing Add:* 7211 County Highway 7 Roscoe NY 12776-2568

DEPAOLA, TOMIE
DESIGNER, ILLUSTRATOR
b Meriden, Conn, Sept 15, 34. *Study:* Pratt Inst, BFA, 56; Calif Col Arts & Crafts, MFA, 69; Lone Mountain Col, Doctoral Equivalency, 70; also with Ben Shahn & Richard Lindner; Colby-Sawyer Col, LHD, 85; St Anslem Col, DH(hon). *Hon Degrees:* hon degrees, Colby-Sawyer Col, 85, St Anselm Col, 94, Notre Dame Col, 96, Enevson Col, 99, Univ Conn, 99, Georgetown Univ, 02, New Eng Col, 03. *Work:* Kerlan Collection, Univ Minn, Minneapolis; Worcester Art Mus, Mass; Osborne Collection, Toronto; Thomas J Dodd Res Ctr, Univ Conn, Storrs. *Comn:* Mural, Dominican Sisters Retreat House Chapel, Schenectady, NY, 58; two murals, Conception Abbey Retreat House, Mo, 59; renovation, design & murals, St Sylvester's Church, Graniteville, Vt, 61; murals, Glastonbury Monastery, Hingham, Mass, 62; altar painting, Newman Cult Ctr, Rensselaer Polytech Inst, 68. *Exhib:* Children's Bk Illusr, Everson Mus, 77; Art and the Alphabet, 78 & A Peaceable Kingdom: Animals in Art, 82, Houston Mus Fine Arts; The Original Art Ann, Master Eagle Gallery, NY, 80-83; A Decade of the Original Art of the Best Illustrated Children's Books, 1970-1980, Univ Conn Libr, Storrs, 82; Illustrators Exhib, Metrop Mus Art & NY Pub Libr, 82-83; Kraft Educ Ctr, Art Inst Chicago, Ill, 92; Tomie Turns 60, Cedar Rapids Mus, Mich, 94; Coves Gallery, Mass, 98; and others. *Collection Arranged:* Kerlan Collection, Univ Minn, Minneapolis, 81. *Pos:* Designer & tech dir speech & theater, Colby-Sawyer Col, 73-76. *Teaching:* Asst prof design & painting, Newton Col of Sacred Heart, Mass, 62-66; asst prof design, Lone Mountain Col, San Francisco, 67-70; instr art, Chamberlayne Jr Col, 72-73; assoc prof, Colby-Sawyer Col, 73-76; assoc prof illus & graphic design, New Eng Col, Henniker, 76-79. *Awards:* Caldecott Honor Bk Award, Am Libr Asn, 76; Regina Medal, Cath Libr Asn, 83; Smithsonian Medal, Smithsonian Inst, 90; Newbery Honor Book Award, Am Libr Asn, 2000. *Bibliog:* Something About the Author, Volume 59, Gale Res, 90; Major Authors and Illustrators for Children and Young Adults, Gale Res, 92; Barbara Elleman (auth), Tomie de Paola: His Art and His Stories, 99; and others. *Mem:* Authors Guild; Soc Children's Bk Writers. *Media:* Mixed. *Publ:* Auth & illusr, The Clown of God, Harcourt Brace Jovanovich, 78; illusr, Tomie de Paola's Mother Goose, 85, Bonjour, Mr Satie, 91, Jingle, the Christmas Clown, 92, Strega Nona Meets Her Match, 93, The Legend of the Poinsettia, 94, GP Putnam's Sons; auth/illusr, 26 Fairmount Avenue, GP Putnam's Sons, 99, Strega Nona Takes a Vacation, 00, Meet the Barkers, GP Putnam's Sons, 01. *Mailing Add:* c/o G P Putnam's Sons 345 Hudson St New York NY 10014

DE PEDERY-HUNT, DORA
SCULPTOR, DESIGNER
b Budapest, Hungary, Nov 16, 13. *Study:* State Lyceum, Budapest, 32; Royal Sch Appl Art, Budapest, MA, 43. *Work:* Nat Gallery Can, Ottawa; Art Gallery Ont, Toronto; Smithsonian Inst; Royal Cabinet Medals, Brussels, Belg & The Hague, Netherlands; Mus Contemp Crafts, Charlottetown, PEI; and others. *Exhib:* Can Pavillion, Expo '67; Sculpture Symposium, Toronto, 78; Prince Arthur Gallerie, 78; Hamilton Art Gallery, 79; Gallery Stratford, 79; and others. *Awards:* Can Govt Centennial Medal, 67; Queen's Jubilee Medal, 72; Civic Award Merit, 79. *Mem:* Royal Can Acad; Sculptors' Soc Can; Ont Soc Artists. *Mailing Add:* 84 Carlton St Apt 613 Toronto ON M5B 2P4 Canada

DEPILLARS, MURRY N
ADMINISTRATOR, ILLUSTRATOR
b Chicago, Ill, Dec 21, 38. *Study:* Kennedy-King Community Col, AA (fine arts); Roosevelt Univ, BA (art educ) & MA (urban studies); Pa State Univ, Univ Park, PhD (art educ). *Work:* Paul Roberson Cult Ctr, Pa State Univ, University Park; Art Inst Chicago, Inst Positive Educ, Chicago; Consolidated Bank, Richmond; Studio Mus, Harlem, NY. *Comn:* Mural, African & African-Am Studies Ctr, Univ Mich, Ann Arbor, 71; illusr, J Negro Educ, Howard Univ, 74; illusr, Destruction of Black Civilizations, 74 & Steps to Break the Circle, 75, Third World Press; illusr, Story of Kwanza, Inst Positive Educ, Chicago, 75. *Exhib:* Mus Sci & Indust, Chicago, 70; The Indignant Eye, Whitney Mus Am Art, NY, 71; Am Greeting Card Gallery, NY, 72; Rainbow Sign Gallery, Los Angeles, 74; World Expo '74, African-Am Pavilion, Spokane, 74; Huntsville Mus Art, 79; Miss Mus Art, Jackson, 80; Heckscher Mus, Huntington, NY, 86; NY State Mus, Albany, 87; Alfred & David Smart Galleries, Univ Chicago, Ill, 87; Fay Gold Gallery, Atlanta, Ga, 88; Geme Festival of Cult, SERMAC, Ft DeFrance, Martinique, 88; Lee Hall Gallery, Clemson Univ, 90; Mus Sci & Indust, Chicago, 92; Norman Parrish Gallery, Washington, DC, 93; Lyons Matrix Gallery, Austin, Tex, 95; Betty Rymer Gallery Sch Art Inst, Chicago, Ill, 95; Newcomb Hall Artspace, Univ Va, Charlottesville, 95; Satori Fine Art Gallery, Chicago, Ill, 96. *Pos:* Asst dir, Educ Asst Prog, Univ Ill, Chicago, 68-71, asst dean, Sch Arts, Va Commonwealth Univ, 71-76, dean, 76-. *Teaching:* Instr, Chicago Comt of Urban Opportunity, 68; asst prof art, Va Commonwealth Univ, 71-76, assoc prof 76-84, prof, 84-95. *Awards:* Man of Excellence Plaque, Rep China, 80; Nat Endowment Arts, 81, 82 & 83; Alumni Fel, Penn State Univ, 90; and others. *Bibliog:* F D Cossitt (auth), DePillars is Artist with message, Richmond Times Dispatch Newspaper, 6/15/70; Semella Lewis & Ruth Waddy (auth), Black artists on art, Contemporary Crafts, Inc, Vol II; Robert Doty (auth), Contemporary Black Artists in America, Whitney Mus Am Art, 72. *Mem:* Nat Conf Artists (pres, 73-); Nat Art Educr Asn; Pan African Artists Alliance; Afri-Cobra; and others. *Media:* Acrylic, Oil. *Publ:* Illusr, A People of the Sun, 73; auth, Emerging Voice of the Black Visual Artists, Black Art, 76; Art history and Black culture, 77 & Renaissance to Renaissance, 80, Minority Voices; Wanted: A role for the Black visual artists, Western J Black Studies, 82; Multiculturalism in Visual Arts Education: Are America's Educational Institutions Ready for Multiculturalism, Art, Cult & Ethnicity, 90; The Visual Arts: Obsession of Indifference and Intolerance, The Washington Review, 91. *Dealer:* Third World Press 7524 S Cottage Grove Chicago Ill 60619. *Mailing Add:* 8101 Cavendish Ln Richmond VA 23227

DE PIÑA RAMOS, THEODORE SANCHEZ See Ramos, Theodore

DE PUMA, RICHARD DANIEL
HISTORIAN, EDITOR
b DuBois, Pa, May 15, 42. *Study:* Swarthmore Col, BA(art hist), 64; Bryn Mawr Col, MA(archeol), 67, PhD(archeol), 69. *Collection Arranged:* Etruscan & Villanovan Pottery (auth, catalog), Univ Iowa Mus Art, 71; Roman Portraits (auth, catalog), Univ Iowa Mus Art, 88; Art in Roman Life: Villa to Grave (auth, catalog), Cedar Rapids Mus Art, 2003. *Pos:* Res assoc, Field Mus Natural Hist, Chicago, Ill, 84-; adv bd, Am J Archaeol, 85-98, Etruscan Found, 91-; ed, Studies in Classics Monograph Series, Univ Wis, 93-2004. *Teaching:* Instr classical art, Univ Iowa, Iowa City, 68-69, from asst prof to assoc prof, 69-86, prof, 86-, F Wendell Miller Distinguished prof, 2000-2004. *Awards:* Nat Endowment Humanities Grant, 85, 99; Am Inst Indian Studies, 87; Res Fel, Deutsches Archaologisches Inst, 94. *Mem:* Archeol Inst Am; Col Art Asn; Soc Promotion Roman Studies; Inst di Studi Etruschi ed Italici. *Res:* Etruscan pottery & bronzes; Greek vase painting; mosaics; Etruscan forgeries. *Publ:* Auth, Etruscan Tomb-Groups: Ancient Pottery and Bronzes in Chicago's Field Museum of Natural Hist, Mainz, 86; Corpus Speculorum Etruscorum, USA 1 & 2,

Ames, 86 & 93, USA 4, Rome, 2005; co-ed, Rome and India: The Ancient Sea Trade, Madison, 91; Murlo and the Etruscans: Art and Society in Ancient Etruria, Madison, 94; auth, Corpus Vasorum Antiquorum: J Paul Getty Mus 6, Malibu, 96; and others. *Mailing Add:* 409 Hutchinson Ave Iowa City IA 52246

DERBY, MARK
CERAMIST, INSTRUCTOR
b E Lansing, Mich, Jan 1, 60. *Study:* Calif State Univ, Long Beach, BFA, 84 & MFA, 89. *Work:* Mus Ceramic Art Alfred, NY State Col Ceramics; San Angelo Mus Art, Tex; Nora Eccles Harrison Mus Art, Utah State Univ, Logan. *Exhib:* Ameen Art Gallery, Nicholls State Univ, Thibodaux, La; Northwestern State Univ, Natchitoches, La, 96; Sylvia Schmidt Gallery, New Orleans, La, 97; Contemp Craft, La Villa Meilleur, New Orleans, La 98; Living with Tile, Wayne Art Ctr, Wayne, Pa, 98; Columbus Cult Arts Ctr, Columbus, Ohio, 1999; Erth Gallery, New Orleans, La, 2001. *Teaching:* Instr ceramics, Braille Inst, Anaheim, Calif, 87-88, Palos Verdes Art Ctr, Calif, 88, Clay Studio Sch, Philadelphia, Pa, 92-95 & Univ City Arts League, Philadelphia, Pa, 92-95; vis asst prof ceramics, Newcomb Col Art, Tulane Univ, 95-98; adj prof ceramics, La State Univ, Baton Rouge, 98. *Awards:* Individual Fel, Nat Endowment Arts, 90; Individual Fel, Ariz Comn Arts, 91; Individual Fel, La Div Arts, 98. *Bibliog:* Jimmy Clark (auth), Whimsical Clay, Ceramics: Art & Perception, issue 5, 91; Keely Coghlan (auth), Quiet Symmetry Speaks Volumes in Ceramics, San Angelo Standard Times, 4/17/92; Chris Waddington (auth), vessels apt works for sculptor's, The Times Picayune, New Orleans, La 4/20/97; Gerry Williams (auth), Louisiana Gumbo, The Studio Potter, Vol 29, No 2, June 2001; Doug MacCash (auh), Ceramics capture Feel of the City, Times Picayune, New Orleans, 9/21/2001. *Mem:* ACC; Nat Coun Educ in Ceramic Arts. *Dealer:* Rhino Contemp Crafts New Orleans La; Derby Pottery & Tileworks New Orleans La. *Mailing Add:* 2029 Magazine St New Orleans LA 70115

DEREMER, SUSAN RENÉ
PAINTER, ILLUSTRATOR
b Atlanta, Ga, Jun 29, 59. *Study:* Inst Fine Arts, Rio De Janeiro, Brazil, cert, 78; Univ Ga, BFA, 82; Art Students League NY, with Nelson Shanks, 98. *Work:* Hist Mus Smyrna, Ga. *Comn:* portrait, Tryon Publ Co, Atlanta, 97; portrait, Dr Morton S Silberman Zoo, Atlanta, 2001. *Exhib:* One-woman show, South Cobb Arts Alliance, Inc, Mableton, Ga, 92; Fine Arts Soc Kennesaw, Ga, 95; AAPL Grand Nat, Salmaguni Club, New York City, 97, 98 & 2003; two-person invitational, The Art Place-Mt View, Marietta, Ga, 99; one-woman show, A Retrospective Exhib Paintings Pastel & Drawings,The Cult Arts Ctr, Douglasville, Ga, 2004. *Pos:* art dir, Exec Printing Inc, Marietta, Ga, 88-90; graphic artist, IBM, Atlanta, 92-93; pres, Deremer Studio Inc, 93-. *Teaching:* drawing instr, Artists Atelier of Atlanta, 1995; painting instr, Douglasville Sch Art. *Awards:* First Place Illustration, Ga Scholastic Press Asn, 77; First Place, Atlantic Artists Club, 94; Third Place, Fine Arts Soc Kennesaw, 95. *Bibliog:* Suzanne Smith (auth), Susan Deremer-Spotlight, PSA Folio, 97; Master pastel artists of the world, Pastel Artist Int, Marcy/April 2002. *Mem:* Fel Am Artists Prof League Inc; Am Soc Classical Realism; Am Soc Portrait Artists; Portrait Soc Am; Portrait Soc Atlanta Inc (treas, 95-97, pres, 97-99). *Media:* Oil, Pastel, Charcoal, Graphite, Ink. *Publ:* Auth, Atlanta An Historical Sketchbook, Tryon Publ Co, 98; auth, Folio, Portrait Soc Atlanta Newsletter, 97-2000. *Dealer:* The Portrait Group PO Box 8067 Reston Va 30134. *Mailing Add:* 8341 Timberlane Dr Douglasville GA 30134

DERGALIS, GEORGE
PAINTER, SCULPTOR
b Athens, Greece, 28; US citizen. *Study:* Painting with DeChirico & Morandi, 48-50; Acad Belle Arti, Rome, MA, 51; Sch Mus Fine Arts, Boston, dipl, 58. *Work:* De Cordova Mus, Mass; Boston Pub Libr; Camara de Comercio & Museo de Arte, Medellin, Colombia; US Army Ctr Military Hist, Washington, DC; and others; Print Research Found. *Comn:* Nine watercolors, Boston, 78 & mural, Norwood, 78, Citizen's Bank; portrait, Worcester Acad, 88; sculpture & murals, Finca El Porvenir, 90 & 96. *Exhib:* Through the Looking Glass traveling show, 89-90; Fantasy, Boston Pub Libr, 92; South Shore Art Ctr, 94; Cambridge Art Asn, 94; Wayland/Artspace, 94; Boston Corp Art, 95; and others; Watercolor USA, Springfield Art Mus, Mo, 2002; Landscapes Seen and Imagined, DeCordova Mus, Lincoln, Mass, 2003; In Good Company, The Harvard Club of Boston, 2003; Rocky Mt NH Watermedia Exhibition, Foothills ArtCenter, Golden, CO, 2000, 03 & 05; Attleboro Mus, 2004 & 06; Biennial Juried Underground Railroad Exhib, Northern KY Univ, KY, 2004. *Pos:* combat artist US Army Hist Dept, Vietnam, 67; Artist-in-residence, Partners of the Americas, 79; master, Copley Soc Boston, 81; designer, Wayland Veterans Memorial. *Teaching:* Instr painting, De Cordova Mus, 61-94; art instr, Sch Mus Fine Arts, Boston, 61-70; pvt art classes, Wayland, Mass, 69-. *Awards:* Gold Medal, Acad Italia delle Arti e del Lavoro, 80; Best of Show, Holiday Card Contest, Commonwealth Mass, 2000; Juror's Award, Attleboro Mus, 2004; Top People of Year Award, Wayland Town Crier, 2005; others. *Bibliog:* Freedom of Expression, Marilyn Bauer (auth), The Cincinatti Enquirer; Susan L Sherwood (auth), Artist Pours Heart into Design, Wayland Town Crier, 6/30/2005; Liz McGeachy (auth), A Memorial for Wayland, Slippery Rock Gazette, 2/2006; many others. *Mem:* DeCordova Mus. *Media:* All. *Mailing Add:* 72 Oxbow Rd Wayland MA 01778

DERN, F CARL
SCULPTOR
b Salt Lake City, Utah, Apr 24, 36. *Study:* San Francisco Art Inst, 1969; Univ Calif, Berkeley, 1971-1972. *Work:* In many pvt collections. *Exhib:* San Francisco Art Inst Centennial Exhib, de Young Mus, 70; New Mus Mod Art, Oakland, 70-73; 1st & 2nd Soap Box Derby, San Francisco Mus Mod Art, 75 & 78; San Jose Mus Art, 78; Syntax Corp Outdoor Sculpture Exhib, 79-80; San Mateo Arts Coun, Proarts Gallery, Oakland, 80; Richmond Art Ctr, 81; and others; Univ Calif Nelson Art Gallery, 1988; Esprit Sculpture Park, 1990; Bolinas Mus, 1993-2003; Fresno Art Mus, 2003. *Teaching:* Lectr sculpture, Univ Calif, Berkeley, 75 & Univ Calif, Davis, 83; lectr art, Sonoma State Univ, 77 & 78. *Awards:* Anne Bremer Prize in Art, Univ Calif, Berkeley, 69 & 72; First Prize, 1st Int Contemp, Jon Morehead Gallery, Chico, Calif, 71; Hand Hallow Found Fel, 82 & 83. *Mem:* Artists Equity. *Mailing Add:* 58 Park Rd Fairfax CA 94930

DERNOVICH, DONALD FREDERICK
PAINTER, EDUCATOR
b Rock Springs, Wyo, April 9, 42. *Study:* Univ Wyo, BA(art educ), 66, MA(art), 67; Ft Hays State Univ, MFA(painting), 83. *Work:* Birger Sandzen Mem Gallery, Lindsborg, Kans; Halseth Co Community Arts Ctr, Rock Springs, Wyo; Wayne State Col, Wayne, Nebr; Ella Carothers Dunnegan Gallery, Bolivar, Mo; Mus Nebr Art, Kearney. *Comn:* Two watercolors, Law Enforcement Acad, Douglas, Wyo, 85; painting, Chadron St Col, Chadron, Nebr, 90; painting, Beard Oil Co, Gemini Div, 92; painting, Am First Bank, McCook, Nebr, 94, 2000; painting, State Bank, Benkleman, Nebr, 94. *Exhib:* Arts for the Parks, Nat Wildlife Art Mus, Jackson, Wyo, 93, 96, 98-2001, 2003 & 2005; Am Watercolor Soc 128th, 135th 138th, Int, Salamagundi Club Galleries, 95, 2002, 05; 171 St Nat Acad Design, Nat Acad Galleries, NY, 96; Oil Painters Am, Greenhouse Gallery Fine Art, San Antonio, Tex, 96; CM Russell Art Auction, Great Falls, Mont, 97-2006; Phippin Mus Art Show, Prescott, Ariz, 1997-2005; Zantman Galleries, Palm Desert, Calif, 2001; Buffalo Bill Art Show, Cody Wyo, 2004-06; Dana Gallery, Bozeman, Mont, 2006. *Pos:* Dir, McCook Area Arts Coun, 75-78; exhib bd, Asn Nebr Arts Clubs, 86-90. *Teaching:* Art dir & instr, McCook Community Col, Nebr, 75-2004. *Awards:* Purchase Award-Best Show, Mus Nebr Art, Kearney, 89; Award for Excellence, Arts For Parks Ann-Top 100 Traveling, 93, 98; Best Watermedia, Ann Western Spirit Art Show, Cheyenne, 94-98; 2nd Place in Watermedia, Phippen Western Art Show, Prescott, Ariz, 99; Artists Favorite Award, Spirit of the Great Plains Invit, Mus of Nebr Art, Kearney, Nebr, 2000; Doc Smith Award, Blackfoot Valley Art Exhib, Lincoln, Mont, 97, Silver Award, 2000; Peoples Favorite and Artists Favorite Awards, Platte River Valley Western Art Show, Saratoga, Wyo, 2000; First Place in Oil, Phippen Mus Western Art Show, Prescott, Ariz, 2002; Best of Show, High Plains Art Festival, Oberlin, Kans, 2006. *Bibliog:* Up the river with a paint brush, Am Artists Mag, 92; The art of Don Dernovich, Contact-News-N-Viewslett, 94. *Mem:* Am Watercolor Soc (sig mem); Oil Painters Am (sig mem); McCook Art Guild (life mem); Nat Watercolor Soc (sig mem); Kans Watercolor Soc (sig mem); Rocky Mountain Plain Air Painters; IMPACT, Nebr. *Media:* Watercolor, Oil. *Publ:* Auth, Splash Four, Northlight Bks, 96; Best In Watercolor, Watercolor Places, Rockport Publ, 1987, 96; Splash Five, 1998. *Dealer:* Blackhawk Gallery Saratoga Wyo; Spirits In The Wind Gallery Golden Colo. *Mailing Add:* 210 Taylor PO Box 163 Culbertson NE 69024

DE ROTHSCHILD, ELIE ROBERT
COLLECTOR
b Paris, France, May 29, 1917. *Study:* Univ de Paris, Lycee Louis le Grand, Fac of Law. *Pos:* pres, Rothschild Bank, Zürich, Switz, Assicurazioni Generali, Trieste & Venice, Italy, formerly. *Awards:* Named Officier, Legion d'honneur; named one of Top 200 Collectors, ARTnews Mag, 2004; recipient Croix de guerre, Ufficiale Ordine al Merito della Repubblica Italiana. *Collection:* Old Masters, Impressionism & Modern Art. *Mailing Add:* 32 Ormonde Gate London United Kingdom SW3 4HA

DE ROTHSCHILD, ERIC ALAIN ROBERT DAVID
COLLECTOR
b NY City, Oct 3, 40. *Study:* Poly Sch, Zürich, 63. *Awards:* Named one of Top 200 Art Collectors, ARTnews Mag, 2004. *Mem:* Rothschild Found, Paris (pres, currently); Nat Found, graphic & plastic Arts, Paris; Smithsonian Inst, Wash, DC (admin coun, 96). *Collection:* Old Masters, Modern & Contemporary Art. *Mailing Add:* Rothschild & Cie Banque 17 Ave Matignon Paris 75008 France

DEROUX, DANIEL EDWARD
PAINTER, SCULPTOR
b Juneau, Alaska, Oct 25, 51. *Study:* NS Col Art & Design, Halifax, Can, 74 75. *Comn:* 3 murals, Univ Alaska, Fairbanks; 2 murals, City of Anchorage, Alaska; 3 murals, city of Junca, Alaska; 26 paintings, City of Palmer, Alaska. *Exhib:* San Francisco Mus Mod Art, 79-80; 15th Ann Nat Small Sculpture & Drawing Exhib, Corpus Christi, Tex, 81; Collage & Assemblage, traveling exhib, 81-82; Los Angeles Int Art Competition, 88; NY Int Art Competition, 88; and others. *Pos:* Cur visual arts, Alaska State Mus, 78-79. *Awards:* Most Accomplished Artist, Los Angeles Int Art Competition, 81; Best of Show, Calgene W Coast Art Competition, Davis, 84; Third Place, NY Int Art Competition, 88. *Bibliog:* Margaret Firmin (auth), Only painting what he sees, Alaska Advocate, 2/79; art ed (auth), Whimsical images are his delight, Anchorage Times, 2/79; Marianna Woodward (auth), Dan DeRoux Juneau buckaroo, Alaska J, 1/80. *Mailing Add:* 19191 Randall Rd Juneau AK 99802

DERRICKSON, STEVE BRUCE
PAINTER
b Baltimore, Md, Mar 21, 52. *Study:* Ohio Univ, BFA, 74; Tyler Sch Art, Temple Univ, MFA, 77. *Work:* Bank of Am; Principal Financial Group; Univ NC; Security Pac Bank. *Exhib:* solo exhib, Stephen Wirtz Gallery, San Francisco, 89; Sue Spaid Fine Art, Los Angeles, Calif, 90; Insect Politics, Body Horror, Social Order, Hallwalls, Buffalo, NY, 90; Invitational, Berland/Hall Gallery, NY; Eye Flower Drawings, PPOW Gallery, NY, 94; and others. *Teaching:* Instr art, Univ Tex, Austin, 77-80; asst prof art, Univ Tex, Austin, 80-84; vis artist, Ohio State Univ, Columbus, Ohio, 87. *Awards:* Installation for Text Sculpture Symp, Tex Comm Arts, Austin, 83; Fel, Nat Endowment Arts, 87-88; Residency, MacDowell Colony, Petersborough, NH, 91.

Bibliog: Eleanor Heartney (auth), Art & the electronic fishbowl, Art News, 12/86; Kate Linker (auth), Review of cinemaobject, Artforum, 12/86; Robert Mahoney (auth), Review of a romantic distance, Arts Mag, 5/88. *Dealer:* Sue Spaid Fine Art Gallery 7454 1/2 Beverly Blvd Los Angeles Calif 90036. *Mailing Add:* 572 Plutarch Rd Highland NY 12528

DERRYBERRY, VIRGINIA TAYLOR
PAINTER, EDUCATOR
b Morristown, Tenn, Jan 10, 50. *Study:* Vanderbilt Univ, Nashville, BA, 73; Peabody Col, Nashville, MA, 76; Univ Tenn, Knoxville, MFA, 84. *Work:* Carnegie Mus Art, Pittsburgh; Tenn State Mus, Nashville; Morris Mus, Augusta, Ga; State W Va Permanent Collection, Charleston; Metrop Airport, Nashville, Tenn. *Comn:* Paintings, First Union Tower, Greensboro, NC, 93; paintings, S Cent Bell, Nashville, Tenn, 94; 16 site spec paintings, Hartsfield Atlanta Int Airport, 96. *Exhib:* Am Drawings, Forum Gallery, NY, 86; Drawings from the 80's, Carnegie-Mellon Univ Art Gallery, Pittsburgh, 87; one-man show, Southeastern Ctr Contemp Art, Winston-Salem, NC, 86, Ashville Art Mus, NC, 93, McIntosh Gallery, Atlanta, Ga, 96 & Cumberland Gallery, Nashville, Tenn, 98; The Figure, Marcia Wood Gallery, Atlanta, 98; Circumnavigation (with catalog), Nationsbank Plaza Gallery, Atlanta, 98. *Teaching:* Asst prof drawing & painting, WVa Univ, Morgantown, 84-88 & Univ NC, Asheville, 96-; prof drawing & painting, Savannah Col Art & Design, Ga, 88-93. *Awards:* Governor's Award, State of WVa, 85; Individual Artists Grant, State of Ga, 91-94; Assoc Artists Southeastern Spectrum Best of Show, Winston-Salem, NC, 98. *Bibliog:* Frances McDougal (auth), Land of a different color, Southern Accents, 7/94; Bill Alexander (auth), Virginia Derryberry, Art Papers, Atlanta, 4/95. *Mem:* Col Art Asn. *Media:* Oil. *Dealer:* Cumberland Gallery 4107 Hillsboro Circle Nashville TN 37215

DESANTIS, DIANA
PAINTER
b Brooklyn, NY. *Study:* Traphagen Sch Art, cert, 46; Parsons Sch Design, dipl, 49; Art Students League, with Harvey Dinnerstein & David Leffel, 91-92. *Comn:* Portrait, Brushstroke Design Asn, NY, 94. *Exhib:* Soc of Illustrators Nat, NY, 92; Catherine Lorillard Wolfe Nat, NY, 92-94; Open Juried Nat, Nassau Co Mus, 92-94; Hudson Valley Art Asn Nat, Hastings, NY, 93; Pastel Soc Am Nat, NY, 94; and others. *Awards:* Norman Rockwell Mus Award, Soc Illustrators, 92; Gold Medal, Knickerbocker Artists, 92; David & Elsie Ject Key Mem Award, Audubon Artists, 94. *Bibliog:* Article in Artspeak, 4/91; article in Williston Times, 6/93; article in News Day, 9/93. *Mem:* Knickerbocker Artists USA; Pastel Soc Am; Audubon Artists; Catherine Lorillard Wolfe Art Club; Am Artist Prof League. *Media:* Pastel, Oil. *Mailing Add:* 81 Bay Ave Huntington NY 11743

DE SANTO, STEPHEN C
PAINTER
b Louisville, Ky, May 27, 1951. *Study:* Huntington Col, BA(art), 74; Ball State Univ, MA(art), 78. *Work:* Wichita Art Mus, Kans; Anderson Fine Arts Ctr, Ind. *Exhib:* Mid-Year Show, Butler Inst Am Art, Youngstown, Ohio, 80-82; Am Watercolor Soc Traveling Exhib, 10 museums across the US, 80, 82 & 85; 157th Ann Exhib, Nat Acad Design, NY, 82; Navy Pier Int Art Expo, Chicago, 85-88. *Pos:* Full-time fine artist. *Awards:* Ed Whitney Award, 80 & High Winds Award, 85, Am Watercolor Soc Ann Exhib; Merit Award, Watercolor USA Ann, 85. *Bibliog:* Michael Ward (auth), Letter from the editor, Artist's Mag, 1/91; Rachel Wolf (auth), SPLASH II-Watercolor Breakthroughs, Northlight Bks, 93; David Pyle (auth), The Swipe File, Artist's Mag, 7/94; and others. *Media:* Acrylic, Mixed Media. *Mailing Add:* 1325 Kensington Blvd Fort Wayne IN 46805

DESCHAMPS, FRANCOIS
PHOTOGRAPHER
b Nov 18, 46. *Study:* Sorbonne, Paris, 64-65; Univ Ill, Champaign, BS(Phi Beta Kappa), MS, ABD (mathematics), 65-70; Ill Inst Technol, Inst Degisn, MS(photog), 72. *Work:* Mus Contemp Art, Chicago; Metro Mus; Houston Mus Fine Arts; Mus Mod Art, NY; Brooklyn Mus. *Teaching:* Aegean Sch Fine Arts, Paros, Greece, 73; Bradley Univ, Peoria, Ill, 72-80; teacher & dir Photog Option, State Univ NY at New Paltz, 80-; prof art dept, State Univ NY, New Paltz. *Awards:* Nat Endowment for Arts, Photog Fel, 83 & 87; Photogr's Fel, NY Found Arts, 88 & 98; Intcr Arts Travel Fel, Nat Endowment Art, 94; Fel, Univ Auckland Res Found, 95; Residence Cite' des Arts, Paris, 2002. *Media:* Offset Books, Photographic Boxes. Collection: Metropolitan Museum, Museum of Modern Art, NY. *Publ:* Auth, Life in a Book, VSW Press, 86; coauth, Particle Theory, Nexus Press, 91; auth, A Guide to Antipodia, Univ Arts, Philadelphia, 92; auth, Memoire d'un Voyage en Oceanie, Photoforum, NZ, 95; auth, Sombras Rojas, USW Press, 99. *Mailing Add:* 120 Hasbrouck Rd New Paltz NY 12561

DESIDERIO, VINCENT
PAINTER
b Philadelphia, Pa, 1955. *Study:* Haverford Col, BA(fine arts/art history), 77, Acad di Belle Arti, Florence, Italy, 77-78, Pa Acad Fine Arts, cert, 79-83. *Work:* Sammlung Ludwig Neve Galerie, Aachen, WGer; Denver Art Mus; Everson Mus, Syracuse, NY; Metrop Mus Art, NY; Greenville Co Mus Art, SC; The Solomon R Giggenheim Mus, NY; Mus of Fine Arts, Boston, Mass; Hirshhorn Mus & Sculpture, Wahington, DC; Pa Acad of Fine Arts, Phila, PA; Seven Bridges Foundation, Conn. *Exhib:* Solo exhibs, Lawrence Oliver Gallery, Philadelphia, 86, Lang & O'Hara Gallery, NY, 87, 89 & 90, Greenville Mus, SC, 88, Queens Mus, NY, 91, Marlborough Gallery, NY, 93, 97, 99, 2001, 02 & Very Spec Arts Gallery, Washington, DC, 93; Marlborough Gallery, 2004; In the Looking Glass: Contemp Narrative Painting, Mint Mus Art, Charlotte, NC, 91; On Paper, Marlborough Gallery, NY, 92, Summer Show, Marlborough Gallery, 2001, Oil on Paper, Marlborough Gallery, 2002; The Anxious Salon, Mass Inst Technol, 93; List Visual Arts Ctr, Cambridge, Mass, 93; The Seer, O'Hara Gallery, NY, 94; Queens Artists: Highlights of the 20th Century, Queens Mus Art, NY, 97; Art 1997 Chicago: 5th Ann Expo of Int Galleries Featuring Modern and Contemp Art, Navy Pier, Chicago, 97; Forma Y Figuracion: Obras Maestras De La Coleccion Blake-Purnell, Guggenheim Bilbao, 98; 1998 Collector's Show: The Ark Arts Ctr, Little Rock, Ark, 98; 1998 Collector's Show, Ark Arts Ctr, Little Rock, Ark, 98; The Cantor Fitzgerald Gallery, Haverford Coll, Pa, 2002; group exhibs, Modern and Contemp Portraits, Forum Gallery, NY, 2003, Transforming the Commonplace, Susquehanna Art Mus, Pa, 2003. *Awards:* Pollock/Krasner Found Grant, 87; Fel, Nat Endowment Arts, 87; Grand Prize SAS Prince Rainier III, 30th Ann Show Contemp Art, Monte Carlo, Monaco, 96. *Bibliog:* David Zimmerman (auth), Art exhibit casts a critical eye at common concepts of heroism, rev, USA Today, 10/29/96; Phillipe Cruysmans (auth), Dix Artistes Couronne's a Monaco, Le Figaro, 5/14/96; Carol King (auth), realism: The new hip, ARTnews, 2/97. *Media:* Oils. *Mailing Add:* c/o Marlborough Gallery 40 W 57th St New York NY 10019

DESJARLAIT, ROBERT D
MURALIST, WRITER
b Red Lake Chippewa Reservation, Redlake, Minn, Nov, 18, 1946. *Study:* Self taught. *Work:* NDak Mus Art, Grand Forks; Meridel Le Sueur Libr, Augsburg Col, Minneapolis; Anoka-Hennepin Educ Admin Ctr, Anoka; Robbinsdale Educ Admin Ctr, New Hope. *Comn:* Illus, Anoka-Hennepin Am Indian Lang & Cult Prog, 89-90; mural, Saturn Sch Tomorrow, St Paul, 92; mural, Phillips Neighborhood Safe Art Proj, Minneapolis, 95; mural, Minneapolis Indian Educ Proj, 96; mosiac, Phillips Gateway Prog, Minneapolis, 96. *Exhib:* Homecomings, NDak Mus Art, Grand Forks, 85; Minn Chippewa Art Exhib, Am Indian Community House Gallery, NY, 86; In Defense of Sacred Lands, Harcus Gallery, Boston, Mass, 87; Pictures from Home: Minnesota Illustrators of Children's Books, Univ Art Mus, Minneapolis, 88; Metaphorical Fish, Univ Art Mus, Minneapolis, 90. *Pos:* Art dir/curric specialist, Northern Winds Arts Educ Proj, Minneapolis, 92-95. *Teaching:* Art instr, Am Indian Art Hist & Drawing, Heart of the Earth Survival Sch, Minneapolis, 89-90, Native Am Educ Serv Col, Minneapolis, 94-95, Lacourt Orielles Community Col, 96; instr traditional arts, Am Indian OIC Col, Minneapolis, 96. *Awards:* First Place, Drawing, Ojibwe Art Expo, Minneapolis, 88; Percy Fearing Award for Illus, Minn Coun Teaching of Foreign Lang, Minneapolis, 88; CUE Award, Minneapolis Comn Arts, 95. *Bibliog:* Kathy Thornes (auth), DesJarlait depicts Ojibwe vision, Red Lake Times, 87; Interview with Robert DesJarlait (video), Northern Lights & Insights, Hennepin Co Libr, Minneapolis, 92; Beverly Slapin & Doris Seale (ed), Through Indian Eyes: The Native Experience in Books for Children, Philadelphia, 92. *Mem:* Native Cult Arts Prog/Native Arts Circle; Minn State Arts Bd Artists in Educ. *Media:* Acrylic, Graphite Pencil. *Publ:* Auth, Nimiwin, A History of Ojibway Dance, 90, Rethinking Stereotypes: Native American Imagery in Art & Illustration, Anoka-Henn Press, Coon Rapids, 93; Art of the Ojibway, Northern Winds Desktop Press, 94; auth & illusr, Nimiwin: An Ojibway Dance Curriculum Coloring Book, Northern Winds Desktop Press, 96; auth, Traditional powwow vs contest powwow and the role of the Native American community, Wicazo Sa Rev, Univ Minn Press, 96; illusr, The First American Series, 88-90, auth & illusr, Ni-mi-win: A History of Ojibway Dance, 90 & illusr, Traditional Indian Stories, 92, Anoka-Hennepin Press, Coon Rapids. *Dealer:* Art Lending Gallery 2500 Groveland Terr Minneapolis Minn

DE SMET, LORRAINE
PAINTER
b Passaic, NJ, May 5, 1928. *Study:* Art Students League, study with Issac Soyer, Harvey Dinnerstein, David Leffel, Hillary Holmes, Richard Goetz, 79-84; Montclair Art Mus, 86. *Work:* US Coast Guard Collection; Union Trust, Stamford, Conn; Univ Conn Health Ctr, Farmington. *Exhib:* Focus on Art, NJ, 88, 89 & 90; Ridgewood Art Inst, 89-2004; Caldwell Col, 90, 94-2005 & 2006; Catherine Lorillard Wolfe, Nat Arts Club, NY; With Coast Guard on Governors Island, Hudson Valley Art Asn, NY; Am Artists Prof League; Salmagundi Club, NY; Pen & Brush Club, NY; Best of the Best, Trenton Mus, 2001. *Pos:* Bd dir, Pen & Brush Club, 85-92, brush chmn, 87-89, co-chair brush sect, 94-95 & 97; bd govs, West Essex Art Asn, 92-98; bd dir, Art Ctr NJ, 94-, secy & mem chair, currently. *Awards:* Ann Waldon Award, Am Artists Prof League, 98, Merit Award, 2000 & 2002; Merit, Livingston Art Asn, 99-2002, 1st place, 2004; Millburn-Short Hills Award of Excellence, 2001 & 02, Award of Merit, 2004 & 05; Oakside Cult Award, 2004; 1st Pl, W Essex Art Assn, 2005 & Art Ctr NJ, 2005; Caldwell Progress Award, 2006. *Bibliog:* Joseph Merkel (auth), article, Artspeak, 84; Will Grant (auth), article, Artspeak, 87; Howard Farber (auth), Artspeak, 90. *Mem:* Pen & Brush Club (vpres, 89-92); life mem Art Students League, NY; Am Artists Prof League; West Essex Art Asn; Art Ctr NJ; and others. *Media:* Oil. *Specialty:* Still life & portraits. *Mailing Add:* 33 Campbell Rd Fairfield NJ 07004

DESMETT, DON
CURATOR, GALLERY DIRECTOR
b Philipsburg, Pa, May 20, 54. *Study:* Univ Mass, Amherst, MFA, 84. *Collection Arranged:* Jerry Kearns: Deep Cover (auth, catalog), Tyler Sch Art, 91; The Price of Power, (auth, catalog), Cleveland Ctr Contemp Art, 91; Michele Blondel, Tyler Sch Art, 92; Beth B (auth, catalog), 95; Mike Glier: Garden Court (auth, catalog), 95. *Pos:* Dir, Tyler Galleries, Tyler Sch Art, 90-. *Teaching:* Instr Mus Studies, Tyler Sch Art, currently. *Mailing Add:* 1000 Melrose Ave Elkins Park PA 19027-3014

DESMIDT, THOMAS H
PAINTER, EDUCATOR
b Sheboygan, Wis, Sept 6, 44. *Study:* Lincoln Col, AA; Layton Sch Art, BFA; Syracuse Univ, MFA. *Work:* Milwaukee Art Inst, Wis; Francis & Sidney Lewis Collection Contemp Art; F&M Corp, Richmond, Va; Miller Brewing Co, Milwaukee, Wis; Everson Mus Art, Syracuse; and others. *Exhib:* Solo exhibs, Mem Art Gallery,

Univ Rochester, 72, Everson Mus, 73 & Va Mus Fine Arts, 78; James Yu Gallery, NY, 73 & 74; 19th Corcoran Biennial, Washington, 74; Va Artists, Va Mus, Richmond, 77. *Teaching:* Instr painting, Va Commonwealth Univ, 70-73, dir, Art Found, 73-76, asst prof art, 73-, asst dean, 76-. *Awards:* One-Man Exhib Award, Rochester Mem Gallery, 70; Fac Res Grant, Va Commonwealth Univ, 73. *Media:* Canvas, Acrylic. *Dealer:* James Yu Gallery 393 W Broadway New York NY 10012. *Mailing Add:* c/o Aaron Gallery 1717 Connecticut Ave NW Washington DC 20009

DE SOTO, LEWIS D
SCULPTOR, EDUCATOR
b San Bernardino, Calif, Jan 3, 54. *Study:* Univ Calif, Riverside, BA, 78; Claremont Grad Sch, Calif, MFA, 81. *Work:* Los Angeles Co Mus Art, Calif; San Jose Mus Art; Mus Mod Art, NY; Mus Contemp Art, Los Angeles; San Francisco Arts Comn, Calif; and others; Des Moines Art Ctr. *Comn:* Photomural, San Francisco State Univ, 88 & 89; sculpture, Phoenix Art Comn, 90 & 91; Design Team Sculpture, San Francisco Arts Comn, 94, 97 & 98; Arrivals Lobby, San Francisco Int Airport, 2000; Gateway sculpture, Univ Tex, San Antonio, 2001. *Exhib:* Photog Memory, Seattle Art Mus, 88; One-man show, Univ Art Mus, Berkeley, 91, Artists Space, NY, 91, Pétúkmiyat Pé Túkmiyat, San Jose Mus Art, 91, Mod Museet, Stockholm, 93, Ctr Contemp Arts, Santa Fe, NMex, 94, Nelson Atkins Mus, Kansas City, 96 & Artpace, San Antonio, Tex, 96, Ship, Bill Maynes Gallery, NY, 2000, 02, Paranirvana, Mus of Contemp Religious Art, Saint louis Univ, 2000, Samek Art Gallery, Pa, 2002, Coll of the Holy Cross, Mass, 2002; The Spatial Drive, New Mus Contemp Art, NY, 92; Landscapes as Metaphor, Columbus Mus Art, 94; Nowhere, La Mus, Humelback, Denmark, 96; Recital, List Visual Art Ctr, Mass Inst Technol, Cambridge, 98. *Teaching:* Instr photogr, Otis Art Inst, Parsons Sch Design, Los Angeles, Calif, 83-85; chmn, Art Dept, Cornish Col Arts, Seattle, Wash, 85-88; prof art, San Francisco State Univ, 88-; dir grad studies, Calif Col Arts & Crafts, Oakland, Calif, 93-95; artist in residence, List Visual Arts Ctr, MIT, Mass, 97-98. *Awards:* Affirmative Action Award, San Francisco State Univ, 89 & 90 & Meritorious Prof promise & achievement, 90; Fel in Installation, Calif Arts Coun, 92; Nat Endowment Arts Fel, 96; Eureka fel, 99. *Bibliog:* Rebecca Solnit (auth), Living Places, Art Space, 92; Jean Fisher (auth), Fragments of a Fictional Body/Lewis Desoto, Turning the Map (UK), 92; Rebecca Solnit (auth), Lewis deSoto, Visions of America, Abrams, 94; and others. *Mem:* San Francisco Camerawork (bd mem, 92-95); Yerba Buena Ctr Arts (bd mem, 94-95). *Media:* Miscellaneous Media. *Publ:* Auth, Tahualtapa project, 9-1-1 Seattle, 5/86; Haypatak, Witness, Kansatsusha, San Francisco Arts Comn, 90; coauth (with Rebecca Solnit), Kingdoms, 92; auth, Don Anton, Centro de la Raza, Sacramento, Calif, 95; coauth, Heat & Cold, Tate Mag, London, winter 96. *Dealer:* Bill Maynes Gallery 529 W 20th St New York NY 10011. *Mailing Add:* 2696 W 7Th St San Bernardino CA 92410

DESPORTES, ULYSSE GANDVIER
PAINTER, HISTORIAN
b Winnsboro, SC, Apr 12, 20. *Study:* Richmond Prof Inst, Col William & Mary, with Julien Binford, Marion Junkin & Theresa Pollack, BFA; Ecole Normale Superior Beaux-Arts, Paris, France, with Maurice Brianchon; Inst Art & Archeol, Univ Paris, with Pierre Lavedan & Andre Chastel. *Work:* Va Mus Fine Arts, Richmond; Washington & Lee Univ, Lexington, Va; Va Commonwealth Univ, Richmond. *Comn:* painting, Va Mus Fine Arts; mural, Bridgewater, Va, 85, Post Office Staunton, Va, 86. *Exhib:* Va Artists 1961 & Va Artists 1963, Va Mus Fine Arts; SC Artists, Gibbs Art Mus, Charleston, 62. *Pos:* Dir catalogues, Kende Galleries, New York, 46-48; dir, Florence Mus, SC, 57. *Teaching:* Asst prof art hist & painting, Hollins Col, 57-62; prof art & chmn dept, Mary Baldwin Col, 62-87, emer. *Awards:* Second Prize, SC Artists Asn, 62; Cert of Merit, Va Mus Fine Arts, 63. *Mem:* Staunton-Augusta Art Ctr. *Media:* Oil. *Res:* Neoclassic art; sculptor Guiseppe Ceracchi; painter Louis David. *Publ:* Contribr, Bulletin Mus Bernadotte, 62; Princeton Libr Chronicle, 62; Art Quart, 63 & 64; Antiques Mag, 69. *Mailing Add:* 322 N New St Staunton VA 24401-3640

DES RIOUX (DE MESSIMY), DEENA VICTORIA (COTY)
GRAPHIC ARTIST, PHOTOGRAPHER
b Cambridge, Mass, Dec 7, 41; French & US citizen. *Study:* RI Sch Design, 59-62; Brown Univ, 60-62; Univ Paris at Sorbonne, 61, 63-64. *Work:* New Orleans Mus Art, La; Milwaukee Art Mus, Wis; Austin Mus Art, Tex; Int Ctr Graphic Art, Ljubljana, Slovenia; Mus Art, RI Sch Design; Grand Forks Art Gallery, Vancouver, BC, Canada. *Exhib:* solo exhibs, Psychoanalytic Inst, Boston, 74, Art Inst, Boston, 75, Mus Sci, Boston, 78, Ward-Nasse Gallery, New York City, 78, Helander Gallery, Palm Beach, Fla, 85, Columbia Univ, NY, 92, Univ Wyo Art Mus, Laramie, 94, Silicon Gallery, Phila, 96, 00, Bunkier Sztuki Art Ctr, Krakow, Poland, 97, Mus Gornoslaskie, Bytom, Poland, 97, Northlight Gallery, Everett Community Col, Wash, 98, 00, Kans State Univ Gallery, Manhattan, 98, Grants Pass Mus Art, Ore, 98, Cent Wash Univ, Sarah Spurgeon Gallery, Ellensburg, 98, Firehouse Gallery, Nassau Community Col, Garden City, NY, 99, RI Col, Bannister Gallery, Providence, 99, Wash State Univ, Tricities, Richland, 2000, Hockaday Mus Art, Kalispell, Mont, 2000, Columbia Basin Col, Esvelt Gallery, Pasco, 2000, Herkimer Co Community Col, Cogar Gallery, NY, 01, Elmhurst Art Mus, Ill, 01, Schoolhouse Hist and Art Mus, Colstrip, Mont, 01, Mont State Univ, Northcutt-Steele Gallery, Billings, 01; Dahl Arts Ctr, Ruth Brennan Gallery, Rapid City, SD, 2004; Can/Grand Forks Art Gallery, Vancouver, BC, 2005; Texarkana Regional Arts & Humanities Ctr, Texarkana, Tex, 2005; Zanesville Art Ctr, Zanesville, Ohio, 2006; invitational group shows, Mokotoff Gallery, New York City, 86, Warwick Mus, 91, Mus Art RI Sch Design, 94, Cartier/Fifth Ave, 94, Fuller Mus Art, 95, Ea Wash Univ, USA Mus Tour, Cheney, Wash, 94-2000, Midwest Photog Invitational, IX, X, XI, two-yr, ten-venue sponsored by Univ Wis, Green Bay, 96-2002; NY; Hofstra Univ Mus, Hofstra Mus at 40/Work on Paper, Hempstead, 2003; Portugal; IV Print Festival of Evora, Teoartis & Town Council (Region-Lisbon) 2004; Japan; Tama Art Univ Mus, Tokyo Int Print Triennale, Tokyo, 2005; represented in permanent collections Cent Acad Art, Kuala Lumpur, Malaysia, Hofstra Univ Mus, Hempstead, NY, Int Ctr Graphic Art, Ljubljana, Slovenia, Southern Ill Univ Mus, Carbondale, Ind Univ Art Mus, Boise State Univ, Idaho, Mus Art at RI Sch Design, Austin Mus Art, Tex, Alexandria Mus Art, La, Downey Mus Art, Calif, Eastern Washington Univ, Fuller Mus Art, Brockton, Mass, Internat Soc Graphic Art, Krakow, Nat Ctr Fine Arts, Cairo, NY Pub Libr, Palm Springs Desert Mus, Calif, Tama Art Univ Mus, Tokyo, Univ Ala at Birmingham, Univ Pa, Phila, Univ Wyo Art Mus, Laramie, New Orleans Mus Art, La, Elmhurst Art Mus, Ill, Elvehjem Mus Art, Univ Wis, Madison, Milwaukee Art Mus, Wis, Mont State Univ, Billings; competitive exhibs, At The Edge II, Wendy Weitman, Laguna Gloria Art Mus, Austin, Tex, 90-92, Int Triennale of Graphic Art, Krakow, Poland/Nuremberg, Ger, 91-92, 94-95, 00-02, Nat Fine Arts Ctr/Giza, Egypt, guest/cultural ministry, 1st Egyptian Int Print Triennale, 94, 2nd triennale 97, 3rd triennale, 00, 4th triennale, 03, Palm Springs (Calif) Desert Mus, 26th Nat Exhib, Henry T Hopkins, 95, Franklin Inst, Philadelphia, 95; Tama Art Univ Mus, Tokyo, 95, Silvermine Guild Galleries, Spectra '97, Robert Sobieszek, New Canaan, Conn, 97, 26th Nat Exhib, juror R John Bullard, Masur Mus Art, Monroe, La, 99, Internat Ctr Graphic Art, Ljubljana, Slovenia, Biennale 22, 97, Pitti Immagine srl, Stazione Leopolda, Florence, Italy, 98, Brooklyn Mus Art, Digital: Printmaking Now, Marilyn S Kushner, 01, Museo Nacional de Bellas Arte, IV and V Salon and Colloquium of Digital Art, Havana, Cuba, 02, 03, Boston Printmakers 2003 N Am Print Biennial Clifford S Ackley, Boston Univ 808 Gallery, Mass, 03, numerous others; Poland; Int Triennale Soc, Int Graphic Triennale 2003-2005, Krawkow; Washington DC; Fraser Gallery, 8th Ann Georgetown Inter Kristen Hileman, 2004; Vt; Studio Place Arts, One Earth, Barre, 2004; Poland; Triennale 2003, Sponsor; SMTG, Horst-Janssen Mus, Oldenburg, Ger, 2003-2004. *Pos:* Package designer, illusr, pvt teacher, freelance artist, Boston, 62-63, 64-70; founder & dir, 7 at Large, NE Women Artists' Collab, Boston, 75-78; exhib consult, Asn Artist-Run Galleries, NY, 80-82, pub relations dir, 83-84; exhib coordr, NY Alumni Chap, RI Sch Design, 85-86, Women Exhib in Boston Inc, 73-75; juror Heritage Plantation Mus, Cape Cod, Mass, 77; coord exhibitor (grants), Art Inst, Boston, 75, Mus Sci, Boston, 77-78; spec exhib cons, Mus City of NY, 83-84; guest exhibitor, Danvers Art and Hist Soc, Attleboro Mus, Mass, Nashua Arts and Sci Ctr, NH; Co-Juror, DIGITALSPLASH, Rockaway Artists Alliance, Fort Tilden, New York City, 2003. *Teaching:* guest lectr, Mass Col Art, Boston, 75, Harvard Grad Sch Design, Lesley Col, Cambridge, Mass, 76, 77, UN Photog Soc, NY, 93, Univ Wyo Art Mus, Laramie, 94, Nassau Community Col Firehouse Gallery, Garden City, NY, 99, RI Col Bannister Gallery, Providence, 99, Rockaway Artists Alliance, Queens, NY, 99, Hockaday Mus Art, Kalispell, Mont, 00, Herkimer Co Community Col, NY, 01 & Elmhurst Art Mus, Ill, 01; International Graphic Triennale 2003, SMTG-Krakow, Internet Panel Discussion; Dahl Fine Art Ctr & Sch of Mines and Technol, Rapid City, SD, 2004. *Awards:* Named One of NY Outstanding Artists, Ethel Scull, New York City, 83; Travel citation, Mid-Am Arts Alliance, 90-92; Juror/Roberta Waddell award, Boston Printmakers, Mass, 93; Grant, Duggal Color Projects Inc, NY, 92; Juror/Sachi Yanari award in Poly Grams, sponsored by Ind Univ, Purdue Univ, Ft Wayne, 99; Touring Program; Washington State Arts Commisssion/ EWU-ETS, Cheney, WA, 97-2001. *Bibliog:* Eileen Watkins (auth), High Tech & Myth, photo/review, Sunday Star-Ledger, Newark, NJ, 92; Alaks & Decker, Solo review/colorplate, Grants Pass Daily Courier, Ore, 98; William Zimmer (auth), Digital Exhibition Updates in the Medium, Sunday NY Times, 2000; Digital; Printing Now/ Cat Intro, Marilyn S. Kushner, Cur/ Prints, Brooklyn Mus, NY, 2001; Sunday New York Times/ Nov, Hofstra Mus at 40, Works on Paper, Helen A. Harrison, LI, NY, 2003; Exploring Color Photography, 4th Edition, Robert-Hirsch, Mc Graw-Hill, NY, 2004. *Mem:* Boston Visual Artists Union (coord, 73-75); Cambridge Art Asn (juror, 73-74); RISD NY Alumni Chap; Art and Sci Collaborations Inc, NY. *Media:* Electronic Imaging. *Interests:* Cinema, Computer Animation, Dance, Language, Psychology, Robotics, Science Fiction, Theater, Travel. *Dealer:* Silicon Gallery 139 N 3rd St Philadelphia Pa 19106; 10 Jay St Brooklyn NY 11201. *Mailing Add:* 251 W 19th St Apt 3B New York NY 10011-4039

DESSNER, MURRAY
PAINTER
b Philadelphia, Pa, Nov 11, 34. *Study:* Pa Acad Fine Arts, William Emlen Cresson Traveling Scholar, 65 & J Henry Schiedt Traveling Scholar, 66; also with Franklin C Watkins & Hobson Pittman. *Work:* Pa Acad Fine; Pittman Collection, Bryn Mawr Col, Pa; Pa Fed Collection; Cornell Fine Arts Ctr Mus; Philadelphia Mus Art; and others. *Exhib:* One-man shows, Peale Galleries, Pa Acad Fine Arts, 70, Marion Locks Gallery, Philadelphia, 72, 75, 78 & 84, Barbara Gillman Gallery, Miami, 83, Vorpal Gallery, NY, 84 & 86, Levy Gallery, Philadelphia, 91 & Locust Ct, Philadelphia, 96, Peng Gallery, Philadelphia, Pa, 99, Peng Gallery, Phila, PA, 2003; Davis Dominguez Gallery, Tucson, Ariz, 2005. *Teaching:* Prof painting, Pa Acad Fine Arts. *Awards:* Philadelphia Mus Art Purchase Prize, Cheltenham Art Ctr; Pa Acad Fine Art Purchase Prize, Philadelphia. *Bibliog:* Two Philadelphians, Time Mag; article, Art News; article, Philadelphia Inquirer, 96. *Media:* Acrylic. *Dealer:* Peng Gallery Philadelphia PA; Davis Dominguez Gallery Tuscon Ariz. *Mailing Add:* 802 Sansom St Philadelphia PA 19107

DESTABLER, STEPHEN
SCULPTOR
b St Louis, Mo, 33. *Study:* Princeton Univ, AB, 54; Univ Calif, Berkeley, MA, 61. *Work:* San Francisco Mus Mod Art; Oakland Mus, Calif; Am Craft Mus, NY; Fine Arts Mus San Francisco; Minneapolis Inst Arts. *Comn:* Birthplace, Old St Louis Post Off, 85-87; Pieta, New Harmony Inn & Conf Ctr, Ind, 88; Winged Guardians, San Jose Conv Ctr, Calif, 93; winged figure, Grad Theological Union, 94. *Exhib:* Solo exhibs, Oakland Mus, 74, Emily Carr Col Art, Vancouver, BC, 83, San Francisco Mus Art, 88 & Mus Contemp Religious Art, 93; CDS Gallery, NY, 94; Essential Gesture (with catalog), New Harbor Art Mus, 94; New Bronzes, CDC Gallery, NY, 95. *Teaching:* Prof art, San Francisco State Univ, 67-92. *Awards:* Am Craft Coun Fel, 94;

Fourth Rodin Grand Prize Exhib, Utsukushi-gahari Open Air Mus, Japan, 92. *Media:* Clay; Metal, Cast. *Dealer:* Franklin Parrasch Gallery 20 W 57th St New York NY 10019; Paul Thiebaud Gallery 718 Columbus Ave San Francisco Calif 94133. *Mailing Add:* 21 Bret Harte Rd Berkeley CA 94708

DETMERS, WILLIAM RAYMOND
PRINTMAKER, EDUCATOR
b Pontiac, Mich, June 20, 42. *Study:* Miami Univ, Ohio, BFA, 64, MEduc, 68; Cranbrook Acad Art, MFA, 70; Univ Cincinnati, EdD, 78. *Work:* Miami Univ, Oxford, Ohio; Univ Southern Colo, Pueblo; Herron Sch Art, Indianapolis; Univ Hawaii, Manoa; Culver-Stockton Col, Canton, Mo; Univ Ark, Pine Bluff; and others. *Comn:* Drawings, Methodist Church, Fredericktown, Ohio; drawings, Methodist Church, Canton, Mo; and others. *Exhib:* Ann Midyear Show, Butler Inst Am Art, Youngstown, Ohio, 64; one-man shows, Bd Room, Nova Scotia Col Art & Design, 70, Gallery, Southern Colo State Col, Pueblo, 73, Litho Constructs, Matrix Gallery, Ind Univ, Bloomington, 79, Mabee Foundation Gallery, Culver-Stockton Col, 91 & Keokul Art Ctr, Iowa, 92; Wakonda Art Guild Group Shows, Mo, 88-92; Juried Exhib, Novinger, Mo, 89 & 90; Hannibal Arts Club, Mo, 90-92; Quad States Art Exhib, Quincy, Ill, 91-92; Images 92, Highland CC, Kans; Exhibs, 95-: Delta Art Exhib, Pine Bluff Art League, Ark Senate Offices, Little Rock, Ark Art Center, Arts & Science Center for Southeast Ark, Univ Ark, Pine Bluff, Taylor's Contemporanea, Hot Springs, Ark; and others. *Pos:* gallery dir, Culver-Stockton Col, 88-95; gallery dir, Univ Ark, Pine Bluff, 95-2002. *Teaching:* Art Teacher, Preble Co Schs, Ohio, 65-68; vis instr printmaking, Nova Scotia Col Art & Design, summer 70; instr printmaking & art educ, Southern Colo State Col, 70-73; art teacher, Fredericktown, Ohio Schs, 73-74; vis lectr, Ind Univ, Bloomington, 76; prog chmn art educ, Herron Sch Art, Ind Univ-Purdue Univ, Indianapolis, 76-80; area head art educ, La State Univ, 80-85; art educ, Univ Hawaii, Manoa, 85-88; assoc prof art, Culver-Stockton Col, 88-94; instr art, Canton R-V Sch, 94-95; prof art & coord art educ, Univ Ark, Pine Bluff, 95-. *Awards:* Educ Improvement Fund Grant, Univ Hawaii, 86-87; Fac Devt Awards, Culver-Stockton Col, 89-92; Title III Project Grant. *Bibliog:* Mildred Monteverde (auth), Art display limited to plastic and wood, Pueblo Star J, 73; Lauretta Fox (auth), Litho Constructions and other prints by Detmers, Mt Vernon News, 75. *Mem:* Nat Art Educ Asn; Mo Art Educ Asn; Wakonda Art Guild; Canton Area Arts Coun, Mo (past pres); Quincy Art Club, Ill; Pine Bluff Art League; Nat Asn Sch Art & Design. *Media:* Lithography, Intaglio. *Res:* Curriculum development & evaluation in the visual arts. *Publ:* Auth, A Conceptual Model for the Planning of Curricula for the Visual Arts in Higher Education, Dissertation Abstracts Int, 79; A Conceptual Model for Curriculum Planning and Evaluating in Visual Arts, Studies in Art Educ, 80; AV Reviews, Sch Arts, Davis Publ; Red Line Group Recommendations, Teachers Arts, La State Univ, 85; coauth (with K Marantz), The liberal education component of art teacher education: a response, Visual Arts Res, spring, 88; and others, 96-. *Mailing Add:* 2 Sutton Pl Pine Bluff AR 71603-7528

DETTWILLER, KATHRYN KING
PAINTER
b Nashville, Tenn, Dec 3, 47. *Study:* Vanderbilt Univ, Nashville, BA, 68; George Peabody Col, 68-69; Santa Fe Inst Art, NMex, with Nathan Oliveira, 92. *Work:* Bank Nashville, Metrop Airport Authority, DET Distributing Co, C A Howell & Co, Nashville, Tenn; Sen Bill Frist's Washington Off, DC; Columbia State Community Col, Tenn. *Exhib:* One-woman show, Parthenon Mus, Nashville, 93 & Indivisible: New Work by Kathryn Dettwiller, Renaissance Cen, Dickson, Tenn, 2002; Tennessee: From the Mountains to the Mississippi, Cheekwood Mus Art, Nashville, 93 & About Face, 94; Scene/Unseen III Nat Exhib, Eastern NMex Univ, Portales, 94; Priva B Gross Int, Queensborough Community Col, City Univ NY, Bayside, 96; Combined Talents: The Fla National, Appleton Mus Art, Ocala, & Fla State Univ Mus, Tallahassee, 98; Interpretations, Ceramics by Bill Capshaw & Paintings by Kathryn Dettwiller, Tenn Arts Comn, Nashville, 98; A Sense of Place, Nashville Int Airport, Nashville & Belfast Waterfront Hall, Belfast, Northern Ireland, 2001; Women Beyond Borders, Frist Ctr for Visual Arts, Nashville, Tenn, 2003; Fragile Species: New Art Nashville, Frist Ctr for Visual Arts, Nashville, Tenn, 2005. *Pos:* Asst dir educ, Tenn Fine Arts Ctr, Cheekwood, 68-69; bd mem, Metrop Nashville Arts Comn, 88-94; juror, Countdown 2001, Summer Lights Art Exhib, 91; bd mem Visual Artists Coun, Frist Ctr for Visual Arts, 99-; bd mem, Arrowmont Sch Arts & Crafts, Gatlinburg, Tenn, secy, 2005-. *Awards:* Best of show, Northern Nat Art Competition, 91; Hon Mention, Women's Works, 96; Second Place, 47th Spiva Ann Competition, 97; Gallery Award, Best of Tenn, Tenn State Mus, 2001; Second Place, 5th Ann DIG Through Art Conf, Nashville, Tenn, 2003. *Bibliog:* Susan Chappell (auth), Artists offer bridge to oasis, Nashville Banner, 2/24/93; Susan Knowles (auth), Changing subjects, Nashville Scene, 6/30/94; Louise Lequire (auth), Laughing with Nashville Artists, Nashville Life, 10/94; Kaaren Engel (auth), A conversation with Kathryn Dettwiller, VAAN newsletter, 11-12/2000; Encaustic art, Nashville Lifestyles, Oct-Nov/2002. *Mem:* Visual Arts Alliance, Nashville (bd mem, 95); Nat Mus Women Arts; SESAC. *Media:* Oil, Encaustic. *Mailing Add:* 108 Savoy Cir Nashville TN 37205-5013

DEUTSCH, RICHARD
SCULPTOR
b Los Angeles, Calif, 53. *Study:* Univ Calif, Santa Cruz, BA(art), 76. *Work:* Patrick J Lannon Foun, Los Angeles; Renwick Gallery, Smithsonian; Mill's Col, Oakland; McDonald's Corp, Chicago; Shell Oil Corp, Houston. *Comn:* Terrazza sculpture/Ocean View Park, Santa Cruz Arts Comn, Calif, 84; Marble sculpture Shelton Police Acad, Wash State Arts Comn Art in Pub Places, Shelton, 87; Terrazzo pavement medallion, San Francisco Arts Comn Pub Places, 88. *Exhib:* Renwick Gallery, Smithsonian, Washington, DC, 80; Gray Art Mus, NC, 82; Monterey Peninsula Mus Art, Calif, 82; San Jose Inst Contemp Art, Calif, 83; Art Mus Santa Cruz, Calif, 85; Jewish Community Mus, San Francisco, 87; Palo Alto Cult Ctr, Calif, 88. *Awards:* Exemplary Arts Education Residency, Calif Arts Coun, 83; Visual Artist Fel, Nat Endowment Arts, 84; Vis Sculptor, Am Acad Rome, 87. *Bibliog:* Paul Sutor (auth), Artist in the development process, Urbanland, 9/2/91; Elizabeth Broadrup (auth), Richard Deutsch: motion, Sculpture Mag, 11/12/92. *Media:* Marble. *Mailing Add:* 340 Swanton Rd Davenport CA 95017

DEUTSCHMAN, LOUISE TOLLIVER
DEALER, CURATOR
b Taylorville, Ill, Sept 6, 21. *Study:* MacMurray Col, BA; Northwestern Univ Sch Journalism, Univ Paris, Sorbonne. *Collection Arranged:* Seven Decades of Twentieth-Century Art From the Sidney and Harriet Janis Collection, Mus Mod Art & Sidney Janis Gallery Collection, La Jolla Mus Contemp Art & Santa Barbara Mus Art, Calif, 80. *Pos:* Assoc dir, Waddell Gallery, New York, 66-74; assoc cur, Sidney Janis Gallery, New York, 75-78, assoc dir, 80-2000; dir, Alex Rosenberg Gallery, New York, 78-80; curator, Pace Wildenstein, NY, 2000-. *Specialty:* Contemporary art; 20th century masters, American & European. *Mailing Add:* 36 E 68th St No 3B New York NY 10021

DEVEREUX, MARA
PAINTER
b Brooklyn, NY, Jun 9, 25. *Study:* Great Neck, NY Studio, 50; Art Students League, 52; Otis Art Inst, MFA, 64; Liverpool Col Art, Eng; NY Acad Art, NY. *Comn:* Plaster Sculpture, Saks Fifth Ave, NY, 90; Plaster Sculpture, Bloomingdales, NY, 90; Works on paper, Lipton Tea Co, Inglewood, NJ, 91; Oil Canvas, Canon Communications, Santa Monica, Calif, 2000; Acrylic Canvas, Bret Mosher Builder, Los Angeles, Calif, 2004; Acrylic & Oil Canvas 60″x108″, comn by Dr & Mrs Alex Gershman, Beverly Hills, Calif, 2006. *Exhib:* Brooklyn Mus, NY, 51; Hecksher Mus, Huntington, NY, 80; Santa Barbara Mus, Calif, 74; Jeju Int, Seogwipo Kidang, Jeju Island, 2004; Art Festival Mus, Korea, 2004; Gwang Wha Moon Int Art Festival, Korea, 2006. *Collection Arranged:* Frederick Wiseman Collection, Calif; Dr & Mrs Alex Gershman, Calif; Matthew Egan, Tex; William Brun, Calif; Dr & Mrs Victor Bekbosunov-Kazakhstan. *Awards:* Otis Parsons Inst, MFA, Los Angeles, Calif; Inst Classical Art, NY. *Bibliog:* Elizabeth Gorcy (auth), An Artists Life, Film Documentary, 2003; Laurence Vittes (auth), The Invisible Made Visible, Sr Life, 2004; Tanya Shifman (auth), 10 Physicists & an Abstract Painter (film documentary), 2006; William Wilson (auth), A Critical Guide to Galleries, Los Angeles Times; Rita Riff (auth), In Philadelphia, Artists Cast a Pop Eye, NY Times. *Mem:* Metrop Artist Asn, Los Angeles, Calif. *Media:* Oil, Acrylic, Clay. *Publ:* ed, Invisible Made Visible, Article, Calif Sr Life, 2004. *Dealer:* Gallery Asto Pearl Park 923 East Third St Los Angeles Calif 90013. *Mailing Add:* 661 Shatto Pl Unit 100 Los Angeles CA 90005

DEVINE, NANCY
PAINTER
b Hyannis, Mass, Feb 8, 49. *Study:* Univ Mass, Amherst, 1967-70. *Comn:* Calendar, USPS, Wash DC, 2000. *Exhib:* Northern Arts Nat Competition, Rhinelander, WI, 1991; Homage to Norman Rockwell, Fraser Art Gallery, Wash DC, 2001; All New England Exhib, Cape Cod Art Assoc, Barnstable, Mass, 1993, 95 & 2005. *Pos:* Layout artist, Rosen Textile Engraving, Agawam, MA, 1970-72. *Awards:* 2nd Place, Mashpee Arts Council, 1997-98. *Bibliog:* Alan Petrucelli (auth), Real Life Art of Nancy Devine, Cape Cod Times, 1997; Saundra Tobins (auth), Painting Cape Cod the Devine Way, Cape Cod Mag, 2001. *Mem:* Cape Cod Art Assoc; Nat Assoc Women Artists. *Media:* Acrylic, Oil. *Mailing Add:* 20 Delta St Hyannis MA 02601

DEVLIN, LUCINDA ALICE
PHOTOGRAPHER, EDUCATOR
b Ann Arbor, Mich, Dec 18, 47. *Study:* East Mich Univ, BS, 70, MFA, 73. *Work:* Mint Mus, Charlotte; Biblio Nat, Paris; Princeton Univ Art Mus; Macht/OnMacht, Int Cult centrum, Antwerp, Belgium, 98-99; Under/Exposed, Stockholm Underground, Sweden, 2000; and others. *Exhib:* Lightwork Photos Over the 70's & 80's, Everson Mus Art, Syracuse, 85; Working with Tradition, NY State Mus, Albany, 93; The Omega Suites, Tartt Gallery, Washington, 93; Evidence of Death, Light Factory, Charlotte, 94; Discipline & Photograph - The Prison Experience, Chicago, 95; Int Cult Ctr, Antwarp, Belg, 96; solo exchange, Un-raume, M bochum, Kunstvermittlung, Bochum, Ger, 98; Maqtters of a Fine Wall, Bakalar Gallery, Mass Sch Art, Boston, 97; Under/Exposed, Stockholm, Underground, Sweden, 98-99; Paul Rodgers / 9W, NY, 2000; Venice Birnnale, 2001; solo exhib, The Omega Suites und Water Rites, Daadgalerie, Berlin, 2001, Paul Rodgers/9W, NY, 2001; and others. *Teaching:* Asst prof photog, Syracuse Univ, 77-88 & State Univ NY, New Paltz, 89-94; Artist Residency, Ger Academic Exchange, Berlin, Ger, 99. *Awards:* Creative Artists Pub Serv Fel, NY State Coun Arts, 79, 82 & 83; Aaron Siskind Fel, 92; Nat Endowment Arts Fel, 92; Catalog Proj, NY Found Art, 96; Miss Inst for Arts and Letters, 99. *Bibliog:* The Omega Suites, Creative Camera Mag, Lon, 94; Portfolio, Catalog Contemp Photog, Lon, 95; Lucinda Devlin (auth), The Omega Suites, Zeit Mag, Hamburg, Ger, 98; The Omega Suites, Steide, 2001. *Mem:* Soc Photog Educ. *Publ:* Clean Death/Der saubere Tod, 2000; Katastrophen und Desaster-Das Jahrhundert am Ende, 2000; and others. *Mailing Add:* 10779 Tallow Wood Lane Indianapolis IN 46236

DEVON, MARJORIE LYNN
ADMINISTRATOR
b Jersey City, NJ, Dec 2, 45. *Study:* Univ Calif, Berkeley, BA, 67. *Collection Arranged:* Tamarind Impressions: Recent Lithographs (traveling), Arts Am Prog, US Information Agency, 85; Tamarind: 25 Years (traveling, with catalog), NMex Art Mus, 85; Mexico Nueve (traveling, with catalog), 87; Collaborations: Artists + Printers (traveling), Arts Am Prog, US Information Agency, 91; Tamarind: 40 Years (ed, catalog), Univ NMex Art Mus, 2000. *Pos:* From asst dir to dir, Tamarind Inst, Albuquerque, 80-. *Teaching:* Pub art, Univ NMex. *Mailing Add:* c/o Tamarind Inst 108 Cornell Dr SE Albuquerque NM 87106

DE VORE, RICHARD E
CERAMIST
b Toledo, Ohio, 33. *Study:* Univ Toledo, Ohio, BE, 55; Cranbrook Acad Art, Mich, MFA, 57. *Work:* Yale Univ Art Gallery, New Haven, Conn; Victoria & Albert Mus, London, Eng; Philadelphia Mus Art, Pa; Los Angeles Co Mus Art, Calif; Cleveland Mus Art, Ohio; Metrop Mus Art, NY. *Exhib:* Solo exhibs, Hill Gallery, Birmingham, Mich, 87, 93, 95 & 99, Max Protetch Gallery, NY, 87, 89, 91, 94, 96 & 98 & Greenberg Gallery, St Louis, Mo, 88, Kruithuis Mus, The Neth, 99, San Francisco Mus Art, 99, Los Angeles Co Mus Art, 2000, World Ceramics Exposition, Korea, 2001; East-West Contemp Ceramics, Seoul, Korea, 88; Ten Am Ceramicists, US Embassy Exhib, Univ Hong Kong, 89; De Vore, Price, Turner, Hill Gallery, Birmingham, Mich, 90; 28th Ceramic Nat Exhib, Everson Mus Art, Syracuse, NY, 90; and others. *Collection Arranged:* Am Craft Mus, New York City; Ark Art Ctr, Little Rock; Butler Inst Am Art, Youngstown, Ohio; Contemp Mus Art, Honolulu; Detroit Inst Art; Joslyn Art Mus, Omaha, Nebr; Houston Mus Fine Arts; Metrop Mus Art; Nat Mus Am Art, Washington, DC; Newark Mus, NJ; Philadelphia Mus Art; Yale Univ Art Gallery, New Haven, Conn; Los Angeles Co Mus Art; Denver Art Mus; and others. *Awards:* Nat Endowment Arts Grant, 76, 80 & 86; Am Craft Coun Fel, 87. *Bibliog:* Garth Clark (auth), American Potters, Watson-Guptill, New York, 81; Florence Rubenfeld (auth), Pottery of Richard De Vore, Am Craft, 83; Janet Kopolos (auth), article, Art Papers, Vol VIII, No 2, 84; Sarah Bodine & Michael Dumas (coauth), Am Ceramics, 89. *Publ:* Auth, Ceramics of Betty Woodman, Craft Horizon, 78; Color, Texture & Light, Studio Potter, 86. *Dealer:* Max Protech 511 22nd St New York NY 10012. *Mailing Add:* 1617 Sheely DR Fort Collins CO 80526

DE VORE, SADIE DAVIDSON
PRINTMAKER, PAINTER
b Wheaton, MO, Jun 12, 37. *Study:* Southwest MO State Univ, BS(art), 58; RI Col, MAT(drawing); NY Univ, post grad; Skidmore Univ, summer studies. *Comn:* Portrait, Stanton Terranova, Westerly, RI, 2000; portrait, Desa Buffum, Weekapaug, RI, 2000; Portrait, Bradie Metheny Padenarum, 95; portrait, Catherine Barrington, RI, 2000. *Exhib:* Art Exhib, Springfield, Mo Art Mus, 59; Lyme Acad Fine Arts Asn, Lyme Conn, 2002, 2003, 2006; NAC Gallery, Norwich, Conn, 87-2005. *Collection Arranged:* Hoxie Gallery, Westerly, RI, 2002; Monotype Show, Watercolor Soc, Pautucket, RI, 2004; Emporium Gallery, Hamden, Conn. *Teaching:* Instr, painting, printmaking & art hist, Stonington Sch, 72-2005; instr, monotype workshops, printmaking, RI, Conn, NY & Weekapaug, RI, 90-; instr, watercolor, Fla & Saratoga, NY, formerly; art educ, Art Asn bds (juror), 1972-. *Awards:* First Place Award, Westport Show, KC Art Dealer, 91; first place, 30 Miles of Art, Essex; MAA Triplett Award; Essex Ann WHIS ACGOW Award. *Mem:* South Co Art Asn; Mystic Art Ctr; Monotype Guild New Eng (secy, bd, 95-2005); Lyme Art Asn; ACGOW, Westerly, RI (2001, 2002); Am Asn Marine Artists. *Media:* Watercolor, Silver, Monotypes, Oil. *Res:* 19th Century drawing, Beardsley, Kandinsky design; Monotypes by hand and intagli press, abstract, litho press, landscape & design. *Mailing Add:* 137 High St Mystic CT 06355

DE WAAL, RONALD BURT
COLLECTOR, PATRON
b Salt Lake City, Utah, Oct 23, 32. *Study:* Univ Utah, BS, 55; Mexico City Col, summer 55 & 58; Univ Denver, MA, 58. *Collection Arranged:* Beethoven in the Arts, Univ Utah, 65 & Colo State Univ, 66, 67, 70, 83 & 85. *Pos:* Humanities librn & exhibs chmn, Colo State Univ, Ft Collins, 66-88. *Awards:* John H Jenkins Award for best work of bibliography published in US during 74; Colo Libr Asn Lit Award, 87. *Mem:* Beethoven Soc; Col Art Asn Am; Nat Sculpture Soc. *Interests:* Painting and Sculpture, Classical Music, Writing, Dancing. *Collection:* Beethoven statuary and paintings; pewter, porcelain, and wood figure sculptures; Sherlock Holmes statuary, paintings and prints. *Publ:* Auth, The World Bibliography of Sherlock Holmes and Dr Watson, NY Graphic Soc, 74; Bramhall House, 77; The International Sherlock Holmes, Shoe String Press, 80; The Universal Sherlock Holmes (5 vols), Metrop Toronto Reference Libr, 94; A Bibliography of Published and Unpublished Writings, The Shoso-in Bulletin, Tokyo, Vol 10, 8/2000. *Mailing Add:* 638 12th Ave Salt Lake City UT 84103

DE WAN-CARLSON, ANNA
PRINTMAKER, PAINTER
b Dec 29, 49. *Study:* Art Inst Pittsburgh, 71; Syracuse Univ; Univ Col, Syracuse. *Work:* Carrier Corp-UTC; Print Club Albany; Onondaga Savings Bank; Onondaga Hist Asn; Maria Regina Col. *Exhib:* Print Club Albany 17th Nat Competition, NY; Space Group Korea 6th Int Miniature Print Biennial, Seoul, Korea; Ball State Ann Drawing & Small Sculpture Exhib, Muncie, Ind; Art Ctr Grand Prairie Nat Miniature Exhib, Stuttgart, Alaska; Fine Arts Inst San Bernardino Co Mus 27th Ann Exhib, Redlands, Calif; 66th Nat Exhib, Art Asn Harrisburg, Pa. *Collection Arranged:* Proof of the Print-Syracuse Printmakers, A Retrospective Exhib, Onondag Hist Asn, Syracuse, NY, 92. *Pos:* Exhib cur, Syracuse Printmakers; contrib writer, J of the Print World, 92; guest cur, Onondaga Hist Asn, Syracuse, NY, 92; dir, 12 RMS-4 Gallery, Syracuse, NY, 92-94, Cent NY Art Open, 95. *Teaching:* Artist in residence, Marie Regina Col, 75-76. *Awards:* Best in Show-Graphics, Women's Art Gallery, NY; First Prize-Graphics, Allentown Festival Arts, Buffalo, NY; First Prize, Popular Photog Mag. *Bibliog:* Syracuse Herald Am Stars Mag, 7/94; Art & Understanding, Vol 3, No 3, Issue 12, 8/94; The Mediator-Eye on the Arts, Vol 1, Issue 9, 9/94. *Mem:* Syracuse Printmakers (pres, formerly); Print Club Philadelphia; Everson Mus; Print Club Rochester; Print Club Albany. *Media:* Serigraph; Miscellaneous Media. *Publ:* Proof of the Print, J of the Printworld, Charles Stewart Lane Publ, Vol 15, No 2, spring 92. *Mailing Add:* 145 Avon Rd Syracuse NY 13206

DEWITT, EDWARD
PAINTER - ACRYLIC, OIL, SCULPTOR
b Jersey City, NJ, Aug 1, 38. *Study:* Self taught. *Work:* Bronx Zoological Soc; Palisades Amusement Park. *Comn:* Am Pres Sculptures, Bass Relief Series 2003, Chesapeake Reproductions, Mappsville, Va; Sir Winston Churchill; Louis Armstrong; Babe Ruth; US Pres Gerald Ford, John F Kennedy, Dwight Eisenhower & Harry Truman; Official 3rd Millennium Commemorative Double Eagle (bronze sculpture), US Hist Soc; Lewis & Clark (sculpture), Chesapeake Reproductions, 2004; Robert Kennedy (medallion). *Collection Arranged:* Boy Scouts Am; Nat Asn Theater Collection; Anheuser-Busch, Am Series, 5 yr series, sterling silver comermorative plates; Gen Motors Fisher Body; Playboy, road to the gold medallians. *Bibliog:* Artist in Our Midst, 21st Century Pro. *Media:* Oil. *Publ:* Collectors Mart, 76; New Art Int, 99; Direct Art Buyer, 99. *Dealer:* CJ Mugavero 201 Farnsworth Ave Bordentown NJ 08505; Swain Galleries 703 Watchung Ave Plainfield NJ 07060. *Mailing Add:* 411 N Carolina Tr Browns Mills NJ 08015

DEWITT, KATHARINE CRAMER
MUSEUM DIRECTOR
Study: Manhattenville Col of Sacred Heart, BA. *Pos:* Docent, Cincinnati Art Mus; co-chmn, Presidential Inaugural Comt, 2001. *Mem:* Nat Coun Arts; Nat Endowment for Arts; Cincinnati Fine Arts Fund (co-chmn, Individual Gifts 85, 93, mem, Allocation Comt, 91-94). *Mailing Add:* Cincinnati Art Mus 953 Eden Park Dr Cincinnati OH 45202

DEWOODY, BETH RUDIN
PATRON
b NYC. *Study:* Univ Calif, Santa Barbara, Studied Anthropology & Film Studies; New Sch Social Res, BA. *Pos:* Pres, May & Samuel Rudin Found Inc; exec vpres, Rudin Mgt Co; contrib ed, Hampton's Cottages & Garden's Mag; Dir, asst dir: (TV series) Born Free; prod asst, Annie Hall, The Front, Hair, co-prodr, Enter Juliet. *Mem:* Whitney Mus Am Art. *Mailing Add:* c/o Whitney Mus Am Art 945 Madison Ave New York NY 10021

DEZZANY, FRANCES JEAN
ASSEMBLAGE ARTIST, SCULPTOR
b Chicago, Ill, Aug 2, 42. *Study:* Kean Univ, NJ, BA, 70; Montclair State Univ, NJ, MA, 75; Art Students League, studied anat with Anthony Palumbo, 80-85. *Work:* Bergen Community Mus, Paramus, NJ. *Comn:* Three geometric wall pieces, Interior Decorator, Livingston, NJ, 79. *Exhib:* Between Art & Craft: The Fine Line, Del Art Mus, Wilmington, 75; Visual Interplay, Bergen Community Mus, Paramus, NJ, 77; Contemp Fiber Art, Newark Mus, NJ, 78; Leather Art/Leather Work, Montclair Art Mus, NJ, 79; Pieces in Space, Atelier Gallery/Snug Harber, Staten Island, NY, 86; Selected Works, D-Art Visual Art Ctr, Dallas, Tex, 90; Montclair State in Manhattan, Westbeth Gallery, NY, 94; La Chapelle Des Penitents, Gourdes, France, 2000; Longview Mus of Fine Arts, Longview, Tex, 2001; one person show, Bath House Cult Ctr, Dallas, Tex, 2001. *Pos:* Dir exec bd, Double Tree - Artist Inc Gallery, 76-77; art demonstr/lectr, Mus & Schs, NJ & Tex, 76-90; sculpture juror & pub relations, Nat Asn Women Artists, New York, 81-82; art dept chairperson & asst principal, Bending Oaks High Sch, Dallas, Tex, 89-92. *Teaching:* Instr arts & crafts, Rutgers, Newark, 76, Newark Mus, 76-77. *Awards:* Cert of Excellence in Art, St John's Contemporary Relig Art, Pastor Hourihan, 86; First Place Paper City Wide, On My Own Time, Dallas Bus Com Arts, 94; Hazel Witte Collage Award, Nat Asn Woman Artist, 97. *Bibliog:* Nita Leland & Virginia Lee Williams (auth), Creative College Techniques, Northlight Books, 94; Hartly, Bellinger & Williams (auth), Bridging Time & Space, Markowitz Pub, 98; Mary Carrol Nelson (auth), Fiberarts, 3-4/99. *Mem:* Nat Asn Women Artists; Soc Layerists Multi Media; Tex Sculpture Asn. *Media:* Assemblage. *Publ:* Auth, Moth-Proofing Techniques for Weavers & Spinners, Fiberarts No 1, 80; auth & ed, Society Layerists in Multi Media Nat Newslett No 23, Soc Layerists, 89. *Mailing Add:* 5403 Ridgedale Ave Dallas TX 75206-6011

DHAEMERS, ROBERT AUGUST
SCULPTOR, EDUCATOR, PRINTMAKER
b Luverne, Minn, Nov 24, 1926. *Study:* Calif Col Arts & Crafts, BFA, 52, MFA, 54. *Work:* City San Francisco Art Comn, Calif; First Christ Lutheran Church, Burlingame, Calif; San Jose State Col; Mills Col, Oakland, Calif; St Catherine Indian Sch, Santa Fe, NMex. *Comn:* Wrought iron wall mural, Jerry's Restaurant, San Leandro, Calif, 60; sculpture crucifix, First Christ Lutheran Church, 61; fountain, Frank Hunt Archit, Oakland, Calif, 63; Sundial Cor-Ten (steel 2 ton), Sci Complex, Mills Col, 70; bronze tabernacle, Holy Cross Hosp, San Fernando, Calif, 77. *Exhib:* Am Fedn Arts Traveling Exhib of New Talent, 59; San Francisco Art Comn, Calif Palace Legion, 61; M H DeYoung Mus, San Francisco, 62; Columbia Univ, 64; Mus Contemp Crafts, Creative Casting, NY, 64; Bertrand Russell Centenary Int, Nottingham, Eng, 73; Brigham Young Univ, Utah, 76; 12th Int Sculpture Conf, Mills Col, 82; Pub Sculpture Exhib, San Francisco Art Comn, 85-86; Brigham Young Univ, Utah, 76; and others. *Pos:* Adv, Kala Inst, 81-88. *Teaching:* Asst prof art, Calif Col Arts & Crafts, 51-56; assoc prof art, Mills Col, 57-75, prof, 75-, actg head dept art, 63-64, head dept, 73-76 & 79-80. *Awards:* First Award Sculpture Gold Metal, Oakland Mus Art, 52; First Award Metal Work, Calif State Fair, 62; Mellon Found Grant, 77, 80 & 83; Nat Endowment Arts Grant, 88-89. *Bibliog:* New Talent, Art Am, 66. *Mem:* Western Col Asn (accreditation comt, 69-); Western Asn Schs & Cols; Accrediting Comn Sr Cols & Univs; Int Sculpture Asn; Bay Area Consortium Visual Arts (steering comt, 87-89). *Media:* Metal, Etching. *Res:* Linear form and computer graphics. *Interests:* Metal casting and fabrication. *Publ:* Coauth, Simple Jewelry Making for the Classroom, 58; contribr, Metal Techniques for Craftsmen, 68; Craftsmen of the Southwest, 65 & The Crafts of the Modern World, 68; Lunar Suite I, The Hamptons Publ Dans Papers Ltd, 7/81; Sculpture 12, Int Sculpture Ctr, 82; Calif Art Review, 88; 2004 Modernist Jewelry 1940-60; auth: Mar Beth, Wearable Art movement. *Mailing Add:* 6 Ascot Ln Piedmont CA 94611

D'HARNONCOURT, ANNE
HISTORIAN, MUSEUM DIRECTOR
b Washington, DC, Sept 7, 43. *Study:* Radcliffe Col, BA magna cum laude, 65; Courtauld Inst Art, Univ London, MA with distinction, 67. *Collection Arranged:* Marcel Duchamp, Philadelphia Mus Art, Mus Mod Art & Art Inst Chicago, 73-74; Philadelphia: Three Centuries of American Art, Philadelphia Mus Art, 76; Eight Artists, Philadelphia Mus Art, 78; Violet Oakley, Philadelphia Mus Art, 79; Futurism and the International Avant-Garde, Philadelphia Mus Art, 80; John Cage: Scores and Prints, Whitney Mus Am Art, Albright-Knox Mus, Philadelphia Mus Art, 82. *Pos:* Cur asst, dept painting & sculpture, Philadelphia Mus Art, 67-69, cur, 20th cent art, 72-82, dir, George D Widener, 82-96, dir & Chief Exec Officer, 97-; asst cur, 20th cent art, Art Inst Chicago, 69-71; regent, Smithsonian Instn, Washington; vis com, J Paul Getty Mus, Malibu, Calif; bd dir, Luce Found, Inc New York City; bd overseers, Grad Sch Fine Arts, Univ Pa, Philadelphia; bd dir, The Fabric Workshop, Philadelphia; mem adv bd, Found French Mus, Inc; mem mus panel, NEA, 76-78, visual arts panel, 78-80, indemnity panel, 85-88, & mus overview panel, 86-87; bd trustees, Hirshhorn Mus & Sculpture Garden, Washington, 74-86; bd trustees Japan Soc New York City; and others. *Awards:* Chestnut Hill Col Medal, 87; James D Burke Prize Fine Arts, St Louis Art Mus, 87; Women's Hist Award, Mayor's Comn Women, 88; Chevalier l'Ordre Arts & Lettres, France, 95; Philadelphia Award, 97; Founder's Award for Exemplary Service to History 2001, Officer de l'Orde des Arts et des Lettres, France, 2002. *Mem:* Fairmount Park Art Asn Philadelphia (bd trustees); Grad Sch Fine Arts, Univ Pa, (bd overseers); Col Art Asn; Am Asn Mus; Int Coun Mus; Phi Beta Kappa; Am Philosophical Soc; Fel AAAS; Asn Art Mus Dirs. *Publ:* The first of Boccioni meets Miss FlicFlic ChiapChiap, Art News, 11/80; contribr, Futurism and the International Avant-Garde (exhib catalog), Philadelphia Mus Art, 80; Marcel Duchamp, Notes, GK Hall & Co, Boston, 83; Marcel Duchamp, Manual of Instructions for Etant Donnes, Philadelphia Mus Art, 87; Paying Attention (exhib catalogue), Los Angeles Mus Contemp Art, 93. *Mailing Add:* Philadelphia Mus Art PO Box 7646 Philadelphia PA 19130

DIAL, GAIL
METALSMITH, EDUCATOR
b Tulsa, Okla, Aug 23, 47. *Study:* Pittsburg State Univ, Kans, MA, 71; Ind Univ, Bloomington, with Alma Eikerman, MFA, 74. *Work:* Mus Plains Ind, Browning, Mont; Idaho First Nat Bank, Boise; Ind Mus Fine Arts, Bloomington; Pittsburg State Univ, Kans. *Exhib:* Goldsmith: 74, Renwick Gallery, Smithsonian Inst, Washington, DC, 74; Forms in Metal: 275 Yrs of Metalsmith, Mus Contemp Crafts, NY, 74; Contemp Crafts Am, Colo State Univ, Ft Collins, 75; Crafts for Am, Phillipines Design Ctr, Manila, 77; Copper, Bronze & Brass, Tuscon, Ariz, 77; Lake Superior Nat, Duluth Art Inst, Minn, 81. *Collection Arranged:* Marilyn Levine: Ceramics, 79; William Wiley Prints, 80. *Teaching:* Prof metal & crafts, Idaho State Univ, Pocatello, 74-. *Awards:* Cash Awards, Indianapolis Mus, 73 & Boise Art Gallery, 75 & 76. *Mem:* Prof mem Soc North Am Goldsmiths; Northwest Designer Craftsmen. *Media:* Gold, Silver. *Publ:* Contribr, Contemporary Jewelry, Holt Rinehart, 75; Contemporary Crafts of the Americas: 1975, Regnery, 75. *Mailing Add:* 533 Appaloosa Ave Pocatello ID 83201-7013

DIAMOND, JESSICA
GRAPHIC ARTIST
b Bronx, NY, Jun 6, 57. *Study:* Sch Visual Arts, NY, BFA, 79; Columbia Univ, MFA, 81. *Work:* Stedelijk Mus Voor Actuele Kunst, Ghent, Belgium; Whitney Mus Am Art, NY; Mus Het Domein, Sittard, Netherlands; Montreal Mus Fine Arts; Mus Modern Art, NY. *Comn:* The Mystic Leaves, Kouter, Gent, Belgium, 2000. *Exhib:* Solo exhibs, Hallwalls, Buffalo, NY, 85, Am Fine Arts Co, NY, 89-90 & 92, Artspace Annex, San Francisco, 91, Jablonka Galerie, Koln, Ger, 91, Galerie Fahnemann, Berlin, Ger, 91, Galleria Massimo De Carlo, Milan, 93 & Deitch Projects, NY, 96, Galerie Analix, Geneva, 96, Le Consortium, Dijon, France, 97, Vera Van Laer Gallery, Antwerp, Belg, 98, Stedelijk Mus Het Domein, Sittard, The Neth, 99, Birmingham Mus of Art, Ala, 2000, Art Gallery of York Univ, Toronto, Ont, Can, 2001, Montreal Mus Fine Arts, 2002; Group exhibs, On View, New Mus Contemp Art, NY, 86, Venice Biennal, 93 & Mus van Hedendaagse Kunst, Ghent, 93; Nostalgia as Resistance, Pop Project IV, Clocktower, NY, 88; Just Pathetic, Rosamund Felsen Gallery, Los Angeles, 90; Biennial, Whitney Mus Am Art, NY, 91; Nachtregels/Nightlines, Centraal Mus, Ultrecht, The Neth, 91; Heart, Mind, Body, Soul: Am Art in the 1990's, Selections from the Permanent Collection, Whitney Mus Am Art, 97; De Beurs van Judocus Vijdt, Kunstkapital in Gent, Bijlokemuseum, Gent, Belgium, 98; Zeitwenden, Kunstmuseum Bonn, Ger, 99; Zeitwenden, Kunstlerhaus Wien, Vienna, Austria, 2000; Sonsbeek 9, Arnhem, The Neth, 2001; Ota Fine Arts, Tokyo, 1999; Power, Casino Luxembourg, 2002. *Awards:* John Simon Guggenheim Meml Found Fel, 2000; Nat Endowment for the Arts Fel, 89. *Bibliog:* Susan Morgan (auth), and that's the way it is--the works of Applebroog, Diamond, Wegman, Artscribe, 6-7/86; Thomas Lawson (auth), Nostalgia as Resistance, Modern Dreams: The Rise and Fall and Rise of Pop, Mass Inst Technol Press, 88; Lydia Dona (auth), The memo on the wall: recent works by Jessica Diamond, Arts Mag, 10/90; Francesco Bonami (auth), Who is Jessica Diamond & Why Is She Saying Those Terrible Things About Us?, Flash Art, 1-2/93. *Media:* Wall Drawings/Wall Paintings, Conceptual Art. *Mailing Add:* 549 83rd St Brooklyn NY 11209

DIAMOND, MARY E B
PAINTER
b Detroit, Mich, Sept 2, 51. *Study:* Self-taught; Charles Sovek Workshop: Develop Your Natural Abilities-Oil Painting, 94. *Work:* Islip Art Mus, East Islip, NY; Cent Suffolk Hosp, Riverhead, NY; Marine Midland Bank, Southampton, NY. *Comn:* Wildlife (duck), comn by June Kujawa, Southampton, NY, 92; Estate Series (landscape), comn by M Rose Browne, NY, 93; Mr & Mrs Lustbader (portrait), comn by Robert P Diamond, NY, 93; Portrait of Fred, comn by Morgan Monceaux, Southampton, NY, 93; landscape mural, comn by Betsy Nichol, Sag Harbor, NY, 94. *Exhib:* 39th Ann Long Island Artist Juried Exhib, Hecksher Mus, Huntington, NY, 94; Landscape Today: East End Views, Guild Hall Mus, East Hampton, NY, 94; 5th Ann Nat Juried Exhib, Harve de Grace Mus, Md, 95; This Land is My Land Invitational Exhib, Elaine Benson Gallery, Bridgehampton, NY, 96; Sundance Gallery Invitational Season Opening Exhib, Bridgehampton, 96; and others. *Pos:* Judge all schs art festival, Parrish Art Mus, Southampton, NY, formerly; awards panelist, NY Coun Arts, Riverhead, 93-95; guest cur exhib, Long Island MacArthur Airport Upper Level Gallery, 96; admin asst, East End Arts & Humanities Coun, 96; auditor, NY State Coun Arts, 96-. *Awards:* Spec Opportunity Stipend, NY State Coun Arts, 94; First Place & Peoples Choice Awards, North Shore Art Guild, Farmingville, NY, 94; First Place, NY Cult Ctr, 95. *Bibliog:* Jay Thorne (dir), Thoughts of an Artist, Cablevision, 2/94; Marion Wolberg Weiss (auth), Honoring the artist, Dans Papers, 8/26/94; Renee Dahl (auth), Mary EB Diamond - Jewel of the East End, Independent Newspaper, 7/3/94. *Mem:* Founding mem Onyx Group (treas, 94, pres, 94); Nat Soc Painters Casein & Acrylic; Smithtown Township Arts Coun Inc; East End Arts Coun; Southampton Artists Asn (vpres 91, pres 92). *Media:* Oil, Acrylic. *Dealer:* Rose Marie Sampat 52 Ayers Rd Locust Valley NY 11560. *Mailing Add:* 83 N Side Dr Sag Harbor NY 11963

DIAMOND, PAUL
PHOTOGRAPHER
b Brooklyn, NY, June 20, 42. *Study:* Pratt Inst, BFA, 65; Purdue Univ, MA, 80. *Work:* Int Mus Photog, George Eastman House, Rochester, NY; Nat Gallery Can, Ottawa, Ont; Fogg Art Mus, Cambridge, Mass; Boston Mus Fine Arts. *Exhib:* 60s Continuum, George Eastman House, 72; one-man shows, Sq Bromides, Gallery Optica, Montreal, Que, 73 & Floating Found of Photog, NY, 74; Peculiar to Photog, Univ NMex, 76; Five, St Charles on the Wazee, Denver, Colo, 77; Contemp Photog, Fogg Art Mus, 77. *Teaching:* Instr photog, Calif Col Arts & Crafts, Oakland, 77-78; guest lectr photog, Univ Colo, Boulder, 77; instr, Moore Col Art, Philadelphia, currently. *Awards:* Guggenheim Found Fel, 75-76; Nat Endowment for the Arts Grant, 78. *Mem:* Soc Photog Educ. *Publ:* Contribr, Photographer's Choice, Addison House, 75, Ctr for Creative Photog, Vol 4, Univ Ariz, 77 & Grotesque in Photography, Ridge Press, 77. *Dealer:* Witkin Gallery 41 E 57th St New York NY 10022

DIAMOND, STUART
PAINTER
b Brooklyn, NY, April 8, 1942. *Study:* Pratt Inst, BFA, 59-63. *Work:* Mus Mod Art, NY; Mus Contemp Art, Chicago; Samual P Harn Mus Art, Univ Fla, Gainesville; Southwest Regional Mus, Corpus Christi, Tex; Ft Lauderdale Mus Art, Fla; Frederick R Weisman Art Found, Los Angeles; Bowdoin Mus, Brunswick, Maine; Ballinglen Archive, Ballinglen Arts Found, Ballycastle, Co Mayo, Ireland; Robert Hull Fleming Mus. *Exhib:* Great Wall Gallery, Toronto, 91; Japan Arts Gallery, Tokyo, 91; Baltimore Co Campus Fine Arts Gallery, Univ Md, 92; Bare Bone, curated by Nima Yankowitz, TZ Art & Co, NY, 96; After the Fall: Aspects of Abstract Painting Since the 1970s, Newhouse Ctr Contemp Art, Staten Island, NY, 97; Am Portraits, George Sherman Union Gallery, Boston Univ, Mass, 98; A Selection of Works from the Edward R Broida Collection (with catalog), Orlando Mus Art, 98; Vt Studio Ctr Press, Helen Day Art Ctr, Stowe, 98; The Children in Crisis, Invitational Benefit (with catalog), 99; Drawing in the Present Tense (with catalog), Drawing Ctr, NY, 99; ND Mus Art, Grand Forks, 2000; The Figure: Another Side of Modernism, Lily Wei, Cur, Newhouse Ctr for Contemp Art, Snug Harbor, 2000; 3 person drawing show, Western Wyo Comm Col Art Gallery, Rock Springs, 2001. *Teaching:* Assoc prof art, Cooper Union, NY, 88-97; instr painting, Parsons Sch Design, NY, 92-; full-time prof, Columbia Univ, 1992-2002, Univ Arts, 2003, Pratt Inst, 2003; instr art, RI Sch Design, 80-88, guest critic, Rome prog, 2000. *Awards:* Nat Endowment Arts Fel, 80-81 & 87-88; Solomon Guggenheim Fel, 87-88; Ballinglen Arts Found Artist-in-residence, Ballycastle, Ireland, 97-98; Vt Studio Ctr guest artist, 98-2001; Gladys E Cook Prize in Painting, Nat Acad Design, 2002. *Bibliog:* Lois Trulow (auth), interview, Art New Eng, June-July 98; Debra Balkin (auth), essay, Drawing in the Present Tense, full color catalog, Parsons, 99; Ken Johnson (auth), Objects of Desire, 125 Views of the Human Figure, NY Times, 9/1/2000. *Mem:* Skowhegan Sch Art. *Publ:* Joan Crowder, New York art comes to Auchincloss Gallery in a classy exhibition, Santa Barbara News-Press, 7/19/86; Dana Saulnier, Stuart Diamond, Q: A J of Art, Dept Art Col Archit, Art, & Planning, Cornell Univ, 5/90; Painting Faculty Show (catalog), Cooper Union, 96; Bare Bones (catalog), Tex Art & Co, New York, 96; After the Fall: Aspects of Abstract Painting (catalog), 97; The Figure: Another Side of Modernism (catalog), Newhouse Ctr, 2000; Catalog of Prints, Distinguished Artists at Vermont Studio Center, Vt Studio Ctr Press, color & black/white, 99. *Mailing Add:* 454 Broome St New York NY 10013

DIAMONSTEIN-SPIELVOGEL, BARBARALEE
WRITERTELEVISION INTERVIEWER, PRODUCER
Study: NY Univ, Doctorate, 63. *Hon Degrees:* Baltimore Col Art, Hon LHD, 90; Md Inst Col Art, Hon Dr; Longwood Col, Hon LHD, 95. *Collection Arranged:* Buildings Reborn: New Uses, Old Places, traveling, 76-; American Architecture Now (auth, catalog), Leo Castelli Gallery, New York, 80; Visions and Images, Int Ctr Photog, New York, 81-; Handmade in America, Leo Castelli Gallery & Metrop Mus Art, New York, 83; The Landmarks of New York (auth, catalog), 88; 8 Wonders of the NY World, 92; cur, Landmarks of New York, NY Hist Soc, 98. *Pos:* Staff asst, The White House, 63-66 & first dir New York City cult affairs, 66-71; writer, Sat Rev, 65-68 & Harpers Bazaar, 69-71; spec proj ed, Art News, 74-, Ladies Home J, 77-81, Int Commun Agency, 78, Partisan Rev, 78-79 & Interiors, 80; interviewer & producer, ABC-ARTS Cable Network, CBS-TV, WNYC-TV, Manhattan Cable Television & Arts & Entertainment Network; comnr, NY Landmark Preserv Comt, 72-87, Cult

Affairs Coun, 74-86, Landmarks Conservancy vice-chairperson, 83-, chmn, 87-95; assoc, Am Craft Mus, 81-; dir, Munic Art Soc, NY, 73-83 & Fresh Air Fund, 87-; adv comt hist & theory of design, Grad Sch Design, Harvard Univ, 90; bd dir, Corcoran Gallery & NY Hist Soc; mem, US Holocaust Mus Mem Coun, 90; comt mem, US Comn Fine Arts, 95; mem, NY State Hist Archives Partnership Trust, 95; chmn, Hist Landmarks Preserv Ctr, 95-; appointee, US Comn Fine Arts, 96- & Gov Pataki's Comn Hon Achievements Women, 97-. *Teaching:* Adj assoc prof, City Univ NY, Hunter Col, 74-77; vis prof, New Sch-Parsons Design, 76-82, Duke Univ, 78 & 83. *Awards:* Founders Day Award, Pratt Inst, 94; Visionary in the Arts Award, Mus Contemp Crafts, 95; Good Citizens Award, Coun Sr Ctrs & Serv NYC Inc, 96; and others. *Mem:* Munic Art Soc (mem bd dir, 72-); NY Landmark Conserv (bd gov); Am PEN; Women's Forum; Art Comn NY; and many others. *Publ:* Auth, Interior Design, 3/81; American photographers on photography, 11/81; Handmade in America, Harry N Abrams Publ, 83; American Architecture Now, Part I & II, 84; Fashion: The Inside Story, 85; Remaking America, 86; auth, The Landmarks of New York I & II, 89 & The Landmarks of New York III, 98. *Dealer:* Leo Castelli Gallery 420 W Broadway New York NY. *Mailing Add:* 720 Park Ave New York NY 10021

DIAO, DAVID
PAINTER, CONCEPTUAL ARTIST
b Sichuan, China, Aug 7, 43; US citizen. *Study:* Kenyon Col, AB, 64. *Work:* Whitney Mus Am Art, NY; San Francisco Mus; Art Gallery Ont, Toronto; Va Mus, Richmond; High Mus, Atlanta, Ga; Brooklyn Mus; Danforth Art Mus; Hirshhorn Mus; Mod Mus Art, St Etienne, France. *Exhib:* Biennial Exhib, Whitney Mus Am Art, NY, 69 & 73; Postmasters Gallery, NY, 85, 86, 88, 89, 91, 93 & 95, Galeria Westersingel 8, Rotterdam, The Neth, 88, Mus d'Art Moderne, St Etienne, France, 89, Galerie Joseph Dutertre, Rennes, France, 89, Provincial Mus voor Moderne Kunst, Oostende, Belg, 90, Het Kruithuis, Musvoor Hedendaagse Kunst, s-Hertogenbosch, The Neth, 90, Claire Burrus Gallery, Paris, 90; Avant-Garde in the 80's, Los Angeles Co Mus Art, Calif, 87; Generations of Geometry, Whitney Mus Art at Equitable Ctr, NY, 87; Post-Abstract Abstraction, Aldrich Mus, Ridgefield, Conn, 87; Wind and Matter: New Am Abstraction, USIA traveling exhib to Asian capitals, 89; Jet Lag, Turon Travel, Inc, 89; one-man shows, Provincial Mus voor Mod Kunst, Oostende, Belg, 90, Het Kruithuis, Mus voor Hedendaagse Kunst, The Neth, 90, Claire Burrus Gallery, Paris, 90, Selections 1972-1991, Cherng Piin Gallery, Taipei, Taiwan, 91 & 94; Slow Art: Painting in NY Now, PS1 Mus, Queens, NY. *Teaching:* Independent Study Prog, Whitney Mus, New York, 70-, Cooper Union, 94-; assoc prof, Hampshire Col, Amherst, Mass. *Awards:* Guggenheim Fel, 73-74; Nat Endowment Arts, 80, 87 & 93; Gottleib Fel, 92; and others. *Bibliog:* Kees Broos (auth), David Diao (essay catalog), Mus voor Hedendaagse Kunst Het Kruithuis,s-Hertogenbosch, Netherlands & Provincial Museum voor Moderne Kunst, Oostende, Belg, 90; Marjorie Welish (auth), Abstraction, Advocacy of, Tema Celeste, 1-21/92; Bruce Ferguson (auth), From Vision to Text a Re-Action (catalog), St Etienne, 89. *Dealer:* Postmasters Gallery. *Mailing Add:* c/o Postmasters Gallery 459 W 19th St New York NY 10011

DIAS-JORGENSEN, AURORA ABDIAS
PAINTER
b Belem, Brazil, June 10, 18; US citizen. *Study:* St Josephs Col, Brooklyn, NY, 39; Bank Street Col, New York, MA; Art Students League. *Exhib:* invitational show, Mocha Mus Contemp Hispanic Art, NY, 85; solo exhib, Broome St Gallery, NY, 93, Ceres Gallery, NY, 95, 97, 2000, Koener Gallery, West Hampton Beach, NY, 99 & 2000; group shows, Nabisco Gallery, NJ, 89, Bergen Mus Art & Sci, NJ, 90, Dupont Gallery Washington & Lee Univ, Lexington, Va, 93 & Wilkes Gallery, Wilkesboro, NC, 93; Art Students League Juried, Mus Provincetown, Mass, 93; Kunstler Forum, Bonn, Ger, 98; Midwest Mus Am Art, Elkhart, Inc, 99. *Teaching:* Art, Pub Sch 108, New York, 60-80. *Awards:* Merit Award, Annual Exhib, Nat Acad Design, New York, 79; Ralph Mayer Mem Award, Nat Asn Women Artists 98th Annual Exhib, 87; First Prize Medal of Honor & Elzabeth Stanton Blake Mem Award, Nat Asn Women Artists 103rd Annual, 92, Clara Shainess Award, 97, Gretchen Richardson Mem Award, 98, First Prize Medal of Honor Amelia Peabody Mem Award (Sculpture), 2000. *Mem:* Nat Asn Women Artists (vpres, 87-89 & 95-96); life mem Art Students League; Artists Equity, NY (bd dir). *Media:* Acrylic on Paper, Acrylic on Paper. *Dealer:* Koener Gallery. *Mailing Add:* 220 E 17th St New York NY 10003-3661

DIAS GRIFFIN, ANNE
PATRON
Study: Harvard Bus Sch, MBA; Georgetown Univ (summa cum laude). *Pos:* Analyst, Banking Dept Goldman Sachs; investment analyst, Fidelity Investment Ltd, London; analyst & portfolio mgr, Soro Fund Mgt; analyst Viking Global Investors; founder, vpres, managing partner, Aragon Global Investors. *Mem:* Chicago Symphony Orchestra (trustee); Whitney Mus Am Art. *Mailing Add:* c/o Whitney Mus Am Art 945 Madison Ave New York NY 10021

DIAZ, LOPE (MAX)
PAINTER, EDUCATOR
b Santurce, PR, Dec 13, 43. *Study:* Univ PR, BA, 66; Hunter Col, New York, MA, 71. *Work:* Museo DeArte, Ponce, PR; Mus Latin Am Print, PR Inst Cult, San Juan; Glaxo, RPT, Raleigh, NC; Museo De Arte, Univ De Puerto Rico, Rio Piedras, PR; Mint Mus Art, Charlotte, NC. *Exhib:* Solo shows, Mus Univ PR, Rio Piedras, 83; Galeria Botello, Hato Rey, PR, 88-94; Greenville Mus Art, Greenville, NC, 93; Mint Mus Art, Charlotte, NC, 94; Hodges Taylor Gallery, Charlotte, NC, 94 & 97; Lee Hansley Gallery, Raleigh, NC, 97; and others. *Teaching:* Asst prof art, Sch Archit Univ PR, 84-88 & assoc prof, Sch Design, NC State Univ, 88-. *Awards:* First Prize for Watercolor, Christmas Art Festival, Ateneo, PR, 66; First Prize for Painting, IBEC Group Show, 68; Honorary Award, Second Latin Am Graphic Biennale, Int PR Cult, 73. *Bibliog:* Tom Patterson (auth), Painter Diaz turns conventional framing inside out, The Charlotte Observer, NC, 7/31/94; Enrique Garcia Gutierrez (auth), Lope Max Diaz Para Pensar y Disfrutar, Nuevo Dia, 11/5/95; Tom Patterson (auth), New works show Diaz and painting outside the box, Charlotte Observer, 1/26/97. *Media:* Acrylic, Oil. *Publ:* Contribr, Kasimir Malevich: Revolucionario, Frente, 78. *Dealer:* Maud Duquella Galeria Botello 314 FD Roosevelt Ave Hato Rey PR 00918; Hodges Taylor Gallery 401 N Tyron St Charlotte NC 28202. *Mailing Add:* PO Box 10012 Raleigh NC 27605

DIBERT, RITA JEAN
PAINTER, PHOTOGRAPHER
b Flint, Mich, Feb 25, 46. *Study:* Flint Community Jr Col, AA(art), 66; Univ Mich, Ann Arbor, BFA, 69, MFA, 71; also studied with Gerome Kamrowski, Albert Mullen & Ted Ramsey; Univ Calif, Los Angeles, 67-68 & Nathan Lyons, Joan Lyons, Scott McCarney, 91-93; State Univ NY, Brockport, MFA(elec media), 94. *Work:* Detroit Inst Art; Calif Mus Photog; Munson-Williams-Proctor Inst; Polaroid Corp, Cambridge, Mass; Toledo Mus Art; Pratt Art Inst; and many others. *Comn:* Hyatt Hotels; Hayworth Furniture; Detroit Renaissance Ctr Restaurant; Blue Cross/Blue Shield, Mich; Raddison Hotels; and others. *Exhib:* One-person shows, Upper Catskill Coun Art, 91, Clausen Gallery, Chicago, 91, Cooperstown, NY, 91, Charlotte-Douglas Airport, 94, Mercer Gallery, 94, Monroe Col, Rochester, NY, 94 & Cone Univ Ctr, Univ NC, Charlotte, 94; Mich Directions Invitational, Flint Art Inst, 94; Alumni Invitational, Univ Mich Slausser Gallery, Ann Arbor, 94; New Impressions Photo Ann, Light Impressions Gallery, Rochester, NY, 94; Southern Visions Traveling Photog Exhib, 94; 25 Yr Retrospective, No Sense of Time, Quiz Gallery, 97; and others. *Teaching:* Lectr & area coordr photog & printmaking, Residential Col, Univ Mich, Ann Arbor, 72-74; asst prof, Hartwick Col, 74-79; asst prof & artist-in-residence, Pomona Col & Claremont Grad Sch, 79-86; asst prof arts, Claremont Grad Sch, 79-86; vis assoc prof, Hartwick Col, Oneonta, NY, 89-90; adj, State Univ NY at Brockport, 92-93; prof electronic media, Univ NC, Charlotte, 93-95; prin, acad tutor, head photog dept, Quay Sch Arts, Wanganui, NZ, 95-. *Awards:* Polaroid Grant, 83-92 & 98; Ruth Chenven Found Painting Grant, 90; New York State Coun Arts Decentralization Grant, 91; Grant Wanganui Regional Community Poly, 99; Top Festival Print Festival of Photography, Wanganui Camera Club, 96 & 98; Best in Show Annual Women's Show, UNCC, Charlotte, NC, 94. *Bibliog:* Article, Trends Section, Time-Life, 82, Popular Photog Ann, 86; Series of 5 Detroit full color 24x30 Lithographs, Univ Lithoprinters, Ann Arbor, Mich. *Mem:* Col Art Asn; Women's Caucus Art; Soc Photog Educ; Friends of the Sargeant Gallery (Whanganui, New Zealand); Artists Alliance (Auckland, New Zealand). *Media:* Acrylic. *Publ:* Illusr back cover, European Photography, Polaroid Corp, 83; infrared photog, Photo District News, 3/91; infrared photog, Pop Photo Discoveries, 7/92; James McGinnis Hand Coloring Photographs, AMPHOTO, 94; Marshalls Hand Coloring, 95. *Dealer:* Artist Trait Claremont Calif; Gallery 53 Cooperstown NY. *Mailing Add:* 113 Somme Parade Wanganui New Zealand

DICE, ELIZABETH JANE
CRAFTSMAN, ILLUSTRATOR, WEAVER
b Urbana, Ill, Apr 3, 19. *Study:* Univ Mich, BDesign, 41, MDesign, 42; Ind Univ, MA, 66; Int Sch Art, Mex; Inst Allende, Mex; Columbia Univ Teachers Col; Norfolk Art Sch; painting with Jerry Farnsworth; Penland Sch Crafts, 71 & 73. *Comn:* Woven Hanging, Carrier Chapel, Miss Univ for Women (Gift of class of 82). *Exhib:* Miss Art Asn, 48-51, 67 & 68; Nat Crafts Exhib, Wichita, Kans, 50; Nat Watercolor Show, Jackson, Miss, 51; New Orleans Art Asn, 55; Craftsmen's Guild Miss, 75; Path of the Weaver, Memphis, 78 & 80; and many others. *Teaching:* Assoc prof art, Miss State Col Women, 45-79, prof, 80-82; retired; Weaving Workshop for Chimmneyville Weavers, Jackson, Miss, 85. *Awards:* Prizes, Jackson, Miss, 46 & 51; Miss River Craft Exhib Award, 63; Horn Lake Libr Purchase Award. *Mem:* Archaeol Inst Am; Handweavers Guild Am (state rep, 72-77); Miss Mus Art; Southeastern Col Art Conf; Columbus Art Asn. *Media:* Weaving, Polymer Clay. *Specialty:* General; Columbus Arts Council. *Interests:* paper. *Mailing Add:* 134 King St Columbus MS 39702-6345

DI CERBO, MICHAEL
PAINTER, PRINTMAKER
b Paterson, NJ, 1947. *Study:* Pratt Inst, BFA & MFA. *Work:* Brooklyn Mus; Victoria & Albert Mus, London; Detroit Art Inst; Portland Art Mus, Ore; Brit Mus. *Comn:* Mural, Next City Corp, 82 & In Business Corp, 82. *Exhib:* Brooklyn Mus, 78; Print Club, Philadelphia, 80 & 85; Sotheby Park Bernet, NY, 81-84; solo exhib, Union St Gallery, San Francisco, 82, Portland Art Mus, Ore, 92, Phillips Fine Art, NY, 94, Chicago Print Fair, 94-96, Int Fine Print Dealers Asn Print Fair, 93-96, Old Print Shop, NY, 94, 96, Fitzwilliam Mus, Cambridge, Eng, 94, Seton Hall Univ, South Orange, NJ, 95; World Print Coun, San Francisco, 82; Kanagawa Prefectural Mus, Yokohama, 82, 84, 85, 88-90 & 92; Albany Inst Art Hist, NY, 86; De Cordova Mus, Lincoln, Mass, 86, 90, 92 & 2000; Taipei Fine Arts Mus, Taiwan, 87, 89, 93 & 2005; Schweinfurth Mem Art Ctr, Auburn, NY, 89; Aldrich Mus Contemp Art, Ridgefield, Conn, 90; Fred Baker Gallery, Chicago, 96; 2nd Int Trennial, Bitola, Macedonia, 97; Int Print Exhib, Portland Art Mus, Oreg, 97; Silvermine Guild, New Canaan, Conn, 98; Broom Street Gallery, NY, 99; Florean Mus, Carbunari, Romania, 2000; Atlantic Gallery, NY, 99, 2000; The Old Print Shop, 98, 2000, 2002; Springfield Art Mus, Mo, 99 & 2005; Rennsselaerville Inst, 2001; NY Hist Soc, 2004; Hollar Soc Gallery Prague, 2006; and others. *Pos:* Pres, Soc Am Graphic Artists 89-94; curator twentieth century, Old Print Shop, 2000-. *Teaching:* Prof art, Seton Hall Univ, South Orange, NJ, 92-99. *Awards:* Beveled Edge Award, Saga Nat, 98; Presentation Print Award, Print Club Albany, 2001; John Taylor Arms Award, Audubon Artists', 2002. *Bibliog:* City Lights Exhib, Art & Antiques Bull, 5/2000; article, Ink Images & Impressions, Newark Star Ledger, 4/15/2001; The Opposties, Jour of the Print World, spring 2001. *Mem:* Soc Am

Graphic Artists; Boston Printmakers & Artists Equity; Print Consort; Am Print Alliance. *Media:* Acrylic, Watercolor, Etching. *Publ:* Architectural Fantasies, Symmetry 2, VCH, 89. *Dealer:* Corp Art Directions 41 E 57 St New York NY 10022; Old Print Shop 150 Lexington Ave New York NY 10016. *Mailing Add:* 143 Bennett Ave Apt GA-3 New York NY 10040

DICKERSON, BRIAN S
PAINTER
b Middleburgh, NY, May 3, 51. *Study:* Pa Acad Fine Arts, 71-72; pvt study with Paul Rotterdam, 94-96; Beaver Col, BFA; Vt Col, MFA, 96. *Work:* US Mint, Philadelphia, public & private collections. *Exhib:* solo exhib, Nat Acad Design, NY, 80, Hahn Gallery, Philadelphia, Pa, 85-91, Del Community Col, 87, Visual Arts Gallery, Cobleskill, NY, 88 & Landscape as Mystical Metaphor, State Univ NY, Cobleskill, 89; Woodmere Gallery, Philadelphia, 80 & 81; Butler Mus Am Art, Youngstown, Ohio, 81; Hahn Gallery, Philadelphia, 82; Inst Man & Sci, Rennselaerville, NY, 83; Juried Exhib, Knickerbocker Artists Group, Salmagundi Club, NY, 87; Honorable Mem Painting Juried Exhib, Woodmere Mus, Philadelphia, Pa, 88; Fel Pa Acad Fine Arts Exhib, 88, 92-94 & 97; Woodmere Mus, Philadelphia, Pa, 88-93; Butler Inst Am Art, Pittsfield, Mass, 89; Nat Arts Club, NY, 90; Vt Col, Wood Gallery, Montpelier, 95; Family Values Rhetoric vs Reality, Wood Gallery, Vt Col, Montpelier, 96; The Unbroken Line, Centennial Exhib Fel, Pa Acad Arts, 97; NY State Mus, Albany, 99-. *Pos:* Artist, Inst Man & Sci, Rensselaerville, NY. *Teaching:* Fac mem, Art Inst Philadelphia, currently; Antonelli Inst, 94-97. *Awards:* First Prize, Woodmere Mus; Ralph Fabri Medal of Merit, Nat Soc Painters Casein & Acrylic, 80. *Mem:* Fel Pa Acad Fine Arts. *Media:* Oil, Drawing, Graphite. *Mailing Add:* 151 W Durham St Philadelphia PA 19119

DICKERSON, DANIEL JAY
PAINTER, INSTRUCTOR
b Jersey City, NJ, Dec 22, 22. *Study:* Cooper Union Art Sch, 41-43 & 45-46; Cranbrook Acad Art, BFA, 47, MFA, 49. *Work:* Joseph H Hirshhorn Collection; Adelphi Univ Mus; Ill Wesleyan Mus; Corcoran Gallery; Weatherspoon Gallery, Univ NC. *Comn:* NVE Bank mural, Leonia, NJ; art prog, US Coast Guard. *Exhib:* Whitney Mus Am Art Ann, 47; Pa Acad Fine Arts, 53; Audubon Artists Exhib, 64; Nat Inst Arts & Lett, 68; Nat Acad Design, 74; and others. *Teaching:* Lectr art, Manhattanville Col, 65-69; chmn dept art, Finch Col, 69-78; instr, Nat Acad Design Sch Art, 77-88 & Art Students League, 78-96. *Awards:* First Prize, Springfield Art Mus, 54; Emily Lowe Award for Painting, Audubon Artists, 64; Henry Ward Ranger Purchase Award, Nat Acad Design, 74; and others. *Mem:* Artists Fel; US Coast Guard Artists; Nat Acad Design; Nat Acad. *Media:* Acrylic, Oil. *Mailing Add:* 104 High St Leonia NJ 07605

DICKERSON, VERA MASON
PAINTER, INSTRUCTOR
b Radford, Va, July 28, 46. *Study:* Radford Univ, BFA, 68; Am Univ, MFA, 70; studied with Wayne Thiebaud, Daniel Greene (workshop) & Carla O'Connor. *Work:* Miller Brewing Co, Eden, NC; Gannett Publ Co, Arlington, Va; Marriott Corp; Clarion Hotels. *Comn:* Portraits, Fed Judges James Hill, Atlanta, Ga, Adrian Spear, San Antonio, Tex & John Jamison, Fredericksburg, Va, comn by Bar Asn, Darlington Co, SC, 81-83; portraits, Gen Marion Kinon, Dillon, SC, 85 & Clara Black, comn by Roanoke City Schs, Va, 86. *Exhib:* Traveling Exhib, Over the Blue Ridge, Roanoke Mus Fine Arts, Va, 81; More Than Land or Sky, Nat Mus Am Art, Washington, DC, 81; Southeast Print & Drawing Show, Belle Air Gallery, Fla, 82; Va Mus Fine Arts, Richmond, 83; After Her Own Image, Salem Col, Winston-Salem, NC, 85; Henley Spectrum, Winston-Salem, NC, 92; 28 one-person shows; Nude, Lexington Art League, KY, 2001; and others. *Collection Arranged:* Roanoka Coll, Longwood Univ. *Pos:* Artist-in-residence pastel drawing, Va Mus Fine Arts, Richmond, 83-84; dir, Sketchbook Tour Scotland, 90, 98 & 99, Ireland, 2001. *Teaching:* Asst prof art, Va Western Community Col, Roanoke, Va, 72-78, dept art chmn, 78-81; founded The Studio Sch, Roanoke, Va, 90-. *Awards:* Nat Endowment Arts Grant, 81; Best in show, Kaliedoscope Festival, 88 & Showcase for the Arts, 87, 88; First Prize Bristol Community Arts, 2000; Am Watercolor Soc, 2002; Rocky Mt Nat Watermedia Exh, 2002. *Bibliog:* More than Land & Sky, Nat Mus Am Art Publ, 79; Over the Blue Ridge, Roanoke Mus Fine Arts Publ, 81; A Treasury of Southern Art & Literature, MacMillan, 93. *Mem:* Va Watercolor Soc (found mem, bd dir, pres, 98-99); signature mem, Nat Watercolor Soc; Balt Watercolor Soc. *Media:* Oil, Mixed. *Interests:* Travel & gardening. *Dealer:* Signature 9 Gallery Roanoke Va; Corporate Art Source Montgomery Ala. *Mailing Add:* 148 W Arrowhead Ct Troutville VA 24175

DICKINSON, ELEANOR CREEKMORE
PAINTER, GRAPHIC ARTIST
b Knoxville, Tenn, Feb 7, 31. *Study:* Univ Tenn, with C Kermit Ewing, BA, 52; San Francisco Art Inst, with James Weeks, 61-63; Univ Calif, 67, 71 & 81; Academie de la Grande Chaumiere, Paris, France, 71; Calif Col Arts & Crafts, MFA, 82; Golden Gate Univ, 84. *Work:* Libr Cong, Nat Mus Am Art, Corcoran Gallery Art, Washington; San Francisco Mus Mod Art; Library of Congress; numerous privat collections including Senator Edward Kennedy, Senator Herschel Rosenthal, and numerous others. *Comn:* Wall installation (bronze), Univ San Francisco, 91. *Exhib:* Solo exhibs, San Francisco Mus Modern Art, 65, 67, Santa Barbara Mus, 66, Judah Magnes Mus, Berkeley, 68, Fine Arts Mus, San Francisco, 69 & 75, Knoxville Mus Art, Knoxville, 70, Corcoran Gallery Art, 70 & 74, Poindexter Gallery, NY, 72 & 74, J B Speed Art Mus, Louisville, Ky, 72, Wash State Mus, 75, Cheney Cowles Mus, Spokane, Wash, 75, Triton Mus, Santa Clara, 75 & 77, Smithsonian Inst Traveling Exhib, 75-81, Huntsville Mus Art, 77, Montgomery Mus Fine Arts, 78 & Oakland Mus, 79, Menil Mus/Screen Memories Gallery, Houston, Tex, 88, Michael Himovitz Gallery, Sacramento, 88, 89, 91, 93, 98, Hatley Martin Gallery, San Francisco, 86, 89, Gallery 10, Washington, DC, 89, Diverse Works Gallery, Houston, 90, Ewing Gallery, Univ Tenn, 91, Mus Contemp Religious Art, St Louis, 95, Thacher Gallery, Univ San Francisco, 2000; Diverse Works Gallery, Houston, Tex, 90; 20th Century Women Artists, Queensboro Community Col, NY, 90; Am Religions, Smithsonian Inst, 90-91; A Salute To Women, Nat Mus of Women in Arts, 91; Recent Acquisitions, Fine Arts Mus San Francisco, 91; Witness to Dissent, Art In General, NY, 92; 500 Yrs Since Columbus, Triton Mus, Santa Clara, 92; Images of Us, Bedford Gallery, Walnut Creek, 92; 16th Nat Invitational Drawing Exhib, Emporia State, 92; Michael Himovitz Gallery, Crocker Art Mus, 94; New Perceptions of the Spirit, GTU Gallery, Berkeley, 95; Global Focus, UN World Conf, Women, Beijing, Moscos, 95; Searching for the Spiritual, Hope Col, Mich, 97; Mary, St Mary's Col, Maraga, Calif, 97; Radiant Object, Cheney Cowles Mus, Spokane, 97; Dorothy Gillespies Collection, Orlando Mus, Art Mus Western Va & Art Mus Radford Univ, 97 & 98; Preserving the Past Securing the Future, Nat Mus Women in Arts, 98; Artists of Western States, Artcore Gallery, Los Angeles, 99; The Female Gaze, Ohlone Col, Fremont, 2000; Truth and Lies, Triton Mus, 2000; Art by Women, Goethe Inst, Kathmandu, Nepal, 2001; Like A Prayer, Tryon Gallery, Charlotte, NC, 2001; Bay Area Figurative Art, Univ California, Berkeley, Calif, 2004; Violence Against Women/Women Against Violence, Nexus Gallery, Berkeley, 2004; Gender in Motion, 3TEN HAUSTUDIO, Atlanta, GA, 2005; Traveling Restropective, Downtown Gallery, Univ Tenn, 2005; Ells Gallery, San Francisco, 2005; Ohlone Col, 2006; A Madel, Lewis Pohl Gallery, Honolulu, 2005; Revisioning, Maifland Art Ctr, Fla; Artcard, Shariah Art Mus, United Arab Emirates; Highly Favored (traveling exhibit), Gordon Col, Mass, 2006-. *Collection Arranged:* Howard Finster, Fine Arts Mus San Francisco, 2006. *Awards:* Mid-Career Award, Womens Caucus, Col Art Asn, 95; Lifetime Achievement Award, Women Art Caucus Col Art Asn, 2003; and others. *Bibliog:* Marsha Maguire (auth), Confirming the word: artist and social documentarian, Quarterly J Libr Cong, 81; Dr Peter Selz (auth), San Francisco: Eleanor Dickinson at Hatley Martin, Art Am, 89; Martina R Norelli (auth), Allgemeines Kunstler Lexikon, 2001. *Mem:* Artists Equity Asn (nat vpres); Women's Caucus Art (Nat affirmative action off/bd mem, 2000-2006); Col Art Asn (CAA chair Committee for Women in the Arts); Calif Lawyers Arts (state vpres 86-). *Media:* Ink, Pastel on Velvet. *Publ:* Auth, Tennessee revival services, Libr Cong Arch Folk Song, 71; illusr, Complete Fruit Cookbook, Scribner, 72 & Human Sexuality: A Search for Understanding, West Publ, 84; coauth (with B Benziger), Revival!, 74 & illusr, That Old Time Religion, 75, Harper & Row, Elkmont, 2005; and others. *Mailing Add:* 2125 Broderick St San Francisco CA 94115

DICKINSON, NORMAN
PAINTER
b Liverpool, Eng, May 8, 21. *Study:* Liverpool Col Art, 35-39; Royal Col Art, London, ARCA, 46-49. *Comn:* Portrait, Tony O'Reilly, Pittsburgh, 73; portrait, Trammell Crow, Dallas, Tex, 84; portrait, David Rockefeller, NY, 85; portrait, Elizabeth Koch, 87; portrait, Elizabeth Johnson, 90. *Media:* Oil

DICKSON, JANE LEONE
PAINTER
b Chicago, Ill, May 18, 1952. *Study:* Sch of Boston Mus Fine Arts, dipl, 76; Harvard Univ, BA(magna cum laude), 76. *Work:* Metrop Mus Art & Mus Mod Art, NY; Whitney Mus Am Art; Victoria & Albert Mus, London, Eng; Libr Cong, Washington; Art Inst Chicago, Ill; Brooklyn Mus Art, NY. *Comn:* MTA Arts for Transit Poster, New York City, 90; Radio Shack, 2004; MTA Mosaics, Times Square Station, 2006. *Exhib:* solo exhibs, Brooke Alexander Gallery, NY, 86, 88, 90 & 92, Joe Fawbush Gallery NY, 83 & Whitney Mus at Philip Morris, 96, Marlborough Gallery, NY, 2003, 05, Almost There, Jersey City Mus, NJ, 2006; On 42nd Street, Whitney Mus-Philip Morris, NY, 84; Biennial Exhib, Whitney Mus, NY, 85; Pub & Pvt: Am Prints Today, Brooklyn Mus, NY, Carnegie Inst, Pittsburgh & Walker Art Ctr, Minn, 86-87; A Graphic Muse, Prints By Contemp Am Women, Yale Univ Art Gal, Mt Holyoke Col MA & Richmond VA, 87-88; Ean Keuze/A Choice KunstRai Amsterdam, 88; Portraying the Night, Kansas City Art Inst, 88; Life Under Neon, Moore Col Art, Philadelphia, Pa, 89; retrospective, Ill State Univ (auth, catalog), Normal (traveling), 94; Paradise Alley, Whitney Mus at Philip Morris, 96; Saints Grown Up, Temple Univ Tyler Sch Art Gallery, Philadelphia, 97; Out of Here, Ft Lauderdale Mus of Art, 01; East Village, New Mus, 2005; Downtown, Grey Art Gallery, NY Univ & Warhol Mus, Pittsburg, Pa, 2006; Caja Granada, Spain. *Pos:* Art/Omi residency, 99. *Teaching:* Sch Visual Arts NY 88-89, Temple Univ, Tyler Sch Art, Philadelphia Pa, 90, Cooper Union, State Univ NY, Purchase, 96; prof art Pace Univ, 2000-, Calif State Northridge, 98. *Awards:* Grants, Nat Endowment Arts, Washington & Ariana Found, 85; Dewars Young Artist Award, 90. *Bibliog:* Ken Gonzalez Day (auth), Jane Dickson at Long Beach Mus Art, Art Issues, 3-4/96; Holland Cotter (auth), A romantic haze on dead-end lives of the city, NY Times, 6/14/96; Vincent Katz (auth), Jane Dickson at Black & Herron, Art Am, 7/96. *Media:* All. *Dealer:* Marlborough Gallery 40 W 57th St NY 10019. *Mailing Add:* 17 Hubert St New York NY 10013

DICKSON, JENNIFER JOAN
PHOTOGRAPHER, LECTURER
b Piet Retief, Repub SAfrica, Sept 17, 1936; Can citizen. *Study:* Goldsmith's Col Sch Art, Univ London, 54-59; Atelier 17, Paris, with S W Hayter, 60-65. *Hon Degrees:* LLD (hon) Univ Alta, 88. *Work:* Victoria & Albert Mus, London; Nat Gallery Can, Ottawa; Metrop Mus Art, NY; Montreal Mus Fine Arts; Smithsonian Inst; Royal Acad Arts, London, Eng. *Comn:* The Secret Garden (collabr: Henry J Kahanek & Ray Van Dusen), 76 & Paradise, 80, Nat Film Bd Can; The Last Silence, Can Mus Contemp Photog, Ottawa, 93, & Palazzo Te, Mantua, Italy, 93. *Exhib:* Salon des Realites Nouvelles, Musee d'Art Moderne, Paris, 62 & 66; Biennale de Paris, Mus Mod Art, Paris, 63; Modern Prints, 65 & Contemp Prints, 66, Victoria & Albert Mus, London; Salon Int de la Gravure, Montreal Mus Fine Arts, 71; Folio Seventy Three Traveling Exhib, San Francisco Mus Art, 74; Forum 76, Montreal Mus Fine Arts, 76; Celebration of the Body, Agnes Etherington Art Centre, Queen's Univ, Ont; Tendances

Actuelles au Quebec, 79 & L'estampe au Que 1970-1980, 80, Musee d'Art Contemporain, Montreal; 14th Int Biennial of Graphic Art, Ljubljana, Yugoslavia, 81; solo exhibs, Il Tempo Classica, Saidye Bronfman Centre, Montreal, 82, A Journey to Cythere, Wallack Art Ed, Ottawa, 82, Jennifer Dickson: A Continuum, Edward Monaghan Art Consult, Ottawa, 83 & Versailles: Through the Crystal Wall, Wallack Galleries, Ottawa, 83; The Thief of Time, Wallack Galleries, 2006. *Collection Arranged:* Imprint 76 (current Can graphic art), Ont Arts Coun; Nat Libr and Archives, Can; Can Mus Contemp Photography. *Teaching:* Vis prof fine arts, Univ Wis, Madison, 72; vis artist fine arts, Queen's Univ, Kingston, Ont, 77-78; instr dept visual arts, Univ Ottawa, formerly; freelance lectr & photographer. *Awards:* James A Reed Award, Can Painters-Etchers & Engravers, 73; Special Purchase Award, World Print Competition, San Francisco Mus Art, 73; Prize, 5th Norwegian Int Print Biennale, 80; and others. *Bibliog:* Michael Rothstein (auth), Frontiers of Printing, Studio Vista, 70; Anthony Gross (auth), Etching, Engraving & Intaglio Printing, Oxford Univ Press, 72; Edward-Lucie Smith (auth), Art in Seventies, Phaidon/Cornell Univ Press, 80; and others. *Mem:* Academician Royal Acad Arts; Print & Drawing Coun Can; Can Artists Representation; fel Royal Soc Painter-Etchers & Engravers. *Media:* Photography. *Res:* Syrian Orthodox monasteries in Turkey. *Specialty:* Canadian art. *Interests:* gardening, vintage fashion. *Publ:* Auth, The Hospital for Wounded Angels, Porcupines Quill Inc, 87. *Dealer:* Wallack Galleries 203 Bank St Ottawa ON K2P 1W7 Can. *Mailing Add:* 20 Osborne St Ottawa ON K1S 4Z9 Canada

DICKSON, MARK AMOS
PAINTER, PRINTMAKER
b Boulder, Colo, Mar 4, 1946. *Study:* Metrop State Col, BA, 69; Pratt Inst, 69-70; Univ Denver, MFA, 73. *Work:* Plains Art Mus, Morehead, Minn; Colo Graphic Arts Ctr, Denver, Colo; Denver Ctr Performing Arts, Colo. *Comn:* Oil on canvas, Texaco Oil, White Plains, NY; oil, American Airlines; oil, Kennedy Int Airport, NY; oil, Hakodate Hotel, Tokyo, Japan. *Exhib:* Nat Audubon, Nat Acad Design, NY, 70; Artist Exchange, Joslyn Art Mus, Omaha, Nebr, 73; Arts 80, Nat Boulder Arts Ctr, 80; Colorado Print Invitational, Colo Graphic Arts Ctr, Denver, Colo, 84; Draw 82, Boulder Arts Ctr, Colo, 82; Creativity 86, Art Direction Mag, NY, 86; Graphics 86, Am Inst Graphic Arts, NY, 86; Artist of Taos, Stables Art Ctr, Taos, NMex, 87; Downtown Ctr Visual Art, 25 Yrs, 25 Artists, Metrop State Col, Denver, Colo, 90; Near North & Northwest Art Coun Gallery, Printmakers Coop Ann Exhib, Chicago, 92. *Teaching:* Instr printmaking, Univ Denver, Colo, 73; assoc prof fine art, St Thomas Col, Denver, 75-79; instr painting, Rocky Mountain Col Art, Denver, Colo, 87. *Awards:* Research & Travel Grant, Am Asn Theological Schs, 79; Award of Merit, Graphics 86, Inst Graphic Arts, 86; Award of Distinction, Creativity 86, Art Direction Mag, 86. *Bibliog:* Mystique Mag Northern NMex, 8/84; Where Chicago Mag, 9/91; Colorado Expression Mag, summer 92. *Media:* Oil; All Media. *Dealer:* Mary Bell Gallery Chicago IL; Friesen Gallery Seattle WA. *Mailing Add:* 101 Ash Denver CO 80220

DICORCIA, PHILIP LORCA
PHOTOGRAPHER
b Hartford, Conn, 53. *Study:* Sch Mus Fine Arts, Boston, dipl, 75, post grad cert, 76; Yale Univ, New Haven, MFA, 79. *Work:* Bertelsmann Music Group, NY; Benesta Corp, Madrid; Bibliotheque Nationale, Paris; Fogg Art Mus, Harvard Univ; Gemeente Mus, Helmond, Holland. *Exhib:* Contemp Photog VI, Fogg Art Mus, Harvard Univ, Cambridge, Mass, 77; Witnesses: Against Our Vanishing, Artists Space, NY; Pleasures and Terrors of Domestic Comfort, Mus Mod Art, NY, Baltimore Mus Art, Los Angeles Co Mus Art, Contemp Art Ctr, Cincinatti, 91; Our Town, Burden Gallery, NY, 92; Family Matters, Northlight Gallery, Ariz State Univ, Tempe, 93; Prospect 93, Frankfurter Kunstverein & Schirn Kunsthalle, Ger, 93; Down Town, The Neth Photo Inst, Rotterdam, The Neth, 94; Present/Future, Jackson Fine Art, Atlanta, 94; Flesh and Blood, Fotofeis, Edinburgh, Scotland, Ansel Adams Ctr Photog, San Francisco, Foto Manifestabe, Eindhoven, The Neth, 94; Art & Public, Geneva, Switz, 95; Pace Wildenstein MacGill, NY, 96 & 98; Whitney Biennial, Whitney Mus Am Art, NY, 97; Galerie Almin Rech, Paris, 98; Galerie Rodolphe Janseen, Brusels, 98; Philip-Lorca diCorcia, Museo Nacional Centro de Arte Reina Sofia, Madrid, 98; Streetwork, Galerie Klemens Gasser und Tanja Grunert, Cologne, 98; and many others. *Awards:* Artist Fel, Nat Endowment Arts, 80, 86 & 89; John Simon Guggenheim Mem Found Fel, 87. *Bibliog:* Alice Rose George (auth), Flesh and Blood: Photographers Images of their Own Families, Picture Proj Inc, New York, 92; Chris Bruce (auth), After Art: Rethinking 150 years of Photography, Henry Art Gallery, Univ Wash, Seattle, 94; Vince Aletti (auth), Short List, Village Voice, 12/8/98. *Mailing Add:* 55 Hudson St Apt 8D New York NY 10013

DI COSOLA, LOIS BOCK
PAINTER, PRINTMAKER
b Brooklyn, NY, Jan 23, 35. *Study:* Early Master classes, Mus Mod Art, NY, grant, 51, BFA, 53; New Sch, R Pousette-Dart, 60; Pratt Graphics Ctr, 73-75; State Univ NY, Bachelor of Prof Studies for life's work in art, 85. *Work:* Guild Hall Mus, East Hampton, NY; Mus Mod Art, NY; Sophia Smith Collection, Smith Col, Northampton, Mass; int & pvt collections. *Exhib:* Carnegie Fine Art Inst, 53; Asn Am Artist Galleries, NY, 54; Art & Design Exhib, 33rd Ann Int Art Dir Club, NY, 54; NY World's Fair, 64; Hecksher Mus, 64 & 78; Guild Hall Mus, E Hampton, NY, 63-64 & 80-81; X12, Pioneer Feminist Art Exhib, NY, 70; Traveling Print Exhib, Pratt Graphics Ctr, NY, 75; Provinciaal Mus, Bel, 82; Born to Survive, Mus Het Toreke, Belg, 84; Elaine Benson Gallery, Bridgehampton, NY, 89, 91 & 96; Mus Mod Art, NY; Life of the City, Mus of City of NY, 2002; 9/11 exhib, Virtual Union Square, 2002; Reactions, Exit Art, 2002; and others. *Pos:* Graphic Artist, Norcross, Seventeen Mag, 53-56, Sesame St, 69-70 & Time-Life Bks, 73; bd mem, Prof Artist Guild, 66 & Nat Drawing Asn, 89; arts ed, Sunstorm Artst, 82. *Teaching:* Prof art, Hofstra Univ, Hempstead, NY, 90-. *Awards:* Augustus St Gaudens Medal for Draftsmanship, 53; Printmaking Award, Carnegie Inst Fine Art, 53; First Prize-Drawing, Seventeen Mag, 53; Art Dir's Club Award, 54; Painting & Drawing, Guild Hall Mus, Harold Rosenberg, 63; Mus Mod Art Curator's award, 63; Finch Col Mus, James Brooks' selection, 64; Guggenheim Mus Curator's Award, 64; Whitney Mus Curator's Award, 64. *Bibliog:* Art Kane (auth), We know what we like, Seventeen Mag, 6/53; Manuel De La Torre (auth), Lois DiCosola, 82; Helen Harrison (auth), Best of Long Island Graphics, NY Times, 9/81; Dr Saul Levine (auth), Portrait of an Artist: Lois DiCosola, Sunstorm Arts, 82; Elaine Booth Selig (monogr), Lois Di Cosola, 2005; Feminists Who Changed America: 1963-1975, Univ Ill Press, 2006. *Mem:* Drawing Soc; Mus Mod Art. *Media:* All. *Interests:* Literature, theatre. *Dealer:* Aldona M Gobuzas 215 E 79th St New York NY 10021. *Mailing Add:* 25 Arch Ln Hicksville NY 11801

DIDOMENICO, NIKKI
CONCEPTUAL ARTIST, ASSEMBLAGE ARTIST
b Newark, New Jersey, June 8, 48. *Study:* Douglas Col, BA, 71; d'Ecole de Beaux Art Paris, 71-72; Scuola di Torano, Carrara, Italy, Masters, 73-78. *Work:* Pagani Found, Milano, Italy; Banco di Lavoro, Carrara, Italy; pvt collections. *Comn:* Sculptures, comn by J Blum, San Francisco, 76, E Marucci, NJ, 85. *Exhib:* Salon du Mai, Palais Royale, Paris, 73; Incontri, Pietrasanta, 76; Biennale della Spezia, The City, La spezia, 75; Tentazioni, Forte di Belvedere, Firenze, 85; Expos Grup, Italy, 93. *Teaching:* Vis instr, Stockton State Col, NJ. *Awards:* Recognition, Icontri, I Noguchi, 76. *Bibliog:* Laura Grahm (auth), Avanti, 80; Mirko Puccerelli (ed), Arte Now, 84. *Mem:* Artist Equity, NY; Il Gruppo, Italy; Art Police (co-pres, 88-). *Media:* Mixed Media. *Dealer:* Stephen H Jones 357 W 54th St New York NY 10019. *Mailing Add:* 252 W 21 St No 54 New York NY 10011-3426

DIEHL, GUY
PAINTER, INSTRUCTOR
b Pittsburgh, Pa, Feb 1, 49. *Study:* Diablo Valley Col, Pleasant Hill, Calif, 70; Calif State Univ, Hayward, BA, 73; San Francisco State Univ, MA, 76. *Work:* Fine Arts Mus San Francisco, Calif; Caldwell Banker, West Palm Beach, Fla; Bank of Am, San Francisco, Calif; Princeton Univ, NJ; Progressive Insurance Co, Cleveland, Ohio; and others. *Comn:* Princess Cruise Lines; Peninsula Hotel, NY; MGM Mansion, Las Vegas, Nev. *Exhib:* Group exhibs, Millard Sheets Gallery, Pomona, Calif, 2001, Bank of Am, San Francisco, 2001, Anne Reed Gallery, Ketchum, Idaho, 2002, Conn Graphic Arts Ctr, Norwalk, 2002, Edith Caldwell Gallery, Sausalito, Calif, 2003, San Jose Mus Art, Calif, 2003, Gallery Henoch, New York City, 2004, Pasadena Mus Calif Art, 2004, Paula Brown Gallery, Toledo, Ohio, 2004, Hackett-Freedman Gallery, San Francisco, 2004, Piaza Gallery, San Francisco, 2004, Mendenhall Sobieski Gallery, Pasadena, Calif, 2004, Charles Campbell Gallery, San Francisco, 2005, Gallery C, Hermosa Beach, Calif, 2005, George Krevsky Gallery, San Francisco, 2005-2006, Judson Gallery Contemp & Traditional Art, Los Angeles, 2005, Bedford Gallery, Walnut Creek, Calif, 2005, Sonoma Valley Mus Art Biennial 2005, Sonoma, Calif, Sullivan Gross, Santa Barbara & Montecito, Calif, 2006, Klaudia Marr Gallery, Santa Fe, NMex, 2006; Solo exhibs, Modernism, San Francisco, 93-94, 97, Fletcher Gallery, Santa Fe, NMex, 95, Hackett-Freedman Gallery, San Francisco, 98, 2001, 03, Hunsaker/Schlesinger Gallery, Santa Monica, Calif, 2004. *Teaching:* Instr painting, Diablo Valley Col, Pleasant Hill, Calif, 77-82; instr painting, Chabot Col, Livermore, Calif, 80; Las Positas Col, Livermore, Calif, 80-90; Ft Mason Art Ctr, San Francisco, 92-98. *Awards:* Purchase Award, Alameda Co Art Commission, 72; Marin Art Coun Individuaal Artists Grant, 94; Biennial Exhib Award, Sonoma Valley Mus Art, 2005. *Bibliog:* Dottie Indyke (auth), Less is more in Diehl's Seductions of light, The Santa Fe New Mexican, Pasatiempo, 7/7/95; Richard Tobin (auth), Short reviews, THE magazine, Santa Fe, NMex, 8/95; Steven Nash, Guy Diehl and History, Hackett Freedman Gallery, San Francisco, Calif, 98; Christopher Willard (auth), The Details on Details, American Artist Mag, 8/02; others. *Media:* Acrylic, Watercolor. *Dealer:* Hackett-Freedman Gallery 250 Sutter St San Francisco Calif 94108; Magnolia Editions 2527 Magnolia St Oakland Calif 94607. *Mailing Add:* 188 W Blithedale Ave Mill Valley CA 94941

DIEHL, HANS-JURGEN
PAINTER
b Hanau, Ger, May 22, 40. *Study:* Ecole Nationale Superieure des Beaux-Arts, Paris; Akademie der bildenden Kunste, Munich; Hochschule fur Bildende Kunste, Berlin, 59-66. *Work:* Mus Preusischer Kulturbesitz, Nat Gallery, Berlin, Ger; Ulmer Mus, Ulm, Ger; Sprengel Mus, Hannover, Ger; Kunsthalle Kiel, Kiel, Ger; Mus Witten, Witten, Ger. *Exhib:* Solo shows, Ulmer Mus, Ulm, Ger, 77, Kunsthalle, Berlin Ger, 85; Ugly Realism, Inst Contemp Arts, London, 78; Utopian Visions in Modern Art: Dreams and Nightmares, Hirshhorn Mus, Washington, DC, 83; Stationen der Moderne, Berlinische Galerie, Berlin, Ger, 89; Hugh Lane Munic Gallery Mod Art, Dublin, 91; Galerie Limmer, Köln, Ger, 99; Kesselhaus, Hannover, Ger, 2000. *Teaching:* Prof painting, Hochschule der Kunste, Berlin, 77. *Mem:* Deutscher Kunstlerbund. *Dealer:* Galerie Limmer Venloer Str 21 50672 Koln Germany. *Mailing Add:* 47 Clinton St New York NY 10002

DIETRICH, BRUCE LEINBACH
MUSEUM DIRECTOR, ADMINISTRATOR
b Reading, Pa, Oct 10, 37. *Study:* Kutztown Univ, BS, 60; Univ Denver, 61; Temple Univ, 62-67; Millersville Univ, 67, State Univ NY, MS, 70; George Washington Univ, 81-83; Am Legal Inst/Am Bar Asn, 81-87; Kellog Proj/Smithsonian Inst, 84, 85 & 87. *Collection Arranged:* The Sea, 76, Winter Winds, 78, Master Prints, 78, Spectrum, 78 & Director's Choice, 83, Reading Pub Mus & Art Gallery; Fractal Dimension, 88. *Pos:* Cur space sci, Reading Pub Mus & Art Gallery, 67-69, mus dir, 76-92; dir, Reading Planetarium, 69-93; mus management consult, 92-93; retired. *Mem:* Middle Atlantic Planetarium Soc; Asn Planetariums Can; Asn Sci Mus Dirs; Am Asn Advan Sci; and others. *Mailing Add:* 1546 Dauphin Ave Wyomissing PA 19610-2118

DIETRICH, LINNEA S
HISTORIAN, EDUCATOR
b Lebanon, Pa, July 26, 44. *Study:* Am Univ, AB, 66, Univ Del, MA 67, PhD, 73. *Teaching:* From asst prof to prof art hist, Univ SFla, 68-89; prof, Miami Univ, Oxford, Ohio, 89-. *Awards:* Hampton Int Travel Grant to Egypt-Effective Educ, Nat Sci Found, 89. *Mem:* Col Art Asn; Women's Caucus Art; Historians 19th Century Art; Mid-west Art Hist Asn. *Res:* 19th and 20th century art history and theory; pedagogy and critical thinking; Women in art; Islamic art. *Publ:* Auth, On Audrey Flack, Arts Mag, 81; Form & Content, In: Death of Art, Arthur Danto, 84; Gauguins' Notebook for Aline, Art Criticism, 91; 6 books on art history, Reinderr Co, 96; Aging & Contemporary Art, J Aging & Identity; auth, Arab & Persian Women Artists, Woman's Art J. *Mailing Add:* 4080 Shollenbarger Rd Oxford OH 45056

DI FATE, VINCENT
ILLUSTRATOR, PAINTER
b Yonkers, NY, Nov 21, 45. *Study:* Phoenix Sch Design, cert, 67; Sch Visual Arts, 68; Art Students League, 68-70; MA, Syracuse Univ, 2003. *Work:* NASA Mus, Cape Canaveral, Fla; NASAM, Smithsonian Inst, Washington; Soc Illusr, NY; Univ Kans; New Brit Mus, Conn. *Exhib:* Solo shows, Reading Pub Mus, Pa, 78 & Mus Sci & Natural Hist, St Louis, Mo, 82; New Brit Mus Am Art, Conn, 80; Bronx Mus Arts, NY, 80; Stadthalle Limburg, WGer, 80; Am Mus-Hayden Planetarium, 88. *Teaching:* Instr, Univ Bridgeport, Conn, 79 & Sci Fiction & Fantasy Illus, Fashion Inst Technol, 93-. *Awards:* Hugo Award, World Sci Fiction Asn, 78; Skylark Award, New Eng Sci Fiction Asn, 87; Artistic Achievement Award, Asn Sci Fiction/Fantasy Artists, 98. *Bibliog:* George Magnan (auth), Science fiction art, Today's Art & Graphics, 3/81; Ellen Datlow (auth), Stellar technician, Omni Mag, 5/81; Brian M Fraser (auth), All the colors of space and time, Questar Mag, 10/81. *Mem:* Soc Illusr (pres, 95-97); Graphic Artists Guild; Int Asn Astronomical Artists; Am Sci Fiction/Fantasy Artists (pres, 78). *Media:* Acrylic, Oil. *Publ:* Co-auth & illusr, Di Fate's Catalog of Science Fiction Hardware, Workman Publ, 80; contribr, The Science Fiction Reference Book, Starmont House, 81; auth & ed, Infinite Worlds: The Fantastic Visions Sci Fiction Art, Penguin Studio Books, 97; The Science Fiction Art of Vincent Difate, Paper Tiger, 2003. *Mailing Add:* 12 Ritter Dr Wappingers Falls NY 12590

DIFRONZO, FRANCIS G
PAINTER
Study: Calif State Univ, Fullerton, BFA, 94; Pa Acad Fine Arts, Philadelphia, MFA, 98. *Exhib:* Solo exhibs, Common Disaster, Artists' House Gallery, Philadelphia, 99, Philadelphia Cathedral, 2000, Segue, 2000, Rosenfeld Gallery, Philadelphia, 2002, 2004. *Awards:* Recipient Art in Am Scholarship Award, Liquitrex, 93; Stobbart Found Fel in the Arts, 98; Pew Fel in the Arts, 2004

DIGBY, LYNNE
PAINTER, WRITER
b Gloucester, Eng; US citizen. *Study:* Gloucester Col Art, Eng, 56-57; Ont Col Art, 58-59; studied with Can abstr expressionist Harold Town, 58. *Work:* McGraw Hill. *Exhib:* Mt Aramah Invitational, Orange Co Hist Soc, Clove Furnace Historic Site, 86; NE Watercolor Soc Ann Exhib, Harness Racing Mus, Goshen, NY, 95-96; 104th Ann Open Exhib, Catherine Lorillard Wolfe Art Club, 2000; solo exhib, Port of Call Gallery, Warwick, 2002 & 2004, Exec Suite Gallery, Gov Bldgs, Goshen, NY, 2005. *Pos:* Pres, Orange Co Sub-chap, Graphic Artists Guild NY, 82-87; vpres Graphic Artists Guild NY Inc, 85-87. *Awards:* Best Oil Painting, Actinolite Ann Exhib, Can, 63; Harness Racing Mus Award, Northeast Watercolor Soc Int Ann Exhib, 96; Best in Show, Orange, Colo, Day Exhib, 2005. *Bibliog:* Warwick Valley Dispatch, 6/2000; preview, Daily Freeman, 5/2002; Warwick Advertiser, 11/2002; Chronicle, 4/16/04 & 6/22/05. *Mem:* Exhib mem, Woodstock Artists Asn, NY; exhib mem, Garrison Art Ctr, NY; Woodstock Artists Asn & Mus. *Media:* Oil, Mixed Media. *Dealer:* Flying Pig Gallery Sussex NJ; Art4business 161 Leverington Ave Philadelphia Pa 19127; Port-of-Call Gallery Warwick NY 10990; Woodstock Artists Asn & Mus Woodstock NY. *Mailing Add:* 153 Montgomery St Goshen NY 10924

DI GIACINTO, SHARON
PAINTER
Study: Ohio Univ, Athens, BFA, 81; Tex Woman's Univ, Denton, MFA, 83. *Work:* Hill Country Arts Found, Ingram, Tex; Glendale Pub Libr, Ariz; Paradise Valley Community Col, Phoenix, Ariz; Glendale Community Col, Ariz; Peru State Col, Nebr; City of Mesa Water Dept, Ariz. *Exhib:* solo exhib, Sun Cities Art Mus, Sun City, Ariz, 89, The Return to Animal Imagery, Visual Arts Gallery, Phoenix, Ariz, 90 & Peoria City Hall, Ariz, 95, Phoenix Col, Ariz, 2000, Heffernan Room, West Valley Art Mus, Surprise, Ariz, 2001, Fine Art Gallery, Phoenix Col, Ariz, 2000; two person exhib, Chandler Ctr Arts, Ariz, 91 & Casa Grande Art Mus, Ariz, 97; 23rd Ann Nat Exhib, San Bernardino Co Mus, Redlands, Calif, 88; 53rd Ann Nat Midyear Exhib, Butler Inst Am Art, Youngstown, Ohio, 89; Hoyt Nat Painting & Drawing Exhib, Hoyt Inst Fine Arts, New Castle, Pa, 89; Am Realism Competition, Parkersburg Art Ctr, WVa, 92; 35th Chautauqua Nat Exib Am Art, NY, 92; Stockton Nat Print & Drawing Exhib, Haggin Mus Art, Calif, 92; Beyond Drawing, Sheemer Art Ctr & Mus, Phoenix, 94; Drawn West Fourth Biennial Drawing Exhib, Norra Eccles Harrison Mus Art, Utah State Univ, Logan, 94; Primates in Art & Illustration, Univ Wis, Madison, 96; Good Night, Art After Dark, Ariz Mus Youth, Mesa, 97; Southwest Color Juried Exhib, Poway Ctr Performing Arts, Calif, 98. *Pos:* Co-chmn, Peoria Arts Comn, 88-91; juror Fine Arts Exhib, Ariz State Fair. *Teaching:* Instr, painting & color theory, Phoenix Col, 83-84; Instr, drawing & color theory, Glendale Community Col, 85-88. *Awards:* First Prize, St Hubert Giralda Animal Imagery Nat Exhib, 87; Best of Show, Don Ruffin Mem Statewide Exhib, 89; Glendale Municipal Art Gallery First Prize for Drawing and Prints, 31st Ann Juried Fine Arts Exhib, Glendale, Ariz, 94. *Mem:* Col Art Asn of Am; Phoenix Art Mus. *Media:* Oil, Graphite. *Publ:* Illusr, The Best of Colored Pencil 2, 94, The Best of Oil Painting, 96 & The Best of Drawing and Sketching 98, Rockport Publ, Gloucester, Mass

DI GIACOMO, FRAN
PAINTER
b Miami, Ariz, Oct 24, 44. *Study:* Scottsdale (Ariz) Artist's Sch, studies with Paul Leveille, 1985, David Leffel, 1995 & 96 & Howard Terpning, 2000. *Work:* Nat Ctr States Cts, Williamsburg, Va; Henry Wade Justice Ctr, Dallas; City Hall, Auburn, Maine; St Plus A Cath Ch, Dallas; Rasor Elem Sch, Plano, Tex. *Comn:* 2 portraits, Dallas Morning News, 1987 & 93; 13 telephone book covers, Area Wide Directory Co, Carrollton, Tex, 1988-94; 9 portraits, Haggar Apparel, Dallas, 1994; portrait Chief Justice Warren Burger, comn by Charles Noteboom, 1994; 3 portraits, Home Interiors & Gifts, Dallas, 1997-2001. *Exhib:* various ann exhibs, Oil Painters Am, 1992-2002; Women Artists of the West ann int, Las Vegas, 1992; ann nat, Acad Artists Asn, Springfield, Mass, 1992 & 94; Texas & Neighbors ann 5 state, Irving, Tex, 1995, 7 & 2000; ann nat, Salmagundi Club, NY, 1998. *Teaching:* pvt instruction. *Awards:* 1st Place, Asn Creative Artists, 1994; 1st Place, Plano Art Asn, 1996; 2nd Place, Richardson Civic Art Soc, 2002. *Bibliog:* Rasmi Simhan (auth), High profile, Dallas Morning News, 6/2002; Steve Carter (auth), Elegance articulated, Dallas Home Design, 10/2002; Charlotte Berney (auth), Gallery tour, Cowboys & Indians, 12/2002. *Mem:* Am Soc Classical Realism; Oil Painters Am (signature); Asn Creative Artists (signature); Portrait Soc Am. *Media:* Oil. *Specialty:* Classical Realism. *Publ:* Contribr (book), The Best of Portrait Painting, North Light Books, 98; auth, I'd Rather do Chemo than Clean out the Garage: Choosing Laughter Over Tears, Brown Books, 2003; Contribr, Am Artist Magazine, 2004; Contribr, Am Artist, Still Life Highlights, 2005. *Dealer:* Southwest Gallery 4500 Sigma Dallas Tex 75244; Gallerie Amsterdam Carmel Calif. *Mailing Add:* 16806 Club Hill Dr Dallas TX 75248

DIGNAC, GENY (EUGENIA) M BERMUDEZ
SCULPTOR, ENVIRONMENTAL ARTIST
b Buenos Aires, Arg, June 8, 32; US citizen. *Work:* Mus Mod Art, Cali, Colombia; Mus del Banco Cent Guayaquil, Ecuador; Latin Am Art Found, San Juan, PR; Fundacio Joan Miro, Barcelona, Spain; Palazzo Dei Diamanti, Ferrara, Italy. *Exhib:* Many one-women shows, 87-71 & produced 33 fire gestures, US, Europe & SAm, 1970-2000; Some More Beginnings, Exp in Art & Technol, Brooklyn Mus, NY, 68; IX Festival Art, Cali, Columbia, 69; Earth, Air, Fire, Water, Elements of Art, Boston Mus Fine Arts, 71; Arte de Sistema, Centro de Arte y Communicacion, Mus Mod Art, Buenos Aries, 71; III Biennial of Art Coltejer, Medellin, Colombia, 72. *Awards:* Uranus II (light & plastic sculpture), IX Festival of Art, Mus Mod Art, Cali, Colombia, 69. *Bibliog:* Charlotte Strifer Rubenstein (auth), American Women Artists, GK Hall & Co, 82, Del Pop Art A La Nueva Imagen; Jorge Glusberg (auth), Ediciones de Arte Gaglianome, Argentina, 85; Jules & Nancy G Heller (auths), Encyclopedia of XX Century North American Artists, Garland Publ, New York & London, 95; Douglas Davis (auth) Art and the Future, Praeger Pubs, 73. *Media:* Light, Plastics, Fire, Temperatures. *Publ:* Del Pop Art a La Nueva Imagen; Kans Quart Vol 17 No 3, 85; Performance and Environmental Art, Kans Quarterly, 85. *Dealer:* Osuna Art, 7200 Wisconsin Ave, Bethsda, MD, 20814. *Mailing Add:* 4109 E Via Estrella Phoenix AZ 85028

DIKER, CHARLES & VALERIE
COLLECTOR
b New York, NY. *Study:* Harvard Univ, BA, 56, MBA, 58. *Pos:* Managing partner, Diker Mgt LLC, currently. *Awards:* Named one of Top 200 Collectors, ARTnews Mag, 2004. *Mem:* Antique Tribal Art Dealers Asn Inc, George Gustav Heye Ctr (co-chmn bd, mem nat bd, currently); Nat Mus Am Indian. *Collection:* Native American Art; Modern & Contemporary Art

DILL, GUY
SCULPTOR, EDUCATOR
b Duval Co, Fla, May 30, 46. *Study:* Chouinard Sch Art, Los Angeles, BFA, 70. *Work:* Mus Mod Art, Whitney Mus Am Art, NY; Calif State Univ, Long Beach; Long Beach Mus Art, Calif; Mus Contemp Art, Los Angeles, Calif; Newport Harbor Art Mus, Calif. *Comn:* Prudential Ins Co, Canoga Park, Calif, 77; Fed Bldg, Huron, SD, 79; Pac Corp Towers, El Segundo, Calif, 86-87; Hughes Ctr, Las Vegas, Nev, 91; Sony Music Campus Arboretum in Santa Monica, Lowe Develop, Los Angeles, Calif, 92; and many pvt comns. *Exhib:* Solo shows include Flow Ace Gallery, Los Angeles, Calif, 82, 83, 84 & 86, Ace Contemp Exhibs, Los Angeles, Calif, 88, Ochi Gallery, Boise, Idaho, 88, Annex Gallery, San Diego, Calif, 89, San Diego Design Ctr, Calif, 89, Kay Kimpton Gallery, San Francisco, Calif, 90, Jan Turner Gallery, Los Angeles, Calif, 92, Denny Vaughn Gallery, Aspen, Colo, 95, Ellips Exhib, Brussels, Belgium, 96, 97 & 98, Bobbie Greenfield Gallery, Los Angeles, Calif, 97, 99 & 2000 & Meyerovich Gallery, San Francisco, Calif, 2000, Peter Findlay Gallery, NY, 2006; group shows include Guggenheim Mus, 71; Ace Gallery, Los Angeles, 71, 73 & 77; Pace Gallery, NY, 74 & 76; Biennial Show, Whitney Mus Am Art, 74; Sculpture Made in Place, Walker Art Ctr, Minneapolis, Minn, 76; Calif Sculpture Show, Bordeaux, France, 84 & Mannheim, Ger, West Bretton, Eng & Hovikodden, Norway, 85; Ooldonk Sculpture Exhib, Ooldonk Castle, Belg, 94. *Pos:* mem artists adv coun, Mus Contemp Art, Los Angeles, Calif, 81-82; mem selection panel, Calif Arts Coun, 82-83; mem adv coun arts, Cedars Sinai Med Center, Los Angeles, Calif, 85-2001. *Teaching:* Instr, Sculpture Dept, Univ Calif, Los Angeles, 77-78 & head, 78-82; vis artist-lectr, Wright State Univ, Dayton, Ohio, 77. *Awards:* Theodoron Award, Guggenheim Mus, 71; Nat Endowment Arts Fel, 74 & 81; First Prize, Am Show, Chicago Inst Art, 74; Stars Design Lifetime Achievement Award, Pacific Design Center, 2000. *Bibliog:* Peter Frank & Phyllis Tuchman (auths), Guy Dill, Black Innes (catalog), p 1-20; Jan Butterfield (auth), About the Collection Artists, Art Collection of Pacific Enterprises (catalog), p 36, 111 & 186; Jan Butterfield (auth), Guy Dill sculpture is about proof, Artspace, p 55-57 & 71, 9-10/92. *Mem:* Calif Art Coun; Cedars Sinai Med Ctr, Los Angeles, Calif (adv coun arts, 85-92). *Media:* Mixed. *Collection:* Mus Collections: Albright-Knox Mus, Buffalo, Long Beach Mus Art, Calif, LA Co Mus Art, Minneapolis Inst Art, Mus of Contemp Art, LA. *Mailing Add:* 1321 Innes Venice CA 90291

DILL, LADDIE JOHN
PAINTER, SCULPTOR
b Long Beach, Calif, Sept 14, 43. *Study:* Chouinard Art Inst, BFA, 68. *Work:* Mus Mod Art, NY; Mus Contemp Art, Los Angeles; San Francisco Mus Mod Art, Calif; Smithsonian Inst, Washington; Oakland Mus Art, Calif; Chicago Art Inst. *Comn:* Glass fountain, Los Angeles Pub Libr, Cent Br, 93. *Exhib:* One-man shows, Pasadena Mus Mod Art, Calif, 71, Portland Univ Gallery, Ore, 71, Sonnabend Gallery, NY, 72, Calif Inst Technol, 82, Laica, 82, Charles Cowles, 83, Ochi Gallery, Sun Valley, Idaho, 89, 93, 95 & 99, Persons & Lindell Gallery, Helsinki, Finland, 89, Works Gallery S, Costa Mesa, Calif, 90 & 91, Conejo Valley Art Mus, Thousand Oaks, Calif, 92, Andrea Marquit Fine Arts, Boston, Mass, 94, Chac Mool Contemp Fine Art, Los Angeles, Calif, 96 & Bakersfield Mus Art, Calif, 99 & 2001; The Mod Era, San Francisco Mus Mod Art, 76 & Smithsonian Inst, Washington, 77; Calif Painting & Sculpture, San Francisco Mus Mod Art, 77; Painting of the 70's, Albright-Knox Gallery, Buffalo, 78-79; Corcoran Biennial, 83-84; Fredrick R Weisman Mus Art, Malibu, Calif, 97; Downey Art Mus, Calif, 98; Nev Mus Art, 98; Calif Ctr Arts, Escondido, 99; Norton Simon Mus, Pasadena, Calif, 99; Armory Ctr Arts, Pasadena, Calif, 99 & 2000. *Teaching:* Lectr painting, Univ Calif, Los Angeles, 75-88; chair visual arts, Santa Monica Col Design, Art & Archit, 90-. *Awards:* Nat Endowment Arts Grant, 75 & 82; Guggenheim Fel, 80. *Bibliog:* Robert Hughes (auth), Los Angeles, Time Mag, 71; Judy Goodman (auth), Laddie Dill new work, Arts Mag, 75; Michael Smith (auth), Laddie John Dill, Baxter Art Gallery, Calif Inst Technol, Pasadena, 78. *Media:* Cement, Polymer, Glass; Oil on Canvas. *Mailing Add:* 1625 Electric Ave Venice CA 90291

DILL, LESLEY
SCULPTOR
b Bronxville, NY, 1950. *Study:* Skidmore Col, 68-70; Trinity Col, BA (English, cum laude), 72; Smith Col, MA (art educ), 74; Md Inst Art, MFA (painting), 80. *Work:* Libr Cong, Washington, DC; Whitney Mus Am Art, Metrop Mus Art & Mus Mod Art, NY; Joslyn Art Mus, Omaha, Nebr; Art Inst Chicago; Achenbach Found, MH de Young Mem Mus, San Francisco, Calif; Am Embassy, Geneva; Contemp Mus, Honolulu, Hawaii; and others. *Exhib:* Solo exhibs, Queens Mus Bulova (with catalog), NY, 92, Arthur Roger Gallery (with catalog), New Orleans, 93, 94, 97 & 2000, Ann Jaffe Gallery, Miami, Fla, 93, Sandler Hudson Gallery, Atlanta, Ga, 93, Bernard Toale Gallery, Boston, Mass, 1993, 96 & 99, Frumkin/Adams Gallery, NY, 93 & 95, Gracie Mansion Gallery, NY, 94 & George Adams Gallery, 95, 97, 98 & 2000, Byron Cohen Gallery for Contemp Art, Kansas City, Mo, 2002, A Ten Yr Survey: Dorsky Mus, SUNY, New Paltz, The Art Gallery, Univ of Colo, Boulder, Cult Ctr, Chicago, Ill, Contemp Mus, Honolulu, Scottsdale Ctr for Contemp Art, 2002-04; Voice, Ken Kirshman Artspace, New Orleans, La, 2004; New Works, Equinox Gallery, Vancouver, BC, 2005; I Heard as if I Had No Ear: Lesley Dill & Tom Morgan, Montalvo Arts Center, Saratoga, Calif, 2006; and others; Fall From Fashion (with catalog), Aldrich Mus Contemp Art, 93; The Body Human, Nohra Haime Gallery, NY, 94; Material Concerns, Rotunda Gallery, Brooklyn, NY, 94; Paint, Props & Process, Castle Gallery, Col New Rochelle, NY, 94; 5 Women Sculptors (with catalog) XI Valparaiso Biennial, Chile, 94-95; In the Flesh, Freedman Gallery, Reading, Pa & Aldrich Mus Contemp Art, Ridgefield, Conn, 95-96; Alliance for Contemp Art: Auction 98, Denver Art Mus, 97; Contemp Narratives in Am Prints, Whitney Mus Am Art, Champion, NY, 99-2000; Uncommon Threads: Contemp Artists and Clothing, Herbert F Johnson Mus, Cornell Univ, Ithaca, NY, 2000; New York, New Work, Now! Currier Mus of Art, Manchester, NH, 2002; From Stone to Foam, Nohra Haime Gallery, NY, 2002; Me, Myself, & I, George Adams Gallery, NY, 2002; Word/Image, Westport Arts Center, Westport, Conn, 2003; Cut Bite Stroke: Techniques in Printmaking, Firehouse Art Gallery, Nassau Community Col, Garden City, NY, 2004; Clothesline: Art, Clothing, Identity, Santa Fe Art Inst, NMex, 2005; Words & Images, The Hebrew Home Riverdale, Riverdale, NY, 2005-2006; Full House: Views of the Whitney's Collection at 75, Whitney Mus Am Art, NY, 2006; and others. *Pos:* Cur, Fall Show, Condeso/Lawler Gallery, New York, 84; artist-in-residence, Altos de Chavon, Dominican Repub, 84; cur, Traps: Elements of Psychic Seduction, Carlo Lamagna Gallery, New York, 87; fac, Parsons Sch Design, 91-. *Teaching:* Instr art, St Ann's Sch, Brooklyn, NY, 84-91; Parsons Sch Design, 90-91. *Awards:* Zaner Corp Purchase Award, Small Works 83, Patterson Sims, 83; Fel, Nat Endowment Arts, 90; Proj Residency Award, Hillwood Art Mus & NY State Coun Arts, 92; NY Found Arts Drawing, Printmaking Category, 1995; Grant, Joan Mitchell Found, 96; and others. *Bibliog:* Louise Sheldon (auth), Lesley Dill's Sculptures are Sensual and Spiritual, Baltimore Chronicle, 1/3/90; David Hirsh (auth), AIDS: Challenging Art, NY Native, 1/29/90; Rose Slivka (auth), From the Studio, E Hampton Star, 11/15/90. *Mem:* Nat Acad. *Mailing Add:* c/o George Adams Gallery 41 W 57th St 7th Fl New York NY 10019

DILLOW, NANCY ELIZABETH ROBERTSON
ADMINISTRATOR, HISTORIAN
b Toronto, Ont, June 26, 28. *Study:* Univ Toronto, BA. *Collection Arranged:* J E H MacDonald, RCA, 1873-1932 (with catalog), 65; Piet Mondrian and the Hague School of Landscape Painting (with catalog), 69; Saskatchewan: Art and Artists (with catalog), 71; Marilyn Levine-Donovan Chester (with catalog), 74; Frank Nulf (with catalog), 76; Transformation of Vision, H Eric Bergman (catalog), 83, Tony Tascona (catalog), 84. *Pos:* From asst cur to cur exten & educ, Art Gallery Ont, 56-67; dir, Norman Mackenzie Art Gallery, 67-79; chief cur, Winnipeg Art Gallery, 80-86. *Teaching:* Prof hist Can art, Univ Regina, 72-79. *Mem:* Fel Can Mus Asn (coun, 67-70). *Res:* Canadian art history. *Mailing Add:* 99 Estelle Ave Toronto ON M2N 5H4 Canada

DI MEO, DOMINICK
PAINTER, SCULPTOR
b Niagara Falls, NY, Feb 1, 1927. *Study:* Art Inst Chicago, four year dipl, 50, BFA, 52; Univ Iowa, MFA, 53. *Work:* Art Inst Chicago; Whitney Mus Am Art, NY; Ill Bell Tel Co, Chicago; Univ Mass, Amherst; Nat Collection Am Art, Smithsonian Inst. *Exhib:* Ann Exhib Contemp Am Painting, Whitney Mus Am Art, 67-68; Fantasy & Figure, Am Fedn Arts, NY & Traveling Show, 68-69; Violence in Recent Am Art, Mus Contemp Art, Chicago, 68-69; The Crowd: Exhibit of Sculpture, Paintings & Graphics, Arts Club Chicago, 69; Visions/Painting & Sculpture: Distinguished Alumni 1945-Present, Art Inst Chicago, 76; 16th Joan Miro Int Drawing Prize Competition, Barcelona, Spain & Sala de Cult de la Caja de Ahorros de Navarra, Pamplona, 77; 100 Artists--100 Yrs, Alumni of the Sch of Art Inst Chicago, Centennial Exhib, Art Inst Chicago, 79-80; Momento Mori, Centro Cult/Arte Contemp, Mexico City, Mex, 86-87. *Teaching:* Instr, Chicago Acad Fine Arts, 67-69; vis artist, Art Inst Chicago, 77. *Awards:* Guggenheim Mem Found Fel Graphics, 72-73; Nat Endowment Arts Sculpture Fel, 82-83. *Bibliog:* Whitney Halstead (auth), Introd, In: Di Meo, Work: 1959-1966, Galaxie, 67. *Media:* Mixed. *Mailing Add:* 429 Broome St New York NY 10013

DIMSON, THEO
DESIGNER, ILLUSTRATOR
b London, Ont, Apr 8, 30. *Study:* Ont Col Art, Toronto, 50; Danforth Tech Sch. *Work:* Typomundus 20, France; Publ archives, Ont, Can; Metro Toronto Cent Libr; Harvard Univ. *Exhib:* Am Inst Graphic Arts, NY; Montreal Art Director's Show, 51-75; Graphica Club Toronto; Graphica Club Montreal; Int Poster Art, Bulgaria; one-man poster show, Toronto, 78; Posters Biennial, Warsaw, Poland, 80; Lahti Poster Biennial, Finland, 81; 1st Int Triennial of Posters, Japan, 85; Int Litfass Biennial, Munich, Ger, 92; Greatis Festival, Russia, 93; one-man show, Royal Ont Mus, 93-94; Greatis Festival, Russ, 93; Art Gallery Beijing China, 2001. *Pos:* Vpres creative design, Art Assocs Ltd, Toronto, 59-65; pres & creative dir, Dimson & Design, 65-83; pres & creative dir, Theo Dimson Design, Inc, Toronto, 83-. *Teaching:* Seneca Col, Toronto, Can, 94-2000; George Brown College, Toronto, Can, 95-2000. *Awards:* Medal Awards, Arts Directors Club, Toronto & Montreal; Award of Excellence, Am Inst Graphic Arts; First Winner, Usherwood Award for continuous outstanding contribution to the Visual Arts, Can, 86; Outstanding Achievement Award, Premio Int Diseno, Mex, 2003. *Bibliog:* Hara (auth), Designers, Graphic Design Mag, 62; Republic of Childhood, Oxford Univ, 67. *Mem:* assoc mem Ont Col Art; Alliance Graphique Int; fel Graphic Designers Can; Advertising & Design Club, Toronto. *Media:* Graphic. *Publ:* Illusr, The Sunken City, 60 & The Double Knights, 63, Oxford; Rubaboo Five, Gage, 65; auth, Great Canadian Posters, Oxford Univ Press. *Mailing Add:* PO Box 131 Brechin ON L0K 1B0 Canada

DINC, ALEV NECILE
PAINTER, DESIGNER
b Turkey; US citizen. *Study:* Inst Technol, Ankara, Turkey, 56-61; Ridgewood Art Sch, NJ, 68, Fashion Inst Technol, New York, 69. *Work:* Turkish Embassy, NY; Kismet Furniture, Paterson, NJ; NY Sch Interior Design; Clifton H S; Osterreiche Kommunal Kreditbank, Vienna. *Teaching:* Tchr art, Clifton & Wayne H S. *Awards:* First Prize, Turkey, 60; Danielle Ruebel, Mental Health Orgn, 89. *Bibliog:* Abraham Ilein (auth), Art Review, Artspeak, 87; Ernie Garcia; Robert F Lanzetti; Films by Matt Bora, Eric Rubel. *Mem:* Salute to Women in the Arts; Clifton Asn Artist; Art for Mental Health; Studiomontclair NJ. *Media:* Oil, Acrylic; Watercolor. *Publ:* Auth, Artists in the 1990's, Manhattan Arts Int Mag, 94; Art Ctr artist, interview with John Sgull, Channel 24 Cable, 93; contribr, Healing Art, Cable TV, Newark, NJ, 93; Spanish Cable TV, Channel 47, Spanish Newspaper, Secaucus, NJ, 96; N T N Network, Cable TV, NJ, 97; USA Turkish Times, 2006; Herald Newspaper, 2001; Dateline Jour. *Mailing Add:* 90 Day St Apt G-4 Clifton NJ 07011

DINE, JIM
PAINTER, SCULPTOR, PHOTOGRAPHER
b Cincinnati, Ohio, June 16, 35. *Study:* Univ Cincinnati and Boston Mus Sch, 53-55; Ohio Univ, BFA, 57, grad study, 58; studied drawing with Frederick Leach. *Hon Degrees:* Calif Col of Arts and Crafts, PhD (hon), 97. *Work:* Whitney Mus Am Art, Mus Mod Art & Metrop Mus Art, NY; Tate Gallery, London, Eng; Nat Collection Fine Art; Albright-Knox Art Gallery, Buffalo; Walker Art Ctr, Minneapolis; and others. *Comn:* At the Wedding, Seibu Dept Store, Tokyo, Japan; Second Nuveen Painting, John Nuveen & Co, Chicago, 92; Ape & Cat, Battery Park City Authority for Robert Wagner Park, NY, 96; Three Red Spanish Venuses (lg scale sculpture), Guggenheim Mus Bilbao; Jerusalem Heart (painting, prints & posters), comn by Andrea & Charles Bronfman, 98; banner for the Palio, Mayor of Siena, Italy, 2000. *Exhib:* Masters of Am Print, Margaret Lipworth Fine Art, Boca Raton, Fla, 93; The Portrait Now, Nat Portrait Gallery, London, 93-94; NY on Paper, Galerie Thaddaeus Ropac, Paris, 94; Marlborough Graphics, NY, 94; Sculptors' Maquettes, Pace Gallery, NY, 94; Art to Art: Paley, Dine And Statom Respond to Toledo's Treasures, Toledo Mus Art, Ohio, 96; solo exhib, Galerie Inge Baecker, Cologne, 97, Galerie de Bellefeuille, Montreal, Can, 97, Galerie im Traklhaus, Salzburg, 97, Museo Regional de Guanajuato, Mex, 97, Richard Gray Gallery, Chicago, 98, Galeria Ramis Barquet, Mex, 98, Solomon R Guggenheim Mus, New York, 99; Pace Wildenstein, Los Angeles, 98 & 99; Wheatfields, Denver Art Mus, Colo, 98; Ideal & Reality - The Classical Nude in XX Century Art from Bonnard to Warhol, Rupertinium Salzburger Landesmuseum, Salzburg, 98; Pop Art: Selections from the Mus of Modern Art, High Mus Art, Atlanta, 98 & NY State Mus, Albany, 99; Time Magazine 75th Anniversary Exhib, Nat Portrait Gallery, traveling exhib, 98-; Contemp Classicism, Neuberger Mus Art, NY, 99; Jim Dine Mois de la Photo à Paris, Maison Europeenne de la Photographie, 98-99; Jim Dine New Photographs: Kali in NY, PaceWildenstein, MacGill, 98; Jime Dine: New Color Photographs, PaceWildenstein, 99; Jim Dine, Galerie Daniel Templon, Paris,

2000. *Teaching:* Vis prof, Oberlin Col, 65 & Cornell Univ, 66-67; instr, Rhodes Sch, 58; instr, Royal Col Art, London, 1967-68; artist-in-residence, Williams Col, Williamstown, Mass, 76. *Awards:* Norman Harris Silver Medal & Prize, Art Inst Chicago, 64; Pyramid Atlantic Award of Distinction, 92; Elected to Akademic der Kunste, Berlin. *Bibliog:* Robert Mahoney (auth), Reviews: Jim Dine/Pace, Flash Art, 3/94; Thomas Padon (auth), Reviews: New York, Sculpture, 5/94; Martha Langford (auth), Ancien Regime, Border Crossings, fall 94. *Mem:* Am Acad Inst Arts & Letts, NY; Nat Acad (assoc, 83, acad, 2002). *Publ:* Illusr, The Poet Assassinated, 68; auth & illusr, Welcome Home Lovebirds, 69; coauth, Work from the Same House, 69; coauth & illusr, The Adventures of Mr & Mrs Jim & Ron, 70; illusr, Ape and Cat, Arion Press, Calif, 97. *Mailing Add:* 59 Barrow St New York NY 10014-3701

DINGUS, MARITA TERESA
SCULPTOR
b Seattle, July 13, 56. *Study:* Temple Univ, BFA, 80; San Jose State Univ, MFA, 85. *Work:* Seattle Art Mus; Microsoft Corp, Redmond, Wash; Safeco Corp, Seattle; Seattle Arts Comn; Wash State Arts Comn; Bailey-Boushay, Seattle, Wash; Mundt MacGregor, Seattle, Wash. *Exhib:* Collabr, Tacoma Art Mus, Wash, 90; Come to Your Senses, Bellevue Art Mus, Wash, 91; Transformation, Knoxville Mus of Art, Whatcom History Art Mus, Bellingham, Wash, 97, New Bedford Mus Art, Portmouth, Mass, 2000; Passion for Possession, Seattle Art Mus, 98-99; Stop Asking, We Exist, Am Craft Mus, NY, 99-2000; solo exhibs, Francine Seders Gallery, Seattle, Wash, 2000, 03, Henie Onstad Kunstsenter, Norway, 2002; group exhibs, Rush Arts Gallery and Resource Ctr, Ny, 2003, City Space, Bank of Am Tower, Seattle, Wash, 2003, Rental Sales Gallery, Seattle Art Mus, Wash, 2003. *Teaching:* Assoc prof Art, Seattle Cent Community Col, 88-94, Green River Community Col, Auburn, Wash, 89; Asst prof Art, Ga Southern Univ, Statesboro, 99-2000. *Awards:* Recipient NEA Travel Grant, 92; Named Visual Arts fel, Arrut Trust, 94; Named fel John Simon Guggenheim Meml Found, 99-2000. *Bibliog:* Leslie King Hummond (auth), Gumbo Ya Ya; Contemporary Women African American Artists, Midmarch Press, 90; Lois Allan (auth) Contemporary Art in the Northwest, Crafstman House, 95. *Mem:* Docent Seattle Art Mus. *Media:* Miscellaneous Media. *Dealer:* Francine Seders Gallery. *Mailing Add:* 5812 S 331st St Auburn WA 98001

DINGUS, PHILLIP RICK
PHOTOGRAPHER
b Appleton City, Mo, Jan 3, 51. *Study:* Univ Calif, Santa Barbara, BA, 73; Univ NMex, MA, 77, MFA, 81. *Work:* Ctr Creative Photog, Tucson, Ariz; Mus Mod Art, Metrop Mus Art, NY; San Francisco Mus Mod Art; Mus Fine Arts, Houston, Tex; Buddy Holly Ctr Fine Arts Gallery, Lubbock, Tex; plus many others. *Exhib:* James Gallery, Houston Int Foto Fest, 88 & 90; Phoenix Art Mus, Ariz, 90; Dine'tah-Hajiinei: Place of Emergence, SW Mus, Los Angeles, Calif, 91; Between Home & Heaven, Smithsonian Inst, Washington, DC, 92; Dickinson State Univ, NDak, 92; plus many others. *Teaching:* Grad Teaching asst art photogr & fundamental, Univ NMex, 76-79; lectr photogr drawing & art hist, NMex Tech, 79-81; vis lectr, Univ Colo, Boulder, 81-82; assoc prof, Tex Tech Univ, 82-. *Awards:* Nat Endowment Art/Mid Am Art Alliance Reg Fel, 87; Proj Grant photog India, 87-88; plus many others. *Bibliog:* Michael Costello (auth), Alternate views: A recent film by Roger Sweet and Rick Dingus, Artspace, summer 78. *Mem:* Soc Photog Educ; Friends Photog. *Media:* Photography. *Publ:* Auth, The Photographic Artifacts of Timothy O'Sullivan, 82, Second View: The Rephotographic Survey Project, 84, Marks in Place, 88, Between Home & Heaven: Contemporary American Landscape Photo, 92, NMAA, Smithsonian, Univ NMex Press; author, Techne: A Candid Look, Spot, 2000. *Mailing Add:* 3201 45th St Lubbock TX 79413-3513

DINGWALL, KENNETH
PAINTER, INSTRUCTOR
b Devonside, Clockmamanshire, Scotland, Jan 13, 38. *Study:* Edinburgh Col Art, Scotland, studied with Sir William Gilles and John Maxwell, DA, 59, MFA, 69; studied at Athens Sch Fine Art, Greece. *Work:* Scottish Nat Gallery Mod Art, Edinburgh; Brit Coun Collection, London; Saatchi Collection, London; Mpls Art Inst; Glasgow Art Gallery & Mus, Scotland. *Exhib:* Modern Kunst Fran Skottland, Amons Anderson Mus, Helsinki, Finland, 80; Scottish Art, Scottish Nat Gallery Mod Art, Edinburgh, 85; one-man shows Peter Noser Galerie, Zurich, 87, Cleveland Ctr Contemp Art, 97, Katharina Rich Perlow Gallery, NY, 99; Scottish Art Since 1900, Barbican Art Ctrs, London, 90; Cleveland Mus Invitation, 91; Knoedler & Co Invitational, NY, 98; Musee des Beaux-Arts, de Tourcoing, France, 2001. *Pos:* mem art com, Scottish Arts Coun, 84-88; mem bd trustees, Cleveland Ctr Contemp Art, 99-. *Teaching:* prof & chmn painting dept, Cleveland Inst Art, 88-. *Awards:* Daad Award Berlin, Scottish Arts Coun, 77; Ohio Arts Coun Fel, 95; Cleveland Arts Prize, 97. *Bibliog:* Keith Hartley (auth), Scottish Art Since 1900, Scottish Nat Gallery, 89; Duncan MacMillan (auth), Scottish Art 1460-1990, Mainstream Publ, Edinburgh, 90 & Kenneth Dingwall, Edinburgh Univ, 96; Mudro MacDonald (auth), Scottish Art, Thames & Hudson, 2000. *Media:* Oils, Drawings, Wood Constructions. *Dealer:* Katherina Rich Perlow 41 E 57th St New York, NY 10022; Peter Noser Clansinsstrasse 65 Zurich Galerie

DINNERSTEIN, HARVEY
PAINTER
b Brooklyn, NY, Apr 3, 28. *Study:* With Moses Soyer, 44-46; Art Students League, 46-47; Tyler Art Sch, Temple Univ, cert art, 50. *Hon Degrees:* Lyme Acad Fine Arts, Old Lyme, CT, DHL, 98. *Work:* Metrop Mus Art (Lehman Collection) & Martin Luther King Labor Ctr, NY; New Britain Mus Art, Conn; Fleming Mus, Univ Vt, Burlington; Nat Mus Am Art, Washington; Butler Inst Am Art, Youngstown, Ohio; Nat Acad Design, NY; Whitney Mus Am Art, NY; plus others. *Exhib:* Contemp Am Paintings, Whitney Mus Am Art, NY, 55 & Contemp Drawings, 64; Childe Hassam Award Exhib, Am Acad & Inst of Arts & Lett, NY, 74, 78 & 87; Living Am Artists & the Figure, Pa State Univ Mus Art, University Park, 74; 3 Centuries of Am-Nude, NY Cult Ctr, 76; Bicentennial Exhib of Am Illus, NY Hist Soc, 76; one-man show, Sindin Galleries, NY, 83; retrospective, Butler Inst Am Art, Youngstown, Ohio, 94; Wunderlich Galleries, NY, 97; Frey Norris Gallery, San Francisco, Calif, 2003, 05; plus many others. *Pos:* Academician, Nat Acad Design, New York, 74. *Teaching:* Instr drawing & painting, Sch Visual Arts, New York, 65-80, Nat Acad Design, 75-92, Art Students League, 80-. *Awards:* Temple Gold Medal, Pa Acad Fine Art, 50; Hassam & Spelcher Purchase Award, Am Acad & Inst of Arts & Lett, 74, 78 & 87; Ranger Purchase Award, Nat Acad Design, 76; Obrig Prize, Nat Acad Design, 86; and others. *Bibliog:* Susan E Meyer (auth), 20 Figure Painters and How They Work, Watson-Guptill, 79; How We Lived, Esquire Mag 50th Anniversary Issue, 6/83; The Seasons, Am Artist Mag, 8/83. *Mem:* Audubon Artists; Allied Artists. *Media:* Oil, Pastel. *Publ:* Coauth, New look at protest, the eight since 1908, Art News, 2/58; illusr, Drawings of the Montgomery Bus Boycott, 12/64 & illusr & auth, The face of protest, 12/68, Esquire Mag; illusr, A Portfolio of Drawings, Kenmore Press, 68; illusr & auth, Harvey Dinnerstein--Artist at Work, Watson-Guptill, 78; On pastel, Am Artist Mag, 5/88; Int Artist Magazine, 12/05-1/06. *Dealer:* Frey Norris Gallery 456 Geary St San Francisco CA. *Mailing Add:* 933 President St Brooklyn NY 11215

DINNERSTEIN, LOIS
HISTORIAN, LECTURER
b New York, NY, Oct 24, 32. *Study:* NY Univ Wash Sq Col, BA, 53; NY Univ Inst Fine Arts, MA, 60; City Univ New York Grad Ctr, PhD, 79. *Pos:* Res cur, Benjamin Sonnenberg Collection, NY, 57-58, Daniel & Rita Fraad Collection, NY, 62-63 & Montclair Art Mus, NJ, 75-76. *Teaching:* Instr art hist, Vassar Col, 59-61, City Univ NY, Brooklyn Col, 64-77; adj prof, Brooklyn Ctr, Long Island Univ, 82-84; adj prof, Am Civilization Prog, Grad Sch Arts & Sci, New York Univ, 88; lect, Art Students League, 90-91. *Awards:* Rockefeller Found fel, City Univ New York, 77. *Mem:* Asn Historians Am Art. *Res:* Eighteenth and 19th century American art. *Publ:* Auth, Thomas Eakins' Crucifixion as Perceived by Mariana Griswold Van Rensselaer, 5/79, The iron worker and King Solomon: Some images of labor in American art, 9/79, Beyond revisionism: Henry Lerolle's The Organ, 1/80 & The industrious housewife: Some images of labor in American art, 4/81, Arts Mag; John Singleton Copley's Portrait of Elizabeth Allen Stevens (art mus catalog), Res Supplement, Montclair, 79; Artists in their studios, Am Heritage, 2/83; When Liberty was Controversial, In Support of Liberty: European Paintings at the 1883 Statue of Liberty Pedestal Fund Art Loan Exhibition (exhib catalog), Parrish Art Mus, Southampton & Nat Acad Design, New York, 86; and others. *Mailing Add:* 933 President St Brooklyn NY 11215-1603

DINNERSTEIN, SIMON A
PAINTER
b Brooklyn, NY, Feb 16, 43. *Study:* Brooklyn Mus Art Sch, with David Levine & Louis Grebenak, 64-67; City Col New York, BA, 65; Hochschule für Bildende Kunst, Kassel, Ger, Fulbright fel, 70-71. *Work:* Minn Mus Art, St Paul; Palmer Mus of Art, Penn St Univ; Nat Mus Am Art, Smithsonian Inst; Martin Luther King Jr Labor Ctr, Nat Acad Design, NY; and others. *Comn:* Staempfli Gallery, NY, 79 & 88. *Exhib:* one-man shows, Am Acad in Rome, 77, New Sch, 81 & 93; St Paul's Sch, Concord, NH, 91; An Am in Rome, NJ Ctr Visual Arts, Summit, NJ, 94; ACA Gallery, NY, 99; Bread & Roses Gallery, NY, 99; Walton Arts Ctr, Univ Ark, 99; Gallery 1199, 85 & 99; Texarkana Regl Arts Ctr, Tex/Ak, 2000; plus others. *Teaching:* Instr painting, Brooklyn Mus Art Sch, 71-72; instr painting & drawing, The New Sch, New York, 75-; instr, New York City Tech Col, 79-88; lectr, Am Acad Rome, 77-78, US Info Serv, Spain, 79, Pa State Univ, 84, Port Washington Pub Libr, Long Island, 90, St Paul's Sch, NH, 91 & Nassau Community Col, 94; vis prof, Pratt Inst, 86-87; Instr, drawing & painting, New Sch/Parsons Sch, NY, 75-2005. *Awards:* Fulbright Fel, Ger, 70-71; Ralph Fabri Prize, Nat Acad Design, 97 & Bertelson Prize, 98; Artists Fel, New York Found Arts, 87; Rome Prize Fel, Am Acad in Rome, 76-78; Ingram Merrill Award for Painting, 78-79; Cannon Prize, Nat Acad Design, 88; plus others. *Bibliog:* The Art of Simon Dinnerstein (monogr), Univ Ark Press, 268 pps, 140 reproductions, 90; Sandy Brooke (auth), Hooked on Drawing: Illustrated Lessons & Exercises for Grades 4 and up, Prentice Hall, 96; Cynthia Dantzic (auth), Drawing Dimensions, Prentice Hall; Roy Proctor (auth) Exploring the edge: no slave to fashion, artist draws us into other states of mind, Richmond Times, 2000. *Mem:* Soc Fel Am Acad Rome; Nat Acad Design. *Media:* Miscellaneous, Oil, Drawing, Engravings. *Specialty:* Contemporary Art. *Publ:* Auth, (monograph), The Art of Simon Dinnerstein, Univ Ark Press, 90; Anthology: Drawing from Life, Harcourt, Brace & Jovanovich, 92 & 96; Centennial Directory, Am Acad Rome, 95; Community of Creativity: A Century of MacDowell Colony Artists, Currier Gallery Art, 96; Simon Dinnerstein: A Retrospective, Ont Rev, 98; monograph, Simon Dinnerstein: Paintings and Drawings, Hudson Hills Press, 99; monograph, Simon Dinnerstein: survey of the artist's work, Hanging Loose Press, NY; St Ann's Review, 2000; Brooklyn Jews, 2001; 100 New York Painters, 2006. *Dealer:* ACA Galleries New York NY 529 W 20th St New York NY 10011. *Mailing Add:* 415 First St Brooklyn NY 11215

D'INNOCENZO, NICK
SCULPTOR, PAINTER, PRINTMAKER, DESIGNER
b Rochester, NY, Dec 12, 34. *Study:* State Univ NY Buffalo, BS(art educ), 60; Cranbrook Acad Art, MFA(sculpture/design), 63. *Work:* State Univ NY Buffalo; Smith-Corona-Marchant Corp, Syracuse, NY; private collections in NY, Mich & Fla. *Comn:* Welded bronze reliefs, State Univ NY State Univ NY Oswego, City of Oswego & Oswego Co Savings Bank; 2 O'clock-Tower, 80' Fountain, State Univ NY; Multiple computer facilities, State Univ NY Oswego. *Exhib:* Artists of NY, Everson Mus, Syracuse, 75; Artists of NY State, State Fairgrounds, Syracuse, 81 & 89; Pyramid Gallery, Rochester, NY, 96; Arnot Mus Art, Elmira, NY, 2005; Arts and Cult,

2004; Artists Pallete, 2004; numerous one-man shows, 1963-2004. *Teaching:* Prof sculpture & design, State Univ NY Col Oswego, 63-2000. *Awards:* Best of show, NY Open, 96; 1st Prize Graphics, Pyramid Artists, Rochester, NY, 97; 1st Prize Sculpture, NY State Fair, 96 & 2nd Prize Graphics, 97; Artist of the Yr, Oswago Co, 2004. *Mem:* Int Sculpture Ctr. *Media:* Steel, Mixed Media; Computer-imagery. *Collection:* State University New York, Buffalo; Smith-Corona Corporation, Syracuse, New York. *Mailing Add:* Edwards Cir Rd 3 Oswego NY 13126

DINSMORE, JOHN NORMAN
EDUCATOR, ADMINISTRATOR
b Trenton, Mo, Jan 18, 40. *Study:* Truman State Univ, BS, 63; Univ Northern Colo, MA, 68; Univ Kans, EdD, 78. *Work:* Sheldon Mem Art Gallery, Lincoln, Nebr; Univ Nebr at Kearney; Univ Northern Colo; Mountain State Telephone, Denver, Colo. *Comn:* Weaving, Broadway State Bank, Council Bluffs, Iowa, 75; weaving, First National Bank, Kearney, Nebr, 76; graphic design, The Cellar Shoe Store, Geneva, Nebr, 77; weaving, Nye, Hervert, Jorgensen & Watson Law, Kearney, Nebr, 79; weaving, Prof Bldg (Med), Gillette, Wyo, 83. *Exhib:* Fibers 1977, SW Mo State Univ, Cape Giradeau, Nebr, 77; Nebr Crafts Exhib, Sheldon Gallery, Lincoln, Nebr, 77; Nebr Art Educators Show, Elder Gallery, Lincoln, Nebr, 87; Nebr Crafts Coun, Mus Nebr Art, Kearney, 91; Fac Exhib, Mus Nebr Art, Kearney, 95, 19th Ann Nebr Art Educators Juried Exhib, 2001, UNK Art Dept Fac Exhb, 2003; Phelps Fine Art Gallery, Hastings, Nebr, 97. *Teaching:* Prof fibers & art educ, Univ Nebr Kearney, 68-, dept chairperson, 93-2001. *Awards:* Second Place, Midwest Weavers Conf, 74; 3-D Art Educators Award, Nebr Art Teachers Asn, 86. *Mem:* Nat Art Educ Asn; Nebr Art Teachers Asn (pres & vpres, 92-93); Nat Educ Asn; Handweavers Guild Am; Midwest Weavers Asn. *Media:* Fiber. *Res:* Exploration of patterns through weaving. *Publ:* Auth, Conceptual Crafts, Craft Range, 79; Nebraska midwife, Nebr Crafts, 83; The American avant-garde: A comparison of quilt & painting design, 83, Design influences on Hawaiian appliqued quilts, 85 & Amish quilts: A comparison of the old and the new, 89, Platte Valley Rev. *Mailing Add:* Univ Nebr Dept of Art/Art History 25th St & 9th Ave Kearney NE 68849

DINSMORE, STEPHEN PAUL
PAINTER
b Omaha, Nebr, July 7, 52. *Study:* Univ Nebr, Lincoln, BA, 74. *Work:* Lydon Fine Art, Chicago, Ill; William Havv Gallery, Denver, Colo; Arden Gallery, Boston, Mass; Groveland Gallery, Minn; Kiechel Fine Arts, Lincoln, Nebr. *Comn:* Fairmount Hotel, Kansas City, Mo; numberous corporate and private commissions. *Exhib:* Robert Kidd Gallery, Birmingham, Mich, 2000 & 2002; William Harv Gallery, 2001; Arden Gallery, Boston, Ma, 2001 & 2005; Haydon Gallery, Lincoln, Nebr, 2001; William Harv Fine Arts, Denver, Colo, 2004; Lydon Fine Art, Chicage, Ill, 2001 & 2003 - 2005; Anderson O'Brien Gallery, Omaha, 2004. *Awards:* Artist Residency, Bemis Found, Omaha, Nebr, 92. *Media:* Oil on Canvas. *Publ:* Reproduction, Country Home Mag, 6/91; Article, Chicago Tribune, 4/2/92; Article, Rocky Mountain News, 12/4/99; New American Paintings, 97; Grand Image Poster, Seattle; Boston Globe, 7/23/01; Lincoln Journal Star, 4/18/04; Phoenix House and Garden, Fall 04. *Mailing Add:* 2840 Sherman St Lincoln NE 68502

DIPASQUALE, PAUL ALBERT
SCULPTOR, LECTURER
b Perth Amboy, NJ, June 29, 51. *Study:* Univ Va, BA with hons, 73; Va Commonwealth Univ, MFA (sculpture), 77. *Work:* Va Hist Soc, Richmond; Black His Mus of Va, Richmond; Nat Air & Space Mus, Smithsonian Inst, Washington, DC; Baltimore Aquarium, Md; Billings/Rockafeller Mus, Woodstock, Vt. *Comn:* Native Am monument, Richmond Metro Authority, Va, 86; Headman monument, Va Comn for Arts, Richmond, 91; Arthur Ashe monument, Va Heroes Inc, Richmond, 96; Arthur Ashe Mem medallion, ESPN-Disney Corp, Washington, DC, 2000; Oliver Hill monument bronze bust, Richmond Convention Ctr Authority, 2001. *Exhib:* Paul Dipasquale, NC Mus Art, Raleigh, 84; Stars, Nat Air & Space Mus, Washington, DC, 91; Civil Rights - Virginia, Black Hist Mus Va, Richmond, 98; Story of Virginia, Va Hist Soc, Richmond, 99. *Pos:* vis artist, Arts Coun Richmond, Va, 89-92 & Am Acad Rome, Italy, 96 & 98; vis artist pub sculpture, Va Commonwealth Univ, Richmond, 87-98; bd dir, Black Hist Mus Va, Richmond, 96-98. *Teaching:* instr fine arts, N Va Community Col, Annandale, 79-81; vis prof sculpture, Col of William & Mary, Williamsburg, Va, 91-92. *Awards:* Fathers in Prison Grant, Fed Weed and Seed Program, 96; Richmonder of the Year, Style Mag, 96; Social Justice Award, Va Commonwealth Univ Dept Social Work, 2000. *Bibliog:* Ben Forgey (auth), Voyages of the Indian sculpture, Washington Post, 7/19/87; Scott Mason (auth), The monumental debate (doc), Cent Va Television, 96; S Driggs & RG Wilson, Richmond's monument ave, Univ NC Press, 3/1/01. *Mem:* NSS, NY; Int Sculpture Ctr, Washington, DC. *Media:* Bronze. *Publ:* contribr, Working With Plastics, Time Life Books, 82; contribr, City Secrets Rome, Little Book Room, New York, 2000; contribr, City Secrets Florence, Venice and the Towns of Italy, Little Book Room. New York, 2001. *Dealer:* Addison/Ripley Fine Art 1670 Wisconsin Ave NW Wash DC 20007; Bazzanti Gallery Florence Italy. *Mailing Add:* 1408 National St Richmond VA 23231-1533

DIPERNA, FRANK PAUL
PHOTOGRAPHER, INSTRUCTOR
b Pittsburgh, Pa, Feb 4, 47. *Study:* Ctr of the Eye, Aspen, Colo, with Gary Winogrand, 71; Visual Studies Workshop, Rochester, NY, with Ralph Gibson, Syl Labrot, Nathan Lyons & Alice Wells, 71-72; Goddard Col, MA(photog), 77. *Work:* Polaroid (Europa), Amsterdam, The Neth; Libr Cong, Smithsonian Inst, Corcoran Gallery Art, Washington; Bibliot Nat, Paris; Nat Mus Am Art, Washington; Metrop Mus Art, NY; Ctr Creative Photography, Univ Ariz, Tucson. *Comn:* State of Art Inc, Vancouver. *Exhib:* one-man shows, Bushes, 74 & Color Photographs, 77, Corcoran Gallery Art, Photographs, Diane Brown Gallery, Washington, 77 & 81, Color Photographs, Sebastian Moore Gallery, Denver, Colo, 78, Kathleen Ewing Gallery, Washington, 82 & 84, Color Landscape Photographs, Rice Univ, Houston, Tex, 86 & The Presence of Things, Kathleen Ewing Gallery, Washington, DC, 98 & 2000, In The Studio, Kathleen Ewing Gallery, 2006; Va Photogr, Va Mus Fine Arts, 73 & 75; One of a Kind (traveling exhib), Mus Fine Arts, Houston, Univ Ariz, Los Angeles Inst Contemp Arts & Art Inst Chicago; Eye of the West: Camera Vision & Cult Consensus, Hayden Gallery, Mass Inst Technol, Cambridge, 77; Washington Photog: Images of the Eighties, 82, Terra Sancta, (with catalog) 90, Corcoran Gallery Art, Washington; Light Work, Photog Over the 70s and 80s, Everson Mus Art, Syracuse, NY, 85; Comfort Gallery, Haverford Col, Pa, 86; Rice Univ, Houston, Tex, 86; Kathleen Ewing Gallery, Washington, 89 & 94; Between Home and Heaven, Contemp Am Landscape Photog, Nat Mus Am Art, Washington; Carnegie Mus Art (with catalog), Pittsburgh, Pa; Longwood Invitational, Virginia Photographers (with catalog), Longwood Ctr Visual Arts, Farmville, Va, 97; Mary, McLean (Va) Project for the Arts, 2000; Southern Exposure Contemp Photo in Virginia, Mus Western Va, Roanoke, 2002; Images of Italy Kathleen Ewing Gallery, 2004; Road Trip Gallery, Smithsonian Mus Am Art. *Pos:* artist in res, Vt Studio Center, 2002. *Teaching:* Instr photog, Northern Va Community Col, Alexandria, 73-78; instr photog, Corcoran Col Art & Design, 74-78, asst prof & chmn dept, 78-81, asst prof, 81-84, assoc prof & chmn dept, 84-87, assoc prof, 87-94, prof, 94-, prof, chmn photg dept, 99-2001; vis prof, Univ Ga, study abroad Cortona, Ital, 2005. *Awards:* Cert of Distinction, Va Photog, 73; Artist-in-Residence Fel, Camargo Found, Cassis, France, Lightwork, Syracuse, NY, 82. *Bibliog:* David Taunous (auth), Frank DiPerna at the Corcoran, Mark Power at Diane Brown, Art in Am, 1-2/78; Owen Edwards (auth), SX-70: Land's painless epiphany machine, Sat Rev, 7/22/78; Jo Ann Lewis (auth), Galleries, The Washington Post, 4/89; Ferdinand Protzman (auth), Galleries, Washington Post, 9/2000; Jessica Dawson (auth), Galleries, Wash Post, 4/29/2006; Nord Wennerstrom (auth), Frank Di Perna, Artforum, 2006. *Mem:* AAUP. *Media:* Traditional & Digital Color Photographs. *Publ:* Auth, Color Photographs, Corcoran Gallery Art, 77; One of a Kind: Recent Polaroid Color Photography, Godine; SX-70, Lustrum Press, 79; contribr, Washington Photography: Images of the Eighties (catalog), Corcoran Gallery Art, 82; Between Home & Heaven: Contemporary Am Landscape Photography, Nat Mus Am Art, 92; Contact Sheet 97, 25th Anniversay Ed, Lightwork, 98. *Dealer:* Kathleen Ewing Gallery 1609 Connecticut Ave NW Washington DC 20009. *Mailing Add:* 37559 Allder School Rd Purcellville VA 20132

DIRGO, RAY ROBERT
CARTOONIST, ILLUSTRATOR - CHILDRENS BOOKS
b Bridgeport, Conn, Aug 5, 31. *Study:* Pratt Inst; Yale Univ. *Pos:* Adv art & graphics, Exec Off White House, formerly; developer, Flintstones, Top Cat, Magilla Gorilla & Quick Draw McGraw; freelance adv art, formerly

DIRKS, JOHN
SCULPTOR, CARTOONIST
b New York, NY, Nov 2, 1917. *Study:* Art Students League, New York, 36; Boston Sch Practical Art; Yale Univ, BA, 39; Columbia Univ Painting & Sculpture, 45. *Work:* Ogunquit Mus Am Art. *Comn:* Over 400 pvt comns in 40 states (sculptures), 66-. *Pos:* Cartoonist assisting his father on "The Captain and the Kids" comic, better known as "Katzenjammer Kids", took over completely for father, 1958.; Dir, Ogunquit Mus Am Art, 88-98. *Mem:* Ogunquit Art Asn, Maine, 60-92; Lyme Acad Fine Arts, Old Lyme, Conn (trustee 83-91). *Media:* Non-Ferrous Metal with water. *Dealer:* Ogunquit Mus Am Art 181 Shore Rd Box 815 Ogunquit ME 03907. *Mailing Add:* 10 Hillwood E Old Lyme CT 06371

DIRSMITH, RONALD
ARCHITECT
Study: Univ of Ill, BS (archit engineering); Univ of Il, MA (archit design). *Pos:* Licensed architect in Ill and Fla; architect, Perkins & Will; principal, Ed Dart & Assoc; cofounder (with Suzanne Roe Dirsmith), principal archit Dirsmith Group, 1971—. *Awards:* Named Nat Acad; Nat Acad of Design, 99; fel, Rome Prize in Archit. *Mem:* Nat Acad; fel, Am Acad Rome. *Mailing Add:* c/o The Dirsmith Group 318 Maple Ave Highland Park IL 60035

DISKA, (P)
SCULPTOR
b New York, NY. *Study:* Vassar Col, BA; Acad Jullian, Paris. *Work:* Cornell Art Mus, Ithaca, NY; Mus Art & Indust St Etienne, France; Int Sculpture Parks, Austria, Israel, Czech, Yugoslavia & France; Palm Springs Desert Art Mus, Calif; Paris Open-air Sculpture Mus; French Ministry Cult; and others; Pub Park, Fredericksburg, Va. *Comn:* Over 20 commissioned works in stone, wood, cast iron and brick for public spaces in France, including eight fountains & seven play sculptures; Monument to the French Resistance, cast iron on rough-cut stones, St Ouen Region, Paris, 85. *Exhib:* One-man shows, Galerie Suzanne de Coninck, Paris, 65, Galerie Les Contards, Lacoste, 65, Southern Methodist Univ, Dallas, Tex, 65, Galerie Jacques Casanova, Paris, 66, Ruth White Gallery, NY, 69; Munic Mus, Mainz, WGer, 86; Ecole Des Hautes Etudes Commerciales, France, 88; Galerie Hansma, Paris, 92. *Teaching:* Instr sculpture, Sarah Lawrence Summer Sch, Lacoste, France, 74 & 75. *Awards:* Competition for fountain, New Town Melun-Senart, France, 79; Portes-les-Valence, France, 83. *Bibliog:* Virginia Watson Jones (auth), Contemporary American Women Sculptors, Oryx Press, 88; Charlotte Streier Rubinstein (auth), Women Sculptors of America, G K Hall, Boston; Dr Penny Dunford (auth), Biographical Dictionary of Women Artists in Europe and America Since 1850, Harvester/Wheatsheaf (Eng), Univ Pa Press, 89. *Mem:* Maison des Artistes, France; Réalités Nouvelles, France. *Media:* Mixed

DISTEFANO, DOMENIC
PAINTER, INSTRUCTOR
b Providence, RI, Mar 27, 24. *Study:* Florence V Canon Art Sch, Philadelphia, Pa, 1947-1951; Acad Fine Arts, Philadelphia, Pa, 1950-1954. *Work:* Springfield Art Mus, Watercolor USA, Springfield, Mo; Pa Bank, Philadelphia, Pa & various locations in US & Europe. *Exhib:* Woodmere Art Mus, Germantown, Pa, 1959; Salmagundi Art Club, NYC, 1975-; Audubon Artists Art Soc, 1980-1999; Allied Artists of Am Exhib, Nat Arts Club, NYC, 1990-2000; Hist Asn Calender Exhib, The White House, Washington, DC, 2000; 100th Anniversary Exhib of Philadelphia Watercolor Soc, Berman Mus, Philadelphia, Pa, 2001; Traveling Ann Int Exhib, 2005. *Pos:* Juror of selections & awards, Am Watercolor Soc, NY, 1995-2006. *Teaching:* Demonstr, Workshops in Watercolor, Bucks Co, Pa & Rockport, Mass, 2006. *Awards:* Gold Medal in Aquamedia, Audubon Artists Art Society, NY, 1996; Medal Creative Arts, Rockport Art Asn, Mass, 2000; Watercolor Award, Penn Watercolor Society, 2005; Bryan Mem Award, Am Watercolor Society 139th Int Exhib at Salmagundi Club, NYC, 2006. *Bibliog:* Am Artist Mag; Palette Talk; Watercolor Your Way; Techniques of 23 Int artists. *Mem:* Allied Artists of Am; Audubon Artists Art Society, NYC; Philadelphia Sketch Club (pres 1954); Am Watercolor Society (Dolphin Fel/board dirs); Rockport Art Asn, Mass; Philadelphia Watercolor Soc. *Media:* Watercolor. *Publ:* Auth, Painting Dynamic Watercolors, Art Instr Asn, 2000. *Mailing Add:* 51/2 Prospect St Apt #3 Rear Rockport MA 01966

DI SUVERO, MARK
PAINTER, SCULPTOR
b Shanghai, China, 33. *Study:* San Francisco City Col, 53-54; Univ Calif, BA, 56. *Work:* Wadsworth Atheneum, Hartford, Conn; Whitney Mus Am Art; Hirshhorn Mus; Dallas Mus Fine Arts; Art Inst Chicago. *Exhib:* Continuity and Change, Wadsworth Atheneum, 62; Contemp Ann, Art Inst Chicago, 63; Contemp Am Sculpture Section I, Whitney Mus Am Art, 66; 1966 Ann Exhib: Contemp Am Sculpture & Prints, Whitney Mus Am Art, 66; Park Place Show, Hayden Gallery, Mass Inst Technol, 66; Sculpture Int, Solomon R Guggenheim Mus, 67; Am Sculpture of the Sixties, Los Angeles Co Mus Art, 67; 1968 Ann Exhib: Contemp Am Sculpture, Whitney Mus Am Art, 68; Plus by Minus, ALbright-Knox Gallery, 68; Martin Luther King Benefit, Mus Mod Art, NY, 68-69; NY Painting and Sculpture: 1940-1970, Metrop Mus Art, NY, 69-70; 1970 Ann Exhib: Contemp Am Sculpture, Whitney Mus Am Art, 70-71; Works for New Spaces, Walker Art Ctr, Minneapolis, 70-71; Am Drawings 1963-1973, Whitney Mus Am Art, 73; one-man shows, Hill Gallery, Birmingham, Mich, 96, Weigand Gallery, Belmont, Calif, 96, Galerie Jeanne-Bucher, Paris, France, 96, Gagosian Gallery, 97, Orange Co Mus Art, 98 & Hiroshima Mus Contemp Art, Japan, 98; Calif: 3 x 8 twice, Honolulu Acad Arts, 78; Homage to Picasso, Walker Art Ctr, 80; Am Sculpture/Collection of Howard & Jean Lipman, Whitney Mus Am Art, 80; The First Show: Painting & Sculpture from Eight Collections, 1940-1981, Mus Contemp Art, Los Angeles, 83-84; Int Exhib VII, Solomon R Guggenheim Mus, 85; The Third Dimension, Whitney Mus Am Art, 85; Aspects of Collage, Assemblage and the Found Object in the 20th Century, Solomon R Guggenheim Mus, 87; Sculpture since the Sixties, Whitney Mus Am Art, 88; "The Junk" Aesthetic Assemblage of the 1950's and Early 1960's, Whitney Mus Am Art, 89; Akira Ikeda Gallery, Taura, Japan, 92; Hill Gallery, Birmingham, Mich, 92; Socrates Sculpture Park, Long Island City, NY, 94; New Sculpture, LA Louver, Venice, Calif, 94; The Essential Gesture, New Port Harbor Art Mus, Newport Beach, Calif, 94; plus many others; Piece Tower, Day for Night, Whitney Biennial, 2006. *Awards:* Doris C Freedman Award, 87; Albert S Bard Award Merit in Archit & Urban Design, City Club New York, 88; Spec Recognition Award, Art Comn City New York, 95. *Bibliog:* Robert Hughes (auth), Truth amid steel and elephants, Time, 7/71; Carter Ratcliff (auth), article, Artforum, 11/72; EC Baker (auth), Mark Di Suvero's Burgundian Season, Art Am, 5/6/74

DITOMMASO, FRANCIS
DIRECTOR
b Genoa, Italy, July 9, 53; US citizen. *Study:* Int Univ Arts, Florence, Italy, cert, 72. *Pos:* Dir, Student Galleries, Sch Visual Arts, New York, formerly, Visual Arts Mus, 94-. *Mailing Add:* c/o Sch Visual Arts SVA Galleries 209 E 23rd St New York NY 10010

DITTMER, FRANCES R
COLLECTOR
Pos: Cur, Refco Collection, formerly; pvt consult, cur, of modern & contemp art Art Inst Chicago; bd dir, Drawing Ctr Inc, Whitney Mus Am Collectors, currently. *Awards:* Names one of the top 200 Collectors, ARTnews Mag, 2004. *Mem:* Diamond Art Found; Art Inst Chicago. *Collection:* Contemporary Art. *Mailing Add:* Art Inst Chicago 111 S Michigan Ave Chicago IL 60603-6110

DIVOLA, JOHN MANFORD, JR
PHOTOGRAPHER
b Santa Monica, Calif, June 6, 49. *Study:* Calif State Univ, Northridge, BA, 71; Univ Calif, Los Angeles, MA, 73, MFA, 74. *Work:* Mus Mod Art & Metrop Mus Art, NY; Int Mus Photog, George Eastman House, Rochester; New Orleans Mus Art; Fogg Mus Art, Mass; Univ Calif & Getty Mus, Los Angeles; others. *Comn:* 11 photographs, US Info Agency, 74. *Exhib:* 24 from Los Angeles, San Francisco Mus Art, 73; Mirrors & Windows, Mus Mod Art, NY, 78; New Presences at the Fogg, Fogg Mus Art, Mass, 78; one-man shows, Blue Sky Gallery, Portland, Ore, 79, Freidas Gallery, NY, 80, New Image Gallery, Harrisonburg, Va, 80, Photographers Gallery, Melbourne, Australia, 80, Los Angeles Munic Art Gallery, Calif, 85, Galerie Niki Diana Marquardt, Paris, 90 & Rena Bransten Gallery, San Francisco, 96; 1981 Biennial Exhib, Whitney Mus Am Art, NY; La Jolla Mus Contemp Art, Calif, 85; group exhib, Calif Photog: Remaking Make Believe, Mus Mod Art, NY, 89; Individual Realities in the California Art Scene (traveling), Sezon Mus Art, Tokyo, Japan, 91; More Than One Photog, Mus Mod Art, NY, 92; Multiple Images: Photographs since 1965 from the Collection, Mus Mod Art, NY, 93; After Art: Rethinking 150 Yrs of Photog, Henry Gallery, Seattle, 94; The Photog Condition, San Francisco Mus Contemp Art, 95; Perpetual Mirage: The Desert in Am Photog Books and Prints, Whitney Mus Am Art, 96. *Teaching:* Instr photog, Calif Inst Arts, 78-88; prof, Univ Calif, Riverside, 88-, chmn, Art Dept, 91-96. *Awards:* Nat Endowment Art Grants 73, 76, 79 & 91; Guggenheim Fel, 87; Flintridge Found Fel, 98. *Bibliog:* Photography Year 1980, Time-Life, 80; Andy Grundberg & Julia Scully (auths), Currents: American photography today, Mod Photog, 10/80; Mark Johnstone (auth), article in Camera, 11/80. *Mem:* Soc Photog Educ. *Publ:* Illusr, Three images reproduced, New West Mag, 11/6/78; John Divole, "Continuity", Smart Art Press, 97; Isolated Houses, Nazraeli Press, 2000. *Dealer:* Janet Borden Galler 560 Broadway New York NY 10012. *Mailing Add:* 245 Ruth Ave Venice CA 90291

DIXON, GLENN
CRITIC
Pos: Art ed, Wash City Paper, formerly; art critic Wash Post.com, 2004-. *Awards:* Recipient 3rd Place for Art Criticism; Asn of Alternative Newsweeklies, 97; Hon Mention for Art Critisism, 2003. *Publ:* Contrib to Artnet.com Magazine. *Mailing Add:* Wash Post 1150 15th St Washington DC 20071

DIXON, JENNY (JANE) HODLEY
ADMINISTRATOR
b Montreal, Que, Oct 1, 50; US citizen. *Study:* Univ Colo, BFA & BA, 72; Univ Stranieri, Perugia, Italy, 72; Columbia Univ, MBP, 83. *Collection Arranged:* Adminr & organizer of temporary installations of large-scale sculpture by: Jean Dubuffet, Isamu Noguchi, Jeffrey Owen Brosk, Mrvin Torffield, Richard Serra, Linda Howard & Sandro Martini; also assisted in installation of work by: Arthur Weyhe, George Sugarman, Pierre Clerk & others. *Pos:* Dir, Pub Art Fund Inc, formerly; moderator & producer of weekly radio prog, Artists in the City, WNYC-AM, 79-; exec dir, Lower Manhattan Cult Council, NY, currently. *Teaching:* Assoc prof, Visual Arts Admin, New York Univ, 98 & Dept Libr Studies, Parsons Sch Design, 98. *Publ:* Ed, Walking tour guide of public art in Lower Manhattan, Pub Arts Coun, 76. *Mailing Add:* 394 Union Ave Brooklyn NY 11211

DIXON, KEN
PAINTER
b St Clair, Mo, May 30, 43. *Study:* Drury Col, Springfield, Mo, BA, 65; SW Mo State Univ, Springfield, 66; Univ Ark, Fayetteville, MFA, 68, with David Durst & Howard Whitlach. *Work:* Nelson-Atkins Mus, Kansas City, Kans; San Antonio Mus Art, Tex; Kalamazoo Inst Arts, Mich; Mus Mod Art, Miami, Fla; US Govt, Dept Treasury; plus others. *Exhib:* One-man shows, Camden Inst, London, 73, Univ Ky Gallery, 90; Tex Fine Arts Nat, 84; Words as Images, 84 & Texas Currents, 85, San Antonio Inst; New Tex Art, Cheney Cowles Mus, Spokane, WA, 92; Wlm Campbell Cont Art, FT Worth, Tex 2002; Collins Gallery, Houston, Tex, 2004. *Pos:* Gallery dir, Baldwin-Wallace Col, 69-72 & Tex Tech Univ, 77- 90. *Teaching:* Instr painting, Kalamazoo Col, 66-69 & Baldwin-Wallace Col, 69-72; prof painting, Tex Tech Univ, 75-2003. *Awards:* Purchase Award, Miami Graphics Inst Mus Mod Art, Fla, 77; Outstanding Emerging Artist Nat Competition, Galveston Art Ctr, 84; Tex Award, Mid-Am Arts Alliance. *Bibliog:* Ken Dixon; Order & Disorder Art Papers, Jan. 95 Glen R. Brown, p.63; Ken Dixon, New American Painting, 2000, Number 30, Open Studio Press, Wellesley, MA pp 38-41; Sacred Landscapes, Art Mus South Tex, 2006. *Media:* Acrylic, oil. *Interests:* ornithology, geology, hiking & new science. *Dealer:* Campbell Gallery Ft Worth TX. *Mailing Add:* 1920 32nd St Lubbock TX 79411

DIXON, WILLARD
PAINTER
b Kansas City, Mo, Mar 31, 42. *Study:* Cornell Univ; Brooklyn Mus Sch; San Francisco Art Inst, MFA, 69. *Work:* Metrop Mus Art, NY; Oakland Mus, Calif; Utah Mus Fine Art, Salt Lake City; San Francisco Mus Mod Art; San Francisco Int Airport, Calif. *Comn:* Storm Source (mural), Oakland Mus, Nat Hist Dept, Calif, 84; Fire Road, Trans America Corp, 88; Missouri Countryside (mural), Commerce Bancshares, Kansas City, Mo, 97; The Eastern Sierra in Fall (mural), Calif Supreme Court, San Francisco Civic Ctr, 98; Red Rock Canyon Fed Courthouse, Las Vegas. *Exhib:* SECA Contennial Exhib, San Francisco Mus Mod Art, Calif, 70; Landscape, Seascape, Cityscape, Contemp Arts Ctr, New Orleans, La, 86; Contemp Landscapes, William Sawyer Gallery, 88; The Modern Pastoral, Robert Scholekopf Gallery, NY; The Landscape in Twentieth Century Am Art, Metrop Mus Art, 92; Rediscovering the Landscape of the Americas, Gerald Peter Gallery, Santa Fe, NMex, 96; Facing Eden: 100 Yrs of Landscape Art in the Bay Area, DeYoung Mus, San Francisco; and many others. *Teaching:* Instr, Calif State Univ, Hayward, 71-72, Calif Col Arts & Crafts, 73-76 & San Francisco State Univ, 89-90. *Awards:* Purchase Award, San Francisco Art Festival, 76 & 77; Fel, Nat Endowment Asn, 89. *Bibliog:* Bill Berkson (auth), Willard Dixon, Recent Landscape Paintings (catalog), Hackett-Freedman Gallery, 98. *Media:* Oil on Canvas. *Dealer:* Fischbach Gallery NY; Hackett Freedman Gallery San Francisco Calif; Earl McGrath Gallery Los Angeles Calif; Dolby Chadwick Gallery San Francisco Calif; I Wolk Gallery St Helena Calif. *Mailing Add:* 5 Belloreid San Rafael CA 94901

DIXSON, WENDY FAY
PAINTER, GRAPHIC ARTIST
b London Eng, Sept 18, 31. *Study:* Regent St Polytech Sch Art, London, 48-51; Boston Mus Sch Art, 53; Corcoran Sch Art, 72 & 77. *Work:* Nat Mus Women in the Arts & Nat Mus Am Art, Smithsonian Inst, Washington, DC; Montgomery Co Collection, Rockville, Md; The Frederick & Lucy S Herman Found, Norfolk, Va. *Exhib:* Label Women, Nat Women's Caucus for Art, Fed Bldg, 79; Southern Graphics,

traveling, 83-85; 1st Ann Artists Equity Show, Washington, DC, 85; Focus Int: UN Women's Conf, Nairobi, Kenya, 85. *Awards:* First Prize Drawing, Md Co Art Exhib, 79; Citation, Am Album, 86. *Mem:* Philadelphia Print Club; Artists Equity; Coalition Washington Artists; Montgomery Co Arts Coun. *Media:* Silverpoint, Mixed Media. *Dealer:* Franz Bader Gallery 1701 Pennsylvania Ave Washington DC 20006

DLUHY, DEBORAH HAIGH
EDUCATOR, ADMINISTRATOR
b Summit, NJ, Mar 4, 40. *Study:* Wheaton Col, Norton, Mass, BA, 62; Karl-Ruprecht Univ, Heidelberg, Ger; Harvard Univ, Cambridge, Mass, PhD, 76. *Pos:* Develop officer, Mus Fine Arts, Boston, Mass, 78-84, asst dir, 84-86; assoc dean admin, Sch of Mus Fine Arts, Boston, 86-87, dean acad progs & admin, 87-93, dean of sch, 93-, deputy dir, 99-; pres Alumni Asn, Wheaton Col, 94-2000, trustee, 2000-; trustee Cult Educ Collab Boston, 87-90; Wheaton Col, Norton, Mass, 88; mem exec comt, v chair fin and facilities, 2001-2002; chair fac/staff comt, mem goverance bd, 2004; vchair pres search comt; pres Wheaton Col Alumni Assoc, 94-2000; visitor Walnut Hill Sch, Natick, 96; pres Pro Arts Consortium, 99-2000; bd dir Boston Arts Acad, 99; exec comt & sec, Nat Asn Shcs Art & Design, 2001-07. *Teaching:* Lectr art hist, Wheaton Col, Norton, Mass, 75-76, Boston Col, Newton, Mass, 76-78 & Radcliffe Seminars, Radcliffe Col, 77. *Awards:* Woodrow Wilson Fel, 63. *Mem:* Nat Asn Schs Art & Design; Pro Arts Consortium; Asn Ind Cols Art & Design; St Botolph Club. *Res:* Medieval art; 13th century wallpainting, Germany. *Mailing Add:* Sch Mus Fine Arts 230 Fenway Boston MA 02115-5534

DMYTRUK, IHOR R
PAINTER, EDUCATOR
b Ukraine, Feb 11, 38; Can citizen. *Study:* Univ Alta; Vancouver Sch Art. *Work:* Alta Art Found; Univ Calgary, Alta; Ukranian Inst Mod Art, Chicago; Art Gallery, Windsor, Ont; Art Bank, Can Coun; plus others. *Exhib:* Alta Contemp Drawings, Edmonton Art Gallery, 73; one-man shows, Extension Ctr Gallery, Univ Alta, Edmonton, 2006; Alberta Art Found, Hokkaido Mus Mod Art, Japan, 79; Painting in Alberta: A Historical Survey, Edmonton Art Gallery, 80; Recent Acquisitions by Alta Art Found, Beaver House Gallery, 84; Mechanics of Vision: Drawing in Alberta, Ext Ctr Gallery, Univ Alberta, 2000; PULSE, A Northern Alberta traveling Drawing Exhibition, 2002-04. *Teaching:* Instr drawing & painting, Fac Exten, Univ Alta; Retired, 2002. *Awards:* All Alberta 1966 Award, Reeves & Sons Ltd; Can Coun Travel Grant, 66 & Arts Grant, 72 & 74. *Bibliog:* Myra Davies (auth), Recent work by Ihor Dmytruk, 10-11/71, Arts Can; Karen Wilkin (auth), Painting in Alberta-An Historical Survey, Edmonton Art Gallery Publ, 80; V Kubijovyc (ed), Encyclopedia Ukraine, vol 1, 84. *Media:* Multimedia. *Mailing Add:* 9801-92 Ave Edmonton AB T6E 2V4 Canada

DO, KIM V
PAINTER, EDUCATOR
b New York, NY, May 23, 54. *Study:* New York Studio Empire State Col, 75; State Univ NY, BFA, 76; Univ Pa, MFA, 79. *Work:* Cargill Int; Johnson & Johnson, NJ; Mid Atlantic Bank, NJ; Reader's Digest, NY; Citicorp, NY; many others. *Comn:* mural, Beacon Restaurant, NY, 99; mural, Beacon Restaurant, Stamford, Conn, 2000; landscape, comn by Horace Mann Sch, 2000; portrait of Frederick Phineas Rose, Coun For Relations, 2000. *Exhib:* Bodies and Souls, Artists Choice Mus, NY, 83; 167th Ann Exhib, Nat Acad Design; Eubie Blake Nat Mus, Baltimore, MD, 93; Independence Seaport Mus, Philadelphia, Pa, 96; Colleagues in the Landscape, Paramount Ctr for Arts, 97; New Hudson River Sch, Union Col, Schenectady, NY, 99; Faces of Courage, Heroes of 9/11, touring exhib, 2002-; portrait donation, Faces of Courage, Heros of 9/11, touring exhib, 2002-04. *Teaching:* Lectr painting, State Univ NY, Purchase 82-83; dept chmn, Visual Arts, Horace Mann Sch, NY, 85-. *Awards:* Horace Mann Travel Grant, Italy, 95. *Bibliog:* Ronny Cohen (auth), Kim Do, Artforum, 4/91; M Stephen Doherty (auth), Exploring One Location, Am Artist, 7/91; Gerrit Henry (auth), Kim Do, Art In Am, 1/92. *Mem:* Col Art Asn; Nat Art Educ Asn. *Media:* Oil, Gouache. *Interests:* landscape, portraiture, non-objective abstraction. *Publ:* Illusr, Hudson Valley Cookbook (cover), Addison Wesley. *Dealer:* Gross McCleaf Gallery 127 S 16 St Philadelphia PA 19102. *Mailing Add:* 53 Spring St New York NY 10012

DOBARD, RAYMOND GERARD
HISTORIAN, PAINTER
b New Orleans, La, Sept 13, 47. *Study:* Xavier Univ La, with Numa Rousseve, BA, 70; Johns Hopkins Univ, with Penelope Mayo, MA, 73 & Phoebe B Stanton & Charles F Stuckey, PhD, 75. *Work:* Tougaloo Col Gallery, Miss; Howard Univ Gallery, Washington; Prairie View, A&M Univ Tex; Amerika Haus Hamburg, Ger; City of Lubeck, Ger. *Exhib:* one-man shows, Evans-Tibbs Gallery, Washington, 80; Hamburg Media Ctr, Ger, 87; Black Hist Resource Ctr, Alexandria, Va, 92; Uncommon Beauty in Common Objects, 93-95; Made by Men: African Am Quilts, Univ Md Gallery, 96 & Smithsonian, Analostia Mus, 99; Stop Asking, We Exist: African Am Craft Art, 1998-2000. *Teaching:* Prof art hist, Howard Univ, Washington, DC, 75-96. *Awards:* Mellon Scholar-in-Residence, Tougaloo Col, 81; artist-in-residence, Thomas Mann Fel, Lubeck, Ger, 86. *Mem:* Col Art Asn; Am Quilt Study Group; Nat Quilters Asn. *Media:* Watercolor, Quiltmaking. *Res:* Death iconography in the works of Kaethe Kollwitz; quilt patterns, symbols & African-American spirituals as signals on the Underground Railroad; the iconography of heritage. *Publ:* Lady's Circle-Patch Work Quilts Mag, 9-10/91; Communal emblems and personal icons, Int Rev African Am Art, 94; Connecting Stitches: Quits in Illinois Life, 95; Hidden in Plain View: A Secret Story of Quilts and the Underground Railroad, 99; While on the Way to Canaan: Survival Skills, Washington Antiques Catalogue, 2000; auth, introd, A Piece of My Soul: Quilts of Black Arkansas, 11/2000

DOBBS, JOHN BARNES
PAINTER
b Passaic, NJ, Aug 2, 31. *Study:* Brooklyn Mus, Skowhegan. *Work:* Syracuse Mus Art, NY; Fairleigh Dickinson Univ; Butler Inst Am Art, Youngstown, Ohio; Univ Mass; Springfield Mus Art, Mass; Hirshorn Col, Washington, DC; Neuberger Col, Purchase, NY; and others. *Exhib:* one-man shows (32) in US & France; Mud Mod Art, NY; Nat Inst Arts & Letters, NY; Nat Acad Design; Whitney Mus, NY; Salon Des Independents, Paris; Salon Populiste, Paris; many others. *Teaching:* Instr, Brooklyn Mus Art Sch, 56-59; instr, New Sch Social Res, 65-; instr, City Col NY, 70-71; prof, John Jay Col Criminal Justice, 72-96, Art Students League, 82-83. *Awards:* Ranger Fund Purchase Prize, Nat Acad Design, 74 & 80; Thomas Proctor Prize, 74 & Benjamin Altman Prize, 78, Nat Acad Design; Art Award, Am Acad Arts & Lett, 93; many others. *Mem:* Nat Acad; Century Asn. *Media:* Oil. *Publ:* Illusr, Death and Justice Frescoes, 70; Fortune Mag, 70; Liberation Mag, 4/72; Common Elligies, 78 & What Rhymes with Cancer, 82, New Rivers Press; many others. *Dealer:* ACA Galleries NYC; George Krevsky Gallery, San Francisco. *Mailing Add:* 463 West St New York NY 10014

DOBKIN, JOHN HOWARD
ADMINISTRATOR, CONSULTANT
b Hartford, Conn, Feb 19, 42. *Study:* Yale Univ, BA, 64; Inst d'Etudes Politiques, Paris, France, 65; NY Univ, JD, 68. *Collection Arranged:* Paintings of the Figure, Nat Acad Design, 79; Landscape Paintings, Nat Acad Design, 80; Edwin Dickinson: Draftsman Paints, 81; Artists by Themselves, 83. *Pos:* Exec asst to secy, Smithsonian Inst, Washington, DC, 68-71; adminr, Cooper-Hewitt Mus Design, 71-78; dir, Nat Acad Design, NY, formerly; adv comt, Archives Am Art, NY; bd dir, Municipal Art Soc, Arthur Ross Found & Sch Am Ballet; pres, Historic Hudson Valley, 89-99; philanthropic cons, 99-. *Awards:* Exceptional Serv Award, Smithsonian Inst, 71. *Mailing Add:* PO Box 12 Annandale-on-Hudson NY 12504

DOCKTOR, IRV
PAINTER, ILLUSTRATOR, PRINTMAKER
Study: Univ Arts, Philadelphia, Pa, graduated; Barnes Found, Merion, Pa. *Comn:* Brochure booklet, 40th Anniversary of Kansas City Lyric Opera Co. *Teaching:* instr, High Sch of Art & Design, New York City, formerly; instr, Newark Sch of Fine Art, formerly. *Awards:* Best in Show, Edgewater Arts Festival, 99; Award, NJ Watercolor Soc; Best in Show, Philadelphia Color Club. *Mailing Add:* 100 Old Palisade Rd Apt 3010 Fort Lee NJ 07024

DODD, H(ELEN) C(AROLYN)
PAINTER
b Greenwich, Conn, July 9, 24. *Study:* Swarthmore Col, BS, 45; studies, Glassell Sch Art, 91-. *Work:* Am Bd Radiology, Tucson, Ariz; Koch Industs, Wichita, Kans; Bank Newport, Portland, Ore; U Tex, Austin & San Antonio; MD Anderson Hosp, Houston, Tex. *Exhib:* Grand Nat Exhib, Miss Mus Art, 97, 98, 99, 2000; Watercolor USA, Springfield Art Mus, Mo, 95, 96, 98, 99, 2000; NWWS Retrospective Exhib, Frye Art Mus, Seattle, Wash, 2000; KWS Seven State Exhib, Wichita Art Mus, Kans, 96, 97, 98, 99, 2000; Taos Nat Watercolor, Taos Mus Art, NMex, 97, 98, 99, 2000; Midwest Nat Exhib, Neville Pub Mus, Greenbay, Wis, 92, 94, 95; Philadelphia Watercolor Club, Woodmere Art Mus, Philadelphia, Pa, 95, 99; 173 Ann Exhib, Nat Acad Mus, NY, 98. *Awards:* Bronze Medal, Am Watercolor Soc, 2000; Silver Medal of Honor, Audubon Artists, 2000; Best of Show, Philadelphia Watercolor Club, 2000; Gold Medal, Am Watercolor Soc, 2003. *Mem:* Nat Watercolor Soc; Audubon Artists Inc; Philadelphia Watercolor Club; Midwest Watercolor Soc; NW Watercolor Soc. *Media:* Watercolor. *Publ:* Contribr, Color Right From The Start, Watson Guptill, 94; contribr, Painting Composition, Rockport Publ, 97; contribr, The Best Of Watercolor 2, Rockport Publ, 97; auth, Create A Model For Your Vision, Watercolor Magic, 97; contribr, The Best Of Watercolor 3, Rockport Publ, 99. *Dealer:* Gallery A 105-107 Kit Carson Rd Taos NM 87571; Joyce Petter Gallery 161 Blue Star Douglas Mich 49406. *Mailing Add:* 1749 South Blvd Houston TX 77098

DODD, LOIS
PAINTER, EDUCATOR
b Montclair, NJ, Apr 22, 27. *Study:* Cooper Union, with Byron Thomas & Peter Busa, 1948. *Hon Degrees:* Lyme Acad, Col Fine Arts. *Work:* Cooper Union Mus, First Nat City Bank, Chase Manhattan Bank Collection, AT&T, NY; Kalamazoo Art Ctr, Mich; Ciba-Geigy Chem Corp, Ardsley, NY; RJ Reynolds, Winston-Salem, NC; Commerce Bank Shares, Inc, Kansas City, Mo; Security Pac Nat Bank; Nat Acad of Design; Metrop Life Insurance Co; Reader's Digest, Pleasantville, NY; Museo dell'Arte, Udine, Italy; Bowdoin Col Mus, Maine, 2004. *Exhib:* Fischbach Gallery, NY, 1978-2002; Lyman Allyn Mus, New London, Conn, 80; NJ State Mus, Trenton, 81; Anne Weber Gallery, Georgetown, Maine, 87; Caldbeck Gallery, Rockland, Maine, 90, 94, 95, 98, 2001-03; Dartmouth Col, Hanover, NH, 1990, & 2004; Rider Col, Lawrenceville, NJ, 92; Montclair Art Mus, NJ, 96; Farnsworth Mus, Rockland, Maine, 96; Trenton City Mus, 96, 2002-, 2004. *Pos:* Co-founder, Tanager Gallery, New York, 52-62; bd of gov, Skowhegan Sch of Painting & Sculpture, 80, chmn, 86-88. *Teaching:* Instr, Wagner Col, 63-64, Philadelphia Col Art, 63 & 65; instr, Brooklyn Col, 65-72, assoc prof, 75-85, prof, 85-92. *Awards:* Ital Govt Study Grant, 59-60; Longview Found Purchase Award, 62; Ingraham, Merrill Found Grant, 71; Am Acad & Inst Arts & Letts Award, 86; Nat Acad of Design, 87 & 90; Cooper Union, Distinguished Alumni Citation, 87. *Bibliog:* Madeleine Keller (ed) Bench Press Series on Art, 85; Am Artist Mag, 4/91; Yankee Mag, 4/92; Down East Mag, 6/96. *Mem:* Nat Acad, 88; Am Acad Arts & Letters, 98. *Media:* Oil. *Dealer:* Alexandre Gallery 41 E 57th St New York NY 10022. *Mailing Add:* c/o Alexandre Gallery 41 East 57th St New York NY 10022

DODD, M(ARY) IRENE
PAINTER, EDUCATOR
b Athens, Ga, Dec 30, 41. *Study:* Duke Univ, AB, 64; Univ Ga, with Lamar Dodd, Howard Thomas, Irving Marantz Everett Kinstler and others, MFA, 67. *Work:* Smithsonian Art & Space Mus, Washington, DC; High Mus Art, Atlanta, Ga; Macon Mus Arts & Sci, Ga; Univ Tenn, Martin; Ga Mus Art, Athens. *Exhib:* Solo exhibs, Lamar Dodd Art Ctr, LaGrange, Ga, 85 & 88, Swan Gallery, Atlanta, 87 & Vadasta Cult Gallery, Ga, 97; Hay House, Macon, Ga, 84; Fifty Outstanding Am Artists, Foster Harmon Galleries, Sarasota, Fla, 84; Woodruff Art Ctr, Atlanta, Ga, 84; Valdosta State Col, Ga, 84; Southern Watercolor Exhibition, Jackson, Miss, 85; Georgia Watercolor Exhibition, Macon Mus Arts, Ga, 86; Nat Arts Club, NY, 86-90. *Teaching:* Prof hist, painting & drawing, Valdosta State Col, 67-, dept head, 72-80. *Awards:* Prize, Ga Watercolor Exhibition, 84; Prizes, Southern Watercolor Exhibition, 84 & 85. *Mem:* Nat Arts Club; Southern Watercolor Soc; Ga Watercolor Soc; Southwest Watercolor Soc. *Publ:* Illusr, Darien, The Death and Rebirth of a Southern Town, Mercer Univ Press, Macon, Ga, 81. *Mailing Add:* 316 Oak Trace Dr Valdosta GA 31602

DODDS, ROBERT J, III
COLLECTOR
b San Antonio, Tex, Sept 19, 43. *Study:* Yale Univ, BA, 65; Univ Pa Sch Law, LLB, 69. *Pos:* Term trustee, Mus Art, Carnegie Inst, 71-82; pres, Pittsburgh Plan Art, Pa, 82-85; trustee, Westmoreland Co Mus Art, Greensburg, Pa, 83-91; chmn, Carnegie-Mellon Univ Art Gallery, Pittsburgh, Pa, 85-91. *Collection:* Post-minimal and conceptual art and contemporary photography. *Mailing Add:* 3101 Old Pecos Tr No 687 Santa Fe NM 87505

DODGE, ROBERT G
PAINTER, SCULPTOR
b Boston, Mass, Aug 14, 1939. *Study:* Univ Pa, BA, 63, BFA, 65, MFA, 66. *Work:* McDonalds Corp, Chicago, Ill; TRW Corp, IBM & Equitable Corp, NY; James A Michener Mus. *Exhib:* Philadelphia Furniture, Pa Acad Fine Arts, 91; In Our Circle, James A Michener Mus, Doylestown, Pa, 91; New Abstraction, Rabbet Gallery, New Brunswick, NJ, 92; Sansar Gallery, Washington, DC, 92; Furniture of the 90's, Am Soc Furniture Arts, Houston & Parsons Sch Art, NY, 92. *Teaching:* Prof drawing & sculpture, Bucks Co Community Col, 68-. *Awards:* Prix de Rome Sculpture, Am Acad, Italy, 74-76. *Bibliog:* Portfolio, Am Craft, 88; Collaboration sparks creativity in wood, NY Times, 8/9/87; An exhibit fills a mansion, Philadelphia Inquirer, 8/21/87; Exhibition Review, Philadelphia Inquirer, 5/13/94. *Media:* Mixed. *Dealer:* Sansar Gallery 4200 Wisconsin Ave Washington DC 20016; Rabbet Gallery 120 Georges Lane New Brunswick NJ 08901. *Mailing Add:* c/o Rabbet Gallery 120 Georges Rd New Brunswick NJ 08901

DODRILL, DONALD LAWRENCE
PAINTER, ILLUSTRATOR
b Richwood, Ohio, Aug 28, 22. *Study:* Marion Bus Col, cert, 41; Ohio State Univ, Columbus, BFA(cum laude), 49; Syracuse Univ, MFA(illus), 75. *Work:* Schumacher Gallery, Capital Univ; Zanesville Art Ctr, Ohio; Wagnall Found Gallery, Lithopolis, Ohio; Ger Village Soc Hist Mus, Columbus; First Methodist Church, Hilliard, Ohio; St Anthony Med Ctr, Columbus. *Comn:* Union Station (painting), Ohio Bell Tel, Columbus, 78; Neil House (painting), Columbus Dispatch, 81; paintings, Huntington Bank, Washington Court House, Ohio, 81, EV Bischoff Co, Columbus, 83 & Borden Co, Columbus, Ohio, 83; Marysville Methodist Church, 87; Newark Advocate, Newark, Ohio, 91; Licking Co Hosp, Newark, Ohio, 92 & 96. *Exhib:* Ohio Watercolor Soc Exhibs, 74-87, 2003; Nat Waterclor Soc Exhib, Palm Springs Desert Mus, Calif, 81 & Laguna Beach Mus Art, Calif, 82; Midwest Watercolor Soc, Neville Mus, Green Bay, Wis, 84; Am Watercolor Soc, Salmagundi Club, NY, 86, 87, 88 & 92; Miss Watercolor Soc, Jackson, Miss, 91; and others. *Pos:* Partner, Dodrill Design, 54-; dir, Windon Gallery, 79-99. *Teaching:* Instr graphic design, Capital Univ, 76-83; instr watercolor, Adult Educ Prog, 77-2006, Upper Arlington, Ohio. *Awards:* Smithe Schnacke Award, Ohio Watercolor Soc, Cincinnati, 85; Hardy Gramatky Mem Award, Am Watercolor Soc, 86 & Ogden Pleisner Mem Award, 87; Karl Wolfe Award, Miss Watercolor Soc, Miss Mus Art, Jacksonville, 91. *Bibliog:* Jacqueline Hall (auth), Dodrill blends sensitivity, realism, Columbus Dispatch, 1/27/85; Susan Porter (auth), Book Dedicated to Local Cancer Victim, Worthington News, 9/27/89; Susan Stonick (auth), For Watercolor Artist Everything is a Subject, Dublin News, 9/20/89. *Mem:* Watercolor Soc, Nat, Ohio; Cent Ohio Watercolor Soc (vpres, 68, pres, 69); Upper Arlington Art League (pres, 75); Bexley Area Art Guild (pres, 80); Ohio Watercolor Soc (bd dir, 83-85); Am Watercolor Soc; Pa Watercolor Soc; Worthington Art League. *Media:* Watercolor. *Publ:* Illusr cover, Columbus Bus Forum, 75 & 76, Better Living Mag, 75 & 76 & Ohioana Libr Quart, 76-86; auth, The Transparent Touch, Watson Guptill, New York, 89; Splash 3, North Light Books, 1994; and others. *Mailing Add:* 4853 Nugent Dr Columbus OH 43220

DODWORTH, ALLEN STEVENS
CONSULTANT, CURATOR
b Long Beach, Calif, Nov 19, 38. *Study:* Stanford Univ, BA(fine arts & design), 62; Portland State Univ; Univ Utah. *Collection Arranged:* Ann Exhibs for Artists of Idaho, 69-75, Painters of the Idaho Scene, 72 & American Masters in the West, 74, Boise Gallery Art; Am Abstracts, 76; The Grand Beehive, Salt Lake Art Ctr, 80; V Douglas Snow Retrospective, Utah Mus Fine Arts, 94. *Pos:* Chmn, White Gallery, Portland State Univ, 67-69; dir, Boise Gallery Art, Boise Art Mus, 69-76; dir, Salt Lake Art Ctr, 76-81; dir, Western Colo Ctr Arts, 81-85; independent art appraiser, Salt Lake City, Utah, currently. *Awards:* Mus Prof Fel, Nat Endowment Arts, 73. *Mem:* Utah Lawyers for the Arts; Salt Lake City (design bd); Friends of the Wagnerian Opera; Alta Club Arts Found, Salt Lake City (pres, currently). *Publ:* Auth, To Be in this Country, Univ Utah Press, 94

DOE, WILLO
CRITIC, WRITER
b Pusan, Republic of Korea; US Citizen. *Study:* Yonsei Univ, Korea, BA (philos), 79; Heidelberg Univ, Ger; E Lansing Col, Mich, 83. *Collection Arranged:* Stonechime Images (auth, catalog), New York City Gallery, 95, Light and Darkness, 96, Across the Divide, 97 & Distinguished Criteria, 98. *Pos:* Contrib ed, Art Monthly, Seoul, Korea, 95; mus critic, Space: Archit, Art Design, 96; cur, Korean Cult Serv, NY, 98; contrib ed NY Art World, NY, 99; contribr writer, Fiber Arts Mag, Asheville, NC, 2001-03; contribr editor, Nat Mus Contemp Art, Korea, 2003-. *Teaching:* Fac brush painting, Art Ctr Northern NJ, 94-95. *Awards:* Nat Award for Art Criticism, 95. *Res:* Independent Artists that don't belong to a specific art movement or sch, therefore easily misplaced and displaced in the history of art and the art world. *Publ:* auth, Crossing Boundaries: The Art of Lidia Syroka, Fiberarts, Fiberarts Mag, 2002; Sang Soo Kim and Ot Painting: The Korean Cultural Serv, NY, 2003; Rothko, Stamos, Viante, and Sharf: The NY Sch, Nat Mus Contemp Art, Korea, 2004; Masae Uezmis Art (exhib catalog), Walter Wickeiser Gallery, NY, 2004; The Unknown Artists' communities in NY city, Nat Mus Contemp Art, Korea, 2004. *Mailing Add:* 355 W 85th St New York NY 10024

D'OENCH, ELLEN GATES
CURATOR, EDUCATOR
b New York, NY, Oct 2, 30. *Study:* Wesleyan Univ, BA, 73; Yale Univ, PhD, 79. *Collection Arranged:* Darkness into Light (with catalog), Yale Univ Art Gallery, 76; The Conversation Piece: Arthur Devis & Contemporaries (auth, catalog), Yale Ctr Brit Art, 80; Jim Dine Prints 1977-1986 (coauth, catalog), Wesleyan Univ, national tour, 86. *Pos:* Cur emer, Davison Art Ctr, Wesleyan Univ, 79. *Teaching:* prof emer hist art, Wesleyan Univ, Middletown, Conn, 79-98. *Mem:* Print Coun Am. *Res:* 18th century French and British prints; contemporary prints. *Publ:* Coauth, Rembrandt in 18th Century England, Yale Ctr Brit Art, 83; auth, Robert F Sheehan: Color Photography 1948-1955, Davison Art Ctr-Wesleyan Univ, 87; coauth with Sylvia Plimack, Mangold: Works on Paper 1968-1991, catalog, Davison Art Ctr-Wesleyan Univ, 92; Prodigal Son Narratives 1480-1980 (catalog), Yale Univ Art Gallery, 95; Copper Into Gold: Prints by John Raphael Smith, 1751-1812, Yale Univ Press, 99. *Mailing Add:* Davison Art Ctr-Wesleyan Univ 301 High St Middletown CT 06457

DOERNBACH, MARGUERITE
PAINTER
b Germantown, Pa. *Study:* Beaver Col, Pa; Am Artists Sch, NY; studied with Benton Spruance, Robert Gwathmey, Milton Hebald, & Hananiah Harari; self taught. *Work:* 7 paintings, Seven Main Aspects of NJ Pine Barrens; NJ Captial Bldg Annex; Under the Turnpike Bridge, James A Michener Art Mus, Doylestown, Pa; Sunlit Branches in Cadwalader Park, Trenton City, Mus, 97; Electricity of a Fores, NJ State Mus, 2000. *Exhib:* solo exhib, NJ State Mus, Artists League Central NJ, S Brunswick, Strawbridge & Clothier Dept Store, Jenkintown, Pa; 50 small watercolors, NJ State Mus, 99-2000; Rutgers Univ, Newark, NJ; The Alternate Space Gallery, New York City; Rotunda Gallery, London, Eng. *Awards:* Jurors' Merit Award, Mercer Co Cult & Heritage Comn; Eleanore Lust Prize, Ctr for the Arts in So Jersey; third place, Garden State Watercolor Soc. *Mem:* Trenton Art Works Asn, NJ. *Media:* Acrylic, Oil, Watercolor and India Ink. *Mailing Add:* 333 West State St apt 3G Trenton NJ 08618

DOEZEMA, MARIANNE
MUSEUM DIRECTOR, HISTORIAN
b Grand Rapids, Mich, Sept 8, 50. *Study:* Mich State Univ, BA, 73; Univ Mich, MA, 75; Boston Univ, PhD (Smithsonian Predoctoral Fel, Nat Mus Am Art), 90. *Collection Arranged:* The Public Monument and Its Audience, Cleveland Mus Art, Ohio, 77-78; American Realism and the Industrial Age, Cleveland Mus Art, 80-81 & Columbus Mus Art, 81; Davis Cone: Theatre Paintings, Ga Mus Art, 83 & Hunter Mus Art, Chattanooga, Tenn, 83; Painting Abstract: Gregory Amenoff, John L Moore, Katherine Porter, Mt Holyoke Col Art Mus, 96, Boston Univ Art Gallery, 97, Maier Mus, 97 & Cedar Rapids Mus Art, 97; The Sporting Woman: The Female Athlete in American Culture, Mount Holyoke Col Art Mus, 2004; Jane Hammond: Paperwork, Mount Holyoke Col Art Mus, 2006. *Pos:* Cur educ, Ga Mus Art, Univ Ga, 81-83, assoc dir, 83-85; prog officer, Mus, Div Pub Prog, Nat Endowment Humanities, 90-92; dir, Mt Holyoke Col Art Mus, 94. *Teaching:* Instr & asst cur, Dept Art Hist & Educ, Cleveland Mus Art, 76-81; asst prof & adj cur art dept, Maier Mus, Randolph-Macon Woman's Col, 92-94. *Awards:* Ralph Henry Gabriel Dissertation Prize, Am Studies Asn, 90. *Mem:* Am Asn Mus; Am Studies Asn; Col Art Asn Am. *Publ:* Auth, Americans and Paris, Colby Col Art Mus, 90; George Bellows: Paintings, Los Angeles Co Mus Art, 92; George Bellows and Urban America, New Haven, 92 & Reading American Art, 98, Yale Univ Press; ed, Changing Prospects: The View from Mt. Holyoke, 2002. *Mailing Add:* Mount Holyoke Col Art Mus South Hadley MA 01075-1499

DOGANCAY, BURHAN
PAINTER, SCULPTOR
b Istanbul, Turkey, Sept 11, 29. *Study:* Acad Grande Chaumiere, Paris, France; Univ Paris, France. *Work:* Guggenheim Mus, NY; Metrop Mus, NY; Natl Gallery Art, Washington, DC; Mus Modern Art, NY; Whitney Mus, NY; Mich Univ Mus Art, Ann Arbor, Mich; Georges Pompidon Ctr, Paris, France. *Comn:* Alucobond Shadow Sculpture, Zurich, 83. *Exhib:* Palais des Beaux-Arts, Brussels, 82; Gallery Engstrom, Stockholm; Galerie Baukunst, Cologne, 82; Centre Georges Pompidou, Paris, 82; Seibu Mus-Yurakucho Art Forum, Tokyo, 89; The State Russian Mus, St Petersburg, 92; Artists' Union, Moscow, 92; JFK Int Airport, NY, 98-99; and many others. *Collection Arranged:* John & Mable Ringling Mus Art, Sarasota; Kennedy Mus Art, Athens, Ohio; Maier Mus Art, Lynchburg, Va; Mus of Modern Art, NYC; Brooklyn Mus Art; Ga Mus Art. *Awards:* Tamarind Lithography Workshop Fel, 69; Medal of

Appreciation, Russian Ministry Cult, 92; Nat Medal Arts Life Time Achievement & Cult Contrib, Pres of the Repub Turkey, 95. *Bibliog:* Louise Schultz (auth), Dogancay and His Work, 71; E G Bowles & Tony Russell (auth), This Book is a Movie, 71. *Mem:* NY Artists Equity Asn. *Media:* Acrylic, Gouache; Collage. *Collection:* Dogoncay Mus, Istanbul. *Publ:* Dessine-moi L'Amour, Editions Syros Alternatives, 92; Dogancay (monogr), Hudson Hills Press, New York, 86; Bridge of Dreams, Hudson Hills Press, New York, 99; Dogancay: A Retrospective, Buran Edits, Istanbul, 2001; Dogancay: Works on Paper 1951-2000, Hudson Hills Press, NY, 2003; Burhan Dogancay: Walls of the World, Kerber, Dusseldorf, 2003. *Dealer:* Radio House Gallery, New York; John Stevenson Gallery New York. *Mailing Add:* 220 E 54th St New York NY 10022

DOHERTY, MICHAEL STEPHEN
EDITOR, PRINTMAKER
b New Orleans, La, Mar 9, 48. *Study:* Knox Col, Galesburg, Ill, BA, 70; Cornell Univ, Ithaca, NY, MFA, 72. *Work:* Smithsonian Inst. *Exhib:* Young Printmakers, Herron Sch Art, Indianapolis, Ind, 70; Bradley Nat Print & Drawing, Bradley Univ, Peoria, Ill, 77; Drawing Biennial, Muscarelle Mus, Col William & Mary, Williamsburg, Va, 88; solo exhibs, Ferris State Univ, Mich, 94, Bryant Gallery, New Orleans, 94 & Bryant Gallery, Jackson, 95; John Pence Gallery, San Francisco, 2000; Tree's Place Gallery, Orleans, Mass, 2001. *Pos:* Art critic, WHCUAM, Ithaca, NY, 72-76; copy supervisor & ed, Advance Process Supply Co, 77-78; ed in chief, Am Artist Mag, New York, 79-. *Teaching:* Adj prof art, Tompkins-Cortland Community Col, 73-76; instr art & art hist, Knox Col, Galesburg, Ill, 76-77. *Mem:* Am Soc Mag Ed; Col Art Asn; Portrait Soc Am; Fla Watercolor Soc. *Media:* Oil Painting. *Publ:* Auth, The romance in Mario Cooper's watercolors, 79, Robert Cottingham: An unabashed realist, 79 & Working with light-sensitive materials, 80, Am Artist Mag; Paul Ortlip: his heritage & his art, 83; Developing ideas in artwork, 88; Business Letters For Artists, Watson-Guptill Publ, 93; Creative Oil Painting, Rockport Publ, 96; auth, The Watson Guptill Handbook of Landscape Painting, 98. *Mailing Add:* Am Artist Mag 770 Broadway New York NY 10003

DOHERTY, PEGGY M
MUSEUM DIRECTOR, CURATOR
b Chicago, Ill. *Study:* Columbia Col Chicago, BA; Sch Art Inst Chicago, MA. *Collection Arranged:* Choice Impressions, 94; Recycled & Reassembled, 94; Home: Domestic Narratives, 95; Figures, 96; Addendum, 97. *Pos:* Res asst photo collections, Art Inst Chicago, 88-89; dir, Northern Ill Univ Art Mus Gallery, 90-94, Northern Ill Univ Art Mus, 94-. *Mem:* Am Asn Mus; Ill Asn Mus; Col Art Asn; Chicago Artists Coalition. *Res:* Contemporary art. *Mailing Add:* Northern Ill Univ NIU Art Mus Altgeld Hall De Kalb IL 60115

DOIG, PETER
ARTIST
b Edinburgh, Scotland, 59. *Study:* Studies at Wimbledon Sch Art, 79-80; St Martin's Sch Art, BA, 83; Chelsea Sch Art, MA, 90. *Exhib:* solo shows, Concrete Cabins, Miro Gallery, London, 94; Homely Gesellschaft für Aktuelle Kunst, Bremen, Ger, 96; Blizzard seventy seven, Kunsthalle Kiel, 98; wing-mirror, Gavin Brown's enterprise, NY, 99; Almost Grown, The Douglas Hyde Gallery, Dublin, 2000; Mus Contemp Art, Miami, 2000; Nat Gallery Can, 2001; 100 Years Ago, Victoria Miro Gallery, London, 2002; Charley's Space, Bonnefanten Mus, Maastricht, 2003; Metrop, Pinakothek der Moderne, Munich, 2004; group shows, New Contemporaries, ICA, London, 82; Barclay's Young Artist Award, Serpentine Gallery, London, 91; Twelve Stars, Barbican Ctr, London, 93; Here & Now, 94; The Turner Prize Exhib, Tate Gallery, London, 94; About Vision: New British Painting in the 1990's, The Fruitmarket Gallery, Edinburgh, 98; Alpenblick, Kunsthalle Wien, Austria, 97; Twisted: Urban & Visionary Landscapes in Contemp Painting, Can Abbermuseaum, Eindhoven, 2000; Hier ist dort, Salzburger Kunstverein, Austria, 2001; Dear Painter, paint me, Schirn Kunsthalle, Frankfurt, 2002; Days Like These, Triennial Exhib Contemp Painting British Art, Tate Gallery, London, 2003; Bearings: Landscapes from the IMMA Collection, Irish Mus Mod Art, Dublin, 2004; Day from Night, Whitney Biennial, NY, 2006. *Pos:* trustee, Tate Gallery, London, 95-2000. *Awards:* John Moores Found Prize, 93. *Mailing Add:* Michael Werner Gallery 4 E 77th St New York NY 10021

DOLAN, MARGO
DIRECTOR, ART DEALER
b Philadelphia, Pa, Mar 19, 46. *Study:* Conn Col, BA(art hist). *Collection Arranged:* Ballinglen Archive, Co Mayo, Ireland. *Pos:* Docent, Univ Mus, Philadelphia, Pa, 68-70; asst dir, Print Club, 70-73, dir, 73-77; dir, Asn Am Artists, Philadelphia, 78-84; co-owner, Dolan-Maxwell Gallery, Philadelphia, 84- & NY, 88-90; co-founder, Artist in Rural Ireland Fund, Pa & Ballinglen Arts Found, Ballycastle, Co Mayo, Repub Ireland, 92-. *Mem:* Int Fine Print Dealers Asn; Philadelphia Art Dealers Asn (vpres, 82-84 & pres, 84-85). *Specialty:* Modern and contemporary works on paper. *Mailing Add:* Dolan/Maxwell 2046 Rittenhouse Sq Philadelphia PA 19103

DOLE-RECIO, LECIA
ARTIST
b San Francisco, Ca, 71. *Study:* RI Sch Design, BFA; Art Ctr Col Design, MFA. *Work:* Rep in permanent collections, Mus Contemp Art, Los Angeles, Walker Art Ctr, Minneapolis, Los Angeles Co Mus Art. *Exhib:* Group shows, Whitney Biennial, Whitney Mus Am Art, 2004; one-woman shows, Richard Telles Fine Art, Los Angeles, Adamski Gallery Contemp Art, Aachen, Ger. *Mailing Add:* c/o Whiney Mus Am Art 945 Madison Ave New York NY 10021

DOLL, CATHERINE ANN
PAINTER, DESIGNER
b San Jose, Calif. *Study:* San Jose City Col, with Joseph Zirker, 72; Univ Wis, 82. *Work:* United Auto Workers Regional Hq, Milwaukee, Wis; mural proj, Viaduct at Field Mus, Chicago. *Exhib:* Wisconsin Directions, Milwaukee Art Mus, 82-84; 10th Yr Anniversary, ARC Gallery, Chicago, Ill, 85; Haggerty Mus Art, Milwaukee, 88; Topeka Gallery, Chicago, Ill, 88; Edinburgh Festival, 369 Galley, Scotland, 89; Tokyo Art Fair, Japan, 90; Lloyd Shin Gallery, Chicago, Ill, 90. *Collection Arranged:* Art by Auto Workers, United Auto Workers, Local 72, Kenosha, Wis, 81; Products of Society, NAB Gallery, 83 & ARC Gallery, 85, Chicago, Ill; Furniture/Furniture, Haggerty Mus, 88. *Pos:* Independent artist-designer, 82-; artist-designer hand painted clothing, workshop Very Special Art Fair, Ctr Learning Disabilities, Waukegan Ill & Univ Wis, Kenosha, 85; vpres, ARC Gallery, Chicago, Ill, 85-86. *Awards:* First Place Awards, Art by Auto Workers, United Auto Workers Union, 81 & 82; Assistance Grant, Chicago Off of Fine Arts, 85, 89 & 90. *Bibliog:* Barry Benson (reporter), Six O'Clock News, NBC, 5/83; Anne Beaton (auth), Unemployed paint painful picture, 5/83 & Margaret Hawkins (auth), Weekend plus, 12/85, Chicago Sun Times; Marlo Danato (auth), Chicago Tribune, 89; Ginny Holbert (auth), Chicago Sun Times, 90. *Mem:* Chicago Artist Coalition; Artists Residents Chicago. *Media:* Mixed. *Publ:* Contribr, United Auto Workers Calendar, 80 & 81; cover, Law & Justice, Nelson-Hall, 87; Lloyd Shin Gallery, Selected Works (catalog)

DOLL, DONALD ARTHUR
EDUCATOR, PHOTOGRAPHER
b Milwaukee, Wis, July 15, 37. *Study:* St Louis Univ, BA, MA. *Work:* Sheldon Art Gallery, Lincoln, Nebr; Mid-Am Arts Alliance, Kansas City, Mo; Rochester Inst Technol, NY. *Exhib:* Crying for a Vision, A Rosebud Sioux Trilogy (traveling exhib), Nat Endowment Arts, 76-78. *Teaching:* From assoc prof photog to prof, Creighton Univ, 69-, chmn fine & performing arts dept, 76-88. *Awards:* World Understanding Through Photog, Univ Mo Sch Journalism, Nat Press Photog Asn & Nikon, 76. *Mem:* Soc Photog Educ; Nat Press Photog Asn. *Publ:* Coauth & ed, Crying for a Vision, Morgan & Morgan, 76; contribr, Photojournalism, Nat Geographic & Nikon, 76. *Mailing Add:* Dept Fine & Performing Arts Creighton Univ Omaha NE 68178

DOLL, LINDA A
PAINTER, INSTRUCTOR
b Brooklyn, NY, May 5, 42. *Study:* Palomar Col, AA; San Diego State Univ, BA(art), 77; Univ Calif, San Diego Extension, cert(teaching), 78; studied with Rex & Joan Irving Brandt, Millard Sheets & Robert E Wood. *Work:* Scripps Hosp, La Jolla, Calif; Redlands Hospital, Riverside, Calif; Campbell River Community Coun, Campbell River, BC, Can. *Exhib:* San Diego Int Exhib, 78, 79, 82, 83 & 84; La Int Exhib, New Orleans, 82; Nat Arts Club Ann Exhib, NY, 82; Allied Artist Ann Exhib, Salmagundi Club, NY, 82; Adirondacks Nat Exhib Am Watercolors, Old Forge, NY, 83; Watercolor West Ann Exhib, Riverside, Calif, 82, 84 & 85-88; Rocky Mountain Nat Exhib, Golden, Colo, 84, 85; Nat Watercolor Soc Ann Exhib, Brea, Calif, 84, 85 & 88; Am Watercolor Soc Ann Exhib, NY, 85-90; Watercolor West Members Ann, Calif, 87 & 88. *Pos:* US Coast Guard Artist, 85-. *Teaching:* Instr workshops & sems, US, Can, Mex & Europe; instr drawing & painting, Poway Unified Sch Dist, 78-82 & Palomar Col, 80-. *Awards:* Harry Hulett Jr Award, Watercolor Okla, 84; E Gene Crain Purchase Award, Watercolor West Ann Exhib, 85; Elsie & David Wu Ject-Key Award, Am Watercolor Soc Ann Exhib, 88. *Bibliog:* article, An American Artist, Watercolor; 2/86; Artists in Southern Calif, 88. *Mem:* Life mem San Diego Watercolor Soc (pres, 80-81); La Jolla Art Asn (vpres, 79-80); Am Watercolor Soc, NY (bd dir, 90-92, 2000-2001 & juror, formerly); Nat Watercolor Soc, Calif (bd dir, 91-94 & pres, 94-95); Watercolor West (bd dir, 86-); life mem Fedn Can Artist, Vancouver. *Media:* All Media. *Dealer:* 11956 Bernardo Plaza Dr No 332 San Diego CA 92128

DOLL, NANCY
DIRECTOR
b Chicago, Ill. *Study:* Mundelein Col, Chicago, BFA, 69; Univ Iowa, Iowa City, MA, 71; Getty Mus Mgmt Inst, Berkeley, Calif. *Exhib:* Home Show II, 97; One Word: Plastic, 2003; Manic, 2004; Jessica Stockholder: kissing the Wall, 2005. *Pos:* cur 20th Cent Art, Santa Barbara Mus Art, 86-92; exec dir, Santa Barbara Contemp Arts Forum, 92-98; dir, Weatherspoon Art Mus, 98-. *Teaching:* Instr, Univ Tenn at Chattanooga, 74-75; instr, Boston Archit Ctr, 77-78; instr, Tufts Univ, 85-86 (summers). *Mem:* AAM; SE Mus Dirs Consortium; Art Table; Am Asn Col and Univ Mus&Gal. *Specialty:* Contemporary Art. *Collection:* Modern & contemporary art. *Publ:* 25 Years of De Bris, 6B Contemporary Arts Forum, 02. *Mailing Add:* Univ North Carolina Weatherspoon Art Mus Spring Garden St at Tate St Greensboro NC 27402

DOLMATCH, BLANCHE
PAINTER
b New York, NY, Dec 14, 25. *Study:* Brooklyn Col, BA (magna cum laude), 47; Univ Wis, MA, 48; Nat Acad Design, Art Students League, 48-50. *Work:* Nat Mus Women Arts, Washington; Yad Vashem (Nat Mus Israel), Jerusalem; Inst Strategy Develop, Washington; Mudge Rose Guthrie Alexander & Ferdon, NY; Butler Inst Am Art, Youngstown, Ohio; Hoffman-La Rouche, NJ. *Exhib:* Spring Show, Weatherspoon Gallery, Univ NC, Greensboro, 80; Collectors Exhib, McNay Mus, San Antonio, 80; Mem Gallery Ann, Albright-Knox Gallery, Buffalo, 81-82; Archit Images Contemp Ptg, Summit Art Ctr, NJ, 82; solo exhib, Hudson River Mus, Yonkers, NY, 87 & Butler Inst Am Art, Youngstown, Ohio, 2000; Conversations between Cultures, Readers Digest Asn, Pleasantville, NY, 93; City/Country, Park Ave Atrium, NY, 94; Artist of Month, Artists Space, NY, 98; solo exhib, New York Publ Exhib Libr, 03. *Awards:* First Prize (Oils), Nat Asn Women Artists, 73; Top Award for Painting, 24th New Eng Exhib, Silvermine Guild, 73; Award for Painting, Katonah Mus Artists Asn,

2000. *Bibliog:* Helen Hennessey (auth), Interview, NEA Newspaper Syndicate, 4/20/70; Holland Cotter (auth), Review of solo show, NY Arts J, 11/12/78; William Zimmer (auth), Neighbor artists, NY Times, 10/11/92; The Vindicator (review of solo show), Youngstown, Ohio, 12/17/00; Visions (interview), Katonah Mus Newsletter, fall 2002. *Mem:* Coun Arts Westchester; Katonah Mus Artists Asn. *Media:* Acrylic, Oil on Canvas

DOMINGUEZ, EDDIE
CERAMIST
b Tucumcari, NMex, Oct 17, 57. *Study:* Cleveland Inst Art, BFA, 81; Alfred Col Ceramics, MFA, 83. *Work:* Roswell Mus & Art Ctr, NMex; Albuquerque Mus Fine Art, NMex; Mus Fine Art, Santa Fe, NMex; Cooper-Hewitt Mus, NY; Kohler Arts Ctr, Sheboygan, Wis. *Comn:* Tile mural, City Tucson, Ariz; tile mural, Phoenix Airport, Ariz; tile mural, Great Brook Valley Health Ctr, Wooster, Mass. *Exhib:* New Orleans Mus Art, La, 94; solo exhibs, Firehouse Art Ctr, Norman, Okla, 94, Munson Gallery, Santa Fe, NMex, 94, 95, 99, Jan Weiner Gallery, Kansas City, Mo, 95 & 96, Joanne Rapp Gallery/The Hand and the Spirit, Scottsdale, Ariz, 95, Kavesh Gallery, Sun Valley, Idaho, 95, Munson Gallery, Santa Fe, NMex, 97, Morthern Clay Ctr, Minn, 98; Margolis Gallery, NY, 95; Margo Jacobson Gallery, Portland, Ore, 96; Jane Haslem Gallery, Washington, 96; Karen Ruhlen Gallery, Santa Fe, NMex, 96; Johnson Co Community Col, Overland Parks, Kans, 96; Site Santa Fe Gallery, NMex, 96; Bruce Kapson Gallery, Santa Monica, Calif, 96; Very Special Arts Gallery, Albuquerque, NMex, 97; Joanne Rapp Gallery/The Hand and the Spirit, Scottsdale, Ariz, 97; Buddy Holly Fine Arts Ctr, Tex, 99; Qualita Gallery/Nancy Hoffman, NMex, 2000. *Pos:* Lectr, Southern Ill Univ, Carbondale, 91; Eastern NMex Univ, Clovis, 91; Cleveland Inst Art, Ohio, 92. *Teaching:* Artist in residence & lectr, Ohio State Univ, 84; Cleveland Inst Art, Ohio, 86; Univ Mont, Missoula, 88; vis artist & lectr, various US & Can Schs, Cols & Univs, 93-97; asst prof fine arts, Univ Nebr, Lincoln, 98. *Awards:* Fel, NEA, 86 & 88; Artists in Res, Roswell Mus & Art Ctr Grant, 87; Kohler Arts-in-Industry Grant, 88. *Media:* Clay, Metal. *Publ:* Contr, Ceramics Month. *Dealer:* Munson Gallery 225 Canyon Rd Santa Fe NM 87501; Joanne Rapp Gallery/The Hand & The Spirit 4222 N Marshall Way Scottsdale AZ 85251. *Mailing Add:* c/o The Munson Gallery 225 Canyon Rd Santa Fe NM 87501

DOMJAN, EVELYN
PAINTER, PRINTMAKER
b Budapest, Hungary, Mar 25, 22. *Study:* Hungarian Royal Acad Fine Arts, BA, 45. *Work:* Birger Sanzen Mem Gallery, Linsborg, Kans; Saddleriver Valley Cult Ctr, NJ; Am Mus Folk Art, NY; Skylands, Ringwood, NJ; Hungarian Heritage Ctr, New Brunswick, NJ. *Comn:* Fish and Shells of Seven Seas, Wagstaff Residence, Tuxedo Park, NY. *Exhib:* Ringwood Manor Spring and Fall, NJ, 92-94; Skyland Centennial, NJ, 92; The Best is yet to be, Ramapo Col, Mahwah, NJ, 93; Creative Imagery, Small Work Show, Cult Ctr, Demarest, NJ, 93 & Olympia, 95; Black & White, Watchung, NJ, 95. *Teaching:* Lectr graphic arts, art hist, hist world folk art. *Awards:* Nat Endowment Arts, 68; First Prize for Wood Carved Images, Budapest Publ Gondolat, 86. *Bibliog:* Cassidy Enoch-Rex (auth), Of Gardens, Gauguin, and Greece, 1/28/2006. *Mem:* Soc Am Graphic Artist; Salute Women Arts; Ringwood Manor Asn Arts; Metrop Mus Art; Asn Int Des Arts Plastiques, UNESCO; Circle Francais Print Club, Albany. *Media:* woodcuts, exlibko, exhibitions. *Publ:* Auth, Parta, Hungarian Folk Mus, 72; Edge of Paradise, Domjan Studio, 75; Eternal Wool, Domjan Studios, 76; Woodcarved Images, Budapest, 86; Panorama of Hungarian Peasant Painting, 87; Pavologia, Domjan Studios, 88. *Dealer:* Mus Am Hungarian Found 300 Somerset St New Brunswick NJ. *Mailing Add:* West Lake Rd Tuxedo Park NY 10987

DONAHUE, PHILIP RICHARD
PAINTER, EDUCATOR
b Detroit, Mich, Apr 1, 43. *Study:* St Peters Col, AB(art hist), 69; Spring Hill Col, MA, 72; Grad Theological Union, PhD, 83; painting and visual hermeneutics with Jay DeFeo, John Boyle & Jane Dillenberger. *Comn:* Donahue Painting Series, Soc Jesus, New Orleans, La, 70-82; St Ignatius Mural, St Charles Col, Grand Coteau, La, 72; Presidential Series, Spring Hill Col, Mobile, Ala, 74; Ordination Card Series, Jesuit Sch Theology, Berkeley, Calif, 74-82; covers (Japanese poetry bk), Tokyo, 82-83. *Exhib:* Allied Arts Competition, Metrop Mobile Mus, Ala, 74; The Holy in Art, St Alberts Col, Oakland, Calif, 75; Religious Art Ann, Grad Theological Union, Berkeley, Calif, 75-82; Emergence Art Xian Thought, Grace Cathedral, San Francisco, Calif, 76; one-man show, Jesuit Art Ctr, Baltimore, Md, 78; Ann US Exhib, AT Gallery, Tokyo, 82-; Grad Theological Union, Berkeley, 83; Calif Small Works, Sonoma Mus Visual Arts, Santa Rosa, Calif, 2001; Arts on Fire 5, Sanchez Art Center, Pacifica, Calif, 2001; Revealing/Concealing, Taking the Leap Heritage Square, Emeryville, Calif, 2001; 10 Artists Revealed, Sight & Insight Art Center, Mill Valley, Calif, 2001; Showcase 2002, Berkeley Art Center, Berkeley, Calif, 2002; Spring Thing, Sight & Insight Art Center, Mill Valley, Calif, 2002; Coming Together, Art Guild of Pacifica, Calif, 2003; Columbarium, Sun Gallery, Hayward, Calif, 2003; mem only, Richmond Art Ctr, Calif, 2003; Showcase 2004, Berkeley Art Ctr, 2004; Light Shows to Canvas, Cafe Galleria, 2004; Dia De Los Muertos, Sun Gallery, 2004; Showcase 2005, Berkeley Art Ctr, 2005; Paint Behaving Badly, UC Berkeley, 2005; Sakai-Berkeley, Sakai Mus, Osaka, Japan, 2006; Dia de Los Muertos, Oakland Mus, Calif, 2006; Picasso at Lapin Agile, Bainbridge Island, Wash, 2006; Showcase, Berkeley Art Center, Calif, 2006. *Collection Arranged:* Artworks 82, Int Hunger Proj, 82; Link Art Int, Tokyo, Osaka, Hiroshima, 82 & Hakuhodo, Sapporo, 83; 10 Artists Revealed, Mill Valley Art Ctr, Calif, 2001; Spring Thing, Mill Valley Art Ctr, Calif, 2002. *Pos:* Acting chmn, art hist, St Peter's Col, Jersey City, NJ, 67-68; artist-in-residence, St Charles Col, Grand Coteau, La, 70-72 & Jesuit Sch Theology, Berkeley, Calif, 74-82; dir spec events & art educ, Link Art Int Ltd, Oakland, 82-; writer, Meaning in Painting, Finearts, 91-; chief cur, studio visit, Mus of Calif, Oakland, 2003. *Teaching:* Asst instr art hist & drawing, St Peters Col, Jersey City, NJ, 64-68; asst prof painting, Spring Hill Col, Mobile, Ala, 72-74; Link Art Int, 82-. *Awards:* Full Patronage, Soc Jesus, 70-82; First Place, Asn Educ Tech, 72; First Place, Allied Artist Coun, 74; Oscar d'Italia, Academia Italia, Calvatone, Italy, 92; World Culture Prize, Centro Studio, Richerche Della Nazione, Parma, Italy, 94. *Bibliog:* C J McNaspy (auth), American Jesuits in the Arts, The Jesuit, fall 76; K G Connolly (auth), Art & belief, New Catholic World, 1-2/80; T Anzai & A Donahue (auth), Link art international, Motions, Tokyo, 11/81. *Mem:* Am Soc Aesthetics; Int Soc Artists; Art Guild of Pacifica; Int Soc Experimental Artists; Berkeley Art Ctr, Sanchez Art Ctr & Richmond Art Ctr; Mill Valley (Sight & Insight) Art Ctr. *Media:* Oil, Mixed Media. *Res:* Iconological hermeneutics: symbolic interpretation of the levels of meanings in paintings. *Publ:* Illusr, Bom Pastor, Brazil, Catholic Voice, 77; auth, Iconological Hermeneutics, Am Acad Religion, 80; Visual Art, Society & Religion, New Catholic World, 80; Greco-Roman Influences in Early Xian Iconology, Calif Classic Asn, 81; contribr to cover, Oasis (Japanese Poetry), Tokyo, Japan, 90. *Mailing Add:* 11591 Berry Patch Ln NE Bainbridge Island WA 98110

DONATI, ENRICO
PAINTER, SCULPTOR
b Milan, Italy, Feb 19, 1909; US citizen. *Study:* Univ Pavia, Italy, Dr, 29; Art Students League, 40; New Sch Social Res, New York, 41. *Work:* Albright-Knox Art Gallery, Buffalo, NY; Univ Art Mus, Univ Calif, Berkeley; Mus Mod Art, NY; Whitney Mus Am Art, NY; Baltimore Mus Art. *Exhib:* Eight Carnegie Int Exhibs, 45-61; Embellished Surfaces, Mus Mod Art, NY, 53-54; Younger Am Painters, Solomon R Guggenheim Mus, 54-55; Palais des Beaux-Arts, Brussels, Belg, 61; Friends Collection, Whitney Mus Am Art, 64, Staempfli Gallery, NY, 62-82 & Grand Palais, Paris, 80; One man exhibs, Gimpel & Weitzenhoffer, NY, 84, 86 & 87, Carone Gallery, Ft Lauderdale, Fla, 84, 90 & 92, Georges Fall, Paris, 85, Zabriskie Gallery, NY, 87, Galerie Zabriskie, Paris, 89 & Louis Newman Gallery, Beverly Hills, 86, 89 & 91, Retrospective: 1942-2001, Weinstein Collection, 2006. *Pos:* Mem adv bd, Brandeis Univ, Waltham, Mass, 56-72; mem pres coun arts & archit, Yale Univ, 62-72; chmn nat comn, Univ Art Mus, Univ Calif, Berkeley, 70-72. *Teaching:* Vis lectr & critic, Yale Univ, 62-72. *Bibliog:* John Gruen (auth), Enrico Donati, Mus de Poche, 65. *Dealer:* Gimpel & Weitzen Hoffer 1040 Madison Ave New York NY 10021. *Mailing Add:* 222 Central Park S New York NY 10019-1408

DONEGAN, CHERYL
PAINTER
b New Haven, Conn, 1962. *Study:* RI Sch Design, Providence, BFA(painting), 84; Hunter Col, New York, MFA, 90. *Exhib:* Solo exhibs, Nice Fine Arts, France, 94, Galerie Rizzo, Paris, France, 94, TENT, Basilco Fine Arts, NY, 96, Line, Baurngartner Galleries, Washington, DC, 97 & Scenes plus Commercials: A Retrospective Development - The Movie, Basilco Fine Arts, NY, 97, Lotta Hammer, London, 98; ACC Galerie Weimar, 98; 1998 Video Room Video Festival, Salon 75, NY, 98; 98 Made in US, Galleria II Capricorno, Venice, 98; Educating Barbie, Trans Hudson Gallery, NY, 98; Positioning, Bard Ctr Curatorial Studies, NY, 99. *Awards:* Grant, Anonymous Was a Woman Foundation, 97. *Bibliog:* Carol Kino (auth), Educating Barbie, Time Out, 9/17-24/98; Heinz-Norbert Jocks (auth), I Love New York, Kunstforum, 1-2/99; Milena & Thiel Noikolva & Wolf Gunter (coauths), Crossover, Flash Art, 2-3/99

DONER, MICHELE OKA
SCULPTOR
Study: Univ Mich, BA, 1966; Univ Mich, MA, Teaching Fellowship, 1968; Univ Detroit (post grad work) 1969. *Work:* City of Trees, Evanston Pub Libr, Evanston, Ill, 1994; Positron, Arthur Rich Mem Univ Mich, Ann Habor, Mich, 1996; Medallion Flight, Wash Nat Airport, Alexandria, Va; Poplar & Iris Garden of Justice, US Courthouse, Greenville, Tenn, 2001; US Courthouse, Gulfport, Mich, 2002. *Exhib:* Body Language, Nat Design Mus, NY, 1995; Bare Witness Clothing & Nudity, Metrop Mus of Art, NY, 1996; Illuminations, Mus of Contemp Art, N Miami, Fla, 1997; Acts of Faith, Abraham Lubelski Gallery, NY, 1998; Heroines & Heroes, Cynthia Broan Gallery, NY, 1999; Women Designers in the USA 1900-2000 Diversity & Difference (traveling), Bard Grad Ctr, NYC, 2000. *Collection Arranged:* Metrop Mus of Art, NY; Art Inst of Chicago; Am Mus of Natural Hist, NY; Va Mus of Fine Arts, Va; Children's Mus of Manhattan, NY. *Awards:* Award of Excellence, UN Soc of Artists & Writers; Distinguished Alumni Award, Univ Mich. *Bibliog:* Mildred Constantine & Laurel Reuter (auths), Whole Cloth, Monacelli Press, 1997; Frank Lloyd Wright (auth), Fifty Favorite Rooms, Archetype Press, 1998; Peter Whoriskey (auth), Three Seconds to Decide on the Famous, Unknown, Miami Herald, 1996. *Media:* Installation. *Publ:* Portraits Michele Oka Doner, Hubertus Raben Int, pages 54-57, Aug, 1995; Michele Oka Doner Muscheim am Miami Beach, Juliana Balint, Wohnen, pages 38-45 & cover, May, 1996; Michele Oka Doner at MoCA, Entertainment News & Views, page 15, Nov-Dec, 1997. *Mailing Add:* 94 Mercer St 2nd Fl New York NY 10001

DONHAUSER, PAUL STEFAN
SCULPTOR, PAINTER
b Berlin, Ger, May 6, 36; US citizen. *Study:* Univ Wis-Milwaukee, BS(art); Univ Wis-Madison, MS(art); Ill State Univ, PhD(art). *Work:* Int Mus Ceramics, Faenza, Italy; Nat Mus Art, Gdansk, Poland; Maison des Metiers d'Art Francais, Paris; Everson Mus Art, Syracuse, NY; Smithsonian Inst, Washington, DC. *Comn:* Relief mural (6ft x 15ft), Student Union, Wis State Col, Oshkosh, 71; series of five free standing outdoor sculptures, Univ Wis Campus, 78; Ceramic mural (6 ft x 40 ft), Hughes Hall, Winn City Health Ctr, 84; Paintings (4 ft x 8 ft), Columba Correctional Inst, Portage Wis. *Exhib:* Wis Directions, Milwaukee Art Ctr, 76; Landscape: New Views, Johnson Mus, Cornell Univ, Ithaca, NY, 78; Int Biennial Exhib of Ceramic Sculpture, Vallauris, France, 78; Clay & Fiber, Wustum Fine Arts Mus, Racine, Wis,

78; Donhauser Retrospective: 1957-1977, Paine Art Mus, Oshkosh, 77; Int Ceramics Exhib, Tejimi, Japan. *Teaching:* Instr ceramics, Madison Area Tech Col, Wis, 60-63; instr drawing & ceramics, Ill State Univ, Normal, 63-65; prof ceramics, Univ Wis, Oshkosh, 65-. *Awards:* Nat Award for Ceramic Sculpture, 8th Miami Ceramic Nat Exhib, Coral Gables Art Asn, Fla, 72; Grand Prize of Faenza, 35th Int Exhib of Ceramics, Int Mus of Ceramics, 76; Nat Endowment Arts, Visual Artist Fel, 84. *Bibliog:* Sergio Cavina (auth), Emilia Romagna, Regione, Bologna, Italy, 9/76; Linda Witt (auth), Donhauser wins Italy's top ceramic prize, People Weekly, 10/11/76; James Auer (auth), Uncommon clay, Milwaukee J, 9/77. *Mem:* Int Acad of Ceramics, Geneva, Switz; Am Crafts Coun; Wis Designer Craftsmen. *Media:* Acrylic, Ceramics. *Publ:* Co-auth, New Ceramics, St Martins, London, 74; auth, History of American ceramics, The Studio Potter, Kendall/Hunt, 78. *Dealer:* Ruth Volid Gallery 225 W Illinois St Chicago IL 60610; Tori Folliard Gallery Milwaukee WI. *Mailing Add:* 5724 I Ah May Tah Rd 210 Museum Pl Oshkosh WI 54901

DONLEY, RAY
PAINTER
b Austin, Tex, Dec 4, 50. *Study:* Univ Tex at Austin, BFA, 1981; Univ Tex at Austin, MA, 1983. *Exhib:* One man shows, Jack Meier Gallery, Houston, Tex, 1995, 1999-2000, & Wright Gallery, NY, 2001, among others; Marshall Gallery, Scottsdale, Ariz, 2004; f8 Fine Art Gallery, Austin, Tex, 2005; Principle Gallery, Alexandria, Va, 2005; Montana Gallery, Palm Beach, Fla, 2005; Sarah Bain Gallery, Anaheim, Calif; Trinity Gallery, Atlanta, Ga. *Pos:* artist in res, St Edward's Univ, Austin, Tex; artist in res, Univ Tenn, Knoxville. *Awards:* First Prize, San Remo Biennale, 2003. *Bibliog:* Michael Barnes (auth), Last Word on the Arts, Austin Am Statesman, 2001; Jared Schroeder (auth), Exhibit: Paintings Evoke Dark Side, San Angelo Standard Times, 2003; Molly Beth Brenner (auth), A Piece of Work: A Painting by Ray Donley, Austin Chronicle, 2004; and others. *Media:* Oil & Mixed Media. *Dealer:* Sarah Bain Gallery, Anaheim, Calif; The Marshal Gallery, Scottsdale, Ariz; and others. *Mailing Add:* PO Box 4391 Austin TX 78765

DONLEY, ROBERT MORRIS
PAINTER, EDUCATOR
b Cleveland, Ohio, July 5, 34. *Study:* Sch Art Inst, BFA, 60, MFA, 66. *Work:* Ill State Univ, Normal; Northern Ill Univ, DeKalb; Mobil Oil Corp, NY; Smithsonian Inst, Washington, DC; Boeing Corp; and others. *Exhib:* Los Angeles Mus Ann, Los Angeles Co Mus, 59-61; Nat Traveling Exhib Chicago Artists, Crocker Mus Art, Sacramento, Calif, 76; 76th & 77th Exhib Artists Chicago & Vicinity, Art Inst Chicago, 77 & 78; New Visions, Aldrich Mus Contemp Art, Ridgefield, Conn, 81; Crimes of Compassion, Chrysler Mus, Norfolk, Va, 81; 36th Ill Invitational, Ill State Mus, Springfield, 84; Intersections: Artists View of the City, Laguna Gloria Art Mus, Austin, Tex, 86; Fetish Art: Obsessive Expressions, Rockford Art Mus, Ill, 86; Chicago Art 1945-1995, Mus Contemp Art, 96-97. *Teaching:* Prof painting & drawing, De Paul Univ, Chicago, Ill, 67-. *Awards:* Logan Prize, 77, Nat Endowment Arts Grant, 80; Pauline Palmer Prize, Chicago Show, 90. *Bibliog:* Carrie Rickey (auth), Chicago, Art in Am, 7-8/79; Judith Wilson (auth), The last detail, Village Voice, Vol XXV, No 49, 80; Michele Vishny (auth), Robert Donley, Arts Mag, 10/83. *Media:* Oil, Acrylic. *Dealer:* Corbett Us Dempsey Chicago IL. *Mailing Add:* 1101 N Damen Ave Chicago IL 60622

DONMEZ, YUCEL
PAINTER, SCULPTOR
b Kars, Turkey, Jan 5, 46, US citizen. *Study:* Applied Fine Arts Acad, Istanbul, BA, 74. *Work:* UN Plaza, NY; High Flt Found, Colorado Springs, Colo; Vestel Electronics Corp, Manisa, Turkey; Truman Col, Int Press Ctr, Chicago; plus others. *Comn:* Snow paintings, Chicago Grand Park, Chicago, Ill 93; 15,000 meter square snow paintings, Fuji Film Istanbul, Mount Uludag, Bursa, Turkey, 96; Mediterranean Art Festival, Miami & Boca Raton, Fla, 1987; Turkish Art Ministry Comn. *Exhib:* Int Art Fair, Navy Pier, Chicago, 73; Sculpture Exhib, Chicago Pub Libr Cult Ctr, 74; Meditteranian Weeks, Bloomingdale Support, Miami, 87; Turkish Art Gallery, UN Plaza, NY, 87; Turkish Am Artist, Art Inst Chicago, 87; First Contemp Exhib, Topkadi Palace Mus, Turkey, 92; Istanbul Art Expo, 90, 97, 98, 99, 2000, 2002; Middletown Art Fest 2000, Middletown, Ohio; Gallery 2000 Chicago, 2002; plus others. *Collection Arranged:* Bahceschir Univ, Istanbul, Turkey, 2000. *Pos:* adviser for 21 centuries Art Rsch, Bahcesehir Univ, Istanbul, Turkey. *Teaching:* Artist workshops, Urban Gateways, Chicago, 88-97. *Awards:* 21st Century's Artist Award, North Am Turkish Asn Price Commn. *Bibliog:* Interview with Maureen Wolf, WGN TV, 7/87; Margaret Sheridan (auth), Chicago Tribune, 6/26/88; Alan G Artner (auth), Chicago Tribune, 8/24/89; Brian Clifford (auth), The Middletown Jour, 10/1/2000. *Mem:* Plastic Arts Found, Turkey; Urban Gateways, Chicago. *Media:* Acrylic, Glass, Metal, Rock, Snow, Digital Works. *Publ:* Auth, Canvas and Digital Works, Zerdust Publ, 2001. *Dealer:* Gallery 2000 Chicago 2246 N Clark St Chicago IL 60614. *Mailing Add:* 5520 N Artesian Ave Apt 3 Chicago IL 60625

DONNANGELO, DAVID MICHAEL
PAINTER, ART DEALER
b Bethlehem, Pa, Sept 3, 57. *Study:* Studied sculpture under Italo Scanga; Moravian Col; Tyler Sch Art; Baum Sch Barnes Found. *Work:* Rome, Italy; RCA Weaversville Prog, Northampton, Pa; Musikfiest Collection, Bethlehem, Pa. *Comn:* Murals, Super Value, Laneco, Inc, Allentown, Bethlehem & Easton, Pa, 93; Catholic Oils, Wegmans. *Exhib:* Governor's Exhib, William Penn Mus, Harrisburg, Pa, 74; Art Gallery Award, Kemerer Mus, Bethlehem, Pa, 75; Lehigh Art Alliance Exhib, 80; Hazelton Art League Regional Exhib, 81; 9th Nat Print Show, Moravian Col, Payne Gallery, Bethlehem, Pa, 94. *Awards:* First Place, Bethlehem Art Show Comt, 76; Purchase Award, Pa State Univ, 81; Purchase Award, Morovian Col, 94. *Media:* Oil, Acrylic. *Dealer:* Contemporary Fine Art. *Mailing Add:* 1881 Abington Rd Bethlehem PA 18018

DONNELLY, MARIAN CARD
HISTORIAN, EDUCATOR
b Evanston, Ill, Sept 12, 23. *Study:* Oberlin Col, AB, 46, MA, 48; Yale Univ, PhD, 56. *Pos:* Art librn, Univ Rochester, 51-53; res assoc, Art Inst Chicago, 56-57. *Teaching:* Instr art hist, Upsala Col, 48-50; from asst prof to prof art hist, Univ Ore, 66-; retired. *Mem:* Archaeol Inst Am; Soc Preserv New Eng Antiquities; Royal Soc Arts, London; Soc Archit Historians (dir, 64-67, 78-, second vpres, 72-74, first vpres, 74-76, pres, 76-78). *Res:* Vernacular and technological architecture in North Europe and America, particularly during the sixteenth, seventeenth and eighteenth centuries. *Publ:* Theaters in the Courts of Denmark & Sweden, J Soc Archit Historians, 84; New England Meeting Houses of the Seventeenth Century, Wesleyan Univ Press, 68; Materials in Early New England, Old Time New Eng, 71; A Short History of Observatories, Univ Ore Bks, 73; Architecture in the Scandinavian Countries, MIT Press, 92. *Mailing Add:* 2175 Olive St Eugene OR 97405

DONNELLY, TRISHA
ARTIST
b San Francisco, Calif, 74. *Study:* Univ Calif, Los Angeles, BFA, 95; Yale Univ, Sch Art, MFA, 2000. *Exhib:* one woman shows, Air de Paris, 2002, Casey Kaplan, NY, 2002 & 2004, Art Positions, Art Miami Beach, 2003, The Wrong Gallery, NY, 2004, Art Pace, San Antonio, Tex, 2005, Kunsthalle Zürich, 2005, Gallery Modern Art, Bolgona, 2006 & Special Project Portikus, Frankfurt a Main, 2006; group exhibs, Minty, Richard Telles Gallery, Los Angeles, 99; Found Louis-Jeantet de Médecine, Geneva, 99; Echo, Artist's Space, NY, 2000; The Dedalic Convention, MAK Mus, Vienna, 2001; Moving Pictures, Solomon R Guggenheim Mus, 2002; Hello, My Name Is., Carnegie Mus Art, Pittsburgh, 2002; 50th Int Exhib Art, Venice Biennial, 2003; Peripheries become the center, Prague Biennial, 2003; Biennial Contemp African Art, Obrist, Dakar, 2004; Collection (or How I Spent a Year), PS1 Contemp Art Ctr, Long Island City, 2004; Moscow Biennial Contemp Art, 2005; The Imaginary Number, Kunst Werk, Berlin, 2005; 4tth Berlin Biennial Contemp Art: Of Mice & Men, 2006; and many others. *Pos:* vis fac, New Genres dept, San Francisco Art Inst. *Awards:* recipient, Central-Kuntspreis, Cologne, Ger, 2004. *Mailing Add:* San Francisco Art Institute 800 Chestnut St San Francisco CA 94133

DONNESON, SEENA
SCULPTOR, GRAPHICS ARTIST
b New York, NY. *Study:* Pratt Inst; Art Students League, with Morris Kantor; Pratt Graphic Arts Ctr, with Michael Ponce de Leon. *Work:* Mus Mod Art, NY; Phillip Morris Int, NY; Los Angeles Co Mus Art; Smithsonian Mus, Washington, DC; Ft Lauderdale Mus Art; Boca Raton Mus Art, Fla. *Comn:* Ed prints, Touchstone Press; tapestry design, Equitable Life & Insurance Co, NY, 76; ed prints, Ft Lauderdale Mus Fine Arts, Fla, 77; outdoor sculpture, Snug Harbor Cult Ctr, Grow-Kiewit-Mk, NY, 79; outdoor sculpture, Jersey City State Col, NJ, 81. *Exhib:* The Collograph, Pratt Graphic Arts traveling exhib, NY State Coun Arts; Material & Metaphor, Wm Paterson Col, Ben Shahn Gallery; Norfolk Mus Arts & Scis; Ann City Mus Art Gallery, Hong Kong; Paper Works, State Univ NY, Stonybrook, 94; and others. *Pos:* App mem, Nassau Co Fine Arts Comn, 70-; exhib cur coordr, Dept Parks, Recreation & Cult Affairs, NY, 71-74. *Teaching:* Lectr hist mod art, New York Univ, 61-63; in-sch-artist, Nassau Co Cult Coun, 71-79; lectr, Nassau Co Off Cult Develop, 71-79 & New Sch Social Res, 74-; painting & drawing, New Hampshire Col, 80-83; private students. *Awards:* Fel, MacDowell Found, 63, 64; Clayworks, NY, 81; Creative Artists Serv Prog Grant, NY State Coun Arts, 83-84; Queens CounArts, 89. *Bibliog:* John Perreault (auth), Up the river, Soho Weekly News, 78; Grace Glueck (auth), Sculpture under a city sky, New York Times, 78; Mary Anne Pennington (dir), Seena Donneson, Relief Sculpture (film), Greenville Mus Art, NC, 87; Phyllis Braff (auth), Uses of paper, New York Times, 97; Nat Asn Women Artists (photo), Newsday, 97. *Mem:* Artists Equity Asn, NY; Long Island City Artists Inc. *Media:* Metals, Paper; Collographs, Etchings. *Specialty:* Sculpture. *Publ:* Beata Thackeray (auth), Paper: Making-Decorating (photo, review, listing), Conran Octopus, Ltd, London, Eng, 10-97; contribr, American Printmakers, Graphics Group, 74; Women Artists in America, 75; Exploring The Visual Arts, Davis Publ, 76. *Dealer:* Quietude Sculpture Gallery Garden 24 Fern Rd East Brunswick NJ; Spring Gallery Belgrade Lakes ME. *Mailing Add:* 43-49 Tenth St Long Island City NY 11101

D'ONOFRIO, BERNARD MICHAEL
GLASS BLOWER, SCULPTOR
b Medford, Mass, Jan 7, 51. *Study:* Univ Mass, Amherst, BFA, 73; Pilchuck Sch, Stanwood, Wash, 81, 82; Kent State Univ, MFA, 83. *Work:* Moderne Int Glaskunst, Ebeltoft, Denmark; Pilchuck, Stanwood, Wash; Headley Whitney Mus, Lexington, Ky; Milwaukee Art Mus, Wis; Kogawezaki Glass Mus, Shizvoka, Japan; Tampa Art Mus. *Comn:* Bank One, Akron, Ohio, 82; Network World, Framingham, Mass, 90; Meditech Corp, Westwood, MA, 2004. *Exhib:* Boston Now, Inst Contemp Art, Boston, Mass, 89; Contemp Glass, Milwaukee Art Mus, Wis, 90; one-man exhib, Snyderman Gallery, Philadelphia, Pa, 90 & Sanske Gallery, Zurich, Switz, 92; 10th Anniversary Exhibition, Helander Gallery, West Palm Beach, Fla, 91; World Glass Exhib, Gallery Nakama, Tokyo, Japan, 91; Garland Gallery, Santa Fe, NMex, 93; William Traver Gallery, Seattle, Wash, 94; Holsten Gallery, Stockbridge, Mass, 99 & 2000; Habatat Galleries, Boco Raton, Fla, 2000; Sofa, Chicago Navy Pier, 2000; Habatat Galleries, Chicago, 2002; Morgan Gallery, Pittsburgh, 2003. *Collection Arranged:* Bronfman Collection; Pritzker Collection. *Pos:* dir, Donofrid Studio. *Teaching:* Instr design, Cranbrook Sch, Bloomfield Hills, Mich, 73-80; vis lectr glass, Mass Col Art, Boston, 83-; vis artist glass, Tokyo Glass Art Inst, Japan, 92 & 98. *Awards:* Finalist Award, Mass Artists Fel, 89; Visual Artist Fel, Nat Endowment Arts, 90; Silver Prize International Glass Kanazawa, Japan, 92. *Bibliog:* Susan Barahal

(auth), Sculptural perspectives, Art New Eng, 88; Paul Hollistr (auth), Delicate and bold, NY Times, 89; James Yood (auth), review, Galss Magazine, winter 2002. *Mem:* Glass Art Soc. *Media:* Glass. *Dealer:* Imago Art 73-970 El Paseo Palm Dessert, CA 92260; Holsten Gallery Elm St Stockbridge MA 01260. *Mailing Add:* 299 Village St Millis MA 02054

DONOHOE, VICTORIA
HISTORIAN, CRITIC
b Philadelphia, Pa. *Study:* Rosemont Col, BA; Univ Pa Grad Sch Fine Arts, MFA; Pius XII Inst Fine Arts Advan Study, Florence, Italy, cert(scholar), 53; Am Fedn Arts Workshop Art Criticism, scholar(with Max Kozloff), 68. *Hon Degrees:* Villanova Univ, PhD (fine arts). *Collection Arranged:* Religious & Liturgical Art from the Eastern US, Philadelphia Civic Ctr, 63. *Pos:* Art critic, Standard & Times, Philadelphia, 59-62; art critic, Philadelphia Inquirer, 62-; guest cur, Into Storage Exhib, Univ Mus, Univ Pa, 74; corresp, Art News, 75-; dir for selection, Exhib Liturgical Art, 41st Int Eucharistic Cong, Philadelphia, 76 (for this exhib chose artists for 25 commissioned works); adv, Philadelphia Craft Show, 77; adv fac, Franklin & Marshall Col, 79; mem comt, Nat Millennium Scared Art Project. *Teaching:* Lab asst studio art & art hist, Rosemont Col, 50-52, lectr, 54-55. *Awards:* Award, Catholic Fine Arts Soc, 76. *Mem:* Int Asn Art Critics/Am Sect; Soc Archit Historians; Irish Georgian Soc, Dublin; Medieval Acad Am; Am-Italy Soc. *Res:* Late 19th & early 20th century American sculpture; figurative painting & sculpture; contemporary crafts; American architecture. *Publ:* Contribr, Sculpture of a City: Philadelphia's Treasures in Bronze and Stone, 74; contribr, Knight-Ridder Newswire, 73-; also contribr to anthologies, mags, encyclopedias & Sunday supplements; contribr, Invisible Philadelphia: Community Through Voluntary Organizations, 95; contribr, From Style to Program: Evolution of Taste and Aesthetics in Liturgical Art from the Mid-19th Century to the Post-World War II Era, Stained Galss in Catholic Phila, 2002. *Mailing Add:* 34 Narbrook Park Narberth PA 19072-2124

DOO DA POST, EDWARD FERDINAND HIGGINS III
PAINTER, MAIL ARTIST
b LaCrosse, Wis, Nov 10, 59. *Study:* Western Mich Univ, Kalamazoo, BA(art), 72; Univ Colo, Boulder, MFA, 76. *Work:* Electroworks Collection, Eastman House, Rochester, NY; US Post Off, Boulder, Colo; Univ Mich, Ann Arbor; Artists Stamps & Stamp Images, Simon Frasier Univ Gallery, Burnaby, BC; Jean Brown Arch, Shaker Seed House, Tryingham, Mass; Swiss Postal Mus, Bern, Switz; and others. *Comn:* Business Face Issue (portrait), Paul Schorr; portrait & sheets, Doo Da Stamps of Portrait, Sue Blair. *Exhib:* Fourteenth Midwest Joslyn Art Mus, Omaha, Nebr, 76; Timbres, Et Tampons, E' Artistes Cabnet des Extampes, Mus d'Art & d'Histoire, Geneva, Switz, 76; 4th Denver Metro Show, Denver Art Mus, 76; 6th New York City Doo Da Art Show & Auction, XOXO Gallery, NY, 94; Stamp Art Gallery, San Francisco, 96; Baby Jakes, NY, 96; and others. *Collection Arranged:* First New York City Stamp Invite (auth, catalog), 34 Artists' Stamp Images, 77; Commonpress Number 18 (auth, catalog), 79; Third Int Doo Da Stamp Invite (catalog in prep), 384 Artists stamps. *Pos:* 3rd Grand Poo Ba, Order Triangle-Glue (sea tech # 5). *Teaching:* Prof painting, Rivington Sch Artists, NY; prof, Elberta Sch Art, Elberta, Mich. *Awards:* CT Chew Schwendelmarken Rug Award, 96. *Bibliog:* Peter Frank (auth), Artists Stamps, Art Express 1, Vol 1, 81; Alexandra Anderson (auth), Portfolio 3, Vol 3, 5-6/81; Ronnie Cohen (auth), article, Art News, 12/81. *Mem:* Rivington Sch; Knights Templar Carver Rubber-Eraser Division. *Media:* Acrylic, Color Xerox. *Publ:* Auth & illusr, To Grow an Asparagus (under pen name Sam Scotland), 70, & A Piece of Licorice and Other White Elephants, 72, Glotco; contribr, The Rubber Stamp Album, Workman Publ, 78; auth, Artists' stamps, Print Collectors' Newslett, 11-12/79; Artistamp News, Vancouver, BC, Can, vol 1 No 2, 8/92; The 3rd International Doo Da Stamp Invite, 2000. *Dealer:* Gracie Mansion Gallery New York City. *Mailing Add:* 153 Ludlow St New York NY 10002-2241

DOOGAN, BAILEY
PAINTER, INSTRUCTOR
b Philadelphia, Pa, Oct 24, 41. *Study:* Moore Col of Art, Pa, BFA, 63; UCLA, MA, 77. *Work:* Tucson Mus Art; Univ of Ariz Mus Art; Ariz State Univ Art Mus, Nelson Fine Arts Ctr, Tempe; Pensacola Jr Col, Fla; Annaghmakerrig, Tyrone Guthrie Ctr, Co Monagham, Ireland. *Exhib:* Phoenix Triennial, Phoenix Art Mus, Ariz, 90; Original Sin, Hillwood Mus Long Island Univ, 91; Mea Corpa Artists of Conscience Series, Alternative Mus, NY, 92; Int Critics Choice, Mitchell Mus, Ill, 93; Signs of Age: Representing the Older Body, Santa Barbara Contemp Art Forum, Calif, 97-98; Theatre of Self Invention: Self Portrature in Contempory Art, Speed Art Mus, Ky, 98; A Survey of Drawings 1988-98, Univ Ariz Mus of Art, 98; Picturing the Modern Amazon, The New Mus Contemp Art, NY, 2000. *Pos:* prof painting/drawing, Univ Ariz, 82-99, prof emerita, 99-. *Teaching:* visiting prof painting/drawing, Univ Nevada, 92. *Awards:* Fel in Painting Nat Endowment for the Arts, 96; Ariz Arts Award Southern Ariz Community Found, 96; Contemp Forum Grant Phoenix Art Mus, 98. *Bibliog:* Ann Wilson Lloyd (auth) Report from Tucson: The New West, Art in Am, 10/92; Joanna Frueh, Arlene Raven Langer (auths), New Feminist Criticism: Art Identity Action, Harper Collins, 93; Joanna Frueh (auth) Erotic Faculties, Univ Calif Press, 96. *Mem:* Col Art Asn (bd dir national 97-). *Media:* Oil. *Publ:* contribr Conversation: Picturing the Modern Amazon, Art Journal, 2000. *Dealer:* Etherton Gallery 135 South 6th Ave Tucson Ariz 85701. *Mailing Add:* 521 E 2nd St Tucson AZ 85705

DOOLEY, DAVID I
PAINTER, EDUCATOR
b Olney, Ill, Jan 15, 40. *Study:* Eastern Ill Univ, BS, 68, MS, 72; Univ Ill, post grad, 79; Am Acad Art, Chicago, 80. *Work:* Citizens Bank Collection, Evansville, Ind; George Koch Sons Inc, Evansville, Ind; Dining Oil Collection, Lawrenceville, Ill; Bristol-Myers Squibb Co, Evansville, Ind. *Comn:* Point of Purchase (illus), Berol, Brentwood, Tenn, 93. *Exhib:* Wabash Valley Exhib, Sheldon Swope Art Mus, Terre Haute, Ind, 84-94; Realism Today, Evansville Mus Arts, Ind, 84-92; Masters of Colored Pencil Nat, Massey Fine Arts, Santa Teresa, NMex, 93; New Harmony Gallery Contemp Art, Ind, 94; Lana Competition Exhib, Campbell-Thiebaud Gallery, San Francisco, Calif, 94. *Teaching:* Prof art drawing, Vincennes Univ, Ind, 82-94; workshop instr mixed media, Discover Art, San Diego, Calif, 92-94 & Nat Art Mat & Trade, 92-94. *Awards:* Purchase Award, Realism Today, Bristol-Meyers Squibb, 87; Third Place, Masters Colored Pencil Nat, Massey Fine Arts, 92; Purchase Award, Border to Border, Larson Biennial Nat Drawing, 93. *Bibliog:* Doris Replogle Porter (auth), Illinois artist David Dooley, Ill Mag, 88; Stephen Doherty (dir), Reflections of Excellence (video), 92; Sandra Angelo (dir), Special Effects with Colored Pencils (video), 94. *Media:* Colored Pencil. *Publ:* Coauth, Isolated in the Absurd, Prairie Press Publ Co, 69; auth, Applying colored pencil over an acrylic wash, Am Artist, 89; contribr, Colored Pencil Basics, Walter Foster & Co, 94; Painting with colored pencils, Artist's Mag, 7/94; Colored-pencil artists get it together, Am Artist, 94. *Mailing Add:* RR 3 Box 384 Lawrenceville IL 62439

DOOLEY WALLER, M L
PAINTER
b Kansas City, Mo, Mar 20, 1936. *Study:* Rockhurst Col, Kansas City, Mo, 57; Kansas City Art Inst & Sch Design, BFA, 58; Univ Kans, MFA candidate, 71; Univ Mich, MFA, 82 (scholar Sch Art, 80). *Work:* Mem Art Gallery, Rochester, NY; Indianapolis Mus Art; Morris Mus, Morristown, NJ; Arthur Anderson, Rochester, NY; Bank One, Indianapolis; Lilly Research Clinic, Indiana Univ Hospital, Indianapolis; and many others. *Comn:* Lilly Research Clinic, Ind Univ Hosp, Indianapolis; nine oil painting, pvt comn. *Exhib:* Solo exhibs, Inman Page Libr, Jefferson City, Mo, 55, Contemp Art Gallery, Kansas City, Mo, 58, Central Col, Fayette, Mo, 58, Rockhurst Col, Kansas City, Mo, 58, Kans City Art Inst & Sch Design, 58, Rackham Gallery, Univ Mich, 80, Shahin Requicha Gallery, Rochester, NY, 82, 84 & 85, Rush Rhees Gallery, Univ Rochester, 85, Ruschman Gallery, Indianapolis, 93, 98 & 2004, Ind Univ E, Richmond, 96; LA Art, Los Angeles, Calif, 92; Ruschman Gallery, Indianapolis, 92-2005; The Graphics Generation 1940-1965, Indianapolis Mus Art, 93; The Act of Painting, Mem Art Gallery, Rochester, NY, 98; Collectors Vision: Selections from Collection of Edmund Pease & Nurak Israsena, Morris Mus, Morristown, NJ, 2000; Whispers to Shouts, Ind State Mus, Indianapolis, 2005; and many others. *Pos:* Bd mem, Friends of Herron, Herron Sch Art, 97, 98-99; selection comt mem, Contemp Art Soc, Indianapolis Mus Art, 97-98; juror, Arts Ind Postcard Series 15, 94, Circle Ctr Painting Project, Symphony in Color, Indpls Symphony Orch, 94 & Herron Sch Art Sr Show, 2000. *Teaching:* Instr two dimensional design, Univ Mich Sch Art, 79-80; instr painting, Univ Rochester, NY, 85, Kansas City Mus, St Teresa's Acad, Plus X Sch, Kansas City, 58-59. *Awards:* Honorable Mention, Midwest Biennial Exhib, Joslyn Art Mus, Omaha, Nebr, 58 & 8th Mid Am Ann Exhib, Nelson-Atkins Mus, Kansas City, Mo, 58; Margaret Allen Barnett Award, 1958; Diane Waldman Juror's Special Mention, Nat Midyear Exhib, Butler Inst Am Art, 83; and others. *Bibliog:* National Midyear Exhib 1983 (exhib catalog), Butler Inst Am Art, Youngstown, OH; Robert C Morgan, Art Review, Democrat & Chronicle, Rochester, NY, 84; Visions Magazine Art Quarterly, LA Artcore, Los Angeles, 92; Rachel Berencon Perry, (auth), Whispers to Shouts: Indian Women who Create Art (exhib catalog), Indiana State Mus, 2005. *Mem:* Contemp Art Soc; Friends of Herron Sch Art, Indianapolis, Ind (bd mem, 97-); Nat Mus Women Arts; Indianapolis Mus Art. *Media:* Oil, Miscellaneous Media. *Publ:* auth, Nat Midyear Exhib (exhib catalog), Butler Inst Am Art, Youngstown, Ohio, 83; auth, The Graphics Generation: Am Abstract Prints (exhib catalog), Indianapolis Mus Art, 93. *Dealer:* Ruschman Gallery 946 N Alabama Indianapolis Ind 46205. *Mailing Add:* 4035 N Pennsylvania Indianapolis IN 46205

DORAY, AUDREY CAPEL
PAINTER
b Montreal, Que, June 4, 31. *Study:* McGill Univ, Montreal,with John Lyman & Arthur Lismer, BFA, 52; Atelier 17, with SW Hayter, Paris, France,56. *Comn:* Electronic mural, Mazda Motors, Vancouver, BC, 73; two paintings, Mandarin Hotel, Vancouver, 84. *Exhib:* Solo exhib, Vancouver Art Gallery, 61; Nat Art Gallery, Ottawa, Ont, 66; Intermedia Nights, 68 & Inaugural Show, 83, Vancouver Art Gallery; Vancouver Print Show, Heidelberg, Ger, 69; Mus Contemp Crafts, NY, 72; Arteder '82, Bilbao, Spain, 82. *Teaching:* Instr painting & graphics, Vancouver Art Sch, 59-62. *Awards:* Bursary Award, Can Coun, 68-70. *Bibliog:* Tony Emery (auth), The Vancouver explosion, Art Int, 10/68; Michael Rhodes (auth), Audrey Capel Doray, Arts Can, 12/68; Doris Shadbolt (auth), Canadian Art Today, Studio Int, 70. *Media:* Acrylic on Canvas, Paper. *Dealer:* Bau Xi Gallery 3045 Granville St Vancouver BC V6H 3J9 Canada. *Mailing Add:* 4441 W First Ave Vancouver BC V6R 4H9 Canada

DOREMUS, SUSANNE
EDUCATOR
Study: Elmira Col, BA, 65, Univ Wis-Madison, MFA, 68. *Exhib:* Zolla/Lieberman Gallery, Chicago; Bill Maynes Gallery, NY; Mus Contemp Art, Chicago; The Drawing Center, NY; Art Inst Chicago; Nat Acad Mus, NY 2006; represented in permanent collections of Chase Manhattan Bank, NY, NIU Art Mus, DeKalb, Mus Contemp Art, Chicago, and Yale Univ Art Mus. *Collection Arranged:* Chase Manhattan Bank, NY; Northern Ill Univ, DeKalb; Mus Contemp Art, Chicago; Yale Univ Art Mus, Conn. *Teaching:* Prof, chair painting & drawing, Sch Art Inst Chicago, 93-. *Awards:* Nat Educ Asn grant; Ill Arts Coun fel. *Bibliog:* Artforum, Art in Am, NY Times. *Mailing Add:* Sch Art Inst Chicago 37 S Wabash Chicago IL 60603

DOREN, HENRY J T
PAINTER, EDUCATOR
b New York, NY, May 20, 29. *Study:* Sch Educ, NY Univ, BS, 48; Fac Arts, Ottawa Univ, MA, 59; Art Students League, 59-62; Frank Reilly Sch Art, New York, 62-64; Inst Allende, Univ Guanajuato, San Miguel de Allende, Mexico, MFA, 65. *Work:* Mother and Child, Polish Mother's Hosp Gallery, Lodz, Poland; Environment & 20th

Century Man, Dom Polonii Mus, Pultusk Castle, Poland; Consulate Repub Poland, 91; US Collections of former US Sen Bradley & Gov Byrne, NJ. *Comn:* Portrait, comn by Prof W Wagner, 94. *Exhib:* showcase, Theatre Gallery, Montclair State Col, NJ, 83; Riker Hill Artists, Schering-Plough Gallery, Madison, NJ, 88; Polish-Am Artists, Galleria del Arte, Petroleas Mexicana, Mexico City, 89; Nabisco Gallery, 96; Art Teachers NJ, Monmouth Mus, 96. *Pos:* Ed, PS Arts, Co Col of Morris Libr, Randolph, NJ, 76-83; ed & publ, NJ Artform, 79-83. *Teaching:* Assoc prof art, Co Col of Morris, Randolph, NJ, 68-83. *Awards:* First Prize, Westfield Art Asn, 69; Fulbright Comn, Madrid, Spain, 71; Exchange Scholar Grant, Polish Acad Sci, Warsaw, 74-75. *Bibliog:* Ester Singer (auth), Doren show is forceful, Jersey J, 12/4/71; Dr W Carl Burger (auth), Doren, the humanist view, NJ Artform; Madison artist honored, Independent Press, 12/89. *Mem:* Life mem Art Students League, NY. *Media:* Acrylic, Oil. *Publ:* Contribr, NJ Music & Art Mag, 70-71; auth, Tresures of Polish Art, Interpress, Warsaw, Poland, 76. *Mailing Add:* 4822 E Water St Tucson AZ 85712

DORETHY, REX E
ADMINISTRATOR, EDUCATOR
b Macomb, Ill, Mar 14, 38. *Study:* Ill State Univ, MS, 65, PhD, 72; Univ Ill, PostGrad, 68. *Pos:* Faculty & head dept, Art Ball State Univ, 72-84; chair dept of art/design, Univ Wis, 84-92; asst to dean, Coll Fine Arts, Univ Wis, 92-. *Teaching:* Asst prof, Art Educ, Ill State Univ, 67-72; prof, Ball State Univ, Muncie, Ind, 72-84; prof art, Univ Wis, Stevens Point, 84-. *Mem:* Nat Art Educ Asn; Wis Art Educ Asn; Nat Arts Policy Coun; Col Arts Asn. *Publ:* Auth, Teacher Action-Student Response, 70 & Motion Parallax in Spatial Abilities of Young Chile, Studies Art Educ, 78; coauth, Mental Function, Perceptual Differences, Achievement in Art, Studies Art Educ, 78; auth, Research Priorities in Visual Arts Educ, Rev Res Visual Arts, 81; Questions/Positions Concerning the Gifted in Art, Viewpoints: Art Educ, 83. *Mailing Add:* 124 Maple Bluff Rd Stevens Point WI 54481-8441

DORFMAN, BRUCE
PAINTER, ASSEMBLAGE ARTIST, INSTR (STUDIO/ART SCH)
b New York, NY, Aug 15, 36. *Study:* Art Students League, with Yasuo Kuniyoshi, Arnold Blanch, Charles H Alston; Univ Iowa, with Mauricio Lasansky, Stuart Edie, BS, 58. *Work:* Butler Inst Am Art, Youngstown, Ohio; Skirball Mus, Los Angeles; Carnegie Mus, Pittsburgh, Pa; Rockefeller Found, NY; Govt Israel; Smithsonian Inst, Washington, DC; Sewall Gallery, Rice Univ, Houston, Tex; Everson Mus, Syracuse, NY; McNay Mus, Houston, Tex; Arco Collection, Los Angeles, Calif; Mus of Loule, Loule, Portugal and others. *Comn:* Rockefeller Found, 79; mural, Dutchess Co Art Asn, NY State Coun on the Arts, 80; Stedman Collection, Houston, Tex, 88; Gov Monaco, Permanent Mission United Nations, 96. *Exhib:* Norton Mus Art, W Palm Beach, Fla, 62; NY World's Fair Invitational, 64; Butler Inst Am Art, 71-72 & 75; Arras Gallery, NY, 82, 86 & 88; Albright-Knox Art Gallery, Buffalo, NY, 87-88; Hunter Mus, Tenn, 87-88; Addison-Ripley Gallery, Washington, 90 & 94; Mus des Beaux-Arts, Mons, Belg, 94; Hal Katzen Gallery, NY, 94; Bergen Mus, NJ, 95; Korean Cult Ctr, NY, 95; JJ Brookings Gallery, San Francisco, Calif, 1998-99; The Reece Galleries, NY, 99, 2001; Process, Art Students League of NY, 2003; Kouros Gallery, NY, 2003, 2005; Gallerie Dionisi, Los Angeles, Calif, 2004-2004. *Collection Arranged:* Korea in America (6 Korean Artists), Art Ctr, North NJ, 88. *Pos:* Artists Talk On Art, Panel Moderator, NY, 91; lectr, Pompidou Ctr, Musee D'Orsay, Musee Picasso and L'Orangerie, Paris, France, 94; trustee, Am Fine Arts Soc, Art Students League, NY; chair, Forum Series, Art Students League, NY, 97-98. *Teaching:* Fac, Art Students League NY, 64-; guest artist, Norton Mus, WPalm Beach, Fla, 62-64, Schenectady Mus, 65-66, Everson Mus, Syracuse, NY, 72; resident artist, Syracuse Univ, 71; mem fac, New Sch Soc Res, NY, 79-95 & Art Ctr Northern NJ, 82-96; Master Class, NY, 80-94; Int Sch Art, Loule, Portugal, 93; Guest artist, Instituto de Arte Frederico Brandt, Caracas, Venezuela, 96. *Awards:* Fulbright Fel, 61; New York World's Fair Exhib Award, 64; Purchase Award, Butler Inst of Am Art, 72; Arts East Found Individual Grant, 88 & 90; The Artists Fel Inc individual Grant, NY, NY, 2004. *Bibliog:* Lois Katz (auth) Exhib Catalog Text, Nightsongs and Placefields, 89; Ingrid Periz (auth), article, ARTnews, 7/2001; Gerrit Henry (auth), article, Art in Am, 5/2000; Phyllis Braff, New York Times, 8/1999; N Berkowitz (auth), The NJ Commuter, 2003; Jonathan Goodman (auth), Exhib Catalog Text, NY Times, 2005. *Mem:* Life mem Art Students League; Fedn Mod Painters & Sculptors. *Media:* All Media. *Collection:* Smithsonian Inst, Wash, DC; Butler Inst of Am Art, Youngstown, OH; Atelier Mourlot, Paris, FR; Loule Mus, Loule, Port; Searle Collection, Chicago, ILL; Everson Mus, Syracuse, NY; Rockefeller Found, NY; others. *Publ:* Color Mixing, Grosset & Dunlap, 67. *Dealer:* Kouros Gallery, 23 E 73 St New York NY 10021; Roseline Koener Gallery, Westhampton NY 11978; Broadhurst Gallery, Pinehurst, NL. *Mailing Add:* 355 West 85 St #45 New York NY 10024

DORFMAN, ELISSA
PAINTER, PRINTMAKER, SCULPTOR
b Brooklyn, NY, May 12, 50. *Study:* CUNY, 69 71, Brooklyn Mus Art Sch, with I Soyer, 69-72; Art Students League, with John Havannes & I Soyer 70-72, Pratt Graphic Ctr, 72, New Sch Social Res & Parsons, with Robert Conover, 76-79. *Exhib:* One-man show, Collector's Gallery, NY, 79, Galerie Raymond Duncan, Paris, 79, Univ Md, 80, Art Space Gallery, Hyogo, Japan, 82 & Galler Fuji, Osaka, Japan, 82, Ny Carlsberg Glyptotek Mus, Copenhagen, Denmark, JustOriginals.com Artist Directory, 99-2000, Galeria d'Art Zero, Barcelona, Spain, 2002, Vanderbilt Mus (Planetarium), NY, 2006, Museo del Banco Central del Equador, 2006, Iowa Biennial Exhib, 2006; Salon des Surindependents, Musee de Luxembourg, Paris, 80; Int Graphic Arts Exhib (auth, catalog), Feria Int de Muestres, Bilbao, Spain, 82; Cabo Frio Int Print Biennial, Brazil, 83; group show, Tokyo Mus, 83, Mills Pond House Gallery, St James, NY, 94 & 97; The Sharjah Arts Mus, United Arab Emirates, 00; Celebrity Art Auction, Ireland, 00; Galeria d'Art Zero, Barcelona, 2002; London Biennale 2002, 291 Gallery, London; and numerous others. *Awards:* Soc of Arts Acad Award, 2001; Fine Arts Award, Art Domain.Ibiza, 2001; Digital Color Artists Award, Digital Consciousness, 2001. *Bibliog:* Olga Lomelin (auth), The Agenda, Del Arte, 1996; Mantle Fielding's Dictionary of Am Painters, Sculptors & Engravers, 2001; Artprice Intl Art Market Directory, 2003; Davenport's Art Reference, 2003. *Mem:* Artists Equity; Visual Artists and Galleries Asn; Art Students League (life); Nat Mus Women in the Arts; Soc of Arts Acad UK. *Media:* Oil. *Collection:* Autograph Mus, Poland, 2003. *Publ:* Contribr, A Personal Journal with Quotes & Art by Women, Running Press, 92; How to Program Well (cover), Richard De Irwin, 92; Computer Systems Architecture, Organization & Programming (cover), 92. *Dealer:* Karel Stoop Galeria D'Art Zero Cap de Mon 6 Barcelona Spain (affiliated with gallery). *Mailing Add:* 345 East 81 St No 18E New York NY 10028

DORFMAN, ELSA
PHOTOGRAPHER, WRITER
b Apr 26, 37. *Study:* Tufts Univ, Medford, BA, 59; Boston Col, Chestnut Hill, Mass, MEd, 62. *Work:* Portland Mus Art, Maine; Wellesley Col, Mass; Mus Fine Arts, Boston; San Francisco Mus Art, Calif; Princeton Univ, NJ; Fogg Art Mus-Harvard Univ. *Comn:* numerous, 80-2003. *Exhib:* Portraits of Women, Everson Mus, Syracuse, NY, 73; Women of Photog, San Francisco Mus Art, Calif, 75; Boston Artists, Boston Mus Fine Arts, 78 & 81 & 90; Boston Now, Inst Contemp Art, Boston, 83; Self Portraits, Zurich Art Mus, Switz, 85 & Lausanne Art Mus, Switz, 85; Am Photog, Fogg Mus, 86; Decordova Mus, 2000. *Pos:* Portrait photogr at own studio in Cambridge, Mass, currently. *Teaching:* Lectr at various US universities & cols. *Awards:* Bunting Fel, Radcliffe Col, 74. *Mem:* Am Civil Liberties Union. *Media:* Portraits. *Interests:* Rare Polaroid 20x24. *Publ:* Auth, Elsa's Housebook, Godine, 74; article, Womens Rev Books, Wellesley Col, 85-90; article, Views, Photog Resource Ctr; article, Famille Granary Press, 99; En Fanukke, Nohairday, 2003. *Mailing Add:* 607 Franklin St Cambridge MA 02139

DORFMAN, FRED
ART DEALER, GALLERY DIRECTOR
b Chicago, Ill, Feb 19, 46. *Study:* Am Univ, 69; Chicago Art Inst, 71-72. *Pos:* Owner, Dorfman Gallery, currently. *Mem:* Visual Artist & Gallery Asn; Int Art Dealers Asn. *Media:* Paintings, Sculptors. *Specialty:* International contemporary art; sculpture, drawings, paintings, multiples and graphics. *Publ:* Article, New York Arts J, 79. *Mailing Add:* 529 W 20th St New York NY 10011

DORFMAN, GEOFFREY
PAINTER, WRITER, MUSICIAN
Study: Cooper Union, BFA; Syracuse Univ, MFA. *Work:* painting, Tree of Life (Henry Ward Ranger Purchase award, Nat Acad). *Exhib:* Nat Acad Mus, NY City, 2006; concerts and recitals at Weill Hall at Carnegie Hall, Columbia Univ, Westminster Choir Col, Stevens Inst Tech, Marlborough Summer Festival, England, 97. *Teaching:* Assoc prof painting, drawing, modern culture CUNY Col Staten Island, 78-; vis asst prof art Dartmouth Col, 2000. *Awards:* Individual Fellowship Grant, Nat Educ Asn, 78. *Mailing Add:* 232 Mercer St Trenton NJ 08690-1406

DORN, PETER KLAUS
DESIGNER, GRAPHIC ARTIST
b Berlin, Ger, June 30, 32; Can citizen. *Study:* Journeyman compositor, Berlin; Ont Col Art, Toronto; Hochschule für Grafik & Buch Kunst, Leipzig. *Hon Degrees:* Distinguished Service Award, Queens Univ. *Work:* Toronto Pub Libr Fine Arts Sect; Douglas Libr, Special Collections, Kingston; Massey Col, Toronto; Carlton Univ Art Gallery, Ottawa. *Comn:* 200 Anniversary Commemorative Postage Stamp, New Brunswick; Canada, XIII Biennale di Venecia (catalogue), 86. *Exhib:* Royal Can Acad, 70; Agnes Etherington Art Ctr, Kingston, 71; Look of Books, 74, 76 & 77; Design Can, 75; Spectrum Can, 76; Group Exhib, Toronto, 79; and others. *Pos:* Proprietor, Heinrich Heine Press, Toronto, 63; typographer, Univ Toronto Press, 66-71; dir, Graphic Design Unit, Queen's Univ, 71-95, pres, 96-; dir, Graphic Serv, King Abdulaziz Univ, Camberley, Eng, 82-83. *Teaching:* Teaching master typography, St Lawrence Col, Kingston, 78-; guest lectr, NS Col Art & Design, Univ Man, Sheridan Col, 80. *Awards:* Awards, Ont Asn Art Galleries, 80-83; Awards, Am Inst Graphic Arts, 80 & 83; Distinguished Serv Award, Queen's Univ, 91; Ont Volunteer Serv Award, 2006. *Bibliog:* Applied Arts Quart, Vol 3, No 1, spring 88. *Mem:* Royal Can Acad; Guild Hand Printers (dir); fel Graphic Designers Can (nat past pres, Kingston past pres); Am Inst Graphic Arts; Pittsburgh Hist Soc (exec). *Media:* Typography/Letterpress Printing. *Publ:* DA, A Journal of Painting Arts, Vol 55, pg 57-60. *Mailing Add:* Graphic Design 2924 Hwy 2 Kingston ON K7L 5H6 Canada

DOROSH, DARIA
PAINTER, SCULPTOR
b Ukraine, Mar 21, 1943; US citizen. *Study:* Fashion Inst Technol, AAS, 63; Cooper-Union Sch Art & Archit, cert, 68. *Work:* Libr Cong, Washington, DC. *Exhib:* Purchase Fund Exhib, Am Acad Arts & Letts, NY, 73; New Art II: Textures and Surfaces, Mus Mod Art, NY, 81; AIR Group, Kunsthalle, Lund, Sweden, 81; Patterns, San Jose Inst Contemp Art, Calif, 81; Photo Start, Bronx Mus, NY, 82; Homeless at Home, Storefront for Art Archit, NY, 86; Competition Diomede, Clocktower Gallery, NY, 89. *Teaching:* Prof fashion design portfolio, Fashion Inst Technol, 69-; instr painting, Parsons Sch Design, New York, 76-85. *Awards:* Nat Endowment Arts Grant, 86; NY State Coun Arts Grant, 88. *Bibliog:* Patricia Phillips (auth), review, Art Forum, 5/84; N F Karlins (auth), Tribeca sidwalk sculpture gets Soho Gallery preview, Battery News, 4/88. *Media:* Mixed Media, Computer Arts. *Publ:* Auth, Art And Context: A Personal View, Leonardo J Int Soc Arts, Sci & Technol, Pergmamon Press, 88

DORRIEN, CARLOS GUILLERMO
SCULPTOR

b Buenos Aires, Arg, Oct 8, 48; US citizen. *Study:* Univ de la Plata, Arg, 67; Lowell Technol Inst, Mass; Montserrat Sch Visual Art, Mass, BFA, 73. *Work:* Bentley Col, Waltham, Mass; John Hancock Insurance Co, Boston; Mus 20th Century, Medellin, Colombia. *Comn:* Portal (sculpture), Bentley Col, Waltham, Mass, 78; Cutting Object (marble), City Medellin, Colombia,81; Granite Ribbon, Mass Transit Authority, Porter Sq Sta, Cambridge, Mass, 82. *Exhib:* Arts on the Line, Hayden Gallery, Mass Inst Technol, Cambridge, 79; Art in Pub Places, Carpenter Ctr, Harvard Univ, Cambridge, Mass, 80; Biennial Art Medellin, Colombia, 81; Mus 20th Century, Colombia, 81; Brocton Art Mus Trienial, Mass, 83. *Pos:* Guest sculptor, City Medellin, Colombia, 81. *Teaching:* Lectr, Sch Mus Fine Arts, Boston, 80-81; instr sculpture, Art Inst Boston, 82-86. *Awards:* Traveling Grant, Partners Am, 81; Purchase Award, IV Biennial Art Medellin, Colombia, 81; WBZ-TV Fund for the Arts Grant, 83. *Bibliog:* Mary Sullivan (auth), Carlos Dorrien: An interview, Back Bay View, Vol 3, 78; Gerald Ryan (auth), Sculptures for business, Boston Today, 9/79. *Media:* Granite, Bronze. *Dealer:* Clark Gallery Lincoln Sta Lincoln MA 01773. *Mailing Add:* 156 Weston Rd Wellesley MA 02181-5727

DORSEY, DEBORAH WORTHINGTON
PAINTER

b Alexandria, Va. *Study:* Radcliffe, BA; Columbia Univ, MA MPhil; Nat Acad Sch Design. *Work:* Commerce Bank NJ; Pfizer; Pew Charitable Found; Johnson & Johnson, NJ; Merrill Lynch. *Exhib:* Invitational Exhibition Former Prize Winners, Nat Arts Club, NY, 78; Adirondack Nat Exhib Am Watercolors, Community Arts Ctr, Old Forge, NY, 82; Am Watercolor Soc, Nat Acad Design & Salmagundi, NY, 82 & 88; one-man shows, Philadelphia Art Alliance, Pa, 89, Brownstone Gallery, NY, 93, Adobe Gallery, Edgewater, NJ, 95 & Educ Testing Serv, Princeton, NJ, 95; Magenta Gallery, Princeton, NJ, 91; Newman Gallery, Philadelphia, 92; For Us and About Us, Nat Asn Women Artists, ARC Gallery, Chicago, 92; Three Rivers Arts Festival, Pittsburgh, 1996, 98 & 2001; Audubon Artists, 1997, 99, 2001. *Pos:* Art researcher, Time Life Films, 70-73; art critic, Art News, 71-72; writer, Filmstrip House, 1974-75. *Teaching:* Adj prof art hist & painting, CW Post & Long Island Univ, 74-78 & 82; instr drawing, State Univ NY-New Paltz, 82-83; instr portrait painting, Craft Students League, New York, 83-85. *Awards:* First Prize, 83 & Portrait Prize, 87, Ann Mem Exhib, Nat Arts Club, NY; Mem Award Portrait, Nat Asn Women Artists, Elizabeth Stanton Blake, 90; Solveig Stromsoe Palmer Award, Nat Asn Women Artists, 1996, 99, 2003; Elias Newman Mem Award, Audubon Artists, 99. *Bibliog:* Cathy Viksjo (auth), Magenta Art Gallery a gem, Trenton Times, 3/4/90; Eileen Watkins (auth), Exploring new dimensions, Newark Star Ledger, 4/14/95; Biographical Encyclopedia of American Painters, Sculptors and Engr, Dealers Choice Books. *Mem:* Nat Asn Women Artists; Audubon Artists. *Media:* Watercolor, Oil. *Publ:* Draw like Seurat, Artist's Mag, 2/96; Giving life to your landscapes, Artist's Mag, 2/99. *Dealer:* Sales & Rental Gallery Philadelphia Mus Art PA; DSA Fine Arts Beacon NY; Windham Fine Arts Windham NY. *Mailing Add:* 156 E 74th St New York NY 10021

DORSEY, MICHAEL A
PAINTER, ADMINISTRATOR

b Findlay, Ohio, July 31, 49. *Study:* Eastern Ill Univ, BS, 71; Bowling Green State Univ, MA 72, MFA, 73. *Work:* Miss Mus Art, Jackson; Meridian Mus Art, Miss; Cotton Landia Mus Art, Greenwood, Miss; Southeast Ark Arts & Sci Ctr, Pine Bluff, Ark; Bowling Green State Univ, Ohio; Univ Perugia, Italy; Burroughs Wellcome Company, NC; plus numerous public & pvt collections in USA, Wales, Japan, France & Scotland. *Comn:* East Carolina Univ. *Exhib:* 17th Ann Piedmont Graphics, Greenville Mus Art, SC, 81; Of On & About Paper, Columbia Mus Art & Sci, SC, 82; SPAR Nat, Barwell Art Ctr, Shreveport, La, 83; 26th Ann Delta Exhib, Ark Art Ctr, Little Rock, 84; 19th Ann Nat Exhib, Coos Art Mus, Coos Bay, Ore, 84; 9th Ann Nat Southern Watercolor Soc, Miss Mus Art, Jackson, 85; Nat Ark Exhib, Ark Arts & Sci Ctr, Pine Bluff, 85; Artists Who Teach, Fed Reserve Bldg, Washington, DC, 87; solo exhibs, Swope Art Mus, Terre Haute, In, 89, Hinds Jr Col, Jackson, Miss, 90, Albers Art Gallery, Memphis, Tenn, 90, Miss State Univ, 92, East Carolina Univ, 93 & Greenville Mus Art, 94. *Collection Arranged:* guest curator, Watercolors from the Permanent Collection, Greenville Mus Art, NC. *Teaching:* Dean & prof art, Sch Art & Design, East Carolina Univ, 91-; assoc prof & dept head, Miss State Univ, 82-86, prof & dept head, 86-91. *Awards:* Outstanding Alumni, Bowling Green State Univ, 89; Outstanding Art Alumni, Eastern Ill Univ, 92; Best in Show Award, Nat Dimensions Exhib, Winston-Salem, NC, 93. *Bibliog:* Paul Grootkerk (auth), The beauty parlor mirror, J Am Cult, 88 & Historical permanence of Fantastic, 89; Michael Duffy (auth), The Beauty Salon Series, Greenville Mus Art, NC, 2005. *Mem:* Col Art Asn; Miss Watercolor Soc (pres, 86-88); Nat Art Educ Asn; Miss Art Asn; NC Watercolor Soc. *Media:* Mixed Media, Drawing. *Interests:* History & film. *Dealer:* Nicholas Dorsey, St. Petersburg, Fla. *Mailing Add:* East Carolina Univ Sch Art Greenville NC 27858-4353

DORSKY, NATHANIEL
FILMMAKER

b New York, NY, 43. *Study:* Antioch Col, 61. *Comn:* Ctr Georges Pompidou, France; archives in Japan, Australia, France, Holland & Can. *Pos:* Ed & camera person, film ind. *Teaching:* Instr, Univ Calif, Berkely & Stanford Univ. *Awards:* Emmy Award, Gauguion in Tahiti, 68; Guggenheim Fel, 97; 3 Grants, Nat Endowment Arts; Best Documentary New Spirit Award, 2000. *Bibliog:* rev, NY Times, 97 & 98. *Publ:* Triste (film), 74-76; Alaga (film), 74-76; Ariel (film), 83; 17 Reasons Why (film), 85-87; Variation (film), 92-98; ed, Arborzitae, Night Waltz: The Music of Paul Bowles. *Mailing Add:* 751 1/2 16th Ave San Francisco CA 94118

DORST, CLAIRE V
PAINTER, PRINTMAKER

b Plymouth, Wis, June 4, 22. *Study:* Beloit Col, BA, 49; Univ Iowa, MA, 53; Univ Wis-Madison, United Lutheran Church Am Scholar, 62-63, MFA, 63. *Work:* Univ Iowa; Univ Wis; also in pvt collections; Disney; McDonald's Corp. *Exhib:* Wisconsin at Work, 50 & Wisconsin Painters & Sculptors Ann, 64, Mem Mus, Milwaukee; Fla State Fair Show, Tampa, 65; Nat Exhib Contemp Painting, Soc Four Arts, Palm Beach, Fla, 66, 70, 85, 94, 96; Hortt Mem Exhib, Mus Arts, Ft Lauderdale, Fla, 68, 70 & 87; Fla Watercolor Soc, 2006; and others; Retrospective, Polk comm Coll Art Gallery, Winter Haven, Fla 2006. *Pos:* Chmn Art Depts, Carthage Col & Fla Atlantic Univ; Independent watercolor workshop leader, 91-; juror, Art Fairs, Exhibns, 85-. *Teaching:* Asst prof studio art, Wayne State Col, 53-59; prof art & art hist & chmn dept art, Carthage Col, 59-64; prof studio art, Fla Atlantic Univ, 64-91, chmn Dept Art, 68-84, emer prof, 91-; instr Boca Mus of Art, 93-04; workshops, 93-. *Awards:* Tellus Madden Award, Wis Spring Show, 63; First Prize in Painting, Winter Park Art Fair, 65; Atwater Kent Award, Soc Four Arts Nat Exhib, 66; over 100 awards in major art fairs, 67-98. *Mem:* Hon mem Palm Beach Watercolor Soc (founding pres, 83); Fla Watercolor Soc, 91-; Gold Coast Watercolor Soc. *Media:* Oil, Watercolor; Acrylics. *Res:* specialty study for book. *Interests:* giving workshops. *Publ:* Auth, Artists Guide to Sidewalk Exhibiting, Watson/Guptill, 80; Expand Your Watercolor Horizons (video), 98. *Mailing Add:* 618 High St Boca Raton FL 33432-3646

DORST, MARY CROWE
GRAPHIC ARTIST, CRAFTSMAN

b Wis, June 5, 27. *Study:* Beloit Col, BA(art; cum laude); Northern Ill Univ, MA(drawing). *Work:* McDonald Corp; Vero Beach Ctr for Arts. *Exhib:* Colored Pencil Soc Am, 95; Int Soc Exp Artists, 94, 97; plus others. *Collection Arranged:* The Other Side of the Generation Gap, Constructions in Flexible Materials, Printmakers of the Americas & Edward S Curtis, Fla Atlantic Univ Art Gallery, 73-77; Florida Heritage, Contemporary Women Artists of the Gold Coast & Art in Fiber and Clay, Palmetto Gallery; Points of Color, 1st All-Fla Color Pencil Competition,Cornell Mus., Del Ray Beach, 98. *Pos:* Gallery dir, Fla Atlantic Univ, 73-77; art reviewer, Boca Raton News, Fla, 75-76 & 85-86; art dir, Palmetto Gallery, NCNB Banks, Boca Raton, 79-87; art/writer for local publ, 88-89. *Teaching:* Instr art, Marymount Col, Fla, 65-67, & Broward Community Col, Fla, 73-75; Palm Beach Jr Col, 75-83; adj instr, Atlantic Univ, Fla, 87-. *Awards:* Hon Mention, Nat Exhib Am Painting, Soc Four Arts, 83; Spec Award, Palm Beach Watercolor Soc, 87 & 92; Broward Art Guild, 90 & 91. *Bibliog:* Featured artist (calendar), Broward Arts Coun, 86. *Mem:* Hon mem Fla Craftsmen (area dir, 75-78 & 82-84); Am Crafts Coun; Palm Beach Co Coun Arts; hon mem Palm Beach Watercolor Soc (pres 89-91); Soc Experimental Artists; and others. *Media:* Pencil, Color Pencil. *Publ:* Auth, A Day in Mino, Crafts Horizons, 6/71; contribr, art articles, local monthly mag; Reviews in Art Voices, South; art critic, Boca Raton News, 77 & 87. *Mailing Add:* 618 NW High St Boca Raton FL 33432

DOS SANTOS, JONAS ALVES
ENVIRONMENTAL ARTIST, SCULPTOR

b Recife, Brazil, Nov 7, 47. *Study:* Atelier de Artes Livres, Recife, Brazil, 65-66; Escola de Arte, Recife, Brazil, BA, 66-68; Corcoran Sch Art, Washington, 68-72. *Work:* Corcoran Mus Art, Smithsonian Inst Mus Am Art, Brazilian-Am Cult Inst, Washington; Philadelphia Mus Art, Pa Acad Fine Arts, Philadelphia. *Exhib:* Americas, Pa Acad Fine Arts, Philadelphia, 82; Bay of All Saints/Bahia, Afro Am Mus Philadelphia, 84; Sacred and Profane, El Mus del Barrio, NY, 88; Shrine of the Immigrant, Socrates Sculpture Park, Long Island, 90; Back to Eden/Guerre, Alternative Mus, NY, 91; Artists Choose Artists, Inst Contemp Art, Philadelphia, 91; Oxygen Share, Smithsonian Inst, Washington, 91; The Crossing, Hillwood Mus, Long Island, 92; ECO/LOGICA 93, Mex Mus, San Francisco, 93; Helios the Nearest Star/the Sun 94, Sci Ctr, Philadelphia, 94; ECO:ACCA/MAM 95,Montclair Art Mus, NJ, 95; Laboratory Earth/Ritual for the Conferee 96, Int Performance Symposium, Pa State Univ, University Park, 96; Project Brazil/USA 2001, Nexus Gallery, Philadelphia, 98; Myhelan Millennium Project, Myhelan Art Ctr, Long Valley, 99; DANCA/NATA (installation), Art in City Hall, Philadelphia, 99; Cult Politics/The Century's Assessment (performance), Annenberg Performing Arts Ctr, Philadelphia, 2000; Artists & Communities: Am Creates for the Millennium (exhib & residencey), Roswell Mus Art, NMex, 2000; SEA.COM (installation, performance), Museu da Praia, Ponta do Mangue, Maragogi, Alagoas, Brazil, 2001; .COM Series, Levy Gallery, Moore Col Art, Philadelphia, 2001. *Pos:* Bd dir, Nexus Found, 93- & Prints in Progress, 94. *Teaching:* Residency performance, Art Inst Chicago, 79, Univ Colo, Boulder, 91 & Arco, Lisbon, Portugal, 93-94. *Awards:* Nat Endowment Arts Fel, 91; Arts Int-Lila Wallace Found, 93; Mid-Atlantic Found Fel, 94. *Bibliog:* Susana T Leval (auth), Jonas dos Santos, Intar Gallery, 89; Judith McWillie (auth), A Source Book, Intar Gallery, 92; Luis Cannitzer (auth), Artists Page, Col Art Asn, 92. *Mem:* Smithsonian Inst; Nat Asn Arts Orgns. *Media:* Interdisciplinary. *Mailing Add:* 1242 N Lawrence St Philadelphia PA 19122-4428

DOUDERA, GERARD
PAINTER, EDUCATOR

b Sharon, Conn, Dec 29, 32. *Study:* Hartford Art Sch, BFA 56; Univ Ill. *Work:* Wadsworth Atheneum, Hartford; Butler Inst Am Art, Youngstown, Ohio; New Britain Mus, Conn. *Exhib:* One-man shows, DeCordova & Dana Mus, Lincoln, Mass, 59, Conn Comn Arts' Showcase Gallery, Hartford, 85, Slater Mus, Norwich, Conn, 89 & 93, Pindar Gallery, NY, 89 & 90, Mus Art, Univ Conn, 90 & New Canaan Soc Arts, Conn, 93; New Britain Mus Am Art, Conn, 61; Univ Hartford, 71. *Teaching:* Prof painting, Univ Conn, 62-87, head art dept, 74-77; emer prof art, Univ Conn, 87-; artist-in-residence, Camargo Found, Cassis, France, 87; vis artist, Weir Farm Heritage Trust, 92-93. *Awards:* First CAFA Award, Conn Artists Ann, Slater Mus, Norwich, 86, First Prize, 2003. *Bibliog:* C Libov (auth), A Painter's World in Bigelow Hollow,

Conn Sect, NY Times, 8/18/85; J Brodsky (auth), A Landscape Sensibility, Gerard Doudera A Retrospective (catalog), William Benton Mus, Univ Conn, 90; S Doherty (auth), Painting at the Site of American Impressionism, Am Artist, 5/93. *Mem:* Conn Acad Fine Arts (pres, 81-86). *Media:* Oil, Watercolor. *Dealer:* Kerygma Gallery 38 Oak St Ridgewood NJ. *Mailing Add:* 490 Lewis Hill Rd Coventry CT 06238

DOUGHERTY, PATRICK T
SCULPTOR
Study: Univ NC, Chapel Hill, BA, 67, Art Dept, 82; Artist Schol, 98: Univ Iowa, Iowa City, MA, 69. *Exhib:* Solo exhibs, Spirit Square Art Ctr, Charlotte, NC, 86, Second St Gallery, Charlottesville, Va & NY Univ, Broadway Windows, 88, St Andrew's Gallery, Sewanee, Tenn & NC Mus Art, Raleigh, 89; Biennial, Mint Mus, Charlotte, NC, 88; Birmingham Mus Art, 88; High Mus, Atlanta, Ga, 89; Dittmer Collection, Aspen, Colo, 94; Assen City Proj, The Neth, 94; SC State Mus, Columbia, 94; Salina Art Ctr, Kans, 94; John Michael Kohler Arts Ctr, Sheboygan, Wis, 95; Am Craft Mus, NY, 96; Copenhagen Botanical Gardens, Denmark, 96; Spoleto Festival, Charleston, SC, 97; Tallaght Community Art Ctr, Dublin, Ireland, 97; San Jose Art Mus, 98; Univ Mich at Ann Arbor, 98; Nat Mus Natural Hist, Smithsonian Inst, Washington DC, 2000; many others. *Pos:* Lectr various mus, cols & univs, 87-93; artist-in-residence, Univ NC, Chapel Hill, 93, Anderson Ranch, Snowmass Village, Colo, 94, 95, 99 & NC State Univ, Raleigh, 99,; visual arts panel Nat Endowment Arts, 89, Art Mid-West, 91, Mid-Atlantic Arts Found, 91, NC Arts Coun, 90-91, Pa Arts Coun, 93, Mid-Am Arts Alliance, 95, Southern Arts Fedn, 95, 96, Bush Artist Fels, 97 & Ill State Arts Coun, 98. *Awards:* NC Artist Fel Award, 86, 98; Nat Endowment Arts Fel, 90, 91 & 94; Pollock-Krasner Found Sustaining Grant, 94. *Bibliog:* photos & article, Ann Arbor News, 4/12/98; photo & article, Chicago Sun-Times, 5/27/98; Artwork that Branches Out, Philadelphia Inquirer, 10/5/2000. *Mailing Add:* 9007 Dodsons Crossroads Chapel Hill NC 27516

DOUGHERTY, RAYMOND EDWARD
PAINTER, INSTRUCTOR
b Wildwood, NJ, June 15, 42. *Study:* Pa Acad Fine Arts, dipl, 68; Univ Pa Grad Sch Fine Arts, BFA, 70. *Work:* Ocean City Art Ctr, NJ; Noyes Mus, Ocean View, NJ; NJ Univ of Med & Dentistry, Camden; Atlantic Co Special Serv Sch Dist, Hostler Hall, NJ. *Exhib:* 27th Nat Soc Painters Casein & Acrylic, Am Acad & Inst Arts & Lett, NY, 79-90; 111th Am Watercolor Soc, Nat Acad Design, NY, 78; 2nd Biennial, NJ State Mus, Trenton, 79; Audobon Artist Ann, Nat Arts Club, NY, 80-89; NJ Art Educ Exhib, Trenton State Col, 82. *Collection Arranged:* 20th, 21st & 22nd Nat Traveling Exhib, Nat Soc Painters in Casein & Acrylic, 77-80; Old Bergen Art Guild, Bayonne, NJ Group Nat Tour, 79-80. *Teaching:* Instr fine arts, NJ Pub Schs, 70-78, Am Inst Ment Studies, Vineland, NJ, 79 & Secondary Parochial School System, 80; instr art, Helmbold Educ Ctr, 84; instr, Atlantic Co Special Serv Dist, 90. *Awards:* Lotos Club Exhib Award Paintings, 90-91; Cert Merit, Nat Soc Painter in Casien & Acrylic, 91; Morecai Newman Mem Award, 85. *Mem:* Cape May Co Art League (pres, 77-78); Nat Soc Painter Casein & Acrylic (bd dir, 79, vpres, 84, pres, 89); Audubon Artists; Nat Artists Equity; Painters & Sculptors Soc NJ; and others. *Media:* Oil & Acrylic; Demonstration & Criticism

DOUGLAS, EDWIN PERRY
PAINTER, INSTRUCTOR
b Lynn, Mass, June 18, 35. *Study:* RI Sch Design, BFA; San Francisco Art Inst, MFA. *Work:* Montreal Mus Fine Arts, Can; Dayton Art Mus, Ohio; Cincinnati Art Mus; Lincoln Land Community Col Art Mus, Springfield, Ill; Portland Mus Art. *Exhib:* San Francisco Art Inst Nat Painting & Sculpture Tour, 63; 81st Ann Spring Exhib, Montreal Mus Fine Arts, 64; 31st Ann Can Soc Graphic Art, Kingston, Ont, 64; Cincinnati Biennial, Cincinnati Art Mus, 69; Portland Mus Art, Maine, 74; Walt Kuhn Gallery, Maine, 83; Joan Whitney Payson Gallery, Maine, 84; Papendrecht Mus Contemp Art, The Neth, 85; Icon Gallery, Brunswick, Maine, 90; Greenhut Gallery, Maine, 91. *Teaching:* Instr painting, Univ Man Sch Art, 63-64; instr drawing & painting, Cincinnati Art Acad, Ohio, 64-68; vis prof art, Wash Univ Sch Fine Arts, 69-72; vis lectr painting, Univ Cincinnati, 72-73; prof, Portland Sch Art, 73-, head painting dept, 73-93; guest lectr, Joan Whitney Payson Gallery, Maine, 84 & Mt Holyoke Col, Mass, 88. *Awards:* Convocation & Commencement Addresses, 84 & 85. *Bibliog:* Dialogue on Painting (film), Miami Univ TV, 67. *Media:* Oil. *Mailing Add:* 31 Gertrude Ave Portland ME 04103-3827

DOUGLAS, LEAH
GALLERY DIRECTOR, CURATOR
b Carlisle, Pa. *Study:* Tyler Sch Art, BFA, 85. *Collection Arranged:* Gregory Botts: Villa of the Sun (paintings); Colin Chase: Alchemy of Thought (sculpture); The Impulse to Abstract: Recent Work by Ritzi Jacobi (textile; coauth, catalogue), Univ Arts, Philadelphia, 94; Renewing the Spirit: Paintings from the Harlem Horizon Art Studio (auth, catalog), Univ Arts, Philadelphia, 94; Process of Form: Drawings by Judith Shea, Univ Arts, Philadelphia, 94; Willie Cole: Iconic Structures, 95; Elaine Reichek: Guests of the Nation, 96; Jon Kessler: Unplugged, 97. *Pos:* Dir exhib, Univ Arts, Philadelphia, 90-; independent cur, 92-. *Mem:* Am Asn Mus. *Publ:* Auth, Albert Paley: Sculpture (exhib catalog), Univ Arts, 90. *Mailing Add:* 4579 Fleming St Philadelphia PA 19128-4720

DOUGLAS, L(INDA) J
PAINTER, INSTRUCTOR
b Sellersville, Pa, Dec 16, 48. *Study:* Philadelphia Col Art, with Ree Morton & Cynthia Carlson, BFA, 75; Art Inst Chicago, MFA, 77. *Work:* Mus Contemp Art, Chicago; Ill State Mus. *Comn:* Pub Art Proj, Leafgate Garden Park, Evanston, Ill. *Exhib:* Gallery A, Chicago, Ill; Ctr Contemp Art, Chicago, Ill; Art Mus Southeast Tex; Convergence, Mind, Myth & Material, Peter Miller Gallery, Chicago, 85; Krannart Mus, Champaign, Ill, 86. *Pos:* Asst dir acad advising, Art Inst Chicago. *Teaching:* Columbia Col, Art Inst Chicago. *Awards:* Individual Artist Award, Ill Arts Coun Grant. *Bibliog:* Jeff Abel (auth), New Art Examiner, 11/87; James Yood (auth), Art News, 11/87; John Brunetti, Dialogue, 1-2/91. *Media:* Oil. *Publ:* Auth, Speakeasy, 2/84 & A message in darkness, 6/84, New Art Examiner. *Dealer:* Gallery A 300 W Superior Suite 102 Chicago IL 60610; Bennett Gallery 4515 Kingston Pike Knoxville TN 37919

DOUGLAS, TOM HOWARD
PAINTER, SCULPTOR
b Lexington, Tenn, Nov 23, 57. *Study:* Austin Peay State Univ, BFA, 80; Univ Miss Oxford, MFA, 83. *Work:* Tenn State Mus, Nashville; Parthenon Mus, Nashville; Tupelo Artist Guild Gallery, Tupelo, Miss; Univ Miss, Oxford; Austin Peay State Univ, Clarksville, Tenn; Nashville Int Airport, Tenn. *Comn:* bronze bust, Davis Center, Itawamba Community Col, Fulton, Miss, 2006. *Exhib:* Mid Am Exhib, Owensboro Fine Arts Mus, Owensbor, Ky, 80; Two Visions of Landscape, C W Woods Gallery, Hattiesburg, Miss, 85; Recent Works, Margaret F Treahorn, Clarksville, Tenn, 85; A Glimpse of the South, Brent Wood Gallery, St Louis, Mo, 86; ICC Faculty Show, Univ Ark at Littlerock, 88; Numbers Invitational, Cooper Ave Gallery, Memphis, Tenn, 88; 2 x 4, Carnegie Arts Ctr, Leavenworth, Kans, 88; Constellations, Ark State Univ, Jonesboro, 89; Oratory, Robinson-Willis Gallery, Nashville, Tenn, 89. *Pos:* Artist-in-Residence, Itawamba Co (Miss Arts Commn, NEA), 84-85. *Teaching:* Chair, dept art, painting, Itawamba Community Col, 91-, instr, 83-. *Awards:* Best of Show, Crossties, Crossties Asn, 85; Best of Show, Redlands Festival, 87; Best of Show, Gum Tree Arts Fair, Gum Tree Asn, 88; Best of Show, Gumtree, 2003; Art Educ of the Year, Miss Asn Art Educ, 2004. *Bibliog:* Alec Clayton (auth), Review, Art Papers, 3-4/86. *Media:* Acrylic, Enamel on Wood, Tin, Clay, Monoprints. *Publ:* My Hearts in the High Lands, Recent Work of Ron Dale, Ceramics Monthly, 2003. *Mailing Add:* Chmn Dept Art Itawamba Community Col 602 W Hill St Fulton MS 38843

DOUMATO, LAMIA
LIBRARIAN, HISTORIAN
b Aug 26, 47; US citizen. *Study:* RI Col, BA; Pa State Univ, MA(art hist); Simmons Col, Boston, MLS; Boston Univ; Columbia Univ; George Washington Univ. *Exhib:* Retrospective 1972-1982, Women's Caucus for Art, Moore Col Art, 83. *Collection Arranged:* Rhode Island Architecture, Providence Pub Libr; Raphael, Nat Gallery Art Libr, 81; American Architecture: Hist View, Nat Gallery of Art Libr, 84; Beaux Arts et Belles Lettres, Nat Gallery Art Libr, 97; Clothing For The Soul Divine, Nat Gallery Art, 2002; Spectacles, Natl Gallery of Art, libr, 2004 & 2005. *Pos:* Art librn, Providence Pub Libr, 70-71; ref librn, Boston Univ Libr, 71-74 & Mus Mod Art Libr, New York, 74-78; reference librn, Nat Gallery Art, Washington, DC, 81-88, head of reader servs, 88-. *Teaching:* Teaching asst art hist, Pa State Univ, 70; prof & head, Art & Archit Libr, Univ Colo, Boulder, 78-81; teacher res methods, Univ Colo, 79-81. *Awards:* Coun Creative Work Grants, Univ Colo, 79-81; Robert H Smith Fel, 97-98; HW Wilson Award, 2000; Arms Fel, 2001; ALSA Mellon Bruce Fel, CASVA 2001; Bibliogrpahical Soc, Oxford, Eng, 2002. *Mem:* Col Art Asn; Art Librn Soc NAm; Art Librn Soc Washington, DC; Asn Archit Librn; and others. *Res:* Production of Syriac manuscripts in 11th-13th century and the interrelations of Crusader and Indigent Artists of the Area. *Interests:* Illuminated manuscripts, architectural bibliography and women architects; History of Jewelry. *Publ:* auth, Museum Design, Chicago Coun Planning Librn, 80; Women in literature of art, Oxford Art J, Vol 3, 4/80; contribr, The Comfortable House, Mass Inst Technol Press, Cambridge, 86; Architecture and Women, Garland Pub, 88; Architecture a Place for Women, Smithsonian Press, 89; Art of Bishop Dioscorus Theodorus, Arte Cristiana, 99; Opening the Door to Paradise, Al-Masaq, 2000; Patriarch Michael the Great, Cahiers Archeologiques, 2001; P.C. England Col of Artists Books, 2001; auth, Pontifical of Ignatius II Arte Cristiana, 2003. *Mailing Add:* 3001 Veazey Terr NW Washington DC 20008

DOUTHAT, ANITA S
PHOTOGRAPHER
b Cincinnati, Ohio, June 27, 50. *Study:* Inst Design, Ill Inst Technol, BS(design), 72; Sch Art Inst Chicago, courses in video & art hist; Univ NMex, MA(art), 81, MFA(art), 86. *Work:* Albuquerque Mus Art & Hist; Univ Art Mus, Univ NMex; Columbus Mus Art, Ohio; Cincinnati Art Mus, Ohio; Mus Fine Arts, Houston, Tex. *Exhib:* Solo exhibs, Orange Coast Col, Costa Mesa, Calif, 86, Bucks Co Community Col, Pa, 87, Greenfield Community Col, Mass, 89, Houston Ctr Photog, 92, Robert C May Gallery, Univ Ky, 93 & Carnegie Arts Ctr, Covington, Ky, 94, Kenyon Col, Gambier, Ohio, Barat Col Lake Forest, Ill, 96; group shows, Vertical Axis, Mus Contemp Photog, Columbia Col, Chicago, 94, The Shelf-Life of Objects, Univ Tex, Dallas, 00; Experimental Vision, Denver Art Mus, 94; Inside/Outside, Hood Mus, Dartmouth Col, Hanover, NH, 96; Shadows & Light, Columbus Mus Art, Columbus, Ohio, 98; 2x2: Photographs by Anita Douthat and Cal Kowal, Cincinnati Art Mus, Ohio, 00, Houston Ctr for Photog, 02; Lost & Found, Weston Art Gallery, Ohio. *Pos:* Assoc cur exhibs, John Michael Kohler Arts Ctr, Sheboygan, Wis, 83-84; cur, Photog Resource Ctr, Boston, Mass, 85-92; registr, Carl Solway Gallery, Cincinnati, Ohio, 93-. *Teaching:* Instr photog, Northern Ky Univ, 93-95 & 97-99; vis artist, Ohio State Univ, 95. *Awards:* Fel, Nat Endowment Arts, 91 & 92; Fel, Ky Fedn for Women, 2000. *Mem:* Soc Photog Educ; Nat Campaign Freedom Expression. *Publ:* Auth, Fabricated categories, Views, winter 88; Transforming with light, Art New Eng, 6/89; Commentary: photography at the Univ NMex, PhotoEduc, A Polaroid Newsletter for Teachers Photog, spring 90; coauth, Censorship and obscenity, Art New Eng, 11/90; auth, Fearful symmetries: the Berlin Wall reconsidered, Views, spring 92. *Mailing Add:* 3521 Reitman St Alexandria KY 41001

DOVE, TONI
VIDEO ARTIST
b New York, NY. *Study:* RI Sch Design, BFA, 68. *Work:* Mus Fine Arts, Boston, Mass; Worcester Art Mus, Mass; Achenbach Found Graphic Arts, Fine Arts Mus, San Francisco, Calif; Santa Cruz Co Art Mus, Calif; Mus of Modern Art, NY, 98; The Wexner Ctr for the Arts, Columbus, Ohio, 98-99; Electronic Music Found, Ltd, NY; ISA Computing Commons Gallery, Ariz State Univ; and others. *Exhib:* Fugitive Concepts (slides), Corcoran Armand Hammer Gallery, Washington, 89; Pyramid Atlantic & Brandywine Workshop Print Show, Md Art Place, Baltimore, 89; Pyramid Atlantic Benefit, Washington, 89 & 91; Contemp Book Art, the Print Club, Philadelphia, Pa, 90; The Blessed Abyss (slide, film & sound piece), Whitney Mus at Philip Morris, NY, 92; Keepers of Secrets & Truths Otherwise Unknown, Berman Mus Art, Collegeville, Pa, 94; Mesmer-The Book & Beyond, Forum Ctr Arts, St Lewis, Mo, 95; Artificial Changelings, Int Film Festival, Rotterdam, 98, The Wexner Ctr, Columbus, Ohio, 98, 99, Aris Ctr for the Capital Region, Troy, NY, 00. *Teaching:* Instr, watercolor workshops, Brown Univ, RI, 74, Pine Manor Col, Brookline, Mass, 75-79, Boston Col, Newton, Mass, 79-86; vis critic & lectr, Pine Manor Col, 74, Worcester Art Mus Sch, 74, 79, Mass Col Art, 78-82, 85, Sch Mus Fine Arts, 78-82, NY Univ, Tisch Sch Performing Arts, 91-94, Trinity Col, Conn, 93-94, Sch Visual Arts, NY, 94, Brown Univ, RI, 94; lectr series new tech, Mus Modern Art, NY, 98. *Awards:* Artist in Residence Grant, Harvestworks Inc, New York, 93-94; Rockefeller Found MAP Grant, 2000; Greenwall Found Grant, 2000; NY State Coun on the Arts Media Grant, 2000; Nat Endowment for the Arts Multidisciplinary Grant, 2000; Langlois Found Grant, 2001; NY Found for the Arts Fel, 2001; Map Grant, Rockefeller Foun, 01; LEF Found Grant, 02. *Bibliog:* Terence Grieder (auth), Artist & Audience, Brown & Benchmark, 96; Richard Zvonar (auth), Artificial changelings (rev), Interactivity Mag, 9/96; Margo Lovejoy (auth), PostModern Currents, Art & Artists in the Age of Electronic Media, Prentice Hall, 96; Stephen Johnson (auth), Artificial Changelings (rev), Feedmag.com, 98; Margaret Morse (auth), Virtualities (book of essays), Ind Univ Press, 98; Conversation with Ton Dove and Brian Massumi, Artbyte Mag, Jan/Feb 98-99; The Art of the X-Files, Harper Collins, 99; and numerous revs. *Media:* Performance, Installation. *Mailing Add:* 115 W Broadway New York NY 10013

DOW, JIM D
PHOTOGRAPHER
b Boston, Mass, July 26, 42. *Study:* RI Sch Design, BFA, 65, MFA, 68. *Work:* Addison Mus Am Art, Andover, Mass; Art Inst Chicago, Ill; High Mus Art, Atlanta, Ga; Metrop Mus Art & Mus Mod Art, NY; Mus Fine Arts, Boston. *Comn:* New Eng Sports Mus, Boston; Yale Univ Law Sch; Polaroid Corp & Close-Up Mag; Los Angeles Olympic Arts Festival, Mus Contemp Art; Robert Freidus Gallery Publ; Joseph E Seagram's Corp Bicentennial Project, The Co Court House, 76; Target Stores, 85; Univ NDak, 85. *Exhib:* One-person exhibs, Film in the Cities, St Paul, 88, Robert Klein Gallery, Boston, 87, Worcester Art Mus, 85, Univ Art Gallery, Amherst, Mass, 84, Mus Art, Colobne, 83, Univ Art Galleries, Grand Forks, NDak, 81, Thorne Sagendorph Art Gallery, NH, 80, Janet Borden Inc, NY, 90, 93 & 95, Oriole Park at Camden Yards, Baltimore, Md, 92, Univ Rochester, NY, 92, traveling exhib, Smithsonian Inst, Nat Touring Exhib, Minor League Baseball Park Panoramas, 93-95, Md Sci Ctr, Baltimore & Commonwealth Mus, Boston, 93-95, Int Mus Photog, Rochester, NY, 97 & RI Hist Soc, Providence, 98; Sales Gallery, Metrop Mus Art, NY, 90; Addison Mus Am Art, Andover, Mass, 91; group exhib, Thorne, Sagendorph Art Gallery, 80, Jorgenson Art Ctr, Univ Conn, 81, Mus Art, Cologne, Ger, 83, Brooklyn Mus, 84, Mus Contemp Photog, Chicago, 85, Julie Saul Gallery, NY, 93; two-person exhibs, Paul Kopeikin Gallery, Los Angeles, 93 & Light Impressions Gallery, Rochester, NY, 94; The Puck Stops Here, NHL All Star Game, San Jose Art Mus, 95; Janet Borden, Inc, NY, 2003; and others. *Teaching:* Art hist/hist photog, Mus Sch, Tufts Univ, 73-; photog, Sch Mus Fine Arts, Boston, Mass, 73-; numerous lectures & workshops, 82-94. *Awards:* Nat Endowment Arts Fel, 72, 79 & 90; Mellon Found, 88; New Eng Found Arts Fel, 97; Sch of Mus Fine Arts Enrichment Grant, Boston, 2000; LEF Found Grant, Somerville, Mass, 2003. *Bibliog:* Kohtaro Tizawa & Natsuki Ikezawa (auths), New Landscape, Tokyo, Japan, 91; Sports Stadiums, Saison J, Tokyo, Japan, 7/15/92; John Pastier (auth), Diamonds Aren't Forever, Hist Preserv Mag, 7-8/93; Court House, Horizon Press, 78; The American and National Leagues, 82; Court House, RFG Pub, 83; Sleeping Giants, Camera Arts Mag, 83; New Color, New Work, Abbeville Press, 84; Ten Photographers, Olympic Arts Festival, Los Angeles Ctr for Photographic Studies & Mus Contemporary Art, 84; Constance Sullivan (ed),The Spirit of Sport, 85. *Mem:* Art Inst Boston. *Publ:* Fields of Dreams, Playboy, Japan, 5/5/93; Buenos Aires: City of Longing, Vol 81, Simzu Bull, Tokyo, Japan, summer 93; Dream Fields (calendar), Chronicle Books, San Francisco, 9/94; The Sun Slowly Sets on the English Corner Shop, Telegraph Mag, London, 1/14/94; Hot Spots: The Curry Restaurant in England, Telegraph Mag, London, 7/23/94. *Dealer:* Janet Borden Inc 560 Broadway New York NY 10012; Bonni Benrubi Fine Arts 148 E 74th St New York NY 101021. *Mailing Add:* 95 Clifton St Belmont MA 02478

DOWD, JACK
SCULPTOR
b New York, NY, Mar 23, 38. *Study:* Adelphi Univ, art educ, 60; Arts Students League. *Comn:* HBE Corp, St Louis; New England Bio Laabs, Boston; Mountain Top Mall, St Thomas, Virgin Island; David Cohen Symphony Hall, Sarasota; Rapa Nui, Inc, Hawaii. *Exhib:* Expressions, Art & Cult Ctr Mus, Hollywood, Fla, 90; Artstravaganza, Asn Visual Artists, Chattanooga, Tenn, 91; All Fla Juried Exhib, Boca Raton Mus Art, 92 & 96; The Fla Nat, Fla State Univ Mus, Tallahassee, 92; Brevard Art Mus, Melbourne, Fla, 93, Montgomery Mus Fine Arts, 92; Nat Sculpture Soc, New York City, 95, 96, 99; Ellen Noel Art Mus, Tex, 2000; High Desert Mus, Calif, 2000; Exposed Ann Outdoor Exhibit, Stowe, Vt, 2000; Ringling Mus Fine Art, Sarasota, 2001. *Pos:* Chmn, Sarasota Pub Art Comt, 91-92. *Teaching:* Artist-in-Residence, Asn Visual Artists, Cattanooga, Tenn, 92. *Awards:* Helen Gapen Oehler Award, Allied Artist Show, 93; Award Scene Unseen, East NMex Univ, 95; Visual Art Ctr, Sarasota, Fla, 99. *Bibliog:* New York Times, 99; New York Post, 99; Sarasota HeraldTribune, 96, 99. *Mem:* Sarasota Visual Arts Ctr; Sarasota Co Arts Council; Nat Sculpture Soc; Art Students League. *Media:* Wood, Clay. *Dealer:* Jack Dowd Studios 1331 10th St Sarasota FL 34236. *Mailing Add:* c/o Jack Dowd Ltd Editions 1311 10th St Sarasota FL 34236-5518

DOWDEN, ANNE OPHELIA TODD
PAINTER, WRITER
b Denver, Colo, Sept 17, 1907. *Study:* Univ Colo; Carnegie Inst Technol, BA, Art Students League. *Hon Degrees:* Moore Col Art, Hon Dr Fine Arts, 88. *Work:* Hunt Botanical Libr, Pittsburgh, Pa; NY Botanical Garden; Brooklyn Botanical Garden. *Comn:* Paintings for reproduction as facsimile prints, Frame House Gallery, Louisville, Ky, 69-79; painting, three azaleas, Callaway Gardens, Pine Mountain, Ga, 71; painting, tulip tree flowers, NY Botanical Garden, 72; painting, rhododendron, Holden Arboretum, Cleveland. *Exhib:* Am Textiles, Metrop Mus Art, NY, 48; one-man shows, Brooklyn Botanical Gardens, 57, 77 & 85, Hunt Botanical Libr, 65, NY Pub Libr, 83; Int Group Shows, Hunt Botanical Libr, 64, 68, 72 & 77; Denver Botanical Gardens, 2002; Contemp Botanical Art, Denver Mus Art, 2002; Hunt Inst, 2003; Smithsonian, 2003; and other group & one-man shows. *Teaching:* Instr drawing, Pratt Inst, 30-32; head dept art, Manhattanville Col, 32-53. *Awards:* Tiffany Found Fel, 29-31. *Bibliog:* Ronald King (auth), Botanical Illustration, Potter, 78; Something About the Author, Vol 10, Gale Research Inc, 90. *Mem:* Am Soc Botanical Artists. *Media:* Watercolor. *Publ:* Auth & illusr, Look at a Flower, 63, Wild Green Things in the City, 72, The Blossom on the Bough, 75, From Flower to Fruit, 84 & The Clover and the Bee, Crowell, 90; illusr, Shakespeare's Flowers, Crowell, 69; This Nobel Harvest, Collins, 77; Wild Flowers and the Stories Behind their Names, Scribner, 77; auth & illusr, Poisons in Our Path, Harper-Collins, 94; and many others. *Mailing Add:* 350 Ponca Pl Boulder CO 80303

DOWELL, JAMES THOMAS
PAINTER, FILMMAKER
b Greenville, Tex, Sept 11, 49. *Study:* New York Studio Sch, 69; Southern Methodist Univ, BFA, 72; Univ Iowa, MA & MFA, 74. *Work:* Univ Iowa Mus; Southern Methodist Univ, Dallas, Tex. *Exhib:* Solo exhib, Anoka-Ramsey State Col, Minneapolis, Minn, 73, Univ Gallery, Southern Methodist Univ, Dallas, Tex, 79, Warehouse Arts Ctr, Corsicana, Tex, 82, Waco Art Ctr, Tex 83, Soho Ctr Visual Arts (with catalog), NY, 85 & Richland Col Art Gallery, Dallas, Tex, 92; Still Life: A Selection of Contemp Paintings, Kent State Univ, Ohio, 80; In Search of the Am Experience, Jacob Javits Bldg, NY, 89; Paper Ball Section-Pavel Tchelhchew - The Landscapes of the Body, Katonah Mus Art, NY, 98; Object as Metaphor, Marymount Manhattan Col, NY; James Dowell: Portrait as Self-Portrait, McKinney Ave Contemp, Dallas, 2002; Object Lessons, Valley House Gallery, Dallas, 2003; Still Lifes, Tyler Mus Art, Tex, 2003; Sleep in a Nest of Flames, RAI network, Ital, 2006; Ned Rorem: Word & Music, Aspen Music Festival, Aspen, Colo, 2006. *Awards:* Elmer B Ischoff Award, Mus NMex SW Biennial, 70. *Media:* Oil on Canvas. *Dealer:* Valley House Gallery 6616 Spring Valley Rd Dallas TX 75225. *Mailing Add:* 777 W End No 2B New York NY 10025

DOWELL, JOHN E, JR
EDUCATOR, PRINTMAKER
b Philadelphia, Pa, Mar 25, 41. *Study:* Temple Univ Tyler Sch Art, BFA(printmaking, ceramics), 63; John Herron Art Inst, Indianapolis, advan lithography with Garo Antreasian, 63; Tamarind Lithography Workshop, Los Angeles, artist-printer fel, 63 & sr-printer fel, 66; Univ Wash, Seattle, MFA(printmaking, drawing), 66. *Work:* Mus Mod Art, NY; Brooklyn Mus Art, NY; Boston Mus Fine Art, Mass; Art Inst Chicago; Corcoran Gallery Art, Washington, DC; and many others. *Exhib:* One-man shows, Venice Biennale, 70, Corcoran Gallery Art, DC, 71 & Ft Worth Art Mus Ctr, Tex, 72; Whitney Biennial, 75 & Printmaking New Forms, 76, Whitney Mus Am Art; Recent Am Drawings, Mus Mod Art, NY, 76; 30 yrs Am Printmaking, Brooklyn Mus Art, NY, 76; Three Centuries Am Art, Philadelphia Mus Art, 76; Drawings of the 70's, 35th Exhib of Soc Contemp Art, Art Inst Chicago, 77; Collectors Collect Contemp: A Selection from Boston's Collections, Inst Contemp Art, Boston, 77; A J Wood Galleries, Philadelphia, 80; and many others. *Teaching:* Assoc prof art & printmaking, Tyler Sch Art, Temple Univ, Rome, Italy, 71-74, Philadelphia, 74-76, prof, 76-82. *Awards:* Univ Ill, Champaign Fac Summer Fel, 70; Nat Endowment Arts Fel Painting, 74-75; Temple Univ Res Grant, 75-77; and others. *Bibliog:* Henry Martin (auth), Scribble, Art Int, 3/73; Donna Stein (auth), Musicianly painting, Art News, 11/73; John Dowell's sound perspective, Arts Exchange, 5/77; and others. *Mailing Add:* 1516 N 15th St Philadelphia PA 19121-4310

DOWLER, DAVID P
SCULPTOR, DESIGNER
b Pittsburgh, Pa, Feb 1, 44. *Study:* Syracuse Univ, BID, 69. *Work:* Leigh Yawkey Woodson Mus Art, Wausau, Wis; Corning Mus Glass, NY; Hokkaido Mus Mod Art. *Exhib:* Mus Mod Art, Kyoto, Japan, 81; Americans in Glass, Leigh Yawkey Woodson Art Mus, Wausau, Wis, 81 & Cooper-Hewitt Mus, NY, 81; Good As Gold, Smithsonian Inst, Washington, DC, 81; Production Lines, Philadelphia Col Art, 83; Glass Now, Hokkaido Mus Mod Art, 83. *Awards:* Furniture Design Award, Progressive Archit Mag, 82. *Bibliog:* Elliot Erwit (auth), Assignment in Glass (film), 78. *Mailing Add:* 249 Pine St Corning NY 14830-3147

DOWLEY, JENNIFER
DIRECTOR
Study: Denison Univ, Granville, Ohio, BA(theater arts), 70, grad studies. *Pos:* Apprentice, Film Study Ctr, Mus Mod Art, NY, 69; asst dir, Nat Cinemas, Dublin, Ireland, 71-72; admin asst, Mus Children, Denver, Colo, 73-74; fundraising consult, Boston Ballet, Mass, 75; assoc dir, Artists Fel Prog, co-dir, Taking Care Bus Artists

Found, Boston, Mass, 75-78; dir, Arts on the Line, Cambridge Arts Coun, Mass, 78-81 & Headlands Ctr Arts, Saulsalito, Calif, 86-94, formerly; coordr, Art Pub Places Prog, Sacramento Metrop Arts Comn, 81-86; dir, Headlands Ctr for Arts, Sausalito, Calif, 86-94; dir, Visual Arts & Mus Prog, Nat Endowment Arts, Washington, 94-99; Chmn Pew Fel Arts, 95-; pres, Berkshire Taconic Community Found, 99-. *Awards:* Am Inst Architects Award for Arts on the Line, 87; Distinguished Service Award, Nat Endowment for Arts, 96 & 99. *Mem:* Art Table (bd dir N Calif Chap, 88-90 & DC chap, 96-99); Alliance of Artists Communities (co-founder & chair, 91-94); Arts Advisory Bd; Civitella Found (bd dir, 2001-). *Publ:* Contribr, Money Business: Grants and Awards to Creative Artists, 1st ed, 78; Arts on the Line-a case study for the Urban Mass Transportation Administration, 80; Sculpture Sacramento (catalog), 82. *Mailing Add:* Berkshire Taconic Community Found 271 Main St Great Barrington MA 01230

DOWNER, SPELMAN EVANS
PAINTER, PHOTOGRAPHER
b Pasadena, Calif, Aug 25, 54. *Study:* Stanford Univ, BA(environ design), 77; San Francisco State Univ, MA(painting), 82. *Work:* Libr Congress, Washington, DC; Univ Alaska, Fairbanks; Nat Park Serv, Bettles, Alaska; Am Asn Advan Sci, Washington, DC; Brit Petroleum Corp, Anchorage. *Comn:* Petersburg Quadrants, Petersburg Sch Dist, Alaska, 87; Siberia Meets Alaska, State of Alaska & Alaska Airlines, Provideniva, USSR, 88; North Pacific Arc, Anchorage Mural Comt, 89; Cent Brooks Range, Gates of the Artic Nat Park, Bettles, Alaska, 90; Kenai Peninsula Portrait, Alaska Wildland Adventures, Cooper Landing, Alaska, 93; Geraldine R Dodge Found, Morristown, NJ, 98; Lawrenceville Sch, NJ, 98. *Exhib:* Solo-exhibs, Kenai Fine Art Ctr, Alaska, 91, Hudson River Mus, Westchester, NY, 95, Arsenal Gallery, NY, 96, Mus Hudson Highlands, NY, 97 & Mus of City NY, 98, Education Testing Svc, Princeton, NJ, 99, NJ Ctr Visual Arts, Summit, 99; Anchorage Mus Hist & Art, Alaska, 92, 94-95; Rochester Mus & Sci Ctr, NY, 94; Mesa Southwest Mus, Ariz, 94; All-of-a-Piece, Katonah Mus Art, 95; Seoul Int Art Fair, Korea, 96; New Am Talent 13, Tex Fine Art Asn, Austin, 97-98; Aerial Perspectives: Reality, Imagination and Abstraction, DC Moore Gallery, NY, 97; Landscapes Seen & Unseen, Pratt Manhattan Gallery & Pratt Brooklyn, NY, 97-98; Scale, Rudolph Poissant Gallery, Houston, 98; US Fed Reserve, New York City, 99. *Collection Arranged:* Geraldine R Dodge Found, Morristown, NJ; Lawrenceville Sch, NJ. *Teaching:* Univ Alaska, Kenai Peninsula Col, 90-94. *Awards:* Best of Show, Int Juried Show 1996, NJ Ctr Visual Arts, 96; Dodge Found Fel Grant, Vt Studio Ctr, 97; NY State Coun Arts, Arts Educ Grant, Accessing Cult/Hist Infor, 98. *Bibliog:* Chris Farlekas (auth), Giving landscapes new form, Times Herald Record, 1/10/97; Richard Polsky (auth), Contemp Am Art, Art Market Guide, 97; Roberta Smith (auth), The Metropolis, glimpses of the first 100 years, The New York Times, 98. *Media:* Oil, Drawing; Photography. *Publ:* Auth, Second Manifesto of Maximalism, Alaska Artistic License, 94. *Dealer:* Dru Arstark Gallery 568 Broadway No 403 New York NY 10012. *Mailing Add:* PO Box 825 Cooper Landing AK 99572

DOWNES, RACKSTRAW
PAINTER, CRITIC
b Kent, Eng, Nov 8, 39; US citizen. *Study:* Cambridge Univ, Eng, BA, 61; Yale Univ, BFA, 63, MFA, 64. *Work:* Hirshhorn Mus, Washington, DC; Pa Acad, Philadelphia; Whitney Mus Am Art, Brooklyn Mus, Chase Manhattan Bank, Metrop Mus Art, Equitable Life Insurance & Mus Mod Art, NY; Mus Fine Arts, Houston, Tex; Witherspoon Mus, NC; Carnegie Inst, Pittsburgh; Nelson Atkins Mus, Kansas City, Mo, Biennial Exhib, Whitney Mus Am Art, NY, Contemp Art Realism, Philadelphia, Pa, Real Really Real, Super Real, San Antonio Mus, 1981; solo exhib, Chinati Found, 1999; Fresh Kills Snug Habor Cult Center, Stanton Island, 2001. *Comn:* Painting, US Dept Interior, 76. *Exhib:* Carnegie Int, Carnegie Inst, 83; The Realist Landscape, Rutgers Univ, New Brunswick, NJ, 85; Drawing and Drawings, Hudson River Mus, Yonkers, NY, 86; solo exhib, Weatherspoon Art Gallery, 92; The Long View, Mus Mod Art, NY, 94; Reinterpreting Landscape, Maier Mus Art, Lynchburg, Va, 96; Modern Art Despite Modernism, Mus of Modern Art, NY, 2000. *Pos:* Gov, Skowhegan Sch Painting & Sculpture, 1981-1995. *Teaching:* Asst prof fine arts, Univ Pa, Philadelphia, 67-79; Grad Sch Fine Arts, Yale, 1979-1980; Harvard Univ, 1997-1998. *Awards:* Creative Artists Pub Serv Award, 78; Individual Grant, Nat Endowment Arts, 80; Guggenheim Found Fel, 98. *Bibliog:* Robert Storr (auth), Rackstraw Downes: Painter as Geographer, Art in Am, 10/84; Peter Schjeldahl (auth), True Views, New Yorker, 10/2004; Samford Schwartz (auth), Rackstraw Downes, Princeton Univ Press, 2005. *Mem:* NY Artists Equity Asn; Nat Acad. *Media:* Oil. *Specialty:* Contmporary American and European Art. *Collection:* The Artist's Eye, Colby Col Mus Art, Waterville, Maine, 1992. *Publ:* ed, Fairfield Porter: Art in its Own Terms, 1979; auth, Claude's sermon on the mount, Art News, 10/81; Impressionists vs the salon: Modern & not, Art Am, 1/96; Auth, In Relation to the Whole, Edgewise, 2000; auth, Under the Gowanvs adn Razor-Wire Journal, Turning The Head, 2000. *Dealer:* Betty Cuningham Gallery, NY, NY. *Mailing Add:* 16 Greene St New York NY 10013

DOWNIE, ROMANA ANZI
SCULPTOR
b Rome, Italy, May 9, 25; US citizen. *Study:* Liceo Artistico Accademia Belle Arti, maturita, 45; San Francisco State Univ, BA(cum laude), 61, MA, 63; Univ Calif, Berkeley. *Work:* Museo de Roma, Italy; San Francisco Libr, Mus Photog & San Francisco State Col, San Francisco; Bidwell Libr, Southern Methodist Univ, Dallas. *Comn:* Portrait, Free Masons of Rome, 45; F DeBellis (portrait), comn by DeBellis Found, San Francisco, 68; George Moscone (portrait) & Harvey Milk (portrait), comn by Joseph Dee, San Francisco, 78 & 82; mural, Herrick's Hospital, Berkeley, Calif, 81; bronze statuette, Sammy Davis Jr, comn by Joseph Dee-Brooks, Mus Photography. *Exhib:* 1st Women's Show, Palazza Brancaccio, Rome, 47; San Francisco Art Festival, 64-81; Italian Am Artists, Mus Italo Americano, San Francisco, 79-82. *Bibliog:* Michael Robertson (auth), A sculptor caught in the politics of art, San Francisco Chronicle, 7/9/82; Lucy Harris & Stephanie Johnson (auths), Artist extraordinaire, Viewpoint, Oakland, 2/84; Mark Luca (auth), Italian American artists in the Bay Area, Il Caffe, Sacramento, 2-3/86. *Media:* Clay, Wax. *Dealer:* Greenwooper Gallery & Garden Shop Elk CA 95432. *Mailing Add:* 27800 N Hwy One Fort Bragg CA 95437

DOWNS, DOUGLAS WALKER
SCULPTOR
b Pomona, Calif, May 30, 1945. *Study:* Whittier Col, BA, 67; Claremont Grad Sch, 67-68, study with Aldo Casanova & Jean Ames; Ariz State Univ, 69-70. *Work:* King Karl Gustav XVI, Stockholm, Sweden; The White House; King Don Juan Carlos I & Queen Sofia, Seville, Spain; Long Island Chess Mus, Commack, NY. *Comn:* Bust of a Scholar (bronze), Collier Art Corp, Los Angeles, 74; Abstract Family (bronze), Am Asn Marriage & Family Therapy, Washington, DC, 75; Hawk on Rock (bronze), Tor House Found, Carmel, Calif, 79; Joseph Smith (bronze), 83 & Emma Smith (bronze), 85, Monterey Sculpture Ctr, Calif; Eagle gates (bronze), Ronald M Abend Inc, 89. *Exhib:* Solo exhib, Southwestern Arts Ltd, Carmel, 78; Favell Mus, Klamath Falls, Ore, 77; George Phippen Mem Exhib, Prescott, Ariz, 77; Westerman and Downs, Galerie de Tours, San Francisco, Calif, 84; The New Masters, May Gallery, Scottsdale, Ariz, 86; Artists of the West, Trails West Gallery, Laguna Beach, Calif, 88; Networks by Weers, Downs and Burns, May Gallery at Borgata, Scottsdale, Ariz, 96; Downs, Oliver and Thomas, May Gallery at El Pedregal, Ariz, 98; Worldwide Exhib of Fine Arts in Miniatures, Smithsonian Inst, Wash, DC, 2004. *Awards:* Best Art with Western Theme, Mont Miniature Art Soc, 15th Ann, 93; 1st Prize, Sculpture, Sage Gallery, Atlanta, Ga, 93; 1st Prize, Sculpture, 61st & 62nd Ann Int Exhibs, Washington, DC, 94 & 95; 1st Prize, Sculpture, 18th Ann North Am Exhibs, Baltimore, 2001. *Bibliog:* D W Armstrong (auth), Bronze artist Douglas Downs, Acquire, 5/74; L Longstaff (auth), Sculptor of 1000 faces, Southwest Arts, 11/77; H Sutliff (auth), Sculpture by Douglas Downs, Key, Calif Art Rev, 9/79; A survey of the state's museums, galleries and leading artists, 88; 2000 Outstanding Artists and Designers of the 20th Century, 1999; Biographical Encyclopedia of American Painters, Sculptors and Engravers of the US Colonial to 2002. *Mem:* Carmel Art Asn (bd dir, treas, 83-84, 87-88 & 93-94); sig mem, Miniature Artists Am, 96. *Media:* Bronze. *Dealer:* Carmel Art Asn Gallery, Calif; Caravan Bookstore, Los Angeles. *Mailing Add:* 405 Alder St Pacific Grove CA 93950

DOWNS, LINDA ANNE
CURATOR, HISTORIAN
b Detroit, Mich, May 30, 45. *Study:* Monteith Col, Wayne State Univ, PhB, 69; Univ Mich, MA(art hist), 73; Mus Mgt Inst, Univ Calif, Berkeley, 79; post grad studies, Am Univ, Washington, DC. *Collection Arranged:* Student Art Exhibs, Detroit Inst Arts, 69-77, Barbara Chase Ribaud Sculpture, 72, Diaghilev & Russian Stage Design, 72, Caravaggio's Conversion of the Magdalene: An Analysis of the Painting, 73, African Art of the Dogon, 74; The Rouge: The Image of Industry in the Art of Charles Sheeler and Diego Rivera (auth, catalog), Detroit Inst Arts, 78; Diego Rivera: A Retrospective (auth, catalog), Detroit Inst of Arts, 86. *Pos:* Spec asst, Proj Outreach, Detroit Inst Arts, Mich, 68-69, jr cur educ, 69-73, asst cur educ, 73-76, cur educ, 76-89; head, education div, Nat Gallery Art, Washington, 89-; bd trustee, Am Fed Arts, currently. *Teaching:* Adj asst prof art hist, Wayne State Univ, Detroit, Mich, 76-89. *Awards:* Best Cult Film Award for Only Then Regale My Eyes, Midwest Pub Broadcasting Serv, 76; Cine Golden Eagle for the Frescoes of Diego Rivera film, 86. *Mem:* Am Asn Mus; Mus Educators Round Table; Art Table; Col Art Asn; Int Coun Mus. *Publ:* Coauth, Gallery Activities for Unguided Groups, Mus News, 89; Diego Rivera, International Dictionary of Art and Artists, London, 90; A Recent History of Women Educators in Art Museums, Gender Perspectives: Essays on Women in Museums, Smithsonian Inst Press, 94; The need for learning research in museums, In: Public Institutions for Personal Learning (John Faulk & Lynn Dierking, eds), Am Asn Mus, Washington, 95; Diego Rivera: The Detroit Industry Murals, 99. *Mailing Add:* Nat Gallery Art Washington DC 20565

DOWNS, STUART CLIFTON
ADMINISTRATOR, EDUCATOR
b Arlington, Va, Nov 11, 50. *Study:* Hampden-Sydney Col, BA, 73; Western Ky Univ, MA, 77; Univ NC, Chapel Hill, cert, 85. *Collection Arranged:* Folios, Quartos & Costumes: From the Folger Shakespeare Libr, 84; Philip Pearlstein: Personal Selections, 86. *Pos:* Dir, Sawhill Gallery, James Madison Univ, Harrisonburg, VA, 83-. *Teaching:* Instr, introd to mus work & mus studies, James Madison Univ, 79-, internship art, 81-. *Mem:* Am Asn Mus; Va Asn Mus (bd mem, 84-). *Mailing Add:* 655 S Dogwood Dr Harrisonburg VA 22801

DOYLE, JOE
PAINTER, EDUCATOR
b Manhattan, NY, Feb 27, 41. *Study:* San Francisco State Univ, Calif, BA, 69, MFA, 71. *Work:* Oakland Mus, Calif. *Comn:* Dallas, Tex. *Exhib:* Option 73/30, Contemp Art Ctr, Cincinnati, Ohio, 73; Interstices, Cranbrook Acad Art, Bloomfield Hills, Mich, 75; 6 EBay Painters, Oakland Mus, Calif, 77; Aesthetics of Graffiti, San Francisco Mus Art, 78; one-man show, San Jose Mus Art, Calif, 79, Foster Goldstrom Fine Arts, San Francisco, 83 & 85, Route 66 Gallery, Philadelphia, J Rosenthal Fine Arts, Chicago, 86, Ill Metrop Ctr, Chicago, 86, Merging One Gallery, Santa Monica, 87 & Harcourt's Contemp Gallery, San Francisco, 88; Reality of Illusion, Denver Art Mus, Colo, 79; Three Bay Area Painters, Chico State Univ, Calif, 79; Selections from the Contemp Art Collection of the Oakland Mus, Kaiser Ctr, Calif, 80; Midwestern Mus Art, Elkhorn, Ind, 81; Icons of Contemp Art, Foster Goldstrom Fine Arts, Oakland, Calif, 83; The Gallery Collection, J Rosenthal Fine Arts, Chicago, 84; Shadows, Univ Calif, Davis, 85; Dallas Collects, Concord Bank, Tex, 86; Merging One Gallery, Santa

Monica, Calif, 87; The Goldstrom Collection, Davenport Art Ctr, Davenport, Iowa, 88. *Teaching:* Instr painting, Laney Col, Oakland, Calif, 71-73; co-chmn fine arts, Acad Art, San Francisco, 75-76; adj prof fine arts, Univ San Francisco, 75-76; instr, spray painting, Calif Col Arts & Crafts Exten Prog, Oakland, 79-80, painting, drawing, figure drawing, San Francisco Acad Art, 78-79,. *Bibliog:* David Berreth (auth), Art Museum, Miami Univ, Oxford, Ohio, 9/85; Thomas Albright (auth), Art in the San Francisco Bay Area 1945-1980, Univ Calif Press, 85; Daniel E Stetson (auth), New Acquisitions, Davenport Mus Art, Davenport, Iowa, 4/88. *Mem:* Calif Fedn Art Teachers. *Media:* Mixed. *Dealer:* Harcourts Contemporary 535 Powell St San Francisco CA 94108. *Mailing Add:* 4545 Toyon Pl Oakland CA 94619

DOYLE, JOHN LAWRENCE
PRINTMAKER, PAINTER
b Chicago, Ill, Mar 14, 39. *Study:* Art Inst Chicago, BAE, 62; Northern Ill Univ, MA, 68. *Work:* Libr Cong; Smithsonian Inst Collection Traveling Exhib; Art Inst Chicago; Cody Mus Western Art; Midwest Mus Am Art; and others. *Comn:* Poster, Denver Mus Natural Hist. *Exhib:* 22nd Boston Printmakers Exhib, De Cordova Mus, Lincoln, Mass, 70; Images on Paper, Miss Art Mus, Jackson, 70; Prints & Drawings, Los Angeles Co Mus Art, Los Angeles, Calif, 73; Rahr W Mus, Manitowoc, Wis, 79; Scottsdale Art Ctr, Ariz, 79; Harvard Med & Law Libr, Cambridge, Mass; Nat Libr Med, Bethesda, Md; Nat Gallery Art, Washington; Milwaukee Art Ctr; Welcome Inst, London; and others. *Awards:* Eisendrath Prize, 73rd Chicago Show, Art Inst Chicago, 72; Purchase Prizes, 24th Am Drawings Biennial, Norfolk Mus Arts & Sci, 72 & Images on Paper, Miss Art Mus, 72. *Bibliog:* Mendelowitz (auth), Drawings (Illustration), Univ Iowa, 76; Ben Dallas (auth), Mysticism through visual metaphor, SW Arts Mag, 77; Scott E Dial (auth), John L Doyle, Art Voices S, 11/79. *Media:* Lithograph, Watercolor, Acrylic. *Mailing Add:* c/o Joan Cawley Gallery 7135 E Main St Scottsdale AZ 85251

DOYLE, MARY ELLEN
PAINTER
b Hartford, Conn, Oct 8, 38. *Study:* Vassar Col, 56-58, Boston Univ Sch Fine Arts, BFA, 62, study with Walter Murch; Columbia Sch Painting & Sculpture, 64-65, study with John Heliker. *Work:* Wadsworth Atheneum, Hartford, Conn; Ark Art Ctr, Little Rock; The Phillips Collection, Washington, DC; Achenbach Found for the Graphic Arts, Fine Arts Mus of San Francisco, Calif; Albuqueque Mus, NMex; New Orleans Mus Art, La; Nat Mus Am Art, Washington, DC; and others. *Exhib:* Solo exhibs, New Sch Social Res, NY, 82 & 89, Susan Conway Gallery, Washington, 92, 94, 97, 2000 & 2002, The Phillips Collection (with catalog), Washington, DC, 97; Towards the Horizon: Recent Works on Paper (with catalog), Montgomery Mus FIne Arts, Ala, Miss Mus Art, Jackson & Columbus Mus Art, Ga, 99-2000. *Teaching:* Instr studio art, Barnard Col, New York, 62-65; instr children's art classes, Mus Mod Art, New York, 63-71; instr drawing, New Sch Social Res, New York, 78-94, Continuous Ser Award, 95. *Awards:* Walter Biggs Mem Award, Nat Acad Design, 89; Adolf & Clara Obrig Prize, Nat Acad Design, 94; Distinguished Alumni Award, Boston Univ Sch for Arts, 2000. *Bibliog:* Janet Wilson (auth), Galleries: Mary Ellen Doyle and the beauty of the beach, Long Island Lights, Wash Post, 1/92; Weil, Rex (auth), Mary Ellen Doyle, Artnews, 12/97; Greben Deidre Stein (auth), Artist's East End Landscapes Lead to Overdue Recognition, NY Times, 11/97; Ferdinand Protzman (auth), Galleries: Geometry's Pretty Picture, Washington Post, 3/2000. *Media:* Watercolor. *Dealer:* Susan Conway Gallery 716 Acequia Madre Santa Fe New Mexico 87501. *Mailing Add:* 41 Union Sq W New York NY 10003

DOYLE, NOEL FRANCIS
PAINTER, SCULPTOR
b Kingston, Ont, Dec 18, 61; Can & Irish citizen. *Study:* Univ Toronto; Univ Ottawa; Univ BC. *Work:* Absolute Vodka, Stockholm, Sweden; Molsons Brewing Co, Toronto, Can; Jones Brewing Co, Tenn; The Sleeman Collection, Guelph, Canada; Philips Electronics, Toronto, Can. *Comn:* The Jury (painting series), comn by Daniel Stripinis, Ottawa, 90; Absolute Paintings, Absolute Vodka, Sweden, 94. *Pos:* Dir, Blast Gallery, 91-92, NF Doyle Gallery, 92-93; owner, Galerie Voltaire, 93-95. *Teaching:* Lectr art, Univ Ottawa, 88 & Univ Toronto, 90. *Bibliog:* Kate Taylor (auth), Noise Off, Globe & Mail, 94. *Mem:* Soc Voltaire. *Media:* Wood, Paint. *Publ:* Auth, Bounce Off-Jeff Wall, Art Focus, 92; Horoscopes of Art World, Art Focus, 94-95. *Dealer:* Lory James Gallery Voltaire 3 Rosemount Ave M6K IY4. *Mailing Add:* 196 Bathurst St Toronto ON M5T 2R8 Canada

DOYLE, TOM
SCULPTOR, EDUCATOR
b Jerry City, Ohio, May 23, 28. *Study:* Ohio State Univ, BFA, 52, MA, 53, MFA, with Roy Lichtenstien & Stanley Twardewicz. *Work:* Carnegie Inst, Pittsburgh; Kley Collection, Ger; City Beautiful Project, Dayton, Ohio; Allentown Cedar Parkway, Allentown, Pa, 87. *Comn:* Fiberglass sculpture, Pub Arts Coun, City of New York, 72; Fed Bldg & Courthouse, Fairbanks, Alaska, 80; Cooper Sq Housing, NY, 85; Queens Col/City Univ NY, Science Bldg, Flushing, NY, 88; Jean Widmark Mem, Roxbury, Conn, 97. *Exhib:* Vanishing Points, Moderna Museet, Stockhom, Sweden, 84; Portes Ouvertes, Foundation d'-Art De Lanapoule, Lanapoule, France, 89; solo exhibs, Allen Stone Gallery, NY, 61 & 62, Dwan Gallery, New York City, 66 & 67, Picker Art Gallery, Hamilton, NY, 76, Miami Dade Community Col, Fla, 82, Sculpture Ctr, New York City, 88, Bill Bace Gallery, 94, Longhouse Found, E Hampton, NY, 95, Mattatuck Mus, Waterbury, Conn, 96, Paris/NY/Kent Gallery, Kent, Conn, 96 & Kouros Gallery, NY, 99, Kouros Gallery, 99, Nicolaysen Art Mus & Discovery Ctr, Casper, WY, 2001, New Arts Program, Kutztown, Pa, 2001, Paessaggio Gallery, W Hartford, Conn, 2001, New Arts Gallery, 2003 & 05, Shirley/Jones Gallery, 2006; Sculptors and Their Environments, Pratt Manhattan Gallery, NY, 98; Wash, Pride and Place, The Gunn Hist Mus, Wash, Conn, 2000; Six Great Families, Paris-NY-Kent Gallery, Kent, Conn, 2000; Chesterwood Mus, Stockbridge, Mass, 2002. *Teaching:* Instr sculpture, Brooklyn Mus Art Sch, 60-68 & New Sch Social Res, 61-68; assoc prof sculpture, Queens Col, 70-92, prof sculpture, 82, retired. *Awards:* Fel Sculpture, Nat Endowment Arts, 90-92; Jimmy Ernst Award for Lifetime Achievement, Am Acad Arts & Letts, 94; Ohioana Career Award, 96. *Bibliog:* Lucy R Lippard (auth), Tom Doyle, Kunsthalle, Dusseldorf, 65 & Space embraced: Tom Doyle's recent sculpture, Arts, 4/66; Robert Pincus-Witten (auth), Tom Doyle: Things patriotic and union blue, Arts, 9/79; and others. *Mem:* Am Abstract Artists; Nat Acad. *Media:* Wood, Bronze. *Dealer:* Kouros Gallery; Paesaggio Fine Arts; Shirley/Jones Gallery

DOYON, AURORA S
PAINTER
b New Delhi, India, Apr 14, 62. *Study:* Mus Fine Art, Boston, 94-95; studied with Joshua Graham, Graham Sch Art, 94-95. *Comn:* Portrait, comn by Mary Wilson, NY, 98; portrait, comn by Nicholas Evans, San Francisco, 98; portrait, comn by Mayor Willie Brown, City of San Francisco. *Exhib:* Celebration of Fine Art, San Francisco, 98; John Muir Art Show, Walnut Creek, Calif, 98. *Awards:* Honorable Mention, John Muir Art Show, 98. *Mem:* Portrait Soc Am; Wash Soc Portrait Artists; LaMorinda Arts Alliance; Las Juntas Artists. *Media:* Oil on Canvas, Charcoal. *Mailing Add:* 1126-D Reeves Ct San Francisco CA 94130

DRACHNIK (CAY), CATHERINE MELDYN
PAINTER, EDUCATOR
b Kansas City, Mo, June 7, 24. *Study:* Kansas City Art Inst, 41-42; Univ Md, BS, 45; Calif State Univ, Sacramento, MA (art therapy), 75; studied at Parsons Sch Design, NY, 45, Carmel Art Inst, Old Dominion Univ, Long Beach State Col, Am River Col. *Work:* Aerojet Corp Gallery, Folsom, Calif. *Comn:* portrait, comn by Ms Kelly Netto, 95; comn by James Jenkins, 98; comn by Mr & Mrs James Glasscock, 98; comn by Susan Baxter, 99; comn by Mrs Robert Trathen, 2000; comn by Joan Gann, 2000; comn by John Haynes, Capt USN Ret. *Exhib:* Int Art Exhib, Saigon Art Mus, Vietnam, 62, Vietnamese Spring Exhib, 62; Capitol Area Exhib, Smithsonian Inst, Washington, DC, 64; 43rd Ann Exhib, Haggin Art Mus, Stockton, Calif, 94, 95, 96, 97, 98, 2002, 03 & 06; Calif Watercolor Asn, San Francisco, 98, 2001 & 05; Watercolor West, Brea Cult Ctr, Calif, 99; West Coast Soc Portrait Artists, Sacto Fine Arts Ctr, Sacramento, 99; Rocky Mt Nat Exhib, Colo, 99-; Biennial Statewide Watercolor, Triton Mus Art, Santa Clara, Calif, 2000 & 02; Am Watercolor Soc, Salmagundi Club, New York City, 2000. *Teaching:* instr art, Calif State Univ, Sacramento, 75-92 & dir Art Therapy Program, 99; instr metaphors, Coll Notre Dame, Belmont, Calif, 75-90; instr children's art class, Sacramento Fine Arts Center, 94-95; instr fashion illustration, Sacramento City Coll, 96-2006. *Awards:* Award of Excellence, Calif State Fair, 2000 & 05; Award of Excellence, Northern Calif Artist Open, 2000; Pres award Calif Watercolor Soc, San Francisco, Calif, 2001; Most Outstanding Watercolor, Calif State Fair, 2001; Award of Excellence, Magnum Opus, Sacto Fine Arts Ctr, 2002; First Place, Watercolor, Primere Graphics, 2002; Award of Excellence, No Calif Artists, 2003; Special Award, Haggin Mus, 2003; Best of Show, Vacaville Art League, 2004; First Place, Watercolor, KR Gallery, 2004. *Bibliog:* Holly Heyser (auth), Therapeutic Drawing, Sacramento Bee, 6/88; Chris Astone (auth), One Generation Helping Another, The Key, Spring 96; Gladys Agell (auth), Art Therapists Who Are Artists, AMC J Art Therapy, 5/99. *Mem:* Am Art Therapy Asn (hon life mem, pres, 87-89); Northern Calif Art Asn (publicity chair, 2000-2001, signature mem); Calif Watercolor Asn (signature mem); Calif State Univ Art Alumna Asn; Am Watercolor Asn; Nat Assistance League; Crocker Kinsley Art Club. *Media:* Watercolor. *Specialty:* Paintings. *Publ:* auth, The History of the Licensing of Art Therapists as Marriage & Family Counselors, Arts in Psychotherapy, 89; auth, Interpreting Metaphors in Children's Drawings, Abbeygate Press, 95; auth, The Artwork of Art Therapy Pioneers, AMC J Art Theraphy, 96; contribr, Working With Images-The Art of Art Therapists, Charles C Thomas, 2001; Illustrating the Problem, Inside Arden News, 7/03. *Dealer:* Elliott Fouts Art Gallery 4749 J St Sacramento Ca 95819; CJE's Art & Fiber Gallery 10239 Fair Oaks Blvd Fair Oaks CA 95628. *Mailing Add:* 4124 American River Dr Sacramento CA 95864-6025

DRAKE, JAMES
PRINTMAKER, SCULPTOR
b Lubbock, Tex, Sept 12, 46. *Study:* Art Ctr Col of Design, fel, BFA with Hons, 69, MFA, 70. *Work:* El Paso Mus Art, Tex; Phoenix Art Mus, Ariz; Univ NMex Art Mus, Albuquerque; Univ Tex, El Paso; Mathews Art Ctr, Ariz State Univ, Tempe. *Exhib:* New Visions, Amarillo Art Ctr, Tex, 81; one-man exhib, Galveston Arts Ctr on the Strand, Tex, 82; Southern Fiction, Contemp Art Mus, Houston, 83; New Orleans Triennal, New Orleans Mus Art, 83; and others. *Teaching:* Instr life drawing, Art Ctr Col of Design, Los Angeles, 69-70 & Univ Tex, El Paso. *Bibliog:* Barbara Cortright (auth), Sculpture & graphics, Art Week, 2/76. *Mailing Add:* c/o Adair Margo Gallery 415 E Yandell Suite 10-B El Paso TX 79922-1726

DRAKE, PETER
PAINTER, DRAFTSMAN
b Garden City, NY, July 29, 57. *Study:* Pratt Inst, BFA, 79. *Work:* Mus Contemp Art, Los Angeles, Calif; Los Angeles Co Mus, Calif; Mus Mod Art Mex, Mexico City; Phoenix Mus Art, Ariz; J Patrick Lannen Found, Miami, Fla. *Exhib:* East Village Art in Berlin, Zellermayer Gallery, Berlin, 84; Nueva Pintura Narrativa, Mus Tamayo, Mexico City, 84; Blue Condition, Greenville Co Mus, SC, 85; NY/Seattle, Seattle Ctr Contemp Art, Wash, 85; Romanticism/Cyncism in Contemp Art, Haggerty Mus, Milwaukee, Wis, 86; Avant Garde in the 80's, Los Angeles Co Mus, Calif, 87; solo exhibs, Elizabeth Leach Gallery, Portland, Ore, 97 & Lowe Gallery, Atlanta, Ga, 97; The Liars (III) Frightful Paint Arti et Amicitiae, Amsterdam, 98; Small Works-The Sequel, Susan Cummins Gallery, San Francisco, Calif, 98. *Pos:* Artist/consult,

Drawing Ctr, New York, 84-; staff writer, Flash Art, 86. *Awards:* Nat Endow Arts, 87. *Bibliog:* Michael Kohn (auth), Romantic Vision, Flash Art, 85; Michael Cone (auth), Peter Drake, Flash Art, 86; Michael Brenson (auth), The ink drawing of Peter Drake, NY Times, 87. *Media:* Oil. *Dealer:* Curt Marcus Gallery. *Mailing Add:* 520 Second Ave Apt 15C New York NY 10016

DRAPALIK, BETTY R
PAINTER, CONSULTANT
b Cicero, Ill. *Study:* workshops under Phil Austin, Bridget Austin, Catherine Wilson Smith, Tony Van Hasselt, Rose Edin, Tom Trausch, Tom Lynch, Tom Francesconi, Diane Maxey, John Dioszegi, Ratinda Das, Ingrid Albrecht. *Work:* Spring Blossoms I, Col of Lake Co, Grayslake, Ill; Cana Light, Assoc Bank of Sister Bay, Wis; School House Path, Greenbelt Cult Ctr, N Chicago, Ill; Lady Slipper, Lake Villa Pub Libr, Ill; Reflections and Shadows, Waukegan Township Supv Office, Ill; Ill Tall Grass Prairie, Aurora Hist Mus; Garden Guardian, M/M Dittman, Cana Island Light House I, Lynn Ackerman, Tinley Park, Ill; Cana Light to Doctor Rodger Welker, Waukegan, Ill, 98; Sweetie Pie to Mrs Ron Hlavin, 98. *Comn:* Garden Guardian Angel, Grace Missionary Church, Zion, Ill; The Glowing, Jane Sherman; Arnie's Garden Guardian, Rev & Mrs David Eikenberry; In the Garden, First Presbyterian Church of Waukeegan, Ill; Fence Gardian, Patricia Ann Ryan, Beach Park, Ill; Maiden Hair, The Clearing in Door Co, Wis. *Exhib:* Recent Works, Cmty Gallery of Art, Grayslake, Ill, 93, 94, 96-98, 00, 03; 34th-40th Ann Juried Exhib, Hardy Gallery, Ephraim, Wis, 96-00; 9th Ann Nat Exhib, Truman State Univ, Kirksville, Mo, 96; NW NMex Arts Coun Exch Nat, Farmington, NMex, 97; Watercolor 99, 00, 01, 04, 05 & 06, Dellora A Norris Cult Ctr, Saint Charles, Ill, 99, 00, 01, 03; Red River Watercolor Soc, Minn State Univ, Moorhead, Minn, 99; Celebrating Door Co Ridges Book Project, Guenzel Gallery, Fish Creek, Wis, 00, Pushing the Boundaries of Watercolor, 02; Anderson Art, Cedar Ctr, Kenosha, Wis, 2004 & 2005; Pikes Peak, Watercolor Int, Watermedia XIII 2003; Western Colo Watercolor Soc, 12th Ann Exhib, March 2004; solo exhib, Lake County Discovery Mus, 2005, Jack Benny Cult Art Ctr, 2006. *Collection Arranged:* Retrospective of Phil Austin's Work, Jck Benny Cultural Arts Ctr, Waukegan, IL, May 2004. *Teaching:* instr art, Girl Scouts USA, 45-55; instr art, Boy Scouts Am, 45-55; subst tchr Waukegan Visual Arts Ctr, 02; One day class, Walkerville School, MI, 2003-. *Awards:* 1st Place in watercolor, Lake Co Art League Fine Arts Festival/ Door Co Art League, 1996; Best of Show, Kenosha Art Asn/Lake Co Art League Ann Art Event, 1997; Purchase award, 36th Ann Juried Exhib, Hardy Gallery, 1998; 2nd place, Impression in Watercolor, Dr William M Sch Col of Podiatric Medicine at Rosalind Franklin Univ of Med & Sci. *Bibliog:* Melissa May Dobbins (auth), The art clinic, Artist Mag, 5/1997; Laini Zinn (auth), From budding to blooming artist, Lake Co & Its Arts, 4/1997. *Mem:* Nat Mus Women in the Arts; Transparent Watercolor Soc Am (life mem); Red River Watercolor Soc; Lakes Region Watercolor Guild; Lake County Art League (former pres). *Media:* Watercolor. *Interests:* To promote "transparent" watercolor as a recognized medium, to promote public interest in fine art, and to share nature's beauty. *Collection:* Watercolors by Phil Austin, Win Jones, Tom Lynch, Sharon Crosbie, Tony Van Hasselt; Hummel and Lladro figurines; artist collector plates. *Publ:* contbr, Celebrating Door County's Wild Places, Prairie Oak Press, 2001. *Dealer:* Avenue Art Shop Racine WI; Deerpath Art Gallery Lake Forest IL. *Mailing Add:* 2018 W Grove Ave Waukegan IL 60085

DRAPELL, JOSEPH
PAINTER, FILMMAKER
b Humpolec, Bohemia, Czech, Mar 13, 40; Can citizen. *Study:* Cranbrook Acad Art, with Donald Willett & George Ortman, MFA, 70. *Work:* Guggenheim Mus; Mus Fine Arts, Boston; Mus Mod Art, Vienna, Austria; Brit Mus, London; Nat Gallery, Prague. *Comn:* Outdoor sculpture, Halifax, NS; mural, Cineplex Odeon Theatres, Toronto, Ont. *Exhib:* New Acquisitions, Guggenheim Mus, 72; New Abstract Art, Edmonton Art Gallery, 77; Color Abstractions, Mus Fine Arts, Boston, 79; The Threshold of Color, Edmonton Art Gallery, 82; retrospective, Art Gallery Windsor, Ont, 84 & Moore Gallery, Hamilton, Ont, 96; Island Paintings, Shippee Gallery, NY, 88; New New Painting, Galerie Gerald Piltzer, Paris; The Archetypal Figures, Gallery One, Toronto, 94; Gallery Ism, Seoul, Korea, 95; Fine Art 2000, Greenwich, Conn, 96; Flint Inst Arts, Mich, 98; New New Painters, The Real Avantgarde Armory Show, New York City, 2000; New New Painters, Nat Gallery, Prague, 2002. *Collection Arranged:* Drapell at 65, Mus New Painters, Toronto, 2005; High Stakes the Crisis in Art, 2006. *Teaching:* Instr artistic methods, York Univ, Toronto, 70-71; vis artist in residence, Syracuse Univ, 73; guest artist, Triangle Artists' Workshop, Pine Plains, NY, 84, Emma Lake Artists' Workshop, Univ Saskatchewan, 88. *Awards:* Can Coun Grant, 71; Ont Arts Coun Grants, 75 & 76. *Bibliog:* Karen Wilkin (auth), The Recent Work of Joseph Drapell (catalog essay), New York, 86; Kenworth Moffett (auth), New New Painting (book), Nouvelles Eds Francaises, Paris, 92; Donald Kuspit (auth), Painting Beside and Inside Itself (catalog essay), Art 2000, Conn, 96. *Media:* Acrylic on Canvas; Bronze; Film. *Dealer:* Moore Gallery 80 Spadina Ave Toronto ON; Mus New New Painting, 128 Claremont St, Toronto, Canada. *Mailing Add:* 123 Bellwoods Ave Toronto ON M6J 2P6 Canada

DRAPER, JOSIAH EVERETT
PAINTER, WRITER
b East Orange, NJ, Oct 17, 15. *Study:* Pratt Inst, Brooklyn, advert design & illus; Grand Cent Sch Art, New York, with Harvey Dunn; also with Edgar Whitney, Paul Strisik & John Pike. *Work:* Cummer Gallery Art, Jacksonville, Fla; Jacksonville Univ; US Navy; City of Bahia Blanca, Arg; Jacksonville Mus of Arts & Sci; and others. *Comn:* Painting, Jacksonville Area Chamber of Commerce, 72 & 81; ten paintings, Sea Pines Co, Amelia Island, Fla, 73, 5 paintings, Indian River Plantation, Stuart, Fla, 81; painting, District Court Appeals, Daytona Beach, Fla. *Exhib:* Am Watercolor Soc Ann, NY, 62-74; one-man shows, Fla Gulf Coast Art Ctr, Clearwater, 73 & Jacksonville Art Mus, 74; District Court Appeals, Tallahassee, Fla, 82; Indian River Plantation, Stuart, Fla, 83; and many others. *Pos:* Artist, Prudential Ins Co Am, 35-50, art dir, 51-72; retired; pres, J E Draper, AWS, Inc, 81. *Teaching:* Instr watercolor technique, Jacksonville Art Mus, 70-88; spec watercolor workshops in US, West Indies, Europe & Mexico. *Awards:* Ann Traveling Exhib, Am Watercolor Soc, 66 & 69 & Carolyn Stern Award, 69. *Mem:* Am Watercolor Soc; Fla Watercolor Soc (bd dirs, 72-, pres, 77-78); St Augustine Art Asn (pres, 72-74, bd dir, 75-81); Jacksonville Watercolor Soc; Salmagundi Club, NY. *Media:* Transparent Watercolor, Drawing. *Publ:* Auth, Putting People in Your Paintings, 85, People Painting Scrapbook, 88, contribr, Basic Drawing Techniques, 91, Basic Watercolor Techniques, 91, Basic People Painting Techniques & Splash II, 92, North Light. *Dealer:* Ponte Vedra Club Ponte Vedra Beach FL 32082. *Mailing Add:* 20 Ponte Vedra Circle Ponte Vedra Beach FL 32082

DRASLER, GREGORY J
PAINTER
b Waukegan, Ill, June 7, 52. *Study:* Univ Ill, BFA, MFA. *Exhib:* Cave Painting (auth catalog), Queens Mus Art, NY, 94. *Teaching:* Princeton Univ, Williams Col. *Awards:* New York Found Arts Fel, 91; Nat Endowment Arts Fel, 93. *Mailing Add:* 137 Duane St Apt 4B New York NY 10013

DREIBAND, LAURENCE
PAINTER, LECTURER
b New York, NY, Nov 8, 44. *Study:* Chouinard Art Inst, Los Angeles, 61; Art Ctr Col Design, Los Angeles, BFA(with distinction), 67, fel & MFA, 68. *Work:* Home Savings & Loan Collection; Container Corp Am Collection; Chase Manhattan Bank. *Comn:* Great Ideas of Western Man, Container Corp Am, 70. *Exhib:* West Coast 70, E B Crocker Art Gallery, Sacramento, Calif, 70; Beyond the Actual, Pioneer Mus, Stockton, Calif, 70; one-man shows, David Stuart Galleries, 70-72, Los Angeles Inst Contemp Art, 80 & Allen Stone Gallery, NY, 81; California Artists, Long Beach Mus Art, 71; Galerie Quatres Mouvements, 74; Janus Gallery, 83. *Teaching:* Instr painting & photog, Art Ctr Col Design, 70-, chmn dept fine arts, 72-. *Awards:* First Prize, Fine Arts Gallery San Diego, 70; Great Ideas of Western Man Purchase Award, Container Corp Am, 70; 19th All City Festival Purchase Award, Munic Art Gallery, Los Angeles, 71. *Bibliog:* Joseph Young (auth), Los Angeles artist--Laurence Dreiband, Art Int, 70; Barbara Witus (auth), Paintings of Laurence Dreiband, Los Angeles Free Press, 3/31/72; Udo Kulterman (auth), New Realism, New York Graphic Soc, 72. *Media:* Oil, Acrylic. *Publ:* Auth, Laurence Dreiband, Paintings and Drawings, David Stuart Galleries, 72. *Mailing Add:* Art Ctr Col Design 1700 Lida St Pasadena CA 91103

DREIKAUSEN, MARGRET
PAINTER
b Cologne, Ger, Jan 9, 37. *Study:* Fashion Inst Technol, AAS, 67; Hunter Col, BA, 75, MA, 78, study with Robert Swain, Mary Miss & Robert Morris. *Work:* Staedtische Mus Heilbronn, Heilbronn, Ger; IBM Corp; Westchester & Sterling Forest, NY; Citibank, Long Island City, NY; Hong Kong & Shanghai Banking Corp, NY. *Exhib:* Stadtbuecherei, Heilbronn, Ger, 91; Nat Art Competition, Northeast Mo State Univ, Kirksville, Mo, 92; Gallery 84, NY, 93; Artists Choose Artists, Flushing Arts Coun, 94; Fac Leave Show III, Parsons Sch Design, NY, 95; East Bank Artists, Henry DeFord Gallery, Long Island, NY, 96; Women's Hist Month, Fed Bldg, Jamaica, NY, 97; From Our Side of the River, Henry DeFord Gallery, Long Island, NY, 98; and others. *Teaching:* Instr design, Parsons Sch Design, 79-. *Awards:* Second Prize, Nat Art Competition, Northeast State Univ, Kirksville, Mo. *Bibliog:* Barbara Haag (auth), Die Erde von oben gesehen, 4/10/84; Ten Artists (catalog), Second Long Island City Open Studios; Heilbronner Stimme (auth), Das Truegerische im Foto, 1//10/91 & Landschafts-Design, 1/17/91. *Mem:* Col Art Asn Am; Long Island City Artists Inc. *Media:* Miscellaneous Media. *Publ:* Auth, Aerial Perception, The Earth as Seen From Aircraft and Spacecraft and its Influence on Contemporary Art, Art Alliance Press, Philadelphia, 85; contribr, Essays on Creativity and Science, ed by Diana DeLuca, Hawaii Coun Teachers English, Honolulu, 86

DRESKIN, JEANET STECKLER
PAINTER, EDUCATOR
b New Orleans, La, Sept 29, 21. *Study:* Newcomb Col, Tulane Univ, with Will Henry Stevens, BFA, 42; John Hopkins Univ, med art cert, 43; John McCrady Sch, New Orleans; Clemson Univ, MFA, 73; Art Students League, NY. *Hon Degrees:* South Carolina Governor's School for the Arts & Humanities, Lifetime Achievement Award, 98; The Governor's Award for the Arts: 2004, Elizabeth Verner Lifetime Achievement Award, 2004. *Work:* Smithsonian Nat Mus of Art, Washington; Ga Mus Art, Athens; Greenville Co Mus Art, SC; Guild Hall Mus, East Hampton, NY; State Art Collection, SC State Mus, Columbia; Gibbes Mus, Charleston, SC; Zimmerli Mus, Rutgers Univ, NJ. *Comn:* Seals & plaque, SC State Bd Health, Columbia, 57; McDonald Corp, Chicago, 82; Merrill Lynch, Atlanta, Ga, 85; painting, Nat Mus Illus, NY, 86; Fed Reserve Bank Richmond, Charlotte, 88. *Exhib:* Chautauqua Exhib Am Art, NY, 70; 38th Ann Mid-Yr Show, Butler Inst Am Art, Youngstown, Ohio, 74 & 83; Art in Medicine, Nat Mus Illus, NY, 86; Nat Print & Drawing Exhib, Rudolph Lee Gallery, Clemson Univ, SC, 87, 89, 91, 93, 2002 & 2005; traveling show, Centennial Exhib, Nat Asn Women Artists, 89-90, Invitational Drawing Exhib USA, Mid Am Arts Alliance, Kansas City, Mo, 89-91; Nat Women's Exhib, India, 89-90; National Works on Paper, Univ Miss, Oxford, Miss, 91; many others; 100 Years/100 Artists: SC State Mus, 99-2000; Greenville Co Mus of Art, 62, 64, 70, 75, 85, 99 & 2005. *Pos:* Staff artist, Am Mus Nat Hist, New York, 43-45; staff artist, Univ Chicago Med Sch, 45-50. *Teaching:* Painting & graphics, Greenville Co Mus Sch Art, 50-52 & 62-, head sch, 68-74; adj prof art, Univ SC, 73-96, Governor's Sch, 81-2000. *Awards:* Merit Award, Int Grand Prix, Cannes, France, 73; Award, Southern Watercolor, Univ Miss, 85, 88 & 97; Merit Award, San Diego Int Watercolor, 97; award, Am Soc Contemporary Artists, NYC, 97, 2000 & 2002. *Bibliog:* Jack A Morris, Jr (auth), Contemporary Artists of

South Carolina, Tricentennial Comn, 70; Patricia Robbins (auth), Jeanet Dreskin, Art Voices S, 5-6/79; Feature, Art's the Thing, SC Educ TV, 87; and others; Martha Severens (curator), Greenville County Museum of Art Catalogue, 99. *Mem:* Guild SC Artists (mem bd, 55-, treas, 68, vpres, 71, pres, 72); Nat Asn Women Artists (mem comt, 71-); SC Watercolor Soc (pres, 83-84); Nat Asn Med Illusr; Southern Graphics Coun (secy-treas, 74-76, treas, 88-90, mem bd, 74-92); plus others. *Media:* Goauche; Watercolor; Collage. *Publ:* Illusr, Anatomy of the Gorilla, Am Mus Nat Hist, Columbia Univ, 43-46; What's New, Abbot Labs (& Latin Am ed), 46, 47 & 49; Surgery of Repair, Lippincott, 50; Williams Obstetrics, Stander-Appleton, 50; Surgical Anatomy, BC Decker (Mosby), 90; many others. *Dealer:* Hampton III Gallery Ltd 11 Hampton Ctr Taylors SC 29687. *Mailing Add:* 60 Lake Forest Dr Greenville SC 29609

DREWAL, HENRY JOHN
HISTORIAN, EDUCATOR
b Brooklyn, NY, Mar 11, 43. *Study:* Hamilton Col, BA; Inst African Studies, Columbia Univ, cert, MA, PhD. *Collection Arranged:* Dimensions in Black Art, African, Afro-American & Afro-Brazilian Art at Cleveland State Univ, 75 & African Fabrics: Tradition and Change, 76, Cleveland State Univ; Traditional Art of the Nigerian Peoples: the Ratner Collection (auth, catalog), Mus African Art, 77; African Artistry: Technique and Aesthetics in Yoruba Sculpture (auth, catalog), High Mus Art, Atlanta, 80; Object and Intellect: African Art from the Neuberger Mus, State Univ NY, Purchase, 86; Shapes of the Mind: African Art from Long Island Cols (auth, catalog), Hofstra Univ; Yoruba: Nine Centuries of African Art & Thought, (auth, catalog), 89; African Permanent Collection, Cleveland Mus Art, 90. *Pos:* Vis prof art hist State Univ of NY Purchase, 86, Univ Calif, Santa Barbara, 88. *Teaching:* Asst prof African, Oceanic, Am Indian & Afro-Am art, Cleveland State Univ, 73-77, assoc prof, 77-81, chmn dept, 82-85, prof, 82-90; consult African Art, Cleveland Mus Art, 88-90; Erjue-Bascom prof art hist, Univ Wis, Madison, 90-. *Awards:* Cleveland State Univ Res Grants, 74, 75, 76, 79, 80, 81 & 89; Nat Endowment Humanities Grant, 77-78, 81, 85, 89 & 90; Andrew W Mellon Fel, Metrop Mus Art, 85-86, 86-87; Rockefeller Found Grant, 88; NY State Coun on Arts, 89; Univ Wis-Madison, Fac Grants, 91; Fulbright-Brazil, 97; Nat Endowment Humanities fel, 98; Ford Found Grant, 2000; AIIS fel, 2001; Fulbright-Benin, 2003; Fel Guggenheim Mem Found, 2004. *Mem:* Col Art Asn; Triennial Symp Traditional African Art; Midwest Art Hist Asn; Soc Study Visual Anthrop; Art Coun African Studies Asn; Soc Africanist Archeologists; Wis Acad of Scis, Arts, and Letters, Midwest Art Soc, Congress on Research in Dance, Col Art Asn, African Studies Asn. *Res:* History of art among the Yoruba, Fon and Ewe of West Africa and the African Diaspora of Brazil, Cuba, Puerto Rico, Panama, Mexico and India; principles of performance aesthetics; iconology. *Publ:* Flaming Crowns, Cooling Waters: Masks of the Ijebu Yoruba, 86; Art and Divination Among the Yoruba, Design and Myth, 87; Mermaids, Mirrors, and Snake Charmers, Igbo Mami Wata Shrines, 88; Beauty and Being: Aesthetics and Ontology in Yoruba Body Art, 88; Performing the Other: Mami Wata Worship in West Africa, The Drama Rev, 88; Art or Accident: Yoruba Body Artists and their Deity Ogun, 89; The Meaning of Osugbo Art, Man does not go naked, 89; Yoruba: Nine Centuries of African Art and Thought, 89; Yoruba Art and Aesthetics, 91; The Yoruba Artist, 94; Beads, Body, and Soul, 98. *Mailing Add:* Elvehjem Mus Art Univ Wis Madison WI 53706

DREYER, CLARICE A
SCULPTOR
b Missoula, Mont, Sept 10, 46. *Study:* Mont State Univ, BFA(art educ), 79; Univ Calif Berkeley, MFA, 81. *Exhib:* Solo shows, Marilyn Butler Gallery, Santa Monica, Calif, 90, Cheney Cowles Mus, Spokane, Wash, Owings/Dewey Fine Art, Santa Fe, NMex & South East Ctr Contemp Arts, Winston Salem, NC, 91; Arvada Ctr Arts, Colo, 91; Boise Art Mus, Idaho, 91; Boulder Art Ctr, Colo; and others. *Awards:* Pub Sculpture Comn Finalist, Mill Valley Sculpture Fountain, Calif, 84; Nat Endowment Arts Fel, 84 & 90; Pub Art Comn, Arvada Ctr Arts, Colo, 91. *Bibliog:* Lyn Smallwood (auth), Art, Seattle Post-Intelligencer, 7/15/88; Doloris Targan Ament (auth), At the edge, Seattle Times, J3, 7/17/88; Chris Schnoor (auth), Ordinary people, Reflex, 20, 9-10/88; and others. *Mailing Add:* 4750 Jordon Spur Rd Bozeman MT 59715

DREZNER, A L
SCULPTOR, ARCHITECT
b Trenton, NJ, May 27, 59. *Study:* St Lawrence Univ, BA(fine arts), 81; Johnson Atelier Tech Inst Dept Sculpture, 82; Univ Calif Los Angeles, 94; Harvard Univ Grad Sch Design, 97; Univ Calif Los Angeles,; Master in Arch UCLA, 2002. *Work:* Mass Inst Tech Visual Art Ctr, Cambridge, Mass; Rose Art Mus, Brandeis Univ, Waltham, Mass; Norton Family Found & Collection, Santa Monica, Calif; Johnson & Johnson Found, Lawrenceville, NJ. *Comn:* Proj ser, Santa Monica Mus Art, Calif, 97; Univ of Texas @ Dallas, 2005. *Exhib:* Triennial, Fuller Mus Art, Brocton, Mass, 90; solo exhib, Santa Monica Mus Art, Calif, 97; 97 Kunsthalle, Kunsthalle Lophem, Belgium, 97; Lance Fung Gallery, New York City, 2001; C Luckman Gallery Calif State Univ, Los Angeles, 2000; Univ of Tex, Dallas, 2005. *Collection Arranged:* Mit List @ Visual Arts Ctr, Buandeis Univ. *Teaching:* Teaching asst, Univ Calif Los Angeles, 94-95. *Awards:* Nat Endowment Arts Lottery grant, Boston Womens Installation Artist, 88; Project grant, Art Matters Inc, NY, 89; Colman Found grant, Boston Univ, 90; Pollock-Krasner Found Award, 99; Open Nat 9/11 Mem Competition, Los Angeles Int Airport, 3rd Place, 2003. *Bibliog:* Miles Unger (auth), A L Drezner, Art New England, 2/91; Amy Drezner, 1/95 & Beauty and intrique, 3/96, Los Angeles Times. *Media:* Installation, Sculpture. *Dealer:* Marc Foxx Gallery 3026 Nebraska Ave Santa Monica CA 90404. *Mailing Add:* PO Box 49-1801 Los Angeles CA 90049

DRIESBACH, DAVID FRAISER
PRINTMAKER
b Wausau, Wis, Oct 7, 22. *Study:* Univ Ill, Beloit Col; Univ Wis; Pa Acad Fine Arts; State Univ Iowa; Atelier 17, with S W Hayter, 69. *Work:* Seattle Mus, Wash; Dayton Art Inst, Ohio; Columbus Gallery Fine Arts, Ohio; Bibliot Nat, Paris, France; Boston Mus Fine Arts. *Comn:* Fiscal Flight (ed, 150 color etchings), Sears Roebuck Co, 67; series of bronze reliefs, Asn Am Artists, NY, 68; color intaglio ed, Checker Cab Co, Kalamazoo, Mich, 74; color intaglio, Soc Am Graphic Artists; color viscosity, Gemarts, Knoxville, Tenn. *Exhib:* Young Printmakers of America, Mus Mod Art, NY, 53; Ten Printmakers of USA, Purdue Univ, 66; one-man show travels Yugoslavia 5 months with US Info Agency, 85; Grafica Contemporanea Americana, Venice, Italy, 77; retrospective show, Univ Md, Baltimore Co, 79; Seventh British Int Print Biennale, Bradford, Eng, 82. *Teaching:* Prof printmaking, Northern Ill Univ, 64-91 (retired). *Awards:* Ford Found Purchase Prize for Intaglio, 60; 10th Ann Colorprint USA Purchase Prize, Tex Tech, 83; Second Int Exhib of Prints & Drawings Award, Wesleyan Col, Macon, Ga. *Bibliog:* Bob White (auth), David Driesbach, Chicago Art Scene, 1/68; The complex world of David Driesbach, Northern Alumnus, 3/68; David Driesbach Retrospective (catalog), Northern Ill, Univ, Dekalb. *Mem:* Midwest Col Art Asn; Soc Am Graphic Artists; Boston Printmakers. *Media:* Intaglio. *Dealer:* Edenside Gallery Louisville, KY; Sylvia Schimdt Gallery New Orleans LA; Annex Gallery, Santa Rosa, Calif. *Mailing Add:* 200 Wyndemere Circle Apt # W106 Wheaton IL 60187

DRIESBACH, WALTER CLARK, JR
SCULPTOR, INSTRUCTOR
b Cincinnati, Ohio, July 3, 29. *Study:* Sch Dayton Art Inst, 47-52, with Robert Koepnick; studio asst to Joseph Kiselewski, New York, 54-55; Art Acad Cincinnati, 55-56, with Charles Cutler. *Hon Degrees:* Sch Dayton Art Inst, diploma, 51. *Work:* Citizen (bronze figure), Pyramid Hill Sculpture Park & Mus, Hamilton, Ohio; Bell Tel Co; Gen Elec Co; Raymond Walters Col; Figure of a Bull, Mus Arts and Crafts, Zagreb, Croatia. *Comn:* Life of St Teresa (limestone entablature), St Teresa Church, Cincinnati, 62; The Lord's Supper (walnut relief), Good Shepherd Church, Cincinnati, 64; Firefighters' Mem (granite figure), Cincinnati, 68; Limestone portrait, (Harriet Beecher Stowe) Mercantile Libr, Cincinnati, 2002. *Exhib:* Ohio Sculptors, Akron & Canton Art Insts, 60; Northwest Territory Sculpture Show, Cincinnati Art Mus & John Herron Inst Art, Indianapolis, Ind, 61; Univ Cincinnati Regional Sculpture, 68; Invitational Exhib, Cincinnati Art Mus, Ohio, 72 & 81; Figure '82, Contemp Art Ctr, Cincinnati, 82; retrospective, Art Acad Cincinnati, 88; and others. *Teaching:* Instr drawing & sculpture, Memphis Acad Arts, 56-58, Wilmington Col, 63-66, Thomas More Col, 70-71 & 78-93; instr sculpture, Dayton Art Inst Evening Sch, 58-60 & Col Mt St Joseph, 72; instr sculpture, drawing & 3-D design, Univ Dayton, 66-72; instr sculpture, 3-D design & found, Art Acad Cincinnati, 70-87; instr wood carving, Communiv, Univ Cincinnati, 80-81; stone carving workshop, Community Educ, Art Acad Cincinnati, 90-. *Awards:* Fleischmann Purchase Prize, Zoo Arts Festival, Cincinnati, 64; First Prize, Prof Sculpture Div, Ohio State Fair Fine Arts Exhib, 66, Second Prize, 68. *Mem:* Cincinnati Carvers' Guild. *Media:* Wood, Cast Bronze. *Specialty:* Sculpture. *Publ:* Contribr, Contemporary Stone Sculpture, 70 & Creating Small Wood Objects as Functional Sculpture, 76, Crown; Masters of Wood Sculpture, Watson-Guptill, 80; Sculpture: Technique-Form-Content, Davis Publ, 89; The Sculpture Refrence, Sculpture Books Publ, 04. *Dealer:* Barbara Beatrice Gallery 562-C Buttermilk Pike Crescent Springs KY 41017. *Mailing Add:* 2541 Erie Ave Cincinnati OH 45208

DRIESSEN, ANGELA KOSTA See Kosta, Angela

DRISCOLL, EDGAR JOSEPH, JR
CRITIC
b Boston, Mass, Sept 1, 20. *Study:* Cambridge Sch Weston; Univ Iowa, with Grant Wood; Yale Univ Sch Fine Arts. *Pos:* Art critic, Boston Globe, 46-73; Boston corresp, Art News, 73-. *Mem:* Cambridge Art Asn (secy & bd dir). *Mailing Add:* 75 Hancock St No 1 Boston MA 02114

DRISCOLL, ELLEN
SCULPTOR, INSTRUCTOR
Study: Wesleyan Univ, BA(studio art) cum laude, 74. *Work:* Met Mus Art; Whitney Mus of Am Art; Addison Gallery of Am Art; New Sch for Social Rsch; Detroit Inst of Art. *Comn:* Mid-Atlantic States Arts Consortium Virginia Ctr Creative Arts, Sweet Briar, Va, 86; Oliver Ranch, Geyserville, Calif, 88; Ellyn & Saul Dennison, Bernardsville, 90; Mr Robert Orto, La Jolla, Calif, 91; Pub Art Comn for Grand Central Station, Metrop Transportation Authority, 92-98; As Above, So Below, 20 mosaic and glass works for Grand Ctrl Terminal North, Met Transp Authority and Met-North Railroad, 99; Circuitstream, 9'x22' sandblasted glass mural, Bank of Am, 2000. *Exhib:* A Contemp View of Nature, 86 & Innovations in Sculpture, 88, Aldrich Mus Contemp Art; Solo exhibs, Stavaridis Gallery, Boston, Mass, 87, Tim Hill Gallery, Birmingham, Mich, Whitney Mus Am Art (with catalog), 91-92, Contemp Art Ctr, Cincinnati, 92, New Work, Huntington Gallery, Mass Col Art, Boston, 93, Threadwaxing Space, NY, 95, Univ Mich Mus of Art, Ann Arbor, 97, The African Am Mus, Fresno, Calif, 2000, Green St Gallery, Boston, 2001, Univ Mass, 2001; 1980: A New Generation, Metrop Mus, NY, 88; Totem, 89 & Am Abstraction at the Addison, 91, Addison Gallery Am Art; 55 Ferris Street Exhib, Brooklyn, NY, 93; Art en Route: MTA/Arts for Transit Paine Webber Gallery, NY & The Mus Stony Brook, Long Island, 94; Threadwaxing Space, NY, 94; Equal Rights & Justice, High Mus, Atlanta, Ga, 94; In Three Dimensions: Women Sculptors of the 90s, Snug Harbor Cult Ctr, Staten Island, NY, 95; Lehman Col Art Gallery, Bronx, NY, 96; Paraphotography, Maier Mus of Art, Lynchburg, Va, 98; Recent Projects: Ellen Driscoll and Lesley Dill, Bernard toale Gallery, Boston, 99; Marilyn Monroe X Times, Emily Peterson Gallery,

NY, 99; Ellen Driscoll, Lesley Dill, Ambreen Butt, DNA Gallery, Provincetown, Mass, 99; Forms in Motion, Cooper Union, 2000. *Teaching:* Asst dir admissions, Parsons Sch Design, 80-83; dir, Parsons Sch Design, 85-89; vis lectr & critique, numerous museums, universities, & cols, 86-; vis artist, Univ NC, Chapel Hill, 88 & Sch Mus Fine Arts, Boston, 89; instr, sophomore & jr sculpture, RI Sch Design, 92, assoc prof sculpture, 92-98 & prof sculpture, 98-. *Awards:* Nat Endowment Arts, 84 & 86; Guggenheim Fel, 87; Grant, LEF Found, 92; Les Arques France, EEC & Local Govt, 94; Anonymous Was a Woman Fel, 98-99; Mass Cult Coun Fel in Sculpture, Pilchuk Sch of Glass Artist-in-Residence, 99; Rockefeller Found Bellagio Residency, Italy, 2001; Banff Ctr for the Arts Residency, Can, 2001. *Bibliog:* Goings on About Town/Art, New Yorker, 2/10/92; William Zimmer (auth), review, NY Times, 95; Nancy Princenthal (auth), review, Art Am, 6/95; Patricia Phillips (auth), The Proportions of Paradox, Sculpture Mag, Nov 2000; Janet Koplos (auth), Ellen Driscoll's Passages, Art in Am, June 2000; Barbara Rodriguez (auth), Autobiographical Inscription: Form, Personhood and the American Woman Writer of Color, Oxford U Press. *Mailing Add:* 8 Stinson Ct Cambridge MA 02139

DRISCOLL, JOHN PAUL
DEALER, ART HISTORIAN
b Madison, Minn, Oct 28, 49. *Study:* Univ Minn, BA, 71; Pa State Univ, MA, 74, PhD, 85. *Exhib:* Hans Coper (with catalog), 94; Lucie Rie (with catalog), 94; Warren MacKenzie (with catalog), 95; Six Master Potters of the Modern Age (with catalog), 95; Gutte Eriksen (with catalog), 95; Seeking the Spiritual: The Paintings of Marsden Hartley (with catalog), 98. *Collection Arranged:* Charles Sheeler: Works on Paper (catalog), 74, Checklist of the Permanent Collection, 77, American Paintings from Collection of Daniel J Terra, 77, Arthur B Davies from the Brill Collection, 79 & All That Is Glorious Around Us, 81, Pa State Univ Mus Art; Paintings from William H Lane Foundation, Munson-Williams-Procter Inst, 78; Contemporary British Ceramics, Fitchburg Art Mus, 82; John F Kensett: An American Master, Worcester Art Mus, 85. *Pos:* Registr, Pa State Univ Mus Art, 75-78; cur, William H Lane Found, 78-82; guest cur, Kensett Exhib, Worcester Art Mus, 83-85; owner & dir, Driscoll & Walsh Fine Art, Boston, 83-88 & Babcock Galleries, 86-. *Teaching:* Instr, Fitchburg State Col, 79-84; adj instr, New York Univ Cont Educ, 96-. *Awards:* Alumni Achievement Award, Pa State Univ. *Bibliog:* Hilton Kramer (auth), Charles Sheeler, NY Times, 4/13/74; Outstanding exhibitions, Apollo Mag, 6/74. *Mem:* Nat Arts Club; Am Asn Mus; Am Antique Soc; Am Numismatic Asn; Archives Am Art. *Res:* Emphasis on American art with current focus on John F Kensett and Edwin Dickinson. *Specialty:* 19th and 20th century American painting and sculpture. *Publ:* A Marsden Hartley of 1908, Am Art J, 80; John Stuart Ingle: Paradigms of reality, Am Artist, 82; John F Kensett: An American Master, Norton, 85; All that is Glorious Around Us, Cornell Univ Press, 97; The Artist and the American Landscape, First Glance Bks, 98. *Mailing Add:* Babcock Galleries 724 Fifth Ave New York NY 10019

DRISKELL, DAVID CLYDE
PAINTER, EDUCATOR
b Eatonton, Ga, June 7, 31. *Study:* Skowhegan Sch Painting & Sculpture, with Jack Levine & Henry V Poor, scholar, 53; Howard Univ, with James A Porter & Morris Louis, BA, 55; Cath Univ Am, with Nell Sonnemann & Ken Noland, MFA, 62; Riksbureau voor Kunsthistorisches Documentatie, The Hague, Neth, cert, 64. *Work:* Corcoran Gallery Art, Smithsonian Inst, Washington, DC; Birmingham Mus Art; Corcoran Gallery Art, Washington, DC; Carl Van Vechten Gallery Fine Arts, Fisk Univ, Nashville, Tenn; Ark Fine Arts Ctr, Little Rock; and others. *Comn:* Mountain and Tile Suite (10 woodcuts-color), Tenn Arts Comn, 72. *Exhib:* Baltimore Mus Area Exhib, 65; Corcoran Area Exhib, 66; Birmingham Festival Exhib, 72; Cent South Ann, Nashville, 72; Mid-South Exhib, Memphis, 75; Painting Across the Decade, DC Moore Gallery, NY, 2006. *Pos:* Mem bd adv, Mus African Art, 67-; mem visual arts adv panel, Tenn Arts Comn, 69-, mus adv bd, 73-; guest curator, Smithsonian Inst, 72; guest curator, Los Angeles Co Mus Art, 74-76; mus adv panel, Nat Endowment Arts, 74-77; bd gov, Skowhegan Sch Painting & Sculpture, 75-. *Teaching:* Prof painting & art hist, Talladega Col, 55-62; prof painting & art hist, Howard Univ, 62-66; prof art & chmn dept, Fisk Univ, 66-76; vis prof, Univ Ife, Nigeria, 70; vis prof, Bowdoin Col, 73; vis prof, Bates Col, 73; prof art, Univ Md, College Park, 76-82, chmn dept art, 78-83. *Awards:* Model of Excellence Award in Art, Colgate-Palmolive, 93; Amistad Research Award, 93; Am Acad Arts & Letters, 93 & 94. *Mem:* Col Art Asn Am; Nat Conf Artists; Am Mus Asn; Am Fedn Art. *Media:* Oil, Tempera. *Res:* Role of the Black artist in American society and traditional African art, its impact on Afro-American art. *Mailing Add:* 4206 Decatur St Hyattsville MD 20781-2127

DROEGE, ANTHONY JOSEPH, II
PAINTER, DRAFTSMAN
b Philadelphia, Pa, Sept 22, 43. *Study:* Pa State Univ, BA, 65; Univ Iowa, MA, 67, MFA, 68. *Work:* Kemper Ins Co Collection, Long Grove, Ill; Clara Eagle Gallery, Murray State Univ, Ky; Art in the Embassy Prog, US State Dept; Indianapolis Mus Art, Ind; South Bend Art Ctr, Ind; and others. *Comn:* Numerous pub & pvt portrait comns. *Exhib:* Mid-Year Show, Butler Inst Am Art, Youngstown, Ohio, 70; The Emerging Real, Storm King Art Ctr, Mountainville, NY, 73; The Big Show, JB Speed Art Mus, Louisville, Ky, 75; Panorama Am Art, Midwest Mus Am Art, Elkhart, Ind, 79; Thirteenth Union League Club, Chicago Art Show, 81; 68th Ind Artists Show, Indianapolis Mus Art, 81; Master-Apprentice: The Indiana Art Tradition Carries On, Ind State Mus, 85; Realism Today, Evansville Mus Arts & Sciences; Performance: Action Painting, Fountain Head Tanz Theatre, Berlin, Ger, 94. *Collection Arranged:* Indianapolis Mus Art; South Bend Regional Mus Art; Northeast Normal Univ, Chanchun, China; Shaanxi Teachers Univ, Xian, China, Univ Iowa, Murray State Univ; Fountainhead Tanz Theatre, Berlin; Midwest Mus Am Art. *Teaching:* Instr painting & drawing, Murray State Univ, Ky, 68-71; prof painting & drawing, Ind Univ, South Bend, 71-. *Awards:* Commendation from Elmer Bishoff, Mid-Am Show, Joslyn Art Mus, Omaha, 68; First Place Painting, 7th Biennial Michiana Regional Art Competition, South Bend Art Ctr, 72; Best of Show at 8th Biennial Michiana Regional Art Competition, First Bank & Trust Co, 74, 22nd Elkhart Regional, Midwest Mus Am Art. *Bibliog:* Byron Burford (auth), View from the Midwest, Readers & Writers, summer 68; Gene Porter (auth), Mirrors repeated in Droege paintings, Ft Wayne News-Sentinel, 4/73; Dennis Shapiro (auth), article, New Art Examiner, Chicago, 4/75. *Media:* Oil, Gouache; Pastel, Watercolor. *Dealer:* Gruen Gallery Chicago IL; Padulo Longstreth & Goldberg Naples FL. *Mailing Add:* 16169 Waterside Dr Granger IN 46530

DROHOJOWSKA-PHILP, HUNTER
WRITER, ART CRITIC, JOURNALIST
b Schenectady, NY, Sept 5, 52. *Study:* Ohio State Univ, Columbus, 70-72; Ariz State Univ, Tempe, 73-75; Inst Allende, San Miguel de Allende, Mex, BFA, 76. *Pos:* Art ed, Los Angeles Weekly, Calif, 80-84; columnist, Los Angeles Herald Examiner, 83-86; W Coast corresp, Artnews, 85-; chair, Dept Lib Arts & Sci, Otis Col Art & Design, 87-95; contribr, Archit Dig, 87-, Los Angeles Times, 87-, Western Interiors & Designs, 2001-; Artnet, 2001. *Mem:* Int Asn Art Critics; Art Table; Author's Guild Pen. *Res:* Biography of Georgia O'Keeffe. *Interests:* American modern contemporary art. *Publ:* Full Bloom: The Art and Life of Georgia O'Keeffe, WW Norton, 2003; Undiscovered O'Keeffe, Artnews, 4/2000; Alfred Stieglitz at the National Gallery of Art, Washington DC, Artnews, 1/2001; other articles and essays. *Mailing Add:* 9822 Millboro Pl Beverly Hills CA 90210

DRONZEK, LAURA ANN
PAINTER
b Litchfield, Ill, Nov 14, 61. *Study:* Univ Wis, BA, 82, MFA, 93. *Work:* Madison Art Ctr & Univ Wis Union, Madison; Gardiner Art Gallery, Stillwater, Okla. *Exhib:* The Exquisite Corpse, Transmission Gallery, Glasgow, Scotland, 94; Cimarron National Works on Paper, Gardiner Art Gallery, Stillwater, Okla, 95; Intimus, Dean Jensen Gallery, Milwaukee, Wis, 96; Sullivan & Dronzeke, Steinway Gallery, Chappel Hill, NC, 97; Wisconsin Triennial, Madison Art Ctr, Wis, 96; Food Glorious Food, Wustum Mus, Racine, Wis, 97; Three Wise Women, Vorpal Gallery, San Francisco, Calif, 97; Undefining Painting, Detroit Artists Market, Mich, 98; Nat Ctr for Children's Illus Lit, Dallas Mus Art, Texas, 2000; Watercolor Wisconsin, Charles A Wustum Mus, Racine, Wisc, 2000; Under Light, Underlight, Dean Jenen Gallery, Milwaukee, WI, 2002; Artists & the Uncultivated Landscape, Wustum Mus, Racine, WI, 2003; A Decade of Art from the Wisconsin Acad Gallery, James Watrous Gallery, Madison, WI, 2004. *Teaching:* Lectr life drawing, Univ Wis, Madison, 94. *Awards:* Purchase Award, Cimarron Nat Works on Paper, Gardiner Art Gallery, 93; Individual Artists Grant, Wis Arts Bd, 94 & Individual Fel, 98. *Bibliog:* Nathan Guegulerre (auth), The world around us: challenging perceptions of geography, Shepard Express, 96; N Steven Zevitas (auth), New American Painting, Open Studios Press, 97; James Aver (auth), A Feast for the eyes, Milwaukee J Sentinel, 97; Snow Business, New York Times Book Rev, 11/21/99. *Media:* Acrylic on Paper. *Mailing Add:* c/o Dean Jensen Gallery 759 N Water St Milwaukee WI 53202

DROWER, SARA RUTH
PAINTER, CRAFTSMAN
b Chicago, Ill, Oct 15, 1938. *Study:* Roosevelt Univ, BS, 59; Univ Ill, Chicago, MS, 61; Art Inst Chicago. *Work:* Ill State Mus, Springfield; Minn Mus Art, Minneapolis; Borg-Warner Corp, DePaul Univ, Standard Oil, Chicago. *Exhib:* Inedible Cakes & Souvenir Shows, 82, Am Politics, 84, Renwick Gallery, Smithsonian Inst; New Elegance, Newark Mus, NJ, 84-85; Artwear '85, Bellevue Art Mus, Wash; Designed to Wear, Ore Art Mus, Arts & Crafts, 85-86; Wearable Fibers A Revolution Bodywear, Milwaukee Art Mus, 86; plus many others. *Pos:* Sci illusr, Turtox-Biol Supply, 62-64. *Awards:* First Prize Watercolors, Union League Club, Chicago, 72; Ill Coun Grant: Crafts, 86; Best of Show, Fine Art Exhib, Artists Guild Chicago, 74. *Mem:* Surface Design; Am Crafts Coun. *Media:* Miscellaneous Media. *Mailing Add:* 127 Laurel Wilmette IL 60091-2830

DRUM, SYDNEY MARIA
PAINTER, PRINTMAKER
b Calgary, Alta, Nov 20, 52. *Study:* Univ Calgary, BFA(with distinction in art), 74; York Univ, MFA, 76. *Work:* Mus Mod Art, NY; Philadelphia Mus Art, Pa; Nat Mus Am Art, Washington; Mus Am Ostwall, Dortmund, Ger; Can Coun Art Bank, Ottawa, Ont. *Comn:* Pope, Ballard, Shepard & Fowle, Chicago, 82; Zimmerli Mus, Rutgers Univ, New Brunswick, NJ, 89; Harmann-Reimer Corp, NY, 90. *Exhib:* One-woman shows, Name Gallery, Chicago, 79, Getler/Pall Gallery, NY, 81, Hart House Art Gallery, Univ Toronto, Ont, 81 & 95 Gallery Pascal, Toronto, Ont, 81 & 83, Jan Cicero Gallery, Chicago, 82 & Mus am Ostwall, Dortmund, Ger, 94; World Print III, San Francisco Mus Mod Art, Calif, 80; Bau-Xi Gallery, Toronto, Ont, 87, 90, 92 & 95; 55 Mercer Gallery, NY, 93, 96, 98, 2000, 02, 04, 06; Woodlands Art Gallery, London, Eng, 99; Gallery Surge, Tokyo, Japan, 99; CAS Gallery, Osaka, Japan, 99; Kunstverein Alte Feuerwache, Dresden, Ger, 02; Optisches Mus, Jena, Ger, 2004. *Teaching:* Sessional lectr studio art, Univ Alta, Edmonton, Can, 76-77; instr studio art, Nova Scotia Col Art & Design, Halifax, Can, 77-78; asst prof studio art, Univ Ill, Chicago Circle, 78-83; univ lectr studio art, Governors State Univ, Ill, 83-84; asst prof studio art, Rutgers Univ, 84-87. *Awards:* Can Coun Arts Grant, 76-77; A-N-W Prof Prize, 55th Ann Members Show, Print Club, Philadelphia, Pa, 79; Artist Fel, Yaddo Found, 80 & 85. *Bibliog:* Joyce Zemans (auth), Beyond the border at Harbourfront Art Gallery, Artmag, 2-3/80; Liz Wylie (auth), Sydney Drum at Gallery Pascal & Hart House Art Gallery, Artmag, 5-6/81; Jonathan Goodman (auth), Sydney Drum, Exhibition Essay, 55 Mercer Gallery, New York, NY, 9 10/98; Gerrit Henry (auth), Sydney Drum, Art in America, July 2003. *Mem:* Col Art Asn Am; Print Club; Printmaking Coun NJ. *Dealer:* Birch Libralato Gallery Toronto. *Mailing Add:* 138 W 120th St New York NY 10027

DRUMM, DON
SCULPTOR, CRAFTSMAN
b Warren, Ohio, Apr 11, 35. *Study:* Hiram Col; Kent State Univ, BFA & MA. *Work:* Cleveland Mus Art; Bowling Green State Univ; Columbus Gallery Fine Arts; Pan Am Airlines; Goodyear Tire & Rubber Co; and others. *Comn:* Reliefs, walls, aluminum & steel sculpture & fountains, Alcoa Co, Pittsburgh, Episcopal Diocese, Sao Paulo, Brazil, Richard Gossar Mem Sculpture, Toledo, Ohio, Curtain Bluff Hotel, Antigua BWI & City of Akron, Ohio; 2 cement murals, Bowling Green State Univ, Ohio, 66; corten steel sculpture, Baltimore, Md & Miami, Fla, 75; corten steel sculpture, City of Miami, Fla, 75; 14 cement wall relief murals, Quaker-Hilton, Akron, Ohio, 80; and many others. *Exhib:* Group shows, 64 & 65 & Traveling Exhib circulated by Am Fedn Arts, 65-67 & 72, Mus Contemp Crafts, NY; Cleveland Mus Art, 64-68; Columbus Gallery Fine Arts, 66 & 67; and others. *Pos:* Owner, Don Drumm Studios & Gallery, Akron, Ohio, 71-. *Teaching:* Artist in residence, Bowling Green State Univ, 66-71; instr, Penland Sch Crafts, 66-79. *Awards:* Purchase Prize, Cleveland Mus Art, 64; Prize, Nat Soc Interior Design, 65; Prize, Columbus Gallery Fine Arts. *Mem:* Ohio Designer Craftsmen; Am Craftsmen's Coun; Fine Arts Comn, Akron, Ohio. *Media:* Cast Metals, Miscellaneous Media. *Res:* Investigation into the use of contemporary materials and construction techniques to create urban sculpture specializing in the use of cast aluminum and concrete. *Dealer:* Don Drumm Studios & Gallery 437 Crouse St Akron OH 44311. *Mailing Add:* Don Drumm Studio Gallery 437 Crouse St Akron OH 44311-1220

DRUMMER, WILLIAM RICHARD
GALLERY DIRECTOR
b Ottawa, Ohio, Feb 17, 25. *Study:* Ohio State Univ, BA, 50, MA, 57. *Exhib:* Piranesi, Miss State Mus, Jackson, 80-81 & Brooks Mem Art Gallery, Memphis, 82; Pensacola Art Mus, Fla, 83; New Orleans Mus Art, La, 84; Mario Villa Gallery, New Orleans, La, 89; Maguerite Oestreicher Fine Art Gallery. *Pos:* Dir, Gallery 539, New Orleans, 75-. *Mem:* Int Fine Print Dealers Asn. *Specialty:* Japanese woodblock prints, Piranesi etchings, fine architectural prints and drawings, rare architectural books. *Mailing Add:* 539 Bienville St New Orleans LA 70130

DRUMMOND, SALLY HAZELET
PAINTER
b Evanston, Ill, June 4, 24. *Study:* Rollins Col, 42-44; Columbia Univ, BS, 48; Inst Design, Chicago, 49-50; Univ Louisville, MA, 52. *Work:* Mus Mod Art, Metrop Mus Art, Whitney Mus Am Art, NY; Hudson's Dept Store, Detroit; J B Speed Mus Art, Louisville; Weatherspoon Art Gallery, Univ NC, Greensboro; Corcoran Gallery Art, Hirshhorn Mus & Sculpture Garden, Washington, DC; and others. *Exhib:* Solo exhibs, Tanager Gallery, NY, 60, Green Gallery, NY, 62, Fischbach Gallery, NY, 68 & 78, Aldrich Mus, 81, Artist Space, 84, Cornell Fine Arts Ctr, Rollins Col, Winterpark, Fla, 89 & Louisville Visual Arts Asn, Ky, 90, Mitchell Algus Gallery, NYC, 2003; Am Artists Ann, Whitney Mus Am Art, NY, 60; Americans 63, Mus Mod Art, NY, 63; Recent Acquistions, Whitney Mus Am Art, 64; Albright-Knox Art Gallery, 69; Retrospective, Corcoran Gallery Art, Washington, DC, 72; A Change of View, Aldrich Mus, 75; Underknown, PS1, NY, 86; The Kentuckians 1987, Nat Arts Club, 87; 5 Points Gallery, East Chatham, NY, 94; Nat Acad Arts & Letts, NY, 95; 175th Ann Exhibn, Nat Gallery Design, NY, 2000; Armory Show, NY, 2001; Group Show, Seeing Red, Hunter Col, NYC, 2004; 2 person show, Alexandre Gallery NYC, 2005; and many other one-man & group exhibs. *Teaching:* Instr, Skowhegan Sch Art, 73. *Awards:* Fulbright Grant, Venice, 52; Guggenheim Grant, France, 67. *Bibliog:* Lawrence Campbell (auth), Dotted light, Art News Mag, 4/72; Gene Baro (auth), Forward to "Retrospectives" Catalogue, Corcoran Gallery Art, 72. *Media:* Oil. *Dealer:* Philip Alexandre. *Mailing Add:* 129 Camp Creek Rd Germantown NY 12526

DRUTT, HELEN WILLIAMS
DEALER, LECTURER
b Winthrop, Mass, Nov 19, 30. *Study:* Tyler Sch Art, Temple Univ, BFA; Barnes Found; Moore Col Art, Philadelphia, hon DA, 90. *Collection Arranged:* Two British Goldsmiths, Ramshaw & Watkins, 73; UICA: Craft Faculty, 74; Soup Tureens: 1976 (ed, catalog), 76; Olaf Skoogfors Retrospective (ed, catalog), 79; Robert Arneson: Self-Portraits 1966-1978 (ed, catalog), 79; Ruth Duckworth & Claire Zeisler (ed, catalog), 79; Contemporary Ceramics: A Response to Wedgewood (ed, catalog); Robert L Pfannebecker (ed, catalog); Claus Bury (ed, catalog); Contemporary Arts: An Expanding View (catalog), 86; Broaching it Diplomatically: A Tribute to Madeleine K Albright (int traveling exhib), 98-99. *Pos:* Curatorial consult, Mus Philadelphia Civic Ctr, 67, 70 & 73; exec dir, Philadelphia Coun Prof Craftsmen, 67-73; mem, Acquisition Comt, Montreal Mus Decorative Arts, Can; founder & dir, Helen Drutt Gallery, 74-; gallery consult, Moore Col Art, 78; consult, Nat Endowment Arts, 79-; selected panelist & juror for numerous exhibs, 68-89. *Teaching:* Mod craft hist, Philadelphia Col Art, 72-80; prof, Moore Col Art, Philadelphia, 74-84 & prof hist art, 82 & 87; vis scholar, Am Academy, Rome, Italy. *Awards:* Award Advan Mod Ceramics, Int Ceramics Symp, 81; Grant, Pa Coun Arts, 85-88; Founders Day Award, Fleisher Art Mem, Philadelphia Mus Art, 95. *Bibliog:* Carol Saline (auth), Crafty lady, Philadelphia Mag, 75; Professional Women (film), ABC-TV, Philadelphia, 76. *Mem:* Collab 20th Century, Philadelphia Mus Art; Am Crafts Coun (Pa state rep, 75-); Pa State Coun on the Arts (crafts panel, 75-78). *Specialty:* Twentieth century work in fiber, ceramics & metal; contemporary crafts. *Publ:* Contribr, Craft Horizons, Am Crafts Coun, 70; Contemporary Jewelry: 1964-96 HWD Collection, Philadelphia Mus Arts, Stedeliek, Montreal Mus Arts; coauth, Jewelry of Our Time, Thames & Hudson, 95. *Mailing Add:* 2222 Rittenhouse Sq Philadelphia PA 19103-5505

DUBACK, CHARLES S
PAINTER, PRINTMAKER
b Fairfield, Conn, Mar 10, 26. *Study:* Whitney Sch Fine Arts, New Haven, Conn; Newark Sch Fine & Indust Arts, NJ; Skowhegan Sch Painting & Sculpture, Maine; Brooklyn Mus Art Sch. *Work:* Corcoran Gallery Art, Washington, DC; Emory Collection, Emory Univ, Atlanta, Ga; Columbia Mus Art, SC; Butler Mus Am Art; Am Tel & Tel, New York; and others. *Exhib:* Prints & Drawings, 53, Trends in Watercolor Today, 57, 20th Biennial Int Watercolor Exhib, 59 & Print Show, 70, Brooklyn Mus, NY; Whitney Ann Exhib of Contemp Am Painting, New York, 59-60; Mus Mod Art, New York, 62; 20th Ann Exhib Contemp Am Painting, Lehigh Univ, Bethlehem, Pa, 74; Works on Paper, Weatherspoon Art Gallery, Greensboro, NC, 75; Ft Wayne Mus of Art, Ind, 76; one-man show, Landmark Gallery, 79-82, Susan Gross Gallery, Philadelphia, Pa, 85, Anne Weben Gallery Georgetown, Maine, 86; New Dimensions in Drawing, Aldrich Mus, Conn, 81; two-man show, Farnsworth Mus, Rockland, Maine, 84; Art in Embassies, US Govt, 85; Austin Peny State Univ, Clarksville, Tenn, 87. *Collection Arranged:* Ten Painters of Maine, Landmark Gallery, New York, 77. *Bibliog:* Connie Smith (auth), A sentimental journey, Village Voice, 4/76; Laura Pipune (auth), Window exhibit at museum, Ft Wayne Jour-Gazette, 10/76; Holland Cotter (auth), Charles DuBack, Arts Mag, 11/77. *Media:* Multimedia. *Mailing Add:* Greenhut Galleries 146 Middle St Portland ME 04101

DUBASKY, VALENTINA
PAINTER
b Washington, DC, Mar 1, 51. *Study:* Goddard Col, BA, 74, MA, 77. *Work:* Newark Mus, NJ; Orlando Mus, Fla; HF Johnson Art Mus, Cornell; Nat Mus Women Arts, Washington; Jane Voorhees Zimmerli Art Mus, Rutgers U, NJ. *Comn:* Fuzhou Int Ctr, China. *Exhib:* New Acquisitions, Aldrich Mus Contemp Art, Conn, 81; Albright-Knox Mus, Buffalo, NY, 82, 83 & 87; Art of the 70's & 80's, Aldrich Mus Contemp Art, Conn, 85; solo exhibs, Hodges Banks Gallery, Seattle, 86, Oscarsson-Siegeltuch Gallery, NY, 86, Empire Bronze Art Gallery, Long Island, 87, Ruth Siegel Gallery, NY, 90 & 91, Rena Haveson Gallery, Pittsburg, 95, Hodges Taylor Gallery, Charlotte, NC, 97, Cheryl Pelavin Fine Art, NY, 98, Thailand Art Ctr Gallery, Silpakorn Univ, Bangkok & Friesen Fine Arts, Seattle; Documenta, 34 Raumes, Berlin, Ger, 92; Animal Imagery, Champion Paper, Hartfield, Conn, 93; ES Painting Space, NY, 93; Art in Embassy Exhib, United States Embassy, Oslo, Norway, 93; and many others. *Awards:* Pollock-Krasner Found grant, 1986 & 2001; Art Amb to the Baltics, Art in Embassies Program, 2002; Cult Exch fellow, US Dept State, Bangkok, 2001. *Bibliog:* Christian Sci Monitor, 11/23/92; Ancient Futures: Cave-wall Landscape Paintings, Bangkok Post, 2001; Elizabeth Ash (auth), The art of visual diplomacy, State Mag, 2003. *Media:* Oil on Canvas. *Publ:* Contribr, Women in Print (exhib catalog with essays), 90; Intaglio Printing in the 1980's (exhib catalog), Jane Voorhees Zimmerli Art Mus, 90 & Surface Printing in the 1980's (exhib catalog with essays), 90; photographs, Soul Survivors: Stories of Women and Children in Cambodia, Carol Wagner (auth), Creative Arts Books, 2002; Art in Embassies Exhibition, Residence of the American Ambassador, Riga, US Dept State, 2002; Toxic Landscapes: Artists Examine the Environment, Puffin Cult Forum, 2002. *Dealer:* Cheryl Pelavin Fine Arts 13 Jay St New York NY 10013; Friesen Fine Art PO Box 1613 Sun Valley ID 83353; Friesen Fine Art 1210 2nd Ave Seattle WA 98101; Hodges Taylor Gallery 401 N Tryon St Charlotte NC 28202; Galerie Timothy Tew 309 East Paces Ferry Rd # 130 Atlanta GA 30305; Robert L Kidd Gallery Birmingham MI 48011. *Mailing Add:* 463 West St Apt D1016 New York NY 10014

DUBEN, IPEK AKSUGUR
PAINTER, SCULPTOR
b Istanbul, Turkey, 41. *Study:* Univ Chicago, MA, 65; NY Studio Sch, 4 yr cert, 76; Mimar Sinan Univ, Istanbul, Turkey, PhD, 84. *Work:* Rotterdam Mus, Holland; City of Istanbul Mus & Turco-British Asn, Istanbul, Turkey. *Comn:* Pvt collections in US, Turkey, United Kingdom, France, Japan. *Exhib:* New York - Istanbul, Ataturk Cult Ctr, Turkey, 92; Women Artists from the Beginning of the Republic to the Present, Istanbul Archeol Mus, Turkey, 93; Ephesus, Imagination of History, Ephesus, Turkey, 95; OpPositions, Mus Voor Volkenkunde, Rotterdam, The Neth, 95-97; Karamustafa Import-Export, Mus fur Volkerkunde, Vienna, Austria, 98; The Fifith Sharjah International Arts Biennial, UAE, 01; Reading the City of Signs: Istanbul Revealed or Mystified?, Aksanat Gallery, Istanbul & London Col Communication, Eng, 2003; Bibliotheca Alexandrina's First Int Biennial for Hand Printed Artists' Books, Alexandria, Egypt, 04; Call Me Istanbul, ZKM, Karlsruhe, Ger, 04; Nations and Origins, Galerie Nord, Berlin, Ger, 05; 8th Int Multimedia Art Festival, Serbia & Montenegro, 06; Contemp Art from Turkey & Korea, Incheon Centre Contemp Art, Korea, 06; Sinopale: 1st Int Sinop Arts Biennial, 06; 4th Int Artist's Books Exhib, King St Stephen Mus, Hungary, 06; Substance & Light: Ten Sculptors use Cameras, Munson-Williams-Proctor Art Inst, Mus Mod & Contemp Art, Utica, NY, 06. *Pos:* Secy gen, Asn Int des Arts Plastiques, Istanbul, Turkey, 90-91; artist-in-residence, Sculpture Space, Utica, NY, 98. *Teaching:* Lectr at various galleries & mus in Turkey & US, 84-98; instr art hist, Bosphorus Univ, Istanbul, 86; instr art appreciation, Yildiz Univ, Istanbul, 90; adj prof, Istanbul Tech Univ, 2000-2004; instr, Istanbul Bilgi Univ, 2005. *Awards:* Brit Coun Arts Grant, Burgh House Exhib, London, 85; Painting Award, Contemp Istanbul Artists, Istanbul Mus Painting and Sculpture, 80; artists-in-residence, Sculpture Space, Utica, NY, 98; Turkish Ministry cult Exhib Grant, 01; Moon & Stars Project Exhib Grant, NY, 01 & 06. *Bibliog:* Ali Akay (auth), Sentences from a Body Multiplied, Gosteri, Istanbul, 11/94; Carol Naggar (auth), Scrolls of the Future, I Publ, 94; Beral Madra (auth), Roundtrip: cat essay, Borusan Pubs, 10/00; Von Thomas Joerdens (auth), Wir-Gefül sorgt für Ausgrenzung, Oranienburger Generalanzeiger, Berlin, 4/05. *Mem:* Artists Equity Asn; Asn Int Arts Plastiques (secy gen, 90-91). *Media:* Mixed Media, Metal, Wood, Video, Artist's books. *Publ:* Numerous articles in art magazines & newspapers, 78-91; auth, Painters

of Pera, Beymen Publ, 90; ed, Contemporary Thought and Art, PSD Publ, 91; auth, Turk Resmi ve Elestrisi 1880-1950 (Turkish Painting and its Criticism 1880-1950), Bilgi Univ Press, Istanbul, 06. *Dealer:* Nev Gallery Macka Caddesi Instanbul Turkey. *Mailing Add:* Serdari Ekrem Sok 56 Dogan Apt A/14 Beyoglu Istanbul Turkey

DUBIEL, CAROLYN MCPEEK
COLLAGE ARTIST
b Ploesti, Romania, Aug 16, 30; US citizen. *Study:* Okla State Univ, BS, 52; Univ Pittsburgh, MR, 54. *Work:* Mt St Marys Col, Newburg, NY; Bridgeport Hosp, Bridgeport, Conn. *Exhib:* Small Works, NY Univ, 85-90; Color Box Series, Danville Mus, Va, 87; Works on Paper, Univ Tenn, Knoxville, 90, Perkins Mus, Moorestown, NJ, 90 & Univ Tex, Tyler, 93; Nat Asn Women Artists traveling exhib, 91; Oklahomans Come Home, Oklahoma City Arts Place, 92. *Teaching:* Art, El Paso High Sch, 52-53. *Awards:* Presidents Award, North Coast Col Soc, 88; Genius Foundation, Nat Asn Women Artists, 90. *Mem:* North Coast Col Soc; Soc Layerists & Multi-Media; Nat Asn Women Artists; Artists Equity, NY. *Media:* Collage. *Publ:* Cover artist, Sunshine Artists, 8/91; Creative Collage, Watson-Guptill, 94; contribr, Creative Collage Techniques, Northern Lights, 94. *Mailing Add:* 60 Moore Rd Sussex NJ 07461

DUBINSKIS, ANDA
PAINTER
b Bethesda, Md, 1952. *Study:* Cooper Union, New York, BFA, 74; Univ Pa, Philadelphia, MFA, 77. *Comn:* Bus stop poster, Philadelphia Art Now, Pa, 89. *Exhib:* Solo exhibs, Maine State Coun Arts, Augusta, 84, More Gallery, Philadelphia, Pa, 85, Janet Fleisher Gallery, Philadelphia, Pa, 88, 91 & 93, Icon Contemp Art, Brunswick, Maine, 96, Fleisher/Ollman Gallery, Philadelphia, Pa, 2002; Summer Shows, 87-90 & 93 & Four Women Painters, 89, Janet Fleisher Gallery, Philadelphia, Pa; A Telling Impulse, Morris Gallery, Pa Acad Fine Art, Philadelphia, 87; Figuring, Woodmere Art Mus, Philadelphia, Pa, 93; New Directions, Fricke Gallery, Belfast, Maine, 94; A Feminine Mystique, Freedom Gallery, Allbright Col Ctr Arts, Reading, Pa, 95; Six Ways of Seeing, Conduit Gallery, Dallas, 96; Four Contemp Philadelphia Painters, Gettysburg Col Art Gallery, Pa, 96; group exhibs, Pictura Lucida, Philadelphia Art Alliance, Pa, 2000, Fifty Yrs, Fleisher-Ollman Gallery, Philadelphia, Pa, 2003. *Teaching:* Instr advanced figure drawing, Moore Col Art, Philadelphia, Pa, 85-86; instr drawing, La State Univ, Baton Rouge, 89; instr art, Kutztown Univ, Pa, 91-92. *Awards:* Pa Coun Arts Fel for Painting, 85 & 88; Nat Endowment Arts Grant for Painting, 89 & 91; Leeway Fel Award, 2000. *Bibliog:* Searching Out the Best, Morris Gallery, Philadelphia Fine Arts, Pa, 88. *Mem:* Col Art Assoc. *Media:* Oil on Wood Panel

DUBLAC, ROBERT REVAK
PAINTER
b Farmington, Conn, Nov 28, 38. *Study:* Hartford Art Sch, Univ Hartford, BFA(painting, cum laude), 63 & grad study, 68; Yale Univ, with Scully & Nodleman, 67; Temple Univ, Rome, Italy, with Richard Callner, Roger Anliker, Barbara LaPenta & Dmitri Hadzi, 68-69. *Work:* Vanveldon Ltd, London, Eng; Marriott Hotel Corp; Cigna Corp, Hartford, Conn; Aetna Insurance Co, Hartford, Conn; Bank of Hartford, Conn; and many pvt collections in US, Canada, Italy, Ger, France & Eng. *Exhib:* Wadsworth Atheneum; one-man exhibs, Images Art Gallery, Briarcliff Manor, NY, 85, Aires E Gallery, Brewster, Mass, 85, Portfolio Gallery, Stamford, Conn, 86, Saugatuck Gallery, Westport, Conn, 86, Unionville Mus, Farmington, Conn, 88, Hurlbutt Gallery, Greenwich, Conn, 96 & Chase/Freedman Gallery, W Hartford, Conn, 97; The Saugatuck Gallery, Westport, Conn, 86; Unionville Mus, Unionville-Farmington, Conn, 88; Images Gallery, Toledo Ohio, 89; Berkshire Mus, Pittsfield, Mass, 98; Nat Acad Design, NY. *Pos:* Chmn art dept, Avon High Sch, Conn, 65-67 & Litchfield High Sch, Conn, 69-80; co-dir, Fortman Studio, Florence, Italy, 77-78; self-employed artist/painter, 80-. *Teaching:* Art instr, Avon High Sch, Conn, 65-67, adj prof art hist, 67; art instr, Litchfield High Sch, Conn, 69-80. *Awards:* Grant, Adolph & Esther Gottlieb Found, 90; Elizabeth Found Grant, New York, 95; Pollock-Krasner Found Grant, 99. *Media:* Watercolor, Oil-Gouache. *Mailing Add:* Brookside 62 Cottage St Unionville CT 06085

DUBNAU, JENNY
PAINTER
Study: Barnard Col, BA, 85; Yale Univ, MFA, 96. *Exhib:* One-man shows, Clifford-Smith Gallery, Boston, 2000, & 2002, The Dealership, Brooklyn, 2002, Bucheon Gallery, San Francisco, 2003, Black & White Gallery, Brooklyn, 2003; exhib in group shows, MMC Gallery, New York City, 89, Women View Women, Brooklyn YMCA, 91, Hot, K&E Gallery, 95, Heads, 96, Portraits, Graham Modern Gallery, 96, Little, Jeffrey Coploff Gallery, 98, Go! Figure, Clifford-Smith Gallery, 99, Winter White, 2004, Six Degrees of Separation, Forrest-Scott Gallery, 99, Where are All the People, DeChiara Stewart Gallery, 2000, Smile, HERE, 2001, Artists to Artists, Ace Gallery, 2002, Sympathetic Nerves, Capsule, 2004, Portraits, Esso, 2004; Open House: Working in Brooklyn, Brooklyn Mus Art, 2004, Head Games, Revolution Gallery, 2004. *Awards:* Grantee Louis Comfort Tiffany Found, 2002; Guggenheim Found Fel, 2004; Pollock-Krasner Grant, 2004. *Mailing Add:* Black & white Gallery 483 Driggs Ave Brooklyn NY 11211

DUBOIS, ALAN BEEKMAN
CURATOR, ADMINISTRATOR
b Forest Glen, NY, Dec 14, 35. *Study:* State Univ NY, New Paltz, BS, 58; Ind Univ, MFA, 66. *Work:* Ringling Mus Art, Sarasota, Fla; New Orleans Mus Art. *Exhib:* Light Seven, Mass Inst Technol. *Collection Arranged:* Fans a la Mode, 88; Masterpieces of American Photography, 1899-1982, 89, Good, Better & Best: Decorative Arts from Mid-American Museum Collections, 90; European Fans 1700-1920 from the Colin Johnson Collection, 91; Color-Cut-to-Clear and Engraved Glass, 91; Elsa Freund: An American Studio Jeweler, 91; American Art Jewelers: 1950s, 91; National Objects Invitational, 91; American Glass: Carder and Steuben, 92; Flights of Fancy: Audubon Prints and Porcelain Birds, 92; Working in other Dimensions: Objects and Drawings, 93; American Arts and Crafts 1900-1920, 93; National Objects Invitational (auth, catalog), 93; Arkansas: Year of American Craft (auth, catalog), 93; Contempory Crafts from the Horn Collection, 93; Contemporary Jewelery 1964-1993; Selected Works: Helen Williams Drutt Collection, 93; Connections: Objects and Drawings from the Permanent Collection, 93; Exploring Sources: Objects and Drawings from the Permanent Collection, 94; Working in Other Dimensions: Objects and Drawings II (auth, catalog), 94; National Objects Invitational, 95; Leaning into the Wind: Ceramic Works by Bennett Bean, 96; Moving Beyong Tradition, A turned-Wood Invitational, 97; Born of Ashes: Woodfired Ceramics, 99; Making Difference: Fiber Sculpture by Jane Sauer, 2000. *Pos:* Dir, Wash Co Mus Fine Arts, 64-66; asst dir, Mus Fine Arts, St Petersburg, Fla, 66-84 & Orlando Mus Art, Fla, 84-89; cur decorative arts, Ark Arts Ctr, Little Rock, 89-. *Teaching:* Adj prof photog & art hist, Eckerd Col, St Petersburg, Fla, 84-. *Awards:* Nat Endowment Arts Fel, 72 & 75. *Mem:* Col Art Asn; Am Asn Mus. *Media:* Clay, Fiber, Glass, Metal, Wood. *Res:* contemporary objects in craft media. *Specialty:* Contemporary Objects of Craft Media. *Interests:* photography. *Publ:* Elsa Freund: An American Studio Jeweler & National Objects Invitational, Ark Arts Ctr, Little Rock, 91; Bennett Bean, Leaning into the Wind: Ceramic Works, 96; Moving Beyond Tradition: A Turned-Wood Invitational, 98; Earl Pardon: Joy in the Making, 98; Jeri Au: Works in Clay, 98. *Mailing Add:* Arkansas Arts Ctr Little Rock AR 72203

DUBOIS, MACY
ARCHITECT, DESIGNER
b Baltimore, Md, Dec 20, 29; Can citizen. *Study:* Md Inst; Tufts Univ, BSE; Harvard Univ, MArch. *Comn:* Ont Pavilion, Expo 67, Ont Govt, 66; Lakehead Sci Bldg, Lakehead Univ, 66; Albert Campbell Libr, Scarborough Pub Libr Bd, 73; George Brown Col Applied Arts & Technol, Toronto, 73; Govt Can Bldg, North York, Ont, 78. *Exhib:* Toronto City Hall Competition, 58; Sao Paolo Exhib, 64; Massey Medals for Archit, 64 & 67; Amsterdam City Hall Competition, 69. *Pos:* Archit critic, Can Architect, 63-. *Mem:* Ont Asn Architects; fel Royal Archit Inst Can; academician Royal Can Acad Arts (pres, 88-91). *Mailing Add:* 175 Carlton St Toronto ON M5A 2K3 Canada

DUBROW, JOHN
ARTIST
b Salem, Mass, Oct 14, 58. *Study:* San Francisco Art Inst, BFA, 80, MFA, 83. *Work:* represented in public collection Metrop Mus Art, NY City. *Exhib:* One man shows incl Forum Gallery, New York City, 1985, 87, 90; exhib in group shows Am Acad Arts and Letters, Nat Acad Design, NY Studio Sch, Hackett Freedman Gallery, permanent collections, Salander-O'Reilly Galleries. *Teaching:* Prof NY Studio Sch of Drawing, Painting, and Sculpture. *Awards:* Recipient Pollock Krasner Found award, 86-87. *Mem:* Nat Acad. *Mailing Add:* Lori Bookstein Fine Art 37 W 57th St 3rd Floor New York NY 10019

DUCKWORTH, RUTH
SCULPTOR, CERAMIST
b Hamburg, Ger, Apr 10, 19; Brit & US citizen. *Study:* Liverpool Sch Art, 36-40; Hammersmith Sch Art, 55; Cent Sch Art & Crafts, London, 56-58; De Paul Univ, Hon Dr, 82. *Hon Degrees:* Hon Doctorate, DePaul Univ, Chicago, Ill, 82. *Work:* Boston Mus Art; Smithsonian Inst, Washington; Philadelphia Mus Art; Art Inst Chicago; Metro Mus Art; and others; Mus Mod Art, Tokyo, Japan. *Comn:* Wall panel, St Mary's Church, Walsingham, Eng; porcelain wall panels, State of Ill; 15' Bronze, Chicago Bd Options Exchange, 81; Beth Israel Synagogue, Hammond, Ind, 82; mural, Animal Care Ctr, Chicago, 83; and others. *Exhib:* One-woman shows, Boyman's Mus, Rotterdam, 79, Exhib A, Chicago, 80, 82 & 84, Am Porcelain, Renwick Gallery, Washington, 80, Garth Clark Gallery, NY, 90, 96, Bellas Artes Gallery, Santa Fe, NMex, 92, 93 & 96, Keramik-Galerie Bowig, Hannover, Ger, 93, Jewish Mus, Rendsburg, Ger, 94; and others. *Teaching:* Instr ceramics, Cent Sch Arts & Crafts, London, 59-64; asst prof ceramics, Midway Studio, Univ Chicago, 64-77; vis artist, Corsham Sch Art, Eng, 65; various workshops & seminars, 72-. *Awards:* Lifetime Achievement Award, Nat Mus Women in Art, Washington, DC, 93; Gold Medal, Nat Soc Arts & Letts, St Louis, 96; Lifetime Achievement, Gold Medal, Am Craft Coun, 97; Master of the Medium Renwick, Smithsonian, 2002. *Bibliog:* Tony Birks (auth), The Art of the Modern Potter, Country Life, 67; Heinz Spielmann & Karin Heise (auth), Ruth Duckworth Keramische Objekte, Rendsburg, 94. *Mem:* Arts Club Chicago; World Crafts Couns; Union Leaque Club. *Media:* Stoneware, Porcelain. *Dealer:* Thea Burger 651 North Rd PO Box 68 Barnard Vermont 05031-0068. *Mailing Add:* c/o Thea Burger Assoc PO Box 68 651 North Rd Barnard VT 05031-0068

DUERWALD, CAROL
PAINTER, ILLUSTRATOR
b Brooklyn, NY. *Study:* Studied with artist William C Kautz, 75-81; Parson Sch Design, 76; Huntington Art League, New York, 85-89. *Comn:* Mural, comn by Mr & Mrs B Cohen, Oyster Bay, NY, 89; portrait, comn by Mr & Mrs T Brennan, Chester, NJ, 91; portrait, comn by Mr & Mrs G Baker, Oyster Bay, NY, 92; portrait, comn by Mrs D Coleman, Charlottesville, Va, 92; portrait, comn by Mrs M Geenman, Upper Brookville, NY, 92. *Exhib:* Rochester Art Club Open Juried Exhib, Mem Art Mus, Rochester, 84; Huntington Township Art League Open Juried Exhib, Heckscher Mus, Huntington, NY, 85; Pastel Soc Am Juried Open, NY, 89-92; Am Artists Prof League Grand Nat, 91 & Salmagundi Open Juried Exhib, Salmagundi Club, NY, 92; Pastel Soc Am Open, NY, 94; Am Artists Prof League Grand Nat, 94; and others. *Pos:* Sketch & design artist, Blum Folding Paper Box, Rosedale, NY, 56-57; sketch &

design artist, Cellucraft Inc, New Hyde Park, NY, 57-61; illus & design, freelance, 65-70. *Teaching:* Instr drawing, Pittsford High Sch, NY, 83-84; instr pastel painting, Pittsford Art Club, NY, 83-84; instr pastel portraits, Penny Sch, Cutchoque, NY, 88 & Somerset Art Asn, NJ, 94; instr pastel still life, Somerset Art Asn, 94-. *Awards:* Best Painting in Show, Am Artist Prof Grand Nat League, 91; George Innes Mem Award for Pastel, Salmagundi Club Open Exhib, 92; Hon Mention, Am Artist Prof NJ & others. *Mem:* Pastel Soc Am; Am Artist Prof League; Huntington Township Art League; Somerset Art Asn; Morris Co Art Asn. *Media:* Pastel. *Publ:* Contribr, Hampton Scene, 89; Observer Tribune, 91 & 94; Currier News, 91; Star Ledger, 92; Best of Pastel II, Rockport Publ, 99. *Mailing Add:* 46 Mile Dr Chester NJ 07930

DUESBERRY, JOELLYN
PAINTER
b Richmond, Va, June 30, 44. *Study:* Smith Col, BA(art hist), 66; Inst Fine Arts, New York Univ (Woodrow Wilson fel), MA, 67; Art Students League, New York, 69-79; Pietrasanta, Italy, 74-77; New York Acad, 84-85; New York Studio Sch, 94-95. *Work:* AT&T Chemical Bank & Shearson-Lehamn Brothers, NY; Nat Parks Collection, Washington; Smith Col art Mus, Northhampton, Mass; First Bank Boston, Mass; Security Pac Bank, Los Angeles; Denver Art Mus & Fed Couthouse, Denver; and numerous pvt collections. *Comn:* Denver Fed Courthouse, 92. *Exhib:* Solo exhibs, Tatistcheff & Co, NY, 82, 83 & 85, Reynolds-Minor Gallery, Va, 84, Gerald Peters Gallery, Santa Fe, NMex, 86 & 88, Graham Mod, NY, 89, 91 & 94, Joellyn Duesberry: Landscapes 1972-1992, Denver Art Mus, 92-93, Duesberry's Garden Paintings, Robinschon Gallery, Denver, A Covenant of Seasons Traveling Exhib, Va Mus Fine Art, Arvada Art Ctr, Denver Art Mus, Marsh Gallery, Univ Richmond, 98-, Landscape Paintings, James Graham & Sons, NY, 2000, Joellyn Duesberry, Landscapes, Gleason Fine Art, Camden, Maine, 2001, Joellyn Duesberry, Points of View, Gerald Peters Gallery, Sante Fe, NMEx, 2002; Contemp Romantic Landscape Painting, Orland Mus Art, Loch Haven, Fla, 86; The Landscape Observed, Md Inst Col Art, 89; Hubbard Mus Invitational, Ruldoso, NMex, Soviet Union, WGer & Japan, 90; Robischon Gallery, Denver, 94; Gerald Peters Gallery, Santa Fe, 95; Graham Gallery, NY, 96, 98, 2000; Illuminating Words, Singer Gallery, Denver, 2000; The Virginia Landscape, Va Hist Soc, 2001; Random Acts of Beauty, Foothills Art Center, Golden, Colo, 2002; The Am River, Nat Juried & Invitational Exhib, Great Rivers Arts Inst, Walpole, NH, 2002-04; Virginia Lynch Gallery, Providence, 2003. *Teaching:* guest lectr, NY Studio Sch, Spring Island Trust, Arapahoe Community Col, Loveland Mus. *Awards:* Resident fel, Rocky Mountain Nat Park 91; Comn Awards, Ct Appeals; Distinguished Alumni Award, Col Schs, Va, 94; Benjamin Altman Landscape Painting Prize, 97. *Bibliog:* May Brawley Hill (auth), Joellyn Duesberry, Arts Mag, 9/85; Michael Brenson (auth), Joellyn Duesberry, New York Times, 10/18/85; Carl Little (auth), Duesberry at Graham Modern, Art in Am, 3/92; David Park Curry (auth), A Covenant of Seasons; Rose Glaser (auth), Painting Colorado, Southwest Art Mag, 2003. *Mem:* Century Asoc. *Media:* Oil on Linen, Monotype on Paper. *Publ:* Auth, Joellyn Duesberry: Contemporary Colo Artists Poster Series, Denver Art Mus, 96; Women Artists Calendars; Up in the Air, Lower Manhatten Cultural Council, World Trade Center Residency. *Dealer:* James Graham & Sons New York NY 10021; Gerald Peters Santa Fe NM. *Mailing Add:* 2800 Williamette Ln Littleton CO 80121

DUFF, ANN MACINTOSH
PAINTER, PRINTMAKER
b Toronto, Ont, Can. *Study:* Cent Tech Sch; Queen's Univ Summer Sch Fine Arts. *Work:* Nat Gallery Can, Ottawa; Art Gallery Ont, Toronto, Agnes Etherington Gallery, Queen's Univ; City Toronto Arch; Ore State Univ, Corvallis; Univ Toronto Art Centre. *Comn:* Watercolor painting, Reader's Dig for Expo 67, Montreal. *Exhib:* Five Toronto Painters, Montreal Mus Fine Art; Can Soc Painters in Watercolour & Am Watercolor Soc Joint Exhib, 72; Fifty Yrs of Watercolour, Art Gallery, Ontario, 75; Watercolours Japan-Canada, Tokyo-Montreal, 76-77; Robarts Libr Univ Toronto, 97; On Paper, Univ Toronto Art Center, 2002; twenty-one solo shows in Toronto. *Awards:* Queen Elizabeth Silver Jubilee Medal, 77; Curry Award, 80 & 81; Loomis & Toles Award, 84; Hon Award, Can Soc Painters Watercolour, 84. *Bibliog:* Frances Duncan Barwick (auth), Pictures from the Douglas M Duncan Collection, Univ Toronto, 75; Rebecca Sisler (auth), Passionate spirits, Clarke Irwin, Toronto, 80; DA 41 A Journal of the Printing Arts, Porcupine's Quill Publ, Erin, Ont, 97. *Mem:* Royal Can Acad Arts; Can Soc Painters Watercolour (exec, 70-75). *Media:* Watercolor, Wood Engraving. *Dealer:* D&E Lake Ltd 1199 Yonge St Toronto ON Canada M4T 3A8. *Mailing Add:* 133 Imperial St Toronto ON M5P 1C7 Canada

DUFF, JAMES H
MUSEUM DIRECTOR
b Pittsburgh, Pa, Oct 11, 43. *Study:* Washington & Jefferson Col, BA, 65; Univ Mass, MA, 70. *Collection Arranged:* Wildlife in Art, Brandywine River Mus, Chadds Ford, Pa, 73; Maxfield Parrish: Master of Make-Believe, 74; Harvey Dunn, 74; Peter Hurd, 77; The Collection of Amanda K Berls & Ruth A Yerion, 80; An American Vision: Three Generations of Wyeth Art (auth, catalog), 87. *Pos:* Dir, Mus Hudson Highlands, 66-73; consult, NY State Coun Arts, 70-72; dir, Brandywine River Mus, 73- & Nat Mus Serv Bd, 86-95. *Mem:* Asn Art Mus Dirs (pres, 96-97); Am Asn Mus; Mid-Atlantic Asn Mus (pres, formerly). *Interests:* American art & Chinese ceramics. *Publ:* Auth, Not for Publication: Landscapes, Still Lifes and Portraits by NC Wyeth, Brandywine River Mus, 82; An American Vision, Little, Brown, 87. *Mailing Add:* PO Box 297 Chadds Ford PA 19317

DUFF, JOHN EWING
SCULPTOR
b Lafayette, Ind, Dec 2, 43. *Study:* San Francisco Art Inst, BFA, 67; with Manuel Neri, Paul Harris & Ron Nagle. *Work:* Kaiser Wilhelm Mus, Krefeld, Ger; Guggenheim Mus Art, Whitney Mus Am Art & Mus Mod Art, NY; Inst Contemp Art, Boston, Mass; Metropolitan Mus, NY. *Exhib:* Anti-Illusion, Procedures & Materials Show, Whitney Mus, 69, David Whitney Gallery, 70 & 71, John Meyers Gallery, 72 & 73 & Willard Gallery, 75, 76, 77 & 78, NY; Daniel Wienburg Gallery, 73, 75, 77, 79 & 81; Margo Leavin Gallery, Los Angeles, Calif, 81; Development in Recent Sculpture, Whitney Mus Am Art, 81 & Enclosing the Void, 88; Blumhelmar Gallery, 86 & 88; one-man exhib, David McKee Gallery, 93 & 95. *Awards:* Theodor Award, Guggenheim Mus, 77; Brandis Award for Visual Arts, 87. *Bibliog:* Barbara Rose (auth), Where we are & what we like, NY Mag, 4/72 & 4/75; John Russell (auth), current shows in NY Times, 3/75; J Tannenbaum (auth), rev in Arts Mag, 6/75. *Media:* Fiberglass, Steel. *Publ:* Contribr, Art Now: New York, 72. *Mailing Add:* 5 Doyers St New York NY 10013-5140

DUFFY, MICHAEL JOHN
PAINTER, PRINTMAKER
b Chicago, Ill, Dec 29, 45. *Study:* Colo Col, Colorado Springs, BA, 72. *Work:* Denver Art Mus; Mesa Col, Grand Junction; Colo Col, Colorado Springs; Columbia Mus Art, SC. *Comn:* Viet Nam Vets Art Mus, Chicago. *Exhib:* Solo exhibs, Colo Col Packard Gallery, Colorado Springs, 83, Glastonbury Gallery, San Francisco, 85 & Columbia Mus Art, SC, 90; 46th Ann, Soc Four Arts, Palm Beach, Fla, 84; Chicago Print Show, Northwestern Univ, Evanston, Ill, 85; Small Paintings & Sculpture, Univ Denver, 87; Crescent Art Centre, Belfast, Ireland, 93; and others. *Awards:* Atwater Kent Award, 46th Ann Soc Four Arts, 84; Best of Show, Colorado Springs Fine Art Ctr, 85. *Bibliog:* Irene Clurman (auth), Intensity intact, Rocky Mountaint News, 5/30/86; New prints, Print Collectors Newsletter, 7/87; Abrams (auth), The Art of the Vietnam Veterans Art Mus, 11/98. *Mem:* Chicago Art Inst; Chicago Art Coalition. *Media:* Oil. *Dealer:* A Clean Well Lighted Place New York NY; Lovely Fine Art Oakbrook Terr FL. *Mailing Add:* 193 Country Commons Cary IL 60013

DUFOUR, PAUL ARTHUR
PAINTER, DESIGNER
b Manchester, NH, Aug 31, 22. *Study:* Univ NH, BA, 50; Yale Univ, BFA, 52; also with Takahiko Fujita & Ikuo Hirayama, Japan, 64. *Work:* Masur Mus Art, Monroe, La; Springfield Art Mus, Mo; La State Collection, Baton Rouge; La Bicentennial Collection; Centraplex Munic Collection, Baton Rouge. *Comn:* Stained glass sculpture & mosaic, St Joseph Prep Sch, Baton Rouge, La, 68; stained glass windows, Holy Ghost Church, Hammond, La, 74; stained glass windows & bronze sculpture, Our Lady of Mercy, Baton Rouge, 74; stained glass, St Patrick Church, Lake Providence, La; glass windows & bronze doors, St Mary of Pines, Shreveport, La, 79; and many others. *Exhib:* Stained Glass Invitational, Mus Fine Arts, Jacksonville, Fla, 79; 20 Yr Retrospective, La State Univ Art Gallery, 79; Glaskunst, Int Expo of Glass, Kassel, Ger, 81; Vicointer, Glass Invitational Expo, Valencia, Spain, 83; A Rebirth of A Medium, Nat Glass Invitational, Univ Tex, San Antonio, 83; 21st through 34th Ann State Exhib Prof Artists, 66-79; Contemp Glass, Corning Mus, 79 & 80; Southeast Craft, Lemoyne Art Found, 80; Am Glass Invitational, Kansas City, Mo, 80; Int Glass Art Exposition, Kassel, Ger, 80; and many others. *Pos:* Supvr educ, Currier Gallery Art, Manchester, NH, 52-55; artist-in-residence, Viterbo Col, 68. *Teaching:* Asst prof painting, St John's Univ, 55-58; vis prof design, Sienna Heights Col, 57; prof design & stained glass, La State Univ, Baton Rouge, 58-. *Awards:* Top Award, La Int Watercolor Exhib, 69; First Purchase Award, 4th Int Watercolor, 72; Hon Mention, Vicointer, Valencia, Spain, 83. *Bibliog:* Corning Mus Glass Microfiche Prog, 78; New Glass Rev I, Corning Mus Glass, 80; Jensen & Conway (auths), Ornamentalism, Potter, 82. *Mem:* Am Glass Guild; Col Art Asn; Am Craft Coun; La Watercolor Soc. *Media:* Multimedia. *Dealer:* Baton Rouge Gallery 205 N Fourth St Baton Rouge LA 70801; Matrix Gallery 912 W 12th St Austin TX 78713. *Mailing Add:* 20535 Narrow Rd Covington LA 70435-0424

DUFRESNE, ISABELLE COLLIN See Violet, Ultra

DU JARDIN, GUSSIE
PAINTER, PRINTMAKER
b San Francisco, Calif, Feb 19, 18. *Study:* Univ Colo, BA; Univ Iowa, MA. *Work:* NMex Mus Art, Santa Fe; NMex Highlands Univ; Univ Iowa; Roswell Mus, NMex; Univ Colo Mus; Mus NMex, Albuquerque. *Exhib:* Butler Inst Am Art 26th Ann, 61; NMex Biennial, 71, 73 & 75; Mus NMex Southwest Biennial Exhib, 72, 74 & 76, Invitational, 78; one-woman exhibs, Roswell Mus, 78, 92 & 96, Gov Gallery, NMex State Capitol, Santa Fe, NMex, 79, Western State Col, Gunnison Colo, 91, Art Inst Permian Basin, Odesa, Tex, 93, SW 96 Mus NMex & Invitational Clines Gallery, Sante Fe, 96. *Pos:* Artist-in-Residence Prog, Roswell Mus, 77-. *Awards:* First Purchase Award, Mus NMex, 61. *Media:* Acrylic, Oil. *Mailing Add:* 1403 W Berrendo Rd Roswell NM 88201

DUKE, LEILANI LATTIN
ADMINISTRATOR
b Aug 27, 43. *Study:* Denison Univ, BA, 65; Syracuse Univ, MA, 66; Arts Admin Inst, Harvard Univ, 78; Eastman Sch, Hon Dr. *Pos:* Res asst, Onondoga City, Syracuse, NY, 66-69; staff asst, US Senate Labor & Pub Welfare Comt, Washington, DC, 68-69; fed aid coordr, Senator Jacob Javits, US Senate, Washington, DC, 69-71; exec secy, Fed Coun Arts & Humanities Nat Fdn on Arts & Humanities, 71-78; coordr, Design Educ Prog, Nat Endowment Arts, 71-76, Spec Constituencies Prog, 76-78; exec dir, Calif Confederation Arts, 79-81; prog develop officer, J Paul Getty Trust, 81-; dir, Getty Ctr Educ Arts, 83-; independent consult, currently. *Mem:* Am Craft Coun (bd mem); Col Art Asn; Nat Art Educ Asn. *Mailing Add:* 1030 Glenhaven Dr Los Angeles CA 90272

DUKES, CAROLINE
PAINTER, PRINTMAKER
b Ujpest, Hungary; Can citizen. *Study:* Sigiesmund de Strobl Studio, Hungary; Acad Fine Arts, Budapest; Sch Art, Univ Man, Winnipeg, dipl, 72, with Ivan Eyre. *Work:* Winnipeg Art Gallery; NDak Mus Art; Yad Vashem Art Mus, Jerusalem, Israel; Budapest Mus Fine Arts, Hungary; Montreal Mus Fine Art; MacKenzie Art Gallery,

Regina; Can Coun Art Bank, Ottawa; and others. *Comn:* Mosaic: A Journal for the Comparative Study of Literature and Ideas (cover & 11 reproductions), 77; No Longer Two People (cover), Turnstone Press, 79; Print edition, Winnipeg Art Gallery, Man, 81 & 88; Prairie Fire (Can mag), 92 & 96. *Exhib:* Solo exhibs, Melnychenko Gallery, Winnipeg, 91, Winnipeg Art Gallery, 91, Plug In Gallery, Winnipeg, Can, 92, Vasarely Mus, Budapest, Hungary, 93, McKenzie Art Gallery, Regina, Sask, 94, NDak Mus Art, 95; Plains Mus, Moorehead, Minn, 91; NDak Mus Art, 91 & 95; Autoren Galerie 1, Munich, Ger, 94; Royal Canadian Acad Art Exhib, Winnipeg, 97; MacKenzie Art Gallery, Regina, 98; Triangle Gallery, Calgary, 98; Instituto Cabanas, Guadalajara, Mex, 98; Robert McLaughlin Art Gallery, Oshawa, Ont, Can, 96; Architecture 2 Gallery, Univ Manitoba, Winnipeg, 2000; plus others; AGSM, Manitoba, Can, 2002; MacKenzie Art Gallery, Regina, 2002; Concordia Univ, Montreal, 2002; Carlton Univ Art Gallery, Ottawa, 2002; Hart House, Univ Toronto, 2003; Sir Wilfred Grenfell Col Art Gallery, Meml Univ Newfoundland, 2003-. *Pos:* Juror (art); lectr. *Teaching:* Mentor, Manitoba Artist Women's Art, formerly. *Awards:* Outstanding Painting Award, Winnipeg Art Gallery, Man Soc Artist, 76; B Grant, Canada Coun, 90, 93; Major Arts Grant, Man Arts Coun, 92, 93, 94, 2002. *Bibliog:* Gary Genosko (auth), Building Blocks of Memory, Border Crossings, No 1, Jan/99; Lisa Young Kutsukake (auth), Intiuting the Past, Style Manitoba, summer 2001; Loren Lerner (auth), Memories & Testimonies, catalogue, 2002. *Mem:* Can Artist Representation; Plug In Inc; Manitoba Printmaking Asn; Ace Art; Royal Can Acad Art; Mentoring Artists for Womens Art. *Media:* Acrylic, Oil; Charcoal, Linocut, lino/woodcut. *Publ:* Gallerie, Women's Art, 12/89. *Dealer:* SITE Gallery 55 Arthur St Winnipeg Canada R3B 1H1; Caroline Dukes Artwork Trust 736 Waverley St Winnipeg Manitoba Canada. *Mailing Add:* 736 Waverley St Winnipeg MB R3M 3L7 Canada

DUMAIS-BERUBE, YVETTE
PAINTER, SCULPTOR
b St Joseph de Lepage, Que, July 18, 30. *Study:* Ecole Normale: pedagogie, 49; Comn Scolaire: certificat decoration interieure, 68; Ministere education: attestation arts plastiques, 69. *Work:* Govt of Can, Hon Benoit Bouchard, Ambassaduer, Ottawa; Hydro-Quebec, Denis St-Pierre, Montreal, Que; Govt of Que, Lavoie-Roux; Quebecor, Pierre Peladeau,Montreal, Que; Gaz Metropolitain Marcel La forest, Que, Govt of Que, Minister of Roads & Transport, Jacques Brassard Montreal. *Exhib:* Aux Racines du Temps, jumele avec les dieux de L'Egypte, Shawinigan Cult Ctr, Royal Ont Mus, Can, 87; Isis-deesse de la Verite, Louis-Hemon Mus, Peribonka, Que, 89; Morin-Miller Galleries, NY, 88; Centre Cult AMORC, Montreal, 94; Mutation, Gallery Jardin Oeil, Chicoutimi, Que, 95; and others. *Awards:* Gold Medal, Collective & Trophy of Excellence, Nat Circle of Artists & Painters, 86; Bourse for solo exhib, Minister of Culture, 87. *Bibliog:* Guy-Marc Fournier, Mieux Connaitre, Mieux Connaitre Inc, 86; Marche de l'art (fine art market), Guide Vallee, 93-94; Repertoire 95, Perspectives Peinture, Conseil Peinture Que, 95. *Mem:* Regional Culture Coun. *Publ:* Auth, Guy-Marc Fournier, Mieux Connaitre, Mieux Connaitre Inc, 86; auth & ed, Jean-Claude Larouche, Yvette Dumais-Berube Exprime son Art sur Papyrus, Editions JCL, 90; auth, Biennial of Female Artist (exhib catalog), Art Addiction, Stockholm, 93 & 94. *Dealer:* La Maison Richelieu 451 Richelieu St Marc sur Richelieu PQ J4H 2W1. *Mailing Add:* 112 Ave Gagne Roberval PQ G8H 1E5 Canada

DUMAS, ANTOINE
PAINTER
b Quebec City, Que, Dec 8, 1932. *Study:* Col des Jesuites, Quebec City, Baccalaureate Rhetorique, 53; Ecole des Beaux-Arts, Quebec City, dipl, 58; Acad Art Col, San Francisco, 69-70; Ecole des Arts Visuels. *Work:* Collection Alcan, Montreal; Rothmans Collection & Imperial Oil, Toronto; CIL Collection & Soquip Collection, Montreal; Musee Du Quebec, Quebec City; and others. *Comn:* Stained glass mural, Dorval Airport, Montreal, 60; painted mural, RSW & Assoc Consult Engineers, Montreal, 75; four stamps, Can Post, Ottawa, 76, 78, 79 & 92; tapestry, Aetna Can Bldg, Montreal, 83. *Exhib:* Many solo exhibs, 77, 78, 80, 85 & 91; Traveling Exhib, Nancy Poole's Studio, Toronto, 80, Rodman Hall, St Catharines, 80, Laurentian Univ Mus, Sudbury, 80, & Univ Western Ont, 80, 85, 91; Galerie Bernard Desroches, Montreal, 81, 83 & 87; Livres d'Artistes, Bibliot Nat du Que, Montreal, 82; Galerie Madeleine Lacerte, Quebec City, 82, 83, 89, 92, 96, 99, 02; group exhib, Forum 76, Mus des Beaux-Arts, Montreal, 89 & 92; and others. *Teaching:* Prof graphic design, Ecole des Beaux-Arts, Quebec City, 62-65; dir, prog commun arts, Ecole des Arts Visuels, Univ Laval, 70-73, prof illus design, 70-. *Awards:* Lt Gov's Silver Medal, Ecole des Beaux-Arts, Que State Dept, 58. *Bibliog:* Michele Marchand (auth), Painters Series (film), Can Broadcasting Corp TV, 81; Roland Bourneuf (auth), Antoine Dumas, Ed Int Stanke, 83; Laurent Laplante (auth), catalog, Ed Lacerte, 89. *Mem:* Hon mem Soc Graphistes du Que; Royal Can Acad Art; hon mem, Quebec Garrison Club; Asn des Illustrateurs de Québec. *Media:* Oil, Acrylics. *Publ:* Auth, A l'Enseigne d'Antan, Ed Pelican, 70. *Dealer:* Galerie Madeleine Lacerte 1 Cote Dinan Quebec City PQ G1K 3V5 Canada; Nancy Poole's Studio 16 Hazelton Toronto On M5R 2E2 Canada

DUMOUCHELLE, ERNEST J
APPRAISER
Study: Univ Detroit Col, BA; Wayne State Univ; Gemological Inst. *Pos:* Vpres, DuMouchelle Art Gallery Co, Detroit, currently; Appraiser, Antiques Roadshow, WGBH-PBS, currently. *Mem:* Am Gemological Inst; Am Soc Appraisers. *Mailing Add:* DuMouchelle Gallery 409 E Jefferson Detroit MI 48226

DUMOUCHELLE, LAWRENCE F
APPRAISER
Pos: pres, Detroit & Canada Tunnel Corp, formerly; pres, Founders' Soc, Jr Coun, Detroit Inst Arts, formerly; appraiser, Antiques Roadshow, WGBH-PBS, currently; Chief Exec Officer, DuMouchelle Art Galleries, Detroit, 57-. *Mem:* Int Soc Appraisers; Nat Auctioneers Asn; Mich Auctioneers Asn; Am Soc Appraisers; Meadowbrook Arts Comn. *Mailing Add:* DuMouchelle Gallery 409 E Jefferson Ave Detroit MI 48226

DUNBAR, MICHAEL AUSTIN
SCULPTOR, ADMINISTRATOR
b Santa Paula, Calif, Sept 21, 47. *Study:* Ill State Univ, Normal, BS, 71, MS, 78; Univ Ill, Springfield, MA, 74. *Work:* Ill State Mus; Krasl Art Ctr, St Joseph, Mich; Eastern Ill Univ, Charleston; Southern Ill Univ, Carbondale; Ill State Univ, Normal; Univ Notre Dame, Ind; and others; Nathan Manilow Sculpture Park, Chicago, Ill; Pyramid Hill Sculpture Park, Hamilton, Ohio. *Comn:* Univ Wis, Stevens Point; Western Ill Univ, Macomb; Eastern Ill Univ, Charleston; Southern Ill Univ, Carbondale; sculpture, Pier Walk 96, Univ Notre Dame, Chicago, 96; Time Equities Inc, NY; Lewis and Clark Col, Godfrey, Ill; South Western Ill Col, Belleville, Ill; Univ Ill, Champaign, Ill. *Exhib:* Three Illinois Sculptors, Northwestern Univ, Evanston, Ill, 89; Sculpture Walk, Chicago River Park, Ill, 91; Out of Time, Bloomington, Ill, 91; Abstract Works, Struve Gallery, Chicago, Ill, 91; Chicago: The Third Dimension, Ukrainian Inst Mod Art, Chicago, Ill, 94; Six Ill European Sculptors Tour, Rome Italy, 2000; Sculpture on the prairie, Wandell Sculpture Park, Urbvana, Ill, 99; Michael Dunbar Machinist Sudies, Ill State Mus, JRT Ctr, Chicago, 96; The Univ Notre Dame Sculpture Project, Notre Dame, Ind; Heavy Equiptment, Flint Institute of Art, Flint, MI; Six AM Sculprores in Rome, Rome, Italy; Machinist Studies, Maiden Lane Exhib Space, NY. *Collection Arranged:* IL Collection Fine the James R Thompson Ctr, Chicago, IL; Portrait of IL for the IL State Libr, Springfield, IL. *Pos:* coordr, Art in Archit, State of Ill, 77-. *Teaching:* Instr, Univ Ill, Springfield, 76 & Lincoln Land Community Col, 78 & 86. *Bibliog:* Alumni news, Ill State Univ, 9/91. *Mem:* Chicago Sculpture Soc; Asn Corp Art Curs; Arts Club of Chicago. *Media:* Sreel, Bronze. *Mailing Add:* 912 S Park Springfield IL 62704-2341

DUNCAN, RICHARD (HURLEY)
DRAFTSMAN, PRINTMAKER
b Daytona Beach, Fla, Feb 11, 44. *Study:* Southern Ill Univ, Edwardsville, BA, 66, MFA, 73; study with John Adkins Richardson, Robert Malone, and James Butler. *Work:* Aukland City Art Gallery, NZ; Springfield Civic Collection, Ill; Southeast Ctr Contemp Art, Winston-Salem, NC; Printclub Albany, Cooperstown Art Asn, NY; Dulin Gallery, Knoxville, Tenn; Barnett Bank and Sunbank, Fl. *Comn:* Two lithographs, Verein Originalgraphik, Switz, 74. *Exhib:* 35 Artists of the Southeast, High Mus & traveling, 76-78; Worldprint 77, San Francisco Mus Mod Art, 77; one-person exhibs, Hunter Mus, 77 & Ritter Art Gallery, Fla Atlantic Univ, Boca Raton, 85; 25th Nat Exhib Prints, Nat Collection Fine Arts & Libr Cong, 77-78; 100 Worldprints, Smithsonian Traveling Exhib, 77-79; Honolulu Nat Print Exhib, Hawaii, 82; 62nd Nat Print Exhib, Soc Am Graphic Artists, NY, 86-87; Printmakers 98, Pittsburgh Ctr Arts, 98; Printwork 98 Nat, Poughkeepsie, NY, 98; Best of Years Retrospective, Dulin Gallery, Knoxville, Tenn, 2004. *Pos:* vpres, Fla Printmakers, -2004. *Teaching:* Instr printmaking, Univ South, 73-78; assoc prof printmaking & drawing, Fla Int Univ, 78-. *Awards:* Ford Found Grants, 74 & 77; Merit Award, 18th Nat Printmaking & Drawing Exhib, 81; Nat Endowment Arts Grant, 85; S Fla Cult Consortium Grant, 85. *Bibliog:* Coleman, Richardson & Smith (auths), Basic Design: Systems, Elements, Applications, Prentice-Hall, 83. *Mem:* Fla Print makers (bd mem, 98-), Southeast Col Art Asn; So Graphics Coun Conf (co-chmn Miami, 2000). *Media:* Etching, Drawing & Painting. *Publ:* Contrib, Florida printmakers (auth), Impressions, spring-fall 95-. *Mailing Add:* 8700 SW 149th Terr Miami FL 33176

DUNHAM-GRIGGS, MARGARET
PAINTER, SCULPTOR
b Atlanta, Ga, May 30, 22. *Study:* Finch Col, New York, with Leon Kroll, 42; Art Students League, with Yasuo Kuniyoshi, 44; Columbia Univ, with John Heliker, 57. *Work:* Hudson River Mus, Yonkers, NY. *Comn:* Mural, comn by L Abernathy, Mt Kisco, NY, 57. *Exhib:* Wadsworth Atheneum Ann, Hartford, Conn, 68; Ann Invitational, Finch Mus, NY, 69; Gallery at Hastings-on-Hudson, NY, 82 & 85; solo exhibs, Hudson River Mus, Yonkers, NY, 67-86, Maine Art Gallery, Wiscasset, Maine, 75 & Maine Coast Artists, Rockport, 85; Lever House, NY, 87; and others. *Awards:* First Prize Painting, 5th Ann Adirondack Exhib, W Adams Sch Art, 58, Westchester Art Soc Nat Exhib, 68 & Nat Exhib, White Plains, Whitney Mus, 71. *Bibliog:* Suzanne Kiplinger (auth), Margaret Dunham, Village Voice, 58; Eve Medoff (auth), River scene, Herald Statesman, 67; K Beale (auth), On-the-line, Gannett Papers, 85. *Mem:* Maine Art Asn; Hudson River Contemp Artists; Union Maine Visual Artists. *Media:* All. *Dealer:* Stark Gallery 594 Broadway New York NY 10012

DUNIGAN, BREON NINA
SCULPTOR
b New York, NY, Apr 13, 61. *Study:* Atlanta Col Art; Mass Col Art, BFA, 84; Rutgers Univ, NJ, MFA, 86, with W Gary Kuehn. *Comn:* Sculpture, Univ Va, Charlottesville, 93. *Exhib:* Provincetown Group Gallery, 90, 91 & 92; Better Homes & Monuments Show, Brooklyn, NY, 91; Berta Walker Gallery, Provincetown, Mass, 92; Black & Herron Gallery, NY, 95; DNA Gallery, Provincetown, Mass, 95-2004; Provincetown in Hudson, Carrie Haddad Gallery, NY, 97 & The Nude, 98; Southeastern Ctr Contemp Art, Winston-Salem, NC, 98; Sex Pots, the Erotic Life of Clay, San Francisco State Univ Art Mus, San Francisco, Calif, 2002; Gregory Lind, New Field, New Territories Gallery, San Francisco, Calif, 2002. *Pos:* Freelance sculptor;

carpentry. *Awards:* Nat Endowment Arts Grant, 90; Pollock-Krasner Grant, 91; New Eng Found Arts Award, 97. *Bibliog:* Sara London (auth), article, Art New Eng, 10/95. *Mem:* Provincetown Art Assoc. *Media:* Miscellaneous. *Dealer:* DNA Gallery Provincetown MA; Carrie Haddad Hudson NY. *Mailing Add:* PO Box 722 Truro MA 02666

DUNITZ, JAY
PHOTOGRAPHER
b Reading, Pa, Feb 4, 56. *Study:* Kansas City Art Inst, 74; San Francisco Art Inst, BFA, 78. *Work:* Mus Mod Art, Int Ctr Photog, NY; Nat Mus Am Art, Corcoran Gallery Art, Washington, DC; Cornell Univ Art Mus; Indianapolis Mus Art, Ind; Cincinnati Art Mus, Ohio; Santa Barbara Mus Art, Calif; Newport Harbor Art Mus, Newport Beach, Calif. *Exhib:* New Acquisitions in Graphic Arts, Nat Mus Am Art, Washington, DC, 88; Present Tense, Los Angeles Munic Art Gallery, 88; solo exhibs, Santa Monica Col Photog Gallery, Calif, 88 & Fitchburg Art Mus, Fitchburg, Mass, 90; Photographs from EF Hutton Collection, Contemp Art, NY, 88; Photographs from the Collection, Corcoran Gallery Art, Washington, DC, 89; Ansel Adams Gallery, Yosemite Nat Park, Calif, 92. *Teaching:* Lectr, Santa Monica Col, Calif, Calif State, Long Beach, Rochester Inst Technol, Nat Aeronautics & Space Admin. *Bibliog:* Kathryn Livingston (auth), Making found objects, Am Photog, 9/84; Dinah Berland (auth), Dunitz zaps steel for light series, Los Angeles Times, 11/29/85; Larry Stein (rev), Arts LA, KCRW-FM, Nat Pub Radio, Santa Monica, 10/31/88. *Publ:* Auth, Pacific Light, Light Press, Inc, 89; illusr, A current affair, Confetti, 90. *Dealer:* Lumina 251 W 19th St 7-B New York NY 10011; Susan Spiritus Gallery 3333 Bear St Costa Mesa CA 92626. *Mailing Add:* 20585 Seaboard Rd Malibu CA 90265-5351

DUNKELMAN, LORETTA
PAINTER
b Paterson, NJ, June 29, 37. *Study:* Douglass Col, BA, 58; Acad Belle Arti, Florence, Italy, 60-61; Hunter Col, MA, 66. *Work:* Chase Manhattan Bank; Bellevue Med Ctr, NY; Dana Art Ctr, Colgate Univ; Univ Cincinnati; Univ Kans Art Mus, Lawrence. *Exhib:* Whitney Biennial Contemp Art, 73 & Am Drawings 1963-73, Whitney Mus Am Art, NY; Of Paper, Newark Mus, NJ, 73; Women Choose Women, NY Cult Ctr, NY, 73; AIR Gallery, NY, 73, 74, 78, 81, 83 & 87; Waves: An Artist Selects, Cranbrook Acad Art, Bloomfield Hills, Mich, 74; Cornell Artists Past & Present, Johnson Mus, 77; NY Now, Phoenix Art Mus, 79; Structure, Narrative, Decoration, McIntosh-Drysdale Gallery, Washington, DC, 80; Konsthall, Lund, Sweden, 81; Let's Play House, Bernice Steinbaum Gallery, NY, 86; Michael Walls Gallery, NY, 89; Artist on the Edge, Mary H Dana Women Artist Series, Mabe Smith Douglass Libr, Rutgers Univ, NJ, 2005; and others. *Teaching:* Vis artist, Univ Cincinnati, 74; asst prof art, Univ RI, 74-75; asst prof art, Cornell Univ, 77-80; vis artist, Ohio State Univ, 84; asst prof painting, Virginia Commonwealth Univ, 86-88; vis artist, Sch Art Inst Chicago, 90, Univ Calif, Berkeley, 93-94. *Awards:* Visual Artist Fel Grant, Nat Endowment Arts, 76, 82, 93-94; Adolph & Esther Gottlieb Found Individual Grant, 91; NY Found for the Arts, Artist's Fel, 91. *Bibliog:* Ellen Lubell (auth), article, Arts Mag, 5/74; Peter Frank (auth), Gifts of the imagi, Village Voice, 1/8/79; Tiffany Bell (auth), article, Arts Mag, 2/79; Robert Merritt (auth), Romantic Views: Light and dark, Richmond Times Dispatch, 10/3/87. *Mem:* Col Art Asn. *Media:* Oil, All Media. *Mailing Add:* 151 Canal St New York NY 10002

DUNLAP, LOREN EDWARD
PAINTER, INSTRUCTOR
b Anderson, Ind, Feb 2, 32. *Study:* Herron Art Sch, BFA; Oqunquit Sch Painting & Sculpture, Tulane Univ, MFA. *Work:* Addison Gallery Am Art, Andover, Mass; Santa Barbara Mus, Calif; Univ Calif Collection; NY Times Bk Collection, Notre Dame Univ; Fine Arts Ctr, Anderson, Ind. *Comn:* Mural, comn by Jane Blaffer Owen, Blaffer Trust, New Harmony, Ind, 65; three panel paintings, comn by Jane Arneberg, NY, 70; painting, Pfizer Chemical Co, NY, 74; mural, comn by Kenneth Owen, New Harmony, Ind, 90; mural, comn by Joan Quillin, Palm Beach, Fla, 92. *Exhib:* One-man shows, Purdue Univ, West Lafayette, Ind, 59 & Santa Barbara Mus Art, Calif, 63; Drawing Ann, Norfolk Mus, Va, 60; Albright-Knox Art Gallery, Buffalo, NY, 60; Boston Mus Contemp Arts, Mass, 60; Univ Calif Fac Show, 63; 10 Yr Retrospective, Columbia Club, Indianapolis, Ind, 85; and others. *Pos:* cons architecture & design. *Teaching:* Instr studio & art hist, Herron Sch, Indianapolis, 58-62; lectr studio & art hist, Univ Calif, Santa Barbara, 63-65. *Awards:* Louis Comfort Tiffany Grant, 55 & 65. *Media:* Oil. *Publ:* Auth, Traditions of the East, Revolutions of the West, Herron J, 60. *Mailing Add:* Box 332 Sagg Rd Sagaponack NY 11962

DUNLAP, WILLIAM
ART EDUCATOR
Study: Univ Miss, MFA. *Exhib:* one-man shows incl, Corcoran Gallery Art, Nat Acad Sci, Aspen Mus Art, Southeastern Ctr Contemp Art, Mus Western Va, Albany Mus Art, Cheekwood Fine Arts Ctr, Mint Mus Art, Miss Mus Art, Contemp Art Ctr, New Orleans; In Spirit of the Land; Winding River: Contemp Painting from Vietnam, Meridian Int Ctr, Washington DC, 97-98, Outward Bound: Am Art Brink of 21st Century, writer Art & Antiques, Washingtonian, Arts Review; exhib incl, Reconstructed Recollections, Inaugural Exhib: Story of South, Ogden Mus Southern Art, New Orleans, 2003-04; What Boys Draw & Other Works, Soren Christensen Gallery, New Orleans, 2004; Panorama Am Landscape, Gibbes Mus Art, Charleston, SC, 2004-05. *Collection Arranged:* Rep in permanent collections, Metrop Mus Art, Corcoran Gallery Art, Lauren Rogers Mus, Mobil Corp., Riggs Bank, IBM Corp., Fed Express, Equitable Collection, Arkansas Art Ctr, U.S. State Department, U.S. Embassies throughout the world, Rogers Ogden Collection. *Teaching:* Prof Appalachian State Univ, NC, 70-79; Memphis State Univ, 79-80; Art Commentator, "Around Town": WETA-TV, Arlington, Va; Speaker in field: Lectr on art related subjects at coll, univ, inst, and prof conf. *Mailing Add:* WETA TV 2775 Quincy St Arlington VA 22206

DUNN, FONTAINE
PAINTER
b 1946. *Study:* Tulane Univ, New Orleans, BFA, 70, State Univ NY, Fredonia, 72, Whitney Mus Am Art, 73, Carnegie-Melon Univ, MFA, 74. *Work:* First Nat City Bank, Boston, Mass. *Exhib:* One-person shows, Art Latitude Gallery, NY, 80 & 81, Gray Art Gallery, Jenkins Fine Arts Ctr, ECarolina Univ, Greenville, NC, 85 & Condeso-Lawler Gallery, NY, 86; New Abstract Paintings, Cork Gallery, Avery Fisher Hall, NY, 86; Abstract Images, Art in General, NY, 87; Dwellings, Althea Viafora Gallery, NY, 87; Five Painters, PS 122, NY, 88; group show, 48 Laight Gallery, NY, 88; New Abstraction, Weatherspoon Art Gallery, Winston-Salem, NC, 89. *Teaching:* Guest lectr painting, Sarah Lawrence Col, Bronxville, NY, 86-89; vis lectr painting, Princeton Univ, NJ, 86 & spring 90; adj instr painting, Trenton State Col, NJ, spring 90. *Awards:* Nat Endowment Arts Fel in Drawing, 87; Adolph & Esther Gottlieb Found Grant, 88; Pollock-Krasner Found Grant, 88. *Bibliog:* Ken Sofer (auth), An exhibition of abstract painting, Artnews, 11/82; Valentin Tatransky (auth), Art in general, rev, Arts Mag, 10/85; Stephen Westfall (auth), rev of one-person show at Condeso-Lawler, Arts Mag, 5/87; Ellen Handy (auth), Abstract painting, Arts Mag, summer, 87. *Mem:* Col Art Asn. *Mailing Add:* 165 W 91st St Apt 16E New York NY 10024

DUNN, PHILLIP CHARLES
EDUCATOR, ADMINISTRATOR
b Chicago, Ill, Mar 1, 47. *Study:* Univ Ill, BFA(art educ), 68; Inst Design, Ill Inst Techol, MS(visual educ), 70; Ball State Univ, EdD(art educ), 78. *Comn:* Sculpture, Univ SC, Spartanburg, 83, 85 & 87. *Exhib:* Photog 79, Ariz State Univ Gallery, Tempe, 79; four-person show, Presby Col, Clinton, SC, 79; two-person show, McKissick Mus, Columbia, SC, 79; Columbia Col Gallery, SC, 80; one-person show, USC Coastal Gallery, Conway, SC, 82, McMaster Gallery, Columbia, SC, 2005. *Pos:* Prog officer, Getty Ctr Educ Arts, 88-90 (vis appointment). *Teaching:* Instr photog, Col DuPage, 71-76; vis prof photog, St Xavier Col, 74-76; prof art educ, Univ SC, 78-, dir grad studies in art, 80-85 & chmn dept art, 2002-. *Awards:* Mary J Rouse Award, 81; Higher Educator of the Year, SC Art Educ Asn, 81; Southeastern Art Educator of Year, Nat Art Educ Asn, 87; Nat Art Educator of the Year, Nat Art Educ Asn, 99. *Mem:* Nat Art Educ Asn; Guild SC Artists; Columbia Artist Guild; SC Art Educ Asn (treas, 80-82). *Media:* Digital photography. *Res:* Curriculum develop in art. *Publ:* co-ed, A True Likeness: The Black South of Richard S Roberts, 1920-1936, Algonquin Press, 86; auth, Promoting School Art: A Practical Approach, Nat Art Educ Asn Press, 86; The Curriculum Navigator for Art: Middle Sch, 94 & The Curriculum Navigator for Art: Elementary Sch, 95, Dale Seymour Publ; Creating Curriculum in Art, Nat Art Educ Asn, 95; InFolio: An Electronic Portfolio, President Develop Group, 2000. *Mailing Add:* Dept Art Univ SC Columbia SC 29208

DUNN, ROGER TERRY
HISTORIAN
b Bethesda, Md, Feb 24, 46. *Study:* Am Univ, Washington, DC; Pa State Univ, BA(art hist & painting); Pratt Inst, MFA(painting), 70; Northwestern Univ, PhD(art hist), 78. *Exhib:* Shanxi Teachers Univ, Linfen, China, 88; Anderson Gallery, Bridgewater, Mass, 97; Visual Arts Gallery, Boston, Mass, 99; Galerie 8, Aubeterre, France, 2006. *Collection Arranged:* Quilts from the Plymouth Antiquarian Soc, 74; John J Enneking: American Impressionist (ed, catalog), 75; The Boston Painting Invitational, 75, Michael Mazur: Vision of a Draughtsman, 76; Craftforms (ed, catalog), 76; American Pastimes (ed, catalog), 77; On the Threshold of Modern Design: The Arts and Crafts Movement in America (auth, catalog), Danforth Mus, 84. *Pos:* Cur, Brockton Art Ctr, Mass, 74-77; dir, Gallery at OUI, Boston, 76-80. *Teaching:* Prof art hist, Bridgewater State Col, 80-. *Mem:* Col Art Asn; Met Mus Art; MOMA; Mus Fine Arts Boston. *Res:* Monet, Rodin and their symbolist circle; exhibition research on 19th century American art. *Publ:* Auth, Lawrence Kupferman: A Retrospective Exhibition, 74; ed, Landscape and Life in 19th Century America, 74; The Ikat weavings of Joan Hausrath, Fiberarts, 11/81. *Mailing Add:* 871 Main St Hingham MA 02043-3503

DUNN, TOM (THOMAS) CHARLES
PAINTER, ILLUSTRATOR
b Brooklyn, NY. *Study:* Pratt Inst, Brooklyn, 41, cert, 48. *Work:* US Marine Corps Mus Bldg 58, Navy Yard, Washington. *Comn:* Mimosan (mural), comn by Mr O'Rielly, Atlantic Highlands, 47; murals, comn by James Snyder, 70-. *Exhib:* Evolution of Am Publ in Paperbacks, Columbia Univ, 55; one-man show, Monmouth Univ Gallery 800. *Teaching:* Instr illus/figure drawing, Newark Sch Fine Art, 58; teacher landscape/seascape, Studio in Belford, 60-69. *Awards:* Henry Luhrs Award, Guild Creative Art, 85 & 87; Col J W Thomason Award, US Marine Corps Hist Found, 97. *Media:* Multimedia. *Publ:* Illusr, US Marines on Iwo Jima, Battery Press, 45; mag ad campaign, Fortune Mag, 60's; Piet Schreuders, Dolphin Enterprises, 81; Iwo Jima Legacy of Valor, Vanguard, 85; cover illusr, Fortitudine, Marine Corps, 97

DUNNIGAN, MARY CATHERINE
LIBRARIAN
b Tazewell Co, Va, May 7, 22. *Study:* Mary Washington Col, BA; Columbia Univ, MLS. *Pos:* Librn, Col of Archit, Va Polytech Inst, Blacksburg, 66-73; librn, Fiske Kimball Fine Arts Libr, Univ Va, Charlottesville, 73-87. *Mem:* Soc Archit Historians; Art Libr Soc NAm; Asn Archit Sch Librn (pres, 80-81); Spec Libr Asn Arts & Humanities Div (chmn mus, 73-74). *Res:* Inventory-computation: Architectural drawings of University of Virginia buildings. *Interests:* Development of research library for support of art, architecture and drama curriculum. *Mailing Add:* 1643 Rugby Ave Charlottesville VA 22903

DUNNING, JEANNE
PHOTOGRAPHER, VIDEO ARTIST
b Granby, Conn, 60. *Work:* Mus Modern Art, NY; Art Inst Chicago, Ill; Mus Contemp Art, Los Angeles, Calif; Mus Contemp Art, Chicago, Ill. *Exhib:* Venice biennial, Venice Beinnial, Italy, 95; Feminin-Maxculin, Ctr Georges pompidov, Paris, France, 95; Sydney Biennial, Art Gallery New South Wales, Sydney, Australia, 96; Jeanne Dunning, Konstmuseet, Malmo, Sweden, 99; James Harris Gallery, Seattle, 2000; Bodybuilder & Sportsman Gallery, Chicago, 2001; Wanderings of the Mind's Eye: Photog by Ill Artists, Mus Contemp Art, Chicago, 2004. *Awards:* Comm Arts Asst Grant, Chicago Off Fine Arts, 89; Individual Artist Fel, Ill Arts Coun, 91-92; Grantee, Louis Comfort Tiffany Found, 93. *Mailing Add:* Mus Contemp Art 220 East Chicago Ave Chicago IL 60611

DUNOW, ESTI
PAINTER, HISTORIAN
b New York, NY, June 12, 48. *Study:* Brandeis Univ, BA, 66-70; Skowhegan Sch Painting & Sculpture, 71; New York Studio Sch, with Phillip Guston & Mercedes Matter, 70, 70-72, New York Univ-Inst Fine Arts, with Robert Goldwater, Gert Schiff, Robert Rosenblum, William Rubin, 70-81. *Exhib:* One-person show, Bowery Gallery, NY, 81, 83, 85, 87 & 90. *Pos:* Coauthor, Chaim Soutine Catalog Raisonne, 76-78, 84-. *Awards:* Ford Found Fel in Mus Work, Inst Fine Arts & Metrop Mus Art, 72; Mus Training Fel, Nat Endowment Arts, 76-77. *Bibliog:* Freddy Kaplan (auth), Regional landscapes, Artist, 2/84; Gerrit Henry (auth), New York reviews, Art News, 2/86; Jed Perl (auth), Houses, fields, gardens, hills, The New Criterion, 2/86. *Media:* Oil. *Res:* Early twentieth century painting; School of Paris, emphasis on Chaim Soutine. *Publ.* Auth, Chaim Soutine (exhib catalog) Arts Coun of Great Britain, 82; Soutive Galleri, exhib catalog, Bellman, NY, 84. *Dealer:* The Bowery Gallery 121 Wooster St New York NY 10012. *Mailing Add:* 225 W 86th St New York NY 10024-3330

DUNYE, CHERYL LYNN
FILMMAKER, VIDEO ARTIST
b Monrovia, Liberia, May 13, 66; US citizen. *Study:* Temple Univ, BA, 90; Rutgers Univ, MFA, 93. *Work:* Norton Family Collection, Santa Monica, Calif; and others. *Exhib:* Whitney Biennial, Whitney Mus Am Art, NY, 97; Berlin Film Festival. *Teaching:* Fac media studies, Pitzer Col, 96-2000; lectr, Adv Flim Issues, Calif Inst Arts, 96; adj fac video art, Univ Calif, Riverside, 97-99. *Awards:* Teddy Award, Berlin Film Festival, 96; Rockefeller Fel & Anonymous Was A Woman Award, Rockefeller Found, 97; 3 Sapphie Awards, Girlfriends Mag, Best Dir, Best film, Lifetime Achievement Award; Nom Best Dir, Ind Film Project, 2002. *Bibliog:* Marc Mauceri (dir), Lavender Limelight, First Run Features, 97; Jacqueline Bobo (auth), Black Women Film & Video Artists, 97; Alexandra Juhasz (auth), Women of Vision, Univ Minn, 99. *Media:* Film; Screenplay, Video. *Publ:* Contribr, Building Subjects, Movement Res, 92; Possessed, Mass Inst Technol Press, 94; Vanilla Sex in the Wild, Anchor Bks, 96; coauth, The Fae Richards Photo Archive, Art Space Bks, 97. *Dealer:* Prefered Artist 16633 Ventura Blvd Suite 1421 Encino CA 91436. *Mailing Add:* 566 N Chester Ave Pasadena CA 91006

DUPUIS, DAVID
b Holyoke, Mass, 1959. *Study:* Univ Washington, Seattle, BFA, 1982, BA (in theatre), 1982. *Exhib:* One man shows at Simon Watson Gallery, NY, 1989, Karsten Schubert, Ltd, London, 1991, Petersberg Gallery, 1991, Rubenstein/Diacono, NY, 1992, Turner & Byrne, Dallas, Tex, 1994, Mario Diacono Gallery, Boston, 1995, White Columns, NY, 1997, Derek Eller Gallery, NY, 1999, 2001, 2003, 2005, 2006, Schmidt Contemporary Art, LA, Calif, 2000, and others; Group shows include Outer Limits, Holly Solomon Gallery, NY, 1989; Black, White & Grey, Petersberg Gallery, NY, 1990; Synthesis, John Good Gallery, NY, 1991; Primal Abstraction, Mario Diacone, Boston, 1992; Contextures and Constructures, Rubenstein/Diacono, 1992, Summer Group Exhib, 1993; Paint Royale, Ed Thorpe Gallery, NY, 1994; Schmidt Contemporary Art, St Louis, Mo, 1995, 1996; Geoffrey Young Gallery, Mass, 1997, 1998, Pencil Me In, 2004; Free Coke, Greene Naftali Inc, NY, 1999; Superorganic Hyroponic Warfare, Derek Eller Gallery, Ny, 2000, Back to Nature, 2000, Nina Bovasso, David Dupuis, Andrew Masullo, 2002, Drawings, 2003, Inaugural Group Exhib, 2006, Summer Group Exhib, 2006; Not a Lear, Gracie Mansion Gallery, NY, 2001; Drawn, Dinter Fine Art, NY, 2006; The Name of This Show is Not GAY ART NOW, Paul Kasmin Gallery, NY, 2006; Variegated Radiant Dream Plot, Gregory Lind Gallery, San Francisco, 2006; and others; represented in collections of San Francisco Mus Modern Art, Jan Voorhees Zimmerli Art Mus at Rutgers Univ, New Mus of Contemporary Art. *Mailing Add:* Derek Eller Gallery 615 West 27 St New York NY 10001

DUQUE, ADONAY
PAINTER, DRAFTSMAN
b Coro, Venezuela, Apr 13, 54. *Study:* Sch Fine Arts Cristobal Rojas, Caracas, Venezuela, 72-75; Sch Fine Arts Univ Complutense, Madrid, 78-83; Atelier Hachette, Paris, 85. *Work:* Mus Fine Arts, Caracas, Venezuela; Mus Contemp Art, Caracas, Venezuela; Nat Gallery, Caracas, Venezuela; Philadelphia Mus; Studio Arts Ctr Int, Florence, Italy. *Exhib:* Nat Biennial of Art, Alejandro Otero Mus Visual Arts, Caracas, 92; The Purloined Image, Flint Inst Art, 93; Memories of Vision, Mus Contemp Art, Caracs, Venezuela, 93; New Acquisitions 20 Yrs, Mus Contemp Art, Caracs, 93; New Acquisitions, Mus Fine Arts, Caracas, Venezuela, 93; Changing Faces, Nassau Co Mus Art, Roslyn Harbor, NY, 97. *Awards:* First Prize Salon Arturo Michelena, 91; First Prize (drawing), IV Nat Biennial & Second Prize, Nat Biennial Visual Arts, Alejandro Otero Mus Visual Arts, 92. *Media:* Acrylic on Canvas. *Mailing Add:* c/o Ambrosino Gallery 769 Northeast 125th St Miami FL 33161

DURANT, SAM
EDUCATOR
b Seattle, 61. *Mailing Add:* Calif Inst Arts 24700 McBean Pkwy Valencia CA 91355

DUREN, STEPHEN D
PAINTER
b Fairfield, Calif, Apr 8, 48. *Study:* San Francisco Art Inst, BFA, 74; Calif State Univ, Sacramento, MA, 77. *Work:* Grand Rapids Art Mus, Mich; Muskegon Mus Art, Mich; Frey Found, Mich; Grand Valley State Univ, Mich; Austin Peay State Univ, Tenn. *Comn:* Paintings, Steelcase Inc; drawings, Herman Miller, Inc; poster design, Grand Rapids Arts Coun, Mich. *Exhib:* Solo exhibs, Grand Rapids Art Mus, Mich; Muskegon Mus Art, Mich; Dennos Mus Center, Mich; Midland Ctr Arts, Mich; Krasl Art Center, Mich; Battle Creek Art Center, Mich; Interlochen Arts Acad, Mich; Creative Arts Center, Central Mich Univ, Mich; Byron Roche Gallery, Chicago, IL; Robert Allen Gallery, San Francisco, Calif; Patricia Carlisle Gallery, Santa Fe, NM. *Teaching:* Asst prof, Kendall Col Design, Mich, 79-84. *Awards:* Artist's Grant, Mich Coun Arts, 87; Artist Residency Fel, Ucross Found, Wyo, 88; Artist's Grant, Adolf & Esther Gottlieb Found, NY, 88. *Bibliog:* Duren, Grand Rapids Press, 12/90; Artist at work, Mich Coast Mag, 22-27, 36, 4/92; Stephen Duren/Artistic anomaly, Grand Rapids Mag, 11/94; Chicago Tribune, IL, 7/02; New City, 6/00. *Media:* Oil. *Dealer:* Art Endeavors Grand Rapids MI; Monroe Fine Art Grand Rapids MI; Byron Roche Gallery Chicago IL; Robert Allen Gallery San Francisco CA. *Mailing Add:* 6087 100th St Caledonia MI 49316

DURHAM, JEANETTE R
PAINTER
b Plainfield, NJ, June 17, 45. *Study:* Montclair State Col, BA, 67; Art Students League with Bruce Dorfman, 71-72; Westchester Art Workshop with Gregory Lysun, 80-81; S Univ Col Oneonta, MSEd, 91. *Work:* Kingsley Sch, Boston, Opto Generic Devices, Van Hornesville, NY; private collections. *Comn:* Lorna Altemus (painting), 93; M/M James Wilson (painting), 96. *Exhib:* Solo exhibs, Birds of the Air and Other Phenomena, Gannett Gallery, State Univ NY, Utica, 88, Waterfalls, South Shore Arts, Little Falls, NY, 91, The Meditative Landscape, Pleiades Gallery, New York, 93 & Land & Sky, Mohawk Valley Ctr Arts, Little Falls, NY, 94, Rocks, Rensselaer Polytechnic Inst, Troy, NY, 97, In Midstream: 1967-1997, Herkimer Co Comm Col, Herkimer, NY, 97 & The Meditative Landscape, Art Ctr at Old Forge, NY, Recent Work, Mohawk Valley Ctr Arts, Little Falls, New York, NY, 2004; Art of Northeast USA, Silvermine Guild, New Canaan, Conn, 86, 98 & 2006; WHMT Exhib, NY State Mus, Albany, 88; Ann Nat Exhib, Cooperstown Art Asn, 91, 94, 97, 99; Pleiades Gallery, NY, 91-2002; 56th Ann Nat Midyear, Butler Inst Ann, 92; Mohawk-Hudson Regional, Albany Inst Hist & Art, 93 & 96, Current Works, Arts Coun Cent NY, Utica, 94 & Made in NY, Schweinfurth Mem Art Ctr, Auburn, NY, 98; Gallery 210, Syracuse 99; Canajoharie Libr and Art Gallery Regional, 2000; two-person show, Cazenovia Col, 2001; Artists Who Happen to be Women, Tex A&M Univ, College Station, Tex. *Teaching:* Instr painting, drawing, Mohawk Valley Ctr Arts, Little Falls, NY, 83; instr art, Owen D Young C S, VanHornesville, NY, 87-92; adj instr humanities, Herkimer Co Comm Col, NY, 98-. *Awards:* Award, Nat Asn Women Artists, 91 & 98; Award, Mohawk Hudson Regional, Albany Inst Hist and Art, 96; Award, Silvermine Guild, 98; SOS grant NYFA, 98. *Bibliog:* Christine Temin (auth), Discovering art off the beaten path, Boston Globe, 11/15/84; Keith Benman (auth), Artist Makes Her Mark, Herkimer Evening Telegram, 12/9/96; Jonas Kover (auth), Durham in Her Prime with a Hilly Place, Utica Observer Dispatch, 10/10/97; and others. *Mem:* Nat Asn Women Artists; Col Art Asn; Decentralization Grants Panel, CNYCAC, 1999-2001; Mohawk Valley Ctr for the Arts (exhib comt, 95-). *Media:* Oil. *Mailing Add:* 111 Hoke Rd Jordanville NY 13361

DURHAM, JIMMIE
ARTIST
b Ark, 40. *Study:* Ecole des Beaux-Arts, Geneva, BFA (sculpture), 72. *Work:* Volpinum Kunstsammlung, Vienna; MuHKA, Antwerp; Stedelijk Mus voor Actuele Kunst, Belgium; Irish Mus Mod Art, Dublin; Zerynthia Roma; Mus het Domein, Neth. *Exhib:* Souvenirs of Site-Seeing: Travel & Tourism in Contemp Art, Whitney Mus Am Art, 91; Land, Spirit, Power, Nat Gallery Can, Ottawa, 92; Crossings, 98; Antwerp Cultural Capital of Europe, 93; A Certain Lack of Coherence, Palais des Beaux-Arts, Brussels, 93-94; Original Re-runs, Inst Contemp Art, London, 93-94; Cocida y Crudo, Nat Ctr Art Mus Reina Sofia, Madrid, 94; Transformers, Illingworth Kerr Gallery, Alberta Col Art & Design, 96; Interruptions, Nat Mus Contemp Art, Lisbon, 99; Venice Biennial, 99, 2001, 2003, 2005; Stoneheart, Ctr Contemp Art, Kitakyushu, 2000; Gallery Nordenhake, Stockholm, 2000; Int Triennial Contemp Art, Tokyo, 2001; Through a Sequence of Space, Gallery Nordenhake, Berlin, 2002; Sydney Biennial, 2004; Off Grid, Ottawa Art Gallery, 2005; Ordering the Ordinary, Timothy Taylor Gallery, London, 2005; Tirana Biennial, 2005; Guangzhou Triennial, 2005; Carnets du Sous-Sol, Galerie Michel Rein, Paris, 2006; Day for Night, Whitney Biennial, 2006; Designing Truth, Stiftung Wilheim Lehmbruck Mus, Duisburg, 2006; Saudades, Crac Alsace, Altkirch, 2006. *Pos:* writer & ed, Art & Artists Newspaper, 82-86; founder, exec dir, International Indian Treaty Coun, United Nations; exec dir, Foundation Community Artists, NY. *Bibliog:* Pascale Cassagnau (auth), Jimmie Durham; Calais, Vienna, Reims, Art Press, Vol 214, 96, 68-69; Joane Cardinal-Schubert (auth), In the red, in: Borrowed Power: Essays on Cultural Appropriation, Rutgers Univ Press, NJ, 97; Beverly Koski & Richard William Hill (auths), The Centre of the World is Several Places (Part 1), FUSE Magazine, Vol 21, No 3, summer 98, 24-33; and many others. *Dealer:* Christine König Gallery Vienna; Barbara Wien Gallery Berlin; Exit Art New York NY. *Mailing Add:* Galerie Barbara Wien Linienstr Berlin 158 10115 Germany

DURHAM, JO ANN FANNING
PAINTER
b Sulphur Springs, Tex, May 31, 35. *Study:* Tex Women's Univ, Tex A&M, BS, 56; studied with Glenn R Bradshaw, Mary Todd Beam, Ed Blackburn, Maxine Masterfield, Marilyn Hughey Phillis & Bror Utter. *Hon Degrees:* Acad Int des Arts Contemporains, Belg, Hon Dr, 94. *Work:* Huntsville Mus Art, Ala; Cannon Gallery,

Bismarck State Col, NDak; Univ N Tex Health Science Ctr, Fort Worth; Fort Worth Women's Club, Tex. *Exhib:* National League of Am Penwomen, Summer Art Mus, Washington DC, 92 & 96; Belgium Grand Prix, 93-96, 2004; Salon D'Automne, Grand Palais, Paris, France, 92, 93 & Soc Int Des Beaux Arts, 94, 96; A Fresh Look at Tex Art, McKinney Ave Contemp, Dallas, 99; Int Soc Experimental Artists, Huntsville Mus Art, Ala, 99; Soc Layerists in Multi Media, Chapelle Des Penitents Blancs, Gordes, France, 2000; Salmagundi Club, NY, 2002, 2003, 2005; Wales Cynon Valley Mus, Aberdare, Wales, 2004; Cardiff Whales, UK, 2005. *Pos:* dir, Atrium Gallery, Forth Worth, Tex, 79-82; artist in residence, Tex Comn on Arts, 90-91 & 94-95. *Teaching:* instr art, FWISD, Fort Worth, Tex, 68-69 & Kennedy Ctr Imagination Celebration, 90-93; instr painting, Templeton Art Ctr, Fort Worth, Tex, 86, Carrizo Lodge Art Sch, Ruidoso, NMex, 87-88 & Women's Club Art Dept, Fort Worth, 2000. *Awards:* Citation Award, John L Clardy, 86; Tom Lynch Award, 87; Best of Abstracts, Phillip Isenberg, 96; Nautilus fel, Int Soc Experimental Artists, 2000; Samuel Leitman Mem Award, Salmagundi Club, NY, 2006. *Mem:* Soc Watercolor Artists (vpres, 89, signatore); Int Soc Experimental Artists (pres, 98 & 99, signatore); Tex Fine Arts Asn, Region XV (pres & regional dir, 79, 80 & 81); Tex Visual Arts Asn (asst vpres, 93); Salmagundi Club; Southwestern Watercolor Soc Dallas (signatore); Society of Hayerists in Multi Media (signatore). *Media:* Mixed Water Media and Encaustics, Sand, Watercolor. *Specialty:* Comtemporary, Abstract. *Interests:* The mysteries of the cosmos. *Collection:* Tex A & M Tarleton; Fort Worth Pub Libr; Permanent Collection & Woman's Club of Fort Worth First United Methodist Church. *Publ:* Art and Healing, 1999; Master Painters of the World, International Artist Magazine, 2000; Splash 8, 2004; The Art of Layering Making Connections, 2004; Plus many others magazines & books articles. *Dealer:* Upstairs Gallery 1038 W Abram St Arlington TX; Kens Gallery 5922 Wedgewood Dr Fort Worth TX. *Mailing Add:* 4300 Plantation Dr Fort Worth TX 76116

DURHAM, WILLIAM
PAINTER, SCULPTOR

b Flint, Mich, Mar 14, 37. *Study:* Mich State Univ, BA, 60; painting with Morris Kantor, Boris Margo & Abraham Rattner. *Work:* Guild Hall, East Hampton, NY; Warnaco Inc, Park Ave, NY; Mich State Univ, East Lansing; Butler Inst Am Art; Stony Brook Mus, NY; Emelin theater, Mamaroneck NY; South Hampton Hospital, NY; Woodside Church, Mich. *Comn:* Painting, NY World's Fair, 64. *Exhib:* One-man shows, Benson Gallery, Bridgehampton, NY, 67, 71, 72 & 74 & Art Placement Int, NY, 81, Blue Heron Art Ctr, New York City, 2002; Am Acad Arts & Lett, NY, 74; Heckscher Mus, Huntington, NY, 74; Artist of the Hamptons, Guild Hall, Easthampton, NY, 75; Chicago Art Inst; Kaber Gallery, New York City 1982; Bologna Lanoi Gallery, East Hampton, NY, 83, 85, 92; 50 Year Retrospecitve, Asawaugh Hall, East Hampton, NY, 2006. *Pos:* guest curator, Bologna Landi Gallery, East Hampton, NY, 92. *Teaching:* Grad asst, Mich State Univ, 61. *Awards:* Adolph & Ester Gottlieb Found Emergency Assistance Grant, 98; Pollack-Krasner Found Inc, 98. *Bibliog:* Article, NY Herald Tribune, 64, NY Times, 64-75 & 2006 & East Hampton Star, 2005; Art in America. *Media:* Acrylic; Aluminum. *Dealer:* Butler Fine Art East Hampton NY. *Mailing Add:* PO Box 316 Amagansett NY 11930

DURR, PAT (PATRICIA) (BETH)
PAINTER, PRINTMAKER

b Kansas City, Mo; US & Can citizen. *Study:* Univ Kans, BA(educ), 61; Univ Southampton, 62; Kansas City Art Inst, 63; Ottawa Sch Art, with Duncan deKergommeaux, 65. *Work:* Can Coun Visual Art Bank, Can Embassy in Kiev; Univ Toronto Art Gallery, Ont; Biogen Inc Cambridge, MA; Goodwin Procter, NYC, NY; Hinshaw & Culbertson, Boston, Mass; EMC Corporation, Boston, MA; Can Embassies Kiev & Berlin. *Comn:* Mural, Ottawa Sch Bd, First Ave Sch, Ont, 79; Serigraph, 75th Anniversary Portfolio, Royal Trust Co, Ottawa, Ont, 80; mural, City of Ottawa Heron Rd Multiservice Ctr, 90; mural & frieze, Churchill Alternative Sch, Ottawa Bd Educ, 91; patterned concrete walkways & mural, Ottawa/Carleton Transpo Heron Rd Transitway Sta, 92-95. *Exhib:* solo-exhibs, Art Gallery Algoma, Sault Ste Marie, Ont, 90, MacLaren Art Ctr, Barrie, Ont, 92, Centre d'Exposition L'Imagier, Alymer, Que, 93, Libr Gallery, Cambridge, Ont, 94 & The Gallery, Univ Toronto, Scarborough Campus, 96, CAC Gallery, North Adams, Mass, 97, 2005, Univ Winnipeg, Manitoba, 99' Tremaine Gallery, Hotchkiss Sch, Lakeville, Conn, 2003; group shows, CAC Art Gallery, North Adams, Mass, 96, In Situ, Sightline, Univ Alta, 97 Freedom, Diversity, Pluralism, Mu de Arte Contemporaneio de la Univ de Chile, Santiago, 98, Big Impressions: the large-scale contmporary print, The Art Galleries of the Fine Arts Ctr, Univ RI, Kington, 99; The Spirit of Drawing, the Ottawa Art Gallery, On Can; Printtypes Dickeson State Univ, Dickenson, ND, 2003; Directors Choice, Missouri Western State Col, St Joseph, MO, 2004; Made in NAMA, CAC, N Adams, Mass, 2005. *Pos:* Consult, Mayor's Adv Comt Arts & Cult, 79-82, Revenue Can Visual Arts Adv Bd Customs Regulations, 80-82, Ottawa Visual & Performing Arts Ctr Steering Comt, 81-84, vchmn, Health & Welfare Can Adhoc Comt Health Hazards Arts & Crafts, 82 & 86, chmn, Jack Chambers Found, 84-86 & Munic Ottawa Visual Arts Adv Comt, 86-91; vchmn, Ottawa Arts Ctr Found, 87-88; cur, Govt Can Persons Award Exhib, 87-88; consult, Arts-Peat Marwick, 89; art comn adv, Ottawa/Carleton Regional Govt, 92-94, Cent Can Exhib Asn, 94, Can Inst Planners, 94; guest cur, Ottawa Art Gallery, 92-93. *Teaching:* Fine arts coordr, Algonquin Col Visual Art, Ottawa, Ont, 75-78, teaching master painting, 79-82; guest lectr, Univ Manitoba, NASCAD, 82, Ottawa Sch Art, 86, Alberta Col Art, 87, Banff Ctr, 87, Holland Col Sch Visual Arts, PEI, 89, Georgian Col, Ont, 92; drawing & painting inst, Alpen Sch Art, summer 87; guest lectr, Holland Col Sch Visual Arts, PEI, 89 & Yukon Art Gallery, 95; Guest Lecturer for workshops at Gallery 101, Canada, 98-2002. *Awards:* Grant, Can Coun Travel Grants, 81-82 & 99; Victor Tolgesy Award, 89; Whitton Art & Cult Award, City of Ottawa, Can, 1996; City of Ottawa Senior Artist Grant, 2003; Keith Kelly Award for Cult Leadership, National, Can, 2006. *Bibliog:* Heidi Geraets (auth), Pat Durr, Ottawa Art Gallery, 93 & The Library Gallery, Cambridge, 94; Judith Tolnick (auth), the Phenomenon of the Large-Scale Contemporary Print (catalog), Univ RI, 99; Jennifer Gibson (auth), Culture Trash (catalog), Univ Winnipeg, Can, 99; Julie Dault Its ok to have a crush on Art, National Post, 11/06/2003. *Mem:* Can Artists Representation-Les Front des Artistes Canadians (pres, Ottawa, 79-80, nat vpres, 80-82, nat pres, 82-84); Royal Can Acad Arts (exec coun, 85-87, 90-91 & 96-2000); Ottawa Arts Ctr Found (found mem & bd mem, 86-91); City of Ottawa Arts Advisory Committee, Co-Chair, 2001-2003; Can Artist Representation- Nat'l Pres, 2002-2005. *Media:* Acrylic & Mixed Media; Printmaking. *Publ:* The not so impossible dream, Artviews, Vol 9, No 3, 83; Death & taxes, Parallelogamme, Vol 9, No 3, 2/84; The Ottawa Arts Court Project, Recreation Canada, Vol 46, No 4, 11/88; Don Wright in the National Gallery, Arts Atlantic 49, Vol 13, No 1, 94; Past, Present, Future, Arts Atlantic #66, spring 2000; Landscapes with Thighs, Charlotte Wilson-Hammond, Acts Atlantic, #73, Fall 2002; Past Present, Future, Calendar, vol8 # 1 Spring, 2005. *Dealer:* Edward Day Gallery 33 Hazelton Ave Toronto ON Can M5R 2E3; Thérèse Dion Consultation 372 Rue Ste Catherine Ouest Montréal PQ Can H3B 1A2; Galerie St. Laurent & Hill 333 Cumberland St Ottawa ON Can K1N 7J3; Morgan Lehman Gallery 24 Sharon Rd Rte 41 Lakeville CT 06039; Boston Art, 330 Congress Street, Boston, MA, 02210. *Mailing Add:* 167 First Ave Ottawa ON K1S 2G3 Canada

DUSARD, JAY
PHOTOGRAPHER, WRITER

b St Louis, Mo, Feb 18, 37. *Study:* Univ Fla, BArch, 61. *Work:* JC Penney; Eastman Kodak; Ctr for Creative Photog; Fed Reserve Bank San Francisco, Los Angeles; Snell & Wilmer, Phoenix, Tucson, Irvine. *Exhib:* La Frontera, Centro Cult de Tijuana, Mex, 87; Consejo Mexicano de Fotografia, Mexico City, 88; The Cowboy West: 100 Yrs of Photog, CM Russell Mus, Great Falls, Mt, 92; Art Mus S Tex, Corpus Christi, 97; Jay Dusard's West, Desert Caballeros Western Mus, Wickenburg, Ariz, 98; Int Photog Hall of Fame, Oklahoma City, Okla, 2000; Folio Gallery: Whyte Mus of the Canadian Rockies, Alberta, 05. *Pos:* Designer & draftsman, Ellery Green Archit, Tucson, Ariz, 64; designer & lithographer, Northland Press, Flagstaff, Ariz, 66-68. *Teaching:* Asst prof light graphics, Prescott Col, Ariz, 68-75. *Awards:* Guggenheim Mem Found Fel Photog, 81; Four Corners Book Award for Nonfiction for La Frontera, Northern Ariz Univ, Flagstaff, 88; Third Place Award, Photog Book of the Year Competition, New York, 94. *Bibliog:* Michael Saltz (producer), segment, MacNeil-Lehrer News Hour (TV film), PBS-TV, 83; Sheilah Britton (producer), Arizona Artforms: The Art of Jay Dusard (TV film), KAET-TV, Tempe, Ariz, 90. *Mem:* Ctr for Photog Arts, Carmel (adv bd); Malpai Borderlands Group, Cochise Co, Ariz & Hidalgo Co, NMex; Central Ariz Land Trust (adv bd). *Media:* Photography. *Interests:* playing jazz, raising quarter horses, ranch work. *Publ:* Contribr, Photographers & Their Images, Conran Octopus, London, 88; auth & illusr, Open Country, Gibbs Smith Publ, 94; illusr, Beyond the Rangeland Conflict: Toward a West that Works, Gibbs Smith/Grand Canyon Trust, 95; illusr, Cowboy Island: Farewell to a Ranching Legacy, Santa Cruz Island Foundation, 2000; auth & illustr, Horses, Rio Nuevo Publishers, 05. *Dealer:* Etherton Gallery 135 S Sixth Ave Tucson AZ 85701. *Mailing Add:* PO Box 3923 Douglas AZ 85608

DUSENBERY, WALTER
SCULPTOR

b Alameda, Calif, 1939. *Study:* San Francisco Art Inst, 61; ceramics with Marguerite Wildenhain, 62-66; Calif Col Arts & Crafts, MFA, 71. *Work:* Carnegie Inst, Pittsburgh; Columbus Mus Art, Ohio; Guggenheim Mus & Metrop Mus Art, NY; San Francisco Mus Mod Art. *Comn:* Sculpture, Justice Ctr, Portland, Ore, 83; sculpture, Dept Art, Univ Northern Iowa, in prep. *Exhib:* One-man exhib, Univ Northern Iowa, Cedar Falls, 85, Fendrick Gallery, Wash, DC, 86 & 88, Barbara Fendrick Gallery, NY, 89; Metrop Mus Art, NY, 79; Int Sculpture Conf, Washington, DC, 80; Yorkshire Sculpture Park, Bretton Hall, Eng, 81-82; Hamilton Gallery, NY, 81; Grad Sch Design, Harvard Univ, 82; Anderson Gallery, Va Commonwealth Univ, 83; Laumeier Sculpture Park, St Louis, 83; Pratt Mus Art, NY, 87; and others. *Pos:* Pres, Digital Stone Proj, Mercerville, NJ, currently. *Teaching:* Instr ceramic sculpture, Univ Calif, San Francisco, 69; vis sculptor, Sch Landscape Archit, Grad Sch Design, Harvard Univ, 79-. *Awards:* Grants, Creative Artists Pub Serv, 80 & Nat Endowment Arts, 80. *Bibliog:* Nina French-Frazier (auth), Walter Dusenbery, Arts Mag, 6/78; David L Shirey (auth), Creations that bridge the passage of time, NY Times Long Island Ed, 9/13/81; Ann Sargent-Wooster (auth), Dusenbery at the Nassau County Museum, Art in Am, 1/82. *Mem:* Artists Equity Asn; Archit League. *Publ:* Auth, The Story of the Bed, Natoma Soc, Santa Barbara, Calif, 70; Dusenbery interviewed by Howard Greenfeld, 57th St Rev, 1/76. *Mailing Add:* PO Box 144 Fly Creek NY 13337

DUTTON, ALLEN A
PHOTOGRAPHER, PAINTER

b Kingman, Ariz, April 13, 22. *Study:* Art Ctr Schs, Los Angeles; Ariz State Univ, BA, MA, 49. *Work:* Mus Mod Art, NY; Bibliot Nat, Paris; Tokyo Col Photog Mus, Japan; Il Diaframma, Milano, Italy; Santa Barbara Mus Art; Northlight Ariz State Univ, Tempe; Ctr Photog Univ Ariz, Tucson; Univ NMex, Albuquerque; Univ Ky, Louisville. *Exhib:* Solo exhibs, Il Diaframma Gallery, Milano, Italy, 71, Northlight Gallery, Ariz State Univ, 79, 80-88, Photog Southwest Gallery, Scottsdale, Ariz, 79, Shinju Gallery, Tokyo, 79, Nagase Photo Salon, Tokyo, 84, Hayden Libr, Ariz State Univ, 85 & Hal Martin Fogle Gallery, Scottsdale, Ariz, 92. *Pos:* Art ed & photog head, Phoenix Point West Mag, 63-66. *Teaching:* Prof photog & head dept, Phoenix Col, Ariz, 61-82; prof, Tokyo Col Photog, Japan, 72-73. *Awards:* John Hay Fel, 60. *Bibliog:* A D Coleman (auth), Grotesque in Photo, Ridge Press, 78; Jim Stone (auth), Darkroom Dynamics, Curtain & London, 79. *Mem:* Soc Photog Educ. *Publ:* Auth, The Great Stone Tit, Little Wonder Press, 72; A A Dutton's Compendium, Buse Press, 74; coauth, Arizona Then and Now, AG2 Press, 82; Phoenix Then and Now, First Interstate Bank Press, 85; Mythology for the 21st Century, Zeckwough Press, 90. *Dealer:* Etherton Gallery 424 E Sixth St Tucson AZ 85705. *Mailing Add:* 767 W Lee Blvd Prescott AZ 86303-6728

DUVAL CARRIE, EDOUARD
PAINTER, SCULPTOR
b Port Au Prince, Haiti, Dec 12, 54. *Study:* Univ Loyola, Montreal, Que, BA, 78. *Work:* Miami Art Mus, Fla; Davenport Mus Art, Iowa; Detroit Inst Art, Mich; Mus de Col, St Pierre, Port-Au-Prince, Haiti. *Comn:* Jefferson Reaves, Miami Pub Health Dept, 94. *Exhib:* Sacred Arts of Vaudou, Fowler Mus, Univ Calif, Los Angeles, 95; Out of Bounds, Nexus Art Ctr, Atlanta, 96; one-man show, Musee de Col, St Pierre, Port Au Prince, Haiti, 96; From the Edge of Paradise, Polk Mus, Fla, 97; Landscapes; Real and Imagined, Bernice Steinbaum Gallery, Miami, 2000; Migrations, Installation in the New Works Room, Mus Art Of Miami, 2000, Des Migrations sous L Eau, Generous Miracles Gallery, NY, 99, Spirits, Altars & Others, Quintana Gallery, Miami, 97, From The Edge of Paradise, Polk Mus Art, Lakeland, Fla, 97, Musee du Coll St Pierre, Port-au-Prince, Haiti, 96, Silver Linings, Gutierez Fine Arts, Miami Beach, 95; Porter Troupe Gallery, San Diego, 99, Miami Dade Cult Ctr, Miami, 99, Lyle O Reitz Gallery, Santo Domingo, 99, Lakaye Gallery, Los Angeles, 98, David Beitzel Gallery, Project Room, NY, 97. *Awards:* Southern Arts Fedn/Nat Endowment Arts Regional Arts Fel, 96. *Bibliog:* Charles Merewether (auth), Edouard Duval Carrie, Marco Mus, 92; Gerald Alexis (auth), Edouard Duval Carrie, Mus de Col St Pierre, 96; Edward Sullivan (auth), Spirit Altered, Quintana Gallery, 97; David C Driskell (auth) African American Visual Aesthetics, 95; Richard J Powell (auth) Black Art and Culture in the 20th Century, 95; Eric Sarner (auth) La Passe Du Vent- Une histoire Haitienne, 94. *Mem:* 1996 Southern Arts Fedn, Nat Endowment Arts Regional Visual Arts Fel. *Publ:* Contribr, Vodou & Soul, Elle Decor, 90; Matters of spirit, Latin Am Art, 94; Myth magic & monsters, Art News, 95; El pintor y su Compromiso, Atlantica, 97; Edouard Duval Carrie, Artension, 98. *Dealer:* Fernando Quintana 3200 Ponce de Leon Miami-Coral Gables FL 33134; Bernice Steinbaum Gallery 3550 North Miami Ave Miami FL 33127. *Mailing Add:* 3717 Royal Palm Ave Miami FL 33140

DUVEEN, ANNETA
SCULPTOR, DESIGNER
b Brooklyn, NY, May 21, 24. *Study:* Adelphi Acad, watercolor with Anna G Morse, 38-41; Columbia Univ, sculpture with Oronzio Maldarelli, 42; also graphics with Charles L Goslin, 63; St Francis Col, Pa, DHH, 86. *Work:* Civic Ctr, Brooklyn; Mt Scott, Cape Palmas, Liberia WAfrica. *Comn:* John W Olin Memorials, Olin Corp, Stamford, Conn & East Alton, Ill, 72; St Maximilian Kolbe, The Vatican, 82; Francis Cardinal Cooke, Cardinal Cooke Guild, NY, 85; Christopher Columbus, Ital Heritage Ctr, Portland, Maine, 93; 45 stained glass window designs, St Anthony's Sanctuary, Brasilia, 93. *Exhib:* God's Minstrel: St Francis of Assisi, The Walters Art Gallery, Baltimore, 82; retrospective, Santa Croce Basilica Mus, Florence, Italy, 85 & MMC Gallery, Marymount Manhattan Col, NY, 86; Artiste, Dante Alighieri Soc, Palazzo Firenze, Rome, Italy, 86. *Mem:* Greenwich Art Soc. *Media:* Bronze. *Publ:* Illusr, McGraw Hill Encyclopedia of Sci & Technol, 71-86; coauth & illusr, Essentials of Astronomy, Columbia Univ Press, 77

DUZY, MERRILYN JEANNE
PAINTER, LECTURER
b Los Angeles, Calif, Mar 29, 46. *Study:* Pvt study with Vern Wilson, Los Angeles; Calif State Univ, Northridge, BA, 74; Otis Art Inst, MFA 88. *Exhib:* Women Artists in History, Tampa Mus Art, Fla, 86; Contemp Expressions from Los Angeles, Taipei, Taiwan, 89; Of Nature & Nation Yellowstone Summer of Fire, Los Angeles, 90; Elements, Woodland Hills, Calif, 90; Women Artists in History, Platt Gallery, Los Angeles, 91; and others. *Collection Arranged:* Erotic Visions, George Sand Gallery, Los Angeles, 77; Autobiographies, Palos Verdes Art Ctr, Calif, 78; Erotica 88, Gorman Fine Arts, Santa Monica, Calif; Angels, Ancestors & Spirit Guides, Burbank, Calif; Elemental Forces, Sherman Oaks, Calif. *Pos:* Founder & pres, Fla Chapter, Women's Caucus Art, 83-84, adv bd mem, Nat Women's Caucus Art, 84-87 & vpres, new chapters, 86-88; comt Women in the Art, Col Art Asn. *Teaching:* Educator, Artspace Gallery, City of Los Angeles, 91-94; Los Angeles High Sch Arts. *Awards:* First Place, Nat Women's Caucus Art, Lehigh Univ, Pa, 84; Artists Award, Otis Art Inst, Los Angeles, 88. *Bibliog:* Linda Saul (auth), Walking through history, Tampa Mus Newlett, 5/86; Laurel Paley (auth), Merrilyn Duzy & Margaret Lazzari, Artweek, 5/90; Steve Appleford (auth), Artspace's larger view of portraits, Los Angeles Times, 91; Nancy Kapitanoff (auth), Art notebook, Los Angeles Times, 91; and others. *Mem:* Women's Caucus Art; Artists Equity; Artists Alliance; Col Art Asn; Group Nine, Lela Clanterns of the East, Los Angeles, CA. *Media:* Oil, Pastel, Mixed media. *Collection:* Contemporary artists; Vern Wilson, Bruno Bruni, Leonor Fini, Mario Casilli, Norma Jean Squies, Emerson Woelfer & Hannah Wilke. *Publ:* Contribr, Contemporary Women Artists-Datebook, Bo-Tree, 87. *Mailing Add:* 8356 Capistrano Ave West Hills CA 91304-3319

DVERIN, ANATOLY
PAINTER
b Dnepropretrovsk, Ukraine, July 23, 35; US citizen. *Study:* Art Col, Dnepropetrovsk, Ukraine, BA, 50-55; Com & Indust Arts Inst, Leningrad, 55-56; Kharkov Inst Fine Arts, Ukraine, MFA, 56-62. *Work:* Paintings approved, selected & purchased by the govts & comts of the former USSR and/or Ukraine for public display at different mus & galleries, locations unknown. *Comn:* Soldiers Dream (oil), 67, Songs of the Civil War, 69, Ministry Cult USSR, Moscow, Russia; New England (oil), Delta Airlines, 87; Portrait of John Adams (oil), John Adams Venture Capital, Boston, 89. *Exhib:* Artist Mag Nat Competition, 95 & 96; 24th Ann Open Exhib-Pastel Only, Pastel Soc Am, NY, 96; 4th Biennial Nat Exhib Pastels, Pastel Soc N Fla, 96; Pastels USA, Pastel Soc W Coast, Sacramento, Calif, 96; Madison Ave Art Gallery, 96; one-man show, Creative Art Resource & Design, Birmingham, Mich, 98 & Marin Price Galleries, Chevy Chase, Md, 98, Marin-Price Gallerie, 2000; Chevy Chase MD, Marin-Price Galleries, 98; Gallery 1000, Carmel, Calif, 2001. *Awards:* Canson Award of Excellence, 92; Artist Mag Award, Nat Exhib Pastel, Pastel Soc N Fla, 94; Nat Exh Pastel Only, Klimberger Memorial Award, 94; Joseph V Giffuni Mem Award, Best in Show, 96; Canson Award, Best in Show, 98 & 00. *Bibliog:* Carole Katchen (auth), 200 Great Painting Ideas for Artists, 97 & Rachel Rubin Wolf (ed), The Best of Portrait Painting, N Light Bks; Portrait Inspirations, 97 & Landscape Inspirations, 97, Rockport Publ; The Best of Pastel, Quarry Bks. *Mem:* Pastel Soc Am; Oil Painters Am; Knickerbocker Artists; Cassat Pastel Soc; Pastel Soc of N Fla. *Media:* Oil, Soft Pastel. *Publ:* Illusr, When Animals Used to Speak, Childrens Bks, Kiev, USSR, 67; contribr, Ron Lister, Drawing with Pastel, Prentice-Hall Inc, 82; Designing Greeting Cards & Paper Products, by Ron Lister, Prentice-Hall Inc, 84; illusr, Spirit of the Hills, Dan O'Brien (auth), Pocket Bks, 88; Getting a feel for portraits, Artists Mag, 10/98; Kenneth M Bailey (auth), The Power of Personality, Am Artist Mag, 9/2000. *Dealer:* Marin-Price Galleries Chevy Chase Md; Gallery 1000 Carmel CA; Boston Art, Mass; Gallery at Lagerfield NH; Gallery on Marshant Square, Williamsburg, Va; Gallery on the Green, Vt. *Mailing Add:* Nine Oak Dr Plainville MA 02762

DWYER, EUGENE JOSEPH
HISTORIAN
b Buffalo, NY, Sept 14, 43. *Study:* Harvard Univ, BA(classics, cum laude); NY Univ Inst Fine Arts, MA, 67, PhD, 74. *Teaching:* Prof art hist, Kenyon Col, Gambier, Ohio, 73-. *Awards:* Tatiana Warsher Award for the Archaeol of Pompeii, Herculaneum & Stabia, Am Acad Rome, 73-74; Nat Endowment Humanities Fel, 80-81 & 87-88. *Mem:* Col Art Asn Am; Archaeol Inst Am; Am Numismatic Soc. *Res:* Greek and Roman art and classical tradition. *Publ:* The subject of Durer's four witches, Art Quart, 71; Augustus and the Capricorn, Roemische Mitteilungen, 73; auth, Sculpture and its Display in Houses of Pompeii, In: Pompeii and the Vesuvian Landscape, 79; Pompeian Oscilla Collections, Roemische Mitteilungen, 81; Pompeian Domestic Sculpture, 82; The Temporal Allegory of the Tazza Farnese, Am J Arch, 92. *Mailing Add:* Dept Art Hist Bailey House Kenyon Col Gambier OH 43022

DWYER, JAMES
PAINTER, EDUCATOR
b Tulsa, Okla, Oct 24, 21. *Study:* Art Inst Chicago, BFA, 47; Acad Grande Chaumiere, Paris, 47-48; Syracuse Univ, MFA, 50; Univ Chicago; De Paul Univ; study with Boris Anisfeld. *Work:* Everson Mus, Syracuse, NY; Munson-Williams-Proctor Inst, State Univ, Utica, NY; Syracuse Univ, NY; Ashland Col, Ohio. *Comn:* 3100 sq ft mural decoration, Onondaga Co Civic Ctr, Syracuse, NY, 76. *Exhib:* Art Inst Chicago, 47; Metrop Mus Art, NY, 51; City Ctr Gallery, NY, 55; Silvermine Guild Artists Conn, 56; Univ Maine, Portland-Gorham, 74; Lubin House, NY, 77; solo exhib, Krasner Gallery, NY, 81; and others. *Teaching:* Prof painting & drawing, Syracuse Univ, NY, 49-82; retired. *Media:* Acrylic. *Mailing Add:* 223 DeForest Rd Syracuse NY 13214-1926

DWYER, NANCY
SCULPTOR, PAINTER
b New York, NY, Oct 7, 54. *Study:* State Univ NY, Buffalo, BFA(cum laude), 76. *Work:* Chase Manhattan Bank, NY; Israel Mus, Jerusalem; Brooklyn Mus; Albright-Knox Art Gallery, Buffalo; Memphis-Brooks Mus. *Comn:* Obsession Overruled (billboards), NY State Coun Arts, NY, 85; Its Better Live (subway posters), Pub Art Fund, NY, 89; Multiple Choice (outdoor seating), 91-95, Hallway Highways (linolium tiled flooring), New York Bd Educ, 91-95; Who's on First? & Meet Me Here (granite seating), Gateway Corp, 92-94; Word Landscapes (etched precast stone), Criminal Justice Ctr, Philadelphia, 93-95. *Exhib:* 1987 Biennial Exhib, Whitney Mus Am Art, NY, 87; Prospect 1989, Kunsthalle Frankfurt, Ger, 89, Word as Image, Milwaukee Art Mus, 90-91, Okla City Art Mus, 90-91 & Contemp Art Mus, Houston, 90-91; Beyond the Frame, Am Art, 1960-1990, Setagaya Art Mus, Tokyo, 91; Night Lines, Centraal Mus, Utrecht, The Neth, 91; Am Artists of the 80's, Mus D'Arte Contemp, Trento, Italy, 91; The Language of Art, Kunsthalle Wein, Vienna, Austria, 92; Bad Girls I, New Mus Contemp Art, NY, 94; Bad Girls II, Wright Gallery Univ Calif Los Angeles, 94. *Teaching:* Sch Visual Arts, NY. *Awards:* Creative Arts Pub Serv Grant, NY State Coun Arts, 80; Nat Endowment Arts Fel Grant, 82; NY State Sponsored Projs Grant, NY State Coun Arts, 85. *Bibliog:* Marcia Tucker (auth), Nancy Dwyer Makes Trouble, Artforum, 89; Ellen de Bruijne (auth), Night Lines Cent Mus, Utrecht, Neth, 91; Rosetta Brooks (auth), Lost for Words (catalog), 98. *Media:* All Media; Acrylic, Oil. *Mailing Add:* 168 E Seventh St Apt 5B New York NY 10009-6271

DYENS, GEORGES MAURICE
SCULPTOR
b Mar 18, 32; Fr & Can citizen. *Study:* Ecole Nat Super Beaux Arts, Paris, dipl, 61, studied with painter Balthus; Concordia Univ, Montreal, MFA; Holographic Lab. *Work:* Mus Mod Art & Hotel Hilton, Paris; Mus Art Contemp, Montreal; Mus Quebec; Mus Holography, NY; Permanent outdoor installations in Montreal & Quebec City. *Comn:* Public Art Montreal, Quebec City; Repentigny, Joliette, Can. *Exhib:* Mus Rodin, Paris, 66; Int Biennial New Delhi, India, 68; solo exhib, Mus Que, 81 & 95-96; Images du Futur, Montreal, 87, 89 & 92; Alternative Mus, NY, 88; Bienniale Paris 1961-1963, Mississippi Mus Art, Jackson, 95; ART-COM Gallery, Paris, 95; and others. *Pos:* artist-in-residence, Mus Holography, NY; cur, Saidye Bronfman Ctr, Montreal. *Teaching:* Prof sculpture, Univ Que, Montreal, 69-; invited prof & artist, Univ Dauphine, Paris, 92-93. *Awards:* Grand Prix De Rome, Paris, 61; Prix Susse, Bienniale Paris, 63; Shearwater Found Award Art Holography, Ft Lauderdale, Fla, 94. *Bibliog:* Diulio Morosini (auth), La Revincita Della Vita, Paese Sera, Rome, 7/1/65; Gerald Gassiot-Talabot (auth), Dyens, Arts, Paris, 10/20/65; Frank Popper (auth), Art of the Electronic Age, Harry N Abrams, New York, 93. *Mem:* Asn Sculptors Que, Montreal; Asn Arts & Techniques Holographics, Paris; Europ Ctr Technocult, Paris; Europ Acad Sci, Arts & Lit. *Media:* Multi Media, Holography Installation. *Res:* Photonics and Holography. *Mailing Add:* Dept Plastic Arts Univ Que CP 8888 Succ A Montreal PQ H3C 3P8 Canada

DYER, M WAYNE
PAINTER, DESIGNER
b Roanoke, Va, Aug 6, 50. *Study:* Va Western Community Col, AAS(design), 70; Hollins Col, Va, 71-72; James Madison Univ, Harrisonburg, Va, BS(fine arts, paintings, drawing & printmaking), 73; Va Art Inst, with Hartwell Priest, Charlottesville, 74; Radford Univ, Va, MFA(painting & Drawing), 83: workshop, with Robert Farber, 85; Varityper Opers Training Ctr, Atlanta, 86; Arrowmont Sch Arts & Crafts, with Beverly Plummer, 88; Calif State Univ, summer arts prog, 89. *Work:* Lykes Enrichment Ctr, Lykes Hosp, Brooksville, Fla; Ctr for New Creation, Nashville, Tenn; Slocumb Galleries, ETenn Univ, Johnson City; Radford Univ Found, Va; Mary Wash Col, Fredericksburg, Va. *Exhib:* Solo exhibs, Watkins Inst Art, Nashville, 88, Tempo Gallery, Brooksville, Fla, 88, Jacksonville Univ Gallery, Ala, 90, Lincoln Mem Univ Mus, Harrogate, Tenn, 89-90, Kiosk, Johnson City, Tenn, 91, Keene Gallery, Jonesborough, Tenn, 92-93 & Libr Gallery, Wise, Va, 95; Humbolt Univ, Calif State Univ, Arcada, 91; Slocumb Galleries Fac Exhib, 94; The Land on which We Live, Oscar Howe Art Ctr, Mitchell, SDak, 94; 1st Arg Int Art Proj, Capital Fed, Buenos Aires, 94; Akim Masks USA, Sotheby's, NY, 96. *Pos:* Tenn Arts Commission, Media Panel, 85-89, chmn 87-89. *Teaching:* Assoc prof to prof, Dept Art & Design, ETenn State Univ, 83-present. *Awards:* Award of Merit, First Tenn Exhib, Johnson City Area Arts Coun, 86; Award of Merit, First Am Exhib, Kingsport, Tenn, 87; Harvey Award Industrial Advertising, 87; Best Show, Cabaret VI, Johnson City Area Arts Coun, 88; Outstanding Art Faculty Award, 91; Tash 97' Nat Collaboration Award, 97; Pres Award, Nat Down Syndrome Congress, 98; Distinguished Faculty Award, East Tenn State Univ, 1999-2000. *Mem:* Col Art Asn; Southeastern Ctr Contemp Art; Johnson City Area Arts Coun; Am Inst Graphic Design. *Media:* Acrylic, Oil. *Mailing Add:* Dept Art Box 70708 1809 Oakland Ave Johnson City TN 37601

DYYON, MARIO
PAINTER, SCULPTOR
b Ft Meyers, Fla, May 2, 46. *Work:* Mus Mod Art, Whitney Mus Am Art, NY; Larry Aldrich Mus, Conn; Case Western Reserve Univ. *Exhib:* Cleveland Top Artists, In Town Club, 69; Int Exhib Art, Cleveland, 70; Whitney Mus Am Art Ann, 72; Reflections, Larry Aldrich Mus, 72-73; one-man show, Mather Gallery, Case Western Reserve Univ, 83. *Awards:* Printmaker Workshop Bd Scholar, New York, 82. *Mailing Add:* 155 W 73rd St New York NY 10023

DZIERSKI, VINCENT PAUL
PAINTER, DESIGNER
b Pittsburgh, Pa, Jan 1, 30. *Study:* Studied drawing & painting with Armando Del Cimuto, 48-52. *Pos:* Creative dir, Town Studios, Inc, 70-. *Media:* Egg Tempera, Alkyds. *Mailing Add:* 1229 Parkside Dr Bridgeville PA 15017

E

EADES, LUIS ERIC
PAINTER, EDUCATOR
b Madrid, Spain, June 25, 23; US citizen. *Study:* Bath Sch Art, Eng; Slade Sch, Univ London; Inst Polytech Nac, Mexico City, Mex; Univ Ky, Lexington, BA. *Work:* Whitney Mus Am Art, NY; Mus Fine Arts, Houston; Dallas Mus Fine Arts; Ft Worth Art Ctr; Mus Fine Arts, Holyoke, Mass; Denver Art Mus; US West, Denver; Kaiser Permanente; Amoco. *Comn:* Airport mural, Govt Honduras, Toncontin, Tegucigalpa, 48; mural, Mesa Col, Grand Junction, Colo, 79; mural, US W Communications, Denver, Colo, 89. *Exhib:* Recent Painting USA: The Figure, Mus Mod Art, NY, 62; Forty Artists Under Forty, Whitney Mus Am Art, 62; State of Man, New Sch Social Res, NY, 64; 2nd Intermountain Biennial Exhib, Salt Lake Art Ctr, Utah, 65; Colorado Springs Fine Arts Ctr, 69; Purdue Univ, West Lafayette, Ind, 1992; Awada Ctr for Arts and Humanties, Colo, 93; Lincoln Ctr, Foot Collins, Colo, 93; 20/20 Vision, Arvada (Colo) Ctr for the Arts & Humanities, 1996; Digital Images, Regis Univ, Denver, 1996; Egypt of the Mind, Denver Art Mus, 98. *Teaching:* Prof painting & drawing, Univ Tex, 54-60; prof painting & drawing, Univ Colo, 61-90, prof emer, 90-. *Media:* Oil, Acrylic, digital prints. *Publ:* Illus, The Precipice, Univ Tex, 69. *Dealer:* William Havu Gallery 1040 Cherokee St Denver CO 80204. *Mailing Add:* 3857 Orion Ct Boulder CO 80304-1024

EAGEN, CHRISTOPHER T
DIRECTOR
b Ohio, Feb 18, 56. *Study:* Kansas City Art Inst, BFA, 78. *Collection Arranged:* Beyond the Surface: Abstract Illusionists, 82, Art of the Emotionally Disturbed Adolescents, 83, Sculpture from the Ceiling, 84, Live TV: Television as It Happened, 86, Tangeman Fine Arts Gallery, Cincinnati, Ohio. *Pos:* Dir publicity, Contemp Art Ctr, Cincinnati, 78-79; pres, Cincinnati Artists Group Effort, 79-80; asst dir, Tangeman Fine Arts Gallery, Cincinnati, 80-81. *Teaching:* Instr & gallery internship art appreciation, Univ Cincinnati, 82-86. *Publ:* Contribr, Fragments, 83-84, coauth, Contemporary African Sculpture, 84, contribr, Emeritae, 85 & Art Deco Cincinnati, 85, Univ Publ, Univ Cincinnati. *Mailing Add:* 1828 N O St Lake Worth FL 33460-6653

EAGERTON, ROBERT PIERCE
PAINTER
b Florence, SC, Mar 17, 40. *Study:* Atlanta Sch Art, BFA; Acad Fine Arts, Vienna, Austria; Cranbrook Acad Art, Bloomfield Hills, Mich. *Work:* Nat Collection Fine Art, Smithsonian Inst, Washington, DC; Art Inst Chicago; Lessing J Rosenwald Collection, Jenkintown, Pa; Sheldon Swope Gallery Art; Norman McKenzie Mus Art, Regina, Sask; Lincoln Conf Ctr, Indianapolis, Ind. *Exhib:* One-man show, Norman McKenzie Mus Art; Lithographs de la Collection Mourlot, PR, 71; Prints: USA 1974, Univ Pittsburgh; Image South Gallery, Atlanta, Ga, 81; Ruschman Gallery, Indianapolis, Ind, 88 & 90; and others. *Pos:* Co-founder, Transfigurations Press, Sarasota, Fla, 64-66. *Teaching:* Prof painting, Herron Sch Art, Ind-Purdue Univ, Indianapolis, 66-88; guest artist printmaking, Univ Ill, Champaign, 70; vis prof printmaking, Tyler Sch Art, summer 72; vis artist, Univ Sask, Regina, 73, Univ Mich, Ann Arbor, 77, Louisville Sch Art, Ky, 79, Cincinnati Sch Art, Ohio, 81 & Emma Lake Wkshp, Regina. *Bibliog:* Robert Eagerton (video), Indiana Univ, 90. *Media:* Oils. *Publ:* Contribr, Horizon, 87. *Mailing Add:* 7010 Wildridge Dr Indianapolis IN 46256-2130

EARDLEY, CYNTHIA
SCULPTOR
b Trenton, NJ, Mar 18, 46. *Study:* Douglass Col, Rutgers Univ, New Brunswick, NJ, BA (with honors), 68; Sch Visual Arts, New York, 68-69. *Comn:* Peeling Wall, comn by pres Sydney Lewis, Best Products Inc, Richmond, Va, 72. *Exhib:* The Power of Scale, Art Mus S Tex, Corpus Christi, 91; Emerging from NY, Klienert James Art Ctr, Woodstock, NY, 95; Woman Sculptors of the 90's, Snug Harbor Cult Ctr, Staten Island, NY 96; NY Acad of Art, Fac Show, 2001 & 2003; Five Fresh Voices, Franklin Parrasch Gallery, NY, 2001; SOFA Chicago: Int Exposition of Sculpture and Functional Art, 2002. *Pos:* Co-dir, Site Inc, NY, 69-73. *Teaching:* Asst prof, Pratt Inst, Brooklyn, 72; instr sculpture, Newark Mus Sch, 74, Philadelphia Col Art, 89; Figure sculpture, anatomy, art hist; instr grad and continuing educ div, NY Acad Art, 94-2005. *Awards:* First Place Award, Enviro-Vision, Everson Mus, 72; Semi-finalist, Municipal Servs Bldg Plaza Competition, Philadelphia, 92. *Bibliog:* Roberta Smith (auth) Sculpture in the City:; Blankets to Bronze, The New York Times, 4/20/90; Antonin Tenzer (auth) Kransni s i lena Site, Rubrika Architektura, 1/22/99; Cynthia Nadelman (auth), Middle-Aged Gods and Giant Babies, ART News Mag, 12/04. *Mem:* Women's Caucus for Art. *Media:* Bronze, Ceramic. *Publ:* Auth, Creativity & madness, Women's Caucus for Art Newsletter, New York, fall 94; Artists are tougher, Letters to the Ed, NY Times, 5/6/94; In 3 Dimensions: Women Sculptors of the 90s, WCA Update, Vol 6, No 4, 96; Memorialinzing 9/11, Letters to the Ed, NY Times, 12/03/03; Editor's Choice: Helga von Eichen, Bomb Magazine, summer 2004. *Mailing Add:* 115 W Broadway New York NY 10013

EARL, JACK EUGENE
CERAMIST
b Unioplis, Ohio, Aug 2, 34. *Study:* Bluffton Col, BA, 56; Ohio State Univ, MA, 64. *Work:* Butler Mus Art, Youngstown, Ohio; Milwaukee Art Mus, Wis; Mus Contemp Crafts, NY; Nat Mus Am Art, Smithsonian Inst, Washington; Chicago Art Inst; and others. *Comn:* Mural, Kohler Co, Kohler, Wis, 76. *Exhib:* Int Exhib Ceramics, Victoria & Albert Mus Art, London, Eng, 72; Clay Things, Whitney Mus Am Art, NY, 74; one-man shows, Am Craft Mus, NY, 88, Charles A Wustum Mus, Racine, Wis, 88, Octagon Ctr, Ames, Iowa, 88, Perimeter Gallery, Chicago, Ill, 88, Kansas City Art Inst, Mo, 89, Miami Univ, Oxford, Ohio, 90 & Dorothy Weill Gallery, San Francisco, Calif, 90-92; Peremater Gallery, Chicago, 92; Garth Gallery, Los Angeles, Calif, 95; Margolis Gallery, NY, 95; Recent Works, Perimeter Gallery, Chicago, 96; and others. *Collection Arranged:* Objects USA, 68; The Plastic Earth, John Michael Kohler Arts Ctr, Sheboygan, Wis; Decade of Ceramic Art, San Francisco Mus Art, Calif, 73. *Teaching:* Instr ceramics, Toledo Mus Art, 64-72; from asst prof to assoc prof ceramics, Va Commonwealth Univ, 72-78. *Awards:* Merit Award, Louisville Art Ctr, 68-70; Purchase Award, Columbus Gallery Fine Arts, 72; Nat Endowment Arts Award, 75-89; Ohio Coun Arts Award, 81, 83, 85 & 90; and others. *Bibliog:* Down Home, Arts in Va, 74; Art in industry, Crafts Horizon, 74; Lee Nordness (auth), Jack Earl - The Genesis and Triumph, Survival of an Underground Ohio Artist, 86; and others. *Mem:* Hon mem Nat Coun Educ Ceramic Arts. *Mailing Add:* 11173 Evandale Lake Ave Lakeview OH 43331

EARLE, EDWARD W
CURATOR, HISTORIAN
b New Orleans, La, Aug 19, 51. *Study:* Univ Notre Dame, BA, 74; Visual Studies Workshop, State Univ NY, Buffalo, MA(mus studies), 78. *Collection Arranged:* Points of View (ed, catalog), 79; Hand Camera in History, 82; The Orient Viewed, 82; Philip Brigandi, Photographer, 83; Prof Joseph Jastrow, 84. *Pos:* Cur, Visual Studies Workshop, Rochester, NY, 77-79; librn & archivist, Photog Resource Ctr, Boston, 80-82; cur, Calif Mus Photog, Univ Calif, Riverside, 82-. *Teaching:* Instr photog, Swain Sch Design, New Bedford, Mass, 79-80; instr hist photog, Boston Col, Chestnut Hill, 82-83. *Mem:* Col Art Asoc; Soc Photog Educ; Am Cult Asn. *Res:* History of photography, relating aesthetic trends to social and cultural conditions. *Publ:* Contributing articles in Afterimage and New England J Photog, 77-; Points of View, The Stereograph in America: A Cultural History, VSW Press, 79; ed, Philip Brigandi, Calif Mus Photog Bulletin, 83; contribr, The Photographic Vision (TV ser), KOCE-TV for PBS. *Mailing Add:* Senior Cur UCR-Calif Museum of Photography Univ of Calif Riverside Riverside CA 92521

EARLS-SOLARI, BONNIE
CURATOR
b Fallbrook, Calif, Oct 4, 51. *Study:* Univ Calif, Berkeley, BA, 73. *Pos:* Asst cur, Univ Art Mus, 74-77; prog coordr, Cooper Hewitt Mus, 77-78; cur, dir, art prog, Bank Am Corp, 79-. *Mem:* Asn Prof Art Adv; Graphic Arts Coun; Foto Forum; Art Table (Women Visual Arts). *Mailing Add:* 64 Surrey St San Francisco CA 94131

EASTCOTT, ROBERT WAYNE
PRINTMAKER, PAINTER
b Trail, BC, July 20, 43. *Study:* Emily Carr Col Art & Design, (Vancouver Sch Art), with J Shadbolt, D Jarvis & R Kiyooka, Senior Cert (painting & printmaking, hons), 66. *Work:* Nat Gallery, Ottawa; Art Gallery Greater Victoria, BC; Winnipeg Art Gallery, Man; Robert MacLaughlin Gallery, Oshawa, Ont; Kanagawa Prefectural

Gallery, Yokohama, Japan. *Comn:* Portfolio of 5 editions, Generation 84 Youth Soc, Vancouver, BC, 83; portrait of Mr Belzberg (serigraph), New Play Ctr, Vancouver, 83; Edition of 125 (serigraph), Adovocat Structured Settlements; wall relief on riveted aluminum, Rienhard Derreth Graphics Ltd, Vancouver, BC, 89. *Exhib:* Solo exhibs, Can & Japan, 69-91, Crown Gallery, Vancouver, BC, 97, Wayne Escott: The Printed Painting, Burnaby Art Gallery, BC, 98, Generation-Before and After, Lookout Gallery, Regent Col, Univ BC, Vancouver, 98; Fomento de las Artes Decoratives, Barcelona, Spain, 85; Burnaby Art Gallery (with catalog), BC, 88; North of the Border-Contemp Canadian Art, Watcom Co Mus, Wash, 90; Triennale '94 (catalog), Krakow, 94; Int Print Triennial, Kanagawa Perfectural Gallery, Yokohama, Japan, 98. *Pos:* Founding mem & pres, Dunderave Print Soc, 71-76. *Teaching:* Instr painting, Vancouver Sch Art, BC, 65-70; head dept printmaking, Capilano Col, NVancouver, BC, 71-. *Awards:* Can Coun Grant, 68. *Bibliog:* A Perry & K Kritzweiser (auths),Wayne Eastcott, Okui Assoc, Tokyo, Japan, 79; Printed Painting-Ted Lindberg Burnaby Art Gallery, 88; Ted Linberg (auth), The curator's statement, Capilano Rev, 88. *Mem:* Royal Can Acad Arts; Dunderave Print Soc; World Print Coun; Can Print & Drawing Soc; Malaspina Printmakers. *Media:* All Media, Acrylic, Enamel. *Mailing Add:* 2748 Lougheed Hwy No 402 Port Coquitlam BC V3B 6P2 Canada

EASTERSON, SAM PETER
VIDEO ARTIST, CONCEPTUAL ARTIST
b Hartford, Conn, Jan 24, 72. *Study:* Cooper Union, with Tony Ourster, BFA(scholar), 94; Univ Minn, with Lance Neckar, MS, 99. *Comn:* Video, Walker Art Ctr, Minneapolis, 98. *Exhib:* Fuzzy Logic, Inst Contemp Art, Boston, 96; 1997 Biennial Exhib (with catalog), Whitney Mus Am Art, NY, 97; Station to Station, Artists Space, NY, 97; Dialogues, Walker Art Ctr (with catalog), Minneapolis, 98; Benefit Exhib, New Mus, NY, 98; Niet de Kunstvlaai, Sanburg Inst, Amsterdam, The Neth, 98; Scope, Artists Space, NY, 98; Pandaemonium (with catalog), London Electronic Arts, Eng, 98; World Wide Video Festival (with catalog), Sledeljk Mus Modern Art, 99; Art in General (with catalog), NY, 2000; Rare Gallery, NY, 2000. *Pos:* dir, Animal Vegetable, Video. *Teaching:* Guest artist video art, Mass Col Art, Boston, 95 & Grinnell Col, Iowa, 97; instr video art, Art Inst Minn, 98-. *Awards:* Bk Prize, RI Sch Design, 90; Tiffany Prize, 99. *Media:* Video. *Publ:* auth, various articles in NY Times, Village Voice, Flash Art & Timeout NY. *Mailing Add:* 11255 Huston St Apt 211 North Hollywood CA 91601; 11255 Huston St Apt 211 North Hollywood CA 91601

EASTMAN, GENE M
PAINTER
b Council Grove, Kans, Jan 1, 26. *Study:* Univ Kans, BFA; Art Inst Chicago; Univ Iowa, with Stuart Edie, MFA. *Exhib:* Houston Mus Fine Arts, Tex, 58 & 61; Dallas Mus Fine Arts Ann, 59, 63 & 66; Seven States Artists Ann, Delgado Mus, New Orleans, 61; Watercolor USA, Springfield, Mo, 64; 24-64 Nat Exhib Small Paintings, Purdue Univ, 64. *Teaching:* Prof drawing & painting, Sam Houston State Univ, 58-, chmn art dept, 72-79; guest instr drawing & painting, Mus Fine Arts Sch, Houston Mus Fine Arts, Tex, 68-70. *Awards:* First Prize, Painting, Tex Fine Arts Asn, 58; Purchase Award, Okla Printmaker Soc, 64; First Prize, Painting, Tri-State Exhib, Beaumont Mus, Tex, 67. *Media:* Oil, Watercolor. *Mailing Add:* 7191 Hwy 75 South Huntsville TX 77340-7283

EATON, THOMAS NEWTON See Eaton, Tom

EATON, TOM
CARTOONIST, WRITER
b Wichita, Kans, Mar 2, 40. *Study:* Univ Denver, 58; Univ Kans, BFA, 62. *Comn:* Mag covers, Boy's Life, Scholastic Voice, Scholastic Scope, Child Life, and others; posters, Scholastic Mag Inc, 74-79, plus others. *Pos:* Artist-writer Contemp Cards dept, Hallmark Cards, Inc, Kansas City, Mo, 62-66; art ed, Scholastic Mag Inc, New York, 66-68; free lance cartoonist-writer, 68-; regular contrib comic features Dink and Duff, Webelos Woody, Tiger Cubs, The Wacky Adventures of Pedro, Mazes & More, Boys' Life Mag, 84-. *Awards:* Cert of Excellence for Cover, Catch the Eye, 75, Am Inst Graphics Arts. *Bibliog:* Eleanor Van Zandt (auth), A cartoonist looks at the comics, Practical Eng Mag, 68. *Mem:* Am Mensa; Am Anti-Vivisection Soc; Serra Club; Green Peace. *Media:* Pen, Ink. *Publ:* Auth & illusr, Flap, Delacorte Press, 72; Tom Eaton's Book of Marvels, 76, Holiday Greeting Cards, 78 & Super Valentines, 79, Scholastic Bk Serv; Rufus and the Earth Patrol, Sat Eve Post, 78; Captain Ecology, 74; Otis G Firefly's Phantasmagoric Almanac, 74; and others. *Mailing Add:* 911 W 100th St Kansas City MO 64114

EBERLE, EDWARD SAMUEL
CERAMIST, DRAFTSMAN
b Tarentum, Pa, Oct 3, 44. *Study:* Edinboro State Col, BS, 67; NY State Col Ceramics, Alfred Univ, MFA, 72. *Work:* Carnegie Mus Art, Pittsburgh, Pa; Los Angeles Co Mus Art; Newark Mus Art; Nat Gallery Australia, Canberra; Fine Arts Mus San Francisco; Nelson-Atkins Mus Art, Kansas City. *Exhib:* One-man shows: Columbus Mus Art & Carnegie Mus Art. *Teaching:* From instr to asst prof ceramics, Philadelphia Col Art, 71-75; from asst to assoc prof, Carnegie-Mellon Univ, Pittsburgh, Pa, 75-85. *Awards:* Fel, Nat Endowment Arts, 87; Fel, Pa Coun Arts, 86 & 89. *Bibliog:* Gary Wells (auth), A mythic realm in black and white, Am Ceramics, 6/1/87; Michael Odom (auth), Edward Eberle: in the realm of myth, Am Craft, 5-6/92. *Media:* Ceramic. *Dealer:* Garth Clark Gallery 24 W 57th St New York NY 10019. *Mailing Add:* PO Box 5844 Pittsburgh PA 15209

EBERLY, VICKIE
PAINTER
b Washington, DC, May 28, 56. *Study:* Md Inst Col Art, BFA(painting), 78; City Univ New York, Queens Col, NY, MFA(painting), 81. *Work:* Image Communications Inc, NY. *Exhib:* Queens Community Mus, NY, 81; Queens Col Gallery, City Univ NY, 81; Ball State Univ Art Gallery, Ind, 82; El Paso Mus Art, Tex, 82; Barrett House, Poughkeepsie, NY, 85; Central Hall Gallery, NY, 86; 22 Wooster Gallery, NY, 87; Tradition 3 Thousand Gallery, NY, 87. *Media:* Oil on Canvas, Mixed Graphics. *Dealer:* Tradition 3 Thousand Gallery 273 E 10th St New York NY 10009. *Mailing Add:* 8421 110th St Jamaica NY 11418-1243

EBIE, WILLIAM DENNIS
ADMINISTRATOR, PAINTER
b Akron, Ohio, Feb 7, 42. *Study:* Akron Art Inst Sch Design, scholar, 60, Univ Akron & Akron Art Inst Sch Design, BFA, 64; Calif Col Arts & Crafts, scholarships, 67-68, MFA, 68. *Work:* Calif Col Arts & Crafts Gallery. *Exhib:* The Figure: An Invitational Painting Exhibition, Kans State Col Gallery, Pittsburg, 75; Territorial Gallery, Roswell, NMex, 76 & 78; 20th Nat Sun Festival, El Paso Mus Art, Tex, 79; Santa Fe Festival of Arts, 79; Upstairs Gallery, Albuquerque, NMex, 80; Albuquerque United Artists Downtown Ctr Arts, NMex, 81; Fine Arts Gallery, NMex State Fairgrounds, Albuquerque, 85; Stables Art Gallery, Taos, NMex, 86; Carlsbad Art Mus, NMex, 88. *Pos:* Ceramic specialist, Peace Corps, Cuzco, Peru, 64-66; graphic artist, Alameda Co Health Dept, Oakland, Calif, 67-68; asst dir, Roswell Mus & Art Ctr & managing dir, Roswell Mus Artist in Residence Prog, 71-; dir, Roswell Mus & Art Ctr, 87-. *Teaching:* Instr painting, Fla A&M Univ, 69-70; instr painting, Roswell Mus Adult Educ, NMex, 71-78. *Mem:* NMex Asn Mus; Mountain Plains Mus Asn

EBITZ, DAVID MACKINNON
MUSEUM DIRECTOR, HISTORIAN
b Hyannis, Mass, Oct 5, 47. *Study:* Williams Col, BA, 69; Harvard Univ, AM, 73, PhD, 79. *Collection Arranged:* The Baroque Print, Univ Art Collection, 85; Art of Fixing a Shadow, J Paul Getty Mus, 89; Maiolica to Monstrance, Ringling Mus, 94; A Heritage of Collecting, Mus Fla Hist, 95. *Pos:* Interim dir, Univ Art Collection, Univ Maine, 86-87; head dept educ & acad affairs, J Paul Getty Mus, 87-92; dir, John & Mable Ringling Mus Art, 92-. *Teaching:* Asst prof art hist, Univ Maine, 78-84, assoc prof, 84-87. *Mem:* Asn Art Mus Dirs; Fla Art Mus Dirs Asn; Col Art Asn; Am Asn Mus; Int Ctr Medieval Art. *Publ:* Auth, Secular to sacred: The transformation of an oliphant in the Musee de Cluny, Gesta, 86; Fatimid style and Byzantine model in a Venetian ivory carving workshop, Studies in Medieval Culture, 86; The oilphant: It's function and meaning in a courtly society, Houston German Studies, 86; Connoisseurship as practice, Artibus et Historiae, 88; DBAE: Opening a bridge between art history and art education, Alaska J Art, 89; Four Sculptors, Univ Art Collection, 87. *Mailing Add:* c/o John and Mable Ringling Mus Art 5401 Bay Shore Rd Sarasota FL 34243

EBONY, DAVID
EDITOR
Pos: Writer, ArtNet Mag; assoc managing ed, news ed, Art in America Mag, currently managing ed. *Publ:* Auth, Curve: The Female Nude Now, Carlo Maria Mariani, 2003. *Mailing Add:* Art in America Brant Art Publications 575 Broadway New York NY 10012

EBSWORTH, BARNEY A
COLLECTOR
Pos: Founder, chmn, pres, Chief Exec Officer, INTRAV, 59-99, Royal Cruise Line, 72-86, Clipper Cruise Line, 81-97; founder, chmn, Chief Exec Officer, Windsor Inc, St Louis, 79-; trustee, St Louis Art Mus, Seattle Art Mus, Nat Gallery, co-chmn, 96-; dir, Build-A-Bear Workshop Inc, 2000-2006, dir emeritus, 2006-; comnr, Am Art Mus, Smithsonian Inst, currently. *Awards:* Named one of Top 200 Collectors, ARTnews Mag, 2004, 2005, 2006. *Collection:* American modern & contemporary art

ECCLES, TOM
ADMINISTRATOR
Study: Glasgow Univ, Scotland, MA in philos and Italian; Bologna Univ, Italy, Studied for 2 years with Umberto Eco. *Pos:* devel. dir, Proj Ability, Scotland; pub. art consultant, proj mgr Art in Partnership, Edinburgh, Scotland; joined Pub Art Fund, New York City, 93, dir, 96-; founder, In the Pub Realm prog for emerging artists, founder, Tuesday Night Talks lecture series. *Teaching:* instr, moral philos Univ Glasgow, Scotland; instr, critical theory Glasgow Arts Sch, Scotland, 90-92; Lectr, on pub art. *Awards:* Recipient Award for Best Show in an Alternative or Pub; Space as cur of Janet Cardiff: Her Long Black Hair, Int Asn Art Critics/USA, 2005. *Publ:* Co-auth: (book) Plop: Recent Proj of the Public Art Fund, 2004; written articles and reviews for Art in Am. *Mailing Add:* Pub Art Fund 1 E 53rd St New York NY 10022

ECHELMAN, JANET
SCULPTOR, PAINTER
b Tampa, Fla, Feb 19, 66. *Study:* Harvard Col, Harvard Univ, AB (magna cum laude), 87; Milton Avery Sch Arts, Bard Col, MFA, 95. *Work:* Mus Centre Europe/Europas Parkas, Vilnius, Lithuania; Tampa Mus Art, Tampa, Fla; Harvard Univ Film Arch, Cambridge, Mass; Fields Sculpture Mus and Park, Omi, NY; John Michael Kohler Art Center, Sheboygan, Wis. *Comn:* sculpture, Harvard Univ Art Mus, 98; sculpture, Buffalo Bayou Art Park, Houston, Tex, 2000; sculpture, Florence Lynch Gallery at IFEMA, Madrid, Spain, 2001; sculpture, Casa del Cordon, Burgos, Spain, 2001. *Exhib:* one-woman show, Works from Bali, Fung Ping Shan Art Mus, Hong Kong Univ, 90; one-woman show, New Vision, Tampa Mus Art, Tampa, Fla, 93; Wax Hands, Sackler Art Mus, Harvard Univ, Cambridge, Mass, 96; one-woman show, Bellbottoms: Sculpture Combining Net and Bronze, Birla Art Mus, Calcutta, India, 97; Trying to Hide with Your Tail in the Air, Mus Centre Europe, Vilnius, Lithuania, 98; Inside Outside, Fogg Art Mus, Harvard Univ, Cambridge, Mass, 98; Open Spaces, ARCO, Madrid, Spain, 2001. *Pos:* southeast asia regional coordr, Rauschenberg Overseas Culture Interchange, 89-91. *Teaching:* instr visual studies, Harvard Univ Grad Sch Design, 92-96; resident tutor fine arts, Harvard Col, Harvard Univ, 93-2000;

senior lectr, adj prof, Lesley Univ, 98-. *Awards:* artist grant, Pollock-Krasner Found, 99; artist grant in sculpture, Mass Cult Coun, 99; artist fel, Japan Found, 2001. *Bibliog:* Stephen Westfall (auth), Janet Echelman: New Vision, Tampa Mus Art, 93; Adrian Randolph and John Welchman (auths), Two Essays on the Painting of Janet Echelman, Harvard Univ Bow and Arrow Press, 95; Esther David (auth) Janet Echelman (contribr), Bellbottoms: Sculpture Combining Bronze and Net by Janet Echelman, Nat Inst Design India, 97. *Mem:* Int Sculpture Center; Col Art Asn. *Publ:* auth, An Artists Journal from Bali, Hong Kong Univ Dept Fine Arts, 88; auth, Radcliffe Quarterly, Radcliffe Inst Harvard Univ, 92. *Dealer:* Florence Lynch Gallery 147 W 29th St New York NY 10001

ECHOHAWK, BRUMMETT
PAINTER, ILLUSTRATOR
b Pawnee, Okla, Mar 3, 22. *Study:* Sch Arts & Crafts, Detroit, 44; Art Inst Chicago, 44-48. *Work:* Gilcrease Mus Am Hist & Art, Tulsa. *Comn:* Truman Mem Libr (mural, with Thomas Hart Benton), Independence, Mo, 59-60. *Exhib:* Gilcrease Mus, Tulsa; Amon Carter Mus, Ft Worth, Tex; M H De Young Mem Mus, San Francisco; Imperial War Mus, London; Karl May Theater Mus, Bad Segeberg, WGer; Art Through the Embassies, US State Dept, Pakistani, India. *Pos:* Auth & illusr, articles in Western Horseman, Colorado Springs, 50-, Tulsa Sunday World, 50- & Okla Today, 60-; bd mem, Gilcrease Mus Am Hist & Art, Tulsa, 80-. *Bibliog:* Whose Children Are These (film), ABC-TV Network, NY. *Media:* Oil, Tempera. *Publ:* Auth & illusr, Blue book, McCalls Mag, 49. *Mailing Add:* 2525 W Easton Tulsa OK 74127

ECKART, CHRISTIAN
PAINTER
b Calgary, Alta, Can, Jan 9, 59. *Study:* Hunter Col, City Univ New York, MFA, 86. *Work:* Mus Mod Art, NY; Chicago Art Inst; List Visual Art Ctr, Mass Inst Technol; New Sch Soc Res, NY. *Exhib:* Galerie Tanit, Munich, Ger, 89 & 92; Galerie 'T Venster, Rotterdam, The Neth, 88; Galerie Thaddaeus Ropac, Paris & Salzburg, 90 & 91; Rubin Spangle Gallery, NY, 90 & 92; Eli Broad Family Found, Santa Monica, Calif, 92; Thaddaeus Ropac Gallery, Salzberg, Austria, 95 & Paris, 95; Sidney Janis Gallery, NY, 95; Ten-Year Survey Show (traveling), Univ Western Ont, 96-98. *Teaching:* Nova Scotia Col Art & Design, Halifax, NS, Can, 89, Art Ctr Col Design, Pasadena, Calif, 90, Univ Hartford Dept Art, Conn, 91, Alta Col Art, Calgary, Can, 91, Int Art His Conf, NY, 91, Aldrich Mus Contemp Art, Ridgfield, Conn, 92, Univ RI, 92, Sch Visual Arts, NY, 92; studio instr, Sch Vis Art, 94; studio instr, Sch Visual Art, 94-. *Bibliog:* Alexander Puhringer (auth), 9 Fragen am Christian Eckart, Noema Mag, 4/91; Hiromi Honda (auth), Christian Eckart, Agora Mag, 6/91; Balcon Mag, Andachtsbild Studies, No 7, 12/91. *Dealer:* Sidney Janis 110 W 57th St New York NY 10019. *Mailing Add:* 118 N 9th St Brooklyn NY 11211

ECKE, BETTY TSENG YU-HO See Yu-ho, Tseng

ECKER, ROBERT RODGERS
PAINTER, PRINTMAKER
b Waynesboro, Pa, Apr 30, 1936. *Study:* Pa State Col, Shippensburg, BS, 1958; Pa Acad of Fine Arts, 1959-61; Pa State Univ, MFA, 1965. *Work:* Denver Art Mus, Colo; Smithsonian Am Art Mus, Washington, DC; Libr of Congress, Wash, D.C,; NY Pub Libr, NY; Crocker Collection, Sacremento, Calif. *Comn:* Benzinger Winery Imagery Series Label. *Exhib:* Denver Art Mus, Denver Colo, 1991; Am Cult Ctr, Belgrade, 1981; Int Print Exhib, Portland Art Mus, Portland, Ore, 1997; Int Meszzotint Exhib, Davidson Galleries, Seattle, Wash, 1999; Wash State Univ Art Mus, Pullman, Wash, 2003; Artist House Gallery, Philadelphia, 2004 & 2006. *Teaching:* Asst prof drawing and printmaking, Wash State Univ, 1965-72; prof, drawing and painting, Univ of Colo, Boulder, 1972-2001. *Awards:* DH Lawrence Fel, Univ of NMex, 1976; Artists Fel Nat Endowsment for the Arts, 1981-82; Recognition Award in Painting, Colo Council on the Arts, 1995. *Mem:* Soc of Am Graphic Artists (SAGA). *Media:* Acrylic, Oil, Mezzotint Printmaking. *Res:* Mezzotint Prints. *Interests:* All phases of art. *Publ:* Patirck Frank, Robert Ecker, Denver Art Mus, 1991; Susan Edwards, Contemp Icons, Hunter Col NY, 1992; Richard Nalley, Rear Window, Forbes FYI Mag, 2004; Bob Nugent (auth), Imagery: Art for Wine, 2006. *Dealer:* Artist House Gallery 57 N 2nd St Philadelphia Pa 19106. *Mailing Add:* 2143 Royal Lytham Gln Escondido CA 92026-1089

ECKERT, WILLIAM DEAN
PAINTER, HISTORIAN
b Coshocton, Ohio, Oct 10, 27. *Study:* Ohio State Univ, BA(with distinction), BFA(cum laude) & MA; Univ Iowa, PhD. *Work:* Butler Inst Am Art, Youngstown, Ohio; State Hist Soc Mus, Columbia, Mo; Bristol-Myers, Pharmaceutical Collection, Evansville, Ind; The Theodora Pottle Collection, Macomb, Ill (catalog), 78; Evansville Mus of Arts & Sics, In; Western Ill Univ Art Gallery. *Exhib:* MOAK 4 State Regional Exhib, Springfield (MO) Art Mus, 93; 36th, 37th & 41st Delta Art Exhib, Ark Arts Ctr, Little Rock, 93, 94 & 98; 6 state juried show, Art Guild Burlington, Iowa, 95 & 96, 99, 01; 46th & 47th Spiva Ann, Joplin, Mo, 96 & 97, 01; 49th Mid-States Exhibit, Evansville Mus, 98, 00. *Teaching:* Assoc prof art hist, Western Ill Univ, Macomb, 59-65 & Union Col, Schenectady, NY, 65-68. *Awards:* Third Award in Painting, Quincy Art Ctr Regional, Ill, 71; Twentieth Century Art Club Ann prize, St Louis Artists' Guild, 88; Bader Prize, St Louis Artists' Guild, 91; and others; Purchase Award, Evansville Mus of Arts & Sci, 98. *Mem:* Art St Louis; Soc Archit Historians; St Louis Artists Guild; Decorative Arts Trust. *Media:* Acrylic. *Res:* Renaissance stage in Italy; evolution of the perspective scene. *Publ:* Contribr, The college gallery & the liberal arts, Symposium, summer 67

ECKSTEIN, RUTH
PAINTER, PRINTMAKER
b Nuremberg, Ger, May 11, 16; US citizen. *Study:* New Sch Social Res, New York, with Stuart Davis; Art Students League, with Harry Sternberg, Julian Levy & V Vitlacyl; Pratt Graphic Ctr, New York, with Seong Moy & Roberto Delamonica. *Work:* Philadelphia Mus Art; Brooklyn Mus Art; Solomon R Guggenheim Mus; Israel Mus, Jerusalem; Metrop Mus Art, Mus Modern Art, NY; Whitney Mus Am Art; Foss Art Mus; many others. *Exhib:* Neuberger Mus State Univ NY, 89; Andre Zarre Gallery, NY, 92; Suzuki Gallery, NY, 94; Nese Alpan Gallery, Roslyn, NY, 96; Sidney Mishkin Gallery, Baruch Col, City Univ NY, 96; Nassau Co Mus Art, Roslyn, NY, 97; Fed Reserve Bank Hq, NY, 97; Bryant Libr, Heckscher Mus Art, Roslyn, NY, 98; AIR Gallery, NY, 2000; Hillwood Art Mus, LIU, Brookville, NY, 2000; Martin Art Gallery, Muhlenberg Col, Allentown, Pa, 2002; Swope Art Mus, Terre Haute, Ind, 2002. *Awards:* Village Art Ctr Award, NY, 63; Audubon Artists Awards, 77, 78 & 85; Art of Northeast USA Award, 83. *Bibliog:* Art Int, 72; Art News, 72; review, New York Times, 80, 83, 84, 85, 90, 91 & 99. *Mem:* Am Abstr Artists (hon, secy, 70-80); Art Students League (life); Silvermine Guild of Artists (life). *Media:* Acrylic; Collage. *Publ:* Am Abstr Artists 50th Anniv Print Portfolio, 87; A Living Tradition, Bronx Mus Arts, 88; The Persistence of Abstraction, Edwin A Ulrich Mus, Wichita, Kans, 92; Am Abstr Artists 60th Anniv Exhib, Kean Col, Union, NJ, 96; Pioneers of Abstr Art, Baruch Col, City Univ New York, 96; The Way, Ruth Eckstein, 99. *Dealer:* Anita Shapolsky Gallery 152 E 65th St New York NY 10012; Nese Alpan Gallery 1499 Old Northern Blvd Roslyn NY 11576

ECONOMOS, MICHAEL E
EDUCATOR, PAINTER
b Athens, Greece, March 13, 36; US citizen. *Study:* Worcester Art Mus Sch, 59; Yale Art & Architecture, BFA, 61, MFA 64. *Work:* Mich Univ Mus, Ann Arbor; Goutcher Col Mus, Baltimore, Md; Republic of China, Peking; Yale Collection, New Haven, Conn. *Comn:* Street mural, City of Baltimore, Md, 88. *Exhib:* Solo exhib, Baltimore Mus, Md, 70; Light Sound and Motion, Hudson River Mus, NY, 72. *Collection Arranged:* Art Scape (with catalogs), 86, 87 & 88. *Teaching:* Prof painting drawing printmaking, Md Inst Col Art, 62-. *Awards:* Fullbright Grant, 62-63; Ford Found Grant, 83; Nat Endowment Arts, 89-90. *Bibliog:* Bernard Chaet (auth), The Art of Drawing, Holt Rinehart & Winston, 79. *Publ:* Gregory Battock, Super Realism--A Cultural Anthology, E P Dutton & Co. *Mailing Add:* Dept Fine Arts Md Inst Col Art 1300 W Mt Royal Ave Baltimore MD 21217

EDDY, DON
PAINTER
b Long Beach, Calif, Nov 4, 44. *Study:* Univ Hawaii, Honolulu, BFA, 67, MFA, 69; Univ Calif, Santa Barbara, 69-70. *Work:* Cleveland Mus Art, Ohio; Toledo Mus Art, Ohio; St Etienne Mus, France; Neue Galerie, Aachen, Ger; Williams Col Mus Art, Williamstown, Mass. *Exhib:* Fogg Art Mus, Harvard Univ, Cambridge, Mass, 73; Storm King Art Ctr, Mountainville, NY, 73; NY Avant-Garde, Saidye Bronfman Centre, Montreal, Que, 73; Hyper-realisme Americaine, Realism Europ, Centre Nat d'Art Contemporain, Paris, 74; Wadsworth Atheneum, Hartford, Conn, 74; Tokyo Biennial, Japan, 74; Baltimore Mus Art, Md, 76; Realist & Illusionist Art Traveling Exhib, Australia, 77; and others. *Teaching:* Sch Visual Arts, NY. *Bibliog:* Udo Kulterman (auth), New realism, NY Graphic Soc, 72; Peter Sager (auth), Realismus, Verlag M DuMont Schauberg; Virginia Bonito (auth), Don Eddy - The Resonance of Realism in the Art of Post War America. *Media:* Acrylic. *Dealer:* Nancy Hoffman Gallery 429 W Broadway New York NY 10012. *Mailing Add:* 543 Broadway New York NY 10012

EDELL, NANCY
PAINTER, PRINTMAKER
b Omaha, Nebr, Nov 12, 42; Can citizen. *Study:* Univ Nebr, Omaha, BFA, 64; Univ Bristol, Eng, studied film with George Brandt, 68-69. *Work:* Can Coun Art Bank, & Nat Gallery of Can, Ottawa, Ont; Art Gallery Nova Scotia, Halifax; Robert McLaughlin Art Gallery, Oshawa, Ont; Winnipeg Art Gallery, Man; Mt St Vincent Univ Art Gallery, Halifax, NS; Dalhousie Univ Art Gallery, Halifax, NS. *Comn:* Survivors in Search of a Voice, Royal Ont Mus, 95; Mid Northumberland Arts Group, Ashington, Eng, 97. *Exhib:* Innovation: Subject & Technique, Univ Toronto, Scarborough, Ont, 87; 80/20: 100 Yrs of NSCAO, Art Gallery Nova Scotia, Halifax, 88 & Subject Matter: Contemp Painting & Sculpture in NS, 92; solo shows, Univ Nebr Omaha Art Gallery, 88, Univ Moncton Art Gallery, NB, 89, Art Nuns: Recent Work by Nancy Edell, Art Gallery NS (touring), 91, Bemidji Arts Ctr, Minn, 97 & Bricabra, Dalhousie Univ Art Gallery, Halifax, 98, Bricabra, Dalhousie Univ Art Gallery, Art Gallery of Wouthwestern Manitoba, Mus for Textiles, Toronto, Confedn Ctr, Charlottetown, PEI, 99, plus others; 4th Int Biennial Print Exhib, Taipei, Taiwan, 90; Boston Printmakers, 42nd NAm Print Exhib, Fitchburgh Art Mus, 90; Subversive Crafts, Mass Inst Technol Visual Arts Ctr, Cambridge, 93; The Female Imaginary, Agnes Etherington Art Ctr, Kingston, Ont, 94; On Paper of Paper, Kupio, Finland, 96 & Pforzheim, Ger, 97; Layers of Meaning, Woodhorn Colliery Mus, Ashington, Eng, 97, Bradford Industrial Mus, 98, Collins Gallery, Glasgow, 98, & Cleveland Arts Centre, Eng, 98. *Teaching:* part-time fac, Nova Scotia Col Art & Design, Halifax, NS, 82-2000; vis artist printmaking, St Michael's Printshop, St Johns, Nfld, 87; vis fac visual art, Banff Sch Fine Arts, Alta, 88; vis artist, Univ Windsor, Ont, 92, Alta Col Art, Calgary, 92, Mid Northcumberland Arts Group, Ashington, Eng, 97 & Mus Civilization, Hull, Que, 98. *Awards:* Can Coun grant, 74, 80, 84, 87, 88, 90, 92, 94 & 97,99; Manitoba Arts Coun Grant, 77 & 78; Can Coun, Paris Studio, 90; Nova Scotia Arts Coun Grants 97, 2000. *Bibliog:* Bricabra (exhib catalog) Dalhousie Univ Art Gallery. *Mem:* Can Artists Representation (secy, 84-85); Visual Arts NS; NS Printmakers Asn (secy-treas, 87-88). *Media:* Miscellaneous Media. *Publ:* Auth, Art Gallery of Nova Scotia (exhib catalog) 91; Subversive Crafts (exhib catalog), MIT Vis

Arts Ctr, Cambridge, Mass, 93; The Female Imaginary, Agnes Etherington Art Ctr (exhib catalog), Queens Univ, Kingston, Ont, 94; Uses of the Vernacular in Contemporary Nova Scotian Art (exhib catalog), Dalhouse Univ Art Gallery, 94. *Mailing Add:* RR 1 Hubbards NS B0J 1T0 Canada

EDELMAN, ANN
PAINTER, LECTURER
b New York, NY. *Study:* Brooklyn Col, NY; Am Univ, Washington, DC; spec study with Leon Berkowitz & Jacob Kainen. *Work:* US Dept Transportation. *Exhib:* Area Show, Corcoran Gallery Art, Washington, DC, 56; Society of Washington Artists, Smithsonian Inst, Washington, DC, 59; Maryland Artists, Baltimore Mus Art, Md, 70 & 71; Corcoran Gallery Art, Washington, DC, 73. *Teaching:* Lectr contemp art, Exten Course, Univ Md, 72-78, Am Univ, Washington, DC, 79. *Awards:* First Prize, Soc Washington Artists, 72. *Mem:* Artists Equity; Washington Womens Art Ctr. *Media:* Acrylics, Oil. *Mailing Add:* 12919 Crisfield Rd Silver Spring MD 20906-5135

EDELMAN, JANICE
PAINTER - WATERCOLOR, INSTRUCTOR
b Philadelphia, Pa, Apr 13, 33. *Study:* Art Inst Philadelphia, BA, 56; Thomas Edison State Col, Dr Boris Blai and Henry Hensche. *Work:* Woodmere Art Mus, Philadelphia. *Comn:* Watercolor Portrait, Philadelphia, 99; Watercolor Portrait, Fall River, Mass, 00; Watercolor Portrait, Elkins Park, Pa, 02. *Exhib:* Solo-exhib, Woodmere Art Mus, 97-98, Congregation Beth Ore, 03. *Pos:* advert, Illus designer, Art dir, Philadelphia, Pa, 58-78. *Teaching:* Dept Head, Montgomery Co Vocational Sch, 78-80; instr, watercolor, Woodmere Art Mus, Philadelphia, Pa, 91-05; lectr, 98-03. *Awards:* Grumbacher award, 68; Award of Excellence, 39th Ann, Art Dirs Club of Philadelphia, 79; Salmagundi Club NY award, 88. *Mem:* Philadelphia Watercolor Soc; Pa Watercolor Soc. *Publ:* Schlemm & Nicholas, The Best of Watercolor, Rockport, 95; Why I Paint, Artist Mag, 99. *Mailing Add:* 3505 Hale Rd Huntingdon Valley PA 19006-3230

EDELMAN, RITA
PAINTER
b New York, NY, 30. *Study:* Traphagen Sch Design, cert, 51; Silvermine Col Art, 67; also with Victor Candell, Leo Manso & Robert Reed. *Work:* General Electric, Fairfield, Conn; Fairfield Univ, Conn; Gen Foods, White Plains, NY; Deloitte Haskins & Sells, Stamford, Conn; Wichita State Univ, Kans; Fitchburg (Mass) Art Mus. *Exhib:* Stamford Mus, Conn, 73, 77, 78, 82, 90 & 91; solo exhibs, Silvermine Guild Galleries, New Canaan, Conn, 76 & 81, Pindar Gallery, NY, 78, 80, 82, 85 & 87, Stamford Mus, Conn, 90 & Univ Mass, Amherst, 99; Grey Galleries, NY, 80; Aldrich Mus Contemp Art, Ridgefield, Conn, 81; Hampshire Col, Amherst, Mass, 2003; Forbes Libr, North Hampton, Mass, 2005. *Awards:* Judges Choice, Greenwich Art Soc, 72; First Prize, New Haven Paint & Clay Club, 75; Painting Award, New Eng Exhib Painting & Sculpture, Silvermine Guild Artists, 80. *Bibliog:* George Albert Perret (auth), essay, 10/80 & Robert Yoskowitz (auth), review, 12/80, Arts Mag; Cynthia Nadleman (auth), rev, Art News Mag, 1/81. *Mem:* Westport Weston Arts Coun; New Haven Paint & Clay Club; Silvermine Guild Artists. *Media:* Oil, Acrylic. *Dealer:* Oscar Edelman, Hadley, Mass, 01035. *Mailing Add:* 18 Shattuck Rd Hadley MA 01035-9659

EDELSON, GILBERT S
ADMINISTRATOR, LECTURER
b New York, NY, Sept, 15, 28. *Study:* NY Univ, BS, 49; Columbia Univ Sch Law, LLB, 55. *Pos:* Officer, Art Dealers Asn Am, vpres and counsel, currently; mem, com on art law, Asn Bar, City NY, 64-67, 72-75, 84-87 & 89, chmn, 92; dir, Col Art Asn, 69-89, Artforum Mag, 70-77 & Art Quart, 78-80; trustee & mem exec comt, Am Fedn Art, 82-93; trustee, Archives Am Art, Int Found Art Res & NY Studio Sch. *Mem:* Am Fedn Art; Archives Am Art; Int Found Art Res; NY Studio Sch

EDELSON, MARY BETH
CONCEPTUAL ARTIST, PAINTER
b East Chicago, Ind. *Study:* DePauw Univ, BA, 55; NY Univ, MA, 59. *Hon Degrees:* DePauw Univ, DFA, 92. *Work:* Guggenheim Mus Art & Mus Mod Art, NY; Walker Art Ctr, Minneapolis, Minn; Corcoran Gallery Art & Nat Collection, Washington, DC; Indianapolis Mus Art; Seattle Art Mus; Malmo Museum, Sweden; and others. *Comn:* Mural, Danforth Mus, 86; mural, Musee du Quebec, Can 87; mural, London Regional Gallery, 87; mural, Mendel Gallery, 88; mural, WPA, 89; mural, Gilford Col, 90. *Exhib:* Solo exhibs, Washington Proj Arts, 89, Nicole Klagsbrun & A/C Proj Room, NY, 93, Creative Time, NY, 94, Nicolai Wallner Gallery, Copenhagen, Denmark, 96, Trickster, The Agency, London, 98, Home-made Root Beer, Malmo Museer, Sweden, 2000 & Re-scripting the Story, Traveling Exhibition, 2000-02; A/C at 303, 303 Gallery, NY, 93; In-Significance, The Agency, London, 95; Sniper's Nest: Art That Has Lived with Lucy R Lippard, Bard Col Travels, 95-97; Vraiment Feminisme et Art Magazen, Ctr Nat d'Art Contemp, Grenoble, France, 97; Original Visions, McMullen Mus Art, Boston, 97; Contemp Classicism, Neuberger Mus Art & Tampa Mus, 99-2000; Picturing the Modern Amazon (catalog), New Mus, 2000; Century City: Art and Cult in the Modern Metropolis, Tate Mod, London White Columns, NY, 2001; Goddess, Lelong Galerie, New York City, 2002; Person and Political, Guild Hall Mus, LI, NY, 2002, Chelsea Mus, 2003; Making Peace, Shedhalle, Zurich, 2003; Mothers of Invention, Mumok Mus of Contemp Art, 2003; A Life Well Lived, A Survey of Mary Beth Edelson's Work, Malmo Mus, Sweden, 2006. *Teaching:* Instr, Corcoran Sch of Art, 71-76; lectr in 45 cols and universities in the US, Can, Europe & Iceland, 77-86, Danish Royal Acad, 2001-2004; artist-in-residence, Univ Ill, Chicago, 82 & 88, Univ Tenn, 83, Ohio Univ, Columbus, 84, Md Inst Art, 85 & KC AI, Kansas City, 86, Danish Royal Acad, Copenhagen, 2000, 2003. *Awards:* Nat Endowment for the Arts, 1999-2000; Andy Warhol Found for the Visual Arts, 2001-2002; Int Artists Studio Prog in Sweden (IASPIS), 2006. *Bibliog:* The Shaman as a Gifted Artist, High Performance, autumn 1988; Open Letter to Thomas McEvilley, New Art Examiner, 1989; Politiken, Review of Malmo Exhibition, 2000; The Art of Mary Beth Edelson, 2002; 19 Reviews in Sweden of Retrospective Exhibition at Malmo Museum, 2006. *Mem:* Founder Conf Women in Visual Arts, Washington, DC; Original Collective Mem Heresies; Women Artists Coalition; Women's Action Coalition, New York; Founding Mem Int Team to Provide an Artists Contract. *Media:* Photography, Mixed Media. *Publ:* auth The Politics of Women's Spirituality: Essays on the Rise of Spiritual Power Within the Feminist Movement, 1982; Firsthand: Photographs by Mary Beth Edelson 1973-1993, 1993; Women's Culture: New Era of Feminist Revolution?, Scarecrow, 2005; and others. *Mailing Add:* 110 Mercer St New York NY 10012

EDELSTEIN, TERI J
MUSEUM DIRECTOR, HISTORIAN
b Johnstown, Pa, June 23, 51. *Study:* Univ Pa, BA, 72, grad fel, Stouffer Col House, 72-74, teaching fel hist art, 73-75, Penfield scholar, 75-76, MA, 77, PhD, 79. *Pos:* Asst dir dept acad prog, Yale Ctr Brit Art, New Haven, Conn, 79-83; dir, Mt Holyoke Col Art Mus, 83-90; dir, David & Alfred Smart Mus Art, Univ Chicago, 90-92; deputy dir, Art Inst Chicago, 92-. *Teaching:* Lectr art hist, Univ Guelph, Ont, 77-79, Yale Univ, 79-83, Mt Holyoke Col, 83-90, Sr lectr, Univ Chicago, 90-. *Awards:* Fel Mus Prof, Nat Endowment Arts, 88; Resident Fel, Yale Ctr for British Art, 88; Trustee, Williamstown Regional Conserv Lab, 89-91 & Am Fed Arts, 97. *Mem:* Col Art Asn; Chicago Network. *Res:* Iconology of British art. *Publ:* Auth, Berthe Morisot-The Forgotten Impressionist (video), Electronic Field Serv Productions, 89; Colin's Masaniello: Revolutionary Hero, Mt Holyoke Col Art Mus Newsletter, 90; Vauxhall Gardens, Cambridge Guide to the Arts in England, Cambridge Univ Press, 90; Dorothea Hoffmann: Drawings, Philadelphia, 91; ed & contribr, Imagining an Irish Past: The Celtic Revival 1840-1940, Univ Chicago Press, 92; auth, The Stage Is All The World: The Theatrical Designs of Tanya Moiseiwitsch (exhib catalog), David & Alfred Smart Mus, Univ Chicago, 94. *Mailing Add:* c/o Art Inst Chicago 111 S Michigan Ave Chicago IL 60603-6110

EDEN, F(LORENCE) BROWN
COLLAGE ARTIST, PAINTER
b Jericho Center, Vt, Oct 10, 1916. *Study:* Univ Fla, 53-55; Univ Mich, spec studies with Frank Cassara, 62-63. *Work:* Jacksonville Art Mus & Southern Bell Collection, Jacksonville, Fla; Fed Reserve Bank of Atlanta; Coopers and Lybrand, Jacksonville, Fla; Barnett Banks Collection, Fla. *Comn:* Collage & collage triptych Edwin & Ruth Kennedy Mus Am Art, Ohio Univ, 44; landscape watercolor pair, Touche Ross, Jacksonville; landscape watercolor, Atlantic Nat Bank, Jacksonville; collage painting, Designers Showhouse, Ponte Vedra, Fla, 44. *Exhib:* Solo exhibs, Ga Inst Technol, Atlanta, 72, Le Moyne Found Art, Tallahassee, Fla, 75, Alexander Brest Mus, Jacksonville, Fla, 69, 70, 71 & 78, Daytona Art Ctr, Daytona Beach, 80 & Gallery Contemporanea, Jacksonville, 85; Am Painters in Paris, Ctr Int Paris, France, 75; Contemp Am Paintings, Soc Four Arts, Palm Beach, Fla, 77; Nat Soc Painters in Casein & Acrylics, Nat Arts Club, NY, 80; Betty Parsons Exhib, City Hall, Naples, Fla, 80; Mus Arts & Sci, Macon, 82 & 86 & Mem Art Ctr, Atlanta, 83, Ga Nat Watercolor Exhibs IV, V & VII; Major Fla Artists, Harmon Galleries of Am Art, Sarasota, 83, 86 & 88; Audubon Artists 42nd Ann Exhib, Nat Arts Club, NY, 84; Southeastern Watercolorists, Deland Mus, Fla, 84 & 89; The Mus Collection, Jacksonville Art Mus, Fla, 85; Barnett Banks Collection, Polk Mus, Winter Haven, Fla, 86; Fla Competitive, Ctr Arts, Vero Beach, Fla, 87; Ala Nat Watercolor Exhib, 89. *Pos:* Judge of paintings, area shows; Chmn Northeast Fla Artist Group. *Teaching:* Painting, City Club, Ann Arbor, Mich, 62-63 & Art Mus, Jacksonville, Fla, 63-68; instr printmaking, Art Mus, Jacksonville, 68-69. *Awards:* First Award, Ann Juried Exhib, Fla Artist Group, 71 & 79; McDaniel Painting Award, Major Fla Artists, Harmon Galleries, 79. *Bibliog:* Elihu Edelson (auth), JU show classy and complete, Fla Times Union, 12/14/79; Rex Allyn (auth), Works by a dozen women artists, Sarasota Herald Tribune, 8/21/83; Ann Hyman (auth), Well-done exhibits can be evocative, Fla Times Union, 3/18/88. *Mem:* Audubon Artists Am; Ga Watercolor Soc; Fla Watercolor Soc; Soc Painters in Casein & Acrylics; Fla Artist Group (area chmn, 68-85). *Media:* Polymer Collage; Watercolor. *Dealer:* Hodgell Gallery 46 Palm Ave South Sarasota Fl 34236; Gallery Contemporanea 11 Aviles Street St Augustine FL 34236. *Mailing Add:* 5375 Sanders Rd Jacksonville FL 32211

EDEN, GLENN
DRAFTSMAN, PAINTER
b Atlanta, Ga, 51. *Study:* DeKalb Community Col, AA, 71; Ga State Univ. *Work:* High Mus, Atlanta, Ga; Gibbes Mus, Charleston, SC; Columbia Mus, SC; Huntsville Mus, Ala; Mus Arts & Sci, Macon, Ga. *Comn:* Painting, Mariott Marquis, Atlanta, Ga, 85; drawing, Coca-Cola Co, Atlanta, Ga, 86; painting, Wilma, Atlanta, Ga, 87. *Exhib:* Wizard of Oz Drawings, Mint Mus, 76; Artists in Ga, High Mus Art, Atlanta, 81; The Human Figure, New Orleans Contemp Art Inst, La, 82; Ten Pens, Southern Arts Fedn, Atlanta, Ga, 82; Narrative Drawings, Nexus Gallery, Atlanta, 83. *Awards:* Atlanta Bureau of Cult Affairs Grant, 82; Outstanding Alumnus, Dekalb Col, 85; Artists Fel Southeastern Ctr Contemp Art, Winston-Salem, NC, 87-88. *Bibliog:* Jeff Kipnis (auth), Glenn Eden at the Gibbes, Art in Am, 81; Jeff Kipnis (auth), Profile, Art Voices, 81. *Media:* Ballpoint Pen, Prisma Color; Oil on Canvas. *Mailing Add:* 173 Middlesex Ln Marietta GA 30064-1729

EDER, JAMES ALVIN
PRINTMAKER, PAINTER
b Buffalo, NY, Jan 9, 42. *Study:* State Univ NY, Buffalo, BS, 63; Univ Nebr, Lincoln, MS, 66; Northern Ariz Univ, Flagstaff, MA, 75. *Work:* Valley Nat Bank, Mesa, Ariz; First Interstate Bank, Honeywell Corp & Talley Industries, Phoenix, Ariz; Quanex Corp, Houston, Tex; Monoprint, Heritage Art Collection, City Tempe, 96; Nelson Art

Ctr, Ariz State Univ; Hunt Inst Botanical Doc, Carnegie Mellon Univ; Sky Harbor Airport, Phoenix, Ariz; US Embassies, Moscow & Conakry & Guinea. *Comn:* Zona Mona (anamorphic mural on roof), City of Tempe, Tempe Arts Ctr, Ariz, 94. *Exhib:* One-man shows, Univ Ariz, Tucson, 80 & Scottsdale Community Col, Ariz, 81, Ariz State Capitol, Phoenix, 90, Sedona Arts Ctr, 91, Scottsdale Col, 91; Eder-Kollasch, touring southwest, 86-88; Contemp Nature (travelling), Tempe Arts Ctr, 89-90; Northern Ariz Images, Coconino Arts Ctr, Flagstaff, 90; 7th Int Exhib Botanical Art & Illustr, Hunt Inst Botanical Doc, Carnegie Mellon Univ, 92; Jurors Choice, Shemer Art Ctr, Phoenix, Ariz, 95. *Teaching:* Instr art, Evening Div, Phoenix Col, 78-81 & Scottsdale Community Col, 87-92. *Awards:* First Place Printmaking, Ariz State Fair, 76, 77 & 81; Relief Print, Selected Prize, Governors Art Awards, 96. *Bibliog:* Jim Eder: A unique western artist, Sedona Life Mag, winter 78; Mary Carroll Nelson (auth), James A Eder (profile), Art Voices, 9-10/81; Mary Carroll Nelson (auth), Jim Eder: Making woodcut prints, Am Artist, 11/81; The Geologic Art of Eder & Kollasch, Ariz Highways, 11/87. *Media:* Woodcut, Collagraph; Acrylic. *Publ:* Auth, Capturing the Realism of Rocks, Artists Mag, 3/85; A puzzling approach to printmaking, Am Artist Mag, 8/94. *Dealer:* Agnisiuh Gallery Box 910 Hillside Ctr Sedona AZ 86336. *Mailing Add:* 1026 E Carter Dr Tempe AZ 85282-7106

EDGE, DOUGLAS BENJAMIN
SCULPTOR, PAINTER

b Fennimore, Wis, Aug 4, 42. *Study:* San Fernando Valley State Col, BA. *Work:* Mus Mod Art, NY; Arco, Washington, DC; Security Bank, Los Angeles; Patrick Lannon Mus, Fla. *Comn:* Constructionist Pagoda, Imperial Bank, Costa Mesa, Calif, 79. *Exhib:* West Coast Now, Seattle Art Mus, 68; Violence in Am Art, Mus Contemp Art, Chicago, 69; Continuing Surrealism, La Jolla Mus Art, 71; Calif Prints, Mus Mod Art, NY, 72; Separate Realities, Los Angeles Munic Art Gallery, 73; Santa Barbara Mus, 77. *Teaching:* Instr sculpture, Calif Inst Art, Valencia, 70-72; instr painting workshop, Art Ctr Sch Design, Los Angeles, 73-74; lectr sculpture & drawing, Univ Calif, Santa Barbara, 75-76. *Awards:* Cassandra Found Grant, 70. *Bibliog:* Thomas Garver (auth), rev, 10/69 & Peter Plagens (auth), rev, 11/73, Artforum; Milinda Terbell (auth), Art News, 10/73. *Mailing Add:* 1556 Michael Ln Los Angeles CA 90272

EDGERTON, DEBRA
PAINTER, EDUCATOR

b Junction City, Kans, Mar 15, 58. *Study:* Am Acad Art, 79; Univ Kans, BFA, 81; San Francisco Art Inst, 01; Vt Col, 01. *Work:* Kans Gas and Electric, Wichita; Northern Ariz Univ, Flagstaff. *Comn:* Great Kings and Queens of Africa, Anheuser Bush 84 Worlds Fair, New Orleans, La, 84. *Exhib:* Impressions of China, Old Main Mus, Flagstaff, Ariz, 95; Adirondacks Nat Exhib Am Watercolors, Old Forge, NY, 96; State of the Art Int Invitational, Parkland Coll, Ill, 97; Interpreting Surroundings: Works by 4 African Am Artist, Parkland, Ill, 98; Midwest Watercolor Soc 20th Ann Nat Exhib, 99; Allied Artista Am Juried Exhib, NY, 99. *Pos:* pres, Lawrence Art Guild Asn, 91-92; mayoral appointee, Lawrence Art Commn, Kans, 92-93. *Teaching:* instr watermedia, painting, figure painting, Northern Ariz Univ, Flagstaff, 93-; instr painting, Lawrence Art Ctr, Kans, 91-93. *Awards:* Award Excellence, Geary Co Sch Dist; Carolyn Barnard Award 18th Midwest Watercolor Soc Exhib, 94; Award Merit Ariz Aqueous 9th Annual Exhib, 95; Dolan Found scholar, 2001-03; Grad fel San Francisco Art Inst, 2001-03. *Bibliog:* Erik Schutz (auth), Mastering the Moment, Topeka Capital Jour, 4/93; Brian Johnson (auth), China Inspires Art Teacher, Ariz Daily Sun, 10/93; Becky Ramsdell (auth), Small Scale Drawings Capture Little Slices of Life, Ariz Daily Sun, 3/96. *Mem:* Am Watercolor Soc; Nat Watercolor Soc; Midwest Watercolor Soc; Allied Artists Am. *Media:* Watercolor, Oil, Video. *Publ:* auth, article The Watercolor Page, Am Artist Mag, 91; contrib, book Transparent Watercolor Wheel, Watson-Guptill, 94. *Dealer:* Strecker-Nelson Gallery 332 Poyntz Ave Manhattan Tex. *Mailing Add:* 3000 W Brenda Loop Flagstaff AZ 86001

EDGREN, GARY ROBERT
PAINTER, CRAFTSMAN

b Chicago, Ill, Jan 27, 47. *Study:* Southern Ill Univ, BA 70, MFA, 72. *Work:* State of Ill Ctr, Chicago; Byer Mus Art & Nat Hist, Evanston, Ill; Ill Art Mus, Springfield; Univ Galleries, Southern Ill Univ, Carbondale; Kemper Insurance Corp, Chicago, Ill. *Exhib:* Painting & Sculpture, mid-west fac, Univ Ill, Champaign, 76; one-man shows, Deson-Zaks Gallery, Chicago, 75, Krannert Art Gallery Univ Ill, 76, Zaks Gallery, Chicago, 79 & 83 & Univ Galleries Southern Ill Univ, 84; George Irwin Collection, Krannert Art Mus, 79; 29th Ill Invitational, Ill State Mus, Springfield, 79; Survey of 16 Abstract Artists, Springfield Art Asn, 84. *Pos:* Self employed artist, 72-; owner, Special Effects Painting. *Teaching:* Consult acquisition, Univ Galleries Southern Ill Univ, 74-75, vis artist painting & drawing, 77, instr, 77-78. *Media:* All. *Dealer:* Sonia Zaks-Zaks Gallery 620 N Michigan Ave Chicago, IL. *Mailing Add:* 1785 Cedargrove Buncombe IL 62912

EDISON, DIANE
PAINTER, EDUCATOR

b Piscataway, NJ, Sept 3, 49. *Study:* Sch Visual Arts, NY, BFA, 76; Skowhegan Sch Painting & Sculpture, 84; Grad Sch Fine Arts, Univ Pa, Philadelphia, MFA, 86. *Work:* Ark Art Ctr, Little Rock; Am Embassy, Moscow; Dana Gallery, Agnes Scott Col, Decatur, Ga; Leeway Found, Philadelphia, Pa, 00. *Exhib:* Solo exhibs, Univ Ga, Athens, 94, Chattahoochee Valley Art Mus, Lagrange, Ga, 95, Nexus Contemp Art Ctr, Atlanta, 97, George Adams Gallery, 97 & Macon Mus Arts & Sci, Ga, 98; A Second Look, George Adams Gallery, NYC, 2000, 2003; Diane Edison: Drawings, Lamar Dodd Sch Art, Univ Ga, Athens, 2002; SAF/Nat Endowment Arts Fel Exhib, Southeastern Ctr Contemp Art, Winston-Salem, NC, 94; Around the House, Frumbkin/Adams Gallery, NY, 94; Reaffirming the Media, Art Gallery, Univ Mo, Kansas City, 94; Figurative Drawing, Charles More Gallery, Philadelphia, 94; Frumkin/Adams Gallery, NY, 95; Portraits and Self-portraits, George Adams Gallery, 96; Large Drawings and Objects, Ark Art Ctr, Little Rock, 96; Illumination, George Adams Gallery, 98; In Her Voice: Self Portraits by Women, Phillip & Muriel Berman Mus Art, Ursinus Col, Pa, 98-99; The Likeness of Being: Contemporary Self-Portraits by 60 Women, DC Moore Gallery, NYC, 2000; About Face: The Collection of Jackye & Curtis Finch, Jr, Arkansas Art Center, Little Rock, 2001; The Art of Collecting, Flint Inst Arts, Flint, Mich, 2002; Refusing to Dance Backwords, Spruill Gallery, Ga, 2005; The Figure in American Painting & Drawing 1985-2005, Ogunquit Mus Am Art, Maine, 2006. *Pos:* lectr, Telfair Acad Arts & Sci, Savannah, 1991; Assoc dir, Univ Ga, Athens, 97-. *Teaching:* Asst prof Art, Savannah Col Art & Design, 1990-1992; prof painting/drawing, Univ Ga, Athens, 92-97, assoc prof, 97-; prof Painting & Watercolor Studies Abroad Prog (Cortona, Italy), Univ Ga, fall 1993-. *Awards:* Ga Artist Grant, Ga Coun Arts, 93; Nat Endowment Arts Fel, 94; Residency Millay, Milton Avery Found, 95. *Bibliog:* Robert W Duffy (auth), Beyond the innocence, St Louis-Dispatch, 92; Townsend Wolfe (auth), National Drawing International, Ark Art Ctr, 94; Arlene Raven (auth), Diane Edison, Ark Art Ctr, 95; Edward Sozanski (auth), Viewing Women Artists Looking at Themselves, Philadelphia Inquirer, 1/1999. *Mem:* Col Art Asn; Womens Caucus Art; Southeastern Col Art Conf; Am Asn Univ Prof. *Media:* Acrylic, Oil. *Publ:* Kathleen Baxter (auth), Drawing Attention to Museum Collections, Am Artist, 1/2000. *Dealer:* George Adams Gallery 41 W 57th St New York NY 10019. *Mailing Add:* c/o George Adams Gallery 41 W 57th St New York NY 10019

EDLIS, STEFAN T & H GAEL NEESON
COLLECTOR

Pos: Pres, Apollo Plastics Corp, Chicago, currently; trustee, Mus Modern Art, New York City, currently. *Awards:* Named one of Top 200 Collectors, ARTnews Mag, 2004. *Mem:* Whitney Mus Am Art (nat comt, currently). *Collection:* Contemporary art. *Mailing Add:* Apollo Plastics 5333 N Elton Ave Chicago IL 60630

EDMINSTON, SCOTT
DIRECTOR, EDUCATOR

Work: Dir: (plays) Brian Friel's Molly Sweeney, 1998 (Elliot Norton Award Outstanding Dir), Harold Pinter's Betrayal, 2003 (Elliot Norton Award Outstanding Prod, 2003), Jacques Brel is Alive & Well & Living in Paris, 2003. *Pos:* Dir, off of arts Brandeis Univ, 2003-; artistic assoc, Huntington Theatre Co, Boston. *Teaching:* Asst prof - dramatic lit Boston Univ Col Fine Arts, chrmn MFA Dir Pro. *Awards:* Named one of region's ten best theatre dir, Boston Herald. *Mem:* Alliance Boston Theatre Artists & Producers (pres bd, StageSource 98—). *Mailing Add:* Brandeis Univ Dir Off of Arts MS 051 Waltham MA 02454

EDMISTON, SARA JOANNE
EDUCATOR, DESIGNER

b Independence, Mo, June 21, 35. *Study:* Univ Kans, BAE; ECarolina Univ, MA. *Work:* NC Mus Art, Raleigh; NC Nat Banks, several cities in NC; Wachovia Banks, several cities in NC; Duke Univ. *Comn:* Door knocker, NC Nat Bank, Charlotte, 74; and others. *Exhib:* NC Mus Art, Raleigh, 65-67, 71, 73 & 76; Enamels 70 Nat, Crafts Alliance, St Louis, Mo & William Rockhill Nelson Gallery Art, Kansas City, Mo, 70; Piedmont Crafts, Mint Mus Art, Charlotte, 70-73; Crafts Invitational, Jacksonville Mus, Fla, 72; Southeastern Crafts Exhib, Greenville Co Mus, SC, 74; New Directions in Fabric Design, Fine Arts Gallery, Towson State Univ, 76; and others. *Teaching:* Prof textiles & design, ECarolina Univ, 66-. *Awards:* Purchase Award, 5th Ann Piedmont Graphics Exhib, Mint Mus Art, 69; Purchase Award, 39th Ann NC Artists Exhib, NC Art Soc, 76. *Mem:* Surface Design Asn (treas & nat mem chmn, 76-80); Am Crafts Coun; Piedmont Craftsmen Inc; Carolina Designer-Craftsmen; NC Crafts Asn (mem bd dir, 76-79). *Media:* Dye, Enamel. *Dealer:* Piedmont Craftsmen Inc Sales Gallery 936 West Fourth St Winston-Salem NC 27101. *Mailing Add:* 406 W Fourth St Greenville NC 27834-1930

EDMONDS, NICK
SCULPTOR

b 37. *Study:* Student, Ogunquit Sch of Painting & Sculpture, 53-56; Boston Mus Sch, Grad with hon, 61. *Teaching:* Prof, sculpture Mus Sch and Milton Acad, 62-65, Boston Univ, 65-2003, prof, emer, 2003-. *Awards:* Named Nat Acad, Nat Acad, 94; first prize for sculpture, 171st Annual Exhib, Nat Acad, 96; Nat Acad, 2001. *Mem:* Nat Acad. *Mailing Add:* PO Box 86 Sharon MA 02067

EDMONDS, TOM
MUSEUM DIRECTOR, PAINTER

b Lawrence, Kans, July 29, 56. *Study:* Ohio State Univ, BFA, 78; Art Inst Chicago, MFA, 80; postgrad, NY Univ, 93. *Pos:* curator, Monroe Co Hist Soc, Stroudsburg, Pa, 92-93; curator, Andover Hist Soc, Andover, Mass, 93-99; exec dir, Whister House Mus Art, Lowell, Mass, 99-2000. *Bibliog:* Articles in Boston Globe and Lowell Sun, 2000. *Mem:* Northeast Mass Regional Libr Asn (bd mem, 96-2000); Am Asn Mus. *Media:* Oil. *Specialty:* co-dir, Off Broadway Coop Gallery, Lawrence, Mass. *Mailing Add:* 243 Worthen St Lowell MA 01852

EDMONSON, RANDALL W
CERAMIST

b Washington, DC, Jan 30, 47. *Study:* Drury Col, BA, 69; Univ Mo, Columbia, MA, 76; Southern Ill Univ, Carbondale, MFA, 78. *Work:* Monterey Peninsula Mus Art, Calif; Evansville Mus Arts & Sci, Ind; Owensboro Mus Fine Arts, Ky; San Angelo Art Mus, San Angelo, Tex; Museo Internazionale delle Ceramiche, Faenza, Italy; Shepparton Art Gallery, Shepparton, Australia. *Exhib:* The Shape Between Continuity and Innovation, Faenza; Salzbrand 2002, Koblenz, Ger; 2002 Sydney Myer Fund Int Ceramics Award Exhib, Shepparton. *Teaching:* Prof art, Longwood Univ, Farmville, Va, 79-. *Awards:* Cash Award, Va Watercolor Ann, Mead Corp, 83; Hon Mention, 11th Ann Works on Paper, 2nd Street Gallery, Charlottesville, Va, 83; Cash Award, 9th Ann San Angelo Ceramic Competition. *Mem:* Nat Coun Educ Ceramic Arts. *Media:* Clay

EDMONSTON, PAUL
EDUCATOR, EDITOR
b Newton, Mass, Nov 15, 22. *Study:* Mass Sch Art, with Ernest L Major & Cyrus Dallin; Boston Univ, AB(Eng lang & lit), with George Levitine, William Jewell, Edgar Brightman, Gerald Brace & Edward A Post; Fla State Univ, MA(art educ), with Karl Zerbe & Ivan Johnson; Ohio State Univ, PhD(fine art), with Hoyt Sherman, Sydney Chafetz, Manuel Barkan, Jerome Hausman & Ross L Mooney; Post Doctoral Fel, South India, 68; Univ Pa, S Asian studies, 72-73. *Work:* Sch Visual Arts, Ohio State Univ; Kenyon Col. *Exhib:* One-man shows, Kenyon Col Gallery, 60, Ohio State Fine Arts Gallery, 64, Lowe Gallery, Univ Miami, 65, Fla A&M Gallery, 66, Art Gallery, Pa State Univ, 70, 74, 75 & 76 & Monhegan Themes, Visual Arts Gallery, Univ Ga, 86; 8th Ann Drawing/Small Sculpture Show, Ball State Univ, 62, 63 & 64; Drawing USA, St Paul Art Ctr, Minn, 63; Cent Pa Artists, State Mus, Harrisburg, Pa, 63; Sacred Arts X, Wheaton, Ill, 89; National Exposures 90, Winston-Salem, NC, 90; Photographer's Forum Ann, 90-91. *Pos:* Assoc ed, Sch Arts, 62-65; ed, Monograph Series, Vols 1-7, Pa State Papers in Art Educ, 68-74 & An Anthology of Faculty Papers, Pa State Univ, 77; founding ed, Appelles: Ga Art J, 79-. *Teaching:* Instr art/Eng, Manatee Co High Sch, Bradenton, Fla, 49-51; instr art, Fla State Univ, 51-55 & Ohio State Univ, 56-60; from assoc prof to prof art appreciation, printmaking & art ed, Pa State Univ, 60-77; prof art appreciation, drawing & painting & art educ, Univ Ga, 77-88 & prof emer art, 88-; sr Fulbright lectr & scholar, 20th Century Am painting & sculpture, Univ Nijmegen, Neth, 92. *Awards:* Southeast Region Higher Educ Award (Teacher Yr), Nat Art Educ Asn, 87-88; Auroville, S India World Parliament Religions, Chicago, 94; and others. *Mem:* US Soc for Educ Through Art (vpres, 79); Nat Art Educ Asn (res sem, 70-); Asn for Asian Studies; Ga Art Educ Asn (pres, 81-83); Int Soc Educ Art; and others. *Media:* Watercolor; Brush & Ink on Rice Paper. *Res:* Angels & angel intervention in art from Old Testament to present; art appreciation and criticism; pre-Muslim art and architecture of South India; rasa theory of Indian aesthetics; English romantic watercolor painters; 20th Century American painting and sculpture. *Publ:* Auth, A conceptual model of creative visual intelligence, J Creative Behavior, 75; Myth and symbol in Indian art, Australia Soc Educ Art Bul, 77; A proposal for a curriculum in the visual arts, J Art & Design Educ, 82; Participant observation and visual documentation as modes of inquiry in the visual arts, Visual Arts Res, 83; On witnessing a name-giving ceremony of the Oglala Sioux, S Cross-Cult Res Art Educ, 86; and 50 others. *Mailing Add:* 100 Torrey Pine Pl Athens GA 30605-3350

EDMUNDS, ALLAN LOGAN
PRINTMAKER, ADMINISTRATOR
b Philadelphia, Pa, June 7, 49. *Study:* Tyler Sch Art, Temple Univ, Philadelphia & Rome; also with Romas Viesulas & John Dowell, BFA & MFA, Cardiff Art Sch, Wales, UK. *Work:* Philadelphia Mus Art; Nat Collection of Fine Art, Libr of Cong; Pa Acad Fine Arts; Yale Univ; Studio Mus Harlem. *Comn:* Photosilkscreen ed, Philadelphia Mus Art, 71-72. *Exhib:* Silkscreen: History of a Medium, Philadelphia Mus Art, 71-72; Expanded Photograph, Philadelphia Civic Ctr Mus, 72; one-man shows, Univ Md, Baltimore, 72, Alternative Mus, NY, Klein Gallery, Univ Calif, Santa Clara, 98; Inst Contemp Art, Philadelphia, 92; Beyond Aesthetics, Alternative Mus, NY, 93. *Pos:* founder-pres, Brandywine Graphic Workshop, Inc, 72-; visual arts panelist, Ohio, Fla, Md & Pa Coun Arts, 82-91; vis artist, Bloomsburg State Col, 80-, Ariz State Univ, 92; mem adv panel, William Penn Mus Fine Arts Collection, 81; Assoc, A L Edmunds Assoc, 81. *Teaching:* Instr graphics, Haystack Mountain Sch Crafts, Maine, 74; lectr printmaking, Philadelphia Col Art, 75; art coordr, Parkway Prog Sch Dist Philadelphia, 72-. *Awards:* Visual Artist's Fel, Pa Coun, 90; Nat Endowment Arts Fel, 90; Arts Mgt Award, Drexel Univ Int Forum, 94. *Bibliog:* Choosing Mus Sci and Industry, Chicago, 86; Int Rev African Am Art Vol 7, No 4, 88, Artists Choose Artists, Contemp Art, Philadelphia, 91. *Mem:* Brandywine Workshop, Greater Philadelphia Cult Alliance; Arts & Cult Coun, Greater Philadelphia CofC; Mayor's Cult Adv Coun; Pa Acad Fine Art. *Media:* Lithography, Serigraphy. *Res:* Continuous research project on the history of the Black graphic artist; collection of slides, manuscripts and original works as well as developing video documentation. *Publ:* Family Album Series, Univ Calif, Santa Cruz, 98. *Dealer:* Hahn Gallery 8439 Germantown Ave Philadelphia PA 19118. *Mailing Add:* 1520 Kater St Philadelphia PA 19146

EDOUARD, PIERRE EDWARD MAUSSION
PAINTER, SCULPTOR
b Oct 28, 59; French citizen. *Study:* Ecole nationale superieur des Arts decoratif, Dipl, 81; study painting with Zao Wouki. *Exhib:* Musee des arts Decoratif, Paris, France, 84; Autoportraits, Musee de la Seita, Paris, France, 86; Galerie Claude Bernard, 94 & 2000. *Awards:* Prinde dessin des Salon de Montrouge, 80; Prise du Prince Rainier du Monacó, 2004. *Bibliog:* Pierre Cabanne (auth), Gravite et intersite, Elle, 3/89; Jean Marie Tasset (auth), Le style des cimes, Le Figaro, 3/89. *Media:* Oil, Egg Tempera, Bronze, Charcoal. *Mailing Add:* c/o Claude Bernard 7 Rue des Beaux Arts Paris 75006 France

EDSON, GARY F
MUSEOLOGIST, MUSEUM DIRECTOR
b Bethany, Mo, Sept 5, 37. *Study:* Kansas City Art Inst, BFA(sculpture), 60; Newcomb Art Sch, Tulane Univ, MFA(ceramics), 62. *Work:* Stifel Fine Arts Ctr, Wheeling, WVa; WVa Univ, Morgantown; Newcomb Art Sch, Tulane Univ, New Orleans. *Comn:* Ceramic art, Ft Benjamin Harrison Hosp, Indianapolis, 73; sculpture, Robert Borns Assocs, Indianapolis, 74; ceramic art, Fairmont Hotel, New Orleans, 74; sculpture, Pickwick Place Development, Indianapolis, 75; ceramic art, Mignon Faget Ltd, New Orleans, 75-78. *Exhib:* Crosscurrents, Stifel Fine Arts Ctr, Wheeling, WVa, 83; Texas Tech Univ Mus, Lubbock, 85; Univ North Dakota, Grand Fork, 85; Gallery Eighty-Six, Belfast, Maine, 85; Texas 2-D Competition, Tex A&M Univ, Col Station, 85; Univ NMex, Albuquerque, 85; Edson, Kreneck & Murrow, Lubbock Fine Arts Ctr, Tex, 86. *Collection Arranged:* Mochawa: Indian Pottery, Gatlinburg, Tenn, 72; Mexican Market Pottery, Indianapolis, 77 & Morgantown, WVa, 81. *Pos:* Chmn, div art, WVa Univ, Morgantown, 80-84; chmn, dept art, Tex Tech Univ, Lubbock, 84-86; exec dir, the Mus Tex Tech Univ, Lubbock, 86-. *Teaching:* Prof art & ceramics, Herron Sch Art, Indianapolis, 70-80; prof art, WVa Univ, 80-84; prof art, drawing & printmaking, Tex Tech Univ, Lubbock, 84-86, prof mus sci, museology & mus admin, 86-. *Mem:* Am Asn Mus (bd mem, 93-); Int Coun Mus (bd mem, 93-); Tex Asn Mus; Art Mus Asn Am; Nat Asn Sch Art & Design (bd mem, 86-). *Publ:* Auth, Open pit firing, 72 & Silla pottery, 73, Ceramics Monthly; Mexican Market Pottery, Watson-Guptill, 79; Handbook for Museums, Routledge, 94; International Directory of Museum Training, Routledge, 95; Museum Ethics, Routledge, 97. *Mailing Add:* Tex Tech Univ 3206 56th St Lubbock TX 79413-4811

EDWARDS, ETHEL
VISUAL ARTIST
b New Orleans, La. *Study:* Newcomb Col Art Sch; Student of Xavier Gonzalez. *Work:* Chase Manhattan Bank, IBM, NY; Commerce Trust Bank, Kansas City; Baltimore Mus Art, Md; Nat Gallery Art, DC; Newark Mus, NJ; Univ Nebr; Tex Eastern Co, Houston. *Comn:* Ser paintings, comn by Dept Interior, Colo & NMex. *Exhib:* Whitney Mus Am Art, 64 & 65; Watercolor: USA, Springfield, Ill, 67-69; Cape Cod Art Asn, 69; Nat Gallery, Washington, DC; Am Embassy, Paris; Galerie Jeanne Boucher, Paris; Mus Mod Art, NY; Pa Acad, Philadelphia. *Teaching:* Instr, Truro Ctr Arts & mem exec comt. *Awards:* Larry Aldrich Prize, Silvermine Guild Artists; Prizes, Watercolor: USA, Springfield, Ill, 67 & Ball State Univ, Muncie, Ind, 67; Nat Arts Club Ann, NY. *Mem:* Fel McDowell Colony; Cosmopolitan Club, NY. *Media:* Oil, Mixed Media

EDWARDS, GARY MAXWELL
ART DEALER, WRITER
b Southampton, NY, June 11, 34. *Study:* Tufts Univ, BA, 56. *Mem:* Asn Int Photog Art Dealers. *Specialty:* Nineteenth century photographs. *Publ:* Contribr, Athens 1839-1900, A Photographic Record, Benaki Mus, Athens, 85; auth, W J Stillman, an American philhellene, Dialogos, Athens, 87; International Guide to 19th Century Photographers, G K Hall, Boston, 88; Early photographers of Greece in the Musée d'Orsay & BN, Hist Photog, 90. *Mailing Add:* 1711 Connecticut Ave NW Washington DC 20009

EDWARDS, JAMES F
PAINTER, EDUCATOR
b New York, NY, July 25, 48. *Study:* Univ Calif, Santa Barbara, BA, MFA. *Work:* Everson Mus Art, Syracuse, NY; SC State Arts Collection; Am Consulate, Osaka, Japan; Am Embassy, Ahman, Jordon; IBM Corp, Gaitherburg, Md. *Comn:* Collage, Huntsville Mus Art; mural, Atlanta Festival of Art, Atlanta Legal Aid, 88; painting, Embassy Suites Corp, Deerfield, Mich. *Exhib:* One-man shows, Greenville Co Mus Art, SC, 76 & Everson Mus Art, Syracuse, 77; Huntsville Mus Art, Ala, 81; Southeastern Ctr Contemp Art, Winston-Salem, NC, 81; Heath Gallery, Atlanta, 85; Hodges Taylor Gallery, Charlotte, 86; Southern Exposure, The Alternative Mus, NY, 85; Portrait of the South, Palazzo Venezia, Rome; and others. *Teaching:* Prof drawing & painting, Univ SC, 72-. *Awards:* Nat Endowment Arts Fel, 74-75; Proj Grant, SC Arts Comn, 76-77; Individual Artist Fel, SC Arts Comn, 81; and others. *Bibliog:* Kenneth Friedman (auth), James Edwards video tapes, Grossmont Col, El Cajon, Calif; Jane Kessler (auth), James Edwards: Profile, Art Papers, Atlanta, 1-2/82. *Mem:* Southeastern Col Art Asn. *Media:* Miscellaneous, Computer. *Publ:* Auth, Getting into video, Contemp Art-Southeast, 77; Art, language and criticism, Contemp Art-Southeast, Vol II, Number 4-5. *Mailing Add:* Univ SC Dept Art Columbia SC 29208

EDWARDS, JONMARC
PAINTER, CONCEPTUAL ARTIST
b Leavenworth, Kans, Mar 11, 59. *Study:* Minneapolis Col Art & Design, BFA, 83. *Work:* AT&T, Chicago; First Bank System, General Mills, Walker Art Ctr, Minneapolis, Minn; Consulate General of Ger, Los Angeles. *Exhib:* Consumerism & Am, Univ Art Mus, Minneapolis, Minn, 90; 42nd Ann Int Juried Exhib, San Diego Art Inst, 98. *Pos:* Gallery dir, Medium West Gallery, 84-88. *Awards:* Louis Comfort Tiffany Found Award, 87; Jerome Emerging Artist Award, Jerome Found, 88; Bush Found Artist Fel, 89-90. *Bibliog:* Ned Rifkin (auth), Jerome Group Exhibit, Jerome Found, 88; Mason Riddle (auth), Initial View, Ctr Contemp Art, 89; Susan Kandel (auth), Word painting, Los Angeles Times, 95. *Media:* Acrylic, Mixed Media. *Publ:* Contribr, Louis Comfort Tiffany Catalog, Louis Comfort Tiffany Found, 87; coauth, How we talk about abstraction, Artweek, 95. *Mailing Add:* 2337 Observatory Ave Los Angeles CA 90027

EDWARDS, MELVIN
SCULPTOR, EDUCATOR
b Houston, Tex, May 4, 37. *Study:* Los Angeles Co Art Inst; Los Angeles City Col; Univ Southern Calif, BFA. *Work:* Brooklyn Mus, Metrop Mus Art & Mus Mod Art, NY; Los Angeles Co Mus Art; Wadsworth Atheneum, Hartford, Conn. *Comn:* Confirmation, US Social Security Bldg, Fed Plaza, Jamaica, NY; Tomorrow's Wind, Thomas Jefferson Park, East Harlem, NY; Passage, Kingsborough Community Col, Brooklyn, NY; Safe Journey, Motor Vehicle Inspection Sta, Eatontown, NJ; Breaking of the Chains, Martin Luther King, Jr Promenade, Calif. *Exhib:* Los Angeles Co Mus, 65 & 83; solo exhibs, Walker Art Ctr, Minneapolis, Minn, 68, Whitney Mus Am Art, NY, 70, CDS Gallery, NY, 94 & 96, Parchman Stremmel Gallery, San Antonio, Tex, 95, Porter Troupe Gallery, San Diego, Calif, 95 & Montclair Art Mus, NJ, 96; Mus Mod Art, NY, 70, 71, 76, 77 & 88; Whitney Mus Am Art, NY, 70 & 90; Aldrich Mus Contemp Art, Ridgefield, Conn, 71; Storm King Art Ctr, Mountainville, NY, 72; Art

Inst Chicago, 72; Wadsworth Atheneum, Hartford, Conn, 74; Everson Mus, Syracuse, NY, 81; Walker Art Ctr, Minneapolis, Minn, 88; Corcoran Gallery Art, Washington, 89; retrospectives, Montclair State Col Art Gallery, NJ, 90 & Neuberger Mus, Purchase, NY, 93, Hood Mus Art, Hanover, NH, 94, Fla Int Univ, Miami, 94 & McNay Art Mus, San Antonio, Tex, 95; Skoto Gallery, NY, 96; Twentieth Century Am Sculpture at the White House, First Ladies' Garden, Washington, 96; Tragic Wake, Spirit Sq Ctr Arts & Educ, Charlotte, NC, 96. *Teaching:* San Bernardino Valley Col, 64-65, Calif Inst Arts, 65-67 & Orange Co Community Col, 67-69; asst prof, Univ Conn, 70-72; Rutgers Univ, Livingston Col, Mason Gross Sch Arts, Visual Art Dept, 72-. *Awards:* NJ State Arts Coun/Nat Endowment Arts Fel, 84; Fulbright Fel to Zimbabwe, 88 & 89. *Bibliog:* Brooke Kamin Rapaport (auth), Welded poetry, Sculpture Mag, 10/96; Amei Wallach (auth), Melvin Edwards, ArtNews, 10/96; Nancy Princenthal (auth), Melvin Edwards at CDS, Art Am, 1/97. *Mem:* Nat Acad. *Mailing Add:* Mason Gross Sch Arts Visual Arts Dept 33 Livingston Ave New Brunswick NJ 08901-1959

EDWARDS, PAUL BURGESS See Pablo

EDWARDS, SUSAN HARRIS
DIRECTOR
b Baltimore, Md, Sept 26, 1948. *Study:* Univ SC, BA, 79, MA, 83; Grad Ctr, City Univ NY, MPh, 90, PhD, 95. *Collection Arranged:* Hunter College Permanent Collection, 87; Systems and Abstraction, 88; New York Area MFA Exhibition, 90; Formulation & Representation, 90; Physical Relief, 91; Contemporary Icons, 92; Ben Shahn and the Task of Photography in Thirties America, 95. *Pos:* Managing ed, Sheep Meadow Press, Riverdale, NY, 84-85; asst dept paintings & sculpture, Brooklyn Mus, NY, 82-84; cur, Hunter Col, City Univ NY, 87-98; dir, Katanah Mus Art, 98-2004; exec dir & ceo, First Ctr Visusal Arts, Nashville, Tenn, 2004-. *Teaching:* instr art hist, Newberry Col, SC, 81; instr, Queens Col, City Univ NY, 86-89 & NY Univ, 90-98; adj assoc prof, Vanderbilt Univ, 2006-. *Awards:* Bogliasco Fel, 96-97. *Bibliog:* Joshua Dector (auth), Systems & Abstraction, Arts Mag, 3/89; Roger, Denson (auth), A Feminism without Men, Tema Celeste 4-5/92. *Mem:* Col Art Asn; Am Asn Mus. *Publ:* Auth, A Debate on Abstraction, 88, Formulation and Representation in Recent Abstract Art, 90, Hunter Col; Ben Shahn: Focus on America. *Mailing Add:* 401 Bowling Ave # 23 Nashville TN 37205

EDWARDS-TUCKER, YVONNE LEATRICE
CERAMIST, EDUCATOR
b Chicago, Ill, Jan 19, 41. *Study:* Univ Ill, Urbana, BFA(art educ; summa cum laude), 62; Univ Calif, Los Angeles, 62-64; Otis Art Inst, BFA, MFA, 68; studied with Charles White, Michael Frimkess & Helen Watson; numerous other workshops. *Work:* Fisk Univ, Nashville, Tenn; Otis Art Inst; Hampton Univ, Va; Syracuse Univ, NY; Fla A&M Univ, Tallahassee. *Exhib:* Contemp African-Am Crafts, Brooks Mem Art Mus, 79; Power Objects: Ancient & to the Future, Howard Univ Art Gallery, 80; Dimensions & Directions: Black Artists of the South, Miss Art Mus, 80; Forever Free: Art by African-Am Women, 1862-1980, Joslyn Art Mus, Montgomery Mus Fine Arts, Indianapolis Mus, & Univ Md, 81-82; Magic of Clay, Calif Mus Afro-Am Hist & Cult, Los Angeles, 82; Traditional Crafts, Mus Nat Ctr Afro-Am Artists, Boston, 82; Surrealism and the Afro-Am Artist, Evans-Tibbs collection, Washington, DC, 83; Voices: Afro-American Ceramics, Syracuse Univ, 88; JB Speed Mus, Louisville, Ky, 88; Ceramic Traditions, NCECA, Contemp Art Ctr, Kansas City, Mo, 89; African Images in Am Craft, Folk Art Ctr, Asheville, NC, traveling, 92-93. *Collection Arranged:* Florida Craftsmen, 73, Impact 79: Afro-American Women Artists, 79 & Tallahassee Tribute, 81, Fla A&M Univ Art Gallery; Harambee at Lemoyne, 85; Harambee Invitational II, 86; Fla A&M Univ Centennial Art Exhib, 87; Celebration of African-American Art. *Teaching:* Asst prof ceramics & drawing, Miami-Dade Community Col, 68-73; adj prof art, Miami Exten, Shaw Univ, 72-74; prof ceramics & art, Fla A&M Univ, 73-. *Awards:* Award Ceramic Sculpture, Fiftieth Anniversary Exhib, Otis Art Inst, 69; Best in Show, Clay Works 72, Grove House Gallery, Miami, 72; Purchase Award, Syracuse Univ Ceramics Collection, New York, 87. *Bibliog:* Ellen A Ashdown (auth), Afro-Raku: The ceramics of Yvonne & Curtis Tucker, Black Art Int Quart, winter 79 & The ceramics of Yvonne & Curtis Tucker, Art-Craft, 2-3/80; Arna Bontemps (ed), African-American Art History: The Feminine Dimension, In: Forever Free, Stephen Sun Inc. *Mem:* Nat Conf Artists; Nat Conf Educ Ceramic Arts; founding mem Harambee Arts Coun; Fla Folk Life Coun; Fla Craftsmen. *Media:* Clay, Raku Clay, Mixed Media. *Res:* African and Afro-American folklore; Black Art of the South; Black aesthetics; folk art. *Publ:* Illusr, Le theme de la violence, African Arts, Arts d'Afrique, Vol 1, No 1, 67; auth, African, Indian & Oriental Influences in the Aesthetics of Two Contemporary Craftspeople: First National African-American Crafts Conference: Shelby State Community Col, 80; John T Scott & the black aethetic, Int Review African Am Art, Vol 6, No 2, 85; Afro-Raku Ceramics & Y&C Tucker, NCECA J, Vol 10, 51-54, 89-90. *Dealer:* Gallery Antigua 5138 Biscayne Blvd Miami FL 33134. *Mailing Add:* 3007 Kevin St Tallahassee FL 32301-6915

EDWARDSON, JOHN ALBERT
PATRON
b Terre Haute, Ind, Jul 23, 49. *Study:* Purdue Univ, BS(industrial eng), 71; Univ Chicago, MBA(fin & int bus), 72. *Pos:* Commercial banking off, First Bank-St, Paul, 72-77; vpres, treas, Ferrell Cos. Inc, Kansas City, Mo, 77-83, sr vpres fin serv's group, 83-85; exec vpres fin, chief fin off, Northwest Airlines Inc & NWA Inc, St Paul, 85-88; exec vpres, chief fin & admin off, Int Minerals & Chems. Corp, Northbrook, Ill, 88-90; chief fin off, United Airlines Employees Acquisition Corp, Chicago, 90; exec vpres, chief fin off, Ameritech, 91-94; pres, Chief Operating Officer UAL Corp, Elk Grove Village, 94-; chmn, pres & Chief Exec Officer, Burns Int Svcs Corp, Chicago, 99-2000; chmn, Chief Exec Officer, CDW, Vernon Hills, 2001-; trustee, pres, Ravina Festival Asn, Highland Park, Ill, bd trustees, Art Inst Chicago, currently. *Awards:* Recipient Distinguished Eng Alumnus Award Purdue Univ, 88. *Interests:* Sailing, hiking & bicycling. *Mailing Add:* CDW 200 N Milwaukee Ave Indian Creek IL 60061

EGAN, LAURY AGNES
PHOTOGRAPHER, INSTRUCTOR
b Long Branch, NJ, June 29, 1950. *Study:* Carnegie Mellon Univ, BFA, 1972; Color Photog Workshop, Sam Abell, Princeton, NJ. *Work:* Montclair Art Mus (permanent collection), Montclair, NJ; Graphic Arts Collection, Princeton Univ, Princeton, NJ; Southern Methodist Univ, archives, Dallas, Tex; Opera Co of Philadelphia, archives, Philadelphia, Pa; Philip Glass Archives, The Voyage, world premiere opera, NY. *Comn:* Photos of Southern Methodist Univ, SMU Press, 1991. *Exhib:* Views of Princeton, Graphic Arts/Rare Books, Princeton Univ, Princeton, NJ, 1984; Mercer Co Photographic Show, Trenton State Col Mus, Trenton, NJ, 1985-1988; Three-Person Show, Stuart Co Day Sch, Princeton, NJ, 1986; Greek Images, Alkit Digital Collection, Inc, NY, 2000; Three-Person Show, Williams Gallery (representation), Princeton, NJ, 2001-2006. *Pos:* Book Designer/photo illusr, Princeton Univ Press, Princeton, NJ, 1972-1985; Book Designer/photo Illusr, Laury A Egan Design & Photog (various addresses), 1984-2006; Freelance photogr, Opera Company of Philadelphia & all Lincoln Center Orgns, 1991-1999. *Teaching:* Instr design photo, Guild of Creative Art, Shrewsbury, NJ, 1999; instr/private lectr photog, Highlands, NJ (private assignments & portfolio reviews), regional & int (Venice) workshops, 1999-2006; instr, Brookdale Community Col, Lincroft, NJ, 2000-2006. *Awards:* Guild of Creative Art, ann photo, 1983-2006; Purchase Award, Mercer Co Photog Show, Mercer Co, 1986-1987. *Media:* Photography, Fine Arts. *Publ:* Illusr, approx 35 book jackets/covers for 20+ univ presses, Ohio, Princeton, Johns Hopkins, 1977-2003; illusr, Princeton Reflections (participating Illus, Princeton Univ Press, 1990; illusr, SMU Reflections (participating illusr & designer), SMU Press, 1991; illusr, Opera Company of Philadelphia, Lincoln Center Orgns, brochures, publicity, 1992-2000; illusr, Wines & Wineries of the Hudson River Valley (solo photog), Countryman Press, 1993. *Dealer:* Frederick Gallery 401 Spier Ave Allenhurst NJ 07711; Chamot Gallery 111 First Ave Jersey City NJ 07302. *Mailing Add:* 8 Mountain St Highlands NJ 07732

EGBERT, ELIZABETH FRANCES
SCULPTOR, EDUCATOR
b Charleston, WVa, May 10, 1945. *Study:* Mt Holyoke Col, South Hadley, Mass, BA, 67; New York Univ, MA, 70. *Work:* Lab Theater, Mt Holyoke Col; Nassau Co Mus Fine Arts, Roslyn, NY; Biblioteque Nationale, Paris, France; Foreign Arts Mus, Sofia, Bulgaria. *Comn:* Courtyard design, Third St Music Sch, NY, 79; Play Sculpture, NY Dept Cult Affairs, Community Arts Develop Fund & NY State Coun Arts, NY, 84-85. *Exhib:* Contemp Reflections, Aldrich Mus, Ridgefield, Conn, 77; Scuplture on Shoreline Sites (outdoor installation), Roosevelt Island, NY, 80; one-person shows, Women's Interart Ctr, NY, 81, Nassau Co Mus Fine Art, Roslyn, NY, 83 & Sculpture Ctr Gallery, NY, 83; Four Sculptors, Sid Deutsch Gallery, NY, 83; one-person show, Seven Yr Survey, Snug Harbor Cult Ctr, Staten Island, NY, 85. *Pos:* Educ & exhib consult, Jacques Marchais Ctr Tibetan Ctr, Staten Island, NY, 85-86; assoc bd mem, Snug Harbor Cult Ctr, Staten Island, 85-88. *Teaching:* Instr sculpture, Sch Continuing Educ, NY Univ, 78-79; instr sculpture, Philadelphia Col Art, Pa, 85-87. *Awards:* Individual Artists Award, Staten Island Coun Arts, 84 & 85; Pub Art Award, NY State Coun Arts, 85. *Bibliog:* Michael Brenson (auth), What's new around town in outdoor sculpture, 7/19/85 & A bountiful season in outdoor sculpture, 7/18/86, New York Times; Tsipi Ben-Haim (auth), Letter from New York, Int Sculpture, 11-12/85. *Mem:* Sculptors Guild (secy, 85-86); Orgn Independent Artists, NY. *Publ:* Ed & photogr, Shopping center art, On Site, 71. *Mailing Add:* 354 Van Duzer St Staten Island NY 10304-2722

EGELI, CEDRIC BALDWIN
PAINTER, INSTRUCTOR
b Shady Side, Md, Aug 10, 36. *Study:* Principia Col, AA, 55; studied with Bjorn Egeli, 55-84; Corcoran Sch Art with Edmund Arden, 56; Art Students League, New York with Sidney Dickenson, Frank Mason & Frank Reilly, 57-60; Cape Sch with Henry Hensche, summers 78-87. *Work:* Pentagon, Alexandria, Va; Johns Hopkins Hosp, Baltimore, Md; State Capitol, Annapolis, Md; US Dist Court, Washington. *Comn:* Portrait, Arleigh Burke, Am Ordinance Asn, Washington, 67; portrait, Stanfield Turner, CIA, Washington, 79; portrait, Jackie Presser, Teamsters Union, Washington, 83; portrait, Morris Abrahm, Brandeis Univ, Boston, 84; portrait, H Keith Brody, Duke Univ, Durham, NC, 90. *Exhib:* Nat Portrait Sems, NY, Washington, DC & Chicago hotels, 80-83; Egeli Family Exhib, Md Life Bldg, Baltimore, 86; Wohlfarth Galleries, 97-2005, yr show. *Pos:* Pres, Md Portrait Soc, 83-86 & 90-92; Coun Leading Am Portrait Painters, 96. *Teaching:* Portrait painting & figure drawing, Egeli Studios Fall Session, 79-2005; outdoor portrait painting, Cape Sch Art, Provincetown, Mass, summers, 89-2002; Honorary Portrait Instr Nat Portrait Soc, Chicago, 2000. *Awards:* Best Show, Grand Prize, Nat Portrait Sem, John Howard Sanden, 79; Gold Medal for Oil, 80 & Grumbacher Award, 81, Am Artists Prof League; Annie Award, Anne Arundel Co Cult Award, 2001. *Bibliog:* Papperfuse (auth), History of Maryland, State of Md, 78; Steven Doherty (auth), Artists & sons, Am Artist, 88; Portraits as Art, Dossier, 89. *Mem:* Md Portrait Soc (pres, 84-86 & 90-92); Am Artists Prof League; Art Students League; Charcoal Club, Baltimore; Beachcomers Club, Provincetown, Mass. *Media:* Oil. *Specialty:* Portrait Painters of Am in Birmingham, Ala; impressionistic (outdoor), Wohlfarth Gallerie Portraits. *Interests:* Figure & Landscape. *Publ:* Auth, Impressionist Outdoor Painting, 95. *Dealer:* Wohlfarth Gallery 3418 Ninth St NE Washington DC 20017. *Mailing Add:* 111 Fiddlers Hills Rd Edgewater MD 21037

EGELI, PETER EVEN
PAINTER, ILLUSTRATOR
b Miami, Fla, Apr 19, 34. *Study:* Corcoran Sch Art; Md Inst, BFA; Art Students League; George Washington Univ; 3 yrs study with Jacques Maroger. *Work:* US Dept Agriculture; US State Dept; US District Court, Washington; Md State Capitol; US Navy Dept; US Dept Energy; Embassy of USA, London; Colonial Williamsburg Found; plus numerous other collections. *Comn:* Portrait of Judge Robert Bork, US District Ct, 95; portrait of Richard Cheney, US Dept Defense, 95; portrait of William Richardson, Johns Hopkins Univ, 96; portrait of Charles Corry, 96; portrait of Daniel Nathans, Johns Hopkins Univ, 96; portrait of Lloyd Bentsen, US Dept Treas, 97; portrait Donald Coffey, Patrick Walsh, Johns Hopkins Hosp, 99; Royal Norwegian Embassy, DC, 01; Whitten Peters, Sec Air Force, 2001; William Cohen, Sec Defense, 2002; Lawrence Silberman, US Court Appeals, Washington, DC, 2003; Jacob Handlesman, Johns Hopkins Hosp, 2004; John Jumper, USAF, 2005; portrait, Gen Michael Hague, USMC, 2006; portrait, Bishop Michael Bransfield, WVa, 2006; Sidney Kimmel, Johns Hopkins Hosp; and others. *Exhib:* Mystic Int Marine Art Shows, Mystic, Conn, 81-84; Mariners Mus, Newport News, Va, 85; Md Hist Soc, Am Soc Marine Artists, 89; Mystic Seaport Schaefer Gallery, Am Soc Marine Artists, 92; solo shows incl Md Fedn Art, Annapolis, 72, Grand Gallery, Wilmington, Del, 78, South Street Seaport, NY, 80; Cummer Mus & Gardens, Jacksonville, Fla, 97; Grand Central Gallery, NY, 80; Md Hist Soc, Baltimore, 88; Frye Mus, Seattle, Wash, 97; plus others; Cape Mus Fin Arts, Dennis, Ma; Del Art Mus, Downtown Gallery, Wilmington, Del, 01; Vero Beach, Mus Art, Vero Beach, Fla, 2004. *Pos:* Illusr, Marine Corps Inst, Washington, 53-56; pres, Am Soc Marine Artists, 86-89, fel, 95; pvt critiques, 77-, pvt classes 67-77. *Teaching:* Instr painting, St Mary's Col of Md, 61-67; lectr, NC Ctr Advan Teaching, Portraits & Profiles, 92. *Awards:* Best of Show, Mystic Int Marine Art Show, 81; Iron Man Award, Am Soc Marine Artists, 02. *Bibliog:* Ann Powell (auth), Artists Home on the St Mary's River, Mid-Atlantic Country Mag, 6/88; Amiad J Finkel (auth), Captured on Canvas, Chief Exec, Nov/Dec 88; Geoffrey Loftus (auth), Your Best Shot, For a Really Lasting Impression Across the Board, 10/94; Peter J Wrike (auth), Westbank, Egeli and Art, Pleasant Living, 10/96; Rachel Rubin Wolf (auth) Painting Ships, Shores and the Sea, North Light Books, 97; plus others. *Mem:* Am Soc Marine Artists (pres, 86-89, fel, 95). *Media:* Oil, Pastel, Watercolor. *Res:* 17th century English ships, 19th and early 20th century Chesapeake Bay craft. *Interests:* Sailing, history, antiques. *Publ:* Auth/Illusr of seven prints of maritime subjects. *Dealer:* Mystic Seaport Museum Gallery Mystic CT; Admiralty Gallery, Vero Beach, Fla. *Mailing Add:* Westbank Drayden MD 20630

EGER, MARILYN RAE
PAINTER, EDUCATOR
b Offett AFB, Nebr, Jan 2, 53. *Study:* Chapman Col, Single Subject Teaching Credential (art), 90; Calif State Univ, Stanislaus, BA (art), 87; Kansas City Art Inst, 78-80; Acad Art, San Francisco, Calif, 2006-. *Work:* Kaiser Permanente, Stockton & Modesto, Calif; Gulf Oil Chemicals, Pittsburg, Kans; KCRA Channel 3, Sacramento, Calif; Dragonlady Gallery; UC Davis Med Center, Sacramento, Calif; and others. *Comn:* Wine Country (oil painting), comn by Susan Mitchel, Stockton, Calif, 94; Elk Creek Spring (oil painting), comn by Hazel Cottrel, Lodi, Calif, 94. *Exhib:* Realism '93, 5th Ann Exhib, Parkersburg, WVa, 93; SAL Ann, Haggin Mus, Stockton, Calif, 93; State of the Art '93, Woburn, Mass, 93; Nat League Am Pen Women, Redwood City, Calif, 93; 98th Ann, Catharine Lorillard Wolfe, NY, 94; Calif State Fair, 2006. *Pos:* Gibson Greetings Inc, Cincinnati, Ohio, 92-96. *Teaching:* Advan Placement & Introd to Art, Bear Creek High School, 90-. *Awards:* Award of Excellence, Haggin Mus, 92; Ben Day Mem Award, Unitarian Fall Arts Festival, 93; Mellon Grant, Nat Col Bd, 94; Awards of Merit, Calif State Fair, 2006. *Bibliog:* Brian Gold (auth), Art is life for Marilyn Eger, Lodi News-Sentinel The Entertainer, 9/30/94; Les Krantz (auth), Calif Art Review, 89; Greg Schaber (auth), Playing your cards right, Artist Mag, 2/95; Tricia Tomiyoshi (auth), A Life in Art, Lodi News-Sentinel Lodi Living, 10/1/2005. *Mem:* Lodi Art Center; Stockton Art League; Calif Art Educators Asn. *Media:* Oil, Acrylic, Pastels & Miscellaneous Media. *Interests:* antique art glass, french cameo glass, tiffany & antique lamps. *Collection:* high-end antique & contemporary art glass. *Dealer:* Knowlton Gallery 115 S School St #14 Lodi Calif 95240; Iron Door Gallery 458 Main St Murphys Calif 95247. *Mailing Add:* 1295 E Peltier Rd Acampo CA 95220

EGLESTON, TRUMAN G
PAINTER
b Westfield, Mass, Oct 14, 31. *Study:* Mass Col Art, BFA, 58; Calif Col Arts & Crafts, MFA, 59. *Work:* Mus Fine Arts & Wellington Collection, Boston; Framingham State Col, Mass; Salem State Col. *Exhib:* Painting & Sculpture, 58 & Drawing, 59, San Francisco Mus Fine Arts; Boston Arts Festival, Boston Common, 64; Boston Now, Inst Contemp Art, 83; one-man exhib, Ann Plumb Gallery, 89; 3-man exhib, Space Attitudes, Holly Solomon Gallery, 91. *Teaching:* Asst prof drawing & painting, State Univ NY, Fredonia, 60-63; prof, Boston State Col, 64-82 & Univ Mass, Boston, 82-87. *Bibliog:* Erik Saxon (auth), Truman Egleston at Ann Plumb, Art in Am, 4/90; Rick Kreiner (auth), Points of Contact, Metroland Mag, 4/94; Light, Geometry and Color, a conversation with the Artist, Home & Style Mag, 98. *Media:* Oil. *Specialty:* 5 Points.com, Art&Sciencewebsite-includesimages (digital exhib) Plus Conversation. *Collection:* BASS MANOR MUS-Malth, NY; Private Mus Dedicated to my Art 1970's Collection, and 1990 Collection. *Mailing Add:* 3044 Rte 9 East Chatham NY 12060

EGLITIS, LAIMONS
PAINTER, EDUCATOR
b Asite, Latvia, Nov 15, 29; US citizen. *Study:* With Joblovskis, 46-47; Tyler Sch Art, BFA, 69, MFA(fel), 71. *Work:* Philadelphia Mus Art; Virginia Beach Art Ctr Collection; Ottawa Art Collection; Albright Col Collection; Latvian State Mus, Riga; Mus Arsenals, Riga. *Comn:* Mural for Latvian Mus, Rockville, Md. *Exhib:* New Directions, Civic Ctr Mus, Philadelphia, 71; New Acquisitions, Philadelphia Mus Art, 71; Baltimore Film Festival Invitational, Baltimore Mus Art, 75; Md Regional Water Color, Johns Hopkins Univ, 75 & 80; Bicentennial Events, Univ Pa Mus, 76; Overseas Artists, Riga Mus, Latvia, 81; Global Latvian Art Exhib, State Mus, Riga, 90; G Skilter Mem Mus, Riga, 99. *Teaching:* Retired. *Awards:* Hon Award Visual Arts, Latvian Global Cult Found, 73; Gold Medal, Maryland Regional Watercolor Exhib, 86; and many others. *Bibliog:* Arnolds Treibergs (auth), Laimons Eglitis--a painter in exile, Latvju Maksla, Latvian Inst, 12/75. *Media:* Oils, Watercolors. *Mailing Add:* 8 Arbutus Ave Catonsville MD 21228

EGRI, TED
SCULPTOR, PAINTER
b New York, NY, May 22, 1913. *Study:* Master Inst Roerich Mus, dipl, 31-34; Duncan Phillips Mem Gallery Art Sch, 42; Hans Hofmann Sch Art, New York & Provincetown, Mass, 48. *Work:* William Rockhill Nelson Mus, Kansas City, Mo; Mus NMex, Santa Fe; Simon Wiesenthal Holocaust Mus, Los Angeles; Roswell Mus, NMex; Northern Iowa Univ. *Comn:* monument on pedestal, City Albuquerque, NMex, 69; 10 sculptures, Temple B'Nai Israel, Albuquerque, 79; 6ft outdoor St Mary, Ave Maria Parish, Parker, Colo, 88; 20ft fiberglass sculpture, Southwest Tex State Univ, San Marcos, 89; Metal 3D Sculpture, Facade of Taos, NMex, 98. *Exhib:* Colorado Springs Fine Arts Ctr, Colo, 50 & 52; Stables Gallery, 53-88; Religious Art Western World, 58 & Southwestern Art Show, 60, Dallas Mus Fine Arts, Tex; Roswell Mus, NMex, 58, 72 & 81; Shidoni 6th, 7th & 8th Ann Outdoor Show, Tesuque NMex, 80, 81 & 82; Harwood Mus, 98; group exhib, Kuumba: Creativity, Taos, 99, yearly exhibs, New Directions Gallery, Taos, 2001, 02, 03 & 04. *Teaching:* Instr oil painting & life drawing, Kansas City Art Inst, 48-50; lectr art sculpture, life drawing & painting, Univ Wyo, 59-60; instr painting, Philbrook Art Ctr, 5/56 & 5/57; vis lectr art, Univ Ill, Champaign, 60-61; vis artist teacher sculpture, Northern Iowa Univ, summer 63 & 64; lectr, Las Palomas Educ Convention Ctr, Taos, NMex, 82-. *Awards:* Top Award for Sculpture, Mus NMex, 65 & 69 & Honorable Mention for Drawing, 65; Gov Award, Harwood Mus, 96; Community Volunteer Award, from Mayor & Town Coun, Taos, NMex, 2002, outstanding achievement in Fine Arts & Serv to Community Award, 2003. *Bibliog:* Louis G Redstone (auth), Art in Architecture; John Baldwin (auth), Contemporary Sculpture Techniques; John Rood (auth), Sculpture with a Torch; Ted Egri Day (auth), Service to Taos Minorities and Children, 2006; and others. *Mem:* Nat Artists Equity Asn Inc; Taos Art Asn, NMex; Nat Mus Women in Arts, Washington. *Media:* Sculpture, Painting. *Publ:* Contrib 7 illus, Ted Egri: the survival of a sculptor, Am Artist, 6/77; 6 illus, Ted Egri: Sculptor of symbols, Southwest Art, 2/79; cover and 9 illus, Sculptured sentinels, Now Mag, 5/11/80; Art in Agriculture, Louis G Redstone; Contemporary Sculpture Techniques, John Baldwin. *Dealer:* New Directions Gallery 107-B N Plaza Taos NM 87571; Envision Gallery Taos NM 135 N Plaza & North Highway 522 El Prado; HCR 74 PO Box 20612 El Prado 87529. *Mailing Add:* HC 74 Box 22410 El Prado NM 87529

EGUCHI, YASU
PAINTER
b Japan, Nov 30, 38. *Study:* Horie Art Acad, Japan, 58-65. *Work:* Frye Art Mus, Seattle; Heidenheim, WGer; Giengen, WGer; Am Embassy, Paris; and others. *Comn:* Paintings & relief, Sandpiper Golf Course, Santa Barbara, Calif, 72; painting, Deer Valley, Park City, Utah, 81; collage, Eye Bank Sight Restoration Inc, 81. *Exhib:* Austin Gallery, Scottsdale, Ariz, 68-86; Santa Barbara Mus Art, 72-74 & 85; Frye Mus, Seattle, Wash, 74, 84 & 98; Hammer Galleries, NY, 77, 79, 81 & 93; City of Heidenheim, WGer, 80 & 2000; Everson Mus Art, Syracuse, NY, 80; Nat Acad Design, NY, 80-87; Artique Ltd, Anchorage, Alaska, 81-2006; Forest Lawn Mus, 2006; and many others. *Awards:* Artist of the Yr Award, Santa Barbara Arts Coun, 79; Honorary City Award, Heidenheim, WGer, 80; Adolph & Clara Obrig Prize, Nat Acad Design, 83; The Adolph and Clara Obrig prize National Acad of Design, 1983, Cert of Merit Nat Acad of Design, 1985, 87. *Bibliog:* America's sunset coast, Nat Geographic, 78; article, Arts Mag, 78; article, Santa Barbara Mag, 78; article, American Artist, 80. *Mem:* Nat Acad. *Media:* Watercolor, Oil. *Publ:* Auth, Der Brenz Entlang, City of Heidenheim and Austin Gallery, 80; Auth: Yasu Eguchi, Kunsmuseum Heidenheim, 2000; contr to jours in field. *Mailing Add:* PO Box 30206 Santa Barbara CA 93130

EHLERS, CAROL A
ART DEALER
b Birmingham, Mich, May 10, 52. *Study:* Wheaton Col, Norton, Mass, BA, 74. *Pos:* Asst dir, Allan Frumkin Gallery-Photographs Inc, Chicago, 75-78, dir, 78-79; Pres & dir, Carol Ehlers Photographs Inc, 88-90; Pres & dir, Carol Ehlers Gallery Ltd, 90-2000. *Mem:* Asn Int Photog Art Dealers (vpres, 82-86). *Specialty:* 20th century photographs

EHRENKRANZ, JOEL S & ANN
COLLECTOR
b Newark, NJ, Mar 25, 35. *Study:* Univ Pa, BS, 56, MBA, 57; NY Univ, LLB, 61, LLM, 64. *Pos:* Accountant, Peat, Marwick, Mitchell & Co, 57-62; sr partner, Ehrenkranz & Ehrenkranz, Atty at Law, 62-; Blythedale Childrens Hosp (trustee & treas, 66-74); Fedn Jewish Philanthropies (trustee & mem, distrib comt, 71-82); Whitney Mus Am Art (trustee, 73-, vchmn 2004-); adv bd, Wheelchair Found; vpres, Whitney Mus Am Art, 73-2002, pres, 98-2002; trustee, NYU Law Sch, 92-, chmn investment comt, 2003-; grad bd, Wharton Sch Univ Pa, 85-2004; Archives Am Art (trustee, 73, pres, 84-86); trustee, Estee Lauder Co Inc; trustee, distrib comt Fedn Jewish Philanthropies, New York City, 79-83, United Jewish Appeal/Fedn Jewish Philanthropies, New York City, 82-92, pres, 87-92; trustee, Archives Am Art, 73-, pres, 84-86; trustee, Whitney Mus Am Art, 73-; trustee, vchmn, mem exec comt, Mt Sinai Med Ctr, New York City, 87-92, chmn, financial budgets and accountants comt,

92-95; trustee, New York Univ, 98-2001, 2003-; bd overseers, Calif Inst Arts, 2001-; trustee, Archives Am Art, 73, pres, 84-86; trustee & treas, Blythedale Children's Hosp, 66-74. *Awards:* Named one of Top 200 Collectors, ARTnews Mag, 2004. *Mem:* Century Club (White Plains, NY). *Collection:* Contemporary art. *Mailing Add:* 375 Park Ave New York NY 10152

EHRLICH, GEORGE
HISTORIAN
b Chicago, Ill, Jan 28, 25. *Study:* Univ Ill-Urbana, BS, 49, MFA, 51, PhD, 60. *Pos:* Chmn dept art & art hist, Univ Mo-Kansas City, 64-75. *Teaching:* Prof art hist, Univ Mo-Kansas City, 54-92. *Mem:* Hon mem Inst Architects, Kansas City; Soc Archit Historians (pres, Mo Valley chap, 71 & 72). *Res:* Architectural history of Kansas City, Missouri; interrelationship of art to science and technology. *Publ:* Auth, Kansas City, Missouri: An Architectural History, 1826-1990, Univ Mo Press, rev ed, 92; Partnership practice & the professionalization of architecture in Kansas City, Mo, Mo Hist Rev, 7/80; The Bank of Commerce by Asa Beebe Cross: A building of the latest architecture, J Soc Archit Historians, 5/84; The 1807 Plan for an illustrated edition of the Lewis & Clark expedition, The Pa Mag Hist & Biog, 1/85; coauth (with Sherry Piland), The Architectural Career of Nelle Peters, Mo Hist Rev, 10/89; coauth, Guide to Kansas Architecture, 96. *Mailing Add:* 5505 Holmes Kansas City MO 64110

EICHEL, EDWARD W
PAINTER, DRAFTSMAN
b Brooklyn, NY, June 8, 32. *Study:* Art Inst Chicago, BFA(G & I Brown Fel), 58; Oskar Kokoschka Acad, Salzburg, Austria, 59. *Hon Degrees:* Medical Univ Americas, LHD. *Work:* Lyman Allyn Mus, New London, Conn; New York Drawing Soc. *Exhib:* Young Painters Int Biennale, Mus Mod Art, Paris, France, 61; Animal Drawings from the 15th to 20th Centuries, Seiferheld Gallery, NY, 62; Drawing & Print Club Exhib, Detroit Inst Art, Mich, 66; Painters & Sculptors 27th Ann, Jersey City Mus, NJ, 68; Drawings: A Reinvestigation, Joseloff Gallery, Univ Hartford, Conn, 75; 156th Ann Exhib, Nat Acad Design, NY, 81; 43rd Anniversary Exhib, Fedn Mod Painters & Sculptors, 83. *Teaching:* Instr painting & drawing, Eastern Mich Univ, Ypsilanti, 65-66; instr drawing & illustration, Hartford Art Sch, Univ Hartford, Conn, 81-82. *Awards:* Tiffany Found Grant, 67; 27th NJ Ann Medal Merit, Syndicate Mag, 68. *Bibliog:* Sketches of a journey: Israel on the line of a pen, L'Arche, Paris, 7/61; Stuart Hilton (auth), Medal of merit in New Jersey Annual, Today's Art, 12/68. *Mem:* Fedn Mod Painters & Sculptors; Westbeth Artists Community; Creativity Laboratories (dir, 70-); Am Asn Artist-Therapists. *Media:* Oil, Watercolor; Pencil, Pen & Ink. *Publ:* Illusr, The Glass Cage: The Eichmann Trial, Hakibbutz Hameuchad, 62; Israel Sketchbook, Dvir, 62; The Beast Book, Harper & Row, 64; The Perfect Fit: How to Achieve Mutual Fulfillment and Monogamous Passion through the New Intercourse, Donald I Fine Inc, 92 & Signet, 93; video, The Coital Alignment Technique, 2000. *Dealer:* Allan Stone Gallery 48 E 86th Street New York NY 10028. *Mailing Add:* Studio A-1106 463 West St New York NY 10014

EICKHORST, WILLIAM SIGURD
EDUCATOR, CURATOR
b Hackensack, NJ, Mar 4, 41. *Study:* Parsons Sch Design, BFA(advert graphics), 62; Montclair State Univ, BA(art educ), 69, MA(art educ), 70; Ball State Univ, EdD(art educ), 72; Univ Mo, Kansas City, 85; Kansas City Art Inst, 86 & 87. *Work:* Nelson-Atkins Mus Art, Kansas City, Mo; Albrecht-Kemper Art Mus, St Joseph, Mo; Portland Mus Art, Ore; Spencer Mus, Lawrence KS; Quincy Art Ctr, Quincy I. *Exhib:* Art Horizons, Art 54 Gallery, NY, 88; 41st Ann Midstates Exhib, Evansville Mus Art, 88; 19th Biennial Jury Show, Muscatine Art Ctr, 88; 18th Nat Works on Paper, Minot State Univ, 88; 3rd Ann Fla Nat, Fla State Univ, 88; Kansas 13th Nat, Fort Hays State Univ, 88; 5th Ann Maritime Nat, Univ Maine, 88; William Eickhorst, Albrecht Art Mus, 89. *Pos:* Founder & exec dir, Print Consortium, Kansas City, Mo, 83-; vpres, Gallery on the Square, Kansas City, Mo, 85-86. *Teaching:* Prof art educ & studio art, Frostburg State Univ, Frostburg, Md, 72-75; head, grad & undergrad art educ progs, Univ Maine, Orono, 75-78; prof art theory & criticism, Mo Western State Col, St Joseph, Mo, 78-. *Awards:* Juror's Award, 38th Spiva Ann Competitive, 88; Cert of Excellence, Int Art Competition, 88; Mus Purchase Award, Central States Exhib, 89; and others. *Mem:* Boston Printmakers; Nat Art Educ Asn; Mo Art Educ Asn; Mo Alliance Arts Educ (bd dir, 81-82); Soc Am Graphic Artists; and others. *Media:* Mixed Media, Photography. *Specialty:* Contemporary American graphics by established and emerging artists. *Publ:* Auth, rev of Children's Art Judgment by Gordon S Plummer, Art Teacher, 75; Art education and the seventeen years war, 77, Science explains modern art, 85, rev of Art Law by Leonard DuBoff, 85 & From abacus to art, 86, Art Educ-Nat Art Educ Asn. *Mailing Add:* 6121 NW 77th St Kansas City MO 64151

EIDE, JOHN
PHOTOGRAPHER, EDUCATOR
b Minneapolis, Minn, Jan 28, 43. *Study:* Lawrence Univ, BA; Univ Minn, MFA; also with Jerome Liebling, Elaine Mayes & Allan Downs. *Work:* Portland Mus Art. *Exhib:* One-man shows, Wentz Gallery, Portland Art Inst, Ore, Photo Gallery, Portland Sch Art, 79 & Brockton Arts Ctr, Mass, 80; Cyanotypes--Boston Visual Artists Union; Thayer Acad, Braintree, Mass; Worchester Art Mus, Bowdoin Col, Brunswick, Maine, 79; and others. *Pos:* Hon cur photog, Portland Mus Art; dir, Photo Gallery, Maine Col Art, currently. *Teaching:* Prof & area head photog, Maine Col Art, 70-. *Mem:* Soc Photog Educ. *Publ:* Contribr, Io Mag, Earth Geog Issue, No 2, 72

EIDELBERG, MARTIN
HISTORIAN
b New York, NY, Jan 30, 41. *Study:* Columbia Univ, BA, 61; Princeton Univ, PhD, 65. *Pos:* Ed, Decorative Arts Soc Newslett (quart mag), 78-80. *Teaching:* Prof art hist, Rutgers Univ, New Brunswick, 64-2002, prof emeritus; Sothebys Works of Art Prog, New York, currently. *Awards:* Robert C Smith Award, Decorative Arts Soc, 82; Charles F Montgomery Prize, Decorative Arts Soc, 84; George Wittenborn Mem Award, Art Libr Soc NAm, 91. *Res:* 18th century French painting and drawing; modern decorative arts. *Publ:* Masterworks of Louis Comfort Tiffany, Thames & Hudson & Abrams, 89; ed & coauth, Design 1935-1965; What Modern Was, Musee des Arts Decoratifs de Montreal, Abrams, 91; coauth, The Dispersal of the Last Duke of Mantuas Paintings, Vol 123, Gazette des Beaux-Arts, 94; auth, Watteau's Italian Reveries vol 126, Gazette des Beaux-Arts, 95; ed, Messengers of Modernism: American Studio Jewelry, 1940-1960, 96 & Designed for Delight, Alternative Aspects of Twentieth-Century Decorative Arts, 97, Flammarion & Montreal Mus Decorative Arts, Paris & New York; ed, Design for Living, Furniture and Lighting, 1950-2000, Flammarion & Montreal Mus Decorative Arts, Paris and NY, 2000; auth, The Ceramic Forms of Leza McVey, Philmark, 2002; coauth, Watteau et la fête galante, Réunion des musées nationaux, 2004; coauth, The Lamps of Louis Comfort Tiffany, Vendome, 2005

EINREINHOFER, NANCY ANNE
GALLERY DIRECTOR, CURATOR
b Paterson, NJ, Sept 8, 43. *Study:* William Paterson Univ, NJ, MA; Univ Leicester, PhD(Mus Studies) studied with Susan Pearce. *Collection Arranged:* Five Views (auth, catalog), William Paterson Col, 79; Bladen, Kipp, Witkin (auth, catalog), 79; Illusion and Material (auth, catalog), 79; New New York (auth, catalog), 80; Language in the Visual Arts (auth, catalog), 81; Painting About Painting (auth, catalog), 81; Anti-Apocalypse (auth, catalog), 81; The Vogel Collection (auth, catalog), 82; Aspects of Contemporary Realism (auth, catalog), 83; The Great Illusionists (auth, catalog), 83; Legacy of Surrealism (auth, catalog), 88; Hand, Body, House (auth catalog), 90; Tobias Collection: (auth catalog), Africa, 99, (auth catalog), Intuitive Abstraction, 2000, (auth catalog), Oceania, 2001; Interior Views: The Artists Book as a Personal Journal, 2000. *Pos:* Dir, Ben Shahn Gallery, Wm Paterson Univ, Wayne, NJ, 79-. *Teaching:* Instr gallery & mus studies, Wm Paterson Univ. *Awards:* NJ Historical Comn Grant, 90; NJ Com for the Humanities Grant, 90; NJ State Coun on the Arts Grant, 2000-2003. *Mem:* Am Asn Mus; Mid Atlantic Asn Mus; Asn of Col & Univ Mus & Galleries; Col Art Asn; NJ Asn Mus (bd mem). *Res:* Contemporary art, all media; museum interpretation. *Interests:* artists' books, contemp prints, African & Oceanic. *Publ:* Auth, Nineteenth Century Painting of the New Jersey Landscape, 85, Nineteenth Century Maritime New Jersey, 86, Ninteenth Century New Jersey Collection, 88 & Ninteenth Century New Jersey Architecture, 89, Wm Paterson Col Press; The American Art Museum: Elitism and Democracy, Univ of Leicester Press, 99. *Mailing Add:* 1 Cheyenne Tr Sparta NJ 07871

EINS , STEFAN
CONCEPTUAL ARTIST, PAINTER
b Prague, Bohemia; Austrian citizen. *Study:* Univ Vienna, Austria, MA, 65; Acad Fine Arts, Vienna, BA, 67. *Work:* Nat Galerie, Vienna; New Mus, NY; Landesmuseum, St Polten; City of Vienna, Austria; Mus of Modern Art, Vienna, Austria; The Federal Goverment, Austria. *Comn:* Project Vertebrae, comn by Gresten Initiative, Gresten, Noe, Austria. *Exhib:* Documenta 6, 77, Documenta 7, 87; Fashion Moda, 78, 81, 85, 91 & 92; Times Sq Show, 80 & 2001; Oesterreichische Galerie, Vienna, 91; Liquid Steel/Life, outdoor present, NY, 72 & 2004; Trees, NY, 99; Lust/Pain-Pain/Lust, NY, 2004; The Downtown Show, Gret Art Gallery, NY, 2006; Andy Warhol Mus, Pittsburgh, 2006; Austin Mus, 2006. *Collection Arranged:* John Ahearn, 79, Jenny Holzer, 79, Graffiti, Art Success, 80 & Keith Haring, 81, Fashion Moda Mus; Fashion Moda (auth, catalog), New Mus, New York, 80-81 & Documenta 7, Kassel, WGer, 82; Lady Pink, Lady Heart, 83; Ron English, 87; Counting Coup, Democracy at Stake, Theater for New City, NY, 2001. *Pos:* Founder & exec dir, 3 Mercer, NY, 72-79 & Fashion Moda Mus, Bronx, 78-84 & 88-93; pres, Collab Proj Inc, 88, 2001-. *Awards:* Nat Endowment Arts Fel, 80 & 87; CAPS Fel, NY, 70; NY Found for the Arts, 2002; Adolph and Efther Gottlieb Found, 2004. *Bibliog:* Carey Lovelace (auth), S Bronx art, Los Angeles Times, 9/2/84; Karin Kuoni (auth), Stefan Eins: Fashion Moda, Kunstforum, 3-4/91; David Ebony (auth), Eloquent Corrosions, Art in America, 7/2000. *Mem:* Collab Proj Inc. *Media:* Ideas, Liquids, Time/Space, Pattern Repetition. *Publ:* Ed, Some posters from Fashion Moda by Ingrid Sischy, Artforum, 1/81; auth, Francesca Alinovi-Arte di Frontiera, (Italian ed), Flash Art, 2/82; Gabriele von Arnim-Atelier in Den Slums, Art, Ger, 4/82; Lucy Lippard-Get the Message, Dutton, 84; Alan Moore & Marc Miller-ABC No Rio Dinero, ABC No Rio, 85; One/Stefan Eins Exhibitions Catalog, Nat Galerie, Vienna, 91; Suzi Gablik, Has Modernism Failed?, 1984, Chris Townsend, Rapture, Arts Seduction by Fashion, 2002, Thames & Hudson; Peter Rosenstein, Brau Madden, Tatooed Walls, Univ Press Miss, 2006; The Downtown Book, The New York Art Scene 1974-1984, Princeton Univ Press, 2006. *Mailing Add:* PO Box 33 Canal Street Station New York NY 10013-0033

EISENBERG, DANIEL
FILMMAKER, VIDEO ARTIST
b Israel, 1954. *Study:* Studied film with Ernie Gehr, Larry Gottheim, Klaus Wyborny, Saul Levine & Ken Jacobs, State Univ NY, Binghamton. *Work:* Am Fedn Arts, Mus Mod Art, NY; San Francisco Art Inst, Calif; Neth Filmmuseum, Amsterdam; Art Inst Chicago; Australian Sch Film TV & Radio. *Exhib:* Biennial Exhib, Whitney Mus Am Art, NY, 89; Displaced Person, Hampshire Col, Northampton, Mass, 90, Int Found Footage Film Festival, Vienna, Austria, 91, Jerusalem Film Festival, Israel, 92, Univ Calif, Berkeley & San Diego, 93, Middlebury Col, Vt, 94, Univ Wis, Milwaukee, 95, and several other film festivals and museums in the US and abroad; one-man shows, Univ Iowa, Iowa City, 96, Art Inst Chicago, Berkeley, Calif, 97, Calif Inst Arts, Valencia, 97 & 2001, Mus Modern Art, NY, NY, 98, Rocky Mountain Film Center, Boulder, Colo, 98, Harn Mus Art, Univ Fla, Gainesville, 99, Mus Nat Art Moderne, Paris, France, 2000, Nat Univ Mex, Mexico City, 2001 & Bunkier Stuki, Krakow, Poland, 2001; Persistance, Sydney Int Film Festival, 97, Berlin Int Film Festival, 97, Vue Sur Les Docs Festival, Marseilles, 98; Journeys to Berlin, Goeth Inst, NY &

Chicago, 99; Not On My Map, Art Inst Chicago, 99; Whitney Mus Am Art, NY 99; Los Angeles Co Mus Art, 99; Guggenheim Mus, 2000. *Pos:* sound editor, WGBH, Boston, 79-81 & 83, asst ed, 76-78 & 81-82, ed, 81-90 & film res, 81-85. *Teaching:* Instr film, Boston Film/Video Found, 79; asst prof, Mass Col Art, Boston, 79-82, instr video, 87, asst prof film, 93-94; spec instr film & photog, Univ RI, Kingston, 84; vis artist, San Francisco Art Inst, 93; asst prof film & chair, Filmmaking Dept, Art Inst Chicago, 94-97, assoc prof, 98-2000 & prof, 2001-. *Awards:* New England Reg Fel, Nat Endowment Arts, 82 & Media Arts Grant, 89-92; Film Fel, Mass Artists Found, 82 & 91; Production Grant, Mass Coun Arts, 86-88; Grand Prize, Black Maria Film and Video Festival, 88-89; Media Arts Grant, Nat Endowment Arts, 89-92; Artist Fel, MacDowell Colony, 90 & Ill Arts Coun, 2001; Faculty Enrichment Grant, Sch Art Inst, 95, 97 & 99; Fel, John Simon Guggenheim Mem Found, 99-2000. *Bibliog:* Rachel Schreiber (auth), Seized images: Photography, memory and the Holocaust, New Art Examiner, Vol 24, No 7, 22-25, 56, 4/97; Edward E Crouse (auth), Persistence, San Francisco Bay Guardian, 11/18/97; Jeffrey Skoller (auth), Reconstructing Berlin, Afterimage, Vol 26, No 1, 12-13, 7-8/98; William Wees (auth), Old images, new meanings: recontextualizing archival footage of Nazism and the Holocaust, Spectator, Vol 20, No 1, 2000. *Publ:* contrib ed, Joan Robinson, One Woman's Story, 79-80; dir, The Conjuror, 83; contrib ed, Turtle Dreams, 83

EISENBERG, JEROME MARTIN
DEALER, COLLECTOR
b Philadelphia, Pa, July 6, 30. *Study:* Boston Univ, AB, 51; Columbia Univ, with Otto Brendel, Edith Porada & Henry Fischer, 60-63; Pa State Univ, with Jiri Frel, 69-71, PhD, 83. *Pos:* Dir, Royal-Athena Galleries, 58-; founder, Eisenberg Mus Biblical Archeol, Louisville, 61; chmn, Herodium Archeol Expedition Fund, 62; founder, publ, editor-in-chief, Minerva, 1990-. *Teaching:* Lectr forgery & fraud in ancient art, NY Univ, 69-70; vis prof, forgery & fraud in ancient art, Univ Leipzig, 1996. *Bibliog:* Barbara Pollack (auth), Royal-Athena: Access to antiquities, Collectors Quart, 63. *Mem:* Archeol Inst Am (life mem); Appraisers Asn Am; Am Numismatic Soc (life mem); Int Asn Dealers Ancient Art; fellow Royal Numismatic Soc; Int Asn Egyptologists; Int Asn Classical Archaeology. *Specialty:* Egyptian, Near Eastern, Greek, Roman, Etruscan art. *Collection:* Ancient Egyptian faience figurines; Egyptian stone vessels; Green & South Italian pottery; Roman glass; Pre-Columbian and tribal art. *Publ:* Auth, A Guide to Roman Imperial Coins, 57; Art of the Ancient World, 65, 67 & 85; The Age of Cleopatra, 1988; Gods and Mortals: Bronzes of the Ancient World, 1989; 1000 Years of Ancient Greek Vases, 1990; Art of the Ancient World, 1992, 1995, 1997, 1999-2006; Gods & Mortals II, 2004; Images of Warfare, 2004; Mythologies of the Classical World & Ancient Egypt, 2005. *Mailing Add:* c/o Royal-Athena Galleries 153 E 57th St New York NY 10022

EISENBERG, MARC S
PAINTER, SCULPTOR
b New York, NY, Feb 17, 48. *Study:* Sch Visual Arts, BFA, 71. *Work:* Chase Manhattan Bank, NY; Prudential Life Insurance Co, Edison, NJ; Equitable Life Insurance Co, NY; Berley & Co, NY; Weatherspoon Art Gallery, Greensboro, NC. *Exhib:* 19th Nat Print Exhib, 76 & Decade of Am Drawing, 81, Brooklyn, NY; Paper as Medium, Smithsonian Inst, Washington, DC, 78; Painting & Sculpture Today, Indianapolis Inst Art, Ind, 79; Art on Paper, Weatherspoon Mus, Greensboro, NC, 86. *Bibliog:* Corrine Robbins (auth), Works of Marc Eisenberg, Arts Mag, 76; Ronnie Cotrone (auth), Spotlight, Interview Mag, 76; Charles Gatewood (auth), Outlaw artists, Gallery Mag, 85. *Media:* Miscellaneous. *Mailing Add:* 40-60 Douglaston Pkwy Douglaston NY 11363

EISENBERG, MARVIN
EDUCATOR, HISTORIAN
b Philadelphia, Pa. *Study:* Univ Pa, BA, 43; Princeton Univ, MFA, 49, PhD, 54. *Hon Degrees:* Dlitt honorary, Univ St Andrews, 2003. *Pos:* Pres, Col Art Asn, 68-69; mem, Inst for Advan Study, winter 70; mem vis comt, Freer Gallery Art, Washington, DC 70-96, Dept Fine Arts, Harvard Univ, 75-80 & Ga Mus Art, 97-2003; ed, Bulletin Mus Art & Archeol, Univ Mich, 78-88; mem adv comt, Ctr Advanced Study Visual Arts, Nat Gallery, Washington, DC, 79-83. *Teaching:* Instr art hist, Univ Mich, 49-53, from asst prof to assoc prof, 54-61, prof, 61- & chmn dept, 61-69, prof emer, 89; vis prof, Stanford Univ, 73; Berg prof, Colo Col, 90, 93, 95 & 97; lectr, McMaster Univ, 94, Mt Holyoke Col, 94, St Andrews, 98, Gakushuin Univ, Tokyo, 98 & Kyoto Univ, 98. *Awards:* Guggenheim Fel, 59; Star of Solidarity, Ital Govt, 69; Distinguished Teaching in Art History, Col Art Asn Am, 87. *Res:* Italian late medieval and early renaissance painting. *Publ:* Auth, articles on early Italian painting in journals and museum bulletins; Lorenzo Monaco, Princeton Univ Press, Princeton, 89; Confraternity Altarpiece by Mariotto di Nardo, Tokyo, 98. *Mailing Add:* Univ Mich Dept Hist Art Ann Arbor MI 48109

EISENBERG, SONJA MIRIAM
PAINTER
b Berlin, Ger; US citizen, 26. *Study:* NY Univ, BA, 54; Nat Acad Sch Fine Arts, with Leon Kroll, 61; also with Daniel Dickerson, 62-68 & Sidney Delevante, in 60's. *Work:* Palm Spring Desert Mus; Fordham Univ Mus, NY; Archives Am Art, The Jewish Mus, NY; The Cathedral St John the Divine, NY; United Nations Headquarters, NY. *Comn:* Designer cachet for United Nations, Int Year Disabled Persons; book, Seeing the Gospel According to St John, (text & 41 paintings), The Cathedral St John the Divine, NY; Die Kristall Nacht (painting), Briefmarkenhaus Krüger, Munich, Ger, 93; AKIM-USA, NY, 96. *Exhib:* One-woman shows, Galerie de Sfinx, Amsterdam, 74 & Am Mus Hayden Planetarium, NY, 80, Archives of Am Art, Smithsonian Inst, 78; The 14th Int Art Friendship Exhib, Tokyo Metrop Art Mus, Tokyo, Japan, 89; Gallery Park Hotel, Vitznau, Switz, 94; Park Hotel Bürgenstock, Switz, 95; Park Ave Armory, NY, 96; Dussman Kulturhaus, Berlin, 98. *Pos:* Artist-in-residence, Cathedral St John the Divine. *Awards:* Accademia Italia delle Arti e del Lavoro, Medaglio d'Oro, 81; Gold Medal for Artistic Merit, Int Parliament Safety & Peace, 83; World Prize for Culture; Palma d'Oro d'Europa, 86. *Bibliog:* Jan deCarpentier (auth), Kijk's kunst, De Typhoon, 6/74; Gordon Brown (auth), Sonja Eisenberg, Art Mag, 4/75; Nina Brodsky (auth), Miniature Collector, 4/82; Ray Fashora (auth), Taconic Newspapers, 6/89; Berliner Zeitung, Stefan Elfenbein (auth), New York!, 2002. *Mem:* Res Bd Adv, The Am Biog Inst. *Media:* Oil, Watercolor; Pastel. *Interests:* music; wood work miniatures; writing; poetry. *Publ:* auth, From Here to There and Back Again, 2000; auth, Poems and Paintings, 2001; auth, The Red Painted House, 2002. *Dealer:* Cathedral St John the Divine New York NY 10025. *Mailing Add:* 1020 Park Ave New York NY 10028

EISENSTAT, JANE SPERRY
PAINTER
b New York, NY, Mar 2, 20. *Study:* Sculpture Studio Antonio Cortizas, 34-37; Penn Acad Fine Arts, 37-40. *Work:* William Penn Charter Sch & Pub schs & bldgs, Philadelphia; James Michner Mus, Doylestown, Pa. *Comn:* Murals & illus, William Penn Asn Art Proj, Pa, 38-40; Gimbel Brothers, Philadelphia, 40; murals, Santa Clara Asn League, 96. *Exhib:* Philadelphia Acad Fine Arts, 30-50; Juried Exhib, Art Inst Chicago, Detroit Inst Art & Rutgers Univ, Camden, NJ, 60-80; one-woman show, Philadelphia Art Alliance 50-80; Downtown Gallery, Delaware State Mus, Willington, Del, 80; Euphrate Gallery, DeAnza Col, Cupertino, Calif, 88; Triton Mus Bi Ann, Triton Mus Art, Santa Clara, Calif, 98. *Teaching:* Instr & asst prof painting, Philadelphia Col Art, 50-85; assoc prof painting, Moore Col Art, Philadelphia, 67-69; assoc prof drawing, Glassboro Univ, NJ, 72-82. *Awards:* Mary Smith Prize, 60 & Thornton Oakley Medal, Penn Acad Fine Arts, 70; Council Grant, State of NJ, 80; Penn Acad Fine Arts Fel. *Bibliog:* E T Wherry (co-illus), Wildflower Guide, Double Day Publ, 48; Charles LeClair (auth), Art of Watercolor, Prentis Hall, 85; Reproductions, Japanese Idea Art Mag, 92. *Mem:* Philadelphia WC Club. *Collection:* 1000 original Am & Eng illustrations from Darley Rowlandson to Sloan and Rockwell. *Publ:* Auth & illusr, The Challenge of AAB, Harper & Row, Almquist, Sweden, 67; coauth, Jessie W Smith-Step By Step Graphics, Dell Yearling, 87; Illustration In America, Graphis, 90. *Dealer:* Newman Gallery 1625 Walnut St Philadelphia Pa 19103. *Mailing Add:* 3639 Bryant St Palo Alto CA 94306

EISENSTEIN, (MR & MRS) JULIAN
COLLECTORS
Mr Eisenstein b Warrenton, Mo, Apr 3, 21. *Study:* Mr Eisenstein, Harvard Univ, BS, 41, MA, 42, PhD, 48. *Pos:* Mr Eisenstein, Nat res fel, Oxford, 52-53; physicist, Nat Bureau Standards, 57-66; pres & trustee, Washington Gallery Mod Art, 61-65. *Teaching:* Mr Eisenstein, instr, Univ Wis, 48-52; from asst prof to assoc prof, Pa State Univ, 53-57; prof, George Washington Univ, 66-. *Collection:* Contemporary art. *Mailing Add:* 82 Kalorama Cir NW Washington DC 20008-1616

EISENTRAGER, JAMES A
PAINTER
b Alvord, Iowa, Sept 3, 29. *Study:* Augustana Col, Sioux Falls, SDak, BA, 51; Univ Md in Wiesbaden, Ger, 52-53; Univ Northern Iowa, 55; Univ Iowa, Iowa City, MFA, 61; with Stewart Edie, Byron Burford & Mauricio Lasansky. *Work:* Univ Iowa, Iowa City; Sheldon Mem Art Gallery, Lincoln, Nebr; Millersville State Univ, Pa. *Exhib:* Ann Exhib, Springfield Art Mus, Mo, 64-72; one-man shows, Sheldon Mem Art Gallery, 66, Univ Del, Newark, 75 & Northern Ariz Univ Art Gallery, Flagstaff, 77; 31st Mid-Yr Show, Butler Inst Am Art, Youngstown, Ohio, 66; Mid-Am Exhib, William Rockhill Nelson Gallery of Art, Kansas City, Mo, 66 & 70; Mid-W Biennial, Joslyn Art Mus, Omaha, Nebr, 66 & 70; Ten Artists W of the Mississippi, Colorado Springs Fine Art Ctr, 67. *Teaching:* Prof painting, Univ Nebr-Lincoln, 61-; prof & lectr, Vail Summer Workshop, Colo, 71-76; vis prof art, Univ Colo, Boulder, summer 67. *Awards:* Purchase Award, May Show, Sioux City Art Ctr, Iowa, 63; Best Painting Purchase Award, Images on Paper Nat Competition, Springfield Art Asn, Ill, 73; Jesse Loomis Award, Waterloo Ann, Waterloo Munic Gallery, Iowa, 73. *Mem:* Mid-Am Col Art Asn; Col Art Asn. *Media:* Polymer, Oil. *Mailing Add:* Univ Nebr at Lincoln 7501 Whitestone Dr Lincoln NE 68506-1774

EISINGER, HARRY
PAINTER
b Berlin, Ger, Apr 23, 32; US citizen. *Study:* Calif Sch Fine Arts, San Francisco, 57-59; also with Ralph Putzker, Nathan Oliveira & Wayne Thiebaud. *Work:* Slides, Whitney Mus, NY. *Comn:* Drawings, Territorial Gazette, San Francisco, 59; posters, Marin Co Art Ctr, Calif, 60. *Exhib:* One-man shows, Panoras Gallery, NY, 73 & Gallery 84, 77; 32nd & 33rd Nat Audubon Exhibs, Nat Acad Galleries, 74 & 75 & Allied Artists Am Exhib, 75; Gallery 84, NY, 75 & 77. *Awards:* Spinaker Award, Sausalito Mayor, Calif, 60. *Bibliog:* Herb Caen (auth), article, San Francisco Chronicle, 60. *Mem:* Allied Artists Am; Audubon Artists. *Media:* Oil. *Dealer:* Gallery 84 30 West 57th St New York NY 10019. *Mailing Add:* 90 Eaton St Stratford CT 06497-3704

EISNER, CAROLE SWID
PAINTER, SCULPTOR
b New York, NY, Oct 30, 1937. *Study:* Syracuse Univ, AB, 58; Int Sch Photog, 76-78. *Work:* Guggenheim Mus & Knoll Int, NY; Syracuse Univ; Southeast Banking Corp, Miami; Northstar Reinsurance Co, Seattle; Nat Assocs Inc; and others. *Comn:* Set designs for four plays, Theater XII, NY, 78. *Exhib:* Art of the Northeast, Silvermine Guild, New Canaan, Conn, 83; Recent Acquisitions, Guggenheim Mus, NY, 86; Images Gallery, Norwalk, Conn, 86; Sculpture by Guild Artists, Silvermine, Conn, 88; New Am Art Invitational, London, 88; First Womens Bank, 88; David Findlay Galleries, NY, 90; Gallery Sagan, Tokyo, 92; Gallery Tanishima, Tokyo, 92; and

others. *Awards:* Rosenthal Award, Outdoor Sculpture, All New Eng Show, Silvermine, Conn, 78; Sculpture Award, Champion Int, 80; Finalist, Johnson Atelier Nat Sculpture Competition, Princeton, NJ, 80. *Bibliog:* William Pellicone (auth), article, Artspeak, 5/21/81; Jacqueline Moss (auth), article, Arts Mag, 10/84; Will Grant (auth), article, Artspeak, 7/1/86. *Mem:* Silvermine Guild Artists; Weston-Westport Arts Coun. *Media:* Acrylic; Welded Metal. *Publ:* Contribr, Contemporary Women Artists Calendar, Bo Tree Productions, 67 & 87; The Antiques J, 6/79 & 2/80. *Dealer:* David Findlay Gallery 984 Madison Ave New York NY 10021. *Mailing Add:* 1107 5th Ave New York NY 10028-0145

EISNER, ELLIOT WAYNE
EDUCATOR
b Chicago, Ill, Mar 10, 33. *Study:* Roosevelt Univ, BA; Ill Inst Technol, MS; Univ Chicago, MA, PhD. *Teaching:* Instr art educ, Ohio State Univ, 60-61; asst prof educ, Univ Chicago, 61-65; prof educ & art, Stanford Univ, 65-. *Awards:* Hon Dr, Univ Oslo, 86; Hon Dr, Hofstra Univ, 88; hon Dr, Maryland Inst Col Art, 89. *Mem:* Hon fel Nat Art Educ Asn (pres, 77-79); Am Educ Res Asn; Int Soc Educ Through Art (pres, 87-90); Am Educ Res Asn (pres, 92-93). *Res:* Children's artistic development; the uses of art criticism for the study and evaluation of educational practice. *Publ:* Auth, The Educational Imagination, MacMillan, 78; Cognition and Curriculum, Longmans, 82; The Art of Educational Evaluation, Falmer, 85; Qualitative Inquiry: The Continuing Debate (with Alan Peshkin), Teachers Col Press, 90; The Enlightened Eye: Qualitative Inquiry and the Enhancement of Educational Practice, Macmillan, 91. *Mailing Add:* Stanford Univ Sch of Educ Stanford CA 94305-3096

EISNER, GAIL LEON
PAINTER, SCULPTOR
b Detroit, Mich, Oct 17, 39. *Study:* Wayne State Univ, BFA, 66; Art Students League New York with Xavier Gonzalez, 83. *Work:* 47th Dist Ct, Farmington Hills, Mich; DOC, Pontiac, Mich; Resurrection Hosp; Sch Art Inst Chicago, Ill; Rabobank Netherland, Chicago, Ill. *Exhib:* XXI Ann Mich Artists, Art Ctr, Mt Clemins, 93; All Mich/All Media, Krasl Art Ctr, St Joseph, 93; Fantasy and Reality, Art Ctr Battle Creek, Mich, 93 & 94; Cheekwood Mus Art, Nashville, 94; 10,000 Plus Exhib, Art Inst Chicago, 94; Solo exhib, Sinclair Col, Dayton, Ohio, 95, Univ Mich, Ann Arbor, 97, Collin Co Col, Plano, Tex, 97, The Art Ctr, Mt Clemens, Mich, 98, Bus Relief Oils, Collin Co Coll, Plano, Tex, OK Harris, David Klein Gallery, Birmingham, Mich, Stark Weather Art Cen, Romeo, Mich, Shiawassee Art Cen, Owosso, Mich, Fantasy & Frolic, Art Cen Mt Clemens, Mich, Griswold Art Cen, Worthington, Ohio & Go Figure, Sinclair Col, Dayton, Ohio; The City Gallery, WM Costick Ctr, Famington Hills, Mich, 2004; Collages-City Halls Walls, Farmington Hills, Farmington, Mich, 2006. *Pos:* artist in residence, Farmington Area Arts Comn, 2005. *Awards:* Adrian Zahn Nat Arts Club Award, Pastel Soc Am, 87; Sara Winston Mem Award, Nat Asn Women Artists, 92 & Epstein Mem Award, 97; Epstein Mem Award, Nat Asn Women Artists, 97; Detroit Soc Women Sculptors & Painters Award of Merit; Sidney Dickinson Mem Award. *Bibliog:* Mary Klemic (auth), Dark side is bright, folded scenes open up, Eccentric, 2/95; David Grayson (auth), A new dimension on still life, Artists Mag, 12/96; Ellen Piligan (ed), Artist in focus, Metrop Woman Mag, 10/97; Cheryll Warren, Artist Exhibits Work at Shiawassee Art Cen, 3/2002; Rashun Rucker (auth), Folded Art, The Detroit News, 7/18/2004. *Mem:* Nat Asn Women Artists; New York Artist Equity Asn; Art Students League New York; Michigan Soc Painters & Sculptors. *Media:* Oil. *Publ:* Illusr, Making a Living as an Artist, Art Calendar, 92; Am Artists of the Bookplate, James P Keenan, 96, Cambridge Bookplate, Mass. *Dealer:* Outside the Lines 8410 Macomb St Ste 108 Grosse Ile MI 48138; Gwenda Jay Gallery N Wells Chicago IL. *Mailing Add:* 27600 Farmington Rd Ste 108 Farmington MI 48334

EISWERTH, BARRY
ARCHITECT, EDUCATOR
b Williamsport, Pa, Sept 16, 42. *Study:* Pa State Univ Park, BArch, 65. *Comn:* Archit works incl Children's Hosp, Philadelphia, bldgs. Philadelphia '76 Bicentennial, Philadelphia Bourse Bldg, Cypress Sq. Townhouse Complex Philadelphia (recipient Design award Old Philadelphia Devel Corp, Preservation Alliance award for Design Offices and Montgomery McCracken Warker & Rhodes), Constitutional Pavillion for We The People 200, Master Plan and New Classroom Admin Bldg Cairo Am. Col, Engineering and Computer Sci Campus-Am. Univ Cairo, Master Plan Am. Int Sch, Tel Aviv, Master Plan and New Classroom Bldgs, Am Embassy Sch, New Delhi, Master Plan and Design new campus Am, Sch of Warsaw, Brit Int Sch, Cairo; Master Plan and Expansion Am Sch Paris; design of hdqrs Arab Bank, Cairo. *Pos:* Assoc, H2L2 Archits/Planners, Philadelphia, 67-77, partner, 77-88, sr partner, 88-; pres H2L2 Design Co, 80-. *Teaching:* asst prof, archit design Drexel Univ, 75-81; mem fac, thesis advisor Philadelphia Col Art. *Awards:* Recipient awards for archit designs, Alumni Achievement award Pa State Univ, 2000. *Mem:* Am Inst of Archits; Pa Soc Archits; Nat Acad; Philadelphia Club. *Mailing Add:* H2L2 Architects/Planners 714 Market St 6th fl Philadelphia PA 19106-2372

EITNER, LORENZ E A
HISTORIAN, MUSEUM DIRECTOR
b Brno, Czech, Aug 27, 19; US citizen. *Study:* Duke Univ, AB, 40; Princeton Univ, MFA, 48, PhD, 52. *Collection Arranged:* Masterdrawings, Guggenheim Mus, New York & Univ Gallery, Univ Minn, 60; Gericault, Los Angeles Co Mus, Detroit Inst Art & Philadelphia Mus Art, 71-72; numerous art exhibs at Stanford Mus. *Pos:* Dir, Stanford Mus, 63-89. *Teaching:* Prof art, Univ Minn, 49-63; prof art & chmn dept, Stanford Univ, 63-89. *Awards:* Fullbright Fel, 52-52, Guggenheim Fel, 56-57; NEH grant, 79-81; Mitchell Prize, 84; Charles Rufus Morey Prize, 85; Gold Cross of Merit of the Rep of Austria, 89. *Mem:* Col Art Asn Am (vpres, dir, 56-71 & 76-). *Res:* European painting of the latter half of the eighteenth century and the beginning of the nineteenth century. *Publ:* Auth, Gericault, His Life and Work, Cornell Univ Press, 83; 19th Century European Painting, David to Cezanne, Harper-Collins, 87-88; Gericault, sa vie et son oeuvre, Paris, Gallimard, 91; La Peinture du XIXe Siecle en Europe, Paris, Hazan, 93; The Drawing Collection, Stanford Mus Art, Stanford, 93; French Paintings, Nat Gallery Art, Washington, DC, 2000. *Mailing Add:* 684 Mirada Ave Stanford CA 94305

EKDAHL, JANIS KAY
LIBRARIAN
b Topeka, Kans, Dec 7, 46. *Study:* Occidental Col, BA, 68; Columbia Univ, MLS, 69. *Pos:* Art librn, Vassar Col, Poughkeepsie, NY, 71-81; asst dir, Mus Mod Art Libr, New York, 81-94, actg dir, 94-96, chief libr adminr, 96-. *Mem:* Art Libr Soc North Am (Eastern regional rep, 81-83); Art Libr Soc New York; Col Art Asn; Am Libr Asn. *Interests:* Modern and contemporary art; sculpture; American art and architecture. *Publ:* Auth, American sculpture: A guide to information sources, Gale, 77. *Mailing Add:* 107 W 86th St New York NY 10024-3409

ELA, PATRICK H
DIRECTOR
b Oakland, Calif, June 20, 48. *Study:* Occidental Col, Los Angeles, BA, 70; Grad Sch Art Hist, 70-71; Anderson Sch Mgt, MBA, 73, Univ Calif, Los Angeles. *Pos:* Admin dir, Craft & Folk Art Mus, Los Angeles, 76-84, dir, 85-; int consult, 84-. *Teaching:* Prof, arts mgt, Calif State Univ Fullerton, 78-80; Instr, sociology of art world, Occidental Col, 80. *Mailing Add:* Craft & Folk Art Museum 5814 Wilshire Blvd Los Angeles CA 90036

ELDER, DAVID MORTON
SCULPTOR
b Windsor, Ont, July 3, 36; US citizen. *Study:* Wittenberg Univ, BA, 57; Ohio State Univ Grad Sch, MA, 61. *Work:* Denver Art Mus, Colo; Long Beach Art Mus, Calif. *Comn:* Sculpture (metal), Gloria Christi Chapel, Valparaiso Univ, 62, St Paul Lutheran Church, Glenn Bermie, Md, 63, Coconut Grove Ambassador Hotel, Los Angeles, 69 & Barnsdall Park, Los Angeles, 74; sculpture (resin), Pac Home Burbank, 74. *Exhib:* Long Beach Mus Art, 66, 70 & 71; Calif Sky Scape Show, Calif Col Arts & Crafts, Oakland, 69; Calif Landscape Show, La Jolla Mus Art, 69; San Francisco Centennial Show, De Young Mus, 71; Last Plastics Show, Calif Inst Arts, Valencia, 72. *Teaching:* Asst prof sculpture, Calif State Univ, Los Angeles, 68-71; prof sculpture, Calif State Univ, Northridge, 71-, chmn dept 3-d art, formerly assoc dean sch arts, formerly, prof, currently. *Awards:* Fourth Ann Long Beach Mus First Prize, 66; Purchase Award Comn, Southwestern Col, 67; Artist of the Year, Pasadena Arts Coun, 71. *Media:* Bronze, Polyester Resin. *Dealer:* Orlando Gallery 17037 Ventura Blvd Encino CA 91316. *Mailing Add:* Dept Art 3-D Media Calif State Univ 18111 Nordhoff St Northridge CA 91330-8300

ELDER, GENE WESLEY
COLLAGE ARTIST, WRITER
b San Antonio, Tex, Jul 4, 49. *Study:* Trinity Univ, BA, 73; San Antonio Mus Contemp Art, MFA, 92. *Work:* San Antonio Mus Art, Tex; Bonham Exchange, San Antonio, Tex; Alamo Videos, San Antonio, Tex. *Comn:* Time Capsule 2181AD, San Antonio Mus Art, Tex, 84. *Exhib:* Time Capsule, San Antonio Mus Modern Art, San Antonio, Tex, 76. *Collection Arranged:* Power to the Pulp, Artist made paper, 87. *Pos:* Property Mgr, Blue Star Art Complex, 85-93; cur, San Antonio Mus Contemp Art, 87-2005; archives dir, Happy Found, 88-2005. *Teaching:* instr, handmade paper, Southwest Craft Ctr, 85-93. *Mem:* Blue Star Art Ctr (bd mem, 88-90); Knights of Isosceles Triangle (green knight, 2000-2005). *Media:* Collage, found objects. *Publ:* article, Wall Street J, 8/20/99; contribr, Voices of Art, David Freeman, 99-2003; Auth, Murder by Collage with Found Object, Artist Edition, 2000; contribr, MUD Underground, Covert Internet, 2000-2005. *Dealer:* Joan Grona Gallery 116 Blue Star San Antonio TX 78210. *Mailing Add:* 411 Bonham San Antonio TX 78205

ELDER, R BRUCE
FILMMAKER, CRITIC
b Hawkesbury, Ont, June 12, 1947. *Study:* McMaster Univ, Hamilton, Can, BA(hons), 69; Univ Toronto, Can, MA, 70; Ryerson Polytechnic Inst, Toronto, BAppArt, 72-76; Univ Film Studies Ctr, Amherst, Mass, with Ed Emshwiller, Shirley Clarke & Standish Lawder, summers 73-75; modern dance with members of Merce Cunningham Co; political theology of language, with Jacques Derrida, summer 86, courses in mathematics & computer prog, Ryerson Polytech Univ & York Univ, 87-98. *Work:* Numerous prints of films in public lending libraries, schools & universities. *Exhib:* The Art of Worldly Wisdom, Mus Mod Art, NY, 81; retrospectives, Art Gallery Ont, Toronto, 85 & La Cinematheque Quebecoise, Montreal, 86, Can, Anthology Film Archives, 88 & 95, Senzatitolo, Trento, Italy, 96, Images 97, Toronto & Antechamber, Regina, 2000; Illuminated Texts, Mus Mod Art, NY, 86; Toronto Festival of Festivals, 88 & 91; Museo Reina Sofia, Madrid, 90; Exultations, George Eastman House, 94; Et Ressurrectus Est, Stadt Mus, Munich, 95; Anthology Film Archives, NY & Festival International Nouveau Cinema, Montreal, 2000; Cinematheque Ontario, Toronto, 2003; Eros & Wonder, Cinema Nouvelles Ecritures, Paris, 2005; Crack, Brutal, Grief, Festival des Toutes les Cinema, Paris, 2005 & Winnipeg Cinematheque, 2006; and numerous solo shows in Europe, US & Can. *Collection Arranged:* The Photographic Image (auth, catalog), Toronto World Film Festival, 84; Film from Three Continents, Art Gallery Ont, 86; Osnabruck Experimental Media Festival, 88; Int Experimental Film Cong, Toronto, 89; and others. *Pos:* Independent critic aesthet, photog & film, 78-; independent cur avant-garde film, 80-. *Teaching:* Prof human figure & film, Ryerson Polytechnic Univ, Toronto, Can, 72-; dir, grad prog communications & culture, Ryerson Polytechnic Univ; adj prof, Grad Prog Film & Video, York Univ, 98. *Awards:* Best Experimental

Film, Can Film Awards Found, 76; Best Independent Film, Los Angeles Film Critics Asn, 81; Study Tour Award, Auswartiges Amt, Govt Fed Repub Ger, 86; New Media Initiative Grant, Can Coun INSERC, 2003; Ryerson Univ Research Ch, 2004; SSHRC Creation Fine Arts Grant, 2004. *Bibliog:* Lianne McLarty (auth), The films of R Bruce Elder, Take Two, Irwin Publ, 84; Loretta Czernis (auth), Elder: Artaud after Telsat, Can J Political & Social Theory, Vol X, No 1-2, 86; Bart Testa (auth), monograph, Bruce Elder Anthology, Film Archives, 88; Aysegul Koc (auth), Interview with R. Bruce Elder, Cineaction, No 61, 2003; Brett Kashmere (auth), R. Bruce Elder: In the Realm of Mystery & Wonder, Take One, Vol 12, No 45, 2004. *Mem:* Film Studies Asn Can (exec comt, 76 & 83-85); Forth Interest Group; Toronto Semiotic Circle. *Res:* Art and technology; Canadian film, especially the avant-garde in its philosophical context; aesthetics; international avant-garde cinema; the image of the body. *Publ:* Auth, Image and Identity Reflections on Canadian Film and Culture, WLU Press; The Body in Film, Art Gallery Ont, 89; On Sound, Sound Recording, Making Music of Recorded Sound, A dialogue between Bruce Elder and Michael Snow, the Michael Snow Prog, Art Gallery Ont, 94; A Body of Vision: Representations of the Body in Recent Film and Poetry, WLU Press, 98; The Films of Stan Brackhage in the American Tradition of Ezra Pound, Gertrude Stein and Charlie Olson, 98; plus many others. *Dealer:* Canadian Filmmakers Distribution Ctr 37 Hanna Suite 220 Toronto ON Can M6K 1W8; New York Film-makers' Cooperative Clock Tower Gallery 13th Fl 108 Leonard St New York NY 10013. *Mailing Add:* 692 St Clarens Ave 5 Toronto ON M6H 3X1 Canada

ELDERFIELD, JOHN
HISTORIAN, CURATOR
b Yorkshire, Eng, Apr 25, 43. *Study:* Univ Leeds, BA & MPhil; Courtauld Inst Art, Univ London, PhD. *Hon Degrees:* Univ Leeds, Hon Dr Letters, 2006. *Collection Arranged:* Morris Louis (auth, catalog), London Arts Coun Gt Brit, 74; The Wild Beasts: Fauvism and Its Affinities (auth, catalog), 76, European Paintings from Swiss Collections: Post-Impressionism to World War II (auth, catalog), 76, Matisse in the Collection of the Museum of Modern Art (auth, catalog), 78, The Masterworks of Edvard Munch (auth, catalog), 79 & New Work on Paper (auth, catalog), 81, Mus Mod Art, NYk; Contrasts of Form: Geometric Abstract Art 1910-1980, 85-86; The Heroic Century: The Mus of Mod Art Masterpieces, 200 Paintings & Sculptures, Mus Fine Arts, Houston, Tex, 2003-2004; rev ed, Das MoMA in Berlin, Neue Nationalgalerie, Berlin, 2004; Painting & Sculpture: Inaugural Installation, 2004-; Manet & the Execution of Maximillian, 2006; and many others. *Pos:* Harkness fel, Yale Univ, New Haven, Conn, 70-72; Guggenheim Found Fel, 72-73; contrib ed, Artforum, 72-74 & Studio Int Mag, 73-75; cur painting & sculpture, Mus Mod Art, NY, 75-93, dir dept drawings, 79-93, chief cur at large, 93-2003, dep dir curatorial affairs, 95-98; Chief cur painting & sculpture dept, Mus of Modern Art, 2003-. *Teaching:* Lectr hist art, Winchester Sch of Art, Eng, 66-70; instr art hist, Univ Leeds, Eng, 73-75; adj prof, Inst Fine Arts, New York Univ, 95-. *Awards:* Guggenheim Fel, 72-73; Mitchell Prize, 86; Walter Neurath Award, 95; Chevalier des Arts et Lettres, Fr Govt, 89; 100 Most Influential People of the Year, Time Magazine, 2005; Officier dans l'Ordre des Arts et des Lettres, 2006. *Bibliog:* Hugo Ball (auth), The Flight from Time--A Dada Diary, viking, 75. *Mem:* Int Asn Art Critics; Col Art Asn; Fel Royal Soc Arts. *Res:* Twentieth century art. *Publ:* Auth, The Cutouts of Henri Matisse, Braziller, 78; Drawings of Richard Diebenkorn, 88; Helen Frakenthaler, 88; coauth, Matisse in Morocco, A Retrospective, 92; coauth, Modern Starts: People, Places, Things, Mus Modern Art, NY, 99; coauth, Matisse.Picasso, Mus Modern Art, NY, 2002; coauth, Manet & the Execution of Maximillian, Mus Mod Art, NY, 2006. *Mailing Add:* c/o Mus Mod Art 11 W 53rd St New York NY 10019

ELDREDGE, BRUCE B
MUSEUM DIRECTOR, ADMINISTRATOR
b Van Wert, Ohio, July 1, 52. *Study:* Ohio Wesleyan Univ, Delaware, BA, 74; Tex Tech Univ, Lubbock, MA(mus admin), 76; State Univ Albany, NY, 80-81. *Pos:* Dir, Geneva Hist Soc, 76-78, Schenectady Mus, 78-80, Frederic Remington Art Mus, Ogdensburg, NY, 81-84, Muskegon Mus Art, Mich, 84-87, Tucson Mus Art, Ariz, 87-90, Portsmouth Mus, Va, 91-92, Stark Art Mus, Tex, 92-96 & Mus Horse, NMex, 96; coordr arts & humanities, Capitol Dist Humanities Prog, State Univ Albany, NY, 80-81; chmn, Art Comn, Ruidoso, NMex, 96-98; ceo, exec dir, NW Mus Arts & Cult, current bd trustee, Group Health, 2006-. *Mem:* Am Asn Mus; Tex Asn Mus; NMex Mus Asn; Asn Youth Mus (treas, 92-93). *Publ:* Ed, Sourcebook, Tex Asn Mus, 93-96. *Mailing Add:* 2316 W First Ave Spokane WA 99204

ELDREDGE, CHARLES C, III
HISTORIAN
b Boston, Mass, Apr 12, 44. *Study:* Amherst Col, BA, 66; Univ Minn, PhD, 71; Phi Beta Kappa. *Collection Arranged:* Gene Swenson: Retrospective for a Critic (contribr & ed, catalog), 71; Marsden Hartley Lithographs & Related Works (auth, catalog), 72; The Arcadian Landscape: Nineteenth Century Am Painters in Italy (coauth & ed, catalog), 72; John Ward Lockwood, 1894-1963 (auth, catalog), 74; Am Imagination & Symbolist Painting (auth, catalog), 79; Charles Walter Stetson: Color and Fantasy (auth, catalog), 82; Helen Foresman Spencer Mus Art, Univ Kans, Lawrence; Art in New Mexico, 1900-1945 (co-auth, book), Nat Mus Am Art, 86; Pacific Parallels: Artists and The Landscape In New Zealand (auth, catalog), NZ-US Arts Found, 91; Georgia O'Keeffe: Am & Modern, 93; Tales from the Easel: Am Narrative Paintings from Southeastern Mus, Circa 1800-1950 (auth, catalog), 2004. *Pos:* Cur asst, Minn Hist Soc, St Paul, 66-68; Cur collections, Univ Kans Mus Art, Lawrence, 70-71, dir & chief cur, Helen Foresman Spencer Mus Art (formerly Univ Kans Mus Art), 71-82; mem ed bd, Mid-Continent Am Studies Asn, 71-77; assoc ed, Art J, 79-81; mem ed bd, American Art, 87-; dir, Nat Mus Am Art, 82-88; trustee, Amherst Col, 87-93; prof am art, Hall distinguished, Univ Kans, 88-; bd trustees, Amon Carter Mus, 2003-06; dir, Georgia O'Keeffe Found, 89-95; Smithsonian res assoc, 88-. *Teaching:* Prof art hist, Univ Kans, 70-82 & 88-; vis fel, Univ Aukland, 93; vis prof, Buffalo Bill Hist Ctr, Cody, Wyo, 96. *Awards:* Smithsonian Fel, 79 & 95; Fulbright Scholar-New Zealand, 83; Outstanding Achievement Award, Univ Minn, Minneapolis, 86; WT Kemper Fel for Teaching, excellence award, 2003. *Bibliog:* Marsden Hartley (auth), Lithographs and Related Works, 72; Ward Lockwood (auth), 1894-1963, 1974, American Imagination and Symbolist Painting, 79. *Mem:* Asn Art Mus Dirs (treas, 81-82, trustee, 87-88, hon mem, 90-); Col Art Asn; Mid-Continent Am Studies Asn; Am Studies Assoc; Authors Guild. *Res:* American art. *Publ:* contribr, Georgia O'Keeffe: Natural Issues 1918-1924, Williams Col; Georgia O'Keeffe, Abrams, 91; Georgia O'Keeffe, American and Modern, Yale, 93; Life Cycles: The Charles E Burchfield Collection, Buffalo State Col, 96; Reflections on Nature: Small Paintings by Arthur Dove 1942-43, AFA, 97; Tales from the Easel: American Narrative Paintings circa 1800-1950, Ga, 2004. *Mailing Add:* Univ Kans Dept Art Hist 209 Spencer Mus Art 1301 Mississippi St Lawrence KS 66045-0001

ELDREDGE, MARY AGNES
SCULPTOR
b Hartford, Conn, Jan 21, 42. *Study:* Vassar Col, with Concetta Scaravaglione & Juan Nickford, BA; Pius XII Inst, Florence, Italy, with Josef Gudics, MFA. *Work:* Hood Mus Art, Dartmouth Col. *Comn:* Mary the Mother of us All, Our Lady of the Snows Curch, Woodstock, Vt, 90; Mary and Child, Christ the King Cath Community, Las Vegas, Nev, 91; Our Lady of Peace, St Joseph and Christ Child, Blessed Scarament Church, Greenfield, Mass, 92-97; Processional Candlesticks, Paschal Candlestand, St Vincent Ferrer Church, NY City, 97 & 2001; Processional Cross, SS Mary and Joseph, Presentation Relief, Church of Presentation, Stockton, Calif, 2001-03. *Exhib:* Nat Arts Club Religous Art Exhib, NY, 66; Acad Artists Asn Nat Exhib, Springfield, Mass, 67; Modern Art and the Religious Experience, Fifth Ave Presby Church, NY, 68; 6th Biennial Nat Religious Art Exhib, Cranbrook Acad Art, 69; 42nd Nat Interfaith Conf Relig, Art and Archit, Chicago, 81; 42nd Nat Fall Exhib, Southern Vt Art Ctr, Manchester, 98. *Pos:* Dir, Springfield Art & Hist Soc, Vt, 88-90. *Awards:* 16th Ann Bldg Awards Prog Award of Excellence, Staten Island Chamber Com, 77; Miller Award Best Sculpture, Southern Vt Art Ctr, 90; Bene Award, Permanent Visual Arts, Modern Liturgy, 92; and others. *Bibliog:* Virginia Watson-Jones (auth), Contemporary American Women Sculptors, Oryx Press, 86. *Media:* Copper, Stone, Wood. *Dealer:* Garden Gallery Rtell Londonberry Vt 05148; Vermont Fine Art Gallery Gale Farm Center 1880 Mountain Rd #3 Stowe Vt 05672. *Mailing Add:* 408 Parker Hill Rd Springfield VT 05156

ELECTROS See Vekris, Babis A

EL HANANI, JACOB
PAINTER
b Casablanca, Morocco, Mar 14, 47. *Study:* Aveni Sch Arts, Tel Aviv, Israel, 66-69; Ecoles des Beaux Arts, Paris, 69-71. *Work:* Guggenheim Mus, Mus Mod Art, Metrop Mus Art, NY; Centre Georges Pompidou, Paris, France; Nat Gallery Art, Washington, DC. *Exhib:* New Acquistions, Guggenheim Mus, NY, 77; Constructivism and the Geometric Tradition, Albright Knox Gallery, 77; Micrography, Israel Mus, Jerusalem, 81; Printing and Writing, Cooper-Hewitt Mus, NY, 82; New Acquisitions, Hirshhorn Mus, Washington, DC, 86; Trends in Geometric Abstract Art, Tel Aviv Mus, 87. *Awards:* Louis Comfort Tiffany Found Award, 97. *Media:* Ink. *Dealer:* Yoshii Gallery 20 W 57th St New York NY 10019. *Mailing Add:* 473 Broadway New York NY 10013

ELIAS, SHEILA
PAINTER
b Chicago, Ill. *Study:* Art Inst Chicago, 60-68; Columbus Col Art & Design, BFA, 74; Calif State Univ, Northridge, MA, 78. *Work:* Brooklyn Mus, NY; Chase Manhattan Bank, NY; First Los Angeles Bank; Kunsan Contemp Mus, Korea; Laguna Beach Mus Art, Calif. *Comn:* Jeffries Residence, comn by Pasqualle Vazzana, Laguna, Calif, 74; Hilton Hotel, Barbara Dorn & Assoc, Newark, Calif, 83; Exec Life Corp, Los Angeles Co Mus Art Rental & Sales, 84; Spago Restaurant, comn by Wolfgang Puck & Barbara Lazaroff, Tokyo, Japan, 85; Segerstrom Residence, Balboa, Calif, 85. *Exhib:* Liberty: The Official Exhib Commemorating the Centenary of the Statue of Liberty, NY Pub Libr & Louvre, Institude des Decoratifs, Paris, France, 86; The Embellishment of the Statue of Liberty, Cooper-Hewitt Mus, NY, 86; solo exhibs, New Eng Ctr Contemp Art, Capital Bank, Miami, 94, Metro Dade Cult Resource Ctr, Miami, 94, Soho West Gallery, Hollywood, Calif, 95, Barnard Biderman & Worth Gallery, NY, 96, Lowe Mus, Univ Miami, Fla, 97, Edison Comm Col, Ft Myers, 98 & Art & Public Places, Orlando, 98; Kim Foster Gallery, NY, 2001; Bass Mus, Miami Beach, 2002; Michelle Rosenfeld Gallery, NY, 2002. *Awards:* Metro Art Int Medal, New York, 86; Women of Yr, CofC, Tarzana, Calif, 86. *Bibliog:* Harold Mass (auth), Art explosion, Miami Herald, 4/30/92; Vani Chetty (auth), Channel mag, 1999. *Mem:* Artists Equity (mem bd dirs, 81); Col Art Asn; Women's Caucus Art. *Media:* Miscellaneous. *Publ:* Marlena Donohue (auth), Cover Mag, 4/96 & Art News, 10/02. *Dealer:* Michelle Rosenfeld Gallery 16 East 79. *Mailing Add:* 1510 NE 130 St Miami FL 33161

ELIASON, BIRDELL
PAINTER, ILLUSTRATOR
b Molalla, Ore. *Study:* Painting Holidays, with John Pellew, 85-88; Portrait Inst, with John Howard Sanden, 87; Advertising Art Sch, Portland, Ore, 3 years; Study with Tony Van Hasslet, outdoor painting, 1990-91. *Hon Degrees:* Hon member Natl Portrait Soc. *Work:* Village Hall, Hist Soc & Mt Prospect Pub Libr, Mt Prospect, Ill; Arthur's Int, Las Vegas; Nat Women's Libr, Washington, DC, 1990s; mural, Church of Holy Trinity, Anapro, Mex, 2001-2002, Mission Anapra Mex, 2001-2006. *Comn:* Mural, Dr Vanoucek, Mt Prospect, Ill, 76; mural, Mt Prospect Hist Soc, Ill, 82; painting We The People, Dolores Haugh, Mt Prospect Hist Soc, 97; church bulls, St

Paul's Lutheran Church, 1980-2002. *Exhib:* Gold Coast Art Fair, Chicago's Biggest Art Show, 80-92; Am Indians, Prism Gallery, Evanston, Ill, 92; Art Originale, Lutheran Gen Hosp, Park Ridge, Ill, 92; one-man show, Palatine Gallery, Ill, 94; St Johns Uhlein-Peter Gallery, Milwaukee, 95. *Collection Arranged:* Mt Prospect Village Hall; Zion Lutheran Church, Chicago; mural, orthodontist office, Mt Prospect. *Pos:* art dir, artist in residence, Mt Prospect Hist Soc. *Teaching:* Instr religious symbols, Zion Lutheran Sch, Chicago, 67-69, Presbyterian Church, Mt Prospect, Ill, 80-81; handicapped & stroke victims, Americana Health Care Ctr, Arlington Heights, Ill, 79-80. *Awards:* Statue of Victory Cult World Art, Cremona, Italy, 85; Grand Prize, US Bicentennial Comn, 86; Premio Milano Award, Italy, 88; Grand Prize, We the People Award; Outstanding Woman of the 20th Century, Am Biog Inst; 100 Top Educator, Cambridge, Eng, 2005. *Bibliog:* Nicolo Panepinto (auth), Academia Italia Delle Artie Del Lavoro, Salsomaggiore Terme, Italy, 80; Internat Encyclopedia Dictionary of Modern Contemporary Art, 2001-2002. *Mem:* Munic Art League Chicago; Oil Painters Am; Mt Prospect Hist Soc; Arlington Heights Art League; Troutdale Ore Hist Soc; Ore Hist Soc; Mt Prospect Hist Soc. *Media:* Oil, Watercolor. *Res:* Am Indians in Oreg 1936-40, Wisc Indians, Idaho & other cliff dwellers, Indian Paintings; Oregon Historical Soc, Portland, OR. *Interests:* sketching outdoors. *Collection:* Skip Farley (Mt Prospect mayor); St Paul's Ch. *Publ:* Illusr, Around the Home, Rand McNally Co, 57; Artists USA, 85; Where Town & Country Meet, Mt Prospect Hist Soc, 92; The Story of a Community Mt Prospect, Mt Prospect Hist Soc, 92-94; contrib paintings Ency of Living Artists 1989-2001. *Dealer:* Marvin Arthur Arthur's Internat Las Vegas NV. *Mailing Add:* 12 N Owen St Mount Prospect IL 60056-2532

ELIASOPH, PHILIP
HISTORIAN, CRITIC, CONSULTANT
b New York, NY, 51. *Study:* Adelphi Univ, BA, 72; State Univ NY, Binghamton, MA, 75, PhD, 79, study with Kenneth C Lindsay. *Collection Arranged:* Paul Cadmus: Yesterday and Today (auth, catalog), Miami Univ & traveling, 81; Robert Vickrey: Lyrical Realist, ACA Galleries & traveling, 82; Stevan Dohanos: Images of America, New Britain Mus Am Art, 85; American Art: Past & Present, Kennedy Galleries, 88; Mark Balma: Drawing From Tradition, Electa, Milan, 93. *Pos:* Educ consul, Art of the Western World (TV ser), Pub Broadcasting System, 87-; Conn ed, Art New England (mo) 84-87; alternate mem & art adv comt, Stamford, Conn, Pub Arts, 86-88. *Teaching:* From instr to prof art hist & art criticism, Fairfield Univ, Conn, 75-, chmn fine arts dept, 84-89; dir, Walsh Art Gallery, Quick Ctr Arts, 89-97. *Awards:* Fac Res Grant, Fairfield Univ, 84; CINE Golden Eagle (Robert Vickrey: Lyrical Realist), Int Film Jury, 86. *Mem:* Col Art Asn Am; Int Asn Art Critics; New Eng Appraisers Asn. *Res:* 20th century American art; Italian renaissance painting; propaganda; art & politics; mass media & criticism; American figurative painting. *Publ:* Producer, Robert Vickrey: Lyrical Realist and Steven Dohanos: Images of America (doc films), 86; Valor & Vainglory: French Military Art, Forbes Mag Collection, 87; Mastering egg tempera-techniques of Robert Vickrey, Artist's Mag, 11/87; co-auth, Art of the Western World Faculty Guide, Pub Broadcasting System & Annenberg Found, 89; Robert Cottingham: Rolling Stock Series (exhib catalog), Harcourt's Contemp Art, San Francisco, 91; contribr, Am Arts Quarterly, Am Art Jour, Smithsonian, Antiques & Fine Art Magazine, 2000-. *Mailing Add:* c/o Dept Visual & Performing Arts Fairfield Univ Fairfield CT 06430

ELIOT, LUCY CARTER
PAINTER
b New York, NY. *Study:* Vassar Col, BA; Art Students League with Bridgman, Brackman, Raphael Soyer & Kantor; Columbia Univ, with Ralph Mayer; studied with William Von Schlegell, Ogunquit, Maine. *Work:* Rochester Mem Art Gallery, NY; Munson-Williams-Proctor Inst, Utica, NY. *Exhib:* Pa Acad Fine Arts, Philadelphia, 46, 48-50, 52 & 54; Va Biennial, 48; Corcoran Biennial, Washington, DC, 47 & 51; Ringling Bros Mus, Sarasota, Fla, 58; Nat Acad Design, NY, 71, 78 & 90; Butler Inst, Youngstown, Ohio, 65, 67, 69, 70, 72, 74 & 81; Upland Idyll, Everson Mus, Syracuse, NY, 76; Cooperstown Art Asn, 78, 81 & 90. *Pos:* Mem bd, Artists' Tech Res Inst, 75-79. *Teaching:* Instr painting & drawing, Dept Occupational Therapy, Bronx Vet Hosp, NY, 50-52. *Awards:* Moore-Greenblatt Mem Award, Nat Asn Women Artists, 93; Michael M Engel Mem Award, 94; Robert Philipp Mem Award, 95. *Mem:* Artists Equity Asn; Audubon Artists; Am Soc Contemp Artists; Nat Asn Women Artists; NY Soc Women Artists; and others. *Media:* Oil, Casein. *Mailing Add:* 131 E 66th St New York NY 10021

ELKINS, LANE
EDUCATOR, CERAMIST
b McDonald Co, Mo, Mar 26, 25. *Study:* Southwest Mo State Col, BSEd(with hon), 49; Columbia Univ, MAFA & FAEd, 50; with Marquerite Wildenhain, 56 & 63; Cranbrook Acad Art, MFA, 62. *Work:* Springfield Art Mus, Mo. *Comn:* Pottery and jewelry comns for individuals. *Exhib:* Springfield Art Mus Ann Regional Show, 53-72; Wichita Art Asn Galleries Decorative Arts & Ceramics Exhib, 60 & 62; Ann Drawing & Sculpture Show, Ball State Univ Art Gallery, 63; Am Jewelry Today, Ala Mus Fine Arts, 64; Am Craftsmen Show, Smithsonian Inst, 70. *Teaching:* Prof ceramics, Southwest Mo State Univ, 50-82, prof art, 62-87; retired. *Awards:* Protective Image (cast bronze) Award, Edmund F Ball, Nat Sculpture Show, 63. *Mem:* Am Craftsman Coun; Mo Craftsman Coun. *Media:* Clay, Metals. *Publ:* Contribr, Walker Art Quart, spec issue, 59. *Mailing Add:* 29 Swiss Ct Florissant CO 80816

ELKINS, TONI MARCUS
PAINTER, DESIGNER
b Tifton, Ga, Feb 22, 46. *Study:* Boston Univ, 65-66; Univ Ga, ABJ, 68; Columbia Col, 78-80. *Work:* Springfield Art Mus, Mo; Randolph Macon Woman's Col, Lynchburg, Va; Richland NE High Sch; Clemson Univ; Asheville Mus Art, NC; Cent Carolina Community Found, Columbia, SC. *Exhib:* Rocky Mountain Nat, Foothills Art Ctr, Golden, Colo, 83; Watercolor West, 84-2000; San Diego Watercolor Soc Int, 84 & 85-2000; SC State Mus traveling exhib, 85; Nat Watercolor Soc, Brae, Calif; Watercolor USA Honor Soc, Springfield, Mo; Eastern Wash Watercolor Soc, 2000; Northeast Watecolor Soc, NY, 2000. *Collection Arranged:* SC First Miniature Show (auth, catalog), Cameo Gallery, 80; Southern Watercolor's 24th Ann, McKissick Mus, 2001. *Pos:* Supt fine arts, SC State Fair; exec dir, SC Crafts Asn, 86-96; chmn, Sculpture Pub Places, 95-97; Wine Festival adv Coun, Columbia, SC. *Awards:* President's Award, Soc Watercolor Painters, Joshua, Tex, 92; Meyer Hardware Award, Rocky Mountain Nat, Golden, Colo, 92; Howard B Smith Award, SC Watercolor Ann, Marion, 92; John Richeson Award, San Diego Watercolor Soc, Linda Doll Purchase Award, Golden Artists Colors Merit Award, 2000; Elizabeth O'Neill Verner Award for Contribn to SC Art, 99; Toni Milyard REMAX Merit Award, Western Colo Watercolor Soc, 2000; 2000 Women of Distinction Award, Congaree Girl Scouts, Inc, 2000. *Mem:* Cult Coun Richland & Lexington Counties; Southeastern Arts & Crafts Expos (adv bd coun); Cent Carolina Community Found; SC Watercolor Soc (pres 2005-06). *Media:* Watercolor, Photograph; Mixed Media. *Publ:* Contribr, Miles Batl's Complete Guide to Creative Watercolor; Les Krantz (auth), The New York Art Rev, 89; Community Tour Mag (cover), SC Arts Comn, 92; Lake Murray Mag, 8/2006; and others. *Dealer:* City Art 1224 Lincoln St Columbia SC 29201. *Mailing Add:* 1511 Adger Rd Columbia SC 29205-1407

ELLENZWEIG, ALLEN BRUCE
WRITER, CRITIC
b New York, NY, Nov 4, 50. *Study:* Cooper Union, with Dore Ashton, BFA, 1973; New York Univ, MFA (dramatic writing), 1985. *Collection Arranged:* Private Myths: Unearthings of Contemporary Art (auth, catalog), Queens Mus, NY, 78; Visual Diaries: A Personal Use of Words and Images (auth, catalog), Alex Rosenberg Gallery, 80; Prejudice & Pride: The New York City Lesbian & Gay Community, World War II-Present (auth, catalog), Tweed Gallery, City Hall, New York, 88. *Pos:* Contrib ed, Arts Mag, NY, 1974-79; contrib reviewer, Art Am, 1980-86; lectr & panelist, The History of Homoerotic Themes in Photography, Ethics & Evidence in Lesbian & Gay Studies, Ctr for Lesbian & Gay Studies, City Univ NY Grad Ctr, 1989; moderator & panelist, The Homoerotic at Risk: Censorship of Gay Sensibility in Photography, 4th Ann Lesbian, Bisexual & Gay Studies Conf, Harvard Univ, 1990; Queering the Movies, Outwrite, 6th Ann Gay & Lesbian Writers Conf, 1996; NY corresp, PASSION: Mag of Paris, 1983-85, contrib ed, 1985-85; Paris corresp, NY Native, 1985; contrib writer, critic, Gay & Lesbian Rev Worldwide, 1995-; pres, bd of trustees, The Robert Giard Found, 2003-. *Teaching:* part-time lectr expository writing, Rutgers Univ, 1999-2000; educator guide, NY Hist Soc, Fall 2004. *Awards:* Writer in residence, Michael Karolyi Mem Found, Vence, France, 72 & Edward Albee Found, Montauk, NY, 79; Writing Fel, Vt Studio Ctr, 98; Writing fel, Vt Studio Ctr, 2003. *Bibliog:* John Russell (auth), When art imitates anthropology, 4/9/1978 & Grace Glueck (auth), Visual diaries, 2/22/1980, NY Times; Robert Julian (auth), Bodies of Evidence, Bay Area Reporter, 10/15/1992; Julian Bell (auth), Decency and Delusion, Times Literary Supplement, 3/19/1993. *Mem:* Nat Writers Union; Publishing Triangle. *Res:* Male homoerotic themes throughout the history of photography. *Publ:* Auth, The Homoerotic Photograph: Male Images from Durieu/Delacroix to Mapplethorpe, Columbia Univ Press, 1992; Anne Frank: The Secret Annex and the Closet, Response: Contemporary Jewish Rev, winter/spring 1997; Picturing the Homoerotic, in: Queer Representations, NYU Press, 1997; The Athena Galleria, in: Men on Men 7, Dutton/Signet, 1998; A Fine Point, in: Kosher Meat, Sherman Asher Publ, 2000. *Mailing Add:* 200 W 15th St New York NY 10011

ELLER, EVELYN ELLER ROSENBAUM
COLLAGE AND BOOK ARTIST, PAINTER
b New York, NY, Apr 17, 33. *Study:* Art Students League, NY, with Morris Kantor & W Barnet, 51-54; Acad De Belle Arte, Rome Italy, 54-55; Sch for Visual Arts, New York, 89. *Work:* Indianapolis Mus Fine Art, Ind; Nat Mus Women Arts, Washington, DC; Libr Mus Mod Art, NY; King St Stephens Mus, Hungary; Libr Brooklyn Mus, NY; Yale Univ, Arts of the Book Collection; Univ Western Mich; Newark Public Libr, NJ; Tyler Mus of Art, Tex Univ of Vt, UCLA, Calif; Queens Mus, NY; Mus of the City, NY; Univ Calif, Los Angeles. *Exhib:* Juried Ann, Queens Mus, NY, 74-75 & 89; Works on Paper, Brooklyn Mus, NY, 75; Int Book Exhib, King St Stephens Mus, Hungary, 87, 94, 2000 & 2006; Book as Art IV, Nat Mus Women Arts, Washington, 91 & 96; Artist Book, Islip Art Mus, Long Island, NY, 91; My Vision, Sumner Sch Mus, Washington, 91; Corcoran Gallery Art, Washington, 93, 97 & 99; Art of the Book, Univ Indianapolis, Indiana, 2002; Flushing Town Hall Biennial, 2002; and others; Krasdale Gallery, NY, 2003; New York City Health & Hospital Corp, 2003; Ctr for Book Arts, NY, 2004; Queens Mus, 2005-2006; Brooklyn Public Library, 2006. *Pos:* Admin asst, Art Sch Mus Mod Art, New York, 58-59. *Teaching:* Workshop & sem instr, Alliance Queens Artists, NY, 89-99. *Awards:* Juror Award, Small Works Ann, 83; Showcase Award, Queens Borough Pub Libr, New York, 85; Lever House Lobby Gallery Award, New York, 96. *Bibliog:* John Arthur Shanks (auth), Evelyn Eller, techniques of landscapes collage, Artists Mag, 4/84; John & Joan Digby (auth), The Collage Handbook, Thames & Hudson, 85; B Ommerman (auth), Around Town, Newsday, 4/7/91; Shreen La Plantz (auth), The Art and Craft of Handmade Book, Lark, 2001; Orí Soltes (auth), Fixing the World, Brandies Univ Press, 2002; Covers of 4 jours, 2000, Am Speech-Language Hearing Asn; Orisoltes (auth) Fixing the World, Jewish American Painters in the 20th Century, 2003; Artist Has the Gift, The Queens Courier, 2006. *Mem:* Ctr Bk Arts. *Media:* Handmade Papers, Acrylic. *Specialty:* Artist's Books. *Interests:* Music, Literature. *Dealer:* Joshua Heller Rare Books Washington DC; Vamp & tramp, Books Dealer, LLC, Birmingham, AL. *Mailing Add:* 165 West End Ave Apt 16R New York NY 10023

ELLINGER, ILONA E
PAINTER, EDUCATOR
b Budapest, Hungary, June 12, 13. *Study:* Royal Hungarian Univ Sch Art, MFA; Royal Swedish Art Acad; Johns Hopkins Univ, with David M Robinson & W F Albright, PhD; Univ Freiburg; Univ Wis; Phi Beta Kappa. *Work:* Pvt Collections, Illus of Book Hindu Hythology in Art. *Exhib:* Soc Washington Artists; one-man show, Am-Brit Art Ctr, George Washington Univ, 50; Silver Spring Art Gallery, 51; Corcoran Gallery Art, 58; Batiks, Gallery N, Setauket, 77; and others; State Univ of NJ Faculty Show, 2001. *Teaching:* Prof art & head dept, Trinity Col, Washington, DC, 43-78, Fulbright prof hist art & archit, Nat Col Arts, Lahore, W Pakistan, 63-64; vis prof, State Univ NY Stony Brook, 69-79, prof emer; prof, SUNY, 79-85, Emer, currently. *Awards:* Cornelia Harcum Award, Johns Hopkins Univ; Fulbright Award, 63-64. *Mem:* Soc Washington Artists; Archaeol Inst Am. *Media:* Oils, Watercolor, Pen. *Res:* Hindu mythology as depicted in sculpture & painting. *Interests:* Hindu and Buddhist Art history. *Publ:* Auth, Hindu Mythology in Art; Hindu Divinities, 2002. *Dealer:* Trafford 2333 Government St Victoria BC Canada. *Mailing Add:* 67 Quaker Path Stony Brook NY 11790

ELLIOT, CATHERINE J
PAINTER, GRAPHIC ARTIST
b New York, NY, July 26, 47. *Study:* Sarah Lawrence Col, BA, 69; Creative Arts Workshop, New Haven, Conn, 73; Otis Art Inst, Los Angeles, 76-77; Univ Col Los Angeles, 80. *Work:* BBDO Advert; Cutter's Restaurant; New West Corp; Scitex America. *Comn:* Large outdoor sculpture, comn by Keith Williamson, Los Angeles. *Exhib:* Moon St Gallery, Westport, Conn, 74; Am Ceramics Soc, Brand Art Gallery, Los Angeles, 75 & 88; Otis Art Inst Group Show, Los Angeles, 77; one-man shows, RGA Gallery, Los Angeles, 77 & 26th St Gallery, Santa Monica, Calif, 79; 4th Ann Great Lakes Show, Chicago, Ill, 90; The Fifth Monarch Tile Nat Ceramic Competition, San Angelo Mus Fine Arts, Tex, 90. *Teaching:* Instr ceramics, Moon St Pottery, Westport, Conn, 73; instr pvt ceramics lessons, 74-77; instr, The Color Ctr, Los Angeles, 93-94. *Awards:* Purchase Award, Am Ceramic Soc Group Show, 75. *Bibliog:* Carole Katchen (auth), Artist's Mag, 90; Sara Scribner (auth), Faces, Designer's West Mag, 90. *Mem:* Am Ceramic Soc; Artists Equity Asn. *Media:* Miscellaneous Media; Computer Graphics. *Publ:* Macdigest Mag, 2/94, 4/94, 6/94, 9/94 & 11/94. *Mailing Add:* 9528 Dalegrove Dr Beverly Hills CA 90210-1711

ELLIOT, JOHN THEODORE
PAINTER, WRITER,TEACHER
b London, Eng, May 25, 25; US citizen. *Study:* Acad Fine Arts, Italy, 47-50; NY Univ, Film Sch, 51-54; Sch Visual Arts, 58-59; also pvt study in Europe. *Work:* Chesterwood Mus & Naumkeag, Trustees of Reservations, Stockbridge, Mass; Ala Space Ctr, Huntsville; Nat Trust Hist Preserv, Washington, DC. *Comn:* Hist Preserv, comn by Mrs Onassis, K Hepburn, A Baxter & Nat Trust, NY, Los Angeles & DC; murals, Village of Nyack & Haverstraw, NY; Pres Ronald Reagan Portrait, Republican Party; cards, BAI Int, 96 & 97; and others; Finkelstein Libr Meml Portrait. *Exhib:* French Retrospective, Metrop Mus Art, NY, 76, Nat Collection Fine Arts, Smithsonian Inst, 77, Detroit Inst, Mich, 77 & Fogg Art Mus, Cambridge, Mass, 78; 20th Ann Int, Soc Illustr, NY, 77; Knickerbocker Nat, Nat Arts Club, NY, 79; Pastels Only, Copley Soc, Boston, 79; and others. *Pos:* Pres visual commun, Graphics for Industry Inc, Dover, Del & Tenafly, NJ 67-2000, JE-GFI Ince, NY: Vpres, Hist Soc Nyacks, 99-2000. *Teaching:* Workshops and videos, The Total Pastelist, Art & Design in Action & Tools of the Trade. *Awards:* Gold Medal, Freedoms Found Valley Forge, 70; Ten Best Awards, Soc Illustrators, 77; numerous nat exhib awards. *Bibliog:* Freedom to innovate, Indust Photog, 7/70; Hudson Valley Mag, 98. *Mem:* Pastel Soc Am; Soc Illustrators; PSA Nat Arts Club; Salmagundi Club; Oil Pastel Asn Int Ltd. *Media:* Oil, Pastel. *Publ:* The Night the Animals Talked, Am Broadcasting Co, 75; American Phenomenon, Nat Found, 77; Learning from the Pros, Watson-Guptill, 84; Introduction to Oil Pastels, 87; Pastels & the Portrait, 88; Painting Solutions, Hands, Faces & Figures, Quarto, 90; Pastels & the Landscape, 90; Painting Solutions, Hands, Faces & Figures, Quarto, 90; contrib ed, numerous articles, The Artist's Mag; Oil Pastel for the Serious Beginner, Watson-Guptill, 2002. *Dealer:* JE-GFI Inc. *Mailing Add:* c/o JE-GFI Inc 304 Highmount Terr Upper Nyack NY 10960

ELLIOT, SHEILA
ARTS, WRITER, ADMINISTRATOR
b Philadelphia, Pa, Mar 25, 46. *Study:* Vassar Col, AB, 67; Fairleigh Dickenson Univ, MA, 79; studied and New York Univ & Columbia Univ, NY. *Work:* Oil Pastel for the Serious Beginner, Watson-Guptill, 2002. *Pos:* Dir pub relations, Pastel Soc Am, NY, 81-83; exec dir, Oil Pastel Asn NY, 83-86; ed, Art & Artists USA, 83-86; contrib ed, The Artist's Magazine, 86-; publicity dir, Pen & Brush Inc, NY, 87-90; webmaster, OPAI.org, 2001-2004; Managing Ed & Staff writer on Art The Hook Mag, 2005-; publicity dir & trustee, Hopper House Art Ctr, NY, 2006-. *Bibliog:* Oil Pastel for the Serious Beginner, Watson-Guptill, 2002; Chinese Art & Architecture, Mason Crest Pub, 2004; Ancient History of China, Mason Crest Pub, 2004; The Artists Mag, American Artists, Pastel Journal, etc. Numerous Articles, 2001-2004. *Mem:* Oil Pastel Asn Int (treas 2001-2004. *Res:* Working methods and procedures of current American artists. *Publ:* Contribr, Painting for the Pros, Watson-Guptill, 83; coauth, Introd to Oil Pastel, Holbein, 86 & Pastels & the Portrait, 88; numerous articles, The Artists' Mag, 85-; Decorative Artist's Workbook, 90; Pastels & the Landscape, 90. *Mailing Add:* 304 Highmount Terr Upper Nyack NY 10960

ELLIOTT, ANNE
SCULPTOR, PAINTER
b Pittsburgh, Pa, Aug 9, 44. *Study:* Sarah Lawrence Col, BA, 66; Art Students League, 67; Parson Sch Design, 69; Pratt Inst, Cert, 92. *Work:* Westmoreland Mus, Greensburg, Pa; Alternative Mus, NY. *Exhib:* One-person exhibs, Graham Gallery, NY, 78 & 80, Westmoreland Mus Art, Greensburg, Pa, 82, Summerfare, Ctr Arts, State Univ NY, Purchase, 83 & 84, Pittsburgh Pub Theater, Installation for Production of K2, 84, Hewlett Gallery, Carnegie-Mellon Univ, 84, Johnston Art Mus, Johnstown, Pa, 88 & Blair Art Mus, Hollidaysburg, Pa, 88; Originals, Graham Gallery, NY, 80 & Selections from Gallery Artists, 83; Exchanges III, Abrons Art for Living Ctr, Henry St Settlement, NY, 81; Candidates for Awards, Am Acad & Inst Arts & Letts, NY; Nature: Images & Metaphor, Views by Women Artists, Greene Space Gallery, NY, 82; Papyrus Abstractus, Westport-Weston Art Alliance, Westport, Conn, 82; The New Explosion: Paper Art, Fine Arts Mus Long Island, Hempstead, NY, 82, Byer Mus Arts, Evanston, Ill, 83; Seven New Artists, Pittsburgh, Today, Carnegie, Pittsburgh, 84; Sculpture by Women in the Eighties, UP Gallery, Pittsburgh, 85; Columns by Artists, 14 Sculptors' Gallery, NY, 86; Paper: Form & Substance, NJ Ctr Vis Arts, Summit, NJ. *Teaching:* Col NJ, 93-94. *Awards:* Fel, Pa Coun Arts, 85. *Bibliog:* Hilton Kramer (auth), Art at Guggenheim: Niche for Favorites, NY Times, 5/31/80; John Perrault (auth), Anne Elliot, Westmoreland Mus, Gettysburg, Pa, 82; John Caldwell (auth), Seven New Artists, Pittsburgh Today, Carnegie, 84. *Mem:* Col Art Asn; Nat Sculpture Ctr. *Media:* Aluminum Mesh & Paper; Acrylic, Oil. *Dealer:* Leslie Ava Shaw 110 W 87th St New York NY. *Mailing Add:* 2775 Main St Trenton NJ 08648

ELLIOTT, BETTE G
PAINTER, INSTRUCTOR
b Mansfield, Ohio, Sept 22, 20. *Study:* Otterbein Col, with Marc Moon, Barse Miller & others, BFA & BA, 42. *Work:* Canton Art Inst, Ohio; N Canton Libr, Ohio; US Embassy, Nepal; Ohio State Univ; numerous pvt collections. *Comn:* 26 paintings for Gordon, Formet & Clevenger, Canton, Ohio. *Exhib:* one-women shows, Duke Univ Libr, Durham, NC, 80, Ashtabula Art Ctr, Ohio, 88, Mansfield Art Ctr, Ohio, 88, Zanesville Art Ctr, Ohio, 88, Canton Mus, Ohio, Ctr Gallery, Parma, Ohio, & others; Watercolor Ohio '89, Brit Petroleum Atrium, Cleveland; Pittsburgh Aqueous, Arts & Crafts Ctr, Cleveland, Ohio, 89; Art Expo, 92; Canton Mus, 97; Marsilleir Mus, 98; Kent State Univ. *Teaching:* Instr adult classes, Alliance Art Ctr, 69-80, North Canton Little Art Gallery, 1969-80, Kent State, 1979-80 & Wayne Gen Col, 1979; instr adult classes, Wayne Gen Col, Orville, Ohio, 1979, instr drawing, 1980-81; studio instr, 80-92; workshop, 80-2000. *Awards:* First Place, Pittsburgh Aqueous, 89 & Cuyahoga Falls Abstr Sch, 2000; Third Place, Canton Art League, 2000, Award of recognition, 2005. *Mem:* Ohio Watercolor Soc (show coordr, 82 & 86, vpres, bd dir); assoc mem Am Watercolor Soc; Canton Art League. *Media:* Watercolor, Acrylic. *Publ:* Am Artist Mag, 7/92; Cover of Fla Eye Bank Ann Report; Ohio Artist Catalog, 92. *Mailing Add:* 806 Portage St North Canton OH 44720

ELLIOTT, DOROTHY BADEN
CONSERVATOR
b Brookfield, Md, July 18, 14. *Study:* Mt Holyoke Col, hons in course, AB, 36; Brooklyn Mus, prof training by Caroline Keck, 60-63. *Pos:* Asst to conservator, Whitney Mus, 61-62; assoc conservator, Brooklyn Mus, 62-63; conservator painting pvt studio, Sarasota, Fla, 63-; assoc conservator, Walters Art Gallery, Baltimore, 66-79. *Mem:* Fel Am Inst Conserv; fel Int Inst Conserv; Am Asn Mus; Int Coun Mus. *Mailing Add:* 700 John Ringling Blvd No 308 Sarasota FL 34236-1542

ELLIOTT, LILLIAN
WEAVER, TAPESTRY ARTIST
b Detroit, Mich. *Study:* Wayne Univ, BA; Cranbrook Acad Art, Bloomfield Hills, Mich, MFA. *Work:* Mus Contemp Crafts, NY; Detroit Inst Arts; San Francisco City Art Collection; Objects, USA--Johnson's Wax Collection, Smithsonian Inst Travelling Exhib, 70-72; Univ Art Collections, Ariz State Univ, Tempe. *Exhib:* Calif Design Exhibs, Pasadena Art Mus, 62-71; Fabric Collage Invitational, Mus Contemp Crafts, NY, 65; Collagen--Collage Invitational Exhib, Kunstgewerbe Mus, Zurich, Switz, 68; Objects, USA--Johnson's Wax Collection, Smithsonian Inst Traveling Exhib, 70-72; Tapestry, Tradition & Technique Invitational, Los Angeles Co Mus Art, 71. *Pos:* Fabric designer, Ford Motor Co Styling Div, Dearborn, Mich, 56-59. *Teaching:* Instr art, Univ Mich Col Archit & Design, Ann Arbor, 59-60; lectr textiles, Univ Calif, Berkeley, 66-76. *Awards:* San Francisco Art Festival Purchase Award, 65 & 69; Founder's Soc Purchase Award, Mich Craftsmen's Show, Detroit Inst Arts, 69; Calif Arts Coun Grant/Artist in Residence, 79-80. *Media:* Textile. *Publ:* Auth, Chap, In: The New American Tapestry, Van Nostrand Reinhold, 68. *Mailing Add:* 1775 San Lorenzo Ave Berkeley CA 94707-1824

ELLIS, ANDRA
PAINTER, CERAMIST
b New York, NY, Mar 3, 48. *Study:* Queens Col, City Univ New York, BFA, 71. *Work:* Mint Mus Art, Charlotte, NC; Karen Johnson Boyd, Racine, Wis; Sanford Besser, Little Rock, Ark; Luwa Corp, Charlotte, NC; Nations Bank, Charlotte, NC. *Exhib:* The Collector's Eye, Am Craft Mus, NY, 91; one-person exhib Hodges Taylor Gallery, Charlotte, NC, 92 & 95; B'nai B'rith Klutznick Mus, Washington, DC, 95; Miriam Cup, Hebrew Union col Skirball Mus, Exhib, 97; Helander Gallery, Palm Beach, Fla, 92; Works Southern Women, Fay Gold Gallery, Atlanta, Ga, 92; Spotlight, Miss Mus Art, Jackson, 91. *Pos:* Dir, Ceramics Dept, West Side YMCA, NY, 74-82, dir/producer, Int Clay Film Festival, Greenwich House Pottery & traveled to NY State Col Ceramics, Alfred, NY, 81-85; spec projs coord, Greenwich House Pottery, NY, 82-84; proj designer & dir, Children's Mural/Children's Law Ctr, Charlotte, NC, fall 91. *Teaching:* Instr Intermediate to advanced ceramics, two dimensional design, mixed media sculpture & apprenticeship progs in clay, 74-82; lectr, Viewpoints: Four Artists on Art, Mint Mus Art, Charlotte, NC, 91; lectr, Surface Exploration in Clay, Sawtooth Ctr Visual Arts, Winston-Salem, 91-92 & Queens Col, Charlotte, NC, 91-92; Philadelphia Sch Dist, currently. *Awards:* Nat Endowment Arts Visual Artists Fel, 90-91; NC Arts Coun Artist Proj Grant, 92-93. *Bibliog:* Vanessa Lynn (auth), Andra Ellis, Am Ceramics, winter 89; Pamela Blume Leonard (auth), Figurative clay, Art Papers, 11-12/91; John Rodgers (auth), Andra Ellis, Art Papers, 9-10/92. *Dealer:* Hidges Taylor Gallery 401 N Tyron St Charlotte NC 28202. *Mailing Add:* 7535 Woodcrest Ave Philadelphia PA 19151

ELLIS, GEORGE RICHARD
MUSEUM DIRECTOR
b Birmingham, Ala, Dec 9, 37. *Study:* Univ Chicago, BA & MFA, Univ Calif, Los Angeles, candidate in PhD prog. *Pos:* Art supvr, Jefferson Co Schs, 62-64; former asst dir, Birmingham Mus Art; dir develop & asst dir, Mus Cult Hist, Univ Calif, Los Angeles, presently; dir, Honolulu Acad Arts. *Mem:* Los Angeles Ethnic Art Coun; Am Mus Asn; Art Mus Dirs Asn; Hawaii Mus Asn; Pac Arts Asn. *Mailing Add:* Honolulu Acad Arts 900 S Beretania St Honolulu HI 96814

ELLIS, LOREN ELIZABETH
PAINTER, PHOTOGRAPHER
b Binghamton, NY, Dec 12, 53. *Study:* Univ SFla, BA, 74; Fla State Univ, MFA, 77. *Work:* Eastman Kodak Collection, Pharmaceutical Br, Philadelphia, Pa; House of Reps, Capitol Bldg, Tallahassee, Fla; Mus of Modern Art; NY Public Libr; 13 Mus Szcerin, Poland; Queens Mus; Park Ave Bank, NY NY; Mus Photog Krakow, Poland; Santa Barbara Mus Art. *Comn:* Mural, Hillsborough Parks Dept, 82,; mural, Johnson & Johnson Co, 83; mural, Tampa Electric Co, 83; mural, Fund for Dance, 20th Anniversary, NY; mural, Lee Co Electric Co, Ft Myers, Fla, 84; mural, My Yankees; Joyce Theatre Dance, New York City; Yar Mural Russ Adv, New York City. *Exhib:* Solo exhib, Hillsborough Co Mus, Tampa, Fla, 74, M Ingban Gallery, Soho, NY & Chasama Times Sq 9/11; Professional Women Artists, Lowe Art Mus, Miami, Fla, 74; Tampa Mus Art, 79, 80 & 82 & Nostalgia, Tampa Mus W, Fla, 84; Mus Choice, Lock Haven Arts Ctr, Orlando, Fla, 81; Phoenix Gallery Invitational, Soho, 95; group exhib, Exit Art 9/11. *Pos:* Art cur, Photo Exhib, Youth Mus Charlotte Co, Fla, 77 & Womens Survival Ctr, 82-83; dir & founder, Art for Healing Inc, NY. *Teaching:* Inst art & photomontage, Parsons Sch Design, NY, 89-96. *Awards:* Fine Arts Coun Fel, Fla, 77; Merit Award, Tampa Mus, 78; Grants, Arts Coun Tampa & Hillsborough Com 90; Grant, Puffin Found Ecology Works; Centrum Port Townsend Residency, WA; Grant, Lower Manhattan Cultural Council, book on 9/11. *Bibliog:* Articles in Art South, Tampa Times, Photo Dist News, Szicine News & Full Page in Poland. *Mem:* Prof Women Photogrs; Photog Administrators Inc; Puffin Found NY; PAI; Fla State Alumni. *Media:* Photographic Painting. *Res:* chernobyl for ecology series, 98-; Holocaust for project, 2000-. *Specialty:* Photog; Mixed Media; Murals; Corp Identity Art. *Publ:* Contribr, cover art, Tampa Bay Mag, 79 & Organic Mag, 89. *Dealer:* Omega Art New York City. *Mailing Add:* 2350 Broadway New York NY 10024

ELLIS, RAY
PAINTER, LECTURER
b Philadelphia, Pa, Apr 24, 21. *Study:* Philadelphia Mus Sch Art, 39-42. *Work:* Farnsworth Mus, Rockland, Maine; Columbus Mus Art, Ga; Telfair Mus Art, Savannah, Ga; Morris Mus Arts & Sci, Morristown, NJ; Charles Russell Mus, Great Falls, Mont; Heckscher Mus, Huntington, NY; Univ Nebr Mus, Lincoln, Nebr; Harrisburg Art Mus, Pa; Cooperstown Hall of Fame Mus, NY. *Comn:* One Man's Island (watercolor), McGraw-Hill Co, NY, 67; series of watercolors, Midlantic Bank, Newark, NJ, 68; Polo (watercolor), Dun & Bradstreet, NY, 73; River Man (watercolor), AT&T Co, Bedminster, NJ, 77; Island Overlook, Allied Corp, Morristown, NJ; After Colors, Johnson-Higgins Inc, NY. *Exhib:* One-man shows, Pa Acad Fine Arts, Philadelphia, 47, Columbus Mus Art, Ga, 72, Columbia Mus Art, SC, 72, Charles Russell Mus, Great Falls, Mont, 74, Morris Mus Arts & Sci, Morristown, NJ, 76 & MacCullough Mus, Morristown; Am Watercolor Soc, Nat Acad Design, NY, 65-71; Nat Arts Club Ann, NY, 72-77; Fayetteville Mus, NC, 85; Chris Beetles Gallery, London, Eng, 87 & 89, Audubon Artists, 69-74; Closson's Gallery, Cincinnati, 95; Telfair Mus Art, 76-99; Jensen Fine Art, NY, 2000; Telfair Mus Art, Morris Mus, Butler Inst Am Art, 2004. *Teaching:* Instr workshops, Ga, Mass, Montana, NJ, Leicester Polytech - UK, NY & Fla, Miss Watercolor Soc. *Awards:* Winsor & Newton Medal, Audubon Artists, 72; Gold Medal of Honor, Hudson Valley Art Asn, 74; Medal Honor, Nat Arts Club; Medal of Honor, Salmagundi Club, 2004. *Bibliog:* Walter Cronkite (co-auth), South by Southeast, 83, North by Northeast, 86, & Westwind, Oxmoor House, 90; Ben Wright (co-auth), Spirit of Golf, Longstreet Press, 92; Arthur Gordon (co-auth) Ray Ellis' Savannah & The Low Country, 94; Robert Ballard (co-auth) Coastal Images of America, Abbeyville, 98; Fishing the Vineyard, Compass PBLG, 2000. *Mem:* Am Watercolor Soc; NJ Watercolor Soc (pres, 66-67); Salmagundi Club (first vpres, 72-73); Artists Fel Found (pres, 72-73); Philadelphia Watercolor Club Century Asn; Nat Arts Club; Lotus Club. *Media:* Watercolor, Oil. *Interests:* Golf, tennis, Baseball, traveling. *Publ:* Sail, NxNE paintings, 9/86; Downeast SxSE paintings, 9/86; Southern Accents, 9/86; Yankee, 5/87; Cape Cod Mag, 6/87; US Art, White House Paintings, 11/00; auth, Ray Ellis Retrospect: A Painter's Journey, 2004; auth, Ray Ellis Paints Flowers, Abbeville Press, 2005; plus others. *Dealer:* www.rayellis.com. *Mailing Add:* c/o Ray Ellis Gallery-Compass Prints Inc 205 W Congress St Savannah GA 31401

ELLIS, RICHARD
PAINTER, ILLUSTRATOR
b New York, NY, Apr 2, 38. *Study:* Univ Pa, BA. *Work:* New Bedford Whaling Mus, Mass; Philadelphia Zoological Garden; Denver Mus Natural Hist; Kendall Whaling Mus; Sea Life Park, Hawaii. *Comn:* Mural of whales, Denver Mus Natural History, 78; mural of Moby Dick, New Bedford Whaling Mus, Mass, 86; mural of blue whale, New Bedford Whaling Mus, 2000. *Exhib:* Whale paintings, New Bedford Whaling Mus, 75, Mystic Seaport, 75 & Am Mus Natural Hist, 76; Animal Art Show, Los Angeles Co Mus, 77; shark paintings, Am Mus Natural Hist, 78; Acad Natural Sci, Philadelphia, 81; Museo del Mare, Genoa, Ital, 2005. *Pos:* Exhib designer, Am Mus Natural Hist, 65-68 & res assoc, 2002-. *Teaching:* Lectr, Am Mus Natural Hist, 82-83. *Bibliog:* T Walker Lloyd (auth), Richard Ellis, Am Artist Mag; Steve Blount (auth), Richard Ellis, Sport Diver Mag; Derek S B Davis (auth), Richard Ellis, Pa Gazette. *Mem:* Soc Animal Artists; Explorers Club. *Media:* Mixed. *Interests:* Photography, Conservation. *Publ:* Auth & illusr, The Book of Whales, Knopf, 80; Dolphins and Porpoises, Knopf, 82; Men and Whales, 91; Great White Shark, 91; Monsters of the Sea, 94; Deep Atlantic, 96; Search for the Giant Squid, 98; Imagining Atlantis, 98; Encyl of the Sea, 2000; Aquagenesis, 2001; The Empty Ocean, 2003; Sea Dragons, 2003; Tiger Bone & Rhino Ham, 2005; Singing Whales & Flying Squid, 2006; and others. *Dealer:* Sportsman's Edge Ltd 136 E 74th St New York NY 10021; Coast Gallery Hwy One Big Sur CA 93920. *Mailing Add:* 17 E 16th St No 9 New York NY 10003

ELLIS, ROBERT M
PAINTER
b Cleveland, Ohio, 22. *Study:* Western Reserve Univ, Sch Archit, 40-42; Cleveland Sch Art, 46-48 (grad); Mexico City Col, Mexico City, BA, 49; Univ Southern Calif, MFA, 52. *Work:* Amoco Production Co, Houston; Mus Albuquerque; Mus Fine Arts, Santa Fe; Robert Walz & Assocs, Hollywood, Calif; numerous pvt collections. *Exhib:* Occidental Col Art Gallery, Los Angeles, 57; one-man shows, Pasadena Art Mus, Calif, 61, Hollis Gallery, San Francisco, 64, James Yu Gallery, NY, 75, Hills Gallery, Santa Fe, NMex 77, Wildine Gallery, Albuquerque, 81, Kauffman Galleries, Houston, 86, Retrospective, Univ NMex Art Mus, Albuquerque, 91; Greenhill Gallery, Fort Lauderdale, Fla, 73; Santa Barbara Mus Art, Calif, 79; Jill Youngblood Gallery, Los Angeles, 84; one person exhib, Kauffman Galleries, Houston, Tex, 86, Contemp exhib, Philip Bareiss Fine Arts, Taos, NMex, 91, Cafe Gallery, Albuquerque, NMex, 91, Univ NMex Art Mus, Albuquerque, 91; Statements, A perspective on Contemp Art in NMex, Albuquerque, NMex, 85 & 86; Landscape Invitational, Kron/Reck Gallery, Albuquerque, NMex, 86; Modern Monoprints, An Exhibi of Monotypes, Kimo Gallery, Albuquerque, NMex, 98. *Pos:* Cur educ, Pasadena Art Mus, 56-64; asst dir, Univ Art Mus, Univ NMex, 64-68, dir, 68-71; interim dir, The Harwood Found, Taos, NMex, formerly, dir, currently; award juror, Nat Exhib Am Watercolor IV, Taos, NMex, 98; mem, Site Santa Fe Advisory bd, 98; oversaw renovation & expansion, The Harwood Mus, Supervised Permanent Collection, 95-98. *Teaching:* prof dept art & art hist, Univ NMex, 64-87, prof emer, currently. *Awards:* Special Recognition Award, Univ NMex, Taox, 97; Regents Meritorious Service Medal, Univ NMex, 97; NMex Governor's Award, Individual Support of the Arts, 98. *Bibliog:* James A Moore (auth), Robert M Ellis/A Painter's Space, Paintings and works on Paper 1951-1990, Univ NMex Art Mus Catalog, 91; Louis Ribak (auth), The Late Drawings (with catalog), The Harwood Mus, 92; Robert Ellis (auth), The Harwood Found of the Univ of NMex/Taos 1923-1993, History & Collection, 93. *Publ:* Viewpoints, poster for benefit art auction, Dept Art & Hist, Univ NMex, 87

ELLIS, SALLY STRAND See Strand, Sally Ellis

ELLIS, STEPHEN
PAINTER
b High Point, NC, 1951. *Study:* Cornell Univ, Ithaca, NY, BFA, 73; New York Studio Schs, 73-74. *Work:* Denver Art Mus. *Exhib:* One-man shows, Galerie Nathalie Obadia, Paris, France, 93 & 96, Galerie Thomas Von Lintel, Munich, Ger, 95, 97 & 99, Galerie Barbara Farber, Amsterdam, The Neth, 96, Andre Emmerich Gallery, NY, 96, Marella Arte Contemporanea (with catalog), Sarnico, Italy, 97, Patrick De Brock Gallery, Knokke, Belg, 98 & Rosamund Felsen Gallery, Los Angeles, Calif, 98; Just a Story from Am, Galleria in Arco, Turin, Italy, 94; NY Abstract Painting, Ala Gallery, NY, 94; Tavelli Gallery, Aspen, Colo, 94; Reveillon '94, Stux Gallery, NY, 94; Drawings and Prints, Byron Cohen Gallery, Kansas City, Mo, 95; Abstraction from Two Coasts, Douglas Lawing Gallery, Houston, Tex, 95; New York on Paper, Galerie Thomas von Lintel, Munich, Ger, 95; Stephen Ellis and Lydia Dona, Manfred Baumgartner Gallery, Washington, DC, 95; Made in USA: Original Works on Paper, Galerie Bob van Orsouw, Zurich, Switz, 95; NY Abstraction, Macdonald Stewart Art Ctr, Guelph, Ont, Can, 95 Transatlantica: The Am-European Nonrepresentational (with catalog), Museo de Artes Visuales Alejandro Otero, Caracas, Venezuela, 95; Nuevas Abstracciones (with catalog), Museo Nacional Centro de Arte Reina Sofia, Madrid, Spain, 96; After the Fall: Aspects of Abstract Painting Since the 1970s (with catalog), Snag Harbor Cult Ctr, Staten Island, NY, 97; Abstraction/Abstractions: Conditional Geometries (with catalog), Musee d'Art Moderne de Saint Etienne, France, 97; Graphite on Paper, Galerie Thomas von Lintel, Munich, Ger, 97; Das Abstrakte, Galerie Thomas Rehbein, Cologne, Ger, 97; Paintings, Manfred Baumgartner Gallery, Washington, DC, 97; Small Paintings, Green & Red Galleries, Dublin, Ireland, 97; Vertical Painting, PS 1 Contemp Art Ctr, Long Island, NY, 97; New York Stories (with catalog), Diatonia, Commune di Faenza Assessorato alla Curltura, Faenze, Italy, 98; Six Painters (Baroque Geometry) (with catalog), Marlborough Chelsea Gallery, NY, 98; One by One, Galerie Thomas von Lintel, Munich, Ger, 99; Four Painters, Carpenter Ctr, Harvard Univ, Boston, Mass, 99; Elge Wimmer Gallery, NY, 99; Marella Arte Contemporanes, Milan, 00; and others. *Pos:* Assoc ed, Art Am Mag, 88-89, contrib ed, 89-94; ed asst, Parkett Mag, 89 & Artforum Int Mag, 93-96. *Teaching:* Adj instr painting, State Univ NY, Old Westbury, 82-83; vis artist, Louisville Arts Coun, Ky, 88, Univ Tenn, Knoxville, 89, Kent State Univ, Ohio, 90, RI Sch Design, 94 & 95, Parsons Sch Design, 95 & 96, Akademie voor beeldende Kunst, Enschede, Holland, 96, Ecole regionale des Beaux-Arts de Valence, France, 97, Calif Inst Arts, Valencia, 97 & Harvard Univ Dept Visual & Environmental Studies, spring 99; instr, NY Univ, 92- & Bard Col, 94 & 95. *Awards:* Painting Grant, NY Found Arts, 85; Painting Grant, Nat Endowment Arts, 91. *Bibliog:* Luk Lambrecht (auth), Index van abstracte schilderkunst, De Morgen, Brussels, 8/14/98; Tinga Horny (auth), Hier Regiert die Vielfalt, Kunstmarkt, 2/11/99; Anne Erfle (auth), Krafte gegen neue Medien, Suddeutsche Zeitung, (SZ extra), 2/11/99. *Publ:* Auth, Irony and exploration, Issue Mag, no 1, 84; The Bronze Age, the Iron Age, the Age of Gold, Issue Mag, no 3, 85; Something different, Bomb Mag, spring 87; Theory of practice/practice of theory, Code Mag, Amsterdam, 87; After the fall, Team Celeste Mag, 12/91. *Dealer:* Andre Emmerich Gallery 41 E 57th St New York NY 10021. *Mailing Add:* 44 White St New York NY 10013

ELLIS-TRACY, JO
PAINTER, DEALER
b Tulsa, Okla. *Study:* Univ Southern Calif, BFA; Stanford Univ, 64. *Work:* Philbrook Art Mus; Exquisite Visions on a Theme of Balanchine, Harvard Univ Theatre. *Comn:* 20 Drawings for Apollo 17 Mission, CBS, NY; Female Athlete (sculpture), Calif Sports Inc, The Forum, Los Angeles; Bronze Man Walking (sculpture), Conn Gen Life Insurance, Hartford; Space Life (painting & film), Nat Aeronautics & Space Admin, Goddard Space Ctr, Md; Commemorative Award (steel plaque), Armco Steel Corp, Ohio; Corp Imagery & Commun Proposals & Models. *Exhib:* Calif Design Show, Pasadena Art Mus; Calif Artists Group, Newport Harbor Art Mus, Newport Beach; Fisher Gallery, Univ Southern Calif, Los Angeles; Philbrook Art Mus, Tulsa, Okla. *Pos:* Founder, Jet-Art, NY, 66; critic, Pasadena Star News; pres & creative dir, The Eye Int Group, Inc, NY, Eye Int Gallery, Fine Arts Bldg, 89, Eye Int Gallery, Fine Arts Bldg, Los Angeles, 92; Pres, Eye Int, Fine Art Co, NY. *Bibliog:* Jo Ellis Tracy-Variations on a theme of the dance, KCET Television, Los Angeles; Jo Ellis Tracy-Artist, Pasadena Mag; Jo Ellis Tracy-American Artist, London Times. *Media:* Mixed Media, Oil, Drawing. *Specialty:* Contemp paintings, sculpture & drawings, realism & romantic realism; specific projects; commissions in painting & sculpture; decorative items of unusual design; fine art furniture. *Publ:* Illusr, Exquisite visions on a theme of Balanchine, Forbes Mag, 86 & American Business & the Arts, brochure, Forbes, 86. *Dealer:* The Eye International Group Inc New York NY. *Mailing Add:* 30 E 70th St New York NY 10021

ELLISON, ROBERT W
SCULPTOR
b Detroit, Mich, Dec 13, 46. *Study:* Mich State Univ, BFA, 69, MFA, 71. *Comn:* Sculpture, Untitled, Universal Steel Corp, Lansing, Mich, 69; sculpture, Point to the Time, Kincaid Elementary Sch, Municipality of Anchorage, Anchorage, Alaska, 96; sculpture, Mr Zebra & Friends, Alameda Co Recorders Office, Oakland, Calif, 99; sculpture, Chase, City Park Lincolnshire Shopping Ctr, ECD Corp, Chicago, Ill, 2002; Sculpture, Impact, Stockton Teen Ctr, Calif, 2005; Bay Area Rapid Transit, Enbarcadero Sta, San Fran, Calif. *Exhib:* Solo Exhibs, San Francisco State Univ, Calif, 88, Victor Fischer Galleries, San Francisco, 91, Am Pres Lines Hq, Calif, 92, Contract Design Center, San Francisco, 95, Sculptural Invitational, Meuso Valle D' Aosta, Torino, Italy, 95; People's Choice Proj, Concord, Calif, 90; Oakland City Ctr, Calif, 90; Fermi Lab, US Dept Energy, Batavia, Ill, 91; Northshore Sculpture Park, Skokie, Ill, 93; City of Palm Desert, Calif, 94; La Quinta Sculpture Park, Calif, 94; Mountain View City Hall, Calif, 94; Olive Grove Sculpture Garden, Calif, 98; William Zimmer Gallery/Stevenswood, Calif, 98; Group Exhib, Oakland City Ctr, Calif, 92; North Shore Sculpture Park, Skokie, IL, 93; William Zimmer Gallery/Stevenswood, Mendocino, Calif, 98; Mill Valley Sculpture Garden, Mill Valley, Calif, 2002; solo shows, James WIllis Gallery, San Francisco, Calif, 76; San Francisco State Univ, San Francisco, Calif, 88; Victor FIscher Galleries, San Francisco, Calif, 91; Sculpture Invitational, Museo Valle D'Aoasta, Torino, Italy, 95. *Collection Arranged:* Bourborbygmi, 28th Ann San Francisco Art Festival, 74; Grey Streak, 21st Ann Calif Show, 74; Riccochet, Palo Alto Outdoor Sculpture Exhib, 77; Four Times Daily, San Francisco Civic Ctr Plaza, 79; Arch Tworain, Donut Diorama, San Francisco Redevelopment Agency, 81. *Pos:* Pres, Lookout Sculpture Park West. *Teaching:* Instr sculpture design & drawing, Mich State Univ, 70-71; Lansing Community Col, Mich, 71-72; Col Marin, Kentfield, Calif, 72-77; San Francisco Acad Art Col, Calif, 96. *Awards:* First Place, 21st Ann All Calif Show, 75; Feature Exhib, Bicentennial San Francisco Art Festival, 76; Purchase Recommendation, People's Choice Project, Concord, Calif, 90. *Bibliog:* Mervin Gilbert (auth), The Big Cheese on the Highway: Bill Zimmer's Solution for Art That's Just Too Big for Walls, Steppin Out Mag, vol 34, 99; Diane Peterson (auth), County's Artists Make Lives an Open Studio, Press Democrat, 10/10/99; Pubic Art, The Guild, vol 13, 202, 98. *Mem:* Pacific Rim Sculpture Group; Sonoma Co Cult Arts Coun; Int Sculpture Ctr, Petaluma Arts Council. *Media:* Welded Steel Painted, Aluminum. *Interests:* Growing cactus and succulents. *Dealer:* Alison Bies Fine Art. *Mailing Add:* 6480 Eagle Ridge Rd Penngrove CA 94951

ELLOIAN, CAROLYN AUTRY See Autry, Carolyn

ELLOIAN, PETER
GRAPHIC ARTIST
b Cleveland, Ohio, Apr 20, 36. *Study:* Cleveland Inst Art, BFA; Univ Iowa, MFA; Pratt Graphic Ctr. *Work:* Toledo Mus Art; Libr Cong, Washington; Philadelphia Mus Art; Mus Mod Art Gallery, Yerevan, Armenia; Yugoslav Portrait Gallery, Tuzla, Bosnia; House of Humor & Satire, Gabrovo, Bulgaria. *Exhib:* Nat Exhib Prints, Libr Cong, 71, 73 & 77; Drawings & Prints, Am Cult Ctr Gallery, Belgrade, Yugoslavia, 86; Inst per la Cult e l'Art, Catania, Sicily, 87; Int Print Biennale, Varna, Bulgaria, 89, 91 & 93; Kochi Int Triennia Exhib Prints, Japan, 90; Int Invitational L'Utopie, Sans Illusion, Atelier Contrast, Fribourg, Switz, 92; Int Exhib, Portland Art Mus, Ore, 97; Nat Print Biennial, Univ, Minn, 98; McNeese Nat Works on Paper, 2000; Int Biennial of Mini Prints, Tetovo, Republic of Macedonia, 2001; Master Exhib, Minsk, Belarus, 2002; Int Small Engraving, Salon Carbunari, Romania, 2003; Pacific Rim Int Print Exhib, Univ Hawaii, Hilo, Hawaii, 2005; Mini Print Int, Cadaques, Spain, 2005. *Teaching:* Instr, Toledo Mus Art, Sch of Design, 66-87; Instr, Village des Arts en France, Lacoste, France, 84 & 87; prof printmaking & drawing, Art Dept, Univ Toledo, Ohio, 87-2001. *Awards:* Ismet Mujezinovic Award, Fourth Int Biennial Portrait Drawings & Graphics, Tuzla, Yugoslavia, 86; Lynd Ward Mem Award, Print Nat, Hunterdon, NJ, 92; Gascar Award, House of Humor & Satire, Gabrovo, Bulgaria, 95; and others. *Mem:* Soc of Am Graphic Artists; Boston Printmakers. *Media:* Drawing, Printmaking. *Mailing Add:* 26114 W River Rd Perrysburg OH 43551

EL MAE See Lorelli, Elvira Mae

ELOWITCH, ANNETTE
DEALER
b Portland, Maine, Dec 24, 42. *Study:* Boston Univ, 61; Westbrook Col, Portland, Maine, AA, 63;. *Pos:* Co-owner, Barridoff Galleries, 75-. *Specialty:* Nineteenth and twentieth century paintings. *Mailing Add:* Barridoff Galleries PO Box 9715 Portland ME 04104-5015

ELOWITCH, ROBERT JASON
DEALER, PATRON
b Portland, Maine, Apr 8, 43. *Study:* Amherst Col, BA. *Pos:* Drama/film critic, Portland Press Herald & Eve Express, 67-69, Maine Times, 70-75; owner & pres, Barridoff Galleries, 75-. *Mem:* Maine State Comn Arts & Humanities (comnr, 73-75); Skohegan Sch Painting & Sculpture (dir, 68-80); Portland Sch Art (sch comt mem, 74-75); United Portland Regional Orgn of Arts Resources (vchmn, 74). *Specialty:* 19th and early 20th century American oils and contemporary regional oils, watercolors, etc. *Interests:* Promotion and support of the arts in the state of Maine; purchase and sale of American and European art of the 18th, 19th & 20th centuries. *Mailing Add:* PO Box 9715 Portland ME 04104-5015

ELOZUA, RAYMON
SCULPTOR
b Ger, 47; US citizen. *Study:* Univ Chicago, 65-69. *Work:* Mus Fine Arts, Houston, Tex; Am Craft Mus, New York, NY; San Francisco Mus Mod Art, Calif; Wadsworth Atheneum, Hartford, Conn; Carnegie Mus Art, Pittsburgh, Pa; and others. *Exhib:* New Visions, Aldrich Mus Contemp Art, Ridgefield, Conn, 81; Brooklyn 1984, Brooklyn Mus, NY, 84; solo exhibs, Carlo Lamagna Gallery, NY, 88, Braunstein/Quay Gallery, San Francisco, Calif, 88 & 89, Cleveland Ctr Contemp Art, The Galleria, Ohio, 89, Ariz Mus Art, Tucson, 90, Demons and Sirens, Habatat-Shaw Gallery, Detroit, 92 & Music of Abstract Expressionism, Pfizer Gallery, NY, 98; Art and the Law: 15th Ann Exhib, West Publ Co, St Paul, Minn, 90; Steel & Silver, 20th Century Photogs of Indust, Carnegie Mus Art, Pittsburgh, Pa, 92; 29th Ceramic Nat Exhib, Everson Mus Art, Syracuse, NY, 93; Confrontational Clay: The Artist as Social Critic (traveling), Am Craft Mus, Flint Inst Arts, Mich, others, 2000; Color and Fire: Defining Moments in Studio Ceramics 1950-2000 (traveling), Los Angeles Co Mus Art, others, 2000; many others. *Pos:* studio asst, Vittore Bochetta, Chicago, 68-70; Properties designer, Julliard Theatre, NY, 71-73; designer & photog, Daniel Negrin Film & Dance, NY, 74-75; independent designer, Am Craft Coun, Baltimore, Md, 75-77; cur, Allan Chasanoff Ceramic Collection, 79-99; artist-in-residence, Sarasota Sch Visual Arts, 80, Juniata Col, Pa, 80, SUNY, New Paltz, 81 & La State Univ, 99. *Teaching:* fac ceramic sculpture, NY Univ, NY, 82-86 & Calif Col Arts & Crafts, Oakland, 83; Fac grad sem, RI Sch Design, Providence, RI, 83-84; instr grad sem, Pratt Inst Design, Brooklyn, NY, 84-85. *Awards:* Fels, Nat Endowment Arts, 80, 81 & 87 & NY Found Arts, 88; Fel for Arts, CINTAS, 81. *Bibliog:* Joyce Lovelace (auth), The Ubiquitous Teapot, Am Craft, 4/94; Chiori Santiago (auth), Still Clay, Am Craft, 98; Judith Schwartz (auth), Confrontational Clay: The artist as social critic, Exhibits USA, 2000. *Media:* All. *Publ:* catalog, Allan Chasanoff Ceramic Collection, Mint Mus Crafts, Charlotte, NC, 2000. *Mailing Add:* 292 Elizabeth St New York NY 10012-2832

ELSE, ROBERT JOHN
PAINTER, EDUCATOR
b Wayne, Pa, Nov 26, 18. *Study:* Columbia Univ, BS & MA. *Work:* Crocker Art Mus, Sacramento; Univ of Calif-Los Angeles Libr; Calif State Libr Prints Rm. *Comn:* City Hall, Sacramento, 87. *Exhib:* 4th Print Ann Exhib, Brooklyn Mus, 50; Kingsley Ann Exhib for Northern Calif Artists, Crocker Art Gallery, 50-64; Oakland Art Gallery's Ann Exhib, 51; Survey of Pac Coast Painting, Walnut Creek, Calif, 51; 17th Ann Watercolor Exhib, San Francisco Mus of Art, 53; retrospective, Crocker Art Gallery, 77, Robert Else Gallery, Calif State Univ, Sacramento, 90; Sacramento Valley Landscapes, Univ Calif, Davis, 79; Picturing California's Other Landscape: The Great Central Valley, The Haggin Mus, Stockton, Calif, 99. *Pos:* Coun mem, Comt on Art Educ, Mus of Mod Art, 49-52; mem joint bd trustees, Crocker Art Mus, 73-75; mem, Sacramento Metrop Arts Comn, 80-82. *Teaching:* Prof art pract, painting & drawing, Calif State Univ, Sacramento, 50-79, emer prof, 79-. *Awards:* Purchase Award, 1st Int Biennial of Contemp Color Lithography, Cincinnati Mus of Art, 50; First Prize Oil Painting, Kingsley Club, 64. *Media:* Acrylic, Watercolor. *Dealer:* Solomon Dubnick Gallery 2131 Northrop Ave Sacramento CA 95825

ELY, TIMOTHY CLYDE
BOOK ARTIST
b Snohomish, Wash, Feb 9, 1949. *Study:* Western Wash Univ, Bellingham, BA(drawing & printmaking), 72, Univ Wash, Seattle, MFA(design), 75. *Work:* Victoria & Albert Mus, London, Eng; Libr Cong, Washington, DC; John Paul Getty Mus, Los Angeles, Calif; Spencer Collection, New York Pub Libr, NY; Rijksmuseum Meermanno-Westreenianum Den Haag, Neth; Mus Mod Art, Brooklyn Mus, The Grolier Club, NY; Yale Univ, Princeton Univ & Harvard Univ. *Comn:* Artist Book, Polar Rare Book Rm, Univ Alaska, Fairbanks, 84; Book of Roses, Sony Music, NY. *Exhib:* Solo exhibs, Eaton/Shoen, San Francisco, 84, NY Acad Sci, 87, Contemp Crafts Gallery, Portland, Ore, 88, Granary Bks, NY, 89, 91, 92 & 93, Minn Ctr Bk Arts, Minneapolis, 89 & Victoria & Albert Mus, London, Eng, 89; Folger Libr, Washington, DC, 87; Univ Arts, Philadelphia, Pa, 88; Ctr for Bk Arts, NY, 88-92; Maison du Livre de l'Image et du Son, Ville de Villeurbanne, France, 88; Am Craft Mus, NY & Boston Athenaeum, Mass, 88; Cult Ctr, Boulogne-Billancourt, France, 89; Biblioteque de l'Arsenal, Paris, France & Bibliotheca Wittocklana, Brussels, Bel, 90; Grolier Club, NY, 91; Anchorage Hist & Fine Arts Mus, Alaska, 91; Princeton Univ, NJ, 92; Gallery Tinka, San Jose, Costa Rica, 92; Nat Col Art & Design, Bergen,

Norway, 92; The World of Maps, Mus Art, Anchorage, Alaska, 94; Smithsonian Inst Libr, Science & Artists Book, Washington, DC, 95; The New Storytellers: One-of-a-Kind artists' books in Boston Libr Mus, Wildener Libr, Harvard Univ, 96; Alphabet Book II Chicago, Ill, 97. *Teaching:* Instr book art, Ctr for Book Art, NY, 84-. *Awards:* Pollack-Krasner Found Grant, 86; Art Matters Grant, 88 & 90; Nat Endowment Arts Reg Grant, West States Art Fedn, 94. *Bibliog:* Roy Harley Lewis (auth), Fine Bookbinding in the Twentieth Century, Arco Publ, 85; Martha Bergman (auth), An interview with Timothy C Ely, The New Bookbinder, UK, 87; Lois Allan (auth), Complex and simple mysteries, Artweek, 5/88. *Mem:* Designer Bookbinders, Eng. *Media:* Painting, Drawing. *Publ:* Auth, Portfolio (article), Am Crafts Mag, 6/86; Martina Margetto (auth), International Crafts, Thames & Hudson, 91; Synesthesia, Granary Bks, 93; The Flight into Egypt, Chronicle Bks, 95. *Mailing Add:* 504 N Mill Stn Colfax WA 99111

EMBIRICOS, EPAMINONDAS GEORGE (PANDY EMBIRICOS)
COLLECTOR
b Athens, Greece, July 15, 43. *Study:* MIT, BS, MS, 65. *Pos:* Chmn Embiricos Shipping Agency, Ltd, London, 69-91; vchmn, Greek Shipping Coop, Com NTERCARGO, 86-99; Embiricos Shipbrokers Ltd, London, 91-; chmn, Greek Shipping Coop Com, 99-. *Awards:* Named one of top 200 collectors, ARTnews Magazine. *Collection:* Old masters, impressionism & modern art. *Mailing Add:* Embiricos Shipbrokers Ltd 1-19 New Oxford St London WC1A 1NU United Kingdom

EMBREY, CARL RICE
PAINTER, INSTRUCTOR
b Hamilton, Tex, Oct 28, 38. *Study:* Univ Tex, Austin, BFA, 63, MFA, 64, with Everett Spruce. *Work:* Marion Koogler McNay Mus, San Antonio; San Antonio Art League, Tex; Ark Arts Ctr, Little Rock; Emerson Gallery, Hamilton coll, Clinton, NY. *Exhib:* Am Arts Nat Exhib, Butler Inst, Youngstown, Ohio, 65; Artists of the Southeast & Tex, Isaac Delgado Mus, New Orleans, 67; 60 Tex Artists, Inst Texan Cult, San Antonio, 68; Tex Artists Invitational, Longview Mus, Tex, 68-70; Art Teachers, Witte Mem Mus, 77; one-man shows, Marion Koogler McNay Art Inst, San Antonio, 74 & fifteen-year survey, San Antonio Art Inst, 88; and others. *Collection Arranged:* Paintings of Carl Embrey (auth, catalog), Five Year Retrospective, 74; The Work of Carl Embrey Retrospective (with catalog), McNay Art Mus, San Antonio, 97; Carl Embrey, The Artist and the American Landscape, McNay Art Mus, San Antonio, Tex, 2004; The Work of Carl Embrey, Forty Years, 1965-2005, Art Ctr Waco, Tex, 2005. *Teaching:* Prof painting & drawing, San Antonio Art Inst, 64-93. *Awards:* Onderdonk Mem Award, San Antonio Art League, 65; Honorable Mention, Arts Nat, Tyler Mus, 67; Merit Award, Tex Artists Invitational, Longview Art League, 72. *Bibliog:* Gail Falbo Smith (auth), Embrey--A Documentary, Trinity Univ, 78; Nanette Simpson (auth), Carl Embrey, Southwest Art, Houston, 79; Dan Goddard (auth), Carl Embrey, Southwest Art, Houston, 89; Steve Bennet (auth), Southwest Art: Carl Embrey, 97; Michael J. Smith (auth), A Point of Origin, Carl Rice Embrey, documentary, Pub Svc Television. *Media:* Acrylic Emulsion, Water colour; Graphite Pencil, Silverpoint. *Res:* silverpoint and painting panel construction. *Specialty:* eclectic. *Interests:* Art History: Painter's materials and techniques. *Publ:* John Driscoll & Arnold Skolnick (auths), The Artist and the American Landscape, Chameleon Books, Inc, 1998. *Dealer:* contact Carl Embrey. *Mailing Add:* 9319 Nona Kay Dr San Antonio TX 78217-5020

EMERICK, JUDSON J
HISTORIAN
b Kingston, NY, July 3, 41. *Study:* Hope Col, Holland, Mich, BA, 63; Univ Mich, Ann Arbor, MA, 65; Univ Pa, PhD, 75. *Teaching:* Instr art hist, Pomona Col, 73-75, asst prof art hist, 75-80, assoc prof, 80-, chmn dept art, 80-87 & 96-, prof, 97-. *Awards:* Samuel H Kress Found Fel, 71-73; Nat Endowment Humanities Fel, 81. *Mem:* Col Art Asn; Soc Archit Historians; Int Ctr Medieval Art. *Res:* Late antique and medieval art with special emphasis on Italian architecture and painting. *Publ:* Coauth, Early Sixth Century Frescoes at San Martino ai Monti in Rome, Romisches Jahrbuch fur Kunstgestschichte, Vol XXI, 84; The Tempietto del Clitunno near Spoleto, Penn State Press, 98; The Column Display inside S Prassede, Rome, Mededelingen van het Nederlands Inst te Rome, 2001. *Mailing Add:* 154 N Mountain Ave Monrovia CA 91016

EMERY, LIN EMERY BRASELMAN
KINETIC ARTIST, SCULPTOR
b New York, NY. *Study:* Ossip Zadkine Studio, Paris; Sculpture Ctr, NY. *Hon Degrees:* Loyola Univ, New Orleans, 2004, Doctor of Letters. *Work:* Nat Collection Am Art, Washington; New Orleans Mus Art; Norton Art Galleries, West Palm Beach, Fla; Huntington Mus Art, WVa; Walter P Chrysler Mus, Norfolk, Va; Mus Foreign Art, Sofia, Bulgaria; Fine Arts Mus South, Mobile, Ala; Brevard Art Mus, Melbourne, Fla; Ogden Mus Southern Art, New Orleans. *Comn:* Kinetic sculpture, City of Virginia Beach, 89; City of Oxnard, Calif, 90; Hofstra Univ, NY, 90; Sterling Drug Co, Collegeville, Pa; Daytona Beach Airport, Fla; Financial Guaranty Insurance Co, NY; Neiman Marcus, Short Hills, NJ; L R Nelson Corp, Peoria, Ill, 95; Menorah Hosp, Kansas City, Mo, 96; Izumisano Hosp, Japan, 96; Osaka Dome, Japan, 97; Stirling Corp, Irving, Tex, 2000; Mitre Corp, McLean, Va, 2001; Knight Oil Co, Lafayette, LA, 2005. *Exhib:* Solo shows, Contemp Arts Ctr, New Orleans, 78 & 81 & Max Hutchinson Gallery, NY, 82, retrospective, New Orleans Mus Art, 96 & Imperial Calcasieu Mus, Lake Charles, La, 97; Int Sculpture Conf Exhib, 80; GSA Art in Archit, Nat Collection Fine Art, 80; World Expo, Brisbane, Australia, 88; Alexandria Mus, La, 89; Mus SE Tex, Beaumont, 91; Brevard Art Mus, Melbourne, Fla, 92; Arthur Roger, New Orleans, 93 99, 2003; Kouros Gallery, NY, 2000, 2006; Meadows Mus, Shreveport, La, 2001; Masur Mus, Monroe, La, 2001; Arthur Roger; Kouros Gallery, 2005. *Pos:* Vis critic, Tulane Univ Sch Archit, 67-68; fel, Va Ctr Creative Arts, 81. *Teaching:* Vis artist, Newcomb Art Sch, Tulane Univ, 81 & Univ Maine, 88. *Awards:* Mayor's Award Excellence in the Arts, New Orleans, 80; Young Womens Club Am Role Model Award, 89; Lazlo Aranyi Award, Pub lic Art, 90; Grand Prize, Pub Art, Osaka Prefecture, Japan, 97; Gov's Arts Award, 2001. *Bibliog:* Pierce (auth), Lin Emery's aquamobiles, Art Int, 69; Roger Green (auth), The kinetic sculpture of Lin Emery, Arts Mag, 12/79; Bill Goliantly (auth), Tubular Bells, Horizon, 4/85; Josef Marker (auth), Lin Emery, InSite, 90; V Watson-Jones (auth), Contemp Am Woman Sculptors; Charlotte Rubenstein (auth), Am Women Artists; Edward Lucie-Smith (auth), Lin Emery: Borrowing the Forces of Nature, 96; Judy Collischan (auth), Welded Sculpture of 20th Century, 2000. *Mem:* Sculptors Guild NY; Int mem Royal Soc Brit Sculptors; Century Asn NY; Int Women's Forum; Nat Acad; Nat Acad. *Media:* Kinetics, Metals, Installations. *Publ:* Co-auth, Kinesone I, Leonardo, Vol 19, Issue No 3. *Dealer:* Kouros Gallery 23 E 73rd St New York NY 10021; Arthur Roger Gallery 432 Julia St New Orleans LA 70130. *Mailing Add:* 7520 Dominican St New Orleans LA 70118

EMIL, ARTHUR D
COLLECTOR
b New York, NY, Dec 29, 24. *Study:* Yale Univ; Columbia Law Sch. *Mem:* Int Coun Mus Mod Art; Am Fedn Arts. *Collection:* Modern painting; ancient sculpture, southeast asian art. *Mailing Add:* 420 Lexington Ave New York NY 10170

EMMERICH, ANDRE
ART DEALER, WRITER
b Frankfurt, Ger, Oct 11, 24. *Study:* Amsterdam Lyceum, Neth; Kew Forest Sch, New York; Oberlin Col, BA, 45. *Awards:* Distinguished Citizen's Award, Nassau Co Mus Fine Art Asn, 87; Medal, Arch Am Art, 2002. *Bibliog:* Wall St Journal. *Mem:* Century Asn, NY. *Publ:* Auth, Art Before Columbus, Simon & Schuster, 63, 71, 78 & 83; Sweat of the Sun and Tears of the Moon--Gold and Silver in Pre-Columbian Art, Univ Wash Press, 65 & 77; also numerous articles in Art Am, Arts, Am Heritage, Washington Post and many others. *Mailing Add:* 30 E 72nd St Apt 16 New York NY 10021

EMMERT, PAULINE GORE
PAINTER, EDUCATOR
b Marks, Miss, July 1, 23. *Study:* Long Island Univ, BA, 70, MA, 78. *Work:* Long Island Univ, Greenvale, NY; New York Univ Hosp, NY; Daniel Gale, Sotheby Parke Bernet; Coldwell-Banker Realty, Cold Spring Harbor, NY; Lloyd Harbor Village, NY. *Comn:* Lloyd Harbor (painting), comn by Mrs D Kent Gale, Huntington, NY, 78; Centerport Harbor (painting), comn by Capt & Mrs Victor Grubbs, Monroe, Ga 83; Cold Spring Harbor (painting), comn by Dr & Mrs Richard H Sand, Huntington, NY, 89; No--Five Cordwainer Lane, comn by Mr & Mrs Harold Paul family; Cordwainer Lane (painting), comn by Harold Paul Family. *Exhib:* Cold Spring Harbor Whaling Mus, 81 & 93; Nat Asn Women Artists-Jacob Javits Fed Bldg & Nationwide Tours, 88-96; Cold Spring Harbor Community Room, 90 & 92; Miss Mus Art, 91; Long Island MacArthur Airport Terminal, 95. *Pos:* Lectr, Art Relig-Cult, Nat Asn Univ Women, 86, Huntington Art League & Huntington Methodist Church, 78-79; Cur, TianJin Art Col, Huntington, NY, 83; Lectr, Nat Asn Univ Women, Huntington, NY, 84. *Teaching:* Mux Lane Studio, Huntington, NY Pub Schs, Cold Spring Harbor Dist 2, Huntington Dist 3. *Awards:* William Meyerowitz Memorial-Award, Nat Asn Women Artists, 94; Heckscher Mus Long Island Show Award; Silver Brush Award, Nassau Co Mus Art, 94. *Bibliog:* David Shirey (auth), Nuances of Seasons, NY Times, 8/21/81; Ronald Pisano (auth), Long Island Paintings of the 20th Century, 90; Diane Ketchum (auth), Emmert Paintings in Airport Terminal, NY Times, 8/13/95. *Mem:* Nat Asn Women Artists (judge oils, 86-88); NY Artists Equity; Suburban Art League; Art League Long Island. *Media:* Oil, Watercolor. *Res:* Art religion and culture in 70 countries. *Mailing Add:* 61 Preston St Huntington NY 11743-2054

ENCINIAS, JOHN ORLANDO
PAINTER
b San Miguel Co, NMex, Nov 24, 49. *Work:* Millicent Rogers Mus, Taos, NMex; Frye Art Mus, Seattle, Wash; US W Direct Corp Collection, Denver, Colo; United Mo Bank, Kansas City, Mo; Wichita Art Asn, Kans. *Exhib:* Solo exhibs, Frye Art Mus, Seattle, Wash, 93-; Govs Invitational, Loveland Mus, Colo; Am Art in Miniature, Gilcrease Mus, Tulsa, 92-94; Nat Acad Western Art, Nat Cowboy Hall Fame, Oklahoma City, 85-94 & Prix de W Invitational, 95-; Western Visions Miniature Show, Nat Mus Wildlife Art, Jackson Hole, Wyo, 92-98; Albuquerque Mus Miniature, NMex, 95-98. *Bibliog:* Walter Gray (auth), Metrop Library System, The Quiet Paintings of John Encinias, 86 & Painting on Location, 87. *Media:* Oil. *Publ:* Contribr, John Encinias, Artists Rockies, fall 79; coauth, Masterworks of Impressionism, Masterworks Art Publs, 85; contribr, Introduction-John Encinias, SW Art, 4/87; Beyond reality, Art of the W, 9-10/88; Six colors & white, Am Artist, 8/98. *Mailing Add:* 2081 W 52nd Ave Denver CO 80221

ENDE, ARLYN
DIRECTOR
b New Orleans, La. *Study:* La State U, 49-51; Tulane Univ, 51; Art Inst Chicago, 53. *Comn:* Tapeta, Bridgestone-Firestone Nat Hdqs, Nashville, 91; Tapetas, West End Eynagogue, Nashville, 00; Fabric Collages, IBM, Atlanta, 98. *Exhib:* Uncommon Thread, Spruill Ctr Gallery, Atlanta, 99; Side By Side, Nashville, Belfast, Ireland Airports, 01; Am Women in the Arts, Art in Embassies, Lima, Peru, 00-02. *Collection Arranged:* Full Bleed, Works of Brad Thomas, 01; Tradition in Transition, Tapestries and Constructions, 01; Mining the Surface, Works of George Dunbar, 01; Vanderbilt Univ, Nashville; Little Havana Community Ctr, Miami; Shalom Theatre, Nashville; Bradley Mem Hosp, Cleveland, Tenn. *Pos:* exec dir and cur, Art Ctr of Cannon Co, Tenn, 90-95; dir, Univ Art Gallery, Univ of the South, 99-03. *Awards:* Grand Prize,

Am Crafts Awards, NY, 1989; Best of Show, Fiber Art in the 90's, Sawtooth Ctr for Visual Arts, Winston-Salem, NC, 89. *Bibliog:* Anna Fariello, Three Approaches to Contemporary Hooking, Fiber Arts Mag, 91; Fiberarts Design Books 1,3, and 6; Guild 4 and Guild 5; A Celebration of Hooked Rugs; Contemporary Crafts for the Home; Surface Design Jour; Am Craft; Fiberarts; Interior Design. *Mem:* Tenn Asn Craft Artists; Surface Design Asn; ACC. *Mailing Add:* Univ of South Univ Art Gallery 735 University Ave Sewanee TN 37383-1000

ENDERS, ELIZABETH
PAINTER
b New London, Conn, Feb 18, 39. *Study:* Conn Col, BA, 62; New York Univ (MA), New York, NY, 87. *Work:* Addison Gallery Am Art, Andover, Mass; Dow Jones Art Collection; Florence Griswold Mus, Old Lyme, Conn; Graham Gund, Cambridge, Mass; Lyman Allyn Art Mus, New London, Conn; Agnes Gund, New York City; Pfizer Inc; Wadsworth Atheneum, Hartford, Conn. *Comn:* Children's Dance Ctr; Lyman Allyn Mus Art, New London, Conn. *Exhib:* One-woman shows, Paul Schuster Gallery, Cambridge, Mass, 66, Ulysses Gallery, NY, 92 & 94, Lyman Allyn Mus, New London, Conn, 94, Cowles Gallery, NY, 95, Norbert Considine Gallery, Princeton, NJ, 97 & UNTITLED / FOLIO, Artists Space, New York City, NY, 2001; Artists Space Multiple, 95; Human/Nature, New Mus Contemp Art, NY, 95; Image & Eye, NY Studio Sch Benefit Exhib, 95; New Talent, New Ideas, Charles Cowles Gallery, NY, 96; Nightmare on Broome St, Dieu Donne, NY, 97; The Winter Show, Works on Paper & Gotham Group, Charles Cowles Gallery, 98; Painterly Abstraction, Lyman Allyn Art Mus, 98; Look at Art, Charles E Shain Libr, Conn Col, New London, Conn, 2004; Charles E Shain Libr, Conn College, New London, Conn, 2004 & 2006; Real Art Ways, Hartford, Conn, 2004; Alva Gallery, New London, Conn, 2006; and others. *Awards:* Medal, Conn Col, 93. *Bibliog:* Carol Vogel (auth), Inside Art, Miniature Golf for Art's Sake, NY Times, 10/8/93; Janet Purcell (auth), Abstract Language at Stuart, Trenton Times, 3/14/97; Peter Slatin (auth), Elizabeth Enders/Ulysses, ARTnews, 10/94; and many others; Elizabeth Enders Measures Art & Language, Connecticut College Alumni Magazine, Sept 2004; Elizabeth Enders, The Buzz, Kathleen Edgecomb (auth), The Day, New London, CT, 2004; Pat Serenet (auth), JAVA, The Hartford Courant, 11/22/04; Alva gallery to present recent work by Elizabeth Enders in Attachment, Antiques and the Arts Weekly, 3/10/06; Conn Calendar, NY Times, 2006. *Mem:* Artists Space (bd trustees, 86-95); Col Art Asn. *Media:* Oil, Acrylic. *Publ:* Co-auth, Elizabeth Enders, John Sailer Ulysses, 92; Ulysses Gallery, Lyman Allyn Mus, 1994; Connecticut, The Spirit of America, by Patricia Harris and David Lyon, Hary N Abrams Inc. Publ, New York, NY, 2000. *Dealer:* Charles Cowles Gallery 537 W 24th St New York NY. *Mailing Add:* 307 Seventh Ave # 601 New York NY 10001

ENGELBERG, GAIL MAY
PATRON
Pos: Trustee, Engelberg Charitable Found; bd trustee, Solomon R Guggenheim Mus, New York City; bd dir, Jazz at Lincoln Ctr. *Mailing Add:* Engelberg Found 30 W 68th St New York NY 10023

ENGELHARDT, THOMAS ALEXANDER
EDITORIAL CARTOONIST
b St Louis, Mo, Dec 29, 30. *Study:* Denver Univ, 50-51; Ruskin Sch Fine Arts, Oxford Univ, 54-56; Sch Visual Arts, New York, 57. *Work:* State Hist Soc Mo, Columbia. *Comn:* Mural (humorous animals), Pediat Assoc, Mo, 73. *Exhib:* One-man shows, Fontbonne Col, Mo, 72 & Decade of the Environment 1970-1980, Old Courthouse, St Louis, 81 & Mark Twain Bank, St Louis, 88; Sch Visual Arts Alumni Exhib, Hansen Gallery, NY, 75; plus numerous group shows. *Pos:* Free-lance cartoonist, New York, 57-60 & 98-; ed cartoonist, Newspaper Enterprise Asn, Cleveland, Ohio, 60-61 & St Louis Post-Dispatch, 62-97. *Awards:* Ethical Humanist of the Year, St Louis Ethical Soc, 87. *Media:* Pen & Ink, Crayon. *Publ:* Auth, Cartoonist Profiles, 69; Dateline 1976, Overseas Press Club, 76; Cartoonist Profiles, 91. *Mailing Add:* 900 N Tucker Blvd St Louis MO 63101

ENGELSON, CAROL
PAINTER
b Seymour, Ind, 1944. *Study:* Carnegie-Mellon Univ, Pittsburgh, Pa, BFA, 66. *Work:* Calouste Gulbenkian Found, Lisbon; Aldrich Mus, Ridgefield, Conn; Found Art This Century, Paris; San Diego Art Ctr; Chase Manhattan Bank, NY; Carnegie-Mellon Univ, Pittsburgh, Pa. *Exhib:* Solo exhibs, 112 Workshop, Inc, NY, 77, Ruth Schaffner Gallery, Santa Barbara, Calif, 78, Oscarsson-Hood Gallery, NY, 80 & Univ Conn, Hartford, 85; Third Ann Contemp Reflections, Aldrich Mus, Ridgefield, Conn, 74; Selections from the Aldrich Mus, Am Fedn Arts Traveling Exhibition, 74-77; New Dimensions in Drawing, 1950-1980, Aldrich Mus, Ridgefield, Conn, 81; Nat & Int tour, Am Painting the 80's, 79-83; Color Abstraction in the 1980's, Baruch Col Gallery, NY, 85; Minus 40 Plus, Haenah Kent Gallery, NY, 91. *Teaching:* Vis lectr painting, Carnegie-Mellon Univ, 78, Univ Wis-Milwaukee, 82, Univ Conn, Hartford, 85, Pratt Inst, 87 & Parsons Sch Design, 88. *Awards:* Edward MacDowell Colony Fel, 71, 72, 74 & 75; Grant, Comt Visual Arts, New York, 74; Nat Endowment Arts Grant, 77-78; Am Acad Arts & Lett Grant, 83. *Bibliog:* Annette Nachumi (auth), Carol Engelson, Arts Mag, 11/80; John Yau (auth), Carol Engelson and Rick Klauber at Oscarsson-Hood, 3/81 & Deborah Rosenthal (auth), First underground show, fall 84, Art in Am; Vivien Raynor (auth), The gathering of the avant-garde: The Lower East Side, NY Times, 85; Claire Gravel (auth), A Baie Saint-Paul, l'Art Contemporian Descend dans l'Arene, Le Soleil, 8/20/88; Barbara Rose (auth), Autocritique, 88; Hilton Kramer (auth), American painting the eighties, NY Times, 1/90; Grace Gluck (auth), New Debates on Jackson Pollock, New Biography. *Media:* Oil on Canvas, Pastel on Paper. *Publ:* Auth, Jackson Pollock, The Man and the Myth, J of Art, Vol 2, No 3, 12/89, 28. *Dealer:* David Anderson Gallery Martha Jackson Pl Buffalo NY 14214. *Mailing Add:* 131 Allen St New York NY 10002

ENGERAN, WHITNEY JOHN, JR
PAINTER, EDUCATOR
b New Orleans, La, Feb 1, 34. *Study:* Spring Hill Col, BA & MA; St Louis Univ, STL; Art Students League. *Work:* Cunningham Mem Libr, Terre Haute, Ind; Vincennes Univ; Harold E Simon Collection; Michael Gardes Collection; La State Univ, Lafayette. *Comn:* Fire ritual mural, St Marys Col, 62; suffering servant mural, Martin Army Hosp, Columbus, Ga, 66; Terre Haute First Nat Bank, 74; sci ctr mural, WVa Inst Technol, 88. *Exhib:* Ind State Univ, Turman Art Gallery, Terre Haute, Ind, 71-98; Circling the Apocalypse, Tondi paintings, Pierce Gallery, Montgomery, WVa, 88; painting, Wholely, Holy, Wholely, Bicentennial Art Mus Paris, 90; Grapevine Gallery, 98-99 & Swope Art Mus 98, Terre Haute; Disking Millenium Prints Paintings, Univ Art Gallery, Terre Haute, Ind, 2001; Millennial Pulses, Drawings Prints, Pierce Gallery, Montgomery, WVa, 3/2000; Hulman Union Gallery, 2001. *Collection Arranged:* Ida Kohlmeyer Retrospective, 72, Images of Our Time, 73 & American 6 Pak: Six Bicentennial Exhibits, 74-75, Turman Gallery, Terre Haute; I Kohlmeyer Retrospective, Mint Mus, 82-84. *Pos:* Cur permanent collection & dir, Turman Gallery, 71-75. *Teaching:* Asst prof aesthet & chmn dept art, Loyola Univ, 66-68; assoc prof aesthet, Stephens Col, 68-71; prof art theory & criticism, Ind State Univ, Terre Haute, 1971-2002, prof emeritus, 2002-, chmn dept, 71-78. *Awards:* First Prize Watercolor, Kans Artists' Exhib, 62 & 65. *Bibliog:* Margaret Harold (ed), Prize Winning Watercolors of America, Allied Publ, 63; Jason Berry (auth), Rev, Ida Kohlmeyer: 30 years, New Orleans Mag, 19-20, 1/85; David Kiehl (auth), Ida Kohlmeyer: Recent Works, Morris Mus, 96. *Mem:* Col Art Asn Am; Nat Coun Art Admin; Mid-Am Col Art Asn. *Media:* Enamel, Acrylics, Serigraphy. *Specialty:* Regional Artists of theMidwest, all media. *Publ:* article in Arts Update, 2/83; Ida Kohlmeyer (catalog), Mint Mus, 12/83; article, Full circle for Dick Hay--sculptor in clay, Butlleti Informatiu de Ceramica, Barcelona, Spain, 86; articles in Ceramic Art Monthly, 12/97. *Dealer:* Diane Mann and Assoc RR1 Box 116 Merom In 47861; Swope Museum Purchase Gallery 25 South 7th St Terre Haute IN 47807; Farrington Gallery 1540 S 3rd St Terre Haute IN 47802. *Mailing Add:* 1509 S Center St Terre Haute IN 47802

ENGLE, STEVE
SCULPTOR, PAINTER
b Honolulu, Hawaii, Dec 27, 50. *Study:* Santa Barbara Art Inst, Calif, BFA(sculpture), 71-73; Ind Univ, Bloomington, MFA(sculpture), 77-80; Pa Acad Fine Art, Philadelphia, figure painting class, 82-84. *Work:* Microsoft Corp, Redmond, Wash; First Hawaiian Bank, Honolulu; Wash State Arts Comn; Sch Dist, Lacey, Wash; Seattle Arts Comn. *Comn:* sculpture comn by Laila & Thurston Twigg-Smith, Honolulu, Hawaii, 84 & 94; sculpture, Seattle Arts, Comn, Wash, 90. *Exhib:* Sculpture & photog, Contemp Arts Ctr, Hawaii, 81; solo exhibs, Passing Through, 90, Figurative Compulsions, 92, Lisa Harris Gallery, Seattle, Wash & Steve Engle-Sculptures, Contemp Mus, Honolulu, 96, Davis & Cline Gallery, Ashland, Ore, 2000, Hypotenuse Gallery, Sinclair Community Col, Dayton, Ohio, 01; Thirty Yrs of the Honolulu Advertiser Gallery 1961-1991, Honolulu Advertiser Gallery, 91; Exhibition 6, Microsoft Corp, Redmond, Wash, 92; Spirit of the West, A Celebration of the Arts, WestOne Bank, Wash, Ore & Idaho, 92; Nat Showcase V, Alternative Mus, NY; Thorndike Gallery, Southern Ore Univ, Ashland, 01; Hypotenuse Gallery, Sinclair Cmty Col, Dayton, Ohio, 01; Davis & Cline Gallery, Ashland, 00; The Contemp Mus, Honolulu, 96. *Teaching:* Sculpture clay figure sculpture, woodcarving sculpture workshop, Sonoma State Univ, 93. *Awards:* Visual Artists Fel Sculpture, Nat Endowment Arts, 90; Seattle Artists Proj Grant, Seattle Arts Comn, 90; Wash State Arts Comn Slide Registry, Olympia, 91. *Bibliog:* Gretchen Faust (auth), Syncretism: art of the 21st century (exhib, catalog), Arts Mag, 5/91; Doug Margeson (auth), Artwork for AIDS, J Am, 3/19/93; Joan Rose (auth), Contemporary museum exhibits spiritual, sensual, Honolulu Advertiser, 9/96. *Media:* Wood, Clay, Oil. *Mailing Add:* 1065 Benson Way Unit 11 Ashland OR 97520

ENGLER, KATHLEEN GIRDLER
SCULPTOR
b Indianapolis, Ind, Jan 30, 51. *Study:* John Herron Sch Art, Ind Univ, 69-70; Univ Ga, 80; Med Col of Ga, 80; Augusta Col, BFA, 81. *Work:* Southern Bell Corp Collection, AFCO Corp Collection, Atlanta, Ga; Osbon Med Syst Int; So Bell, Atlanta Ga; Creative Arts Guild, Dalton, Ga; plus others. *Comn:* Cultural Triad (bronze fountain), Maxwell Performing Arts Theater, Augusta, Ga, 86; Bronze Women of Excellence Awards, 88-98; The Graduate (bronze), Med Col of Ga, 89; Life's Advocate, Univ Hosp Women's Ctr, Augusta, Ga, 98; 3 piece monumental bronze, Children's Med Ctr, Augusta, Ga, 99. *Exhib:* Mobile Mus Art, Ala, 96; Celebrating the Torch; A Run of Grecian Images Phorum, Augusta, Ga, 96; Red Clay Survey, Huntsville Mus Art, Ala, 98; Resurrected Forms, Spartanburg Mus Art, SC, 99 & Gertrude Herbert Art Inst, Ga, 99; Mother/Nature, B Rust and K Groler Engler, 2002; Mary Pauline Gallery, Augusta, Ga, 2002; The Nature of Change, Oconee Cult Arts Found, Watkinsville, Ga, 2003. *Teaching:* artist in res, Children's Med Ctr, Med Col of Ga. *Bibliog:* Jeffrey Day (auth), Powerful sculpture: The State, 8/93; Rich Coply (auth), Sculptor inspired by nature, Augusta Chronicle, 9/94; The Source Book of Artists: Architects, Ed 10, The Guild, 95; On the Outside: Public Sculpture, Augusta Chronicale, 2/2000. *Media:* Bronze, Paper, Pulp. *Dealer:* The Mary Pauline Gallery, Augusta, Ga, 30901. *Mailing Add:* 753 Aumond Rd Augusta GA 30909-3258

ENGLER, SHERRIE LEE
PAINTER, ILLUSTRATOR
b Paducah, Ky, July 9 62. *Study:* Ark State Univ, BS, 1985. *Exhib:* Equine Art Guild 4th Ann Art Exhib (online exhib), Mustard Creek Art Gallery, LaCrosse, Wis, 2002. *Pos:* Graphic Artist Illusr, Carson Graphics, Jackson, Tenn, 1985-1987; Illusr, Equine Res Inc, Tyler, Tex, 1999-2001; Equine Artist, Headed W Studios, Tenn, 2001-2005-. *Teaching:* Instr Art, Univ Sch Jackson (Col Prep Sch), 1991-1996. *Awards:* Top 3

Selling Items, Am Horse Publ, Horseman's Corral, 2002; Cover Artist (22 covers), Horseman's Corral, Sherrie Engler, 2000-2005. *Mem:* Nat Mus of women in the Art, Wash, DC; Blue Book of N Am Artists; Equine Art Guild; Equine Arts Protection League (pres). *Media:* Mixed Media, Paint Pencil/Watercolor. *Publ:* (Ed), Todays Horse Trader Design Assoc Inc NMex, 2002; (ed), Equine Marketeer, The Equine Marketeer, Pa, 2003; (ed), Mid-South Horse Review, Apr 2003 Review, Horse Review, Somerville, Tenn, 2003; (illus), Photos & Drawings for Conformation & Anatomy (496 pgs), 1999; (illus), True Horse Stories, Equine Res Inc, 2001. *Mailing Add:* 2797 Stafford Stone Rd Greenfield TN 38230

ENGLISH, HAL (HAROLD) J
PAINTER
b Buffalo, NY, Nov 21, 1910. *Study:* Albright Art Sch, Univ Buffalo. *Comn:* 249 Pvt Portraits. *Exhib:* Pastels Only-Pastel Soc Am, Nat Arts Club, NY, 79-84, 86-91 & 2000, PSA Master Pastelist, 87; National Small Paintings Exhib, NMex Art League, Albuquerque, 82-94; Artists of Am, Colo Hist Mus, Denver, 83 & 90; Pastels USA, Sacramento Fine Arts Ctr, Carmichael, Calif, 87-89; Ann Exhib-Oil Painters Am, Prince Gallery, Chicago, 92; Miniatures, Albuquerque Mus, NMex, 93, 94, 95, 96, 97 & 98. *Pos:* Advert, 35-65. *Teaching:* Instr design, State Univ Col Buffalo, 65-66; artist-in-residence drawing, Hilbert Col, Hamburg, NY 74-76. *Awards:* Russell Award, Pastels Only, Pastel Soc Am, 80 & Heydenrick Award, 87; Best of Show, Nat Small Paintings Exhib, NMex Art League, 82-83 & 89; Best of Show, 2nd Nat, Pastel Soc, NFla, 92; Acad Artists Asn Medal of Honor, Springfield, Mass, 87. *Bibliog:* Dale C English & Pat Yungbluth (coauths), Hal English, Artists Rockies, 84. *Mem:* Pastel Soc Am; Acad Artists Asn; Fine Arts League Buffalo (pres, 90-92); Pastel Guild, Buffalo. *Media:* Pastel. *Dealer:* Art Dialogue Gallery Linwood Ave Buffalo NY. *Mailing Add:* 6055 Armor Rd Orchard Park NY 14127-3150

ENGLISH, HELEN WILLIAMS DRUTT See Drutt, Helen Williams

ENGLISH, JOHN ARBOGAST
PAINTER
b Trenton, NJ, Nov 7, 13. *Study:* Trenton Sch Indust Art; Trenton State Col, BS. *Comn:* Numerous marine paintings & yacht portraits comn by pvt individuals. *Exhib:* Miami Int Boat Show Marine Exhib, 74-75; Am Soc Marine Artists Ann Show, 78-79; Greenwich Workshop Ann Marine Show, 79; Mystic Seaport Ann Marine Show, 79; 3rd Ann Exhib, Am Soc Marine Artists, 81; and others. *Pos:* Publ lithographic reproductions marine subj, Riverside Studio, Island Heights, NJ. *Awards:* Gold Medal, Franklin Mint; First Award Oil Painting, Ocean Co Artist Guild; Second in Show, Miami Int Boat Show Exhib. *Mem:* Ocean Co Artist Guild; Grove House, Miami; charter mem Am Soc Marine Artists. *Media:* Oil. *Dealer:* Newman Galleries 1625 Walnut St Philadelphia PA 19103

ENMAN, TOM KENNETH
PAINTER, MUSEUM DIRECTOR
b Salt Lake City, Utah, Feb 22, 28. *Study:* Univ Wash, Exten, 48-49; Chicago Acad Fine Arts, cert, 52; Cape Sch Art, Provincetown, Mass, scholar, 52; Calif Col Arts & Crafts, Oakland, 53-54; Univ Calif, Los Angeles, Exten, 58-61; Laguna Beach Sch Art, Calif, 69; also with Alex Villumsion & Playa Del Ray, Calif, 62. *Exhib:* 19th Newport Ann, Newport Beach, Calif, 64; Laguna Beach Art Gallery Ann Fall Mem, 64; All Calif Exhib, Laguna Beach, 65; 7th Nat Ann Art Round Up, Las Vegas, 66; Laguna Beach Art Asn Graphic & Drawing Exhib, 67. *Pos:* Dir, Artist Guild Laguna Beach, 64-65 & Laguna Beach Mus Art, 65-80; consul, Plein Air Painters, 82 & 86. *Awards:* First in Graphic (pen & ink), 64 & hon mention in oil, 65, Laguna Beach Art Asn. *Mem:* Laguna Beach Art Asn (dir); Monterey Hist & Art Asn, Calif. *Media:* Oil, Watercolor. *Res:* American artist from 1890-1940. *Dealer:* Redfern Gallery 1540 South Coast Hwy Laguna Beach CA 92651; Maureen Murphy Fine Arts 1187 Coast Village Rd Montecito CA 93108

ENOS, CHRIS
PHOTOGRAPHER, ASSEMBLAGE ARTIST
b Calif, Aug 21, 44. *Study:* Foothill Col, AA, 65; Univ Am, Mexico City, 67; San Francisco State Univ, BA(sculpture), 69; San Francisco Art Inst, MFA(photog), 70. *Work:* George Eastman House, Rochester, NY; Bibliot Nat, Paris; Polaroid Corp, Amsterdam, Holland; Shaklee Corp, Calif; Seagrams Collection, NY; DeCordova Mus & Sculpture Park, Lincoln, Mass; and many others. *Exhib:* Mass Inst Technol, Cambridge, 71, 73 & 80; San Francisco Mus Art, 71 & 80; Fogg Art Mus, 74, 76, 78 & 80; one-person shows, Somerville Community Access Ctr, Somerville, Mass, 90, Barn Gallery, Oqunquit, Maine, 90 & Pagosa Springs Art Ctr, Colo, 92; Recent Acquisitions, Boston Mus Fine Arts, 76; Univ Vt, Burlington, 80; Int Ctr Photog, NY; Inst Contemp Art, Boston, 81 & 83; Sonnabend Gallery, NY, 81; Artist Found Gallery, Boston, Mass, 91; Photog Resource Ctr, Boston, Mass, 91; Robinson Gallery, Denver, Colo, 93; Denver Art Mus, Colo, 93. *Pos:* Founder & pres, Photog Resource Ctr, Boston, 76-81; Gallery dir & coordr lect series, New Eng Sch Photog, 77-78; artist in residence, Lightwork Workshop, Syracuse Univ, 78 & Int Ctr Photog, NY, 80. *Teaching:* Instr photog, Sonoma State Univ, 71-73, San Francisco Acad Art, 72-73, Univ Calif, San Francisco, 72-73 & New Eng Sch Photog, 77-78; asst prof, Windham Col, 74 & Hampshire Col, 74-75; instr, Harvard Univ, 77 & MA prog, summer 80; vis artist, Univ Colo, Boulder, 80 & Smith Col, Northampton, Mass, 82-83; vis lectr, Univ Calif, Los Angeles, 83; assoc prof, Univ NH, 86-; lectr, Tufts Univ, Medford, Mass, 91; lectr, Pagosa Springs Art Ctr, Colo, 92. *Awards:* Liberal Arts Fac Summer Res Fel, Univ NH, 91; Somerville Arts Coun Artists Fel, 93; Mass Cult Coun Fel, 98. *Bibliog:* Alfred A Knopf (auth), Legacy of Light, NY, 87; Simon & Schuster (auths), Flora Photoraphicia, NY, 91; Photography in Boston 1955-1985, MIT Press, 2001. *Mem:* Soc Photog Educ; Visual Studies Workshop, NY; Photog Resource Ctr Boston; and others. *Media:* Mixed Media. *Publ:* Contribr, Camera 35 Mag, New York, 73; Camera Mag, Bucher/Switz, 75; Horticulture Mag, Boston, 77; Women See Women, Crowell, 77; auth, Landscape as Photograph, Yale Univ Press, New Haven, Conn, 85

ENRIGHT, JUDY A
PAINTER, PRINTMAKER
b Canton, Ohio, May 16, 39. *Study:* St Mary's Col, Notre Dame, Ind, BA, 61; Univ Mich, with Jerome Kamrowski & Rudolf Arnheim, BFA (cum laude), 85; Kyoto Seika Univ, Japan, 90. *Work:* Capital Commons Ctr, Lansing, Mich; R P Scherer Corp, Troy, Mich; Spectrum Health Hosp, Grand Rapids, Mich; Swords into Plowshares Mus, Detroit; Bank of Ann Arbor. *Exhib:* Award Show, Saginaw Art Mus, Mich, 78; Ann Show, Massillon Art Mus, Ohio, 91-92; Ann Award Show, Art Ctr Battle Creek, Mich, 92-94; Ann Award Show, Ella Sharp Mus, Jackson, Mich, 93; Galeria Biegas, Detroit; Shiawasee Arts Coun. *Teaching:* Pvt art tchr. *Awards:* Bob Typsinski Mem Award, Gold Medal Exhib, Scarab Club, 86; Pauline Angle Award, All Media Show, Left Bank Gallery, Flint, Mich, 94; Outstanding Achievement Award Visual Arts, Livingston Arts Coun, 94. *Bibliog:* Robert Romaker (auth), Brighton artist puts visual questions on big canvases, Ann Arbor News, 1/91; Joy Hakanson Colby (auth), Enright exotica, The Detroit News, 4/21/94; John Carlos Canto (auth), Cleared for takeoff, Ann Arbor News, 7/17/94. *Mem:* Ann Arbor Women Painters (treas, 86); Brighton Art Guild. *Media:* Oil. *Publ:* Auth, Environment & Art Letter, Chicago, IL, 1/97; Metropolitan Women Mag, Detroit, 95, 96. *Mailing Add:* 5620 Bauer Rd Brighton MI 48116

ENRIQUEZ, GASPAR
PAINTER, METALSMITH
b El Paso, Tex, July 18, 42. *Study:* East Los Angeles Jr Col; Univ Tex, El Paso, BA; printmaking with Loren Janzen & jewelry with Walt Harrison; NMex State Univ, metalsmithing with Kate Wagle & Peter Voris, MA. *Work:* State Nat Bank; Univ Tex, El Paso; NMex State Univ Gallery; Southwestern Bell. *Exhib:* Fresno Art Mus, 91; San Francisco Mus Art, 91; Albuquerque Mus, 91; Denver Art Mus, 91; Plains Art Mus, Fargo, NDak; Univ Minn Art Mus, Minneapolis; Nat Mus Am Art, Washington, DC; El Paso Mus Art, La Rosa Dolorosa, 95; The Col Santa Fe 1995 Sculpture Proj, 95; Assistance League of Houston, Celebrates Texas Art, 95-96; Figurative Foundation, Martin-Rathburn Gallery, San Antonio, Tex, 96; Texas Dialogues, Blue Star Art Space, San Antonio, Tex, 97; Tres Proyectos Latinos, Laguna Gloria, Austin, Tex, 97; Una Pagina Mas, Adair Margo Gallery, 99; and others. *Awards:* Hon Mention, El Paso Int, 85; Juniors Award, Tex Fine Arts Asn Exhib, 87; Siqueiros-Pollock Award, 96. *Mem:* Juntos Art Asn (pres); Int Designers Craftsman; Am Craft Coun. *Media:* Acrylic, Oil; Precious Metals. *Dealer:* Mi Casa Studio Gallery San Elizario TX 79849; Janson-Perez Gallery 417 8th St San Antonio TX 78215. *Mailing Add:* Box 17112 El Paso TX 79917

ENSRUD, WAYNE
PAINTER, PRINTMAKER
b Albert Lea, Minn, Apr 4, 34. *Study:* Minneapolis Col Art & Design, BFA, 56; with Oskar Kokoschka, 56-79; with Ben Shahn, Joseph Albers & Vaclav Vitlacyl. *Work:* Bristol Mus Art, RI; New Eng Ctr Contemp Art, Brooklyn, Conn; French Inst Gallery, NY; Gallery Collection of Gov Trinidad, West Indies; Galleria of Contessa Borghese, Rome, Italy. *Comn:* Seagram's Taste of the Nation (poster), 93, 94 & 95; Domaine del la Romanee-Conti, France, 95; Domaine Le Flaive, France, 95; Sassicaia, Italy, 97; Robert Mondavi, 2001; and many others. *Exhib:* One-man shows, Oakland Art Mus, Bristol Art Mus, French Inst, NY Galerie Esmeralda, Paris, Galerie Damien, Paris, Sansio Gallery, Tokyo, Artistic Galleries, Scottsdale, Ariz, 93, Paintings of Paris bistros, 93, Grand Fetes Medoc, 94, Celebration of Burgundy, 95, Top NY Ital Restaurants, 96 & Famous Grand Cru Chateaux Medoc, 97, many others; Washington Ave Gallery, Minneapolis, Minn, 93; Beard Gallery, Minneapolis, Minn, 93; French Vineyard Series, Horseneck Inc, Greenwich Conn, 93; Gallery & Co, Tokyo, Japan, 93; Famous Ital Vineyards, 97; Art Collection Inc, Miami, Fla, 98; and numerous others. *Collection Arranged:* Lever House Coll, New Eng Ctr for Contemp Art; Bristol Art Mus; Musee D'Art, Callionoe, France. *Pos:* Art dir, Univ Calif, Berkeley, 58-61; exec art dir, Channel 13 TV, New York, 64; art dir, Gemini Space Program, ABC, New York, 65-66. *Teaching:* Instr film animation, Pratt Inst, New York, 67-72; painting & drawing, Cumberland Sch, Great Neck, NY, 67-79; guest prof figure painting, Simon's Rock Early Col, Great Barrington, Mass, 78. *Awards:* permanent marble plaque, Hotel de Medicis, Paris, 87; Soc of Grappileurs of Beaujolais, France, Inductee, 90; Commanderie du Bontemps de Medoc et des Graves, France, Inductee, 97. *Bibliog:* Monika Pichler (auth), Wayne Ensrud: Life of an artist, In: Work in Progress, 81; Lisa Doherty (auth), Wayne Ensrud: Life of an Artist, In: Work in Progress, 96. *Mem:* Coffee House Club. *Media:* Oil, Watercolor; Lithography, Etching. *Publ:* Contribr, Wine J; auth, Wine Journal with Paintings by Wayne Ensrud, Galison Press, New York, 96. *Dealer:* Peter Hastings Falk. *Mailing Add:* 65 Central Park W New York NY 10023

ENSTICE, WAYNE
ASSEMBLAGE ARTIST, WRITER
b Irvington, NJ, Dec 16, 43. *Study:* Pratt Inst, BFA, 65; Univ NMex, MA, 69. *Work:* Univ NC, Chapel Hill; Univ Ark, Art Gallery, Fayetteville; Roswell Mus & Art Ctr, NMex; Ariz Commun on Arts, Yuma Art Mus; Univ NMex, Albuquerque; Univ Ariz, Mus Art. *Exhib:* Alternative Mus, New York City; Drawing Ctr, New York City; Diverse Works Gallery, Houston, Tex; Saper Gallery, New York City; Space Gallery, Los Angeles. *Teaching:* Prof, chmn, Dept Art, Ind State Univ, Terre Haute, 90; prof, dir, Sch Art, Univ Cincinnati, Ohio, 95-2000; prof, Univ Cincinnati, 2000-. *Awards:* Artist-in-Residence Grant, Roswell Mus & Art Ctr, 84-85; grant Summerfair, Inc, 2001. *Bibliog:* Robert Murdock (auth), essay, Univ Ark Press, 79; William Peterson (auth), article, Artspace, 80; John Perreault (auth), Art in Am, 81; Peter Frank (auth), essay, Roswell Mus & Art Ctr Catalog, 85. *Publ:* Auth, Performance Art's Coming of Age, Performance Art, Dutton Press, 84; coauth, Drawing/Space, Form and Expression, 90, Prentice-Hall, ed, 96, 2003; co-auth, Jazz Spoken Here, La State Univ Press, 92 (hard cover), Da Capo Press, NY, 94 (soft cover); Reading Jazz, Robert Gottlieb (auth), Pantheon Books, NY, 96; co-auth, Jazzwomen, Indiana Univ Press, 2004. *Mailing Add:* 7310 Kirby Dr Burlington KY 41005-9687

ENTERLINE, SANDRA
JEWELER
b Oil City, Pa, 1960. *Study:* Rochester Inst Technol, Sch Am Craftsmen, AD, 80; RI Sch Design, BFA(jewelry & metalsmithing), 83. *Work:* Oakland Mus Art, Calif. *Exhib:* Solo exhibs, Susan Cummins Gallery, Mill Valley, Calif, 90, 94 & 96, Shaw Gallery, Northeast Harbour, Maine, 93; Americky Sperk (with catalog), Mus Decorative Arts, Prague, Czechoslavakia, 91; Good as Gold, The Hand & The Spirit Gallery, Scottsdale, Ariz, 92; Crossroads (with catalog), Artwear, NY, 92; Design Visions, Australian Int Crafts Triennial (with catalog), Art Gallery of Western Australia, Perth, 92; Jewelry Invitational, Mobilia Gallery, Cambridge, Mass, 93; 7 for 10, Susan Cummins Gallery, Mill Valley, Calif, 93; Am Jewelers, Perimeter Gallery, Chicago, Ill, 93; Sculptural Concerns: Contemp Am Metal working (with catalog), Contemp Arts Ctr, Cincinnati, Ohio, traveling, 93-94; Contemp Am Jewelry, Edinburgh Int Festival, Scottish Gallery, Scotland, 96; New Times, New Thinking: Jewelry in Europe and Am Traveling Exhib, Craft Coun Gallery, London & Nat Mus Wales, UK, 96; Cross Currents, Shipley Art Gallery Traveling Exhib, Birmingham Sch Jewelry & Silversmithing, Eng, Surrey Inst Art, Eng, Cleveland Craft Ctr, Eng & Soc Contemp Crafts, Pa, 96; Celebrating Am Art, Kunstindustrie Mus, Copenhagen, Denmark, 97; Brooching It Diplomatically: A Tribute to Madelaine K Albright, Helen Drutt Gallery traveling exhib, Mus Contemp Art, The Neth, Mus Applied Art & Design, Finland, 98; Jewelry Moves, Nat Mus Scotland, Edinburgh, 98; and others. *Teaching:* Vis artist, Mass Col Art, Boston, 91; vis prof, Sch Mus Fine Arts, Boston, 91-92. *Awards:* Visual Arts Fel, Nat Endowment Arts, 88. *Publ:* Auth, article, Jewelers Circular Keystone, 1/86; Metalsmith Mag, fall 88, spring 91 & winter 98

ENYEART, JAMES LYLE
HISTORIAN, DIRECTOR
b Auburn, Wash, Jan 13, 43. *Study:* Kansas City Art Inst, BFA, 65; Univ Santiago, Chile, cert(Orgn Am States Fel), 66-67; Univ Kans, MFA, 72. *Work:* Int Mus Photog, George Eastman House, Rochester, NY; Bibliot Nat, Paris, France; Sheldon Mem Gallery, Univ Nebr, Lincoln; Albrecht Mus Art, St Joseph, Mo; Nat Mus Am Art. *Comn:* Nineteenth Century archit of St Joseph, 74 & stained glass windows of St Joseph, 75, Albrecht Mus Art, St Joseph, Mo. *Pos:* Staff photog, Nelson Gallery Art, Kansas City, Mo, 65-66; charter dir, Albrecht Gallery Art, St Joseph, Mo, 67-68; cur photog, Helen Foresman Spencer Mus Art, Univ Kans, Lawrence, 68-76; comnr, Kans Arts Comn, 73-74; dir, Ctr Creative Photog, Univ Ariz, 77-89, ed, The Archive, 77-89, George Eastman House: Int Mus Photog & Film, Rochester, NY, 89-95; leader hist sect, Friends of Photog, Carmel, Calif, 76-77 & Rencontres Int de la Photog, Arles Festival, France, 79; visual arts rev panel, Nat Endowment for Arts, 79, panel mem design excellence proj, 84, grants panel spec exhibs category, 85, visual arts consult, 86, challenge grants/spec projs panel, 86 & 93 & peer panel mus challenge grants, 93; rev panel, 1980 Bush Found Fels, St Paul, Minn, 80; nominating comt, MacArthur Found, 82-; consult, Polaroid Corp, 83-89; adv comt, W Eugene Smith Mem Fund, 83-89 & Site Santa Fe, NMex, 98-; selection comt, Ariz Gov's Arts Awards, 84; ed, Image, 89-; mem creative arts award comn, Brandeis Univ, 90-95; adv bd Aaron Siskind Found, 91, Am Photog Inst, New York Univ, 91-, ITP & Columbia Univ, 92; adv panel, Eliot Porter Arch, Amon Carter Mus Art, 91 & Ctr for Am & Commonwealth Arts & Studies, Univ Exeter, Eng, 86-93; sr adv, Harold & Esther Edgerton Estate, Boston, Mass, 95-; dir, Marion Ctr, Col Santa Fe, 95-. *Teaching:* Instr drawing & design, Mo Western State Col, Univ Mo, 67-68; lectr art hist, Univ Kans, 68-70, asst prof, 69-75, assoc prof, 76, instr photog, 71-75; adj prof art, Univ Ariz, 77-89; consult, dept art, Cornell Univ, 93; Anne & John Marion prof photog arts, Coll Santa Fe, 95-. *Awards:* Nat Endowment for Arts Grant, 73, 74, 75, 76-94 & 95; Photokina Obelisk Award for photog contrib, Cologne, WGer, 82 & 94; John Simon Guggenheim Mem Fel, writing, 87, many others. *Bibliog:* profile, Ariz Highways, 1/86; Tamara Scalera (auth), Interview with James Enyeart, Photo Metro, 12/87; The 100 Most Important People in Photography, Am Photo, 5-6/98. *Mem:* Nat Soc Photog Educ (bd dir, 78-82, publ comt, 73-76, nat conf chair, 76); Friends Photog (exec dir, 76-77, vpres, 78-81); hon corresp mem Deutschen Gess für Photog. *Res:* Conservation and restoration of photographs; nineteenth and twentieth century photographers. *Publ:* Ansel Adams Legend and Legacy: Ansel Adams and Nineteenth Century Landscape Photographers, Pacific ress Serv, Japan, 93; The Nature of Photographs, Johns Hopkins Univ Press, 98; Land, Sky and All That Is Within: Visionary Photographers of the Southwest, Mus NMex Press, 7/98; William Christenberry: Absolute Essence (essay), in: William Cristenberry:Adams House in the Black Belt, Landfall Press, 99; Mirrors of Marginal Thought (essay for Jim Dine exhib), PaceWildenstein Gallery, New York, 9/99. *Mailing Add:* 46 Bonanza Trail Santa Fe NM 87505

EPSTEIN, MITCH (MITCHELL) D
PHOTOGRAPHER
b Holyoke, Mass, Aug 23, 52. *Study:* Union Col, Schenectady, NY, 70-71; RI Sch Design, 71-72; Cooper Union, New York, with Garry Winogrand, 72-74. *Work:* Metrop Mus Art, NY; Whitney Mus Am Art, NY; San Francisco Mus Mod Art, Calif; Mus Mod Art, NY; Mus Fine Arts, Houston, Tex; J Paul Getty Mus, Los Angeles, Calif; Art Inst Chicago, Ill; Corcoran Gallery Art, Washington, DC. *Exhib:* Contemp Urban Color, Addison Gallery Am Art, Phillips Acad, Andover, Mass, 80; Recent Acquisitions Exhib, Mus Fine Arts, Boston, Mass, 80; Recent Acquisitions Exhib, Corcoran Gallery Art, Washington, 80; Color Photographs: Recent Acquisitions, Mus Mod Art, NY, 84 & 87; Romance of the Taj Mahal (traveling exhib), Los Angeles Co Mus Art, 90-91; one-man exhibs, Fogg Art Mus, Cambridge, Mass, 91, Julie Saul Gallery, NY, 94, Tenri Gallery, NY, 95, Gallery Contemp Photog, Los Angeles, 96, Wooster Gardens/Brent Sikkema, NY, 96 & Ctr Doc Studies, Durham, NC, 98; This Sporting Life (traveling exhib), High Mus Art, Atlanta, 92-93; India: A Celebration of Independence, Philadelphia Mus Art, Pa, 97; Photog after Modernism: Extensions into Contemp Art, San Francisco Mus Mod Art, Calif, 98; Eggleston and the Color Tradition, J Paul Getty Mus, Calif, 99; Yancy Richardson Gallery, NY, Photo Espana, Madrid, Jackson Fine Art, Atlanta, 2004; Sikkema Jenkins & Co, NY, 2005. *Teaching:* lectr color photog, Carpenter Ctr, Harvard Univ, 77; Lectr, Int Ctr Photog, winter 97, assoc prof photog, Bard Col, Sch Art, 97; vis lectr, grad photog prog, Sch Visual Arts, 2004. *Awards:* Individual Photog Grant, Nat Endowment Arts, 78 & NY State Coun Arts, 80; Grant, Pinewood Found, 94; John Simon Guggenheim Memorial Found, Fel 2002-2003; Kraszna-Kraus Photog Book Award, 2004. *Bibliog:* Charles Hagen (auth), Art in Review: Mitch Epstein, Julie Saul Gallery, NY Times, 4/94; Peter von Ziegesar (auth), Mitch Epstein at Julie Saul, Art in Am, 7/94; Jim Lewis (auth), review, George Mag, 10/96. *Publ:* Photogr, In Pursuit of India, Aperture, New York, 87; auth, Fire, Water, Wind: Photographs from Tenri, Doyusha, Tenri, Japan, 95; Doubletake, In Vietnam and Versailles, Ctr Doc Studies at Duke Univ, Durham, NC, 95; A New Life: Stories and Photographs from the Suburban South, WW Norton/Double Take, NY, 96; Vietnam: A Book of Changes, W W Norton/Doubletake, 96; The City, Powerhouse Books, 2001; Family Business, Steidl, 2003; Recreation: American Photographs 1973-88, Steidl, 2005. *Dealer:* Brent Sikkema Gallery 530 West 22nd St New York NY 10011; Sikkema Jenkins & Co 530 W 22nd NYC 10011. *Mailing Add:* 6 Rivington St No 2 New York NY 10002

EPSTEIN, YALE
PAINTER, PRINTMAKER
b New Haven, Conn, Jan 26, 34. *Study:* Brooklyn Mus Art Sch, 55-58 & Rosenthal Scholar, 59; Brooklyn Col with AD Reinhardt & Marc Rothko, MFA, 58; Pratt Graphics Ctr, 72-75. *Comn:* Hyatt Hotel, NY; Marriot Hotel, Palm Springs, Calif; Pfizer Corp, NY; Royal Caribbean Cruise Lines. *Exhib:* Art 14, Basel Int, Switz, 83 & 90; Prints USA, Univ Wis, La Crosse; Woodstock Artists Asn; Hudson River Mus, Yonkers, NY; Brooklyn Col. *Collection Arranged:* Brooklyn Mus, NY; Albright-Knox Gallery, Buffalo, NY; Bibliot Nat, Paris, France; City of Chicago; Univ Wis; Yale Univ. *Teaching:* Instr art, Brooklyn Col, NY, 76-83 & Sch Visual Arts, 82-90. *Awards:* First Prize Graphics, Hudson River Mus, 84. *Bibliog:* Rev, Print Collector's Newslett, 9/81. *Mem:* Nat Art Educ Asn; Col Art Asn; Artists Equity; Woodstock Artists Asn; Soc Am Graphic Artists. *Media:* Pastel; Etching, Monoprint, Painting. *Interests:* travel. *Publ:* Auth, article, Art J, Col Art Asn, winter 67-68; Tom Boutis, rev, Arts Mag, 6/80; Artspeak, 6/16/88; Aspects of Nature, Domberger Stuttgart Ger Publ, 90. *Dealer:* Somerhill Gallery 3 Eastgate E Franklin St Chapel Hill NC 27514; Suma Gallery 527 Amsterdam Ave NY NY 10024; Michele Birnbaum Fa PO Box 286232 NY NY 10128. *Mailing Add:* 20 Wiley Ln Woodstock NY 12498

EPTING, MARION AUSTIN
PRINTMAKER, EDUCATOR
b Forrest, Miss, Jan 28, 40. *Study:* Los Angeles City Col, AA; Los Angeles Co Art Inst, Otis, MFA, 69; also with Ernest Freed, Lee Chesney, Shiro Ikegawa & Charles White. *Work:* Oakland Mus, Calif; Seattle Art Mus; Libr Cong, Washington, DC; Achenbach Found, DeYoung Mus, San Francisco; Whitney Mus, NY; Smithsonian Inst; and others. *Comn:* Intaglio prints comn by John Wilson, Lakeside Studios, Mich, 72 & 74. *Exhib:* 1st Nat Print Exhib, San Diego Fine Arts Soc, 69; Northwest Printmakers, Seattle Art Mus, 69; Oakland Art Mus, 73; traveling exhib, Western Asn Art Mus, 73-75; Smithsonian Inst Traveling Exhibs, 80-84. *Collection Arranged:* Black Untitled III, Western Asn Art Mus; Chico Group, Old Bergen Art Guild, NJ. *Pos:* Resident artist, Lakeside Studios, Mich, 70-; art dir, J-Squared B-Squared Consult, Los Angeles, 71-. *Teaching:* Prof art, Calif State Univ, Chico, 69-. *Awards:* Calif South 7 Best of Show, San Diego Fine Arts Guild, 69; Northwest Printmakers Purchase Award, Seattle Art Mus, 69; First Place for Graphics, Cal Expo, Del Mar, Calif, 69. *Bibliog:* J Edward Atkinson (auth), Black Dimensions in Contemporary American Art, Times Mirror, 71; Theresa Dickason Cederholm (auth), Afro American Artists, Boston Pub Libr, 73; Waddy/Lewis (auth), Art: African American, Harcourt Brace Jovanovich, 78. *Media:* Intaglio, Serigraphy. *Mailing Add:* Calif State Univ Art Dept Chico CA 95929-0820

ERBE, CHANTELL VAN
GRAPHIC ARTIST, PAINTER
b Jersey City, NJ, Dec 31, 68. *Study:* Self taught. *Comn:* computer presentations, computer illus, graphic art, pvt comns. *Exhib:* Nat Arts Club, NY, 95, 96, 98, 99, 2000-2004; Salmagundi Mus, NY, 2000; Butler Inst Art, Youngstown, Ohio, 2001; Audubon Artists Inc, 2000, 2001, 2002; Nat Arts Club, 2001, 2002; Catharine Lorillard Wolfe Art Club, 2001, 2002; J Wayne Stark Gallery, College Station, Tex, 2003; Mus Tex Tech Univ, Lubbock, 2003; McInich Art Gallery, 2006. *Awards:* Art Award most creative artist, Ramapo Co, 1987; Strathmore Award, Allied Artists Am, 96; Am Biog Award, 2000. *Bibliog:* Martin Parsins (auth), Allied artists, a plethora of pleasures, Artspeak Mag, 95-96. *Mem:* Allied Artists Am (exec sec, 95-98, bd dir, 99-2001); Colored Pencil Soc Am. *Media:* Colored Pencil. *Publ:* Brian H Peterson (auth), The Cities, The Towns, The Crowds: The Paintings of Robert Spencer, 2004; Jessic Salisbury (auth), Exhibit Proves Fine Art Can Spring from the Humble Colored Pencil, Tel News, 4/2004; Nikki Moustaki (auth), Parrots for Dummies, 2005; Anton Souza (auth), Top 3 Friendliest Birds, Bird Talk Mag, 8/2005; Samuel Buckle (auth), Escape from Samsara, Cancer of the Tribe, Island, Revolve Mag, 2005

ERBE, GARY THOMAS
PAINTER
b Union City, NJ, Sept 2, 44. *Study:* Self-taught. *Comn:* Butler Inst Am Art, Ohio. *Exhib:* Solo Exhibs, Summit Art Ctr, NJ, 76, New Britain Mus Am Art, Conn, 76, Alexander Gallery, NY, 82 & 85, NJ State Mus, Trenton (with catalog), 83, Butler Inst Am Art, Youngstown, Ohio (with catalog), 85, Sordini Art Gallery, 85, ACA Gallery, NY, 98, Harmon-Meek Gallery, Fla, 2003; Baseball Hall Fame, Cooperstown, NY, 91; NJ Fine Arts Ann, Noyes Mus, Oceanville, 92; traveling retrospective (with catalog), New Britian Mus Am Art, Conn, Butler Inst Am Art, Ohio, James A Michener Art Mus, Pa & Boca Raton Art Mus, Fla, 95; Boca Raton (Fla) Art Mus, 95; Springfield Art Mus, 99; Nat Arts Club, NY, 2000. *Awards:* First Prize, Nat Arts Club, 97; Gold

Medal, Audubon Artists, 98; The Salzman Award, Nat Arts Club, 98; Lifetime Achievement Award, The Butler Inst Am Art. *Bibliog:* Levitational realism, Am Artist, 74; Gary T Erbe, Arts Mag, 82; An artist who captures the eye, then the mind, New York Times, 83; Local heroes, NJ Monthly, 84. *Mem:* Allied Artists Am (pres, 94-); Assoc Artists NJ; Conn Acad Fine Arts; Audubon Artists; Nat Arts Club; fel Salmagundi Club; Trompe L'Oeil Soc Artists. *Media:* Oil. *Collection:* The Butler Institute American Art, Ohio; Montclair Art Museum, NJ, NJ State Museum; Archives of American Art, DC. *Publ:* NY Art Review & Am Artists, Krantz Pub; Int Artists Mag. *Mailing Add:* 600 Hudson St Apt #5A Hoboken NJ 07030

ERBE, JOAN
PAINTER, SCULPTOR
b Baltimore, Md, Nov 1, 26. *Study:* Md Inst Col Art. *Work:* Munic Court, Washington; Peale Mus, Baltimore; Baltimore Mus Art; Morgan Col; Mus de Barrio, Caracus, Venezuela. *Exhib:* Seven shows, Baltimore Mus Art, 54-65; Smithsonian Inst, 56; Corcoran Gallery Art, 57-60; Butler Inst Am Art, 60 & 61; Am Acad Arts, 76; Acad Arts, Easton, Md, 86; Rehoboth Art League, 87; Partners Gallery, Bethesda, Md, 88-91; 6 one-person shows, Gomez Gallery, Baltimore, Md, 89-94. *Teaching:* Pvt lessons, 70-. *Awards:* Artists Equity Asn, 60 & 61; Corcoran Gallery Art, 60 & 62; Baltimore Mus Art, 63, 64 & 66; plus others. *Media:* All Media. *Dealer:* Gomez Gallery 3600 Clipper Mill Rd No 100 Baltimore MD 21211; Hand Artes Truchas NM

ERBES, ROSLYN MARIA See Rensch, Roslyn

ERBURU, ROBERT F
PATRON
b Ventura, Calif, Sept 27, 30. *Study:* Univ Southern Calif, BA, 52; Harvard Univ Law Sch, JD, 55. *Pos:* Chmn bd, Chief Exec Officer, pres, Times Mirror Co, Los Angeles, bd dir, formerly; chmn, Reserve Bank of San Francisco, 89-91; bd dir, Marsh & McLennan Co, Inc, New York City, 96-, lead dir, 2004-, non-exec chmn, 2005-; trustee coun, Nat Gallery Art, Wash, DC, 2000-; chmn, emer, J Paul Getty Trust, currently. *Mem:* CofC of US & Los Angeles Area CofC (dir, formerly); Newspaper Asn Am (bd govs, exec bd, exec comt, bd dir, 80-92, off, 88-92, chmn, 91-92); Art Collections & Botanical Gardens. *Mailing Add:* Marsh & McLennan Co Inc 1166 Ave of Americas New York NY 10036

ERDELAC, JOSEPH MARK
COLLECTOR, PATRON
b Cleveland, Ohio. *Exhib:* Ohio Collectors, A Nations Legacy, Toung, Japan. *Mem:* Life mem Cleveland Mus Art, Butler Inst Am Art, Youngstown, Ohio & Royal Photographic Soc Brit. *Interests:* Donor of art works to local and national museums, universities, schools and educational television. *Collection:* Oils, watercolors and graphics by local and national Washington Project for the Arts artists; oils, watercolors, drawings and graphics by Rockwell Kent; watercolors, drawings and collages by Stephen Longstreet; also work by Henry Miller, Charles Bukowski, Kenneth Patchen and Udinotti. *Mailing Add:* 19630 Center Ridge Rd Rocky River OH 44116-3635

ERDLE, ROB
PAINTER, EDUCATOR
b Selma, Calif, Aug 17, 49. *Study:* Reedley Col, Calif, AA; Calif State Univ, Fresno, BA; Bowling Green Univ, Ohio, MFA. *Exhib:* Ala Nat Watercolor Exhib, Birmingham Mus Art, 75-76; Toledo May Show, Toledo Mus Art, Ohio, 75-76; Southern Watercolorist Nat Exhib, Cheekwood Arts Ctr, Nashville, Tenn, 77; Rocky Mountain Nat Watercolor Exhib, Foothills Arts Ctr, Golden, Colo, 77; one-man show, Del Mar Col, Corpus Christi, Tex, 77; Tex Fine Arts Nat Exhib, Laguna Gloria Art Mus, Austin, 77; and others. *Pos:* Dir, Chautauqua Inst Art Gallery, Chautauqua, NY. *Teaching:* Asst prof watercolor works on paper, NTex State Univ, 76-80, assoc prof, 80-. *Awards:* Outstanding Painting Award, May Show, Toledo Mus Art, 75 & 76; First Prize Purchase Award, Ala Nat Watercolor Exhib, Birmingham Mus Art, 76; Watercolor USA, Springfield Art Mus, 77. *Mem:* Nat Watercolor Soc, Los Angeles; Tex Watercolor Soc, San Antonio; Watercolor Soc Ala, Birmingham; Southern Watercolor Soc, Memphis; Southwestern Watercolor Soc, Dallas. *Media:* Mixed. *Mailing Add:* 1701 Greenwood Dr Denton TX 76201

ERENBERG, SAMUEL JOSEPH
PAINTER, PRINTMAKER
b Los Angeles, Calif, 1943. *Study:* Univ Calif, MFA, 76. *Work:* Mus Fine Arts, Kunstmuseum, Bern, Switzerland, Lucern, Switzerland; Univ Calif Berkeley Art Mus; San Diego Mus Art; Santa Barbara Mus Art. *Exhib:* Sam Erenberg, Univ Art Mus, Santa Barbara, Calif, 75; Maxwell's Law, Santa Barbara Mus Art, 78; Sam Erenberg: Recent Work, Santa Barbara Contemp Arts Forum, Calif, 84; PLANETSprocketpaintings, Skirball Cult Ctr Mus, Los Angeles, 89; Die Sammlung Toni Gerber, Mus Fine Arts, Kunstmuseum, Bern, Switz, 96; Invitational, The Jewish Mus San Francisco, 97; In Search of the Absolute, Sheldon Mem Art Gallery, Lincoln, Nebr, 97; Sam Erenberg: Painting, Nora Eccles Harrison Mus, Logan, Utah, 2000; Craig Krull Gallery, Santa Monica, Calif, 2003. *Teaching:* vis artist, The Ohio State Univ, Columbus, 78-79. *Awards:* Artists fel Calif Arts Coun, 99; Artists fel Durfee Foundation, 2003. *Bibliog:* Barbara Gilbert (auth), Tabernacle, 87; Rosanna Albertini (auth), The Complete Works of R.B., 99; Frances Colpitt (auth), The Ash Paintings, catalog for exhib at Craig Krull Gallery, Santa Monica, Calif, 2004. *Mem:* Am Asn Mus. *Media:* Painting. *Specialty:* Painting, Photography. *Dealer:* Craig Krull Gallery 2525 Michigan Ave B-3 Santa Monica CA 90403. *Mailing Add:* 947 25th St Santa Monica CA 90403-2109

ERES, EUGENIA
PAINTER
b Winiza, Ukrania, Apr 28, 28; US citizen. *Study:* Fine Art Sch, Sao Paulo, Brazil, with Prof Murillo, 54-58; Famous Artists Sch, Westport, Conn, with Norman Rockwell, Fletcher Martin & Doug Kingman, 66-69; Nat Acad Fine Arts, New York, with Hugh Cumpel, 70-71. *Work:* Galleria de Artes IV Centenario, Sao Paulo; Russian Am Hist Mus, Lakewood, NJ; pvt collection of Jacqueline Kennedy-Onassis, H Bartow Farr Jr Dep Gen Counsel, and others. *Exhib:* One-man show, Galleria de Artes IV Centenario, Sao Paolo, Brazil, 56-58, Int Art Expo NY Coliseum, 83-85, Int Art Expo, Wash, DC, 83, Hommond Mus North Salem, NY, 68; Am Artists Prof League Grand Nat, 68-94; Nat Art League, NY, 74-81; Knickerbocker Artists, 74-81; Hudson Valley, 76-94; Pen & Brush, 77-79; Salmagundi Club, 77-78; Custom House Mus Area, World Trade Ctr, NY, 79-81; Le Salon des Nations, Paris, 83. *Awards:* First Prize, Russian Am Soc, 75-78; Gold Medal of Honor, Nat Art League, 77; Gold Medal, Accademia Italia, 79; and others. *Mem:* Life fel Am Artists Prof League; Knickerbocker Artists; Nat Art League; Catharine Lorillard Wolfe Art Club; Accademia Italia; Hudson Valley Art Asn. *Media:* Oil, Lithographs. *Interests:* Traditional impressionist. *Mailing Add:* 109-10 Park Line S No A-10 Richmond Hill NY 11418

ERICKSON, JOY M
PAINTER, GRAPHIC ARTIST, PHOTOGRAPHER
b Princeton, Ill, June 18, 32. *Study:* Northern Ill Univ, with Jack McCarthy, 61; Univ Ill, with William J Kennedy, 62. *Work:* Rotunda, United Methodist Bldg, Capitol Hill, Washington, DC; Funderburg Libr, Manchester Col, North Manchester, Ind; Everett Free Libr, Pa; Int Serv Ctr, Md. *Comn:* Beauty in Aging, mural, comn by the directors, Fahrney Keedy Chapel, Boonesboro, Md, 73; Ashton 1910, hist mural, Ashton Hist Soc, Ill, 74; portrait of Dorothy Johnson, comn by Dr John Baker, Juniata Col, Huntingdon, Pa, 89; portrait, Elizabeth Baker, comn by John Baker, Ohio Univ, Athens, 91; portrait, Dr C C Ellis, comn by Dr Calvert N Ellis for Juniata Col, Huntingdin, Pa, 92; portrait, H B Brumbaugh, comn by Harold Brumbaugh for Juniata Col, Huntingdin, Pa, 92. *Exhib:* Nat Asn Women Artists, Jacob Javitts Fed Bldg, New York City, 85, 86 & 89; Women Artists Invitational, Hodson Gallery, Hood Col, Frederick, Md, 86; Nabisco Figurative Show, Corporate Gallery, Morristown, NJ, 87; NAPCA, Nat Arts Club, NY, 86, 87 & 90; Arts Invitational, City Hall Gallery, Frederick, Md, 88; Nat Asn Women Artists Mems Show, Northwood Univ, West Palm Beach, Fla, 95. *Collection Arranged:* Digital Art & Photog by Joy Erickson, UU Gallery, Sarasota, Fla, 2004-05. *Pos:* Pres & publ ed, Nat Asn for the Arts, Elgin, Ill, 73-83; interim dir arts & relig, Church of the Brethren, Elgin, Ill, 77-78; vpres communs, NRPRC of Washington, DC, 83-86. *Awards:* Best of Show, Phidian Art Club Ann Exhib, 71; Award of Distinction, Nat Asn Women Artists, 95; Northern Ill Univ Blue Ribbon, Town & Country Dist. *Bibliog:* David Boul (auth), Find out about refugees in art, Baltimore Sun, 12/11/81; Susan Mix Schank (auth), Art that reflects the spirit, Church Woman, 12/86; Linda Greely (auth), Fine arts highlight invitational, Frederick News Post, 5/88. *Mem:* Nat Asn Painters in Casein and Acrylic; Nat Asn Women Artists; Sarasota Co Arts Coun. *Media:* Acrylic. *Res:* restoration of genealogical resources. *Specialty:* digital art and photog, acrylic on canvas. *Publ:* Auth, In Straw and Story, 77, illusr, A is for Angels, 78 & ed, Let Not the Music that is in Us Die, 78, Brethren Press; illusr, A Christmas Eve Smorgasboard, 35, 1997; Skräddare Sven Jonasson, 35, 1997. *Dealer:* G L Gannett 3652 Allenwood St Sarasota FL 34232. *Mailing Add:* 3652 Allenwood St Sarasota FL 34232

ERICKSON, MARGARET JANE See Goodwill, Margaret

ERICKSON, MARK D
PAINTER
b Alta dena, Calif, 52. *Study:* Art Ctr Col Design, Los Angeles, Calif, 68-70; Ore Sch Arts & Crafts, Portland, Ore, 83-84; Calif Col Arts & Crafts, Oakland. *Work:* Western Colo Ctr Arts. *Exhib:* Contemp Wood '90, Banaker Gallery, Walnut Creek, Calif, 90; The Shapes & Colors of Wood 1990, ACCI Gallery, Berkeley, Calif, 90; solo exhibs, New Work, Meredith Gallery, Baltimore, Md, 90, Western Colo Ctr Arts, Grand Junction, Colo, 92; Top of the Table, Virginia Breier Gallery, 90, Calif Crafts Mus, Ghiradelli Sq, San Francisco, Calif, 92; Benchmark: Studio Furniture for the Nineties, traveling exhib, 90; Multimedia Southwest, Ten Arrow Gallery, Cambridge, Mass, 90; Richmond Art Ctr, Calif, 90-91; Gallery Fair, Mendocino, Calif, 90 & 92; New Am Furniture, Oaklans Mus, Calif, 91. *Teaching:* Ore Sch Arts & Crafts, Portland, 84-85; lectr & woodshop technician, Calif Col Arts & Crafts, 85-90. *Awards:* Nat Endowment Arts, 88; First Place: Golden Bear Award, Calif Works, Sacramento, 88; First Place Award, Sun Gallery Exhib, Hayward, Calif, 88. *Media:* Enamel on Glass. *Publ:* Numerous articles in various magazines, 86-90. *Mailing Add:* 1694 Highland St Seaside CA 93955

ERICKSON, MARSHA A
DIRECTOR, ADMINISTRATOR
b Ancon, Panama, Feb 1, 1945; US citizen. *Study:* Univ Hawaii, Manoa, 63-65. *Exhib:* Hawaiian Quilts, Mus Am Folk Art, NY, 78. *Pos:* Founder, Volcano Art Ctr, Hawaii, 74, prog dir, 74-81, exec dir, 81-86; Kokee Natural Hist Mus, 87-. *Bibliog:* Thelma & Jay Newman (auths), Container Book, 77 & Barbara Stephan (auth), Decorations for Holidays & Celebrations, 78, Crown Publ. *Mem:* Arts Coun of Hawaii (mem bd, 85-86); State Found on Cult & Arts (comt mem, 80-86); Nat Asn Interpretation; Hawaii Environ Educ Asn (co-founder). *Res:* Intersection of arts and sciences. *Specialty:* Hawaiian landscapes, cultures and world views. *Publ:* Ed, The Volcano Gazette, Volcano Art Ctr, 74-84; At Canyons Edge, Kokee Mus, 88-

ERIKSEN, GARY
SCULPTOR, MEDALIST
b Jackson, Mich, Sept 11, 43. *Study:* Oberlin Col, BA, 66; Kent State Univ, MA, 68; Univ Chicago, 71-73; Acad Belle Arti Roma, 73-77; Scuola Dell'Arte Medaglia, Rome, dipl licenza, 77. *Work:* Nat Gallery Art, Budapest; Smithsonian Inst Numismatics Collection; Cooper-Hewitt Mus; Zecca Roma, Italy; Am Numismatic Soc, NY. *Comn:* American Eagle, Kurt Wayne Inc, NY, 80; Church God in Christ, NY & Memphis, 81; thirty bas-relief portraits, Basketball Hall Fame, Springfield, Mass, 85; Gate Relief, Erasmus Hall High Sch, Brooklyn, NY, 87. *Exhib:* First Ann Open Sculpture Exhib, Salmagundi Club, NY, 82; Fedn Int Editeurs Medailles Int Biennial, Palazzo Medici Riccardi, Florence, 83; Carnegie Mansion Embellishments, Cooper-Hewitt Mus, NY, 83; Am Numismatic Asn, Colorado Springs, 87. *Pos:* Consult hand tools design, Sculpture House Inc, New York, 81-82. *Awards:* First Prize, Salmagundi Club First Ann Open Sculpture Exhib, 82; Fountains Proj Grant, NY State Coun Arts, 82. *Bibliog:* Ed Reiter (auth), article, New York Times, 8/15/82. *Mem:* Col Art Asn; Visual Artists & Galleries Asn. *Media:* Bronze, Terra Cotta. *Publ:* Illus, Village Voice, 5/1/84; auth, Alex Ettl, master artisan, Sculpture Rev, Fall 84; co-auth, Medals to the fore, Sculpture Rev, Fall 86

ERIKSON, CHRISTINE
EDUCATOR
Study: Parson Sch Design; Bank St Col Ed, BS(arts admin), 89. *Teaching:* Asst prof art, Univ Alaska Anchorage, 81-. *Mailing Add:* Dept Art Univ Alaska Anchorage 3211 Providence Dr Anchorage AK 99508

ERLEBACHER, MARTHA MAYER
PAINTER, EDUCATOR
b Jersey City, NJ, Nov 21, 37. *Study:* Gettysburg Col, Pa, 55-56; Pratt Inst, Brooklyn, NY, BID, 60, MFA, 63. *Hon Degrees:* NY Acad Art, Hon Dr Fine Arts, 2006. *Work:* Philadelphia Mus Fine Art, Pa; Pa Acad Fine Arts; Art Inst Chicago, Ill; NJ State Mus, Trenton; Libr Cong, Washington. *Comn:* Portrait, Most Reverend Joseph McShea, Allentown, Pa, 80; portrait, Dr William Hagerty, Drexel Univ, Philadelphia, Pa, 84; portrait, Dr Willys Silvers, Univ Pa Med Sch, Philadelphia, 90; portrait, James Bennett Straw, Pres, Union League Club of Philadelphia, 2000. *Exhib:* Philadelphia-Three Centuries Am Art, Philadelphia Mus Art, Pa, 76; Contemp Am Realism Since 1960, Pa Acad Fine Arts, Philadelphia, 81; Representational Drawing Today: A Heritage Renewed, Univ Art Mus, Santa Barbara, Calif, 83; Am Realism: 20th Century Drawings & Watercolors from the Glenn C Janss Collection, San Francisco Mus Mod Art, Calif, 85-86; Philadelphia Collects Art Since 1940, Philadelphia Mus Art, Pa, 86; Modern Myths, Boise Gallery Art, Idaho, 87; Realism Today: Am Drawings from the Rita Rich Collection, Nat Acad Design, NY, 87-88; The Figure, Ark Arts Ctr, Little Rock, 89-90. *Teaching:* Univ Arts, Philadelphia, 66-94; Grad Sch Figurative Art, NY Acad Art, 93-. *Awards:* Ingram Merrill Found Grant, 78; Sr Fel, Nat Endowment Arts, 82; Pa Coun Arts, Fel visual arts, 88. *Bibliog:* Anne D'Harmoncourt (auth), Philadelphia: Three Centuries Am Art, Philadelphia Mus Art, Pa, 76; Frank H Goodyear, Jr (auth), Contemp Am Realism Since 1960, NY Graphic Soc, 81; Charles Jencks (auth) Past Modernism, the New Classisism in Art and Achit, Rizzoli, NY, 87. *Media:* Oil. *Dealer:* Forum Gallery, 745 5th Ave, New York, NY 10151. *Mailing Add:* 7733 Mill Rd Elkins Park PA 19027

ERMAN, BRUCE
PAINTER, EDUCATOR
b Los Angeles, Calif, Mar 14, 45. *Study:* Univ Calif, Berkeley & Los Angeles, with James Melchert & Ibram Lassaw, BArch, 63-69; San Francisco Art Inst, with John Komisar, 74-75; Calif Col of Arts (CCAC), Oakland, with Arthur Okamura, Jason Schoener, Jack Mendenhall & Ronald Dahl, MFA, 74-79. *Work:* Calif Col of Arts(CCAC), Oakland; Davidson Col, NC. *Comn:* Favorite Toy & Under the Sea (murals), San Francisco Sch, Calif, 81; Nicacio Elementary School Mural, 82 & Black Mountain Theatre (mural), Point Reyes Station, 83, Youth-in-Arts, Greenbrae, Calif; Alamo Square Victorians (mural), Synergy Sch, San Francisco, 90-91; An Alvarado Alphabet (mural), Alvarado Arts Workshop, Alvarado Elem Sch, San Francisco, 96-97. *Exhib:* one-person exhibs: Time Pieces, Calif Col of Arts (CCAC), Oakland, 77; New Work, Davidson Col Chambers Art Gallery, NC, 80; Dwellings and Details, San Mateo Co Arts Coun, Belmont, Calif, 81; New Work-The Same Old Paintings, Art Space, Univ Nev Community Col Southern Nev, Las Vegas, 83; New Work, Valley Art Gallery, Walnut Creek Art Ctr, Calif, 85 & Unreal Estate, Christa Faut Gallery, Davidson, NC, 91; group exhibs: Rainbow Show (with catalog), de Young Mus Art, San Francisco, Calif, 75; All California '84, Laguna Beach Mus Art; Layering/Connecting, Zanesville Art Ctr, Ohio & Stifel Fine Arts Ctr, Wheeling, WVa, 87; 27th Ann, Fairfield, Calif, 89; Gallery Artists, Christa Faut Gallery, Davidson, NC, 92-99, Cornelius, NC, 2000-04; Calif Col of Arts (CCAC), Alumni Exhib, Oakland, Calif, 98. *Collection Arranged:* Peter MacLaird, Sausalito, CA. *Pos:* Guest cur, Calif Col of Arts (CCAC), Oakland, 77 & Chabot Col, Hayward, 80, Calif. *Teaching:* Lectr painting, Calif Col of Arts (CCAC), Oakland, 79 & 85, lectr exten fac, dept painting, 83-87; lectr painting, artist-in-residence, Alvarado Arts Workshop, Alvarado Elem Sch, San Francisco, 96-97. *Awards:* First Prize Painting, Univ Calif Los Angeles, Westwood, 64; Jurors Award, Fairfield, Calif, 27th Ann, 89. *Bibliog:* Thomas Albright (auth), At the end, Currant Mag, 75; Cathy Curtis (auth), Undeveloped premises, Artweek, 82; Jill Santuccio (auth), Unreal estate at Christa Faut Gallery, Mecklenburg Gazette, 91. *Mem:* Col Art Asn, NY; San Mateo Co Arts Coun, Belmont, Calif. *Media:* All. *Res:* Materials, Methods & Techiques of Painting. *Collection:* Bill and Elizabeth Shea, San Francisco, CA. *Publ:* Art Workshop, Berkeley Monthly, 74; Introduction to Woodcarving Tools, Whole Earth Epiloque & Co-Evolution Quar, 74. *Dealer:* Christa Faut Gallery Cornelius NC 28031. *Mailing Add:* 546 Shotwell San Francisco CA 94110

ERMAN, GERALDINE
SCULPTOR
b Detroit, Mich. *Study:* Wayne State Univ, Detroit, Mich, BFA, 75; Cranbrook Acad Art, Bloomfield Hills, Mich, MFA, 78. *Exhib:* One-woman shows, Kingsborough Col Gallery, Brooklyn, NY, 89, Petrosino Park, Lower Manhattan Cult Coun & NYSCA, 90, Watson Gallery, Wheaton Col, Mass, 93, White Columns, NY, 95 & Sculpture Ctr, NY, 95; Boston Now Ten, Inst Contemp Art, Boston, 91; The Pop Body, Sally Hawkins Gallery, NY, 92; Emerging Sculptors, Sculpture Ctr, NY, 92. *Pos:* Vis artist sculpture, Md Inst, Col Art, 97. *Teaching:* Asst prof, Bard Col, 88-92; vis lectr, Dept Archit, Mass Inst Technol, 93-94. *Awards:* Fel Grant Sculpture, Nat Endowment Arts, 86; Rome Prize Fel Sculpture, Am Acad in Rome, 90-91; Fel Sculpture, Guggenheim Found, 94. *Bibliog:* Peter Walsh (auth), A Delicate Balance, rev, Art New Eng, 5/90; Roberta Smith (auth), Three Group Shows, NY Times, 5/92; Catherine Liu (auth), The Pop Body, Flash Art, 10/92. *Mailing Add:* 91 Java St Brooklyn NY 11222

ERNSTROM, ADELE MANSFIELD
HISTORIAN
b Scranton, Pa, June 25, 30; Can citizen. *Study:* Univ Utah; Univ Calif, Los Angeles, BA, PhD. *Pos:* Co-ed, RACAR (Revue d'art canadienne/Canadian Art Review), 90-93; bd mem, Can Fedn Humanities, 94-95; mem gen assembly, Humanities & Social Sci Fedn Can, 95; pres, Univ Art Asn, Can, 94-97, adv bd mem, 98-2000; English lang book review ed, Racar, 2000-2004. *Teaching:* Asst prof, Hamline Univ, St Paul, Minn, 66-68 & State Univ NY Col, Brockport, 68-71; asst & assoc vis prof, Univ Guelph, Ont, Can, 75-77; assoc prof & chairperson, Bishop's Univ, Lennoxville, Que, 77-82, chairperson, 82-88 & 90-92, prof, 82-96,. *Awards:* Am Coun Learned Soc One-Yr Res Fel, 71-72; Res Grants, Bishop's Univ, 79 & 80; Social Scis & Humanities Res Coun Can Grant, 83 & 85; and others. *Mem:* Col Art Asn; Univ Art Asn Can (pres, 94-97); Asn of Art Historians (UK). *Res:* Interconnections of Art Hist as practiced inside and outside institutions; Women Art Hist as "Outsiders, Gertrude Bell and the Iraq Mus in Baghdad. *Publ:* Equally Lenders and Borrowers in Turn: The Working and Married Lives of the Eastlakes, Art Hist, 92; Anna Jameson and George Eliot, RACAR, 93; The Afterlife of Mary Wollstonecraft & Anna Jameson's, Winter Studies & Summer Rambles in Canada, Women's Writing, 97; Why Should We Be Always Looking Back?, "Christian" Art in Nineteenth Century Historiography in Britain, Art History, 99; Art Hist Inside and Outside the Univ, (guest ed and contribr auth), RACAR XXVIII, 2001-03. *Mailing Add:* c/o Dept Fine Arts Bishop's Univ Lennoxville PQ J1M 1Z7 Canada

ERTMAN, EARL LESLIE
HISTORIAN, EDUCATOR
b Parma, Ohio, Nov 13, 32. *Study:* Univ Southern Miss, BS, 65; Case Western Reserve Univ, MA, 67; Cleveland Mus, Egyptian art with John D Cooney, 67-71; Univ Akron, classics with TT Duke, 67-70. *Collection Arranged:* Egyptian Mus Collection: Studies for the Centennial of the Egyptian Mus, Cairo, Vol 1, 03. *Pos:* Art historian & field photogr, Johns Hopkins Exped to pyramid area, Giza, Egypt, summer 72 & 74, Tell el Rataba, 78; dir, Sch Art, Univ Akron, 81-90; art historian/site supv, Univ Ariz, Egyptian Exped to West Valley (WV-24), summer 92, Main Valley of King's (KV-10), 92-94; Can Final Clearance KV-55, summer 93; assoc dir, Univ Memphis (KV-10 & KV-63), 92-. *Teaching:* Instr Western art, Dept Art Hist & Educ, Cleveland Mus Art, 65-67; prof art hist, Univ Akron, 67-98, prof emer art, 98-. *Bibliog:* Geoffrey Martin (auth), The Memphite Tomb of the Horemheb Commander-in-Chief of Tutankhamun, London, 89; Geoffrey Martin (auth), A Bibliography of the Armana Period & its Aftermath: The Reigns of Akhenaten, Semenkhkre, Tutankhamun & Ay, London, 91; Nicholas Reeves & Richard Wilkingson (auths), The Complete Valley of the Knigs, London, 96; Z Hawass (ed), The Identity of the King & Queen on Tutankamum's Golden Throne, Egyptology at the Dawn of the Twenty-first Century: Proceedings of the Eight Int Congress of Egyptologists, Vol 2, Am Univ Cairo, 2003; G Knoppers & A Hirsch (eds), Dead as a Duck: A Royal offering scene?, Egypt, Israel and the Ancient Mediterranean World: Studies in Honor of D B Redford, Brill, Leiden, Boston, 2004; contrib w/ R Wilson & O Schaden (auths), Unraveling the Mysteries of KV-63 KMT, Mod J Ancient Egypt, 2006. *Mem:* Egypt Explor Soc; Archaeol Inst Am; Am Res Ctr Egypt; Soc Study Egyptian Antiquities, Toronto. *Res:* Iconographic and stylistic analysis of ancient Egyptian art, espec Amarna art. Analysis & pub objects from newly discovered tomb (KV63) Valley of Kings, Luxor, Egypt, and others. *Publ:* A rediscovered sandstone head of Tutankhamun in the Rosicrucian Egyptian Mus San Jose, Calif, In: Essays in Egyptology in Honor of Hans Goedicke (B Bryan & D Lorton, eds), San Antonio, Tex, 94; Evidence of the Alterations to the Canopic Jar Portraits & Coffin Mask from KV55 (R Wilkinson, ed), 95; Valley of the Sun Kings, New Explorations in the Tombs of the Pharaohs, Tucson, Ariz, 95. *Mailing Add:* 1148 E Howe Rd Tallmadge OH 44278

ERVIN, KATHEY
CERAMIST
b Raymond, Wash, Nov 10, 52. *Study:* Peinsula Col, 72-74; Kansas City Art Inst, BFA(ceramic art), 81; Univ Ill, Champaign-Urbana, MFA, 83. *Exhib:* Solo exhib, Merwin Gallery, Ill Wesleyan Univ, Bloominton, Ill, 85; Pewabic Pottery, Detroit, Mich, 85, 86 & 87; A Spote O' Tea, The Clayhouse, Santa Monica, Calif, 87; Dinner at Eight, Gallery Eight, La Jolla, Calif, 87; At the Table, Soc Arts & Crafts, Boston, Mass, 87; The Teapot: Form & Functions, Artworks, Seattle, Wash, 87; The Form of Fuction, Nat Clay Invitational, Creative Arts Workshop, New Haven, Conn, 88; Form and Fuction: Teapots, Craft Alliance, St Louis, Mo, 88. *Teaching:* Instr, Kansas City Art Inst, Mo, 79-81, Thornburn Community Ctr, Champaign, Ill, 83 & Penland Arts & Craft Ctr, NC, 91. *Awards:* Creative & Performing Arts Fel, Univ Ill, 81-83; Nat Endowment Arts Grant, 86. *Bibliog:* Article, Am Craft Mag, 12/86; Art, money and the NEA, Ceramics Monthly, 2/87; Kathey Ervin (auth), Limitations and focus, Ceramics Monthly, 2/88. *Mailing Add:* 330 Carlsborg Rd Sequim WA 98382

ERWIN, FRAN (FRANCES) SUZANNE
PAINTER, SCULPTOR
b Stockton, Calif. *Study:* St Mary's Col, Walnut Creek, Calif, certificate, 75-76; Thomas Leighton Acad Fine Art, San Francisco, Calif, 76-82; Can Fed Watercolor Artists, Salt Spring, 77. *Work:* Rosecrucian Egyptian Mus, San Jose, Calif; Nat Maritime Mus, Fort Bragg, Ky; Alameda Co Court House, Calif; Diocese of Oakland, Calif; Hayward Area Recreation Dept Off & Facilities, Calif; and others. *Comn:* contemp painting state symbol, Alameda, Calif, 90. *Exhib:* Invitational, City of Quincy Mus, Ill, 89; solo exhibs, Amador Hist Soc Mus, Pleasanton, 90 & San Ramon Community Ctr, Calif, 92; Soc Western Artists, Hall of Flowers, San Francisco, Calif, 90; Calif State Fair, Sacramento; San Francisco World Trade Club, 94. *Pos:* adv bd, Pastel Soc West Coast, currently. *Teaching:* Lectr, portraiture, Merced Col, Calif, 91. *Awards:* Best of Show, Rosicrucian Mus, Soc Western Artists, 88 & Alameda Co Fair, Air Comt, 89. *Bibliog:* Eleanor Chroman (auth), Lifestyles, Castro Valley Forum, 89; Pastel Artists, Southwest Art, 89; Noted Artist showing work at Mus, San Ramon Times, 90. *Mem:* Pastel Soc West Coast (chmn exhibs & events, 85-86, vpres, 87-88, pres, 89-); Pastel Soc Am (signature mem); Knickerbocker Artists, New York (signature mem); Nat League Am Penwomen (active mem); Soc Western Artists (signature mem); Allamo/Danville Art Soc. *Media:* Pastel, Oil. *Publ:* articles Bay Area News Publ. *Dealer:* Main Street Gallery Pleasanton Calif; Phantom Gallery Hayward Calif. *Mailing Add:* 22125 Orange Ave Castro Valley CA 94546

ESAKI, YASUHIRO
PAINTER, PRINTMAKER
b Omuta, Japan, June 8, 41. *Study:* Acad Art Col, BFA, 72; Lone Mountain Col, MFA(painting), 75, MFA(printmaking), 78. *Work:* Achenbach Found, Fine Art Mus, San Francisco; Boston Mus Fine Arts; Brooklyn Mus; Cincinnati Art Mus; Metrop Mus & Art Ctr, Miami, Fla. *Comn:* Etching, Mark Hopkins Hotel, San Francisco, 78. *Exhib:* MIX Graphic I, San Francisco Mus Mod Art, 73; Acquisition Shows, Achenbach Found, Fine Art Mus, San Francisco, 75, 78 & 79; Nat Drawing Exhib, Rutgers State Univ, Camden, 77; Third Int Graphic Biennial, Metrop Mus & Art Ctr, Miami, Fla, 77; Contemp Am Artist Exhib, Cent Mus, Tokyo, 78; 2nd Nat Drawing Competition, Miami Univ Mus, Oxford, Ohio, 78; solo exhibs, Lone Mountain Col, San Francisco, 78, Monterey Peninsula Mus Art, Calif, 80, Collectors Gallery, Oakland Mus, Calif, 87-91, Gallery Azuchi, Osaka, Jap, 88-97, Gallery Asuka, Tokyo, Jap, 89-91; 21st Nat Print Exhib, Brooklyn Mus, 79; Am Print Survey, Truman State Univ, Kirksville, Mo, 97 & World Print Survey, 98; Print Types, Abeline Tex Univ, 97 & Indian Hills Community Col, Ottumva, Iowa, 98; Mixed Media 97, Stage Gallery, Merrick, NY, 97. *Teaching:* Instr printmaking, Acad Art Col, San Francisco, 78-91. *Awards:* Purchase Prize, Belknap Mem Int Print Competition, Columbia-Greene Community Col, 78; Purchase Prize, Stockton Nat '78, Univ Pac & Pioneer Mus & Haggin Art Gallery, 78; Purchase Award, 17th Bradley Nat Prints & Drawing Exhib, Bradley Univ, Peoria, Ill, 79. *Bibliog:* Robert McDonald (auth), Drawing by Yasuhiro Esaki, Artweek, 77; Nancy C Pierce (auth), Third Miami graphic biennial, Graphics, 78; Gene Baro (auth), Twenty-First National Print Exhibition, Brooklyn Mus, 79. *Mem:* Calif Soc Printmakers. *Media:* Acrylic, Color Pencil; Etching. *Mailing Add:* 11 San Antonio Ct Walnut Creek CA 94598

ESCALET, FRANK DIAZ
PAINTER, SCULPTOR
b Ponce, PR, Mar 16, 30. *Study:* Self taught. *Work:* Naprstek Mus, Nat Gallery, Prague, Czech; SE Mus Fine Arts, Beaumont, Tex; Bratslavia Primitive Mus, Slovakia; Frydek-Mistek Mus, Northern Moravia; Orgn Am States Art Mus, Washington; Art Mus of SE Tex, Beaumont; Ellen Noel Mus of the Permian Basin, Odessa, Tex; History Mus of New York City; New Britain Mus Am Art, Conn. *Exhib:* Solo exhibs, Naprstek Mus, Prague, 90-91, Union Artists, Moscow, 91-92, Mus Chicano, Phoenix, 96; One-man traveling show Czechoslovakia, Russia, Poland, Yugoslavia, Hungary, Ukraine, 1991-; represented in permanent collections at Naprstkovo Mus, Prague, Union of Artists, Moscow, Bratslavia Primitive Mus, Slovakia, Frydek-Mistek Mus No Moravia, Museo Chicano, Phoenix, Southeast Tex Art Mus, Beaumont, Archit M Huntington Gallery, Austin, Tex, Housatonic Mus, Bridgeport, Conn, Orgn of Am States Art Mus, Washington, Maryknoll (NY) Sisters Ctr, Museum City NY, 1998; featured on pub TV, 1978, 82, 89; works in permanent collections Museum City of NY, Ellen Noel Mus Art of Permian Basin, Odessa, Tex, Dowd Fine Arts Mus, Cortland, NY, New Britain Mus Am Art; artist: Song and Dance Man acrylic, 1996. *Pos:* Owner, operator Talent Shop, New York City, 1955-58; House of Escalet, New York City, 1958-71; Pandora's Box, Eastport, Maine, 1971-73; Cobbler's Bench Art Gallery, Pembroke, 1973-82; House of Escalet Gallery, Kennebunkport, 1982-84, House of Escalet Studios, Kennebunkport, 1984-. *Teaching:* instr leathercraft, Pasamaquoddy Reservation, Perry, Maine, 1971-72; instr, Vocational Sch, Maine, 1972-73. *Awards:* Award of Excellance, Manhattan Arts Mag, 92; Represented USA at the Meeting of Two Worlds Exhib, Prague, Czech, 92. *Bibliog:* Subject of numerous television progs, 78-89; Manhattan Arts Mag, Rene Phillips Assoc, 91. *Mem:* World Peace Advocates. *Media:* Paintings; Sculpture. *Publ:* Contribr, New York Art Review--An Illustrated Survey of the City's Museums Galleries & Leading Artists, Les Krantz Publ, 90. *Mailing Add:* c/o House of Escalet Studios 24 Fletcher St Kennebunk ME 04043-1901

ESCALLON, ANA MARIA
MUSEUM DIRECTOR, CURATOR, WRITER
b Columbia. *Exhib:* curator exhibs: 18 sculptures by Colombian artist Fernando Botero positioned along Constitution Ave in Wash, DC, 1996; An Architect of Surrealism, works by Roberto Matta, 2004; (with Twylene Moyer), Sculpture in Four Dimensions, Mus of the Americas, 2004. *Pos:* dir Art Mus of the Ams, Washington, 95-2004. *Publ:* auth, Gerchman, 94, Mejla-Guinand, 02. *Mailing Add:* Art Mus of the Americas 1889 F St NW Washington DC 20006

ESCOBAR, MARISOL See Marisol

ESCOBEDO, HELEN
ENVIRONMENTAL ARTIST
b Mexico City, Mex, July 28, 36. *Study:* Univ Motolinia, BA(humanities); ARCA, 3 yr scholar. *Hon Degrees:* Asn Royal Col of Art. *Work:* Mus Mod Art, Mex; Prague Nat Gallery, Czech; Palacio de Bellas Artes, Mexico City; also in pvt collection of Stanley Marcus, US; Ordrup Samlung, Copenhagen. *Comn:* Coatl (steel), Univ Mex, 80; Reaseguradora Patria Bldg, 80; Barda Caida, Univ Mex, 81; The Great Cone (steel), City of Jerusalem, Israel, 86; El Reposo del Sol, Santiago, Cuba, 88; Seaview, Arlington House Lobby, London, Eng, 89. *Exhib:* One-man shows, Prague Nat Gallery, 69, Park Lazienkowsky, Warsaw, Poland, 70, Mus Mod Art, Mexico City, 75, Helsingin Kaupungin Taidemuseo, Helsinki, Finland, 91, Balliol Col, Univ Col, St Johns Col & Mus Mod Art, Oxford, Eng, 92; Kunstindustri Mus, Oslo, Norway, 70; Middelheim Sculpture Bienale, Antwerp, Belg, 71; Ordrupgaard Mus, Copenhagen, 90; Mus du Que, Can, 92; The Artists Studio Gallery, Tel Aviv, Israel, 93. *Pos:* Dir, Dept Mus & Galleries, Nat Univ Mex, 61-77; tech dir, Mus Nat Arte, Mex, 82; dir, Mus Arte Mod, Mex, 83. *Teaching:* Artist-in-residence, Tulane Univ, 76, Hartnell Col, 77, Newcomb Col, 81, Kunsterhaus Betanien, Berlin, 81, Scripps Col, 83; res fel, Fac humanities, Ctr Sculptural Space, Univ Mex, 78; pentiment, Fachhochschule, Hamburg, Ger, 94; Centro Nacional para las Artes, Mexico, 98 & Mus Posada Ags, 99. *Awards:* Guggenheim Fel, 81; Acad Sci Letts et Beaux Arts, Belgium, 88; FONCA Fel, Mexico, 90. *Bibliog:* Alfredo Gurrola (dir), Helen Escobedo - Ambients Totales (film), Color Mex; Rita Eder (auth), Helen Escobedo, Nat Univ Mex; Escobedo Derouin, Mus Du Que, Can; Graciela Schmilchuk (auth), Helen Escobedo - Pasos en la Arena, Turner Libros, Madrid. *Mem:* Int Nat Sculpture Ctr, Washington, (mem bd, 71-); Int Coun Mus (mem bd, 75-); Sculptor's Guild, NY; Academie Royale de Sciences Lettres et Beaux Arts, Belgium. *Media:* Multimedia. *Mailing Add:* la Cerrada de San Jeronimo 19 Mexico DF 10200 Mexico

ESHOO, ROBERT
PAINTER
b New Britain, Conn, 26. *Study:* Boston Mus Fine Arts Sch Mass, cert & dipl; Vesper George Sch Art, Boston; Syracuse Univ, BFA & MFA. *Work:* Wadsworth Atheneum, Hartford, Conn; Currier Gallery Art, Manchester, NH; Munson-Williams-Proctor Inst, Utica, NY; Addison Gallery Am Art, Andover, Mass; New Britain Mus Am Art. *Exhib:* Recent Drawings USA, Mus Mod Art, NY, 56; Chicago Art Inst Ann, 57; Young Artists, Whitney Mus, 57; Selections 1959, 59 & View 1960, 60, Inst Contemp Art, Boston; Am Painting 1962, Va Mus Fine Arts, Richmond, 62; The Dana Collection, 62 & Potlatch, 63, Inst Contemp Art, Boston; 28th Biennial, Corcoran Gallery, Wash, DC, 63; Northeastern Regional: Art Across Am, 65 & Art for Embassies, 66, Inst Contemp Art, Boston; one-man shows, Rigelhaupt Gallery, 68, Pucker-Safrai Gallery, Boston, 72 & 75, Manchester, NH, 76 & 79, Currier Gallery Art, 81 & 86 & 94, Dartmouth Col, 86, St Paul's Sch, 88, New England Col, 89 & 94, Hatfield Gallery, Manchester, NH, 90; Pucker Gallery, Boston, 2004; New Britain Mus Am Art, 2004. *Teaching:* Sch Mus Fine Arts, Boston, 54-55, Syracuse Univ, 56-57, Phillips Acad, Andover, 60 & 62-64 & Derryfield Sch, 65-80; supvr, Currier Art Ctr, 58-95. *Awards:* McDowell Colony. *Bibliog:* New Talents USA, Art in Am, 2/56; American artists coming to the fore, Harper's Bazaar, 3/60; Emerging reputations, Art in Am, summer 62. *Media:* Watercolor & Constructions. *Specialty:* paintings, sculpture, ceramics. *Dealer:* Pucker Gallery Boston MA. *Mailing Add:* 16 Liberty Square #374 Bloomfield CT 06002

ESMAN, ROSA
GALLERY DIRECTOR, DEALER
b New York, NY, Nov 29, 27. *Study:* Smith Col, BA. *Work:* Mus Mod Art, NY Int, Whitney Mus Am Art, Metrop Mus Art, NY; Brit Arts Coun, London. *Pos:* Pres & dir, Tanglewood Press, New York, 64-69 & 72-; dir, Abrams Original Editions, 69-72; pres & dir, Rosa Esman Gallery, 72-94; partner, Ubu Gallery, 94-. *Mem:* Art Dealers Asn Am. *Specialty:* Contemporary European paintings, drawings, modern contemporary and surrealist photography, sculpture, prints and multiples; Russian avant-garde material, 1911-1933; American art, 20th Century. *Publ:* Ed, Seven objects in a box, 66 & New York, 10/69, Ten from Leo Castelli, 67, 9 Pyramios, Sol Lewitt, 91

ESPENSCHIED, CLYDE
PAINTER
b St Louis, Mo. *Study:* With Valentine Vogel portrait painter, 44-46; St Louis Sch Fine Arts, Washington Univ, 46-49; Manhattan Graphics, New York, 93. *Work:* Peat Marwick Montvale Art Collection, Montvale, NJ; Bulgari, NY. *Exhib:* St Louis Mus, Mo, 49; Omaha Mus, Nebr, 60; Audubon Show, Nat Acad, NY, 62; Trenton Mus, NJ, 66, 68 & 74; Millhouse-Bundy Arts Ctr, Waitsfield, Vt, 83; Heidi Jones Gallery, NY, 84; one-person shows, Noho Gallery, NY, 84, 86, 88, 91 & 93, Mukaida Fine Arts Gallery, 91; Three Rivers Art Festival, Pittsburgh, Pa, 86 & 88; Morris Mus Fel Show, NJ, 87; Drawing Exhibition (Alternative Space), Noho Gallery, 2000; Westbeth Invitational, NY, 99; Myungsook Lee Gallery, NY, 95. *Awards:* Nat Endowment Arts Fel Grant, 85; NJ Coun Arts Grant, 85; Honorable Mention, Three Rivers Art Festival, Pittsburgh, Pa, 86. *Bibliog:* Vivien Raynor (auth), article, Arts Mag, 60; Frederic Schwartz (auth), article, Artspeak, 84; Mark Brennan (auth), article, Art & Oxygen, 84; Sanford Sivit Shaman (auth), Pa State Univ, 87. *Media:* Oil on Canvas, Pastel on Paper, Ink on Paper & Acrylic. *Mailing Add:* 265 Main St Spotswood NJ 08884

ESS, BARBARA
PHOTOGRAPHER
b Brooklyn, NY, 1948. *Study:* Univ Mich, Ann Arbor, BA, 69; London Sch Film Technique, 71. *Work:* Art Inst Chicago; List Visual Art Ctr, MIT, Cambridge Mass; Nat Mus Am Art, Smithsonian Inst, Washington; San Francisco Mus Mod Art; Whitney Mus Am Art; The Carnegie Mus of Arts, Pittsburgh; San Francisco Mus

Modern Art; New Orleans Mus of Art; Mus Contemp Art, Los Angeles; Modern Art Mus of Ft Worth; Mus of Fine Arts, Houston. *Exhib:* Tate Gallery, 82; Inst Contemp Art, Boston, 85; Whitney Mus Am Art (two exhibs); 87; Baltimore Mus Art, 87; solo exhibs, High Mus Art (with catalog), 93, Queens Mus, Flushing, NY (traveling, with catalog), 93, Curt Marcus Gallery, 94, 96 & 98, 2000, Faggionato Fine Arts, London, 94 & 98, Stills Gallery, Edinburgh, Scotland, 96 & Kohn Turner Gallery, Los Angeles, 97; Nat Mus Am Art, Washington, 89; Art Gallery Western Australia, Perth & Nat Art Gallery NZ, Wellington, 90; Everson Mus, 90; Nat Mus Mod Art, Tokyo & Kyoto, 90; Victoria & Albert Mus, 91; Wadsworth Atheneum, 92; Kunsthaus Zurich, Switz, 93; Alice's Looking Glass, Apex Art, NY, 96; The Baseball Show, Curt Marcus Gallery, NY, 96; Blind Spot Photog, Paolo Baldacci Gallery, NY, 96; Making Pictures, Nicole Klagsburn, NY, 96; With a Different Camera, Aspen Art Mus, Colo, 97; Disappearing Act, Bound & Unbound with Leslie Tonkonow Gallery, NY, 98; From the Heart: The Power of Photog - A Collectors Choice, Art Mus S Tex, Corpus Christi, Tex, 98; Wessel and O'Connor Gallery, NY, 99; Galeria Pepe Cobo, Seville, 2000; Hayward Gallery, London, 2000. *Awards:* Nat Endowment Arts Regional Photog Fel, Mid Atlantic Arts Found, 90-91; Nat Endowment Arts, 94. *Bibliog:* David Lillington (auth), Creative Camera, 10-11/96; David Lillington (auth), Metropolis M, 10/96; Nancy Princenthal (auth), Barbara Ess at Curt Marcus, Art Am, 12/96; Glueck, Grace (auth.) Barbara Ess New York Times, 98; Blind Spot #13, 6 pages reproductions, 99; Bollen, Christopher (auth.) Barbara Ess, She Woke with a Start, Time-Out, 2000. *Publ:* Contribr, Thought Objects, 87; auth, Camera Austria, 10/88. *Mailing Add:* c/o Curt Marcus Gallery Inc 2 Fifth Ave #17N New York NY 10011

ESSER, JANET BRODY
HISTORIAN
b New Haven, Conn. *Study:* Univ Iowa, with John Rosenfield & William Heckscher, BFA, 51; Kent State Univ, BS, 53; Calif State Univ, Long Beach, MA, 70; Univ Calif, Los Angeles, with Rubin & Nicholson, PhD, 78. *Collection Arranged:* San Diego Collects: African Art, 78; Faces of Fiesta: Mexican Masks in Context, 80; sr consult, Behind the Mask in Mexico, Mus Int Folk Art, Santa Fe, 88-90. *Teaching:* From asst prof to assoc prof, San Diego State Univ, 75-83, prof, 83-. *Awards:* Nat Endowment Humanities Summer Inst Fel, 78, 92; Hubert B Herring Mem Award for Best Scholarly Bk on Latin Am, 88. *Mem:* Col Art Asn Am; Latin Am Studies Asn; Latin Am Art Historians Asn; African Studies Asn; Ethno-Hist Soc; Pac Coast Coun on Latin Am Studies. *Res:* Pre-Columbian, European and African antecedents of masking traditions in contemporary rural Mexican communities; African imagery in Iberia; Social History of Mexican Folk Art. *Publ:* Mask Making and Mask Use in Michoacan, Mex Fine Arts Ctr Mus, Chicago, 90; Auth, Mascaras rituales de la sierra tarasca, Michoacan, Inst Nac Indigenista, Mex; Tarascan Masks of Women as Agents of Social Control, Univ BC Press, Vancouver, 83; The Functions of Folk Art in Michoacan, Memphis State Univ, 84; ed, Behind the Mask in Mexico, Mus NMex, Santa Fe, 88. *Mailing Add:* Ctr Latin-Am Studies San Diego State Univ San Diego CA 92182-4446

ESSL, KARLHEINZ, SR
COLLECTOR
b Apr 16 1939 Hermagor Austria. *Pos:* Schömer Co 1959-73; Schömer L+S 1973-76; pres Schömer L+S Do It Yourself Co (now Build Max) 1976-99. *Awards:* Named one of top 200 art collectors, ARTNews mag 2004, 2005, 2006. *Mailing Add:* bauMax AG Aufeldstrasse 17-23 Klosterneuburg A-3400 Austria

ESSLEY, ROGER HOLMER
PAINTER, GRAPHIC ARTIST
b Rochester, NY, Jan 11, 49. *Study:* Syracuse Univ, 66-69; Goddard Col, MA, 81. *Work:* Metrop Mus Art, NY; Indianapolis Mus Art, Ind; Joslyn Art Mus, Omaha, Nebr; Ind Univ Mus Art, Bloomington; Mem Art Gallery, Rochester, NY. *Exhib:* One-man show, Southeastern Ctr Contemp Art, Winston-Salem, NC, 84; Large Figurative Drawing, Va Mus Fine Arts, Richmond, Va, 85; The Figure in 20th Century Art, Nat Acad Design, NY, 85-86; Motion & Arrested Motion Contemp Figure Drawing, Chrysler Mus, Norfolk, Va, 87; Contemp Wing, Metrop Mus Art, NY, 87-88; Uncommon Ground, Va Mus Fine Arts, Richmond, 90. *Awards:* Regional Fel, Works on Paper, Mid Atlantic Arts Found, 88; Va Prize for the Visual Arts, 90. *Bibliog:* Paul Richard (auth), Together again, Washington Post, 84; Edward Lucie-Smith (auth), Am Art Now, Phaidon Pr, 85. *Publ:* Illus, Appointment, Simon & Schuster/Green Tiger, 93; auth/illus, Reunion, Simon & Schuster, 94; Under the Pear Tree, Cobblehill, 97; Angles in the Dust, Troll/Bridgewater, 97. *Dealer:* Reynolds Gallery 1514 W Main St Richmond VA 23220. *Mailing Add:* 30 N Main St Newmarket NH 03857-1210

ESTABROOK, REED
PHOTOGRAPHER, INSTRUCTOR
b Boston, Mass, 44. *Study:* RI Sch Design, BFA, 69; Art Inst Chicago, MFA, 71. *Work:* Mus Mod Art, NY; Art Inst Chicago; Int Mus Photog, Rochester, NY; J Paul Getty, Santa Monica, Calif; Minneapolis Inst Arts, Minn; Art Inst Hawaii. *Comn:* San Jose Mus Mod Art. *Exhib:* Mirrors & Windows, Mus Mod Art, NY, 78; one-man shows, Sioux City Art Ctr, Iowa, 81, Klein Gallery, Chicago, 82 & James Madison Univ, Harrisburg, Va, 83; Recent Color, San Francisco Mus Mod Art, Calif, 82 & 84; Recent Aquisitions, Fogg Art Mus, Harvard Univ, Cambridge, Mass, 83; Road & Roadside: Am Photographs 1930-1986, Ill State Univ Art Gallery, Art Inst Chicago, San Francisco Mus Mod Art, 87; Big Pictures, San Francisco Mus Mod Art, Calif, 90; Translations, Mappin Art Gallery, Sheffield, Eng, 91; Three Decades of Midwestern Photog, Davenport Art Mus, Iowa, 92; Am Made: The New Still Life, Isetan Mus Art, Tokyo, Japan, Hokkaido Obihito Mus Art, Japan, 93, Royal Col Art, London, Eng, 94; Forecast: Shifts in direction, Mus Fine Arts, Santa Fe, NMex, 94; Picturing Modernity, San Francisco Mus Mod Art, 96; Location-Location, San Jose Inst Contemp Art, 96; Image & Object, Sheppard Fine Art Gallery, Reno, Nev, 2001. *Teaching:* Instr photog, Univ Ill, Urbana-Champaign, 71-74; asst prof photog, Univ Northern Iowa, 74-78, assoc prof, 78-83; photog chmn, Kansas City Art Inst, 83-84; prof & coordr photo, Sch Art Design, San Jose State Univ, 84-. *Awards:* WR French Fel Competition, Art Inst Chicago, 71; First Place, Am Photographics, Andromeda Gallery, Buffalo, 76; Photog Fel, Nat Endowment Arts, 76. *Mem:* Soc for Photog Educ. *Media:* Photography. *Collection:* The Art Institute Chicago, Ill; Boise Gallery Art, Boise, Idaho; National Museum of American Art, Washington, DC; International Museum of Photography, Rochester, NY; Walker Art Center, Minneapolis, Minnesota. *Publ:* Contribr, New American Nudes, Morgan & Morgan, 81; Picture Mag No 17, 81; American Photography, 83; New DIrections, Weston Naef, 84; The Making of a Collection: The Minneapolis Institute of Arts, Aperture, Millerton, 85; Photokina 1986, Cologne, W Ger, 86; Peninsular Mag, Vol 10, 87. *Mailing Add:* 482 Chetwood St Oakland CA 94610

ESTERN, NEIL
SCULPTOR
b New York, NY, Apr 18, 26. *Study:* Barnes Found, 46-47; Tyler School Fine Arts of Temple Univ, BFA & BS(educ), 47. *Comn:* Portraits, J Robert Taft, Danny Kaye, John F Kennedy, J Edgar Hoover, Pres Carter, Prince Charles, Lady Diana, Jack Nicholson, Eleanor Roosevelt, Fiorello La Guardia, La Guardia Memorial, Greenich Village, NYC, Miguel de la Madrid, David Levine; portrait bust of John F Kennedy, Kennedy Mem, Grand Army Plaza, Brooklyn, 65; Franklin D Roosevelt & Eleanor Roosevelt, FDR Mem, Washington, DC, Nat Cathedral, Washington, DC; Irving Berlin (relief portrait), Muxic Box Theater & Nat Portrait Gallery, Washington, DC. *Exhib:* Numerous one-man and group shows in Conn, NY, NJ, Philadelphia, NH & Italy; Claude Pepper Statue, Tallahasse, Fla. *Pos:* Pres, Nat Sculpture Soc, 94-96 & 2005-. *Awards:* Mildred Vincent Prize, Nat Sculpture Soc, 88 & 92; Greenwich Village Soc Hist Preserv Award, La Guardia Statue, 96; Nat Acad Award, Franklin D Roosevelt Scale Model, 98; Pres Design Award, FDR Mem, 2000. *Mem:* Fel Nat Sculpture Soc; Nat Acad; Century Asn. *Media:* Clay, Bronze. *Mailing Add:* 82 Remsen St Brooklyn NY 11201

ESTEROW, MILTON
EDITOR, PUBLISHER
b New York, NY, July 28, 28. *Study:* Brooklyn Col, NY. *Pos:* Asst cult news dir, New York Times, 6/3/68; ed & publ, ARTnews, 72-; publ, ARTnewsletter, 75-. *Teaching:* Lectr art, mus, col & univ. *Awards:* George Polk Award, 81 & 92; Nat Mags Award, 81; Clarion Award, 81, 84, 98, 2000 & 2001; Investigative Reporters & Editors Award, 84; Page One Award, 85; Nat Headliner Award, 85 & 94; and others; Lifetime Achievement Award, Col Art Asn, 2003. *Publ:* The Art Stealers, 66. *Mailing Add:* ARTnews 48 W 38th St New York NY 10018

ESTES, RICHARD
PAINTER
b Kewanee, Ill, 32. *Study:* Chicago Art Inst, 52-56. *Work:* Whitney Mus Am Art & Mus Mod Art, NY; Rockhill Nelson Mus, Kansas City, Mo; Toledo Mus, Ohio; Art Inst Chicago; Des Moines Art Ctr; Hirshhorn Mus, Washington, DC; and many others. *Exhib:* Solo exhibs, Carpenter Ctr Vis Arts, Harvard Univ, Cambridge, 90, Richard Estes 1990, traveling exhib, Mus Art, Kinetsu, Osaka & Hiroshima City Mus Contemp Art, Japan, 90, Richard Estes: Urban Landscapes, Portland Mus Art, Maine & Foster Goldstrom Gallery, NY, 91, Richard Estes: The Complete Prints, Canton Art Inst, Ohio, Los Angeles Arts & Sci Mus, Baton Rouge, Columbia Mus Art, SC, Huntsville Mus Art, Ala, 92, Marlborough Gallery, NY, 93, 95, 97 & 98 & Galleria Marlborough, Madrid, Spain, 98, Marlborough Gallery, NY, 2001; On Paper, galleria d'arte il gabbiano, Rome, Italy, 96; La Ville Moderne en Europe: Visions Urbaines d'Artistes et d'Architectes, 1870-1996, Mus Contemp Art, Tokyo, 96; Realism After Seven Am, Hopper House, NY, 96; Art 1997 Chicago: 5th Ann Expo of Int Galleries Featuring Modern and Contemp Art, Navy Pier, Chicago, 97; City Scapes, Marlborough Gallery, NY, 97; Landscape: The Pastoral to the Urban, Ctr for Curatorial Studies & Art in Contemp Cult, Bard Col, NY, 97; NY Perspectives, MB Modern, NY, 98; Le Futur du Passe, Lieu d'Art Contemporain Corbieres Maritimes, France, 98; Transforming the Commonplace: Masters of Contemp Realism, Susquehanna Art Mus, Pa, 2003; and many others. *Awards:* MECA Award for Achievement as a Visual Artist, Maine, 96. *Bibliog:* Carol King (auth), Realism, The new hip, ARTnews, 2/97; Jaime Fernandez (auth), Sauray Estes, doe visiones diferentes del arte actual, Ya de madrid, 1/16/98; Jose Luis Gallero (auth), Richard Estes la otra orilla de la realidad, ABC Cutl, 1/16/98. *Mem:* Nat Acad. *Media:* Oil. *Publ:* Meisel Lars (auth), Richard Estes The Complete Painting 1966-1985, Harry Abrams Inc, 1986; John Arthor (auth), Richard Estes Paintings & Prints, Chameleon Books, San Francisco, CA, 1993; John Wilmerding (auth), Richard Estes, Rizzoli Intenat Publ, NYC, 2006. *Dealer:* Marlborough 40 W 57th St New York NY 10019

ETCHISON, BRUCE
CONSERVATOR, PAINTER
b Washington, DC, Dec 19, 18. *Study:* Am Univ, BA; Yale Univ Sch Fine Arts, BFA & MFA. *Work:* Washington Co Mus Fine Arts, Hagerstown, Md; Chesapeake Bay Maritime Mus, St Michaels, Md; Merrick Art Gallery, New Brighton, Pa. *Exhib:* Merrick Art Gallery, New Brighton, Pa; Washington Co Mus Fine Arts, Hagerstown, Md. *Pos:* Dir, Washington Co Mus Fine Arts, 50-64 & Abby Aldrich Rockefeller Folk Art Collection, 64-66; conservator for pvt collectors mus, univs, cols, hist soc & the State of Pa, formerly; currently retired. *Mem:* Int & Am Insts Conserv Hist & Artistic Works; Washington Conserv Guild. *Media:* Oil, Etching, Sculpture. *Publ:* Coauth, Roentgen Examination of Painting, 60; auth, Radiant Heat for Vacuum Tables, 69. *Mailing Add:* 3830 Farmstead Dr Fayetteville PA 17222

ETROG, SOREL
SCULPTOR, PAINTER
b Jassy, Romania, Aug 29, 33; Can citizen. *Study:* Tel Aviv Art Inst, Israel, 53-55; Brooklyn Mus Art Sch, 58. *Work:* Nat Gallery Can, Ottawa; Art Gallery Ontario & Hart House, Univ Toronto; Tate Gallery London; Musee en Plein Air & Musee d'Art Moderne, Paris; Mus Mod Art & Guggenheim Mus, NY; Hirshhorn Mus, Washington, DC; Storm King Art Ctr, Mountainville, NY; UCLA; Montreal Mus Fine Arts; Kroller-Muller, Holland. *Comn:* EXPO, Montreal, 67; Olympia & York Ctr, Toronto, 72; Bow Valley Sq, Calgary, 75; SunLife Ctr, Toronto, 84; Olympic Park, Soeul, Korea, 88; and others. *Exhib:* Solo exhibs, Walter Moos Gallery, 59, 61, 63, 65, 67, 81, 84 & 90, Dominion Gallery, Montreal, 63, 67, 73 & 89 & Pierre Matisse Gallery, NY, 65; one-man retrospective, 1958-68, Pallazzo Strozzi, Florence, 68; Etrog - A Decade, 15 Ont Cols, touring exhib, 68-69; Fine Arts Mus, Montreal, 68; Dunkelman Gallery, Toronto, 70, 71 & 72; Winnipeg Art Gallery, Man, 71; 4th Int Exhib Contemp Sculpture, Mus Rodin, Paris, 71; City Hall, Toronto, 72; Marlborough Gallery, NY, 77; Singapore Art Mus, 97; Buschlen Mowatt Gallery, Vancouver & Palm Desert, 2001. *Collection Arranged:* Spectrum Canada, Royal Can Acad Arts, Montreal, 76; Contemporary Outdoor Sculpture at the Guild, Scarborough, Ontario, 82. *Awards:* Chevalier of Arts & Letters, Govt France, 97. *Bibliog:* William Withrow (auth), Etrog: Sculpture, Wilfred, Toronto, 67; Theodore A Heinrich (auth), The Painted Constructions 1952-1960, Staempfli et Cie, Berne, 68; Pierre Restany (auth), Sorel Etrog, Prestel, NY, 2001. *Mem:* Royal Can Acad Arts. *Media:* Bronze, Steel. *Publ:* Illusr, Imagination Dead Imagine, London, 72 & Chocs, NY, 69-72; auth, Dream Chamber (Joyce & the Dada Circus), Black Brick Press, London, 82; Hinges, a play, Calder, London, 83; L'Aquilone/The Kite, All'insegna del pesce d'oro, Milan, 84. *Mailing Add:* Box 67034 2300 Yonge St Toronto ON M4P 1E0 Canada

ETTENBERG, FRANKLIN JOSEPH
PAINTER, PRINTMAKER
b Brooklyn, NY, May 7, 45. *Study:* Univ Mich, BS(design), 66, with Milton Cohen, Fred Bauer & John Stephenson; Univ NMex, MA, 71, with John Kacere. *Work:* Detroit Inst Art; Roswell Mus & Art Ctr, NMex; Fine Arts Mus, Santa Fe; Minnesota Mus Art, St Paul; Anderson Mus Art, Roswell, NMex. *Comn:* Paired Paintings, NMex Arts Comn, 78; Taos Watershed Mural, Mary Medina Bldg, Taos, NMex, 78. *Exhib:* Solo exhibs, Janus Gallery, Santa Fe, 86 & 88 & Wright Gallery, Dallas, 84 & 85; Conlon Gallery, Santa Fe, 89; Artists Discover Columbus, Castillo Ctr, NY, 92; Galerie Rondula, Vienna, Austria, 94; Austria Tabakmus, Vienna, 97; Five Allies, NMex State Capitol, 2002; Kunst Forum, Hallein, Austria, 2004. *Pos:* Exec comt, Advocates for Contemp Art, Santa Fe, 73-75; cert graphoanalyst, Int Graphoanalysis Soc, Chicago, 77. *Teaching:* Instr, Santa Fe Workshops of Contemp Art, 74; pvt painting instr, 79-. *Awards:* Roswell Mus Artist-in-Residence Grant, NMex, 71; Southwest 85, Purchase Award, (monotype), Merit Award, (painting), Mus Fine Art, Santa Fe, 85; Contemporary '98 Best in Show, Fuller Lodge, Los Alamos, NMex, 98; Certificate of Recognition, State Legis, NMex, 2002. *Bibliog:* W Peterson (auth), Critique of painted low-reliefs, spring 82, W Peterson (auth), review, fall 86, Abstract painting in New Mexico, fall 88, Artspace; W Clark (auth), Artist profile, Sunday Arts, Albuquerque Journal, 3/6/88; Dr Miro Klivar (auth), FE-Master of Gestural Meditatiion (essay), Am Soc Aesthetics, Prague, CZ, 2005. *Media:* Acrylic, Linen; Monotype on Rives BFK. *Collection:* Capital Art, Santa Fe, NMex, Anderson Mus, Roswell, NMex. *Publ:* Contribr, Santa Fe Fine Arts Calendar, 93 & 94. *Dealer:* Silvia Stenitzer Santa Fe NM Tel #505-983-6934. *Mailing Add:* c/o Frank Ettenberg Studio 2001 Ft Union Dr Santa Fe NM 87505

ETTINGER, SUSI STEINITZ
PAINTER, LECTURER
b Berlin, Ger, July 29, 22; US citizen. *Study:* Univ Louisville, BFA(cum laude art hist), 43; with Dr Justus Bier. *Work:* Springfield Art Mus, Mo; State Hist Soc Mo, Columbia; Sch of the Ozarks, Point Lookout, Mo; Greenwood Lab Sch, Springfield; Margaret Harwell Art Mus, Poplar Bluff, Mo. *Exhib:* one-artist shows, Springfield Art Mus, 75, Southwest Mo Univ, 80, Drury Col, 84, Sch Ozarks, 87, Mabee Art Ctr; Women Artists 77 Exhib, Kansas City, Mo Univ, 77; Watercolor USA, 79; Springfield Area Artists Exhib, Springfield Art Mus, 90; Moak, Springfield Art Mus, 96. *Teaching:* Dir children's art classes, Springfield Art Mus, 60-66; lectr art, Southwest Mo State Univ, 64-84, emer prof, 84-. *Awards:* Regional Ten State Competition Purchase Award, 69 & Purchase Award, Watercolor USA, 90, Springfield Art Mus; First Prize Painting, Mo Col Fac Show, 70; Award in recognition of creative accomplishments in the visual arts, Am Asn Univ Women, 74. *Media:* Acrylic, Collage. *Mailing Add:* 1080 Paterson St Apt 801 Eugene OR 97401

ETTL, GEORG
PAINTER, SCULPTOR
b Nittenau, Ger, Mar 3, 31. *Study:* Sorbonne, Paris, France, 63-65; Wayne State Univ, BA, 65, MA, 67, MFA, 68. *Work:* Mus Abteiberg, Möchen Gladbach, Ger; Kaiser Wilhelm Mus, Krefeld, Ger. *Comn:* Amphitheater, 81 & Murals for City Co Bldg, Vierson, Ger, 83-84. *Exhib:* All Mich Exhib, Flint Inst Arts, 72; solo exhib, Mus Abteiberg, Mönchen Gladbach, Ger, 77-78; With a Certain Smile, Zurich, Switz, 79; Kick Out the Jams: Detroit's Cass Corridor 1963-77, Detroit Inst Arts & Mus Contemp Art, Chicago, 81; With a Certain Smile, Krefeld, Ger, 83. *Awards:* Purchase Prizes, 58th Exhib Mich Artists, Detroit Inst Arts, 70 & All Mich Exhib, Flint Inst Arts, 72. *Bibliog:* Johannes Cladders (auth), Georg Ettl, Städtisches Mus Mönchen Gladbach, 77; Julian Heyden (auth), Georg Ettl: Hausordnung, Krefelder Kunstmus, 83; Nena Dimitrijevic (auth), Sculpture and Its Double, Sculpture Show, Greater London Coun, 83. *Media:* All. *Mailing Add:* Rahserstr 14 Viersen 406 1 Germany

EUREN, BARRY A
PAINTER
b Sacramento, Calif, Oct 4, 48. *Study:* Calif State Univ, BA, 1972, 1973; Calif Community Col. *Work:* White House Collection, Washington, DC; CM Russell Mus, Great Falls, Mont; Oakland Mus, Calif; Calif State Univ, Sacramento, Calif; Calif State Archives, Sacramento, Calif. *Comn:* Bicenntenial 1976, Bur of Indian Affairs, Washington, DC, 1976; Book of Healing, Jesus Christ, Worldwide, 2005. *Bibliog:* Constance Smith (auth), Living Artists, Art Network Press, 2003. *Mem:* Am Inst of Fine Art; Am Asn of Printing House Craftsman; Print Club of Albany. *Media:* Etching, Oil, Printmaker. *Interests:* Painting under the pseudonym, Nerue. *Dealer:* Wills Gallery 222 N Locust St Carlisle Ky 40311. *Mailing Add:* 3220 Watt Ave #58 Sacramento CA 95821

EURICH, JUDITH
APPRAISER
Pos: Cur asst, 19th Century Photography, San Francisco Art Mus. *Teaching:* Teacher, Acad Art College, Hearst Art Gallery, St Mary's College, Moranga, Calif. *Mailing Add:* Bonham & Butterfields 220 San Bruno Ave San Francisco CA 94103

EVANGELINE, MARGARET
PAINTER, COLLAGE ARTIST
b Baton Rouge, La. *Study:* La State Univ, 61-63 & 65; Univ New Orleans, BA, 75, MFA, 78. *Work:* Texaco, Houston, Tex; Simone, Peregine, Smith & Redfern, New Orleans; IBM, Tenn; Bank of the South, Atlanta, Ga; Pensacola Mus, Fla. *Comn:* Painting, Entergy Collection, Jackson, Miss, 94. *Exhib:* one-man shows, Pensacola Mus Art, Fla, 91, Res Nova, NY, 92, Byron Roche Gallery, Chicago, Ill, 2000, Alva Gallery, New London, Conn, 2001, Palm Beach Inst Contemp Art, Palm Beach, Fla, 2001, ACA Galleries, NY, 2001, Galerie Simonne Stern, New Orleans, La, 93, 94, 96 & 99; Galerie Simonne Stern, New Orleans, La, 93; Nave Mus, Victoria, Tex, 98; Howard Scott/M13, NY, 99; group exhibs, The Drawing Ctr, NY, 2000, Fluid Flow, James Graham Gallery, NY, 2000, Fall Group Show, Betty Wasserman Art & Interiors, NY, 2000 & Younger Artists, Anita Shapolsky Gallery, NY, 2001. *Awards:* Artist-in-Residence, Villa Montalvo Found, Saratoga, Calif, 91; Painting Fel, NY Found for the Arts, 96; Artist-in-Residence, ART/OMI Found, Omi, NY, 99. *Bibliog:* Dominique Nahas (auth), Margaret Evangaline, New Art Examiner, 57-58, 9/98; Michael Rush (auth), The Confessions of MLLE G (catalog), The Drawing Ctr; Lilly Wei (auth), Margaret Evaneline, Galerie Simonne Stern, Art in Am, 1/2000. *Media:* Acrylic, Oil; Found Objects. *Publ:* Illusr, cover, The critical state of visual art in New York, Review Mag, 12/1/98

EVANS, BOB JAMES
PAINTER, EDUCATOR
b Chicago, Ill, May 2, 44. *Study:* Parsons Col; Univ Iowa; Northeast Mo State Univ, BEd; Drake Univ; Southern Ill Univ, Carbondale, MFA. *Work:* Southern Ill Univ, Carbondale; Western Ill Univ, Macomb; Ill State Univ, Normal; Quincy Art Club; Lakeview Mus Arts & Sci; Rockford Art Mus, Ill; Block Gallery, Northwestern Univ. *Comn:* Subscription print series, Plucked Chicken Press, Evanston, Ill, 86. *Exhib:* 16th Midwest Biennial, Joslyn Art Mus, Omaha, Nebr, 80; Irwin Collection, Krannert Art Mus, Univ Ill, 80; Watercolor USA, Springfield Art Mus, Mo, 80; one-man shows, Zaks Gallery, Chicago, Ill, 81 & 84; Chicago Int Art Expos, 82-87; Fabrications, Chicago Sculpture Soc, 83; Sound/Light, ARC, Chicago, 87; one man shows, Endicott Col, MA, 97, Hess Gallery, Pine Manor Col, 2004. *Collection Arranged:* Emergence of Modernism in Illinois 1914-1940, 76; Illinois Photographers 1978, 80; Illinois Invitationals, 71-84; Contemporary American Photography, 88; White Mountain Painters, 92; Art Forms in Nature: The Prints of Ernst Haeckel, 2000. *Pos:* Res asst, Univ Galleries, Southern Ill Univ, Carbondale, 69-70; cur art, Ill State Mus, Springfield, 70-, head dept art, 81-85; gallery dir & dept chmn, Rockford Col, 85-88; dir, Danforth Mus Art, Framingham, Mass, 88-95. *Teaching:* Instr drawing & painting, Springfield Art Asn, Ill, 71-76; adj asst prof arts mgt, Sangamon State Univ, 73-78; assoc prof, Rockford Col, 85-88; adj fac, Framingham State Col, Mass, 88-95; prof visual commun, Endicott Col, Beverly, Mass, 95-, chmn visual comm, 95-98; prof visual art, Pine Manor Col, Chestnut Hill, MA, 2001-. *Awards:* Best in Show, Quincy Art Club Ann Exhib, 72 & 78; Governors Art Award, Ill Arts Coun, 80; Merit Award, Miss Corridors, Davenport Art Mus, Iowa, 81. *Bibliog:* David Elliott (auth), article, Chicago Sun Times, 6/21/81; Alan G Artner (auth), article, Chicago Tribune, 7/3/81. *Mem:* Col Art Asn; Am Asn Mus. *Media:* Mixed, Painting. *Publ:* Auth, articles in Living Mus, 70- & Craft Horizons & Mus News; plus numerous exhib catalogs. *Mailing Add:* 11 Willowbrook Dr Framingham MA 01702

EVANS, BURFORD ELONZO
PAINTER, LECTURER
b Golinda, Tex, July 20, 31. *Study:* Sorbonne Univ, cert 55; Echole de Beaux Arts, Paris, France. *Work:* Mus Fine Arts, Lubbock, Tex; Black Arts Ctr, Waco, Tex; Northwood Inst, Midland, Mich; Bishop Col, Dallas, Tex. *Comn:* Josephite Black Arts Calendar, Josephite Pastoral Ctr, Washington, DC, 74. *Exhib:* Mobile Arts Festival, Ala, 70; Discovery 70, Nat Black Arts Festival, Cincinnati, Ohio, 70; Nat Black Arts Festival, Normal, Ill, 73; one-man show, State Capitol, Austin, Tex, 73, Abajan Ivory Coast, Africa, 95, Southside Cult Ctr, Chicago, Ill, 2001; Tex Fine Arts Festival, Houston, 74. *Awards:* Second Award, Dimension IV Houston Art League, Humble Oil Co, 68; Betty McGowan Award, Mobil Arts Festival, 70; Distinguished Artist Award, Nat Coun Negro Women, 72. *Bibliog:* James Kennedy (auth), Ethnic American Art, Slide Libr, Univ Ala, 70-75; Charolette Phelen (auth), Evans remembers June tenth, Houston Chronicle, 71; Theresa Dickason Cederholm (auth), Afro American Artist, Boston Pub Libr, 73. *Mem:* Art League Houston; Tex Fine Arts Asn; Contemp Arts Asn. *Media:* Multimedia. *Specialty:* Contemporary. *Interests:* Impressionist. *Dealer:* Claude Smith 3917 Art Gallery Houston TX. *Mailing Add:* 5327 Knotty Oaks Tr Houston TX 77045-4018

EVANS, DICK
PAINTER, SCULPTOR
b Roswell, NMex, July 10, 41. *Study:* Tex Tech Univ, Lubbock, 59-62; Univ Utah, Salt Lake City, BFA, 64, MFA, 66. *Work:* Nat Mus Am Art, Smithsonian Inst; Sheldon Mem Art Gallery, Univ Nebr, Lincoln; Milwaukee Art Mus, Wis; Ariz State Univ, Tempe; Herbert F Johnson Mus Art, Cornell Univ, Ithaca, NY; and others. *Comn:* ceramic murals, Deloitte, Haskins & Sells, 86, Warshafsky, Rotter, Tarnoff, Gesler & Reinhardt, 86 & Milwaukee Art Comn, 88, Milwaukee, Wis; RTE Corp, 87; Firstar, 87. *Exhib:* Landscape: New Views, Johnson Art Mus, Cornell Univ, Ithaca, NY, 78; Poetic Image, Elements Gallery, NY, 80; Sheldon Mem Art Gallery, Univ Nebr, Lincoln, 82; solo shows, Michael H Lord Gallery, Milwaukee, Wis, 84 & 89, Elaine Horwitch Galleries, Santa Fe, NMex, 90, Tory Folliard Gallery, Milwaukee, Wis, 93, 95 & 2006, Robins Hyder Gallery, Santa Fe NMex, 96; Joyce Robins Gallery, Santa Fe, NMex, 1997-2006; Shadid Fine Art, Edmond, Ok, 2003, 2004, 2005, 2006; and others. *Teaching:* Instr art, Texas Tech, Lubbock, 66-70; asst prof art, Univ Tenn, Knoxville, 71-72 & Univ NMex, Albuquerque, 72-75; prof art, Sch Fine Arts, Univ Wis, Milwaukee, 75-87, assoc dean, 81-83. *Awards:* NMex Disting Artists Calendar Award, NMex Mag, 99. *Bibliog:* Margaret L Brown (auth), The abstracted landscape, Southwest Art, 9/97; Susan Hallsten McGarry (auth), Inside Out: The landscape of memory, 6/99; Marsha McEuen (auth), Art Pairs, Santa Fean Mag, 5/99; Dotte Indyke (auth), Dick Evans National Reviews, Art News, 9/2//02; Kristen Buckner (auth), Best of the West- Exploring Nature's Enigmas, Southwest Art, 5/04; Kristen Buchner (auth), Best of the West-Mellow Yellow, Southwest Art, 5/04; Judith Fein & Paul Ross, Emerging Artists, Art 7 Antiques, 4/05. *Media:* Acrylic. *Dealer:* Joyce Robins Gallery 201 Galisteo St Santa Fe NM 87501; Shadid Fine Art 19 N Broadway Edmond OK 73034; Tory Folliard Gallery 233 N Milwaukee St Milwaukee Wis 53202. *Mailing Add:* 47 Coyote Mountain Rd Santa Fe NM 87505

EVANS, GARTH
ARTIST AND EDUCATOR
b Stockport, Cheshire, Eng, Nov 23, 1934; arrived in US, 79. *Study:* Studied at Manchester Jr Col Art, 51; Manchester Regional Col Art, 57; Univ Col London, diploma fine art, 60. *Exhib:* Solo shows include Rowan Gallery, London, 62, 64, 66, 68, 69, 72, 74, 76, 78, 80, Minneapolis Inst Arts, 79, Mt Holyoke Col Art Mus, South Hadley, Mass, 83, Robert Elkon Gallery, NY City, 83, Tibor de Nagy Gallery, NY City, 84, Robert Brown Contemp Art, Washington, 88, Compass Rose Gallery, Chicago, 89, Hill Gallery, Birmingham, Mich, 90, Wrexham Mus and Art Ctr, Rhyl, Wales, 91, Rosemary Hall, Wallingford, Conn, 93, Dana Arts Ctr, Colgate Univ, Hamilton, NY, 95, Korn Gallery, Drew Univ, Madison, NJ, 96, Claudia Carr Gallery, NY City, 97; group shows include Air Gallery, London, 62, Stone Gallery, Newcastle Upon Tyne, Eng, 64, Camden Arts Ctr, London, 66, Whitechapel Art Gallery, London, 68, Hayward Gallery, London, 71, 75, Redfern Gallery, London, 77, Oporto Sch Fine Art, Portugal, 80, Robert Elkon Gallery, NY City, 81, Newhouse Gallery, NY City, 83, John Davis Gallery, Akron, 86, NY Studio Sch, NY City, 89, Charles Cowles Gallery, NY City, 91, PMW Gallery, Stamford, Conn, 92, Skidmore Col, Saratoga Springs, NY, 93, Am Acad Arts and Letters, NY City, 96; represented in public collections Tate Gallery, London, Welsh Art Council, Brooklyn Union Gas, Merthyr Tydfil Art Gallery, Wales, Victoria & Albert Mus, London, Mus Modern Art, NY Metrop Mus, NY City, Brooklyn Mus, Joseph H Hirshhorn Mus, Washington, DC, Nat Mus Modern Art, Brazil, Power Gallery Contemp Art, Sydney, Gulbenkian Found Lisbon, Portugal, Yale Ctr British Art. *Teaching:* Vis lectr Central Sch Art, London, 60-65, Camberwell Sch Art, London, 60-69, St Martin's Sch Art, London,65-79, Chelsea Sch Art, London, 78-79, Yale Sch Art, Yale Univ, 83, 85, 86; vis prof Minneapolis Col Art and Design, 73; external examiner Maidstone Col Art, Kent, Eng, 77-79, Nat Col Art and Design, Dublin, Ireland, 78, Goldsmiths Col, Univ London, 78-81; vis tutor Slade Sch Fine Art, Univ Col, London, 70-81; vis artist sculpture dept Royal Col Art, 70-81; vis artist Mt Holyoke Col, South Hadley, 79-81, Manchester Poly, 78-83; assoc lectr in sculpture Camberwell Sch Art, London, 71-83; faculty mem NY Studio Sch, NY City, 88-. *Awards:* Sabbatical Awrd, Arts Council Great Britian, 66; Major Prize, 75; Film Bursary Award, 79; Bursary Award, Greater London Arts Asn, 78; Pollock-Krasner Found Award, 96; Newcastle Cruddas Park Sculpture Competition, 61; British Steep Corp Fellow, 69; John S Guggenheim Memorial Found Fellow, 86; British Council Exhib Abroad, 79. *Mailing Add:* NY Studio Sch 8 W 8th St New York NY 10011

EVANS, JOHN
COLLAGE ARTIST, PAINTER
b Sioux Falls, SDak, Aug 24, 32. *Study:* Art Inst Chicago, BFA, 61, MFA, 63. *Exhib:* Pa Acad Fine Art Ann, 64; one-man shows, Eastern Mont State Univ, Billings, 80, Cordier & Ekstrom, NY, 80 & 81 & Arts Club, Chicago, 82; 100 Yrs Art on the Lower Eastside, NY, 88; Works on Paper, 128 Rivington Gallery, 88; Gracie Mansion Gallery, NY, 90; Artstar, Los Angeles, 91; Dietrich Gallery, NY, 94; Knoedler Gallery Invitational, 97; Mary Delahoyd Gallery, NY, 98; NY Historical Soc, 2002-2003; Constellation, Pavel Zoubok Gallery, 2006; and others. *Pos:* Artist-in residence, Decenter, Glums, Denmark, 71; artist-in-residence, Villa Arson, Nice, France, 86. *Awards:* Nat Endowment Arts Grant, 85; Pollack-Krasner Grant, 89. *Bibliog:* Lynn Zelevansky (auth), Art & Auction, 10/84; Victoria Donohue (auth), Philadelphia Inquirer, 2/28/87; Michael Andre (auth), Art in America, 10/98. *Media:* Acrylic, Oil; Mixed & Mail art. *Specialty:* Collage. *Publ:* Auth, Collection of 38 Collage Books, privately publ, 76; Remnants of an Unknown Woman-with Ursule Molinero, Red Dust Press, 87; John Evans Collage, Quantuck Lane Press, 2005. *Dealer:* Pavel Zoubok 533 W 23 St New York NY 10011. *Mailing Add:* 199 E 3rd St 2B New York NY 10009

EVANS, JUDITH FUTRAL
PAINTER
b Ft Smith, Ark. *Study:* Univ Ark, Fayetteville, BA, 61; Univ Iowa, Iowa City, MFA, 64. *Work:* Shearson Lehman Hutton, NY; Avon Corp, NY; US Air, Philadelphia, Pa; Towers Perrin, Stamford, Conn; Giro Credit Bank, Vienna, Austria & NY. *Comn:* After Diego Rivera, comn by Al Solokov & Co, NY, 86; Golden Gate with Wildflowers Comn, Tafapolsky & Smith LLP, San Francisco, 02; Portrait, Sylvia Barker Comn, Mt Sinai Medical Ctr, NY, 04; JRB Art, Oklahoma City, OK 2004-2006. *Exhib:* Blue Mountain Gallery, NY, 80-94; Nat Mid-Year Am, Butler Inst Am Art, Ohio, 85, 88, 92; Nat Soc Painters Casein & Acrylic, NY, 89; Park Avenue Atrium, NY, 96; Heckscher Mus Art, NY, 96; Gatehouse Gallery, Glasgow, Scotland, 97; Ethel Sergeant Smith Gallery, Wayne, Pa, 97; Sherry French Gallery, NY, 97-06; Doran Gallery, Tulsa, Okla, 02-06; Albright Knox Gallery, Buffalo, NY, 99; Hurlbutt Gallery, Greenwich, Conn, 98; New London Art Soc, Conn, 98; Ctr for the Arts, Vero Beach, Fla, 98; Ark Art Ctr, Little Rock, 97; Pastel Soc Am, 34th Ann Exhib, NY, 2006. *Collection Arranged:* Avon Corp, NY; US Air, Philadelphia; Tafapolsky & Smith LLP, San Francisco; Towers Perrin, Stamford, Conn; Giro Credit Bank, Vienna, Austria; Shearson Lehman Hutton, Frankfort, Ger; Dewey, Ballantine, NY; Maimonides Med Ctr, NY; Hunter Col, NY; Cedar Crest Col, Allentown, Pa; Castrol Corp, NJ; Southern Ark Univ, Magnolia; Columbia Presbyterian Hosp, NY; Cary Ellis Co, Houston; Broadacre Mgmt Co, Chicago; Mt Sinai Medical Ctr, NY; Thatcher, Proffit & Wood, NY; McCown & Evans, San Francisco, CA; Arkansas Art Center, Little Rock, AR. *Pos:* Founder, Blue Mountain Gallery, New York, 79-; Scenic Artist, Major Motion Pictures, Network Television, Broadway Shows, Metropolitan Opera, NY, 84-. *Bibliog:* Jeff Stinson (auth), Arkansas puts works on display, Wash Gazette, 5/91; Diane Freedman (auth), Artists celebrate their environment, Artspeak, 3/16/96; Paulette Weiss (auth), French's American on 57th, Where Mag, 7/99. *Mem:* United Scenic Artists, Local 829, NY; Am Women in Radio & Television, NY. *Media:* Oil, Acrylic, Watercolor, Pastel, Portrait, Landscape, Still Life. *Specialty:* realism. *Publ:* Best of Acrylic Painting, 96, Best of Oil Painting, 96 & Landscape Inspirations, 97, Rockport Publ Inc, 97. *Dealer:* Sherry French Gallery 601 W 26th St, New York, NY; JRB Art, 2810 N Walker, Oklahoma City, OK. *Mailing Add:* 34 Plaza St Apt 808 Brooklyn NY 11238

EVANS, KENYA
ARTIST
b Sumter, NC, 74. *Exhib:* Hannah Höch, Mit Pinsel, Feder und Schere, Galerie Remmert und Barth, Duesseldorf, 98; Day for Night, Whitney Biennial, NY, 2006. *Pos:* gallery supv, Contemp Arts Mus, Houston, Tex; mem, Otabenga Jones & Assoc. *Mailing Add:* Contemporary Arts Museum Houston 5216 Montrose Blvd Houston TX 77006

EVANS, RICHARD
PAINTER, EDUCATOR
b Chicago, Ill, Oct 1, 23. *Study:* Otis Art Inst, dipl; Calif Col Arts & Crafts; Studio of George Miller, New York; Univ Wyo, MA; Stacey Found Fel, 47; Tiffany Found Fels, 48 & 50. *Work:* San Francisco Fine Arts Comn; Univ Wyo; Col Southern Utah. *Comn:* Tile mural, Univ Wyo, 68; portrait of Sam S Knight, Univ Wyo Geol Mus; twenty sculptures of prominent personages for private comns. *Exhib:* One-man show, Yellowstone Art Ctr, Billings, Mont, 74; retrospective, Univ Wyo Mus, 76; Santa Fe Art Festival, 77; Directions Gallery, Colo State Univ, 79; 57th Mid-Year, Butler Inst, 81; Drawing Ann, Rutgers Univ, 81; and others. *Teaching:* Instr drawing, Calif Col Arts & Crafts, Oakland, 50-52; instr drawing & painting, Miami Univ, Oxford, Ohio, 56-57; prof printmaking, drawing & painting, Univ Wyo, 57-. *Awards:* Ford Found Grants, 64 & 66; 26th Cedar City Invitational Purchase Award, 66; Anonymous Donor Award, Otis Art Inst 50th Anniversary Exhib, 68. *Bibliog:* Victor Flach (auth), The Making of Ikon 13 (film & TV tape), Univ Wyo, 70; Victor Flach (auth), By these presents: Richard Evans, A retrospective, 76. *Media:* Oil, Acrylic; Intaglio. *Publ:* Auth, On large scale prints, Am Artist, 11/62. *Mailing Add:* 150 Corthell Rd Laramie WY 82070-4369

EVANS, ROBERT GRAVES
EDUCATOR, SCULPTOR
b Rawlins, Wyo, Nov 19, 44. *Study:* Atlanta Sch Art, BFA; French Govt Fel, Paris, 69; with Stanley Hayter; Tulane Univ, with Julius Struppeck, MFA. *Work:* Evansville Mus Arts & Sci, Ind; Sheldon Swope Art Mus, Terre Haute, Ind; Ind State Univ, Terre Haute; Central Mich Univ, Mt Pleasant; The Univ of the South, Swanee, Tenn. *Comn:* Man of Year Award (sculpture), Atlanta, Ga, 69; Film Festival Award (sculpture), Atlanta, Ga, 69; bronze bust of Pres Rankin, Ind State Univ, 75; outdoor sculpture, Cent Mich Univ, 75; outdoor monumental sculpture comn, Indianapolis, Ind, 82. *Exhib:* Mid-States Art Exhib, Evansville Mus Arts & Sci, Ind, 78; New Harmony Gallery of Contemp Art, New Harmony, Ind, 82; Wabash Col, Outdoor Sculpture Exhib, Crawfordsville, Ind, 85; Solo Sculpture Exhib, Herr-Chambliss Fine Arts Gallery, Hot Springs Nat Park, Ark, 90; Sculpture Exhib at Mid-Am Mus, Hot Springs Nat Park, Ark, 91. *Pos:* Prof of Art. *Teaching:* Prof sculpture, Ind State Univ, Terre Haute, 72-78, assoc prof art, 78-84, prof art, 84-. *Awards:* Sculpture Acquisition, Swope Art Gallery, 77; Mus Guild Purchase Award, Evansville Mus Arts & Sci, 78; Beautification Award, Terre Haute CofC, 81. *Mem:* Southern Sculpture Asn; Arts Illiana; Col Art Asn. *Media:* Bronze, Aluminum. *Mailing Add:* Ind State Univ Dept of Art Terre Haute IN 47809

EVANS, TOM R
PAINTER
b St Paul, Minn, June 4, 43. *Study:* Univ Minn, BA, 65, MFA, 68. *Work:* Grey Gallery, New York Univ; Chase Manhattan Bank, London, Eng; Gen Mills, Minneapolis, Minn; IBM, White Plains, NY. *Exhib:* Walker Biennial, Walker Art Ctr, Minneapolis, Minn, 68; Contemp Reflections, 71 & Best of Contemp Reflections, 73, Aldrich Mus,

Ridgefield, Conn; one-person exhibs, John Bernard Myers Gallery, NY, 73 & 74 & Max Hutchinson Gallery, NY, 79; New Work-NY, New Mus, NY, 81; Gimpel & Weitzenhoffen Gallery, NY, 86; Paint as Primal Substance, Painting Ctr, NY, 97; Marymount Col, NY, 97; Solo: 55 Mercer Gallery, 2004; 55 Mercer Gallery, 2005; Group: Looking Back & Moving Forward, Univ of Minn. *Teaching:* Asst prof, Fashion Inst Tech. *Media:* Oil on Canvas or Linen. *Mailing Add:* 115 W Broadway New York NY 10013

EVAUL, WILLIAM H, JR
PAINTER, PRINTMAKER
b Philadelphia, Pa, July 2, 49. *Study:* Fleischer Mem Sch Art, Syracuse Univ, Pratt Inst, BFA, 81; Whitney Mus Am Art, Grad Studies, 81. *Work:* The Library of Congress, Provincetown Art Asn & Mus, Mass; Sunrise Art Mus, Charleston, WVa; Printmaking Workshop, NY; Jane Vorhees Zimmerli Art Mus, New Brunswick, NJ. *Comn:* Arts Foundation of Cape Cod-Pops-by-the-Sea Artists-Original painting and limited print edition commissioned 2002. *Exhib:* Provincetown & the Art of Printmaking, Smithsonian Inst Traveling Exhib, 90-92; Int Fine Print Dealers Asn Ann Print Fair, 90-2000; solo exhibs, Printmaking Coun, NJ, 94 & Inter-active Virtual Painting, SMA Real Time, NY, 98; Modernism, Park Ave Armory, NY; Innovative Printmaking from an Am Art Colony, Zimmerli Art Mus; Int Miniature Print Exhib, 2001, Conn Graphic Arts Ctr, Norwalk, Conn; Southcoast New Eng Printmaking 1939-2003, Univ of Mass, Dartmouth; North Am Print Biennial 2005, Boston Univ. *Pos:* Dir/cur, Provincetown Art Asn & Mus, 86-90; guest cur, Cape Mus Fine Arts, 92. *Teaching:* Asst inst lithography, Pratt Graphics Ctr, 80-82; instr printmaking, Truro Ctr Arts, 92-; guest lectr, Ga Mus Art, Ogleby Inst & others; tchr Penn Acad Fine Art, Charles Demuth Found, Zimmerli Art Mus. *Awards:* Fel, Fine Arts Work Ctr, Provincetown, 70-72; Finalist, Elizabeth Found, NY, 95. *Bibliog:* Ann Brigham (auth), Contemporary artists, Orthodox traditions, Antiques & Arts, 1/90; Joe Burn (auth) Block printing undergoes an Evaul-lution The Provincetown Banner, Nov 98; Scott Dalton (auth) White-Line Woodcut Artist bill Evaul Carves Out More Than a Niche A-Plus-Art/Antiques/Design, July, 2002; Viginia Reiser (auth), The Kindest Cut-White-Line Woodcuts, Cape Arts Review Annual 2002. *Mem:* Asn Am Mus; Nat Artists Equity; Art Fedn Am; Col Art Asn. *Media:* Oil, Woodcut. *Res:* American Art-Provincetown White-Line Woodblocks. *Publ:* Auth, The Genesis of a unique woodcut tradition, Pratt Graphics Ctr, 84; The Eye of the Collector, Cape Mus Fine Art, 92. *Mailing Add:* PO Box 958 Truro MA 02666

EVEN, ROBERT LAWRENCE
EDUCATOR
b Breckenridge, Minn, June 7, 29. *Study:* Valley City State Col, BS; Univ Minn, MA & PhD; Art Inst Chicago; Minneapolis Col Art & Design. *Teaching:* Instr art, Univ Minn, 52-54; prof art, Northern Ill Univ, 63-, chmn dept, 74-. *Awards:* Res Grant, State Ill, 64 & Dean's Fund, Northern Ill Univ, 65 & 73. *Mem:* Col Art Asn Am; Mid-Am Col Art Asn; Nat Coun Art Adminr; Nat Asn Sch Art. *Mailing Add:* 413 Fairmont Dr De Kalb IL 60115-2336

EVERGON
PHOTOGRAPHER
b Niagara Falls, Ont, Dec 28, 46. *Study:* Mt Allison Univ, Sackville, NB, BFA, 70; Rochester Inst Technol, MFA (photog), 74. *Work:* Nat Gallery Can, Can Mus Contemp Photog & Can Art Bank, Ottawa, Ont; Found Cartier pour l'Art Contemp, Jouy-en-Josas, France; Mus de Que, Quebec City. *Exhib:* Solo exhibs, Galerie Séquence, Chicoutimi, Québec, Can, 89, Recent Works by Evergon, Glenn/Dash Gallery, Los Angeles, 89, Evergon 1971-1987 Traveling Exhib, 89-90, Richard Feign Gallery, Chicago, Ill, 90, Art 45, Montreal, Que, Can, 90, Recent Polaroids, Jack Shainman Gallery, NY, 90; The Photog of Invention: Am Pictures of the 80's, Nat Mus Am Art, Washington, DC, 89; Prospest Photographie, Frankfurt Kunstverein, Frankfurt, WGer, 89; Andreas Serrano, Andrea Rugieri Gallery, Washington, DC, 90; Selection III, Polaroid Collection, Houston Foto Fest, Tex, 90; Selections V, Polaroid Collection, Photokina, Stuttgart, Ger, 90; PRET, Collection D'Oeurves D'Art, Mus du Que, Can, 90; and others; Photographies: Pour célébrerle 150e anniversaire de la naissane de la photographie, Found Cartier pour l'art contemporain, Jouy-en-Josas, France, 90. *Teaching:* Lectr photog, Louisville Sch Art, Ky, 72-73; part-time lectr photog, drawing & design, Univ Ottawa, 74-90. *Awards:* Ont Arts Coun Grants, 80 & 89; Can Coun Arts Grants, 82-90; Can Coun Art A Grant, 90. *Bibliog:* Peter Weiermair (auth), Evergon-Homo Barocco, Cliches, No 48, Belg, 88; Christie Day (auth), The wit and wisdom of a remarkable Canadian artist, Can Photog, No 1, Toronto, Can, spring 90; Martin B Pendersen (auth), Graphis Photo 90, Graphis Corp, Zurich, Switz, 90. *Mem:* Can Artists Representative, Ont & Ottawa; Visual Arts Ont. *Media:* Polaroid, Holography. *Publ:* Contribr, Artifacts at the End of a Decade, 80; Canadian Portfolio, 80; Ottawa Portfolio 1983, The Company of Artists and Patrons, 83; The New Photography: A Guide to New Images, Processes and Display Techniques, Prentice-Hall, 85. *Dealer:* Art 45 2155 Guy St Montreal PQ H3G 1K4 Canada. *Mailing Add:* c/o Jack Shainman Gallery 513 W 20th St New York NY 10011-2819

EVERHART, DON, II
SCULPTOR, MEDALIST
b York, Pa, Aug 19, 49. *Study:* Kutztown State Univ, BFA(painting), 72. *Work:* Smithsonian Inst; Brit Mus; Nat Sculpture Soc; Georgetown Univ; Am Numismatic Soc; Brookgreen Gardens. *Comn:* The Dance of the Dolphins (art medal), 106th Issue Soc Medallists, 82; Hermit Crab (art medal), Brookgreen Gardens, SC, 91; 24 installed sculptures, (Sports Hall of Fame) Georgetown Univ, Washington, 92-; The Fossil Collection (6 art medals), 128th Issue Soc Medallists, 94; 1997 Off Inaugural Medal for Clinton/Gore, Medallic Art Co, 96; Sculpted Obverse, Buffalo Nickel, 2005; Califronia State Quarter Reverse, 2005; Reverse, Jackie Robinson Congressional Medal, 2005. *Exhib:* Reliefs & Medals Expos, Nat Sculpture Soc, NY, 85; Am Medallic Sculpture Asn, Newark Mus, NJ, 90; Expos Fedn Int de la Medaille, British Mus, London, 92, Hungarian Nat Gallery, Budapest, 94; Traveling Show, New Medal, Am Medallic Sculpture Asn, Franklin Mint Mus, Nat Sculpture Soc, NY, Am Numismatic Soc, Colorado Springs, 94; FIDEM 94, Hungarian Nat Mus, Budapest, 94 & FIDEM 98, The Hague, Amsterdam, 98; and many others. *Pos:* Illusr, Int Design Orgn, Moorestown, NJ, 72-73; sculptor-in-residence, Franklin Mint, 73-80; freelance sculptor & medalist, 80-2004; Sculptor-Engraver, US Mint, 2004-, sculpted: Calif state quarter, 2005, nickel obverse, 2006, sculpted & designed: Nevada state quarter, 2006, Franklin the Elder silver dollar, 2006. *Teaching:* Instr sculpture, Chester Co Art Asn, 85-88 & W Chester Univ, 97-98. *Awards:* First Prize, Nat Sculpture Soc, 85; Numismatic Art Award for excellence in Medallic Sculpture, Am Numismatic Soc, 94; Best of Show, The New Medal Traveling Show, Franklin Mint, 94; and others. *Bibliog:* Kari Stone (auth), Opening up to medals, Coinage, 5/94; George Cuhaj (auth), Don Everhart II: A natural talent for Medallic art, The Numismatist, 10/94; Kari Stone (auth), Dinosaur medals, Coinage, 11/94. *Mem:* Am Medallic Sculpture Asn (pres, 92-94); Fedn Int de la Medaille; Nat Sculpture Soc; Knickerbocker Artists; Am Artists Prof League; and others. *Media:* Bronze, Clay; Plaster, Urethane. *Interests:* bicycling, tropical fish. *Mailing Add:* 1047 Niels Ln W West Chester PA 19382-7176

EVINS, PATSY JEAN
PAINTER
b Port Lavaca, Tex, Mar 10, 52. *Study:* NTex State Univ, Denton, BFA, 75; Lyme Acad Fine Art, Old Lyme, Conn, 85-86; Silvermine Sch Art, New Canaan, Conn, 87-88. *Work:* John Marlor Arts Ctr, Milledgeville, Ga; Gen Electric Capital, Atlanta, Ga; St Joseph Hosp, Augusta, Ga; Univ Hosp, Augusta, Ga; NBC, NY. *Comn:* Painting, Ritz Carlton, San Juan, 97; painting, Hyatt Regency, Wichita, Kans, 97. *Exhib:* Am Watercolor Soc Traveling exhib, 91-92; solo-shows, Gertrude Herbert Inst, Augusta, Ga, 92, John Marlor Art Ctr, Milledgeville, Ga, 93 & Chattahoochee Valley Art Mus, La Grange, Ga, 94; Takarazuka Int & Cult Ctr, Japan, 94, 96 & 98; Davidson Co Mus Art, Lexington, 95; Artexpo, NY, 95; Madison Showcase at Mercy Ctr, Conn, 95. *Teaching:* Expanding Art Boundaries, Gertrude Herbert Inst Art, Augusta, Ga, 94 & Pushing Beyond Your Boundaries, 98. *Awards:* 12th Exhib-Ga Watercolor Soc Award, 1st Union Nat Bank, 91; 14th Ann SC Watercolor Soc Award, Dutch Door Art Express, 91. *Bibliog:* Painter strives to convey positive images in works, Augusta Chronicle, 2/21/91; Through the eyes of the artist, Augusta Mag, 2-3/92; Jennifer Gipson (dir), Femme Nouvelle, Charlotte Soutter Roe, 94. *Mem:* SC Watercolor Soc; Gertrude Herbert Inst Art; Arts & Healing Network. *Media:* Two-D Casein; Oil, Pastel. *Mailing Add:* 108 Springlakes Cir Martinez GA 30907

EWALD, ELIN LAKE
FINE ART SPECIALIST APPRAISER
b Raleigh, NC. *Study:* Art Students League with Edwin Dickinson; Am Acad Art; Art Inst Chicago; grad prog, NY Univ & Metrop Mus Art; Nat Acad Design, NY; NY Univ, PhD(Phi Beta Kappa). *Pos:* Lectr in field; appraiser, O'Toole-Ewald Art Assoc Inc, 74-78, ASA sr appraiser, vpres, partner, 78-82, pres, 82-; adv cur Am Mus Nat Hist, NY, Walters Art Gallery, Baltimore, Md, Afro-Am Mus, Philadelphia; art adv, US Army Corps Engineers, Off Pub Adminr, Manhattan & Albany, Off Atty Gen & Dist Atty, NY & Westchester, FBI, Govt Can, Tax Revenue. *Mem:* Am Soc Appraisers (pres, 92-93, sr appraiser, bd dir, NY Chap, ed/columnist, NY Chap Newsletter); Am Asn Mus; Int Coun Mus; Costume Soc Am; Am Arbitration Asn; Am Bankruptcy Inst; Corp Art Mgt; plus others. *Specialty:* Consultants and fine art/antiques appraisers, specialists in damage/loss/fraud cases involving fine/decorative art. *Interests:* For over 60 years, firm has appraised and assembled private collections for individuals, corporations and museums; additionally, it has arranged donations of individual works of art and collections to museums; specialists in damage/loss reports and appraisals of corporate collections, expert witness testimony. *Publ:* Auth, Hester Bateman and English Women Silversmiths of the 18th Century, Ms Mag, 76; articles In: Valuation Mag, Fairshare, Ms Mag, Evaluation, CPPC Newsletter; contrib ed, Personal Property J. *Mailing Add:* 1185 Park Ave New York NY 10128-1308

EWALD, WENDY T
CONCEPTUAL ARTIST, EDUCATOR
b Detroit 1951. *Study:* Antioch Col, BA(art), 74; New Sch Social Rsch Vera List Ctr Art & Politics, Sr Fel, 2000-2003. *Hon Degrees:* Doctorate Bank St Sch of Eductaion, 2005. *Work:* Int Ctr Photog, Metrop Mus, NY; Addison Gallery Am Art, Andover, Mass; Polaroid Collection, Cambridge, Mass; Hallmark Collection; Cleveland Ctr Contemp Art; RISD Mus, RI. *Comn:* Constructing Identity, Mondrian Found, Amsterdam, Holland, 96; World Faiths Proj, Ackland Mus, Chapel Hill, NC, 97; Artist in an Archive, Am Joint Distribution Comn, 98. *Exhib:* Solo exhibs, George Eastman House, Rochester, NY, 93, Ansel Adams Ctr, San Francisco, 93, Ctr Creative Photog, NY, 94, Southeast Mus Photog, Daytona Beach, Fla, 94 & Addison Gallery Am Art, NY, 96, Partobject Gallery, NC, 2000, Stills Gallery, Edinburgh, 01, Museet for Fotokunst, Odense, Denmark, 01, Corcoran Gallery of Am Art, 02, RI Sch Design Mus, 02, Kemper Mus of Contemp Art, Kansas City, 02, Queens Mus of Art, New York City, 03, Yossi Milo Gallery, New York City, 03, Morocco Scalo Gallery, New York City, 03; Biennial, Whitney Mus Am Art, NY, 97; Fotomus, Winterthur, Switz, 2000; Addison Gallery Am Art, 2001; group exhibs, Miami Mus Art, 99, Art Gallery, New South Wales, Australia, 2000, Ctr for Art and Vis Cult, Univ Md, 03; Handworkshop, Richmond, Va, 04; Art Angel, Toward A Promised Land, London, England, 04-06. *Collection Arranged:* Detroit Art Inst; Addison Gallery of Am Art; Metrop Mus Art; Hallmark Collection; Int Ctr Photog; Polaroid Corp; Libr Congress; Franklin Ctr, Duke Univ; RI Sch Design Mus. *Pos:* Creator & dir, Literacy through Photog, Durham, NC, 90-. *Teaching:* Sr res assoc photog educ, Duke Univ, 91-; vis assoc prof photog, Bard Col, 96. *Awards:* Nat Endowment Arts Fel, 88; NY Found Fel, NY Found Arts, 90; MacArthur Found Fel, 92-97; Artist Residency, Cleveland Ctr for Contemp Art, 2000; Comn, RI Sch Design Mus, 02. *Bibliog:* Vicki Goldberg

(auth), Family Circle Mag, 89; Anne Higgonet (auth), Pictures of Innocence, Thames & Hudson, 97; Penny Woolcock (dir), Kids, Channel 4-Britain, 97. *Media:* Photogrpahy, Video. *Publ:* Ed & contribr, Appalachia: A Self-Portrait, Gnomon, 79; auth, Portraits & Dreams, Writers & Readers, 85; Magic Eyes: Scenes from an Andean Girlhood, Bay Press, 92; I Dreamed I Had a Girl in My Pocket, W W Norton, 96; contribr, Constructing Identity/Photoworks in Progress, Snoek-Ducajut Zoon, 97; Wendy Ewald Secret Games, Scalo, Berlin, Zurich & New York, 00; American Alphabets Scalo, 05; In Peace & Harmony: Carver Portraits, Handworkshops, 05. *Dealer:* Scalo 560 Broadway New York NY. *Mailing Add:* PO Box 582 Rhinebeck NY 12572

EWING, LAUREN
SCULPTOR
b Ft Knox, Ky, 46. *Study:* Skidmore Col, BA, 64-68; State Univ, MS; Univ Ca, Santa Barbara, MFA. *Work:* Metrop Mus Art; Chase Manhattan Bank; Walt Disney Co; Mus Contemp Art, San Diego, Calif. *Exhib:* The New Mus, 80; Hirshhorn Mus, Wash, DC; De Cordova Mus; Ulrich Mus, 95; solo exhib, Kunstralleu Daeuse, Denmark, Diane Baum Gallery, Interim Art, London. *Teaching:* instr, Williams Col, formerly; instr, RI Sch Design, formerly; instr, Fine Arts Work Ctr, Provincetown, Mass, formerly; instr, Int Summer Acad Fine Arts, Salzburg, Austria, formerly; instr, Rutgers Univ, New Brunswick, NJ, currently. *Awards:* Nat Endowment for the Arts, 82. *Mem:* Col Art Asn; Am Asn Univ Prof. *Media:* Bronze, Stone, Steel & Wood. *Specialty:* Installations and Site Sculpture. *Mailing Add:* 146 Franklin St New York NY 10013

EWING, SUSAN R
EDUCATOR
b Lawrenceville, Ill, 55. *Study:* Stephens Col, AA(music), 74; Ind Univ, BA(jewelry & metalsmithing), 76, MFA(jewlery & metalsmithing), 80. *Work:* White House Collection of Am Crafts. *Exhib:* Solo exhib, Hans Hansen Solv, Copenhagen, Denmark; Aspects Gallery, London, Eng; Park Ryu Sook Gallery, Seoul, Korea; Schweizerisches Landesmuseum, Zurich, Switz; Mus fur Kunsthandwerk, Frankfurt, Ger; Mathildenhohe Mus, Darmstadt; Fortunoff's, NY; Am Craft Mus. *Pos:* Head, Metals Prog, Miami Univ, 81-. *Teaching:* Prof metals, Fine Arts Dept, Sch Art, Miami Univ. *Awards:* Ohio Arts Coun Individual Artists Fel, 87, 89 & 91; Ohio State Bd Regents Grant, 93; Fulbright Grant, 97. *Bibliog:* Articles in NY Times, Christian Science Monitor Metrop Home, Am Craft Mag, Mirabella, Metaismith, Art Aurea & Gold Und Siber; European Journal (televised segment), PBS & INFAS-TV, Tokyo. *Mailing Add:* School Art-Fine Arts Dept Miami Univ Oxford OH 45056

EYERMAN, CHARLOTTE
CURATOR, ART HISTORIAN
Study: Holy Cross Col, BA (English), 1987; Univ Calif Berkeley, PhD (history of art), 1997. *Pos:* Asst cur paintings, J. Paul Getty Mus, LA, 2002-05; cur modern art, St. Louis Art Mus, Mo, 2005-; founder, elucidART, Inc. *Teaching:* Lectr impressionism in context, Southern Methodist Univ, 1993; teacher art hist, Univ Southern Calif, LA and Art Center Col Design, Pasadena; vis instr, Union Col, Schenectady, NY, 1994-96, asst prof Visual Arts Dept, 1996-2001, John D and Catherine T. MacArthur asst prof, 1996-97; Flagstaff Forum lectr, Smithsonian Assocs, 2000. *Mailing Add:* Saint Louis Art Mus Forest Park One Fine Arts Drive Saint Louis MO 63110-1380

EYRE, IVAN
PAINTER
b Tullymet, Sask, Apr 15, 35. *Study:* Univ Sask, 52; Univ Man, BFA, 57; Univ NDak, 58. *Work:* Nat Gallery Can, Ottawa, Ont; Mackenzie Art Gallery, Regina, Saskatchewan; Edmonton Art Gallery, Alta; Winnipeg Art Gallery, Man; Pavilion Gallery, Assiniboine Park, Winnipeg. *Comn:* Resurrection, (painting) Can Cath Conf, Ottawa, Ont, 76; Black Arrow Plain, (painting) Can Indust & Com Bank, Edmonton, Alta, 80; The Canadian Art Portfolio comm for the Nfld Hist Parks Asn, 95; North Northwest (painting) Teron Int, Ottawa, Ont, 86. *Exhib:* One-man shows, Nat Gallery Can, Ottawa, Ont, 78, 88, Robert McLaughlin Gallery, Ivan Eyre Expos, Oshawa, Ont, 80 (travelled To Paris, London & Edinburgh) 81, Art Gallery Greater Victoria Traveling, 82 & Winnipeg Art Gallery, Winnipeg, 82 & 88; Mira Godard Gallery, Toronto, 78, 79, 81, 90, 92, 94, 96 & 99; Ivan Eyre: Personal Mythologies: Images of the Milieu Nat, Gallery Can, Ottawa, Ont, 88; Pavilion Gallery, Winnipeg, 98, 99, 2000, 02 & 04; Ivan Eyre, Loch Mayberry Fine Art, Winnipeg, 2000. *Teaching:* Prof design, Univ NDak, 58-59; prof drawing & painting, Univ Man, Winnipeg, 59-93, prof emeritus, 94-; prof painting, Banff Centre, Alta, summer 72. *Awards:* Sr Arts Awards, Can Coun, 66 & 78; Queens Silver Jubilee Medal, Gov Gen of Can, 77; Univ Man Jubilee Award, 82; Queen's Golden Jubilee medal, 2002. *Bibliog:* E Zuk (producer), Visual Thinker (film), CBC, Winnipeg, 81; George Woodcock (auth), Ivan Eyre, Fitzhenry & Whiteside, 81; Visions (film), TV Ont, 83; Terrence Heath (auth), Beginning with One Work, Personal Mythologies/Images of the Milieu-Ivan Eyre, Winnipeg Art Gallery, 88; Tom Lovatt (auth), Ivan Eyre Drawings, Pavilion Gallery, 2003; Ivan Eyre (auth), Ivan on Eyre, Pavilion Gallery, 2004; and many other films & articles in various mags. *Mem:* Royal Can Acad Arts. *Media:* Acrylic, Drawing; Sculpture. *Dealer:* Loch Gallery 306 St Mary's Rd Winnipeg Manitoba Canada R2H 1J8. *Mailing Add:* 1098 Des Trappistes St Winnipeg MB R3V 1B8 Canada

F

FABBRI, ANNE R
CURATOR, CRITIC, ART WRITER
b Norristown, Pa. *Study:* Radcliffe Col, AB(cum laude); Bryn Mawr Col, MA(art hist), 71; Univ Calif, Berkeley, 79; Princeton Univ, NEH Scholar, Dept Art & Archaeol, 80, Winter Inst, Winterthur Mus, Del. *Collection Arranged:* Seven Afro-American Artists of the Delaware Valley (auth, catalog), 81; Tradition and Innovations, 81; Five Hispanic Artists of Pennsylvania (auth, catalog), 82; Social Realism and the Figure, 82; Celebration of New Jersey Artists (auth, catalog), 83; Landscapes Here and Now, 87; Gerald Lynch, Sculptor, 88; Recent Oil Paintings by Glenn Rudderow, 89; Recent Sculpture by Charles Searles, 89; Artists' Gardens, 90; The Urban Scene, Philadelphia Through the Eyes of Its Artists, 92; What a Beautiful View, Ten Different Approaches to Nature, 92; Saludos Latinos, 92; Viewpoints I, II & III, 93; Artists of Germantown and Mount Airy, Phildelphia, 93; Viewpoints IV & V, 94; Floored Art: Off the Floor on to the Walls, 94; Artists of Manayunk & East Falls, Philadelphia, 94; Rome & Philadelphia: Three Viewpoints, 94; 1 Screen, 2 Souls, 4 Hands, Art In City Hall, 96; Wild Life, Art in City Hall, 99; New Frontiers, 2000. *Pos:* Art critic & art ed, The Drummer, Philadelphia, 76-79; art critic, The Bull, Philadelphia, 79-80, WXPN Express, 80-81, Philadelphia Daily News, 99-, The Contrarian, Art Matters, Art Newspaper, Art in Am Art News, Am Artist; dir & cur, Alfred O Deshong Mus, Widener Univ, Chester, Pa, 80-82, Noyes Mus, Oceanville, NJ, 82-91; dir, Paley Design Ctr, Philadelphia Col Textiles & Sci, 91-2000. *Teaching:* Lectr hist art, Villanova Univ, Pa, 71-73, Drexel Univ, Philadelphia, 74-76 & arts management prog, Rosemont Col, 98-02. *Awards:* John Cotton Dana Award, Mus Coun NJ, 92. *Bibliog:* Article, Art Matters, 6/83. *Mem:* Print Club, Philadelphia (bd govs); MUSE Found Visual Arts; Int Asn Art Critics; Am Asn Mus; Col Art Asn; Art in City Hall (adv coun, chair). *Res:* Art theory; Mannerist art and iconography. *Interests:* Music, Antiquity, Theatre. *Publ:* Auth, Patience pays at Dr Barnes's Bks & Arts, 1/80; Three sculptors, 1/80, Harry Bertoia, 2/80 & Judith Ingram, 3/80, Arts Mag

FABBRIS, VICO
PAINTER, ENVIRONMENTAL ARTIST
b Northern Italy, 50. *Study:* Scuola Regionale Toscana, Florence, Italy, dipl, 73; L'Academia di Belle Arti, Florence, Italy, MFA, 78. *Work:* De Cordova Mus and Sculpture Park, Lincoln, Mass; Provincetown Art Asn and Mus, Mass; Suffolk Univ, Boston; Fidelity Investment Corp, Boston. *Comn:* mural, Univ Florence, Italy, 77, Psychiatric Hosp San Salvi, Florence, 78; outdoor floor mosaic, Judith Thurman, NY, 97; monoprint marathon, Fine Arts Work Center, Provincetown, Mass, 99; print project, Muka Studio, Aukland, New Zealand, 2000; Botanica, Cape Mus Fine Art, Dennis, Mass, 2002. *Exhib:* Juried Mem Exhib, Provincetown Art Asn and Mus, Mass, 79-91; Exploring The Corners: Box Works, Islip Art Mus, NY, 93; The Artist's Garden, Boston Ctr for the Arts, 97; Botanica, Truro Ctr for the Arts, Mass, 98; Annual Exib, De Cordova Mus, Lincoln, Mass, 98; Forum Gallery, New York City, 2001-. *Teaching:* adj fac in drawing and painting, New Eng Sch Art and Design, Boston, 95-, Lorenzo de Medici, Florence, Italy, 96, The Art Inst Boston, 96-98, 2000-. *Awards:* finalist, Blanche Coleman Award, 97, 2000; Mass Cult Council Award, 2000. *Bibliog:* Mary Behrens (auth), Botanical Unknown, Artsmedia, 96; Christine Temin (auth), Bold De Cordova Annual, Boston Globe, 98; Patricia J Williams (auth), Fresh Eggs, Fried Baloney, The Nation, 4/5/99; Botanical Unknown, Our Place, HGTV, 6/2001. *Media:* Watercolor. *Publ:* New American Paintings, Northeast vol 20, 1999. *Dealer:* Forum Gallery, 745 Fifth Ave, NYC. *Mailing Add:* c/o Rice Polak Gallery 430 Commercial st Provincetown MA 02657

FABIANO, DIANE FABIAN
PAINTER - MISCELLANEOUS MEDIA
b Winthrope, Mass, Oct 7, 52. *Study:* Calif Col Arts & Crafts, BA(summa cum laude, painting), 76; Calif State Univ, Northridge; Boston Univ, Mass; Worcester Art Mus Sch, Mass; Sch of Mus Fine Arts, Mass. *Work:* Ventura Mus, Calif; Laser Inst, Van Nuys, Calif; San Francisco Arts Comn Gallery, Calif; Calabasas Art Pub Places Gallery, Calif; Mass Gen Hosp, Boston. *Comn:* Site specific painting, Trade Wind Tours Hawaii, Las Vegas, Nev, 80; six site specific paintings, Benjamin Jay Stores & Salons, Woodland Hills, Calif, 90-91. *Exhib:* Dangerous/Endangered Animals, Circa 9 Gallery, San Diego, Calif, 91; Endagered Species & Rainforests, Calabasas Art Pub Places Gallery, Calif, 92; Conejo Valley Art Mus, Thousand Oaks, Calif, 94; solo exhib, Alley Gallery, Santa Barbara, Calif, 94, Paris Sketches & Paintings, Sweet Art Gallery, Oja, Calif, 97, Universal Languages, Bova Gallery, Los Angeles, 98 & BGH, The Loft Gallery, Santa Monica, Calif, Major & Minor, BGH Loft Gallery 4, Bergamot Station, Santa Monica, Calif, 2002; Downey Mus Art, Calif, 96; group exhib, Bova Gallery, Universal Language, Los Angeles, Calif, 98, Art Share Los Angeles, 40th Ann Art Exhib, Los Angeles, Calif, 2001, SCWCA Gallery, Small Works, Los Angeles, Calif, 2003, Long Beach Arts Gallery, Summer Group Exhib, Calif, 2004, Gallerie Yoramgil, Group Photog Exhib, Beverly Hills, Calif, 2005. *Pos:* Art dir, Eara Advert Resources, 90-91, gallery dir, 99-. *Bibliog:* Lisa McKinnon (auth), Planet myths, symbols mix (2 page interview), Press-Courier, 2/91; Beth Farnsworth (interviewer), Art & the Endangered, Midday News Show, KEY TV, Santa Barbara, Calif, 10/6/94; Ron Soble (auth), An artist's odyssey with the LA Philharmonic, Ojai Valley Times, 6/5/97. *Mem:* City of Calabasas, Parks, Rec & Cult Comt (arts coun liaison, 91); Artist Equity Asn; Womens Caucus Arts; Los Angeles Arts Coun. *Media:* Mixed. *Specialty:* Calif artists. *Publ:* Contribr, Encyclopedia of Living Artists, Dirs Guild Publ, 87; California Artists Review, Am References, 89; auth, The Planets, The Queens of Space, Golden Era Legacy Prod, 92; contribr, Art/Life Mag, Art/Life Eds, 2/92, 1/94 & 1/96. *Dealer:* East Side/West Side Art 597 Route 118 Warren NH 03279

FABING, SUZANNAH J
DIRECTOR
b Cincinnati, Ohio, Oct 1, 42. *Study:* Wellesley Col, BA, 64; Harvard Univ, MA, 65. *Pos:* head division of research on collections, Nat Gallery of Art, Washington, DC, 83-92; vis comt Wellesley Col Mus, 1988-; Mem Art Info Task Force, Getty Art Info Prog, 1990-94; surveyor, AAM Mus Assessment Prog, 1991; dir & chief cur, Smith Col Mus of Art, Northampton, Mass, 92-2005; reviewer, Nat Endowment of the Humanities, 1992-94; Overview panel, Nat Edu Assoc, 1993-94; Fitchburg Art Mus, chrmn, 1983-88; trustee, Fitchburg Art Mus, 1975-82, Revels, Inc, 1981-82, 88-92),

others; dir, Summer Inst in Art Mus Studies, Smith College, 2006. *Mem:* Asn Art Mus Dirs; Art Table; Am Asn Mus; Col Art Asn; Archaeological Inst Am. *Publ:* The Gods Delight, Cleveland Mus Art, 88; Nat Gallery of Art, Cambridge Univ Press, 87; Image and Word: Art and Art History at Smith Col, 03. *Mailing Add:* Smith Coll Hillyer Hall 114 Northampton MA 01063

FACCINTO, VICTOR PAUL
PAINTER, FILMMAKER
b Albany, Calif, Oct 30, 45. *Study:* Calif State Univ, Sacramento, BA, 69, MA, 72; Creative Artists Pub Serv Prog Fel, NY, 77, NC Artist Fel, 1980, 1986, 2000. *Work:* Film Study Collection, Mus Mod Art Collection, NY; Wake Forest Univ, Winston-Salem, NC. *Exhib:* New Am Filmmakers, Whitney Mus Am Art, NY, 72-74; Cineprobe, Mus Mod Art, NY, 75; Circulating Film Program, Am Fedn Arts, NY, 72-; Am Experimental Cinema 1905-1984, Pompidou Ctr, Paris, 85; one-man shows, NC Mus Art, 86, Phyllis Kind Gallery 1980, NY, 82, 2004, Bruce Helander Gallery, NY, 90, New Films, Millennium, NY, 96, Southeastern Ctr Contemp Art, NC, 2000 & Madison Art Ctr, Wis, 2000, Millennium, NY, 2003. *Collection Arranged:* Gladys Nilsson Retrospective, Wake Forest Univ Art Gallery, 79 & Video Sculpture, 95. *Pos:* Gallery dir, Wake Forest Univ, 78-. *Teaching:* Instr multi-media, Wake Forest Univ, Winston-Salem, NC, 81-82; lectr art, painting & drawing, 84-. *Awards:* NC Visual Artist Fel, 81, 86 & 2000. *Bibliog:* Grace Glueck (auth), New York Times, 4/4/80; Kay Larson (auth), Village Voice, 4/7/80; Victoria Lautman (auth), Exhibition review, Chicago Sun Times, 4/17/87. *Media:* Oil Acrylic; Film, Video & Digital Photography. *Publ:* Co-producer & photographer, Howard Finster: Stranger from Another World, Abbeville Press, New York, 89. *Dealer:* Phyllis Kind Gallery 136 Greene St New York NY 10012. *Mailing Add:* Dept Art Wake Forest Univ Winston-Salem NC 27109

FACEY, MARTIN KERR
PAINTER, EDUCATOR
b Colorado Springs, Colo, Apr 25, 48. *Study:* Univ Calif, Los Angeles, with William Brice & Charles Garabedian, BA, 71, with Richard Diebenkorn, MA, 73, MFA, 74. *Work:* Security Pacific Bank Collection, Los Angeles, Calif; Bank Am Collection, San Francisco, Calif. *Exhib:* Solo exhib, Los Angeles Munic Gallery, 79, Ivory-Kimpton Gallery, San Francisco, 81, 83-85, 87, Tortue Gallery, Santa Monica, 80, 82-83, 86 & 88, Univ Art Mus, Albuquerque, NMex, 87; two-person show, Claremont Grad Sch Gallery, 85; Jean Albano Gallery, Chicago, 88 & 91; Zimmerman-Saturn, Nashville, Tenn, 89; Sena East Gallery, Santa Fe, NMex, 90. *Teaching:* Instr painting & drawing, Santa Monica Col, Calif, 78-85; vis lectr painting & drawing, Univ Calif, Los Angeles, 83-85; assoc prof painting & drawing, Univ NMex, 86-. *Awards:* Gugenheim Fel in Painting, 82-83; Burlington Northern Found Award for Meritorius Teaching, Univ NMex, 87. *Bibliog:* Judith Spiegel (auth), Revitalizing abstraction, Artweek Mag, 6/25/88; Michael Laurence (auth), Martin Facey at Tortue, Artscribe Int, 10/86; David Winter (auth), Martin Facey at Ivory-Kimpton, Art News, 1/86; Peter Frank (auth), Pick of the Week, Los Angeles Weekly, 6/16/88; Sandy Ballatorxe (auth), Painter Centers Himself in Images. *Mem:* Col Art Asn; Los Angeles Contemp Exhib; Albuquerque United Artists. *Media:* Oil. *Dealer:* Sena East Gallery 125 East Pl Santa Fe NM 87501; Works Gallery 106 W 3rd St Long Beach CA 90802. *Mailing Add:* c/o Jean Albano Gallery 215 W Superior St Chicago IL 60610-3528

FADEN, LAWRENCE STEVEN
PAINTER, PRINTMAKER
b Brooklyn, NY, Oct 21, 42. *Study:* Brooklyn Mus student scholar; Sch Visual Arts; NY Studio Sch; and with Nicholas Carone. *Work:* Chase Manhattan Bank, NY; Smith Kline Beecham Corp, NJ; The Educ Allianco Art Gallery, NYC, 98; New Orleans Mus, L-Anna. *Comn:* Painted procelain mask of James Ensor Akim Masks, Southbys, NY, 96; Alumni Exhib, Bill Jensen: Juried NY Studio Sch, 03; The Continuous Mark: 40 years of the NY Stud Sch, 2005, Juried by Jennifer Sachs Samet. *Exhib:* one-man shows, GW Einstein Gallery, 80, 85, 92 & 96; The Mask in Contemp Art, Sewall Art Gallery, Rice Univ, 93; Conviviality and Confetti, The Noyes Mus of Art, NJ, 99, Feast for the Eyes, 99; Aspects of Realism, Main St Gallery, Dobbs Ferry, NJ, 11/2000. *Teaching:* Instr, Educ Alliance Art Sch, 82-84; vis artist, Parson Sch Design, 92. *Bibliog:* Brett Busang (auth), Am Artist Mag, 92; Gail Levin (auth), His Legacy For Artis; Edward Hopper The American Imagination, Whitney Mus Am Art, 95. *Mem:* Alliance Figurative Artists (prog dir, 75); Fedn Mod Painters & Sculptors. *Media:* Windsor Newton Oil, Watercolor; Etching, Litholgraphy. *Dealer:* Gilbert W Einstein Co 98 Riverside Dr New York NY 10025. *Mailing Add:* 184 E Seventh St No 7 New York NY 10009

FAEGENBURG, BERNICE K
PAINTER, PRINTMAKER
b Philadelphia, Pa. *Study:* Tyler Sch Fine Arts, Temple Univ, Philadelphia, BS; Nat Acad Design; CW Post Col, Long Island Univ, Brookville, NY, MS(art educ), 72. *Work:* Jane Voorhees Zimmerli Art Mus, NJ. *Comn:* Seascape (triptych), Nature's Bounty, Bohemia, NY. *Exhib:* Reflections of Winter, Nassau Co Mus Fine Arts, Roslyn Harbor, NY, 78; 37th Ann Exhib, Audubon Artists, NY, 79; 28th Ann Exhib, Parrish Art Mus, Southampton, NY, 81; traveling painting exhib, Mus Southwest, Midland, Tex, 91; traveling painting exhib, Richmond Art Mus, Ind, 91; Art of the Northeast, Silvermine Guild of Artists, New Canaan, Conn, 92; Fine Arts Mus Long Island, Hempstead, NY, 92; A View of One's Own, Zimmerli Art Mus, New Brunswick, NJ, 94; Tokyo, Japan, Onward Gallery, 2001; NY Col Insights, 2003. *Awards:* First Prize, Manhasset Art Asn, 79; Molly Canaday Mem Award, Nat Asn Women Artists, 87 & Beatrice Jackson Mem Award, 94; Best Show, Visual Artists Alliance Long Island, 95. *Bibliog:* M Milet (auth), L'Art A L'Etranger, La Revue Mod, 4-5/80; Helen Harrison (auth), In pursuit of meaning, NY Times, 12/13/92; East Hampton Star, Aug 5, 99, Sanscgundc, Sheridan; TV Thursday, Dec 11, 2003, Wigren's Crib, Ch 56. *Mem:* Nat Asn Women Artists (prog chair, 87-89, vpres, 89-91 & pres, 91-93); Viridian Gallery Artists (treas, 81-83); Hempstead Harbor Artists Asn; Jimmy Ernst Artists Alliance. *Media:* Acrylic, Oil; Serigraphy, Silkscreen. *Collection:* Zimmerli Art Mus, Rutgers Univ, NJ; Queenboro Community College, New York City; Steelcase Inc, New York City; Natureis Bounty, Bohemia, NY. *Mailing Add:* 31 Canterbury Ln Roslyn Heights NY 11577

FAFARD, JOE (JOSEPH) YVON
SCULPTOR
b Ste Marthe, Sask, Sept 2, 42. *Study:* Univ Man, BFA; Pa State Univ, MFA. *Work:* Winnipeg Art Gallery, Man; Glenbow Mus, Calgary, Alta; Brock Collection, Vancouver; Montreal Mus Fine Arts; Nat Art Gallery Can, Ottawa; and others. *Comn:* The Pasture (7 bronze cow sculptures), Toronto Dominion Ctr, 85. *Exhib:* Joe Fafard's Pensee, Winnipeg, Calgary, Vancouver, Regina, 73; solo exhibs, Edmonton, Calgary, Saskatoon, Surry, Lethbridge, Kingston, Hamilton, Banff, Oshawa, Charlottetown & Regina, 79. *Awards:* Order of Can, 81. *Bibliog:* Mike McKinnery (auth), I Don't Have to Work that Big, Nat Film Bd, 73. *Media:* Mixed. *Dealer:* Susan Whitney Art Gallery 1627 Victoria Ave Regina SK Can; Downstairs Gallery 10154-103 St Edmonton AB Can. *Mailing Add:* c/o Susan Whitney Gallery 2220 Lorne St Regina SK S4P 2M7 Canada

FAGALY, WILLIAM ARTHUR
CURATOR, HISTORIAN
b Lawrenceburg, Ind, Mar 1, 38. *Study:* Ind Univ, Bloomington, BA, 62, MA, 67. *Collection Arranged:* He's the Prettiest: A Tribute to Big Chief Allison "Tootie" Montana's Fifty Years of Mardi Gras Indian Suiting, New Orleans Mus Art, 97; Preacher Art, Phyllis Kind Gallery, NY, 97; Watercolor USA 99, Springfield Art Mus, Mo, 99; Nat Works on Paper, McNeese State Univ, Lake Charles, La, 99; Its a Wonderful World, Contemporary Art Ctr, New Orleans, 03; Speculative Grammar Artistides Logothetis, CUE Art Foundation, NYC, 03; Tools of Her Ministry: Art of Sister Gertrude Morgan, Am Folk Art Mus, NYC, 04; Resonance from the Past: African Sculpture from the New Orleans Mus of Art, Mus for African Art, NYC, 05; In the Congl: An Introduction to the Field Research Archives of Frere Joseph Cornet, Loyala Univ and New Orleans Mus Art, 2006; and many others. *Pos:* Registrar, New Orleans Mus Art, 66-67, cur collections, 67-72, chief cur, 73-80, asst dir art, 81-2001, Francoise Billion Richardson cur African Art, 67-. *Teaching:* Assoc prof art hist, Delgado Col, 67-69; vis assoc prof, Univ New Orleans, 80. *Awards:* Charles E Dunbar Jr Career Svc Award, La Civil Svc League, 99; Isaac Delgade Meml Award, The Fel New Orleans Mus Art, 2001; Chevalier de l'Ordre des Arts et des Lettres, Republique Francaise, 2006. *Bibliog:* profile, Start to Finish Prog, Discovery Channel, 94; Marda Burton (auth), Every Nook & Cranny, Veranda, 95. *Mem:* Arts Coun of African Studies Asn; Ctr African & African American Studies (adv bd); Southern Univ, New Orleans. *Res:* Art and life of self-taught artists Sister Gertrude Morgan and Roy Ferdinand. *Collection:* Contemporary American self-taught art; Northwest Coast Native American baskets; Japanese ikebana baskets; African art. *Publ:* The gifted amateur: The art and life of Charles Woodward Hutson, Folk Art Mag, fall 97; Sister Gertrude Morgan, Self-Taught Artists of the 20th Century: An American Anthology, San Francisco Chronicle Bks, 98; Sister Gertrude Morgan, Charles W Hutson, Encyclopedia of American Folk Art, NY Am Folk Art Mus, 03; Perfect Greek Island, New Orleans Times-Picayune, 03; Gumbo Ya-Ya and Hey Pockey Way, Louisiana Cultural Vistas, 04; Jesus is my Airplane: Life and Art of Sister Gertrude Morgan, Louisiana Cultural Vistas, 04; Ancestors of Congo Square: African Sculptures from the New Orleans Mus of Art, Art Tribal, 04. *Mailing Add:* New Orleans Mus Art PO Box 19123 City Park New Orleans LA 70179

FAGAN, ALANNA
PAINTER, PRINTMAKER
b New Bedford, Mass, 39. *Study:* Silvermine Guild Sch Art, New Canaan, Conn, painting & sculpture. *Comn:* Portrait, pres, Istituto Geografico de Agostini, Novara, Italy, 81; portrait, founder, Cohen & Wolf, PC, Bridgeport, Conn, 83; portrait, Ctr Creative Leadership, Wilmington, NC, 84; portrait, former dean, New Eng Sch Law, Boston, Mass, 84; portrait, retired pres, Harvard Club, NY, 91. *Exhib:* Am Painters in Paris, Palais de Congres, France, 75; Pastel Soc Exhib, Copley Mus, Boston, 79; Painters of St Barthelemy, Cent Falls Gallery, NY, 84; Group of 5, Galerie du Mus, Paris, France, 85; 161st Ann Exhib, Nat Acad Design, NY, 86; Art of the Northeast, 95, 99 & 2000; Am Watercolor Soc, 97. *Teaching:* Instr portrait & pastels, Silvermine Guild Sch, 77-81. *Awards:* Stamford Art Asn Award of Excellence, Faber Birren Nat Color Award Show, 98. *Mem:* Allied Artists Am; Salmagundi Club; Silvermine Guild Artists; Ctr for Contemp Printmaking. *Media:* Oil, Pastel, drypoint etching, monotype. *Publ:* Auth & illusr, Drawing People (filmstrip) & Drawing Animals (filmstrip), Troll Assocs, 81. *Mailing Add:* 73 Housatonic Dr Milford CT 06460

FAGER, CHARLES J
CERAMIST, SCULPTOR
b Osage City, Kans, Feb 3, 36. *Study:* Kans State Univ, Manhattan, BArch, 59; Univ Kans, Lawrence, MFA(ceramics), 63. *Work:* Nat Collection Fine Art; Nat Mus Am Art, Smithsonian Inst. *Comn:* Ceramic installation, Tampa Pub Libr, 70; ceramic wall, Arbor Off Ctr, Clearwater, Fla, 73; hanging sculpture installation, GTE Fla, Tampa, 83; sculpture, Fla Dept of Law Enforcement Regional Crime Lab, Jacksonville, Fla, 87; hanging sculpture installation, Opus South Corporation, Tampa, Fla, 89. *Exhib:* Piedmont Craftsman, Mint Mus, Charlotte, NC, 76; Ceramics Conjunction, Long Beach Mus Art, Calif, 77; Craftsmen of the Southeast Invitational Exhib, Birmingham Mus Art, Ala, 78; Am Porcelain: New Expressions in an Ancient Art, Renwick Gallery, Smithsonian Inst, 81; Cast Clay, Nat Invitational Exhib, Pinch Pottery, Northhampton, Mass, 85; Tampa Triennial, Tampa Mus Art, Fla, 85; and numerous other group & one man shows. *Pos:* Consult archit, Rowe Holmes Assoc Archits Inc, Tampa, Fla, 73-74. *Teaching:* Art instr, Kans State Univ, Manhattan, 60-61; grad asst

instr, Univ Kans, Lawrence, 61-63; prof art, Univ S Fla, Tampa, 63-. *Awards:* Irving Hill First Award for Ceramics, Ninth Ann Kans Designer-Craftsman Exhib, Lawrence, 62; Ceramics Purchase Award, Wichita Nat Decorative Arts & Ceramics Exhib, Wichita, 62; Award of Excellence, Ann State Fla Craftsmen Exhib, 76; Fla Individual Artist Fel Award, 87-88. *Bibliog:* Lloyd E Herman (auth), American Porcelain: New Expressions in an Ancient Art, 80; Charlotte F Speight (auth), Images of Clay Sculpture, 83; Donald Frith (auth), Mold making for ceramics, 85. *Media:* Clay, Metal. *Res:* Application of industrial clay form processes to art; slip casting ceramic figures from life; photoceramics. *Mailing Add:* c/o Albertson-Peterson Gallery PO Box 1900 Winter Park FL 32790

FAHLEN, CHARLES C
SCULPTOR, EDUCATOR
b San Francisco, Calif, 39. *Study:* Calif State Univ, San Francisco, BA, 62; Otis Art Inst, Los Angeles, MFA, 65; Slade Sch, Univ London, Eng, 67. *Work:* Denver Art Mus, Colo; Mus Mod Art, NY; Oakland Mus, Calif; Philadelphia Mus Art, Pa Acad Fine Arts, Prudential Life Insurance, Philadelphia Conv Ctr; plus many others. *Comn:* Tidal Park, City of Port Townsend, Wash, 88; Devil's Tower, Inst Contemp Art, Univ Pa, 90; Colter's Hell, Inst Contemp Art, Univ Pa, 91; Diamond Park, Philadelphia Redevelopment Authority, 94; NJ Transit, 96 & 98; plus many others. *Exhib:* One-man shows, Richard Feigen Gallery, NY, 71, Henri 2, Washington, DC, 74, Marianne Deson Gallery, Chicago, 79, Lawrence Oliver Gallery, Philadelphia, 89 & ICA, Philadelphia, 91; Biennial of Contemp Am Painting & Sculpture, Whitney Mus Am Art, 73; Philadelphia: Three Centuries of Am Art, Philadelphia Mus Art, 76; Contemp Drawings: Philadelphia, Pa Acad Fine Arts, 78; Philadelphia Collects: European and Am Art since 1940, Philadelphia Mus Art, 86; Contemp Philadelphia Artists, Philadelphia Mus Art, 90; In & Out of the Landscape: A Site Specific Outdoor Sculpture Exhib, Penn State Univ, Berks Campus, Reading, 94; Non-Traditional Prints: Sculptors Projects at the Fabric Workshop, Lukaes Gallery, Loyola, Pa, Fairfield Univ, Conn, 94; Options: Selections from the Contemp Collection, Denver Art Mus, 95; Biennial '96, Del Art Mus, 96; and many others. *Teaching:* Prof sculpture, Moore Col Art & Design, Philadelphia, Pa, 67-, head, 3-D Dept, currently. *Awards:* Nat Endowment Arts, 80 & 88; Grants, Moore Col Art & Design, 82, 84, 86 & 94; Individual Grant, Pa Coun Arts, 82, 85 & 91; Hazlett Mem Award for Excellence in Arts, Pa Coun Arts, 85. *Bibliog:* Artists try new directions, Philadelphia Inquirer, 6/25/88; Ron Glowen (auth), Port Townsend: Tidal Park revives old port, Public Art Revi, winter/spring 89

FAHLMAN, BETSY LEE
HISTORIAN
b Wolfeboro, NH, July 18, 51. *Study:* Mt Holyoke Col, Mass, BA, 73; Univ Del, Newark, MA, 77, PhD, 81. *Teaching:* Lectr art hist, Franklin & Marshall Col, 77-79; asst prof art hist, Old Dominion Univ, Norfolk, Va, 80-88; assoc prof art hist, Ariz State Univ, 88-. *Mem:* Col Art Asn; Soc Indust Archaeol; Soc Archit Historians; Victorian Soc Am. *Res:* American Art, 1850-1930, architecture, painting, sculpture and photography. *Publ:* From Connecticut to France: New Haven Painters in Paris, Barbizon, Brittany and Giverny, J New Haven Colony Hist Soc, Vol 41, No 1, fall 94; Guy Pene du Bois: The Twenties at Home and Abroad (exhib catalog), Wilkes Univ, Sordoni Art Gallery, Wilkes-Barre, Pa, 95; Arnold Ronnebeck and Alfred Stieglitz: Remembering the Hill, Hist Photog, Vol 20, No 4, Winter 96; Cotton Culture: Dorothea Lange in Arizona, Southeastern Col Art Conf Rev 13, No 1, 96; John Ferguson Weir: The Labor of Art, Newark: Univ Del Press, 97. *Mailing Add:* Sch Art Ariz State Univ PO Box 871505 Tempe AZ 85287-1505

FAILLACE, RACHAEL
ARTIST
Study: RI Sch of Design, BFA,; Mason Gross Sch of the Arts, MA. *Exhib:* Life with Pocket Change & Pleasures, Ben Shahn Galleries at William Paterson Univ, Wayne, NJ, 2002, First Year Graduate Exhib, Mason Gross Galleries, New Brunswick, NJ, 2003; Prints & Drawings, MPG Contemp, Boston, Mass, 2004; Diagram & Scribble Archive, SAC Gallery, Stony Brook, NY, 2005; Structural Integrity, Arts Guild of Rahway, NJ, 2006. *Mailing Add:* 95 Hillside Ave Berkeley Heights NJ 07922

FAIRBANKS, JONATHAN LEO
CURATOR
b Ann Arbor, Mich, Feb 19, 33. *Study:* Brigham Young Univ & Univ Utah, BFA, 53; Univ Pa & Acad Fine Arts, MFA, 57; Univ Del, MA(Winterthur Fel), 61; Inst Patologia Libro, Rome, cert conservation, 68. *Exhib:* North Point Gallery, San Francisco, 1999; Tivioli Galleries, Salt Lake City, 1999; The Crane Collections, Wellesley, Mass, 2000. *Collection Arranged:* WyeHouse, Alhambra, Spain; Acad Nat Sci, Phila; Nat Portrait Gallery; also pvt collections. *Pos:* Cur asst, Winterthur Mus, 61-62, asst cur, 62-67, assoc cur, 67-; Katharine Lane Weems Cur, Am decorative arts & sculpture, Mus Fine Arts, Boston, 71-, emeritus, 99-; app Comt Preservation The White House. *Teaching:* Teaching fel, Pa Acad Fine Arts, 55-57; adj prof, Univ Del, 61-70 & Am & New Eng Studies Prog, Boston Univ, 71-. *Awards:* Mural Award, Acad Natural Sci; Robert H Lord Award Excellence Hist Studies, Emmanuel Col, 83; Charles F Montgomery prize, 83. *Mem:* Hon mem New Eng Chap, Am Soc Interior Designers; Soc Archit Historians; fel Am Inst Conserv; fel Pilgrim Soc; Colonial Soc Mass; hon fel, Am Crafts Coun, 86. *Publ:* Auth, forward, Art and Commerce: American Prints of the Nineteenth Century, Univ Press Va, 78; ed, Boston Furniture of the Eighteenth Century, Colonial Soc Mass, Vol 48; coauth, American Furniture 1620 to the Present, Richard Marek Inc, 81; coauth, New England Begins, The Seventeenth Century, Boston Mus Fine Arts, 82; auth introd, Sam Maloof, Woodworker, New York, 83; and others. *Mailing Add:* 580 Harrison Ave Ste 301 Boston MA 02118-2440

FAIRFIELD, RICHARD THOMAS
PRINTMAKER, EDUCATOR
b Peoria, Ill, Aug 7, 37. *Study:* Bradley Univ, BFA, 61; Univ Ill, MFA, 63. *Work:* Howard Univ, DC; St John's Univ, Jamaica, NY; B Carroll Reece Mem Mus, E Tenn Univ, Johnson City; Ball State Univ, Muncie, Ind; Albion Col, Mich. *Exhib:* Northwest Printmakers, Seattle Art Mus, 70; Ball State Small Sculpture & Drawings, Ball State Univ, Muncie, Ind, 73; Am Miniature Printmaker, San Diego State Univ, Calif, 88; Interprint LVIV 90, LVIV Mus Hist Relig & Atheism, USSR, 90-92; Int Independents Exhib Prints, Kanagawa, Japan, 90; Paper Invitational, John F Kennedy Mem Union Art Gallery, Univ Dayton, Ohio, 90; solo exhib, Albion Col, Mich, 91; and others. *Teaching:* Prof printmaking, Eastern Mich Univ, Ypsilanti, 63- & Santa Reparata, Florence, Italy, spring 74; Paris, France, spring 87, 89 & 98; Florence, Italy, spring 90 & 95; Madrid, Cardoba, Barcelona, Spain, spring 92 & 96, London, Eng, 94 & Athens, Greece, 97. *Awards:* Purchase Awards, NDak Ann, Univ NDak, 66, Imprint, Kutztown State Col, 67 & Drawing USA, St Paul Art Ctr, 67; Alma Col, 88. *Media:* Etching, Screen. *Dealer:* River Gallery Chelsea MI 48118. *Mailing Add:* Eastern Mich Univ Dept Art Ypsilanti MI 48197

FAIRLIE, CAROL HUNTER
EDUCATOR, PAINTER
b White Plains, NY, Dec 14, 52. *Study:* Pa Acad Fine Arts, with Lois Sloan & Dan Millar, 1974; Tex Woman's Univ, BFA, 1990; Sch Visual Arts, Univ N Tex, with Vernon Fisher & Rob Erdle, MFA, 1993. *Work:* Sui Ross State Univ, Alpine, TX. *Comn:* Mural, Tex Woman's Univ, Denton, TX, 1986; interior, Tetra Pak Co, Denton, TX, 1996; interior, SOHO Salon, Denton, TX, 1996; mural, Alpine Pub Libr, TX, 2003; portrait, comn by Jean Hardy, Alpine, TX, 2004. *Exhib:* Watercolor USA, Springfield Mus Art, MO, 1992 & 2005; Arizona Aqueous, Tubac Center Arts, Mesa, AZ, 1994; Side by Side, Berman Mus, PA, 2002; Noyes Mus, Oceanville, NJ, 2003; Watercolor MO III, Winston Churchill Mus, Fulton, MO, 2003; 15 Exposures, Pa Acad Traveling Exhib, PA, 2004. *Teaching:* Adj prof painting & drawing, Univ N Tex, Denton, TX, 1993-1995; lect, 1995-1996; assoc prof painting & drawing, Sui Ross State Univ, Alpine, TX, 1996-. *Awards:* Rita Phoenix Mem, 1993; Barnet Mem, Philadelphia Watercolor Soc, 2002. *Mem:* Nat Watercolor Soc (newsletter ed, 2002-2004); Philadelphia Watercolor Soc (signature mem); Watercolor Art Soc, Houston; College Arts Assoc; Tex Art Educ Assoc (VASE juror, 2003-2005). *Media:* Acrylic, Oil, Watercolor. *Mailing Add:* 502 East Ave 1 Alpine TX 79830

FAIRWEATHER, SALLY H
ART DEALER, CONSULTANT
b Chicago, Ill, Sept 29, 17. *Study:* Art Students League, 36; Art Inst Chicago, BA, 39. *Pos:* Co-dir & owner, Fairweather-Hardin Gallery, Chicago, 47-91, Art Dealers Asn Am, 62-63 & Found Arts Scholar, Chicago, 64-; co-founder, Chicago Art Dealers Asn, 66. *Teaching:* Instr life drawing, Katherine Lord Sch, Evanston, Ill, 39-43. *Specialty:* Modern paintings, graphics and sculpture. *Publ:* Auth, Picasso's Concrete Sculpture, Hudson Hills Press, 82. *Mailing Add:* 180E Pearson St No 5206 Chicago IL 60611

FAISON, SAMSON LANE, JR
HISTORIAN, MUSEUM DIRECTOR
b Washington, DC, Nov 16, 1907. *Study:* Williams Col, BA, 29; Harvard Univ, MA, 30; Princeton Univ, MFA, 32; Williams Col, Hon LittD, 71. *Hon Degrees:* Mass Col Lib Arts, DFA, 97. *Collection Arranged:* The New England Eye, 83, and other permanent collections & temporary exhibs, Williams Col Mus Art. *Pos:* Exec secy, Comt on Visual Arts, Harvard Univ, 54-55; dir, Williams Col Mus Art, 48-76; trustee, Bennington Mus, Vt, Hancock Shaker Village, Inc, Mass; art vis comt, Mt Holyoke Col, Mass. *Teaching:* From instr to asst prof art, Yale Univ, 32-36; from asst prof to prof art, Williams Col, 36-76, chmn dept, 40-69; vis prof, Univ Pa, New York Univ, Columbia Univ, Univ Calif, Berkeley & Harvard Univ, summers; vis res prof, Univ Ga, spring 68 & Western Carolina Univ, spring 2000. *Awards:* Chevalier, Legion of Honor, Fr Govt, 47; Guggenheim Fel, 60-61. *Mem:* Col Art Asn Am (pres, formerly); Asn Art Mus; Int Asn Art Critics; Mass Coun Arts & Humanities. *Res:* German eighteenth century architecture; nineteenth and twentieth century French and American painting. *Publ:* Auth, Dominikus Zimmermann, Mag Art, 52; Manet, Abrams, 53; Guide to Art Museums of New England, Harcourt Brace, 58; Art Tours and Detours in New York State, Random House, 64; Art Musems of New England, Godine, 82. *Mailing Add:* 1611 Cold Spring Rd Williamstown MA 01267

FALCKENBERG, HARALD
COLLECTOR
b 1943. *Study:* JD, Freibourg U, Geneva, Switzerland. *Pos:* Managing dir, Sammlung Falckenberg, 1979-; hon judge, Hamburg Constl. Ct., currently; pres, Hamburg Kunstverein art assn, currently; creator, PhoenixArt Cultural Found, Hamburg, 2001-. *Awards:* Named one of top 200 art collectors, ARTnews mag, 2004, 2005, 2006. *Mailing Add:* Sammlung Falckenberg Phoenix Fabrikhallen Tor 2 Wilstorfer Strasse 71 Hamburg 21073 Germany

FALCONER, MARGUERITE ELIZABETH
PAINTER, INSTRUCTOR
b Boston, Mass, July 5, 19. *Study:* Mus Fine Arts, Boston, 28-30; studied with Emile Gruppe, Roger Curtis & Robert Douglas Hunter, 63-70, with George Dergalis, 68-70; DeCordova Mus, Lincoln, Mass, 68, 69 & 70. *Work:* Cape Cod Mus Fine Art, Dennis, Mass; St Christopher's Episcopal Church Libr, Eldredge Pub Libr, Chatham, Mass; Fleet Banks, Cape Cod, Mass; Nat Mus Am Art, Smithsonian Inst, Washington; Nat Mus Women in Arts, Washington, DC; Bank of Am, Cape Cod & Boston, Mass; Rockland Trust Co, Cape Cod, Mass. *Comn:* Sea & Sand, comn by Mrs William Gale Curtis Jr, Grosse Pointe, Mich, 73; Old Mill Point, comn by Mr & Mrs Paul McAdams, Chatham, Mass, 86; Chatham Fish Pier, comn by Mr & Mrs Dellapenta,

Rye, NY & Chatham, Mass, 93; Summer View of Mill Pond, comn by Mr & Mrs Henry Weintraub, Stamford, Conn, 94; Pleasant Bay Shore, Lower Cape Outreach Coun, Orleans, Mass, 97. *Exhib:* One-person shows, Brockton Pub Libr, Mass, 63, Forge Art Gallery, Quincy, Mass, 66, Thomas Crane Pub Libr, North Quincy, Mass, 67 & Club House Gallery, West Hartford, Conn, 92; Nyack Gallery, NY, 75-82; Christmas Juried Show, Los Angeles Contemp Gallery, Los Angeles, 86; An Exhib of Paintings by Marguerite Falconer, Churchill Gallery, Newburyport, Mass, 88, 2004-05; Reflections, Cahoon Mus Am Art, Cotuit, Mass, 90; Salmagundi Artists, Beacon Hill West Gallery, Carmel, Calif, 95. *Pos:* Judge for numerous exhibs, 65-2001; co-proprietor, McElwain-Falconer Gallery, Chatham, Mass, 68-87; bd dir, Creative Arts Ctr, Chatham, Mass, 83-85; proprietor, Falconer Gallery, Chatham, Mass, 87-93. *Teaching:* Instr oil painting, Brockton & Bridgewater YWCA, 65-71, Quincy Evening Practical Arts, 67-71 & var art asn, 68-89; instr, demonstr workshops for art asns on south shore Boston, Cape Cod, corp programs, 68-2000. *Bibliog:* Barbara W Foote (auth), Marguerite E Falconer-Painting Cape Cod, Nauset Calendar, 90; Barbara W Foote (auth), Painting Her Beloved Cape Cod for the Past 35 Years, Nauset Calendar, 91; Edward F Maroney (auth), A gallery is passed on as an artist focuses on her canvas, Cape Cod Chronicle, 93. *Mem:* Am Artists Prof League; Cape Cod Mus Fine Arts; Creative Arts Ctr, Chatham, Mass (founder, 69); charter mem Nat Mus Women in Arts; Copley Soc Boston; Mus Fine Arts Boston. *Media:* Oil. *Interests:* travel, music, writing. *Collection:* paintings, sculpture; Dr & Mrs David Knauss, Chatham, M&M Robit Dubis, Chatham, M & Mrs Mark Kerwin, Boston, MA, Judge Philip Zandt, New Paltz, NY, Mr Robert Redford, Provo, Utah & Mr & Mrs Gil Sparks, Del, Julie Harris, Chatham, Mass & Los Angeles, Calif, Mr & Mrs Robert Tarnow, Chatham, Mass & Naples, Fla. *Publ:* An African Quest, Soundings, St Christopher's Church, 88. *Dealer:* Falconer's Chatham MA. *Mailing Add:* PO Box 54 Chatham MA 02633

FALSETTA, VINCENT MARIO
PAINTER, EDUCATOR
b Philadelphia, Pa, Nov 5, 49. *Study:* Temple Univ, Philadelphia, Pa, BA, 72; Tyler Sch Art, Philadelphia, Pa, 72-73; Tyler Sch Art, Rome, Italy, MFA, 74, Special Study with Prominent Professors John Wade and David Pease. *Work:* El Paso Mus Art, Tex; United Bank Denver, Los Angeles; Utah Mus Fine Arts, Salt Lake City; Mus Fine Arts, Houston, TX; Mus SE Texas, Beaumont, TX. *Comn:* Neiman Marcus, Newport Beach, CA. *Exhib:* Solo exhibs, Amarillo Art Ctr, 83, OK Harris Works of Art, NY, 86, 87, 90 & 96, Longview Mus, Tex, 92 San Angelo Mus Fine Arts, Tex, 93, Univ North Tex Denton, 93, Conduit Gallery, Dallas, Tex, 95, 98 & 2000, 2002, 2004, Galveston Arts Ctr, 96, Vincent Falsetta-Field of Vision (with catalog), El Paso Mus Art, 96 & Art Ctr, Waco, Tex, 96, Univ Texas, Arlington, Tex, 2002, Mus East tex, Lufkin, Tex, 2003; Group exhibs, Works on Paper: Southwest, Dallas Mus Fine Arts, Tex, 78, Gateway Exhib, Dallas Mus Art, 84, Laguna Gloria Art Mus, Austin, Tex, 84; Mostra 91: Six Ital Am Artists, Mus Italo Americano, San Francisco; Chaos to Order, Art Mus Southeast Tex, Beaumont, 92; Signs and Symbols (traveling exhib in Africa & Near East), 94-96; The Myth of Baseball, Arlington Mus Art, Tex, 94; Art Patterns, Austin Mus Art, Tex, 97; Contemporaries of the Great Southwest, El Paso Mus Art, Tex, 99; A Hot Show: Abstract Paintings, Arlington Mus Art, Tex, 99; Univ Texas, Dallas, Tex, 2001; Texas Works, Buddy Holly Ctr, Lubbock, Tex, 2002; The Grid Unlocked, Fort Worth Community Art Ctr, Fort Worth, Tex, 2003; Haley Martin Galleries, San Francisco, Calif, 2004. *Teaching:* Asst prof painting & drawing, Ind Univ, Bloomington, 74-75; instr, Univ Utah, Salt Lake City, 75-77; asst prof, Univ NTex, Denton, 77-84, assoc prof, 84-92, prof, 92-. *Awards:* Vis Artist Fel Brandywine Workshop, Philadelphia, Pa, 83, 89; Pollock-Krasner Found Grant, 92-93; Mid Am Arts Alliance Grant, Nat Endowment Arts, 96. *Bibliog:* Michael Odom (auth), Art Papers, 11/2002-12/2002; John Zotos (auth), Art Lies, summer 2002; John Zotos (auth) Artlies, Winter 2003-2004; Three Decades of American Printmaking (The Brandywine Workshop Collection), Hudson Hills Press, 2004; New American Paintings, Open Studio Press, 2005. *Media:* Acrylic, Oil. *Dealer:* OK Harris Works of Art 338 W Broadway New York NY; Conduit Gallery 1626 C Hi Line Dr Dallas TX 75207; Anya Tish Gallery Houston TX. *Mailing Add:* 202 Forest St Denton TX 76209

FALSETTO, MARIO
EDUCATOR
b Italy, May 17, 50; Can citizen. *Study:* Carleton Univ, Ottawa, Can, BA, 71; NY Univ with Jay Leyda, Annette Michelson, Stan Brakhage, Manny Farber, VF Perkins & P Adams Sitney, MA, 76, PhD, 90. *Pos:* Chmn dept cinema & photog, Concordia Univ, 81-84, asst dean, Fac Fine Arts, 84-87 & chair, Cinema Dept, 96-97, assoc & acting dean, Fac Fine Arts, 87-90, grad prog dir, 98-2001. *Teaching:* Lectr film studies, Univ Manitoba, Winnipeg, Can, 77-78; lectr film studies, Concordia Univ, Montreal, Can, 78-82, asst prof, 82-87, assoc prof, 87-99, prof 99-. *Awards:* Social Sciences and Humanities Research Council Award, 2002-. *Mem:* Film Studies Asn Can (pres, 85-87); Soc for Cinema Studies; L'Association Quebecois des Etudes Cinematographiques. *Media:* Writer. *Res:* Recent American and experimental films; Films of Stanley Kubrick & Nicolas Roeg; Independent narrative film. *Publ:* Auth, The Mad & the Beautiful: A Look at Two Performances in the Work of Stanley Kubrick in Making Visible the Invisible, Scarecrow Press, 90; Stanley Kubrick: A Narrative & Stylistic Analysis, Greenwood Press, 94; ed, Perspectives on Stanley Kubrick, GK Hall, 96; Personal Visions: Conversations with Contemporary Film Directors, Silman-James Press, 2000; Stanley Kubrick: A Narrative & Stylistic Analysis, 2d edit, 2001. *Mailing Add:* Hoppenheim Sch Am Cinema Concordia Univ 1455 De Maisonneuve Montreal PQ H3G 1M8 Canada

FANARA, SIRENA
PAINTER, LECTURER
b White Plains, NY. *Study:* Self taught. *Work:* Mus Campidoglio, Mus Mod Art, Rome, Italy; Mus Castello Sforzesco, Milano, Italy; Mus Eureka, Ill; Regione Fruili Venezia Giulia, Regione Siciliana; Regione Sarda; Voorhees Zimmerli Art Mus, NJ; New England Ctr Mus; Mus Art & Sci, Daytona, Fla. *Comn:* Paintings for Federico Fellini, Frankie Laine, Gina Lollobrigida, Vittorio de Sica, The Vatican, Pope Paul XI & Pope John Paul II, Vatican Mus; 3 paintings, Family Bible Encycl, Vol 19-20, Curtis Bks & Copylab, 72. *Exhib:* One-woman shows, Gallerie Andre Weil, Paris, 68, Mike Douglas TV Show Exhib, 68, Palazzo delle Esposizioni, Comune di Roma, Rome, 69 & State Gallery in Teatro Massimo, Palermo, Sicily, 70; C W Post Univ Gallery, 77; Lowenstein Gallery, NY, 83; Wapner Gallery, NY, 86; Wash Mus Fine Art, 66; Hostra Mus, 87; Pace Univ, 89. *Pos:* Dir, Sirena Art Studios, New York, formerly. *Teaching:* Lectr, Fordham Univ, NY, 85-. *Awards:* Gold Medal Award, Acad of Paestum; Medal of Vatican, Pope John Paul II, Vatican Mus, 84; Artist of Love Trophy, 86. *Bibliog:* Guilio Bolaffi (auth), Bolaffi on modern art, Torino, Italy, 70 & 72. *Mem:* Acad of Paestum; Acad dei 500; Acad Tiberina; Int Comt Cult, Rome; Metrop Mus Art; Acad Burgkart, Rome (deleg for USA, 90). *Media:* Acrylic, Oil. *Publ:* Illusr & auth, autobiography, MPH Publ, 76; The Roses and the Thorns, pvt publ, 89; Visions of Women Artist, pvt publ, 89. *Mailing Add:* 1035 Fifth Ave New York NY 10028

FANE, LAWRENCE
SCULPTOR
b Kansas City, Mo, Sept 10, 33. *Study:* Harvard Univ, AB, 55; Boston Mus Sch, 56; with George Dimetrios, 56-59. *Work:* Corcoran Gallery; Mus Contemp Art, Udine, Italy; New York City Bd Educ; De Cordova Mus, Lincoln, Mass; Brooklyn Mus, NY; and others. *Comn:* Bronze & concrete fountain, comn by Villa San Lorenzo, Assisi, Italy, 66; portrait, Union of Am Hebrew Congregation, NY, 67; concrete sculpture, Trent Univ, Peterboro, Ont, 71; outdoor sculpture (8 ft), comn by Nichol Home, Milwaukee, 74; steel & concrete sculpture, Secker & Warburg Publ, London, 78. *Exhib:* one-person shows, Zabriskie Gallery, New York City, 69 & 2006, Marilyn Pearl Gallery, New York City, 76, 78, 82, 85, Bard Col Mus, NY, 77, Duke Univ, NC, 77, Spazio Oolp, Turin, Italy, 80, Bill Bace Gallery, New York City, 91, 93, 95, Sch Design, Raleigh, NC, 93, Ben Shahn Galleries, Wm Patterson Col, NJ, 96, Jaffe-Friede & Straus Galleries, Dartmouth Col, NH, 97, Kouros Gallery, New York City, 99, 2003, Machines of the Mind, Marsh Gallery, Univ Richmond, VA, 2000, Muscarelle Mus Art, Williamsburg, VA, 2000; Solare Arte, Piacenze, Italy, 2006; Drawings The Baltimore Mus of Art, 69, New Acquisitions, Univ Mass, 70, New, Zabriskie Gallery, New York City, 71; Operation Re-build, Mus of Contemp Am Art, Udine, Italy, 78; Largescale Outdoors, De Cordova Mus, Mass, 74; Allegoria dell Inpronte Digitale, Galleria Sale, 79; Arte Contemporanea Americana, Palazzo Venezia, Rome; Aspects of Abstraction, Colby Col Mus, Maine, 83; Courtyard Sculpture, Hudson River Mus, 87; The Significant Surface, Philadelphia Art Alliance, 90; Friends of DAniel Robbins, Mus of RISK, Providence, 96; Sit on This: Artists' Chairs, Palm Beach Mus Art, Fla; Recent Acquisitions, Brooklyn Mus Art, NY; Am Acad Arts and Leters, New York City, 98, 2000; Nat Acad Design Invitation, New York City, 2002. *Teaching:* Instr design, RI Sch Design, Providence, 63-66; prof sculpture, Queens Col, City Univ NY, 66-98; vis artist Yale Univ, Boston Univ, Dartmouth Col, NY Studio Sch, and others. *Awards:* Prix de Rome, 60-63; Ingram Merrill Found Fel, 73 & 84; Dept Housing & Urban Develop Grant, 73; Res Found Grant, City Univ New York, 86 & 94. *Mem:* Am Acad Rome (exec comt, 79-); Nat Acad; Soc Fel; Am Acad Rome. *Media:* Steel, Bronze; Wood, Concrete. *Dealer:* Kouros Gallery Inc 23 E 73rd St New York NY 10021. *Mailing Add:* 10 Beach St New York NY 10013

FANGOR, VOY
PAINTER
b Warsaw, Poland, Nov 15, 22; US citizen. *Study:* Warsaw Acad Fine Arts, MFA. *Work:* Guggenheim Mus, NY; Mus Mod Art, NY; Univ Calif Art Mus, Berkeley; Muzeum Sztuki, Lodz, Poland; Stedelijk Mus, Amsterdam, Holland. *Exhib:* The Responsive Eye, Mus Mod Art, 65; 34th Biennale Venezia, Padiglione Centrale, 68; Guggenheim Mus, 70. *Teaching:* Asst prof painting, Warsaw Acad Fine Arts, 53-61; prof painting, Fairleigh Dickinson Univ, 65. *Bibliog:* R C Kennedy (auth), Notes on Fangor, Art Int, 66; Jay Jacobs (auth), Pertinent and impertinent: illusionist, Art Gallery Mag, 69; John Canaday (auth), Fangors romantic op, New York Times, 2/15/70. *Media:* Oil. *Mailing Add:* 2006 Conejo Dr Santa Fe NM 87505

FANTAZOS, HENRYK MICHAEL
PAINTER, PRINTMAKER
b Kamionka Strumilowa, Poland, Jan 18, 44; US citizen. *Study:* Acad Fine Art, Cracow, Poland, MA(painting), 69. *Work:* Nat Mus, Poznan, Poland; Mus Gornoslaskie, Bytom, Poland; Nat Mus, Lublin, Poland; Kosciuszko Found, NY; George Washington Univ, DC. *Exhib:* The Eccentrics, Southeastern Ctr Contemp Art, Winston-Salem, NC, 83; Southeast VIsual Art, Ga State Univ, Atlanta, 86; Fantasy Landscape, Tampa Mus Art, Fla, 87; Fact, Fiction, Fantasy (traveling exhib), Univ Tenn, 87-88; one-man shows, Philadelphia Art Alliance, Pa, 89, Waterworks Art Ctr, Salisbury, NC, 96, Weems Gallery, Meredith Col, Raleigh, NC, 97, Mus Art, Greenville, NC, 97. *Awards:* Best of Show Durham Art Guild Competition, 87; Int Print Competition Winner, San Diego Art Inst, 94; Artist Fel Award, NC Arts Coun, 97. *Bibliog:* Olga Wickerhauser (auth), Describing the incessant obstinate sight, Charleston Gazette, 1/83; Deborah Winsteadman (auth), Fantazos: Artist follows visionary muse, Durham Sun, 5/18/89; Max Halperen (auth), Fantazos at Meredith, Spectator, 3/26/97. *Mem:* Art Space Artist Asn, NC. *Media:* Oil, Egg Tempera; Copper. *Mailing Add:* 227 W Hill Ave Hillsborough NC 27278

FARAGASSO , JACK
PAINTER, INSTRUCTOR
b Brooklyn, NY, Jan 23, 29. *Study:* Art Students League, with Frank J Reilly, 48-52. *Work:* George Washington Carver Mus, Tuskegee Inst, Ala; The Nat Mus of Am Art, Newport, RI. *Comn:* Peter Marcelle, Clare Booth Luce, Judy Goffman & James Rodgers. *Exhib:* Gallery Mod Art, NY, 69; Am Artists Prof League, 69-71 & 73-79;

The Nude in Fine Art, O'Brien's Emporium, Scottsdale, Ariz, 91-92; Modern Masters of Figuative Painting, Leslie Levy Gallery, Scottsdale, Ariz, 92; Fletcher Gallery, Woodstock, NY, 2002. *Pos:* Illusr, many book co, 57-. *Teaching:* Instr drawing, painting & illus & dir, treas & trustee, Frank Reilly Sch Art, NY, 67-68; instr drawing, painting & illus, Art Students League, 68-; instr drawing & painting, Woodstock Sch Art, 81 & Scottsdale Artist Sch, Ariz 84-86. *Bibliog:* Kent Steine (auth), The Art of Jack Faragasso, Illus Mag, No 1, 2002; articles in NY Daily News & Am Artist Mag. *Mem:* Art Students League; fel Am Artists Prof League; Am Portrait Soc; Artists Fel Inc; Am Renaissance 21st Century. *Media:* Oil, Gouache. *Collection:* early 20th century Am fine artists & illustrators. *Publ:* Auth, The Students Guide to Painting, North Light Publ, 79; For Edward Munch Aquaoil, Watercolor Magic, fall, 97; On choosing an art insturctor, Art Ideas, Vol 4, No 4, 98, article on Mastering drawing the human figure from life, memory, imagination, spring 2000; Mastering Dreaing the Human Figure from Life, Memory, Imagination, Stargarden Press, 99. *Mailing Add:* 340 E 55th St New York NY 10022

FARBANISH, THOMAS
SCULPTOR
b Endicott, NY, Mar 21, 63. *Study:* Rochester Inst Technol, NY, BFA, 86. *Work:* Huntsville Mus Art, Ala; Am Craft Mus, NY; Prescott Collection & Davis Wright & Jones, Wash; Huntington Mus Art, WVA; Wheaton Mus Am Glass, NJ; Pilchuck Glass Sch, Rochester Inst Technol, NY. *Exhib:* Selected one & two man & group exhibs, World Glass Exhib, Gallery Nakama, Tokyo, Japan; NYEGW Auction, Christies, NY; Rochester Finger Lakes Exhib, Mem Art Gallery, Rochester, NY, 84; Robert L Kidd Gallery, Mich; Glass Am, Heller Gallery, NY, 86 & 96; William Traver Gallery, Seattle, 87, 90, 93 & 95; Sarah Squeri Gallery, Cincinnati, Ohio; Artspace, Kohler Art Ctr, Sheboyban, Wis; Grohe Gallery, Boston, Mass; Snyderman Gallery, Philadelphia, Pa; Breaking the Mold: New Directions in Glass, Huntsville Mus Art, Ala; AVA Gallery, Lebanon, NH, 91; Am Glass Now, Leedy Voulkos Gallery, Kansas City; Pilchuck in NY, Miller Gallery, NY, 93; Butlers Gallery, Portland; Paint and Glass - The Expressive Connection, Philabaum Gallery, Tucson; Glass as Art: Celebrating the 25th Anniversary of the Glass Art Society, Blue Spirel, Ashville, NC, 94; and many others. *Teaching:* Workshops & lect, Tyler Sch Art, Pa State Univ, Penland Sch, NC, Rhode Island Sch Design, Ontario Col Art, Canada, Univ Ill Champaign, Mass Col Art, Pilchuck Glass Sch, Wash, Bucks Co Community Col, Pa, Golden Glass Studio & Sch, Kent State Univ, Ohio State Univ, Chataugua Art Inst, Rochester Inst Technol & Urban Glass, NY, Portland Sch Art & Haystack Sch Crafts, Maine; Fac, Penland Sch, NY, Haystack Sch Crafts, Maine, Pilchuck Glass Sch, Wash; fac/lectr, Rochester Inst Technol, Sch Am Crafts, NY. *Awards:* Creative Glass Ctr Am Fel, NJ, 85; Visual Artist Fel, Nat Endowment Arts, 88. *Bibliog:* Kangas, Matthew (auth), Exhibit at Trevor Gallery reflects the many facets of glass art, Seattle Times, 92; Mary Douglas (auth), Glass Mag, No 53, spring 93; Eleanor Heartney (auth), Thomas Farbanish, Traditionalist, Glass Mag, No 57, fall 94; and others. *Mailing Add:* c/o William Traver Gallery 110 Union St 2nd Fl Seattle WA 98101

FARBER, AMANDA
PAINTER, SCULPTOR
b New York, NY, May 13, 57. *Study:* Cooper Union, BFA, 78; Univ Calif, San Diego, MFA, 86. *Exhib:* One-woman shows, Mandeville Annex Gallery, Univ Calif, San Diego, 84, Patty Aande Gallery, San Diego, 86 & 87, Boehm Gallery, Polomar Col, San Marcos, 88, Dietrich Jenny Gallery, San Diego, 89, Soma Gallery, San Diego, 92 & Porter Troupe Gallery, San Diego, 96; Frustrated Blonde, Univ Art Gallery, San Diego State Univ, 93; Diderot and the Last Luminaire, Southern Exposure, San Francisco, Calif, 94; Common Ground, Mus Contemp Art, San Diego, 95; Kidstreet, Children's Mus, San Diego, 95. *Teaching:* Asst teacher, Walden Sch, New York, 79-81; teaching asst, Visual Arts Dept, Univ Calif, San Diego, 83-86, lectr, 91, 92, 96, 97 & 98; art teacher, The Child's Primary Sch, San Diego, 86-88; instr, Palomar Col, San Marcos, Calif, 87-88 & 89-97 & Design Inst San Diego, La Jolla, Calif, 94-97; lectr, San Diego State Univ, 87-90, instr, 88-89. *Awards:* Grand Recipient, Art Matters Inc, 89 & 92; Fel, Nat Endowment Arts, 89. *Bibliog:* Leah Ollman (auth), Sculpture that touches spirit, Los Angeles Times, 5/22/91; Ann Jarmusch (auth), Three dimensions and beyond, San Diego Tribune, 5/24/91; Robert Pincus (auth), Exhibit shows force, San Diego Union-Tribune, 6/13/93; Robert Pincus (auth), Show is ground, San Diego Union-Tribune, 11/12/95; Robert Pincus (auth), Witty inventiveness spawns a presence of mind, San Diego Union-Tribune, 7/10/97. *Mailing Add:* 3629 Arnold Ave San Diego CA 92104-3441

FARBER, MAYA M
PAINTER
b Timisoara, Rumania, Jan 24, 36; US citizen. *Study:* Pratt Inst, privately with Edwin Oppler; Hunter Col; Hans Hoffman Sch; Art Students League, with Reginald Marsh. *Work:* Butler Inst Am Art, Youngstown, Ohio; Int Tel & Tel, NY; Columbia Mus Art, SC; Ga Mus Art, Athens; Jacksonville Art Mus, Fla; Primex Plastics Corp, Richmond, Ind. *Exhib:* One woman shows, Rockefeller Ctr, NY, 79, Mountain Top Gallery, 80, Ugarit Gallery, Tel Aviv, Israel, 80, NY State Fair, 84-85, River House, NY, 84 & 86, Nelli Aman Gallery, Tel Aviv, Israel, 92; group shows, Great Expectations, Madison Ave, 78, Mountain Top Gallery, Windham, NY, 79 & 94, & Twilight Part Art Asn, Collage, 79 & Northcoast Collage Soc, 94; Small works show, Catskill Gallery, 2000; Collage & Assembledge Soc, 2000-05; Leman Studio Gallery, Palm Beach, Fla, 2005; Windham Fine Arts, NY, 2005; Charlotte Fin Gallery, Vero Beach, Fla, 2004. *Awards:* Second Prize, Jamaica Festival Art, 67; Judges Special Merit, Nat Collage Soc, 88; Judges Special Merit, 16th Annual Exhib, Nat Collage Soc, 2000. *Bibliog:* Nita Leland & Virginia Williams (auths), Creative Collage Techniques, 94; B Bierbaum & Petrina Gardner (auths) Collage in all Dimensions, 2005. *Mem:* Nat Collage Soc. *Media:* Collage, Acrylic. *Dealer:* Chase Gallery Inc 31 E 64th St New York NY 10021; Windham Fine Arts Windham NY 12424. *Mailing Add:* 435 E 52nd St New York NY 10022

FARES, WILLIAM O
PAINTER
b Compton, Calif, July 16, 42. *Study:* San Francisco Art Inst, BA & MFA. *Work:* Chase Manhattan Bank; Va Mus Fine Arts; State Univ NY Col Purchase; Yale Art Gallery; Muhlenberg Ctr for the Arts, Allentown, Pa; Guggenheim Mus & Mus Mod Art, NY. *Exhib:* Biennial, Whitney Mus Am Art, NY, 75; Albright-Knox Art Gallery, Buffalo, NY, 75; Paperworks, Mus Mod Art, NY, 76; Am Drawing 1927-1977, Minn Mus Art, St Paul, 77; one-man exhib, Zolla/Lieberman Gallery, Chicago, 77; Stamford Mus, Conn, 78; Va Mus Fine Arts, 79; Jefferson Co Hist Soc, Watertown, NY, 79; Tex Gallery, 79; and many others. *Awards:* Nat Endowment Arts Grant, 79-80. *Bibliog:* David Bourdon (auth), article, The Village Voice, 12/6/76; Barbara Cavaliere (auth), article, Arts Mag, 2/77; Kenneth Whal (auth), On abstract literalist works, Arts Mag, 4/77; articles in: Art in Am & Art Forum. *Media:* Acrylic. *Dealer:* Dannenburg 44 Broone St New York NY 10012. *Mailing Add:* 110 W 26th St 5th Flr New York NY 10001

FARHI, JEAN CLAUDE
SCULPTOR
b Paris, France, Feb 11, 40. *Study:* Sch Beaux Arts, Nice, France, 68. *Work:* Mus Contemp Art, Antwerp, Belg; Mus Mod Art, Beaubourg Mus, Paris, France. *Comn:* Monumental sculpture, Palace Cong, Nice, France, 85; monumental sculptures, Atalanta Capitol, NY, 86; monumental sculpture, comn by Nathan Senota, Long Island, NY, 87; monumental sculpture, comn by Martin Sosnoff, New Canaan, Conn, 88; bldg facade, City of Nice, France, 88. *Exhib:* Solo exhibs, Maeght Found, St Paul, France, 73 & FIAC, Paris, France, 86; Silverman Collection, Cranbrook Acad Art Mus, Mich, 81; Les Mains Regardent, Mus Picasso, Antibes, France, 81; Chicago Int Art Fair, 84; Intermedia Between Painting & Sculpture, 84 & Innovation in Sculpture, 1985-1988, 88, Aldrich Mus Contemp Art, Ridgefield, Conn; Antwerp Mus Contemp Art, Belg, 87. *Awards:* Young Sculptor First Prize, Prix de Jeune Sculpture, Mediterranean Union Mod Art, 64. *Bibliog:* William Zimmer (auth), Three shows, three styles, New York Times, 84; Rene Predal (dir), Farhi Plastique Broadway 561, Nice Cinema, 85; Farhi-Sculptor, Tele-Monte-Carlo, Italy, 88. *Media:* Methacrylate. *Publ:* Auth, Iris Time, Pendel, 78; ed, Larousse Dictionary of Painting, Larousse, 80; Grand Dictionary-Encyclopedia Larousse, Vol VIII, Larousse, 85; auth, New York Face A Son Patrimoine, Pierre Mardgha, 86; Notre Observatoire, Martano. *Mailing Add:* 561 Broadway New York NY 10012

FARIAN, BABETTE S
PAINTER, GRAPHIC ARTIST
b New York, NY, June 6, 16. *Study:* New York Sch Fine & Appl Art, two years; Cooper Union, three years; Art Students League, three months, with Bridgman; Mus Mod Art, three years; additional study with Donald Stacy, Addison Lamar, Joseph Margulies & Morris Kantor. *Work:* Brooklyn Botanic Garden, NY; US Fine Arts Registry; Women's Fine Arts Mus; Sloan-Kettering Mem Ctr; Archives, Nat Mus Women, Washington; also in many pvt collections. *Comn:* Bookplate, Stanford Univ, 94. *Exhib:* Metrop Mus 81 St Gallery, NY, 77; Flushing Coun Cult & Arts, 86, 94-97; Composers, Authors & Artists: 1986-1998, Nat League Am Pen Women, 97-98; Lever House, 88 & 95; Katherine Lorillard, 90 & 92; Broome St Gallery, 92; Audubon Artists Nat Asn Painters in Casein & Acrylic, 93-98; Nat Arts Club, 94-98; Brownstone Gallery, 94; and others. *Pos:* Color consult, Addison Lamar, 37-40; designer, Krasom Co, NY, 55-57; freelance designer, 58-59; asst head studio, Manhattan Shirt Co, NY, 60-65; designer, Hanscom Fabrics. *Teaching:* Instr color & design, Cooper Union Art Sch, 37-41; pvt classes, 73-74. *Awards:* Award of Merit, Watercolor Nat League Am Pen Women, 89 & 90; First Prize Short Story, 81 & First Prize Watercolor, 83, Composers, Authors & Artists Am; First Prize Oil, Jackson Hts Art Club 89- & Hon Mention, 90; Award of Merit, Community Col, 93; and many others. *Bibliog:* Article & photos in Vineyard Gazette, 74; articles & photos in World Mag, 89 & Catholic Fine Arts Mag, 90; Photo's in Composers, Authors & Artists Mag, Art News, Newsweek & local papers. *Mem:* Burr Artists; Nat Asn Am Pen Women; Composers, Authors & Artists Am; Audubon Artists; Nat Asn Painters in Acrylic & Casein; and others. *Media:* Acrylic, Pen & Ink. *Interests:* sketching, painting, writing. *Publ:* Auth, The pendulum of time and the arts, 68; article, Artist's Equity Mag, 75, 86 & 88; auth, First Prize Short Story: Composers, Authors, Artists; Am Mag, 81. *Mailing Add:* 34-48 81st St Jackson Heights NY 11372-2821

FARIS, PETER KINZIE
WRITER, HISTORIAN
b Washington, DC, Oct 7, 43. *Study:* Nat Col Art, Lahore, Pakistan, 62; Colo State Univ, Ft Collins, BA, 65; Univ Colo, Boulder, MFA, 70. *Exhib:* 1974 All-Calif Exhib, Laguna Beach Art Mus; One-man show, Hatton Gallery, Colo State Univ, Ft Collins, 79; Aspen Art Found Exhib, Colo, 75; Assistance League All-Media Competition, Houston Art Mus, Tex, 76; 8-West Biennial, Western Colo Ctr for the Arts, Grand Junction, Colo, 76; and others. *Collection Arranged:* Pattern and Sources of Navajo Weaving, Navajo Rug Exhib, 77; Life on the High Plains (auth, catalog), Hist Photos from Black Hills, 78. *Pos:* Gallery dir & educ progs coordr, Arvada Ctr for Arts & Humanities, Colo, 76-78; exec dir, Western Colo Ctr for Arts, Grand Junction, 78-81; exhib designer, Aurora Hist Mus, Colo, 95-. *Teaching:* Instr fine arts, Prestonburg Community Col, Ky, 70-72; asst prof studio art, Chapman Col, Orange, Calif, 72-74; instr, Univ Colo, Denver, 84 & Redrocks Community Col, Lakewood, Colo, 85-90. *Mem:* Colo Archeol Soc; Utah Rock Art Res Asn; Colo/Wyo Asn Mus. *Publ:* Auth, A fertility cermony illustrated in The Cave of Life, Petrified Forest National Park, Arizona, Southwestern Lore, 3/86; Postclassic vernal abstraction: The evolution of a unique style in Late Fremont rock art in Dinosaur National Monument, Utah, Southwestern Lore, 3/87; auth, chapt In: Design Aspect in Uinta and San Rafael Fremont rock art; compiled paper, In: Rock Art of the Western Canyon, Johnson Publ & Colo Archeol Soc & Denver Mus Natural Hist, 89; Petroglyph chronology in southeast Colorado, SW Lore, spring 95. *Mailing Add:* 18603 E Crestridge Dr Aurora CO 80015-5128

FARM, GERALD E
PAINTER, SCULPTOR
b Grand Island, Nebr, Mar 8, 35. *Study:* Famous Artist Sch, Westport, Conn; Nebr State Col, BA(educ). *Work:* Deming Fed Savings, NMex; Olney Savings & Loan, Tex; Bank Beaver City, Okla; plus many pvt collections. *Comn:* First Nat Bank, Uvalde, Tex. *Exhib:* CM Russell Auction, Great Falls, Mont, 73 & 75; Real Show, Grand Cent Art Galleries, NY, 79; Mus Nebr Art, Kearny, Nebr, 88; Nat Finals Art Auction, Las Vegas, Nev; Cheyenne Frontier Days Art Show, Wyo, 91-98; Miniatures, Fine Arts Mus, NMex, 92; Celebrate Am Realism, San Diego, 92; Western Rendezvous of Art, Helena, Mont, 92. *Awards:* Peter Hassrick Merit Award, Western Rendezvous Art, 92. *Bibliog:* Byron Jones (auth), The story teller's art of Gerald Farm, Southwest Art, 79; Patti Jones Morgan (auth), G Farm, tinged with nostalgia, Southwest Art, 88; Patricia O'Connor (auth), Gerald Farm-Accentuating the Positive, Art West, 92. *Media:* Oil. *Dealer:* Settlers West Gallery Tucson AZ; Trailside Galleries, Scottsdale, Ariz & Jackson, Wyo. *Mailing Add:* 5609 Foothills Dr Farmington NM 87402

FARMER, JOHN DAVID
MUSEUM DIRECTOR, EDUCATOR
b Washington, Ga, Jan 25, 39. *Study:* Columbia Univ, BA, 60; Univ NC, Chapel Hill, MA, 63; Princeton Univ, MFA, 65, PhD, 81. *Collection Arranged:* Virtuoso Craftsman (with catalog), 69; Concepts of the Bauhaus (with catalog), 72; German Master Drawings of the 19th Century (with catalog), 72-73; Rubens and Humanism (with catalog), 78; Rowing/Olympics (with catalog), 84; Rosa Bonheur (with catalog), 97. *Pos:* Curatorial asst, Worcester Art Mus, Mass, 67-69; cur, Busch-Reisinger Mus, Harvard Univ, 69-72; cur earlier painting, Art Inst Chicago, 72-75; dir, Birmingham Mus Art, 75-79 & Univ Art Mus, Univ Calif, Santa Barbara, 81-90; dir exhibs, Am Fedn Art, 90-92; dir, Dahesh Mus, NY, 93-. *Teaching:* Instr art hist, Clark Univ, 68-69; lectr, Harvard Univ, 71; adj prof, Univ Calif, Santa Barbara, 81-90, NY Univ, 94-, Christie's, NY, 96- & Pratt Inst, Brooklyn, 97-. *Awards:* Charles F Montgomery Prize, 84; Fulbright Fel, 66-67. *Mem:* Col Art Asn; Am Asn Mus; Int Coun Mus. *Res:* Art of the Northern Renaissance, especially painting and decorative arts of early Sixteenth Century Low Countries. *Publ:* coauth, Catalogue of European paintings, Worcester Art Mus, 74; auth, Gerard David's lamentation and an anonymous St Jerome, Mus Studies, 75; Ensor, Braziller, 75; coauth, Design in America, The Cranbrook Vision 1925-50, Abrams, 83; editor, Picturing the Middle East, Dahesh Mus, 96

FARNHAM, ALEXANDER
PAINTER, WRITER
b Orange, NJ, May 5, 26. *Study:* Art Students League, with George Bridgman, W C McNulty & Frank Vincent DuMond; also with Van Dearing Perrine & Anne Steel Marsh. *Work:* Newark Mus, NJ; Nat Arts Club, NY; Monmouth Col; James A Michener Collection; Morgan Guaranty Trust Co, NY. *Comn:* Murals, Naval subjects, Naval Repair Base, New Orleans, 45; portrait of dir, Am Found for Blind, 50; painting of off bldg, NJ Mfrs Ins Co, Trenton, 69, 83; Washington Crosses the Delaware (pewter plate design), Franklin Mint, 76. *Exhib:* Methods and Materials of the Painter, Montclair Art Mus, circulated in Can, 54; Nat Acad Design 135th Ann Exhib, NY, 60; Eastern States Art Exhib, Springfield, Mass, 65-67; NJ Award Artists Exhib, Montclair Art Mus, 66; NJ Artists, Newark Mus Invitational, 68. *Pos:* Artist, US Navy, 45-46; pres, Associated Artists NJ, 72-77; writer, Maine Antique Digest, 76-2005. *Teaching:* Taught classes in painting The Hunterdon Art Center, Clinton, NJ, 1979; Rider College, Lawrenceville, NJ, 1989. *Awards:* 2nd Award, Nat Arts Club, 48, Elisha Boudinot Kieth Award, 50; Best in Show, Monclair Art Mus, 50; Purchase Award, Newark Mus, 68; NJ State Coun Arts Fel, 80; First Award, Summit Art Ctr Nat Exhib, 81. *Bibliog:* Diane Hamilton (auth), Painters of the Valley, Country Mag, 12/81; Palette Talk #51, M Grumbacher, Inc, 82; Dorris Brandes (auth), Artists of the River Towns, 2002. *Mem:* Assoc Artists NJ (pres, 72-77). *Media:* Oil. *Publ:* Auth & illusr, Tool collectors handbook, 70, 72 & 75; auth, Architectural patterns, subjects for the artists brush, 74; Early Tools of NJ & the Men Who Made Them, 84; Search for Early New Jersey Toolmakers, 92. *Dealer:* The Coryell Gallery 8 1/2 Coryell St Lambertville NJ. *Mailing Add:* 78 Tumble Falls Rd Stockton NJ 08559

FARNSWORTH, HELEN SAWYER
PAINTER, WRITER
b Washington, DC. *Study:* Masters Sch, Dobbs Ferry; Nat Acad Design Sch, with Charles Hawthorne. *Work:* Whitney Mus Am Art; Pa Acad Fine Arts; Toledo Mus; Atlanta Mus; Indianapolis Mus. *Comn:* Paintings, Blue Ridge Spring, Chesapeake & Ohio RR, NY, First Nat City Bank & Circus Parade, G Lister Carlyle. *Exhib:* Carnegie Nat & Int, Pittsburgh; Am Painting Today, Metrop Mus Art; Century of Progress, Chicago; San Francisco World's Fair; NY World's Fair; and many others. *Teaching:* Instr, Art Students League, New York Farnsworth Sch Art, Cape Cod & Fla. *Awards:* Award for The Bareback Rider, Ringling Mus; First Hon Mention for Trees by the Turn, Art Inst Chicago; First Prize for landscape & still life, Atlanta Mus. *Bibliog:* Ernest Watson (auth), Helen Sawyer, Am Artist. *Mem:* Nat Acad Design; Fla Artists Group; Audubon Artists; Nat Asn Women Painters & Sculptors; Fel, Royal Acad. *Media:* Oil, Watercolor. *Res:* Material on life and work in Syracuse University Archives and Archives of American Art. *Publ:* Auth, Paintings in oils on paper, Am Artists; Living Among the Modern Primitives, Scribner; Peter Sawyer (auth), Master Mariner, Cape Cod Compass. *Mailing Add:* 3482 Flamingo Ave Sarasota FL 34242-1004

FARRELL, PATRICK
PAINTER, PRINTMAKER
b Escanaba, Mich. *Study:* Self-taught. *Work:* Rahr-West Art Mus, Manitowoc, Wis; Charles A Wustum Mus Fine Arts, Racine, Wis; Milwaukee Pub Libr, Wis; Univ Wis, Stevens Point; Miller Art Ctr, Sturgeon Bay, Wis; Woman's Club Wis, Milwaukee, Wis. *Exhib:* One-man shows, Bergstrom-Mahler Mus, Neenah, Wis, 74, Oshkosh Pub Mus, Wis, 77, Rahr-West Art Mus, Manitowoc, Wis, 86, John Michael Kohler Arts Ctr, Sheboygan, Wis, 87, Marin-Price Galleries, Chevy Chase, Md, 99 & 2002, Tory Folliard Gallery & Milwaukee, Wis, 2000 & 2003, 2005, Craven Gallery, West Tisbury, 2002, Martha's Vineyard, Ma, Hidell Brooks, Charlotte, NC, 2001, RiverEdge Galleries, Mishicot, Wis, 2004, Grace Chosy Gallery, Madison, Wis, 2006; Wisconsin Impressions, Milwaukee Art Mus, 82; Patrick Farrell Retrospective, Wis Acad Sci, Arts & Letters, Madison, 92 & Charles Allis Art Mus, Milwaukee, 98; 84th Allied Artists Am, Nat Arts Club, NY, 97. *Awards:* Festival of Art Purchase Award, Friends Milwaukee Art Mus, 73; Milwaukee Art Comn Award of Excellence, 84; John Young - Hunter Mem Award, 84th & 97th Allied Artists Am, NY. *Bibliog:* James M Auer (auth), The Magic World of Patrick Farrell (film), Auer Art Films, 77; Scott S Stewart (auth), The Art of Patrick Farrell, Ivy House Publ, 80; Margaret Fish Rahill (auth), Patrick Farrell Paintings, Charles Allis Art Mus, 84; Heidi Levy (auth), Famous Wis Artists & Architects: Patrick Farrell, Badger Books, 2004. *Mem:* hon mem, Allied Artists Am, NY. *Media:* Oil. *Publ:* Contribr, Oil Paintings of Patrick Farrell, Tre Art Publ, 72; Painter Patrick Farrell reveals best secret, Milwaukee Sentinel, 77; Milwaukee 1980, New Art Examiner, 80; Exhibit unveils the fruit of Farrell's labor, 95 & The artful survivor, 98, Milwaukee J Sentinel; auth, Master of Illusion: Patrick Farrell, Milwaukee Mag, 2006. *Dealer:* Marin-Price Galleries 7022 Wisconsin Ave Chevy Chase MD 20815; Tory Folliard Gallery 233 N Milwaukee St Milwaukee WI 53202; Carol Craven New York NY; RiverEdge Galleries Mishicot WI. *Mailing Add:* 2752 N Summit Ave Milwaukee WI 53211

FARRENS, JUANITA G
PAINTER, SCULPTOR
b Philippine Republic; US citizen. *Study:* Bukidnon Inst, Mindanao, Philippines, BSE, 39; Md Univ Exten, Ankara, Turkey, 53-54; La Tech Univ, 83-86, 87 & 88; Univ New Orleans, 88-92; Delgado Community Col, 88-92. *Work:* Westminster Abbey, Spencer, Mass; St Alphonso Church, Philippine Republic; St Dominic Church, Mother Cabrini High Sch & Knights of Columbus, New Orleans; Colo Gold Mine Sch, Golden; New Orleans Mus Fine Arts. *Comn:* Garden scene, comn by Joe Barhill, Boulder, 60; landscape, Shepherd Ctr, Mt Carmel Acad, New Orleans, 82; Knight Columbus, New Orleans, La, 84; Joseph Clementine, New Orleans, 85; William Sork, New Orleans, 85; The Crucifixtion (life size sculpture), Courtland, Minn, 94. *Exhib:* Biennial Exhib Piedmont Painting & Sculpture, Mint Mus Art, 77-79; Joslyn Art Mus Ann, 78; Pastel Soc Am Ann, Nat Arts Club, NY, 78-80 & 83; Ga Second Ann Exhib, Columbus Mus Arts & Sci, 81; Aqueous, JB Speed Art Mus, 82; First Patron Watercolor Gala, Kresge Fine Art Ctr, Oklahoma City, 83; Springville Mus Fine Art, Utah, 84-85; 47th Contemp Am Art, West Palm Beach, Fla, 85; Kans Pastel Soc Nat, 85-86; Degas Pastel Soc First Open Nat, New Orleans, La, 86; 45th Nat Watercolor, Birmingham Mus Art, Ala, 86. *Teaching:* Instr art, Farrens Art Sch, New Orleans, 60- & Sheperd Ctr, Mt Carmel Acad, New Orleans, 78-83; lectr & demonstr painting, New Orleans Art Asn, 64-83 & Holy Cross Col, 68. *Awards:* Merit Award, Tenth Nat New Orleans Art Asn, 84; Pastel Soc Award Excellence, 86. *Mem:* Allied Artists Am; Am Portrait Soc; founding mem La Watercolor Soc (vpres, 71-72); New Orleans Art Asn; Am Pastel Soc. *Media:* Watercolor, Pastel. *Publ:* NY Art Review, American Publishing Corp, 10/88; article, Times Picayune, 85-86 & 94. *Dealer:* Archives Nat Found New York NY; Art South Inc PA. *Mailing Add:* 6164 Marshal Foch New Orleans LA 70124

FARRIS, GREER
SCULPTOR
b Ft Smith, Ark, June 24, 42. *Study:* Western State Col, Colo, BA, 1965; Pratt Inst, studied with Robert Natkin, 1965-66; Northeastern State Col, MEd, 1970; Southern Ill Univ, MFA, studied with Nick Verqette, 1972. *Work:* Joslyn Art Mus, Omaha; Ark Arts Ctr, Little Rock. *Comn:* Ferro/Cement sculpture, Ark Arts Ctr, Mount Burg, Ark, 1981; steel sculpture, VA Hosp, Little Rock, 1982-83; wood sculpture, Ozark Woodland Sculpture Garden, Univ Ozarks, Huntsville, Ark, 2000. *Exhib:* 6th Biennial Beau Arts, Columbus, Ohio 1972; La Bicentennial, Old State Capitol, Baton Rouge, 1973; Texas Ann, Laguna Gloria Mus, Austin, 1973; Carft Invitational, Univ NMex, Albuquerque, 1973; Baroque '74, Mus Contemp Crafts, NY, 1974; Looking at Earth, Smithsonian Inst, Washington, 1986-87. *Teaching:* instr art & clay, Tulane Univ, 72-76, Westark Community Col, 77-87. *Awards:* Fel, Ark Arts Coun, 1985. *Dealer:* Diamond G Gallery 200 N 21 St Fort Smith AR 72901. *Mailing Add:* 200 N 21st St Fort Smith AR 72901

FARRIS, JOSEPH
CARTOONIST, PAINTER
b Newark, NJ, May 30, 24. *Study:* Art Students League; Biarritz Univ; Whitney Sch Art. *Work:* Paintings in private collections; painting, Cocktails (Emily Lowe award). *Exhib:* One-man show, Ward Eggleston Gallery, NY; and many group exhib. *Pos:* Contract artist, New Yorker, 71-. *Mem:* Cartoonists Asn. *Media:* All. *Publ:* Contribr cartoons & covers to The New Yorker, Sat Eve Post, Barrons, Ladies Home J, Playboy, Penthouse, New Woman, Punch & other nat mag; illusr, Slave boy in Judea; bk jackets for others; auth & illusr, Phobias & Therapies (cartoon bk), Grosset & Dunlap; contribr, Pilgrim's Progress (cartoon bk), Thomas More Press; The New Yorker 1975-1985 Anniversary Album; illusr, The Latin Riddle Book; cartoon collections, They're a Very Successful Family, 89 & Just a Cog in the Wheel; cartoon strip, Phipps, United Media, 89-92; auth, Money, Inc, 2001; auth, Elm Street (memoir)

FARROW, PATRICK VILLIERS
SCULPTOR
b Los Angeles, Calif, Nov 27, 42. *Study:* Univ Calif, Los Angeles; Loyola Univ; study under Archemedes Giocomantonio. *Work:* Norton Simon Mus, Pasadena, Calif; Middlebury Col, Vt; City of Rutland, Vt; City of Ishidoriya, Japan; pvt collections; Frick Mus, Long Island NY. *Comn:* Sculpture, City Rutland, 84; presentation piece, Crossroads Arts Coun, 86; pub sculpture, Middlebury Col, 88; City Ishidoriya, Japan,

89. *Exhib:* Nat Art Club; Nat Acad Design, 77; Nat Sculpture Soc Ann, NY, 78-92; Am Acad Arts & Lett, NY, 80-; Am Soc Interior Designs, 85; Audubon Artists, NY, 86; and others. *Collection Arranged:* Norton Simon Mus, Pasadena, Calif; Frick Mus, Long Island, NY. *Teaching:* Guest lectr, Am Acad Arts and Letters, New York, 78. *Awards:* Award of Distinction, 77 & Memoriam Award, 85, Allied Artists Am; Bronze Medal, 78 & Edith & Richmond Proskauer Award, 80; Pietro Montana Mem Prize, 88; awards, NSS, 78, 80 & 88; Community award, Crossroads Arts coun, Rutland, Vt, 94. *Bibliog:* Rex Reed (auth), article, Cosmopolitan, 68; Theodora Morgan (auth), articles, Nat Sculpture Rev, 78, 80, 83, 84, 86 & 93; articles in Vt Mag, 89, Boston Globe, 89, New York Times, 89, Time Mag, 89, House and Garden Mag, 93, & others. *Mem:* Fel Nat Sculpture Soc; Allied Artists Am (jury of mem & selection 84, 87); Rutland Area Art Asn (bd dir, 83-88). *Media:* Steel, Bronze. *Specialty:* Sculpture & Jewelry by Patrick Farrow. *Interests:* Kayacking Short-Wave Radio. *Collection:* Worldwide. *Publ:* Narional Sculpture Review 78-95, House & Garden Mag, 91; William & Mary College Review, 94; Vermont Mag, 95; Contribr, New York Daily News, 79, New York Post, 80, People Mag, 5/80, Sculpture Rev, 83, Southern Vt Mag, 86 & 95, Boston Globe, 89, NY Rev, 88, Time Mag, 89 & New York Times, 89. *Dealer:* Farrow Studio & Gallery Castleton VT 05735. *Mailing Add:* PO Box 1503 Castleton VT 05735

FARVER, JANE
CURATOR, MUSEUM DIRECTOR
Work: Curator Global Conceptualism: Points of Origin, 1950s-1980s. *Pos:* Dir, Lehman Col Art Gallery, City Univ of NY, 1989-1992; dir exhib Queens Mus Art, 1992-1997; dir, List Visual Arts Ctr, Mass Inst of Technol, 1999-. *Mailing Add:* List Visual Arts Ctr 20 Ames St Bldg E15 Cambridge MA 02139

FARVER, SUZANNE
ADMINISTRATOR, COLLECTOR
b Pella, Iowa, Feb 22, 55. *Study:* Grinnell Col, BA(Phi Beta Kappa), 78; Univ Denver, JD, 83. *Pos:* Trustee, Denver Art Mus, 88-93; dir develop & pub affairs, Anderson Ranch Arts Ctr, Snowmass Village, Colo, 90-92; dir, Aspen Art Mus, Aspen, 92-; collections comt, Denver Art Mus, 93-. *Mailing Add:* Aspen Art Mus 590 N Mill St Aspen CO 81611

FARWELL, BEATRICE
HISTORIAN, EDUCATOR
b Santa Barbara, Calif, Oct 9, 20. *Study:* Knox Col, BA(art), 42; NY Univ, MA(art hist), 65; Univ Calif, Los Angeles, PhD(art hist), 73. *Pos:* Mem bd trustees, Santa Barbara Mus Art, 71-76, 93-96. *Teaching:* Lectr & sr lectr, Metrop Mus Art, New York, 43-66; vis lectr art hist, Univ Calif, Santa Barbara, 66-67, lectr, 67-74, assoc prof, 74-77, prof, 77-91, emer prof, 91. *Mem:* Col Art Asn (bd dir, 77-81); Southern Calif Art Historians (vpres, 80-81); Arch Am Art. *Res:* French 19th century painting and graphic art; emphasis on realism and popular imagery. *Publ:* Auth, A Manet masterpiece reconsidered, Apollo, 7/63; Courbet's Baigneuses & the rhetorical feminine image, Art News Ann, 72; Manet's Nymphe Surprise, Burlington Mag, 4/75; French Popular Lithographic Imagery 1815-1870, Vols 1-12; Univ Chicago Press, 81-97; Manet and the Nude, Garland Press, 81; The cult of images: Beaudelaire and the 19th century media explosion, Univ Calif Art Mus, Santa Barbara, 1977, The charged image, Santa Clara Mus Art, 1989. *Mailing Add:* 4523 Auhay Dr Santa Barbara CA 93110-1705

FASNACHT, HEIDE ANN
SCULPTOR
b Cleveland, Ohio, Jan 12, 51. *Study:* RI Sch Design, BFA, 73; New York Univ, MA. *Exhib:* Sculpture on the Wall, Aldrich Mus Contemp Art, Ridgefield, CN, 86-87; Figurative Impulses: Six Contemp Sculptors, Santa Barbara Mus Art, Calif, 88; Enclosing the Void, Whitney Mus Am Art at Equitable Ctr, 88; Making Their Mark: Women Artists Move Into the Mainstream 1970-1985, Cincinnati Art Mus, New Orleans Mus Art, Denver Art Musw & PaAcad Fine Arts, 89; Contemp Collectors, La Jolla Mus Contemp Art, Calif, 90; Breaking Ground, Contemp Arts Ctr, Cincinatti, Ohio, 87; Mapping, Mus Mod Art, NY, 94; Suspended Instants, Sculpture Ctr, NY, 97-98; These Things Happen, Bill Maynes Gallery, NY, 98, one person show, Galeria Trama, Barcelona, Spain, Galeria Trama, Barcelona, 2003, Strange Attractors, Richmond, 04, Bernard Toale Gallery, Bosotn, 05 & Pan-Am Gallery, Dallas, 06; Yale Univ Art Gallery, Looking at Am, New Haven, Conn, 2002; NC Mus Art, Defying Gravity (with catalog), 2003; Tableau Ecrans, Galerie les Filles du Calvaire, Paris & Brussels; Dallas Mus Art; Mus Fine Arts, Boston; Philadelphia Mus Art, Pa; High Art Mus, Atlanta, Ga; Booklyn Mus Art. *Teaching:* Adj prof sculpture & drawing, State Univ NY, Purchase, 81; artist-in-residence, Bennington Col, Vt, 81 & 86; lectr, Yale Univ, 81, RI Sch Design, 87, 91 & 92, Parsons Sch Design, 89 & Whitney Mus Am Art, 90; vis artist & lectr, Cleveland Inst Arts, 81, Md Inst Col Art, 85 & RI Sch Design, 85; vis lectr, Princeton Univ, 87 & 92; asst prof sculpture, Harvard Univ, 94- & instr, 96; instr, Parsons Sch Design. *Awards:* Yaddo Fel, 80, 85 & 90; MacDowell Colony Fel, 81-82, 86-87 & 2005; Guggenheim Grant, 90; Nat Endowment Arts, 94; Pollock-Krasner Grant, 99; Rockefller Fndtn Fel, Bellagio, Italy, 2003 & Montalvo Ctr Arts, 06. *Bibliog:* N Princenthal (auth), Drawing to Sublime, Kent Publs, 2003; R Rubenstein & Edward Albee (auths), Strange Attractors, Va Commonwealth Univ, 2003. *Mem:* Col Art Asn; Int Sculpture Soc. *Media:* Drawing, Sculpture. *Dealer:* Kent Gallery, New York, NY; Galeria Thama, Barcelona, Spain; Bernardo Toale Gallery, Boston, MA. *Mailing Add:* 4 White St New York NY 10013

FASOLDT, SARAH LOWRY
ADMINISTRATOR, CURATOR
b Evanston, Ill, Feb 7, 50. *Study:* Ecole du Louvre, Paris, 69; Univ Colo, Boulder, BA, 72. *Pos:* Cur Homstead, Farnsworth Art Mus, Rockland, Maine, 83; dir, Maine Coasts Artists, Rockport, 84-89; assoc dir, Farnsworth Art Mus, Rockland, Maine, 94-. *Mem:* Maine Community Cult Alliance. *Publ:* Auth, But is it art?, 1/81 & Monhegan: 100 years of island painting, 8/84, Down East Mag. *Mailing Add:* Farnsworth Art Mus PO Box 466 Rockland ME 04841

FAUBION, S MICHAEL
ADMINISTRATOR
b Tex, May 10, 52. *Study:* Univ Tex, BA, 74, LBJ Sch Pub Affairs, MPA, 76. *Pos:* Asst dir visual arts, Nat Endowment Arts, Washington, DC, 85-88, coordr, 98-. *Mailing Add:* 4016 18th St NW Washington DC 20011-5325

FAUDE, WILSON HINSDALE
DIRECTOR, CURATOR
b Hartford, Conn, Feb 20, 46. *Study:* Hobart Col, BA, 69; Trinity Col, MA. *Work:* Wadsworth Mus, Hartford, Conn; Mark Twain Memorial, Hartford, Conn; Old State House, Hartford, Conn. *Pos:* Exec dir, Old State House, 85-; cur, Mark Twain Mem, 71-79. *Mem:* Century Asn; Nat Arts Club. *Mailing Add:* 42 Fulton Pl West Hartford CT 06107

FAUDIE, FRED
PAINTER, ILLUSTRATOR
b DuBois, Pa, May 29, 41. *Study:* Cornell Univ, AB(art hist), 63; Univ Iowa, Iowa City, MA(painting), 65, photogr with John Schulz, 67-68; Syracuse Univ, MFA(illus), 79. *Work:* Addison Gallery Am Art; Lincoln Co Heritage Trust; Lincoln State Monument. *Exhib:* Brockton Triennial, Brockton Art Mus, Mass, 81 & 84; Billy the Kid, Lincoln Co Heritage Trust, 84; Something Human, Univ Mass, 87; Ninth Ann Boston Drawing Show, 88; Black in the Light, Genovese Gallery, Boston, 88; New Eng Impressions, Art of Printmaking, Fitchburg Art Mus, Mass, 88. *Teaching:* Prof painting & drawing, Univ Mass Lowell, 68-, chairperson art dept, 80-83. *Bibliog:* Allara (auth), New Editions, Vol 81, No 9, Art News, 9/82; Billy, the myth and image, Print Collectors Newsletter, Vol 13, No 3, 83; Erdman (auth), Fred Faudie: Mixed themes, Art New Eng, Vol 9, No 2, 2/88. *Mem:* Boston Visual Artists Union; Lowell Art Asn. *Media:* Oil, Acrylic. *Mailing Add:* Dept Art Univ Mass Lowell 1 University Ave Lowell MA 01854

FAULCONER, MARY (FULLERTON)
PAINTER, DESIGNER
b Pittsburgh, Pa. *Study:* Pa Mus Sch Art; also with Alexei Brodovitch. *Work:* Paul Mellon pvt collection; Duchess of Windsor pvt collection; plus many others. *Comn:* Paintings, Steuben Glass; designed six stamps, US Postal Serv, 74; designed Rose stamp, US Postal Serv, 78; designed Love stamp, US Postal Serv, 82; Franklin Mint, 84; Katherine Hepburn; Jacquine Kennedy. *Exhib:* Alex Iolas Gallery, NY, 55, 58 & 61; Philadelphia Art Alliance, 62; Bodley Gallery, NY, 64, 66, 69 & 72; Tenn Fine Arts Ctr, Nashville, 67; De Mers Gallery, Hilton Head, SC, 71-72; Ursus, Hotel Carlyle, NY. *Pos:* Art dir, Harper's Bazaar Mag, 40; art dir, Mademoiselle Mag, 45. *Teaching:* Instr advert, Philadelphia Mus Sch Art, 36-40. *Awards:* Distinctive Merit Award, 54, 57 & 61, Silver Medal, 58 & 59, Art Dir Club; Gold Medal, Am Rose Soc, 78. *Media:* Gouache. *Dealer:* URSUS Art Dealer Madison Ave NY City. *Mailing Add:* 20 Beekman Pl New York NY 10022

FAULDS, W ROD
ADMINISTRATOR, DESIGNER
b Rexdale, Ont, May 28, 53; US citizen. *Study:* Humbolt State Univ, BA, 77; Calif State Univ, Fullerton, MA, 80. *Exhib:* Sothebys Mus of NY, Hong Kong. *Collection Arranged:* Catherine Howe Paintings 1988-97, Univ Galleries, Fla, Atlantic Univ, Boca Raton. *Pos:* Dir, Brattleboro Mus & Art Ctr, 81-84; assoc dir, Williams Col Mus Art, 84-92; asst dir, Guggenheim Mus, 93-94; chief designer, Brooklyn Mus Art, 95-96; dir, Univ Galleries, Fla Atlantic Univ, 96-. *Teaching:* Mus Studies, Fla Atlantic Univ, 96-. *Mem:* Am Asn Mus; Asn Col Univ Mus Galleries (NE rep, 86-89). *Res:* Contemporary art with emphasis in sculpture and photography. *Publ:* Coauth, Object/Illusion/Reality-12 American Photographers, Calif Univ, Fullerton, 79; contribr, Mary Cassatt: The Color Prints, Abrams, 89; Black Photographers Bear Witness: 100 Years of Social Protest, Williams Col Mus Art, 89; Stitching Memories: African American Story Quilts, Williams Col Mus Art, 89; Sites of Recollection: Four Altars and a Rap Opera, Williams Col Mus, 92, Nu Art South Fla, 2000, South Fla Cultural Consortiumn Visual and Media Artists Fellowship Winners, 2000. *Mailing Add:* 722 SW 27th Wy Boynton Beach FL 33435

FAULKNER, FRANK
PAINTER
b Sumter, SC, July 27, 46. *Study:* Univ NC, Chapel Hill, BFA, 68, MFA, 72. *Work:* Hirshhorn Mus, Washington, DC; Nat Collection of Fine Arts, Washington, DC; Albright-Knox Art Gallery, Buffalo, NY; Smith Col, Northampton, Mass; Chase Manhattan Bank, NY. *Comn:* Urban wall proj, South Eastern Ctr Contemp Arts-Nat Endowment Arts, Winston-Salem, NC, 74; Orlando Int Airport, 81. *Exhib:* Whitney Mus Am Art Biennial, NY, 75; Slocumb Gallery, Univ Tenn, 76; one-man shows, Knowlton Gallery, 76-81; Material Dominant, Univ Pa, Philadelphia, 77; Southeast 7, Southeastern Ctr Contemp Art, Winston-Salem, NC, 77; Painters & Sculptors SE, High Mus Art, Atlanta, Ga, 77. *Awards:* Individual Artist Grant, Nat Endowment Arts, 75; Regional Artist Grant, South Eastern Ctr Contemp Arts-Nat Endowment Arts, 76; NC Architects Award, 76. *Bibliog:* William Zimmer (auth), Frank Faulkner, Arts Mag, 10/76. *Media:* Acrylic, Mixed Media. *Dealer:* Monique Knowlton Gallery 19 E 71st St New York NY 10021. *Mailing Add:* c/o Arden Gallery 129 Newbury St Boston MA 02116

FAUNCE, SARAH CUSHING
MUSEUM CURATOR
b Tulsa, Okla, Aug 19, 29. *Study:* Wellesley Col, BA; Washington Univ, MA; Columbia Univ. *Collection Arranged:* New Black Artists, 69; Peruvian Colonial Painting, 71; Pearlman Collection of Post-Impressionist Painting, 74; Anne Ryan Collages (auth, catalog), 74; Folk Sculpture USA (contribr, catalog), 76; Belgian Art 1880-1914 (contribr, catalog), 80; Northern Light: Realism and Symbolism in Scandinavian Painting 1880-1910, 82; Carl Larsson (contribr, catalog), 82; Malcolm Morley, 84; Jennifer Bartlett, 85; Courbet Reconsidered (contribr, catalog), 88; In the Light of Italy, Corot & Early Open-Air Painting (contribr, catalog), 96. *Pos:* Cur art collections, Columbia Univ, 65-69; exhib consult, Jewish Mus, 68-70; cur painting & sculpture, Brooklyn Mus, 69-98; dir Courbet Catalogue Raisonme Project, 98-. *Teaching:* Lectr art theory & criticism, Barnard Col, 64. *Mem:* Col Art Asn Am; Am Asn Mus; Int Coun Mus. *Publ:* auth, The domestic art of Carl Larsson, In: Carl Larsson, 82; Eugene Delacroix, In: European Writers, The Romantic Century, Vol 1, 85; Reconsidering Courbet, In: Courbet Reconsidered, 88; Gustave Courbet, Abrams, 93; Rome and Its Environs: Painters, Travelers, and Sites, 96; auth, Seurat and The Soul of Things, Belgian Art 1880-1914, 80; auth, Courbet: Feminist in Spite of Himself, Body, ArtGallery of New South Wales, 97; auth, Courbet's Java Landscape with Shepherd and Donkey, New York, Salander-O'Reilly, 98; auth, Courbet's Concept of Realism, The Battle for the Earth, in barbizon, Malerei der Natur, Natur der Malevei, 99

FAUSEL, ALAN
APPRAISER
Study: UCLA, BA(art hist); Stanford Univ, MA(art hist). *Pos:* Asst cur, European sculpture, decorative arts Fine Arts Mus, San Francisco, 86-89; cur, Frick Art Mus, Pittsburgh, 89-91; dir, European painting dept & mus serv's dept Butterfield & Butterfield, San Francisco, 91-94; sr vpres, dir, painting & drawing dept Doyle, NY, 94; lectr, Appraisal Asn Am, currently. *Teaching:* adj lectr, NYU Grad Sch Educ, currently. *Mailing Add:* Doyle NY 175 E 87th St New York NY 10128

FAUST, JAMES WILLE
PAINTER, SCULPTOR
b Lapel, Ind, May 22, 49. *Study:* Herron Sch Art, Indianapolis, Ind, BFA, 71, Univ Ill, Champaign-Urbana, MFA, 74. *Work:* Minn Mus Art, St Paul; Snite Mus Art, South Bend, Ind; Ind Univ Art Mus, Bloomington; Indianapolis Mus Art, Ind; Emporia State Univ, Kans. *Comn:* Absolut/Carillon Importers Ltd; Herb & Diane Meyer Simon; Melvin Simon & Assocs; Eli Lilly & Co; structured steel sculpture, SMT Realty/Allison Pointe, Indianapolis, Ind. *Exhib:* Brazil Works on Paper Partnership Int, Mus De Arte Do Rio Grande Do Sul, Porto Allegre, S Am, 84; solo show, Indianapolis Mus Art, 85 & 92; Contemp Am Drawing, Wichita Mus Art, Kans, 87; Am Drawing Biennial, Muscarelle Mus Art, Williamsburg, Va, 88; Chicago Int New Art Forms Expos, Navy Pier, Ill, 89; and others. *Awards:* Krannert Creative & Performing Arts Fel, Univ Ill, 73; Purchase Awards, 28th & 31st Ann Drawing & Small Sculpture Show, Ball State Univ Art Mus, 82 & 85; John Gordon Mem Award, 45th Ann Exhib Contemp Am Paintings, 83. *Bibliog:* A Conversation with James Faust (documentary), Indianapolis Art League; Absolut Indiana, Absolut Statehood Campaign, USA Today, 7/23/91. *Media:* Acrylic, Graphite & Prismacolor Pencils. *Publ:* Illusr, The American Story, Sat Evening Post, 75; Sat Evening Post Cover 3/76; Rock & Romance (record album), Faith Band, Village Records, Inc, 78; Arts Indiana (magazine cover), 6/88. *Dealer:* Martha S Faust 8457 Union Chapel Rd Indianapolis IN 46240. *Mailing Add:* 8457 Union Chapel Rd Indianapolis IN 46240-4331

FAVRO, MURRAY
SCULPTOR
b Huntsville, Ont, Dec 24, 1940. *Study:* H B Beal Tech Sch, London, Ont, 58-64. *Work:* Art Gallery Ont, Toronto; Nat Gallery Can, Ottawa, Ont; Can Coun Art Bank, Ottawa, Ont. *Comn:* Sculpture, Ministry Transport Bldg, Cornwall, Ont, 78. *Exhib:* Solo shows, Carmen Lamanna Gallery, 68, 71-73, 76, 77, 80, 82 & 83; Musee d'Art Mod Ville, Paris, 73; Mt Allison Univ & Rutgers Univ Art Gallery, 75; Changing Visions: The Canadian Landscape (with catalog, travelling show), Europe, 80; London Art Gallery, Ont, 76; Ten Canadian Artists in the 1970's (with catalog, traveling exhib), Europe, 76; A Retrospective, Art Gallery Ont, 83; Outdoor Sculpture Exhib, Quebec City, 84; 49th Parallel, NY, 86; Havana, Cuba, 89; McKenzie Gallery, Saskatoon, Sask, 91; Obscure Gallery, Quebec City, Que, 92. *Awards:* Can Coun Grants, 68-72; Can Coun Senior Grant, 74, 78, 80 & 83. *Bibliog:* France Morin (auth), Icarus: The Vision of Angels, 86. *Mem:* Can Artists Representation; Royal Canadian Acad. *Publ:* Auth, Heart of London, Ottawa, 68; Biographical Information About the Influences on My Work, 71, Windmill Electric Generator, 75 & The Flying Flea and Henri Mignet Its Designer, 77, Carmen Lamanna Gallery, Toronto. *Mailing Add:* 783 Queens Ave London ON N5W 3H7 Canada

FAY, MING G
SCULPTOR, EDUCATOR
Study: Columbus Col Art & Design, dipl, 65; Kansas City Art Inst, BFA, 67; Univ Calif, Santa Barbara, MFA, 70. *Work:* Columbus Art Mus, Ohio; Hong Kong Mus Art; Sidney Lewis Found, Va; Mobile Hq, NY; Justice Ctr, Philadelphia; Teipei Mus Art, China. *Comn:* Conrad Hilton, Hong Kong, 90. *Exhib:* Solo exhib, Keen Gallery, NY, 93, Alisan Fine Arts Ltd, Hong Kong, 94, Butters Gallery, Portland, Ore, 94, Kim Foster Gallery, NY, 94 & 96, Broadway Windows, NY, 96 & Stone Quarry Hill Art Park, Cazenovia, NY 97; Elusive Source, Corcoran Gallery Art, Washington, DC, 95; Feast for the Eyes (with catalog), John Michael Kohler Art Ctr, Sheboygan Arts Found, Wis, 96; Lings, Bulova Corp Ctr, Queens Mus Art, NY, 97; Biennial Exhib Pub Art, Neuberger Mus Art, State Univ NY, Purchase, 97; Ancient Emblems, Contemp Signifiers, Jersey City Mus, NJ, 97; Gardens of Urban Delight: The Lower East Side, Henry Street Settlement Art Ctr, NY, 97; Garden of Quin, Whitney Mus at Phillip Morris, NY, 98; Paper: The State of Connection, Bergstrom Mahler Mus, Neenah, Wis, 98; Sculpture Leedy Voulkos Art Ctr Gallery, Kansas City, Mo, 98. *Pos:* Adv bd, Asian Am Art Ctr, NY, 88-92; artist adv bd, New Mus, NY, 89-92; bd, Alternative Mus, NY, 91 & Chinese Am Arts Coun, NY, 92. *Teaching:* Inst, Chinese Univ Hong Kong, 68-69; Columbus Col Art and Design, Ohio, 70-71; Univ Pittsburgh, Pa, 71-74; Hong Kong Polytechnic, Hong Kong, 75; Pratt Inst, Brooklyn, New York, 78-80; Semester at Sea, UCIS, Univ Pittsburgh, 82; William Paterson Univ, Wayne, NJ, 83-99. *Awards:* Per Cent for Art, Criminal Justice Ctr, 93; New York Experimental Glass Workshop, Vis Artist Residency, 94; Mid-Atlantic Arts Found, Visual Residency Prog, Rutgers Ctr Printmaking, 94; and others. *Bibliog:* Kathleen Finley Magnan (auth), The alchemist of spirits, Asian Art News, 7-8/94; Fay Hirsch (auth), Ming Fay - A Feast for the Eyes, John Michael Kohler Arts Ctr, 96; John Yau (auth), The Garden of Earthly Delights, The Work of Ming Fay, Whitney Mus Am at Philip Morris, NY, 98; Brook Barrie (auth), Contemporary Outdoors Sculpture, Rockport Pub, 99. *Mem:* Epoxy Art Group. *Media:* Mixed Media; Metal. *Res:* fantasy gardens. *Dealer:* Butters Gallery Portland OR. *Mailing Add:* Power Art Ctr 25 Power Ave Wayne NJ 07470

FAZZINO, CHARLES
PAINTER, PUBLISHER
b New York, NY, Dec 26, 55. *Study:* Sch Visual Arts, with S Chuast, Sue Coe, Jack Potter, BFA, 77. *Work:* NBC Experience Store, NY; The Eisner Found, Burbank, Calif; Newark Beth Israel Childrens Med Ctr; Circus World Mus, Baraboo, Wis; Muscular Dystrophy Assn Hq, Tucson. *Comn:* Spl Olympics 25th Ann, Spl Olympics Internat, 96; murals, Newark Beth Israel Med Ctr, Childrens Hosp, 98; Ofcl Art, Sachsiluute Festival, Zurich, 99; NY Times Square Celebration, Mayors Office, NY, 2000; Today Show Concert Series, NBC, NY, 2000 & 2002. *Pos:* owner, Individual Self-Pub, NY, 78-94; owner, Mus Editions, Ltd, 94 -. *Mem:* Muscular Dystrophy (nat vpres). *Media:* Acrylic, Oil, All Media. *Dealer:* Museum Editions Ltd 32 Relyea Pl New Rochelle NY10801. *Mailing Add:* 32 Relyea Pl Ste 2 New Rochelle NY 10801

FEAR, DANIEL E
CONSULTANT, EDITOR
b Tacoma, Wash, Mar 28, 49. *Pos:* Dir & pres, The Silver Image Gallery Inc, 73-93; dir, Art Support, 96-. *Mem:* Founding mem Asn Int Photog Art Dealers Inc. *Media:* Photography. *Publ:* Ed, Northwest Photographer's Resource Guide, 90; Creating a Successful Career in Photography, 92; Creating a Successful Career in Visual Art, 97. *Mailing Add:* Art Support 300 Queen Ann Ave N No 425 Seattle WA 98109-4599

FEARING, WILLIAM KELLY
EDUCATOR, PAINTER
b Fordyce, Ark, Oct 18, 18. *Study:* La Tech Univ, BA; Columbia Univ, MA. *Work:* Dallas Mus Fine Arts; Ft Worth Art Ctr; Mus Fine Arts Houston; Inst Contemp Arts, Boston; Marion Koogler McNay Art Mus, San Antonio; Milwaukee Art Mus; Jack S Blanton Mus Art, Univ Tex, Austin; Longview Art Mus, Tex. *Exhib:* Mary Moffett Gallery, La Tech Univ, 81; A Retrospective of Drawings and Other Works on Paper 1945-1985 (with catalog), Old Jail Art Ctr, Albany, Tex, 85 & (with catalog) Marion Koogler McNay Art Mus, San Antonio, 86; solo exhibs, Valley House Gallery, Dallas, Tex, 92 & 96, Flat Bed Press Gallery, Austin, 95 & Robinson Galleries, Houston, 95; Prints of The Fort Worth Circle 1940-1960, Archer M Huntington Art Gallery, Univ Tex, Austin, 92; Valley House Gallery, Dallas, Tex, 94; Pascal Robinson Galleries, Houston, Tex, 99; and others. *Teaching:* Prof studio art, Univ Tex, Austin, 47-87, Ashbel Smith emer prof, 87-2000. *Awards:* Archives Am Art, Smithsonian Inst, Washington, 84. *Bibliog:* New talent USA, Art in Am, 62; John Palmer Leeper (auth), The Texas hill country: Interpretations by 13 painters, Texas A&M Press, 81; Stephen Pinson (auth), Prints of the Ft Worth Circle, Archer M Huntington Art Gallery, Univ Tex, Austin, 92; Amy Freeman Lee (auth, cur), Winging with the Wild White Bird. *Mem:* Nat Soc Lit & Arts; lifetime mem Tex Art Educ Asn. *Media:* Oil, Etching. *Publ:* Coauth, Our expanding vision, 60, The creative eye, 2nd ed, 79 & Art and the creative teacher, 71, Benson; ed, Creativity and the human spirit, Tex Quart, spring 73 & spec issue, 75; coauth, Helping children see art and make art, Vol I & II & The Way of Art, Vol I & II, 86, Benson; contribr forward, in: We Are Not Alone, Tex Lutheran Univ, 2000. *Dealer:* Valley House Gallery Spring Valley Rd Dallas TX 75240; Pascal Robinson Galleries 2307 W Alabama St Houston TX 77098. *Mailing Add:* 914 Calethea Austin TX 78746

FEATHERSTONE, DAVID BYRUM
CRITIC, CURATOR
b Iowa City, Iowa, Jan 23, 45. *Study:* Univ Calif, Berkeley, AB, 67; Univ Ore, Eugene, MA, 71. *Exhib:* Celebrations, Hayden Gallery, Mass Inst Technol, Cambridge, 74; Northwest Invitational, Seattle Art Mus, Wash, 75; Attitudes: Photog in 70's, Mus Art, Santa Barbara, Calif, 80. *Collection Arranged:* Bernard Freemesser, A Retrospective Exhib, 78; Photographs by Vilem Kriz (auth, catalog), 79; The Diana Show, Pictures Through A Plastic Lens (auth, catalog), 80; Aerial Photographs by William Garnett, 80; Photographs by Marsha Burns (auth, catalog), 81; Mount St Helens, the Photographer's Response, 83; Point Lobos: Place as Icon, 84; The Painted Image: Applied Color in Photography, 85; Edward Weston: A Mature Vision, 86; Holly Roberts - Painted Photographs (auth, catalog), 90; Yosemite: A Lifetime, Photographs by Ansel Adams, 90; Reagan Louie, Photographs of China 1980-1190, 91; This Is The American Earth, 92. *Pos:* Cur photog, Historical Photog Collection, Univ Ore Libr, Eugene, 74-76; exec assoc, The Friends Photog, Carmel, Calif, 77-87, dir publs, 87-91; independent cur & ed, 91-. *Awards:* Art Critics Fel, 76 & 78 & Mus Prof Fel, 82, Nat Endowment Arts; Residency Fel, Wurlitzer Found, Taos, NMex, 82. *Mem:* Soc Photog Educ; Am Asn Mus; Oracle Conference of Photog Curators; Houston Fotofest (int adv bd). *Res:* Contemporary photography. *Publ:* Auth, Doris Ulmann:

American Portraits, Univ NMex Press, 85; Photographs of Mother Teresa's Mission's of Charity in Calcutta, Friends of Photog, 85; ed, Close to Home, Seven Documentary Photographers, 89 & Of Time and Place: Walker Evans and William Christenberry, 90, Friends of Photography; Holly Roberts, Photographs, Friends of Photography, 90. *Mailing Add:* 1820 Vallejo St No PH-1 San Francisco CA 94123-4902

FEBLAND, HARRIET
SCULPTOR, PAINTER
b New York, NY. *Study:* Pratt Inst; NY Univ; Art Students League; Am Artists Sch; Atelier 17, Paris. *Work:* Westchester Co Court House, White Plains Civic Plaza; Cincinnati Art Mus; Emily Lowe Mus, Coral Gables, Fla; Jane Voorhees Zimmerli Art Mus, Rutgers Univ, NJ; Hempstead Bank of Long Island Collection of Am Art; Pepsico Corp, Somers, NY; State Univ NY, Potsdam; Hudson River Mus, Yonkers, NY; State of Hawaii Arts and Cult Found, Hilo, Art in Pub Places Collection; Gibson Mus, Potsdam, NY; Grounds for Sculpture Mus, Hamilton, NJ. *Comn:* Sculpture, Haverly Collection, NY; sculpture, comn by Hon & Mrs Irwin Davidson collection, New Rochelle, NY; Metromedia HQ, Los Angeles, LA; Westchester Co Courthouse, Civic Plaza, White Plains, NY. *Exhib:* Solo retrospectives, Hudson River Mus, NY, 63, Silvermine Guild, Conn, 73, Bridge Gallery, Munic Art Ctr, White Plains, NY, 76, Brainerd Art Gallery, State Univ NY, 86, Va Ctr for the Creative Arts, Camp Gallery, 91, Berkeley Col Gallery, NYC, 2006; One-women exhibs, Katonah Gallery, 70, 80, Vincent Price Gallery, Chicago, 71, Rutgers Univ Gallery, NJ, 75, Va Ctr Creative Arts, 91, Contemp Illusr Gallery, 98, Janer 81 Gallery, 98, Nat Space Soc, Houston, 99, VAHC Galleries 2000, Donnell Libr Ctr, New York City, 03, Interchurch Ctr Galleries, NJ, 2004, Berkeley Col Gallery, NYC, 2006; group invitationals, Cincinnati Art Mus, 68, Mus d'Art Mod, Paris, 70, Alwin Gallery, London, 70, Hudson River Mus, 70-83, Woman Choose Women, NY Cult Ctr, 73, Potsdam Plastics, State Univ NY, 74 & Carnegie Inst; Krasdale Gallery, White Plains & NY, 97 & 98; Zimmerli Art Mus, New Brunswick, NJ, 98; Univ Hawaii, Hilo; Sarah Lawrence Col Gallery, 2000; Hunterdon Mus Art, Clinton, NJ, 02, Jamison-Carnegie Heritage Mus, Talladega, Ala, 01, UN Gallery, NYC, 02, Grounds for Sculpture Mus, Hamilton, NJ, 02, Stephen Gang Gallery, NYC, 02, Univ Wis, Kenosha, 03, Heuser Art Ctr, Bradley Univ, Peoria, Ill, 03, Valdosta Fine Arts Gallery, Valdosta State Univ, Ga, 03, Binney and Smith Gallery, Banana Factory, Bethlehem, Pa, 02, Springfield Art Mus, MO, 03; Univ Nebraska, Lincoln, NE, 04, Poughkeepsie Art Mus, Poughkeepsie, NY, 04; Moon Song Grounds for Sculpture Mus, Hamilton, NJ, 2005; New Arts Prog, Invitational Salon Exhib Small Works, Lehigh Valley & Berks, Pa, 2006; Nat Asn Women Artists (NAWA), 117th Ann Exhib, Goggle Works Center for the Arts, Reading, Pa, 2006. *Collection Arranged:* Cincinnati Art Mus; Pepsico Corp; New Sch for Social Rsch, Art Ctr, NYC; Nat Asn Women Artists Collection; Agnes K Haverly Found; Va Ctr for the Creative Arts. *Pos:* Dir, Harriet FeBland Art Workshop (painting), Chelsea Sch Art, London Univ, 62-95, teacher, 85; Bennington Col, 88 & Santa Fe NMex, 93; artist-in-residence (printmaking), State Univ NY, Potsdam, 86. *Teaching:* Instr & lectr, NY Univ, 60-62; instr & dir, Harriet FeBland Art Workshop, 62-95, Pelham Art Ctr, NY 62-95; instr, Westchester Art Workshop, White Plains, 65-72. *Awards:* Andrew Nelson Whitehead Award, Am Soc Contemp Artists, 85, 87, 89, 93, 94, 96, 97, 99 & 2000-2006; Elizabeth Morse Genius Found Award, Nat Asn Women Arist, 86-98 & Gretchen Richardson Freelander Mem Award, 97; Agnes K Haverly Found, Award Video for TV, 86; Robert Conover Award, Soc Am Graphic Artists, 99; artist-in-residence, SUNY Potsdam Col, NY, 86; fel, Tyrone Guthrie Ctr, Ireland, 87, Woodstock Sch Art, NY, 89, Va Ctr for the Creative Arts, 83, 87. *Bibliog:* Newman (auth), Plastics as sculpture, 74 & Plastics as an art form, Chilton; Dona Meilach (auth), Collage and Assemblage, Doubleday, 75; Harriet FeBland (film), AK Haverly Found, 83; Charlotte S Rubinstein (auth), Women in Am Sculpture; and others. *Mem:* NY Artists Equity Asn (vpres, 70-76, pres, 89-90, chmn & prog dir); Am Soc Contemp Artists (pres emer, 1983-2005, ed 2003, pres 2005-); Int Art Asn UNESCO, United Nations (secy, 80-82); Nat Asn of Women Artists; Soc Am Graphic Artists; Womens Inst Art, and others. *Media:* Construction Sculpture; Monotypes; painting. *Specialty:* Gallery 81, Sculpture & Painting, NY. *Interests:* Space sci, astronomy. *Publ:* Encyclopedia of Polymer Sci, 69-; and many others (35 bks). *Mailing Add:* 245 E 63rd St Apt 1803 New York NY 10021

FECHTER, CLAUDIA ZIESER
CURATOR, WRITER
b New York, NY, Mar 14, 31. *Study:* Case Western Reserve, AB, 52; Columbia, MA, 54. *Collection Arranged:* The Loom and the Cloth, Fabrics of Jewish Life (catalog), Temple Mus, 88; Sacred Landmarks, Cleveland State Univ Gallery, 90; For Everything a Season, Cleveland State Univ, 02. *Pos:* Dir, Temple Mus, 84-97; cur, Cleveland State Univ, 97-. *Awards:* Northern Ohio Live - Cult Exhibs, 01. *Mem:* Coun Am Jewish Mus (steering comt); Northeast Ohio Mus Coun. *Res:* Judaic ritual fabrics. *Interests:* Judaica and antiquities of the Holy Land region. *Publ:* Auth, The Loom and the Cloth, Temple Mus, 88; Custom, costume & ceremonial cloth, Creative Needle, 9/88; The fabric of Jewish Life, Vol XVIII, No 1, Coun Am Embroideres, 2/89; From Generation to Generation: Fabrics of Jewish Life, 88; For Everything a Season, 2000. *Mailing Add:* 2541 Richmond Rd Cleveland OH 44122

FEDER, BEN
DESIGNER, PAINTER
b New York, NY, Feb 1, 23. *Study:* Parsons Sch Design; Vet Ctr, Mus Mod Art, with Prestopino. *Exhib:* Stamford Mus Art, Conn, 60; Bodley Gallery, NY, 64; Inst Allende, San Miguel Allende, Mex. *Pos:* Designer & graphic arts consult, New Bk Knowledge, Grolier Inc; pres, Ben Feder Inc, NY; owner & design consultant, Clinton Vineyards Dutchess Co, NY. *Mem:* Am Soc Enologists. *Media:* Guache, Acrylic. *Mailing Add:* 65 E 76th St Apt 9E New York NY 10021

FEDER, PENNY JOY
PRINTMAKER, ILLUSTRATOR
b New York, NY, Oct 13, 49. *Study:* CW Post Col, Long Island Univ, Brookville, NY, with James Lewicki & Harry Hohen, BA(art educ), 71 & with Arthur Leipsig & Alfred van Loen, MA(printmaking), 75; Brooklyn Mus Art Sch, printmaking, 72. *Work:* Nynex Corp; Cunard Lines Int; Holland Am Shipping Lines Int; Nat Mus Am Art; Nat Mus Art, Smithsonian Inst. *Comn:* Catalog cover & poster design, Wash Sq Outdoor Art Exhib, NY, 75; woodcut, Collectors Guild, NY, 76; woodcut, Calhoun's Collectors Soc, Minneapolis, 81. *Exhib:* Ann, Audubon Artists Soc, Inst Arts & Letts, 80; Nat Acad Design, 81; Knickerbocker Artists, Nat Arts Club, NY, 81; Brooklyn Mus, 85; Fed Plaza, NY, 86; Lever House Gallery, NY, 96; James Beard Gallery, NY, 96. *Teaching:* Lectr-demonstr, Suffolk Co Sch System, NY, 70 & Salamagundi Club, New York, 79; and at various other art groups in NY. *Awards:* John Taylor Arms Award, Audubon Artists 39th Ann, 81; Knickerbocker Award, 32nd Knickerbocker Artists Ann, 83; Gold Medal, Salmagundi Club, 83. *Bibliog:* Jeanne Paris (auth), Diaries of creativity & Malcolm Preston (auth), Flourishing symbiosis, Newsday Newspaper, Long Island, NY, 2/77. *Mem:* Philadelphia Print Club; Audubon Artists Soc. *Media:* Woodcuts, Etchings. *Publ:* Auth, Original Printmakers, Art Expo Preview Mag, 1-2/93; article in Art Business News; article in Decor Mag. *Mailing Add:* 80-90 Dumfries Pl Jamaica NY 11432

FEDERHEN, DEBORAH ANNE
CURATOR, HISTORIAN
b Shirley, Mass, June 19, 54. *Study:* Col William & Mary, BA(art hist), 76; Univ Mo-Columbia, MA(art hist), 81; Univ Del, MA(Am cult, Lois F McNeil Fel), 85. *Collection Arranged:* Accumulation & Display: Mass Marketing Household Goods in America, 1880-1920 (coauth, bk), Winterthur Mus, 86; Classical Taste in America, 1800-1840, Baltimore Mus Art, 93; Extinct Specie: Money in Maine from Colony to Capitalism, York Inst Mus, 93; Garden of the East: Life in Maine - 1604-1713, York Inst Mus, 94; Memory is a Painter: The Art of Grandma Moses (traveling exhib), Richard Nixon Libr, Calif, Gerald Ford Mus & Libr, Mich, New Britain Mus Am Art, Conn, Newport Art Mus, RI, Soc Four Arts, Fla & LB Johnson Libr, Tex, 98-99. *Pos:* Cur, Soc Preserv Long Island Antiquities, Setauket, NY, 87-88; res assoc, Baltimore Mus Art, 88-91; cur, York Inst Mus, Saco, Maine, 92-96; cur collections, Bennington Mus, Vt, 96-99. *Teaching:* Instr decorative arts, Winterthur Mus, Del, 85-87. *Awards:* McCormick Scholarship, Victorian Soc, 82; Nat Mus Act Internship, Yale Univ Art Gallery, 82-83. *Mem:* Soc Winterthur Fels; Decorative Arts Soc. *Res:* American Decorative arts and material culture; specializing in furniture; silver, quilts and ceramics. *Publ:* Coauth, Paul Revere - Artisan, Businessman & Patriot, Paul Revere Mem Asn, 88; contribr, Decorative Arts & Household Furnishings in America, 1650-1920: An Annotated Bibliogrphy, (book), Winterthur Mus, 89; Politics & furniture: The patrons & products of Jonathan Gostelowe & Thomas Affleck, Winterthur Mus, 94; coauth, Colonial Massachusetts Silversmiths: A Biographical Dictionary, Yale Art Gallery, 98; co-auth (with Ellen Denker), The Bennington Porian Project: An analytical reevaluation of the Bennington Museum Collection, Antiques Arts Weekly, 10/23/98. *Mailing Add:* Bennington Mus W Main St Bennington VT 05201

FEDERICO, FRANK
PAINTER, PASTEL
b New Orleans, LA, July 3, 28. *Study:* Southwest LA Inst; New Orleans Accad of Art; John McCrady Art School. *Work:* John Hopkins Univ; Gulf Oil Corp; IBM; Hart Develop Corp. *Comn:* New Orleans Vista, YWCA, New Orleans, LA, 1964; Scenes of Yesteryear, Gortons Seafood, Glouchester, Mass, 1973; Transcendence, Univ of Conn, 1994. *Pos:* Pres, Kent Art Asn, Kent, Conn, 1990-1992, pres, CT Pastel Soc, 1998-2000. *Teaching:* Instr watercolor, oils, figure, Fl Gulf Coast Art Ctr, Clearwater, 1976-1980; instr, W Hartford Art League, W Hartford, Conn, 1985-2006. *Awards:* Nat Watercolor Soc Open Juried (2nd prize), Best in Show, PSA Ann, Hahnemuhle Co, 2000; CPS Rennaisance, JR Reeves, 2002. *Bibliog:* Colin Fry (auth), Make Color Work for You, Am Artist Mag, 2004. *Mem:* Pastel Soc Am (master pastelist); Int Asn Pastel Painters (master circle); Allied Artists Am (signature); Nat Watercolor Soc (signature); Am Watercolor Soc (mem). *Media:* Watercolor, Oil. *Res:* Conduct painting workshops locally & abroad. *Interests:* Art interest is having a cognizance of the world I live in. *Publ:* Ed, U Conn Mural Marks Change, Hartford Courant, 1992; ed, Profile of an Artist, Litchfield Living, 1994; auth, A Workshop Experience: A Colorist Approach to Pastel, Pastel J, 1999; auth, Plein Air Painting, Pastel Soc Am, 2000. *Dealer:* The Gallery 309 Primrose Rd Burlingame Calif 94010. *Mailing Add:* PO Box 363 Goshen CT 06756

FEDERIGHI, CHRISTINE M
CERAMIST, SCULPTOR
b San Mateo, Calif, June 22, 49. *Study:* Cleveland Inst Art, BFA, 72; Alfred Univ Col Ceramics, NY, MFA, 74. *Work:* Ariz State Univ Mus, Tempe; Monsanto Corp, Washington, DC; Mus Arts & Sci, Daytona, Fla; John Michael Kohler Jr Collection, Sheyboygan, Wis; Ft Lauderdale Mus Art, Fla; and others. *Comn:* Art State Pub Bldgs, 89; Fla Int Univ Libr NMiami; Biscane Nature Ctr, Key Biscayne, Fla, 98. *Exhib:* Ceramic Sculpture, Ore Sch Arts & Crafts, Portland, 90; solo exhibs, Grossmont Col, El Cajon, Calif, 94, SDFA-Esther Saks Fine Art, Chicago, 94, Harris House, Atlantic Ctr for Arts, 2001, Transcending Dimensions, Ormond Beach Mus, Fla, 2003 & Layers of Hands, Tenn Tech Col, Appalachian Ctr for Arts, Smithville, 2005; Objects & Drawings, Ark Arts Ctr, Little Rock, 94; Boca Raton Mus Art, Fla, 97; Lowe Art Mus, Coral Gables, Fla, 98; R Duane Reed Gallery, St Louis, 2000; Elaine Baker Gallery, Boca Raton, Fla, 2000; A Rendevous, Mus Nebr Art, Kearney, 2001; Southern Women of Influence, Ky Ctr Art, Louisville, 2001; Visual Perspectives, Sofa Chicago Gallery, 2002; Univ Fla Mus, 2002; Int Perspectives in Ceramics, Susan St Gallery, Solano Beach, Calif, 2001; Summer Dene Gallery, San

Diego, 2003; NCECA Exhib, Yingee Ceremics Mus, Taiwan; Particles & Passions, Acad Art, Easton, Md, 2005; The Figure, Cervene Haas Gallery, Scottsdale, Ariz; Dunedin Art Ctr, Dunekin, Fla; Sherrie Gallerie, Columbus, Ohio, 2006-; Human Nature, Col Notre Dame, Balitmore. *Teaching:* Prof art & ceramics/design, Univ Miami, 74-. *Awards:* Grant, Fla Fine Arts Coun, 83, 79, 91 & 98; Nat Endowment Arts, 88 & 89; Virginia A Groot Fdn, 90; Cooper Fel, Univ Miami, 2006-. *Bibliog:* Ann Prospero Reban (auth), article, Am Ceramics, Vol 5, 86; Frank Boyden (auth), 18 Ceramic Artists, Studio Potter, 88; Ricardo Pav-Louza (auth), Miami Artists, Art Int, 89. *Mem:* Nat Coun Educ Ceramic Arts; Fla Craftsmen. *Media:* Ceramics; Clay. *Publ:* Auth, Is anybody home?, New Art Examiner, 85; Bombs & oranges, discovering Miami's explosive art scene, Arts Mag, 11/90; Helen Kohen, Miami Herald, 1/11/91; Ceramics Monthly (cover & article), 2/92. *Dealer:* Sandy Carson Gallery Denver CO; Elaine Baker Gallery Boca Raton FL. *Mailing Add:* 1315 Obispo Ave Coral Gables FL 33134-3511

FEHER, TONY
ARTIST
b Albuquerque, 56. *Exhib:* Solo shows include Wooster Gardens, NY, 93, Gramercy Int, NY, 94, Acme, Santa Monica, Calif, 95, New Mus Contemp Art, NY, 96, Zilkha Gallery, Wesleyan Col, Conn, 97, Richard Telles Fine Art, LA, 98, Numark Gallery, Washington, DC, 99, Anthony Meier Fine Arts, San Francisco, Calif, 2000, Red Room and More, Ctr Curtorial Studies, Bard Coll, NY, Univ Calif, LA Hammer Mus, 2001, Maybe/Enjoy, Worcester Art Mus, Mass, 2002, I'm Tired of Toast, Univ Calif Berkeley Art Mus, 2002; group shows include Foundation Show, Art Mus, Southern Tex, Corpus Christi, 80; Atomic Art, Max Fish, NY City, 89; AIDS/SIDA, Real Art Ways, Hartford, Conn, 90; Gulliver's Travels, Galerie Sophia Ungers, Koln, Ger, 91; Queer Show, Minor Injury, Brooklyn, NY, 91; The Auto-Erotic Object, Hunter Col, NY City, 92; Art Around the Park, Tompkins Square Park, NY City, 93; Gramercy Int, NY, 94; Inaugural Exhib, Paul Morris Gallery, 95; Simple Matter, Numark Gallery, Washington, DC, 98; Beyond Minimalism, Koyanagi Gallery, Tokyo, 98; Hindsight, Whitney Mus Am Art, NY, 99; Deja Vu, Art Miami, 2000; New Work, Addison Gallery, Am Art, Andover, Mass, 2001; Leisure Theory, Coleccion Jumex, Mexico City, 2002; Basic Instinct, Mus Contemp Art, Chicago, 2003; Poetic Justice: 8th Int Istanbul Biennial, Turkey, 2003; State of Play, Serpentine Gallery, London, 2004; Nat Acad Mus, NY City, 2006; represented in permanent collections of Addison Gallery Am Art, Andover, Mass, Art Inst Chicago, Baltimore Mus Art, Henry Art Gallery, Seattle, Israel Mus, Jerusalem, La Colllecion Jumex, Mexico City, Modern Art Mus, Ft Worth, Tex, Mus Fine Arts, Houston, San Francisco Mus Modern Art, Solomon R Guggenheim Mus, NY City, Walker Art Ctr, Whitney Mus Am Art, NY City. *Mailing Add:* ACME Spaces 1 & 2 6150 Wilshire Blvd Los Angeles CA 90048

FEIFFER, JULES
CARTOONIST, WRITER
b New York, NY, Jan 26, 29. *Study:* Art Students League, 46; Pratt Inst, 47-51. *Pos:* Asst to syndicated cartoonist, Will Eisner, 46-51; cartoonist, Village Voice, 56-97; cartoons publ weekly, London Observer, Eng, 58-66 & 72-80 & Playboy Mag, 59-; syndicated nationally, 59-. *Awards:* Acad Award Animated Cartoon, Munro, 61; George Polk Mem Award, 62; Pulitzer Prize for Editorial Cartoons, 86. *Bibliog:* Lisa Schwarzbaum (auth), Jules Feiffer in season, Daily News Mag, 3/5/89; Maralyn Lois Polak (auth), interview, Philadelphia Inquirer, 10/15/89; John Douglas (auth), Grand Rapids Press, 10/6/1. *Mem:* Authors Guild. *Publ:* Auth, 11 collections cartoons including, Feiffer's Marriage Manual, 67, Feiffer on Nixon, 67, Tantrum: A Cartoon Novel, 79, Jules Feiffer's America: From Eisenhower to Nixon, 82 & Marriage is an Invasion of Privacy, 84; Fieffer's Children, 86; and plays & novels

FEIGEN, RICHARD L
DEALER, COLLECTOR
b Chicago, Ill, Aug 8, 30. *Study:* Yale Univ, BA, 52; Harvard Univ, MBA, 54. *Pos:* Chmn & dir, Richard L Feigen & Co, Inc, 57-; trustee, John Jay Homestead, Katonah, NY & Lincoln Univ, Pa, 82-90; dir, Art Dealers Asn Am, 74-78, 86-91 & 97-. *Mem:* Life fel Metrop Mus Art; life fel Minneapolis Soc Fine Arts; gov life mem Art Inst Chicago. *Specialty:* European and American paintings, drawings and sculpture, 1400 to the present. *Collection:* Old Master paintings and drawings; Beckmann, Ernst, Tanguy, Cornell, Dubuffet, Rosenquist. *Publ:* auth, Dubuffet and the Anticulture, 69; contribr, Office Design, 70; auth, George Grosz: Dada Drawings, 72; auth, Tales from the Art Crypt, Knopf, 2000. *Mailing Add:* 34 E 69th St New York NY 10021

FEIGENBAUM, HARRIET
SCULPTOR, ENVIRONMENTAL ARTIST
b Brooklyn, NY, 39. *Study:* Nat Acad Sch Fine Arts, New York, 59-61; Sch Gen Studies, Columbia Univ, 68-71; study art hist with Howard Hibbard, 73-74. *Work:* Nat Mus Women in Arts, Corcoran Gallery Art, Washington; Herbert F Johnson Mus, Cornell Univ, Ithaca, NY; Andrew Dickson White Mus, Colgate Univ, Hamilton, NY; Hillwood Art Mus, Long Island Univ, Brooksville, NY. *Comn:* Willow Rings, Reclamation Proj, 85, The Greenwood Colliery Sundial, 88, Scranton Chamber Com, Pa; Holocaust Mem, Appellate Courthouse, NY, 90; relief sculpture, Dormitory Authority, NY, 94. *Exhib:* Land Structures Built Where the Petroglyphs are Made by Children, Artpark, Lewiston, NY, 77; Women in Am Archit: A Historic & Contemp Perspective, Brooklyn Mus, NY, 77; Dwellings, Inst Contemp Art, Philadelphia, Pa, 78; The Presence of Nature, Whitney Mus Am Art, NY, 78; Dwellings Travels to, Neuberger Mus, Purchase, NY, 79; solo exhib, Pa Acad Fine Arts, Philadelphia, 86; Office of the Dead, Wheaton Col, Norton, Mass, 97, Women of Stone, Neuberger Mus, Purchase, NY, 2000-01; Art and the Law, Am Bar Asn, traveling US, 87-89. *Awards:* Artists Fel, Erosion & Sedimentation Control Plan Ned Ash & Coal Silt Area, 84 & Art in Pub Places, Greenwood Colliery Sundial, 87, Nat Endowment Arts; Excellence in Design Award, Art Comn of City New York, 91. *Bibliog:* Lucy Lippard (auth), Architectural complexes in nature, Art in Am, 1-2/79; Michael Brenson (auth), The state of the city as sculptors see it, New York Times, 7/27/90; Joan Marter (auth), Nature redox: Recent reclamation art, Sculpture, 11-12/94; Ann H Murray (auth), Artin America, Harriet Feigenbaum at the Neuberger Mus, 7/01. *Mem:* Pub Art Fund. *Media:* Stone, Mixed Media. *Collection:* City of NY (Holocaust Mem, Appellate Courthouse, 1st Dept New York City). *Publ:* Auth, The influence of Galileo on Bernini's Saint Mary Magdalen and Saint Jerome, Art Bull, 3/77; Where should land art go?, No 13, 81 & Reclamation art, No 22, 88, Heresies. *Mailing Add:* 49 W 24th St 11th Fl New York NY 10010

FEIN, B(ARBARA) R
EDUCATOR, PAINTER
b Brooklyn, NY, Dec 11, 41. *Study:* Brooklyn Col, BA, 62; Univ Md, 64-66; City Univ New York, MA, 67, PhD, 69; Univ NH, 70-80. *Work:* NY Pub Libr; Seacoast Regional Coun Ctr, Portsmouth, NH; York Co Coun Ctr, Sanford, Maine; Deaconess Hosp, Boston; Kittery Art Asn, Maine; Harber Home, Maine. *Comn:* Child at a Circus (mural), USN Hosp, Portsmouth, 71. *Exhib:* Copley Soc, Boston, 69-75, Walt Kuhn Mem-Norton Hall Gallery, Cape Neddick, Maine, 69-76; Drawings '71, Minn Mus Art, Minneapolis, 71; 6th Ann Drawing & Small Sculpture Exhib, Del Mar Col, Corpus Christi, Tex, 72; Wadsworth Atheneum, Conn Acad Fine Arts, Hartford, 72; 33rd & 34th Ann Nat Art Exhib, Southern Utah State Col, Cedar City, 73 & 74; Mike Levitan Gallery, NY, 86. *Pos:* PS Gallery, Ogunquit, Maine, 87 & 88. *Teaching:* Guest lectr abstract painting, Univ Maine, Orono, 71; vis lectr drawing, oil painting & watercolor, Univ NH, Durham, 73-87; prof visual studies, NH Vocational Technol Col, Stratham, 82-. *Awards:* Third Place Prof, Manchester Art Asn, NH, 70; First Place Oil-Acrylic & Hon Mixed Media, Newbury Port Art Asn, Mass, 71; Graphics Award, York Art Asn, Maine, 71, 73, 76 & 79. *Mem:* Maine State Art Asn (bd dir, 73-74); Copley Soc; York Art Asn (pres, 88-90). *Media:* Watercolor; Pencil. *Publ:* Illusr, Dora Young's Tatting Manuals, 74 & 75; Single's Circle, 74; MCAT: New Medical Admissions Test, Barnes & Nobles, 81. *Dealer:* Kennedy Gallery New York NY; Fry Gallery York ME. *Mailing Add:* NH Community Technol Col Dept Art & Sci 277 R Portsmouth Ave Stratham NH 03885-2297

FEIN, STANLEY
PAINTER, DESIGNER
b Brooklyn, NY, Dec 21, 19. *Study:* Parsons Sch Design; NY Univ. *Work:* NY Univ Collection; pvt collection Dr Timothy Costello, Pres Adelphi Univ; The Bank of NY Collection; Bank of NY; NY Univ. *Comn:* NY Hist (paintings), 71, Cities of NY (paintings), 72, Historic Interiors (paintings), 78 & Cols of NY (paintings), Bank NY. *Exhib:* Phoenix Gallery, 1963; Nat Acad Design, 2000 & 2001; 55 Mercer Gallery, 2005 & 2006. *Pos:* Art dir, Doremus & Co, formerly; creative dir, Pesin Sydney & Bernard, formerly, Stanley Fein, Advertising, currently. *Teaching:* Instr design & color, Pratt Inst, 56-58. *Awards:* Art Dirs Club NY, 56-65; Wall Street Art Asn, 60; Soc Illusrs, 70 & 71. *Mem:* Fedn of Mod Painters & Sculptors. *Media:* Multimedia. *Mailing Add:* 313 DeGraw St Brooklyn NY 11231

FEINBERG, ELEN
PAINTER
b New York, NY, Jan 22, 55. *Study:* Cornell Univ, Ithaca, New York, BFA, 76; Indiana Univ, Bloomington, MFA, 78. *Work:* Los Angeles Co Mus Art; Israel Mus, Jerusalem; Milwaukee Mus, Wis; Univ Calif, Santa Cruz Art Mus; Fresno Art Ctr, Calif; Morgan Guarantee Trust, NY; IBM, Atlanta, Ga; many others. *Exhib:* Solo shows, Roger Ramsay Gallery, Chicago, 87, Mekler Gallery, Los Angeles, 89, Bill Bace Gallery, NY, 90, Mulvane Art Mus, Topeka, Kans, 93, Locus Gallery, St Louis, Mo, 96 & 98, The X Prize, St Louis Sci Ctr, Mo, 96, Impost Gallery, Albuquerque, NMex, 97, Dist Fine Arts, Washington, DC, 99, Ruth Bachotner Gallery, Los Angeles, Calif, 99 & Sarah Morthland Gallery, NY, 99, Plains Art Mus, 2000, Lost City Arts, NY, 2002, District Fine Arts, Washington, DC, 2003, 05, Chiaroscuro Gallery, Santa Fe, 2004, Scottsdale, Ariz, 2005, Price Dewey Contemp, Santa Fe, NM, 2006, and many others; Gallery A, Chicago, 95; Pleasure, Artemisia Gallery, Chicago, 96; Cedar Rapids Mus Art, Iowa, 96; Inferno, Iowa Cedar Rapids Mus Art, 96; The Smallest Show on Earth, Richard Levy Gallery, Albuquerque,NMex, 97; Locust Gallery, St Louis,Mo, 97 & 99; Abuquerque Mus, NMex, 97; Holter Mus Art, Helena, Mont, 97; Ruth Bachofner Gallery, Santa Monica, Calif, 97 & 98; US Dept of State, Art Embassies Prog, Lilongwe, Malawi, 98; Preview/Review, Byran Cohen Gallery Contemp Art, Kansas City, Mo, 98; District Fine Arts Contemp Art, Washington,DC, 98; Remembering Beauty: Am Landscape, South Bend Regional Mus Art, Ind, 98; Albuquerque/Santa Fe, Cedar Rapids Mus Art, 98; Metaphor Contemp Art, Brooklyn, NY, 2002; Johnson Gallery of Fine Arts Mus, Univ NMex, 2003; many others. *Collection Arranged:* Champion Int Corp, Chicago; Shell Oil Co, Houston; Delta Airlines, Orlando; Arbor Group, NY; Madison Financial Svcs, Nashville; OCI Chemical Corp, Shelton, Conn. *Pos:* Artist-in-residence, Montalvo Ctr for Arts, Saratoga, Calif, 81 & 82, Hambidge Ctr for Creative Arts & Scis, Rabun Gap, Ga, Roswell Mus & Art Ctr, NMex, 85-86, 93, MacDowell Colony, 86 & Va Ctr for Creative Arts, Sweet Briar, 98; guest artist, Tamarind Inst, Albuquerque, NMex, 84 & 89; Regents prof art, Dept Art & Art Hist, Univ NMex, 94-97; rep for NMex, Friends of Art & Preservation in Embassies, 2000. *Teaching:* Vis assoc prof, Art Wash Univ, 86-87; lectr, St James Calvier Ctr for Creativitiy, Valletta, Malta, 2001, Int Soc Cult Economists, Rotterdame, The Netherlands, 2002, Oxford Univ, Eng, 2003. *Awards:* Basil H Azkazzi Award, Painting, 97; Bundeskanzleramt Fed Chancellery Fel in Painting, Vienna, Austria, 98; Fulbright Scholar Award, Ger, 2000; Fulbright Scholars Award, Ger, 2000; Fel in painting, St James Cavalier Ctr for Creativity, Valletta, Malta, 2001; Presdl Tchg Fel, Univ NMex, Albuquerque, 2002; fel in painting, Hungarian Multicult Ctr, Balfound; and others. *Bibliog:* B Waterman Peters (auth), New Art Examiner, Chicago, 94; C F Shepley (auth), St Louis Post Dispatch, 96; H Glick (auth), New American Paintings, Open Studio Press, Wellesley, Mass, 97. *Mem:* Col Art Asn Am. *Media:* Painting.

Publ: Profile: Elen Feinberg, Pulsar, Internat Asn Astronomical Artists, 2001; Elen Feinberg, The Independent, Valetta, Malta, 2001; Elen Feinberg, Image and Analog: The Nature of Space, The Inspiration of Astronomical Phenomena: Edition Malta, 2002; Michael Coris, Ad Reinhardt, A Monograph, 2003. *Mailing Add:* 613 Ridge Pl NE Albuquerque NM 87106

FEINBERG, JEAN
PAINTER
b New Rochelle, NY, 1948. *Study:* Skidmore Col, BS (Fine Arts), 70; Hunter Col, MA (Painting, MacDowell Colony Fel), 77. *Work:* Best Products Co; IBM Corp; Amerata-Hess Corp; Rich & Tang Investment Banking, Inc; Peat, Marwich, Main & Co; Weatherspoon Art Gallery; Guess Jeans, Inc; and others. *Exhib:* Cadavre Exquis, Drawing Ctr, NY, 93; Remotion, ES Vandam NY, 94; Sculpture Ctr, Benfit, NY, 94; solo shows, Rosa Esman Gallery, NY, 81, 84, John Davis Gallery, Akron, Ohio & NY, 84, 85, 87, Stux Gallery, 94 & Beth Urdang Gallery, Boston, 94; 10th Anniversary Celebration, Beth Urdang Gallery, Boston, 99; Materializing, Fashion Inst Tech, NY, 99; Yaddo Benefit, NY, 2002; Works on Paper, Fashion Inst Tech Art and Design Faculty, Mus at Fashion Inst Tech, NY, 2002; Finely Drawn: A Recent Gift of Contemp Drawings, Weatherspoon Art Gallery, Greensboro, NC, 2002; and others. *Teaching:* Adj fac, Parsons Sch Design, 80-99, Fashion Inst Technol, 85-; artist-in-residence, MFA Prog, Bard Col, 84-94; vis lectr, artist RI Sch Design, Princeton Univ, Art Inst Chicago, Univ RI, Brown Univ, Kent State Univ, Syracuse Univ, Pratt Inst, Sch Visual Arts, SUNY, Fredonia, 81-97. *Awards:* Nat Endowment Arts, 78, 83 & 89; Edward Albee Found Residence, 79 & 95; Yaddo Fel, 97. *Bibliog:* Barry Schwabsky (auth), Jean Feinberg at John Davis, Arts Mag, 5/87; John Yau (auth), Jean Feinberg, Victoria Munroe Gallery, Artforum, 3/90; Vivien Raynor (auth), For a Sophisticated Audience, NY Times, 9/27/92; Jeanette Fintz (auth), Departures, Arrivals, Pit Stops- Three Artists at ADD Gallery, The Artful Mind, 1-2/03; D. Dominick Lombardi (auth), Keeping It Simple, in Color and Form, NY Times, 2/16/03; and others. *Media:* Oil, Miscellaneous Media. *Publ:* Heresies Mag, winter 78; 54 Pages, New York, 78; Roof X, A Quarterly Journal of Poetry, summer 79. *Mailing Add:* 10 Leonard St New York NY 10013-2962

FEINGOLD, KEN
ARTIST
Study: Studied, Antioch Col, 70—76; Studied, Calif Instit of Arts. *Work:* One-man shows incl Whitney Mus, 79, exhibs incl Signs, The New Mus Contemp Art, 85, Contemp Art in Context, Mus Mod Art, 88, Between Word and Image, 93, 2002 Biennial Exhib, Whitney Mus Am Art, 2002, Art, Lies, and Videotape: Exposing Performance, Tate Liverpool, 2004, digital works, Subject with Four Footnotes, 1975, Jimmy Charlie Jimmy, 1992, Eros and Thanatos at Sea, 2004; auth: New Screen Media: Cinema/Art/Narrative, 2002. *Exhib:* One man shows incl Whitney Mus, 79; Exhibs incl Signs, The New Mus Contemp Art, 85; Contemp Art in Context, Mus Art, 88; Between Word and Image, 93, 2002; Biennial Exhib, Whitney Mus, Am Art, 2002; Art, Lies and Videotape: Exposing Performance, Tate Liverpool, 2004; digital works, Subject with Four Footnotes, 75; Jimmy Chrlie Jimmy, 92; Eros and Thanatos at Sea, 2004; auth: New Screen Media: Cinema/Art/Narrative, 2002; Recipient Bonn Videonalle, Videonale-Preis, 92; fel Guggenheim Mem Found, 2004; grantee NEA, 79, NY Found for Arts, 88, Rockefeller Found; Media Arts fel, 2003. *Pos:* Assoc prof fine arts Minneapolis Col Art & Design, 77-85; adj assoc prof, Princeton Univ, Visual Arts Prog 89-94, Cooper Union Sch of Arts, 1993-94; prof computer art Sch Visual Arts, NY, 1993-98; Vis artist Bard Col, 2001; guest fac The Royal Univ Col Fine Arts, Stockholm, 2002; Adj assoc prof Princeton Univ; Visual Arts Prog, 89-94; Cooper Union Sch of Arts, 93-94; prof computer art sch; Visual Arts NYC, 93-98; Vis Arts Bard Col, 2001; guest fac, The Royal Univ Col Fine Arts, Stockholm, 2002. *Awards:* Recipient Bonn Videonalle, Videonale-Preis, 1992; fel Guggenheim Mem Found, 2004; grantee Nat Educ Assoc, 79, NY Found for Arts, 88, Rockefeller Found Media Arts Fel, 2003. *Mailing Add:* 140 Fifth Ave New York NY 10011

FEININGER, T LUX
PAINTER, WRITER
b Berlin, Ger, June 11, 1910; US citizen. *Study:* Bauhaus, Dessau, Ger, 26-32; stage design with Oskar Schlemmer; also with Paul Klee, W Kandinsky & Josef Albers, dipl, 29; Inst Fine Arts, NY Univ, with Salmony, Lopez-Rey, Cook & Friedlaender, 46-47. *Work:* Mus Mod Art, NY; Busch-Reisinger Mus & Fogg Art Mus, Harvard Univ; Altonaer Mus, Hamburg, Ger. *Exhib:* Am Realists and Magic Realists, Mus Mod Art, NY, 43; Revolution and Tradition in Modern Am Art, Brooklyn Mus, 51; Whitney Mus Am Art Ann, NY, 51; Four Am Painters, Mass Inst Technol, 54; Retrospective, Busch-Reisinger Mus, 62; Wheaton Col, 73; Wamsutta Club, New Bedford, Mass, 74; Photographs of the 20's & 30's, Prakapas Gallery, NY, 80; Gallery on the Green, (with essay), Lexington, Mass, 86, 88, 90 & 92; Achim Mueller Fine Art Gallery, NY, 95; retrospective Mus Moritzburg, Halle, Ger, 98; retrospective Altona Mus, Hamburg, Ger, 98-99. *Teaching:* Instr design, Sarah Lawrence Col, 50-52; lectr drawing & painting, Harvard Univ, 53-62; instr, Boston Fine Arts Mus Sch, 62-75; retired. *Awards:* Hon Mention, Arts & Crafts Club, New Orleans, 48; Hon Mention, Cambridge Art Asn, 63. *Bibliog:* Thomas B Hess (auth), Profile, Art News, 2/47; Feininger family, Life Mag, 11/51; E Bitterman (auth), Art in modern architecture, Van Nostrand Reinhold, 52. *Mem:* Westport Art Group. *Publ:* Auth, The Bauhaus: Evolution of an idea, Criticism, summer 60; Lyonel Feininger: City at the edge of the world, Praeger, 65; Address on modern art, Harvard Art Rev, 66; The heritage of Lyonel Feininger, Am-Ger Rev, 66. *Mailing Add:* Achim Moeller Fine Art 36 East 64th St New York NY 10021

FEINMAN, STEPHEN E
DEALER, PUBLISHER
b New York, NY, Sept 29, 32. *Collection Arranged:* cur Andre Masson, Johnny Friedlander, Miljenko Bengez, Felix Sherman, Nick Kosciuk. *Pos:* Pres, Gary Arts Ltd, 65-72; pres, Multiple Impressions Ltd, 72-93; Pres, S E Feinman Fine Arts Ltd, 93-; pres, GSL Arts Corp, 2004. *Mem:* Fine Arts Retail Trade Syst; Panther Org. *Specialty:* Twentieth Century European and American prints, drawings and paintings. *Collection:* Andre Masson, Johnny Friedlander

FEINSTEIN, ROCHELLE H
PAINTER, PRINTMAKER
Study: Pratt Inst, BFA, 75; Univ Minn, MFA, 78. *Work:* Mus Mod Art, NY; Libr Cong, Washington, DC. *Exhib:* Solo shows include Emily Sorkin Gallery, 87, 89, David Beitzel Gallery, 93, Max Protetch Gallery, NY, 94, Paintings, Halsey Gallery, Charleston, NC, 95, Copycats, BillMaynes Gallery, NY, 96, The Wonderfuls, Jersey City Mus, NJ, 96, Men, Women and Children, Max Protetch Gallery, 96, Pictures, Ten in One Gallery, NY, 2002; group shows include Exit Art, NY, 86; To Make the Visible Seen, Studio Sch, NY, 87; The Debate on Abstraction: The Persistance of Painting, Hunter Col, NY, 89; The Painting Project, 91; Abstraction, Schmidt Contemp, St Louis, 92; Works on Paper/Faculty, Yale Univ Sch Art, 95; Just What Do You Think You're Doing, Dave? Williamsburg Art & Historical Soc, NY, 97; The Drawing File, Pieroji, 2000; The Gasworks, London, 97; Conversation, Art Resources Transfer, NY, 99; Liste Art Fair, Basel, Switzerland, 2002; A More Perfect Union, Max Fish, NY, 2004; Nat Acad Mus, NY City, 2006. *Pos:* Pub Arts Proj, CETA/NY Artists Prog, 78-79. *Teaching:* Instr, Bennington Col, 79-94; assoc prof painting & printmaking, Yale Univ, Conn, 94-98, prof painting & printmaking, 98-. *Awards:* Nat Endowment Arts Grant, 90; Joan Mitchell Found Grant, 94; John Simon Guggenheim Mem Found Painting Fel, 96; Biennial Competition, Louis Comfort Tiffany Found, 97; Found Contemp Performance Art Grant, 99; Teseque Found Grant, 2000; Civitella Raineri Residency, 2001; Marie Walsh Sharpe Found, 2002; Giverny Artists Residency, 2003. *Dealer:* Max Protech Gallery 511 W 22nd St New York NY 10011. *Mailing Add:* c/o Max Protetch Gallery 511 W 22nd St New York NY 10011-1109

FEIST, HAROLD E
PAINTER, SCULPTOR
b San Angelo, Tex, 45. *Study:* Univ Ill, Champaign-Urbana, BFA, 67; Col Art, Md Inst, MFA, 69. *Work:* Mus Fine Arts, Boston; Edmonton Art Gallery, Alta; Art Gallery Hamilton, Ont; Mendel Art Gallery, Saskatoon, Sask; Mem Univ Newfoundland Arts & Cult Ctr. *Exhib:* 25 Canadians, Birmingham Arts Festival, Ala, 79; The New Generation: A Curator's Choice, Andre Emmerich Gallery & traveling, 80-82; The Hines Collection, Univ Place, Boston, 84; Abstraction X Four, Can House, Can High Comn, London, toured Europe, 85; Toronto 3, Eva Cohon Gallery, Highland Park, Ill, 86; Curator's Choice: A Ten Yr Retrospective--Feist, Drapell, Sutton, Buschlen-Mowatt Gallery, Vancouver, 88; solo exhibs, Virginia Christopher Gallery, Calgary, 82 & 90, Gallery One, Toronto, 82-91, Galerie Elca London, Montreal, 83-86, 88 & 90, Buschlen-Mowatt Fine Art, Vancouver, 84 & 90, Eva Cohon Galleries, Chicago & Highland Park, Ill, 88, Agnes Etherington Art Centre, Queens Univ, Kingston, Ont, 88-90 & Kathleen Laverty Gallery, Edmonton, 90. *Teaching:* Mem fac, Alta Col Art, Calgary, 68-74, Univ Saskatchewan, Regina, 74-75 & Mt Allison Univ, Sackville, NB, 75-78, Univ Guelph, Ont, 78-80, Sheridan Col, Brampton, Ont, 79-80. *Bibliog:* Gary Michael Dault (auth), Paint, Can Art, fall 84; Karen Wilkin (auth), Harold Feist: Genesis of an image, Artpost, spring 88; Karen Wilkin (auth), Harold Feist: Genesis of an Image (exhib catalog), Agnes Etherington Art Centre exhib, 88. *Media:* Acrylic on Canvas; Acrylic Sheet, Wood. *Dealer:* Gallery One 121 Scollard St Toronto ON; Galerie Elca London Montreal. *Mailing Add:* 374 Delaware Ave Toronto ON M6H 2T8 Canada

FEKETE, BRIAN
PAINTER
b Dearborn, Mich, June 10, 55. *Study:* Wayne State Univ, BFA, 79, Alumni Teaching Fel, 90, Grad Prof Scholar, 91, MFA, 92. *Work:* Miller, Canfield, Paddock & Stone, Detroit Inst Arts, Detroit, Mich; Mr & Mrs S Brooks Barron, Southfield, Mich; Mr & Mrs Frank Piku, Mich; Robert Kobetis & Patricia Miller, Detroit, Mich; and others. *Exhib:* Solo-exhibs, Detroit Inst Arts Sales Gallery, 83, Broadway Gallery, Detroit, 88; Viewpoint 84-Out of Square, Cranbrook Acad Art, 84; Ann Printmaking Exhib, Ann Arbor Art Asn, 94; Mich Fine Arts Competition, Birmingham-Bloomfield Art Asn, 94; 8th Ann Celebrate Mich Artists, Paint Creek Ctr Arts, 94; Interventions, Detroit Inst Arts, 95; and many others. *Teaching:* Part-time instr painting, Wayne State Univ, 90-91 & 94. *Awards:* Jurors Award Excellence, Mich Fine Arts Competiton, Birmingham-Bloomfield Art Asn, 89; Scholar, Detroit Artists Market, 91; Best in Show, Mich Fine Arts Competition, Birmingham-Bloomfield Art Asn, 94. *Bibliog:* Joy Hakanson Colby (auth), Four ways that art lovers can spend the weekend, Detroit News, 10/88; Marsha Miro (auth), Juror makes Michigan fine arts competition a fine, personal show, Detroit Free Press, 5/1/94; Marsha Miro (auth), Defining Michigan through its artists, Detroit Free Press, 9/4/94. *Mem:* Col Art Asn. *Media:* Oil. *Publ:* Annual Guide to Galleries, Museums, Artists, Art in Am, 86 & 87; Wayne State Univ in Michigan, Alumni Exhib, 86; Other Space: An Exhibition of Recent Art Work, Detroit Artist Market, 86; Choices: Twenty Painters from the Midwest, Minneapolis Col Art & Design; Art for Life, 90

FELD, AUGUSTA
PAINTER, PRINTMAKER
b Philadelphia, Pa, Apr 18, 19. *Study:* Fleisher Art Mem & Music Settlement Sch, Philadelphia; Philadelphia Col Art, BA; Tyler Sch Fine Arts, Temple Univ; Pa Acad Fine Arts, MA. *Work:* Acad Fine Arts, Hahnemann Hosp, Sch Dist Permanent Collection, Woodmere Art Mus, Philadelphia; Marple-New Town Libr, Broomall, Pa;

Widerner Col, Chester, Pa; and others. *Comn:* Tree of Life (mural of wood inlays, gold paint and vinyl, with Joseph Brahim), Delaware Co Community Ctr, Springfield, Pa, 64; dance mural (oil painting), Melita Dance Studio, Philadelphia, 68; also portraits & murals comn by individuals. *Exhib:* Woodmere Art Mus, 61-88; Artist Equity Asn, Philadelphia, 74; Philadelphia Art Alliance, 74-75; Philadelphia Civic Ctr, 74 & 80; Cheltenham Art Ctr, Pa, 79-88; Abington Art Ctr, Jenkintown, Pa, 79-88; Beaver Col, Glenside, Pa, 84-85; Philips Mill Art Ctr, New Hope, Pa, 87-88; and others. *Pos:* Dir art, Hillview-Trout Nursery Sch, Broomall, Pa, 61-; art coordr, Abington Art Ctr, Jenkintown, 79-87. *Teaching:* Instr art, Philadelphia Sch Dist, 54-65, Wallingford Art Ctr, Pa, 63-64 & Haverford, Pa, 63-65. *Awards:* First Prize for oils, Atlantic City C of C, 68; First Prize, print exhib, Cheltenham Art Ctr, 71; First Prize in Portraiture, La Lomita Mus, Mission, Tex, 79; Best in Show, Perkiomen Valley Art Ctr, 84; First Prize in Oil Painting, Cheltenham Art Ctr, 85; Painting Award, Phillips Mill Art Exhib, New Hope, Pa, 88; First Prize (graphics), Doylestown Art Ctr, 90. *Bibliog:* Article, La Rev Mod, 64. *Mem:* Philadelphia Watercolor Soc; Philadelphia Watercolor Club; Doylestown Art League; Woodmere Art Mus; fel Pa Acad Art. *Media:* All Media. *Mailing Add:* 102 Berlin-New Freedom Rd Berlin NJ 08009

FELD, MARIAN PARRY See Parry, Marian

FELD, STUART P
DEALER
b Passaic, NJ, 35. *Study:* Princeton Univ, AB, 57; Harvard Univ, AM, 58. *Exhib:* Three Centuries of Am Painting, 65, 200 Yrs of Watercolor Painting in Am, 66, Metrop Mus Art; Am Paintings & Historical Prints from the Middendorf Collection, Metrop Mus Art & Baltimore Mus Art, 67; Neo-Classicism in Am Inspiration and Innovation 1910-1840 (auth, catalog), Hirschl & Adler Galleries, NY, 91; Boston in the Age of Neo-Classicism 1810-1840 (auth, catalog), Hirschl & Adler Galleries, NY, 99; Of the Newest Fashion Masterpieces of Am Neo-Classical Decorative Arts (auth with Elizabeth Feld, catalog), Hirschl & Adler Galleries, NY, 2001; In Piontal Style: The Gothic Revival in America, 1800-1860 (auth with Elizabeth Feid), Hirschland Adler Galleries, NY, 2006. *Pos:* Var curatorial positions leading to assoc cur-in-charge, Dept Am Painting & Sculpture, Metrop Mus Art, 61-67. *Awards:* Bryant fel, Metrop Mus Art, NY. *Mem:* Am Antiquarian Soc. *Specialty:* American and European art of 18th, 19th and 20th centuries. *Publ:* Coauth (with Albert Ten Eyck Gardner), American Paintings: Painters Born by 1815 (Catalogue of the Permanent Collection of the Metropolitan Mus of Art), Vol 1, NY Graphic Soc, 65; and more than fifty exhibition catalogues and articles about American paintings, decorative arts, and architecture. *Dealer:* Hirschl & Adler Galleries 21 E 70th St New York NY 10021. *Mailing Add:* Hirschl & Adler Galleries Inc 21 E 70th St New York NY 10021

FELDHAUS, PAUL A
EDUCATOR, PRINTMAKER
b Cincinnati, Ohio, July 19, 1926. *Study:* Cincinnati Art Mus; Miami Univ, Oxford, Ohio, BFA, 50; Bradley Univ, Peoria, Ill, MA, 52; study with Edwin Fulwider & Ernest Freed, printmakers. *Work:* Carroll Reece Mus, ETenn State Univ; Friends Meeting House, Boston, Mass; Montgomery Mus Fine Arts, Ala; Mobile Pub Lbir, Ala; Ford Times Col; Achenbach Found, San Francisco; Turner Print Gallery, CSU, Chico; Art Gallery, Calif State Poly Univ, Pomona; Chico Art Center, Calif; and others. *Comn:* Mural, Mastin Sch Nursing, Mobile, Ala, 66; mural, Woman's Clinic, Mobile, Ala, 67; and others. *Exhib:* Int Biennial Graphic Art, Mus Mod Art, Ljubljana, Yugoslavia, 75; Int Exhib Graphic Art, Frechen, WGer, 76; Seventh Premio Int Biella of Printmaking, Italy, 76; US Embassy Traveling Exhib, Yugoslavia, 83; Crocker-Kingsley Exhib, Sacramento, 83; one-man print exhib, Chico Art Ctr, Calif, 89; US-UK Print Connections traveling exhib, Eng, 89-90; Invitational Woodcut Print show, Goldenwest Coll, Huntington Beach, Calif, 89; and others. *Teaching:* Assoc prof art, Spring Hill Col, Mobile, Ala, 52-71; prof printmaking & drawing & coordr printmaking dept, Calif State Univ, Chico, 71-91, prof emer, 91-. *Awards:* First Place Purchase Award, Dauphin Island Nat Competition, 65, 66, 68 & 70; First Place Graphics, Mobile Watercolor & Graphic Arts Show, 69; Purchase prize, Ink & Clay XVI, Cal State Poly, Pomona, 90; Meritorious Performance Award, Calif State Univ, Chico, 88; Outstanding Artist Award in Chico, 96; designated Nat Treasure of Chico, 99. *Mem:* Col Art Asn; Graphics Soc; Ala Art League (pres, 69-70); Calif Soc Printmakers; Los Angeles Printmaking Soc; Print Consortium. *Media:* Lithography, Engraving, Gouache. *Publ:* Univ J, CSU, Chico woodcut or linocut included in every publ 85-91 with commendation & award, 90. *Dealer:* Marilyn Sousa Vagabond Rose 236 Main St Chico CA 95926. *Mailing Add:* 310 Legion Ave Chico CA 95926-4517

FELDMAN, ALINE M
PRINTMAKER, PAINTER
b Leavenworth, Kans, May 11, 28. *Study:* Washington Univ, St Louis, Mo, with Werner Drewes, 46-49; Indiana Univ, BS, 51; Studied woodcut & sumi painting with Unichi Hiratsuka, 62. *Work:* Nat Mus Am Art, Washington, DC; Worcester Art Mus, Mass; McNay Art Mus, San Antonio, Tex; Contemp Mus, Honolulu, Hawaii; UCLA Art Mus, Los Angeles. *Comn:* woodcut mural panel, Mutual of NY, Purchase, NY, 85; woodcut murals, Hyatt Regency Hotel, Kauai, Hawaii, 90. *Exhib:* 22nd Area Exhib Works on Paper, Corcoran Gallery of Art, Washington, DC, 80; Nat Print & Drawing Exhib, Haggin Mus, Stockton, Calif, 85; Earth Views, Nat Air & Space Mus, Washington DC 86; Grabadores USA, Museo de Arte Moderno, Buenos Aires, 87; A Graphic Muse, Santa Barbara Art Mus, Calif, 87-88; New Acquisitions, Nat Mus Am Art, Washington DC, 88; Press Work: Art of Am Printmakers, Nat Mus Women Arts, Washington DC, 91; A World of Maps, Anchorage Mus Hist & Art, Alaska, 94-95. *Awards:* Purchase Prize, Duxbury Art Mus, Mass, 97; Woodcut Award, World Print Festival, 98; Veloric Award, Cynthia & Micheal Veloric, 99. *Bibliog:* Capital Edition, A Cut Above, CBS-TV, 4/29/90; Various art reviews in Washington Post. *Mem:* Southern Graphics Coun; Boston Printmakers; Los Angeles Print Soc; Washington Print Club; Mid-America Print Coun. *Media:* Woodcut; Pastel. *Dealer:* Mary Ryan Gallery 24 W 57th St New York NY 10019; Marsha Mateyka Gallery 2012 R Street NW Washington DC 20009; Locus Gallery 7700 Forsyth Blvd St Louis MO 63105. *Mailing Add:* 5013 Eliots Oak Rd Columbia MD 21044

FELDMAN, ARTHUR MITCHELL
MUSEUM DIRECTOR, ART AND ANTIQUES DEALER
b Philadelphia, Pa, Dec 22, 42. *Study:* Villanova Univ, BS, 64; Univ Pa with George Tatum; Univ Mo, MA(art hist & archaeol), 70. *Pos:* Vis cur, Victoria & Albert Mus, London, Eng, 70-71; assoc cur & asst adminr, Renwick Gallery, Smithsonian Inst, Washington, DC, 71-73; dir, Spertus Mus of Judaica, 73-85; exec dir, Jewish Mus Chicago, 86-; pres, Arthur M Feldman Gallery, Highland Park, 86-. *Teaching:* Lectr, Col Lake Co, 86-92. *Specialty:* antique & contemporary judaica. *Publ:* Auth, Jewish Artists of the 20th Century, 75, The Hill Page Collection, 75, The Jews of Yemen, 76 & Faith and Form: Synagog Architecture of Illinois, 76, Spertus Col Press; The Sons of Zebulan: Jewish Maritime History, 79. *Mailing Add:* 667 Central Ave Ste 1 Highland Park IL 60035-5620

FELDMAN, BELLA
SCULPTOR, EDUCATOR
b New York, NY. *Study:* Queens Col, City Univ New York, BA; Calif Col Arts & Crafts; Calif State Univ, San Jose, MA. *Work:* Oakland Mus, Calif; Berkeley Art Mus, Univ Calif. *Comn:* Sculptures, Marshal Tulin, Hydronautics Inc, Silver Spring, Md, 64, Sasaki-Walker Landscape Architects, Newport Shopping Ctr, Newport Beach, Calif, 65, Royston Hanamoto Landscape Architects, Potrero Park, Richmond, Calif, 66 & Fountain Fed Home Loan Bank, San Francisco, Calif, 90. *Exhib:* Palace Legion Honor, San Francisco, 61; Summer Series, San Francisco Mus, 64; San Francisco Art Inst, 75; San Jose Mus Art, 82; Jan Baum Gallery, 2000; Bryan Ohno Gallery, Seattle, WA, 2004; Habatat Gallery, Chicago, IL War Toys Redux, Aug-Oct, 2004. *Pos:* Cult specialist, US Info Agency to Uganda, 90. *Teaching:* Prof, Calif Col Arts & Crafts, 64-, grad dir, 75-79, prof emer, 2000; lectr art, Makerere Univ Col, Fine Art Sch, Uganda, 68-70. *Awards:* Calif Mus Trustees Award, 67; First Prize, San Francisco Women Artists, 67; E L Cabot Trust Fund Award, Harvard Univ, 75; Nat Endowment Arts Grant, 86-87; Florsheim Grant, 96. *Bibliog:* Gloria Frym (ed), Second Stories, Chronicle Bks; Kate Regan (auth), Possibility and paradox, Mus of Calif Mag, 9/87 & 10/87. *Mem:* Women's Caucus Art; Committee-West, East Bay; Col Art Asn. *Media:* Welded Medal, Cast Medal, Glass. *Dealer:* Jan Baum Gallery, 170 S La Brea, Los Angeles, 90036; Habatat Gallery, 222 W Superior St, Chicago, 60610; Bryan Ohno Gallery, Seattle, WA; Buchlen Mowatt Gallery, Palm Desert. *Mailing Add:* 12 Summit Ln Berkeley CA 94708

FELDMAN, EDMUND BURKE
EDUCATOR, CRITIC
b Bayonne, NJ, May 6, 24. *Study:* Newark Sch Fine & Indust Arts, with John R Grabach & Emile Alexay, dipl, 41; Syracuse Univ, BFA, 49; Univ Calif, Los Angeles, with Karl With, Stanton MacDonald Wright & Abraham Kaplan, MA(art hist), 51; Columbia Univ, with Lyman Bryson & George Counts, EdD, 53. *Pos:* Cur paintings & sculpture, Newark Mus, 53. *Teaching:* Assoc prof art, Livingston State Col, 53-56; assoc prof painting, sculpture & design, Carnegie-Mellon Univ, 56-60; chmn art div, State Univ NY Col New Paltz, 60-66; prof art, Ohio State Univ, summer 66; prof art, Univ Ga, 66-92; vis prof, Univ Calif, Berkeley, winter 74. *Awards:* Named Alumni Found Distinguished Prof Art, Univ Ga, 73. *Mem:* Kappa Pi; Col Art Asn Am; Nat Art Educ Asn (pres-elect, 79-81 & pres, 81-83). *Res:* Art history and criticism. *Interests:* Visual literacy. *Publ:* Auth, Art as Image and Idea, 67, Becoming Human Through Art, 70, Thinking About Art, 85 & Practical Art Criticism, 94, Prentice-Hall; Varieties of Visual Experience, Prentice-Hall & Abrams, 72, second ed, 81, third ed, 87, fourth ed, 93; The Artist: A Social History, 95; Philosophy of Art Education, 96. *Mailing Add:* 140 Chinquapin Pl Athens GA 30605

FELDMAN, FRANKLIN
PRINTMAKER, WRITER
b New York, NY, 27. *Study:* Columbia Law Sch, LLB, 51; Art Students League (study with Howard Trafton, Ivan Olinsky & Byron Browne); New Sch Soc Res, Parsons Sch Des (study with John Ross & Herman Zaage). *Work:* Princeton Univ, Rare Book Libr; Brown Univ, John Hay Libr; Dance Collection, NY Publ Libr; Harvard Univ, The Houghton Libr; Yale Univ, Sterling Mem Libr; British Mus; Victoria & Albert Mus. *Exhib:* Silvermine, Prints Int, 90; Int Miniature Show, 90; Contemp Am Printmakers, Thomas J Walsh Gallery, Fairfield Univ, 94; East/West Printmakers Show, 96; Nat Print Show, Club Albany Exhib, 98. *Pos:* vis artist, The Am Acad in Rome, 2006. *Teaching:* Lectr law, Columbia Law Sch, 1979-2002. *Awards:* Fel, Yaddo, Saratoga Springs, NY, 83; Ledyard Cogsworth Purchase Prize, Nat Print Show, Print Club Albany, 98. *Mem:* Int Found Art Res (pres & dir 71-96); Grolier Club; Century Asn; Soc Am Graphic Arts. *Media:* Etching, Lithography, Transferred Prints. *Res:* Legal aspects of art. *Publ:* Coauth, Art Works: Law, Policy, Practice, Practising Law Inst, 74; Art Law, Little, Brown & Co, 86; also, various articles in legal publications relating to art & law. *Mailing Add:* 15 W 81st St New York NY 10024

FELDMAN, JOEL BENET
PRINTMAKER, EDUCATOR
b Richmond, Va, Dec 9, 42. *Study:* Carnegie Inst Technol, with Robert Gardner, BFA, 65; Ind Univ, with Rudy Pozzati & Roy Sieber, MFA, 67. *Work:* Mary & Leigh Block Gallery, Northwestern Univ, Evanston, Ill; New York Pub Libr Print Collection; Brooklyn Mus, NY; Grunwald Collection, Univ Calif, Los Angeles; Spertus Mus, Chicago. *Exhib:* Under Her Brothers Eyes, Contemp Arts Ctr, New Orleans, 88; Mid Am Print Coun Figurature Show, Purdue Univ Gallery, West Lafayette, Ind, 93; 69th

Int Competition, Print Club, Philadelphia, 94; one-person show, Ill State Mus, 94 & Forum Continuing Art, St Louis, 94. *Teaching:* Instr printmaking, Univ Ga, Athens, 67-70; vis instr, Ohio Univ, Athens, 72-73; prof, Southern Ill Univ, Carbondale, 73-. *Awards:* Ill Arts Coun Visual Arts Fel, 91-92; Arts Midwest Visual Arts Fel, Nat Endowment Arts, 92-93; Visual Arts Fel, Nat Endowment Arts, 93-94. *Bibliog:* Michael Bulka (auth), Review, Art in Am, 4/91; Hamza Walker (auth), Review, New Art Examiner, summer 93. *Mem:* Mid Am Print Coun; Paint Club Ctr Prints & Photographs. *Media:* Woodcut, Drawing. *Dealer:* R Duane Reed Gallery 1 N Taylor St Louis MO 63108; SK Josefsberg 403 NW Eleventh Ave Portland OR 97209. *Mailing Add:* 1925 Brown Pl Murphysboro IL 62966

FELDMAN, KAYWIN
MUSEUM DIRECTOR, CURATOR
Study: Univ Mich, BA; Univ London, MA in Mus mgt and art hist. *Pos:* Educational cur, British Mus Art; dir, Fresno Metrop Mus Art, Hist and Sci, Calif, 1996-1999, Memphis Brooks Mus Art, Tenn, 1999-. *Awards:* Recipient Central Calif Excellence in Bus award, 1996. *Mailing Add:* Memphis Brooks Museum of Art Overton Park 1934 Poplar Ave Memphis TN 38104

FELDMAN, ROGER LAWRENCE
SCULPTOR
b Spokane, Wash, Nov 19, 49; US citizen. *Study:* Univ Wash, Seattle, BA, 72; Fuller Theological Seminary, 72-73; Regent Col, Vancouver, BC, studied with Hans Rookmaaker, 77; Claremont Grad Univ, Calif, MFA, 77. *Work:* Concordia Univ, Mequon, Wis & Irvine, Calif, 1999; Union Univ, Jackson, Tenn, 2000; George Fox Univ, Newberg, Ore, 2001; Seattle Pacific Univ, Wash, 2002; Barrington Ctr for Arts, Gordon Col, Wenham, Mass, 2002. *Comn:* Bronze sculpture, East Hill Community Ctr, Gresham, Oregon, 79-80; Site spec steel sculpture, Wash State Arts Comn Renton Vocational Tech Inst, Renton, 87-89; Wrtie Stuff, Margery Wheaton, Pasadena, Calif, 99. *Exhib:* Cornerstone, Bushnell, Ill, 96; Gallery W, Sacramento, 96; Roberts Wesley Col, Rochester, NY, 97; Bethel Col, Ind, 98; Tacoma Art Mus, Wash, 04; Rock Suyama Space Mus, 05; Mittersill, Austria, 05. *Teaching:* Prof sculpture & design, Biola Univ, La Mirada, Calif, 89-2000, Seattle Pacific Univ, Wash, 2000-. *Awards:* Fel, Nat Endowment Arts, 86; Fel, Connemara Found, 91; Artist Residency, Yaddo, Saratoga Springs, NY, 93. *Bibliog:* Karen Mulder (auth), The art of true inquiry, a profile of Roger Feldman, Mars Hill Rev, winter/spring, 96; Cathy Curtis (auth), To have and have not, Los Angeles Times, 4/97; Theodore Prescott (auth), Nature and nature's God in late twentieth century American art, Cresset, 98; Theodore Prescott, David Morgan, Terrence Dempsey & Z Ori Soltes (coauths), Like a prayer: A Jewish and Christian presence in contemporary art, Tryon Ctr for Visual Art, Charlotte, NC, 2001; Sheila Farr (auth), How Spaces we Live in Come to Inhabit us, The Seattle Times, 04. *Mem:* Christians in Visual Arts; Int Sculpture Ctr; Seattle Art Mus. *Media:* Metal, Welded; Wood, Concrete. *Publ:* auth, Off-Centered Consequences,Image: J of Arts & Religion, 2001. *Mailing Add:* Seattle Pacific Univ 3307 3rd Ave W Seattle WA 98119

FELDMAN, RONALD
DEALER
Study: Syracuse Univ, BA, 59; NY Univ, JD, 62. *Pos:* Co-owner & founder, Ronald Feldman Gallery, NY, 71-; overview panel, Nat Endowment for Arts, 83, critics sem, 83, panelist Art Bank, 79; adv bd, Res Ctr Arts & Culture, Columbia Univ, 85-; bd dir, Friends of List Art Ctr, Brown Univ, 85-90, Exit Art, NY, 87- & Creative Capital Found, 99-,; dealer's comt for ann benefit auction, New Mus, NY, 89-92, chmn, 89; artist's prize panel, Brandeis Univ, Waltham, Mass, 89; co-chmn, Artists for Freedom of Expression, 90-; mem nat coun, Washington Univ, Sch Fine Arts, St Louis, Mo, 93-. *Teaching:* Adj prof art hist, Brown Univ, 91. *Awards:* Larry Award, Aldrich Mus Contemp Art, Ridgefield, Conn, 97. *Bibliog:* Robert Atkins (auth), Scene and Heart, Village Voice, 4/12/94; Carol Vogel (auth), Are Happy Days Here Again? Art World Prepares for a Test, NY Times, 4/29/94; Barbara A MacAdam (auth), Close to Bill, ARTnews, 1/97. *Mem:* Nat Coun Arts; Art Dealers Asn Am (vpres 94-97, bd dir, 91-97); Social Venture Network; Bus for Social Responsibility. *Specialty:* Contemporary artists; European and American masters, painting, sculpture and prints from Impressionism forward. *Mailing Add:* 31 Mercer New York NY 10013

FELDMAN, WALTER (SIDNEY)
PAINTER, PRINTMAKER
b Lynn, Mass, Mar 23, 25. *Study:* Yale Univ Sch Fine Arts, BFA, 50, Sch Design, MFA, 51; also with W de Kooning, Stuart Davis & Josef Albers. *Hon Degrees:* Brown Univ, Hon MA, 56. *Work:* Addison Gallery Am Art, Andover, Mass; Metrop Mus Art, NY; Fogg Art Mus, Cambridge, Mass; Israel Mus, Jerusalem; Mus Mod Art, NY; Bezalel Nat Mus; Decordova & Dana Mus; Gulbenkian Found, Lisbon, Portugal; Victoria & Albert Mus, London; and many others. *Comn:* Color woodcut, Int Graphic Arts Soc, 57; mosaic pavements, Temple Beth-El, Providence, RI, 57; stained glass windows, Sugarman Mem Chapel, Providence, RI, 61; World's Fair poster, IBM Corp, 63; Quezalcoatl (mural), Pembroke Col, Brown Univ, 66; 32 panel mural, Temple Emanu-El, Providence, RI, 68; commemorative silver plate, Gorham Silver Co, 73; mosaic mural, Temple Beth-El, Providence, RI, 99; portrait, Barnaby Keeny; portrait, Robert Warren Morse. *Exhib:* Am Watercolors, Drawings and Prints, Metrop Mus Art, 52; Recent Drawings USA, Mus Mod Art, NY, 55; Mostra Int, Milan, Italy, 57; 26th Biennial, Corcoran Gallery, Washington, DC, 59; Nat Inst Arts & Lett, NY, 61; one-man show, Hopkins Ctr, Dartmouth Col, 78. *Pos:* Dir, Brown/Ziggurat Press, 90. *Teaching:* Instr painting & design, Yale Univ Sch Design, 50-53; prof painting & printmaking, Brown Univ, 53-; vis prof drawing, Harvard Univ, 68; artist in residence, Hopkins Ctr, Dartmouth Col, 78; John Hay prof bibliography, Brown Univ, 93-. *Awards:* Metrop Mus Art Award, 52; Gold Medal, Mostra Int, Milan, Italy, 57; First Painting Award, Boston Arts Festival, Mass, 64; Governor's Award for Art, RI, 80. *Bibliog:* G Y Loveridge (auth), Providence practitioner of ancient art, The Rhode Islander, 4/25/54; Michael Forster (auth), The color of Mexico is black, Nivel 41, German P Garcia (Mexico City), 5/25/62; Jane Shelton (auth), Walter Feldman, Harvard Art Rev, spring 66. *Mem:* Am Color Print Soc. *Media:* All. *Publ:* Coauth (with J Schevill), Ghost Names, Ghost Numbers (woodcuts), Handmade Bks. *Dealer:* Joshua Heller Washington DC; Bromer Booksellers Boston MA. *Mailing Add:* 107 Benevolent St Providence RI 02906-3154

FELGUEREZ, MANUEL
PAINTER, SCULPTOR
b Zacatecas, Mex, Dec 12, 28. *Study:* Academia de la Grande Chaumier, with Ossip Zadkine, Paris, 49-50. *Work:* Museo de Arte Moderno, Mex; Museo Tamayo, Mex; Museo Espanol de Arte Contemporaneo, Madrid; Museo de Arte, San Antonion, Tex; Biblioteca Miguel Arango, Bogota, Colombia. *Comn:* Mural de Hierro, Cine Diana, Mexico City, 61; escultura, Espacio Escultorico UNAM, Mexico City, 78; mural policromado, Centro Cult Alfa, Monterrey, NL Mex, 82; El Cerro Nultivara (escultura), Gobierno de Colombia, Medellin, Colombia, 83; escultura metal policromado y vidrio, Gobierno de Corea, Seoul, Korea, 88. *Exhib:* Troix Artistes Mexicains d'Aujourd'hui, Palais de Beaux Arts, Bruselas, Belgica, 75; XIII Bienal de Sao Paulo, Brazil, 75; La Maquina Estetica, Carpenter Ctr Visual Arts, Cambridge, 76; solo exhibs, Museo Espanol de Arte Contemporaneo, Madrid, Spain, 80, Fundacion Calouste Gulbenkian, Lisboa, Port, 81, Lalit Kala Acad, Neuva Delhi, India, 83; XLII Bienal, Pabellon Mexicano, Venecia, Italy, 86. *Teaching:* Instr visual arts, Univ Iberoamericana, Mex, 56-61, Univ Nat Autonoma Mex, 69-92. *Awards:* Premio de Pintura, Trienal de India, Nueva Delhi, 68; Gran Premio de Honor, XIII Bienal, San Paulo, Brazil, 75; Premio Nacional de Artes, Mex Govt, 88. *Bibliog:* Damian Bayon (auth), America Latina en sus Artes, Siglo XXI-UNESCO Paris Barcelona, 74; Octavio Paz (auth), Los Privilegios de la Vista, Centro Cult de Arte Contemoraneo, 90; Juan Garcia Ponce (auth), Manuel Felguerez, Ediciones del Equilibrista, 92. *Mem:* Acad Artes Mex; Sistema Nacional de Creadores de Arte. *Publ:* Auth, El Espacio Multiple, UNAM, Mex, 78; coauth, Diferencia y continuidad, Multiarte, Mex, 82; La Maquina estetica, UNAM, Mex, 85. *Dealer:* Galeria Ramis Barquet Av Real San Agustin No 304-L-2B Residencial San Agustin Garza Garcia Mexico 66260. *Mailing Add:* Calle 10 de Mayo No 15 Olivard de los Padres Mexico City Mexico DF 01780

FELISKY, BARBARA ROSBE
PAINTER, PRINTMAKER
b Chicago, Ill, Mar 24, 38. *Study:* Univ Mich, studied drawing under Frederick O'Dell, BA, 60; Laguna Sch Art, with Hans Burchardt, 75, Calvin Goodman, 1982. *Work:* City of Orange Civic Ctr, Calif; City of Brea Civic Ctr, Calif. *Comn:* Murals, Home Savings & Loan, Los Angeles, 84, Gen Tel Co, Sacramento, 84, Breakers Hotel, Long Beach, 85, Off Nat Educ, Irvine, 86; Folding Screen, New Seoul Hotel, Los Angeles. *Exhib:* California Traditionalist, Redlands Mus, Calif, 80; Catharine Lorillard Wolfe, Nat Arts Club, NY, 82; The Traditionalist's Exhib, Brea Civic Ctr Gallery, Calif, 84; 51st Int Exhib, Arts Club, Washington, 84; Int Miniature Art Shows, Min Art Soc, Fla & NJ, 85. *Teaching:* Oil painting, YWCA, Santa Ana & Orange, Calif, 74-80; teacher & consult, pvt studio, 76- & City of Orange Sch Dist, 76-84. *Awards:* First Place Still Life, In Miniature Ann Exhib, 79; First Place Landscaping, Nat Western Small Painting Show, NMex, 83; Purchase Award, City of Brea, 84. *Bibliog:* Searching for Levitan, Am Artist, 7/88; Am Artist, 5/84. *Mem:* Artist mem Laguna Mus; California Art Club; Los Angeles Co Art Mus. *Media:* Oil, Monotype. *Interests:* Travel, photography. *Publ:* Contribr, Flower painting then and now, Am Artist, 5/84; illusr, Los Angeles Times Home Mag, 4/28/85; auth, The Search for Levitan, Am Artists, 7/88; contribr, Painting Gardens, Art Trends Mag, 3/96. *Dealer:* Chermers Gallery 17300 Seventeenth St Tustin CA 92680; Simic Gallery P O Box 5687 Carmel CA 93921; Bev's Fine Art, Raleigh, NC; Sher Galleries, 135 NE First, Hallandale, Fla. *Mailing Add:* 2942 Lake Hill Dr Orange CA 92667

FELKER, DAVID LARRY
SCULPTOR, GALLERY DIRECTOR
b Spokane, Wash, July 6, 40. *Study:* Eastern Wash Univ, BA, 75; Wash State Univ, MFA, 78. *Work:* Anchorage Mus Hist & Art, Alaska; Mus Judetean, Bistrita, Romania. *Exhib:* Solo exhibs, Intersections of Time & Space, 82, Three Coordinates Plus Time, 86, The Arc, Anchorage Mus Hist & Art, 87, Arc of the Alembic Current, Goldsmith's Mus, London, Eng, 90, Generator Bistrita, Mus Judetean, Generator Bucharest, Univ Bucharest Mus, Romanis, 90 Alaska Generator, Visual Arts Ctr, Anchorage, 92; US Cult Exhib, Magadan Mus Art, Russia, 92-93; Anchorage Mus Hist & Art; Int Gallery Contemp Art, Minneapolis, 96; Brighton Festival/Tichborn Gallery, Eng, 01. *Collection Arranged:* International (sculpture), 84; Dennis Oppenheim (drawing/sculpture), 85; Colour (paintings), 86, Altered Images, Eng, 92; Interaction 20 (paintings/sculpture), Europe, 90; Diva Galleries, Seattle, 03. *Pos:* Dir sculpture, Visual Arts Ctr Alaska, 81; dir, Int Gallery Contemp Art, Minneapolis, Minn, 95-98; dir, cur, Kerf Int Exhib, Seattle, Wash, 2003-05. *Teaching:* Instr drawing, Chapman Col, Alaska, 79-86; asst prof painting, drawing & sculpture, Univ Alaska, Anchorage, 86, adj fac, 91-93; instr, 3-dimensional, Col St Catherine, St Paul, Minn, 99; instr, 3-dimensional design, Shorline Community Col, Seattle, Wash, 05. *Awards:* Nat Endowment Arts Fel 89 & 91, Arc Alembic Current Goldsmith's, London, 90, Theurgic Helmet, VACA, 92; Ken Gray Contemp Arts Award, 94; The Minneapolis Award, 96. *Bibliog:* Ron Glowen, We Work in the Dark, Anchorage Mus, 93; J Decker(auth), Ice Breakers-Alaska's Most Innovative Artists, Book Publ, 99; Julie Decker (auth), Found And Assembled in Alaska, 2001. *Media:* All. *Mailing Add:* 16147 Stone Ave N Shoreline WA 98133-5745

FELLER, ROBERT L
CONSERVATION SCIENTIST
b Newark, NJ, Dec 27, 1919. *Study:* Dartmouth Col, AB, 41; Rutgers Univ, MS, 43 & PhD, 50. *Pos:* Head, Nat Gallery Art Res Proj, Carnegie-Mellon Inst Res, Pittsburgh, 50-76, dir, Ctr on the Materials of the Artist & Conservator, 76-88, dir emer, 88-; ed, Int Inst Conserv Hist & Artistic Works, Am Group Bulletin, 60-74. *Teaching:* Vis scientist, Conserv Ctr, NY Univ Inst Fine Arts, spring 61. *Awards:* Pittsburgh Award, Am Chemical Soc, 83; Col Art Asn/Nat Inst Conserv Award, Distinction in Scholar & Conserv, 92; University projects Award for Distinguished Achievement in Conservation, 2000. *Mem:* Fel Int Inst Conserv Hist & Artistic Works (pres, Am Group, 64-66); Int Coun Mus, Comt Conserv (pres, 69-78); Nat Conserv Adv Coun (pres, 76-79); Inter Soc Color Coun; Fedn Soc Paint Technol; and others. *Res:* Picture varnishes; effects of light on museum objects; analysis of pigments in works of art. *Publ:* Coauth, On Picture Varnishes and Their Solvents, 59, rev ed, 71; ed, Artists' Pigments, Vol I, Cambridge Univ Press, 85; auth, Accelerated Aging: Photochemical & Thermal Aspects, J Paul Getty Trust, 94. *Mailing Add:* 220 N Dithridge St Pittsburgh PA 15213

FELLOWS, ALICE
PAINTER
b Atlanta, Ga, Sept 14, 35. *Study:* Syracuse Univ, BFA (magna cum laude), 57; Antioch Univ, MAP, 92. *Work:* NC Mus Art, Raleigh; Southeastern Ctr Contemp Art (SECCA), Winston-Salem, NC; Mint Mus Art, Charlotte, NC; Eli Broad Corp Collection, Los Angeles; Norton Family Collection, Los Angeles; many others. *Exhib:* One-woman shows, Art Gallery Chapel Hill, 68, 69, 73, Mint Mus Art, Charlotte, NC, 74, Los Angeles Munic Art Gallery, 80, Artspace Gallery, 80, Susan Gersh Gallery, Los Angeles, 80, Roy Boyd Gallery, 82, Kirk de Gooyer Gallery, 84, 85, Santa Monica Col Gallery, Calif, 88 & Hiromi Int, Santa Monica, 2000; A Sense of Being, Claremont Grad Sch Gallery, Calif, 91; Vital Signs (with catalog), Barnsdall Munic Gallery, Los Angeles, 95 & Landscape: The Continuum (with catalog), 95; Still Life.Still Here, Hunsaker-Schlesinger Gallery, 96; Drawn in LA, Armory Ctr Arts, Pasadena, Calif, 96; Supplications, El Camino Col Art Gallery, Los Angeles, 97; Vessels: Form and Function, Palos Verdes Art Ctr, Rancho Palos Verdes, Calif, 98; COLA Individual Artists Grants Exhib (with catalog), Los Angeles Munic Art Gallery, 98; Pure de(Sign), Otis Col Art & Design, Los Angeles, 2000; many others. *Pos:* Resident, Dorland Colony, Temecula, Calif, 83 & Yaddo, Saratoga Springs, NY, 91; pvt consult for artists & writers, 87-96; facilitator, Palms Middle Sch, Los Angeles, 96 & Crossroads Sch, Santa Monica, 96; comnr, City of Santa Monica Arts, 94-99; ed adv, Barnsdall Munic Art Gallery, 95-96; Santa Monica Pub Arts Comt, 95-2000; artists adv comt, Los Angeles Munic Art Gallery, 99-2000. *Teaching:* In-studio sems for art grad students, Univ Calif Los Angeles, Univ Southern Calif, Claremont, 80-96; guest lectr, Univ Calif Los Angeles, 90-91; Seniors Making Art Workshops, Southern Calif, 96. *Awards:* Nat Endowment Arts Fel Painting, 91; Individual Artis's Fel, City of Los Angeles Cult Affairs, 97; Durfee Found Grant, 2000. *Bibliog:* Phillis Rosenzweig (auth), Painting into Nature, 86 & Directions 1986, catalog, 86, Hirshhorn Mus; Howard Fox (auth), 1990 Regional Fellowships, WESTAF-Nat Endowment Arts, 90; Anne Ayres (auth), Charting New Currents, Celebrating 10 Years of Grant Making, Calif Community Found, J Paul Getty Trust Fund Visual Arts, 98. *Mailing Add:* 656 Copeland Ct Santa Monica CA 90405

FELLOWS, DEBORAH LYNNE See Copenhaver-Fellows, Deborah Lynne Fellows

FELLOWS, FRED
PAINTER, SCULPTOR
b Ponca City, Okla, Aug 15, 35. *Comn:* Portfolio of prints, Winchester on the Frontier, Winchester Firearms; Paintings/Bronze Sculptures for Nat Finals Rodeo, Pro Rodeo, Hesston Corp. *Exhib:* Cowboy Artists Am Show, Phoenix & Okla, 68-; Cowboy Hall of Fame; Whitney Gallery; Gran Palais, Paris; First Western Art Show, China; Los Angeles Co Mus Art; Cowboy Artists Am Mus, Kerrville, Tex. *Pos:* Commercial artist & art dir. *Teaching:* Painting workshops for Cowboy Artists of Am Mus. *Awards:* Award for Contrib to Fine Art in Am, Grumbacher, 76; Silver Medal, Cowboy Artists of Am, 78; Gold Medal Sculpture and Best of Show, Cowboy Artist Asn Ann Exhib, 91. *Bibliog:* Brave New Cowboy (doc), Nat Pub TV; Great Plains Massacre (doc), BBC; article, Southwest Art, 10/82. *Mem:* Cowboy Artists Asn (secy-treas & vpres, 74-75, pres, 75-76 & 94-95, dir, 92-94). *Publ:* Auth, Saddles of the early west, Mont Hist Soc Mag, 68; Art of the West, 6/92. *Mailing Add:* PO Box 8053 Bigfork MT 59911

FELSEN, ROSAMUND
ART DEALER, GALLERY DIRECTOR
b Pasadena, Calif, Feb 28, 34. *Pos:* Owner, Rosamund Felsen Gallery, Santa Monica, Calif, currently. *Specialty:* Contemporary art. *Mailing Add:* Bergamot Station B-4 2525 Michigan Ave Santa Monica CA 90404-4014

FELTER, JAMES WARREN
PAINTER, PRINTMAKER
b Bainbridge, NY, Aug 25, 43; Can citizen. *Study:* Univ S Fla, Tampa, BA(painting), 64; Univ Wash. *Work:* City of Vancouver, BC; BC Prov Collection, Can; Manawatu Art Gallery, NZ; Mildura Arts Centre, Australia; Mus Contemp Art, Quito, Ecuador; and others. *Comn:* Trademark, OCEPA-Ecuadorian Handcrafts, Quito, 65; posters, Seattle Opera Asn, Wash, 67; Simon Fraser Univ Arts Centre, Burnaby, BC, 70 & 72. *Exhib:* The Seventies, Mus Mod Art, Sao Paulo, Brazil, 76; 37th Venice Biennale (ECART Invitational), Italy, 76; Four Can Artists, Moderna Galerija, Liubljana & touring Yugoslavia, 76-77; Sixth Int Miniature Print Competition, Pratt Graphics Ctr, NY & touring US, 77-78; Cabo Frio Int Print Biennial, Brazil, 82; Images du Futur, Montreal, 87. *Collection Arranged:* Simon Fraser Collection, Simon Fraser Univ; The British Columbia Craft Exhibition (with catalog), Vancouver, BC, 72; Artist's Stamps and Stamp Images (circulated 1975-80), 74. *Pos:* Dir, Galeria de Ocepa, Quito, Ecuador, 65-66 & Jas Cyberspace Mus, 95-; cur-dir exhib, Simon Fraser Univ, 70-85. *Teaching:* Vis artist, Escuela de Bellas Artes, Univ Cent Ecuador, 66; resident visual arts, Simon Fraser Univ, 69. *Awards:* Finalist-Major Work of Art Competition, Univ Calgary, Alta, 74; Winner, Trademark Competition, Craftsmen's Asn BC, 75; Can Coun grant, 79. *Bibliog:* Article, La Rev Mod, Paris, 8/63; Mario Leon Meneses (auth), James W Felter en la Galeria Siglo XX, El Comercio, Quito, 2/24/66; Francoise Le Gris (auth), article, Vie des Arts 69, Montreal, 73; article, Vie des Arts, Montreal, 6/86. *Mem:* Western Can Art Asn (chmn, 75-76 & 78-80); Can Mus Asn; Int Coun Mus; W Vancouver Community Arts Coun (bd dir). *Media:* Ink, Acrylic. *Res:* Pre-Columbian and indigenous arts. *Publ:* Auth, 450 Desinos Del 500 DC, Span, Quito, 66; ed, Paul Rand 1896-1970, Vancouver, BC, 72; contribr, Contemporaries of Emily Carr in British Columbia, Vancouver, 74; contribr, Vehicule Art: in Transit, Montreal, PQ, 75

FELTER, JUNE MARIE
PAINTER, PRINTMAKER
b Oakland, Calif, Oct 19, 19. *Study:* Oakland Art Inst, Calif, 37-40; Calif Sch Arts & Crafts, Oakland, 37-40, Calif Sch Fine Arts, San Francisco, with Richard Diebenkorn, 60-61. *Work:* Nat Mus Am Art, Washington, DC; San Jose Mus Art, Calif; Oakland Art Mus; San Francisco Art Comn; Am Fedn Arts, NY; 871 Fine Arts Gallery, 99; Kennedy Gallery, Oakland, Calif, 2000. *Comn:* Suite of six etchings, comn by Dana Reich & Brian Jones, San Francisco, 81; three ed lithographs, Meridien Hotel, San Francisco, 83; plus 200 portraits comn by various indiviuals 54-58 & stage sets for various school programs in the 50's. *Exhib:* De Young Mus, San Francisco, 59; The Painted Flower, Oakland Mus, Calif, 60; Calif Soc Etchers, San Francisco Mus Mod Art, 63; Nat Drawing Show, San Francisco Mus Mod Art, 70; Elegant Miniatures, San Francisco Mus Mod Art, 84; 871 Fine Arts Gallery, San Francisco, 89, 90, 92 & 96; Art in Embassies Program, Washington for Vienna, Austria, 94. *Teaching:* Instr watercolor, painting & figure drawing, San Francisco Mus Mod Art, 64-79; instr painting, Univ Calif, San Francisco, 79-80. *Awards:* Purchase Award, Oakland Art Mus, 60; Purchase Award Oil Painting, San Francisco Art Comn, 64. *Bibliog:* Susan Felter (dir), June Felter, A Painter (film), Univ Calif, Los Angeles, 69-70; Arthur Bloomfield (auth), A stir at the beach, San Francisco Chronicle, 8/3/78; Thomas Albright (auth), Art in the San Francisco Bay Area 1945-80, Univ Calif Press, Berkeley, 85; Kathan Brown (auth), Why Draw a Live Model, Crown Point Press, San Francisco, Calif. *Mem:* Calif Soc Printmakers (coun mem, 83-84). *Media:* Acrylic, Watercolor, oil painting. *Specialty:* Fine arts; books. *Publ:* Contribr, Prize Winning Paintings, Allied Publ, 66; Auth, Musicality with poet Barbara Guest & illusr June Felter, Kelsey St Press, Berkeley, Calif, 88; Ourer in the Duer in the Window with Barbara Guest, Roof books, 2003; illust, The Confetti Trees with poet Barbara Guest, 99, Sun & Moon Press, Los Angeles; Calif Watercolors 1850-1970, Hillcrest Press. *Dealer:* 871 Fine Arts Gallery 49 Geary St San Francisco CA 94168. *Mailing Add:* 1046 Amito Ave Berkeley CA 94705

FELTUS, ALAN EVAN
PAINTER, EDUCATOR
b Washington, DC, May 1, 43. *Study:* Tyler Sch Fine Arts, Temple Univ, Philadelphia, 61-62; Cooper Union, NY, BFA, 66; Sch Art & Archit, Yale Univ, MFA, 68. *Work:* Univ Va Art Mus; Nat Mus Am Art, Am Med Asn & Hirshhorn Mus, Washington, DC; NJ State Mus; Nat Acad Design, New York City. *Comn:* Murals, Am Med Asn, 85. *Exhib:* Wash Figurative Painters, Corcoran Gallery Art, Washington, DC, 73-74; Forum Gallery, NY, 76, 80, 83, 86, 91, 94, 96, 98, 2002 & 2005; Nat Acad Design, 77, 78, 82, 86, 88, 90, 95, 97, 99, 2001 & 2005; Am Acad & Inst Arts & Lett, NY, 77, 79, 81 & 94; Okla Art Ctr, 78; Wash Painting, Corcoran Gallery Art, 82; Wichita Art Mus, 87; Ann Nathan Gallery, Chicago, Ill, 94, 98, 2000 & 2003; Huntington (WVA) Mus Art, 2000; Hemphill Fine Arts, Washington, DC, 2001-. *Pos:* artist, 1984-. *Teaching:* Instr art, Dayton Art Inst, Ohio, 68-70; assoc prof art, Am Univ, Washington, DC, 72-84. *Awards:* Rome Prize Fel Painting, Am Acad Rome, 70-72; Tiffany Found Grant, 80; Nat Endowment Arts Individual Grant, 81; Pollock-Krasner Found Grant, 92 & 2005. *Bibliog:* Charles Jencks (auth), Post-Modernism, New York, Rizzoli, 87; Alan Feltus (auth), Inside the painter's mind, the Artist's Mag, 1/92; Alan Feltus (auth), Living and working in Italy, Am Artist Mag, 8/92; Howard DaLee Spencer (auth), Alan Fedltus in Italy, Am Arts Quar, winter, 92; Edward Lucie-Smith, Am Art Now, William Morrow & Co, NY, 85, London, 95; Edward Lucie-Smith, Art Today, Phaidon Press, 95; Edward Lucie-Smith, Art Tomorrow, Editions Pierre Terrail, Paris, 2002. *Mem:* Nat Acad. *Media:* Oil. *Dealer:* Forum Gallery 745 Fifth Ave New York NY

FENG, YING
PAINTER, PHOTOGRAPHER
b Chengdu City, Si Chuan Province, China, Mar 16, 51. *Study:* Si Chuan Norman Univ, BFA (art), 1986-94; Pastel School/Nat Art Club with Jason Chang, 1999-2002. *Work:* Su Zhou Pastel Mus, China; Amerasia Bank Gallery, Flushing, NY; Chengdu Arts Mus, China; Queens Art Inst, Flushing, NY; Si Chan Mus of Art, China. *Comn:* Portrait of Mr. Wu, Chinese Culture Ctr, Flushing, NY, 2000; Portrait of Bank President, Lin's Gallery, Hong Kong, 2001; Portrait of Actor, Lin's Gallery, Hong Kong, 2001; Portrait of Musician, Taiwan Ctr, Flushing, NY, 2001; Mural of Chinese Culture, Lin's Gallery, Hong Kong, 2002. *Exhib:* 89th Allied Artists of Am (juried), Nat Art Club, New York City, 2002; 74th Am Artists Prof League, Salmagundi Club, New York City, 2002; Collected Works of China 1st Pastel Exhib, Suzhou Art Mus, Su Zhou, China, 2003; 61st Audubon Artists (juried), Salmagundi Club, New York City, 2003; Taiwan Ctr 1st & 2nd Int Pastel Exhib (juried), Flushing, NY, 2005 & 2006; 63rd Audubon Artists Show (juried), Salmagundi Club, New York City, 2005; Joyce

Duka Arts Found, Nat Art Club, New York City, 2005; 33rd Pastel Soc of Am Show (juried), Nat Art Club, New York City, 2005. *Pos:* prog dir, North Am Pastel Artists Asn, Flushing, NY, 1998-. *Teaching:* instr pastel, Golden Eagle Inst, Flushing, NY, 2004-. *Awards:* Silver Metal, 89th Allied Artists of Am, Dianne B. Barnhard, 2002; Gold Metal, 61st Audubon Artists, 2003, 63rd Audubon Artists, 2005. *Mem:* Audubon Artists Inc; The Am Artists Prof League Inc; Pastel Soc of Am; North Am Pastel Artists Assoc (prog dir 1997); The Allied Artists of Am Inc. *Media:* All Media. *Publ:* ed, Allied Artists Award Winer: Ying Feng, World Journal, 2002; contribr, Collected Works of China Pastel Exhib, Gu Wu Xian Pub, 2003; ed, Art Times: Audubon Artist Award Winer, Art Time, 2003; ed, Excellent Pastelist: Ying Feng, World Journal, 2005; L'Art du Pastel, Art Du Pastel En France, 2006. *Mailing Add:* 141-25 Northern Blvd Apt C11 Flushing NY 11354

FENG, Z L
PAINTER, EDUCATOR
b Shanghai, China, Oct 23, 54. *Study:* Shanghai Teacher's Univ, BFA, 82; Radford Univ, MFA, 89. *Work:* Springfield Art Mus, Mo; Art Mus, Radford Univ, Va; Walt Disney World, Orlando; Gulfstream Aerospace Ctr; Orlando Int Airport. *Comn:* Maya Angelou (portrait), Radford Univ, 90; Mr Ferlin (portrait), Va Tech, Blacksburg, 92; Judge Jame Sprouse (portrait), Fed Ct House, Richmond, Va, 97; portrait, CarilionHealth System, Radford, Va, 99; portrait, Dr. Douglas Covington, pres Radford Univ, 2005. *Exhib:* Shanghai Mus Fine Arts, 81; Contemp Chinese Artists, Mod Art Mus, Paris, 82; Nat Mus Fine Arts, Beijing, 86; The Face of Am, Arts Ctr Galleries, Old Forge, NY, 94; Tresors, World Trade Ctr, SIngapore, 94; Nat Art Club, NY, 99; Salmagundi Club, NY, 1999, 2000; one-man show, The Art of Feng, Art Mus Radford Univ, 2000. *Pos:* Master panelist, PSA, NY, 95-. *Teaching:* Asst prof studio art, Shanghai Teacher's Univ, 82-86; prof, Radford Univ, 91-. *Awards:* Best Show award, Grand Nat Watercolor Exhib, Mississippi Mus Art, 2002; Best in Show Award, Int Juried Competition, Soc Watercolor Artist, Ft Worth, Tex, 2003; AAPL Award, Allied Artists Am, NY, 2004; Best in Show Award, Hilton Head Art Festival, SC, 2005-2006. *Bibliog:* Phil Eastey (auth), West Meets East, PBS-TV Sta, Harrisonburg, Va, 91. *Mem:* AWS; Allied Artists Am; Audubon Artists; Nat Watercolor Soc; PSA. *Media:* Oil, Watercolor, Pastel, Egg Tempera. *Publ:* Illusr, Creative Watercolor, 95, Best of Watercolor-Painting Texture, 97 & The Best of Watercolor 2, Rockport Publ Inc, 97; illusr, The Artistic Touch 2, The Artistic Touch 3, Creative Art Press, 99 & China-Watercolor, 2001. *Dealer:* Little Gallery on Smith Mt Lake 30 Booker T Washington Hwy Moneta VA 24121. *Mailing Add:* 1006 Walker Dr Radford VA 24141

FENSCH, CHARLES EVERETTE
ADMINISTRATOR, EDUCATOR
b Mansfield, Ohio, Dec 11, 35. *Study:* Kent State Univ, Ohio, BS(art), 58; Wayne State Univ, Detroit, Mich, MAE, 65; Univ Mich, Ann Arbor, Mich, MA, 75. *Work:* Univ Tex, El Paso. *Comn:* Mural series, Kent State Univ, Ohio, 58. *Exhib:* Mich Craftsmen, Detroit Inst Art; Fourth Invitational, Henry Ford Col, Dearborn, Mich; 16th Regional Exhib, Univ Mich, Ann Arbor; 15th Ann Exhib, Canton Inst Art, Ohio; Mich-Ind exhib, Nazareth Col, Ind; Brigham Young Univ, Provo, Utah; Museo de Arte, Mex; Univ Texas, El Paso, Tex. *Teaching:* Prof art, Eastern Mich Univ, 65-81; prof & chmn, Dept Art & Theatre Arts, Univ Tex, El Paso, 82-, assoc dean. *Awards:* Artist Teacher Yr, State Mich, 73; Best in Show, Mich Artists Exhib, Mich State Comn, 74; Kennedy Art Ctr Fel, 2001. *Mem:* Nat Art Educ Asn (vpres); Mich Art Educ Asn (pres); Tex Asn Sch Art (bd dir); Nat Coun Arts Adminr (sec, treas & pres, 94); Col Art Asn; Texas Art Ed. *Publ:* Auth, Art, a return to structure, E'lan; Art conference proposals, Art Educ, Nat Art Educ Asn. *Mailing Add:* Univ Tex Dept Art El Paso TX 79968

FENTON, HOWARD CARTER
PAINTER, EDUCATOR
b Toledo, Ohio, July 2, 1910. *Study:* Chouinard Art Inst; Univ Calif, Los Angeles, BA & MA; also with S McDonald Wright; also studies in Japan, Eng, & Italy. *Work:* Santa Barbara Mus Art Calif; Univ Calif, Santa Barbara; Univ Ill. *Exhib:* One-man shows, Santa Barbara Mus Art, 61 & 64, Esther Bear Gallery, 66 & 75, Univ Calif Art Galleries, 67, 74, 90, 93, Galleria Piazza di Spagna, Rome, 68, Alwin Gallery, London, 68 & Hartnell Col, 76, 81 & 94. *Teaching:* Prof art, Univ Calif, Santa Barbara, 48-78, chmn dept art, 50-60, prof emer, 78-. *Bibliog:* David Gebhard (auth), Howard Fenton, Haagen Press, 68; Phyllis Plous (auth), Howard Fenton, Bollinger & Peters, 90. *Mem:* Contemp Art Forum; Santa Barbara Art Asn; Santa Barbara Mus Art. *Media:* Oil, Acrylic. *Res:* Traveled to India, China and Japan for research. *Specialty:* Contemporary Painting Abstract. *Interests:* Asian and 19th Century French. *Collection:* Contemporary American artists, Asian Influence, and So. African Sculpture. *Dealer:* Dept Art Univ Calif Santa Barbara. *Mailing Add:* 1000 Ladera Ln Montecito CA 93108

FENTON, JULIA ANN
CURATOR, CONCEPTUAL ARTIST
b Tupelo, Miss, Feb 11, 1937. *Study:* Millsaps Col, Jackson, Miss, BA(relig), 58; Pa State Univ, grad study in philos & visual arts, 62-65; Atlanta Col Art, 70-74. *Exhib:* Transcripts for Justine, High Mus Art, Heath Gallery, 77; Encuentro Int de Video 1977, Mus de Arte Contemporaneo de Caracas, Venezuela, 76-77; The Avant-Garde: 12 in Atlanta, High Mus Art, 79; one-woman shows, Reductions, Atlanta Women's Art Collective, 80; You Are Here, Callanwolde Art Ctr Gallery, Atlanta, Ga, 90; Baby, Blackfish Gallery, Portland, Ore, 99; Foul is Fair, Calif State Univ, Chico, 2001; Trench, Mark Woolley Gallery, Portland, Oreg, 2001; Devices and Desires, Mark Woolley Gallery, 2003; In the Garden, Adams St Univ, Alamosa, Colo & Emory Univ, Atlanta, Ga, 2006; Emerging Artists 2006, Spruill Gallery, Atlanta, Ga, 2006; Change: Works by Lucinda Bunnen, Anette Cone-Skelton, Donald Locke and Rocio Rodriguez, Spruill Gallery, Atlanta, Ga, 2006. *Pos:* Ed, Contemp Art-Southeast Mag, 75-77 & Atlanta Art Workers Coalition Newspaper, 77-78; ed & vpres ed affairs & mem bd dir, Contemp Art/Southwest, 76-77; dir activities & ed newspaper, Atlanta Art Workers Coalition, 77-78, dir info resources & bd dir, 79-80, Southeastern Women's Caucus Art (prog chairperson, 79); acting co-dir, Nexus Contemp Art Ctr Gallery, Atlanta, Ga, 89-90; dir, Chastain Gallery, Atlanta, Ga, 90-93; gallery dir, Nexus Contemp Art Ctr, Atlanta, Ga, 93-95; dir, Newport Visual Art Ctr, Ore, 96-98; mem, City Coun, Toledo, OR, 2004-2006; exhibs dir, Spruill Gallery, Atlanta, Ga, 2006-. *Awards:* Named Outstanding Woman in the Arts, Atlanta Women Film, 82; Named Outstanding Woman in the Arts, Ga Soc Hist Preserv, 96. *Bibliog:* John Howett (auth), Julia Fenton at the Atlanta women's art collective, Art in Am, 4/81; Lois Allan (auth), Julia Fenton at Blackfish Gallery, Artweek, Vol 30, No10, 10/99; Sue Taylor (auth), Trench, Arrt In America, 2/2002. *Mem:* Col Art Asn; Ga Asn Mus & Galleries; Am Asn Mus. *Media:* Multi-Media and Site Specific Installations. *Publ:* Contribr, John Y Fenton (ed), Theology and Body, Westminster, 74; ed, Contemporary art Vol 1, No 1 & 2, Southeast Mag, 76; ed, Thirty-Six Women Artists, Atlanta Women's Art Collective, 4/6/78; Annette De Meo Carlozzi and Julia A Fenton, Out of Bounds: New Work by Eight Southeastern Artists, Nexus Contemp Art Ctr, Atlanta, 96. *Dealer:* Mark Woolley Gallery Portland OR. *Mailing Add:* 2367 Autumn Dr Snellville GA 30078

FENWICK, ROLY (WILLIAM ROLAND)
PAINTER, EDUCATOR
b Owen Sound, Ont, Feb 4, 32. *Study:* Mt Allison Univ, NB, with Alex Colville & Lawren Harris Jr, scholar, 54. *Work:* McIntosh Gallery, Univ Western Ont; Owens Mus, Mt Allison Univ, NB; London Regional Art & Hist Mus, London Free Press, Ont; Sir George Williams Univ, Montreal; Art Gallery Hamilton. *Comn:* President portrait, Univ Western Ont, 94. *Exhib:* Montreal Spring Exhib, Montreal Mus Fine Arts; solo exhibs, Nancy Poole Studio, London, Ont, 70, 72 & 76, London Regional Art Gallery, Ont, 78, Bau-Xi Gallery, Toronto, 84, 86, 88, 89, 90, 91, 92 & 95, Gairloch Gallery, Oakville, Ont, 90, Tom Thomson Gallery, Owen Sound, Ont, 90 & Thielsen Galleries, London, Ont, 92 & 95; Experiencing Drawing, McIntosh Gallery, Univ Western Ont, London, 87; Landscape, Bau-Xi Gallery, Toronto, 87; Personal Visions, Bau-Xi Gallery, Toronto, 89; Love for the Land, Homer Watson Gallery, Kitchener, Ont, 94; Watermarks, Bau-Xi Gallery, Toronto, 97; Oil and Water Works, Michael Gibson Gallery, London, Ont, 98; James Baird Gallery, Newfoundland, 98; Art Mart 98, with Tony Urquhart, London Reg Art Gallery, London, Ont, 98; Scanning the Contemp Landscape, Gallery Lambton, Sarnia, Ont, 98. *Pos:* Art dir, Simpsons-Sears, Toronto, 56-66. *Teaching:* Prof visual arts, Univ Western Ont, 68-89, prof emer, 90-. *Mem:* Univ Art Asn Can; Royal Can Acad; Ont Soc Artists. *Media:* Oil, Watercolor. *Publ:* Illusr, War and Other Measures, House Anansi, 77; Wintering Over, Quadraut Ed, 80. *Dealer:* Bau-Xi Gallery 340 Dundas St W Toronto ON M5T 1G5; Michael Gibson Gallery Carling St London ON. *Mailing Add:* 755 Maitland St London ON N5Y 2W4 Canada

FEODOROV, JOHN
ARTIST
b Los Angeles, Calif, 60. *Study:* Calif State Univ, Long Beach, BFA (drawing & painting); Vt Col, Montpelier, MFA. *Work:* Road to Heaven, 2004; Heaven, 2004; Origin of Religion, 2005; Chose One, 2005; Breath of Life, 2005; Myth Today, 2005; Office Shaman, 2005; Gods Feeding, 2005; Sacrement, 2006; Temple, 2006; Alphabet, 2006. *Exhib:* What Makes the Red Man Red?, King Co Art Comn, 95; Here/After, SOIL, Seattle, 99; Office Shamans & Other Mythologies, Sacred Circle Gallery, Seattle, 2001; Myths & Prophesies, Howard House, Seattle, 2002; Four Sacred Spaces, 911 Media Arts Ctr, Seattle, 2005. *Pos:* arts comnr, Seattle, 2000-2003. *Teaching:* art teacher, Fairhaven Col, Western Wash Univ, Bellingham; arts educator, Arts Corps, Seattle, 2001-. *Awards:* Sheldon Bergh Award, Basil H Alkazzi Found, NY, 95; GAP Grant, Artist Trust, Seattle, 2000; Artist Assistance Award, Jack Straw Found, Seattle, 2002. *Mailing Add:* Fairhaven College Western Washington University 516 High St Bellingham WA 98225-9118

FERBER, LINDA S
CURATOR, HISTORIAN
b Suffern, NY, May 17, 44. *Study:* Barnard Col, New York, BA, 66; Columbia Univ, New York, MA, 68 & PhD(Wyeth Endowment Am Art fel), 80. *Pos:* Cur Am painting & sculpture, Brooklyn Mus, New York, 76-85, chief cur, 85-99; Andrew W Mellon cur Am art, 99-. *Teaching:* Adj prof art hist, Columbia Univ, 78-98 & CUNY, 2003. *Awards:* Phi Beta Kappa, 66; Fleishman Award, Smithsonian Archives Am Art, 2002. *Mem:* Col Art Asn; Am Asn Mus; Int Found Art Res; Archives Am Art; Asn Art Mus Cur; Am Studies Asn. *Res:* Am art with a special interest in painting and sculpture of the nineteenth century. *Publ:* Coauth, The New Path: Ruskin and the Am Pre-Raphaelites, The Brooklyn Mus, 85; auth, Never at Fault: The Drawings of William Trost Richards, The Hudson River Mus, 86; coauth, Albert Bierstadt: Art & Enterprise, The Brooklyn Mus in assoc with Hudson Hills Press, Inc, 91; coauth, Masters of Color and Light: Homer, Sargent and The American Watercolor Movement, Brooklyn Mus in assoc with Smithsonian Inst Press, 98; coauth, America: The New World in 19th Century Painting, Prestel Verlag, 99, Pastoral Interlude: William T Richards in Chester County, 2001 & In Search of a National Landscape: William T Richards in the Adirondacks, 2002. *Mailing Add:* Dept Am Art Brooklyn Mus 200 Eastern Pkwy Brooklyn NY 11238

FERBERT, MARY LOU
PAINTER
b Cleveland, Ohio, Sept 21, 24. *Study:* Duke Univ, BA, 45; Cleveland Inst Art, 68-78 & 95. *Work:* Cleveland Mus Natural Hist, Cleveland State Univ, Ohio; Nat Mus Women Arts, Washington, DC; Zimmerli Art Mus, Rutgers Univ; Am Numismatic Soc, NY; El Paso Mus of Art; plus numerous pub collections; Butler Inst Am Art,

Youngstown, Ohio; Fed Res Bank of Cleveland; and others. *Comn:* Painting 641/2 x 421/2, Richard E Jacobs Group, 1987; Painting 48" x 96", Cleveland-Cliffs Inc, Cleveland, Ohio, 88; painting 4 x 471/2, Lakewood Hos, Ohio, 1990; three paintings 60" x 36", Key Bank, Cleveland, Ohio, 92; 75th Anniversary Commemorative Medal, Cleveland Mus Natural Hist, 95; painting, 53 1/2 X 34 3/4, RPM Inc, 97; painting (36" X 96"), Rocky River Pub Libr, Ohio, 98; painting (40: X 32"), Rocky River Pub Libr, Ohio, 2002; painting (48" X 48"), Am Diabetes Asn, Celebrity Art Auction, Cleveland, 2002. *Exhib:* Centennial Traveling Exhib, Catherine Lorillard Wolfe Art Club Ann, 82-90, 92-93 & 1995-2002; solo exhibs: Butler Inst Am Art, Youngstown, Ohio, 93, Bonfoey Gallery, Cleveland, Ohio, 2001, 2005; Watercolor USA, Springfield Art Mus, Mo, 94; Catherine Lorillard Wolfe Art Club Ann, 1995-2006; Nat Asn Women Artists Exhib, Athens, Greece, 96; Nat Asn Women Artists, Athens, Greece, 96; Gallery BAI, Barcelona, Spain, 98; State of the Art Biennial Watercolor Invitational, 1st Venue Siena Hts, Ill, 2003, 2nd Venue Parkland Col, Champaign, Ill, 2004; NEO Show, Cleveland Mus Art, 2005. *Teaching:* Instr watercolor, Cleveland Inst Art, 86 & 89-98. *Awards:* Bronze Medal of Hon, 120th Ann Exhib, Am Watercolor Soc, 87; Special Mention for Painting, 69th Ann Exhib, May Show, Cleveland Mus Art, 88; Medal Hon, 93 & Hon mem, 98, Catharine Lorillard Wolfe Art Club; Golden Achievement Award, Golden Age Ctrs of Greater Cleveland, Inc, 99; Award NJ Watercolor Soc, 2000; Honored Guest, Cleveland Artists Found, 2005; plus others. *Bibliog:* Elizabeth McClelland (auth), The Art of Mary Lou Ferbert, Ohio Artists Now, Cleveland, 93; Rachel Wolf (auth), Splash 4: The Splendor of Light, 96 & Splash 5: Best of Watercolor, 98, N Light Bks, Cincinnati; Katheryn Kipp (auth), the Best of Flower Painting, N Light Bks, Cincinnati, 97; Adelene Flethcer (auth) The Flower Painter Pocket Palette Book 2, Chartwell Books, Inc, Edison, NJ, 2000; Glencoe Lit Readers Choose, Glencoe/McGraw-Hill, NY, 2000; Nina Gihans (auth), Creative Essence: Cleveland's Sense of Place, Kent State Univ Press, 2005. *Mem:* Am Watercolor Soc; Catharine Lorillard Wolfe Art Club, Inc; Nat Asn Women Artists; charter mem Watercolor USA Honor Soc; Artists Archives of the Western Reserve; Nat Watercolor Soc; Transparent Watercolor Soc Am. *Media:* Transparent Watercolor. *Specialty:* Ohio Artists. *Interests:* Natural History, Sports, Cooking, Gardening. *Publ:* Auth, Nature in the City, Cleveland Mus of Nat Hist, 1979; auth, Book of Hearts, 4-Chamber Press, 2006. *Dealer:* Bonfoey Gallery 1710 Euclid Ave Cleveland OH 44115. *Mailing Add:* 334 Parklawn Dr Cleveland OH 44116

FERGUSON, ALICE C
PAINTER
b New Brunswick, NJ, Feb 7, 47. *Study:* Rutgers Univ, 65-66; various workshops for oil painting, 94-95. *Exhib:* Art by the Sea, Bethel Creek House, Vero Beach, Fla, 94-98; Grand Nat Exhibs, Salmagundi Club, NY, 95-97, 99; Allied Artists Ann, Nat Arts Club, NY, 96 & 98; Am Artists Prof League Invitational, Sun Bank Int, Miami, 96; Regional Exhib Fine Art, Martin Co Cult Ctr, Stuart, Fla, 97. *Awards:* Best in Show, Martha Lincoln Gallery, 97; 1st Place Award, Vero Beach, 2000. *Mem:* Fel Am Artists Prof League; assoc mem Allied Artists Am. *Media:* Oil. *Dealer:* KC Kelly Gallery 1 Railroad Ave Goshen NY. *Mailing Add:* 22 Watercrest Dr Doylestown PA 18901

FERGUSON, CHARLES B
MUSEUM DIRECTOR, PAINTER
b Fishers Island, NY, June 30, 18. *Study:* Williams Col, AB; Art Students League, painting with Frank Dumond & graphics with Harry Sternberg; Trinity Col, MA. *Work:* New Britain Mus Am Art, Conn; Mattatuck Mus, Waterbury, Conn; DeCordova Mus, Lincoln, Mass; Amerind Found, Ariz; Scoville Corp, Waterbury, Conn. *Comn:* Stained glass window, Fishers Island, 71; murals, Williston Acad, East Hampton, Mass, Renbrook Sch, West Hartford, Conn, pvt home, Fishers Island, NY & Henry L Ferguson Mus, Fishers Island, NY; 7 murals, Fishers Island, NY, 94. *Exhib:* Conn Acad Fine Arts; Conn Watercolor Soc; Greater Hartford Civic Arts Festival; Williams Col Mus, Williamstown, Mass, 91; Red Barn Gallery, Fishers Island, NY; one-man exhibs, New Britain Mus, Conn, Mattatuck Mus, Conn & Farmington Mus Village Libr, Seabury, Bloomfield, Conn. *Collection Arranged:* Aaron Draper Shattuck, 70; Robert B Brandegee, 71; William T Richards, 73; Dennis Miller Bunker, 78; Three Generations of Wiggins, 1870's-1970's, 79; Three Centuries of Connecticut Art, 81; Allan Butler Talcott, Painter of Landscapes, 83; paintings & etchings in many pvt collections in US, Eng, the Carribbean & Bejing, China. *Pos:* Dir, New Britain Mus Am Art, Conn, 65-84; trustee, Hillstead Mus, Farmington, Conn, currently; pres, Henry L Ferguson Mus, Fishers Island, NY, currently; art adv, Hartford Steam Boiler Insurance Co, Conn. *Teaching:* Instr hist art & studio painting, Trinity Col & Loomis Sch, Eaglebrook Sch, Mass & The Hillschool, Pa. *Awards:* New Britain Herald Prize, 70; Sanford Low Prize, Conn Acad Fine Arts, 71; First Place in Oil, Int Maritime Exhib, Mystic, Conn, 78; First Prize for Oils, Mystic Marine Exhib, Conn, 81. *Mem:* Conn Acad Fine Arts; Art Guild Framington; New Britain Mus; HL Ferguson Mus New York; Hill-Stead Mus Conn. *Media:* Acrylics; Watercolor. *Publ:* 67 years of the Fishers Island Golf Club Links, pvt publ, 94; 27 Views of Rare Rock Lighthouse in the Four Seasons, 2000. *Mailing Add:* 33 Farmstead Ln Farmington CT 06032

FERGUSON, GERALD
PAINTER
b Cincinnati, Ohio, Jan 29, 37. *Study:* Wilmington Col, Ohio, BS, 62; Ohio Univ, Athens, MFA, 66. *Work:* Mus Mod Art, NY; Mus Stuzki, Lodz, Poland; Art Gallery Ont, Toronto; Glenbow Mus, Calgary, Alta; Art Gallery NS, Halifax; Vancouver Art Gallery; Nat Gallery of Can. *Comn:* Sculpture, Halifax Commons, 69. *Exhib:* Mus Mod Art, NY, 70; solo shows, Anna Leonowens Gallery, Halifax, NS, 74 & Art Gallery Ont, Toronto, 76 & 77; Galeria Foksal, Warsaw, Poland, 77; Glenbow Mus, Calgary, Alta, 81; Dalhousie Art Gallery, Halifax, 84; and others. *Teaching:* Asst prof, Kansas City Art Inst, 67-68; prof, NS Col Art, Halifax, 68-; mentor art, Calif Inst Arts, Valencia, 73-74. *Bibliog:* Eric Cameron (auth), Gerald Ferguson, Studio Int, spring 75; Dennis Young (auth), Task Oriented Art, Dalhousie Univ, 76 & Speculate to Appreciate, Vanguard, 85; Diana Nemiroff (auth), Late Style, Jour of Can Art History, 2000. *Media:* Miscellaneous Media. *Publ:* Auth, The Standard Corpus of Present Day English Language Usage by Word Length, 70; publ, Cleophas and His Own, Marsden Hartley (auth), 82. *Dealer:* Wynick/Tuck Gallery, Toronto, ON, Can. *Mailing Add:* Dept Art NS Col Art & Design 5163 Duke St Halifax NS B3J 3J6 Canada

FERGUSON, LARRY SCOTT
PHOTOGRAPHER, CURATOR
b North Platte, Nebr, May 16, 54. *Study:* Univ Nebr, Lincoln, BFA, 77; Rochester Inst Technol, NY, sem 78. *Work:* Sheldon Mem Art Gallery, Lincoln, Nebr, Libr of Cong, DC; Western Heritage Mus, Omaha, Nebr; Univ Okla, Norman; Murray State Univ, Ky; and others. *Comn:* Photograph, collab Sachio Yamashita, Metrop Arts Coun, Omaha, Nebr, 79 & photograph, murals & sculpture, 79; photograph, Bldg Reborn, Smithsonian Inst, DC, 79; photograph, Tube Walkway, Omaha Airport Auth, Nebr, 80. *Exhib:* Am Vision, Nat Artists Alliance, NY Univ, 79; Juried Exhib, Friends of Photog Gallery, Carmel, Calif, 79 & Diana Camera Show, 80; Omaha: Then & Now, Western Heritage Mus, 79, Omaha: Then & Now II, 80 & Omaha: Then & Now III, 81; one-man shows, Sheldon Mem Art Gallery, Lincoln, Nebr, 79 & Southern Light Gallery, Amarillo, Tex, 80; Walker Art Ctr, Minneapolis, 81; and others. *Pos:* Cur photographs, Adams Co Hist Soc, Hastings, Nebr, 77-78, Nebr Arts Coun & Nat Endowment for Arts artist-in-residence grants & cur photographs, Bostwick-Frohardt Collection, Western Heritage Mus, Omaha, 78-81. *Teaching:* Instr photography, Univ Nebr, Omaha, 81-, Bellevue Col, 82-. *Awards:* Jurors Award, Nat Artists Alliance, 79; Jurors Award, 2nd St Gallery, Charlottesville, Va, 80; Artist in residence Grant, Nebr Arts Coun, 81-82. *Bibliog:* Shawn P Leary (auth), Arts scan, 79 & Art Simmering (auth), Dodge Street, 80, Omaha Mag; Joanne Stanwick (auth), Suitable for framing, Omaha Mag, 81; article, Artweek, 9/5/81; and others. *Mem:* Soc Photog Educ; Friends of Photog; Visual Studies Workshop, Rochester, NY. *Publ:* Contribr, Twelve Photographers: A Contemporary Mid-America Document, Mid-Am Arts Alliance, 78; contribr, Self-Portrayal: The Photographers Image, 79 & Untitled Number 21, by Jim Alinder, 80, Friends of Photog; Object and Image, by George Craven, Prentice-Hall, 82. *Mailing Add:* 1701 Vinton St Omaha NE 68108-1432

FERGUSON, MAX
PAINTER, PRINTMAKER
b New York, NY, 1959. *Study:* New York Univ, BS, 80. *Work:* Metrop Mus Art, NY; Forbes Mag Collection, NY; NY Hist Soc; Brooklyn Hist Soc; City Amsterdam, Holland; Forbes Magazine Coll, NY. *Comn:* Portrait, comn by Edward Asner, NY, Richard Brown Baker, Estate of H W Janson, Alex Cooper & Martin Margulies. *Exhib:* Starved for Art, Sch Visual Arts Mus, NY, 85; Urban Visions: The Contemp Artist, Adelphi Univ, Garden City, NY, 87; Coney Island, Gallery Henoch, NY, 90; Art Cologne, Galerie Ulrich Gering, Cologne, Ger, 91-. *Awards:* Pratt/Silvermine Award, Int Print Competition, New Caanan, Conn, 86. *Bibliog:* John Loughery (auth), Arts Mag, 11/86; Patrick Pacheco (auth), The new faith in painting, Arts & Antiques, 5/91; Vivien Raynor (auth), New York Times, 3/92. *Media:* Pencil, Intaglio; Oil on wood, Masonite Panel

FERGUSON-HUNTINGTON, (LADY) KATHLEEN E
SCULPTOR, ENVIRONMENTAL ARTIST
b Chicago, Ill, Jan 31, 45. *Study:* Stephens Col, Columbia, Mo, 63-64; Layton Sch Art, Milwaukee, Wis, BFA, 69; RI Sch Design, Providence, MFA, 71; Md Inst Col Art, Digital Arts, 99. *Work:* Russell Courthouse, Atlanta. *Comn:* J B Speed Mus, 87; Honeywell Corp, Minneapolis, Minn. *Exhib:* One-person shows, Univ Cincinnati, 81, Graham Mod Gallery, NY, 85, High & Mus Art, Atlanta, Ga (with catalog), 86, Kozmic Kingdom, An Environmental Installation, JB Speed Mus, Louisville, Ky, 87, Southeastern Ctr Contemp Art, Winston-Salem, NC, Sun Cities Art Mus, Ariz, 92, Angeles Gate Art Ctr, Los Angeles, 94, Milwaukee Inst Art & Design, 97, Mus Modern Art, Machynlleth, Wales, 2002, Centre Culture Francais, Doha, Qatar, 2002; Va Mus Fine Arts, Richmond, 73; Biennial of Contemp Am Art, Whitney Mus Am Art, NY, 75; Southern Abstractions, traveling to Contemp Arts Ctr, New Orleans; The Santa Fe Sculpture Project 1993, NMex, 93; New Mexico 93, Mus Fine Arts & Mus NMex, Santa Fe, 93; Ernesto Mayans, Santa Fe, NMex, 96; 40 American Artists, Mus de Arateau de Rochefort-En-Terre, France, 2003; Women & Art, A Global Perspective, Sharjah, UAE, 2005. *Teaching:* Vis artist, Conn Col, 79; asst prof, Univ Ky, 80-82; teaching fac, Va Commonwealth Univ, Doha, Qatar, 2000-. *Awards:* Ky Arts Coun Grant; Fel, Helene Wurlitzer Found, Taos, NMex; Ky Found for Women Grant, Sally Bingham, La. *Bibliog:* John Yau (auth), article, Art Am, 79; William Zimmer (auth), article, Soho Weekly News, 79; Grace Glueck (auth), article, NY Times, 85; Peter Frank (auth), article, Press-Telegram, 5/94. *Mem:* Col Art Asn Am Int Sculpture Ctr. *Media:* Cast Metal; Mixed. *Publ:* Contribr, Milton Klonsky (auth), Speaking Pictures, Crown, 74; auth & illusr, Natti's Navigations, pvt publ, 78. *Mailing Add:* Virginia Commonwesth Univ PO Box 8095 Doha 21210 Qatar

FERHOLT, ELEANORE HEUSSER See Heusser, Eleanore Elizabeth Heusser Ferholt

FERN, ALAN MAXWELL
MUSEUM DIRECTOR
b Detroit, Mich, Oct 19, 30. *Study:* Univ Chicago, AB, 50, MA, 54 & PhD, 60; Courtauld Inst, Univ London, res scholar. *Collection Arranged:* Diverse print, poster & photo shows, Libr Cong, 62-82; Leonard Baskin, Nat Collection Fine Arts, Smithsonian Inst, 70; var exhibs at Nat Portait Gallery, 82-00. *Pos:* From asst cur to cur, asst chief to chief, Prints & Photographs Div, Libr Cong, 61-76, dir, Res Dept, 76-78, dir, spec collections, 78-82; dir, National Portrait Gallery, Smithsonian Inst, 82-2000. *Teaching:* From asst to asst prof, Univ Chicago, 52-61. *Awards:* Chevalier,

Ordre de la Couronne, Belgium, 80; Chevalier, Ordre des Arts et des Lettres, France, 85; Commander, Royal Order of Polar Star, Sweden, 88. *Mem:* Print Coun Am (dir, 63-69, pres, 69-71); Col Art Asn Am (dir, 84-88); Am Antiquarian Soc; Double Crown Club, London; Grolier Club, New York City. *Res:* History of prints, posters, book design, 19th and 20th century art. *Publ:* Auth, A note on the Eragny Press, Cambridge Univ Press, 57; coauth, Art nouveau, 60 & Word and image, 69, Mus Mod Art, NY; Leonard Baskin, Smithsonian Press, 70; Revolutionary Soviet film posters, Johns Hopkins Press, 74; Arnold Newman's Americans, Little Brown, 92. *Mailing Add:* 3605 Raymond St Chevy Chase MD 20815

FERNANDEZ, (JULES) JAKE
PAINTER; PHOTOGRAPHER
b Havana, Cuba, May 13, 51. *Study:* Univ Fla, BA, 76; Univ S Fla, MFA (Grad Teaching Fel), 79. *Work:* Ringling Mus Art, Sarasota, Fla; Fla State Capitol Bldg, Tallahassee; Contemp Art Mus, Univ S Fla, Tampa; St Petersburg Community Col, Fla; Am Express Corp, Jacksonville, Fla. *Exhib:* Ann Exhib Contemp Am Painting, Soc Four Arts, Palm Beach, Fla, 75, 76, 78; The New Floridians, Jacksonville Art Mus, Fla, 77, 78; Seven Realists from the Southeast, Southeastern Ctr Contemp Art, Winston-Salem, NC, 78; Selection from Fla Collections, Dunedin Art Ctr, Fla, 91; Screen Plays, Ormond Meml Art Mus, Ormond Beach, Fla, 95, Fla Craftsman Gallery, St Petersburg, 95, Appleton Mus, Ocala, Fla, 95, Ctr Arts, Vero Beach, Fla, 96; one-man show Frances Wolfson Art Gallery, Miami Dade Co Community Col, 98, Mus Art, Ft Lauderdale, Fla, 2000. *Teaching:* Instr pastel, Armory Art Ctr, West Palm Beach, Fla, 2000. *Awards:* Merit Award, Sarasota Art Asn, 79; State Fla Individual Artist Fel, Fla Div Cult Affairs, 99. *Bibliog:* Sheldon Lurie (auth), Abstration: Four From Latin America, Miami Dade Community Col, 86; Juan Martinez (auth), Jake Fernandez, Sites & Composites, Miami Dade Community Col, 98; Allys Palladino-Craig (auth), Jake Fernandez: Etheral Journeyman, Mus Art, Ft Lauderdale, 2000. *Media:* Oil, Pastel. *Dealer:* Westwood Gallery 578 Broadway First Floor New York NY 10012; Cole Pratt Gallery 3800 Magazine St New Orleans LA 70115. *Mailing Add:* 223 E 11th St 2B New York NY 10003

FERNIE, JOHN CHIPMAN
SCULPTOR
b Hutchinson, Kans, Oct 22, 45. *Study:* Colo Col, 63-65; Kansas City Art Inst, BFA, 68; Univ Calif, Davis, grant, 69, teaching fel & MFA, 70. *Work:* San Francisco Mus Art; Univ Calif Mus, Berkeley. *Exhib:* One-man shows, Nova Scotia Col Art, 74 & John Gibson Gallery, 77; group shows, Documenta 5, Kasel, Ger, 72; 8th & 9th Biennale de Paris; Israel Mus, 76; Houston Mus of Contemp Art, 77; Whitney Mus, NY, 78; Denver Art Mus, 78; Boulder Art Ctr, Colo, 79; plus others. *Teaching:* Asst, Univ Calif, Davis, 69; instr sculpture, Calif Col Arts & Crafts, 70-72, Stephens Col, 72-75 & Nova Scotia Col Art & Design, 75-. *Bibliog:* Richardson (auth), article in Arts Mag, 2/71; Albright (auth), Exciting, compelling show, San Francisco Chronicle, 7/1/71; Jochimsen (auth), Magazin Kunst, 7/74. *Media:* Wood, Cardboard, Photo, Plaster. *Publ:* Auth, Petit trianon, twikkel, I worship you, God bless your symmetry, 70; Masters survey, 70. *Mailing Add:* 1950 Tincup Ct Boulder CO 80303

FERO, SHANE
GLASS BLOWER, COLLAGE ARTIST
b Chicago, Ill, Sept 10, 53. *Study:* Plattsburg State Univ, 74-76; Penland Sch Crafts, NC, with Stephen Dee Edwards, Fred Birkhill & Paul Marioni, 88-89; Pilchuck Glass Sch, Seattle, Wash, with Kurt Wallstab, 91. *Work:* Mus Am Glass, Wheaton Village, Millville, NJ; Glasmuseum, Ebeltoft, Denmark; New Orleans Mus Art; Huntsville Mus Art, Ala; Ashville Mus Art, NC. *Exhib:* Craft of the Carolinas, Gibbes Mus Art, Charleston, 93; solo exhib, Ariodante Gallery, New Orleans, 93, 95 & 97; Breaking the Mold: New Directions in Glass (with catalog), Huntsville Mus Art, 96; The Glasmuseum-The First Ten yrs, Ebeltoft, Denmark, 96-97; Contemp Flameworked Glass, Mus Am Glass, Millville, NJ, 97; 15th Int Glass Invitational, Habatat Galleries, Boca Raton, Fla, 97; Venezia Biennial of Glass, Centro Studio Vetro, Venice, Italy, 98; Sofa: Chicago, 1995-2000. *Teaching:* Penland Sc Crafts, NC, 90-99; Urban Glass, Brooklyn, 96-98; instr flameworking glass, Corning Mus Glass, NY, 97-. *Bibliog:* Joan Falconer Byrd (auth), Glass from North Carolina, Glasmuseum, Ebeltoft, Denmark, 95 & Shane Fero: Myth, Magic & Spirit, Urban Glass Mag, 97/98. *Mem:* Piedmont Craftsmen; Am Craft Coun; Glass Art Soc. *Media:* Glass, Mixed Media. *Dealer:* Albertson-Peterson Gallery 329 Park Ave S Winter Park FL 32789. *Mailing Add:* c/o Penland Sch PO Box 266 Penland NC 28765

FERRARA , ANNETTE
EDITOR, EDUCATOR
Study: Sch of Art Inst, MA. *Pos:* Found ed, writer TENbyTEN, Chicago, 99-. *Teaching:* Lectr, Columbia Col, DePaul, SAIC; teacher, art hist Mus of Contemp Art. *Mem:* Chicago Art Critics Asn. *Publ:* Co-auth: Xtreme Interiors, 2003; contributor writings to Artforum, zingmagazine, provinceton Arts. *Mailing Add:* TENbyTEN 222S Morgan 3E Chicago IL 60607

FERRARA, JACKIE
SCULPTOR
b Detroit, Mich. *Work:* Chase Manhattan Bank, Solomon R Guggenheim Mus, Whitney Mus Am Art, Mus Mod Art & Metrop Mus Art, NY; Los Angeles Cjo Mus of Art; Dallas Mus Fine Art; High Mus Art; Nat Mus Am Art, Washington. *Comn:* Wash Conv & Trade Ctr, Seattle, 89; Stuart Collection, Univ Calif, San Diego, 91; Pittsburgh Int Airport, 92; Tang Ctr, Mass Inst Technol, 95; MTA Arts for Transit, Grand Central Subway, NY, 2000. *Exhib:* Biennial Exhib, Whitney Mus, 73 & 79; Recent Acquisitions, Mus Mod Art, NY, 83; solo exhibs, Moore Col Art, Philadelphia, 87, San Antonio Art Inst, 87, Genovese Gallery, Boston, 90, Michael Klein Inc, NY, 91, 94 & 96, Hudson River Mus Westchester, Yonkers, NY, 93 & Freedman Gallery, Albright Col Ctr Arts, Reading, Pa, 93, In Focus: Jackie Ferrara, Mus of Contemp Art, Chicago, 98, Univ Conn, Storrs, 2000; MoreThan Minimal: Women's Work in the 70s, Rose Art Mus, Brandeis Univ, 96; Max's Kansas City, 65 Thompson Street, NY, 96; Constructions, Michael Klein Gallery, NY, 96; Outdoor Exhibition, Woodson Art Mus, Wausau, Wis, 96; Red Arches, Frederieke Taylor/TZ Art, NY, 98; one-woman retrospective Frederieke Taylor/TZ' Art Gallery, NY, 2000; Sculptures and Drawings, Frederieke Taylor Gallery, 2002; Long-Bin Chen: Redaing Sculpture, Frederieke Taylor Gallery, 2003. *Awards:* Grants, NY State Coun Arts, 71 & 75 & Nat Endowment Arts, 73, 77 & 87; Guggenheim Found Fel, 76; Award for Excellence in Design, Art Comn City NY, 88; Inst Hon, Am Inst Architects, 90; Tucker Award for Design Excellence, Building Stone Inst, 91. *Bibliog:* Kirby Gookin (auth), Jackie Ferrara, Artforum, 9/94; Davie Rimanelli (auth), Constructions, New Yorker, 2/12/96; Nancy Stapen (auth), Feminism meets minimalism, Boston Globe, 4/30/96. *Publ:* Jackie Ferrara Drawings, 6 & 7/77, Lapp Princess Press, New York, 77; Jackie Ferrara Sculpture, A Retrospective, Ringling Mus, Sarasota, 92. *Dealer:* Frederieke Taylor 535 W 22d St New York NY 10011. *Mailing Add:* 121 Prince St New York NY 10012

FERRARI, DOUGLAS
ARTIST
Study: Rutgers Univ, BA, 1992; Montclair State Col, MA, 1994; Brooklyn Col, MFA, 1997; Drew Univ, Dr of Letts in Contemp issues, 1999-. *Exhib:* Solo exhibs, Relic Quarries, Chuck Levitan Gallery, NY, 1997, Exhib of Sculpture & Prints, Lockjaw Gallerly, Philadelphia, Pa, 1998, Rittenhouse Gallery (Rittenhouse Hotel), Philadelphia, Pa, 1999, Thompson Park Gallary, Middletown, NJ, 2000. *Pos:* Exec dir & pres, Shore Inst of the Contemp Arts. *Teaching:* Grad Asst, Art dept, Montclair State Univ, 1993-1994; Adj fac, Art Dept, Brookdale Community Col, 1994-; Adj fac, Bloomfield Co, spring, 1997; Adj fac, Ocean Co Community Col, fall, 1999-2002. *Mailing Add:* 110 Norwood Ave Long Branch NJ 07740

FERRARI, VIRGINIO LUIGI
SCULPTOR, EDUCATOR
b Verona, Italy, Apr 11, 37. *Study:* Scuola d'Arte N Nanni, Verona, Italy; Acad Cignaroli, Verona, Italy. *Hon Degrees:* Master of Art/Sculpture. *Work:* Biennale Nazionale di Verona; High Mus Art, Atlanta, Ga; Univ di Parma Mus, Italy; Ravinia Park, Highland Park Ill; City of Verona Public Gardens; City of Chicago, Corner of State and Washington St. *Comn:* Bronzes, Pick Hall for Int Studies, Univ CHicago, 71; Vanderbilt Univ Med Ctr Hosp, 80; Being Born(sculpture), City of Chicago, 83; Revenue Bldg, Springfield Ill, 85. *Exhib:* Brooklyn Mus, 68; Art Inst Chicago, 68; traveling exhibs, State Ill Arts Coun, 69, Ill Bronzetto Ital, 71, Int Art Expo, Chicago, 81-86 & Mile of Sculpture, 82-84; Sears Tower Bank, Chicago, 77; Seven Sculptors, DePaul Univ, 78; retrospective, Paris Art Ctr, France & Cult Ctr, Ill, 85; V Ferrari - 1959-2003 Ombre della Sera, Gallery d'Arte Moderna, Verona, Italy, 2003; and many others. *Collection Arranged:* 6 Sculturi Americani Dall'Illinois in Europa, Baur, Dunbar, Emser, Ferrari,Rojek, Scarff, EUR Lake and park, Rome, 2000. *Pos:* Sculptor in residence, Univ Chicago, 66-76; Liceo Artistico, Verona, 63-66; Loyola Univ, Rome Ctr, 99-01. *Teaching:* Asst prof sculpture, Univ Chicago, 67-76. *Awards:* Nostra Ministero Publica, Istruzione Roma, Italy, 64; Biennale Nazionale di Verona, 65; Ill Coun of Am Inst Architects Award, 77; Man of the Yr, Ital Cult Ctr, Ill, 86; Cavaliere Officiale Republica Italiana, Offical Knight of the Itralian Republic, 93; Ill Governors Award, IAC, 2003. *Bibliog:* Arturo Quitavalle (auth), Ferrari Gocce d'Amor Pop, Univ di Parma, 70; article, Cimaise Mag, 82; V Ferrari sculpture, Paris Art Ctr, Rizzoli Publ, 85. *Mem:* Sindacato Artisti; Arts Club Chicago; Hyde Park Art Ctr (bd mem). *Media:* Metal, Marble. *Mailing Add:* 5429 S Eastview Park Chicago IL 60615-5980

FERREIRA, ARMANDO THOMAS
EDUCATOR, SCULPTOR
b Charleston, WVa, Jan 8, 32. *Study:* Chouinard Inst; Long Beach City Col; Univ Calif, Los Angeles, BA & MA. *Work:* Wichita Art Mus; State Calif Collection; Univ Utah Art Mus. *Exhib:* Los Angeles Co Mus, 58, 60 & 66; Pasadena Mus Art, 68; Univ Calif, Santa Barbara, 73; Northern Ill Univ, 86; Beckstrand Gallery, Palos Verdes, Calif, 87; Univ Madrid, 92; and other group & one-man shows. *Teaching:* Prof ceramic sculpture, Calif State Univ Long Beach, 57-85, assoc dean, Sch Fine Arts, 85-91, acting dean, Col Arts, 91-; Fulbright lectr, Brazil, 81. *Awards:* Purchase Awards, Calif Expos, 61 & Wichita Art Asn, 66; Fel, Nat Asn Schs Art & Design. *Mem:* Nat Asn Schs Art Comn Accrediting; Int Video Art Network. *Media:* Clay, Mixed. *Mailing Add:* c/o State Univ Dept Art 1250 N Bellflower Blvd Long Beach CA 90840-0006

FERRELL, CATHERINE (KLEMANN)
SCULPTOR
b Apr 27, 47; US citizen. *Study:* Fla Atlantic Univ, BA(sculpture), 69; Univ Miami, MA(sculpture), 72; further study, Pietrasanta, Italy; apprenticeship, Montoya Intl Art Studios; studied with Blair Buswell, Stanley Bleifield, Jill Burkee, Lincoln Fox, Jerry Balciar, Kirsten Kokkin, Jo Saylors, Zahourek & Veryl Goodnight; further study, Pietrasanta, Italy; apprenticeship, Montoya Int Art Studios. *Work:* Delray Beach Pub Libr, Fla; Brevard Art Ctr & Mus, Fla; Norton Gallery Art; Bennex Int, Norway; Cornell Mus of Art and History, Fla; pvt collections of Dr. Paul Gingras & Gunter Schultz-Franke. *Comn:* Black African Stone Fish, John H Surovek Fine Arts, Palm Beach, Fla, 82-83; Alabaster Self-Portrait, comn by Artine Artinian, Palm Beach, Fla, 83; Mythical Fish, comn by Mr & Mrs Gunter Schulz-Franke, Osnäbruck, WGer, 83; archit sculpture & wall reliefs, comn by Sally Gingras, West Palm Beach, Fla, 83 & 84; sculpture, comn by Mr & Mrs Marshall Brumer, Bellevue, Wash, 98; United World Col, Montezuma, NMex, 2002. *Exhib:* Solo exhibs, Elliot Mus, Fla, 87, 35 Yr Retrospective, J Sexton Gallery, Fla, 96, McCreeless Fine Arts Gallery, Ashbury Col, Kent, 96, Univ Mich, Flint, 96, Art from the Heart (with catalog), Cornell Mus Art &

Hist, Fla, 98, Cornell Mus, Delray Beach, Fla, 99; Emerging Realism, Trade St Gallery, 90; Simply Fish, Munson Gallery, Fla, 93; Wildlife, The Artists View, Leigh Yawkey Woodson, Wis, 97; Benson Sculpture Garden, 97-98; Cornell Mus Inspirations, 2000; Art of the Animal Kingdom, Bennington Ctr for the Arts, Vt; plus others. *Pos:* Sculptor in residence, Brookgreen Garden, 2000-01; owner & pres, Art Equities Inc. *Awards:* Elliot Liskin Mem Award, Salmagundi Club, NY; Pen & Brush Award, Pen & Brush Exhib NY, 92; Salmagundi Award, Pen & Brush Exhib, NY, 93; Cornell Mus Award, Inspirations, 2000; Coun of Am Artists Award, Acad Artists of Am; Silver Medal of Honor, Audubon Artists of Am, 99. *Bibliog:* Gary Schwan (auth), New exhibits worth taking in, Palm Beach Post, 2/6/83; Helen Colella (auth), Catherine Ferrell, capturing nature in a variety of mediums, Art Rev Mag, Vol VII, No 1, 8/96; Wildlife Art Mag, 99; plus others. *Mem:* Catherine Lorilland Wolfe Art Club Asn, NY; Pen & Brush, NY; assoc mem Audubon Artists Am, NY; Am Soc Marine Artists; Salmagundi Club, NY; Am Acad Women Artists; fel Am Artists Profl League, Inc; Knickerbocher Artists, Inc; plus others. *Media:* Bronze, Stone. *Interests:* Traveling, reading, painting & sketching. *Dealer:* Cheryl Newby Gallery Rawley's Island SC. *Mailing Add:* 12546 N Hwy A1A Vero Beach FL 32963-9411

FERRIS, DANIEL B
GALLERY DIRECTOR, CURATOR
b Columbia, SC, Sept 10, 47. *Study:* Univ SC, BS, 69; Alliance Francaise, Paris, 73. *Collection Arranged:* Spirit of the Object, Humphrey Fine Arts, 92. *Pos:* Dir, Amos Eno Gallery, New York, 90-; cur, YWCA Gallery, Brooklyn, NY, 90-91. *Bibliog:* The Amos Eno Performance Arm, Downtown, 3/91; Plenty of Energy, The Villager, 2/28/91; Downtown Essentials, Best of the Week - Spirit of the Object; Downtown Express, 4/26/92. *Mem:* Asn Artist Run Galleries; Coalition Independent Artists (exec dir, 85-); BWAC, 91-. *Specialty:* Contemporary. *Mailing Add:* 210 E 15th St No 11A New York NY 10003

FERRIS, (CARLISLE) KEITH
ILLUSTRATOR, PAINTER
b Honolulu, Hawaii, May 14, 29. *Study:* Tex A&M Col; George Wash Univ; Corcoran Sch Art; spec study with Tad Crawford & Gerald McConnell, Pratt Inst, 79. *Hon Degrees:* Daniel Webster Col, Hon DHL, 95. *Work:* USAF Art Col, Pentagon; Nat Air & Space Mus, Smithsonian Inst; US Airforce Mus, US Airforce Acad. *Comn:* Boeing; Gen Electric; Lockheed Martin; Pratt & Whitney; Mural (25ft x 75ft), Fortresses Under Fire, World War II Gallery, 76, & mural (20ft x 75ft), Evolution of Jet Aviation, 81, Nat Air & Space Mus, Smithsonian Inst, Washington DC; Painting of Mem, USAF Mem Found, 2006; and others. *Exhib:* USAF Exhib, NY Soc Illusr, 61-; one-man shows, Nat Air Space Mus, Smithsonian Inst, Washington, 69-70, NY Soc Illusr, 70 & 79, US Air Force Mus, 83, US Air Force Acad, 83, Am Airlines C R Smith Mus, Ft Worth, 95, Simuflight Corp, Ft Worth, 96 & Mighty Eighth Air Force Heritage Mus, Savannah, 98; Colo Springs Fine Art Mus, 90; Royal Air Force Mus, 91; Daniel Webster College, 2000; George Bush Pres Libr, Tex A&M Univ, Col Station, Tex, 2003. *Collection Arranged:* Pacific Air Forces, Royal Hawaiian Hotel, Honolulu, 2002; US Air Force Mus, 2003; Simuflie, Fort Worth, 2003; Soc illusrs, New York, NY, 2003; George Bush Pres Library, College Station, TX, 2003; The Mighty 8th Air Force Mus, Savannah, GA, 2003. *Pos:* Art dir-prod mgr, Cassell Watkins Paul Art Studio, St Louis, 52-56; freelance artist/illusr, 56-; chmn, Air Force Art Comt, Soc Illusr, 68-70 & 79-91, hon chmn, 91-; pres, Am Soc Aviation Artists, 88-90, 99-2000. *Teaching:* Workshop, in conjunction with Am Soc Aviation Artists Ann Forum, 89, 90, 92, 94, 95 & 96, 99, 2000, 2002, 2004. *Awards:* Citation of Hon, Air Force Asn, 78; Dean Cornwell Recognition Award, Soc Illusr, 92; Best Show, Am Soc Aviation Artists, 95 & 96; Laureate for Life Time Achievement, Aviation Week & Space Technol Laureate Hall Fame, Nat Air & Space Mus, 2004; Laureate, Illusr Hall Fame, Soc Illustrators, NY, 2006. *Mem:* Life mem NY Soc Illusr; founding mem Am Soc Aviation Artists. *Media:* Oil. *Specialty:* aviation art. *Interests:* aviation technol & history. *Collection:* over 2,000 books, tech manuals, drawings, & slide/photog reference files. *Publ:* The Aviation Art of Keith Ferris, Peacock Press, Bantam Bks, 78; Real trouble, Aviation Art Mag, Vol 2, 94; Global workhorse, Flight Mag, 11-12/96; auth, Life, Flight and Art, Air Power History, Vol 52, No 1, Spring 2005. *Dealer:* Keith Ferris Galleries. *Mailing Add:* 50 Moraine Rd Morris Plains NJ 07950

FERTITTA, ANGELA
EDUCATOR, ADMINSTRATOR
Study: Univ Colo, BFA, MFA. *Exhib:* Exhib incl Fac Honorarium Exhib. *Teaching:* Dean, academic affairs Art Inst Boston at Lesley Univ, Boston, adjunct prof drawing & painting/found. *Mailing Add:* Art Inst of Boston at Lesley Univ 700 Beacon St Boston MA 02215-2598

FESSLER, ANN HELENE
VIDEO ARTIST, WRITER
b Toledo, Ohio, Oct 2, 49. *Study:* Ohio State Univ, Columbus, BA, 72; Webster Col, St Louis, MA(media), 75; Univ Ariz, MFA(photog), 82. *Work:* Whitney Mus Am Art; Ctr Creative Photog; Mus Contemp Art, Chicago; Franklin Furnace Book Arch, NY; Mus Mod Art. *Comn:* MAPTAP, Maryland Arts Place, 85; billboards, Art Against Aids, NY, 90; roadside installation, She Rode Horses, Washington Proj Arts, DC. *Exhib:* Going for Baroque, Walters Art Mus, Baltimore, Md, 95; Ex/Changing Families, Calif Mus Photog, Riverside, Calif, 97; Close to Home, Bell Gallery, List Ctr, Brown Univ, Providence, RI, 2001; Everlasting, Md Inst Col Art, Balitmore, Md, 2003; Everlasting: New Eng, Radcliffe Inst, Harvard Univ, Cambridge, Mass, 2004. *Collection Arranged:* Expanding Committment: Diverse Approaches to Socially Concerned Photography, Meyerhoff Gallery, MD Inst Col Art, 86. *Teaching:* Instr photog & video, Webster Col, St Louis, 74-79; vis artist photog, Tyler Sch Art, 81-82; instr photog & books, Md Inst Col Art, 82-92; head, Photography Dept, RI Sch Design, 93-97; prof, photog dept, RI Sch Design, 97-. *Awards:* Artist's Fel, Md State Arts Coun, 85, 88 & 92; Artist's Fel, Nat Endowment Arts, 89; Production grant, LEF Found, 2002; Radcliffe Fel, Radcliffe Inst, Harvard Univ, 2003-2004. *Bibliog:* Bella English (auth), The Girls Who Went Away, The Boston Globe, 7/28/2003; Robert Speer (auth), Deprived of a chance to be Mothers, San Francisco Chronicle, 5/7/2006; Kathryn Harrison (auth), In Trouble, NY Times Book Review, 6/11/2006. *Media:* Video, Audio. *Res:* Current work addresses the long-term impact of surrendering a child for adoption. Writing & artwork gives voice to the surrendering mothers. *Publ:* Auth, Guide to Coloring Hair, Tyler Offset Press, 82; First Aid for the Wounded, 87, Life Saving & Water Safety, Visual Studies Workshop, 89; Art History Lesson, copublished with Nat Mus Am Art, Washington, DC, 91; Genetics Lesson, Nexus Press, Atlanta, 92; auth, The Girls Who Went Away: The Hidden History of Women Who Surrendered Children for Adoption in the Decades Before Roe v Wade, The Penguin Press, 2006. *Mailing Add:* RI Sch Design 2 College St Providence RI 02903

FETCHKO, PETER J
MUSEUM DIRECTOR
b Yonkers, NY, July 3, 43. *Study:* Westminster Col, Fulton, Mo, BA, 65; George Washington Univ, Washington, DC, MA, 72; Univ Paris, Sorbonne, 72. *Collection Arranged:* Stone Age New England (coauth, catalog), 75; Japan Day by Day (coauth, catalog), 77; Christian Art of an African Nation, Ethiopia (coauth, catalog), 78. *Pos:* Cur, Peabody Mus, Salem, 68-80, dir, 80-. *Mem:* Japan Soc Boston; Tattoong Club Japan; Am Ceramic Circle. *Res:* New Guinea and Pacific material culture; Japanese crafts. *Publ:* Auth, Pacific Collections of the Peabody Mus, S Pac Bull, 74; Salem Trading Voyages to Japan During the Early Nineteenth Century, Peabody Mus, 86; ed, Salem: To the Farthest Part of the Rich East, Maritime America, Peter Neill, 88

FETT, WILLIAM F
INSTRUCTOR, PAINTER
b Ann Arbor, Mich, Sept 22, 18. *Study:* Sch Art Inst, Chicago. *Work:* Mus Mod Art, NY; Chicago Art Inst; Mus Mod Art, Mexico City; Weatherspoon Art Gallery, Univ NC, Greensboro; McNay Mus, San Antonio, Tex; San Carlos Art Mus, Mexico City, Mex, 88; Amon Carter Mus, Ft Worth, Tex. *Exhib:* Romantic Paintings in Am, Mus Mod Art, NY, 43; one-man shows, Int Watercolor Show, Art Inst Chicago, 44, De Young Mus, San Francisco, 54 & Weatherspoon Art Gallery, Univ NC, Greensboro, 71; Seattle Art Mus, Wash, 45; Mex-Am Cult Inst, Mexico City, 65 & 92; Watercolor USA, Springfield Art Mus, Mo, 71; Texas Watercolor Soc, San Antonio, Tex, 82; Messing Gallery, St Louis, Mo, 92; one-man retrospective, UNAM Galleries, Mexico City, 96. *Teaching:* Prof drawing & painting, Art Sch, Wash Univ, St Louis, Mo, 46-81, prof emer, 81. *Awards:* Anna Louise Raymond Grad Student Award, Art Inst Chicago, 41-43; Fulbright Scholar to Italy, US Govt, 50-51. *Media:* Watercolor, Oil; Charcoal. *Publ:* Articles, View Mag, View Inc, New York, 43; Romantic Paintings in American, Mus Mod Art, New York, 44; article, Dyn Mag, Wolfgang Paalen, Mex, 45; article, Arts Mag, St Louis, 81; Agenda Mag UNAM, Mexico City, Mex, 96. *Mailing Add:* Colonia Banjidal Sur 69-A 217-2 Deleg Iztapalapa-09450 DF Mexico

FETTING, RAINER
PAINTER
b Wilhelmshaven, Ger, Dec 31, 1949. *Study:* Hochschule der Kûnste, Berlin, Meisterschûler, 77; Columbia Univ, New York, 78-79. *Work:* Mus Gegenwartskunst, Basel, Switz; Portland Art Mus, Ore; Mus Contemp Art, Sydney, Australia; Musée des Beaux Arts, Toulon, France. *Exhib:* A New Spirit in Painting, Royal Acad Arts, London, Eng, 81; Image Innovations, Va Mus, Richmond, 83; An Int Survey of Recent Paintings, Mus Modern Art, NY, 84; Origen y Vision, Museo de Arte Moderno, Mexico City, 84; States of War: New Am Painting, Seattle Art Mus, Wash, 85; 1945-1985 Kunst in BRD, Nat Galerie Berlin, WGer, 85; one-man shows, Kunsthalle Basel, Switz & Mus Folkwang, Essen, WGer, 86. *Bibliog:* Christo Joachimides (auth), Zeitgeist, Katalog, 82; Giovanni Testori (auth), Rainer Fetting, Flash Art, Italy, 4/86; Jean Christopher Ammann (auth), Rainer Fetting, Kunsthalle Basel Katalog, 86. *Dealer:* Marlborough Gallery 40 W 57th St New York NY. *Mailing Add:* c/o de Andino Fine Arts 2450 Virginia Ave NW Washington DC 20037-2679

FEUERHERM, KURT K
PAINTER
b Berlin, Ger, Mar 22, 25. *Study:* Albright Art Sch; Univ Buffalo, BFA; Cranbrook Acad Art, MFA; Yale Summer Sch, Norfolk, Conn, with NaumGabo, Peter Blume & Ben Shahn; Yale Univ, with Josef Albers, Stuart Davis & Abraham Rattner. *Work:* Cranbrook Art Mus, Bloomfield Hills, Mich; Mem Art Gallery, Rochester, NY; Albright-Knox Art Gallery, Buffalo, NY; Henry Gallery, Univ Wash, Seattle; Am Fedn Art. *Comn:* Ceramic abstract mural, Midtown Plaza, Rochester, NY, 64; Stations on the Cross, Our Lady of Mercy Church, Rochester, 64; St John's the Evangelist Church, Rochester, 65; Liberty Pole (consult designer), City of Rochester, 66. *Exhib:* Am Painting Today, Metrop Mus Art, NY, 50; Cranbrook Painting Exhib, Bloomfield Hills, Mich, 52; Columbia Mus of Art Painting Biennial, SC, 57; Everson Mus Art, Syracuse, NY, 57-70; one-man show, Henry Gallery, Univ Wash, Seattle, 69; NY Crafts, Munson-Williams-Proctor Inst, Utica, NY, 61; four-man show, Mem Art Gallery, Univ Rochester Fac Show, 70; and others. *Pos:* Conservator, Intermuseum Lab, Oberlin, Ohio, 71-72. *Teaching:* Asst prof painting, Univ Rochester, NY, 60-71; assoc prof studio arts, Empire State Col, Rochester, 73-87; design instr, Polimoda Fashion Sch, Firenze, Italy, 95-97. *Awards:* Purchase Awards (painting & watercolor), Cortland Art Mus, 53; Award of Merit, Columbia Painting Biennial, 57; Henri Projansky Award, Rochester Finger Lakes Exhib, 69. *Media:* Collage, Acrylic. *Dealer:* Malton Gallery 2709 Observatory Ave Cincinnati OH 45208. *Mailing Add:* 42 Wilmer St Rochester NY 14607

FEUERMAN, CAROLE A
SCULPTOR, PAINTER
b Hartford, Conn, Sept 21, 45. *Study:* Hofstra Univ, NY, 63; Temple Univ, 64; Sch Visual Arts, BFA, 67. *Work:* Forbes Mag & Malcolm Forbes Mag Collection, New York, NY; Tampa Mus Art, Fla; Mr Pierre Cornette de Saint-Cyr, Paris, France; private collections of Pres Bill & Hillary Clinton, Dr Henry Kissinger & Mr & Mrs Norman Bramen; Ambassador William Schwartz, Longboat Key, Fla; and many other pvt collections. *Comn:* Attitude (sculpture), Rouse & Assoc, Columbia, Md, 88; Absolut Vodka (6 sculptures), Carillon Importers Ltd, Teaneck, NJ, 89, 90 & 92; Frederick Weisman Art Found (5 sculptures), Los Angeles, Calif, 92 & 93; V and S, The Swedish Wine & Spirits Corp (1 sculpture), Stockholm, Sweden, 92; sculpture, comn by Mr & Mrs Theodore Baum, Palm Beach, Fla, Southampton, NY & Englewood, NJ, 92-93. *Exhib:* Solo exhibs, Arnesen Gallery, Vail, Colo, 90, Hokin Gallery, Palm Beach, Fla, 92, Carillon Importers, Teaneck, NJ, 93, Int Swimming Hall of Fame, Ft Lauderdale, Fla, 93, Neptune, Baritzer/Gray/Hamano Gallery, Santa Monica, Calif, 97, New Blue Works, RVS Fine Art, Southampton, NY, 98 & Selected Works, Galerie Facade, Paris, France, 98; Ft Lauderdale Mus Art, Fla, 92; Heroism, Peconic Gallery, Riverhead, NY, 92; New York City by Day, City by Night, Gallery Henoch, NY, 92; NAm Sculpture Exhib, The Foothills Art Ctr, Golden, Colo, 92; The 2nd Fujisankei Biennale Exhib, Hakone Open Air Mus, Kanagawa-Ken, Japan, 94; Summer Exhib, Ekerum Konsthall, Leif Holmar Gallery, Oland, Sweden, 94 & 96; Batter Up: The Art of Baseball, Pelham Art Ctr, NY, 94; 60th Ann Nat Exhib, Cooperstown Art Asn, NY, 96; Selections from the Frederick R Weisman Collections, Frederick R Weisman Mus Art, Pepperdine Univ, Malibu, Calif, 96 & 98; Contemp Realism 95, Medici Ctr Visual Arts, Philadelphia, Pa, 96; The Florida National, Mus Fine Arts, Fla State Univ, Tallahassee, 96; Going for the Gold, Nat Sculpture Soc, Am Tower, NY, 96; The 35th Juried Exhib, Parrish Art Mus, Southampton, NY, 96; The Anxious Image: New Psychological Realism, Cleveland Univ Art Mus, Ohio, 97; Illusions: Trompe l'oeil and Sleight of Hand, Riverside Art Mus, Calif, 98; Feverman and Graziani, Creiger/Dane Gallery, Boston, Mass, 99; and others. *Collection Arranged:* Dr & Mrs Philip Sassauer, Mr & Mrs Ron Katz, Mr Sid Singer. *Awards:* Finalist, Sculpture Competition, 80; Charles D Murphy Sculpture Award, 81 & Amelia Peabody Sculpture Award, 82, Nat Asn Women Artists; First Prize, US Nat Fine Arts Competition, 84. *Bibliog:* Turning Resin into Gold, Leaders Mag, Vol 20, No 2, 250-251, 4-6/97; Art Exhibitions, NY Times, 6/22/97; On Record, Sculpture, 3/98. *Mem:* Int Sculpture Ctr; Nat Asn Women Artists. *Media:* Bronze, Marble; Resin, Oil. *Dealer:* Steffan Stux Gallery Art, Chelsea, NY

FEW, JAMES CECIL
PAINTER
b Orangeburg, SC, Aug 24, 30. *Study:* Clemson Col, BS(elec eng), 53; Univ Chicago, MBA, 64; also workshops with Albert Handell, PSA, 88 & 90, Ben Konis, PSA, 89, Marilyn Simpson, PSA, 83, 84 & 85 & William Hook, 99. *Work:* USAF Art Collection, Washington; Air Force Armament Mus Art Collection, Eglin AFB, Fla. *Comn:* Acrylic painting, comn by Richard Pike, Lynn Haven, Fla, 90; pastel, USAF Art Collection, 92; acrylic, US Air Force Art Collection, 97. *Exhib:* Pastel Soc Am Ann Open Exhib, Nat Arts Club, NY, 88, 90, 91, 92 & 94; Knickerbocker Artists USA Nat Open Exhib, NY, 89, 92, 95 & 96; Am Artists Prof League Grand Ann Exhib, 90, 91 & 92, Salmagundi Club, NY, 90, 91 & 92; Allied Artist Am 76th & 78th Ann Exhib, Nat Arts Club, NY, 89 & 91; Salmagundi Nat Open Exhib, Salmagundi Club, NY, 93. *Teaching:* Pvt lessons. *Awards:* Award Merit, Degas Pastel Soc 2nd Biennial Nat Exhib, Degas Pastel Soc, 88; Art Student's League-NY Award, Knickerbocker Artists 39th Nat Open Exhib, Art Student's League, 89; Ballin Award, Salmagundi Nat Open, Salmagundi Club, 93. *Mem:* Pastel Soc Am; Knickerbocker Artists, USA; Degas Pastel Soc; Pastel Soc NFla (bd dir, 88-); Am Artists Prof League. *Media:* Pastel, Acrylic. *Publ:* Pastels with Zing, Artist's Mag, 06/95. *Mailing Add:* 9620 Sunnybrook Dr Navarre FL 32566-2530

FICHTER, ROBERT W
EDUCATOR
b Ft Myers, Fla, Dec 30, 1939. *Study:* Univ Fla, BFA (printmaking & painting), 63; Ind Univ, MFA, 66. *Work:* Int Mus Photog, George Eastman House, Rochester, NY; Pasadena Art Mus, Calif; Nat Gallery of Can, Ottawa; Mus Fine Arts, Boston, Mass; Princeton Univ, NJ; and others. *Exhib:* Contemp Photog from the Collections, Boston Mus Fine Arts, 74; The Art of Offset Printing, Sch Art Inst Chicago, 78; Northern Ky State Col, 81; Whitney Biennial, Whitney Mus Am Art, 81; Robert Freidus Gallery, NY, 81; Photog in Calif 1945-1984, San Francisco Mus Mod Art, Calif, 84; Extending the Perimeters of Twentieth-Century Photog, San Francisco Mus Mod Art, 85; Photog & Art: Interactions since 1946, Los Angeles Co Mus, Calif, 87; Capturing an Image: Collecting 150 Yrs of Photog, Mus Fine Arts, Boston, Mass, 89; The Cherished Image: Portraits from 150 Yrs of Photog, Nat Gallery Can, Ottawa, 89; Graphic Studio, Contemp Art From the Collaborative Workshop at the Univ S Fla, Nat Callery Art, Washington, DC, 91; one-person exhib, Photog & Other Questions, Int Mus Photog, Rochester, NY, 82 traveled to FSU Fine Arts Gallery, Tallahassee, Fla, 83, Frederick White Gallery, UCLA, 84, Mus Contemp Photog, Columbia Col, Chicago, Ill, 84, Mus Mod Art, San Francisco, Calif, 84, Univ NMex, Albuquerque, 84 & Brooklyn Mus, NY, 85 & New Work, Univ Gallery, Memphis State Univ, 89. *Teaching:* Prof art, Fla State Univ, 1972-2006, prof emeritus, 2006-. *Awards:* Fels, Nat Endowment Arts, 79 & 84; Fla Visual Arts, 81. *Mem:* Col Art Asn Am; Soc Photog Educ. *Publ:* Auth, Robert Fichter, Photography and Other Questions (exhib catalog), Univ NMex Press & George Eastman House Mus; contribr, Graphics Studio, Univ S Fla, Tampa, 12/10/84; Tamarind Inst, Albuquerque, NMex, 11/9/87; Rolling Stone Press, Atlanta, Ga, 88-90; illus, James Huginin, (auth) A-X Cavation, Dept Art, Univ Colo, 88. *Mailing Add:* 710 Waverly Rd Tallahassee FL 32313

FICK, WILLIAM GEORGE
PRINTMAKER
b Lirik, Sumatra, Indonesia, Oct 19, 63; US citizen. *Study:* Duke Univ, BA, 86; Univ NC, Greensboro, MFA, 90. *Work:* New York Pub Libr; Zimmerli Art Mus, Rutgers Univ, New Brunswick, NJ; Weatherspoon Art Gallery, Univ NC, Greensboro; Bradley Univ, Peoria, Ill. *Exhib:* One-man show, Southeastern Ctr Contemp Art, Winston-Salem, 91; 24th Bradley National, Bradley Univ, Peoria, 93; Hooligans, Anderson Gallery, Richmond, 94; EuroAmericana de Grabado 4, Sala Munic de Exposiciones, La Coruña, Spain, 94; Colorprint USA, Tex Tech Univ, Lubbock, 94; New Am Talent: 10, Laguna Gloria Art Mus, Austin, 94. *Awards:* E D Found Grant, 92; Best of Show for Printmaking, 24th Bradley Nat, 93; Nat Endowment Arts Fel Grant, 93. *Mem:* Col Art Asn; Southern Graphics Coun; Mid-Am Print Coun; Philadelphia Print Club. *Media:* Prints. *Mailing Add:* 1121 Rotary Dr High Point NC 27262

FIDLER, SPENCER D
PRINTMAKER
b Detroit, Mich, Nov 20, 44. *Study:* Calif State Univ, Northridge, BA, 66; Univ Iowa, MA, 76 & MFA, 78. *Work:* Univ Iowa; Hallmark Fine Art Collection; Musee de Petit Format, Couvin, Belg; Biblioteque Nationale, Paris; El Paso Mus Art, Tex; NMex State Univ Art Gallery. *Exhib:* Premio Internazionale Biella per l'Ineisione, Bienale, Italy, 97; Fresh Ink, Austin Mus Art, Tex, 97; Liberte, Egalite Fraternite, Mus Arts, Los Angeles, 98; 15th Nat LAPS, Los Angeles, 99; 22nd Int, Kyoto City Mus, Japan, 2002. *Teaching:* Prof printmaking, N Mex State Univ, Las Cruces, 78-. *Bibliog:* Clinton Adams (auth), Printmaking in New Mexico, Univ NMex Press, Albuquerque, 91. *Mem:* Col Art Asn; Boston Printmakers; Southern Graphics Coun. *Dealer:* Spencer Fidler Las Cruces NM; Flatbed Austin Tex; 416 West Gallery Denison Tex. *Mailing Add:* NMex State Univ Dept Art Las Cruces NM 88003

FIELD, MARSHALL
PATRON
b Charlottesville, Va, May 13, 41. *Study:* Harvard Col, BA, 63. *Pos:* With NY Herald Tribune, 64-65; dir, Field Enterprises, Inc, Chicago, 65-84, dir, mem exec comt, 65-84, chmn bd, 72-84, The Field Corp, 84-, Cabot, Cabot & Forbes, 84-, chmn exec comt, 85-89, sr dir, chief exec off, 1989-; publ, Chicago Sun-Times, 69-80, Chicago Daily News, 69-78; publ World Book-Childcraft Int Inc, 73-78, dir, 65-80; Trustee, Art Inst Chicago, Rush-Presbyn, St Lukes Med Ctr, Chicago Community Trust; chmn bd trustees, Chicago Pub Libr Found; chmn bd, Terra Mus Am Art; chmn bd trustees, Field Mus Natural Hist; adv bd, Brookfield Zoo. *Mem:* Nature Conservancy; River Club; Chicago Club; Harvard Club; Racquet Club; Onwentsia Club; Jupiter Island Club; Shore Acres Club. *Mailing Add:* 225 W Wacker Dr Ste 1500 Chicago IL 60606-1235

FIELD, PHILIP SIDNEY
PAINTER, PRINTMAKER
b Brooklyn, NY, Sept 17, 42. *Study:* Art Students League, with Arnold Blanch; Yale Norfolk Summer Sch Music & Art, 62; Syracuse Univ, BFA, 63; RI Sch Design, with Michael Mazur, MFA, 65; Vienna Acad Fine Arts, Fulbright Grant, 65-67. *Work:* Hunterdon Art Ctr, Clinton, NJ; Syracuse Univ; Univ Dallas; Tulsa City-Co Libr, Okla. *Exhib:* one-man shows, Shunjyo Gallery, Tokyo, Japan, 78, Tex Women's Univ, Denton, Tex, 82, Pan Am Univ, Edinburg, Tex, 86 & 88, Robinson Galleries, Houston, Tex, 90, Tex A&M Kingsville, 2003, Univ Tex Pan Am, 97, 98, 99, 2000; Texas Printmakers, N Tex State Univ, Denton, 81; Xochil Art Inst, Mission, Tex, 82; Kansas Eight Nat Small Painting, Drawing & Print Exhib, Fort Hayes State Univ, 83; Across Texas, Patrick Gallery, 84; Dia de los Muertos Exhib, Xochil Art Inst, Mission, Tex, 87 & 88; Arte Rio Grande, McAllen Int Mus, McAllen, Tex, 2001; Native Spirits, Palawan Island, Phillipines, 2002; Digital Interactions, Waseda Univ, Tokyo, 2002; Int Fac Exhib, Embassy of Phillipines, Khala Lampur, Malaysia, 2002; Art on the Move, McAllen Int Mus, 2002; Digitally Propelled Ideas, Pomona, Calif, 2002; Siggraph, San Diego, Calif, 2003. *Pos:* Critic, For Art's Sake, column, McAllen Monitor, 80-81. *Teaching:* Instr art studio, Juniata Col, Huntingdon, Pa, 69-70; from instr to assoc prof, Univ Tex, Pan Am, 71-90. *Awards:* Augusta Hazard Award, Lowe Art Ctr, Syracuse Univ, 63; Merit Award, McAllen Int Mus, Tex, 88, Best of Show, 89 & 91; Art Fac of STex, McAllen Int Mus, 88. *Bibliog:* Al Brunelle (auth), article, Art News, 5/73; Maurice Schmidt (auth), Reflections on art, 1/76 & Art, light and history 6/76, Corpus Christi Caller. *Mem:* Col Art Asn. *Media:* Intaglio; Oil. *Mailing Add:* Dept Art Pan American Univ 1201 West Univ Drive Edinburg TX 78539

FIELD, RICHARD SAMPSON
CURATOR, HISTORIAN
b New York, NY, Aug 26, 31. *Study:* Harvard Univ, AB, AM & PhD. *Collection Arranged:* 15th Century Woodcuts & Metalcuts from the National Gallery of Art (with catalog), 65; Jasper Johns: Prints 1960-1970 (with catalog), 70 & Silkscreen: History of a Medium (with catalog), 71, Philadelphia Mus Art; The Fable of the Sick Lion: A Fifteenth Century Blockbook (with catalog), 74, Gabriel de Sanit-Aubin (with catalog), 75, Jasper Johns: Prints 1970-1977, 78, Prints Drawings and Paintings by Philip Pearlstein, 79 & The Prints of Armand Seguin (1869-1903), 80, Davison Art Ctr, Wesleyan Univ; Fifteenth Century Woodcuts, Metrop Mus Art, 77. *Pos:* Asst to dir, Fogg Art Mus, Cambridge, Mass, 61-62; asst cur of prints, Alverthorpe Gallery-Nat Gallery Art, 62-68 & Philadelphia Mus Art, 69-72; cur, Davison Art Ctr, Wesleyan Univ, Middletown, Conn, 72-79; cur prints, drawings & photographs & assoc dir, Art Gallery, Yale Univ, New Haven, Conn, 79-. *Teaching:* Assoc prof art, Wesleyan Univ, 72-79. *Awards:* Fulbright Grant, France, 59-60; Finley Fel, Nat Gallery Art, 65-67. *Mem:* Print Coun Am (dir, 70-72). *Res:* Fifteenth century woodcuts; Gauguin; contemporary prints. *Publ:* Auth, Gauguin's Noa Noa suite, Burlington Mag, 68; auth, Woodcuts from Altomunster, Gutenberg-Jahrbuch, 69; auth, Gauguin's Monotypes, 73; auth, The Prints of Richard Hamilton, 73. *Mailing Add:* 46 Mountain View Terr North Haven CT 06473

FIERO, GLORIA K
EDUCATOR, HISTORIAN
b New York, NY, May 19, 39. *Study:* Univ Miami, Coral Gables, AB, 60; Univ Calif, Berkeley, MA, 61; Fla State Univ, Tallahassee, PhD, 70. *Teaching:* Prof hist, Univ La at Lafayette, 69-96, emer, 96-. *Awards:* Fulbright Fel to Belg, 66-67; Amoco Found Award Outstanding Teaching, 83; Honoree, Gloria K Fiero Friends of the Humanities Arts Series, 96. *Mem:* Col Art Asn Am; Southeastern Col Art Conf; Nat Asn Humanities Educ; South-Central Renaissance Conf (pres, 85-86). *Res:* Late Medieval, northern Renaissance painting and manuscripts; early 20th century painting. *Publ:* Courtier and commoner: Two styles of fifteenth century manuscript illumination, Explorations Renaissance Cult, 77; Geertgen tot Sint Jans & the Dutch manuscript tradition, Oud Holland, 82; Death Ritual in Fifteenth Century Manuscript Illumination, J Medieval Hist, 84; Three Medieval Views of Women, Yal Univ Press, 89; The Humanistic Tradition, 6 vols, WC Brown & Benchmark, 92 & 94; 3/e, McGraw-Hill, 98; 5th ed 2006; LANDMARKS in Humanities, McGraw Hill, 2005

FILIPACCHI, DANIEL
PATRON
b Paris, France, Jan 12, 28. *Pos:* French corresp, Ebony Mag, Paris; photog, Paris Match mag; jazz disc jockey, radio prod Europe 1, Paris, 1955-60; chmn, principal owner, Publ Filipacchi, 60-; founder, owner, ed var mag, France, 63-; chmn, Chief Exec Officer, Warner-Filipacchi Music, SA, Paris, 70-85; chmn, Hachette Filipacchi Mag, New York City, 90-; co-artistic dir, Sidney Bechet Centennial, New Orleans, 97; prod, Musisoft/Masters of Jazz; trustee, SR Guggenheim Mus, currently; chmn, principal owner, Paris Match, other French consumer mag, currently. *Awards:* Named one of top 200 collectors, ARTnews Mag, 2004. *Collection:* Modern art, especially surrealism. *Publ:* Ed, Surrealism: Two Private Eyes, The Nesuhi Ertegun & Daniel Filipacchi Collections, 99. *Mailing Add:* Hachette Filipacchi Mags 1633 Broadway 40th Fl New York NY 10019-6708

FILIPOWSKI, RICHARD E
SCULPTOR, EDUCATOR
b Poland, May 29, 23; US citizen. *Study:* Inst Design, Ill Inst Technol, with L Moholy-Nagy, BA. *Work:* Addison Gallery Am Art, Andover, Mass; State St Bank & Trust Co, First Nat Bank, Boston Safe Deposit & Trust Co, Mus Fine Art, Boston, NY; Chase Manhattan Bank, NY; Mus Fine Arts, Boston. *Comn:* Sculptural ark, Temple B'rith Kodesh, Rochester, 62; sculptural cross, Trinity Evangel Lutheran, Philadelphia, 65; sculpture, Echo, Revere Copper & Brass Corp, NY, 65; Winter Pine Sculpture, Town of Lexington, MA, 79; Pinecone, Small Scale Sculpture, SPNEA, 2003. *Exhib:* Art for US Embassies, Inst Contemp Art, Boston, 66; Nat Exhib Art, Ogunquit, Maine, 67; one-man shows, Fitchburg Art Mus, Mass, 68 & State Univ Oneonta, NY, 69; Outdoor Sculpture Exhib, De Cordova Mus, Lincoln, Mass, 72; Mass Inst Technol, 84; Arch Am Art, Boston, Mass, 89 & 90; Art Career: Photos Sculpture Reviews & Exhibs, Archives Am Art Smithsonian, 89-90; Gift to the Nation, Libr of Congress, 2002. *Teaching:* Assoc prof visual design, Mass Inst Technol, 53-88, prof emer, 88. *Awards:* First Prize Sculpture, Boston Arts Festival, 58; Aleck & Ruth McLean Award, Nat Exhib Art, Ogunquit, 67. *Bibliog:* Katherine Kuh (auth), Abstract and surrealist American art, Art Inst Chicago, 48; Patricia Boyd Wilson (auth), The home forum, Christian Sci Monitor, 65; Phoebe Cutler (auth), Richard Filipowski's sculpture, Harvard Art Rev, 67. *Media:* All Media. *Mailing Add:* 10 Round Hill Rd Lexington MA 02173

FILLERUP, MEL
PAINTER
b Lovell, Wyo, Jan 28, 24. *Study:* Art Students League; study with Paul Bransom, Serge Bongart, William Reese, Conrad Schwiering, Robert Meyers & Robert Lougheed. *Work:* Nat Cowboy Hall Fame, Okla City. *Comn:* Husky dogs, Husky Oil Co; mural, Vis Ctr, Cody, Wyo; 2 murals, Utah Valley State Col, Heber City. *Exhib:* Western States Show, Cody Country Art League, 65-75; Springville Art Mus Show, 70-2003; CM Russell Auction, Great Falls, Mont; Wind River Artists Asn; NY Life Ann Calendar Competition; Nat Cowboy Hall Fame, Wild Animal Art Exhib, 79; Western Rondezvous of Art, Bozeman, Mont; Buffalo Bill Art Show, Cody, Wyo. *Teaching:* Oil painting, North West Community Col, 74-75. *Awards:* Best of Show, Cody Country Art League Western Show, 91; Nick Eggenhoffer Award, 92; Peter Hassrick Award, Western Rondezvous of Art, 92; Artist of the Yr Award, Buffalo Bill Art Show, 2005; Gold medal Award, AICA, San Dimas, Calif; William E. Weiss Award, Buffalo Bill Art Show, 2005. *Bibliog:* Carl Belhtold (auth), The Artristry of Melvin M. Fillerup. *Mem:* Cody Country Artist Asn (pres, 68-70); Soc Animal Artists. *Media:* Oil, Watercolor. *Specialty:* Western art. *Interests:* Drawing, painting, hunting, fishing. *Collection:* Northwest Community College. *Publ:* Auth & illusr, Sidon: The Canal that Faith Built; articles, Southwest Art, 9/80 & Palette Talk, No 54; Art of the West, The Studio, 7-8/93; Am Artists, 2/2000. *Dealer:* Big Horn Gallery Cody Wyoming; Ericson Gallery Salt Lake City UT. *Mailing Add:* 2007 Kerper Blvd Cody WY 82414

FILLIN-YEH, SUSAN
MUSEUM DIRECTOR, CURATOR
b New York, NY. *Study:* Grad Ctr, City Univ New York, PhD, 81. *Collection Arranged:* Charles Sheeler: American Interiors, The Technological Muse & American Art in the 1950's (auth, catalog), 87. *Pos:* Cur, Douglas F Cooley Mem Art Gallery, Reed Col, Portland, Ore, 91-92, dir, 92-. *Teaching:* Asst prof, Yale Univ, New Haven, Conn, 82-89; adj prof, Hunter Col NY, 91. *Awards:* Ann Achievement Award, PhD Alumni Asn City Unvi NY, 92. *Mem:* Col Art Asn Am; Alliance of Independent Cols Art. *Publ:* Auth, The Serpentine Lattice, Herbert Newton Cooley Gallery, 93 & Modern Art in America, 96, Reed Col. *Mailing Add:* Douglas F Cooley Mem Art Gallery Reed Col 3203 SE Woodstock Blvd Portland OR 97202-8199

FILMUS, MICHAEL ROY
PAINTER
b New York, NY, May 12, 43. *Study:* Boston Univ, BA, 66; Art Students League. *Work:* Berkshire Mus, Pittsfield, Mass; Minneapolis Inst Art; Art Inst Chicago; Denver Art Mus; Hunter Mus Art, Chattanooga, Tenn. *Exhib:* Drawings USA, Minn Mus Art, 75; one-man shows, Hirschl & Adler Galleries, NY, 75, 77 & 79, David Findlay Jr, NY, 84, 96 & 98, Welles Gallery, Lenox, Mass, 90; Albrecht Mus Art, 76; 200 Yrs of Am Art, Berkshire Mus, Pittsfield, Mass, 76; Flint Inst Arts, Mich, 77; Art of the State, Rose Art Mus, Waltham, Mass, 79; Contemp Naturalism, Nassau Co Mus Fine Art, Roslyn Harbor, NY, 80. *Awards:* Purchase Prize, 40th Ann Midyear Show, Butler Inst Am Art, 76. *Bibliog:* John Arthur (auth), The temperament of nature: Recent paintings by Michael Filmus, Arts Mag, 4/84; Michael Brenson (auth), Michael Filmus, NY Times, 4/84; Eunice Agar (auth), The Filmus Family, Am Artist, 12/95. *Mem:* Life mem Art Students League. *Media:* Oil, Pastel. *Mailing Add:* 221 Castle Hill Ave Great Barrington MA 01230

FILMUS, STEPHEN I
PAINTER
b New York, NY, Feb 4, 1948. *Study:* Univ Pittsburgh, BA, 70; Columbia Univ, MA, 71; Art Students League, 72. *Work:* Ball State Mus, Muncie, Ind; Bank New Eng, Springfield, Mass; Berkshire Mus, Pittsfield, Mass. *Exhib:* Solo shows, Still-Lifes, Berkshire Mus, Pittsfield, Mass, 80 & 84, Welles Gallery, Lenox Mass, 89 & 2004-06, Lenox Gallery of Fine Arts, 2002, 2003; Still Life: Five Visions, David Findlay Jr, NY, 84; Works on Paper, David Findlay Jr, NY, 85; 2 plus 4 Artists Working, Clark-Whitney Gallery, Lenox, Mass, 86; Berkshire Art Gallery & Art Ctr, Great Barrington, Mass, 96; Norman Rockwell Mus, Stockbrdige, Mass, 2001. *Pos:* Trustee, Becket Arts Ctr. *Awards:* First Place, Works on Paper, Berkshire Art Mus, 79. *Bibliog:* Gerrit Henry (auth), Still Life: Five Visions, Arts Mag, 9/84; Charles Bonenti (auth), Filmus, Works on Paper, Arts Mag, 6/85; Eunice Agar (auth), The Filmus family, Am Artist, 12/95. *Mem:* Great Barrington Cult Coun. *Media:* Oil. *Dealer:* Lenox Gallery of Fine Arts 69 Church St Lenox MA 01240. *Mailing Add:* 4 Fern Hill Rd Great Barrington MA 01230

FINCH, RICHARD DEAN
PRINTMAKER, EDUCATOR
b Springfield, Mo, Apr 16, 51. *Study:* Southern Ill Univ at Edwardsville, BA, 74, MFA, 76. *Work:* Brooklyn Mus; Detroit Inst Art; Ill State Mus; Lakeview Mus Arts & Sci, Peoria, Ill; Luxun Acad Fine Arts, Sheyang, China. *Exhib:* Drawings: 81st Exhib, Art Inst Chicago, 85; one-man shows, Shledon Swope Art Mus, 89, Univ Mass, 93; Contemp Ill Artists, Lakeview Mus, Peoria, Ill, 94; Telling It Like It Is, Peltz Gallery, Milwaukee, Wis, 94; 19th Ann Art on Paper, Md Fedn Art, 96. *Pos:* Dir, Normal Editions Workshop, Ill State Univ, Normal, 77-96. *Teaching:* Prof printmaking, compos & life drawing, Ill State Univ, Normal, 77-96. *Awards:* Artist Fel, Nat Endowment Arts, 83; Artist Fel, Ill Arts Coun, 92. *Mem:* Mid Am Print Coun; Print Consortium; Fla Printmaking Soc. *Publ:* Coauth, Experiments in affordable custom lithography, Print News, Vol 3, 81; Lithography Lab Manual, pvt publ, 91; Lithography & Monotype: A Manual of Simplified Techniques for Student Use, pvt publ, 94. *Dealer:* Peltz Gallery 1119 E Knapp Milwaukee WI 53202. *Mailing Add:* 12 Swan Lake Rd Bloomington IL 61704-1297

FINCH, SPENCER
PAINTER, SCULPTOR
Study: Doshisha Univ, Kyoto, Japan, 83-84; Magna Cum Laude, Hamilton Col, NY, BA(comparative lit), magna cum laude, 85; RI Sch Design, MFA(sculpture), 89. *Work:* Whitney Biennial, Whitney Mus Am Art, 2004. *Exhib:* One-man shows incl with Paul Ramirez Literal Truth, Real Art Ways, Hartford, Conn, 1993, one-man shows include, Postmasters Gallery, NY, 1994, 1995, 1997, 1998, 2000, 2002, 2004, Matrix 133, Wadsworth Atheneum, Hartford, Conn, 1997, Rhona Hoffman Gallery, Chicago, 2001, Artpace, San Antonio, Texas, 2003, exhib in group shows at Home for June, Home of Contemp Theater & Art, NY, 1991, Vacation Show, Four Walls, Brooklyn, 1992, Part II, Sandra Gering Gallery, NY, 1994, Four Views From Earth, Ctr Arts, San Francisco, 1995, Between the Acts, Ice Box, Athens, Greece, 1996, Paradise 8, Exit Art, 1999, Conceptual Art As Neurobiological Praxis, Thread Waxing Space, NY, 1999, Made You Look, Austin Mus Art, Tex, 2000, Art on Paper, Weatherspoon Art Gallery, NC, 2000, NY Paper Sculpture Show, Sculpture Ctr, NY, 2003, Indivisible Cities, Bill Maynes Gallery, NY, 2004, Nothing Compared to This, Contemp Arts Ctr, Cincinnati, 2004; exhib in group shows at Home for June, Home of Contemp Theater & Art, NY, 1991, Vacation Show, Four Walls, Brooklyn, 1992, Part II, Sandra Gering Gallery, NY, 1994, Four Views From Earth, Ctr Arts, San Francisco, 1995, Between the Acts, Ice Box, Athens, Greece, 1996, Paradise 8, Exit Art, 1999, Conceptual Art As Neurobiological Praxis, Thread Waxing Space, NY, 1999, Made You Look, Austin Mus Art, Tex, 2000, Art on Paper, Weatherspoon Art Gallery, NC, 2000, NY Paper Sculpture Show, Sculpture Ctr, NY, 2003, Indivisible Cities, Bill Maynes Gallery, NY, 2004, Nothing Compared to This, Contemp Arts Ctr, Cincinnati, 2004. *Mailing Add:* c/o Postmasters Gallery 459 W 19th St New York NY 10011

FINCHER, JOHN H
PAINTER, ASSEMBLAGE ARTIST
b Hamilton, Tex, Aug 4, 41. *Study:* Hardin-Simmons Univ, Abileen, Tex Tech Col, BA, 64; Univ Okla, MFA, 66. *Work:* Dallas Mus Fine Arts; Univ Okla Mus Fine Arts; Wichita Mus Art; Albuquerque Mus, NMex; St Louis Art Mus; and others. *Exhib:* Second Western States Exhib, Corcoran Gallery, Washington, DC, 83; Cold Springs Fine Arts Ctr, 86; Elaine Horwitch Gallery, 87; Albuquerque Mus, NMex, 88; J Cacciola, NY, 90; Elaine Horwitch, Santa Fe, 91; Collages, Monotypes and Paintings, Gerald Peters Gallery, Santa Fe, 2006. *Teaching:* Assoc prof art, Wichita State Univ, 66-77. *Awards:* Wurlitzer Found Grant, Taos, NMex, 72. *Media:* Oil. *Publ:* Auth, articles in Art Space, Arts, Art News & Art in Am; plus various catalogs. *Mailing Add:* 610 Don Canuto St Santa Fe NM 87501-4269

FINDLAY, DAVID B, JR
DEALER
b Kansas City, Mo, June 30, 33. *Study:* Cornell Univ, BME & MBA. *Pos:* Pres, David Findlay Jr Fine Art, currently. *Mem:* Art Dealers Asn Am. *Specialty:* American 19th and 20th Century paintings and sculpture including Hudson River Sch; impressionism, 1920s, 1930s, 1940s modernism; contemporary realism. *Mailing Add:* 41 East 57th St Suite 1115 New York NY 10022

FINDLAY, JAMES ALLEN
LIBRARIAN
b Saginaw, Mich, Aug 13, 43. *Study:* Wayne State Univ, BA, 70, MSLS, 72; Univ Calif, Los Angeles, MA, 75. *Pos:* Reference & cataloging libr, Univ Calif, Los Angeles Art Libr, 75-79; Latin Am archivist, Mus Mod Art Libr, New York, 79-82; dir, RI Sch Design Libr, 82-87; dir, Fashion Inst Tech, New York City Libr, 87-89; head librn, The Wolfsonian Found, Miami Beach, Fla, 89-95 & Broward Co Libr, Bienes Ctr Lit Arts. *Mem:* Art Libr Soc NAm. *Res:* Modern Latin American art; design; decorative arts; propaganda arts; rare books & special collections. *Interests:* Modern art; architecture; fashion; decorative arts; propaganda arts, commercial art, typography. *Publ:* Dorothy Porter Wesley (1905-1995), 2001; Pop-up, Peek, Push, Pull, 2001; Auth, Florida, The Making of a State, 2002; Big Little Books, 2002; Modernism for the Masses: Artist-Designed Postcards, 2003. *Mailing Add:* 702 13th St No 305 Miami Beach FL 33139

FINE, ELSA HONIG
HISTORIAN, EDITOR
b Bayonne, NJ, May 24, 30. *Study:* Syracuse Univ, BFA, 51; Tyler Col Fine Arts, MEd(art), 67; Univ Tenn, EdD(art hist), 70. *Pos:* founding ed, publ, Woman's Art J, Glenside, Pa, 80—. *Teaching:* Asst prof, art Knoxville Tenn Col, 70—75; adj prof, various univs & col, Knoxville, Tenn, 75—80. *Awards:* Recipient Woman of Achievement Award, Woman's Caucus for Art, 96; Status of Women Award, Col Art Asn, 2001; Alumni Award, Tyler Col, 2002. *Mem:* College Art Asn; Women's Caucus for Art. *Publ:* Auth, The Afro-American Artist: A Search for Identity, 73, Women and Art: A History of Women Painters & Sculptors from the Renaissance to the 20th Century, 78. *Mailing Add:* Woman's Art Journal 1711 Harris Rd Laverock PA 19038

FINE, JANE
PAINTER
b Forest Hills, NY, Sept 25, 58. *Study:* Harvard Univ, BA (magna cum laude), 80, Sch Mus Fine Arts, Boston, 81-83; Skowhegan Sch Painting & Sculpture, 89. *Work:* Brooklyn Union Gas Co, NY; Advanta Progressive Corp, NY; Saks Fifth Ave Collection, NY. *Exhib:* Solo Show, White Columns, NY, 92, Hudson Walker Gallery, 93, Casey Kaplan, 95 & 96 & Pierogi Gallery, Brooklyn, 2000; Other Rooms, Ronald Feldman Fine Art Gallery, NY, 95; Arena, Brooklyn, NY, 95; Wacko, Workspace, NY, 95; Schmidt Contemp Art, St Louis, Mo, 96; PPOW Gallery, NY, 99, 2000; Compelled, Hunterdon Mus Art, Clinton, NJ, 2000; others. *Teaching:* Visiting prof, Alfred Univ, NY, 97-99, SUNY, Purchase, 99-2000; resident, Cite Int des Artes, Paris, 98; instr, Vassar Col, 02; instr, RI Sch of Design, 03. *Awards:* Yaddo Artist Residency, 90, 96, 98 & 2001; Visual Arts Fel, NY Found Arts, 94; Pollock-Krasner Found, 2001; and others. *Bibliog:* Carol Vogel (auth), Inside Art, NY Times, 6/9/2000; Galleries: Brooklyn, Jane Fine, New Yorker, 11/27/2000; Holland Cotter (auth), For Hikers Seeking Art, Brooklyn is a Left Bank, NY Times, 12/15/2000. *Mem:* Col Art Asn; Skowhegan Alumni Asn. *Media:* Acrylic. *Dealer:* Joe Amerhein Pierogi 177 N 9th St Brooklyn NY 11211. *Mailing Add:* 179 Grand St Brooklyn NY 11211

FINE, JUD
SCULPTOR, EDUCATOR
b Los Angeles, Calif, Nov 20, 44. *Study:* Univ Calif, Santa Barbara, BA, 66; Cornell Univ, MFA, 70. *Work:* Minneapolis Inst Art; Los Angeles Co Art Mus & Mus Contemp Art, Los Angeles; Mus Stuki, Lodz, Poland; Art Inst Chicago & Mus Contemp Art; Power Inst Fine Arts, Sydney, Australia; Guggenheim Mus, NY; Yale Univ Art Mus, New Haven, Conn; San Diego Mus Contemp Art, Calif. *Comn:* Security Pac, Costa Mesa Gallery, Calif; Mem Garden Carnation Co, Glendale, Calif; Spine, Los Angeles Cent Libr, 93; Scan, Culver City, Calif, 96; Mission Trail, San Antonio, Tex, 97; Venice Beach, Civic Plaza, Modesto, Calif, 98; San Francisco Zoo, 98. *Exhib:* Solo exhib, Ronald Feldman Gallery, 72, 73, 76, 78 & 81, Margo Leavin Gallery, Los Angeles, 77, 79, 81 & 84, Anderson Gallery, Va Commonwealth Univ, Richmond, 82, Thomas Segal Gallery, 83 & Los Angeles Munic Art Gallery, 85, and many others; Los Angeles Co Mus, 72; San Diego Mus Contemp Art, 73 & 88; 71st Am Exhib, Art Inst Chicago, 74; Inst Contemp Art, Boston, 74; Indianapolis Mus Art, 76; Santa Barbara Mus Art, 78; San Diego Mus Contemp Art, 93 & 98; Univ Calif Fine Arts Gallery, Irvine, 87; and others. *Teaching:* vis prof, Ohio Univ, Athens, 75; prof art, Univ Southern Calif, 88-. *Awards:* Contemp Art Coun New Talent Grant, Los Angeles Co Art Mus, 72; Laura Slobe Mem Award, Art Inst Chicago, 74; Individual Artist Fel, Nat Endowment Arts, 82; Grant, Calif State Arts Coun, Sculpture Comn, Exposition Park, Los Angeles, 83; 53rd Ann Western Bks Award. *Bibliog:* Arts Mag, 5/72, 10/73, 9/74 & 3/75; Articles, Arts Mag, 9/74 & 3/75 & Artforum, 4/75; Robert McDonald (auth), Poles Remain as Theme in Sculptures by Fine, Los Angeles Times, 2/24/87. *Media:* Mixed. *Publ:* Auth, Or: An Introduction, 74 & Walk, 75, pvt publ; Walk, Chicago, 76; Revolutions, the Art Record, Green St Recording & Ronald Feldman Fine Arts, NY, 81; Judd Fine, La Jolla Mus Contemp Art, Calif, 88; coauth, Spine, Los Angeles Libr Asn, 94. *Dealer:* Ronald Feldman Gallery 31 Mercer St New York NY 10013. *Mailing Add:* 1366 Appleton Way Venice CA 90291

FINE, RUTH E
CURATOR, PRINTMAKER
b Philadelphia, Pa, May 10, 41. *Study:* Skowhegan Sch Painting & Sculpture; Philadelphia Col Art, BFA, 62; Univ Pa, MFA, 64. *Work:* Philadelphia Mus Art; Nat Gallery Art, Washington, DC; Fleming Mus, Univ Vt, Burlington; Hunterian Art Gallery, Glasgow Univ, Scotland. *Collection Arranged:* Lessing J Rosenwald: Tribute to a Collector (auth, catalog), 82 & Gemini GEL: Art & Collaboration (auth, catalog), 84-, Nat Gallery Art, Washington, DC; Drawing Near: Whistler Etching from the Zelman Collection (auth, catalog), Los Angeles Co Mus Art, 84-; The 1980's: Prints from the Collection of Joshua P Smith, Nat Gallery, 89; The Art of John Marin, Nat Gallery, 90. *Pos:* Cur, Lessing J Rosenwald's Collection, Alverthorpe Gallery, 72-80; cur modern prints & drawings, Nat Gallery Art, Washington, DC, 80-. *Teaching:* Lectr, Philadelphia Col Art, 65-69, Beaver Col, 69-72 & Univ Vt, 76 & 77. *Awards:* Ingram Merrill Found Grant. *Mem:* Col Art Asn; Print Coun Am (mem bd dir, 85-88). *Media:* Etching, Watercolor. *Res:* American and British graphic arts, 18th-20th centuries. *Publ:* Coauth, The Prints of Benton Spruance: A Catalogue Raisonné (with R Looney), Pa Press & Free Libr, Philadelphia, 86; contribr, In Honor of Paul Mellon: Collector & Benefactor, Nat Gallery Art, 86; ed, James McNeill Whistler: A Reevaluation, Nat Gallery, 87; coauth, The Drawings of Jasper Johns, Nat Gallery Art, 90. *Dealer:* Dolan Maxwell Gallery Philadelphia Pa. *Mailing Add:* Curator Mod Prints & Drawings Nat Gallery Art 6th St & Constitution Av Washington DC 20565

FINEBERG, GERALD S
COLLECTOR
Pos: Founder, mgr, The Fineberg Companies, Wellesley, Mass, currently, chmn bd; mem bd overseers. Rose Art Mus, 97, chmn, 2001; chmn, Fine Hotels Co. *Awards:* Gerald S and Sandra Fineberg Gallery, The Rose Art Mus, Brandeis Univ, named in their honor, 2002. *Collection:* Modern & Contemp Art. *Mailing Add:* The Fineberg Companies 1 Washington St Ste 400 Wellesley MA 02481

FINK, AARON
PAINTER, PRINTMAKER
b Boston, Mass, Mar 10, 55. *Study:* Skowhegan Sch Painting & Sculpture, 76; Md Inst Col Art, BFA, 77; Yale Univ Col Art, MFA, 79. *Work:* Mus Mod Art, Metrop Mus Art & NY Pub Libr, NY; Metrop Mus Art, NY; Philadelphia Mus Art, Pa; Mus Fine Arts, Boston, Mass; Art Inst Chicago, Ill; Prudential Life Insurance Co; Libr Cong & Nat Gallery Art, Washington. *Exhib:* A Feast for the Eyes, Mus Mod Art, NY, 92; The Art Collection of the Federal Reserve Board: Five Yrs of Accessions, Bd Gov Bldg, Washington, 92; Magidson Fine Art, Aspen, Colo, 95; retrospective, Aaron Fink 1984-1995, Rockford Art Mus, Ill, 95-96; Paintings & Counterproofs, Lisa Sette Gallery, Scottsdale, Ariz, 96; Face & Figure, Mus Fine Arts, Boston, 96-97; Stillife: The Object in Am, Selections from Mus Mod Art (traveling), Marsh Art Gallery, Richmond, Va, 97; solo exhibs, N, Aaron Fink Contemp Master, Galerie D'Avignon, Can, 2001, New Paintings, Alpha Gallery, Boston, Mass, 2002, Aaron Fink, Magidson Fine Art, Aspen Colo, 2002, Pamela Auchincloss, NY, 2002. *Awards:* Fel, Nat Endowment Arts, 82 & 87; Fel, Mass Coun Arts & Humanities, 84. *Bibliog:* Lea Saslav (auth), Open Season, Boston, 10/91; Nancy Stapen (auth), Two Artists Who View Nature & Culture, Boston Globe, 11/21/91; Gary Susman (auth), Artists on Art, Boston Phoenix, 5/15/92; Lois Tarlow (auth), Profile: An Interview with Aaron Fink, Art New Eng, 3/89. *Media:* All. *Dealer:* Alpha Gallery 14 Newbury St Boston MA 02116

FINK, ALAN
ART DEALER
b Chicago, Ill, July 17, 25. *Study:* Univ Ill, BA. *Pos:* Dir, Alpha Gallery Inc. *Mem:* Art Dealers Asn Am; Boston Art Dealers Asn. *Specialty:* Twentieth century painting, sculpture and graphics; modern master prints. *Mailing Add:* c/o Alpha Gallery 14 Newbury St Boston MA 02116

FINK, HERBERT LEWIS
PAINTER, EDUCATOR
b Providence, RI, Sept 8, 21. *Study:* Carnegie Inst Technol, 41; RI Sch Design, BFA, 49; Yale Univ, MFA, 56; Art Students League; also with John Frazier, Gabor Peterdi, Arshile Gorky & Rico Lebrun. *Work:* Boston Mus Art; Art Inst Chicago; Baltimore Mus Art; Md Inst; Brown Univ; Corcoran Gallery, Washington; Philadelphia Mus Art. *Comn:* Mural, RI Post Off Lobby, Providence, 59; metal sculpture, Sen Green Airport, 60; archit screen, Hartford Bank & Trust Bldg. *Exhib:* Philadelphia Mus Art; Merrill-Chase Galleries, 79; Farnsworth Mus, 82; Republic China, 86; State Ill Bldg, Chicago, 86; and others. *Pos:* Print ed, Int Graphic Arts Soc; trustee, Tiffany Found & Mitchell Found, Mt Vernon, Ill. *Teaching:* Instr painting & drawing, RI Sch Design, 51-61; instr, Yale Univ, 56-61; prof art & chmn dept, Southern Ill Univ, Carbondale, 61-83, distinguished prof, 83-; lectr, univs in Chancum, Chandu, Guanju, Julin & Sezvan Province, Cult Ministry, Peoples Repub China, 85. *Awards:* Purchase Prizes, Soc Am Graphic Artists, 59 & Libr Cong, 59; Guggenheim Fel, 65-66; Visual Artist of the Year, State of Ill, 86; Tiffany award, 60. *Mem:* Nat Acad of Design. *Publ:* Auth, Graphic Artist, Univ Southern Ill Press; book with 100 full page illus, China, 91; Auth, Contemporary American Printmaking, 99. *Dealer:* Huston Tuttle Gallery. *Mailing Add:* 35 Pascal Ave Rockport ME 04856-5914

FINK, JOANNA ELIZABETH
ART DEALER, GALLERY DIRECTOR
b Boston, Mass, Aug 8, 58. *Study:* Wellesley Col, Mass, 76-78; New York Univ, BA, 80; Inst Fine Arts, New York Univ, MA, 83. *Pos:* Admin asst & photogr, Dept Fine Arts, New York Univ, 80-82; res consult, art prog, Chase Manhattan Bank, New York, 83; dir, Alpha Gallery, Inc, Boston, Mass, 83-. *Teaching:* Teaching asst, art hist, New York Univ, 82. *Mem:* Art Dealers Asn Am; Boston Art Dealers Asn; Asn Boston Pub Libr (bd dir, currently). *Specialty:* Contemporary American painting, sculpture and works on paper; 20th century American and European works; modern master prints. *Publ:* Auth, Georg Baselitz: Selected Prints, 1963-1985 (exhib catalog), Alpha Gallery, Boston, 85; auth, The Orphic Art of Varujan Boghosian, Provincetown Arts, 95; auth, various book rev, AA New Eng, 92-95. *Mailing Add:* Alpha Gallery Inc 14 Newbury St Boston MA 02116

FINK, LARRY (LAURENCE) B
EDUCATOR, PHOTOGRAPHER
b Brooklyn, NY, Mar 11, 41. *Study:* With Lissette Model, 59; Coe Col; New Sch Soc Res. *Work:* Mus Mod Art, NY; Corcoran Gallery Art, Washington, DC; Mus Fine Arts, Boston; New Orleans Mus Art; Seattle Mus Art. *Exhib:* Broxton Gallery, Los Angeles, 76 & Case Solway Gallery, Cincinnati, 77; one-man shows, Light Gallery, NY, 77 & 80, Lehigh Univ, Bethlehem, Pa, 78, Sander Gallery, Washington, DC, 78-79, Mus of Mod Art, NY, 79 & Gallery Forum, Spain, 85; San Francisco Mus Art, 81; retrospectives, Harrison Gallery, 86 & Light Gallery, 86. *Teaching:* Instr, Parson Sch Design, 67-72, Kingsborough Community Col, City Univ NY, 69-73, Inst Contemp Photog, Lehigh Univ, 76, Int Ctr Photog, NY, 77; prof photog, Yale Sch Fine Arts, 77-78; prof, Cooper Union, 79; prof photog, Lehigh Univ, 84-87, Bard Col, 87. *Awards:* Creative Artists Pub Serv Fel, 71-72 & 73-74; Guggenheim Fels, 76-77 & 79-80; Nat Endowment Arts Photog Fel, 78-79; Hazlett Award for Excellence in Art, Governor Pa, 85. *Dealer:* Lieberman & Saul Gallery New York NY; Light Gallery 724 Fifth Ave New York NY 10019. *Mailing Add:* PO Box 295 Martins Creek PA 18063

FINK, LOIS MARIE
HISTORIAN, CURATOR
b Michigan City, Ind, Dec 30, 27. *Study:* Capital Univ, BA, 51; Univ Chicago, MA, 55, PhD, 70; Capital Univ, Hon Dr Humanities, 82. *Collection Arranged:* Academy: The Academic Tradition in American Art (auth, catalog), Nat Collection Fine Arts, 75. *Pos:* Cur res, Nat Mus Am Art, 70-93, emer cur, 93-. *Teaching:* Instr art hist & sociology, Lenoir Rhyne Col, 55-56; instr art hist & educ, Midland Col, 56-58; instr, Roosevelt Univ, 58-64, asst prof, 64-70. *Mem:* Col Art Asn; Am Studies Asn; Soc Arts, Relig & Contemp Cult. *Res:* Nineteenth and early twentieth century American art; relationship of French art to American art. *Publ:* Auth, American artists in France, 1850-1870, Am Art J, 73; coauth, Academy: The Academic Tradition in American Art, Smithsonian, 75; auth, French art in the United States, 1850-1870, Gazette Beaux Arts, 78; American participation at the Paris salons, 1870-1900, Int Comt Hist Art 24th Cong, 82; contribr, Elizabeth Nourse, 1859-1938: A Salon Career, Smithsonian, 83; Am Art at the Nineteenth Cent Paris Salons, Cambridge Univ Press, 90. *Mailing Add:* Off Res & Fel Nat Mus Am Art Smithsonian Inst Washington DC 20560

FINKE, LEONDA FROELICH
SCULPTOR, DRAFTSMAN, EDUCATOR
b Brooklyn, NY, 22. *Study:* Art Students League, NY, 45. *Work:* Butler Inst Am Art, Youngstown, Ohio; Nat Portrait Gallery Smithsonian Inst, Washington; Brookgreen Gardens, SC; Brit Mus, London, Eng; City Univ NY; Kingsboro (Ohio) Community Col; Bates Col Mus, Lewiston, Maine; Sculpture Garden; Grounds For Sculpture 2001, Hamilton, NJ. *Comn:* Soc Medalists, The Prodigal Son, 88; Three 6 ft figures (sculpture), Women in the Sun, Atlanta, Ga, 88; Virginia Woolf, British Art Medal Soc, 89; 7 ft figure bronze (sculpture), pvt collection, Conn, 90; Max Som Medal, Otolaryngology Dept, Montefiore Hosp, NY, 92; Centennial metallic sculpture, Am Acad Otolaryngology; Aiken Taylor Award Sewahee Review, 2002. *Exhib:* Images of Am, US Info Agency (traveling exhib bronze figure sculpture selected); NY Botanical Gardens, 81; Int Fedn Medalists, Stockholm, 85 & Brit Mus, London, 92; Port Hist Mus, Philadelphia, Pa, 87; Sculpture Garden, Stamford Mus, Conn; FIDEM, London, 92; Stages of Creation Pub Sculpture, Nat Acad Mus, NY, 98; FIDEM 2000, Goethe Nat Mus, Weimar, Ger; Contemp Sculpture at Chesterwood, Stockbridge, Mass; Mus Contemp At, Los Angeles; Megaro Mus of Art Tokyo Japan, 2001; Grounds for Sculpture Hamilton NJ, 2002; 200 Years of Art Figure Art by Artists Long Island Mus at Stony Brook NY 2003; Challenging Tradition Women fo the Academy Nat'l Academy of Design, 2003; Sculptors guild at White Plains, NY Outdoors exhib for one yr, 2004. *Collection Arranged:* Nat'l Portrait Gallery of Smithsonian Mus, Wash. DC; Butler Institute of American Art, Youngtown, Ohio; British Mus, London, England; Grounds for Sculpture, Hamilton, NJ; The City Univ of NY, Kingsboro, Brooklyn; The Century Assoc. NY; Nat'l Academy of Design, NY; Chrysler Mus, Norfolk, VA; Mus of Foreign Art, Sofia Bulgoria; and more. *Pos:* Adj Prof. *Teaching:* Adj prof sculpture & drawing, Nassau Community Col, 70-95; vis lectr, Hartford Univ Conn, Fordham Univ, NY, Brookgreen Gardens, SC & Brit Art Medal Soc, Loughborough (Eng) Univ, 89. *Awards:* Agop Agapoff Award, Nat Sculpture Soc, 93; Silver Medal, Nat Sculpture Soc, 94; J Sanford Saltus Award, Am Numismatic Soc, 97; and many others; Sculpture House Award-Lifetime Adievement, Nat Sculpture Soc 2005. *Bibliog:* Watson Jones (auth), Contemp Am Women Sculptors; Stella Pandell Russel (auth), Art in the World. *Mem:* Sculptors Guild; Art Medal Soc; fel Nat Sculpture Soc; Am Medallic Sculptors Asn; Nat Acad; Century Asn. *Media:* Plaster for Bronze, Silverpoint, Drawing. *Interests:* Reading, Plants, Gourmet Food, Dance Performances. *Publ:* National Sculpture Review, 93; Brooklyn Journal, 2004. *Dealer:* Fisher Galleries 807 15th St NW Washington DC 20036; Shidoni Bronze Gallery Tesuque NM. *Mailing Add:* 10 The Locusts Roslyn NY 11576

FINKEL, BRURIA
DESIGNER, SCULPTOR
b Jerusalem, Israel, Aug, 2, 32, US citizen. *Study:* Seminar Hakibutzim, Tel Aviv, BA, 53; Alfred Univ, NY, 55; Santa Monica City Col, 71-73. *Work:* Renwick Gallery, Smithsonian; The Stadmuseum, Dusseldorf, Ger; Skirball Mus Art, Los Angeles; Sussman-Preja Collection, Culver City, Calif; Tom Patchett Collection, Track 16, Santa Monica. *Comn:* Natural Elements Sculpture Park, City Santa Monica, 83-; Verona Bldg, Lewi Ceta Partnership, Santa Monica Mus Art, 88-91; Celebration tapestry, Temple Alyah, Woodland Hills, Calif, 93-94; Wall of Water Curtain of Light, Step Up on Second, Santa Monica, 94-95. *Exhib:* The Complete Head Series, De Saisset Art Mus, Santa Clara, Calif & Desert Mus, Palm Springs, Calif, 80-81; Am Porcelain, Renwick Gallery, Smithsonian Inst, Wash DC, 80-84; Tradition in Transition (with Catalog), Univ Calif, Irvine, 82; The Divine Chariot Series (with catalog), Skirball Mus Art, Los Angeles, 85, Jewish Mus, San Francisco, 86; Across Time Space & the Ages (with catalog), Stadmuseum, Dusseldorf, Ger, 93-94; Santa Monica Mus Art, 98; Susret Art, Galerie Kunstmanufaktur Auftragswerkstatte, Austria, 2000; Texturen von Susret Art, Statthalle, fur Kunst Raum, Austria, 2000; Los Angeles Angel Project, 2001; 1001 Reasons to Love the Earth, World Art Collection & Exhib, The Neth and Korea, 2001; Jewish Fed New Bldg, Los Angeles, 2001; 2000 Reasons to Love the Earth (traveling), Essen, Ger, Amsterdam, Los Angeles, Buenos Aires, Tokyo, Johannesburg, Sydney, 2000-03; solo shows, Jacueline Anhalt Gallery, Los Angeles, 72-86, The Erosion Series, Roberts Gallery, Santa Monica, 75, The Complete Head Series, Desert Mus, Palm Springs & DeSaisset Art Mus, Santa Clara, 80-81, Tradition in Transition, Univ Calif, Irvine, 82, The Transformation Series, Tom Luttrell Gallery, San Francisco, 82, New Work in Handmade Paper, Meredith Niles Gallery, Santa Barbara, 82, The Divine Chariot Series, Hebrew Union Col, Skirball Mus Art, Los Angeles, 85, Nine Books for the Poet, Univ Calif Art Libr, Los Angeles, 85, Permutations on the Letters Alef and A, Bertha Urdang Gallery, NY, 86, The Divine Chariot Series, Jewish Mus, San Francisco, 86, Artbooks from the Divine Chariot Series, Artworks Gallery, Los Angeles, 87, Paintings and Artbooks from the Divine Chariot Series, Artemesia Gallery, Chicago, 88, Tarmac Gallery, Santa Monica, 90, Aspects of the Divine Chariot, Sherry Frumkin Gallery, Santa Monica, 91, Back on Broadway, Santa Monica, 98; Mail Art, Sharajah Art Mus, United Arab Emirates, 2005. *Awards:* Calif Arts Coun Award, 76-78 & 88-91; Dorland Mt Colony, 84; Honor Award, Nat Terrazzo & Mosaic Asn, 94. *Bibliog:* Paul S Donlauser (auth), History of American Ceramics, Hunt Kendall, 75; Virginia Watson Jones (auth), Contemporary American Women Sculptors, Oryz Press, 86; Susan Wilson (auth), Bruria Finkel leaves her artistic mark, The Outlook, 9/20/96. *Mem:* Santa Monica Arts Comn (founding mem, chair, 91-93); Nat Women Polit Caucus W Los Angeles (treas, 95-96); Children's Mus, Santa Monica (bd mem, 86-89); Womanspace (founding mem, bd mem, 71); Los Angeles Coun Women Arts (founding mem, bd mem, 70). *Publ:* Auth, The Book of the Letter, Tree Trigram Press, 67. *Mailing Add:* 1225 Hill St Santa Monica CA 90405

FINKELPEARL, TOM
MUSEUM DIRECTOR
Study: Princeton Univ, BA; Hunter Col, MFA. *Pos:* cur dir, PS 1's Clocktower Gallery, 1982-90; exec dir, Percent for Art Progressive, Dept Cultural Affairs, New York City, 1990-96; dir, artist colony Maine, 1996-99; deputy dir, PS 1 Contemp Art Ctr, Long Island City, 1999-2002; exec dir, Queens Mus Art, 2002-. *Mailing Add:* Queens Mus Art NYC Bldg Flushing Meadows Corona NY 11368-3398

FINKELSTEIN, HENRY D
PAINTER, EDUCATOR
b Bar Harbor, Maine, Sept 3, 58. *Study:* Cooper Union, with Reuben Kadish & Nicolas Marsicano, BFA 80; Yale Sch Art, with Lester F Johnson, MFA 83. *Exhib:* Solo exhibs, Prince Street Gallery, NY, 86, 88 & 91, Andrews Gallery, Williamsburg, Va, 89, Parkerson Gallery, Houston, Tex, 89, Wash Art Asn, Conn, 91, Mus du Chateau de Rochefort en Terre, France, 93, Bengert MacRae Gallery, Wyckoff, NY, 93, Gleason Fine Art Gallery, Portland, Maine, 93, Simon Gallery, Morristown, NJ, 2000, Valley House Gallery, Dallas, Tex, 2002, 04 & Kraushaar Galleries, NY, 2001, 03, 05; group exhibs, On the Edge: 40 Yrs of Maine Painting, Portland Mus Art, Maine, 92-93 & Mostly Maine, Tibor de Nagy Gallery, NY, 93; Bengert MacRae, Wyckoff, NJ, 93; Gleason Art Gallery, Portland, Maine, 93. *Teaching:* Asst prof, Hartford Art Sch, 84-92; vis asst prof, Pratt Inst, NY, 86-87; vis artist, Col William & Mary, Williamsburg, Va, 89; instr, Nat Acad Design, NY, 96-; Lyme Acad, Old Lyme, Conn, 2003. *Awards:* Fulbright Fel, Italy, 83-84; Julius Hallgarten Prize, Nat Acad Design, 88; Klots Found Residency Grant, Chateau de Roche Forten Terre, France, 92 & 2000; Carnegie Prize, Nat Acad Design, 03. *Bibliog:* Jean-Pierre Chedaleux (auth), Ouest France, 7/28/92; Philip Isaacson (auth), Maine Sunday Telegram, 5/30/93; Carl Little (auth), Art New Eng, 10/93. *Mem:* Nat Acad. *Media:* Oil. *Dealer:* Kraushaar Galleries New York NY. *Mailing Add:* 46 W 22nd St New York NY 10010

FINKELSTEIN, MAX
SCULPTOR, PAINTER
b New York, NY, June 15, 15. *Study:* Los Angeles City Col; Sculpture Ctr, New York; Calif Sch Art, Los Angeles; Univ Calif, Los Angeles. *Work:* Krannert Art Mus, Univ Ill, Champaign; Hirshhorn Mus, Washington, DC; Univ Calif Mus, Berkeley; Santa Barbara Mus Art, Calif; Los Angeles Co Mus Mod Art; and others. *Exhib:* Highlights of the 1967-1968 Art Season, Larry Aldrich Mus Contemp Art, Ridgefield, Conn, 68; one-man shows, La Jolla Mus Art, Calif, 68 & Esther Robles Gallery, 70; Microcosm, Long Beach Mus Art, 69; Painting & Sculpture Today, Indianapolis Mus Art, Ind, 70; and many others. *Teaching:* Instr sculpture, Univ Judaism. *Awards:* Los Angeles Munic Gallery, 65; Long Beach Mus, 65 & 67; Krannert Mus, Univ Ill, Champaign, 67. *Bibliog:* Ray Faulkner & Edwin Ziegfield (auths), Art Today, Holt, 69. *Media:* Metal, Wood Construction. *Mailing Add:* 621 N Curson Ave Los Angeles CA 90036-1811

FINKLER, ROBERT ALLAN
EDUCATOR, PAINTER
b Chicago, Ill, Nov 22, 36. *Study:* Ill Wesleyan Univ, with Rupert Rilgore & Fred Brian, BFA, 59; State Univ Iowa, with Byron Burford & Robert Knipschild, MFA, 62. *Work:* St Cloud State Col, Minn; Waldorf Col, Iowa; Wis State Univ, Oshkosh; Mankato State Univ; Gen Mills, Minn; West Point, NY. *Exhib:* Drawings USA, St Paul Art Ctr, Minn, 66; Minn Artists Biennial, Minneapolis Art Inst, 67 & 70; Akron Art Inst, Ohio, 70; Rochester Art Ctr, Minn, 77; Minn Artists Compt, 79, 81, 84 & 86; MAEP Minneapolis Inst Arts, 82 & 96; Artbanque (Minneapolis) Gallery, Minn, 86, 87 & 89. *Pos:* Art dept chairperson. *Teaching:* Prof art, Mankato State Univ, 61-. *Awards:* Pres lectureship, Winter Holidays, Presidents Fund, Mankato State Univ, 77

FINLEY, DONNY LAMENDA
PAINTER
b Goodwater, Ala, Oct 7, 51. *Study:* Jacksonville State Univ, BS, 75. *Work:* Birmingham Mus Fine Arts, Ala; Columbus Mus Arts & Sci, Ga; Fine Arts Mus of the South, Mobile, Ala; LaGrange Mus Fine Arts, Ga; Fayette Mus Fine Arts, Ala. *Comn:* Painting, Ala Cattleman's Asn, Talladega, 76. *Exhib:* Am Watercolor Soc, Nat Acad Design, NY, 78, 80 & 82; Alabama Art, US Senate Bldg, 79; Watercolor USA, Springfield Art Mus, Mo, 80; Rocky Mountain Nat, Foothills Art Ctr, Golden, Colo, 81; Nat Watercolor Soc, Palm Springs Desert Mus, 83 & 84; Salmagundi Club, NY, 85; Nat Acad Design, 88, Sonat, Birmingham, 90. *Awards:* Larry Quackenbush Mem Award, Am Watercolor Soc, 80; Strathmore Award, Nat Watercolor Soc, 83; Charlotte Livingston Award, Salmagundi Club, NY, 85; Walter Biggs Mem Award, Nat Acad Design, NY, 90. *Bibliog:* Marda Kaiser Burton (auth), Just a country boy, Southwest Art, 79; Joyce Deaton (auth), Down home Donny, Birmingham Mag, 79; Nell Luter (auth), Donny Finley's Moments Captured, Royal Publ, 87. *Mem:* Am Watercolor Soc. *Media:* Watercolors, Egg Tempera. *Publ:* Contribr, The Tennessee Conservationist, Tenn Dept Conserv, 78, Southwest Art, Art Mag, 79 & Birmingham Mag, 79; illusr, A Catalogue of the South, Oxmoor House, 79; Watercolor page, Am Artist Mag, 81; auth, He Restores My Soul, Harvest House Publ, 2000; contribr, Peace Like A river, 2001, The Heart of Loveliness, 2001, Haravest House Publ. *Dealer:* Marin Price Galleries Bethesda MD; Trees Place Orleans MA. *Mailing Add:* 5057 Greystone Way Birmingham AL 35242-6476

FINLEY, GERALD ERIC
HISTORIAN
b Munich, Ger, July 17, 31; Can citizen. *Study:* Univ Toronto, BA, MA; Johns Hopkins Univ, PhD. *Exhib:* Turner and George IV Edinburgh, Tate Gallery, London/Nat Gallery Scotland, Edinburgh, 81; George Heriot, Painter of the Canadas, Nat Gallery Canada, Ottawa, 78. *Teaching:* Lectr art & archeol, Univ Toronto, 59-60; lectr art, Univ Sask, Regina, 62-63, actg dir, Norman Mackenzie Art Gallery, 62-63; from asst prof to prof art hist, Queen's Univ, 63-95. *Awards:* Gustav Bissing Rotating Fel, Johns Hopkins Univ, 61; Inst Advan Studies Humanities Fel, Edinburgh Univ, 79-80; Fel, Royal Soc of Can, 84. *Mem:* Royal Can Acad Art; fel Royal Soc Canada, 84. *Res:* British late eighteenth and early nineteenth centuries painting; landscape, especially J M W Turner; history of ideas. *Publ:* Auth, Landscapes of Memory: Turner as Illustrator to Scott, 80; Turner and George the Fourth in Edinburgh, 1822, 81; George Heriot: Postmaster Painter of the Canadas, 83; The Deluge Pictures: Reflections on Goethe, JMW Turner and Early Nineteenth-Century Science, Zeitschrift fur Kunstgeschichte, 97; Angel in the Sun: Turner's Vision of Hist, 99; and others. *Mailing Add:* 52 Earl St Kingston ON K7L 2G6 Canada

FINLEY, KAREN
WRITER
Publ: Auth, Shock Treatment, 90; illusr, Enough is Enough: Weekly Meditations for Living Dysfunctionally, 93; A Certain Level of Denial, 99; Living it Up, 99. *Mailing Add:* City Lights Bks Inc 261 Columbus Ave San Francisco CA 94133

FINN, DAVID
PHOTOGRAPHER
b New York, NY, Aug 30, 21. *Study:* City Col Univ New York, BA. *Exhib:* Oceanic Sculptures, Metrop Mus Art, NY, 74; Henry Moore Photographs, l'Orangerie, Paris, France, 77. *Collection Arranged:* Exploring Sculpture, Canova (auth, catalog) & Cellini, Andrew Crispo Gallery, NY; Henry Moore Sculpture and Environment (photographs), Fischer Fine Art Ltd, London, 77; Large Two Forms (auth, catalog), Fairweather-Hardin Gallery, Chicago; Henry Moore, Am Cult Ctr, Madrid. *Awards:* Herbert Adams Mem Medal, Nat Sculpture Soc. *Mem:* MacDowell Colony; Artists for Environ Found; Int Ctr of Photog; Parsons Sch of Design. *Publ:* Auth, Sculpture at Storm King, 79 & New Rochelle, Portrait of a City, 80, Abbeville Press; The Florence Baptistery Doors, Viking Press, 80; Henry Moore at the British Museum, Brit Mus Publ Ltd, 81; Monumental Greek Bronze Sculpture, Abbeville Press, 83. *Mailing Add:* c/o Ruder & Finn 301 E 57th St 3rd Flr New York NY 10022

FINN, DAVID
SCULPTURE
b Urbana, Ill, 1952. *Study:* Cornell Univ, Ithaca, NY, BS, 74; Mass Col Art, Boston, MFA, 82. *Work:* Fondation Cartier, Paris, France; Weatherspoon Art Gallery, Univ NC, Greensboro; Leeds City Art Gallery, Eng; Herbert F Johnson Mus Art, Cornell Univ, Ithaca, NY; Bemis Found, Omaha, Nebr; Mint Mus Art, Charlotte, NC. *Comn:* New Works, Pub Art Fund, NY, 85; Diggs Tower, Winston Salem, NC, 2005. *Exhib:* Solo exhibs, Weatherspoon Art Gallery, Univ NC, Greensboro, 90, Atrium Gallery, Univ Conn, Storrs, 91, Watermans Art Ctr, Brentford, W London, Eng, 92, Leeds City Art Gallery, Eng, 92, NDak Mus Art, Grand Forks, 93 & ES Vandam Gallery, NY, 97; Atlantic Sculpture, Art Ctr, Col Design, Pasadena, 87; Art on Paper 1989, Weatherspoon Art Gallery, Univ NC, Greensboro, 90; Lost and Found, Sculpture Ctr, NY, 91; de'Persona, Oakland Mus Art, Calif, 91; Disjuntive, Valencia Community Col Gallery, Orlando, Fla, 91; Depersona, Oakland Mus Art, Calif, 91; Assemblage, Southern Ctr Contemp Art, Winston Salem, NC, 92; Resurrections: Objects with New Souls, William Benton Mus Art, Univ Conn, Storrs, 94; Body and Soul, ES Vandam Gallery, NY, 96; Thresholds: Spiritual Art, 2003-2006, South Carolina Mus Art, Columbia, SC. *Teaching:* Vis asst prof sculpture, Wake Forest Univ, Winston-Salem, NC, 88-91 & 95-98 & assoc prof, 98-; asst prof sculpture, Kutztown Univ Pa, 94; vis artist, Univ NC, Chapel Hill, 94; asst prof, Wake Forest Univ, Winston-Salem, NC, 2000-. *Awards:* Fel, New York Found Arts, 88; Fel, Nat Endowment Arts, 90; Fel, ZS Reynolds Found, 2001-2005; Fel, NC Arts Coun, 2006-2007. *Bibliog:* Greg Booth (auth), Artist's Children carry a weight beyond their lightness of being, Grand Forks Herald, NDak, 11/12/92; Tom Paterson (auth), Sculptor's works is highlight of faculty exhibit at WFU, Winston-Salem J, 12/10/95; Bill Arnig (auth), David Finn (rev), Time Out, New York, 1/23/97. *Mem:* S Eastern Ctr Contemp Art, Winston-Salem, NC (mem bd dir, 2000). *Media:* Trash, Marble, Newspaper, Publ Art, Installation. *Publ:* Auth, David Finn, Salvatore Ala Gallery, New York, 86; David Finn: Newspaper Children, Third Eye Centre, Glasgow, 88; David Finn Masked Figures, Weatherspoon Art Gallery, Univ NC, Greensboro, 90; Newspaper Children, Watermans Art Centre, Brentford, Gr Brit, 92. *Mailing Add:* 716 S Hawthorne Rd Winston-Salem NC 27103

FINNEGAN, SHARYN MARIE
PAINTER
b New York, NY, Aug 16, 46. *Study:* Art Students League, New York; Acad de Belli Arti, Rome, Italy; Marymount Col, Tarrytown, NY, BFA; NY Univ, studied with Esteban Vicente, MA. *Exhib:* Report from Soho, Grey Art Gallery, NY, 75; Artists' Choice: Figurative Art in NY, Bowery Gallery, and four others, NY, 76; one-woman exhibs, Roswell Mus & Fine Arts Ctr, NMex, 77, Prince St Gallery, 74, 75, 77, 80, 86 & 89 & Interiors, One Penn Plaza, 86, NY, Long Island Univ, NYC, 2006; Painted Light, Queens Mus, 83; Am Women Artists, Cornwall Painting Ctr, New York City, 2003. *Pos:* Gallery coordr, Prince St Gallery, NY, 74-75 & 77-79. *Teaching:* Instr art & art hist, Parsons Sch Design, NY. *Awards:* Artist-in-residence, Roswell Mus & Fine Arts Ctr, 76; Palisades Artist-in-Residence, NY, summer 79; Residency, MacDowell Colony, Peterborough, NH, 79; Artist-in-residence, Brisons Veor, Cornwall, Eng, 2000-02 & 04; AIR, Seydisfjordor, Iceland, 2003. *Bibliog:* J Mellow (auth), Rev, New York Times, 1/74; P Frank (auth), Rev, Soho Weekly News, 1/74; J Dreiss (auth), Rev, Arts Mag, 4/74, 3/78 & 4/81; Ellen Lubel (auth), Views by Women Artists, NY Women's Caucus for Art, 82, and others. *Mem:* Women in the Arts, NY; Col Art Asn. *Media:* Oil, Charcoal. *Publ:* Claire Moore, Women's Art Jrnl, Spring/Summer 81. *Dealer:* Blue Mountain Gallery 530 W 25th St NYC 10001. *Mailing Add:* 5550 Fieldston Rd No 9E Bronx NY 10471-2532

FINOCCHIARO, PINO
PRINTMAKER, PAINTER
b Catania, Italy. *Study:* Inst Art Catania, Italy; Inst Art Urbino, Italy. *Work:* Sassoferrato Mus Art Cont-Nea, Sassoferrato, Italy; Exlibris Mus, Corsico Milan, Italy; Gabinetto Stampe Mod & Antique, Baenacauallo, Italy. *Comn:* Mural, BPA, NY, 86; mural, PS, Catania, Italy, 87; mural, SB, Albissola, Italy, 90; mural, SJ Ex Convento 1600, Donnalucata, Italy, 93. *Exhib:* Int Exlibris, Comunedi Pescara, Italy, 88; Grafica Originale, Casanatale Raffaello, Urbino, Italy, 91; Incisione Ital, New Art, S Benedetto Del Tronto, Italy, 92; Repertorio Incisori Italini, Comune Di Baenacauallo, Baenacauallo, Italy, 93. *Awards:* Ambrogino Artistic Merit, City Milan, Italy. *Bibliog:* Capoferri (auth), Incisione Italiana, New Art Capoferri, 92; Mariani (auth), Trompe L'Oeil, Devecchi, 93. *Mem:* Presidente Associazione Italiana Graf Originale. *Media:* Etching

FIORAVANTI, JEFFREY PAUL
ARTIST
b Saugus, Mass. *Study:* Salem State Col, BSBA, 1980; Clark Univ, 2000. *Work:* Care Ann, North Shore Hist Mus, Gloucester, Mass. *Comn:* Painting, Carroll Ray, N Andover, Mass, 2004. *Exhib:* Images of Civil War RattleRelds, Nat Mus of Civil War Medicine, Frederick, Md, 2003, Am Landscape, 2004; Story Telling, Art Three Gallery, Manchester, NJ, 2003; In Memory of Deeds Past, Lynn Hist Mus; History Meets the Arts, Gallery thirty, Gettysburg, Pa, 2004; Painting the Soul of Am, ARA Gallery, S Hamilton, Mass, 2004; Impressions of New Eng, Bennington Ctr Arts, Bennington, Vt, 2004; 7th Ann Juried Exhib, For Pastels Only, Pastel Soc ME, Kennebunk, ME, 2006; 11th Ann Juried Exhib, For Pastels Only Cape Cod, Soc of Cape Cod, Chatham, Mass, 2006. *Pos:* Sr materials planner, Teradyne, Inc, Boston, 1984-96; production scheduler, Compensated Devices, Inc, Melrose, 1997-99; web specialist Attunity, Inc, Burlington, 2000-01; graphic designer, advertising copywriter TK Keith Co, Wakefield, 2001-; prin, owner Fioravanti Fine Art, 2003-. *Teaching:* Instr, pastel painter, Chelmsford Ctr Arts, Mass, 2003. *Awards:* Olympian Corp award, Pastel Soc W Coast Int Open Exhib, 2000; Best in Show award, Con Pastel Soc, 2000; Terry Ludwig Gold Award, 2006. *Bibliog:* Master Pastelist of the World USA Showcase, Pastel Artist Int, 5-7/2000; This Hallowed Ground, North Shore Sunday, 2003; Lyme Artist Recreater Civilian, The Boston Globe, 2003; Help is on the Way, Art Bus News, 2004; Inspired by Historic Landscapes, Am Artist Magazine, 11/2005. *Mem:* Pastel Soc Am (signature), NY; Conn Pastel Soc (signature), Conn; Pastel Painters Soc Cape Cod (signature), Mass; North Shore Art Asn, Mass; Degas Pastel Soc, LA. *Media:* Pastel. *Dealer:* Art Res Assoc Gallery 300 at Main S Hamilton Mass 01982; Art Three Gallery 44 South St Manchester NH; Gallery Thirty 30 York St Gettysburg Pa 17325. *Mailing Add:* 49 Pennybrook Rd Lynn MA 01905

FIORE, JOSEPH ALBERT
PAINTER, INSTRUCTOR
b Cleveland, Ohio, Feb 3, 25. *Study:* Black Mountain Col, with Josef Albers, Ilya Bolotowsky & William De Kooning, 46-48; Calif Sch Fine Arts, 48-49. *Work:* Whitney Mus Am Art, Chase Manhattan Collection, NY; Corcoran Gallery, Washington; Nat Acad Design NY; State Mus Art, Raleigh, NC; Hofstra Mus, Hempstead, NY, 2001; Black Mountain Col: Experiment in Art Museo Nacional Centro De Arte Renia Sofia, Madrid, 2002-03; Farnsworth Mus, Rockland, ME. *Exhib:* Whitney Mus Am Art Ann, 59; solo exhibs, Staempfli Gallery, 60, Schoelkopf Gallery, 65 & 69, John B Myers Gallery, 74 & Fischbach Gallery, 77 & 81; Six Maine Artists, Farnsworth Mus, Rockland, 83; Art at Black Mountain, Grey Gallery, NY Univ, 87; one-man retrospective, Black Mountain Col Mus & Arts Ctr, Zone One Contemp, Asheville, NC, 95; Cathedral St John the Divine, 97; Round Top Ctr for the Arts, ME, 97, 2002; Rider Univ Art Gallery Lawrenceville, NJ; Ctr for Maine Contemp Art, Rockland, ME, 2004. *Teaching:* Instr painting & drawing, Black Mountain Col, 49-56, chmn dept art, 51-56; instr painting, Philadelphia Col Art, 62-70

& Md Inst Col Art, 70-75; vis instr, Artists Environ Found, NJ, 72-83; instr landscape painting, Nat Acad Design, NY, spring 79 & Parsons Summer Painting Prog, France, 80; resident critic, Vt Studio Sch, Johnson, 87. *Awards:* First Prize, Metrop Young Artists First Ann, Nat Arts Club, 58; Hassam-Speicher Fund Purchase Award, 81 & 98; Edwin Palmer Mem Prize, Nat Acad Design 170th Ann, 95; Recipient prize for painting San Francisco Mus Ann, 1949, 1st prize Metrop Young Artists 1st Ann Nat Arts Club, New York City, 1958, Adolph and Clara Obrig Prize, Nat Acad of Design 178th Ann, 2003; Artists for Environ Found Residence Grantee, 1976; Nettie Marie Jones Fel Ctr Music, Drama and Art, Lake Placid, NY, 1983, purchase award Am Acad Arts and Letters, 1998; Carnegie Prize, Nat Acad of Design, 2001; Obrig Prize, 2003. *Bibliog:* Fairfield Porter (auth), The Oriental in American Art, Art in its Own Terms, Taplinger, 79; Mary E Harris (auth), The Arts at Black Mountain College, Mass Inst Technol Press, 87; James Thompson (auth), Imagining the Landscape: Joseph Fiore's Structures of Rhythm and Sentiment, Black Mountain Col dossiers No 1, Black Mountain Col Mus & Art Ctr, 95; Vincent Katz (auth), Black Mountain Coll; Experiment in Art, Madrid, Spain, 2002. *Mem:* Nat Acad (cert of merit 168th Ann Exhib 1993, Edwin Palmer Mem prize 170th Ann 1995, Cannon prize 175th Ann 2000, Andrew Carnegie prize 176th Ann 2001, Adolph and Clara Obrig prize 178th Ann, 2003); Artists Equity Asn NY, Nature Conservancy, Maine Audubon Soc, Natural Resources Coun Maine. *Media:* Oil, Watercolor

FIRER, SERGE
PRINTMAKER, GRAPHIC ARTIST
b Gorky, Russ, Oct 26, 54; Can citizen. *Study:* Gorky Art Sch, MA, 73. *Work:* Pushkin Mus, Moscow; Altai Mus, Barnaul, Russ; Gorky Art Mus, Russ; State Mus Israel, Jerusalem. *Comn:* Old Gorky Etchings, Artist's Union, Moscow, 82; The Portrait Gallery of Underground Workers, Artist's Union, Moscow, 87. *Exhib:* one-man shows, David Gallery, Jerusalem, Israel, 92, Klim Gallery, Toronto, 96; Art Expo, NY, 95; Art Multiple, Dusseldorf, Ger, 95-96. *Teaching:* Instr etching print, Bezalel, Jerusalem, Israel, 92-94. *Bibliog:* Young Artists of 80 in Russia, Ministry Cult Russ, 89; Jerusalem Post, 92. *Media:* Etching. *Mailing Add:* c/o Klim Art Publ Ltd 1238 Centre St Thornhill ON L4J 3M9 Canada

FIRESTEIN, CECILY BARTH
PAINTER, AUTHOR
b Brooklyn, NY, Apr 25, 33. *Study:* Art Students League, Adelphi Univ, BA, 53; with Hans Hofmann, New York, 54; New York Univ, cert advanced study, 58, MA, 55. *Work:* Corcoran Gallery Art, Washington, DC; Yale Univ Art Gallery, New Haven, Conn; Rose Art Mus, Waltham, Mass; Skirball Mus, Los Angeles, Calif; Brooklyn Mus, NY; Delaware Mus, Wilmington, Del; Jane Voorhees Zimmerli Mus, NJ; Freud Mus, London & Vienna; City Without Walls, NJ; Art in Embassies Program, Kuwait, San Jose, Costa Rica, Dhaka, Bangladesh, Dumascus, Syria, Ansuncion, Paraguay, Islamabad, Pakistan; Johnson & Johnson, NJ. *Comn:* Illustrations for handbook, The Central Synagogue, NY, 78 & 79; rubbing of monument, Tarrytown Historical Soc, NY, 79; art deco door, Miami Design Preservation League, Miami, Fla, 80; rubbing illusration for notepapers, South Street Seaport Mus, NY, 81; Jewish Calendar, Nat Jewish Mus, 99; US Dept of State, Bishkek, Krygyztan. *Exhib:* One-woman shows, Phoenix Gallery, NY, 1962-2005, Joseph Wahl Gallery, Calif, 2006, In Loving Memory, Mus City NY, 78, South St Seaport Mus, NY, 81, Spanish Inst, NY, 83, Farleigh Dickenson Univ, 92; Galerie Meissner, Hamburg, Ger, 83; Gwangji Biannual, Korea. *Pos:* Printmaker & art consult, District 24, Valley Stream, NY, 53-60; arts coordr, Cent Synagogue NY, 75-78; critic, Artspeak, 82-90. *Teaching:* Lectr, many univ, 1972-2003; instr/lectr rubbings, Cooper Hewitt Mus, NY, 80, South St Seaport Mus, NY, 2002 & Parsons Sch Design, NY, 83, Univ SC, 89, YMCA NY, 90, Montclair State, NJ, 92 & Connecticut Graphics Art Center, Norwalk, Conn, 96, Mus City NY, 2000, Ctrl Park Conservancy, 2002. *Awards:* Traveling Exhib Am Art, Am Fedn Arts, 68; Grant, Unique New York, Nat Coun Arts, 74; Artist-in-Residence, Bronx Co Hist Soc, 75-81; Medal of Honor for Printmaking, Nat Asn Women Artists, 2000; Elizabeth Stanton Lake Memorial Award for Printmaking, 2000. *Bibliog:* Angela Taylor (auth), She teaches a modern form of an ancient art, New York Times, 76; Jerry Talmer (auth), Art among the headstones, New York Post, 78; Barbara B Buchholz, article, House & Garden Guides, 79; Gallery & Studio Notebook, Mar 2003; interview, Paintingsdirect.com, Mar, 2000. *Mem:* Life mem Art Students League; NY Soc Women Artists; Baltimore Printmakers; Soc Am Graphic Artists; Nat Soc Women Artists; Pi Lambda Theta (Nat Hon Kappa Delta Pi). *Media:* Work on paper. *Publ:* Auth & illusr, Rubbing Craft, Quick Fox, NY, 77; Rub a Landmark, Nat Trust Hist Preserv, 78; Rubbing brass & stone, New World Book of Knowledge, Grolier, Inc, 80; The Art of making rubbings, Seaport Mag, 80; Reach Out and Touch Something, New York Daily News, 88; Artists Equity Awards J, 2002; Making Paper and Fabric Rubbings, Lark Books, 2000. *Dealer:* Phoenix Gallery Inc 568 Broadway New York NY. *Mailing Add:* 8 E 96th St New York NY 10128

FIRESTONE, EVAN R
ADMINISTRATOR, HISTORIAN
b Richmond, Va, Nov 21, 40. *Study:* Kent State Univ, BA, 62; Univ Wis-Madison, MA, 65, PhD, 71. *Teaching:* From instr to assoc prof, Univ Mass, Dartmouth, 68-77, chmn, dept art hist, 73-77; prof & head, dept art, Western Carolina Univ, 77-83; prof & chmn, dept art & design, Iowa State Univ, 83-90; prof & dir, Lamar Dodd Sch Art, Univ Ga, 90-97 & prof art hist, 97-. *Awards:* Throne-Aldrich Award, State Hist Soc Iowa, 92. *Mem:* Col Art Asn. *Res:* Twentieth century art, especially abstract expressionism. *Publ:* Auth, John Linnell: The eve of the deluge, Cleveland Mus Art Bull, Vol 62, 4/75; Herman Melville's Moby Dick and the abstract expressionists, Vol 55, No 7, 3/80, Color in abstract expressionism: sources and background for meaning, Vol 55, No 7, 3/81, James Joyce and the first generation New York school, Vol 56, No 10, 6/82 & In praise of steel: Notes on some recent direct-metal sculpture, Vol 60, No 4, 4/86, Arts Mag; Fritz Bultman (auth), The case of the missing Irascible, Arch Am Art J, Vol 34, No 2, 94; The death of Moby Dick: Vincent Desiderio's The Progress of Self Love, Am Art, Vol 10, No 2, summer 96; Fritz Bultman: Collages, exhib at Georgia Museum of Art, 97; Fritz Bultman (auth), Actaeon paintings: sexuality, punishment, and oedipal conflict, Genders 34, Fall 2001; Barnett Newman's Onement I: the way up and down is one and the same; source, Vol 24, No 1, Fall 2004. *Mailing Add:* Univ Ga Lamar Dodd Sch Art Athens GA 30602-4102

FIRSTENBERG, JEAN PICKER
DIRECTOR
Study: Boston Univ, BS(summa cum laude), 58. *Pos:* Dir, Am Film Inst, 80- & Trans-Lux Corp, currently; adv bds, Big Sisters of LA, Will Rodgers Inst & Scott Newman Found, currently; trustee, Boston Univ. *Awards:* Alumni Award, Boston Univ, 82; Women in Film Crystal Award, Women in Film, Los Angeles, 90. *Mem:* Acad Motion Picture Arts & Sci; Women in Film; Women's Trusteeship for Betterment of Women. *Mailing Add:* American Film Inst 2021 N Western Ave Los Angeles CA 90027

FISCH, ARLINE MARIE
JEWELER, EDUCATOR
b Brooklyn, NY. *Study:* Skidmore Col, BS(art); Univ Ill, Urbana, MA(art); Fulbright student grant to Denmark, 56-57; Fulbright res grant to Denmark, 66-67; Sch Arts & Crafts, Copenhagen, Denmark; also with Bernhard Hertz Guldvaerefabrik, Copenhagen. *Hon Degrees:* Doc Humane Letters, Skidmore Col. *Work:* Victoria & Albert Mus, London; Vatican Mus, Rome; Am Craft Mus NY; Royal Scottish Mus, Edinburgh; Schmuckmus, Pforzheim; Houston Mus Fine Arts; Nat Gallery Australia; Dauner Collection, Munich. *Exhib:* Schmuck-Objekte, Mus Bellerive, Zurich, Switz, 71; Goldsmith, 74, 76 & 79; Tokyo Int Jewelry Art Exhib, 77, 80 & 83; Mus Für Angewandt Kunst, Vienna, 82; Jewelry USA, 84; Solo Retrospective, Elegant Fantasy, 2000. *Pos:* Trustee, Am Craft Coun, 72-75 & 94-2000; bd dir, Haystack Mt Sch Crafts, 73-82 & 91-2000; vpres, World Crafts Coun, 77-81; pres, SNAG, 82-85. *Teaching:* Instr design & weaving, Skidmore Col, 58-61; prof jewelry & weaving, San Diego State Univ, 61-2000; guest lectr design, Guldsmedshojskole, Copenhagen, Denmark, 67 & 71; vis lectr, Crafts Coun of Australia, 75; vis prof, Boston Univ, 75-76; Fulbright lectr, Inst Applied Arts, Vienna, Austria, 82; Fulbright lectr, Mus Fine Arts, Montevideo, Uruguay, 89. *Awards:* Gold Medal, Int Handicraft Fair, Munich, 71; Distinguished Alumni Award, Skidmore Col, 86; Living Treasure of Calif Declaration, 85; Outstanding Prof, San Diego State Univ, 96; Distinguished Craft Educator Award, James Renwick Alliance, 2000; Gold Medal, Am Craft Coun, 2001. *Bibliog:* J Keefer Bell (auth), Metalsmith, summer 88; Dormer & Turner (auth), The New Jewellery, 85; Elegant Fantasy: the Jewelry of Arline Fisch, publ Arnoldsche Art Publishers; and others. *Mem:* World Crafts Coun (dir, 74-76, vpres for NAm, 76-81); founding mem Soc NAm Goldsmiths (pres, 82-85); fel Am Crafts Coun (Calif rep, southwest regional assembly, 69-72, craftsman-trustee, 72-75); Allied Craftsmen San Diego. *Media:* Jewelry. *Res:* Textile structures in metal including weaving, braiding, kniting & crochet. *Interests:* Travel, reading & opera. *Publ:* Auth, Textile Techniques in Metal, Van Nostrand Reinhold, 75, 2nd ed, Lark Books, 96; Contemporary Dutch Jewelry, 4/91 & Ronald Pearson, Silversmith, 6/92, Am Craft; auth, Crocheted Wire Jewelry, Lark Books, 2006. *Dealer:* Mobilia Gallery, Cambridge, MA; Electrum Gallery, London, UK. *Mailing Add:* 4316 Arcadia Dr San Diego CA 92103

FISCHER, HAL (HAROLD) ALAN
WRITER, CONSULTANT
b Kansas City, Mo, Dec 18, 50. *Study:* Univ Ill, Champaign-Urbana, BFA, 73; San Francisco State Univ, with Jack Welpott, MA, 76; Univ Calif, San Diego, with David Antin, MFA, 88. *Work:* San Francisco Mus Modern Art. *Exhib:* Photo-Linguists, Santa Barbara Mus Art, Calif, 77; Camerawork Gallery, San Francisco, 78; Photographs and Words, San Francisco Mus Mod Art, 81; Photog in Calif, 1945-1980, San Francisco Mus Mod Art, 84; Made in Calif, Los Angeles Co Mus Art, 2000-01. *Pos:* Contrib ed, Artweek, 77-83; reviewer, Artforum, 78-82; develop assoc, Fine Arts Mus, San Francisco, 82-84; dir exhib, Tinken Mus Art, 85-; project dir, Asian Art Mus, 88-2003; develop planner, Balboa Art Conservation Ctr, 92-. *Teaching:* Lectr photog, Calif Col Arts & Crafts, Oakland, 78-80; instr, City Col San Francisco, 79-82. *Awards:* Art Critics Fel, 77, Photogr Fel, 80, Critic-in-Residence Grant, 81, Art Writers Fel, 84, Nat Endowment Arts. *Bibliog:* Joan Murray (auth), Reading the structure of a subculture, 8/13/77 & Judith Dunham (auth), Messages on the skyline, 10/6/79, Artweek; Jeff Perrone (auth), Hal Fischer, Artforum, 10/19/77; Stephen Hannook (auth), Space & Time, 98. *Mem:* Int Asn Art Critics. *Res:* Contemporary photography and art. *Publ:* Auth, Gay Semiotics, 78; 18th Near Castro, 79; contribr, The Still Photograph: The Problematic Model, NFS Press, 81; auth, Don Worth: Photographs 1955-1985, Friends of Photog, 86. *Mailing Add:* 117 Pierce St San Francisco CA 94117

FISCHER, HENRY GEORGE
HISTORIAN, CURATOR
b Philadelphia, Pa, May 10, 23. *Study:* Princeton Univ, BA, 45; Univ Pa, PhD, 55. *Pos:* Asst, Egyptian Sect, Univ Mus, Univ Pa, 49-56; from asst cur to cur, Dept Egyptian Art, Metrop Mus Art, NY, 58-70, Wallace cur Egyptology, 70-79, research cur, 79-91, cur emeri, 92-. *Teaching:* Adj prof Egyptian art & lang, Inst Fine Arts, NY Univ, 62-79. *Awards:* Fel, Guggenheim Found, 56-57; Ordentliches Mitglied, Deutches Archol Inst, 82; Corresp Fel, Brit Acad, 96. *Res:* Palaeography; iconography; sculpture; minor arts of ancient Egypt. *Publ:* Auth, L'écriture et l'Art de l'Egypte Ancienne, Presses Univ France, 86; Egyptian Studies III: Varia Nova, Metrop Mus Art, 96; Tomb of Ip at El Saff, Metrop Mus Art, 96

FISCHER, JOHN
PAINTER, SCULPTOR
b Antwerp, Belg, Aug 11, 30; US citizen. *Study:* City Univ New York, 48-49. *Work:* Fond De Decoration Du Canton De Genève, Geneva, Switz; Univ Ky, Louisville; Everson Mus, Syracuse, NY. *Comn:* Decorative mural (20 ft), Keebler Co, Chicago, 69. *Exhib:* Jewelry by Contemp Artists, Mus Mod Art, NY, 67; The Baker's Art, Mus

Contemp Crafts, NY, 68; solo shows, Everson Mus, Syracuse, 72, NY Cult Ctr, NY, 73 & Musée Cantonal, Lausanne, Switz, 87; one-man retrospective, Scholoss Hardenberg, Velbert, Ger, 83; Community Arts Special Events Festivals at various galleries, mus, parks & many other locations, 1960-70. *Media:* Oil, Computer; Bread. *Dealer:* Brö & Kase Galerie L'Anciene Laiterie Soral Geneva Switz. *Mailing Add:* 75 Warren St Apt 1 New York NY 10007

FISCHER, R M
SCULPTOR
b New York, NY, Mar 21, 1947. *Study:* Long Island Univ, NY, BA, 71; San Francisco Art Inst, Calif, MFA, 73. *Work:* Whitney Mus Am Art; Dallas Mus Art; Cincinnati Art Mus; Tamayo Museo Mexico City; Mus Mod Art, NY; Carnegie Mus Art, Pittsburgh, Pa. *Comn:* Double gateway to park, comn by MacArthur Park Proj, Los Angeles, Calif, 85; Rector Gate, Battery Park City, NY, 89; State House clock, Boston, Mass, 90; Brooklyn Battery Tunnel Clock, NY, 92; Sky Stations, Kansas City, Mo, 94. *Exhib:* One-man show, Contemp Arts Ctr, Cincinnati, Ohio, 81, Whitney Mus Am Art, 84, Musee de La Ville de Toulon, France, 84, Inst Contemp Art, Boston, Mass, 85, Whitney Mus Am Art, 84, Daniel Weinberg Gallery, Los Angeles, 85 & 88, Inst Contemp Art, Philadelphia, 85, Baskerville & Watson Gallery, NY, 85, 87, Arthur Rogers Gallery, New Orleans, 88, Galerie Beaubourg, Paris, 88, Donald Young Gallery, Chicago, 88, Galerie Barbara Farber, Amsterdam, The Neth, 89, Jay Gorney Modern Art, NY, 89, & 94, Sidney Janis Gallery, NY, 91, Deitch Projects, NY, 98, Lever House, NY, 99; Whitney Mus Am Art, 83, 85 & 88; Chicago Sculpture Int, 85; Fundaca Bienal de Sao Paulo, Brasil, 85; Lafonct Mus, Tokyo, 85; High Style, Whitney Mus Am Art, 85; Modern Detour, Wiener Secession, Vienna, Austria, 90 & Sidney Janis Gallery, 91; Jay Gorney Mod Art, 94; Mus Mod Art, NY; Whitney Mus Am Art; Carnegie Mus Art, Pittsburgh, Pa; Cincinnati Art Mus, Ohio; Eli Broad Found, Los Angeles, Calif; Nelson-Atkins Mus, Kansas City, Mo; group exhibs W whitney Mus Am Art, 95, Serralves Found, 95; Nat Gallery, Alexander Soutzos Mus, 96, Athens Sch Fine Arts, 96; Queens Mus Art, Carnegie Mus Art, San Jose Mus Art, Calif, 97; Texas Gallery, Houston, 1998; Lennon, Weinberg Gallery, NY, 1998; PaineWebber Art Gallery, NY, 1999; TIAA CREF, NY, 1999; John Weber Gallery, 2000; Univ Mass, Amherst Univ Gallery, 2000; Sandra Gering Gallery, NY, 2002. *Teaching:* Instr, Sch Visual Arts, NY, 85-86, Skowhegan Sch Painting & Sculpture, 87. *Awards:* Nat Endowment Arts, 82, 86 & 94; Creative Artists Pub Serv Fel, 82; Tiffany fel, 84; CAPS, NY Coun Arts, 83; Award for Excellence in Design, Art Comn City of NY, 87; Asn Lighting Engrs Award, Kansas City Chap, 95; Allied Arts and Craftsmanship Award, AIA, Kansas City Chap, 95. *Bibliog:* Suzanne Stesin (auth), Home Furnishings, 82; Denise Domerque (auth) Artist Design Furniture, 85; Dan Cameron (auth), High-Tech Redux, Flash Art, summer 88. *Media:* All Media. *Dealer:* Carl Solway Gallery, Cincinnati. *Mailing Add:* 390 Wythe Ave # 101 Brooklyn NY 11211

FISCHER, ROBERT A
SCULPTOR
b Minneapolis, 68. *Study:* Escuela Salmintina, Spain, degree, 1989; Minneapolis Col Art & Design, Degree Interdisciplinary Studies (Hon) Prog, 1993. *Exhib:* One-man shows incl Hiding Places for a Dense City, Art in General, NY, 1999; New Work, Conductor's Hallway Gallery, London, 1999; Light/House, Franklin Art Works, Minneapolis, 2000; My Winnebago Travels, Vox Populi Gallery, Philadelphia, 2000; Mirrored Boat, Macalester Col Art Gallery, St Paul, 2000; In Site, Madison Art Ctr, Wis, 2000; Dee/Glasoe, NY, 2001; Elizabeth Dee Gallery, NY, 2002; Mary Goldman Gallery, Los Angeles, 2004; Cohan and Leslie, NY, 2005; exhib in group shows at Five Jerome Artists, Minneapolis Col Art & Design, 1996, Reimaging the Landscape, Katherine E Nash Gallery, Minneapolis, 1997, One Hundred Yrs of Sculpture, Walker Art Ctr, Minneapolis, 1998, Interval, Sculpture Ctr, NY, 1999, Door as Metaphor in Contemp Art, NJ Ctr Visual Art, 2002, Druid: Wood as a Superconductor, Space 101, Brooklyn, 2003, Soft Cell, Foxy Productions, Brooklyn, 2003, I Feel Mysterious Today, Palm Beach Inst Contemp Art, Fla, 2004. *Awards:* Grantee Visual Arts Fel, Minnesota State Arts Board, 1996; Jerome Found Fel, 1995; Visual Arts Fel, Bush Found, 1999. *Mailing Add:* c/o Cohan and Leslie 138 Tenth Ave New York NY 10011

FISCHER, THOMAS JEFFREY
PHOTOGRAPHER, EDUCATOR
b Glendale, Calif, May 7, 46. *Study:* Calif State Univ, Northridge, BA, 73; Stanford Univ, MFA, 87. *Work:* Savannah Col Art & Design, Ga; Greenwood Mus, SC; Libr Cong, Washington; Interlochen Ctr Arts, Mich; Nat Maritime Mus, Norfolk, Va. *Exhib:* Photograph as Document, Downey Mus Art, Calif, 88; Recent Landscapes, Stanford Univ Photo Gallery, Calif, 89; Nat Landscape Exhib, Mus Rockies, 89; Contemp Southeastern Photog, Crealde Inst Art, Orlando, Fla, 93; Southern Landscapes, Mobile Townhouse, Univ Southern Ala, 96; Waters of the Southeast, Nat Maritime Mus, 96; Jewels in the Crown, Nat Gallery, Washington, 2001; Paradise/Paradox, Nathan Wilson Ctr for Arts, Jacksonville, Fla, 2002; G-8 Summit, 2003; Mem Univ Gallery, 2006. *Pos:* Dean, Sch Media Art, Savannah Col Art & Design, 1998-; Prof of photog, 1990-present. *Teaching:* Instr fine art, Lucia Mar Unified Schs, Arroyo Grande, Calif, 1973-85; lectr photog, Stanford Univ, Calif, 1986-88; prof, Savannah Col Art & Design, Ga, 1990-, ch photog dept, 2006-. *Awards:* Designation Award in Art, Cult Olympiad, US Olympic Comt, 95; James Borelli Fel, Stanford Univ, 96; Prof of Yr, Savannah Col Art & Design, 97 & 98; US Prof of the Yr Selection, 2004. *Mem:* Soc Photog Educ; Col Art Asn; Nat Art Educ Asn; Soc Photog Educ (nat bd mem). *Media:* Photog. *Publ:* Illusr, Rodin J, Stanford Univ Press, 88; illusr & auth, Waters of the Southeast, Savannah Col Art & Design, 96. *Dealer:* Gallery Lumiere 124 Oglethorpe Ave Savannah Ga 31401. *Mailing Add:* 307 Washington Savannah GA 31405

FISCHL, ERIC
PAINTER
b New York, NY, 1948. *Study:* Calif Inst Arts, Valencia, BFA, 72. *Work:* Metrop Mus Art & Dominique DeMenil, NY. *Exhib:* Solo exhibs, Whitney Mus Am Art, NY, 86, Ctr Fine Arts, Miami, Fla, 92, Galeria Soledad Lorenzo, Madrid, Spain, 93, Galerie Daniel Templon, Paris, France, 94, 97, Daniel Weinberg Gallery, San Francisco, 94, Laura Carpenter Fine Arts, Santa Fe, NMex, 94, Gagosian Gallery, NY, 98, Galleria Lawrence Rubin, Milan, Italy, 98, Galerie Daniel Templon, Paris, 99, Mary Boone Gallery, NY, 84, 86, 87, 88, 90, 92, 94, 96, 99, 00, Mus fur Moderne Kunst, Frankfurt, Ger, 99, Mary Ryan Gallery, NY, 99, Mario Diacono Gallery, Boston, 99, Gagosian Gallery, London, 00, Jablonka Galerie, Koln, Ger, 01; Biennial, Whitney Mus, NY, 85 & 91; Mus Art, Ft Lauderdale, Fla, 86; Cincinnati Art Mus, Ohio, 86; Ludwig Mus, Cologne, WGer, 86; Mus Contemp Art, Los Angeles, 86 & 98; Michael Kohn Gallery, Los Angeles, 86; Inst Contemp Arts, London, Eng, 87; Los Angeles Co Art Mus, 87; Sara Hilden Art Mus, Tampere, Finland, 88; Whitney Mus Art at Equitable Ctr, NY, 89; Inst Contemp Art, Philadelphia, Pa, 91; Aldrich Mus Contemp Art, Ridgefield, Conn, 92; Nat Mus Am Art, Washington, DC, 97; Cleveland Mus Art, Ohio, 98; Parrish Art Mus, Southampton, NY, 98; Michael C Carlos Mus, Emory Univ, Atlanta, 98; Joseloff Gallery, West Hartford, Conn, 98; Turner & Runyon Gallery, Dallas, 98; Aspen Art Mus, Colo, 99; Whitney Mus Am Art, NY, 99; Nassau Co Mus Art, Roslyn Harbor, NY, 00; Newhouse Ctr for Contemp Art, NY, 00; Barbara Gladstone Gallery, NY, 00; Peter Blum/Blumarts Inc, 00; Brooklyn Mus Art, 01; Mus Contemp Art, North Miami, Fla, 01; AXA Gallery, NY, 01; Thomas Ammann Fine Art, Zurich, 2006; and many others. *Teaching:* Lectr in painting, Nova Scotia Col of Art & Design, 74-78. *Awards:* Nat Acad, Nat Acad of Design, 1994. *Bibliog:* Phoebe Hoban (auth), Artists on the beach, NY Mag, 7/1/91; Kristine McKenna (auth), Cozy connection, Los Angeles Times, 2/2/92; Phyllis Braff (auth), On the ocean fair and or at seasides here and in Euorpe, NY Times, Long Island Weekly, 8/2/92; Grace Glueck (auth), Eric Fischl, The NY Times, 2/6/98; Robert Taplin (auth), Eric Fischl at Gagosian, Art in America, May 98; Paolo Falcone (auth), Palermo vive, Tema Celeste, July 98; Phyllis Braff (auth), The Works of Art That Inspire the Artist, The NY Times, 11/15/98; Stephen Wright (auth), Eric Fischl: Inside Out, 1982, Artforum, May 99; Francesco Poli (auth), Eric Fischl, Tema Celeste, May 99; Steven Vincent (auth), Mary Boone Shows Eric Fischl Portraits, Art & Auction, 5/1/99; Lee Klein (auth), Eric Fischl, The NY Art World, June 99; Lilly Wei (auth), Eric Fischl, Art News, Sept 99; Donald Kuspit (auth), Eric Fischl, Artforum, Oct 99; Louisa Buck (auth), Fischl's phases at Gagosian, The Art Newspaper, July 2000; Willia Feaver (auth), Eric Fischl, Art News, Sept 2000; Martin Herbert (auth), Eric Fischl, Tema Celeste, Oct 2000; Richard Polsky (auth), Polsky's Pick, Art & Auction, Nov 2000; Robert Smith (auth), Eric Fischl, The NY Times, 12/15/2000; James Kalm (auth), Figuratively Speaking: Eric Fischl, NY Arts, Feb 2001; Edward Leffingwell (auth), Eric Fischl at Mary Boone, Art in Am, Mar 2001; Carly Berwick (auth), A Comedian Goes into an Art Gallery, Art News, June 2001. *Mem:* Am Acad Arts and Letters; Nat Acad. *Mailing Add:* c/o Mary Boone Gallery 745 Fifth Ave New York NY 10151

FISCHMAN, BARBARA J
PAINTER
Study: City Univ, NY, MFA; NY Univ, studied; Christie's NY, studied. *Comn:* Chow Chow, Pastel Mus China. *Exhib:* Europastel, Ital, 2002; Art du Pastel, France, 2002-03; The Butler Inst Am Art, Youngstown, Ohio, 2003; St Petersburg, Russia, 2003; Suzhou, China; Pastel Soc of China. *Pos:* art appraiser & pastelist, NY, currently. *Teaching:* instr, Giffuni Atelier for Pastels, NY. *Mem:* Pastel Soc Am (PSA) (mem, pres, currently). *Media:* Pastels. *Mailing Add:* 315 W 39th St New York NY 10018

FISH, ALIDA
PHOTOGRAPHER
b May 2, 44. *Study:* Univ Florence, Italy, 65-66; Smith Col, Northampton, Mass, BA, 67; Harvard Univ, Cambridge, Mass, 69; Rochester Inst Technol, NY, MFA, 76. *Work:* Philadelphia Mus Fine Arts; State Mus Pa; George Eastman House, Int Mus Photog, Rochester, NY; Murray State Univ; Del Mus Art. *Exhib:* Albright-Knox Art Gallery, 80; Huntsville Mus Art, Ala, 82; Pa Acad Fine Arts, 84; solo exhibs, Centre Gallery, Jamestown Community Col, Olean, NY, 90, Schmidt-Dean Gallery, Philadelphia, 90, 92, 94 & 98, Penn State Univ, Harrisburg, 91, Pa Acad Art, 93 & Aronson Gallery, Univ Arts, Philadelphia, 96; Digital Dialects, New Paradigms, Creiger-Dane Gallery, Boston, 95; Objects of Personal Significance (traveling), Hunter Mus Art, 96; Photoworks, Nexus Found Today's Art, Philadelphia, 96; Complexity & Contradiction, Postmodernism in Philadelphia Photog, Paley Design Ctr, Philadelphia Col Textiles & Sci, 96; Biennial 96, Del Art Mus, Wilmington; Sloan Gallery, Lockhaven Univ, 97; Photog Mus Thessaloniki, Greece, 97; Schmidt-Dean Gallery, Philadelphia, 98. *Pos:* Consult, Polaroid Corp, Cambridge, Mass, 86 & 88, Sch Art & Design, NY State Col Ceramics at Alfred Univ, 93 & Conn Col, New London, 94. *Teaching:* Workshops, various art schs & universities, 74-96; vis artist & photog prog adv, Penland Sch, NC, 83-87; lectr & panelist, various schs, universities & museums, 77-96; prof photog & chmn media arts, Univ Arts, Philadelphia 81-. *Awards:* Nat Endowment Arts Fel Photog, 94-95; Venture Fund Grant, Univ Arts, 95; Biennial '96 Award, Del Art Mus, Wilmington, 96. *Mem:* Soc Photog Educ; Print Ctr, Philadelphia. *Dealer:* Schmidt-Dean Gallery 1636 Walnut St Philadelphia PA 19103. *Mailing Add:* 1816 Millers Rd Wilmington DE 19810

FISH, JANET I
PAINTER
b Boston, Mass, May 18, 38. *Study:* Smith Col, BA; Yale Sch Art & Archit, MFA; Skowhegan Summer Sch. *Hon Degrees:* Lyme Acad, Conn, hon DFA, 200. *Work:* Whitney Mus Am Art, NY; Dallas Mus Art, Tex; Metrop Mus Art, NY; Art Inst Chicago; Pa Acad Fine Arts; and others. *Exhib:* Art Inst Chicago, 72 & 74; Am

Drawings 1963-1973, Whitney Mus Am Art, 73; The Liberation, Corcoran Gallery, Washington, DC & US Info Agency Traveling Exhib, Europe, 76-77; Am 76 (traveling exhib), Brooklyn Mus, NY & US Dept Interior, 76-78; Eight Contemp Am Realists, Pa Acad Fine Arts & NC Mus Art, 77; Butler Inst Am Art, 79; Collector's Ann Contemp Art, Boca Raton Mus Art, Fla, 90; Selections from the Glenn C James Collection, Spiva Art Mus, Joplin, Ohio; New Viewpoints, Seville World Expo, US Pavillion, 92; Yale Collects Yale, Yale Univ Art Gallery, 93; Yellowstone Art Ctr, Mo Traveling Exhib, 95-97; Janet Fish Selected Works, Mus Art, Ft Lauderdale, Fla; The Prints of Janet Fish, Traveling, Exhib, 98-99; Albright-Knox, Buffalo, NY; Cleveland Mus Art; Met Mus Art, NY; The Australian Nat Gallery, Canberra; Minneapolis Mus Art, Minn; plus others. *Pos:* Bd governors, Skowhegan Sch Painting & Sculpture; artist adv bd, Marie Walsh Sharpe Art Found. *Teaching:* instr, The Marie Walsh Shapre Art Found Summer Sessions, 89-2000. *Awards:* MacDowell Fel, 68, 69 & 72; Australia Coun Arts Grant, 75; Am Acad Arts & Letts Award Art, 94; Henry Ward Ranger Purchase Prize, Nat Acad Design, 2001; William A. Paton Prize for Watercolor, Nat Acad Design, 2005; and others. *Bibliog:* Garret Henry (auth), Janet Fish, Burton Skira Publ; Linda Konheim Kramer (auth), The Prints of Janet Fish, John Szoke Publ. *Mem:* Artists Equity; Century Asn; Nat Acad. *Media:* Oil, Watercolor. *Dealer:* DC Moore Gallery 724 5th Ave New York NY 10019. *Mailing Add:* 101 Prince St New York NY 10012

FISH, JULIA A
PAINTER
b Toledo, Ore, 50. *Study:* Pac Northwest Col Art, BFA, 76; Col Art, Md Inst, MFA, 82. *Work:* Art Inst Chicago, Mus Contemp Art & Harold Washington Libr Ctr, Chicago, Ill; State Ore; Seattle City Light Collection, Wash; Ill State Mus, Springfield; Mus Modern Art, New York City. *Exhib:* Solo exhibs, Robbin Lockett Gallery, Chicago, 91, Amy Lipton Gallery, NY, 92, Christopher Grimes Gallery, Santa Monica, Calif, 93, 95 & 96, 2001, Feigen, Inc, Chicago, 94, Lipton-Owens Co, NY, 95, Ill Art Gallery, Chicago, 95 & Renaissance Soc, Univ Chicago, 96, Ten in One Gallery, Chicago, 98, Feigen Contemp, New York City, 99; Drawing in Chicago Now, Columbia Col Art Gallery, 96; Mist, Hermetic Gallery, Milwaukee, Wis, 96; Art in Chicago, 1945-1995, Mus Contemp Art, Chicago, 96; New York: Drawings Today, San Francisco Mus Mod Art, 97; Zeichnungen (4)-Drawings 4, Galerie Klaus Fischer, Berlin, Ger, 97, Bauen and Bauten: Kunst in der Architektur, 98; No Ill Univ, DeKalb, 2000; Trancending Earth and Sky, Univ Art Gallery, San Diego State Univ, 2000; Entry: Plan, Fragments, Reconstructions, Christopher Grimes Gallery, Santa Monica, Calif, 2001; Out of Place: Contemp Art and the Archit Uncanny, Mus Contemp Art, Chicago, 2002; Speculative Chicago: A Compendium of Archit Innovation, Gallery 400, Univ Ill Chicago, 2003; The World Becomes a Private World: The Cooper and Rosenwasser Collection, Mills Col Art Mus, Berkeley, Calif, 2004; Living Rooms, Anthony Grant, New York, NY, 2005; 181st Ann Invitational Exhib, Nat Acad Design, New York, NY, 2006; Figures in the Field: Figurative Sculpture and Abstract Painting from Chicago Collections, Mus Contemp Art, Chicago, 2006. *Teaching:* Instr painting & drawing, Pac Northwest Col Art, 78-80 & 82-83; instr drawing, Mt Hood Community Col, Gresham, Ore, 82-83 & 84; vis artist & asst prof painting & drawing, Univ Iowa, 83-85; vis artist, Art Inst Chicago, 86-89; asst prof, Sch Art & Design, Univ Ill, Chicago, 89-95, dir grad studies, 91-94, assoc prof, 95. *Awards:* Louis Comfort Tiffany Found Award, 91; Visual Artist Fel, Nat Endowment Arts, 93; Robert H Mitchel/Univ Ill Scholar Award, 96; Campus Research Bd Grant, Univ Ill at Chicago, 97, Research award in Arts, Archit and Humanities, 2000-01; Individual Artist award, Richard H Driehaus Found, 2006. *Bibliog:* Susan Snodgrass (auth), Julia Fish at the Renaissance Soc, Art in Am, 4/96; John Brunetti (auth), View: Julia Fish/The Renaissance Soc, Dialogue, 4-5/96; Laurie Palmer (auth), Julia Fish/The Renaissance Soc, Frieze, 5/96; Mahoney, Robert, Julia Fish and Claudia Matzko, Time Out New York, 99; Pincus, Robert L, Landscapes Old Passion with New Darker Side, San Diego Union Tribune, 2000; numerous others. *Dealer:* Christopher Grimes Gallery 916 Colorado Ave Santa Monica CA 90401-2717. *Mailing Add:* 1614 N Hermitage Ave Chicago IL 60622

FISH, RICHARD G
DESIGNER, PAINTER
b Philadelphia, Pa, Apr 7, 25. *Study:* Univ Pa, BA(appl arts); Philadelphia Mus Sch Art, with Azio Martinelli, dipl(advert design); Haverford Col. *Work:* Frito Lay Corp; Col Southwest Art, Dallas, Tex; Rocky Mountain Nat Park, Colo. *Comn:* Paintings, Dravo Corp, Pittsburgh, Pa, 69; Caleco, West Chester, Pa, 79-86. *Exhib:* Butler Inst Am Art, Youngstown, Ohio, 68, 70 & 74; Norfolk Mus Art, Va, 69; Philadelphia Mus Art, 69; Cummer Gallery Art, Jacksonville, Fla, 69; one-man shows, Gross-McCleaf Gallery, Philadelphia, 75, 78 & 83; Munson Gallery, Santa Fe, NMex, 84, 89 & 90; Central High Sch Alumni at the Woodmere Art Mus, Chestnut Hill, Pa, 2002. *Pos:* Freelance designer & owner, Richard Fish Assoc, Havertown, 52-. *Teaching:* Artist-in-residence, Rocky Mountain Nat Park, Colo, 91-92. *Awards:* Gold Medal, Philadelphia Graphic Arts, 62-65 & 76; Gold Medal, Philadelphia Art Dirs, 65; Silver Medal, Pennational Arts Ann, State of Pa, 67. *Mem:* Print Club, Philadelphia; Art Dir's Club. *Media:* Ink, Watercolor; Egg Tempera, Acrylic. *Publ:* One Day in Summer, Random House, 69; auth, The Artist in Scotland, Small World-Volkswagen Am, 72; illusr, Pathways to Independence, Chatham Press, 75; Haym Salomon, Liberty's Son, Jewish Publ, 75; Return to Big Grass, Ducks Unlimited, 87; Exploring Old Cape Cod, Parnassus Imprints, 95. *Mailing Add:* 1733 Academy Ln Havertown PA 19083

FISHER, CAROLE GORNEY
PAINTER, SCULPTOR
b Minneapolis, Minn. *Study:* Minneapolis Col Art & Design, BFA, 64; Pa State Univ, MFA, 66. *Work:* Roanoke Fine Arts Ctr, Va. *Comn:* Print ed, Minn State Arts Coun, 70; sculpture, Univ Minn, Morris, 73. *Exhib:* Pa State Univ, 72; Two Nations, Six Artists, Minn-Can, 74; Walker Art Ctr, Minneapolis, 74; Whitney Biennial Contemp Am Art, NY, 75; Woman as Viewer Exhib, Winnipeg Art Gallery, 75. *Pos:* Comnr, Minneapolis Art Comn, 75-. *Teaching:* Instr printmaking & drawing, Minneapolis Col Art & Design, 68-69; artist in residence printmaking, Bemidji State Univ, 69-70; instr drawing, Col St Catherine, 73-82. *Bibliog:* Cindy Nemser (auth), Whitney Biennial, Changes, New York, 75; Amy Goldin (auth), The New Whitney Biennial, Art in Am, 5-6/75; Chris Kohlmann (auth), 1975 Whitney Biennial, Mid West Art, 5/75. *Mem:* Col Art Asn Am. *Media:* Miscellaneous. *Dealer:* One Hundred Eighteen: An Art Gallery 1007 Harmon Minneapolis MN 55400. *Mailing Add:* 2524 Stevens Ave S Apt 2 Minneapolis MN 55404-4346

FISHER, DONALD G & DORIS
COLLECTOR
Study: Univ Calif, 50. *Pos:* partner, Fisher Property Investment Co, formerly; With, M Fisher & Son, 50-57; co-founder, Gap Stores, San Bruno, Calif, 69; chmn, Gap Inc, 69—2004, pres, 69-83; mem adv coun, Off of US Trade Rep, 87-98; trustee, Presidio Trust, 97-; dir, Schwab Charles Corp; bd mem, Calif State Bd Educ. *Awards:* Named one of Top 200 Collectors, ARTnews Mag, 2004. *Collection:* Contemporary & american art, especially German. *Mailing Add:* Gap Inc 2 Folsom St San Francisco CA 94105

FISHER, JAMES DONALD
SCULPTOR, MUSEUM DIRECTOR
b Houghton, Mich, July 24, 38. *Study:* Corcoran Sch Art, with Richard Lahey, 56-61; George Washington Univ, 68-73, with H Irving Gates, BA, 71, MFA, 73. *Exhib:* Washington Area Exhib, Corcoran Gallery Art, Washington, DC, 67; Prince Georges Community Col, Largo, Md, 68. *Collection Arranged:* Dual Retrospective-Peter Hurd-Millard Sheets, Amarillo Art Ctr, 74, When You Say Cowboy-Survey of Western Art in Texas (with catalog), 74 & Elisabet Ney in Austin, 81. *Pos:* Technician Mus Hist & Technol, Smithsonian Inst, 60-68; dir, Amarillo Art Ctr, 73-77; dir, George Washington Carver Mus, Elizabeth Ney Mus & O Henry Mus, 77-2000, ret. *Teaching:* Grad teaching asst & asst prof lectr design & drawing, George Washington Univ, 71-73. *Mem:* Am Asn Mus. *Media:* Welded Steel, Vacuum-Formed Plastics. *Res:* 19th century industrial design and 20th century non-objective sculpture. *Publ:* Auth, Two Centuries of American Quilts and Coverlets, Amarillo Art Ctr, 76; coauth, Central Texas rural schs, Tex Heritage Mag, 87; WPA projects in Texas, Tex Heritage Mus, fall 93

FISHER, JEROME & ANNE
COLLECTOR
Pos: Chmn emer, Nine West Group; Jerome & Anne C Fisher Charitable Foundation. *Awards:* recipient, Humanitarian Award, 97; humanitarian of the yr, Shoes on Sale, 2003; Named one of top two hundred collectors, ARTnews magazine, 2004. *Collection:* Modern art. *Mailing Add:* Nine West Group 1129 Westchester Ave White Plains NY 10604

FISHER, JOEL
SCULPTOR
b Salem, Ohio, June 6, 47. *Study:* Kenyon Col, AB(magna cum laude, phi beta kappa). *Work:* Mus Mod Art, NY; Stedelijk Mus Amsterdam; Victoria & Albert Mus, London, Eng; Tate Gallery, London; Ctr George Pompidou, Paris; Kunst Mus Bern, Switz. *Exhib:* One-man shows stadtisches Mus Mônchengladbach, 74, Mus Mod Art, Oxford, 77, Stedleuk Mus, Amsterdam, 78, Kunst Mus Luzern, 86, Galerie Farideh Cadot, 91, Diane Brown Gallery, 92, Ben Shawn Gallery, Paterson Col, NJ, 94 & Lawrence Markey Gallery, NY, 94; An Int Survey of Contemp Painting and Sculpture, Mus Mod Art, NY, 84; Structure to Remblance: 8 Sculptors, Albright Knox Gallery, Buffalo, 87; Four Am, Brooklyn Mus, 89; Chance, Choice & Irony, Todd Gallery, London, 94; 5th Paper Biennale, Leopold Hoesch Mus, Duren, Ger, 94. *Teaching:* Goldsmiths Col, London Univ, 79, Bath Acad Art, Eng, 80-82, RI Sch Design, 85 & 90, Vt Studio Sch, 88-, Sch Visual Arts, 89-; prof, Ecole des Beaux Arts, Paris, 95-; Philadelphia Acad Art MFA prog, 93-. *Awards:* George A & Eliza Gardner Howard Found, 86-87; Fel, Pollock-Krasner Found, 93; John Simon Guggenheim Fel, 93-94. *Bibliog:* Simon Field (auth), Joel Fisher on Paper, Art & Artists, 1/72; Lisa Bear (auth), Strong as a Spider's Web, Avalanche, 12/74; Robin White (auth), View Mag, 81. *Mem:* Col Art Asn Am. *Publ:* Auth, Double Camouflage, Mansfield Fine Arts Ctr, 70; The Berliner Book, Berlin Kunstler Prog des DAAd, 73; Instances of Change, Bonomo Diffusione, Bari, Italy, 75; Dissolution, Stadt Mus Monchengladbach, 75; An Image in Blankness, Mus Mod Art, Oxford, 77. *Mailing Add:* PO Box 349 River Rd North Troy VT 05859-0349

FISHER, KIM
PAINTER
Study: UCLA, BFA, 96; Otis Col Art & Design, MFA, 98. *Work:* 21 Paintings from Los Angeles, Robert V Fullerton Art Mus, San Bernardino, Calif, 2002; Whitney Biennial, Whitney Mus Am Art, 2004. *Exhib:* One-woman shows, China Art Objects, Los Angeles, 99, 2001, Midway Contemp Art, St Paul, 2003, John Connelly Presents, New York City, 2004, Shane Campbell, Oak Park, Ill, 2004, Modern Inst, London, 2005; group shows, LA-LV-LA, Donna Beam Fine Art Gallery, Univ Nevada, 97, The Comestible Compost, Gallery 207, West Hollywood, Calif, 98, Young & Dumb, ACME LA, 2000, Platypus, Lawrence Rubin Greenberg Van Doren Fine Art, NY, 2001, Selections, Bolsky Gallery, Otis Col Art & Design, Los Angeles, 2001, Cancelled Art Fair!, China Art Objects, Los Angeles, 2001, The Stray Show, boom, Chicago, 2002, Fair, Royal Col Art, London, 2002, Works for Giovanni, China Art Objects, Los Angeles, 2003, Still or Sparkling?, John Connelly Presents, NY, 2003, A Red Letter Day, Fredericks Freiser Gallery, NY, 2003, such things I do just to make myself more attractive to you, Peres Projects, Los Angeles, 2004. *Mailing Add:* c/o John Connelly Presents 526 W 26th St Ste 1003 New York NY 10001

FISHER, LEONARD EVERETT
PAINTER, ILLUSTRATOR
b Bronx, NY, June 24, 24. *Study:* With Moses Soyer, New York, 39; Art Students League, with Reginald Marsh, 41; Brooklyn Col, with Olindo Ricci & Serge Chermayeff, 41-42; Yale Univ Sch Fine Arts, BFA, 49, MFA, 50. *Hon Degrees:* Paier Col Art, Diploma, 98. *Work:* Butler Inst Am Art, Youngstown, Ohio; Libr of Cong, Washington, DC; Mt Holyoke Col, S Hadley, Mass; New Brit Mus Am Art, Conn; NY Publ Libr; and others. *Comn:* Am Bicentennial (four block eight cent commemorative postage stamps), 72, Legend of Sleepy Hollow (ten cent commemorative postage stamp), 74, Liberty Tree (thirteen cent embossed envelope), 75 & Skilled Hands for Independence (four block thirteen cent commemorative stamps), 77, US Postal Serv, Washington, DC; mural, Norwalk Transit Authority Admin Building, US Govt & Conn state, 2002. *Exhib:* Painters Panorama, Am Fedn Arts Sponsored Tour, 54-56; New Eng Painting Ann, Silvermine Guild Artists, 68, 69 & 71; Butler Inst Am Art, Youngstown, Ohio, 72; retrospective, New Brit Mus Am Art, Conn, 73 & Am Mus Illus, NY, 91; one-man shows, Rotunda, Free Libr Philadelphia, 76, Univ Hartford, Conn, 76, Gen Elec Corp, 76, NY Hist Soc: 200 Yrs of Am Illus, 76 & Story Lines-Scatchboard Illus, AA Resources Ore, Ore Arts Comn & Nat Endowment Arts, 93-94, NY Pub LIbr, 2000; Soc Illustr Mus Am Illus, NY, 90-92; Milk and Eggs: The Am Revival of Tempera Painting 1930-1950, Brandywine Mus, Chadus Foro, Pa, 2002. *Pos:* Illusr & auth, children's books for major publ, 54-; bd dir, Silvermine Guild Artists, 70-74; deleg-at-large, White House Conf, Libraries & Info Serv, 79; Pres, Westport, Conn Pub Libr, 86-89. *Teaching:* Dean studies, Whitney Sch Art, 51-53; instr art hist, painting, life drawing & bk illus, Paier Col Art, 66-78, dean acad affairs, 77-81, dean emer, 82-. *Awards:* Pulitzer Scholar Art, 50; Kerlan Award, Univ Minn, 91; Arbuthnot Citation, Am Libr Asn, 94-95. *Bibliog:* Charles M Daugherty (ed), Six Artists Paint a Still Life, North Light, 77; Howard Munce (ed), Magic and Other Realism, Hastings House, 81; Norman D Stevens, Patricia Cianciolo & Ellen Embargo (auths), Leonard Everett Fisher: A Life of Art, Univ Conn, 98. *Mem:* Soc of Illusr; Silvermine Guild Artists; Authors Guild; PEN; Soc Children's Bk Writers & Illustr. *Media:* Acrylic, Soft Engraving. *Publ:* Auth & illusr, The Great Wall of China, Atheneum, 86; Cyclops, 91; Gutenberg, 93; Kinderdike, 94, Atheneum; William Tell, Farrar Straus & Giroux, 96; Gods and Goddesses of the Ancient Maya, Holiday House, 2000; Sky, Sea, the Jetty, and Me, Marshall Cavandish, 2001. *Dealer:* Cavalier Galleries 405 Greenwich Ave Greenwich CT 06880. *Mailing Add:* 7 Twin Bridge Acres Rd Westport CT 06880

FISHER, PHILIP C
PAINTER, ART DEALER
b Oil City, Pa, Nov 17, 30. *Study:* Graceland Col, 50; Univ Nebr, 55; studied with Norman Rockwell, Stevan Dohanos, Albert Dorne & Al Capp, 58-61. *Work:* Sagendorf Int Dollhouse Mus. *Exhib:* Int Platform Asn Invitational Art Show, Hyatt Regency Hotel, Washington, DC, 86; The Great Colo Showcase, Denver, 89. *Pos:* Cartoonist-illusr, 'Brenda Starr' syndicated comic strips, Chicago, Ill, 77-78; portrait artist, Omaha, Nebr & Denver, Colo, 80-88; art dealer, Fisher's Master Artists, Inc, Golden, Colo, 86-88. *Mem:* Am Portrait Soc; Int Platform Asn. *Media:* Oil on Linen, Pen & Ink. *Specialty:* Realist oils on canvas, portraiture, genre, landscapes, still lifes, seascapes, impressionism. *Publ:* An illustrated survey of leading contemporaries, Am Artists, Chicago, Ill, 89; An illustrated survey of the city's museums, galleries and leading Artists, New York Art Rev, 90. *Mailing Add:* 1180 S Yerba Santa Dr Pueblo West CO 81007

FISHER, ROB (ROBERT) NORMAN
SCULPTOR, LECTURER
b Cleveland, Ohio, May 28, 39. *Study:* Mass Inst Technol, with Gyorgy Kepes, BSc, 61; State Sch Design, Oslo, Norway, cert, 62; Univ Rome, Italy, cert, 63; Syracuse Univ, with Arthur Pulos, MS(indust design), 65. *Hon Degrees:* Disting Fel, Studio Creative Inquiry, Carnegie Mellon. *Work:* Indianapolis Mus Art; Joslyn Art Mus, Omaha, Nebr; Grounds in Sculpture, NY; Southern Alleghanies Mus of Art, Pa; Colo Mus of Outdoor Art. *Comn:* A Page from the Book of skies, suspended sculpture, Medical Ctr, Saudi Arabia, 88-89; Protos, Booz Allen Hamilton, Va, 2001; Osaka-Skyharp suspended sculpture, Osaka Hilton Int, Osaka, Japan, 86; Dihedrals, Gateway Ctr, Md, 2002; Slice of Life, AstraZeneca Pharmaceuticals, Del, 2002; Reigning Knowledge, Nat Educ Asn, Washington, DC, 2003, American Dream, Pub Art Roj, Philadelphia Int Airport, 2003; Orgonelle, Fla Atlantic Univ, 2004-05; Jet Stream, new Indianapolis Int Airport, 2006; Horizon Suite Hotel, Hong Kong, 2006; Royal Carribean Cruise Line, Springfield, Ore, 2006; City of Hope Nat Med Ctr, 2006; Univ Utah, Salt Lake City, 2006. *Exhib:* 14th Midwest Biennial, Joslyn Art Mus, Omaha, 69; Electra 83, Musee d'Art Modern, Paris, 83; One-man show, Computer-Aided-Environmental Sculpture, Recruite G-7 Gallery, Tokyo, Japan, 88; Infinite Illusions, Ripley Gallery, Smithsonian Inst, Washington, DC, 90; Nexus Found for the Arts, Philadelphia, Pa, 2000; NICAF Yokohama '92, Int Contemp Art Fair, Japan, 92; The Fujisankei Biennale Excellent Maquettes, The Hakone Open Air Mus, Japan, 92; Elastic Visions, Computers and Art Exhib, Zoller Gallery, Penn State Univ, 94; Influenced by Architecture: 9 Artists, Fitchburg Art Mus, Mass, 94; Susquehanna Art Mus, Harrisburg, Pa, 96; 20th Century Matrix, NTT Intercomm Ctr Mus, Tokyo, Japan, 1997-2004; Artists Select Artists, Exhib, Century Asn, New York City, 2003; Momentum Kinetic Art Invit, Grounds for Sculpture, NJ, 2006. *Pos:* Res fel, Materials Res Lab, Pa State Univ, 82-; res affil, Ctr Advan Visual Studies, Mass Inst Technol, 83-; artist-in-residence, Col Engineering, Pa State Univ, 88; Visual Arts Panelist, Nat Found for Advancement in the Arts, 2001-04; res Fel, Studio for Creative Inquiry, Carnegie Mellon Univ, Pittsburgh, Pa, 93-2003; Prog Chmn, 19th Int Sculpture Conf, Pa, 2001; bd dir, Int Sculpture Ctr, 96-; keynote speaker, Science & Art 4th Int Symposium, Rutgers Univ, 2005; lecturer, 3rd Int Symposium Interactive Media Design, Istanbul, Turkey. *Teaching:* Dir, Visual Eng Lab, Penn State Univ, 89 & 90; invited lectr, Technol & Art, Japan & China 86, Nat Computer Graphics Asn, Calif, 87, 89 & 91, Inter Sculpture Symposium, Washington, DC, 90 & 2nd Int Symposium Electronic Art, Netherlands, 90; smithsonian studio arts lectr, Washington, DC, 91; speaker, ACM-Siggraph, Los Vegas, Nev, 91; vis lectr, Taliesin West, Ariz, 92; artists in residence, Inst Studies in the Arts, Ariz State Univ, 92; instr & lectr, Tsukuba, Dept Art, Tokyo, Japan, 94, Waseda Univ, Dept Archit, Tokyo, Japan, 94, Int House of Japan, Tokyo, Japan, 94, Kansai Comptuers & Archit Asn, Osaka, Japan, 94; chmn, Computers & Sculpture panel, Fourth Int Symp Electronic Art; sr rsch artist, Carnegie Mellon Univ, Pittsburgh, Pa, 97-; lectr in field; Lectr, 3rd Int Symposium of Interactive Media Design, Yeditepe Univ, Istanbul, Turkey, 2005; moderator/speaker, coordr, Int Sculpture Symposium, New Orleans, LA, 2004-. *Awards:* Merit Award, Vietnam Vet Mem Competition, 81; Special Projects Fel Pa Coun Art, 86, 87 & 90; Fulbright Asn, 92; Nat Sci Found Grants for Artistic Director, Carnegie Mellon Univ, 94-95, 97-2000; Distinguished Fel, STUDIO for Creative Inquiry, Carnegie Mellon Univ; Merit Award, Beijing Sculpture Exhib, 2006. *Bibliog:* Richard Childers (auth), Infinite Illusions, 90; Lillian Schwartz (auth), the Computer Artists Handbook, 92; television revs, CNN Science & Technology Report - Computer Sculpture, 89, 90; The Sculptor's Apprentice, Computer Graphics World, 8/91; High-Tech Sculpture, 3/92; Stanley W Angrist (auth) article Wall Street Jour, 6/17; Peter Deisler (auth), Interactive planetariums, CHIP Mag, 98; R Friedhoff & Harry N Abrams (auth), Visualization: The Second Computer Revolution, 89; Art Matters, Philadelphia, Pa, 2002; Art News, Nat Reviews, 2002; Philadelphia Inquirer, 2002; S Atwood, Decleration of an Artist, Technology Review, MIT, 2004; R Babcock (auth), Art in Architecture, Buildings Magazine, 2004; American Dream, USA Today, Aug 29, 2003. *Mem:* Pa Coun on the Arts (spec proj panel, 84-87); Hist & Archit Rev Bd, Bellefonte, Pa, 76-86; Int Sculpture Ctr, 87. *Media:* Metal, Light, Electronic Media. *Res:* Interactive planetarium shows about the brain; science & nature as subject matter for sculpture. *Publ:* Coauth, Understanding Visual Forms, Van Nostrand Reinhold, 76; Computer-aided sculpture, Leonardo, J Sci & Art, Pergamon Press, Oxford, Eng, 85; Escultura Asistida por Ordendor: Considerciones Visuales y Tecnicas, Telos, Spain, 86; Computer-aided Sculpture: Implications for the Design Professions, conf Proceedings, Nat Computer Graphics Asn, 87; Computers & Sculpture, Sculpture Mag, 91; auth & ed, The Computer: A Tool For Sculptors, Van Nostrand Reinhold Publ Corp, N4, 94-95; coauth series of columns Sculpture Mag, May/June 91; Declaration of an Artist, Technology Review, 2004; Symposium Proceedings, 3rd Int Symposium Interactive Media Design, Istanbul, Turkey, 2006. *Mailing Add:* 228 N Allegheny St Bellefonte PA 16823-1630

FISHER, SARAH LISBETH
CONSERVATOR
b Washington, DC, Nov 1, 45. *Study:* Wellesley Col, BA(art hist), 67; Florence, Italy, with pvt painting conservator, 67-68; Inst Technol Paintings, Stuttgart, Ger, with Dr R Straub, 69-70; Swiss Inst Art Res, Zurich, Switz, with Dr T Brachert, cert in conserv, 72; with T Hermanes, Canton of Vaud, Switz, 69 & 70; Cent Inst Art Res, Amsterdam, Holland, with Dr J Mosk, 73; Inst Royal du Patrimoine Artistique, Brussels, Belg, with N Gortghebeur, cert in conserv, 75. *Pos:* Conservator & asst to the dir, Swiss Inst for Art Res, Zurich, Switz, 72-74; conservator, Intermus Lab, Oberlin, 75-77, Balboa Art Conserv Ctr, San Diego, Calif, 77-81 & Nat Gallery Art, Washington, DC, 81-. *Teaching:* Instr painting conserv, Intermus Conserv Asn, Oberlin, Ohio, 75-77. *Mem:* Am Inst Conserv Hist & Artist Works; Int Inst Conserv Hist & Artistic Works; Western Asn Art Conserv; Washington Conserv Guild. *Publ:* Ed, Rubens' The finding of Erichthonius: Examination and treatment, Allen Mem Art Mus Bulletin, Oberlin Col, XXXVIII, No 1, 80-81. *Mailing Add:* Nat Gallery Art Painting Conserv Dept Fourth & Constitution Ave NW Washington DC 20565

FISHER, VERNON
CONCEPTUAL ARTIST
b Ft Worth, Tex, 43. *Study:* Hardin-Simmons Univ, BA, 67; Univ Ill, MFA, 69. *Work:* Hirshhorn/Smithsonian Inst, Corcoran Gallery Art, Washington, DC; Guggenheim Mus & Mus Mod Art, NY; Albright-Knox, Buffalo. *Exhib:* Bronx Mus Arts, NY, 84; Hirshhorn Mus & Sculpture Garden, Washington, DC, 84; New Orleans Mus Art, La, 86; Brooklyn Mus, NY, 86; Walker Art Ctr, Minneapolis, Minn, 87; Los Angeles Co Mus Art, 87; Inst Contemp Arts, London, 87; solo exhib, Asher-Faure Gallery, Los Angeles, 86, Barbara Gladstone Gallery, NY, 87, Hiram Butler Gallery, Houston, Tex, 87, Lannan Mus, Lake Worth, Fla, 87, Fred Hoffman Gallery, Buffalo, NY, 89 & Hiram Butler Gallery, Houston, 90; Karsten Schubert Ltd, London, 89; Mus Fine Arts, Houston, 90; Asher-Faure Gallery, Los Angeles, 91; Rena Bransten Gallery, San Francisco, 92; and others. *Teaching:* Assoc prof art, Austin Col, Sherman, 69-78; prof art, NTex State Univ, 78-. *Awards:* Visual Artist Award Grant, SECCA, 81, 88; Louis Comfort Tiffany Found Grant, 80-81, 84. *Bibliog:* John Habich (auth), Past/imperfect Kroust marathon, Minneapolis Star & Tribune, 4/11/87; Colleen O'Conner (auth), High profile: Vernon Fisher, Dallas Morning News, 9/20/87; Gary Schwan (auth), Lannan's walls teach perspective, Palm Beach Post, 10/23/87. *Publ:* Ed, Five stories, No 2, winter-spring 79 & A childhood friend, No 4, summer 80, White Walls; The Paris Review, Paris Review Inc, Vol 23, No 80, summer 81; auth, Navigating By the Stars, Landfall Press, Chicago, 89; ed, Navigating by the stars, Neon, summer 92. *Mailing Add:* Charles Cowles Gallery 537 W 24th St New York NY 10011

FISHMAN, BARBARA (ELLEN) SCHWARTZ
PAINTER, PRINTMAKER
b Brooklyn, NY, May 3, 46. *Study:* Sch Fine Arts, Boston Univ, BFA, 68; NY Univ, with Chuck Close, MA(painting), 73. *Work:* Boston Univ Traveling Art Show. *Comn:* Several pvt commissions. *Exhib:* Nat Asn Women Artists For Exhib to India, Jehangir Art Gallery, Bombay, India, 89; 100 Yrs/100 Works, Kirkpatrick Ctr, Tulsa, Okla, 90; Audubon Artists, Nat Arts Club, NY, 91; The Tree An Artist's Gift, Bergen Mus Art, Paramus, NJ, 91; North By South, Nassau Co Mus Art, Roslyn, NY, 92. *Pos:* Chair scheduling, Graphic Eye Gallery, Port Washington, NY, 86-; juror painting, Nat Asn Women Artists, New York, 93-; mem & chmn, Stan Brodsky Exhib, Art Adv Coun,

Port Washington, NY, 93-. *Teaching:* Teacher art, Simon Baruch Jr High, New York, 68-70. *Awards:* Louis Lozowick Award, Audubon Artists Nat Art Club, 90; Stelly Sterling Mem, Nat Asn Women Artists, 92; Long Beach Art League/Art Club Rockville Ctr Gold Award, Nassau Co Mus Art, 92. *Mem:* Nat Asn Women Artists; Manhasset Art Asn; Audubon Artists; Art Adv Coun. *Media:* Acrylic, Oil. *Mailing Add:* 4 Woodcleft Ave Port Washington NY 11050

FISHMAN, LOUISE
PAINTER
b Philadelphia, Pa, 39. *Study:* Philadelphia Col Art, 56-57; Pa Acad Fine Arts, 58; Tyler Sch Fine Arts, BFA & BS, 63; Univ Ill, MFA, 65. *Work:* Art Inst of Chgo; Carnegie Mus of Art, Pitts; High Mus of Art, Atlanta; Jewish Mus, NY; Metrop Mus of Art, NY. *Exhib:* Whitney Mus Am Art, 87; solo exhibs, Olin Art Gallery, Kenyon Col, Gambier, Ohio, 92, Temple Gallery, Tyler Sch Art, 92 & 93, Morris Gallery, Pa Acad Fine Arts, 92-93, Robert Miller Gallery, NY, 93, 95 & 96, Bianca Lanza Gallery, Miami, 94, Cheim & Read, New York City, 98 & 2000, Paule Anglim Gallery, San Francisco, 98 & 2000; 25 Americans: Painting in the 90's, Milwaukee Art Mus, Wis, 95; Artist's Choice: Elizabeth Murray, Mus Mod Art, NY, 95; Carnegie Mus Art, 95; Severed Ear: The Poetry of Abstraction, Creiger-Dane Gallery, Boston, 99; Walking, Danese, NY, 99; Abstraction: Realism, Susquehanna Art Mus, 99; Drawing in the Present Tense, Parsons Sch of Design, 99; 17th Ann Exhib, Nat Acad of Design, 2000; Snapshot, Balt Mus of Contemp Art, Md, 2000; The Perpetual Well: Contemp Art from the Collection of the Jewish Mus, Parrish Art Mus, 2000. *Awards:* Nat Endowment Arts, 75-76, 83-84 & 94; NY Found Arts, Fel, 86; Adolph & Esther Gottlieb Found, Grant, 86. *Dealer:* Cheim & Read Gallery 521 W 23rd St New York, NY 10011. *Mailing Add:* c/o Robert Miller Gallery 526 W 26th St #10A New York NY 10001-5541

FISKIN, JUDY
PHOTOGRAPHER, VIDEO ARTIST
b Chicago, Ill, April 1, 1945. *Study:* Pomona Col, with John Mason, BA, 66; Univ Calif, Berkeley, 66-67; Univ Calif, Los Angeles, MA(art hist), 69. *Work:* Bibliot Nat, Paris, France; Dallas Mus Fine Arts, Tex; Mus Contemp Art, La Jolla, Calif; Mus Fine Arts, Houston, Tex; Mus Contemp Art, Los Angeles. *Comn:* What We Think About When We Think About Ships, Los Angeles Co Mus Art, 2000. *Exhib:* Solo shows, Castelli Graphics, NY, 76, Curt Marcus Gallery, NY, 91 & 94, Asher-Faure Gallery, Los Angeles, 91, Mus Contemp Art, Los Angeles, 92 & Patricia Faure Gallery, 94; Los Angeles in the 70's, Ft Worth Art Mus, Tex, 77; Group Material: Democracy, DIA Art Found, NY, 88; Typologies: Nine Contemp Photogrs, Newport Harbor Art Mus, Newport Beach, Calif, San Francisco Mus Mod Art, Akron Art Mus & Corcoran Gallery Art, Washington, 91; Special Collections: The Photog Order from Pop to Now, Int Ctr Photog, NY, 92; Diary of a Midlife Crisis (film), San Francisco Film Fest, Bonn Videonale, Kassel Film & Video Fest & Mus Contemp Art, Los Angeles; producer, My Getty Ctr (Silver Award, Worldfest, Houston, Best of Festival, Berkeley Video & Film Fest, Impakt Festival, Utecht, The Neth). *Collection Arranged:* 50 Ways to Set the Table (video), Mus of Modern Art, NYC, 2004; Anthology Film Archives NYC, 2004; Angles Gallery, Santa Monica, 2004. *Pos:* Co-dir, Womanspace Gallery, 73-74. *Teaching:* prof photog, Calif Inst Arts, Valencia, 77-, assoc dean, 79-84. *Awards:* Nat Endowment Arts Grant, 80 & 90; Lifetime Achievement Award in Photog, Los Angeles Ctr Photog Studies, 95; Silver Spire Award, San Francisco Int Film Fest, 98. *Bibliog:* Richard Armstrong (auth), Judy Fiskin's Photographs JS Calif Art Mag, 9-10/79; Robert L Pincus (auth), Judy Fiskin: some questions of aesthetics visions, winter 89; Terry R Myers (auth), Judy Fiskin, Arts, 4/91. *Mem:* Soc Photog Educ; Los Angeles Ctr Photog Studies. *Media:* Black & White Video. *Dealer:* Angles Gallery Santa Monica CA. *Mailing Add:* c/o Calif Inst Arts 24700 McBean Pkwy Valencia CA 91355

FISS, CINTHEA
PHOTOGRAPHER, VIDEO ARTIST
b New York, NY. *Study:* Antioch Univ, BFA, 78; Nova Scotia Col Art & Design, 78-80; Calif Inst Arts, MFA, 93. *Work:* San Francisco Arts Comn, Calif; Los Angeles Pub Libr; Ctr Creative Photog, Tucson, Ariz. *Exhib:* Solo exhib, Side Street Gallery, Santa Monica, Calif, 94; ISP Open Studios, Whitney Mus, NY, 96; Deadly Responses: Murder & Suicide, Longwood Arts Gallery, NY, 96; Buck Stop: Pro-Vanities in the Bathroom, Spot Gallery, NY, 96; Joint Ventures, Basillico Fine Arts, NY, 96; Open Circuits, Contemp Art Mus, Tampa, 96. *Collection Arranged:* Women Artists at Work, Eye Gallery, 90. *Pos:* Cur & bd dir, Eye Gallery, San Francisco, 84-89; facilities mgr, Headlands Ctr Arts, Sausalito, Calif, 88-89; artist-in-residency, Calif Arts Coun, 94-95; co-dir, Internet Agency, NY, 95-. *Teaching:* Vis prof photog, Univ Ariz, Tucson, 94-95; asst prof electronic media, Univ SFla, Tampa, 95-. *Awards:* Visual Artist fel New Genres, Nat Endowment Arts Regional WESTAF, 94; Artist Equip Access Award, Bay Area Video Coalition, 94. *Bibliog:* David A Greene (auth), Women at work, Los Angeles Reader, 11/25/94; C Brue and K Shields (auths), Withinsight: Visual Territories of Thirty Artists, 95; Vivien Raynor (auth), Deadly responses, NY Times 2/11/96. *Mem:* Col Art Asn. *Media:* Photography; Electronic Media. *Publ:* Contribr, Tradeswomen Mag, San Francisco, 85-88; Honeycakes for Cerebus, Art Press, 93; Women and Work, New Sage Press, 87 & 94; auth, Pump, Rethinking Marxism, 95; Implications of recent technological changes, API J, 96

FITCH, BLAKE
MUSEUM DIRECTOR, PHOTOGRAPHER, CURATOR
b Greensboro, NC, 1971. *Study:* Pratt Inst, BFA, 94; Art Inst Chicago, 98; Boston Univ, MS, 2001. *Work:* Cur Photobooth, Jan Staller: A Retrospective. *Pos:* Exec dir, Griffin Mus of Photog, Winchester, Mass, currently. *Mailing Add:* Griffin Mus Photog 67 Shore Rd Winchester MA 01890

FITCH, STEVE (STEVEN) RALPH
PHOTOGRAPHER, INSTRUCTOR
b Tucson, Ariz, Aug 16, 49. *Study:* Univ Calif, Berkeley, BA, 71; San Francisco Art Inst, 77; Univ NMex, Albuquerque, MA, 78. *Work:* Mus Mod Art, NY; Mus Fine Arts, Boston; Fogg Art Mus; Oakland Mus; Houston Mus Fine Arts. *Exhib:* Solo exhib, Art Mus, Univ Calif, Berkeley, 75; The Aesthetics of Graffiti, 79 & Beyond Color, 80, San Francisco Mus Mod Art; Color as Form: History of Color Photog, George Eastman House, Rochester, NY, 82; Exposed & Developed: Photog Sponsored by Nat Endowment Arts, Smithsonian Inst, Nat Mus Am Art, 84; Marks & Measures: Linda Connor, Rick Dingus, Steve Fitch & Charles Roitz, Spencer Art Mus, Univ Kans, Lawrence, 85; Road and Roadside, Art Inst Chicago, 87; Arts '93, Fine Arts Mus, Santa Fe, NMex, 93; Perpetual Mirage, Whitney Mus Am Art, 96. *Teaching:* Instr, Asn Students Univ Calif Studio, Berkeley, 71-77; teaching asst, Univ NMex, Albuquerque, 78-79; instr, Univ Colo, Boulder, 79-85; vis assoc prof, Univ Tex, San Antonio, fall 85; vis lectr, Princeton Univ, 86-90; asst prof art, Col Santa Fe, NMex, 90-. *Awards:* Nat Endowment Arts Fel, 73, 75 & 81. *Bibliog:* Lois Fishman (auth), article, Creative Camera, 8/77; Jonathon Greene (auth), American Photography: A Critical History, Abrams, New York, 84; Rick Dingus (auth), article, Artspace Mag, spring 84. *Publ:* Auth, Diesels and Dinosaurs, Long Run Press, 76; Highway as Habitat, Univ Art Mus, Santa Barbara, Calif, 86; Marks in Place, Univ NMex Press, 88; Night Photography: A Survey of 20th Century Night Photography, Hallmark Photog Collection, Kansas City, Mo, 89; New Dimensions, Agfa Corp, 90. *Mailing Add:* HC63 Box 5 Pena Blanca NM 87041

FITERMAN, DOLLY
GALLERY DIRECTOR, COLLECTOR
b Minn. *Study:* Univ Minn; St Cloud Bus Col; Hon Dr, Univ St Thomas, 97. *Pos:* Dir & Chief Exec Officer, Dolly Fiterman Fine Arts; guest cur, Milton Avery Exhib, Boca Raton, Fla; trustee, Frederick R Weisman Art Mus, Univ Minn, formerly; livetime adv, Minn Opera, Minneapolis Inst Art; trustee, Am Ctr Photog. *Teaching:* Guest lectr, Univ Minn & Boca Raton Mus, Fla; lectr, Minneapolis Woman's Club, Am Asn Univ Women & Minn Mus Am Art; symp, Minneapolis Col Art & Design. *Awards:* App by Gov to Minn State Arts Bd, 91-96; Guest of USSR Cent Union of Artists at Tretyakov Mus, Moscow, 90; Alexandrine Award, Col St Catherine, 90. *Bibliog:* Daniel Farson (auth), Referenced in with Gilbert and George in Moscow, Minneapolis Star Tribune (cover story), 9/91; This Old Library, Minneapolis Skyway News, 9/91; Hello Dolly, St Paul Pioneer Press, 11/91. *Mem:* Minneapolis Inst Art; Walker Art Ctr, Minneapolis. *Specialty:* Paintings; fine prints and drawings; sculpture--American and European. *Publ:* Auth, Dialogue: Alchemy of the Word (exhib catalog), 93; An Exhibition of North American and European 20th Century Chairs (exhib catalog), Dolly Fiterman Fine Arts, 96; Painting Album of Yikai (exhib catalog), Dynasties Art Consult, Singapore, 97. *Mailing Add:* Dolly Fiterman Fine Arts 100 University Ave SE Minneapolis MN 55414

FITZGERALD, ASTRID
PAINTER, PRINTMAKER, WRITER
b Wil, Switz, July 28, 38; US citizen. *Study:* Col St Agnes, Fribourg, Switz, 55; Art Students League, New York, 62; Fashion Inst Technol, New York, 68; Pratt Graphics Ctr, New York, 72; Polytechnic Sch, London, Eng, 58-59. *Work:* Aldrich Mus, Ridgefield, Conn; Wellesley Col, Mass; Marymount Col, Tarrytown, NY; Rockefeller Ctr Collection; Educ Mgt Ctr, Atlanta, Ga. *Comn:* Kindercare Corp, Montgomery, Ala; IBM, Boca Raton, Fla; Ashley Plaza Hotel, Tampa, Fla; Union Bank Switz, NY. *Exhib:* Albright-Knox Mus, Buffalo, NY, 73; Contemp Reflections, Aldrich Mus, 78; Pietrasanta Fine Arts, NY, 86; Galerie Neue Kunst, Wil, Switz, 93; Harmony by Design Exhib, traveling to Chicago, Washington, DC & NY, 94; Hyposwiss, Zurich, Switz, 96; Murakami Gallery, NY, 96-97; Muroff Kotler Visual Arts Gallery, SUNY at Ulster, Stone Ridge, NY, 2000; Galerie Raubach, St Gallen, Switz, 01, 02; Artcanal, 02; Lelandcrow, Switz, 02; Lo River Arts, Beacons NY, 2005; Wuersch & Gering, NY, 2005-2006. *Awards:* Michael M Engel Mem Award, Nat Arts Club, New York, 73; Charles Levitt Award, Nat Asn Women Artists Ann, 78; Juror's Award, Fourth Ann Small Works Competition, NY Univ, 80. *Bibliog:* Roger Lipsey (auth), The Art of Astrid Fitzgerald-New Images, Old Faith, 85; Richard H Pichler (auth), Swiss Artist in New York, 85; Adrian Frost (auth) Probing the mysteries, Woodstock Times, NY, 2000; Art Canal 02 Catalog, Internat Sculpture Exhibition, Switzerland. *Mem:* NY Artists Equity Asn; Swiss Inst NY; Women's Studio Workshop. *Media:* Oil, Watercolor, Eucaustic. *Publ:* Contribr, Traveler's Key to Ancient Greece, Knopf, 89; Auth, Harmony by Design, Parabola, winter 91; An Artist's Book of Inspiration, Lindisfarne Press, 96; auth, Being Consciousness Bliss - A Seeker's Guide, 2002. *Dealer:* Ellen Price New York NY. *Mailing Add:* 650 West End Ave New York NY 10025

FITZGERALD, BETTY JO
PAINTER, PRINTMAKER
b Colusa, Calif, Jan 10, 42. *Study:* Univ Northern Calif, Chico, BA, 63; Univ Wash, MS, 66; Evergreen State Col (printmaking & design), 90-92. *Work:* Sch Admin Ctr, Hampton, Pa; North Kansas City Hosp, Mo; Seattle Art Mus Rental Gallery, Wash. *Comn:* Watercolor painting, Sovrain Financial, Baltimore, Md, 88; watercolor painting, Allen Womens Ctr, Denver, Colo, 89; 2 mixed media collages, Olympia Golf & Country Club, Wash, 90; 2 paintings watercolor, Samsun Med Ctr, Santa Barbara, Calif, 90; watercolor collage, Telco Credit Union, Seattle, Wash, 91; acrylic/canvas painting, Swedish Med Found, 04. *Exhib:* Nat Watercolor Soc Ann, Brea Civic Ctr, Calif, 91; Water Music Festival Invitational, Ilwaco Heritage Mus, Wash, 93; NW Watercolor Soc Signature Mem Invitational, Wash State Conv Ctr, Seattle, 93; SW Wash 40th Exhib, State Capital Mus, Olympia, 93; 11th Ann Greater Midwest Int, Art Ctr Gallery, Cent Mo State Univ, 96; Art for Environmental Advocacy, Adell McMillan Gallery, Univ Ore, Eugene, 98; NW Expression, Coos Art Mus, Ore, 98;

NW Watercolor Soc Invitational, Maryhill Mus Art, Goldendale, Wash, 97; 1st Int Exhib, Salisbury State Univ, Md, 97; Frye Mus, 60th Anniversary, Seattle, 2000; Coos Art Mus, Oreg, 2001-04; Bellevue Art Mus, Wash, 01; Watcom Mus History & Art, Bellingham, Wash, 05. *Pos:* pres, Northwest Watercolor Found. *Teaching:* La Conner Workshops, 95 & 97; Sunshine Coast Sch Arts, Coupeville, Wash, 99; Spokane Watercolor Sco Workshops, 2006. *Awards:* Ewwg Gold Award, Ea Washington Watercolor Soc, 00; 3rd Pl Pa Art League Nat, Gig Harbor Gallery, Wa, 03; Best of Show, PAL Nat, Gig Habor, Wash, 2006; and others. *Bibliog:* Doug Margeson (auth), Women painters art on display, J Am, 3/6/92; Hand Made for the Holidays, Olympian, 10/6/96; Curt Dewees (auth), The Artful Cup, Fresh Cup Mag, 8/98. *Mem:* Women Painters Wash (pres, 92-93, treas, 1996-2001); Nat Watercolor Soc; signature mem NW Watercolor Soc (vpres, 98-99, pres, 1999-2000); signature mem NCoast Collage Soc; Arts Olympia (treas, 95 & 96-98). *Media:* Watermedia, Monotypes, Acrylic. *Specialty:* contemporary mixed media & monotype. *Interests:* travel, native plants, art advocate in the community. *Publ:* Auth, Abstracts in Watercolor (ed by Lou Schlemm), Rockport Publ, Mass, 96; Road Tableaux, catalogue of watercolor paintings, 02. *Dealer:* Seattle Art Mus Sales & Rental Gallery 1334 First Ave Suite 140 Seattle WA 98101-2902; Coos Art Mus Rental & Sales Gallery Coos Bay Oreg; Childhood's End Gallery Olympia Wash. *Mailing Add:* 3327 Windolph Ln NW Olympia WA 98502

FITZGERALD, JOAN V
PAINTER, COLLAGE ARTIST
b Batavia, NY, Jan 24, 1930. *Study:* Rochester Inst of Tech, 1948-49; Buffalo State College, BS (Art Educ), 1964; MS (Art Educ), 1969. *Work:* Canisius col, Buffalo, NY; Marble House Editions Publ Co, New York, NY; Harry & Jeanette Weiberg Campus, Getzville, NY; Roswell Park Cancer Inst, Buffalo, NY; Carolyn House (Niagara Falls YWCA), Niagara Falls, NY. *Exhib:* Summer Salon Series Invitational Exhib, Broome St Gallery, New York, NY, 2000; Collage Artists of America Juried Exhib, Brand Exhib Ctr, Glendale, CA, 2003; Recent Paintings by Joan Fitzgerald, Peter & MaryLou Vogt Gallery, Canisius College, Buffalo, NY, 2003; Viridian Artist's 15th National Juried Exhib, Viridian Gallery, New York, NY, 2004; Catherine Lorillard Wolfe Nat Juried Exhib, Nat Arts Club, New York, NY, 2005; Nat col Soc 21st Annual Juried Exhib, Butler Inst of Am Art, Salem, OH, 2005. *Pos:* Pres, Buffalo Soc of Artists, Buffalo, NY, 1980; chwn, Western NY Artists Group, Buffalo, NY, 2002-2003. *Teaching:* asst prof, Humanities drawing/painting, 1985-92 (PT), Erie Community col, Buffalo, NY, 1992-98, acting asst academic dean, 90-92, instr, drawing/painting, 1992-1998. *Awards:* Dir Choice, Small Juried New Eng Regional, Main St Gallery, Groton, NY, 2004; Spec Recognition Award, Landscape V (Int Juried Internet Exhib), Period Gallery, Lincoln, Nebr, 2005; Special Recognition Award, Abstract VI (Int Juried Internet Exhib), Period Gallery, Lincoln, Nebr, 2005. *Bibliog:* Larry Bradshaw (auth), Period Gallery Summer Nat Invitational Exhib, Period Gallery Newsletter, Lincoln, Nebr, 2000; Katherine Rushworth (auth), Small Works/Big Show (Small Works New Eng Regional Exhib), Syracuse Post Standard, Syracuse, NY, 2003; Katherine Rushworth (auth), Good Things in Small Packages (Small Works New Eng Regional Exhib), Syracuse Post Standard, Syracuse, NY, 2004. *Mem:* Buffalo Soc of Artists, Buffalo, NY (pres 1980); Western NY Artist's Group, Buffalo, NY (chwn 2002-2003); Nat Collage Soc, Hudson, OH, (signature mem). *Media:* Acrylic, Collage. *Publ:* auth, The Magic Lunch Box, Marble House Editions (in press), 2004; auth, Not Another Christmas, Marble House Editions (in press), 2004; auth, Glamour (poetry chapbook), Word Runner Press (in press), 2004; auth, The Iris House, Marble House Editions (in press), 2005. *Dealer:* Donald J. Siuta Art Dialogue Gallery One Linwood Ave Buffalo NY 14209-2203. *Mailing Add:* Box 245 Athol Springs NY 14010

FITZGERALD, JOE
PAINTER, PRINTMAKER
b Washington, DC, 50. *Study:* Univ Md, College Park, BA, 72; State Univ NY, Oswego, studied printmaking with George O'Connell, 73. *Work:* US Embassy, Ankara, Turkey; US Embassy, St George's, Granada; Montgomery Co, Rockville, Md; US Embassy, Bahrain; Designs chosen by US Mint for Obverse & Reverse 2005 Nickel. *Comn:* Mural, Hyatt Hotel, Pittsburgh, Pa, 90. *Exhib:* Benefit Auction, Corcoran Gallery, Washington, DC, 85; one-man shows, Studio Gallery, Washington, DC, 87, 89 & 93, Audubon Soc, Chevy Chase, Md, 89, Franz Bader Gallery, Washington, DC, 94, Studio Gallery, Washington, DC, 96, Galerie Ingrid Cooper, Kensington, Md, 98 & George Meany Int Ctr, Silver Spring, Md, 98; Heart Works, Washington Proj Arts, Washington, DC, 90; Eight DC Artists, Nat Press Club, Washington, DC, 91; invitational show, George Meany Int Ctr, Silver Spring, Md, 94; Foxhall Gallery, Washington, DC, 1999, 2001, 2002, 2005. *Pos:* Illusr, US Consumer Proj Safety Comn, 72-80; art dir, Nat Libr Med, Bethesda, Md, 80-2005. *Awards:* Montgomery Co Purchase Award, 85; Honarium, US Mint, for 2005 Coin Design. *Bibliog:* Michael Welzenbach (auth), Paint for paint's sake, Washington Post, 3/4/89; Mary McCoy (auth), Dark and lovely, Washington Post, 11/24/90; Lee Fleming (auth), Joe Fitzgerald at studio, Washington Post, 3/6/93; Karen Schafer (auth), Jack of all Trades, Montgomery Gazette, 7/3/98; William L Hamilton (auth), His 5 Cents' Worth, NY Times, 3/24/05. *Mem:* Us Mint Artistic Infusion Prog. *Media:* Oil, Pastels & woodcuts. *Dealer:* Foxhall Gallery Washington DC. *Mailing Add:* 828 Sligo Ave Silver Spring MD 20910

FITZPATRICK, ROBERT JOHN
MUSEUM DIRECTOR
b Toronto, Ont, May 18, 40; naturalized, 62. *Study:* Spring Hill Col, BA, 63, MA, 64; Woodrow Wilson Fel, Johns Hopkins Univ, 64-65. *Collection Arranged:* Roy Lichtenstein at CalArts--Drawings and Collages from the Artist's Collection, 77; Roy Lichtenstein: Interiors, Mus Contemp Art, Chicago, 99. *Pos:* Pres, Calif Inst Arts, 75-87; vpres cult affairs, Los Angeles Olympic Organizing Comt, 81-84; dir, Olympic Arts Festival, Los Angeles, 84, Los Angeles Festival, 85-87; pres, EuroDisney, Paris, 87-93; dir & chief exec officer, Mus Contemp Art, Chicago, 98-; trustee, Archeworks, Chicago, Am Ctr Fedn Paris; mem Balt City Coun, 71-75; mem Md Democratic State Cent Comt, 70-74; trustee Craft and Folk Art Mus, Los Angeles, 76-82; trustee Dunn Sch, Los Olivos, Calif, 80-84, Bennington Col, Vt; pres Calif Inst Arts, Valencia, 75-87, Euro Disneyland, Burbank, Calif, 87-93; Chief Exec Officer, Reconstruct Finance Corp, Paris, 93-95. *Teaching:* chmn dept modern languages Gilman Sch, Balt, 68-72; dean of students John Hopkins Univ, 72-75; dean sch of arts Columbia Univ, New York City, 95-01. *Awards:* Officer, l'Order des Arts et des Lettres, France; chevalier, Ordre National de Merite, France. *Mailing Add:* Mus Contemporary Art 220 E Chicago Ave Chicago IL 60611

FITZPATRICK, TONY
PAINTER
b Chicago, Ill, 58. *Work:* Art Inst Chicago; Mus Mod Art, NY; Nat Mus Am Art, Washington; Philadelphia Mus Art; Portland Art Mus, Ore. *Exhib:* One-man shows, Janet Fleisher Gallery, Philadelphia, 93 &94, Loomis Chaffee Sch, Richmond Art Ctr, Windsor, Conn, 94, Art Inst Chicago, 95, Adam Baum Gold Gallery, NY, 96, Monique Knowlton Gallery, NY, 96, Contemp Art Ctr, Cincinnati, 96. *Bibliog:* Jonathan Demme (auth), The Hard Angels (exhib catalog), Janet Fleisher Gallery, Philadelphia, 88, The Real Deal (exhib catalog), World Tattoo Gallery, 94 & The Secret Birds and Other Subjects (exhib catalog), Augen Gallery, Portland, Ore & Janet Fleisher Gallery, Philadelphia, 94

FITZSIMONDS, CAROL STRAUSE
PRINTMAKER, GALLERY DIRECTOR
b Richmond, Va, Mar 13, 51. *Study:* Hollins Col, Va, BA, 73; Art League Sch, Torpedo Factory Art Ctr, 84-85. *Work:* Libr Congress, Nat Mus Am Hist, Smithsonian Inst, Nat Mus Women in Arts, Washington, Newport Art Mus, RI; Jane Voorhees Zimmerli Art Mus, New Brunswick, NJ. *Exhib:* 23rd Nat Invitation Drawing Exhib, Emporia State Univ, Kans, 96; A Collection at Rutgers: Recent Acquistions, Zimmerli Art Mus, 99; Aud Artists 58th Nat Exhib, NY, 2000; Silvermine Guild 23rd Nat Print Biennial, New Canaan, Conn, 2000; Time Pieces, Newport Art Mus, 2000, Contemp Highlights: 21st Century Acquisitions to Permanent Collection, 2005. *Pos:* Partner, Spectrum Gallery, Washington, 85-87, Printmaker's Inc, Alexandria, Va, 86-87 & 92-2001 & Spring Bull Gallery, Newport, RI, 99-2006. *Teaching:* monotype Providence Art Club, 02; printmaking Newport Art Mus Sch, 02, Providence Art Club, 2003-; bookbinding for artists Newport Art Mus Sch, 03. *Awards:* CLWAC Medal Hon, 92; AAPL Leila Gardin Sawyer Mem Award, 2000; Bruce Crane Mem Award, 99. *Bibliog:* John Pantalone (auth), Artistic life of a traveling printmaker, Newport this Week, 5/4/89; The Best of Printmaking, An Int Collection, Rockport Publ Inc, 97; Mark St. John Erickson (auth), Printmaking, Daily Press, 12/10/2000. *Mem:* Catharine Lorillard Wolfe Art Club Inc; Copley Soc Art; Am Artists Prof League; Boston Printmakers; Soc Am Graphic Artists. *Media:* Aquatint Etching. *Publ:* Auth, Imagined journeys, J Print World, fall 89 & Eye Wash, 10/89; Auth, Exploring Aquating, Artists Mag, 99; auth, The Art of Printmaking, J Print World, spring 2006. *Dealer:* Old Print Barn, 343 Winona Rd New Hampton NH 03256; Green River Gallery 297 Hope St Bristol RI 02809. *Mailing Add:* 251 Water St Portsmouth RI 02871

FIX, JOHN ROBERT
SCULPTOR, SILVERSMITH
b Pittsburgh, Pa, Oct 31, 34. *Study:* Rochester Inst Technol, Sch Am Craftsmen, BFA; Conn Col, MAT; study with Lawrence G Copeland, Hans Christianson, William A McCloy & Frances Felten. *Comn:* Host box, Glenwood Lutheran Church, Minn, 57; chalice, St Andrew's Episcopal Church, New Kensington, Pa, 62; chalice, 68 & menorah, 71, Harkness Chapel, Conn Col, New London; altar set, St Paul's Episcopal Church, Westbrook, Conn, 79; plus many pvt comn in sculpture & metalsmithing. *Exhib:* Assoc Artists Pittsburgh Ann, Carnegie Mus, 57-80; New Eng Invitational, De Cordova Mus, Lincoln, Mass, 62; RI Arts Festival, Providence, 64; Soc Conn Craftsmen Traveling Show, 66; Three Rivers Arts Festival, Pittsburgh, 71, 73 & 74; 25th Anniversary Exhib, Brookfield Craft Ctr; one man show, Metal Works, Lyman Allyn Art Mus, New London, Conn, 90; Katheryn Forrest Trust Ann Exhib, Slater Mus, Norwich, Conn, 85-2000. *Teaching:* Metalsmithing, Norwich Art Sch, The Norwich Free Acad, Conn, 60-92 (retired), head art dept, 89-92; instr sculpture & art hist, Upward Bound, Conn Col, 69; dir young peoples art prog, Lyman Allyn Art Mus, New London, 74-82; jewelry workshops, Guilford Handcraft Ctr, Conn, Wesleyan Potters, Brookfield Craft Ctr, Conn; adj fac, Three Rivers Community Col, Norwich, Conn, 96-. *Awards:* First Prize in Crafts, 58, Mrs Roy A Hunt Award, 61 & Jury Award for Distinction in Crafts, 68, Assoc Artists Pittsburgh; Award for Excellence in Silver, Katheryn Forrest Trust Crafts Invitational, Slater Mus, Norwich, Conn, 86; Award in Sculpture, Mystic Art Asn, juried exhib, 86; Purchase Prize, Katheryn Forrest Trust, 89, 92 & 2000. *Bibliog:* John D Morris (auth), Creative Metal Sculpture, Bruce Pub Co, NY, 71; Shirley Charron (auth), Modern Pewter, Van Nostrand Reinhold Co, 73; Gold Smiths J, 79. *Mem:* Mystic Art Asn Inc (pres, 74); Assoc Artists Pittsburgh; Lyman-Allyn Art Mus (bd dir, 88-94), New London, Conn. *Media:* Silver, Gold, Pewter. *Mailing Add:* PO Box 362 Stonington CT 06378

FLACH, VICTOR H
DESIGNER, WRITER
b Portland, Ore, May 31, 1929. *Study:* Univ Ore, Sch Archit & Allied Arts, with Jack Wilkinson, BS & MFA; Univ Pittsburgh, Henry Clay Frick Fine Arts Dept, with Walter Read Hovey; also with R Buckminster Fuller, 53 & 59. *Comn:* Three-wall mural, Clearlake Sch, Eugene, Ore, 56; The Heritage Series Interview with American Painter Ben Shahn, PBS-TV, 65; two-wall, three-story mosaic tile mural, Sci Ctr, Univ Wyo, 67-68; The Arts in Practice, TV prog, with Richard Evans, UW-TV, 71; relief ceramic-tile mural sect, Springcreek Sch, Laramie, 95. *Exhib:* One-man, group &

traveling shows, incl: Portland Art Mus, 52, Denver Art Mus, 71, Contextualist Arts Gallery, 84-85 & Univ, Mus & Galleries from various cities across the US; 40 yr Photo Retrospective, Black Hills State Univ, SDak, 89. *Pos:* Ed, In/sert: Active Anthology for the Creative, 55-62; cur, Cathedral of Learning-Frick Fine Arts Gallery, Pittsburgh, 59-64. *Teaching:* Prof painting, design & theory, Univ Wyo, 65-92, prof emer, 93. *Res:* Toward a comprehensive tetradic typologic systems programming as model for archetypal-prototypal iconographic and colorfielding structural morphology. *Publ:* Auth, Gloss of the Four Universal Forms, The Eyes' Mind, Anatomy of the Canvas: R Wells Paintings, Univ Pittsburgh; By These Presents: Richard Evans Retrospective, 76 & The Stage: Joseph Deadrick Drawings, Univ Wyo, 78; Indigenous Image, 79 & Contextualist Manifesto, 82; Displacings & Wayfarings, North Atlantic Bks, 2nd Ed, 88; Iconography of Wilkinson's Orientation Mural, Univ Ore, 90; History & Nextory, 2000. *Mailing Add:* 1618 Custer Laramie WY 82070

FLACK, AUDREY L
PAINTER, SCULPTOR
b New York, NY, May 30, 31. *Study:* Cooper Union, grad, 48-51; Cranbrook Acad Art, Yale Univ, scholar & study with Josef Albers, 52; NY Univ, Inst Fine Arts, 53. *Work:* Whitney Mus Am Art, Mus Mod Art, Metrop Mus Art & Guggenheim Mus, NY; San Francisco Mus Fine Art, Calif; St Louis Mus, Mo; Nat Mus Women Arts, Smithsonian Inst, Washington, DC; Nat Mus Arts, Canberra, Australia. *Comn:* Family portrait comn by Oriole Farb, Dir, Riverside Mus & Stuart M Speiser Collection, Smithsonian Inst, Washington, DC; Civitas: Four Visions (Gateway to the City of Rock Hill), four bronze figures (13' ea), Rock Hill, SC, 91; 10-story-high monument to Catherine of Braganza (1638-1705), Princess of Portugal & Queen of England, Hunter's Point, Queens, NY, 92. *Exhib:* 22 Realists, Whitney Mus Am Art, 70; Whitney Mus Am Art, 72 & 78; Illusion & Reality, Australia Coun Traveling Exhib, 77-78; Nat Gallery Art, 80, Guggenheim Mus, 81 & Contemp Am Realism since 1960, Pa Acad Fine Arts, 81-83; Sacred Images in Secular Art, Whitney Mus Am Art, 86; solo exhibs, Saints & Other Angeles: The Religious Paintings of Audrey Flack, traveling exhibs, sponsored by Cooper Union, NY, 86-88, A Pantheon of Female Deities (catalog), Louis K Meisel Gallery, NY, 91; Classical Myth & Imagery in Contemp Art (catalog), Queens Mus, Flushing, NY, 88; In Sharp Focus: Super Realism (catalog), Nassau Co Mus Art, Roslyn, NY, 91; Six Takes on Photo-Realism, Whitney Mus Am Art at Champion, Stamford, Conn, 91-92; Photo-Realism: Revisited, Mus Art, Ft Lauderdale, Fla, 91-92; retrospective, Breaking the Rules, 1950-1990, traveling exhib, Wight Art Gallery, UCLA, Calif, Butler Inst Am Art, Youngstown, Ohio, Nat Mus Women Arts, Washington, DC, JB Speed Art Mus, Louisville, Ky, 92-93; Art Mus Western Va, Roanoke, 96, Guild Hall Mus, East Hampton, NY, 96; Joy Tash Gallery, Scottsdale, Ariz, 97; Miami Univ Art Mus, Oxford, Ohio, 97. *Collection Arranged:* Akron Art Mus; Albright-Knox Art Gallery, Buffalo, NY; Australian Nat Gallery, Canberra; Dallas Mus Art; Mint Mus Art, Charlotte, NC; Nat Mus Am Art, Smithsonian Inst, Washington, DC; Nat Mus Women in the Arts, Washington, DC; NYU Collections; San Francisco Mus Modern Art; St Louis Art Mus; Butler Inst Am Art, Youngstown, Ohio; Metrop Mus Art; Mus Modern Art; Guggenheim Mus; Walker Art Ctr, Minneapolis; Whitney Mus Am Art. *Teaching:* Pratt Inst, Brooklyn, NY, 60-68; prof anat, NY Univ, 60-68; Sch Visual Arts, NY, 70-74; Mellon prof anat, Cooper Union, 82; Albert Dorne prof, Univ Bridgeport, Conn, 75; Riverside Mus Master Inst, New York City, 66-67; C&R Smith Disting vis prof, George Wash Univ, DC, 92; vis prof, Univ Pa Inst Contemp Art, Philadelphia, 94; lectr, Nat Acad Design, New York City, 87-. *Awards:* Albert Dorne Prof, Univ Bridgeport, 75; Nat Exhib Paintings Award of Merit, Butler Inst Am Art, 74; The Cooper Union Citation, Cooper Union, 77 & St Gaudens Medal, 82. *Bibliog:* Laurie S Hurwitz (auth), A Bevy of Goddesses: Paintings & Sculptures by Audrey Flack, Am Artist, 9/91; Amy Fine Collins & Bradley Collins (auth), Audrey Flack, Art Am, 11/91; Arthur C Danto, Books & the Arts: Our Holiday Lists, The Nation, 12/30/91; Carol Strickland (auth), Individualist-Idealist Breaks the Rules, NY Times, 9/27/92; Thalia Gouma-Peterson (auth), Breaking the Rules: Audrey Flack, a Retrospective 1950-1990, Harry N Abrams, Inc, New York, 92. *Media:* Oil, Bronze. *Publ:* Illusr, Tokyo Biennale (catalog), 74; Art in Am, 74; Vanitas (exhib catalog), L K Meisel Gallery, 78; auth, Audrey Flack on Painting, Harry N Abrams Inc, 81; Audrey Flack, Art and Soul, E P Dutton, 86; auth, Photorealism (vol I & II), Harry N Abrams Inc, 80 & 93. *Mailing Add:* c/o Louis K Meisel Gallery 141 Prince St New York NY 10024

FLACKMAN, DAVID J
PAINTER
b New York, NY, Mar 3, 34. *Study:* Stanford Univ, BA, 55; Art Students League, 56-58; studied with Maestro Pietro Annigoni & Nerina Simi, Florence, Italy, 58-67. *Work:* Washington Nat Gallery; Bruce Mus, Greenwich; Parish Mus, Southampton, NY. *Comn:* Portrait of Richard Nixon, Time Mag, NY, 68; Apollo 8 Astronauts, NASA, Orlando, Fla, 69; portrait of Carlos Montoya, comn by Carlos Montoya, NY, 75; portrait of St Agnes, St Agnes Church, Greenwich, Conn, 80; portrait of St Lucy, St Ignatius Church, Tarpon Springs, Fla, 94. *Exhib:* Apollo 8, Washington Nat Gallery, DC, 70; Weiner Gallery Artists, Weiner Gallery, NY, 74; Nat Arts Club Show, NY, 74-75; Salmagundi Club Show, NY, 74-75; solo exhib, Bruce Mus, Greenwich, Conn, 77 & Tarpon Springs Cult Ctr, Fla, 94. *Bibliog:* Gordon Schmidt (auth), David Flackman, Artist, Bruce Mus, Conn, 77; Marion M White (auth), Artist cultivates then paints, Greenwich Time, 9/11/89; Ann Bakkalapulo (auth), Still life, Tampa Tribune, 1/10/94; Bruce Hosking (auth), Work of a saint, Tampa Tribune, 11/23/94. *Media:* Oil. *Mailing Add:* 4600 Riverview Blvd Bradenton FL 34209

FLAHAVIN, MARIAN JOAN
PAINTER, SCULPTOR
b Colton, Wash. *Study:* Holy Names Col, BA(art), 59. *Work:* Deaconess Hosp, Ronald MacDonald House, St Anne's Children's Home, Valley Gen Hosp, Spokane, Wash; Leanin' Tree Publs, Boulder, Colo; Sacred Heart Children's Hospital; St John the Baptist Church, Salt Lake City. *Comn:* Plate/figurine series, comn by Goebel, Ger, 84; many portraits throughout US; Garden sculpture & fountain series. *Exhib:* Salmagundi 14th & 18th Ann, NY, 91 & 95; Pastel Soc Am 22nd Ann, NY, 94 & San Francisco, 96; Conn Pastel Soc Ann, Wallingford, 94; Int Asn Pastel Soc, Denver, 95; Am Artists Prof League, NY, 95 & 97; and others; Pastel Soc West Coast, 2002; Catherine Lorillard Wolfe 106th Ann, New York City, 2002; Butler Institute Am Art, 2003. *Teaching:* Instr, Pastel, Portraiture and Sculpture, currently. *Awards:* Best of Show/People's Choice, Northwest Pastel Soc Ann, 89; Merit/People's Choice, Md Ann, 90; Merit Award, Salmagundi Ann, 91. *Mem:* Signature mem Pastel Soc Am; signature mem Pastel Soc West Coast; signature mem Northwest Pastel Soc; emer mem Women Artists Am West. *Media:* Pastel, Oil; Bronze. *Publ:* Contribr, Southwest Art Mag, 82; Collectors Mart Mag, 84; Art Talk mag, 84; Midwest Art Mag, 85. *Dealer:* The Painters Chair 330 Sherman Coeur D'Alene ID 83814. *Mailing Add:* 4714 S Schafer Rd Spokane WA 99206

FLAM, JACK D
HISTORIAN, EDUCATOR
b Paterson, NJ, Apr 2, 40. *Study:* Rutgers Univ, BA, 61; Columbia Univ, MA, 63; New York Univ, PhD, 69. *Collection Arranged:* Henri Matisse Paper Cut-Outs (auth, catalog), Nat Gallery, 77; Matisse Image into sign, St Louis Art Mus, 93; Matisse The Dance (catalog), Nat Gallery, 93; Judith Rothschild, An Artist's Search, Metrop Mus, New York, NY, 98; Matisse-Derain, Collioure, Musée d'Art Moderne de Ceret, 2005; Matisse in Transition: Around Laurette, Norton Mus Art, West Palm Beach, Fla, 2006. *Pos:* Ed, The Documents of 20th Century Art, 81-; art critic, Wall Street J, 84-92. *Teaching:* Instr art hist, Rutgers Univ, 62-66; assoc prof art hist, Univ Fla, 66-70; prof art hist, Brooklyn Col & Grad Ctr, City Univ New York, 75-91; distinguished prof, City Univ New York, 91-. *Awards:* Guggenheim Fel, 79-80; Nat Endowment Humanities Fel, 87-88; Charles Rufus Morey Award, Col Art Assoc, 88; and others. *Bibliog:* Eric de Chassey (auth), Jack Flam à la Source de l'Art, Beaux-Arts, 3/94. *Mem:* Int Asn Art Critics; Col Art Asn. *Res:* Currently working on a major critical study of Matisse and on a series of articles on early Modernist painting. *Publ:* Auth, Matisse on Art, Phaidon, 73, Dutton, 78 & Calif, 95; Matisse, The Man & His Art, Cornell Univ Press, 86; Motherwell, Rizzoli, 91; Richard Diebenkorn, Rizzoli, 92; Robert Smithson: Collected Writings, Calif, 96; and others; Judith Rothschild: An Artist's Search, Hudson Hills, 98; The Modern Drawing, Morgan Libr, 99; Matisse and Picasso: The Story of Their Rivalry and Friendship, Westview, 2003; Primitivism and Twentieth-Century Art: A Documentary History, 2003; Matisse in Transition: Around Laurette, 2006. *Mailing Add:* 35 W 81st St New York NY 10024

FLANAGAN, BARRY
SCULPTOR
b Flintshire, North Wales, 1941. *Study:* Birmingham Col Art Crafts (fine art dept), 58; St Martin's Sch Art, 60 & 63. *Work:* Art Inst Chicago; Arts Coun Gt Brit; Mus Mid Art, NY; Nat Gallery Canada, Ottowa; San Francisco Mus Mod Art. *Exhib:* One-man exhib, Waddington Galleries, 80, 81, 83 & 85, Pace Gallery, NY, 83, Richard Gray Gallery, Chicago, 85; Inner Worlds, British Arts Coun Exhib, London, 82; British Drawings and Watercolour, Traveling exhib, People's Repub China, 82; Hayward Gallery, London, 82. *Bibliog:* Michael Compton (auth), Barry Flanagan: Recent Sculpture, The Pace Gallery, 83; William Feaver (auth), Alice doesn't live here, The Observer, 6/9/85; Sandra Miller (auth), On Barry Flanagan, No 2, Irish Arts Re 3, summer 86. *Media:* Bronze. *Mailing Add:* 505 LaGuardia Pl No 3C New York NY 10012

FLANAGAN, MICHAEL
PAINTER
b Buffalo, NY, Dec 24, 43. *Study:* Northwestern Univ, 62; Parsons Sch Design, 63-66; Yale Univ, 66-67. *Work:* Chicago Mus Contemp Art, Chicago, Ill; Ark Art Ctr, Little Rock; Hood Mus, Hanover, NH. *Exhib:* One-person exhib, Cordier & Ekstrom Gallery, NY, 81 & 83, PPOW, NY, 91 & 95, The Chrysler Mus, Norfolk, Va, 92-93; New Visions, Aldrich Mus Contemp Art, 81; The Seer, O'Hara Gallery, NY, 94; Transport, Maier Mus Art, Randolph Macon Woman's Col, Lynchburg, Va, 94; Insights: A Distant View, Worcester Art Mus, 94-95; Art from the Drivers Seat, Hudson River Mus, Yonkers, NY, 96. *Teaching:* Instr painting, Sch Visual Arts, 90-. *Awards:* Nat Endowment Arts Fel, 87; Yaddo Fel, 88; Visual Arts Fel, Nat Endowment Arts, 93. *Bibliog:* Christopher Sweet (auth), rev, Artnews, 9/91; Norman Oder (auth), Railroads enshrined in pantheon hybrid, Publs Weekly, 6/13/94; The imaginary railroad, New York Times Mag, 9/25/94. *Publ:* Auth, Stations, Pantheon, 94; Images of a displaced past, Art J, 96

FLANERY, GAIL
PAINTER, PRINTMAKER
b Cleveland, Ohio, May 7, 47. *Study:* Cooper Union, New York, BFA, 72. *Work:* Citicorp, Chemical Bank, Lehman Bros & Solomon Bros, NY; IBM Collection, Fla. *Exhib:* Kornblee Gallery, NY, 77; Tanglewood Gallery, NY, 78; Nat Drawing Show, Holman Gallery, State Col, Trenton, NJ, 79; Landscapes, 83 & Invitational, 86, Painting Space 122, NY; Contemp Am Landscapes, Hudson River Mus, Yonkers, NY & Tucson Mus Art, Ariz, 84; K Caraccio Collection, Montgomery Col, Rockville, Md, 85. *Bibliog:* Rev, Arts Mag, 10/76; Today's landscape, NY Times, 2/84; Comtemporary American Landscapes, New Vistas, Hudson River Mus, 84. *Media:* Oil; Miscellaneous. *Dealer:* Orion Editions 270 Lafayette St New York NY 10012. *Mailing Add:* 511 Eighth St Brooklyn NY 11215

FLANSBURGH, EARL ROBERT
ARCHITECT
b Ithaca, NY, Apr 28, 31. *Study:* Cornell Univ, BArch, 54; Mass Inst of Technol, MArch, 57; Harvard Univ Sch Bus, SCMP, 82. *Pos:* Job captain, designer The Archits Collaborative, Cambridge, Mass, 58-62; partner Freeman, Flansburgh & Assoc, 61-63; consult, Arthur D Little, Inc, Cambridge, 64-70; prin, Earl R Flansburgh & Assoc,

63-69, pres, dir design, 69-. *Teaching:* vis prof, archit design Mass Inst Tech, 65-66; instr, art Wellesley Col, 62-65, lectr art, 65-69. *Awards:* Fulbright Res Grantee Bldg Res Station, Eng, 57-58; William Candill Award, Am Col & Univ Mag 93; Award of Hon, Boston Soc Archit, 99. *Mem:* Fel Am Inst of Archit; Nat Acad; Royal Inst Brit Archit Boston Soc Archit (chmn prog comt, 1969-71, comnr pub affairs 71-73, comnr design, 73-74, dir, 71-74, pres, 80-81). *Mailing Add:* 77 N Wash St Boston MA 02114-1908

FLATTAU, JOHN W
PHOTOGRAPHER
b New York, NY, Nov 26, 40. *Study:* Brown Univ, AB, 62; Harvard Univ, LLB, 65. *Work:* Int Ctr Photog, NY; Tour de Paris, Villeneuve-Sur Lot, France. *Exhib:* Photographs, Gallerie Agathe Ballard, Gaillard, France, 90; Witkin Gallery, NY, 91; Athens Ctr, Greece, 97; Havana, Cuba, 2000; Leica Gallery, NY, 2002. *Specialty:* Photography. *Publ:* Auth, Bridges, Lustrum Press, 85; Photographs, Witkin Gallery, 93; coauth, Les Rendez-vous de Margaret, Lustrum Press, 94; auth, Rue Obscure-Vague Regret, Ianda, 96; Recent Memories, Ianda, 02. *Dealer:* Leica Gallery, 670 Broadway, NY, 10012. *Mailing Add:* 714 Broadway New York NY 10013

FLATTMANN, ALAN RAYMOND
PAINTER, INSTRUCTOR
b New Orleans, La, Aug 6, 46. *Study:* John McCrady Art Sch, 64-66. *Work:* Okla Art Ctr, Oklahoma City; Lauren Rogers Mus Art, Laurel, Miss; Miss Mus Art, Jackson; Longview Mus Art, Tex; New Orleans Mus Art. *Comn:* Murals, Old Zion Baptist Church, New Orleans, 67 & Grace Episcopal Church, 72. *Exhib:* Solo exhibs, Lauren Rogers Mus Art, 70, 75 & 81 & Okla Arts Ctr, 79; Pastel Soc Am, NY, 76-2005; Degas Pastel Soc, New Orleans, 83-2005; Soc des Pastellistes de France, Lille, France, 87; Southeastern Pastel Soc, Atlanta, 92-2005; others. *Teaching:* Instr painting & drawing, John McCrady Art Sch, New Orleans, 67-82; pvt workshops in oil, pastel, watercolor. *Awards:* Elizabeth T Greenshields Found Grant Award, 73; Master Pastelist Designation, Pastel Soc Am, 91 & 1st Place Landscape Award for Worldwide Pastel Excellence, 2000; Am Artist Art Masters Award/Pastel, Am Artist Mag, 96; Hall of Fame Honoree, Pastel Soc Am, 2006; and others. *Bibliog:* Joyce Kelly (auth), The Poetic Realism of Alan Flattmann, ACM Publ Co, 80; Linda Price (auth), Learning from Today's Art Masters, Am Artist, 6/96; John R Kemp (auth), Alan Flattmann's French Quarter Impressions, Pelican Publ, 2002. *Mem:* Pastel Soc Am; Degas Pastel Soc; Hellenic Arts Soc; Southeastern Pastel Soc. *Media:* Pastel, Oil. *Publ:* Auth, The Art of Pastel Painting, Watson-Guptill, 87; Combining sketching and watercolor painting, Watercolor, winter 95; Impressions of the City, Pastel Artist Int, 8-10/99; Heightened Atmosphere, Pastel Journal, 6/2006. *Dealer:* Bryant Galleries 3010 Lakeland Cove Suite A Flowood MS 39232. *Mailing Add:* 822 Heather Hollow Covington LA 70435

FLAX, FLORENCE P (ROSELIN POLINSKY)
PHOTOGRAPHER, WRITER
b Brockton, Mass, June 23, 36. *Study:* Chandler Sch Women, Boston, cert, 55; Northeastern Univ, Boston; Adult Educ Ctr, Boston. *Work:* Smithsonian Inst, Smithsonian Castle, Nat Arboretum, Smithsonian Nat Mus Am Hist, Supreme Court & Nat League Am Pen Women, Washington, DC. *Exhib:* Int Platform Asn Art Group Exhibs, Washington, DC, 1992-2001; An Odyssey into Infrared, Washington, DC, Home of Steward Mott, Washington, DC, 96 & The World as Seen Through Infrared, 98; US Nat Arboretum, Washington, DC, 1999; Flowers Forever--The Washington Home of Stewart Mott, The Invisible World of Infrared Photog, 2000; Chrome Inc, Washington, DC, 2003-. *Collection Arranged:* Photog (black & white), Capital Hill Art League, Washington, DC, 1996; M Frisby (photog), Wall St J (corresp to White House), Northeastern Univ, Boston, 1998; infrared photogs, Nat Arboretum, Washington, DC, 1998. *Pos:* Photo ed, contribr, Old Dominion, Sierra Club, 94-96; contribr, photo column, Times Community Newspaper, 98-. *Teaching:* Various workshops; seminar on infrared film. *Awards:* Judge's Choice 1st Prize, Int Platform Asn Ann Art Show, 93, 1st & 2nd Prize, 94, 95, 97 & 98, 1st Prize, 1999, 2001; Best in Show Award, Capitol Hill Art League, 96. *Bibliog:* Carole Lee Morgan (auth), Fantasy of Infrared, Hill Rag, 95; Gwen Landry Impson (auth), Simply flowers, Hill Rag, 97; Amy Guerrero (auth), Hot images - photographer focuses in on hidden world, Enterprise, 98; Baltimore Sun; Washington Post. *Mem:* Am Soc Med Photogs (bd mem, 95-96); Nat League Penn Women Am; Int Platform Asn (adv com, 92-98); Capitol Hill Art League; Washington Ctr Photog; Rocky Creek Art League. *Media:* Infrared Photog, Macro Photog. *Res:* Infrared film as tool to detect plant disease. *Publ:* Auth, Ektachrome infrared photography, ASMP Mag, 95; Washington Beyond the Monuments, Capital Hill Art League, 96. *Mailing Add:* 104 Saratoga Waye NE Vienna VA 22180-3663

FLECKER, MAURICE NATHAN
PAINTER, EDUCATOR
b Brooklyn, NY, Feb 27, 40. *Study:* State Univ NY Col, New Paltz, with Ilya Bolotowsky, Gabriel Laderman, George Wexler & George Wardlaw, BS; Brooklyn Col, with Philip Pearlstein, Ad Reinhardt, Carl Holty & R J Wolff, MFA; Art Students League, painting scholar; New Sch Social Res; Brooklyn Mus, painting scholar; Pratt Inst. *Work:* Fed Savings Bank, State Univ NY Col, New Paltz; Brooklyn Mus. *Exhib:* One-man shows, Aegis Gallery, NY, 62, Icarus Gallery, NY, 66, Bank Gallery, NY, 69 & First Street Gallery, NY, 77; Wadsworth Atheneum, Hartford, Conn, 65; W V Smith Art Mus, Springfield, Mass, 65; Brooklyn Mus, NY, 68-75; Vered Gallery, East Hampton, 84; East End Arts Coun, NY, 86; Mill Pond Exhib, Haupaugeny, 88; Col Gallery, Selden, NY, 88. *Teaching:* Instr, Brooklyn Mus Art Sch, NY, 68-75; prof life drawing & sculpture, head art, music & philos, 72-82, Suffolk Co Community Col. *Bibliog:* Amei Wallach (auth), One road to realism, Newsday, 77; Maria Latona (auth), Inspiration from Life, Long Island Press, 77; Ellen Frisina (auth), Artist believes in taking time, Mid Island News, 10/18/79. *Mem:* Soho Ctr for Visual Arts; Col Art Asn. *Media:* Oil, Watercolor. *Mailing Add:* 101 Cooper Ct Port Jefferson NY 11777

FLEISCHER, ARTHUR, JR
PATRON
b Harford, Conn, Jan 27, 33. *Study:* Yale Univ, BA, 53. *Hon Degrees:* Yale Univ, LLB, 58. *Pos:* Assoc Strasser, Spiegelberg, Fried & Frank, New York City, 58-61; legal asst, Securities & Exchange Comn, Wash, 61-62, exec asst to chmn, 62-64; assoc, Fried, Frank, Harris, Shriver & Jacobson, New York City, 64-67, partner, 67-, chmn, 89-97, sr partner, 97-; adv to adv, comt Fed Securities Code Proj, Am Law Inst, 70-78; legal adv com, bd dir, NY Stock Exchange, 87-91. *Teaching:* Vis lectr, law Columbia Univ, New York City, 72-73. *Mem:* Am Bar Asn (mem comt on fed regulation of securities regulation 69-); Asn Bar City New York (mem special comt on lawyers role in securities transactions 73-77, chmn comt securities regulation 72-74); Century Country Club (New York City); Ind Cur Int, (trustee, 90-2002); Whitney Mus Art, (trustee, mem photog comt, currently). *Collection:* Primarily photography, drawings & prints. *Publ:* Coauth, Tender Offers, 78, 6th edition, 2002, Board Games, 88; co-ed, Ann Inst on Securities Regulation, 70-81; contribr, articles to prof jours. *Mailing Add:* Fried Frank Harris One New York Plaza Fl 27 New York NY 10004-1980

FLEISCHER, ROLAND EDWARD
HISTORIAN, EDUCATOR
b Baltimore, Md, Feb 12, 28. *Study:* Western Md Col, BA, 52; Johns Hopkins Univ, MA, 54, PhD, 64. *Hon Degrees:* Western Md Col, Hon DFA, 93. *Teaching:* Assoc prof art hist, Univ Miami, Fla, 56-66; prof art hist, George Washington Univ, 66-74; prof art hist, Pa State Univ, 74-, prof emer, 96. *Awards:* Fulbright Award, Univ Amsterdam, 54-55; Hon Dr Fine Arts, Western Md Col, 93. *Mem:* Col Art Asn; Historians Netherlandish Art; Historians Am Art; Penn State Inst, Arts & Humanities (fel emeritus). *Res:* Colonial painting in America; Dutch painting of the 17th century. *Publ:* Auth, Ludolf de Jongh and the Early Work of Pieter de Hooch, Oud Holland, 78; co-ed & contribr, The Age of Rembrandt: Studies in Seventeenth Century Dutch Painting, In: Vol III, Papers in Art History from The Pennsylvania State University, Univ Park, Pa, 88; auth, Gustavus Hesselius: Face Painter to the Middle Colonies, NJ State Mus, Trenton, 88; Emblems & Colonial Am Painting, The Am Art J, Vol XX, No 3, 88; Ludolf de Jongh (1616-1679): Painter of Rotterdam, Davaco Publ, 89; and others. *Mailing Add:* 30355 Falcon Ln Big Pine Key FL 33043

FLEISCHMAN, AARON I
COLLECTOR
Study: Trinity Col, Conn, BA, 60; Harvard Law Sch, LLB, 63. *Pos:* Bd dirs, Whitney Mus Am Art; trustee, Miami Art Mus; sr partner, Fleischman & Walsh LLP, 76-, managing partner. *Awards:* Named one of Top 200 Collectors, ARTnews mag, 2006. *Collection:* Modern & contemporary art. *Mailing Add:* Fleischman & Walsh LLP Ste 1600 1919 Pennsylvania Ave NW Washington DC 20006

FLEISCHMAN, BARBARA GREENBERG
PATRON
b Detroit, Mich, Mar 20, 24. *Study:* Univ Mich, BA 44. *Pos:* psychoanalyst's secy, 47-49; secy, Greenberg Insurance Agency, 47-49; customer/pub relations consult, Kennedy Galleries, New York City, 76-; bd trustees, NY Pub Libr, 1980-, Mus Television & Radio, 88-92 & J Paul Getty Trust, 2000-06. *Teaching:* Teacher, Detroit Pub Schs, 44-45. *Awards:* Archives of Am Art Award Smithsonian, 2005. *Mem:* Cosmopolitan Club; Detroit Instit Arts, (mem women's comt, 57-66); Off the Record Luncheons, Foreign Policy Asn, (gov bd, 78-85); Planned Parenthood, New York City, 90-96; Archives of Am Art, (pres, 98-2002, chmn bd 2002-). *Mailing Add:* 870 United Nations Plaza New York NY 10017

FLEISCHMAN, STEPHEN
MUSEUM DIRECTOR, CURATOR
b Newton, Mass, July 7, 54. *Study:* Univ Wis-Madison, BS(fine arts), 77; MA(arts admin), 83. *Collection Arranged:* Highlights from the Permanent Collection, 91; Self-Portraits from the Permanent Collection, 92; Sculpture by Mark Lorenzi, 92; Jim Dine: Drawing from the Glyptothek (auth, catalog), 93; Deborah Butterfield: Sculpture 1980 to 1992, 94; Wis Trienial, 96, 99, 2002; Claes Oldenburg: printed stuff, 97; Ursula von Rydingsvard: sculpture, 98; Donald Lipski: A Brief History of Twine, 2000; Truman Lowe: Remembrance, 2001. *Pos:* Spec asst dir, Walker Art Ctr, Minneapolis, 83-86, dir prog planning, 86-90; dir, Madison Mus of Contemp Art, Wis, 91-; reviewer, Accreditation prog of Am Asn Mus. *Mem:* Am Asn Mus. *Publ:* Auth (catalog) Donald Lipski: A Brief History of Twine, 2000. *Mailing Add:* Madison Museum of Contemporary Art MMOCA 222 W Washington Ave Suite 350 Madison WI 53703

FLEISCHNER, RICHARD HUGH
ENVIRONMENTAL ARTIST, SCULPTOR
b New York, NY, July 1, 1944. *Study:* RI Sch Design, BFA, 66, MFA, 68. *Work:* Albright-Knox Art Gallery, Buffalo, NY; Whitney Mus Am Art, Guggenheim Mus, NY; Dallas Mus Art, Tex; Mus Art, RI Sch Design; Los Angeles Mus Contemp Art; and others. *Comn:* Mass Inst Technol, 85; MBTA, Arts on the Line, Cambridge, 85; Temple Univ, Philadelphia, 85; General Mills, Minneapolis, 85-87; Becton Dickinson Project, Franklin Lakes, NJ, 87; East Capital Plaza, St Paul, Minn, 91; and many others. *Exhib:* Drawings/Structures, Inst Contemp Art, Boston, 80; The Figurative Tradition, 80, Whitney Biennial, 81, New Am Art Mus, 82, Whitney Mus Am Art, NY;

Form and Funtion--Proposals for Pub Art for Philadelphia, Pa Acad Fine Arts, 82; Artist as Social Designer, Los Angeles Co Mus Art, 85; one-man shows, Harcus Gallery, 86, MacIntosh Drysdale Gallery, Washington, 87, Gerald Peters Gallery, Dallas, Tex, 91 & 95, Des Moines Art Ctr, 92 & Bell Gallery, Brown Univ, RI, 95; Individuals, A Selected Hist of Contemp Art-1945-86, Mus Contemp Art, Los Angeles, 86-88; Vanguard Gallery, Philadelphia, Pa, 87; Ten Sites, Laumeier Sculpture Park, St Louis, Mo, 91; Things for the Home, 92, & Summer Stock 1993, 93, Gerald Peters Gallery, Dallas; Différentes Natures-Visions de l'art contemporain, La Défense de Paris, France, 93. *Teaching:* Asst prof art, Brown Univ, Providence, 70-74; vis guest lectr & critic, many schs & museums throughout US. *Awards:* Am Acad Art & Letts Grant, 74-75; Nat Endowment Arts Fel, 74, 80 & 90; Gov's Award Art, RI Gov Edward Di Prete, 86. *Bibliog:* Ann Jarmusch (auth), La Jolla Institution discovers life downtown, San Diego Union Tribune, 2/7/93; Regina M Flanagan (auth), That 'beauty' problem: four artists on 'beauty' in public art, Pub Art Rev 6, fall/winter 94; Julia Brown Turrell (auth), Richard Fleischner: Works on Paper, Gerald Peters Gallery, 95. *Media:* Miscellaneous. *Mailing Add:* 224 Williams St Providence RI 02906

FLEISHER, PAT
DESIGNER, CURATOR
b Toronto, Ont. *Study:* Univ Toronto, BA; painting, Skowhegan, Maine; Ont Col Art; St Adele, Quebec; printmaking, York Univ, 71. *Work:* Palm Springs Desert Mus, Calif; Harbourfront Art Gallery, Toronto; Robert McLaughin Art Gallery, Oshawa; Univ Col Cape Breton, Niagara Col. *Exhib:* Aaron Berman Gallery, NY; Arnold Gottlieb Gallery, Toronto, Ont; Roschar Gallery, Toronto, 89; Forsyth Gallery, Toronto, 89; 291 Gallery, Toronto, 90. *Collection Arranged:* Toronto Women Artists: Three Decades, 83; Horoscope Paintings by Noel F Doyle, Absolut Vodka, Can, 94; Angel Orensanz, Beta Shee Mus, 95. *Pos:* Founder-ed, Art Mag, 69-82, Toronto Int Art Fair, 80, Art Expo, Toronto, 83, Discovery, 85 & Artfocus Mag & Toronto Indoor Art Show, 92-; pres, Art Mag, Inc, 74-87; publ & ed, Art Post, 83-92; dir, 291 Gallery, Toronto, 89-92; pres, Fleisher Fine Arts Inc, 92-. *Teaching:* Lectr & art guide, Toronto & NY galleries & studios, 71-; Toronto bd educ, Koffler Art Gallery. *Awards:* Merit Award, Art Mag, Soc Publ Designers New York, 75; Queen Elizabeth Silver Jubilee Medal, awarded by Jules Leger, Gov Gen of Can, 78; Ont Asn Art Galleries Design Award, 80. *Bibliog:* Joan Murray (auth), Pat Fleisher: Photoartist, Canadian Women's Studies, 81. *Mem:* Int Asn Art Critics; Can Periodical Pub Asn; Friends Can Mus Asn; Ont Periodicals Artistic Expression & Criticism. *Media:* Cibachrome and Colour Xerox Photography. *Publ:* Auth, A western pilgrimage, 77 & The mystery of the Maya, Art Mag, 79; The woman as artist, Ave Mag, 83; Artist Rose Lindzon: A profile, City & Co Home Mag, 84; Botero review, Latin Am Art, USA, 90; Daniel Bartridge, Pastel Paintings, Allmart Ltd, 95. *Mailing Add:* 15 McMurrich St Apt 706 Toronto ON M5R 3M6 Canada

FLEMING, FRANK
SCULPTOR
b Bear Creek, Ala, June 17, 40. *Study:* Univ Ala, BS, 62, MA, 69, MFA, 73. *Work:* City of Birmingham, Five Points South; Montgomery Mus Art, Ala; Nat Mus Am Art, Smithsonian Inst; Nelson Rockhill Mus, Kansas City, Mo; Utah Mus Fine Art, Salt Lake City. *Comn:* rabbit sculpture, 90, porcelain sculpture, 92, Birmingham Botanical Gardens, Ala; Five Points South Fountain, City of Birmingham, Ala, 91; bronze sculpture, Barney Ellis Plaza, Kansas City, Mo, 95; bronze deerman, Buckhead Park, Atlanta, 98; eagle sculpture, Assurance Corp, Miami, Fla, 98. *Exhib:* Contemp Crafts of the Americas, Ft Collins, Colo, 75; Am Porcelain, 81 & Animal Imagery, 81, Renwich Gallery, Smithsonian Inst; Art from Appalachia, Nat Mus Art, Washington, 81; one-man shows, Birmingham Mus Art, Ala, 82 & Montgomery Mus Art, Ala, 83; Poetry of the Physical, Mus Am Crafts, NY, 86; Fourth Int Shoebox Sculpture Exhib, Univ Hawaii Art Gallery, 91. *Awards:* Harriet Murray Award, Birmingham Mus Art, 90; Ala State Arts Coun Fel, 90; Southern Arts Fedn Sculpture Fel, 91. *Bibliog:* R M N McAusland (auth), Frank Fleming's fantasy in porcelain, Am Artist, 4/79; Annette Hatton (auth), Frank Fleming, Ga Rev, summer 85; Janet Kopolos (auth), Frank Fleming, Am Ceramics, 4/2/85. *Media:* Clay, Bronze. *Mailing Add:* 1309 Saulter Rd Birmingham AL 35209

FLEMING, LEE
WRITER, CURATOR, CRITIC
b Philadelphia, Pa, Jan 26, 52. *Study:* Yale Col, BA, 72; Univ Toronto, MA, 74. *Exhib:* Strange (auth, catalog), Rockville Arts Place, Md, 91. *Collection Arranged:* Critics Picks, Md Art Pl, 92; Family Matters, Tartt Gallery, Washington, DC, 92. *Pos:* Sr ed, Mus & Arts Mag, formerly; Art & film ed, Washington Rev Arts, 79-89; Washington Correspond, Artnews, 83-88; visual arts commentator, Nat Pub Radio, 88-; sr ed, Garden Design Mag, formerly; art critic, Washington Post, currently; managing ed, Landscape Architecture, currently. *Awards:* Washington, DC Comn Arts & Humanities Fel Lit & Criticism, 81 & 84; Ucross Found Residency Fel, 85; Larry Neal Writer's Award, 89. *Publ:* On metaphor, Washington Rev, 82; Biennial directions: Direction 1983, ARTNews & What's at issue is the issue, Artnews, 83; Art, Am Quart, 83; Manon Cleary (Gulbenkian Indth, Lisbon), 84. *Mailing Add:* WETA TV 2775 S Quincy St Arlington VA 22206

FLEMING, MARGARET NIELSEN
GRAPHIC ARTIST, ILLUSTRATOR
b Brooklyn, NY, May 10, 24. *Study:* Parsons Sch Design, with John Rogers, Stuart Klonis & Edgar Whitney, 43. *Comn:* JW Red & JW Black Packaging, Nat Distillers, London, Eng, 74-84; Christmas card designs, Am Artists Group, NY, 75-85; portrait of Bryant Park, Deloitte, Haskins & Sells, NY, 86; credit card designs, Affinity Marketing, Rye, NY, 87-95; admin off & pavilion, US Merchant Marine Acad, Kings Point, NY, 91. *Exhib:* Catharine Lorillard Wolfe Art Club, Nat Arts Club, NY, 80; Am Watercolor Soc Ann, Nat Acad, NY, 81 & 83; Art League Nassau Co Members, CW Post Col, Westbury, NY, 85, Lever House, 88, Molloy Col, Rockville Ctr, NY, 91; Visual Art Alliance Long Island, Nassau Co Mus, Roselyn, NY, 89; Chelsea Art Ctr, 98. *Pos:* Illusr, Lester Beall Inc, NY, 43-47, Hanzl & Hanzl Inc, NY, 47-60; free lance illusr, 60-96. *Awards:* Award of Excellence, Art League Nassau Co Member's Show, 91; Grumbacher Medal, Floral Park Art League, 92; Award of Excellence, Village Art Club Rockville Ctr, 96. *Mem:* Art League Nassau Co, NY; Village Art Club Rockville Ctr, NY; Tri-Co Art League, NY. *Media:* Watercolor, Acrylics. *Publ:* Illusr, Hotel, Doubleday, 65; Cooking for Two-Betty Crocker, Western Publ, 75; Skill Builders & Condensed Books, Readers Digest, 75-85; Holidays & Special Occasions, Food Borders, Dover Publ, 93-96; and others. *Mailing Add:* 15 St Paul's Pl Garden City NY 11530

FLEMING, RONALD LEE
DESIGNER, ADMINISTRATOR
b Los Angeles, Calif, May 13, 41. *Study:* Pomona Col, BA(cum laude), 63; Harvard Univ, MCP, 67. *Comn:* Developed art plans & strategies, Carriagetown & Flint, Mich; James Ctr, Richmond, Va; Bethesda Meridian, Prince Georges Co, Md; highway corridor megalithic landscape with sculptor William P Reimann, Radnor, Pa; cultural landscape with artist Greg Lefeure, Smith Students Center, Pomona Col, Claremont, CA. *Exhib:* On Common Ground, 81; What So Proudly We Hailed: America's Threatened Cult Landscapes, 90-92. *Pos:* First chmn, Cambridge Arts Coun, 75-79, Cambridge One Percent Pub Art Comn, 79-85; pres, Townscape Inst, 79-. *Teaching:* Lectr, Columbia Univ, Harvard Univ, Yale Univ & Univ Calif, Los Angeles. *Awards:* Merit Award, Am Soc Landscape Architects, 80; Commendation Design Excellence, Dept Transportation-Nat Endowment Arts, 81. *Mem:* Founding mem Cambridge Arts Coun (chmn, 74-79); fel Royal Soc Arts, London; Tavern Club, Boston; Century Asn, NY; Knickerbocker Club, NY; Somerset Club; Sprouting Rock Beach Asn, Newport, RI. *Publ:* Coauth, Place Makers, Creating Public Art that Tells You Where You Are, 81, second revised ed, 87; On Common Ground, Harvard Common Press, 82; auth, Facade Stories, Hastings House, 82; New Providence: A Changing Cityscape, Harcourt Brace Jovanivitch, 87; Saving Face, How Corporate Franchise Design Can Respect Community Identity, 94. *Mailing Add:* 8 Lowell St Cambridge MA 02138-4726

FLEMING, STEPHEN
PAINTER, CERAMIST
b Oxford, Pa, Apr 6, 50. *Study:* Royal Acad, London, cert(painting), 74; Calif State Univ, Sacramento, BA, 77; Univ Calif, Davis, MFA, 85. *Work:* Roswell Mus & Art Ctr, NMex; Kemper Collection, Kansas City, Mo. *Exhib:* Solo exhibs, Campus Gallery, Chemeketa Col, Salem, Ore, 88, Himovitz/Solomon Gallery, Sacramento, Calif, 88, Allrich Gallery, San Francisco, Calif, 88 & 90, Munson-Williams Proctor Inst, Utica, NY, 88, Univ Art Gallery, Calif State Univ, 88, Michael Himovitz Gallery, Sacramento, 89, Morgan Gallery, Kansas City, Mo, 89; Apocalyptic Vision, Sioux City, Iowa, 89; Charlotte Crosby Kemper Gallery, Kansas City Art Inst, 89; Expo at Chicago Navy Pier, 90; Roswell Mus & Art Ctr, NMex, 92; Joseph Nease Gallery, Kansas City, Mo, 2001. *Pos:* Artist-in-residence, Roswell Mus & Art Ctr, NMex, 86-87 & Bemis Found/Alternative worksite, Omaha, Nebr, 88; preparator, Stephen Wirtz Gallery, San Francisco, Calif, 85-86; dir, Roswell Artist-in-Residence Prog, NMex, 94-. *Teaching:* Asst prof painting, Kansas City Art Inst, 88-93 & fall 95 & 97; vis asst prof ceramics, La State Univ, 98. *Awards:* Nat Endowment Arts, 86; Grant, Roswell Mus & Art Ctr Found, 86-87 & 92. *Media:* Oil, Mixed Media; Clay. *Dealer:* John Natsoulas Gallery Davis CA; Joseph Nease Gallery Kansas City MO. *Mailing Add:* 1404 W Berrendo Rd Roswell NM 88201

FLEMING, THOMAS MICHAEL
SCULPTOR, PAINTER
b Philadelphia, Pa, May 12, 51. *Study:* Harrisburg Area Community Col, AA(with honors), 72; Pa State Univ, BFA(with honors), 75; Univ Minn, MFA, 78. *Work:* Musee des Arts, Lausanne, Switz; Int Glasmuseum, Ebeltoft, Denmark; Univ Minn Art Mus, Minneapolis; Corning Mus, NY; Ga State Univ, Urban Life Plaza, Atlanta, Ga. *Comn:* Ceramic sculpture, Wausau Insurance Cos, Wis, 83; sculpture, McDonald's Corp, Houston, Tex, 87. *Exhib:* Americans in Glass 1981, LY Woodson, Wis & Cooper-Hewitt Mus, NY; Int Directions Glass, Art Mus W Australia, Perth, 82; Order/Chaos, Minn Mus Art, St Paul, 83; Directions IV, Milwaukee Art Mus, Wis, 84; Glass from USA & Japan, Mus Basel, Switz, 86; Expressions En Verre, Musee des Arts, Lausanne, Switz, 86. *Pos:* Co-founder & dir, SoHo Studio Ctr, NY, 87-99; pres, Art Shoot, NY, 88-92; artistic prog consult, Anglo-Am Workshops, NY, 88-89; founder, www.artnyc.com, 96-. *Teaching:* Prof art, Univ Wis Marathon, Wausau, 78-; inst, Anglo-Am Workshops, London, Eng, 88. *Bibliog:* Robert Silberman (auth), Americans in Glass: A Requiem?, Art in Am, 3/85; Dan Klein (auth), Glass: A contemporary art, Rizzoli Int, 90; Olivier Royant (auth), Les Milliardaires Americans: Scope 90, Didier Hatier, 90. *Mem:* Int Sculpture Soc; Glass Art Soc; Nat Coun for Educ in Ceramic Arts. *Media:* Miscellaneous; Acrylic, Oil. *Publ:* coauth, Recyclable Ceramics, 78 Coun Educ Ceramic J, 87; Auth, Studio Molds--Three Approaches, 83, Interview with artist Ron Nagle, 87, Nat Coun Educ Ceramic J. *Mailing Add:* 518 S Seventh Ave Wausau WI 54401

FLEMINGER, SUSAN N
ADMINISTRATOR, EDUCATOR
b New York, NY, Nov 23, 41. *Study:* Hofstra Univ, BA, 65; Hunter Col, MA, 67. *Collection Arranged:* Riding on a Blue Note; In-Site Series (designs for community improvement project); Exchanges I, II & III, Artists Select Artists; and many others. *Pos:* Consult, NY State Coun Arts; freelance cur, Harper Collins Gallery, Fordham Univ/Lincoln Ctr, Dittengass Gallery, Brooklyn Mus/Community Gallery, Educational Alliance, Craft Students League; educ dir, Yeshiva Univ Mus, NY, 78-80; dir, visual

arts & arts in educ, Henry St Settlement Arts Ctr, NY, 85-; arts ed, Prospect Press, Brooklyn, NY, 84-85; Deputy Dir /Dir of Visual Arts & Art in Education. *Teaching:* Instr art hist & arts educ, NY Community Col, Kingsborough Community Col, Stern Col & Yeshiva Univ. *Awards:* Sch & Culture Award, NY Comn Cult Affairs, 88; Very Special Arts Award, Educator Yr, Doctoral Asn, 92; Coming up Taller from Presidents Committee on Arts and Educations, 2002. *Mem:* Art Table; Nat Art Educ Asn; Nat Alternative Arts Orgns; Arts in Educ Roundtable. *Specialty:* Contemporary art. *Interests:* Creating artists books. *Publ:* Auth, Art Reviews, Prospect Press Newspaper, 82-85; Joseph Delaney: An Interview, Arts & Artists, 3/82; Laura Schechter, 86 & Bert Hasen (monogr), 87, Arts Mag; Emilio Cruz: Spilled Nightmares, Revelations & Reflections (catalog essay), Studio Mus Harlem, 87; Presentation on Community Arts Education, Nat Asn Art Educ, 96. *Mailing Add:* 571 Ninth St No 1 Brooklyn NY 11215

FLESCHER, SHARON
HISTORIAN, ADMIN
b New York, NY. *Study:* Barnard Col, BA; NY Univ, MA; Columbia Univ, Grad Sch Arts & Sci, MA & PhD, 77. *Pos:* Exec Dir, Int Found for Art Research, NY, 98-; ed-in-chief, IFAR Journal, NY, 98-. *Teaching:* Adj Assoc Prof Arts, NY Univ, NY, 93-. *Bibliog:* Amy Gale, Art Guardian:Sharon Flescher, Art & Antiques, Feb, 2003; Simon de Burton, IFAR, TRACE magazine, Feb 2003; Philip Eliosoph (auth), Art Sleuth: IFAR and its Direction, Dr. Sharon Flescher, Antiques & Fine Art, 1-2/2006. *Mem:* Col Art Asn; Am Asn Mus; ArtTable. *Res:* Ethical, legal, and scholarly issues concerning acquisition, ownership & authenticity of art; 19th & 20th Century European paintings. *Publ:* Auth, Zacharie Astruc: Critic, Artist, Japoniste (1833-1907), Garland Publ, 78; auth, More on a Name: Manet's Olympia, The Art Journal, 85; auth, Zacharie Astruc, Grove Dictionary Art, McMillan, 96; auth, Beware: Heliogranures Can Fool the Unwitting, IFAR Journal, 2002; The Intl Foundation for Art Research, Expert vs the Object, Oxford, 2004; auth, Anatomy of an Art Fraud: Ely Sakhais Two-Decade Long Scheme, IFAR Journal, 2005. *Mailing Add:* IFAR 500 5th Ave Ste 935 New York NY 10110

FLETCHER, HARRELL
EDUCATOR, FILMMAKER
Study: San Francisco Art Inst, BFA in Photog, 1990; Calif Col Arts & Crafts, MFA, 1994; Univ S Calif, Cert in Ecological Horticulture & Sustainable Food Systems, 1996. *Work:* Mus Pieces, MH de Young Mem Mus, San Francisco, 1999, Whitney Biennial, Whitney Mus Am Art, NY, 2004. *Exhib:* Exhib incl Garage Sale, Gallery Here, Calif, 1993, Some People We Metrop, Richmond Art Ctr, Va, 1996, Anthony, McBean Project Room, San Francisco Art Inst, 1997, Wanderings & Observations, Bedford Gallery, Walnut Creek, Calif, 1998, The Boy Mechanic, Yerba Buena Ctr Arts, San Francisco, 1999, Saying I Love You or Something Like That, Inst, San Francisco, Calif, 2000, Every Sunshine, Portland Inst Contemp Art, 2001, The Sound We Make Together, DiverseWorks, Houston, 2003, Now Its A Party, Hartford, Conn, 2003, A Moment of Doubt, Christine Burgin, NY, 2004, Happiness Follows Us Like a Shadow, New Langton Arts, San Francisco, 2004 Tender Feelings, Gas Works, London, 2005; exhib in group shows at Urban Renewal Laboratory, Southern Exposure, San Francisco, 1998, We're Excerpts, Andrew Kreps Gallery, NY, 2002, Street Selections, The Drawing Ctr, NY, 2003; cur (exhibs) Whipper Snapper Nerd, Yerba Buena Ctr Arts, San Francisco, 1998, Survivalist, Southern Exposure, San Francisco, 1999, A Love For All Animals, San Francisco Art Comn Gallery, 2001, Hello There Friend, Christine Burgin, NY, 2003. *Pos:* Co-found, Gallery HERE, Oakland, Calif, 1993-94; video & mag co-coord, Creativity Explored, 1994-98; guest lectr, Calif Col Arts & Crafts, San Francisco, 1999, Henry Art Gallery, Seattle, 1999. *Teaching:* guest lectr, Calif Col Arts & Crafts, 1994, San Francisco Art Inst, 1994; asst prof, Portland State Univ, Ore, 2004; instr, Beginning Sculpture Stanford Univ, 1998; guest lectr, Univ Calif- Berkeley, 1998; instr, Interdisciplinary Seminar, 1999; Salon Lect, Series Prog Headlands Ctr Arts, 1999; guest lectr, Calif Col Arts & Crafts, San Francisco, 2000, San Francisco State Univ, 2000, White Chapel Gallery, London, 2001, Yale Univ, 2002, Pratt Inst, Brooklyn, 2002, Otis Sch Art & Design, Los Angeles, 2003, Univ Calif-Irvine, 2003; instr, sculpture Cooper Union, New York City, 2004. *Awards:* Recipient Post-Grad Studio Award, Headlands Ctr Arts, 1994, Headlands Ctr Arts Residency, 1998; Residency Grant, Calif Arts Coun, 1994, Creative Work Fund Grant, 1996, 2000, Artists & Communities Millenium Grant, 1999, Creative Capital Grant, 2002, Artslink Grant, 2003, Gunk Grant, 2003

FLETCHER, LELAND VERNON
PAINTER, SCULPTOR
b Cumberland, Md, Sept 18, 46. *Study:* Univ Minn, BS, 72. *Work:* Victoria & Albert Mus, London; Mus D'Art Mod, Barcelona, Spain; Minneapolis Inst Art, Minn; Mus Ludwig, Cologne, Ger; Mus De Arte Contemp Da Univ De Sao Paulo, Brazil; Art Mus of Calf State Univ, Long Beach; Bradford Mus, England; Civico Mused Revoltella, Trieste, Italy; Mus Plantin-Moretus, Antwerp, Belgium; and others; Kunsthalle Bremen, Ger; Kunsthalle Hamburg, Ger. *Comn:* Art Zone Maubeuge (200' x 300' urban environmental sculpture) & Construction 1A:11 (16' x 10' x 10' painted steel sculpture), Ministry Cult & Ville de Maubeuge, France, 87. *Exhib:* Solo exhibs, San Jose State Univ Union Gallery & City of San Jose, Calif, 78, Univ Art Gallery, Calif State Univ, Hayward, 89 & Lake Co Mus, 95; Electroworks, Cooper-Hewitt Mus, NY, 79; Recent Acquisitions, Wolfgang-Gurlitt Mus, Neue Galerie der Stadt Linz, Austria, 82; Intergrafik 84 Triennale, Berlin, Ger, 84; 9th Int Brit Print Biennale, Victoria & Albert Mus, London, Eng, 86; 11th Graphic Biennale, Krakow, Poland, 86; Exhib Diomede, Inst Contemp Art, The Clocktower Gallery, NY, 89; Books: Inside & Out, Anchorage Mus Hist & Art, Alaska, 91; 10th Biennale Int, Mus d'Art Contemp d'Eivissa, Spain, 91; 6th Am Drawing Biennial, Muscarelle Mus Art, Col William & Mary, Williamsburg, Va, 98; and others; Int Exhib, Sharjah Arts Mus, United Arab Emirates, 2000 & 2005; Reactions, Wiluamson Gallery, Art Ctr Col of Design, Pasadena, Ca, 2002. *Pos:* Fine art specialist, City of San Rafael, Calif, 77-78; artist in residence, Lake Co Arts Coun, Calif, 98-99. *Awards:* Hon Mention, Minn State Fair Fine Arts Exhib, 70. *Bibliog:* Stephen Moore (auth), Leland Fletcher, Wordworks, Vol 3, No 2, 79; Carl Loeffler (auth), Performance Anthology, Contemp Arts Press, 80; Leland Fletcher, La Voix du Nord, 7/87; Books: Inside & Out, David Edelfsen, Anchorage Mus Hist & Art. *Media:* Miscellaneous Media. *Mailing Add:* 3288 Konocti Lane Soda Bay Kelseyville CA 95451

FLETCHER, STEPHEN L
APPRAISER
Pos: Partner, exec vpres, chief auctioneer, appraiser, Skinner, Inc, Boston, Mass, 75-; dir, Am Furniture & Decorative Arts, currently; appraiser, Antiques Roadshow, WGBH-PBS, currently; contribr, writer, Art & Antiquities in Estates, currently. *Teaching:* lectr, in field, currently. *Mem:* Provincetown Art Asn Mus (bd trustees, currently); Mus Fine Arts, Boston, Mass. *Mailing Add:* Skinner Inc 63 Park Plaza Boston MA 02116

FLETCHER, VALERIE J
CURATOR, HISTORIAN
b Madison, Wis, Aug 26, 51. *Study:* Conn Col, BA, 73; Columbia Univ, MA, 77, MPh, 79, PhD, 94. *Collection Arranged:* Josef Albers, Hirshhorn Mus, 80, Barbara Hepworth, 81, Dreams & Nightmares: Utopian Visions in Modern Art (auth, catalog), 83-84, 20th Century Sculpture, 85, Surrealist Art (auth, catalog), 86-87, Alberto Giacometti 1901-66 (auth, catalog), 88-89, Crosscurrents of Modernism: Latin American Pioneers (auth, catalog), 92, Alexander Calder, 93-94, Paul Gauguin 96-97, Henry Moore, 98, Shahzia Sikander, 2000 & Tim Hawkinson, 2001; Human Figure Interpreted (auth, catalog), Taiwan Mus Fine Art & Shiga Mus, Japan, 95. *Pos:* Res asst, Metrop Mus Art, New York, 76-78; cur sculpture, Hirshhorn Mus, Smithsonian Inst, 78-. *Teaching:* Lectr, dept educ, Mus Mod Art, New York, 77-78; vis prof Utopian art, Continuing Educ, Georgetown Univ, 86. *Res:* 19th and 20th century painting and sculpture. *Publ:* Alberto Giacometti (exhib catalog), Hiroshima Art Mus, Japan, 97; coauth, Hishhorn Mus: 150 Works, 96, Alberto Giacometti, Vienna Kunsthalle & Royal Acad, London, 96 & Julio Gonzalez (exhib catalog), Kunstmuseum Bern, 97; A Garden for Art, Hirshhorn Mus, 98; Alberto Giacometti, Montreal Mus, 98; Giacometti's Paintings, Columbia Univ & UMI, 99; coauth, Hishhorn Mus: 150 Works, 96. *Mailing Add:* c/o Hirshhorn Mus & Sculpture Garden Dept Painting & Sculpture Washington DC 20560

FLICK, FRIEDRICH CHRISTIAN
COLLECTOR
Pos: Founder & chmn, FC Flick Found against Xenophobia, Racism and Intolerance. *Awards:* Named one of top 200 Collectors, ARTnews Magazine, 2004. *Media:* C. *Collection:* Old masters, European sculpture, modern & contemporary art. *Mailing Add:* FC Flick Foundation Am Neuen Markt Potsdamn 14467 Germany

FLICK, PAUL JOHN
COLLECTOR, PAINTER
b Rock Island, Ill, Feb 5, 43. *Study:* Univ Minn, BA & MFA(printing & printmaking); studied with Herman Cherry & Mario Valpe. *Work:* Univ Minn. *Exhib:* Univ of Minn Studio Art Gallery, 70 72; Rochetser Arts Ctr, Minn, 89; Group show, Minneapolis Inst Arts, 80, 90 & 2000; one man shows, Univ of Minn, 72, Twin Cities Metrop Art Alliance, 75, Northland Gallery, St Louis Park, 76, West Bank Gallery, Minn, 76. *Pos:* Freelance artist, 69-. *Teaching:* Instr drawing & color, Bur Engraving, 72-83. *Mem:* Artist Equity Asn (pres, 76-77); Twin Cities Metrop Arts Alliance; Vietnam Vets Art Group. *Media:* Assemblages, Constructives, Paintings. *Interests:* Primitive African Art & Contemp Ceramics. *Collection:* The Courage Ctr, Golden Valley, Minn, Univ of Minn, Univ of Tenn, Numerous Pvt Collections. *Dealer:* LRM Designs 3317 Minneha Ha Ave S Minneapolis MN 55409. *Mailing Add:* 4032 Lyndale Ave S Minneapolis MN 55409

FLICK, ROBBERT
PHOTOGRAPHER, EDUCATOR
b Amersfoort, Holland, Nov 15, 39; US citizen. *Study:* Univ BC, BA, 67; Univ Calif, Los Angeles, MA, 70, with Robert Heinecken & Robert Fichter, MFA, 71. *Work:* Ctr Creative Photog, Tucson, Ariz; Chicago Art Inst, Ill; Hallmark Collections, Kansas City, Mo; Mus Mod Art, NY; Oakland Mus Art, Calif; San Francisco Mus Mod Art. *Exhib:* Art Inst Chicago, Ill; Ctr Creative Photog, Tucson, Ariz; Fine Arts Gallery, Univ Calif, Davis; Fine Arts Gallery, Univ BC, Can; Frederick S Wight Art Gallery, Univ Calif, Los Angeles; Henry Art Gallery, Univ Wash, Seattle; Light Gallery, NY; Los Angeles Co Mus; Min Gallery, Tokyo; Musee d'Art, Mod de la Ville de Paris, France; Mus Mod Art, Lodz, Poland; Photo-Kina, Koln, WGer; Vancouver Art Gallery. *Teaching:* Prof art, Univ Ill, Champaign-Urbana, 71-76 & Univ Southern Calif, Los Angeles, 76-. *Awards:* Nat Endowment Arts Survey Grant, 79; Nat Endowment Arts, Individual Artist Fel, 82 & 84; Nat Endowment Arts Individual Artist Grant, 83. *Bibliog:* Article, Afterimage, Vol 8, No 5, 12/80; article, Journal, Southern Calif Art Mag No 29; Berger, Searle & Wadden (coauths), Radical, Rational, Space, Time, Idea Networks in Photography, Henry Art Gallery, Univ Wash, Seattle, 82; Van Deren Coke (auth), Facets of Modernism: Photographs from the San Francisco Museum of Modern Art, Hudson Hills Press, NY, 86. *Mem:* Soc for Photog Educ; Col Art Asn. *Media:* Silverprint. *Publ:* Auth, Camera, Nos 2 & 10, C J Bucher Ltd, Lucerne, Switz, 72 & 81; Photographer's Choice, Addison House, Danbury, NH, 75; Robbert Flick, Selected Work: 1980-1981 (exhib catalog), Los Angeles Mun Art Gallery, Calif, 81; The Photographic Vision, Tele Course, Coast Community Col, Fountain Valley, Calif, CBS/Holt, Rinehart & Winston, 84; Robbert Flick, MIN Gallery, Tokyo, Japan, 87. *Dealer:* Photoman Inc 42 E 76th St New York NY 10021. *Mailing Add:* c/o Craig Krull Gallery Bergamont Sta 2525 Michigan Ave Bldg B-3 Santa Monica CA 90404-4014

FLOMENHAFT, ELEANOR
CURATOR, CONSULTANT
b Brooklyn, NY, Aug 21, 33. *Study:* Hofstra Univ, Hempstead, NY, BA(art hist), 76; Queens Col, NY, MA(art hist), 84. *Collection Arranged:* British Watercolors and Drawings 1750-1910 (auth, catalog), 80 & CoBrA, 81, Emily Lowe Gallery, Hofstra Univ; The New Explosion: Paper Art (auth, catalog), Nat Traveling exhib, 82; Celebrating Contemporary American Black Artists (auth, catalog), 83; Adja Yunkers: A Twentieth Century Master (auth, catalog), 84; Transit: Russian Artists Between East & West (auth, catalog), 89; Faith Ringgold: 25-Year Survey (auth, catalog), 90-93; Beverly Buchanan: ShackWorks, 94-96; Elizabeth Catlett, 98. *Pos:* Cur art, Emily Lowe Gallery, Hofstra, 78-80; dir, Fine Arts Mus, Long Island, NY, 81-92; independent cur, 92-; trustee, Anne Frank Ctr. *Awards:* Pres Award, Long Island, 84; Women of Year, Hemstead Chamber of Commerce, 89; Pathfinder Award, Hempstead, 90. *Bibliog:* Phyllis Braff (auth), Many ideas meet in Yunkers' art, New York Times, 6/3/84; Karen Lipson (auth), Back in the USSR, a hit from Long Island, Newsday, 3/13/90; Betty Freudenheim (auth), An artist traces her life on quilts, New York Times, 5/27/90. *Mem:* Am Asn Mus; Art Table. *Res:* Art of the Cobra group 1948-1951: the abstract experimentalists of Europe; The Barcelona School, Post World War II; contemporary Russian art; contemporary American art; contemporary women in the arts. *Publ:* Auth, The Roots & Development of Cobra Art, Hempstead, NY, FAMLI, 85; Josep Guinovart, essay in catalog for retrospective exhib, Hempstead, NY, FAMLI, 87; Karel Appel, The Dupe of Being, ed by Roland Hagenberg NY: Ed Lafayette, 89, pp 243-259; Outside the USSR, essay in catalog, Transit: Russian Artists Between East & West, NY: Eduard Nakhamkin Fine Arts, 89; Interviewing Faith Ringgold: A Contemporary Heroine, essay in catalog for exhib, Hempstead, NY, FAMLI, 90; auth, Beverly Buchanan: Shacks Architecture Catalog, 94; auth, (essay) Burhan Dogancay, Dolmabahce Cult Ctr, Istanbul, Turkey, 2001. *Mailing Add:* 1294 Seawane Dr Hewlett NY 11557

FLOOD, RICHARD SIDNEY
WRITER, CURATOR
b Philadelphia, Pa, Nov 10, 43. *Study:* St Joseph's Col, BA, 65; Univ Pa, Annenberg Sch Commun, MA, 67. *Collection Arranged:* PSI (Inst Art & Urban Resources), Figuratively Sculpting, 81; Franklin Furnace, The Page as Alternative Space: The Last Decade, 81; Memento Mori, Centro Cultural/Arte Contemporaneo, Mexico City, 86. *Pos:* co-founder, ed, Art Exchange, Philadelphia, 1976-79; managing ed, books ed, Artforum, NY, 1980-83; dir, Barbara Gladstone Gallery, NY, 1983-94; chief cur, Walker Art Ctr, Minneapolis, 1994-2005, New Mus Contemp Art, NY, 2005-. *Res:* Contemporary art; particularly as it relates to popular culture. *Publ:* Contribr, Robert Gober, An Interview, The Print Collector's Newsletter, 4-5/90, 6-9; The Knickers' Effect, SHIFT, Vol 3, No 4, 90, 16-23; Down the Airshaft, Parkett, No 17, 88, 152-160; Go Fetch the New Yorker, Parkett, No 21, 89, 62-66; The Dog & the Suicide, Parkett, No 23, 90, 146-151. *Mailing Add:* New Mus Contemp Art 556 W 22nd St New York NY 10011

FLORES, CARLOS MARINI
ARCHITECT, HISTORIAN
b Ciudad, Mex, May 28, 37. *Study:* Univ Nac Autonoma de Mex, Arquitecto, 60, Historiador, 64; Univ de Roma, Italy, Restaurador, 62. *Comn:* Alcazar de Colon, Dominican Repub, 65; Antiqua, Guatemala, 72; rtagena de Indias, Columbia, 75; Portobelo - Panama Viejo, Panama, 78. *Collection Arranged:* El Quijote, Mus Iconografico, 88; Chavez Morado, Mus del Pueblo, 89. *Pos:* Dir monumentos coloniales, Inst Nac de Antropologia e Hist, 62-66; dir monumentos artisticos, Inst Nac de Bellas Artes, 77-81; dir centro hist cd Mex, Distrito Fed, 82-85. *Teaching:* Historia arquitectura, Univ Nac Autonoma de Mex, 60-90; restauracion monomentos, Univ de Roma, Italy, 70- & Univ Fla, Gainesville, 80-92. *Awards:* Academico Nacional, Acad de Arquitectura, 78 & Academico Emerito, 88 & Piemio Nacional, 96. *Bibliog:* Homenaje - F de la Mazatlan, Inv Esteticas, Univ Nac Autonoma de Mex, 74; Rest de Monumentos, Cuadernos de Arquitectura, Inst Nac de Bellas Artes, 79; Cons Pat Monumental Inst Nac Autonoma e Hist, ICOMOS Mexicano, 96. *Mem:* Int Coun Monuments & Sites, Paris; Acad de San Jorge, Barcelona; Consejo del Gran Caribe para los Monumentos y Sitios, Dominican Repub; Acad Nac de Arquitectura, Mex; Acad Mexicana de Arquitectura, Mex. *Res:* Hist de la arquitectura, restauracion de monumentos, art contemporaneo. *Publ:* Auth, Santigo Tianguitenco, 64; Casas Virreinales de la Ciudad de Mex, 70; Restauracion de Cuidades, 72; contribr, Arquitectura Mexicana del S XVI, 83; coauth, El Palacio de Iturbide, Banco Nac de Mex, 92. *Mailing Add:* Mazatlan 190 Ciudad de Mex Col Cuauhtemoc #06140 Mexico

FLORET, EVELYN
SCULPTOR
b France. *Study:* Wash Univ, St Louis, BA; Nat Acad School of Fine Arts studied with Anthony Antonios. *Exhib:* Nat Sculpture Soc Ann Exhibs, 1998 & 2001; Allied Artists of Am 86th ann exhib, 1999; Sculpture & Medallic Art Exhib (Pen & Brush), 2000-2001 & 2003-2006; In Remembrance: Sept 11 (Nat Sculpture Soc), 2002; Audubon Artists Ann Exhib, 2003-2006; Allied Artists of Am An Exhib, 2004. *Awards:* Elliot Liskin Mem Award, Pen and Brush, 2000, 2004; Gold Medal of Honor for Sculpture, Audubon Artists, 2003. *Mem:* Audubon Atists Inc; The Pen and Brush, Inc; Am Society of Media photogrs; Soc of N Am Goldsmiths. *Media:* Clay, Bronze. *Interests:* Photography, computer for photographic art & printing, piano playing. *Mailing Add:* 8 E 83rd St Apt # 14D New York NY 10028

FLORIN, SHARON JUNE
PAINTER
b Brooklyn, NY, Feb 16, 52. *Study:* Art Students League, with David Leffel, Issac Soyer, among others, 69-77; Adelphi Univ, BA, 73. *Work:* Mus City NY; Nawa Collection, Zimmerli Art Mus, Rutgers Univ, NJ. *Exhib:* Nat Asn Women Artists Ann Exhib, 90-2004, 2006; 55th Ann Nat Midyear Exhib, Butler Inst Am Art, Youngstown, Ohio, 91, 2003, 2005; 35th Chautauqua Nat Exhib Am Art, Chautauqua Inst, NY, 92; Her Artworks, South Bend Art Ctr, Ind, 92; 11th Sept Competition Exhib, Alexandria Mus Art, La, 92; Braithwaite Fine Arts Gallery, Southern Utah Univ, 94; Drawing the Lines, NY Transit Mus, Brooklyn, 97; Int Juried Show, NJ Ctr Visual Arts, 98; Liberty Enlightning the World, Hudson Waterfront Mus, Brooklyn, NY, 98; Annual Exhib, Nat Arts Club, NY, 2000; Catharine Lorillard Wolfe Art Club, 2000-2006, Ann Exhib; Poughkeepsie Art Mus, NY, 2005. *Awards:* Nat Asn Women Artists, NY, 1989,1990, 1992, 1995, 1996, 1998, 2000 (medal hon), 2001, 2004, 2006; Catharine Lorillard, Wolf Art Club, NY, 1998, 2000, 2004, 2005; Georgetown Int Art Competition, Fraser Gallery, Washington, DC, 2001; Pen & Brush Club, NY, 2002. *Bibliog:* New York Through Artists Eyes, The NY Times, 10/14/83; A Picturesque Neighborhood, NY Daily News, 5/19/91; Here's A Stroke of Genius, Park Slope Courier, Brooklyn, NY, 8/28/00; Unforgettable Places to Create, Artist's Mag, spring 2006. *Mem:* Women Arts, Inc; Nat Asn Women Artists; Catharine Lorillard Wolfe Art Club; Org of Independent Artists; NY Artists Equity. *Media:* Oil. *Mailing Add:* 339 E 19th St New York NY 10003

FLOWER, MICHAEL LAVIN
ART DEALER, PHOTOGRAPHER
b Queens, NY, Aug 31, 58. *Study:* Simon's Rock Early Col, AA, 77; Dartington Col Art, UK, dipl, 78; Philadelphia Col Art, BFA, 80. *Work:* Mednick Gallery, Philadelphia Col Art. *Comn:* Balloon's at Lake Placid, Winter Olympic Games, comn by Dr Clayton Thomas, Brimfield, Mass, 80; The Mayans (photograph), comn by Gladys Carbo, Stockbridge, Mass, 81; Berkshire Landscapes (photograph), Arcadian Shop, Lenox, Mass, 83. *Exhib:* Year End, Fed Bldg, Philadelphia, 80; TV Veg, Main Gallery, Philadelphia Col Art, 80. *Collection Arranged:* City Reception, 84, Photo & Pencil, 84, China: The People and Landscape, 84, Photographic Silkscreens, 84 & Photographic Installations, 85, Chiaroscuro Gallery, Lenox, Mass. *Pos:* Supvr dept photog, Moore Col Art, Philadelphia, 81; owner & dir, Chiaroscuro Gallery, Lenox, Mass, 83-. *Teaching:* Substitute prof experimental photog, Simon's Rock, Great Barrington, Mass, 86; internship dir, photog, Lenox Mem High Sch, Mass, 86; photo instr, Miss Ponters Sch Interim Prog, 87. *Specialty:* Fine art photography

FLOWERS, THOMAS EARL
PAINTER, EDUCATOR
b Washington, DC, Feb 17, 28. *Study:* Furman Univ, BA; Univ Iowa, MFA. *Work:* Greenville Co Mus Art, SC; Columbia Mus Art, SC; Chase Manhattan Bank, NY; Vincent Price Enterprises, Chicago; Fed Reserve Bank Va, Charlotte, NC, Nations Bank. *Comn:* Mural, Vince Perome, Greenville, SC, 62; mural, Saad Rug Co, Greenville, 63; mace & medallion, Furman Univ, Greenville, 65; mural, City Hall, Greenville, SC. *Exhib:* Eighteenth Ann Guild SC Artists Exhib, 68; 11th Ann Southern Contemp Art Exhib, Mobile, Ala, 69; Best in Show, Springs Art Exhib, Lancaster, SC, 81; Atlanta Artists Club, Nat 1, Ga, 70; Southeastern Painter's Choice Exhib, Ga Col, Milledgeville, Ga, 71. *Pos:* Co-owner, Tate Gallery, Liberty, SC. *Teaching:* Asst prof art & chmn dept, Ottawa Univ, 56-58; instr sculpture, E Carolina Col, 58-59; assoc prof art & chmn dept, Furman Univ, 59-89; retired. *Awards:* Purchase Award, SC Arts Comn, 71; Second Award, Franklin Mint, 72; Art in Archit Award, SC Chap, Am Inst Architects, 77; Spartanburg Art Asn Bureau Award, 91. *Bibliog:* Jack A Morris (auth), Contemporary artists of South Carolina, Greenville Co Mus Art, 70; R Smeltzer (auth), article, Southern Living Mag, 12/70; M Hays (auth), article, Furman Univ Mag, spring 72. *Mem:* Guild SC Artists (pres, 61-62, bd dir, 71-72); Greenville Artists Guild (pres, 72-73); Southeastern Col Art Asn; Am Craftsman's Coun. *Media:* Mixed. *Publ:* Illusr covers, Furman Univ Mag, winter 67, summer 68 & 5/69; illusr cover, Springs Cotton Mill Ann Report, 69; illusr, Images, Univ NC, Asheville, summer 69. *Dealer:* Hampton III Gallery Ltd 10 Gallery Ctr Taylors SC 29687. *Mailing Add:* 803 Shoals Creek Church Rd Easley SC 29640-9532

FLOYD, CARL LEO
SCULPTOR, ENVIRONMENTAL ARTIST
b Somerset, Ky, Oct 12, 36. *Study:* Kansas City Art Inst, BFA, 64; Cranbrook Acad Art, MFA, 67. *Work:* Praltown Park, Lexington, Ky; Vt Freeway, St Albans; Hogback Nature Park, Madison, Ohio; Mand Corning Prof, Holden Arboretum, Mentor, Ohio; Univ Vt Art Mus, Burlington. *Comn:* Steel & wood sculpture, Willoughby Fine Arts, Ohio, 72; Stone Earth, Inner City, Bad Kreuznach, WGer, 75; All People's Park, Lake Co Metrop Parks, 76-77; Earth-Stone, Cleveland Pub Libr, 79; One Acre Proj, Ohio Arts Coun, Madison, 80. *Exhib:* Contemp Sculpture, J B Speed Mus Art, Louisville, Ky, 68; Environ Sculpture, Dulin Gallery Art, Knoxville, Tenn, 69; 2nd Cincinnati Biennial, Cincinnati Art Mus, 69 & Biennial Awards Exhib, 70; Sculpture of New Era, Chicago Fed Plaza, 76; Sculpture on the Green, Columbus Arts Coun, Ohio, 79; Nature Environ, Minn State Univ, Bemidji, 79. *Teaching:* Instr sculpture & archit, Univ Ky, Lexington, 67-71; instr sculpture, Cleveland Inst Art, 71-. *Mailing Add:* Dept Sculpture Cleveland Inst Art 11141 East Blvd Cleveland OH 44106-1700

FLUDD, REGINALD JOSEPH
PAINTER, CRAFTSMAN
b New York, NY, June 10, 38. *Study:* Ind Univ, BS(art); Queens Col, MS(art); study with Kenneth Campbell & Barse Miller; Art Inst Chicago; New York City Col. *Work:* Alcoa Aluminum Corp, NY; Norton Mus, Palm Beach, Fla; Nassau Community Col, Garden City, NY; Ocean City Cult Arts Ctr, NJ; Rose Art Mus, Brandeis Univ, Waltham, Mass; and others. *Exhib:* Am Drawing Biennial, Norfolk Mus, 71; Okla Art Ctr, Oklahoma City, 72; Aldrich Mus, Ridgefield, Conn, 74; New Britian Mus Contemp Art, Conn, 74; one-man show, Hecksher Mus, Huntington, NY, 75; and others. *Teaching:* Instr art, Syosset High Sch, NY, 64-; asst prof painting, Suffolk Community Col, 74-77. *Awards:* Best in Show, Bayshore CofC, 68 & Patchoque

CofC, 70; Grand Prix, Locust Valley Art Show, Operation Democracy, 73. *Bibliog:* Laurie Anderson (auth), article in Art News, 1/72; Malcom Preston (auth), article in Newsday, 3/12/75; Jean Paris (auth), article in Long Island Press, 7/6/75. *Mem:* Nat Educ Asn; Nat Art Educ Asn; Huntington Art League. *Media:* Oil, Watercolor. *Mailing Add:* 24 W Sanders Greenlawn NY 11740

FLUEK, TOBY
PAINTER, GRAPHIC ARTIST
b Czernica, Poland, Feb 20, 26; US citizen. *Study:* Art Students League, with Robert Beverly Hale; also with Joe Hing Lowe & Irving Koenig. *Work:* David Mamet pvt collection. *Exhib:* Bronx Mus Arts Ann, NY, 72 & 74-76; Hudson Valley Art Asn Ann, White Plains, NY, 73, 75-84 & 86; Queensborough Community Col Art Gallery, NY, 85, 87 & 88; Rockland Ctr Holocaust Studies, Spring Valley, NY, 90; Yeshiva Univ Mus, NY, 94; The Holocaust Mem & Educ Ctr, Nassau Co, 96; Fla Holocaust Mus; Holocaust Mem Resource & Educ Center, Maitland, Fla, 2006. *Teaching:* Instr oil painting, Woodside Jewish Ctr, NY, 72. *Awards:* Best Show, Art League Nassau Co, 79; Prix du Roman Historique, Hist Novel Prize, 91; Chosen Best Book for Young Adults 1991 by Am Libr Asn, Young Adults Servs Div; and others. *Bibliog:* Images of Life, Loss, Orlando Sentinel, Orlando, Fla, 5/18/2006; Memories of My Life in a Polish Village, Orlando Weekly, Orlando, Fla, 4/3/2006. *Media:* Oil, Charcoal, Watercolor. *Publ:* Passover As I Remember It, Alred A. Knopf, 94. *Mailing Add:* 60-10 47th Ave Woodside NY 11377

FLUME, VIOLET SIGOLOFF
DEALER, RESTORER
b Huntington, WVa. *Study:* Trinity Univ, with Phillip Wilson. *Work:* Paintings & portraits in pvt collections, US & Mex. *Exhib:* San Antonio Art League, 64-70; one-woman shows, Southwestern Fine Arts Exhib, Univ Tex, 67, HemisFair, 68 & Trinity Univ, 68. *Pos:* Owner & dir, Wonderland Gallery, 66-72 & Wonderland Art Sch, 69-72; owner, Sigoloff Fine Art Galleries, 72-. *Awards:* Watercolor & Miniature Award, Composers, Authors & Artists Exhib, New York, 65; San Antonio's Outstanding Woman in Art, San Antonio Express & Eve News, 67. *Mem:* Tex Fine Arts Asn; San Antonio Art League. *Media:* Oil. *Specialty:* Fine art, contemporary and antique paintings. *Publ:* Auth, The Last Mountian, Branden Publ, Boston. *Mailing Add:* 3835 Morgan Creek San Antonio TX 78230

FLYNN, JOHN (KEVIN)
PAINTER, RESTORER
b Los Angeles, Calif, Nov 7, 53. *Study:* Pvt study with Clyde Johnson, 68-74, Art Center Col Des, with Lorser Feitelson, 75-76 & Harry Carmean, 75-78; Pratt Inst, with Joseph A Smith, BFA, 83; New York Univ, cert appraisal studies, 92. *Work:* Permanent Collection, Pratt Inst, Brooklyn, NY. *Exhib:* 45th Ann Nat Midyear Show, Butler Inst Am Art, 82; 15th Anniversary Exhib, Brooklyn Mus, 83; Artists in the Marketplace, Bronx Mus, 87; 1988 Stockton Natl Print & Drawing Exhib, Hagin Mus, Calif, 88; 165th Ann Exhib, Nat Acad Design, NY, 90; 28th Ann Open Exhib, San Bernadino Co Mus, Calif, 93; The 33rd Irene Leache Mem Exhib, Chrysler Mus, Norfolk, 96; 2000 Reasons to love the Eart, Milennium Exhib, The Hague, The Neth, 2000. *Pos:* Paintings restorer, J K Flynn Co, 74-, appraiser of paintings, sculpture & works on paper, 85-. *Teaching:* Instr painting-pastels & composition-drawing, Craft Students League, 90-94. *Awards:* David Humphries Mem Award, Allied Artists Am Inc, 82; Joseph S Isidor Mem Medal Excellence in Figurative Composition, Nat Acad Design, 90; William Henry Lowman Award, Silvermine Guild Ctr Arts, 92; Wheeler Page Memorial Award, Wayne Art Ctr, Wayne, PA, 97. *Bibliog:* Malcom Preston (auth), Displaying works by five, Newsday, 83; Karin Lipson (auth), Artwork by prizewinners, Newsday, 86; Vivien Raynor (auth), The drive to be topical, The urge to compete, The NY Times, 92. *Media:* Oil on Linen, Charcoal/Graphite, Ink & Watercolor on Paper. *Publ:* Auth, Technical answers-discovering the oil medium of the masters, The Artists Mag, 9/92; Technical answers-keeping color mixing organized-saving premixed colors, The Artists Mag, 5/93; Seeing your way to better oils - Don Wards eight step painting process lets you push your paintings in any direction, The Artists Mag, 3/95; Technical answers-the art of scumbling-dealing with mildew and insects on canvas, The Artists Mag, 7/94; Technical answers-uncover old masters secrets for creating form with contrast, learn to keep your oil painting from cracking, The Artists Mag, 10/96. *Dealer:* JK Flynn Company 471 Sixth Ave Park Slope Brooklyn NY 11215-4020. *Mailing Add:* 471 6th Ave Brooklyn NY 11215-4020

FLYNN, PAT L
JEWELER, GOLDSMITH
b Edinboro, Pa, Oct 29, 54. *Study:* Edinboro State Col, 73-76; State Univ Col New York, New Paltz, BFA, 78. *Work:* Chicago Art Inst; Nordenfjeldske Kunstindustt Mus, Trondheim, Norway; Renwick Gallery, Smithsonian Inst; Am Mus Art; Mus Arts and Design, NY; RI Sch Design; also pvt collections of Mr & Mrs Ron Abramson, Mr & Mrs Malcolm Knapp & Robert Pfannebecker. *Exhib:* Silver in Service, Castle Gallery, New Rochelle, NY, 87; Goldsmithing, Louisiana State Univ, 88; 20th Century Decorative Art, Naval Pier, Chicago, 87, 88 & 89; Jewelers Work, Washington, 96; The Poetry of Passion, DeNova Gallery, Palto Alto, Calif; Falling Gracefully, Susan Cummins Gallery, Mill Valley, Calif; Pat Flynn, Gallery Materia, Scottsdale, Ariz, 2002, Patina Gallery, Sante Fe, NMex, 2003; Nat Invitational, Bowling Green State Univ, Ohio, 2002; At Arms Length, Saybains Gallery, Royal Oak, Mich. *Pos:* Freelance jeweler, goldsmith & modelmaker, 82-85; owner, Pat Flynn Inc, 85-. *Teaching:* Arrowmont Sch Arts & Crafts, Ball State Univ, Boston Univ, Brookfield Craft Ctr, Chautauqua Inst, Creative Arts Workshop, Greenwood Galleries, Haystack Mountain Sch Crafts, La State Univ, 92nd St YMWHA, Northern Ariz Univ, Nova Scotia Sch Art & Design, Ore Sch Arts & Crafts, Parsons Sch Design, Penland Sch Crafts, Pa Guild Craftsman, Peters Valley, San Diego State Univ, Sch Fine Arts, Saide Brofman Ctr, Skidmore Col, Southwest Craft Ctr, Summer Vail Metalsmithing symp, Univ Houston, Univ Wis & Worchester Craft Ctr. *Awards:* Craftsman Fel, Nat Endowment Arts, 85, 88 & 94; Christofle Prize, Philadelphia Craft Show, 87; NY State Found Arts Fel, 88; Nat Ornamental Metal Mus, Master Metalsmith, 98. *Mem:* Am Crafts Coun. *Publ:* Ornament Mag, 1/93; Lapidary J, 6/93; Metalsmith Mag, fall 93 & summer, 94. *Dealer:* Susan Cummins Gallery 12 Miller Ave Mill Valley CA 94941; Jewelers Work 2000 Pennsylvania Ave Washington DC 20006. *Mailing Add:* 480 Mohonk Rd High Falls NY 12440-5301

FLYNT, ROBERT
PHOTOGRAPHER
b Williamstown, Mass, Mar 27, 56. *Study:* Skowhegan Sch Painting & Sculpture, 74 & 76; NY Studio Sch, Paris, 75; Tyler Sch Art, BFA, 78. *Work:* Mus Mod Art, Metrop Mus Art, NY; Los Angeles Co Mus Art; Mus Fine Art, Houston; Baltimore Mus Art; Int Ctr Photog, NY; Worcester Art Mus, Mass. *Comn:* Dance set (co-collaborator), Bebe Miller Co, Brooklyn Acad Mus, NY, 89; Theatre set/projections (co-collaborator), Los Angeles Contemp Exhibs, Calif, 90; The Yellow Room, Dahghda dance co, Ireland, 2003. *Exhib:* Interactions, Inst Contemp Art, Philadelphia, 91; New Photog 8, Mus Mod Art, NY, 92; Bathers, Washington Ctr Photog, Washington, DC, 96; Bodies in Flux, Weatherspoon Art Gallery, Univ NC, Greensboro, 98; Waterproof, Centro Cult de Belem, Lisbon, Port, 98; San Francisco Camerawork, 99; Wessel & O'Connor Gallery, NY, 2000; Anatomically Incorrect, Mus Mod Art, NY, 2000; Partial Disclosures, Univ RI, Kingston, 2000 & Centro Cult de Belem, Lisbon, Portugal, 2000; solo exhib, Maus Habitos Gallery, Porto, Portugal, 2001 & 04, Clamp Art, New York City, 2004; Anxiety & Desire, Metrop State Col Denver, Colo, 2004; Hidden Histories, New Art Gallery, Walsall, UK, 2004; New to View, Worcester Art Mus, Mass, 2006; Body Familiar, Griffin Mus Photography, Winchester, Mass, 2006; Body Lanuages, Katzen Arts Ctr, Am Univ, Washington, 2006; and others. *Pos:* Co-cur, Space Case Gallery, PS 122, New York, 89-94. *Teaching:* Univ Nev, Las Vegas, 96 & Sch Visual Arts, NY, 98-. *Awards:* Photog Fel, Blind Trust, Mid-Atlantic Arts Found, 95; Residency Fel, MacDowell Colony, 98; Peter S Reed Found Grant, 2004; and others. *Bibliog:* D Bright (auth), The Passionate Camera, Routledge, 98; Emmanuel Cooper (auth), Male Bodies, Pastel, 2004; Michael Petry (auth), HiddenHistories, Artmedia, 2004. *Mem:* Soc Photog Educ. *Publ:* Auth, Life Jacket, pvt publ, 92; coauth, Blind Trust, pvt publ with Temple Univ, 94; auth, Compound Fracture, Twin Palms Publ, 96; auth, Numbered Days, pvt publ, 2001. *Dealer:* Clamp Art 531 W 25th St New York NY 10001; GZ Gallery 4200 N Marshall Way Scottsdale AR 85751. *Mailing Add:* 383 Spring Lake Rd Red Hook NY 12571

FOGG, MONICA
PAINTER, EDUCATOR
b Belaire, Tex. *Study:* Washington Univ, 73; Principia Col, Elsah, Ill, BA, 74; St Cloud Univ, Minn, MA, 86. *Work:* General Mills & Honeywell, Minneapolis; Prudential Insurance Co Am, Plymouth, Minn; Principia Col, Elsah, Ill; Marathon Oil Co, Midland, Tex. *Comn:* Minn Protective Life, Eden Prairie, 75; Woodhill Country Club, Wayzata, 82; AMFAC-City Ctr, Minneapolis, 82; Univ Minn Hosp, 86. *Exhib:* Metamorphose-One, Minn Mus Art, St Paul, 76; Midwest Watercolor Ann, Tweed Mus, Duluth, Minn, 77 & 78; Northstar Soc Ann, Minneapolis, 77-83; Aqucous Open, Pittsburgh Watercolor Soc, Pa, 78; one-woman show, Expressive of Alaska, Artique, Anchorage, 81; Minn Artist Asn, Minneapolis, 82; Expressive Chroma on Paper, Kieale Gallery, St Cloud, Minn. *Teaching:* Instr, St Louis Watercolor Soc, 74, Northstar Watercolor Soc, 77, Univ Minn, 80-86, Edina Art Ctr, 80-81, Fogg Studio, 81-83, Art Ctr Minn, 83 & St Cloud State Univ, 84-86. *Awards:* Second Prize, Minn 77, State Arts Coun, 77; Award Excellence, Northstar Watercolor Soc Ann, 77, 80, 82 & 83; Award of Excellence, Minn Artists Asn, 82; and others. *Bibliog:* Fredric Appel (auth), Watercolor: When it's good, Minn Star & Tribune, 78; Cindy Rumsey (auth), Artist on the move (film), WCCO-TV, Minneapolis, 81; Warren Martin (auth), Watercolor-An Art (film), WTCN-TV, Minneapolis, 81. *Mem:* Minn Soc Fine Arts; Northstar Watercolor Soc (treas, 78-81 & bd mem, 78-81); Midwest Watercolor Soc; Twin Cities Watercolor Soc; Women's Caucus Arts. *Media:* Watercolor. *Mailing Add:* 3790 Pasture Ridge S Rd Afton MN 55001

FOGG, REBECCA SNIDER
PRINTMAKER, PAINTER
b Washington, DC, Dec 16, 49. *Study:* Rochester Inst Technol, summer 72; RI Sch Design, BFA, 72. *Work:* Rochester Inst Technol, Henrietta, NY; Am Fed Savings & Loan, Sacramento, Calif; Resorts Unlimited, Atlantic City, NJ. *Comn:* Etching, Columbia Bank, Newark, NJ, 74; etchings with Michael Harris, Rickey's Calif Hyatt, Palo Alto, Calif, 83. *Exhib:* Printmakers Regional Exhib, Rochester Mem Art Gallery, 75; Kala Inst Printmakers, Hearst Mus, St Mary's Col, Moraga, Calif, 79; Biennial Exhib, Mus Munic de las Artes Graphicas, Maracaibo, Venezuela, 81. *Teaching:* Instr drawing & graphic design, Genesee Community Col, Batavia, NY, 75-77; instr computer graphics & design, Ohlone Col, Fremont, Calif, 91-. *Awards:* Community Prog Grant Award, Burlington in Transition, Mayor's Coun Arts, Burlington, Vt, 86. *Media:* Etching; Watercolor. *Dealer:* San Francisco Mus Mod Art Rental Gallery Bldg A Ft Mason San Francisco CA 94123. *Mailing Add:* 982 Kiely Blvd Unit H Santa Clara CA 95051-5047

FOHR, JENNY
PAINTER, PRINTMAKER
b New York, NY. *Study:* Hunter Col, BA; Alfred Univ; Univ Colo, MA; City Col. *Work:* Norfolk Mus, Va; Long Beach Island Found Arts & Sci, NJ; Dr Wardell Pomeroy, NY; Oakland Mus, Calif; Charles Suter, Ciba-Geigy, NY. *Exhib:* One-man show, Chautauqua Art Asn Galleries, NY, 60 & Brooklyn Mus, 61; Nat Asn Women Artists, Chateau de la Napoule, France, 65; Nat Asn Women Artists Traveling Show, India, 66; NJ State Mus, Trenton, 68; Am Color Print Soc Traveling Show, 72. *Teaching:* Asst instr sculpture, Brooklyn Mus, 49-51; instr art, Beekman Hill Sch,

69-81. *Awards:* Samuel Mann Award, Am Soc Contemp Artists, 71; May Granick Award, Nat Asn Women Artists, 75; Doris Kreindlr Award, 81; The Alvin & Co Award, 83. *Bibliog:* Article, New York News, 76. *Mem:* Am Soc Contemp Artists (pres, secy, bd dir); Nat Asn Women Artists (secy, jury chmn, dir); Painters & Sculptors Soc NJ (selection jury, bd); Am Color Print Soc; New York Soc Women Artists (dir, cat chmn). *Media:* Miscellaneous Media. *Mailing Add:* 165 E 32 St Apt 5E New York NY 10016

FOLDA, JAROSLAV (THAYER), III
HISTORIAN
b Baltimore, Md, July 25, 40. *Study:* Princeton Univ, AB, 62; Johns Hopkins Univ, PhD, 68. *Teaching:* From asst prof to prof medieval art, Univ NC, Chapel Hill, 68-78, prof, 78-, chmn, 83-87 & N Ferebee Taylor prof art hist, 96-. *Awards:* Nat Endowment Humanities, 73-74, 81-82 & 98-99; Guggenheim Fel, 88-89; Nat Humanities Ctr Fel, 88-89, 98-99; Haskins Medal, Medieval Acad Am, 99. *Mem:* Medieval Acad Am; Col Art Asn Am; Int Ctr Medieval Art; Soc for the Study of the Crusades and the Latin East; ASOR; US Nat Byzantine Comt. *Res:* Medieval art of the High and Late Middle Ages, especially Crusader art, 1098-1291. *Publ:* Auth, Crusader Manuscript Illumination at St Jean d'Acre, Princeton Univ Press, 76; contribr, K M Setton (ed), A History of the Crusaders, Vol 4, Univ Wis Press, 77; auth, The Nazareth Capitals and the Crusader Church of the Annunciation, CAA Monograph, 42, 86; The Art of the Crusaders in the Holy Land: 1098-1187, Cambridge Univ Press, 95; Crusader Art in the Holy Land, from the Third Crusade to the Fall of Acre: 1187-1291, Cambridge Univ Press, 2005; and others. *Mailing Add:* Dept Art Hanes Art Ctr Univ NC Chapel Hill NC 27599-3405

FOLEY, DAVID E
PAINTER
b New Orleans, La, Mar 16, 54. *Study:* Univ New Orleans, BA, 77; Univ Colo, MFA, 80. *Work:* Payne Weber, Boulder; ATT, Denver; USA Ins Corp, Colo Springs; Dushanbe Hall of Econ Achieuments, Tajikistan. *Comn:* Painting, Theodore Gentner, Portland, Ore, 2001; Painting, Ted & Robin Haughland, Denver, 2002; Painting, Pinnocol Insurance, Denver, 02. *Exhib:* Colo State of the Art, Aspen Art Mus, 89; A Celebration of the Desert, Desert Caballeros Western Mus, Wickenburg, Az, 99; Paintings of the West Landscape, Aruada Ctr for the Arts, Colo, 94; The New West, Sangre de Christo Art Center, Pueblo, Colo, 96. *Awards:* Purchase Award, 8th Nat Print & Drawing Exhhib, Minot State Col, 78. *Mem:* Denver Art Mus. *Media:* Acrylic. *Collection:* Paintings throughout US as well as: Puerto Rico, Canada, Mexico, Australia, China, Israel, Germany, France, England & Tajikistand. *Publ:* Emily Van Cleve (auth), David Foleys Work, Santa Fe Newspaper, 97; Michael Paclia (auth), Seasonal Winds, West Word/Newtimes, 99; The Artist and the Am Landscape, First Glance Books, 98; Focus Santa Fe/The Beauty of Nature, Focus Santa Fe, 02. *Dealer:* Charlene cody Gallery Ltd 130 W Palace Ave Santa Fe NM 87501. *Mailing Add:* 5045 Ingersoll Pl Boulder CO 80303

FOLEY, TIMOTHY ALBERT
ART DEALER
b New Orleans, La, May 11, 47. *Study:* Loyola Univ, New Orleans; Univ New Orleans, BA(anthrop), 71. *Awards:* Distinguished Alumni, Univ New Orleans, 91. *Mem:* Am Soc Appraisers. *Specialty:* Quality contemp art as well as important 19th and 20th century art; Southern artists of the 19th and early 20th centuries. *Mailing Add:* 6374 Pratt Dr New Orleans LA 70115-2750

FOLK, TOM C
ART DEALER, HISTORIAN
b Oct 30, 55. *Study:* Seton Hall Univ, with Petra Chu, BA, 1977; Rutgers Univ with Matthew Baigell, MA, 1980; City Univ NY with William Gennis, PhD, 1987. *Work:* James Michener Mus, Doylestown, Pa. *Exhib:* The Pa School of Landscape Painting: An Original America Impressionism, Allentown Art Mus & Corcoran Gallery, Wash, DC, 1983; A Woman of Genius, NJ State Mus, Trenton, 1990; Father of Neer Hope Modernism, Allentown Art Mus, 2003. *Teaching:* adj prof, Rutgers Univ, Newark, NJ, 1995-2000; adj prof, Caldwell Col, NJ, 1998-2001; adj prof, St Peter's Col, Jersey City, NJ, 2001-. *Awards:* Juror for Allied Artists Exhib, NYC, 2001. *Bibliog:* Denise M Topolnicki (auth), The Fine Art of Fraud, Money Magazine, 9/1986; Ann E Berman (auth), Bucks County Impressionists, Architectural Digest, 11/1994. *Mem:* Appraiser's Assoc of Am (assoc mem); Potteries of Trenton Soc. *Publ:* auth, The Pennsylvania Impressionists, Assoc Univ Presses, 1997. *Mailing Add:* PO Box 501 Bernardsville NJ 07924

FOLKUS, DAN (DANIEL) ALAN FREDRICKSON
DESIGNER, ILLUSTRATOR
b Rice Lake, Wis, Oct 1, 46. *Study:* Lawrence Univ, BA(philos & art), 68; assisted muralist Granville Bruce, Dallas, 72. *Work:* Kenosha Pub Mus, Wis; Charleston Mus, SC; West Fla Int Airport, main terminal. *Comn:* Mural, NJ State Trout Hatchery; McDonalds Steam Engine Mural, Pa Turnpike at King of Prussia; mural, Discoverer's of Flight, Dayton Airport. *Exhib:* Philadelphia Acad Nat Sci, 100 ft sculpted rock formations; Saks 5th Ave Prosceniums for Spaeth Design, 99, 2000. *Pos:* Preparator, Dallas Mus, 72-74; freelance illusr, 74-78; cur exhibs, Kenosha Pub Mus, Wis, 78-79; chief exhibs planner-designer, Charleston Mus, SC, 79-80; asst film dir, WCBD-TV, SC, 80-81; pres, Visual Syntax, Collingswood, NJ, 82-. *Teaching:* Vis lectr, Rutgers Univ. *Awards:* Exhib Builders Asn Award, Dupont Print Show, 85. *Mem:* ASIFA-EAST Animation Soc. *Media:* Latex Casting, Acrylic Painting. *Publ:* Illusr, Pests Control, auth, Dr E P Cheatum, Prestige Press, 73; Dust storms of Mars, Astronomy Mag, 77; Biologic Cardiac Assit, In: Assisted Circulation, Springer-Verhag, 88

FOLMAN, LIZA
PRTINTMAKER, PAINTER
b New York, NY, Feb 25, 51. *Study:* State Univ New York, BFA, 72; Boston Univ, MFA, 76. *Work:* Mus Fine Arts, Boston, Mass; Boston Pub Libr, Boston, Mass; Bibliotheque Nationale, Paris, France; The Col Board Collection, NY; The Reader's Digest Collection, NY. *Exhib:* Collector's Gallery Exhibit, McNay Art Inst, San Antonio, Tex, 82; The Drawing Show, Boston Cen for Arts, Boston, Mass, 84 & 93; Drawings from Boston, DeCordova Mus, Lincoln, Mss, 87; 165th Ann Exhib, Nat Acad of Design, NY, 90; Estampes et Livres d'Artistes du Xxeme Sicle: Enrichissements du Cabinet des Estampes, 78-88, Bibliotheque Nationale, Paris, France, 92; Women in Watercolor, Boston Pub Libr, Boston, Mass, 93, 96 & 99; Immortalized, The Art Complex Mus, Duxbury, Mass, 98; Group exhib, Randall Beck Gallery, Boston, 87, 89 & 94, Proof in Print, Boston Pub Libr, 2001. *Teaching:* instr etching/drawing, Mass Col Art, Boston, Mass, 82-83 & 86-88; teaching assoc, Boston Univ, 89-91; assoc prof, Art Inst Boston, Lesley Univ, Boston, Mass, 90-. *Awards:* Fulbright Fel, 84-85; MacDowell Colony Artist's Fel, 84 & 85; Blanche E Colman Award, 98. *Mem:* Boston Printmakers. *Media:* Etching, Watercolor. *Publ:* Christine Temin, Perspectives, 89 & Artists share feelings.,The Boston Globe, 99; Cate McQuaid, Prints Charming & Significant, The Boston Globe, 97. *Mailing Add:* Art Inst Boston Lesley Univ 700 Beacon St Boston MA 02215

FOLSOM, FRED GORHAM, III
PAINTER, CONSERVATOR
b Washington, DC, July 31, 1945. *Study:* Pratt Inst, NY, with Martha Erlebacher, 64-67; Sch Visual Arts, NY, 67; Corcoran Sch Art, Washington, 69. *Work:* Corcoran Gallery, Washington; Lyndon B Johnson Libr, Austin, Tex; Dimock Gallery, George Washington Univ; Hickory Mus Art, NC; Wells Col, Aurora, NY; Mayor of Silver Spring, Md, 91. *Comn:* Superior Court, Washington, DC; Fred Folsom Sculpture, Univ Colo, Boulder, Colo, 2004. *Exhib:* Md Biennial Exhib, Baltimore Mus Art, 74 & 85; one-man shows, Gallery K, Washington, 80, 82, 84 & 88, WPA, 92 & Md Art Place, Baltimore, 93; Wash-Moscow Art Exchange, Tretya Kov-Gallery, Russia, 85; The Washington Show, Corcoran Gallery Art, 85; Black Art, Rockville Art Place, Md, 95; Gallery Stendahl, NY, 97; Artists Mus, Washington, 97; Montgomery Col, Md, 99; Strathmore Hall, Md, 2002; Arts Club of Washington, DC, 2002; True Colors, Meridian House, DC, Atlanta, Cairo, Casablanca, Berlin, Vienna, Dallas, 2002-2006; Folsom Sc;ulpture, Univ Colo, Boulder, Colo, 2004. *Pos:* Actor, Robert Wilson Theater Productions, New York, 66; conservator & owner, Art Restoration Ctr, Wheaton, Md, 73-. *Awards:* Md State Arts Coun, 81, 82, 87, 89, 96 & 2000; Mayor's Comn Arts, Baltimore, 82; Individual Grant Visual Arts, Nat Endowment Arts, 85; Md Gov's Citations, 1982, 1996, 2000. *Bibliog:* Articles in Washington Post, 82, 84, 85, 87, 91, 92, 97, 99 & 2000, 2002, Art Internat, 79, 81, 83; JW Mahoney (auth), Fred Folsom, Art in America, 80, 81, 93; Brand & Chaplin (auths), Christians in the Arts, Art & Soul, 2000; G Wolfe (auth), Image Mag, 1992. *Media:* Oil, Linen. *Publ:* Cover illusr, The poet John Pauker, Art Int, 1/79; auth, (cover story) The Man Who Made New York, Financial Hist Mag, 2000. *Mailing Add:* 212 Hillsboro Dr Wheaton MD 20902

FOLSOM, ROSE
CALLIGRAPHER, WRITER
b Madison, Wis, July 31, 53. *Study:* Pvt study with Sheila Waters, 74-75; Rochester Inst Technol, calligraphy master class with Hermann Zapf, 79-80. *Work:* H M Queen Elizabeth II; Artery Orgn, Bethesda; Houghton Rare Book Libr, Harvard Univ. *Comn:* Nat Gallery Art, Washington; US Dept State. *Exhib:* Solo exhibs, Foundry Gallery, Washington, & Minn Ctr Book Arts, 96; Scene in DC, Amos Eno Gallery, NY, 88; Traditions of the Pen, Smithsonian Inst, 94; The Book as Art VIII, Nat Mus Women Arts, 96. *Collection Arranged:* Calligraphic Books, Nat Mus Women in the Arts, 92. *Pos:* Owner, Folsom Calligraphy Studio, 73-; Washington corresp, Calligraphy Rev Mag, Norman, Okla, 85-93. *Teaching:* Instr, Washington Calligraphers Guild, 78-; lectr hist calligraphy, Nat Mus Am Art, Renwick Gallery, 90, Smithsonian Inst, 92 & 94. *Awards:* Hermann Zapf Educ Fund Scholar, 93. *Bibliog:* Jane Snow (auth), Living treasures, Washingtonian Mag, 8/88; Michael Welzenbach (auth), Bare bones beauty, Washington Post, 10/7/89; Paul Richard (auth), The soul of the scribe, Washington Post, 8/11/96. *Mem:* Washington Calligraphers Guild. *Media:* Ink on Paper. *Publ:* Illusr, International Calligraphy Today, Watson-Guptill, 82; auth, The Calligraphers' Dictionary, Thames & Hudson, 90; illusr, The Creative Stroke, Rockport, 93; Brush Lettering, Lyons & Burford, 94. *Mailing Add:* 212 Hillsboro Dr Silver Spring MD 20902-3126

FONDAW, RON
SCULPTOR
b Paducah, Ky, Apr 25, 54. *Study:* Memphis Col Art, Tenn, BFA, 76; Univ Ill, Champaign, MFA, 78. *Work:* Renwick Gallery, Smithsonian Inst, Washington; Columbus Mus Fine Art, Ohio; Tenn State Arts Comn, Nashville; John Michael Kohler Arts Ctr, Sheboygan, Wis; Richard & Joy Haft, Miami, Fla; Dr Carl Djerassi, Woodside, Calif; Martin Z Margulies, Grove Isle, Fla. *Comn:* Art in Public Places, Ghost Islands, Key Biscayne, Fla, 87; outdoor sculpture, Fragments, Southeastern Ctr Contemp Art, Winston-Salem, NC, 87; outdoor sculpture, NAOS, Coconut Grove, Fla, purchased by City of Miami, Coconut Grove Asn, 88; outdoor sculptures, Earth Structures, EHampton Ctr Contemp Art, NY, 88; Now and Never, Socrates Sculpture Park, Long Island City, NY, 89; Ferro's Dream, Fla Int Univ, Miami, 90; The Giving Tree, St Louis Art Mus, 98; Whisper Walls, Cedarhurst Sculpture Park, Mt Vernon, IL; Who We Are, Arts in Transit, St Louis, 99; The Langlow Brisge, Henry Lay Sculpture Park, Los Angeles, MO, 2001; The Vertical Loop, Bi-State Development, St Louis, MO, 2003. *Exhib:* Am Ceramics Now, Everson Mus Art, Syracuse, NY, traveling juried exhib: Am Craft Mus, NY & Crocker Art Mus, Sacramento, Calif, 87; Am Ceramics Now, traveling, De Cordova & Dana Mus & park, Lincoln; Birmingham

Mus Art, Ala, 89; one-man exhibs, Of Iron and Earth, Atlantic Ctr Arts, New Smyrna Beach, Fla, 89, Ron Fondaw, drawings, Nat Acad Sci, Washington, 90 & Fusion, Clay Studio, Philadelphia, 95; BMW Gallery, NY, 90; Twenty-Five in Miami, Miami Dade Community Col, S Campus Gallery, Fla, 90; Abstraction, Eve Mannes Gallery, Atlanta, Ga, 90; Buildings with Clay, Hoffman Gallery, Ore Sch Art & Crafts, 90; 3 Sampson Gallery, Stetson Univ, Deland, Fla, 90; Art in Industry, John M Kohler Art Ctr, Sheboygan, Wis, 90; and others; Kansas City Artists Coalition, Kansas City, MO, 2002; Ron Fondaw, Northern Clay Ctr, Minn, MN, 2004. *Teaching:* Vis instr art, Ohio Univ, 78; assoc prof art, Univ Miami, Coral Gables, Fla, 79-; lectr, Ohio State Univ, 83, Univ Gainesville, Fla, 84, Chicago Art Inst, Ill, 86, Ft Lauderdale Mus Art, Fla, Ormond Mem Art Mus & Tokyo Nat Univ Fine Art, Japan, 87, Chautauqua Sch Art, NY, 88 & Chicago Art Inst, Ill 89 & Hollufgard Kulturcenter, Odense, Denmark, 90; vis prof sculpture, Univ NC, Chapel Hill, 94-; prof art, Washington Univ, St Louis, currently. *Awards:* Guggenheim Fel, 85; Nat Endowment Art Fel, 88 & 89; Awards in Visual Arts 8, 89; New Forms, Fla, 90; Fla Arts Coun Fel, 92; Kranzberg Award, 98; Pollack-Krasner Award, 97; Kransberg Award, St Louis Art Mus, MO, 98. *Bibliog:* Paula Harper (auth), Sculpture-Ron Fondaw, Am Ceramics, Vol 2, 4, 84; Helen Kohen (auth), Staring and shivering, Art News, 6/81; Susan Peterson (auth), The Art and Craft of Clay, 91, Contemporary Ceramics, 2001, Prentice Hall; Julie Stevenson (auth) Weathering Change, Sculpture Magazine, Sept 2000. *Media:* Ceramics. *Mailing Add:* 2004 Stemler Rd Columbia IL 62236

FONG, WEN C
EDUCATOR
b Shanghai, China, Dec 9, 30. *Pos:* Res asst, Cleveland Mus Art, 53; vis cur oriental art, Yale Art Gallery, 58-59. *Teaching:* From instr to asst prof, Princeton Univ, 55-60, fac 60-, chmn PhD prog Chinese & Japanese art & archeol, 64-, prof art & archeol & cur oriental art, 67-, chmn dept art & archeol, 70-73, chmn exec com art mus, 70-75 & Sanford Edwards prof art & archeol, 71-. *Awards:* Bollingen Found Fel, 56-57; Guggenheim Fel, 61-62; McCosh Fac Fel, Princeton Univ, 65-66. *Mem:* Am Col Art Asn (bd dir, 71-76); Chinese Art Soc Am; Am Philos Soc; Chinese painting delegation to People's Repub China, 77; Acad Sinica. *Publ:* Auth, Images of the Mind: Selections from the Edward L Elliott Family and John B Elliott Collections of Chinese Calligraphy and Painting, 84; Beyond Representation: Chinese Painting and Calligraphy 8th - 14th Century, 92; Possessing the Past: Treasures from the National Palace Museum, 96; and many others. *Mailing Add:* 83 Allison Rd Princeton NJ 08540

FONTAINE, JOHN C
ADMINISTRATOR
Study: Univ Mich, BA, 53. *Hon Degrees:* Harvard Univ, LLB, 56. *Pos:* Pres, Knight-Ridder, Inc, Miami, Fla, formerly; bd mem, Samuel H Kress Found, 75-, chmn, 94-; partner, Hughes Hubbard & Reed LLP, New York City, 97-. *Mem:* Nat Gallery Art, Wash, DC, (mem bd trustees, 84-2000 & 2002-). *Mailing Add:* Samuel H Kress Found 174 E 80th St New York NY 10021

FOOLERY, TOM
ASSEMBLAGE ARTIST
b Green Bay, Wis, Aug 29, 47. *Study:* Self-taught. *Work:* Clorox Corp, Oakland; Ara Mark Corp, Los Angeles; Kaiser Permanente; Imagery Estate Winery; and others. *Comn:* Murals, St Francis Mem Hosp, San Francisco, 79-81. *Exhib:* Humor in Art, Los Angeles Inst Contemp Art, 81; one-man shows, William Sawyer Gallery, San Francisco, 81 & Jacqueline Anhalt Gallery, Los Angeles, 82; Dobrick Gallery, Chicago, 83, Tortue Gallery, Santa Monica, 90 & 92, Fresno Art Mus, 91, Holter Art, Helena Mont, 94; Anxious Interiors, Laguna Beach Mus Art, Calif, & traveling, 84; Miniature Environments, Whitney Mus at Phillip Morris, 89; 40 Yrs of California Assemblage, Univ Calif Los Angeles, (traveling), 89; Tortue Gallery, Santa Monica, Calif, 90, 92; Napa Valley Col, 91; Fresno Art Mus, 91; Holter Mus Art, Helena, Mont, 95; Mont Arts Coun, 2001; Botanica, Bozeman, Mont, 2002; Sutton West Gallery, Missoula, Mont, 2004; Hallie Ford Mus Art, Willamette Univ, Salem, Ore, 2006; group exhibs, Paris Gibson Square Mus Art, 2001, Sutton West Gallery, Missoula, Mont, 2002, Holter Mus Art, Helena, Mont, 2002-2003, Custer Co Art Ctr, Miles City, Mont, 2003-2004; Hallie Ford Mus, Salem, Ore, 2006; Nicolayen Mus Art, Casper, Wyo, 2006; Micaela Gallery, San Francisco, 2006. *Awards:* fel, Mont Arts Coun, 2002. *Bibliog:* John Russell (auth), NY Times, 8/11/89; Andrew Olds (auth), Miniature Environments, ID, 11/89; Elaine de Mann (auth), Carrot & Schtick, Air & Space, 2/91. *Media:* All. *Mailing Add:* Ravin' Raven Rd Dillon MT 59725

FOOSANER, JUDITH
EDUCATOR, PAINTER
b Sacramento, Calif, Aug 10, 40. *Study:* Univ Calif, Berkeley, BA, 64 & MA, 68. *Work:* Newport Harbor Art Mus, Newport Beach, Calif; Everson Mus, Syracuse, NY; Albuquerque Mus, NMex. *Exhib:* Laguna Beach Mus, Calif, 67; Calif Palace Legion Honor, San Francisco, 69; Bellevue Art Mus, Wash, 76; M H DeYoung Mem Mus, San Francisco, 77; Oakland Mus, Calif, 81; Ark Arts Ctr, 90; Space Gallery, Los Angeles, Calif, 90. *Teaching:* Prof fine arts, Calif Col Arts & Crafts, Oakland, 70-82; vis asst prof art, Univ Calif, Berkeley, 75-77. *Media:* Oil. *Mailing Add:* 2667 21st St Sacramento CA 95818

FOOTE, HOWARD REED
ARTIST, PAINTER
b Richmond, Ind, Dec 15, 36. *Study:* Toledo Mus Art, Ohio, 54-55; Sch Mus Fine Arts, Boston, 55-57; San Francisco Art Inst, BFA, 60; Stanford Univ, MA, 70; additional study with Nathan Oliveira. *Work:* Achenbach Found, Palace of the Legion of Honor, San Francisco; City of Leeds, Eng; City of San Francisco; Stanford Univ. *Exhib:* Bay Area Printmakers Soc Fourth Nat Exhib, Oakland Mus, Calif, 58; 1970 Peace Exhib, Philadelphia Mus Art, 70; San Francisco Art Inst Centennial Exhib, Palace of the Legion of Honor, San Francisco, 71; Four Printmakers, San Francisco Mus Art, 71; 18th Nat Print Exhib, Brooklyn Mus, NY, 72; San Francisco Area Printmakers, Cincinnati Art Mus, Ohio, 73; Interstices, San Jose Art Mus, Calif & Cranbrook Acad Art Mus, Bloomfield Hills, Mich, 75; Gallery Route One, Point Reyes Station, Calif, 98. *Teaching:* Instr printmaking, Acad Art, San Francisco, 70-90 Calif State Univ, Hayward, 71-72; instr printmaking, drawing & 3-D design, Col Notre Dame, Belmont, Calif, 75-84. *Media:* Artist, Painter, Paintmaker, Woodworker. *Publ:* Contribr, Ramparts Mag, 6/70; BYTE, 9/81. *Mailing Add:* PO Box 311 Tomales CA 94971

FORBES, DONNA MARIE
MUSEUM DIRECTOR
b Albion, Nebr, Mar 19, 1929. *Study:* Mont State Univ; Pratt Inst; Eastern Mont Col, BS(art educ), 52; Harvard Summer Inst in Arts Admin; Univ Calif, Berkeley, Mus Mgt Inst, 83. *Collection Arranged:* The Christmas Story, 78, The Cowboy, 78, Using Paper, 80, Chinese Robes: 1750-1900, 82 & The William Andrews Clark Collection: Treasures of a Copper King, 88, Yellowstone Art Ctr, Billings, Mont. *Pos:* Dir, Yellowstone Art Ctr, Billings, Mont, 74- & 98-; mem, Eastern Mont Col Found Bd, 74-79 & 82-, pres, 78; mem selection comt, Downtown Redevelopment Bd, Billings, Mont, 86; mem, Downtown Coordr Coun, Billings, Mont, 86. *Teaching:* Instr design & art educ, Eastern Mont Col, 52-53. *Mem:* Art Mus Asn; Am Asn Mus; Mont Art Gallery Dirs Asn (adv exec bd, 78-, pres, 80-82); Mountain-Plains Mus Asn; Am Fedn Arts (bd dir, 87-97). *Mailing Add:* 1116 Eighth St W Billings MT 59101

FORBES, JOHN ALLISON
HISTORIAN, PAINTER
b Evansburg, Alta, Sept 19, 22. *Study:* Univ Alta, BEd, 48, MEd, 51; Univ London, associateship, 56; Univ Iowa, MA, 67. *Collection Arranged:* Bart Pragnell-Watercolours, Univ Art Gallery, Edmonton, 67; J B Taylor-Memorial (auth, catalog), Edmonton Art Gallery, 73. *Teaching:* prof emeritus, art & design, Univ Alberta. *Mem:* Royal Soc Arts, London; Univs Art Asn Can; Friends Univ Alberta Mus & Collections; Canadian Aviation Hist Soc. *Media:* Watercolor, Acrylics. *Res:* Western Canadian landscape painters; military art. *Publ:* Coauth, Mountain landscapes of J B Taylor, Can Alpine J, Vol 57, 74; auth, Douglas Haynes (exhib catalog), Glenbow Art Gallery, Calgary, 74; Robert Sinclair (exhib catalog), Aggregation Gallery, Toronto, 76. *Mailing Add:* 11523-77 Ave Edmonton AB T6G 0M2 Canada

FORD, HARRY X
EDUCATOR, ADMINISTRATOR
b Seymour, Ind, Jan 12, 21. *Study:* John Herron Art Inst, 40-41; Univ Calif, Los Angeles, AB, 50; Sacramento State Univ, MA, 53. *Hon Degrees:* Kans Art Inst, Hon Dr Fine Arts, 74. *Exhib:* Two Am Artists, America Haus, Stuttgart, Ger, 55. *Pos:* Chmn teacher educ dept, Calif Col Arts & Crafts, Oakland, 58-59, actg pres, 59-60, pres, 60-85; hon bd mem, Osaka Univ Arts, Japan, hon prof emer. *Teaching:* Instr art, Placer Union HS, Auburn, Calif, 50-53 & Stuttgart Am HS, Ger, 53-58; hon prof emer, Naniwa Col, Osaka. *Mem:* Nat Asn Schs Art & Design. *Media:* Oil

FORD, JOHN
PAINTER, SCULPTOR
b Washington, DC, Mar 2, 50. *Study:* Self-taught. *Work:* Oakland Mus Art; Prudential Insurance Co, Newark, NJ; Nashville Med Corp, Tenn; Sidney Lewis Collection, Richmond, Va. *Comn:* Trap sculpture, Kenmare Sq, NY. *Exhib:* Whitney Mus Am Art Biennial, 75; Aspects of Abstract, Crocker Art Mus, Sacramento, Calif, 79; Coastal Currents, Ctr Arts, Corpus Christi, Tex, 81; Sacramento Connection, Laguna Gloria Mus, Laguna Beach, Calif, 82; Jersey City Art Mus, NJ, 82; solo exhib, State Univ NY, Purchase, 82. *Teaching:* Lectr, Bakersfield State Univ, 77, Sacramento State Univ, 78 & C W Post Ctr, Long Island Univ, 83. *Awards:* Artists Fel, Nat Endowment Arts, 82. *Bibliog:* Thomas Albright (auth), Sleepers and spectacles, Art News, 9/79; Vivien Raynor (auth), article, New York Times, 82; Thomas Albright (auth), Art in the San Francisco Bay Area, Univ Calif Press, 85. *Media:* Acrylic, Oil; All Media. *Mailing Add:* 28 Overlook Terr Simsbury CT 06070

FORD, LISA COLLADO See Collado, Lisa

FORD, ROCHELLE
SCULPTOR
b New Kensington, Pa, Jul 18, 36. *Study:* Allegheny Col, Meadville, Pa, 54-56; Univ Pittsburgh Pa, BS, 56-58. *Work:* Abstract Sculpture, Ramsell Corp, Pleasantry, Calif; Claremont Sch, Gate to bldg entrance, Claremont, Calif; Endowed Chair, Mass Inst Technol, Cambridge, Mass; Multiple Tree Sculpture, City of Oakland, Calif; ITT, NY City. *Comn:* Congresswoman Barbara Lee, Oakland Calif; Dr & Mrs Bill Cosby, Santa Monica, Calif. *Exhib:* Group exhib, Long Beach Mus Art, Calif, 98, Triton Mus Art, Santa Clara, Calif, 99, San Jose Inst Contemp Art, San Jose, Calif, 2000, San Jose Mus Art, Calif, 2000, Iris Gerald Ctr for Visual Arts, Stanford, Calif, 2001, Can Col, Cupertino, Calif, 2002-2004; Solo exhib, Palo Alto Medical Found, Palo Alto, Calif, 94, 3COM Corp, Santa Clara, Calif, 99, Stanford Univ, Calif, 2001, Gallery Blu, Santa Clara, Calif, 2004. *Awards:* Nat Art Calendar Mag Award, Sallsbury, Md, 2000; Soho Int Art Award, NY, 2001; Distillery Literary J Cover Award, Lynchburg, Tenn, 2002. *Media:* Recycled Metal, Mixed Media. *Publ:* Sitting Pretty, Sunset Mag, 98; auth, Artistic Splendor, Fine Living TV, 2003; Garden Rooms, Better Homes & Gardens, 2003. *Dealer:* Lillian White Shamwari Gallery 4176 Piedmont Ave Okland CA 94611. *Mailing Add:* 1155 Waverley St Palo Alto CA 94301

FORD, WALTON
PAINTER, PRINTMAKER
b Larchmont, NY, 60. *Study:* RI Sch Design, Providence, BFA, 82, Europ Honors Prog, Rome, 82. *Work:* Univ Art Mus, Calif State Univ, Long Beach; Whitney Mus of Am Art, NY; New Britain Mus of Am Art, Conn; Spencer Mus of Art, Kans. *Comn:* Percent for Art, NY; murals, Jane Addams Vocational High Sch, Bronx, NY. *Exhib:*

Solo shows, Bess Cutler Gallery, NY, 90, 91, Contemp Arts Ctr, Cincinnati, Ohio, 93, Nicole Klagsbrun Gallery, NY, 93 & Va Beach Ctr for Arts, 93, Southeastern Ctr Contemp Arts, NC, 97, Aspen Art Mus, Colo, 98, Univ Art Mus, Calif State Univ, Long Beach, 99, Kohn-Turner Gallery, Los Angeles, Calif, 99, Paul Kasmin Gallery, NY, 2000 & Bowdoin Col Mus of Art, Maine, 2000; Marion Locks Gallery, Philadelphia, Pa, 92; Michael Klein Gallery, NY, 93; John Berggruen Gallery, San Francisco, 94; Ho Gallery, Hong Kong, 95; Next of Kin, List Visual Art Ctr, MIT, 95; Heroic Painting, Southeastern Ctr Contemp Art, Winston-Salem, NC, 96; Animal Tales: Contemp Bestiary and Animal Painting, Whitney Mus Am Art, Champion, Conn, 97; Wild Thing: Artists views of the Animal World, John Berggruen Gallery, San Francisco, 98; Summer Show: 1999, Paul Kasmin Gallery, NY, 99; The Great Drawing Show 1550 - 1999, Kohn Turner Gallery, Los Angeles, 99; Collectors Gallery XXXIII, The McNay Gallery, San Antonio, Tex, 99; Deja Vu: Reworking the Past, Katonah Mus of Art, NY, 2000; Brutal Beauty, Bowdoin Col Mus Art, Maine, 2000; Bitter Gulfs, Paul Kasmin Gallery, NY City, 2004. *Awards:* Grant, Mid-Atlantic Arts Found, 90; Nat Endowment Arts Fel, 91; John Simon Guggenheim Mem Found Fel, 92. *Bibliog:* Neville Wakefield (auth), Walton Ford, Elle Decor, 6-7/97; Raphael Rubinstein (auth), Walton Ford at Paul Kasmin, Art in Am, 12/97; Edward Gomez (auth), Past is present, Art & Antiques, 12/98; Kaylan Melik (auth), The Natural, Town & Country, 1/99; Meg Linton (auth), Inside the Watercolor World of Walton Ford, Juxtapoz, May/June 99; Faye Hirsch (auth), Working Proof, Art on Paper, Vol 3, No 5, May-June 99; Dodie Kazanjian (auth), Animal Magnetism, Vogue, July 99; Edith Newhall (auth), King of the Beasts, New York Mag, 5/5/2000; Steven Vincent (auth), Kasmin Shows Walton Ford, Art & Auction, 5/2000; Ashley East (auth), Brutal Beauty: Where the wild things are, The Bowdoin Orient, 9/29/2000; Philip Isaacson (auth), Ford's paintings embrace Audubon - but with a twist, Maine Sunday Telegram, 11/19/2000; Edward Liffingwell (auth), review, Art in Am, 1/2001; and many others. *Dealer:* Paul Kasmin Gallery 293 Tenth Ave New York NY 10001. *Mailing Add:* PO Box 238 Southfield MA 01259

FORD NUSSBAUM DRILL, SHEILA
ART DEALER, CONSULTANT
b Philadelphia, Pa, Mar 9, 40. *Study:* Univ Pa; New York Univ; New Sch Social Res, New York. *Pos:* Owner, Sheila Nussbaum Gallery, Millburn, NJ, currently; trustee, Montclair Art Mus. *Teaching:* Guest Lectr, Parsons Sch Design, NY. *Awards:* 1987 Woman of the Year, Bus & Prof Women Millburn-Short Hills, Inc; Bus Watch Award, Business J, NJ, 88. *Bibliog:* Patricia Malarcher (auth), New luster for Essex, NY Times, 11/7/82; Yolanda Cifarelli (auth), New Jersey gallery targets, Crafts Report, 1/85; Katherine Kaye (auth), Sheila Nussbaum: At Home with Art, Star Ledger, 11/17/89. *Mem:* Am Craft Coun. *Specialty:* Contemporary Art American crafts and art jewelry; young emerging artists. *Mailing Add:* Sheila Nussbaum Gallery 325 Ravine Dr South Orange NJ 07079

FOREMAN, LAURA
CONCEPTUAL ARTIST, SCULPTOR
b Los Angeles, Calif. *Study:* Parsons Sch Design, New York, ongoing studies since 1979. *Work:* Antwerp Mus, Belg; Storefront for Art & Archit, NY; Vermont Studio Colony, Vt. *Comn:* Time Coded Woman (art video), Channel 13 WNET-TV, NY, 78 & Brooklyn Acad Mus, 82; art video installation, New Sch Social Res, NY, 78; art holograms, Holographic Film Found, NY, 83; public art sculptor, 5 parks in New York City, JBR Found, 90. *Exhib:* Souyun Yi Gallery, NY, 89 & 91; Barbara Krakow Gallery, Boston, 91; Cityarts Show, Bronx Mus, 91-92; Kleinert Arts Ctr, Woodstock, 92; Wustum Mus, Wis, 93; Lookout Mountain Sculpture Park Maquette Traveling Exhib, Italy, Ger, Denmark & Bulgaria, 94-96. *Pos:* Consult, Nat Endowment Humanities, 70-75; judge, Television Emmy Awards, 79-81; visual arts juror, Ill Arts Coun, 85, Seattle Arts Comn, 95. *Teaching:* Instr conceptual art, performance art & creative thinking, New Sch Social Res, New York, 79-; performance art, Chapin Sch, New York, 92, conceptual art, 92 & 93, Metrop Mus Art, 94. *Awards:* Residency, Lookout Mountain Sculpture Park, Pa, 94; Contemp Artists Ctr, Mass, 96; Leighton Artists Colony, Banff, Can, 99. *Bibliog:* Georgia Dullea (auth), Artfully built nests await feathering, NY Times, 4/12/90; Leslie Garisto (auth), From Bauhaus to Birdhouse, Harper Collins, 2/92; Tucker J Coombe (auth), The Artists' Life, Artist's Mag, 4/92. *Mem:* Artists Talk on Art, NY. *Media:* Mixed Media. *Publ:* Confrontation, Literary Mag, fall 92; Santa Clara rev, Another Chicago Mag, fall 93; Pig Iron Anthology, spring 94; Collection of Foremans Work, Sundown Books, spring 96. *Mailing Add:* c/o Rich Keene 262 Mott St Apt 5 SR New York NY 10012-6108

FORESTA, MERRY A
CURATOR
b New York, NY, Aug 3, 50. *Study:* Cornell Univ, BA(eng lit), 71, MA(art hist), 79. *Pos:* Asst cur, painting & sculpture, Nat Mus Am Art, Smithsonian Inst, Washington, DC, 78-82, assoc cur, 83-88, cur, 88-93, sr cur, 94-; chmn, Smithsonian Comt Photog, 95-. *Teaching:* Various lectrs, sumposia & conferences, 84-96. *Awards:* Smithsonian Res Opportunity Fund Recipient, spring 85; Smithsonian Workshop Grant, 2/86; Smithsonian Scholarly Studies Res Grant, 2/86, renewed 2/87 & 2/92. *Mem:* Soc Photog Educ; Col Art Asn. *Publ:* Auth, Perpetual motif: The art of Man Ray, 12/88; Irving Penn: The Passion of Certainties, for Irving Penn: Master Images at the Smithsonian, Smithsonian Inst Press, 90; Between home and heaven: Contemporary American landscape photography, 5/92; coauth (with John Wood), Secrets of the dark chamber: The art of the American daguerreotype, 6/95; American photographs: The first century, 11/96. *Mailing Add:* c/o Nat Mus Am Art 8th & G St NW Washington DC 20560

FORESTER, RUSSELL
PAINTER, SCULPTOR
b Salmon, Idaho, May 21, 20. *Study:* Inst of Design, Chicago, 50. *Work:* Guggenheim Mus & McCrory Corp, NY; Mus Contemp Art, San Diego, Calif; Security Pac Bank & Cedars-Sinai Med Ctr, Los Angeles; Bank of Am, San Francisco; Zurich Insurance Co, Switz; Sheldon Mem Art Gallery, Lincoln, Nebr; Aerojet-Gen Corp, La Jolla, Calif; Flint Inst of Art, Mich. *Exhib:* Houston Mus Fine Art, Tex, 62; Nat Drawing Exhib, San Francisco Mus Art, 70; Santa Barbara Mus Art, Calif, 74; Phoenix Art Mus, Ariz, 75; Sheldon Mem Art Gallery, 76; San Diego Mus of Art, 76 & Drawing Show, 77 & 78; Everson Mus Art, Syracuse, NY, 77; New Acquisitions, Guggenheim Mus, 77; La Galerie, Paris, France, 77; La Jolla Mus of Contemp Art, 79, 81 & 83; Mod Art Ctr, Zurich, Switz, 88; Iracu 16, 30 Year Retrospective, Bergamont Station, Santa Monica, 97; The Atuenquem, LaJolla, Calif, 99. *Awards:* Fel, Am Inst Archit. *Bibliog:* Melinda Wortz (auth), articles, Art News, 9/79 & 4/83; Betty Brown (auth), article, Arts Mag, 1/83; Russell Forester: An Unauthorized Autobiography, Smart Art Press, Santa Monica, 97; numerous art catalogues. *Mem:* Grand chambellan, Chevaliers of the Tastevih; Artist in collection, life mem, Guggenheim Mus. *Media:* Mixed. *Mailing Add:* 2025 Soledad Ave La Jolla CA 92037

FORGE, ANDREW MURRAY
WRITER, PAINTER
b Hastingleigh, Kent, Eng, Nov 10, 23. *Study:* Camberwell Sch Art, London, 57-59, with William Coldstream & Kenneth Martin. *Work:* Tate Gallery, London; Arts Coun Gt Brit. *Exhib:* Retrospective, Bristol Mus, Eng, 64; Inst Contemp Arts, Boston, 75. *Pos:* Trustee, Tate Gallery, London, 64-72, Nat Gallery, London, 66-70 & Am Acad Rome, 82-88. *Teaching:* Lectr painting, Slade Sch, London, 50-64; prof painting, Yale Sch Art, 75-94. *Awards:* Guggenheim Fel, 79-80. *Media:* Oil. *Res:* 19th and 20th century art. *Publ:* Auth, Soutine, 65; Rauschenberg, Abrams, 69; Monet, Abrams, 83. *Mailing Add:* 22 Shinar Mountain Rd Washington Depot CT 06794

FORGEY, BENJAMIN FRANKLIN
ARCHITECT, CRITIC
b Ashland, Ky, July 31, 38. *Study:* Princeton Univ, BA, 60. *Pos:* Art critic, Wash Star, 67-81, art/archit critic, Wash Post, 81-. *Awards:* Fulbright fel, Japan, 1985-86. *Mem:* Int Art Critics Asn (Am sect). *Res:* 20th century art, architecture. *Publ:* Var articles in Art News Mag, 70-, Smithsonian Mag, 75-, Portfolio Mag, 78- & Aperture Mag, 79-. *Mailing Add:* Wash Post 1150 15th St NW Washington DC 20071-0002

FORMAN, ALICE
PAINTER
b New York, NY, June 1, 31. *Study:* Cornell Univ, with Kenneth Evett & Norman Daly, BA; Art Students League, with Morris Kantor. *Exhib:* Whitney Mus Am Art, 60; White Mus Art, Cornell Univ, 61; Phoenix Gallery, NY, 66, 68, 71, 74 & 75; Marist Col, 68 & 71; Butler Inst Exhib, 72; Kornblee Gallery, 77 & 79; Am Still Life, Contemp Arts Mus, Houston, 83; and others. *Teaching:* Lectr, Marist Col, 77; vis asst prof painting & drawing, Vassar Col, 80-81. *Awards:* Nat Student Asn Regional Awards; Daniel Schnackenberg Merit Scholar, Art Students League. *Media:* Oil. *Dealer:* Kornblee Gallery 20 W 57th St New York NY 10019. *Mailing Add:* 130 E 63rd St New York NY 10021

FORMAN, KENNETH WARNER
PAINTER
b Landour, India, June 5, 25; US citizen. *Study:* Wittenberg Col, AB, BFA; Ohio State Univ, MA. *Work:* Wittenberg Col, Springfield, Ohio; Univ RI, Kingston; Conn Com on the Arts; Univ Zagazig, Cairo, Egypt; Off of the Treas, State Conn; Moldex Corp, Putnam, Chimerix Corp, Glastonbury, Conn. *Exhib:* Nat Drawing Exhib, Ball State Teachers Col, Muncie, Ind, 65; 12th Biennial Exhib Contemp Am Prints, Brooklyn Mus, 65; 23rd Int Exhib Soc Printmakers, US Nat Mus, 66; Monotypes Today IV, Artworks Gallery, Hartford, Conn, 78; A Kademia Sztuk Piekynch, Krakow, Poland, 87; Legislative Off Bldg, State Conn, Hartford; Bradley Int Airport, Conn Comn Arts, 89; Four Decades (Retrospective), William Benton Mus Art, Univ Conn, Storrs, 92; Monotypes Today, Housatonic Mus Art, 93. *Teaching:* Instr media & techniques, painting, Am Archit & art hist, Univ Conn, 57-, prof art, 68-89, (retired). *Awards:* First Painting Award, Mystic Art Asn, Conn, 63; Hartford Art Festival Purchase Award, Hartford CofC, 72; Third Ann Prints Exhib Award, Shippee Gallery, NY, 86. *Media:* Oil, Watercolor. *Res:* Victorian architecture in England and New England; traditional media with synthetic media in painting. *Publ:* Auth, Understanding in the Arts, 59 & illusr, 61, Fine Arts Mag; illusr, spec ed, Penny Paper, 64; auth, Salvador Dali's moustache, Floating Opera, 67; Connecticut Architecture During the Growth of the Nation, William Benton Mus of Art, Univ Conn, 76

FORMICOLA, JOHN JOSEPH
PAINTER, EDUCATOR
b Philadelphia, Pa, Dec 27, 41. *Study:* Fleischer Art Mem, 56-59; Pa Acad Fine Arts, cert(Cresson Award, Schiedt Award), 64. *Work:* Philadelphia Mus Art; Cleveland Mus Art, Ohio; Miami Mus Mod Art, Fla; Mus Art, Carnegie Inst, Pittsburgh; Prudential Insurance Co Am; Exxon Corp; Mus Philadelphia Civic Ctr; Noyes Mus, NJ. *Comn:* Brandywine Graphic Workshop, Philadelphia, 82. *Exhib:* Del Art Mus, Wilmington, 78; Contemp Drawings, Philadelphia Mus Art & Pa Acad Fine Arts, 78; solo exhibs, Frank Marino Gallery, NY, 80 & Marian Locks Gallery, Philadelphia, 80 & 84; 20th Anniversary Del Biennial Exhib, Univ Del, Newark, 82; Decades of Design, Baltimore, 88; Images and Objects, Boston, 90. *Pos:* Owner & dir, Gallery Pane Vino, 65-68; dir, Marian Locks Gallery, Philadelphia, 68-73; designer & consult, Danhart-Heim Architects, 76-77; partnr-dir, Chew and Formicola Gallery, 83-. *Teaching:* Instr design, Drexel Univ, Philadelphia, 70-; instr painting, Cleveland Inst Art, Ohio, 79-80. *Awards:* First Hallgarten Award, Nat Acad Design, 65. *Bibliog:*

Frank Goodyear & Anne Percy (auth), Pa Academy Fine Arts, Contemp Drawing, 78; Patterson Sims (auth), The 20 Univ Del Biennial Exhib Introd 82. *Media:* Oil, Fabric. *Publ:* Images, Arts Mag, 69; John Canada (auth), New York Times, 70; Lenore Malen (auth), Arts Mag, 9/80; Michael Stolback (auth), Arts Mag, 10/80. *Dealer:* Chew and Formicola Gallery, Philadelphia, PA. *Mailing Add:* 725 Carpenter St Philadelphia PA 19147-3933

FORNAS, LEANDER
PRINTMAKER, INSTRUCTOR
b Gardner, Mass, June 18, 1925. *Study:* Pratt Inst, cert, 50; Kunstgewerbeschule, Zurich, 51; Ateneum, Helsinki, 51-53; Univ Mass, MFA, 73 & currently, Doctorate candidate, 90. *Work:* Mus Mod Art, NY; Ateneum, Helsinki; Libr Cong; Rockefeller Collection; NY Pub Libr. *Comn:* Developed new glass engraving methods, Steuben Glass, NY, 55; designed & instituted graphics facilities, Pratt Inst, NY, 58, Fine Arts Ctr, Univ RI, 66 & Holyoke Community Col, 72-75; graphic indust illus, portrait comns & misc design, Finland, 59-65. *Exhib:* One-man shows, New Talent, Mus Mod Art, 55 & Sao Paulo Biennial Prints, 59; Curator's Choice, Print Club, Philadelphia, 56; Printmakers Soc Finland Traveling Exhib, US, Europe & Far East, 59-66. *Pos:* Dir, Design & Graphics Studio, Helsinki, 58-66; chmn art dept, Holyoke Community Col, 70-74. *Teaching:* Instr printmaking & drawing, Holyoke Community Col, 70-96. *Mem:* Printmakers Soc Finland (bd dir, 59-61); Lit Soc Finland; Finno-Urgarian Soc Finland. *Media:* All Media. *Res:* Multicultural: North Eurasians (Siberia), Subarctic Cree, (Canada). *Mailing Add:* Moores Cor Leverett MA 01054

FORNELLI, JOSEPH
SCULPTOR, PAINTER
b Chicago, Ill, May 21, 43. *Study:* Art Inst, Chicago. *Work:* Cornell Univ, Ithaca, NY; Columbia Mus, SC; Nat Vietnam Vets Art Mus, Chicago; Park Ridge Pub Libr, Ill; Alice Forrester Miniatures Collection, Leigh Yawkey Woodson Mus, Wausau, Wis. *Comn:* Dell Publ for Pres Nixon, NY, 74; Encycl Britannica for Pope Paul VI, Chicago, 74; Columbus Hosp, Chicago, 76; Ducks Unlimited, Memphis, Tenn, 89; US Hist, Richmond, VA, 91; Nat Rifle Asn, 93 & 94. *Exhib:* LBJ Mus, Austin, Tex, 83; Lincoln Ctr, Cork Gallery, NY, 84; Am Mus Fly Fishing, Manchester, Vt, 91; Southeastern Wildlife Expos, Charleston, SC, 92; Nat Vietnam Vets Art Mus, Chicago, 96; and others. *Pos:* Painter & sculptor, Richard Rush Studio, Chicago, 73-74; art dir, Monastery Hill Bindery, Chicago, 74-77; design coordr, Ducks Unlimited, Chicago, 79-83; bd dir, Chicago Munic Art League, 79-92; pres, Vietnam Veterans Arts Group, 81-, Fornelli Design Studio, 89-, Nat Vietnam Vets Art Mus, Chicago, 96-. *Awards:* Gold Medal, Chicago Munic Art League, 79; Award of Merit, Soc Animal Artists Denver Mus, 82; Blue Ribbon, Nat Wildlife Fedn, 83. *Bibliog:* Ann Keegan (auth), Art snares wild spirt, The Treasures of Vietnam, Chicago Tribune, 5/87; Art reflects Vietnam War, NY Times, 10/81; Joan Johnson (producer), Good Morning America, ABC TV, 10/81; Niki Barrie (auth), Tuesday's child, Wildlife Art News, 9/93. *Mem:* Chicago Munic Art League; Chicago Artists Guild; assoc Am Watercolor Soc; Oil Painters Am; Vietnam Vet Arts Group. *Media:* Watercolor, Oil; Bronze, Stone. *Publ:* Illusr, Moving Along with Charlie Dickey, Charles Dickey, Winchester Press, 85; Fly Fishingest Gentleman, Keith Russel, Winchester Press, 86; The Wildfowler's Quest, George Reiger, Lyons Burford, 89; Steel Barbs, Wild Waters, Jerry Gibbs, Outdoor Life Books, 90; A Rough Shooting Dog, Charles Fergus, Lyons & Burford, 91. *Mailing Add:* c/o Fornelli Studio 1017 S Prospect Park Ridge IL 60068-4728

FORREST, CHRISTOPHER PATRICK
PRINTMAKER, PAINTER
b Trenton, NJ, Oct 2, 46. *Study:* Va Polytechnic Inst, BS, 68; NC State Univ, MS, 74. *Work:* Nat Acad Sci, Washington, DC; NJ State Mus, Trenton; Ferrum Col, Va; Metro-Goldwyn Mayer, Los Angeles; Bausch & Lomb, Rochester, NY. *Exhib:* Easton Waterfowl Festival, Md, 96; Soc Animal Artists Exhib, Acad Nat Sci, Philadelphia; one-man shows, Golden Door, New Hope, Pa, Town Plaza, Brea, Calif, & Chabot Galleries, Campbell, Calif; Soc Animal Artists Ann, Denver Mus Nat Hist; Nat Wildlife Fedn Wildlife in Art Show, Vienna, Va; Sterling Fine Arts Gallery, Laguna Beach, Calif; Soc Am Artists Exhib, Cleveland Mus Natural Hist; Hang Ups, Orange, Calif. *Pos:* Gen production mgr, Evergreen Publ Inc, 80-81. *Bibliog:* Cathy Lyons Colletti (auth), All-enveloping moods, Southwest Art Mag; article, The Artist-Chris Forrest, Prints Mag; Judy Hughes (auth), Lasting impressions lithography, Wildlife Art News. *Mem:* Soc Animal Artists; Buzzard Coun Am. *Media:* Lithography, Intaglio; Acrylic, Oil. *Publ:* Duck Unltd Mag, 78, Readers Digest, 82, Outdoors, 83, & Conservationist Mag, 84. *Dealer:* Hang Ups 1319 W Katella Ave Orange CA 92667; Primrose Press PO Box 302 New Hope PA 18938. *Mailing Add:* 6 Cranberry Ln Vincentown NJ 08088

FORRESTALL, THOMAS DE VANY
SCULPTOR, PAINTER
b Middleton, NS, Mar 11, 36. *Study:* Mt Allison Univ, 54-58, Hon DFA; Can Coun grant to travel & study in Europe, 58-59, sculpture grant, 67; King's Col, Hon Dr Civil Law. *Work:* Can Coun; Winnipeg Art Gallery; Art Gallery Windsor; Confederation Mem Gallery; Nat Gallery, Hungary; and others. *Comn:* Kennedy & Churchill Mem, Prov NB, 64; steel sculpture, Atlantic Pavilion, Expo 67; welded relief mural, Centennial Bldg Fredericton, 68; two large welded steel sculptures, Can Govt, Fed Bldg, Antigonish, NS, 70; mural abstract for playhouse, Beaverbrook Can Found, Fredericton, 72. *Exhib:* One-man shows, Montreal Mus Fine Arts, 72, Nat Mus Art, Bulgaria, 80, Nat Gallery Art, Romania, 81, Nat Mus Art, Transylvania, Nat Mus Art, Hungary, 81 & Bayard Gallery, NY, 81; Can Cult Centre, Rome, Italy, 83; Habema Centre Tel Aviv, 84; Nat Mus Art Prague, 85; Nova Scotia Pavilion, Expo '86 Vancouver; and others. *Pos:* Asst cur, Beaverbrook Art Gallery, 59-60. *Awards:* Can Coun Lectr Tour Grants, 77-79; Queen's Jubilee Medal, 78; Can 125 Medal, Order Can, 86. *Bibliog:* P Murphy (auth), Shaped paintings, article, Art Mag, 78. *Mem:* Royal Can Acad Arts; St Vincent De Paul Soc; Order Can. *Media:* Tempera; Steel, Iron. *Publ:* Coauth, Shapes, 72; Returning the Favor Dr N Webb, Lancelot Press. *Mailing Add:* c/o Forrestall Fine Arts Ltd 3 Albert St Dartmouth NS B2Y 3M1 Canada

FORRESTER, CHARLES HOWARD
SCULPTOR
b Jersey City, NJ, Sept 30, 28. *Study:* Univ Wash, BFA, 58; Univ Ore, MFA, 60. *Work:* Bundy Art Gallery, Waitsfield, Vt; Shakespeare Mem Theatre, Ashland, Ore; Medford Pub Parks, Ore; Western Ky Univ, Bowling Green. *Comn:* Family Group, Bowling Green Hosp, Ky; sculpture (wood), Northern Telecom Bldg, Nashville, Tenn, 85; sculpture (wood), Dr Iwrin Eskind, 92; sculpture (cast aluminum), Nelson Metals Products Corp, Glasgow, Ky, 94; Lilly Corp, Bowling Green, Ky, 96. *Exhib:* The Nude, Lexington Art League, 88; Sculpture Indoors and Out, Lexington Art League, 88; Water Tower Ann, Louisville, Ky, 89; CofC Gallery Art, Bowling Green, Ky, 93; Jewish Community Ctr Exhib, Nashville, Tenn, 94; and others. *Teaching:* Lectr sculpture, Salford Tech Col, Eng, 63-65; prof sculpture, Western Ky Univ, Bowling Green, 65-92. *Awards:* Citizens Nat Bank Purchase Award, Capitol Arts Ctr, Bowling Green, Ky, 81. *Bibliog:* Anon (auth), Some Younger Northwest Sculptors, NW Rev, 61; M Harold (ed), Prize-Winning Sculptures, Allied Publ Inc, 67. *Mem:* Southern Asn of Sculptors (vpres, 66-70). *Media:* Cast Metal, Wood. *Mailing Add:* 1623 Franklin Ave Nashville TN 37206-2521

FORRESTER, PATRICIA TOBACCO
PAINTER, PRINTMAKER
b Northampton, Mass, Sept 17, 40. *Study:* Yale Summer Sch Music & Art, 61; Smith Col, BA, 62; Yale Univ Sch Art, BFA, 63, MFA, 65. *Work:* Brooklyn Mus; San Antonio Mus Art; Achenbach Found, Legion Hon; Oakland Mus; Mem Art Gallery, Univ Rochester; Corcoran Gallery Art & Nat Mus Women Arts, Washington, DC; Art Inst Chgo; Nat Mus Am Art; and others. *Comn:* Duke Univ Hosp. *Exhib:* Solo exhibs, San Francisco Mus Art, 68, MH De Young Mem Mus, 77, Fischbach Gallery, NY, 85, 87 & 88, Fendrick Gallery, Washington, 86, Reynolds/Minor Gallery, Richmond, Va, 87, Steven Scott Gallery, Baltimore, Md, 92 & 97, Addison/Ripley Gallery, Washington, 93 & 96, Gerald Peters Gallery, Santa Fe, NMex, 94 & 97, Braunstein/Quay Gallery, San Francisco, 94 & 98 & Salander O'Reilly Galleries, NY, 96; Ten Plus Ten Plus Ten Washington Painters, Corcoran Gallery, 82; Am Realism, Davidson Collection, Pa Acad Fine Arts, 83; Washington Watercolor, Corcoran Gallery, 84; Fruits, Flowers and Vegetables; The Contemp Still Life, Kavesh Gallery, Ketchum, Idaho, 93; Am Masters of Watercolor, Southern Alleghenies Mus Art, Loretto, Pa, 94; Prize Winners 171st Ann Exhib, Nat Acad Design, NY, 96; Salander-O'Reilly Galleries, NY, 96; Addison-Ripley Gallery, Washington, 96. *Teaching:* Asst prof printmaking, Calif Col Arts & Crafts, 72-81; guest artist painting, Kent State Univ, 81, Art Inst Chicago, 82, New Orleans Acad Fine Art, 84. *Awards:* Guggenheim Fel Printmaking, 67; Yaddo Fel, 79 & 81; MacDowell Colony Fel, 80; and others. *Bibliog:* Robert Merritt (auth), Watercolor: in a new light, Times-Dispatch, 11/21/87; Seasons and Days of Trees, Christian Sci Monitor, 4/18/90; Michael Welzenbach (auth), Patricia Tobacco Forrester at Fendrick, Washington Post, 2/17/90. *Mem:* Nat Acad. *Media:* Watercolor. *Dealer:* Salander-O'Reilly 20 E 79th St New York NY 10021; Addison-Ripley 9 Hillyer Ct NW Washington DC 20008. *Mailing Add:* Addison Ripley Fine Art 1670 Wisconsin Ave NW Washington DC 20007

FORSMAN, CHUCK (CHARLES) STANLEY
PAINTER, EDUCATOR
b Nampa, Idaho, May 5, 1944. *Study:* Univ Calif, Davis, study with Wayne Theibaud & William Wiley, BA, 67, MFA, 71; Skowhegan Sch Painting & Sculpture, Maine, 70. *Work:* Phoenix Art Mus, Ariz; Metrop Mus Art, NY; Yellowstone Art Mus, Billings, Mont; Wichita Art Mus; Denver Art Mus; and others. *Exhib:* Whitney Mus Am Art, Stamford, Conn, 81; Hudson River Mus, Yonkers, NY, 85; one-man show, Yellowstone Art Mus, Billings, Mont, 83, 95, Boulder Ctr Visual Arts, Colo, 83, Denver Art Mus, Colo, 85, Tucson Mus Art, 85, Paine Art Ctr, Oshkosh, Wis, 86, Rahr-W Mus, Manitowok, Wis, 86, Univ Colo Galleries, Boulder, 90, Mint Mus, Charlotte, NC, 91, St Johns Col, Santa Fe, NMex, 91, Nat Acad Sci, Washington, 91, Univ NV Las Vegas, 94, Nev Mus Art, 94, Art Mus S Tex, Corpus Christie, 95, Cheney Cowles Mus Art, Spokane, Wash, 95, Wichita Ctr Arts, Kans, 95, William King Regional Art Ctr, Abingdon, Va, 97 & Kenyon Col, Ohio, 97, Robischon Gallery, Denver, Colo, 2000,2004, 2005: Gerald Peters Gallery, Santa Fe, NMex, 1999, 2002; Am Mus Natural Hist, NY, 85; Va Mus Fine Arts, Richmond, 90; and others. *Teaching:* Asst painting & sculpture, Univ Calif, Davis, 70-71; prof fine arts, Univ Colo, Boulder, 71-. *Awards:* Nat Endowment Arts Grant, 79, 85 & 95; Fac Fel, Univ Colo, Boulder, 79 & 88; Mus Purchase, Am Acad Arts & Lett, 79; Covisions Recognition Award, Colo Coun Arts, 95; W Publishing, Art and the Law, Purchase Award, 96; Univ Colo Fac Fel, 2002. *Bibliog:* Gerrit Henry (auth), Art News, 11/83; Carter Radcliffe (auth), Art Int; Richard Martin (auth), articles, Arts Mag. *Media:* Oil on Masonite. *Publ:* auth, Arrested Rivers, Univ Press Colo, 94. *Dealer:* Robischon Gallery 1740 Wazee Denver CO 80202; Gerald Peters Gallery 1011 Paseo Del Peralta Santa Fe NM 07501. *Mailing Add:* 511 Pleasant St Boulder CO 80302

FORSYTH, ILENE H(AERING)
EDUCATOR, HISTORIAN
b Detroit, Mich, Aug 21, 28. *Study:* Univ Mich, AB, 50; Columbia Univ, AM, 55, PhD, 60. *Teaching:* Lectr, Barnard Col, 56-58; instr, Columbia Univ, 59-61; asst prof, Univ Mich, Ann Arbor, 61-68, assoc prof, 68-74, prof, 74-84, Arthur F Thurnau prof emerita, 84-; vis prof hist art, Harvard Univ, 80; Andrew W Mellon prof, Univ Pittsburgh, 81; vis prof hist art, Univ Calif, Berkeley, 96. *Awards:* Inst Advan Study Fel, 77; Warner G Rice Humanities Award, 91; Kress Prof, Ctr Advan Study Visual Arts, Nat Gallery Art, Washington, DC, 98-99. *Mem:* Int Ctr Medieval Art (dir, 70,

vpres, 81-85); Acad Arts, Sci & Belles Lett, Dijon; Midwest Hist Soc (mem bd dir, 79-81; Col Art Asn (mem bd dir, 80-84, mem exec comt, 82-84); Medieval Acad Am (mem bd adv, 85-). *Res:* Medieval art, especially Romanesque sculpture. *Publ:* Auth, Magi and majesty: Romanesque sculpture and liturgical drama, Col Art Asn Bulletin, 68; Throne of Wisdom, Princeton Univ Press, 72; Ganymede capital at Vezelay, Gesta, 76; Cockfighting in Burgundian Romanesque sculpture, Speculum, 78; The Uses of Art: Medieval Metaphor in the Michigan Law Quadrangle, Univ Mich Press, 93. *Mailing Add:* 5 Geddes Heights Ann Arbor MI 48104

FORSYTHE, DONALD JOHN
PRINTMAKER, EDUCATOR
b Pittsburgh, Pa, July 2, 55. *Study:* Ind Univ Pa, BS, 77; Rochester Inst Technol, MFA, 79. *Work:* Bank of NY, Wilmington, Del; Franklin Mint, Philadelphia, Pa; Graham Ctr Mus, Wheaton, Ill; Philadelphia Savings Fund Soc, Philadelphia, Pa; Rochester Inst Technol, NY; Atlantic Richfield Corp, Phila, Pa; Ballinglen Archive, Ballinglen Arts Found, Ballycastle, County Mayo, Ireland; Am Bible Soc. *Comn:* 6 choir windows, stained glass, Cathedral St Stephen, Harrisburg, Pa; 8 sanctuary windows, Mission Hills Baptist Church, Littleton, Colo. *Exhib:* La Grange National VI, CUAA Gallery, Ga, 81; 6th NC Printing & Drawing Society Exhib, Charlotte, NC, 82; Tactile Vision, William Penn Mus, Harrisburg, Pa, 84; New Drawings, Dolan/Maxwell Gallery, Philadelphia, Pa, 85; Visions of the World, Shoemaker Mus, Juniata, Pa, 86; 44th Ann Juried Exhib, Woodmere Art Mus, Philadelphia, 86; Sacred Arts IX, Graham Ctr Mus, Wheaton, Ill, 87; Christian Imagery in Contemp Art, Albany Inst Art, NY, 88; New Am Talent, Laquana Gloria Art Mus, Austin, Tx, 89; Perspectives from Pennsylvania, Carnegie Mellon Univ Mus, Pittsburgh, Pa; Art of the State, William Penn Mus, Harrisburg, Pa; Anno Domini: Jesus Through the Centuries, Provincial Mus Alberta, Edmonton, Can, 2000; One-man Show, Burning Lights, monotype & collage, Union Univ, Jackson, Tenn, 2002, Time Uncertain Box Constructions 1986-2003, Penn Col Gallery, Pa Col Tech, Williamsport, 2003; The Next Generation Contemp Expressions of Faith, Mus Biblical Art, NYC, 2005. *Pos:* Dir, Louise Aughinbaugh Art Gallery, Messiah Col, 85-88 & 92-2000; pres, Christians Visual Art, 91-93. *Teaching:* Distinguished prof art, Messiah Col, Grantham, Pa, 81-. *Awards:* Best of show, Sacred Arts XII, Graham Ctr Mus; Hon Mention, New Am Talent, Tex Fine Arts Asn, 89; Artworks Award, Art of the State, Pa Juried Mus Exhib, Univ Pa Mus; First Prize, sculpture, 1995 & Second Prize, works on paper, 1999, Art of the State, Pa, Wm Penn Mus, Harrisburg. *Bibliog:* John Skillen (auth), The Reconstructive Art of Donald Forsythe, IMAGE: a journal of arts & religion, No 18, 1998; Ena Heller, Marcus Burke (auths), The Word as Art: Contemporary Renderings, 2000; Marcus Burke (auth), Why Art Needs Religion, Why Religion Needs the Arts, pp 154-157, 2004; Ena Giurescu (auth), Reluctant Partners: Art and Religion in Dialogue, 2004; Wayne Roosa (auth), The Next Generation: Contemporary Expressions of Faith, Eerdmans Pub, 2005. *Mem:* Christians in the Visual Arts (mem bd, 85-); Int Soc Christian Artists; Southern Graphics Coun; College Art Assoc. *Media:* Mixed Media, Collage. *Mailing Add:* Messiah College One College Ave Box 3004 Grantham PA 17027

FORT-BRESCIA, BERNARDO M
ARCHITECT
b Lima, Peru, Nov 19, 51. *Study:* Princeton Univ, BA(archit), 73; Harvard Univ, March, 75. *Comn:* Babylon, Pacific Developers, Miami, Fla, 77; Atlantis, Stonecrest Development, Miami, Fla, 78; The Palace, Helmsley Enterprises, Miami, Fla, 78; Imperial at Brickell, Harlon Group, Miami, Fla, 79; Overseas Tower, Overseas Finance Corp, Miami, Fla, 80. *Exhib:* New Americans, Inst Archit & Urban Studies, Rome, Italy, 79; Work of Arquitectonica, Cooper-Hewitt Mus, NY, 79, Pa State Univ, 80 & Univ Va, 81; and others. *Pos:* Principal, Arquitectonica, Coral Gables, Fla, 77-. *Teaching:* Vis prof archit, Univ Miami, Coral Gables, Fla, 75-77. *Awards:* Citation, Progressive Archit Ann Design Awards, 78 & 80. *Bibliog:* Articles, Wall St J, 7/7/83, Archit Rec, 7/83, Global Archit Document 7, 8/83 & others. *Mem:* Am Inst Architects; Architectural Club of Miami (pres, 78-80). *Mailing Add:* 550 Brickell Ave Suite 300 Miami FL 33131

FORTSON, BEN J
PATRON
Pos: Pres, Fortson Oil Co; vpres, trustee, Kimbell Art Found & Mus, 1975-; trustee emeritus, Tex Christian Univ. *Mailing Add:* Fortson Oil Co Ste 3301 301 Commerce St Fort Worth TX 76102

FORTSON, KAY KIMBELL CARTER
PATRON, ADMINISTRATOR
Study: Univ Tex, BA, 1956. *Pos:* pres, chmn bd trustees, Kimbell Art Found & Mus, 1975-; trustee, Tex Christian Univ; hon trustee, Modern Art Mus, Fort Worth, Tex. *Mailing Add:* Kimbell Art Found Ste 2240 301 Commerce St Fort Worth TX 76102

FORTUNATO , NANCY
PAINTER, ILLUSTRATOR
b Highland Park, Ill, Nov 29, 41. *Study:* Studied with Ed Betts, 80, Dong Kingman, 85; Zhejiang Inst Fine Arts, with Lu Yanshao, Hangzhou, China, 84. *Hon Degrees:* AAPL, elected a Fellow; Royal Coatimundi, Ariz Watercolor Assoc; Purple Sage, Texas Watercolor Soc. *Work:* Leigh Yawkey Woodson Art Mus, Wausau, Wis; Int Crane Found Mus, Baraboo, Wis; People of the Century Goldblatt Collection, Chicago; also pvt collections of Reverend Billy Graham & Winston Lord. *Comn:* People of the Century Goldblatt Found. *Exhib:* Impressions in watercolor, Elliott Mus, Stuart, Fla, 89; 19th Ann Watercolor Exhib, W Riverside Art Mus, Calif, 89; Soc Animal Artists, Cleveland Mus Nat Hist, Ohio, 91; Soc Animal Artists, Roger Tory Peterson Inst, Jamestown, NY, 92; 1st Naval Air Mus Show, Pensacola, Fla, 93-94; and others. *Pos:* Pres emeritus, Midwest Watercolor Soc, 97-99; pres, Int Soc Marine Painters, 2002-. *Teaching:* Instr beginning & advanced watercolor, Dist 211 & 214, Palatine & Arlington Heights, Ill, 75-; instr advanced watercolor Elgin Community Col, nat workshops. *Awards:* M Grunbacher Award, Int Soc Artists, 80; Windsor & Newton Award, Cuyahoga 4 State Nat, 85; Ill State Fair, Prof Exhib, First Place, 91; 12th Ann Miniature Exhib Award, Art Gallery Fells Point, Md, 95; Award of Excellence Tex Watercolor Soc, 99; Merchandise Award 60th Ann Exhib Northwest Waterocolor Soc, 2000; merit, 26th Ann Nat Exhib of trans Watercolors at Midwest Watercolor Exhib, Kanakee, IL, 2002; merit, 27th Nat Exhib Midwest Watercolor Society, West Bend, WI, 2003. *Bibliog:* James Auer (auth), Mountaintop gave artist new outlook on her art, Milwaukee J, 87; Pam & Ed Menaker (coauths), She doesn't paint inside the lines, N Shore Mag, 88; Mark Mandernach (auth), Brush with greatness, Chicago Tribune, 96. *Mem:* Midwest Watercolor Soc (bd mem, 89-, vpres 95-97); Am Soc Marine Artists; Catharine Lorillard Wolfe Art Club; Whiskey Painters Am; Soc Animal Artists; US Coast Guard Artist; fel Am Artists Prof League; Acad Artists Am. *Media:* Watercolor; Ink. *Collection:* Zhejiang Academy of Fine Arts, China; Leigh Yawkey Woodson Art Mus, WI; Rev Billy Graham; Winston Lord; The Loon Foundation, Naval Air Mus. *Publ:* Cover illusr, Birdwatcher's Digest, 84, 86 & 87; US Lighthouse Log Mag, Lighthouse Soc, 85-95; Wildbirds, Japan, 94; cover illusr, The US & Northeast Asia Nelson Hall, 93; auth, Capture Movement in Your Paintings, Quarto Publ, 96; The Artistic Touch III, 99; Texas 50th Anniversary Album, 99. *Dealer:* Nippersink Gallery Richmond IL; Wildes Art Gallery Tomah WI & Camden ME. *Mailing Add:* 249 N Marion St Palatine IL 60074

FOSTER, APRIL
PRINTMAKER, EDUCATOR
b Berwyn, Ill, Oct 9, 47. *Study:* Univ Ill, Champaign-Urbana, BFA, 70, MA(art educ; fel), 71; Tyler Sch Art, Temple Univ, MFA(printmaking; fel), 73. *Work:* Cincinnati Art Mus, Ohio; Boston Mus Fine Art, Mass; Univ Mich Art Mus; Dayton Art Inst, Ohio; Miami Univ Art Mus. *Exhib:* Prints & Drawings, Thomas More Col, 88; Invitational Exhib, Closson's Gallery, 90, Col Mt St Joseph, 90; solo exhib, Xavier Univ, 94, Sabbatical exhib, Art Acad, Cincinnati, Ohio, 1/2000; sabbatical exhib, Art Acad Cincinnati, Ohio, 2000. *Teaching:* Asst printmaking, Temple Univ, 71-72, instr printmaking, summer 73; prof printmaking & drawing, Art Acad Cincinnati, 73-. *Awards:* Award for Excellence in Teaching, Greater Cincinnati Consortium of Cols & Univs, 89. *Mem:* Col Art Asn; Mid-Am Print Coun; Southern Graphics Coun. *Media:* Lithography, Egg Tempera. *Dealer:* Closson's Gallery Cincinnati OH. *Mailing Add:* Art Acad Cincinnati Dept Fine Art 1125 St Gregory St Cincinnati OH 45202-1799

FOSTER, MAELEE THOMSON
EDUCATOR, PRINTMAKER, COLLAGE ARTIST, WRITER
b Milford, Conn, Sept 19, 32. *Study:* Univ Bridgeport, BS(art educ), 64; Tyler Sch Art, Temple Univ, MFA, 69. *Work:* Collagraphic series includ, Early philosphical works, Spanish Series, Maya Myth Series & Time Cycle Glyph Series. *Comn:* Collagraphs, Honeywell Int, Philadelphia, Pa, 69-74; cover & logo, Vupak Control System, Honeywell Int, Philadelphia, Pa; collage & cover designs, Technical Publ Co, Chicago, Ill, 71-72. *Exhib:* Stonehenge Series, Bi-Ann Nat Photog Exhib, Southwestern La Univ, 84; solo exhibs, Crime in Alachua Co, Copier Print Collages, Gainesville City Hall, Gainesville Sun, Col Law, Univ Fla, 85 & 85; Traveling Exhib, Italy, Int Soc of Copier Artists under auspices of Post Machina Group & Am Consulate in Florence, 86; Works-A Visual Arts Celebration, Iscagraphics Exhib, Edmonton, Alta, Can, 88; Past & Present Works: Collagraphs and Photographs, 2004; AIA Gallery, Tampa, Fla, 2005. *Collection Arranged:* State Fla, State Senate Bldg, Tallahassee; Champion Paper Co, Stamford, Conn; Barnett Bank, Fla Artists Collection, Jacksonville; Trans-Co Company Public, Houston, Tex; Housatonic Community Col, Bridgeport, Conn; E.F. Hutton & Co; Fla Hosp Asn; Xerox Corp; Delta Air Lines. *Pos:* Art dir, State Conn, Long Lane Sch, 64-67; distinguished chmn, Archit Preserv, 99-2003. *Teaching:* Instr drawing & design, Univ Bridgeport, Conn, 69-71; prof communications/design/prehist, Univ Fla, Col Archit, Gainesville, 71-92; distinguished prof, Asn Collegiate Sch Archit, 2000; prof Emer, Sch Archit, Univ Fla, 2000-. *Awards:* First Prize, Barnum Arts Festival, Mus Art, Sci & Indust, Bridgeport, Conn, 62, 66, 67, 68 & 71; Am Inst Architects Educ Honors, 89 & 95; Graham Found Grant, Advanced Studies Fine Arts, 96. *Bibliog:* Creative Spatial Exploration: Process Drawing, Representation J Graphic Educ, Vol 3, No 3, 86; Diane Greer (auth), A link to the profession, Fla Architect, 7-8/89; Tom Porter (auth), Archispeak, Sacred Space, Spon Publ, London & NY, 2004. *Mem:* Archeol Inst Am; New Eng Antiquities Res Asn. *Media:* Collage, Collagraph. *Res:* On site investigation of the prehistoric sites of Mesoamerica, South America, North America and Megalithic sites of Europe in preparation for text Prehistoric Placemaking; Middle East, Asia. *Interests:* Travel related to prehistoric research; film and cooking. *Publ:* auth, Creative Spatial Exploration: Process Drawing, Representation, J Graphic Educ, Vol 3, No 3, 86; Experiencing a Creative High, J Creative Behavior, Vol 26, No 1, 92; Megalithic Sites Reexamined as Spatial Systems, Power of Place, 91; Diagramming of the Visual Design Process, 99; 27 publ papers & articles on design, communications & prehist

FOSTER, STEPHEN C
HISTORIAN, WRITER
b Princeton, Ill, Dec 3, 41. *Study:* Northern Ill Univ, BA; Univ Ill, MA; Univ Pa, PhD. *Pos:* Dir, Prog for Mod Studies, Univ Iowa, Iowa City. *Teaching:* Asst prof art hist, Bowdoin Col, Brunswick, Mass, 72-74, mem fac, Am Painting Summer Inst, 74 & 76; prof art hist & criticism, Univ Iowa, Iowa City, 74-. *Awards:* Smithsonian Fel, 85; Taipei Fine Arts Mus Grant, 87; Getty Grant, 92; and others. *Mem:* Col Art Asn Am. *Res:* Sociology of modern art with research emphasis in the areas of Dada and Abstract Expressionism; folk art. *Publ:* The Critics of Abstract Expressionism, Ann Arbor: UMI Research Press, 85; contrib ed, Event Art and Events, Ann Arbor: UMI Research Press, 88; The World According to Dada, TFAM, 88; Franz Kline: Art and the Structure of Identity (exhib catalog), Electa, 94; Dada: The Coordinates of Cultural Politics, GK Hall & Co New York, 96. *Mailing Add:* Dept Art & Art Hist Univ Iowa Iowa City IA 55242

FOSTER, STEVEN DOUGLAS
PHOTOGRAPHER
b Piqua, Ohio, Sept 10, 45. *Study:* Nathan Lyons Home Workshop, Rochester, 64-66; Rochester Inst Technol, AAS, 65; Inst Design, Ill Inst Technol, BS, 68; Univ NMex, MFA, 72. *Work:* Art Inst Chicago; Int Mus Photog at George Eastman House, Rochester; Univ NMex Art Mus; Mus Mod Art, NY; Huston Mus Art; Walker Art Ctr, Mus Contemp Photog, Chicago; and others. *Exhib:* Vision & Expressions, Int Mus Photog at George Eastman House, Rochester, 69; Artists in Ga, High Mus, Atlanta, 74; Wis Dirs II, Milwaukee Art Ctr, 78; Am Photog in the 70's, Art Inst Chicago, 79; Perception: Field of View, Los Angeles Ctr for Contemp Photog, 79. *Teaching:* Instr, Ga State Univ, Atlanta, 72-75; prof, Univ Wis-Milwaukee, 75-. *Awards:* Grad Sch Res Grant, Univ Wis-Milwaukee, 79; Milwaukee Co Individual Artist Fel, 90; Wis Arts Bd Individual Artist Grant, 94. *Mem:* Soc Photog Educ. *Media:* Black, White, Color and Silver Print. *Publ:* Contrib, Wisconsin Directions II, Milwaukee Art Ctr, 78; The Lake Series, Art Inst Chicago, 82; New American Photography, Chicago Ctr Contemp Photog, 81; Five Photographers, Milwaukee Art Mus, 87; Swimmers, Aperture, 88. *Dealer:* Ehler Crudill Gallery Chicago; Michael Lord Gallery Milwaukee

FOTOPOULOS, JAMES
FILMMAKER
b Norridge, Ill, 76. *Work:* Whitney Biennial, Whitney Mus Art, 2004, and others. *Pos:* founder, Fantasma Inc, 98. *Teaching:* Guest lectr, "Film One" prod class Univ Tex, Austin, 2001 & 2003; guest lectr, NJ City Univ, 2003. *Publ:* Dir.: (films) ZERO, 1997, Migrating Forms, 1999 (Best Feature Award, NY Underground Film Festival, 2000, Made in Chicago Award, Chicago Underground Film Festival, 2000), Back Against the Wall, 2000, Consumed, 2001 (Chicago Underground Film Fund Grant, Chicago Underground Film Festival, 2001), Christabel, 2001, The Lighthouse, 2004 (No Budget Award, Cinematexas Inte Short Film & Video Festival, 2004), Spine Face, 2005; exhib include with Cory Arcangel Fotopoulos/Arcangel Part 5, NY Film Festival, 2004. *Mailing Add:* Fantasma Inc 1400 W Devon 440 Chicago IL 60660

FOULADVAND, HENGAMEH
PAINTER, CRITIC
b Tehran, Iran; US citizen. *Study:* Studied painting under masters of Persian art in Iran; San Jose State Univ, BA, 76, MA, 79. *Work:* Encyclopedia Iranica Found, Line & Tone Typographics, NY; Found Iranian Studies, Washington. *Exhib:* Middle Eastern Studies Invitational, NY & Mem Libr Invitational, Long Island Univ, NY, 89 & 91; Persian Artists in US, Strathmore Hall Arts Ctr, Md, 90; Long Island Artists Exhib, Heckscher Mus, NY, 90; Transcending the Immediate Surrounding, Port Washington Pub Libr, NY, 91; Essence & Attributes, Huntington Arts Coun, NY, 92 & 94; MacArthur Airport, Islip, Long Island, 97; Gallery Gora, Montreal, Can, 99; CIMA, Inc, NY, 99; Drawing the Line, La Mason Frances, Columbia Univ, 2000. *Pos:* Exec dir, Ctr for Iranian Mod Arts, 98-; ed bd, Tavoos Art Mag, 99-. *Teaching:* Vis artist, Creativity Workshop, Columbia Univ Dept Middle Eastern Cult, 96 & 97. *Bibliog:* Les Krants, New York Art Rev, 88; Encyclopedia of Living Artists, 94; Who's Who in the East, 97. *Mem:* Huntington Township Art League; Smithtown Arts Coun; Huntington Arts Coun. *Media:* Acrylic, Oil; Watercolor, Mixed Media. *Dealer:* Mir Enterprise 179 New York Ave Huntington NY 11743. *Mailing Add:* 525 Caledonia Rd Dix Hills NY 11746

FOULGER, RICHARD F
PAINTER, PRINTMAKER
b Kamloops, BC, Apr 30, 49. *Study:* Alta Col Art, 67-70; Vancouver Sch Art, dipl, 72; Notre Dame Univ, BFA, 75; Simon Fraser Univ, teaching cert, 76. *Work:* Soc Can Painter Etchers & Engravers, York Univ, Can, Toronto Dominion Bank Collection Can Art, Toronto, Can; Vancouver Art Gallery, Can; Print Club, Philadelphia, Pa; Alberta Col Art, Can; BC Art Bank, Victoria, Can. *Exhib:* Solo shows, Vancouver Art Gallery, BC, 72, Cloudscape Gallery, BC, 1990-2000, Hummingbird Gallery, Nelson, BC, 92 & 97; group shows, Kootenay Baindary Regional Juried Exhib, Nelson, BC, Can, 95-97, Nelson Centennial Gallery, 97, Carr Inst Art & Design, Alumni Show, Vancouver, BC, Can, 98, ArtWorks, Tenth St Campus, Nelson, BC, Can, 2000, Open Water, John B Aird Gallery, toronto, Ont, Can, 2000, 100 Artists for 100 Yrs; Netidea Gallery, Nelson, BC, Can. *Teaching:* Art instr, Art & Stage Craft, LV Rogers Sec, 75-2000. *Awards:* Visual Arts & Crafts Scholar, Govt Alta, Can, 69 & 70. *Mem:* Brit Columbia Art Teachers Asn; Can Inst Theatre Tech; The Can Trail Soc; Nelson Pub Art Gallery Soc. *Media:* Mixed Media, Serigraphy. *Dealer:* Cloudscapes Gallery & Studio

FOULKES, LLYN
PAINTER
b Yakima, Wash, Nov 17, 34. *Study:* Univ Wash, 53-54; Cent Wash Col Educ, 54, Chouinard Art Inst, 57-59. *Work:* Whitney Mus Am Art, Mus Mod Art, Guggenheim Mus, NY; Art Inst, Chicago; Los Angeles Co Mus Art, Mus Contemp Art, Calif; Oakland Mus Art, Calif; San Francisco Mus Mod Art, Calif. *Exhib:* solo exhibs, Kent Fine Arts, Forum, Zurich, 87, Hooks-Epstein Gallery, Houston, Tex, 88, Herter Art Gallery, Univ Mass, Amherst, 89, POP: The First Picture, Kent, NY, 90, I Space, Univ Ill, Chicago, 93, Patricia Faure Gallery, Santa Monica, Calif, 94, 96, Laguna Art Mus, Calif, 95, Gallery Paule Anglim, San Francisco, 97, Peter Blake Gallery, Laguna Beach, Calif, 01, Post POP, Kent Gallery, NY City, 2004; LA Hot and Cool, Stux Gallery, NY, 88; Art of the 70's, Manny Silverman Gallery, Los Angeles, Calif, 88; Am Pie, Bess Cutler Gallery, NY, 89; Real Allusions, The Whitney Mus Am Art, NY, 90; Helter Skelter, Mus Contemp Art, Los Angeles, 92; retrospective Between a Rock and a Hard place (traveking), 95-98; Norton Simon Mus, Pasadena, Calif, 99, 01, Patricia Faure Gallery, Santa Monica, Calif, 99, Orange Co Ctr for Contemp Art, Santa Ana, Calif, 00, Laguna Mus Art, 01, Frye Art Mus, Seattle, 01, Mus Modern Art, 01, Los Angeles Post Cool, San Jose Mus Art, Calif, 2002, Paperwork, Patricia Correia Gallery, 2003, POP from San Francisco Collections, San Francisco Mus Modern Art, 2004, 181st Ann Invitational Exhib, Nat Acad Mus, NY City, 2006. *Collection Arranged:* Cur, Imagination, Los Angeles Inst Contemp Art, Calif; Guggenheim Mus, New York City; Mus Modern Art; Art Inst Chicago; Whitney Mus Am Art, New York City; Musee Boymans, Rotterdam; Los Angeles Co Mus Art; Norton Simon Mus, Pasadena, Calif; San Francisco Mus Modern Art; Oakland Mus Calif; Mus Contemp Art, Los Angeles. *Teaching:* Prof painting & drawing & artist in residence, Univ Calif, Los Angeles, 65-71; resident painter, Painting workshop, Art Ctr Sch, Los Angeles, 71-77; vis prof art, Univ Calif, Irvine, 81-82, Santa Barbara, 83-84; prof, Otis Art Inst, Los Angeles, 86-87. *Awards:* New Talent Purchase Grant, Los Angeles Co Mus Art, 64; Medal of France (first award for painting), 5th Paris Bienniale, Mus Mod Art, Paris, 67; Guggenheim Found fel, 77-78; Fel Grant, Nat Endowment Arts, 86. *Bibliog:* Hilary Dole Klein (auth), Time out: sticking up the one-man band, Santa Barbara News & Rev, 1/23/88; Mark Van Proyen (auth), Navigating the semiotic mire, Artweek, 8/20/88; Robert Taylor (auth), LA hot and cool: A rewarding exhibit, Boston Globe, 1/88; Peter Frank (auth), Forty Years of California Assemblage, Wright Gallery, Sculpture, 1-2/90; Peter Plagens (auth), Welcome to Manson High, Newsweek, 3/22/92; David Pagel (auth), The Importance of Being Earnest, LA Times, F36, 3/2/2000; Bernard Cooper (auth), Vulgarian Rhapsody, LA Mag, 128-132, 12/2001. *Media:* Oil, Acrylic. *Mailing Add:* c/o Kent Gallery 541 W 25th St New York NY 10001

FOURCARD, INEZ GAREY
PAINTER
b Brooklyn, NY. *Study:* Pratt Inst, Brooklyn, NY; McNeese State Univ, Lake Charles, La, BFA, 63. *Work:* Bertrand Russell Peace Found, London, Eng; Gallery Ancient & Mod Art, Salsomaggiore, Italy. *Comn:* Landscape with Pond, New Emanuel Baptist Church, Lake Charles, La, 75; Jesus & The Nativity, Mt Pilgrim Baptist Church, Lake Charles, 83. *Exhib:* La State Art Comn, traveling exhib, 64; one-woman shows, Lynn Kottler Galleries, NY, 71 & Art Mus Southwest La, Lafayette, 72; Eminent Black Artist of Louisiana, Cent La Art Asn Inc, Alexandria, 76; Prominent Black Artists of Louisiana, La Black Legislators Caucus, State Capitol, 87; Black Heritage Festival, Civic Ctr, Lake Charles, La, 88; and others. *Awards:* Cash Award, First Prize, Mother & Son, La State Art Comn, 64; Gold Medal First Prize, The Connoisseur, Acad Italia dell Artie del Savro, 80; Statua della Vittoria, The Connoisseur, Centro Studie Ricerche Dalle Nazioni, 85. *Bibliog:* Herbert Lieberman (auth), Artist-USA, Artists Equity Asn, Inc, 70, 72 & 74; Bernadine Proctor (auth), Black Artist of Louisiana, 88. *Media:* Oil. *Publ:* Contribr, International Artist Directory, 75; The History of Contemporary Art, Int d'Arte Mod, 82. *Mailing Add:* 1414 St John St Lake Charles LA 70601

FOWLE, BRUCE S
ARCHITECT
Study: Syracuse Univ, Sch of Archit, BA(archit), 60. *Pos:* Assoc, Edward Larrabee Barnes, FAIA, 70-77; co-founder, senior principal Fox & Fowle Archits, Prof Corp, 78—; Co-founder, Archits, Designers & Planners for Soc Responsibility, New York City, 82; chmn, Syracuse Univ Sch Archit Adv Commun. *Awards:* named to Am Inst of Archits Col of Fel, 85; recipient George Arents Pioneer Medal, Syracuse Univ, 2001. *Mem:* Fel, Inst for Urban Design; Am Inst of Archits Design Commun; Nat Acad (acad, 94). *Mailing Add:* Fox & Fowle 22 W 19th St New York NY 10011

FOWLE, GERALDINE ELIZABETH
HISTORIAN
b Grand Rapids, Mich, Jan 3, 29. *Study:* Am Univ, 53-58; Univ Mich, Ann Arbor, MA(art hist), 60, PhD(art hist), 70. *Pos:* Newslett ed, Midwest Art Hist Soc, 77-80 & Soc Archit Historians, 80-86; archivist, Midwest Art History Soc, 86-. *Teaching:* Asst lectr English art, Univ Manchester, England, 63-66; vis instr Baroque art, Univ Pittsburgh, 67; assoc prof, Univ Mo, Kansas City, 67-. *Mem:* Col Art Asn; Soc Archit Historians; Midwest Art Hist Soc; Mid-Am Col Art Asn (treas, 74-75). *Res:* Sebastien Bourdon, French artist of the 17th century. *Publ:* Contribr, Two pendants by Sebastien Bourdon, Bulletin, Boston Mus Fine Arts, 73; Sebastien Bourdon's acts of mercy, Hortus Imaginum, 74; The lady who got Tassi thrown into prison, Helicon Nine, 80; Crucifixion of St Peter, Mus Art, Univ Kans, 87. *Mailing Add:* 5726 Charlotte St Kansas City MO 64110-2762

FOWLER, ERIC NICHOLAS
ILLUSTRATOR, PAINTER
b Morristown, NJ, Feb 14, 1954. *Study:* Syracuse Univ, NY, 72-74; illusr workshop (First Scholar award), 77; Pratt Inst, Brooklyn, NY, BFA(hons), 78. *Work:* Soc Illustrs permanent collection; Mercer Co Cult & Heritage Comn; The Princeton Junior Sch. *Comn:* Comn by Robert A Black, Los Angeles. *Exhib:* Graphis Ann, Switz, 83-84; Diaz-Marciall Gallery, NY, 84; Art Dirs Club Ann, NY, 86; one-man shows, Frenchtown, NJ, 89 & Princeton Trenton Artworks, 94; Larsen-Dulman, New Hope, Pa, 89-91; Bristol Myers Squibb, 91; and others. *Awards:* Certificates Merit, Soc Illusr Ann Show 77, 82, 86, 89, 91 & Soc Publ Designers, 82 & 86; Print Regional Design Ann, 86 & 88; Distinguished Artist Grant, NJSCA, 90-91; and many others. *Mem:* Soc Illusr (bd dir 1990-, chmn permanent collection 1998-); Artworks, Trenton Artist Workship Asn NJ; Trenton Mus Soc (bd dir, chmn acquisitions com); Philadelphia Sketch Club. *Media:* Oil; Mixed. *Publ:* The Directory of Illustrations vol 8, 92 & vol 12, 95. *Dealer:* Rhinehart-Fischer Gallery Trenton NJ. *Mailing Add:* 417 Beatty St Trenton NJ 08611

FOWLER, FRANK EISON
ART DEALER, CONSULTANT
b Chattanooga, Tenn, June 2, 46. *Study:* Univ Ga, BBA, 69. *Comn:* Produced Inaugural Portfolio, 76 & Presidential Portfolio, 80, comn by Pres Jimmy Carter. *Pos:* Mem adv bd, John F Kennedy Ctr Performing Arts, formerly & Ga Mus Art, Athens, currently. *Mem:* Appraisers Asn Am; Int Soc Appraisers. *Res:* Represent Andrew Wyeth. *Mailing Add:* 120 Swatauqa Ln Lookout Mountain TN 37350-1442

FOWLER, MARY JEAN
WEAVER
b Ames, Iowa, Feb 5, 34. *Study:* Iowa State Univ, Ames, BS(appl art), 56, MS, 57; Arrowmont Sch Arts & Crafts, Gatlinburg, Tenn; also various workshops under nationally known artists. *Comn:* 3 landscape blankets, Hilton Hotel, Bryan-College Station, Tex, 55; Flyers in the Breeze (hanging), First Nat Bank Quail Valley, Houston, 83; 3 woven landscape panels, First City Bank Forum NAm, San Antonio, 83; 6 woven landscape panels, First City Bank Gulf Gate, Houston, 84. *Exhib:* One-man shows, Archway Gallery, 81, Travels in Quiet Landscapes, 84 & Watkins, Carter & Hamilton Archit, 85, Houston, Tex; Dimension Houston, Houston Art League, Tex, 82; Instr Show, Convergence Fibers for Architectural Spaces, Southern Methodist Univ, Houston, 83 & Dallas, 84; Five Fiber Artists, Baylor Univ, Waco, Tex, 84; Concepts: Work and Wearables, Owatonna Arts Ctr, Minn, 85. *Pos:* Vchmn, Arrowmont Bd Govs, Arrowmont Sch Arts & Crafts, Gatlinburg, Tenn, 72-88. *Teaching:* Independent weaving consultant working with sch syst on contract basis; instr, St John's Sch Art, Houston, Tex, 86-, Arrowmont Sch Arts & Crafts, 90-92 & Rice Univ Summer Sch for high sch students, Houston, Tex, 91-. *Awards:* Master chair in Primary Educ, 92, St John's Sch, Cullen Found, 92. *Mem:* Am Craft Coun; Handweavers Guild Am

FOX, CARSON
SCULPTOR - MISCELLANEOUS MEDIA
b Oxford, Mass, 68. *Study:* Pa Acad Fine Arts, 87-91; Univ of PA, BFA; Rutgers Univ, MFA. *Work:* Pa Acad Fine Arts; Hofstra Mus, Hempstead, NY; NJ Acad of Med, Princeton, NJ; Rider Univ, Lawrenceville, NJ. *Exhib:* Main Line Art Ctr, Haverford, Pa; Pa Acad Fine Arts; Mason Gross Gallery, Rutgers Univ, NJ; Artist House Gallery, Philadelphia, Pa, 2001; solo exhib, Artist House Gallery, Philadelphia, Pa, Women's Studio Workshop Gallery, Rosendale, NY, Montgomery Co Col Gallery, Pa, OK Harris Gallery, New York City, 2001. *Teaching:* instr, screen printing, NY Univ, currently. *Awards:* Grumacher Award for Printmaking, 92; NJ State Mus Soc Award, 2000; Coun on Arts Sculpture Grant, 2001. *Mailing Add:* 945 Berkeley Ave Trenton NJ 08610

FOX, FLO
PHOTOGRAPHER, LECTURER
b Miami, Fla, Sept 26, 45. *Study:* With Lisette Model, 80-83 & Andre Kertesz, 85. *Work:* Focus Gallery, San Francisco; Brooklyn Mus, NY. *Comn:* Three-dimensional photography, Minn Mus Art, 86. *Exhib:* Asphalt Garden, Canon Gallery, Paris, 81, Camden Arts Ctr, Eng, 81; Auto-Focus Photog, Boston Mus Fine Art, 82 & Philadelphia Mus Art, 83; Beyond Limitations, The Nikon House, NY, 87; two-person show with Weegee the Famous, Agathe Gaillard Galerie, Paris, France, 87; IBM Building, Nat MS Soc, NY, 89; Times Square Hotel, 2000. *Teaching:* Instr photog, Lighthouse for Blind, NY, 79-80, Village Nursing Home, 84 & YWCA, 85-86, NY; 18 seminars including, Philadelphia Mus Art, Boston Mus Fine Arts & Park West Camera Club. *Awards:* Cert Merit, Boston Mus Fine Art, 82 & Philadelphia Mus Art, 83. *Bibliog:* Georgia Dullea (auth), A camera does the seeing, New York Times, 4/80; Elizabeth Mehren (auth), Trades sight for insight, Los Angeles Times, 9/81; article in The Plain Dealer, Cleveland, Ohio, 6/85. *Mem:* Park West Camera Club. *Publ:* Photogr, The Picture Book of Greenwich Village, 85; The Human Animal, by Phil Donahue; Art of the Eye, Minn Mus Art, 86; Black & White New York & What She Wants-Women Artists Look at Men, Life Mag, 9/94; Sculpture Review Mag, spring 94. *Mailing Add:* 135 W 23rd St No 607 New York NY 10011

FOX, JUDITH HOOS
CURATOR
b Oakland, Calif, June 13, 49. *Study:* Bryn Mawr Col, BA, 71; Univ Minn, MA, 74. *Collection Arranged:* S & Y Ombra: An Autobiography in Form, Beverly Pepper, MIT, 88; Ericson Ziegler: The Wellesley Method, Wellesley Col Mus, 90; The Matter of History: Selected Work by Annette Lemieux (with catalog), Davis Mus, 94; The Body As Measure (with catalog), Davis Mus, 94; Re:formations/design directions at the end of a century (with catalog), Davis Mus, 96; William de Koonings Door Cycle (with catalog), Davis Mus & Whitney Mus, 95-96; Surrounding Institutions: Views Inside the Car, Daris Mus (with Catalog), 2002; Over & Over: Passion for Process (with Catalog) Krannert Art Mus, Univ Illinois, 2005; Pattern Language: Clothing As Communicator (with catalog), Tufts Univ Art Mus, 2005. *Pos:* Cur intern, Walker Art Ctr, Minneapolis, 73-74; cur, Inst Contemp Art, Boston, 74-75; asst dir, Wellesley Col Mus, Mass, 77-82; cur painting & sculpture, Mus Art, RI Sch Design, Providence, 82-84; adj cur, 20th century dept, Mus Fine Arts, Boston, independent cur, 84-88; cur, Davis Mus & Cult Ctr, Wellesley Col; independent cur & consult. *Teaching:* Instr mus studies, Wellesley Col, 84; vis Assoc Cur in Am Art, Harvard Univ Art Mus. *Mem:* Art Table. *Publ:* Contribr, Naives and Visionaries, Walker Art Ctr, 74; The Railroad in the American Landscape: 1850-1950, Wellesley Col Mus, 81; Handbook of the Museum of Art, Rhode Island Sch of Design, 86. *Mailing Add:* 21 Myrtle St Jamaica Plain Boston MA 02130

FOX, JUDY (JUDITH) C
SCULPTOR, CERAMIST
b Elizabeth, NJ, Feb 14, 57. *Study:* Skowhegan Sch Painting & Sculpture, 76; Yale Univ, BA(Jonathan Edwards Art Award), 78; Ecole Superior des Beaux Arts, Paris, 79; NY Univ Inst Fine Arts, MA(art hist), 83, cert conserv, 84, RI Sch Design. *Comn:* Sculpture, City Univ NY, 94. *Exhib:* Portrait of Our Times, Revolution, Ferndale, Mich, 95; Herter Art Gallery, Univ Mass, Amherst, 95; one-woman show, Kunst werk, Berlin, Ger, Yale Univ Art and Architecture Gallery, New Haven, Conn, 77, Bruno Fachetti Gallery, New York City, 87, Calof Lamagna Gallery, New York City, 89, PPOW, New York City, 93, 96, 2000, Christine Konig Galerie, Vienna, Austria, 94, Rena Branston Gallery, San Francisco, Calif, 96, Gallery Joe, Philadelphia, Pa, 96, Kunsthalle Palazzo, Leistal, Switz, 97, Ace Gallery Los Angeles, Calif, 98, Rupertinum, Salzburg, Austria, 98, Galerie Thaddaeus Ropac, Paris, France, 2000, God Lover, PPOW, New York City, 2001, Love & War, John Michael Kohler Arts Center, Sheboygen, Wisc, 2001 & Vigeland Mus, Oslo, Norway, 2004; Identita e Alterita, Venice Bienannle, Italy, 95; Narcissim, Calif Ctr Arts, Escondido, 96; Sphinx Chapel, PPOW, NY, 96; Premasculine, Rena Branston Gallery, San Francisco, 96; Prefeminine, Gallery Joe, Philadelphia, 96; To Be Real, Cen for Arts Yerba Buena Gardens, San Francisco, Calif, 97-98; Aldrich Mus Contemp Art, Ridgefield, Conn, 98; Twenty-Six Am Artists, Campo & Campo, Antwerp, Belgium, 99; Collector's Choice, Exit Art, New York City, 2000; Olympia Redux, The Contemp Mus, Honolulu, Hawii, 2000; The End An Indpenedent Vision Contemp Art, Syracuse, NY, 2000; Oh Baby!, Exhibit A, NY, 2000. *Pos:* Vis artist, Empire State Prog, 89, Middlebury Col, 89, Tyler Sch Art, 92, Md Inst Art, Baltimore, 2002, NY Acad Art, 2002 & Univ Tex, Austin, 2003. *Teaching:* Fac, Yale Univ, 90-92 & Tyler Sch Art, 92, Mus Contemp Art, Chicago, 97, RI Sch Design, 2000, NY Acad Art, 2000, others. *Awards:* Residency, NY Acad Art, 86; Individual Artist grant, Nat Endowment Arts, 88 & 94. *Bibliog:* Rainer Metzger (auth), Kunstforum Int, 6/95; Christian Kravagna (auth), Art Forum, 9/95; Nancy Princenthal (auth), Art in America, 10/96; Christopher Reardon (auth), Fox's Fables, ARTnews, 6/2000; Genevieve Breerett (auth), La Corps Perdue, Dans Les Images, LeMonde, 5/2000; and others. *Media:* Fired Clay, Casien Paint. *Dealer:* PPOW Gallery NY. *Mailing Add:* 270 Lafayette St No 1306 New York NY 10012

FOX, LINCOLN H
SCULPTOR
b Morrilton, Ark, June 14, 42. *Study:* Univ Tex, Austin, with Charles Umlaf, BFA, 66; Univ Dallas, with Heri Barscht, MA, 67; Univ Kans, Lawrence, with Elden Tefft, MFA, 68. *Work:* El Paso Art Mus; Mus Southwest, Midland, Tex; Land of the Four Seasons Collection, Lake of the Ozarks, Mo. *Comn:* Child of Prague, Cistercian Prep Sch, Irving, Tex; Turn of the Century Cable Tool Workers, Permian Basin Petroleum Mus, Midland, Tex, 76; wall relief, First Christian Church, Ruidoso, NMex, 82. *Exhib:* One-man show, Smithsonian Inst, 75, Fine Arts Mus Albuquerque, 78 & El Paso Art Mus, 79; Nat Acad Western Art Ann, Nat Cowboy Hall Fame, Oklahoma City, 75, 79 & 80; Nat Sculpture Soc Ann Exhib, Equitable Bldg, NY, 82 & 83; Nat Western Artists First Ann Exhib, Civic Ctr, Lubbock, Tex, 82 & 83; and others. *Teaching:* Instr sculpture, Univ Kans, Lawrence, 67-68; instr sculpture & drawing, Amarillo Col, 69-71. *Awards:* Purchase Award, 60th Ann Nat Competition Am Art, 70; Bronze Medal, Solon Borglum Mem Sculpture Exhib, Nat Cowboy Hall Fame, 75; Misner Award, 49th Ann Exhib Nat Sculpture Soc, 82. *Bibliog:* Morgan Catherine Merrill (auth), Lincoln Fox: Mood, media and idea, Southwest Art Mag, 5/80; Peggy & Harold Samuels (auths), Contemporary Western Artists, Southwest Art Publ, 82; article, Nat Sculpture Rev, summer 82. *Mem:* Nat Sculpture Soc; Nat Western Artist Asn. *Media:* Bronze, Stone; Pastel. *Dealer:* Christine's Gallery Sante Fe NM

FOX, MICHAEL DAVID
SCULPTOR, PROFESSOR,PHOTOGRAPHER
b Cortland, NY, Dec 29, 37. *Study:* State Univ NY, New Paltz, with Ilya Bolotowsky & Ken Green; State Univ NY, Buffalo, with Robert Davidson & George Stark, BS, 62, MS, 69; Brooklyn Mus Sch, with Tom Doyle, Rueben Tam & Toshio Odate, cert, 64. *Work:* State Univ NY, Buffalo, Cortland, Oswego & New Paltz; Brooklyn Mus; Morehead State Univ, Morehead, Ky; Pvt collections through out the world. *Exhib:* Finger Lakes Ann, Rochester Mem Art Gallery, 63-93; Ann Prof Exhib, Brooklyn Mus, 64; JB Speed Art Mus, Louisville, Ky, 65-67; Cent NY Ann, Everson Mus, Syracuse, 68-84; Artists Cent NY, Munson-Williams-Proctor Inst, Utica, 68-89 & 95; Visual Image Gallery, New York City, 70-71; OK Harris, NY, 71; State Univ Ark Nat, Univ Gallery, 73; Cooperstown Art Mus Nat, NY, 81; 16 solo exhibs incl, Elmira Col, 78, Oswego Art Guild 78 & 88, Univ Vt, State Univ NY, Oswego & others in NY, Toronto & Rome; Mich Watercolor Nat, 85; State Univ NY Painters Invitational, Geneso, 88. *Pos:* Dir, Popular Image Gallery, Oswego, NY, 73-; proj dir, Nat Endowment Arts Grant, State Univ NY, Oswego, 78-2000. *Teaching:* Teacher art, Rochester City Schs, NY, 62-65; instr, Morehead State Univ, Ky, 65-67; prof art, State Univ, Oswego, NY, 67-2000, retired, 2000. *Awards:* Sculpture Award, Ann Exhib, Brooklyn Mus, 64; Painting Awards, Finger Lakes Exhib, Rochester Mem Art Gallery, 78 & NY State Fair, Syracuse, 78-81, 92, 93, 94 & 97; Best of Show, Art Asn Oswego; and many more. *Bibliog:* Sculpture (feature), CBS TV, 76, 78 & 80; Sculpture (feature), Can Nat Television, 79; PM Mag (feature), CBS TV, 81; Arthur Williams: Beginning Sculpture, Technique, Form & Content (feature), 95. *Media:* Plastic, Polyester Resin. *Publ:* Contrib, Evergreen Review (bk), Cavalier Sch Arts, NY Times; articles in Nat Lampoon & Scanlons Monthly. *Mailing Add:* 38 W End Ave Oswego NY 13126

FOX, TERRY ALAN
CONCEPTUAL ARTIST, SCULPTOR
b Seattle, Wash, May 10, 43. *Study:* Self taught. *Work:* Univ Art Mus, Berkeley; Mus Modern Art, San Francisco; Kuntzmuseum, Luzern, Switz; Folkwang Mus, Essen, Ger; Mus Contemp Art, Vienna, Austria. *Comn:* Sculpture (stone), Podio del Mondo di Arte, Middelberg, Holland, 78. *Exhib:* Solo exhibs, Univ Art Mus (with catalog), Berkeley, 73, Everson Mus, Syracuse, 74, Long Beach Mus Art, 75, Kunstmuseum (with catalog), Luzern, Switz, 82, Folkwang Mus (with catalog), Essen, Ger, 82, DAAD Galerie, Berlin, Ger, 82 & Kunstraum, Munich, Ger, 85. *Pos:* Artist-in-residence, DAAD, Berlin, WGer, 82-83. *Publ:* Auth, Catch Phrases & Hobo Signs, Kunstraum, Munich, Ger, 85. *Mailing Add:* c/o Ronald Feldman Fine Arts 31 Mercer St New York NY 10013

FRABEL, HANS GODO
SCULPTOR
b Jena, Ger, June 9, 41. *Work:* Smithsonian Inst, White House & Nat Bldg Mus, Washington, DC; Wertheim Mus, WGer; Botanical Mus, Harvard Univ, Cambridge, Mass; Dusseldorf Mus, WGer; Headly-Whitney Mus, Lexington, Ky. *Comn:* Gift to Deng Xiaoping, comn by City Atlanta, Ga, 79; gift to people of Berlin, comn by VPres Rockefeller, Washington, DC; gift to Lord High Mayor, London, Delta Airlines, Atlanta, Ga, 79; gift to Pres Carter, Ga Democratic Party, Atlanta, Ga; Gardens for Peace, Moscow, 88; Queen Elizabeth II, 91. *Exhib:* Jr Art Gallery, Louisville, Ky, 75; New Glass, traveling, 79-; Contemp Glass Gallery, NY, 80; Westlake Gallery, White Plains, NY, 81; Glass Gallery, Bethesda, Md; Crystal Fox, Carmel, Calif; Global Gallery, Tampa, Fla; Foster-White, Seattle, 92. *Pos:* Bd, Ga Coun on Int Visitors. *Awards:* Phoenix Award, Atlanta Chamber of Commerce, Ga; Peoples Choice Best in Glass, Artists Soc Int, 87; Am Interfaith, Silver Award, 92. *Bibliog:* Sampling of contemporary picture, Cleveland Plain Dealer, 80; Creating art in glass, Dallas Times-Herald, 80; Frabel's glass meets the flame, Southern Living, 5/81. *Mem:* Glass Art Soc; Am Sci Glassblowers Soc. *Media:* Borosilicate Crystal. *Dealer:* 309 East Paces Ferry Rd. Ste. 101 Altanta, GA, 30305, 11-5 Tue-Sat. *Mailing Add:* 695 Antone St NW Atlanta GA 30318-7601

FRACE, CHARLES LEWIS
PAINTER
b Mauch Chunk, Pa, Feb 18, 26. *Study:* Philadelphia Col Art, Pa. *Work:* Nat Wildlife Fedn, Washington, DC. *Comn:* Official portrait of Morris the Cat, 9-Lives Cat Food, 76; paintings for reprod of ltd ed prints, Frame House Gallery, 73-80 & Am Masters Found, 81-92. *Exhib:* one-man show, Cumberland Mus & Sci Ctr, Nashville, 78, 81 & 89 & Houston Mus Nat Sci, Tex, 60 original paintings, 91; Ann Orginal Art Showcase, Mississauga, Ont, Can, 89, 90 & 91; Royal Ont Mus, Ornitholology Gallery, Toronto, Can, 87; Northeastern Wildlife Expos, Albany, NY, 87, 88; Nat Mus Natural Hist, Smithsonian Inst, Washington, DC, 35 original paintings, The Am Wildlife Image and Charles Frace, 92-93; and others. *Awards:* Spec Award of Merit, Denver Mus Natural Hist, Colo, 82; Inducted into publication's First Ann Hall of Fame (wildlife category), US Art Mag, 91; Spec Honored guest at official opening ceremonies, Nashville Zoo, Tenn, 91. *Mem:* Soc Animal Artists, NY. *Media:* Oil, Acrylic. *Publ:* Illusr, Last Chance on Earth, Chilton 5096, 66; The Life of the Jungle, McGraw-Hill, 70; Wonders of Island Life & Animals in Action, Readers Digest, 72; The Wolf, Coward, McCann, 73; The Art of Charles Frace, 82; Nature's Window, 92. *Dealer:* Somerset House Publ Houston TX. *Mailing Add:* c/o Somerset House Publ 10688 Haddington Houston TX 77043

FRACKMAN, NOEL
CRITIC, HISTORIAN
b New York, NY, May 27, 30. *Study:* Mt Holyoke Col, Sarah Williston Scholar, 48-50; Sarah Lawrence Col, BA, 52, MA, 53; Columbia Univ, 64-67; Inst Fine Arts, NY Univ, MA, 76, PhD, 87. *Pos:* Lectr, Aldrich Mus Contemp Art, Ridgefield, Conn, 67-75; partic, Art Critics Workshop, Am Fedn Arts, 68; lectr, Gallery Passport Ltd, New York, 68-; contrib ed, Arts Mag, New York, 68-92; cur educ, Storm King Art Ctr, Mountainville, NY, 73-75; contractural lectr, Metrop Mus Art, New York, 94-95. *Teaching:* Instr, Continuing Educ Div, Purchase Col, State Univ NY, Purchase, 88-, adj assoc prof humanities, 98-. *Awards:* Mademoiselle First Prize, Col Publ Contest, 61. *Mem:* Int Asn Art Critics; Art Table; Friends of Newberger Mus Art. *Publ:* Auth, Super-chair, Art Voices, fall 66; The Stein family and the era of avant-garde collecting, 2/71 & The enticement of watercolor, 6/74, Arts Mag; Jump into the New York art world, Harper's Bazaar, 2/72; plus art rev in Scarsdale Inquirer, 62-67, Patent Trader, 62-71 & Arts Mag, current issues; John Storrs retrospective catalog, Whitney Mus Am Art, 86. *Mailing Add:* 3 Hadden Rd Scarsdale NY 10583

FRAENKEL, JEFFREY ANDREW
ART DEALER
b Shreveport, La, Jan 28, 55. *Study:* Antioch Col, BFA, 77. *Pos:* Pres, Fraenkel Gallery, San Francisco. *Mem:* Art Dealers Asn Am; Asn Int Photography Art Dealers. *Specialty:* 19th and 20th century photographs. *Publ:* Photography in Spain in the Nineteenth Century, 83; The Kiss of Apollo: Photography & Sculpture 1845 to the Present; Seeing Things, 94; Open Secrets: Seventy Pictures of Paper 1815 to the Present, 96; Under the Sun, 96. *Mailing Add:* 49 Geary St San Francisco CA 94108

FRAILEY, STEPHEN A
PHOTOGRAPHER
b Chicago, Ill, Sept 3, 57. *Study:* San Francisco Art Inst, 77; Bennington Col, BA, 79. *Work:* Fogg Art Mus, Harvard Univ, Boston, Mass; Chase Manhattan Bank, NY; Int Ctr Photog, NY; Mus Fine Arts, Houston; Princeton Univ Art Mus; and others. *Exhib:* Art & Advertising, Int Ctr Photog, NY, 87; Avant Garde in 80's, Los Angeles Mus, Calif, 87; Contemp Diptychs, Whitney Mus/Equitable, NY, 87; Photog Fabrications, Carpenter Ctr, Cambridge, 88; The Photog of Invention, Nat Mus Am Art, Washington, DC, 89; Thin Air, Julie Saul Gallery, NY, 99. *Pos:* Dir, Mary Boone Gallery, 80-85; artist-in-residence Chinati Found, Marfa, Tex, 2000. *Teaching:* Chmn, Photo Dept, Sch Visual Arts, NY, 85-, Int Ctr Photog, NY & Bard Col, Annandale, NY, 93-98; vis prof, Benington Col, 97, fac chiar grad photography dept, 94-. *Awards:* Macdowell Colony Fel, 88 & 95; Nat Endowment Arts, 88; Aaron Siskind Found Grant, 92. *Bibliog:* Portfolio, Paris Rev, spring 89; David Robbins (auth), Stephen Frailey, Arts Mag, 9/89; Portfolio, Art Forum, 10/90; and others; Genuine Initiation, Art on Paper, 1-2/99. *Publ:* Auth, Richard Avedon, Print Collector, 5/86; Ray Metzger, Art News, 9/87; Thin Air: The Photographs of Adam Fuss, Art Forum, 11/93; Murder, Mystery & Mayhem, Apature, 97; and others. *Mailing Add:* 11 Charlton St New York NY 10014

FRAME, JOHN
SCULPTOR
b San Bernardino, Calif, Nov 27, 50. *Study:* San Diego State Univ, BA, 75; Claremont Grad Sch, MFA, 80. *Work:* California Collection, Crocker Ctr, Los Angeles, Calif; Collection of Los Angeles Community Redevelopment Agency; Los Angeles Co Mus Art. *Comn:* Sculptural tableau, Cedars Sinai Hosp, Los Angeles, Calif, 87. *Exhib:* Return of the Narrative, Palm Springs Desert Mus, Palm Springs, 84; Crime and Punishment, Triton Mus, Santa Clara, Calif, 84; Three Sculptors, ARCO Ctr Visual Art, Los Angeles, Calif, 84; Sprektrum Los Angeles, Galerie Hartje, Berlin, WGer, 85; Kindred Spirits, Los Angeles Munic Art Gallery, 86; Avante-Garde in the 80's, Los Angeles Co Mus, 87; solo exhib, Los Angeles Co Mus Art, 92. *Awards:* Visual Artists Grants, Nat Endowment Arts, 84 & 86; Young Talent Award, Los Angeles Co Mus Art, 85; J Paul Getty Mus Individual Artists Fel, 95. *Bibliog:* K Zimmerer (auth), Fools and fallacies, Visions Mag, 87; Mac Mcleod (auth), Small sculptural dramas, Artweek, 87; William Wilson (auth), Ruminations on the resistance to nature, LA Times, 94. *Media:* Wood. *Mailing Add:* 2421 S Santa Fe No 21 Los Angeles CA 90058

FRANCES, (SHERANA) HARRIETTE
PRINTMAKER, PAINTER
b San Francisco, Calif. *Study:* San Francisco Sch Fine Arts, 42-45; San Francisco Art Inst, 63 & 65-66; James Weeks, Painting Instructor, Tamarind Inst, Univ NMex, 88-90 & 92. *Work:* Fresno Art Ctr, Calif; Charles D Clark Collection, McAllen, Tex; Achenbach Found Graphic Arts; San Francisco Legion of Honor Fine Arts Mus. *Exhib:* one-woman show, Haggin Mus, Stockton, Calif, 64 & Calif Palace Legion Hon, 68; James D Phelan Award Exhib, De Young Mus, San Francisco, 63 & Palace Legion of Honor, 65; Americana-Bicentennial, San Francisco Mus Modern Art, 76; Brandts-Klaenfabrik Mus, Funen, Denmark, 89; 8th Nat Juried Exhib, Berkeley, Calif, 92; Calif Small Works, Luther Burbank Ctr for Arts, Santa Rosa, Calif, 96; Beyond Boundaries, Richmond Art Ctr, Calif, 97; Inst Franco-Am Rennes, France, 98; Contents & Contexts: Lithography After 200 Yrs - Honolulu, Hawaii; Radical Printmaking, San Francisco Comn Gallery, 2000; Int/Invitational Exh of Prints, Chung/Shan Nat Gallery, Taiwan, 2005; Printmakers Today, Somarts, San Francisco, Calif, 2006. *Teaching:* Instr life drawing, Exten, Univ Pac; instr lithography, Artists Proof Graphics Workshop, Larkspur, Calif; instr monotype, Col of Marin, Kentfield, Calif. *Awards:* Calif State Fair Award, 64; James D Phelan Award in Art, 65; Calif Small Works Annual, Lother Burbank Ctr for Arts, Santa Rosa, Calif, 96; 2nd Biennial, Janet Turner Nat Print Competition, 97. *Bibliog:* George Christy (auth), Are you with it, Town & Country Mag, 67; Martin Fox (ed), A graphic artist depicts her LSD trip, Print Mag, 67; Joan Lisetor (auth), Reviving an ancient art, Independent J, 75. *Mem:* San Francisco Mus Mod Art; Calif Soc of Printmakers; Marin Arts Coun. *Media:* Lithography, Acrylic. *Collection:* Charles & Nancy Curley Collection, Marin Cty, Calif. *Publ:* Contribr, Ramparts Mag, 66; contribr, Print Mag & Psychedelic Art, 67; Erotic Art of the Masters, 18th, 19th & 20th Centuries, Lyle Stewart Publ; contribr, The Spirit of Shamanism, Tarcher Publ, 90; auth, Drawing It Out, Maps Publ, Fla, 2001. *Mailing Add:* 105 Rice Lane Larkspur CA 94939

FRANCIS, JEAN THICKENS
ASSEMBLAGE ARTIST, PAINTER
b Laurel, Miss, Mar 15, 43. *Study:* Millsaps Col, 61-63; Memphis Art Acad, BFA(sculpture), 66. *Work:* South Central Bell, Miss; Deposit Guaranty Nat Bank, Tupelo & Jackson, Miss; First Nat Bank, Miss; Boyle Investment CO, Memphis Tenn; Int Paper Co, Memphis, Tenn. *Comn:* N Mississippi Women's Health Ctr, Tupelo; Peoples Bank and Trust, Tupelo; Community Federal Savings & Loan, Tupelo; US Embassy, Riyadh, Saudi Arabia, 94. *Exhib:* Mississippi River Crafts Exhib, Brooks Mem Art Gallery, 77; Papermakers & Paperusers, Southeastern Artists, Southeastern Ctr Contemp Art, Winston-Salem, NC, 80; one-person shows, The 500 lb Paper Project, Miss Mus Art, Jackson, Open Gallery, Miss Mus Art, Jackson; Prints, Drawings & Crafts Show, Ark Art Ctr, Little Rock, 81; Artsite Invitational, New Orleans, La, 80; More Than Land or Sky: Art from Appalachia, Nat Mus Am Art, Smithsonian Inst & traveling, 81-84; The State of The Art: Mississippi, Contemp Art Ctr, New Orleans, La, 83; Papermakers Invitational, Western Carolina Univ, Cullowhee, NC, 85; Paper Art-New Directions, Texas Tech Univ Mus, Lubbock, Tex, 85; 100 Gloves: And Then Some, Univ Mus, Oxford, Miss, 85. *Pos:* Self-employed artist, currently. *Teaching:* Instr art, Memphis City Sch, Tenn, 66-67; instr sculpture, Memphis Acad Art, Tenn, summer 74; vis artist, Jackson City Sch, Miss, 76; guest artist, papermaking, Nat Mus Am Art, 81, Miss Mus Art, Jackson, 81, Arrowmont Sch Arts & Crafts, Gatlinburg, Tenn, 84 & Itawamba Jr Col, Fulton, Miss, 85; instr, papermaking, Appalachia Ctr Crafts, Smithville, Tenn, 83; artist in residence, Tupelo City Sch, Miss, 83-84, Bellazio Study Ctr, Italy, 90. *Awards:* Grand Prize, 76 & Second Prize, 77, Miss Artist Competitive Exhib, Miss Art Asn; Merit Award, Greater New Orleans Int Art Exhib, 77; Grant, Rockefeller Found, 90. *Bibliog:* Articles, Art Voices South, 5/79, Cityscape, 81 & 82 & Art Papers, 7-8/82; Annette Cone-Skelton (auth), Southeastern artists today: a cross section, Contemp Art/SE, 78; Gary Witt (auth), Ke & Jean Francis of Tupelo, Mississippi: A union of opposites, Art Voices/South, 5/79; Stephen Flynn Young (auth), A visit with Jean Thickens Francis, Art Papers, 82. *Media:* Mixed Media. *Dealer:* Albers Fine Art Gallery 1102 Brookfield Rd Suite 101 Memphis TN 38119. *Mailing Add:* 512 Magnolia Dr Tupelo MS 38801-3530

FRANCIS, MADISON KE, JR
SCULPTOR, PRINTMAKER
b Memphis, Tenn, Aug 19, 45. *Study:* Miss State Univ, Starkville; Memphis State Univ, Tenn; Memphis Acad Art, Tenn; Cleveland Inst Art, Ohio, BFA(sculpture), 69; Cape Sch Art, Provincetown, Mass, study painting with Henry Hensche. *Work:* Southeastern Ctr Contemp Art, Winston-Salem, NC; Mint Mus, Charlotte, NC; New

Orleans Mus, La; Mus Fine Arts, Boston, Mass; Rose Mus, Brandeis Univ, Waltham, Mass. *Comn:* Steel sculpture, People's Bank, Tupelo, Miss, 73; sculpture, Itawamba Jr Col, 78; time capsule sculpture, North Miss Med Ctr, Tupelo. *Exhib:* Southern Exposure: Not a Regional Exhib, Alternative Mus, NY, 85; A Sense of Place: Contemp Southern Art, Minneapolis Col Art & Design Gallery, Minn, 86; Fact/Fiction/Fantasy: Recent Narrative Art in the Southeast, Traveling exhib, Ewing Gallery, Univ Tenn, Knoxville, 87; Southern Arts Fedn Touring Sculpture Exhib, Atlanta, Ga, 87- 89; Solo exhibs, Recent Works, Memphis Ctr Contemp Art, Tenn, 88, Recent Prints, Drawings & Sculpture, Marcia McCoy Gallery Contemp Art, Santa Fe, NMex, 89 & Reconstruction: Tornado Series, Clara Eagle Gallery, Murray State Univ, Ky, 89; Looking South: A Different Dixie, Touring Exhib, Birmingham Mus, Ala, 88; Freneticism, Valencia Community Col, Orlando, Fla, 88; The Blues Aesthetic: Black Cult & Modernism Touring Exhib, Washington Pro Arts, Washington, DC, 89; and others. *Teaching:* Instr, Cleveland Inst Art, 69-71; instr sculpture, Memphis Acad Art, summer 73; instr graphics, Penland Sch, NC, 78-79. *Awards:* SAF/NEQ Regional fel sculpture, Southern Arts Fedn, 87; Award for visual arts, Mississippi Inst Arts and Letters, 87; Rockefeller Found Grant, Bellagio Study Ctr, Italy, 90. *Bibliog:* Becky Hendrick (auth), El Paso/Las Cruces Letter, Art Space, winter 87-88; Jane Bedno (auth), Tornadoes in Beulah Land, Vol 2, No 3, winter 89; Stephen Flinn Young (auth), Post-southernism: The Southern Sensibility in Postmodern Sculpture, Southern Quarterly, Vol XXVIII, No 4, fall 89. *Media:* Miscellaneous Media; Intaglio, Silkscreen. *Dealer:* Galerie Simone Stern New Orleans La; Morgan Gallery Kansas City Mo. *Mailing Add:* 801 Temple Terr Oviedo FL 32765

FRANCIS, TOM
PAINTER
b Sheboygan, Wis, Mar 12, 51. *Study:* Univ Wis, BS, 73, MA, 75, MFA(Henry Vilas Fel), 76. *Work:* State Wis, Madison; Chase Manhattan Bank, NY; Omni Int, Atlanta; Europco Corp, Fla; Coca Cola Corp, Atlanta, Ga; and others. *Comn:* Paintings, Made in Heaven (film), comn by Alan Rudolph, dir; Hyatt Corp, Aruba & Puerto Rico; Embassy Suites, Orlando, Fla; Omni Corp, Miami, Fla. *Exhib:* Columbia Mus, SC, 82; Atlanta in France, Paris, Toulouse France, 85; Volte del Sud, Rome, Italy, 85; Sandler/Hudson Gallery, Atlanta, 90; McIntosh Gallery, Atlanta, 92; Zinc Gallery, Bluewater Bay, Fla; Mary Pauline Gallery, 97; Montgomery Mus Art, Ala, 97; Spruell Ctr Arts, Atlanta, 98; & many others. *Teaching:* Chmn dept painting, Atlanta Col Art, 78-. *Media:* All. *Mailing Add:* Dept Art Atlanta Col Art 1280 Peachtree NE Atlanta GA 30309

FRANCO, BARBARA
MUSEOLOGIST
b New York, NY, Mar 16, 45. *Study:* Bryn Mawr Col, BA; Cooperstown Grad Progs, MA. *Collection Arranged:* White's Utica Pottery (catalog), 69-70 & Shaker Arts & Crafts (catalog), 70-71, Munson-Williams-Proctor Inst, Utica, NY; Masonic Symbols in American Decorative Arts (catalog), Mus of Our Nat Heritage, 75-76; Decorated Masonic Aprons (catalog), Mus of Our Nat Heritage, 80-81; Fraternally Yours (catalog), Mus Our Nat Heritage, 86. *Pos:* Cur decorative arts, Munson-Williams-Proctor Inst, 66-73; cur, Mus of Our Nat Heritage, 73-90; asst dir, Minnesota Hist Soc, 90-95; exec dir, Hist Soc Washington, currently. *Res:* Symbolism and history of Fraternal Organizations in America; American hooked rugs; American 19th-century decorative arts and cultural history. *Publ:* Auth, Stoneware made by the White Family in Utica, NY, 71 & New York City furniture bought for Fountain Elms, 73, Antiques; John Henry Belter; A Rococo Revival Cabinetmaker in the Limelight, Nineteenth Century, Vol 6 No 2, summer 80; A Treasury of Hooked Rugs, Country Living, 87; Masonic Imagery, Aspects of American Printmaking, 1800-1950, James F O'Gorman (ed), Syracuse Univ Press, 88

FRANK, CHARLES WILLIAM, JR
WOOD CARVER, WRITER
b New Orleans, La, June 8, 22. *Study:* BChemEng. *Exhib:* New Orleans Mus Art, 75; Hillsborough Co Mus, Tampa, Fla, 76; Univ New Orleans Fine Arts Mus, 76; Huntsville Mus Art, Ala, 76-77; West Baton Rouge Hist Asn, 76; Nat Crafts Coun, Winston-Salem, NC, 77. *Pos:* Auth & contribr, NAm Decoys, 72-77; auth, La Duck Decoys, 75-79; La Out of Doors, 77-78 & Ward Found Mag; Anatomy of a Waterfowl, Pelican Publ, 81 & Wetland Heritage, 85. *Awards:* Best of Show, Catahoula Lake Wildfowl Festival, 75 & 76; First Place, La Wildfowl Carvers Exhib, 76; La Master Craftsman, 77. *Bibliog:* Article in La Conservationist, State of La, 73 & 75; Phillips Petroleum Co (auth), Louisiana's Wetland Heritage, The Decoy, 76. *Mem:* La Crafts Coun; La Wildfowl Carvers & Collectors; Int Wildlife Carvers; Nat Wood Carvers Asn. *Media:* Wood, Polychrome. *Collection:* Definitive collection of several thousand Louisiana and world wide duck decoys. *Publ:* Auth articles, Am Shotgunner, 76 & Southern Outdoors, 77. *Mailing Add:* 3112 Octavia New Orleans LA 70125

FRANK, DAVID
ADMINISTRATOR, EDUCATOR
b St Paul, Minn, Sept 13, 40. *Study:* Univ Minn, Duluth, with Glenn C Nelson, BS(art); Tulane Univ La, MFA. *Work:* Tweed Gallery, Duluth; Newcomb Art Sch Collection; Mid Tenn State Univ Collection, Murfreesboro; Miss Univ for Women, Columbus; Miss Dept Archives & Hist. *Comn:* Pohl Gym, Miss Univ for Women, Columbus & St Ignatius Catholic Church, Mobile, Ala. *Exhib:* Mid South Ceramics & Crafts Exhib, Tenn; 14th Ann Delta Art Exhib, Ark; Crafts Invitational, Univ Ala; Invitational Exhib, Nat Endowment Arts; Miss River Crafts Exhib, Brooks Gallery, Memphis, Tenn; 13th Bi State Exhib, Meridian Mus Art, Miss. *Teaching:* Prof art, Miss Univ for Women, 65-, head div fine arts & performing arts, currently. *Mem:* Craftsmen's Guild Miss; Am Craftsman's Coun. *Media:* Clay

FRANK, HELEN GOODZEIT
PAINTER, PRINTMAKER
b Jersey City, NJ, May 29, 30. *Study:* Tyler Sch Fine Arts, Temple Univ; Cooper Union; New Sch, with Abraham Rattner & Seymour Lipton, 48; Art Students League, with George Grosz, 50. *Work:* NJ State Mus, Trenton; Newark Public Libr Print Collection, NJ; Am Mus Immigration, NY; UNICEF; Libr Congress. *Comn:* Portfolio, Grant Union Co, NJ, 80-81. *Exhib:* NJ State Exhib, Montclair Mus, 63; Am Watercolor Soc, NY, 65; Pratt Graphic Int, NY, 75 & 77; Morris Mus, Morristown, NJ; NJ Watercolor Soc, Morristown; Rutgers Univ, NJ. *Teaching:* Artist-in-residence, Springfield Pub Sch. *Mem:* Artists Equity. *Mailing Add:* 445 Meisel Ave Springfield NJ 07081

FRANK, MARY
SCULPTOR, PAINTER
b London, Eng. *Study:* Am Artists Sch with Max Beckmann, 50; studied with Hans Hofmann, 51 & 54. *Work:* Hirshhorn Mus and Sculpture Garden, Washington; Metrop Mus Art, Mus Modern Art, NY; Mus Fine Arts, Boston; Art Inst Chicago; Brooklyn Mus Art. *Exhib:* 10 Independents, Solomon R Guggenheim Mus, NY, 72; Whitney Sculpture Ann, 72, Whitney Bienniel, 73 & 79, Small Objects, Whitney Mus Am Art, NY, 77; Drawings of the 70's, Art Inst Chicago, 77; Contemp Women: Conciousness and Content, 77 & Pub and Private: Am Prints Today, Brooklyn Mus, 86; one-woman show, Neuberger Mus, State Univ NY, Purchase, 78, 2000, Brooklyn Mus, 87, DeCordova and Dana Mus and Park, Lincoln, Mass, 88, Everson Mus Art, Syracuse, 88, Pa Acad Fine Arts, Philadelphia, 88, DC Moore Gallery, 96, 98 & 2000 & Allentown Art Mus, 2001; 8 Artists, Philadelphia Mus Art, 78; Mysterious and Magical Realism, Aldrich Mus Contemp Art, Ridgefield, Conn, 80; The Painterly Print, Metrop Mus Art, NY, 80; The Painterly Print Traveling Exhib, Mus Fine Arts, Boston, 80; Sculpture in the 70's - The Figure, Pratt Inst, NY, 80; The Figurative Tradition, Whitney Mus Am Art, NY, 80; The Clay Figure, Am Craft Mus, NY, 81; Am Printmaker's Show, Brooklyn Mus, 83; Contemp Am Monotypes, Chrysler Mus, Norfolk, Va, 85; Body and Soul: Recent Figurative Sculpture, Contemp Arts Ctr, Cincinnati, 85; Disarming Images, 86, Standing Ground: Sculpture by Am Women, Contemp Arts Ctr, Cincinnati, 87; The Jewish Mus Collects, Jewish Mus, NY, 88; Committed to Print, Mus Modern Art, NY, 88; The 1980's: Prints from the Collection of Joshua P Smith, Nat Gallery Art, Washington, 90; Shadows of Africa, Cent Park Zoo Gallery, NY, 92; Print and Drawing Society 25th Anniversary Exhib, Baltimore Mus Art, 93; The Second Dimension: Twentieth-Century Sculptor's Drawings, Brooklyn Mus, 93; Likeness of Being, DC Moore Gallery, 2000; Pasadena Col, 1995; Nielsen Gallery, Boston, 1996; Elena Zanz Gallery, Woodstock, 1995, 98, 2002; Reynolda House Mus, Winston-Salem, 1999; Allentown Art Mus, 2001; Marsh Art Gallery, Richmond, 2003. *Teaching:* Distinguished prof, Bard Col, Annandale-on-Hudson, NY, 92; grad fac, Pa Acad Fine Arts, Philadelphia, 92-93. *Awards:* Guggenheim Award, 73 & 83; Am Acad Arts and Letts Electee, 84; Lee Krasner Award, Pollock/Krasner Found, 93. *Bibliog:* Jerry Thompson and Hilton Kramer (auth), The sculpture of Mary Frank, The Eakins Press, 77; Margaret Moorman (auth), In a timeless world, Artnews, 5/87; Hayden Herrera (auth), Mary Frank, NY: Abrams, 90; Linda Nochlin (auth), Marty Franki Encounters, NY: Abrams, 2000. *Mem:* Am Acad Arts & Letts; Nat Acad. *Dealer:* DC Moore Gallery 724 Fifth Ave New York NY 10019. *Mailing Add:* c/o DC Moore Gallery 724 Fifth Ave New York NY 10019

FRANK, PETER SOLOMON
CRITIC, CURATOR
b New York, NY, 50. *Study:* Columbia Col, BA(art hist), 72; Columbia Univ, MA(art hist), 74. *Collection Arranged:* Artists' books section of Documenta 6, Kassel, WGer, summer 77; Artists' Books USA Traveling Exhib, 78-80 & Mapped Art: Charts Routes Regions Traveling Exhib, 81-83, Independent Curators Inc; Young Fluxus, Artists Space, New York, 82; Indiana Influence-The Modern Legacy, Fort Wayne Mus Art, 84; To the Astonishing Horizon, Los Angeles Visual Arts, 85; Earsights: Visual Scores & Musical Images, Nexus Gallery, Philadelphia and Southern Alleghenies Mus, Johnstown, Pa, 85; Southern Abstraction, City Gallery of Contemp Art, Raleigh, NC, 87 & Contemp Arts Ctr, New Orleans, 88; Line and Image, Independent Curators, Inc, 88-90; The Theater of the Object, 1958-1972, Alternative Mus, NY, 89; Visual Poetry, Otis/Parsons Art Inst, Los Angeles, 90; Los Angeles Art, Foreign Artists, Kilkenny Castle, Ireland, 92; The Sticking Place; Space & Image in Contemporary Collage, Long Beach City Col, 92; Multiple World, Atlanta Col Art, 94; Fluxus Scores, Col Creative Studies, Univ Calif, Santa Barbara, 94; Reconstructivism: New Geometric Painting in NY, Space 504, 95; Grins: Humor and Whimsy in Contemporary Art, Lost Angeles Co Fair, 97; Edge, Image, Informatgion, ARTernatives, San Luis Obispo, 98; Fluxus Film & Video, Museo Reina Sofia,Madric, 2002. *Pos:* Art critic, SoHo News, 73-76, Village Voice, 77-79 & Diversion Planner, 83-90, Los Angeles Weekly, 88-, Long Beach Press Telegram, Calif, 93-96 & Art Commotion, 96-98, Book Radio, 2000-, Angeleno Mag, 2003-; cur assoc, Independent Curators Inc, 74-81; assoc ed, Tracks, 74-78, Nat Arts Guide, 79-81 & Art Express, 80-81; cur sound & mus, Inst Art & Urban Resources at PS1, 79-80; cur, Exxon Nat Exhib, 19 Emergent Americans, Guggenheim Mus, 81; contrib ed, Art Economist, 81-83; ed, Re Dact, 83-87; Am cur adv, Documenta 8, Kassel, WGer, 87; Los Angeles Corresp Contemp, 88-90; ed, Visions, 90-95; contrib ed, Artspace, 90-93; gallery coordr, Long Beach City Col, Calif, 92. *Teaching:* Vis asst prof contemp arts, Pratt Inst, Brooklyn, NY, 75-76; adj assoc prof, Sch Arts, Columbia Univ, 78; adj lectr, Tyler Sch Art, Temple Univ, 83; lectr, Univ Calif, Irvine, 88-90; lectr, Claremont Grad Sch, 89 & 92-97; vis critic, Calif State Univ, Fullerton, 90-91; vis lectr, Univ Calif, Santa Barbara, 94. *Awards:* Nat Endowment Arts Grant, 78 & 81; Fluxus Res Fel, Royal Norwegian Ministry For Affairs, 87. *Bibliog:* Jacqueline Brody (auth), Peter Frank: A Case for Marginal Collectors, Print Collectors Newsletter, 6/78; Grace Glueck (auth), How emerging artists really emerge: Getting the biennials together, Art News, 5/81; Katherine Cook (auth), Talking Art: A Conversation with Peter Frank &

Peter Selz, Artspace, summer 91. *Mem:* Int Asn Art Critics; Poets & Writers; Col Arts Asn of Am; Int Künstlers Gremium. *Publ:* Something Else Press: An Annotated Bibliography (document text), MacPherson & Co, Kingston, NY, 83; New, Used & Improved: Art for the '80s, Abbeville Press, 87; Intermedia: Die Verschmelzung der Künste, Benteli Verlag, 87; Roller: The Paintings of Donald Roller Wilson, Chronicle Books, 88; Lawrence Gipe: Paintings, Karl Bornstein, 89. *Mailing Add:* PO Box 24A36 Los Angeles CA 90024-1036

FRANKEL, DEXTRA
EDUCATOR, DESIGNER
b Los Angeles, Calif, Nov 28, 24. *Study:* Long Beach State Col. *Work:* Philadelphia Free Libr; La Jolla Art Mus, Calif; St Paul Art Ctr, Minn; Pac View Mem Park, Corona Del Mar, Calif; Kennecott Copper Co, Salt Lake City, Utah; also in pvt collections. *Exhib:* Los Angeles Co Mus Art, 59, 62 & 66; Cincinnati Art Mus; Newport Harbor Art Mus, Newport Beach, Calif; Butler Inst Am Art, Youngstown, Ohio; Calif Palace of Legion of Honor, San Francisco; Denver Art Mus, Colo; Seattle Art Mus, Wash; Portland Art Mus, Ore; San Francisco Mus Art, Calif; H M De Young Mus, San Francisco; Smithsonian Inst, Washington, DC; and many others. *Collection Arranged:* Recorded Images/Dimensional Media, 67, Intersection of Line, 67, Frazer/Lipofsky/Richardson, 68, Transparency/Reflection, 68 & others, Art Gallery, Calif State Univ, Fullerton; and numerous others. *Pos:* Dir art gallery, cur & designer exhib, Calif State Univ, Fullerton, 67-91; owner & founder, Dextre Frankel Assoc, 91-. *Teaching:* From asst prof to assoc prof art, Calif State Univ, Fullerton, 64-79, prof art, 79-91. *Awards:* 8 Nat Endowment Arts Grants, 75 & 77-82; Design Award, Soc Typographic Arts Union Bank Hist Mus, 81. *Mem:* Am Asn Mus; Am Craft Coun; Art Mus Asn. *Media:* Exhibits. *Publ:* Auth, article, Pasadena Mus, 65 & 68 & Crafts Horizons Mag, 73. *Mailing Add:* PO Box 5307 Santa Monica CA 90409

FRANKEL, STUART & MAXINE
COLLECTOR
Study: U Mich, BBA, 61, AB, 66. *Pos:* Bd directors Chinati Found, Marfa, tex, and Independent Curators Int; bd and exec comt Children's Hospital of Mich; nat adv bd Storm King Art Ctr, Mountainville, NY, and UMMA; chair bd governors Cranbrook Acad Art and Cranbrook Art Mus; pres Stuart Frankel Development Co, Troy. *Collection:* modern & contemp art, especially Latin Am, ceramics & sculpture

FRANKENTHALER, HELEN
PAINTER, PRINTMAKER
b New York, NY, Dec 12, 28. *Study:* Horace Mann, Brearly & Dalton Sch: Bennington Col, Vt, BA, 49; Studied with Rufino Tamayo, Wallace Harrison, Paul Freeley & Hans Hoffman; twenty hon degrees from US univs and cols, 69-94. *Work:* Brooklyn Mus, Cooper Hewitt Mus, NY Univ Art Collection, Solomon R Guggenheim Mus, Whitney Mus of Am Art, Metrop Mus Art & Mus Mod Art, NY; Art Inst Chicago; Cleveland Mus Art; Pasadena Art Mus, Calif; Nat Gallery Art, Washington, DC; Mus Fine Art, Boston; Carnegie Inst, Pittsburgh; Philadelphia Mus Art, Pa; Baltimore Mus Art, Md; San Francisco Mus Art; Seattle Art Mus; Butler Inst Am Art, Youngstown, Ohio; Milwaukee Art Inst, Wis; Walker Art Inst; plus many others. *Comn:* Shield (acrylic on canvas), First Wis Nat Bank, Milwaukee, 73; installation (7' x 17'), North Cent Bronx Hops, NY, 73-74; design for tapestry (10' x 45'), Fourth Nat Bank, Wichita, Kans, 73-74; tapestry design (10' x 57'), Hong Kong Club, Hong Kong, 84. *Exhib:* NY Painting & Sculpture: 1940-1970, Metrop Mus Art, NY, 69-70; Retrospective, Whitney Mus Am Art, NY, 69 & Berggruen Gallery, San Francisco, Calif, 72; Albright-Knox Art Gallery, Buffalo, NY, 70; Abstract Painting in the 70's, Mus Fine Arts, Boston, 72; Block Prints, Whitney Mus Am Art, 82; From Munch to Johns: Modern Prints from the Collection, Fogg Art Mus, 83; Changes: The 1960's into the 1980's, Aldrich Mus Contemp Art, 83; Am Print Renaissance 1958-1988, Selections from the Permanent Collection, Whitney Mus Am Art, Stamford, Conn, 88; Made In the Sixties, Painting and Sculpture from the Permanent Collection, Whitney Mus Am Art, NY, 88; Twentieth Century Paintings and Sculpture: Selections for the Tenth Anniversary of the E Bldg, Nat Gallery Art, Washington, DC, 88; The Gestural Impulse 1945-60, Whitney Mus Am Art, NY, 89; Projects and Portfolios; the 25th National Print Exhib, Brooklyn Mus, 89; Baltimore Collects: Painting and Sculpture since 1960, Baltimore Mus Art, 90; The Unique Print, Mus Fine Arts, Boston, 90; one-woman exhibs, Knoedler & Co, NY, 92, 94 & 95, Nat Gallery Art, Wash, 93, Robert Kidd Gallery, Birmingham, Mich, 93, Meredith Long & Co, Houston, 93 & 94, Dennos Mus Ctr, Traverse City Mich, 95, Tyler Graphics Ltd, Mt Kisco, NY, 95 & Bobbie Greenfield Gallery, Santa Monica, Calif, 95; 30th Anniversary Show-The First 15 Yrs, Heath Gallery Inc, Atlanta, 94; Ken Tyler: Thirty Yrs of Printmaking, The Gallery, Halls Crown Ctr, NY, 95; Seven from the Seventies, Knoedler & Co, NY, 95; Some Very Important Am Artists, Am Arts Festival, 95; Masters of Am Watercolor: A 100 Year Survey, Southern Alleghenies Mus Art, St Francis Col, Loretto, Pa, 95; Artist's Choice: Elizabeth Murray: Modern Women, Mus Mod Art, NY, 95; Art Works: The Paine Webber Collection of Contemp Masters, Mus Fine Arts, Houston, 95. *Pos:* Trustee, Bennington Col, 67-; fel, Calhoun Col, Yale Univ, 68-. *Teaching:* Instr contemp painting sem, Yale Univ, spring 70; instr contemp painting sem, Hunter Col, 70 & Princeton Univ, 71; lectr, Univ Ariz, Tuscon, 78, Graphics Art Coun NY, Nat Arts Club, 79, Duke Univ & Art Inst Chicago, 83 & 91, Lowe Art Mus, Miami, Fla, 84 & Fla Int Univ, Miami, 92; slide lect, Aspen Art Mus, Colo, 91; slide lect & questions & answers, Phillips Col & New York Pub Libr, 92; plus many other lectures & seminars. *Awards:* Distinguished Artist Award for Lifetime Achievement, Col Art Asn, 94; Lotos Medal Merit, Lotos Club, NY, 94; Artist of Yr Award, Art Resources in Teaching, Chicago, 95; Jerusalem prize, 99; Lifetime Achievement award, 99. *Bibliog:* Holland Cotter (auth), Helen Frankenthaler, review, NY Times, 11/27/92; Nancy Malloy (auth), Helen Frankenthaler, review, Artnews, 2/93; Eric Gibson (auth), Breaking the Rules, Wash Times, 4/16/93; Hilton Kramer (auth), An Interview with Helen Frankenthaler, Partisan Review, spring 94; Robert C Morgan (auth), Helen Frankenthaler Prints and Works on Paper, Contemp Art, summer 94. *Mem:* Nat Educ Asn, Am Acad (vice-chancelor 1991), Am Acad Arts and Scis, Nat Coun Arts, Nat Inst Arts and Letters, Nat Acad. *Publ:* Auth, Letters to the editors, Print Collectors Newsletter, Vol 16, No 2, 5-6/85; Artist' Choice, Art & Antiques, 12/86; Did we spawn an arts monster?, NY Times, 7/17/89; Profile, Visual Arts, 89; Hans Namuth; an appreciation, 12/90; and others. *Dealer:* Knoedler & Co Inc 19 East 70th St New York NY 10021

FRANKFURTER, JACK
PAINTER, DESIGNER
b Vienna, Austria, Mar 25, 29; US citizen. *Study:* Cooper Union Sch Art, 50-51; Col City NY, BS, 51; Columbia Univ, BA, 52; Accademia di Francia, Villa Medici, Rome, 58-59. *Work:* Springfield Mus Fine Arts, Mass; Wichita Art Mus, Kans; Univ Cincinnati Art Mus, Ohio; Malcolm Forbes Collection, NY; Museo Mario Praz, Rome. *Exhib:* Allied Artists Am, Nat Acad Design, NY, 54 & 56; Am Artists Ann, Whitney Mus, NY, 55; Soc of the Four Arts, Palm Beach, Fla, 68; Biennial Int, Biennale Di Lignano, Italy, 70; X Quadriennale Di Roma, Galleria D'Arte Mod, Rome, Italy, 77; San Francisco Int Airport, 93; Empire State Building Galleries, NY, 94; solo shows, Galleria 88, Rome, 60-72, La Zagara, Napoli, 61, Country Art Gallery, NY, 62, 71, Alwin Gallery, London, 69, 72, Palm Beach Gallery, 70, Mus Fine Arts, Springfield, Mass, 70, Piccola Barcaccia, Cagliari, 71, Galleria Arno, Firenze, 73, Findlay Galleries, NY, 73, Findlay Galleries, Palm Beach, 74, Kama Studio, Rome, 74, Galleria Doria, Porto Ercole, 75, 80, Galleria Ca' d'Oro, Rome, 76, 77, 79, 82, 83-89, 2001, Bodley Gallery, NY, 76, Mickelson Gallery, Washington, DC, 76, Janice Throne Gallery, Springfield, Mass, 76, The Gallery, LA, 77, Galleria Cortina, Milano, 83, Tiffany & Co, NY, 92, 92, Empire State Bldg Galleries, NY, 94. *Pos:* Designer, Tiffany & Co, New York, 56-57; stage designer, Bayrisches Schauspielhaus, Muenchen, Ger, 77-79. *Teaching:* Auburn Univ, Ala, 55-56. *Awards:* Gold Medal, Premio Campidoglio, Roma, 69; Premio Via Conndotti, Rome, 79. *Bibliog:* Sterling McIlhany (auth), American Artist in Rome, Am Artist, 6/61; Mario Praz (auth), Paintings of Frankfurter, Agraf Art Editions, 73; Antonio Porcella (auth), Frankfurter Galeria Ca d'Ora, Roma, 76. *Media:* Oil on Canvas. *Publ:* Contribr, numerous articles in NY Times, 60-71; cover art, Am Artist, 9/65 & 11/68; title page, Arts & Leisure, NY Times, 12/5/71; auth, article for UNICEF Art Calendar, 72; auth & cover art, Wichita, Wichita Chamber Commerce, 76. *Dealer:* Galleriea Ca d'Oro Plazza Di Spanga 81 Roma Italy 00187; Marcelle Fine Arts South Hampton LI. *Mailing Add:* 90 Park Terrace E New York NY 10034

FRANKLIN, DON
PAINTER, PHOTOGRAPHER, SCULPTOR
b Uniontown, Pa, Mar 16, 31. *Study:* Art Inst Pittsburgh, 49-50. *Work:* Locust Hill Gallery, Pittsford, NY; Six Nations Mus, Onchiota, NY; Akwesasne Mus, Hogansburg, NY; Dick Moll's Gallery, Mendon, NY; Mill Gallery, Honeoye Falls, NY. *Comn:* Period painting, Dick Moll's Gallery, 75. *Exhib:* Arts for Greater Rochester, Nazareth Arts Ctr, Pittsford, NY, 89; solo exhib, 1570 Gallery, Rochester, NY, 90; Fine Art Showcase, Wilson Arts Ctr, Rochester, NY, 90-91, Mem Art Gallery, Rochester, NY, 92; Art Inst Pittsburgh, Pa, 2003. *Collection Arranged:* Spectrum Labs Caricature Col, Rochester, NY. *Pos:* Art dir, Bausch & Lomb, 70-73 & creative dir, 77-94, self-employed, 94-. *Teaching:* Instr art, Univ Rochester Mem Art Gallery, Rochester, NY, 77-82. *Awards:* Award Excellence, Fine Art Showcase, WXXI Pub Television, 90; Award Excellence, Fine Art Showcase, Archit Inst Am, 91. *Media:* Miscellaneous Media, Watercolor, Graphite, Pastel, Acrylic. *Publ:* Pastel Artists Int, 1 2/2002; Int Artist's, 101 Ways to Paint People & Figures, How Did You Paint That, series. *Dealer:* The Mill Gallery Honeoye Falls NY. *Mailing Add:* 160 Chelmsford Rd Rochester NY 14618

FRANKLIN, HANNAH
SCULPTOR, PAINTER
b Poland, June 20, 37; Can Citizen. *Study:* Montreal Mus Fine Art Sch, BA, 68; studied with Arthur Lismer. *Work:* Montreal Mus Art, Que; Musee d'Art Contemporian, Montreal; Musee du Quebec, Ont; Can Coun Art Bank, Ottowa; Cabinet du Quebec; Simon Fraser Univ, Vancouver, BC. *Comn:* Sculptures, Jacque Cartier, 84 & Vancouver Centenniel Comn, 86; St Jean Port Joli (sculpture), Mus Que, 84. *Exhib:* Small Sculpture Biennial, Budapest, Hungary, 71; Saidye Bronfman Ctr, Montreal, 73; Biennial, Basel, Switz, 74; Fete du Fleuve, Que, 84; 3 Sculptors & 12 Sculptors, Palais de Cong Montreal, 85. *Teaching:* Instr sculpture, Saidye Bronfman Ctr, Montreal, 74-76. *Awards:* First Prize Sculpture, Hadassah Wiz Exhib, 70, 72 & 74; Purchase Award Que Concour, Govt Que, 70. *Bibliog:* Guy Robert (auth), l'Art au Quebec, La Presse, 73; Art Actuel Quebec, Iconia, 83; Arthur Williams (auth),The Sculpture Reference, 2004; and others. *Mem:* Soc Sculptors Que (vpres, 72); Vancouver Sculptors Asn; Int Sculptors Asn. *Media:* Plastic, Bronze; Acrylic, Oil. *Publ:* La Sculpture et le Vent, Women Sculptors of Quebec, 2004. *Mailing Add:* 85 Holton Ave Montreal PQ H3Y 2G1 Canada

FRANKLIN, PATT
PAINTER, SCULPTOR
b 1941. *Study:* Pratt Inst, BFA, 62; Tulane Univ, MFA, 70. *Work:* Boston Libr Print & Drawing Collection & New Eng Med Ctr Lobby Collection, Boston, Mass; Int Telephone & Telegraph, NY; Colby Col, Waterville, Maine; Gilette Corp, Boston; LL Bean, Maine; Ogunquit Mus, Maine; Bowdoin Coll Mus Art, Maine; Honeck O'Toole, Maine. *Comn:* Painted murals, Doctors of Touro Hospital, New Orleans, La, 68. *Exhib:* Cranbrook Art Mus, 76; one-person shows, Varley & Stevens Gallery, Portsmouth, NH, 85, Portland Stage Co, Maine, 86, Unity Col, Maine, 89, Cong Sq Gallery, Portland, Maine, 89, Merrimack Col, N Andover, Mass, 90, Rissho Univ, Tokyo, 92, Ogunquit Mus Am Art, Maine, 94; Presence of Women, Bowdoin Mus, Brunswick, Maine, 92; O'Farrell Gallery, Brunswick, Maine, 93; June Fitzpatrick

Gallery, Portland, Maine, 93 & 98; Ratliff Gallery, Sedona, Ariz, 95-96; Mathias Fine Art, Maine, 2000; Mathias Fine Art, 2000-2003. *Teaching:* Prof drawing & ceramics, Univ South Maine, Gorham, 70-2000; instr ceramics, Mass Col Art, summer 73 & Haystack Sch Art & Crafts, Deer Isle, Maine, 77. *Awards:* Fellar Award, Silvermine Competition, 73. *Bibliog:* Beem, Edgar Allen, Maine Art Now, Gardiner, Maine; Docear Press, 90, pages, 202,224-225; Jacks, Shirley, Art New England, Oct-Nov 94; Temin, Christine, Boston Globe, Nov, 84. *Mem:* Am Craft Coun; Women's Caucus Art; Nat Coun Educ Ceramic Arts; Col Art Asn. *Media:* Oils; Clay. *Publ:* Allgemeines Kunst Lerlexikon. *Dealer:* June Fitzpatrick Gallery Portland ME; Mathias Fine Art Boothbay, ME. *Mailing Add:* PO Box 94 Gorham ME 04038

FRASCONI, ANTONIO
GRAPHIC ARTIST, PAINTER
b Buenos Aires, Arg, Apr 28, 1919; arrived in US in 1945; US citizen. *Study:* Archit Acad, Montevideo, 36-37; Art Students League, 45; New Sch Social Res, 47. *Work:* Bibliotheque Nat, Paris, France; Mus Mod Art, NY; Metrop Mus Art; Casa Americas, Havana, Cuba; Univ Puerto Rico. *Comn:* Snow Flakes, Christmas ornaments, Metrop Mus Art, NY, 72. *Exhib:* Solo exhib, Books & Posters of Antonio Frasconi, State Univ NY, 85; Univ Puerto Rico Mus, San Juan, 86; Repression, Exilio y Democracia-La Cultura Uruguaya Univ Md, 86; 1986 Biennial, Orgn Int Biennial Illus, Tokyo, Japan, 86; 196 Fiera del Libro, Bologna, Italy, 86; Museo d' Arte Contemporanea, Bologna, Italy, 86; Mus Contemp Art, NY, 86; Commission Arts Showcase Gallery, Conn, 87; over 100 Nat & Int exhibs. *Teaching:* Distinguished teaching prof art, State Univ NY, Purchase, 73-77 & 86-, assoc prof, 77-79, prof, 79-; prof visual arts, State Univ NY, Purchase, 1980. *Awards:* Annual Childrens Lit Auth & Artist Award, Libr Cong Children's Lit Ctr, 89; Lee Krasner Award for Lifetime Achievement, Pollack-Krasner Found, 97; Gov Art Award, Conn Comn on Arts, 98. *Bibliog:* Margit Varga (auth), Woodcuts by Antonio Frasconi, Am Artist, 10/74; Nat Hentoff & Charles Parkhurst (auth), Frasconi-Against the Grain, MacMillan, 75; Jane Sterett (auth), Interview with Antonio Frasconi, Print Rev 17, 83. *Mem:* Nat Acad. *Media:* All. *Publ:* Illusr, The Salamander, Red Ozier Press, 82; Yentl the Yeshiva Boy, Farrar, Straus, 83; Monkey Puzzle and Other Poems, Atheneum, 84; Prima Che tu Dica Pronto, Plain Wrapper Press, 85; Sat at Midnight, Nadja, 86. *Dealer:* Terry Dintenfass Gallery 50 W 57th St New York NY 10019. *Mailing Add:* 26 Dock Rd Norwalk CT 06854

FRASER, ANDREA R
CONCEPTUAL ARTIST, MUSEOLOGIST
b Billings, Mont, Sept 27, 65. *Study:* Sch Visual Arts, 82-83; Whitney Mus Am Art, independent study prog, 84-85. *Work:* Antoni Tàpies Found, Barcelona; Mus Boymans, Rotterdam; Centre Georges Pompidou, Paris; Sprengel Mus, Hanover; Wadsworth Atheneum, Hartford. *Exhib:* Damaged Goods, Gallery Talk, New Mus Contemp Arts, NY, 86; Mus Highlights, Philadelphia Mus Art, 89; Welcome to the Wadsworth, Wadsworth Atheneum, 91; Aren't they lovely? (auth, catalog), Univ Art Mus, Berkeley, Calif, 92; A Society of Taste (auth, catalog), Kunstverein Munich, 93; Biennial Exhib, Whitney Mus Am Art, 93; Venice Biennale, Austrian Pavilion, 93; A Project in Two Phases, EA-Generali Found, Vienna, 95. *Teaching:* Guest artist sculpture, Cooper Union, 90 & 96; part-time fac performance, Tyler Sch Art, 92. *Awards:* Fel, Art Matters Inc, 87 & 89; NY Found Arts, 91; Nat Endowment Arts, 91. *Bibliog:* Marcia Tanner (auth), Inside information: aren't they lovely? in UAM, Berkeley, Artweek, 8/20/92; Hanne Weskott (auth), I provide services: Ein Gesprach mit Andrea Fraser, Artis, 5/93; Johanna Hofleitner (auth), Feldforschung in der Direktion: Andres Fraser in der Wiener EA-Generali Foundation, Neie Zuricher Zeitung, 5/30/95. *Media:* Performance, Installation. *Publ:* Auth, Woman 1/Madonna and Child 1506-1967, Andrea Frutsen, 84; In and out of place, Art Am, 85; Individual Works, John Weber Gallery, 88; Notes in the museum's publicity, Lusitania, 90; Museum highlights: a gallery talk, October, 91. *Dealer:* Colin De Land American Fine Arts 40 Wooster St New York NY 10014. *Mailing Add:* c/o New Mus Contemp Art 210 Eleventh Ave New York NY 10001

FRASER, CATRIONA TRAFFORD
GALLERY DIRECTOR, PHOTOGRAPHER
b Reading, England, Jan 8, 72. *Study:* Wallingford Sch, Oxfordshire, England, Grad, 88; Plymouth Col Arts and Design, Diploma, Devon, Eng, 88-89. *Work:* Glamis Castle, 92; Brusque Mus, Santa Caterina Brazil, 93; Photographer Dunnottar Castle, 92; Kinnaird Castle, 92; Photography Competition, Calif, Fleur No II, 92. *Exhib:* Nat Art Competition, 96, Castlegait Gallery, Scotland, 92, Sacramento Fine Arts Ctr, 92, New Image Gallery, Va, 92, Carnegie Mus, Pittsburgh, 92, St Helena Art League, Calif, 93, Brusque Mus, Santa Caterina Brazil, 93, Art League Gallery, Va, 94, 95, Va Commonwealth Univ, 95, Eklektikos Gallery, Wash DC, 96, Fraser Gallery, Wash DC, 96, 97, 99, 2000, 2002, Infrared Gallery, Chicago, 98, Bruce Gallery, Edinboro Coll, Pa, 2001, Am Ctr Physics, Md, 2004. *Pos:* Asst photog trainee, Reading Evening Post, Reading, Eng, 87; Found, Cairn Photog, Fettercairn, Scotland, 91; Dir, Fraser Gallery, Wash, 96-, Bethesda, Md, 2002-; Found, Secondsight, 2003-. *Awards:* Recipient Hon Award, 42d Ann Boardwalk Int Arts Festival, 98. *Mem:* Art Dealers Asn Greter Wash, Bethesda CofC. *Mailing Add:* Fraser Gallery 7700 Wisconsin Ave Ste E Bethesda MD 20814

FRASER, MARY EDNA
ENVIRONMENTAL ARTIST, CRAFTSMAN
b Fayetteville, NC, Mar 20, 1952. *Study:* E Carolina Univ, Greenville, NC, BS (textiles & interior design), 74; Arrowmont Sch Crafts, Univ Tenn, Gatlinburg, Tenn, 75-76; Univ Ga, Surface Design Southeast, 77, with Chungi Choo; pvt study with Fred Andrade & Dr. Orrin Pilkey. *Work:* Smithsonian Inst, Nat Air & Space Mus, Washington; Nat Aeronautics & Space Admin, Washington; Am Embassy, Bangkok, Thailand; George Wash Univ; New Eng Aquarium; NASA; First Union Nat Bank; Charleston Int Airport; Roper Hospital. *Comn:* two batiks, Charleston Int Airport, SC, 86; 70 yds batik sculpture, Charleston Int Airport, SC, 88; 15 yds batik sculpture, Symmes Libr, Greenville, SC; 5 batiks, SC Visitor Ctr, Charleston, 90; Ponds (3'x9' batik on silk), New Eng Aquarium, Boston, 96; and others. *Exhib:* Solo exhibs, Islands from the Sky, Surroundings, NY, 82, Spoleto Festival USA, Charleston, 85, Islands from the Sky, Gibbes Mus Art, 89, A Celebration of Barrier Islands, Duke Univ Mus Art Nat Science Found, 99 & Nat Acad Sci, 2001, Naturescapes, Mass Audubon Visual Arts Center, Canton, Mass, 2005, Silk Tableaus, Peabody Essex Mus, Salem, Mass, 2005; Batik Exhib, Donnell Libr, NY, 85; Earth Views, Nat Air & Space Mus, Washington, 86; Contemp Batik Artists, Southern Ohio Mus, Portsmouth, 90; Aerial Inspirations, Nat Air & Space Mus, Washington, 94-95; Fashion is a VERB, Mus Fashion Inst Technol, NY, 95; Wax Eloquent, Mass Col Art, Boston, 2005; Celebrating Women Artists of the Lowcountry, Wells Gallery, Kiawah, SC, 2005. *Pos:* Design consult, City Charleston; lectr, AATCC Symp, Smithsonian Inst; plus numerous lectures at museums and conferences. *Teaching:* Instr batik, Textile Mus, Washington, DC, summer 84 & 96; instr, World Batik Conf, Boston, Mass, 2005; instr, Gibbes Mus Art, Charleston, SC, 2006. *Awards:* Third Place, Nat Air & Space Mus, 86; Third Place, Eros Data Ctr, 98; SC Art Coun Fel, 98. *Bibliog:* Hank Burchard (auth), A Seamless Show of Fabric, Wash Post, 9/9/94; Diane M Bolz (auth), Lofty Perspectives: The Silk Batiks of Mary Edna Fraser, Smithsonian Mag, 11/94; Aida Rogers (auth), Spiritual Link: Artists Join to Save the Earth with their Shared Creativity, Chicago Tribune, 12/17/97; Susan Haynes (auth), Artist With an Attittude, Coastal Living Mag, 9/2000. *Mem:* Surface Design Asn. *Media:* Batik, Monotype. *Interests:* Music, Poetry, Sculpture, Science & Travel. *Publ:* Contribr, Artcraft, 80; Art with architecture in mind, Am Inst Architects, 2/91; Textile Designs: Ideas and Applications, PBC Int, 92; Women & Flight, Bulfinch Press, 97; contribr, A Celebration of the Worlds Barrier Islands, Columbia Univ Press, 2003; coauth, What the Water Gives Me, BookSurge Publ, 2004. *Mailing Add:* PO Box 12250 Charleston SC 29422

FRASER, PAMELA
PAINTER, SCULPTOR
b Smyrna, Tenn, 1965. *Study:* Sch Visual Arts, New York, BFA, 88; Univ Calif, Los Angeles, MFA, 92. *Exhib:* Lotus Motel, Inglewood, Calif, 95; solo shows, Casey Kaplan Gallery, NY, 96 & 98; The Strange Power of Cheap Sentiment (or a Bientot to Irony), White Columns, NY, 96; From here to Eternity, Max Protetch, 98; The Stroke, Exit Art, NY, 99; Do Paintings Dream of Veronese Green, Elga Wimmer Gallery, NY, 99. *Awards:* Skowheghan Sch Painting & Sculpture Fel, 88; Louis Comfort Tiffany Award, 97. *Bibliog:* Ken Johnson (auth), Art in review: Pamela Fraser, NY Times, 1/30/98; Kim Levin (auth), Voice choices: Pamela Fraser, Village Voice, 2/10/98; Maia Damianovic (auth), article, Tema Celeste, 9/98. *Mailing Add:* c/o Casey Kaplan Gallery 416 West 14th St New York NY 10014

FRATER, HAL
PAINTER
b New York, NY, Mar 3, 1909. *Work:* Southern Alleghenies Mus Art, Loretto, Pa. *Exhib:* Minnesota Mus, 80 & 82; Nat Acad Design; Brooklyn Mus; Allied Artists Am; Chrysler Mus, Provincetown, Mass; Seton Hall Univ; Permanent collection & exhib of 24 works, Thundering Seas Mus, Ore State Univ; and others. *Teaching:* Instr, Sch Art & Design & Educ Alliance, NY. *Awards:* Jane Peterson Award, Allied Artists, 59; Award, Audubon Artists, 2000. *Mem:* Painters & Sculptors Soc NJ; Allied Artists Am; Soc Illusr; Artists Equity Asn; Audubon Artists. *Media:* Acrylic, Oil. *Dealer:* Am Gallery Carmel Calif

FRATKIN, LESLIE
PHOTOGRAPHER
b Schenectady, NY, 1960. *Study:* State Univ New York, Albany, BA, 83. *Work:* Corcoran Gallery Art, Washington, DC. *Exhib:* Red Windows, Barney's, NY, 95; Image Workshop Series, Foster Goldstrom Gallery, NY, 95; Bosnia: The War Tour, Foster Goldstrom Gallery, NY, 95; House/Scene, traveling exhib, Ger, 97; Seeing the Other, Riverside Studios, London, Eng, 98; Volare: The Icon of Italy in Global Pop Cult, Florence, Italy, 99. *Pos:* Freelance photogr, 83-; creator & proj dir, Sarajevo Self-Portrait: The View from Inside, 95-. *Awards:* Grant, Trust for Mutual Understanding, 97, 99; Soros Found/Open Soc Inst Individual Proj Fel & Grant, 97, 2000; The Righteous Persons Found grant, 99. *Publ:* Auth, Sarajevo Self-Portrait: The View from Inside, Umbrage Ed, 2000. *Mailing Add:* 416 Lafayette St No 3H New York NY 10003

FRAUGHTON, EDWARD JAMES
SCULPTOR
b Park City, Utah, Mar 22, 39. *Study:* Univ Utah, BFA, 62; studied under Dr Avard T Fairbanks & Justin Fairbanks. *Work:* Riveredge Found, Calgary, Can; Leanin' Tree Mus Western Art, Boulder, Colo; Valley Bank, Las Vegas, Nev; Nat Cowboy Hall of Fame & Western Heritage Ctr, Oklahoma City, Okla; Favell Mus Western Art, Klamath Falls, Ore. *Comn:* Mormon Battalion Monument, Sons of Utah Pioneers, Prisidio Park, San Diego, Calif, 69; Ben H Bohac (relief portrait), Talman Savings & Loan, Chicago, 70; All is Well, Family Monument, Sons of Utah Pioneers, Brigham Young Cemetery, Salt Lake City, 74; Truman O Angell Portrait, Church of Jesus Christ of Latter-day Saints, Salt Lake City, Utah, 77; Spirit of Wyo, 15 ft major monument, Capitol Grounds, Cheyenne, 80; Official Inaugural Medal, President Ronald Reagan. *Exhib:* Nat Acad Western Art, Oklahoma City; Nat Sculpture Soc, NY; Whitney Mus Western Art, Cody, Wyo; Bohemian Club, Bohemian Grove, Monte Rio, Calif; Nat Acad Design, NY; Artists of Am, Denver. *Teaching:* Instr, Scottsdale Artist's Sch, 86. *Awards:* Lance Int Prize, Nat Sculpture Soc, 79; Artist of the West, San Dimas Festival of Western Arts, 81; The Tallix Foundry Prize, Spirit of Man, Nat Sculpture Soc, 81; and others. *Bibliog:* Pat Broder (auth), Bronzes of the American

West, Abrams, 74; Peggy & Harold Samuels (auths), Contemporary Western Artists, Southwest Art Publ, 82; Profiles in American Art (film), Ken Meyer Prod. *Mem:* San Francisco Bohemian Club; Nat Sculpture Soc; Nat Acad Western Art. *Media:* Bronze & Stone Carving. *Mailing Add:* 10353 S 1300 W South Jordan UT 84095-8876

FRAZE, DENNY T
COLLAGE ARTIST, EDUCATOR
b Weatherford, Tex, May 28, 40. *Study:* Univ Tex, Austin, BFA(studio, art hist), 62; Univ Colo, MFA(painting), 64, study with Luis Eades & Roland Reiss. *Work:* Univ Colo, Boulder; Dishman Art Gallery, Beaumont, Tex; Museo Internacional De Electro Grafica, Cuenca, Spain. *Comn:* Collage Amarillo Art Ctr, Tex. *Exhib:* Over 200, incl one-man shows, Odessa Col, 80, Mus Art, Norman, Okla, 83, Koenig Art Gallery, Seward, Nebr, 87, Tex Tech Mus, Lubbock, Tex, 87, Art Inst Permian Basin, Odessa, Tex, 89, Meadows Gallery, Denton, Tex, 90, Tarleton State Univ, Stephenville, Tex, 99 & Tex Luth Univ, Seguin, 2002; Cent States Exhib, Pratt, Kans, 95; 1st Great Plains Nat, Fort Hayes, Kans, 95; Nat Works on Paper, Tyler, Tex, 96; Works on Paper '96, Houston, Tex, 96; and others. *Pos:* Pres, Tex Asn Sch Art, 70-72, 84-86, bd mem 70-74 & 83-86; bd mem, Tex Coun Arts Educ, 70-72. *Teaching:* Prof art & chmn dept, Amarillo Col, Tex, 65-2000. *Awards:* Best Show, Cent States Exhib, 95; Recommended for Purchase, Amarillo Art Ctr, Tex, 93 & 95; Juror's Choice Award, Nat Works on Paper, Tyler, Tex, 96; and others. *Bibliog:* Southwest Art Review. *Mem:* Tex Asn Sch Art (pres, 70-72 & 86-88); hon mem Amarillo Fine Arts Asn; Tex Coun Arts Educ. *Media:* Collage, Drawing. *Publ:* Auth, Denny Fraze Collages: A Retrospective Exhib (exhibit catalog), Art Ctr, Amarillo, Tex, 88. *Mailing Add:* 2219 S Hayden Amarillo TX 79109

FRAZER, JAMES (NISBET), JR
ASSEMBLAGE ARTIST, WRITER
b Atlanta, Ga, Oct 6, 49. *Study:* Amherst Col, BA(cum laude), 71; Ga State Univ, MFA, 73; also with Fairfield Porter. *Work:* High Mus Art, Atlanta; Corcoran Gallery; Chase Manhattan Bank; Addison Gallery of Am Art; J Paul Getty Mus. *Comn:* Southern Bell Telephone Co, 80; Veterans Admin Med Ctr, Atlanta, 83; Omni Int Hotel, Atlanta, 85. *Exhib:* South Am Traveling exhib, Arte EUA: El Sur, US Info Agency, 76-77; 35 Artists in the Southeast, High Mus Art, 76-78; Art Patron Art, Southeastern Ctr for Contemp Art, Winston-Salem, NC, 78; one-man shows, High Mus Art, Ga & Southeastern Ctr Contemp Art, Winston-Salem, NC, 81; Contemp Panoramic Photog, Addison Gallery Am Art, Andover, Mass, 84; Iron Bridge Show, Appalachian Environ Art Ctr, Highlands, NC, 89-90; Vital Signs, Nexus Contemp Art Ctr, 91; 20 Artists/20 Yrs, Nexus Contemp Art Ctr, 93; Avant-Garde revisited, Nexus Contemp Art Center, Atlanta, Ga, 98; Rocky Mountain Biennial, Mus Contemp Art, Ft Collins, Colo, 2002; Artists of Heath Gallery, Mocaga, Atlanta, Ga, 2002; Digital Splash, Studio 6 Gallery, Queens, NY, 2003; Inadventently, Kayo Gallery, Salt Lake City, Utah, 2005. *Pos:* Pres, Nexus Inc, Atlanta, 73-74, mem bd dir, 73-81; dir, New Visions Gallery, Salt Lake City, UT, 2002-2004. *Teaching:* Instr photog, Atlanta Col Art, Ga State Univ, 72-76 & Mercer Univ, 77-81. *Bibliog:* Peter Morrin (auth), Jim Frazer: Hand-Colored Photographs, High Mus Art, Atlanta, 81; Laura Lieberman (auth), Jim Frazer, Southern Accents, 5-6/88. *Media:* Digital Imagery. *Publ:* Journey to the natural bridge, Belize Currents, No 16, 93; Macal River trip, Belize Currents, No 20, 94; Jocassee Jour, River, Vol 1, No 6; Confederates in Brazil, South American Explorer, 2003; Pharmaceutical El Dorado, Fact or Fancy? South American Explorer, 2004. *Dealer:* Sandler-Hudson Gallery 1831 Peachtree Rd NE Atlanta GA 30309. *Mailing Add:* 1897 South 1600 East Salt Lake City UT 84105

FRAZER, JOHN THATCHER
FILMMAKER, PAINTER
b Akron, Ohio, Apr 2, 32. *Study:* Univ Tex, BFA; Yale Univ, MFA; with Joseph Albers; Wesleyan Univ, Hon MA. *Work:* Davison Art Ctr, Wesleyan Univ, Middletown, Conn; Libr Cong, Washington, DC; Cullinan Collection, Houston Mus Fine Arts; Nicholson Mem Libr, Longview, Tex. *Exhib:* Tex Ann, Dallas Mus Fine Arts, 58; New Haven Arts Festival, Conn, 60; Boston Arts Festival, Mass, 61; Flaherty Film Festival, Lakeville, Conn, 66; Am Film Festival, NY, 68. *Teaching:* Prof art, motion pictures & drawing, Wesleyan Univ, 59-. *Bibliog:* New talent, USA, Art in Am, 62; Bernard Chaet (auth), The Art of Drawing, Holt, 70. *Mem:* Am Asn Univ Prof; Col Art Asn Am; Am Film Inst. *Media:* Acrylic, Oil. *Interests:* Motion pictures. *Publ:* Auth, Documentary films & books on documentary films, Choice Mag, 69; Artificially Arranged Scenes, The Films of George Melies, G K Hall, 79. *Mailing Add:* 7 Bretton Pl 238 Washington Terr Middletown CT 06457-4108

FRECKELTON, SONDRA
PAINTER
b Dearborn, Mich, Jun 23, 36. *Study:* Art Inst Chicago; Student, Sch of Art Institute of Chicago, 1956; Student, Univ Chicago, 1956; LittD (hon), Hollins Col, 1994. *Hon Degrees:* LHD, Hollins Col, Va, 94. *Work:* Va Mus Fine Arts, Lewis Collection; Nat Mus Am Art, Washington, DC; Springfield Art Mus, Mo; Kalamazoo Inst Art, Mich; Okla City Mus. *Exhib:* One-woman shows, LoGuidice Gallery, Chicago, 70, Brook Alexander Gallery, NY, 76 & 79-81, Allan Frumkin Gallery, Chicago, 77, Fendrick Gallery, Washington, DC, 80, John Berggruen Gallery, San Francisco, 82, Robert Schoelkopf Gallery, NY, 86, 88 & 90, Maxwell Davidson Gallery, NY, 93 & Sunrise Mus, Huntington, WVa, 98-99, Huntington (WVa) Mus, 98; Mod Am Realism: Sara Roby Found Collection, Nat Mus Am Art, Washington, DC, 87 & 98- & Madison Art Ctr, Wis, 98-; Collaboration in Print, Stewart & Stewart Prints 1980-1990, Traveling Exhib (with catalog), 91-92; Hollins Col, Roanoke, Va, 95; Emory & Henry Col, Emory, Va, 96; Four Artists, Four Objects, Ten Yrs Traveling Exhib, 98-; John Pence Gallery, San Francisco, 2000; Contemp Am Realist Drawing, The Davidson Collection, Art Inst Chicago, 1999-2000. *Teaching:* Vis artist & lect at many schs & univs; McAndless Distinguished Prof Chair, Eastern Mich Univ, Ypsilanti, Mich, 92, Hollins Col, Va, 93, 95, 96, 97 & 98. *Awards:* Bradford Print Prize, 79; Art Masters Award, Watercolor, Am ARtist Mag, 95; Fac Fel, Hollins Col, Va, 97, 98 & 99; Pollock-Krasner Award, 2002. *Bibliog:* Janice Oresman (auth), Article, Arts Mag, 12/82; Paul Cummings (auth), article, Drawing Mag, 11/83; Thomas Bolt (auth), article, Arts Mag, 1/86. *Mem:* Nat Acad. *Media:* Watercolor. *Publ:* contribr, Realist Drawings and Watercolors, NY Graphic Soc, 81; contribr, Dynamic Still Life in Watercolor, Watson Guptill, 83. *Dealer:* Alice Simsar Gallery, Mich, Stewart and Stewart Prints, Mich. *Mailing Add:* 331 Epps RD Oneonta NY 13820

FRECON, SUZAN
PAINTER
b Mexico, Pa, Feb 12, 41. *Study:* Univ Strasbourg, 62; Pa State Univ, BFA, 59-63; L'ecole Nat Super des Beaux Arts, Paris, 63-66. *Work:* Mus Mod Art, Whitney Mus Am Art, NY; Nat Gallery Art, Washington, DC; Kunstmuseum, Bern, Switzerland; Fogg Art Mus, Cambridge, Mass. *Exhib:* solo exhibs, Kunsthalle Bern, Switz, 86, 94, Julian Pretto Gallery, NY, 88, Univ Art Mus, Berkeley, Calif, 89, 95, Lawrence Markey Gallery, NY, 92, 93, 96, 99, 01, 03, Hirschl & Adler Mod, NY, 96, Hausler, Munich, 98, Galerie Franck & Schulte, Berlin, 99, Galerie Philippe Casini, Paris, 99, Friedrich Gallery, Bern, Switz, 2000, The Drawing Ctr's, Drawing Room, NY, 2002 & Lawrence Markey Gallery, NY, 99, 2001 & 2003; Lawrence Markey Gallery, New York City, 2004; Peter Blum Gallery, New York City, fall 2005; Kunst Mus Bern Switz, fall 2005; Undercurrents & Overtones, Oliver Art Ctr, CCAC, Oakland, Calif, 98; Geistes Gegenwart, Diozesan Mus, Freisig, Ger, 98; Whitney Biennial 2000, Whitney Mus Am Art, NY, 2000; group exhib, Works on paper and drawings, Galerie paul Andreisse, Amsterdam Whitney Biennial, Whitney Mus Am Art, NY, 2000; group exhib, The Fall Line, OSP Gallery, Boston, Watercolor, NY Studio Sch, NY, Drawings of Choice from a NY Collection, Krannert Art Mus, Urbana-Champaign, Ill, 2002, Ark Art Center, Little Rock, 2003, Ga Mus of Art, Univ of Ga, Athens, The Bowdin Col Mus of Brunswich, ME & Cincinatti Art Mus, Cincinatti, Ohio, 2003. *Collection Arranged:* Ark Arts Ctr, Little Rock; Diözesanmus, Freising, Ger; Fogg Art Mus, Harvard Univ, Cambridge, Mass; Kunstmus, Bern, Switzerland; Mus Mod Art; Nat Gallery Art, Washington, DC; Univ Art Mus, Berkeley, Calif; Whitney Mus Am Art, NY. *Bibliog:* Kenneth Baker (auth), Berkeley Art Mus, Art News, San Francisco, 10/95; Charles Dee Mitchell (auth), Suzan Frecon, Art in Am, 3/97; John Yau (auth), Suzan Frecon Paintings, Richter Verlag, 99; Ken Johnson (auth), NY Times, 3/5/99; NY Rev of Art, 2/94. *Media:* Oil, Watercolor. *Dealer:* Lawrence Markey, 311 6th St, San Antonio, TX, 78215; Peter Blum, 99 Wooster St, New York, NY, 10012; Fredrick Galerie, Grenzacher Strasse 4 CH 4058 Basel. *Mailing Add:* PO Box 391 New York NY 10013

FREDELL, GAIL
CRAFTSMAN
b San Francisco, Calif, Aug 13, 51. *Study:* Univ Calif, Berkeley, AB, 74; Rochester Inst Technol, NY, MFA, 80. *Comn:* Sculpture, Fire-Storm Mem Gardens, Berkeley, Calif. *Exhib:* Am Craft Mus, traveling tour, 87; Axis 20 Gallery, Atlanta, 89; Oakland Mus, Calif, 90 & 94; Univ Calif, Art Mus at Blackhawk, 92; San Francisco Mus Mod Art, Calif, 95; Joanne Rapp Gallery, Scottsdale, Ariz, 95. *Pos:* Dir woodworking & furniture prog, Anderson Ranch Arts Ctr, Snowmass Village, Colo, 94-. *Teaching:* Instr furniture design, Univ Calif, Davis, 85 & Penland Sch, NC, 86; vis lectr, San Diego State Univ, 87 & 90 & Univ Calif, Berkeley, 90; instr, Calif Col of Arts & Crafts, Oakland, Calif, 80-88; guest instr, various workshops, 84-. *Awards:* Nat Endowment Arts, 88; Focus Design Award, 89; Firestorm Mem Sculpture Competition Award, 92. *Media:* Furniture

FREDENTHAL, RUTH ANN
PAINTER
b Detroit, Mich, 38. *Study:* Philadelphia Mus Col Art, 57; Yale-Norfolk Sch Art with Bernard Chaet, 58; Bennington Col with Paul Feeley, Tony Smith & Vincent Longo, BA, 60. *Work:* Chase Manhattan Bank, NY & Albany; Aldrich Mus Contemp Art, Ridgefield, Conn; Brooklyn Mus, NY; Donazione Panza Di Biumo Museo Cantonale d'Arte, Lugano, Switzerland; Villa Menafoglio, Litta Panza, Panza Collection, Varese, Italy; Karl Ernst Osthaus Mus, Hagen, Ger. *Exhib:* Mus Cantonale d'arte, Lugano, Switz, 95; Palazzo Ducale, Gubbio, Italy, 98-2003; Borromini Arte contemporanea, Ozzano Monferrato, Italy, 2000-01; Mart, Rovereto, 2002; Aganahuei Arte Contemp, Alba, Italy, 2004; Villa Lagarina, Port Venere, Italy, 2004; Karl Ernst Osthaus, Mus Der Stadt Hagen, Hagen, Ger, 2005. *Awards:* Fulbright Fel Painting & Graphic Arts to Florence, Italy, US State Dept, 60-61. *Bibliog:* Stephen Westfall (auth) article, Art Am, 3/90; Reegan Upshaw (auth), article, Art Am, 11/93; Donald Kuspit (auth), catalog essay, Stark Gallery, 95; David Sotnik (auth) video documentary, New York, 90-99. *Media:* Oil. *Interests:* Dance, music, travel, yoga, pilates. *Dealer:* Stark Gallery 555 W 25th St New York, NY 10001. *Mailing Add:* 438 W 37th St 5B New York NY 10018

FREDERICK, DELORAS ANN
PAINTER, INSTRUCTOR
b Fletcher, Okla, Jan 25, 42. *Study:* Central State Univ, 75; with Joseph Mugnaini, 79-80; with M Doug Walton, 79-80. *Work:* Presbyterian Hosp, Baptist Mem Hosp, Patrick Petroleum & CMI Corp, Oklahoma City, Okla; CCI Corp, Tulsa, Okla. *Exhib:* Artist Salon, Okla Mus Art, Oklahoma City, 75-80; Okla Territorial Mus, Guthrie, 78-80; Nat Small Painting Exhib, W F Mullaly Galleries, Birmingham, Mich, 78; The Miniature Painter, Sculptors & Gravers Soc, Art Club Washington, Washington, DC, 80; Ann Art Exhib, Mus Great Plains, Lawton, Okla, 80-81; and others. *Pos:* Instr watercolor, Art Supply Shop, Oklahoma City, Okla, 75-79; instr, Wkshps for Art Club in Okla, Oklahoma City, 77-81. *Teaching:* Instr water, Nichels Hills Elementary Sch, Oklahoma City, Okla, 81. *Awards:* Best of Show, Mid-Del Art Guild, 77, 79 & 80; Best Still Life Award, Founders Arts Club, Washington, DC, 80; Artist Holiday Award,

Tri State Kans, 83. *Bibliog:* Deloras Frederick, Okla Art Gallery Mag, 80; Peggy Ridgeway (auth), Deloras Frederick, Art Voices, 81. *Mem:* Mid-Del Art Guild (1st vpres, 76-77); Oklahoma Watercolor (1st vpres, 77-78); Watercolor Oklahoma (1st vpres, 78-79); Oklahoma Art Guild (1st vpres, 79-80); Nat League Am Pen Women, Inc. *Media:* Watercolor, Acrylic. *Dealer:* House Gallery 5536 N Western Oklahoma City OK 73116; Studio Gallery 2020 E Eleventh Tulsa OK 74104. *Mailing Add:* RR 1 Box 19760 Porum OK 74455-9610

FREDERICK, HELEN C
PRINTMAKER, CONCEPTUAL ARTIST
b Pottstown, Pa, 45. *Study:* RI Sch Design, BFA, 67, MFA, 69. *Work:* Fogg Mus, Cambridge, Mass; Nat Mus Am Art, Washington, DC; USA Today Nat Hq, Arlington, Va; Whitney Mus Art, NYC; Nat Gallery Art; and others; RI Sch Design. *Exhib:* Solo exhibs, Sequences, Steven Scott Gallery, Baltimore, Md, 89, Treading Water, David Adamson Gallery, Washington, 91, Collaborations on Paper, Va Polytech Univ, Blacksburg, Va, 93, Under Construction: Relay, Rewind, Record, Dieu Donne Gallery, NY, 96, Revealing Conditions, Art Ctr, South Fla, 2000, The View is Daunting, Lamardodd Gallery, Univ Athens, Ga, 2002; Innovative Prints & Paperworks, Baltimore, Mus Art, Md, 87; Object D'Art: Contemp Screens, traveling exhib, Va Mus Fine Arts & the Hand Workshop, Richmond, 90; Prints Washington, Corcoran Gallery Art, Washington, DC, 92; Seven-up, Master Printers of Pyramid Atlantic Montgomery Col, Rockville, Md, 94; Helen Frederick, Rick Hungerford & Ken Polinskie, Colombo Americano Cult Ctr, Medillin, Columbia, S Am, 95; Fine Prints, Washington Printmakers Gallery, Washington, DC, 95; Evolution of the Print, Addison Ripley Gallery, Washington, DC, 95; Graphic Legacy, Nat Mus Women Arts, Washington, DC, 95; Mountain Lake Series, Emerson Gallery Art, 96, McLean Project for the Arts, Va, 96; Group Print Show, Washington, DC, 98; Art Cnt South Fl Revealing Conditions, 2001; Southwest Craft Center Scieran Suspension, 2001; Univ of Georgia Solo Exhib The View Is Daintry, 2002. *Pos:* vis critic, Sch Design; exec artistic dir, Pyramid Atlantic. *Teaching:* Assoc prof, art & visual tech dept, Col Visual & Performing Arts; Assoc prof, George Mason Univ, Fairfax. *Awards:* Fulbright Grant & Am Scand Fel, Munch Mus, Oslo, Norway, 73-74; Mid Atlantic Arts Found Residency Fel, 88; Rutgers Ctr for Innovative Printmaking, 95; Governor's Award for the Arts as leading Maryland Artist, 2000; Recipient of Gov's Award for Excellence and Leadership in the Arts in Maryland, 2000. *Bibliog:* Mary McCoy (auth), Earthviews at RAP, Washington Post, 1/16/93; Joann Moser (auth), Paper alchemy at Pyramid Atlantic, Handpapermaking, summer 93; Susan Davidson (auth), Profile, Art & Antiques, 5/94; Milena Kalinovska (interview), The View is Daunting, 2003. *Media:* Paper, Print Media, Digital Art Installations. *Publ:* Auth, Crossing Over/Changing Places, USIA Traveling Exhib, 1990-1995. *Dealer:* Addison Ripley Gallery Washington DC; Paul Bridgewater New York. *Mailing Add:* 8707 Reading Rd Silver Spring MD 20901

FREDERICK, ROBILEE
PAINTER, SCULPTOR
b Evansville, IN, Oct 08, 31. *Study:* Wellesley Col, BA, 1953; Classes at Calif Col of ARt, Oakland, Calif, 1970; Classes in welding & glass, 1990-2005. *Work:* Hess Collection (Donald Hess), Napa, Calif; Achenbach Ctr for the Graphic Arts, Fine Arts Mus, San Francisco, Calif; di Rosa Preserve, Napa, Calif; Doris & Don Fisher collection, San Francisco, Calif; The Buck Collection, Newport Beach, Calif. *Comn:* Light Pieces, Hess Winery, Donald Hess, Colome, Chile, 2002; Light Pieces, Quintessa Winery, Napa Valley, Calif, 2003; Light Pieces, Hess Collection, Napa, Calif, 2006. *Exhib:* Veiled Memories, San Francisco Arts Comn Gallery & Ariz State Univ Art Mus, 96 & 99; Toward the Millennium, Monterey Mus of Art, Monterey, Calif, 1997; An Art Odyssey, Univ Art Gallery at Sonoma State Univ, Santa Rosa, Calif, 2001; Burn, Norton Mus Art, West Palm Beach, Fla & Columbia Mus Art, SC, 2001; On the Surface: Contemp paintings by Bay Area Women, Monterey Mus, 2002; Parallel Convergence, Napa Valley Mus, Yountville, Calif, 2004; Circle of Memory, Mus of Photog Arts, San Diego, Calif, 2004; Santa Fe Art inst, Santa Fe, NMex, 2005. *Awards:* Grants, Veiled Memories, Zellerbach Family Fund, Friends of the San Francisco Pub Libr, Poets & Writers Grant, Nat Endowment for the Humanities, 1996. *Bibliog:* Donna Schumacher (auth), Veiled Memories, Sculpure Magazine, 97; Gary Brady-Herndon (auth), A Studio Built for Two, Napa Valley Register, Napa, CA, 8/2002; Stephanie Salter (auth), Stones of Sorrow for the Missing, San Francisco Chronicle, 2003; Robert Pincus (auth), Food for the Soul, San Diego Tribune, 2004; Gary Brady (auth), Along Similar Lines, Napa Valley Register, 2004; and others. *Mem:* Calif Soc of Printmakers (CSP), (vpres speaker, 1970); Art Coun of Napa Valley. *Media:* Mixed Media. *Publ:* Auth, Fie de Siecle Painting (art), Artweek, 1997; coauth, Art by Gail Chase-Bien & Robilee Frederick, Napa Valley Mus, 2004; and others. *Dealer:* Braunstein/Quay 430 Clementina San Francisco, CA 94103 4107; Ruth Bachofner Gallery Bergamot Station G2 2525 Michigan Ave Santa Monica Calif 90404. *Mailing Add:* 1417 Hudson St Saint Helena CA 94574

FREDERICK, SARADELL ARD See Ard, Saradell

FREDERICKS, BEVERLY MAGNUSON
PAINTER, RESTORER
b Colorado Springs, Colo, June 14, 28. *Study:* Colorado Springs Fine Arts Ctr, Archie Music, Boardman Robinson, Emerson Woelffer & Vaclav Vytlacil, 46-54; Magnuson Antiques Restoration, Oscar & India Magnuson Co; Antelope Valley Col Calif, Paul Greenlee; Santa Monica Col Lucille Brown Green; UCLA; Emerson Ctr, Printmaking, Nancy Grenier, Calif; Kala Inst, San Francisco, World Print Coun, 85 & Uno Grafico, Milan Italy, Geogio Upiglio, 85. *Work:* Nat Burn Ctr, Univ Tex, Galveston; Lawrence Welk Mus, Escondido, Calif; Univ Akron, Ohio; Bank of America, permanent collections, Calif; Toyota Corp, Mich; Home Savings Am. *Comn:* Rocky Mountains suite, Universal City Bank, Calif, 83; Turn of the Century Oils, 86 & Constable's England, 88, Las Vegas Hilton; monotype diptychs, Marriott Hotels, Los Angeles, New Orleans & Newport, 88; 1890's Figurative Series, TRW Corp, Calif, 89; Spirit of Freedom (oil), Tianamen Square, Florence Jean Goodman, Calif, 89. *Exhib:* Los Angeles Co Mus, 59; Ringling Mus Art, Fla, 59; Ambassador Col, Calif, 77 & 80; Riverside Mission Inn, Robertson, Calif, 82; Wilshire Miracle Mile, Warner, Calif, 82; retrospective, Am Inst Fine Arts, Calif, 88; Barton Galleries, Akron, Ohio; Newman Galleries, Beverly Hills, Calif. *Pos:* Restorer, selected works by Benton, Prendergast, Burkhardt, Kline, Kollwitz, Dixon, Kuntz, Cauduro, Stamos, Vicente, Goya, Reynolds, Moore, Aronson, Gilot, Zuniga, Scholder, Donti, Piranesi, Lubner (LACMA), Stella (MMOA), Lidow. *Teaching:* Lectr, monotype hist & technoc, Calif, 88 & instr & narrator monotype, HRP Video (2 hrs), Calif, 90. *Awards:* Fel, Am Inst Fine Arts, Calif, 80; Hall of Fame, Palmer Alumni Asn, Colo, 85; The Ten Best Teachers on Tape, Elliot, Artists Mag, 91; Fel, Nat League Am Pen Women, 82. *Bibliog:* Robin Longman (auth), American tonalist, Am Artist, 82; Les Krantz (auth), Calif Art Review, Am References, 88; Calvin Goodman (auth), The Art Marketing Handbook, 91; Art Marketing in the 21st Century, 7th ed. *Mem:* Artists Equity Asn, Los Angeles; Am Inst for Conserv, Washington, DC; Am Inst Fine Arts, Calif (bd dir & treas, 78-85); Intern Inst for Conserv, London, Eng; Nat Mus Women Arts, Washington, DC; Int Who's Who of Prof & Bus Women, 89. *Media:* Oils, Printmaking. *Publ:* Contribr, Watercolor Monotypes, Watercolor, 88; prod/dir, Harvey Ray Fredericks, video, with companion book (auth) John Stafford Fredericks, The Art of Creating Monotypes, HR Productions, 90; auth, Mary Carroll Nelson; The Art of Creating Monotypes, Am Artist, 90; M Stephen Doherty, Watching Monotypes Being Made, Am Artist, 91; Calvin Goodman, from the studio to the boardroom, Am Artist, Co. *Dealer:* Art Studio of Beverly Fredericks 8227 Westlawn Ave Los Angeles CA 90045. *Mailing Add:* 8227 Westlawn Ave Los Angeles CA 90045

FREDMAN, FAIYA R
SCULPTOR, PAINTER
b Columbus, Ohio, Sept 8, 25. *Study:* Calif State Univ, San Diego; Univ Calif, Los Angeles. *Work:* Chicago Art Inst, Ill; Mus Mod Art, NY; Cedars-Sinai, Los Angeles, Calif; Oakland Mus, Calif; Mus Photog Arts, Luce-Forward, Permanent Collection Mus Contemp Art, San Diego; Getty Ctr, Santa Monica, Calif; Banff Ctr for Arts, Canada; and others. *Comn:* Sardina (sculpture), Comn by Robert Orton Sculpture Garden, 98. *Exhib:* Solo shows, La Jolla Mus Contemp Art, 68, 74 & 81, Thomas Babeour Gallery, La Jolla, 81, Univ Calif, San Diego & Irvine, 84, Ruth Bachofner Gallery, Los Angeles, 85 & 88 & Univ Calif, Riverside, 85; Mus Photog Arts, La Jolla, Calif, 88; Ruth Bachofner Gallery, Los Angeles, 90; Palomar Col Boehm Gallery, San Marcos, Calif, 90; Athenaeum, La Jolla, Calif, 94; Porter-Troupe Gallery, San Diego, 96; and others. *Collection Arranged:* AZ State Univ, Tempe, Az; Athenaeum, LA Jolla, CA; Brandes Investment, San Diego, CA; Banff Ctr for the Arts, Canada; Chicago Art Inst.; LA Jolla Sculpture Garden, LA Jolla, CA; Getty, Rare Book Special Collections, Santa Monica; Luce-Forward, San Diego; Mus Contemp Art San Diego; Mus Modern Art, NY; Mus Photographic Art, San Diego; Nat'l Mus of Women in Arts, Washington, DC; Oakland Mus, Oakland, CA; Peter Farrell Collection, San Diego, CA; San Francisco Mus, Modern Art; Seacrest Village, Encinitas, CA; Suzanne Stanford Collection, LA Jolla, CA; Joseph & Elaine Monsen, Seattle, WA; Dana Fayman, San Diego; U.C. CA, Los Angeles, Artist Book, Collection; UC CA, San Diego, Artist Book Collection. *Teaching:* Instr, Exten, Univ Calif, San Diego, 77-. *Awards:* US Dept Housing & Urban Develop Nat Community Art Competition Award, 73; First Prize, San Diego Pub TV Program, 78. *Bibliog:* Lucy Lippard (auth), Body, Nature & Ritual in Women's Art, Chrysalis Mag, 77; Jean Luc Bordeaux (auth), Unstretched surfaces Southern Calif, Los Angeles Inst Contemp Art J, 11/77. *Media:* Mixed, Oil; Photography, Metal All. *Publ:* Auth, Faiya Fredman Akroteri Series Catalog, Univ Calif, 84, Faiya Fredman Selected Works 1968-1989 (with catalog), Palomar Col Boehm Gallery, 90. *Mailing Add:* PO Box 2735 La Jolla CA 92038

FREDRICKSON, DANIEL ALAN See Folkus, Dan (Daniel) Alan Fredrickson

FREED, DAVID
PRINTMAKER, PAINTER
b Toledo, Ohio, May 23, 36. *Study:* Miami Univ; Univ Iowa; Royal Col Art, London. *Work:* Art Inst Chicago, Ill; Nat Am Mus Arts, Washington, DC; Va Mus Fine Arts, Richmond; Victoria & Albert Mus, London; Mus Mod Art, NY; and others. *Exhib:* Photog in Printmaking, AAA Gallery, NY, 68-70; one-man shows, Franz Bader Gallery, Washington, DC, 68, 70, 73, 76 & 82 & Va Mus Fine Arts, Richmond; Albright-Knox Art Gallery, Buffalo, NY; Biennial Graphic Art, Moderna Galerija, Ljubljana, Yugoslavia; Il Bisonte, Florence, Italy, 89; Retrospective, Anderson Gallery & Cabell Libr, Va Commonwealth Univ, 2001; Common Ground, Corcoran Gallery, Washington, DC, 2005. *Pos:* prof emeritus, Virginia Commonwealth Univ. *Teaching:* Prof printmaking, Va Commonwealth Univ, 66-, prof, 78-; guest lectr etching, Cent Sch Art, London, 69-70; prof, Va Commonwealth Univ, 1966-. *Awards:* Fulbright grant, 63-64; Va Mus Fine Arts Fel, 83-84; Natie Marie Jones Fel, Lake Placid, NY, 84; Thersea Pollak award in Visual Arts, 2001; Svc Award, Va Commonwealth Univ. *Bibliog:* David Freed-Printmaker; David Freed, film by David Williams. *Mem:* Soc Am Poets; Sierra Club; Southern Graphics Coun. *Media:* Works on Paper. *Res:* Studio. *Collection:* Prints & Small Sculpture. *Publ:* Collaborations and Artists Books with Poets Charles Wright, Larry Levis, Steven Lautermilch and Philip Levine. *Dealer:* Reynolds Gallery Richmond Va. *Mailing Add:* 1825 W Grace Richmond VA 23220

FREED, DOUGLASS LYNN
PAINTER, EDUCATOR, CURATOR, MUSEUM DIRECTOR
b Garden City, Kans, Dec 24, 44. *Study:* Ft Hays Kans State Univ, BS, 67, MA, 68; Rotary Int Group Study Exchange to Italy, 78. *Work:* Univ Mo Mus Art & Archeol, Columbia; St Louis Art Mus; Steinburg Art Mus, Wash Univ, St Louis; Newark Mus, NJ; Emporia State Univ, Kans; Wichita Ctr for Arts; Kemper Mus Contemp Art,

Kansas City, Mo; Daum Mus Contemp Art, Sedawa, Mo. *Comn:* Oil painting, KEO Bldg Corp, Sedalia, Mo, 91; oil paintings, Deloitte & Touche, St Louis, 96. *Exhib:* Visions, Mid Am Arts Alliance, 81 & traveling; Vorpal Gallery, NY, 81-84, 86 & 88; one-man shows, Vorpal Gallery, San Francisco, 82 & 90, Batz-Lawrence Gallery, Kansas City, 83, 85; Zola-Lieberman Gallery, Chicago, 85; Greenberg Gallery, St Louis, 85; St Louis Design Ctr, 86; Mus Art & Archeol, Univ Mo, 92, Elliot Smith Contemp Art, St Louis, 92, 95, 96, 2000; Leedy Voulkos Arts Ctr, Kansas City, 93, 97; Sherry Leedy Contemp Art, Kansas City, 2000; Kathryn Markel Fine Arts, NY, 2004; Olsen-Larson Gallery, Des Moines, IA, 2004; ETRA Fine Arts, Miami, Fla, 2005; Lanoue Fine Art, Boston, MA, 2005. *Collection Arranged:* Works on Paper, Mo State Coun on Arts (contribr, assembled 12 sites), 80-81; Mid America Art Alliance, 24 sites, 82-83; Missouri Painters, 12 sites, Mo Coun Arts, 85; cur, 42 solo exhib, Goddard Gallery, 1995-2000; cur, Daum Mus Contemporary Art, Sedalia, Mo, 2001-03. *Pos:* Dir, Daum Mus Contemp Art, 2001-. *Teaching:* Chmn dept art, State Fair Community Col, Sedalia, Mo, 68-2001. *Awards:* Biannual Grant, Mo Art Coun, 84; Design Arts Grant, Nat Endowment Arts, 87; Creative Artists Grant, Mo Arts Coun, 90. *Bibliog:* Patterson Sims (auth), catalog, Mo Artist's Exhib, 84; Nancy N Rice (auth), Doug Freed, New Art Examiner, 3/85; Jim White (auth), Douglas Freed, Abstract Painter, Dept Art Hist, Univ Mo, Columbia, 92. *Mem:* Am Asn Mus. *Media:* Oil. *Specialty:* Contemporary art. *Publ:* auth catalog, Betty Woodman, 2002; auth catalog, Sculptural Clay Invitational, 2002; auth catalog, Awakenings, 2002; auth catalog introduction, Jan Kankeko, 2003. *Dealer:* Sherry Leedy Contemp Art Kansas City MO; Elliot Smith Contemp Art St Louis MO. *Mailing Add:* 1100 W Fourth Sedalia MO 65301

FREEDLAND, BARRY
SCULPTOR
b Nov 19, 68. *Study:* Ariz State Univ, Tempe, BFA, 90; Sch Mus Fine Art, Tufts Univ, MFA, 94. *Exhib:* Artists Invite Artists, Kingston Gallery, Boston, Mass, 94; 1996 Exhib Painting & Sculpture, Berkshire Art Mus, Pittsfield, Mass, 95; North Eng/North Amsterdam II, Real Art Ways, Hartford, Mass, 97; Art/RGGES, Mobius-Alternative Art Space, Boston, Mass, 97; Cements in Clothing, Revolving Mus, Boston, Mass, 98. *Pos:* Guest critic, Harvard Univ, Cambridge, Mass, 95. *Teaching:* Part-time instr, Bridgewater State Coll, Mass, 94-; vis lectr, Sch Mus Fine Arts, Boston, Mass, 96-98. *Awards:* Scottsdale Film Festival Best Animated Short Film, Ariz, 92; Traveling Scholar, Sch Mus Fine Arts, Boston, 98; Artist Grant, Mass Cult Coun, 99. *Mem:* Col Art Asn. *Media:* Metal, Bubblegum. *Dealer:* 123 Anawan Ave Boston MA 02132

FREEDMAN, DEBORAH S
PAINTER, PRINTMAKER
b New York, NY, May 1, 47. *Study:* Studied Art Students League, 67 & New York Univ, BS, 70. *Work:* NY Pub Libr; NY State Facilities Corp. *Comn:* Touch Sanitation Map NY, Ronald Feldman Gallery, 84; waterfall suite folding screen, comn by Jeff Winant, Short Hills, NJ, 89; monoprint etching, KOP Finnish Bank, NY, 90. *Exhib:* Alternative Imaging Systems, Everson Art Mus, Syracuse, NY, 79; Electro Works, Int Mus Photog, Rochester, NY, 79 & Cooper Hewitt Mus, NY, 80; Artists Books, Rutgers Univ, New Brunswick, NJ, 82; Abstract Energy Now, Islip Art Mus, NY, 86; Projects & Portfolios, Brooklyn Mus, NY, 89; Works on Paper '90, Long Island Univ, Brooklyn Campus, NY, 90; Garbage Out Front, Munic Arts Soc, NY, 90; Retakes, Canadian Coun Prints & Drawings, Toronto, 90. *Awards:* MacDowell Colony fel, 90. *Bibliog:* Video Portrait, interview, Asaaiti Broadcasting, Tokyo, 88; Jack Anderson, rev, That was fast, NY Times, 88; Jackie Brody (auth), Deborah Freedman-Monoprints, Print Collectors Newsletter, 89. *Media:* Monoprint etching. *Publ:* Contribr, The great goddess, Heresies, 78; auth, Flue--a painter testifies to the glory of xerox, Franklin Furnace, 82. *Dealer:* Betsy Senior 55 Crosby St New York NY 10012. *Mailing Add:* 121 Wooster St No 5 New York NY 10012

FREEDMAN, JACQUELINE
PAINTER
Study: New Sch Social Res, New York, 65; Sch Visual Arts, 70. *Work:* Everson Mus Art, Syracuse, NY; Hudson River Mus; Queens Mus; Mus Mod Art, Art Lending Serv; Air France. *Comn:* 5 Clay Totem (50 clay paintings), pvt, 88. *Exhib:* Solo shows, Painted: Over Pages, Ctr Book Arts, NY, 82, Found Gallery, 82, Painted Photographs of Queens Streets & Neighborhoods, La Guardia Community Col, Long Island City, 85 & Recent Paintings, Flushing Gallery, Flushing Coun on Cult & Arts, NY, 87; group show, Art By The Book, Islip Mus, NY, 88; Queens Artists (with catalog), Queens Mus, 89; Works on Paper, Queensboro Community Col, 90; Long Island City Artists, Queens Coun Arts, NY, 92; OIA Benefit Exhib, Org Independant Artists, Brooke Alexander Gallery, N, 93; Women's Art, Women's Lives, Women's Issues, New York City Comn Status of Women, Tweed Gallery, 93; Open Studios, Independent Studios I, Long Island City, NY, 94-98; Henri Gallery, Washington, DC, 94-96; Cow Parade, NY Cent Park, 2000; The Garden Revisited, Islip Mus, Flowers, Petals and Seeds, Painted Book, 2000; plus others. *Teaching:* Instr painting & drawing, Jamaica Arts Ctr, 75-85. *Awards:* Nat Endwoment Arts Proj Grant, 80-81; Fel, Creative Arts Pub Serv, 82-83; Arts Apprenticeship Prog, Dept Cult Affairs, NY, 84. *Bibliog:* Helen A Harrison (auth), Work in miniature challenges the power of perception, New York Times, 11/81; Just above midtown, Black Current, vol 2, 9/82; William Peterson (auth), Jaqueline Freedman, Artspace Mag, winter 83. *Media:* Acrylic, Oil. *Dealer:* Independent Studios I 10-27 46th Ave NY NY 11101. *Mailing Add:* 41-06 Case St Elmhurst NY 11373

FREELAND, BILL
SCULPTOR, PAINTER
b Pittsburgh, Pa, June 16, 29. *Study:* Philadelphia Mus Sch Art, 51-55; Hans Hofmann Sch, Provincetown, Mass, 56-. *Work:* Wilmington Mus & Soc Fine Arts, Del; Int Tel & Tel Collection, NY; Pa Acad Fine Arts; Philadelphia Mus Art, 87; Westtown Sch, Westtown, Pa; Allied Irish Bank, Dublin, Ireland; Mayo Co Coun, Castlebar Co Mayo, Ireland; Allied Irish Bank, Dublin, Ireland; American Express, NY; Arco Co, Philadelphia, Pa; Delaware Art Mus, Wilmington, Del; ITT Collection, NY; Lannan Found, Los Angeles, Calif; Montclair Mus, NJ; Pa Accad Fine Arts, Philadelphia; Philadelphia Mus Art, Pa; Univ Del, Newark, Del; Ballinglen Found, Ballycastle, Mayo Co, Ireland; Hawkswell Theatre, Sligo, Ireland. *Comn:* Sculpture, South St Develop Co, Philadelphia, Pa. *Exhib:* Color Show, Birmingham Mus, Ala, 63; Nat Watercolor Show, Pa Acad Fine Arts, Philadelphia, 69; One-man shows, Touchstone Gallery (with catalog, 80), NY, 78 & 80, Dolan/Maxwell (with catalog), NY, 89; From the Winston Malbin Collection Traveling Exhib (with catalog), 80; Pa Acad Fine Arts, 85; Iontas 97, Royal Hibernian Acad, (with catalog) Dublin, 99; Garrubbo/Bazan Gallery, West Chester, PA, 2004; Taylor Gallery, Dublin, Ireland, 2005; List Gallery, Swathmore Gallery, 2006. *Teaching:* Prof emer fine arts, Moore Col Art, 69-90. *Awards:* Pa State Grant, 87; Pollock-Krasner Found Grant, 89; Ballinglen Arts Fel, Co Mayo Ireland, 92; Hereward Lester Cooke Found Grant, 78. *Bibliog:* Theodore F Wolf (auth), articles, Christian Sci Monitor, 3/24/81 & 1/16/84; Robert M Murdock (auth), The Sculpture of Bill Freeland, 89; Conor Fallon, Patrick Murphy (auths) Bill Freeland Process and Ritual, 99. *Media:* Wood, Steel; Oil, Stone. *Collection:* Color Show, Birmingham Mus, Ala, 63; Nat Watercolor Show, Pa Acad Fine Arts, Philadelphia, 69; One-man shows, Touchstone Gallery (with catalog, 80), NY, 78 & 80, Dolan/Maxwell (with catalog), NY, 89; From the Winston Malbin Collection Traveling Exhib (with catalog), 80; Pa Acad Fine Arts, 85; Iontas 97, Royal Hibernian Acad, (with catalog) Dublin, 99; Garrubbo/Bazan Gallery, West Chester, PA, 2004; Taylor Gallery, Dublin, Ireland, 2005; List Gallery, Swathmore Gallery, 2006; List Gallery, Swathmore Col, 2006. *Dealer:* Taylor Galleries Dublin Ireland. *Mailing Add:* 1170 Valley Creek Rd Downingtown PA 19335

FREEMAN, DAVID L
PAINTER, GRAPHIC ARTIST
b Columbia, Mo, Nov 10, 37. *Study:* Univ Mo, BA & MA; State Univ Iowa, MFA; Penland Sch Crafts & Penland Weavers. *Work:* Mint Mus Art, Charlotte, NC; Minn Mus Art, St Paul; SC Nat Bank, Columbia; SC State Art Collection; NCNB Corp, Charlotte, NC; Dupont, Atlanta, Ga; US Teledsta, Atlanta, Ga; SC State Art Collection, Columbia; Fannie Mae, Atlanta, Ga; Bank Mecklenburg, Charlotte, NC. *Comn:* Painting, RJ Reynolds Inc, Winston, Salem, 85; painting, Swanston Fine Arts, Atlanta, Ga, 86; painting, GE/Electrical Distribution & Control, 90. *Exhib:* Eleventh Piedmont Painting & Sculptor Show, Mint Mus Art, NC, 71; three-man show, Mint Mus Art, NC, 78; two-man show, Greenville Co Mus Art, SC, 81, Asheville Mus Art, NC, 87; Three SC Painters, Waterworks Gallery, Salisbury, NC, 82; solo shows, High Point Theater Galleries, NC, 84 & Carlson Lobrano Gallery, Atlanta, Ga, 90; Columbia Col, SC, 87; SC Arts Comn Triennial, 92-93. *Teaching:* Asst prof studio art, Univ Wis, Madison, 63-70; prof studio art, Winthrop Univ, Rock Hill, SC, 70-. *Awards:* Purchase Awards, Drawings USA, Minn Mus Art, St Paul & 8th Ann Piedmont Graphics Exhib, Mint Mus Art, 71; Spring Mills Exhib & Traveling Show Award, New York, 78. *Mem:* Nat Col Art Asn. *Media:* Acrylic. *Specialty:* Mod Art. *Interests:* Music, Gardening. *Dealer:* Modern Eye Gallery Charlotte NC. *Mailing Add:* 630 University Dr Rock Hill SC 29730

FREEMAN, GERTRUDE
COLLECTOR
b Newark, NJ, July 20, 27. *Study:* Newark Sch of Fine & Indust Arts, NJ; Univ Miami, Fla, BA(art hist). *Collection Arranged:* Miami Beach Conv Ctr, Miami Beach, Fla, 80; Hollywood Art Ctr, Hollywood, Fla, 81; Walter Heller Bldg, Miami, Fla, 83; Bacardi Bldg, Miami, Fla. 85; Seminole Community College, Orlando, Fla, 91 & 94; Mus Art, Rollins College, WInter Park, Fla, 2000; Orlando Mus Art, Orlando, Fla, 2002. *Pos:* Consultant & purchasing agent for corporate collections, specializing in Contemp prints, watercolors (works on paper) & sculpture; advisor & coordr for art show for regional artists; artist representative for painter Ivy Volpe; exclusive representative for multi-media artist Leon Gordon Miller & surrealistic artist Mark Freeman; collector of Modern & Contemp 20th century art in all media, recent acquisitions: John Grauback, James Carlin, Matthew Geddes, David Maxwell. *Mailing Add:* 3192 Yattika Pl Longwood FL 32779-3113

FREEMAN, JEFF(REY VAUGHN)
PAINTER, EDUCATOR
b Bismarck, NDak, Oct 19, 46. *Study:* Moorhead State Univ, Minn, BS(art), 70; Univ NDak, Grand Forks, MA(art), 72; Univ Wis-Madison, MFA(painting), 80. *Work:* Sheldon Mem Art Gallery, Lincoln, Nebr; Madison Art Ctr, Wis; SDak Art Mus, Brookings; Plains Art Mus, Fargo, NDak; Joslyn Art Mus, Omaha, Nebr. *Exhib:* Art For a New Century, SDak Art Mus, Brookings, 89; Midlands Invitational, Joslyn Art Mus, Omaha, Nebr, 90; Off the Wall, 91 & Midwest Visions: Constructed Realities, 89, Sheldon Mem Art Gallery, Lincoln, Nebr; SDak Sculpture Invitational, Lincoln Gallery, Northern State Univ, Aberdeen, 92; SDak Art Mus, Brooking, SDak, 95; SDak Sch Mines & Technol, Rapid City, 96; Univ SDak Art Fac Exhib, Mus der Stadt, Ratingen, Ger, 97, SDak Art Mus, Brooking, 97; Gus Lucky Gallery, Minn, 98; 38th, 39th & 41st Midwest Artist Invitational, Rourke Gallery, Minn, 98, 99 & 2001; 55th Souix City Regional Exhib, Souix City Art Center, 99; Printed & Painted Gallery 72, Omaha, Nebr, 2001; solo exhibn, Eclecticism, Univ SDak Art Gallery, 2001. *Teaching:* Assoc prof art, Univ SDak, Vermillion, 80-93, prof, 96-. *Awards:* Visual arts fel (painting), SDak Arts Coun, 88-89; visual arts fel (painting), Arts Midwest/Nat Endowment Arts, 90-91; visual arts fel (painting), Nat Endowment Arts, 91-92. *Bibliog:* Patrick White (auth), The Painting as Artifact, Sioux City Art Ctr, Iowa, 86; Mason Riddle (auth), Jeff Freeman: Constructions, Univ SDak Art Galleries, Vermillion, 90. *Mem:* Col Art Asn Am; SDaks Arts. *Media:* Oil, Acrylic. *Dealer:* Gallery 72 Leavenworth Omaha NB. *Mailing Add:* 900 W Main St Vermillion SD 57069

FREEMAN, KATHRYN
PAINTER, INSTRUCTOR, ILLUSTRATOR
b Elmira, NY, Oct 28, 1956. *Study:* Univ NH, BFA 79; Brooklyn Col, MFA, 81; Skowhegan Sch Painting & Sculpture, 81. *Work:* Arnot Mus, Elmira, NY; Miller d Chevalier, Washington DC; Van Ness Feldman, Washington DC; Chase Manhattan Bank, NY; Swiss Bank, NY. *Comn:* murals, Orlando City Hall, Fla, 91; mural, Williams & Connolly, Washington, 95; murals, Jacksonville Pub Libr, 2005; and numerous pvt collections. *Exhib:* Solo exhibs, First Street Gallery, NY, 83, Rozbrat-Warsaw, Warsaw, Poland, 86, Tatistcheff Gallery & Co, NY, 86, 91 & 94 & Pepper Gallery, Boston, 95, Hanmon-Meek Gallery, Naples, Fla, 99, David Findlay Gallery, NY, 99; Bodies & Souls, Artist Choice Mus, NY, 83; The New Am Scene, Squibb Gallery, Princeton, NJ, 85; New Talent-NY, Sioux City Ctr, Iowa, 86; Artsites, Emerson Gallery Art, McClean, Va; Trees, Nat Acad Scis, Washington DC, 97; Catching the Shimmer, Nancy Hoffman Gallery, NY, 97; Dedicated to Art, Corcoran Mus Art Design, Washington DC, 2000. *Pos:* illusr, Loon Chase, 2006. *Teaching:* Instr design & color, Brooklyn Col, 82; instr painting, NY Acad Art, 82-84; adj prof painting & drawing, Corcoran Sch Art Design, Washington DC, 98-; instr, Corcoran Col of Art & Design, 98-. *Awards:* Ingram Merrill Fel, 87; Individual Artist Award, State Md, 98, 99. *Bibliog:* Susan Koslow, Kathryn Freeman, Arts Mag, 83; Ronny Cohen, Kathryn Freeman, Art Forum, 89; Michael Brenson, Kathryn Freeman, NY Times, 91. *Media:* Oil, Egg Tempera, Watercolor. *Dealer:* Lonstreet-Goldberg Art 5640 Taylor Rd Naples FL 34109; Osterville Fine Arts Osterville MA. *Mailing Add:* 6917 Woodside Pl Chevy Chase MD 20815

FREEMAN, ROBERT
PAINTER
b May 8, 46. *Study:* Boston Univ, Mass, MA, BFA, 71, MA, MFA, 81. *Work:* Brown Univ; Nat Ctr AFO Am Artist. *Exhib:* Solo exhibs, Smith & Mason Gallery, Washington, 70, Nat Mus Afro-Am Artists, Roxbury, Mass, 81, Chapel Gallery, W Newton, Mass, 82, Addison Gallery Am Art, Andover, Mass, 82, Wendell St Gallery, Cambridge, Mass, 83, 86 & 87, Clark Gallery, Lincoln Mass, 83, 86, 88, 90, 2004 & 2006, Zenith Gallery, Washington, 84, Isabel Neal Gallery, Chicago, 89, June Kelly Gallery, NY, 89; Carpenter Ctr Visual Arts, Harvard Univ, Cambridge, Mass, 88; Boston Collects: Contemp Painting & Sculpture, 86, Massachusetts Masters: Afro-Am Artists, Mus Fine Arts, Boston, Mass, 88; Selections: Six Contemp African-Am Artists, Williams Col Mus Art, Williamstown, Mass, 89. *Teaching:* Art dir, Weston Pub Schs, Mass, 73-81; artist-in-residence & painting instr, Noble & Greenough Sch, Dedham, Mass, 81-; lectr/instr, Harvard Univ, Cambridge, Mass, 88-94. *Bibliog:* Petty Peyton (auth), Portrait of the artist as a rising star, Tab, 1/17/88; Marty Carlock (auth), Electric Lady Land, Lincoln J, 1/21/88; Allan Gold (auth), Boston Curator Defends Black Artists' Exhibition, NY Times, 1/26/88. *Media:* Oil. *Mailing Add:* 28 Seaverns Ave Boston MA 02130

FREEMAN, ROLAND L
PHOTOGRAPHER
b Baltimore, Md, July 27, 36. *Study:* Self taught. *Hon Degrees:* Millsaps Col, LHD, 97. *Work:* Baltimore Mus Art; Corcoran Gallery; High Mus Art; Int Ctr Photog; Smithsonian Inst, Washington. *Exhib:* Crossroads: Black Am, Mass Inst Technol, 75; Something to Keep You Warm, Calif Afro-Am Mus, Los Angeles, 86; Alabama Quilters, Ala State Coun Arts & Humanities Gallery, Montgomery, 86-87; More Than Something to Keep You Warm, Bergen Mus Art & Sci, Paramus, NJ, 88; The Arabbers of Baltimore, Baltimore Mus Art, 90; one-man shows, Acad Arts, Easton, Md, 90, Nat Afro-Am Mus & Cult Ctr, Wilberforce, Ohio, 91, Springside Sch, Philadelphia, King-Tisdell Cottage Found, Savannah, Ga, Nat Civil Rights Mus, Memphis, Mus Am Quilter's Soc, Paducah, Ky, 92, Nat Black Arts Festival, APEX Mus, Atlanta, 92, Jackson State Univ, Miss, 92, 1996 Centennial Olympic Games, Atlanta, 96. *Pos:* Research photog, Smithsonian Inst Ctr for Folklore Progs & Cult Studies, 72-; freelance photog, currently; cur, Festival American Folklife, Smithsonian Inst, Washington, DC, 84, 86, 87 & 98, Nat Mall, Washington, DC, 86, King-Tisdell Col, Savannah, Ga, 87 Bergen Mus Art and Sci, Paramus, NJ, 88, African Am Mus, Cleveland, Ohio, 88, Baltimore Mus Art, Md, 90, Acad Arts, Easton, Md, 90, Nat Afro-Am Mus and Cult Center, Wiberforce, Ohio, 91, Nat Civil Rights Mus, Memphis, Tenn, 92 & Word Ct Women Against War, Cape Town, South Africa, 2001; cons, Fed Govt Nigeria, 81-82, Piney Woods School project and book, Miss, 82, Farish St Historic Dist preservation project, Jackson, Miss, 82-83 & Diana N'Diaye, Smithsonian Inst, Washington, DC, 96-97. *Teaching:* Instr, doc photog, George Washington Univ; photog-in-residence/res assoc, Inst for the Arts & Humanities at Howard Univ, Smithsonian Inst Ctr Folklife Progs & Cult Studies; Eudora Welty vis prof Millsaps Col, Jackson, Miss, 97. *Awards:* Nat Endowment Arts, Young Humanist Fel, 70, Masters Photog Visual Arts Fel, 82 & 91; Chmn's Grant, Nat Found Humanities, 72; Visual Folklore award Asn African and African Am Folklorists, 89; Contemp Contrib Pan Africanism Pyramid Award, Pan African Movement, 93; Living Legend Award for outstanding achievement photog, Nat Black Arts Festival, 94. *Mem:* Am Soc Media Photogrs; White House News Photogrs Asn; African-Am Mus Asn; Asn Study Afro-Am Life & Hist; Friends Photog. *Publ:* Auth, Stand By Me: African American Expressive Culture in Philadelphia, Smithsonian Inst Off Folklife Progs, 89; The Arabbers of Baltimore, Tidewater Publ, Centreville, Md, 89; Margaret Walker's For My People: A Tribute, Photographs by Roland L Freeman, Univ Miss Press, Jackson, Miss, 92; A Communion of the Spirits: African-American Quilters, Preservers, and Their Stories, Rutledge Hill Press, Nashville, 96; The Mule Train: A Journey of Hope Remembered, 98. *Mailing Add:* 117 Ingraham St NW Washington DC 20011

FREEMAN, TINA
PHOTOGRAPHER, CONSULTANT
b New Orleans, La, May 5, 51. *Study:* Art Ctr, Col Design, BFA, 72; Rochester Inst Technol, 78; also with Helmet Gernsheim & Beaumont Newhall. *Work:* New Orleans Mus Art; Bibliot Nat, Paris; Nat Mus Photog, Film & Television, Bradford, Eng. *Comn:* NEA Art in Pub Places, Pascagoula, Miss. *Exhib:* Solo exhibs, Cunningham-Ward Gallery, NY, 77, Galerie Simonne Stern, New Orleans, 78, 80 & 84, Newcomb Art Gallery, Tulane Univ, New Orleans, 83 & Southeastern Ctr Contemp Art, Winston-Salem, NC, 85, Univ Ore Mus Art, 88; Contemp Art Ctr, New Orleans, 79-86; Clouds and Trees, 84 & A Tribute, 85, Witkin Gallery, NY; A Sense of Place: Contemp Southern Art, Minneapolis Col Art & Design, Minn, 86; Arthur Roger Gallery, New Orleans, La, 92; The Academy Gallery, New Orleans, La, April 2, 2005-May 12, 2005. *Collection Arranged:* Paris After the Great War, 77; Diverse Images (auth, catalog), Photog Collection of New Orleans Mus Art, 78; Hard Times, Farm Security Administration Photography, 79; Women in Photography, 79; Deep Ocean Photography (with assistance from US Navy), 80; Lisette Model: A Retrospective (auth, catalog), Washington, DC, 81; New Acquisitions: New Directions in Black and White, 81; The Photographs of Mother St Croix (auth, catalog), 82 & Leslie Gill: A Classical Approach to Photography (auth, catalog), New Orleans Mus Art and traveling, 83-. *Pos:* Assoc cur photog, New Orleans Mus Art, 77-79, sr cur, 79-, consultant, 82-85; vpres arts, Contemp Arts Ctr, New Orleans, 85-86. *Teaching:* Lectr, Free Univ, New Orleans, 80. *Awards:* Nat Endowment Art, Purchase Prize; Culver Artist Hall of Fame, 2004. *Bibliog:* John Lawrence (auth), monograph, Women Artists News, 80; Kathleen Moak (auth), The enduring appeal of portraits, Contemp Arts Southeast, 80; Eric Bookhardt (auth), Tina Freeman photographing artists, Uptown, 83; John Lawrence (auth), Tina Freeman: A sense of place and mortality, New Orleans Art Rev, 3-4/83. *Mem:* Soc for Photog Educ; Am Soc Mag Photogrs. *Publ:* Auth, Diverse Images, Amphoto, Garden City, 78; The Photographs of Mother St Croix, New Orleans Mus Art, 82; Leslie Gill: A Classical Approach to Photography, New Orleans Mus Art, 84; contribr, Arts Quart, New Orleans; Photographer for Color, Natural Palletts for Painted Rooms, Clarkson Potts, 92

FREER, FRED-CHRISTIAN
PAINTER, SCULPTOR
b Cortland, NY, Dec 17, 56. *Study:* State Univ NY, Cobleskill, AAS, 77. *Comn:* Mug, KUAC TV & Radio 104-7, Fairbanks, Alaska, 94. *Exhib:* Group exhib, Anchorage Mus Fine Arts, Alaska, 90, The Bear Gallery, 90 & 93; solo exhib, Schweinfurth Art Ctr, Auburn, NY, 94. *Mem:* Fairbanks Art Asn. *Media:* Acrylics. *Publ:* Auth, Christmas Raven Series, 94, 95 & 96. *Mailing Add:* 1610 Kennedy St Fairbanks AK 99709-5103

FREHM, LYNNE
PAINTER
Work: Black Sails, 75-78; Clown, 76; King Bill, 92; Wedding, 93; Secret Places, 95-96; Night Sail, 97. *Exhib:* Solo shows include Norwalk Mus, Conn, 73, Bruce Mus, 74, Ruth Siegel, NY City, 91, Andre Arre, 96, 97, 2002, Exhibit A, 2000; group shows include Yale Univ, 68; Federal Courthouse, NY City Organization Independent Artists, 77; Landmark, NY City, 78; Attitude Art, 87; Blondies Contemp Art, 91-94; Allan Stone, 95; Beatrice Conde Gallery, 97; The Fanelli Show, OK Harris Gallery, NY City, 97; Nat Acad Mus, NY City, 2006

FREILICHER, JANE
PAINTER, PRINTMAKER
b Brooklyn, NY, Nov 29, 24. *Study:* Brooklyn Col, BA, 47; Hans Hofmann Sch Fine Arts, 47; Columbia Univ, MA, 48. *Work:* Brooklyn Mus, NY; Metrop Mus Art & Mus Mod Art, NY; Brandeis Art Mus, Mass; NY Univ; Hirshhorn Mus, Washington, DC; Descriptions of a Masque, woodcuts, Limited Eds Club, 98; cur, Nat Acad, 2002. *Comn:* Book Cover, Homage to Frank O'Hara, Creative Arts Bk Co, Berkeley, Calif, 80; sets, The Heroes, Eye & Ear Theatre, NY, 81; lithograph, Self-Portrait in a Convex Mirror, Arion Press, San Francisco, 84. *Exhib:* Whitney Mus Am Art Ann, 55-; one-woman shows, Tibor de Nagy Gallery, NY, 52-70, 98, 2000, 2002, 2004, Fischbach Gallery, NY, 75, 77, 79, 80, 83, 85, 88, 90 & 95, Wadsworth Atheneum, Hartford, Conn, 76, Utah Mus Fine Arts, Univ Utah, Salt Lake City, 79, Kornbluth Gallery, Fairlawn, NJ, 81 & 89, Parrish Art Mus (traveling), 86-87, Heath Gallery, Atlanta, 90 & Reynolds Gallery, Richmond, 93, Tibor de Nagy Gallery, NY, 98, 2000; Traveling Retrospective, Currier Gallery, NH, Parrish Art Mus, Southampton, NY, Contemp Art Mus, Houston & Marian Koogler McNay Mus, San Antonio, Tex, 86-87; Whitney Biennial, NY, 94-95; Women in the Visual Arts, Hollins Col Art Gallery, Roanoke, 96; By the Sea, Fotouhi Cramer Gallery, East Hampton, NY, 96; group exhibs, Master Art Workshop Exhib, Avram Gallery, Southhampton, NY, 2000, Personal Space: the Domesticated Long Island Landscape, Parrish Art Mus, Southhampton, NY, 2000, Am Views: Memory, Nostalgia, and the Idea of Place, Parrish Art Mus, Southhampton, NY, 2002. *Teaching:* Vis critic & lectr, Univ Pa Grad Sch Fine Arts, 68, Skowhegan Sch Art, 68-88, Carnegie-Mellon Inst, 71, Mus Fine Arts, Boston; Parsons Sch Design, MFA Prog, 89 & 90; and others. *Awards:* Nat Acad Design (academician) (Saltus Gold medal 1987, Benjamin Altman landscape prize 1995, Edwin Palmer prize 2003); Eloise Spaeth Award for Distinguished Achievement in Painting, Guild Hall Mus, 91; Southampton Cult & Civic Ctr Award, 92; 12th Ann Acad Arts Lifetime Achievement Award, Guild Hall, East Hampton, NY, 96. *Bibliog:* Hilton Kramer (auth), The New York Observer, 3/29/99; Jane Freilicher & Fairfield Porter, Modern Painters, fall 99; Charles Simic (auth), catalog essay for tibor de Nagy exhib, 2000. *Mem:* Nat Acad; Am Acad of Arts and Letters, NY (vpres, bd dir, 99). *Media:* Oil. *Dealer:* Tibor de Nagy Gallery 724 5th Ave New York NY. *Mailing Add:* 51 Fifth Ave New York NY 10003

FREIMARK, BOB (ROBERT)
PRINTMAKER, PAINTER
b Doster, Mich, Jan 27, 22. *Study:* Univ Toledo, BEd; Cranbrook Acad Art, MFA; independent study in Mex,Czech Republic, Guatemala & Cuba. *Work:* Nat Gallery, Prague, Czech; Smithsonian Inst & Libr Cong, Washington; Los Angeles Co Mus, Calif; Brit Mus; Portland Art Mus, Ore. *Comn:* Brenton Banks, Des Moines, 74; Kundalini Found, NY, 74; Impressions Workshop, Boston, 74-75; tapestry, Olympic Games, Moscow, 80; Hotel Cosima, Tokyo, Japan, 95. *Exhib:* Drawings of 12 Countries, Art Inst Chicago, 52; Pa Acad Fine Art Painting Ann, 52-53; Brooklyn Mus Biennial Watercolor Exhib, 64; Tokyo Munic Mus, 95 & 96; Mus Contemp Art, Sao Paulo, Brazil, 96; Nat Parliament, Praha, Czech Repub, 96; Beyond Boundaries, Richmond Art Ctr, 97; Int Print Exhib, Portland Art Mus, 97. *Pos:* Guest artist, Joslyn Mem Mus, Omaha, Nebr, 61, Huntington Galleries, WVa, 63 & Riverside Art Ctr, Calif, 64; guest artist & lectr, Columbia Univ, 63; vis prof, Harvard Univ, 72-73. *Teaching:* Instr drawing, Toledo Mus Art, 52-55; instr painting, Ohio Univ, 56-59; resident artist, Des Moines Art Ctr, 59-63; prof graphics, San Jose State Col, 64-86, prof emer, 86-; artist-in-residence, Mus Regla, Cuba, 2001, Mus Guayasamin, Quito, Ecuador, 2002, Balatonfured, Hungary, 2002. *Awards:* New Talent in USA Award, Art in Am, 57; Ford Found Grant, WVa, 65; Spec Creative Leave, Calif State Col Syst, 67. *Bibliog:* Roberta Loach (auth), In conversation with Robert Freimark, Visual Dialog, 76; Dan McGuire (auth), Kaleidoscope, TV video, KTEH, 79-8080; David Howard (auth), Bob Freimark (video), Channel 16, New York & Channel 25, San Francisco. *Mem:* Am Print Alliance; Los Angeles Printmaking Soc; South East Conference Latin Am Studies (SECOLAS). *Media:* Painting, Lithography; Tapestry. *Res:* Mexican popular culture; rehabilitation through art; environmental planning for contemporary living; Art Protis tapestries. *Interests:* Graphics, film and video. *Publ:* video, Arte Cubano: Contemporary Art and Culture in Cuba, 2000; video, film, El Dia Tarasco: The Day of the Dead among the Tarascan Indians; Royal Chicano Air Force; Los Desaparecidos-The Disappeared Ones, World Fest Houston, Tex. *Dealer:* Haus Wiegand Munich Germany; Windermere Gallery Seal Rock Ore; Hart Gallery Palm Desert Carmel Chicago; Parish Gallery Wash DC. *Mailing Add:* Rte 2 Box 539A Morgan Hill CA 95037

FREITAG, WOLFGANG MARTIN
LIBRARIAN, LECTURER
b Berlin, Ger, Oct 27, 24; US citizen. *Study:* Univ Freiburg, Ger, PhD; Simmons Col, Boston, MS(libr sci). *Pos:* Chief librn, Fine Arts Libr, Harvard Col Libr, Fogg Art Mus, 64-91. *Teaching:* Lectr bibliog & art historiography, Harvard Univ, 67-75, sr lectr, 75-91. *Awards:* Distinguished Serv Award, Art Libr Soc NAm, 90. *Mem:* Col Art Asn; charter mem Art Libr Soc NAm (pres, 80); Asn Col & Res Libr; Metrop Mus Art, NY; Syracuse Univ Sch Info Studies; and others. *Res:* History of the critical reception and fluctuating popular fame of major artists, due to changing perspectives of scholars and shifts in public attitudes towards art. *Publ:* Auth, Tapping a serviceable reservoir: The selection of periodicals for art libraries, Art Libr J, 76; Early uses of photography in the history of art, Art J, 79; Monographs on Artists, Garland, NY, 85 & 97; Cooperative Collection Development, 87; Art Reproductions in the Library in The Documented Image, Syracuse UP, 87; and others

FRENCH, CHRISTOPHER CHARLES
PAINTER, WRITER
b St Louis, Mo, 57. *Study:* Univ Calif, Davis, BA, 80. *Work:* Hewlett-Packard, NY & Atlanta; Sallie Mae Inc, Wash; Hirshhorn Mus & Sculpture Garden, Washington, DC; McNeese State Univ, Lake Charles, LA; Richard L Nelson Gallery, Univ Calif at Davis. *Comn:* Painting, comn by Dean & Paul Shatz, Wash, 93; painting, Hewlett Packard, Atlanta, 94; painting, Goethe-Inst, Wash, 97. *Exhib:* Cité Int Arts, Paris, 96; Transformal, Wiener Secession, Vienna (with catalog), 96; Md Art Place (with catalog), 98; Galveston Art Ctr, Tex, (with catalog) 2003; Blue Star, San Antonio, Tex, 2003; solo exhib, Bill Maynes Gallery, NY, 2000, Devin Bolden Hiram Butler Gallery, Houston, 2003; Devin Borden Hiram Butler Gallery, 2005. *Pos:* Contrib ed, Artweek, 83-87 & J Art, 88-91; bd trustees, Washington Proj Arts, 94-96; bd trustees, DiverseWorks, Houston, 2001-; contribr, ARTnews, FlashArt, Glasstire.com. *Teaching:* Adj prof, Univ Md, College Park, 97-99; vis prof, Univ Houston, Tex, 2000-2001; tchr, Glassell Sch, Houston, 2002-. *Awards:* Fel, Nat Endowment Arts, 93; Cité Int Arts, Paris, 96; Joan Mitchell Found, 99; Grant CACCH, Houston, 2003. *Bibliog:* Brigitte Borchhardt-Birbaumer (auth), Von ästhetik und Verwandlung, Wiener Zeitung, 4/4/96; David Pagel (auth), Redefining the borders of abstraction, Los Angeles Times, 11/14/96; Ferdinand Protzman (auth), In Paris, an artist regains his touch, 11/16/96. *Mem:* AICA, NY. *Media:* Oil. *Publ:* Ed, Facing History, Corcoran Gallery Art, 90; contribr, Beyond the Frame, Setagaya Art Mus, Tokyo, 91; auth, The Human Factor, Albuquerque Mus, 93; Like a Body Without a Shadow, Marsha Mateyka Gallery, 93. *Dealer:* Devin Borden Hiram Butler Gallery, Houston. *Mailing Add:* 2626 Morrison St Houston TX 77009

FRENCH, STEPHEN WARREN
PAINTER, SCULPTOR
b Seattle, Wash, Sept 6, 34. *Study:* Univ Wash, BA, 56; MFA, 60. *Work:* San Francisco Mus Art, Calif; Johnson Wax Found, Racine, Wis; Univ Okla, Norman; Univ Wis, Madison; San Francisco Art Comn, Univ Pacific; and others. *Exhib:* Prints of the Sixties, Smithsonian Inst, Washington, DC, 65; Nat Print Exhib, Brooklyn Mus, NY, 65; Painters Behind Painters, Palace of Legion of Honor, San Francisco, Calif, 67; British Int Graphics Exhib, Bradford Mus, Eng, 69 & 71; two person exhib, San Francisco Mus, 70, Triangle Gallery, San Francisco, 2006; one person shows, Redding Mus, 80 & San Jose Art Mus, 80, Calif; Bridge Gallery, San Francisco, 1981; plus others. *Pos:* Adv bd, Inst Contemp Art, San Jose, 89-; pub art adv comt, City of San Jose, 90; comnr, Fine Arts Comn, San Jose, 90-93, chmn, 93-94; collections comt, San Jose Mus Art, 90; exec com San Jose Mus of Art, 99-; vice-pres bd Ctr for Literacy Arts, 99-2005. *Teaching:* Asst prof painting & prints, Univ Wis, Madison, 61-66; asst prof to prof, San Jose State Univ, 66-, chmn art dept, 86-90, assoc dean humanities & art, 90-98 & actg dean, 98; vis artist, Mont State Univ, 70 & Univ Wash, 70-71. *Awards:* Ford Found Purchase Award, Walker Biennial, Minn, 64; Art in Embassies Purchase Award, US Information Agency, 65-66; Am Graphics Award, Univ Pac, 69. *Mem:* Col Art Asn; Nat Conf Art Admin; Nat Asn Schs of Art & Design. *Media:* Acrylic, Silk Screen. *Dealer:* Triangle Gallery San Francisco CA. *Mailing Add:* 736 N 17th St San Jose CA 95112-3030

FRERICHS, RUTH COLCORD
PAINTER, LITHOGRAPHER
b White Plains, NY. *Study:* Conn Col, BA; Art Students League. *Work:* Thunderbird Bank, Phoenix, Ariz; First Nat Bank, Continental Bank, Valley Nat Bank, Ariz; permament collection, Mus State Univ Southeastern Mo; and others. *Exhib:* Watercolor West Nat Exhib, Riverside, Calif, 72; Southwestern Fedn Watercolor Exhib, Mus Albuquerque, 76; Nat Watercolor Soc Ann, 76; Scottsdale Watercolor Biennial, Ariz, 78; Conn Col Alumni Exhib, New London, 78; and others. *Mailing Add:* 321 E Pomona Rd Phoenix AZ 85020

FRESKO, COLLEENE
APPRAISER
Study: Bucknell Univ, BA. *Pos:* appraiser, Childs Gallery, Boston, currently; consult, Vespi Corp; fac, Skinner, Inc, Boston, 87, vpre, & dir, Am European paintings & prints dept, currently; appraiser, Antiques Roadshow, WGBH-PBS, currently; founder, Firewall Gallery Skinner, Inc. *Teaching:* Teacher, art hist Mount Ida Col, formerly. *Mem:* Art Table women in arts orgn. *Mailing Add:* Skinner Inc 63 Park Plaza Boston MA 02116

FREUD, LUCIAN MICHAEL
PAINTER
b Berlin, Dec 8, 22. *Study:* Ctr Sch Arts & Crafts, London, 39; East Anglian Sch Painting and Drawing. *Work:* Tate Gallery, Nat Portrait Gallery, Arts Coun of Great Britian, Brit Coun, Brit Mus, Fitzwilliam Mus, Cambridge, Nat Mus Wales, Cardiff, Scottish Nat Gallery Modern Art, Edinburgh, Hartlepool Art Gallery, Walker Art Gallery, Liverpool, Liverpool Univ, City Art Gallery, Whitworth Gallery, Art Gallery South Australia, Mus Western Australia, Beaverbrook Art Gallery, New Brunswick, Can, Centre Georges Pompidou, Paris, Bibliotheque Nat, Paris, Victoria and Albert Mus, Sigmund Freud Mus, London, Centro Cult Arte Contemporaneo, Mexico City, Nat Gallery, Capetown, Republic South Africa, Art Inst Chicago, Mus Modern Art, New York City, Metrop Mus Art, Carnegie Inst, Pittsburgh, Hirshhorn Mus, Washington, numerous others. *Exhib:* one-man, Lefevre Gallery, 44, Nishimura Gallery, Tokyo, 79, Thomas Agnew & Sons, 83, Hirshhorn Mus and Sculpture Garden Smithsonian Inst, Wash, 87, Mus Nat d'Art Moderne, Paris, 87-88, Hayward Gallery, London, 88, Neue National Gallery, Berlin, 88, Scottish Nat Gallery Modern Art, Edinburgh, Eng, 88, The Fruitmarket Gallery, Edinburgh, 88, Berggruen Gallery, Paris, 90, Saatchi Collection, London, 90, Nishimura Gallery, Tokyo, 91, Thomas Gibson Fine Art Ltd, London, 91, Palazzo Ruspoli, Rome, 91, Castello Sforzesca, Milan, 91-92, Tate Gallery, Liverpool, 92, Queen's Gallery Buckingham Palace, 2002-03. *Collection Arranged:* rep in pub. collections Tate Gallery, Nat Portrait Gallery, Arts Coun of Great Britian, Brit. Council, Brit. Mus, Fitzwilliam Mus, Cambridge, Nat Mus Wales, Cardiff, Scottish Nati Gallery Modern Art, Edinburgh, Hartlepool Art Gallery, Walker Art Gallery, Liverpool, Liverpool Univ, City Art Gallery, Whitworth Gallery, Art Gallery S Australia, Mus Western Australia, Beaverbrook Art Gallery, New Brunswick, Can., Centre Georges Pompidou, Paris, Bibliotheque Nat, Paris, Victoria and Albert Mus, Sigmund Freud Museum, London, Centro Cultural Arte Contemporaneo, Mexico City, Nat Gallery, Capetown, Republic South Africa, Art Inst Chicago, Mus Modern Art, NY City, Metrop Mus Art, Carnegie Inst, Pittsburgh, Hirshhorn Mus, Wash, numerous others. *Teaching:* Instr, Slade Sch Art, 48-58; vis, asst Norwich Sch Art, 64-65. *Awards:* named Companion of Honor, 83; recipient Order of Merit, 93. *Mem:* Am Acad and Inst Arts and Letters; Am Acad Arts & Sci's. *Mailing Add:* c/o James Kirkman 46 Brompton Sq Lonfon United Kingdom SW3 2AF

FREUDENHEIM, NINA
DEALER, COLLECTOR
Pos: Owner, Nina Freudenheim Gallery; art cons, Baird Music Hall, SUNY, Buffalo, 86, Rochester Swsquicentennial, Inc, 87, Buffalo and Erie Co Pub Lib, 95 & Highland Hosp Rochester, NY, 98 & others; corp art cons, Westwood Pharmaceuticals, Inc, Marine Midland arena, Buffalo, Mark IV Industries, Buffalo, Headquarter Cos/Olympic Mgt, Buffalo & others; art appraiser Albright-Knox Art Gallery, AT&T, Castellani Art Mus, Nat Gallery Can, IRS, Mem Art Gallery Univ Rocheste & others. *Awards:* Community-Univ Award Outstanding Woman in the Arts, SUNY, Buffalo, 82; Award Outstanding Individual Arts Prof, Arts Coun and Greater Buffalo CofC, 89. *Mem:* Appraisers Asn Am. *Specialty:* Contemporary, national and international art. *Collection:* Works by Pol Bury, Jules Olitski, Georges Noel, Lucas Samars, Fontana and many others. *Mailing Add:* 140 North St Buffalo NY 14201

FREUDENHEIM, TOM LIPPMANN
MUSEUM ADMINISTRATOR
b Stuttgart, Ger, July 3, 37; US citizen. *Study:* Harvard Col, AB; NY Univ, MA. *Hon Degrees:* Univ Md, DFA, 79. *Collection Arranged:* Pascin (with catalog), 66 & Arnaldo Pomodoro (with catalog), 70, Univ Art Mus, Berkeley, Calif; Alfred Leslie, Worcester, 84. *Pos:* Cur, Jewish Mus, NY, 62 65; asst dir, Univ Art Mus, Berkeley, 66-71; dir, Baltimore Mus Art, 71-78; dir, Mus Prog, Nat Endowment Arts, 78-82, Worcester Art Mus, 82-86; asst secy, Smithsonian Inst Mus, 86-92; asst secy arts & humanities, Smithsonian Inst, 92; deputy dir & chief operating officer, Jewish Mus,

Berlin, Ger, 99-2000; dir, Gilbert Collection, London, 2000-. *Mem:* Col Art Asn Am; Am Asn Mus; Am Fedn Arts; Nat Found Jewish Cult. *Publ:* Auth, Myer Myers, American Silversmith, 65; Illuminated Hebrew Manuscripts, 65; Persian Faience Mosaic Wall, Kunst Orients, 68; Holocaust art, 78; ed, American Museum Guide, 83. *Mailing Add:* Gilbert Collection Somerset House Strand London United Kingdom WC2R 1LA

FREUDENSTEIN, ELLIE (ELEANOR) T(ERENYI)
PAINTER, ENVIRONMENTAL ARTIST
b Detroit, Mich, Feb 4, 36. *Study:* Univ Calif, Los Angeles, with Lucille Brown Green Jan Stussey, Rico Lebruu & Sam Amato, BFA (honors, art), 58. *Work:* Santa Barbara Bank & Trust; David Zukor Prodns, Hollywood, Calif; Transamerica Life, San Francisco; Westcap Investors Inc, Los Angeles; Cynthia Wood Found. *Comn:* EDS Unigraphics, Cypress, Calif, 96; Cynthia Wood Found; Transamerica Life, San Francisco, Calif, 2000; Santa Barbara Bank Trust, Calif, 2001; Barbie Benton, Aspen co, select personnel serv, Santa Barbara, Calif; Peppertree art show, Santa Ymez, Calif, 2006; Grop show Tirage Gallery show, Pasadena, Calif, 2006. *Exhib:* One-woman show, Gallery Los Olivos, Calif, 93, Doubletree Gallery, Ventura, Calif, 93, Faulkner West, Santa Barbara, Calif, 93 & Waterhouse Gallery, Santa Barbara, Claif, 2000-2001, Am Impressionist Soc Nat Exhib, 2001, 2002, 2003; Watercolors, Hahn & Horn Gallery, Santa Barbara, Calif, 93-94; Women Artists of West, Gallery Liz Montana, Los Olivos, Calif, 94; Under the Oaks, Santa Barbara Natural Hist Mus, Calif, 95; Label Art Exhib, Cent Coast Wine Classic, 95; 87th Calif Art Club Gold Medal Exhib, Los Angeles Arboretum, Calif, 96; Small Painting Show, Watercolor Gallery, 98; Mission San Juan Capestrano Show, 98, 99 & 2000; Oil Painters of Am Nat Show, Americana Gallery, Carmel, Calif, 2000; 1st Ann Spring Salon, Edenhurst Gallery, 2000; Ronald Reagan Presidential Library & Mus, 2003; 7th nat AIS, Rockport, Tex, 2006; others. *Teaching:* Instr watercolor, Sea Pines Studio, 83-96. *Awards:* Bronze Award, Discovery 93, Art Calif Mag, 93; Ojai Spring Competition 3rd Prize, Cent Coast Watercolor Soc, 94; Best of Show, Santa Barbara Mus Nat Hist, 97; Award Joan Irvine Smith Competition, 99. *Mem:* Am Impressionist Soc; Calif Art Club; Oil Painters Am; Gold Coast Watercolof Soc; Women Artists West; Conservancy Painters. *Media:* Watercolor, Oil. *Specialty:* Traditional Works of Art, Oil, Watercolor. *Publ:* Women in the arts, Southwest Art Mag, 11/96; Guide book of Western artists, Art of West Mag, 97. *Dealer:* Waterhouse Gallery 1114 State St Santa Barbara CA 93110; Tirage Gallery One West California Blvd Pasadena Calif; Huntsman Gallery 410 East Hyman Ave Aspen Colo; Zantman Gallery Carmel & Palm Desert Calif. *Mailing Add:* 4595 Via Huerto Santa Barbara CA 93110

FREUND, PEPSI
PAINTER, COLLAGE ARTIST
b New York, NY, Oct 17, 38. *Study:* Self taught. *Work:* Citibank & Chase Bank, NY; Long Island Jewish Med Ctr, New Hyde Park, NY; Franklin Gen Hosp; St James Nursing Home; 9/11 Mem, Hofstra Univ, Hempstead, NY; and various corps. *Exhib:* Long Beach Mus, Long Island; Fine Arts Mus, Long Island; Guggenheim Mus, Long Island; one person shows, St John's Univ, Oceanside Libr & W Hempstead Libr; Long Beach Celebrity Arts, Nat Art League. *Pos:* workshop instr, Watermill, NY and Sarasota, Fla. *Teaching:* Instr at var Nassau Co Schs; Boces Demonstr, Venice & Sarasota, Fla; instr, workshops, Riverhead & Watermill, Long Island, NY. *Awards:* Gold & Silver Awards, Nat Art League; Bronze Award, Nassau Mus Fine Art. *Bibliog:* Articles in Mag & newspapers. *Mem:* 30 Artists; Nat Asn Women Artists Am. *Media:* Collage, Watercolor; Acrylic. *Specialty:* fine art. *Publ:* Illustrator 4 books, The spirit of Jezebel, Offenses-Diane Ford, Abuse-Theresa Duffy, God's Little Tomatoes, Joan Ann Warnell. *Dealer:* Soundview Art Gallery 35 Chandler Sq Port Jefferson New York NY; Galerie des Hamptons Hampton Beach NY. *Mailing Add:* 15 Penn Commons Yaphank NY 11798

FREUND, TIBOR
PAINTER, MURALIST
b Budapest, Hungary, Dec 29, 10; US citizen. *Study:* Fed Tech Univ, Zurich, dipl archit, 32; Vilmos Aba-Novak Art Sch, Budapest, 34; studies Oriental techniques of mosaics, Meshed, Iran, 40. *Work:* Mus Fine Arts, Budapest; James A Michener Collection, Univ Tex, Austin; Goucher Col, Md; Ravinia Art Festival Asn, Chicago, Ill; Ball State Univ, Muncie, Ind. *Comn:* First moving mural on ridged surface, Bd Educ, Pub Sch 111, NY, 63; first moving mural on flat surface, Bd Educ Sch 162, NY, 70. *Exhib:* Seven one-man shows, NY, 60-76; Am Fedn Arts Traveling Exhibs, 63-67, & 71-72; Abstract Art, Riverside Mus, NY, 65; An Am Report on the Sixties, Denver Art Mus, Colo, 69; Painting & Sculpture Today, Indianapolis Mus Art, Ind, 70. *Awards:* First Prize, 19th Ann New Eng Exhib, Silvermine Guild, 68. *Bibliog:* John Canaday (auth), Tibor Freund, NY Times, 10/4/69; Peter Schjeldahl (auth), Fourth show in New York, 69 & Phyllis Derfner (auth), Sixth show in New York, 74, Art Int; and others. *Mem:* Nat Soc Mural Painters. *Media:* Acrylic. *Res:* Developed motion painting from a crude nineteenth century invention called three-sided picture. *Publ:* Auth, Motion in painting--a new art form, Am Artist Mag, 11/64. *Mailing Add:* 34-57 82nd St Jackson Heights NY 11372

FREUND, WILL FREDERICK
PAINTER, EDUCATOR, WRITER
b Madison, Wis, Jan 20, 1916. *Study:* Univ Wis, BS, MS; Univ Mo; Tiffany Found Fel, 40 & 49. *Work:* William Rockhill Nelson Gallery Art, Kansas City, Mo; Joslyn Mus Art, Omaha, Nebr; Okla Art Ctr, Oklahoma City; Mulvane Mus Art, Topeka, Kans; Univ Nebr Art Galleries, Lincoln; and others. *Exhib:* Mo Pavilion, NY World's Fair, 64; New Talent USA, Art in Am Mag, 65; Watercolor USA, Springfield Art Mus, Mo, 70 & 72; Evansville Mus Art, Ind; Denver Art Mus; Butler Inst Art; Nat Gallery Art, Washington, DC; and others; Windsor Gallery, Stephens Col, Columbia, Mo; Columbia Art League Gallery; Southern Ill Univ, Edwardsville. *Teaching:* Instr art, Stephens Col, 46-64; prof fine art, Southern Ill Univ, Edwardsville, 64-81. *Awards:* First Prize Watercolor, Ruth Renfro Award, St Louis City Art Mus, 63; Purchase Prize & Bronstein Award, Evansville Mus Art; First Prize Watercolor, Quincy's 24th Ann. *Bibliog:* article, Will Freund, painter, potter, woodworker, boombass player, Wis Alumnus, 1/61; Eileen B Saarinau, New Talent USA, NY Times; La Revue Moderne, French Arts Mag. *Mem:* life fel Int Arts and Letters; Int Inst Arts and Letters. *Media:* Oil, Watercolor. *Mailing Add:* PO Box 182 Watersmeet MI 49969

FREUNDLICH, AUGUST L
ADMINISTRATOR, COLLECTOR
b Frankfurt, Ger, May 9, 24; US citizen. *Study:* Antioch Col, BA, 49, MA, 50; New York Univ, PhD, 60. *Collection Arranged:* All in Line (linear drawings,auth, catalog), Joe & Emily Lowe Art Gallery, Syracuse Univ & Terry Dintenfass Inc Gallery, New York, 80; Self Portraits (auth, catalog), Tampa Mus Art, 88; Robert Gwathmey (auth, catalog), Butler Inst Am Art, Mus Fine ARts, St Petersburg, Fla, Va Hist Mus, Telfair Mus, Pa Acad Fine Arts, 98-2000; and others. *Pos:* Consult, Nat Found Advan Arts; pres & exec dir, RA Florsheim Art Fund; bd, Exec Serv Corps, Tampa; trustee & pres, Richard Florsheim Art Fund, 87-; cur, Work of Richard Florsheim, Contemp Tableau (Beal, Goodman, Witkin). *Teaching:* Head art dept, Eastern Mich Univ, 54-58; chmn arts div, George Peabody Col, 58-64; dir & chmn art dept, Lowe Art Mus, Univ Miami, 64-70; dean, Sch Art, Syracuse Univ, 70; dean, Col Visual & Performing Arts, 71-82; dean, Col Fine Arts, Univ SFla, 82-86, prof fine arts, 86-91. *Awards:* Kress Found grant (2); Ford Found grant. *Mem:* Int Coun Fine Art Deans; Col Art Asn; Am Asn Mus; Nat Art Club; Life Fel Nat Art Educ Asn. *Res:* Social commentary art, American & German; American graphics and sculpture. *Collection:* Self-portraits; 20th century prints; American drawings. *Publ:* Auth, William Gropper, Ward, Richie Press, 63; Frank Kleinholz, Univ Miami, 66; Karl Schrag, 70 & 80; Richard Florsheim, AS Barnes, 76; auth, Federico Castellon, Syracuse Univ, 78; S Rosenblum, Nogorme Press, 89; The Sculpture of James Earle Fraser, Universal Press, 2000; and others. *Mailing Add:* 18407 Timberlan Dr Lutz FL 33549-5830

FREY, BARBARA LOUISE
CERAMIST, EDUCATOR
b Bloomington, Ind, Apr 28, 1952. *Study:* Ind Univ, Bloomington, BFA, 76; Syracuse Univ, MFA, 78. *Work:* Columbia Col Art Collection, SC; Ark Art Ctr, Little Rock; Grant Arnold Print Collection, State Univ NY, Oswego; Purple Sand Factory #5, Yixing, China. *Comn:* Ceramic tile mural, comn by Dr Karl F Frey, Harlingen, Tex, 85. *Exhib:* A Tea Party, Ferrin Gallery, Northampton, Mass, 89, 91-92, 94 & 97; The Tea Party, Am Crafts Mus, NY, 91 & 93; Teapot Invitational, Dorothy Weiss Gallery, San Francisco, 91, 93 & 94 & Craft Alliance Gallery, St Louis, 93, 94 & 96; Rituals of Tea, Garth Clark Gallery, NY, 91; The Tea Party: An Exhib of Contemp Teapots, Nat Mus Ceramic Art, Baltimore, 93; Purple Sands: 21 Western Potters in China, JBK Gallery, Amsterdam, The Neth, 97; Contemp Clay in Texas, Austin Mus Art, 97; Clay Traditions: Texas Educators and their Teachers, Dallas Mus Art, 98; Eight Texas Artists, Arlington Mus Art, 98; Confluence, Australian, Bolivian and Am Artists Exhib, Kyoto Munic Arts & Crafts Gallery, Japan, 98. *Teaching:* Instr ceramics, State Univ NY, Oswego, 78-80; assoc prof, Tex A&M Univ, Commerce, 80-. *Awards:* Bankers Trust Co Award, 49th Cooperstown Art Asn Nat, 84; Merit Award, NCECA Juried Member's Exhib, 88; Ceramics Prize, 55th Cooperstown Art Asn Nat, 90; and others. *Mem:* Nat Coun Educ Ceramic Arts; Col Art Asn. *Media:* Ceramics. *Publ:* Contribr, Porcelain: Traditions and New Visions, Watson-Guptill, 81; Electric Kiln Ceramics, 81 & 94, 2nd ed, Ceramics: Mastering the Craft, 90 & Hand-Formed Ceramics, Chilton Bk Co, 95; The Best of New Ceramc Art, Hand Bks, Madison, Wis, 97. *Dealer:* Dorothy Weiss Gallery 256 Sutter St San Francisco CA 94108; Ferrin Gallery 179 Main St Northampton MA 01060. *Mailing Add:* 1513 Park St Commerce TX 75428

FREY, MARY E
PHOTOGRAPHER
b Yonkers, NY, Nov 25, 48. *Study:* Col New Rochelle, NY, BA(fine arts), 70, Yale U, MFA(photog), 79. *Work:* Art inst Chicago; Mus Fine Arts, Houston Ctr Photog, Houston, Tex; Mus Mod Art, NY; Smith Col Mus Art, Northampton, Mass; Int Polaroid Corp & Carpenter Ctr Visual Arts, Harvard Univ, Cambridge, Mass. *Exhib:* New Photog 2, Mus Mod Art, NY, 86; Arrangements for the Camera, Baltimore Mus Art, Md, 87; solo exhibs, Northfield Mt Hermon Sch, Northfield, 89, Blatent Image/Silver Eye, Pittsburgh, Pa, 89, Ledel Gallery, NY, 89, Arno Maris Gallery, Westfield State Col, Mass, 91, Springfield Mus Fine Arts, 93, Laelia Mitchell Gallery, Boston, 95, Northlight Gallery, Ariz State Univ, 96, Springfield Tech Comm Col, Springfield, 97, Marlboro Col, Vt, 98, Donaldson Gallery, Miss Porter's Sch, Farmington, Conn, 2001; Pleasures and Terrors of Domestic Comfort, Mus Mod Art, NY, 91 & Baltimore Mus Art, 92; Los Angeles Co Mus Art, 92; Arno Maris Gallery, Westfield Col, Mass, 2001; Gameface, Arts & Industry Bldg, Smithsonian Instn, Washington, 2001. *Teaching:* prof, Hartford Art Sch, Univ Hartford, 79-; vis artist, Smith Col, 94-95. *Awards:* Fel, Nat Endowment Arts, 81, 92; Guggenheim Fel, 84; Mass Coun Cult Grant, 96; Springfield Cult Coun Artist Grant, 97, 99. *Bibliog:* Gloria Russell (auth), Photography, sculpture exhibits explore grand themes, 5/17/92 & Real life through a lens, 4/4/93, Sunday Republican, Springfield, Mass; Kathryn Marx (auth), Right Brain/Left Brain Photography, Watson-Guptill, New York, 94. *Mem:* Soc for Photog Educ

FRIBERG, ARNOLD
PAINTER, PUBLISHER
b Winnetka, Ill, Dec 21, 13. *Study:* Art Instr Schs; Chicago Acad Fine Arts; Am Acad Art, Chicago. *Work:* Tweed Mus, Duluth, Minn; Prince Wales Northern Heritage Ctr, Yellowknife, Can; Leaning Tree Mus, Boulder; Sheldon Mus, Lincoln, Nebr; Temple Square, Salt Lake City; Favell Mus, Ore. *Comn:* 100 Years of American

Inter-collegiate Football (series of paintings), Chevrolet Sports Art Collection, 69; The Northwest Mounted Police (series over 200 paintings), Northwest Paper Co, Tweed Mus, Duluth, Minn, 37-72; Winners and Losers (painting), comn by Steve Wynn, 76; life size portrait of Prince Charles with horse Centenial, comn by Govt Northwest Territories, Can, 79; Golden Nugget Casino, Las Vegas, Nev. *Exhib:* Ten Commandments Series, toured every continent, 57-58; Motion Picture Indust Exhib, NY World's Fair, 64-65; De Mille Dynasty Exhib, Los Angeles, 85-86; Expo-86, Vancouver, BC, Can. *Pos:* Chief artist-designer, Cecil B De Mille, 54-57. *Teaching:* Lectr vitality in relig painting, art as serv & Russell & Remington. *Awards:* Hon Best Artist of 1991 Western Heritate Art Show, Salt Lake City, 91. *Bibliog:* Vern Swanson (auth), Southwest Art Mag, 12/81; Ted Scharz (auth), Arnold Friberg, Northland Press, 84; Vicki Stavig (auth), Art of the West, 1/92. *Mem:* Life mem Royal Soc Arts, London; Chelsea Arts Club, London; Newcomen Soc, Philadelphia. *Publ:* Auth & illusr, The Ten Commandments, 57 & Arnold Friberg's Little Christmas Book, 58. *Mailing Add:* c/o Friberg Fine Arts Inc 5206 Pinemont Dr Salt Lake City UT 84123

FRICANO, TOM S
PAINTER, PRINTMAKER
b Chicago, Ill, Oct 28, 30. *Study:* Bradley Univ, BFA, 53; Univ Ill, Urbana, MFA, 56. *Work:* Libr Cong, Washington; Philadelphia Mus; Art Inst Chicago; Los Angeles Co Mus Art; Seattle Art Mus; Utah Mus Fine Art; Brooklyn Mus Art, NY; Univ of Tex, Austin, Tex; Univ of Lethbridge, Can; Ohio State Univ, Athens, Ohio. *Exhib:* One-man shows, Harmon Fine Arts Ctr, Drake Univ, Des Moines, Iowa, 77, Fresno State Univ Gallery, Calif, 78, Pepperdine Univ, Malibu, Calif, 79, Univ NDak, Grand Forks, 80, Bibo Gallery Art, Peoria, Ill, 81, Arts Place II, Okla Arts Ctr, Oklahoma City, 83, A Survey: 25 Yrs of Printmaking, Fairweather Hardin Gallery, Chicago, Ill, 88; Carnegie Art Mus, Oxnard, Calif, 94; Millard Sheets Gallery, Pomona, Calif, 95; Calif State Univ, Northridge, 96; Gilkey Ctr Graphic Arts, Portland Art Mus, Ore, 97. *Teaching:* Instr painting & printmaking, Bradley Univ, Peoria, Ill, 58-63; prof painting & printmaking, Calif State Univ, Northridge, 63-; vis artist, Ohio State Univ, Columbus, 69, Univ Utah, 71, Univ Mont, Bozeman, & Art Inst Chicago, 75, Univ NDak, Grand Forks, Cranbrook Acad Art, Bloomfield Hills, Mich & Eastern Mich Univ, Ypsilanti, 80. *Awards:* Fulbright Grant, Florence, Italy, 60-61; Louis Comfort Tiffany Res Grant, 65; Calif State Univ Found Res Grant, 66, 68, 74 & 78; Guggenheim Found Fel, 69 & 70. *Bibliog:* Lawrence C Goldschmidt (auth), Watercolor Bold and Free, NY/Pitman Publ, 80; John Ross & Claire Romano (coauths), The Complete Collagraph, Free Press, 80; Leonard Edmondson (auth), Etching, Van Nostrand Reinhold. *Mem:* Hon mem Los Angeles Printmaking Soc (vpres, 64-65). *Publ:* Auth, Thoughts Emerging, 91; Contemporary Flight, 91; Book, Thoughts Emerging,91: Portfolio, Contemporary Flight, 91; It All Adds Up, 92. *Mailing Add:* 9820 Aldea Ave Northridge CA 91325-1916

FRICK, JOAN
PAINTER, CONCEPTUAL ARTIST
b Toronto, Ont, Mar 11, 42. *Study:* Univ de Montreal: Ecole Beaux-Arts, 63. *Work:* Art Gallery Ont; Gallery Stratford, Ont; Can Coun Art Bank, Ottawa; Can Art Arch, Vancouver Art Gallery; Norman McKenzie Art Gallery, Regina, Sask; Art Gallery Peterborough, Ont; Univ Toronto; Carleton Univ. *Comn:* Art Gallery Northumberland, 88; Art Gallery Hamilton, 88; Art Gallery Algoma, 92; Kitchener-Waterloo Art Gallery, 92; The Gallery/Stratford, 94; and others. *Exhib:* Ontario Now, Art Gallery Hamilton, Ont & Kitchener, Waterloo Art Gallery, Ont, 76; Abstractions, Place Bonaventure, Montreal, Gallery-Stratford, Ont & Can Cult Ctrs, London & Paris, 76; Summer Show, Royal Acad, London, 77; Markings, Can Embassy, Washington, Ga State Univ Art Gallery, Atlanta & Can Consulates, Chicago & Boston, 78-79; Future Traditions Ontario 81 Traveling Exhib, 80-82. *Pos:* Archit Designer, 64-69. *Awards:* Can Coun Proj Costs Grants, 72, 74, 86 & 87; Ont Arts Coun Grants, 82, 84, 85, 88, 93 & 96. *Bibliog:* Mark Frutkin (auth), Hidden lines of colour, Beau Joust, 12/14/82; David Burnett & Marilyn Shiff: Contemporary Canadian Art, Hurtig, 83; Robert Reid (auth), Artist Combines Mirrors, Lights for KW, Art Gallery Exhib, Kitchener-Waterloo Record, 6/12/92; and others. *Mem:* life hon mem Art Gallery Ont; Int Sculpture Ctr. *Media:* Miscellaneous Media, Non-Static Light & Space. *Publ:* OA Publication of the Arts, Winter 76; Works by Offset, Artists in Books, 78; Light line drawing, 95; Mary Jo Hughes (auth) Agnes, E Therington Art Ctr. *Dealer:* Fran Hill Gallery, 230 Queen St E, Toronto, Can, M5A 1S3. *Mailing Add:* 648 Richmond St W Toronto ON M6J 1C3 Canada

FRIED, HOWARD LEE
SCULPTOR
b Cleveland, Ohio, June 14, 46. *Study:* Syracuse Univ, 64-67; San Francisco Art Inst, BFA, 68; Univ Calif, Davis, MFA, 70. *Work:* Cleveland Mus Art, Ohio; Syracuse Univ, NY; Univ Calif, Davis; Ft Worth Art Mus, Tex; San Francisco Mus Mod Art, Calif. *Comn:* Mural, Syracuse Univ, 66. *Exhib:* Looking West, Joslyn Art Mus, Omaha, Nebr, 70; The 80's, Univ Art Mus, Univ Calif, Berkeley, 70; Projection, Kunsthalle, Dusseldorf, Ger, 71 & Louisiana Mus, Denmark, 72; Documenta 5, Kassel, Ger, 72; and many others. *Teaching:* Instr sculpture, San Francisco Art Inst, 68-, chmn performance & video dept, 83-. *Awards:* Augusta Hazard Award, Syracuse Univ, 66; Adeline Kent Award, San Francisco Artist's Comt, 71-72; Nat Endowment Arts Grant, 75. *Bibliog:* Grace Glueck (auth), New York: Big thump on the bass drum, Art in Am, 5-6/71; Brenda Richardson (auth), Howard Fried: Paradox of approach-avoidance, Arts Mag, 6/71; Steve Davis (auth), Howard Fried installation piece, Art Week, 3/25/72. *Publ:* Auth, Inside the harlequin, Flash Art, 71; auth, Studio relocation, Breakthroughs in Fiction, 72; auth, Cheshire cat 4, Avalanche. *Mailing Add:* 1101 Georgia St Vallejo CA 94590

FRIED, NANCY
SCULPTOR
b Philadelphia, Pa, Nov 7, 45. *Study:* Univ Pa, Philadelphia, BA, 68. *Work:* Brooklyn Mus; Metrop Mus Art, NY; also several pvt collections. *Exhib:* Solo exhibs, Graham Modern Gallery, 91 & 93, New Arts Prog, Kutztown, Pa, 92, Janus Avivson Gallery, London, 94, Russell Sage Col, Troy, NY, 95, Art in Gen, NY, 96 & DC Moore Gallery, 97; Aldrich Mus Contemp Art, 95; (Real)ist Women, Selby Gallery, Ringling Sch Art & Design, Sarasota, Fla, 97; Terra-Firma, Art Gallery, Univ Md, Col Park, 97; The Discovered Breast: From Myth to Science, Padova Mus, Italy, 97; The One Chosen Christ in Recent NY Art, Thomas Walsh Art Gallery, Fairfield Univ, Conn, 97; Born of Clay, Garth Clark Coll, 99; Confronting Cancer through Art, Univ Pa, 99; Ark Art Ctr, Little Rock, 2000; Flint (Mich) Inst, 2001; DC Moore, NY, 2001. *Teaching:* Vis artist sculpture, Univ NMex, Albuquerque, 90, State Univ NY, Purchase, 91 & 93 & Univ Albany, 94; sculpture fac, Dept Fine Arts, Fashion Inst Technol, 94-. *Awards:* Pollock-Krasner Found Award, 91; Elizabeth Found Award, 93; Nat Endowment Arts Sculpture, 94. *Bibliog:* Edward Lucie-Smith (auth), Art Today, Phaidon, 95; Curating the 90's, Village Voice, 4/30/96; Joanna Isaak (auth), Feminism & Contemporary Art, The Revolutionary Power of Women's Laughter, Routledge, 97. *Media:* Terra Cota. *Dealer:* DC Moore Gallery 724 Fifth Ave New York NY 10019

FRIEDBERG, RACHEL (RAY)
PAINTER, DIRECTOR
b Brooklyn, NY, Jan 9, 29. *Study:* Art Students League, with Reginald Marsh; also with Leon Goldin & George Picken. *Work:* Newark Mus. *Exhib:* Enigmatic Image, Newark Mus, NJ, 84-85; Dunev Gallery, San Francisco, Calif, 86-92; Vered Gallery, NY, 86, 87, 88, 89 & 90; Guildhall Mus, NY, 86; Jersey City Mus, 87; Nassau Co Mus, 88; Judy Youens Gallery, Houston, Tex, 89, 90 & 91; Hal Katzen Gallery, NY, 90; Avanti Galleries, NY, 91 & 92; Lieberman/Saul Gallery, NY, 92; Palo Alto Cult Ctr, Calif, 92. *Pos:* Dir, Edward Williams Gallery, Fairleigh Dickinson Univ, 74-, Becton Hall Gallery, 89-. *Teaching:* Artist in residence, Fairleigh Dickinson Univ, 73-. *Awards:* Northshore Competition First Prize, Mus Mod Art, 71; NJ Coun Arts Fel Painting, 83; First Prize, Guild Hall, 88, Mus Award, 89, 91 & 92. *Bibliog:* Vivian Raynor (auth), article, NY Times, 79, 85 & 87; Phyllis Braff (auth), article, NY Times, 86, 87, 88 & 90; Karen Lipson (auth), article, Newsday, 1/29/88 & 8/22/86; Patricia Johnson (auth), article, Houston Chronicle, 7/13/89. *Media:* Encaustic. *Publ:* Dona Meilach, (auth), Box Art Assemblage, 73; Kayliss, Sunstorm Art Mag, 11/87, 10/88; Jeremy Kramer, Hampton Mag, 8/88; Image Forecast, Nikkei Publications, Tokyo, Japan, 89. *Dealer:* Avanti Galleries 22 E 72nd St New York NY; Michael Dunev Gallery 77 Geary San Francisco CA

FRIEDBERG, RICHARD S
SCULPTOR, EDUCATOR
b Baltimore, Md, Aug 10, 43. *Study:* Antioch Col, BA, 65; Yale Univ, BFA & MFA(Graham Found Fel), 68. *Work:* Citicorp Bank, Chase Manhattan Bank, NY. *Comn:* Sculpture, Rutgers Univ, NJ, 70; sculpture, Mobil Corp, Va, 79. *Exhib:* Whitney Ann, 71 & Whitney Biennial, 73, Whitney Mus Am Art, NY; Munson-Williams Proctor Inst, NY, 77; Storm King Art Ctr, NY, 79; Prospect Mountain Sculpture Show, Lake George, NY, 79; Alexander Milliken Gallery, NY, 81. *Teaching:* Assoc prof fine art, Fairleigh Dickinson Univ, Rutherford, 70-. *Awards:* Nat Endowment Arts Fel, 74. *Bibliog:* Ellen Schwartz (auth), Richard Friedberg, Art News, 78; Carter Ratcliff (auth), Richard Friedberg, Arts Mag, 79. *Mem:* Col Arts Asn. *Media:* Steel, Aluminum. *Mailing Add:* 62 Green St No 5 New York NY 10012

FRIEDEBERG, PEDRO
SCULPTOR, PAINTER
b Firenze, Italy, Jan 11, 36; Mex citizen. *Study:* Chauncy Hall Sch, Boston, 52-53; Univ Iberoamericana, Mexico City, Archit, 60. *Work:* Mus Des Arts Decoratifs Du Louvre, Paris; Rose Art Mus, Brandeis Univ, Waltham, Mass; Worcester Art Mus, Mass; Mus Mod Art (Print Dept), NY; Mus Contemp Art, New Orleans, La. *Comn:* Garden sculptures, comn by Andre Bloc, Paris, France, 65; mural, Hotel Camino Real, Mex, 68; Hands (3 wood sculptures), J Patrick Lannan Found, Palm Beach, 70; mural, Inst Mex Comercio Exterior, Mex, 79; sculptures, K&B Corp Collection, New Orleans, 88. *Exhib:* 11th Int Biennale, Mus Mod Art, Tokyo, Japan, 74; Biennale of Puerto Rico, San Juan, 80; Biennale of Oslo, Mus Mod Art, Norway, 85; Clepsidra & Babilometro, Mod Art, Mex City, 86; 100 Artistas Mexicanos, Mus Marco, Monterrey, 94; Palacio de Bellas Artes, Mex City, 98; Casa del Risco, Mex City, 2000. *Collection Arranged:* Microbienal I (collective show 70 artists), 77; Expo Chinchismo, Galeria La Chinche, 82; Microbienal II (collective show 70 artists), 85; Galeria Pedro Friedeberg, San Miguel Allende, Gto, Mex. *Pos:* Art ed, Mex This Month, 58-63; dir, Galeria La Chinche, 78-81. *Awards:* 2nd Prize, Biennale of Cordoba, Arg, 69; First Prize, Biennal of San Juan, PR, 79; 2nd Prize, Triennale De Grabado, Buenos Aires, 80. *Bibliog:* Ida Rodriguez P (auth), Pedro Friedeberg, Univ Mex, 72; Conaculta, 99. *Mem:* Consejo Nac De Las Artes. *Media:* Wood; Miscellaneous Media. *Publ:* Tarot, 96. *Dealer:* Galeria De Arte Mexicano GOB Rafael Rebollar 43 Mexico DF 11850 Mexico

FRIEDLANDER, LEE
PHOTOGRAPHER
b Aberdeen, Wash, July 14, 34. *Work:* Mus Mod Art Metrop Mus Art, NY; Art Inst Chicago; Victoria & Albert Mus, London; San Francisco Mus Mod Art, Calif; Fogg Art Mus, Cambridge, Mass; George Eastman House, Rochester, NY. *Exhib:* The Photographers Eye (with catalog), Mus Mod Art, NY, 64; Twelve Photographers Toward a Social Landscape (with catalog), Rose Art Mus, Brandeis Univ, Waltham, 67; New Documents (with catalog), Mus Mod Art, 67; Mirrors & Windows: Am Photog Since 1960 (with catalog), Mus Mod Art, NY, 78; Three on Technology (with catalog), Mass Inst Technol, Cambridge, 88; solo exhibs, Robert Miller Gallery, NY,

96, Fraenkel Gallery, San Francisco, 96, Ctr of Creative Photog, Tucson, 97, Janet Borden Inc, NY, 98, 99, 2000 & 2001, Fraenkel Gallery, San Francisco, 98, Rencontres d'Arles, 99 & Andrea Rosen Gallery, 2001; In Camera, Mus of Fine Arts, 93; One Hundred Yrs of Street Photog, Wright State Univ, Dayton, Ohio, 94; Hidden Faces, Paul Kopeikin Gallery, Los Angeles, 94; Janet Borden, Inc, NY, 2002; Galerie Micheline Swajcer, Antwerp, Belgium, 2002; Am Musicians, The Sheldon Galleries, St Louis, 2003. *Awards:* John D & Catherine T MacArthur Found Award, 90; French Chevalier of Order of Arts and Letters, 99; Skowhegan Medal in Photograph, 2000. *Bibliog:* Maria, Smithsonian Press, Mass, 92. *Publ:* Letters from the People, 93, Self Portrait, 98, Am Musicians, 99, DAP. *Mailing Add:* c/o Janet Borden Inc 560 Broadway New York NY 10012

FRIEDMAN, ALAN
SCULPTOR, DESIGNER
b Philadelphia, Pa, Sept 9, 44. *Study:* Rochester Inst Technol Sch Am Craftsman, BFA, 67; Univ Wis, Madison, MFA(sculpture), 69. *Work:* Univ Wis, Union Galleries, Madison, 69; Ind State Univ, Terre Haute, 72; Indianapolis Mus of Art, 77. *Comn:* Entrance doors (wood), St Paul's Univ Cath Church, Madison, 68; sculpture (plywood), Cunningham Mem Libr, Ind State Univ, Terre Haute, 73. *Exhib:* Retrospective, Wis Directions, Milwaukee Art Ctr, 75; Indianapolis Mus Art Traveling Exhib & Mus Gallery Exhib, 75-76; New Handmade Furniture, Mus Contemp Crafts, NY, 79; Contradictions, Fendrick Gallery, DC, 79; Fine Arts Comt Visual Arts, Program of the XIII Olympic Winter Games, Lake Placid, NY, 80; Recent Art Furniture, Niagara Univ, 82; and others. *Pos:* Designer furniture, E A Roffman Co, NY, 72; AF Works, Mansfield Rd Studio, Hillsdale, NY, 78. *Teaching:* Vis asst prof art, Univ Wis, Madison, 69-70; assoc prof furniture design & sculpture, art dept, Ind State Univ, Terre Haute, 72-79; guest lectr, State Univ NY, New Paltz, 83; lectr, The Creative Process, NY Found Art Grant, Hudson River Mus, Yonkers, 89. *Awards:* Nat Endowment Arts Individual Fel Grant, 76-77; Design Award for Excellence, Daphne Found, NY, 82; Individual Fel Grant, NY Found Arts, 88-89. *Bibliog:* Thelma Newman (auth), Woodcraft, Chilton Bks, NY, 78; Nicholas Rookes (auth), Masters of Wood Sculpture, Watson-Guptill, NY, 80; Dona Meilach (auth), Woodworking, The New Wave, Crown, New York, 81. *Mem:* Am Crafts Coun. *Publ:* The Designer, NY, 80; Progressive Archit, 81; Archit Record, 81. *Mailing Add:* 61 Mansfield Rd Hillsdale NY 12529

FRIEDMAN, B H
WRITER
b New York, NY, July 27, 26. *Study:* Cornell Univ, BA, 48. *Pos:* Adv coun mem, Cornell Univ Arts Col & Herbert F Johnson Mus; trustee, Am Fedn Arts, 58-64 & Whitney Mus Am Art, currently; dir, Fine Arts Work Ctr, Provincetown, Mass, 68-82. *Teaching:* Lectr Eng, Cornell Univ, 66-67. *Awards:* Fels, Coord Coun Lit Mag, 75; Nelson Algren Award, 83. *Mem:* Century Asn. *Publ:* Auth, Whispers, 72; auth, Jackson Pollock: Energy Made Visible (biog), 72; auth, Alfonso Ossorio (monogr), 73; auth, Museum, 74; auth, Almost a Life, 75; auth, Gertrude Vanderbilt Whitney (biog), 78; plus many others. *Mailing Add:* 439 E 51st St New York NY 10022

FRIEDMAN, BENNO
PHOTOGRAPHER
b New York, NY, Mar 28, 45. *Study:* Brandeis Univ, BA. *Work:* Mus Mod Art, NY; Boston Mus Fine Arts; Fogg Mus, Cambridge, Mass; Nat Mus Am Art Smithsonian Inst; Va Mus, Richmond; and the pvt collections of Belinda Rathbone, William Turnage, Frank Kolodny, Micky Ruskin & Claude Picasso; and others. *Exhib:* Recent Acquisitions, Mus Mod Art, NY, 70; Being Without Clothes, Hayden Gallery, 71; Points of View, Inst Contemp Art, Boston, 72; Octive of Prayer, Hayden Gallery, 72; Recent Acquisitions, Fogg Mus, Harvard Univ, 72; Baltimore Mus Art, 72; Exposure: Objects/Events, Inst Contemp Art, Boston, 73; Private Realities, Boston Mus Fine Arts, 74; solo exhibs, Light Gallery, 75, 76, 77 & 78, Asher-Faure Gallery, Los Angeles, Calif, 80, Yajima Gallery, Montreal, 81 & 84, Photograph Gallery, NY, 81, Film in the Cities Gallery, St Paul, Minn, 82, Harcus-Krakow Gallery, Boston, Mass, 82, Charles Cowles Gallery, NY, 82 & Marcuse PFeiffer Gallery, NY, 86 & 89; Fogg Mus, 77; Whitney Biennial, Whitney Mus Am Art, NY, 81; Photo-Collage, Contemp Arts Mus, Houston, Tex, 82; Butler Inst Am Art, Ohio, 83; Extending the Perimeters of 20th Century Photog, San Francisco Mus Mod Art, 85; The Photog Print, Mus Fine Arts, Houston, 86; Photog and Art, Harcus Gallery, Boston, 89; New Images in Photog, Andrea Marquit Fine Arts, Boston, 90. *Teaching:* Instr, Col Art & Design, Minneapolis, Minn, 82, Sch Mus Fine Arts, Houston, 82, Smith Col, North Hampton, Mass, 83 & Anderson Ranch, Aspen, Colo, 83. *Awards:* Mass Coun Arts & Humanities Fel Grant, 75; grant, Creative Artists Publ Serv, NY State. *Bibliog:* Jim Stone (ed), Darkroom Dynamics, 79; articles, Photoshow Mag, 80 & Popular Photography, 8/82. *Publ:* Contribr, Art in Am, 70 & Aspen Mag; Idea, NY Photogr, 74; illusr, Bad Behavior (by Mary Gaitskill), Vintage Books, NY, 89; Nightmares and Human Conflict (by John E Mack), Columbia Univ Press, NY, 89; plus others. *Mailing Add:* 120 Kellogg Rd Sheffield MA 01257

FRIEDMAN, LYNNE
PIANTER, INSTRUCTOR
b Panama City, Fla, Feb 26, 45. *Study:* Queens Col, with John Ferren, BA (art), 65, with Rosemary Beck & Louis Finkelstein, MFA, 74; Brooklyn Mus Art Sch, 68; Columbia Univ, EdD (art), 79. *Exhib:* One-woman show, Noho, Gallery, 1996, 1998, 2001, 2005, Land's End, 2003; Fire & Ice, Attleboro Mus, Mass, 97; Thunder & Lightning, Salisbury State Coll, Md, 97; Visions of the Land, Del Valley Art Center, NY, 99; Dancing Ground of the Sun, 2004; Booth, Mus Western Art, Ga. *Pos:* Pres, Noho Gallery, New York City, 97-99; Board, Art Soc,Kingston, NY. *Teaching:* Prof art, Kean Col NJ, Manhattanville Col, Purchase, NY, Ulster Co Community Col, 2002; Sierra Club tups, 2004-2006; artist-in-residence: Helene Wurlitzer Found, 2003, Va Ctr for Creative Arts, 2000, Erpf Ctr, 2001; Fundacion Valparais, 2005; Moulin a Nef, Auvillar, France, 2006. *Mem:* NY Soc Women Artists (pres, 96-2000); Artists Equity; Nat Asn Women Artists; Orgn Independent Artists. *Media:* Oil, Watercolor, Pastel. *Collection:* Albright Knox Gallery, Buffalo, NY; Pace Univ; IBM; Dillon Read; Pfizer Corp; Columbia Presbyterian Hosp; Ritz Carlton Hotal, Rbtwood Johnson Hospital. *Publ:* Artists in the 90's, Manhattan Arts, 9/94; Deciphering the secret landscapes, Queens Courier, 11/98; Panoramic landscapes, Arts Letter, 4/99; Water as Metaphor, Gallery & Studio, 4/2001. *Mailing Add:* 414 Circle Ave Kingston NY 12401

FRIEDMAN, MARTIN
MUSEUM DIRECTOR
b Pittsburgh, Pa, Sept 23, 25. *Study:* Univ Pa; Univ Wash, BA, 47; Univ Calif, Los Angeles, MA, 49; Columbia Univ, 56-57; Belg-Am Found Grant, Brussels, 57-58; Univ Minn, Am Art Fel, 58-60; numerous honorary degrees, nationally & internationally. *Exhib:* Jean Dubuffet: Monuments, Simulacres, Practicables, 73; Nevelson: Wood Sculpture, 73; Naives & Visionaries, 74; Projected Images, 74; Oldenburg: Six Themes, 75; The River: Images of the Mississippi, 76; Scale & Environ: 10 Sculptors, 77; Noguchi's Imaginary Landscapes, 78; George Segal Sculptures, 78; Picasso: From the, Musee Picasso, Paris, 80; Hockney Paints the Stage, 83; Tokyo: Form and Spirit; Jan Dibbets, 87; Sculpture Inside Outside, 88. *Pos:* Fel, Brooklyn Mus, 56-57; sr cur, Walker Art Ctr, 58-60, dir, 61-; co-chmn mus panel, Nat Endowment Arts, 77-78; mem, Nat Coun Arts, 78-84; arts adv to mus & educ inst. *Awards:* Ford Found Fel, 61-62; Intellectual Interchange Fel, 82. *Mem:* Am Fedn Arts; Nat Collection Fine Arts Comn; Asn Art Mus Dirs (pres, 78-79); Century Asn. *Publ:* Auth, Charles Sheeler, Watson-Guptill; Hockney Paints the Stage, Abbeville Press co-publ, 83; Tokyo: Form and Spirit, Harry N Abrams co-publ, 86; Jan Dibbets, 87 & Sculpture Inside Outside, 88, Rizzoli Int, co-publ; Sculpture Inside Outside, Rizzoli Int, co-publ, 88. *Mailing Add:* 18 E 12 St Apt 12 New York NY 10003

FRIEDMAN, MARVIN ROSS
DEALER
b Minneapolis, Minn. *Study:* Univ Miami, BA, 63, JD, 66. *Awards:* Guest cur, James Rosenquist Metrop Mus, Antoni Tapias Metrop Mus & Komar & Melamid Metrop Mus. *Bibliog:* Joan Kleinman (auth), The Art Market: Interview with Leading Dealers, Metrop Mus, 79; Tim Harris (auth), Great art dealers, Venture Mag, 9/83. *Specialty:* Major modern and contemporary pictures. *Publ:* Auth, Antoni Tapias (exhib catalog). *Mailing Add:* 2600 Douglas Rd Coral Gables FL 33134

FRIEDMAN, SABRA
PAINTER
b New York, NY. *Study:* New York Univ. *Work:* Bellevue Hospital; Islip Art Mus. *Exhib:* Primordial Elementaire, Caidoz Gallery, 83; Emblems of Imaginations, Islip Art Mus, 84; Affirmations of Life, Kenkeleba House; Chain Reaction, 55 Mercer St, 85; Queens Artists Salon, Flushing Gallery, 86; Second Ann Long Island City Open Studios, 87; Laguardia Community Col, 87. *Bibliog:* Margaret Betz (auth), New York reviews: Fourteen artists, ArtNews, 12/80. *Mailing Add:* 243 W 70 St No 9A New York NY 10023

FRIEDMAN, SALLY
PAINTER
b New York, NY, Jan 21, 32. *Study:* Queens Col, City Univ New York, BS, 53, MA, 59; Ruskin Sch Art, Oxford Univ, Eng, 62-64; Art Students League, 65-70. *Work:* Okla Art Ctr; New Eng Ctr Contemp Art, Brooklyn, Conn; Berkshire Bank & Trust Co, Pittsfield, Mass; Mitsubishi Paper Int & Warwick, Welsh & Miller Inc, NY; Allianz Risk Transfer Inc, NY; Mus Arts & Scis, Daytona Beach, Fla. *Exhib:* Works on Paper, Brooklyn Mus, 75; Butler Inst Am Art Ann, 75 & 76; Pratt Inst, 85; Donnell Libr Ctr, NY, 87, 91, 96 & 97; Long Island Univ, NY, 92; Fairleigh Dickinson Univ, NJ, 93; Coach Gallery, East Hampton, NY, 2000; Clayton, Libertore Gallery, Bridgehampton, NY, 2002; others. *Pos:* Secy, Phoenix Gallery, New York, 80-81, pres, 82-83. *Teaching:* Elem sch, New York City, 85-. *Awards:* Grumbacher Award, 80, Sara Winston Mem Prize, 82 & Erlanger-Seligson Mem Prize, 86, Nat Asn Women Artists. *Bibliog:* Artists stick to their guns, 6/90, Art values both the home and the exotic, 9/91 & Three solos of artists at their peak, 5/92, Pursuing a single concept, 10/93, Art Speaks; Behind the Walls of Artists Studios, 7/2000. *Mem:* Art Students League; Artists Alliance East Hampton. *Media:* Oil. *Interests:* Subject of my work stems from nature, the intimate & familiar settings of the home, city & country life. *Publ:* Contribr, Art Now--color slides, Vol VI, No 3 & 4, 78. *Dealer:* Paintings Direct Inc. *Mailing Add:* 255 W 88th St Apt 4D New York NY 10024

FRIEND, PATRICIA M
PAINTER
b Philadelphia, Pa, May 4, 31. *Study:* Goucher Col, BA, 54; Am Univ, MFA, 75; studied with Laura G Douglas. *Work:* Deke Perrerea Int Bank, NY; Fed Reserve Bank Richmond, Baltimore; Arent, Fox, Kintner, Plotkin & Kahn Col, Washington, DC; Squires, Sanders & Dempsey Col & Watkins Collection, Am Univ, Washington, DC; C&P Tele Co, Exec Off, Arlington. *Comn:* Large oil painting, exec lobby, Am Physical Therapist Asn, Alexandria, 83; painting for advertising, Nat Security Bank, Washington, DC, 86; Delta Airlines. *Exhib:* One-woman shows, Emerson Gallery, McLean, Va, 67, Plum Gallery, Kensington, Md, 80, 82, 84 & 86 & Franz Bader Gallery, Washington, DC, 86, 89, 91 & 92; Landscape in Art, Int Monetary Fund, Wash, 81; Painting: A Decade, Art Place, Rockville, Md, 90; Landau Gallery, Bethesda, Md, 2002; NIH, Gallery One, Bethesda, Md, 2002; Daystar Gallery, Wash, DC, 2004; Orchard Gallery, Bethesda, Md, 2005; Washington Theological Union, Wash, DC, 2006. *Pos:* Corresponding secy, Washington Soc Artists, 70-71; art in embassies prog, State Dept, 78-88; reproduction of work for 1991 calendar, Women

Art. *Teaching:* instr, co-founder, Kensington Workshop, 77-; Mt Vernon Col, Washington DC, 79-83; pvt instr, currently. *Awards:* Master Fine Art, Nat Security Bank; Top 10 Finalist, Search for Jesus 2000 Int Competition. *Mem:* Wash Soc Artists (corp secy, 70-71); Artists Equity. *Publ:* DC Area Artists Publication, Lab Sch Washington, 89-94; and others. *Mailing Add:* 7206 45th St Chevy Chase MD 20815

FRIESE, NANCY MARLENE
PAINTER, PRINTMAKER
b Fargo, NDak, Sept 1, 48. *Study:* Yale Univ Summer Sch Music & Art, with Louis Finkelstein Fel, summer 76; Art Acad Cincinnati, studied with Stewart Goldman, April Foster, Diploma of Art, 77; Univ Calif, Berkeley, studied with Sylvia Lark, Hassell Smith, Elmer Bischoff, One Year Grad Sch, 77-78; Yale Univ Sch Art, studied with Gabor Peterdi, Gretna Campbell, Andrew Forge, MFA, 80. *Work:* NDak Mus Art, Grand Forks; Grunwald Ctr Graphic Arts, Univ Calif, Los Angeles; William Benton Mus Art, Storrs, Conn; Yale Univ Gallery Art, New Haven; Housatonic Mus Art; Federal Reserve Bank; Boston Public Libr; NY Public Libr; Muscarelle Mus Art; RI Sch Design Mus Art; Grunwald Ctr for Graphics Art, UCLA; Colby Col Mus Art; World Art Bank, Washington DC. *Comn:* Theodore Roosevelt Found; Ina Mae Rude Entre Neur Ctr. *Exhib:* Solo shows, Giannetta Gallery, 89, NDak Mus Art, Grand Forks, NDak, 90, Univ Mont Gallery, Missoula, 90, Cornell Univ Gallery, 92, Pepper Gallery, Boston, 94, 96, 97 & 2000, Prints, Korn Gallery, Drew Univ, Madison, 97 & Under Brittany Skies, Nancy Moore Fine Art, NY, 97; Virginia Lynch Gallery, Tiverton, RI, 95; Kristina Wasserman Gallery, Providence, RI, 95; Gallery BAI, Barcelona, Spain, 96; Nancy Moore Fine Arts, NY, 97; Generations, New Bedford Art Mus, Mass, 97; PSA, NY; Pepper Gallery, Boston, Mass, 98; Jaffe-Friede & Strauss Gallery, NY, 99; Gross McCleaf Gallery, Phildelphia, 99. *Pos:* Artist-in-residence, Millay Colony for the Arts, Austerlitz, NY, 81, Artists for the Environ Found, Walpack, NJ, fall 81, Theodore Roosevelt Medora Found, ND, summer 92, Anderson Ranch, 97, MacDowel Colony, NH, 97, I-Park, CT, 02. *Teaching:* Drawing, Bennington Col, VT, 80-81; asst prof, Printmaking, Univ Tulsa, 83-87; vis asst prof, Visual Art Dept, Princeton Univ, NJ, 86; head, Printmaking Dept & prof, RI Sch Design, Providence, 90-; Dean of Grad Studies, Full Prof of Graduate Studies, 2004-. *Awards:* Nat Endowment for Arts painting grant, 91 & 92; US-Japan Grant, Nat Endowment Arts, 93; Blanche E Colman Award, 95; Residency, City of Pont-Aven, Brittany, France, 97 & 99; George Sugarman Found Award, 2005. *Bibliog:* Jude Schwendenwein (auth), article, Art New Eng, 88; Michael Jones & Betty Collings (auth), Moving the Margin Catalog, Emily Davis Gallery, Akron, 90; William Zimmer (auth), Bound By Light Catalog, 94; Cate McQuaid (auth), Friese's Wild Color, The Boston Globe, 98; Art on Paper 2000 Auth Faye Hirsch. *Mem:* Col Art Asn; Women's Caucus for Art; Calif Soc Printmakers; Los Angeles Soc Printmakers; Printmakers Network of Southern New England, (co-founder, 92); Art Table; Bd of Govs Risd Mus of Art; Found bd mem NDak mus of Art. *Media:* Oil, Watercolor. *Publ:* Auth, The Poetic Etchings of Mary Nimmo Moran, Gilcrease Mus & Univ, Tulsa, 84; coauth, Prints of Thomas Moran, Gilcrease Mus, 86; New American Painting, The Open Studio, 99. *Dealer:* Pepper Gallery 38 Newbury St Boston, MA. *Mailing Add:* 92 Columbia Ave Cranston RI 02075-3818

FRIGERIO, ISMAEL
PAINTER
b Santiago, Chile, 1955. *Exhib:* Solo exhibs, Galeria Visuala, Santiago, Chile, 86, Terne Gallery, NY, 87, Intar Gallery, NY, 87, Galeria Plástica Nueva, Santiago, Chile, 89, Galeria Botello, Hato Rey, PR, 90, Galeria Bass, Caracas, Venezuela, 91 & Scott Alan Gallery, NY, 91; Mus Fine Arts, Houston, 89; Corcoran Gallery, Art, Washington, 89; Los Angeles Co, Mus, Calif, 89; Brooklyn Mus, NY, 89; Bass Mus Art, Miami, Fla, 89; Museo del Barrio, NY, 89; Earth: Latin Am Vision, Mus de Bellas Artes, Caracas, Venezuela, 90; The Decade Show, Studio Mus Harlem, NY, 90. *Awards:* Nat Endowment Arts, 89

FRINTA, IRENA ALTMANOVA
PAINTER
b Plzen, Czech, Sept 3, 23: US citizen. *Study:* Graphic Sch, Prague, Czech Repub, cert, 43, Col Art, 47; Ecole Des Beaux - Arts, Paris, France, Cert, 50; Acad Andre Lhote, Paris, France, cert, 48; New York State Univ, Albany, MA, 70. *Work:* Albany Inst Hist Art, NY; State Univ New York Art Mus; Empire Blue Cross & Blue Shield, Albany, NY; Gallery Western Bohemia, Plzen, Czech Repub; Four Winds, Saratoga Springs, NY. *Exhib:* Landscapes, Int Monetary Fund, Washington, 81; Pastel Artists, Cooperstown Libr, NY, 90; Nat Asn Women Artists: 100 Yrs, Albany, NY, 90; Nature & People, Gallery J Trnka, Plzen, Czech Repub, 92; Les Urbach Gallery, Albany, NY, 96; The Arts Ctr Gallery, Saratoga Springs, NY, 2000. *Pos:* Mem, Art Coun, Schenectady Mus; pres, Graphic Artists New York, Albany, Schenectady, Troy. *Teaching:* Art instr pastel, State Univ NY, Albany, 76-81, Col at Oswego, Pisa, Italy, 78. *Awards:* Thomas Leighton Mem-Dier Award, Pastel Soc Am, 79; Guest Artist at Yaddo, Saratoga Springs, NY, 84; Honorable mention, The Pastel J, 6th Annual Pastel 100 Competition, 2005. *Mem:* Graphic Artist NY (pres, formerly); Ctr Galleries, Albany, NY; Albany Mus Hist Art; Pastel Soc Am, NY. *Media:* Pastels. *Publ:* The Pastel J, The Years Best Art, issue 37, April, 2005. *Dealer:* Rice Gallery Albany NY. *Mailing Add:* c/o Pastel Soc Am National Arts Club 15 Gramercy Park S New York NY 10003

FRINTA, MOJMIR SVATOPLUK
HISTORIAN, EDUCATOR
b Prague, Czech, July 28, 22; US citizen. *Study:* Col Fine & Appl Arts, Prague; Karlova Univ, Prague, BA; Ecole des Beaux Arts, Paris, France; Ecole du Louvre, Paris; Univ Mich, MA, 53, PhD(hist art), 60. *Pos:* Sr restorer, Metrop Mus Art, New York, 55-63. *Teaching:* Prof art hist, State Univ NY, Albany, 63-93, prof emer, 93. *Awards:* Nat Endowment Humanities Grant, 77-78 & 82-84; Mellon Senior Fel, CASVA; Fulbright Fel Yugoslavia. *Mem:* Col Art Asn; Int Inst Conserv Art; Int Ctr Medieval Art; Medieval Acad Am. *Res:* Late medieval & Byzantine painting & sculpture; early Netherlandish painting; art technology. *Publ:* Auth, Master of the Gerona martyrology & Bohemian illumination, 64, auth, Investigation of the punched decoration of medieval Italian & non-Italian panel paintings, 65, The quest for a restorer's shop of beguiling invention: Restorations and forgeries in Italian panel paintings, 78, Art Bulletin; Genius of Robert Campin, Mouton, 66; The puzzling raised decoration in the paintings by Master Theodoric, Simiolus, 76; Punched Decoration on Late Medieval Painting, Maxdorf, 98. *Mailing Add:* 150 Maple Ave PO Box 854 Altamont NY 12009

FRITZ, CHARLES JOHN
PAINTER
b Mason City, Iowa, Feb 20, 55. *Study:* Iowa State Univ, BS, 77. *Work:* Denver Art Mus; Macnider Art Mus, Mason City, Iowa; Rohr-West Mus, Monitowoc, Wis, 99; CM Russell Mus, Great Falls, Mont, 02; Buffalo Bill Hist Ctr, Cody, Wy. *Comn:* Painting, Iowa Vet Hosp, Des Moines, 83. *Exhib:* Artists of Am, Colo Hist Mus, Denver, 94-96; Am Art in Miniature, Thomas Gilcrease Mus, Tulsa, Okla, 95; In the Mountains and Under the Sky, Charles H Macnider Mus, Mason City, Iowa, 95; Great Am Artists, Cincinnati Mus Ctr, Ohio, 96; Prix de West, Nat Cowboy Hall Fame, Oklahoma City, 96-04; Western Visions Exhib, Nat Mus Wildlife Art, Jackson, Wy; Charles Fritz, An Artist with the Corps of Discovery, Mont Mus Art & Cult, Missoula, Ore Hist Soc, Portland, Nat Cowboy & Western Heritage Mus, Oklahoma City, CM Russell Mus, Great Falls, Mont, Booth Mus Western Art, Cartersville, Ga, Macnider Art Mus, Mason City, Iowa. *Awards:* Dale Hawkins Mem Award, Western Heritage Ctr, 90; Best of Show, CM Russell Mus, 92, 96, 97, 2000; Lee M Loeb Mem Award for Landscape, Salmagundi Club, New York, 93; and others. *Bibliog:* Nancy Gillespie (auth), A healthy tension, Art of the West, 2/92; Carol Dickinson (auth), rev, Rocky Mountain News, 4/92; Gayle Shirley (auth), Charles Fritz, Big Sky J, 3/97; Nancy Gillespie (auth), Big Country, Big Talent/Art of the West, 5/99; Vicki Stanig (auth), An Artist's Eyes: The Lewis and Clark Expedition, 11/04; Donna Healy (auth), The Art of Exploration, Billings Gazette, 8/15/04; Dan Hays (auth), Epic Adventure, Statesman Journal, 12/26/04. *Media:* Oil, Watercolor. *Publ:* Illusr, Places of Spirit-Canyon de Chelley, Gibbs-Smith, 96; Donald Hagerty (auth), Lending the West-100 Contemporary Artists, Gibb-Smith; auth, Charles Fritz - An Artist with the Corps of Discovery, Farcountry Press, 04. *Dealer:* Stuart Johnson 6420 N Campbell Ave Tucson AZ 85718. *Mailing Add:* 8912 Susanna Dr Billings MT 59101

FRITZLER, GERALD J
PAINTER, WATERCOLOR
b Chicago, Ill, Aug 27, 53. *Study:* Am Acad Art, Chicago, AA(graphic art), 74, AA(fine art, scholar), 76; Studied under Irving Shaprio & Bill Parks. *Work:* Am Acad Art, Chicago; Am Western Art Collection, Peking; Pvt collection of Pres & Mrs Reagan; Rocky Mountain Nat Park, Estes Park, Colo; CM Russell Mus, Great Falls, Mont. *Exhib:* A Brush with Reality, CM Russell Mus; Salon D'Arts, Artists of Am, & Colo Watercolor Soc, Colo Hist Mus,; Laguna Plein Air Painters Invitational, Laguna Art Mus; Nat Acad Western Art, Nat Cowboy Hall of Fame; Colo Governors Invitational Exhib, Loveland Mus; Am Watercolor Soc, NY; Transparent Watercolor Soc Am, Ill; Nat Watercolor Soc, Calif; Northwest Rendevous Exhib, Mont; Maynard Dixon Country Exhib, Utah. *Pos:* Art Dealer, Historian, Juror. *Teaching:* Instr outdoor watercolor painting wkshps & figure painting & drawing, Western Colo Ctr Arts, 83-98; Jackson Hole Acad Art, 90; Western State Col, Gunnison, Colo, 90. *Awards:* Strathmore Paper Award, Am Watercolor Soc, 86; Artist in Residence, Rocky Mountain Nat Park, 90 & 94; Colo Watermedia Award, Colo Watercolor Soc, 92 & 96. *Bibliog:* Walter Gray & Dan Blanchard (auth), Gerald Fritzler, Southwest Art, 6/91; Peggy & Harold Samuels (auth), Contemporary Western Artists; Rachel Wolf (auth), Splash III, 94, Splash IV, 96 & Splash V, 98, Northlight Books, F & N Pub; Stephen Doherty (auth) The Force of Inspiration-Watercolor Mag Winter 2004. *Mem:* Colo Watercolor Soc; Am Watercolor Soc; Nat Watercolor Soc; Transpartent Watercolor Soc of Am; Int Soc Marine Painters; Laguna Plein Air Painters Asn. *Media:* Watercolor. *Specialty:* Fine traditional art, watercolors, oils, bronze sculpture, ceramics, drawings, pastels. *Collection:* traditional work in oil, watercolor & pastel, as well as bronze; Raku ceramics. *Publ:* Auth, The Best of Watercolor, 95 & Marine Art, 98, Rockport Publ; Watercolor Expressions, Rockport Publ Inc, 99; The Simple Secret to better Painting, North Light Books, 2003; Enchanted Isle, a History of Plein Air Painting on Santa Catalina Island, The Soc for the Advan Plein Air Painting, 2003. *Dealer:* Claggett/Rey Gallery, Vail, Colo; Fritzler Fine Art, Mesa, Colo; Grapevine Gallery Oklahoma City OK. *Mailing Add:* PO Box 253 Mesa CO 81643

FROMAN, ANN
SCULPTOR, DESIGNER
b New York, NY, Apr 7, 42. *Study:* Fashion Inst Technol, NY, AA, 61; Palace of Fontainebleau Sch Fine Art, France, cert, 61; Nat Acad Sch Fine Art, New York; Art Students League. *Work:* Radcliff Col; Butler Mus Art, Youngstown, Ohio; Richmond Libr, Wichita, Kans; Brooklyn Col, NY; Time Warner Inc, NY. *Comn:* Queen Esther (bronze), Temple Israel, Wilkes Barre, Pa, 79; Women of the Bible (bronze), Temple DeHirsch Sinai, Seattle, Washington, 80; Swirl (bronze), Bankers Trust Co & Footwear Asn of New York, 82; Holy Family, St Raphael Church, Livingston, NJ, 83; American Bounty (bronze), Culinary Inst Am, Hyde Park, NY, 83. *Exhib:* Art of Relationships, Wisser Libr, NY Inst Technol; Fashion Inst Technol; NY Artists, Brooklyn Mus, 71; one-woman shows, Berkshire Mus, Pittsfield, Mass, 77, Col Misericordia, Dallas, Pa, Bennington Mus, Vt, 81 & Judaica Mus, Phoenix, Ariz, 82; US Customs Mus, NY, 80; and others. *Teaching:* Hunter Col. *Awards:* Mortimer C Ritter Award, Fashion Inst Technol, 71; Watson Guptill Award, Nat Art Club, 76; First Prize Sculpture, Salmagundi Club, Am Soc Contemp Artists, 80. *Bibliog:* Sculpture & poetry unite in Ann Froman's art, Art Speaks, NY; Images in Art, Jewish J; Richard

Lesser (auth), Bronze dance from sculptor's mind, Ariz Repub, 1/30/82; Sculptor Ann Froman proves Bible relations are relevant today. *Mem:* Am Soc Contemp Artists; Artists Equity Asn. *Media:* Plastic, Cast Metal. *Dealer:* Froman Studios Anson Rd Stanfordville NY 12581-0367. *Mailing Add:* Ann Froman Galleries 22 E Market St Rhinebeck NY 12572

FROMBOLUTI, SIDEO
PAINTER
b Philadelphia, Pa, Oct 3, 20. *Study:* Tyler Col Fine Art, Philadelphia, Pa. *Work:* Philadelphia Mus Art, Pa; Mus Art, Carnegie Inst, Pittsburgh, Pa; The Nelson Rockefeller Collection; Corcoran Gallery, Washington, DC; Allentown Mus, PA; Allegheny Col Mus, Pa; Southern Ill Univ; Ciba-Geigy Corp, Ardsley, NY; First Nat Bank, Chicago; Boston Mutual Life Insurance Co, Mass Hyatt Hotel, NY; Fidelity Bank, Philadelphia, Pa. *Exhib:* Solo exhibs, Galerie Darthea Speyer, Paris, 70-74, Landmark Gallery, NY, 73, 75, 78, 80 & 82, Brownson Art Gallery, Purchase, NY, 83, Gross McCleaf Gallery, Philadelphia, 83, Maurice M Pine Libr, Fairlawn, NJ, 84 & Ingber Gallery, NY, 87; Art on Paper, Weatherspoon Gallery, Greensboro, NC, 75; Butler Inst Am Art, Youngstown, Ohio, 78; A Gray Day, Longpoint Gallery, Provincetown, Mass, 82; Woman Artists, Paris, France, 84; Knowing What I like, John Myers, Kouros Gallery, NY, 87; Jerald Melberg Gallery, Charlotte, NC, 87. *Awards:* Drawing Award, Acad Design Juried Exhib, NY, 84. *Bibliog:* Sandler (auth), article, Aujourd'hui; Oeri (auth), article, Quadrum; Kingsley (auth), article, Art Int. *Mem:* Century Club, NY; Nat Acad. *Media:* Oil on Canvas. *Dealer:* Barbara Ingber Gallery 415 West Broadway New York NY 10012. *Mailing Add:* 178 Prince St New York NY 10012-2905

FROMENTIN, CHRISTINE ANNE
PAINTER, GRAPHIC ARTIST
Study: Elmira Col, NY, BFA, 75; New York Univ, MFA, 77, studied figurative painting with John Kacere, realism with Don Eddie & Idelle Webber. *Work:* Gelmart Indust, NY; Cole of Calif, Los Angeles; and many pvt collections. *Comn:* Paintings, Essilor Co Inc, Joinville, France, Gellis & Mellinger Inc, NY, Prisma-Sun Bow, Inc, Los Angeles & Logo-Paris, Inc, Novato, Calif, World Market Equities, Inc, NY. *Exhib:* Martin Molinary Galleries, NY, 82; Gallerie Jean Pierre Lavignes, Paris, 83; Yve Arman Gallery, NY, 84; Vered Gallery, East Hampton, NY, 85; De Marigny Gallery, NY, 86; Joseph Bruck Artists Management, NY, 89-90; New Eng Fine Art Inst, Boston, 93; and others. *Pos:* Illusr, Joseph Bruck Artist's Rep, 84-85 & Joseph Mendola Inc, 85-86, NY; graphic designer, The Gap, NY, 89-90, Wathne Ltd, 90-92 & Polo Ralph Lauren, NY, 93-96; art dir, Bugle Boy Ind, NY, 97-98; acct mgr Christie's Auction House, Estates & Appraisals dept, 99-2002. *Awards:* Hample Ctr Scholar Prize, Contemp Paintings Exhib, Arnot Art Mus, 75; Juror's Award Pavilion, New Eng Fine Art Inst, Boston, 93. *Bibliog:* Josette Malze (auth), Christine Fromentin: The myth of women, Paris-Scope, Le Matin & Vital Mag, Paris, 83; Toni Canger (auth), Christine Fromentin, NJ Art Forum, 85. *Media:* Oil on Linen. *Publ:* Illusr, Lee Iacocca, Time Mag, Switch, Signet Bks, Allesandro, Bantam Bks, 85, Dark Side, Berkley Bks & Point of Purchase, Smirnoff Liquors, 86. *Mailing Add:* 395 Broadway #15A New York NY 10013

FRONCKOWIAK, ARTHUR
PAINTER
b Buffalo, NY, Aug 1, 49. *Study:* Univ Buffalo, NY, 69-70; Canisius Col, BA, 71. *Work:* Raymond James Financial Corp, St Petersburg, Fla; Empire Savings of Am, Deland, Fla; Belleview-Mido Gallery, Clearwater, Fla; The Gallery, Sarasota Visual Arts Ctr, Fla; over 500 works in corp & pvt collections. *Comn:* Murals & paintings, US Home Corp, Ft Myers, Fla, 91; murals & paintings, Arthur Rutenberg Corp, Naples, Fla, 93; painting series: Olde Florida Country Club, Naples, 96; murals & paintings, Quail West Country Club, Bonita Springs, Fla, 94; murals & paintings, Checkers Restaurants NAm, Clearwater, Fla, 95; and others. *Exhib:* Regional Design Show, ASID, Sarasota, Fla, 93; Annual Open, Sarasota Visual Arts Ctr, Fla, 94; Bicentennial Exhib, Orlando Mus Art, Fla, 95; Art-Reach '95, Nat Cong Art & Design, Salt Lake City, Utah, 95; Artists of Fla, Sarasota Visual Arts Ctr, Fla, 95. *Awards:* Best in Show, Artist of Fla, Sarasota Visual Arts Ctr, 95. *Bibliog:* Aaron Fodiman (auth), Classical art-mastery of paint-an acquired skill, Tampa Bay Mag, 95. *Mem:* Sarasota Visual Arts Ctr. *Publ:* Contribr, Fla Archit Digest Ann Ed, 94; A touch of Tuscanny, Open House Mag, 96. *Mailing Add:* 165 E Venice Ave Ste E Venice FL 34285-1926

FRONTZ, LESLIE
PAINTER
b Cleveland, Ohio, Aug 23, 50. *Study:* Muskingum Col, BA (cum laude), 1972; Southern Ore State Col, BS(suma cum laude), 1981; Univ NC-Greensboro, MFA(Holderness Fel), 1986. *Exhib:* Arts for the Parks, Wyo and Washington, 1987; Nat Oil & Acrylic Painters, Mo, 1993; Oil Painters Am, Ill, 1994; Southern Representational Exhib, Comer Mus, Ala, 1995; Davidson Co Mus Art, NC, 1997; Salem Col Fine Arts Center, NC, 2003; Soc of Women Artists, London, 2006; Southern Watercolor Soc Ann, Charlottesville, Va, 2006. *Teaching:* Instr oil painting, Davidson Co Community Col, Lexington, NC, 86-87; adj fac art hist, Front Range Community Col, Fort Collins, Colo, 89-90; instr drawing, 2-d design & art appreciation, Wash State Community Col, Marietta, Ohio, 91-92; instr art, Southwest Sch, Lexington, NC, 97-2003; adj fac, Davidson Co Community Col, Lexington, NC, 95-96, 2006. *Awards:* Award of Excellence, Ohio Watercolor Soc, Ohio, 92; Mason Mem Award, Batavia Soc Artists, 93; Best of Show, Comer Mus, 95; Canson Award, Watercolor Soc, 2006. *Bibliog:* Shelly Fling (auth), pvt showings: Leslie Frontz, US Art, 12/89. *Mem:* Southern Watercolor Soc; Soc Womens Artists, Plein Air. *Media:* Watercolor. *Publ:* Painting for Impact, Artist's Mag, 1/95. *Dealer:* Fountainside Fine Art Gallery, 1904 Eastwood Rd # 44, Wilmington NC 28403; Heart of Living Gallery 5588-A Garden Village Way Greensboro NC 27410; Broadhurst Gallery 2212 Midland Rd Pinehurst NC 28374. *Mailing Add:* 296 Peace Haven Dr Lexington NC 27292

FROST, STUART HOMER
EDUCATOR, PAINTER
b Arendtsville, Pa, Nov 22, 25. *Study:* Pa State Univ, BA; Brooklyn Mus Sch; Skowhegan Sch Painting & Sculpture. *Work:* Pa Acad Fine Arts, Philadelphia; Butler Art Inst, Youngstown, Ohio; Dulin Gallery Art, Knoxville, Tenn; Mus Art, Pa State Univ, University Park; Mansfield Univ, PA. *Exhib:* Am Watercolors, Drawings & Prints, Metrop Mus Art, 62; Recent Drawings USA, Mus Mod Art, 64; Watercolor USA, 66; Butler Art Inst Mid-Yr Show, 75; 9th Dulin Nat Print & Drawing Competition, 75; Drawings from Four Decades, Stuart Frost Babcock Galleries, 88; Drawn to Constructions, Stuart Frost Babcock Galleries, 93. *Pos:* Mural Assist. to Henry Varnum Poor, Allyn Cox. *Teaching:* Emer Prof of Art, Pa State Univ, University Park, currently. *Media:* Pen, Ink. *Dealer:* Babcock Galleries 725 Fifth Ave New York NY. *Mailing Add:* 139 E Hubler Rd State College PA 16801-7918

FRUDAKIS, ANTHONY P
SCULPTOR
b Bellows Falls, Vt, July 30, 53. *Study:* Pa Acad Fine Arts, cert, 76; Univ Pa, MFA, 91. *Work:* Brookgreen Gardens Mus, SC. *Comn:* Summer (male & female runners), Tropicana Hotel & Casino, Atlantic City, NJ, 86; Otter Fountain (lifesize cold cast bronze), Bally Hotel & Casino, Atlantic City, NJ, 86; Mother & child (cold cast bronze), Atlantic City Day Nursery, Atlantic City, NJ, 88; Justice (bas relief), Cape May Ct House, NJ, 89; Dr Charles Drew (bust), Drew Ct, Atlantic City, NJ, 89; Jonah (monument), Ocean City Cult Ctr, NJ, 90; Ascension, St Mary's Cathedral, Saginaw, Mich, 99; Andromeda (monumental bronze), East Lansing, Mich, 2000; George Washington (monumental bronze statue), Hillsdale, Mich, 2003. *Exhib:* Nat Sculpture Soc, NY, 76-89; Brookgreen Gardens Mus, SC, 83; Accent Gallery, Northfield, NJ, 88; Aaron's Gallery, Indianapolis, Ind, 88; Philadelphia Sketch Club, Pa, 88; Image of Women in Art, Renaissance Gallery, Philadelphia, Pa, 88; Corporate Art, Trammel & Crow, Philadelphia, Pa, 89; Grand Central Art Gallery, NY, 90, 92; Ocean City Cult Ctr, NJ, 92; Sturgis Civic Ctr, Mich, 92; Hillsdale Col, Mich, 93, 97, 99; Toledo Art Mus, Ohio, 94; Nat Sculpture Soc NY, 97; Nat Acad Design Ann Show, NY, 2001; Sculptors of Mich, Hillsdale Col, 2001; and others. *Teaching:* Instr sculpture, Frudakis Acad Fine Arts, Philadelphia, Pa, 74-77, Stockton State Col, Pomona, NJ, 77 & Fashion Inst Technol, NY, 81-82; adj prof, Atlantic Community Col, 90-91; assoc prof fine arts, Hillsdale Coll, 91-. *Awards:* Best Portrait, Lantz Award, 78 & 88, Gold Medal, 82, Gloria Medal, 83 & L Miselman Prize, 86, Nat Sculpture Soc, NY; First Prize for Sculpture, NJ State Art Show, 79; M B Hexter Award, Allied Artists Am, 82; finalist, NJ Vietnam Meml Competition, 90, Chatham Fishermen's Monument, Mass, 90; prize, Nat Acad Design Artist Fund, NY, 91; Daniel Chester French award, Nat Acad Design, NY, 2001. *Mem:* Nat Sculpture Soc, NY; Nat Acad (artist fund prize 1991). *Media:* bronze. *Interests:* guitar, billiards. *Mailing Add:* 36 Highland Ave Hillsdale MI 49242-1540

FRUDAKIS, EVANGELOS WILLIAM
SCULPTOR, INSTRUCTOR
b Rains, Utah, May 13, 21. *Study:* Greenwich Workshop, NY, 35-39; Beaux Arts Inst Design, NY, 40-41; Pa Acad Fine Arts, Cresson, Scheidt & Tiffany Scholar; Am Acad Rome, Italy, Prix de Rome Fel, 50-52. *Work:* Pa Acad Fine Arts, Philadelphia; Smithsonian Inst; Weizmann Inst, Israel; Nat Acad Fine Arts, NY; Airlie Found, Va; Woodmere Art Mus. *Comn:* Icarus & Daedalus Fountain, Little Rock, Ark; Welcome Fountain, Philadelphia, Pa, 88; Minute Man, Washington, 91; Minute Man, Arlington, Va, 94; Reaching Found, Brookgreen Gardens, 97; bronze figure, Welcome Fountain, Nat Gaurd Bldg, Wash DC; bronze memorial, Stephen F Hyde, Trump Castle, Atlantic City, NJ; Greek Relief, Greek Orthodox Archdiocese, NY City & Ellis Island; bronze monument, The Signer, Independence Nat Hist Park, Philadelphia, Pa; bronze figure, Naiad Fountain, Philadelphia Civic Ctr, Philadelphia, Pa; and others. *Exhib:* Nat Sculpture Soc Ann, 41-85; Pa Acad Fine Arts Ann, 41-62; Nat Acad Design Ann, 48-86; Philadelphia Mus Art, 59 & 62 & Twenty-three Sculptors Exhib, 72; one-man shows, Atlantic City Art Ctr, 56 & 61, Woodmere Art Mus, 57 & 62, Philadelphia Art Alliance, 58, Pa Acad Fine Arts, 62 & Briarcliff Col Mus Art, 74. *Teaching:* Instr, var art ctrs, NY, NJ & Pa, 41-63; instr, Nat Acad Design, Sch Fine Art, New York, 70-76, Old Church Cult Ctr, Demarest, NJ, 75-78; sr instr, Pa Acad Fine Arts, Philadelphia, 72; founder & instr, Frudakis Acad Fine Arts, Philadelphia, 76-90; instr, Loveland Academy Fine Art, 89-96. *Awards:* Gold Medal, Nat Acad Design, 64, 84; Gold Medal, Nat Sculpture Soc, 72; Artists Fund Prize 75, 79 & 90; and others. *Mem:* Fel Pa Acad Fine Arts; fel Am Acad Rome; fel Nat Sculpture Soc; academician Nat Acad Design; Allied Artists Am; Nat Acad. *Media:* Bronze, Marble. *Res:* Statues of the Roman Forum; Michelangelo's Rondanini Pieta. *Mailing Add:* 312 Valley Dr Kerrville TX 78028

FRUDAKIS, ZENOS
SCULPTOR
b San Francisco, Calif, Jul 7, 51. *Study:* Pa Acad Fine Arts, Philadelphia, 73-76; Univ Pa, Philadelphia, BFA, 81, MFA, 83. *Hon Degrees:* Acad Int L'Unita Cult, Rome, Academician. *Work:* LBJ Libr, Tex, King Ctr, Philadelphia, Brookgreen Gardens, SC; two over life size bronze figures, Utsukushi-Ga-Hara Mus, Japan; K Leroy Irvis (bust), State Mus, Harrisburg; Nat Acad Design, NY. *Comn:* Portraits, Dilworth, Paxson, & Kalish, Philadelphia, 80-81; Workers Mem, Bethlehem, Pa, 91; Reaching (monumental bronze figures), Indianapolis; Dream to Fly (monumental bronzes), Cherry Hill, NJ; bronze portrat busts, Martin Luther King Jr, Douglas MacArthur,

Dinah Shore, Arnold Palmer, and many others; Pa Anthracite Miners Mem, Shenandoah; Arnold Palmer & Bobby Jones, August, Ga; Former Mayor Frank Rizzo, Philadelphia, Pa; Gov Ellis Arnall, Atlanta; Arch Bishop Cavvadas (portrait), Brookline, Mass, 96; Air Force Memorial, Arlington Nat Cemetery, Va; Convergence, Secaucus Transportation Ctr, NJ. *Exhib:* Nat Sculpture Soc, 79-2000; Allied Artists Am, NY, 80-81; Nat Acad Design, NY, 80, 84, 86 & 90; Pa Acad Fine Arts Fel Ann, 81; Inst Contemp Art, Philadelphia, 81-83; Rutgers Univ Fac Show, 84-86; Invited artist, Utsukushi-Ga-Hara Open Air Mus, Japan, 90. *Pos:* Mem bd dir, Nat Sculpture Soc; mem, ed bd, Nat Sculpture Rev Mag; Nat Academician. *Teaching:* Coadj prof sculpture & drawing, Rutgers Univ, 84-85; guest lectr anat & sculpture, Med Col Pa, Philadelphia, 86 & 87, Scottsdale Artist's Sch, Ariz, 90; invited artist, Utsukushi-Ga-Hara Open Air Mus, Japan, 1990. *Awards:* John Spring Art Founder Award, Nat Sculpture Soc, 81, Gloria Medal, 81, Tallix Award, 82, President's Prize, 85, Silver Medal Honor, 86; Liskin Award, Knickerbocker Artists, 85; Henry Hearing Art-in-Archit Award, 90; Hakone Open-Air Mus Award, Japan, 90. *Mem:* Fel Nat Sculpture Soc (bd dir, 1988-, Art-in-Archit award 1990, edit pro-tem Nat Sculpture Rev, 1991-2002); Allied Artists Am; Fel, Pa Acad Fine Arts; Knickerbocker Artists; Am Artists Prof League; Fel, Nat Acad. *Media:* Bronze. *Publ:* Drawing, Nat Sculpture Rev Mag, 86; The National Sculpture Society Celebrates the Figure, Dr Jean Henry, 87. *Dealer:* Portraits Incorporated New York NY. *Mailing Add:* 2355 Mt Carmel Ave Glenside PA 19038

FRUEH, DEBORAH K A (DEBI)
PAINTER, SCULPTOR

b St. Louis, MO Nov 24, 51. *Study:* St Louis Col, AA, studied painting with George Bartko, 1969-1971; Fontbonne Col, Advan Studies, studied sculpture with Rudi Torrini, 1971-1972; St Louis Univ, Advan Studies, studied Baroque Art, 1972-1973. *Work:* The White House, Washington, DC; Off of Congressman Ed Whitfield, Paducah, Ky; Waterstreet Gallery, Seamans Church Inst Hq, NY; Museu Carmin Miranda, Mus, Rio de Janerio, Brazil; Wis Barge Lines Collection, Cassville, Wis. *Comn:* Portrait (30″x40″), Dr Everett Lerwick, comn by friends of Dr Lerwick, Mis Baptist Hosp, St. Louis, Mo, 1980; Portrait (20″x24″), Dr Zemlyn, comn by Bd Dirs, Chester Mem Hosp, Chester, Ill, 1989; Portrait (50″x60″), Susan Lengsfield Kasper & Children, comn by Diane Lengsfield (Paducah Ky), Washington, DC, 1993; Portrait (20″x24″), Len O'Hare, Pres, comn by bd Dirs W Ky Col, Paducah, Ky, 2002; Pencil 24″x30″), M V Jayne Hougland, comn by Asn Retired Marine Personnel, Paducah, Ky, 2004. *Exhib:* Solo exhibs, The Art of Debi Frueh, Paducah Art Guild, Market House Mus, Paducah, Ky, 1973, Debi Frueh Paintings/Sculptures, Arts Coun Gallery, Paducah, Ky, 1979; 26th Midstates Art Exhib, Evansville Mus Arts & Sci, Evansville, Ind, 16th Ann Art Exhib, Paducah Art Guild, Market House Mus, Paducah, Ky, 1973; Gallantly Streaming (artists respond to 9/11), Yeiser Art Center Mus, Paducah, Ky, 2002; Torrit Grey, 10th Ann, Gamblin Artists Colors Co, Portland, Ore, 2003; Size Matters, Yeiser Art Center Mus, Paducah, Ky, 2006. *Pos:* Gallery asst, St. Louis Col, St. Louis, Mo, 1971-1972. *Teaching:* Lectr Sculpture, Paducah Art Guild Market House Mus, 1973; instr sculpture, Paducah Col, Paducah, Ky, 1977-1979. *Awards:* Best of Show (oil painting), 41st Ann Art Exhib, City of Paducah, 1976; 1st Place (oils), Celebrating Women, Lourdes Found, 2002; Special Award for Creativity (Torrit Grey), 10th Ann Gamblin Artists Color, Co, 2003. *Bibliog:* Berry Craig (auth), Artist Enjoys Reactions to Her Sculptures, Sun Democrat, 1979; Erin Green (auth), Debi Frueh, Portrait Artist, Film/Interview WPSD TV. 2000; Darlene Mazzone (auth), From Wickliffe to the White House, Paducah Life Mag, 2003. *Mem:* Mus Women in the Arts; Am Soc Portrait Artists; Yeiser Art Center. *Media:* Acrylic, Oil, All Media; Clay. *Publ:* Auth, Illusr (art), Christmas Wish, Millennium Tribute, Paducah Life Mag, 2000; auth, illusr (art), Love Lady Liberty, Paducah Life Mag, 2002; contribr, illusr (art), From the Gallery, (From Wickliffe to the White House), Paducah Life Mag, 2003; auth, illusr (art), Lets Give Thanks, Paducah Life Mag, 2003; auth, illusr (web), Torrit Grey, Allegory of Painting, Gamblin Artist Colors Co, 2004. *Dealer:* The Artist's Palate 40 Avenida Goya Tubac AZ 85646. *Mailing Add:* Debi Frueh Portrait Studio 1985 Deerfield Rd Wickliffe KY 42087

FRUEH, JOANNA
CRITIC

b Chicago, Ill, 48. *Study:* Sarah Lawrence Col, BA, 70; Univ Chicago, MA, 71, PhD, 81. *Exhib:* Retrospective, Joann Frueh (auth), 2005; Retrospective, Tanya Augsburg, (auth), Nev Mus Art, 2005. *Pos:* Dir, Artemisia Gallery & Fund, Chicago, 74-76. *Teaching:* Asst prof mod art, Oberlin Col, Ohio, 81-; asst prof contemp art & art criticism, Univ Ariz, Tucson, 83-85; prof art hist, Univ Nev, Reno, 90-. *Awards:* Susan Koppelman Award for Feminist Art Criticism: An Anthology, 89; Artist Fel Lit Arts, Nev Arts Coun, 2001. *Bibliog:* Robert Christgau (auth), Children of the Porn, Village Voice, 67-68, 7/30/96; Maria Elena Buszek (auth), Monster/beauty: building the body of love, BUST, spring 2002; Carol Siegel (auth), Practicing what they teach, Rhizomes, issue 3, 2002. *Mem:* Col Art Asn (bd dir, 97-2001). *Media:* Performance art, photography. *Res:* Contemporary art, with a special interest in women artists and feminist art theory. *Interests:* Yoga, bodybuilding. *Publ:* Auth, Brumas: A Rock Star's Passage to a Life Re-Vamped, Freshcut Press, 83; Hannah Wilke: A Retrospective, Thomas H Kochheiser (ed), Univ Mo Press, Columbia, 89; New Feminist Criticism: Art, Identity, Action, Harper Collins, NY, 94; Erotic Faculties, 96, & Monster/Beauty: Building the Body of Love, 2001, Univ Calif Press; Picturing the Modern Amazon, Rizzoli Int, 2000; Maria Elena Buszek, Pin-Up Grrrls: Feminism, Sexuality, Popular Culture, Duke Univ Press, 2006, 14-16; Swooning Beauty: A Memoir of Pleasure, Univ Nev Press, 2006. *Mailing Add:* c/o Univ Nev - Reno Dept Art 224 Reno NV 89557-0007

FRY, JUDY ARLINE
PAINTER, JEWELER

b Great Falls, Mont, July 25, 38. *Study:* Wash State Univ Exten, 1957-58. *Work:* Carnegie Inst, Pittsburgh, Pa. *Comn:* Mural, Spokane Coliseum, Spokane, WA, 1957. *Exhib:* Studio Gallery of Utah, Springdale, Utah, 1982-83. *Pos:* Vpres, Pac NW Art League, 1967-68. *Awards:* First Place scholar, Carnegie Inst, 1953-54, 55-57. *Mem:* Ore Crafted, Eugene, Ore. *Media:* Acrylic, Oil, Watercolor. *Mailing Add:* 1334 Oak Patch Rd Apt 85 Eugene OR 97402-3267

FRYBERGER, BETSY G
CURATOR

b Chicago, Ill, May 7, 35. *Study:* Bryn Mawr Col, BA, 56; Radcliffe Col, MA, 58; Harvard Univ, MA, 57-58. *Collection Arranged:* Gavarni: Prints (auth, catalog), Stanford Univ, 71, Toulouse-Lautrec: Prints and Drawings (auth, catalog), 72, Morris and Company (coauth, catalog), 75, Whistler: Themes and Variations (coauth, catalog), 78, Paul Klee: In Celebration of/50 Prints (coauth, catalog), 79 & Gwen John (coauth, catalog), 82, Two Decades of American Prints from the Anderson Collection 1967-87 (catalog exhib), 87, Mark Tobey: Works on Paper (coauth, catalog), 90, Stanford University Musuem of Art / Drawing Collection (coauth, catalog), 93, Picasso: Graphic Magician / Prints from the Norton Simon Museum, (auth, catalog), 98, The Changing Garden: Four Centuries of European and American Gardens (auth, catalog), 2003. *Pos:* Asst cur prints & drawings, Art Inst Chicago, 60-67; cur prints & drawings, Stanford Univ Mus Art, 70-. *Teaching:* lect in Continuing Studies, exhib, The Changing Garden, 2003, & exhib, The Artist Observed: Portraits & Self-Portraits, 2004; lect, Gertrude Jekyll and William Morris, The Huntington, San Marino, Calif, 96; lect, Monet and the Influence of Japanese Prints on his Garden, Elizabeth F Gamble Garden, Palo Alto, Calif, 96; lect, French 17th and 18th century Gardens, Norton Simon Mus, 2002; lect, The Changing Garden, Filoli, Woodside, Calif, Elizabeth F Gamble Garden, & the Calif Garden & Landscape Hist Soc ann meeting at Standfor Univ, 2003; lect, Three Garden Heriones: Gertrude Jekyll, Beatrix Jones Farrand & Vita Sackvill West, Elizabeth F Gamble Garden, Libr Assoc, Ann Arbor, Mich, 2004; lect, Versailles: Example and Influence, Univ Mich Mus Art, Ann Arbor, 2004; lect, 18th century Artists Exploring the Roman Countryside: Views of Hadrain's Villa and Villa d'Este at Tivoli by Piranesi Fragonard and Hubert Robert, Cantor Ctr for the Arts at Stanford Univ, 2005. *Mem:* Print Coun Am (bd mem, 79-, vpres, 81-); Col Art Asn; adv bd & chair of the educ committee, Elizabeth F Gamble Garden, Palo Alto, Calif. *Interests:* Gardens. *Mailing Add:* Iris & B Gerald Cantor Ctr for Visual Arts at Stanford Univ Museum Way Stanford CA 94305-5060

FUENTE, LARRY
SCULPTOR

b Chicago, Ill, Sept 29, 47. *Study:* Kansas City Art Inst, 66-68. *Exhib:* Oakland Mus, Calif, 87; Mus Fine Arts, Boston, 88; Va Mus Fine Art, Richmond, 89; Renwick Gallery, Smithsonaian Inst, Washington, 90; Calif State Fair, Sacramento, 93; Smithsonaian traveling exhib, 93; Mendocino Art Ctr, Calif, 93; Regional Ctr Arts, Walnut Creek, Calif, 94; Whats Afoot Gallery, Casper, Calif, 94; Natural Hist Mus, Los Angeles, 94. *Awards:* Nat Endowment Arts Fel, 80 & 88

FUERST, SHIRLEY MILLER
SCULPTOR, PRINTMAKER

b Brooklyn, NY, June 3, 28. *Study:* Brooklyn Mus Art Sch, with Reuben Tam; Pratt Ctr Contemp Printmaking; Art Students League, with Roberto DeLamonica; Hunter Col, MFA, 71. *Work:* James A Michener Found Collection of Twentieth Century Am Art, Univ Tex, Austin; Exxon Corp, NJ; Allentown Art Mus, Pa; Portland Mus Art, Maine. *Comn:* Translucent sculpture, comn by Marcia Frazier, Beverly Hills, Calif, 84; Double Cloud Column (translucent sculpture), comn by Michael Jacobs, Sausalito, Calif, 96; Small Cloud translucent sculpture, comn by George Van Deventer, Washington, Maine. *Exhib:* 32nd Midyear Show, Butler Inst Am Art, 68; sol shows incl Underwater Gardens, Steinhardt Conservatory Exhib Gallery, Brooklyn Botonic Garden, 90, Reef and Cloud Gardens, Broadway Windows, NY, 91, Tide Pool Series, Ednl Testing Svc Conf Ctr, Princeton, NJ, 93, Wind Spirits and Microcosms, Space Between Gallery, Bangor, Maine, 96, New/Now, New Britain Mus of Am Art, New Britain, Conn, 2000, Shirley Fuerst: Translucent Sculpture, Flinn Gallery, Greenwich, Conn, 01, Translucent Sculptures, St Peter's Church, Citigroup Bldg, NY, 02; Women Artist Series, Douglas Col Libr, Rutgers Univ, 78; Underwater Gardens, Steinhardt Conserv Gallery, Brooklyn Botanic Garden, 90; Reef & Cloud Gardens, Broadway Windows, NY Univ, 91; Tide Pool Series, Educ Testing Serv, Princeton, NJ, 93; 24th Juried Show, Allentown Art Mus, 94; Solstice 97, Portland Mus Art, Maine; Island Invitational, Blum Gallery, Col Atlantic, Maine, 98; solo shows incl New/Now, New Britain Mus of Am Art, Conn, 2000; Shirley Fuerst: Translucent Sculpture, Flinn Gallery, Greenwich, Conn, 01; Translucent Sculptures, St Peter's Church, Citigroup Bldg, NY, 02. *Awards:* Oil Competition First Prize, Village Art Ctr, NY, 63; Merit Award with Distinction, Enjay Chem Co, NJ, 66; Eric Schwartz Graphics Award, Nat Asn Women Artists, 70. *Bibliog:* Conversation with an artist, Shirley Fuerst, Joy Goodman (videotape), Channel 31, 77; Anna Marie Saintonge (auth), Shirley Fuerst: Shaping nature's fragile moments, Hardwood Mag (http://www hrdwood com/art/sfuersthtml); Carl Little (auth), Wind spirits and micro cosms: sculpture by Shirley Fuerst, Art New Eng, 97. *Mem:* Orgn Independent Artists; Am Asn Mus. *Media:* Plastic, Miscellaneous Media. *Publ:* Auth, Health hazards in art, Art Workers News, 75; videotape documentaries of women artists, 70 & Women Artists Newsletter, 76; ed, Feminism and ecology, Heresies, 80. *Mailing Add:* PO Box 145 Mt Desert ME 04660

FUGLIE, GORDON LOUIS
GALLERY DIRECTOR, HISTORIAN
b Los Angeles, Calif. *Study:* Univ Calif, Los Angeles, MA(art hist), 91. *Collection Arranged:* Early 20th Century German Prints, Univ Calif, Los Angeles, 82-84; Tamarind Lithography Workshop & Inst, Univ Calif, Los Angeles, 83-85; Max Thalmann Graphics, Loyola Marymount Univ, 91-94; LMU Art Collection, res and exhib, 2005. *Pos:* Asst cur & actg cur, Grunwald Ctr Graphic Arts, Univ Calif, Los Angeles, 81-86; dir, Laband Art Gallery, Loyola Marymount Univ, 89-. *Mem:* Col Art Asn; Am Art Mus Asn. *Res:* Figurative art, 1950-2000; Contemp Art. *Publ:* Attending To the Earth: Robert Glenn Ketchum, Loyola Marymount Univ, 90; co-auth, Burning Lights, Loyola Marymount Univ, 94; contrib auth, The Art of Michael Schrauzer, Image, 95; Representing LA: Recent Pictorial Currents in Southern California Art, Seattle, 2000; auth, John Frame: Enigma Variations, Long Beach, 2005. *Mailing Add:* 1 LMU Dr Los Angeles CA 90045-8346

FUHRMAN, ESTHER
SCULPTOR, JEWELER
b Pittsburgh, Pa, Feb 25, 39. *Study:* Pa State Univ, 56-57; Frick Dept Fine Arts, Univ Pittsburgh, BA, 60; also with Sabastiano Mineo & Hana Geber, NY. *Work:* Port NY Authority; World Trade Ctr, NY; Am Crafts Coun, NY; UAHC Architects Adv, NY; Deere & Co, Moline, Ill; and others. *Comn:* Gemstone & bronze memorial, Temple Sinai, Pittsburgh, 78; bronze memorial, Temple Keneseth Israel, Philadelphia, 79; pvt residential comns, NY, Philadelphia, Pittsburgh, Miami, NJ, Los Angeles, Paris, Sydney, 79-81; bronze figure, Scott Paper Co, Philadelphia, 81; and others. *Exhib:* Nat Asn Women Artists, NY; Sculptors League, NY; Equitable Life Assurance, NY; Lever House, NY; Jewelers of Am, Javits Ctr, NY; and others. *Pos:* Head Designer, Outasight Jewelry Coll, 94-. *Teaching:* Lectr sculpture today, Sands Point Acad, Long Island, 71 & Kimberley Sch, NJ, 72; lectr studio secrets, Montclair Mus Art. *Awards:* New Designer Award, Jewelers Am; Sculpture Award, Nat Asn Women Artists. *Bibliog:* Marilyn Goldstein (auth), Massive sculpture shapes her life, Newsday, 3/69; article, La Rev Mod, 3/72; Jewelers Circular Keystone, 6/88; Modern Jeweler, 7/88; Accent Mag, 3/89; Accessories Mag, 3/4/5-89. *Mem:* Nat Asn Women Artists; Sculptors League (vpres, currently). *Media:* Bronze, Gold, Sterling Silver. *Dealer:* Lavon Art Gallery Cambridge Square Union Hill Rd Morganville NJ 07751. *Mailing Add:* Rivá Pointe 600 Harbor Blvd Apt 1022 Weehawken NJ 07086

FUJIMARA, MAKOTA
PAINTER
b Boston, 60. *Study:* Cum laude, Bucknell Univ, BA, 83; Toyko National Univ of Fine Arts and Music, MFA, 89. *Exhib:* Exhibs incl Contemp Nihonga Exhib, Contemp Mus Toyko, 98, One Hundred Yrs of Nihonga, Toyko Nat Univ of Fine Arts and Music Mus, 2000, Like a Prayer, Tryon Ctr Visual Arts, 2003, Considering Peace, Sato Mus, 2003, one-man shows include Gravity and Grace, Bellas Artes, 2002, Columbines, Gallery at Matsuya Ginza, 2002, Four Quartets, Kristen Frederickson Contemp, 2003, Golden Pines, Dillon Gallery, 2003, The Still Point, Takashimaya Gallery, 2003-04, exhibited in group shows at Art as Prayer, Cooper Union Gallery, 2001, TriBeCa Temporary Exhibits, 2001, WATERwalks, Ise Cult Found, 2002, The Return of Beauty, Kristen Frederickson Gallery, 2002, The WRONG Exhibit, Birmingham, Eng, 2003, Represented in permanent collections Contemp Mus Tokyo, Nerima Mus Art, Oxford House, Sato Mus, St Louis Art Mus, Tamaya Collection, Toyko Nat Univ of Fine Arts and Music, Yamaguchi Prefecture Mus. *Pos:* Member National Council on Arts, National Endowment for Arts, 2003—. *Mailing Add:* Nat Endowment for Arts 1100 Pennsylvania Ave Northwest Washington DC 20506

FUJITA, KENJI
SCULPTOR
b New York, NY, 1955. *Study:* Bennington Col, BA, 78; Whitney Mus Independent Study Prog, NY, 78; Queens Col, NY, MFA, 98. *Exhib:* Solo exhibs, Cable Gallery, NY, 85 & 86, Daniel Weinberg Gallery, Los Angeles, 87 & 88, Jean Bernier, Athens, 89 & Luhring Augustine, NY, 88, 91 & 92; Aldrich Mus, Ridgefield, Conn, 86; Venice, Bienniale, Italy, 88; Sculpture, Kruygier/Landau Gallery, Santa Monica, 89; Luhring Augustine Gallery, NY, 90; Drawings, Luhring Augustine Hetzler, Santa Monica, 90; Recent Acquisitions of Prints & Drawings by Contemp Artists, Brooklyn Mus, NY 92; Contemp Wood Sculpture, Brooklyn Mus, NY, 92. *Teaching:* instr, Sch Visual Arts, Bard Col, 93 & vis asst prof visual arts, 98. *Awards:* Nat Endowment Arts Fel Sculpture, 84, 88 & Works on Paper, 91; NY Found Arts Fel, 87; Pollock/Krasner Found Grant, Scullpture, 96; John Simon Guggenheim Mem Found Fel, Visual Art, 98. *Bibliog:* Joshua Decter (auth), Kenji Fujita, Arts, 4/92; Holland Cotter (auth), Kenji Fujita: Luhring Augustine Gallery, New York Times, 7/24/92; Roberta Smith (auth), Kenji Fujita: The merge of sense and nonsense, NY Times, 88. *Media:* Sculpture, Works on Paper. *Mailing Add:* PO Box 205 71 Old Post Rd Staatsburg NY 12580

FUKUHARA, HENRY
PAINTER, INSTRUCTOR
b Los Angeles, Calif, Apr 25, 1913. *Study:* With Edgar A Whitney, 72; with Rex Brandt, 74; with Robert E Wood, 74; with Carl Molno, 76. *Work:* Heckscher Mus, Huntington, NY; Abilene Mus Fine Art, Tex; Nassau Community Col, Garden City, NY; San Bernardino Co Mus Art, Calif; Hiroshima Mod Mus Art, Japan. *Exhib:* One-man shows, Dowling Col, Oakdale, Long Island, 78 & Friends World Col, Lloyds Neck, NY, 80; Elaine Benson Gallery, Bridgehampton, NY, 79; Nat Invitational Watercolor, Zaner Gallery, Rochester, NY, 81; Kawakami Gallery, Tokyo, Japan, 86; Setagaya Mus Art, Tokyo, 87-96; and others. *Pos:* Watercolor instr, Venice High Sch, Calif, 92-93. *Teaching:* Instr painting workshops, Cutchogue, Long Island, 81-83, Mont Miniature Art Soc, 82, Islip Art Mus, NY, 82, Parrish Art Mus, Southampton, 83, Fullerton Col, Santa Monica Col & Palos Verdes Art Ctr, Calif, 88 & Yosemite Nat Park, Calif, 89-92. *Awards:* Purchase Award, Nassau Community Col, 76; Elise Brown Mem, Mamaroneck Art Guild, NY, 78; Best in Show Watercolor, Strathmore Paper Co, 79; Life Time Achievement Award, Nat Watercolor Soc and Watercolor West, 2004. *Bibliog:* Janice Loyoos (auth), Painting with abanded control, Am Artist Mag, 5/93; Ron Ranson (auth), Learn to Paint Watercolor the Edgar Whitney Way, Northlight, 94; Rachel Wolf (auth), Splash 3 & 4, Northlight, 94-95; Watercolor Magic (auth), Fall Issue, 2000, 01; Show the Shapes, International Artist, issue 25, 2002; The Road to Freedom, Artist's Mag., Oct. 2002. *Mem:* Pittsburgh Watercolor Soc; Ala Watercolor Soc; Nat Watercolor Soc. *Media:* Watercolor, Acrylic. *Dealer:* William Anderson Gallery Pacific Coast Hwy Sunset Beach CA. *Mailing Add:* 1214 Marine St Santa Monica CA 90405-5815

FUKUI, NOBU
PAINTER
b Tokyo, Japan, US citizen. *Study:* Art Students League, 64-65. *Work:* Indianapolis Mus Art, Ind; Larry Aldrich Mus, Conn; Nat Mus Mod Art, Tokyo & Kyoto; Chase Manhattan Bank, NY; and others. *Exhib:* One-man shows, Daniel's Gallery, 1965, Max Hutchinson Gallery, 1970, 72, 73, 75 & 79, Patricia Hamilton Gallery, 1987 & 1988, Marisa Del Re Gallery (with catalog), NY, 1989-90 & 1993, Richard Green Gallery, Santa Monica, Calif, 1990, Hokin Gallery, Fla, 1992 & 1993; Painting & Sculpture Today, Indianapolis Mus Art, 1970, 1972 & 1974; David Klein Gallery, Mich, 1993 & 1997; Central Fine Arts, NY, 1999; Camino Real Gallery, 1991 & 2004; Stephen Haller Gallery, 2004 & 05. *Bibliog:* David Shirley (auth), Art downtown: Construction shifts, The NY Times, 1/15/72; Carter Ratcliff (auth), Notes on line, Art Am, 90; Priya Malhotha (auth), A Man of Spiritual Exploration, Asian Art News, Nov 2004; Grace Glueck (auth), Nobu Fukui, The NY Times, 5/14/2004; Carter Ratcliff (auth), States of Stability, Art in America, 5/2005. *Media:* Oil. *Dealer:* Stephen Haller Gallery, 542 W 26th St, New York, NY 10001. *Mailing Add:* 141 W 26th St New York NY 10001

FUKUTAKE, SOICHIRO
COLLECTOR
Pos: Pres, Benesse Corp, Japan, 86-2003, dir, chmn & ceo, 2003-. *Awards:* named one of Top 200 Collectors, ARTnews Mag, 2004. *Mem:* pres, Naoshima Fukutake Art Mus Foundation. *Collection:* Impressionism & contemp art. *Mailing Add:* Benesse Corp 3-7-17 Minamigata Okayama-si Okayama 700-8686 Japan

FULD, RICHARD SEVERIN, JR.
COLLECTOR, PATRON
Study: Univ Colo, BA, 69; NYU Stern Sch Bus, MBA, 73. *Pos:* Joined Lehman Brothers, New York City, 69, managing dir, 69-84; vice chmn Shearson Lehman (merger Shearson and Lehman Brothers), 84-90; pres, co-CEO Shearson Lehman Brothers Inc, 90-93; pres, COO Lehman Brothers Holdings, Inc., 93-94, CEO, 93-, chmn, 94-; Mem PSA Govt and Fed Agency Securities Com; dir Fed Reserve Bank of NY; mem exec com Partnership for New York City, Bus. Roundtable and Bus Coun. *Awards:* Named one of Top 200 Collectors, ARTnews, 2006. *Mem:* Trustee Mt Sinai Med Ctr, New York City, Middlebury Coll.; former chmn Mt. Sinai Children's Ctr Found, mem exec com; bd dir Ronald McDonald House. *Collection:* Collects works on paper, especially postwar and contemporary

FULLER, DIANA
CURATOR, EDITOR
b New York, NY, Jan 14, 34. *Study:* Sorbonne, art hist. *Pos:* Co-owner, dir, Hansen Fuller Gallery, 60-77, Hansen Fuller Goldeen Gallery, 78-90, Fuller Goldeen Gallery, 82-87, Fuller Gross Gallery, 87-90; trustee, Headlands Ctr Arts, San Francisco Art Inst; co-founder, Bacva and 80 Langton St; pres, Performing Arts Workshop, formerly; founder & pres, Proj Sculpture Pub Site, 82-86; owner/dir, Creative Arts Enterprises, 90-; dir, Greg Jubileum: Norway Celebrates the Arts, 92-94; int arts comt, Exploratoreum, 95-; bd dir, Pub Art Works, 99-. *Publ:* Co-ed, proj dir, Parallels & Intersections: The Remarkable History of Women Artists in California 1950-2000, UC Press, 2001. *Mailing Add:* 2173 15th St San Francisco CA 94114

FULLER, EMILY
PAINTER
b New York, NY, Aug 9, 41. *Study:* Garland Jr Col, Boston, Mass, Assoc BD, 62; Mus Sch Fine Arts, Boston, Mass, 62-66; Tufts Univ, BS(art educ), 66; Art Students League, New York, study with Richard Mayhew, 68-69; Sch of Visual Arts, NYC, 88-89. *Work:* Mus Mod Art, Chase Manhattan Bank, NY; Aldrich Mus Contemp Art, Ridgefield, Conn; Prudential Ins Corp Am; Indianapolis Mus Art, Ind; City Bank NAm, NY; Miami Dade Pub Libr System, Fla; IBM Corp, NY; and others. *Exhib:* One-person shows 55 Mercer, NY, 72, 75, 78 & 79, Soho 20, NY, 77, Webb & Parsons, Bedford Village, NY, 77, Frank Marino Gallery, NY, 80, Cardet Gallery, Coral Gables, Fla, 81, New Materialism, Frauen Mus, Bonn, Ger, 85, Stanford Mus & Nature Ctr, Conn, 88, Maine Coast Artists, Rockport, 89, Foxhall Gallery, Washington, DC, 90 & Bergen Mus Art & Sci, Paramus, NJ, 92; Art in Transition: A Century of The Mus Sch, Mus Fine Arts, Boston, Mass, 77; Paper as Medium, Smithsonian Inst Traveling Exhib Serv, 78-79; Gifts of Drawings: European Acquisitions, Am Acquisitions, Mus Mod Art, NY, 79; and other group & one-person shows @ mashitvilla Gallery, Millbrook, NY, 2005-2006. *Pos:* Trustee, Bergen Mus Arts & Sci, Paramus, NJ, 93-94. *Bibliog:* Michael Florescu (auth), Emily Fuller, article in Arts Mag, 4/79; John Russell (auth), Art: New drawings at the Modern, New York Times, 8/10/79; Linda Rohr (auth), Emily Fuller, Bergen Mus Arts & Sci, 92. *Mem:* NY Artists Equity. *Media:* Oil, Pastels. *Interests:* archit; antiques; glass. *Collection:* Mus Mod Art; JP Morgan Chase; Indianapolis Mus Art; Prudential Insurance Co Am; IBM; Deutsche Bank; and others. *Publ:* Contribr, Emily Fuller pioneers in art, Garland Mag, Garland Jr Col, 74. *Dealer:* Mabbettsville Gallery Millbrook NY 12545. *Mailing Add:* 130 W 24th St Apt 3A New York NY 10011

FULLER, JEFFREY P
DEALER, GALLERY DIRECTOR
b Chicago, Ill, May 14, 50. *Study:* Univ Vienna, 70-71; Holy Cross Col, Mass, BA, 72. *Pos:* Asst, Hokin Gallery, Inc, Chicago, 74-78, dir, 78-79; dir, Jeffrey Fuller Fine Art, Ltd, 79; accredited sr appraiser, Am Soc Appraisers, 84-. *Mem:* Philadelphia Art Dealers Asn (pres, 87-88); Am Soc Appraisers; Philadelphia Art Alliance (bd mem, 82-85); Swedish Am Hist Mus (art adv panel, 82-85); Philadelphia Volunteer Lawyers for Arts (bd mem, 84-); and others. *Specialty:* Twentieth century American and European art. *Mailing Add:* Jeffrey Fuller Fine Art Ltd 730-32 Carpenter Ln Philadelphia PA 19119

FULLER, MARY (MARY FULLER MCCHESNEY)
SCULPTOR, PUBLISHER
b Wichita, Kans, Oct 20, 22. *Study:* Univ Calif, Berkeley, AA, 43. *Work:* State Calif; Children's Sculpture Garden, Community Ctr, Salinas, Calif; San Francisco Art Comn; Petaluma Pub Libr; San Francisco Gen Hosp; and others. *Comn:* Calabi-Whismand Totem, Sebastopol, Calif, 92; Shakti, Pac Sch Healing Arts, Gualala, Calif, 92; Santa Cruz Art Comn, 93; Berkeley, Calif, 2002; Reno, Nev, 2002; and others. *Exhib:* San Francisco Mus Art, 47-50 & 60; Gump's Gallery, San Francisco, 65; Calif State Univ, Sonoma, at Cotati, 71; Santa Rosa City Hall, Calif, 74 & 86; Fremont, Calif, 80; Lafayette, Calif, 82; Portland, Ore, 88; Carmel, Calif, 88; San Francisco, 2002. *Collection Arranged:* Period of Exploration (with catalog), Oakland Mus, 73. *Pos:* Researcher, Arch Am Art, 64-65; staff writer, Currant Mag, San Francisco, 75-76; ed & publ, Sonoma Mt Publ Co, 96. *Awards:* First Prize Ceramic Sculpture, Pac Coast Ceramic Ann, 47 & 49; Ford Found, 65; Merit Award, San Francisco Art Festival, 71; Nat Endowment Arts art critic grant, 75. *Media:* Carved concrete. *Publ:* Auth, articles in Art Digest, 54, Artforum, 62, 63, 70 & 71, Art in Am, 63 & 64 & Craft Horizons, 73, 76, 77 & 78; A Period of Exploration, 73. *Dealer:* Quicksilver Forestville, CA. *Mailing Add:* 2955 Sonoma Mountain Rd Petaluma CA 94954

FULLER, SUE
SCULPTOR, PRINTMAKER
b Pittsburgh, Pa. *Study:* Carnegie Inst Technol, BA, 36; Columbia Univ Teachers Col, MA, 39; and with Hans Hofmann, S W Hayter & Josef Albers. *Work:* Metrop Mus Art & Whitney Mus Am Art, NY; Nat Collection Fine Arts, Smithsonian Inst, Washington, DC; Tate Gallery, London; Guggenheim Mus, NY; plus others. *Comn:* String Composition 52, comn by M Greef for bd rm, Com Investment 200; String Composition T-250, Emerson Crocker Mem for Gail Borden Pub Libr, Elgin, Ill, 72; String Composition T252, All Souls Unitarian Church, NY, 79; String Construction No 253, McNay Art Inst, San Antonio, 83. *Exhib:* First Biennial Sao Paulo, Brazil, 50; Abstract Art in Am, Mus Mod Art, NY, 51; Edward Root Collection, Metrop Mus Art, NY, 53; Plastics USA, US Info Agency traveling exhib, USSR, 61; Responsive Eye, Mus Mod Art, NY, 65. *Teaching:* Instr mobile design, Mus Mod Art, NY, 45-47; guest artist, Univ Ga, 51-52; instr art, Columbia Univ Teachers Col, 52 & 58; instr two-dimensional design, Pratt Inst, 65-66. *Awards:* Carnegie Mellon Univ Alumni Merit Award, 74; Women's Caucus Art Hon Award, 86; Honoree, First Women Sculptors Conf, Cincinnatti, Ohio, 87. *Bibliog:* Rosalind Browne (auth), Sue Fuller: Threading transparency, Art Int, 1/20/72; David Shirey (auth), Esthetic magic of geometry, New York Times, 4/23/78; Harry A Broadd (auth), The String Constructions of Sue Fuller, Arts & Activities, 4/82. *Mem:* Soc Am Graphic Artists (vpres Soc Am Etchers, 46-51); Artists Equity Asn NY (vpres, 52-53); Sculptor's Guild. *Media:* Plastic, String. *Publ:* Auth, Mary Cassatt's use of soft-ground etching, Mag Art, 2/50, 20th century cat's cradle, Craft Horizons, 4/54; dir, String Composition (film), NY State Coun Arts, 70; co-dir (with film maker Maurice Amar), String Composition (video), 74

FULLERTON, MARY See Faulconer, Mary (Fullerton)

FULTON, HAMISH
CONCEPTUAL ARTIST
b London, Eng, 1946. *Study:* Hammersmith Col Art, London; St Martin's Sch Art, London; Royal Col Art, London. *Work:* Mus Mod Art, NY; Tate Gallery, London; Stedelijk Mus, Amsterdam; Van Abbemuseum, Eindhoven. *Exhib:* Solo exhibs, Stedelijk Mus, Amsterdam, 73, Kunst Mus, Basel, 75, Cent d'Art Contemp, Geneva, 78 & Gallery Beauborg, Cent Georges Pompidou, Paris, 81; ARS, 83, Helsinki, 83; As of Now, Walker Art Gallery, Liverpool, Eng, 83-84; A Contemp Focus 74-84, Hirshhorn Mus, Washington, DC, 84; Second Nature, Common Ground, London, 85; Retrospective 1975-1985, Stedelijk Van Abbemuseum, Eindhoven & traveling, Europe, 85; The Real Picture, Queens Mus, NY, 86; and many others. *Bibliog:* Michael Auping (auth), Moral landscape, Art in Am, 2/83; Earthworks & beyond, Abbeville Press, 84; Robert Morgan (auth), The residue of vision, Arts Mag, 3/86. *Media:* Photography. *Publ:* Photogr, Nepal 1975, Van Abbemuseum, Eindhoven, 77; Roads and Paths, Schirmer Mosel, Munich; Twilight Horizons, CAPC, Bordeaux, France, 83; Coast to Coast Walks, Coracle, London, 85

FULTON, JACK E
PHOTOGRAPHER, INSTRUCTOR
b San Francisco, Calif, June 30, 39. *Work:* San Francisco Mus Mod Art, Calif; Bibliotech Nat, Paris, France; Oakland Mus, Calif. *Comn:* NFL Football, 68. *Exhib:* 2 Saunters, Summer & Winter, Port Photog Fest, 89; Halsted Gallery West, San Francisco, Calif, 91; Suite Nevada, Nev Hist Soc, Las Vegas, 91. *Teaching:* Prof, San Francisco Art Inst, 69- & Univ Calif, Santa Cruz, 78-. *Awards:* Art Fel, 80 & 92 & Publ Fel, 2 Saunters: Summer & Winter, 86, Nat Endowment Arts; Residency Award, Nev State Coun Arts, 91. *Mem:* Soc Photog Educ (Western regional conf coordr), 89. *Media:* Photography, Writing. *Dealer:* Stremmel Gallery Reno NV; Linda Wolcott-Moore Mill Valley CA. *Mailing Add:* 109 Orange St San Rafael CA 94901

FULTON ROSS, GALE
ARTIST
b Medford, MA, July 28, 47. *Study:* Studied with: Melvin Johnson, Melvin George Sch Art, Boston, 1965-1976; Cleveland Bellow, DeYoung Mus, Oakland, Calif, 1976-1981; Pierre Parsus, France, 1993; studied, Berlin, 1996. *Work:* Am Mus African Am Artists; Calif Mus African Am Art; Forbes Gallery, NYC; Arthur Ashe Found; Thurgood Marshall Estate, NC Univ. *Comn:* Archbishop Desmond Tutu; Jackie Robinson, comn by Mrs Rachel Robinson; Dr Arthur Logan, comn by Marion Logan; Ambassador Bradlet Holmes; Gov Michael Dukakis. *Exhib:* Earth N' Arts Gallery, Oakland, 1971-1976; Black Expo, San Francisco, 1972; The Gallery, Los Angeles, 1978; Brockman Gallery, 1984; Calif African Mus, 1986; Chuck Levitan Gallery, NYC, 1996; SoBo Fine Art, Tulsa, 1999; One-women shows: Nat Coun Chas Hdqs, NYC, Castillion Fine Art, 1991; Zora Neal Hurston Mus, Monique Knowlton Gallery, NYC, 1994; Don Roll Gallery, Sarasota, African Am Mus, 1995. *Pos:* Trustee, Nat Urban League, 1976-1978; local/state judge, Miss Am Pageant, 2000; actor roles in: Blue Hill Ave & The Crucible (films). *Awards:* Atlanta Life Painters award, 1990; Nat Coalition of 100 Black Woman Artistic Achievement Award, 1995; Humanitarian award W Coast Center Human Develop, 1996. *Mailing Add:* PO Box 15022 Sarasota FL 34239

FUMAGALLI, BARBARA MERRILL
PRINTMAKER
b Kirkwood, Mo, Mar 15, 26. *Study:* Univ Iowa, Iowa City, BFA, 48, MFA, 50, with Mauricio Lasansky; Univ NMex, 80-81, with Garo Antreasian, John Sommers & Jim Kraft. *Work:* Mus of Mod Art, NY; Nelson A Rockefeller Collection, NY; Univ Ill, Urbana; Univ Iowa, Iowa City; Hamline Univ, St Paul, Minn; St John's Univ, Collegeville, Minn. *Exhib:* Walker Art Ctr, Minneapolis, Minn, 49, 56 & 63; Young Am Printmakers, Mus Mod Art, NY, 53; solo exhibs, Tweed Gallery, Univ Minn, 65 & 82, Concordia Col, Moorhead, Minn, 65, Suzanne Kohn Gallery, St Paul, 67, Hamline Univ, St Paul, 69 & 84, Paine Art Ctr & Arboretum, Oshkosh, Wis, 73 & St John's Univ, Minn, 84; Smithsonian Inst, traveling exhib, 66-68; NW Printmakers, Seattle Art Mus, Wash, 66-69; One West Contemp Arts Ctr, Ft Collins, Colo, 94; Truman State Univ, Kirksville, Mo, 98; Indian Hills Community Col, Ottumwa, Iowa, 98; Southeast Mo State Univ, Cape Girardeau, Mo, 99; Wayland Baptist Univ, Plainview, Tex, 99; Studio Channel Islands, Camarillo, Calif, 2000 & 2001; Univ Ctrl Ark, Conway, 2001; Focus on the Masters, Ventura Calif, 2002 & 2003; Mo Western State Col, St. Joseph, 2003; Ventura Co Arts Coun, 2004; Dickenson State Univ, NDak, 2004; Ashford Univ, Clinton, IA, 2005; Art & Jazz Festival, Studio Channel Islands Art Center, Calif State Univ, Camarillo, Calif, 2006. *Teaching:* Instr, Univ Wis, Stout, 79 & 81. *Awards:* Post Facto Prize, City Art Mus, St Louis, Mo, 47; Purchase Prize, Univ Ill, 54; Best Show, Arrowhead Art Exhib, 63. *Bibliog:* Donald M Anderson (auth), Elements of Design, Holt, Rinehart & Winston, 61. *Media:* Engraving, Serigraphy; Oil, Watercolor. *Publ:* Illusr, Swing Around the Sun, Lerner Publ, 65. *Mailing Add:* 352 E Calle La Sombra Camarillo CA 93010

FUNDERBURK, AMY ELIZABETH
PAINTER, PHOTOGRAPHER
b Charlotte, NC, Feb 16, 66. *Study:* Appalachian State Univ, BS, 88; Assoc Artists Winston-Salem Pastel Workshop with Wolf Kahn, 91, Vermont Studio Center, April 2005. *Work:* The Artinian Self-Portrait Collection, Appalachian State Univ, Boone, NC; Babcock School for Business Management, Wake Forest Univ, Winston-Salem, NC, 97. *Comn:* Portraits, Legends Entertainment Ctr, Appalachian State Univ, 88; many pvt portraits, 88-; Brighid at the Forge (oil on linen painting), Student Govt Asoc Permanent Art Collection, Forsyth Tech Community Col, Winston-Salem, NC, 96. *Exhib:* The Red Clay Survey, Huntsville Mus Art, Ala, 90; Spotlight 95 Art Exhib, Davidson Co Mus Art, Lexington, NC, 95; Whose Body is it Anyway, Mills Pond House Gallery, Smithtown Twp Arts Coun, St James, NY, 95; Holy Baloney, Woman Made Gallery, Chicago, 95; Magic Casements: A Mixed-Media View of Lit, Tuttle Gallery, McDonogh Sch, Baltimore, 95-96; one-woman show, Wisdom of the Ancient Lore: Symbolic Interpretation of Spiritual Knowledge, Parsons Gallery, Spartanburg Co Mus Art, SC, 96; solo exhibs, Durham Art Guild, Central Carolina Bank Gallery, NC, 98, Mars Hill Col, ars Hill, NC, 199, Wisdom of the Ancient Lore: Selectios from Two Symbolic Series and Related Works, Ctr for Creative Arts, Yorklyn, DE, 2002; group exhibs, Creating Ceremony, Main Gallery, theatre Art Galleries, High Point, NC, 2000, Hickory Mus of Art, Hickory, NC and McColl Ctr Vis Art, Charlotte, NC, 2004. *Collection Arranged:* Journeys: Work from Artists' Intl Travels,. Milton Rhodes Gallery, Winston-Salem, NC, 2002 & 2003; Allegory, Milton Rhodes Gallery, Winston Salem, NC, 2003. *Pos:* Exhib coordr, Winston-Salem Forsyth Co Arts Coun, 92-96, Greater Winston-Salem Chamber Com, 93-; art reviewer, Now Mag, Winston-Salem, 94; exhib coordr, Worell Prof Ctr for Bus Mgt, Wake Forest Univ, Winston-Salem, 96-; exhibs coordr, Sch of Law, Wake Forest Univ. *Teaching:* Instr art, Sawtooth Ctr Visual Arts, 89-; instr oil painting, Forsyth Tech Community Col, 89-. *Awards:* Emerging Artist Fel Grant, Winston-Salem Forsyth Co Arts Coun, 90-91; Solo Show Award, 6th Juried Show, Ctr/Gallery, Carrboro, NC, 91; first place, 26th Annual Spotlight, Juried Exhib, Davidson Co Mus Art. *Bibliog:* Jill Doss (auth), Art features artists' friends & family, The Dispatch, 8/4/94; Tom Patterson (auth), Exhibition to highlight emerging artists who received small arts council grants, The Winston-Salem J, 5/14/95; Tom Patterson (auth), A Sampling of NC's Finest, Winston-Salem Journal, 8/15/04. *Mem:* Asn Artists of Winston-Salem (vpres, 94-95; pres, 96). *Media:* Oil, Pastels; Black & White Photo. *Publ:* Illusr, Candle Lovefeast, Old Salem, Inc, 90; auth, Imagery in Celebration of the Divine Feminine on Display, The Winston Salem Chronicle, 3/23/95; auth, Alternative Location: the Hidden Market, Art Calendar Mag, Jul-Aug, 2002. *Mailing Add:* 416 Corona St Winston-Salem NC 27103-2817

FUNDORA, THOMAS
PAINTER
b Havana, Cuba, March 7, 35; US citizen. *Study:* Candler Col (art), 58, Escuela San Alejandro (oil painting), 59, Wash Sch Art (drawing & oil), 61, Escuela de Arte Bologna (restoration), 65, Sch Art, Bologna, Italy (art restoration), 65. *Work:* Mama Leone's Art Gallery, NY; Spanish Pavillion, New York World's Fair; Record World Art Collection, NY; J Cayre Art Exhib, NY; Coleccion Arte Latinoamericano, Rio de Janeiro, Brazil. *Comn:* Gran Canal, Venice, Mama Leone's Restaurant, NY, 68; Plaza Catedral de La Habana, Ital Art Gallery, Miami, Fla, 90; Jose Marti, Fundacion Cubanoamericana, Miami, Fla, 90; Balseros, Garces Com Col, Miami, Fla, 91. *Exhib:* Bienal Latinoamericana, Instituto Arte Latino, Washington, DC, 68; Los 10 Grandes, Instituto de Puerto Rico, NY, 69; Bienal de Sao Paulo, Arte Latinoamericano, Brazil, 71; Int Art Exhib, Int Art Gallery, Miami, Fla, 89; European & Latin Masters, Martin's Art Gallery, Coral Gables, Fla, 90; CatalinaArt Gallery, Kendall, Fla, 96; Domingo Padron Art Gallery, Coral Gables, Fla, 97; Frames USA Gallery, Kendall, Fla, 97; Catalina Art Gallery, Coral Gables, Fla, 98; Izzo's Artery Gallery, Chicago, Ill, 98; Ocean Reef Art League, Key Largo, Fla, 02. *Awards:* Int Grand Prize, Mama Leone's Art Show, 66; Painter Year, Carteles Mag, 67; Second Prize, CCIA Art Show, 69. *Bibliog:* Don Galaor (auth), Fundora Pinta Milagros, Diario Las Americas, 10/65; Ramon Cotta (auth), Obra Pintor Cubano en NY, El Imparcial, Puerto Rico, 5/66; Efrain Hidalgo (auth), Cristo se Movio, Diario La Prensa, 11/68. *Mem:* Asn Pintores Latinoamericanos, NY; Circulo Pintores de Miami; Thomas Fund Art Ctr, Coral Gables; Monroe Coun Arts (adv bd mem). *Media:* Watercolor, Oil. *Mailing Add:* 100 Bahama Rd Key Largo FL 33037

FUNK, CHARLOTTE M
TAPESTRY ARTIST, WEAVER
b Milwaukee, Wis, Sept 27, 34. *Study:* Univ Wis-Whitewater, BS, 71; Ill State Univ, Normal, MS, 75, MFA, 76. *Comn:* Passage to the Sea: Land, Sand & Sea, Corpus Christi Nat Bank, Tex, 81; Wind in the West, Lubbock Munic Bldg, 86; Sunset Winds, Mem Hosp, Midland, Tex. *Exhib:* Seventh Int Biennial Tapestry, Lausanne, Switz, 76; Clay, Fiber, Metal--Women Artists, Bronx Mus Arts, NY, 78; Contemp Tapestry, Pratt Inst, NY, 80-81; Fiber Structure Nat, 87; Nine in Texas, Houston, 89; solo show, Hueser Art Ctr, Bradley Univ, 90; Funk and Funk - Fired & Woven, Albany, Tex, 96. *Teaching:* Instr textiles, Tex Tech Univ, Lubbock, 78-97; instr, Arrowmont Sch Arts & Crafts, 81-88. *Awards:* Judges' Choice Award, Contemp Crafts Americas, Handweavers Guild Am, 75. *Bibliog:* Geometric Design in Weaving, Regensteiner, 86; Art Space, 1-2/90; Handwoven Mag, 5-6/94. *Mem:* Am Craftsmens Coun; Handweavers Guild Am. *Media:* Miscellaneous Fibers. *Mailing Add:* 15422 Kid Run San Antonio TX 78232-4043

FUNK, ROGER L
EDUCATOR, DESIGNER
b White Hall, Ill, Sept 2, 34. *Study:* Univ Ill, BFA, 57; Syracuse Univ, MID(indust design), 64. *Pos:* Designer, Gen Elec Co, 57-63; pres, Midwest Design Inc, 81-86; pres, Funk & Assocs Design, Inc, 86-. *Teaching:* Prof design, Mich State Univ, 65-81, 89-; prof & chmn dept design, Kansas City Art Inst, 81-86; dir, Sch design, Univ Cincinnati, 86-89. *Mem:* Indust Designers Soc Am (chmn educators comt, 84-86); Inter-Soc Color Coun

FUNK, VERNE J
CERAMIST, SCULPTOR
b Milwaukee, Wis, July 19, 32. *Study:* Univ Wis-Milwaukee, BS, MS & MFA. *Work:* Milwaukee Art Ctr; Mus Contemp Crafts, NY; Columbus Gallery Fine Arts, Ohio; Ariz State Univ, Tempe; Charles A Wustum Mus of Fine Arts, Racine, Wis; Mus of Tex Tech Univ, Lubbock, Tex; San Angelo Mus of Fine Arts, San Angelo, Tex; plus others; Natl Decorative Arts Mus, Riga, Latvia; Canton Art Inst, Ohio. *Exhib:* Objects: USA; Clayworks, 20 Americans, Mus Contemp Crafts, NY; solo exhibs, The Dance, W Tex Mus; The Figure in Clay, Craft Alliance, 91 & Steppin' Out, Canton Art Inst; Ceramics Now-1989, Downey Mus, Calif; Third Ceramic Nat Invitational, Canton Art Inst; Verne Funk: Thirty Yr Rev, NAU, Flagstaff, Ariz; Earth and Fire: Ceramic Sculpture, San Antonio Mus Art; Tex Clay III, San Marcos, Tex; Red Heat, Univ Tulsa, Okla; Tex Mud, Dallas Ctr Continuing Art; 21st Century Ceramics, Columbus Col Art & Design; Big Head, SW Ctr Art & Craft, Tex; 14th Ann Ceramics Compilation, San Angelo, Tex. *Pos:* Pres, Wis Designer-Craftsmen, 64-66; chmn, Visual Arts II, Wis Arts Found & Coun, 67. *Teaching:* Instr, Carthage Col, 66-69 & Univ Wis-Whitewater, 69-73; guest artist ceramics, Calif State Univ, Fresno, 72; prof ceramics & dir art sch, Bradley Univ, Peoria, Ill, 73-77; assoc prof ceramics, Tex Tech Univ, Lubbock, 77-81 & prof, 81-97. *Bibliog:* Donald Key (auth), Prominent Wisconsin potters, Milwaukee J, 71; Elizabeth Sasser (auth), Verne Funk: The dance, Ceramics Mo, 1/87; Gene Kleinsmith (auth), Clay's the Way, Victor Valley Press, 2nd Ed, 88. *Mem:* Am Craft Coun; NCECA; ISC. *Media:* Clay. *Specialty:* Contemporary Art. *Publ:* Craft & Art of Clay, 2nd ed, 3rd ed & 4th ed; History of American Ceramics: the Studio Potter; Objects: USA; Spirit of Clay; Surface Decoration, Lark Books, 99; Working with Clay, 2nd Edition Prentise Hall, 2003; contrib, Electric Kiln Ceramics, 3rd Edition, 2004; Making Marks, Ceramics Surface, KP Books, 2004. *Dealer:* CODA Gallery Palm Desert CA. *Mailing Add:* 15422 Kid Run San Antonio TX 78232-4043

FURINO, NANCY V
PAINTER
b Chicago, Ill, Nov 19, 28. *Study:* Sch of Mus Fine Arts, Boston (summa cum laude, traveling fel) 51. *Comn:* Landscape painting, comn by Rosabeth Moss Kanter, Edgartown, Mass, 89; landscape painting, comn by Thomas Nessa, Mass, 92. *Exhib:* Brooklyn Mus, 50; Allied Artists of Am, Nat Arts Club, NY, 87, 88, 89; Copley Master's Show, Pittsburgh Ctr for Arts, 86, New Eng Regional, Fed Reserve Bank, Boston, 88; 12 Copley Masters, Fitchburg Art Mus, Mass, 89; Audubon Artists, Nat Arts Club, Salmagundi Club, NY, 90, 92, 97, 2000, 2005; Carol Craven Gallery, 2006. *Teaching:* Masters Workshops for the Copley Soc of Boston. *Awards:* Originality Award, Copley Soc, 81; Beatrice Jackson Mem, Audubon Artists, 2000. *Bibliog:* Elaine Lembo (auth), Nancy Furino, Vineyard Gazette, 85; Nancy Furino, Cape Cod Life, 87; Edward Feit (auth), Am Artist, 88; Jacqueline Sexton (auth), 87-90; Marthas Vineyard Times, 2005. *Mem:* Audubon Artists Inc; Copley Soc Boston. *Media:* Oil. *Specialty:* Carol Craven Gallery, American Modernist Paintings. *Publ:* Cover, Arts, Mathas Vineyard Times, 2005; Two covers, 2006 Marthas Vineyard mag. *Dealer:* Carol Craven Gallery Holms Hold Rd Vineyard Haven Ma 02568

FURMAN, (DR & MRS) ARTHUR F
COLLECTORS, PATRONS
b Scranton, Pa; Mrs Furman, b Hazleton, Pa. *Study:* Dr Furman, Temple Univ, DMD; Mrs Furman, Pa State Univ. *Pos:* Trustees, Furman Family Trust; pres & vpres, Found Visual Arts. *Interests:* Arranging and exhibiting items from collection in various institutions, museums, galleries and schools. *Collection:* American contemporary masters painting and sculpture; ancient Thai, Cambodian and Indian bronzes; Chinese incense burners, Oriental artifacts. *Mailing Add:* 1250 S Washington St No 611 Alexandria VA 22314-4455

FURMAN, DAVID STEPHEN
SCULPTOR, EDUCATOR
b Seattle, Wash, Aug 15, 45. *Study:* Univ Ore, BA(ceramics), 69; Univ Wash, MFA(ceramics & glass blowing), 72. *Hon Degrees:* Escuela Nac de Bellas Artes, Hon PhD, 2000. *Work:* Univ Puget Sound Mus Art; Security Pac Nat Bank; Los Angeles Co Mus Art; World Ceramic Foundation Mus, Icheon, Korea; Fulbright Comn, Lima, Peru; Marietta Col Art Mus; US Embassy, Lima, Peru; San Francisco Mus of Art; and others. *Exhib:* Clay (ceramic sculpture), Whitney Mus, 74; Small Scale in Contemp Art, Chicago Art Inst, 75; Hard and Clear, Los Angeles Co Art Mus, 75; Seattle Art Mus; MH De Young Mem Mus; one-person shows, OK Harris Works of Art, NY, 90, Margulies Talpin Gallery, Miami, 90, Tortue Gallery, 91, Judy Yovens Gallery, 93, Sherry Frumkin Gallery, 96, S Ore State Univ, 96, Gallery 221, NY, 04, Dubnick gallery, Sacramento, Calif, 05; Sherry Frumkin Gallery, 93; Los Angeles, 93; Dorothy Weiss Gallery, 94; Laguma Art Mus, 94; Navy Pier, Chicago, 94; Frumkin Duvall Gallery, 2000. *Teaching:* Prof art, Claremont Grad Sch, Pitzer Col, 73-, prof art, Studio Arts Prog; instr clay sculpture, Otis Art Inst, 75-; lectr, Univ Utah, Boston Univ, Ind State Univ, Univ Ga, Univ Washington, Univ Calif, Los Angeles & Irvine; Peter, Gloria Gold Endowed Prof Art prog, Pitzer Col, Claremnt, Calif, 2003-2008. *Awards:* Craftsman's Fel, Nat Endowment for Arts, 75, Interdisciplinary Fel, 86-87 & vis artist fel, 96; Fulbright Fel, Peru, 79-80, 2000 & Fulbright Sr Artist Fel, Costa Rica, 90 & Peru, 99; Fac Dev Fel, Pitzer Col, 81-83. *Bibliog:* C H Hertel (auth), David Furman-Biographical Narrative Sculpture, 74; W C Hunt (auth), David Furman-miniature environments, Ceramics Monthly, 1/75; article in Am Ceramics, 8/2/90. *Mem:* World Crafts Coun; Am Crafts Coun; Nat Coun Educ Ceramic Arts; Artists Equity. *Media:* Ceramics, Sculpture. *Res:* Pre Colombian History of Peru. *Specialty:* Art. *Collection:* Los Angeles County Mus Art; Long Beach Mus Art; Garland Mus Art; San Francisco Mus Mod Art; Yixing Ceramic Mus, Yixing, China; Racine Art Mus; Mus Ceramics, Faenza, Italy; US Embassy, Lima, Peru. *Publ:* Studio Potter, Vol 14, No 1, Las Lineas De Nazca. *Dealer:* Sherry Frumkin Gallery Santa Monica CA; Gallery 221 New York City; Solomon Dubnick Gallery Sacramento CA. *Mailing Add:* Pitzer Col Art Dept 1150 Mills Ave Claremont CA 91711

FURNAS, BARNABY
PAINTER
Study: Sch Visual Arts, NY, BFA, 95; Columbia Univ, BFA, 2000. *Work:* War (What Is It Good For?), Mus Contemp Art, Chicago, 2003, Go Johnny Go, Kunsthalle Wien, Austria, 2003, Watercolor Worlds, Dorsky Gallery, Long Island City, 2004, Whitney Biennial, Whitney Mus Am Art, 2004, 179 Ann: Invitational Exhib Contemp Art, Nat Acad Design, NY, 2004, Seeing Other People, Marianne Boesky Gallery, 2004. *Exhib:* One-man shows, Marianne Boesky Gallery, NY, 2002, 2003, Modern Art Inc, London, 2004; group shows at Urban Romantics, Lombard Fried Gallery, NY, 1999, All Terrain, Freidrich Petzel Gallery, NY, 1999, @, PPOW Gallery, NY, 2000, Project Room, Artists Space, NY, 2000, Collectors's Choice, Exit Art, NY, 2000, All Am, Bellwether, Brooklyn, 2001, The Fourth Ann Altoids Curiously Strong Collection, Los Angeles Contemp Exhib, 2002, Officina Am, Galleria d'Arte Moderna, Bologna, Italy, 2002, Drawings, Metro Pictures, 2003, Transnational Monster League, Derek Eller Gallery, NY, 2003, Funny Papers: Cartoons & Contemp Drawing, Daniel Weinberg Gallery, Los Angeles, 2003. *Mailing Add:* c/o Marianne Boesky Gallery 535 W 22nd St New York NY 10011

FURR, JIM
PAINTER, PRINTMAKER
b Camden, Tenn, Aug 14, 39. *Study:* Univ Tenn, BFA; Tulane Univ, MFA; Tamarind Inst Lithography. *Work:* Montgomery Mus Fine Arts, Ala; Equitable Life Assurance Soc US, Bank Am Corp; Kans State Univ, Lawrence; R J Reynolds Corp; IBM Corp; and others. *Comn:* Colony Sq Hotel Corp, Atlanta, 78; Loew's Anatole Hotel Corp, Dallas, 79; Cannon Chapel, Emory Univ, Atlanta, 81; Marriott Marquis, Atlanta, 87. *Exhib:* Drawings, Mint Mus Art, NC, 79; one-person show, Tex A&I Univ, Kingsville, 74 & Montgomery Mus Fine Arts, 81; Southeast Seven IV, Southeastern Ctr Contemp Art, 81; Continuum III, Dulin Gallery Art, Knoxville, Tenn, 81; Red Clay Survey: Southeastern Biennial, Huntsville Mus, Ala, 90; Southern Abstraction: Contemp Arts Ctr, Raleigh, NC & traveling, 89; Lagrange Nat Biennial, Ga, 94; and many others. *Teaching:* Sabbatical replacement printmaking, Tulane Univ, New Orleans, La, 73-74; vis artist printmaking, Tex A&I Univ, Kingsville, 74-75; prof painting & drawing, Auburn Univ, Ala, 77-. *Awards:* Southeastern Ctr Contemp Art/Nat Endowment Arts

Grant, 80; Nat Endowment Arts Individual Artists Fel Grant, 81; Special Merit Award, Southeastern Exhib, Spartanburg, SC, 82. *Bibliog:* Mark Price (auth), Jim Furr, Artpapers, 3-4/81; Norman Pendergraft (auth), Southeastern Seven at SECCA, Art Voices, 7-8/81. *Media:* Oil; Charcoal, Oilstick. *Dealer:* Heath Gallery 416 E Paces Ferry Rd Atlanta GA 30305. *Mailing Add:* Auburn Univ Dept Art Auburn AL 36849

FURTH, KAREN J
PHOTOGRAPHER
b New York, NY, 61. *Study:* Univ Pa, BA(am hist), 83; NY Univ, Int Ctr Photog, MA(photog), 88. *Work:* JP Morgan; Mount Sinai Hosp; also pvt collections of Frank & Mary Ann Arisman, Valle Furth & Dr Yael Danielli. *Exhib:* Solo exhibs, 494 Gallery, 91, 92 & 94 & Pulse Art Gallery, 97; Domestic Landscapes, Sullivan Co Mus, 95; Artwalk NY, Puck Bldg, 95; The Furor of Change, Pulse Art Gallery, 96; Play, Dance Theater Workshop, 98; A Room With a View, Golin/Harris, 98, Face Value, 2002; The Current, AIR Gallery, 2004; Artists Work, The Creative Ctr, 2005. *Collection Arranged:* JP Morgan, Mt Sinai Hosp, Frank and Valle Furth, Dr Yael Daneili; Vantagepoint 13 "Community", ICP at the Point, Bronx, NY, 2005; Still Life: A Documentary Photography Project for Cancer Survivors, The Creative Center, NY, 2006. *Pos:* Biomedical photogr, Rockefeller Univ, 88-89; photogr, Smithsonian Intst, Nat Mus Am Indian, 89-94; freelance photogr, 94-. *Teaching:* Lectr, Int Ctr Photog, 89-90, instr, 98-2005; instr/consult, Ctr Urban Community Serv, Times Sq, 94-2002; fac, New School Univ, Eugene Lang College, 99-2005; instr, The Creative Ctr: Arts for People with Cancer, 2003-. *Awards:* Int Outreach Grant, 93 & 94; Gilbert Graphic Paper Award, 93; Open Soc Inst Individual Proj Fel, Soros Found, 97. *Bibliog:* Greg Emmanuel (auth), This Week Around Town, Photography in Motion, Time Out NY, Vol 43, No 172, 1/7/99-1/14/99; Geoff Carter (auth), The Passenger's Picks for the Week, Squaring the Circle, Circling the Square, 2/17/99. *Mem:* Col Art Asn; Soc Photog Educ. *Media:* Photography, Video. *Publ:* auth, Still Life: Documenting Cancer Survivorship, Umbrage Editions, 2006; auth, Through the Front Door, The Turtle, Vol 5, No 1, 28-33, winter 1993; plus many others. *Mailing Add:* 790 Riverside Dr Apt 12P New York NY 10032

FUSCO, LAURIE S
HISTORIAN, EDUCATOR
b Boston, Mass, Oct 31, 41. *Study:* Wellesley Col, Mass, with John McAndrew & Curtis Shell, BA(art hist), 63; NY Univ Inst Fine Arts, with Colin Eisler, Ludwig Heydenreich, Craig Smyth, Richard Krautheimer & Charles Sterling, MA & PhD(art hist), 77. *Pos:* Sr lectr & head scholarly progs; J P Getty Mus, 78-. *Awards:* Fulbright-Hays Grant, 72-73; Samuel H Kress Res Grant, 74-75; Harvard Fel, Villa I Tatti, 83. *Mem:* Col Art Asn Am; Art Historians of Southern Calif (secy-treas, 79-80). *Res:* Study of anatomy and movement by fifteenth century Italian artists; New documents for Lorenzo de Medici as a collector of antiquities. *Publ:* Auth, Antonio Pollaiuolo's use of the antique, J Courtauld & Warburg Inst, Vol 42, 257-263; The use of sculptural models by painters in fifteenth century Italy, Art Bulletin, Vol 65, 175-194; An unpublished Fra Filippo Lippi, J Paul Getty Mus J, Vol 10, 1-16; Pollaiuolo's Battle of the Nudes, In: M Natale, Scritti di storia dell'arte in onore di Federico Zeri, Vol 1, 196g, Milan, 84

FUSCO, YOLANDA
PAINTER, PRINTMAKER
b Ben Kovce, Czech, Oct 24, 22; US citizen. *Study:* Art Students League of New York, 40-45; Pratt Inst, Brooklyn, NY; studied with Ernest Fiene, Vaclao Vytlaci & Harry Sternberg. *Work:* Michael Waldorf Asn, Los Angeles, Calif; Donald Commors Asn, Duxbury, Mass; many private and corp collections. *Comn:* Portrait, comn by Nassau Co, NY, 81; many portraits comn by various individuals. *Exhib:* Group shows, Columbia Univ, NY, 65, Heckscher Mus, Huntington, NY, 76; Traveling watercolor exhib, Butler Inst of Am Art, Youngstown, Ohio, 82; two-person shows, Hewlett_Woodmere Pub Libr, Long Island, NY, 85, Art League Daytona Beach, Fla, 86; one-woman shows, Daytona Art League Gallery, Daytona Beach, Fla, 92 & Adelphi Univ, NY, 91; group exhibs, Gallery by the Sea, Port Clyde, Maine, 95, Lupine Gallery, Monhegan, Maine, 96 & Governor's Mansion-Maine Arts Coun, Augusta, 96, Backroads Gallery, Damariscotta, Maine, 2000; solo exhibs, Village Art Ctr Gallery, NY; Backroads Gallery, Damaroscola, Maine; Monhegan Modernists from the collection of John M Day, Susquehanna Univ, Lore Degenstein Gallery, Selinsgrove, Pa; and others. *Pos:* Dir, Washington Co Mus. *Teaching:* Pvt art teacher, Adult Ed, 60-87. *Awards:* Sadie & Max Tesser Award, Audubon Artists, Nat Arts Club, NY, 81; R W Rall Award, Daytona Beach, Fla, 90; Award for Oil, Nassau Co Mus Art, 93. *Bibliog:* reviews, Allied Publications, Art News, Herald Tribune, Newsday, Village Voice. *Mem:* Nat Asn Women Artists; NY Artists Equity; Life mem, Art Students League; Monhegan Artists; Art League of Daytona Beach, Fla. *Media:* Watercolor, Oil; Lithography. *Publ:* Prize Winning Watercolors, Allied Publ, 62; NAWA Catalog, 79; Audubon Artists Catalog, 81. *Mailing Add:* 48 Alden Ave Valley Stream NY 11580

FUSSINER, HOWARD
PAINTER, EDUCATOR
b New York, NY, May 25, 23. *Study:* Am Peoples Sch, 38-42; Art Students League, 46-47; Cooper Union, 47-49; Hans Hofmann Sch, 48; NY Univ, 49-52. *Work:* Everhart Mus, Scranton, Pa; Staten Island Inst Mus, NY; Slater Mus, Norwich, Conn; Mattatuck Mus, Waterbury, Conn; Hobart & William Smith Cols, Geneva, NY; Yale Univ Art Gallery. *Comn:* Mural, NY Univ, 51-52. *Exhib:* Pa Acad Fine Arts Biennial, Philadelphia, 62; Boston Arts Festival, 63; Am Acad & Inst Arts & Lett Art Awards Show, 84; one-man show, Georgetown Univ, Washington DC, 88; Retrospective, Slater Mus, Norwich, Conn, 91; Erector Sq Gallery, 95, 98, 99; and others; Slifka Ctr, Yale Univ, 98, 2002. *Collection Arranged:* Slater Mus, Norwich, Conn; Heublein Corp and many other banks in New Haven; Slifka Ctr, Yale Univ, New Haven, Conn. *Pos:* Bd mem, New Haven Paint & Clay Club. *Teaching:* Instr humanities, Morehouse Col, 52-55; instr art, Colby Jr Col, 58-60; prof art, Southern Conn State Univ, 60-88, prof emer, 88-. *Awards:* Best in Show, New Haven Arts Festival, 61, Hartford Plaza 7, 64, Waterbury Arts Festival, 68 & Conn Artists, Slater Mus, 77; Painting Today Award, Erector Sq Gallery, New Haven, 95; 1st Prize, Berkshire Art Asn, 62; 2d Prize, Boston Arts Festival, 63; 3d Prize, RI Arts Festival, 62. *Bibliog:* Erich Fleischmann (auth), Fussiner, conversation with an artist, New Haven Register, 11/18/90; Review of exhibition, Munson Gallery, New Haven, NY Times, 11/11/90; Jude Schwendenwein (auth), Exhibit shows maturation in Fussiner, Hartford Courant, 10/15/95; Judy Birke (auth), Landscapes He Has Loved, New Haven Register, 7/28/02; Cheever Tyler (auth), Artists Next Door, Partnership for Conn Cities, 2006; Arnold Skolnick & Carl Little (auths), More Maine Painters, Chameleon, 2006; Cheever Tyler (ed), Artists Next Door, The Partnership for Conn Cities, 2006. *Mem:* New Haven Paint & Clay Club. *Media:* Oil, Acrylics. *Res:* John Constable, 88-89. *Interests:* piano & classical music. *Publ:* Auth, Organic integration in Cezanne's painting, summer 56 & Use of subject matter in recent art, spring 61, Art J; John Sell Cotman, A modernist before his time, Conn Rev, summer 90; many newspaper articles, New Haven Register. *Dealer:* Turtle Gallery Deer Isle ME; Clark House Gallery, Bangor, ME. *Mailing Add:* 1 Everit St New Haven CT 06511

FYFE, JO SUZANNE (STORCH)
INSTRUCTOR, PAINTER
b Omak, Wash, May 8, 41. *Study:* Wash State Univ, BA(fine arts), 64, MFA, 68; Whitworth Col, Spokane, Wash & Eastern Wash State Univ, Cheney, grad studies. *Work:* Mt Vernon Sch Dist, Wash; Oak Harbor Sch Dist, Wash; Cashmere High Sch, Wash; Wash State Univ, Pullman; 27 works, Wash State Arts Comn. *Comn:* Triptych-painting/mixed-media, Wash State Arts Comn, Cashmere, 84; sculpture, Spokane Art Comn, Spokane Fire House, 92. *Exhib:* Women in Art, Eastern Wash State Univ Art Gallery, Cheney, Wash, 81; Juried Show, Carnegie Art Ctr, Walla Walla, Wash, 83; Works on Paper, The Art Gallery, Longview, Wash, 86; Works of Heart, Cheney Cowles Mus, Spokane, Wash, 86-2003; Western Art Show, Ellensburg & Spokane, Wash, 86-88; Works on Paper, Evergreen State Col, 87-89; Past Presence, A Circle of Women's Vision, Corvallis, Ore, 87; Art on the Green, Coeur D'Alene, Ind, 90; Art Walk, Sand Point, Ind, 90; Jumping the Fence, Spokane Art Sch, Wash, 92, Play, 2000; 25th Anniversary, Gallery One, Ellensburg, Wash, 95; Interpretations: A Celebration of Native Am Heritage Month, Lewis-Clark Ctr, Lewiston, Idaho, 98; Earth Day Exhib, Chase Gallery, Spokane, 2000, 2003; Two in-Two Out, Spokane Community Col, 2002. *Teaching:* Part-time instr design, Wash State Univ Exten, Spokane, 64-72; instr art, design, & sculpture, Spokane Falls Community Col, 65-2002, chmn dept, 75-84, 88-; retired, 2002. *Awards:* 1st Prize, acrylic, Clarkson Valley Ann, Lewis & Clark Art Asn, 81; Painting Award, Art on the Green, 90-94; Community Purchase Award, Art on the Green, 94, 2000, 2002. *Bibliog:* Dodie Murphy Wagner (auth), Painting and sculpture said good combination, Pullman Herald, 83; other newspaper articles. *Mem:* Artists Trust. *Media:* Acrylic, Miscellaneous Media. *Dealer:* Cheney Cowles Mus W2316 First Ave Spokane WA 99204; Northwest Mus Arts & Culture Spokane WA. *Mailing Add:* S 8017 Ramona Rd Spokane WA 99224-9617

G

GABELER, JO
PAINTER - WATERCOLOR
b Baton Rouge, La, Feb 14, 31. *Study:* Stephens Col, with John Pike, Ray Ellis, Fred Messersmith, Dong Kingman, Tony van Hasselt, Tom Hill, Millard Wells, Miles Batt, Al Brouillette, Christopher Schink, Judi Betts, Jeanne Dobie, Edward Betts, Charles Reid & Stephen Quiler. *Work:* Elliott Mus, Stuart, Fla; Moody Found & Rosenberg Libr, Galveston, Tex; Transco Energy Co, Houston; Allied Bank of Seabrook, Tex. *Comn:* Nine Watercolors, Lily Pulitzer, Palm Beach, Fla, 65; Commemorative plaque, Corps Diplomatic, Vientiane, Laos, 68; Christmas cards, Am Womens Club, Vientiane, Laos, 68-71; Lao Silk Pavilion, Mme Tao Peng Sananakone, Vientiane, Laos, 70; watercolor, City of Galveston, 82, presented to City of Nigata, Japan. *Exhib:* Group shows with Fla Watercolor Soc, Mus Arts & Sci, Daytona, 78, Brevard Art Ctr & Mus, Melbourne, 81, State Capitol, Tallahassee, 82 & Boca Raton Mus Art, 84; Watercolor Art Soc, Houston Pub Libr, 81; Galveston Art League, Rosenberg Libr, 83; Prof Artists Guild, Boca Raton Mus Art, 84-86; one-woman shows, Elliott Mus, Stuart, Fla, 86 & Scarborough House, Savannah, Ga, 88; John Tucker Fine Arts, 2000; 2-person show, Al Stine Gallery, Anderson, SC, 2002. *Teaching:* Instr, Landings Art Asn, 93, 95, 97, 98, Savannah Art Asn, 2000, 03 & 04. *Awards:* Pres Award, Fla Watercolor Soc, 81 & 82; Purchase Award, Galveston Art League, 82; Merit Award, Watercolor Art Soc Houston, 82 & Fla Watercolor Soc, 86. *Bibliog:* Eileen B Flaum (auth), Watercolorist-Jo Gabeler, Focus, 3/86. *Mem:* Salmagundi Club, NY; Signature mem Fla Watercolor Soc; Galveston Art League (pres, 81-82); Landings Art Asn Savannah, Ga (pres 90). *Media:* Watercolorist. *Interests:* Ceramics, needle point design. *Publ:* Illusr, The Galley Collection, 97; illusr (with others), The Golf Courses of the Landings, 93. *Dealer:* Gallery 209 209 River St Savannah Ga; Savannah and the Dolphin and the Mermaid thunderbolt Ga. *Mailing Add:* 11 Mainsail Crossing Savannah GA 31411-2723

GABIN, GEORGE JOSEPH
PAINTER, INSTRUCTOR
b Brooklyn, NY, Apr 16, 31. *Study:* Brooklyn Mus Art Sch; Art Students League, with Reginald Marsh, Ivan Olinsky & Will Barnett. *Hon Degrees:* Montserrat Col Fine Art, DFA. *Work:* Bank Boston, Boston Pub Libr, Mass; Tenn Botanical Garden & Fine Arts Ctr, Cheekwood; Grunwald Ctr Graphic Arts, Los Angeles, Calif; Jane Voorhees

Zimmerli Art Mus, New Brunswick, NJ; Brush Art Gallery, Canton, NY; and others; Deloitte-Touche, Boston, Mass; Samuel P Horn Mus, Gainesville, Fla; John D Merriam Collection, Boston Pub Libr; Rockport Pub Libr, Mass; Peter & Virginia Benin, Wilton, Conn, Robert & Graziella Singer, Milan, Italy. *Exhib:* Nat Acad Design, Allied Artists Am & Audubon Artists, 60-91; one-man shows, Carl Seimbab Gallery, 63 & 67, Guild Boston Artists, 72, Doll & Richards Gallery, 75, Montserrat Col Art, 83, Edna Stebbins Gallery, Cambridge, Mass, 86, Pingree Sch, Hamilton, Mass, 90 & Chase Gallery (with catalog), Boston, Mass, 91, 94, Sherry French Gallery (with catalog), NY, 03; Am Fedn Arts Nat Traveling Show, 64-65; Albright Mus, Buffalo, NY, 66; Montserrat Col Art, Beverly, Mass, 90, 98; retrospective, 35 Yrs (with catalog), Chase Gallery, Boston, Mass, 94; and others; Parallel Lives, Two Person Show, Montserrat Col of Art, 98; Chase Galleries, Boston, MA, 98, 2001 & 2004; and others. *Teaching:* Instr illus & drawing, New Eng Sch Art, Boston, 63-70; instr drawing & painting, Montserrat Col Art, 70-, prof, chmn, dept painting & drawing, founding fac; landscape painting, La Scoula del Vedere, Trieste, Italy, 89-95; prof emer, Montserrat Col of Fine Art. *Awards:* Grumbacher Gold Award, Holyoke Art Coun, 81; Stow Wengenroth Award, Rockport Art Asn, 82; Ralph Fabri Medal Merit, Allied Artist Am, 83; and others. *Mem:* Allied Artists Am; Guild Boston Artists; Brickbottom Artist Asn. *Media:* Oil, Pastel. *Publ:* Auth, The World & I, monograph, Imaginary Idyll, 7/97; auth essay, Report From Boston, Art in America, 6/99. *Dealer:* Chase Gallery, Boston, MA. *Mailing Add:* Studio B554 One Fitchburg St Somerville MA 02143

GABLE, JOHN OGLESBY
PAINTER, MURALIST
b Frankfort, Ky, Mar 7, 44. *Study:* Univ Ky; Art Ctr Col Design, BS(indust design), 66. *Work:* Oxford Univ; Union Mutual; Charles S Payson collection; Peabody Mus; Bank New Eng. *Comn:* Watercolors, comn by Alan Bond, Australia, 83, Boston Classical Orch, 83, Dennis Conner, 87, Oxford Univ, 89, Philip Morris, USA, 94; Portraits: Smithsonian Inst, Washington, DC; Kennedy Family, Boston, 99; Murals: Audi Corp, Ger, 99; Volkswagen Corp, Ger, 2000; Automotive Hall of Fame, Greenfield Village, Dearborn, 97; Clydes, Washington, DC, 94; MBNA, 2001; Paintings: Clydes, Washington, DC, 2005. *Exhib:* 46th Nat Ann, Butler Inst Am Art, 82; 161st Ann Exhib, Nat Acad Design, NY, 86 & 88; Coe Kerr Gallery, NY, 82; Payson-Weisberg Gallery, NY, 83 & Barridoff Galleries, Portland, Maine; Portland Mus Art, Maine; Forum Gallery, NY, 86; Guild of Boston Artists, 93. *Awards:* Wurdemann Prize, Nat Watercolor Soc; William A Paton Prize, Nat Acad Design, NY; Artist Mag Award, Am Watercolor Soc. *Bibliog:* Alexander Bridge (auth), Am Artist, 83; Philip Isaacson (auth), Maine Sunday Telegram, 83; Martha Thomas (auth), Archit Digest, 07/2005. *Media:* Watercolor, Oil, Acrylic. *Specialty:* Contemp Realism. *Interests:* The Human Condition. *Collection:* Smithsonian Inst, Peabody Mus; MBNA, Nat Bank of Detroit; Princeton Univ; Charles S Payson; Audi Corp. *Dealer:* Guild of Boston Artists 162 Newbury St Boston MA 02116

GABLIK, SUZI
PAINTER, WRITER
b New York, NY, Sept 26, 34. *Study:* Black Mountain Col, NC, summer 51; Hunter Col, BA, 55, with Robert Motherwell. *Exhib:* Solo exhibs, Alan Gallery, NY, 63 & 66, Landau-Alan Gallery, NY, 67, Henri Gallery, Washington, DC, 71, Terry Dintenfass, 72 & 78 & Hester Van Royen Gallery, London, 78; Photog Image, Guggenheim Mus, NY, 66; Young & Fantastic, Inst Contemp Arts, London, 69; After Surrealism: Metaphor & Simile, Ringling Mus Art, Sarasota, Fla, 72; Women Choose Women, NY Cult Art Cts, 73; Menagerie, Mus Mod Art Lending Serv, 75. *Pos:* Vis artist & lectr, Univ Colo, Syracuse Univ, Yale Univ, Univ Wis, Boston Col, San Francisco Art Inst, Oberlin Col, Bard Col & Md Inst Art, 74-75. *Teaching:* Vis prof fine arts, Univ South, Sewanee, Tenn, fall, 82 & 84, Univ Calif, Santa Barbara, spring, 85, 86 & 88 & Va Tech, Blacksburg, fall, 89 & spring, 90. *Awards:* Lifetime Achievement Award, Women's Caucus for Art, 03. *Bibliog:* London Correspondent, article in Art in Am. *Mem:* Col Art Asn. *Media:* Miscellaneous Media. *Publ:* Coauth, Pop Art Redefined, 69 & auth, Magritte, 70, New York Graphic Soc; auth, Progress in Art, Rizzoli, 77; Has Modernism Failed?, 84, The Reenchantment of Art, 91 & Conversations Before the End of Time, 95, Thames & Hudson; Living the Magical Life: An Oracular Adventure, 02, Phanes. *Mailing Add:* 3271 Deer Run Rd Blacksburg VA 24060

GABRIEL, JEANETTE HANISEE
CURATOR, HISTORIAN, CONSULTANT
b Long Beach, Calif, 40. *Study:* Calif State Univ, BS, 76, MS, 78; Univ Calif - Santa Barbara, MA, 88. *Work:* Los Angeles Co Mus Art, Calif; Gilbert Collection (auth catalog), Los Angeles, Calif & London, Eng. *Pos:* Cur, LACMA, 89-92; cur, Gilbert Collection Mus, Los Angeles, 94-2000; hon cur, Somerset House, London, 2001-. *Mem:* Reform Club, London; Churchill Ctr. *Interests:* Mystery writing. *Publ:* Coauth, Mosaic tables in the Gilbert collection, 11/89 & Mosaic mementoes, 5/93, Antique Collector Mag, By judgement of the eye: The Varya and Hans Cohn collection, Los Angeles County Mus Art, 91, The World of Jade, Marg Publs, 92, Silver, gold boxes and decorative objects in the Gilbert collection, Apollo, 1/97 & The Winston Churchill portraits of Alfred Egerton Cooper, Finest Hour: The J of Int Churchill Soc, 97, Gilbert Collection, Micromosaics and Hard Stones, 2000, The Open Portrait Winstin Churchill, Spring, 2003, No 118, Summer, 2003, No 119. *Mailing Add:* 3150 31 St San Diego CA 92104

GABRIELSON, WALTER OSCAR
PAINTER
b Orr, Minn, July 25, 35. *Study:* Univ Calif Los Angeles, BS, 58; Chouinard Art Inst, 61-63; Otis Art Inst, BFA, 63, MFA, 65. *Work:* Chase Manhattan Bank, NY; Crocker Bank, Los Angeles Co Mus Art, Cedars-Sinai Hosp & Capitol Group, Los Angeles; Hilton Hotel, Burbank, Calif. *Comn:* Burbank Airport Hilton Hotel, Los Angeles. *Exhib:* Six Calif Artists, Saskatoon, Sask Mus, Can, 78; Karl Bornstein Gallery, 81-82 & 84-85; Los Angeles Mus Art, 82; Car Show, Sherry Frumkin Gallery, Santa Monica, 92; Alternatives, San Luis Obispo, Calif, 94; Jill Thayer Gallery, 97, 2002. *Pos:* Printer, Tamarind Lithography Workshop, 64-66; writer, Artweek, Art in Am, 74-79; vis artist, Univ Hawaii, 79, Claremont Grad Sch, 80, Wash State Univ, 84, Murray State Univ, Ky, 86; co-cur, Addictions, Santa Barbara Contemp Arts Forum, 91. *Teaching:* Asst prof, Calif State Univ, Northridge, 66-82. *Awards:* Tamarind Grant, Ford Found, 64-66. *Bibliog:* Article in Artnews, 4/83, Images & Issues, 5/6/83 & Los Angeles Times, 12/10/83; and others. *Mem:* Los Angeles Inst Contemp Art (chmn jour comt, 74-75); Santa Barbara Contemp Arts Forum, 89-92. *Media:* Oil; Wood. *Publ:* Auth, Why suck the mainstream if you don't live in New York, Art in Am, 1-2/74; Winged beauty, Air Progress, 11/75; The ironic Los Angeles artist, Los Angeles Inst Contemp Art J, 10-11/76; CAF Addictions Catalogue, 91; Persistence (autobiog), 93. *Dealer:* Jill Thayer Gallery 1700 20th St Bakerfield CA 93301. *Mailing Add:* 375 Pine Ave No 2 Goleta CA 93117

GAGE, BEAU
SCULPTOR; PHOTOGRAPHER
b Rye, NY, Dec 3, 45. *Study:* St John's Col, BA, 71; Art Students League, 84-87. *Work:* Jacksonville Mus Sci & Hist, Fla; Interbank of NY. *Comn:* sculpture, Jacksonville Jaguars Inc, Fla, 96. *Exhib:* A Valentine For Martha Graham, Sotheby's, NY, 90. *Mem:* Orgn Independent Artists, NY; Internat Sculpture Ctr, NY; Internat Ctr Photog, NY; Poets House, NY; Fel Mus Mod Art, NY. *Media:* Bronze; Iris Prints. *Mailing Add:* 320 E 46th St Apt 34E New York NY 10017

GAGNON, CHARLES EUGENE
SCULPTOR, CONSULTANT
b Minneapolis, Minn, Feb 24, 34. *Study:* Univ Minn, AA, 56, BS, 58 & MEd, 60; Minneapolis Sch Art, 59; with Berthold Schiwetz, Florence, Italy, 64-65; Jacques Lipchitz, 68. *Work:* Numerous pub and pvt collections throughout the US, Can, Japan, UK & Europe. *Comn:* St Francis and the Birds (heroic size sculpture), St Marys Hosp, Rochester, Minn, 69; Hubert H Humphrey (life size portrait), New Govt Ctr, Worthington, Minn, 79; Vatican Collection, Rome, Italy, 84; 12 ft Peace Fountain, Rochester, Minn, 89; Emergence of Life, Chicago, Ill, 92; Guardian Angel, Houston, 2000; Ascension of Christ, Demontreville Jesuit Retreat House, St Paul, Minn, 2000; St Francis and the Birds, Franciscan Art Mus, Assisi, Italy, 2000; Peace Fountain, Mulheim, Ger; plus others; St Olaf Angel, St Olaf Catholic Church, Minneapolis, Minn, 2004; Crucifixion 6FT, St Olaf Catholic Church, Minneapolis, Minn, 2005. *Exhib:* Nat Acad Galleries, NY, 62; Nat Arts Club, NY, 62; Walker Art Ctr Biennial, Minneapolis, 62; Minneapolis Art Inst, 63. *Collection Arranged:* 40 small bronzes, life size string quartet in studio galleries, 2005. *Pos:* Full-time, self-employed working sculptor & dealer. *Teaching:* Instr sculpture, Univ Minn, Rochester, 72. *Awards:* One of ten students from US chosen to teach art in Europe, Univ Minn, 57-58; Purchase Award & Two-Man Show Award, Madison Ave Art Gallery, NY, 62; Mayor's Gold Medal Honor, Artistic Cult Achievement, 87. *Bibliog:* Kling (auth), The Sculpture of Charles E Gagnon, Preview, Collegeville, Minn, 68; Hardie (auth), Charles E Gagnon, Mohave, Kingman, Ariz, 73; Ehrbar (auth), A Ten-year Dance to the Music of Bronze, Kenyon Col, 83; Dugan (auth), Artists Speak the Language of Love, Focus, Rochester, Minn, 95. *Media:* Bronze. *Res:* Figurative bronze sculpture; working predominantly in the field of large architectural commissions. *Specialty:* Figurative bronze sculpture. *Interests:* Small and large bronze sculpture commissions for pvt collectors, churches, bus, pub spaces indoors or outdoors. *Collection:* 40 small bronzes Life size "string quartet" in studio galleries 2005. *Publ:* Contribr, An artist fulfilled, 71; Progeny, 73; Kenyon College, Its Third Half Century, 75; An Art Tour of Saint Mary's, 75; Voice of a New Age, 76; UNESCO Courier, 91, plus others. *Dealer:* Full time prof, self-employed working studio sculptor & dealer. *Mailing Add:* PO Box 4 Rochester MN 55903

GAINES, ALAN JAY
PRINTMAKER, PUBLISHER
b New York, NY, Aug 23, 42. *Study:* NY Univ, BS, 65; New Sch, Parsons Sch Design, with John Ross, 72-74. *Work:* South Street Seaport Mus, Mus Gallery, NY; and others. *Comn:* Historic American Ship, Franklin Mint, Pa, 75; Nantucket Whalers & New Bedford Whalers, 77 & Develop of Am Transportation, 78, Collector's Guild, NY; Gloucester Schooners (etching), Bk of Month Club & 260 Club, 77; marine etchings, 77 & two railroad etchings, 78, Graphics Guild, Div of Doubleday, NY; spec series five important & hist Am ships, Am Express, 78; America's Maritime Heritage (four etchings), Franklin Mint, Pa, 81; and others. *Exhib:* One-man shows, South Street Seaport Mus, 74, Oestreicher Gallery, NY, 74, Wiseman Gallery, Newport, RI, 76, Redwood Libr & Atheneum, Newport, RI, 79 & Providence Pub Libr, RI, 81. *Bibliog:* Joseph Patrick Henry (auth), Artist of the sea, The Franklin Mint Almanac, 7/75; article, RI Mag, 9/80. *Media:* Mixed. *Mailing Add:* 40 Franklin St Newport RI 02840

GAINES, WILLIAM ROBERT
PHOTOGRAPHER, PAINTER
b Madison, Va, Aug 12, 27. *Study:* Pa Mil Col; Va Commonwealth Univ, BFA; Columbia Univ, MFA; and with Renato Guttuso, Italy, 56-57. *Work:* Univ Va, Charlottesville; Va Polytech Inst & State Univ, Blacksburg; Retreat for the Sick, Richmond; Philip Morris Inc; First & Merchants Nat Bank; St Mary's Hosp, Richmond. *Exhib:* Five Va Artists Biennials, 49-63; Abingdon Sq Painters, NY, 53; Va Beach Boardwalk Exhib, 58; Va Commonwealth Univ, 64; one-man exhib, Tappahannock, Va, 72. *Collection Arranged:* Art Nouveau (with catalog); Francisco Goya: Portraits in Paintings, Prints & Drawings (with catalog), 72; Sculpture by Willi Gutmann, 72; 12 American Painters (with catalog), 74. *Pos:* Registr, Va Mus, 51-53, artmobile cur, 53-54, supvr educ, 54-56, 57-62, head progs div, 62-82; dir, Inst Contemp Art Va Mus, 80-82; interim dir, Anderson Gallery, Va Commonwealth Univ,

87; exhib originator, Marine Resources Coun, Brevard Co, Fla; mem adv bd, S Mainland Libr, Brevard Co, Fla. *Teaching:* Instr painting, drawing & art hist, Va Mus, Richmond, 54-56, 57 & 62; dir, Gov Sch Gifted, Mus Ctr, 73; instr, painting, drawing, art history, Rappahannock Community Col, Warsaw, Va, 82-87; instr, Va Commonwealth Univ, Richmond, 78-84. *Awards:* Best in Show Awards, Va Beach Boardwalk Exhib, 58 & Thalhimers Invitational, 63; James R Short Award, SEMC, 81; Distinguished Alumnus, Va Commonwealth Univ, Richmond, 91. *Mem:* Am Asn Mus; Coun Va Mus. *Media:* Acrylic. *Publ:* Auth, Art kits, Arts Va, Vol VI, No I; auth, Virginia Museum: Two pioneer programs, Mus News, Vol 50, No 2; producer, 12 American Painters (TV), 74 & Style & Expression: Encounter I (TV), 75

GAITHER, EDMUND B
MUSEUM DIRECTOR, HISTORIAN
b Great Falls, SC, Oct 6, 44. *Study:* Morehouse Col, BA, 66; Ga State Col; grad study, art history, 66-68, Northeastern Univ, 84, Framingham State Col, 93, RI Col, 94. *Collection Arranged:* Afro-Am Artists: New York & Boston (with catalogue), Jamaica Art Since the Thirties, Henry O Tanner, A Romantic Realist, Home Folks Africa, For Us, Abdias Do Nascimento: A Brazilian Brother, African Gods in Brazil, Our Elders, Crite & Dames, Ah Haiti, Glimpses of Voudou, Haiti-Haiti, Bannister & Duncanson, Twentieth Century Afro-Am Artists, Mus Fine Arts, Boston; Richard Yarde: Watercolors, 93; Blues Paintings of George Hunt, 93; traveling exhib, Treasures of the MNCAAA, 93; Struggles Against Racism, 94; Rashid Diab: A Retrospective, 94; A Selection of Paintings & Drawings by Afro-American Artists, 94; Holy War in the Sudan/Relics of Mahdist Era, 94; Aspelta: A Nubian King's Burial Chamber, 94; Carlos Byron: Renaissance Artist, 95. *Pos:* Dir & cur, Mus Nat Ctr Afro-Am Artists, Boston, 69-; dir visual arts prog, Elma Lewis Sch Fine Arts, Boston, 69-; spec consult, Mus Fine Arts, Boston, 69-; curric consult, Urban Gateways, Ctr Arts Educ, 90 & Miami Pub Schs, 88. *Teaching:* Asst prof art hist, Boston Univ, 70-78; lectr art hist, Wellesley Col & Harvard Col, 71-76. *Bibliog:* An American Collector, Mus Art, RI Sch Design, Providence, 68; Robert H Glauber (auth), Black American Artists, Ill Bell Tel Co, 71; Leo Twiggs (auth), Opinion, Mus News, 5/72. *Mem:* Nat Conf Artists; Col Art Asn; Pan-African Conf Artists; Boston Black Artists Asn. *Res:* Historical and critical discussion of Afro-American art. *Publ:* Ed, Affairs of Black Artists, 71; contribr, Artists Proofs, The Annual of Prints and Printmaking, NY Graphic Soc, 72; Afro-American Art, in: Negro Reference Book, Phelps-Stokes Found, New York, NY, 73; auth, Afro American Art in: Dialogue, John Wilson/Joseph Norman (article), Mus Fine Arts, 95; and numerous others. *Mailing Add:* c/o Mus Nat Ctr Afro Am Artist 300 Walnut Ave Boston MA 02119

GALE, NESSA
SCULPTOR, PAINTER
b Chicago, Ill, Aug, 2, 37. *Study:* Studied sculpture with Brian Quinn. *Work:* Tucson Mus Art, Ariz; Ariz State Univ, Tempe; Northern Ariz Univ, Flagstaff; Univ NMex, Albuquerque. *Comn:* Sculpture, Western Properties, Phoenix, Ariz, 86; painting, Median Inst, Pittsburgh, 87; painting, Practice Outlook Inc, Phoenix, Ariz, 88; mural, Har Zion Temple, Paradise Valley, Ariz, 90; sculpture, IB Goodman, NY, 91. *Exhib:* Ariz Biennial, Tucson Mus Art, 80-84; Midwestern Invitational, O'Rourke Gallery, Moorhead, Minn, 84; Pedestal I, Scottsdale Art Ctr, Ariz, 93. *Dealer:* Wiseman & Gale 4015 N Marshall Way Scottsdale AZ 85251. *Mailing Add:* 7011 E Doubletree Ranch Rd Paradise Valley AZ 85253

GALE, PEGGY
WRITER, CURATOR
b Mackenzie, Guyana, May 18, 44; Can citizen. *Study:* Univ degli Studi, Florence, Italy, 65-66, Univ Toronto, Can, BA, 67. *Pos:* Educ officer, Art Gallery of Ont, Toronto, 67-74; asst film & video officer, Can Coun, Ottawa, 74-75; video dir, Art Metropole, Toronto, 75-79, spec proj coordr, 85-87; exec dir, A Space, 79-81; contrib ed, Canadian Art (mag), Toronto; guest cur Nat Gallery, Art Gallery Ont, Toronto & other Can & Int mus. *Teaching:* Instr, Nova Scotia Col Art & Design; lectr video & performance art, var schs, mus & galleries, 75-. *Awards:* Canada Coun A Grant, 83; Toronto Arts Award, 2000; Governor General's Award, Vis & Media Arts, 2006. *Mem:* Int Asn Art Critics; The Writers Union of Canada. *Res:* Media art, specializing in performance, video, installations, thematic assessment and development of critical language, 65-. *Publ:* Auth, Muntadas, Searching Between the Frames, spring 93; Videotexts, Wilfred Laurier Univ Press & The Power Plant 95; ed, (with Lisa Steele) Video re/View the (best) source for critical writings on Canadian Artists' Video, Toronto Art Metrop, 96; Tout le temps/Every Time, Le Biennale de Montreal (catalog), Montreal Ctr Int d'art Contemporain, 2000; Artists Talk, Press Nova Scotia Col Art & Design, 2004. *Mailing Add:* 176 Cottingham St Toronto ON M4V 1C5 Canada

GALEN, ELAINE
PAINTER
b New York, NY, July 12, 28. *Study:* Philadelphia Mus Sch Art, dipl, 50; Univ Pa, BA, 51; Art Students League, 55-59; NY Univ, MA, 63; major study with Morris Kantor. *Work:* Brooklyn Mus; Miss Mus, Jackson; Tampa Mus, Fla; Neuberger Mus, NY; NY Pub Libr; Univ Ariz Mus; Michener Mus, Doylestonw, Pa; Israel Mus, Jerusalem; corp and pvt collections; Univ of Arts Libr, Nat Liberty Mus, Free Library, Phila; Wellesley College, Mass; Pepperdine College, Calif. *Exhib:* Whitney Mus Am Art, NY, 61; Brooklyn Mus Int, 63 & 78; one-person show, Pa Acad Fine Arts, Peale House, 72; Art Inst Chicago, 78; The Jewish Mus, 88; Soho 20, NY, 88, 90, 92 & 94; Rathbone Gallery, Albany, NY, 88; Neuberger Mus, Purchase, NY, 92 & 94; Tampa Mus Art, Fla, 94; Gallery 1756, Chicago, 96 & 99; Art in Embassies, Nicosia, Cypris, 97; Michener Mus, Doylestown, Pa, 2000; Miss Mus, Jackson, 2000; plus numerous others; Neuberger Mus, NY, 01; Gallery 1756, 98, 99, 02; Monique Goldstrom, 02; The Studio, NY, 2004-2006; Concordia Gallery, 04, 05. *Collection Arranged:* The Arts Exchange, Pfizer Coll, New York, NY; Metro Media Corporate Coll, New York, NY. *Pos:* Consult Developing, NJ Schs, 68-72, lectr-instr painting & drawing, 73 & assoc prof, 84-96; vis prof, Ben Gurion Univ, Israel, 98, Kaye Col, Israel, 99. *Teaching:* Lectr hist art, painting & drawing, NY Univ, 70-73, Prairie State Col, Chicago Heights, Ill, 74-, Lake Forest Col, 78-80, Manhattanville Col, 81-88, NY, Purchase, 81-; Columbia Univ, 84-90; assoc prof drawing & design, State Univ New York, Purchase, 90-96. *Awards:* Nat Print Award, Hunterdon Ctr, NJ, 70; Am Iron & Steel Inst Award for Design Excellence, 72; Florsheim Art Fund Grant, 92. *Bibliog:* Conversation with the Artist, Channel 19, NY State Coun Arts. *Mem:* Print Club, Philadelphia (artist mem). *Media:* Oil, Multi-Media. *Publ:* Auth, Deborah Portfolio, Haybarn Press, 96; auth, Miriam Portfolio, 98; auth, Lilith Portfolio, 2004. *Dealer:* Gallery 1756 Chicago IL. *Mailing Add:* 512 Millwood Rd Mt Kisco NY 10549

GALINSKY, NORMAN
PAINTER, GRAPHIC ARTIST
b Charleston, WVa, Jan 28, 42. *Study:* Univ Cincinnati, BS, 64; Columbia Univ, with Philip Guston, Stamos, Malcolm Morley & Jack Tworkov, MFA, 73; Art Students League, printmaking workshop with Bob Blackburn. *Work:* Columbia Univ, NY; Mobil Oil Corp, NY; Four Seasons Hotel, Washington, DC; IBM, Armonk, NY; Pepsico, Purchase, NY. *Exhib:* Solo exhibs, Truman Gallery, NY, 78 & Katonah Gallery, NY, 79; Five on Paper, Spencer Mus, Univ Kans, Lawrence, 78; Small Works, 6th Ann Juried Show, Washington Sq Gallery, NY Univ, 82; Paperworks '80, Hudson River Mus, Yonkers, NY; The Abstract Vision, Cork Gallery, Lincoln Ctr, NY, 85; Constructions, Wooden Tent Gallery, Vineyard Haven, Mass, 90. *Pos:* Bd dir, Rockland Ctr Arts, West Nyack, NY, 84-. *Awards:* Contemp Artist Prize, Paperworks 80, Hudson River Mus, 80; NY Tele Award, Mt Aramah Exhib, Arden, NY, 86. *Bibliog:* Gordon Brown (auth), rev, Arts Mag, 9/78; Martin Filler (auth), Remodeled house-remodeled lives, House & Garden, 5/80; Steve Bush (auth), Salon West 3, Artspeak, 2/16/86. *Media:* Miscellaneous. *Dealer:* Orions Editions 270 Lafayette St New York NY 10012; Katonah Gallery 28 Bedford Rd Katonah NY 10536. *Mailing Add:* 20 Lawrence Ln Box 636 Palisades NY 10964

GALLAGHER, CAROLE
PHOTOGRAPHER, WRITER
b New York, NY, July 16, 50. *Study:* Col New Rochelle, BA, 72; New Sch, with Philippe Halsman, 73; Hunter Col, City Univ New York, with Tony Smith, Robert Morris, Doug Ohlson & Rosalind Krauss, MA, 77. *Work:* Bibliot Nat, Paris; State Mus, Pazin, Yugoslavia; World Image Ctr Photog; Fuji Art Mus, Tokyo. *Exhib:* The Nuclear Half Century-Witnesses Testify, Hiroshima, Japan; Visa Pour L'Image, Perpignan, France, 94; Am Ground Zero, Int Ctr Photog, Midtown Gallery, NY, traveling, 94-97; Latent August: the Legacy of Hiroshima & Nagasaki, Japanese-Am Hist Soc, San Francisco, 95; From Nuclear Bombs to Nuclear Bullets, Edge Gallery, London, 95; Perpetual Mirage: Photog Narratives of the Desert West, Whitney Mus Art, 95; Future Perspectives, World Image Ctr Photog, Fuji Art Mus, Tokoyo, 97. *Pos:* Dir Nuclear Towns Doc Proj, Utah State Hist Soc, 85-90; consult & researcher, ABC-News Turning Point, 93; consult, The Peoples Century, BBC Series, 94; syndicated journalist/photojournalist, SYGMA, 94; writing memoirs, Lust for Light. *Teaching:* Instr photog, Col New Rochelle, NY, 77-78 & Kingsborough Col, City Univ NY, 77-79 & Univ Utah Commun Dept, Salt Lake City, 88-90; vis prof, Univ Utah Art Dept, 88-90. *Awards:* Nev Humanities comt, 92; Pope Found Award for Investigative Journalism, 93; Fel in nonfiction literature, New York Found Arts, 93; and others. *Bibliog:* Paul Stimson (auth), Between the signs, Art in Am, 10/79; Rene Denizot & R Barry (auths), Il Est Temps--It's About Time, Yvon Lambert, Paris, 80; Carole Gallagher at Leo Castelli, Express, fall 81; Susan Lyman (auth), Fallout: picturing the downwind survivors, The Deseret News, 2/25/87; Judy Rollins (auth), Clouds of Creation, The Salt Lake Tribune, 6/19/88. *Publ:* Illusr, Muscles, 83 & Punch, 83, Avon; Nuclear Test's Legacy of Anger: Workers See Betrayal on Peril, New York Times, 12/14/89; American Ground Zero: The Secret Nuclear War, Cambridge: MIT Press, 93, Elefanten Press, Berlin, spring 95. *Dealer:* Ronald Feldman Gallery 31 Mercer St New York NY 10013; SYGMA Photo News Inc 322 Eighth Ave New York NY 10001. *Mailing Add:* 79 Mercer St New York NY 10012-4430

GALLAGHER, CYNTHIA
PAINTER, EDUCATOR
Study: Philadelphia Col Art, BFA, 72; Queens Col, Flushing, NY, MFA, 74. *Work:* Metro Mus Art, NY; First Nat Bank of Chicago; Shearson-Lehman American Express, NY, San Francisco; also pvt collections of James & Beth Rudin DeWoody, Curt Marcus & Robin Tewes and Mary Ryan & Bruce Liebowitz; Skadden, Arps, Meagher & Flom. *Exhib:* One-woman shows, 55 Mercer St, NY, 76 & 78, Grace Borgenicht Gallery, NY, 81, Luise Ross Gallery, NY, 88, Edward Thorden Gallery, Göteborg, Sweden, 89, Charles More Gallery, Philadelphia, 90 & 91, Mary Ryan Gallery, NY, 92 & Espace Croix Barangon, Toulouse, 94; Art on Paper, Weatherspoon Mus, Greensboro, NC, 82; Collectors Choice, Ark Art Ctr, Little Rock, 88; Parrish Art Mus Design Biennial, Southampton, Long Island, NY, 91; Fanfare, 150 Anniversary NY Philharmonic; Montclair (NJ) Mus, 97; Nabisco Gallery, E Hanover, NJ, 98; Elsa Mott Ives Gallery, New York City, 99. *Pos:* Graphics consult, NY State CAPS; vis critic, Brown Univ, RI Sch Design, 94. *Teaching:* Asst prof, Queens Col, City Univ NY, 74-89; vis critic, NY Univ, 74-75; Philadelphia Col Art, Philadelphia, Pa, 76-77; Yale Univ, Summer Sch of Music & Art, Norfolk, Conn, 80; vis critic, Brandeis Univ Alumni Asn, NY, 84; guest lectr, Stanford Univ Alumni Asn, 85; life drawing, two-dimensional painting, drawing, design, Fashion Inst Technol, NY, 88; instr, Found Dept, Parsons Sch Design, NY, 94-. *Awards:* Creative Artists Pub Serv Prog, 81; Nat Endowment Arts, 83 & 89; NY Found Arts, 89. *Bibliog:* Articles in NY Times, 1/18/87 & Philadelphia Inquirer, 4/13/90; Mary Cummings (auth), Southampton Press, 8/29/91; Edward Sosanski (auth), On galleries, Philadelphia Inquirer, 10/31/91; Kenneth Leslie, (auth book) Oil Pastel, 90. *Dealer:* Kristina Wasserman Gallery Providence RI. *Mailing Add:* 800 Valley Rd Montclair NJ 07043

GALLAGHER, ELLEN
PAINTER
b Providence, RI, 65. *Study:* Sch Mus Fine Arts, Boston, 92, student, Skowhegan Sch Art, Maine, 93; Oberlin Col, student. *Work:* Mus Mod Art, Whitney Mus Art, Metrop Mus Art, Guggenheim Mus, NY; Mus Fine Art, Boston; Mus Contemp Art, Los Angeles; Denver Mus Art, Denver; Moderna Museet, Stockholm. *Exhib:* Solo exhibs, Akin Gallery, Boston, 92, Mario Diacono Gallery, Boston, 94, Mary Boone Gallery, NY, 96, Anthony d' Offay Gallery, London, 96, Gagosian Gallery, NY, 98, Ikon Gallery, Birmingham, 98, Galerie Max Hetzler, Berlin, 99, Anthony d'Offay Gallery, London, 2000, Watery Ecstatic, ICA, Boston, 2001, Ellen Gallagher: Preserve, Drawing Ctr, NY City, 2002, Currents 88, St Louis Art Mus, 2003, Murmur, Galerie Max Hetzler, Berlin, 2003, Orbus, Fruitmaker Gallery, Edinburgh, 2004, deLuxe, Whitney Mus Am Art, NY City, 2005, Fluidity of Time, Mus Contemp Art, Chgo, 2005-06; Whitney Biennal, Whitney Mus Am Art, NY, 95; Inside the Visible, Inst Contemp Art, Boston, 96 & Whitechapel Art Gallery, London, 96; Project Painting, Basilico Fine Arts, 97 & Irish Mus Mod Art, Dublin, 97; The Body Pointing, Mario Diacano Gallery, 97; Postcards from Black Am, De Beyerd Ctr Contemp Art, Breda, The Neth, 98. *Awards:* Provincetown Fine Arts Fel, 95; MacDowell Colony, New Hampshire, 96; Joan Mitchell Fel, 97; Am Acad award in Art. *Bibliog:* Martin Coomer (auth), Ellen Gallagher, Flash Art, 1-2/97; Eric de Chassey (auth), La Peinture est Vivante, L'Oeil, No 489, 10/97; Roberta Smith (auth), Ellen Gallager, NY Times, 3/98. *Dealer:* Mario Diacono Gallery 207 South St Boston MA. *Mailing Add:* c/o Gagosian Gallery 555 W 24th St New York NY 10011

GALLAGHER, KATHLEEN ELLEN
PRINTMAKER, PAINTER
b New York, NY, Dec 18, 49. *Study:* Marymount Manhattan Col, New York, BA, 71; Herbert H Lehman Col, Grad Sch, New York, with Arun Bose, MA, 75. *Work:* Brooklyn Mus, Mus Mod Art & Pratt Graphics Ctr, NY; DeCordova Mus, Lincoln, Mass; Philadelphia Mus Art, Pa; Portland Mus, Ore; Housatonic Mus Art, Bridgeport, Conn; Mus of City of NY, 2002. *Comn:* Etching editions, Lyndhurst, Tarrytown, NY & Drayton Hall, Charleston, SC, Nat Trust Hist Preserv-Christie's, London & NY, 82; Surface & Diversity, Housatonic Mus Art, Bridgeport, CT, 98. *Exhib:* Grunwald Ctr, Univ Calif, Los Angeles, 86; NY Inspired: Past & Present, John Szoke Gallery, NY, 88; Lynd Ward Exhib, Soc Am Graphic Arts, NY, 92; NY Icons: Michael Ingbar Gallery, NY, 93; Thomas J Walsh Art Gallery, Fairfield Univ, Conn, 94; Lore Degenstein Gallery, Susquehanna Univ, 95; 479 Gallery, NMex, 96; Old Print Shop, NYC, 2001; Nat Taiwan Normal Univ (NTNU), Taiwan, 2004. *Collection Arranged:* Atlantic Richfield Co, Citibank NA, IBM Corp, Mellon Bank, NY Times, others. *Teaching:* Instr watercolor, Elizabeth Seton Col, Yonkers, NY, 84-88; instr printmaking & painting, Col New Rochelle, NY, 86-92; vis artist watercolor & printmaking, Westchester Arts Coun, NY, 86-; instr printmaking, Herbert H Lehman Col, 92 & 97-; instr art, Albert Leonard, New Rochelle, NY, 90-; instr watercolor, Herbert H Lehman col, 2001-02. *Awards:* Stuart M Egnal Award, 55-65, Print Club, 80; Purchase Award, Prints USA, Pratt Graphics Ctr, New York, 82. *Mem:* Printmaking Workshop; Westchester Arts Coun; Soc Am Graphic Artists NY (Adv Coun). *Media:* Etching; Watercolor. *Dealer:* Michael Ingbar Gallery Archit Art 568 Broadway New York NY 10012. *Mailing Add:* 6 Brookside Ave Pelham NY 10803

GALLANDER, CATHLEEN S
ART DEALER, REPRESENTATIVE
b San Antonio, Tex, Feb 4, 31. *Study:* Univ Tex, Austin, BA(hist); Harvard Univ, scholar art hist; Harvard Bus Sch, Inst Arts Admin. *Pos:* Dir, Art Mus S Tex, Corpus Christi, 61-80 & Newport Harbor Art Mus, Calif, 80-83; panelist, Nat Endowment Arts; pvt consult & fine arts appraisals, currently. *Mem:* Col Art Asn Am; Am Asn Mus; Am Fedn Arts; Western Asn Art Mus; Art Table. *Mailing Add:* 529 W 42nd St #2R New York NY 10036

GALLES, ARIE ALEXANDER
PAINTER, EDUCATOR
b Tashkent, Russia, Oct 2, 44: US citizen. *Study:* Temple Univ, BFA, 68; Univ Wis, MFA, 71. *Work:* NJ State Mus, Trenton. *Comn:* Charles Allen, NY; Edgar Kaiser Jr, Vancouver, Can. *Exhib:* Solo exhibs, O K Harris Gallery, NY, 77, 79 & 82, Zolla-Libermman Gallery Chicago, Ill, 79 & NJ State Mus, Trenton, 89; Abstract, Material, Pictorial, Illusionism, O K Harris West, Scottsdale, Ariz, 80; Contemp Painting, Del Mus, Wilmington, 80; Five Decades: Recent Works by Alumni of the Dept Art, Elvehjem Mus Art, Univ Wis, Madison, 80; Art of Fashion, Bernice Steinbaum Gallery, NY, 90; Painting: NJ Benjamin Gallery, William Paterson Col, Wayne, NJ, 92; and others. *Pos:* Dir, Madison Acad of Art & Morris Gallery, 77-80, Phyllis Rothman Gallery, Fairleigh Dickinson Univ, 88-. *Teaching:* Prof art & chmn fine arts dept, Fairleigh Dickinson Univ, Madison, NJ, 72-81, assoc prof, 81-84, prof, 84-. *Bibliog:* Article in Chicago Sun Times, 9/23/79 & Phoenix Gazett, 12/27/80; Robert Paschal & Robert Anderson (auths), Advanced Air Brush The Techniques-Art of the Dot, Van Nostrand Rineholt, 84. *Media:* Flourescent Acrylic on Aluminum Extrusions, Caran D Ache Oil Pastel. *Publ:* Auth, Air Brush Action, Mag, 10/88. *Dealer:* O K Harris 383 W Broadway New York NY; Zolla-Lieberman Gallery 356 W Huron Chicago IL 60610. *Mailing Add:* 116 Blue Lagoon Laguna Beach CA 92651-4233

GALLI, STANLEY WALTER
PAINTER
b San Francisco, Calif, Jan 18, 1912. *Study:* Calif Sch Fine Arts, San Francisco; Art Ctr Sch, Los Angeles. *Work:* Air Force Mus, Colo; Baseball Hall of Fame Mus, Cooperstown, NY; Palm Springs Desert Mus; Hall Fame Soc Illusr, NY. *Comn:* Conserv series, Weyerhaeuser Co, Tacoma, Wash, 52-68; wildlife paintings, Calif Casualty Group Collection, San Mateo, 73-78. *Exhib:* One-man shows, Nut Tree Gallery, Calif, 76, Crocker Art Mus, Sacramento, Calif, 80, Robert Mondavi Winery, Calif, 81, Charles & Emma Frye Art Mus, Seattle, 83, Espacio Gallery, Larkspur, Calif, 90, Riverside Mus, Baton Rouge, La, 92, Mus Italo Americano, San Francisco, 95, Solano Bank, Vacaville, Calif, Vacaville Mus, 2002; NY Hist Soc, 77; group show, Oakland Mus, Calif, 78, Gallery Imago, San Francisco, Calif, 88, Marin Art Coun, Larkspur, Calif, 93 & Calif Art Mus, Santa Rosa, Calif, 93; two-man exhib, Palm Springs Desert Mus, Calif, 78; Calvin R Vander Woude Gallery, Palm Springs, Calif, 85; JJ Brookings Gallery, San Francisco, 96-97, 98, 99, 2000; and others; Bergelli Gallery, Larkspur, Calif, 2001; Kentfield for Women, Sausalito Womens Club, 2001; Sausalito Womens Club, 2003. *Pos:* Illusr, Saturday Evening Post, 50-68, McCalls Mag, 60-67, Reader's Digest Mag & Condensed Bks, 60-78 & US Postal Serv Stamp Design, 68-78. *Teaching:* San Francisco City Col Art Dept, Prof Practices for Adv Students, 68, 69, 71, 72 & 73. *Awards:* Silver Medal, Dillon Lauritzen Award, Los Angeles Art Dir Club, 58; Best US Postage Stamp of Yr, Postal Commemorative Soc, 68, 72 & 78. *Bibliog:* 200 Years of American Illustration, Random House, 77; The Illustrator in America, Madison Sq Press, NY, 84; Outstanding American Illustrators Today, Graphic Sha Publ Co, Tokyo, 84. *Mem:* Soc Illusr New York & San Francisco. *Media:* Acrylic, Oil. *Mailing Add:* PO Box 66 Kentfield CA 94914

GALLO, ENZO D
SCULPTOR
b Italy, Oct 25, 27. *Study:* San Alejandro Univ Fine Arts, Havana, Cuba, MFA; Senatus Univ Verae Arademirus, BA; study with Jose Sicri & Ramos Blanco, sculptor & Augusto Valderama, painter, Havana. *Work:* Pagani Mus, Milan, Italy; Young Circle, Hollywood, Fla; Town of Padula, Italy; Art Mus the Amercias, Washington, DC; Port Everglades Park, Ft Lauderdale, Fla. *Comn:* Sculpture & mosaic murals, Hollywood Mem Gardens, Fla; mosaic murals, Am Savings & Loan, Miami Beach; sculpture, Doral Beach Club, Miami Beach; sculpture (bronze), Hallandale Pub Libr. *Exhib:* Metrop Mus, Miami, 75; one-man shows, Heller Bldg, 87, Omni Int, Miami, 78, West Palm Beach Art Gallery, 79, Inter-Am Art Gallery, Coral Gables, 80, Fedn of Cuban Teachers of Fine Arts, Miami, Fla, 86; Latin Am Artist of the Southeastern US, Lowe Art Mus, Miami, 78; First Ann Art Competition, Nova Univ, 79. *Teaching:* Prof sculpture, San Alejandro Inst Fine Arts, Havana, Cuba & Broward Adult Educ, 62-65. *Awards:* Selected by US Dept of HUD for Environ Art in Pub Places, 73; First Monumental Proj Assigned by Pres Reagan for Christopher Columbus Quincentenary, Port Everglades, Fla, 88; Medallion Design Accepted as the Off Medallion of Grand Regatta Columbus 1992 Quincentenary, Wash, DC, 89. *Bibliog:* John R Thompson (auth), Traveling Tribune Reporter Pays Visit to Sculptor in Exile, The Chicago Tribune, 69; Marian Vynne (auth), Italian Artist Works, The Miami News, 2/73; Thomas Lawrence (auth), Enzo Gallo Reduces Natural Data to Pure Forms, Manhattan Arts Mag, 9/91. *Mem:* Fla Sculpture Asn; Artist Equity Asn Fla (pres, 75-78); Am Fedn Arts; Fla Artist Group; Broward Art Guild. *Media:* Marble, Bronze. *Publ:* Auth, Columbus Rediscovered, The Miami Herald, 8/87; The Man of the Mountain, The El Nuero Miami Herald, 92

GALLO, FRANK
SCULPTOR, EDUCATOR
b Toledo, Ohio, Jan 13, 33. *Study:* Toledo Mus Sch Art, BFA, 54; Cranbrook Acad Art, 55; Univ Iowa, MFA, 59; Univ Ill, 85, sr scholar. *Work:* Mus Mod Art & Whitney Mus Am Art, NY; Art Inst Chicago; Los Angeles Mus Art; Cleveland Mus Art; plus others. *Comn:* Portrait, Daniel Pope Cook, Ill, 69; portraits, String Teachers of Am, 69-72; seven life-size concrete figures, Bicentennial Comn, Champaign, Ill, 76; stained glass wall, Harry Thoroue, 80; ed paper castings, Beethoven Found, 85. *Exhib:* Ann, Whitney Mus Am Art, 64-67, Young Am, 65; Alliance on Art, Smithsonian Inst, Washington, DC, 68; Venice Biennale, 68; Works in Paper, Art Inst Chicago, 78; retrospective, Paine Art Ctr, Oshkosh, Wis, 83; and others. *Teaching:* Prof sculpture, Univ Ill, 60-94. *Awards:* Guggenheim Found Fel, 66; Best Illus of the Year, Soc Publ Designers, 79. *Bibliog:* Peter Plagent (auth), article, Schlock Elite, New York, 12/3/78; Frank Gallo, Famous Artists Ann I (catalog), NY Hastings House, 80; Frank H Goodyear (auth), Contemporary American Realism since 1960, Archives of American Art Series, Little Brown, Boston, 81. *Publ:* Illus, cover, Raquel Welch, Time Mag, 11/69, The faint, Playboy Mag, 1/78 & Illus 21, NY Hastings House, 80. *Mailing Add:* c/o TRA Art Group 1700 Stutz Dr No 98 Troy MI 48084-4500

GALLO, RUBEN A
CRITIC, CURATOR
b Guadalajara, Mex, Dec 22, 69. *Study:* Yale Univ, BA, 91; Columbia Univ, MA, 96. *Collection Arranged:* Video Faz, Museo Regional Guadalajara, Mex, 96; The Conceptual Trend, Museo del Barrio, New York, 97. *Pos:* Dir, Forum Int Art & Theory, Guadalajara, Mex, 97-98. *Teaching:* Preceptor humanitites, Columbia Univ, NY, 95-; adj Latin Am art, Lehman Col, City Univ NY, 97-. *Res:* Latin American art; contemporary art; photography. *Publ:* Auth, The Labyrinths of Mexican Art, Flash Art 186, 96; El Intelectual Arte el Memoricidio, 1/97 & Manuel Alvarez Bravo y el Andante con Moto, 9/97, Vuelta, Mex; The Necessity of Revolt Interview with Julia Kristeva, Trans, 98. *Mailing Add:* 401 W 118th St Apt 25 New York NY 10027

GALLO, WILLIAM VICTOR
CARTOONIST, ILLUSTRATOR
b New York, NY, Dec 28, 22. *Study:* Columbia Exten Cartoonists & Illusr. *Work:* Baseball Hall Fame, Cooperstown, NY. *Exhib:* One-man show, Spectrum Art Gallery, NY, 80. *Pos:* With NY Daily News, 41-, sports cartoonist, 60-. *Awards:* Page One Awards, NY Newspaper Guild, 65, 68-70, 72-73, 75, 77-81, 85-86; Best Sports Cartoonist, Nat Cartoonist Soc, 68, 69, 70, 72, 73, 78, 85 & 86; Outstanding Achievement, Alumni Soc Sch Visual Arts, 75; and others. *Mem:* Nat Cartoonists Soc; Soc Silurians; and others. *Mailing Add:* 1 Mayflower Dr Yonkers NY 10710

GALLOWAY, STEVE
CONCEPTUAL ARTIST
b Los Angeles, Calif. *Study:* Calif Inst Arts, Valencia, BFA, 74. *Exhib:* One-man shows, Los Angeles Inst Contemp Art, 82, Mus Contemp Art, Los Angeles, 85, Monterey Peninsula Mus Art, Calif, 86, Acme Art, San Francisco, Calif, 87, James Corcoran Gallery, 87, 90 & 93, Gallery Paule Anglim, San Francisco, Calif, 93, Hunsaker/Schlesinger Gallery, Santa Monica, Calif, 98 & Armory Ctr Arts, Pasadena, Calif, 2000; Works on Paper, Ctr Contemp Art, Chicago, Ill, 90; Painting, Rosa Esman, NY, 91; Drawings, James Corcoran Gallery, Santa Monica, Calif, 92; Beyond Appearance, Armory Ctr Arts, Pasadena, Calif, 94; Nev Inst Contemp Art, Las Vegas, 95; Riverside Art Mus, Calif, 98. *Awards:* Fel, Nat Endowment Arts, 87. *Bibliog:* Susan Sanford Whitehead (auth), article, Visions, winter 87; Ben Marks (auth), Artweek, 2-3/90; Cathy Curtis (auth), Los Angeles Times, 2/23/90. *Mailing Add:* 2508 2nd St Santa Monica CA 90405

GAMMON, JUANITA L
EDUCATOR, GRAPHIC ARTIST
b New Orleans, La. *Study:* Univ Ill, BFA & MFA; advanced study. *Work:* Work in many pvt & pub collections. *Comn:* Many pvt comns. *Exhib:* Dream Mus, Champaign, Ill, 70; McKinley Found, Urbana, Ill, 70; Nat Acad Design, NY, 70-71; Univ Ill, 71; Parkland Col, 75, 79-2003; Quincy Art Gallery, 94; Springer Art Ctr, 2006; Artist Guild, St Louis, Mo, 2006; and others. *Pos:* Judge, local, regional & nat art exhibs, 67-; art lectr & critic & consult curric design, 67-; supvr, Champaign Co Art Show, 69-89; exhibitor, cur & spec tour guide, Nat Drawing Invitational, Parkland Gallery, 94. *Teaching:* Prof art & chmn Fine & Applied Arts Dept, Parkland Col, Champaign, 67-; serving on many col comts, teaching specialities (painting, drawing, illus, art hist). *Awards:* Many prof hons & awards. *Mem:* Colored Pencil Soc Am; many other prof organizations. *Media:* Acrylic, Colored Pencils; Watercolor. *Interests:* Photography; research pub & private gardens (for artist's panoramic style garden paintings). *Publ:* Ed, Parkland Intercom, Story Shop Book; contrib (drawing), A Stroke of Genius: The Best of Drawing, 2007. *Dealer:* Rocking Chair Studio 711 W Healey Champaign IL 61820. *Mailing Add:* 711 W Healey Champaign IL 61820

GAMWELL, LYNN
CURATOR, HISTORIAN
b Chicago, Ill, June 24, 43. *Study:* Univ Ill, BA, 67; Claremont Grad Sch, MFA, 70; Univ Calif, Los Angeles, PhD, 77. *Pos:* dir, Art Mus, State Univ NY, Binghamton, currently. *Teaching:* Lectr art hist, Univ Calif, Los Angeles, 72-74; asst prof art hist, Saddleback Col, Mission Viejo, Calif, 84-87; lectr, Science, Sch of Visual Arts, NY, currently. *Mem:* Col Art Asn; Art Table. *Res:* Contemporary art. *Publ:* ed contribr, Sigmund Freud and Art: His Personal Collection, Abrams, NY, 89; coauth, Madness in America: Cultural & Medical Perceptions of Mental Illness Before 1914, Cornell Univ Press, 95; Health and Happiness in Twentieth-Century Avant Garde Art, Cornell Univ Press, 96; co-auth; Dreams 1900-2000: Science, Art and the Unconscious Mind, Cornell Univ Press, 2000; auth, Exploring the Invisible: Art, Science and the Spiritual, Princeton Univ Press, 2002. *Mailing Add:* 101 W 80th St Apt 10A New York NY 10024-7102

GANAHL, RAINER
CONCEPTUAL ARTIST
b Bludenz, Austria. *Study:* Univ Innsbruck, MA, 85; Akademie Dusseldorf, MA, 90; Whitney Independent Study Prog, 90-91. *Work:* Pompidov Collection, Ctr George Pompidou, Paris, France; Guggenheim Mus (web site project), NY; Mus Mod Art & General Found, Vienna, Austria; Mus Contemp Art, Oslo, Norway. *Exhib:* One-man shows, Persons Weekend Mus (auth, catalog), Toyko, 93, Dallas Mus Art, 92, Kunsthaus Bregenz (auth, catalog), 98 & Mus Modern Art, Vienna, 99; Educational Complex (auth, catalog), General Found, Vienna, 97; Venice Biennial - Austrian Pvillion, Venice, 99; Kunstwelten Im Dialog, Mus Ludwig, Cologne, 99-2000; Vernaculars: Speaking Performances, Pompidou Ctr, Paris, 2000-2001. *Teaching:* assoc prof, Sch/Acad Fine Arts, Esav, Geneva, 96-98. *Bibliog:* Barry Schwarsky (auth), Rainer Ganahl: Windows on the World, Cambridge Univ Press, 97; George Baker (auth) Rainer Ganahl: Max Protetch Gallery, Artforum, 4/99; Roberto Costantino (auth), Broken Language, Flash Art Ital, summer 2000; Gregory Williams (auth), Artforum, summer 2001. *Media:* Video, Paper. *Publ:* Coauth, Rainer Ganahl, Imported - A Reading Seminar, Semidtext New York, 98; auth, Reading Karl Marx, Bookworks, London, spring 2001. *Dealer:* Galerie Nachst St Stephan Grunzngerg 1/2 1010 Vienna Austria; Baumgartner Gallery New York NY. *Mailing Add:* 1255 Fifth Ave Apt 3H New York NY 10029

GANDERT, MIGUEL ADRIAN
PHOTOGRAPHER, LECTURER
b Espanola, NMex, Jan 12, 56. *Study:* Univ NMex, BA, 77, MA, 83. *Work:* Mus Fine Arts, Santa Fe; Phoenix Art Mus, Ariz; Mass Col Art, Boston; Getty Ctr Hist Art & Humanities, Santa Monica, Calif; Ctr Creative Photog, Univ Ariz, Tucson. *Comn:* Martineztown/Santa Barbara, Community Photog Survey, City Albuquerque, 92; Retratos Mestizaje: A Photographic Survey of the Indo-Hispano Traditions of the Rio Grande Corridor, Rockefeller Found, 92-93; Latino Diversity, Use of 20 inch by 24 inch instant camera; Photographic collaboration with Sonaran photog Oscar Monroy (photog colonias in Nogales, Mex), Ariz Comn Arts, 94; From the West: Chicano Narrative Photography (narrative photog series), Mex Mus, San Francisco, Calif, 94. *Exhib:* Contemp-Am Photog, Galeria Licht, Oslo, Norway, 77-78; Boxers & Wrestlers, Blue Sky Gallery, Portland, Ore, 78; Let's Boogie at Okies, ASA Gallery, Univ NMex, Albuquerque, 80; Burque, Santa Fe Ctr Photogr, NMex, 84; The New Photog Survey, Mus Fine Arts, Santa Fe, 85; Statements, NMex State Fair Gallery, Albuquerque, 85 & 86; VSJ/Scenes from an Urban Chicano Experience, Nev State Mus Am Hist, Smithsonian Inst, Washington, DC, 90 & Univ NMex Art Mus, Albuquerque, 93; Hispanic Scenes from the Southwest, Kenyon Col, Gambier, Ohio, 91; La Frontera: A Way to Survive, MARS Art Space, Phoenix, Ariz, 94; Homeland/Use and Desire, Mass Col Art, Boston, 94; From the West: Chicano Narrative Photog, Mex Mus, San Francisco, Calif, 95-. *Teaching:* Instr photogr, Univ NMex, Albuquerque, 82-83, asst prof, currently. *Bibliog:* Kathy Livingston (auth), Riding low, Am Photogr, 4/84; Bart Ripp (auth), The south valley knows the photographer, Albuquerque Tribune, 8/12/85; Hal Rhodes (dir), The Illustrated Daily, 85 & Miguel Gandeft photographer-on assignment, KNME TV. *Mem:* Hispanic Cult Found. *Publ:* Contrib, Contemporary Identities: The Phoenix Triennial, Phoenix Art Mus, 93; 1993 Biennial Exhibition, Whitney Mus Am Art, Harry N Abrams Inc, Publ, NY; Three Generations of Hispanic Photographers Working in NMex, Harwood Found Univ NMex, Taos, 93; coauth, Flow of River, Hispanic cult Found; photogr, Los Tesoros del Espiritu: Familia y Fe, Academia El Norte Publ, 94. *Dealer:* Andrew Smith Gallery 76 E San Francisco St Santa Fe NM 87501. *Mailing Add:* c/o Andrew Smith Gallery 203 W San Francisco St Santa Fe NM 87501

GANEK, DAVID KENT
COLLECTOR
Study: Franklin & Marshall Col, 85, Grad. *Pos:* Risk arbitrage trader Donaldson Lufkin & Jenrette, NYC; partner Strategic Air Command Capital Advisors LLC, Stamford, CT; co-founder, principal Level Global Investors LP, Greenwich, 2003—. *Awards:* Named one of Top 200 Collectors, ARTnews magazine, 2004, 2006. *Collection:* Contemporary art & photography. *Mailing Add:* Level Global Investors LP 537 Steamboat Greenwich CT 06830

GANEK, DOROTHY SKEADOS
PAINTER, SILVERSMITH
b Athens, Greece, Aug 8, 46; US Citizen. *Study:* NY Sch Interior Design, 65-68. *Work:* Schearing Plough Corp, NJ; Sheraton, Needham, Mass; Cigna Corp; PSE & Gas Co, Warner Lambert Inc; Caldwell Banker; Kenwood Electronics; Kessler Institute, NEC; and others. *Exhib:* Zheijiang Mus, Hangzhou, China; Nat Asn Women Artists (traveling), 88; Los Angeles Artcore Invitational, Nat Watercolor Soc, 88; Am Watercolor Soc, 91-92. *Pos:* Interior designer, Dorothy Ganek Interiors, 69-85. *Awards:* Silver Medal Honor, NJ Watercolor Soc; Cecil Shapiro Award, Nat Asn Women Artists, 91; John Young Hunter Award, Am Watercolor Soc, 92. *Mem:* Nat Asn Women Artists; NJ Watercolor Soc; Allied Artists Am; Audubon Artists; Am Watercolor Soc. *Media:* Watermedia. *Publ:* Splash (watercolor book), 90; Goodlife Mag, 90; Am Artist Mag-Watercolor, spring 94; The Best of Watercolor & The Best Compositions, Rockport Publ; and others. *Dealer:* Kerygma Gallery Ridgewood NJ; Art Forms Red Bank NJ. *Mailing Add:* 125 Rynda Rd South Orange NJ 07079

GANES, LUCY
SCULPTOR, EDUCATOR
b Plainfield, NJ, Nov 18, 49. *Study:* Art Students League, 70; Lake Erie Col, BFA, 71; Pratt Inst, with Calvin Albert & George McNeil, MFA, 74. *Work:* Lehigh Univ, Westtown Sch, Pa; ARA Services. *Exhib:* May Show, Cleveland Mus Art, 74; Drawings USA, Smithsonian Inst Traveling Exhib, 76-79; solo exhib, Westchester State Col, Pa, 79; For the Love of Drawing, Kemerer Mus, Bethlehem, Pa, 81; Del Biennial, Univ Del, Newark, 81 & 83; Installation of Drawings & Sculpture, Muse Gallery, Philadelphia, 83 & 85; Installation of Sculpture and Drawings, Lehigh Univ, 85; Allentown Art Mus, 86; Southern Vt Art Center, 86. *Collection Arranged:* Womens Caucus Art Nat Exhib (auth, catalog), 84. *Teaching:* Vis lectr sculpture & drawing, Lake Erie Col, Ohio, 74-75; instr sculpture, Univ SAla, 76-77; assoc prof sculpture, drawing & painting, Lehigh Univ, Pa, 81-. *Mem:* Col Art Asn; Women's Caucus Art. *Dealer:* Muse Gallery 1915 Walnut St Philadelphia PA 19103. *Mailing Add:* Dept Art & Archit Lehigh Univ 17 Memorial Dr E Bethlehem PA 18015

GANLEY, BETTY
ARTIST
b Rahway, NJ, Sept 18, 42. *Exhib:* 20th Ann Exhib, Southern Watercolor Soc, Delf Norna Mus, Moundsville, WV, 97; Mid-Atlantic Regional Watercolor Exhibition, Rockville, MD, 97; Va Watercolor Soc, VA, 2000 & 2004; Rocky Mountain Nat Watermedia Exhib, Colo, 2000; The Manor House, Green Spring Gardens Park, Alexandria, Va, 2002; Blackrock Center for the Arts, Germantown, Md, 2003. *Awards:* Best of Show, Potomac Valley Watercolor Soc, Quiet Waters Gallery, 2004; North Light Award, Virginia Watercolor Soc, North Light Publ Co, 2004; Top Ten, Australian Artist Magazine, Still Life Competition (International), 2004; Best of Show, Wash Watercolor Soc, 2005; Peoples Choice Award, Vienna Art Soc, Small Works Show, 2005. *Bibliog:* Alice Ross (auth), A Matter of Perspective, Elán Magazine, 2000. *Mem:* Southern Watercolor Soc; Virginia Watercolor Soc, Dir At Large, 2004; Potomac Valley Watercolor Soc; Washington Watercolor Soc; Baltimore Watercolor Soc; Vienna Art Soc. *Media:* Watercolor. *Publ:* Contrib, Fresh Flowers, The Best of Flower Painting, North Lights Publ, 96; contrib, Splash 5, The Glory of Color, North Light Publ, 98; contrib, The Artists Touch III, Creative Art Press, 99; contrib, Splash 7, A Celebration of Light, North Light Publ, 2002; auth, Secret Gardens in Watecolor, Intl Artist Publ, 2005; contrib, Splash 9, Watercolor Secrets, North Light Publ, 2006; auth & illustr, Artists Projects You Can Paint, 10 Secret Gardens in Watercolor, Int Artist, 2005. *Mailing Add:* 713 Forest Park Rd Great Falls VA 22066

GANNON, LANIE E
SCULPTOR
b Mar 2, 59. *Study:* Memphis Col Art, BFA(painting), 81; Appalachian Ctr for Crafts, with Wendy Maruyama & Trent Whitington, 83-86. *Exhib:* Sculpture in the Garden, Cumberland Gallery, Nashville, Tenn, 92; Gallery 500, Philadelphia, Pa, 91; From the Mountains to the Mississippi, Nat Mus Women Arts, Cheekwood Fine Arts Ctr,

Nashville, Tenn, 93; Garden Sculpture, Bennett Gallery, Knoxville, Tenn, 94; solo exhibs, Zeitgeist Gallery, Nashville, 94 & Virtual Gallery, 98; Bennet Gallery, Knoxville, 94 & 95; Fac Exhib, Belmont Univ, Nashville, 98; Oasis Ctr, Nashville, 98 & 99; An Evening With the Arts, Tenn Performing Arts Ctr, Nashville, 98. *Pos:* Visual arts consult, FAST Track Educ Proj, Vanderbilt Univ, 93-. *Teaching:* Adj prof fine art, Belmont Univ, Nashville, Tenn, 90-; artist-in-residence & visual arts prog coordr, Nashville Inst/Arts, 92-93; FAST Track Ed Prog, Vanderbilt Univ, 93-94. *Awards:* Visual Artists Fel, Nat Endowment Arts, 88 & 98; Owens-Corning Visual Arts Fel, Tenn Arts Comn, 94; Greater Knoxville Advertising Award, Gold Medal for four color poster illus. *Bibliog:* Show Review, New Art Examiner, 10/91; Guide to Maintenance of Outdoor Sculpture, Am Inst Conserv Hist Artistic Works, 93; A Bicentennial Tribute to Tennessee Women, 1796-1996, Univ Tenn Press, 95. *Media:* Aluminum, Wood. *Mailing Add:* 4211 Idaho Ave Nashville TN 37209

GANTZ, ANN CUSHING
PAINTER, INSTRUCTOR
b Dallas, Tex, Aug 27, 35. *Study:* Memphis Acad Art; Southwestern Univ, Memphis; Newcomb Col Tulane Univ, New Orleans, La, BFA, 55. *Work:* Dallas Mus Fine Arts, Tex; Denver Mus, Colo; Smithsonian Inst, Washington; Boston Mus, Mass; Los Angeles State Mus; Okla City Mus, Okla; others. *Comn:* KERA-TV, 88; Trammell Crow Co, 88; Alpha Omicron Pi Hq, 95; Dallas Opera, 96; Design Ctr, 96. *Exhib:* Oklahoma City Art Ctr, 56-58; Painting & Sculpture Ann, Nat Acad Design, NY, 57, 60; Norfolk Mus, Va, 58, 59; Printmaking Today, Brooklyn Mus, NY, 59; Ann Shows, Ark Art Ctr, Little Rock, 59, 60 & 61; retrospective, Dallas Visual Art Ctr, 96; Tennison Gallery, 99; Valley House, 2003; David Dike Gallery, 2002 & 2003; Tex Art Collectors, 2002 & 2003; MAC Mus, Group, 2004, 05, 06; One-man show, Pland Art Ctr, 2006 & Monticello Gal, Fort Worth, 2006; and others. *Collection Arranged:* various families. *Pos:* Pres, Cushing Galleries Inc, 63-79; owner, Cushing Studio, 79-. *Teaching:* Instr printmaking & painting, Dallas Mus Fine Arts Sch, 56-62; instr painting, printmaking & drawing, Cushing Galleries Sch Studio Art, 62-79, instr, Cushing Studio, 79-. *Awards:* TFAA Artist of Yr Award, 79; Oak Award, 81; McMurray Found Award, 83; Delta Kappa Award, 87. *Mem:* Dallas Print & Drawing Soc (pres, 58-60); YWCA Art Comt; Tex Printmakers (pres, 60-63); Dallas Art Gallery Asn (founder, 78); Cushing Atelier (founder, pres, 90-2003); TV Visual Arts Asn (hon); Dallas Arts Coalition. *Media:* Oil, Woodcut; Acrylic, Serigraphy. *Mailing Add:* 4654 Edmondson Dallas TX 75209

GANZ, JULIAN, JR
PATRON
b Dec, 29. *Pos:* Pres, McMahan Furniture Stores, Los Angeles, currently; trustee, Los Angeles Co Mus Art, currently; Nat Gallery Art, Wash, DC. *Mailing Add:* McMahan Furniture Stores 2237 Colby Ave Los Angeles CA 90064

GANZ, SYLVIA SQUIRES See Squires Ganz, Sylvia (Tykie)

GANZI, VICTOR FREDERICK
PATRON
b NY City, Feb 14, 47. *Study:* Fordham Univ, BS, 68; Harvard Univ, JD, 71; NYU, LLM(taxation), 81. *Pos:* Tax accountant, Touche Ross & Co, Denver, 71-73; assoc, Rogers & Wells, New York City, 73-78, partner, 78-86; managing partner, Rogers & Wells (now Clifford Chance Rogers & Wells), 86-90; vpres, secy, gen counsel, Hearst Corp, New York City, 90-92, Chief Financial Officer, chief legal off, sr vpres, 92-97; pres, Hearst Books/Bus Pub Group, 95-99; exec vpres Hearst Corp, New York City, 97-2002, Chief Operating Officer, 98-2002, pres, Chief Exec Officer, 2002-. *Mem:* Am Bar Asn; Am Inst of CPA; Colo Soc CPAs; William Randolph Hearst Found (bd dir, currently); Whitney Mus Am Art (trustee, currently). *Mailing Add:* The Hearst Corp 959 8th Ave New York NY 10019-3795

GAON, SIMON
PAINTER, SCULPTOR
b New York, NY, 43. *Study:* Art Students League, 62-63; Adad, Harlem, Holland, 63; studied with Arthur Bressler; self taught. *Work:* Yeshiva Univ Mus, NY; Mus City NY; NY Hist Soc; Frances Loisirs, Paris. *Exhib:* Peter Findlay Gallery; Galeri Rubens, Sweden, 99; Yeshiva Univ, 2001; Solo exhib, Nicolas Roerich Mus, New York City, Susan Conway Gallery, Washington, DC, Art Students League, NY, Galerie Rose, Hamburg, Ger, 99. *Awards:* Edward G MacDowell Award. *Mem:* Arts & Crafts Alliance; St Painters; Art Students League. *Media:* Oil. *Specialty:* Cityscapes, people in Cafes. *Mailing Add:* 425 Riverside Dr New York NY 10025

GARABEDIAN, CHARLES
PAINTER
b Detroit, Mich, 23. *Study:* Univ Calif, Los Angeles, MA, 61. *Work:* Metrop Mus Art & Whitney Mus Am Art, NY; Los Angeles Co Mus Art & Mus Contemp Art, Los Angeles, Calif; Rose Art Mus, Brandeis Univ, Waltham, Mass; San Diego Mus Contemp Art, Calif. *Exhib:* Biennial, Whitney Mus Am Art, 75 & 85 (with catalog); solo exhibs, Whitney Mus Am Art (with catalog), NY, 76, Holly Solomon Gallery, NY, 82, Twenty Yrs of Work (with catalog) Rose Art Mus, Waltham, Mass, 83, La Louver, Venice, Calif (with catalog), 83, 86, 88, 90, 92 & 94, Hirschl & Adler Mod (with catalog), NY, 84 & 87, Gallery Paule Anglim, San Francisco, 85 & 93, Arts Club Chicago (with catalog), Ill, 85; Painting & Sculpture in Calif: The Modern Era (with catalog), San Francisco Mus Mod Art, Calif, 76; National Collection of Fine Arts, Smithsonian Inst, Washington, DC, 76; Contemp Art from Southern Calif, High Mus, Atlanta, Ga, 80; First Newport Biennial, Los Angeles Today (with catalog), Newport Harbor Art Mus, Newport Beach, Calif, 84; Content: A Contemp Focus, 1974-1984 (with catalog), Hirshhorn Mus & Sculpture Garden, Smithsonian Inst, Washington, DC, 84; The Classical Tradition in Painting & Sculpture (with catalog), Aldrich Mus Contemp Art, Ridgefield, Conn, 85; The Figure in 20th Century Am Art: Selections from the Metrop Mus, Metrop Mus Art, traveling, 85; Conn Collects: Am Art Since 1960, Whitney Mus Am Art/Fairfield Co, Stamford, Conn, 86; Projects & Portfolios: 25th Ann Print Exhib, Brooklyn Mus Art, NY, 89; Spirit of Our Time, Santa Barbara Contemp Arts Forum, Calif, 90; LA When it Began, James Corcoran Gallery, Los Angeles, Calif, 90; On Water, Ruth Bachofner Gallery, Santa Monica, Calif, 93; 43rd Biennial Exhib Contemp Am Painting, Corcoran Gallery Art, Washington, DC, 93-94; Persistance of the Human Image, Fresno City Col Art Space Gallery, Calif, 93; Three Visions, Riva Yares Gallery, Scottsdale, Ariz, 94; and many others. *Awards:* Nat Endowment Arts Fel, 77; Guggenheim Fel, 80. *Dealer:* La Louver 45 N Venice Blvd Venice CA 90291. *Mailing Add:* c/o LA Louvre Gallery 45 N Venice Blvd Venice CA 90291

GARBUTT, JANICE LOVOOS
PAINTER, WRITER
b Dubuque, Iowa. *Study:* Chouinard Art Inst. *Comn:* Mural, comn by Mr & Mrs Walter Frey, San Clemente, Calif. *Exhib:* Los Angeles Co Art Mus; Calif Art Club; solo exhibs, Circle Gallery, San Diego, Descanso Gardens, Carol Hard's Rancho Mirage Gallery & the Gallery, Palm Springs, Calif. *Pos:* Narrator, Visions of Calif (doc film), KCOE Pub Television, 95. *Teaching:* Instr fashion promotion, Chouinard Art Inst, 47-48. *Awards:* Merit Award; First Prize for Short Story, Ann Conf Mary & Donald Decker, Royal Lit; Selected as one of Ten Living Legends Exhib, Kluglak Gallery, Miracosta Col; Svc Award Am Artists mag. *Mem:* Am Soc Composers, Authors & Publishers; Author's Guild; Dramatist's Guild Am. *Media:* All. *Res:* Archived writings on Calif art by the Smithsonian. *Publ:* Auth & illusr, Design is a Dandelion; co-auth, Making Pottery without a Wheel, Prentice Hall, in prep; many articles in Los Angeles Times, Am Artist, Westways, Christian Sci Monitor, Charm, Parade, Toledo Star News & Southwest Art; Antiques & Fine Arts. *Dealer:* ART Beasley Gallery 2802 Juan St San Diego CA 92110. *Mailing Add:* 3357-P Monte Hermoso Laguna Hills CA 92653-2940

GARCHIK, MORTON LLOYD
PAINTER, PRINTMAKER
b Brooklyn, NY, June 25, 1929. *Study:* Brooklyn Mus, painting with Max Beckmann & printmaking with Gabor Peterdi; Sch Visual Art, NY. *Work:* Minn Mus Art; Libr Cong. *Comn:* Book cover for Gimpel the Fool, Avon Paperback, 63. *Exhib:* One-man show, Union of Am Hebrew Congregations, 63; 7th Ann Contemp Am Printmakers Exhib, DePauw Univ, 65; Ohio Univ 7th Ann, 66; Seattle Art Mus Int Exhibs, 66 & 67; two-man show, Art Corner, Milburn, NJ, 75; Artists Equity, NY, 78. *Pos:* Art dir, Commun Channels, Inc, NY, 72-77. *Awards:* First Prize, Drawing, Sch Visual Arts, 55; Purchase Award, Olivet Col 5th Nat Print Exhib, 65. *Media:* All. *Publ:* Auth, Art Fundamentals: Basics of Drawing, Painting, Sculpture & Printmaking, Stravon Educ Press; Creative Visual Thinking: How to Think Up Ideas Fast, Art Direction Bk Co; illusr, in: Harpers, Avon paperback, Farrar, Straus & Cudahy, Parents Mag Press. *Mailing Add:* 163 Sewall Ave Winthrop MA 02152-1557

GARCIA, OFELIA
ADMINISTRATOR, PRINTMAKER
b Havana, Cuba, Feb 12, 41; US citizen. *Study:* Escuela Nacional de Bellas Artes, Havana, Cuba, 58-60; Manhattanville Col, BA, 69; Tufts Univ & Boston Mus Sch, MFA(printmaking), 72; Duke Univ, Post-Grad. *Hon Degrees:* Atlanta Col Art, Hon Dr (fine arts), 91. *Work:* Princeton Univ Graphic Arts Col; NJ State Mus, Trenton; Free Libr Philadelphia; Museo Grafico, Inst Puerto Rican Culture, San Juan; Barnard Col, NY. *Exhib:* Third Miami Graphics Biennial, Metrop Mus & Art Ctr, Fla, 77; 53rd Ann Juried Show, The Print Club, Philadelphia, 77; NJ State Mus, Trenton, 78; Barnard Col, NY, 79; solo shows at Colegio Universitario, Santurce, PR, 70, Cohen Arts Ctr, Tufts Univ, 72 & Duke Univ Gallery, 74; Five Hispanic Artists, Deshong Mus, Pa, 82; A Growing Am Treasure, Pa Acad Fine Arts, William Penn Mus, 83. *Collection Arranged:* Invitational Print Exhib in honor of Lessing J Rosenwald (auth, catalog), Print Club, Philadelphia, Pa, 80; Contemp Prints from Lehigh Univ Collection (auth, catalog), Bethlehem, Pa, 80; Recent Gifts: Print at Univ Pa (auth, catalog), Grad Sch Fine Arts, 81; Printed by Women (auth, catlog), Philadelphia, Pa, 83; Int Mezzotint Comptetion, The Print Club & Pratt Graphic Ctr, New York, 84. *Pos:* Dir, The Print Ctr, Philadelphia, 78-85; critic, Pa Acad Fine Arts, 82-85; pres, Atlanta Col Art, 86-91, Rosemont Col, 91-95; art adv comt, Barnes Found, 91-94; bd dir, Am Coun Educ, 92-95; bd dir, Haverford Col, 92-; sr fel, Am Council Edu, 95-97; dean, Col of Arts & Commun, William Paterson Univ, 97-. *Teaching:* Asst prof printmaking & drawing, Newton Col Sacred Heart, 69-73, chmn dept, 70-73; asst prof, Boston Col, 75-76; prof (art dept), William Paterson Univ, 97-2006. *Awards:* First Prize, All-Sch Competition, Escuela de Bellas Artes, Havana, Cuba, 59; Am Bk Builders Scholar Prize, Boston Mus Sch, 69; Kent Fel, Danforth Found, 75-80; citation, City of Philadelphia, 85. *Bibliog:* Ross Romano (auth), The Complete Collagraph, Macmillan, 80; articles in Philadelphia Inquirer, 79-95, Atlanta Constitution, 86-91 & Print Collector's Newsletter. *Mem:* Fel Soc Values Higher Educ; Woman's Caucus Art (pres, 84-86); Col Art Asn Am (bd dir, 86-90); Haverford Col (bd mem, 1992-2004); ArtPride NJ (mem, 2005-); Jersey City Mus (bd chmn, 2001). *Media:* Prints, Drawings. *Dealer:* The Print Ctr 1614 Latimer St Philadelphia PA 19103. *Mailing Add:* 299 Pavonia Ave No 2-5 Jersey City NJ 07302

GARCIA, RUPERT (MARSHALL) R
PAINTER, EDUCATOR
b French Camp, Calif, Sept 29, 41. *Study:* San Francisco State Univ, with John Gutmann, BA, 68, with Richard MacLean & Robert Bechtle, MA, 70; Univ Calif, Berkeley, with Peter Selz, Herschel Chipp & T J Clark, MA, 81. *Work:* Nat Mus Am Art, Smithsonian Inst, Washington, DC; Oakland Mus, Calif; Univ Art Mus, Berkeley, Calif; San Francisco Mus Mod Art, Calif; The Mex Mus, San Francisco. *Comn:*

Posters and Society (poster), San Francisco Mus Mod Art, 74; posters for Amnesty Int, San Francisco, 76; Mex Mus, San Francisco, 76; Nat Chicano Coun Higher Educ, Berkeley, Calif, 79; pastel painting, Ruben Libr, Sonoma State Univ, Rohnert Park, Calif, 79. *Exhib:* One-man show, Oakland Mus, 70, San Francisco Mus Mod Art, 78, Univ Art Gallery, State Univ NY, Binghamton, 81, Univ Art Mus, Berkeley, Calif, 84, Mex Mus, San Francisco, 86 & The Haggin Mus, Stockton, Calif, 88; Images of an Era: The Am Poster 45-75, Nat Collection Fine Arts, Smithsonian Inst & Corcoran Gallery Art, Washington, DC, 75; Raices Antiquas/Visones Nuevas, Tucson Mus Art, Ariz, 77; Prelude to the Fifth Sun, Univ Art Mus, Berkeley, Calif, 77; Mex-Am Artists San Francisco Bay Area, Mex Mus, 78; Das Andere Am, Staaliche Kunsthalle, Berlin, WGer, 83; The Human Condition, Mus Mod Art Biennial III, San Francisco, 84; Close Focus, Nat Mus Am Art, Washington, DC, 87; Committed to print, Mus Mod Art, NY, 88; Latin Am Presence in US, Bronx Mus Arts, NY, 88; and others. *Collection Arranged:* Arte de la Revolucion Cubana: Silkscreens by Rene Mederos, Galeria de La Raza, San Francisco, 73; Realismo Chicano: Drawings by Juan Fuentes, Chicano Students Libr, Univ Calif, Berkeley, 76. *Pos:* Artist in residence, Calif Arts Coun, 86, Inst Cult Commun EW Ctr, Honolulu, Hawaii, 87. *Teaching:* Lectr silkscreen, printmaking, painting & drawing, San Francisco State Univ, 78, 79 & summer 81; lectr art hist Mex, Univ Calif, Berkeley, 79-81, lectr graphic design, 82-85; vis asst prof art hist Mex, Wash State Univ, Pullman, 84; vis artist, Ill State Univ, Bloomington, 88; assoc prof art, San Jose State Univ, 88-. *Awards:* Printmaking, San Francisco Arts Comn, 86; Purple Globe Award, San Francisco State Univ, 86. *Bibliog:* Ramon Favela (auth), The Art of Rupert Garcia, The Mexican Mus, San Francisco, 86; Peter Selz, (auth), Rupert Garcia: The Moral Fervor of Painting and its Subjects, Arts, 4/87; Bill Berkson (auth), Rupert Garcia, The Haggin Mus, 88. *Media:* Oil, Pastel. *Res:* Art and culture of the Chicano and Mexican. *Publ:* Coauth, Recent Raza murals in the US, Radical Am, 78; auth, Politics of Popular Art, Chimearte, Los Angeles, 78; Murales Recientes de La Raza en Estado Unidos, Plural, Mex, 79; Mexican Movie Poster Art, Myth, Illusion, Deception, Galeria de la Raza, San Francisco, 79; Frida Kahlo, A Bibliography and Biographical Introduction, Univ of Calif, Berkeley, 83. *Dealer:* Iannetti-Lanzone Gallery 310 Grant Ave San Francisco CA 94108; Saxon-Lee Gallery 7525 Beverly Blvd Los Angeles 90036. *Mailing Add:* c/o Aurobora Press 147 Natoma St San Francisco CA 94105-3710

GARCIA GUERRERO, LUIS
PAINTER
b Guanajuato City, Mex, Nov 18, 21. *Study:* Escuela Nac de Artes Plasticas, UNAM, 49; Escuela de Pintura, Escultura y Grabado, INBA, 50; Taller de Tecnicas y Materiales, IPN, 51. *Work:* Galeria de Arte Mexicano, Mus Nac de la Estampa, INBA, Galeria Lopez Quiroga, Mexico City. *Comn:* Stained-glass window, Zoquiapan, Mex, 53-56. *Exhib:* Los Surrealistas en México, Mus Nac de Arte, INBA, Mexico City, 86; Divertimentos, Galeria de Arte Mexicano, Mexico City, 86; one-man show, Mus del Pueblo, Guanajuata City, 87. *Bibliog:* Luis Cardoza Y Aragon (auth), Luis Garcia Guerrero, State of Guanajuato, 82; Carlos Monsivais (auth), Garcia Guerrero, Promexa, 87; Sergio Pitol (auth), Luis Garcia Guerrero, State of Guanajuato, 93. *Media:* Oil. *Mailing Add:* c/o Galeria De Arte Mexicano Gobernador Rafael Rebollar 43 San Miguel Chapultepec 11850 Mexico

GARD, SUZANNE E
PAINTER
b Seattle, Wash. *Comn:* Benton's Heavenly Serenade, comn by FE Everett Jr, Pres DAPC, 94; Animal Portraits, comn by Dr C Hunter, OD Seattle, Wash, 94. *Exhib:* Mamaroneck 36th Ann Nat Open Exhib, Westbeth Gallery, NY, 94; Special Voices, Thunder Spirit Lodge, Jahn/Matter Arts, Minneapolis, Minn, 94; solo exhibs, Sidney Gallery & Mus, Port Orchard, Wash, 94, Moss Bay Gallery, Kirkland, Wash, 95 & Kent Arts Comn Exhib, City Hall, Wash, 95-96; Children's Hosp, Seattle, 95; AKIM, MASK's 96, Sotheby's, NY, 96. *Teaching:* Instr drawing & inks, City of Kent Cult Arts, 95-. *Awards:* Award Excellence, Manhattan Arts Int Artists 90s, 95 & 96; First & Third Places, Auburn Juried Fine Art, Wash, 96. *Bibliog:* Catherine Drillis (auth), Suzanne Gard explores natures evolutions, Manhattan Arts Int Artists in the 90's, 11-12/93; JM Lewis (auth), About the cover artist Suzanne Gard, The Entertainer, 3/94; Thomas Lawrence (auth), Suzanne Gard blends detail with drama, Manhattan Arts Int Artists in the 90's, 11/12/94. *Mem:* Catherine Lorillard Wolfe Art Club; Oil Pastel Asn/United Pastelists Am; Knickerbocker Artists USA; NW Watercolor Soc, Seattle. *Media:* Watercolor; Mixed Inks on Paper. *Mailing Add:* 24301 138th Ave SE Kent WA 98042-5185

GARDINER, HENRY GILBERT
ART DEALER, MUSEUM DIRECTOR
b Boston, Mass, Aug 27, 27. *Study:* Harvard Col, AB, 50, Harvard Univ, MA, 59. *Collection Arranged:* Color & Form, 1909-1914, & Cross & Sword, 76, San Diego Mus, 76. *Pos:* Cur paintings & sculpture, Philadelphia Mus Art, 60-69; dir, San Diego Mus Art, 69-79 & Mitchell Wolfson Mus, Miami, 83-84. *Teaching:* Prof mus studies, Univ Southern Calif, 81. *Specialty:* European and American art from 1850 to 1950, with emphasis on abstract painting 1900-1915. *Mailing Add:* PO Box 3121 Palm Beach FL 33480

GARDINER, T MICHAEL
PAINTER, INSTRUCTOR
b Seattle, Wash, Feb 5, 46. *Study:* St Thomas Seminary, BA, 69; Cornish Col Arts, 73; Univ Wash, teaching cert, 78. *Work:* Seattle Water Dept & City Light; SAFECO, Seattle; Nordstrom, Seattle; US West, Seattle. *Comn:* Painting on a City Bus, Art Project, Metro-Seattle, 92; Painting, Ballard High School, Seattle, 2005. *Exhib:* Seattle Art Mus, 75; one-man shows, Polly Friedlander Gallery, Seattle, 77, Manolides Gallery, 79-85, MIA Gallery, 88 & 90, Augen Gallery, Portland, 89, Susan Cummins Gallery, Mill Valley, Calif, 89 & 91 & Monte Clark Gallery, Vancouver, BC, 92; Sea-First Bank Gallery, 91, Linda Cannon Gallery, Seattle, Wash, 94; Monte Clark Gallery, Vancouver, BC, 94; and others. *Teaching:* Vis artist, Painting, Drawing, Cent Wash Univ, Ellensburg, 91; painting, Sch Visual Concepts, Seattle, Wash, 93-94. *Awards:* Nat Endowment Arts, 89. *Media:* Acrylic, Mixed Media. *Publ:* Revs, Art in Am, 7/91; Black Uhura at the Apollo Theatre, 4/5/93, The Winters Tale at BAM, 4/18/94 & Bastille Day on Gansevoort St, 7/18/94, New Yorker Mag; Am Illus, 94. *Dealer:* Linda Cannon Gallery 520 Second Ave Seattle WA 98104. *Mailing Add:* 3023 NW 63rd St Seattle WA 98107-2566

GARDNER, ANN
CERAMIST
Study: Univ Ore, Portland & State Univ, Maude Kerns Art Ctr (ceramics & fine arts). *Work:* Am Craft Mus, NY; Nordstrom, Montgomery, Md; Saks Fifth Ave; City of Seattle; Detroit Inst Arts, Mich; Am Craft Mus; Seattle Art Mus; Renwick Gallery Nat Mus Am Art, Washington. *Comn:* Washington State Convention and Trade Ctr; London Club, Las Vegas; Port of Seattle. *Exhib:* One-woman shows, Sculpture in Glass & Mixed Media, Esther Saks Gallery, Chicago, 87, William Traver Gallery, Seattle, Wash, 87, 88 & 89, Art Gym, Maryhurst Col, Portland, 87, Familiar Rhythyms, Linda Farris Gallery, Seattle, Wash, 92, Butters Gallery, Portland, William Travers Gallery, Seattle, 99, 2001; group shows, Bellevue Art Mus, 88 & 91, Linda Ferris Gallery, Seattle, 88 & 91; Spirit of the West, traveling exhib, 92; Dreams & Sheilds, Salt Lake Art Ctr, Utah, 92; Seattle Art Mus, 95; Huntsville, (Ala) Mus, 96; Renwick Gallery, Smithsonian, 99. *Teaching:* Artist in residence, Kohler Foundry, 84 & 86, Pilchuck Glass Sch, 85 & 87, Centrum Found, printmaking, 89; lectr, Univ Wash, Seattle, 90. *Awards:* Nat Endowment Arts Grant, 86, fcl, 94-95; Louis Comfort Tiffany award, NY, 93. *Bibliog:* Linda Humphrey & Fred Albert (auths), The Northwest, 91; Ronnie Miller (auth), Out of the Fire, p 44-46, 91; Ann Gardner shows a tender side, Seattle PI, 2/91; Vicki Harper (auth.) American Craft, 98. *Mailing Add:* c/o William Travers Gallery 100 Union St 2nd Fl Seattle WA 98101

GARDNER, JOAN A
PAINTER, BOOK ARTIST
b Joliet, Ill, May 3, 33. *Study:* Univ Ill, BFA & MFA(Kate Neal Kinley Mem fel), 55; Norfolk Summer Art Sch, Yale Univ, with Rico Lebrun & Gabor Peterdi, fel, 56. *Work:* Univ Ill; Am Fedn Art; Art Inst Chicago; Yale Univ; Lyman Allyn Mus, New London, Conn; Harvard Univ; Mus Modern Art, NY. *Exhib:* New Britain Mus Art, Conn, 73; 55 Mercer Gallery, NY, 74-80 & 2001; Slater Mem Mus, Norwich, Conn, 77; retrospective, Lyman Allyn Mus, New London, Conn, 81; Film, 55 Mercer Gallery, NY, 2001; one person shows 55 Mercer Gallery, NY, 82, 85, 86, 88, 90, 92, 95 & 97, Kent State Univ Art Gallery, Kent, Ohio, 83, Fairleigh Dickinson Univ, Hackensack, NJ, 85, Ohio Perspectives, Akron art Mus, 86, People Paintings, Art Space, New Haven, Conn, 89, Promenade Gallery, Bushnell Auditorium, Hartford, Conn, 90, The Emily Davis Gallery, Akron, 90, Stocker Ctr, Elyria, Ohio, 92, Erector Square, New Haven, Conn, 98, Here Arts Ctr, NY, 2000, and others; retrospective, John Slade Ely House, New Haven, Conn, 94. *Teaching:* Instr art, Southern Conn State Col, 65-77; asst prof, Univ New Haven, 78-81; assoc prof, Kent State Univ, 82-93; retired prof painting, Kent State Univ, Kent, Ohio. *Awards:* Fulbright-Hays Award, 74-75; Conn Comn Arts Grant, 79-80. *Bibliog:* Joan Gardner, A Painting Retrospective, New Haven ARTS, cover, Vol 7, No 4, 9/1994; Micahel Rush (auth), The John Slade Ely House/New Haven Joan Gardner retrospective, Art New England, 9/1994; Hank Hoffman (auth), Open art searchery, The New Haven Advocate, 5/28/1998. *Mem:* Conn Acad Fine Arts; Women's Caucus on Art; Col Art Asn; Conn Women Artists; Spaces, Cleveland, Ohio. *Media:* Paintings, Collage. *Collection:* MOMA, Yale, Harvard, etc. *Publ:* Coauth, Robot (film), 72; Rooms (bk of drawings), 79; If I Were, poetry-picture bk, 81; Cast of Characters (bk of drawings). *Dealer:* 55 Mercer Gallery New York NY. *Mailing Add:* 10-735 Silver Sands Rd New Haven CT 06512

GARDNER, SHEILA
PAINTER
b Jersey City, NJ, Mar 31, 33. *Study:* Endicott Col, AA, 52; Art Students League, 54-57; New Sch, 56-59. *Work:* AT&T, Mobil Oil & Chemical Bank, NY; Portland Mus Art, Maine; Boise Art Mus, Idaho. *Comn:* Arthur Anderson, Boston, Mass, 87; Westone Bank, Boise, Idaho. *Exhib:* Contemp Images: Watercolor, Allen Priebe Gallery, Univ Wis, Oshkosh, 83; Traveling Exhib, Am Realism-20th Century Drawings & Watercolors, San Francisco Mus Mod Art, Calif, 85-86, De Cordova & Dana Mus, Lincoln, Mass, 86, Akron Art Mus, Ohio & A M Huntington Art Gallery, Univ Tex, Austin, 87; The Monumental Image: Watercolor USA, Springfield Art Mus, Mo, 86; Boise Art Mus, 88-90; Univ Idaho, Moscow, 90; Green Woods and Crystal Waters: The Am Landscape Tradition Since 1950, Philbrook Mus Art, Tulsa, Okla & 3 Mus, 99-. *Teaching:* Workshops, Sun Valley Ctr Arts & Humanities, 85, 89, 90, 93-95, 2006; instr painting & drawing, Univ Maine, 86. *Bibliog:* Women Artists and American Watercolors, Abbeville Press, 88; John Arthur (auth), Spirit of Place, Bullfinch; Abrams (auth), American Realism-Janss Collection; John Driscoll (auth), The Artist and the American Landscape, Chameleon Press, 98. *Media:* Oil, Watercolor. *Dealer:* Gail Severn Gallery 400 Firts Ave, No Ketchum ID 83340. *Mailing Add:* 748 Eastlake Dr Spring Creek NV 89815

GARDNER, SUSAN ROSS
PAINTER
b New York, NY, Oct 25, 41. *Work:* Metrop Mus Art, NY; Southern Ill Univ; Northern Ill Univ; Atlantic Richfield Corp; Woman's Interart Ctr; Art Embassies Prog, Washington, DC; other private collections. *Comn:* Two wall murals, Pub Sch 94, Dept Cult Affairs Percent for Arts Prog, NY; Noah's Ark, St Peters Church, Citicorp, NY. *Exhib:* Seattle Art Mus, 71; De Cordova Mus, Lincoln, Mass, 71; Cook Gallery, Lincoln Ctr, 81; Brooklyn Mus, 72, 78, 79, 82 & 84; 55 Mercer St, NY, 82;

one-person shows, Webb & Parsons Gallery, Conn, 82, Twinning Gallery, NY, 83, LaGuardia Community Col, 84, 94 & 97 & Saint Peter's, Citicorp, NY, 86; The Doll Show, Hillwood Art Gallery, CW Post Col, NY, 85; City Without Walls, Newark, 1986, 87, 88 & 90; Goddard Gallery, NY, 1991 & 94; Animals, Animals, Anita Shapolsky Gallery, NY, 1995; Art and the Law (traveling), univ galleries acroos USA, 1996-97; Earthquake, Mus Moving Image, Astoria, NY, 1997; Fed Reserve, NY, 1998; Outsider (invitational), Bittersweet Gallery, New Haven, Conn, 1998; Art and Humor invitational, NY, 1999; You Are What You Eat (invitational), Peekskil (NY) Art Ctr, 1999; The Dirt Show (invitational), Tobey Fine Arts, NY, 2000; SmallWorks Invitational, Blue Mountain Gallery, NY, 2001. *Teaching:* Asst prof studio & art hist, Manhattan Community Col, New York, 66-70; assoc prof, head of Art Dept, Yeshiva Univ, 75-. *Awards:* Purchase Award, Northern Ill Univ, 71. *Bibliog:* interview, NY Times, 5/27/1973; photo & article, Long Island Press, 4/27/73, East Hampton Star, 5/73 & Arts, 6/83; article, Daily News, 3/1970, 4/1973 & 10/1987. *Mem:* Col Art Asn Am. *Media:* Acrylic, Rhoplex, Metal; Mosaic, Tiles, Beadwork. *Mailing Add:* 108 Wyckoff St Brooklyn NY 11201-6307

GAREY, PATRICIA MARTIN
CERAMIST, PAINTER
b State College, Miss, Nov 11, 32. *Study:* Tex Woman's Univ, BS(costume design & fashion illus); Tex Tech Univ, Lubbock, MFA, with Jim Howze, Terry Morrow, Lynwood Kreneck, Hugh Gibbons, 2-Dimensional Studio & Minor Art Hist; Art Students League, 77; Villa Maria Ctr Arts, Perugia, Italy, 85. *Work:* Home Econs Dept, Tex Tech Univ, Lubbock; NMex Jr Col, Hobbs. *Exhib:* Santa Fe Festival of Arts, 79 & 80; Sangre Cristo Art Ctr, Pueblo, Colo, 79; one-woman shows, NMex Jr Col, Hobbs, 81 & Univ Tex Permian Basin, Odessa, 81, Dallas Mus Fine Art, Beaux Arts Ball Art Auction & Exhib, Dallas, Tex, 86-88 & 90; Clayworkers of NMex Invitational Exhib, Governors Gallery, Round House State Capitol, Santa Fe, 95; and many others. *Collection Arranged:* The Round House, State Capitol Bldg, Santa Fe. *Pos:* Artist in sch prog, HEW Emergency Sch Aid Proj, Hobbs, 74-; artist, bd dir, Southwest Symphony, Hobbs, NMex, 88, 90; West States rep, Villa Maria Ctr Arts, Perugia, Italy; arts comnr, NMex, 99-02. *Teaching:* Instr drawing & painting, Col Southwest, NMex, 67-70, instr art hist, 74; instr, Dossant Meadows Mus Art, Dallas, Tex, 90; summer workshops, Cloud Croft, NMex, 89, 91 & 92; drawing instr, Villa Maria Ctr for the Arts, Perugia, Italy, 96; prof, NMex Jr Col, 96-97. *Awards:* Cash Award, Figure Study No 1, 72; First Prize Ceramics, 74 & First Prize Graphics, 75, Llano Estacado Art Asn; Best of Show, ceramics, Llano Estacado Art Asn, 98; Best of Show, oil painting, Llano Estacado Art Asn, 04. *Media:* Drawing; Acrylic, Oil, Clay. *Collection:* Black Gold Casino Race Track; painting, sculpture, etc, NM state capitol bldg, The Round House, Santa Fe, NM. *Dealer:* De-Lis Galleries Hobbs NMex; Old Pecos Gallery Carlsbad NM. *Mailing Add:* 315 E Alto Hobbs NM 88240-3905

GARFIELD, PETER
PAINTER, PHOTOGRAPHER
b Stamford, Conn, 61. *Study:* Dartmouth Col, BA (cum laude), 84; Ecole Nationale Superieure des Beaux-Arts, Paris, France, 85-87; Pratt Inst, Brooklyn, NY, 87. *Work:* San Francisco Mus Mod Art; Los Angeles Co Mus Art; Progressive Corp, Cleveland, Ohio; Howard Stein Collection, NY. *Exhib:* Solo shows, Am Cathedral, Paris, France, 87, Strauss Gallery, Dartmouth Col, 93, Plerogi 2000, Brooklyn, 96 & Felgen Gallery, Chicago, 96, Feigen Contemp, NY, 98,Queens Mus Bulova Cen, NY, 98, Kaplnos Galerie, Berlin, Ger, 99, 2000, Vaknin Schwartz, Atlanta, Ga, 99, Art & Pub, Geneve, Switz, 2000; Planie-Galerie Guth & Maas, Reutlingen, Ger, 96, Feigen Contemp, NY, 98, Queens Mus Bulova Ctr, NY, 98; High Anxiety, Ctr Photog Woodstock, NY, 96; Blind Spot: The First Four Years, Paolo Baldacci Gallery, NY, 96; The Lie of the Land, Univ Art Mus, Univ Calif Santa Barbara, 96; Making it Real (traveling), Aldrich Mus Contemp Art, Reykjavik Munic Art Mus, Iceland, Portland Mus Art, Maine, Yukon Arts Ctr, Can, Virginia Beach Ctr Arts, 97-98; Exterior/Interior: The Way I See It: Five Photographers Working in Brooklyn, Brooklyn Mus Art, NY, 98; Neiborhood Watch, Julie Saul Gallery, NY, 98; NY State Biennial, NY State Mus, Albany; MAYDAY, Cen Art, Neuchatel, Switz, 99; Threshold, Contemp Art Cen Va, Virginia Beach, 2000; WestWecheel-Zum Wert des Junstwerks, Mus Angewandte Kunst, Cologne, Ger, 2001; others. *Collection Arranged:* Bankers Trust Co, New York City; The Equitable Corp, New York City; FRAC Bourgogne, Dijon, France; Los Angeles Co Mus Art, Calif; MacArthur Found, Chicago, Ill; MIT List Visual Arts Cen, Cambridge, Mass; Progressive Corp, Cleveland, Ohio; San Francisco Mus Modern Art, Calif. *Awards:* Visual Arts Fel, Edward F Albee Found, Montauk, NY, 92 & 94; Fel, Nat Endowment Arts, 93-94; MacDowell Colony Studio Residency, Peterboro, NH, 96. *Bibliog:* Ken Johnson (auth), Peter Garfield at Feigen Contemp, NY Times, (p E38), 2/20/98; Vince Aletti (auth), Stuck Inside of Mobile: Peter Garfied, after the fall, Village Voice (p137), 3/10/98; Grady T Turner (auth), House of Shards, World Art, Issue No 18, 64-68, 9/98. *Mailing Add:* 70 Skillman Ave Brooklyn NY 11211-2209

GARHART, MARTIN J
PAINTER
b Deadwood, SDak, July 2, 46. *Study:* student, Univ Wyo, 64-66; SDak State Univ, BA, 69; WVa Univ, MA, 70; Southern Ill Univ, Edwardsville, MFA, 72. *Work:* Libr Cong, Smithsonian Inst, Washington, DC; Brit Mus, London; Calif Palace Legion of Honor, San Francisco. *Exhib:* Drawings USA, 72; Colorprint USA, 73; Bradley Print Show 15th Nat, 74; 2nd NH Int Print Competition, 74; Davidson Nat Print & Drawing Competition, 74; group shows, Flanders Gallery, Minneapolis, Minn, 96, 98 & 99, Place of the Mind, Mansfield Arts Ctr, Ohio, 00, Purdue Univ, West Lafayette, Inc, 00, Foster Art Ctr, Peoria, Ill, 00, others. *Teaching:* From asst to assoc prof art, Kenyon Col, 72-. *Awards:* Spec Purchase Award, Davidson Print & Drawing Competition, 74; Purchase Award, Bradley Print Show 15th Nat, 74; Jurors Award of Merit, 2nd NH Int. *Mem:* Col Art Asn Am; NH Graphic Soc. *Media:* Oil, Watercolor. *Mailing Add:* 100 Woodside Dr Gambier OH 43022

GARMAN, ED
PAINTER, WRITER
b Bridgeport, Conn, July 4, 14. *Study:* Self-taught. *Work:* Sheldon Mem Art Gallery, Univ Nebr, Lincoln; Mus NMex, Santa Fe; Metrop Mus Art, NY; Salt Lake Art Ctr, Utah; Nat Mus Am Art, Washington, DC. *Exhib:* Painters & Sculptures of the Southwest Ann, Mus NMex, 41-44; Solomon Guggenheim Found 5th Ann, NY, 43; Lure of the West, Salt Lake Art Ctr, 70; Masterpieces from the Mus of NMex, Marion Koogler McNay Art Inst, San Antonio, Tex, 70. *Bibliog:* Marilyn Hagberg (auth), Hot Geometry of Ed Garman, San Diego Mag, 9/68; Tiska Blankenship (auth), Ed Garman: Ideal-Modern, Jonson Gallery, Univ NMex. *Mem:* Transcendental Painting Group. *Media:* Acrylic, Gouache. *Res:* 20th century as it pertains to its ideal (Eutopian) aspects. *Publ:* Auth, Art of Raymond Jonson, Painter, 75. *Dealer:* Michael Rosenfeld Gallery 50 W 57th St New York NY 10019

GARNER, JOYCE (CRAIG)
PAINTER
b Covington, Ky, Dec 4, 47. *Study:* Univ Ky, BS, 68. *Work:* University Hosp, Cincinnati, Ohio; US Mission to Europ Community, Brussels, Belg; St Lukes Hosp, Newport, Ky; Southern Progress Collection, Birmingham, Ala. *Comn:* Mural, Balke Properties; St Louis, Mo, 91; 1915 Reminicense, Mackey/Mitchell Architects; Rain or Shine painting & poster, Asn Metrop Sewage Agencies, Washington, 95. *Exhib:* Art Forms 90, Greater Lafayette Mus Art, Ind, 90; All Ky Women's Art Exhib, Headley-Whitney Mus, Lexington, Ky, 91; solo exhib, Headley-Whitney Mus, 92, Jewish Community Ctr, Louisville, 95, Marin-Price Gallery, Chevy Chase, Md, 98; Ladies Lunch: Exploring the Tradition, New Harmony Gallery Contemp Art, Ind, 92; The Marriage Project: a midlife perspective traveling exhib, 95-96; Midwest Mus Am Art, 97. *Awards:* Alternate Visions Grant, Nat Endowment Arts, Rockefeller Found, Warhol Found & NC, SC & Ky Coun Arts, 93; Resident Fel, Hambidge Ctr, 94; The Best Oil Painting, Rockport Publ, 96, The Landscape Inspirations, 97. *Bibliog:* Judy Look (auth), Thats where you'll find me, Louisville Eccentric Observer, 10/23/94; Barney Quick (auth), The big and little enchantments of Joyce Garner, Nuvo, Indianapolis, 6/27/96; Benita Heath (auth), Visual metaphors play in Joyce Garner's work, Lexington Herald-Leader, 9/13/98. *Media:* Oil. *Dealer:* Malton Gallery 2709 Observatory Cincinnati OH 45208; Hot House Gallery 546 S Meridian Suite 511 Indianapolis IN 46225. *Mailing Add:* 7300 Happy Hollow Ln Prospect KY 40059

GARNETT, WILLIAM ASHFORD
PHOTOGRAPHER, EDUCATOR
b Chicago, Ill, Dec 27, 16. *Work:* Smithsonian Inst, Washington; Mus Mod Art & Metrop Mus Art, NY; George Eastman House, Rochester. *Comn:* Photographic mural, Mus Mod Art & State Dept, US Pavillion, Osaka World's Fair; The Searching Eye (film), comn by Saul Bass & Eastman Kodak & From Here to There (film), comn by Saul Bass & United Airlines, NY World's Fair, 64-65; America Begins in New England (aerial essay), Life Mag, 67 & Splendors Where the Eagles Soar (aerial essay), 68. *Exhib:* William Garnett, Aerial Photog, Eastman House, Rochester; The Family of Man & Diogenes IV, Mus Mod Art; Photog & the Am Landscape & photog from mus collection, Mus Mod Art; Smithsonian Air & Space Mus, 82. *Teaching:* Prof design & photography, Univ Calif, Berkeley, 68-84. *Awards:* Ctr Advan Visual Studies Fel, Kepes, Mass Inst Technol, 67-68; Guggenheim Fel, 53, 56 & 75; Lifetime Achievement in Landscape Photog Award, Am Soc Mag Photogr, 83. *Bibliog:* Beaumont Newhall (auth), The History of Photography, Mus Mod Art; Peter Pollack (auth), The Pictorial History of Photography, Abrams; Walker Evans (auth), Over California, Fortune, 3/54. *Collection:* Aerial photography from US, Can, Mex, Japan, Hong Kong, Manila and Australia. *Publ:* Auth, The Extraordinary Landscape: Aerial Photographs of America, New York Graphic Soc, 82; William Garnett Aerial Photographs, Univ Calif Press, 94. *Mailing Add:* 1286 Congress Valley Rd Napa CA 94558

GARNSEY, CLARKE HENDERSON
HISTORIAN, EDUCATOR
b Joliet, Ill, Sept 22, 13. *Study:* Cleveland Inst Art, dipl, 47; Western Reserve Univ, BS(art educ), 47, MA(art hist), 48 & PhD(art hist), 62. *Comn:* Fourteen murals, Volusia Co Schs, Fla, 34-38 & series of etchings of historic locations, Eastern Fla, WPA Fed Art Proj; watercolors, Amarillo Col, Tex. *Exhib:* Daytona Beach Art League Ann Exhib, 34-42; Southern States Art League Ann Exhib, 35-38; Wichita Art Asn Exhib, Kans, 37-38; May Show, Cleveland Mus Art, 49 & 58; Nat Exhib Relig Art, Rochester, NY, 69. *Pos:* Chmn studio work, Amarillo Col, 49-63; chmn art hist, Wichita States Univ, 63-66. *Teaching:* Lectr, Cleveland Mus Art & Cleveland Inst, 57-59; prof art, Univ Tex, El Paso, 66-79, emer prof, 79-. *Awards:* Numerous awards and mentions nationally. *Mem:* Col Art Asn Am; Soc Archit Hist; Tex Fine Arts Asn; Tex Asn Sch of Art; Rio Bravo Watercolorists. *Media:* Watercolor, Enamel. *Res:* Latin American colonial architecture with emphasis on Neo-Classicism. *Mailing Add:* 607 Linda Ave El Paso TX 79922-2018

GAROIAN, CHARLES RICHARD
CONCEPTUAL ARTIST, EDUCATOR
b Fresno, Calif, Nov 7, 43. *Study:* Calif State Univ, Fresno, BA(art), 68, MA(art), with Allen Bertoldi, 69; Stanford Univ, with Elliot W Eisner, PhD(educ), 84. *Exhib:* SECA Exhib, San Francisco Mus Mod Art, 74; Circumstancial Evidence, Birmingham Loft, Pittsburgh, 91; Flayed Ox, Paul Robeson Cult Ctr, Penn State Univ, 92; Butt of the Media in the Face of the Publ, Cleveland Performance Art Festival & Ward-Nasse Gallery, NY, 92; Naked Controversy, Pittsburgh Ctr Arts, Kutztown Univ Art Series, 94; Requiem March, Studio for Creative Inquiry, Carnegie Mellon Univ, 94; and others. *Teaching:* Art, Los Altos High Sch, 69-86; lectr art educ, Univ Washington, Seattle, summer 77; educ dir, Palmer Mus Art, Penn State, 86-90, asst dir, 90-91, assoc prof art educ, Sch Visual Arts, 91-; lectr performance art, Deep Creek Sch, Ariz State

Univ Summer Inst, 92-96. *Awards:* Teacher of the Year Mountain View/Los Altos High Sch Dist, 1976; Pa Coun on Arts grantee, 1986, 87, 88, 90, 91; recipient Creative Prog award Nat Univ Continuing Educ Assoc, 1990, 91; Interdisciplinary Arts Fel, Pa Coun Arts, 93; Fulbright Scholar to Armenia, 94; Research Grant, Getty Educ Inst Arts, 96. *Bibliog:* Paul Blaum (auth), The lonely passion of Charles Garoian, Ararat Quar, spring 91; Amy Sparks (auth), Cleveland Performance Art Fest: Community Outreach or Shotgun Wedding?, summer, 93; Frank Green (auth), Dialogue, Arts in the Midwest, 9/93. *Mem:* Nat Art Educ Asn; Col Art Asn; Int Soc Educ Through Art. *Publ:* Coauth, The Deep Creek School: Technology, Ecology and the Body as Pedagogical Alternatives in Art Education, J Soc; Theory in Art Educ, 94; Censorship in the art classroom, Sch Arts, 1/96, 3/96 & 1/97; A Common Impulse in Art and Science, Leonardo J, 96; auth, Art Education and the Aesthetics of Land Use in the Age of Ecology, Studies in Art Educ, 97; Performance Art: Repositioning the Body in Postmodern Art Education, J Multicultural & Cross-cult Res Art Educ, 97. *Mailing Add:* Pa State Univ Sch of Visual Arts 210 Patterson Bldg State College PA 16802-2502

GARRARD, MARY DUBOSE
HISTORIAN, EDUCATOR
b Greenwood, Miss, July 25, 37. *Study:* Newcomb Col, BA, 58; Harvard Univ, MA, 60; Johns Hopkins Univ, PhD, 70. *Teaching:* From asst prof to prof art hist, Am Univ, Washington, DC, 64-. *Awards:* Mid-Career, Achievement Award, Women's Caucus for Art, 91. *Mem:* Women's Caucus for Art (pres, 74-76); Col Art Asn Am (bd dir, 77-81); Am Asn Univ Prof; Miss Inst Arts & Letters. *Res:* 16th century and 17th century Italian art; feminist and gender studies, 15th-18th century. *Publ:* Auth, Artemisia Gentileschi: The Image of the Female Hero in Italian Baroque Painting, Princeton Univ Press, 89; co-ed, Feminism and Art History: Questioning the Litany, Harper & Row, 82; auth, The liberal arts and Michelangelo's first project for the tomb of Julius II, Viator: Medieval & Renaissance Studies, 84; co-ed, The Expanding Discourse: Feminism and Art History, Harper Collins, 92; The Power of Feminist Art, Abrams, 94. *Mailing Add:* 2915 NW University Terr Washington DC 20016

GARRETT, JOHN
CRAFTSMAN
b El Paso, Tex, 50. *Study:* Claremont McKenna Col, Calif, 72; Univ Calif, Los Angeles, MA, 76. *Work:* High Mus Art, Atlanta; Oakland Mus, Calif; Am Craft Mus, NY; Craft & Folk Art Mus, Los Angeles; Albuquerque Mus Art, NMex; and many others. *Exhib:* Renwick Gallery, Nat Mus Am Art, Washington, DC, 88; Union des Arts Decoratifs, Paris, 89; solo exhibs, Katie Gingrass Gallery, Milwaukee, 91, Suzanne Brown Gallery, Scottsdale, Ariz, 91, Schneider-Bluhm-Loeb Gallery, Chicago, 92, Worth Gallery, Taos, NMex, 92 & Connell Gallery, Atlanta, 93; Third Ann Basketry Invitational, Sybaris Gallery, Royal Oak, Mich, 92; Fittings, Farrell Collection, Washington, 92; Baskets: Redefining Volume & Meaning, Manoa Art Gallery, Univ Hawaii, Honolulu, 93; USA Today, The Neth Textile Mus, Tilburg, 93. *Teaching:* Scripps Col, Claremont, Calif, 78-79; instr, Univ Calif, Los Angeles, 81-88. *Awards:* Nat Endowment Arts Fel, 83

GARRISON, BARBARA
PRINTMAKER, ILLUSTRATOR
b London, Eng, Aug 22, 31. *Study:* Wellesley Col, Mass, BA, 53; Columbia Univ, MA, 56; Pratt Graphics Ctr. *Work:* De Grummond Collection, Univ Southern Miss; Mus Am Illust, NY; Mazza Collection, Univ Findley, Ohio; Mus of Am Illustration, NY; Skirball Mus, Los Angeles, Calif. *Comn:* Unicef Cards, Carnegie Hall Stage Bill (cover), Unum (Mag Cover). *Exhib:* Mini-Gravat Int, Barcelona, Spain, 84; Int Miniature Print, Seoul, Korea, 84; Int Miniature Print, Pratt Graphics Ctr, NY, 84-85; Statue of Liberty Traveling Exhib, 86; Soc Illusrs Ann, NY, 86. *Teaching:* Instr art, Spence Sch, 63-69, Nightingale-Bamford Sch, 70-78, NY. *Awards:* IAGA Award, 78; New York Times 10 Best Illus Books, 92; Ezra Jack Keets Unicef Award, 92; ALA Pick of the Lists Award, 95, 96 & 97. *Mem:* Soc Illusrs; Artists Equity NY; Graphic Artists Guild. *Media:* Etching, Collagraph. *Publ:* Only One, Cobble Hill, 92; My First Book of Jewish Holidays, Dial, 94; Josiah True & the Art Maker, Simon & Schuster, NY, 95; Look at the Moon, Mondo Publ, 96; One Room School, Boyds Mills, 97; The Frog House, Dutton, 04. *Mailing Add:* 12 E 87th St No 3C New York NY 10128

GARRISON, DAVID EARL
PAINTER, MURALIST
b Jacksonville, Ill, Mar 23, 40. *Study:* Am Acad Art, studied pastel with Daniel Green & watercolor with Irving Shapiro, 64-68; Anatomy with Bill Parks; Iowa Wesleyan Col, BA, 87; art study in Mex. *Work:* Marriott Hotel Corp; Holiday Inn Corp; United Airlines; Iowa's Sesquicentennial Mural. *Comn:* Hist mural, Iowa Welcome Ctr; Iowa Sesquicentennial Mural. *Exhib:* Nat Artists Prof League Exhib, NY, 87-90 & 92-94; Xi'an China Exhib, Pastel Soc Am, NY, 88-98; Oil Painters Am Exhibs, Chicago, Ill, 2000 & San Antonio, Tex, 2000; Pastels toured France, 2002, Italy & Russia, 2003; Butler Inst Am Art, 2003; Pastel Soc France, 2003. *Teaching:* Instr, Iowa Arts Coun, Des Moines, 79, 94, 98; Attitude for Artist, workshops across country; Teach the Teachers, Amana (Iowa) Colonies. *Awards:* Pastel Soc Am Award, 96 & 97; Wyo Conservation Stamp, 2000. *Mem:* Am Artist Prof League (signature mem, award, 2000); Pastel Soc Am (signature mem); Hudson Valley Art Asn. *Media:* Oil, Pastel; Acrylic. *Publ:* Auth, The Best of Oils, The Best of Pastels, Rockport Publ, 96; article, Artist's Mag, 3/98. *Dealer:* Carol Brown 2009 S Central Ave Burlington IA 52601. *Mailing Add:* 831 S Garfield Burlington IA 52601

GARRISON, GENE K
PHOTOGRAPHER, PAINTER, WRITER
b Aug 11, 25. *Study:* Ariz State Univ; Phoenix Col, AFA; Glendale Community Col; study with Bill Ahrendt, Jason Williamson, Finae Frei, Jan Sitts, Helen del Grosso, Linae Frei & Joella Jean Mahoney; Yavapari Community Col. *Exhib:* Art Barn ana Art Room, Cave Creek, Ariz; Conrad's Imagine & Es Posible, El Pedregal, N Scottsdale, Ariz; Cactus Shadows Fine Art Ctr, Cave Creek, Ariz; Cave Creek Mus, Ariz; Sedona Arts Center, Ariz; Cactus Shadows Fine Arts Ctr; Sedona City Hall, Ariz. *Pos:* Cur, various art shows. *Teaching:* Volunteer art teacher, spec educ handicapped children, Desert Arroyo Middle Sch, Cave Creek, Ariz; tutor The Literacy Ctr, Sedona, Ariz. *Mem:* Sedona Art Center; Soc Layerist in Multi-Media; Oak Creek Canyon Camera Club; Prof Writers Prescott. *Media:* Photography, Oils, Acrylics, Multi-Media. *Specialty:* Eclectic Galleries. *Publ:* Various articles on artists & art shows published in magazines such as Carefree Enterprise & Antiques World; coauth, From Thunder to Breakfast, 77; auth, Javelina Have-uh-What?; auth, Widowhood Happens, Xlibris Corp, 2002; auth, There's Something About Cave Creek, 2006. *Mailing Add:* 495 Rodeo Rd Sedona AZ 86336-3369

GARTEL, LAURENCE M
COMPUTER ARTIST, PHOTOGRAPHER
b New York, NY, June 5, 56. *Study:* Art Students League, with Knox Martin, 75; Sch Visual Arts, with Al Brunelle, George Trakas, Bill Beckley & Cora Kennedy, BFA, 77. *Work:* Calif State Univ, Long Beach; Polaroid Corp, Cambridge, Mass; Lending Collection, Mus Mod Art, NY; Universita Degli Studi Di Camerino, Italy; Dept Housing, City Univ New York. *Comn:* Absolut Gartel, Absolut Vodka; Miami Int Airport. *Exhib:* Exchange of Information, Mus Mod Art, NY, 90; Nuvo Japonica & Other Cybernetic Romances, Norton Gallery Art, West Palm Beach, Fla, 91; Nuvo Japonica & Other Cybernetic Romances, Ringling Sch Art, Sarasota, Fla, 92; Masur Mus Art, Monroe, La, 94; A Cybernetic Romance, Palm Beach Int Airport, Fla, 95; Am Haus, Frankfurt & Berlin, 97; Galerie Posteria, Milan, Italy, 98; Palm Beach Photog Mus, DelRay Beach, Fla, 2001; Gallery of Fine Art, Edison Col, Ft Myers, Fla, 2003; Colo Springs Mus of Art, Fla, 2004; Gallery of Fine Art, Edison, Col, Ft Myers, Fla, 2003; Coral Springs Mus of Art, Fla, 2004. *Collection Arranged:* Bibliotheque Nationale, Paris; Smithsonian Inst Mus of Am History, Wash DC. *Awards:* Residency Grant, Experimental Television Ctr, Owego, 78-92; Poster Award, Art Director's Club, NJ, 85; Artist-in-Residency Grant, NY State Coun Arts, 85. *Bibliog:* End of artistic barbarians, Computerworld, Australia, 85; Mary Ann Marger (auth), Computer art, St Petersburg Times, Tampa, Fla, 87; Helen Harrison (auth), Mod Romance, Via Computer, NY Times, 10/88; Gartel: Arte and Technologia, Edizioni Mazzotta, Italy, 98. *Mem:* Electronic Design Ast, Boca Raton, Fla. *Media:* Computer Graphics. *Publ:* Auth & illusr, The incubation of electronic imaging, Photomethods, 82; illusr, Laurence Gartel video, fantasy or future?, Camera Weekly, Eng, 82; coauth & illusr, Fantasia Ben Calcolata, PM Mag, Italy, 83; auth, Laurence M Gartel: A Cybernetic Romance, Gibbs Smith, Utah, 89; Laurence Gartel, the CD, Diamar, Seattle, 97. *Dealer:* Corporate Art Directions New York. *Mailing Add:* PO Box 970761 Boca Raton FL 33497

GARTEN, CLIFF
SCULPTOR
b Ridgewood, NJ, May 3, 54. *Study:* State Univ NY, Col Ceramics, Alfred, NY, BFA, 74; RI Sch Design, MFA, 78. *Work:* Everson Mus Art, Syracuse, NY. *Comn:* Ceramic Installation, Meyer, Scherer and Rockcastle Ltd Archit Offices, 88; study garden, Brainerd Community Col, Minn, 91; entry plaza, Beaverton City Hall, Ore, 92; design & sculpture, St Paul Cult Garden, Minn, 92-93; coordr, Rising From the River, Places in St Paul, Minn, 94-95. *Exhib:* Solo exhibs, Rochester Art Ctr, Minn, 81, Paired Vases, Minneapolis Col Art & Design, Minn, 85, Situations, Thomson Gallery, Minneapolis, Minn, 86 & New Sculpture, Carleton Col, Northfield, Minn, 90; Nat Endowment Arts Regional Fel Exhib, traveling exhib, 86; Midwestern Sculpture Competition, South Bend Art Ctr, 90; The Evasive Vase, ProArt Gallery, St Louis, Mo, 91; Am Ceramics, Tweed Mus Art, Duluth, Minn, 93; Architectural Clay, Clay Studio, Philadelphia, Pa, 93; and others. *Pos:* Mem bd dir, Pub Art, St Paul, Minn, 87-. *Teaching:* Teaching fel ceramics, RI Sch Design, Providence, RI, 75-78; prof art, Hamline Univ, St Paul, Minn, 78-. *Awards:* Visual Artists Fel Grant, Nat Endowment Arts, 86; Bush Found Artist Fel, 94-95; Hist Preservation Award, Am Inst Art, St Paul Cult Garden, 94. *Bibliog:* Podas-Larson residence, Archit Minn, 9-10/91; Conversation with Regina Flanagan, Archit Minn, 3-4/92; Regina Flanagan (auth), Artists Cultivate New Garden Forms, Pub Art Rev, fall/winter/93. *Mem:* Pub Art St Paul (bd dir, 87-). *Publ:* The History of American Ceramics: 1607 to the Present, Harry N Abrams, Inc, New York, 88; American Ceramics, The Collection of the Everson Museum of Art, ed, Barbra Perry, Rizzoli, New York, 89; The Avant Garde & The Landscape, Can They Be Reconciled, Landworks Press, Minneapolis, Minn, 90

GARVENS, ELLEN
PHOTOGRAPHER
b Omro, Wis. *Study:* Univ NMex, Albuquerque, MA, 82, MFA, 88. *Exhib:* Solo exhibs, Am Cult Ctr, Cameroon, WAfrica, 80, New Ctr Contemp Arts, Santa Fe, NMex, 85, Jayne H Baum Gallery, 87, 89 & 93, Fine Art Ctr Galleries, Univ RI, 93 & Art Mus, Col Wooster, 94, 1st St Gallery, 01, Dolby Chadwick Gallery, San Francisco, 01; Spaces Gallery, Cleveland, Ohio, 92; In Camera, Mus Fine Arts, Santa Fe, NMex, 93; The Global Environment, Fotofest, Houston, Tex, 94; Certain Uncertainties, Bowdoin Col Mus Art, New Brunswick, Maine, 95; Jacob Lawrence Gallery, Univ Wash, Seattle, 96. *Teaching:* Asst prof art, Oberlin Col, Ohio, Univ Wash, Seattle, currently. *Awards:* HC Powers Grant, Oberlin Col, 90; B Wade & Jane B White Fel in Humanities, Oberlin Col, 91; Royalty Res Fund, Univ Wash, 96; Artists Trust Fel, 00. *Bibliog:* Barry Schwabsky (auth), NY reviews, Sculpture Mag, 3/93; William Messer (auth), New Art Examiner, 95; article, Creative Camera, 10-11/98; Geoffrey Camera (auth), Creative Camera, 99; Ellen Garvens (auth) Morphic Resonance Creative Camera, 98. *Mem:* Soc Photogr Educ; Col Art Assoc. *Publ:* Article, Art on Paper, 1-2/99. *Dealer:* Jayne H Baum New York NY. *Mailing Add:* Univ Wash Sch Art Seattle WA 98195

GARVER, FANNY
ART DEALER
b Racine, Wis, Apr 3, 27. *Study:* Univ Wis, BA, 49, BLS, 50; Middlebury Col, Vt. *Collection Arranged:* Regional Artists of Wisconsin (auth, catalog), 77 & Nineteenth Century British Watercolour Drawings, Fanny Garver Gallery, Madison, Wis; John Wilde and His Students; Harold Altman Retrospective. *Pos:* Dir, Jane Haslem Gallery, 69-72; founder, dir & pres, Fanny Garver Gallery, 72-2000; vpres, Garver Crafts, 85. *Awards:* Artful Woman of the Year, Nat Women's Political Caucus Dane Co, 96. *Mem:* Art Inst Chicago; Am Craft Coun; Madison Print Club (mem chmn); Milwaukee Art Ctr; Madison Art Ctr. *Specialty:* 19th century British, Wisconsin and regional artists; American fine arts crafts; Oil. *Publ:* Auth, Master Prints, 82 & Fanny Garver Collection of American Crafts, 85, Fanny Garver Gallery, Madison, Wis. *Mailing Add:* 230 State St Madison WI 53703

GARVER, THOMAS H
CONSULTANT, CURATOR
b Duluth, Minn, Jan 23, 34. *Study:* Barnes Found, Merion, Pa; Haverford Col, BA; Univ Minn, MA; Mus Mgt Inst, Univ Calif, Berkeley, 79. *Collection Arranged:* George Tooker Retrospective, Fine Arts Mus San Francisco, 74; New Photography: San Francisco & Bay Area, 74; Representations of America (co-organized with Henry Geldzabler, co-auth, catalog), traveling USSR, 77-78; Joseph Raffael, The California Years, 1969-78 (auth, catalog), San Francisco Mus Mod Art, 78 & Nathan Oliveira, 84; Sylvia Pilmack Mangold, Madison Art Ctr, 82; Corp Art Collection, Rayovac Corp, Madison, Wis, 85; Regarding Art: Artworks about Art, John Michael Kohler Arts Ctr, Sheboygan, Wis, 90; Mind and Beast: Contemporary Artists and the Animal Kingdom (auth, catalog), Leigh Yawkey Woodson Art Mus, Wausau, Wis, 92; Flora, Contemporary Artists and the world of flowers, Leigh Yawkey Woodson Art Mus, Wausau, Wis, 95; Trains that passed in the night, the Railroad Photography of O Winston Link, Sheldon Mem Art Gallery, Univ Nebr, Lincoln, Nebr, 98; Water: A Contemporary American View, Gibbes Mus Art, Charleston, SC, 99. *Pos:* Asst to dir, Krannert Art Mus, Univ Ill, 60-62; asst dir, Seattle World's Fair, 62 & Rose Art Mus, 62-68; dir, Newport Harbor Art Mus, Newport Beach, Calif, 68-72 & 77-80 & Madison Art Ctr, Wis, 80-87; consult art gallery design, Univ Chicago, Calif Inst Arts, 69 & ARCO Ctr Visual Arts, 73; cur exhibs, Fine Arts Mus San Francisco, 72-77; site visitor, Mus Accreditation Prog, Am Asn Mus; Consulting Org Cur, O Winston Link Mus, Roanoke, VA, 2002-04. *Teaching:* Hist of art & museology, Calif State Univs, Long Beach & Fullerton, San Quentin Prison, through Col Marin, Kentfield & Univ Wis, Madison. *Res:* Contemporary American art. *Publ:* Auth, Nathan Oliveira, Survey Exhib (catalog essay), San Francisco Mus Mod Art, 84; George Tooker, Clarkson N Potter, Inc, Publ, 85, rev 92; Mind and Beast: Contemporary Artists and the Animal Kingdom, Leigh Yawkey Woodson Art Mus, Wausau, Wis, 92; The Last Steam Railroad in America: Photographs by O Winston Link, Harry N Abrams Inc, 95; Intro to Invisible New York: The Hidden Infrastructure of the City, John Hopkins Univ Press, Baltimore, 98; intro to In The Traces: The Railroad Paintings of Ted Rose, Ind Univ Press, Bloomington, 2000; Intro to Doubletake- A Rephotographic Survey of the City of Madison, WI, 1925-2000, Univ Wisc. Press; Intro to Joseph Goldyne, Washington, DC, The Corcoran Gallery of Art, 2003; O Winston Link The Man and The Mus, O Winston Link Mus, 2004. *Mailing Add:* 1962 Atwood Ave Madison WI 53704

GARVER, WALTER RAYMOND
PAINTER, WRITER
b Medina, NY, 27. *Study:* State Univ NY Buffalo, BFA, 55; also with Charles Burchfield, 50. *Work:* Butler Inst Am Art, Youngstown, Ohio; Minn Mus Art, St Paul; Cincinnati Univ; Indiana Univ Pa; Burchfield-Penney Ctr, Buffalo, NY. *Exhib:* Nat Acad Design Ann, NY, 56, 60, 70, 71 & 75; Chautauqua Nat Exhib, NY, 58-; one-man show, Albright-Knox Art Gallery, 72 & 90; Okla Art Ctr Ann, Oklahoma City, 81 & 83; Audubon Artists Ann, NY, 83-2003; Am Watercolor Soc, 85 & 86; and many others. *Pos:* Contrib ed, Artist's Mag, 86-06. *Teaching:* Teacher art hist, drawing, painting & photog, Amherst Sr High Sch, Snyder, NY, 58-85, chmn art dept. *Awards:* Remy Award, Am Watercolor Soc Ann Exhib, 85; Gilmore-Romans Mem Award, Allied Artists Ann Exhib, 94; Gold Medal of Hon, Audubon Artists Annual Exhib, 2003. *Mem:* Buffalo Soc Artists (pres, 64); Audubon Artists; Nat Watercolor Soc; Allied Artists Am; Copley Soc Boston. *Media:* Oil, Watercolor. *Res:* Continued research on the lives of master watercolor painters for the Meet the Masters column in Watercolor Magic Magazine. *Publ:* Numerous articles & reviews in The Artist's Mag & Watercolor Magic; contrib ed, Watercolor Magic mag, 1999-, Artist's Mag, 1986-1999, Magic Mag, 99-2006. *Dealer:* Vern Stein Fine Arts 5747 Main St Williamsville NY 14221; Oxford Gallery 267 Oxford St Rochester NY 14607. *Mailing Add:* 4230 Tonawanda Creek Rd East Amherst NY 14051

GARWOOD, AUDREY
PAINTER, PRINTMAKER
b Toronto, Ont, July 7, 27. *Study:* Ont Col Art; Rijksacad, Amsterdam, scholar; Le Chaumiere, Paris. *Work:* London Gallery & Art Mus, Ont; McLaughlin Art Gallery, Oshawa, Ont; Burnaby Art Gallery, BC; Hamilton Art Gallery, Ont; Ont Art Gallery, Toronto. *Exhib:* Royal Can Acad; Ont Soc Artists; York Univ Hayward State, Calif; San Francisco Univ, Calif; Nat Gallery Showcase, Ottawa. *Teaching:* Life painting & printmaking, Central Tech, Toronto, 65-71; Calif Col of Arts, Crafts, Advan Painting, Landscape painting, 76-78. *Awards:* Can Graphic Art Soc Award; Sterling Trust Award, Can Painters & Etchers; J Forester Award, Ont Soc Artists. *Mem:* Royal Can Acad Art; Ont Soc Art. *Media:* Oil, Watercolor

GARWOOD, DEBORAH A
CONCEPTUAL ARTIST, WRITER
b Camden, NJ, July 8, 56. *Study:* Oberlin Col, BA, 78; Hunter Col, City Univ of NY, MFA, 88. *Hon Degrees:* Nova Scotia Col Art & Design, Halifax, Can, cert, 76; Brooklyn Mus Art Sch, NY, cert, 79. *Work:* Evans Pond, NJ; A Long Term Study of a Single Place, 1997-on going; Paris Solstice, 2003 (photography). *Exhib:* Western Agenda, Artists Space, NY, 91; Salon Show, Art in General, NY, 92; solo exhib, Franklin Furnace, New York City, 84, Scott Pfaffman Gallery, New York City, 98; 4 Walls Slide & Film Club, Brooklyn, NY 2001; A Ramona Studio, 01; Lindsey Brown Gallery, 02; Magdalena Col, Oxford, Eng, 03; Makor Gallery, NY, 2004; Sullivan Co Art Mus, NY, 2004; Artist In Residence, Chashama, Inc NY. *Collection Arranged:* Hunter Col Print Gallery, New York; Mus Mod Art Libr, New York; Haddonfield Hist Soc, Haddonfield, NJ; NY Pub Libr, Spencer & Berg Collections, New York; El Archivero Museo De Ante Carrillo Gil, San Angel, Mex; Pierogi Flat Files, Brooklyn, NY; Sewing, 84. *Teaching:* Instr Cooper Union Continuing Edn, NYC, 93. *Awards:* Robert Smithson Meml Scholarship for sculpture, Brooklyn Mus, 78. *Bibliog:* Connie Butler (auth), Western Agenda, Artists Space, 91; Calvin Reid (auth), Mo' Art, Art in General, 93. *Mem:* Col Art Asn. *Media:* Photography, Drawing, New Media. *Res:* Interdisciplinary 19th century studies; theatrical innovation and early modernism in Paris; contemporary cultural theory. *Interests:* Philosophy, natural history, history of science. *Publ:* William Henry Fox Tabot at ICP and Susan Derges at Paul Kasmin, www.artcritical.com, 3/03; Bower of Bliss (catalog essay), Cynthia Broan Gallery, 02; Stephen Mueller (catalog essay), Bill Maynes Gallery, 01; A Liturgy of Division (article), PAJ: A Journal of Performance and Art, 9/01; The Dining Room as Celestial Vault in Marcel Proust's In Search of Lost Time, Memorie della Societa Astronomica, Italy, 2004; Paris Solstice, Canopus Press, Bristol, 2005. *Dealer:* Leslie Lund, New York, NY. *Mailing Add:* 432 E 11th St Apt 3RB New York NY 10009

GARY, JAN (MRS WILLIAM D GORMAN)
PAINTER, PRINTMAKER
b Ft Worth, Tex, Feb 13, 1925. *Study:* Art Ctr Sch, Los Angeles; San Antonio Art Inst, Tex; Art Students League. *Work:* Butler Inst Am Art, Youngstown, Ohio; Pensacola Art Ctr, Fla; Wis State Univ, Eau Claire; Brandeis Univ, Waltham, Mass; Rosenberg Libr, Galveston, Tex. *Exhib:* One-person show, Caldwell Col, NJ, 78; Am Acad Arts & Lett, 67-68; Four NJ Artists, Canton Art Inst, Ohio, 71; Cent Wyo Mus Art, Casper, 75; Charles & Emma Frye Mus Art, Seattle, Wash, 77; and others. *Pos:* Assoc dir, Old Bergen Art Guild, Bayonne, NJ, 62-90. *Awards:* Childe Hassam Fund Purchase Award, Am Acad Arts & Lett, 68; Dorothy F Seligson Mem Prize, Nat Asn Women Artists Ann, 75; David Soloway Mem Award, Allied Artists Am, 85. *Bibliog:* Henry Gasser (auth), article, Am Artist, 10/70. *Mem:* hon mem, Audubon Artists; hon mem Allied Artists Am; hon mem Am Watercolor Soc. *Media:* Acrylic, Casein; Woodcut. *Mailing Add:* 43 W 33rd St Bayonne NJ 07002

GARZA LAGUERA, EUGENIO
COLLECTOR
b Monterrey, Dec 18, 1926. *Study:* Studied industrial chemical engineering at Instituto Tecnologico y Estudios Superiores de Monterrey. *Pos:* Laboratorist, Tecnica, 47, pres, 63; mem bd dirs, Visa Group, 96, pres bd, 81; joined FEMSA, Mexico, 46, chmn, Mexico, formerly, hon life chmn bd, Mexico, 2001-; chmn, Bancomer, SA, formerly, hon life chmn, currently; chmn, Financiera de Credito de Monterrey, formelry, Valores Industriales, S.A., Banca Serfin; hon life chairman ITESM; pres, EISAC, currently. *Awards:* Named one of Top 200 Collectors, ARTnews magazine, 2004, 2006. *Collection:* Contemporary and 20th-century Mexican art. *Mailing Add:* FEMSA General Anaya No 601 Pte Col Bella Vista Monterrey Nuevo Leon Mexico CP 64410

GARZIO, ANGELO C
POTTER, CRAFTSMAN
b Campobasso, Italy, July, 22, 22. *Study:* Syracuse Univ, NY, BA, BS (libr sci), 49; Univ Iowa, MA (art hist), 54, MFA (ceramics), 55; Arabia Pottery, Helsinki, Finland, 56-57; Hochsch Keramicks, Höhr-Grenzhausen, Ger, 60-61, postgrad, Faenza, Italy, 65. *Work:* Mus Contemp Crafts, NY; Wichita Art Asn; Univ Art Mus, Hong Ik, Seoul, SKorea; Art Mus, Univ Benin, Benin; Everson Mus, Syracuse, NY; and others. *Exhib:* Biannual Nat Ceramic Exhib, Syracuse Mus Art, NY, 56, 58, 62, 64 & 66; Fiber-Clay-Metal Nat Craft Exhib, St Paul Art Mus, Minn, 57; Invitational Int Exhib, Brussel's World Fair Art Pavillion, Belg, 58-59; Smithsonian Inst, Washington, 60, 62 & 63; Ceramic Arts USA, Int Mineral Corp Mus, Skokie, Ill, 66; 24th, 25th, 28th & 31st Int Ceramic Competition, Int Ceramic Mus, Faenza, Italy, 68, 69, 72 & 75; Sargadelos Gallery, Madrid, Spain, 89. *Collection Arranged:* Syracuse Everson Mus, NY; Univ Iowa Mus Fine Art; Wichita Art Asn Collection, Kan; Utah State Univ, Logan; Univ Utah, Salt Lake City. *Teaching:* Prof ceramic art, Kans State Univ, 57-92, prof emer, 92-; vis lectr & prof ceramic art, Hong Ik Univ, Seoul, Korea, 73-74; lectr & dept head, Dept Indus Design, Ahmadu Bello Univ, Nigeria, 77-78; lectr & prof ceramic art, Univ Misiones, Arg, 92. *Awards:* Faculty Res Grant, Kans State U., 66. *Bibliog:* Sandra B Ernst (auth), Angelo Garzio, Ceramics Monthly, Vol 29, No 1, 81; LuAnn F Culley (auth), Angelo Garzio: Life as the ultimate art form, Kans Quart, Vol 14, No 4, 82; Antonio Vivas (auth), Angelo Garzio, Ceramica, Madrid, Spain, Vol 6, No 22, 85. *Mem:* Nat Conf Educ Ceramic Art; Kans Artist Craftsman Asn (vpres, 63-64). *Media:* Clay. *Res:* Faculty Res Grant; State Univ, 1962; Salt Glazing Teniques at Cones. *Publ:* Auth, German salt glazing, Craft Horizons, Vol 13, No 3, 63; Raku (portfolio feature article), Ceramics Monthly, Vol 15, No 6, 67; Kansang Mus Collection of Koryo Celadons, Korea J, Vo 14, No 7, 74; A Man & A Kiln: Mark Zamantakis, NZ Potter, Vol 26, No 1, 84; Antonio Prieto: In retrospect, Ceramica, Spain, Vol 6, No 23, 86. *Dealer:* Pewabic Pottery 10125 E Jefferson Detroit MI 48214; Clay Pidgeon Gallery Denver CO; Collections Gallery, Topeka, Kans. *Mailing Add:* 1902 Blue Hills Rd Manhattan KS 66501-4503

GARZON-BLANCO, ARMANDO
DESIGNER, PAINTER
b Havana, Cuba, Feb 1, 41. *Study:* La State Univ, BA, 66, MA(design), 68, MA(art hist), 69, PhD(theatre-art), 76; Fulbright-Hays Res Grant, Spain, 72-73, La State Univ Coun on Res & Rodriguez-Acosta Fund Grants, Spain, 74. *Work:* Centroplex, Baton Rouge; Anglo-Am Mus & Univ Libr, La State Univ, Baton Rouge; Cath Student Ctr, Baton Rouge. *Comn:* Baptistry murals, St Paul Cath Church, Baton Rouge, 70; sanctuary & chapel, Christ the King Chapel, Baton Rouge, 73-75; altarpiece, St James Lutheran Church, Gonzales, La, 77. *Exhib:* Jay Broussard Mem Gallery, State La Dept Art, Hist & Cult Preserv, 72; US Cult Ctr of Am Embassy, Madrid, Spain, 73; Fundacion Rodriguez-Acosta Banco de Granada Gallery, Spain, 73. *Teaching:* From instr to prof design, painting & art hist, La State Univ, Baton Rouge, 68-77; prof design, painting & art hist & head art dept, Nicholls State Univ, Thibodaux, 77-. *Awards:* Purchase Award, 2nd Ann Int La Watercolor Soc, 71. *Bibliog:* Miguel Rodriguez-Acosta Carlstrom (auth), Los artistas por el sureste espanol, Banco de Granada & Fundacion Rodriguez-Acosta, Spain, 73. *Mem:* La Watercolor Soc; SCent Renaissance Asn; Col Art Asn Am; Northeastern Mod Lang Asn; Nat Coun Art Adminr. *Media:* Watercolor, Mixed Media. *Res:* Interrelation of the theatre arts and visual arts; Spanish Jesuit theatrical practice in the 16th and 17th century; Afro-Cuban art. *Publ:* Auth, Note on the authorship of the Spanish Jesuit play of San Hermenegildo, Theatre Survey, 74; The Tragedia de San Hermenegildo, Seville, 1590, Explorations in Renaissance Culture, 76; La Tragedia de San Hermenegildo en el teatro y en el arte, Estudios sobre literatura y arte dedicados al profesor, Emilio Orozco Diaz, II, Universidad de Granada, 79. *Mailing Add:* PO Box 31 Tucson AZ 85702

GASPARRO, FRANK
SCULPTOR, INSTRUCTOR
b Philadelphia, Pa, Aug 26, 09. *Study:* Pa Acad Fine Arts; also with Charles Grafly. *Comn:* Designed reverse of Kennedy Half-Dollar, Am Numismatic Asn Medal, 69, obverse & reverse of President Richard M Nixon Medal, 69, obverse & reverse of Eisenhower Dollar & reverse of Lincoln Mem US One Cent; designed obverse & reverse of Susan B Anthony One Dollar, 79; Statue of Liberty Commemorative Medal Series, 86; reverse of Isabella & Columbus $2500 Proof Gold Coin, Bahamas, 87; also many medals for US mint. *Exhib:* Philadelphia Mus Art Sculpture Exhib, 40; Pa Acad Fine Arts, Philadelphia, 46; Medals at French Mint, Paris, 50; Spanish Int Medallic Art Exhib, Madrid, 52 & 68; Woman on the Medal, Int Medallic Exhib. *Pos:* Engraver, US Mint, Philadelphia, 42-65, chief engraver, 65-81. *Teaching:* Instr, Fleisher Art Sch, Philadelphia, 46-; instr, Pa Acad Fine Arts, 81. *Awards:* Order of Merit, Ital Repub (Cavaliere Ufficiale), 73; Citation for Super Performance of the US Treasury, 77; Percy Owenx Award Outstanding Artist, Pa, 79; plus others. *Mem:* Soc Medalists; Fr Soc of the Medal. *Media:* All. *Mailing Add:* 216 Westwood Park Dr Havertown PA 19083

GAST, CAROLYN BARTLETT (LUTZ)
ILLUSTRATOR, ILLUMINATOR
b Cambridge, Mass, Apr 30, 29. *Study:* Col Practical Arts & Lett, Boston Univ, BS(bk illus), 50. *Work:* Nat Mus Natural Hist, Smithsonian Inst & US Geol Surv, US Dept Interior, Washington. *Exhib:* Seventeenth Area Exhib Corcoran Gallery Art, Washington, 65; Scientific Illus, Nat Mus Natural Hist, Smithsonian Inst, 68; Ann Exhibs Asn Med Illusr, 69-79; one-women shows, Kotor, Yugoslavia, 70 & Tyler Gallery, NVa Community Col & Cosmos Club, Washington, 85; Nat Exhibs, Guild Natural Sci Illusr, 79 & 81-85; 30 Yr Retrospective, Nat Mus Nat Hist, Smithsonian Inst, 84; invitational exhib, Guild Natural Sci Illusr, Nat Acad Sci, 85; Nat Exhib, Calligraphers Guild, Washington, 86; Eyes on Sci: Illustrating Natural Hist, Nat Mus Nat Hist, Smithsonian Inst, 96. *Pos:* Scientific illusr, US Geol Surv, Dept Interior, 52-56 & Nat Mus Natural Hist, Smithsonian Inst, 59-85. *Awards:* Hon Mention in Sculpture, 17th Area Exhib Corcoran Gallery Art, Washington, 65; First Place, Nat Exhibs, Guild Nat Sci Illusr, 79 & 82. *Mem:* Founding mem Guild of Natural Sci Illusr (vpres, 71-73, pres, 73-75); Nat Stereoscopic Asn. *Media:* Mixed. *Publ:* numerous scientific publications and journals, 59-85; Illusr, Smithsonian Contributions to Zoology, 67-85; Mary S Gardiner's The Biology of the Invertebrates, McGraw-Hill, 72; The Guild Handbook of Scientific Illustration, New York, Van Nostrand Reinhold, 89; auth & illustr, Stero World, Vol 18, No 1, 3/4-91. *Mailing Add:* 5730 First St S Arlington VA 22204

GAST, MICHAEL CARL
PAINTER
b Chicago, Ill, June 11, 30. *Study:* Sch Art Inst Chicago, BFA, 52; Univ Am, Mex, MFA(cum laude), 60. *Exhib:* Washington Watercolor Asn 66th Ann Nat Exhib, Smithsonian Inst, 63 & Metrop Area Exhib, Howard Univ, Washington, DC, 70; Soc Washington Artists 70th & 71st Ann Exhib, Smithsonian Inst, 63 & 64; four-man show, Mickelson Gallery, Washington, DC, 66; Foundry Gallery, Washington, DC, 80; Downtown Gallery, Del Art Mus, Wilmington, Del, 80; Portraits, Gallery 10 Ltd, Washington, DC, 85; A Tribute to Isobel MacKinnon, Sch Art Inst Chicago Gallery, 85; Art Inst Chicago Alumni Exhib, Parish Gallery, Washington, DC, 98. *Pos:* Mus technician, div ceramics & glass, Nat Mus Hist & Technol, Smithsonian Inst, 61-64 & mus specialist, Nat Collection Fine Arts, 69-71. *Teaching:* Asst prof painting, George Washington Univ, 71. *Bibliog:* Andrea O Cohen (auth), article, Washington DC Gazette, 4/19/72. *Mem:* Artists Equity Asn (chap vpres, 73-77, nat secy-treas, 75-79, nat pres, 79-81). *Media:* Polymer, Oil. *Publ:* Contribr, Fed Art Patronage Notes, 77, Ceramics Monthly, 78 & Artists Equity Asn Nat Newsletter, 77-81. *Mailing Add:* 5730 First St S Arlington VA 22204

GATES , BILL (WILLIAM HENRY) & MELINDA FRENCH, III
COLLECTOR
b Bill, Seattle, Wash, Oct 28, 55 b Melinda, Dallas, Tex. *Study:* Bill: Harvard Univ, 75; Melinda: Duke Univ, BS(computer sci & econ), 86, MBA, 87. *Pos:* Bill: Co-founder, Traf-O-Data Co, Seattle, 72-73, Microsoft Corp (formerly, Micro Soft), Albuquerque, 75; gen partner, Microsoft Corp, 75-77, pres, 77-82, chmn bd, 81-, exec vpres develop activities, 82-83; founder, Corbis, 89; chief, software archit, Redmond, Wash, 99-; bd dir, ICOS Corp, 1990-, Berkshire Hathaway Inc, 2004-; Melinda: with Microsoft Corp, 87-96; Co-founder, Bill & Melinda Gates Found, Seattle, 2000-; bd dir, Drugstore.com, The Wash Post Co, 2004-. *Awards:* Nat medal, Tech US Dept Commerce Tech Admin, 92; named CEO of Year, Chief Exec Mag, 94; named one of Top 200 Collectors, ARTnews Mag, 2004. *Collection:* 19th Century American Art. *Publ:* Bill: (auth) The Future, 94, The Road Ahead, 95, Business at the Speed of Thought, 99. *Mailing Add:* Microsoft Corp 1 Microsoft Way Redmond WA 98052-8300

GATES, HARRY IRVING
SCULPTOR, EDUCATOR
b Elgin, Ill, Dec 8, 34. *Study:* Univ Ill, BFA, 58, MFA, 60. *Work:* Chase Manhattan Bank, NY; Corcoran Gallery Art, Washington; Int Art Prog Div, Nat Collection Fine Art, Washington; Washington Co Mus Fine Arts, Hagerstown, Md; Baltimore Mus Fine Art, Md; Washington & Lee Univ, Va. *Exhib:* One-man shows, Baltimore Mus Fine Art, 64, Western Md Col, Westminster, 95, Wash Co Mus Fine Arts, Hagerstown, 95, Japan Info & Cult Ctr, Embassy of Japan, Washington, 96 & Higgins Armory Mus, Worcester, Mass, 97; Small Sculpture Purchases for Int Art Prog, Nat Collection Fine Art, 69; New Sculpture, Corcoran Art, Washington, 70; Five Maryland Artists, Md Arts Coun, 72-73; Sculpture Invitational, Rochester Inst Technol, 75; The Object as Poet, Renwick Gallery, Washington, & Mus Contemp Crafts, NY, 77; 18 yr retrospective, Washington Co Mus Art, Md, 78; two-man exhib, Dimock Gallery, George Washington Univ, 79. *Teaching:* Asst prof sculpture, George Washington Univ, 64-78, assoc prof, 78-98, prof, 98-. *Awards:* First Prize, 21st Ann Contemp Art, Palm Beach, Fla, 59; Artists Coun Award, 25th Ann Exhib for Sculpture, 61; Gov Prize, Md Ann, 70. *Mailing Add:* Smith Hall of Art Rm 101 George Washington Univ 801 22nd St NW Washington DC 20052

GATES, HENRY LOUIS, JR
PATRON
b Keyser, WVa, Sept 16, 50. *Study:* Yale Univ, BA(summa cum laude), 73; Univ Cambridge, Eng, MA, PhD(eng Lang & Lit) 79; Phi Beta Kappa. *Hon Degrees:* Numerous hon degrees from US & foreign univ, 89-2002. *Pos:* pres Afro-Am Acad, 84-; Chmn, Dept of Afro-Am Studies, 91-, dir WEB DuBois Inst, 91-; trustee, Whitney Mus Am Art, currently; bd dir, Lincoln Ctr Theatre, currently. *Teaching:* Lectr Eng & Afro-Am studies Yale Univ, New Haven, 76-79, asst prof, 79-84, assoc prof, 84-85; prof Eng, comparative lit & Africana studies Cornell Univ, Ithaca, NY, 85 88, WEB DuBois prof lit, 88-90; John Spencer Bassett prof, Eng & Lit Duke Unv, 90-91; WEB DuBois prof humanities, prof Eng Harvard Univ, 91-. *Awards:* Fac prize, Yale Afro-Am Cult Ctr, 84; Nat Humanities Medal, 98; Teachers Col Medal for Distinguished Serv, Columbia Univ, 2000. *Mem:* Am Acad Arts and Scis; African Lit Asn; Am Studies Asn; Modern Language Asn; Asn for Study of Afro-Am Life & Hist; Col Language Asn; Caribbean Studies Asn; Coun on Foreign Relations; PEN. *Publ:* Auth, Figures in Black, 87, Signifying Monkey, 88, Loose Canons, 92, Colored People: A Memoir, 94, (with Cornel West) The Future of the Race, 96, Thirteen Ways of Looking at a Black Man, 97, Wonders of the African World, 99, Africana: The Encyclopedia of the African American Experience, 99, (with Cornel West) The African-American Century, 2000, Little Known Black History Facts, 2000, The Trials of Phillis Wheatley: America's First Poet and Her Encounters with the Founding Fathers, 2003; ed, Black is the Color of the Cosmos: Charles T. Davis's Essays on Black Literature and Culture, 42-81, 82, Our Nig, 83, The Slave's Narrative, 85, Black Literature and Literary Theory, 85, Race, Writing, and Difference, 86, The Classic Slave Narratives, 87, The Souls of Black Folk, 89, Reading Black, Reading Feminist, 1990, Bearing Witness, 91, The Norton Anthology of African American Literature, 96, The Dictionary of Global Culture, 97, Hannah Crafts, The Bondwoman's Narrative, 2002; series ed, Oxford-Schomburg Library of the 19th Century Black Women, 88; co-ed, Encarta Africana Encycl, 1999 (Outstanding Contrib to Pub., Black Caucus of Am Libr Asn, 2000). *Mailing Add:* Harvard Univ Dept Afro-Am Studies Barker Ctr 12 Quincy St Cambridge MA 02138-3804

GATES, JAY RODNEY
MUSEUM DIRECTOR
b Kansas City, Mo, Nov 21, 45. *Study:* Inst European Studies, Vienna, Austria, 67; Col Wooster, Ohio, BA, 68; Univ Rochester, NY, MA, 70. *Exhib:* Mitthoefer Collection of African Sculpture, Col Wooster Mus, Ohio, 74; Prints & Drawings by Sculptors, Cleveland Mus Art, Ohio, 75; Tenn Quilts, Brooks Mem Art Gallery, Memphis, 79; Arts of Ancient Egypt: Treasures on Another Scale, Memphis & Washington, DC, 81. *Pos:* mus curator, Col Wooster, 71-73; asst cur art hist & educ, Cleveland Mus, 73-76; cur educ, St Louis Art Mus, 76-78; dir, Brooks Mem Art Gallery, Memphis, 79-81, Seattle Art Mus, 87-93, Dallas Mus Art, 93-98 & Phillips Collections, Washington, DC, 98-; asst dir & cur Am art, Nelson Gallery, Atkins Mus, 81-83; dir, Spencer Mus Art, Univ Kans, Lawrence, 83-87. *Teaching:* Instr art hist, Col Wooster, Ohio, 71-73; Case Western Reserve Univ, Cleveland, 73-76; prof art hist, Univ Kans, 83-87. *Mem:* Am Asn Mus; Col Art Asn; Asn Art Mus Dirs. *Res:* Public education in art museums; American painting. *Publ:* Auth, Television from the galleries, Mus News, 75; co auth, Teaching advanced placement art history in a museum, Art J, 75. *Mailing Add:* Phillips Collection 1600 21st St NW Washington DC 20009

GATES, JEFF S
PHOTOGRAPHER, DESIGNER
b Los Angeles, Calif. *Study:* Mich State Univ, East Lansing, BA, 71; Univ Calif, Los Angeles, MFA, 75. *Work:* Ctr Georges Pompidou, Paris; Victoria & Albert Mus, London; Los Angeles Co Mus Art; Seattle Art Mus; J Paul Getty Mus, Los Angeles; and others. *Exhib:* In Our Path, online; Solo exhibs, Midtown Y, NY, 89, Baltimore Mus Art, 92, Grey Art Gallery, NY, 92, Sheppard Col, Sheppardstown, WVa, 93, El Camino Col, Torrance, Calif, 95, Downey Mus Art, Calif, 95 & Millersville Univ, Pa, 96; Outcry: Artists Answer AIDS (traveling), Mus Contemp Art, Baltimore, 91; Siggraph '91, Nat Siggraph Conf, Las Vegas, 91; Wit & Wisdom: Humor in Art, Forum Gallery, Jamestown, NY, 92; Multi Media Grunderziet: Computergraphics State of the Art, Univ Wuppertal, Ger, 92; and others. *Pos:* Dir, ArtFBI, 88-. *Teaching:* Keynote speaker, Nat Conf Art Admin, Anchorage, Alaska; Instr, Md Inst, Col Art, 85-; online web design instr, Minneapolis Col Art & Design, 84-85 & 95-. *Awards:* Photog Fel, Md State Arts Coun, 91; Travel Grant, Brit Coun, Washington, 92; Photog Fel, Nat Endowment Arts, 84 & 90, Arts Admin Fel, 90. *Bibliog:* Ayofemi Folayan (auth), article, High Performance, spring 93; Blake Lange (auth), Artists on exhibit, J Washington Apple Pi, 9/94; Patricia Riedman (auth), Artists make best use of the net, Adobe Mag, 2/97; and others. *Media:* Web Design, Internet Art. *Mailing Add:* PO Box 2769 Silver Spring MD 29015

GATES, MIMI GARDNER
MUSEUM DIRECTOR
b Dayton, Ohio, July 30, 42. *Study:* Stanford Univ, BA, 64; Univ Iowa, MA, 70; Yale Univ, PhD, 81. *Collection Arranged:* co-cur Stories of Porcelain, From China to Europe, 00; Ancient Sichuan: Treasures from a Lost Civilization, 01. *Pos:* Cur Asian Art, Yale Univ 75-87, dir 87-94; Illsley Ball Nordstrom dir, Seattle Art Mus, 94-. *Teaching:* instr Chinese art hist, mus studies, Yale Univ; fac mem Univ Wash. *Mem:* Asn Art Mus Dirs (pres, 90). *Publ:* Contribr, Bones of Jade, Soul of Ice, Yale Art Gallery, 85; Coauth, Real & Imaginary Beings, Yale Art Gallery, 80; Ed, Communion of Scholars: Chinese Art at Yale, Chinese Inst, 87. *Mailing Add:* 100 University St Seattle WA 98101

GATTEN, DAVID
FILMMAKER
b Ann Arbor, Mich, 71. *Study:* Sch Art Inst Chicago, MFA, 98. *Work:* Whitney Mus Am Art; Art Inst Chicago. *Exhib:* Whitney Biennial, 2002 & 2006; The Am Century, Whitney Mus Am Art, Art Inst Chicago; San Francisco Cinémathèque; Art Gallery of Ont; Cinémathèque Française; Helsinki Film Co-Op; Mus Contemp Cinema; Contemp Cinema, Lisbon; Millenium Film Workshop; First Person Cinema; Anthology Film Archives; Cinema Project Chicago; Filmmakers, Views from the Avant Garde, NY Film Festival, 2005. *Teaching:* assoc prof, Cinema & Photog, Ithaca Col, NY. *Mailing Add:* 14 Verona St 4C Brooklyn NY 11231

GATTO, PAUL ANTHONY
PAINTER, INSTRUCTOR
b Brooklyn, NY, Sept 19, 29. *Study:* Self taught fine artist. *Work:* Jennings Hall, S Oaks Hosp, Amityville, NY; Kramer Lane Sch, Bethpage, NY; Garden City Inn, NY; Manhasset High Sch, NY; Methodist Church Community Ctr, NY. *Comn:* The Visitation, The Annunciation, The Parable, The Ministry & The Shepherd, (oil panels) Maria Regina RC Church, Seaford, NY, 89-. *Exhib:* Ninth Art Festival, Two Flags, Douglas, Ariz, 81; 61st Ann Nat Exhib, Ogunquit Art Ctr, Maine, 81; 59th Ann Nat Apr Salon, Springville Mus, Utah, 83; Pro Art Exhib, Utah Pageant Arts, Am Fork, 83; Artists at Work, Nassau Co Mus Art, Roslyn, NY, 90; The Morsel, Nat Mus Catholic Art & History, NY; and others. *Pos:* Pres & bd trustees, Farmingdale Pub Libr, 77-; pres, Ital Cult Soc, 75-78; art damage appraiser, Royal, Home, Aetna & Utica Mutual Insurance, 70-. *Teaching:* Lectr demonstr fine arts, painting, 67-; teacher fine arts, painting, Paul Gatto Gallery, Farmingdale, NY, 67-; teacher fine arts, painting, NY Inst Technol, Islip, 88-. *Mem:* Hechscher Mus, Huntington, NY, Artists Regist, 82. *Media:* Oils, Watercolor. *Interests:* music, piano. *Publ:* Illusr, Published prints, 11/76 & Times Square-New Years Day, 82, Paul A Gatto; poster, portrait Alexander, Fundraiser, Polish Gift Life Charity, 91. *Mailing Add:* Paul Gatto Gallery 300 Main St Farmingdale NY 11735

GATTO, ROSE MARIE
PAINTER
b Brooklyn, NY, Apr 11, 31. *Study:* Brooklyn Col, 49; Art Students League, 80. *Work:* Cranford Pub Libr, NJ, 80. *Exhib:* Summit Art Ctr, NJ, 83; Nat Asn Women Artists, 89-90. *Teaching:* Instr, Jane Law Gallery, 86-; Teen Festival Union Col, 86-89; Westfield Adult Sch, 87-88. *Awards:* First Place, NJ Watercolor Soc, 86. *Bibliog:* Three Generations of Artists, Daily J, 82. *Mem:* NJ Watercolor Soc (asst nat chmn, 89); Nat Asn Women Artists (record secy 89). *Media:* Watercolor, Mixed Media. *Mailing Add:* 29 Alden St Apt 2A Cranford NJ 07016

GAUCHER, YVES
PRINTMAKER, PAINTER
b Montreal, Que, 34. *Study:* L'Ecole des Beaux Arts, Montreal, 54-56. *Work:* Mus Mod Art, NY; Libr of Cong, Washington, DC; Victoria & Albert Mus, London, Eng; Mus d'Art Contemp, Montreal; Nat Gallery of Can, Ottawa, Ont. *Exhib:* Contemp Painters as Printmakers, Mus Mod Art, NY, 64; Expo 70, Japan; Aspects of Can Art, Members Gallery, Albright-Knox Art Gallery, Buffalo, NY, 74; Thirteen Artists from Marlborough Gallery, NY, 74; one-man shows, Mural Installation, Nova Corp, Calgary, Alberta, 82, Centre Cult Can, Bruxelles, Belg, 83, Can House, London, Eng, 83, Centre Cult du Can, Paris, 83, Galerie Esperanza, Montreal, 86, Olga Korper Gallery, Toronto, 85, 86 & 88 & 49th Parallel Centre Contemp Can Art, NY, 89; 15th Anniv Show, Olga Korper Gallery, Toronto, 88; Waddington & Gorce Inc, Montreal, 88; Montreal Painting of 1960's, Americas Soc Art Gallery, NY, 89; Living Impressions, Art Gallery, Hamilton, Ont, 89; and others. *Teaching:* Asst prof fine arts, Sir George Williams Univ, Montreal, 63-69, assoc prof, 70-; prof, Concordia Univ, Montreal, 66-. *Awards:* First Prize, Nat Print Competition, Burnaby, BC, 61; Second Prize, Int Triennale of Colored Prints, Grenchen, Switz, 64; Grand Prize, Sandage 68, Montreal Mus Fine Arts, 68. *Bibliog:* Donald Brackett (auth), Yves Gaucher & Christopher Kier, Arts Report, 3/8/88; Perceiving painting through the pores, Now Mag, 3/10/88; Norman Theriault (auth), Art: Style over story, Forces, winter 88. *Publ:* Auth, Living Impressions (exhib catalog), Art Gallery Hamilton, Ont, 89. *Mailing Add:* Dept Art Concordia Univ George Williams Campus Dept Studio A 1455 De Maissoneuve W Montreal PQ H3G 1M8 Canada

GAUCHER-THOMAS, NANCY A
PAINTER, INSTRUCTOR
b Marlboro, Mass. *Study:* New York Phoenix Sch Design, 73-75; with Paul Wood, Dorothy Watkeys Barberis, Thomas Sgouros, Irwin Greenberg & Pat Sansoucie. *Work:* Newport Hosp, RI; Bank of Newport, Middletown, RI; Newport Nat Golf Club, RI; Vis Nurse Serv, Middletown, RI; Ocean Plaza Hotel, Ocean Grove, NJ. *Comn:* Watercolor painting, Newport Nat Golf Club, RI, 94; watercolor painting, comn by Mrs M Rohrmann, Guatamala, 94; portrait, KVH, 2006. *Exhib:* Nat Asn Women Artists Showcase, Lever Gallery, NY, 95; NE Watercolor Ann, Goshe, NY, 96; Springfield Art League 78th Nat, Mus Fine Arts, Mass, 97; Newport Art Mus Mem Show, RI, 98; Acad Artists 48th Nat Exhib Contemp Realism Art, First Church Gallery, Springfield, Mass, 98; Art NE-USA 43rd Ann, Silvermine Arts Guild, New Canaan, Conn, 98; 102nd Ann Catherine Lorillard Wolfe Art Club Nat, Nat Arts Club, NY, 98. *Teaching:* Studio workshop, watercolor painting, 90-. *Awards:* JD Ayers Art Diversified-Springfield Art League 78th Nat Exhib Award, Mus Fine Arts, Springfield, Mass, 97; First Place Watercolor, Newport Art Mus, 98; Jack Richeson Merchandise Award, Northwest Watercolor Soc, 2000. *Mem:* Nat Asn Women Artists; Am Artist Prof League (pres emerita RI chap); signature mem Northeast Watercolor Soc; Nat Watercolor Soc; Acad Artists. *Media:* Watercolor

GAUDARD, PIERRE
PHOTOGRAPHER, GRAPHIC ARTIST
b Marvelise (Doubs), France, Oct 6, 27; Can citizen. *Study:* Ecole Estienne, Paris, France. *Work:* Can Mus Contemp Photog, Ottawa, Ont; Musee Art Contemporain, Montreal, Que; Galerie FNAC, Paris, France; Bibliotheque Nationale, Paris, France; Winnipeg Art Galerie, Can; Can Coun Bank of Ottawa; Nat Art Galerie, Ottawa. *Exhib:* One-man shows, Les Prisons, Galerie de L'Image, Ottawa, 77, Musee d'Art Contemporain, Montreal, 80, Galerie Canon, Amsterdam, The Neth, 80, Univers Carceral, Galerie FNAC Forum, Paris, 80, En France, Galerie de L'Image, Ottawa, 82, Place des Arts, Montreal, 83 & Exercises de Style, Galerie Dazibao, Montreal, 84; Exposure, Art Gallery Ont, Toronto, 75; Tendances Actuelles au Quebec, Musee d'Art Contemporain, Montreal, 78; 66-Photographes-Actuels, Palais des Beaux Arts, Brussels, Belg, 81; Photographie au Quebec, Galerie du Rip, Arles, France, 82; Photographie Actuelle au Quebec, Galerie Quebec, Paris, France, 82; Le Mois de la Photo Á Montréal, Maisons de la Cult, (invité d'honneur), 89; and others. *Teaching:* Photo workshop, Col Bois de Boulogne, Montreal, Can, 88-. *Awards:* Medaille de la Fedn Int d'Art Photo-graphique, Montreal, 69; Carveth Award, Hamilton Camera Club, Can, 70; Medaille d'or ONF, Ottawa, Nat Film Bd, 72; Ministere des Affaires Cult du Que Grants, 82 & 86; and many others. *Bibliog:* Jacque Giraldeau (auth), La Toile d'Araignee, Films Nat Film Bd, Can, 79; Francois Caillat (auth), Pierre Gaudard, Zoom, Paris, 3/80; Serge Jonque (auth), Photo a l'Air Libre, Vie des Arts, 7/83. *Publ:* Coauth, Canada du Temps Qui Passe, ONF, 67; auth, Image-10-Les Ouvriers, Nat Film Bd, Ottawa, 72; coauth, Exposure, Art Gallery, Toronto, 75; Entre Amis, ONF, 76; auth, Les Prisons, OVO, 77. *Mailing Add:* 10255 Jeanne Manee Montreal PQ H3L 3B7 Canada

GAUDEAMUS See Jordan, John L

GAUDIERI, ALEXANDER V J
MUSEUM DIRECTOR
b Columbus, Ohio, Apr 23, 40. *Study:* Ohio State Univ; Univ Paris, Sorbonne; Colgate Univ; Barton Kyle Yount Scholar, Am Grad Sch Int Com; Inst Fine Arts, NY Univ, with Robert Rosenblum, Sir Francis Watson & James Parker. *Exhib:* Picasso: Meeting in Montreal, 85 & Miro: Works on Paper & in Bronze, 86, Montreal Mus Fine Arts. *Pos:* Dir, Telfair Acad Arts & Sci, 76-83, Montreal Mus Fine Arts, 83-87, Locust Grove (Samuel FB Morse hist site, 94-95) & Marietta-Cobb Mus Art, 97. *Teaching:* Adj prof mus studies prog, Grad Sch Arts & Sci, NY Univ, 92-97. *Mem:* Asn Art Mus Dirs; Am Asn Mus; Soc Archit Historians; and others. *Res:* European decorative arts--wood marquetry; development of geometric forms into curvilinear and floral motifs from circa 1715 to mid-century; French romantic painting--the horse paintings of Alfred de Dreux and the influence of Gericault on his oeuvre. *Collection:* Decorative arts including Georges II & III furniture, silver and porcelain. *Mailing Add:* PO Box 3 Palm Beach FL 33480

GAUTHIER, NINON
CURATOR, HISTORIAN
b Verdun, Que, Nov 9, 1943. *Study:* Studied with Georges-Henri Riviere; Univ de Montreal, BS, 67; MS, 68; Ecole des Hautes Etudes, 72-74; Univ Paris IV-Sorbonne, MA (contemporary art history), 95, DEA (contemporary art history), 96, PhD (art history), 2004. *Exhib:* Color & Light & Drawing Illusions (auth catalog), Century Gallery, Sylmar, Calif, 94. *Collection Arranged:* Marcel Barbezv: Mastering The Accidental Churchill (coauth, catalog), Col Arts Gallery, Cambridge, Eng, 98; Josef Albers Hommage au carre: de la science a la magie, Galerie HEC, Univ Mtl, 85; Color & Light & Drawing Illusions (auth catalog), Century Gallery, Sylmar, Calif, 94;

Marcel Barbeau en filigranes, Domaine Cataraqui, Quebec City, 99; marcel Barberau Derives et variations, Galerie Montcalm, Hull 2000; Gaz Metrop, Montreal, Can; Union Vie, Drummoned Ville, Can; Via Rail Mil, Can; Marcel Barbeua Comprehensive Draings 1954-1982 (auth, catalog), Paintings 1944-1977, Scultpure 1944-2000; plus others. *Pos:* Asst dean, Fac Fine Arts, Univ du Que Montreal, 74-76; dir, Centre d'etude et ed communication sur l'art, 89-; corresp, Paris Sculpture, 2005-. *Teaching:* Lectr, Dept Art Hist & Dept Fine Arts, Univ Que, Montreal, 86, 87 & 89-90. *Awards:* Spec Collab Award, Nat Bus Writing Award, Toronto Press Club, Royal Bank Can, 87; Cult Journalism Excellency Award, Can Conf Arts, Samuel & Saydie Bronfman Found, 89. *Bibliog:* Marie-Claude Fortin (auth) Mine d'art, Voir, 12/19/90; Ann Duncan (auth), New art-book venture defying the odds, The Gazette, 2/2/91; Gerald Needam (auth) Loyal to abstraction, Books in Canada, Vol XX, No. 2, 91; Jean Dumont (auth), Marcel Barbreau: retour a Paris, Le Devoir, Montreal, 91; Theo Barbu and Marcel Barbeau (coauths) a Canadian in Paris, Art Speak, New York, 6/91. *Mem:* Asn Art Critics Can (secy, 89-92); Art Collectors Asn Que (dir, 88-92); Centre d'etude et de communications sur l'art (pres, 88-93). *Res:* Canadian art of fifties and sixties; history of Canadian Contemporary art scene and market; interraction between critics, institutions, media and art market on artist's works, career and on art works prices; history of comtemporary sculpture. *Publ:* Coauth, Le marché de l'art et le statut de l'artiste, Ministere des affaires culturelles du Que, 82; Le Mecenat prive au Quebec: mythe ou realite?, Possible, 85 & 86; auth, Vivre des arts visuels, Publs du Que, 87; Code d'ethique des sculpteurs, Conseil de la sculpture du Que, 90; coauth, Marcel Barbeau: le regard en fugue, CECA, 90; plus others. *Mailing Add:* 11 Rue Sesto Fiorentino Batiment TH5 18E Étage Apt 101 Bagnolet France

GAUTHIER, SUZANNE ANITA
PAINTER
b Saint-Boniface, Man, Aug 12, 48. *Study:* Univ Man, Winnipeg, BFA(hons), 69. *Work:* Can Coun Art Bank & Mus of Man, Ottawa; Winnipeg Art Gallery, Man; Collection Pre05t d'Oeuvres d'Art, Mus Québec; Bemis Foundation, Omaha; Musée D'Art Contemporaine, Collection Lavalin, Montréal. *Exhib:* Palazza Della Esposizioni, Faenza, Italy, 85-86; 37th Salon de la Jeune Peinture, Grand Palais, Paris, 86; Jane Corkin Gallery, Toronto, 88; Exten Print & Drawing Coun of Can, Toronto, 90; Subject/Matter, Art Gallery NS, 92; and others. *Teaching:* Lectr printmaking, Sch Art, Univ Man, 77-79; asst prof painting, NS Col Art & Design, 88-92. *Awards:* B Grant, Can Coun, 87; Soutien Aux Artistes, Ministér des Affaires, Culturelles, Que, 88; Travel Grant, Can Coun, 89. *Bibliog:* Françoise Legris-Berggman (auth), L'ouevre polymorphe de Suzanne Gauthier, Vie des Arts, 88; Bernard Mulaire (auth), Chien, Les Editions du Blé, 85; Gérard Xuriguera (auth), Le dessin, le pastel, l'aquarelle dans l'art, Éditions Mayer, Paris, 87. *Mem:* Can Artists Representation/Front des Artistes Canadiens. *Media:* Encaustic Painting; Photography. *Publ:* Illusr, Canadian Artists in Exhibition, 1973-1974, Roundstone Coun, 74; Le Nu, La Lumiére et Les Ombres, Les Editions du Blé, 75; coauth & illusr, Vortex, Les Editions du Blé, 85; Figures Nomades, Migrant Images, Les Ed Ink, Inc, 89. *Mailing Add.* 5654 Harris St Apt 2 Halifax NS B3K 1H2 Canada

GAUVIN, CLAUDE E
PAINTER
b Bathurst, NB, June 14, 39. *Study:* Ecole Beaux Arts Montreal, dipl, 60; Univ Que, Montreal, BA(spec educ), 74; Tyler Art Sch, 76. *Work:* Banque Art NB, Fredericton; Consolidated Bathurst, Montreal; Univ Moncton, NB. *Exhib:* Solo exhibs, Radio-Can, Moncton, NB, 80 & Rothmans Gallery, Moncton, NB, 83; Collections, Art Bank NB, Dieppe, 81; Univ Maine, 82; Art Collections, Univ Moncton, NB, 83. *Teaching:* Instr art, Montreal Sch Design, 60-63 & Philadelphia Sch Bd, 74-77; prof painting, Univ Moncton, NB, 78-. *Awards:* Constance Carlston Award, Univ Maine, 82. *Bibliog:* Bernard Levy (auth), Le plaisir de l'objet, Vie Arts, 80. *Mem:* Can Art Rep, Fedn Artistes Can (secy, 81, exec secy, 82-83)

GAUVREAU, ROBERT GEORGE
PHOTOGRAPHER, EDUCATOR
b Renton, Wash, Aug 14, 48. *Study:* Cent Wash State Univ, BA, 70; Ariz State Univ, Tempe, MFA, 73. *Work:* Coos Art Mus, Coos Bay, Ore. *Exhib:* Phoenix Art Mus, Ariz, 73; Spectrum Gallery, Tucson, 76; Creative Eye Gallery, Sonoma, Calif, 76; Cent Wash State Univ, Ellensburg, 77; Coos Bay Mus, Ore, 78; and others. *Teaching:* Lectr photog, State Univ NY, New Paltz, 73-74; instr photog, Modesto Jr Col, Calif, 74-, dean arts, humanities & commun, currently. *Mem:* Soc Photog Educ. *Media:* Color. *Mailing Add:* 35109 Highway 79 SPC 228 Warner Springs CA 92086-9728

GAVALAS, ALEXANDER BEARY
PAINTER
b Limerick, Ireland, Jan 6, 45; US citizen. *Study:* Sch Art & Design, dipl, 63; Manhattanville Col, 69-; Col New Rochelle, BA, 95. *Work:* Tweed Mus Art, Duluth, Minn; and others. *Exhib:* One-man shows, Tweed Mus Art, Minn, 80, Western Ill Univ Libr Gallery, 81, Ft Wayne Mus Art, Ind, 82, Marycrest Col Eberdt Art Gallery, Iowa, 82, Arnot Art Mus, NY, 82 & Queens Col Art Ctr/Paul Klapper Libr, NY, 83. *Teaching:* Instr art & music, St Catherine of Alexandria, Brooklyn, NY, 84-86. *Awards:* Commemorative Award, Men of Achievement, IBC, 85. *Bibliog:* Matt Santoro (auth), At peace with his environment, Queens Ledger, 80; Alan Garfield (auth), Alexander Beary Gavalas Recent Paintings & Drawings, Krasl Art Ctr, 80, Idealism, serenity mark Gavalas' landscapes, Ft Wayne Sentinel, 4/82. *Mem:* Int Platform Asn. *Media:* Oil, Pen & Ink. *Publ:* Auth, articles, Irish Echo, 82 & 83; articles, New York Daily News, 82; articles, Western Queens Gazette, 82

GAWARECKI, CAROLYN ANN See Grosse, C(arolyn) Ann Gawarecki

GAY, BETSY (ELIZABETH) DERSHUCK GAY
PAINTER, INSTRUCTOR
b Philadelphia, Pa, Nov 27, 27. *Study:* Sweet Briar Col, Va, BA, 49; Nat Acad Fine Arts, New York, 56; studied with Edgar A Whitney, Charles Reid, Frank Webb, Gerald Brommer, Virginia Cobb, Nita Engle & others. *Work:* George B Markle Gallery, Penn State Univ Gallery, Pardee Collection Church Gallery, Hazelton, Pa; Sweet Briar Col Gallery, Va; Pelham Art Ctr Gallery, NY. *Comn:* Painting, Eleventh Hole, Whippoorwill Club, Armonk, NY, 72; painting, Creation, Art Comt Church Collection, Hazleton, Pa, 75; painting, Summer Delights, Bedford Gourmet, NY, 90. *Exhib:* New Eng Exhib at Silvermine, Conn; Knickerbocker Artists, NY, 76; Nat Arts Club, NY, 78; Nat Asn Women Artists NY, Ber Community Mus, Bergen, NJ, 82; Katonah NY Mus Art. *Teaching:* Instr water media, Northcastle Adult Educ, Armonk, NY, 77-82, Pelham Art Ctr, NY, 78- & Briarcliff Continuous Educ, New York, 79-83. *Awards:* Catharine Lorillard Wolfe Art Club President's Award, 98th Ann Exhib, Nat Arts Club, NY, 94; CLW Art Club Cash Award, 98th Ann Exhib, Nat Arts Club, NY, 94; First Prize, Mixed Media, Founder's Show, Hurlbutt Gallery, Conn, 97. *Bibliog:* The Best of Acrylic Painting, Rockport Publ, 96; Creative Inspirations, Rockport Publ, Inc, 97. *Mem:* Nat Asn Women Artists; Catherine Lorrilard Wolfe Art Club, NY; Mamaroneck Artists Guild; Katonah Mus Art. *Media:* Watercolor; Mixed Media. *Interests:* Painting, teaching, golf, tennis, gardening, 9 grandchildren, love to be with and help with. *Mailing Add:* 51 Round Hill Rd Armonk NY 10504

GAYDOS, TIM (TIMOTHY) JOHN
PAINTER,SCULPTOR
b New York, NY, Dec 6, 41. *Study:* Univ Calif, Berkeley, 59-61; Accademia Di Belli Arti Di Brera, Milano, Italy, 62-63. *Work:* Rutgers Univ, New Brunswick & Newark, NJ; Vets Admin Hosp, Paramus, NJ; Butler Inst of AM Art Youngstown, Ohio; Metropolitan Opera, New York City; Montclair Art Mus NJ; Jersey City Mus, NJ; Bergen Mus, Paramus, NJ. *Comn:* Painting of Richard Wagner (composer), Bloomfield Libr, NJ, 84; Lady Cow Diva, Sculpture NY, Cow Parade, 2000; The New York Palace/Le Cirque Patrons; Portrait, Jerome Hines, Metrop Opera, NYC. *Exhib:* NJ Biennial, NJ State Mus, Trenton, 83 & Newark Mus, 85; Pastel Invitational, Hermitage Mus, Norfolk, Va, 85 & 87; solo exhib, Montclair Art Mus, NJ, 88-89; Bergen Mus NJ, 98; Univ of Maine at Machias, 2000, 2005; 165th Ann, Nat Acad Design, NY, 90; NJ Arts Ann, Noyes Mus, Oceanville, NJ, 92; Butler Inst of Am Art Ann, 2001, 2003, 2004. *Pos:* Only Fine Artist-Painter & Sculptor. *Awards:* NJ State Coun Arts Fel, 93-94; Gold Medal of Honor Am Watercolor Soc, 95; Top Award Pastel Soc Am, 95; Silver Medal of Honor Am Watercolors Soc, 2002; Nat Arts Club Award, Pastel Soc Am, 2004; Fell for Painting, NJ State Coun Arts, 2006. *Bibliog:* Award Winning Watercolors of 95 by Bebe Raupe The Artist's Mag, 9/95; Guilding The Eye by Kate Bolick, AM Artist Mag, Jan, 2002; Making the Human Connection by Maureen Bloomfield Watercolor Magic, Autumn, 2002. *Mem:* Pastel Soc Am (master pastellist); Am Watercolor Soc-Dolphin Fell NJ, Watercolor Soc. *Media:* Pastel, Acrylic. *Publ:* Contribr, Pastel Interpretations, North Light, 93; Contributor Pastel Portraits, by Watson Guptill, 96. *Dealer:* Woodwind Gallery, Machias, ME

GAYLORD, FRANK CHALFANT, II
SCULPTOR, DESIGNER
b Clarksburg, WVa, Mar 9, 25. *Study:* Carnegie Inst Technol Col Fine Arts; Tyler Sch Fine Arts, Temple Univ, BFA. *Comn:* Firemen Mem (granite), Nyack, NY; Pioneer Family (granite), Akron, Ohio; Arthur Fiedler (granite portrait), Boston Univ Libr, 82; William Penn (granite figure), Pen Treaty Park, Philadelphia, 82; William Shakespeare (granite portrait), Old Globe Theater, San Diego, 83; Nat Korean War Mem on the Mall, Washington, DC, 93. *Exhib:* Nat Sculpture Soc Ann Exhib, 65, 79 & 90. *Bibliog:* Article, The memorial sculpture of Frank Gaylord, Stone Am Mag, 4/82; The Stone Whistle (film), Barre Granite Asn. *Mem:* Assoc Nat Sculpture Soc; Fel, Nat Sculpture Soc. *Media:* All Media. *Publ:* Auth, Why Christ? & A portrait of Hector, 68, Monumental News Rev. *Mailing Add:* 25 Delmont Ave Barre VT 05641-3630

GEALT, ADELHEID MEDICUS
MUSEUM DIRECTOR, HISTORIAN
b Munich, Ger, May 29, 46; US citizen. *Study:* Ind Univ, PhD, 79. *Collection Arranged:* Italian Portrait Drawings, 1400-1800 from North American Collections Traveling Exhib (auth, catalog), 83. *Pos:* Cur, Ind Univ Art Mus, Bloomington, 76-, dir, 89-. *Awards:* Nat Endowment Arts Cur Grant, 80; Nat Endowment Arts Planning & Implementation Grant, 81; Am Philos Soc Grant, 81; Nat Endowment Humanities Grant, 85. *Mem:* Ind Arts Comn(adv panelist, 89-). *Res:* Primarily Italian painting and drawing from 1300-1800. *Publ.* Auth, Looking at Art, A Visitor's Guide to Art Museums, RR Bowker, 83; The Punchinello Drawings of Domenico Teipolo, Braziller, 86; coauth, Art of the Western World, Summit Bks, 89; auth, Painting of the Golden Age: A Biographical Dictionary of Seventeenth-Century European Painters, Greenwood Press, 93; coauth/co-cur, Giandomenico Tiepolo: Maestraia e Gioco, Electra, 96. *Mailing Add:* Ind Univ Art Mus Bloomington IN 47405

GEAR, JOSEPHINE
WRITER, CURATOR
b London, Eng, Nov 24, 38. *Study:* The English equivalent of a degree in museology; the dipl of Mus Asn Gt Brit, 65; Woodrow Wilson Dissertation fel, 73-74, Inst Fine Arts, NY Univ, scholar award, 75-76, PhD, 76; study with Bob Rosenblum & Gert Schiff. *Pos:* Dir, Univ Art Gallery, State Univ NY, Binghamton, 79-87 & Whitney Mus Am Art At Philip Morris, 87-91. *Teaching:* Asst prof art hist, Briarcliff Col, NY, 75-77 & State Univ NY, Bimghamton, 79-87; adj assoc prof mus studies, NY Univ, 92-. *Mem:* Col Art Asn Am; Am Asn Mus; Int Asn Art Critics. *Publ:* Auth, Master or Servant, A Study of Selected English Painters and Their Patrons of the Late 18th and

Early 19th centuries, Garland, 77; Some alternative spaces in New York and Los Angeles, Studio Int, 80; Melvin Edwards: Large Sculpture (catalog, essay), Newberger Mus, State Univ NY, Purchase, 93; Thinking in Wood: C/rary Wood S/ture (catalog), Lowe Art Mus, Univ Miami, 94; and others

GEBHARDT, ROLAND
SCULPTOR, DESIGNER
b Paramaribo, Suriname, Sept 24, 39; US citizen. *Study:* Art Acad Hamburg, Ger, with Theo Ortner; Kuntsgewerbeschule, Zurich, Switz; also apprenticeship in stained glass, Marburg, Ger. *Work:* Art Acad, Hamburg; Brandeis Univ; Storm King Art Ctr, Mountainville, NY; City of Ludwigshafen, Ger; Neuberger Mus, Purchase, NY. *Exhib:* One-man sculpture & painting exhib, Hudson River Mus, 71, Gallery 84, NY, 73 & Robert Freidus Gallery, 78; 20th Century Sculpture in Westchester Collection, Yonkers, NY, 72; Carlton Gallery, NY, 74 & 77; Storm King Art Ctr, 75 & 76; The Minimal Tradition, Aldrich Mus, Ridgefield, Conn, 79; Pumpkins, Art Et Industry, NY, 82; Eight one-day exhibs, Kunstmuseum, Dusseldorf, Fed Repub Ger, 82. *Awards:* Annual Prize, Art Acad Hamburg, 62. *Bibliog:* Fred Salaff (auth), Roland Gebhardt--Sculptor (film), 72; Arlene Krebs (dir), Liniar Void (video), 78. *Media:* Metal, Stone; Fiberglass, Concrete. *Publ:* Auth, Fresh Sculpture, 81. *Mailing Add:* 67 Vestry St New York NY 10013-1734

GECHTOFF, SONIA
PAINTER, DRAFTSPERSEON
b Philadelphia, Pa, Sept 25, 26. *Study:* Philadelphia Mus Col Art, BFA, 50; Ford Found Fel, Tamarind Lithography Workshop, 63; study, CSFA Lithography Studio, 52-53. *Work:* Guggenheim Mus, Mus Mod Art & Metrop Mus Art, NY; Baltimore Mus Art; San Francisco Mus Mod Art; Worcester Art Mus, Mass. *Exhib:* Calif Painting: Mod Era, San Francisco Mus of Art, 76; Drawing Acquisition Shows, Mus of Mod Art, NY, 77 & Extraordinary Women & Am Drawn & Matched, 76-77; solo show, Gruenebaum Gallery, NY, 79, 80, 82, 83, 85 & 87 & Kraushaar Gallery, NY, 90, 92, 95 & 98; New Dimensions in Drawing, 50-80, Aldrich Mus Contemp Art, Conn, 81; Am Women-Am Art, Stamford Mus, Conn, 85; Art on Paper: Weatherspoon Guild, NC, 87; 56th Nat Midyear Exhib, Butler Inst Art, Youngstown, Oh, 92; Paper Trails, Art Mus Santa Cruz, Calif, 93; San Francisco Sch Abstr Expressionists, San Francisco Mus Mod Art, 96; Poindexter Collection, Denver Art Mus, 98-99; Stamp of Impulse - Abstract Expressionist Prints, Worcester (Mass) Art Mus, 2001; The Most Difficult Journey, Yellowstone Art Mus, Billings, Mont, 2002; Expressive Impressions: 3 Decades of Am Abstract Prints, Cummer Mus Art, Jacksonville, Fla, 2003. *Teaching:* Lectr art, Queens Col, 70-74; assoc prof art, Univ NMex, 74-75; artist-in-residence, Skidmore Col, NY, 88, 89, 90 & 95; vis artist, Chicago Art Inst, 89; artist-in-residence, Adelphi Univ, No, 91 & 93; master drawing, Nat Acad Sch Art, NY, 2000-01, 2001-03. *Awards:* Mid-Atlantic Nat Endowment Arts Grant, 88; Pollock-Krasner Found Grant, 94 & 98; Richard Florsheim Art Fund, 95; Charles Eliot Norton award in graphics, Nat Acad Design Mus Art, 2001. *Bibliog:* James Mellow (auth), Sonia Gechtoff: A different kind of knowledge, Arts Mag, 2/82; Michael Brenson (auth), Sonia Gechtoff's New Direction, NY Times, 11/25/83; John Loughery (auth), Sonia Gechtoff: The Theatre of the Visible Kraushaar Galleries Catalogue, 5/92 & Sonia Gechtoff: 4 Decades Works on Paper, Skidmore Col catalog, 95; American Abstract Expressionism of the 1950s: An Illustrated Survey, NY School Press, 2003. *Mem:* Arch Am Art; Nat Acad. *Media:* Acrylic, Oil; Graphite. *Mailing Add:* 463 West St Apt 936 New York NY 10014

GEDDES, ROBERT
ARCHITECT, EDUCATOR
b Philadelphia, Pa, Dec 7, 23. *Study:* Yale Univ, attended, 46; Harvard Univ, MArch, 50. *Hon Degrees:* NJ Inst Tech, LHD, 1998; Univ NY, LHD, 1999. *Comn:* prin works incl; Moore Sch Electrical Engring, Univ Pa, 58, Police Hqs, Philadelphia, 62, resident halls Univ Del, 66, Univ Pa, 67, housing projects, Westchester, Pa, also, Philadelphia and, Trenton, 66-77, Univ Pa Medical Sch and Hosp, 78-84, dining hall and acad building, Sch Natural Scis, 2001, Inst for Advanced Study, Princeton, 71, humanities and social scis. bldg, Southern Ill Univ, Carbondale, 68-74, Stockton State Col, 71-75, Corning (NY) Downtown Renewal, 75; master plan and design Liberty State Park, NJ, 75-77, laboratory bldgs, Mobil Corp, 81, JB Speed Art Mus Louisville, 83; Muhlenberg Col Libr, 86, Ctr City plan, Philadelphia, 85-87, Hosp Univ Pa, 87, Pub. Safety Bldg, White Plains, NY, 85-, Franklin Inst, Philadelphia, 87-90, Stern Sch Bus NY Univ, 87-93, Alexanderpolder urban design, Rotterdam, 93. *Pos:* pvt practice, Robert Geddes, Archit, Princeton & New York City, 90-99; co-dir, Crosstown 116 Upper Manhattan HUD Univ Partnership, 97; consult, Reg Plan Asn, NY; adv on archit and urban design, US Delegation to UN, Habitat II Conference, Istanbul, 96; pvt practice, Geddes Archits, 2000-; found, co-chmn Princeton Future Inc, 2000-. *Teaching:* prof, archit and civic design Univ Pa, 51-65; prof, archit, dean Sch Archit Princeton Univ, 65-82, William Kenan prof, 68-89; lectr, Univ London, 72-98; prof archit, Henry Luce, urbanism & hist New York Univ, 89-98. *Awards:* Fel, NY Inst for the Humanities, 89—; second prize, Nat Opera House, Sydney, Australia, 58; First prize, Int Town Planning Competition for Expansion of Vienna, Austria, 71, award for Excellence in Archit Educ ACSA-AIA, 84. *Mem:* Fel for design Am Inst of Archit (dir educ res proj, 65-67, pres NY chap 97); Harvard Grad Sch Design Alumni Asn (pres, formerly). *Publ:* Contribr, articles on archit to Encyl Brit, 74-79; ed, Principles and Precedents, Process Archit J, 85; ed, Cities in Our Future, 97

GEDEON, LUCINDA HEYEL
MUSEUM DIRECTOR, ADMINISTRATOR
b Port Chester, NY, Oct 13, 47. *Study:* Calif State Univ, Long Beach, BA(art hist), 78; Univ Calif, Los Angeles, MA, 81, PhD(art hist), 90. *Collection Arranged:* Jacob Lawrence, Collaborations & Connections: 20th Century Collaborative Bookworks (with John Risseeuw; auth, catalog), Ann Flaten Pixley, Sharokh Rezvani Workshop, Meeting Ground: Basketry Traditions & Sculptural Form (with Margo Shermeta; auth, catalog), Felice Lucero-Giaccardo: Contemporary Pueblo Painter (with Barbara Loeb; auth, catalog), Univ Art Mus, Ariz State Univ, Tempe, 90-91; Art Detour Exhib, Artlink Inc, Phoenix, Ariz, 90; Alison Saar: Inside Looking In (with Nancy Miller & Francis Sprout; auth, catalog), Neuberger Mus Art, State Univ New York, Purchase, 92; Rebecca Medel: Transcendental Fiber Constructs (auth, catalog), Neuberger Mus Art, State Univ New York, Purchase, 93; Melvin Edwards Sculpture: A Thirty Year Retrospective 1963-1993 (ed, catalog), Neuberger Mus Art, State Univ New York, Purchase, 93; Roy R Neuberger: Patron of the Arts, Neuberger Art Mus (ed, catalog), State Univ New York, Purchase, 93; Color Options, Westchester Community Col Art Gallery, 93; June Wayne: A Retrospective (sculpture; auth, catalog), 96; Elizabeth Catlett Retrospective (auth, catalog), 97. *Pos:* Asst dir, Grunwald Ctr Graphic Arts, Univ Calif, Los Angeles, 81-83, actg dir & cur, 83-85; chief cur, Univ Art Mus, Ariz State Univ, Tempe, 85-91; dir, Neuberger Mus Art, State Univ New York, Purchase, 91-. *Awards:* Afro-Am Studies Fel & Edward A Dickson Hist Art Fel, Univ Calif, Los Angeles, 84; Col Fine Arts Research Grant, Ariz State Univ, Tempe, 90; Arts Exhib Grant, Ariz Comn, 90-91. *Mem:* Am Asn Mus; Art Table; Col Art Asn; Mus Asn Ariz (bd mem, 88-90); Asn Art Mus Dir. *Res:* History of American and African-American art; history of prints. *Publ:* Auth, Rebecca Medel's Transcendental Net Results, Fiberarts, 9-10/91; The Janet Taylor Studio: A Tapestry Workshop in the Arizona Desert, Fiberarts, 3/91. *Mailing Add:* Neuberger Mus State Univ NY-Purchase 735 Anderson Hill Purchase NY 10577-1400

GEE, HELEN
ART CONSULTANT, CURATOR
Collection Arranged: Curated 78 exhibs, 54-88; Stieglitz & the Photo-Secession, NJ State Mus, 78; Bank Tokyo, NY; Indust Bank Japan, NY; Photography of the Fifties (catalog), Ctr Creative Photog, Tucson. *Pos:* Owner & dir, Limelight Gallery. *Teaching:* Parsons Sch Design, 80-. *Interests:* 19th and 20th century painting, sculpture and photography. *Publ:* Photography of the Fifties: An American Perspective, Univ Arizona Press, 83; Limelight: A Memoir, Univ NMex Press, 97

GEE, LI-LAN See Li-lan

GEESLIN, LEE GADDIS
PAINTER, EDUCATOR
b Goldthwaite, Tex, June 28, 20. *Study:* Univ Tex; New Orleans Art & Crafts; Art Inst Chicago, BFA & MFA. *Exhib:* Annually with local & regional shows of the Southwest; one-man shows, Brownsville, San Angelo, Houston, Corpus Christi, Brady, Lufkin, Dallas & Texarkana, Tex, also Shreveport, La, 63-. *Pos:* Dean, Col Fine Arts, Sam Houston State Univ. *Teaching:* Prof art, Sam Houston State Univ, ret. *Mem:* Tex Watercolor Soc; Tex Fine Arts Soc; Tex Art Educ Asn; Am Asn Univ Prof; Col Art Asn Am. *Media:* Oil, Watercolor

GEFFEN, DAVID LAWRENCE
COLLECTOR
b Brooklyn, NY, Feb 21, 43. *Study:* City Univ NY, student. *Pos:* Pres, Geffen-Roberts, Inc, 70-71, Asylum Records, 70-73, Elektra-Asylum Records, 73-76; vchmn, Warner Brothers Pictures, 74, vpres, 75, exec asst chmn, Warner Commun, 77; founder, pres, chmn, Geffen Records & Geffen Film Co, LA, 80-89; founder, pres, David Geffen Co, 90-95; co-founder, (with Jeffrey Katzenberg & Steven Spielberg) Dreamworks SKG, Universal City, 94-,chmn 1994-2006, co-chmn, Glendale, Calif, 2006-; prodr: (films) Personal Best, 82, Risky Business, 83, After Hours, 85, Lost in America, 85, Little Shop of Horrors, 86, Beetlejuice, 88, Men Don't Leave, 90, Interview with the Vampire, 94; co-prodr: (plays) Master Harold.and the Boys, 82, Cats, 82, Good, 82, Dreamgirls, 83, Social Security, 86, Madam Butterfly, 88 (9 Tony awards including best play), (musical) Miss Saigon; co-prodr. (flims) Dreamgirls 2006. *Teaching:* Mem. faculty, Yale U., 78. *Awards:* Named one of Top 200 Collectors, ARTnews Mag, 2004, 2006; named one of the worlds richest people 2001-2005, 50 Most Powerful People in Hollywood, Premiere mag., 2005-06. *Mem:* Los Angeles Co Art Mus (bd dir, currently). *Collection:* Modern and Contemporary Art, especially Abstract Expressionism. *Mailing Add:* Dreamworks SKG 100 Flower St Glendale CA 91201

GEFFERT, HARRY
SCULPTOR
b Live Oak, Tex, July 11, 34. *Study:* SW Tex Univ, San Marcos, Tex, BS, 57; NMex Highlands, Las Vegas, NMex, MA, 61. *Work:* Dallas Mus Fine Arts & Barrett Collection, Tex; Mod Art Mus Fort Worth, Tex; Mus Fine Arts, Houston, Tex; many pvt collections. *Exhib:* Solo exhibs, Kimbell Mus, Ft Worth, Tex, 85, Fort Worth Gallery, Tex, 86, Dallas Mus Art, Tex, 90, Cedar Vallery Col, Lancaster, Tex, 91, Moody Gallery, Houston, Tex, 92, Art Mus SE Tex, Beaumont, 94, Dallas Visual Art Ctr (with catalog), 98, Pillsbury Peters Fine Art, Dallas, 01, Moody Gallery, Houston, 02; The Figure, Valley House Gallery, Dallas, Tex, 98; Univ Tex San Antonio, 99; Houston Mus Fine Arts, 2000; Personal Playgrounds, Austin (Tex) Mus of Art, 01; Red Bud Gallery, Houston, 02; Williams Tower Gallery, Houston, 03. *Collection Arranged:* Mod Art Mus Fort Worth, Tex; Mus Fine Arts, Houston; Barrett Collection, Dallas. *Pos:* Owner, Green Mountain Fine Arts Foundry, Crowley, Tex, 84-. *Teaching:* Assoc prof sculpture, Tex Christian Univ, Ft Worth, 60-87. *Awards:* Visual Artists Fel Grant, Nat Endowment Arts, 90; Legend Award Hon, Dallas Visual Art Ctr, Tex, 98. *Bibliog:* Patricia Johnson (auth), Genesis in fire exhibit revels in the versatility of bronze, Houston Chronicle, 12/27/95; Janet Kutner (auth), article, Dallas Morning News, 9/25/98; Denise Getson (auth), article, ArtLies, winter 98-99; Getson (auth.) ArtLies, 98-99, Weinstein (auth.) 99; Lightman, Victoria, Sculpture in Houston, Sculpture Magazine, 2000; Patricia Johnson (auth), Beyond Borders, Houston Chronicle, 11, 9/24/2000. *Media:* Bronze. *Dealer:* Betty Moody 2815 Colquitt Houston TX 77098. *Mailing Add:* 3037 Eggleston Crowley TX 76036

GEFTER, JUDITH MICHELMAN
PHOTOGRAPHER
b Gloversville, NY. *Study:* Pratt Inst, cert; NY Univ; Univ Fla; Fla State Univ; also with William E Parker & Wilson Hicks Conf, Univ Miami. *Work:* Mint Mus, Charlotte, NC; Jacksonville Art Mus, Fla; Tampa Art Inst, Fla; Southern Bell Collection, 85; Barnett Bank, 90. *Comn:* Two wood carvings, comn by Mem Hosp, Jacksonville, Fla, 84; sculpture, Art-in-Public Places, Housing Urban Develop, 85. *Exhib:* Am Soc Mag Photogr Traveling Show, 62-63; one-woman shows, Pratt Inst, 66 & 67, Breast & Face, Steiglitz Gallery, NY, 75, Phillips Gallery, Jacksonville Univ, Fla, 77, Univ Fla, 78 & Computography, Neikrug Gallery, NY, 92; retrospect, Jacksonville Art Mus, 70; There is No Female Camera Traveling Show, Neikrug Gallery, NY, 75 & Univ NFla, 81; Fabulous Photographs, Cummer Mus, Jacksonville, Fla, 92; JCA Gallery, 98, 99, 2000; Fairfax Gallery, Jacksonville, Fla, 2000; Venice Redux, Haskell Gallery, Jacksonville Airport, 2003. *Teaching:* Adj prof photogr, Fine Arts Dept, Univ NFla, 80-81; Kodak guest artist, Ctr Creative Imaging, Camden, Maine, 92. *Awards:* Best Ann Report (2 yrs), Koger Co, Mead Paper Co, 79-80; Best Cover (photograph) Ann Reports, J Cato Ann Report Dept Cato Inst, 85. *Bibliog:* Elizabeth Kaufman (auth), My life & my art, Arts Assembler, 11/75; portfolio, Charter Issue Kalliope, A Tour of Women's Art, winter 79; Challenge of Freelance Photography (audio-visual prog), Media Loft Inc, 80 & Jacksonville Mag, 10/85; Profile in FL Times Union, March 2003. *Mem:* Am Soc Media Photogr (life); Soc Photogr Commun (pres, NFla chap, 65-70); Nat Soc Lit & Arts. *Media:* Computer Art, Photography, Digital Photography. *Interests:* Computer, Fiction Writing, Art Museums, Classical Music. *Publ:* Illusr, Jacksonville Calendar Diary Bicentennial Ed, 76; contribr, Longman Dict Mass Media & Communication, 82. *Mailing Add:* 2319 Isle Royale Lane Davis CA 95616

GEHRY, FRANK O(WEN)
ARCHITECT
b Toronto, Ont, Feb 28, 29; US citizen. *Study:* Univ Southern Calif Col Fine Arts, 49-51, Col Archit, BArch, 54; Harvard Univ Grad Sch Design, 56-57. *Hon Degrees:* Calif Inst Arts, D, 87; RI Sch Design, DFA, 87; Tech Univ NS, D Eng, 89; Otis Art Inst, DFA, 89; Occidental Col, LHD, 93; Whittier Col, D, 95; So Calif Inst Archit, D Archit, 97; LLD, Univ Toronto, 98; Univ Southern Calif, D, 2000; Yale Univ, D, 2000; Harvard Univ, D, 2000; Univ Edinburgh, D, 2000. *Work:* Mus Mod Art, Metrop Mus Art, NY; Los Angeles Mus Contemp Art; Philadelphia Mus Art. *Comn:* Calif Aerospace Mus, State Calif, Los Angeles, 83; Weisman Art Mus, Minneapolis, 93; Guggenheim Mus, Bibao, Spain, 97; Experience Music Proj, Seattle, 2000; Weatherhead Sch Mgt, Cleveland, 2002. *Exhib:* Los Angeles Co Mus Art, Calif, 65, 66, 68, 78, 80, 81, 83, 94 & 97; Chicago Tribune Late Entries, Inst Contemp Art, Chicago, 80; La Presenza del Passato, Biennale Venezia, Italy, 80; Documenta VII, Kasel, Ger, 82; Shape and Environment, Whitney Mus Am Art, 82; Ten New Buildings, Inst Contemp Art, London, 83; Calif Counterpoint, Nat Acad Design, NY, 83; Art of the Motorcycle, Solomon R Guggenheim Mus, NY, 98. *Pos:* Prin, Frank O Gehry & Assoc, Inc, 62-. *Teaching:* Vis critic, Rice Univ, 76, Univ Calif, Los Angeles, 79, Yale, 82, 85, 87, 88 & 89; William Bishop chair, Yale Univ, 79, Charlotte Davenport prof archit, 82, 85, 87, 88, 89 & 99; vis critic, Eliot Noyes chair, Harvard Univ, 84; vis scholar, Fed Inst Technol, Zurich, Switz, 96; vis prof, Univ Calif, Los Angeles, 98. *Awards:* Premium Imperiale, 92; Dorothy and Lilian Gish Prize, 94; Nat Medal Arts, Nat Endowment Arts, 98. *Bibliog:* Beyond Utopia, Michael Blackwood Productions, 83; Joseph Morgenstern (auth), The Gehry style, NY Times Mag, 5/16/83; Lindsay Stamm Schapiro (auth), A minimalist architecture of allusion, Progressive Archit, 6/83. *Mem:* Fel, Am Inst Archit; Nat Acad. *Publ:* Auth, Frank Gehry: Buildings and Projects, Rizzoli, New York, 85. *Mailing Add:* Frank O Gehry & Assoc 12541 Beatrice St Los Angeles CA 90066-7001

GEIER, PHILIP HENRY, JR
PATRON
b Pontiac, Mich, Feb 22, 35. *Study:* Colgate Univ, BA, 57; Columbia Univ, MS, 58; Delta Kappa Epsilon. *Pos:* With, McCann-Erickson, Inc, Cleveland, 58-60, New York City, 60-68; chmn, McCann-Erickson Int UK Co, London, 69-73; exec vpres, McCann-Erickson Europe, 73-75; vchmn, int operations McCann Worldwide, London, 73-75; vchmn, int Interpublic Group of Cos, Inc, New York City, 75-77, pres, chief operating off, 77-80, chmn, chief exec off, 80-2001, pres, 85-2000. *Mem:* Doubles (New York City); River (New York City); Sloane (London); Hurlingham (London); Whitney Mus of Am Art (trustee, currently). *Mailing Add:* Interpublic Group Cos Inc 1271 Avenue of the Americas Ste 400 New York NY 10020-1459

GEIGER, PHILLIP NEIL
PAINTER, DRAFTSMAN
b Ft Lauderdale, Fla, Feb 26, 56. *Study:* Wash Univ, BFA, 78; Yale Univ, MFA, 80. *Work:* Chemical Bank, New York, NY; Gen Foods, Minneapolis, Minn; CSX Corp, Richmond, Va; Stevens Co, Little Rock, Ark. *Exhib:* Solo exhibs, More Gallery, Philadelphia, 82 & 83, Swarthmore Col, 87 & Tatistcheff & Co, NY, 86, 88, 90, 93 & 95, Hollins Col, 89; Bodies & Souls, Artists' Choice Mus, NY, 83; Drawings, Drawings, Drawings, Forum Gallery, NY, 84; Painterly Realism, Fontbonne Col, St Louis, 84; Contemp Narrative Figure Painting (with catalog), Payne Gallery, Moravian Col, Bethlehem, Pa, 86; Am Art Today: The Figure in Landscape, Art Mus at Ft Lauderdale Int Univ, Miami, 86; Landscape Painting (with catalog), Gibbes Mus Art, Charleston; Reynolds, Richmond, Va, 98, 2001 & 03; Tibor De Nagy, NY, 2005; Hacket-Freedman, San Francisco, Calif, 2000 & 02. *Teaching:* Asst prof art, Colo State Univ, Ft Collins, 80-83 & Univ Va, Charlottesville, 83. *Bibliog:* Kay Larson (auth), New Fares '86, New York Mag, 3/86; Michael Kimmelman (auth), New York Times, 2/26/88; Ronnie Cohen (auth), Art Forum, 5/90. *Media:* Oil. *Dealer:* Peter Tatistcheff 50 W 57th St New York NY 10019. *Mailing Add:* Univ Va Dept Art Charlottesville VA 22903

GEISERT, ARTHUR FREDERICK
PRINTMAKER, ILLUSTRATOR
b Dallas, Tex, Sept 20, 41. *Study:* Concordia Teachers' Col, Seward, Nebr, BS, 63; Univ Calif, Davis, MA, 65; Chouinard Art Inst, Los Angeles; Otis Art Inst, Los Angeles; Art Inst Chicago. *Work:* Mus Art, Lodz, Poland; Freeport Art Mus, Ill; First Nat Bank Chicago; Standard Oil of Ind, Chicago; Calif Col Arts & Crafts, Oakland. *Exhib:* One-man shows, Ill Art Council Gallery, Chicago, 79, Foxley Leach Gallery, Washington, DC, 86, Boston Pub Libr, 86 & The Print Club, Philadelphia, 86; West 79, The Law, Minn Mus Art, St Paul, 79; 5th Univ Dallas Nat Print Invitational, Univ Dallas, 79. *Teaching:* From instr to asst prof art, Concordia Col, River Forest, Ill, 65-70; asst prof art, Concordia Col, Seward, Nebr, 70-71. *Awards:* 10 Recommended Picture Books, Time Mag, 95; Horn Book Honor Book, Boston Globe, 96; Silver Medal, Soc Illustrators, 96. *Mem:* Chicago Artists Coalition; Artists Equity Asn Inc; Boston Printmakers; The Print Club, Philadelphia; Los Angeles Printmaking Soc. *Media:* Etching. *Publ:* Auth & illsr, Oink Oink, 93; After the Flood, 94; Haystack, 95; Roman Numerals I to MM, 96; The Etcher's Studio, 97. *Mailing Add:* 6939 W Guilford Rd Galena IL 61036-9785

GEKIERE, MADELEINE
PAINTER - ACRYLIC, OIL & WATERCOLOR, FILMMAKER
b Zurich, Switz; US citizen, 19. *Study:* Art Students League, with Kantor; Brooklyn Mus Art Sch, with Tamayo; NY Univ, with Sam Adler. *Work:* Worcester Art Mus, Mass; Fogg Mus Art, Cambridge, Mass; NY Univ Collection; Brooklyn Mus, NY; Currier Gallery of Art, Manchester, NH; and others. *Exhib:* Univ Ga, 67; Western Carolina Univ, 72; NY Univ Loeb Ctr; many one-man shows in NY, Babcock Galleries, film showings, Millenium & Artists Space, The Collective for Living Cinema, NY & 2nd Int Women's Film Festival, Donell Branch NY Pub Libr. *Teaching:* Assoc prof painting, NY Univ, 58-67; prof painting, City Col NY, 67-90; vis prof painting, Univ Ga, 67; prof Emer, City Gallery of NY, currently. *Awards:* Best Ill Bk of Year, New York Times, 57, 59 & 63; Audubon Medal of Honor, 69; Childe Hassam Purchase Prize, Soc Art & Lett, 73. *Mem:* Artists Equity Asn. *Media:* Ink, Oil, Watercolor & Pencil. *Publ:* Auth & illusr, Who Gave Us, 53; illusr, Switch on the Night, 57; auth & illusr, The Princess & the Frilly Lilly, 60; illusr, The Reason for the Pelican, 60; illusr, John J Plenty and Fiddler Dan, 63. *Mailing Add:* 427 W 21st St New York NY 10011

GELBER, SAMUEL
PAINTER, EDUCATOR
b Brooklyn, NY, Mar 14, 29. *Study:* Brooklyn Col, BA; NY Univ, MA. *Work:* Purchase Mus, NY; Farnsworth Mus, ME; Brooklyn Mus, NY. *Comn:* painting, Bellevue Hosp, 86. *Exhib:* Brooklyn Mus Biennial, 56; one-man shows, Green Mountain Gallery, NY, 72, 74, 76 & 79, A Sense of Place, Wichita Art Mus, Kans, 73, Springfield Art Mus, Mo, 74 & Joslyn Art Mus, Nebr, 74; Maine Coast Artists, 98, Portland Mus, ME, 2000, Farnsworth Mus, ME, 2001; and others. *Teaching:* Instr drawing, Pratt Inst, Brooklyn, 62-65; prof painting & drawing, Brooklyn Col, 62-, chmn, 88, prof emer, 91-. *Awards:* Crane & Co Award for Painting, Berkshire Mus, 66. *Bibliog:* Lee Wallin (auth), New Realism 70, St Cloud State Col, 70; Alan Gussow (auth), A Sense of Place--the Artist and the American Land, Friends of Earth, 72; Sanford Sintz Shannan (auth), An interview with Philip Pearlstein, Art in Am, 9/81; Samuel Gelber, The Season Suite, Farnsworth Mus, 10/2001. *Media:* Oil, Lithography. *Mailing Add:* 215 W 98th St New York NY 10025

GELERNTER, DAVID H
CRITIC, PAINTER, EDUCATOR
Study: Yale Univ, BA; Yale Univ, MA (classical Hebrew Lit); State Univ NY, PhD (computer sci). *Pos:* Chief scientist, Mirror Worlds Technol. *Teaching:* Prof computer sci, Yale Univ, New Haven. *Mem:* Nat Coun Arts; Nat Endowment for Arts, 2002—. *Publ:* Cultural columnist, NY Post, art critic Weekly Standard; auth: Mirror Worlds, The Muse in the Machine; Computerizing the Poetry of Human Thought, 94, 39; The Lost World of the Fair, 95, Drawing Life, 97, Machine Beauty. *Mailing Add:* Nat Endowment Arts 1100 Pennsylvania Ave NW Washington DC 20506

GELINAS, ROBERT WILLIAM
PAINTER, EDUCATOR
b Springfield, Mass, Mar 1, 31. *Study:* Univ Conn; Univ Ala, BFA & MFA; also with Lawrence Calgagno & Tatsuiko Heima. *Work:* Kelley Fitzpatrick Mus, Montgomery, Ala; Mead Corp Collection, Atlanta, Ga; Fla House of Rep, Tallahassee; Mus Fine Arts, Little Rock, Ark. *Comn:* Chapel sculpture, Wesley Found Student Ctr, Memphis, 60. *Exhib:* Art USA, 58, NY, 58; 26th & 27th Corcoran Biennials, Washington, DC, 59 & 61; Painting of the Yr Ann, Mead Corp, Atlanta, 61; Bon Marche Nat Gallery Exhib, Seattle, Wash, 63; Fla Showcase, Rockefeller Ctr, NY, 64; Soc of Four Arts Exhibs, Palm Beach, Fla, 66, 72, 77, 78 & 79. *Pos:* Art dir, Tuscaloosa News, Ala, 55-57; artist-in-residence, Maitland Res Ctr, 65 & Upham Studio, Naples, 66-69. *Teaching:* Guest artist instr, Allisons Wells Art Colony Workshops, Canton, Miss, 58-62; asst prof art, Memphis State Univ, 58-63; from assoc prof to prof art, Univ SFla, 63-98. *Awards:* First Purchase Prize, Mid South Ann, 61; 18th Ann Purchase Exhib Prize, Carrol Reese Mus, 67; Best of Show, Gulf Coast Art Exhib, Bellaire, Fla, 78. *Bibliog:* Benbow (auth), All out war, St Petersburg Times, 8/65; Gelinas the modern master, Tampa Tribune, 66. *Media:* Acrylic. *Mailing Add:* 1325 Cocoanut Ave Sarasota FL 34236-2533

GELLER, BUNNY ZELDA
WRITER, SCULPTOR
b New York, NY, May 21, 26. *Study:* Univ Calif, Los Angeles, 44-46; studied with Alfred Van Loen & Philip Darling & Berta Margolies, 62-70; Fla Int Univ, 89-87. *Work:* Nat Mus Women Arts, Washington, DC; Broward Co Main Libr, Ft Lauderdale, Fla; Kushi Found, Brookline, Mass; Hallandale Cult Ctr, Fla. *Comn:* Two sculptures,

Hallandale Cult Ctr, Fla, 98. *Exhib:* One-man shows, Bowery Savings Bank, NY, 78, Lynn Kottler Galleries, NY, 78 & Hollywood Art Mus, Fla, 78-79; All Broward Exhib, Ft Lauderdale, Fla, 78; Old Westbury Hebrew Congregation, NY, 78; De Ligny Galleries, Ft Lauderdale, Fla, 79 & 83-84; Int Treasure Fine Art, Plainview, NY, 78, 79, 80 & 81; Int Art Expo (with catalog), NY, 82, 83 & 92; Exhibition of Fine Art, Nassau Mus Fine Art Asn, 85; Nelson Rockefeller Collection Inc, NY, 83; First Ann Int Wildlife Expo, Atlantic City, 83; United Nations Conf, Nairobi, 85; Hallandale Cult Ctr, Fla, 98. *Pos:* Judge, Fine Art & Craft Show, Ft Lauderdale, Fla, 79-81; art adv coun, Westbury Mem Libr, NY, 90-94. *Awards:* First Prize, Carrier Found Auxilary Arts Festival, 85; Ed Choice Award, Nat Libr Poetry, 95; Inductee, Int Poetry Hall Fame, 96. *Bibliog:* Town & Country Mag, 82; Art in Am Mag, 83-84; Sunstorm Arts Mag, 84. *Mem:* Nat Mus Women Arts Asn; distinguished mem Int Soc Poets. *Media:* Bronze, Clay. *Publ:* Auth, Bunny Geller Original Poetry, 95; Choices, 96; contribr, Beyond the Stars, 95 & Best Poems of the 90's, 96; Kaleidoscope, 97; The Monkey and the Parakeet (A Poetic Tale for Children), 97; auth, Impressions, 99. *Mailing Add:* 400 Diplomat Pkwy Apt 711 Hallandale FL 33009-3732

GELLER, ESTHER GELLER SHAPERO
PAINTER, PRINTMAKER
b Boston, Mass, Oct 26, 21. *Study:* Mus Fine Arts Sch, Boston, dipl; also with Karl Zerbe. *Work:* Mus Fine Arts, Boston; Addison Gallery Am Art, Andover, Mass; Brandeis Univ; Walters Gallery, Regis Col; St Mark's Sch Gallery, Southboro, Mass. *Exhib:* Art Inst Chicago Ann; US Info Serv Circulating Exhibs in the US & Far East; one-man show, Am Acad Art Gallery, Rome, 71, Newton Art Ctr, 78, Artworks at the Wayne, 79 & Stonehill Col, 86; Pastel Show, Regis Col, 84; Honored Artists, Danforth Mus, 95; and others. *Teaching:* Instr painting & drawing, Sch Mus Fine Arts, Boston, 43, Boris Mirski Art Sch, 46-48, Natick Art Asn Sch, 55-61 & Wayland Art Asn, 83. *Awards:* Cabot Fel, 49; Fels, MacDowell Colony, Yaddo & Am Acad, 50-71. *Bibliog:* Pratt & Fizell (auth), Encaustic, Lear Publ, 49; Bern Chaet (auth), Artists at Work, Webb, 60; B Hayes (auth), The Layman's Guide to Modern Art; R Lister (auth), Drawing with Pastel; and others. *Media:* Watercolor, Encaustic. *Dealer:* Geller Studio 5 Summer St Natick Mass 01760; Firehouse Studios. *Mailing Add:* 9 Russell Cir Natick MA 01760

GELLER, MATTHEW
SCULPTOR
b New York, NY, Sept 28, 54. *Study:* Conn Col, BA, 76; Univ Del, MFA, 78. *Work:* Mus Mod Art, Whitney Mus Am Art, Franklin Furnace, NY; Stedelijk Van Abbemuseum, Einhoven, Moderna Musset, Stockholm. *Exhib:* The Times Square Show, Collaborative Proj Inc, 80, Mus Mod Art, 82, 87, 88, 94 & 2000, Int Ctr For Photog, NY, 89; Mus Mod Art, Jerusalem, 81; Long Beach Mus, 82, La Jolla Mus, Calif, 87; Whitney Mus Am Art, 83, 90 & 96; Inst Contemp Art, Boston, 84; Laforet Mus, New Orleans, 84; Your Television, Your Home, New Mus Contemp Art, NY, 90; Witte de With, Rotterdam, 99. *Pos:* VPres, Collaborative Proj Inc, NY, 81-82; co-dir, Line Asn, NY, 81-83; consult, Visual Arts, Nat Endowment for the Arts, 84, 85; co-chair media panel, NY State Coun on the Arts, 86-88. *Teaching:* Sch of Visual Arts, NY, 83-84, 86-90, Univ Calif, San Diego, 87, Princeton Univ, 88, William Col, Williamstown, Mass, 90, Pratt Inst, 94- & Parsons Sch Design, 96-. *Awards:* Nat Endowment Arts Fel Visual Arts, 87 & 89; Rome Prize, Am Acad in Rome, 91-92; Fel, Creative Capital Foun, 99-2000. *Bibliog:* Articles in Village Voice, NY Times, Artnews, Art in American & Art Forum. *Mem:* NY State Coun Arts. *Media:* Mixed Media, Installation. *Publ:* Contribr, Difficulty Swallowing: A Medical Chronicle, 81 & 1983 Engagements, 82, Works Press, NY; Hidden away in a musty chamber, Wedge Mag, 83; Windfalls, In: Just Another Asshole, Japanese Artists Asn, 84; From Receiver to Remote Control: The TV Set, New Mus Contemp Art, 90. *Dealer:* Revolution 23257 Woodward Ave Ferndale Mich 48220; Lawrence/Feuer/Lamontagne Gallery 531 West 26 New York NY 10001. *Mailing Add:* 4 White St New York NY 10013

GELLIS, SANDY L
SCULPTOR, ENVIRONMENTAL ARTIST
b Bronx, NY. *Study:* Sch Visual Arts; City Col New York; New Sch Social Res, FIT (AAS). *Work:* Libr Congress, Washington, DC; Brooklyn Mus, Whitney Mus & Spencer Col, NY Publ Libr; Allentown Art Mus, Pa; Fogg Art Gallery, Harvard Univ, Mass; Nat Mus Natural Hist, Washington, DC. *Comn:* River Memory, Work Wall, Children's Room, Helen B Atkinson Health Ctr; Cygnus A: Environment, Pub Libr Plaza, Bronx, NY, 92-94; River Memory, Word Wall, Children's Room, Helen Batkinson Health Ctr; and many others. *Exhib:* Projects and Portfolios, 25th Nat Print Biennial, Brooklyn Mus, NY, 89; Presswork: The Art of 100 Women Printmakers (traveling), Nat Mus Women Arts, Washington, DC, 91; solo exhib, Gallery Three Zero (with catalog), 92, TZArt & Co, 95 & Karen McReady Fine Art, NY, 98; Karen McReady Fine Art, NY, 97, 98 & 2000; Contemp Narratives in Am Prints, Whitney Mus Am Art at Champion, Conn, 2000; Prints & Drawings 1960-2000, Arthur M Sackler Mus, Harvard Univ Art Mus, Cambridge, 2000. *Collection Arranged:* LA Specola Natural History Mus, Florence Italy; United States Dept of State; J P Morgan & Co, NY; Houghton Libr, Harvard Univ, Mass; Prudential Ins Co Am, NY; Mem Art Gallery, Univ Rochester, NY; Whitney Mus Am Art, NY; NY Pub Libr; Fogg Art Gallery, Harvard Univ, Cambridge, Mass; Brooklyn Mus; Northlands Glass Workshop, Scotland. *Teaching:* Instr, Sch Visual Arts, NY, 79-2000 & Fashion Instr Technol, 80-83; vis artist, Sch Visual Arts, 79-2000, Fashion Inst Tech, 80-83, Md Inst Art, Parsons Sch Art & Design, C W Post Univ, Univ Gallery Fine Arts Ctr, Univ Mass, Amherst & Univ Idaho, Moscow; guest artist, printmaking workshop, NY, 86-87 & 93, NY Experimental Glass Workshop, 84. *Awards:* Grants, Sculpture, 79-80 & 81-82 & Drawing & Printmaking, 87-88, Nat Endowment Arts; MacDowell Fel, Sculpture, 79; CAPS Fel, Sculpture, 78. *Bibliog:* Articles, NY Times, 90 & 94; Zahra Partovi (dir), Footsteps (video), 97; Richard Yelle (auth), Glass Art from Urban Glass, 2000; many others. *Media:* Etching, Printmaking. *Interests:* Environment; Computers; Space; Cultures. *Publ:* Earth-Mapping Artists Reshaping Landscape, Edward S Casey; Auth, Intericon 1986 (exhib catalogs, 1 & 2), Charlottenborg, Denmark, 86; Glass (exhib catalog), Soc Arts Crafts, Pittsburgh, Pa, 89; Projects and Portfolios, 25th Nat Print Biennial (exhib catalog), Brooklyn Mus, NY, 89; Political Landscapes (exhib catalog), Hillwood Art Mus, Greenvale, NY, 90; and numerous other exhib catalogs. *Mailing Add:* 39 Bond St New York NY 10012

GELTNER, DANITA SUE
SCULPTOR, PAINTER
b Atlanta, Ga, May 19, 52. *Study:* Studied at Sorbonne, Paris, France, certificat Francaise, 73; Univ Pittsburgh, BA, 76; Md Inst Col Art; MFA, 78. *Work:* K & B Found, New Orleans, La; Verlain Found, New Orleans, La; Prudential Collection, Newark, NJ. *Comn:* Window installation, Charles Jordan Shoes, Trump Tower, NY, 92. *Exhib:* Art Mart Gallery, NY, 85 & 86; PPOW Gallery, NY, 87; Grace Borgenicht Gallery, NY, 88; UP Gallery, Pittsburgh, Pa, 91; Mendelson Gallery, Pittsburgh, Pa, 92. *Awards:* Art Matters Inc, Found Grant, New York, 86 & 88; Committee Award, Biennial Exhib, Fine Arts Mus S, 87. *Bibliog:* Michael Brenson (auth), Danita Geltner, NY Times, 2/7/86; Elizabeth Hess (auth), Faux foe, Village Voice, 6/30/87; Kate Linker (auth), Review, Art Forum, 10/87. *Mem:* Orgn Independent Artists, NY; Artists in Residence, NY; Artists Equity, NY; White Columns, NY (secy bd dir, 90-92); Ringside, NY. *Mailing Add:* 80 Warren St No 19 New York NY 10007-1013

GENAUER, EMILY
CRITIC, WRITER
b New York, NY. *Study:* Hunter Col, grad; Sch Jour, Columbia Univ, BLit; Nat Acad. *Pos:* Staff writer & art feature writer, New York World, 29-31; art critic & ed, New York World-Tel, 32-49; art critic, New York Herald Tribune, 49-66; art critic & ed, New York World Jour Tribune, 66-67; art commentator, Educ TV, New York, 67-77; art critic-columnist, Newsday Syndicate, 67-76; adv bd, Sch Jour, Columbia Univ. *Awards:* New York Newspaper Women's Club Award for Outstanding Column in Any Field, 49, 56, 58, 60 & 69; Columbia Univ Jour Alumni Award, 60; Pulitzer Prize, Distinguished Art Critic in Journalism, 75. *Mem:* Nat Coun Humanities; Int Asn Art Critics; New York Newspaper Women's Club. *Publ:* Auth, Toulouse-Lautrec (monogr), 53, Biography of Chagall, 57, Hommage a l'Ecole de Paris, 62, Biography of Tamayo 74, Metrop Mus Art, NY; Chagall at the Met, 71; and others

GENIUSZ, ROBERT MYLES
PRINTMAKER, FILMMAKER
b Milwaukee, Wis, Aug 30, 48. *Study:* Sch Fine Arts, Univ Wis, Milwaukee, BFA, 74, MFA, 76. *Work:* Kohler Art Ctr, Sheboygan, Wis; Sheboygan Pub Schs, Wis; Performing Art Ctr, Theatre Sch, Milwaukee. *Comn:* Puppet Theatre, Kohler Art Ctr, Sheboygan, Wis, 76. *Exhib:* Strange Tales, Kohler Art Ctr, Sheboygan, Wis, 76; Ann Beloit & Vicinity, Wright Arts Ctr, Beloit, Wis, 76, 77 & 79; Artists/Toys, Milwaukee Art Ctr, 77 & 79; Toys Designed by Artists, Ark Arts Ctr, Little Rock, 78 & 27th Ann Delta Invitational, 79; Form, Fun & Fantasy, Mt Mary Col, Milwaukee 78; one-man show, Printed Worlds, Oshkosh Pub Mus, Wis, 79; Wisconsin Artists, Cudahay Gallery, Milwaukee Art Mus, 83; Int Paper Conference, Kyoto, Japan, 83; and others. *Teaching:* Instr 3-D, 2D & drawing, Univ WisParkside, Kenosha, Jan, 78; instr filmaking, Univ Wis-Milwaukee, Sept, 79; artist in residence filmaking, Performing Art Ctr, Milwaukee, Wis, 79-80, Milwaukee Pub Schs, 81-83. *Awards:* Nat Endowment Arts Grant, Artist-in-Residence Prog, 76-77 & 79-84. *Bibliog:* Evelyn Terry Bridges (auth), Wisconsin artists make toys, Milwaukee, Vol 4, No 12, 12/79. *Mem:* Col Art Asn Am; Artists Equity Asn. *Mailing Add:* 997 Granville Rd Cedarburg WI 53012-9379

GENKIN, JONATHAN
PAINTER
b New York, NY, 57. *Exhib:* Solo exhibs, Damon Brandt Gallery, New York, 86-89, Galeria Bonk, Cologne, Ger, 87 & Daniel Newburg Gallery, NY, 89; Glastnost, Galeria Bonk, Cologne, Ger, 87; From the Monochrome and Beyond, Univ Maine, Orono, 88; The Colour Alone: The Monochrome Experiment, Mus St Pierre, Lyon, France, 88. *Awards:* Nat Endowment Arts Fel, 87. *Mailing Add:* 332 Mount Airy Rd Croton On Hudson NY 10520-1604

GENN, NANCY
PAINTER, SCULPTOR
b San Francisco, Calif. *Study:* San Francisco Art Inst, Calif; Univ Calif, Berkeley. *Work:* San Francisco Mus Mod Art; Mus Mod Art, Brooklyn Mus, NY; Nat Mus Am Art, Smithsonian Inst, Libr Congress, Washington; Los Angeles Co Mus Art, Calif; Mills Col Art Mus, Oakland, Calif; and others. *Comn:* Bronze lectern & five bronze sculptures for chancel table, First Unitarian Church, Berkeley, Calif, 61 & 64; bronze fountain, Cowell Col, Univ Calif, Santa Cruz, 66; bronze menorah, Temple Beth Am, Los Altos Hills, Calif, 68; 17 murals in ceramic glazed tile & two bronze fountain sculptures, Sterling Vineyards, Caligosta, Calif, 72 & 73; bronze fountain sculpture, Expo 74, Spokane, Wash, 74; pair of mixed media paintings on paper, IBM, San Jose, Calif. *Exhib:* Solo shows, MH de Young Mem Mus, San Francisco, 55 & 63, San Francisco Mus Art, 61, New Worlds, Oakland Art Mus, 71, Los Angeles Inst Contemp Art, 76, Harcourts Gallery, San Francisco, 91 & 96, Brendan Walter Gallery, Los Angeles, Calif, 92, Mills Col Art Mus, Calif, 99, Leighton Gallery, Blue Hill, Maine, 2000, Ulivi Gallery, Prato, Italy, 02; Fresno Art Mus, Fresno, Calif, 2003; Bolinas Mus, Bolinas, Calif, 2003; Istituto Ital di Cult & the Chicago Art Inst, Chicago, Ill, 2004; Istituto Italiano di Cult, Los Angeles, Calif, 2004; group show, Twentieth Century Drawings, Stanford Univ, Palo Alto, Calif, 55; Winter Invitational, Calif Palace Legion Hon, San Francisco, 60-63; group show, Contemp Reflections, Aldrich Mus, Ridgefield, Conn, 72-73; group show, Works on Paper, Mus Mod Art, NY, 76;

group show, Paper as Medium Smithsonian Inst Traveling Exhib, 78-80; group show, Making Paper, Am Craft Mus, NY, 82-84; group show, Paper as Image, Arts Coun Gt Brit, 83-84; Paper Works: Seven Perspectives, Tampa Mus, Fla, 86; group show, First Int-Biennale Paper Art, Leopold-Hoesch Mus, Duren, WGer, 86; solo show, Takada Gallery, San Francisco, 99, 03, Michael Petronko Gallery, NY, 97, Fresno Art Mus, 03, Bolinas Art Mus, 03 & Leighton Gallery, Blue Hill, ME, 99 & 2000; group shows, DL Gallery, Seoul, South Korea, 02, Monique Goldstrom Gallery, New York City, 02, Portland Art Mus, Oreg, 97, JJ Bookings Gallery, San Francisco, 97, Albright-Knox Gallery, Buffalo, NY, 93-94, 95. *Collection Arranged:* Albright-Knox Art Gallery, Buffalo, NY; Aldritch Mus, Ridgefield, Conn; Am Craft Mus, New York City; Auckland Mus, New Zealand; Brooklyn Mus, NY; Cincinnati Art Mus; Indianapolis Mus Art; Internat Ctr Aesthetic Rsch, Italy; Libr Congress, Washington, DC; Los Angeles Co Mus; Mills Col, Oakland, Calif; Mus Modern Art, New York City; Nat Mus Am Art, Washington, DC; Smithsonian Inst, Washington, DC; New York Univ Art Collection; Oakland Mus, Calif; San Francisco Mus Art; Univ Calif, Berkeley; New York Public Libr. *Pos:* Univ of CA, Berkeley, Art Alumni, Advisory Board Member; Kala Art Institute, Board Member, Berkeley, CA. *Awards:* Purchase Award Painting, State of Calif, 57; Hon Award for Design Excellence, US Dept Housing & Urban Develop, 68; US-Japan Creative Arts Fel, 78-79. *Bibliog:* David Bourdon (auth), Pulp Artists Paper MOMA, The Village Voice, 106, 8/23/1976; Robert McDonald (auth), Genn and Al-Hilali - Works in Paper, Artweek, Vol VIII, 8, 2/19/1977; Deloris Tarzan (auth), Nancy Genn Grows, Seattle Times, 4/15/1977; Max Wykes-Joyce (auth), Art in London, Internat Herald Tribune, Paris, 4/21/1978; John Perreault (auth), Paperworks, American Craft, 2, 6, 8-9/1982; Alan G Artner, Artcritic-Review, Nancy Genn, Chicago Tribune, May 21. 2004. *Media:* Mixed media on paper; mixed media on canvas, Bronze Sculpture. *Res:* lectures on handmade paper in contemporary art. *Specialty:* contemporary, modern. *Interests:* architecture & aesthetics. *Publ:* Nancy Genn, Paper Paintings, essay by Jane Farmer, 84, Andro Crispo Gallery, New York,; Nancy Genn, Places of Light, Recent Paintings essay, by Bruce Nixon, 97; Catalogue- Nancy Genn, Istituto Italiano di Cultura, Chicago, IL, Curator, Francesca, Valente, 2004. *Dealer:* Takada Gallery 251 Post St San Francisco CA; Flatfile Galleries, 217 North Carpenter, Chicago, IL, 60607. *Mailing Add:* 1515 La Loma Ave Berkeley CA 94708

GENTILE, GLORIA IRENE
DESIGNER, SCULPTOR, PAINTER
b New York, NY. *Study:* Cooper Union, New York, 47-50; Yale Univ, 51-54, BFA & MFA; study with Josef Albers, Will Barnet, Abraham Rattner, Nicholas Marscicano, Stuart Davis, Buckminster Fuller, Philip Johnson, Frederick Kiesler, Louis Kahn, Frank Lloyd Wright & Alvin Lustig. *Exhib:* One-person shows, Art Dirs Club, NY, 68, Young & Rubican Gallery, NY, 68, Ogilvy & Mather Inc Gallery, NY, 68, William Esty Gallery, NY, 68, Batten, Barton, Burstine & Osborne Agency, NY, 69, Cooper Union Gallery, NY, 74, Caffe Latte & Double Rainbow, Calif, 94; Sculpture Happening, Mus Mod Art, NY, 72; Los Angeles Art Asn, 91-94; Contemp Images Gallery, 92; Midway Hosp, Los Angeles, 93; Computer paintings, Cyberspace, Calif, 93. *Pos:* Founder & dir, Gentile Studio Computer Graphics, 75-2005. *Teaching:* Instr concepts & promotion, Sch Visual Arts, New York, 68-74 & Parsons Sch Design, 72-; instr promotional design, Cooper Union, 74-; Queens Col, 78-79; instr, Fashion Inst Technology, 80-81 & Pratt Inst, 82-83. *Awards:* Graphic Design Desi Award. *Bibliog:* Article in New Worlds of Reading, Harcourt Brace Jovanovich, 69. *Mem:* Art Dir Club. *Media:* Articulated Bronze, Ball Joints, sculpture, Watercolors. *Mailing Add:* 333 E 46th St Apt 6F New York NY 10017

GENTRY, AUGUSTUS CALAHAN, JR
PAINTER, PRINTMAKER
b Tyler, Tex, Feb 5, 27. *Study:* Tyler Jr Col, AA, 48; Univ Tex, with Boyer Gonzales, Ralph White & Seymour Fogel, BFA, 52. *Work:* Am Nat Life Collection, Galveston, Tex; Shell Oil Collection, Houston; Repub Nat Bank, Dallas; First City Bank & InterFirst Bank, Tyler, Tex; Spring Valley Collection, Dallas. *Comn:* McKittrick Canyon (16 pieces), comn by Donors of McKittrick Canyon Nat Park, Houston, 70. *Exhib:* NY Int, 70; Southwest Watercolor Soc 100 Best Ann, 73 & 74; Midwest Wildlife Art Show, Kansas City, Mo, 74-75; Outdoors in Ga, Nat Wildlife Show, 76-77 & 79-82; one-man show, Tyler Mus Fine Art, 2006. *Teaching:* Grad asst sculpture, Univ Tex, Austin, 52-53; instr art, Tyler Independent Sch Dist, 53-59; instr watercolor, Tyler Jr Col, 70-73; artist-in-residence, Univ Tex, Tyler, 80-, instr overseas grad studies in watercolor, 83. *Awards:* Tex State Artist, 73; Signature Mem Award, Southwest Watercolor Soc, 74. *Bibliog:* Wilkins (auth), The local gentry, Chronicles, Smith Co Hist Soc, 70; E L Enloe (auth), E Guide, 5/21/98. *Mem:* Southwest Watercolor Soc; Graphics Soc. *Media:* Watercolor; Etching. *Publ:* Illusr, Chronicles of Smith Co, Tex, 70 & 71. *Mailing Add:* 922 S Bois D Arc Ave Tyler TX 75701-1507

GENTRY, WARREN MILLER
PAINTER
b Manville, Wyo, Oct 3, 21. *Study:* Ariz State Univ, with Tom J Harter, BA, 50, MA, 55; Univ Calif, Berkeley, with Frank Lobdell, 64. *Work:* Munic Collection, Orange, France. *Exhib:* Ariz State Fair Fine Arts Exhib, 49-63; 1st Ariz Ann, Phoenix, 59; Fresh Paint Show, MH De Young Mus, 59; Old Phoenix Art Mus. *Pos:* Founding chmn dept art, 63-68, Glendale Col & founding dir, Art Collection, 63-69; owner & founder, The Gentry Gallery, Scottsdale, Ariz. *Teaching:* Prof art hist & painting, Glendale Community Col, 63-83; retired. *Awards:* Valley Bank Purchase Award, 1st Ariz Ann, 59. *Mem:* Scottsdale Beautification Comn (first chmn); founding mem, Scottsdale Fine Arts Comn. *Media:* Oil, Watercolor. *Res:* experimenting with hist painting surface. *Interests:* World travel including South Am, Africa, Asia & Europe. *Collection:* Asian art: Chinese cloisonne and champleve collection of 45 pieces from fifteenth century Ming through the period of Qianlong; Buddha sculpture collection of bronze, stone, and wood (16 pieces); 20 pieces of carved ivory; collection of jade. *Mailing Add:* PO Box 4082 Scottsdale AZ 85261

GENUTE, CHRISTINE TERMINI
PAINTER, SCULPTOR
b Brooklyn, NY, Sept 30, 47. *Study:* Pratt Inst, BFA; Hunter Col, study with Tony Smith & Robert Walker, MFA. *Exhib:* Long Beach Mus, NY, 80 & 81; Nat Soc Painters Casein & Acrylic, 81; one-woman show, Univ Pa, 82; Laguna Beach Mus Art, Calif, 84; Newport Harbor Art Mus, Calif, 84; EAC Gallery, NY, 85-90; Beaux Arts Gallery, Southbury, Conn, 88; Phoenix Gallery, NY, 88; Mahwah Libr, NJ, 99; Ridgewood Art Inst, NJ, 2000; Bergenfield Libr, NJ, 2001. *Pos:* Art dir, Circle Galleries, New York, 76-77, Jack Gallerie, New York, 76-77, Gallerie La Grande Illusion, New York, 77, Neill Gallery, New York, 78-79, Atelier Royce Ltd, 81, Hanover Fine Arts, Mass, 83; bd mem, CHADD of Bergen Co, NJ. *Teaching:* Lectr galleries, New Sch, Sch Visual Arts, New York, 77-78; adj prof, La Guardia Community Col, 89-90. *Bibliog:* Chris Jones (auth), The 24 Hour Room, Am Home Mag, 5/77; New York Art Rev, 88. *Media:* Acrylic, Oil, Clay, Oil Pastel Originals. *Interests:* involvement in creative/multi-sensory/ learning as a learning Consultant. *Collection:* Ridgewood Gallery, 2/2003 Group Show. *Publ:* New York Art Review Les Krantz by American Reference. *Mailing Add:* 81 Malcolm Rd Mahwah NJ 07430

GEOFFREY, IQBAL
CONCEPTUAL ARTIST, SCULPTOR
b Chiniot, Pakistan, Jan 1, 39. *Study:* Govt Col, Lahore, Pakistan, BA; Punjab Univ, LLB (Summa cum Laude), 59, Sangamon State Univ, MA; Harvard Univ, LLM; Read Univ, PhD & Hon LLD; Univ of the Panjab, DLitt, 03. *Work:* Boston Mus Fine Arts; Philips Collection; Tate Gallery; Arts Coun Gt Britain; Cornell Univ Mus Art; St James Palace, London; British Mus, London; Pasadena Mus Art, Lord Baden-Powell House, London; Worcester Art Mus; Smith Col; and others. *Exhib:* Conceptual Occurrences, Hyde Park, London, 60; one-man shows, Arts Coun Pakistan, 64, Cent Wash State Col, 71, Cornell Univ, 72, Los Angeles Municipal Art Gallery, 73 & Everson Mus, Syracuse, NY, 74, among others; Hayward Gallery, 89-90; Embassy of France, Pakistan, 92; The Southall Graveyards, Maddox, 94-; Lahore Art Gallery, 95; Dickinson State Univ Art Gallery, NDak, 03; SUA Sponte Art Fest, Nat Gallery, London, 03. *Pos:* Dir, Mus Conceptual Art, Lahone, 68-70 & Geoffrey tey Khitran, 1960-; Chmn, Geoffrey & Khitran, 60-. *Teaching:* Prof fine arts, St Mary's Col, Ind, 67-68; prof fine arts, Cent Wash State Univ, 70-71; vis prof fine arts, Cleveland State Univ, 71-72; prof art Hist, Hunerkada Col Art, 91-. *Awards:* John D Rockefeller III Award Creative Painting, 64 & 65; Pub Tribute by the President of Pakistan, 64; Paris Biennale Award, 65; Arts Coun of Great Britain Award for Painting, 68; Ctrl Washington State Univ Award for Creativity, 71; Sir Herbert Read Medal, 92; LHCBA Millennium Award, 02; and others. *Bibliog:* Herbert Read-H W Janson (auth), Iqbal Geoffrey, Grand Central Moderns, 63; David Luisi (auth), Re: Iqbal Geoffrey, CWSC, 70; Edward Lucie-Smith (auth), Race, Sex & Gender in Art, London, 94. *Publ:* Grad ed, Harvard Art Rev, 65-66; auth, The Concept of Human Rights in Islam, 80; auth, How to Make Love to a Judge, 83

GEORGE, PATRICIA
PAINTER
b Cheyenne, Wyo. *Study:* Univ Calif, Los Angeles, BA. *Work:* Hilton Hotel, Long Beach, Calif; J C Penney Bus Systems, Dallas, Tex; Instar Corp, Montgomery, Ala. *Comn:* Four major oil paintings, Hilton Hotel Corp, Los Angeles, Calif, 91; numerous interior designs. *Exhib:* Int Invitational, Hellenic Inst, Athens, Greece, 90; Permanent Collection, Commanderie d Unet Mus, Bordeaux, France, 92; Grand Prix de France, Chapelle de la Sorbonne, Paris, France, 92; Permanent Collection, Fayette Mus, Ala, 93; Int Exhib, Int Artists Japan, Tokyo, 93; Int Artists Sapporo, Japan, 97. *Awards:* Lauret Award, Vieux de la Colombier, French Minister of Culture, 90; Spec Award of Jury, Exhib Famboyance, Musee d'Art Moderne, France, 93; Winner Cover Contest, Manhattan Arts, NY, 93. *Bibliog:* Irene Kleist (auth), Patricia George artist, Metro Mag, 89; Alexandra Shaw (auth), Patricia George captures impact of scene, Manhattan Arts, 9/92; Diana Roberts (auth), Patricia George follows the Sun, Manhattan Arts, 9/93. *Media:* Oil. *Mailing Add:* 4141 Ball Rd Studio 221 Cypress CA 90630

GEORGE, RAYMOND ELLIS
PRINTMAKER, EDUCATOR
b Cedar Falls, Iowa, Sept 13, 33. *Study:* Univ Northern Iowa, BA, 55, MA, 62. *Work:* Smithsonian Inst, Washington, DC; The Dupont Corp; Victoria & Albert Mus, London, Eng; Libr Cong, Washington, DC; NY Pub Libr. *Comn:* Ceramic mural, Dubuque Pub Schs, Iowa, 60. *Exhib:* Contemp Am Prints, State Univ NY Col Oneonta, 69; Nat Drawing Exhib, Ark Art Ctr, 88; one-man show, Printworks Gallery, Chicago, Ill, 87-88; Am Miniature Printmakers Exhib, San Diego, Calif, 88; 11th Nat Print Invitational, Univ Dallas, 89; Am Portfolio II, Printmaking Coun NJ, 89. *Teaching:* Prof art, Ill State Univ, Normal, 71-, artist in residence, Munson Williams Proctor Inst, Sch Art, Utica, NY. *Awards:* Purchase Awards, Eight-State Print Exhib, J B Speed Art Mus, 74, 83 & Nat Drawing Exhib, Southern Ill Univ, Carbondale, 75; Visual Artist Award, Nat Endowment Arts, 85. *Mem:* Boston Printmakers; Col Art Asn. *Media:* Intaglio, Drawing. *Publ:* Auth, Graphite Lithography, Tamerind Tech Papers, 77; Chicago Art Rev, 89. *Mailing Add:* 1907 Garling Dr Bloomington IL 61701

GEORGE, SYLVIA JAMES
PAINTER, ILLUSTRATOR
b Syracuse, NY, Oct 13, 21. *Study:* Pratt Inst, 44; Am Univ, 53; pvt study with Robert Gates, 53, John H Sanden 77-78 & Daniel Greene, 82. *Work:* John F Kennedy Libr, Boston, Mass; Howard High Sch, Ellicott City, Md; DuFief Elementary Sch, Gaithersburg, Md; St Louis Church, Clarksville, Md; Howard Community Col, Columbia, Md; S Bauman, Elkridge Hist Soc. *Comn:* Portrait of Milton S Kronheim & the Hon Judge Milton S Kronheim Jr of the Kronheim Co, Alpha Gamma Rho, AB Hamilton Univ Md; eight portraits, Belgian dignitaries; portrait of Mike Cusimano,

Asn Growth Enterprises Inc, 93; portrait of Nicholas B Mangione Sr, Md Health Enterprises, 94; portrait of Charles Kratz & Family, Kratz Auto Parts Inc, 94. *Exhib:* Solo exhib, Howard Community Col, Columbia, Md, 73; Baltimore Watercolor Soc Show, Turner Bldg, Johns Hopkins, 76; Slayton House Gallery, Columbia, Md, 70-88; Life of Baltimore Gallery, Baltimore, 84; Corcoran Gallery, Washington, 85; Faces: A Look Within, Shenandoah Col, Winchester, Va, 85; 100th Anniversary of the Automobile, Daimler-Benz, Stuttgard, WGer, 85; Mansion Art Gallery, Rockville, 96. *Pos:* Chmn registry, Howard Co Arts Coun, Md, 79-80; vpres, Visual Arts Alliance, 80-82; dir publicity, Md Pastel Soc, 86; chmn, art selection comt, Slayton House, Columbia, Md, currently; pres, SJG Art Studio/Gallery, currently. *Teaching:* Pvt adult instr, 70's; instr children, Glenely Co Sch, 70's; art asst, drawing & painting, Palotti High Sch, Md, 80-82; artist-in-residence, Oakland Mills High Sch, Md, 82. *Awards:* Dey Brothers Award, 36; First Prize, Johns Hopkins Univ-APL Art Competition, 79. *Bibliog:* Article in The Sun, Howard Co, 9/29/93; Article in Washington Post, Howard Co, 10/7/93; Article in Columbia Mag, summer 94. *Mem:* Artists Equity; Md Pastel Soc; New Art Ctr; Nat Mus Women Arts; Md Soc Portrait Painters; Portrait Club New York; Visual Arts Alliance; Col Art Asn. *Media:* Oil, Watercolor. *Publ:* Illusr, covers, Guard Mag, Johnson Studios, 76-78. *Mailing Add:* SJG Art Studio/Gallery 8600 Foundry St Savage MD 20763-9512

GEORGE, THOMAS
PAINTER, DRAFTSMAN
b New York, NY, July 1, 18. *Study:* Dartmouth Col, BA, 40; Art Students League; Acad Grand Chaumiere, Paris; Ist Statale Arte, Florence, Italy. *Work:* Guggenheim Mus, Mus Mod Art, Whitney Mus & Brooklyn Mus, NY; San Francisco Mus; Mus Am Art, Washington, DC; Tate Gallery, London, Eng; Mus Fine Arts, Houston; Nat Gallery, Oslo, Norway; Bridgestone Mus, Tokyo; numerous corp collections including Chase Manhattan Bank, AT&T, RCA, Ford Motor Co, Portland Art Mus, Maine, Mus of Contemp Art (Samtidskunst), Oslo, Norway; Princeton Univ, 2005; Rider Univ, NJ, 2006; others. *Comn:* Tapestry, Slatkin Art Gallery, NY, 68; poster/print, US Olympic Comt & Kennedy Galleries, NY, 74; Dodge Found, 87. *Exhib:* Whitney Mus Am Art Ann, 60-62 & 65; Princeton Univ Art Mus, 75; Nat Collection Fine Arts, 77; Betty Parsons Gallery, 68, 70, 72, 74, 76, 78 & 81; Maxwell Davidson, NY, 83 & 85; Retrospective, NJ State Mus, 87, Galleri Riis, Oslo, 84, 86, 88 & 90, Snyder Fine Art, NY, 90, 91, 93 & 96; Hood Art Mus Dartmouth Col, 90; Julian Hartnoll Gallery, London, 90; solo shows incl Princeton Gallery of Fine Art, 71, 73, 81, 83, 85, 87, 89, Jefferson Place Gallery, Washington, 74, Princeton Univ Art Mus, 75, Nat Collection of Fine Arts, Washington, 77, NJ State Mus, 87, Hood Mus Art, Dartmouth Col, 90, Williams Gallery, Princeton, NJ, 97, others. *Teaching:* Vis artist, Univ Tex, 78; artist-in-residence, Dartmouth Col, 79. *Awards:* Award, NJ State Mus, 72; Pres Medal for Life Achievement, Dartmouth Col, 91; Princeton Arts Coun Award, 92. *Mem:* Fel Edward MacDowell Colony. *Media:* Oil, Ink; Pastel. *Publ:* Illusr, A Line of Poetry, A Row of Trees, Jargon, 65; Kweilin's An American artist in China, 76; The Norway Series, Capellen, Oslo, 80. *Dealer:* Snyder Fine Art New York NY

GEORGES, PAUL G
PAINTER
b Portland, Ore, June 15, 23. *Study:* Univ Ore, study with Jack Wilkinson 46; study with Hans Hofmann, New York and Provincetown, 47 & Fernand Leger, Paris, 49-52. *Work:* Mus Modern Art, Whitney Mus, NY; Hirschorn Collection, Smithsonian Inst, Corcoran Art Collection, Washington; Richmond Mus, Sydney & Frances Lewis Wing, Va; Ctr for Figurative Painting, Heckscher Mus. *Exhib:* Mead Art Mus, Amherst, Mass, 85; Greenville Co Mus Art, SC, 85; Slow Art, PS 1 Mus, Long Island City, NY, 92, Salander-O'Reilly Galleries, NY, 92, 94, 96, 98, 00, 03; Galerie Darthea Speyer, Paris, 95; Five Decades, Sordoni Art Gallery, Wilkes Univ, Wilkes Barre, Pa, 95; one man retrospective, Ctr Figurative Painting, NY, 2000. *Pos:* Founder & chmn bd, Artists Choice Mus, NY, 76-84. *Teaching:* Retired prof painting, Brandeis Univ, Waltham, Mass. *Awards:* Hassam Purchase Award, Am Acad, 90; Individual Grant, Adolph & Esther Gottlieb Found, 92; Grant, Pollock-Krasner Found, 93. *Bibliog:* Carter Ratcliff (auth), Paul Georges, ACMJ, fall 83; Jed Perl (auth), Autumn Alphabet, The New Criterion, No 7, 3/89; Lisa Liebmann (auth), Art, The New Yorker, 8/17/92; Hilton Kramer (auth), NY Observer, 5/26/2000; Brooks Adams (auth), Art in Am, 1/2001; Rhonda Lieberman (auth), Catalog 2003. *Mem:* Nat Acad Design (assoc, 79-83, academician, 83-). *Media:* Oil. *Dealer:* Salander-O'Reilly Galleries 20 E 79th St New York NY 10021. *Mailing Add:* 85 Walker St New York NY 10013

GERAN, JOSEPH, JR
SCULPTOR, DESIGNER
b 1945. *Study:* San Francisco City Col, AA, 66; Calif State Univ, San Francisco, BA, 70; Calif Col Arts & Crafts, MFA, 73. *Comn:* Prints of movie stars, Oakland Mus, 74; bronze bust of Dr Martin Luther King Jr, RI State, 87. *Exhib:* Los Angeles Co Mus, Los Angeles, 74; RI Sch Design, 75; Southeastern Mass Univ, 75; Bryant Col, 75; Univ Vt, 75; San Francisco Mus Art, 76; Ctr Art & Cult of Bedford Stuyvesant, 88; plus numerous group & one-man shows. *Pos:* Corp vpres, Col Inc, 70-71; processing chmn, FESTAC 74, 73-74; freelance jewelry designer. *Teaching:* Instr, EOC Summer Youth Prog, 69; lectr, Calif State Univ, San Francisco, 69-71; art consult & sch aide, Galileo High Sch, San Francisco, 70; instr, Booker T Washington Community Ctr, San Francisco, 71; asst prof painting, drawing & sculpture & co-dir ethnic studies div, Calif Col Arts & Crafts, 70-74; adj fac mem, Antioch Col West, 74; dean third world prog, RI Sch Design, 74-; prof art, Community Col RI, 81-; instr, The Jewelry Inst, 85-86. *Awards:* Guy F Atkinson Found Award, 69-71; Ill State Univ Sculpture Award, 73; Distinguished Serv Award, Congressman Ron Dellums, 75. *Mem:* Nat Conf Artists; San Francisco Art Comn Screening Comt. *Media:* Bronze, Wood; Multi. *Publ:* Cover design, Black Art, Black Cult, issue, J Black Poetry, 72; photog of art work, Yardbird Reader, 73; cover design, Blacks on Paper, Brown Univ, fall 75. *Mailing Add:* 85 Newark St Providence RI 02908-5315

GERBARG, DARCY
PAINTER
b Baltimore, Md, May 20, 49. *Study:* NY Studio Sch Drawing, Painting & Sculpture, 73-74, Univ Pa, BA, 76. *Work:* Siemens Mus, Ger; Insurance Co N Am; Polaroid Corp; Sierra Fed. *Exhib:* SIGGRAPH Ann Art Show, US & Int tours, 81-87; Electra, Mus Art Mod de la Ville de Paris, France, 83; Bronx Mus Art, 85, Computers & Art, IBM Mus Sci & Art, 87-89, NY; Siemans Mus, Munchen, Ger, 85; CADRE Exhib, San Jose Mus Art, Calif, 86; artware, Kunst und Elektronik, Landesmuseum Volk und Wirtschaft, Dusseldorf, WGer, 87; one-woman show, Fine Arts Mus Long Island, 89; Everson Mus, Syracuse, NY; Smithsonian Inst, Washington, DC, 90. *Teaching:* Adj fac, Tisch Sch Arts, NY Univ, 81-84; artist-in-residence Courant Inst Mathematics, Robotics & Manufacturing Res Lab, NY Univ, 88-, founding dir MFA prog computer art, Inst Computers Arts, Sch Visual Arts, NY, 84-88; lectr, Computer Graphics Ctr, Pratt, NY & State Univ NY, Stony Brook. *Bibliog:* Digital Portfolio Computer Graphics World, 83; Dale Petersen (auth), Genisis II: Creation & recreation with Computers, Reston, 85; Computer Graphics: Village Voice, 88. *Mem:* Spec Interest Groups Graphics Siggraph Nat (art show chmn, 81); Nat Computer Graphics Asn Arts (bd dir), 85-89. *Media:* Acrylic. *Publ:* Ed, Siggraph 82 Art Show (exhib catalog), Acme Printers, 82; auth, Digital Imaging: Paint Systems, Computer Graphics World, 8/83; contrib, Computers as Artist's Tool, Springer-Verlag, 86; auth, Anniversary Spec: Reflections on a Goldan Decade: Pennwell Publ Co, 12/87. *Mailing Add:* 149 W 24th St New York NY 10011-1917

GERBER, GAYLEN
CONCEPTUAL ARTIST, PAINTER
b McAllen, Tex, June 8, 55. *Study:* New York Studio Sch Painting, Drawing & Sculpture, 78-79; Art Inst Chicago, MFA, 80. *Work:* Neues Mus Weserburg, Bremen, Ger; Mus Contemp Art, Chicago, Ill; Domaine de Kerguehennec, Ctr D'Art Contempotain, Locmine, France; Charlottenborg Exhib Hall, Copenhagen, 2002. *Exhib:* one-man show The Renaissance Soc, Chicago, Ill, 92, High Mus Art, Atlanta, Ga, 98, Neues Mus Weserburg, Bremen, Ger, 2000; Documenta IX, Kassel, Ger, 92; 25 Americans, Milwaukee Art Mus, Wis, 95; DeadPan, Kunstverein Munich, Ger, 96; Kunst in der Stadt, Kunsthaus Bregenz, Ger, 99; Art Inst of Chicago, IL, 2002. *Teaching:* Assoc prof Sch Art Inst Chicago, 87-2000. *Awards:* NEA Arts Midwest Award, 95; Tiffany Found Award, 2000; Art Coun NY Award, 2001. *Bibliog:* J Cullum (auth), Artificially achieved perfection, Atlanta Jour, 4/10/98; M Grabner (auth), Gaylen Gerber, Frieze Issue 40, 98; G Gerber/K Bitterli (auth), Interview, La Biennale de Montreal, 2000. *Dealer:* Chicago Project Room 6130 Wilshire Blvd Los Angeles CA 90048; Galerie Susanna Kalli Davidstrasse 40 CH-9000 St Gallen Switzerland. *Mailing Add:* 1459 W Cortez St Apt 1F Chicago IL 60622

GERBRACHT, BOB (ROBERT) THOMAS
PAINTER, INSTRUCTOR
b Erie, Pa, June 23, 24. *Study:* With Joseph Plavcan, 38-42; Yale Sch Fine Arts, with Rudolph Zallinger, Deane Keller & Josef Albers, BFA, 51; Univ Southern Calif, with Jules Heller, MFA, 52. *Work:* Triton Mus Art, Santa Clara, Calif; Univ S Calif, Los Angeles, 52; Univ Art Acad, San Francisco, Calif, 80 & 96; City of Sunnyvale, Calif, 90; Glide Ch, San Francisco, 90. *Comn:* Stations of the Cross (oil painting) & Creche (sculpture), Queen Apostles Church, San Jose, Calif, 63; portraits, notably, Mrs Bruce Jenner and children, Malibu, Calif, 80 & 82; Rev Jack La Rocca, Los Altos, Calif, 88; Rev Cecil Williams, Glide Mem Methodist Church, San Francisco, 90; Historical Portraits Competition Comn Award to paint John Hendy, City of Sunnyvale, Calif, 90; Mr Austin Warburton for the Triton Mus Art, Santa Clara, Calif; and others. *Exhib:* One-man shows, Fisher Art Gallery, Univ Southern Calif, 51, Laudau Gallery, Los Angeles, 52, Images West Gallery & Montalvo, Saritoga, Calif, 72, San Jose Art Ctr, 79 & 83, Montalvo, 82, Discovery Gallery, La Tarentella, Cupertino, Calif, 84 & Commonwealth Club, Calif, 92, Triton Mus Art, Santa Clara, Calif, 2003 & 2006; group shows, 2nd Ann Open Exhib, Salmagundi Club, NY, 79; San Jose Mus Art, 50th Ann Celebration Exhib of San Jose Art League, 88; San Jose Art League World Without War Exhib, 88; Pastel Soc Am Ann Nat Exhib, NY, 79, 88, 90, 91, 92, 97 & 98; Bedford Biennial, Regional Ctr Arts, Walnut Creek, Calif, 91; Grand Exhib, Akron Soc Artists, Cuyahoga, Ohio, 91; 78th Ann, Allied Artists Am, NY, 91; 6th Ann Open Exhib, Pastel Soc West Coast, Sacramento, Calif, 92; Figurative Paintings, John Pence Gallery, San Francisco, 97; Realism Today, Am Artists Mag Exhib, San Francisco, 2000; Pastel Soc West Coast Dist Pastelist Exhib, Carmichael, Calif, 2002; Pastel Soc Am Invitational Exhib, Butler Inst Am Art, Youngstown, Ohio, 2003; The Group, Odd Fellows Yerba Buena Lodge # 15, San Francisco, 2003-2006; Pinole Artisans, Pinole, Calif, 2004; Bay Area Figurative Art Exhibit, Univ Calif, Calif, 2004. *Pos:* Vpres, Images West Gallery, Saratoga, Calif, 72; trustee, Soc Western Artists, 87-88; judge, Pastel Soc West Coast, Int Exhib, 2004; juror, Sierra Pastel Soc Exhib, 2004; judge, Los Gatos Art Fest, 2004. *Teaching:* Instr art, Col Notre Dame, Calif, 58-60 & San Jose City Col, 68-71; founder & instr, Nat Ann Portrait & Figure Painting Workshops: Univ Calif, Santa Cruz, Asilomar, Pacific Grove, Pleasanton, Walnut Creek, San Jose, Crockett & Sacramento, Calif, 80-; nat sem portrait & figure painting, Calif, Mo, Nebr, Nev, NMex, Tex, Vt, Mex, NY, Colo, Fla, Mass, Ore & SCarolina. *Awards:* Achievement Award, Pastel Teacher, Am Artist Mag, 93; Gold Medal in Pastel, Tools of Trade Show, San Francisco, 98; Lifetime Achievement Award of Sonoma Plain Air Corp, 2002; and numerous others. *Bibliog:* Nat art competition winners, Am Artist Mag, 7/85; Cathy Kosier (auth), Best of show, US ART, 12/88; Pvt showings, US ART, 9/89; The Little Book About Pastel, Zandal Books, 2002; Pure-Color, The Best of Pastel, North Light Books, 2006. *Mem:* Soc Western Artists (trustee, 87-88); Pastel Soc West Coast; Pastel Soc Am; Pinole Artisans. *Media:* Oil, Pastel. *Publ:* Auth, Drawing what you see, Am Artist Mag, 82; Let go and look, Profile Mag Am Portrait Soc, spring 84; Tips on painting the head & figure, Am Artist Mag, 9/92; Realism Today, Am Artist, 10/2000; People & Places, Exhib Catalog of Triton Mus Art, 2003. *Mailing Add:* 1301 Blue Oak Ct Pinole CA 94564

GERDTS, ABIGAIL BOOTH
HISTORIAN, CURATOR
b New Milford, Conn, June 20, 37. *Study:* Radcliffe Col, AB(fine arts), 60; Syracuse Univ, Sch Art, 62-63. *Collection Arranged:* Spec exhib, Charles Sheeler (auth, catalog), Nat Collection Fine Arts, Smithsonian Inst, 68; The Working American (auth, catalog), Dist 1199 & Smithsonian Inst Travelling Exhib Serv, 79. *Pos:* Mem secy, Corcoran Gallery Art, Washington, DC, 59-61; res asst painting dept, Mus Fine Arts, Boston, 61-62; asst cur exhib, Nat Collection Fine Arts, 64-70, coordr bicentennial inventory Am paintings, 70-77, coordr 19th century exhibs index, 77-78; spec asst to dir, Nat Acad Design, New York, 80-87, cur paintings & sculpture, 88-89; dir, Winslow Homer Catalogue Raisonne, City Univ New York Grad Center, 90-. *Mem:* Col Art Asn. *Publ:* Auth, The Working American, Sites, 79; Winslow Homer in Monochrome, Knoedler Galleries, 86; An American Collection: Paintings and Sculpture, Nat Acad Design, 89; auth, Record of the Works of Winslow Homer, 2005. *Mailing Add:* PhD Program in Art History/Graduate Center/ City University of New York 365 Fifth Ave New York NY 10016

GERDTS, WILLIAM H
HISTORIAN, EDUCATOR
b Jersey City, NJ, Jan 18, 29. *Study:* Amherst Col, BA, 49, LHD, 92; Harvard Univ, MA, 50, PhD, 66; Syracuse Univ, Hon Dr fine arts, 96. *Collection Arranged:* Thomas Birch (auth, catalog), 66; and many others. *Pos:* Dir, Myers House, Norfolk, Va, 53-54; cur painting & sculpture, Newark Mus, NJ, 54-66; dir gallery, Univ Md, 66-69; assoc with Coe Kerr Gallery, NY, 69-71. *Teaching:* Assoc prof, Univ Md, 66-69; assoc prof art, Brooklyn Col, 71-74, prof, 74-85; prof, Grad Ctr, City Univ NY, 85-99, prof emer, 99-; lectr, Am art in mus, col, univ & adult schs. *Awards:* Guggenheim Found Fel, 80. *Publ:* Auth, American Still-Life Painting, Praeger, 71; American Neo-Classical Sculpture: The Marble Resurrection, Viking, 73; The Art of Henry Inman, Nat Portrait Gallery, Smithsonian Inst, Washington, 87; American Impressionism, 84, Art Across America: Regional Painting in America Through 1920, 3 vols, 90, Abbeville Press; Monets Giverny: An Impressionist Colony, Abbeville Press, 93; William Glackens: Line and Work, Abbeville Pres, 96; plus others. *Mailing Add:* Dept Art Hist City Univ New York 365 Fifth Ave New York NY 10016

GERHOLD, WILLIAM HENRY
PAINTER, EDUCATOR
b Ashtabula, Ohio, Mar 30, 29. *Study:* Oberlin Col, with Jeanne Miles, BA; Ohio State Univ, MA. *Work:* Army-Navy Club, Charleston, WVa; Marietta Col, Ohio; Marshall Univ, WVa; WVa Univ, Morgantown. *Exhib:* Butler Midyear, Youngstown, Ohio; Appalachian Corridors II, Charleston; Perspectives, Cincinnati, Ohio, 70; Forest Festival, Elkins, WVa; Ohio State Fairs. *Teaching:* Assoc prof educ, Antioch Col, 57-58; assoc prof art, Marietta Col, 62-. *Awards:* First Prize Watercolor, Appalachian Arts & Crafts Fair, 70, Best Prof & Best WVa Landscape, Forest Festival, 71-75. *Mem:* Cent Ohio Watercolor Soc; Am Artists Prof League; WVa Artists & Craftsmen Guild; Allied Artists; Am Watercolor Soc. *Publ:* Auth & illusr, Trinity Rev, 58; WVa Mag, 73 & 74. *Dealer:* Bonfoeys 1710 Euclid Ave Cleveland OH 44115

GERICH, BETTY A JULIETTE
SCULPTOR, CERAMIST
b Danbury, Conn. *Study:* Univ Conn, BFA, 68; Univ Hartford, MAEd, 80; Wesleyan Univ, CAS, 89. *Exhib:* Solo shows, Garrett Gallery, Am Int Col, Springfield, Mass, 80, New Britain Mus Am Art, Conn, 85, Zilka Gallery, Wesleyan Univ, Middletown, Conn, 89 & Artworks Gallery, Hartford, Conn, 91, Artworks Gallery, 9/2001, Behind the Mask, Artworks Gallery, Hatford, Conn, Face Value, Exposure, Manchester, Conn, 2004, Chasing Beauty, Sue & Eugene Mercy, Jr, Gallery, Windsor, Conn, 2005; Society of Conn Crafts, Slater Mem Mus, Norwich, 81; Springfield Art League, George Walter Vincent Smith, Mass; Conn Clay, Slater Mem Mus, Norwich. *Teaching:* Art teacher, Somers High Sch, 76-; art coordr, Somers Schs, 83-91; lectr, Art Hist Survey, Asnuntuck Community Col, 2003-. *Awards:* Third Prize, Charter Oak Ann Exhib, 91; Individual Artist Fel, Greater Hartford Arts Coun, 99; Koenig Art Award, Conn Women Artists, 99; Beatrice G Epstein Mem Award, Nat Asn Women Artists, 2003. *Bibliog:* Heather Nann Davis (auth), Passion for Sculpture, Jour Inquirer, 1999; Indraneel Sur (auth), A Way with Clay, The Hartford Courant, 2001; Richard Guinness (auth), Artist Depicts Power of One Over Others, Jour Inquirer, 2001. *Mem:* Conn Women Artists; New England Sculptors Asn, Boston, Mass; Nat Asn Women Artists, NY; Artworks Gallery, Hartford, Conn. *Media:* Ceramic Sculpture. *Publ:* Contribr, Shaping Space, Holt, Rinehart & Winston, 87; photo & article, Artis Mag, winter, 2004; contribr (sculpture), 500 Figures in Clay, fall 2004; contribr (photo & article), Artis Mag, summer, fall 2005; contribr (photo & article), Up Front, Ceramics Monthly Mag, 2006. *Dealer:* Artworks Gallery 233 Pearl St Hartford CT 06106. *Mailing Add:* 18 Carriage Dr Enfield CT 06082

GERLACH, CHRISTOPHER S
PAINTER
b Wareham, Mass, Dec 8, 52. *Study:* Lake Forest Col, Ill Univ Calif, BA, 74; Calif State Univ, San Diego, MA, 77; Oxford Univ, 79; Royal Acad London, 79. *Work:* Oxford Univ, England; Buckingham Palace, London; Calif State Univ, San Diego. *Exhib:* Exhibition XI, Fine Arts Mus, San Antonio, Tex, 83; Contemp Art, La Jolla Mus, Calif, 85; Art & the Law, traveling, 87-88; Utopian Visions, Mus Mod Art, NY, 88; Am Beach Paintings, Tampa Mus, Fla, 89. *Teaching:* Instr, Calif State Univ, San Diego, 75-77. *Awards:* Bank Am Award, Eggerton Coghill Landscape, Oxford Univ, 69. *Bibliog:* Abigail Wender (auth), Venice--Painting by CG, Diversion, 9/87; Jan Jennings (auth), A World in Oils--Ranch & Coast, 4/90. *Media:* Oil. *Dealer:* William Sawyer Gallery 3045 Clay St San Francisco Calif 94115. *Mailing Add:* c/o Art Space/Virginia Miller Galleries 169 Madeira Ave Coral Gables FL 33134-4515

GERLOVINA & GERLOVIN, RIMMA & VALERIY
CONCEPTUAL ARTIST, PHOTOGRAPHER
b Mrs Gerlovina b Russ, 1951; Mr Gerlovin b Russ, 1945; US citizens. *Study:* Mrs Gerlovina, Moscow State Univ, Russ, 68-73; Mr Gerlovin, Moscow Art Theater Studio, Russ, 62-67. *Work:* Art Inst Chicago; John Paul Getty Mus, Malibu, Calif; Denver Art Mus, Colo; Int Ctr Photog, NY; Zimmerli Art Mus, Rutgers, NY. *Comn:* Changes (photo proj), Progressive Corp, Cleveland, 96-97. *Exhib:* Photems, Art Inst Chicago, 89; Photos, List Visual Arts Ctr, Mass Inst Technol, Cambridge, Mass, 89; Photog of Invention, Nat Mus Am Art, Smithsonian Inst, Washington, DC, 89; Retrospective, Fine Art Mus Long Island, Hempstead, NY, 91; Traveling Retrospective Photoglyphs (with catalog), Jacksonville Mus Art, 93, New Orleans Mus Art, 94 & Telfair Mus Art, Savannah, 96; Portraits, US Embassy, Moscow, Russ, 97-; and others. *Awards:* Best Cover & Top Ten Photographs Award, Black Book, 97; Award of Excellence, Communication Arts Mag, 97; Design Excellence, Print Mag, 97. *Bibliog:* John Jacob (auth), Photoglyphs (monograph), New Orleans Mus Art, La, 93; Phyllis Braff (auth), Photoglyphs, NY Times, Long Island Sect, 4/9/95; Linda Weintraub (auth), Art on the edge and over, Am Showcase, NY, 96. *Media:* Multimedia. *Publ:* Auth, Russian Samizdat Art, Willis Locker & Owens, NY, 86; co-ed, Collective Farm, pvt publ, 82-87; illusr cover & reproductions, NY Times Mag, 7/7/96; cover, Sciences Mag, NY Acad Sci, 5-6/97; Genesis, Doubleday, 96. *Dealer:* Robert Brown Gallery 2030 R St Washington DC 20009. *Mailing Add:* c/o Carson Masuoka Gallery 760 Santa Fe Dr Denver CO 80204

GERMANO, THOMAS
PAINTER, EDUCATOR
b New York, NY, Oct 11, 63. *Study:* Cornell Univ, Scholar, BFA, 85; Yale Univ, Scholar, MFA, 89. *Work:* Arthur Anderson & Co, Int Hqtrs, St Paul, Ill & Melville, NY; Acad Arts, Moscow, Russia; Yale Univ Art Mus, New Haven, Conn; Cape Cod Retreat House, Mass; Am Postal Workers Union, Washington, DC. *Comn:* 1185 Park Ave proj. *Exhib:* Am Labor Mus, Haledon, NJ, 92; Michael Ingbar Gallery, NY, 92-94; Seminole Community Col, Sanford, Fla, 93; Art/La 1993, Contemp Realist Gallery; Art & the Law, West Publ Co, 94; Mus City NY; Heike Pickett Gallery, Ky, 97-05; Dumbo Arts Festival, Brooklyn, NY, 99-06; Small Works Show, East Galleries, New York City, 04-06. *Teaching:* Assoc prof, SUNY, Farmingdale. *Awards:* Traveling Grant to Russia, Int Res & Exchanges Bd, 89; Traveling Grant to Washington, DC, UUP, 2000; Traveling Grant to Amboise, France, UUP, 2001; Travel Grant to Greece, UUP, 2005; Puffin Found Grant, 2006. *Mem:* Col Art Asn; NYC Metro Mus Art. *Media:* Oil. *Res:* Leonardo da Vinci. *Interests:* Oil Painting and Renaissance Art History. *Publ:* Auth, Labor Paintings (catalog), 92; illusr, cover, Wordsmith Mag, 93; American Icons, Lithographic Print Edition of 1500, 2000; Nat Academy Mus (catalog), 2004. *Dealer:* Bachelier-Cardonsky Gallery Kent Conn; Heike Pickett Gallery Versaillies Ky. *Mailing Add:* 191 B Glen Cove Ave Sea Cliff NY 11579

GERNHARDT, HENRY KENDALL
SCULPTOR, CERAMIST
b Salem, Conn, Aug 3, 32. *Study:* Norwich Art Sch, Conn; Sch Am Craftsmen, Rochester Inst Technol, NY, with Frans Wildenhain; Sch Art, Syracuse Univ, NY, BA & MFA; Sch Appl Arts, Helsinki, Finland, study with Kyllikki Salmenhaara, Fulbright Scholar. *Work:* Everson Mus Art, Syracuse, NY; Syracuse Univ; DePauw Univ, Greencastle, Ind; Chrysler Mus, Provincetown, Mass; Univ SDak, Vermillion. *Comn:* Pottery, Imperial House, NY, 60; tile mosaic, Syracuse Univ, 63; vase, State Univ NY, Cortland, 67; baptismal font, Lynnwood Reformed Church, Guilderland, NY, 69; sculpture, comn by Alexander E Holstein, Syracuse, 72. *Exhib:* Ceramic Nat, Everson Mus Art, 54-72; Int Trade Fair, Posen, Poland, 58; Contemp Crafts Exhib, Skidmore Col, Saratoga Springs, NY, 62, 71 & 75; Int Ceramic Exhib, Silvermine Guild Artists, New Canaan, Conn, 64; 22nd Ceramic Ann, Scripps Col, Claremont, Calif, 66. *Teaching:* Prof ceramics, Sch Visual & Performing Arts, Syracuse Univ, 60-96 & Sch Am Craftsmen, summer 71, Munson-Williams Proctor Inst, 2001. *Awards:* Merle Alling Sculpture Award, Rochester Finger Lakes Exhib, Mem Art Gallery, 63 & 71; O Hommel Prize for Pottery, Ceramic Nat, Everson Mus, 68; 1st, 2nd & 3rd Awards, NY State Expos, Syracuse, 71. *Bibliog:* Lewenstein & Cooper (auth), New Ceramics, Van Nostrand Reinhold, 74; Rick Hirsch (auth), Raku, Watson Guptill, 75; article, Craft Horizons, 75; Ulysses Diete (auth), Great Dots, Newark Mus, 2003. *Mem:* Nat Coun Advan Ceramic Arts; Am Crafts Coun; New York Craftsmen; Fla Craftsmen. *Media:* Clay, Glaze. *Mailing Add:* PO Box 975 Cedar Key FL 32625

GERSOVITZ, SARAH VALERIE
PAINTER, PRINTMAKER
b Montreal, PQ. *Study:* McDonald Col; Montreal Mus Fine Arts; Concordia Univ, MA. *Work:* Am Embassy, Ottawa; Libr Cong, Washington, DC; NY Pub Libr; Nat Gallery SAustralia; Israel Mus; Universitat Kaiserslattern, WGer; and many Mus, Univ, Libr Pub & private collections, US, Can, Ger, Brazil, Hungary, France, Poland, Peru, Colombia, Italy, Eng, Venezuela, others. *Exhib:* One-man shows, Montreal Mus Fine Arts, 62 & 65, Confederation Art Gallery, 76, London Art Gallery, 82, l'Universite de Sherbrooke, 78, 83 & 95, Stewart Hall Art Gallery, 84 & 2000, Bibliotheque Nat du Que, 96 & 97, & Galerie de la Ville, Dollard-des-Ormeaux, 99, Galérie Auguste-Chénier, Ville Marie Que, 2003; Art Gallery Victoria, 66, Univ Alberta, 68, Art Gallery Hamilton, 69, Mt St Vincent Univ, 71, St Mary's Univ, 76; Biennales Graphic Art, Ljubljana, Yugoslavia, 79 & 75; Drawing Exhib, Miro Mus, Barcelona, Spain, 79, 82 & 86; Bienal de Arte Valparaiso, Chile, 83, 85, 87, 89, 91 & 94; Int Print Biennale, Taipei, Taiwan, 84 & 86; and many others in USA, France, Spain, Venezuela, Peru, Switz, Italy, Norway, Bulgaria, Korea, Ger, Brazil, Eng, Colombia, Czech, Hungary, Hong Kong, Australia, Scotland, Poland, China, Greece & Macedonia. *Pos:* Critic, Artsatlantic & others. *Teaching:* Instr painting, drawing & printmaking, Saidye Bronfman Ctr, Montreal, 72-85; Visual Arts Ctr; and others. *Awards:* Graphic Art Prize, Winnipeg Art Gallery, 62; Purchase Awards, Mus du Que,

66, Nat Gallery S Australia, 67, Dawson Col, 74, Thomas More Inst, 77 & l'Universite de Sherbrooke, 79; First Prize, Concours Graphique, Univ Sherbrooke, 77 & Int Jury Prize Graphics, 89 Biennale, Gabrovo, Bulgaria; Travel Award, House of Humor & Satire, Gabrovo, Bulgaria, 85 & 91; and others. *Bibliog:* G Daigneault (auth), La Gravure au Quebec, Printworld; Complete Biennial Guide to Canadian Artists, 95-96; North American Women Artists of the 20th Century, Heller; Guy Robert (auth), Le Cercle due Plieralisme, 98; National Archives of Canada. *Mem:* Royal Can Acad Arts (coun mem). *Media:* Acrylic, Oil; Silkscreen. *Interests:* Gardening. *Publ:* Illusr cover, Figures in a Landscape, Oberon, 67; illusr cover, Feminin Pluriel, Masculin Singulier, 80; and others. *Dealer:* Galérie d'art Jean Claude Bergeron 150 Nie St Patrick Ohaua Ontario Kin 5J8. *Mailing Add:* 4360 Montrose Ave Montreal PQ H3Y 2B1 Canada

GERST, HILDE W
DEALER
Study: Ploner Acad, Italy. *Pos:* Owner, Hilde Gerst Gallery, NY. *Mem:* Am Asn Mus; Nat Soc Lit & Arts; Nat Mus Women Arts. *Specialty:* French painting from Impressionist to contemporary; sculpture. *Mailing Add:* 955 Fifth Ave New York NY 10021-1738

GERSTEIN, DAVID STEVEN
FILMMAKER
b Cleveland, Ohio, Sept 23, 51. *Study:* Antioch Col, BA, 74; Art Inst Chicago; San Francisco Art Inst. *Exhib:* One-man shows, NAME to Name Gallery, Chicago, 76 & Canyon Cinematheque, San Francisco, 78, 80 & 82; High Mus Art, Atlanta, Ga, 79; Anthology Film Archive, NY, 81; Newberger Mus, Purchase, NY, 81; Arsenal Cinema, Berlin; Austrian Film Mus, Vicuna; and others. *Pos:* Bd dir, Canyon Cinema Coop, San Francisco, 77-82, Found Art Cinema, 83-. *Awards:* 3rd Place, San Francisco Art Inst Film Festival, 77; Ann Arbor Film Festival, 78; Hon Mention, Athens Int Film Festival, 78. *Bibliog:* Linda Dackman (auth), Kino-Frisco, Cinema News, Found Art Cinema, 77. *Publ:* Auth, Films of Joel Singer, 77, auth, A modest confutation, 78 & ed, Cinemanews. *Dealer:* Canyon Cinema Coop 2325 3rd St 338 San Francisco CA 94133. *Mailing Add:* c/o GALLERIA SILECCHIA 12 S Palm Ave Sarasota FL 34236

GERTJEJANSEN, DOYLE
PAINTER
b Tracy, Minn, Sept 1, 48. *Study:* Mankato State Univ, Minn, BA, 69; Univ Minn, MFA, 71. *Work:* Adams & Reese, New Orleans, La; Ariz State Univ; Hotel Intercontinental, New Orleans, La; New Orleans Mus Art, La; plus many other pvt & pub collections. *Exhib:* Solo exhibs, Arthur Roger Gallery, New Orleans, La, 81, 83 & 85, New Orleans Ctr Performing Arts, La, 84, Susan Abeline Gallery, Zurich, Switz, 86, Galerie Simonne Stern Ltd, Atlanta, Ga, 89 & 96 & Conkling Gallery, Mankato State Univ, Minn, 89; The Red Clay Survey, Biennial Exhib Southern Art, Huntsville Mus Art, Ala, 88; Eighteenth Ann Works on Paper, Southwest Tex State Univ, San Marcos, 88; Art LA 88, Third Int Contemp Art Fair, Los Angeles Convention Ctr, Calif, 88; What's Hot at Gillman-Stein, Gillman-Stein Gallery, Tampa, Fla, 89; Art for Art's Sake, Contemp Arts Ctr, New Orleans, La, 89; Gallery Artists, Galerie Simonne Stern, New Orleans, La, 89, 93 & 94; Louisiana in Black Light, La State Univ Union Art Gallery, Baton Rouge, La, 90 & Newcomb Sch Art, Tulane Univ, New Orleans, La, 90; Art of the 70's and 80's, Works from the Permanent Collection, New Orleans Mus Art, La, 91; Major Works on Paper, Galerie Simonne Stern, New Orleans, La, 90; Major Works-Nine Gallery Artists, Galerie Simonne Stern, New Orleans, La, 90; The Infinite Variety of Abstraction, New Visions Gallery, Ithaca, NY, 91; Louisiana Contemporaries: Selections from the ARCO Collection, Univ Art Mus, Univ Southwestern La, Lafayette, 92; The Red Clay Survey: Third Biennial Exhib of Contemp Southern Art, Huntsville Mus Art, Ala, 92; Asprodites, Dunbar, Gertjejansen & Pijuan, Galerie Simonne Stern, New Orleans, La, 92; Mostly Big, Contemp Arts Ctr, New Orleans, La, 92; Under Glass & In The Round, Galerie Simonne Stern, New Orleans, La, 92; Inaugural Exhib, New Orleans Mus Art Expansion, La, 93; Louisiana Now, New Orleans Ctr Contemp Art, La, 95; Louisiana Competition 85, La Arts & Sci Ctr, Baton Rouge, 95; New Discoveries at the New Gallery, New Gallery, Houston, Tex, 95; Drawing 6, Fine Arts Gallery, Univ New Orleans, La, 95; Louisiana Open, Contemp Arts Ctr, New Orleans, 95; Guns in the Hands of Artists, Positive Space Gallery, New Orleans, La, 96; The La Story (with catalog), Delfina Studio Trust, London, Eng, 96; Southern Arts Fedn/Nat Endowment Arts 1996 Visual Arts Fel Winners, Southeastern Ctr Contemp Art, Winston-Salem, NC, 97; and others. *Teaching:* Instr fine arts, Univ New Orleans, La, 71-75 & prof fine arts, 88-. *Awards:* Silver Circle Artist, Contemp Art Ctr, New Orleans, La, 93; La Educ Quality Support Fund Grant, 96; Nat Endowment Arts/Southern Fedn Arts Fel Painting, 96. *Bibliog:* Chris Waddington (auth), Gallery shows target the art of abstraction, Times-Picayune, 4/12/96; Douglas McCash (auth), A professor longhair monument: Doyle Gertjejansen and Lyn Emery, Offbeat Mag, 5/96; Terrington Calas (auth), Janus subtext, New Orleans Art Rev, Vol XIV, No 5, 5-6/96. *Dealer:* Galerie Simonne Stern 518 Julia St New Orleans LA 70130. *Mailing Add:* 4771 LaFaye St New Orleans LA 70122

GESKE, NORMAN ALBERT
MUSEUM DIRECTOR, EDUCATOR
b Sioux City, Iowa, Oct 31, 15. *Study:* Univ Minn, BA; NY Univ Inst Fine Arts, MA. *Hon Degrees:* Doane Col, Hon D Fine Arts, 69. *Collection Arranged:* Ernst Barlach (first Am mus exhib), 55; American Participation, 34th Venice Biennale, 68; American Sculpture, 70; Ralph Albert Blakelock (auth, catalog), 75. *Pos:* Asst dir, Univ Nebr Art Galleries, 50-53, actg dir, 53-56, dir, 56-83, dir emer, 83. *Teaching:* Prof, Univ Nebr-Lincoln. *Awards:* Distinguished Service Award, Univ Nebr, Kearney, 80; Distinguished Serv Award, Lincoln Found, 91; Founders Award, Mus Nebr Art, 93; Nebraskaland Foundation, Pioneer Award, 2004; Nebraska Arts Council, Leonard Thiessen Award, 2004. *Mem:* Hon mem Asn Art Mus Dirs; Nebr Art Asn (life trustee); Mus Nebr Art Found (trustee). *Res:* Nebraska Blakelock inventory. *Publ:* Auth, The Figurative Tradition in Recent American Art, 68; Rudy Pozzatti, American Printmaker, 71; Ralph Albert Blakelock 1847-1919, 75; Light & Color, Images from New Mexico, 81; The American Painting Collection of the Sheldon Memorial Art Gallery, Univ Nebr Press, 88. *Mailing Add:* 128 N 13th St No 408 Lincoln NE 68508

GETLER, HELEN
ART DEALER, CONSULTANT
b New York, NY, May 30, 25. *Study:* Bryn Mawr Col, BA, 45. *Pos:* Co-dir, Getler/Pall Gallery, New York, currently. *Mem:* Art Table. *Specialty:* Contemporary artists; works on paper, prints, paintings and drawings. *Mailing Add:* c/o Helen Getler Gallery 303 E 37th New York NY 10016

GETTY, NILDA FERNANDEZ
EDUCATOR, SILVERSMITH
b Buenos Aires, Arg, June 2, 1936; US citizen. *Study:* Archit at Buenos Aires Univ, Univ NC, Raleigh & Univ Pa; Stetson Univ, Deland, Fla, BFA(art); Univ South Fla, Tampa; Univ Ga, MFA(metalsmithing & printmaking). *Work:* Deland Mus, Fla; Univ South Fla; Denver Art Mus; Minn Mus of Art, St Paul; Colo State Univ. *Comn:* St Luke's Chalice, St Luke's Episcopal Church; eleven copper emblems, Larimer Co High Sch. *Exhib:* Goldsmiths Invitational (traveling exhib), Minn Mus Art, St Paul, 74; Metals Invitational, Fullerton Gallery, Calif, 75; two-person show, Gryphon Gallery, Denver, 75 & 77; Sheldon Mem Art Gallery, Lincoln, Nebr, 76; NAm Goldsmith Invitational, Phoenix Mus, Ariz, 76-77; Metals Invitational, Henry Gallery, Seattle, Wash, 77; solo exhib, Minn Mus Art, St Paul, 74; and others. *Teaching:* From instr to prof metalsmithing, Colo State Univ, Ft Collins, 70-. *Bibliog:* Donald Willcox (auth), Body Jewelry: International Perspectives, Regnery, 73; Philip Morton (auth), Contemporary Jewelry, Holt, Rinehart & Winston, 2nd ed 76. *Mem:* Soc NAm Goldsmiths; Am Crafts Coun; World Crafts Coun. *Media:* Silver, Gold. *Publ:* Auth, Contemporary Crafts of the Americas, Regnery, 75; auth, articles, Contemporary Crafts, 75 & Ceramics Mo, 75; auth, Crafts in the Americas, Crafts Horizons, 74. *Mailing Add:* c/o Colo State Univ Dept Art Fort Collins CO 80523-1770

GEVAS, SOPHIA
DIRECTOR, PAINTER
b Athens, Ohio, Oct 3, 54. *Study:* L'Univ D'Aix-Marseille, L'Ecole Des Beaux Arts, Aix-En-Provence, France, 74; Miami Univ, Ohio, BFA, 76; apprentice to Reuben Nakian (sculptor), 83. *Work:* Pepsi-Co Int, Purchase, NY; Epic Co, Falls Church, Va; Tower Marketing Systs, Malvern, Pa; Communication Skills Inc, Phoenix, Ariz; Energy Conservation Systs, Arlington, Va. *Comn:* Large scale oil painting, comn by Mr & Mrs Deupi, McLean, Va, 80; large scale oil painting, comn by Mr & Mrs Donald Smith, Vienna, Va, 80; large scale oil painting, comn by Thomas Murphy, Arlington, Va, 85. *Exhib:* Solo exhibs, Gloria Gallery, Nicosia, Cyprus, 86, Antinor Gallery, Athens, Greece, 86 & Adelphi Univ Manhattan Ctr, NY, 91; In the Natural World, Park Ave Atrium, NY, 87; 29th Ann Barnum Exhib, Discovery Mus, Conn, 88; That's What It's All About, Erector Square Gallery, New Haven, Conn, 88; Addressing the Margin, Ferguson Libr Gallery, Stamford, Conn, 94. *Collection Arranged:* Monuments & Memory: Reflections on the Former Soviet Union traveling exhib (auth, catalog), 94; Fictitious Icons Ann Charnow traveling exhib (auth, catolog), 99; Rough (auth, catalog) 2000; The Color Withing, Work by Artists From Luxembourg (auth catolog) 2000. *Pos:* Co-founder & vpres, Loft Artist Asn, Stamford, Conn, 84-89; dir/cur, Gallery Contemp Art, Sacred Heart Univ, Fairfield, Conn, 89-. *Teaching:* Adj instr art hist/life drawing, Sacred Heart Univ, Fairfield, Conn, 84-89; instr painting/sculpture, Stamford Mus, Conn, 87. *Bibliog:* Paris Takopoulos & Dorothy Kosinski (auths), Art news: Sophia Gevas, Political Times (Greece), 4/11/86; Glafkos Xenos (auth), The human relationship to nature (review), O Agon, 5/22/86; Janet Koplos (auth), Artist explores mythic spaces (review), Advocate/Greenwich Time, Times Mirror, 3/10/91. *Mem:* Stamford Art Asn. *Media:* Oils & Mixed Media on Paper & Masonite. *Publ:* Auth, From the Figure: In Black & White (catalog), Sacred Heart Univ, 94. *Mailing Add:* 44 Fairfield Ave Norwalk CT 06854

GHAHARY, ZIA EDIN
CONSULTANT, ART HISTORIAN
b Mar 5, 27. *Study:* Univ Tehran, Iran, BA(lit), 45, BA(law & political sci), 46; Post Grad Studies(Persian & Islamic Art, Antiquities: South & West Asia, India, Iran, Egypt, Iraq, Lebanon, Syria & Israel), 48-49; Sorbonne Univ Paris, PhD(comparative lit & schs art), 50; Univ Rome, PhD(political sci), 53; movie director, Centro Esperimentale Di Cinemtografia, Rome with Roberto Rossellini & Vittorio DeSica; Ind Univ(cert appraiser art/antiques). *Pos:* Minister, acting ambassador Can and Lebanon, 73; ambassador in Venezuela, Brazil, Colombia, Peru, Ecuador, Trinidad & Tobago, 77-79; pres, Zighom Int Fine Arts & AAA (Art, Antique, Authentication & Appraisals, 83-; pres, int studies advisory bd, Bergen Community Col, formerly; platform speaker, Program Corp Am (topics incl, future of mus & art, China, Middle East & oil issues), currently. *Teaching:* Lectr & prof, Univ Tehran, 60-67, Nat Univ Iran, 64-70. *Awards:* Millenum of Avicenna Award; Homayoum of 2nd Order. *Mem:* CAPP Int Soc Appraisers (cert appraiser); World Future Soc; life mem NY Art Students League; Appraisers Asn Am (cert appraiser). *Media:* Photography, Video, Movies. *Res:* Am, Oriental, Europ and Middle Eastern paintings, sculptures, manuscripts and illuminated miniature paintings; Oriental Rugs, Middle Eastern and Europ Tapestry and Carpets; Persian antiquities, Egyptian, Roman, Greek, Islamic, Judaica and Pre-Colombian artworks, decoratives and furniture. *Specialty:* Painting, Period Europ and Am Furniture. *Interests:* Rare coins, Oriental rugs. *Collection:* Am, Eng, Can, Persian and some Israelite coins; 18th & 19th Century Am and Fr furniture,

paintings, sculpture; Persian rugs & tapestry collection. *Publ:* Auth, Noise of Silence, 48; Blue Letters (Surrealist Poems), 48; Series of articles on neorealism in European movies, 54-55; Third world article series (future of social, economic & political development in the world), 57; ed, Catalogues Raisonnee on painter, sculpture, Betty Gilman & Ainslie Burke (American 1922-1991), 93. *Mailing Add:* c/o AAA Appraisals/Zighom Intl Fine Arts 240 Heather Lane Franklin Lakes NJ 07417

GHENT, HENRI
CRITIC, WRITER
b Birmingham, Ala, June 23, 26. *Study:* US Armed Forces Inst, Honolulu, Hawaii, 45-46; New Eng Conservatory, Boston, 47-51; Marian Anderson scholar, 51 & 52; Georges Longy Sch, Cambridge, 51-53; Martha Baird Rockefeller grant, 57; Univ Paris, 58-60; also pvt study in Ger & Eng; Vogelstein Found Fel, 78; Yaddo Found Fel, 79, Cottonwood Found & Jarvil Commonwealth Found. *Hon Degrees:* Allen Univ, Hon Dr Humanities. *Collection Arranged:* The Invisible Americans: Black Artists of the 1930's, 69; 10 Afro-American Artists, Mt Holyoke Col, 69; 15 International Artists, Community Gallery, Brooklyn Mus, 69, Allusions, 2nd Anniversary Exhib, 70 & Native North American Art: Mixed Media Works by Contemporary American Indian Artists, 72; Afro-American Artists: Since 1950, Brooklyn Col, 69; 8 Afro-American Artists (catalog), Rath Mus, Geneva, Switz, 71; 1972 All-Ohio Painting & Sculpture Biennial, Art Inst, Dayton, 72. *Pos:* Consult, Nat Endowment Arts, Minn Mus Art, St Paul, Dayton Art Inst, Mt Holyoke Col, Rath Mus, Geneva & Mus d'Art Haitien, Port-au-Prince, Haiti; with Allen Univ; dir, Community Gallery, Brooklyn Mus, 68-72; corresp, Le Monde de la Musique, Paris, France, 83-. *Teaching:* Vis lectr, Col Finger Lakes Series, 70-71 & Dayton Art Inst, Ohio; Queens Col, NY, 74; lectr, Teachers Col, Columbia Univ, 75-80. *Awards:* Ford Found Res-Travel Grant, 74-75; Crane Found Res-Travel Grant, 81-82; Cottonwood Found Grant, 83. *Bibliog:* Articles in Boston Sunday Globe, 12/7/75, Village Voice, 7/19/76, Los Angeles Times, 10/10/76, Artforum, New York Times, Cleveland Plain Dealer,; plus others. *Mem:* Smithsonian Assocs; Int Soc Educ Through Art; African-American Inst; Nat Art Educ Asn; Nat Soc Lit & Arts. *Interests:* Eclectic art with emphasis on contemporary painting, sculpture and graphics. *Collection:* Contemporary painting, sculpture & graphics. *Publ:* Auth, White is not superior, NY Times, 12/8/68; Black creativity in quest of an audience, Art in Am, 5-6/70; The second generation, Art Gallery Mag, 6/74; Spanish art in transition, Art Int, 10/15/75; contribr, Le Monde de la Musique, Danser Mag, Paris; and others. *Mailing Add:* 310 E 75th St Apt 1-F New York NY 10021

GHIKAS, PANOS GEORGE
PAINTER, EDUCATOR
b Malden, Mass. *Study:* Yale Univ Sch Fine Arts, BFA, 43, MFA, 47; Akad der Bildenden Kunste, Stuttgart, Ger, with Willi Baumeister, 53-54. *Work:* Wadsworth Atheneum, Hartford, Conn; Walker Art Mus, Bowdoin Col; New Britain Mus Am Art, Conn; Colby Col; Art Mus, Waterville, Maine; and others. *Exhib:* Abstract & Surrealist Show, Chicago Art Inst, 47; 2nd Int Salon des Realites Nouvelles, Paris, France, 48; Ann Am Painting, Whitney Mus Am Art, 49; Am Painting Ann, Univ Ill, 50; Worcester Mus Biennial Contemp Am Painting, 52. *Pos:* Asst conservator, Yale Univ Art Gallery, 57-59. *Teaching:* Vis artist design, Carpenter Ctr, Harvard Univ, 64-66; vis prof drawing, Bowdoin Col, 70-71; prof painting, RI Sch Design, Providence, 71-82 & Mass Col Art, 72-. *Awards:* Fulbright Fel, 53; MacDowell Colony Fel, 67; Blanche E Colman Found Grant, 69. *Bibliog:* Chaet (auth), Artists at Work, Webb, 61. *Media:* Egg Tempera. *Publ:* Illusr, Tales of Christophilos, 54; illusr, Again Christophilos, 56; illusr, The Golden Bird, 57; illusr, The Golden Sword, 60. *Mailing Add:* Mass Col Art Boston MA 02115

GHIKAS, PATIENCE HALEY See Haley, Patience

GIACALONE, VITO
PAINTER, HISTORIAN
b Newark, NJ. *Study:* Montclair State Univ, BA, 60; Univ Iowa, MA, 65, MFA, 66. *Work:* Mus Univ Iowa; Guggenheim Mus; Metrop Mus Art; Smithsonian Nat Mus Am Art; Brit Mus; Prudential Insurance Co; Mus Mod Art Study Collection; New York Public Libr; Brooklyn Mus Print Collection; Princeton Univ Libr Graphic Arts Collection. *Exhib:* Howe Gallery, Kean Univ, NJ, 85, 86, 87, 90, 94, 95, 96 & 97; Albright Knox, Buffalo, NY, 87; Philadelphia Mus Art, 88; Benton Gallery, Southampton, NY, 90 & 91; Edwin A Ulrich Mus Art, Wichita, Kans, 92; Ben Shahn Gallery, Wayne, NJ, 93; Castrol World Hq, 93; Nabisco Corp Hq, 94; Noyes Mus, NJ, 94; Schering-Plough Corp Galleries, 94; Am Abstract Artists (auth, catalog), Kean Col, NJ, Westbeth Gallery, NY & Baruch Col, NY, 96; Guild Hall Mus, E Hampton, NY, 97; Hillwood Art Mus, Brookville, NY, 2000; Martin Art Mus, Pa, Westbeth Gallery, NY, 2002, 2003 & 2004. *Collection Arranged:* Chu Ta, Selected Paintings and Calligraphy (auth, catalog), Vassar Col Art Gallery, 72-73 & New York Cult Ctr, 73; Style & Theme in Japanese Art: from the 13th to the 20th Centuries (auth, catalog), 88, Power of the Brush: Calligraphic Painting by Wang Fang-yu (auth, catalog), 89, James Howe Gallery, Kean Col, NJ; The Eccentric Painters of Yangzhou (auth, catalog), China House Gallery, China Inst Am, New York, 90; Bada Shanren at the Smithsonian, Oriental Art Magazine, 2004. *Teaching:* Prof painting, Kean Univ, NJ, 66-2001, prof emer; artist-in-residence, Univ Ill, Urbana, 75-; lectr Chinese painting, China Inst Am, NY, 78-80 & 90, Inst Asian Studies, NY, 82-89; vis artist, Columbia Col, Mo, 84; instr, Detroit Art Inst, 85; adj prof, Studio Arts, Sch Visual Arts, NY. *Awards:* Painting Fels, MacDowell Colony, NH, 84 & 85 & Va Ctr Creative Arts, 86 & 87. *Bibliog:* Suzanne Frank (auth), article, Arts Mag, 72; Karen Lipson (auth), article, Newsday, 86; Eileen Watkins (auth), article, Sunday Star Ledger, 96. *Mem:* China Inst Am; Am Abstract Artists; Int Asn Art Critics. *Media:* All Media. *Res:* Chinese eccentric painting of the 17th and 18th centuries. *Publ:* Auth, Chu Ta (1626-1705): Toward an understanding of his art, 75, Wen Cheng Ming exhibition, 76, Eight dynasties of Chinese painting, 81 & The John M Crawford Jr Collection of calligraphy and painting in the Metropolitan Museum of Art, Part 1, 85, Part 2, 86, Oriental Art Mag; Style and Theme in Japanese Art: from the 13th to the 20th centuries, 88; Power of the Brush: calligraphic paintings by Wang Fang-Yu, 89; The Eccentric Painters of China, 90; Wei Jing Xian, A Unique View of Chinese Art and Culture, Kean Univ, 2000. *Dealer:* Anita Shapolsky Gallery 152 E 65th St New York NY 10021; Arlene Bujese Gallery 66 Newtown Lane East Hampton NY 11937. *Mailing Add:* 463 W St B938 New York NY 10014

GIALANELLA, DONALD G
SCULPTOR, GRAPHIC ARTIST
b Plainfield, NJ, June 9, 56. *Study:* Montclair State Col, 74-77, Cooper Union, BFA, 79, with Jim Dine, Milton Glazer & Louise Bourgeois. *Comn:* The Fire Unleashed, graphics, ABC Documentary Unit, 85; 25th anniversary, opening animation, Wide World of Sports, 86; Superbowl XIX, opening animation, ABC Sports, 87; Good Morning America, opening animation, 87 & 90; Loving, Opening Animation, 90; and others. *Exhib:* Solo shows, City Without Walls, Newark, NJ, 80, ARS Gallery, Ankara, Turkey, 95, Marcella Luiso, Bronxville, NY, 96 & Gallery 53, Cooperstown, NY, 96; Wind & Water, Smithy-Pioneer Gallery, Cooperstown, NY, 96; Luma Gallery, Colorado Springs, Colo, 98; Sommerhill Gallery, Chapel Hill, NC, 98; Icarus Int, Nags Head, NC, 99; Salmagundi Club, Audubon Artists, NY, 2000; 23rd Ann Smithsonian Show, Washington, DC, 2005. *Pos:* Art dir, ABC News, NY, 84-86, ABC Sports/Entertainment, 86-93; creative dir, Turkish Radio & Television Network, 93-95; founder, Wind & Sky Studio, Cooperstown, NY, 96-. *Teaching:* Lectr, Montclair State Col, State Univ NY, Long Island, 86-89; instr, Bilkent Univ, Ankara, Turkey, 93-95. *Awards:* Cleo Hartwig Mem Award, Audubon Artists 58th Ann Exhib, NY, 2000; Domenico Facci Award, Audubon 59th Ann New York City, 2001; Best in Show, Paradise City Arts Festival, 2004. *Bibliog:* Computer manipulation of news, Computer Pictures, 1/85; Computer graphics on television, Computer Graphics World, 4/85; The changing face of news graphics, Technol Rev, 3/87. *Mem:* Broadcast Designers Asn; Am Craft Coun; Audubon Artists, NY City. *Media:* Steel. *Publ:* Auth, Electronic wizardry, computer graphics at ABC, Capitol Cities/ABC, 86. *Mailing Add:* 4861 State Hwy 28 Ste 1 Cooperstown NY 13326-5229

GIAMPIETRO, ISABEL ANTONIA
SCULPTOR, DESIGNER
b Marsicovetere, Potenza, Italy; US citizen. *Study:* Scuola Dell'Arte Della Medaglia, with G Romagnoli, dipl, 50; Fine Arts Acad, Rome, Italy, with Calori, Rivosecchi & Cataudella, degree 51, Stockholm, Sweden, glass with SE Skawonius, cert, 56; Manhattanville Col of the Sacred Heart, BA (humanities); Manhattanville Cum Laude, graduated. *Work:* Smithsonian Inst; Corning Glass Mus; Metrop Mus Art; Mitchell Wolfson Jr collection of decorative arts, Fla; and other mus in Europe and pvt collections. *Comn:* Seal of State of Va (bas-relief), Jr CofC, Oklahoma City, 52; portrait of George Washington (bronze relief 5'x41/2'x3'), George Washington Masonic Nat Mem, Eastman Kodak (1976 Bicentennial Celebration XI Milan Triennale), Alexandria, Va, 1982. *Exhib:* Triennale, Stedelijk Mus, Amsterdam, The Neth, 57; two-person exhib, Leerdam New Glass, Utrecht Mus, The Neth, 57; Expos Int, Brussels, Belgium, 58; Glass 1959, Metrop Mus Art, NY; Corcoran Gallery, Washington; one-woman show: Alan Moss Gallery, 84; Modern Glass, Metrop Mus Art, 95-96; and others. *Awards:* Nominee of the Gold Medal, Triennale XI, 57; Grand Prix, Expo, Brussels, Belgium, 58; Environmental Design Grant, Nat Endowment Arts, 78. *Bibliog:* Renzo Marchelli (auth), Portrait of an artist, Negozi e Vetrine, 57; The Metropolitan Museum of Art: Glass 1959, Corning Mus, 59; Geoffrey Beard (auth), International Modern Glass, Charles Scribner's & Sons, 76. *Media:* Bronze, Glass. *Interests:* Photog. *Mailing Add:* 300 E 40th St Apt 31H New York NY 10016

GIANAKOS, CRIS
SCULPTOR, ENVIRONMENTAL ARTIST
b New York NY, Jan 4, 34. *Study:* Sch Visual Arts, cert. *Work:* Mus Mod Art, NY; Moderna Museet & Nat Mus, Stockholm; Nassau Co Mus Fine Arts; Smithsonian Inst; Fog Art Mus, Cambridge, Mass; Nat Gallery, Athens; State Mus Contemp Art, The Costakis Collection, Thessaloniki, Greece; Johnson Mus Art, Cornell Univ, Ithaca, NY; US Information Agency, Washington, DC; Malmo Mus, Sweden; Brooklyn Mus, NY. *Comn:* Gemini (steel sculpture), City Malmo, Sweden; Styx (large scale interactive sculpture), Col Long Island Univ, 88; Zumikon Ramp, Max Bill George Vontongerloo Found, Zurich. *Exhib:* Mus Mod Art, NY, 71; PS 1, Queens, NY, 78; one-man exhibs, Nassau Co Mus Fine Arts (with catalog), NY, Hal Bromm Gallery, NY, 79 & 81, Galerie Nordenhake, Stockholm, Sweden, 85, Univ Gallery, Univ Mass, Amherst (with catalog), 89 & Stark Gallery, NY, 90, 92 & 93; Los Angeles Inst Contemp Art, 80; Brooklyn Mus, NY, 89; Wynn Kramarsky, NY; Stefan Stux Gallery, NY; Thessalonik, Cult Capital Europe (with catalog), Greece, 97; Retrospective Exhib State Mus Contemp Art, Greece (with catalog). *Teaching:* Prof Sch Visual Arts, New York, 65-. *Awards:* Nat Endowment Arts Award, 80; Adolph & Ester Gottlieb Found Grant, 76, 80, 89; Pollack-Krasner Found Grant. *Bibliog:* Gianakos-4 Scandanavian Exhibitions (catalog, Steven Madoff auth), 85-86; Stephen Westfall (auth), Rev, Art Am, 87 & 89; William Zimmer (auth), New York Times, 90; Thomas McEvilley, Retrospective catalog, 1992; auth William Zimmer exhib catalog, 1980. *Media:* Mixed. *Specialty:* Contemp Art. *Publ:* Contribr, Words and Images, Mus Mod Art, New York, 70; Image of an Era: The American Poster 1945-1975, Nat Collection Fine Art, Smithsonian Inst; Architectural Sculpture, Los Angeles Inst Contemp Art, Calif, 80; Places in Our Llives, Art in Embassies Program, 2001; Modern Odysseys-Greek American Artists of the 20th Century, 1999. *Dealer:* Stux Gallery, 530 W 25 St, New York, NY; Gallery Nordenhake Berlin; Gallery Stefan Anderson Sweden; Alpha Delta Gallery Athens Greece; Pace Editions, 32 East 57th, New York, NY. *Mailing Add:* 93 Mercer St New York NY 10012

GIANGUZZI, JOSEPH CUSTODE
SCULPTOR, PAINTER - OIL PAINTING
b Bronx, NY, Mar 4, 41. *Study:* Art Students League, NY City, 1958-59; Studied under William Zorach, Harry Sternberg, Morris Kantor. *Comn:* Unicorn, Margaret B Freeman Collection, comn by Thomas PF Hoving, NY, 1966; Athletes, 20' Terra Cotta wall, LaGuardia Community Col, Long Island City, NY, 1981; Statue Sam Levinson, Brooklyn Center Performing Arts, Brooklyn, NY, 1985; Statue Helen Kelly, City Univ NY, 1994; Statue David B Steinman, City Univ NY, 1996. *Exhib:* Group shows incl: Burr Galleries, New York City, 1958-61, Sagittarius Gallelry, New York City, Salmagundi Club Galleries, New York, 1963-65, The Barn Gallery, Hartford, Conn, 1979; solo show Queensborough Community Col, 1977; commns from Thomas P F Hoving, La Guardia Community Col, Brooklyn Col, City Univ of NY; Backus Gallery & Mus, Fort Pierce, Fla, 2003; Riverbend Sculpture Beinnial, Owensboro Mus Fine Art, Owensboro, Ky, 2005. *Awards:* First prize sculpture, Salmagundi Club, NY, 1964, 1965; Gruber Award, SUNY at Purchase, Harrison Coun for the Arts, 1983. *Mem:* Burr Artists, Inc. *Media:* Marble & Oil Painting. *Mailing Add:* 724 W Las Olas Blvd Ft Lauderdale FL 33312-7145

GIANLORENZI, NONA ELENA
PAINTER, SCULPTOR
b Virginia, Minn, July 20, 1939. *Study:* Queens Col, 61-65, studied color with John Ferron & Herb Aach; New Sch Social Res, 62-67, studied sculpture with T Doyle & C Guinnivar, painting with A Savelli; Brooklyn Col, 67-68, studied painting with H Holtzman & Carl Holty; studied sculpture with Lee Bonticou, 89; studied color & portraiture with Lois Dodd, 91; studied mod & contemp art hist with Mona Hadler, 92; studied techniques & theories art hist with Susan Koslow, 94; studied art conoisseurship with Jack Flam, 94. *Exhib:* 9th Street Survival Show; Black Velvet Erotic Arts Show, 81; Projective-Kinetic Traveling Exhib, 86; Asage Gallery, NY; Brooklyn Col Exhib, 92; Outdoor Sculpture Exhib, 93. *Pos:* Asst dir, Am Art Gallery, New York, 61-67; dir, ASAGE Art Gallery, New York, 77-88 & Art Space Inc New York, 89-92. *Teaching:* Art teacher, Charles Borromeo, Brooklyn & Mt Carmel & St Francis Sch Deaf, Queens, 68-71. *Awards:* Work Study Grant, St Scholastica, Duluth, Minn; Art Studio Scholar, New Sch Soc Res; Loy Scholar, Ford Found Fel, Brooklyn Col. *Bibliog:* Grace Glueck (auth), No More Raw Eggs at the Whitney, New York Times, 2/13/72. *Media:* Acrylic; Wood, Metal Detritus. *Specialty:* Three-dimensional wall painting existing in real space with movement, light and/or sound (kinetic); contemporary art masterworks, side by side with works by emerging artists. *Publ:* Auth, The Art Market, Jackie Fine Arts, 79; Don Jacobson: Kinetic Art (exhib catalogs), ASAGE Gallery, 81 & 84; Position paper (for an emerging gallery), ASAGE Gallery, 82; coauth, Yudel Kyler: Cool Surrealism (exhib catalog), 85 & Gerald Lindahl and the Creation of Psychological Space (exhib catalog), 86, ASAGE Gallery; Grace Glveck (auth), No More Raw Eggs at the Whithey, NY Times, 2/13/72. *Dealer:* Am State of the Art Gallery Exchange 162 W 4th St New York NY 10014; Art Space Inc 415 Rugby Rd Brooklyn NY 11226. *Mailing Add:* 415 Rugby Rd Brooklyn NY 11226-5611

GIBB, ANN W
PAINTER
b New York, NY, 25. *Study:* Cornell Univ, 41-45; Art Students League; studied with Herb Olsen, Charles Reid, Christian Midjo & Glenora Richards. *Exhib:* Nat Acad Design; Audubon Artists; Allied Artists Am; Hudson Valley Art Asn; Solo exhib, Darien Libr, 57 & 96, Barbizon Gallery, New York City, Acad Our Lady Mercy, Kauffmann-Locke Gallery, Nantucket, Mass, 94. *Teaching:* instr, Silvermine Sch Art. *Awards:* Best Landscaped Award, New Canaan Ctr for Arts; Rothchild Purchase Prize, Allied Artists of Am; Landscape Prize, Art of the Northeast. *Mem:* Knickerbocker Artists; Allied Artists Am; Am Watercolor Soc; Miniature Art Soc NJ. *Mailing Add:* 50 Hanson Rd Darien CT 06820

GIBBONS, HUGH (JAMES)
PAINTER, EDUCATOR
b Scranton, Pa, Oct 26, 37. *Study:* Pa State Univ, with Elaine de Kooning & Robert Mallary, BA(painting), 59, MA(painting), 61. *Work:* WTex Mus, Lubbock; Bucknell Univ Collection. *Exhib:* One-man shows, Univ Tex, Permian Basin, Odessa, Tex, 90 & Charleston Heights Gallery, Las Vegas, Nev, 90; TVAA Citation, Dallas, 91; Amarillo, Tex Competition, 93; New Am Talent, Austin, Tex, 94; 22nd Ann, Confluence, Ingram, Tex, 94; Texas Art Int, El Paso, Tex, 94; and others. *Teaching:* Prof painting & drawing & MFA coordr, Tex Tech Univ, 63-. *Media:* Oil, Pencil. *Mailing Add:* Tex Tech Univ Dept Art Lubbock TX 79409

GIBBONS, JOE
FILMMAKER
Exhib: AFI Video Festival, Los Angeles, 89; Art of the Century, Whitney Mus, 89-91; The Talking Cure, Artist's Space, NY, 90=91; Consumer Tools, Mus Mod Art, 91; The Kitchen, NY, 92; Whitney Biennial, 92, 2000, 2002 & 2006; Impakt Festival, Utrecht, Neth, 94-99; Black Maria Film & Video Festival, 95-2000; NY Video Festival, Film Soc Lincoln Ctr, 95-2002; Int Film Festival, Rotterdam, 95-2003; Viper Festival, Zurich, 98; NY Film Expo, 99; Pacific Film Archive, Calif, 2000. *Pos:* lectr, Vis Arts, MIT. *Awards:* Best Experimental Film, New Eng Film & Video Festival, 86 & 92; Award of Excellence, 27th Sinking Creek Film/Video Festival, 94; Second Prize, Black Maria Film & Video Festival, 96, 98-2001 & 2004; First Prize, Viper Video Festival, 96; and many other fellowships & grants. *Mailing Add:* MIT 265 Massachusetts Ave Cambridge MA 02139

GIBBS, BARBARA
MUSEUM DIRECTOR
b Newton, Mass, Feb 15, 50. *Study:* Brown Univ, AB(fine arts, magna cum laude), 72; Univ Calif, Los Angeles, Grad Sch Mgt, MBA(arts mgt), 79. *Pos:* Deputy dir, Portland Art Asn, Ore, 79-83; dir, Crocker Art Mus, Sacramento, Calif, 83-94 & Cincinnati Art Mus, Ohio, 94-. *Mem:* Asn Art Mus Dir; Am Asn Mus

GIBBS, TOM
SCULPTOR
b Dubuque, Iowa, Sept 17, 42. *Study:* Loras Col, BA(art); Univ Iowa, with Olivier Strabelle, MA(sculpture) & MFA; also with Walter Arno, Ger. *Work:* Tweed Mus, Univ Minn, Duluth, 89. *Comn:* Western Electric Corp, 80; Esterville Pub Libr, 81; Univ Dubuque, 88; Morningside Col, Sioux City, Iowa, 89; Univ Central Ark, 94; Univ Northern Iowa, 95. *Exhib:* Univ Minn, Duluth, 88; Riverwalk Outdoor Invitational, Chicago, 89; Sculpture Tour 91, Walters State Col, Tenn; Ala Bienniel, Univ Ala, Tuscaloosa, 93; Pier Walk 98, Chicago, 98. *Teaching:* Instr art, Clarke Col, 68-69; asst prof sculpture, Ariz State Univ, 70-72. *Awards:* Honorable Mention, Nat Vietnam War Memorial Design Compt, Washington, DC, 81; Nominee, Second Ann Awards in the Visual Arts, 82; Creative Artists Planning Proj Task Force, Iowa, Art Coun, 88-90; Gov's Award for Service to Arts, 89. *Bibliog:* Articles, Chicago Sun Times, 6/29/80 & 5/23/82 & Art News, 11/80; Joan Jeremy Hewes (auth), Worksteads, Tom Gibbs, Sculptor, pp 24-29 & 120, Doubleday, NY, 81. *Mem:* Int Sculpture Ctr. *Media:* Welded & Cast Metal. *Publ:* Auth, Field hearings on the reauthorization of the National Foundation for the Arts on Humanities Act J pp 412-421. *Dealer:* Molly-Rose Gallery 5400 SW 99th Terr Coral Gables FL. *Mailing Add:* 1333 Kaufmann Dubuque IA 52001

GIBBS, Y GALE
PAINTER, SCULPTOR
b Oklahoma City, Okla, Dec 7, 46. *Study:* Cameron Univ, BFA, 88; Univ NTex, grad studies, 90; workshops with James Surls, Dave Hickey & Jack Mims. *Work:* Cameron Univ, Lawton, Okla. *Comn:* Sculpture, Eisenhow High Sch, Lawton, Okla; sculpture, comn by Mr & Mrs Tom D'spain, Duncan, Okla; sculpture, comn by Keith Bishop, Oklahoma City; sculpture, comn by Dr Jack Bowman, Lawton, Okla; drawing, comn by Mr & Mrs Bob Ott, Duncan, Okla. *Exhib:* Solo exhibs, Ill Cen Col, Peoria, 88, Ritual Rhetoric & Resolution & La State Univ, Shreveport, 92, Eastfield Col, Dallas, Tex, 92, Harrisburg Area Community Col, Pa, 94, Bird STories, Dallas Visual Art Cen, Tex, 96 & Farce & Fable, Austin Peay State Univ, Clarsville, Tenn, 99. *Pos:* Secy, Wave, Denton, Tex, 92. *Teaching:* Fel design, Univ NTex, Denton, 89-90. *Awards:* First Place, Clary-Miner Gallery Nat, 89; Third Place, 24th Ann Del Mar Nat, Leisure Time, 90. *Bibliog:* Gibbs work exhibited in New York, Lawton Constitution, 87; Richard Huntington (auth), Woodcuts, pencils, paint, Buffalo News, 4/21/89; Lori Baker (auth), Gibbs bares abstract messages, College Harbinger, 89. *Mem:* Tex Sculpture Asn, Dallas; Dallas Visual Art Cen; Wave. *Media:* Oil on Canvas

GIBRAN, KAHLIL GEORGE
SCULPTOR
b Boston, Mass, Nov 29, 22. *Study:* Boston Mus Sch, 40-43, painting with Karl Zerbe. *Work:* Pa Acad Fine Art, Philadelphia; Cheekwood Art Ctr, Nashville, Tenn; Elmira Col, NY; Swope Gallery, Ind; Rockhill Nelson Gallery, Kans; Boston Mus Fine Arts, Mass; Springfield Mus Fine Arts. *Comn:* Bronze wall mural, Forsythe Dental, Boston, 71; bronze plaque of Judge Francis Ford, Fed Ct House, Boston & poet Kahlil Gibran, Copley Sq, Boston, 77; madonna (bronze figure), Jamaica Plain, Mass, 81; silver medallion of Elliot Norton, Boston Theatre Dist Asn, 83; Port Gibran Kahlil Gibran, Worcester State Col, 87. *Exhib:* Whitney Mus Am Art Ann, 56; Int, Trieste, Italy, 66; New Eng Artists, Provincetown Art Asn & Cyclorama, Boston, 71; one-man show of bronze sculpture, Cambridge Art Asn, 77; Cambridge Art Asn, Mass, 80; Boston Atheneum, 81; Boston Arts Festival, 85; Poet, Clasped Hands, Alimad Inc, 97; contemp sculpture, Chesterwood, 97, St Botolph Club, 98, French Libr, Boston, 98; Art of Spirit, Forest Hills Cemetery, Boston, 98, Provincetown Art asn, 99. *Teaching:* Wellesley Col, 58 & Boston Mus Sch. *Awards:* George Wiedner Medal, Pa Acad Fine Arts, 58; John S Guggenheim Fel, 59-60; Nat Inst Arts & Lett Award & Fel, 61. *Bibliog:* Gregory MacDonald (auth), Kahlil Gibran a Boston sculptor, Boston Globe Mag, 67; Nathan Hale (auth), Welded Sculpture, Watson-Guptill, 68; Donald Irving (auth), Sculpture Material and Process, Van Nostrand Reinhold, 70. *Mem:* Provincetown Art Asn; Copley Soc (Boston chpt); St Botolph Club (Boston chpt). *Media:* Steel, Bronze. *Publ:* Auth, Sculpture in process, Nat Sculpture Rev, 70; Sculpture Kahlil Gibran, 72; coauth, Kahlil Gibran--His Life and World, New York Graphic Soc, 74; revised, Interlink 91, Observations On The Reasons for the Cremona Tone, 93. *Mailing Add:* 160 W Canton St Boston MA 02118-1216

GIBSON, ANN
HISTORIAN, EDUCATOR
b Hagerstown, Md, Apr 30, 44. *Study:* Kent State Univ, BS, 65, MA 70; Univ Pittsburgh, MA, 78; Univ Del, PhD, 84; Phi Kappa Phi. *Comn:* Black Paintings, 1946-1977, 1998. *Pos:* assoc prof, art hist State Univ of NY, Stony Brook, 92-98, acting chmn dept art, 93-94; chmn, dept art hist Univ Del, 98-. *Teaching:* Teacher art pub schs, Hinckley & Wooster, Ohio, 66-69; studio adj, Kent (Ohio) State Univ, 69-72, Akron (Ohio) State Univ, 70-72; art hist adj, Univ Pittsburgh, 79; instr, art Art Inst Pittsburgh, 72-75, Point Park Col, Pittsburgh, 75-79. *Awards:* Andrew W Mellon fel Metrop Mus Art, 81-83; Morse fel Yale Univ, 87-88, senior fel, 90-91; recipient Distinguished Alumna award, Univ Pittsburgh, 95. *Mem:* Int Asn Critics; Col Art Asn. *Publ:* Auth: Issues in Abstract Expressionism, 1990, Abstract Expressionism: Other Politics, 1997, Judith Godwin, Style and Grace, 1997, Norman Lewis, guest editor (with Stephen Polcari), Art Journal; also articles. *Mailing Add:* U Del Dept Art Hist 206 Mechanical Hall Newark DE 19716

GIBSON, BENEDICT S
PAINTER, EDUCATOR
b Grand Rapids, Mich, Sept 21, 46. *Study:* Kendall Sch Design, dipl, 67; Aquinas Col, BA, 70; Univ Nebr, MFA, 73. *Work:* Albright-Knox Art Gallery, Buffalo, NY; Butler Inst Am Art, Youngstown, Ohio; Mem Art Gallery, Rochester, NY; Rutgers Univ, New Brunswick, NJ; Flint Inst Arts, Mich; and others. *Exhib:* 34th Western NY Exhib,

Albright-Knox Art Gallery, 74; Nat Drawing 1994, Trenton State Col, NJ, 94; 71st Ann Spring Show, Erie Art Mus, Pa, 94; 84th Ann Juried Show, Assoc Artists Pittsburgh, Carnegie Mus Art, Pa, 94; Art Fac Exhib, Bruce Gallery, Edinboro Univ Pa, 94; 20th Ann October Evenings Exhib, Meadville Coun Arts, Pa, 94; and others. *Collection Arranged:* Drawing Invitational (cataloged), 76; First Decade, Charles B Burchfield Ctr Col, 76; Penney Collection (cataloged), State Univ NY Upstate Med Ctr, 77; Three Painters, Millersville State Col, 77; Tenth Anniversary Exhibition, Kenan Ctr, Lockport, NY, 77. *Teaching:* Prof art, Edinboro Univ Pa, 76-. *Awards:* Cash Award, 79th Ann Juried Assoc Artists Pittsburgh Show, Pa, 89; Edinboro Univ Fac Res Grant, 90; Cash Award, 71st Ann Spring Show, Erie Art Mus, Pa, 94. *Bibliog:* Edward Booth-Clibborn (ed), American Illustration 2, Harry Abrams, Inc, New York, 83; Susan Krane (auth), Wayward Muse, A Historical Survey of Painting in Buffalo, Albright-Knox Art Gallery, Buffalo, NY, 87; Harry Schwalb (auth), Catching up, state of the art in Pittsburgh, Pittsburgh Mag, 1/94. *Mem:* Asn Artists Pittsburgh, Pa; Copyist Prog, Nat Gallery Art, Washington, DC, 2004. *Media:* Acrylic, Oil. *Publ:* Michael A Tomor (ed), Artists of the Commonwealth, Realism in Pennsylvania Painting, 1950-2000, Southern Alleghenies Mus Art. *Mailing Add:* Edinboro Univ Dept Art Edinboro PA 16444

GIBSON, JAMES D
VIDEO ARTIST, PAINTER
b Milbank, SDak, Dec 13, 38. *Study:* Ill Wesleyan Univ, BFA; Ohio Univ, MFA. *Work:* State Univ NY Col, Fredonia; Univ NDak. *Comn:* Videotape animation, St Mary's Col, Notre Dame, Ind. *Exhib:* Artists of Montana, Senate Off Bldg, Washington, 65; 12th Midwest Biennial, Joslyn Art Mus, Omaha, Nebr, 72; Emerging Expressions, Bronx Mus Arts, 88; Artiste Computer Art Symp, Marycrest Col; SIG Graph, Computer Art Show, Dallas, 86; Transmedia Video, Berlin, 97. *Teaching:* Instr art, Eastern Mont Col, 65-67; prof art, Northern State Univ, SDak, formerly, chmn art dept, 67-86. *Awards:* Purchase Awards, Paintings, 68, SDak Works on Paper, 71-72, & videotape, 89, SDak Mem Art Ctr; Project Grant, SDak Arts Coun, 90. *Mem:* Nat Asn Sch Art (bd dir, 71-72). *Media:* Computers, Ink. *Publ:* Illusr, Motive Mag, Methodist Church, 68-70; auth, Campus Call, Catholic Church, 68; illusr, Composites, Indust Press, NY. *Mailing Add:* 3126 Bell Dr Boulder CO 80301

GIBSON, JOHN STUART
PAINTER, PRINTMAKER
b Northampton, Mass, Oct 14, 58. *Study:* RI Sch Design, BFA, 80; Yale Sch Art, MFA, 82. *Work:* New York Pub Libr; Acklin Mus, Charlotte, NC; Univ Mass, Amherst; Smith Col Mus Art; Mus Fine Arts, Boston. *Exhib:* Beyond Realism, Southern Alleghenies Mus, Loretto, Pa, 92. *Teaching:* Instr art, Smith Col, Northampton, Mass, 85-92. *Media:* Oil. *Dealer:* Miller Block Gallery Newbury St Boston Ma 02116; Wendy Hoff Perspective Fine Arts 19 E 71st St New York NY 10021. *Mailing Add:* 30 Williams St Northampton MA 01060-9703

GIBSON, MICHAEL
PAINTER
b Atlanta, Ga, 62. *Study:* Univ Ga, Athens, BFA, 89. *Work:* Hunter Mus, Chattanooga, Tenn; NBHV, Hamburg, Ger; numerous pvt collections throughout the US & Nantes, France. *Exhib:* Contemp Int Mus Art, 92; Spotlight on Southeastern Artist Ann Exhib, 93, 94 & 95; An Am Renaissance, Lowe Art Gallery, Atlanta, Ga, 93; Nexus Contemp Arts Ctr, 95; November Show, New Mus Contemp Art, NY, 95; Atlanta Collects: Contemp Southern Art in Atlanta Collections, Consult Art, Ga, 97; Watermark, Fay Gold Gallery, Atlanta, Ga, 97; Born Again: Found Objects in Contemp Art, Art Walk, Atlanta, Ga, 98; Body and Soul: Contemp Southern Figures, Columbus Mus, Miss Mus Art, Mobile Mus Art & Cummer Mus Art, 98; Fay Gold Gallery, Atlanta, 99, 2001, 02; LPP Projects, London, Eng, 2000; Kevin Bruk, Miami, Fla, 2002; Cascade of Scales: James Graham & Sons, NY, 2002; Fresh: NoNo, Atlanta, Ga, 2002; Painting as Paradox: Artist Space, NY, 2002. *Awards:* Nat Endowment Arts Fel, Southeastern Ctr Contemp Art/Nat Endowment Arts 96-97. *Publ:* Contribr, Art & Antiques, Jezebel Mag, Atlanta Mag & New Art Examiner, 97; and many others. *Mailing Add:* c/o Fay Gold Gallery 764 Miami Circle Atlanta GA 30324

GIBSON, RALPH H
PHOTOGRAPHER
b Los Angeles Calif, Jan 16, 39. *Study:* US Navy, studied photog, 56-60; San Francisco Art Inst, 60- 61; Univ Md, DFA (hon), Ohio Wesleyan Univ, DFA (hon). *Work:* Mus Mod Art & Metrop Mus Art, NY; Int Mus Photog, George Eastman House, Rochester, NY; Fogg Art Mus, Cambridge, Mass; Corcoran Mus; Bibliotheque National, Paris, France; plus many others. *Comn:* 20 images, Museo del Arte Comtemporanea, Turin, Italy, 2003. *Exhib:* Photog for Collectors, Mus Mod Art, NY, 75, Rooms, 77, Mirrors and Windows, 78 & Penthouse, 80; one-man exhibs, Baltimore Mus Art, 76, Seattle Art Mus, 83, Leica Gallery, NY, 96, Galerie Abelard, Sens, France, 96, Frankfurter Kunstverein, Ger, 96, Leo Castelli, NY, 96 & Whitney Mus Am Art, NY, 96; Counterparts: Form and Emotion in Photog, Metrop Mus Art, NY, 82; Prototypes, Whitney Mus Am Art, NY, 83; Exposed and Developed, Nat Endowment Arts, Nat Mus Art, Washington, DC, 84; Aquisitions Recents, Mus Mod Art, Paris, 84; Das Aktfoto 1840-1985, Kunsthaus, Munich, WGer, 85; L'Autoportrait a L'Age de la Phtoog, Mus Cantonal, Lausanne, Switz, 85; plus numerous others throughout the world. *Teaching:* Lectr at var places including Ont Col of Art, Toronto, Sun Valley Ctr for the Arts, Idaho, Int Festival at Arles, France, Ansel Adams Gallery, Yosemite Valley, Calif & Tyler Sch of Art, Temple Univ, Philadelphia, Pa, 75 & Cranbrook Acad, Detroit, Mich, Inst of Contemp Art, London, Eng, Sydney Acad of Art Australia, Mus Fine Art, Houston, Tex & Frei Univ, Amsterdam, Neth, 77. *Awards:* Grand Medal, City of Arles, France, 94; Commandeur de l'Ordre des Arts et des Letters, 2003. *Bibliog:* Encyclopedie International des Photographes de 1839 a Nos Jours, Camera Obscura, Geneva, 85; Popular Photography, Vol 92, No 7, 85; International Museum of Photography Encyclopedia of Photography, 84; plus many other books and serials, 67-86. *Publ:* Auth, The Spirit of Burgundy, Aperture, NY, 94; Pharaonic Light, Guild Hall, 95; Infanta, Takarajima, NY & Tokyo; Light Years, Editions Stemmie, Zurich, 96; Deus Ex Machina, Taschen Ed, 99. *Dealer:* Leo Castelli 420 W Broadway New York NY 10013. *Mailing Add:* 331 W Broadway New York NY 10013

GIBSON, SANDRA
PAINTER, FILMMAKER
b Portland, Ore. *Study:* RI Sch Design, BFA, 99; Ecole des Beaux, Arts. *Work:* Artist Whitney Biennial, Whitney Mus Am Art, 2004. *Publ:* dir, (films) Cinematheque, ON, Pacific Film Archive, Anthology Film Archive, Rotterdam Film Festival, Ind. Exposure, Empire State Film Festival, Ann Arbor Film Festival, South Beach Animation Festival. *Mailing Add:* c/o Whitney Mus Am Art 945 Madison Ave New York NY 10021

GIBSON, WALTER SAMUEL
EDUCATOR, WRITER
b Columbus, Ohio, Mar 31, 32. *Study:* Ohio State Univ, BFA, 57, MA, 60; res at Kunsthistorisch Inst Rijksuniversiteit, Utrecht, 60-61 & 64-66; Harvard Univ, PhD, 69. *Pos:* Murphy Lectureship, Univ Kans & Nelson-Atkins Mus Art, Kansas City, Mo, 88. *Teaching:* Asst prof art, Case Western Reserve Univ, Cleveland, 66-71, chmn dept & assoc prof, 71-79, Andrew W Mellon prof humanities, 78-97, Andrew W Mellon prof emer, 97-; Clark vis prof art hist, Williams Col, 89 & 92, lectr, 2006. *Awards:* Kress Found Grant, 70; Guggenheim Found Grant, 78-79; Fel in Residence, Neth Inst Advan Study, Wassenaar, Neth, 95-96. *Mem:* Col Art Asn Am; Int Ctr Medieval Art; Midwest Art Hist Soc; Renaissance Soc Am; Medieval Acad Am; Am Asn Netherlandic Studies; Historians Netherlandish Art; Soc Emblem Studies. *Res:* Dutch and Flemish art, 15th-17th centuries; iconography. *Publ:* Hieronymus Bosch: An Annotated Bibliography, G K Hall, 83; Mirror of the Earth: The World Landscape in Sixteenth-Century Flemish Painting, Princeton, 89; Pieter Bruegel the Elder: Two Studies (The Franklin D Murphy Lectures XI), Univ Kans, 91; Pleasant Places: The Rustic Landscape from Bruegel to Ruisdael, Calif, 2000; Pieter Bruegel and The Art of Laughter, Calif, 2006. *Mailing Add:* 938 Mason Hill Rd N Pownal VT 05261-9339

GIFFUNI, FLORA BALDINI
PAINTER, LECTURER
b Naples, Italy, Oct 26, 19; US citizen. *Study:* NY Univ, BFA, 42; Teachers Col, Columbia Univ, MFA, 45. *Work:* Univ Hawaii; Medgar Evers Col, NY; Cabrini Col, Pa; New York City Hall. *Exhib:* Nat Art League, Douglaston, NY, 71; Pastel Soc Am, Nat Arts Club, NY, 72-88; Am Artist Prof League, Grand Cent Gallery, NY, 77; Salmagundi Open, Salmagundi Club, NY, 78-84; Knickerbocker Artists, Salmagundi Club, 80-81; Allied Artists, Nat Arts Club, NY, 88. *Pos:* founder, Flora B. Giffuni Gallery Am Pastel Art, Butler Inst, Youngstown, OH. *Awards:* Best in Show, Catharine Lorillard Wolfe Art Club, Nat Acad, NY, 70, Am Artists Prof League, 77 & Nat Arts Club, 82. *Mem:* Pastel Soc, Nat Arts Club; Pastel Soc Am (founder, pres, 72-88); hon mem Salmagundi Club. *Media:* Pastel. *Res:* History of pastels. *Mailing Add:* 15 Gramery Park S New York NY 10019

GIGLIOTTI, JOANNE MARIE
ADMINISTRATOR, PAINTER
b Pittsburgh, Pa, June 12, 45. *Study:* Carnegie-Mellon Univ, BFA, 67; Penn State Univ, MA, 78; grad courses, George Wash Univ; Trinity Col. *Work:* The Charlotte McCormick Private Collection, Fla; Nat Mus Women Arts; Westinghouse Collection; Penn State Univ; The Anita Shelford Family Collection. *Comn:* The McCormick Collection; Senator Strom Thurmond Information Center, SC; Jay & Addie Edleson Collection; Ann Burger Linden House; Mary and Michael, Buckler Collection. *Exhib:* Carnegie Mus Art, Pittsburgh, Pa, 68 & 71; Beautiful Batik, Arts & Sci Ctr, Nashua, NH, 74, Battle Creek Art Ctr, Mich, 75, Brigham City Mus Art, Brigham City, Utah, 75, Arnut Mus Art, Elmira, NY, 75, Abilene Fine Arts Mus, Tex, 76, Bronx Libr, Manhattan Branch, 76, Fayette Art Mus, Ala, 76; Early Childhood Enrichment Auction, Smithsonian Inst, 94 & Women's Exhib, 95; Tile Heritage Exhib, Santa Barbara, Calif, 96; Coverings, Int Tile Conf, Orlando, Fla, 97; Philadelphia Artists Alliance Tile Exhib, 98; Tile Artist's Today by Susan Werschkul, Tile Heritage Found Symposium, 96; Am Tile Artists by Richard Serving, ITC Coverings, 97. *Collection Arranged:* Etruscan Exhib, Univ Perugia/Oshna Gallery, Wash, DC, 84; Juried 19th Ann 4 State Competition, Masur Mus Art, Monroe, La, 92; Russian Art Project Exhib & auction, Georgetown, DC, 5/2006. *Pos:* Dir, Hub Arts & Craft Ctr, Penn State Univ, 78-80; founder & dir, Fine Arts Connection, Washington, 80-87; dir, Studio Arts Dept, Smithsonian Assoc Resident Prog, dir, Discover Graphics, Smithsonian Inst, Washington, 93-94; chair Smithsonian Inst Women's Coun, 88-95, art specialist, Russian art proj/auction, 2005-06; artist/owner, BatikTile.com, Gaithersburg, Md, 95-. *Teaching:* Instr, Batik-silkscreen-color-design and marketing & bus art, Smithsonian Inst - Resident Assoc Prog, 83-87; lectr, Am Univ, 84-86; guest lectr, George Washington Univ, 93-95, Smithsonian Inst, Yale Univ, 94; teacher, pvt art and computer graphics classes; teacher, mentoring for young artists, 95-; teacher, master classes ceramics; teacher, Women's Issues Project - Women's Informational Needs, 2002-2003; teacher, artist's master classes, 2005-. *Awards:* Best in Category (mixed media), Big Bends Nat Art Competition, Tallahassee, 68; Creative Programming Award, Nat Univ Continued Educ Asn, 90; Smithson Soc Grant, 94-95. *Bibliog:* Artists World, Discovery Channel, 90; article, Wash Home Sect, 92; article with photos, Traditional Home Mag, spring 96; Unique Batik, Decor Mag, 3/2001; Serious about ceramics, Jour Newspapers, 8/99; article, Tile and Decorative Surfaces, 5/98; article, Traditional Buildings Mag, 95, 98; article, Kitchen and Bath Mag, fall 98; article, Kitchen and Bath Design News, 3/98, 5/98; article, Designers Showcase, 96, 97; Washach wave, Restaurant Guide, winter 2001; Unique Batlik, Decor Magazine,

3/2001; Exploring the Art of Balik (Tile to Die for), Expression Magazine, 5-6/2002; Eloise Piper, Batik for Artists & Quilters, North Light Books, Cincinnati, Ohio, 3/2001. *Mem:* Women in Mus Network, 87-; Tile Heritage Found 94-; Tile Coun Am; Int Tile Coun; Art Speak (World Art Asn); Tile Artists Am; Smithsonian Inst (mem Latino Working Com, 93-95); Fine Arts Net work Carnegie Mellon Alumne DC Chap, 96-2006. *Media:* Painting. *Interests:* Political Activist; Mentoring. *Collection:* Nat'l Mus of Woman in the Arts,; The Westinghouse Collection; The McCormack Collection; private collections, USA. *Publ:* Coauth, Time-Life Art Ser, Time-Life Publ, 88; The Business of Art, Prentice-Hall, 89; Eloise Piper (auth), Batik for Artists & Quilters, North Light Books, 2001; Traditional Buildings Magazine, Potfolio Secion, 95 & 98; Exploring the art of Batik, Expression Mag, May/June/2002. *Dealer:* batiktile.com; The Ceramic Tile Store.com. *Mailing Add:* 69 Bralan Ct Gaithersburg MD 20877

GILBERT, ALBERT EARL
PAINTER, ILLUSTRATOR
b Chicago, Ill, Aug 22, 1939. *Work:* Am Mus Natural Hist, NY; Carnegie Mus, Pittsburgh; Ill State Mus, Springfield; Nat Audubon Soc, NY; du Pont Collection, Del Mus Natural Hist, Wilmington; Princeton Univ. *Comn:* Paintings of Am wildlife & plants, Nat Wildlife Fedn, Washington, DC, 67-74; Audubon bird proj (20 color plates of Am birds), Franklin Mint, Pa, 75. *Exhib:* Wildlife in Art, Brandywine River Mus, Chadds Ford, Pa, 73; SAm Birds, Am Mus Natural Hist, NY, 73; one-man show, Wildlife Portraits, Incurable Collector Gallery, NY, 74; Animals in Art, Royal Ont Mus, Toronto, 75; Bird Art Exhib, Leigh Yawkey Woodson Art Mus, Wausau, Wis, 77; and others. *Awards:* Winner, Fed Duck Stamp Competition, 78-79. *Bibliog:* B J Lancaster (auth), Gilbert's birds, Cornell Univ Lab of Ornithology Bulletin, 75; The artist--Al Gilbert, Prints Mag, spring, 79. *Mem:* Soc Animal Artists; Ridgefield Guild Artists. *Media:* Opaque Watercolors, Acrylics. *Publ:* Illusr, The Audubon Illustrated Handbook of American Birds, 68, The Red Book--Wildlife in Danger, 68, Curassows and Related Birds, 73 & Birds of New York State, 74; auth, My studio is the jungle, Int Wildlife Mag, 9-10/76; and others. *Dealer:* Blakeslee Gallery 350 Royal Poinciana Palm Beach Fl 33480; Steep Rock Wildlife Art PO Box 107 Bridgewater CT 06752. *Mailing Add:* 279 New Milford Rd W Bridgewater CT 06752-1029

GILBERT, CREIGHTON EDDY
HISTORIAN, WRITER
b Durham, NC, June 6, 24. *Study:* NY Univ, with Walter Friedlaender, Richard Offner, Lionello Venturi, Erwin Panofsky, Meyer Schapiro & Richard Krautheimer, BA, 42, PhD, 55;. *Hon Degrees:* Adelphi Univ, Hon LHD, 90; Univ Louisville, LHD, 97. *Collection Arranged:* Early Italian Paintings, Yale Univ Art Gallery, 84-2000. *Pos:* Cur, Ringling Mus, Sarasota, Fla, 59-61; ed-in-chief, Art Bulletin, 80-85. *Teaching:* Jr posts, Emory Univ, Univ Louisville, Ind Univ, Bloomington, 46-58; from assoc prof to Sidney & Ellen Wien prof hist art, Brandeis Univ, 61-69; prof hist art, Queens Col, 69-77; vis prof, Univ Leiden, Netherlands, 74-75; Robert Sterling Clark vis prof, Williams Col, 76; Jacob Gould Schurman prof hist of art, Cornell Univ, 77-81; prof, Yale Univ, 81-2000 & prof emer, 2000-; vis Zacks prof, Univ Jerusalem, 85. *Awards:* Mather Award for Best Art Criticism of Year, Col Art Asn Am, 64; Fel, Netherlands Inst Advan Study, 72-73. *Bibliog:* Interviews Rotterdam Courant-Handelsblad, 2/75 & Giornale Dell'Arte, Turin, 11/88. *Mem:* Fel Am Acad Arts & Sci; Col Art Asn Am; Ateneo Veneto. *Res:* history of Italian Renaissance painting and sculpture. *Publ:* Transl, Complete Poems & Selected Letters of Michelangelo, 63, Mod Libr Ed, 65, Vintage, 70, 3rd Revised Ed, Princeton, 80; ed, Italian Art 1400-1500, Sources and Documents, Prentice-Hall, 79, Italian ed, IRSA, 88, rev ed, Northwestern Univ Press, 92; Poets Seeing Artists' Work, Olschki, 91; Michelangelo On and Off the Sistine Ceiling, Braziller, 94; Caravaggio and His Two Cardinals, Penn State Univ Press, 95

GILBERT, HELEN ODELL
PAINTER, PRINTMAKER
b Calif. *Study:* Mills Col, Oakland, Calif, AB, 43; Cent Sch Art, London, 60; Univ Calif, Berkeley; with J Frielander, Paris, Univ Hawaii, MFA, 68; Pratt Graphics, NY. *Work:* Mus Mod Art, NY; Simon Guggenheim Mus, NY; Metrop Mus Art; Brit Mus; Honolulu Acad Arts; Bibliotheque Nat, Paris, Mus for Kunst and Gewerbe, Hamburg, Ger, Berkeley Art Mus, Berkeley, Calif, San Diego Art Mus, Calif, plus many others. *Comn:* Environ Wall Relief Paintings, Kaiser Outpatient Clinic, Honolulu; Environ Installations, King Kalakaua Ctr, Japan Travel Bureau, First Hawiian Bank, Honolulu, Hawaii. *Exhib:* Soc Am Graphic Artists, NY, 79, 83, 87 & 99; Dusseldorf, Basel & Koln Art Fairs, 80, 81, 83, 84 & 86; Meissner Gallery, Hamburg, 84; La Strutture Dela Visualita, Musei Civici Da Varese, Varese, Italy, 84; Exhib Am Abstract Artists Asn, City Gallery NY, 87; Contemp Art Mus, Honolulu, 89; Karen Fesel Galerie, Dusseldorf, 90; Honolulu Acad Arts, 94; Pioneers in Abstract Art, Sidney Mishkin Gallery, NY, 96; Int Print Exhib, Portland Art Mus, 97; Air Gallery, NY, 2000; plus others. *Teaching:* Prof art, Univ Hawaii, 65-; vis exchange prof, Parsons Sch, New York, 78-79; vis prof, Pratt Inst, 83. *Awards:* Res Grant, Univ Hawaii, 69 & 70; Study & Res Grant, Pratt Graphics, Ford Found, 79; Purchase Awards State Found Cult & Arts, Hawaii, 78, 81, 83 & 86; Study & Res Grant, Pratt Graphics, Ford Found, 79; Honolulu Printmakers Merit Award, 83, 84, 85 & 87. *Bibliog:* Virginia Watson-Jones (auth), Contemporary Women Sculptors, Ornyx Press, 86; Hans Heinz Holz (auth), Le Strutture Delia Visualita, Edizioni Milano, 85. *Mem:* Am Abstract Artists Asn; Honolulu Printmakers Asn; Soc Am Graphic Artists. *Dealer:* Fine Art Assoc 1021 Auahi St Bldg 4 Honolulu HI 98614; Karin Fesel Galerie Prinz Georg Stra Dusseldorf Germany

GILBERT, HERB
PAINTER
b Brooklyn, NY, Oct 30, 29. *Study:* Art Career Sch, 48-51; Brooklyn Mus Art Sch, with Reuben Tam, 55-58; Pratt Inst with Walter Murch, Reuben Nakian & George McNiel, 56-57; Univ Calif, 73. *Work:* Mus NMex, Santa Fe; Motorola Corp, Phoenix, Ariz; Am Republic Insurance Co, Des Moines, Iowa; Salt River Proj, Phoenix, Ariz; Bahai Nat Ctr, Wilmette, Ill; Univ Ariz Mus Art. *Exhib:* Own Your Own Regional, Denver Art Mus, 64; Southwest Fine Arts Biennial, Mus NMex, 74; Invitational, Cochise Col, Douglas, Ariz, 77; Birds Eye View Gallery, Newport Beach, Calif, 78; Cochise Fine Arts, Bisbee, Ariz, 79, 82 & 84; Lambert-Miller Gallery, Phoenix, Ariz, 81; Ariz Biennial, TMA, Tucson, Ariz, 82; Dinnerware Gallery, Tucson, Ariz, 82; Galeria Mesa-Chroma-Zone, Mesa, Ariz, 88; Davis Gallery Tucson, Ariz, 89, 90, 92, 93 & 94; Univ Ariz Mus Art, 89. *Teaching:* Instr graphics & drawing, Inst Am Indian Arts, Santa Fe, 71-75, chmn dept commun design, 74-75. *Awards:* Three Distinctive Merit Awards, Two Gold Medals & Eight Honor Awards, Art Dirs Club Denver, 59-69. *Bibliog:* Interview: Six Bisbee Artists, Artspace, winter 79; Michael Cadieux (auth), Herb Gilbert, Artspace, summer 83. *Media:* Acrylic, Collage. *Publ:* Contribr, Impressions of Arizona (painting), Art Am, 4/81. *Mailing Add:* c/o Davis Dominguez Gallery 154 E Sixth St Tucson AZ 85705

GILBERT, SHARON
COLLAGE ARTIST, CONCEPTUAL ARTIST
b Brooklyn, NY, Feb 15, 44. *Study:* Skowhegan Sch, 65; Cooper Union, BFA, 66. *Work:* Biblio Nat France, Paris; Mus Mod Art Libr Book Collection, Whitney Mus Libr, Brooklyn Mus Libr, NY; Archiv Sohm, Staatsgalerie of Stuttgart, Ger; Yale Univ Art Libr, Conn; J Paul Getty Ctr Libr, Calif. *Exhib:* Book Arts in the USA, USIA & Ctr for Bk Arts, Touring Africa, 90-92; Short of Rage, PABA Gallery, New Haven, Conn, 99; Working in Brooklyn: Artist Books, Brooklyn Mus Art, 2000; Far from Secret: Artist Books, Ctr for Book Arts, 02; Working in Brooklyn, Brooklyn Mus Art, 04; Artist Books, Kunst Centret Silkeberg Bad, Denmark, 04; Pressing Issues, Corcoran Gallery, Wash, DC, 05. *Awards:* Womens' Studio Workshop, Rosendale, NY, 82; New York Found Arts, 89; Brooklyn Community Access and TV award, Rotunda Gallery, 99. *Bibliog:* Lucy Lippard (auth), Conspicious Consumption: New Artists Bks, 85; Joan Lyons (ed), Artists Books: A Critical Anthology & Sourcebook, Visual Studies Workshop Press, Rochester, NY, illus, page 52; Handmade Books, Worcester, Davs Publ, 97. *Mem:* Women's Caucus for Art (NY Chaptadv bd, 79-83); Orgn Independent Artists. *Media:* Collage. *Publ:* A Nuclear Atlas, Women's Studio Workshop, Rosendale, NY, 82; artist bks, Poison America, 88, Working Time, 94, Chemical Ways, 97, Police (State) USA, 01, So Quiet, 03, Seeing Amsterdam, 04. *Dealer:* Printed Matter Inc New York NY; PABA Gallery New Haven CT. *Mailing Add:* 323 Atlantic Ave Brooklyn NY 11201

GILBERT-ROLFE, JEREMY
PAINTER
b Tunbridge Wells, Kent, Eng, Aug 4, 45. *Study:* Tunbridge Wells Sch Art, NDD, 65; London Univ, ATC, 67; Fla State Univ, MFA, 70. *Work:* Getty Study Ctr, Santa Monica; Commodities Corp, NJ; Chase Manhattan, NY; Albright-Knox Mus, Buffalo, NY; many pvt collections. *Exhib:* One-man shows, Anne Plumb Gallery, NY, 90, Genovese Gallery, Boston, 90, 93 & 96, Stark Gallery, NY, 94, Merve Verlag, Berlin, 96 & Shoshana-Wayne Gallery, Santa Monica, Calif, 96; Critics as Artists, Andre Zarre Gallery, NY, 95; Surface/Support, Bennington Col, Vt, 96; Trans-Hudson Gallery, NY, 96; Color Field to New Abstraction, Rose Art Mus, Brandeis Univ, 96. *Teaching:* Instr, Fla State Univ, 68-71, Princeton Univ, 72-78, Parsons Sch Design, 78-80, Calif Inst Arts, Valencia, 80-86, Art Ctr Col Design, Pasadena, Calif, 86- & Yale Univ, fall 87-89. *Awards:* Nat Endowment Arts, 74, 80 & 89; Guggenheim Fel, 97. *Bibliog:* Michael Cohen (auth), Jeremy Gilbert-Rolfe (interview), Flash Art, 5-6/95; Saul Ostrow (auth), Une ensemble fragmente, la peinture abstraite apres le modernisme, Art Press, 16, 95; Charles D Mitchell (auth), Works in UNT exhibit are monochromatic but multifaceted, Dallas Morning News, 2/96. *Mem:* Int Asn Word & Image Studies; Int Asn Philos & Lit. *Publ:* Auth, Cabbages, raspberries & video's thin brightness, Art & Design, 5/96; Gehry's houses, gastarbeitenhauslich, GA (in press), spring 96; Sheer without fear, the boys can't take it, Contemp Art Issues, 19-20, 96; introd, In: Seams: Art as a Philosophical Context, Gordon & Breach Publ, Inc, 96; Eugene Kaelin, artist's philosopher, J Aesthetic Educ (in press), 97. *Dealer:* Shoshana Wayne Gallery Bergamont Sta B-1, 2525 Michigan Av, Santa Monica, CA, 90404. *Mailing Add:* 2900C Airport Ave Santa Monica CA 90405-6109

GILBERTSON, CHARLOTTE
PAINTER, LECTURER
b Boston, Mass. *Study:* Boston Univ, BA; Art Students League; Pratt Inst, New York; studied with Fernand Leger, Paris; othee studies included courses in English Literature and English Usage at Cape Code Community Col in Mass and other similar studies at the Univ Dublin. *Work:* Guild Harwich Artists, Cape Cod; many pvt collections USA & Europe. *Exhib:* E A T Show, Brooklyn Mus, NY, 68-69; Erik Nord Gallery, Nantucket, 75; Bodley Gallery, 75 & 77; Irving Galleries, Palm Beach, Fla, 77; Pace Univ Mus & St Peters Col Mus, 78; Galeria Bryna, Palm Beach, 80 & 81; Guild of Harwich Artists, Harwich Port, Mass, 98 & 99; Eissey Campus Gallery, North Palm Beach, 2000; private exhib, Completed Papua New Guinea Series, Harwich Port, Mass, 2002; invitational exhib, Collage Series on paper based on letters A to Z, Palm Beach, Fla, 2003; and several others. *Pos:* Dir, Iolas Gallery, NY, 62-74 & Galeria Bryna, Palm Beach, 79-80; free lance lecturer, 80-; Palm Beach Mirror, Palm Beach, Fla; publ rels, Ann Norton Sculpture Gardens, West Palm Beach, Fla; asst to Cy Coleman, pianist and composer, during engagement at Regency Hotel, NY. *Mem:* Visual Arts Galleries Asn; Am Fedn Arts; Int Women's Writing Guild; life mem, Art Students League; Palm Beach Co Coun Arts. *Media:* Acrylic, Mixed Media. *Publ:* Papua New Guinea: Lik Lik Hap, Club Press, 98. *Dealer:* Art Commun Int 210 Rittenhouse Sq Suite 100 Philadelphia PA 19103; VAGA 350 Fifth Ave Ste 2820 New York NY 10118. *Mailing Add:* 18 Old Sch House Rd Harwich Port MA 02646

GILBOY, MARGARETTA
PAINTER, PRINTMAKER
b Philadelphia, Pa, Aug 10, 43. *Study:* Philadelphia Col Art, BFA, 65; Univ Colo, Boulder, MFA, 81. *Work:* Denver Art Mus; State Mus, Harrisburg, Pa, 99; Philadelphia Mus Art, Pa; Pa Acad Fine Arts; Woodmere Art Mus. *Comn:* Pub Libr, Boulder, Colo, 85; mural, Philadelphia Anti-Grafitti Network, 91; Wistar Inst, 95; Georgetown Univ Sch Medicine, 97. *Exhib:* Biennial, Joslyn Art Mus, Omaha, Nebr, 68; 5th Colo Ann, Denver Art Mus, 79; Colo Women Arts, Arvada Ctr Arts & Humanities, 79; Nat Painting Show, Washington & Jefferson Col, Washington, Pa, 80; Colo Biennial, Colo Springs Art Ctr, 81; Strictly Personal, Del Ctr Contemp Art, Wilmington, 95; Nature Morte: Contemp Still Life, Mus Am Art, Philadelphia, 96; one-woman show, Philadelphia Art Alliance, Pa, 99, Del Ctr for Contemp Art, Wilmington, 2001 & Mizel Ctr Arts and Cult, Denver, Colo, 2003; Aspects of Representation, Univ Western Carolina, 98; Elbows & Tea Leaves, Boulder Mus Contemp Art, 2000. *Pos:* Vis artist, Anderson Ranch Art Ctr; vis artist residency ceramics Anderson Ranch Arts Ctr, 2001. *Teaching:* Instr painting, Univ Colo, Boulder, 76-77, 80-82 & 2002-; lectr drawing & painting, Pa Acad Fine Arts, 86-. *Awards:* Yaddo Fel, 86; Bessie Berman Grant, The Lee Way Found, 94; Helen Lakin Truehart Award, Nat League Am Pen Women, 96. *Bibliog:* Eve Medoff (auth), Realism plus, Am Artist Mag, 3/79; Richard Torchia (auth), Margaretta Gilboy (catalog essay), Marian Locks Gallery, 90; Between Heaven and Earth, The Paintings of Margaretta Gilboy, 99. *Mem:* Col Art Asn. *Media:* Watercolor, Oils. *Dealer:* William Havu Gallery 1040 Cherokee St Denver CO 80204

GILCHRIEST, LORENZO
CONSTRUCTIONIST, EDUCATOR
b Thomasville, Ga, Mar 21, 38. *Study:* Newark Sch Fine & Indust Arts, 57-58; Newark State Col, BA, 62; Pratt Inst, MS, 67; Md Inst, MFA, 75. *Work:* Newark State Col; Fairleigh Dickinson Univ; Edward & Verdi Johnson Collection, Howard Univ; pvt collections of David Driskell, Grace Parks Johnson, Dr. Benjamin Jenkins & Dr. James Tolliver. *Exhib:* Some Negro Artists, Fairleigh Dickinson Univ, 65; one-man shows, Univ Md, 70 & Morgan State Univ, 79; Md Regional, Baltimore Mus Art, 71; Black Art, Towson State Col, 75; three solo & many group shows, Argus Gallery; one-man sabbatical exhib, Towson State Col, 93. *Pos:* Assoc art dir, Sen Robert Kennedy Proj, Bedford Stuyvesant Youth in Action, Brooklyn, NY, 65-67. *Teaching:* Asst prof art, Towson State Col, 67-97; guest prof sculpture, Cornell Univ, summers 72 & 73; teacher constructions, painting & drawing, Baltimore Mus Art, 73-74; guest prof print workshop, Morgan State Univ, summer 77. *Awards:* Afro American Slide Depository for Afro Americans, Samuel Kress Found, 71; Fel Int Arts Sem, Fairleigh Dickinson Univ, 62. *Bibliog:* Barbara Gold (auth), Blackmarks, Black art, Sun Paper Art Sect, 6/75. *Media:* mixed media. *Mailing Add:* 55 Pond Rd Delta PA 17314-8660

GILCHRIST, ELIZABETH BRENDA
EDITOR
b Coulsdon, Eng, US citizen. *Study.* Smith Col, BA(art hist); Art Students League. *Pos:* Asst, Durlacher Brothers Art Gallery, New York, 54-57; art admin asst, Brussels World's Fair, Belg & New York, 57-58; fund raiser, Mus Mod Art, New York, 59-62; reporter, Show Mag, New York, 62-64; staff writer, Am Heritage Publ Co, 64; sr art ed, Praeger Publ, New York, 65-75; ed publ, Cooper-Hewitt Mus, Nat Mus Design, Smithsonian Inst, New York, 76-81; mem adv coun for continuing educ prog, Mus Collaborative Inc, 77 78, publ consult & art ed (freelance), 81-. *Mem:* Drawing Soc (mem bd dir, 60-81, mem exec comt, currently); Soc Archit Historians; Col Art Asn; Am Asn Mus; Victorian Soc Am. *Publ:* gen ed, The Smithsonian Illustrated Library of Antiques, Cooper-Hewitt Mus, 76-81; auth, Yoga Mooseana Book, Filmflam, 2000; auth, For a Nephew: A Tale of Chairs, 2001; auth, Paws for Peace, Gabi's, 2002; auth, guide to Maine, Braceypoint, 2003. *Dealer:* Blue Heron Gallery Deer Isle Maine. *Mailing Add:* 1 Croswell Ln Deer Isle ME 04627

GILDEN, BRUCE
PHOTOGRAPHER
b Oct 16, 46. *Work:* Mus Mod Art, NY; Victoria & Albert Mus, London, Eng; Philadelphia Mus Art; Libr Cong, Washington, DC; Mus Fine Arts, Houston; Brooklyn Mus, NY; Shadai Gallery, Tokyo, Tokyo Met Mus of Photography; The Royal Photographic Soc, Bath, Eng; plus others. *Comn:* Medecins San Frontieres Twentieth Anniversary, 91; Mission Photographique Transmanche, CRP Nord Pas de Calais, France, 93; Gallery Photog, Dublin, Ireland, 96. *Exhib:* Twelve Photographers Look At Us (with catalog), Philadelphia Mus Art, 87; PPS Gallerie, Hamburg, Ger, 91; Mean Streets, Mus Mod Art, NY, 91; Casa des Artes, Vigo, Spain, 92; Mus Mod Art, NY, 93; Uber die Grossen Stadte, Marstall, Berlin, Ger, 93; solo exhibs, Musee de L'Elysee Lausanne, Switz, 93, Galerie Bodo Niemann, Berlin, Ger, 93, Musee de la Photographie, Charleroi, Belg, 93, Leica Gallery, Solms, Ger, 94, Agathe Gaillard Gallery, Paris, France, 94, Royal Photog Soc, Bath, Eng, 97 & Robert B Menschel Photog Gallery, Syracuse Univ, NY, 97; Who's Looking at the Family? (with catalog), Barbican Art Gallery, London, 94. *Teaching:* Instr workshops, Soros Found, Novosibirsk, Russia, 2000. *Awards:* Nat Endowment Arts Photogr Fel, 80, 84 & 92; Villa Medicis Hors les Murs, France, 95; European Publ Award for Photog, 96; Artist's Fel Award, The Japan Found, Tokyo, 99; Award NY Found for Arts, 2000. *Mem:* Magnum Photos (assoc). *Publ:* Illusr, Aperture, New York, spring 92; Facing New York: Photographs by Bruce Gilden, Cornerhouse Publ, Eng, fall 92; British Vogue (portfolio), London, Eng, 2/93; Bleus, Cahier No 13, Mission Photographique Transmanche, CRP Nord Pas de Calais, France, 94; Haiti: Photographs by Bruce Gilden, Dewi Lewis Publ, Braus & Editions Marval, fall 96; photogr, Facing New York, Cornerhouse Pubs, 92; photogr, Go, Muhkendals Magnum, 2000; plus others. *Dealer:* Magnum Photos Paris/London/New York/Tokyo. *Mailing Add:* 25 Mercer St New York NY 10013

GILDZEN, ALEX
WRITER, COLLECTOR
b Monterey, Calif, Apr 25, 43. *Study:* Wagner Col, with Kenneth Koch, 63; Kent State Univ, BA, 65, MA, 66. *Collection Arranged:* The Photographer's Art: An Exhibition of Prints and Books on Photography, 81; The Art of P Craig Russell, 92. *Pos:* Assoc cur, Spec Collections, Libr, Kent State Univ, 77-85, acting cur, Mus, 82-83, cur, Spec Collections, 85-93; ed, Dress: J Costume Soc Am, 82-84; volunteer, Santa Fe Inst Fine Arts, 94-95; bd dir, Santa Fe Cares, 98-. *Teaching:* Prof, Libr Admin, Kent State Univ, 85-93. *Awards:* Exhib Catalog Award, Comt Rare Bk Section, Ala; President's Medal, Kent State Univ, 93; Ohioana Citation, Ohioana Libr, 93. *Bibliog:* Roberta Berke (auth), Bounds Out of Bounds, Oxford Univ Press, 81; Dimitris Karageorgiou (ed), Gildzen at 50, Toucan Press, 93. *Mem:* Costume Soc Am (region III pres, 82-83). *Res:* Film and theater history; modern sculpture. *Collection:* Contemporary sculpture, drawings, prints and photographs. *Publ:* Ed, Six Poems-Seven Prints, Kent State Univ Libr, 71; auth, Haber's shattered landscapes: Studies in nature and time, (exhib catalog), Kent State Univ, 77; Partially buried woodshed: A Robert Smithson log, 78 & Ira Joel Haber: Poolside reflections on coming out of the box, 82, Arts Mag; The Avalanche of Time: Selected poems 1964-1984, 86; Joseph Chaikin: A Bio-bibliography, 92; A Gathering of Poets, 92. *Mailing Add:* 2328 Brother Abdon Santa Fe NM 87505

GILHOOLEY, DAN
PAINTER
Study: Hunter Col, BA, MA; Ctr Modern Psychoanalytic Studies; Boston Grad Sch, MA (psychoanalysis). *Teaching:* Prof, art, Suffolk Co Community Col, currently. *Mem:* Nat Acad. *Mailing Add:* Suffolk Co Cmty Col Asst Dean Instr 121 Speonk-Riverhead Rd Riverhead NY 11901

GILHOOLY, DAVID JAMES, III
SCULPTOR
b Auburn, Calif, Apr 15, 43. *Study:* Univ Calif, Davis, BA, 65, MA, 67. *Work:* Philadelphia Mus Art, Pa; San Francisco Mus Mod Art; Whitney Mus Am Art; Norton Mus Art, West Palm Beach, Fla; Australia Nat Gallery, Canberra; Stedelijk Mus, Amsterdam; and others. *Comn:* Breadwall, Govt Can Bldg, Calgary, Alta; Merfrog Fountain, Stanford Univ, Calif; and others. *Exhib:* Funk Show, Inst Contemp Art, Boston, 67; Realism '70, Montreal Mus Art & Art Gallery, Ont, 70; Whitney Mus Am Art, 70, 71, 74 & 82; Matrix Gallery, Wadsworth Atheneuem, Hartford, Conn, 76; Painting & Sculpture: The Mod Era, San Francisco Mus Art & Nat Collection Fine Art, Washington, 77; Mus Contemp Craft, NY, 78; Ceramic Sculpture: Six Artists, Whitney Mus Am Art, 81 & San Francisco Mus Mod Art, 82; Keepers of the Kiln Traveling Exhib, 91; San Jose Mus Art, Calif, 92; Elvis & Marilyn 2 x Immortal Traveling Exhib, Inst Contemp Art, Boston, 94; var exhibs at maj mus incl Whitney Mus, Los Angeles Co Mus Art, Philadelphia Mus Art & San Francisco Mus Art; Trashformations Traveling Exhib, Whatcom Mus Art, Bellingham, Wash; De Saisset Mus, Santa Clara Univ, 99; Halle Ford Mus, Willamette Univ, Salem, Oreg, 2000; and others. *Teaching:* Instr drawings & watercolor, San Jose State Col, 67-69; instr ceramics & sculpture, Univ Sask, Regina, 69-71; instr ceramic & sculpture, York Univ, 71-75 & 76-77; instr ceramics & drawing, Univ Calif, Davis, 75-76. *Bibliog:* The Artist as Historian, artscanada, 75; Henry Hopkins (auth), 50 West Coast Artists, Chronicle Books, 81; Ceramic Sculpture, Six Artists, Univ Wash Press, 82; David Gilhooly, J. Natsoulas Press, 92; The Not-so-Still Life, Univ Calif Press, 2002; Regina Clay (auth), Worlds in the Making, McKenzie Art Gallery, 2005. *Mem:* Royal Can Acad. *Media:* Plastics, Assemblage. *Publ:* Peter Selz (auth), Funk, Univ Calif Press, 67; David Zack (auth), Nut Art in Quake Times, Artnews, 3/70; J. Arneson (auth), David Gilhooly, Craft Horizons, 8/71; Steve Prokopoff (auth), David Gilhooly, Chicago Mus Art, 76; G.M. Dault (auth), My Beavers and I, Vancouver Art Gallery, 76; Tom Folk (auth), Plasticity & David Gilhooly, Art Magazine, 10/87. *Dealer:* MICAELA Gallery San Francisco Calif. *Mailing Add:* 4385 Yaquina Bay Rd Newport OR 97365

GILL, GENE
PAINTER, CRAFTSMAN
b Memphis, Tenn, 33. *Study:* Memphis State Univ; Chicago Art Inst, Ill; Chouinard Art Inst, Los Angeles, BFA. *Work:* Los Angeles Co Mus, Los Angeles; Palm Springs Desert Mus, Calif; Atlantic Richfield Corp, Los Angeles; Home Savings, Los Angeles; Tee Ridder Mus Miniatures, NY. *Exhib:* 9th Ann Southern Calif Exhib, Long Beach Mus Art, 71; Laguna Beach Art Mus Exhib Ten, Calif, 71; Dimensional Prints, Los Angeles Co Mus Art, 73; Laguna Beach Art Mus, 77; Los Angeles Printmakers 1960-1980, Los Angeles Co Mus Art, 81; one-man shows, Comara Gallery, 70-71 & 74; Orlando Gallery, 95; Ronald Reagan Pres Libr, 2000. *Awards:* Purchase Award, Home Savings, 69; Purchase Award, Westside Jewish Community Ctr, 70; Jurors Award, Laguna Beach Art Mus, 70. *Bibliog:* Gatto, Porter & Selleck (auths), Exploring Visual Design, 78; George Magnan (auth), Today's Art, 79; Gerald F Brommer (auth), Discovering Art History, 81. *Media:* Acrylic, Oil; Serigraphy, Mixed media. *Mailing Add:* 3895 Valley Lights Dr Pasadena CA 91107

GILL, JOHN P
SCULPTOR
b Renton, Wash, Oct 24, 49. *Study:* Cornish Sch Allied Arts, Seattle, Wash; Kansas City Art Inst, Mo, BFA, 73; NY State Col Ceramics, Alfred Univ, MFA, 75. *Work:* Victoria & Albert Mus, London, Eng; Brooklyn Mus, NY; Ark Art Ctr, Little Rock; Kansas City Art Inst, Mo; Los Angeles Mus, Calif; and others. *Comn:* Vase, Mus Mod Art, NY, 88. *Exhib:* One & two man exhibs, Hadler-Rodriguez Gallery, NY, 81, 83 & 85, Univ Colo, 84, DBR Gallery, NY, 84, Dorothy Weiss Gallery, San Francisco, Calif, 86, 88, 90, 92 & 94, Grace Borgenicht, NY, 83, 86, 90 & 93, Revolution Gallery, Mich, 95 & Kraushaer Galleries, NY, 96 & 98; Am Ceramics, Victoria &

Albert Mus, London, Eng, 86; What's New? Am Ceramics Since 1980 (with catalog), JB Speed Art Mus, Louisville, Ky, 87; 28th Ceramic Nation, Everson Mus, 90; Borgenicht 40th Anniversary Show, NY, 91; Nat Object Invitational, Ark Art Ctr, Little Rock, 91; Chthonic Realm, Helen Drutt Gallery, Philadelphia, 92. *Teaching:* Assoc prof, NY Col Ceramics; prof, Alfred Univ, 1984-. *Awards:* Fel, Nat Endowment Arts, 79, 92 & 93; Ohio Arts Coun Individual Artists Grant in Crafts, 83 & 84; Grant, NY State Found Arts Grant, 88. *Dealer:* Kraushaar Galleries 724 5th Ave New York NY. *Mailing Add:* 149 N Main St Alfred Station NY 14802

GILLEN, JOHN
SCULPTOR, PAINTER
b Uniontown, Pa. *Study:* Univ Calif, Los Angeles, 64-68, BA, Univ Calif, Berkeley, 72-74, MA. *Exhib:* One-man exhibs, Davis Art Ctr, Calif, 72, The Clocktower, NY, 80, Wall Constructions, Paul Klein Gallery, Chicago, 87, Wall Sculptures, Laurie Rubin Gallery, NY, 87, New Work, Burnett Miller Gallery, Los Angeles, 88 & Concept Gallery, Pittsburgh, Pa, 92, Jernigan Wicker Fine Arts, 2000; Abstraction: Painting & Sculpture, Angles Gallery, Santa Monica, Calif, 86; Selections from the Berkus Collection, Long Beach Mus Art, Calif, 88; Jernigan Wicker Fine Arts, 2001; and many others. *Teaching:* Asst prof studio arts, Baruch Col, CUNY, 80-84, Univ Pittsburgh, Pa, 88-96. *Awards:* Eisner Prize for Creative Achievement in the Arts, Univ Calif, Berkeley, 74; Creative Artists Pub Serv Grant, NY State Coun Arts, 78; Artists Fel, Nat Endowment Arts, 80, 84 & 86. *Bibliog:* Joan Quinn (auth), LA, Art & Auction, 11/86; Deborah Gimelson, It's all relative, Art & Auction, 3/87; Cathy Curtis (auth), In the galleries, Los Angeles Times, 1/88. *Mem:* Col Art Asn. *Dealer:* Concept Art Gallery Pittsburgh PA; Jernigan Wicker Fine Arts San Francisco CA. *Mailing Add:* 4 Foxglove Ln Yountville CA 94599

GILLESPIE, DOROTHY MURIEL
PAINTER, SCULPTOR
b Roanoke, Va, June 29, 1920. *Study:* Md Inst Col Art, Baltimore; Art Students League; Atelier 17, New York, with Stanley William Hayter; Caldwell Col, NJ, Hon DFA, 76; Niagara Univ, NY, Hon Doctor Pedagogy, 90. *Work:* Guggenheim Mus & NY Univ; Mus Art, Ft Lauderdale, Fla; Birmingham Mus Art; NC Mus Art, Raleigh; Newark Mus Art; Fort Wayne Mus Art; Lafayette Mus, Ind; Brooklyn Mus; Castellani Mus, Buffalo, NY; Virginia Mus Fine Arts, Richmond; Yale Univ Art Gallery, Conn. *Comn:* Forms in Space Concerto (15'9 l/2"x14'13"x1 1/2"), Sprint Inc, Wake Forrest, NC, 94; Wall sculpture, Aerial Concerto (8'5" x 12'9" x 1 1/2") Art Serve, Ft Lauderdale, Fla 94; wall sculpture, Wind Chimes (8' x 11" x 1 1/2"), Mayo Clinic, Rochester, Maine, 95; wall sculpture, Wind Song (15' 10 3/4" x 15' 3/4") Northwest Bank, Rochester, Maine, 95; Encircled Path to the Enchanted Castle (62' x 18' x 18'), City Admin parking garage, Orlando, Fla, 98. *Exhib:* Va Mus Fine Art, Richmond, 63; Brooklyn Mus, NY, 76; Inaugural Awards to Women in the Fine Arts, Alice Barber Art Fund Inc, Helander Gallery, NY, 91; Southern Fla Invitational, George Bolge Selects, Mus Art, Ft Lauderdale, 91; Children in Crisis Benefit Exhib, Lorence Monk Gallery, NY, 91; solo-exhibs, NJ Ctr Visual Arts, Summit, 93, Ann Norton Sculpture Gardens, West Palm Beach, Fla, 93, Washington & Lee Univ, Lexington, Va, 93, Zone One Contemp, Asherville, NC, 93, St Johns Mus Art, Wilmington, NC, 93, Monty Stabler Gallery, Birmingham, Ala, 94 & Harmon-Meek Gallery, Naples, Fla, 94; Methods & Materials in Contemp Sculpture, Columbus Mus, Ga, 93; Univ Cent Fla, Orlando, Fla 95; Cross McLeaf Gallery, Philadelphia, Pa, 95; Mus Western Va, Roanoke, Va, 98; plus many other group and one-woman shows. *Collection Arranged:* Women Artists Paint Women Artists, Virginia Miller Gallery, 78; Artist Choice, Clayworks Gallery, New York, 79; PCA: Invites, Philadelphia Col Art, 83; traveling show, Art in Fashion/Fashion in Art, 87-89; Fordham Univ at Lincoln Ctr, New York, 90; Dorothy Gillespie: Works from Radford Univ Collection (with catalog), Traveling Show, Radford Univ Art Mus, 98. *Pos:* Lectr var univs & mus, 62-93; artist-in-residence, Womens Interart Ctr, NY, 72; co-coordr, Women's Interart Ctr, 73-76; chairperson, Fine Arts Comt, Int Women's Art Festival, 75; dir, Art & Community Inst, Md Inst Col Art, 77-83 & 80, New Sch Social Res, NY, 77-83; artist rep environ art, Clayworks, 78-79; vis comt fine arts, Lehigh Univ, Pa, 81-83; vis fel, Woodrow Wilson, 85-93; art in pub places comt, Broward Cult Affairs Coun, 93-94; vis artists, Md Inst Col Art, Baltimore, 83, Abilene Christian Univ, Tex, 84, Merideth Col, Raleigh, NC, 84, Asheville Mus Art, NC, 84, Radford Univ, Va, 85, Reynolds House Mus, Winston-Salem, NC, 85; dist prof of art, Radford Univ, currently. *Teaching:* Instr, Human Relations Ctr, New Sch Social Res, 72-83. *Awards:* Allied Professions Award, Va Soc, Richmond, 86; Women of Distinction Award, Birmingham-Southern Col, Ala, 87; Grant Award, Alice Baber Art Fund, 90; Honor Award for Lifetime Achievement in Visual Arts, Women's Caucus for Art, 2001. *Bibliog:* James R Nelson (auth), Birmingham News, 2/13/94; Frederick Kaimann (auth), Birmingham News, 2/13/94; Pamela H. Simpson and Elsa Honig Fine (auths.) Women' s Caucus for Art Catalog; Charlotte Steifer Ruenstein, American Women Sculptors, Boston, 90. *Mem:* Col Art Asn; Southeastern Conf Art Cols. *Media:* Painted Sculpture. *Publ:* Contribr, Professionalism & the woman artist, Womens Studies & Arts, 79 & Feminist Collage, 79; Overcoming barriers: The woman artist in the South, Southern Quart, 79; Professionalism & the Woman Artist (Elsa Honig Fine, sr ed), Women's Studies Arts, 79. *Dealer:* Associated American Artists 20 W 57th St New York NY 10019. *Mailing Add:* Radford Univ Art Dept PO Box 6965 Radford VA 24142

GILLESPIE, OSCAR JAY
PRINTMAKER
b McNary, Ariz, Dec 31, 52. *Study:* Arizona Univ, BFA, 77; Ariz State Univ, MFA, 83. *Work:* Fogg Mus,Harvard Univ, Cambrdige, Mass; Bibliotheque Nationale de France, Paris; Kemper Group collection, Chicago, Ill; Plains Mus, Fargo Ndak; NY Pub Libr, NY. *Exhib:* Fabled Impressions, Georgia Mus of Art, Athens, 2000; ECCE Home 2000, rudolph E Lee Gallery, Clemson Univ, SC, 2000; Prints USA, Springfield Art Mus, Mass, 2001; one man shows incl: Printmaking Gallery, Temple Univ, Philadelphia, Pa, 2001; Volunteer State Col, Gallatin, Tenn, 2002; Contemp Art Ctr, Peoria, Ill, 2003; New Faces Exhib, Marshall Arts Gallery, Scottsdale, Ariz, 2002; Sixty Square Inces Exhib, Purdue Univ Gallery, West Lafayette, Ind, 2004. *Teaching:* Prof art, Bradley Univ, Peoria, Ill, 86-. *Awards:* Finalist award, Artist Fel, Ill Arts Coun, 2002; Samuel Rothberg award, Prof Excellence, 2003; Purchase award, Sixty Square Inches Exhib, 2004. *Mem:* Soc of Am Graphic Artsists; Southern Graphics Coun; Mid-Am Print Coun. *Media:* Printmaking (intaglia, monotype), drawing. *Mailing Add:* 5713 N Keenland Ave Peoria IL 61614

GILLIAM, SAM
PAINTER
b Tupelo, Miss, Nov 30, 33. *Study:* Univ Louisville, Ky, BA, 52-55, MA, 58-61, LHD, 80; Northwestern Univ, LHD, 90. *Work:* Mus African Art, Phillips Collection, Nat Collection Fine Arts, Corcoran Gallery Art & Howard Univ, Washington, DC; Mus Mod Art & Metrop Mus Art, NY; Carnegie Inst, Pittsburgh, Pa; Walker Art Ctr, Minneapolis, Minn; Art Inst Chicago, Ill; Princeton Univ, Rutgers Univ, New Brunswick, NJ; Madison Art Ctr, Wis; Baltimore Mus Art, Md. *Comn:* Circles, Circuits, Boxes, Contel Fed Syst Comn, Chantilly, Va, 90; Windows Go Orange (e e cummings), Am Craft Mus, 91; Washington Coulours, Kaempfer Corp, Washington, DC, 91; Riders Blue, Archer Street Station, Metrop Transit Authority, Archer Street Subway Station, Jamaica, NY, 91; Norfolk, USAA Insurance Co, MARO Building, Norfolk, Va, 92; and others. *Exhib:* Art Ctr Ann, J B Speed Mus, Louisville, Ky, 61; Tribute to Martin Luther King, 68, Works on Paper, 70, Cut- Bend-Spindle-Fold, 74 & Handmade Paper, 76, Mus Mod Art, NY; Ann Exhib of Contemp Am Painting, Whitney Mus Am Art, NY, 69; Gilliam-Krebs-McGowan, 69, 34th Biennial of Contemp Am Painting, 75 & 10 plus 10 plus 10, 82, Corcoran Gallery Art, Washington, DC; 69th Am Exhib (with catalog), 70 & 72nd Am Exhib (with catalog), 76, Art Inst Chicago; Works for New Spaces (with catalog), Walker Arts Ctr, Minneapolis, 71; Kid Stuff? (with catalog), Albright-Knox Art Gallery, Buffalo, NY, 71; Works for Spaces: Antonakos, Bladen, Gilliam, Irwin & Rockburne (with catalog), San Francisco Mus Art, 73; 30 Yrs of Am Printmaking (with catalog), Brooklyn Mus, 76; Arts on the Line: Art for Pub Transit Spaces, Hayden Gallery, MIT, Cambridge, Mass, 80; Am Abstraction Now, 82 & Painting in the South, 84, Va Mus Fine Art, Richmond; solo exhibs, Davis/McClain Gallery, Houston, Tex, 86, Alice Simsar Gallery, Ann Arbor, Mich, 86, G H Dalsheimer Gallery, Baltimore, Md, 86, Carl Solway Gallery, Cincinnati, Ohio, 87, Klein Gallery, Chicago, 87 & 88, Robert Kidd Gallery, Birmingham, Mich, 87 & Iannetti-Lanzone Gallery, San Francisco, 88, Frederick Gallery, NY, 91, Gallery Simone Stern, New Orleans, 91 & Smith Andersen Gallery, Palo Alto, Calif, 92; The Experienced Eye, Ownesboro Mus Fine Art, Ky, 88; Looking South: A Different Dixie, Birmingham Mus Art, Ala, 88; African Am Art From the Collection, Philadelphia Mus Art, Pa, 90; Golden Windows Inside Gold, an installation Whitney Mus Am Art, Philip Morris, NY, 93-95; Galerie Simmone Stern, New Orleans, La, Baumgartner Galleries, Washington, DC, 94; Imago Gallery, Palm Desert, Calif, 95; 44th Biennian Exhib Contemp Am Painting, Corcoran Gallery of Art, Washington, DC, 95. *Teaching:* Instr, art, Pub Sch System, Washington, DC, 58-67; Corcoan Sch Art, Washington, DC, 64-67; Md Art Inst, Baltimore, 67-82; prof painting, Univ Md, 82-85; prof art, Carnegie Mellon Univ, 85-89. *Awards:* Individual Artist Grants, 67 & 89, Workshop Activities Grant, 73-75, Nat Endowment Arts, 67, 89; President's Award, Md Col Art & Design, 87; Order of Merit Award, Univ Louisville Alumni Asn, 87. *Bibliog:* John Beardsley (auth), Modern Painters at the Corcoran: Sam Gilliam, Corcoran Gallery Art, 83; Gerrit Henry (auth), A Metaphor for Human Being: New Paintings by Sam Gilliam, Arts Mag, 2/85; Jane Addams Allen (auth), Letting Go, Art in Am, 1/86. *Mem:* Washington Proj Arts (bd dir, 80-85); Col Art Asn (art comt, bd dir, 85-88); Anacostia Community Orgn (pub art work comt, adv bd, 87-88); Nat Acad. *Mailing Add:* 1428 U St NW rear Washington DC 20009

GILLIE, PHYLLIS I DANIELSON
ADMINISTRATOR, TAPESTRY ARTIST
b Marion, Ind. *Study:* Ball State Univ, BA(art), 53; Mich State Univ, MA, 60, EdS, 66; Ind Univ, EdD, 68; Kendall Col Art & Design, Hon DFA, 89. *Work:* Mint Mus Art, Charlotte, NC; pvt collections. *Comn:* Jewish Communtiy Ctr, Indianapolis. *Exhib:* Weatherspoon Gallery, Greensboro, NC, 69 & 70; Stitchery, Pa, 71 & Iowa, 75; Matrix Gallery, Bloomington, Ind, 72; one-person shows, Jewish Community Ctr, Indianapolis, Ind, 72 & Eye-Opener Gallery, Cincinnati, Ohio, 72; Mint Mus Art, 74; Herron Art Gallery, Indianapolis, 74; Sloane O'Stickey Gallery, Cleveland, Ohio, 74; Women in Art, West Bend, Wis, 76; Moonspace Gallery, Wis, 2002. *Pos:* Pres, Kendall Col Art & Design, Grand Rapids, formerly; consult, mus & arts orgns & non-profit orgns; pres, Danielson/Gillie & Assoc & D G Imports & Designs; pres, PDG Gallery. *Teaching:* Asst prof art, Ball State Univ, Muncie, Ind, 66-67; asst prof art educ, Univ NC, Greensboro, 68-70; assoc prof educ & art, Herron Sch Art, Indianapolis, 70-76. *Awards:* Mich Woman of the Yr Arts Award, 84. *Bibliog:* Kathleen Fisher (auth), Women in Action. *Mem:* Fair Trade Fedn; Mus Stores Asn; ArtServ Mich; Grand Valley Artists Mich; Women Made Gallery Chgo. *Media:* Fabric, Fiber, Wood. *Publ:* Auth, Art for the Second & Third Grades, Kimball/Hunt, 66; Paper mache and the elementary teacher, Arts & Activities, 12/70; Selected teacher characteristics of art student teachers, Studies Art Educ, winter 71; The woman administrator in art, Col Art J, 76; and others. *Mailing Add:* 6137 Chamonix Ct SE Grand Rapids MI 49546

GILLING, LUCILLE
PRINTMAKER
b Hamilton, Mo. *Study:* Kansas City Art Inst; New York Sch Fine & Appl Arts in Paris, France, Eng & Italy, dipl; Queens Univ. *Work:* Nat Libr Can, Ottawa; Montreal Mus Fine Art; Victoria & Albert Mus, London, Eng; Ohio State Univ; Wayne State Univ. *Exhib:* Soc Can Painters, Etchers & Engravers, Toronto, Ont, 56-; one-man shows, Pascall Gallery, Toronto, 66, Sobot Gallery, Toronto, 69 & Marjorie

Kauffmann Graphics, 72; Can Fine Art Gallery, Toronto, 74; plus others. *Awards:* Sterling Trust Award, 59; Anaconda Award of Merit, 68. *Mem:* Toronto Heliconian Club (exec coun, 71-75). *Media:* Etching. *Publ:* Portfolios of etchings, The Canterbury Tales, 66 & Don Quixote, 69, Original signed etchings Ed 100. *Dealer:* Campbell Tomi Gallery 210 Gerrard St E Toronto Ont Can

GILLINGWATER, DENIS CLAUDE
SCULPTOR, EDUCATOR
b Glendale, Calif, Feb 15, 46. *Study:* Univ Cincinnati, BFA, 68, MFA, 70. *Exhib:* Eighth West Biennial, Western Colo Ctr Arts, 74; Southwest & Rocky Mountain States Exhib, Scottsdale Fine Arts Comn, 75; solo exhib, Scottsdale Ctr Arts, 78; Ariz Sculpture, Northern Ariz Univ Art Gallery, Flagstaff, 80 & 81; Four Corners State Biannual, Phoenix Art Mus, 81; and others. *Teaching:* Asst prof intermedia, Ariz State Univ, 73-78, assoc prof, 78-. *Awards:* Nat Endowment Arts Artist-in-Residence, Mesa, Ariz, 73; Acquisitions, Phoenix Art Mus, 77 & Scottsdale Ctr Arts, 75; and others. *Mailing Add:* 6701 Clinton St E Scottsdale AZ 85254-5253

GILLMAN, BARBARA SEITLIN
DEALER
b Miami, Fla, Jan 14, 37. *Study:* H Sophie Newcomb Col, 55; Univ Miami, with Dr Virgil Barker, BA(Am art), 58. *Collection Arranged:* Israel 25, contemp Israeli art (auth, catalog), Bacardi Bldg, City of Miami, 79. *Pos:* Panelist, State Fla Grant Panel. *Specialty:* Contemporary original art, paintings and sculpture; Regional artists. *Mailing Add:* c/o Barbara Gillman Gallery 939 Lincoln Rd Miami Beach FL 33139-2601

GILLMAN, DEREK A
MUSEUM DIRECTOR, ADMINISTRATOR
Study: Oxford Univ, Eng, MA; Univ East Anglia, Eng, LLM. *Pos:* Mem Getty Trust Mus Mgt Inst, 91; exec dir & provost, Pa Acad Fine Arts, Philadelphia, 99-2001, pres & Chief Exec Officer, 2001; Cur British Mus; keeper (dir), Sainsbury Centre Visual Arts, Univ East Anglia, Norwich, Eng; dep dir, Nat Gallery Victoria, Melbourne, Australia; exec dir & pres, Barnes Found, 2006. *Bibliog:* Institute of Art and Law (Leilester), The Idea of cultural heritage, 2006. *Mem:* Norfolk Inst Art & Design (gov 90-95). *Mailing Add:* Barnes Foundation 300 N Latches Ln Merion Station PA 19066

GILMAN, BETTY HELLER
SCULPTOR, PAINTER
b Asbury Park, NJ, June 15, 24. *Study:* Fieldston, studies with Victor D'Amico, 41; Roslyn Art Sch, studies with Josef Presser, 57. *Comn:* Escalation (bronze sculpture), Yale New Haven Hosp Art Collection, Conn. *Exhib:* Solo exhib, Bodley Gallery, NY, 78, Artworks Gallery, New Haven, Conn, 81, NY Pub Libr, 87, Montserrat Gallery, NY, 98 & Expressions in Fine Art, Santa Fe, NMex, 99-; Transformation of Matter into Art, NY Acad Sci, NY, 90; The Tree-An Artist's Gift, Bergen Co Mus, Paramus, NJ, 90; Choices 91, Shoreline Alliance Arts, Guildford, Conn, 91; Art Ct, Meadowlands, Rutherford, NJ, 91; Hollycroft Outdoor Sculpture Show, Ivoryton, Conn, 96; Ward-Nasse Gallery, NY, 97; Montserrat Gallery, NY, 99. *Awards:* Medal of Honor & First Prize, Nat Asn Women Artists, 72-75, 79 & 85; Merit Award, 72-74, Artists Craftsmen NY, First Prize, 80, 86 & 87; First Prize, Conn Statewide Juried Show, Conn Comn Arts, 88 & 90. *Bibliog:* Sculptor Gilman Favors Use of Force, New Haven Register, Conn, 81; Cosmic artist tackles the final frontier, Shoreline News, Conn, 97; Journey's through space, Our Town Publ, NY, 97. *Mem:* Nat Asn Women Artists; Artist Craftsmen New York; Artstudio Club New York; Essex Art Asn (bd mem, 84). *Media:* All Media; Acrylic, oil. *Res:* exploring ancient pillars. *Specialty:* abstract connection to nature. *Publ:* Auth, American Women Artists (article), La Revue Moderne, Paris, 71; Members of Association of Women Artists (article), La Revue Moderne, Paris, 75; Earth According to Gilman, Hartford Courant, 81; Sculptor Gilman favors use of force, New Haven Register, 82. *Dealer:* Jerre McGurdy 225 Canyon Rd Santa Fe NMex 87501

GILMOR, JANE E
SCULPTOR, EDUCATOR
b Ames, Iowa, June 23, 47. *Study:* Iowa State Univ, Ames, BS(textiles), 69-70; Sch Art Inst, Chicago, 69-70; Univ Iowa, Iowa City, MA(paint), 76 & MFA(painting), 77. *Work:* Tokyo Univ Mus Art, Japan; Mus Contemp Crafts Libr, NY; Tyrone Gutherie Ctr, Newbliss, Ireland; Los Angeles Co Mus Art Libr; Ragsdale Found, Lake Forest, Ill; Banff Ctr, Can. *Comn:* Davenport Mus Art; Des Moines Art Ctr, Iowa. *Exhib:* Minn Mus Art, Minneapolis, 86; Nat Sculpture Exhib, Cincinnati, 88; Artemesia, Chicago, 89 & 2000, 2001; AIR Gallery, NY, 89, 90, 92, 94, 98 & 2000; Bemis Ctr Contemp Art, Omaha, 93 & 99; Cedar Rapids Mus Art, 94; Univ Minn Gallery Art, 96; Gallerie Rufino Tomayo, Oaxaca, Mex, 96; Olson-Larsen Galleries, Des Moines, Iowa, 98; Banff Int Ctr for the Arts, Can, 2000; A LR Gallery, NY, 2002; and others; A.I.R. Gallery, NYC, 2002, 05; Platformia Revolver Gallery, Lisbon, Portugal, 2006. *Collection Arranged:* Des Moines Art Ctr; Mus Contemp Art, Chgo; LA Co Mus; Cedar Rapids Mus art. *Teaching:* Prof of Art, chmn Art Dept, Mt Mercy Col, Cedar Rapids, IA, 1974-; vis prof, Sch Art, Univ IA, 1986; fulbright vis prof, Univ Evora Portugal, 2003-04. *Awards:* Artist's Proj Grant, Iowa Arts Coun, 95, 2002; McKnight Found/Intermedia Arts Interdisciplinary Artist's Fel, 96; Leighton Studio resident, Banff Ctr, Can, 2000; SOS Grant, Smithsonian Inst, 2001; NEA Creativity Grant, 2002; Sr Fulbright Res Teaching award, Portugal, 2003-2004. *Bibliog:* Hope Palmer (auth), Rev, Tractor, fall 93; Debra Leveton (auth), Three Iowa masters, Iowa Architect, spring 94; Kay Turner (auth), Beautiful Necessity, Thames and Hudson, 99; B Love (auth), Feminists Who Changed America 1963-1973, 2006. *Media:* All Media. *Specialty:* Contemporary Art. *Dealer:* Olson-Larson Galleries Des Moines Iowa; A.I.R. Gallery NYC. *Mailing Add:* 358 Trailridge Rd SE Cedar Rapids IA 52403

GILMORE, ROGER
ADMINISTRATOR, CONSULTANT
b Philadelphia, Pa, Oct 11, 32. *Study:* Dartmouth Col, AB; Univ Chicago Divinity Sch, grad study. *Hon Degrees:* hon DFA Sch Art Inst Chicago, 93; hon DHL Main Col Art, 2002. *Pos:* Dean, Sch Art Inst Chicago, 65-87, provost, 87-89; pres, Ox Bow Summer Sch Art, 87-89; pres, Maine Col Art, Portland, Maine, 89-2001. *Mem:* Nat Trust Hist Preserv; fel & life mem Nat Asn Schs Art & Design (pres, 87-90). *Publ:* Ed, Over a Century: A History of the School of the Art Inst of Chicago, 82. *Mailing Add:* 24 Fairmount St Portland ME 04103-3051

GILMORE FORD, JOHN
COLLECTOR
b Baltimore, Md. *Study:* Baltimore City Col, degree; Johns Hopkins Univ; Loyola Col; Md Inst Col Art, BFA. *Exhib:* Collection Indo-Asian art, Walters Art Gallery, Baltimore, 71. *Pos:* Nat vpres, Am Inst Interior Designers, 70-; Sr appraiser, specializing in Asian art, Am Soc Appraisers. *Bibliog:* P Pal (auth), Indo-Asian art, 71, Walters Art Gallery, Apollo Mag & Connoisseur Mag. *Mem:* Am Fedn Arts; Asia Soc; Am Soc Appraisers. *Interests:* Indian, Nepalese, Tibetan, Javanese, Chinese & Japanese bronzes, stone sculptures and paintings, contemp Asian art. *Collection:* Desire and Devotion: Art from India, Nepal and Tibet from the John and Berthe Ford Collection, Walters Art Mus, 2001; Exhib Santa Barbara Mus Art, 2002; Exhib Albuquerque Mus Art, 2002; Exhib Birmingham Mus Art, 2003; Exhib Hong Kong Mus Art, 2003. *Mailing Add:* 2601 N Charles St Baltimore MD 21218-4586

GILPIN, HENRY EDMUND
PHOTOGRAPHER, EDUCATOR
b Cleveland, Ohio, Nov 10, 22. *Study:* Los Angeles City Col, 46-48; Univ Calif, Los Angeles, 49-50; Cleveland Inst Art, 51; Ansel Adams Yosemite Workshop, 59. *Work:* Monterey Peninsula Mus Art, Calif; The Nat Mus Mod Art, Kyoto, Japan; San Francisco Mus Mod Art, San Francisco, Calif; Art Inst Chicago, Chicago, Ill; Minneapolis Inst Art, Minn. *Exhib:* Friends of Photog, Carmel, Calif, 72; Rockford Art Asn, Ill, 72; Sam Houston State Univ, 74; Art & Sci Mus, Nashua, NH, 78; Photo Gallery Int, Tokyo, Japan, 81; Expo 90, Osaka, Japan; Photographs, Monterey, Mus of Art, 97. *Teaching:* Instr photog, Monterey Peninsula Col, 64-2000, Ansel Adams Yosemite Workshop, 67-73 & 81-82 & Friends of Photog, Carmel, 69-86; Univ Calif, Santa Cruz, 86-. *Bibliog:* Video, The Roots of Calif Photog. *Mem:* Friends of Photog (trustee, 69-79); Photog Ctr of Monterey Peninsula (trustee, 88-90). *Dealer:* Susan Spiritis Gallery 3929 Birch St Newport Beach CA 92660; Ansel Adams Gallery Yosemite & Birlingame CA. *Mailing Add:* 1353 Jacks Rd Monterey CA 93940

GILSON, GILES
SCULPTOR, DESIGNER
b Philadelphia, Pa, July 19, 42. *Study:* Self-taught. *Work:* Metrop Mus Art, NY; Nat Collection, The Renwick, Smithsonian Inst, Washington; Detroit Inst Art, Mich; Los Angeles Co Mus Art, Calif; Contemp Mus Honolulu; and others. *Comn:* Wall sculpture, Lewis Collection, Richmond, Va, 81 & 82; Story Piece, Lipton Collection, Los Angeles, 84; Library Table, Hunter-Stieble Collection, NY, 86; Sculpture- NEC Found, Ronsselear Polytechnical Inst. *Exhib:* 20th Century Decorative Arts, Metrop Mus Art, NY, 81; Art of Woodturning, Am Craft Mus, NY, 83; Nat Wood Invitational, Craft Alliance, St Louis, Mo, 83; Polished Perfection, The Renwick, Washington, 86; Int Turned Object Show, Port of Hist Mus, Pa, 88; Out of the Woods, touring Eastern Europe, 93-97. *Pos:* Consult artist & technician, Creative Advantage, Schenectady, NY, 78-; consult artist, Gen Elec Co, Schenectady, NY, 82 & Harmony Arts Ltd, NY; tech consult, 3M Corp, St Paul, Minn, Harmony Arts Ltd, NY & Steinburger Sound, Newburgh, NY, 85; designer, Formula Honda race car body, 91; tech consult, GE (product test), 96. *Teaching:* Panelist-speaker, Conv Am Soc Interior Designers, Washington, DC, 78; instr, NAm Turning Symp, Philadelphia, 81, State Univ NY, New Paltz, 84-87, Am Asn Woodturners Conv, Gatlinburg, Tenn, 90 & State Univ NY, Purchase, 93 & Woodturning Design Conf, Saskatoon, Can, 92; workshops, Design Prog, State Univ NY; speaker & slides, Carnegie-Mellon Univ, Pittsburgh & Soc Art Craft, Pittsburgh; Am Craft Armory, NY, 87; speaker, Craft Alliance, St Louis, Mo, 88; artist-in-residence, Univ Pa, Ind, 89; guest lectr & instr, Calif State Univ, Fullerton, 90; panelist & instr, Am Crafts Coun Southeastern Conf, Jackson, Miss, 91; keynote speaker & workshops, Asn Woodturners Gt Brit Int Sem, Loughborough, Eng, 93. *Awards:* Spec Award, NAm Turned Object Show, 81; Best Dimensional Display, Upstate NY Ad Club, 85; Artist-in-Residency, Mid-Atlantic Found Arts, 88. *Bibliog:* Design Book II, Taunton Press; Albert Locolf (auth), A Gallery of Turned Objects; Lathe Turned Objects, Wood Turning Ctr; Beyond Wood-Emotional Expressions (video), KATIA-TV, Video Art Production; Speilman (auth), The Art of the Lathe; and others. *Mem:* Am Craft Coun; Am Asn Woodturners. *Media:* Wood, Metal; Plastics, Composites; Paints; Acryllics; Lacquers; Urethanes. *Publ:* Auth, Router rail, Techniques 4, Taubton Press, 82; Polychromatic Turning, Turning Points, 88; introd, Works of the Lathe: Old and New Faces, 88; contribr, Polychromatic Assembly for Woodturning, Linden Publ; Make Money from Woodturning, Guild of Master Craftsmen Publ, Eng. *Mailing Add:* 766 Albany Schenectady NY 12307

GIMBLETT, MAX(WELL)
PAINTER, SCULPTOR
b Auckland, NZ, Dec 5, 35; US & NZ citizen. *Study:* Ont Col Art, Toronto, 64; San Francisco Art Inst, 65. *Work:* San Jose Mus Art, Calif; San Francisco Mus Mod Art, Achenbach Found, San Francisco; Pa Acad Fine Arts, Philadelphia; Getty Ctr, Santa Monica, Calif; Mus Contemp Art, Sydney, Australia, Art Gallery New South Wales, Univ New South Wales; Art Gallery of Queensland, Brisbane, Australia; Mus Mod Art, NY; Whitney Mus Art, NY; Bodleian Library, Oxford Univ, England; Nat'l Art Gallery, Washington; Yale Univ, New Haven, CT; Nat Gallery Australia, Melbourne. *Exhib:* Haines Gallery, San Francisco, Calif, 91, 93, 96, 97, 2000, 2003, 2005; Gow,

Langsford Gallery, Auckland, NZ, 91, 93, 95, 97, 98, 99, 2001, 2003, 2004, 2006; Jan Turner Gallery, Los Angeles, 92; Jensen Gallery, Wellington, NZ, 92, 93, 95, 96, 97 & 98; Getty Ctr, Santa Monica, 92; Sherman Gallery, Sydney, 95; Margaret Thatcher Projects, NY, 99, 2003; Ethan Cohen Fine Arts, NY, 2001. *Pos:* Trustee, Lew Lye Found, New Plymouth, New Zealand. *Teaching:* Vis artist printmaking, Ind Univ, Bloomington, 79; vis assoc prof, Pratt Inst, Brooklyn, 79-89; vis lectr, Univ Canterbury, Christ Church, NZ, 81 & 92; vis assoc prof, Int Honors Program in Japan, India & Kenya; vis artist, City Art Inst, Sydney, Australia, 86; J Paul Getty assoc, Getty Ctr Hist of Art & Humanities, Santa Monica, 91-92; artist-in-residence, Queensland Univ Technol, Brisbane, Australia, 93 & Rockefeller Found Study & Conf Ctr, Bellagio, Italy; Visiting Artist Elam School of Fine Arts, Univ Auckland, New Zealand, 2004. *Awards:* Grant, Queen Elizabeth II Arts Coun NZ, 80, 86; Painting Fel, Nat Endowment Arts, Washington, DC, 89. *Bibliog:* Wystan Curnow, Thomas McEvilley, and Barbara Kirshenblatt-Gimblett, Max Gimblett; The Brush of all Things, Auckland Art Gallery New Zealand, 72 pgs; Wystan Curnow and John Yau Max Gimblett, Craig Potton Publishing Co and Gow Langsford Gallery, New Zealand, 172 pgs, 123 color plates, Anne Kirker, Max Gimblett The Language of Drawing; Kirshenblatt-Gimblett (auth), Art From Start to Finish. *Mem:* Jung Found, NY; Queensland Gallery Art (special patron). *Media:* Acrylic Polymer, All Media. *Publ:* Contribr, In the presence, Art NZ, 80; Max Gimblett and Wystan Curnow, Modernism, San Francisco, 82; Spirit Tracks, Pratt Manhattan Gallery, NY, 86; Sightings & Drawing with Color, Pratt Inst & Instituto de Estudios Norte Americanos, 88; Wystan Curnow, Objects of Alchemy, Artis Gallery, Auckland, NZ, 90. *Dealer:* Haines Gallery 49 Geary St San Francisco CA; Gow, Langsford Gallery Auckland NZ. *Mailing Add:* 231A Bowery New York NY 10002-1218

GINNEVER, CHARLES
SCULPTOR

b San Mateo, Calif, Aug 28, 31. *Study:* With Zadkine & Hayter, Europe, 53-55; Calif Sch Fine Arts, San Francisco, BFA, 57; Cornell Univ, MFA, 59. *Work:* Wadsworth Atheneum, Hartford, Conn; Hirshhorn Mus, DC; State Univ NY, Albany; Walker Art Ctr, Minn; Metrop Mus Art, NY; Australian Nat Gallery, Canberra, Australia; Nat Mus Am Art, Smithsonian Inst, Washington, DC; Seattle Art Mus, Washington; San Francisco Mus Modern Art, Calif. *Comn:* Hewlett-Packard Corp, Calif, 85. *Exhib:* One-man shows, Dag Hammarskjold Plaza Sculpture Garden, NY, 73, Max Hutchinson Gallery, 78-79 & 86, Long Beach Mus Art, 78, Construct, Chicago, 79 & 81, Storm King Art Ctr, 80, Marlborough Gallery, NY, 83, Fuller-Goldeen Gallery, San Francisco, 84 & 86, Dorothy Goldeen Gallery, Santa Monica, 87 & 90, Gerald Peters Gallery, Santa Fe, NMex, 91 & Smith-Anderson Gallery, Palo Alto, Calif, 95; Seattle Art Mus, Wash, 87; Contract Design Ctr, San Francisco, 93; Smith Anderson Gallery, Palo Alto, Calif, 95; Acad Art, San Francisco, Calif, 97; State Univ NY, Purchase, 97; Iris & D Gerald Cantor Ctr Visual Art, Stanford Univ, Calif. *Teaching:* Instr, Cornell Univ, 57-59, Pratt Inst, 63, New Sch Soc Res, 64, Brooklyn Mus Sch, 64-65, Newark Sch Fine & Indust Art, 65, Dayton Art Inst, 66, Aspen Sch Contemp Art, Colo, 66, Orange Co Community Col, NJ, 66 & Windham Col, 67-75; vis artist, Univ Calif, Berkeley, spring semester, 89 & Vt Studio Sch, Johnson, 97. *Awards:* Nat Endowment Arts Grant, 75; Pollock-Krasner Grant, 97-98; Lifetime Achievement Grant, Lee Krasner, 99-00 & 00-01. *Bibliog:* Wayne Anderson (auth), California funk and the American Express, J Art, 6/91; David Bell (auth), Exhibits challenge, define artworks as objects, J North, 10/17/91; Gallery hopping, Pasatiempo, 10/18-24/91. *Media:* Steel. *Dealer:* Gerald Peters Gallery Santa Fe NM

GINSBURG, ESTELLE
PAINTER, SCULPTOR

b St Louis, Mo, Mar 27, 24. *Study:* Univ Mo; Brooklyn Mus Art Sch; Cornell Univ. *Work:* C W Post Univ, NY; Univ Mass, Amherst; Univ Art Gallery, State Univ NY, Stony Brook; pvt collections in Europe, SAm & US. *Exhib:* Ball State Univ, Muncie, Ind, 73; solo exhibs, Cent Hall Gallery, NY, 75, 77-79, Fine Arts Mus Nassau Co, NY, 77 & Royal Acad, Stockholm, Sweden, 79; Invitational, York Col, Pa, 77; Brentano Gallery, NY, 79, 81 & 82; Univ Stony Brook Mus (auth, catalog), NY, 96. *Pos:* Art lectr mus collections, N Shore Community Arts Ctr, NY, 70-73; instr, Five Towns Music & Art Found, NY, 73-83, Nassau Off Cult Develop, 74-77 & Art Resources Ltd, NY, 79-80. *Teaching:* Lectr art, 5 Towns Sch Dist, 80-96. *Awards:* Mixed Media Award, Heckscher Mus, NY, 72; Sculpture Award, North Shore Art Exhib, 74; Painting Award, Port Washington Libr, 75. *Bibliog:* Malcum Preston (auth), rev, Newsday, NY, 76-79; Jeanne Paris (auth), rev, Long Island Press, 77 & 78; articles, New York Times, 79, 86 & 87. *Mem:* Cent Hall Artists, NY; Prof Artists Asn NY (mem chmn, 74-76). *Media:* Wood, Paint; Mixed Media, Silkscreen. *Publ:* J Digby (auth), Collage Handbook, Thames & Hudson. *Mailing Add:* 370 Longacre Ave Woodmere NY 11598

GINSBURG, MAX
PAINTER, ILLUSTRATOR

b Paris, France, Aug 7, 31. *Study:* Syracuse Univ, BFA; Nat Acad Design; City Col New York, MA. *Exhib:* Allied Artists Am, 1956-2003; Am Vet Soc Artists; Audubon Artists, 1962-2003; Harbor Gallery, Cold Spring Harbor, 66, 68, 69, 71, 72, 74, 76, 78 & 80; Reyn Gallery, 80; Grand Central Gallery, 80-81; Soc Illus, 1979-2000; NY Cult Ctr; Martin Luther King Labor Ctr; Cavalier Gallery, Greenwich, CT, 2005. *Collection Arranged:* New Britain Mus Am Art; Martin Luther King Labor Ctr; NY Cultural Ctr Mus; Soc Illustrators Permanent Collection; HJ Heinz Co. *Teaching:* Instr painting & illus, Sch Visual Arts, New York, 84-2000 & Art Students League, New York, 97-99. *Awards:* Prize, 61 & Gold Medal, 62 & 65, Am Vet Soc Artists; Allied Artists Am, 61, 72, 2000 & 2002; Nat Art Club, 63; Gold Medal, Soc Illusrs, 83; Christopher Award. *Mem:* Allied Artists Am; Audubon Artists; Soc Illusrs. *Media:* Oil. *Mailing Add:* 40 W 77th St New York NY 10024-5128

GINZBURG, YANKEL (JACOB)
PAINTER, SCULPTOR

b Alma-Ata, USSR, Mar 23, 45; US citizen. *Study:* Inst Art Israel, dipl, 61. *Work:* Israel Mus, Jerusalem; Hirshhorn Mus; Bat-Yam Mus, Tel Aviv Mus, Israel; Skirball Mus, Los Angeles; Holocaust Mus, Washington, DC. *Comn:* A Hope Fulfilled is a Source of Life (mural), comn by B'nai B'rith, Jerusalem, 73; Freedom Road (tapestry), comn by Bicentennial Comn; Hands & Hearts (monumental mural), Washington, DC, 79; Bicentennial Poster, comn by Pres Reagan, Air & Space Mus, Washington, DC, 83; comn to design 3 graphics commemorating the Bicentennial of the Constitution, 85; Invisible Hands (monumental sculpture), Tampa, Fla, 86. *Exhib:* One-man shows, Washington Gallery Art, 69, Martin Lawrence Galleries, Los Angeles, Calif, 79, 82 & 83, Arthur Charles Galleries, Washington, DC, 82 & 83, Hallowell Gallery, Philadelphia, 83, Dyansen Gallery, San Francisco, Carmel, Beverly Hills & San Diego, Calif, New Orleans, La, NY, Boston, Tokyo, Japan, 89, Bronte Contemp Arts, Boston, 92 & many others; Int Art Fair, Cologne, Ger, 75; Int Art Show, Dusseldorf, Ger, 76; Mod Masters of Israel Show, Philadelphia Mus Art Civic Ctr, 78; Works on Paper, Skiball Mus, Los Angeles, Calif, 78; Washington Light Show, Washington, DC, 80; Gallery Hawaii, 80; Gallery Virgin Islands, St Thomas, 80; Vincent Lee Fine Arts, Hong Kong, 92-94. *Teaching:* Instr, Acad Arts, Israel, 65-67. *Awards:* Silver Medal, Rome Biennale, 62; First Prize, Bat-Yam Mus Art Competition, Israel, 65; First Israeli artists to exhib in Cairo, Egypt as guest of Anwar Sadat, 79 & invited by Soviet Union to exhib in Moscow, 90; Humanitarian Award First Class, hon by Pres Yeltsin & Supreme Soviet of the Russian Fedn, 92. *Bibliog:* The Art of Yankel Ginzburg, Alef Editions, 85; Ginzburg: The Russian Collection, Russian Academy of the Arts, 92; Herman Taube (auth), The Art and Life of Yankel Ginzburg, 94. *Media:* Acrylic, Oil. *Publ:* Art book, Soc of Art Collectors, 75; Treasures of the Sea, 79. *Mailing Add:* 5810 Connecticut Ave Chevy Chase MD 20815-4242

GINZEL, ANDEW H
ARTIST

b Chicago, July 14, 1954. *Study:* Attended State Univ NY, 81, Bennington Col, 74. *Comn:* Kunsthalle, Basel, Switzerland, 89; Oreg Convention Ctr, Portland, 90; Pa Convention Ctr, 94; Battery Park City, NY City, 92; Olympic Arts Festival, Atlanta, 96; Oculus, MTA, NY City, 99. *Exhib:* Solo shows include Polarities Kansas City Int Airport, 2004, Metronome Union Square South Project, NY City, 999, TZ'Art, NY City, 96, Acqario Romano, Rome, 95, Madison Art Ctr, Wis, 92-93, Three Rivers Arts Festival, Pittsburgh, 91, Minneapolis Col Art and Design, 91, Damon Brandt Gallery, NY City, 90, Kunsthalle, Basel, 89; group shows include Contemp Artists and the Am Acad in Rome, 95, 96; Equitable Gallery, NY City, 96; Paine Webber Gallery, NY City, 94; The Drawing Ctr, NY City, 93-94; Nat Acad Mus, NY City, 2006; represented in collections of Brooklyn Mus, Beckton Dickinson and Co, Franklin Lakes, NJ, Centro Corp, Cleveland, Prudential Life Ins, Co. *Pos:* Artistic consultant Hudson River Park Conservancy, NY City, 97. *Teaching:* Sculpture faculty mem Sch Visual Arts, NY City, 86-. *Awards:* Visual Arts Fellowship, Nat Endowment for Arts, 86, 94; Indo-Am Council for Exchange of Scholars Fellowship, 90; Louis Comfort Tiffany Found Award, 91; Pollock-Krasner Found Award, 94. *Mem:* Fel, Am Acad in Rome (Rome Prize, 94-95)

GINZEL, ANDREW See Jones & Ginzel

GINZEL, ROLAND
PAINTER, PRINTMAKER

b Lincoln, Ill, 21. *Study:* Art Inst Chicago, BFA; State Univ Iowa, MFA; Slade Sch, London. *Work:* Univ Southern Calif; Univ Mich; Ill Bell Tel Co; Art Inst Chicago; US Embassy, Warsaw, Poland; Mus of Contemp Art, Chicago, IL; Wooster Art Mus, Wooster, MA; and others. *Exhib:* Art Inst Chicago, 69; Madison, Wis, 69; Notre Dame Univ, 69; one-man show, Phyllis Kind Gallery, 69; Whitney Mus Am Art Biennial, NY, 75; Roy Boyd Gallery Chicago, 85-. *Teaching:* Prof printmaking, Univ Chicago, 57-58; prof prints & painting, Univ Ill, Chicago Circle, 58-69; instr painting, Univ Wis, 60; instr art, Saugatuck Summer Sch, 61-62. *Awards:* Print & Drawing Prize, 67 & Campana Prize, 69, Art Inst Chicago; Fulbright Fel to Rome, 62. *Media:* Painting, Sculpture. *Interests:* Fly Fishing. *Dealer:* Roy Boyd Gallery, Chicago, IL. *Mailing Add:* #'120 Kimball Farms 235 Walker St Lenox MA 01240

GIOBBI, EDWARD GIOACHINO
PAINTER, SCULPTOR

b Waterbury, Conn, July 18, 26. *Study:* Student, Whitney Sch Art, New Haven, 47; Vesper George Sch Art, Boston, 50; Cape Sch Art, Provincetown, Mass, 50; Art Students League, NY City, 56; Acad Fine Arts, Florence, Italy, 54. *Work:* Boston Mus Fine Arts; Whitney Mus Am Art, NY; Hirshhorn Mus; Art Inst Chicago; Albright-Knox Gallery. *Exhib:* One-man exhibs, Neuberger Mus, 77 & Gruenebaum Gallery, NY, 78 & 79; Young Am, Whitney Mus Am Art, 60; Recent Figure USA, Mus Mod Art, NY, 60; 40 Painters under 40, Whitney Mus Am Art, 62; and others. *Teaching:* Artist-in-residence, Memphis Acad, Tenn, 59-60 & Dartmouth Col, 72. *Awards:* Emily Lowe Award, 49; Ford Found Artist-in-Residence Prog, 66; Guggenheim Fel, 72. *Mem:* Westchester Coun Arts, Katonah Gallery (adv bd, currently); Nat Acad. *Media:* Oil; Mixed. *Mailing Add:* 161 Croton Lake Rd Katonah NY 10536-1201

GIOELLO, DEBBIE
PAINTER, DESIGNER

b Jan 1, 35. *Study:* Univ State NY, 68; Oswego State Univ, BS,70; H Lehman Col MA, 72. *Work:* Hudson River Mus, Yonkers, NY; Queens Cult Ctr, NY; Fashion Inst Tech, NY; State Office Building, Albany, NY. *Exhib:* Hudson River Mus, Yonkers, NY; Bronx Mus Arts, NY; Bruce Mus, Greenwich, Conn; Nat Asn Women Artists,

NY; Dickinson State Univ, NDak. *Teaching:* Prof design, Fashion Inst Tech, 68-, chairperson fashion design dept, 89-93. *Awards:* Award, Mamaroveck Int, 74; Award Silvermine Guild, 75; Award for Excellence in Teaching NY State Chacellor, 98; Teacher of the Yr Avalon, 98. *Mem:* Artists Equity Asn; Nat Asn Women Artists. *Media:* Watercolor; Graphics. *Publ:* Coauth, Fashion Production Terms, Fairchild Publ, 79; auth, Profiling Fabrics, 80, Designer Stylist Handbook, Vol I & II and Figures, 80, & Understanding Fabrics, 82, Fairchild Publ; contribr, Random House Dictionary-Fashion & Textile Area, Random House, 83-85; auth, Design Solutions for Fashion Designer, 99; Fashion Figures for Design Solutions, 99. *Mailing Add:* 237 Van Cortland Pk Ave Yonkers NY 10705-1548

GIOIA, DANA (MICHAEL)
CRITIC
b L.os Angeles, Calif, Dec 24, 50. *Study:* Stanford Univ, BA, 73, MBA, 77; Harvard Univ, MA, 75. *Hon Degrees:* St Andrews Col, PhD in Lit (hon), 2003. *Pos:* commentator, BBC Radio, 92-2003; co-dir, West Chester Writers Conf, 95-2002; music critic, San Francisco mag, 97-2003; librettist for opera Nosferatu, 2001; dir, Teaching Poetry Conf, 2001-02. *Teaching:* vis writer, John Hopkins Univ, Sarah Lawrence Col, Colo Col, Wesleyan Univ. *Awards:* Recipient Frederick Bock prize Poetry, 86; Am Book award, 2002. *Mem:* Poetry Soc Am (vpres 92-2003); Nat Endowment Arts, (chmn, 2003—); Nat Fed Coun on Arts & Humanities. *Publ:* Auth: (poetry) Daily Horoscope, 1986, The Gods of Winter, 1991, Interrogations of Noon, 2001, (criticism) Can Poetry Matter? Essays on Poetry an Am Culture, 1992, 2d ed, 2002; editor: The Ceremony and Other Stories, 1984, Poems from Italy, 1985, New Italian Poets, 1990; co-ed: Literature: An Intr to Fiction, Poetry and Drama, 2001, Longman Anthology of Short Fiction, 2000, Selected Short Stories of Weldon Kees, 2002, Twentieth-Century Am Poetry, 2003; translator: Eugenio Montale's Mottetti: Poems of Love, 1990; contribr to periodicals includ New Yorker, Atlantic, Washington Post, Hudson Rev., Poetry. *Mailing Add:* Nat Endowment for Arts 1100 Pennsylvania Ave NW Washington DC 20004

GIORDANO, GREG JOE
PAINTER, PHOTOGRAPHER
b New York, NY, Nov 27, 60. *Study:* Sch Visual Arts; Robert Bateman Master Class, Wausau, Wis, 86. *Exhib:* 1984 Winter Olympic Games, Int Olympic Comt Hq, Saravejo, Yugoslavia, 84; National Art Exhib Alaskan Wildlife, Anchorage, 84 & 85; Group Miniature Exhib, Wild Wings Gallery, San Francisco, Calif, 85; Federal Duck Stamp Competition, Easton Waterfowl Festival, 85 & 86; Trailside Galleries. *Teaching:* Scottsdale Artists Sch. *Awards:* Finalist, Fed Duck Stamp Competition, 84 & 85; People's Choice Award-Best in Show, Alaskan Art Exhib, 85. *Bibliog:* Leonard Lang (auth), Artist vignette, Wildlife Art News, 9/85. *Media:* Gouache, Oil. *Publ:* Field & Stream Mag. *Mailing Add:* 76 Tally Ho Rd Ridgefield CT 06877-2818

GIORNO, JOHN
CONCEPTUAL ARTIST, PRINTMAKER
b New York, NY, Dec 4, 36. *Study:* Columbia Univ, BA, 58. *Work.* Mus Mod Art, NY; Cen Pompidou Mus, Paris, France. *Comn:* Innovated Dial-A-Poem, 68. *Exhib:* Performance, Beacon Theatre, Ritz & Palladium, NY; Poem Print Gallery Exhibs, NY, Paris & Berlin. *Pos:* Founder & pres, Giorno Poetry Systems Inst Inc, 65-. *Media:* CD Video, Silkscreen. *Publ:* Contribr, Balling Buddha, Kulchur Press, 70; Cancer in my Left Ball, Something Else Press, 73; Shit, Piss, Blood, Pus, & Brains, Painted Bride Press, 77; Grasping at Emptiness, Kulcur Press, 85; You Got to Burn to Shine, Serpents Tail Press, 94. *Mailing Add:* 222 Bowery New York NY 10012

GIOVANNI
PAINTER, PRINTMAKER
b Laurence, Mass, March 13, 49. *Study:* Vesper George Art Sch, 69-70; Art Inst Boston, 70 71; Boston Univ Sch Fine & Appl Arts, BFA, 87; Boston Univ Col of Lib Arts (scholarship Renaissance study, Padera, Italy), 87-88. *Work:* Alamo Rent-A-Car headquarters, Ft Lauderdale; Nat Portrait Gallery, Washington, DC; Mus Fine Arts, Boston, Mass; Fogg Mus, Cambridge, Mass; The White House, George Bush Libr Collection, Washington, DC; Pres George Bush Libr, Houston, Tex. *Comn:* Portrait, M I T Hist Collection, Boston, Mass, 89; various canvases, Westwood Int, Caleo, Peru, 89; mural, Boston Redevelopment Authority City Hall, Padua, Italy, 89; American Flag, Bass Energy Corp, Fairlawn, Ohio, 91; The American Spirit, Republican Nat Conv, Houston, Tex, 92. *Exhib:* Dallas Design Center, 89; Ergane Gallery, NY, 91-92; one-man show, Francesco Anderson Gallery, Boston, 89-90, Pierce Galleries Inc, Hingham, Mass, 91-92, Boston Design Ctr, 91, Gallery at 4 India, Nantucket, 92; one-man retrospective, Bridgewater State Col, Bridgewater, Mass, 91; Fuller Mem Art Mus, Brockton, Mass, 96. *Pos:* Owner, Giovanni Studios, Boston, Mass, 88-. *Bibliog:* Patricia Jobe Pierce (auth), Giovanni DeCunto, Nantucket Beacon, 8/7/91; Patricia Jobe Pierce (auth), Italian-American painter makes an impact, Boston Post Gazette, 5/15/92; Patricia Jobe Pierce (auth), The leather district goes "pop" with art of Giovanni, Improper Bostonian, 5/27/92. *Media:* Acrylic, Oil, Lithography. *Mailing Add:* c/o Pierce Galleries Inc 721 Main St Rte 228 Hingham MA 02043

GIOVANOPOULOS, PAUL
PAINTER
b Kastoria, Greece, Nov 11, 39; US citizen. *Study:* New York Univ (Dept Fine Arts Scholar), 58-59; Sch Visual Arts, New York, cert, 61. *Work:* Libr Congress, Washington; Butler Inst Am Art, Youngstown, Ohio; Harvard Univ, Cambridge, Mass; Guild Hall Mus, East Hampton, NY; Bruce Mus, Greenwich, Conn. *Comn:* Newport X 25, Lorillard Loewes Corp, NY, 93; Classic Camel, RJ Reynolds, Holland, 94; Ark Restaurant Corp, 95; Vorres Mus, Greece, 98. *Exhib:* Lower Manhattan Revisited: SoHo, NoHo & Tribeca, Maier Mus Art, Lynchburg, Va, 87; The Purloined Image, Flint Inst Art, Mich, 93; Art after Art, Nassau Co Mus Art, Roslyn Harbor, NY, 94; Food for Thought, Louis K Meisel Gallery, NY, 95; Butler Inst Am Art, 96; Jaffe Baker Gallery, Boca Raton, Fla, 96; Elaine Baker Gallery, Boca Raton, Fla, 99; Galerie Wagner, Switzerland, 2000; Galerie Sechzig, Austria, 2000. *Teaching:* Sch Visual Arts, New York, 69-70, Parsons Sch Design, 70-78 & Pratt Inst, Brooklyn, NY, 80-82. *Awards:* Chaloner Prize Found Fel, 64 & 65; Five Towns Music & Art Award, 94. *Bibliog:* Matthew Rose (auth), Honoring the Artists of the Hamptons, Dans Papers, 8/23/91; Constance Schwartz (auth), Paul Giovanopoulos, Art after Art, 9/94; David Shirey (auth), Paul Giovanopoulos (exhib catalog), Butler Mus Am Art, 10/96. *Media:* Acrylic on Canvas. *Mailing Add:* 119 Prince St New York NY 10012

GIPE, LAWRENCE
PAINTER
b Baltimore, Md, 62. *Study:* Va Commonwealth Univ, BFA, 84; Otis Art Inst/Parsons Sch Design, MFA, 86. *Work:* Worcester Art Mus, Mass; Brooklyn Mus, NY; Orlando Mus Art, Fla. *Exhib:* Va Mus Fine Arts, Richmond, 83; solo exhibs, Joseph Helman Gallery, NY, 96, 98 & 99, Bentley Gallery, Scottsdale, Ariz, 96, Fay Gold Gallery, Atlanta, Ga, 98, Ludwig Found, Havana, Cuba, 2000 & Alan Koppel Gallery, Chicago, Ill, 01; Tampa Mus Art, Fla, 96; Joseph Helman Gallery, NY, 96, 97, 98, 99 & 2000; Boston Univ Art Gallery, Mass, 97; Yoshi Gallery, NY, 99; Alan Koppel Gallery, Chicago, Ill, 2000; and many others. *Pos:* Writer & critic, 85-; bd dir, Found Art Resources, Los Angeles, 86-87; co-cur, Natural Sources, Angel's Gate Cult Ctr, San Pedro, Calif, 87; cur, Cult Fetish, Pasadena City Col Gallery, 89; vis artist, Art Ctr Pasadena, 89; art hist fac, Art Ctr Sch Design, Pasadena, Calif, 96. *Teaching:* Lectr & panelist, numerous col & univ in Calif. *Awards:* Fel, Nat Endowment Arts, 89 & 95; Printmaking Studio Portfolio Grant, Rutgers Archive, 92. *Bibliog:* Martha Donelan (auth), In the Studio with Lawrence Gipe, Santa Barbara News-Press, 3/99; Niki Richards (auth), Making Their Mark, The Independent, 4/99; Robert Mahoney (auth), The Last Picture Show, Time Out New York, 1/2000

GIPS, C L TERRY
PHOTOGRAPHER, EDUCATOR
b Oneida, NY, Mar 4, 45. *Study:* Cornell Univ, BS, 67; Yale Sch Art & Archit, MArch, 71. *Work:* Nat Mus Am Art, Washington; Picker Gallery, Colgate Univ, Hamilton, NY; State Vermont, Montpelier; Nat Mus Women in Arts, Washington. *Exhib:* One-person shows, 112 Workshop, NY, 77, Light Work Gallery, Syracuse, NY, 89, Tweed Mus Art, Duluth, Minn, 90 & Arnold Porter, Washington, 92; Ann Invitational Photog Exhib, Atrium Gallery, Conn, 83; Printed by Women, Port of History Mus, Philadelphia, 83; Selected Photographs 86, Philadelphia Print Club, Pa, 86; AIR Gallery, NY, 88; Am Artists, Deutsch-Amerikanisches Inst, Regensberg, WGer, 88. *Pos:* VPres bd trustees, VT Coun Arts, 83-84; dir, The Art Gallery, Univ Md, College Park, 92-. *Teaching:* Core fac Fine Art, Goddard Col, Plainfield Vt, 76-80; adj fac art & photog, Univ Vt, Burlington, 80-84; asst prof photog, Univ Maryland, 84-89, assoc prof photog, 90-. *Awards:* New York State Council Exhib Grant, 74; Nat Endowment Arts Artist's Fel, 86; Creative and Performing Arts Grant, Univ Md, 90, 92. *Mem:* Col Art Asn; Soc Photog Ed; Womens Caucus Art (chair, nat honor awards comt, 84-86). *Publ:* Guest ed, Computers & Art, Art J, 90; ed, Significant Losses: Artists Who Have Died from AIDS (exhib catalog), Univ Md, 94; Joyce Scott's Mammy Nanny Series, Feminist Studies, 96; Willem de hooper, A Retrospective Exhib 1966-1996 (exhib catalog), Univ Md, 96; Terra Firma (exhib catalog), Univ Md, 97. *Mailing Add:* 9408 Thornhill Rd Silver Spring MD 20901-4834

GIRARD, BILL
SCULPTOR
b Reno, Nev, May 12, 36. *Study:* San Diego State Univ, BS, 58; Ariz State Univ, 64; Scripps Univ, Calif, 66. *Work:* DuPage Art Ctr Mus, Glen Ellen, Ill. *Comn:* Portrait, pvt comn, Austin, Tex, 99; miniature Indian pow-wow dancers, Franklin Mint, Pa, 91; two life-size champion show dogs, pvt comn, Hillsborough, Calif, 92; earthenware Indian, Ray Tracey Gallery, Santa Fe, NMex, 92. *Exhib:* Sculpture in the Park & Invitational, Loveland, Colo, 87-97; Southwest Art in the Wine Country, Sharpsteen Mus, Calistoga, Calif, 90-93; Mountain Oyster 22nd-27th Ann Shows, Tucson, Ariz, 91-94; AICA Western Art Exhib, San Dimas, Calif, 92; Danada/Cantigny Sculpture Invitational, Chicago, 93-94; Classic-Am show, Los Angeles, 94; and others. *Teaching:* Instr, Loveland Art Acad. *Awards:* Best of Show, Heritage Am Show, Heritage Am Mus, 88; Peoples' Choice Award, Southwest Art in Wine Country, Art West Mag, 91; Purchase Award, Loveland Invitational Show & Sale, Colo, 97. *Bibliog:* Katherine Newman (auth), Bill Girard, 91 & Vicki Stavig (auth), Girard Studio, 92, Art West; Shirley Behrens(auth), Profile of Bill Girard, Art West, 94; Rita Simmons (auth), Bill Girard, Southwest Art Mag, 97. *Mem:* NMex Sculpture Guild; Albuquerque United Artists; Albuquerque Arts Alliance. *Media:* Bronze, Stoneware Clay. *Interests:* Travel, computers, family. *Publ:* Auth, Artistic News, Artistic Galleries, 92. *Mailing Add:* 1628 Sagebrush Trail SE Albuquerque NM 87123-4463

GIRARD, (CHARLES) JACK
PAINTER, EDUCATOR
b Ft Knox, Ky, May 15, 51. *Study:* ECarolina Univ, BFA, 73, MFA, 76; Univ SC, 83. *Work:* SC Mus Comn, Columbia; Berea Col, Ky; Appalachian State Univ; Coca-Cola Bottling Co, Atlanta; Cent Bank & Trust Co, Ky; Transylvania Univ, Ky; Eastern Kentucky Univ, Ky. *Comn:* Drawings in collab with writer Jo Carson, Lexington Alzheimers Asn, 90; Aside Show installation in collab with artist Steve Armstrong, Morlan Gallery, Lexington, NJ. *Exhib:* Univ Ky Art Mus, Lexington, 91; Ky Art and Craft Found Gallery, Louisville, 93; Chapman Friedman Gallery, Louisville, 96, 97, 98, 99, 2001, 03, 04; Carnegie Ctr, Covington, 03; Water Tower, Louisville, 03; Vanderbilt Univ, Nashville, 04; Morlan Gallery, Lexington, 05; Ill Central Col, 2006. *Pos:* Asst, Walker Gallery, Columbia, SC, 76-78. *Teaching:* Vis artist, Carteret Tech Col, 78-79; instr art, Berea Col, 79-80; asst prof art, Centre Col, Ky, 80-81; prof art, Transylvania Univ, 81-. *Awards:* Jones Develop Grant, 87, 90, 92, 94, 96, 98, 2002 &

2004-05; Lexington Arts & Cult Coun Grant, 90 & 96; Kenan Grant, 2006. *Bibliog:* Steve Lyon (auth), Keeping tabs on the masquerade, J Seamus, 10/86. *Mem:* Col Art Asn of Am (CAA). *Media:* All Media. *Specialty:* Contemp art. *Publ:* Coauth (with Ann Kilkelly), Confinement and isolation in the art of Edward Kienholz, Med Heritage J, 1-2/86; Asensio Saez Garcia, Literatura de Levante, CAM Fundacion Cult, Murcia, Spain, 93; Asensio Saez Garcia: Symbiosis of word and Image, Literature Film and the other Arts in Modern Spain, Letras Peninsulares, 95. *Dealer:* Chapman Friedman Gallery, Louisville, KY. *Mailing Add:* 145 W Bell Ct Lexington KY 40508

GIRO, R(ALPH) VICTOR GIRONDA
SCULPTOR, PAINTER
b Brooklyn, NY, Dec 3, 36. *Study:* Pratt Inst, BFA; Nat Acad Design; Metrop Col, BS, 72; Art Students League. *Comn:* Sculptures, stainless steel, Kenneth Richardson, 69; stainless steel, Selma Wallace Assoc, 72; bronze, George T Rossi, 72; sculpture, Joseph S Sample, Billings, Mont; and others. *Exhib:* Silvermine Guild, New Canaan, Conn, 63; Nat Acad Design Galleries, 72-75; Brooklyn Mus Show, 73-75; Caravan House, NY, 74; Eric Galleries, 75-88; Giro Galleries, Brooklyn, NY. *Pos:* Owner, Giro Galleries. *Awards:* First Prize, Brooklyn Mus, 73 & 75. *Mem:* Nat Acad Design; Am Inst Archit. *Media:* Carved Bronze, Welded Stainless Steel. *Mailing Add:* 305 Degraw St Brooklyn NY 11231-4710

GIRONDA, R See Giro, R(alph) Victor Gironda

GIROUARD, TINA
SCULPTOR, PAINTER
b De Quincy, La, May 26, 46. *Study:* Univ La, Lafayette, BFA, 68. *Comn:* Contemp Art Ctr, New Orleans, La, 89; Lafayette Reg Airport, La, 90. *Exhib:* One-person shows, Vamonosi, Museo Tamayo, Mexico City, 83, Camellian, World's Fair, New Orleans, La, 84, Five Painters, Artist's Alliance, Lafayette, La, 86, Pane/Pain/Plane, Contemp Arts Ctr, New Orleans, La, 87, Camouflage, Mus Art, Alexandria, La, 89, Atlantic Ctr Arts, 90 & Contemp Arts Ctr, New Orleans, 90; Deeds and Feats, Contemp Art Ctr, New Orleans, 83; Gris Gris, Artist's Alliance, Lafayette, La, 87; Installations, Contemp Art Ctr, New Orleans, La, 87; A Decade of Pattern, Inst Contemp Art, Philadelphia, Pa, 87; Tribute to Excellence, Masur Art Mus, Monroe, La, 88; Making Their Mark, Cincinnati Mus Art, Ohio, 89; 41st Biennial Exhib, Corcoran Gallery, Washington, DC, 89; Louisianna Collection, Univ Art Mus, Lafayette, 90; Mus Gulf Coast, New Orleans, La, 90; Architectural Collaborations, Contemp Art Ctr, New Orleans, La, 90; and many others. *Awards:* Nat Endowment Arts Grant, 76 & 83; Lila Wallace Arts Int Grant, 93; Gottlieb Found Grant, 97. *Bibliog:* Numerous exhib catalogs, 76-89. *Dealer:* Jonathon Ferrah Gallery New Orleans LA. *Mailing Add:* 2274 Main Hwy No 31 PO Box 64 Cecilia LA 70521

GITLIN, MICHAEL
SCULPTOR, DRAFTSMAN
b Capetown, SAfrica, April 23, 43. *Study:* Hebrew Univ Jerusalem, BA, 67; Bezalel Acad Art, Jerusalem, dipl, 67; Pratt Inst, MFA, 72. *Work:* Guggenheim Mus; Stedelijk Mus, Amsterdam; Lenbachhaus, Munich; Israel Mus, Jerusalem; Hirshhorn Mus, Washington, DC. *Comn:* Sculpture (Cor Ten steel), Schmela Gallery, Düsseldorf, 76; Adam's Gate (mahogany), Jerusalem Found, Israel, 83; Sequence, Tel Aviv Mus, Israel, 84. *Teaching:* Instr art, Parsons Sch Design, 79-84; prof, Columbia Univ, NY, 87 & Univ Calif, Davis, 88. *Awards:* Fel, Nat Endowment Arts, 84-85 & 85-86; Guggenheim Fel, 87-88; Pollock Krasner Found, 91-92. *Bibliog:* Stephen Westfall (auth), Humanizing Sculpture (text in Kunstraum exhib catalog), Munich, 86; Annelie Pohlen (auth), From Seeing to Feeling (text in Bonner Kunstverein exhib catalog), Bonn, 88; Maia Damianovic (auth), Silence and Reprieve (text in Muhka Mus catalog), Antwerp, 91. *Mem:* NY Artists Equity Asn. *Media:* Wood, Mixed Media, Copper, Spandex. *Collection:* Solomon R Guggenheim Mus, NY; Hirshhorn Mus & Sculpture Garden; Ludwig Mus, Köln; Stedelijk Mus, Amsterdam; Städtische Galerle, Lenbachhous, Munich. *Mailing Add:* 284 Lafayette St New York NY 10012

GITTLER, WENDY
PAINTER, HISTORIAN
b Manhattan, NY. *Study:* Columbia Univ, New York, BS(art hist), 63; Hunter Col, New York, MA, 67; Brooklyn Col, MFA(painting), 73. *Work:* Pvt collections of, Prof Martin James, Brooklyn, NY, Prof Edward Casey, State Univ NY, Stony Brook, Violet Baxter, NY & Mr & Mrs Sibony, NY; Savannah Col Art & Design, Ga; Barbara Goodstein, Queens, NY; Southeast Mo State Univ Mus; Savannah Col Art & Design, GA. *Exhib:* Nat Exhib, Lehigh Univ, Pa, 84; The Figure Now, NY, 90; Invitational exhibs, Blue Mountain Gallery & Atlantic Gallery, NY, 1996-2006; Fedn Modern Painters & Sculptors, Fordham Univ, NY, 96 & 2000; Benefit Exhib, The Artist Mirrored: Self Portraits, NY Studio Sch, 1996-2006; Benefit Exhib, Mckee Gallery, NY & Royal Col Art, London, 98; solo exhib First Street Gallery, New York City, 1976, 82, 88, 95, 99, 2002, 2005; Benefit exhib NY Studio Sch, 1996-2005; Liman Studio Gall, Palm Beach, Fla, 2004-2005; West Beth Gallery, NY, 2006. *Collection Arranged:* S E Mo St Univ Mus; Savannah Col Art & Design, Ga. *Pos:* Coordr artists meetings, Educ Alliance, NY, 72-74; moderator, Image, Symbol & Sign ann meetings, Artists Equity, 95-2006 & Paths of Narrative Today, 96, vpres; juror, Am Soc Contemp Artists, currently. *Teaching:* Lect Survey Art, Hunter Col, NY, 68-80, 19th-20th century art, Sch Visual Arts, NY, 79-86, aesthetics, Parsons Sch Design, NY, 89-96; NY Studio Sch, NY, 90-2006; Lectures & Critiques 90-2006. *Bibliog:* Albert P Ryder (auth), Under a cloud, Art News, 95. *Mem:* Col Art Asn; Fedn Mod Painters & Sculptors; Artists Equity; Int Asn Art Critics. *Media:* Oil, Watercolor; Gouache. *Res:* Beyond the Frame; Space in the Late Paintings of Matisse, Bonnard & Braque. *Interests:* history; philosophy; archaeology. *Publ:* Auth, Image, symbol, sign, 95 & Paths of narrative today, 96, Artists Equity Bull; Wings & Anchors-Selected Paintings of John Hultberg 1949-93 (exhib catalog), Univ Art Gallery, Stony Brook, NY, 96; Art words-Bonnard & the Space of Inhabited Time, 98; Drawing Without Models, Wiegand Gallery, Belmont, Calif, 99. *Dealer:* First Street Gallery 524 W 26th St New York NY. *Mailing Add:* 780 West End Ave New York NY 10025

GIUFFRE, HECTOR
PAINTER, GRAPHIC ARTIST
b Buenos Aires, Arg, Aug 5, 44, Ital & Arg citizen. *Study:* Escuela Superior Bellas Artes, Buenos Aires; Univ Salvador, Buenos Aires. *Work:* Mus Mod Art Buenos Aires, Arg; Mus Mod Art Bogota, Colombia; Archer-Huntington Coll, Univ Tex, Austin; Citibank NA Collection, NY; Lever Collection, London, Eng. *Comn:* Portrait, comn by Emperor Rezah Pahlevi, Iran; portrait, comn by Jacques Lassaigne, Paris; portrait, comn by Marcos Curi, Buenos Aires; portrait, comn by Ignacio Pirovano, Buenos Aires; many other comn portraits worldwide, 67-. *Exhib:* 10th Biennial Paris, Mus Mod Art, 77; 2nd Biennial Havana, Biennial Bldg, 86; Abstraccion-Figuracion/Figurative-Abstract, Archer-Huntington Art Gallery, Univ Tex, Austin, 89; one-man show, Mus Mod Art, Bogota, Colombia, 89; 12th Biennial-Evanston, Evanston Art Ctr, Ill, 94. *Teaching:* Instr painting & compos, studio, Buenos Aires, 70-89; workshop instr, Mus Mod Art Buenos Aires, 87-89; workshop instr, Art Ctr, Camara Comercio Bldg, Medellin, Colombia. *Awards:* Lever Art Contest First Prize, Instr Contemp Art, London, 80; 4th Biennial Medellin Critic's Award, El Colombiana newspaper, 81; First Prize, Int Artist's Colonies Found Contest, New York, 88. *Bibliog:* Raul Santana (auth), Hector Giuffré, an Opening to the Real, Art Editions Gaglianone, 80; Seymour Menton (auth), Magic Realism Rediscovered, Asn Univ Press, NJ, 83; Jorge Lopez Anaya (auth), A Vision of Contemporary Argentine Art, Patio Bullrich Found, 91. *Mem:* Chicago Artists Coalition; Coll Art Asn, NY; Tex Art Asn; Soc Arg Artistas Plasticos, Buenos Aires. *Media:* Painting, All. *Publ:* Auth, On the Intimate Structure of Reality, Lirolay Gallery, 68; Guidelines to structural realism, Hitos Mag, 75; The realism in which I believe, Pluma y Pincel Mag, 76; Structural realism as a possibility of being of peinture, Artemas Mag, 78; Related and Realist Manifesto, Julia Lublin Gallery, 84. *Mailing Add:* PO Box 14230 Chicago IL 60614-0230

GIURGOLA, ROMALDO
ARCHITECT
b Rome Sept 2, 20. *Study:* Scuola Di Archit Univ di Roma, graduate, (summa cum laude), 48; Columbia Univ, MS (archit), 51. *Pos:* Partner, Mitchell/Giurgola Archit, Philadelphia, New York City, from 58; chmn, dept archit Columbia Univ, 68-71. *Awards:* Gold Medal Award, Fel Am Inst of Archits, 82. *Mem:* Fel Am Inst of Archits; Nat Acad, Am Acad & Inst Arts and Letters, Acad Nazionale di San Luca (corr). *Mailing Add:* 170 W 97th St New York NY 10025-6450

GIUSTI, KARIN F
SCULPTOR
Study: Yale Univ Sch Art, MFA(sculpture). *Comn:* The World is Your Oyster, Long Wharf Park, New Haven, Conn, 90; Pearl Necklace, pvt collection, Philadelphia, Pa, 91; Oyster-Hearts, PECO Energy Co, Philadelphia, Pa, 95; Bon Chance Baby & Par-O-Dise, PECO Energy Co, Philadelphia, Pa, 96. *Exhib:* Absolute Cow, Vt Col Art Ctr, Montpelier, 89; On Site New Eng, Urban Arts Inc, Bank Boston Gallery, Mass, 89; Trouble in Paradise, Mass Inst Technol List Visual Arts Ctr, Cambridge & Art Gallery, Univ Md, College Park, 89; Towards 2000, RI Sch Design & Hartford Art Sch, 91-92; Contemp Sculpture, Chesterwood Mus, Stockbridge, Mass, 91-92; Challenging Utopia, 14 Sculptors, NY, 91-92; Invitational, Real Art Ways, Hartford, Conn, 91-92; Seasons: Passage and Presents (installation), Bradly Int Airport, Hartford, Conn, 93; Alumni III, Univ Mass Fine Arts Ctr, Amherst, 93; Sculpture Ctr at Roosevelt Island, Sculpture Ctr, Roosevelt Island, NY, 93; Garbage, Real Art Ways, Hartford, Conn, 94 & Thread Waxing Space, NY, 95; Contemp Installations, La Quita Open Air Mus, Calif, 94; Faculty Show, Brooklyn Col, City Univ NY, 95; Pop Up Show, Socrates Sculpture Park, Queens, NY, 95; Art in the Anchorage 1995, Creative Time, NY, 95; Investing in Dreams, Conn Comn Arts, Lyman Allyn Art Mus & Statewide Mus Collaborative by Conn Comn Art Individual Grant Recipients, 95; The White House/Green House, Real Art Ways, Hartford, Conn, 95 & Lower Manhattan Cult Coun, NY, 96; Just the Thing, Contemp Outdoor Sculpture & Object Woodson Art Mus, Wis, 98; Art Exchange Show, Anya von Gosslen Gallery, NY, 98; Gothic Distress, Trans Hudson Gallery, NY, 98; EV plus A 98 - Int Biannual Exhib, St Mary's Cathedral, Limerick, Ireland, 98. *Teaching:* Head sculpture dept, Brooklyn Col, City Univ New York, 95-. *Awards:* Nat Endowment Arts Regional Grant, New Eng Found Arts, 91; Guggenheim Fel Installation & Sculpture, 97-98; Fulbright Research Award, Ireland, 98-99. *Bibliog:* Roberta Smith (auth), Anchor and balm for restless souls, NY Times, 8/4/95; Holland Cotter (auth), Sculpture that basks in the summer sunlight and air, NY Times, 8/9/96; Jesephine Gear (auth), Site specific, public sculpture by Armajani and Giusti, Rev Mag, 9/15/96. *Mailing Add:* c/o Guisti Studio 82 Wall St Ste 1105 New York NY 10012

GJERTSON, STEPHEN ARTHUR
PAINTER, WRITER
b Minneapolis, Minn, May 21, 49. *Study:* Univ Minn, 67-70; Sch Assoc Arts, St Paul, 70-71; Atelier Lack, Minneapolis, Minn, 71-75. *Work:* Col St Benedict, St Joseph, Minn; Christ Col Irvine, Calif; Montclair Art Mus. *Comn:* Triptych, Nokomis Heights Lutheran Church, Minneapolis, Minn, 79-86; Peace, Be Still (painting), St John's Lutheran Church, Mound, Minn, 97; Newington-Cropsey Found, Hasting-on-Hudson, NY; portrait of gov Arne H Carlson, Minn State Capitol, 99. *Exhib:* Classical Realism:The Other 20th Century, traveling exhib, 82-83; Classical Realist Conf & Exhib, Heritage Art Gallery, Alexandria, Va, 86, 88 & 92; 63rd & 64th Nat Apr Salons, Springville Mus Art, Utah, 87 & 88; Newington-Cropsey Found, NY, 96, 01 & 06; E Coast Ideals, W Coast Concepts (traveling exhib), 97; Biblical Arts Ctr, Dallas, 02. *Pos:* Ed adv, Classical Realism J; Pres, Am Soc Classical Realism; Ed, Classical Realism Newsletter. *Teaching:* Atelier Lack, 73-88; Atelier N, 84-93; Atelier LeSueur, 91-92. *Awards:* Grant, Elizabeth T Greenshields Found, 73-75; Juror's Award, 63rd Nat Apr Salon, Springville Mus Art, 87; Cash Award, 64th Nat Apr Salon, Friend Grand Central Art Galleries, 88. *Bibliog:* Annette Hathaway (auth), Stephen Gjertson,

Am Artist, 10/83; Carole Katchen (auth), Creating a Joyous Beauty, Painting Faces & Figures, Watson-Guptill, 86; Annette LeSueur (auth), Timeless Treasure: The Art of Stephen Gjertson, Am Soc Classical Realism, 93. *Mem:* Full Guild Mem, Am Soc Classical Realism. *Media:* Oil. *Publ:* Auth, The Necessity of Excellence, Realism in Revolution/Taylor, 85; Hippolyte Flandrin-A Personal Appreciation, Classical Realism Quarterly, summer 88; contribr, Classical Realism J, Am Soc Classical Realism; auth, Richard F. Lack: An American Master, Am. Soc. Classical Realism, 01; co-auth, For Glory and For Beauty: Practical Perspectives on Christianity and the Visual Arts, 02. *Dealer:* Stephen Gjertson Studio 3855 Colfax Ave N Minneapolis MN 55412. *Mailing Add:* 3855 Colfax Ave N Minneapolis MN 55412

GLADSTONE, BARBARA
DEALER, HISTORIAN
b Philadelphia, Pa. *Study:* Univ Pa; Hofstra Univ, BA, 68, MA, 70. *Pos:* Founder, owner & dir, Barbara Gladstone Gallery, New York, 80-; bd mem, Art Dealers Asn, 90-93, 94-95, Printed Mattes, 93-94. *Teaching:* Instr art hist & mod archit, Hofstra Univ, 71-75. *Mem:* Art Dealers Asn Am. *Specialty:* Contemporary painting, sculpture and photography; publisher of contemporary American prints and photographs. *Mailing Add:* Barbara Gladstone Gallery 515 W 24th St New York NY 10011

GLADSTONE, M J
PUBLISHER
b New York, NY, May 4, 23. *Study:* Harvard Univ, SB(anthrop), 44, MA(fine arts), 46. *Pos:* Ed, Print & Print Collector's Quart, 50-53, Merriam-Webster Dictionary, 53-55, Collector's Quart Report, 62-63; assoc dir publ, Mus Mod Art, New York, 63-64; consult, NY State Coun Arts, 67-73; dir, Mus Am Folk Art, New York, 69-70, Publ Ctr Cult Resources, New York, 73-88, ed-in-chief, 88-89; publ, Furthermore Press, Germantown, NY, 91-; consult, JM Kaplan Fund, NY, 96-. *Publ:* Contribr, Britannica Encycl Am Art, 73; auth, A Carrot for a Nose, Scribner, 74; contribr, How to Know American Folk Art, Dutton, 77. *Mailing Add:* PO Box 355 Germantown NY 12526

GLANCY, MICHAEL
SCULPTOR
b Detroit, Mich, Feb 11, 50. *Study:* Univ Denver, BFA(ceramics), 73; RI Sch Design, BFA(sculpture), 77, MFA(sculpture), 80. *Work:* Metrop Mus Art, NY; Victoria & Albert Mus, London, England; Nat Mus Am Hist, Smithsonian Inst, Washington, DC; Philadelphia Mus Art, Philadelphia, Pa; Hokkaido Mus Mod Art, Sapporo, Japan; Chrysler Mus, Norfolk, Va; The High Mus, Atlanta, Ga; Detroit Inst Art, Mich; Carnegie Inst Mus Art, Pittsburgh, Pa; Corning Mus Glass, Corning, NY; Los Angeles Co Mus Art, Los Angeles, Calif; Musee Arts De'coratits, Paris, France. *Comn:* Sculpture (large scale), NY. *Exhib:* Oakland Mus, Oakland, Calif, 86; World Glass Now, Hokkaido Mus Art, Sappora, Japan, 85 & 88; New Works in Glass & Metal, Habatat Galleries, Detroit, Mich, 88; Newport Art Mus, RI, 88; Heller Gallery, NY, 89; Galerie von Bartha, Basel, Switz, 95 & 96; Venice Bienielle in Glass, Venice, Italy, 96; Barry Friedman, NY, 97, 2000. *Pos:* Artist & Artist in Residence. *Teaching:* Assoc fac, Metals Prog, RI Sch Design, 82-2000; instr, Pilchuck Glass Ctr, Seattle, Wash, 82-88 & 96. *Awards:* Nat Endowment Arts Fel, 86; Mass Coun Arts Fel, 87, 99; French Found Int Ctr Contemp Art Fel Grant, Chateau de Beychevelle, 91. *Bibliog:* Sculptural glass, Am Art Glass Quart, fall, 83; Elegant glass made by masters, New York Times, 12/13/84; Breaking into glass, Esquire, 2/85. *Mem:* Gas Soc, Corning, NY. *Media:* Glass, Metal & Stone. *Publ:* Auth, Shadow & Substance, Glancy, Heller & Hampson, 89; Interactions 91, Glancy, Klein, von Bartha, 91; Infinite Obsessions with Maurice Marinot, 99. *Dealer:* Galerie von Bartha Basel Switz; Barry Friedman Ltd 67th St at Madison Ave New York NY. *Mailing Add:* 85 Carpenter St Rehoboth MA 02679

GLANTZMAN, JUDY
PAINTER
b Long Island, NY, May 24, 56. *Study:* RI Sch Design, BFA(Silver Medal: Outstanding Student), 78. *Work:* Franklin Furnace, New Sch Social Res, Grey Art Gallery, Chase Manhattan Bank, NY; Can Imperial Bank; Equitable Bank, NY; Bell Savings Bank, Pa. *Exhib:* Solo exhibs, Civilian Warfare, 83 & 84, Gracie Mansion, 85, NY, Paris Green Gallery, La Jolla, Calif, 86, St Mary's Col, Md & Hudson River Mus, 90; Portraits-East Village, PS 1, Long Island City, NY, 84; Women of Influence, Amerika Haus, Berlin, Ger, 84; Santa Barbara Mus, Calif, 85; Saidye Bronfman Center, Montreal, 85; Ackland Art Mus, Chapel Hill, NC. *Teaching:* Mem fac, part time, Parsons Sch Design, NY; 2-D Design, Sch Visual Arts; RI Sch Design, Providence, 82-83. *Awards:* Silver Award, Royal Soc Arts, London, 78; Artist on Location; NY found Arts, 87; Anonymous Was a Woman Found, 97. *Bibliog:* Donald Kuspit (auth), Climbing, Art Forum, 4/84; Walter Robinson & Carlo McCormick (auths), Slouching towards Avenue D, Art in Am, summer 84; David Bourbon (auth), Sitting pretty, Vogue, 11/85; John Russell (auth), Art: New paintings, New York Times, 1/25/85; Robert Pincus-Witten (auth), The new irascibles, Arts, 9/85; Edward Sozanski (auth), article, Philadelphia Enquirer, 9/87; Elisa Turner (auth), article, Miami Herald, 11/88. *Mem:* CAA. *Media:* Oil on Canvas. *Dealer:* Carol Getz Gallery Miami FL & Da Entlang Germany

GLANZ, ANDREA E
ADMINISTRATOR, CURATOR
b New York, NY, Oct 14, 52. *Study:* Cornell Univ, BS(human develop & expressive arts); Stanford Univ, MA(art educ). *Pos:* Grad asst, Stanford Univ Mus Art, Calif, 74-75; cur educ, Triton Mus Art, Santa Clara, Calif, 75-77, dir, 77-78; from asst cur to cur, San Jose Mus Art, Calif, 78-79; asst dir, Continuing Prof Educ, Mus Collab, New York, 79-80, dir, 80-85. *Teaching:* Instr, West Valley Community Col, Saratoga, Calif, 76. *Mem:* Am Asn Mus; Mus Educators Roundtable; Col Art Asn; Nat Trust for Hist Preserv. *Publ:* Coauth, A Catalog of Paintings by Theodore Wores in the Collection of the Triton Museum of Art, 76 & Two Hundred Years of Santa Clara Valley Architecture: A Stylistic Survey, 76, Triton Mus Art; auth, The Role of Museum Management Training in Developing Effective Museum Managers & In Search of Excellence: The American Museum Experience, Scottish Mus Coun, Edinburgh, 85. *Mailing Add:* 90 Jane St Hartsdale NY 10530-1927

GLASER, BRUCE
HISTORIAN, EDUCATOR
b Brooklyn, NY, Sept 25, 33. *Study:* Columbia Col, BA; Columbia Univ, MA. *Pos:* Dir, Howard Wise Gallery, New York, 60-61 & Gallery of Israeli Art, Am-Israel Cult Found, New York, 65-68; exec dir, Art Ctr Northern NJ, Tenafly, 68-70. *Teaching:* Instr art hist, Pratt Inst, 61-62; instr, Hunter Col, 62-65; prof art hist, Univ Bridgeport, 70-, chmn dept, 70-77, dean, Col Fine Arts, 77-81. *Awards:* Mem Found for Jewish Cult Fel, 70-72; Summer Inst, Nat Endowment Humanities, Chicago, 84; Vis Scholar, Coun for Humanities, 86. *Mem:* Col Art Asn Am; Int Coun Mus; Am Asn Mus. *Res:* Modern and contemporary art; Israeli art. *Publ:* Ed & coauth, Oldenburg, Lichtenstein, Warhol: A discussion, Artforum, 2/66; coauth, Questions to Stella & Judd, Art News, 9/66; ed & coauth, An interview with Ad Reinhardt, Art Int, 12/66; ed & coauth, Modern art and the critics, Art J, winter 70-71; auth, Robert Natkin, Arts, 6/78. *Mailing Add:* 78 Gaybowers Ln Fairfield CT 06430-2011

GLASER, DAVID
PAINTER, SCULPTOR
b Brooklyn, NY, Sept 29, 19. *Study:* Art Students League, scholar, with Wilhelm Von Schlegel, NY Sch Art, NY Sch Contemp Art, with Philip Evergood; Brooklyn Mus Art Sch, with Moses Soyer, Xavier Gonzales & Edwin Dickinson. *Work:* Full-color reproductions of paintings mailed throughout Long Island, New York City. *Comn:* Artist: Civilian Conserv Corps, 36; Created (Giggy F Useless) World War II cartoon character, USA, 42-46; Poster ser for US Army, 43-44; 1950-1985 Fine Art and Graphic Art Promo in all New Space Age Technologies, N Am Philips (Amperex), Gen Signal (Cardion), Polytech Reasearch and Devel, Plessey Inc, Hohner Harmonicas Corp, others. *Exhib:* Munic Galleries, Jackson, Miss, 44; Nat Art Club, 59; ACA Galleries, 60; 3 man show, Heckscher Mus, Huntington, NY, 64; Nassau Community Col, 79 & 81; Hofstra Univ, NY, 80; Adelphi Col, 80; Nassau Co Mus Fine Art, 80; Wantagh Libr, 82; Hempstead Harbor Art Asn, Glen Cove, 82; Islip Mus, 83; Levittown Libr, 86; Freeport Libr, 87; Longbeach Art League, 89; illuminated slide series (projected art) Long Island Cmty Chorus, Warsaw Ghetto Contata, 60. *Pos:* Inventor, art dir & designer, Mosamics Co pres, 46-48; newspaper artist, Bering Breeze, Aleutians, 45-46; treas, Comic Artists Guild, 48; art dir, 54-60; dir & designer, Studio Concepts, 60-; pres, Allied Artists Am, 85. *Teaching:* Instr, Art Ctr Island Jewish Sch, 59; spkr in field, 99. *Awards:* Grand Prize, Redesign of Levitt House, 67 & Printing Indust NY, 73 & 77; Monadnock Mills Graphic Excellence Award, 75; Cert of Merit, Vet Soc Am Artists, 79; Desi Graphics Award, 80 & 82; Inst Elec & Electronics Engrs Award, 83; Award of Excellence, Long Beach, LI, 89. *Mem:* Allied Artists Am; Huntington Township Art League; Int Soc Poets; Nat Libr Poetry. *Media:* Mixed Media; Copper, Illumination. *Res:* Experimental silk screen production for industry; developed Process Mosaic Reproduction; new approaches in advertising and media including all communication skills; architectural sculpture using copper, plastics or electricity; pictorial Map Entire Am Revolution. *Specialty:* Combining poetry, art, and music on tape to tell a complete creative story, using specific lighting/focus on human condition and environment. *Interests:* Mechanics, environment, nature, hiking, long distance swimming. *Publ:* Auth & illusr, American Indian, Crime & Punishment, Superstition & Parapsychology, 47-50; Popular Sci, Popular Mechanics & Electronics Illustrated, 61-65; My Mother Died Dancing; Cross-over, Bridges of the Mind, 93; Poetry anthologies, Nat Libr Poetry, 96-98. *Dealer:* Kennedy Studios 37 Clarendon St Boston MA. *Mailing Add:* 33 Downhill Ln Wantagh NY 11793

GLASER, MILTON
DESIGNER, ILLUSTRATOR
b New York, NY, June 26, 29. *Study:* Cooper Union Art Sch, 51; Acad Fine Arts, Bologna, Italy, with Giorgio Morandi, Fulbright Scholar, 52-53; Minneapolis Inst Art, Hon DFA; Moore Col Art, Hon Degree; Philadelphia Mus Sch, Hon Degree; Sch Visual Arts, Hon Degree; State Univ Col, Buffalo, Hon Degree, 87, Hon Doctorate, Queens Col, City Univ NY & Londons Royal Col Art. *Work:* Mus Mod Art, NY, Chase Manhattan Bank, NY; Israel Mus, Jerusalem; Nat Archives, Smithsonian Inst, Washington; Cooper Hewitt Design Mus, NY. *Comn:* Mural, Fed Off Bldg, Indianapolis, 74; permanent exhib, Port Authority NY, World Trade Ctr, 75; interior elements, signage & graphic theming, Sesame Park, Pa, 81-83; mural, Astor Place Subway Sta, NY, 85; Int AIDS symbol, World Health Orgn, 87. *Exhib:* One-man show, Portland Visual Arts Ctr, Maine, 75, Mus Mod Art, NY, 75 & Wichita State Univ, 75, Ctr Georges Pompidou, Paris, France, 77, Lincoln Ctr, NY, 81, Carpenter Ctr Gallery, NY, 81, others; Mus Mod Art, Liege, Belgium, 82; Houghton Gallery at The Cooper Union, NY, 84; Hammer Gallery, NY, 86; Mus Bellas de Artes of Buenos Aires, Argentina, 87; Galleria d'Arte Maderna, Bologna, Italy; Univ Cent Mus, Barcelona, Spain; Errepidue Evento, Vicenza, Italy; Sch Visual Arts, NY; Nuages Gallery, Italy; Piero della Francesa Exhib, Arezzo, Italy; Creation Gallery, Japan, 95; Sawhill Gallery, James Madison Univ, 98; Pushpin an dBeyong: The Celebrated Studio Transformed Graphic Design, Japan, 97; Brigham Young Univ; and othres. *Collection Arranged:* Mus Modern Art, NY; Israel Mus, Jerusalem; Chase Manhattan Bank, NY; Nat Archve, Smithwonian Inst, Washington, DC; Cooper Hewitt Nat Design Mus, NY; Civic Mus, Vicenza, Italy; Mus Modern Art, Buenos Aires, Argentina. *Pos:* Pres, Push Pin Studios, NY, 54-74; chmn bd & design dir, NY Mag, 68-77; pres, Milton Glaser Inc Design Studio, 74-; vpres & design dir, Village Voice, 75-77; cofounder, WBMG Design Firm, 83-. *Teaching:* Instr design prog, Sch Visual Arts, NY, 61 & Cooper Union, NY, 94-. *Awards:* Gold Medal, Soc Illusr, 78;

Fulbright Award, Metro Int, 92; Prix Savignac, World's Most Mem Poster, 96; Cooper Hewitt Lifetime Achievement Award, 2004. *Bibliog:* Linda Moss (auth), Milton Glaser at 58, Crains' NY Businessman, 7/13/87; Gael Greene (auth), Over the rainbow, the renaissance of a New York classic, NY Mag, 2/88; Ruth Reichl (auth), Heaven's plate Metrop Home, 6/88. *Mem:* Int Graphic Alliance; Cooper Union (bd trustee, vpres chmn), Art Dir's Club Hall Fame; Art Dir Club; Int Design Conf, Aspen; Soc Arts London; Soc Illusrs. *Publ:* Illusr, Art is Work, 2000, The Alphazeds, 2002, The Design of Dissent, 2004 The Big Rave, 2004 & others. *Mailing Add:* 207 E 32nd St New York NY 10016-6305

GLASGOW, VAUGHN LESLIE
CURATOR, HISTORIAN
b Apr 23, 44; US citizen. *Study:* La State Univ, BA; Borso di Studii, Centro Int Studii Archit A Palladio, Vicenza, Italy, cert, 68; Pa State Univ, MA(Nat Defense Act Title IV Fel), 70; Inst Mus Mgt, Univ Calif, Berkeley, fel, 79; Int Partnership Among Mus, La Rochelle, France, fel, 81. *Exhib:* Solo exhib, Rocks of Ages, Central Conn State Univ, New Britain, 92. *Collection Arranged:* Permanent Collection, Anglo-Am Art Mus, La State Univ, 66-67; G P A Healy: Famous Figures and La Patrons (coauth, catalog), 76; Savoir Faire: The French Taste in Louisiana, 77; Played With Immense Success, 79; L'Amour de Maman: The Acadian Textile Heritage (auth, catalog), 80; The Sun King: Louis XIV and the New World (auth, catalog), 84; The Old State Capital, Baton Rouge, 88; and others. *Pos:* Reader youth grants, Nat Endowment Humanities, Washington, DC, 71-76; arts mgr, State Arts Coun, New Orleans, La, 73-75; chief cur, La State Mus, New Orleans, 75-83, assoc dir, 83-86; dir, spec projs, La State Mus, New Orleans, 86-. *Teaching:* Instr art hist & admin asst, Pa State Univ, 70-71; asst prof art hist, Middle Tenn State Univ, 72-73; lectr art hist, Tulane Univ, 74-79; lectr arts mgt, St Mary's Dominican Col, 81-82. *Awards:* Chevalier des Palmes Academiques, French Govt, 84; Chevalier des Arts et des Lettres, French Govt, 86; Am Asn State Local Hist Award, 92. *Mem:* Am Asn Mus; Int Coun Mus (exhib exchange comt); La Asn Mus; Am Asn State & Local Hist (awards comt); Southeastern Mus Conf. *Res:* European post-Renaissance period; Louisiana studies; architectural history; post-revolutionary French painting. *Publ:* Auth, The Sun King: Louis XIV & the New World (with S Reinhardt, R Macdonald & P Lemoine), LMF, New Orleans, 84; Planning a Traveling Exhibition: American Asn State & Local Hist Technical Report No 10; A Social History of the American Alligator, St Martin's Press, NY, 91; and others. *Mailing Add:* La State Mus 751 Chartres St PO Box 2448 New Orleans LA 70176

GLASS, DOROTHY F
HISTORIAN
b New York, NY. *Study:* Vassar Col, BA, 64; Johns Hopkins Univ, PhD, 68. *Teaching:* Asst prof medieval art, Boston Univ, 69-74; assoc prof, State Univ NY, Buffalo, 74-81, prof, 81-, chair, 87-89. *Awards:* Rome Prize, Am Acad Rome, 85-86; Fulbright Fel, Western European Regional, 89-90; Jane & Morgan Whitney Senior Fel, Metrop Mus Art, 91-93. *Mem:* Medieval Acad Am (counr, 94-97); Col Art Asn; Int Ctr Medieval Art (bd dir, 80-83, domestic adv & publ comt, 87-90 & ed newsletter, 92-95, vpres, 96-99); Soc Fels, Am Acad Rome. *Publ:* Auth, Romanesque sculpture in Campania: a problem of method, Art Bulletin, 74; Italian Romanesque Sculpture: An Annotated Bibliography, Boston, G K Hall & Co, 83; Pseudo-Augustine, Prophets & Pulpits in Romanesque Campania, Dumbarton Oaks Papers 41, 87; Romanesque Sculpture in Campania: Patrons, Programs and Style, Pa State Press, 91; Portals, Pilgrimage and Crusade in Western Tuscany, Princeton Univ Press, 97. *Mailing Add:* Dept Art Hist-Rm 601 Clemens Hall State Univ NY-North Campus Buffalo NY 14260

GLASS, WENDY D
DEALER, COLLECTOR
b New York, NY, Aug 28, 25. *Study:* Bard Col, study of art hist with Stefan Hirsch. *Collection Arranged:* Temple Shaaray Tefila, New York; Temple Israel, New Rochelle, NY; Temple Soc Advan of Judaism, White Plains, NY; Waldamar Cancer Res Found, Hilton Hotel, New York, 65. *Pos:* Dir & owner, Glass Art Gallery, 60-. *Mem:* Appraisers Asn Am; Woman Pays Club; Ukiyo-e Soc Am. *Specialty:* Figurative art; American paintings and graphics, 20th Century; Japanese Ukiyo-e prints. *Collection:* Max Weber, Chaim Gross, Raphael Soyer & Benny Andrews; contemporary 20th century painters; Ukiyo-e masters of the 19th century

GLASSER, NORMA PENCHANSKY
SCULPTOR
b New York, NY, Mar 6, 41. *Study:* Leslie Col, BS, 62; Eastern Mich Univ, MFA, 74. *Work:* Marietta Col, Ohio; La Grange Col, Ga; Saginaw Valley State Col, Mich; Boone Sculpture Garden, San Marino, Calif; Pac Enterprises, Los Angeles, Calif; St Joseph's Hosp, Ann Arbor; Univ of MI, Dearborn, Mich; St Joseph's Hospital, Ypsianti, Mich; Blue Cross, Blue Shield, Detroit, Mich; Ann Arbor Pub Libr, Ann Arbor, Mich, 2006; Restorative View Ctr, St Joseph's campus, Ypsilanti, Mich, 2006; and others. *Comn:* Women Waiting, comn by Charles Givens, Oklahoma City, 84; Summer Garden, Ind Univ-Purdue Univ, Ft Wayne, Ind, 91; Martha Graham, Las Sendas, Ariz, 95. *Exhib:* 56th Ann Nat Exhib, Springville Mus, Utah, 80; 16th Ann Drawing & Small Sculpture Exhib, Del Mar Col, Corpus Christi, Tex, 82; Nat Sculpture Soc Exhib, Equitable Gallery, NY, 83; Mich Outdoor Sculpture II, Southfield Civic Ctr, 89; Taubman Gallery, Ann Arbor, Mich, 91; Power Ctr Performing Arts, Ann Arbor, 92; Nat Asn Women Artists, NY, 94; Dennos Mus, Traverse City, Mich, 96; Invitationa Power Ctr Performing Arts, Ann Arbor, 2000; Bronze 2000, Park Gallery, Kalamazoo, Mich; The Figure as Landscape, Ann Arbor Art Ctr, 2002; Pfizer Sculpture Exhib, Ann Arbor, 2002; Pivotal Space: Recent Sculpture & Drawings, Washington Gallery, Ann Arbor, 2002; Celebrating the Figure, Lansing Art Gallery, Lansing MI, 2002 (Judge Commendation Award); 15th Ann Nat Women's Art Exhib Oakland Community Col Farmington Hills, MI, (2nd Place Award); Art Around Town- Outdoor Sulpture Inst, Sauegatuek, MI, 2004; Wall to Wall, A Survey of Current Regional Sulpture, Flatlanders Galleries Blissfield, MI,2004; Equestrian Gestures Washington St Gallery Ann Arbor, Mich, 2004; From Our Perspective, Oakland Community Col, Farmington Hills, Mich, 2006; Art Around Town, Saugatuck, Mich, 2006; and others. *Pos:* Staff, Ann Arbor Street Fair, 87-2002. *Teaching:* Instr sculpture-drawing, Ann Arbor Art Ctr, 73-2001; guest lectr, Univ Mich, 85 Ann Arbor Publ Schs, 86. *Awards:* First Place, Annie Achievement Award, Visual Arts Three Demensional, Washtenaw Coun Art, Ann Arbor, Mich, 91; Shidon Bronze Gallery, Tesuque, NMex; Cleo Hartwig Award for Sculpture, Nat Asn Women Artists, NY, 94; Purchase Award Univ MI, Dearborn, MI, 2003. *Mem:* Ann Arbor Art Asn (bd mem, 82-87); Nat Asn Women Artists; Mich Guild Artists & Craftsmen; Nat Sculpture Soc. *Media:* Bronze. *Specialty:* Fine Art. *Collection:* Womens Ctr, U of MI, Dearborn MI,; Blue Cross Blue Shield of MI; ST Joseph Hospital, Ypsilanti MI,; many Private, state & national. *Publ:* Contribr, Heroic Sculpture, Western Art Digest, 86. *Dealer:* Washington St Gallery 215 E Washington St Ann Arbor MI; Tamrra Gallery, Huron St, Ann Arbor MI,. *Mailing Add:* 2859 Gladstone St Ann Arbor MI 48104

GLASSON, LLOYD
SCULPTOR, EDUCATOR
b Chicago, Ill, Jan 31, 31. *Study:* Art Inst Chicago, BFA, 57; Tulane Univ, MFA, 59. *Work:* New Brit Mus Am Art, Conn; George Walter Vincent Smith Mus, Springfield, Mass; Wichita Art Mus; Univ Hartford, Conn; Hartford Hosp and The Bushnell Auditorium, Hartford, Conn. *Comn:* Shapiro Mem & Herbert Portraits, Karen Horney Clin, NY, 67; Finial angels atop soldiers & sailors mem arch, Hartford, Conn, DeVane Mem, Yale Univ, Conn, 68; Fox Mem & Patterson Mem, Univ Conn Med Ctr, Farmington; Church of St Helena, West Hartford, Conn; Helen & Harry Jack Gray (portraits), Wadsworth Atheneum; ACMAT Corp, Portrait of Henry Nozko. *Exhib:* One-man shows, Dorsky Gallery, NY, 66 & 74, Trinity Col, 77 & Saltbox Gallery, 85, Hartford, Conn; Univ NH, Durham, 76; Manchester Community Col, 90; Cent Conn State Univ, 91. *Pos:* Exhib designer, Newark Mus, NJ, 60-61; co-founder, Artists Tenants Asn, 61-. *Teaching:* Prof sculpture & drawing, Univ Hartford, West Hartford, Conn, 64-, prof emer. *Awards:* First Prizes, Art Asn Regional, Delgado Mus, New Orleans, 59; Gold Medal, Nat Sculpture Soc, 85 & Nat Acad Design, 86; James E & Francis W Bent Award for Creativity, 89. *Bibliog:* Jolene Goldenthal (auth), Adventurous Revivalist, Hartford Courant, 4/77; Anthony Padovano (auth), The process of sculpture, 81; Vernon Mays (auth), Arch has its angels again, Hartford Courant, 8/20/87; Donald M Reynolds (auth), Masters of American Sculpture, Abbevile Press, 93; Constance Neyer and John Long (coauths) Honoered Service, Hartford Courant, 4/16/2000; plus others. *Mem:* Sculptors Guild; Nat Acad; Soc Conn Sculptors; Nat Sculpture Soc. *Media:* Bronze, Ceramic. *Mailing Add:* 229 Grand St New York NY 10013-4240

GLATT, LINNEA
SCULPTOR
b Bismarck, NDak, Sept 8, 49. *Study:* Moorhead State Univ, Minn, BS, 71; Univ Dallas, Irving, Tex, MA, 72. *Work:* Expose, Acknowledge, Reconcile, Dallas Mus Art, 89; Mimi's Garden, Dallas Arboretum, collaboration, 88; Waste Mgt Facility, City of Phoenix, 89-92. *Comn:* Harrow, Lubben Plaza, Dallas, Tex, 92; Passage Inacheve, Buffalo Bayou, Houston, Tex, 90; Moorhead Room, Moorhead State Univ, Minn, 93. *Exhib:* Univ Colo Art Galleries, Boulder, 87-88; Aspen Art Mus, Colo, 87-88; Tex Women Exhib Nat Mus Women Art's, Washington, DC, 88; Archer M Huntington Art Gallery, Austin, Tex, 90; Circum-stance, Blue Star Art Space, San Antonio, Tex, 90. *Pos:* Bd dir, Tex Sculpture Assoc, 86-87; Dallas Mus Awards to Artist Committee, 88-91. *Teaching:* Instr art, Richland Col, Dallas, Tex, 74-84; art, Southern Methodist Univ, Dallas, Tex, 85-88. *Awards:* Fel, Nat Endowment Arts, 86; Individual art grant, Art Matters Inc, New York, 89; Anne Giles Kimbrought Fund Grant, Dallas Mus Art, Tex, 92. *Bibliog:* Watson-Jones (auth), Contemporary American Women Sculptors, Oryx Press, 86; Laurel Jones (auth), 50 Texas Artists: A Critical Selection of Painters and Sculptors Working in Texas, Cronical Books, 86; Charles Dee Mitchell (auth), Linnea Glatt & Francis Merritt Thompson, Art Forum, 120, summer 91. *Mem:* Founding mem, D W Galllery, 75-. *Media:* Miscellaneous Media. *Mailing Add:* 2412 Hardwick Dallas TX 75208

GLAZER, JAY M & MARSHA S
COLLECTORS, PATRONS
Mrs Glazer b Portland, Ore; Mr Glazer b Anderson, Ind. *Study:* Univ Wash, BS, 63-67; Ind Univ, BS(bus), 69; Univ Tex, MBA, 71. *Exhib:* Out of Site: Selections From the Marsha S. Glazer Collection (24 pieces by artists such as Pablo Picasso, Roy Lichtenstein, Jasper Johns, David Hockney, Jackson Pollock and Wayne Thiebuad), Univ Art Mus., Univ Calif Santa Barbara, 2005. *Pos:* Collector's comt mem, Nat Gallery Art, 97-. *Awards:* Named one of the Top 200 Collectors, The ARTnews, 2004, 2006. *Mem:* Seattle Art Mus (bd mem, 91-94); Mus Mod Art, NY; Guggenheim Mus. *Collection:* Modern and contemporary art. *Mailing Add:* PO Box 997 Mercer Island WA 98040

GLENDINNING, PETER
PHOTOGRAPHER
b New York, NY, Sept 23, 51. *Study:* Syracuse Univ, BFA, 76, MFA, 78. *Work:* Int Mus Photog, Rochester, NY; Everson Mus Art & Light Work, Syracuse, NY; Tweed Mus Art; Murray State Univ, Ky; Unicolor Corp; Ctr Creative Photography, Tucson, Ariz. *Comn:* Official portrait, Gov John Engler, State of Mich; Photog, State Capitol Restoration Proj, Lansing, Mich. *Exhib:* One-person shows, Lightsong Gallery, Tucson, 80, CEPA Gallery, Buffalo, NY, 81, Foto Gallery, NY, 82 & Lowe Art Gallery, Syracuse Univ, 84; Proj Art Ctr, Cambridge, Mass, 82; Contemp Photog as Phantasy, Santa Barbara Mus Art, 82; Main Street Gallery, Nantucket, Mass, 90; South African

Consulate, NY, 99; South African Embassy, Washington DC, 99. *Pos:* Dir, Light Fantastic Gallery, Mich State Univ, East Lansing, 78-; portrait photogr for corp & advert, 84-. *Teaching:* Prof dept art & head photog, Mich State Univ, 78-. *Awards:* Res Grant, Mich State Univ, 81; Unicolor Artist Support Grant, 82; Individual Artist Grant, Mich Arts Coun, 89-90; Addy Citation Excellence, 94. *Mem:* Soc Photog Educ; Friends of Photog; Ctr Creative Photog; Lansing Advert Club; Photo Imaging Educ Asn (bd dir). *Media:* Color. *Publ:* Contribr, Fugitive Color (exhib catalog), Univ Mich, 82; Color Photography: History, Theory and Darkroom Technique, Prentice-Hall, 85; Michigan Quilts: 150 Years of a Textile Tradition, Mich State Univ Mus, 88; numerous magazine covers, advertisements & ann reports. *Dealer:* Photography Assocs Inc 2654 Linden Dr East Lansing MI 48823. *Mailing Add:* Art Dept Kresge Art Ctr Mich State Univ East Lansing MI 48824

GLENN, CONSTANCE WHITE
MUSEUM DIRECTOR, WRITER
b Topeka, Kans, Oct 4, 33. *Study:* Univ Kans, BFA; Univ Mo, Kansas City; Calif State Univ, Long Beach, MA. *Collection Arranged:* Lucas Samaras: Photo-Transformations (auth, catalog), 75; Roy Lichtenstein: Ceramic Sculpture (auth, catalog), 77; George Segal: Pastels 1957-1965 (auth, catalog), 78; Jim Dine Figure Drawings: 1974-1979 (auth, catalog), 79; Frederick Sommer at Seventy-Five (auth, catalog), 80; Apropos Robinson Jeffers: Robert Motherwell-Renate Ponsold (auth, catalog), 81; Robert Longo (auth, catalog), 86; Eric Fischl: Scenes Before the Eye (auth, catalog), 86; Imagenes Liricas: New Spanish Visions (auth, catalog), 90; James Rosenquist: Time Dust (catalog raisonne), 93; The Great American Pop Art Store: Multiples of the Sixties (auth, catalog), 97; Double Vision: Photographs from the Strauss Collection, 2001; Tom Wesselmann: The Intimate Images (auth, catalog), 2003; The Artist Observed (auth, catalog), 2003; Candida Höfer: Architecture of Absence (auth, catalog), 2004. *Pos:* Prof & dir, Mus Studies Cert Prog, Univ Art Mus, Calif State Univ, Long Beach, 73-2004, prof & dir emer, 2004-; chmn South Calif adv bd, Arch Am Art, 78-90; art consult, Archit Digest, 80-88; publ & ed, Artexpress, 88-; contrib ed, Angeles Mag, 88-90 & Antiques & Fine Art, 90-91. *Awards:* Distinquished Scholarly & Creative Achievement Award, Calif State Univ Long Beach; Outstanding Contribr to the Field, Calif Mus Photog, 86; Arts Admin of the Year, Long Beach Pub Corp Arts, 89; Woman of Distinction Award, Soroptimist, 99. *Mem:* Am Asn Mus; Assoc Art Mus Dir (trustee 2000-02, emer, 2004-); Col Art Asn; Art Table. *Res:* American art since 1945. *Specialty:* Contemporary art. *Collection:* Art of the Sixties, Contemporary art & photography. *Publ:* Auth, Jim Dine Drawings, 85, Roy Lichtenstein: Landscape Sketches, 86, Lucas Samaras: Doodles, Sketches and Plans, 87, Wayne Thiebaud: Private Drawings, 88 & Robert Motherwell: The Daedalus Sketches, 88, Harry N Abrams, The Great American Pop Art Store: Multiples of the Sixties, 97; ed, Imagenes Liricas: New Spanish Visions, 90; James Rosenquist: Time Dust, The Complete Graphics 1962-1992, Rizzoli, 93; contribr auth, Dictrionary of Art, 96-, Encyl Americana, 96-; co-auth, Pop Art: An International Perspective, 91; contribr auth, Carrie Mae Weems: The Hampton Project, 00; Double Vision: Photographs from the Strauss Collection, 2001; and many others. *Mailing Add:* Californis State Univ Long Beach Dept of Art 1250 Bellflower Blvd Long Beach CA 90840-3501

GLESMANN, SYLVIA MARIA
PAINTER
b Bavaria, Ger, June 8, 23; US citizen. *Study:* Acad Fine Arts, Nurnberg, Ger; Acad Fine Arts, Munich, Ger, 44; Studied with Robert Sakson & Nicholas Reale. *Work:* Ortho Diagnostics, Bridgewater, NJ. *Comn:* Many pvt comns. *Exhib:* NJ WC Soc, Morris Mus, Morristown, NJ, 80; Summer Selections, Nabisco Brands, East Hanover, NJ, 84; Salmagundi Club Gallery, NY, 88-89, 94, 2000-; Nat Asn Women Artists, NY, 91-92 & 94; Barrons Art Ctr; solo exhibs, Ocean Co Col, NJ, Bridgewater Raritan Pub Libr, 96, Bridgewater Libr, NJ, Ziko's Gallery, New Hope, Pa, Jockey Hollow Gallery, Morristown, NJ, and many others; Bridgewater Creative Art Com, NJ, 2006; Trinity United Church, Warren, NJ, 2006. *Pos:* Chair, 10th chap Outdoor Art Show, Somerset Art Asn. *Teaching:* Somerville Adult Educ Classes; Bridgewater Raritan High Sch, Career Day Demo and Speech, 93-94. *Awards:* Many awards from 70-2005; Editors Choice for Poetry, Int Soc Poetry. *Bibliog:* Les Krantz (auth), NY Art Review, 89. *Mem:* Raritan Valley Arts Asn (pres 76-78); Am Artist Prof League (NJ chap, pres 88-91); Nat Asn Women Artists, NY (juror for works on paper 94-96); Garden State Watercolor Soc; charter mem Mus Women Arts, Wash, DC. *Media:* Egg Tempera, Watercolor. *Specialty:* Art. *Interests:* Poetry, music, painting, reading and travel. *Publ:* Auth, She is Hearts and Flowers, 78, From the Heart, 89, Showcase, 90, Messenger Gazette; Heart in Home, Courrier News, 89; On the Towns, Star Ledger, 91. *Mailing Add:* 36 Twin Oaks Rd Bridgewater NJ 08807

GLICK, JOHN P
CERAMIST
b Detroit, Mich, July 1, 38. *Study:* Wayne State Univ, BFA, 60; Cranbrook Acad, MFA, 62. *Work:* Everson Mus Art; Cranbrook Art Acad Mus; Renwick Gallery, Nat Mus Am Art, Smithsonian Inst, Washington, DC; Detroit Inst Arts. *Exhib:* Edmonton, Atla, Can, 73; Everson Mus Art, Syracuse, NY, 79 & 89; Craftsman Potters Asn Gallery, London, Eng, solo exhib, 85; Detroit Inst Arts, Mich, 88; Nat Mus Ceramic Art, Baltimore, MD, 89; solo exhib, Fosdick-Nelson Gallery, Sch Art & Design, Alfred Univ, Alfred, NY, 90; Am Craft Mus, NY, 92. *Awards:* Mich Found Arts, 77; Nat Endowment Arts, 77 & 88. *Mem:* Am Craft Coun; Mich Potters Assoc. *Dealer:* Shaw Guido 7 N Saginaw Flint MI 48343. *Mailing Add:* 30435 W Ten Mile Rd Farmington Hills MI 48336

GLICK, PAULA F
ART DEALER, WRITER, ART HISTORIAN
b Baltimore, Md. *Study:* Am Univ; George Washington Univ, BA & MA; Columbia Univ, MPhil. *Pos:* Assoc dir, Capricorn Galleries, 74-87, co-dir, 87-97, consultant, appraiser & private dealer; consult to var mus, auction houses & dealers; art history res, lectr; Loudown Co VA Art comt, 2003-2010. *Teaching:* Instr art hist, Cath Univ, 85. *Bibliog:* Paul Sample, Ivy League Regionalist. *Mem:* Col Art Asn Am; Art Table: Am Soc of Appraisors, Am Asn Mus; Italian Art Soc; Asn Historians Am Art; and others. *Res:* Paul Sample; American technology and culture 1830-1960; architecture of Michelangelo; American art 1925-1950. *Interests:* Italian Renaissance and Baroque; American Art of the 1930's & 1940's; American contemporary realists; 19th Century American Landscape. *Collection:* Contemporary American realists from 1900 to 1940. *Publ:* Coauth, Paul Sample: Painter of the American Scene, Hood Mus Art, Dartmouth Col; First Cheureul in America, Am Art J, 96; Paul Starrett Sample, Am Nat Biography, 99; essay, Surrounded by Luxury, Objects of Desire; contribr, Sight and Insight: The Art Works of Burton Silvermann, 98; auth, Hightlights of the International Personal Property Conference, Taos, N Mex, 99, Personal Property Jour, Vol 12, No 1, 2000; catalog, Made in California, LACMA, 2000. *Mailing Add:* 42842 Falling Leaf Ct Ashburn VA 20148-6928

GLICKMAN, ARTHUR
SCULPTOR
b New York, NY, Apr 29, 23. *Study:* With Issac Soyer, 53; Nat Acad Design, with Jean DMarco & Envangelo Frudakis, 64-68; New Sch Social Research, with Bruno Luccesi, 69. *Work:* Bergen Community Mus, Paramus, NJ; Collections of Gov & Mrs Mario Cuomo, Senator Joseph R Pisani, Tish Family, and Dave Thomas. *Comn:* Bird in Flight, IBM, NJ, 74; Freedom Series, comn by Roger Williams Mint, Providence, RI, 76; The Lamplighter, Wash Gas, Washington, DC, 92, 94 & 98; Doors to the Holy Ark, New Synagogue of Ft Lee, NJ, 03. *Exhib:* Allied Artists Am, Nat Acad Gallery, NY, 70, 74, 78, 80, 81, 84, 85 & 98; Nat Acad Design, Nat Acad Gallery, NY, 75; Nat Sculpture Soc, Equitable Life Assurance Soc, NY, 76; Newark Mus, NJ, 76; Sculptors Asn NJ, Madison Square Garden, NY, 76. *Pos:* Advocate for children in foster care. *Teaching:* Inst sculpture casting, Old Church Cult Ctr, NJ, 74. *Awards:* First Prize in Sculpture, Bergen Co Artists Asn, 65 & West New York, NJ, 66; Second Prize in Sculpture, Washington Square, New York, 70; Assoc Members Award, Allied Artists Am, 84; In Memoriam Award, Allied Artists Am, 87, 93 & 94; Won C-Span Presidential Life Portraits Contest; Relief of Thomas Jefferson, 00. *Mem:* Allied Artists Am (vpres, 85, pres, 86-89); Sculptors Asn NJ (pres, 98). *Media:* Bonded Bronze on Plexiglass. *Dealer:* Prince Royal Gallery Alexandria VA 22314. *Mailing Add:* 538 Rutland Ave Teaneck NJ 07666

GLIER, MIKE
DRAFTSMAN, PAINTER
b Fort Thomas, Ky, Aug 26, 53. *Study:* Williams Col, BA, 76; Hunter Col, with Robert Morris, MA, 79. *Work:* Addison Gallery Am Art, Andover, Mass; Williams Col Mus Art, Mass; Hartford Atheneum, Conn; Albright-Knos Mus, Buffalo, NY; Mus Mod Art, NY. *Comn:* BAM-Next Wave, set design comn by Tim Miller, Brooklyn, NY, 84; Walls, Norton Gallery Art, West Palm Beach, 86; Green (wall drawings), comn by Wave Hill, Bronx, NY, 89; Goerdler Mem (with Jenny Holzer), City of Leipzig, Ger. *Exhib:* Biennial, Whitney Mus, NY, 83; Hair Breadth: New Wall Drawings (with catalog), La Jolla Mus Contemp Art, Calif, 84; Sydney Biennial, Art Gallery New South Wales, Australia, 84; Am Ne-Expressionists (auth, catalog), Aldrich Mus, Ridgefield, Conn, 84; Ecrans Politiques, Musee d'Art Contemp de Montreal, 85-86; Wallworks, John Weber Gallery, NY, 86; South Africa Drawings, Washington Project for Arts, Washington, DC, 86; one-man shows, Mus Mod Art, NY, 87, (auth, catalog) San Jose Mus Art, Calif, 89, Alphabet of Lili, Drawing Ctr, NY, 92, Garden Court, Tyler Galleries, Tyler Sch Art, Elkins Park, Pa, 95 & Full Moon on the Hoosick (drawing), Mass Mus Contemp Art, N Adams, 2000-01; Committed to Print, Mus Mod Art, NY, 88; Drawings from the Permanent Collection, Addison Gallery, Andover, Mass, 90; I Love My Time: Contemp Art from the Permanent Collection, Williams Col Mus Art, Mass, 95; Cult Economies (with catalog), Drawing Ctr, NY, 96; The Flower Show, Fruitmarket Gallery, Edinburgh, Scotland, 99-2000; many others. *Pos:* Adv bd mem, Printed Matter Inc, 83; artist adv bd, New Mus, New York, 89; vis comt, Williams Col Mus Art, 90; juror, Albany Inst Hist & Art, 99. *Teaching:* Asst prof art, studio & art hist, Williams Col, Williamstown, Mass, currently. *Awards:* Nat Endowment Art Fel, 81; Award in Visual Arts 9, New Eng Region; Guggenheim Mem Found Fel, 96. *Bibliog:* Sally Yard (auth), The shadow of the bomb, Arts Mag, 4/84; Robin Carson (auth), Untamed visitiation, Garden Design, winter 89; Elizabeth Hess (auth), The equalizer, Village Voice, 6/21/89. *Mem:* Col Art Asn. *Media:* Mixed Media. *Publ:* Auth, The 1979 dime store figurine, Art Forum 80; White Male Power, Senators, Game Show Hosts, National Monuments, pvt publ, 82; Patience observation & investigation, Art Forum, 82; Working Watteau, Art Forum, 4/88; Satisfaction, Hallwalls, San Jose Mus Art, 89. *Mailing Add:* Williams Col Spencer Studio Bldg 35 Driscoll Hall Dr Williamstown MA 01267

GLIMCHER, ARNOLD B
DEALER, WRITER
b Mar 12, 38; US citizen. *Study:* Mass Col Art, BA, 60, Hon DFA; Boston Univ, studied fine arts, 60-61; NY Univ, studied 72-73. *Hon Degrees:* Mass Col Art, DFA. *Pos:* Found & dir, Pace Gallery, New York, 60-; metrop regional adv bd, Chase Manhattan Corp. *Mem:* Am Acad Arts & Letts; Writers Guild Am; Art Dealers Asn Am (bd mem); Chevalier des arts et lettres, Govt France; Acad Motion Picture Art & Sci; Directors Guild Am; Isreal Mus (fel). *Specialty:* Twentieth-century art. *Publ:* Producer, Gorillas in the Mist (film), Warner Bros/Universal Pictures, 88; The Good Mother (film), Touchstone Pictures, 88; dir & producer, The Mambo Kings (film), Warner Bros, 92; Just Cause (film), Warner Bros, 95; auth, Adventure in Art-40 Years at Pace, Leonardo Int, Milan, 2001. *Mailing Add:* Pace Wildenstein Gallery 32 E 57th St New York NY 10022

GLOMAN, DAVID I
PAINTER
b Bryn Mawr, Pa, 58. *Study:* Yale Univ Sch Art, Norfolk, 6/82; Ind Univ, Bloomington, BFA, 83; Yale Univ, New Haven, Conn, MFA, 86. *Exhib:* Hudson Walker Gallery, Provincetown, Mass, 86; E End Gallery, Provincetown, Mass, 87; Third Ann Young Artist's Exhib, Provincetown Art Asn & Mus, Mass, 87; Provincetown Group Gallery, Mass, 88; Nat Soc Arts & Lett Exhib, Ind Univ, Bloomington, 89; Julie Heller Gallery, Provincetown, Mass, 89 & 90; solo shows, Belleview Gallery, Bloomington, Ind, 89, Fontbonne Col, St Louis, Mo, 91, Northampton Ctr Arts, Mass, 91 & 93, Eli Marsh Gallery, Amherst Col, Mass, 94 & Rolly-Michaux Gallery, Boston, Mass, 96; Floyd Co Mus Art, New Albany, Ind, 90; 18th Ann Exhib, Lafayette Mus Art, Ind, 90; Babcock Galleries, NY, 91; Hart Gallery, Northampton, Mass, 92; Northampton Ctr Arts, Mass, 92 & 93; Vt Studio Ctr, Johnson, 94; Gallery in Monterey, Mass, 94; Mead Art Mus, Amherst Col, Mass, 95; Bowery Gallery, NY, 95; Rolly-Michaux Gallery, Boston, Mass, 95; WM Baczek Fine Arts, Northampton, Mass, 97; Hackett-Freedman Gallery, San Francisco, Calif, 97; Pepper Gallery, Boston, Mass, 97; Am Acad Arts & Lett Ceremonial Exhib, Purchase Award Winners, Hassam, Speicher, Betts & Symons Purchase Fund, NY, 98. *Teaching:* Asst, Yale Univ Sch Art, 85-86; lectr, Ind Univ, Herron Sch Art, Indianapolis, 88-89, Smith Col, Northampton, Mass, 90 & 95-98 & Amherst Col, Mass, 92-94 & 97-98; vis artist, Vt Studio Ctr, Johnson, 94; vis asst prof, Hampshire Col, Amherst, Mass, 94-95; instr, ASA Studio Art Prog, Amherst Col, 93-97. *Awards:* Williamsburg Arts Lottery Grant, Mass, 92; Louis Comfort Tiffany Biennial Competition, 97; Hassam, Speicher, Betts & Symons Purchase Award, Am Acad Arts & Lett, New York, 98. *Mailing Add:* 220 Prospect St Northampton MA 01060

GLORIG, OSTOR
PAINTER, CRAFTSMAN
b New York, NY, Feb 14, 19. *Study:* Am Art Sch, New York, with Robert Brackman, Raphael Soyer & Gordon Samstag, four yr cert. *Work:* Mark Twain Portrait, Mark Twain Libr & Mem, Hartford, Conn. *Exhib:* One-man shows, Lynn Kottler Galleries, 56, 59, 61, 64 & 72, Clarksville Gallery, 65 & Col Mt St Vincent, 67; Nat Soc Arts & Lett Empire State Chap Showing, 69 & 79. *Awards:* Interior Design Cover Award, 51; Grumbacher Merit Award, 61. *Bibliog:* Elaine Israel (auth), From diamond to canvas, Long Island Star-J, 5/9/67. *Mem:* Life fel Royal Soc Arts Eng; life mem Nat Soc Arts & Lett; hon mem Kappa Pi. *Media:* Oil. *Dealer:* Lynn Kottler Galleries 3 E 65th St New York NY 10021

GLOVER, ROBERT
SCULPTOR, CERAMIST
b Upland, Calif, May 20, 36. *Study:* Los Angeles County Art Inst, with Peter Voulkos & Helen Watson, MFA, 60. *Work:* Security Pacific Bank, First Bank of Los Angeles & Bella Lewitsky Dance Found, Los Angeles; Fluor Corp, Irvine, Calif; Everson Mus Fine Arts, NY; Oakland Mus Art, Calif. *Exhib:* Drawing Exhib, San Francisco Mus Art, 57; Ceramics National, Everson Mus Fine Arts, Syracuse, NY, 60; Design 11, Pasadena Art Mus, Calif, 71; Sculpture Invitational, San Diego Mus Art, 73; duo exhib, Munic Gallery, Los Angeles, 79; Dualism, Otis-Parsons Exhib Ctr, Los Angeles, 82. *Teaching:* Asst prof ceramics, Otis Art Inst, 62-79; instr color & design, Otis-Parson Sch Design, 79-, instr ceramics, 92. *Awards:* Ford Found Fac Grant, 78. *Bibliog:* Peter Clothier (auth), Remembrances of things past, Los Angeles Weekly, Vol 8, No 5, 12/27/84; Kristine McKenna (auth), Galleries, Los Angeles Times, 12/13/85; Mac McCloud (auth), Metamorphosis of form, Artweek, Vol 16, 12/21/85. *Mem:* Los Angeles Contemp Exhibs. *Media:* Clay, Mixed Media. *Dealer:* Space Gallery 6015 Santa Monica Blvd Los Angeles CA 90038. *Mailing Add:* c/o Otis Col Art & Design 9045 Lincoln Blvd Westchester CA 90045-3550

GLUCK, HEIDI
PAINTER, EDUCATOR
b Brooklyn, NY, Dec 30, 44. *Study:* Bennington Col, with D Smith, T Smith, Caro, Londo, Stroud & P Feely, BA, 66; Hunter Col, New York, with E Goosen, T Smith, R Humphrey & R Morris, 66-70. *Work:* Guggenheim Mus, NY; Israel Mus, Jerusalem; State Univ Ohio, Columbus; Picker Art Gallery, Colgate Univ, Hamilton, NY; Bennington Col, Vt. *Exhib:* Sensible Exploration, Univ Gallery Fine Art, Ohio State Univ, Columbus, 70; A Painting Show, PSI Projects Studios One, Inst Art & Urban Resources, NY, 77; A Brooklyn Portfolio, Brooklyn Mus, NY, 80; Contemp Drawings & Watercolors, Mem Art Gallery, Univ Rochester, 80; Creative Artists Pub Serv Prog Grantees, Brooklyn Mus, NY, 81; 19 Artists-Emergent Am, Guggenheim Mus, NY, 81. *Teaching:* Vis artist painting, Princeton Univ, 80-91. *Awards:* Creative Artists Pub Serv Prog Grant, 78-79. *Bibliog:* Robert Pincus-Witten (auth), Entries: Glück, Stephen, Acconci, Arts Mag, 3/78; Donald B Kuspit (auth), Heidi Glück, Arts Mag, 6/79; Donald B Kuspit (auth), Stops & starts in seventies art and criticism, Arts Mag, 3/81. *Media:* Oil, Acrylic. *Mailing Add:* 414 2nd St 1st Fl Apt 1A Jersey City NJ 07302

GLUHMAN, MARGARET A
GRAPHIC ARTIST, PHOTOGRAPHER
b Bethel Park, Pa. *Study:* Univ Pittsburgh; Cleveland Inst Art. *Work:* Rutgers Univ Art Mus; Meidinger Corp, Louisville, Ky; Owensboro Mus Fine Art; Eastman Pharmaceutical, Pa; and others. *Exhib:* JB Speed Art Mus, 86; 19th Nat Works on Paper, Minot, NDak, 89; La Grange Nat, Ga, 89, 91, 92 & 94; Multi-Focus Int, State Univ NY, Plattsburgh, 95; Nat Small Works, Armory Art Ctr, Fla, 95; Tex Int, Univ Tex, El Paso, 96. *Collection Arranged:* New Works Series I-XXV, 81-87; Collectors & Collections (auth, catalog), 85; Mid-South Monotypes (auth, catalog), 86-87; New Works/New Alabamians (auth, catalog), 90-91. *Pos:* Exhib coordr, Capitol Arts Ctr, Bowling Green, Ky, 81-87. *Media:* Paper. *Mailing Add:* 2095 Evergreen Dr S Auburn AL 36830-6934

GLUSKA, AHARON
PAINTER
b Feb 26, 51. *Study:* France Avni Inst Fine Arts, Israel, 73-76; Academie Ecole des Beaux Arts, Paris, 76-77. *Work:* Albright Knox Mus; Brooklyn Mus; Tel Aviv Mus; Cornell Univ Mus; Israel Mus, Jerusalem. *Exhib:* One-man shows, Bertha Urdang Gallery, NY, 83, 86 & 88, Tiro Gallery, Copenhagen, Denmark, 87, Eric Siegeltuch Gallery, NY, 88, Gordon Gallery, Tel Aviv, Israel, 88, Shoshana Wayne Gallery, Los Angeles, 90, CS Schulte Galleries, South Orange, NJ, 91, Estok/Lanza Fine Art, New York, 92 & Robert Mann Gallery, NY 95; Book, Box, Word, NMiami Ctr Contemp Art, 92; Book, Box, Word Volume II, Univ Fla, 93; Four Contemp Artists, Jewish Mus, NY, 94; Burnt Whole, Washington Proj Arts, DC, 94; Carol Rubenstein Assoc, Pitts, 99 & Phila, 2000; and many others. *Awards:* Pollock-Krasner Found Grant, 89; Nat Endowment Arts Grant, 89. *Mailing Add:* 535 Broadway New York NY 10012

GOAD, ANNE LAINE
ART DEALER, PUBLISHER
b Nashville, Tenn. *Study:* David Lipscomb Univ, Nashville, Tenn, BA(magna cum laude), 67. *Collection Arranged:* 10 + 2, The Parthenon Mus, Nashville, Tenn, 1991; Light a Long Time After, The Parthenon Mus, 2002. *Pos:* Partner, ASID Indust. *Awards:* Industry Ptnr of Yr, Tenn Chpt ASID, 2002. *Bibliog:* Pat Swingley (auth), Italian charm, Tennessean, 5/92; Deborah Highland Collins (auth), Art dealer brings city "vibrationism", Tennessean, 7/95; Peggy Krebs (auth), Original art reflects trend among home buyers, Tennessean, 9/98. *Mem:* Visual Artists Alliance Nashville; Nat Asn Women Bus Owners. *Specialty:* Original paintings featuring mid-south regional artists since 1984. *Mailing Add:* Anne Laine Goad Art Inc PO Box 2165 Brentwood TN 37024

GOBUZAS, ALDONA M
ART DEALER, CONSULTANT
b Brooklyn, NY. *Study:* Notre Dame Col, St John's Univ, BA. *Specialty:* Contemporary American art; Modern art; Estates of John Curoi, Gertrude R Schwartz & Libby Robinson. *Collection:* Contemporary paintings; sculpture; drawings, etchings; prints. *Mailing Add:* Galerie Aldonna 215 E 79th St New York NY 10021

GODBEE, GARY
PAINTER
b Coral Gables, FL Jan 20, 52. *Study:* Boston Univ, Sch of Fine Arts, BFA, 1974; Brooklyn Col, grad painting with Lennart Anderson, 1992; Montclair Univ, grad painting with John Czerkowicz, 1993; Painting Fel, NJ State Coun on Arts, 1993, 2004. *Work:* Pfizer Inc Collection, NY,; Boston Univ, Boston, Mass; Whelan Collection, Washington, DC; Ethyl/New Market Corp Collection, Richmond, Va; Chase Mellon Collection, Jersey City, NJ. *Comn:* Antoine DeLaire, DeLaire, Inc, NY, 1991; Jack Funesti, Am Soc of Perfumers, NY, 1992; Two Views of Trenton (5' x 20' each), State of NJ Dept of Labor, Trenton, NJ, 1998-2000; Newark at Dusk, Arcorp, Newark, NJ, 2000; A Tribute to Dr. Minnefore, St Barnabas Hosp, Dept of Pediatrics, Livingston, NJ, 2006. *Exhib:* Nat Portrait Competition, Portrait Inst, NY, 1996; NJ Mural Proposals, NJ State Gallery/NJ State Mus, Trenton, NJ, 2000-2001; 15E: Contemp Art/NJ Turnpike, Robeson Gallery, Rutgers Univ, Newark, NJ, 2001; Jersey Bound, Tomasulo Gallery, Union Co Col, Cranford, NJ, 2003; NJ: Place of Mind/NJ Arts Ann, Montclair Art Mus, Montclair, NJ, 2005; NJSCA Fel Exhib, NJ State Mus, Trenton, NJ, 2006. *Teaching:* Instr figure drawing, Art Students League, 1992-1993; instr painting, Montclair Art Mus/Yard Sch of Art, 1993-; instr, Somerset Art Asn, 2001-. *Awards:* Exceptional Merit Award, 14th & 21st Ann Metro Shows, City Without Walls Gallery, 1995, 2002; NJSCA Painting Fel, 94 & 2004. *Bibliog:* Dan Bischoff (auth), Asphalt Artery, Star-Ledger, 2001; Dan Bischoff (auth), Terrain Fare, Star-Ledger, 2003; Joshua Rose (auth), Gary Godbee's Panoramas, Am Art Collector Mag, 2006. *Media:* Oil, Drawing Media. *Dealer:* J cacciola Gallery 531 W 25th St NY NY 10001. *Mailing Add:* 210 Washington St Westfield NJ 07090

GODDARD, DONALD
EDITOR, WRITER
b Cortland, NY, Apr 16, 34. *Study:* Princeton Univ, BA, 56. *Pos:* Writer & ed, McGraw-Hill Book Co, New York, 66-69; managing ed, Art News Mag, New York, 74-78, contrib ed, 78- 90; ed, Harry N Abrams Inc, 79-82 & Wildlife Conserv Soc, 82-96. *Mem:* Int Asn Art Critics. *Publ:* Auth, Mark di Suvero: An epic reach, 76 & Rothko's journey into the unknown, 79, Art News Mag; Harry Jackson, Harry N Abrams Inc, 81; Sound-Art, Sound Art Found, 83; Am painting, 90; and others; art rev, newyorkartworld.com, 00. *Mailing Add:* 463 West St New York NY 10014

GODFREY, ROBERT
PAINTER, CRITIC
b Mt Holly, NJ, Apr 17, 41. *Study:* Philadelphia Col Art, BFA, 66; Royal Acad Fine Arts, Copenhagen, post grad, 66-67; Ind Univ, MFA, 69. *Work:* Ind Univ Art Mus, Bloomington; Butler Inst Am Art; Asheville Art Mus; Governor's Collection, State of NC; State Mus Pa; and others. *Comn:* Site Specific Installation, NC Mus Art. *Exhib:* Solo exhibs, Blue Mountain Gallery, NY, 80, 82 & 83, More Gallery, Philadelphia, 80 & 82, Butler Inst Am Art, Youngstown, Ohio, 83 & 92, Zone One Contemp, Asheville, NC, 92, 95 & 97, Galerie En Passant, Hamburg, Ger, 98; group exhibs, Del Art Mus, Ind Univ Mus, Krannert Art Mus, Mint Mus Art, Nat Acad Mus, Queens Mus Art, Reading Pub Mus, State Mus Pa & Southeastern Ctr Contemp Art. *Pos:* Dir, Artists' Choice Mus, New York, 79-80, ed, 80-82; art critic, Asheville Citizen Times, 85-89; ed, CRITS: Discourses on the Visual Arts, 88-93. *Teaching:* Vis artist, Univ Pa, Philadelphia, 79-82; prof art, painting, drawing & art hist, Westminster Col, New Wilmington, Pa, 82-85; head art dept, Western Carolina Univ, Cullowhee, NC, 85-. *Awards:* Drawing Award, Philadelphia Col Art, 66; Fulbright-Hays scholar, Denmark, 66-67; Buhl Found grant, 78. *Bibliog:* William Kelly (auth), Robert Godfrey

(monograph), Arts Mag, 80; Rudy Burckhardt (auth), Poetic Narration (catalog essay), Butle; Chris Redd (auth), Robert Godfrey's Psycological Neo- Expressionism (monograph), Arts J, 88; James Thompson (auth), Recent paintings by Robert Godfrey: Between the dog & the wolf (catalog essay), St John's Mus, NC, 91. *Mem:* Int Asn Art Critics; NC Art Coun; Col Art Asn. *Media:* Oil. *Publ:* Auth, Have museums slighted certain types of art--particularly figurative art?, Am Artists Mag, 79; About sentimentality, 83 & A lesson in still life painting, 84, Artists' Choice Mus J; Civilization, Education and the Visual Arts: A Personal Manifesto, Kappan Mag, 92. *Dealer:* Blue Mountain Gallery 121 Wooster St New York NY 10012; Art Gallery Ltd 502 Pollock St Newbern NC 28560. *Mailing Add:* Downtown Sta PO Box 5 Asheville NC 28802

GODFREY, WINNIE (WINIFRED) M
PAINTER, INSTRUCTOR
b Philadelphia, Pa, Nov 21, 44. *Study:* Marycrest Col, Iowa, 61-63; Art Inst Chicago, 62; Univ Wis, Madison, BS, 66, MFA, 70. *Work:* Ill State Mus, Springfield; Portland Mus, Ore; Rochester Art Ctr, Minn; Hollister Inc, Libertyville, Ill; FMC Corp, Chicago, Ill. *Comn:* Oil painting, State Ill, Danville, 83; oil painting, Oakton Community Col, Ill, 86; oil painting, Marshall Fields, Ill. *Exhib:* Two-person show, Art Inst Chicago Sales Gallery, 81; solo exhib, Chicago Botanic Garden, Glencoe, Ill, 86 & 94, Rahrwest Art Mus, Manitowoc, Wis, 88 & 93; Hot House, John Michael Kohler Art Ctr, Sheboygan, Wis, 89; 20th Century Flower Painting, Mus Art, Ft Lauderdale, Fla, 91; Headley-Whitney Mus, Lexington, Ky, 91; Holland Mus, Mich, 96; and others. *Teaching:* Artist-in-residence drawing & painting, Rochester Art Ctr, Minn, 70; vis lectr drawing, Univ Ill, Chicago, 75-76; instr portraits, Evanston Art Ctr, Ill, 80-85. *Awards:* First Prize, Milwaukee Lakefront, Milwaukee Art Ctr, 75 & 78; Best of Show, Arthur Baer Mem Competition, Beverly Art Ctr, 83; Award of Excellence, Flora Exhib, Chicago Botanic Garden, Glencoe, Ill, 86, 88. *Bibliog:* Richard Waller (auth), article, New York Gallery Guide, 5/82; Jim Hatfield (producer), Two on two, CBS, 84. *Mem:* Artists Equity; Chicago Artists Coalition; North Shore Art League. *Media:* Oil. *Publ:* Auth, article, In: Gallery Guide, Art Now Inc, 82; contribr, The New York Art Review, Macmillan, 82; Illustrators 23, Madison Sq Press, 83; Artists Mag, F&W Publ, 86 & 91; American Painting, Open Press Studios, 95. *Dealer:* Winifred Godfrey 2647 N Orchard Chicago IL 60614. *Mailing Add:* 2647 N Orchard St Chicago IL 60614-1548

GODSEY, GLENN
EDUCATOR, PAINTER
b Amarillo, Tex, June 1, 37. *Study:* Okla State Univ; Univ Tulsa, BA & MA; and with Alexandre Hogue. *Work:* Springfield Art Mus, Mo; Okla State Art Collection, Okla Arts & Humanities Coun, Oklahoma City; Gilcrease Mus, Tulsa. *Comn:* Portrait, Univ Tulsa; portraits, Oral Roberts Univ, The Union Depot & Gilcrease Mus, Tulsa. *Exhib:* One-man shows, Philbrook Art Ctr, Tulsa, 71, Amarillo Art Ctr, 85 & Univ Tulsa, 85; Traveling Exhib of Okla Art, Washington, DC, 76; Saltillo, Mex, 77; two-man show, Univ Tulsa, 78; Am Watercolor, Taipei Fine Arts Mus, Taiwan, 85; Aquarelles Americaines, Tours, France, 86. *Teaching:* Assoc prof painting, Univ Tulsa, 67-. *Awards:* Watercolor USA Purchase Award, SMo Mus Asn, 74; Okla Artist Ann Award, 72 & 74. *Bibliog:* Rev Blakey (auth), Delineating the mysterious, Univ Tulsa Mag; Maurice DeVinna (auth), Music & the arts, Tulsa World Mag, 71; Bill Donaldson (auth), Showcase, Tulsa Tribune, 71. *Mem:* Watercolor USA Hon Soc. *Media:* Acrylic, Watercolor. *Publ:* Auth, Hip generation, Univ Tulsa Mag, 68; illusr, Okla State Univ Lit Quart, Nimrod, Tulsa Mag & Univ Tulsa Mag. *Dealer:* M A Doran Gallery Tulsa OK. *Mailing Add:* Phillips Hall Rm 218 Sch Art Univ Tulsa Tulsa OK 74104

GODWIN, JUDITH
PAINTER
b Suffolk, Va. *Study:* Richmond Prof Inst, Col William & Mary, Va, BFA; Art Students League, with Vaclav Vytlacil, Will Barnet & Harry Sternberg; Hans Hofmann Sch, Provincetown, Mass & New York; Va Commonwealth Univ, Hon DFA, Mary Baldwin Col, Staunton, Va. *Hon Degrees:* Virginia Commonwealth Univ, Hon DFA; Mary Baldwin Col, Hon Doc Humane Letters, VA. *Work:* Metrop Mus, NY; Milwaukee Art Ctr, Wis; San Francisco Mus Mod Art; Nat Mus Art, Osaka, Japan; Yale Univ; Nat Mus Wales, Cardiff; Vassar Col Mus; Va Mus, Richmond; Smith Col Mus; Utah Mus, Salt Lake City; Herbert F Johnson Mus, Cornell Univ; Amarillo Mus Art, Tex; Art Inst of Chicago, Ill; Hirsh Horn Mus and Sculpture Ctr, Washington, DC; and others; Nat Mus Women in the Arts, Washington, DC; NC Mus Art, Raleigh; Newark Mus, NJ; Greenville Co Mus, SC. *Comn:* Painter's Themes (fabric design), Bloomcraft Inc, NY, 76. *Exhib:* One-person shows, Betty Parsons Gallery, 59-60, Ingber Gallery (with catalog), NY, 77, 79, 81-82, 84, 90, 93, 94, 97, Womensbank, Richmond, Va, 81, Phoenix II Gallery, Washington, 83, Marisa del Re Gallery (with catalog), NY, 83, 90 & 92, Northern Mich Univ, Marquette, 84, Mukai Gallery, Tokyo & Lockwood Mathews Mansion Mus, Norwalk, Conn, 85; Mary Baldwin Col, Staunton, VA, 76; Am Fedn Art Traveling exhib, Hans Hofmann as Teacher, 79 & 82; Kenkeleba Gallery, NY, 85; retrospective, Va Polytech Inst, 88, Danville Mus Fine Arts, Va, 89 & Amarillo Mus Art, Tex, 95; Art Mus WVa, 97; Albany Mus Art, Ga; Rutgers Univ, NJ, 2001; Del Ctr for Contemp Art, 2001; Towson Univ, Md, 2002. *Pos:* bd trustees, Mary Baldwin Col, 84-89. *Teaching:* Lectr, May Baldwin Col, VA, 92. *Awards:* Popular Prize, Leache Mem Exhib, Norfolk, 51; Sequicentennial Medal, Mary Baldwin Col, 92; Career Achievement Award, Mary Galdwin Col, Va, 2002. *Bibliog:* Sibella Conner (auth), Judith Godwin responds gradually, Richmond Times-Dispatch, 1/31/93; Robert Hobbs (auth), Judith Godwin, Aesthetic mediations between east and west, Women's Art J, spring-summer, 93; Mark Morey (auth), Judith Godwin: an artist out of time, Amarillo Mus Art, 11/18/95. *Mem:* Am Fedn Arts; Col Art Asn; Women's Caucus Art. *Media:* Oil, Acrylic. *Mailing Add:* c/o Davis 2 Horatio St New York NY 10014

GOEHLICH, JOHN RONALD
EDUCATOR, ADMINISTRATOR
b Chicago, Ill, Sept 29, 34. *Study:* Bard Col, with Louis Schanker, BA, 56. *Pos:* Art dir, Doyle Dane Bernbach Inc, New York, 57-64. *Teaching:* Dean admis, Sch Visual Arts, New York, 66-68; head dept visual commun, Ill Inst Art, Chicago, 69-97. *Awards:* Cert Merit, Art Dirs Club, New York, 63 & 64. *Mailing Add:* 8 Cottage St #4 Newport RI 02840-3212

GOELL, ABBY JANE
PAINTER, ASSEMBLAGE ARTIST, PRINTMAKER
b New York, NY. *Study:* Art Students League, with Harry Sternberg & Charles Alston; Syracuse Univ, BA; NY Sch Interior Design, Cert; Columbia Univ, with Robert Motherwell, Stephen Greene & John Heliker, MFA(painting), 65; Attingham Park, Shropshire, UK, 63; Pratt Graphic Ctr, 65; The Yeats Summer Sch, Sligo, Ireland, 90. *Work:* Mus Mod Art, NY; Yale Univ Art Gallery; Chase Manhattan Bank Collection, NY; Kresge Art Ctr, Mich; Atlantic Richfield Oil Co; Neuberger Mus, Purchase, NY; Print Collection, NY Pub Libr; Smith Col Art Mus; Princeton Univ Art Gallery, Grafisches Kabinet, Munich; Univ Alberta, Can, plus others; Sloane-Kettering Meml Ctr, NY; United Negro Col Fund; Zimmerli Mus, Rutgers Univ, NJ; Newark Pub Libr Print Collection; Loeb Art Mus, Vassar col, Poughkeepsie, NY. *Comn:* Original print, Pratt Graphics Ctr, 75. *Exhib:* Grey Gallery & Study Ctr, NY Univ, 77; Am Acad Arts & Letts, 77; Childe Hassam Purchase Prize Exhib, 77; US Mission, Havana, Cuba, 79-81; Sculpture Ctr, NY, 81; TAGA-PRATT Exhib, Caracas, 82; Silvermine, Conn Ann, 81-82; John Szoke Gallery, NY, 88-89; Southeastern Ohio Cult Ct, 92, Kavehaz Gallery, SoHo, NY, 96; Fotouhi-Cramer Gallery, SoHo, NY, 96, Cooperstown, NY Art Asn Ann, 97. *Pos:* Founder & publ, Arcadia Press, NY. *Teaching:* Instr art hist, Hunter Col, 67; lectr, Lab Inst Merchandising, 67-70. *Awards:* Yaddo Fel, Saratoga Springs, NY, 68; Va Ctr Creative Arts Fel, Sweet Briar, 81; Fondation Samuel Buffat, Geneva, Switz, 97; artist-in-residence, The Banff Ctr for Arts, 2001; CAMAC, Marnay-sur-Seine, France, 2006. *Bibliog:* Archive, Am Mus Women Arts, Washington. *Mem:* Life mem, Art Students League; Women's Caucus Art; sr mem Appraisers Asn Am. *Media:* Acrylic, Oil; Collage, Assemblage, Silk Screens. *Publ:* Ed, English Silver 1675-1825, Ensko & Wenham, revised ed, 80. *Mailing Add:* 37 Washington Sq W New York NY 10011

GOERTZ, AUGUSTUS FREDERICK, III
PAINTER, PHOTOGRAPHER
b Greenwich Village, New York, NY, Aug 15, 48. *Study:* High Sch of Music & Art, New York; Carnegie-Mellon Univ, Pittsburgh, Pa; San Francisco Art Inst, BFA; also with Tom Akawie, Jay Defeo, Augustus Goertz Sr, Wally Hedrick, Bruce Nauman & Jim Rienekin. *Work:* San Francisco Art Inst; Chicago Art Inst; Aldrich Mus Contemp Art, Ridgefield, Conn; Huntington Bank of Ohio; Hyatt Collection, NY; Aetna Casualty & Insurance, Harrison, NY; Siemens Electronics: Shersan Lehman, Chubb Avatav Brokerage. *Exhib:* Selections from The Collection, Aldrich Mus of Contemp Art, 78; Arte Fiera, Bologna, Italy, 78; Todd Capp Gallery, NY; Ruth Bachoffner, Los Angeles; one-man shows, NY Law Sch, 77 & Sarah Rentschler Gallery, 78-85; Are You Experienced, Univ Brussels, Belgium, 81; Somers Gallery, Somerstown, NY; Todd Capp 85-86; The Gallery, Bond St, NY, 90; New-Persona, NY, 90; Patricia Correa, Los Angeles; Robin Rice Photo, NY. *Collection Arranged:* Contemporary Reflections, Aldrich Mus of Contemp Art, Ridgefield, Conn, 73; Encounter, Warren Benedek Gallery, New York, 73. *Pos:* Dir, Art Time Found, NY; consultant, Downtown Ventures, NY; corresp, Viva Mag, Ger, Maire-Claire Mag, German edition. *Awards:* Spec Achievement Award, New York Taxi Drivers, Robert Scull, 65; Honor Student Award, San Francisco Art Inst, 67. *Bibliog:* J Wiessman (auth), article, Art News, 75; Ellen Stern (auth), article, New York Mag, 78; Eleanor Blan (auth), article, New York Times, 80; Ellen Handy (auth), article, Arts Mag, 87. *Mem:* Orgn of Independent Artists; NY WPA Artists Inc; San Francisco Art Inst Alumni Asn. *Media:* Oil, Acrylic; Photo Emulsion. *Publ:* Contribr, New York Art Review, 89; photographs, Viva Magazine, Ger & Bilden Suntag, Ger. *Dealer:* Patricia Correia 1355 Abbot Kinney Blvd Venice Los Angeles CA; Romy Barron 95 Horatio St New York NY 10014. *Mailing Add:* 319 Greenwich St No 2 New York NY 10013-3339

GOETZ, INGVILD
COLLECTOR
Pos: Owner Art In Progress, Art Gallery, Zurich, Germany, 69-71, Munich, 71-84, Sammlung Goetz Mus, 93-2006. *Awards:* Named one of Top 200 Collectors, ARTnews Magazine, 2004-2006; recipient Art Cologne Award, 2001, Munchen Leuchtet Award, 2001. *Collection:* Contemporary art, especially British and Conceptual, arte povera, film & video. *Mailing Add:* Goetz Collection Oberföhringerstrasse 10 Munich 81925 Germany

GOETZ, MARY ANNA
PAINTER, INSTRUCTOR
b Oklahoma City, Okla, Oct 7, 46. *Study:* Okla city Univ, BA, 68; Cape Sch Art, Provincetown, Mass, 69-70; NY Acad Art, New York, 81-82. *Work:* Meyers Gallery State Univ NY, Plattsburgh; Union Pac, Union League Club, White & Case, NY. *Comn:* Landscape of golf course, PGA World Hall of Fame, Pinehurst, NC; View from Olana, Hudson River Club. *Exhib:* solo exhibs, Grand Cent Art Galleries, NY, 91, Newman Galleries, Philadelphia, 86; Collector's Choice, Miss Mus Art, Jackson, 86, 87 & 88; Ann Nat Salon, Springfield Mus Art, Utah, 86 & 87; Brooklyn Bounty: Natural Splendor & Domestic Opulence, Mus Borough Brooklyn, NY, 85; Kirk Patrick Ctr, Okla City, 93; James Cox Gallery, Woodstock, NY, 94-95 & 2002-03; Howell Gallery, Okla City, 2005. *Pos:* Bd mem, Nat Asn Women Artists, 89-. *Teaching:* Instr, landscape & still life painting, Woodstock Sch Art, 91-. *Awards:* Pres Award, Nat Arts Club, 2004. *Bibliog:* Stephen Douherty (auth), Survey of Outdoor Painters, Am Artist, 10/88; Joan D'Arcy (auth), The Richly Diverse Art of Mary Anna

Goetz, Santa Fe Focus, 7/92; Stephen Doherty (auth), Pursuing a Landscape Theme, Am Artist Mag. *Mem:* Nat Arts Club; Salmagundi Club (jury of awards); Nat Asn Women Artists (newsletter ed); Artists Fel; Woodstock Artists Asn. *Media:* Oil. *Publ:* Auth, Robert Shultz: In Memoriam, Portraiture, It's Two Irresistable Forces: Artist & Subject, The Illuminator, 79; Painting Landscapes in Oil, North Light, 91; Impact of Brush Strokes, Am Artist, 92. *Dealer:* James Cox Gallery 4666 Rt 212 Willow NY 12495. *Mailing Add:* 4666 Rte 212 Willow NY 12495

GOETZ, PETER HENRY
PAINTER, LECTURER
b Slavgorod, Russia, Sept 8, 17; Can citizen. *Study:* Waterloo Col, 45; Doon Sch Fine Art, with F H Varley; study watercolor in Japan. *Work:* Queen Elizabeth Collection, Windsor Castle, Eng; London Pub Libr & Art Mus, Ont; Sarnia Pub Libr & Art Mus, Ont; Kitchener Waterloo Art Gallery; Univ Waterloo, Ont; Arnot Art Mus, Elmira, NY; 73 paintings, New City Hall, Waterloo, Ont. *Comn:* Series of twelve paintings from around the world, Waterloo Co Health Bldg, 65; painting of Parliament bldgs, Nat Club, Toronto, 67; Peace Tower, comn by Sen John B Aird, Toronto, 69; painting of Budapest, CFTO-TV, Toronto, 69; View of Prague, Toronto Stock Exchange, 69. *Exhib:* Royal Can Acad; Ont Soc Artists; Can Soc Painters Watercolour; Nat Gallery Ottawa; Am Watercolor Soc, NY, 72. *Teaching:* Lectured and demonstrated adult educ classes throughout Ontario for Dept Educ. *Awards:* Watercolor Prize, Western Ont Exhib; First Prize, Brampton Ann Exhib; Purchase Award, Image 76, Ont Soc Artists, 76; Grand Prize, Que Nat Exhib. *Mem:* Ont Soc Artists; Canada Soc Painters Watercolour; Soc Can Artists; Centro Studi & Scambi Int, Rome; fel Int Inst Arts & Lett; Am Fedn Art. *Media:* Watercolor. *Specialty:* Watercolour paintings. *Interests:* World travel. *Mailing Add:* 784 Avondale Ave Kitchener ON N2M 2W8 Canada

GOETZL, THOMAS MAXWELL
LECTURER, EDUCATOR
b Chicago, Ill, May 31, 43. *Study:* Univ Calif, Berkeley, AB(psychology), 65 & Boalt Hall Sch of Law, JD, 69. *Pos:* Mem bd dir, Calif Lawyers Arts, currently; assoc mem, Nat Conf State Legislatures, Arts Tourism and Cult Resources Comt, currently. *Teaching:* Prof Art Law, Golden Gate Univ, Sch of Law, San Francisco, Calif, 72-. *Mem:* Artists Equity Asn; Calif Lawyers Arts; Calif State Bar. *Publ:* Copyright & the Visual Artists Display Right, A New Doctrinal Analysis, 9 Colum VLA J L & Arts, 84; Kennedy Proposal to Amend the Copyright Law; In Support of the Resale Royalty, 7 Cardozo A & E L J 249, 89; Visual Arts and the Public: A Legislative Agenda for the 1990's, 12 Hast Comm/Ent L J 403, 90. *Mailing Add:* Dept Law Golden Gate Univ 536 Mission St San Francisco CA 94105

GOFFMAN, JUDY GOFFMAN CUTLER
ART DEALER, GALLERY OWNER
Study: Univ Penna, BA, 63, Grad Sch Educ, MS, 64. *Collection Arranged:* Norman Rockwell: An American Tradition, Greenville Co Mus, Greenville, SC, 85-86; A Celebration of American Illustration 1920-1950, C-TEC Corp, Wilkes-Barre, Pa, 87; Norman Rockwell: The Great American Storyteller, Miss Mus Art, Jackson, 88-89; American Illustrators 1880-1950, Parkersburg Art Ctr, Parkersburg WVa, 89; Norman Rockwell In Italy, Cortina d'Ampezzo & Rome, 90; Norman Rockwell in Japan, Tokyo, Osaka, Nagoya, 92; The Great American Illustrators, Odakyu Mus, Tokyo, 93; Maxfield Parrish: A Retrospective, Norman Rockwell Mus at Stockbridge, 95. *Pos:* Guest cur for var travel exhibs of Am illstrs; guest lectr at Miss Mus Art, Lotos Club, Nat Arts Club & Norman Rockwell Mus; found, Nat Mus Am Illustration, Newport, RI; lectr, Nat Arts Club, NY; lectr, Carnegie Abbey Club, Portsmont, RI. *Mem:* Norman Rockwell Mus (Nat Steering Comt); Univ Pa Club of NY; Pa Soc. *Specialty:* Norman Rockwell, Maxfield Parrish, Paintings, drawings & watercolors by important American illustrators of the Golden Age (1890-1950); 19th Century American genre & landscape; early 20th century American Moderns, WPA, Ash-Can & American Impressionists. *Collection:* Golden Age of Great American illustrators, including Norman Rockwell, Maxfield Parrish, NC Wyeth, JC Leyendecker & Howard Chandler Christy. *Publ:* Contribr, Currier's Price Guide to American Artists, 1645-1945 at Auction, 87; auth, Artists as Illustrators: An International Directory with Signatures & Monograms, 1800 to the Present, 89; Maxfield Parrish, Brompton Bks, 93 & 99; Parrish & Poetry, Pomegranate Artbks, 95; Maxfield Parrish: A Retrospective, Pomegranate Artbks, 96; and others. *Mailing Add:* 18 E 77th St No 1A New York NY 10021

GOHEEN, ELLEN ROZANNE
HISTORIAN, CURATOR
b New York, NY, Mar 30, 44. *Study:* Univ Kans, Lawrence, BA & MA. *Collection Arranged:* Masters of 20th Century Photography, 73, American Impressionism, 74, Friends of Art Retrospective, 76, Joseph Cornell, 77, Jasper Johns in Kansas City 1967-1977, 78, Thomas Hart Benton An American Original, 89 & The Drawings of Ralph Barton, 91, Nelson Gallery-Atkins Mus, Kansas City, Mo. *Pos:* From asst cur to assoc cur Europ painting & sculpture, Nelson Gallery-Atkins Mus, 70-75, 20th century art, 75-81, sr lectr, 81-85; coordr, Thomas Hart Benton Proj, 85-89, admin spec exhib & collections mgt, 89-98, dir collections & spec exhibs, 98-99. *Awards:* Sir George Trevelyan Scholar, Attingham Park Summer Sch, Shropshire, Eng, 73. *Mem:* Archaeol Inst Am (pres, Kans Chap, 74-77); Nat Trust Hist Preserv; Soc Archit Historians. *Res:* Twentieth century American and European art, European and American architecture. *Publ:* Contrib, Christo: Wrapped Walk Ways, 79, The Collections of the Nelson-Atkins Mus Art, Abrams, 88; Warren Rosser, Turn and Turn About Kansas City Art Inst, 89. *Mailing Add:* 6135 Overhill Rd Shawnee Mission KS 66208

GOHLKE, FRANK WILLIAM
PHOTOGRAPHER
b Wichita Falls, Tex, Apr 3, 1942. *Study:* Univ Tex, Austin, BA, 64; Yale Univ, New Haven, Conn, MA, 66; pvt study with Paul Caponigro, 67-68. *Work:* Nat Gallery Can, Ottawa, Ont; Australian Nat Gallery, Canberra; Bibliotheque Nationale, Paris, France; Mus Mod Art, NY; Cleveland Mus Art, Ohio. *Comn:* Tex Sesquicentennial (photog survey), comn by Tex Hist Found, Austin, 84; Linea di Confine della Provincia di Reggio Emilia, (photog survey), Italy, 94; Photographs of Lake Erie, George Gund Found, Cleveland, Ohio, 97; Comune di Venezia, Italy: Venezia-Marghera, 98-99; Nat Millenium Survey, Col Santa Fe, NMex, 99-. *Exhib:* Solo exhibs, Int Mus Photog, George Eastman House, Rochester, NY, 74, Amon Carter Mus Western Art, Ft Worth Tex, 75, Mt St Helens: Work in Progress, Mus Mod Art, 83, Landscapes from the Middle of the World, Mus Contemp Photog, Chicago, 88 & Living Water: Photogs of the Sundbury River (with catalog), Mt St Helens; Photog by Frank Gohlke, 81-90; DeCordova Mus, Lincoln Mass, 93; New Topographics: Photographs of a Man-Altered Landscape, Int Mus Photogr, George Eastman House, Rochester, NY, 74; Mirrors & Windows: Am Photog since 1960, Mus Mod Art, NY, 78; An Open Land: Photographs of the Midwest 1852-1982, Art Inst Chicago, Ill, 83; Photog Now, Victoria & Albert Mus, London, 89; Photog Until Now, Mus Mod Art, NY, 92; More Than One Photog, Mus Mod Art, NY, 92; Crossing the Frontier: Photographs of the Developing West, 1849 to the Present, San Francisco Mus Mod Art, 96; Mus Mod Art, New York City, 2005. *Teaching:* Vis lectr, Colo Col, Colorado Springs, 79-88, Mass Col Art, 89-, Yale Univ, 92, Princeton Univ, 95 & Harvard Univ, 96-97. *Awards:* Guggenheim Fel, 75 & 84; Photogr Fel, Nat Endowment Arts, 77 & 86; Artists Fel, Bush Found, St Paul, Minn, 78. *Bibliog:* Robert Silberman (auth), Our town: Tulsa murals, Art Am, 7/85; Vicki Goldberg (auth), What landscapes really mean, Am Photog, 12/88; Ingrid Sischy (auth), Frank Gohlke, The New Yorker, 5/17/92. *Media:* Photography. *Publ:* Landscapes from the Middle of the World (exhib catalog), Friends of Photography, 88; auth, Bare Facts: The Photography of Wright Morris, Hungry Mind Rev, fall 86; Measure of Emptiness: Grain Elevators in the American Landscapes (monograph, with a concluding essay by John C Hudson), John Hopkins Univ Press, 92; Looking for Lee Friedlander, In: Photographs from the Real World (exhib catalogue), Die Norske Bokklubene, Lillehammer, Norway, 93; Linea di Confine Della Provincia di Reggio Emilia: Laboratorio di Fotografia 7 (exhib catalogue), Reggio Emilia, Italy, 95. *Dealer:* Howard Greenberg Gallery, New York, NY,. *Mailing Add:* 2 Bridge St Southborough MA 01772-1962

GOIN, PETER
PHOTOGRAPHER, VIDEO ARTIST
b Madison, Wis, Nov 26, 51. *Study:* Hamline Univ, BA, 73; Univ Iowa, MA, 75, MFA, 76. *Work:* Nat Mus Am Art, Washington, DC; Los Angeles Co Mus Art; San Francisco Mus Mod Art; Amon Carter Mus, Ft Worth, Tex; Minneapolis Inst Art, Minn; Whitney Mus Am Art, NY; Princeton Univ Art Mus; Libr Congress, Washington; numerous pub and private collections. *Exhib:* Picturing Calif, Oakland Mus Art, 89; Baltimore Mus Art, Md, 91, Phoenix Mus Art, Ariz, 92, Mint Mus Art, Charlotte, NC, 92 & Seattle Mus Hist & Indust, Wash, 92; Between Home and Heaven, Nat Mus Am Art, Washington, DC, 91; Wasteland, Fotographie Biennale, Rotterdam, 92; New Orleans Triennial, New Orleans Mus, La, 92; Mus Contemp Art, San Diego, 1993; Atlanta Art Festival, 1993; El Maso Mus Art, 1994; Southeast Mus Photog, 1995; Whitney Mus Am Art, NY, 1996; Princeton Univ Art Mus, 1996; San Francisco Mus Modern Art, 1996; Nev Mus Art, 1998; Univ Ore Mus Art, 1998; Tokyo Met Mus Photog, 2000; Los Angeles Mus Art, 2000; Mus Fine Arts, Houston, 2000; Bienal Int de Fotografia de Cordoba, Spain, 2001; Int Ctr Photog, 2002; Houston Fotofest, 2000; Norsk Mus Fotografi, Orten, Norway, 2003. *Teaching:* Prof art, Univ Nev, 84-94, prof, 94-. *Awards:* Nat Endowment Arts Fels, 82 & 90; Nathan Cummings Grant, 92. *Publ:* Auth, Tracing the Line: A Photographic Survey of the Mexican American Border, 87; Nuclear Landscapes, Johns Hopkins Univ Press, 91; Stopping Time: A Rephotographic Survey of Lake Tahoe, Univ NMex Press, 92; ed, Arid Waters, Univ Nev Press, 92; auth, Humanature, Univ Tex Press, 96; co-auth, A Doubtful River, Univ Nev Press, 2000; Changing Mines in America, Center for Am Places, 2004; Black Rock, Univ of Nevada, Press, 2005. *Mailing Add:* 2365 Crescent Cir Reno NV 89509-3512

GOINGS, RALPH
PAINTER
b Corning, Calif, May 9, 28. *Study:* Calif Col Arts & Crafts, Oakland, BFA, 53; Sacramento State Col, Sacramento, MFA, 65. *Work:* Mus Mod Art, Solomon R Guggenheim Mus, NY; Mus Contemp Art, Chicago; Whitney Mus Am Art, NY; Sheldon Art Mus; and many pvt collections. *Exhib:* One-man exhibs, OK Harris, 70, 73, 77, 80, 83, 85, 88, 91 & 96, Mus Mod Art, NY, 77 & Jason McCoy Gallery, 94; Mus Fine Arts, Boston, MA, 86-87; Butler Inst Am Art, Youngstown, Ohio, 90; Paperwork, Louis K Meisel Gallery, NY, 96; A Survey of Contemp Am Realism, Posco Gallery, Seoul, South Korea, 96; CCAC: Past, Present & Future 1906-1996, Oliver Art Ctr, Calif Col Arts & Crafts, 96; Realism 96, van de Griff Gallery, Santa Fe, NMex, 96; and others. *Pos:* Chmn art dept, La Sierra High Sch, Carmichael, Calif, 59-70. *Teaching:* Instr, Del Norte High Sch, Crescent City, Calif, 55-59, Calif State Univ, Sacramento, 71 & Univ Calif, Davis, 72. *Bibliog:* Patricia C Johnson (auth), Lush watercolor works support artistic visions, Houston Chronicle, 3/27/93; Anastasia Aukeman (auth), Rev, ARTnews, 92; Kevin Lynch (auth), Lush watercolor works support artistic visions, Houston Chronicle, 3/27/93; and others. *Media:* Oil, Watercolor. *Mailing Add:* HCR Box 27 Charlotteville NY 12036

GOLBERT, SANDRA
ARTIST, CRAFTSMAN
b San Juan, Puerto Rico, Nov 9, 37. *Work:* Zimmerli Mus, Rutherford, NJ. *Comn:* Condado Plz Hotel, San Juan, 1987; Pierre Hotel, 1990; Mural, Swissotel, Chicago, 2000. *Exhib:* Paper, Silk & Shadow, InterChurch Ctr, NY, 98; Retrospective, Old Church Cult Ctr, Demarest, NJ, 97; Art From My First 1000 Yrs, Presbyterian Church,

Franklin Lakes, NJ, 1999; 9x9x3 Am Craft Mus, New York City, 98. *Teaching:* instr, Rockland Ctr for the Arts, NY, Old Church Cult Ctr, NJ, The Creative Ctr, NY City. *Awards:* Grant, Nat Endowment for the Arts, 90; Grant, NY Found for the arts, 98; Grant, Pollock-Krasner Found, 91. *Mem:* Surface Design Asn; Salute to Women in Arts. *Media:* Paper, Silk, Fiber. *Publ:* Fiberarts; Surface Design; Vogue. *Mailing Add:* 12 Washington Lane Tappan NY 10983

GOLBIN, ANDREE
PAINTER, EDUCATOR
b Leipzig, Ger, June 4, 23; US citizen. *Study:* Art Students League; Parsons Sch Design; Hans Hofmann Sch Art; New Sch Social Res, Printmaking Workshop. *Work:* Indust Bank Japan; Wako Securities Co, Tokyo, Japan; Eastman Kodak; Klopman Mills; Corcoran Gallery Art, Washington; World Trade Ctr, NY. *Exhib:* Los Angeles Co Mus Art Ann, 49-50; solo exhibs, Camino Gallery, 56 & 58, Roko Gallery, 64, Grand Central Moderns Gallery, 64 & 65, Contemp Arts Gallery, NY Univ, 71 & Grace Gallery, New York City Tech Col, 88; group exhib, Women Choose Women, NY Cult Ctr, 73; Works on Paper, Brooklyn Mus, 75; Noah Goldowsky Gallery, 76; Marymount Manhattan Col, 83; Kenkeleba Gallery, 85; Hudson Guild Gallery, 89. *Pos:* Prom art dir, Mademoiselle Mag, 50-52. *Teaching:* Instr graphic design, Kean Col, NJ, 79-80 & Fashion Inst Technol, 80-81; instr drawing animals on location, Parsons Sch Design, 79-81; instr graphic design, New York City Tech Col, 82-85. *Awards:* Ann Cole Phillips Award, Nat Asn Women Artists, 53; Int Women's Year Award, 76. *Bibliog:* Reviews in Art News, Arts Dig, New York Times, Artforum, 3/73, Nation, 6/25/73; article, Artspeak, 2/16/88. *Mem:* Artists Equity Asn NY; Women's Caucus for Art; Fedn Mod Painters & Sculptors. *Media:* Acrylic, Oil; Watercolor. *Publ:* Illusr, New York Sunday Times gardening section, 74-75 & children's books publ by Lothrop, Lee & Shepard Co, 74, Rand McNally, Grossett & Dunlap

GOLD, LEAH
PAINTER, PRINTMAKER
b New York, NY. *Study:* With Ruth Reeves & Hans Hofmann. *Work:* Butler Inst Am Art; Birmingham Mus Art, Ala; Slater Mem Mus, Norwich, Conn. *Exhib:* Montclair Mus, NJ, 73-75; Tirca Karlis Gallery, Provincetown, Mass, 75-; Fordham Univ at Lincoln Ctr, NY, 75; Nat Art Mus of Sports, NY, 75; Cork Gallery, Lincoln Ctr, NY, 76-. *Awards:* Mrs John T Pratt Prize for Woodcut, Nat Asn Women Artists, 57; Prize for Casein Painting, Painters & Sculptors Soc NJ 18th Ann, 59; Award for Stained Glass Sculpture, Brooklyn Soc Artists, 59. *Mem:* Artists Equity Asn NY (bd dir, 65-); Am Soc Contemp Artists; Metrop Painters & Sculptors, NY (publicity & exhib comt, 72-); Painters & Sculptors Soc NJ. *Media:* Casein, Graphics; Stained Glass, Collages

GOLD, LOIS M
PAINTER
b New York, NY, June 2, 45. *Study:* Boston Univ, BA, 67; Columbia Univ, MA, 70; Nat Acad Design, Marymount Col, 86-89; Art Students League, 86-89. *Work:* Herbert F Johnson Mus Art, Ithaca, NY; Bristol Myers Squibb; Bed Bath & Beyond; Brooklyn Union Gas; Imperial Oil; Canyon Ranch; Boston Univ. *Exhib:* Long Island Landscape: A New Era, Lizan-Tops Gallery, 94 & Long Island Landscape Shows, 95-98; Ruzetti & Grow, NY; one-man Show, Lizan-Tops Gallery, 95-97; Lizan -Tops Gallery, 98-2001; Martha Keats Gallery, Santa Fe, NMex, 98-2001; Rice Gallery, Denver, Colo; Ute Stebich Gallery, Lenox, Mo; Helen Jones Gallery, Sacramento, Calif; Laurel Seth Gallery, Santa Fe; Summa Gallery, NY; Claggett Rey Gallery, Denver; Berkeley Gallery, Scottsdale, Ariz; The Flinn Gallery, Greenwich, Conn, 2005; Quogue Libr, Landscapists on Long Island, Quogue, NY; Nutmeg Gallery, Kent, Conn. *Awards:* Works on Paper, Nat Asn Women Artists, 89; Landscape Awards, Artists Mag, 91 & 93; Juried Scholarship Award, Pastel Soc Am, 94-95; Studio Finalist Award, Artists Mag, 95 & 96; Landscape Award, The Artists Mag, 2000. *Mem:* Cassatt Pastel Soc; Nat Asn Women Artists; Pastel Soc Am; Studio Ctr Artists Asn. *Media:* Pastel. *Collection:* Brooklyn Union Gas; Bristol Myers Squibb; Imperial Oil; Canyon Ranch, Lenox, Mass; Pastelagram, Pastel Artist Int. *Publ:* Pastel Sch, Readers Digest; Painting Shapes and Edges, Readers Digest; Best of Flower Painting, Northlight Books; cover art, Dan's Papers, 99, 2000, 01, 02, 03, 04; Pastel Artist Int, vol 2, 99; Southwest Art, 01; Int Book Art Press, 03; Art reproductions Romm Art; Pure Color, The Best of Pastel, North Light Books, 2006. *Dealer:* Lizan-Tops Gallery 8 E 92nd St New York NY 10128; Martha Keats Gallery 644 Canyon Rd Santa Fe NMex 87501; Ruzetti and Gae 162 E 74 St New York NY 10021; Karin Zatt, Los Angeles, Calif. *Mailing Add:* 45 E End Ave New York NY 10028

GOLD, MARTHA B
SCULPTOR, PAINTER
b New York, NY, Sept 20, 38. *Study:* Univ Rochester; Barnard Col, Columbia Univ, BA; Columbia Univ, MA; Nat Acad Sch Fine Arts, cert; Art Students League. *Exhib:* NAm Sculpture Ann, Foothills Art Ctr, Golden, Colo, 80, 83 & 88; Allied Artists Am, Am Acad Inst Arts & Letts, 80, Audubon Artists Ann, Nat Arts Club, 81 & Nat Sculpture Soc Ann, Equitable Life Insurance Bldg, 81, NY; Philadelphia Tricentennial, 82; solo shows, Ward-Nasse Gallery, 87, 89 & 90. *Teaching:* Privately. *Awards:* Mem Award, Audubon Artists, 79; Youth Award, Nat Sculpture Soc, 79 & 80; Gold Medal Hon, Allied Artists Am, 80 & 83; Foondry Award, NAm Sculpture Exhib. *Bibliog:* Article, Nat Sculpture Rev, 80, Sculpture Mag, 87, Manhattan Arts, 87, NY Art Review, 89, Arte el dia, Argentina, 89. *Mem:* Allied Artists Am; Nat Asn Women Artists; Artists Equity. *Media:* Bronze, Clay; Ink, Oil. *Dealer:* Ward-nasse Gallery Prince St New York NY. *Mailing Add:* 315 E 91st St New York NY 10128

GOLD, SHARON CECILE
PAINTER, EDUCATOR
b Bronx, NY, Feb 28, 49. *Study:* Hunter Col, City Univ of NY, 68; Columbia Univ, 69-70; Pratt Inst, BFA, 76. *Work:* McCrory Corp, Chase Manhattan Bank, Norsearch Indust & Chemical Bank, NY; Prudential Insurance Co Am, NJ; Best Products, Inc, Va; Rose Art Mus, Brandeis Univ, Mass; Southeast Bank, Fla, Everson Mus, Syracuse, NY. *Comn:* Painting on aluminum & fiberglass, Humbolt-Hospital Station, Niagara Frontier Transportation Authority, Buffalo, NY, 82-84. *Exhib:* Works on Paper, Mus Mod Art, Art Lending Serv, NY, 81; solo exhibs, Galerie Michael Storrer, Zurich, Switz, 81, John Davis Gallery, Akron, Ohio, 86, Stephen Rosenberg Gallery, NY, 87, 89, 91; Tyler & Penrose Galleries, Tyler Sch Art, Philadelphia, 83; Summer Show, GH Dalsheimer Gallery, Baltimore, Md, 88; Four-person Group exhib, Stephen Rosenberg Gallery, NY, 88; Painting Beyond the Death of Painting, Kuznetsky Most Exhib Hall, Moscow, USSR, 89; The Image of Abstract Painting in the 80's, Rose Art Mus, Brandeis Univ, Waltham, Mass, 90; and many others. *Pos:* Assoc ed, Re-View Mag, NY, 77-. *Teaching:* Lectr, Princeton Univ, 79-80; NY Univ, 83; vis assoc prof, Univ Tex, San Antonio, 80 & Syracuse Univ, 80-81; vis prof, Va Commonwealth Univ, 82; adj prof, NY Univ, 83; assoc prof painting & critical theory, Syracuse Univ, 85-. *Awards:* MacDowell Colony Fel; Nat Endowment Arts Painting Fel, 81-82; Distinguished Artist Award Lifetime Achievement. *Bibliog:* Joseph Masheck (auth), Sharon Gold, Arts Mag, 10/87; Stephen Westfall (auth), Review, Art in America, 1/88; and others. *Mem:* Col Art Asn Comt (chair, 89). *Media:* Oil. *Publ:* Contribr, reviews in Artforum, 77; auth, Statement, Re-View Mag, 79; The Texas Paintings-Modernism: Forms and Concepts, Univ Tex Press (in prep); auth, Statement, Forum, 89. *Mailing Add:* 10 Leonard St New York NY 10013

GOLDBERG, ARNOLD HERBERT
PAINTER, PRINTMAKER
b Brooklyn, NY, May 16, 33. *Study:* Univ Wis, BS(appl arts), 55; Pratt Inst, BArch, 59; Univ Houston, painting, 70-72. *Exhib:* Twelfth Midwest Biennial, Joselyn Mus, Omaha, Nebr, 72; 17th Ann Delta Art Exhib, Ark Art Ctr, 74; 16th Ann Eight State Exhib, Okla Art Ctr, 74; 52nd Exhib, Shreveport Art Guild, 74; Corpus Christi Art Found Ann Exhib, Art Mus STex, 75; Corpus Christi Art Found Ann Exhib, Art Mus STex, 77. *Teaching:* Instr desktop publ, Houston Community Col, 87-. *Awards:* Dimension VI Award, Art League Houston, 71; Eighth Jury Award Art Exhib, Jewish Community Ctr, Houston, 72; Corpus Christi Art Found Grant, Art Mus STex, 75 & 77. *Media:* Acrylic; Silkscreen. *Mailing Add:* 425 White Wing Ln Houston TX 77079-6828

GOLDBERG, GLENN
PAINTER
b Bronx, NY, Aug 31, 53. *Study:* Queens Col, MFA. *Work:* Mus Mod Art, Metrop Mus Art, NY; The Brooklyn Mus; High Mus Art, Atlanta, Ga; Mus Contemp Art, Los Angeles; Nat Gallery Art, Washington. *Exhib:* One-man shows, Willard Gallery, NY, 85, Dart Gallery, Chicago, Ill, 86, Albany Mus Art, Albany, Ga, 89, Knoedler & Co, NY, 94 & 96, Galerie Albrecht, Munich, Ger, 94, Addison/Ripley Fine Art, Washington, 95 & Grand Arts, Kansas City, Mo, 95; retrospectives, Green Gallery (with catalog), St Louis, Mo, 90, Hill Gallery, Birmingham, Mich, 90, Knoedler & Co Inc, NY, 91 & 92, David Beitzel Gallery, NY, 92; Wacko, The Work Space, NY, 95; Galerie Albrecht, Munich, Ger, 95; Edward Hopper House, Nyack, NY, 95. *Teaching:* Fac, NY Studio Sch, 86-, Chautauqua Inst, NY, 91-93, Vt Studio Ctr, 93 & Parsons MFA Prog, NY, 93-94. *Awards:* Guggenheim Fel, 88-89, Nat Endowment Arts, 89. *Bibliog:* Marsha Miro (auth), Painter's work presents studies in contradiction, Detroit-free Press, 3/24/93; Jeff Wright (auth), Moving images: paintings that appear to have a life of their own, Cover, 3/94; Alice Thorson (auth), Space may look like a million, but exhibit is only average, Kansas City Star, 5/3/95. *Mailing Add:* 1819 Grand Blvd Kansas City MO 64108

GOLDBERG, IRA A
ARTIST
b Queens, NY, Sept 27, 55. *Work:* The Art Students League of NY. *Exhib:* Nat Acad of Design Ann Exhib, 96. *Pos:* Exec Dir, The Art Students League of NY, 01-. *Awards:* Best Still-Life, Nat Acad, 96. *Mailing Add:* c/o Art Students League of NY 215 W 57th St New York NY 10019

GOLDBERG, JIM
PHOTOGRAPHER
b New Haven, Conn, June 3, 53. *Study:* Western Washington Univ, BA, 75; San Francisco Art Inst, MFA(photog), 79. *Work:* Akron Art Mus, Ohio; Baltimore Mus Mod Art, Md; Boston Mus Fine Arts, Mass; Addison Gallery Am Art, Andover, Mass; High Mus Art, Atlanta, Ga; Libr of Congress, Washington, DC; Mus Mod Art, NY; San Francisco Mus Mod Art, Calif; Los Angeles Co Mus of Art; Whitney Mus of Art, NY; J Paul Getty Mus, Los Angeles. *Comn:* Photographs (16), Neville Manor Nursing Home, comn by Cambridge Arts Coun, Mass, 87; Market Street Art-in-Transit, San Francisco, San Francisco Arts Comn, 92; Margaret Jenkins Dance Co & World Studio Found: Help Kids Create, 99. *Exhib:* Photographs (with catalog), 79, Photographs from the Theo Jung Collection, 79, Form, Freud and Feeling, 82-83 & Bay Area Collects, 83, San Francisco Mus Mod Art; Photographs from the Mus Collection, Seattle Art Mus, Wash, 84; Photog in California: 1945-1980 (traveling, with catalog), San Francisco Mus Mod Art, 84; Three Americans, Mus Mod Art, NY, 84; Extending the Perimeters of 20th Century Photog (with catalog), San Francisco Mus Mod Art, 85; solo exhibs, Washington Proj for Arts, Washington, DC, 88 & 90, Univ Tex Health Sci Ctr, Houston, 89, Capp Street Proj, 89, Creative Time, NY, 90, Art in General, NY, 91 & Raised by Wolves, Corcoran Gallery Art, 95, Addison Gallery Am Art, 96, Los Angeles Co Mus Art, 97 & San Francisco Mus Art, 97; The Instant Likeness: Polariod Portraits, Nat Portrait Gallery, Washington, DC, 88; Recent Acquisitions, Nat Mus Am Art, Smithsonian Inst, 88; Rethinking Am Myths (traveling), Laurence Miller Gallery, NY, 88-89; IV Fotobienal-90 (with catalog), Vigo, Spain, 90; Who's Looking at the Family? (with catalog), Barbican Art Gallery, London, Eng, 94; The Class, Zurich Mus of Design, Switz, 97; Years Ending in Nine, Mus of Fine Arts, Houston, 98; Hospice: A Photog Inquiry (traveling, catalog), 96-2001; Made in California, Los Angeles Co Mus of Art, 2000; Am Perspectives: Photographs from the Polaroid

Collection, Tokyo Metrop Mus of Photog, 2000; and others. *Teaching:* Asst prof, Univ Mass, Boston, 84-85; instr, Univ Calif, San Francisco, 80-84, vis instr, 91; undergrad instr, Univ Calif, Davis, 97-99; grad, undergrad & tutorial instr, Calif Col Arts & Crafts, 88-, San Francisco Art Inst, 88-. *Awards:* Glen Eagles Found Grant, 92; The Highland Award, 94; Roberts Found Grant, 94; Ernst Haas Award for Photography Book of Yr, 95; Eureka Fel, 96; Wallace A Gerbode Found Grant, 97. *Bibliog:* David Bonetti (auth), How could the artists have survived this?, San Francisco Examiner, 7/18/97; Tessa DeCarlo (auth), Life on the streets, The Wall Street J, 8/22/97; Christopher Millis (auth), Truth or dare, The Boston Phoenix, 2000. *Publ:* Auth, Rich & Poor, Random House, 89, Raised by Wolves, Scalo Publ, 95, (in collaboration with Nan Goldin, Sally Mann, Jack Radcliffe & Kathy Vargas) Hospice: A Photographic Inquiry, Bulfinch, 96; co-auth (with Tom Bonauro), Sublime Intent, 88; contribr to numerous anthologies, catalogues & portfolios. *Dealer:* Pace/MacGill Gallery 32 E 57th St New York City 10022. *Mailing Add:* 32 E 57th St New York NY 10022

GOLDBERG, JUDITH
ART DEALER
b New York, NY. *Study:* City Col New York, BA, 71. *Pos:* Owner, Judith Goldberg Gallery, currently. *Specialty:* 19th and 20th century prints & drawings. *Mailing Add:* Grand Central PO Box 2020 New York NY 10163

GOLDBERG, MICHAEL
PAINTER
b New York, NY, Dec 24, 24. *Study:* Studies with Hans Hofmann, 40-42, 48-50; Art Students League, New York, 46-47. *Work:* Walker Art Ctr, Minneapolis, Minn; Albright-Knox Gallery, Solomon R Guggenheim Mus, Whitney Mus Art, NY; Baltimore Mus Art, Md; Corcoran Gallery, Hirshhorn Mus, Washington, DC; Wadsworth Atheneum, Hartford, Conn; and many others. *Exhib:* Whitney Mus Am Art, 58, 65, 67 & 73; Walker Art Ctr, 60; Mus Mod Art, NY, 63, 68, 74 & 78; Corcoran Biennial, 69, 77 & 98; Albright-Knox Art Gallery, Buffalo, NY, 85; solo exhibs, Gallery Weinberger, Copenhagen, Denmark, 90, 92 & 97, Lennon, Weinburg, NY, 90, 96, 99, 02, Compass-Rose, Chicago, 90, La Memoria dell' antico pittura e scultura a Venzone, Udine, 91, Lauter, Manheim, 91, Torchetto/Plurima, Milano, Italy, 91, Jason McCoy Inc, NY, 91, Galeria Plurima, Udine, Italy, 82, 84, 90, 96, 99, 01, Galerie Biedermann, Munich, 91, 96, 97, 00, Galeria Mirali, Viterbo, Italy, 00, Galleria Peccolo, Livorno, Italy, 01, Thomas McCormick Gallery, Chicago, 02, Manny Silverman Gallery, Los Angeles, 02; The Art of Abstract Painting, Gallery Camino Real, Boca Raton, Fla, 87; Bette Stoller Gallery, NY, 87; Vanderwoude Tananbaum Gallery, NY, 87, 89 & 91; Lennon, Weinberg Inc, NY, 90 & 91; Manny Silverman Gallery, Los Angeles, Calif, 91; Sch Visual Arts, NY, 97; Ark Arts Ctr, Little Rock, 98; Ft Wayne (Ind) Mus of Arts, 99, Joslyn Art Mus, Omaha, Nebr, Kalamazoo (Mich) Inst of Arts, 99-00; Mus Contemp Art, Los Angeles, 99; Grey Art Gallery, NY Univ, 2000; Worcester Art Mus, Mass, 2001-03; Yellowstone Art Mus, Billings, Mont, 2002; and many others. *Collection Arranged:* Albright-Knox Art Gallery, Buffalo, NY; Art Inst Chicago; Baltimore Mus Art; Cleveland Mus Art; Corcoran Gallery Art, Washington, DC; Mus Fine Arts, Houston; Mus Mod Art, Jerusalem; Mus Mod Art; Mus Mod Western Art, Tokyo; Philadelphia Mus Art; San Francisco Mus Mod Art; Walker Art Ctr, Minneapolis; Whitney Mus Am Art, NYC. *Teaching:* Instr art, Univ Calif, Berkeley, 61-62; Yale Univ, 67; Univ Minn, 68, Sch Visual Arts, New York, 79-. *Bibliog:* Irving Sandler (auth), The New York School: The Painters & Sculptors of the Fifties, Harper & Row, 78; John Johnston (auth), Michael Goldberg's new paintings, Artforum, summer 79; V Tatransky (auth), Arts Mag (rev), 5/79; David Shapiro (auth. with others) Michael Goldberg: Goldberg Variations, Italy, Primaprint, Viterbo, 97. *Publ:* Auth, The canvas plane, or onwards and upwards, It Is, spring 58; Michael Goldberg: Anima (Soul), 02. *Dealer:* Lennon-Weinberg Gallery 580 Broadway New York NY 10012. *Mailing Add:* 222 Bowery New York NY 10012

GOLDBERG, NORMA
SCULPTOR
b New York, NY. *Study:* Sculpture instruction with Victor Trapote, 66-68; sculpture instruction with Carma Anderson, Pat Foley & Abraham Gonzalez, 68-70. *Work:* Tel-Hashomer Hosp, Tel Aviv, Israel; Mus Nat de Art, Punta del Este-Montevideo, Uruguay; Medley Distilling Co, Chicago; Int Mex-Israeli, Mex. *Comn:* Golfer, Club de Golf Bellavista, Calacoaya, Mex, 74. *Exhib:* Int Art Fair, Tel-Aviv, Israel, 77; Retrospective del Arte Judeo-Mex, Moltibanco Mercantil por Bnai Brit, Mex, 85; Lillian Heidenberg Gallery, NY, 86; Art Expo, Arte de Mex, 88; Subasta de Arte, David Alfaro Siquieros, Mex, 90; and others. *Awards:* Art Show Second Place, Acapulco, Mex, 78; Dipl of Outstanding Merits, Ash Kenazi Community Mex, 91. *Bibliog:* Lilly Kassner (auth), Diccionario de la escultura Mex Sigloxx, Univ Aut de Mex, 84; Art Diary Int, Giancarlo Politi Editore, 92. *Media:* Metal, Stone. *Publ:* Contribr, Norma Goldberg, The News, 84; Norma Goldberg en torno al ser humano y su problematica, Endiciones Tiempos Modernos, 85; Norma Goldberg and the human presence, Novedades, 85; A Sculptress of Omnipresent Quality, Arte de Mex, 87; Arte Y Artistas, Ignacio Flores Antunez, 89. *Dealer:* Galeria Aura Amberes 38PB Col Juarez 06600 Mexico. *Mailing Add:* Monte Bianco 115-101 Lomas de Chapultepec Mexico #11000 Mexico

GOLDBERG, ROSELEE
HISTORIAN, CURATOR
b Durban, SAfrica; UK citizen. *Study:* Rand Univ, BFA, 68; Courtauld Inst Art, London, with John Golding, MA(art hist), 70. *Collection Arranged:* Record as Artwork, Royal Col Art Gallery, 73; Piero Manzoni, Royal Col Art Gallery, 74; IMPORTS (int performance series), Kitchen Ctr, 78 & 79; Mus Mod Art performance series, 90. *Pos:* Dir, Royal Col Art Gallery, London, 72-75; cur, The Kitchen Ctr, New York, 78-80; Founding Dir, Performa Inc, (nonprofit org) for the research, development and presentation of new visual art performance, 2004. *Teaching:* Lectr performance hist, Archit Asn London, 77-78, Sch Visual Arts, New York, 79-82 & New York Univ, 88. *Awards:* Publ Award, Arts Coun Gt Brit, 75; Nat Endowment for Arts Art Critic's grant, 79; Chevalier of Order Arts & Letters, French Minister of Culture. *Mem:* Int Asn Art Critics; Col Art Asn; Nat Union Journalists, UK; PEN Am Ctr. *Res:* Thesis on Oskar Schlemmer and performance at the Bauhaus; specialist in history of performance art and related contemporary media. *Publ:* Ed & contribr, special issue, Studio Int on Archit-Art, 75 & Performance Studio Int, 76; contribr, Oskar Schlemmer's performance art, Artforum, 77; Performance: a Hidden History, In: Battcock's Anthology, Dutton, 80; auth, Performance Art: Form Futurism to the Present (rev ed), Abrams, 88; Performance: Live Art Since 1960, Abrams, 98; Laurie Anderson, Abrams, 2000. *Mailing Add:* 327 E 18th St New York NY 10003-2802

GOLDBERGER, PAUL JESSE
CRITIC, WRITER, EDUCATOR, EDITOR
b Passaic, NJ, Dec 4, 50. *Study:* Yale Univ, BA, 72. *Hon Degrees:* Pratt Inst, LHD, 92; Ctr Creative Studies, LHD; NY Sch Interior Design, Hon Dr. *Pos:* Staff ed, The New York Times Mag, New York City, 72-73; archit critic, The New York Times, 73—; ed cult news, 90-94, chief cult corr, 94-95, freelance contribr, 1995—; archit critic, Sly Line Column The NY, 1997—; dean, Parsons Sch Design, 2004—. *Awards:* Roger Starr Journalism award Citizens Housing & Planning Coun, 87; Medal of Honor, NY Landmarks Preservation Found, 91; Preserv Achievement Award, New York City Landmarks Preserv Comn, 96. *Mem:* Soc Archit Historians (bd dir, 77-79); Am Inst of Archits. *Publ:* auth, The Skyscraper, 81; auth, On the Rise: Archit & Design in a Post-Modern Age, 83; auth, The World Trade Ctr Remembered, 2001; auth, Up From Ground Zero, 2004; contribr, articles and essays to prof publs. *Mailing Add:* NY Times 2219 W 43rd St New York NY 10036-3959

GOLDEEN, DOROTHY A
DEALER, CONSULTANT
b San Francisco, Calif, Nov 12, 48. *Study:* Univ Calif, Berkeley, BA (sculpture & design), 72. *Pos:* Dir, Hansen Fuller Gallery, 72-79; vpres, Hansen Fuller Goldeen Gallery, 79-82; principle, Fuller Goldeen Gallery, 82-87; pres, Dorothy Goldeen Gallery, Santa Monica, 87-96 & Dorothy Goldeen Art Advisory, 96-. *Teaching:* Instr, Contemp Art Gallery, Col Marin, 75; frequent lectr for mus & univs; Otis Col Art & Design, 97 & 98. *Mem:* San Francisco Art Dealers Asn (prog dir assoc); Santa Monica-Venice Art Dealers Asn (vpres 87-88, pres, 88, 90-); Mus Contemp Art, Los Angeles (cur coun, 90-92); Art Table Women, Los Angeles (chair 92-94). *Specialty:* Contemporary painting, sculpture and works on paper. *Publ:* Auth, California Gold, US Embassy (traveling exhib catalog), beginning Brussels, 75; Joan Brown, Univ Adron, Ohio (traveling exhib catalog); American Eight, Interspace Corp NJ (traveling exhib catalog), 80; American Eight (catalog essay), Interpace Corp, NJ, 80; and others

GOLDEN, EUNICE
PAINTER, FILMMAKER
b New York, NY. *Study:* Univ Wis; Brooklyn Col, MFA; New Sch Social Res; Art Students League; Empire State Col, BFA. *Work:* Hudson River Mus, Yonkers, NY; New York City Dept Parks & Recreation; Bronx Community Col, NY; Mus Mod Art, Whitney Mus & Guggenheim Mus, NY. *Comn:* Portrait of Poet Leon Herald, comn by Leon Herald, 71; murals, Dept of Parks & Recreation, NY, Dept of Cult Affairs, NY & Bronx Mus of Art; Bronx Community Col. *Exhib:* Palacio de Las Bellas Art, Mexico City, 72; Allan Stone Gallery, NY, 73; Nat Acad Design, NY, 73; Indianapolis Mus, Ind, 74; Bronx Mus Art, NY, 75; Works on Paper, Brooklyn Mus, NY, 75; Film exhib, Anthology Arch, 77; Whitney Mus Am Art, NY, 77; film exhib, Gemeente Mus, The Hague, The Neth, 79; Artists Space, NY, 83; Long Beach Mus, Calif, 85; Hudson Ctr Galleries, 86; Committed to Print Traveling Exhib, Mus Mod Art, 88-89; Guild Hall Mus, Easthampton, NY, 91-98, 2002; Sniper's Nest, Bard Col Ctr Cur Studies (traveling), 95-97; Mus Fine Art, Santa Fe, NMex, 97, 2002-03; one-person exhib, Mitchell Algus Gallery, New York City, 2003. *Collection Arranged:* Hudson River Mus, NY; Bronx Mus of Art, NYC; Mus of Fine Arts, Santa Fe. *Pos:* Dir, Walk-On Community Art Proj, Dobbs Ferry, NY, 68; dir, Westbeth Gallery I, NY, 80-82. *Teaching:* Lectr erotic art, New Sch Social Res, 73; instr mural painting, Guggenheim Mus Prog, NY, summer 75; instr painting, Pratt Inst, 80-81; artist-in-residence, Univ SDak, 76 & Cooper Union, 84. *Awards:* Purchase Award, Hudson River Mus, 63; One of Outstanding Women, NY State Women's Unit Exec Chamber, Albany, 68; MacDowell Colony Fel, 69 & 71; Award, Archives Am Art, Smithsonian Inst, Washington; Grant, NY Found for the Arts, 75; Medal of Honor, Veteran Feminiots of Am, 2003. *Bibliog:* Lucy Lippard (auth), From the Center, Feminist Essays on Women's Art, Dutton, 76 & Art in Am, 11/81; Carter Ratcliff (auth), Art Int, 3/77; Lucy Lippard (auth), Overlay, Random House, 83; Judith Fryer Davidov (auth), Women's Camera Work, Duke Univ Press, 97; Holland Cotter, NY Times, 2003. *Mem:* Fel MacDowell Colony; Col Art Asn Am; Women's Caucus Art. *Media:* Oil, Acrylic. *Publ:* Illusr, Ms Mag, 75; auth, article, Art Workers News, New York, 76; coauth, article, An Anti-Catalog, 77; auth, The male nude in womens art, Heresies, spring 81; and others. *Dealer:* Mitchell Algus Gallery, NYC. *Mailing Add:* 463 West St Apt 332B New York NY 10014

GOLDEN, HAL
PAINTER, CONSERVATOR
b Brooklyn, NY, Dec 10, 1925. *Study:* WPA Art classes, Brooklyn, NY, 1939-40; NY Sch of Industrial Art/Sch of Art & Design NY, 1941-1943; The Art Students League, NY, with Ivan Olinsky Vladimir Lebedev & Rolph Scarlett, 45-46,. *Work:* (Conserv) Putnam Co Mus of Art, Cold Spring, NY; (Conserv) NY Med Col (collection, 19th century paintings), Valhalla, NY; (Conserv) Abby Aldrich Rockefeller Folk Art Mus, Williamsburg, Va. *Comn:* Painting, landscape, Dr N Bruno, Providence, RI; Paintings, portraits, D Waldron, Providence, RI, 2003-2005; Painting, estate, W Slocum, Barrington, RI, 2004; Painting, portrait, C Little, Providence, RI, 2006; Painting,

landscape, M Lyle, Madison, Conn, 2006. *Exhib:* Nat Marine Art Show, Stamford Art Asn, Stamford, CT, 1999; East Southeast Regional, Oil Painters of Am Brazier Fine Art, Richmond, Va, 2002; 74th Grand Nat Exhib, Am Artists Prof League, NY, 2002; Open Non-Mem Juried Exhib, Salmagundi Club, NY, 2003-2004; Nat Open Exhib, Community Arts Asn, Ridgewood, NJ, 2003-2005; two person show, Providence Art Club, 2000 & 2005. *Pos:* Art Dir, numerous Ad Agencies. *Teaching:* New Sch Univ, New York City, pvt students. *Awards:* Certificate of Excellence (Int Poster Competition, Latham Found, 1951; Louis Kuriansky Found Award, (Stanley & Vivian Reed Nat Marine Art Show), Stamford, Conn, Art Asn, 1999. *Bibliog:* Providence (RI) Journal; E Side Monthly, Providence, RI; The Advocate and Greenwich Time, Greenwich, Conn; Sun Chronicle, Attle Boro, Mass. *Mem:* Oil Painters of Am (Exhibiting Artist); Am Artists Prof League (Exhibiting Artist); Am Inst for Conserv of Hist & Artist Works (Assoc); Providence Art Club (Exhibiting Artist). *Media:* Oil. *Mailing Add:* 500 Angell St Apt 308 Providence RI 02906

GOLDEN, JUDITH GREENE
PHOTOGRAPHER, MIX MEDIA

b Chicago, Ill, Nov 29, 1934. *Study:* Art Inst Chicago, BFA, 73; Univ Calif, Davis, MFA (Regents Graduate Fel), 75. *Hon Degrees:* Moore Col Art, Philadelphia, Pa, Hon PhD, 90. *Exhib:* One-person show, San Francisco Mus Mod Art, Calif, 81, Mus Photog Arts, San Diego, 86, Tucson Mus Art, 87, Visual Arts Ctr, Anchorage, Alaska, 90, Scottsdale Ctr Arts, Scottsdale, Ariz, 93, Arte de Oaxaca, Mex, 95, Columbia Ctr Arts, Dallas, Tex, 97, Temple Mus Art, Tuscon, Ariz, 97 & Univ Arts, Philadelphia, Pa, 2002; Temple Music & Art, 2005; group exhib, Silver & Ink, Oakland Mus, Calif, 78; Attitudes-Photog in the 70's, Santa Barbara Mus Art, Calif, 79; Geo Pompidou, Paris, 81; Extending the Perimeters of 20th Century Photog & PhotogFacets of Modernism, San Francisco Mus Mod Art, 86; Photog and Art, Los Angeles Co Mus Art, Calif, 87; Selections 5: From the Polaroid Collection, Traveled Europe/US, 90-94; Self Portraits of Contemp Women: Exploring the Self, Tokyo Metrop Mus Photog, 91; Photog Book Arts in the US Today Traveling Exhib, Univ Tex, San Antonio, 91-94; Proff: Los Angeles Art & the Photog 1960-1980 Traveling Exhib, Laguna Art Mus, Laguna Beach, Calif, 92-94; Art of This Century: 30th Anniversary 1963-93, Univ Art Mus, Univ NMex, Albuquerque, 93; The Irmas Collection of Photog Self Portraits, Los Angeles Co Mus Art, 94; Hist Women Photogrs, NY Pub Libr, 96; The Painted Photograph: Hand Colored Photog, 1830-present (traveling exhib), Univ Wyo Art Mus; History of Women Photographers (traveling exhib), Santa Barbara Mus Art, Calif & Akron Art Mus, Ohio; Our Quarter Century, Ctr Creative Photog, Univ Ariz, Tucson, 2000; Idea Photog: After Modernism, Mus Fine Arts, Santa Fe, NMex, 2002; Los Angeles Co Mus Art, 2003; Ctr for Creative Photo, 2004; Santa Barbara Mus Art, 2005. *Pos:* Bd mem, Los Angeles Ctr Photog Studies, Calif, 77-79 & Camera Work, San Francisco, Calif, 81. *Teaching:* Vis lectr photog, Univ Calif, Los Angeles, 75-79 & Univ Calif, Davis, 80; assoc prof photog, Univ Ariz, Tucson, 81-89, prof, 89-96, emer prof, 96-. *Awards:* Nat Endowment Arts Individual Photogrs Fel, 79; Photog Fel, Ariz Comn on Arts, 84; Individual Artists' Fel, Tucson/Pima Arts Coun, 87. *Bibliog:* Claire VC Peeps (auth), Cycles: A Decade of Photographs by Judith Golden, Friends of Photog, 88; Naomi Rosenblum (auth), The History of Women Photographers, 94; Robert Hirsch (auth), Seizing The Light: A History of Photography, 2000. *Mem:* Soc Photog Educ; Women's Caucus Arts; Friends of Photog; Camera Work. *Media:* Collage, Mixed Media, Photography. *Collection:* Oakland Mus of Art, CA; Denver Art Mus, CO; Fogg Mus, Cambridge, MA; Mus Photog Art, San Diego, CA; Art Inst Chicago & Mus Contemp Photog, Chicago; Mus Contemp Art, Los Angeles; Los Angeles County Mus Art, Los Angeles, CA; Tokyo Metro Mus Photography; Newport Harbor Mus, Newport Beach, CA; Seattle Art Mus, WA; and others

GOLDEN, ROLLAND HARVE
PAINTER, PRINTMAKER

b New Orleans, La, Nov 8, 31. *Study:* John McCrady Art Sch, studied with John McCrady. *Work:* Pushkin Mus, USSR; Masur Mus; New Orleans Mus Art; Miss Mus Art; Springfield Mus Art; Ogden Mus of Southern Art; Alexander Mus Art. *Comn:* Fifty watercolors, La State Hwy Dept, Baton Rouge, 59-60; four watercolors, comn by Gov John McKeithen, La, 65; mural, Furash & Co, 88. *Exhib:* Seven Am Watercolor Soc Exhibs, NY, 65-78; Watercolor USA, Springfield, 66-03; Butler Inst Am Art, Youngstown, Ohio, 67-78; Nat Arts Club, NY, 68 & 72-03; Nat Soc Painters in Casein & Acrylics, NY, 72-88; one-man shows, touring USSR, Moscow, Kiev, Leningrad, Odessa & Southern France, 93-94 & over 100 one-man shows in USA. *Pos:* Vpres, Watercolor USA Honor Soc, formerly; adv bd, Watercolor Mag. *Awards:* Eleven Awards, Nat Arts Club, NY; Seven Awards including Thomas Hart Benton, Watercolor USA; Five Awards, Rocky Mountain; Six Awards, Nat Watercolor Soc. *Bibliog:* John R Kemp (auth), Rolland Golden, The Journeys of a Southern Artist, Pelican Publ Co; Don Lee Keith (auth), Golden boy of watercolor, Delta Rev Mag, 68 & World of Rolland Golden, Royal Publ Co, 70; Jim Keyser (auth), Rolland Golden's Southland, WDSU TV, 73; Mel Leavitt (auth), First Person, 86. *Mem:* Nat Watercolor Soc; Nat Arts Club; Allied Artists Am; Watercolor USA Hon Soc (vpres, formerly); hon mem La Watercolor; Rocky Mt Nat Watermedia; Watercolor West. *Media:* Watercolor, Oil; Lithography. *Publ:* article in Louisiana Life Mag, 82 & 03; article in Miss Mag, 5/86; auth, Palette Talk Mag, 5-6/87 & 9-10/88; articles in Int Fine Art Collector Mag, 9/91 & Am Artist Mag, Watercolor, fall 91; article & cover watercolor, Best of Oil Painting, Best of Acrylic Painting, Splash I & America's Best Contemporary Watercolors, Watercolor (mag), Fall 95 & Spring 2000; Country Roads Magazine, 4 different covers; cover & article, Inside Northside, summer 2003, fall 2005. *Mailing Add:* 215 St Charles Ave Natchez MS 39120

GOLDFIELD, EDWARD L
DEALER, COLLECTOR

b Philadelphia, Pa, Dec 3, 30. *Pos:* Pres, Goldfield Galleries, Ltd, currently. *Mem:* Art Dealers Asn Southern Calif. *Specialty:* 19th and early 20th century American impressionists, ash can, Western paintings and sculpture. *Publ:* Contribr, California: The State of Landscape 1872-1981, Newport Harbor Art Mus & Santa Barbara Mus Art, 91; Plein Air Painters of California, The Southland, Westphalia Publ, 82; Americans in Brittany & Normandy 1860-1910, Amon Carter Mus, Phoenix Art Mus & Nat Mus Am Art, 83; publ, Edgar Payne, pvt publ, 87; William Louis Sonntag, pvt publ, 80

GOLDFINE, BEATRICE
PAINTER, SCULPTOR

b Philadelphia, Pa, Aug 17, 23. *Study:* Studied with Jimmy Leuders, Roy Nuse & Will Barnett, 69-74; also pvt instr with Morris Blackburn, 75-80; Pa Acad Fine Arts, 5 yr cert art, 80. *Work:* Blue Cross, Philadelphia, Harrisburg, Norristown; Bell Atlantic, Philadelphia; Merck Sharp & Dohme, West Point, Pa; Philadelphia Co Med Soc; EI DuPont. *Comn:* Bust, Sir Winston Churchilll, Technion-Israel Inst Technol, Haif, 82; bust, Golda Meier, NY, 84; pastel portrait of Phillip Zinman, Phillip Zinman Found, Boca Raton, Fla, 94. *Exhib:* 71st Ann, Allied Artists Am, NY, 84; Philadelphia Watercolor Club, Art Inst, Pa, 86-94; Forms to Figure With, Glassboro State Col, NJ, 89; one-woman show, Nudes & Other Landscapes, Joy Berman Gallery, Philadephia, Pa, 90; Cheltenham Sch Fine Arts Ann, Philadelphia, Pa, 91, 92 & 93; Fel, travel show, Pa Acad Fine Arts, Philadelphia & Pittsburgh, 91, 92 & 93. *Awards:* First Prize, Woodmere Art Mus, 79 & Pa Acad Fine Arts Ann, 93; Bok Award, Harrisburg Mus, 84; First Prize Pastel, Philadelphia Sketch Club, 85. *Bibliog:* Dr Burton Wasserman (auth), Art Matters, 87; Guide to Manhattan's Outdoor Sculpture, Art Comn & Munic Art Soc, 88; Palmer Poroner (auth), Art Speak, Monthly Gallery Rev, NY, 91. *Mem:* Pastel Soc Am, NY; fel Pa Acad Fine Art; Philadelphia Watercolor Club; Friends Bezaiel Acad Arts & Design; Philadelphia Art Alliance. *Media:* Oil, Pastel, Clay. *Interests:* Art History, Chinese culture & history. *Publ:* The Best of Oil Painting, Rockport Publ, Inc, 96, The Best of Pastel, 96 & Portrait Inspirations, 97. *Dealer:* Joy Berman Gallery 2201 Pennsylvania Blvd Philadelphia PA 19130; Philadelphia Mus Art Sales Gallery. *Mailing Add:* 1250 Grelwood Ave Jenkintown PA 19046

GOLDFINGER, ELIOT
SCULPTOR

b New York, NY, Aug 14, 50. *Study:* Pratt Inst, BFA, 74; Nat Acad Sch, New York, 77-78. *Work:* Am Mus Natural Hist; Metrop Opera House; Mus City of New York; Tel Aviv Cult Ctr, Israel. *Comn:* Bust of Mayor John Lindsay, 78, Mayor Abe Beame, 79, Mayor Robert Wagner, 80 & Mayor Ed Koch, Mus City New York, 81; Bust Leonid Brezhnev, comn by Newsweek for cover, 4/12/82; Bust of Judge Henry Friendly, comn by US Court of Appeals, NY, 89. *Exhib:* Ann Exhib, Allied Artists Am, NY, 78, 80 & 82-86; Ann Exhib, Nat Acad Design, NY, 79 & 86; Mem Exhibs, Salmagundi Club, NY, 79-81; Ann Exhib, Nat Sculpture Soc, NY, 80-91. *Pos:* Staff artist, Am Mus Natural Hist, NY, 74-79. *Teaching:* Instr human & animal anat, NY Acad Art, 83-86; instr human anat, Art Students League, NY, 88-90. *Awards:* Gloria Medal, 80 & Meiselman Prize, 84, Nat Sculpture Soc; Dr H Debellis Prize, Salmagundi Club, 81; Allied Artists Mem Award, 85. *Bibliog:* John David Klein, Apple Polishers (film), WOR-TV News, 81; Sculpture in the News, Sculpture Review, 81; Interview, Sculpture Rev, 1st quarter, 92. *Mem:* Nat Sculpture Soc. *Media:* Plastillene, Bronze. *Res:* Human anatomy for artists, research from life & from cadavers; anatomy of the horse; comparative anatomy for artists. *Publ:* Auth, A sculptural approach to a three-dimensional subject, Catasus J Soc Animal Artists, spring 86; Human Anatomy for Artists, Oxford Univ Press, 91. *Mailing Add:* 37 Rolling Way New Rochelle NY 10804-2405

GOLDIN, LEON
PAINTER

b Chicago, Ill, Jan 16, 23. *Study:* Art Inst Chicago, BFA, 48; Univ Iowa, MFA, 50. *Work:* Brooklyn Mus, NY; Va Mus Fine Arts, Richmond; City Mus St Louis, Mo; Pa Acad Fine Arts, Philadelphia; Baltimore Mus Art. *Exhib:* Am Painting at Mid-Century, Metrop Mus Art, NY, 51; Am Drawings, Mus Mod Art, NY, 56; Corcoran Gallery Art Biennial, Washington, DC, 62; Carnegie Inst Int, Pittsburgh, Pa, 64; Pa Acad Fine Arts Ann, 66; Kraushaar, 60, 64, 68, 72, 84, 88, 90, 93, 96, 98, 2001, 2004; Nat Acad Design, 87, 91, 94, 96, 98, 99, 2000, 04; Maine Ctr for Contemp Arts, Rockport, 2002. *Teaching:* Instr painting & drawing, Calif Col Arts & Crafts, 50-55; instr painting & drawing, Cooper Union, 61-64; prof painting, Columbia Univ, 64-91, chmn dept, 73-75 & 77-80, prof emeritus, 1992-. *Awards:* Fulbright fellow, 52-53; Prix de Rome, 55-58; Guggenheim Fel, 59; Award in Painting, Nat Inst Arts & Lett, 68; NEA Sabbatical Leave Grant, 67-68; Nat Endowment Arts Grant, 80; Benjamin J Altman Prize, landscape painting, 93 & 2003, Adolph & Clara Ognig Prize, 2000, Ranger Purchase, 79 & 2006, National Acad Design. *Mem:* Nat Acad. *Media:* Oil, Gouache, Pastel, Charcoal. *Dealer:* Kraushaar Galleries 724 Fifth Ave New York NY 10019. *Mailing Add:* 438 W 116th St Apt 32 New York NY 10027

GOLDIN, NAN
PHOTOGRAPHER

b Washington, DC, 53. *Study:* Boston Mus Fine Arts, BFA, 77. *Work:* Folkwang Mus, Essen, Ger; Victoria & Albert Mus, London; First Bank, Minneapolis; George Eastman House, Rochester; Whitney Mus Am Art, NY; and others. *Exhib:* Solo shows, Parco Gallery, Tokyo, 98, Jablonka Gallery, Cologne, 98, Gagosian Gallery, Los Angeles, 98, Vaknin Schwartz, Atlanta, 98, Catherine Edelman Gallery, Chicago, 98, Galleri Nordenhake, Stockholm, 98 & Galleri Fauschou, Copenhagen, 98, Contemp Art Mus, Houston, 99, Nat Gallery of Iceland, 99, Joseloff Gallery, Hartford, Conn, 99, White Cube, London, 99, Scalo, Zurich, 2000, Matthew Marks Gallery, NY 2001,

Studio Casoli, Milan and Rome, 2001, Marktkirche, Hannover, Germ, 2002, Galerie Krohn, Germ, 2002, Margarete Roeder Gallery, NY, 2002, Gallery N Von Bartha, London, 2003; Rendez-vous 1 and 2, Collection Lambert en Avignon, 2000; Photog Now, Contemp Arts Ctr, New Orleans, 2000; Essenbilder, Dorrie/Priess, Hamburg, 2000; Couples, Cheim and Read, NY, 2000; 46th Biennial Exhib, Corcoran Mus of Art, Washington, DC, 2000; Angles of Incidence, Ctr for Curatorial Studies, NY, 2001; and others; Matthew Marks Gallery, 2006. *Teaching:* Grad photog, Yale Univ, New Haven. *Awards:* Nat Endowment Arts Grant, Washington, DC, 90; Louis Comfort Tiffany Found Award, 91; Brandeis Award inPhotography, 94; Aaron Siskinf Found, Grant in Photog, 2001; French Order Arts and Letters, 2006. *Publ:* Cookie Mueller (catalog), Pace/MacGill Gallery, New York, 91; The Other Side 1972-1992, Scalo Verlag, 92; coauth (with Joachim Sartorius), Vakat, Walther König, Cologne, 93; (with David Armstrong), A Double Life, Scalo verlag, 94; I'll Be Your Mirror, Scalo Verlag in conjunction with Whitney Mus, NY. *Dealer:* Matthew Marks Gallery 523 W 24th St New York NY 10011. *Mailing Add:* 334 Bowery New York NY 10012

GOLDMAN, BEN
PAINTER
b Philadelphia, Pa, Oct 21, 60. *Study:* NY Studio Sch, 80; Vassar Col, AB, 82; NY Univ, PhD, 93. *Work:* Jersey City Mus, NJ. *Exhib:* Arthsma, Bronx River Arts Ctr, NY, 2002; In Response, Savannah col Art & Design, Ga, 2002; Artists in Residence, Newark Mus, NJ, 2002; Fragments, Urban Inst Contemp Art, Grand Rapids, Mich, 2003; Paper Ball, Jersey City Mus, NJ, 2003; Fighting Chance, Lower Manhattan Cult Coun, NY, 2003; True Colors, Allied Mus, Berlin, Ger, 2004; Super Heroine Show, Gallery 128, 2004; Emerge 6, Aljive, 2005; Urban Eviron, CB Richard Ellis, 2006. *Pos:* Exec Dir City Without Walls; Founder & CEO, United Visual Arts, LLC. *Teaching:* lectr, Artist Forum, 2005; lectr, Jersey City Mus, 2005; lectr, Post Modernism, Sch Visual Arts, 2006. *Awards:* Artist in Residence, Newark Mus, 2002; Certification, Artist in Educ, NJ State Coun on Arts, 2003; Artist Grant Vt Studio Ctr, 2003; Fel, Emerge 6, Aljira, 2004; Fel, Strategic Planning Prog, Creative Capitol, 2004. *Bibliog:* Herman Lloyd (auth), Object Lessons, Guild Publ, 2001; Catherine Carlson (auth), Urban Meets Urban Hip, Voices of Lower Manhattan, 4/4/03; Jeff Theödare (auth), Nohu Art Scene on the Rise, Jersey J, 10/30/04; Holland Cotler (auth), Emerge 5, NY Times, 12/9/2005; Ben Genocchio (auth), Renovation & Extra Security, NY Times, 6/25/2006. *Mem:* Col Art Asn; White Columns Curated Artists Register; Artists Space. *Media:* Acyrlic, Oil. *Publ:* On Every Wall: Reproduction & the Future of Art, (article, book) Forthcoming, 2005. *Mailing Add:* 53 Fulton St Weehawken NJ 07086

GOLDMAN, JANE E
PAINTER, PRINTMAKER
b Dallas, Tex, June 26, 51. *Study:* Smith Col, BA (studio art), 73; Univ Wis, MFA (graphic art), 78. *Work:* Brooklyn Mus; Libr Congress, Wasington DC; Smith Col Mus Art, Northampton, Mass; Cleveland Mus Art; Detroit Mus Art. *Comn:* terrazzo floors, Mass Port Authority, Boston, 96, 98; terrazzo floor, RI Transit Authority, Providence, 99; pavement design, City of Cambridge, Mass, 2000. *Exhib:* Am Drawing in Black and White 1970-1980, Brooklyn Mus, 80; Point of Departure: A Portfolio of Prints, Univ Wis, 84; Book Projects: Dieu Donne Paper, Metrop Mus Art, NY, 86; Collaboration in Print: Stewart & Stewart, Detroit Inst Art, 91; Inspired by Nature, Boston Col Art Mus, 95; Women in the Visual Arts, Hollins Col Art Mus, Roanoke, Va, 96; Recent Am Portraits, Boston Univ, 98; The Work Shop Portfolios, Boston Pub Libr, 2000. *Pos:* Co-dir, Artist's Proof Studio, Cambridge, Mass, 80-84, Mixit Print Studio, 86-2000. *Awards:* Golden Trowel Award, Internat Masonry Inst, 99; Honor Award, Nat Mosaic & Terrazzo Asoc, 99. *Media:* Watercolor, Etching, Terrazzo. *Dealer:* Edith Baker Gallery 2404 Cedar Springs Dallas Texas 75201. *Mailing Add:* 32 Clifton St Somerville MA 02144

GOLDMAN, JUDITH
WRITER, CURATOR
b Chicago, Ill. *Study:* Bard Col, Annandale-on-Hudson, NY, printmaking with Louis Schanker, BA(Lit), 64; Inst Design Ill Inst Technol, printmaking with Misch Kohn, 64. *Pos:* Managing ed, Artist's Proof, Pratt Graphics, New York, 67-69; ed, Print Collector's Newslett, New York, 70-72; managing ed, Artnews, New York, 73-75, contrib ed, 75-; adj cur, Print Collection, Whitney Mus Am Art, 76-92; consultant, The Andy Warhol Art Authentication Bd, 1999-, mem bd, 2006-. *Teaching:* Adj instr graphics, Hunter Col, New York, 74-75; asst prof criticism, Pratt Inst, 76-78. *Awards:* Nat Endowment Arts Grant Criticism, 78. *Res:* Twentieth century graphics, painting and photography: biography. *Publ:* Auth, American Prints: Process & Proofs Jasper Johns Prints: 1977-81, 81; Jasper Johns: 17 Monotypes, Universal Art Ed, 82; Frank Stella, Fourteen Prints, Princeton, 83; James Rosenquist, Viking, 85; James Rosenquist: The Early Pictures, Rizzoli, 92; The Pop Image: Prints and Multiples, Marlbourough, 94

GOLDMAN, LESTER
PAINTER
b Philadelphia, Pa, Aug 15, 42. *Study:* Philadelphia Col Art, BFA, 64; Indiana Univ, MFA, 66. *Work:* Univ Maine; Ind Univ; Kans City Art Inst; Albrecht Mem Gallery; H & R Block; Kemper Insurance Co; State Hist Soc; Nelson Gallery Art; Mutual Benefit Life Insurance Co; IBM; Realex Corp; Continental, Twentieth Century Corp. *Exhib:* One-man shows, Pane-Vino Gallery, Philadelphia, 68, Walter Kelly Gallery, Chicago, 75, Unitarian Church, Kansas City, Mo, 80 & Contemp Art Ctr, Kansas City, Mo, 89, Joe Niese Gallery, 01; Works on Paper, Ind Univ, 87 & Athena on Broadway, Kansas City, Mo, 90; Leedy-Voulkos Gallery, Kansas City, Mo, 88; Portrait, Blue Dolphin, 92; Midland Invitational installation, Joslyn Art Mus, 92; Kabalival installation, Leedy-Voulkos Gallery, 93. *Pos:* Lectr, Joslyn Art Mus, 92. *Teaching:* Asst, Indiana Univ, 65-66; prof painting, Kansas City Art Inst, 66-; vis fac, Alliance of Independent Col Art, NY Studio prog, 85; vis artist, Studio Sch, NY, summer 88; Vermont Studio Sch, summer 89; prof, Art Inst, Kansas City, currently. *Awards:* Andrew W Mellon Fac Develop Grants, 84, 87, 88 & 92; Nat Endowment Arts, 86 & 89; Alliance Independent Col of Art Grant, 86; Charlotte Street Fund Award, 01. *Bibliog:* Lily Pruizo (auth), Yard full of art, Kansas City Star, 90; Sybil Zimmerman (auth), A festival of lights, Kansas City Chronicle, 90; Peter Vonziegezar (auth), Article in Kansas City Star, 93. *Dealer:* Leedy-Voulkos Gallery 1919 Wyandotte Kansas City MO 64108. *Mailing Add:* 37 W 57 Kansas City MO 64113

GOLDMAN, MATT
CONCEPTUAL ARTIST, KINETIC ARTIST
b New York, NY, May 2, 61. *Study:* Clark Univ, BA(econ), 83, MBA, 84. *Work:* New Mus Contemp Art (performance), NY; Milwaukee Art Mus (performance), Wis; Contemp Art Ctr New Orleans (performance), Fla. *Awards:* Obie, Tubes, Village Voice, 91; Drama Desk, Tubes, 92; Lucille Lortel Found Award, Tubes, 92. *Bibliog:* Alisa Soloman (auth), Pissing on propriety, Village Voice, 1/15/91; Vicki Goldberg (auth), Hi tech meets God with Blue Man Group, New York Times, 1/17/91; Thomas M Disch (auth), Blue Man Group: Tubes, Nation, 1/20/92. *Media:* Performance. *Mailing Add:* c/o Blue Man Group 434 Lafayette St New York NY 10003

GOLDNER, JANET
SCULPTOR
b Washington, DC, June 6, 52. *Study:* Asgard Sch, Hurup Thy, Denmark, 71; Penland Sch, NC, 72; Antioch Col, BA, 74; NY Univ, MA, 81. *Work:* Rockrose Develop Corp, NY; and many other private collections. *Comn:* Sculpture, Millay Colony Arts, Austerlitz, NY, 81; sculpture, comn by Robert Mitchell, Ridgefield, Conn, 82; Europos Parkas, Vilnius, Lithuania, 2000; Cosa Cosa, Philadelphia, 2003. *Exhib:* New Mus Contemp Art, NY, 89; Show your Metal, Salena Gallery, Long Island Univ, Brooklyn, NY, 90; WAC Collaborative, Art Anchorage & Creative Time, NY, 92; In Three Dimensions (with catalog), Snug Harbor Cult Ctr, Staten Island, NY, 95; Global Sweatshop, Art Gen, NY, 95; Monmouth Mus & Cult Ctr, Lincroft, NJ, 96; one-person shows, Klutznick Mus, Washington, DC, 96, Art Resources Transfer, NY, 2002, 03; Bronx Mus Arts, NY, 96; Text and Identity, State Univ NY, Stony Brook, 97; Suture, Rotunda Gallery, Brooklyn, NY, 97; Artemisia Gallery, Chicago, 97; Michael Petronko Gallery, NY, 97; O'Kane Gallery, Univ Houston, Tex, 97; Ctr Bk Arts, NY, 98; Statements in Steel, Walton Art Ctr, Fayetteville, Ark, 98; Islip Mus, East Islip, NY, 2001; The Granary, Assoc Segou Laben, Segou, Mali, 2002; Susquehanna Art Mus, Harrisburg, Pa, 2003; McLean Project for the Arts, 2003; pvt collection, Garden Gate, Ossining, NY, 2004; American Embassy, Bamako, Mali, 2006; Nathan Cummings Found, NY, 2006; Center for Book Arts, NY, 2006; Libr, Proteus Gowanus, Brooklyn, NY, 2006; Noyes Mus, Oceanville, NJ, 2006; and many others. *Collection Arranged:* South African Mail: Messages From Inside, UN Spec Comt Against Apartheid, 90; Artists on the Home Front (with catalog), Goddard-Riverside Community Ctr, New York, 91; Bridges and Boundaries (panel), Studio Mus, Harlem, NY, 92; Groupe Bogolan Kasobane (mudcloth costumes & paintings from Mali), Lincoln Ctr Performing Arts, New York, 98. *Pos:* Dir, S African Women Artists in Resistance, 88- & Until That Last Breath: Women with AIDS, NY, 88-89; dir, Art & Culture in Mali, Study Abroad Program, Antioch Col, Yellow Springs, Ohio, 2002-2006. *Teaching:* Lectr, Elmira Col, NY, 84, Cornell Col, Mt Vernon, Iowa, 85 & UN Women's Conf, Nairobi, Kenya, 85; vis artist lect series, Cortona, Italy, 87 & Am Cult Ctr, Bamako, Mali, 95; panel moderator, Nat Conf, Women's Caucus Art, NY, 90, 92 & 94, Studio Mus Harlem, NY, 92, Artists Talk on Art, NY, 93 & Col Art Asn Ann Conf, NY, 94; vis artist, Am Cult Ctr, Bamako, Mali, 95; lectr, Women's Studio Workshop, 95 & 96, Women's Caucus Art, NY, 96; lectr pottery workshops, Queens Mus Art, NY & Adirondack Ctr Arts, Blue Mountain Lake, NY, 96; artist residence, COSACOSA, Philadelphia, 94 & Metal Bks workshop, Webster Univ, St Louis, 98, 99, 2000. *Awards:* Visual Artists Exchange Award, NY Feminist Art Inst, New York, 83; UN Comt Against Apartheid Exhib Grant, 89; Fulbright Res Fel, Mali, Africa, 94-95; Ford Found, Three Continents Textile Collaboration, Indonesia, Mali, Nigeria, 2005. *Bibliog:* Vivian Raynor (auth), article, NY Times, 2/26/95; Roberta Smith (auth), article, NY Times, 8/8/97; Amy Blankstein (auth), Commissions, Sculpture Mag, 12/97. *Mem:* Int Sculpture Ctr; Col Art Asn. *Media:* Steel, Mixed Media. *Res:* West Africa & the country of Mali. *Publ:* Auth, South African Mail: Messages from Inside (essay, catalog), 90; Artists on the Home Front (essay, catalog), 91; In praise of the muse, Syracuse Cult Workers Datebook, 96; Connect Mag, Arts Internat, NYC. *Mailing Add:* 52 Warren St New York NY 10007

GOLDRING, ELIZABETH
WRITER, ENVIRONMENTAL ARTIST
b Forest City, Iowa, Feb 13, 45. *Study:* Smith Col, BA, 67; Harvard Univ, MEd, 77. *Exhib:* Artransition (coordr), Mass Inst Technol, Cambridge, 75; Inst Contemp Art, Boston, 76; Centerbeam (coordr), Documenta 6, Kassel, Ger, 77 & Smithsonian Inst, DC, 78; Int Biennial Exhib Graphic & Visual Art (doc), Secession, Vienna, Austria, 79; Int Alarm (with Otto Piene), Munich, 83; Coyote for Desert Sun/Desert Moon (CAVS artists) Lone Pine, Calif, 86; Eye/Sight (with Vin Grabill) for LightsOrot, Yeshiva Univ Mus, NY, 87; Eye/Sight (with Vin Grabill) & Int Alarm (with Otto Piene) for Otto Piene and CAVS, Kunstrevien, Karlsruhe, Fed Repub Ger, 88. *Pos:* Elem educ specialist, Nat Collection Fine Arts, Smithsonian Inst, 71-72; exhib developer, Childrens Mus, Boston, 73-75; exhib & proj dir, Ctr Advan Visual Studies, Mass Inst Technol, 78-. *Teaching:* Lectr, Art & Environment, CAVS/MIT, 75-. *Awards:* Grant, Diabetes Res & Educ Found, 87. *Res:* Sky Art; Visual Language. *Publ:* Contribr, You are Here (exhib catalog), Mass Inst Technol, 76; ed, CAVS Report on Elemental Sculpture in Public-Predominantly Urban-Places, Nat Endowment Arts & Ctr Advan Visual Studies, Mass Inst Technol, 78; auth, Sky Art-Art That Flies, Flying Colors, Braniff, 79; ed & contribr, Centerbeam, Ctr Advan Visual Studies, Mass Inst Technol, 80; Laser Treatment: Poems and Two Stories, Blue Giant Press,

Boston, 83; The Sky Art Conference, Lightworks, No 17, 85; The Sky Art Manifesto, (coauth with Otto Piene and Lowry Burgess), CAVS/MIT, 86; auth, Desert Sun/Desert Moon and the Sky Art Manifesto, Leonardo, Vol 20, No 4, 12/88; The Inner Eye from the Inside Out, 88. *Mailing Add:* Ctr for Advan Visual Studies Mass Inst Technol 265 Massachusetts Ave Cambridge MA 02139

GOLDRING, NANCY DEBORAH
VISUAL ARTIST, EDUCATOR
b Oak Ridge, Tenn, Jan 25, 45. *Study:* Smith Col, Northampton, Mass, BA(art hist), 67, Univ Florence, with Nina Gregori (Fulbright Fel), 67-68; NY Univ, MFA (sculpture, graphics), 70. *Work:* St Louis Art Mus; Mus Fine Arts, Houston; Int Ctr Photog, NY; Bibliot Nat, Paris; Int Ctr Photog, Bombay, India; and many others. *Comn:* Set design for Ode, Nat Choreography Proj, Nat Endowment Arts & Exxon, 85; set design for Ode with Ze' Eva Cohen & dancers, Joyce Theater, NY, 87. *Exhib:* Inside Spaces, Mus Mod Art, NY, 83; Photog of Inventions: Pictures of the Eighties (with catalog), Nat Mus Am Art, Washington, DC, Mus Contemp Art, Chicago & Walker Art Ctr, Minneapolis, 89; Constructed Spaces, Photog Resource Ctr, Boston, 90; New Directions, Fla Int Univ Art Mus, 91; solo exhibs, Elliot Smith Gallery, St Louis, Mo, 94, Duane Reed Gallery, St Louis, Mo, 96, SE Mus Photog, Daytona Beach Community Col, Fla, 99, 2000, Houston Ctr Photog, Tex, 99-, Alva Gallery, 2000 & Web Gallery, Univ Houston, 2000; Making Pictures, Caldwell Col, NJ, 94; Seeking the Sublime: Neo Romanticism in Landscape Photography, SE Mus Photog, Daytona Beach Community Col, Fla, 95; Landscape, Tisch Sch Arts, NY Univ, 95; New in the Nineties, Katonah Mus, NY, 96; Moving On, Soho 20 Gallery, NY, 96; The Archaelogy of Memory, Trinity Col, 97; Diverse Visions, Photog Perspectives, Pittsburgh Ctr Arts, 97; The Avon Collection, Int Ctr Photog, NY, 97; Distillations, Photog as an Art Form, Nat Ctr Performing Arts, Bombay, 97; World Artists for Tibet, Jonathan Schorr Gallery, NY, 98; Fresh Work 2 (with catalog), SE Mus Photog, Daytona Beach Community Col, Fla, 98; Inst Arts, Shanghai, China, 99; PROFIL, Int month of photo, Czech Republic, 03; Lyman Allen Mus, New London, Conn, 02; Sanvitale, Comune di Parma, Italy, 03-04; Houston Ctr for Photo, Fotofest, 02; Palimpest: Nancy Goldring, Palazzo Pigorini, Bk Mazzota, ed Milan; Gakerie Z, Int month of photog, Bratislava, Slovakia, cat repro, Nov 2003; Palinsesto, Palazzo Pigorini, Parma, Feb 2005; Palimpsest, Gallery 138, New York City, Mar 2006. *Pos:* Co-founding dir, SITE, NY, 69-72 & Chamber, NY, 76-; vis artist & critic, Parsons Sch Design, 80, juror, 88; juror, Sch Archit, NJ Inst Technol, 81; judge, State Arts Exhib & Workshop, Ogden, Utah, 93. *Teaching:* prof drawing, Montclair State Univ, NJ, 72-; vis prof contemp art, RI Sch Design, Providence, 74-75; vis prof, Haverford Col, Pa, 78, Dept Environ Design, Parsons Sch Design; lectr at Art Organizations, Schools and Universities for the Past 28 Years; Facolta di Lettere, Instr English Lit & Language, Univ Pisa 67-68. *Awards:* Grant, NY State Coun Arts, 70-73, 77-79 & 86-89; Res Grant, Montclair State Col, 82-87, 92, 98, Alumni Grant, 86-87, 91, Career Develop Grant, 88-89, 97-99 & Global Educ Travel Grant, 98; Fulbright SE Asia Fel, 94-95; and others. *Bibliog:* Jay Tolson (auth), What's After Modern, US News & World Report, 6/7/99; PMR, Review of Reflections ina Glass Eye, 12/99; Ellen Handy (auth), Distillations: Nancy Goldring, SE Mus Photog, 2000; Compagni di viaggio, Gazetta di Parma, 9/12/2003; Tom Wolf (auth), Reviews of Palimpsest, 2006; Erasure and exchange: Nancy Goldring's palimpsest, The Architect's Newspaper, 5/2006. *Media:* Pencil, Gouache. *Publ:* Auth, rev, Deconstructive architecture, 7/88 & George Ranalli: buildings & projects, 3/89, Bldg Design, London; rev, Identity, Arts Mag, 3/89; contribr, Generation of place, Offramp, Univ SCalif, Vol 1, No 3, fall 90; auth, Imagining Egypt, Avant Garde: J Archit & Aesthetics, Univ Colo, Denver, 7/91; Dream Stills, Avant Garde: J Archit & Aesthetics, Univ Colo, 9/93; and others; Nancy Goldring's Installation, Antiques and the Arts Weekly, 02. *Mailing Add:* 463 West St A1112 New York NY 10014

GOLDSLEGER, CHERYL
PAINTER, DRAFTSMAN
b Philadelphia, Pa, Dec 16, 51. *Study:* Tyler Sch Art, Rome, 71; Philadelphia Col Art, BFA, 73; Washington Univ, MFA, 75. *Work:* Albright-Knox Gallery, Buffalo, NY; Tel Aviv Mus, Israel; Israel Mus, Jerusalem; RI Sch Design Mus, Providence; Mus Mod Art, NY. *Exhib:* Palazzo Vagnotti, Cortona, Italy, 93; Nine Women in Georgia, Nat Mus Women Arts, Washington, 96; Women & Geometric Abstraction, Pratt Inst of Art, NY, 99; Interiors NC, Mus Art, NC, 2000; Drawings of Choice, Krannert Mus, Ill, 2002; Improvisation, Halsey Gallery, Col Charleston, SC, 2002; Utopia, Mus Contemp Art Ga, 2003; Nat Acad Science, Wash, DC, 2005. *Teaching:* Asst prof painting, Western Carolina Univ, 75-77; chmn art dept, Piedmont Col, Demorest, Ga, 88-2001; assoc prof, Ga State Univ, Atlanta, 2001-. *Awards:* NEA Fel, 81 & 91; US/France Fel, 93; Fifth Floor Found, 99. *Bibliog:* Donald Kuspit (auth), Cheryl Goldsleger, Artforum, 11/93; Mark Daniel Cohen (auth), Cheryl Goldsleger, Review, 5/99; Tom McDonough (auth), Cheryl Goldsleger at Rosenberg & Kaufman, Art in Am, 2/00; Jerry Cullum (auth), Designing Women, Art in Am, 9/03; Rex Weil (auth), Utopia, Mus Contemp Art Ga, 2003. *Mem:* Col Art Asn. *Media:* Encaustic, Charcoal. *Dealer:* Rosenberg & Kaufman Fine Art 115 Wooster St New York NY 10012; Kidder Smith Gallery Boston Mass. *Mailing Add:* 170 Greenwood Dr Athens GA 30606-4704

GOLDSMITH, BARBARA
WRITER, HISTORIAN
b New York, NY, May 18, 31. *Study:* Wellesley Col, BA, 57; Pace Univ, Hon DLit, 81; Syracuse Univ, Hon DLett, 81; Lake Forest Col, LHD, 96. *Hon Degrees:* Three Hon Dr. *Pos:* Ed, NY Mag, 66-74; sr ed, Harper's Bazaar, 70-74; The New Yorker; appointee, Pres's Comn on Celebration of Women in Am History, Gov NY, NY State Coun Arts; trustee, NY Pub Libr, exec & nominating comts, Pres Comn for Preservation & Access, Permanent Paper Task Force of Nat Libr Medicine; trustee, NY Soc Libr, Am Acad in Rome; former overseer, Ctr for Res on Women, Wellesley Col; founding ed, NY Mag. *Teaching:* lectr, NY Univ, Harvard Univ. *Awards:* Penn Paper-Pres & Access Award, Am Acad Arts & Scis, 92; 2 Emmy Awards; Presidential Citation, NY Univ; many others. *Mem:* Whitney Mus Am Art; Mus Mod Art, NY; Mus City NY (pres coun, 70-); NY Coun Arts; Guggehheim Mus. *Publ:* Auth, articles The New Yorker, Esquire, Vanity Fair & contrib ed Archit Digest; The Straw Man, Farrar, Straus & Giroux, 76; Little Gloria.Happy at Last, Alfred A Knopf Publ, 80; Johnson v Johnson, 87; Other Powers, The Age of Suffrage, Spiritualism & the Scandalous Victoria Woodhull, Alfred A Knopf Publ. *Mailing Add:* Janklow/Nesbit Assocs 445 Park Ave #13 New York NY 10022

GOLDSMITH, BENEDICT ISAAC
GALLERY DIRECTOR, EDUCATOR
b New York, NY, Aug 1, 1916. *Study:* NY Univ, BS, 40; Art Students League, New York & Woodstock, NY, with Arnold Blanch; Teachers Col, Columbia Univ, MA, 50; Inst Del'Arte, Florence, Italy, 64. *Collection Arranged:* Potsdam Prints (with catalog), 63-74; Robert Mallary, 68; Sculpture, NY Six, 69; New Realism, 71; Women in Art, 72, New Realism, Revisited, 74; Potsdam Plastics, 75; African Sculpture Selections, Anspach Collection, 75; Maine Coast Artists Open, 79; Artists as Teachers, 79; Associates Selects, 79; Off the Wall, 80; & Painters, 80; Richard Derby Tucker Mem Retrospective, 80. *Pos:* Gallery dir, State Univ NY Col Potsdam, 65-78; exhib dir, Maine Coast Artists, 79-82. *Teaching:* Prof art, State Univ NY Col Potsdam, 50-78. *Mem:* Gallery Asn NY (exec comt, 75); Asn Exhib & Gallery, NY (pres, 68-69). *Mailing Add:* 45 Lakeview Terr Rockland ME 04841

GOLDSMITH, ELSA M
PAINTER, GRAPHIC ARTIST
b New York, NY. *Study:* Parsons Sch Fine & Appl Art, scholar award, BA; NY Univ; Pratt Graphic Ctr, (lithography); etching with Ruth Leaf; painting with Betty Holiday. *Hon Degrees:* US Com of Women in the Arts, 1971; City of Cannes, 1972; City of Florence, 1972; UNICEF at the UN Gen Assembly Hall, 1974. *Work:* Human Landscapes Collection, 40-; Joan of Arc (Sister Chapel), 78, honored and aired nationally on 20/20, 94-95; July 4th, 76; Women on the March, 76; Suffragettes, 76; Walking Happy, 84; Civil War Series, 90s; Silverpoint Drawings. *Comn:* Human Landscape Portraits. *Exhib:* 15 solo exhibs, 72-73;10 one man exhibs mus and cultural centers nationwide and 4 one man shows, NY, 72-73; GN Libr, Retro # 4, 74, Women on March, 76; Old Bergen Art Guild, solo show, 74; Works on Paper Women Artists, Brooklyn Mus, NY, 75 & 85; Port Wash Libr, Silverpoint exhib, 75; Cayuga Mus, NY, 83; Syosset Libr, NY, 83; Delhi Art Gallery, 84; Guild Hall Mus, 85; Retrospective 5, Huntington Libr, Long Island, 89; Retrospective 6, East Meadow Libr, 90; Les Malmut Art Gallery, 75th Anniversary Show of the League of Women Voters, Union, NJ, 90; 75th Anniversary Show of the League of Women Voters, 90; Nat Exhib, 93; Nassau Co Mus Art, Long Island, 97. *Pos:* Advert artist, Newswk Mag, NY, 40-41; indust designer, Belle Kogan Assoc, NY, 41-48; freelance artist, Book & Mag Illustrating, NY, 42-; US Delegate, organized 2 shows for women artists in Bulgaria and Italy; arranged an exhib for 75 women artists at Palazzo Vecchio, Florence, Italy, 90. *Teaching:* tchr and owner, Elsa Goldsmith's Studio, 50-74 & North Shore Commun Art Ctr, 71-73 (bd dir, art coord, 73-), Great Neck, NY; painting tchr, Adult Educ, Sewanhake High Sch, Floral Manor, NY, 72-74, LaSalle Col, 73-74; lectr, NOW, NY, 1970s & 1980s. *Awards:* Honors at London Art Mus, 69; Canne Int Gold Medal Hon for painting, 69; US Comt of Women in the Arts, 71, City of Cannes, 72, City of Florence, 72, Unicef at the UN General Assembly Hall, 74; 22 major awards, 72-73; won awards and medals in Group Shows in 42 states, 72-73; Eleanor Roosevelt award, 1973; Susa Kahn Award, 74; Doris Krindel Award, 74; Works on Paper Women Artists, Brooklyn Mus, 75; Nat Exhib Award, 93; honored, Nat Asn Women Artists, 94, Nassau Co Mus Art, 97. *Bibliog:* Community Leaders Am 11th Ed; Charlotte Rubinstein (auth), Am Women Artists; Les Krantz (auth), NY Art Review, 4th ed, 1990. *Mem:* Nat Asn Women Artists (chair); Int Art Asn; Women in the Arts, Inc (bd mem & bicentennial chmn, 74-76); North Shore Community Art Ctr (bd dir & art coordr, 73-); UN Int Womens Yr Arts Festival (bd mem, 75-76); Silvermine Guild Artists, 83; Artist & Equity and LI Art Alliance, 85; Nat Woman's Hall of Fame, 94. *Media:* Oil, Drawing, Etching, Silverpoint, Mixed Media & Conté, Watercolor. *Publ:* Southern Quart, Vol XVII, No 2, 79; SM Dunnells interview, NShore Mag, 83; quoted in The Art of Feminine Power, Abrams, 1994. *Mailing Add:* c/o JoAnn Goldsmith 6216 Barton Creek Cir Lake Worth FL 33463

GOLDSTEIN, CARL
HISTORIAN
b New York, NY, June 24, 38. *Study:* Brooklyn Col, BA, 60; Columbia Univ, MA, 62, PhD, 66. *Teaching:* Instr art hist, Wheaton Col, Norton, Mass, 66; asst prof, Brown Univ, 66-71; prof, Univ NC, Greensboro, 71-. *Awards:* Grants, Am Philosophical Soc, 77 & 82. *Mem:* Col Art Asn Am. *Res:* Baroque art; twentieth century sculpture; history of academies of art. *Publ:* Auth, Visual Fact Over Verbal Fiction, A Study of the Carracci and the Criticism, Theory and Practice of Painting in Renaissance and Baroque Italy, Cambridge Univ Press, 88; Teaching Art: Academies and Schools from Vasari to Albers, Cambridge Univ Press, 96. *Mailing Add:* 801 Greenwood Greensboro NC 27410

GOLDSTEIN, CHARLES BARRY
ART DEALER, APPRAISER
b New York, NY, 45. *Study:* Ohio Univ, Athens, BBA, 67; Am Univ, Washington, MPA, 75; Ind Univ Int Soc Appraisers, CAPP Dipl, 91, CAPP Recertification, 95 & 2000; independent art study in forensic appraising, signatures, art fraud & art terminology; Univ Md & Int Soc Appraisers, CAPP dipl, 2000, cert appraiser personal property in fine art & limited ed prints. *Pos:* Art dealer, Charles Barry Int, Rockville, Md, 75-, art appraiser, 79-, court qualified expert witness & trial consult, 92-; arts comnr, City of Rockville, Md, 91-96, chmn Art Pub Places prog, 93-95 & chmn, Cult Arts Comn, 95-96. *Teaching:* Lectr & forums art & appraisals, Int Soc Appraisers,

Hoffman Estates, Ill Nat Confs & Seattle Nat Confs, 89-; forensic guest lectr, George Washington Univ Masters Forensic Scis Prog. *Awards:* Certs Appreciation, Int Soc Appraisers; Cert Appreciation, City Rockville, Md; Learned Res J Hon, Brandeis Univ Libr. *Mem:* Int Soc Appraisers, (nat fine arts comt, 90-97, designation & rev comt, 89-97); Catalogue Raisonne Scholars Asn. *Specialty:* Prints, paintings & sculpture. *Publ:* Appraisers Info Exchange, winter 92; ISA Newsletter, fall/winter 94; PRINTthoughts, 1/95 & 11/95; Art Calendar, 7/98 & 8/98; ISA Appraisers Exchange, 99; Washington Print Club Quart, 99-2000; Auth, ART FRAUD, MISREPRENTATION, GOBBLEDYGOOK, 1999. *Mailing Add:* c/o Charles Barry International 8 Hardwicke Place Rockville MD 20850-3010

GOLDSTEIN, DANIEL JOSHUA
KINETIC ARTIST, SCULPTOR
b Mt Vernon, NY, June 19, 50. *Study:* Brandeis Univ; Univ Calif, Santa Cruz, BA; St Martin's Col, London, Eng. *Work:* Brooklyn Mus, NY; Chicago Art Inst; Achenbach Found, San Francisco, Calif; Oakland Mus Art, Calif; Carnegie Inst; and others. *Comn:* Sculpture, City of Mountain View, Calif, 93; sculpture, Synoptics, 93; sculpture, Colma BART Sta, Colma, Calif; sculpture, Norcal Waste, San Francisco, Calif, 2001; sculpture, Astra Zeneca, Wilmington, Del, 2002. *Exhib:* Achenbach Found, 72; Prints Calif, Oakland Mus Art, 75; Nat Print Exhib, Brooklyn Mus, NY, 76 & 80; one-man shows, Getler-Pall Gallery, NY, 77, ADI Gallery, San Francisco, 77 & Brooklyn Mus, 83; Calif Palace Legion Hon, San Francisco; Foster Goldstrom Gallery, NY, 93; Mus Contemp Relig Art, St Louis, Mo, 94; Richmond Art Ctr, Calif, 94; Nat Gallery Victoria, Melbourne, Australia, 98; Durke chang Gallery, San Francisco, Calif, 2002. *Bibliog:* Barry Walker & Richard Howard (coauths), Daniel Goldstein: Woodblocks & Paper Cut-Outs, Brooklyn Mus, 83; Robert Flynn Johnson (auth), Beyond Belief, Nat Gallery Victoria, 98; Richard Howard, Robert Atkins & David Maxim (coauths), Reliquaries, Foster Goldstrom Gallery, NY, 94. *Media:* Aluminum, Leather. *Mailing Add:* 224 Guerrero San Francisco CA 94103

GOLDSTEIN, ELEANOR
PAINTER
b New York, NY, May 2, 35. *Study:* Bennington Col, BA, 57. *Work:* US State Dept Art in Embassies; IBM, Armonk, NY; Standard & Poors, Pfizer Co, NY; Pepsico, Purchase, NY. *Comn:* Mural, Cathedral St John Divine, NY, 96. *Exhib:* 12th Ann Art Exhib, Salmagundi Club, NY, 89 & 2000; 11th Ann Pastel Exhib, Pen & Brush Club, NY, 92; HRCA at the Hammond, Hammond Mus, Salem, NY, 92; Art of Northeast, Silvermine, Conn, 2002; River Rock Gallery, Woodstock, NY, 2005; Rockefeller Preserve Art Gallery, Pocanitico Hills, NY, 2006. *Teaching:* Instr, Long Beach Island Art Found, Loveladies, NJ, 2004-06. *Awards:* Norman Wenig Purchase Prize, Pastel Soc Am, 91; Philip Glasser Mem Award, Mamaroneck Artist Guild Nat, 94; Nat Arts Club Award, 97; Seascape Award, Salmagundi Club, 2000. *Mem:* Nat Asn Women Artists; Pastel Soc Am; N Artist Equity Asn. *Media:* Pastel, Oil. *Mailing Add:* 1 Chester Terr Hastings-on-Hudson NY 10706

GOLDSTEIN, GLADYS
PAINTER, COLLAGE ARTIST
b Newark, Ohio. *Study:* Md Inst Art; Art Students League; Columbia Univ, New York; Pa State Univ, Univ Park; study with Hobson Pittman. *Work:* Baltimore Mus Art, Md; Pa State Univ; Univ Ariz; Goucher Col, Baltimore; Univ Md; Fed Reserve Bank; and others. *Exhib:* One-man shows, Baltimore Mus Art, Goucher Col, Duveen-Graham Gallery, NY, Galerie Philadelphie, Paris, IFA Gallery, Washington, DC, Western Md Col, Newark Gallery, Del, Richter Gallery, Weisbaden, Ger, 65-75. *Pos:* Co-chmn art festival, City Baltimore, 71-74; art comt, Mayor's Ball, 73-74; exec comt, Mayor's Adv Comt for Arts & Cult, 74-. *Teaching:* Instr painting, Md Inst Col Art, 60-65; instr art, Col Notre Dame, Md, 65-85. *Awards:* Third Award, Md Art Today, H K & Co, 72; First Award, 25th Ann of Israel, JCC, 74; Awards, Baltimore Mus Art & Pa State Univ. *Media:* Oil; Paperwork, Acrylic. *Mailing Add:* 2002 South Rd Baltimore MD 21209

GOLDSTEIN, HOWARD
PAINTER, EDUCATOR
b New York, NY, Feb 10, 33. *Study:* Albright Art Sch, cert; State Univ NY, Col Buffalo, BS; NY Univ, MA; Columbia Univ, EdD. *Work:* NJ State Mus, Trenton; Morris Mus Arts & Sci, Morristown, NJ; YMCA, NY; Univ Frankfurt, WGer; Imperial Chem Industs, US, Wilmington, Del. *Comn:* Painting, Hoechst-Roussel Pharmaceuticals Inc, 94. *Exhib:* 154th Ann Nat Exhib, Pa Acad Fine Arts, Philadelphia, 59 & 65; Ann NJ State Exhib, Newark Mus, 61, 64, 66, 68 & 77; Art from NJ, NJ State Mus, Trenton, 66-73; 32nd Ann Nat Painting Exhib, Butler Inst Am Art, Youngstown, Ohio, 67; Nat Show, Chautauqua Exhib Am Art, NY, 68 & 69; Ann New Eng Exhib, Silvermine Guild Artists, New Canaan, Conn, 70, 72 & 73; one-person exhib, Westbroadway Gallery, NY, 73, 74, 76, 77, & 79; Summit Art Ctr, NJ, 81 & 83; Tenth Anniversary Exhib, Barron Arts Ctr, 88. *Collection Arranged:* Geometric Art: An Exhib of Paintings & Constructions by 14 Contemp NJ Artists, NJ State Mus, 67; Westbroadway Gallery Group, Rundetarn Mus, Copenhagen, Denmark, 73; one-man exhib, NJ State Mus, 74 & Mercer Med Ctr, Trenton, NJ, 90; Viewpoint 76, Morris Mus Arts & Sci, Morristown, NJ, 76; Retrospective Exhib, Trenton City Mus, 89; 50th Anniv Exhib Assoc Artists of NJ, Hunterdon Art Ctr, 90. *Pos:* Exec dir, Comn Study Arts, NJ, 64-66; coordr visual arts prog, Gov's Sch Arts, 82-95; comnr, Mercer Co Cult & Heritage Comn, 71, chmn, 2004. *Teaching:* Prof painting & art, Trenton State Col, NJ, 60-95, chmn art dept, 80-94, prof emer, 94-; The Coll of NJ, 94-. *Awards:* Emily Lowe Award, Emily Lowe Found Competition, 60; Videorecord Corp Am Award, 23rd New Eng Exhib, 72; Purchase Award, Art from NJ, State of NJ, 73. *Mem:* Assoc Artists NJ; Nat Art Educ Asn. *Media:* Acrylic. *Interests:* acting, theatre. *Mailing Add:* 49 Rockleigh Dr Trenton NJ 08628

GOLDSTEIN, NATHAN
PAINTER, WRITER
b Chicago, Ill, Mar 26, 27. *Study:* Art Inst Chicago, BFA, MFA, with Louis Ritman, 52; Art Students League, with Julian Levi. *Work:* Ark Art Ctr; Boston Pub Libr Collection; also numerous pvt collections; Danforth Mus, Framingham, Mass. *Exhib:* Art Inst, Boston, 92; St Botolph Club Gallery, 96; Retrospective Exhib, 2000. *Pos:* Chmn, Found Prog Study, Art Inst Boston, 73-99. *Teaching:* Prof drawing and painting, Art Inst Boston at Lesley Univ, 72-. *Awards:* Acadamician, Nat Acad Design, NY. *Bibliog:* Gerald Monroe (auth), Technical drawing: The personal approach of Nathan Goldstein, Drawing, 5-6/80 & Am Artist, 2/82. *Media:* Oil, Pen and Ink. *Publ:* Auth, The Art of Responsive Drawing, 73, 2nd ed, 77, 3rd ed, 84, 4th ed, 92, 5th ed, 98 & 6th ed, 2005, Figure Drawing: The Structure, Anatomy and Expressive Design of Human Form, 76, 81 & 92 & 5th ed 98, Painting: Visual and Technical Fundamentals, 79, 100 American and European Drawings: A Portfolio, 82 & A Drawing Handbook, Themes, Tools and Techniques, 86, Prentice-Hall; Design and Composition: The Forming of Order, Prentice-Hall, 89; coauth (withHarriet Fishman), Drawing to See, Prentice-Hall, 2004. *Mailing Add:* c/o Art Inst Boston 700 Beacon St Boston MA 02215

GOLDSTEIN, SHELDON (SHELLY)
PAINTER
b St Louis, Mo, 51. *Study:* Univ Mo; studied with James Harmon, St Louis & Val Dunnett, London. *Work:* Off Secy Interior, Washington. *Comn:* Landscapes, portraits & still-lifes, Italy, Ireland & US. *Exhib:* Bibliot Provinciale, Arezzo, Italy, 93; Palazzo Casali, Cortonra, Italy, 93; Embassy Repub SAfr, 94; Royal Geographical Soc, London, Eng, 95; Hotel Martinez, Cannes, France, 95. *Awards:* Artistic Ambassador, People to People Int, Hq, Kansas City, Mo, 94-95. *Bibliog:* Victoria Fowler (auth), Sheldon Goldstein: Paintings 1980-1989 (monogr), 89; Victoria Fowler (auth), Sheldon Goldstein: Un Pittore in Toscana, The Region of Tuscany (catalog), 90; The Zulus and Landscapes of South Africa, Pts I & II (catalog). *Mem:* Fel Royal Geographical Soc, London, Eng. *Dealer:* Kertesz Gallery 521 Sutter St San Francisco CA 94102; Max Bollag Gallery Werdmuhlestrasse 9 Zurich Switzerland. *Mailing Add:* 1139 Indian Trails St Louis MO 63132

GOLDSZER, BATH-SHEBA
PAINTER, GRAPHIC ARTIST
b Warsaw, Poland, Jan 26, 32; US citizen. *Study:* Hertzeliah Teachers Sem, BA(educ), 56; Art Students League, with Gustav Rehberger; also with Joe Hing Lowe & Ludmila Morosova. *Work:* Many pvt collections, US, Israel, Poland & Argentina. *Exhib:* Hudson Valley Art Asn, Westchester Co Ctr; Catherine Lorillard Wolfe Arts Club, Nat Arts Club Gallery; Am Artists Prof League, Salmagundi Club, NY; Chung-Cheng Art Gallery, Sun Yat Sen Hall, St John Univ; and others. *Awards:* First Prize in Oil, Nat Art League, 74 & 82, Queensboro Soc Arts, 74-77 & Art League Nassau Co, 78 & 79; 7 first prizes in oil and numerous others. *Bibliog:* Jack Besterman (auth), Big Six Art League, Chapel & Pension News, 2/72, An accomplished artist, 2/73 & Coop art scene, 4/74 & 5/79, Towers Reporter. *Mem:* Life fel Am Artists Prof League; Hudson Valley Art Asn; Catherine Lorillard Wolfe Arts Club; Nat Art League; Art League Nassau Co; and others. *Media:* Oil. *Mailing Add:* 7583 Granville Dr, Bldg F Tamarac FL 33321

GOLEMBESKI, BEVERLY L
PAINTER, INSTRUCTOR
b Camden, NJ, Oct 20, 40. *Study:* Monclair Univ, BA (art educ), 62; studied with L Geiser, Chas Reid, F Webb, S Szabo, F Peitre, Judi Betts, RC Clark, A Westerman, Don Getz, Nita Engles, Dom DiStefano, M Ahern, N Barch, V Spicer, Roberta Carter Clark. *Work:* Islands Heights Cult Heritage, NJ; paintings, GTECH Int, Mexico City, Mex; paintings, GTECH Int, Buenos Aires, Arg; sports mural, Cent Regional High Sch, Bayville, NJ; watercolor, Baltimore Art Mus, Md; mural, Shore Community Bank, Toms River, NJ. *Comn:* Bathroom/bedroom design, comn by R Efel, Bayville, NJ, 93; rm design, comn by Paul Orni, Seaside Park, NY, 96; mural, Shore Community Bank, Toms River, NJ, 97; nautical design, comn by B Gollob, Basking Ridge, NJ, 99; portraits, comn by Di Santi family, Rutherford, NJ, 2000. *Exhib:* Monmouth Mus, NJ, 80-82, 98, 2000, 2001 & 2002; Allied Artists Nat Juried, Nat Arts Club, NY, 85 & 2002; Adirondack Nat Exhib, Old Forge, NY, 88-89, 92-99; Baltimore Nat Exhib, Johns Hopkins Univ, 88-89, 91-92; Jane Law Int Miniature Exhib, Surf City Gallery, NJ, 89-90; Salmagundi Club, NY, 89-92, 99-2000 & 2002; Trenton Mus Art, NJ, 89-90; Rider Col, NJ, 2002; Johnson & Johnson, Princeton, NJ, 2002; Georgian Ct Col, Lakewood, NJ, 2002; Muriel Berman Mus Art, Collegeville, 2002. *Collection Arranged:* Office Design, GTech, Mexico & Argentina; Murals, Shore Comm Bank, Prof Buildings, Libaries, NJ & PA. *Teaching:* Instructor of classes, demostrations and workshops from Maine to Flordia & Tuscany, Italy. *Awards:* J Bermingham Award, NJ Watercolor Soc, 89; Merit Awards Pine Shores Ann Juried Show, 99; Fel Nat Artists Prof League, 99; Nat Am Art Prof League, 2000 & 2002; Dick Blick Award, Audubon Artist Inc, 2004; AG Edwards Award, NJ Water Color Soc, 2004; Merit Award, RI Water Color So, 2004. *Bibliog:* Susan Ecord (auth), A Watercolor Demo, NJ Cable TV, 91; Wanda Callagy (auth), Local Scenes at Mural, Del Times, NY, 96; Doug Hood (auth), Daily Observer, Toms River, 99. *Mem:* NJ Watercolor Soc (mem bd, 97-99); Pa Watercolor Soc; Garden State Watercolor Soc; Philadelphia Watercolor Club (signature mem); Ocean Co Artists' Guild (pres, 97-99); fel, Am Artists Prof League; Guild of Creative Art, Shrewsbury, NJ (exhibiting mem); Audubon Artist Inc. *Media:* Watercolor, Acrylic. *Res:* Local art publications & writing articles. *Specialty:* Orginals & prints in all medias covering diverse subject matter. *Collection:* NJ shore scenes, boats, ocean, boardwalks, fish, florals, people, race horses, snow scenes, carousels, tropical parrots. *Publ:* Illusr, Central region sports design, Bayville Press, 81-85; illusr, Lifeguard Book, Art Works, 87, 88, 89; auth, illusr, Calendar, Garden State Publ, 88; illusr, contribr, Art Dialog, NJ Watercolor Soc,

99; illusr, To The Shore Once More, Jersey Shore Publs, 2000; fall cover, Jersey Shore Mag, 2002. *Dealer:* Annex Gallery Surf City NJ; Forked River Framing Forked River NJ; Erickson's Gallery Toms River NJ; Anchor & Palette Gallery Bayhead NJ; Watermark Gallery Tuckerton NJ; Jane Law Studio & Gallery Surf City NJ. *Mailing Add:* 16 I St Seaside Park NJ 08752

GOLEY, MARY ANNE
HISTORIAN, DIRECTOR
b Washington, DC, July 1, 45. *Study:* Univ Md, asst to Dr William H Gerdts, BA, 67; Oberlin Col, 70-71; Case Western Reserve Univ, with Wolfgang Steckow & Karal Ann Marling, MA, 73; Cleveland Mus Art, cert, 75. *Exhib:* John White Alexander: 1856-1915, SI Mus Am Art, 76-77; The Hague Sch & its American Legacy, Fed Reserve Bd & Norton Gallery, West Palm Beach, Fla, 82; The Office as Art: Furnishings & Fixtures, Arlington Art Ctr, 86; Paintings of Edward Steichen, 88 & Samuel Halpert, 91, Fed Reserve Bd; Show Me the Money, Trust for Mus Exhibs. *Collection Arranged:* Permanent collections of Fed Reserve Bd, 75 & Fed Reserve Banks, Miami, 79, Jacksonville, 86 & Dallas, 92. *Pos:* Asst registrar, SI Mus Am Art, 68-71; dir, Fine Arts Prog, Fed Reserve Bd, 75-. *Awards:* Lady of the House of Orange-Nassau, Queen of Neth, 82; House of Nassau, Grand Duke of Luxembourg, 88. *Mem:* Am Asn Mus; Asn Prof Art Advisor (Pres, 94); Arlington Arts Ctr (bd pres, 87-90); Mus Trustee Asn (dir comt). *Res:* Late 19th century American artists in the context of their European influences; J W Alexander, Frank Duveneck & Eduard J Steichen. *Publ:* Auth, Gerald Murphy: Toward an Understanding of his Art and Inspiration (exhib catalog), Fed Reserve Bd, 83; Panel for Music Room by John White Alexander, Detroit Inst Arts Bull, 89; auth, The Influence of Velasquez on Modern Painting, The American Experience, Fed Res, 2000; auth, Arquitect ura y Pinturos del Consejo de la Reserva Federal, Banco de Espana, 99; auth, The Hague School and Its American Legacy, Fed Reserve, 82. *Mailing Add:* 4909 Washington Blvd Arlington VA 22205

GOLICI, ANA
ARTIST
b Romania, 55; arrived in US, 87. *Exhib:* NY Hall of Science; Hunter Col Times Square Gallery; East-West Gallery, NY; Int Print Ctr, NY; Holiday Show, Gallery 49, NY City, 2003-2004; Nat Acad Mus, NY, 2006. *Pos:* With Podul Printmaking Workshop, Romania. *Teaching:* Mem faculty continuing educ Hunter Col, NY City. *Mailing Add:* Hunter College Continuing Education East Bldg 10th Floor 695 Park Ave New York NY 10021

GOLICI, NICOLAE
SCULPTOR
Study: Inst Fine Arts, Bucharest, Romania, MFA (scultpure). *Exhib:* Solo shows include Amfra Gallery, Bacau, Romania, 84, Atelier 35 Gallery, Bucharest, 85, 14 Sculptures Gallery, NY City, 89, 91, Mills Pond House, Smithtown Arts Council, St James, NY, 93, Hurlburtt Gallery, Greenwich, Conn, 96, Firehouse Art Gallery, Garden City, NY, 98; group shows include Place as Act and Metaphor, Village Mus, Bucharest, 83; Contemporary Images, Mus Modern Art, Craiova, Romania, 84; Arts of Today, Int Exhib, Budapest, Hungary, 86; Cultural Anthropology: Altar and Symbols, 14 Sculptors Gallery, NY City, 90, Challenging Utopia, 92, Sculptors Drawing, 93, Material Presence, 94; Columns, Lehigh Univ Art Gallery, 91; Springworks, NY Hall of Science, 92; Fulton Ferry Outdoor Sculpture Show, NY City, 93; The Raw and the Uncooked, 95; Drawn to the Third Dimension, 96; Community Warehouse, Interchurch Ctr, NY City, 98; Urban Air Forms, NY City Univ, 99; Nat Acad Mus, NY City, 2006. *Awards:* Frederich Storck Studio Space Award, City of Bucharest, Romania, 80-82. *Mailing Add:* 225 Guy Lombardo Ave Freeport NY 11520-4456

GOMEZ, MIRTA & EDUARDO DELVALLE
PHOTOGRAPHER
Mirta Gomez: b Havana, Cuba, Dec 20, 53; Eduardo Delvalle;: b Havana, Cuba, Sept 14, 51. *Study:* both: Fla Int Univ, BFA, 76; Brooklyn Col, MFA, 81. *Work:* Mus Mod Art, NY; New Orleans Mus Art, La; Brooklyn Mus, NY; Art in Pub Places, Miami, Fla; Bibliot Nat, Paris. *Exhib:* Viva Nada, Blue Sky Gallery, Portland, Ore, 91; Contemp Southern Photog, New Orleans Tri-Annual Exhib, 92; Mayan Dwellings, Univ Calif, San Francisco, 94; Mayan Dwelling, OK Harris Gallery, NY, 97. *Teaching:* Assoc prof art, Fla Int Univ, Miami, 83-. *Awards:* Individual Artist Fel Photog, Nat Endowment Arts, 76 & 90; Oscar B Cintas Fel, 89 & 96; S Fla Cult Consortium Award, 92; John Solomon Guggenheim fellowship, 97. *Mailing Add:* c/o Fla Int Univ Bldg A-1-318A Miami FL 33181

GOMEZ-QUIROZ, JUAN MANUEL
PAINTER, PRINTMAKER
b Santiago, Chile, Feb 20, 39; US citizen. *Study:* RI Sch Design, Fulbright Fel, 62-63; Yale Univ, Fulbright Fel, 63-64; Pratt Graphic Art Ctr, 64-65; Workshop with Justo Mellado, critic, art curator and Claudio Gianconi, writer, author, poet, 89-90. *Exhib:* One-man shows, Schubert Gallery, Marbella, Spain, 77, Sutton Gallery, NY, 80, 83 86 & 88, Held-Koupernikoff Gallery, Boston, 82, Omar Rayo Mus, Rodalnillo, Colombia, 84 & Todd Capp Gallery, NY, 86; The Latin Am Spirit: Art and Artists in the United States 1920-1970, Bronx Mus Art, NY, 88; ST LIFER, Art Exchange, NJ, 89; The Dead Blimpee Show II, NY, 89; IX Biennal Int De Arte, Valparaiso, Chile, 89; Efectos de Viaje, Mus Nat de Bellas Arts Santiago de Chile, 91; printmaking workshop traveling show to Africa, 94; Paula Rieloff Gallery, NY, 96; group exhib, Primer Festival del Grabado, Mus de la Nac, Lima, Peru, 2004; plus many others. *Pos:* pres, HH Silverman Publishing Co, Fine Art Printing, 86-88; Cur & admin asst, Mus Contemp Spanish Art, NY, 90; auth; jury, Premio Internacional de Novela, Casa de la Cultura Dominicana, NY, 2002. *Teaching:* Lectr studio art, Univ Calif, Santa Barbara, 67-68; dir, NY Univ, Photo Etching Workshop, 69-70; adj prof, art dept, NY Univ, 69-76; lectr, Summit Art Ctr, Summit, NJ, 72-77; Escuela de Bellas Artes, Lima, Peru, 75; NJ Ctr Visual Art, 87; Fla Inst Technol & Printmaker Workshop, 88. *Awards:* Second Prize, Painting, Salon de Primavera, Santiago, Chile, 61; Grand Prize, VI Biennial Printmaking, San Juan, PR, 79; Prize Bienal Maracaibo Venezuela, 82; Hispanic Achievers Feria Mundial Hispana, NY, 85; and many others. *Bibliog:* David Shirley (auth), article in NY Sunday Times, 78; Joseph Merkel (auth), The flexibility of sculpture, Artspeak, 86; article in IBM Nachrichten, 6/89, Ger; Javier Martinez de Pinson (auth), La pintura Multidimensional de Gomez-Quiroz, Medico Interamerico, Vol 17, 4/98; and many others. *Mem:* Sociedad de Escritores de Chile. *Media:* Oil, Acrylic; Intaglio. *Collection:* Solomon Guggenheim Mus, New York City; Metrop Mus Art, New York City; Mus Mod Art, New York City; De Menil Collection, Houston, Tex; Mus Fine Arts, Boston, Mass. *Publ:* auth, Crónicas de Literatura Hablada, Novel, Latino Press; auth, Anthology, Plain View Press, Austin, Tex; auth, Hybrido, Arte y Literatura Ano II Numero 2, 98; auth, La Palabra, Revista de Literatura, 98; and many others. *Mailing Add:* 44 Grand St Apt 2 New York NY 10013

GONZALEZ, ARTHUR PADILLA
SCULPTOR
b Sacramento, Calif, July 22, 54. *Study:* Calif State Univ, Sacramento, BA, 77, MA, 79; Univ Calif, Davis, MFA, 81. *Work:* Tempe Mus, Ariz; Crocker Art Mus, Sacramento, Calif; Everson Mus Art, Syracuse, NY; Alta Bates Corp, Emeryville, Calif; Teravel Police Station, San Francisco, Calif. *Comn:* Sculptures, Metrop Transit Authority, Tuckahoe, Crestwood, & Fleetwood, NY, 88; wall mounted bronze sculptures, Sid Singer, NY, 76 & 77. *Exhib:* Solo exhibs, Susan Cummins Gallery, Mill Valley, Calif, 90, Michael Himovitz Gallery, Sacramento, 90, Koplin Gallery, Santa Monica, Calif, 91, Creative Growth Gallery, Oakland, Calif, 91, John Natsoulas Gallery (with catalog), Davis, Calif, 92, Hahnemann Gallery, Albany, Calif, 93 & Monique Knowlton Gallery, Kent, Conn, 94; Acad Art Ctr at Linekona, Honolulu Acad Arts, 93; 2nd Ann Pacific Rim Sculpture Conference Exhibit, Honolulu Acad Arts, 94; Tastes and Trends, Contemp Craft Mus, San Francisco, 94; Tribute to Robert Arneson "Changing the Face of Am Ceramics", Kingborough Community Col, Brooklyn, NY, 94; Myth and Reality, NJ Ctr Arts, 95; The Figure, John Natsoulas Gallery, Davis Calif, 95; and others. *Teaching:* Instr, Univ Ga, Athens, 82 & 84, Studies Abroad Prog, 82; vis artist, La State Univ, Baton Rouge, 83; instr, New Sch Social Res, NY, 84; asst prof, beginning sculpture, Univ Calif, Davis, 85; asst prof adv seminar, Univ Calif, Berkeley, 88; vis artist, San Francisco Art Inst, 89 & 94; assoc prof, Calif Col Arts & Crafts, 91-. *Awards:* Nat Endowment Arts, 82, 84, 86 & 90; San Francisco Art Comn, 93; Calif Arts Coun Fel, 94. *Bibliog:* Katherine Chapin (auth), Arthur Gonzales: At Heart Level, John Natsoulas Press, 92; Contemporary Ceramics: A Step Toward the Future, Hongik Univ Ceramic Research Inst, 93; Charlotte Speight & John Toke (auths), Hands in clay, 94; and others. *Mem:* New Mus Contemp Art; San Francisco Mus Mod Art. *Media:* Clay, Bronze; Metal Cast. *Mailing Add:* c/o Calif Col Arts & Crafts 5212 Broadway Oakland CA 94618

GONZALEZ, JOSE GAMALIEL
ADMINISTRATOR, DESIGNER
b Iturbide, Nuevo Leon, Mex, Apr 20, 33. *Study:* Chicago Acad Fine Arts; Univ Chicago; Am Acad Art, Chicago, dipl; Art Inst Chicago, BFA; Instituto Allende, San Miguel, Mex, study with Jaime Pinto; Univ Notre Dame, MFA candidate. *Collection Arranged:* Hispanic Festival of the Arts, Mus Sci & Indust, Chicago, 74-78; Mexposicion I-25 Paintings from Bellas Artes in Mexico, 76 & Mexposicion II-Agustin Casasola 1910 Mexican Revolution (photog), 77, Univ Ill, Chicago Circle; Anisinabe Waki Aztlan, Truman Col, Chicago, 77; La Mujer-Mexican Women of Mexico plus Midwest Latinas, Cult Ctr Chicago Pub Libr, 78; Raices y Visiones, Mus Contemp Art Chicago, 79. *Pos:* Art dir, Revista Chicano Riquena, Ind Univ NW, 73-80 & Foxlady Mag, Chgo, 75-76; visual consult, Ill Arts Coun, 76-79 & Nat Endowment Arts, Washington, DC, 78-79; nominator, Chicago Art Awards, 78-. *Teaching:* Instr mural painting, Ind Univ NW, Gary, 74; instr Mex crafts, Columbia Col, Chicago, 78-. *Mem:* Chicago Artists Coalition; Movimiento Artistico Chicano (dir, 78-). *Media:* Acrylic, Mixed Media. *Publ:* Contribr, 450 Years of Chicago History, Albuquerque, NMex, 76; contribr, We Americans, 75 & Gallery, 76, Scott Foresman. *Mailing Add:* March Inc PO Box 2890 Chicago IL 60690

GONZALEZ, MARIA ELENA
SCULPTOR
Study: Miami-Dade Community Col, AA, 77; Florence-Italy Prog, Fla State Univ, 78; Fla Int Univ, BFA(sculpture), 79; San Francisco State Univ, MA(Sculpture), 83. *Exhib:* One-person exhibs, Wall Works, Nuyorican Poets Cafe, NY, 91, Works on Paper 1990-92, Port Authority Bus Terminal, NY, 92, Installations/Sculptures, Carla Stellweg Gallery, NY, 94 & 95, In Our Faces, Interamerican Gallery, Miami Dade Community Col, Miami, Fla, 96, Persistance of Sorrow, El Museo del Barrio, NY, 96 & 97, The Illusory Nature of Control, Hall Walls, Buffalo, NY, 98, Resting Spots, The Project, NY, 99, Mnemonic Archit, Ludwig Found of Cuba, 2000, Mnemonic Archit, Bronx Mus of Art, NY, 2000; Vistas Latinas IV-Adios Columbus, Hillwood Art Mus, Long Island Univ, Brookville, 92; Vistas Latinas IX, Univ Wis Art Gallery, Madison, 93; Cubana, Cuban Mus Arts & Cult Inc, Miami, Fla, 93; Composite, Neuberger Mus Art, Purchase, NY, 94; Encuentro Interamericano de Artistas Plasticos Opening Show, Museo De Las Artes, Universidad de Guadalajara, Mex, 94; New Mus Contemp Art, NY, 95; In Three Dimensions: Women Sculptors of the 90's, Snug Harbor Cult Ctr, Staten Island, NY, 95; Westchester Gallery, State Univ NY, Whiteplains, NY, 98; Interpreting, Rotunda Gallery, Brooklyn, NY, 98; Crossing the Line, Queen's Mus of Art, NY, 2001; Locus/Focus, Sonsbeek 9, Arnhem, The Neth, 2001; Gio Marconi Gallery, Milan, Italy, 2001; Cleveland Ctr for Contemp Art, Ohio, 2000; PSI Contemp Art Ctr, NY, 2000; Six Sculptors, Long Island Univ, NY, 2000. *Awards:* Pollock-Krasner Found Inc Grants, 91 & 98; Spec Nomination Grants, Anonymous Was a Woman Found, Louis Comfort Tiffany Found, 97 & Joan Mitchell Found, 98;

Creative Capital Found grant, 99, 2000. *Bibliog:* Carol Vogel (auth), Inside art, NY Times, E34, 2/5/99; Kim Levin (auth), The Village Voice, Voice Choices, 86, 2/16/99; Holland Cotter (auth), article, NY Times, E37, 2/19/99; and many others; Elvis Fuentes Rodriguez, Mnemonic Architecture, Fundacion Ludwig de Cuba, 2000; Rudi C Bleys (auth), Images of Ambiente: Homo Textuality and Latin American Art Today, 2000; Harmony Hammond (auth), Lesbian Art in America - A Contemporary History, Rizzoli, New York, 2000; Bill Arning (auth), Achieving Failure - Gym Culture, 2000; Jean La Marche, The Illusory Nature of Control, Hall Walls, Buffalo, NY, 98; David Hunt (auth), Time Out, Pumping Irony, 4/2000; Calvin Reid (auth), artnet.com, 4/99; Above and Beyond, The New Yorker, 5/17/99. *Publ:* Dr Rudi C Bleys (auth), Images of Ambiente: Homo Textuality and Latin American Art 1810 - Today, 2000; Harmony Hammond (auth), Lesbian Art in America - A Contemporary History, Rizzoli, 2000. *Dealer:* The Project 427 W 126th St New York NY 10027. *Mailing Add:* 272 Sackett St No 1-R Brooklyn NY 11231

GONZALEZ, MAURICIO MARTINEZ
ADMINISTRATOR, GALLERY DIRECTOR
b Mexico City, Mexico, Sept 30, 45. *Study:* Univ Tex at Arlington, BFA, 73; Univ of Americas, MA, 76; Fla State Univ, PhD, 88. *Exhib:* Rio Azul: City of the Storm God, traveling exhib, Univ Tex San Antonio Art Teaching Gallery, Tex, 89, Denver Mus Nat Hist, Colo, 90, Nat Geographic Soc Explorers Hall, Washington, DC, 90, Nat Hist Mus Los Angeles, Calif, 90, Museo Nac de Arqueologia Etnologia, Guatemala City, 91. *Pos:* Gallery dir, Univ Tex, San Antonio, 82-; asst dean, Col Fine Art & Humanities, Univ Tex, San Antonio, 88-; asst vpres, Off of Multicultural Student Develop, Univ Toledo, Ohio, 90-. *Awards:* Fel Nat Endowment Art, 79; Award for minority mus prof, Smithsonian, 88; Grant, USIA, 89. *Mem:* Am Fed Arts; Am Asn Mus. *Publ:* Coauth, The Museum as a field setting for Teacher Education, J of Mus Educ, 87; InterAmerican Cultural Development, Fla State Univ, Ctr Arts Admn, 88. *Mailing Add:* Office Multicultural Student Develop Student Union Rm 2500 2801 W Bancroft Toledo OH 43606-3390

GONZALEZ-FALLA, SONDRA GILMAN
PATRON
Mem: Whitney Mus Am Art, New York City (trustee, currently); Am Theatre Wing (chmn bd, currently). *Collection:* American Photography. *Mailing Add:* c/o Whitney Mus Am Art 945 Madison Ave New York NY 10021

GONZALEZ-TORNERO, SERGIO
PAINTER, PRINTMAKER
b Santiago, Chile, May 22, 27; US citizen. *Study:* Slade Sch, London, England; Atelier 17, Paris, with S W Hayter. *Work:* Metrop Mus Art, NY; Mus Mod Art, NY; Libr Cong, Washington, DC; Mus Fine Arts, Santiago, Chile; Smithsonian Inst, Washington, DC. *Exhib:* High Mus, Atlanta, Ga, 64; Printers & Sculptors as Printmakers, Mus Mod Art, NY, 64; Int Biennial Contemp Drawings, Nat Mus Fine Arts, Santiago, Chile, 93; Retrospective Exhib, Nat Mus Fine Arts, Santiago, Chile, 93; Westchester Community Col, Valhalla, NY, 94; Haida Gwaii Mus, Qay'llnagaay, Skidegate, BC, 96; Gallery Tribal Art, Vancouver, BC, 96; Mus Northern BC, Prince Rupert, 97. *Teaching:* Vis artist, Concordia Univ, Montreal. *Awards:* NY State Coun Arts Fel, 87; Grant, Adolph & Esther Gottlieb Found, 90; First Prize, 10th Biennial Prints, Latin America & the Caribbean & San Juan, Puerto Rico, 93. *Bibliog:* S W Hayter (auth), About Prints, 62 & New Ways of Gravure, 66, Oxford Univ Press; Fritz Eichenberg (auth), The Art of the Print, Abrams, 76. *Mem:* Soc Am Graphic Artists; Philadelphia Print Club. *Media:* Oil, Intaglio. *Dealer:* Eden Gallery 1903 Eden Ln Wichita Falls TX 76306; Annex Galleries 604 College Ave Santa Rosa CA 95404; A Clean Well-lighted Place 363 Bleeker St NY NY 10014; The Studio 2 Maryland Ave Armonk NY 10504. *Mailing Add:* 30 Highridge Rd Mahopac NY 10541

GOODACRE, GLENNA
SCULPTOR
b Lubbock, Tex, Aug 28, 39. *Study:* Colo Col, BA; Art Students League, NY. *Hon Degrees:* Colo Col, Hon Dr; Tex Tech Univ, Hon Dr. *Work:* Tex Tech Mus, Lubbock; Presby Hosp, Denver, Colo; Brigham Young Univ Art Gallery, Provo, Utah; Cleveland Clinic Children's Hosp, Ohio; Denver Mus Natural Hist, Colo; Vietnam Women's Mem, Washington, DC; Nat College Football Hall of Fame; Irish Memorial, Penn's Landing, Philadelphia. *Comn:* Dr Harvie Pruitt, Lubbock Christian Col, 82; Patrick Haggerty, Tex Instruments, 82; Eric Sloan, 83; Erik Jonsson & Cecil Green, Tex Instruments, 83; William B Travis, Sea World, San Antonio, Tex, 88; Sacagawea, US Mint, 2000. *Exhib:* Solo exhib, Read-Stremmel Gallery, San Antonio, Tex, 88; Fifth Ann Sculpture Park, Loveland, Colo, 88; Eighth Ann Artists Am Show, Colo Heritage Ctr, Denver, 88; Twentieth Anniversary Invitational Exhib, NAm Sculpture Exhib, Foothills Art Ctr, Golden, Colo, 88; Borderlands, Second Ann Exhib, Americana Mus, El Paso, Tex, 88; Fifty-fifth Ann Exhib, Nat Sculpture Soc, NY, 88; two-person show, O'Brien's Art Emporium, Scottsdale, Ariz, 88; Artists Choice Show, Nat Acad Western Art, Oklahoma City, 88; Am Art in Miniature, Thomas Gilcrease Mus, Tulsa, Okla, 88. *Teaching:* Scottsdale Artists Sch. *Awards:* Leonard J Meiselman Award, Nat Sculpture Soc, 83; James Earl Fraser Sculpture Award, Prix De West Exhib, 2002; Inductee, Cowgirl Hall of Fame, 2003; Recipient Tex Medal Arts, 2003; Tex Medal of Arts, 2003; NMex Governor's Award, Excellence in Arts, 2005. *Mem:* Allied Artists of Am; fel, Nat Sculpture Soc; Catharine Lorillard Wolfe Art Club; fel, Nat Acad Western Art; Nat Acad Design (acad, 94-); Nat Acad. *Media:* Bronze. *Publ:* Illusr, bronze relief for jacket, The Flamboyant Judge, 73 & Trank Tenny Johnson, 75; illusr, silver relief for jacket, Robbing Banks was My Business, 74. *Mailing Add:* c/o Galleria Silecchia 12 S Palm Ave Sarasota FL 34236

GOODBRED, RAY EDWARD
INSTRUCTOR, PAINTER
b Brooklyn, NY, Dec 7, 29. *Study:* Art Students League, with Robert Brackman, 48-51; Nat Acad Sch Fine Arts, with Ogden Pleissner, 50-51; New York Univ, 53-56. *Work:* Gibbes Mus Art, Charleston, SC; Fine Arts Theatre, Virginia Wesleyan Univ, Norfolk; City Hall Gallery, Charleston, SC; Art Students League Collection, NY; The Pentagon, Washington, DC. *Comn:* Portrait, Mus of Art, Raleigh, NC, 83; Home Federal of Charleston, SC, 74; Finley-Wagner-Kumble Collection, NY, 80; Sch Archit Clemson Univ, SC, 85; Integon Corp, Winston-Salem, NC, 85. *Exhib:* One-man exhib, Gibbes Mus Art, Charleston, SC; Ann exhib, Riverside Mus, NY; Ann exhib, Augusta Richmond Cty Mus, SC; Allied Artists Am, Nat Acad Design, NY, 70-79; Pastel Soc Am, Copley Soc, Boston, Mass & Nat Art Club, NY; South Carolina Artists, Columbia Mus Art, SC. *Teaching:* Instr, portraiture, Hastie Sch Art, Charleston, SC, 70-74; painting & drawing, Art Students League, NY, 75-81; French Inst, NY, 77-79. *Awards:* Trump Award, Pastel Soc Am, 78; First Prize, Salmagundi Club, 78; Medal of Merit, Knickerbocker Artists Am, 79; First Prize, Charleston Artist Guild, 98. *Bibliog:* Jack Morris (auth), South Carolina Contemporary Artists, Greenville Mus Art, 75; Joe Singer (auth), Painting Women's Portraits & Painting Men's Portraits, Watson Guptill Publ, 77. *Mem:* Salmagundi Club; Pastel Soc Am; Charleston Artists Guild (bd dir). *Media:* Oil, Pastel. *Publ:* Illustr, Omni Mag, Omni Int, 6-12/79. *Dealer:* Portraits Incorporated 985 Park Ave New York NY 10028. *Mailing Add:* 85 Montagu St Charleston SC 29401

GOODE, JOE
PAINTER
b Oklahoma City, Okla, Mar 23, 37. *Study:* Chouinard Art Inst. *Work:* Mus Mod Art & Whitney Mus Am Art, NY; Pasadena Art Mus, Calif; Los Angeles Co Mus Art; Victoria & Albert Mus, London; Ft Worth Art Mus, Tex. *Exhib:* Solo exhibs, Contemp Arts Mus, Houston, 73, Arco Ctr Visual Art, 82, James Corcoran Gallery, Santa Monica, Calif, 86, 89, 90 & 92, Karsten Greve Gallery, Paris, 92, Takada Fine Arts, San Francisco, 93, Bobbie Greenfield Gallery, Venice, Calif, 94 & LA Louver, Venice, Calif, 94; American Pop Art, Whitney Mus Am Art, 74; Chicago Art Inst, 74; Calif Painting and Sculpture: The Modern Era, San Francisco Mus Art, 76; Black and White Art Colors, Scripps Col, 78; Am Painting in the Seventies, Albright-Knox Art Gallery, 78; Aspects of Abstract, Crocker Mus, 78; Art Park, Los Angeles/Brazil Projects 90, Los Angeles, Calif, 90; Takada Fine Arts, San Francisco, Calif, 91; Los Angeles Co Mus Art, Calif, 92. *Awards:* Copley Found; Nat Endowment Arts; Maestro Grant, Calif Arts Coun. *Bibliog:* T Henry (auth), Introduction (exhib catalog), Oklahoma City Art Mus, 89; Nora Halpern Brougher (auth), Looking Through the Work of Joe Goode (exhib catalog), James Corcoran Gallery, Santa Monica, Calif, 90. *Media:* Wood; Oil

GOODELL, ROSEMARY W
PAINTER
b Burbank, Calif, May 20, 45. *Study:* Boston Mus Sch, 65-66; Univ Calif Los Angeles, 67; Univ Calif Berkeley, BA, 68, MA, 70. *Work:* Int House, New Orleans, La; In the Garden, Royal Calcasieu Mus, 2004; Mansur Mus, 2005. *Comn:* Large paintings (2), WBRZ-TV, Baton Rouge, La, 90. *Exhib:* Solo show, Ziegler Mus, 82; Women in the Arts, New Orleans World's Fair, 83; Artists in Action, La Arts & Sci Mus, Baton Rouge, La, 86; Off The Walls, Art in Transit, Contemp Art Ctr, New Orleans, 88; Through Her Eyes, Delgado Col, New Orleans, 95. *Pos:* Instr, currently. *Teaching:* Vis artist, E Baton Rouge Parish Schs, 90-91; artist-in-residence, Glasgow Sch, Baton Rouge, La, 93; art instr, Episcopal Sch, Baton Rouge, La, 93-; instr, Art Dept, Baton Rouge Community Col. *Awards:* painting fel, Skidmore Col, 96; Fullbright Mem Fel, Japan, 98; La Div Arts, minigrant, 98 & 2000; La Div of Arts, Visual Art Fel, 2003. *Bibliog:* Rosemary Goodell, Merci, 76; 30 minute doc, WYES-TV, 96. *Mem:* Col Art Asn; Phi Beta Kappa. *Media:* Painting, mixed media. *Specialty:* Baton Rouge Gallery; Contemporary Art; Southernartistry.org, southesastern art. *Publ:* Sch Arts, 4/93. *Dealer:* Baton Rouge Gallery Baton Rouge LA 70816; Caffery Gallery Baton Rouge LA. *Mailing Add:* 16720 Caesar Baton Rouge LA 70816

GOODINE, LINDA ADELE
PHOTOGRAPHER, SCULPTOR
b Watkins Glen, NY, July 29, 58. *Study:* Univ Rochester, NY, 80; Ithaca Col, NY, MS, 81; Fla State Univ, Tallahassee, MFA, 83. *Work:* Light Work, Menschel Gallery, Syracuse Univ, NY; Frederick R Weisman Collection, Los Angeles, Calif; Aaron Siskind Found; Int Sch Photog, Arles, France. *Exhib:* Personal Icon, Los Angeles Ctr Photog Studies, Calif, 86; The Manipulated Environment, Houston Ctr Photog, Tex, 87; Looking South: A Different Dixie, Birmingham Mus Art, Ala, 88; Vernon Fisher & Linda Adele Goodine, Pensacola Mus Art, Fla, 89; New Southern Photog, Burden Gallery, NY, 89-92; traveling shows, Selections from Weisman Collection, Frederick Weisman Found, Los Angeles & Linda Adele Goodine, Southeastern Ctr for Contemp Art, Winston-Salem, NC; Montgomery Bienial, Indianapolis Mus Art, 92; Cibachromes 1982-1992, Linda Adele Goodine, Ind State Mus, 92. *Teaching:* Artist in residence, photog, Lightwork Community Darkrooms, Syracuse, NY, 86; instr 3-D, Delgado Community Col, New Orleans, La, 88-89; vis artist & assoc prof, Herron Sch Art, Indianapolis, Ind, currently. *Awards:* Nat Endowment Arts, Rockefeller Found, 90; Southern Arts Fedn, 91; Aaron Siskind Found Grant. *Bibliog:* Marcia E Vetrocq (auth), Linda Adele Goodine at Res Nova, Art in Am, 88; Jay Murphy (auth), Linda A Goodine & Vernon Fisher, Art papers, 89; Donald Kuspit Art papers, summer 92. *Mem:* Col Art Asn. *Publ:* Illusr, Exploring Color Photography, Wm C Brown, 89; Louisiana Artist's Pages: Love in the Ruins, Contemp Art Ctr, 89; article for Aperture, No 115, Aperture Found, 89; article for Red Bass, No 13, 89; North of Wakulla: An Anhinga Anthology Anhinga, Press, 90. *Mailing Add:* c/o Herron Sch Art 1701 N Pennsylvania St Indianapolis IN 46202

GOODMAN, CALVIN JEROME
CONSULTANT, COLLECTOR
b Chicago, Ill, Mar 1, 22. *Study:* Harvard Univ, AB(hon), 49. *Pos:* Mgt consult to artists & art dealers, 58-; vpres, Tamarind Lithography Workshop, 59-76; nat consult, Artists Equity Asn, 74-76; nat adv bd Portrait Soc Am, 1998-. *Teaching:* Instr bus methods for artists & artisans, Tamarind Lithography Workshop, 61-71; instr prof practices, Calif Inst Arts, 67-71; instr prof practices, Otis Art Inst, 68-71; lectr, seminar & workshops in marketing art for San Francisco Art Inst, Scripps Grad Sch of Art, Pratt Inst, & Portrait Soc Am, Wash, DC, 99-. *Bibliog:* The booming art market, Los Angeles Magazine, 1/82; B Fredericks (auth), The Art of Creating Monotypes, HR Productions, 90; S Doherty (auth), The Art of G Wetmore, Am Artist, 6/2000; L Moss Perricelli (auth), Review Art Martketing Handbook, Am Artist, 10/2004. *Mem:* Portrait Soc Am (nat bd 98-). *Res:* Fine art market; operations of specialized schools of art and music; original print market; making/marketing monotypes; paper specialties & giclée prints market. *Publ:* Auth, Art Marketing Handbook, GeeTeeBee, 7th ed, 2003; Wilson Hurley's Color Theory and Practice, 5/86, Thomas Hart Benton, 12/89 & 1/90, Advice for Portraitists, 6/2000, The Revival of Religious Art, 12/2000, Am Artist; and others. *Mailing Add:* 11901 Sunset Blvd Suite 102 Los Angeles CA 90049

GOODMAN, HELEN
HISTORIAN, CRITIC
b Detroit, Mich, May 18, 39. *Study:* Univ Mich, BA, 60; Wayne State Univ, MA, 66; New York Univ, PhD, 75. *Exhib:* The Art of Rose O'Neill (auth, catalog), The Brandywine River Mus, 89. *Collection Arranged:* Art Rose O'Neill, Brandywine River Mus, Chadds Ford, Pa, 89. *Pos:* guest cur, Brandywine River Mus, 1989. *Teaching:* Asst prof art hist, Stern Col Women, New York, 66-72; asst prof, Fashion Inst Technol, New York, 68-. *Awards:* Research Found Grant, State Univ NY, 83; Nat Endowment Humanities Grant, 85, 89 & 91; John Sloan Mem Found Grant; Swann Found Caricature & Cartoon Grant, 85. *Bibliog:* Elizabeth Buehrmann (auth), History of Photography, Vol 19, No 4, 338-342, 95; Louise Dahl Wolfe, Dictionary of Women Artists, 427-428, Fitzroy Dearborn Publ, London, 97; Frances Benjamin Johnson (auth), Dictionary of Women Artists, 444-447, Fitzroy Dearbourn Publ, 97. *Mem:* Col Art Asn; Asn Hist Am Art. *Res:* American late 19th and early 20th century art. *Publ:* Auth, essay, In: America's Great Women Illustrators: 1850-1950 (exhib catalog), Madison Sq Press, 85; Women illustrators of the golden age of Am illustration, Woman's Art J, spring/summer 87; The Art of Rose O'Neill, Brandywine Riv Mus, Chadds Ford, Pa, 89; Emily Sartain, The Sartain Family and the Philadelphia Cultural Landscape, Barra Found, Univ Press, 97 & 98; numerous articles in Arts Mag, 1977-87. *Mailing Add:* c/o Fashion Inst Technol 227 W 27th St New York NY 10001

GOODMAN, JAMES NEIL
DEALER, COLLECTOR
b Rochester, NY, Apr 11, 29. *Pos:* Dir, James Goodman Gallery. *Specialty:* Modern American and European masters, including Calder, Cornell, de Kooning, Klee, Leger, Lichtenstein, Matisse, Moore, Picasso and Tanguy. *Mailing Add:* c/o James Goodman Gallery 41 E 57th St New York NY 10022-1908

GOODMAN, JANIS G
PAINTER, DRAFTSMAN
b New York, NY, Oct 21, 1951. *Study:* Queens Col, NY, BA, 72; Corcoran Sch Art, Washington, DC, 73-74; Etruscan Found, Siena, Italy, 74; George Washington Univ, MFA, 75. *Work:* Hirshhorn Mus & Sculpture Garden, Corcoran Gallery Art, Washington, DC; Hunter Mus Am Art, Chattanooga, Tenn; Knoxville Mus Art, Tenn; Univ Va, Charlottesville; Allen Mem Art Mus, Allen Meml Art Mus, Oberlin, Ohio; Dept Interior, Acadia Nat Park, Mt Desert Island; Miss Mus Art, Jackson; Epson Europe, Amsterdam, Neth; IDTV, Amsterdam, Neth. *Comn:* paintings, Westin Hotel, Ft Worth, Tex. *Exhib:* Corcoran Gallery Art, Washington, DC, 80; solo exhibs, Jane Haslem Gallery, Wash, 88, 89 & 93, Steven Scott Gallery, Baltimore, 90, Galerie Maas, Rotterdam, The Neth, 94, The Contents of History (with catalog), B'Nai B'rith Klutznick Nat Jewish Mus, Wash, 95, Gordon Fennell Gallery, Coe Col, Cedar Rapids, 96, Kunstler Werkstatt Bahnhof Westend, Berlin, Ger, 97, Wash Project for Arts, DC, 99, Weatherspoon Art Gallery, Greensboro, NC, 99, Peruvian North Am Cult Inst, Lima, Peru, 2000 & Dist Fine Arts, Wash, DC, 2000; Faculty II, Corcoran Gallery Art, 93; Personal Vision, Five Women Artists, Tatem Art Gallery, Hood Col, Md, 94; Three Am Artists, Galerie Witteveen, Amsterdam, 95; Drawing on Washington, Marsha Mateyka Gallery, 95; Indianapolis Jewish Community Ctr, Ind; Dist Fine Arts & Proj Space, Washington, DC, 98; AVC Contemp Art, New York City, 2002; Hay Gallery, Portland, Maine, 2002; 2004 Biennial, Ctr Maine Contemp Art, Rockland, 2004; Massillon Mus Art, OH, 2006; Butte Silver Bow Arts Found, Mont, 2006. *Pos:* arts reviewer, Around Town, WETA/TV, 2003-; faculty develop, Corcoran Mus, 2003 & 2006; artist in res, St Mary's Col of Md & Butte Silver Bow Artist Residency, Mont, 2006. *Teaching:* Instr drawing, Smithsonian Inst, 77-87; instr color theory, Parsons Sch Design, NY, 85-86; assoc prof fine arts & drawing, Corcoran Sch Art, Washington, DC, 87-, Santa Reparata, Florence, Ital, 2002, St Mary's, Md, 2005, Univ Ga, Cortona Ital Prog, fall 2006. *Awards:* Washington Comn Arts Grant, 81 & 90; Montpelier Cult Award, Md State Drawing, 83; Grant to Individual Artists, DC Comn Arts, 95-96; NEA Exhib Support Grant, 98. *Bibliog:* Morris Yarowsky (auth), The Contents of History, Art Papers, Atlanta, 95; Norma Broude & Mary D Garrand (eds), The Power of Feminist Art, The American Movement of the 1970s, History & Impact; Leslie Wright (auth), Art Papers, Janis Goodman, 97; Erin Pustay (auth), The Independent Weekender, Massillon, OH, 5/6/2006; Roberta Forsell Stauffer (auth), Montana Standard, 5/16/2006; and many others. *Media:* Oil, Mixed Media, Graphite. *Publ:* co-auth (with Dennis Weller), Is Seeing Believing, The Real, The Surreal, The Unreal in Contemporary Photography, NC Mus Art, 2000. *Dealer:* CII'I Contemporary Art Brooklyn NY; Lee Hansley Raleigh NC; AVC Contemporary Art NY; Turtle Gallery Deer Isle ME. *Mailing Add:* 512 8th St NE Washington DC 20002

GOODMAN, MARIAN
DEALER, PUBLISHER
b New York, NY, June 15, 38. *Study:* Columbia Univ Grad Sch Art Hist, BA. *Pos:* Dir publ, Multiples Inc, 65-, pres, 74-; dir, Marian Goodman Gallery, currently. *Mem:* Art Dealers Asn. *Specialty:* Publishing limited editions and sometimes books, records, etc by prominent contemporary artists such as Lewitt, Oldenburg, Warhol, Baldessor, Artswager and many others. *Mailing Add:* Multiples Inc 24 W 57th St New York NY 10019

GOODMAN, MARK
PHOTOGRAPHER
b Boston, Mass, May 19, 46. *Study:* Boston Univ, BA, 70; also with Minor White, 70. *Work:* Mus Mod Art, NY; Mus Fine Arts, Boston; George Eastman House, Rochester, NY; Mus Fine Arts, Houston; Samuel A Dorsky Mus, SUNY, New Paltz. *Exhib:* Recent Acquisitions, Mus Mod Art, NY, 78-79; solo exhib, George Eastman House, Rochester, NY, 80-81; Am Children, Mus Mod Art, NY, 81; Contemp Photogrs IX, George Eastman House, Rochester, NY, 82; Capital Improvements, Austin Hist Ctr, Tex, 86; A Kind of History, The Tremaine Gallery, The Hotchkiss Sch, Lakeville, Conn; plus others; Picturing What Matters, George Castman House Traveling Exhib, 2005-. *Teaching:* Artist-in-residence photog, Apeiron Workshops Inc, Millerton, NY, 72-76; asst prof, Univ Tex, Austin, 80-86, assoc prof, 86-02, prof, 2002-, grad advisor studio art MFA program, 2005-. *Awards:* Nat Endowment Arts Fel, 73; Guggenheim Fel, 77. *Bibliog:* Julia Scully & Andy Grundberg (auth), Currents: American photography today, Mod Photog, Vol 44, No 2, 80; James Kaufmann (auth), Works of love: The photographs of Mark Goodman, Exposure, Vol 20, No 1, 82; Jeanne Clare van Ryzin (auth) Portrait of a small town, Austin Am-Statesman, 3/2000; Timothy Cahil (auth) Photographer's book takes heartfelt look at a small town, Albany New York Times Union, 11/5/2000; Vince Aletti (auth), Open Book, Village Voice, 4-5/2000. *Publ:* Contribr, Photographs of Millerton, NY, 1971-1975, Aperture, Vol 19, No 4, 75; Kansas Album, Addison House, 77; Photographing Children, Time-Life Books, 83; A Kind of History, Millerton, NY: 1971-91, Markerbooks, 99; Mark Goodman (auth), Second Thoughts On Questions I Was Asked Twenty Years Ago, SPOT, spring/summer, 2001. *Mailing Add:* PO Box 889 Bastrop TX 78602

GOODMAN, SIDNEY
PAINTER
b Philadelphia, Pa, Jan 19, 36. *Study:* Philadelphia Univ Arts, 54-58; Yale Norfolk Fel, 57. *Work:* Art Inst Chicago; Libr Cong, Washington; Whitney Mus Am Art, Mus Mod Art, NY; Hirshhorn Collection; Metrop Mus Art, NY; and others. *Exhib:* Pa Acad Fine Arts, 59, 61, 64, 65, 67, 69, 77 (traveling, with catalog), 79 (with catalog), 81 (traveling, with catalog), 82-83 & 90; Philadelphia Mus Art, 59 (with catalog), 62, 67 (traveled, with catalog), 68, 70, 76 (with catalog), 77 (with catalog) & 77, 79 (with catalog), 86 & 86 (with catalog); Mus Mod Art, NY, 62 (with catalog), 63 & 67; Whitney Mus Am Art, 62 (traveling, with catalog), 64 (two exhibs, with catalog), 65 (two exhibs, with catalogs), 67-68, 69 (traveled, with catalog), 69-70, 78 (with catalog) & 80 (with catalog); Corcoran Gallery Art (traveling, with catalog), 63 & 76; Brooklyn Mus, 63 (with catalog) & 69 (two exhibs, with catalogs); Goteborgs Konstmus, Gothenberg, Sweden, (with catalog), 70; Joslyn Art Mus (traveled, with catalog), 73; Va Mus Fine Arts (with catalog), 74; Butler Inst Am Art (with catalogs), 75, 76, 80, 81, 82, 83, 86 & 88; Sheldon Mem Art Gallery, Univ Nebr (traveled, with catalog), 78; Minn Mus Am Art (traveling, with catalog), 79, 80 (with catalog) & 90 (traveling, with catalog); Mus Fine Arts, Boston, 83-84; solo exhibs, Philadelphia Mus Art, 85, Flowers East, London (with catalog), 93, Terry Dintenfass Gallery, NY, 94 & 95, More Gallery, Philadelphia, 94, Kauffmann Gallery, Shippensburg Univ, Pa, 95 & Pa Acad Fine Arts, 96; San Francisco Mus Mod Art (traveling, with catalog), 85-86; Silvermine Guild Arts Ctr, 88; Mus Fine Arts, Houston, 92; Art Inst Chicago, 93-94; NY Realism-Past & Present (traveling, with catalog), Kitakyoshu Munic Mus Art, Japan, 94; The Art of Justice, Drasdale Gallery, White Plains, NY, 95; The Spiritual Dimension, Suzanne H Arnold Art Gallery, Lebanon Valley Col, Annville, Pa, 95; Contemp Drawing: Exploring the Territory (with catalog), Aspen Art Mus, Colo, 95; retrospective, Philadelphia Mus Art, 96. *Pos:* Vis artist, Univ Houston, 79; distinguished vis prof, Univ Calif, Davis, 87; Lamar Dodd Prof Chair, Univ Ga, 91. *Teaching:* Instr drawing & painting, Philadelphia Col Art, 60-78; instr, Tyler Sch, Philadelphia, 77 & Pa Acad Fine Arts, 78-. *Awards:* Visual Art Award, Southeastern Ctr Contemp Art, 91; Ford Found Purchase Award, 91; Nat Educ Asn Fel, 91. *Mem:* Nat Acad. *Dealer:* Salander-O'Reilly Galleries 20 E 79th St New York NY 10021. *Mailing Add:* c/o Pa Acad Fine Arts 118 N Broad St Philadelphia PA 19102

GOODNOUGH, ROBERT
PAINTER
b Cortland, NY, Oct 23, 17. *Study:* Syracuse Univ, Hiram Gell fel, 40, BFA; NY Univ, MA; New Sch Social Res; Ozenfant Sch Art; Hans Hofmann Sch Fine Arts. *Work:* Albright-Knox Art Gallery, Buffalo, NY; Solomon R Guggenheim Mus, Mus Mod Art, Metrop Mus Art, Whitney Mus Am Art, NY; Wadsworth Atheneum, Hartford, Conn; plus others. *Exhib:* One-man shows, Univ Minn, 64, Univ Notre Dame, 64, Arts Club Chicago, 64, Andie Emmerich Gallery, 82 & Tibor de Nagy Gallery, NY, 85; Nat Inst Arts & Letts, 64; New Am Painting & Sculpture, Mus Mod Art, 69; Indianapolis Mus Art, 69; Cayuga Mus Hist & Art, Auburn, NY, 69; Venice Biennial, 70; Am Acad Arts & Letts, 71; Nenberges Mus, Purchase, NY, 99; Goodnough, Washington Co Mus, Hagerstown, Md, 2000; Castellani Mus, Niagara Falls, NY, 2001; plus many other group & one-man shows. *Pos:* Art critic, Art News, 50-57; secy, Documents of Mod Art, 51. *Teaching:* Instr, painting, NYU, 53, Fieldston Sch, Riverdale, NY, 53-60, Cornell Univ, 60. *Awards:* Ada Garrett Award, Art Inst Chicago, 61; Ford Found Purchase Prize, 63; Artist of Yr, Westchester Coun of Arts, 96. *Mem:* Nat Acad. *Media:* All. *Publ:* Contribr, articles to nat mag. *Mailing Add:* Gallery at Lincoln Ctr Concourse Shippee Gallery New York NY 10023

GOODRICH, JAMES W
ADMINISTRATOR, COLLECTOR
b Burlington, Iowa, Oct 31, 39. *Study:* Cen Mo State Univ, BS, 62; Univ Mo, MA, 64, PhD, 74. *Collection Arranged:* Mo Decoys, Mo State Mus, 89. *Pos:* Exec dir, State Hist Soc Mo, 85-. *Awards:* Disting Alumi Award, Univ Mo Col Arts and Sci, 99; Alumni Award, Univ Mo Alumni Asn, 99. *Res:* Folk-art research on Missouri-made waterfowl decoys; Missouri artists. *Interests:* Missouri art, folk art. *Collection:* Missouri Decoys, Missouri Artists. *Publ:* Auth, Ben Yeargan of Missouri: "Working" Decoy Carver, 1984 Ann Am Decoys, 84; Factory Decoys, Mo Conservationist, 86; Roy Shoop's Canadas, Decoy Hunter, 90; John Francis: Missouri Decoy Carver, Decoy Mag, 92; JT Beckhart: Father of the Big Lake Call, Decoy Mag, 96; Robert Ormsby Sweeny: some Civil War Sketches, Mo Hist Rev, 89; Missouri's Woodson Roddy: The Carver from Clinton, Decoy Mag, 98; Duane Evans Lyon: A Sketch of an artist, 02. *Mailing Add:* State Historical Soc of Mo 1020 Lowry St Columbia MO 65201

GOODRIDGE, LAWRENCE WAYNE
PAINTER, SCULPTOR
b Cincinnati, Ohio, Mar 18, 41. *Study:* Univ Cincinnati, BFA(with hon), 63; Univ Cincinnati & Art Acad Cincinnati, MFA, 67. *Exhib:* All-Ohio Painting & Sculpture Exhib, Dayton Art Inst, 67; Mid-States Art Exhib, Evansville Mus Arts & Sci, Ind, 70; one-man show & Louisville Biennial, J B Speed Art Mus, Ky, 71; 17th Ann Drawing & Sculpture Show, Ball State Univ, Muncie, Ind, 71. *Pos:* Toy designer, Kenner Prod Co, 63-65. *Teaching:* Instr found design & color theory, Art Acad Cincinnati, 69-, co-dean, 72-. *Awards:* Second Prize, Eastern Fine Paper Graphic Design, 65. *Publ:* Auth & illusr, European diary, 70 & Truck stop, 71, Cincinnati Mag. *Dealer:* Richard Feigen Gallery 226 E Ontario St Chicago IL 60611. *Mailing Add:* 29 Kathryn Ave Florence KY 41042-1535

GOODSPEED, BARBARA
PAINTER
b Gardner, Mass, Sept 1, 19. *Study:* Famous Artists Sch, Westport, Conn, cert; studied with Edgar A Whitney & Frank Webb. *Exhib:* Hudson Valley Art Asn, Hastings-on-Hudson, NY, 83-93; Am Artists Prof League, NY, 84-94; Salmagundi Club, NY, 86-94; Catharine L Wolfe Art Club, NY, 87-94; Allied Artists Am, NY, 88, 94 & 96; others. *Pos:* Dir & trustee, Kent Art Asn, 72-2005; dir, Catharine L Wolfe Art Club, 90-93 & 98-, Soc Creative Arts, Newtown, Conn, 90-94, vpres painting; Hudson Valley Art Assoc- Board, 2001. *Teaching:* Instr watercolor, Washington Art Asn, Conn, 89-93, Wooster Community Arts, Danbury, Conn, 90-93, Soc Creative Arts, Newtown, Conn, 91-93 & Heritage Village, Southbury, Conn, 95-96. *Awards:* Jane Peterson Award, Salmagundi Club, 93; Corp Award, Catharine L Wolfe Art Club, 93; Claude Parsons Award, Am Artists Prof League, 93; others. *Bibliog:* Denise Matteau (dir), Watercolor Demo, Pittsfield Community TV, Mass, 92. *Mem:* Fel Am Artists Prof League; Catharine L Wolfe Art Club; Acad Artists; Kent Art Asn (pres, 85-88 & 89-92, 2004-2005); Conn Watercolor Soc. *Media:* Oil, Watercolor. *Publ:* Illusr, Forever Flowers, Scribners, 79; The Best of Oil Painting & The Best of Watercolor, Light & Shadow/Landscape Inspirations, Rockport Publ; Best of Watercolor, vol 3. *Dealer:* The Lenox Gallery of Fine Art Lenox MA; Fine Line Art Gallery, Woodbury, CT. *Mailing Add:* c/o Oxford Gallery 267 Oxford St Rochester NY 14607

GOODWILL, MARGARET
PAINTER, DESIGNER
b Los Angeles, Calif, Sept 27, 50. *Study:* Carnegie Mellon Inst, cert, 66; Univ Calif, Santa Barbara, 68-70; Calif Col Arts & Crafts, Oakland, BFA (cum laude), 72. *Work:* Oakland Mus Collectors Gallery, Calif; Triple Crown Hall-Hilton Resort Hotel, Plesanton, Calif; Tamarack Beach Resort, Carlsbad, Calif; Na Hoola Spa, Hyatt Regency, Waikiki, Hawaii, 2000; Del Monte, Kunia, Hawaii, 2000; Plantation Spa, Kaaawa, Hawaii, 2002; Hui No'eau, Maui, Hawaii, 2002. *Comn:* Wave Waikiki (mural, 30' x 90'), Honolulu, Hawaii, 91; catalog cover, Benjamin Cummings Publ, Calif, 91; The Breaks (TV show), Pub Television, Hawaii; concept, design, murals & 3 dimensional sculptures, The Pyramids Restaurant, Honolulu, 96; and others; illus, Forest Solutions, Big Island, Hawaii; mural, Curves, Haleiwa, Hawaii, 2003. *Exhib:* Puna hoe Invitational, Honolulu, Hawaii, 2000; Polynesian Cult Ctr, Hauula, Hawaii, 2000; Boutiki, Pearl Harbor, Hawaii, 2000; Garden Biersch Mardi Gras, 2000; Haleiwa Arts Festival, 2003; many others. *Pos:* Graphic artist, City Arts, Oakland, 70-71; creative art dir, Am Analysis Corp, San Francisco, 74-76; dir, Lone Wolf Gallery, 82-84. *Awards:* First Prize, Ossining Woman's Club Competition & Poughkeepsie Art Ctr, 68; Merit Award, Delta Art Show, 71. *Bibliog:* Wayne Herada (auth), Waikiki's new look, Honolulu Advertizer, 7/20/91; Kristine Bucar (auth), A Couple of artists, The East Honolulu Newspaper 12/93; Kristine Bucar (auth), When art goes online, Honolulu Advertizer, 10/18/94. *Mem:* Historic Hawaii Found; Natural Found Materials; Bishop Mus; Contemporary Mus Art; Acad of Art. *Media:* Acrylic on Canvas, Oil Pastel on Handmade Paper. *Publ:* Illusr, Wit and Wisdom of The Coachella Valley, Desert Discoveries Pubs; Palm Parade (poster), publ by Portal, 92; Greeting cards, calendars, gift bags, etc, publ by Island Heritage; shower curtains, publ by The Springs; plus 18 other posters, 1986-93 calendars & t-shirts. *Mailing Add:* 68-234 Au St Waialua HI 96791-9304

GOODWIN, BETTY
GRAPHIC ARTIST, PRINTMAKER
b Montréal, 23. *Hon Degrees:* Dr honoris causa, Univ Montral, Quebec, 92, Univ Guelph, Ontario, 93 & Univ Windsor, Ontario, 97; hon degrees, Ontario Col Art, Toronto, 93 & Emily Carr Inst Art & Design, Vancouver, 99. *Work:* McGill Univ, Musee des Beaux-Arts de Montral, Musee d'art contemorarian de Montral, Concordia Univ, Lavallin, Centre Int d'art Contemporain de Montreal, Montreal; Banque d'oeuvres d'art, Conseil des Arts du Canada, Nat Gallery Can, Dept External Affairs, Ottawa; Art Gallery Ont, Humber Col, Osler Hoskin & Harcourt, Ydessa Hendeles Art Found, Toronto; Nat Mus Women Arts, Washington; Musee du Que, Bradford City Art Gallery, England, Simon Fraser Univ, Vancouver, MOMA, NY, Mackenzie Art Gallery, Regina, Mount Allison Univ, Sackville & many others. *Exhib:* Solo shows, Fawbush Gallery, NY, 95, Sable-Castelli Gallery, Toronto, 95, Art Gallery Windsor, Ont, (with catalog 95), MacKenzie Art Gallery (with catalog), Regina, 95, Nat Gallery Can (with catalog), Ottawa, 96, Winnipeg Art Gallery (with catalog), 96 & Stephen Freidman Gallery, Londres, 96; Rothenberg (with catalog), Galerie du Centre des arts Saidye Bronfman, Montreal, 95; Reflections of the Soul, Art Gallery North York, Ont, 96; Object-Dessin, Galerie d'art ju Centre culturel, Univ Sherbrooke, 96; L'Écart, Centre d'Art Contemporain La ferme du Buisson, Noisiel, France, 96; Sable-Castelli Gallery, Toronto, 97; Pieces of Time: 1963-98, Jack Shainman Gallery, NY, 98; Betty Goodwin: Framing the Century, Yukon Arts Ctr Gallery, Whitehorse, Can, 2000; The Prints of Betty Goodwin, Nat Gallery of Canada Ottawa, Canada, DDalhousie Art Gallery, Halifax & McMaster Mus Art, Hamilton, Can, 2002; and others; Mus Nat des Beau-Arts du Que, Que, 2004; Sable-Castelli Gallery, Toronto, 2004. *Awards:* Nat Award Visual Arts, Banff Ctr Sch Fine Arts, 84; Prix Borduas, Govt Que, 86; Gershon Iskowitz Prize, 95. *Dealer:* Galene René Blouin, 372 Ste Catherine Ovest, #501, Montreal, PQ Canada H3B 1A2. *Mailing Add:* c/o Galerie René Blouin 372 Ste Catherine Ouest No 501 Montreal PQ H3B 1A2 Canada

GOODWIN, GUY
PAINTER
b Birmingham, Ala, June 19, 40. *Study:* Univ Ala; Auburn Univ, BFA, 63; Univ Ill, MFA, 65. *Work:* Patrick Lannen Mus, Palm Beach, Fla; Chase Manhattan Bank, NY; Philadelphia Acad of Fine Arts. *Exhib:* One-person shows, Area X Gallery, NY, 84 & Dolan-Maxwell Gallery (with catalog), Philadelphia, Pa, 86; Abstract Issues (with catalog), D Hood, S French & Tibor Denage Galleries, NY, 85; Drawing with Respect to Painting II, NY Studio Sch Gallery, 86; Thorden/Wetterling Gallery, Sweden, 87, 90; Suzanne Hilberry Gallery, Mich, 92; Bill Maynes Gallery, NY, 98; Lindsey Brown Gallery, NY, 2002. *Teaching:* Vis artist painting, Wayne State Univ, Detroit, Mich, 78 & Art Inst Chicago, Ill, 80; instr painting & drawing, Bennington Col, Vt, 80-; prof painting, Ohio Univ, currently. *Awards:* Nat Endowment Arts, 74 & 80; Creative Artists Pub Serv, 76; Pollock Krasner, 97; Adolf & Esther Gottlieb Found, 94; Guggenheim Found, 93. *Bibliog:* Michael Brenson (auth), Drawing with respect to painting, New York Times, 5/2/86; Tiffany Bell (auth), Drawing with respect to painting, 6/86 & Margaret Berensen (auth), Guy Goodwin, 10/86, Arts Mag; Edward Suzanski (auth), rev, Philadelphia Inquirer, 9/25/86; Robert Murdock (auth), Guy Goodwin, Chauncey Flats, Review Mag, Feb, 98; Tiffany Bell (auth), Guy Goodwin at Bill Maynes Gallery, Art in America, Oct, 98. *Media:* Oil, Watercolor. *Mailing Add:* 83-10 35th Ave #5F Jackson Heights NY 10013-2911

GOODYEAR, FRANK H, JR
ADMINISTRATOR, HISTORIAN
b New York, NY, Jan 5, 44. *Study:* Yale Univ, BA, 66; Univ Del, Winterthur Prog, MA, 69. *Collection Arranged:* Pennsylvania Academicians (with catalog), Pa Acad of Fine Arts, 73, The Beneficent Connoisseurs, Gibson, Harrison (with catalog), 74 & In This Academy: The Pennsylvania Academy of the Fine Arts, 1805-1976 (with catalog), 76; Thomas Doughty: An American Pioneer in Landscape Painting, 1793-1856 (with catalog), Pa Acad, Corcoran Gallery of Art & Albany Inst, 73-74; American Paintings in the Rhode Island Historical Society, 74; Cecilia Beaux (1855-1942): Portrait of an Artist (with catalog), Pa Acad & Indianapolis Mus of Art, 74-75; American Art: 1750-1800 Towards Independence, Yale Univ Art Gallery, 76; Eight Contemporary American Realists: Philip Pearlstein, Alfred Leslie, Stephen Posen, Janet Fish, Duane Hanson, Joseph Raffael, Neil Welliver & Sidney Goodman, 77; Seven on the Figure (with catalog), Pa Acad Fine Arts, 79; A Man of Genius: The Art of Washington Allston, Pa Acad Fine Arts & Mus Fine Arts, Boston, 80; Contemporary American Realism since 1960 (with catalog), Pa Acad Fine Arts, 81. *Pos:* Cur, RI Hist Soc, 69-72; cur & ed exhib catalogs, Pa Acad Fine Arts, 72-82, pres, 83-; actg cur, Am Painting & Sculpture, Yale Univ Art Gallery, 74-75. *Teaching:* Guest lectr, Univ Tex, Austin, 91. *Mem:* Am Asn Mus (mem, Legislative Comt, currently); Fairmount Park Art Asn (dir, currently); Conserv Ctr Art & Hist Artifacts (dir); Yale Univ Coun Comt on the Art Gallery & Brit Art Ctr (chmn). *Publ:* Auth, Welliver, Rizzoli Int Publ Inc, 85. *Mailing Add:* c/o Buffalo Bill Hist Ctr 720 Sheraton Ave Cody WY 82414

GOODYEAR, JOHN L
SCULPTOR, PAINTER
b Los Angeles, Calif, Oct 22, 30. *Study:* Univ Mich, BD, 52, MD, 54. *Work:* Guggenheim Mus, Whitney Mus Am Art, Metrop Mus Art & Mus Mod Art, NY; Bibliot Nat, Paris; Brit Mus, London. *Comn:* State NJ, 81 & 90; Chiron (plaza), Univ Medicine & Dentistry, NJ, 83; Drawn from the Water (stone reliefs), Jewish Ctr, Princeton, NJ, 84; Dawn of Law (marble relief), State House, Trenton, NJ, 91. *Exhib:* solo exhibs, Amel Gallery, NY, 66, Mass Inst Technol Ctr Advan Visual Studies, Cambridge, 76, Pyramid Gallery, NY, 89, Snyder Fine Arts, NY, 92, Muhlenberg Col, 95, Michener Mus, Doylestown, Pa, 2000 & Ericson Gallery, Philadelphia, Pa, 2000, Hunterdon Mus Art, Clinton, NJ, 2005, Rider Univ Art Gal, 2005; Plus By Minus, Albright-Knox Art Gallery, Buffalo, NY, 68; Boston Mus Fine Arts, 71; Mus Mod Art, NY, 72; Geometric Abstraction 1937-1997, Snyder Fine Art, NY, 97; Six Artists in the '90s, NJ State Mus, Trenton, 96; Trace, Rosenwald-Wolf Gal, Phila, PA, 2004; Twister, Blanton Mus Art, Austin, TX. *Collection Arranged:* Iron Works, Univ of Arts, Rosenwald Wolf Gallery, Philadelphia, Pa, 2003. *Pos:* Prof emeritus, Rutgers Univ. *Teaching:* Instr, Univ Mich, Grand Rapids, 56-62 & Univ Mass, Amherst, 62-64; prof art, Mason Gross Sch Art, Rutgers Univ, 64-97, prof emer, 97-. *Awards:* Graham Found Fel, 62 & 70; Ctr Advan Visual Studies Fel, Mass Inst Technol, 70-71. *Bibliog:* Stephen Westfall (auth), Thinking into Form, (catalog essay), Michener Mus Art, Bucks Co, Pa, 2000. *Mem:* Am Abstract Artists. *Media:* Mixed. *Res:* Sculpture & painting. *Mailing Add:* 167 Seabrook Rd Lambertville NJ 08530

GOPNIK, BLAKE
CRITIC
Pos: Chief art critic, Wash Post, Wash, 2003-, art critic, formerly. *Mailing Add:* Wash Post 1150 15th St NW Washington DC 20071

GORBATY, NORMAN
PAINTER, SCULPTOR
b New York, NY, Oct 5, 1932. *Study:* Amherst Col, BA, 1953; Yale Univ, MFA, 1955. *Work:* Yale Mus Fine Arts, New Haven, CT; Baruch Col, New York; Glucksman Ireland House, NY Univ; Mead Art Mus, Amherst Col, Amherst, Mass; Nat Portrait Gallery, Smithsonian, Washington, DC. *Exhib:* Young Am Print Makers, Mus Mod Art, New York, 1953; Nat Print Exhib, Brooklyn Mus, New York, 1954. *Pos:* Designer, James Eng Assoc, 1955-1956; designer, L W Frohlich, 1956-1958; vpres art group supervisor, Benton & Bowles, Inc, 1959-1968; pres designer, Norman Gorbaty Design, Inc, 1968-. *Teaching:* Teaching fel printmaking, Yale Univ, New Haven, CT, 1953-1955; adj prof advan graphic design, Cooper Union Sch Art, New York, 1961-1970; instr graphic design, Silvermine Sch Art, New Canaan, CT, 1971. *Awards:* Heisey Award, Corning Glass; Yale-Norfolk Art Sch Scholar; 50 Best Books Award, AIGA; Award of Distinctive Merit; and others. *Bibliog:* Gabor Peterdi (auth), Printmaking Methods Old & New, MacMillan, 1959; Print Making with a Spoon, Reinhold, 1960. *Media:* All Media. *Publ:* Contribr Designer, Time Mag, US News & World Report, Fortune Mag, CA Mag (Cancer Soc J), Impact 21, Maine Mag, and others. *Mailing Add:* 42 Meadowwoods Rd Great Neck NY 11020

GORCHOV, RON
PAINTER
b Chicago, Ill, Apr 5, 30. *Study:* Art Inst Chicago, 47-50; Univ Ill, 50-51. *Work:* Whitney Mus Am Art,Mus Mod Art, Metrop Mus Art, Guggenheim Mus, NY; Chicago Art Inst. *Teaching:* Prof art, Hunter Col, formerly. *Awards:* Guggenheim Fel, 94. *Media:* Oil on Canvas, Watercolor. *Mailing Add:* 113 Nelson St Brooklyn NY 11231

GORDIN, MISHA
PHOTOGRAPHER, VIDEO ARTIST
b Riga, Latvia, Russia, Mar 12, 46. *Study:* Self taught in art; Aviation Inst, Russia, MEng, 72. *Work:* Nat Mus Mod Art, Georges Pompidou Ctr, Paris, France; Art Inst Chicago; Detroit Inst Art; Int Mus Photog at George Eastman House, Rochester, NY; Toledo Mus Art, Ohio. *Exhib:* Klein Art Works, Chicago, 91-94; solo exhibs, Mark Masouka Gallery, 90 & 91, New Gallery, Bemis Proj, Omaha, Nebr, 90, Klein Art Works, Chicago, 91 & 94, Bentley Gallery, Scottsdale, Ariz, 92 & 95, Dennas Mus Ctr, Northwestern Mich Univ, Traverse City, 93, Morgan Gallery, Kansas City, Mo, 94 & NDak Mus Art, Grand Forks, 94, JJ Brookings, San Francisco, 2000, Lewalen Contemp, Santa Fe, 2000; Thomson Gallery, Minneapolis, 95; Cedar Rapids Mus Art, Iowa, 96; traveling group exhib, West Publ Corp, Eagan, Minn, 96; and others. *Awards:* Visual Arts Fel, Nat Endowment Arts, 86; Mich Arts Award, Art Found Mich, 87; Creative Artist Grant, Mich Coun Arts, 88; Minn Art Bd Photog Grant, 2000. *Bibliog:* C Reeve & M Sward (auth), The New Photography, Spectrum Publ, 89; Afterimage, Vol 15, Visual Studies, 1/88. *Publ:* Cover Story, black & white Photo Metro, Vol 18 2000, Issue II, 2001. *Mailing Add:* 15257 Fruit Farm Rd Saint Joseph MN 56374

GORDLEY, MARILYN CLASSE
PAINTER, PRINTMAKER
b St Louis, Mo, Aug 4, 29. *Study:* Washington Univ, BFA; Univ Okla, MFA; Ohio State Univ. *Work:* Greenville Mus Art, NC; Spring Mills, Lancaster, SC; Univ Okla; Bank of Am, Greenville; James Michener Mus, Doylestown, Pa. *Comn:* Portraits of Gov Kerr Scott, Arthur Tyler, Henry Belk, Elmer Browning & Weldell Smiley, E Carolina Univ, 64-74. *Exhib:* Cent South Exhib, Nashville, Tenn, 69; Nat Drawing Exhib, Southern Ill Univ, Carbondale, 75; Miss Mus Art, Jackson, 78; Fayetteville Mus Art, NC, 79; Southern Exposure, Hanson Gallery, New Orleans, 80; Now & Then, Mus York Co, Rockhill, SC, 90; Arlington Hall, Greenville, NC, 90; The Contemp Eye, James Michens Art Mus, New Hope, Pa, 05; and numerous two person shows. *Collection Arranged:* Greenville Mus, NC; Lowisburg Coll, NC. *Teaching:* Assoc prof drawing & painting, ECarolina Univ, 64-93; retired. *Awards:* 18th Irene Leache Award, Norfolk Mus, 66; Spring Mills First Prize, 67; Cent South Exhib Award, 69; Innovative Printing Award, Noyes Mus, NJ, 2001; Best in Show, Atlantic City Art Ctr, NJ, 2003. *Mem:* Am Asn Univ Women; Woodmere Art Mus; Phila/Tri State Artist Equity; Philadelphia Art Mus; Michens Art Mus. *Media:* Acrylic, Woodcut. *Dealer:* Riverbank Arts Stockton, NV. *Mailing Add:* 5802 Belmont Manor Pipersville PA 18947-1126

GORDLEY, METZ TRANBARGER
PAINTER
b Cedar Rapids, Iowa, May 24, 32. *Study:* Wash Univ, BFA; Univ Okla, MFA; Ohio State Univ; Univ NC, Chapel Hill. *Work:* Greenville Mus Art, NC; E Carolina Univ; NC Print & Drawing Soc; Univ Okla, Norman; Louisburg Col, NC; Bank of Am; Glaxco; Smith Kline Corp. *Comn:* Aycock portrait for E Carolina Univ. *Exhib:* Ball State Univ Art Gallery, 75; Biennial Exhib Piedmong Painting & Sculpture, Mint Mus, Charlotte, NC, 75; one-man shows, Mint Mus, Charlotte, 78; Razor Gallery, NY, 79; 44th Ann, Butler Inst Am Art, Youngstown, Ohio, 80; two-person shows, Greenville Mus Art, 82, Bank of the Arts, New Bern, 84 & Arlington Hall Gallery, Greenville, 85 & 90, Col Albemarle, Elizabeth City, NC, 90, Gaston Col, Dallas, NC, 91, QLM Assocs, Princeton, NJ, 93 & Stover Mill Gallery, E Pa, 94; 30th Irene Leache Mem, Chrysler Mus, Norfolk, Va, 90; 53rd-62nd Ann Exhib, Woodmere Art Mus, Philadelphia, 93-2005, 55th-63rd Ann Mem Exhib, 95-2002; Tri-State Artist Equity Shows, 2001-06; exhib Riverbank Arts, Stockton, NJ, Langman Gallery, Willow Grove, Pa; Innovare Gallery, Easton, PA, 2004; Atlantic City Art Center, Atlantic City, NJ, 2004. *Teaching:* Prof painting, E Carolina Univ, 59-92, retired. *Awards:* Award Excellence, Art with a Southern Draw, Univ Mobile, Ala, 98; Second Prize for Watercolor & Second Prize for Oil, Kinston Art Show, 68; Merit Award, Wake Visual Arts Asn, Raleigh, 86; Cash Sculpture Award, 35th Tenn, All-State Art Exhib, 96; Artist Equity, Cheltasham, PA, 03; Woodmere Art Mus Members Show, Best in Show, Philadelphia, 2003. *Bibliog:* Emily Farnham (auth), Behind a Laughing Mask, Charles Demuth; SECAC Review, Vol V, No 2, 4/72; Philip Fehl, The Classical Monument, SECAC, Vol VII, No 1, spring 74; Lucy Lippard, Overlay: Contemporary Art and Art of Prehistory, SECAC, Vol XI, No 1, spring 86. *Mem:* Philadelphia TriState Artists Equity (vpres). *Media:* Oil. *Dealer:* Riverbank Arts Stockston, NJ; Howard Gallery, New Hope, PA. *Mailing Add:* 5802 Belmont Manor Pipersville PA 18947

GORDON, ALBERT F
ART DEALER
b Antwerp, Belg, June 18, 34; US citizen. *Study:* Sorbonne, Univ Paris; Columbia Univ, MA, 60. *Collection Arranged:* Aspects of the Doubled Image in African Art (auth, catalog), 76; Beauty and the Beast: A Study in Contrasts (auth, catalog), 77; Ekon Society Puppets: Sculptures for Social Criticism (auth, catalog), 77. *Pos:* Pres, Tribal Arts Galleries, Inc, New York, 68-. *Bibliog:* Terry Trucco (auth), Primitive art, Art News, 4/81. *Mem:* Am Appraisers Asn; Explorers Club. *Specialty:* African art. *Publ:* The Tribal Bead, Tribal Arts Gallery Publ Inc, 74. *Mailing Add:* c/o Tribal Arts Gallery 155 Round Mountain Rd Stephentown NY 12168

GORDON, COCO
ENVIRONMENTAL ARTIST, WRITER
b Genoa, Italy, Sept 16, 38; US citizen. *Study:* Univ Mich, 55-57; Adelphi Univ, BA(art), 59. *Work:* Vassari Futurist Collection, Messina, Italy; Getty Ctr Arts & Humanities, Santa Monica, Calif; Am Craft Mus, NY; Smithsonian Mus, Washington; Visual Art Mus, Beer Sheva, Israel. *Comn:* Culture project (hops for beer), Kulturverein Schreams, Steiermark, Austria, 93; Sculpture, Bonotto Collection, Italy, 98-2000. *Exhib:* Solo exhib, Heckscher Mus, Huntington, NY, 78, Real Art Ways, Hartford, Conn, 86, Foro Boario, Reggio Emilia, Italy, 89, World Fair Pavillion, Messina, Italy, 91, Kunstkanzlei, Vienna, Austria, 93, V-Idea, Genoa, Italy, 95 & Gallery One Twenty Eight, NY, 98; group exhib, Am Craft Mus, NY, 81, Fine Arts Mus Long Island, Hempstead, NY, 81-82 & Sandra Gering Gallery, NY, 97, Instituto De Artes Graficas, De Axaca, Mex, 98, elevator audio work, Art-in-General, NY, 2000, plus others. *Pos:* Publ, W Space Books & Water Mark Press, 78-. *Teaching:* art residency, Vienna Pub Sch, 93; residency Dreste, Italy, 98-2000. *Awards:* Women Studio Workshop Grant, Rosendale, NY, 87; Harvestworks Grant for Audio Production, Studio Pass, 93; Djerassi Found Residency, 96. *Bibliog:* Jerome P Frank (auth), Making handmade paper perform, Small Press Mag, 86; Henry Martin (auth), Il sogno del tempo, Apeiron Mag, Messina, Italy, 91; Marie-Therese Pfeiffer, Coco Gordon-radical food, Vernissage Mag, Vienna, Austria, 93. *Mem:* Poetry Soc Am; Poets & Writers; Acad Am Poets and IAWA. *Media:* Installation, Artist Books, Art & Poetry Performance Events. *Interests:* Bioregionalism, Permaculture. *Publ:* Auth, ed & illusr, Radical Food, Kunstkanzlei, 93; Hip-Hop Solarplexus, Kulturverein Schreams, 93; Superskywoman, V-Idea, 95 & New Observations, 97; TIKYSK (things I know you should know), 96. *Dealer:* Rosa Leonardi V-Idea P'zza Campetto 8A/9 16123 Genova Italy; Christine Jones Kunstkanzlei Riemergasse 14/29 Al0l0 Vienna Austria; Rosanne Chiessl Pari Dispari Gallery RE Italy. *Mailing Add:* 138 Duane St New York NY 10013

GORDON, DAVID
MUSEUM DIRECTOR
b London. *Study:* Grad, Balliol Col, Oxford; studied at London Sch Economics and Harvard Univ. *Pos:* Financial journalist; asst editor The Economist, chief exec officer, 81-93; sec Royal Acad Art, 1996-2002; dir Milwaukee Art Mus, 2002-; governor British Film Inst, 82-92; bd mem South Bank Ctr, 88-96; trustee Architecture Found, 1991-2001, Tate Gallery, 93-98; chmn Contemporary Art Soc, 92-98. *Mailing Add:* Milwaukee Art Museum 700 N Art Museum Dr Milwaukee WI 53202

GORDON, DOUGLAS
SCULPTOR
b Glasgow 66. *Study:* Glasgow Sch Art, 84-88; Slade Sch Art, London, 88-90. *Exhib:* WATT, Witte de With & Kunsthal, Rotterdam, 94; Eigen & Art at the Independent Art Space, London, 95; Kopfbanhhof/Termainal, Hauptbahnhof Leipzig, 95; Looking Awry, Brasilian Embassy, Paris; Animal, Ctr Contemp Arts, Glasgow, 97; Hugo Boss Prize, Guggenheim Mus, SoHo, NY, 98; New Art from Scotland, Museet for Samtidskunst, Oslo, 98; View II, Mary Boone Gallery, NY; So Far Away, So Close, Encore, Brussels, 98; solo shows, 24 Hour Psycho, Tramway, Glasgow and Kunst-werke, Berlin, 93, Lisson Gallery, London, 94, Bad Faith, Kunsterhaus, Stuttgart, 95, Douglas Gordon & Rirkrit Tiravanija, FRAC Languedoc-Roussillion, Montpellier, France, 96, Galleri Nicolai Wallner, Copenhagen, Bloom Gallery, Amsterdam & Galerie Micheline Swajcer, Antwerp, 97; and many others. *Teaching:* vis prof Glasgow Sch of Art. *Awards:* Britains Turner Prize, 97; Hugo Boss Award, 98. *Mailing Add:* c/o Gagosian Gallery 555 W 24th St New York NY 10011

GORDON, HARRY H
SCULPTOR
b Ft Leavenworth, Kans, 60. *Study:* Syracuse Univ, BFA, 79-83; Rutgers Univ, New Brunswick, NJ, MFA; studied with Boris Blai & Roger Mack. *Work:* Lehihg Valley Hosp, Allentown, Pa; James A Michener Art Ctr Sculpture Garden, Doylestown, Pa; Plattsburgh Sculpture Park, NY; State Mus of Pa, Harrisburg. *Exhib:* NJ State Mus, Trenton; Art in the Embassies Prog, US Embassy, Vienna, Austria, 98-2001;

Hunterton Mus of Art, Clinton, NJ, 2000; Artsbridge Gallery, Stockton, NJ, 2001; solo exhib, Woodmere Mus, Chestnut Hill, Pa, Chapin Sch, Princeton, NJ. *Teaching:* instr, Pratt Inst, Brooklyn, NY, currently; instr, Raritan Valley Community Col, currently. *Awards:* Pollock-Krasner Found Award; Herk Van Tongeren Mem Award. *Mem:* Artsbridge, Lambertville, NJ; Int Sculpture Ctr, Hamilton, NJ. *Media:* Wood, Stone & Bronze. *Mailing Add:* 17 Old River Rd Lambertville NJ 08530

GORDON, JAMES A
PATRON
Study: Northwestern Univ, BA (umma cum laude). *Pos:* Fac, Gordon's Wholesale, 71-86; founder, managing partner,Edgewater Growth Capital Partners, currently; treas, Whitney Mus Am Art, trustee currently; bd dir, Des Moines Ballet; bd dir, Chicago Mus Am Art, Northwestern Mem Found, John F Kennnedy Ctr Performing Arts, Chicago Cares Inc, Bankers Trust Co, Methodist Medical Adv; bd dir & former pres, Des Moines Art Ctr; bd dir, Iowa Soc to Prevent Blindness, Des Moines Opera; mem bd, Grinnell Col, chmn, investment comt. *Mailing Add:* c/o Whitney Mus Am Art 945 Madison Ave New York NY 10021

GORDON, JOHN S
SCULPTOR, EDUCATOR
b Milwaukee, Wis, Nov 16, 46. *Study:* Antioch Col, BA, 70; Claremont Grad Sch, MFA, 73. *Work:* Prudential Insurance Co. *Exhib:* Whitney Mus Am Art, Biennial Contemp Am Art, NY, 75; one-man shows, Los Angeles Louver Gallery, Venice, Calif, 77 & Artists Space, NY, 79; USC Atelier, Santa Monica, 88; Shidoni Contemp Gallery, Santa Fe, NMex, 91; Jan Weiner Gallery, Kansas City, Mo, 94; Tinsletown Too, Domestic Setting, Los Angeles, 2004. *Pos:* Consult, Community Redevelop Agency, Los Angeles, 84; Southern Calif Rapid Transit Dist Metro Rail Art-in-Transit Comt, 85-90; mem, Mayor's Task Force Arts, 87-88; consult, Los Angeles Co Transportation Comn, 90-91; bd trustees, Santa Fe Chamber Music Festival, 92-93; consult, Metrop Transit Authority, NY, 97-99; mem, Comn on Accreditation, Nat Asn Schs Art and Design, 2000-; moderator, The Work of 20th Century Self-Taught Artists, John Michael Kohler Arts Ctr, Sheboygan, Wis, 5/2000, Aspects of Henry Darger, Mus Am FolK Art, NY, 2001; mem pub art com, Port of San Diego, 2002-04; mem art selection com, N Embarcadero Visionary Plan, San Diego, 2003-05. *Teaching:* instr ceramics, Mt St Mary's Col, Los Angeles, 73; assoc prof sculpture & ceramics, Univ Southern Calif, 73-, assoc prof, Sch Fine Arts, 89-91; vis asst prof, Claremont Grad Sch, fall 79; dean, Sch Fine Art, Univ Southern Calif, 81-87; acad vpres, Calif Col Arts & Crafts, 88; dean fine arts & cult studies, Inst Am Indian Arts, 91-93; Kansas City Art Inst, 93-96; dean, Sch Art and Design, Pratt Inst, Brooklyn, 96-99, provost, 99-02; dir, Sch Art, San Diego State Univ, 2002-04; provost, Otis Col Art & Design, 2004-. *Awards:* Nat Endowment Arts Grant, 76; Mayor's Cert Appreciation, City of Los Angeles, 84. *Bibliog:* Susan C Larsen (auth), John S Gordon, Arts Mag, 3/77; Peter Frank (auth), On the trail of the emergent American, The Nat Gallery Guide, 1/81; Margaret Lazzari (auth), Delving into minor works, Artweek, 2/6/88. *Mem:* Col Art Asn Am; Int Coun Fine Arts Deans. *Media:* Mixed Media. *Publ:* How about some art in next year's Los Angeles festival, Los Angeles Herald Examiner, 10/6/87; References to Political Climate, Fragility of Human Emotions, Santa Fe New Mex, 10/11/91; New Mexico: Growing internationalism, Art News, 4/92; Authenticity and the curatorial dilemma, The Mag, 7/92; National endowments are not as critics see them, Kansas City Star, 8/4/95; The Practical Handbook for the Emerging Artist (2nd ed), 2002. *Mailing Add:* Otis Col Art 9045 Lincoln Blvd Los Angeles CA 90045

GORDON, JOY L
CURATOR, EDUCATOR
b New York, NY, Jan 31, 33. *Study:* NY Univ, BA, 57, MA, 72. *Collection Arranged:* Contemporary Latino Americano Art, 72; Prints from the NYU Art Collection, Hudson River Mus, Yonkers, 73; Paintings & Sculpture from the NYU Art Collection, Art Gallery, Univ Notre Dame, 73; William Benton Mus Art, Univ Conn, 73; Contemp Asian & Middle Eastern Art from the Grey Found Collection, 75; Report from Soho, 75; Aspects of Am Realism, 76; Prints & Techniques (with catalog), 76; Drawing & Collage (with catalog), 76; Contemp Israeli Crafts, 77; Am Impressionist Painting, 77; Am Still Life Paintings, 19th & 20th Centuries, 78; Containers, Mass Crafts, 79; Art in Process, 79; Directions in Realism: Boston, 80; American Artists in Dusseldorf, 82 & On the Threshold of Modern Design, The Arts & Crafts Movement, 84, Danfort Mus. *Pos:* Asst cur educ, cur & researcher pvt collections, NY Univ Art Collection, 72-74; cur, Grey Art Gallery & Study Ctr, NY Univ, 74-77; dir, Danforth Mus, Framingham, Mass, 77-88 & Guild Hall, East Hampton, NY, 88-93; independent cur, 94-. *Teaching:* Adminr mus studies, NY Univ, 72-77 & Framingham State Col, 78-88. *Mem:* Col Art Asn; Am Asn Mus; New Eng Mus Assoc; Art Table. *Mailing Add:* 28 Sandra Dr East Hampton NY 11937

GORDON, P(ATRICK) S(COTT)
PAINTER
b Claremore, Okla, Oct 24, 53. *Study:* Univ Tulsa, BFA, 74, grad studies, 74-75. *Work:* Philbrook Art Mus, Tulsa, Okla; McNay Art Inst, San Antonio, Tex; Boise Mus, Idaho; City of Tulsa Performing Arts Ctr, Okla. *Comn:* Painting, Tulsa Opera Co, Okla, 79; large scale painting, City of Tulsa, Okla, 89. *Exhib:* Am Realism: Twentieth Century Drawings and Watercolors, traveling exhib, San Francisco Mus Mod Art, Calif, 85; Watercolor USA 1986, The Monumental Image, Springfield Art Mus, Mo; New Horizons in Am Realism, traveling exhib, Flint Inst Art, Mich, 90-91; one-man exhibs, Fischback Gllery, NY, 82, 87 & 90, PS Gordon: Paintings of Women, Mary Ann Doran Gallery, Tulsa, Okla, 85, Contemporaries V: PS Gordon, Wichita Ctr Arts, Kans, 91; Sherry French Gallery, NY, 92; Peyton-Wright Gallery, Santa Fe, NMex, 93; Am Realism, Sewal Art Gallery, Rice Univ, Houston, Tex, 93. *Pos:* Bd mem, Arts and Humanities Coun, 77-85; comt mem, Arts in Pub Places Comt, 87-90; bd dir, Philbrook Art Mus, 89-90. *Awards:* Nat Endowment Arts Grant, 79; Season Poster, Metrop Opera Co, New York, 92-93. *Bibliog:* Brandy Whittingham & Peggy Arenz (auths), PS Gordon: American Artist, 5/91; Charles le Clair (auth), Color in Contemporary Painting, Watson-Guptill Publ, 91; Christopher R Young (auth), New Horizons in American Realism, Flint Inst Art, 91. *Media:* Watercolor. *Dealer:* Peter Tatistcheff & Co 50 W 57th St New York NY 10019

GORE, DAVID ALAN
PAINTER, PHOTOGRAPHER
b Ann Arbor, Mich, May 6, 47. *Study:* Tyler Sch Art, Philadelphia, BFA, 68; Acad Fine Art, with Joseph Amerotica, 72; Philadelphia Mus Art, with Theodore Segal, 72-74, Fortessa Di Basso, Florence, Italy, with Umberto Baldini, 73. *Comn:* Empire & Flute Player (murals), comn by Wilbur Pierce, 85; Pompeian Room, comn by Dr James Sullivan, 85; sculpture, comn by Dr R Shafto, 91; conservation mural (6 ft x 19ft), Bur Mus Delaware; mural (10 ft x 76 ft), Sports Club Woodlyn, Pa. *Exhib:* British & Australian Embassy, 85; Very Victorian, Del State Mus, Dover, 88-89; Mixed Media by David Gore, Widener Univ Mus, Chester, Pa, 90; Afterwords, Philadelphia, Pa, 93; Roam, Wilmington, Del, 94. *Pos:* Chief conservator, Bureau of Mus Del, 74-, Henry M Flagler Mus, 75-80, Widener Univ Mus, 87-94 & Classic Conservation, Chester, Pa. *Teaching:* Instr painting, drawing & design, Bucks Co Community Col, Pa, 71-73. *Awards:* French Int Poster Contest, Paris, 63; Nat Designers Award, 68. *Bibliog:* Art Carey (auth), Restoring Masterpieces, Philadelphia Inquire, 81; Rita Beyer (auth), David Gore Works Shown at Schwartz Gallery, Chestnut Hill Local, 92; Patty Mengers (auth), High Tech Endeavor for Chester Artist, Delaware Co Daily Times, 94. *Media:* Oil, Photographer. *Mailing Add:* 3900 N Washington St Wilmington DE 19802-2148

GORE, JEFFERSON ANDERSON
CURATOR
b Selma, Ala, April 25, 43. *Study:* Harvard Col, BA(visual studies), 65; Skowhegan Sch Painting & Sculpture, 66; Grad Sch Fine Arts, Univ Pa, MFA(sculpture), 70. *Collection Arranged:* Sesquicentennial of Railroad in the Arts (auth, catalog), 79; Exquisite Nomads: Seashells Real and in Art (auth, catalog), 80; Season of Mists (auth, catalog), 81; Spacetoys: Fifty Years of Fantasy, 82; Painted Light (auth, catalog), 83; Mushroom Magic: The R Gordon Wasson Collection of Mycological Art. *Pos:* Cur fine arts, Reading Pub Mus, Pa, 78-. *Teaching:* Asst sculpture, Grad Sch Fine Arts, Univ Pa, 68-70; instr, Albright Col, Pa, 70-74. *Mem:* Citizens Arts in Pa; Philadelphia Art Alliance. *Res:* Cross-cultural influences between Europe and Asia in art and philosophy. *Mailing Add:* 73 Hardwood Ln Mohnton PA 19540-7720

GORE, PAUL M See Goreniuc, Mircea C Paul

GORE, SAMUEL MARSHALL
PAINTER, SCULPTOR
b Coolidge, Tex, Nov 24, 27. *Study:* Atlanta Col Art, BFA; Miss Col, BA; Univ Ala, MA; Ill State Univ, EdD. *Work:* Hull Gallery, Hinds Community Col, Raymond, Miss; Ill State Univ; Miss Univ Women; Aven Galleries, Miss Col; Miss Mus Art. *Comn:* Mural, Van Winkle Methodist Church, Jackson, Miss, 74; portrait bust (bronze), US Sen John Stennis, Miss Wing, Civil Air Patrol, 74 & William Faulkner, Sta WJTV, Howard Lett, Jackson, Miss, 74; Bronze Nurse, Miss Baptist Hosp, 88; Bronze Working Man, Miss Mus Agr & Forestry. *Exhib:* One-man shows, Miss Art Asn, 57 & House Admin Off Suite, US Capitol Bldg, 75; Nat Oils Show & Mem show, Miss Art Asn, Jackson 58; Sears Traveling Show, 63. *Teaching:* Prof drawing, painting & sculpture & head art dept, Miss Col, 51-. *Bibliog:* Ruth Campbell (producer), Conversation with Sam Gore (video tape), Miss Educ TV, 11/75. *Mem:* Miss Art Educ Asn (secy, 61, vpres, 62, pres 63); Nat Art Educ Asn; Southeastern Art Educ Asn; Med-Art USA (bd dir); Christians in Visual Arts. *Media:* Oil, Watercolor; Terra Cotta, Bronze. *Publ:* Illusr, Mississippi Game and Fish, 58-59; Freshwater species of Mississippi, 59. *Mailing Add:* Miss Col Art Dept PO Box 4205 Clinton MS 39058

GORE, TOM
PHOTOGRAPHER, EDUCATOR
b Victoria, BC, Aug 7, 46. *Study:* Univ Victoria. *Work:* Prov Collection, Parliament Bldgs, Victoria; Vancouver Art Gallery, BC; Univ Victoria, BC; City Seattle. *Comn:* Illusr, Earth Meditations, Mike Doyle, 70 & Vancouver Island Poetry Soft Press, 74. *Exhib:* Sask Cult Exchange, 86 & 87; Escuela Artos Aplicadas, Ibiza, Spain, 88; Applied Art Sch, Soria, Spain, 91; Ctr of Cult Brno, Czech Repub, 94 & 95; Joigny, France, 94; Rogut Art, Victoria, 95; Bologna, Italy, 95. *Collection Arranged:* Victoria & Victoria Five, Secession Gallery; Polaroid Collaboratory, 78 & The Stereo Show, 80, Open Space; Latitudes and Parallels, Winnipeg Gallery, 81. *Pos:* Ed art mag, Tryste, 66-68; com photogr, 69-71; cur photog, Open Space, Victoria, 75-84; ed, Rhino Press, 79-90; consult, Winnipeg Art Gallery, 81-; photo ed, Malanat Rev 92. *Teaching:* Lectr photog, Univ Victoria, 77-; instr photog, Camosun Col, Victoria, BC, 73-78. *Awards:* Hon Mention, BC Photogr Show, Simon Fraser Art Gallery, 73; First Prize, Vancouver Island Juried Show, Art Gallery of Greater Victoria, 74; Can Coun Grants, 77, 78 & 90; Dept Communications Grant, 90. *Bibliog:* Glen Howarth (auth), Bio-article, Victoria Press, 70; Carolyn Leier (auth), Bio-article, Arts W, 76; Contemporary Personage, Padua, Italy, 80; Photographic Artists & Innovators, 84; International Catalog Of Contemporary Art, 89. *Mem:* Open Space Arts Soc (pres, 78-); Soc for Photog Educ, NW Region (chmn, 78-81); Victoria Civil Liberties Asn (pres, 88-); Can Federation of Rights & Liberties (bd, 92-); BC Civil Liberties Asn (bd, 96). *Media:* Collage, Photography, Digital Photography. *Res:* Criticism of photography; John Thomson biography; the photograph as theatre; evolution of photographic landscape. *Publ:* Contemporary Photography in British Columbia, Ryerson, 79; auth, In perspective: Vancouver art, Arts W, 1/79; Collecting the paradoxical magic mirror, Photo Communique, Pl, 5/79; Portfolio, Camera Mainichi,

Tokyo, 10/81 & 3/83; George Craven's Objects and Images, New York, 88; Portfolio, Camera Canada, Toronto, 84; An Admirable View, Rhino Press, Victoria, 86; Robert Hirsch's Photographic Possibilities, New York, 90; Building Consensus, Democrat, 92. *Mailing Add:* 1653 Dean Park Rd North Saanich BC V8L 4Y7 Canada

GOREE, GARY PAUL
INSTRUCTOR, PAINTER
b Jackson, Miss, Apr 8, 51. *Study:* Southwestern Okla State Univ, BFA, 72; Tex Tech Univ, MA(educ), 80. *Work:* Williams Co, Tulsa, Okla; Presby Hosp, Oklahoma City, Okla. *Exhib:* Greater Fall River Nat, Mass, 78; Nat Cape Coral Ann, Fla, 79; Okla Art Ann, Tulsa, 80; Okla 81, Univ Okla, Norman, 81; one-man shows, Odessa Col, 94 & Rogers State Col, 96. *Pos:* Art supervisor, Tulsa Pub Schs, 82-86, fine arts coordr, 86-. *Teaching:* Instr art, Tulsa Pub Schs, 73-81; teaching asst art, Tex Tech Univ, 77 & vis prof art, 85-95; instr watercolor, Tulsa Jr Col, Okla, 74- & Philbrook Mus Sch, Tulsa, 94-96. *Awards:* Okla Art Educr of Yr, 83; Nat Western Region Art Supervisor of Yr, 87; Gov's Art Award, 99. *Bibliog:* Peg Ridgeway (auth), article, Art Voices Mag, 9-10/81. *Mem:* Nat Art Educ Asn; Okla Art Educ Asn; Southwestern Art Asn; Okla Art Guild; Tulsa Artist Guild. *Media:* Watercolor. *Publ:* Coauth, Found Object Design in Jewelry, 76, Weaving, Soft Sculpture & Natural Dyes, 77 & Plans, Projects and Processes, 80, Tulsa Pub Schs. *Dealer:* Margo Shorney 6616 N Olie Oklahoma City OK 74128. *Mailing Add:* 1541 S Florence Ave Tulsa OK 74104-5208

GORELICK, SHIRLEY
PAINTER, PRINTMAKER
b Brooklyn, NY, Jan 24, 24. *Study:* Brooklyn Col, BA; Teachers Col, Columbia Univ, MA. *Work:* Norfolk Mus, Va; Brooklyn Mus; Post Col; Housatonic Mus, Conn; Aldrich Mus, Ridgefield, Conn; and others. *Comn:* City Univ Grad Ctr, NY. *Exhib:* Solo shows, Angelski Gallery, NY, 61, Cent Hall Gallery, Port Washington, NY, 74, 76 & 78, Soho 20 Gallery, NY, 75, 77, 79, 82, 84 & 86 & Art Gallery, State Univ NY, Stony Brook, 79; 3rd Ann Contemp Reflections, Aldrich Mus, Ridgefield, Conn, 74; 19th Nat Print Exhib, Brooklyn Mus, NY, 74; Nothing but Nudes, Whitney Mus of Am Art, NY, 77; Hassam Fund Exhib, Am Acad-Inst Arts & Letters, NY, 78; 43rd Nat Midyear Show, Butler Inst Am Art, Youngstown, Ohio, 79; Contemp Naturalism, Nassau Co Mus, Roslyn, NY, 80; A Women's Place, Art Mus, Mus at Stoney Brook, NY, 96. *Teaching:* Instr painting, NShore Community Arts Ctr, Great Neck, NY, 61-79; instr drawing, Nassau Co Off Cult Develop, 73-74. *Awards:* RI Arts Festival Award, 64; Purchase Award, Nassau Community Col, 72; Creative Artists Pub Serv Fel-Painting, NY State Coun on the Arts, 75-76. *Bibliog:* Charlotte Streiffer Rubinstein (auth), American Women Artists From Early Indian Times to the Present, 82; Phyllis Braff (auth), article, NY, 83; Norma Broude & Mary D Garrard (ed), The Power of Feminist Art, 94; Jule Heller & Nancy Heller (auth), North American Women, Artists of the 20th Century; and others. *Mem:* Women's Interart Ctr, NY; Woman's Caucus Art; Prof Artist Guild (vpres, 71-75); Central Hall Artists (treas, 74-78); and others. *Media:* Acrylic; Oil, Silverpoint. *Dealer:* Soho 20 Gallery 545 Broadway New York NY 10012. *Mailing Add:* 8100 Connecticut Ave Apt 1117 Chevy Chase MD 20815-2818

GORENIUC, MIRCEA C PAUL
SCULPTOR
b Bucharest, Romania, Dec 12, 42; US citizen. *Study:* Fine Art Acad, Munich, WGer, 70-72; San Francisco State Univ, BA, 75; San Jose Univ, Calif, MA, 76, MFA, 78. *Work:* Palo Alto, San Jose, Concord, Los Altos & Los Gatos, Calif; pvt collections, Romania, Ger, Sidney, Australia, USA, Paris-France, Norway, Finland, Sweden, Denmark & China. *Comn:* Space Dance for Peace, Wolfe-Sesnon & Buttery, San Jose, Calif, 82, Syntex Corp, (outdoor permanent collection), Palo Alto, 83, City of Los Gatos, 87; Homage to the Challenger, Lyncoln Park, Los Altos, Calif, 86; Rock and Roll for Peace, Art in Pub Places, City of Concord, Calif, 90; pub art collection, City Palo Alto, 94; China Int City Sculpture Exhib & Symposium, Beijing, 2002; Intl Sculpture Park, Beijing, China, 2002. *Exhib:* Grands et Jeunes D'au Jourd' Hui-Grand Palais de Champs Elysee Salon, 85; Orgn Am States, Washington, DC, 99; XIV Int Sculpture Biennale, Ravenna Italy, 2003; Int City Sculptire Exhib & Symposium, Beijing, China, 2003. *Pos:* VPres, IAA/UNESCO US chap, W Coast. *Teaching:* Instr sculpture, West Valley Col, Saratoga, Calif, 80-82. *Awards:* Most Controversial Pub Sculpture, Sunnyvale, Calif, Metro News, 89; Phi Kappa Phi, First Prize & People's Choice Concord 1 percent Art in Pub Places Prog, 91; First Prize, Redding Mus, 1983; Prize of Excellence, Chinese Ministry of Cult, 2002. *Bibliog:* Art reviews in numerous publs; Vol V, Enciclopedy of Contemporary Romanian Personalities in America, 2003. *Mem:* Int Art Asn, USA Chap (vpres 87-91); Artist Equity Asn; Calif Confederation for the Arts; Phi Kappa Phi; Union Plastic Artists Romania; Phi Kappa Phi Nat Hon Soc (Lifetime Mem). *Media:* Cast Metals, Granite. *Res:* New methods in bronze casting, lost wax. *Interests:* piano, classical music, beekeeping, gardening. *Publ:* American Romanian Academy Journal, 86; Architectural Arts and Sculpture, vol 14& 15, 99. *Mailing Add:* 1251 Phelps Ave San Jose CA 95117

GOREWITZ, SHALOM
VIDEO ARTIST
Study: Calif Inst Arts, BFA(multimedia), 71; Antioch Int Univ, MA (video art), 86. *Exhib:* High Mus Art, Atlanta, Ga, 81; Whitney Mus Biennial, 81, 83 & 87; Inst Contemp Art, Boston, 87; Mus Mod Art, NY, 92; Saratoga Springs Pub Libr, NY, 94; NY Int Video Festival, 94; Int Video Festival, Brazil, 94; Sheppard Fine Arts Gallery, Reno, Nev, 95; Mus Contemp Art, Rome, Italy, 95; Richard Anderson Gallery, New York City, Mill Valley Film Festival, Calif, 99; 93 South Art Gallery, Nyack, NY, 2000; Solo Exhib Millennium Gallery, New York City, 99; Mus of Modern Art, New York City, 2001. *Pos:* Video assoc, Daniel Nagrin Dance Co, 72-75; guest cur, Image Processing, The Kitchen, 79-82. *Teaching:* Assoc prof electronic media, Ramapo Col, 82-91, assoc dean, Sch Contemp Arts, 91-. *Awards:* Asian Cult Coun Fel, 91; Arts Int Travel Grant, 93; Fel, Nat Endowment Arts, 93. *Bibliog:* Peter Spooner (auth), Interview with Shalom Gorewitz, Behind the Screen, Ill State Univ Gallery Press, 91; Steve Jacobs (auth), Artist profile: Shalom Gorewitz, Videomaker Mag, 92; Rosanna Albertini (auth), Longing for Real Life, 95. *Publ:* Auth, Prophet without honor: Tamas Waliczky, The Independent, 90; Making art after the Holocaust, Felix, 91; Video Abstraction (catalog), 92; The Next Repetition, Felix, 93; Squeezing Blood from Electrons, 94. *Mailing Add:* 310 W 85th St Ste 7C New York NY 10024

GORING, TREVOR
PAINTER, WRITER
b London, Eng, Nov 28, 49; Can & Europ citizen. *Study:* Ecole Des Beaux Arts, Montreal, BA, 70; Univ Que, Montreal, BFA, 72; St Martins Col Art, London, MFA(painting), 74. *Work:* Can Coun Art Bank, Ottawa; NY State Trial Lawyers Asn, New York; Rotunda Gallery, London, Eng; Georgia Supreme Court Body, Atlanta, GA; Osgoode Hall, Toronto, ON; and others. *Comn:* Mural, Univ du Que, Montreal, 71; street installation, Olympic Comt, Montreal, 76. *Exhib:* Forum 76, Montreal Mus Fine Arts, 76; Quebec Drawings Traveling Show, Nat Mus Can, 76-78; Vehicule Artists, Arte Fiera, Bolonga, Italy, 78-79; Art for the Earth, Bonhams Fine Art, London, Eng, 86; Research in Progress, Concordia Art Gallery, Montreal, 91; Boreale Blues, Musee Du Bas St-Laurent, Que, 91; over 300 exhibs at legal confs in Europe & NAm. *Pos:* Pres, Vehicule Art Ctr, Montreal, 75-82; co-founder & treas, Asn Nat Non-Profit Artist Ctr, Can, 76-78; co-founder & art dir, Parallelogram Arts Mag, Can, 78-81; co-founder & publ, Virus Arts Mag, Montreal, 78-83; publ, Just Art Int, 94-. *Bibliog:* Dale McConathy (auth), Instant archaeology in Montreal, Artscanada, 7/76; Marie Michel Cron (auth), Entre l'hallucination et la douceur, Le Devoir, 9/19/92; Michael Molter (auth), Des forets et des hommes, Vie Des Arts, No 157, 95; Randy Chapnick Myers, (auth) A Tapestry of Law, Lawyers Weekly, 2/4/2005. *Mem:* Hon Fel Roscoe Pound Inst. *Media:* Acryhic on Canvas/limited edition prints. *Res:* Visual history of the legal profession and world judicial systems from earliest times. *Publ:* Ed, Real Live Art, Vehicule Art Inc, 75; contribr, Hommage to Marco Duchamp, Forest City Gallery, 87; auth, Boreal Blues, Trevor Goring, 91; Images of Justice - Women In-Law, Justart Int, 96; Images of Justice - Judges in Time, Justart Int, 97. *Mailing Add:* 202 St-Zotique W Montreal PQ H2V 4S9 Canada

GORNEY, JAY PHILIP
GALLERIST
b Brooklyn, NY, Sept 26, 52. *Study:* Oberlin Col, with Ellen H Johnson, BA(art hist), 73; Whitney Mus Independent Study Prog, fall 72. *Pos:* Dir, Contemp Art, Mitchell-Innes & Nash, NY. *Bibliog:* New York Mag, 6/25/90; Flash Art Int, No 154, 10/90; and others. *Mem:* ADAA. *Res:* Contemporary painting, drawing, sculpture, photography, video. *Mailing Add:* 534 W 26th St New York NY 10001

GORNIK, APRIL
PAINTER, PRINTMAKER
b Cleveland, Ohio, Apr 20, 53. *Study:* Cleveland Inst Art, 71-75; NS Col Art & Design, BFA, 76. *Work:* Chase Manhattan Permanent Collection, London, Eng; Metrop Mus Art, NY; Whitney Mus Am Art; Fort Worth Mus, Tex; High Mus Art, Atlanta. *Exhib:* Pub and Pvt: Am Prints Today, 24th Nat Print Exhib, Brooklyn Mus, 86; Spectrum, Natural Settings, Corcoran Gallery Art, 86; A View of Nature, Aldrich Mus Contemp Art, 87; The New Romantic Landscape, Whitney Mus Am Art, 87; Nocturnal Visions in Contemp Painting, Whitney Mus Am Art, 89; Biennial Exhib, Whitney Mus Am Art, 89; Harmony & Discord: Am Landscape Today, Va Mus Fine Arts, 90; Four Friends, Aldrich Mus Contemp Art (traveling), 92; Landscape as Metaphor, Whitney Mus Am Art, 93; one-person exhibs, Mary Ryan Gallery, NY, 93, Frederick R Weisman Mus Art, Pepperdine Univ, Malibu, Calif, 93, Offshore Gallery, East Hampton, NY, 94, Guild Hall Mus, East Hampton, NY, 94, Edward Thorp Gallery, NY, 94, 96 & 2000, Kohn Turner Gallery, Los Angeles, 95, Turner & Runyon Gallery, Dallas, 97, Mus of Am Art of Pa Acad of Fine Arts, Phila, 98, Glenn Horowitz Booksellers, East Hampton, NY, 99 & Harley Baldwin Gallery, Aspen, Colo, 99, Danese, NY, 2001, Huntington Mus of Art, WVa, 2002; Timely and Timeless, Aldrich Mus Contemp Art, 94; Guild Hall Mus, E Hampton, NY, 94; Kohn Turner Gallery, Los Angeles, 95; Turner and Runyon Gallery, Dallas, 97; Univ Arts & Mus Am Art, Philadelphia, 98; Water: A Contemp Am View, Gibbes Mus of Art, Charleston, SC, 99 & Mobil Mus of Art, Ala, 2000; Why Draw A Landscape, Crown Point Press Gallery, San Francisco, 99 & Karen McCready Gallery, New York City, 99; A Place in the Sun, Steven Scott Gallery, Balt, 99; As Far as the Eye Can See, Atlanta Coll of Art Gallery, 99; The Perpetual Well: Contemp Art from the Collection of the Jewish Mus, Harn Mus of Art, Gainesville, Fla, 2000; Works on Paper 2000, Am Ambassador of Slovak Rep, 2000; Group Landscape Exhib, Winston Wachter Fine Art, Seattle, 2000; Art of the 80s, Winston Wachter Mayer Fine Art, New York City, 2000; Drawings 2000, Barbara Gladstone Gallery, New York City, 2000; group exhibs, Univ Gallery, Fine Arts Ctr, Univ of Mass, Amherst, 2001, Danese, NY, 2001, Michael Kohn Gallery, Los Angeles, Calif, 2001, The Parrish Art Mus, NY, 2001, Carrie Secrist Gallery, Chicago, Ill, 2001, Elizabeth Harris Gallery, NY, 2001. *Bibliog:* John Russell (auth), Making pen and ink seem passe: the proliferation of new ways to draw, NY Times, 8/11/2000; Ken Johnson, Art in review: April Gornik, NY Times, 10/6/2000; Nancy Grimes, April Gornik, ARTnews, 11/2000. *Media:* Oil. *Dealer:* Danese Gallery 41 E 57th St New York City, New York. *Mailing Add:* 41 Greene St No 4A New York NY 10013-5917

GORNY, A-P (ANTHONY-PETER)
CONCEPTUAL ARTIST, ILLUMINATOR
b Buffalo, NY, May 3, 50. *Study:* Univ Siena & Inst del'Arte, Italy, 70-71, State Univ NY, Buffalo, BFA, 72; Sch Art, Yale Univ, MFA, 74. *Work:* Solomon R Guggenheim Mus, NY; Victoria & Albert Mus, London, UK; Albright-Knox Art Gallery, Buffalo; Philadelphia Mus Art; Brooklyn Mus, NY; Los Angeles Co Mus; Cleveland Mus Art,

Ohio. *Comn:* Print image, Bookworks--Int Paper Conf, Philadelphia, 82; print ed, Philadelphia Chamber Orchestra, Pa, 85; print ed, Philadelphia Mus Art Friends, 88; Print Club of Rochester Mem Art Gallery, NY, 91. *Exhib:* Impressions: Experimental Prints, Va Mus Fine Arts, Inst Contemp Art, Richmond, 84; The Sympathy of All Things, Pa Acad Fine Arts Mus, Philadelphia, 84; Prints Ensvite, Caramoor Ctr Music & Art, Katonah, NY & Pratt Graphics Manhattan Ctr Gallery, NY, 85; New Horizons in Am Art 1985, Nat Exxon Exhib, 85 & Emerging Artists 1978-1986: Selections from the Exxon Series, 86, Solomon R Guggenheim Mus, NY; Am Graphic Arts: Watercolors, Drawings and Prints, Pa Acad Fine Arts, Philadelphia, 86; Made in Philadelphia 7, Inst Contemp Art, Univ Pa, Philadelphia, 87; Oui C'est la Morte, Locks Gallery, Phildephia, 93 & 95; If You Only Knew, Beaver Col Art Gallery, Philadelphia, 93; solo shows, Beaver Col Art Gallery, Glenside, Pa, 93, Locks Gallery, Philadelphia, Pa, 93 & 95, Mason Gross Sch Arts, Rutgers Univ, NJ, 94, Franklin Inst, Philadelphia, Pa, 95 & Davidson Col, NC, 96; IN:VISIBLE, Franklin Inst, Philadelphia, Pa, 95; Philadelphia Col Textiles & Design, Pa, 95; New Art on Paper II: Acquired with Funds from the Hunt Manufacturing Co, Philadelphia, Pa, 97; Flowers in Mind, Locks Gallery, Philadelphia, Pa, 98. *Pos:* Artist-in-residence, Franklin Inst; cur, Quiet Mus, Philadelphia, 78-81. *Teaching:* Assoc prof prints-photog-drawing, Tyler Sch Art, Temple Univ, Philadelphia, 74-81, prof photog & grad fac, 94-95; fac, prints, Fleisher Art Mem, Philadelphia Mus Art, 86-94; assoc prof photog & performance art, Univ Arts, Philadelphia, 89-94; fac, Bryn Mawr Col, Pa, 92; vis fac mem, Univ Ariz, Tucson, currently. *Awards:* Individual Artists Fel Grant, Nat Endowment Arts, 89-90; Charitable Trusts Proj Grant, 91, Philos East & West & Individual Artists Fel Grant, 94-96; and others. *Bibliog:* Tom Csazer (auth), article, New Art Examiner, 2/94; Robin Rice (auth), AP Gorny: Invisible, Philadelphia City Paper, 6/30/95; Julia Klein (auth), article, Philadelphia Inquirer, 7/17/95. *Mem:* Am Col Art Asn; Friends of Penland; Citizens for Am Way; Asn Independent Scholars; Inst Contemp Art Friends, Philadelphia, Pa. *Media:* Mixed Media. *Publ:* Auth, It's Another Thing All Together, Falcon Press, 78; Re: Pages Contemporary Bookworks, NEng Found Arts, 80; contribr, New American Photographs, Calif State Col, San Bernadino, 82; Emerging Artists 1978-1986, Selections from the Exxon Series, Guggenheim Found, 86; Searching Out the Best: 1978-1988, Pa Acad Fine Arts, 88. *Dealer:* Locks Gallery Sixth & Washington Sq S Philadelphia PA 19106

GORSKI, DANIEL ALEXANDER
PAINTER, SCULPTOR
b Cleveland, Ohio, Oct 26, 39. *Study:* Cleveland Inst Art, dipl, 61; Yale Univ Sch Art & Archit, with Jack Tworkow & Al Held, BFA, 62 & MFA, 64. *Work:* Yale Univ. *Comn:* Mural, comn by Mr & Mrs Barney Kogen, 92; mural, comn by Mr & Mrs Jack Berridge, 94; installation, comn by Ms Bebe Woolley, 96. *Exhib:* Primary Structures, Jewish Mus, NYC, 1966; Cool Art, Larry Aldrich Mus, Ridgefield, Conn, 68; Hanging and Leaning, Emily Lowe Gallery, Hofstra Univ, 70; 26 x 26, Vassar Col Art Gallery, 71; Md Biennial Exhib, Baltimore Mus of Art, 76; Sculpture Outdoors, Temple Univ, Ambler, Pa, 77-80; Elements Style Artscape, Baltimore, Md, 86; Themes and Variations: Cubism, Artscape, Baltimore, Md, 87; Davis McClain Gallery, 95. *Pos:* Dir, Glassell Sch Art, Mus Fine Arts, Houston, Tex, 90-96. *Teaching:* Artist/adminr, Glassell Sch Art; instr & dir, Mus Fine Art, Houston, Tex, 90-96; artist/adminr, Maryland Inst Col Art, Baltimore, 1971-90. *Awards:* Mr & Mrs Jules Horelick Award, Baltimore Mus of Art, 76; Ford Found Grant, Shelter Inst, summer 79; A Mellon Grant, 84; AICA Grant, 85; City Arts Grant, 87. *Bibliog:* L Lippard (auth), Recent sculpture as escape, 2/66 & Escalation in Washington, 1/68, Art Int; U Kalterman (auth), The New Sculpture, Praeger, 68. *Dealer:* Franz Bader Gallery Washington DC; Barbara Davis Gallery Houston TX. *Mailing Add:* 6 Alteza Santa Fe NM 87508

GORSKI, RICHARD KENNY
EDUCATOR, GRAPHIC ARTIST
b Green Bay, Wis, Apr 20, 23. *Study:* Northern Ill Univ, De Kalb, 62-65; Univ Wis, Milwaukee & Madison, MS(art educ), 50. *Work:* Milwaukee Pub Schs collection Wis Artists. *Exhib:* Wisconsin Painters & Sculptors, Wis Union Gallery, Madison, 39, 47, 49 & 53-56; Milwaukee Art Inst, 40, 46, 47, 49, 50, 53, 55-57 & 60; Walker Art Inst, 47 & 49. *Pos:* Cur & dir, Rahr Civic Ctr & Mus, Manitowoc, Wis, 50-53; illusr & designer, John Higgs Studios, Milwaukee, Wis, 56-57; art dir, United Educators Publ Inc, Lake Bluff, Ill, 60-61; dept head, art & design, Northern Mich Univ, Marquette, 65-75. *Teaching:* Instr art educ, Nat Col Educ, Evanston, Ill, 57-60; assoc prof art educ, Northeastern Ill Univ, Chicago, 61-65; prof graphic design, visual commun, Northern Mich Univ, Marquette, 65-94, emer prof, 95-. *Awards:* J Purchase Award, Wis Painters Ann, Milwaukee J Pub Schs Collection, 57; Special Merit Award, Wis Gimbels Salon, Gimbels Inc, 50. *Mem:* Semiotic Soc Am. *Res:* Structural basis of visual communication, and the semiosis of sight. *Publ:* Auth, Color; article, United Educators Encycl & auth, Painting; article, The Wonderland of Knowledge Encycl, United Educ Publ, 60. *Mailing Add:* 211 Sandstone Dr Marquette MI 49855

GOSS, JARED
CURATOR
Pos: Res asst, Metrop Mus Art, New York City, asst cur. *Awards:* Co-recipient Award for Best Archit or Design Show, Int Asn Art Critics/USA, 2005. *Mailing Add:* Met Mus Art 1000 5th Ave New York NY 10028-0198

GOSSAGE, JOHN RALPH
PHOTOGRAPHER
b New York, NY, Mar 15, 46. *Study:* Walden Sch, 67-69. *Work:* Mus Mod Art, NY; Houston Mus Fine Art; San Francisco Mus Art; Philadelphia Mus Art; George Eastman House, Rochester, NY. *Comn:* Nation's Capitol in Photographs, Corcoran Gallery, 76; Photography in America, AT&T, NY, 78; Photography and the City, Seattle Art Comn, 79. *Exhib:* 14 Am Photogrs, Baltimore Mus & traveling, 75; solo exhibs, Castelli Gallery, NY, 76 & Lunn Gallery, Washington, DC, 80; 10th Biennale Paris, Mus Mod Art, France, 77; Contemp Photog Works, Houston Mus Fine Arts, 77; Gardens, Werkstalt Photog, Berlin, 78; Photog & Sense of Order, Inst Contemp Art, Philadelphia, 81; History of Portrait Photog, Mus Art, Bonn, Ger, 82. *Pos:* Vpres, Columbia Arts Inc, 82-. *Teaching:* Assoc prof photog & art, Univ Md, 77-89. *Awards:* Grants, Stern Fund, 74 & Nat Endowment Arts, 74 & 78; Pratt Mem Award, 96. *Bibliog:* Renato Dansse (auth), American Images, McGraw Hill, 79. *Publ:* Auth, Gardens, Castelli Graphics, 78; The Pond, Aperture Publ, 84; Stadt des Schwarz, Loessstrife Ed, 89; There & Gone, Nazraeli Press, 96. *Dealer:* Castelli Uptown 4 E 77 St New York NY 10021; Ram Gallery Los Angeles Tokyo. *Mailing Add:* 2070 NW Belmont Rd Washington DC 20009

GOTTSCHALK, FRITZ
DESIGNER, LECTURER
b Zurich, Switz, Dec 30, 37. *Study:* Kunstgewerbeschule, Zurich, Switz, dipl; Art Inst Orell Fussli, Zurich, dipl; Allgemeine Gewerbeschule, Basel, Switz, post-grad dipl, with E Ruder & A Hofmann. *Exhib:* The Visual Image of the Montreal Mus, Montreal Mus Fine Arts, Que, Can, 68; Swiss Design, Mus du Louvre, Paris, France, 71; Alliance Graphique Int: 107 Int Designers, Milan, Italy, 74; The Work of Gottschalk & Ash Ltd, Ryder Gallery, sponsored by Container Corp of Am, Chicago, 76; Coninx Mus, Zürich, Switz, 95. *Pos:* Designer art & design dir, Gottschalk & Ash Int, Meilen, Zurich, Switz, 77-; dir design & quality control off, Organizing Comt of 1976 Olympic Games, 74-76. *Awards:* Award of Excellence, Swiss Contemp Design, Dept of Interior, Swiss Govt, 62; two Awards of Excellence, Soc Publ Designers, New York, 70; Bronze Medal, Foire Int du Livre, Leipzig, EGer, 77. *Bibliog:* Adrian Gatrail (auth), The Image Makers, The Gazette, Can, 70; Bill Bantey (auth), Gottschalk & Ash Ltd, Graphis, Switz, Vol 148 (1972); Midori Imatake (auth), Gottschalk & Ash Ltd, Idea (Japan), Vol 115 (1973). *Mem:* Que Soc Graphic Artists; Royal Can Acad; Asn of Swiss Graphic Artists; Alliance Graphique Inter; Graphic Designers Can. *Media:* Graphic Design, Books and Corporate Images. *Publ:* Auth & illusr, article, Idea, Seibundo Shinkosha Publ Co, Japan, Vol 115, 72; ed, article, Revue Suisse de l'Imprimerie, Zollikofer AG, Switz, 74; illusr & contribr, article, Communication Arts, Coyne & Blanchard, Inc, 75; ed, article, Graphis, Vol 185, 77. *Mailing Add:* 26 Bocklingerstrasse Zurich 8032 Switzerland

GOUGH, GEORGIA BELLE LEACH
CRAFTSMAN, EDUCATOR
b Oklahoma City, Okla, Dec 21, 20. *Study:* Central Okla Univ, BS, 41; Univ NTex, MS, 45; with Carlton Ball, 48; with Daniel Rhodes, 54; Univ Okla, PhD, 60. *Work:* Campbell Mem Collection, Am Craft Mus, NY. *Comn:* Wall hanging, comn by Greater Denton Arts Coun, Festival Hall Ctr Visual Arts. *Exhib:* Syracuse Mus, NY, 51 & 56; Wichita Decorative Arts & Crafts, Wichita Mus, Kans, 50, 51 & 53; Miami Nat Ceramic Exhib, Fla, 56; Dallas Craft Market, Tex, 81 & 82; Handmade in Tex, 87; A Decade of Dallas Crafts, 88; solo exhib, Earth, Water, Fire, Air, 96 & Family Reunion, 2000. *Collection Arranged:* Materials Hard & Soft, (ann exhib) Greater Denton Arts Coun, 93. *Teaching:* Prof ceramics, NTex State Univ, 47-75, emer prof art dept, currently. *Awards:* Third Place, Tex Fine Arts Asn, 53; Community Arts Recognition Award, Denton, Tex, 95. *Mem:* Am Craft Coun (trustee, 76-80); Nat Coun Educ Ceramic Arts (secy, 70-73); Am Ceramic Soc Design Sect Southwest Region (pres & secy); World Crafts Coun (US delegate, 78 & 80); hon mem Tex Designer-Craftsmen. *Media:* Ceramics. *Publ:* Auth, Use of native clays in high-grade pottery, Ceramic Industry, 53; Computer data processing system calculations of glaze formulae, Am Ceramic Soc Bulletin, 65; coauth, Fine Arts in Texas Colleges & Universities, 65. *Mailing Add:* 1813 Willowwood Denton TX 76205-6992

GOUGH, ROBERT ALAN
PAINTER
b Quebec, PQ, Aug 13, 31; US citizen. *Study:* Am Acad Art, Chicago, with William H Mosby & J Allen St John. *Work:* Am Fedn Arts; Butler Inst Am Art; Univ Nebr; Sheldon Swope Art Gallery; Battelle Inst. *Exhib:* Painting & Sculpture Today, Herron Mus Art, 66; one-man shows, Gilman Galleries, Chicago, 67 & 69; 35 Yrs in Retrospect, Butler Inst Am Art, 71; Mainstreams, Marietta Col, 74, 75 & 77; Art from Appalachia Traveling Exhib, Smithsonian Inst, 81-; and others. *Awards:* Henry Ward Ranger Purchase Prize, Nat Acad Design, 62; Judges Award, Marietta Nat, 78; Ohioana Libr Asn Citation, 81. *Bibliog:* Doc, WBNS-TV, Columbus, Ohio, 70. *Media:* Oil. *Dealer:* Keny Galleries 300 E Beck St Columbus Ohio 43206. *Mailing Add:* 220 Brookside Dr Chillicothe OH 45601

GOULD, CLAUDIA
MUSEUM DIRECTOR
Study: Boston Col BA in Art Hist; NYU, M in Mus Studies. *Pos:* cur, proj dir, cur exhibs Wexner Ctr Arts Ohio State Univ, 89-91; independent cur New York City, 92-94; exec dir Artists Space 94-99, Inst Contemp Art, 99-. *Mailing Add:* Univ Pennsylvania Inst Contemporary Art 118 S 36th St Philadelphia PA 19104-3289

GOULD, KAREN KEEL
WRITER, CONSULTANT
b Austin, Tex, Sept 26, 46. *Study:* Univ Tex, Austin, BS, 68, MA, 70, PhD, 75. *Teaching:* Vis asst prof art hist, Univ Ore, 80; Mellon Fel, Duke Univ, 80-81; lectr hist, Univ Tex, Austin, 81-89. *Mem:* Int Ctr Medieval Art (mem adv bd, 81-83); Southeastern Medieval Asn (mem exec coun, 81-83); Medieval Acad Am. *Res:* Manuscript illumination; history of manuscripts & printed books. *Publ:* The Psalter and Hours of Yolande of Soissons, Medieval Acad, 78; Sequences De Sanctis Reliquiis as Sainte-Chapelle Inventories, Medieval Studies, 81; Terms for book production in a Latin-English nominale, Papers of the Bibliog Soc Am; The Recovery of a Fifteenth-Century Book of Hours, HRC 2, Scriptorium, 89; Jean Pucelle and Northern Gothic Art, Art Bull, 92. *Mailing Add:* 2602 La Ronde St Austin TX 78731

GOULD, NADIA D
PAINTER, WRITER
b Strasbourg, France; US citizen. *Study:* Washington Sq Col, NY Univ, BA, 49; City Univ Sch Educ, MEd, 71. *Work:* Sarah Lawrence Col, Bronxville, NY; Hebrew Home for Age, Riverdale, NY. *Exhib:* West Side Artists, Riverside Mus, NY, 64; Lesser Known Unknown Painters, World's Fair Am Express Pavilion, NY, 65; Future Great, Westchester Art Soc, NY, 65; Conditional Commitment, Long Island Univ Int, 66; Retrospective, Synagogue Space, NY, 96. *Teaching:* instr, Marymount Col, 2003. *Awards:* Yaddo Grant, 74. *Mem:* Bridge Gallery (secy, vpres); Viridian Gallery (asst dir, 80-); Artist Equity. *Media:* Acrylic, Oil. *Publ:* Auth (e-book), Hitler Made Me a Jew, Boson Bks, 2nd ed (print), 2006. *Mailing Add:* 15 Claremont Ave New York NY 10027

GOULD, PHILIP
CURATOR, COLLECTOR
b New York, NY, Oct 17, 22. *Study:* NY Univ, BA, 49; L'Univ Paris, Dr Univ, 53. *Collection Arranged:* Traditional Anatolian Kilims (coauth, catalog), 86, Artists from China - New Expressionism, 87, Sarah Lawrence Col Art Gallery; The Art of Kuba Weaving (textiles from Zaire), Columbia Univ, 98; Africa's Iron and Copper Currency in the Rotunda, Low Meml Libr, Columbia Univ, 2000; Africa's Copper Currency, Uticia Col, 2002. *Pos:* vis cur, Nat Mus Catholic Art & Hist, NY, 2006. *Teaching:* Instr art hist, Columbia Univ, 54-59, lectr, 56-62; prof, Sarah Lawrence Col, 59-92 (ret); vis prof, Fordham Univ, spring 68, Pratt Inst, fall 73 & Col Chinese Cult, Taipei, Taiwan, 75-76; lectr, NY Coun Humanitics, 95-. *Awards:* Sapirstein lect, Cooper-Hewitt Mus, Smithsonian Inst, 87; UN Develop Prog, Sr Tech Adv, Beijing Teacher's Col, PRC, 89; Elected Assoc Mem, Columbia Univ Sem: Traditional China, 92-95, Africa, Pacific Asian, Latin Am Art, 99-2006. *Bibliog:* Nick Natanson (auth), The craft of teaching, Sarah Lawrence Col Bulletin, spring 83. *Mem:* Soc Archit Historians; Am Soc Aesthet; AAM; ICOM; Textile Conservation Group. *Res:* Chinese art in general and comparative occidental and Oriental iconography in particular; Ancient & Modern African material cultures. *Publ:* auth, Exhibition of Chinese Painting, Ming & Ch'ing (catalog), 73 & Exhibition of Chinese Folk & Provincial Ceramics (catalog), 76, Sarah Lawrence Col; contribr, Acad Am Encycl, 80; auth, Jan van Eyck's Arnolfini Wedding Portrait: The mirror image, In: Iris, Notes Hist Art, Vol 2, 12/83; preface, in: Book of Paintings by Yu Chit-Fu; Rita Reif (auth), The Precious and Proverbal Art of African Money, Sunday, 3/12/2000. *Mailing Add:* 15 Claremont Ave New York NY 10027

GOULDS, PETER J
DEALER, DESIGNER
b London, Eng, Oct 5, 48. *Study:* Walthamstow Sch Art, Eng, 65-67; Coventry Sch Art, Eng, 67-70; Sch Advan Studies, Manchester Polytech, BA, 70 & MA, 71; Shell Fel, 72. *Pos:* Owner, LA Louver Gallery, Venice, Calif, 76-. *Teaching:* Lectr, Bolton Sch Art, 71; lectr commun design, Leeds Polytech, Yorkshire, Eng, 72; vis lectr video workshop & design, Univ Calif, Los Angeles, 72-75; vis lectr, Calif Inst Arts, 75-76; trustee, Otis Sch Art & Design, 98. *Awards:* Leverhulme Award, Uni Lever Trust, 71; Univ Res Grants, Univ Calif, 72-74. *Bibliog:* Kristine McKenna (auth), Opening A New Window on LA's Art, Los Angeles Times, 1/15/95. *Specialty:* Contemporary American and European painting & sculpture

GOULET, LORRIE
SCULPTOR, PAINTER
b Riverdale, NY, Aug 17, 25. *Study:* Inwood Potteries Studios, NY, 32-36, with Amiee Voorhees; Black Mountain Col, drawing & painting with Josef Albers; sculpture with Jose de Creeft, 43-44. *Work:* Sarah Roby Found; Joseph H Hirshhorn Mus & Sculpture Garden, Washington, DC; NJ State Mus; Nat Mus Women in the Arts, DC; Ball State Univ Art Gallery. *Comn:* Ceramic relief, NY Pub Libr, Grand Concourse, Bronx, 58; ceramic relief, Nurses' Residence & Sch, Bronx Munic Hosp, 61; stainless steel relief, 48th Precinct Police & Fire Sta, Bronx, 71. *Exhib:* Dimensions 69, Temple Emeth, NJ, 69; Outdoor Sculpture Show, Van Saun Park, NJ, 71; one-artist shows, Contemporaries Gallery, NY, 59, 62, 66 & 68, Kennedy Galleries, NY, 71, 73-75, 78, 80 & 83-86 & Retrospective, Carolyn Hill Gallery, 88, David Findlay Jr Gallery, NY, 2004-2005; Summit Art Ctr, NJ, 78; Nat Arts Club, NY, 78; 50 Yr Retrospective, Nat Mus Women Arts, Wash, DC, 98; Black Mountain - Una Aventura Am, Museo Nat Centro DeAste Reina Sopha, Madrid, Spain, 2002; group exhib, Mus Nat Hist, 36, Whitney Mus Am Art, NY, 48-50, 53, 55, Metrop Mus Art, 51, Detroit Inst Art, 60, Pa Acad, 1950-52, 54, 59, 64, AD, NY, 66, 75, 77, Corcoran Gallery, Wash, 66, Hofstra Mus, NY, 90, McNey Mus, 90, Copley Soc, Boston, 91, Spanish Inst, 92, Lehigh Univ Art Gallery, 92, Iowa State Univ Brunne Gallery, 92, Paine Art Ctr, Oshkosh, Wis, 92, Mitchell Art Gallery, St John's Col, Annapolis, Md, 92, Erie (Pa) Art Mus, 95, Nat Sculpture Soc, 01, Art Students League, New York City, 2003. *Collection Arranged:* Rep in permanent collections Hunter Mus, Chattanooga, NJ State Mus, Wichita Mus Art, Hirschhorn Sculpture Mus, Wash, The Philharmonic Center, Naples, Fla, Art Students League, NY, Savannah Col Arts. *Pos:* Guest demonstr, Around the Corner, NY Dept Educ, CBS-TV, 64-65; pres, NY Artists Equity Inc, 97 & Fine Arts Fedn, NY, 97. *Teaching:* Instr sculpture-var media & staff mem, Mus Mod Art, NY, 57-64; sculpture staff mem, Scarsdale Studio Workshop, 59-61 & New Sch Social Res, 61-75; staff instr sculpture, Art Students League, NY, 81-2006. *Awards:* First Sculpture Prize, Norton Gallery, 49 & 50 & Westchester Art Soc, 64; Soltan Engel Mem Award, Audubon Artists, 67; The Malvina Hoffman Award, Nat Acad Design, 2001. *Mem:* NY Artists Equity (pres, 98-2002); Fedn Fine Arts (pres, 98-2002, hon vpres 2003); founding mem Visual Artists & Galleries Asn; Nat Acad (acad 89, mem coun 94); Art Bank (trustee). *Media:* Stone, Wood; Acrylic. *Specialty:* Fine Art. *Publ:* Contribr, 20th century sculptors look at their work, The Palette; auth article on greenstone, In: Slate & Soft Stones, 71. *Dealer:* Harmon-Meek Gallery Naples Fla; David Findley Jr Gallery, New York City NY

GOUREVITCH, JACQUELINE
PAINTER
b Paris, Oct 28, 33; US citizen. *Study:* Black Mountain Col, NC, 50; Art Students League, 52; Univ Chicago, BA, 54; Art Inst Chicago, 54-55. *Work:* Wadsworth Atheneum, Hartford, Conn; The Menil Collectin, Houston, TX; De Cordova Mus, Lincoln, Mass; Univ Art Mus, Berkeley, Calif; Charles A Wustum Mus, Racine, Wis; Fuller Mem Mus, Brockton, Mass; Univ NMex, Albuquerque; Wesleyan Univ, Middletown, Conn; Yale Univ Art Gallery, New Haven, Conn. *Comn:* Conn Comn Arts, Western Conn State Univ, Danbury, 83. *Exhib:* One-woman shows, Tibor de Nagy Gallery, NY, 71, 72 & 73, Wesleyan Univ, Conn, 74, 77 & 83, Wadsworth Atheneum, Matrix Gallery Hartford, Conn, 75, Condeso-Lawler Gallery, NY, 80, 82 & 84, Aerial Notations, New Brit Mus Am Art, Conn, 93, Paesaggio Gallery, Conn, 93, 96 & 99 & DFN Gallery, NY, 2000, 2002; group shows, De Cordova Mus, Lincoln, Mass, 71 & 78; Painting & Sculpture Today, Indianapolis Mus Art, 72; Whitney Mus Art Ann, 73; Acad Arts & Letts, 73 & 94; Maxwell Davidson, NY, 90; Paesaggio Gallery, Conn, 93, 96 & 99; Nat Acad of Design, New York City, 2002; NY Studio Sch, 2002; Pierogi, NY, 97-2004; Mary Ryan, NY, 2005; 181st Ann: An Invitational Exhib Contemp Art, Nat Acad Mus, NY City, 2006. *Teaching:* Wesleyan Univ, 67-71 & 78-88; Hartford Art Sch, Univ Hartford, 73-78; Univ Calif, Berkeley, 74, Vassar Col, 77, Univ Houston, 78 & Yale Univ, 82; Cooper Union, 89-92; Mt Holyoke Col, 95. *Awards:* Purchase Award, Am Acad Arts & Letts, New York, 73; grants, Nat Endowment Arts, 76 & Conn Comn Arts, 76; Richard Florsheim Art Fund, 95; Obrig Watercolor, Nat Acad of Design, 2002; American Acad of Art & Letters, NY, 2004. *Bibliog:* Annie Dillard & Deborah Frizzell (auths), catalogue, New Britain Mus Am Art, Conn, 94; Jude Schwendenwein (auth), article, Hartford Courant, 6/9/96; Patricia Rosoff (auth), article, Hartford Advocate, 6/13/96; Ken Johnson (auth), NY Times, 4/28/2000. *Media:* Oil, Watercolor. *Publ:* Auth, article, Art Now: New York, fall 71. *Dealer:* Paesaggio Gallery 966 Farmington Ave W Hartford CT 06107; DFN Gallery76 Franklin St New York NY 10013; Mary Ryan, 24 W 57 St, NY, 10019. *Mailing Add:* 120 Duane St Apt 6 New York NY 10007-1113

GOVAN, MICHAEL
MUSEUM DIRECTOR
Study: Williams Col, BA (art history); studied at Univ San Diego; studied Renaissance art in Italy. *Collection Arranged:* Cur, Picasso and Rembrandt, Williams Col Msu Art, 1986; co-cur, Dan Flavin: A Retrospective. *Pos:* Acting cur, Williams Col Mus Art; dep dir, Solomon R Guggenheim Mus, 1988-94; dir, Dia Art Found, 1994-2006, instrumental in establishment of Dia: Beacon, 2003; dir, CEO, LA County Mus Art, 2006-. *Publ:* The Great Utopia: The Russian and Soviet Avant-Garde, 1915-1932. *Mailing Add:* LA County Museum of Art 5909 Wilshire Blvd Los Angeles CA 90036

GOVEDARE, PHILIP
PAINTER
b Yuba City, Calif, 54. *Study:* Albertson Col Idaho, studied music, 72-73; Univ Ore, studied psychology, 73-74; San Francisco Art Inst, BFA, 80; Tyler Sch Art, Temple Univ, MFA, 84. *Work:* Fed Reserve Bank, Philadelphia; Prudential Insurance Co; Wash State's Art in Pub Places Prog, Kent Sch Dist Portable Collection; Wash State's Art in Pub Places Program, Kent Sch Dist Portable Collection, Kent, Wash. *Exhib:* Solo exhibs, La Galleria Temple, Rome, Italy, 84, Samuel S Fleisher Art Mem, Philadelphia, 87, Pa Acad Fine Arts, 91, Paul Cava Gallery, Philadelphia, 92, Francine Seders Gallery, Seattle, 94, 95 & 97 dp Fong Galleries, San Jose, 96, Upstairs Gallery, Francine Seders Gallery, Seattle, 2000, Pierce Col Fine Arts Gallery, Fort Steilacoom Campus, Lakewood, Wash, 2000, Francine Seders Gallery, Seattle, 95, 97, 2001, The Painting Ctr, NY, 2002; Seders Gallery, Seattle, 86, 88, 89, 93 & 94; Paul Cava Gallery, Philadelphia, 94; Francine Seders Gallery, Seattle, 94; Mostra dei Docenti, Temple Univ, 94; Davis/McClain Gallery, Houston, Tex, 96; Rome Selection Temple Gallery, Philadelphia, 97; Francine Seders Gallery, Seattle, 97, 98, 99, 2002; Temple Gallery, Philadephia, 97; group exhibs, Painting Ctr, NY Univ, 2000, Cancer Lifeline, Seattle, Wash, 2001. *Awards:* Russell Conwell Fel, Temple Univ, 83-84; Tobeleah Wecschler Annual Award in Painting, Cheltenham Art Ctr, Pa, 87; Fel, Pa Coun Arts, 88; Grant, Pollack-Krasner Found, NY, 91; Fel, Nat Endowment Arts, 93-94; Royalty Res Fund Scholar, Univ of Wash, Seattle, 2002. *Dealer:* Francine Seders Gallery Seattle; David/McClain Gallery Houston. *Mailing Add:* c/o Francine Seders Gallery 6701 Greenwood Ave N Seattle WA 98103-5294

GRABARSKY, SHEILA
PAINTER
b Brooklyn, NY. *Study:* NJ Ctr Visual Arts, with Philip Sherrod, spec accreditation; Syracuse Univ; Shrewsbury Art Guild, with Georgette Pettit;. *Exhib:* Painting Today, Fairleigh Dickinson Univ, 91; Imaging/Aging, Bucknell Univ, 92; Ellarslie Open XI, Trenton Mus, NJ, 92; solo exhib, Monmouth Univ, West Long Branch, NJ, 94; Flim Flam & Fins, Clymer Mus, Ellensburg, WVa, 96. *Awards:* Best in Show, 36th Regional Juried, Hudson Artists, 89; Hon Men, Bergen Mus Arts & Sci, 89; Award of Merit, Int Cover Art Competition, Manhattan Arts, 95; Best in Show, No Calif Arts Intl Juried Show, 2000; Best Art, Tulane Univ Literary Review, 2000; Townsend Award, Art Alliance, Red Bank, NJ, 2002; Merion Award, 3rd St Gallery, Philadelphia, Pa, 2002. *Bibliog:* Numerous reviews, Artspeak, 90; Renee Philips (auth), Artists of the 90s, Manhattan Arts, 91; Paul Haupt (auth), Breathing life into canvas, The Herald, 93. *Mem:* Nat Asn Women Artists; Soc Experimental Artists; NY Artists Equity Asn; Org Independent Artists; Nat Womens Caucus for Art; Shrewsbury Art Guild; Art Alliance. *Media:* Acrylic. *Dealer:* Beauregard Fine Art Rumson NJ; Evergreen Gallery Spring Lake NJ; Robin Hutchins Gallery Maplewood NJ

GRABEL, SUSAN
SCULPTOR, PRINTMAKER - MISC. MEDIA
b Brooklyn, NY, June 5, 42. *Study:* Brooklyn Mus Art Sch, with Joseph Konzal & Tom Doyle, 61-65; Brooklyn Col, NY, BA, 63. *Comn:* Ceramic mural, Staten Island Children's Mus, 91; Regarding Women, (installation), A Public Work of Art, Ctr Women's Health, Staten Island, NY. *Exhib:* In Three Dimensions: Women Sculptors of the '90s, Newhouse Ctr Contemp Art, Staten Island, NY, 95; One-woman show, Venus, Wagner Col Gallery, Staten Island, NY, 2001, Venus Emerging, Somoza, Chelsea, 2006; Nude Int 2005; Lexington Art League, Lexington, Ky, 2005; One Woman Earth Venus: Sculpture to Collagraph Art Lab Gallery Snug Harbor cultural Cntr, Staten Island, NY. *Teaching:* art hist survey, Wagner Col, 2002-03; life modelling, Chautauque Sch Art, 2000 & 06. *Awards:* Staten Island, Greater NY Arts Develop Fund Award for Sculpture, 95; NY Sculpture Artists Grant, Snug Harbor Cult Arts, 96; Coun on the Arts & Humanities for Staten Island Encore Grant, 2000; Council on the Arts & Humanities for Staten Island, Original Works Grant, 2004. *Bibliog:* William Zimmer (auth), Mansion and former factory offer varied views of women, NY Times, 90; Vivien Raynor (auth), Color relationships in Valhalla, Family ties in Krasdale, NY Times, 93; Michael J. Fressola (auth), Staten Island Advance, 2000; and others. *Mem:* Women's Caucus Art (pres, NY chap, 92-95); New York Artist Circle. *Media:* cast paper, ceramics, collagraph, monoprints. *Publ:* Art as Activism issue, Woman of Power Mag, spring 87. *Mailing Add:* 257 Oakland Ave Staten Island NY 10310

GRABER, STEVEN BRIAN
GRAPHIC ARTIST, PAINTER
b Newton, Kans, Nov 14, 50. *Study:* Univ Redlands, BA, 72. *Work:* Butler Inst Am Art, Younstown, Ohio; State Ala Capitol Bldg, Montgomery, Ala; S Bend Regional Art Mus, Ind; Fine Arts Mus S, Mobile, Ala; Disney World, Orlando, Fla. *Exhib:* Getting Real, S Bend Regional Mus, Ind, 96; Landscape Exhib, Riverside Art Mus, Calif, 96; one-man show, Butler Inst Am Art, Youngstown, Ohio, 99; Arnot Art Mus, Elmyra, NY, 99. *Bibliog:* Bill Machomer (auth), In the galleries, Art Talk Mag, 1/98; Kristin Bucher (auth), Best of the west, Southwest Art, 2/98; Stephen Doherty (auth), Steven Graber, Am Artist Mag, 1/99. *Media:* Charcoal. *Dealer:* M B Modern 41 E 57th 8th Flr New York NY 10022; Bryant Galleries 316 Royal St New Orleans LA. *Mailing Add:* 938 E 1700 Rd Baldwin City KS 66006

GRADO, ANGELO JOHN
PAINTER, INSTRUCTOR
b New York, NY, Feb 17, 22. *Study:* Art Students League, with Robert Brackman; Nat Acad Design, with Robert Philipp & Frank Reilly. *Exhib:* Am Watercolor Soc Exhibs, 58-71; Allied Artists Am Exhibs, 61-78; Nat Acad Design, NY, 63; Am Artists Prof League, NY, 63-2005; Hudson Valley Art Asn, 69-88, 99-2006; Pastel Soc Am; 14 one-man exhibs. *Teaching:* Pvt classes, Nat Art League & von Liebig Art Ctr, Naples, Fla. *Awards:* Salmagundi Club Prize, 69; Eighteen Am Artists Prof League Awards, 69-81 & 83-2004; Hudson Valley Art Asn Awards, 69, 70, 72 & 84-95; 78 Nat Awards. *Bibliog:* Billi Boros (auth), New talent, Art Times Mag, 64; Int Artist Magazine, 2004, Pastelagram Magazine, 2006. *Mem:* Am Watercolor Soc; Am Artists Prof League (pres emer, 89-); Hudson Valley Art Asn; Pastel Soc Am; Fine Arts Fedn New York. *Media:* Oil, Pastel. *Collection:* National Academy Design, New York. *Publ:* Auth, Mastering the Craft of Painting, Watson-Guptill Publ; Int Artist Mag, 10/2004-11/2004. *Dealer:* Harbor Gallery 24 W 57th St New York NY 10019; Alterman Art Gallery 2504 Cedar Springs Dallas TX 75201. *Mailing Add:* 641 46th St Brooklyn NY 11220

GRADUS, ARI
PAINTER, PRINTMAKER
b Karkur, Israel, Oct 26, 43; US citizen. *Study:* New York Univ, 66-70; Art Students League, New York, 71-73. *Work:* Mus Lower East Side, NY; Jerusalem City Hall, Mayor's Off, Israel. *Comn:* Mural, Temple Anshe Emmeth, New Brunswick, NJ, 86; mural, NCZ Corp, NY, 88. *Exhib:* One-man shows, Patricia Judith Gallery, Boca Raton, Fla, 84, Sansiano Gallery, Tokyo, 85, Goldman Gallery, Rockville, Md, 88, Short Hills Community Gallery, NJ, 89, Shainberg Mus, Memphis, 90 & Gallery 2000, Coral Springs, Fla, 92 & 93; Images, Israeli-Am Ctr, Tel Aviv, 86; 20th Century Artists, Brownstone Gallery, NY, 94; Bergen Co YMHA, NJ, 99; Art Warehouse Gallery, Boca Raton, Fla, 2000. *Awards:* Award of Excellence, City of Boca Raton, Fla, 93; Best in Show Award, City of Highland Park, Ill, 98; First Place Award, Washington Square Art Exhib, NYC, 98. *Bibliog:* Ari Gradus - Artist, Miami Herald, 4/92; A Place Called Yesterday, Channel 2 TV, Israel, 95; Artist in the News, PBS Radio, Wickeford, RI. *Mem:* Mich Art Guild. *Media:* Acrylic; Serigraphs. *Mailing Add:* 423 6th St Brooklyn NY 11215

GRADY, RUBY MCLAIN
PAINTER, SCULPTOR
b Bedford Co, Va, Jan 11, 44. *Study:* Corcoran Sch Art, Washington, DC, with Richard Lahey; Md Univ, with Pietro Lazzari. *Work:* Am Fine Art Exhibs, Washington, DC; NASA Gemini Collection, Washington, DC; Imprimerie Arte Galerie Maeght, Paris, France; West Collection, St Paul, Minn. *Comn:* Corrections (painting, cover textbk), West Publ Co, Minn, 97. *Exhib:* Va Mus Art, Richmond; Washington Sq Sculpture Exhib, Pub Art Trust, Washington, DC, 84; solo exhibs, Jack Rasmussen Gallery, DC, 79, Roanoke Fine Art Mus, Va, 80 & VVKR Atrium, Int Architect Firm, Alexandria, Va, 84; Chrysler Mus Biennial, 86; West Art and the Law (travel exhib), USA & Can, 88-89; Shared Visions, IBM Gallery Sci & Art, NY, 90; Art in Pub Places Sculpture, Rockville, Md, 92 & 97; Kennedy Galleries, NY, 93; Nat Travel Show, Paine Webber Gallery, NY, 93; Am Art Group Exhib, Minn Mus Am Art, 94; Creative Will Show, Grey Gallery, NY, 95; Art in Pub Places Sculpture Exhib, Rockville, Md, 97. *Pos:* Art illusr, FBI, Washington, DC, 56-59; exhib coord for 3 Washington, DC restaurants, 61-73. *Awards:* Annapolis Fine Arts Exhib Award for Metal Sculpture, 74; Washington Artist Photog Exhib, Corcoran Gallery, Washington, DC, 77; Two Purchase Awards, West Collection, St Paul, Minn, 82-87. *Bibliog:* Frank Getlein (introd), Ruby Grady, booklet, Brooks Johnson, 72; Allen Smith (dir), Solo Exhibit in Washington (film), WTTG-TV, 72; article, Am Bar Asn J, Chicago, 82; Thomas W Sakolowaki (auth), The Creative Will Book (4 pages), travel show, NY, 96. *Media:* Steel, Acrylic. *Publ:* Contribr, Nat Community Arts Prog Publ, Govt Printing Off, 70, & Art and the Law National Exhibition Book, West Publ, 82, 83 & 86; The West Collection (Coffee Table Bk), West Publ Co, St Paul, Minn, 87; Photograph, Senses, inside cover mag, NY, 94; Artist Calendar, Pomegranate Publ, Calif, 97. *Mailing Add:* Potowmack Bay Studio 431 Broadcreek Dr Fort Washington MD 20744

GRAEB, DON(ALD) (R)
DESIGNER, PAINTER
b Pittsburgh, PA. *Study:* Carnrgie Mellon Univ, BFA, 59. *Work:* Pittsburgh Pub Sch Syst; Ligonier Art Asoc, Town Hall, Ligonier, Pa; Blue Cross of Pa, Pittsburgh; Mellon Bank, Pittsburgh; Commerce Bank, Denver, Colo. *Comn:* Paintings, Denver Corp, Pittsburgh, 79; paintings, Pittsburgh Ctr/Arts, 84; paintings, Ligonier Art Club, Ligonier, Pa, 87. *Exhib:* Watercolor USA, Springfield Art Mus, Springfield, Ill, 95; Southwest Pa Artists, Southwest Alleghenies Mus, Ligonier, Pa 97-98; Winterfest Invitational, Westmoreland Mus Art, Greensberg, Pa; Am Watercolor Soc Salmagundi Club, NY; Adrondacks N Ex/Am WC, NY. *Pos:* Vpres & creative design dir, Creative Productions, Pittsburgh, 65-97; adv commt, Pittsburgh Bd of Educ, formerly; design consult Carnegie Mus Natural Hist, Pittsburgh, 95-. *Teaching:* Instr watercolor, N Hill Ctr/Arts, All'y Co, Pa & Pittsburgh Ctr of Arts, 87-89. *Awards:* Purchase Award, Commerce Bank, 95; Third Place, The Artist Mag Int Competion, 97; Trailsahd Stream Medal, Adirondack's League Club, 99. *Bibliog:* Ann Abbott (auth), Painting Snow Scenes, Watercolor Magic Magazine, 99; Frank Webb (auth), Dynamic Composition, North Light; Phil Metzgar (auth), The Artists Illust Book, North Light, 2001. *Mem:* The Audubon Artists; Watercolor West; Pa Watercolor Soc; Pittsburgh Watercolor Soc (vpres); Whiskey Panters of Am. *Media:* Watercolor. *Dealer:* Bird-in-Hand 427 Broad St Sewickley PA 15143

GRAESE, JUDY (JUDITH) ANN
PAINTER, ILLUSTRATOR
b Loveland, Colo, Nov 8, 40. *Study:* Augustana Col, 58-59; Univ Colo, Boulder, 65-67. *Work:* Nat City Bank, Denver, Colo; Rose Medical Ctr, Denver, Colo; Kent-Denver Day Sch, Colo; Enid Libr, Okla. *Comn:* Ink on stone, comn for Murray Louis, 78 & woodetching, comn for Hanya Holm, 81, by Colo Contemp Dance; ink on stone, Kent-Denver Country Day Sch, Colo, 83; watercolor, Estes Park Music Festival, 85, Children's Hospital, Denver, 89, 90. *Exhib:* One-man shows, Two-Twenty Two Gallery, El Paso, Tex, 71-72 & 73, Artisan, Princeton, NJ, 72 & 74 & Bishop's Antiques & Gallery, Scottsdale, Ariz, 73-96, pvt studio exhib, 93-2000; Adobe01 Patio, Mesilla, NMex, 85; Beeches' Gallery, Carmel, Calif, 88, 91; Savageau Gallery, Denver, 89, 90 & 91; Colo Contemp Dance, 92; Ann Home Studio Exhibit, 94; Kent Denver Alumni Exhib, 95. *Pos:* Designer, display dept, May D&F, 67-69. *Teaching:* Instr contemp dance, Kent-Denver Sch, Colo, 68-87 & 92-95, visual & performing arts, 88, 2006, custumer designer, 89-, Denver Metrop State Col custume designer costumer, 2004. *Awards:* Dick Drew Teacher of Yr Award, Kent Denver Sch, 99; Donald S Merry Award Excellence in Teaching, Kent Denver Sch, 2006. *Bibliog:* Robert Downing (auth), Ad Lib, Denver Post Roundup Sect, 2/2/75; Betty Harvey (auth), Judy Graese, Artists of the Rockies, 5/75; Marie Torrisi (auth), Colo Monthly Mag, 85; Susan Dugan (auth), Washington Park Profile, 4/2005. *Mem:* Colo Resource Guide; Denver Art Students League, Colorado Dance Alliance; Colorado Dance Alliance; Carson-Brierly Dance Libr; Colo Button Club. *Media:* Watercolor; Wood; Bronze,; Stone; Etchings; Silk Screen; Papier Mache. *Interests:* Antiques. *Publ:* Illusr, The Song of Francis, Northland Press, 73; The Treasure is the Rose, Pantheon Press, 73; Art prints, Woodhill Press, 83, Colo Music Festival, 85, Children's Hosp, 89 & 90, Mermaids, Laughing Elephant Bks, 98. *Mailing Add:* 2055 S Franklin Denver CO 80210

GRAF, DEVA
ARTIST
b Lafayette, Ind, 74. *Study:* Sch Art Inst Chicago, BFA, 97; Univ Ill, Chicago, MFA (studio arts), 2002. *Exhib:* The First Parking Lot Biennale, Chicago, 2001; Bad Touch, Ukrainian Inst Mod Art, 2002; What an Art Life, Stadtdalerte Gallery, Bern, 2003; Gone Missing, Milwaukee, Wisc, 2003; New Art Dealers Alliance, Art Fair, Miami, Fla, 2004; Artadia, Cultural Ctr, Ill, 2005; Day for Night, Whitney Biennial, 2006; one woman shows, 12X12, New Artists New Work, Mus Contemp Art, 2004, Post, Chicago, 2004. *Awards:* recipient, Artadia, Chicago, 2004

GRAFF, FREDERICK C
PAINTER, INSTRUCTOR
b Lodi, OH, Oct 15, 45. *Study:* Miami Univ, BS, 1968; Pvt instr with Franklin A Bates, 1962-72. *Work:* Zanesville Art Mus, OH; North Canton Libr, OH; Medina Co Court House, OH; Governor's Mansion, Columbus, OH. *Exhib:* Am Watercolor Soc (juried), Galleries of Salmagundi Club, New York City, 1977; Midwest Watercolor Soc (juried), Tweed Mus of Art, Duluth, Minn, 1977; Nat Watercolor Soc (juried), Brand Libr Art Galleries, Glendale, Calif, 1978; retrospective, Zanesville Art Mus, OH, 1995; Nat Watermedia (juried), Canton Mus Art, OH, 2001; Transparent Watercolor Soc of Am (juried), Elmhurst Art Mus, Ill, 2004. *Teaching:* instr art, Berea City Schools, OH, 1968-2001; watercolor workshop instr, 1972-. *Awards:* Emily Goldsmith, Am Watercolor Soc, 1989; Winsor Newton, Midwest Watercolor Soc, 2000; Millard Sheets Mem Medal, Am Watercolor Soc, 2006. *Bibliog:* Marilyn Hughey Phillis (auth), Watermedia Technique for Releasing the Creative Spirit, Watson-Guptill, 1992; Int Artist Editors (auth) International Showcase of Prize

Winners, Int Artist Mag, 2/2005 & 3/2005; Mark Mehaffey (auth) Creative Watercolor Workshop, North Light Books, 2005. *Mem:* Am Watercolor Soc; Nat Watercolor Soc; Transparent Watercolor Soc of Am; Ohio Watercolor Soc (treas 1978-80); Whiskey Painters of Am. *Media:* Watercolor. *Mailing Add:* 403 E Liberty St Medina OH 44256

GRAFTON, RICK (FREDERICK) WELLINGTON
PAINTER
b Middletown, Conn, May 3, 52. *Study:* Calif Col Arts & Crafts, BFA(high distinction), 76. *Work:* Metrop Mus Art, Chase Manhattan Bank, NY; Art Inst Chicago; Arco Ctr Visual Art, Los Angeles; Bank Am, San Francisco, Calif. *Comn:* Meridian Building (watercolor), comn by J Lee, San Francisco, 83. *Exhib:* Solo exhib, Grapestake Gallery, San Francisco, 80 & 83, Galleria del Cavallino, Venice, Italy, 81 & San Jose Mus Art, 82; Light & Heavy Light, Mem Union Art Gallery, Univ Calif, Davis, 85; Discreet Power: Reductive Issues in Contemp Painting, Rockford Art Mus, Rockford, Ill, 88; Waterworks, Sierra Nevada Mus Art, Reno, Nev, 88; Almost Alchemy, Transamerica Pyramid Gallery, San Francisco, Calif, 96; Hidden Treasurers, Sonoma State Univ, Calif, 98. *Teaching:* Instr watercolor, Asn Students Univ Calif, Berkeley. *Awards:* Watercolor Award, Calif State Expo, 78. *Mem:* Emeryville Artists Coop. *Media:* Watercolor on Paper, Acrylic and Oil on Canvas and Panel. *Mailing Add:* 1420 45 St #30 Emeryville CA 94608

GRAHAM, BOB
PAINTER, MURALIST
b Canton, Tex, Jan 1, 47. *Study:* N Tex State Univ, 66-69; Cape Sch, with Henry Hensche, 71-82. *Work:* New Orleans Mus Art, La. *Comn:* Portrait Alton Oschner, Oschner Found, New Orleans, La, 85; portrait Frank Barker, Nichols State Univ, Thibbodeau, La, 86; Life of Moses (mural) Jerry Katz & Jewish Community Ctr, New Orleans, 87; portraits First Parrish Judges (4) Jefferson Parrish, Metarie, La, 90; History of Kenner (mural) Kenner, La City Coun, 91. *Exhib:* Kansas Pastel Society, Wichita, 85; Seldom Seen Figures, New Orleans Hist Soc, 88; Allied Artist, Nation Arts Club, NY, 89; Texas & Neighbors, Irving, 89; Am Realism Competition, Parkersburg Art Ctr, WVa, 90. *Awards:* Best of Show, Salmagundi Open, New York, 87; Best Painting in Any Medium, Am Artist Prof League, New York, 88; Best Printing in Any Medium, Knickerbocker Artists, New York, 90. *Bibliog:* Satoru Fugii (auth), Outstanding American Illustrators- Graphic-Sha Japan, 84; Stephen Doherty (auth) Southern Plantation, Am Artist, 1/89. *Mem:* Master pastellist, Pastel Soc Am; founder Degas Pastel Soc. *Media:* Oil, Pastel. *Mailing Add:* 509 Big Rock St Canton TX 75103-1201

GRAHAM, DANIEL H
CONCEPTUAL ARTIST, ENVIRONMENTAL ARTIST
b Urbana, Ill, Mar 31, 42. *Work:* Tate Gallery, London; Stadisches Mus, Monchengladbach, Ger; Allen Art Mus, Oberlin, Ohio; Van Abbemuseum, Eindhoven; Art Inst Chicago; Mod Museet, Stockholm; Mus Contemp Art, Tokyo, Japan; and others. *Comn:* Argonne Nat Labs, Ill; Laumier Sculpture Park, St Louis, Mo; Nexus, Atlanta, Ga; Pub Art Fund, Madison Sq Park, New York City. *Exhib:* Solo shows include Mus fur Gegenwartskunst Basel, 96, Marian Goodman, Paris, 97, Neve Galerie am Landesmuseum Joanneum, Graz, 97, Massimo Minini, Brescia, 97, Centro Galego de Arte Contemporanea, Santiago de Compostela, 97, Kunstwerke, Berlin, Ger, 99, Marian Goodman Gallery, NY, 00, 02, Shigemori Residence, Kyoto, 01, Museu Serralves, Porto, Port, 01-02, Massimo Minini Gallery, Brescia, Italy, 02, Galerie Rüdiger Schöttle, Munich, 02; group shows include Information, Mus Mod Art, NY, 70; Berne Kunsthalle, Switz; Musee Nat d'Art Moderne Centre Georges Pompidou, Paris, France, 77, 79, 86 & 87; In anderen Raumen, Mus Haus Lange & Haus Esters, Krefeld, 91; Transform, Kunstmuseum und Kunsthalle, Basel, 92; Passageworks, Rooseum, Malmo, 93; Films on Art, Nat Gallery Art, Washington, DC, 94; Pub Inf, San Francisco Mus Mod Art, Calif, 95; Artists Photographs, John Gibson Gallery, NY, 96; The Crystal Stopper, Lehman Maupin Gallery, NY, 97; Whitney Biennial, Whitney Mus Am Art, NY, 97, 2006; In Visible Light, Mus Mod Art, Oxford, 97; Broken Home, Greene Naftali Gallery, NY, 97; Skulptur, Projekte in Munster 97, Munster Documenta X, Kassel, 97; Documenta 10, Kassel, Ger, 97; Sharawadgi, Felsenvilla, Baden, 98; Breaking Ground, Marian Goodman Gallery, NY, 98; Am Century: Art and Cult (1950-2000), Whitney Mus Am Art, 99; Seeing Time: Selections from the Pamela and Richard Kramlich Collection, San Francisco Mus Modern Art, Calif, 99; Hex Enduction Hour by The Fall, Team Gallery, NY, 00; Dream Machines, Hayward Gallery, London, Eng, 00; Insites, Interior Spaces in Contemp Art, Whitney Mus Am Art at Champion, Stamford, Conn, 2000; 40th Anniversary, John Gibson Gallery, NY, 01; Inst Contemp Art, Boston, 02; Ctr de Arte, Salamanca, Spain, 02; Ludwig Mus, Cologne, Ger, 02; Vancouver Art Gallery, 03; Parsons Sch Design, Dept Archit, New York City, 03; A Sculpture Show, Marian Goodman Gallery, New York City, 03; and many others. *Teaching:* NS Col Art & Design, Halifax, summer 81; Hamburg Hochschnk, 87-88. *Awards:* Nat Endowment Arts Visual Arts Grant, 80; Creative Artists Pub Serv Grant, 81; Skowhegan Medal for Mixed Media, Skowhegan Sch Painting and Sculpture, New York, 92; French Vermeil Medal, City of Paris, 01. *Publ:* Auth, Performance, 70; Films, 77; Buildings and Signs, 80; Theatre, 82; Pavilions, 83; and others. *Mailing Add:* c/o Marian Goodman Gallery 24 W 57th St New York NY 10019

GRAHAM, K M
PAINTER, PRINTMAKER
b Hamilton, Ont, Sept 13, 13. *Study:* Univ Toronto, BA. *Hon Degrees:* Trinity Col, Toronto, hon fel. *Work:* Art Gallery Ont; Art Bank Can, Ottawa; Edmonton Art Gallery, Alta; MacDonald Stewart Centre, Guelph, Ont; J Barnike Gallery Hart House, Toronto, Ont; Nat Gallery, Can; Art Gallery of Hamilton, Ont; plus others. *Exhib:* Art Gallery of Ont, Toronto, 74; Montreal Mus of Fine Arts, Que, 76; Edmonton Art Gallery, Alta, 77; Galerie Wentzel, Hamburg, WGer, 77; Canada House, London; Cult Ctr, Paris; Am Artists Assoc, NY; David Mirvish Gallery, Toronto; Klonaridis Inc, Toronto; Mem Art Gallery, St Johns Nfld, Beaverbrook, NB; Art Gallery Fredericton, NB; and others. *Awards:* Can Coun Travel Award, 73-74 & 79; Hon Fel, Trinity Col, Univ Toronto, 88. *Bibliog:* Karen Wilkin (auth), The late blooming vitality of Toronto Art, Artnews, 2/80; Ingrid Jenkner, KM Graham 1970-85 (catalogue), Macdonald Stewart Art Ctr, Guelph, Ont; Lora Carney (auth), Brick #39: The Art of KM Graham, 90; Patricia Grattan (auth), KM Graham Eternities of Space (catalog), 94. *Mem:* Royal Can Acad of Arts; Arts & Letters Club, Toronto. *Media:* Acrylic, Canvas; Dry Points, Lithographs. *Specialty:* Canadian art. *Interests:* Painting and drawing. *Dealer:* Douglas Udell Gallery of Edmonton Alberta Vancouver BC Canada; Feheley Fine Arts 14 Hazelton Ave Toronto ON M5R 2E2 Canada; Moore Gallery Toronto 80 Spadima Ave Suite 404 Toronto ON M5V2J3 Canada. *Mailing Add:* 26 Boswell Ave Toronto ON M5R 1M4 Canada

GRAHAM, LOIS (M GORD)
PAINTER
b Kewanee, Ill, Aug 27, 30. *Study:* Knox Col, BA(magna cum laude), Phi Beta Kappa, 52; Washington Univ, with Paul Burlin; also with Jack Tworkov, Nathan Oliviera & Lothar Schall. *Work:* City Seattle Portable Works Collection, Wash; Bellevue City Hall Collection, Wash; Santa Barbara Mus Art; Seattle Art Mus; Northwest Special Collection, Seattle Arts Comn; Yaocultural Cen, Microsoft, Osaka. *Comn:* Mural, Knox Col, Galesburg, Ill, 51; Bellevue, Wash, 75; painting, pvt collection, Seattle, Wash, 79; mural, Seattle Opera House, 86. *Exhib:* Seattle Art Mus, 58, 80-81 & 84; Seattle Pac Univ, 79-81; solo shows, Foster White Gallery, Seattle, 81, 82, 84, 85, 89, 91, 94, 98, 2000, 2002, 2004; Bellevue Art Mus, Wash, 82, 83 & 85; E R Squibb Galleries, Princeton, NJ, 82; Portland Ctr Visual Arts, 82; Artemisia Gallery, Chicago, 83; Pacific Lutheran, UNN, 88; Whatcom Art Mus, 86; and others. *Teaching:* St Louis Co Pub Sch. *Awards:* Honors Award, Seattle Arts Comn, 84; Out standing Achievement in The Arts, Bellevue Arts Commission. *Bibliog:* Mathew Kangas (auth), Lois Graham at Foster/White, Art Am, 12/81 & Lois Graham: A decade in review, 85, Bellevue Art Mus; Betty Brown (auth), Southern California, Lois Graham at Kirk deGooyer, Arts, 2/83; M Kangas, Epicenter: Essays on North Am Art; Nichols, Ellen (ed), Northwest Originals: Northwest Women & their Art, Portland, OR; Hot Spor, 89; Marti Media Inc, 90. *Mem:* King Co Arts Comn; Artist Trust. *Media:* Oil, Monotype. *Dealer:* Foster/White Gallery, 123 S Jackson St. *Mailing Add:* 1100 E Union St No 3A Seattle WA 98122-3928

GRAHAM, ROBERT
SCULPTOR
b Mexico City, Mex, Aug 38; US Citizen. *Study:* San Jose State Col, 61-63; San Francisco Art Inst, 63-64. *Work:* Whitney Mus Am Art & Mus Mod Art, NY; Hirshhorn Mus & Sculpture Garden; Los Angeles Co Mus; Dallas Mus Fine Art, Tex; Fed Reserve Bank, San Francisco Mus Mod Art, San Francisco. *Comn:* Fed Reserve Bank San Francisco, Calif, 83; San Jose Fed Bldg, Calif, 84; Los Angeles Olympic Organizing Comt, 84; Joe Louis Mem, Detroit, Mich; Duke Ellington Mem, Cent Park, NY, 92. *Exhib:* Galerie Neuendorf, Hamburg, WGer, 79; one-man shows, Walker Art Ctr, traveling, 81, Los Angeles Co Mus Art, Calif, 88, Robert Miller Gallery, NY, 89, 90 & 92, Gagosian Gallery, New York, 94 & 96, Dorothy Blau Gallery, Bay Harbor Islands, Fla, 96, Olympic Gateway, Atlanta, Ga, 96 & Faye Gold Gallery, Atlanta, 96; Whitney Mus Am Art, 83, 84, 86, 88, 89 & 93-94; Artists' Photographs: A Private View, Blum Helman Gallery Inc, 93; Drawing the Line Against AIDS, Guggenheim Mus Soho, NY, 93; The Figure in Sculpture, Transamerica Pyramid Lobby Gallery, San Francisco, 94; Illusion/Allusion: Sculpture, Mus Fine Arts, Fla State Univ, 94; Art on Paper, Weatherspoon Art Gallery, Univ NC, Greensboro, 94-95; Feminine Image, Nassau Co Mus Art, Roslyn Harbor, NY, 96-97. *Bibliog:* Maurice Tuchman (auth), Robert Graham: The Duke Ellington Mem in Progress, Los Angeles Co Mus Art, 89; John McEwen, Robert Graham Statues, Frankfurt: Galerie Neuendorf; Twenty-one Figures by Robert Graham, NY: Robert Miller Gallery. *Media:* Bronze. *Mailing Add:* c/o Robert Miller Gallery 526 W 26th St #10A New York NY 10001-5541

GRAHAM, ROBERT C, JR
ART DEALER
b New York, NY, Sept 6, 41. *Study:* Middlebury Col, BA, 63. *Pos:* Chmn & pres, James Graham & Sons Inc, New York, 63-2000. *Mem:* Art Dealers Asn Am. *Specialty:* American painting and sculpture. *Mailing Add:* 425 June Rd Stamford CT 06903

GRAINGER, NESSA POSNER
PAINTER, COLLAGE ARTIST
b Atlantic City, NJ. *Study:* Philadelphia Mus Sch Art, BA; Tyler Sch Fine Arts;, Pa Acad Fine Arts. *Work:* Zheijiang Mus, Hangzhow, China; Elliot Mus, Stuart, Fla; Mus Mod Art Libr, NY; Artist Libr Victoria & Albert Mus, London, Eng; Nat Mus Am Art Libr, Washington; many corporate collections and others. *Exhib:* One-man shows, Douglas Col for Women, NJ, 90, The Interchurch Ctr, NY, 92, Elliot Mus, Stuart, Fla, 93 & Somerset Art Asn, NJ, 98; Nat Acad Design, NY, 92 & 96; Allied Artists Am, Nat Arts Club, NY, 92; Philip & Muriel Berman Mus Art, 94 & 96; Am Watercolor Soc, 95. *Teaching:* Workshops, Sonoma & Livermore, Calif, Palm Beach, Fla, Somerset Art Asn, NJ, NJ Ctr Visual Arts, Lafayette Col, Easton, Pa & Hudson River Art Workshops, Greenville, NY. *Awards:* NJ Watercolor Soc Silver Medal, 85; Audubon Artists of America, Silver Medal, 89; Silver Medal, Knickerbacher Artists, 92; Dale Meyers Medal Honor, Audubon Artists, 96. *Bibliog:* Dorothy Hall (auth), Parkeast, Art & Artists, 11/87. *Media:* Mixed Media, Watercolor. *Specialty:* Watercolor, collage, mixed media. *Interests:* Teaching, painting, museums. *Publ:* Splash 3, North Light Books, 94; Collage Techniques (by Gerald Brommer), ed VIII, 96; Best of Watercolor II & The Best of Watercolor Composition, Rockport Publ, 97; Collage in All Dimensions, Nat Col Soc, Malcom Lewellyn Publ, 2005. *Mailing Add:* 5513 Jaclyn Ln Bethlehem PA 18017

GRALNICK, LISA
JEWELER
b New York, 56. *Study:* Kent State Univ, BFA, 77; State Univ NY, New Paltz, MFA, 80. *Work:* Am Craft Mus, NY; Stedijk Mus, Amsterdam; Schenectady Mus, NY. *Exhib:* Solo exhibs, Sculpture to Wear, Los Angeles, Calif & VO Galerie, Washington, DC, 87, Galerie RA, Amsterdam, The Neth, 88, CDK Gallery, NY, 89, Susan Cummins Gallery, Mill Vallery, Calif, 90, Jewelerswerk Galerie, Washington, DC, 91 & Helen Drutt Gallery, Philadelphia, Pa, 92; Craft Today USA, Am Craft Mus, 89; Body Art, Security Pac Corp, 90; For the Tabletop, Galerie RA, Amsterdam, 91; Schmuckszene 92, Int Handwerksmesse, Munich, Ger, 92; Design Visions: The Second Perth Int Crafts Triennial, Art Gallery Western Australia, Perth Cult Ctr, 92; and others. *Teaching:* Vis prof, head enamelling dept, Kent State Univ, 80-81; vis prof, head jewelry dept, NS Col Art & Design, Halifax, 82-83; instr, jewelry, 92nd St, NY, 86-91; fac, Parsons Sch Design, NY, 91-. *Awards:* Fel, Nat Endowment Arts, 88 & 92; Fel, New York Found Arts, 91 & 95; Louis Comfort Tiffany Found Grant, 93. *Bibliog:* Alice Sprintzen (auth), Art Enamelling, 83; Peter Dormer & Ralph Turner (auths), New Jewelry: Trends & Traditions, 85; Roger Kuhn (auth), The Jewelry of Lisa Gralnick, Metalsmith, summer, 92

GRAND, STANLEY I
CURATOR, HISTORIAN
b Washington, DC, Jan 26, 45. *Study:* Univ Wis, Madison, BS, 67, MA, 85, PhD, 93. *Collection Arranged:* Tom Bamberger: Photographs 1978-1992 (with catalog), Carlsten Art Gallery, Univ Wisc, Stevens Point, 93; Drawing on the Figure (with catalog), Carlsten Art Gallery, Univ Wisc, Stevens Point, 93; The City Observed: Barry Carlsen, Douglas Safranek, Stuart Shils (with catalog), Sordoni Art Gallery, Wiles Univ, 94; Drum Lithographs: 1960-1963 (with catalog), Sordoni Art Gallery, Wilkes Univ, 94; Paul Georges: Self-Portraits (with catalog), Sordoni Art Gallery, Wilkes Univ, 95; Guy Pene du Bois: The Twenties at Home and Abroad (auth, catalog), Sordoni Art Gallery, Wilkes Univ, 95; Between Heaven and Hell: Union Square in the 1930's (auth, catalog), Sordoni Art Gallery, Wilkes Univ, 96; Robert L Schultz: Drawings: 1980-1995 (auth, catalog), Sordoni Art Gallery, Wilkes Univ, 96; John Sloan: Works on Paper, Sordoni Art Gallery, Wilkes Univ, 96; Eugene Atget: Photographs, Vieux Paris, Sordoni Art Gallery, Wilkes Univ, 96; Philippe Halsman: Celebrity Photographs from the 1940s and 50s, Sordoni Art Gallery, Wilkes Univ, 96; Seymour Lipton: Drawings, Sordoni Art Gallery, Wilkes Univ, 97; The Tuscan Landscapes of Richard Upton (auth, catalog), Sordoni Art Gallery, Wilkes Univ, 97; Gary Lang: Paintings and Objects 1975-1997, (auth, catalog), Sordoni Art Gallery, Wilkes Univ, 97; Contemporary Realist Art from the Collection of MellonBank (with catalog), Sordoni Art Gallery, Wilkes Univ, 97; Jimmy Ernst: Shadow to Light, Paintings 1942-1982 (auth, catalog), Sordoni Art Gallery, Wilkes Univ, 97; Anthony Sorce: Four Decades (with catalog), Sordoni Art Gallery, Wilkes Univ, 98; Gregory Conniff: Twenty Years in the Field, Sordoni Art Gallery, Wilkes Univ, 99; The Graphic Art of Paul Bacon, Sordoni Art Gallery, Wilkes Univ, 99; The Collector as Bookbinder: The Piscatorial Bindings of SA Neff, Jr, (with catalog) Sordoni Art Gallery, Wilkes Univ, 99; Edward Schmidt: Mythologies, Sordoni Art Gallery, Wilkes Univ, 2000; Hank O'Neal: Portraits (with catalog), Sordoni Art Gallery, Wilkes Univ, 2000; Michael Thomas: Gables, Sordoni Art Gallery, Wilkes Univ, 2001; Audrey Ushenko: Allegories and Myths (with catalog), Univ Mus, Southeast Mo Sate Univ, 2001; A Gift from the Tamara Kerr Art Bank/New York Artists Equity Asn Inc Honoring Placide and George A Schriever (with catalog), Univ Mus, Southeast Mo State Univ, 2002; Violet Baxter: The View From Union Square (with catalog), Univ Mus, Southeast Mo State Univ, 2002. *Pos:* Cur collections, Madison Art Ctr, 86-87; cur, Edna Carlsten Art Gallery, Univ Wis, 91-93; dir, Sordoni Art Gallery, 93-2000; mus dir Southeast Mo State Univ, 2000-. *Teaching:* Vis prof art hist, Beloit Col, 91; asst prof art hist, Wilkes Univ, 93-2000; assoc prof Southeast Mo State Univ, 2000-. *Mem:* Asn Am Art Historians; Am Asn Mus; Col Art Asn; Int Asn Art Critics. *Res:* Twentieth century American figurative art. *Publ:* Auth, Drawing on the Figure (bk), 93; Paul Georges: Self Portraits, Sordoni Art Gallery, 95; coauth, Guy Pene du Bois: The Twenties at Home and Abroad, 95 & Between Heaven & Hell: Union Square in the 1930s, 96, Sordoni Art Gallery; auth, Robert L Schultz: Drawings 1980-1995, Sordoni Art Gallery, 96; and several other exhib catalogs. *Mailing Add:* 1635 Themis St Cape Girardeau MO 63701

GRANDEE, JOE RUIZ
PAINTER, GALLERY DIRECTOR
b Dallas, Tex, Nov 19, 29. *Study:* Aunspaugh Art Sch, Dallas. *Work:* White House, Washington, DC; Xavier Univ Mus, Cincinnati, Ohio; Mont State Hist Soc Mus, Great Falls; Marine Corps Mus, Quantico, Va; Univ Tex, Arlington. *Comn:* Twenty Mules of Death Valley, US Borax Co, Hollywood, Calif, 65; Linda Bird & Chuck Robb Off Portrait, comn by Lyndon B Johnson family & friends, 67; portrait of Johnny Carson, comn by Rudy Tellez, Assoc Producer NBC, NY, 67; portrait of Robert Taylor, comn by US Borax Co for Robert Taylor, Hollywood, 68; portrait of Leander H McNelly, Texas Ranger, East Wing of White House, Washington, DC, 72. *Exhib:* Custer Exhib, Amon Carter Mus Western Art, Ft Worth, Tex, 68; one-man shows, Norton Art Gallery Mus, Shreveport, La, 71, El Paso Mus Fine Arts, Tex, 72 & Tex Ranger Mus Show, Waco, Tex, 72 & US Capitol, 74; and many others. *Pos:* Owner, Joe Grandee Gallery & Mus of Old West, currently. *Awards:* First Official Artist of Texas, Tex Legis & Gov, 71; Franklin Mint Gold Medal Western Art for Pursuit and Attack, 74; and others. *Bibliog:* Wayne Gard (auth), Joe Grandee--painter of the old west, Am Artist Mag, 67; Grandee Paintings (TV film), US Borax Co, 68; Joy Schultz (auth), The West Still Lives: Grandee, Heritage, 70. *Media:* Oil, Ink. *Specialty:* Paintings, drawings and sculpture works of Joe Ruiz Grandee and displays of historical artifacts. *Publ:* Illusr, Indian Wars of Texas, 65, Pictorial History of The Texas Rangers, 69, The Grand Duke Alexis in the USA, 72 & The Life of Jim Baker (mountain man), 1818-1898, 72; contribr, Cowboy Series, In: Time-Life Bks, 72. *Dealer:* Gene McDaniel PO Box 433 Midland TX 79701; Bob Hoff PO Box 231 Houston TX 77001. *Mailing Add:* 2400 W Pioneer Pkwy Suite 123 Arlington TX 76013

GRANDPRÉ, MARY
ILLUSTRATOR
Study: Minn Col Art & Design. *Pos:* Conceptual illusr, various local editorial clients, currently; visionary, environ & scenery dept DreamWorks' prod Antz; illusr, Harry Potter Series, 97—. *Media:* Pastels. *Publ:* illusr, Harry Potter & Sorcerer's Stone, 97, Harry Potter & the Chamber of Secrets, 98, Harry Potter & the Prisoner of Azkaban, 99, Harry Potter & Goblet of Fire, 2000, Harry Potter & the Order of the Phoenix, 2003, Harry Potter & the Half-Blood Prince, 2005, children's books, The Snow Storm, 83, The Vegetables Go to Bed, 94, Curtain of Night, 97, Pockets, 98, The House of Wisdom, 99, The Purple Snerd, 2000, Aunt Claire's Yellow Beehive Hair, 2001, The Sea Chest, 2002, Plum, 2003, The Thread of Life, 2003, Henry and Pawl, 2004, Sweep Dreams, 2004, Tales from Shakespeare, 2004. *Mailing Add:* c/o Scholastic Inc 555 Broadway New York NY 10001-3999

GRANNE, REGINA
ARTIST, EDUCATOR
b NY City, Jan 16, 39. *Study:* Cooper Union, certificate, 56-59; studied at Hunter Col, 59-60; Yale Univ, BFA, 61, MFA, 63. *Exhib:* Solo shows Tatistcheff Gallery, NY City, 89; Genovese Sullivan Gallery, Boston, 91, 96, 97, 99, 2003; AIR Gallery, NY City, 95, 97, 99, 2002; Lehman Wing Sch Int Studies, Columbia Univ, 2000; Contemp Art, Nat Acad, NY City, 2006. *Teaching:* Instr painting and drawing Ridgewood Sch Art, 67-73; asst prof Bard Col, Annandale-on-Hudson, NY, 73-74, mem faculty, 1983-2005; lectr art CUNY Queens Col, Flushing, 73-84; instr painting and drawing Parsons Sch Design, NY City, 79-93, coordinator MFA program, 1993-2002, faculty mem 2001-2005; vis artist Lakehead Univ, Ontario, Canada, 89, Art Acad Cincinnati, 94; vis instr Moore Col Art, Philadelphia, 90-92

GRANNON, KATY
PHOTOGRAPHER
b Arlington, Mass, 69. *Study:* Univ Pa, BA, 91; Harvard Univ, MA, 93; Yale Univ, MFA, 99. *Work:* Girls Night Out, Orange Cty Mus Art, LA, 2003, Moving Pictures, Guggenheim Mus, Bibao, Spain, 2003; Open House: working in Brooklyn, Brooklyn Mus Art 2004, Whitney Biennial, Whitney Mus Am Art, 2004, From NY with Love, Covivant Gallery, Tampa, Fla, 2004, Land of the Free, Jack Hanley Gallery, San Francisco, 2004. *Exhib:* one-woman shows, Dream Am, Kohn Turner Gallery, Los Angeles, 2000, 51 Fine Art, Antewerp Belg, 2001, Morning Call, Salon 94, New York City, 2003, Sugar Camp Rd, Artemis Greenberg Van Doren Gallery, New York City, 2003, Arles Photog Festival, Arles, Frances, 2004, Emily Tsingou Gallery, London, 2005, Jackson Fine Art, Atlanta, Ga, 2005; group shows, ArtSpace, New Haven, Conn, 98, Another Girl, Another Planet, Lawrence Rubin Greenberg Van Doren Fine Art, NY, 99, Reflections Through a Glass Eye, Inter Ctr Photog, NY, 2000, Smile, Here, NY, 2001, Boomerang: Collector's Choice II, Exit Art, NY, 2001, Women by Women, Cook fine Art, NY, 2002, True Blue, Jackson Fine Art, Atlanta, 2002, From NY with Love, Covivant Gallery, Tampa, Fla, 2004, Land of the Free, Jack Hanley Gallery, San Francisco, 2004. *Awards:* Rema Hort Mann Found Grant, 99; Bucksbaum Award, 2004. *Mailing Add:* c/o Artemis Greenberg Van Doran Gallery 730 Fifth Ave 7th fl New York NY 10019

GRANSTAFF, WILLIAM BOYD
PAINTER, ILLUSTRATOR
b Paducah, Ky, May 17, 25. *Study:* Kansas City Art Inst, with Ross Braught & Ed Lanning, grad; Am Acad Art, with William Mosby & Bill Fleming. *Comn:* Mural, Cadet Club, Garden City, Kans, 45; Old Homeplace, B J Farless, Princeton, Ky, 70; Vietnam (painting), comn by Nat Am Legion, 75 & Korea (painting), 78; 1st Bank & Trust, Princeton, Ky. *Exhib:* Mid-S, Nashville, Tenn, 53; one-man show, Planters Bank, Hopkinsville, Ky, 72, 99. *Pos:* Mem, Art Dirs Club, Nashville, 55-58. *Teaching:* Instr illus, Famous Artist Sch, 59-61. *Awards:* Brackman Blue Ribbon, Nashville, 53; Best of Show, Hopkinsville Discover, 2002. *Bibliog:* Meet your instructors, Famous Artist Mag, 61. *Mem:* Princeton Art Guild. *Media:* Oil, Watercolor. *Interests:* flying instructor. *Publ:* Illusr, What's in a Word, Abingdon, 65; The Way Out, Moody, 70; Golden Treasury of Bible Stories, Southern, 71; illusr, Man-US & Americas, 72 & illusr, Americans All, 72, Benefic. *Dealer:* Heritage Gallery Rosemont Gardens Lexington KY 40503; Bennett Gallery 2104 Crestmoor Rd Nashville TN 37215; Riverwind Gallery 10400 W State Rd 662 Newburg IN 47630. *Mailing Add:* 806 S Jefferson St Princeton KY 42445

GRANT, DANIEL HOWARD
WRITER, CRITIC
b Westport, Conn, Sept 5, 1954. *Study:* Northwestern Univ, BA, 76. *Pos:* Art critic, Newsday, Melville, NY, 80-84, Commercial-Appeal, Memphis, Tenn, 84-86, Boston Herald, Mass, 86-. *Teaching:* Instr artists career skills, Greenfield Community Col, Mass, 92-. *Mem:* Amherst Cult Coun (chmn, 92-96); Found Community Artists (advisory bd mem, 78-84). *Res:* Resources and opportunities for financial support for fine artists. *Publ:* Auth, Business of Being an Artist, 91, How to Start and Succeed as an Artist, 93, Artist's Resource Handbook, 94, Writer's Resource Handbook, 97 & Fine Artist's Career Guide, 98, Allworth Press; Artist's Guide to Making It in New York City, 2001; Selling Art Without Galleries, Allworth Press, 2006. *Mailing Add:* 19 Summer St Amherst MA 01002

GRASHOW, JAMES BRUCE
SCULPTOR, PRINTMAKER
b Brooklyn, NY, Jan 16, 42. *Study:* Pratt Inst, BFA, 62, MFA, 65. *Work:* Mus Mod Art, Pub Libr, NY; Greenville Mus, SC; Libr Cong, Washington, DC; Iron Range Mus, Minn; Roanoke Mus Fine Art, Va. *Comn:* Ballet stage sets, San Francisco Ballet Co, 76 & Nat Ballet Cuba, Havana, 78; Book of the Month Club, 86; Cardboard Sources, Bridgeport Discovery Mus., 94; Cottage Ship, Disney Ship, Wonder. 99; Int Paper Co, Installation, 2000. *Exhib:* A City, Am Inst Architect, Washington, DC, 65; Made with Paper, 67 & Tombstones & Monuments, 67, Mus Contemp Crafts, NY; Human Concern, Personal Torment, Whitney Mus Am Art, 69; Hudson River Mus, NY, 72; Univ Conn, Storrs, 79; Ctr Arts, State Univ NY, Purchase, 82; Aldridge, Ridgefield, Conn, 85; Allan Stone Gallery, 98; Aldridge Mus Contemp Art, 98; solo exhib (sculpture, Allan Stone Gallery, New York City, 66, 68, 69, 71, 74, 79, 82, Ctr. of the Arts, SUNY, Purchase, 83, Discovery Mus, Conn Cardboardasaures, 94, Totem Pole, Traffic Jam 99, Yazoo Cardboard Zoo, Aldrich Mus Contemp Art, Stamford, Conn, 98, Corrugated Exposition, Chicago, 2000. *Teaching:* Assoc prof painting & figure drawing, Pratt Inst, 68-81; prof art, Fairfield Univ, 91-95; prof art, Parsons Sch of Design, 95-96; prof, Art Marie Walsh Sharpe Art Found, Co, 95-. *Awards:* Fulbright Travel Grant, 63; Ital Govt Grant, 63; Tiffany Award Graphics, 65; Andy award, 76, Cert Distinction, Cert Merit, Art Dir Club; Annual Award of Excellence, Comm Arts Mag, 81; Award of Excellence, S Newspaper Design, 82-83; Worlds Most Memorable Poster, Best Mus Poster, 86. *Bibliog:* Steven Heller (auth), article, Graphis, 81; Chauncey Howell (producer), Live at Five, NBC-TV, 82; Jane Cottingham (auth), article, Am Artist Mag, 5/82; Auth. Abrams, New York Observed, 87, Cardboardasaurus, 96. *Media:* Fabric Mache; Woodcut. *Publ:* Illusr, Making Vegetables Grow, 75 & Twelve Moons Make a Year, 80, Knopf; NY Times Mag, 83; Peace, A Dream Unfolding, Somerville House. *Dealer:* Allan Stone Gallery 113 E 90th St New York NY 10128. *Mailing Add:* 14 Diamond Hill Rd West Redding CT 06896

GRASSI, MARCO
CONSERVATOR, RESTORER
b Florence, Italy, July 7, 34; US citizen. *Study:* Princeton Univ, BA(art hist), 56; apprenticeships at: Gabinetto del Restauro, Uffizi, Florence, 59-60; Istituto Centrale del Restauro, Rome, 60-62; & Schweitzerisches Institut für Kunstwissenschaft, 62. *Pos:* Vis conservator, Thyssen-Bornemisza Collection, Villa Favorita, Lugano, Switz. *Awards:* Ital Legion of Merit. *Mem:* Am Inst Conserv Hist & Artistic Works; Int Inst Conserv Hist & Artistic Works; fel Pierpont Morgan Libr. *Mailing Add:* 599 Broadway New York NY 10012

GRASSL, ANTON M
PAINTER, PHOTOGRAPHER
b Munich, Ger, Sept 9, 55. *Study:* Opera of Munich, Ger, apprentice (stage design), 74-76; Bavarian Sch Photog, apprentice, 76-78; Acad der Schonen Kunste, Munich, Ger, BFA, 81; RI Sch Design, MFA(photog), 83. *Work:* Mus Fine Arts, Boston; Rose Art Mus, Brandies Univ, Waltham, Mass; Brockton Art Mus, Mass; Polaroid Collection, Cambridge, Mass; Hypo Bank Art Collection, Munich, Ger; and other private collections. *Exhib:* Solo exhibs, Gallerie Lanz, Bern, Switz, 79, Acad der Schonen Kunste, Munich, Ger, 80, City Hall Mannheim, Ger, 81, Woods Gerry Gallery, Providence, RI, 83, Robert Klein Gallery, Boston, 89 & Cambridge Arts Coun, Mass, 91; Gallerie am Maxwehr, Landshut, Ger, 85; Gallery Laughlin & Winkler, Boston, 90; 10 Yrs Artist Coop, Fed Reserve Bank, Boston, 93; Am Outdoor Theaters, Univ Calif, Berkeley, 94; Robert Klein Gallery, Boston, 95; Howard Yezerski Gallery, Boston, 99. *Pos:* Freelance Photogr, currently. *Awards:* Fel, Mass Found Arts, 91; Fel, Nat Endowment Arts, 92, Graham Found Advan Studies Fine Arts Grant, 95. *Mailing Add:* 259 A St Boston MA 02210

GRASSO, DORIS TEN-EYCK
PAINTER, SCULPTOR
b Fremont, NY, May 3, 14. *Study:* Educ Alliance, New York, with Moses Soyer, Alex Dobkin & John Hovannes; N Hudson Arts Sch, with Fabian Zaccone; Rutherford Art Sch, with Lucille Hobbie. *Work:* Paul Whitener Mem Collection, NC Mus Art; George B Burr Collection, NY; Jersey City Mus Art; Staten Island Pub Schs Collection, NY; Women's Club Collection, Lyndhurst, NJ. *Exhib:* Knickerbocker Artists Int, NY, 63-65; Painters & Sculptors Soc NJ Nat, 65-72; Nat Casein Soc, NY, 68; Acad Artists Regional, NJ, 68-71; Am Artists Prof League Nat, NY, 69-70. *Teaching:* Instr art, YWCA, Bayonne, NJ, 50-55, Doris Grasso Sch Fine Arts, 52-62 & Bayonne's Woman's Club Eve Dept, 65-68; instr, Doris Ten-Eyck Grasso Gallery & Studio, Gloucester, Mass, currently. *Awards:* Pauline Wick Award for Oils, Am Artists Prof League, 68; Golden Lady Award, Nat Women of Achievement (Art), Amita, Inc, 69; First Award for Sculpture, State Fedn Women's Clubs, 70; and others. *Mem:* Fel Am Artists Prof League (pres, NJ Chap, nat dir, 60-62); Painters & Sculptors Soc NJ (bd dir & secy, 62-65); Burr Artists (pub rels, 66-68); Assoc Rockport Artists; fel Int Arts & Lett, Ger & Switz; and others. *Media:* Oil, Watercolor

GRASSO, JACK
PAINTER
b White Plains, NY, Jan 15, 27. *Study:* Study with Herb Olsen & Alex Ross, 67. *Work:* Univ Colo Sch Bus, Boulder; US Coast Guard traveling exhib, NY; YMCA, Stamford, Conn. *Exhib:* Allied Artists Show, Mus Fine Arts, Boston, 75; Hudson Valley Art Asn, White Plains, NY, 75-82; Conn Watercolor Soc, Hartford, 75-82; Lever House, NY, 82; Mystic Int, Maritime Gallery, Mystic, Conn, 83-85; Orleans Art Gallery, Mass. *Pos:* Coast Guard & Navy combat artist, New York, 80. *Teaching:* Instr watercolor, East Ridge Jr High Sch, Ridgefield, Conn, 82-. *Awards:* Mem award, Hudson Valley Art Asn, 75 & 82, Lever House Award, 82. *Media:* Watercolor. *Mailing Add:* 36 Catoonah St Ridgefield CT 06877-4401

GRASSO, SALVATORE FORTUNATO
PAINTER, CONCEPTUAL ARTIST
b Boston, Mass, April 27, 45. *Study:* Art Inst Boston, cert, 66. *Work:* DeCordova Mus, Lincoln, Mass; Suffolk Univ; Tom Nicholas Gallery, Rockport, Mass; Guild Boston Artist; Novo Labs, Holland. *Exhib:* Nat Acrylic & Casein Exhib, Nat Acad Design, NY, 78; New Eng Watercolor Soc Exhib, 78-82; Nat Acad Design Exhib, NY, 79; DeCordova Mus Exhib, Lincoln, Mass, 79; Hudson River Artist Nat Exhib, 80. *Awards:* Rockport Art Asn Awards, 77-82; Frank & Annie Shikler Award, Nat Acad Design Ann Exhib, 79; Purchase Prize, DeCordova Mus, 79; and others. *Media:* Acrylic, Egg Tempera. *Publ:* Am Artist; Pallett Talk

GRASTORF, JEAN H
PAINTER, INSTRUCTOR
b Rochester, NY, Oct 24, 1934. *Study:* Ceramic School at Alfred Univ (paper-making & Lithography), 1976; Rochester Inst of Tech, AAS, 1955; Studies with Clara Nelson. *Work:* Neville Public Mus, Green Bay, Wis; State Univ of New York at Alfred; Florida Int Univ, Miami; Nat Watercolor Soc, Brea, Calif; Raymond James, St Petersburg, Fla. *Comn:* paintings, Haas Historical Mus, St. Petersburg, Fla, 1985; paintings, Bayfront Medical Ctr, St. Petersburg, 1985; paintings, St. Anthony's Cancer Care Ctr, St. Petersburg, Fla, 1986. *Exhib:* Am Watercolor Soc, Salmagundi Club, New York City, 1986, 1988, 19991, 1993-94, 2000-02, 2005-06; Adirondacks Nat Exhib of Am Watercolors, Old Forge Arts Ctr, 1993; Nat Acad Open, Nat Acad of Design, New York City, 1994; Florida Watercolor Soc, Mus of Fine Art, St Petersburg, Fla, 1996; Watercolor USA, Springfield Art Mus, Mo, 2002; Fla Watercolor Soc, Leepa-Rattner Mus of Art, 2005. *Pos:* dean Emeritus painting, Alfred Univ. *Teaching:* instr watercolor, The Arts Ctr, St Petersburg, Fla, 1982-92; instr watercolor workshops, several state & nat watercolor socs, 1985-. *Awards:* First Award, Nat Watercolor Soc, 1997; First Award, So Watercolor Soc, 1998; Don W. Dennis Mem, Am Watercolor Soc, Dennis Family, 2006. *Bibliog:* Stephen Doherty (auth), Easy Solutions-Color Mixing, Quarry Press, 1998; Nita Leland (auth), Exploring Color, North Light, 98; Several articles for Watercolor, Watercolor Magic & Int Artist Mag; Christopher Willard, Watercolor-Mixing, Rockport Pub, 2000. *Mem:* Fla Watercolor Soc (2nd vpres, 89 & 1st vpres, 90); Am Watercolor Soc (dir 2002 & 2003, juror 2002 & 2005); Nat Watercolor Soc; Transparent Watercolor Soc of Am; Rocky Mt Nat Watercolor Soc. *Media:* Watercolor & Acrylics. *Publ:* auth, Pouring Light, Layering Transparent Watercolor, North Light, 2005. *Dealer:* Susanne's Gallery 2900 4th St N St Petersburg FL 33704. *Mailing Add:* 6049 4th Ave Saint Petersburg FL 33710

GRAUER, GLADYS BARKER
PAINTER
b Cincinnati, Ohio, Aug 15, 23. *Study:* Art Inst Chicago, 41-45; Rutgers Univ, 80-84. *Work:* Newark Mus; Montclair Mus; Jane Voorhees Zimmerli Art Mus; Smithsonian Art Book Collection. *Exhib:* Emerging & Established, Newark Mus & Jersey City Mus, NJ, 81; one-woman show, The Invincibles, Courtney Gallery, Jersey City, 85; Nat Conference of Artists, Senegal Nat Mus, Dakar, Africa, 85; Tracking the Trends, Pavilion Gallery, Mt Holly, NJ, 86; Celebration, Morristown Mus, NJ, 86; Morristown Atrium, 92-94; 3-woman show, Newark Mus, 92; Johnson & Johnson, 92; and others. *Teaching:* Instr advert design, Essex Co Voc Tech, Newark, NJ, (retired); instr painting, Newark Mus, NJ, currently. *Awards:* First Prize Watercolor, James St Commons, 83; Mixed Media Fel, NJ State Coun Arts, 85; Artist-in-residence, Newark Mus, 91; Inovative Print Fel, Rutgers Univ, 92. *Bibliog:* Edna Bailey (auth), Artists paintings a depiction of blacks, Newark Star Ledger, 1/13/86; Gumbo Ya Ya - Anthology of Contemp African American Women Artists, Art Press, 95; Public Television State of the Arts, Family Focus, 4/96; Art by African Am, In the Collection of NJ State Mus; Transcultural NJ Diverse Artists Shaping Culture & Communities. *Mem:* Newark Arts Coun; Art Inst Chicago Alumni Asn; Black Woman Visual Perspective (pres, 73-75). *Media:* Mixed Media, Collage. *Dealer:* Bellevue Gallery of Fine Art 209 Bellevue Ave Trenton NJ 08618. *Mailing Add:* 352 Seymour Ave Newark NJ 07112

GRAUER, SHERRARD
PAINTER, SCULPTOR
b Toronto, Ont, Feb 20, 39. *Study:* Wellesley Col, 56-59; Ecole Louvre, Paris; Calif Sch Fine Art, BFA(hon), 65. *Work:* Vancouver Art Gallery; Mus Art Contemp, Montreal; Ont Heritage Fund; Can Coun Art Bank; Nat Gallery Can, Ottawa. *Comn:* Relief mural, Worldwide Int Travel, Vancouver, 69; ceiling panels (steel & fiberglass), DPW, Fed Bldg, Powell River, BC, 76; banners, City Vancouver, 76; Brave Birdmen (steel mesh ceiling sculpture), Ministry Transport, Cornwall, Ont, 80; relief sculpture, Cygnus, stainless steel mesh & chromed sheet steel, WESGAR Corp, Vancouver, BC, 90; Requeim, North Growth Mgmt, 98; Seals, North Growth Mgmt, 03. *Exhib:* Art From Canada's West Coast, Vancouver Art Gallery, 71; Some Canadian Women Artists, Nat Gallery Can, 75; Current Pursuits, Vancouver Art Gallery, 76; retrospective, Surrey Art Gallery, 80; New Vancouver Art Gallery Inaugural Exhib, 83; Artropolis, Vancouver, 93; Vancouver Art Gallery, Face to Face: Four Centuries of Portraits, 98. *Pos:* Bd mem, hon secy, Van Art Gallery, 76-77; mem found bd, Arts, Sci & Technol Ctr, Vancouver, 80. *Bibliog:* Joan Lowndes (auth), Modalities of West Coast sculpture, Artscanada, Vol XXXI, No 2, 74; Ted Lindberg (auth), article, Sherry Grauer, Vanguard, 11/85; Jill Pollack (auth), monogr, On Certain Paths, 87. *Mem:* Royal Can Acad Art; Canadian Artists Representation. *Media:* Oil, Acrylic, Canvas, Steel Mesh. *Dealer:* Bau-Xi Gallery 3045 Granville St Vancouver V6H 3J9; Bau-Xi Gallery 340 Dundas St W Toronto M5T 1G5. *Mailing Add:* 106-8828 Heather St Vancouver BC V6P 3S8 Canada

GRAUPE-PILLARD, GRACE
PAINTER, INSTRUCTOR
b New York, NY, 41. *Study:* City Univ NY, BA, 63; Art Students League, George Bridgman Scholar, with Marshal Glasier and Julien Levi, 64-68. *Work:* Malcom Forbes, Forbes Pubs, NY; The New Jersey State Mus, Trenton; City of Orange, Orange, NJ; NJ Transit, Jersey City, Matawan, Aberdeen; Newark Mus, NJ; and many others. *Comn:* Port Authority Bus Terminal, 92; Robert Wood Johnson Med Sch-CAB, New Brunswick, NJ, Porcelain Enamel (9 pcs), 95; City of Orange, NJ, 96; NJ Transit, Garfield Ave Sta, Jersey City (5 sculptures in porcelain enamel, railings, gate), 97-2000; NJ Transit, Matawan Sta, NJ (porcelain enamel sculpture), 98-99; NJ Transit, Hoboken 2d St Sta, Hoboken, NJ (9 sculptures), 2000. *Exhib:* One-woman shows, Sally Hawkins Gallery, NY, 90, Port Authority Bus Terminal, NY, 92, NJ State Mus, Trenton, 93, NJ Ctr Visual Arts, Summit, 93 & Klarfeld-Perry Gallery, Brookdale Col, Lincroft, NJ, 99, Donahue-Sosinki Art, 2000, Frist Ctr for Visual Arts, Nashville, Tenn, 04, The Proposition, New York City, 05, Carl Hammer, Chicago, Ill, 2006; Art & the Law, Traveling show, 94-95; Elga Wimmer Gallery, NY, 95; Noyes Mus, Oceanville, NJ, 96; Donahue-Sosinski Art, 97; 25th Anniversary Benefit Selections, The Drawing Ctr, NY, 02; The Reflected, Refracted Self, Carl Hammer Gallery, Chicago, Ill, 04. *Teaching:* Instr painting & drawing, Monmouth Co Parks, 76-; instr mural workshop, Nat Acad Design Mus, NY, 03, 04, 05 & 06. *Awards:* NJ State Coun Grant, 82-83, 92-93, 99-2000; Nat Endowment Arts, 85-86; Ctr Innovative Printmaking, Rutgers Univ, NJ, 91. *Bibliog:* Berta Sichel (auth), Flash Art, 98; Bzdak & Petersen (auths), Public Sculpture in NJ, 99; Nancy Ruhling (auth), Newsday, 6/11/99; Marie Maber (auth), Digital Fine Art, Fall 2000; Review by William Zimmer, NY Times, 4/28/02; Review-Fellowship Show, Dan Bischoff (auth), The Star Ledger, 1/7/01; Review by Alan Artner, Chicago Tribune, 4/7/06. *Media:* Pastels, Oil and Digital photographs. *Dealer:* The Proposition 559 W 22 St New York NY 10011. *Mailing Add:* PO Box 213 Keyport NJ 07735

GRAUSMAN, PHILIP
SCULPTOR
b New York, NY, July 16, 35. *Study:* Syracuse Univ, BA(cum laude), 57; Skowhegan Sch Painting & Sculpture, summers 56 & 57; Cranbrook Acad Art, MFA, 59; Art Students League, with Jose de Creeft, 59. *Work:* Brooklyn Mus, NY; Pa State Univ; Wadsworth Atheneum, Hartford, Conn; Nat Portrait Gallery, Washington, DC; Metrop Mus Art, Nat Acad Design, NY; and many others. *Comn:* Created Gertrude Vanderbilt Whitney Award, Skowhegan Sch Painting & Sculpture, 71; Graham Gund Assoc, Boston, 87. *Exhib:* Babcock Galleries, NY, 94; Contemp Sculpture at Chesterwood, Stockbridge, Mass, 94; Grounds for Sculpture, Hamilton, NJ, 94; Artists Who Worked in Paris, NY & Conn, Paris/NY/Kent Gallery, 94; Solo exhib, Borgenicht Gallery, New York City, 66, 74, 79, Alpha Gallery, Boston, 68, 75, Dartmouth Col, Hanover, NH, 72, Univ Conn, 76, Pa State Univ, 77, Wash Art Asn, Wash Depot, Conn, 78, 82, Robert Schoelkopf Gallery, New York City, 83, 87, Babcock Galleries, New York City, 93, Ice Gallery, New York City, 98, Frederik Meijer Gardens & Sculpture Park, Grand Rapids, Mich, 2001; group exhib, Aldrich Mus, Whitney Mus Am Art, Am Acad in Rome, Nat Acad Design, Art OMI Int Arts Ctr, Ohio State Univ, Boston Coliseum, Wadsworth Atheneum, Chicago Arts Club, Fine Arts Mus San Diego, Univ NC, Paris/NY/Kent Gallery, Kent, Conn. *Pos:* Artist in residence, Dartmouth Col, 72. *Teaching:* Instr design, Cooper Union, 65-67; instr design & drawing, Pratt Inst, 65-69; artist-in-residence, Dartmouth Col, 72; instr sculpture & drawing, Skowhegan Sch Painting & Sculpture, 73; vis asst prof, Yale Univ, 74-76, critic archit drawing, Grad Sch Archit, 74-. *Awards:* Rome Prize Fel, 62-65; Dessie Greer Prize, Nat Acad Design, 81, Gold Medal, 88; Certificate of Merit Sculpture, Nat Acad Design, NY, 93. *Bibliog:* Hilton Kramer (auth), New York Times, 10-5/79; Michael Brenson (auth), New York Times, 11-20/87; Vivien Raynor (auth), Sculpture Metals from Aluminum to Zinc, at the Mattatuck, New York Times, 6-19/88; Vivien Raynor (auth), New York Times, 8-17 & 22/94. *Mem:* Nat Acad; Fel Am Acad Rome. *Media:* Cast Metal

GRAVES, KENNETH ROBERT
PHOTOGRAPHER
b Portland, Ore, June 27, 42. *Study:* San Francisco Art Inst, with Jerry Burchard & John Collier Jr, BFA, 70, MFA, 71. *Work:* San Francisco Mus Art; Nat Libr, Paris; Ann Bremer Mem Libr, San Francisco Art Inst; Mus Mod Art, NY; George Eastman House, Rochester, NY; Erie Art Mus, Pa. *Exhib:* Three Photographers, San Francisco Mus Art, 71; New Photog in the Bay Area, MH de Young Mus, 73; Exchange DFW-SFO, Ft Worth Art Mus & San Francisco Mus Art, 75; Color as Form, George Eastman House & Corcoran Gallery, 82; solo exhibs, Blue Sky Gallery, Portland, 82 & 85, Portico Gallery, Philadelphia, 83, OK Harris, NY, 89, 91 & 93 & Univ Vt Fleming Mus, 94; Univ Wyo Art Mus, 94; 2 person show with Eva Lipman, Allentown Art Mus, Pa, 95. *Teaching:* Instr photog, San Francisco Art Inst & Photog Film Ctr West, Berkeley; assoc prof photog, Pa State Univ, 77-92, prof, 92-. *Awards:* Nat Endowment Arts Fel, 76; Purchase Award, Alternatives, 83; First Award, Pa Festival Arts, 83-85. *Bibliog:* Joan Murray (auth), interview, Artweek, 1/22/72; Time-Life Photog, 75; Popular Photog Ann, 82. *Publ:* Coauth, American Snapshots, Scrimshaw Press, 77; Ballroom, Milkweed Eds, 89. *Dealer:* Simon Lowinski Gallery 578 Broadway New York NY 10012. *Mailing Add:* 210 Patterson Bldg Penn State Univ Sch Visual Arts University Park PA 16803

GRAVES, MICHAEL
ARCHITECT, EDUCATOR
b Indianapolis, Ind, July 9, 34. *Study:* Univ Cincinnati, BS(archit), 58; Harvard Univ, March, 59; Am Acad in Rome(fel), Prix de Rome, 60-62. *Hon Degrees:* 11 hon degrees from US cols & univs. *Work:* Mus Mod Art, Metro Mus, Smithsonian Inst, Cooper-Hewitt, Brooklyn Mus, NY; Berlin Mus, Ger; Deutsches Architekturmuseum, Frankfurt, Ger. *Comn:* Walt Disney World Swan & Dolphin Hotels, 87; Hotel NY, Disneyland Park, Paris, 89; Denver Cent Libr, 90; Eng Res Ctr, Univ Cincinnati, 95; Int Finance Corp, 97; US Fed Courthouse Annex, 97; NCAA Headquarters and Hall of Champions, 98; Mus of the Shenandoah Valley, 99; Fed Reserve Bank of Dallas, Houston br, 2000. *Exhib:* One-man shows, Johnstown Art Mus, Pa, Syracuse Univ Sch Archit, Syracuse, NY, 90, Marini Marino Mus, Florence, Italy, 91, Mikimoto Hall, Tokyo, Japan, 92 & Cheekwood Fine Arts Ctr, Nashville, Tenn; retrospective, 25 Yrs in Princeton, Princeton Arts Coun, Kirby Art Ctr, Lawrenceville Sch, NJ, 89; Univ Cincinnati, Aronoff Ctr Design & Art, 96; Topeka & Shawnee Co Pub Libr, Topeka, Kans, 96; New Jersey Inst of Tech Architecture Sch, 80. *Pos:* Dir visual studies prof, Princeton Univ, 70-72; architect-in-residence, Am Acad Rome, Italy, 79. *Teaching:* Lectr archit, Princeton Univ, 62-67, assoc prof, 67-72, prof, 72-; vis prof archit, Univ Tex, Austin, 74, Univ Houston, Tex, 78 & Univ NC, Charlotte, 79; prof, Princeton Univ, 72; Robert Schirmer prof of architecture, Univ Calif, Los Angeles, 77. *Awards:* Am Inst Archit Honor Awards, 75, 79, 82, 83, 85, 87, 90, 92 & 98; Progressive Archit Design Awards, 70, 76, 77, 78, 79, 80, 83 & 89; many others including, NJ Soc Archit, Interiors Mag, Progressive Archit Mag, Pa Furniture Design, Inst Bus Design; Nat Medal of Arts, 99; Gold Medal, Am Inst Archit, 01; NJ Gov's Walt Whitman Award for Creative Achievement; Arts Person of the Year, NJ Ctr for Vis Arts; Henry Hering Medal, Nat Sculpture Soc; firm has more than 160 awards and citations including Progressive Archit awards, ten Am Inst Archit Nat Honor awards, and the AIA/Am Libr Asn Award for Denver Cent Libr; and others. *Bibliog:* Auth, Kings of Infinite Space: Michael Graves and Frank Lloyd Wright, Academy Eds, 84; Michael Graves Buildings and Projects: 1982-1989, Princeton Archit Press, 90; Michael Graves Buildings & Projects: 1990-1994, Rizzoli, 95; Michael Graves: Design Monograph, Ernst & Sohn, 94; The Master Architect Series III, Michael Graves, Selected and Current Works, Images Pub, 95. *Mem:* Fel Edward MacDowell Colony; Fel Am Inst Archit; Trustee Am Acad Rome; Dir Inst Archit & Urbanism. *Media:* Pencil, Colored Pencil; Acrylic Paint. *Collection:* Biedermeier furniture & grand tour. *Publ:* Contribr, Catalogue Venice Biennale, 80; Speaking a New Classicism, Smith Col Mus Art, 81; auth, Le Corbusier's drawn references, In: Introduction to Le Corbusier Drawings, Acad Ed, London, 81; A Case for Figurative Architecture, Rizzoli, 82; Ritual, The Princeton Journal, 84. *Dealer:* Max Protetch Gallery 37 W 57th St New York NY 10019; John Nichols Printmakers 83 Grand St New York NY 10013. *Mailing Add:* 341 Nassau St Princeton NJ 08540

GRAY, CAMPBELL BRUCE
MUSEUM DIRECTOR, MUSEOLOGIST
b Australia, Apr 4, 52. *Study:* Alexander Mackie Col Adv Educ, 78; City Art Inst, Sydney Col Adv Educ, BA(art educ), 83; Univ Sussex, PhD(art hist, Brit Coun Vice Chancellors & Principals Overseas Res Scholar), 95. *Exhib:* Reinis Zusters, 84, Lewers Gallery, Sydney, Australia, The Third Dimension, 84, Image and Surface, 84, The Drawn Image, 85, BIP Selection: A Bi-Polar Situation in Venice, 86, Self Image-The Immolation Mirage, 86; Viewers & Audiences: The Mus/Gallery in Context, Reg Galleries Asn NSW Ltd & Wollongong City Gallery, 95; Western Sites Component of the Australian Perspecta 1991, Art Gallery NSW, Sydney, 91. *Pos:* Inaugural dir, Lewers Bequest & Penrith Reg Art Gallery, NSW, Australia, 81-86; cur, Western Sites Component, Sydney, 90-91; coordr, Postgraduate Studies Unit, Univ Western Sydney, 95-96; dir, Mus Art, Brigham Young Univ, Provo, Utah, 96-. *Teaching:* Sr lectr visual arts, Univ Western Sydney, 86-96, grad chair art hist & criticism, 94-96; art theory & arts admin, Univ NSW, 94-96. *Awards:* Nepean Res Grant, Univ Western Sydney, 95; Exhib Grant, Vis Arts & Craft Bd Australia Coun. *Mem:* Am Asn Mus; Western Mus Asn; Mus Australia Inc. *Res:* The Art Museum: critique, design, function, performance, phenomenology, contextual relevance and value, relationship to recent art and art theory, curatorship, site-specificity in art and the museum. *Publ:* Auth, The Dilemma of Change, Contemp Australian Painting, 90; Context, regionalism & the museum/gallery, 94 & Curatorship: political or critical intervention, 95, Australian Art Monthly; Change in the face of the museum's apparent obduracy, Mus Nat, 95; Looking for the Ground, Angels and the City, 96. *Mailing Add:* Brigham Young Univ Mus Art N Campus Dr Provo UT 84602

GRAY, ELISE NORRIS
SCULPTOR
b Burkesville, Ky, Mar 9, 36. *Study:* Western Ky Univ, BS, 58; Univ Tenn, MS, 59; Arrowmount Sch Crafts, 59; study with Phyllis Hammond & Barbara Bisgyer, 72-77; Parsons Sch Design, 82. *Work:* IBM Corp, Burlington, Vt; AcQuest Capital Corp, NY; Am Fed Bank, Greenville, SC; AT&T Corp, Somerset, NJ; United Jersey Bank, Woodbury, NJ; Mus Arts & Sciences, Macon, Ga, 97. *Comn:* Clay wall relief, Fla Nat Bank, Jacksonville, 86; wall sculpture, IBM Corp, Gaithersburg, Md, 87; wall sculpture, Fla Educ Dept, Tallahassee, 89; wall relief, GE Capital, 93; sculpture, Mem Garden, Community Church White Plains, 94; wall sculpture, Theatre Macon, Ga Coun Arts, 95. *Exhib:* Solo exhib, 14 Sculptors Gallery, NY, 79, 82, 84, 86, & 89, Wesleyan Col, Macon, Ga, 92 & Mus Arts & Sci, Macon, Ga, 95; Art of Northeast, Exhib of Painting & Sculpture, Silvermine Guild of Artists, NY, 79, 82 & 83; Works in Clay-Elise Gray, Hudson River Mus, Yonkers, 83; Schick Art Gallery, Skidmore Col, 88. *Pos:* Co-founder, vpres & pres, Artisans Co-op, Westchester, NY, 73-77; chairperson exhibs publicity, 14 Sculptors Gallery, 78-89. *Teaching:* Field fac adv, archit ceramics, Vt Col Norwich Univ, 86-88; artist-in-residence, Macon Pub Sch, currently. *Awards:* Sculpture Award, Mamaroneck Artist Guild, 78 & 79 Glickenhouse Found Award, 81; Pollock-Krasner Found Grant, 90-91; Individual Artist Grant, Ga Coun Artist, 93-94. *Bibliog:* David Shirey (auth), Art View, New York Times, 6/10/79; Robbie Ehrlic (auth), Elise Gray at 14 Sculptors, Arts Mag, 9/79; Rosalind Schneider (dir), Elise Gray-Fragments and Formations (video), Film Workshop of Westchester, 84. *Mem:* Int Sculpture Ctr; Metrop Mus Art; Nat Mus Women Arts. *Media:* Clay, Cement. *Dealer:* http://elisegrayart1.home.att.net. *Mailing Add:* 1483 Oglethorpe St Macon GA 31201-1512

GRAY, JIM
PAINTER, SCULPTOR
b Middleton, Tenn, June 4, 32. *Work:* Carnegie Libr, Regar Mus, Anniston, Ala; Brooklyn Navy Yard; 40 paintings, Loyal Am Life Ins Co, Mobile, Ala; Winsor & Newton, Secaucus, NJ; 16 paintings, Hibernia Nat Bank, New Orleans; 6 paintings, Am Embassy, Oman; Jim Gray Galleries, Knoxville, Tenn, Gatlinburg, Tenn, Pigeon Forge, Tenn; paintings, sculptures, Am Embassy, Tokyo, Japan; painting, Convention Ctr, Knoxville, Tenn; paintings, Am Embassy, Warsaw, Poland; painting, Sen Chamber Office, Washington, DC; and others. *Comn:* Dolly Parton (over lifesize bronze), Sevierville, Tenn; Pres Andrew Johnson (2 bronzes-over life size), Greeneville, Tenn & Capitol grounds, Nashville, 95; Alex Haley (bronze bust), Univ Tenn, Knoxville; Gov John Sevier (bronze bust), Capitol Bldg, Nashville; bronze, Gen John Sevier; oil, Haslam Col, Knoxville, Boyd Col, Knoxville. *Exhib:* Whiting Mus, Fairhope, Ala, 70, 73, 75 & 92; Watercolor USA, Springfield, Mo, 70; Realist Invitational, Gallery Contemp Art, Winston-Salem, NC, 71; Am Soc Marine Artists Ann, Grand Cent Gallery, NY, 80 & Peabody Mus, Salem, Mass, 81; 400 Yrs of Seafaring, Fine Arts Mus, Mobile, Ala, 82; Mystic Maritime Mus, 86-90; Mariners Mus, Newport News, Va, 87; Md Hist Soc, Baltimore, 89; Retrospective, Arrowmont, Gatlinburg, Tenn, 89. *Teaching:* Instr painting, Buckhorn Art Workshop Ann, Gatlinburg, Tenn; instr watercolor, Atlanta Artist Club, Ga, 69-; lectr art & humanities, Univ Tenn, Knoxville, 70-71. *Awards:* Best Show & Permanent Trophy, Azalea Trail Arts Festival, 57, 58 & 59; Best Show, Hammel-Adams Glass, Mobile, 62 & 63; Paul VI Award, Paul VI Inst Arts, Washington, 87; Art in Embassies Program, Washington; Distinguished Artist award; Tenn Arts Comn Friend of Art Educ in Tenn, 2003. *Bibliog:* Video, PBS, Knoxville. *Mem:* Am Soc Marine Artists (bd dir, 83-, vpres, 88-92); Salmagundi Club; and others. *Media:* Watercolor, Oil; Clay, Bronze. *Publ:* Nat Geographic, 10/68; prints, Painting in Alkyds, Contemp Marine Art, 88; Author Jim Gray, Roads I've Traveled (foreword by Sen Howard Baker); Am Artist Mag 4/77; cover and feature article, Jim Gray's Reason for Being, City View Mag, 12/2004. *Dealer:* Greenbriar Inc PO Box 735 Gatlinburg TN 37738. *Mailing Add:* 2405 Alcoa Hwy Knoxville TN 37920

GRAY, LUKE
PAINTER
b NY City, 61. *Study:* RI Sch Design, Providence; Skowhegan Sch Painting & Sculpture, Maine; Univ Pa, BA, 78-82. *Comn:* Ceiling mural, Transmission, 98; lobby, 1500 Broadway, Times Sq, NYC; mural, Universal Health, Robert Wood Johnson Found, Princeton, NJ; mural, Traveler, Rossrock LLC & Phillip Babb, NY. *Exhib:* Holland Tunnel Art Proj, Brooklyn, NY; Tower Gallery, New York City; Bachelier-Kardonsky Gallery, Kent, Conn; Hamburg Mus Fur Kunst und Gewerbe, Ger; Solo exhib, David Klein Gallery, Birmingham, Mich, Thomas Erben Gallery, New York City, Nicole Klagsbrun Gallery, NY, 89, Galerie Ludwig, Krefeld, Germ, 96, Gary Snyder Fine Art, New York City, 96-2001, Addison-Ripley Fine Art, Washington, DC, 97, 2000. *Media:* Acrylic, Oil. *Specialty:* Murals. *Mailing Add:* 159 Taaffe Pl Brooklyn NY 11205

GRAY, MARIE ELISE
PAINTER
b Bremanger, Norway, Oct 7, 14; US citizen. *Study:* Derbyshire Sch Fine Art, 64-65; Cornish Sch Allied Art, 66-70; Olympic Col, 71; and with Rex Brandt, Sergei Bongart, Warren Brandon, Raymond Brose, Richard Yip, Maxine Masterfield, Christopher Schink & Al Brouchette. *Work:* Frye Art Mus, Boeing Co & US Steel Co, Seattle; Univ Ore; AMFAC Inc, San Francisco; Dean Witter & Assoc; and numerous pvt collections throughout US, Japan, Guatemala & Scandinavia. *Comn:* Painting for retired vpres, Pac Lutheran Univ; five paintings, comn by William Dahlberg, DDS, 80; two paintings, Transglobe Travel, 81; 30 paintings for private collection in Norway; painting for crab fishing Co, Seattle, 90. *Exhib:* Solo exhibs, Freemanson Gallery, 65-71, Frye Art Mus, 72 & 79-80, Goodyears Gallery, Edmonds, 75, Matheson Gallery, Seattle, 76, Charles Wright Acad, Tacoma, 78, Stillwater Gallery, Seattle, 82 & 89 & Northwest Artists Gallery, Univ Village, Seattle, 84; Wash State Art Biennial, Nat League Am Pen Women, Unitarian Gallery, Seattle, 83; Nat League Am Pen Women Exhib, Kitridge Gallery, Tacoma, Wash, 87; Western Painters Spring Exhib, 87 & Northwest Watercolor Exhib, 87 & 88, Bellevue, Wash; NW Signature, Intermec Corp, Arts Coun Snohomish Coun, Everett, Wash, 90. *Pos:* Pres, Co-art Art Asn; exhib chmn, NW Watercolor Exhib, 72; state art chmn, Nat League Am Pen Women, 72-75 & 80-81. *Teaching:* Instr art, YWCA, 68, Wash Athletic Club, Women's Univ Club, 73, Seattle & Sandpoint Golf & Country Club, 75-77. *Awards:* Honor Award, Women Painters of Washington Exhib, Peter Kirk Gallery, Kirkland, Wash, 87; Second Award, Co-arts Ann, Seattle, Wash, 88; D D Jeneen Mem Award, Women Painters of Wash, 89; and others. *Bibliog:* Critic's choice, Seattle Times, 9/16/76 & 77. *Mem:* Northwest Watercolor Soc; Nat League Am Pen Women; Women Painters Wash; Olympic Art Asn. *Media:* Multi, Watercolor. *Dealer:* Kirsten Gallery 5320 Roosevelt Way NE Seattle WA 98105; Stillwater Gallery 1900 N Northlake Way #145 Mariner's Sq Seattle WA. *Mailing Add:* 7723 30th Ave NE Seattle WA 98115-4721

GRAY, RICHARD
DEALER
b Chicago, Ill, 28. *Study:* Univ Ill Sch Archit; Northwestern Univ. *Pos:* Managing Partner, Richard Gray Gallery, 63; chmn bd governors, Smart Mus Art, Univ Chicago; pres, Art Dealers Asn Am, formerly; art advisory Comt, IRS, formerly; trustee, Art Inst, Chicago, Ill, currently. *Mem:* Chicago Art Dealers Asn (former pres); Col Art Asn Am; Am Asn Mus; Art Dealers Asn Am; Archives of Am Art. *Specialty:* Paintings, sculpture & drawings by established European and American Modern Masters and the avant garde. *Collection:* Works on Paper: contemporary, classical Modern, 19th Century French & Old Masters. *Dealer:* Richard Gray Gallery 1018 Madison Ave NY 10021. *Mailing Add:* Gallery 875 N Michigan Ave Ste 2503 Chicago IL 60611

GRAY, ROBERT WARD
ADMINISTRATOR
b Tallahassee, Fla, June 26, 1916. *Study:* Univ Fla; Tri-State Col; Grad Sch Am Craftsmen, with Herbert H Sanders. *Work:* Folk Art Ctr Libr Collection. *Collection Arranged:* Co-dir, New Eng Craft Exhib, 55. *Pos:* In charge pottery shop & coordr craft prog, Old Sturbridge Village, 49-51; dir, Worchester Craft Ctr, 51-61; dir, Southern Highland Handicraft Guild, 61-80, dir emer, 80; dir, Development, 80-84; Craft Mgt Consult, 84-. *Awards:* Fine Arts Award, NC, 98. *Mem:* Fel Am Crafts Coun, 80. *Mailing Add:* 3199 Sweeten Creek Rd # 204 Asheville NC 28803-2136

GRAY, THOMAS ALEXANDER
COLLECTOR
b Winston-Salem, NC, Feb 7, 48. *Study:* Duke Univ, BA(hist art), 70; Am Cult Winterthur Prog, Univ Del, MA, 74; Summer Inst Arts Admin, Harvard Univ, 74. *Pos:* Dir, Mus early Southern Decorative Arts, Winston-Salem, 76-79; consult, Graylyn Conf Ctr, Wake Forest Univ, 80-84; chmn bd trustees, Old Salem Inc, 94-97; co-founder, Toy Mus at Old Salem, 2002. *Awards:* Ruth C Cannon Award, Hist Preserv Found NC, 83. *Mem:* Hist Preservation Soc NC Inc (pres exec comt, 76-78); Hist Preservation Fund NC Inc (bd, 76-, vpres, 79-, pres, 80-82); Stagville Preservation Ctr, Durham, NC (bd, 77-84); Piedmont Craftsmen Inc (bd, 85-89); Old Salem Inc (develop dir, 74-76, bd, 81-, exec comt, 82-). *Collection:* Am Decorative Arts; 225 A.D. to 1925 A.D. *Publ:* auth, Old Salem Toy Mus, Winston-Salem, NC, Old Salem, Inc, 2005. *Mailing Add:* 10 West St Winston-Salem NC 27101

GRAZDA, EDWARD
PHOTOGRAPHER
b New York, NY, Mar 27, 47. *Study:* RI Sch Design, BFA, 69. *Work:* Mus Mod Art & Metrop Mus Art, NY; Mus Fine Art, Houston, Tex; New Orleans Mus Fine Art; Corcoran Gallery Art. *Exhib:* solo exhibs, Corcoran Gallery Art, Washington, DC, 93, The Storefront for Art and Archit, New York City, 96-97, Mountian Film at Telluride, 97, The Kent Sch, Conn, 98, Sepia Int, Inc, New York City, 99-2000; group exhibs, Euphrat Gallery, De Anza Col, Cupertino, Calif, 93, Metrop Mus Art, New York City, 94, Queens Col Cult Ctr, New York City, 95, Nat Arts Club, New York City, 97, The 92nd St Y, NY, 98. *Collection Arranged:* Fogg Mus Art, Cambridge, Mass; San Francisco Mus Modern Art; Metrop Mus Art; Nat Mus Am Art, Washington, DC; Corcoran Gallery Art, Washington, DC; Brooklyn Mus, NY; Ctr for Creative Photog, Tucson, Ariz; Int Ctr Photog, NY; NY Pub Libr; Addison Galler Am Art, Andover, Mass; Mus Fine Arts, Houston; New Orleans Mus Art. *Awards:* Creative Artists Pub Svc Grant, 74, 76; Nat Endowment Arts Grant, 80, 86; Light Work Residency, 83; NY Found Arts Grant, 86; MacDowell Colony Fel, 94, 96, 99; NY State Coun on the Arts Grant, 96; Metrop Transit Authority Arts for Transit Award, 97. *Bibliog:* Camera, 5/74 & 7/78; Granta, Eng (issue 21), 87, (issue 50), 95; Katalog, spring 2000. *Mem:* Col Art Asn. *Publ:* auth, Afghanistan 1980-1989, 90; auth, Neighborhoods of Brooklyn, 98; auth, Afghanistan 1992-1998, 99. *Dealer:* Sepia Int Inc 148 W 24 St New York NY 10010. *Mailing Add:* 17 Bleecker St New York NY 10012

GREAR, J(AMES) MALCOLM
DESIGNER, EDUCATOR
b Mill Springs, Ky, June 12, 31. *Study:* Art Acad Cincinnati, Ohio, cert, 58, Hon Dr Commun Design, 94. *Work:* Cooper-Hewitt Mus, NY; Stedelijk, Amsterdam. *Comn:* Atlanta Comt Centennial Olympic Games; HHS Seal, Dept Health & Human Serv, Washington, DC, 80; Vet Admin 50th Anniversary 15-cent Commemorative Stamp, US Postal Serv, Washington, DC; Presby Church (USA) Seal/Symbol, 85; US Inst of Peace Seal, 88; Mayo Clinic. *Exhib:* New Eng Designers, Addison Gallery Contemp Art, Andover, Mass, 64; Commun by Design, Inst Contemp Art, Boston, 64; Malcolm Grear Designers Exhib, List Art Bldg, Brown Univ, 73, AIGA, NY, 74, Calif Col Arts & Crafts, Jorgensen Gallery Univ Conn, 75 & others; Biennale of Graphic Design Brno 74, Czech; Environmental Design: Signing & Graphics, AIGA, NY, 77; Color, Whitney Mus Am Art, NY; traveling exhib, WCarolina Univ, 90; retrospective, Atrium Gallery, Univ Conn, 92. *Pos:* Founder & Chief Exec Officer, Malcolm Grear Designers, Inc, 60-; designer/consult publ, RI Sch Design, 63- & Guggenheim Mus, NY, 69-; design consult, Comt to Rescue Italian Art, 67-68; nat design chmn, Nat Asn Partners of the Americas, 70-; designer, Sci Am Libr Ser, 82-87; designer/Worth Publ, 69-; design consult, RI Tall Ships 76, 75-76 & Mayo Clinic Foun, 83-. *Teaching:* Lectr graphic design, Art Ctr Asn, Louisville, Ky, 58-60, Allen R Hite Inst, Univ Louisville, Ky, 59-60; assoc prof graphic design, RI Sch Design, 60-79, head, Graphic Design Dept, 65-69, prof, 80-94, Helen M Dansforth prof, 88-93, Helen M Danforth emer prof, 93-. *Awards:* Gov's Arts Award, RI State Coun Arts, 69; Art Libr Soc NAm Award, Henri Matisse: Paper Cut-Outs, 77; John R Frazier Award, 86. *Bibliog:* Walter Diethelm (auth), Signs/Signet/Symbol, ABC Ed, Zurich, 70; Eames Morrison (auth), Power of Ten, Sci An Libr, 81; Aaron Siskind (auth), Pleasures and Terrors, NY Graph Soc, 82; Vicki Roland (auth), An Olympic Feat, VSMD, 8/19/94; Bill Van Siclen (auth), The Creativity Game, The Providence Sunday J, 10/2/94. *Mem:* Am Inst Graphics Art, NY; Providence Art Club; Audubon Soc; Soc Environ Graphic Designers; St Botolph Club. *Publ:* Auth, Curtis: Biology, Worth Publ, 68; coauth (with Van Nostrand Reinhold), Inside/Outside: From the Basics to the Practice of Design, 93; contribr, Signs Without Words & Graphic Design: Sign & Symbol, Hospitable Design for Healthcare & Senior Communities, 91

GREAVER, HANNE
PRINTMAKER, PAINTER
b Copenhagen, Denmark, 33. *Study:* Kunsthaandvaerkerskolen, Copenhagen. *Work:* Beloit Col, Wis; Univ Ga; Univ Maine, Orono; Mich State Univ; Univ Nebr. *Exhib:* Univ Maine, Orono, 70; Five Women Printmakers, Kalamazoo Inst Arts, Mich, 69; Boston Printmakers, 76; Mich Printmakers, 77; Northwest Print Coun Inaugural

Exhib, 82. *Awards:* Purchase Award, Boston Printmakers, 76. *Mem:* Print Arts Northwest (formerly Northwest Print Coun) 1982-2003. *Media:* Lithography, Oil. *Specialty:* Paintings, graphics. *Dealer:* Greaver Gallery, Cannon Beach, Ore. *Mailing Add:* PO Box 120 Cannon Beach OR 97110

GREAVER, HARRY
PAINTER, PRINTMAKER
b Los Angeles, Calif, Oct 30, 29. *Study:* Univ Kans, BFA & MFA. *Work:* Amherst Col, Mass; Univ Maine, Orono; NY Pub Libr; Norfolk Mus Arts & Sci, Va; Univ Utah Mus Fine Arts. *Exhib:* Drawings USA, St Paul, Minn, 63; Drawing & Small Sculpture Show, Ball State Univ, Ind, 68; 2nd Nat Print Show, San Diego, Calif, 71; Drawings by Living Am Artists, Univ Utah Mus Fine Arts, 72-73; 10 Yr Print Retrospective, Cannon Beach Gallery, 89. *Collection Arranged:* Paintings by American Masters, Kalamazoo Inst Arts, Mich, 66, Western Art, 67, The Surrealist, 71 & Reginald Marsh, 74; Harvey Breverman, 76. *Pos:* Dir, Kalamazoo Inst Arts, 66-78; dir, Greaver Gallery, 78-. *Teaching:* Assoc prof art, Univ Maine, Orono, 55-66. *Awards:* Purchase Awards, Norfolk Mus, 63 & 64. *Media:* Watercolor; Lithographs. *Specialty:* Paintings, graphics. *Mailing Add:* Box 120 Cannon Beach OR 97110

GREAVES, JAMES L
CONSERVATOR, RESTORER
b Middletown, Conn, Jan 25, 43. *Study:* Col William & Mary, BS; Inst Fine Arts, NY Univ, MA(art hist), 70, dipl(art conserv), 70. *Pos:* Conserv intern, Los Angeles Co Mus Art, 68-70, conservator, 70; chief conservator, Detroit Inst Arts, 70-76; conservator, Los Angeles Co Mus Art, 77-, actg head conservator, 79-80, senior paintings conservator, 80-85; consult conservator, Huntington Libr, Art Gallery & Botanical Gardens, 79-; pvt conservator, 85-. *Teaching:* Instr, Calif State Univ, Fullerton, 80-87; vis lectr, Univ Calif, Los Angeles, 81-85. *Mem:* Fel Int Inst Conserv Hist & Artistic Works; fel Am Inst Conserv; Western Asn Art Conservators (pres, 78-79). *Publ:* Coauth, New findings on Caravaggio's technique in the Detroit Magdalen, Burlington Mag, 74. *Mailing Add:* 1018 Pacific St Apt D Santa Monica CA 90405-1442

GREBLEZNIK See Lyons, Carol

GRECO, ANTHONY JOSEPH
PAINTER, ADMINISTRATOR
b Cleveland, Ohio, Apr 24, 37. *Study:* Cleveland Inst Art, with Louis Bosa, BFA, 60; Kent State Univ, with Joseph O'Sickey, MFA, 66. *Work:* Jimmy Carter Presidential Libr, King & Spalding Attorneys, Atlanta, Ga; Summit Bank Corp, Atlanta, Ga; Kilpatrick & Cody Law Offices, Atlanta, Ga; Chase Manhattan Bank; Nationsbank, Charlotte, NC. *Comn:* Urban Walls Atlanta, one of six inner-city walls. *Exhib:* Butler Inst Am Art Ann; one-man shows, Armstrong State Col, Savannah, Ga, 76 & Javo Gallery, Atlanta, 78; Works on Paper, Kohler Arts Ctr, Sheboygan, Wis, 77; Aug Selection Atlanta Artists, Fay Gold Gallery, Atlanta, Ga, 81 & Unnatural Landscape, 88; Birmingham Biennial, Birmingham Mus Art, Ala, 87; Eighth Ann Auburn Works Paper, Auburn Univ, Ala, 87; Unnatural Landscape, Fay Gold Gallery, Atlanta, 88; Group Show McIntosh Gallery, Atlanta, 91 & 92; and others. *Teaching:* Chmn drawing dept, Atlanta Col Art, 66-75, chmn div advanced studio & asst to pres, 74-76, acad dean, 76-82; vis instr drawing & painting, Univ Wis-Madison, summer 70; prof painting & drawing, currently; prof emeritus, Atlanta Art Col of Art. *Awards:* Purchase Award, Butler Inst Am Art Midyear, 60; Southern Arts Fedn/Nat Endowment Arts Fel, 88; Gallery Affiliation, McIntosh Gallery, Atlanta. *Media:* Miscellaneous Media. *Collection:* Jimmy Carter Presidential Libr, Atlanta; Coca Cola, Atlanta; Nations Bank Headquarters, Charlotte, NC; Chase Manhattan Bank. *Mailing Add:* 825 Clairemont Ave Decatur GA 30030-3502

GRECO, ANTOINETTA See Antoinetta, Greco

GREELEY, CHARLES MATTHEW
PAINTER, SCULPTOR
b Teaneck, NJ, Sept 11, 41. *Study:* New York Sch Visual Arts, with George Ortman. *Work:* NMex Mus Fine Arts, Santa Fe; Mus Contemp Art, Houston, Tex; Longview Mus, Tex; Mus of Mod Art, San Francisco, Calif; Albuquerque Mus, NMex; and others. *Exhib:* Seven Yr Retrospective, Capricorn Asunder Gallery, San Francisco, 71; two-person show, Contemp Arts Mus, Houston, Tex, 79; Ceramic Show, Glorieta Gallery, NMex, 79; Mariposa Gallery, Albuquerque, NMex, 81; one-person show, Elaine Horwitch Gallery, Santa Fe, 88; and others. *Pos:* Screening judge, San Francisco Art Festival, 71. *Teaching:* Instr painting & ceramics, Glorieta Pass Inst, Glorieta, NMex, 73-77. *Awards:* Cash Award, Weatherhead Found, NY, 74; Purchase Prize, Longview Mus Competition, Tex, 75; First Prize Cash Award, Southwest Biennial Weatherhead Found, NY, 76; and others. *Bibliog:* Tom Albright (auth), The Visionaries, Rolling Stone Mag, 71; Dr Roland Fischer (auth), The art of madness & the madness of art: an altered state experience, Md Psychiat Res Ctr, 72; Charlotte Moss (auth), Art in the Southwest, Art News, 8/77. *Media:* Acrylic, Watercolor; Wood. *Publ:* Contribr, Visions of Elsewhere, San Francisco Art Inst, 71. *Dealer:* Kathryn Fleck Gallery 610 Hyman Ave Aspen CO 81611

GREELY, HANNAH
ARTIST
Study: Univ Calif, Los Angeles, BA, 2002. *Exhib:* solo exhib, Andrea Rosen Gallery, NY, 2004-2005; group exhibs, Sentimental Education, Deitch Projects, NY, 2000; Face Off, The Smell, Los Angeles, Calif, 2001; Spoils, Coleman Gallery, Los Angeles, 2001; Drawing Show, Black Dragon Soc, Vienna, 2001; Something of that Nature, Black Dragon Soc, Los Angeles, 2001; Hannah Greely, Elana Scherr, Tom Grimley, Black Dragon Soc, Los Angeles, 2002; Drawing Show, Julius Hummel Gallery, Vienna, 2002; Sculpture Show, Black Dragon Soc, Los Angeles, 2003; Another Sculpture Show, Angstrom Gallery, Dallas, 2003; Clandestine, 50th Venice Biennale, Venice, Ital, 2003; Grant Selwyn Fine Art, Los Angeles, 2003; Trance Plants, Latch Gallery, Los Angels, 2003; Black Dragon Soc, apex Art, NY, 2004; Waste Material, The Drawing Room, London, 2005; Whitney Biennial Am Art, NY, 2006. *Pos:* res, Bangkok Univ Fine & Applied Arts, Thailand, 2004. *Bibliog:* Jerry Saltz (auth), Sentimental Education, Village Voice, 2000; Charles Ray (auth), Before & After, Frieze, 11/2001; Christopher Miles (auth), The Idolater's Revenge, Flash Art, 5-6/2005, 104-108. *Mailing Add:* Andrea Rosen Gallery 525 W 24th St New York NY 10011

GREEN, ART
PAINTER
b Frankfort, Ind, May 13, 41; US & Can citizen. *Study:* Art Inst Chicago, BFA, 65. *Work:* Art Inst Chicago; Nat Gallery Can, Ottawa; Pa Acad Fine Arts, Philadelphia; Mus Mod Kunst, Vienna, Austria; Mus Contemp Art, Chicago. *Exhib:* Five-man group, The Hairy Who, Chicago, 66-68; Personal Torment-Human Response, Whitney Mus Am Art, NY, 69 & Extraordinary Realities, 73; three-man show, Darthea Speyer Gallery, Paris, France, 70; two-man show, Pa Acad Fine Arts, Philadelphia, 74; Can Canvas, Time Mag Travel Show, 75-76; Ann, San Francisco Art Inst, 77; Who Chicago Traveling Show, Sunderland Arts Ctr, Eng, 79; one-man shows, Phyllis Kind Galleries, 74-86; The Chicago Imagist Print, Smart Gallery, Univ Chicago, 87; Second Sight, Block Gallery, Northwestern Univ, 96; Group shows, Jumpin Back Flash, Chicago Cult Ctr, 2000, Chicago Loop, Whitney Mus Champion, Stamford, Conn, 2000, Made in Chicago ca 1970; retrospective, Kitchener-Waterloo Art Gallery & U Waterloo Art Gallery, 2005; Art in Chicago, Pa Acad Fine Arts, Phila, 2006. *Teaching:* Asst prof painting, NS Col Art, Halifax, 69-71; asst prof painting, Univ Waterloo, Ont, 77-84, assoc prof, 84-99, prof, 99-06, chmn fine arts dept, 88-91, 99-02, ret, 2006. *Awards:* Cassandra Award, Cassandra Found, Chicago, 70; Can Coun Arts Bursary, 71-73 & 76-77; Distinguished Teach Award, Univ Waterloo, 90. *Bibliog:* E Lucie-Smith (auth), American Art Now, William Morrow, New York, 85; D Nadel (auth) Article/Interview The Ganzfeld # 3, NY, pg 128-137, 2003; R Enright (auth), Interview Border Crossings # 96, 2005. *Mem:* Royal Canadian Acad Arts. *Media:* Oil. *Dealer:* Corbett Vs Dempsey 1120 N Ashland Ave Chicago IL 60622. *Mailing Add:* 5 Elizabeth St Stratford ON N5A 4Z1 Canada

GREEN, DAVID OLIVER
SCULPTOR, EDUCATOR
b Enid, Okla, June 29, 08. *Study:* Am Acad Art; Nat Acad Art. *Work:* Los Angeles Co Mus Natural Hist. *Comn:* Dragonfly Fountain, Welton Beckett Asn, Hillsdale Shopping Ctr, San Mateo, Calif, 55; five figure group, Lytton Savings & Loan Asn, Hollywood, 60; children's sculpture, Women's Club for Bruggemeyer Mem Libr, Monterey Park, Calif, 68; Owl Tree (wall relief), dedicated to daughters of Maurice Fletcher & Tree of Life (fountain), Guyer Mem, Altadena Libr, Calif, 69. *Exhib:* Los Angeles Co Mus Art Ann, 61; Southern Calif Expos, San Diego Fair, Del Mar, 66; Citrus Col Invitational, Glendora, Calif, 68; 17th Ann All Calif Exhib, Laguna Beach Art Gallery, Calif, 71; Retrospective Exhib, Sculpture & Calligraphy, Walla Walla Col, Wash, 79; Lyons Gallery, Redlands, Calif, 85; San Bernardino Co Mus, Redlands, Calif, 85; and others. *Teaching:* Asst prof sculpture, Otis Art Inst, 47-73 & Scripps Col, 66; instr, Pasadena Art Mus, Calif, 56-59; instr calligraphy, Pasadena City Col, 74-76. *Awards:* First Prize for Sculpture, Laguna Beach Art Asn, 62 & 67; First Prize for Sculpture, Pasadena Soc Artists, 71, 75, 87 & 89. *Bibliog:* Jarvis Barlow (auth), David Green, Pasadena Independent, 7/13/47; Bev Johnson (auth), Owls, cats & bats, Los Angeles Times Sun Sect, 3/13/60; Peg Powell (auth), A way with animals, Independent Star-News, 12/15/63. *Mem:* Int Inst Arts & Lett; Pasadena Soc Artists; Soc Italic Handwriting (Western Am Br); Soc Calligraphy, Los Angeles. *Media:* Stone, Wood. *Mailing Add:* 176 W Jaxine Dr Altadena CA 91001-3818

GREEN, DENISE G
PAINTER
b Melbourne, Australia, Apr 7, 46; US citizen. *Study:* Ecole Nat Superieure des Beaux Arts; Sorbonne Univ, Paris, BA, 69; Hunter Col, New York, MFA, 76. *Work:* Guggenheim Mus, NY; Nat Gallery Australia; Mus Contemp Art Sydney, Australia; Mus Modern Art, NY; Graphische Sammlung Albertina, Vienna, Austria; Solomon R Guggenheim Mus, NY; Mus of Contemp Art, Chicago; Art Gallery of Western Australia, Perth; Nat Gallery of Victoria, Melbourne. *Exhib:* Young Am Artists: 1978 Exxon National, Solomon R Guggenheim Mus, NY, 78; New Image Painting, Whitney Mus Am Art, NY, 78; Surfaces/Textures, Mus Mod Art, NY, 81; solo exhibs, Ado Gallery, Bonheiden, Belgium, 82, Gallery A Sydney, Australia, 83, Christine Abrahams Gallery, Melbourne, Australia, 85-90, Roslyn OxleGallery, Sydney, Australia, 85, 86, 88, 89 & 92, M13 Gallery, NY, 86, Althea Viafora Gallery, NY, 86, 87 & 88, Albert Baronian Gallery, Brussels, Belg, 86, Anand Sarabhai Studio, Ahmedabad, India, 86, Gallery Contemp Art, Ahmedabad, India, 87, Univ Gallery, Melbourne Univ, Australia, 88; Contemp Still Lifes Traveling Exhib, Mus Mod Art, NY, 82; Emerging Artists 1978-1986, Solomon R Guggenheim Mus, NY, 87; Geometric Perspectives, Mus Mod Art, Art Lending Serv, NY, 91; Raab Galerie, Berlin, 93 & 94; Peter Bellas, 94; Barbara Scott Gallery, Bay Harbour Island, Fla, 94; C Abrahams, 94; Nap Exhib Space, 96; and others. *Teaching:* Instr painting, Roger Willams Col, 72; instr studio & art hist, Fairleigh Dickinson Univ, 72-74; instr, Pratt Inst, 74; artist-in-residence, Ill State Univ, 76 & Art Inst Chicago, 77; instr, summer prog art, State Univ NY, Fredonia, 77; artist in residence, Va Commonwealth Univ, 81, Tyler Col Art, Temple Univ, 82 & Calif Inst Arts, 83; lectr, Art Ctr Col Design, 95, Brown Univ, 95, Kent Gallery Art, 95, Md Inst, 96, Kent State Univ, 96 & Mus Mod Art, Vienna, 96. *Awards:* Ingram Merrill Found Grant, 72 & 73; Visual Arts Bd Grant, 74 & Traveling Grant, 77, Australian Coun Arts. *Bibliog:* John Stringer (auth), Denise Green in Perth, Delaney Galleries (catalog), 91; Christine France (auth), Black and

white studies in Green reveal an inner discourse, The Australian, 10/10/92; Virginia Trioli (auth), Green deeply colors a spiritual canvas, The Age, 7/27/94. *Publ:* Auth, Painterly thought and the unconscious, ART PRESS, 2/94; Painting Post Greenberg, Art Monthly, Australia, 3/96. *Dealer:* Sherman Galleris Sydney, Christine Alrehaus Gallery, Melbourne, O'Beatley Gallery, Scottsdale, Az,. *Mailing Add:* 13 Laight New York NY 10013

GREEN, GEORGE D
PAINTER
b Portland, Ore, June 24, 43. *Study:* Okla State Univ BS, 65, Wash State Univ, MFA, 68. *Work:* Guggenheim Mus, NY; Art Inst Chicago; Denver Art Mus; Detroit Inst Arts; Los Angeles Co Mus Art. *Comn:* AT&T Bldg, NY; Home Box Office Bldg, NY; Bulova Bldg, NY. *Exhib:* Solo exhibs, Triangle Gallery, San Francisco, 77, Louis Mus Am Art, Meisel Gallery, 78, 79, 81-83, 85-88, 90-94 & 95-96; Abstract Painting Redefined, Danforth Mus, Munson Williams Proctor Inst; Reality of Illusion, Denver Mus, Oakland Mus, Alain Blondel, Paris; Phillip Johnson Art Ctr, Allentown, Pa, 86; Art Now Gallery, Gottenburg, Sweden, 87-88; Art Mus, Univ Ore, Eugene, 87; Bernaducci Meisel, 2004; Louis K Meisel, 2004. *Teaching:* Instr, Univ Tex, Austin, 68-71; assoc prof painting, State Univ NY, Potsdam 71-78; vis artist, Portland Art Mus, Ore, 77. *Bibliog:* Joe Jackobs (auth), The reality of artifice, Arts Mag, 2/83; Robert Atkins (auth), article, Archit Dig, 4/83; Edward Lucie-Smith (auth), American Art Now, 85. *Mailing Add:* c/o Louis K Meisel Gallery 141 Prince St New York NY 10012

GREEN, JONATHAN
PAINTER, PRINTMAKER
b Gardens Corner, SC, Aug 9, 55. *Study:* Sch Art Inst, Chicago, BFA, 82;. *Hon Degrees:* Univ SC, Columbia, hon DFA, 96. *Work:* McKissick Mus Art, Columbia, SC; Morris Mus Art, Augusta, Ga; Norton Mus Art, West Palm Beach, Fla; Gibbes Mus Art, Charleston, SC; Naples Mus Art, Fla; Mus Würth, Kuenzelsau, Ger. *Comn:* Oil Painting 40″ x 50″, Seagrams Collection, NY, 80; oil painting 36″ x 48″, Harris Collection, Benicia, Calif, 95; oil painting 48″ x 60″, Hilbert Collection, Hilton Head, SC, 96; oil painting 60″ x 48″, Wroble Collection, Charlotte, NC, 99. *Exhib:* The Black Family, Haggerty Mus Art, Milwaukee, 93; one-man shows, Greenville Co Mus, SC, 94, Mus Greenwood, SC, 95, Gibbes Mus Art, Charleston, SC, 95, IFCC Cult Ctr, Portland, Ore, 98, Mus African Am Art, Tampa, Fla, 98, Quinlan Art Ctr Mus, Gainesville, Ga, 98, Danville Mus Fine Arts Hist, Va, 98, Southern Images, Franklin G Burrough-Simeon B Chapin Art Mus, Myrtle Beach, SC, 2003, Echoes of the South, Ritz Theatre and LaVilla Mus, Jacksonville, Fla, 2001 & A Sense of Place, Coral Springs Mus Art, Coral Springs, Fla, 2002; Vividly Told, Gibbes Mus Art, Charleston, SC, 94; Von Liebig Art Ctr, Naples, Fla; Greenville Mus Art, SC; H Lawrence McCrorey Gallery Multicultural Art, Univ Vt, Burlington. *Collection Arranged:* Hewitt Collection African-Am Art, Rhythms of Life: The Art of Jonathan Green, Myth, Memory and Imagination, Universal Themes in the Life and Culture of the South, Myrtle Beach Collects, Off the Wall & Onto the Stage: Dancing the Art of Jonathan Green,The Evolution of a Ballet, Common Ground: Discovering Community in 150 Years of Art, A History of Color, Diversity Within Unity; Jonathan Green, Soul of the South, Suzanne H Arnold Art Gallery, Lebanon Valley Col, Annville, Pa, 2006. *Pos:* Comt bd mem, Acad Arts, Chicago, 84-86; vpres, United Arts Coun, Naples, Fla, 91-94; trustee Mus Am Folk Art, NY, 2000-; bd visitors Col Arts and Scis, Howard Univ, Washington, DC, 2003-. *Awards:* Alberta G Peacock Award, United Arts Coun, Naples, Fla, 96; Borough of Manhattan Proclamation, NY, 96; Clemente C Pickney Award, SC House Reps, 97; Certificate of Honor, City of Portland, Oreg, 98; King-Tisdell Cottage Found Award, Savannah, Ga, 01; History Makers Award in Fine Arts, Hist Makers Nat Archive, Chicago, 01; Key to the City of Columbia, SC, 01; Order of the Palmetto Award, Gov of SC, 01; Man of Distinction Award, Educ Found Collier Co, 03; Century of Achievement Award, Mus of the Ams, Arlington, VA, 2003; Century of Achievement in Art Award, Mus Ams, Arlington, Va, 03; Community Gem, Gem Soc Naples, Fla, 04; Official Int Ambassador, Arts the State Fla, Florida's First Lady, Columba Bush, Sarasota, Fla, 6/2005; Man of the Year, Gulfshore Life Mag, 2005; Eagle Award, SC Asn Community Develop Corps, 2005; Annual Nat Arts Programs Award, LInks Inc, Pa, 7/2006. *Bibliog:* Norman E Pendergraft (auth), Gullah Life Reflections, NC Cent Univ Art Mus, 88; Carroll Greene Jr (auth), Green comes home, Am Visions Vol 5 No 1, 90; Alan Gussow (auth), The Artist as Native, Pomegranate Artsbooks, 92. *Media:* Acrylic, Oil. *Publ:* illusr, Father & Son, Philomel Books, 92; contribr, The Artist as Native: Reinventing Regionalism (book), Pomegranate Art Book, 93; illusr, Noah, Philomel Books, 94; Gullah Images: The Art of Jonathan Green, Univ S Carolina Press; illusr, Crosby, Harcourt Brace & Co, 96; illusr, Amadeus the Leghorn Rooster, Sandlapper Pub Co Inc, Orangeburg, SC, 2004. *Mailing Add:* c/o Jonathan Green Studios Inc 316 Morgan Rd Naples FL 34114

GREEN, JONATHAN (WILLIAM)
MUSEUM DIRECTOR, PHOTOGRAPHER, FILMMAKER
b Troy, NY, Sept 26, 39. *Study:* Mass Inst Technol, 58-60; Brandeis Univ, BA, 63; Harvard Univ, MA, 67. *Work:* Moderna Museet, Stockholm, Sweden; Mus Fine Art, Boston; Mus Art, Houston; Ctr Creative Photog, Tucson, Ariz; Int Ctr Photog, NY. *Comn:* Subway murals MTA, Cambridge Seven Architects, Boston, 66; mural, Cambridge Seven Architects, Rochester, NY, 69; photo projs, Archit Record Mag, 70-75; photo projs, Baumeister, 71-74; Am Images photo proj, Bell System (AT&T), 79. *Exhib:* Four Contemp Photogrs, Fogg Art Mus, Harvard, Cambridge, Mass, 74; solo exhibs, Hayden Gallery, Mass Inst Technol, 76, Carl Seimbad Gallery, Boston, 76 & Art Mus, Ind Univ, Bloomington, 85; Tuseu Och En Bild, Moderna Museet, Stockholm, Sweden, 78; Am Images, Corcoran Gallery, 80; Miami Color, Bass Mus Art, Fla, 86; two-person exhib, Emily Davis, Univ Akron, Ohio, 89; and many other group shows. *Pos:* Ed, assoc, Aperture Quart, New York, 74-76; dir, Univ Gallery & founding dir, Wexner Ctr Arts & Ohio State Univ, Columbus, Ohio, 81-90; dir, Calif Mus Photog, Univ Calif, Riverside, 90-. *Teaching:* Assoc prof photog, Mass Inst Technol, Cambridge, 68-76; prof photog, Ohio State Univ, Columbus, Ohio, 76-90; prof photog & art hist, Univ Calif, Riverside, 90-. *Awards:* Nat Endowment Arts Photogrs Fel, 78; Bell System (AT&T) Photog Fel, 79. *Bibliog:* Hilton Kramer (auth), Camera work, NY Times Bk Rev, 4/21/74; Joan Murray (auth), American photography, Art Week, 9/84; James Hugunin (auth), American Photography, Exposure: 23 1, spring 85. *Publ:* Auth, Camera Work: A Critical Anthology, 73 & The Snapshot, 74, Aperture; contribr, American Images: New Work by 20 Contemporary Photographers, McGraw Hill, 79; A Center for the Visual Arts: The OSU Competition, Rizzoli, 84; auth, American Photography: A Critical History, Abrams, 84 & 92; Auth, with Philip Glass, Kurt Muncasi and Richard Serra, Pink Noise: Three Conversations Concerning a Collaborative Acoustic Installation, 87; Auth, Continuous Replay: The Photographs of Arnie Zane, 99; Auth, Adam Baer: Displaced Perspectives, 2001. *Mailing Add:* 1984 Bonne Brae Riverside CA 92506

GREEN, NANCY ELIZABETH
CURATOR, WRITER
b Pittsfield, Mass, Apr 27, 55. *Study:* Conn Col, BA, 77; Sotheby Parke-Bernet Decorative Arts Prog, 79; Clark Inst Art Inst, Williams Col, MA, 84. *Collection Arranged:* Six in Bronze (with catalog), 84; The Modern Art of the Print: Selections from the Collection of Lois & Michael Torf (with catalog), 84; American Modernism: Precisionist Works on Paper (auth, catalog), 86-87; Bryan Hunt: Falls and Figures, (with catalog), 88-89; Arthur Wesley Dow & His Influence (auth, catalog), 90-91; Nature's Changing Legacy: The Photographs of Robert Glenn Ketchum, (auth, brochure), 92-93; Master Prints in Upstate New York (auth, catalog), 95-96; Susan Rothenberg: Drawings and Prints (auth, catalog), 98-99; Arthur Wesley Doward Am Arts and Crafts (auth, catalog), 99-00; Vincent Smith (auth, catalog), 00; Surrealist Drawings from the Drikier Collection (auth, catalog), 2003; Bydcliffe; An Am Arts and crafts colony (auth, ed, catalog), 2004. *Pos:* Expert print dept, Christies East, New York, 80-82; curatorial asst, Williams Col Mus Art, 82-85; assoc cur prints, drawings & photographs, HF Johnson, Ithaca, NY, 85-89, cur, 89-, chief cur, 93-2000, sr cur, 2000-. *Teaching:* Cornell Adult Univ, 88-89, 91, 93 & 95-. *Awards:* Moe Prize for scholarly research (Arthur Wesley Dow and his Influence) given by the NY State Hist Asn; Winterthur Fel, 2000, 2005; Getty Curational Research Fellowship, 2002; Ragdale Found Residency, 2005 & 2006; Wolfsonian Fel, 2005; Paul Mellon Fel, 2006; Victorian Soc Award, Metrop Chap for Byndcliffe. *Mem:* Olive Press Adv Bd; Print Coun Am; Williamstown Regional Art Conserv Laboratory (trustee); Exhib Alliance (trustee). *Res:* 19th and 20th Century works on paper, Arts and crafts movement. *Publ:* Auth, Arthur Wesley Dow and His Influence, 91; Master Prints from upstate NY Museums, 95; Susan Rothenberg: Drawings and Prints, 97; Arthur Wesley Dow and American Arts and Crafts, 99; Surrealist Drawing from the Driker Collections 2003; Byrdcliffe; An Am Arts and Crafts Colony, 2004. *Mailing Add:* Herbert F Johnson Mus Cornell Univ Ithaca NY 14853

GREEN, ROGER J
CRITIC, HISTORIAN
b New York, NY, Nov 16, 44. *Study:* Cornell Univ, BA, 67; Tulane Univ, MA, 72; Univ Chicago, PhD, 87. *Pos:* Critic art & archit, Times-Picayune, New Orleans, La, 78-92 & Booth News Service, Ann Arbor, Mich, 92-; corresp, Art News Mag, 78-; New Art Examiner, 92-. *Res:* Art and Architecture in Europe, particularly Berlin, 1920-1940. *Publ:* Auth, Max Papart, Rizzoli, 84; contribr, Berlin/New York, Rizzoli, 91. *Mailing Add:* c/o Booth News Serv 217 Sycamore N St Lansing MI 48933-1033

GREEN, TOM
INSTRUCTOR, SCULPTOR
b Newark, NJ, May 27, 42. *Study:* Univ Md, BA, 67, MA(painting), 69. *Exhib:* New Sculpture: Baltimore-Washington-Richmond, Corcoran Gallery Art, Washington, DC, 70; Washington Sculpture, Philadelphia Art Alliance, 73; one-man show, Corcoran Gallery Art, 73; Whitney Biennial, Whitney Mus Art, NY, 75; North, East, West, South & Middle, Traveling Drawing Show, 75. *Pos:* Chair, Fine Arts Dept, Corcoran Sch Art, currently. *Teaching:* Asst prof sculpture & drawing, Corcoran Sch Art, 69-. *Bibliog:* Susan Sollins (auth), Washington report, Arts Mag, 9/73; David Tannous (auth), Tom Green: Words and images, Woodwind Mag, 12/11/73; Ben Forgey (auth), Washington: Pyramid shapes, Grenoble and theatrics, Art News, 1/74. *Mailing Add:* Dept Fine Arts Corcoran Sch Art 500 17th St NW Washington DC 20006-4804

GREEN, WILDER
ADMINISTRATOR, ARCHITECT
b Paris, France, Apr 17, 27; US citizen. *Study:* Yale Col, 45-47; Ill Inst Technol & Design Inst, Chicago, 47-48; Yale Univ Sch Archit, BA(archit), 52. *Pos:* Asst dir & cur, Dept Archit & Design, Mus Mod Art, New York, 57-61, coordr planning for bldg prog, 61-63, coordr prog, 63-67, dir exhib prog, 67-69, dep to actg dir, 69-70, dir exhib prog, 70-71; pres, Cunningham Dance Found, 69-72; dir, Am Fedn Arts, 71-87; spec consult & cur, Metrop Mus Art, 87-89; pvt art consult & archit, 89-; chmn, Grants Rev Comt, Judith Rothschild Found, 95-. *Teaching:* Asst prof, Yale Sch Archit, 56-57 & Hunter Col, 67-68. *Mem:* The Century Asn; MacDowell Colony; Longhouse Found; Village Ctr Care. *Mailing Add:* 20 E 74th St New York NY 10021

GREENAMYER, GEORGE MOSSMAN
SCULPTOR, EDUCATOR
b Cleveland, Ohio, July 13, 39. *Study:* Philadelphia Col Art, BFA; Univ Kans, MFA; Ctr Advan Visual Studies (res fel), Mass Inst Technol, Cambridge. *Work:* Fuller, Brocton Art Mus, Mass; Duxbury Art Complex, Mass, Boston Univ; Laumeier Sculpture Park, St Louis, Mo; Decordova Sculpture Park, Lincoln, Mass. *Comn:* narrative kinetic sculpture/clock tower, Charlotte, Douglas Intl Airport, NC, 97; narrative kinetic, internally lit, sculpture/wind vane, City of Philadelphia Percent for

Art Prog, 98; narrative kinetic clock/sculpture, NJ Dept Labor, Trenton, NH State Coun Arts, 2000; 3 narrative kinetic wind vane/sculptures, Atlantic City Int Airport, Pomona, NJ, South Jersey Trans Auth, NJ State Coun Arts, 99; narrative kinetic, Penn Sta, New York City/NJ Transit, 2002; Internally Lit, Hoboken Terminal, Hudson-Bergen Light Rail, NJ Transit, 2003; Kinetic Gateway, Union Station, Union, NJ, NJ Transit, 2005. *Exhib:* Pub Sculpture in Columbus, Univ Gallery Fine Art, 84; Pub Art Process, Miami, Fla, 86; Chesterwood, Stockbridge, Mass, 87; Woodson Art Mus, Wausau, Wis, 1998-2000, Decordova Mus, Lincoln, Mass, 2000. *Teaching:* Prof sculpture, Mass Col Art, Boston, 81-2004, prof emeritus, 2005. *Awards:* Artists Fel Grant, Artists Found, Boston, Mass & Tiffany Grant, New York, NY, 77. *Bibliog:* Peter Koenig (auth), article, South Shore Mag, summer 88; John Chandler (auth), article, Sculpture mag, 3-4/88; Nick Capasso (auth), article, Sculpture Mag, May, 99; Doug Norris (auth), review, Art New England, 2-3/2003; Article & Photos, Anvil's Ring, Spring, 2004. *Mem:* Artist Blacksmiths NAm; Int Sculpture Ctr. *Media:* Steel, Aluminum. *Mailing Add:* 994 Careswell St Marshfield MA 02050-5637

GREENBAUM, MARTY
PAINTER, SCULPTOR
b New York, NY, Mar 3, 34. *Study:* Univ Ariz, Tucson, BA, 56; Brooklyn Col, NY, Mass, 91. *Work:* Art Inst Chicago & Libr, Art Inst Chicago; Chrysler Mus at Norfolk, Va; The Print Club, Philadelphia, Pa; J Patrick Lannan Found, Santa Fe NMex; The Norman Fisher Collection, Jacksonville Art Mus, Fla, Madison Art Ctr, Wisc & SUNY, New Paltz, NY. *Comn:* Unique Book, comn by J Patrick Lannan Found, Los Angeles, Calif, 68; Sept Calendar (centerfold), Changes Mag, NY, 71; eds of prints, Shenanigan Press at Jones Rd Print Shop, Barneveld, Wis, 74; Cajun Book, comn by James McDonell, NY, 85. *Exhib:* Personal Torment & Human Concern, Whitney Mus Am Art, NY, 69; 4th Ann Contemp Reflections, Aldrich Mus Contemp Art, Ridgefield, Conn, 75; 20th Nat Print Exhib, Brooklyn Mus, NY, 76; The Object as Poet, Renwick Gallery, Smithsonian Inst, Washington, DC, 76-77; New Ways with Paper, Nat Collection of Fine Arts, Smithsonian Inst, 77; solo exhib, Picker Art Gallery, Colgate Univ, 77; Playground PSI, Long Island, NY, 78; Metamorphosis of the Book, Documenta 6, Kassel, Ger; Artists' Books, Georges Pompidou Ctr, Paris, France, 85; Fetishism Contemp & Primitive, Allan Stone Gallery, NY, 92; Talent, Allan Stone Gallery, NY, 97-99; Dog Days, Pacifico Fine Art, NY, 2000; 40th Anniversary, Allan Stone Gallery, NY, 2000; solo exhib, Pacifico Fico Fine Art, NYC, 2001; solo exhib, Artist Books, 5+5 Gallery, Brooklyn, NY, 2002, Safe-T-Gallery, Brooklyn, NY, 2006. *Teaching:* Art, PS 63, New York, 88-95. *Awards:* The Inst for Art & Urban Resources Inc, 83; Creative Artists Pub Serv Prog, NY, 72, 75; Nat Endowment Arts Grant; The Inst for Contemp Art, 83. *Bibliog:* Dorothea Baer (producer), Marty & Lulu's Playground, Independent Film, 65; David Bourdon (auth), Marty Greenbaum, Village Voice, 65; Gene Baro (auth), The Object As Poet, Smithsonian Inst Press, 77; Rose Slivka (auth), Paper as Medium Smithsonian Institution Traveling Exhibition Service, 78; Ed McCormack (auth), No Longer Innocent: Book Art in America, 60-80, Betty Bright, 2005. *Media:* Painting, Drawing, Collage, Photography. *Publ:* 30 Years of American Printmaking, The Brooklyn Mus, 77; RE: Pages, An Exhibition of Contemporary American Bookworks, Hera Educational Foundation, 81; Jones Road Printshop & Stable 1971-81: A Catalogue Raisonne, Madison Art Ctr, 83; Marty Greenbaum: Visionary Mojo Man in the Postmodern Age, 2002. *Dealer:* Allan Stone Gallery 113 E 90th New York NY; Safe-T-Gallery 111 Front St Brooklyn NY 11201; 5+5 Gallery 111 Front St Brooklyn NY 11201. *Mailing Add:* 505 Court St # 6D Brooklyn NY 11231

GREENBERG, IRWIN
PAINTER, INSTRUCTOR
b Brooklyn, NY, Apr 5, 22. *Study:* Art Students League; NY Univ, BS(art educ); study with Yasuo Kuniyoshi, Will Barnet, Hale Woodruff & Paul Gerchik. *Exhib:* Soldier Art, Nat Gallery, Washington, DC, 45; Mus Fine Arts, Boston, 45; Brooklyn Mus, 48; Birmingham Mus, Ala, 70-71; Milbrook Gallery, NY, 89-92; Wyckoff Gallery, NJ, 92; Taggart Art Gallery, Wyo, 92; Mason Gallery, Ohio; Art Works Gallery, Wis; and others. *Teaching:* Instr life drawing, Baruch Col, City Col New York, 53-54; instr painting & illusr, High Sch Art & Design, 68-85 & Sch Visual Arts, New York, 86-90; instr watercolor painting from life, Art Students League, 95-. *Awards:* High Winds Medal, Am Watercolor Soc, 95; Gold Medal, Ridgewood Art Ctr, NJ, 95; Gold Medal, Perry House, Va, 95; and many others. *Mem:* Am Watercolor Soc; Nat Watercolor Soc; Ga Watercolor Soc; Philadelphia Watercolor Soc; Art Students League. *Media:* Oil, Watercolor. *Publ:* Contribr, Working With Body Color, Watercolor, 92, The Best of Watercolor, 95, Your Personal Painting Style, 95 & People In Watercolor, 96, Am Artists Publ; Wipe it out, paint it back, The Artists Mag, 7/94; Painting the grand portrait, Watercolor Magic, 94, 96, 2004. *Dealer:* Wyckoff Art Gallery Wyckoff NJ 07481; Phillips Gallery 444 E 200 South Salt Lake City UT 84111; Kendall Gallery, Cape Cod MA. *Mailing Add:* 17 W 67th St New York NY 10023

GREENBERG, RONALD K
DEALER, COLLECTOR
b St Louis, Mo, July 17, 37. *Study:* Washington Univ, St Louis, Mo. *Mem:* Art Dealers Asn Am. *Specialty:* Contemporary American art. *Collection:* Works by Lichenstein, Warhol, Stella, Kelly, Motherwell, Frankenthaler, Judd, Serra, Chamberlain and Rauschenberg. *Mailing Add:* 3 Brentmoor Park Saint Louis MO 63105

GREENBLAT, RODNEY ALAN
PAINTER, DESIGNER
b Daly City, Calif, Aug 23, 60. *Study:* Sch Visual Arts, BFA(hon), 82. *Work:* Groeniger Mus, Amsterdam; Chrysler Mus, Norfolk, Va. *Exhib:* The Threshold, RI Sch Design, Providence, 82; one-man show, Gracie Mansion Gallery, NY, 83; Familiar Frontiers, Australian Ctr Contemp Art, Melbourne, 85; Biennial Exhib, Whitney Mus Am Art, NY, 85; Reality and Imagination, Contemp Arts Mus, Houston, 88; Land Ho (with catalog), Chrysler Mus, Norfolk, 92. *Teaching:* Prof computer art, Sch Visual Arts, 92-96. *Bibliog:* Sanfor Shaman (auth), Reality & Imagination, Penn State Univ, 87. *Media:* Multi-media. *Specialty:* Contemporary Art. *Publ:* Auth, Uncle Wizzmo's New Used Car, 90, Aunt Ippys Museum of Junk, 91 Slombo The Gross, 93 & Thunder Bunny, 97, Harper Collins. *Dealer:* Gracie Mansion Fine Arts 101 2nd Ave New York NY 10003, tel: 212-505-7055. *Mailing Add:* 61 Crosby St New York NY 10012

GREENE, CHRIS (CHRISTINE) E
CARTOONIST, PAINTER
b Chelm, Poland, Mar 29, 45; US citizen. *Study:* Newark Sch Fine & Industrial Arts, cert 62-65; Moore Col Art, Philadelphia, BFA, 68; Art Students League, 70-71, pvt studio classes with Joe Hing Lowe, 74-75, pvt studio classes with John Howard Sanden, 76-77. *Work:* Northport High Sch, NY; works in numerous pvt collections. *Comn:* Numerous portraits, caricatures & caricature portraits in NY, NJ, Ariz & Fla, 75-92. *Exhib:* Ann Art Show, Nassau Co Mus, Roslyn, NY, 77-78; Huntington Township Art League 25th Ann, Hecksher Mus, NY, 80; Pastel Soc Am Ann Mem Show, Salamagundi Club, NY, 81; Nat Soc Painters in Casein & Acrylic, Nat Arts Club, NY, 83; Kans Pastel Soc 1st Ann Nat Juried Show, Wichita Art Asn, 84. *Pos:* Portrait painter, independent, Hyannis, Mass, 68-69; textile designer, Schwartz & Liebman Textiles, New York, 70-76; Caricatures by Chris Green, independent business, 82-. *Awards:* First Prize, Huntington Township Art League Ann, 80; Grumbacher Art Award, Independent Art Soc Ann, Grumbacher Art Supplies, 81; Award of Excellence, Channel 21 WLIW, Art Show, 82. *Bibliog:* Helen A Harrison (auth), Health building scores, NY Times, 10/4/79; Art around town, Glen Cove Weekender, 11/15/80; Art revs, Sunstorm, 7/15/84. *Mem:* Pastel Soc Am; Nat Caricaturist Network; Nat Caricaturist Network. *Media:* Pastels, Markers. *Dealer:* Norman Mack 12 Kodiak Dr Woodbury NY 11797. *Mailing Add:* 17 Edward Ln Syosset NY 11791

GREENE, DANIEL E
PAINTER, INSTRUCTOR
b Cincinnati, OH, 1934. *Study:* Art Student's League, NY. *Work:* Mrs Eleanor Roosevelt; Bryant Gumbel of CBS; Astronaut Walter Schirra; Coca Cola Co; Dave Thomas, Wendy's; Dept Agriculture, Secy Ann Veneman; Cincinnati Mus Fine Arts, OH; Clinton Presidential Libr, Ark; Columbus Mus Art, Ga; Harvard Univ, Mass; Princeton Univ, NJ; Yale Univ, Conn; West Point, NY; Nat Accad Design, NY; Metrop Mus Art, NY; and many others. *Exhib:* Loring Gallery, NY, 75; Baker Gallery, Tex, 80; Talisman Gallery, Okla, 80; Miller Gallery, OH, 81 & 2004; Subway Series, Gallery Henoch, NY, 85, 92 & 94; Hammond Mus, NY, 87; Galerie Gismondi, Paris, 87; Hollis Taggart Gallery, NY, 99; John Pence Gallery, Calif, 2001 & 2003; Loring Gallery, Mass, 2003; Charter Oak Gallery, Conn, 2003; NY Transit Mus, 2004; Elaine Baker Gallery, Fla, 2006. *Teaching:* instr, painting, Nat Acad of Design, formerly; instr, painting, Art Students League, NY, formerly. *Awards:* Am Soc Hall of Fame, 92; Pastel Hall of Fame, 83; Lifetime Achievement Award, Am Artist's Mag; Artists Fel Benjamin West Clinedinst Medal, 99; Medal Hon, Portrait Soc Am, 2001; Laureate Award, Pastel Soc West Coast, 2003; Herman Margulies Award Excellence, Pastel Soc Am, 2005; Artist in Special Tribute, Hudson Valley Art Asn, 2006. *Bibliog:* Int Artists Mag; articles in Am Artist Mag, 85, 93 & 01; article, Int Artist Mag, 2/99; Articles in Artists Mag, 2001 & 2003; and many others. *Mem:* Artists' Fel; Pastel Soc Am; Portrait Soc Am. *Media:* Pastels and Oil. *Publ:* Best of Pastel, 96; Pure Color: The Best of Pastel, 98; A Painter's Guide to Design & Composition, 2006; and many others. *Dealer:* John Pence Gallery CA; Gallery Henoch NY. *Mailing Add:* Studio Hill Farm Rt 116 North Salem NY 10560

GREENE, LOUISE WEAVER
TAPESTRY ARTIST, LIBRARIAN
b Lancaster, Pa, May 7, 53. *Study:* Haystack Mountain Sch Crafts, 75; Univ Md, BA(art hist), 92, MLS, 94. *Work:* Gannett Co Inc/USA Today, Washington, DC; Fed Home Loan Mortgage Corp, Washington, DC; Bell Canada, Washington, DC. *Comn:* Woven Tapestry, Gateway Int, Baltimore, Md, 86; Woven Tapestry, Gannett Co Inc/USA Today, Washington, DC, 86; Woven Tapestry, Tyson Corp, Springdale, Ark, 87; Woven Tapestry, Int Point, Washington, DC, 88. *Exhib:* For the Floor, Am Craft Mus, NY, 85; Contemp Crafts, Del Art Mus, Wilmington, Del, 85; Fiber Wall Works, Meredith Gallery, Baltimore, Md, 87; Fiber: State of the Art, Atlanta Financial Ctr, Atlanta, Ga, 88; Light Line & Plane, Scheuer Tapestry Gallery, NY, 88; Peripheral Perspectives, Soc Arts & Crafts, Boston, Mass, 89; Mixed Media Invitational, Miriam Perlman Gallery, Chicago, Ill, 89. *Pos:* Reference Librn, Art Libr, Univ Md, College Park. *Awards:* Judges Choice Award, Wash Craft Show, Renwick Gallery, Smithsonian Inst, Washington, DC, 85. *Bibliog:* Nell Znamierowski (auth), For the Floor, Am Craft Mag, 85; Lisa Hammel (auth), Handmade Rugs at Craft, NY Times, 85; Carol Lawrence (ed), Fiberarts Design Book III, 87. *Mem:* Smithsonian Assoc, Wash, DC; Am Craft Coun, NY; Am Tapestry Alliance; James Renwick Alliance Renwick Gallery; Art Libr Soc NAm. *Media:* Woven Tapestry, Fiber. *Publ:* Contrib, Fiberarts Design Book II, & Fiberarts Design Book III, Lark Books, 83 & 87. *Mailing Add:* 2304 Ashboro Dr Chevy Chase MD 20815

GREENFIELD, AMY
FILMMAKER, VIDEO ARTIST
b Boston, Mass, July 8, 40. *Study:* Radcliffe Col, with Anne Sexton & William Alfred, BA(hon), 62. *Work:* Lincoln Ctr Dance Collection, Mus Holography, NY. *Comn:* Resoled (film), 71 & For God While Sleeping (film), 71, Visual Learning Corp; One-O-One (film), comn by Douglas Dunn, NY, 76; Four Solos for Four Women (videotape), Artists TV Proj, NY, 80; Tribute to Charlotte Morman, Comn by Nam June Paik, 94. *Exhib:* Solo exhibs, Womens Avant-Garde Film Festival, Whitney Mus Am Art, 72, New Videodance, Anthology Film Arch, NY, 77, 80 & 83, The Wave:

Film & Holography, Hayward Gallery, London, 79 & Dance-Film-Video, Mus Mod Art, NY, 83; Two Channel Video, Whitney Mus Am Art, 78; Berlin Int Film Festival, 90; Houston Int Film Festival, 90; Howard Film Archives, 90 & 93; Mus Mod Art, 91; Am Film Inst Independent Film Ser, 91; NY Video Festival, 92; Celebration Arts Without Borders, 94. *Teaching:* Instr film, Tufts Univ, 72-74; vis asst prof, Univ RI, 77-78 & Montclair State Col, 78-79; guest lectr, Univ Calif Art, San Diego, 93. *Awards:* Nat Endowment Arts Grants, 75, 78, 81 & 84; Rockefeller Found Grant, 80; Ten Best Arts & Entertainment, New York Times, 94. *Bibliog:* Robert Haller (auth), article, Millennium Film J, 80; Deborah Jowitt (auth), Prisoners of the lens, Village Voice, 80; John Gruen (auth), Dance visions, Dancemag, 83. *Mem:* Independent Feature Project. *Media:* Film, Video. *Publ:* Auth, Verticle roll, Film Libr Quart, 78; The Big Apple: First in video, 80 & The case of the vanishing videotape, 81, Am Film; Video and film and video, Video Roma, 82; Filmdance space, time, energy, Film Dance, 83; The tales of Hoffman, Film Comment, 95. *Dealer:* Filmmakers Coop 175 Lexington Ave New York NY 10016; Mystic Fire Video Broadway New York NY 10012. *Mailing Add:* 135 St Pauls Ave Staten Island NY 10301

GREENFIELD, JOAN BEATRICE
PAINTER, ENAMELIST
b Bronx, NY, Apr 15, 31. *Study:* Adelphi Univ, New York, BA, (art hist), 5/78, MA(studio arts), 5/81; Nat Acad Design, Audrew Flack, 90; studied with Miriam Shapiro, Parish Mus, 97. *Work:* Adelphi Univ, NY; Buffalo Children's Hosp, NY; Helentex Inc, NY; Rubin & Kimche law offices, Jerusalem, Israel. *Comn:* Portraits, comn by H Cytryn, Woodmere, NY, 87 & 88, P Henry, Franklin Square, NY, 84; enamels, comn by M Partem, Jerusalem, Israel, 88. *Exhib:* Solo exhib, R Harley Gallery, Adelphi Univ, NY, 82; group shows, Mus Philos, NY, 82, Figures, Nabisco Brands Gallery, NJ, 86, Salute Women's History Month, Paper Mill Playhouse Renee Foosaner Art Gallery, NJ, 87, Nat Asn Women Artist Fall Collection, Monmouth Mus Fine Arts, NJ, 87, Celebration 89, The Interchurch Ctr, NY, 89, Small works, Marbella Gallery, NY, 89, Roper Gallery, Frostburg State Univ, Md, 90, Hampton Sq Gallery, West Hampton, NY, 91, Galarie des Hampton, 92, Fire House Gallery, Nassau Community Col, Garden City, NY, 92, Parish Art Mus, Southampton, NY, 95; Community Fine Arts Ctr, Rock Springs, Wyo, 98; Stocker Ctr Gallery, ELyria, Ohio, 98; Saginaw Arts Mus, Mich, 98. *Pos:* Coordr, spec events 78-81, Alumni Exhib, 80-83, Adelphi Univ, Traveling painting Nat Asn Women Artists, NY, 84-90; exec bd & new mem chair, Nat Asn Women Artists, 94-98. *Awards:* Greenblatt Mem, Nat Asn Women Artists, Forest Elec-P Rebhum, 4/84; New Concept, Nat Asn Women Artists, anonymous, 4/89; S Kahn Award, Nat Asn Women Artists, 5/96. *Mem:* Kappa Pi; Nat Asn Women Artists (exec bd, 84-92); NY Artist Equity; Women's Caucus for Art; NY Found Community Artists. *Media:* Acrylic, Oil. *Publ:* Auth, Upon Thy Doorposts, B Rosenblum. *Mailing Add:* 876 Central Ave Woodmere NY 11598

GREENFIELD-SANDERS, TIMOTHY
PHOTOGRAPHER
b Miami Beach, Fla, Feb 16, 52. *Study:* Columbia Univ, BA (art hist), 74; Am Film Inst, with Slavko Vorkapich, MFA (film fel), 77. *Work:* Mus Mod Art, Metrop Mus Art, Int Ctr Photog, NY; Australian Nat Gallery; Nat Portrait Gallery, Washington, DC; Whitney Mus. *Exhib:* One-man shows, Marcuse Pfeifer Gallery, New York City, 82, 85, 87, Leo Castelli Gallery, NY, 87, Mary Boone Gallery, NY, 88, 99, Zeit-Foto, Tokyo, Japan, 88, Greene Gallery, Fla, 89, Marimura Art Mus, Tokyo, Japan, 90, Mus Mod & Contemp Art, Trento, 91, Mod Art Mus, Ft Worth, Tex, 91, Mus Design, Leipzig, Ger, 96, Kunst-Station Sankt Peter, Koln, Ger, 96, Mus Contemp, Mex City, 97, Los Angeles Theater Ctr, 98, Emilio Mazzoli Gallery, Modena, Italy, 2000, Miami Art Mus, 02; group shows, Mus Mod Art, New York City, 91, 99, Staley-Wise Gallery, New York City, 91, Int Ctr Photog, New York City, 93, Ctr Photog, Woodstock, NY, 93, The Saatchi Collection, London, 94, Lincoln Ctr, New York City, 95, Photog Resource Ctr, Boston, 96, Robert Miller Gallery, New York City, 97, Mus of the City of NY, 01, Paine Webber Art Gallery, New York City, 02. *Awards:* Fine Arts Photogr, Am Photogr Mag, 83. *Bibliog:* Hilton Kramer (auth), NY Artist of 50's in 80's, New York Times, 3/27/81; Robert Schwalberg (auth), Portfolio, Camera Arts Mag, 3/82; Dore Ashton (auth), Avenue, 11/82. *Media:* Black & White, Color Polaroid. *Publ:* Contribr, Barrons, 81-86 & Vogue, 83-86; auth, Downtown in the fifties, 81 & Art of the Real, 83, Horizon; Clarkson Potter, Artnews, 83; The New Irascibles, Arts Mag, 9/85. *Dealer:* Mary Boone Gallery 745 Fifth Ave New York Ny 10021. *Mailing Add:* 135 E 2nd St New York NY 10009

GREENHALGH, PAUL
b Bolton, Eng. *Study:* Univ Reading, undergrad degree, 78; Courtauld Inst Art, MA (art hist, specialty in design), 80. *Exhib:* chief organizer, Art Nouveau exhib, Nat Gallery Art, Washington, DC, 2000. *Pos:* Tutor, Royal Col of Art; head art hist, Camberwell Col Arts, London; dep keeper of ceramics and glass, Victoria and Albert Mus, head res; pres, Nova Scotia Col Art and Design, 2001-05; dir & pres, Corcoran Gallery of Art and Col of Art and Design, Washington, DC, 2006-. *Publ:* Auth, Ephemeral Visitas, 88; auth, Modernism in Design, 90; auth, Quotations and Sources on Design and Decorative Arts 1800-1990, 94; auth, The Essential Art Nouveau, 2000; auth, Art Nouveau 1890-1914, 2000; auth, The Persistence of Craft, 02; The Modern Ideal: The Rise and Collapse of Idealism in the Visual Arts from the Enlightenment to Postmodernism, 05. *Mailing Add:* Corcoran Coll Art and Design 500 17th St NW Washington DC 20006-4804

GREENLEAF, VIRGINIA
PAINTER
b Chicago, Ill. *Study:* Yale Univ Sch Fine Arts; Am Univ; also with Ivan Olinsky, Robert Brackman & Gene Davis. *Work:* Dept State. *Exhib:* one-person shows, Studio Gallery, Wash, 71-76, Main St Gallery Ann, Nantucket, 71-96, Parsons Dreyfuss Gallery, NY, Gallery 124, NY, 83 & Main St Gallery, Boston; Mus Fine Arts, Brazil; Haller Gallery, NY; Christy Lawrence Gallery, Lyme, Conn; Alva Gallery, New London, Conn; Rittenhouse Fine Arts, Phila, Pa; Cooley Gallery, Old Lyme, Conn, 2003-05. *Mem:* Artists Equity Asn; Who's Who in America; Ct Conservalley; Old Lyme Historical Assoc. *Media:* Acrylic, watercolor, graphite. *Specialty:* contemporary. *Interests:* History & art. *Mailing Add:* PO Box 931 Old Lyme CT 06371

GREENLY, COLIN
ENVIRONMENTAL ARTIST, CONCEPTUAL ARTIST
b London, Eng, Jan 21, 28; US citizen. *Study:* Harvard Col, AB, 49; Columbia Univ Sch Painting & Sculpture, 51-53. *Work:* Mus Mod Art, NY; Corcoran Gallery Art, Washington; Herbert F Johnson Mus, Ithaca, NY; Philadelphia Mus Art; Albright-Knox Art Gallery, Buffalo; and others. *Comn:* 12,000 Feet of Color, Corcoran Sch Art, Washington, DC, 70; Transitional Image, since destroyed, Everson Mus, Syracuse, NY, 71; Participatory murals, NY State Off Bldg, Utica, 73 & Creative Artists Pub Serv Prog, 75; Restoration and Adaptation: The 1878 Hulse Barn, 78-98. *Exhib:* Young Am Printmakers, Mus Mod Art, NY, 53; one-man exhib, Royal Marks Gallery, NY, 68 & 70, Corcoran Gallery Art, 68 & Finch Col Mus, 74; De Cordova Mus, Lincoln, Mass, 65; Des Moines Art Ctr, 67; Smithsonian Am Art Mus, Washington, DC, 68; Contemp Am Painting & Sculpture, Krannert Art Mus, Ill, 69 & 74; Everson Mus, Syracuse, NY, 71; Andrew Dickson White Mus, Cornell Univ, 72; Images, Mus Mod Art, NY, 73; Finch Col, New York City, 74; John Weber Gallery, NY, 75; Whitney Mus Am Art, NY, 78; NY State Mus, Albany, 81; Contr World Trade Ctr Site Mem Competition, 2003; and others. *Pos:* Vis artist, Cent Mich Univ, 72; artist-in-residence, Everson Mus, Syracuse, NY, 72 & Cazenovia Col, 72; Nat Endowment Arts & Humanities artist in residence, Finch Col, 74. *Teaching:* Dana prof art, Colgate Univ, 72-73. *Awards:* Nat Endowment Arts & Humanities Grant for Sculpture, 67; Creative Artists Pub Serv Prog Grant for Intangible Sculpture, New York, 72; Creative Artists Pub Serv Fel, 78; Decentralization Grant for Video, NY Coun Arts, 93. *Bibliog:* James Harithas (auth), Colin Greenly, Libr Cong No 68-19952, Corcoran Gallery Art, 1/68; Thomas W Leavitt (auth), Colin Greenly: Intangible Sculpture, Libr Cong No 72-9042, Andrew Dickson Mus Art, Cornell Univ, 72; Dore Ashton (auth), article, In Coloquio Artes, NY, 10/74. *Media:* Multiple Archival Digital Images, Intangible Sculpture. *Res:* Format of most universal image in nature reflecting energy interactions. *Interests:* Environ inter-relationships; architecture; Art/seeing educ; change. *Publ:* Auth, A changing image of change, A J for Artists, winter 86; contribr, Images of the Whole, the Artist's Sketchbook (CD-ROM), Leaning Post Productions, 98. *Mailing Add:* 487 Hulsetown Rd Campbell Hall NY 10916

GREENSPAN, GLADYS
PAINTER
b New York, NY, Sept 14, 23. *Study:* Studied at Girls Commercial High Sch & Brooklyn Mus, 42, FIT & Art Students League, 55-57 & Queens Col, 56. *Work:* Jane Voorhees Zimmerli Art Mus, Rutgers Univ, New Brunswick, NJ. *Exhib:* Artist Network of Great Neck, Roslyn Mus Fine Art, NY, 81; solo show, L'Avenir Solo, Great Neck, NY, 88 & Emil Leonard Gallery, NY, 91; Nat Asn Women Artists, Richmond Art Mus, Ind & Mus Southwest, Midland, Tex, 91-92; Paul Mellon Art Ctr, Conn, 93; Salmagundi, NY, 93. *Pos:* Textile designer, Steintex, Ameritex, New York, 57-77. *Teaching:* Drawing with pastels, YMHA-YWHA, Flushing, NY, 77-79. *Awards:* Best Show, Bayside Art League, 82; 1st Prize, Artist Network Great Neck, 93; 2nd Prize, Nat Asn Women Artists, 94. *Mem:* Pastel Soc Am; Nat Asn Women Artists; Artist Network Great Neck; Prof Artist Group Boca Raton Mus. *Media:* Pastels. *Dealer:* 604 Artist Guild of Norton Museum. *Mailing Add:* 6080 Huntwick Terr Apt 307 Delray Beach FL 33484-1852

GREENSTONE, MARION
PAINTER
b New York, NY, Mar 30, 25. *Study:* Brooklyn Col, BA(cum laude), 46; Columbia Univ Teachers Col, MA, 47; Cooper Union, dipl(fine arts), 54. *Work:* Art Gallery London, Ont; Queens Col, Kingston, Ont; Exxon Corp, NY. *Comn:* Mural, comn by Bernard Rothzeid & Fine Arts Comn, NY, 76. *Exhib:* Brooklyn Mus Ann Print Show, 53; Whitney Mus Ann, 53; Pittsburgh Int, 55; Can Nat Exhib, 58; Ohio Univ Prints & Drawings Exhib, 63; one-women shows, Long Island Univ, NY, 70 & 76, Sixth Estate Gallery, NY, 76 & 77, Cusano Gallery, South Norwalk, Conn, 85, Owl Gallery, Long Island, 86, Plandome Gallery, NY, 90, Manhasset Libr Gallery, NY, 92; Works on Paper, Brooklyn Mus, 75; Mus Hudson Highlands, 83. *Teaching:* From adj assoc prof art to prof painting & design, Pratt Inst, 68-92. *Awards:* Fulbright Award, 54-56; Montreal Mus Spring Show Award, 60; Baxter Found Award, 61. *Media:* Oil on Canvas. *Mailing Add:* 790 Carrol St Brooklyn NY 11215

GREENWALD, ALICE (ALICE) MARIAN GREENWALD-WARD
CONSULTANT, MUSEOLOGIST
b Oceanside, NY, Jan 2, 52. *Study:* Univ Exeter, Devon, Eng, with Theo Brown, 71-72; Sarah Lawrence Col, Bronxville, NY, BA(anthrop & Lit), 73; Univ Chicago Divinity Sch, Ill, AM(hist relig), 75. *Collection Arranged:* Los Angeles Collects: Works on Paper and Graphic Art from Israel, 78-79; The Five Sense Show, 78; The Custom Cut: Jewish Papercuts, Past & Present, 79; Jewish Marriage Contracts: A Celebration in Art, 79; Bill Aron: Portraits of Life, The Elderly Jews of Venice, Calif, 79-80, The Realm of Torah, 81, Between Holy & Profane: Xerography by Dina Dar, 81, Huc Skirball Mus, Hebrew Union Col, Los Angeles, Calif; The Tallis as a Metaphor of Community: Fiber Sculptures by Laurie Gross, 82 & Odyssey of Freedom: The Canvas Diary of a Soviet Jewish Emigre (paintings & works on paper by Tanya Kornfield), 83, The American Jewish Experience, 89, Mus Am Jewish Hist, Philadelphia; Daniel's Story, US Holocaust Mem Coun, 91-92. *Pos:* Dir, Mus Am Jewish Hist, Philadelphia, Pa, 81-86; consulting cur, US Holocaust Mem Mus,

Washington, DC, 86-; tech adv, The Pew Charitable Trusts, Philadelphia, 87. *Teaching:* Mus educator Jewish art, Hebrew Union Col, Los Angeles, Calif, 75-81. *Awards:* Nat Endowment Arts Fel Mus Prof, 81. *Mem:* Am Asn Mus; Int Coun Mus; Coun Am Jewish Mus. *Res:* All areas of Jewish art, emphasis on European ritual art and near eastern archaelogy; Holocaust studies. *Publ:* Auth, The Mizrach: Compass of the heart, Hadassah Mag, 10/79; The masonic Mizrach: Jewish ritual art as a reflection of cultural assimilation, J Jewish Art, Vol 10, 83; The American Jewish Experience (exhib catalog), 89. *Mailing Add:* 3929 Military Rd NW Washington DC 20015-2927

GREER, JANE RUTH
SCULPTOR
b New York, NY, Jan 28, 41. *Study:* New York Univ, BFA; Art Students League, with John Hovanes. *Work:* Chrysler Mus, Norfolk, Va; Grey Art Gallery, New York Univ, New York, NY; SE Bank of Fla, Miami; photography, Minneapolis Inst Art. *Comn:* Murals, Holiday Inn, Ft Lee, NJ, 86. *Exhib:* Drawing & Collage, Grey Art Gallery, NY Univ, 77; First Anniversary Exhib, 78 & Works on Paper, 82, Drawing Ctr; photographs, Lyman Allyn Mus, Conn; cut paper, Drawing Ctr. *Media:* Wood, Paper; Photography. *Dealer:* Jane Kahan Gallery 922 Madison Ave New York NY 10021; Gallery Henoch 555 W 25 St New York NY 10001. *Mailing Add:* 81 Wooster St New York NY 10012-4375

GREER, JOHN SYDNEY
SCULPTOR
b Amherst, NS, Can, June 28, 44. *Study:* NS Col Art, dipl(bursary), 62-64; Montreal Mus Sch Art & Design, dipl(hon sculpture; scholar), 66; Vancouver Sch Art, dipl, 67. *Work:* Nat Gallery, Ottawa; Art Gallery Ont; Art Gallery NS; Beaverbrook Art Gallery, Fredericton, New Brunswick, Can; MacDonald Stewart Art Ctr Sculpture Garden, Guelph, Ont, Can; plus others. *Comn:* Y D Klein (lithograph), NS Col Art & Design, 74; The Forks (Winnipeg), Parks, Can, 88; Crow Feather (sculpture), MacDonald Stewart Art Ctr Sculpture Garden, 98; plus others. *Exhib:* Solo exhibs, Sculptured Objective, 68-81, Traveling Exhib, Art Gallery NS, 49th Parallel, NY, Mus d'Art Contemp, Montreal & others, 81-83, Dalhousie Art Gallery, Halifax, 87, Ottawa Sch Art Gallery, 87, Southern Alberta Art Gallery, Lethbridge, 90, St Mary's Univ Art Gallery, Halifax, 90, Black Seeds Glendon Gallery, North York, 97, John Greer Nine Grains of Rice, Nat Gallery of Can, Ottawa, 99, Tantalus, Artsplace, Annapolis Royal, 2000, plus others; Art Contemporain 1990 Savoir-Vivre, Ctr Int Art Contemporian, Montreal, 90; Embodied Viewer, Glenbow Mus, 91; and others. *Teaching:* Assoc prof sculpture, NS Col Art & Design, currently. *Awards:* Can Coun Grant, 85, 88 & 90; Victor Martyn Lynch-Staunton Award, Can Coun, 88. *Bibliog:* Gemey Kelly (auth), review, Vanguard, 82; Ron Shuebrook (auth), review, Vanguard, 9-10/87; Robert Pope (auth), review, Arts Atlantic 29, summer/fall 87. *Mem:* Eye Level Gallery, Halifax (vchmn, 75-); Can Artist Representation, Provincial, Nat. *Media:* Stone, Cast Metal. *Publ:* Auth, Sceptical Spectacles, Dalhousie Art Gallery, 74; Waterrings, Dalhousie Art Gallery, 76; Onion Skin Maker Your Eyes Water, Coach House Press, 81; John Greer Sculptural Objective (exhib catalog), Art Gallery NS, 81; Reconciliation (exhib catalog), 90. *Mailing Add:* PO Box 130 La Have NS B0R 1C0 Canada

GREER, WALTER MARION
PAINTER
b Ware Shoals, SC, Aug 11, 20. *Study:* The Citadel, BS, 42; Clemson Univ, BS, 47; Atlanta Sch Art, 59 & 60; Nat Acad Design, New York, with Robert Phillipp; also with Ben Shute, Atlanta, 62 & study abroad. *Work:* Telfair Acad Arts & Sci, Savannah, Ga; SC State Collection, Columbia Mus Art; paintings, Sea Pines Plantation Co, Hilton Head Island, SC; Greenville Mus Art, SC; C & S Collection, Atlanta & Greenville, SC; and others. *Comn:* Oil landscape, Gov Mansion, Columbia, 67; three paintings, Phipps Land Co, Hilton Head Island & NY, 70; portrait of pres, Emory Univ, 71; triptych, Simmons Collection, Atlanta, Ga; ltd ed print for Marriott Hotels, 81. *Exhib:* Mead Paper Show, Atlanta, Ga, 60; Hunter Ann, Chattanooga, Tenn, 62; SC Invitational, Columbia, 69; one-man shows, Columbia Mus Art, 73 & Telfair Acad Arts & Sci, 74, 76 & 82; Guild SC Artists, 81. *Teaching:* Instr pvt classes, 63-66, 78 & 81; instr spec art classes, USMC, Parris Island, SC, 64-65 & Savannah Art Asn Sch, 66. *Awards:* Savannah Arts Festival Award for Rivers, 66; SC Arts Coun Purchase Award for Pond, 69; SC Archit Award for Pond (Grey Phase), 71. *Bibliog:* Virginia Ball (auth), The man that got away, Atlanta Mag, 65; articles & 28 covers, Islander Mag; Jack Morris & Robert Smeltz (auth), Contemporary artists of South Carolina, 70. *Mem:* Guild SC Artists; hon life mem Beaufort Art Asn. *Media:* Oil, Acrylic. *Publ:* Cover and profile, Southern World Mag, 79 & 80; article, Southern Accents Mag, 82. *Dealer:* Tatler Gallery Hilton Head Island SC 29928. *Mailing Add:* 300 Woodhaven Dr Apt 4104 Hilton Head Island SC 29928-7531

GREER, WESLEY DWAINE
EDUCATOR, CRAFTSMAN
b Weyburn, Sask, Nov 25, 37; US citizen. *Study:* Univ BC, BEd, MEd; Stanford Univ, PhD. *Comn:* logo, Chamber Mus Plus Southwest, Tucson, 2006. *Exhib:* Artists Equity Salute to the Bicentennial, Calif Mus Sci & Indust, 80; On the Face of It: 23 Los Angeles Artists, Calif State Univ, Dominguez Hills, 86. *Pos:* Dir, Getty Improving Visual Arts Educ Proj, Los Angeles, 82-92. *Teaching:* Prof art, Univ Ariz, 82-02, prof emeritus. *Awards:* Art Educ Year, Nat Art Educ Asn, 88; Purchard Award, Greater Oro Valley Arts Coun, 2006. *Mem:* Distinguished Fel Nat Art Educ Asn. *Media:* Giglee prints. *Res:* Art curriculum and staff development in public schools. *Publ:* Auth, Discipline based art education: Approaching art as a subject of study, Studies in Art Educ, 84; Structure for DBAE, Studies in Art Educ, 87; Developments in Discipline Based Art Education (DBAE) Studies in Art Education, 93; Art as a Basic: The Reformation in Art Education, Phi Delta Kappa, 97. *Mailing Add:* 1240 W San Lucas Dr Tucson AZ 85704

GREEVES, R V (RICHARD VERNON)
SCULPTOR
b St Louis, Mo, Feb 24, 35. *Work:* Nat Cowboy Hall of Fame, Oklahoma City; Genesee Country Mus, Rochester, NY; Indianapolis Art Mus, Ind; Liberty Hall, Nat Trust Found, Elizabeth, NJ. *Comn:* Story Teller (bronze sculpture), Sheridan Publ Libr, Wyo, 77; The Cock (bronze sculpture), Bartlesville Civic Ctr, Okla, 82; The Unknown (bronze monument), Whitney Gallery of Western Art, Cody, Wyo, 84. *Exhib:* One-man shows, Wyo State Art Mus, Cheyenne, 71, Kennedy Galleries, NY, 73, Barclays Int Bank, Chicago, Ill, 76, Wyo State Capitol Bldg, Cheyenne, 82 & Nicolaysen Art Mus, Casper, Wyo, 82-83; Nat Acad Western Art Show, Nat Cowboy Hall of Fame, 75-90; Peking Exhib Am Western Art, Beijing Exhib Palace, China, 81; 3M Western Art Show, Art Ctr Minn, St Paul, 83-84; Masters of the Am West, 96-2005. *Collection Arranged:* Sheepeaters of The Yellowstone, The Autry Mus Western Heritage, Los Angeles; Washakie, Chief of the Shoshone, Buffalo Bill Historical Center, Cody, Wyo, Crazy Horse, Buffalo Historical Center; Bird Woman, Autry Mus Western Heritage. *Pos:* Mem arts ctr adv comt, Cent Wyo Col, Riverton, 85-86. *Teaching:* Instr, Scottsdale Artists School. *Awards:* Gold Medal, 76 & 79 & Prix de West, 77, Nat Acad Western Art, Nat Cowboy Hall of Fame; James Earle Fraser Award Artistic Merit in Sculpture, Nat Cowboy Hall of Fame, 2000; Gold Medal, for sculpture, Autry Musm Los Angeles, Calif, 2004. *Bibliog:* Will Carson (auth), A Genuine Greeves, Western Horseman, 6/71; Dean Krakel II (auth), My Life's Work, Southwest Art, 7-8/75; John Running (auth), The Unknown: A Monument by R V Greeves, 86. *Mem:* Nat Acad Western Art (mem exec comt, 82). *Media:* Bronze. *Publ:* Contribr, Bronzes of the American West by Broder, Abrams, Inc, 74; Contemporary Western Artists, Southwest Art, 82; Sculpture Review, Nat Sculpture Soc, 82 & 86; Art West Mag, 83; Four Centuries of Sporting Art by Schmitt, Genesee Country Mus, 84; Leading the West: 100 Contemporary Artist's Art of the West, 98. *Dealer:* Legacy Galleries Jackson Way Scottsdale Ariz; Jackson Wyo; Settlers West Tucson Ariz. *Mailing Add:* PO Box 428 53 N Fork Rd Fort Washakie WY 82514

GREGOIRE, MATHIEU A
SCULPTOR
b New York, NY, Sept 3, 53. *Study:* Univ Chicago, 71-73; Portland State Univ, BA, 79-80. *Work:* Lannan Found, Los Angeles, Calif; City of Portland, Ore; Mus Contemp Art, San Diego; Oakland (Calif) Mus. *Comn:* Blue Granite Shift, Calif Ctr Arts, Escondido, 95; Point Loma Treatment Plant Master Plan, 96; River Shift, Regional Arts Comn, Portland, Ore, 98; Equipment Field, Denver, Colo, 2001. *Exhib:* Solo exhibs: Hood/Slot/Section, Boehm Gallery, Palomar Col, San Marcos, Calif, 87, Dietrich Jenny Gallery, San Diego, Calif, 88, Mattress Factory (with catalog), Pittsburgh, Pa, 88, Sculpture, Laguna Mus South Coast Plaza, Costa Mesa, Calif, 89, Winghouse, (with catalog), Artpark, Lewiston, NY, 89; Jan Turner Gallery, Los Angeles, 92 & Thomas Babeor Gallery, La Jolla, Calif, 94; Misplacement: Revision, Univ San Diego, 92; Madison Art Ctr, 94; Southern Exposure, San Francisco, Calif, 94; Insite 95, San Diego, Calif, 95; Stems & Tubes, Donna Beam Gallery, Univ Nev, Las Vegas, 1999. *Collection Arranged:* UCSF Mission Bay, 2001-2006. *Pos:* Consult, Stuart Collection, Univ Calif, San Diego & City of San Diego. *Teaching:* Assoc prof, Univ Nev, Las Vegas, 98-99; lectr, Univ Calif, San Diego, 2000-. *Awards:* Grant, Metro Arts Comn, 82; Tiffany Award, Louis Comfort Tiffany Found, 89; Nat Endowment Art, 88 & 90. *Bibliog:* Robert Pincus (auth), Minimalist sculptor furnishes Art that mimics furniture, San Diego Union, 3/16/89; Victoria Reed (auth), Gregoire Worth a Deeper Look, Los Angeles Times, 3/92; Leah Ollman (auth), Report From San Diego, Art in Am, 97; Making a Point, Kristin Palm (auth), Metropolis, Aug/Sept 2001; Special Team, Robert Pincus (auth), San Diego Union, June 25, 2001. *Media:* Mixed Media. *Mailing Add:* 3629 Arnold Ave San Diego CA 92104

GREGOR, HAROLD LAURENCE
PAINTER, EDUCATOR
b Detroit, Mich, Sept 10, 29. *Study:* Wayne State Univ, BSEd, 51; Mich State Univ, MS(ceramics, painting), 53; Detroit Soc Arts & Crafts, 55-57, Ohio State Univ, PhD(painting, art hist), 60; and with Hoyt Sherman. *Work:* Xerox Collection, Stamford, Conn; Springfield Art Mus, Mo; Rose Art Mus, Brandeis Univ; State Ill Bldg, Chicago; Borg-Warner Collection, Chicago; Chicago Bd Trade; Chicago Art Inst; Mus Am West, Los Angeles, Calif. *Comn:* Two murals, State Ill New Main Libr, Springfield, Ill, 91; Anderson Industries, Rockford, Ill, 94; Mural, McCormick Place-West, Chicago, Ill, 97; Crown Equipment, New Brennan, OH, 2000; Mural, Central Ill Regional Airport, Bloomington, Ill, 2002; Federal Reserve Bank of Chicago, Ill, 2003; Ill Appelate Court Bldg, Springfield, Ill, 2005. *Exhib:* Solo exhibs, Nancy Lurie Gallery, 74-83, Tibor De Nagy Gallery, NY, 77-91, Richard Gray Gallery, Chicago, 83-99, traveling, 91 & 93, MB Mod Gallery, NY, 98, 2000; Land, Sky, Water, Spokane World's Fair, 74; Contemp Midwest Landscapes, Ind Mus Art, Indianapolis, 86; retrospective (with catalog), Lakeview Mus Arts & Sci, Peoria, Ill, 87-88, Rockford Art Mus (with catalog), Rockford, Ill, 93-94; Plain Pictures, Univ Iowa Mus Art, 96-97; Rediscovering the Landscape, Gerald Peters Gallery, Santa Fe, NMex, 96-97; From the Road, From the River, From the Sky, Univ galleries, Ill State Univ (with catalog), 2000; Grossmont Col, El Cajon, Calif, 2001; Gerald Peters Gallery, Santa Fe, NMex, 2001; Art Mus South Tex, Corpus Christi, 2003; Katharina Rich Perlow Gallery, NY, 2003, 2005; Gerald Peters Gallery, Dallas, Tex, 2004; Loveland Mus Art, Loveland, Colo, 2004; Retrospective: Harold Gregor's Illinois, Mitchell Mus at Cedarhurst, Mt. Vernon, Ill, 2006; Park Central Gallery, 2006; Tory Folliard Gallery, Milwaukee, Wis, 2006. *Collection Arranged:* View from Here: Heartland Painters, McClean County Art Center, Bloomington, Ill, 92. *Teaching:* Asst prof painting & art hist, San Diego State Univ, 60-63; asst prof painting, Purdue Univ, 63-66; assoc prof painting & art hist, Chapman Col, 66-70; prof painting & art hist, Ill State Univ, Normal, 70-88, distinguished prof, 88-95; distinguished prof emeritus, art, Ill State Univ. *Awards:* Nat Endowment Arts Grant, 73, 86 & 93-94; Watercolor USA Purchase Award, 84, 85 & 89; Outstanding Teacher & Researcher, Ill State Univ, 85 &

86; Lifetime Achievement Award, Nat Watercolor Hon Soc, 2006. *Bibliog:* Gerald Nordland (auth), Harold Gregor, Rockland, Ill, 93; J Driscoll & A Skolnick (auths), The Artist and the American Landscape, 98; Kevin Sharp (auth), Harold Gregor's Illinois, Cedarhurst, Mt. Vernon, Ill, 2006; and others. *Mem:* Watercolor Honor Soc. *Media:* Watercolor, Acrylic. *Interests:* literature, architecture, museums, travel. *Publ:* Coauth (with K Gregor), Discovering a lost technique, 7/87 & The techniques of a flatscape, 12/86, The Artists Mag. *Dealer:* Richard Gray Gallery 875 N Michigan Suite 2503 Chicago IL 60611; Gerald Peters Gallery 1011 Paseo de Peralta Santa Fe NM 87501 & Dallas, TX; Katharina Perlow Gallery, 41 E 57th St, New York, NY, 10022; Tory Folliard Gallery 221 N Milwaukee Ave Milwaukee Wis. *Mailing Add:* 107 W Market St Bloomington IL 61701

GREGORIAN, VARTAN
PATRON
b Tabriz, Iran, Apr 8, 34. *Study:* Col Armenian, 55; Stanford Univ, BA, 58, PhD, 64; Phi Beta Kappa. *Hon Degrees:* Numerous hon degrees from US cols & univs, 83-2003. *Pos:* Pres, NY Pub Libr, 81-89; chmn bd, vis Grad Sch & Univ Ctr, City Univ NY, 84-90; bd dir, Aaron Diamond Found, 90-97, Brookings Inst, 94-97, Inst for Int Educ, 89-95, Int League of Human Rights, 84-97, Inst for Advanced Study, 87-, J. Paul Getty Trust, 88-2000, Aga Khan Univ, 95-2000, Human Rights Watch, 96-; bd trustees, Mus Modern Art, 94-, Providence Journal, 98-, Cell Therapeutics, Inc, 2001-, Nat Constitution Ctr, 2002-, Qatar Found, 2003-; pres, Carnegie Corp, New York City, 97-. *Teaching:* Tarzian prof, Armenian & Caucasian hist Univ Pa, Philadelphia, 72-80; dean, Univ Pa (Fac Arts & Scis), 74-78, provost, 78-80; prof, New Sch Social Res, 84-89; prof, Hist & Near Eastern studies NY Univ, 84-89; pres, prof Hist Brown Univ, Providence, 89-97. *Awards:* Gold Medal Honor, City & Province of Vienna, Austria, 76; Distinguished Serv to Pub Educ Award, NY Acad Pub Educ, 98; Nat Humanities Medal, Pres William J Clinton, 98, Eleanor Roosevelt Val-Kill Award, Eleanor Roosevelt Ctr, 99. *Mem:* Am Philosophical Soc (grantee, 65, 66); Asn Advancement Slavic Studies (prog chmn, Western Slavic Conf, 67); Am Hist Asn (prog chmn, 72); Int Fedn Libr Asn (co-chmn, prog comt, 85); Fel Acad Arts Scis; Am Antiquarian Soc; Coun Foreign Relations; Mid-East Studies Asn. *Publ:* Auth, The Emergence of Modern Afghanistan, 1880-1946, 69, The Road to Home: My Life and Times, 2003, Islam: A Mosaic, Not a Monolith, 2003. *Mailing Add:* Carnegie Corp Office of the Pres 437 Madison Ave Fl 27 New York NY 10022-7001

GREGOROPOULOS, JOHN
PAINTER
b Athens, Greece, Dec 16, 21; US citizen. *Study:* In Athens; Univ Conn, BA. *Work:* Minn Mus Art, St Paul; Ball State Found, Muncie, Ind; Slater Mus, Norwich, Conn; De Cordova Mus, Lincoln, Mass; Berkshire Mus, Pittsfield, Mass. *Exhib:* Whitney Mus Am Art Ann, 54 & Art USA, NY, 58; Pan Helleml Salon, Athens, 57-63; 1st Biennale Christlicher Kunst Gegenwart, Salzburg, 58; Drawings USA, Minn Mus Art, 71; Retrospective, William Benton Mus, 90 & Drawings, Titanium, Athens, Greece, 98. *Teaching:* Prof emer, Univ Conn, 53-84. *Awards:* Small Drawings & Sculpture Purchase Award, Ball State Teachers Col, 55; Grumbacher Award, Chautauqua Art Asn 2nd Nat, 59; Drawings USA, St Paul Art Ctr, 63. *Bibliog:* F Walkey (auth), John Gregoropoulos, Art in Am, 2/55; John Gregoropoulos, Zygos, Athens, 57; Art & the new patron, WEDN-TV, 68. *Publ:* Auth, Change in art, Nea Estia, Athens, 57. *Mailing Add:* 644 Wormwood Hill Rd Storrs CT 06268

GREGORY, BRUCE
PAINTER, INSTRUCTOR
b Anadarko, Okla, June 27, 17. *Study:* Art Students League; Colorado Springs Art Ctr; and with Fernand Leger. *Comn:* Murals, UN, NY, 52 & Franklin D Roosevelt Sch, NY, 56; map murals, Civil Defense Hq, NY, 57. *Exhib:* Pa Acad Art, Philadelphia, 52; Art USA, NY, 58; Butler Art Inst Ann, 66; one-man show, Woodstock Artists Asn Presentation Show, Albany Inst, Union Coll, 69; Four Arts Soc, Palm Beach, Fla, 84, 86, 90, 91 & 98; Art League of Manatee Co, A Different Muse Invitational Exhib, 95. *Pos:* Color & design consult, Harrison & Abramovitz, NY, 52-56; prof serv contractor, Fine Arts Evan, Gen Serv Admin, 73. *Teaching:* Instr painting, Union Col, 56-57; instr painting, John Herron Art Inst, Ind, 60-61; instr painting, color & design, Ringling Sch Art, Sarasota, Fla, 61-84. *Awards:* Best of Show, Fla Artists Group, 83 & Elizabeth Morse Genius Found Award, 98; 2nd Prize, Venice Art Ctr, Calif, 95; Marcelle L Bear Mem Award, 96; Four Arts Award, Palm Beach, 98; 2nd Prize, Lee Co Alliance for the Arts, Miami, Fla, 2000. *Bibliog:* Aline Louchhien (auth), UN murals, 9/7/52 & Kathleen Teltsch (auth), US painter does UN Coats-of-Arms, 4/30/53, New York Times; Gorden Brown (auth), Bruce Gregory, Arts Mag, 66. *Mem:* Fla Artists Group. *Media:* Oil, Acrylic. *Publ:* Auth, Leger's atelier, UN murals, Col Art J, 62; contribr, New International Encyclopedia of Art, 67; cons, International Encyclopedia of Art. *Dealer:* Peter Wallace Gallery The Ctr Shops No108 5360 Gulf of Mexico Dr Longboat Key FL 34228

GREGORY, JOAN
EDUCATOR, PAINTER
b Montgomery, Ala, Apr 1, 30. *Study:* Univ Montevallo, AB, 52; Peabody Col, MA, 53, EdD, 66; Inst Allende, San Miguel Allende, Mex. *Work:* NC Nat Bank; La State Art Comn; Springs Mills, Lancaster, SC; US Park Serv, Gatlinburg, Tenn. *Exhib:* Huntington Galleries, 56-61; one-woman shows, 63 & 13th Dixie Art Ann, Montgomery Mus Fine Arts; Southeastern Painting Show, Gallery Contemp Art, Winston-Salem, NC, 71 & 79; Ann NC Artists Exhib & Traveling Show, 71-72. *Pos:* Bd dir, Assoc Artists NC, 69-71 & Southeastern Col Art Conf, 74-78; mem state assembly, Nat Art Educ Asn, 71-73. *Teaching:* Instr art, Marshall Univ, 55-61; chmn dept art, Bloomsburg State Col, 63-64; prof art, Univ NC, Greensboro, 64-90, head dept, 74-85; ret. *Awards:* Purchase Awards, Dillard Collection, Weatherspoon Gallery, Univ NC, Greensboro, 66 & Springs Art Show, Lancaster, SC, 72; Merit Award, NC/Va Art Educators, Southeastern Ctr Contemp Art, 75. *Mem:* Nat Art Educ Asn; NC Art Educ Asn (pres, 71-75); Southeastern Col Art Conf (secy-treas, 81-); Assoc Artists NC. *Media:* Collage. *Mailing Add:* 106 Mansfield Cir Greensboro NC 27455-3400

GREGORY, JOSEPH F
DIRECTOR
Study: State Univ of NY, Binghamton, PhD. *Pos:* dir, Design Arts Gallery. *Teaching:* Asst prof, art hist, dept visual studies Drexel Univ, Philadelphia. *Mailing Add:* Drexel Univ Nesbitt Coll Design Arts 33rd and Market Sts Philadelphia PA 19104

GREGORY, STAN
PAINTER
b Tallahassee, Fla, Sept 22, 48. *Study:* Fla Southern Col, BA, 70; Univ South Fla, MFA, 80. *Work:* Solomon R Guggenheim Mus, NY; Brooklyn Mus Art; Chase Manhattan Bank, NY; Herbert F Johnson Mus, Cornell Univ, Ithaca, NY; Jacksonville Art Mus, Fla. *Comn:* Mural Cityscapes, City of Tampa, Fla, 82; Roadworks (hand painted bill-board), Barnett Bank, Jacksonville, Fla, 83. *Exhib:* New Floridians, 79 & Florida Painting, 82, Jacksonville Art Mus, Fla; New Acquisitions, Herbert Johnson Mus, Ithaca, NY, 84; Two-Dimensional Key West, East Martello Mus, Fla, 85; South Fla Collection, Art Mus, Univ SFla, Tampa, 90; Efstathion Fine Art, NY, 93; group show, Nicholas-Alexander Gallery, NY, 94, Hiro Gallery, Tokyo, Japan, Western Art, 95; B Gillman Gallery, Miami, Fla, 99 & 2000; Dialectica Gallery, NY, 2000; Crossroads, 2001; Sundaizam Tagore Gallery, New York City, 2003. *Pos:* Printmaker, Palm Press, Ltd, Tampa, Fla, 80-84; dir, Fla Ctr Contemp Art, Tampa, 84-85; registr, E Nakhamikin Fine Arts, NY, 86-90; preparator, Mus Mod Art, NY. *Teaching:* Instr painting, color theory, Univ South Fla, 80-82. *Bibliog:* Charles Benbow (auth), Experiment a Rich Art Experience, St Petersburg Times, 10/21/84; Garret Henry (auth), article, Art News, 11/84; Theodore F Wolff (auth), A True Heir to the Modernist Tradition, Christian Sci Monitor, 9/8/85. *Media:* Acrylic, Oil. *Publ:* The New York Art Review, 4th Ed, Chicago, 89; Auth, New Floridians, Jacksonville Art Mus, Fla; Critics Choice, Artists Alliance, Tampa, Fla; Abstract Art from the Cigna Collection, Philadelphia, Pa; Primary Sources, Tagore Gallery, NYC, 2002. *Dealer:* Sundaram Tagore Gallery 137 Greene St New York NY 10012

GREGORY-GOODRUM, ELLNA KAY
PAINTER, PRINTMAKER
b Houston, Tex, Oct 3, 43. *Study:* Univ Okla, BFA, 65; NTex State Univ, MFA, 79. *Work:* Rockwell Int, Brown Found & Consult & Atlantic Richfield, Dallas, Tex; Ford-Renaissance Ctr, Detroit. *Exhib:* 29th Tex Watercolor Soc, McNay Art Inst, San Antonio, 78; Pastel Soc Am, Nat Arts Club, NY, 79; Watercolor Invitational, Birmingham Mus Art, Ala, 79; Nat Watercolor Soc, 85, 87 & 88; Women & Watercolor, Transco Energy Ctr, Houston, 88; Rocky Mountain Nat Water Media, Foothills Art Ctr, 86 & 88; Watercolor USA, Springfield Art Mus, 88; and others. *Teaching:* Instr art, Richland Col, 80-. *Awards:* Best Abstract Award, 79 & Mixed Media Award, Pastel Soc Am, 87; Red Sable Award, Southern Watercolor Soc, 79; Southwestern Watercolor Soc Award, 79, 83, 85 & 88; Nat Watercolor Award, Okla, 88. *Bibliog:* Articles in Park E Publ, New York, 79 & Dallas Morning News, 79. *Mem:* Col Art Asn; Pastel Soc Am; Tex Watercolor Soc; Southwestern Watercolor Soc; Nat Watercolor Soc. *Media:* Watercolor. *Publ:* Auth, Watercolor '89, Am Artist. *Mailing Add:* 7214 Lane Park Dr Dallas TX 75225-2454

GRELLE, MARTIN GLEN
PAINTER
b Clifton, Tex, Sept 17, 54. *Study:* Art Instruction Schs, 72; McLennan Community Col, 75. *Comn:* Bosque landscape, Bosque Co Mus, Clifton, Tex, 74; football mural, Cub Stadium, Clifton, Tex, 76; Bosque Autumn (painting), comn by King Olav IV of Norway, 82; mural, Trinity Lutheran Church, Clifton, Tex, 82; Misty Morning Gather (oil mural), Western Savings Asn, Gatesville, Tex, 86. *Exhib:* Am Indian & Cowboy Artists Ann, Sandmas Calif, 77-83; Western Heritage, Houston, Tex, 79, 81 & 84-85; Stamford Art Found, Tex, 79-86; Tex Art Gallery Preview, Dallas, 80-82; First Ann Student Exhib, Cowboy Artists of Am, Kerrville, Tex, 84; one-man shows, Tex Art Gallery, Dallas, Tex, 86 & 88, Overland Trail Gallery, Scottsdale, Ariz, 89, 90, 91, 92. *Awards:* Bronze Medal, Am Indian Cowboy Artists Exhib, 77; Gold Medal, Am Indian Cowboy Artists Exhib, 79; Silver Award for oil & Artist's Award, Tex Ranger Hall of Fame Show, 85. *Bibliog:* Article, Art West Mag, 1-2/83, 9-10/90; article, Southwest Art Mag, 3/86; Western Art Digest Mag, 1-2/87. *Media:* Oil, Arcylics. *Dealer:* Overland Trail Fine Art Gallery 7155 Main St Scottsdale AZ 85251. *Mailing Add:* Rte 2 Box 123 Clifton TX 76634-9617

GRENON, GREGORY
PAINTER
Study: Ctr Creative Studies, Detroit, 68-70; Wayne State Univ, 69-72. *Work:* Seattle Art Mus, Wash; Portland Art Mus, Ore; Ore Arts Comn; Metrop Arts Comn, Portland, Ore; Seattle Arts Comn. *Exhib:* Seattle Art Mus, 84 & 87; solo shows, Seattle Art Mus, 84, Jamison/Thomas Gallery, Portland, Ore, 94, Laura Russo Gallery, Portland, Ore, 95, 96 & 97, William Traver Gallery, Seattle, 95, 96 & 98, Anne Reed Gallery, Ketchum, Idaho, 96 & 98 & Paris Gibson Sq Mus, Great Falls, Mont, 98, Heller Gallery, NY, 2002, Extreme Company, William Traver Gallery, Seattle, Wash, 2003; Fences Project, One Yr Later, Froelick Adelhart Gallery, Portland, 96; The Tool Show, PICA, Portland, 96; Husbands & Wives, Raleigh Gallery, Boca Raton, Fla, 96; Introduction, Sandy Carson Gallery, Denver, 97; The Mane Event, Ann Reed Gallery, Ketchum, Idaho, 96; For/By/About Women, Morgan Mendelson Contemp Glass Gallery, Pittsburgh, Pa, 97; Summer Group Show, Laura Russo Gallery, Portland, Ore, 97; Prints and Drawings, Laura Russo Gallery, Portland, Ore, 98; Back in Belltown, William Traver Gallery, Seattle, Wash, 98; group exhibs, Glass Am, Red White, and

Blue, Heller Gallery, NY, 2002, Summer Group Show, Laura Russo Gallery, Portland, Ore, 2002, NW Notables, Mirror Pond Gallery, Bend, Ore, 2002. *Awards:* Individual Fel Award, Ore Arts Comn, 84-85; Fel Grant, Nat Endowment Arts, 92; AirTouch Cellular Comn Prints, 98; Dahlia, Gordon and Vivian Gilkey Ctr for the Print, Patron Print, Portland Art Mus, Ore, 99. *Bibliog:* D Eric Bookhardt (auth), Some alarming women, New Orleans Wkly Gambit, 1/25/94; Terrington Calas (auth), Gregory Grenon, New Orleans Art Rev, 1-2/94; Chris Waddington (auth), A master of finesse, a connoisseur of expression, Lagniappe, New Orleans, 1/21/94. *Dealer:* William Traver Gallery 110 Union St 2nd Floor Seattle WA 98101. *Mailing Add:* 9707 NW Roseway Ave Portland OR 97231

GRESSER, SEYMOUR GERALD
SCULPTOR, WRITER
b Baltimore, Md, Sept 26, 26. *Study:* Maryland Univ, BS, 46, MA 72; Inst Contemp Art, 48-50; special study with William Taylor, 49-52. *Work:* St John the Divine Gallery, NY; Fairfield Col, Hartford, Conn; Pierson Col (Yale Univ) New Haven, Conn; New Britian Mus Am Art, Conn; Klutznick Nat Jewish Mus, Catholic Univ, Washington, DC. *Exhib:* Religious Art, Sweetbriar Col, Va, 85; Blood Rites/Birth Rites, Duke Univ, Durham, NC, 86; New Sculptures, Montpelier Art Mus, Laurel, Md, 88; Wesley Theology Seminary, Washington, DC, 92; Gomez Gallery, Baltimore, 95; and others. *Pos:* Consultant/Research. *Teaching:* Instr sculpture, Antioch Col (Columbia Campus) 79-81; residency, Colgate Univ, Hamilton, NY, 89, Thomas Jefferson Sch, Frederick, Md, 90. *Media:* Stone, wood. *Specialty:* Contemporeties. *Interests:* China/Poetry. *Publ:* auth, Stone, Wood & Words, Kunming Press, Kunming, PRC, 2006. *Dealer:* Gallery Ch'i, Brooklyn, NY. *Mailing Add:* 1015 Ruatan St Silver Spring MD 20903

GREY, ALEX V
PAINTER, SCULPTOR
b Columbus, Ohio, Nov 29, 53. *Study:* Columbus Col Art & Design, 71-73; Boston Mus Sch, 74-75. *Work:* Mus Contemp Art-San Diego, La Jolla, Calif; Brooklyn Mus Fine Arts, NY; Krannert Art Mus, Champaign, Ill; Islip Art Mus, NY. *Comn:* Cosmic Christ: Joe Firmage. *Exhib:* Disarming Images, Univ Calif Mus Art, Santa Barbara, 85; Choices, New Mus, NY, 86; Revelations, Aspen Art Mus, Colo, 89; Sacred Mirrors, Univ Colo Mus, Boulder, 90; solo exhib, Univ Galleries, Ill State Univ, Normal, 93; Mus Contemp Art, San Diego, 99; Solway/Jones Gallery, Los Angeles, 2001; Feature Inc, NY, 2002; Tibet House, NY, 2002. *Teaching:* Prof anat of artists, NY Univ, 87-98; prof visionary art, Omega Inst, 94-. *Awards:* Fel in Sculpture, Mass Coun for Arts, 84 & NY Found for Arts, 86. *Bibliog:* Lewis MacAdams (auth), It started out with death, High Performance, spring 82; Carlo McCormick (auth), Through Darkness to Light, Sacred Mirrors/Inner Traditions, 90; John Strausbough (auth), X-ray visions, New York Press, 4/7/92; Alex Grey (auth), Transfigurations, Inner Traditions, 2001. *Mem:* Integral Inst Art. *Media:* Oil, Acrylic; Bronze. *Publ:* Coauth, Art in Transformation: Interview with artist Alex Grey, New Frontier Mag, 89; auth, Sacred Mirrors, Inner Traditions, 90; The Life and Art of Alex and Allyson Grey, Tantra Mag, 92; Visions of Body and Soul, Caduceus Mag, 92; The Mission of Art, Shambhala, 98. *Dealer:* Feature Inc 530 W 25th St New York NY 10001. *Mailing Add:* 725 Union St Brooklyn NY 11215

GRIBIN, LIZ
PAINTER, PRINTMAKER
b London, Eng, Mar 3, 34; US citizen. *Study:* Art Students League; Mus Mod Art; Boston Univ, BFA, 56; studied with David Aronson, Paul Wood & Patrick Ireland. *Work:* Emily Lowe Gallery, Hofstra Univ; Manhattan Bowery Corp Collection, NY; and numerous pvt collections. *Comn:* portrait, commn by Beverly Holmes, 2000. *Exhib:* Solo shows, Art Upstairs, East Willison, NY, 89, Gallery Emanuel, Great Neck, NY, 90, 91 & 94, Nassau Co Mus Art, Roslyn, NY, 94, Sholom Gallery, Cherry Hill, NJ, 95, Bridgehampton Cafe, NY, 97 & 98 & Port Wash Libr, NY, 97; Guild Hall Mus, E Hampton, NY, 88-90 & Elaine Benson Gallery, Bridgehampton, NY, 89; Kirkpatrick Art Ctr, Oklahoma City, Okla, 90; 92nd & 93rd Ann Mem Exhib, Nat Arts Club, 90-91; 35th & 37th Ann Exhib, Heckscher Mus, 90 & 92; 159th Ann Exhib, Nat Acad Design; Nat Arts Club, NY, 90-97; Guild Hall, East Hampton, NY, 95-2003; Arlene Bujese Gallery, East Hampton, NY, 95-97; Ashawagh Hall, East Hampton, NY, 97 & 98; Nan Mulford Gallery, Rockport, Maine, 97-2003; Millennium Gallery, East Hampton, NY, 98; Goat Alley Gallery, Sag Harbor, NY, 98; Artist's Choice, BJ Spoke Gallery, Huntington, NY, 98; Club Colette, Southampton, NY, 2000; Gayle Willson Gallery, Southampton, NY, featured artist, 2002. *Pos:* Dir, Gallery Emanuel, Great Neck, NY, 90-2000-. *Teaching:* Lectr, Guild Hall, Long Island Art Leagues & Nassau Co Fine Arts Ctr, currently; Studio Classes, Bridgehampton, NY; Guest Lectr, Boston Univ, Col Fine Art. *Awards:* Various Awards, Audubon Artists, 85, 89, 93, 94 & 95; Pall Corp Award, Heckscher Mus Art Ann, 96; Bruce Stevenson Award, Nat Arts Club, 98th Ann Show, 96 & 2000; US Libr Cong Living Legend, 2000; Nat Arts Club Presidents Award, 2003; and others. *Bibliog:* Feature article, Art & Antiques Mag, 1/2001, Emerging Artists Portfolio, 2001, Southampton Press & Bostonia Mag, 2003; artist spotlight, Originals (TV show). *Mem:* Nat Asn Women Artists; Audubon Artists; Nat Arts Club; Artists Alliance East Hampton. *Media:* Acrylic, Oil; Etching. *Dealer:* Nan Mulford Gallery Rockland ME; Louis Arnow Gallery San Francisco & Sausalito Calif; Gayle Wilson Gallery Southampton NY; Newbury Fine Arts Boston Mass. *Mailing Add:* PO Box 4 Bridgehampton NY 11932

GRIEDER, TERENCE
HISTORIAN
b Cedar Rapids, Iowa, Sept 2, 31. *Study:* Univ Colo, BA, 53; Univ Wis, MS(appl art), 56; Univ Pa, MA(art hist), 60, PhD(art hist), 61. *Teaching:* Instr art, Univ Wis, Milwaukee, 56-57 & Conn Col, New London, 60-61; from asst prof to prof art, Univ Tex, Austin, 61-00, David Bruton Centennial prof art history emeritus, dept art and art history. *Awards:* US Govt Smith-Mundt Fel to Guatemala, 59-60; Am Coun Learned Soc Foreign Area Fel, 65-67. *Mem:* Col Art Asn; Soc Am Archaeol. *Res:* Archaeological study of the history of pre-Columbian art, emphasizing the Andean highlands of Peru. *Publ:* Coauth, Art of Latin America Since Independence, 66; auth, Art & Archaeology of Pashash, 78; Origins of Pre-Columbian Art, 82; La Galgada, Peru: A Preceramic Culture in Transition, 88; Artist and Audience, rev ed 96. *Mailing Add:* 502 W Live Oak St Austin TX 78704

GRIEFEN, JOHN ADAMS
PAINTER, PRINTMAKER
b Worcester, Mass, Nov 24, 42. *Study:* Williams Col, BA, 66; Art Inst Chicago; Bennington Col; Hunter Col, 66-68. *Work:* Hirshhorn Mus & Sculpture Garden; Boston Mus Fine Arts; Whitney Mus Am Art & Mus Mod Art, NY; Brooklyn Mus; Metrop Mus Art, NY. *Comn:* Painting, Gerald Hines Interest, Framingham, Mass. *Exhib:* Lyrical Abstraction, Whiney Mus Am Art, NY, 71; NS Print Show, Mus Mod Art, NY, 74; Recent Aquisitions, Hirshhorn Mus & Sculpture Garden, Washington, 77; Recent Aquisitions Contemp Art, Boston Mus Fine Arts, 77; solo exhibs, Martha Jackson Gallery, NY, Frank Walters Gallery, Sidney, Australia, 79, Moos Gallery, Toronto, Can, 81, Salander O' Reilly Galleries, 81-82 & 84-85, Edmonton Art Gallery, Can, 84 & Swift Current Nat Mus, Can, 93; and others. *Teaching:* Instr painting, Bennington Col, 67-68; pvt lessons, NY, 72-; instr sculpture, Great Neck Pub Schs, NY, 76-; lectr, NY Univ, Ramapo Col, NJ, currently. *Awards:* Ester Forbes Award, Bancroft Sch, Worchester, Mass, 96. *Bibliog:* Larry Aldrich (auth), Lyrical Abstraction, Whitney Mus Am Art, 70; William Zimmer (auth), John Griefen, 76 & Earl Powell (auth), John Griefen, 78, Arts Mag; plus others. *Media:* Acrylics; Drypoint. *Publ:* Auth, Appreciating art, Update Mag, 85. *Dealer:* Salander-O'Reilly Galleries Inc 20 E 79th St New York NY 10021. *Mailing Add:* 57 Laight St New York NY 10013

GRIEGER, DONALD L
PAINTER
b Niles, Mich, Jan 2, 34. *Study:* Univ Mich, BS, 1957; Air Force Inst Tech, MS, 1966. *Work:* US Coast Guard Collection; Nat Warplane Mus, Elmira, NY; Genesee Community Col, Batavia, NY. *Exhib:* Light on the Landscape, Bryan Mem Gallery, Jeffersonville, Vt, 1998-2006; 62nd Grand Nat Exhib, Salmagundi Club, NY, 1999; 67th & 68th Grand Nat Exhib, Salmagundi Club, NY, 2004-05. *Awards:* Mary Fitch award, Salmagundi Spring Auction, 2004; Salmagundi Club award, 67th Grand Nat Exhib, 2004; Antonio Cirino Mem award, Ann Combined Salmagundi Club, 2005; Martin Hannon Mem Award, Salmagundi Ann Thumb-Box Exhib, 2005; Frank Van Steen Mem Award, Hudson Valley Art Asn 75th Ann Exhib, 2006. *Bibliog:* Charles Movalli (auth), A Conversation with Don Grieger, Am Artist, 1992. *Mem:* Salmagundi Club, NY; Am Artists Prof League; North Shore Arts Asn; Rochester Art Club; Oil Painters of Am. *Media:* Acrylic, Oil. *Publ:* Louise Grieger (auth), 50 Miles on the Erie Canal, Am Artist, 1994. *Mailing Add:* 5024 Terry Hills Dr Batavia NY 14020

GRIER, MARGOT EDMANDS
LIBRARIAN, ADMINISTRATOR
b Washington, DC, May 15, 46. *Study:* Old Dominion Univ, with Parker Lesley, BA(magna cum laude), 71; Univ Md, MLS, 72. *Pos:* Serials librn, Nat Gallery Art, Washington, DC, 73-; automation coordr, Nat Gallery Art, Washington, DC, 87-90; adminr, Educ Div Nat Gallery Art, Washington, DC, 90-. *Awards:* Hermitage Found Award, Norfolk, Va, 69 & 70. *Mem:* Art Libraries Soc North Am; Wasington Art Libr Resources Comt; Embroiderers' Guild Am. *Res:* Integrated museum online access systems. *Interests:* 20th century Mexican; contemporary; small press art magazines, textile history. *Publ:* Auth, Old St Paul's, Kent Co, Md, St Pauls Episcopal Church, 71; contribr, ARLIS/NA Newsletter, Art Libr Soc, 79-80; co-ed, Art Serials Union List, 81; contribr, Art Doc, 83-; ed, National Gallery of Art Serials, Nat Gallery Art, 83; contribr auth, Gemini GEL Art and Collaboration, Ruth Fine, Nat Gallery Art & New York, Abbeville Press, 84. *Mailing Add:* 2718 Ontario Rd Washington DC 20009-2154

GRIESEDIECK, ELLEN
MURALIST
b Jan 26, 48. *Study:* Univ Colo, BFA, 70. *Comn:* Four paintings, Gen Motors, NY, 80; five paintings, Times Mirror Publ, NY, 82; mural, Columbia-Presby Hosp, 96; Wall of America, public art exhbit tribute to builders of Am; designer of Newman's Own labels; Wall of Am, Mural in Progress, 99-2005. *Exhib:* Royal Orleans, New Orleans, 78; Spectrum Olympics, Spectrum Gallery, NY, 79; Seagram's Special Exhib, NY, 80; solo exhibs, Gallery Henoch, NY, 85, 89, Tour de France, Galerie de Poche, Paris, 90 & Empire Arts, Grand Forks NDak, 98. *Bibliog:* Richard Martin (auth), Ellen Griesedieck, Arts Mag, 85; Artist's vision of working America, Labors Heritage Quart, 11/96. *Media:* Aliminum, Fiberglass. *Publ:* Illusr, Summer, Addison/Wesley, 90. *Dealer:* Marcel Fleiss Galerie de Poche 3 Rue Bonaparte Paris France 75006; Gallery Henoch New York NY. *Mailing Add:* 173 Low Rd Sharon CT 06069

GRIFFIN, CHRIS A
SCULPTOR
b Boston, Mass. *Study:* Col of New Rochelle, NY, BFA, 72; Columbia Univ, MA, 73. *Work:* Pictogram Gallery, New York, NY; ISCIP Mus, NY; Everson Mus, Syracuse, NY; Prudential Insurance, Newark, NJ; Phillip Morris, New York, NY; Mobil; Aramco Everson Mus; Islip Mus; Jersey City Mus. *Exhib:* Lines of Vision, Long Island Univ, NY, 89; Words & Images, Henry Street Settlement, NY, 89; Issues of Identity, Dowling Col, NY, 92; Sculptors Drawings, E Hampton Ctr Contemp Art, NY; Geometric Sculpture, Tribeca 148 Gallery, NY; solo exhib, Jersey City Mus, 97; and others. *Teaching:* Assoc prof sculpture, State Univ NY, Old Westbury, 78-. *Awards:* Sculptor Grant Award, NY State Found for Arts, 85; Artist in Residence Grant,

Experimental Glass Workshop, New York, 89. *Bibliog:* Ann Kronenburg (auth), Chris Griffin, Women Artists News, spring 85; Helen Harrison (auth), article, NY Times, 96; Barry Schwabsky (auth), article, NY Times, 97. *Media:* Mixed Media. *Mailing Add:* 230 W 105th St Apt 3D New York NY 10025

GRIFFIN, KENNETH C & ANN DIAS
COLLECTOR
b Boca Raton, Fla. *Study:* Harvard Univ, BA(econ), 89. *Pos:* With Glenwood Investment Corp, formerly; founder, pres, Chief Exec Officer Citadel Investment Group, 90-. *Awards:* Named to Top 200 Collectors, ARTnews Mag, 2004, 2006. *Mem:* Chicago Mus Contemp Art (bd trustees, currently); Chicago Pub Educ Fund, (bd dir, 2003-); Chicago Pub Libr Found; Art Inst Chicago (bd trustees, currently). *Collection:* Impressionism & Post-impressionism Art. *Mailing Add:* Citadel Investment Group LLC 131 S Dearborn St Chicago IL 60603

GRIFFIN, SALLIE THOMPSON
PAINTER, PHOTOGRAPHER
b Columbus Co, NC, Sept 2, 40. *Study:* St Mary's Jr Col, AA, 60; Sch Radiological Technol, Duke Univ, AS, 62 & Sch Nuclear Med, 63; Anson Tech Col, 75-80; Cent Piedmont Community Col, NC, 75-80; Wingate Univ, 76-91 & 97; Studies in Europe, New York & Washington DC. *Work:* Wingate Univ, NC; The Bank of Am, First Union Nat Bank, Charlotte, NC; Carolina Bone and Joint, Union Co Libr, United Carolina Bank (BB&T), Union Co Arts Council, Monroe, NC; pvt collection of John Coffey, Curator of NC Mus Art, S Piedmont Community Col E Campus, Polkton, NC; Davidson Col, NC. *Comn:* A Valentine Tribute to St Mary's (collage), St Mary's Sch, Raleigh, NC, 92; Women Like a Flower (watercolor painting), Arts & Heritage Festival, Wadesboro, NC; watercolor painting, Union Regional Med Ctr, 95; Our Hearts (paintings), Am Heart Asn of NC, 98-2006. *Exhib:* One-woman shows, Dove Pottery and Gallery, Monroe, NC, 90, Stanley Co Libr, Albemarle, NC, 92, Artisan Ctr, Kannapolis, NC, 92 & Union Co Arts Coun, 95; Come See Me Show, Mus York Co, Rock Hill, SC, 97; Shelby Nat Show No 23, Shelby Tech Col, NC, 97; Hang-Up-Put-Down Show, Greenhill Gallery, Greensboro, NC, 98; Art on Paper Show, Weatherspoon Gallery, UNC Greensboro, NC, 99; 27th, 28th & 30th Competition for NC Artists, The Fayetteville Mus Art, NC, 99, 2000, 2002; Waccamaw Art Guild Show, Burroughs and Chapin Art Mus, Springmaid Beach, SC, 99; one woman retrospective, Marshville Libr Gallery, 2000; one-woman show, Wingate Univ, 1980; Am Heart Asn, NC, 1998-2006; The Fayetteville Mus Art Competition for NC Artists, 99-2000, 2003 & 2005; Stanly County Invitational, 2005, NC; Union County Libr Show, 2006, NC. *Pos:* Founder & dir, Libr Gallery, Marshville Br Union Co Libr, NC, 98-2006. *Awards:* Blooming Arts Festival Union County's Finest Award, Monroe, NC, 81 & Best of Show, 94, chmn's award, 2001; many others. *Bibliog:* Lex Youngman (auth), 20 Artists of Union County North Carolina; Anna Griffin (auth), The Designer Scrapbook, Sterling & Chapelle, NY. *Mem:* Watercolor Soc NC, Ala & Conn; life mem Union Co Art League (pres, 79 & 2000-2001); Int Soc Experimental Artists; Union Co Art Coun of NC (bd mem, 80-83); Guild Charlotte Artists. *Media:* Acrylic, Watercolor. *Interests:* art education. *Dealer:* Tidwell Art Gallery 323 King St Charleston SC 29401; Hodges Taylor Gallery 401 N Tryon St Charlotte NC 28202. *Mailing Add:* PO Box 206 Marshville NC 28103-0206

GRIFFITH, DENNISON W
EDUCATOR, ADMINSTRATOR, ARTIST
b Delaware, Ohio. *Study:* Ohio Wesleyan Univ, BFA; Ohio State Univ, MFA. *Exhib:* DePauw Univ, 1998; Butler Inst of Am Art, 1998; Hammond Harkins Gallery, 2003, 2005; Studio Art Ctr Int, Florence, Italy, 2006. *Pos:* Artists prog coordr, Ohio Arts Coun, 78-83; exec dir, Ohio Found Arts; deputy dir, Columbus Mus Arts, 88-98; pres, Columbus Coll Art & Design, 98. *Teaching:* prof, painting 98-. *Awards:* Artist fel, Ohio Arts Coun, 1988, 1990, NEA/Arts Midwest, 1991, Greater Cols Arts Coun, 1996. *Mem:* Assoc Ind. Coll Art & Design; Greater Columbus CofC (co-chmn, creative serv comt, bd mem); Rose Art Mus (bd dirs). *Media:* Acrylic, Oil. *Dealer:* Hammond Harkins Gallery 2261 E Main St Columbus OH 43209. *Mailing Add:* Off of Pres Columbus Coll Art & Design 107 N Ninth St Columbus OH 43215

GRIFFITH, ROBERTA
CERAMIST, PAINTER
b Hillsdale, Mich, May 14, 1937. *Study:* Chouinard Art Inst, BFA, 60; Southern Ill Univ, Carbondale, MFA, 62; Massana Sch, Barcelona, Spain with Llorens Artigas, 62-64; permanent cert in art K-12, NY State U. *Work:* Everson Mus Art, Syracuse, NY; Mus Ceramics, Barcelona, Spain; Roberson Ctr Arts & Sci, Binghamton, NY; Gallery State Univ New York, Albany, NY; Inst de Estudios Norte-Americanos & Escuela Massana, Barcelona, Spain; Yager Mus, Hartwick Col, Oneonta, NY; Escuela Massana, Barcelona, Spain; N Am Studies Center, Barcelona, Spain; pvt collections in the US, Spain, Mex, Ger, Eng & Japan. *Exhib:* Ceramic Invitational, Stockholm, Sweden, 72; solo exhibs, Mus Ceramics, Barcelona, Spain, 81 & 99, Munson-Williams Proctor Inst, Sch Art Gallery, Utica, NY, 82 & 88, Ctr Galleries, Albany, NY, 84, Endicott Col Gallery, Beverly, Mass, 85, Foreman Gallery, Hartwick Col, Oneonta, NY, 89, Warren Gallery, Yager Mus, Hartwick Col, Oneonta, NY & Winfisky Gallery, Salem State Col, Mass, 92, Ford Gallery, Eastern Mich Univ, 99, Ctr Galleries, Albany, 2001, The Yager Mus, 2003; Fundacion Miro, Barcelona, Spain, 81, 82 & 84; Channel 13 Television Art Auction, NY, 83 & 84; 41st Ceramic Int, Mus Ceramics, Faenza, Italy, 83; 13th Chunichi Int Exhib Ceramic Arts, Nagoya, Japan, 85; Cooperstown Nat, NY, 87, 88, 89, 90, 91 & 92; Munson-Williams Proctor Inst, Utica, NY, 88; Arlene McDaniel Galleries 7th Nat Invitational Sculpture Show, W Hartford, Conn, 89; Kutani Int Decorative Ceramics, 97; Yager Mus, Hartwick Col, 2000; Shick Gallery, Skidmore Col, 2002; Oceanside Mus Art, Calif, 2001; Univ NC Galleries, 2001; Art Educator Reshaping the Thinking of Our Community, 2005; 2nd Ann Nat Vasefinder Exhib, 2006. *Pos:* Ceramic designer, Design Technics, Stroudsburg, Pa, 65-66. *Teaching:* Arkell Hall Found Prof Art (Endowed Chair), ceramics, drawing, painting, Hartwick Col, Oneonta, NY, 66-, chmn art dept, 75-91, chmn Humanities, 88-89. *Awards:* Nat Endowment Humanities Summer Inst, Ancient Mesoamerican Civilizations, Univ Pittsburgh, 91; Bd Trustees Fac Res Grant, Hartwick Col, 94, 98, 99 & 2005; Teacher/Scholar Award, Hartwick Col, 95-96; Charles B Hunt award for Lifetime Achievements in Arts and Service to Arts Community, UCCCA, NY, 2002. *Bibliog:* Jonathan Fairbanks & Angela Fina (auths), The Best of Pottery, 96; Edmund De Waal (auth), Design Sourcebook CERAMICS, 2000; Susan Peterson (auth), Contemporary Ceramics, 2000; Tom and Jean Latka (auths), Ceramic Extruding, 2001; Richard Zakin (auth), Mastering the Craft, 90, 2001; Hua Yilong (ed), Works by Ceramic Artists from Around the World, Shanghai Fine Arts Publ, 2006. *Mem:* Nat Coun Educ Ceramic Arts; Cooperstown Art Asn; Am Crafts Coun; Artist-Craftsmen NY, Inc; Empire State Craft Alliance (bd dir, 2000-03); MOMA; Everson Mus Art. *Media:* Ceramic Sculpture, Installations, Drawing. *Res:* Pre-Columbian Art. *Interests:* travel. *Publ:* Auth & illusr, Spanish Ceramics, NCECA Newsletter, 84; NCECA Conference Turns Boston into Clay City, Crafts Report, 84; Cahokia; Ramey Incised Pottery, NCECA J, 85; Artigas and Miro, Studio Potter, 85; The Visual Arts, Up Close and Personal, 3 1/2 Plus Phi Theta Kappa Int Soc, 96-97 Ann. *Mailing Add:* 22 Medallion Dr PO Box 112 Otego NY 13825

GRIFFITHS, WILLIAM PERRY
EDUCATOR, JEWELER
b Traverse City, Mich, Sept 20, 37. *Study:* Western Mich Univ, BS, 61; Univ Wis, MFA, 68. *Work:* Mus Contemp Crafts, NY. *Comn:* Silver pendant, comn by Robert Arneson, Davis, Calif, 68; gold & silver pendants, comn by Don Reitz, Marshall, Wis, 85; silver ring, comn by Jack Youngerman, NY, 86; silver chancellor's chain, Univ Wis Ctr System, Madison, 87. *Exhib:* Objects USA (contribr, catalog), Smithsonian-World, Washington, DC, 69; Wisconsin Directions, 75 & All that Glitters: Personal Ornaments, 86, Milwaukee Art Mus, Wis. *Pos:* working as jeweler, craftman, commissions by appointment, currently. *Teaching:* Assoc prof art, Univ Wis Ctr, Fond du Lac, 68-2002, retired. *Media:* Silver & Gold, Precious Stones. *Interests:* Zuni Indians, In Zuni NM. *Mailing Add:* 67 N Lincoln Ave Fond du Lac WI 54935

GRIGORIADIS, MARY
PAINTER
b Jersey City, NJ, June 23, 42. *Study:* Barnard Col, BA, 63; Columbia Univ, MA, 65. *Work:* Guild Hall Mus East Hampton, NY; First Nat Bank Chicago; Nat Mus Am Art & Nat Mus Women Arts, Washington, DC; Va Mus Fine Art, Richmond; Allen Mem Art Mus, Oberlin, Ohio; Parrish Art Mus, Southampton, NY; Vorres Mus, Athens, Ga; and others. *Exhib:* One-woman shows, AIR Gallery, NY, 72, 75, 78, 82, 84, 86 & 89, OK Harris Gallery, NY, 76, Gallery K, Washington, DC, 78, Helen Shlien Gallery, Boston, 78, 81 & 83 & Barnard Col, 88; Biennial Contemp Am Art, Whitney Mus Am Art, 73; Small Works, Albright-Knox Mus Art, 76-77; Pattern Painting, PSI, NY, 77; The Brooklyn Mus, 77; Islamic Allusions, Alternative Mus, NY, 80; Aldrich Mus Contemp Art, Conn, 81; Burning in Hell, Franklin Furnace, NY; Va Mus Fine Art, 90; Establishing the Legacy: Renaissance to Modernism, Nat Mus Women Art, Washington, DC, 95; 25 Yrs of Feminism, 25 Yrs of Women's Art, Rutgers Univ, NJ, 96; Four By Four, 55 Mercer Gallery, NY, 98; Modern Odysseys, Queens Mus Art, NY, 99 & State Mus Contemp Art, Thessaloniki, Greece, 2000; "Personal and Political", Guild Hall Mus, East Hampton, NY, 2002; Art in Embassies, US Embassies, Cape Town and Pretoria, 2003; Modern and Contemp Art: Selections Permanent Collection, Nat Mus Women in the Arts, Washington, DC, 2004; Recent Acquisitions: Framing the Collection, Parrish Art Mus, Southampton, NY, 2004; Vistas & Visions, Nat Mus Women in the Arts, Wash, DC 2006; and others. *Pos:* Founding mem, AIR Gallery, exec comt, 83-86; adv bd AIR Gallery, 2001-06. *Awards:* NY Found for Arts, 89. *Bibliog:* Hayden Herrera, reviews, Art in Am, 3-4/77; Joan Marter (auth), Mary Grigoriadis, Arts Mag, 11/84; C Robins (auth), The Pluralist Era, 1968-1981, Harper & Row, New York, 84. *Media:* Oil, Pastel. *Mailing Add:* 382 Central Park W New York NY 10025

GRIGSBY, JEFFERSON EUGENE, JR
EDUCATOR, PAINTER
b Greensboro, NC, Oct 17, 18. *Study:* Morehouse Col, with Hale Woodruff & Nancy Prophet, BA, 38; Am Artists Sch, with M Hebald, H Harrari & J Groth, 39; Ohio State Univ, with Prof Hopkins & R Fanning, MA, 40; Ecole Beaux Arts, Marseilles, 45; NY Univ, PhD, 63; Philadelphia Col Art, Hon DFA, 65. *Work:* Tex Southern Univ, Houston; Mint Mus, Charlotte, NC; Nat Mus Ghana, Cape Castle; Richmond Pub Schs, Va; Ariz State Univ; Glendale Community Col; Valley Nat Bank; Bank Am; Milwaukee Art Mus. *Exhib:* Am Negro Expos, Tanner Art Galleries, Chicago, 40; Baltimore Mus, 40; Ariz Ann, Phoenix Mus, 64; one-man show, Centennial Celebration, Morehouse Col, 67; Dimensions in Black, La Jolla Mus, Calif, 70; Dallas City Hall, 81; Ariz State Univ, 86; Benedict Col, 87; Retrospect Exhib Phoenix Art Mus, 2000-2001; Hub Gallery, Penn State Univ Feb-March, 2005. *Pos:* Head dept art, Carver High Sch, 46-54 & Phoenix Union High Sch, Ariz, 54-66. *Teaching:* Artist-in-residence, Johnson C Smith Univ, 40-41; prof art educ & drawing, Ariz State Univ, 66-88, distinguished res scholar, 82-83, prof emer, 88. *Awards:* Medallion of Merit, Nat Gallery Art, 66; Educator of the Yr, Nat Art Educ Asn, 88 & Retired Educator of the Yr, 98; Ariz Gov Award, 89. *Mem:* Fel Nat Art Educ Asn (vpres, 72-74); Black Orgn Arts; Ariz Artists Guild; Consortium of Black Orgns for the Arts; Nat Conf Artists; Artists of the Black Community, Ariz; Nat Found for the Arts (visual arts panel, 81-84); NAEA Comt on Minority Concerns. *Media:* Acrylic, Serigraph. *Res:* African art, its history, materials used and style. *Publ:* Auth, Ba Kuba art, In: Africa Seen by American Negroes, 58; Encounters (exhib catalog), J C Smith Univ Exhib, 68; Art & Ethnics, William C Brown Co; ed, Sch Arts Mag, 10/79. *Mailing Add:* Dept Art Ariz State Univ 1117 N 9th St Phoenix AZ 85006-2734

GRILLO, ESTHER ANGELA
SCULPTOR, PRINTMAKER
b Rome, Italy, Jan 28, 1954; US citizen. *Study:* Queens Col, NY, study with Tom Doyle, 72-74; Brooklyn Col, BA(cum laude), 77, study with Terris & D'Archangelo & MFA, 81, study with Bontecou, Samuels & Mehlmen. *Work:* Brooklyn Col Print Collection, NY; Palmer Mus, Pa State Univ. *Comn:* Wall relief (38'), MTA/Creative Stations. *Exhib:* A Gender Show, Group Material, NY, 81; The Wild Art Show, PS 1, NY, 82; Earth Transformed by Fire, Rotunda Gallery, NY, 84; Beginnings & Endings, Mus Borough Brooklyn, NY, 84; Long Island Artists, Islip Art Mus, East Islip, NY, 85; Holocaust Memorial Art Exhib, Queensborough Community Col, NY, 85; Masters of War, Ammo Gallery, Brooklyn, NY, 85; Taking Liberties: Transcendence and Transgression, Pace Univ Art Gallery, Civic Ctr Campus, Pace Plaza, NY, 86; solo exhibs, Narrative Sculpture: Collage and Prints, 14 Sculptors Gallery, NY, 86, Meltdown, Palmer Mus, Pa State Univ, 88 & Esther A Grillo: Installation, Sculpture, Collage, Prints, 14 Sculptors Gallery, Soho, NY, 88; Queens Mus Juried Ann, Queens, NY, 87; and others. *Awards:* Exhibition Award, B J Spoke Gallery, New York, 83. *Bibliog:* Susan Koslow (auth), Esther A Grillo, Arts Mag, 86; David S Martin (auth), Exhib, events meant to raise nuclear awareness, Centre Daily Times, Assoc Press, 1/14/88; Fatal vision, The Palm Beach Post, Meltdown on display, Express-News, Tex & Nuclear art show to feature Meltdown, Cape Coral Press (all from Assoc Press, 1/11/88). *Mem:* Womens Caucus Art; Col Art Asn. *Media:* Mixed. *Publ:* Contribr, Words-Pictures--Collaborative Work of Women Artists, Womens Caucus Art, 82; Sculpting clay, Nigros H, 92. *Dealer:* 14 Sculptors Gallery 164 Mercer St New York NY 10012. *Mailing Add:* 214 Beach 120th St Far Rockaway NY 11694-1957

GRILLO, JOHN
PAINTER, PRINTMAKER
b Lawrence, Mass, July 7, 17. *Study:* Hartford Sch Fine Arts, Conn, 35-38; Calif Sch Fine Arts, San Francisco, 46-47; studied with Hans Hoffman, New York & Provincetown, Mass, 48-51. *Work:* Metrop Mus Art, Solomon R Guggenheim Mus Art, Whitney Mus Am Art & Brooklyn Mus, NY; British Mus, London. *Comn:* Brotherhood (painting), Univ Mass Art Dept, Amherst, 87; Emily Dickinson (painting), Jones Libr Inc, Amherst, Mass, 93; Stage settings, CAPE Theater Co, Provincetown, Mass, 97. *Exhib:* The Whitney Ann, Whitney Mus Am Art, NY, 53 & 59; 40 Post War Painters, Guggenheim Mus, NY, 77; The Circus Series, Springfield Mus Fine Arts, Mass, 83 & Univ NH, 97; Selected Paintings 1963-1988, Provincetown Art Asn & Mus, Mass, 88; The Park Series, Museo de Antoquia, Medellin, Columbia, 91; Paper Trails: San Francisco Abstract, Art Mus Santa Cruz, Calif, 93; The San Francisco Sch of Abstract Expressionism, Laguna Art Mus, Calif, 96. *Pos:* Trustee, Provincetown Art Asn & Mus, Mass, 95-96. *Teaching:* Vis artist drawing & painting, Univ Calif, Berkeley, 62-63 & 73; instr, Pratt Inst, New York, 65-66; prof, Univ Mass, Amherst, 67-91. *Awards:* Samuel S Bender Award, San Francisco, 47; Ford Found Grant, Los Angeles, 64; Res Grant, Univ Mass, Amherst, 76. *Bibliog:* John Furbish (dir), John Grillo: World Scale Artist in the Pioneer Valley (film), Pioneer Valley Cable TV, 87; Tony Vevers (auth), John Grillo, Provincetown Mag, summer 88; Susan Landaver (auth), John Grillo, Art Calif Mag, 5/90. *Media:* Oil, Watercolor. *Publ:* Auth, Artist's Statement, John Grillo, It Is Mag, winter 59; Essay: yellow can be black, Scrap Mag, 4/61; Jan Muller: A Remembrance, Provincetown Arts Mag, 90; Essay: George Karen-Zhouf (exhib catalog), Asz Publ, 92. *Mailing Add:* c/o Cove Gallery Commercial St PO Box 482 Wellfleet MA 02667

GRIMALDI, VINCE
PHOTOGRAPHER, COLLAGE ARTIST, PAINTER
b Brooklyn, NY, July 21, 29. *Study:* Art Students League, NY City, 1950; New Sch Social Res, NY City, 1957. *Work:* Butler Inst of Am Art, Youngstown, Ohio; Int Ctr of Photog, NY; Mus of Modern Art, NY; Wells Col, Utaca, NY; Brooklyn Mus, NY. *Comn:* 2,000 Years in Rome, Rome Ital, 1965; Dance in Black Am Show, NY, 1978; Evening of Photo Maxims, NY 1983; Celebrating Statue of Libr, NY, 1985; Photo Maxims, CBGB Gallery, NY, 1983. *Exhib:* Autofocus, Floating found of Photog, NY, 1982; Liberty's Eye, New Rochelle, NY, 1986; Taking Liberty, NY State, Albany, NY, 1986; Homage to Joseph Cornell, Silvermine Gallery, Conn, 1987; A-Z Group, Vasarely, Budapest Hungary, 1991; Open Wound, Sarajevo, Bosnia, 1993; New Moon Show, Attleboro, Mass, 2002; Blink Gallery, Newport, RI, 2004; Mus Art, Provincetown, Mass, 2006; Cape Cod Mus Art, Dennis, Mass, 2006. *Teaching:* Lectr, Sr Citizens NY & Saratoga Springs, 1992-93; lectr, Wells Col, Itaca, NY, 2002. *Awards:* Artists Space Fund award, 1986; Workshop award, Ma Photo Workshop, Maine, 1988; Residency award, Vt Studio Ctr, 2004-2005; Pollock-Krasner Grant, 2006. *Media:* photography, collage, box constructions, painting. *Mailing Add:* 280 Washington St (509) Providence RI 02903-3605

GRIMES, MARGARET W
PAINTER, EDUCATOR
b New Bern, NC. *Study:* Gov State Univ, BA, 74, MA, 75; Notre Dame Univ, with Alice Neel, 77; Univ Pa, with Neil Welliver, Rudy Burckhaudt, Yvonne Jacquette and Paul Georges, MFA, 80. *Work:* Pittsburgh Plate Glass Co; Conn Insurance Group NAm; Christian Sci Church Ctr, Boston; US Tobacco Co; Bellevue Hosp Ctr, NY; Atlantic Fed Bank, NJ; Ethan Allen Co, Conn; Nat Acad Sci, Washington, Conn; David Hall Gallery. *Comn:* Print, New York Graphic Soc, 85; Calendar Reproduction, Cairo, Calendar Images, 88. *Exhib:* Int Womens Art Festival, Walker Art Inst, 76; one-person exhibs, Green Mountain Gallery, NY, 79, Blue Mountain Gallery, NY, biennially 1980-2006, Fischbach Gallery, NY, 86, Weir Farm Heritage Trust, 2004; Group Shows, Columbus Mus Art, Ohio, 87, Newport Art Mus, RI, 88; Fischbach Gallery, NY, 86; Katherina Rich Perlow, NY, 88; Univ Pa, 92; Am Realism & Figurative Painting, Cline Art Gallery, Santa Fe, NMex, 94; Five Aspects of the Am Landscape, John Arthur (cur), Crieger-Dane Gallery, Boston, Mass, 95; A Chaos of Delight, Ctr Contemp Art, Wilmington, Del, 96; Washington Art Asn, Washington, Conn, 2000; Nat Acad of Sci, Washington, 2001; Green Woods and Crystal Waters: The Am Landscape Tradition, Philbrook Mus Art, Tulsa, Okla, Ringling Mus Art, Sarasota, Fla, Davenport Mus, Davenport, Iowa, 2000; Nat Acad of Design, Juried Invitational, 2004; plus others. *Pos:* presenter, Conf Liberal Arts & Educ Artist, Sch & Visual Arts, NY, 97; coord, MFA Program, Western Conn State Univ, 2000-; artist in residence, American Univ, Corciano, Italy, 2004, Weir Farm Heritage Trust. *Teaching:* Instr drawing & design, Thornton Community Col, Chicago, 74-79; prof painting & drawing, Western Conn State Univ, 80-; visiting critic, Vt Studio Ctr, Johnson, 95, Vt Col Norwich Univ, Montpelier, 95-96, Tanglewood Inst, Lenox, Mass, 97; guest lectr, Moravian Col, Bethlehem, Pa, 90, Britain, Conn, 97, Cen Conn State U, New Britain, Conn, 97, Western Conn State Univ, Danbury, Conn, 98 & Weir Farm Hist Site, Wilton, Conn, 98; presenter, Gunn Mus Pride of Place, Lectr Series, Washington, Conn, 2000; visiting artist, Am Univ, Italy, 2001-06; Am Univ, Wash, DC, 2004, Chaotauqua Inst, 2003 & 05. *Awards:* Res Grant, Conn State Univ, 85 & 90; Henry Barnard Found Distinguished Lectureship Award, 90; Univ Prof, West Conn State Univ, 92; Benjamin Altman Award, landscape painting, Nat Acad Design, 2004. *Bibliog:* Carl Little (auth), Paintings of New England, Down East Press, 96; Jude Schwendenwien (auth), Grimes Paintings Close to Nature, Hartford Courant, 97; John Driscoll (auth), The Artist in the American Landscape, First Glance Press, 98. *Mem:* Col Art Asn; Am Asn Univ Prof. *Media:* Oil. *Publ:* Co-ed, New Art Asn Newsletter, 71; Green Woods and Crystal Waters, John Arthur, Univ Wash Press; John Arthur (auth), Greenwoods and Crystal Waters: The Am landscape Tradition, Univ of WA Press, 99; Steve Starger, Art New England, 8/2003; Paul Smith, Art in Am, 2004. *Dealer:* Blue Mountain Gallery 121 Wooster Street New York NY 10012. *Mailing Add:* 27 Wykeham Rd Washington CT 06793

GRIMLEY, OLIVER FETTEROLF
PAINTER, SCULPTOR
b Norristown, Pa, June 30, 20. *Study:* Pa Acad Fine Arts, William Emlen Clesson traveling scholar, 47, Henry J Scheidt traveling scholar, 50; Univ Pa, BFA & MFA. *Work:* Woodmere Art Galleries, Mus Art, Pa Acad Fine Arts, Philadelphia; Libr Cong, Washington, DC. *Comn:* Murals, Commonwealth Fed Savings & Loan, Norristown, 63, Continental Bank & Trust, 65 & Am Bank, Lafayette Hills, Pa, 72; papier-mache eagle, comn by Leonard Tose, Vet Stadium, Philadelphia, 71. *Exhib:* Whitney Mus Am Art, Libr Cong & Metrop Mus, 52-57; Pa Acad Fine Arts Watercolor Shows, 58-63; Philadelphia Mus Art. *Teaching:* Instr drawing, Hussian Sch Art, 60- & Pa Acad Fine Arts, 65-. *Awards:* Ralph Pallen Coleman Prize for Illus, 73; First Prize for Sculpture, Regional Coun Community Arts Ctr, 74; J W Zimmerman Mem Prize for Work of Distinction, 79. *Bibliog:* Henry Pitz (auth), article, Am Artist, 71. *Mem:* Philadelphia Watercolor Club. *Media:* Pen & Ink, Watercolor; Miscellaneous. *Publ:* Auth, article, Am Artist, 50. *Mailing Add:* 623 Stonybrook Dr Norristown PA 19403-2725

GRIMM, RAYMOND MAX
SCULPTOR, POTTER
b St Louis, Mo, Jun 20, 24. *Study:* Wash Univ Sch Fine Arts, BFA, 53; Southern Ill Univ, with F Carlton Ball in pottery, MS, 55. *Work:* Univ Ore Mus Art, Eugene; Contemp Crafts Gallery, Portland, Ore; Salem Civic Ctr, Ore; Skamania Lodge, Stevenson, Wash; Pioneer Courthouse Sq, Portland, Oreg. *Comn:* ceramic plaque, 13ft x 3ft, Salishan Lodge, Gleneden, Ore, 65; brick mosaic, 60ft x 9ft, Mountain Park Recreation Ctr, Lake Oswego, Ore, 70; seven brick sculptures, Ore State Veterinary Teaching Hosp, Corvallis, 79; Weather Machine, Pioneer Courthouse Square, Portland, 88; clay & glass mosaic (60' series) bas-relief plaques, Skamania Lodge, Stevenson, Wash, 93. *Exhib:* One-man show, Contemp Crafts Gallery, Portland, 57-59, 63 & 75; Fiber, Clay & Metal, St Paul Art Mus, Minn, 66; Int Exhib Ceramic Art, City Mus, Faenze, Italy, 66; Craft Alliance Gallery, St Louis, 67; Pauling Gallery, Clackamus Community Col, 89; retrospective with wife, Jere Meisel Grimm, Contemp Crafts Gallery, 97. *Teaching:* Prof emer art, ceramics & glass, Portland State Univ, 56-. *Awards:* Jr League Award, St Louis Art Mus, 56; Harold Hirsch Award, Ore Ceramics Studio, 64; Merit Award, Mus Contemp Crafts, New York, 66. *Bibliog:* Catherine Jones (auth), Jere and Raymond Grimm, Creative Crafts Mag, 63; Polly Rothenberg (auth), The Complete Book of Ceramics, Crown Publ, 72; Lamar Harrington (auth), Ceramics in the Pacific Northwest, Univ Wash, 79; John Nance (auth), Ray & Jere Grimm, Ceramics Monthly Magazine, 2003 & 2004. *Mem:* Am Craftsmen's Coun (state rep, 58-61). *Media:* Ceramics, Glass. *Interests:* Combining clay with glass, glass with wood, clay and metal. *Mailing Add:* 1734 NW Aspen Ave Portland OR 97210

GRIMMER, MINEKO
SCULPTOR
b Feb 3, 49. *Study:* Iwate Univ, Morioka, Japan, BA, 72; Otis Art Inst, Parsons Sch Design, Los Angeles, Calif, BFA, 79, MFA, 81. *Hon Degrees:* Lafayett Col, Hon Dr, 97. *Work:* Security Pac Bank; Fresno Art Mus; Norton Computing Co; Shamrock Holdings Inc; Auckland Art Gallery. *Comn:* Calif Med Ctr; Los Angeles Co Transportation Comn; City of Palm Desert, 98; Madison Marquette, 98. *Exhib:* Traditions Transformed, Oakland Mus, Calif, 85; Elements: Four Installations, Whitney Mus Am Art Equitable Ctr, NY, 87; solo exhibs, Ruth Siegel Gallery, NY, 89, Fresno Art Mus, Calif, 90, High Mus Art, Atlanta, 92, Haines Gallery, San Francisco, 94, Auckland Art Gallery, NZ, 94, Japan Cult Ctr, Bangkok, Thailand, 94 & Mus Mod Art, Saitama, Japan, 96, Flora of the North, Los Angeles Artcore Ctr at Union Ctr for the Arts, Calif, 99, Mineko Grimmer, Menil Collection, Tex, 2001; The Nature of the Machine, Chicago Cult Ctr, 93; California in Three Dimensions, Calif Ctr Arts Mus, Escondido, 95; A Listening Garden, UNESCO, Paris, 93; Japan Festival, Harbor Front Ctr, Toronto, 95; New Work Japan, Danforth Mus Art, Framingham, Mass, 88; Utsunomiya Mus Art, Japan, 98; Menil Collection, Houston, 2001. *Awards:* Fel, Nat Endowment Arts, 87; Fel, Calif Arts Coun, 88; Grant Saison Found, 90; Calif

Community Found, J Paul Getty Trust Fund for the Visual arts Fel, 99. *Bibliog:* Merle Shipper (auth), Artists the critics are watching--Mineko Grimmer, Artnews, 5/86; Mary MacNaughton (auth), Sound and silence: the sculpture of Mineko Grimmer, Arts Mag, 11/87; Marge Bulmer (auth), Mineko Grimmer, Artscene, 3/88. *Media:* Natural Materials. *Publ:* Jim Jenkins & Dave Quick (coauth), "Motion/Motion Kinetic Art", Gibbs Smith, 89, Kathleen Stoughton (auth), "Mineko Grimmer, Palisade", 90. *Dealer:* Kaplin Gallery Los Angeles CA. *Mailing Add:* 10747 Wilshire Blvd #504 Los Angeles CA 90024

GRINER, NED H
EDUCATOR, CRAFTSMAN
b Tipton, Ind, Dec 14, 28. *Study:* Ball State Teachers Col, BS; State Univ Iowa, MA; Ind Univ, MFA; Pa State Univ, DEd. *Work:* Evansville Mus Art & Ball State Univ Art Gallery, Muncie, Ind. *Exhib:* Midstates Craft Exhib, 66-67; Jewelry Exhib, Purdue Univ, 67; Indianapolis Mus Art, 75; Ind Univ Mus Art, Bloomington, 76; Ind State Mus, Indianapolis, 77; Ft Wayne Art Mus, Ind, 78. *Teaching:* Asst prof art, Ark State Col, 54-60; asst, Pa State Univ, 60-61; prof, Ball State Univ, 61-94, head dept, 70-81. *Awards:* L Whead Teaching Award, Gen Studies, 90; Very Important Volunteer Award, 93. *Mem:* Nat & Ind Art Educ Asns; Col Art Asn Am; Ind Artist Craftsmen (pres, 66-68); Nat Coun Art Adminr. *Media:* Silver, Bronze, Brass. *Publ:* Contrib, Art--search & self discovery, 68; auth, Side by Side with Coarser Plants: The Muncie Art Movement, 1885-1985, Ball State Univ, 85; Gas Society, Minnetrista Cultural Found Inc, 91; J Ottis Adams: A Sense of Place, Minnetrista Cultural Found Inc, 92; Bethel Pike Pottery: The First Thirty Years, Minnetrista Cult Found Inc, 96. *Mailing Add:* 4516 N Gishler Dr Muncie IN 47304

GRINNAN, KATIE
PAINTER, SCULPTOR
b Richmond, Va, 1970. *Study:* Studio Arts Ctr Int, Florence, Italy, 91; Carnegie Mellon Univ, BFA(painting), 92; Skowhega Sch Painting & Sculpture, Main, 92; UCLA, MFA in Sculpture, 99. *Exhib:* Katie Grinnan Alice Konitz christie fields, Guggenheim Gallery, Chapman Univ, Calif, 2000; one-woman shows incl Rock Bottom, Acme, Los Angeles, 2001, 2003; Out of the Ground into the Sky Out of the Sky into the Ground, Pond, San Francisco, 2002; Wit Form Rainbow (Part I), The Project, Los Angeles, 2003; Material Faith, Kontainer Gallery, Los Angeles, 2004; Real World: Dissolving Space of Experience, Modern Art Oxford, Eng, 2004; Art on Paper, Weatherspoon Art Mus, Univ NC, 2004. *Mailing Add:* c/o Acme 6150 Wilshire Blvd #1 Los Angeles CA 90048

GRIPPE, FLORENCE (BERG)
PAINTER, INSTRUCTOR
b New York, NY, Jan 6, 1912. *Study:* Educ Alliance, 32-34; Works Proj Admin Art Courses, 34-38; pottery with William Soini, 39-41. *Work:* Rose Art Mus, Brandeis Univ. *Comn:* Portraits comn by Doris Brewer Cohen, Lexington, Mass, 69, Signora Attilio Roveda, Locarno, Switz, 70, Dr Luis Martinez & Julio Farinos Castillo, Valencia, Spain, 70 & Jose Marina Galvao Telles, Lisbon, Portugal, 71. *Exhib:* Brooklyn Mus, 51; Lower East Side Independent Artists 3rd Ann Exhib, 58; Guild Hall, Easthampton, Long Island, 75 & 87; Provincetown Art Asn & Mus, Mass, 78; Himmelfarb Gallery, Long Island, 80-81; Burnside Gallery, Long Island, 81 & 83; and others. *Pos:* Art critic, Art News & Craft Horizons, 61-63. *Teaching:* Instr drawing, painting, sculpture & puppetry, United Art Workshops, Brooklyn Neighborhood Houses, NY, 47-54; instr design & pottery, Brooklyn Mus Art Sch, 51-57. *Bibliog:* S Sheridan (auth), Native handicrafts, New York Times Mag, 7/52; article in Daily Transcript, Boston, 7/19/79; article in Peconic Bay Shopper, Long Island, 10/81; and others. *Mem:* NY Ceramic Soc; Artist Club. *Media:* All. *Res:* Glazing formulas; Art history. *Publ:* Auth, With the brush, Ceramic Age, 3/56; coauth, Art news from Boston, Art News, 61-63. *Dealer:* 1942 Orrefors Gallery; 46 America House. *Mailing Add:* Acme Fine Arts 4th Floor 38 Newbury St Boston MA 02116

GRIPPI, SALVATORE WILLIAM
PAINTER, SCULPTOR
b Buffalo, NY, Sept 30, 21. *Study:* Mus Mod Art Sch, 44-45; Art Students League, 45-48; Atelier 17, 51-53; Ist Statale d'Arte, Florence, Italy, Fulbright Scholar, 53-55. *Work:* Whitney Mus Am Art & Metrop Mus Art, NY; Joseph Hirshhorn Collection, Washington, DC; St Lawrence Univ; Everson Mus, Syracuse, NY. *Exhib:* Biennials, Corcoran Gallery Art, 59 & 63; Whitney Mus Am Art Ann, 60 & 61; Walker Art Ctr, 60; Recent Painting USA, The Figure, Mus Mod Art, NY & throughout US, 62; Selected Am Painters, Phoenix Art Mus, Ariz, 67; Elvehjem Art Ctr, Univ Wis, 77 & traveling; Brooklyn Mus, NY, 78; Everson Mus, Syracuse, NY, 78; Artists Books, Mus Mod Art, NY, 94; Ital Am Artists, Hunter Col, NY, 94; one-man shows, NY Univ, New York City, 58, Zabriskie Gallery, NYC, 56, 59, Krasner Gallery, New York City, 62, 64, 79, 81, Feingarten Galleries, Los Angeles, Calif, 67, 70, Rex Evans Gallery, Los Angeles, Calif, 65, Everson Mus, Syracuse, NY, 78, Hardwerker Gallery, Ithaca, NY, 78, Wells Coll, Aurora, NY, 72, Hiestand Gallery, Miami Univ, Oxford, Ohio, 84. *Teaching:* Instr painting, drawing & 2-D design, Cooper Union Art Sch, 56-59; instr, Sch Visual Arts, 61-62; assoc prof art, Pomona Col & Claremont Grad Sch, 62-68; prof art, Ithaca Col, 68-. *Awards:* Fulbright Scholarship, 53 & Renewal, 54. *Bibliog:* Brian O'Dougherty (auth), Variety of exhibitions, New York Times, 3/22/62; Larry Campbell (auth), article, Art News, 10/64; Henry J Seldis (auth), Art walk: A critical guide to the galleries, Los Angeles Times, 5/29/70; and many others. *Mem:* Life mem Art Students League (treas, 61-62, bd control, 61-64); Col Art Asn Am. *Media:* Oil, Watercolor; Wood. *Publ:* Auth, Visual impressions of Italy, Inst Int Educ Bull, 56; Turntable kaleidoscope, Mus Mod Art, 56, 57 & 59; contribr, Twenty-one Etchings & Poems, 58; New York School Abstract Expressionists, Artists Choice by Artists, NY Sch Press, 2000. *Mailing Add:* 9 Orchard Hill Rd Ithaca NY 14850

GRISSOM, EUGENE EDWARD
HISTORIAN, WRITER
b Melvern, Kans, May 15, 22. *Study:* Philippine Univ, 45; Kans State Teachers Col, Emporia, BS, 48; State Univ Iowa, with M Lasansky, MFA, 51. *Work:* Samuel P Harn Mus Art; Norman R Eppink Gallery Collection, Emporia State Univ, Kans; Princeton Univ; Philadelphia Mus Art; Ctr Creative Photog, Univ Ariz. *Exhib:* J B Speed Mus, Louisville, Ky; numerous pvt collections; Univ Iowa; Gainesville Currents, Sch Art and Art History, Univ Fla, 2000. *Teaching:* Instr art educ, Kans State Teachers Col, summer 51; instr art, Univ Ky, 51-53; from asst prof to prof art, Univ Fla, 53-87, chmn dept, 62-78, prof emer, 87, ret. *Awards:* Mngmt Grants, Nat Endowment Arts; Lila Wallace - Readers Digest Nat Jazz Network; ext Eugene E Grissom Trombone Libr in Univ Fla/Dept Mus Libr, 80; co-sponsor Frank Rosolino Meml FR Meml Scholar/Jazz Trombone with Int Trombone Asn, 79; plus others; inducted into Friends of Jazz Hall of Fame, 2004. *Mem:* Internat Trombone Asn; Internat Asn Jazz Record Collectors; Int Asn Jazz Educators; plus others. *Res:* Drawing workshops of the early 15th century in Italy; Antonio Pollaiuolo, Florence engraver of the late 1400's; drawing marks & certain contemporary music notation systems; discography of Conrad Herwig, Ray Anderson, Abram Lincoln, Frank Rosolino. *Publ:* Fond Memories of Frank Rosolino/CD & Transcriptions, Doubletime Jazz Publ, 96; ed, Frank Rosolino, 96, Queen of the Blues, Ella Fitzgerald (A Life Through Jazz). *Mailing Add:* 4607 Clear Lake Dr Gainesville FL 32607

GRISSOM, FREDA GILL
PAINTER, GOLDSMITH
b Groom, Tex. *Study:* WTex State Univ, Canyon, BS; Univ Tex, Austin; also watercolor workshop. *Work:* Montgomery Mus Fine Arts, Ala. *Exhib:* Ann Dixie Exhib, Montgomery Mus Fine Arts, 68; Nat Art Roundup, Las Vegas, Nev, 68; Greater New Orleans Nat, 71; 9th Grand Prix Int, Cannes, France, 73; Galerie Rene Borel, Deauville, France, 73. *Pos:* Co-chmn, Nat Sun Carnival Art Exhib, El Paso, Tex, 65-71. *Awards:* Purchase Award, Montgomery Mus Fine Arts, 68; Second Prize, Greater New Orleans Nat Exhib, 71; Medaille de la Ville de Cannes, First Prize, Watercolor, 9th Grand Prix Int, Cote D'Azur, 73. *Mem:* El Paso Art Asn, Inc (dir, 64-65); El Paso Mus Art; Black Range Art Asn; Tex Watercolor Soc. *Media:* Transparent Watercolor, Acrylic, Oil; Gold, Silver. *Mailing Add:* 399 Vinton Rd Anthony NM 88021-8546

GRISWOLD, WILLIAM M
MUSEUM DIRECTOR, CURATOR
Pos: Head dept, drawings & prints Morgan Libr, New York City, 95-2001; assoc dir, collections J Paul Getty Mus, LA, 2001-04, acting dir, chief cur, 2004-. *Mailing Add:* J Paul Getty Mus 1200 Getty Ctr Dr Los Angeles CA 90049-1687

GROAT, HALL PIERCE
PAINTER, MURALIST
b Syracuse, NY, Dec 31, 32. *Study:* Syracuse Univ, BFA, also Grad Sch Painting; Josef Albers. *Work:* Everson Mus Art, Syracuse, NY; Philatelic Mus, Geneva, Switz; Syracuse Univ & Fleet Bank, NY; Skaneatelles Savings Bank, NY; Merrill Ctr, Bangor, Maine; Portrait of John Mulroy, Collection, John Mulroy Civic Ctr, Syracuse, NY. *Comn:* Hist mural, Merrill Trust Co, Bangor, Maine, 75; hist mural (five panels), Fleet Bank, 77; hist mural, Skaneateles, NY, 79; mural, Miller Brewing Co, Fulton, NY, 80; mural, Bristol-Myers Squibb, 81; mural, Mutual of NY; North Med Ctr, Syracus, NY; hist series, Paine Webber, Syracuse, NY, 2000; hist series of Hist of Syracuse, Rudin Mentor, Trivelpiece Law Firm, 2003. *Exhib:* Rochester Finger Lakes Exhib, Rochester Mem Art Gallery, NY, 59 & 63; Springfield Nat, Mass, 62; Everson Mus Regional, Syracuse, 64 & 70; Cooperstown Nat, NY, 67-83; Butler Inst Am Art, Youngstown, Ohio, 68. *Teaching:* Instr advan painting, Berkshire Mus. *Awards:* UN Philatelic Award; Int Award for UN Stamp; Spec Citation Outstanding Portrait, Albright-Knox Mus Art Western Regional, 94; Jurors Award, Olin Fine Arts Ctr, Washington & Jefferson Col, Pa, 94; Gordon Steele Mem Medal, Cazenovia Col, 2000. *Bibliog:* 32nd annual midyear show--Butler, La Rev Mod, 2/68; Review of selected artist, Art Rev, fall 68; An Artist and His Work (film), WCNY, Syracuse, NY. *Mem:* Sarasota Art Asn; Nat Soc Mural Painters. *Media:* Acrylic, Oil; Watercolor. *Dealer:* Hall Croat Art Studios Inc. *Mailing Add:* 8364 Vassar Dr Manlius NY 13104

GRODSKY, SHEILA TAYLOR
PAINTER, COLLAGE ARTIST
b Newark, NJ, May 7, 33. *Study:* Douglass Col, BA(art ed), 54; Md Inst Art, 68-69; also studied with Nicholas Reale, Gerald Brommer, W Carl Burger & Paul St Denis. *Exhib:* Salmagundi Club Ann, NY, 92; Catharine Lorillard Wolfe Art Club Centennial Exhib, NY, 96; Garden State Watercolor Soc, 98; NJ Watercolor Soc, 98; NE Watercolor Soc Ann Juried Exhib, 98; Int Soc Experimental Artists Ann Juried Exhib, 98; Nat Acrylic Painters Asn USA Ann Juried Exhib, 98; Int Soc of Experimental Artists Ann Juried Exhib, 99; Nat Acrylic Painters Asn USA Ann Open Exhib, 99; Nat Asn of Women Artists, Women's Expo, Baltimore, 99, Fall Exhib, Art Ctr Sarasota Gallery, Fla, 2000; NJ Water Color Soc Ann Open Juried Exhib, 2000; and others. *Pos:* Bd mem, Sussex Co Arts Coun, 75-80. *Teaching:* Instr art, Dover High Sch, NJ, 54-56; instr watercolor, Livingston Art Asn, NJ, 90-91. *Awards:* President's Award, Catharine Lorillard Wolfe Art Club, 93; Avery & Nina Johnson Award, NJ Watercolor Soc, 98; Best in Show, Garden State Watercolor Soc, 98. *Mem:* signature mem NJ Watercolor Soc; Pastel Soc Am; Catharine Lorillard Wolfe Art Club Inc (bd dir, 89, vpres, 97); assoc mem Nat Watercolor Soc; assoc mem Am Watercolor Soc; signature mem Nat Acrylic Painters Asn; Nat Asn of Women Artists. *Media:* Watercolor, Acrylic. *Specialty:* Mixed media. *Publ:* Contribr, Creative Watercolor: A Showcase and Step-by-Step Guide, Best of Watercolor: Painting Color & Floral Inspirations, Rockport Publ. *Mailing Add:* 940 W End Dr Newton NJ 07860

GROFF, BARBARA S
PAINTER, GRAPHIC ARTIST
b Hartford, Conn, Apr 10, 43. *Study:* Hartford Art School, 1961; Self taught. *Exhib:* Academic Artist Assoc Annual Nat Exhib, Springfield, Mass, 2001-06; Allied Artists of Am Annual Exhib, New York City, 2003-05; CT Pastel Soc, Renaissance in Pastels Nat Exhib, W Hartford, Conn, 2003 & 05; CT Pastel Soc, Renaissance in Pastels Nat Exhib, Slater Mus, Norwich, Conn, 2004; Pastel Soc of Am Annual Open Juried Exhib, New York City, 2004-05; Hudson Valley Art Asn Nat Juried Exhib, Hastings-on-Hudson, NY, 2004-06. *Awards:* Connecticut Pastel Society Founder's Awards, Renaissance in Pastels, 2004 & 05; Pastel Honor Award (3 time recip), Acad Artists Asn 55th Ann Nat Exhib, Marion Malley Walsh Fam, 2005; Art Spirit Found Award, Conn Acad Fine Art, 2006. *Mem:* Pastel Soc of Am Inc; Conn Pastel Soc; Acad Artists Asn; Conn Acad of Fine Arts; Kent Art Asn Inc. *Media:* Realism, Stilllife, Graphic Design, Print Media. *Publ:* Kathleen Mellon (auth), Pastels That Slip Life's Hold, Daily Hampshire Gazzette (H.S. Gere & Sons Inc), 2005; Joshua Rose (ed), Exhibition Proves That Still Life Is Not Standing Still, Am Art Collector (Int'l Artist Publ Inc), 2006; Quick Sketches-Conn Pastel Soc Announces Award Winners, Am Artist Mag (VNU Bus Publ), 2006. *Dealer:* William Baczek Fine Arts 36 Main St Northampton, MA 01060. *Mailing Add:* 60-197 Old Town Rd Vernon CT 06066

GROGAN, KEVIN
MUSEUM DIRECTOR
b Washington, DC, Oct 4, 48. *Study:* BA Franklin & Marshall Col, MA Am Univ, Vanderbilt Univ, Ctr Non-Profit Mgt. *Exhib:* Red Grooms: The Graphic Work, In Pursuit of Serious Fun; Karl Struss: A Retrospective View of His Photog; The Am Scene, 1900-1950; Glamour Defined: The Photog of George Hurrell; Louise Dahl-Wolfe: A Retrospective; Wolf Kahn: Pastels Retrospective; and many others. *Pos:* Asst cur & asst dir, Phillips Collection, DC, 71-79; dir, Fine Arts Ctr at Cheekwood, Nashville, Tenn, 80-90; dir, Univ Galleries, Fisk Univ, Nashville, Tenn, 92-99; exec dir/pres, Contemp Art Ctr Va, 99-2002; dir, Morris Mus of Art, 2002-. *Teaching:* Adj assoc prof, Dept Fine Arts, Vanderbilt Univ, 82-90 & Art Dept, Fisk Univ, 90-99. *Awards:* Gordon Holl Outstanding Arts Adminr, 87; Brotherhood-Sisterhood Award, Nat Conf Christians & Jews, 89; Award of Merit, Tenn Asn Mus, 90. *Mem:* Am Asn Mus; Asn Fundraisings Prof; Art Mus Partnership; Southeast Mus Conf; Int Coun Mus; SE Art Mus Directors Forum. *Res:* American art of the late 19th and early 20th centuries; American collectors of the same period; southern art & artists. *Publ:* The Phillips Collection in the Making: 1920-30, Smithsonian Inst; Karl Struss: A Retrospective (exhib catalog); ed & auth foreword, Red Grooms: A Catalogue Raissone of his Graphic Work, rev ed, 85; Art in the Embassy, Paris; Reg Grooms: In Pursuit of Serious Fun; many others. *Mailing Add:* 709 Somerset Way Augusta GA 30909

GROM, BOGDAN
SCULPTOR, PAINTER
b Devincina, Sgonico-Trieste, Italy, Aug 26, 18; US citizen. *Study:* Fine Arts Acad, Perugia, Italy, with Gerardo Dottori, Aldo Pascucci, 44; Fine Arts Acad, Venice, Italy, with Guido Cadorin, Armando Pizzinato, Arturo Martini, 44; Fine Arts Acad, Munich, Ger, with Joseph Oberberger, 52. *Work:* Solomon R Guggenheim Mus, NY; Nat Mus Art, Osaka, Japan; Cincinnati Art Mus, Ohio; NJ State Mus, Trenton; Galleria Naz D'Arte Mod, Rome. *Comn:* Sculpture & murals, Winston-Muss Corp, Phoenix, Ariz, 62; glass windows & sculpture, St Vartan Armenian Cathedral, NY, 68; bronze sculpture, New York City Art Comn, Staten Island, 73; stained windows & sculpture, JCC, White Plains, NY, 86; sculpture, Hekemian Co, Hackensack, NJ, 90. *Exhib:* Grom, Opere di Arredo Urbano, 1959-1979, Sala Comunale D'Arte, Trieste, Italy, 79; Art Expo, NY Coliseum, NY, 81; Int Biennial of Graphic Art, Mod Art Mus, Ljubljana, Yugoslavia, 85; Arazzi Mitteleuropei, Palazzo Venezia, Rome, Italy, 87; Int Biennial of Graphic Art, RYU Contemp Art, Kawasaki, Japan, 89; Sefarad 92, Toledo, Spain & Tel Aviv, Israel, 92. *Pos:* Bd mem, North Jersey Art Ctr, Tenefly, 76-78; cur, North Salem Gallery Ltd, New York, 80-84. *Teaching:* Prof art & art hist, PTUJ State Gymnasium, Yugoslavia 45-47; State Teachers Prep Sch & Gymnas, Trieste, Italy, 47-53; vis instr art, Pratt Inst, New York, 60. *Awards:* Am Inst Archit, 85; For Achievement in Art Teaching, Europ Recovery Plan. *Bibliog:* Susan B Hirschfeld (auth), article, Yugoslavia Cult Ctr (catalog), 89; John De Fazio (auth), Grom, 96. *Mem:* Col Art Asn; Am Medallic Sculpture Asn; Int Sculpture Ctr; Sculptors Asn NJ (pres, 76-78). *Media:* All Media; Tapestry Artist. *Publ:* Illustr, Tom Sawyer, 47 & Huckelberry Finn, 48, Mladinska Knjiga; auth, Slovene Ornaments, pvt publ, 49; Trieste and its Karst, pvt publ, 57; illustr, There is No Such Animal, TB Lippincott, 58; St Senan, Pres08ernova Zalo z08ba, 96. *Mailing Add:* 416 Cumberland St Englewood NJ 07631-4702

GROMALA, DIANE
VIDEO ARTIST, CRITIC
b Menominee, Mich, Feb 24, 60. *Study:* Univ Mich, BFA, 82; Yale Univ, MFA, 90. *Comn:* Dancing with the Virtual Dervish: Virtual Bodies, Meat Book, Pain Distraction, Biomorphic Typography. *Exhib:* Virtual Subjectivities (video), Seattle Art Mus, 95 & Los Angeles Contemp Exhib, Calif, 97; Virtual Dervish (video), Meany Theatre, Univ Wash, 95; Virtual Bodies (video), Western Front Gallery, Vancouver, Can, 96; Virtual Bodies, Mus of Contemp Art, Athens, Greece. *Teaching:* Asst prof, Univ Tex, 90-94 & Univ Wash, Seattle, 95-2000; assoc prof, Ga Tech, Atlanta, 2000-. *Awards:* Innovative Teaching, Am Inst Graphic Arts, 92; Foxworth Centennial Fel, Univ Tex, 94; Fulbright Fel, Fulbright Comn, 99. *Bibliog:* Liz McQuiston (auth), Suffragetts to She-Devils, Phaidon Press, 97; Anne Morgan Spalter (auth), The Computer in the Visual Arts, Addison Wesley, 99; Michael Rock (auth), Design in the Academy, American Institute of Graphic Arts Journal, Vol 13, 95. *Mem:* Col Art Asn; Postmodern Cult (ed bd, 97-2000); Am Inst Graphic Art; Mod Lang Asn. *Media:* Virtual reality, electronic media, biomedical technologies. *Res:* Phenomenology of digital technologies. *Specialty:* Media art. *Interests:* Chronic Pain, biomedical visualizations. *Publ:* auth, Dancing with the Virtual Dervish, in: Immersed In Technology, MIT Press, 95, Pain and Subjectivity in VR, in: Clicking In: Hot Links to a Digital Culture, Bay Press, 96 & Learning the Languages of Babel, Education of an eDesigner, 5/2000,; co-auth, Windows and Mirrors, MIT Press, 2003. *Mailing Add:* 34 Daniel Ave SE Atlanta GA 30317

GRONBORG, ERIK
SCULPTOR, CERAMIST
b Copenhagen, Denmark, Nov 12, 31; US citizen. *Study:* Univ Calif, Berkeley, BA, 62, MA, 63. *Work:* Oakland Art Mus, Calif; Everson Mus Art, Syracuse, NY; Am Crafts Mus, NY; Univ Art Collections, Ariz State Univ, Tempe; Contemp Crafts Asn, Portland, Ore. *Exhib:* One-man shows, Mus Mod Art, Paris, France, 65 & Mus Contemp Crafts, NY, 69; Ceramics '70, Everson Mus Art, Syracuse, NY, 70; World Crafts Coun, Int Exhib, Toronto, Can, 74; Americana, San Francisco Mus Art, 76; Philadelphia Crafts Show, Philadelphia Mus Art, 78; Am Porcelain, Renwick Gallery, Smithsonian Inst, 80; Art in Clay, 1950-1980, Municipal Art Gallery, Los Angeles, 84. *Teaching:* Asst prof ceramics & sculpture, Reed Col, Portland, Ore, 65-69; assoc prof, San Diego State Univ, Calif, 73-75; prof ceramics & sculpture, Mira Costa Col, Oceanside, Calif, 75-. *Awards:* Grand Prix, Mus Mod Art, Paris, 63; Nat Endowment Arts Craftsman Grant, 73; Award, Victoria & Albert Mus, London, 73. *Bibliog:* Kent Hall (auth), Erik Gronborg: the history of the present, Univ Portland Rev, 66; Ida Rigby (auth), Erik Gronborg's accessible art, Artweek, 2/3/79; Judi Nicolaidis (auth), Erik Gronborg: Portrait in Clay (video), Nicolaidis, 79. *Mem:* Am Crafts Coun (state rep, 71-73). *Media:* Wood, Ceramics. *Publ:* Auth, The new generation of ceramic artists, Craft Horizons, 69; Man and art in the urban environment, Nat Park & Conserv Mag, 72; Address to World Crafts Council Conference, Mexico, Ceramic Rev, 77; contribr, Ceramic Art, Comment and Review, 1882-1977, Dutton, 78. *Mailing Add:* 424 Dell Ct Solana Beach CA 92075-1419

GRONK
PAINTER
b Los Angeles, Calif, 1954. *Exhib:* Cult Currents, San Diego Mus Art, Calif, 88; solo exhibs, Gronk, Molly Barnes Gallery, Los Angeles, 84, The Titanic & other Tragedies at Sea, Galeria Ocaso, Los Angeles, 85, The Rescue Party, Saxon-Lee Gallery, 86-89, 50 Drawings, Daniel Saxon Gallery, Los Angeles, 91, Hotel Tormenta, Galerie Claude Samuel, Paris, France, 92, Fascinating Slippers/Pantunflas, San Jose Mus Art, Calif (originated by Mex Mus), San Francisco, 92 & Fascinating Slippers/Pantunflas Fascinantes, Daniel Saxon Gallery, Los Angeles, 92; Chicano & Latino: Parallels and Divergence (catalog), Daniel Saxon Gallery, Los Angeles, 91, El Paso Mus Art, Tex, 92 & Kimberly Gallery, Washington, DC, 92; Of Nature & the Human Spirit, Part II, Daniel Saxon Gallery, Los Angeles, 91; Myth & Magic in the Americas: The Eighties (catalog), Contemp Art, Monterrey, Mex, 91. *Awards:* Artist of Year, Mex Am Fine Art Asn, 77; Visual Artist Fel, Nat Endowment for Art, 83. *Bibliog:* Susan Kandel (auth), LA in Review, Arts Mag, 12/91; Suvan Geer (auth), Los Angeles Times, Calendar sect, 3/20/91; Leigh Ann Clifton (auth), Gronk at SJMA, Artweek, 4/9/92. *Mailing Add:* c/o Daniel Saxon Gallery 552 Norwich Dr West Hollywood CA 90048-1904

GROOMS, RED
PAINTER, SCULPTOR
b Nashville, Tenn, June, 37. *Study:* Sch Art Inst, Chicago, 55; George Peabody Col for Teachers, Nashville, 56; New Sch Soc Res, NY, 56; Hans Hoffman Sch Fine Arts, Provincetown, Mass, 57. *Work:* Allen Mem Art Mus, Oberlin, Ohio; Ark Art Ctr, Little Rock; Art Inst, Chicago; Brooklyn Mus, NY; Chrysler Mus, Norfolk, Va; Cleveland Mus Art, Ohio; Del Art Mus, Wilmington; Denver Art Mus, Colo; Everson Mus Art of Syracuse & Onondago Co, NY; Hirshhorn Mus & Sculpture Garden, Washington, DC; Mint Mus, Charlotte, NC. *Comn:* Tut's Fever Movie Palace (environ comn), with Lysiane Luong, Am Mus Moving Image, Astoria, NY, 88; set design for Meilleurs Amis, Nat Dance Inst, 89; set design for The Shooting of Dan McGrew, Nat Dance Inst, 90; set design for The Mysteries & What's So Funny, Serious Fun & Spoleto Festival, 91; set design for Chakra: A Celebration of India, Nat Dance Inst, 91. *Exhib:* Whitney Mus Am Art, 73, 78, 84 (three exhibs), 86-87 & 87-88; Solo exhibs, Brooklyn Mus, 92 & 94-95, Cheekwood Mus Art, Nashville (traveled to Polk Mus Art, Lakeland, Fla, Albany Mus Art, Ga, Michell Art Gallery & St John's Col, Annapolis Md), 95-96, New Brit Mus Am Art, Conn, 96 & Red Grooms, Marlborough & Boca Raton, Fla, 99, 2000, Self Made Men, DC Moore Gallery, NY, 2001, others; Il Cinema Amaggio di Primi 100 Anni del Cinema, Galleria Arte Gabbiano, Rome, 95; Art from the Driver's Seat: Americans & Their Cars (traveling throughout US), incl Hunter Mus Am Art, Tenn, 95-96; Les Champs de la Sculpture II, Champs Elysees Avenue, Paris, France, 98; Outward Bound: Am Art at the Brink of Twenty-First Century, Meridian Int Cen, 99; Deja vu: Reworking the Past, Kotonah Mus Art, NY, 2000; group exhibs incl, Guggenheim Mus New York City, 72, Ruckus Manhattan, New York City, 75-76, 81, State Univ NY, Purchase, 78, Lowe Art Mus Univ, Miami, Fla, 80, The New Gallery, Cleveland, 82, Int Cooperation Admin, Philadelphia, 82, Allen Frumkin Gallery, New York City, 85, Open Air Mus Sculpture, Middelheim, Antwerp, Belg, 85, Sewell Art Gallery Rice Univ, Houston, 85, Artists' Choice Mus, New York City, 86, Mus Art, Ft Lauderdale, Fla, 86, Wilson Art Ctr, Rochester, NY, 86, Allentown, Pa, Art Mus, 86, NY Acad Art, 86, Whitney Mus Am Art at Philip Morris, New York City, 86-87, National Mus Am History Smithsonian Inst, Wash, 86-, Saxon Lee Gallery, Los Angeles, 1988, Baruch Col, New York City, 88, Lockport Gallery, Ill, 88-89, Bucknell Univ, Lewisburg, Pa, 89. *Collection Arranged:* The Boooklyn Mus, NY; Solomon R Guggenheim Mus, HY; The Hudson River Mus Westchester, NY; Nagoya City Art Mus, Japan; The Met Mus Art, NY; Moderna Museet, Stockholm, Sweden; Mus Art, Kochi, Japan; NJ State Mus, Trenton; Philadelphia Mus Art, Pa; Whitney Mus Am Art, NY. *Teaching:* Vis artist, Syracuse

Univ, 80, Southern Ill Univ, 80 & Colo State Univ, 81; Albert Dorne Prof, Univ Bridgeport, 82. *Awards:* New York Times Ten Best Illus Children's Bks Award, 86; Gov's Award Arts, State Tenn, 86; Mayor's Award Honor, Art & Cult, NY, 88; Founders Medal, Pa Acad, 90. *Bibliog:* Patrick Pacheco (auth), The art collector as activist: Stewart & Linda Resnick, Art & Antiques, 3/96; Jenifer P Borum (auth), rev, Artforum, 4/96; Terry Sullivan (auth), When influence becomes inspiration, Art Masters, 6/96. *Mem:* Nat Acad. *Publ:* Coauth, Rembrandt Takes a Walk, Potter, New York, 87; auth, Ruckus Rodeo, Abrams, New York, 88; illusr, An artist, present at the Creation, reports (cartoon), NY Times, 7/7/91; cover, New Yorker, 10/19/92

GROOT, CANDICE BETH
CERAMIST
b Berwyn, Ill, Mar 4, 54. *Study:* Gustavus Adolphus Col, BA, 76; Tex Tech Univ, with Verne Funk, MFA, 80. *Work:* Contemp Mus NMex, Santa Fe. *Exhib:* 9th Marietta Col Crafts Nat, Ohio, 80; Clay Work/New Work, D W Gallery, Dallas, Tex, 80; Clay Workers Guild, Ill, 81; Small Work Nat, Zaner Gallery, Rochester, NY, 81; Westwood Clay Nat, Calif, 81. *Teaching:* Asst prof ceramics, Gustavus Adolphus Col, St Peter, Minn, 81-. *Awards:* Purchase Prize, Southwest Fine Arts Biennial, Hill Gallery, 78; Juror's Awards, Tex Col Art Show, 78 & Midland Col, 78. *Mem:* Am Crafts Coun; Nat Coun Educ Ceramic Arts. *Media:* Clay, Paper. *Mailing Add:* 911 Edgemere Ct Evanston IL 60202

GROOVER, JAN
PHOTOGRAPHER
b Plainfield, NJ, Apr 24, 43. *Study:* Pratt Inst, BFA(painting), 65; Ohio State Univ, MA(art educ), 69. *Work:* Metrop Mus Art, Mus Mod Art, Whitney Mus Am Art, NY; Baltimore Mus Art, Md; Mus Fine Art, Minneapolis, Minn. *Exhib:* One-man exhibs, Nancy Drysdale Gallery, Washington, 93, Hamiltons Gallery, London, Eng, 93, Fahey/Klein Gallery, Los Angeles, 93, Fraenkel Gallery, San Francisco, 93, Jacksonville Art Mus, Fla, 93, Photo Gallery Int, Sata Corp, Tokyo, 94 & Janet Borden Inc, NY, 96, 98 & 2001 & Toulouse, Espace Eureuil, France, 99; Whitney Mus Am Art, NY, 78; Counter Parts, Metrop Mus Art, NY, 82; retrospective, Mus Mod Art, NY, 87; Am Made: The New Still-Life, Japan Art & Cult Asn, Isetan Mus, Tokyo, Japan, 93; Photographs from the Real World, Lillehammer Art Mus, Norway, 93; A Sense of Place, Elizabeth Leach, Portland, Ore, 94; Pictures of the Real World, Paula Cooper, NY, 94; Defining Eye: Women Photographers of the 20th Century (traveling exhib), St Louis Art Mus, 98; Under Construction, Milwaukee Art Mus, 99; Galleri Bo Bjeggaard, Copenhagen, 2000; Janet Borden, Inc, NY, 2002; and many others. *Teaching:* Asst prof, Art Sch, Univ Hartford, Conn, 70-73; adj fac, State Univ, NY, Purchase, 79-91. *Awards:* Photog Grant, Nat Endowment Arts, 78 & 90; Guggenheim Mem Found Grant, 79; Artists Fel, Nat Endowment Arts, 90. *Bibliog:* Contemporary American photographs, Bull Cleveland Mus Art, Vol 79, 92; Jan Groover: Photographs, Bulfinch Press, Little, Brown & Co, Boston, 93; After Art: Rethinking 150 Years of Photography, Univ Wash Press, Seattle, 94. *Publ:* Auth, Jan Groover: Color Photographs, Milwaukee Art Mus, 80; The New Color Photography, Abbeville Press, 81; Counterparts: Form & Emotion in Photographs, Metrop Mus Art, 82; Jan Groover, Photographs, Neuberger Mus, 83. *Dealer:* Janet Borden Inc 560 Broadway New York NY 10012. *Mailing Add:* c/o Janet Borden 560 Broadway New York NY 10012

GROPPER, CATHY
PAINTER, SCULPTOR
b Cleveland, Ohio. *Study:* New York Univ, BS, 76; Columbia Univ, MA, 78 under Larry Rivers, Elaine de Kooning, Jane Wilson & Milton Resnick. *Work:* Nathan Cummings Collection & Mrs Harvey Meyerhoff Collection, Baltimore, Md & NY; Lillian Berkman, NY; Nathan Goldman Collection, Palm Beach, Fla & NY; Greek Embassy; George S Kaufman Collection. *Comn:* Nate & Me, 82, Nathan Cummings, NY; sculpture, Schermerhorn Inc, Chicago. *Exhib:* Solo exhibs, Am Merchant Marine Mus, Kings Point, NY, 79, Weintraub Gallery, NY, 86 & 95, Penson Gallery, NY, 89; group shows, Hungers 1990's: Not by Bread Alone, Carson Co Sq House Mus, Panhandle, Old Jail Art Ctr, Abilene, Mus Mod Art, Santa Fe, Amon Carter Mus, Fort Worth, Tex & Denver Art Ctr, Colo 90-92 & Elena Zang Gallery, Woodstock, NY, 95; Helen Drutt Gallery, NY, 92; Galerie Sculptures, Paris, France, 1996-2003; Jonathan Poole Gallery, Oxfordshire, Eng, 93-96; Edinburgh Fringe Festival, 2001. *Pos:* Dir, Artists Exchange, television interviews & documentaries, Conn & NY, 79-; dir, Orgn Independent Artists, NY, 90-94; playwright, 2001-2004. *Teaching:* Exec coun, Teachers Col Columbia Univ, 82-97; guest lectr, Fairfield Co, Conn & Antioch Writers Workshop. *Awards:* First Award, Mid-Western States Col Art Competition, Univ Wis, Madison. *Bibliog:* Lynn Seeney (auth), India theme, Art World, 5-6/85; Amy Penn (auth), Brushing up on young talent, New York Post, 11/8/85; Anita Gates (auth), NY Times, 2/2002; Sara Willcock (auth) The Scotsman, 2/2002. *Mem:* Artists Equity; Visual Artists & Galleries Asn; Dramatists Guild; Conn Soc Sculptors. *Media:* Oil, Welding. *Specialty:* Sculpture. *Collection:* Nathan Cummings. *Publ:* Night Mag, 6/2003. *Dealer:* Jacob Weintraub Galerie Sculptors Paris. *Mailing Add:* 110 Lyons Plain Rd Weston CT 06883

GROSCH, LAURA
PAINTER, PRINTMAKER
b Worcester, Mass, Apr 1, 45. *Study:* Wellesley Col, Mass, BA(art hist), 67; Univ Pa, Philadelphia, BFA(painting), 68; study with Gertrude Whiting, James Rayen, Sigmund Abeles, Neil Welliver. *Work:* Libr Cong & Smithsonian Inst, Washington, DC; New York Pub Libr, Brooklyn Mus, NY; Boston Mus Fine Arts & Boston Pub Libr, Mass; Calif Palace Legion Honor, San Francisco; Victoria & Albert Mus, British Mus, London, Eng; Kohler Art Ctr, Sheboygan, Wis; Carnegie Mellon Univ, Pittsburgh, Pa; Univ Calif, Los Angeles; Newark Pub Libr, Rutgers Univ, New Brunswick, NJ; Free Libr Philadelphia, Pa; Greenville Co Mus Art, SC; Honolulu Acad Arts, Hawaii; Madison Arts Ctr, Wis; Asheville Art Mus, NC; Western Carolina Univ, Culcowee, NC; Wilmington Art Mus, NC; and numerous others. *Exhib:* 30 Yrs of Am Printmaking (with catalog), Brooklyn Mus, NY, 76; solo exhibs, Jerald Melberg Gallery, Charlotte, NC, 87, Hodges Taylor Gallery Charlotte, NC, 89 & Christa Faut Gallery, Davidson, NC, 90, 93 & 96, A Prismatic Presence, Milennium Exhib, Rock Sch Arts Found, Valdese, NC, 2000, 250th Ann State of Art, Asn Artists of Winston-Salem, NC, 2004; Goddess/Woman of God, Christa Faut Gallery, Davidson, NC, 97; Solstice Exhib, Les Yeux du Monde, Charlottesville, Va, 97; Garden Gala, Morris Gallery, Columbia, SC, 97; 20th Ann Exhib, Greenhill Ctr NC Ar, Greensboro, 99; 20th Century NC Masters, Lee Hansley Gallery, Raleigh, NC, 2000; Queen Charlotte's Birds of Paradise, Chairs on Parade, Tryon Ctr for Visual Art, Charlotte, NC, 2001; The Legacy of Romare Bearden, Mint Mus Art, Charlotte, 2002; 15x15, Christa Fau Gallery, Cornelius, NC, 2003; Tribute to Alice Ehrlich, Lee Hansley Gallery, Raleigh, NC, 2003; War Charlotte, The Steeple, Charlotte, 2003; Memories of Kitty, Christa Faut Gallery, 2004; and others. *Teaching:* Community classes, 64-97. *Awards:* Teaching Grant, Mint Mus. *Bibliog:* Larry David Perkins (auth), Collaborative American Printmaking (exhib catalog), Lowe Art Gallery, Syracuse Univ, 87; Lawrence Toppman (auth), Music flows through artist's paintbrush, The Charlotte Observer, 5/9/96; Lawrence Toppman (auth), Art of the possible, The Charlotte Observer, 10/6/96. *Mem:* Col Art Asn. *Media:* Acrylic; Hand-made Litho. *Publ:* The True Essentials of a Feast, Libr Cong, 87; Luminous Impressions (film), Univ NC Pub Television, Grasberg/Littletown, 97. *Dealer:* Christa Faut Gallery 19818 N Cove Rd Suite E3 Setton Village Cornelius NC 28031; Somerhill Gallery 3 Eastgate E Franklin St Chapel Hill NC 27514-5816. *Mailing Add:* 497 S Main St PO Box 10 Davidson NC 28036

GROSS, CHARLES MERRILL
SCULPTOR, PAINTER
b Cullman, Ala, Sept 18, 35. *Study:* Atlanta Col Art, BFA; Univ GTO, MFA, Univ GTO via Clayton Univ, PhD. *Work:* Jackson State Univ, Miss; Univ Southern Miss; Marion Military Inst, Ala; Miss Delta Jr Col; Judson Col, Ala; Hinds Jr Col, Miss; City of West Point, Miss. *Exhib:* Mid-South Exhib, Brooks Mem Art Gallery, Memphis, Tenn, 69, 70 & 72; Nat Arts & Crafts Exhib, Jackson, Miss, 69 & 71; Delta Art Exhib, Ark Arts Ctr, Little Rock, 69-71, 74-75 & 78; Regional Sculpture Exhib, Carroll Reece Mus, Jackson City, Tenn, 72; Monroe Nat Ann Art Exhib, Masur Mus Art, La, 73; Mus de Arte, Brazil, 94. *Teaching:* Instr drawing, painting & sculpture, Miss Col, 68-69; asst prof art, Univ Miss, 69-73, assoc prof art, 73-80, prof art, 80-97, prof emer, 97. *Awards:* Merit Awards, 14th Mid-South Exhib, Seventh Ann Southeastern Competition, Rome, Ga & Fifth Nat Arts & Crafts Exhib, Jackson. *Mem:* Nat Art Educ Asn; Southern Asn Sculptors (regional vpres, 72-76). *Media:* All Media. *Mailing Add:* 300 Longest Rd Oxford MS 38655

GROSS, ELISSA FRANCES
ADMINISTRATOR, EDUCATOR
b Wheeling, WVa, Mar 24, 54. *Study:* Chatham Col, 72-74; Case Western Reserve Univ, Cleveland, BA, 76; Univ Chicago, MA, 77. *Pos:* Artists rep, Arts & Humanities Div, WVa Dept Cult & Hist, Charleston, 78-81; cult arts dir, Memphis Jewish Community Ctr, 81-85; dir artists-in-educ prog, Ark Arts Coun, Little Rock, 85-87; invited consult, Nat Endowment Arts-Nat Assembly State Arts Agencies, 85 & 86, Gov's HIPPY Comt, Nat Parent Teacher Asn Conf, Little Rock, 86 & Getty Ctr Educ Round Table Meeting, Chicago, 86; exec dir, Quapaw Quarter Asn, Hist Pres Org, 89-91; dir educ, Family Serv Agency, 91-. *Teaching:* Art Appreciation, Univ Ark, Little Rock, 92; facilitator (long-range planning), Ark Craft Guild. *Awards:* Leadership Award, Nat Consumer Educ, 93, Citation Award, 94. *Bibliog:* Dale Carpenter (dir), The Eyes of the Beholder (film), Ark Educ TV Network, 7/86. *Mem:* Words. *Media:* Arts Administration; Development. *Mailing Add:* 522 Patio Village Way Weston FL 33326-1612

GROSS, JULIE
PAINTER
b July 24, 43. *Study:* Pratt Inst, Brooklyn, NY, BFA, 65; Hunter Col, New York, MA, 74. *Work:* Chase Manhattan Bank; Prudential Life Insurance Co; AT&T Corp; Chait/Chasen, Prepare Inc; Chicago Title; Gulf & Western Corp; Lucent Technol; Suntrust Corp; Pfizer Corp. *Comn:* Bronson Fine Art, 99, 2000. *Exhib:* Solo shows, State Univ NY, Rockland Community Col, Suffern, 76, Frank Marino Gallery, NY, 79, Stephen Rosenberg Gallery, NY, 85 & 87, City Univ NY, Kingsborough Community Col, 93 & 55 Mercer St Gallery, 95, Kathryn Markel Gallery, New York City, 2000, Del Valley Arts Alliance, 2003; Nahan Contemp Gallery, NY, 90; Jessica Berwind Gallery, Philadelphia, 91; Eastern Mont Col, Billings, 92; Police Bldg, 94; Aldrich Mus Contemp Art, Ridgefield, Conn, 96; Parsons Sch of Design Gallery, New York City, 94, 96, 98; Kathryn Markel Gallery, New York City, 99; Margaret Thatcher Projects (3 person show), New York City, 2000; Kenise Barnes Gallery (3 person show), Larchmont, NY, 2001; Delaware Ctr for Contemp Art Struct groupshow, 2005. *Pos:* Fac consult, SADI, Seoul, Korea & KIDI, Kanazawa, Japan, 95 & 96; Ctr for Advan Design, Kuala Lumpur, 97. *Teaching:* Painting, drawing & art hist survey; vis instr, Kutztown State Col, Pa, 75 & Cent Univ NY, Manhattan, 78-79; vis asst prof, Pratt/Manhattan, 75-81 & 86-90; instr, State Univ NY, Rockland Community Col, Suffern, NY, 75-76, Ramapo Col, Wayne, NJ, 76-7, Bloomfield Col, NJ, 77; master teacher painting, State Univ NY, Fredonia, 76-79; instr painting, Metrop Mus Art, 81, RI Sch Design, 81-83; vis instr, Hunter Col, NY, 83-85 & Ctr Advan Design/CENfAD, Malaysia, 97; instr art, Parsons Sch Design, 81- & Fashion Inst Technol, 89-. *Awards:* New Sch, Fac Develop Fund Grant, 89; Nat Endowment Arts Grant, Painting, 91 92; Caps grant; MacDowell Colony Residence, 92; Grantee The New Sch Faculty Devel Fund, 89, 95; Ucross Found Residency, 96; Nat Acad Mus Mural Painting Fel, 2006. *Bibliog:* Judith Page (auth), Ground Works (catalog essay), Valencia Community Col, 89; Peggy Cyphers (auth), rev, Arts Mag, 12/90; Meyer R

Rubinstein (auth), Isn't It Romantic (catalog essay), 94; Jeff Wright (auth.) Review, Cover Mag., 95; New York Contemporary Art Report, 2000. *Media:* Oil. *Interests:* Travel; Design; Reading; Gardening. *Publ:* Coauth, Women and textiles in five cultures, Heresies, New York, No 4, 78; auth, Sustenance, Appearances, New York, No 3, 79. *Dealer:* Kathryn Markel Fine Arts 529 W 20th St New York NY 1001; Kenise Barnes fine Art, Larchmont, NY; Anderow Shire Gallery, Los Angeles. *Mailing Add:* 166 W 22nd St 4F New York NY 10011

GROSS, MARILYN A
PAINTER, PRINTMAKER
b Rolla, Mo, Jan 23, 37. *Study:* St Louis Univ, BS, 58; Wash Sch Art, Port Washington, NY, 75-78, cert, 78; Sch Art Inst Chicago Oxbow; Saugatuck, Mich, 81; Numerous seminars & workshops with leading teachers around the country, 1978-2003. *Work:* Schiff, Hardin & Waite Corp, Chicago, Ill; Com Nat Bank Corp Collection, Peoria, Ill; Magna Bank Corp Collection, Peoria, Ill. *Exhib:* Ala Watercolor Soc Exhib, Ctr Arts, Fairhope, Ala, 98; Am Watercolor Soc Int Juried Exhib, Salmagundi Club, NY, 98; Watercolor USA, Springfield Mus Art, Mo, 98; Flamingo Exhib, Hilton Leach Studios, Sarasota, Fla, 98; 19th Ann Faber Birren Nat Color Award Exhib, Univ Conn, Stamford, 1999; Int Soc Exp Artists, Huntsville Mus Art, Ala, 1999; Ariz Aqueous, Tubac Ctr for Arts, Tubac, Ariz, 1999; Northern Trust Exhib, Longboat Key, Fla, 2000; Int Soc Exp Artists, Dennos Mus, Traverse City, Mich, 2001; Nat Acrylic Painters Asn Exhib, Segretto Contemp Gallery, Santa Fe, NMex, 2002; Challenge of the Champions, Watermedia, Continental Center, Houston, Tex, 2003; Multi Media Nat Exhib, Lexington, Ky, 2006. *Awards:* nominated for Woman of the Year 1999, American Biographical Institute, Raleigh, NC, 1999; nominated for International Woman of the Year 2000/2001, International Biographical Centre, Cambridge, England, 2000; nominated for Twentieth Century Award for Achievement, International Biographical Centre, Cambridge, England, 2000. *Bibliog:* Kathleen Baxter (auth), Entering Another Dimension, Watercolor Mag, spring 2001; Marsha Fottler (auth), Mateial Girls, Sarasota Mag, 6-2003. *Mem:* Sarasota Arts Council; Chicago Artists Coalition; signature mem, Ala Watercolor Soc; assoc mem Am Watercolor Soc; signature mem, Nat Collage Soc; signature mem Nat Asn Acrylic Painters; signature mem Int Soc Exp Artists; and others. *Media:* Watercolor, Mixed Media; Acrylic. *Publ:* The Art of Layering: Making Connections, Society of Layerists in Multi-Media, 2004; The Collected Best of Watercolor, Rockport Art Publs, 2002; Splash 7: The Qualities of Light, North Light Publs, 2002; Am Artist Watercolor Mag, Spring 2001; The Complete Best of Watercolor, Rockport Publs, 2000; Creative Inspirations, Rockport Publs, 1997; Painting Color-Best of Watercolor Series, Rockport Publs, 1997; Painting Composition-Best of Watercolor Series, Rockport Publs, 1997; Watercolor: Abstracts, Rockport Art Publs, 1996; Creative Watercolor, Rockport Art Publs, 1996; Best of Watercolor, Rockport Art Publs, 1995. *Mailing Add:* 374 MacEwen Dr Osprey FL 34229

GROSS, RAINER
PAINTER
b Cologne, Ger, Apr 23, 51. *Study:* Art Acad Col, 71-73. *Work:* Bell Atlantic, Arlington, Va; Chase Manhattan Bank, NY; Hirschhorn Mus, Washington, DC; Kunsthalle, Emden, Ger; Ludwig Collection, Aachen, Ger; Mus Folkwang, Essen, Ger. *Exhib:* NY Now, Kestner Gessellschaft, Hannover, Ger, 82-83; solo exhibs, Musé Cantonal des Beaux Arts, Lausanne, Switz, 84, Kunsthalle Emden (traveling), Ger, Kunstverein Salzburg (traveling), Austria, 89, Mus Gesenkirschen (traveling), Ger, 91, Anderson Gallery, Richmond, Va, 93, Mus SFla, Univ Tampa, 93 & Folkwang Mus, Essen, Ger, 93; Krannert Mus, Champaign, Ill; and various galleries in Ger. *Bibliog:* Gerhard Finch (auth, catalog), Breast Exam, Kunsthalle Emden, 89; Noel Frackman (auth, catalog), Without Words, Ruth Siegel Gallery, NY, 91. *Media:* Oil, Acrylic. *Publ:* Auth, Une Collection s'Anime, Le Musee Cantonal des Beaux-Arts, 84; Ut Poesis Pictura, S D Sauerbier, 86; Without Words, Ruth Siegel Gallery, 91. *Dealer:* Gallery Moos Toronto Can; Gallery Oz Paris France. *Mailing Add:* 122 Second Ave New York NY 10003

GROSS, SANDRA LERNER See Lerner, Sandra

GROSSE, C(AROLYN) ANN GAWARECKI
PAINTER, INSTRUCTOR
b Rahway, NJ, Oct 30, 31. *Study:* Douglass Col, BA, 53; Univ Calif, Berkeley; Univ Colo. *Work:* COMSAT, Washington; Indust Col Armed Forces, Ft McNair, Washington; James River Corp, Richmond, Va; Georgetown Univ; Texaco; Md Casualty Co; Dunnegan Gallery Mus, Bolivar, Mo. *Comn:* Pvt comn by Nancy Dickerson, Merrywood, Va; painting, comn by Mr & Mrs Paul Tagliabue. *Exhib:* One-person shows, Atlantic Gallery, Georgetown, Washington, 78-81, & 91 & 93 Art League Gallery, Alexandria, Va, 88; McBride Gallery, Annapolis, Md, 91; 20th Century Gallery, Williamsburg, Va, 92, Nat Inst Health, 96, Douglass Col Alumnae Artist Show, 99, French Embassy, 00; Va Watercolor Soc State Show, 80-95; Nat Watercolor Soc, Brea, Calif, 87, 89 & 95 (award); Rocky Mt Nat, Golden, Colo, 89 & 98; Aqueous 90, Murray, Ky; Allied Artists Am, NY, 90; 22nd La Nat Watercolor, New Orleans, 92; Knickerbocker Artists, NY, 92; Mid-Atlantic Regional, 97 & 98. *Pos:* Exhibits artist, Mus Nat Hist, Smithsonian Inst, 56-57; partic, Art in Embassies Prog, US State Dept; judge, Nat & Area Watercolor Shows. *Teaching:* Instr watercolor, City of Falls Church, 66-; instr watercolor workshops, Del, Md, WVa, Eng, Acapulco, Mex & Ireland, France, Grand Tetons, Wyo, Greece, Italy & Spain; Art League Sch, Alexandria, Va, 95-. *Awards:* WVa Watercolor Soc Award, 94 & Southern Watercolor Soc Award, 94; 1st Award, Washington Watercolor Soc, 94; Purchase Award, Watercolor USA, 96 & 98; WUSA award, 2003; Va Watercolor Soc, 2004; Mid Atlantic Show Award, Baltimore Watercolor Soc, 2006. *Mem:* Va Watercolor Soc & Art League; Southern Watercolor Soc; Potomac Valley Watercolorists (pres, 74-77); signature mem, Nat Watercolor Soc (Wash, Baltimore, chpts); Watercolor Hon Soc. *Media:* Watercolor, Casein. *Publ:* Art Voices South, 7-8/80; Cover Hill Rag Cong Guide, 1/85, 1/89, 4/89 & 1/90; Texture Watercolor with Casein, Artist's Mag, 1/91; Best of Watercolor-Places, Artist's Mag, 96; Versatile Vignette, Watercolor Mag, Summer 97; Artistic Touch, Artist's Mag, #3, 98; cover design, A Virginia Village Revisited Inc. *Dealer:* Atlantic Gallery Washington DC; Art League Gallery Alexandria Va; Byrne Gallery Middleburg Va; McBride Gallery Annapolis MD. *Mailing Add:* 7018 Vagabond Dr Falls Church VA 22042

GROSSMAN, BARBARA
PAINTER, EDUCATOR
b New York, NY, Nov 10, 43. *Study:* Yale Sch Music & Art, 64; Cooper Union, BFA, 65; Fulbright Grant, Academie der Kunst, Munich, Ger, 67-68. *Work:* Corcoran Collection, Washington, DC; Bryn Mawr Col Lib, Pa; Weatherspoon Art Gallery, Univ NC, Greensboro; Nat Acad Mus, NY; Col Art Collection, Norwalk Community Col, Conn; Housatonic Mus of Art, Conn; Ark Art Ctr; Western Carolina Univ, Cullowhee, NC; Hood Mus Art, Dartmouth Col, Hanover, NJ; Portland Community Col, Portland, Oreg; Johnson and Johnson; Hollins Univ, Roanoke, Va. *Exhib:* Drawing Invitational, Ind Univ, Bloomington, 87; Figure Invitational, Col William & Mary, Williamsburg, Va, 87; Quest, NY Studio Sch, 89; Muscarelle Mus Art, Williamsburg, Va, 94; Western Carolina State Univ, Cullowhee, NC, 98; Mangel Gallery, Philadelphia, Pa, 98; Figurative Painting Now, 55 Mercer, NY, 2000; Wayne Art Ctr, Pa, 2000; solo exhib, Bowery Gallery, NY, 73, 77, 81, 85, 88, 92, 95, 98, 01, Hollins Univ, Roanoke, Va, 03, Taft Sch, Watertown, Conn, 06; Dartmouth Col, Hanover, NH, 2002, Union Col, Schenectady, NY, 03, New Arts Gallery, Litchfield, Conn, 04, 06, Wright State Univ, Dayton, Ohio, 04, Lafayette Col, Easton, Pa, 04, Washington & Lee Univ, Lexington, Va, 05, NY Studio Sch, 05. *Pos:* Applied arts adv comt, Tunxis Community Col, 79-85; vis critic, Yale Univ, 86-2005; chmn exhib comt, Wash Art Asn, 88-; vis artist, Knox Col, 99-2004, Brandeis Univ, 99-2004, Colby Col, 2000. *Teaching:* Adj prof, drawing, Western Conn State Univ, Danbury, 81-94; resident fac, Chautauqua Inst Art Sch, 87-2006; fac, painting & drawing, NY Studio Sch, 88-2001; prof fac, Vt Studio Ctr, 91-95; Hartford Art Sch, Univ Hartford, Conn, 92-; Grad Sch Fine Arts, Univ Pa, 93-2000; Univ Conn, 2000; Yale Sch Art, 2003 & 2005; Western Carolina Univ, NC, 2004-06; Nat Acad Sch Fine Art, NY, 2005. *Awards:* Ingram Merrill Found Award Painting, 82-83; Nat Acad Design Award for painting, 95; Award, Nat Acad Design, 00; Award, Conn Commn on the Arts, 78, 2002; Fulbright Grant, Munich, Ger, 67-68; Henry Ward Ranger Purchase Award, Nat Acad, 2001. *Bibliog:* Robert Godfrey (auth), Aspects of Representation: 9 Painters (catalog), 98; interview, Philadelphia Inquirer, 99; Lynn Munson (auth), Exhibitionism, 00; Jennifer Bell (auth), Art News, 1/2005; Ken Johnson (auth), NY Times, 10/2001; Andrew Forge & Linda Konheim Kramer (auths), Catalogue, Dartmouth Col, 2002; Barbara Grossman A Survey, (catalogue), 2004-2005. *Mem:* Col Art Asn; Nat Acad. *Media:* Oil Paint, Oil Pastel. *Dealer:* Bowery Gallery 530 W 25 St New York NY 10001. *Mailing Add:* 2338 Litchfield Rd Watertown CT 06795

GROSSMAN, BONNIE
GALLERY DIRECTOR
Pos: Founder, Ames Gallery of outsider art, Berkeley, Calif, 70-. *Teaching:* kindergarten teacher, formerly. *Mem:* Calif (formerly Bay Area) Lawyers for the Arts (found mem). *Publ:* Exec prod, co-dir, prod nine TV programs on Calif artists; contribr articles to prof publ; lectr on antiques. *Mailing Add:* Ames Gallery 2661 Cedar St Berkeley CA 94708

GROSSMAN, MAURICE KENNETH
EDUCATOR, CERAMIC ARTIST
b Detroit, Mich, Sept 16, 27. *Study:* Wayne State Univ, Detroit, with J Foster, BS(art educ), 50; Alfred Univ, NY, with Dan Rhodes, 51; Ohio State Univ, Columbus, with Paul Bogatay, MFA(ceramics), 53. *Work:* Detroit Mus Art; Phoenix Mus Art; El Paso Mus; Utah State Mus, Salt Lake City; Albuquerque Mus Art, NMex; Tucson Mus of Art, Ariz. *Comn:* commn by Joan Mannheimer, Des Moines, Iowa, Elizabeth Wainstock, NY, Adolph-Berta Wright, Tucson, Ariz, Robert & Mary Wrenm, Tucson, Judity Goldman, Houston. *Exhib:* Ceramic Nat, Everson Mus Art, Syracuse, 50-68; Clay Invitational, Smithsonian Inst, 53 & 59; Westwood Clay Nat, Otis Art Gallery, Los Angeles, 80; Int Invitational, Arabia & Finland, 84; Possessions, Harrison Mus, Logan, Vt, 89; Raku Kansas City Contemp Art, 89; East West Ctr, Honolulu, 90; Int Gallery, San Diego, Calif, 93. *Teaching:* Instr ceramics, Western Wash Col, Bellingham, 53-54; prof ceramics, Univ Ariz, Tucson, 55-88, prof emer, 88-. *Awards:* Alumni Award, Wayne State Univ, 82; Craft Fel, Nat Endowment Arts, 84; Ariz Art Award, 97. *Bibliog:* John Conrad (auth), Contemporary Ceramic Techniques, Prentice Hall, 79; Robert Peipeuburg (auth), Raku Pottery, Pebble Press, 91; Susan Peterson (auth), Craft and Art of Clay, Prentice Hall, 92. *Mem:* Am Crafts Coun (southwest area rep, 63-66), Ariz Designer-Craftsmen (pres, 60); Tucson Art Ctr (bd dir, 68, adv 88); Nat Coun Educ for Ceramic Arts (regional rep, 72); World Crafts Coun. *Media:* Ceramics. *Publ:* Auth, American ceramics, Tanko Mag, Kyoto, Japan, 56; Clay in the Hand, an American in Japan, Inst Int Educ, 56. *Dealer:* Craft Shop Tucson Mus Art 140 N Main Ave Tucson AZ85701. *Mailing Add:* Univ Ariz Dept Art Tucson AZ 85721

GROSSMAN, NANCY
PAINTER, SCULPTOR
b New York, NY, Apr 28, 1940. *Study:* Pratt Inst, BFA, 62. *Work:* Whitney Mus Am Art, Metrop Mus Art, NY; Princeton Univ Art Mus; Univ Mus, Berkeley, Calif; Dallas Mus Fine Arts; Israel Mus, Jerusalem; Phoenix Art Mus, Ariz; Nat Mus Am Art, Smithsonian Inst, Washington, DC; Va Mus Fine Art, Richmond; Contemp Arts Mus, Honolulu; Greenville Co Art Mus, Greenville, SC. *Exhib:* one-woman shows, Krasner Gallery, New York City, 64-67, Cordier & Ekstrom, New York City, 68-71, 73, 75, 76, Church Fine Arts Gallery, Univ Nevada, Reno, 78, Barbara Gladstone Gallery, New

York City, 80, 82, Heath Gallery, Atlanta, 81, 86, Terry Dintenfass Gallery, 84, Exit Art, New York City, 91, Sculpture Center, New York City, 91, Hillwood Art Mus, New York City, 91, Artemisia, Chicago, 92, Beacon St Gallery, Chicago, 92, Ark Art Ctr, Little Rock, 92, Contemp Mus, Honolulu, 92, Binghamton Univ Art Gallery, 92, Hooks-Epstein Galleries, Houston, 93, 95, LedisFlam, New York City, 94, Weatherspoon Art Gallery, Greensboro, NC, 94, Greenville Cty Mus Art, 2004; numerous group shows, incl, Whitney Mus Am Art, New York City, 68-69, 73, 80, 81, 93 & 95; Contemp Arts Mus, Honolulu, 92; Firefields, Hawaii Ctr, Honolulu, 2000; Gloria: An Exhibit, White Columns, NY, 2002; True Grit: Seven Female Visionaries Before Feminism, Univ Richmond Mus, Va, 2002. *Teaching:* Instr sculpture, Boston Fine Arts Sch, 85; instr drawing, Cooper Union, 89. *Awards:* NY Found Arts Fel, Sculpture, 91; Joan Mitchell Found Award, 96; The Pollock-Krasner Found award, 2000 & 01; and others. *Bibliog:* Cindy Nemser (auth), Art Talk, Conversations with 12 Women Artists, Scribners, 75; Charlotte Streifer Rubenstein (auth), American Women Artists, Avon, 82; Arlene Raven (auth), Nancy Grossman, Hillwood Art Mus, 91; Nancy Grossman (auth) Loud Whispers, Four Decades of Assemblage, Collage & Sculpture, Michael Rosenfeld Gallery, Essay by Lonery Stokes Sims. *Mem:* Nat Acad. *Media:* Sculpture; Drawing; Collage. *Specialty:* Am Abstractionist; Early Abstractionist Expressionist; Underrepresented Am/Modernist Art; Realism; Surrealism; Social Realism. *Dealer:* Michael Rosenfeld Gallery New York NY; Hooks Epstein Galleries Houston TX

GROSSMAN, SHELDON
MUSEUM CURATOR, HISTORIAN
b New York, NY, Aug 30, 40. *Study:* Hunter Col, BA, 62; NY Univ Inst Fine Arts, MA, 66. *Collection Arranged:* Cur, Art in the Age of Petrarch, 74, Venetian Drawings from American Collections, 74, From Caravaggio to Giordano, Painting in Naples 1606-1705 (coauth, catalog), 83 & Caravaggio, The Deposition from the Vatican Collections (auth, catalog), 84, Nat Gallery Art, Washington, DC. *Pos:* Asst cur, Photographic Archives, 71-74 & cur, Northern & Later Italian Paintings, 74-85, Nat Gallery Art, Washington, DC; owner & oper, Grossman Fine Arts Inc, 85-; sr research fel, Corcoran Gallery, Washington, DC, 96. *Teaching:* Rutgers Univ & The State Univ, New Brunswick, NJ, 65 & 66; Manhattanville Col Sacred Heart, Purchase, New York, 66; George Washington Univ, Washington, DC, 74. *Awards:* Fulbright-Hays Travel Grant, 66; Ital Govt Study Grant, 66; Chester Dale Fel, 67-69 & Paul Mellon Vis Sr Fel, 97, Nat Gallery Art, Washington, DC; and others. *Bibliog:* Review, From Rome to Eternity: Catholicism and the Arts in Italy, SF Ostrow, CAA Online Reviews, April 2004. *Res:* Problems in Florentine painting in the late fifteenth and early sixteenth century; analysis of problems of style; archival research; early Baroque art in the context of social, religious and political phenomena; Europena drawing and the Corcoran Gallery. *Publ:* Auth, National Gallery of Art report and studies in the history of art, 68; Mitteilungen des kunst-historischen institutes in Florenz, 69; Master drawings, 72; National Gallery of Art, Studies in the History of Art, 74; Auth, Ghir landaio's Madonna and Child in Frankfurt and Leonardo's Beginnings as a Painter, Stadel Jahrbuch, Vol 7, 79; Titian and Moroni in Trent, Apollo, Vol 109, 79; The Sovereignty of the Painted Image: Poetry and the Shroud of Turin, in From Rome to Eternity. *Mailing Add:* 2312 Tunlaw Rd NW Washington DC 20007-1816

GROSVENOR, ROBERT
SCULPTOR
b New York, NY, 1937. *Study:* Ecole des Beaux Arts, Dijon, France, 56; Ecole Superieure des Arts Decoratifs, Paris, 57-59; Univ di Perugia, Italy, 58. *Work:* Whitney Mus, NY; Storm King Art Ctr, Mountainville, NY; Mus Mod Art, NY; Hirshhorn Mus, Washington, DC; Walker Art Ctr, Minneapolis. *Comn:* Storm King Art Ctr, Mountainville, NY. *Exhib:* Sculpture for the 60's, Los Angeles Co Mus, 67; Plus by Minus, Albright-Knox Art Gallery, Buffalo, NY, 68; Sculpture Ann, Whitney Mus Am Art, NY, 68, Biennial Exhib Am Painting & Sculpture, 73 & 200 Yrs Am Sculpture, 76; 14 Sculptors: the Industrial Edge, Walker Art Ctr, Minneapolis, 69; Contemp Am Art, Whitney Mus Am Art, 69, biennial 73, 200 yrs Am Sculpture, 76; Art on Paper, Inst Contemp Art, Boston, 70; one-man exhibs, Paula Cooper Gallery, NY, 70, 71, 75, 78, 81, 86, 88, 91, 93, 96 & 98, PS1 Inst Art & Urban Resources, Long Island City, NY, 84, Centre d'Art Contemporair du Domaine de Kerguehennec a Bigan Locmine, France, 89, Margo Leavin Gallery, Los Angeles, 90, Galerie Max Hetzler, Cologne, 92 & 95, Kunsthalle, Bern, Switz, 92 & Lawrence Markey, NY, 96; Works on Paper, 31st Ann Exhib, Soc Contemp Art, Art Inst Chicago, 71; Biennial Exhib Am Painting & Sculpting, Whitney Mus Am Art, 73; 200 Yrs of Am Sculpture, Whitney Mus Am Art, 76; Private Images: Photographs by Sculptors, Los Angeles Co Mus Art, Contemp Art Galleries, Lytton Halls, 77-78; Minimal Tradition, 79 & PostMINIMALISM, 82, Aldrich Mus Contemp Art; Art on Paper Weatherspoon Art Gallery, 93; 25 Yrs (Part I), Paula Cooper Gallery, NY, 93; Country Sculpture, le consort, Dijon, France, 94; From Minimal to Conceptual Art: Works from the Dorothy & Herbert Vogel Collections Nat Gallery Art, Washinton, 94; Holiday Exhib, Paula Cooper Gallery, 94; Am Sculptors in the 1960s: Selected Drawings from the Collection, Mus Mod Art, NY, 95; Forum: Robert Grosvenor, Andreas Gursky, John Wesley, Carnegie Mus Art, Pittsburgh, Pa, 99; and many others. *Awards:* Guggenheim Fel, 69; Nat Endowment Arts & Humanities Grant, 70; Nat Acad Arts & Lett Grant, 72. *Bibliog:* Jeremy Gilbert Rolfe (auth), Robert Grosvenor: Specific Clarity, Art in Am, 3-4/76; John Russel (auth), Critics Choice: Galleries, New York Times, 4/21/78; Deborah Perlberg (auth), Reviews in New York, Artforum, summer 78; Donald Kupsit (auth), Robert Grosvenor, Artforum, summer 84; John Russell (auth), Robert Grosvenor, New York Times, 4/18/86. *Mailing Add:* c/o Paula Cooper Gallery 534 W 21st St New York NY 10011

GROTJAHN, MARK
PAINTER
b Pasadena, Calif. *Study:* Univ Colo, Boulder, BFA; Univ Calif, Berkeley, MFA. *Exhib:* Mus Contemp Art, Los Angeles; UCLA Hammer Muss; London Inst Gallery, 54th Carnegie Internat; Carnegie Mus Art, Pitts, Pa, 2005; Whitney Biennial, Whitney Mus Art, NYC, 2006; Mus Modern Art, NYC; one-man shows: Stephen Friedman Gallery, London; Anton Kern Gallery, NYC; Blum & Poe, Los Angeles; Boom, Chicago; The Saatchi Gallery. *Mailing Add:* UCLA Hammer Gallery 10899 Wilshire Blvd Los Angeles CA 90024

GROWDON , MARCIA COHN
ADMINISTRATOR, HISTORIAN
b San Francisco, Calif, Dec 17, 45. *Study:* Stanford Univ, BA, 67, PhD, 76; Univ Mich, BA, 68. *Collection Arranged:* Treasures of the Middle Ages (auth, catalog), 78, The New York School 1940-1960 (ed, catalog), 79, Computers and the Visual Arts: Research & Drawings of H Cohen (auth, catalog), 79, Artists in the American Desert, Nat Tour (auth, catalog), 80-81 & Sierra Nevada Museum Biennial: The Best of Nevada's Contemporary Art (auth, catalog), 86, Nev Mus Art. *Pos:* Cur, Nev Mus Art, Reno, 78-81, dir, 81-87; vchmn, CITY 2000, Reno Arts Comn, 90-96, chmn, 94-95; chmn, Nev Comn for Cultural Affairs, 91-95; coll comt mem, Nev Mus Art, Reno; mem, Nev Hist Preservation Bd, 85-93, chmn, 89-93; vchmn, Nev State Mus Bd, 93-95. *Teaching:* Lectr art hist, Univ Nev, Reno, 89-; lectr, Nev Mus Art, Reno, 2002-. *Awards:* Samuel Kress Found Fel & Travel Grants, 68-70; Governor's Award for Serv to Arts, Nev, 92. *Bibliog:* article, Designed by Will Bruder: Nevada Museum of Art, 2003. *Mem:* Art Table. *Res:* 19th and 20th century art, particularly in the Far West. *Mailing Add:* PO Box 10752 Reno NV 89510

GRUBER, AARONEL DEROY
PAINTER, SCULPTOR, PHOTOGRAPHER
b Pittsburgh, Pa. *Study:* Carnegie Inst Technol. *Work:* Smithsonian Inst; Rose Art Mus, Brandeis Univ; Butler Inst Am Art; De Cordova Mus, Lincoln, Mass; Aldrich Mus Contemp Art; Frederick R Weisman Found Art, Los Angeles; Westinghouse Elec Corp Collection; Kawamura Mem Mus Mod Art, Sakura, Japan; Carnegie Mus Art; Grand Rapids Mus; City of Pittsburgh, Pa. *Comn:* Steelcityscape (steel sculpture, 21 ft), Fort Duquesne Park, Pittsburgh, 77; plexiglas sculpture, Westinghouse, Pittsburgh, Pa; 32 ft cor-ten sculpture, Gen Mills Corp, Minneapolis, 71; two sculptures, comn by DeBartolo, Melbourne Mall, Fla; Par Progress, Grand Cent Mall, Parkersburg, WVa; Blue Cross Blue Shield, Pittsburgh, Pa; Hillman Libr, Univ of Pittsburgh, Pa; Bayer Corp; Mobil Oil. *Exhib:* Solo show, Carnegie Mus Art, 77; Twenty-Five Pennsylvania Women, Southern Alleghenies Mus Art, 79; A Look Back-A Look Forward, Aldrich Mus Continuing Art, 82; Butler Inst Am Art, Youngstown, Ohio, 88; World Expo '88, Brisbane, Australia, 88; Photo Forum, 91-92, 94, 95, 97, 98; Rated "X" Show, Neikrug Gallery, 92; and others; Pittsburgh Ctr for the Arts Biennial, 94; Concept Gallery, Pittsburgh, Pa, 90; Photo Metro, San Francisco, Calif, 93; Westport Arts Ctr Photo Biennial, Conn, 94; Oakland Mus "Architecture in Focus II", Calif, 95; Rena Bransten Gallery, San Francisco, 97; Carnegie Mus of Art, Pittsburgh, 98; Columbus Mus of Art, Ohio, 99. *Awards:* Int Award, Women in Photog, traveling US, Europe & Far East, 89-90; Natural World Photog Competition Prize, Carnegie Mus, 88; Purchase Award, 100 Friends Art, 92; Gloria Fitzgibbon Award in Photography in Miles for Women, Greater Pittsburgh Commn for Women, 93; Westmoreland Co Arts Nat, John Sonafelt Award and Photograph of the Yr Award, 99; Pittsburgh Tribune Review-Photograph of the Yr, Westmoreland Arts and Heritage Festival, Latrobe, Pa, 99. *Bibliog:* Donald Miller (auth), Arts Mag, 5/78; Virginia Watson-Jones, Contemporary American Women Sculptors, Oryx Press, 88; Donald Miller (auth), Artists will create, Pittsburgh Post Gazette, 9/3/88; Donald Miller (auth), Aaronel. The Art of Aaronel deRoy Gruber, 99. *Mem:* Western Pa Soc Sculptors (pres, 74-78); Group A (pres, 79-85); Assoc Artists of Pittsburgh (bd dir, 67-69); PhotoImagers Guild; Nat Mus Women in Arts; Silver Eye, Pittsburgh Ctr Arts (bd mem, 74-85); Women Photog. *Media:* Oil; Steel, Aluminum, Panoramic Photography. *Dealer:* Photo Forum. *Mailing Add:* 2409 Marbury Rd Pittsburgh PA 15221

GRUBER, J RICHARD
ADMINISTRATOR, HISTORIAN
b Louisville, Ky, Mar 30, 48. *Study:* Xavier Univ, BA(Eng), 71; Univ Colo, MA(cum laude), 80; Univ Kans, MPH, 82, PhD, 87. *Collection Arranged:* Memphis in Memphis, 83, Sheffield Silver: The Kirby Collection, Australian Art in Our Time & Kentucky Shaker Furniture, 84, Memphis: 1948-1958 (with catalog), 86, Memphis Brooks Mus Art, Tenn; In Plain View: The Collages of Irwin Kremen (catalog), 87; George Wardlaw: Transitions (catalog), 88; We Like Ike, The Eisenhower Presidency & 1950's America (auth, catalog), 90; Ancient Echos/Silent Messenger: Steve Kestrel, 91; The Dot Man: George Andrews of Madison, Ga (auth, catalog), 94. *Pos:* Cur of collections, Memphis Brooks Mus Art, Tenn, 83-85, interim dir, 84-85, dir, 85-89; dir, Wichita Art Mus, 89-91, Ctr Study Southern Painting, 93-; co-dir, Peter Joseph Gallery, 92; deputy dir, Morris Mus Art, 93-. *Teaching:* Lectr art hist, Univ Colo, Colorado Springs, 79-81; lectr art hist, Augusta Col, 95. *Awards:* Smithsonian Res Fel, Nat Mus Art, 82-83; Kress Found Fel, Kans, 82-83. *Mem:* Am Asn Mus; Am Inst Archit; Col Art Asn. *Res:* Nineteenth and twentieth century American art and architecture, emphasis on Thomas Hart Benton and regionalism. *Publ:* Memphis: 1948-1958, 86. *Mailing Add:* Morris Mus Art One 10th St Augusta GA 30901-0100

GRUCZA, LEO (VICTOR)
PAINTER, EDUCATOR
b Erie, Pa, Jan 3, 35. *Study:* Cleveland Inst Art, dipl, 57; Tulane Univ, MFA, 61, with George Rickey & others. *Work:* Ill State Mus, Springfield; Krannert Art Mus, Univ Ill, Champaign; Ill State Univ, Normal. *Exhib:* Art Inst Chicago, 80-81 & 84; Zriny Gallery, Chicago, 83; Am Acad & Inst Arts & Letters, 83; Nihon Univ, Tokyo, 83;

Viridian Gallery, NY, 85; one-man shows, Zriny Gallery, Chicago, 84, Artemisia Gallery, Chicago, 86, Renner Gallery, Blackburn Col, Carlinville, Ill, 87, ARC Gallery, Chicago, 88, Space Gallery, Chicago, 2001, Lazzare Fine Arts, Stoughton, WI, 2003, Texas Nat, Nacogdoches, Tex, 2003; Gallery U, Cleveland, Ohio, 2004. *Teaching:* Asst prof painting, Univ Ill, Champaign, 66-70, assoc prof painting, 70-84, prof, 85-2003, prof emer, 2003-. *Awards:* First Prize-Painting, Ann Exhib, Delgado Mus, New Orleans, 61; Tiffany Found Grant, NY, 61; Nat Endowment Arts Grants, 82 & 83; Governor's Purchase Award, State of Ill Prof Exhib, Springfield, 82; Yaddo Fel, Hand-Hollow Found, East Chatham, NY, 83; fel, Ctr for Advan Study, Univ Ill, 84-85. *Media:* Oil. *Dealer:* Carolyn Baxley Cinema Gallery Urbana IL 61801. *Mailing Add:* 2204 Blackthorn Dr Champaign IL 61821

GRUEN, JOHN
CRITIC, WRITER
b Enghien-les-Bains, France, Sept 12, 26; US citizen. *Study:* City Col New York; Univ Iowa, BA & MA. *Pos:* Critic of music & art, New York Herald Tribune, 62-68; art critic, New York Mag, 69-73 & Soho Weekly News, 74-; contribr ed, Art News, 76-; sr ed, Dance Mag, 79-. *Teaching:* Lectr, Metrop Mus Art, 79-. *Publ:* Auth, Close-Up Viking Press, 69, The Private World of Leonard Bernstein, 69, The Party's Over Now, 73, The Private World of Ballet, 75 & Erik Bruhn: Danseur Noble, 79; The World's Greatest Ballets, Harry N Abrams, 82; People Who Dance, Princeton Bks, 88; The Artist Observed, A Cappella Bks, 91; Keith Haring, The Authorized Biography, Prentice Hall/Simon & Schuster, 91; and others. *Mailing Add:* 317 W 83rd St New York NY 10024

GRUEN, SHIRLEY SCHANEN
PAINTER
b Port Washington, Wis, Dec 2, 23. *Study:* Univ Wis, Madison, BS(art educ) 45; Art Ctr Sch, LosAngeles, Calif, 46; Cardinal Stritch Col, Milwaukee, 72-88. *Work:* West Bend Fine Arts Gallery, Wis; Milwaukee Art Comn, Wis; Ozaukee Bank, Port Wash, Wis; Heritage Ins, Sheboygan, Wis; Wis Conservatory Music, Milwaukee. *Comn:* three paintings, Port Washington State Bank, 92; two paintings, Marshall & Ilsley Bank, Wis, 93; two paintings, First Financial Savings Bank, 93; Three paintings, Ozaukee Bank, Wis, 94; Heritage Insurance Co, 95. *Exhib:* Solo exhibs, West Bend Gallery Fine Arts, Wis, 81 & Water St Gallery, Moraine Bank, Milwaukee, 84; Salamagundi 11th, 15th, & 18th Ann, NY 88, 92 & 95; Oil Pastel Int Exhib, NY, 89 & 90; WWIA Expressions and Commentary, Neville Mus, Green Bay, Wis, 91; Cedarburg Cult Ctr, Wis, 92; Ariz Aqueous, 93 & 97; Getting There, Neville Mus, Green Bay, Wis 95; Milwaukee Sesquicentennial, 96; Cyberspace, Internet, Virtually the First, WPS, 96; and many others. *Pos:* Owner, Shirley Gruen Studio, Port Wash, Wis, 72-. *Teaching:* Instr watercolor & portrait, Milwaukee Area Tech Col, Wis. *Awards:* Purchase Award, Response 83, Milwaukee Arts Comn, 83; Award, Pa Watercolor Soc, 85; Oil Pastel Award, Salmagundi Club, Oil Pastel Assoc, New York, 88; Citizen of Year, Port Wash Chamber Com, 2003; Citation Historical Art Work of Port Wash, State Leg Wis, 2003. *Bibliog:* West 80-Art and Law, Am Bar Asn Journal, 7/80; Sally Prince Davis (auth), Selling Your Art, North Light Books, Spring 89; articles in Milwaukee J, Wis, 91 & 92, Sheboygan Press, 11/2001. *Mem:* Wis Painters and Sculptors; Wis Watercolor Soc. *Media:* Acrylic, Watercolor. *Specialty:* 20 limited edition prints & various scenes Port Wash. *Mailing Add:* 303 N Franklin Port Washington WI 53074

GRUNBERG, SLAWOMIR
FILMMAKER
b Lublin, Poland. *Study:* Polish Film Sch, Lodz, Poland. *Pos:* Founder, Log-In Productions, 87-. *Awards:* Nat Endowment Arts Fel, 85 & Production Grant, 87; Emmy Award Best Doc, 90; John Simon Guggenheim Fel Doc Filmmaking, 97. *Publ:* Producer of over 40 television docs. *Mailing Add:* Log-In Productions 4 LaRue Rd Spencer NY 14883

GRUNDBERG, ANDY (ANDREW) JOHN
CRITIC, CURATOR
b Bryn Mawr, Pa, June 25, 47. *Study:* Cornell Univ, BA, 69; Univ NC, Greensboro, MFA, 71. *Pos:* Picture ed, Mod Photog, 74-; photog critic, Soho Weekly News, 79-81 & New York Times, 81-91; dir, the Friends Photog, San Francisco, 92-97. *Teaching:* Vis critic, RI Sch Design, Providence, 85; instr art hist, Sch Visual Arts, NY, 86-91 & instr grad photog prog 88-91; vis instr grad photog prog, San Francisco Art Inst, 92; adj prof, Dartmouth Col, 98-99, Univ Hartford, 99-. *Awards:* Reva & David Logan Found Grant, Photog Resource Ctr, 85; Manufacturers Hanover Art/World Award, 89; Infinity Award Int Ctr Photog, 99. *Mem:* Soc Photog Educ (bd dir, 83-88); AAM; Independent Curators Inc. *Res:* Twentieth century American photography, with emphasis on contemporary practice and theory. *Publ:* Contribr, The Camera Viewed, Dutton, 79; contribr, Reading into Photography, Univ NMex Press, 82; auth, Grundberg's Goof-Proof Photography Guide, Fireside, 89; Mike and Doug Starn, Harry N Abrams Inc, 90; Crisis of the Real: Writings on Photography, 1974-1989, Aperture, 90, rev ed, 99. *Mailing Add:* 1102 E Capital St NE Washington DC 20002-6225

GRUNWALDT, CARMELA C
PAINTER
b Chicago, Ill. *Study:* Art Inst Chicago. *Work:* Brand Libr Art Gallery, Glendale, Calif; Carville Marine Hosp, La. *Exhib:* Nat Watercolor Soc Traveling Exhibs, 88-89 & 94-95; Fine Arts Fedn, Burbank, Calif, 93; Los Angeles Art Asn, Calif, 93; Foothills Artcenter, Golden, Colo, 94; Muckenthaler Mus, Fullerton, Calif, 94; and others. *Awards:* Experimental Painting Award, Nat Watercolor Soc, 87; Gold Award, 93, Bronze Award, 93, Art of Calif Mag; Alexander Nepote Award, Nat Watercolor Competition, Muckenthaler Mus, Fullerton, Calif, 94; and others. *Bibliog:* Joseph Mugnaini (auth), Expressive Drawing, Davis Publ, 88; Margerita Nieto (auth), Art Scene, Los Angeles, 93; John Adams (auth), Downey Eagle, Downey, Calif, 94. *Mem:* Los Angeles Art Asn; signature mem Nat Watercolor Soc; Calif Collagists Los Angeles; Pasadena Soc Artists. *Media:* Mixed Media. *Mailing Add:* 772 Linda Vista Ave Pasadena CA 91103-2769

GRUPP, CARL ALF
PAINTER, PRINTMAKER
b Moorhead, Minn, Sept 11, 39. *Study:* Minneapolis Col Art & Design, BFA, 64; Vrije Acad, Netherlands, Vanderlip Scholar, 65; Ind Univ, MFA(with hons), 69; and with Rudy Pozzatti, Urban Couch, Marvin Lowe, William Bailey & James McGarrell. *Work:* Minneapolis Inst Art & Univ Minn Gallery, Minneapolis; Am Embassy, London; Chicago Art Inst; SDak Mem Art Ctr, Brookings. *Comn:* Meditation Mountain, Augustana Col Libr, Sioux Falls, SDak; Parable Paintings, Gloria Dei Lutheran Church, Sioux Falls, SDak. *Exhib:* Joslyn Art Mus 12th Biennial, Omaha, Nebr, 72; Pratt Graphic Art Exhib, NY, 72-73; Am Printmakers, Ind Univ, US Info Agency Tour Eng, 73; Drawings USA, Minn Mus Art, St Paul, 75; Boston Printmakers, 81; plus many others. *Teaching:* Asst lithography, Minneapolis Col Art & Design, 64-65; asst intaglio printmaking, Ind Univ, Bloomington, 68-69; asst prof art, Augustana Col, 69-81, prof art, 88-, emeritus prof. *Awards:* Gustave Krollman Award for Draftsmanship, Minneapolis Col Art & Design, 63; Purchase Awards, SDak Mem Art Ctr, 73 & Silvermine Guild, New Canaan, Conn; Individual SDak State Arts Coun Grant, 88. *Bibliog:* Spotted talents in America, Frasconi, Grupp, Tendensen, 11/65; Craig Volk (auth), Art of Carl Grupp (video tape), KUSD-TV, Univ SDak, 3/75; Carl Grupp: A Look Back, Northern, State Univ, 91. *Media:* Oil, Printmaking. *Dealer:* Eastbank Art Gallery Sioux Falls. *Mailing Add:* 1614 S Phillips Ave Sioux Falls SD 57105

GRUPPE, CHARLES
PAINTER
b New York, NY, July 1, 28. *Study:* Yale Univ; Nat Univ Mex; Columbia Univ, BFA, 54, MFA(Brevoort Fel), 55; Huntington Hartford Found, Pacific Palisades, 56; Fulbright Fel, Italy, 57. *Work:* over 5,000 pvt collections. *Comn:* Paintings, Am Pres Lines, Coolidge, Jackson & Wilson, 65; Yale Divinity Sch, New Haven, Conn, 65; Dolly O'Brien Estate, Palm Beach, 64; First Nat Bank, New Haven, 65; apt complexes, Palm Beach, 72-73. *Exhib:* Silvermine Guild Artists, New Canaan, Conn, 65 & 77; Provincetown Art Asn, 65 & 77 & Rockport Art Asn, Mass, 70 & 77; Butler Mus Am Art, Youngstown, Ohio, 72 & 75; Lord & Taylor, NY, 75; Witte Mus, San Antonio, Tex. *Teaching:* Workshop instr, Marco Isalnd, Fla & Greenwich, Conn, 87-89; Workshops, Cincinnati, Ohio, Acapulco, Mex, Scotsdale, Ariz, Northern Mich, Pocono Mountains, Pa, 94-95; Workshops, Portugal, 1999, Spain, 2000, France, 2001, Italy, 2002. *Awards:* Hudson Valley Award, 86; Silvermine Guild Award, 87; Winsor Newton Nat Competition Award, 94. *Media:* Oil, Acrylics

GRUSKIN, MARY JOSEPHINE
CONSULTANT, COLLECTOR
b Trani, Italy; US citizen. *Study:* Cooper Union, NY Sch Design. *Bibliog:* Art Times, 5/90. *Mem:* Metrop Mus Drawing Soc. *Publ:* Auth, article, Art & Auction, 12/85

GRUSS, MARTIN DAVID
PATRON
b New York, NY, Mar 1, 43. *Study:* Univ Pa, BSE, 64; NY Univ, LLB, 67. *Pos:* Sr partner, Gruss Partners, New York City; bd dir, Mack Cali Realty Corp, NJ; bd trustee, Solomon R Guggenheim Mus, New York City; part-owner, Cleveland Indians MLB team, formerly. *Mem:* NY Bar Asn. *Mailing Add:* Gruss & Co 667 Madison Ave New York NY 10021

GRUVER, MARY EMMETT
PAINTER, INSTRUCTOR
b Leavenworth, Kans, Nov 9, 1912. *Study:* Univ Calif, Berkeley, BA(fine arts), 34, studied landscape painting with Robert Rishell, portrait with Peter Blos. *Work:* Main Lobby, Martinez Vets Hosp, Calif. *Comn:* Portrait commd by Knights of Columbus/a founder of San Francisco Cath Ch; Portrait Gordan Van Vlek, Calif Sec of Agr, Stockmans Bank in Sacramento. *Exhib:* Calif State Fair-Exhib, Fairgrounds, Sacramento, Calif, 65 & 67; Jack London Sq Art Festival, 14th Ann Outdoor, Oakland, Calif, 68; Santa Cruz Statewide Exhib, Santa Cruz League Bldg, Calif, 70-71; San Francisco 26th Art Festival, Civic Ctr Plaza, 72; Soc Western Artists, 31st Ann Hall of Flowers, San Francisco, 78; and others. *Teaching:* Instr art, State Calif, Adult Educ, 61-75. *Awards:* First & Second Representational Oil, Livermore Art Asn 9th Ann, 65; First Pastel Portrait, Santa Cruz Art Ann, 70-71; First Watercolor & Purchase Award, Placerville Art Ann, 76. *Mem:* signature mem Pastel Soc West Coast, Sacramento, Calif; signature mem Soc Western Artists, San Francisco; PSA, NY. *Media:* All Media. *Publ:* Illusr, Weekend Sect, Mountian Democrat, Placerville, Calif, 9/30/94. *Mailing Add:* 5471 Gold Hill Rd Placerville CA 95667

GRYGUTIS, BARBARA
SCULPTOR, ENVIRONMENTAL ARTIST
b Hartford, Conn, Nov 7, 46. *Study:* Univ Ariz, BFA, 68, MFA, 71. *Work:* Standing Leaves, Falling Light, Light Sculpture, King Co Public Art Prog, Seattle, Wash, 2002; The Illuminated Page, City of Santa Clara Public Art Collection, Calif, 2004; Journeys Sculptural environment for WMATA, Washington, DC, 2004; Life Lines, Philadelphia PA, Sculptural environment for SEPTA, City Ctr, Philadelphia, Completion date, 2005; The Seasons, Twin Rivers Community Park, Greeley, Colo, 2006; Luminarias, Phoenix, City of Phoenix Public Art Prog, Ariz, 2006. *Comn:* Portal, General Servs Admin, Los Indios, Tex, 93-95; Garden of Constants, Ohio State Univ Percent for the Arts, 94; Never Does Nature Say One Thing & Wisdom Another, West Toledo Branch

Libr, OH, 97; Front Row Center, Univ Ariz Col Fine Arts, Tucson, 99; Railgate, NJ Transit, NJ, 99; Camelback Bridge Over US Interstate I-17, Phoenix Arts Commision, Ariz, 2000; River Run, Ohio Arts Coun, 2002; Common Ground, Gates Family Found, Denver, Colo, 2001; The Weather, Northwest Light Rail Transit Project, Calgary, Can. *Exhib:* Am Crafts at the White House, Renwick Gallery, Smithsonian Inst, Washington, DC, 76; Mus Contemp Crafts, NY, 76; Everson Mus Art, Syracuse, NY, 76; Landscape, New Views, Herbert Johnson Mus, Cornell Univ, Ithaca, NY, 78; Women Artists: Clay, Fiber, Metal, Bronx Mus, NY, 78; The Parker Collection for the Vice-President's House, Washington, DC, 78; Southwest Sculpture, Scottsdale Ctr Arts, Ariz, 86 (group), 88 (individual); Ceramics in the Urban Setting, 2nd Int Quadriennal Competition, Faenza, Italy, 89; Architectural Clay, Found Archit & Clay Ctr, Philadelphia, Pa, 93; Ala Biennial, Univ Ala, Tuscaloosa, Ala, 93; Socrates Sculpture Park, Long Island City, NY, 94. *Pos:* Artist-in-residence, Tucson Sch Dist 1, 73 & Haystack Mountain Sch Crafts, Deer Isle, Maine, 78. *Teaching:* Master artist workshop, Art in Pub Places, Tucson Mus Art Tucson, Ariz, 86; pub art workshop, Mesa Cummunity Col, Mesa, Ariz, 93. *Awards:* Nat Endowment Arts, 75 & 87; Governor's Award, Ariz Women's Partnership, 85; Nat Adv Comt: The Pub Art Rev, 93-97; Indiv Artist Fel, Ariz Comm Arts, 97; Ariz Alumni Asn Profl Achievement Award, 2002; Best New Pub Art for Common Ground, Denver, by Westword, 2002; Orchid award, with Estrada Land Planning for Robb Field, City of San Diego, Orchids and Onions, 2000; Ariz Artist Award, Tucson Community Found, 1998. *Bibliog:* John Perreault (auth), Impressions of Arizona, Art in America, 4/81; Wayne King (auth), Tucson: Art, Sand, Mules and Taillights, International Herald Tribune, 85; Fabio Bianchetti (auth), La Cermaica Nell, Arredo Urbano, 89; Charlotte Lowe (auth), A Talk with Barbara Grygutis & Peter Warshall, Public Art Review, 90; Albuquerque Art Project, CNN News, 7/13/91; Tucson's Tiled '54 Chevy Sparks Albuquerque Art Flap, Assoc Press, 7/14/91; Work Ethic was Inspiration for New St Paul Sculpture, Union Advocate, Vol 95, No 10, 10/7/91; Data Book/Int Contemp Art Fair, Int Sculpture Ctr, Yokohama, 3/92; Architecturama, Philadelphia Inquirer, 93; Mary Voelz Chandler (auth), Sculpture Invites Folks Down by the River, Rocky Mountain News, Oct 18, 2002; Robert Neuwirth (auth), Government Issue Art, LIMNW17 Mag Internat Design Issue 3, 1999; Tony Sykes (auth *Media:* Public Art. *Mailing Add:* PO Box 3028 Tucson AZ 85702

GUALTIERI, JOSEPH P
MUSEUM DIRECTOR, PAINTER
b Royalton, Ill, Dec 25, 16. *Study:* Norwich Art Sch, Conn, dipl; Sch Art Inst Chicago, Ill, dipl. *Work:* Pa Acad Fine Arts, Philadelphia; Wadsworth Atheneum, Hartford, Conn; RI Sch Design Mus Fine Arts, Providence; Lyman Allyn Mus, New London, Conn; Slater Mem Mus, Norwich, Conn. *Comn:* Wall mural, New London Co Mutual Ins Co, Norwich, Conn; portrait, Gov John Dempsey, State of Conn. *Exhib:* Chicago Art Inst, Ill, 41; Pa Acad Fine Arts, Philadelphia, 48 & 51; Whitney Mus Am Art, NY, 52; Corcoran Gallery Art, Washington, DC; Nat Acad Design, NY; Albany Inst Hist & Art, NY; Wadsworth Atheneum, Hartford, Conn; Calif Palace of the Legion of Honor, Lincoln Park, San Francisco. *Collection Arranged:* Retrospective, Converse Art Gallery, Slater Mus, 92. *Pos:* Dir, Slater Mem Mus, Norwich, Conn, 62-. *Teaching:* Instr art, oil painting, figure & portrait, The Norwich Free Acad, Conn, 43-79. *Awards:* First Prize & Logan Medal, Chicago Art Inst, 41; Purchase Prize, Pa Acad of Fine Arts, 48 & 51; Conn Artists Eastern States Expo Award, 51. *Mem:* Conn Acad Fine Arts Asn; Am Asn Mus; New Eng Conf, Am Asn Mus. *Media:* Oil, Mixed. *Mailing Add:* c/o Slater Mem Mus & Converse Art Gallery 108 Crescent St Norwich CT 06360

GUASTELLA, C DENNIS
PAINTER, INSTRUCTOR
b Detroit, Mich, July 8, 47. *Study:* Macomb Co Community Col, 67; Wayne State Univ, BFA, 72; Eastern Mich Univ, MFA, 75. *Work:* Sheldon Mem Art Galleries, Univ Nebr, Lincoln; NDak Univ, Grand Forks; SDak Mem Art Ctr, Brookings. *Exhib:* Northwest Biennial III, SDak Mem Art Ctr, Brookings, 76; Biennial, Joslyn Art Mus, Omaha, Nebr, 76, 78 & 80; one-man shows, Sheldon Mem Art Galleries, Univ Nebr, Lincoln, 76 & Univ Mich, Slusser Gallery, Ann Arbor, 81; Mich Artists 80/81, Detroit Inst Arts & Flint Inst Arts, 81; and others. *Teaching:* Asst prof art, SDak State Univ, Brookings, 75-80; instr visual arts, Washtenaw Community Col, Ann Arbor, Mich, 80-. *Awards:* Purchase Award, Rutgers Univ, Camden, NJ, 75; Best of Show/Purchase Award, 16th Joslyn Biennial, Joslyn Art Mus, Omaha, Nebr, 80. *Bibliog:* Interview, Detroit Artist Monthly, 11/77; Mike Odom (auth), Exhibit Reflexs 80's Mood, Uno Gateway, Univ Nebr, 1/23/81; Robert Igelhardt (auth), Close examination, distance needed to appreciate works, Ann Arbor News, 8/9/81. *Mem:* Col Art Asn; Midwest Col Art Asn. *Media:* Acrylic, String. *Mailing Add:* Dept Visual Arts Washtenaw Community Col 4800 E Huron River Dr Bldg TI 214 Ann Arbor MI 48106

GUBERMAN, SIDNEY
PAINTER, SCULPTOR
b Greenville, SC, Aug 24, 36. *Study:* Princeton Univ, with Stephen Greene, BA, 58; Univ Pa, with Robert Venturi, MA(archit), 67. *Work:* Nat Mus Am Art, Corcoran Gallery Art, Washington, DC; High Mus Art, Atlanta; Princeton Univ Art Mus; Birmingham Mus Art; and others. *Comn:* Coke USA, 89, McMaster-Carr Atlanta, 90. *Exhib:* One-man show, Greenville Co Mus, SC, 76, Princeton Univ Art Mus, 83, Southeastern Ctr Contemp Art, 84, McKissick Mus, Univ SC, Columbia, 87, Weslyan Col, Ga, 98 & Jacksonville Contemp Art, Fla, 99; William Seitz Mem, Princeton Univ Art Mus, NJ, 77; Artists in Ga, High Mus, Atlanta, 80, 82 & 85; Small Sculpture, Del Mar Col, Corpus Christi, Tex, 81 & 83; Atlanta in France, Paris, & Toulouse, 85; Ten Yrs of Visual Arts at Princeton, 85; Galerie von der Milwe, Aachen, Ger, 90; Susan Conway Carroll Gallery, Washington, DC, 91; Looking South, A Different Dixie, 22 Artists, Four Southern museums; Hodges-Taylor Gallery, Charlotte, NC, 90, 93; Marcia Wood Gallery, 98 & 2000. *Pos:* Exhib dir, Govt Services Savings & Loan, 76-79. *Teaching:* Prof painting, l'Ecole Cantonale Beaux Arts, Lausanne, Switz, 71-73; asst prof drawing, l'Ecole Polytech Fedn Lausanne, Switz, 73-75; vis lectr painting, Princeton Univ, NJ, 81-82; vis prof painting, Univ SC, Columbia, 86-87; vis artist, Atlanta Col Art, 89, 91. *Awards:* Individual Artist's Grant, Nat Endowment Arts, 80-81; Guggenheim Found Fel for Painting, 88-89. *Bibliog:* Benjamin Forgey (auth), An exhilarating abstract painter, Washington Star, 10/78; Mary Swift (auth), Sidney Guberman, Art Voices South, 4/80; Iris Welch (auth), Sidney Guberman, Art Papers, 8/82; Artists New Work Exhibs Maturity & Consistancy, Atlanta Constitution, 88. *Mem:* The Ivy Club. *Media:* Acrylic; Steel, Wood. *Publ:* Auth, Frank Stella's polar coordinate series, Art Papers, 2/82; Sensation, Art Papers, 5-6/84; Frank Stella-An Illustrated Biography, Rizzola, 95; Frank Stella through the Eyes of a Fellow Artist, Book Rev, Jan 96; Frank Stella/Imaginary Landscapes, catalog, 2001. *Dealer:* Marcia Wood Gallery Atlanta Ga. *Mailing Add:* 131 NE Montgomery Ferry Dr Atlanta GA 30309

GUCCIONE, JUANITA
PAINTER
b Chelsea, Mass. *Exhib:* One-person exhibs, Recent Paintings and Watercolors, Colony Arts Ctr, Woodstock, NY, 78, Galerie Liliane Francois, Paris, France, 86; La Galerie Mouffe, Paris, France, 76; Metrop Painters and Sculptors, Manufacturers Hanover Trust Bldg, NY, 78; 46th Ann Exhib, Metrop Painters and Sculptors, NY, 83. *Awards:* Gold Medal, Academia Italia, Calvatone, Italy, 79; Golden Flame of the World Parliament, Academia Italia, Calvatone, Italy, 86. *Bibliog:* Raymond F Pier & Lila K Piper (co-auths), Cosmic Art, Hawthorn Books, New York, 75; Anniversary for Guccione, Ulster Co Gazette, 77. *Media:* Oil, Acrylic. *Dealer:* Wohlfarth Galleries Ninth St NE Washington DC 20017. *Mailing Add:* 60 Sutton Pl S Apt 14KNO New York NY 10022-4168

GUERIN, JOHN WILLIAM
PAINTER, EDUCATOR
b Houghton, Mich, Aug 29, 20. *Study:* Am Acad Art, Chicago; Art Students League; Escuela Bellas Artes, San Miguel, Mex; Colorado Springs Fine Arts Ctr. *Work:* Dallas Mus Fine Arts; Chrysler Mus, Provincetown, Mass; Joslyn Art Mus, Omaha, Nebr; Colorado Springs Fine Arts Ctr; Houston Mus Fine Arts; and others. *Exhib:* One-man shows, Kraushaar Gallery, NY, 59, 63 & 68; Galeria Realities, Taos, NMex, 60; Corcoran Gallery Art, 61; Whitney Mus Am Art, NY; retrospective, Ft Worth Art Ctr, 64; and others. *Teaching:* Instr painting, Dallas Mus Fine Arts, 50-52; prof art, Univ Tex, Austin, 53-80, prof emer, 80-; artist in residence, Skowhegan Sch Painting & Sculpture, 60. *Awards:* Am Acad Arts & Lett Grant, 59; Univ Tex Res Inst Grant, 60 & 66; Ford Found Grant, 79. *Mem:* Tex Fine Arts Asn; life mem Art Students League; Nat Acad Design. *Media:* All. *Mailing Add:* 3400 Stoneridge Rd Austin TX 78746

GUERRA, KONRADO AVINA
PAINTER, SCULPTOR
b Mexico City, Mex, May 12, 50. *Study:* Inst Nacional Bellas Artes, La Esmeralda, 71; Univ Nacional Autonoma de Mex, Acad de Sn Carlos, Facuttad de Artes, Lic (artes & plasticas), 71-79. *Work:* Palacio de Bellas Artes, Mex; Rockford Ill-Int Prints, Chicago; OEA, Dept Artes Visuales, Washington; Art Pocket Mus Art Muvment, Kobe, Japan; Intergrafik-76 Aites Mus, Berlin, Ger. *Comn:* Dise'n10o-Decoracio'n01, 4 Pedastalos-Salada Go Bernadores, Palacio de Goblerno Chiapas, Chiapas, Tuxtla, 83. *Exhib:* Solo exhibs, Inst Nacional Bellas Artes-Palacio, 88, Mus Art Poket, Art Muvment, 95, B David Gallery, 96, Pan Am Health Orgn, 96, Interamerican Develop Bank, 96; Tokyo Int Art Show, 92; Arte Objeto, Museo de la Cd de Mex, 95; Dalí-Mirí, B David Gallery, 95. *Awards:* 1er Lugar, VNAM, 75; Mension Onorifica, Inst Nacional Bellas Artes, 76. *Bibliog:* Konrado-Work Art, Canal-34, Hollywood, Calif, 80; Kop-Art, Canal-11, IPN, 90; Arte del Surrealismo, Canal-4, Tele-Visa, 91. *Media:* Grabado en metal; oil on canvas, Escttura Bronce. *Publ:* Ed, Inter Grafik, 76, Mus für deutschd, 76; Intergrafik 80-Ausstellungszentrum, am Fernehturm, Berlin, 80; auth, Elgrabado Mexicano en el Siglo XX-1922-81, Hugo Covantes, 81; Diccionario de Escultura Mexicana del Siglio XX, Lily Kassner, 84; coauth, Diccionario de las Artes Plasticas, Francisco del Rio, 94. *Dealer:* Suzuki Minoru 2-13-13 Yamamoto D o10i Chuo-Ku Kobe Japan. *Mailing Add:* Juan Sarabia 153 Mexico DF 02800 Mexico

GUERRERO, RAUL
PAINTER, SCULPTOR
b Brawley, Calif, Oct 9, 45. *Study:* Chouinard Art Sch, Los Angeles, BFA. *Work:* Phoenix Art Mus, Ariz; Long Beach Mus Art, Calif; La Jolla Mus Contemp Art, Calif; Security Pacific Bank, Los Angeles; Scripps Clinic, La Jolla. *Exhib:* Solo exhibs, Contemp Arts Forum, Santa Barbara & Los Angeles Inst Contemp Art, 82, Barbara Braathen Gallery, NY, 84, Boehm Gallery, Palomar Col, San Marcos, Calif, 86, Saxon-Lee Gallery, Los Angeles, 87 & 88, Linda Moore Gallery, San Diego, 92 & 95; A San Diego Exhib: 42 Emerging Artists, La Jolla Mus Contemp Art, 85; 1987 Phoenix Biennial, Phoenix Art Mus, Ariz, 87; From the Back Room, Saxon Lee Gallery, Los Angeles, 88, 89 & 90; La Frontera/The Border, Centro Cult de la Raza, San Diego, 93; Mus Contemp Art, San Diego, 95; and many other solo & group exhibs. *Pos:* Guest lectr, Univ Calif, San Diego, 92-. *Awards:* Photography Fel, Nat Endowment Arts, 79. *Bibliog:* Melinda Wortz (auth), Psychological manipulations, Artnews, 5/77; Hunter Drohojowska (auth), Raul Guerrero, Los Angeles Inst Contemp Art, Flash Art Int, 3/83; Christopher Knight (auth), Guerrero's art comes close to B-movie mysticism, 6/2/85, Exhibit of works by Raul Guerrero borders on being retrospective, 10/5/86 & Phoenix joins major leagues in art, 8/25/87, Los Angeles Herald Examiner; Judith Spiegel (auth), Nostalgia: The world flattened, Artweek, 4/30/88; and many others. *Mailing Add:* 1610 Myrtle Ave San Diego CA 92103-5121

GUEST, RICHARD G
PAINTER, CONSULTANT
b Pasadena, Calif, Nov 30, 24. *Study:* Chouinard Art Inst, Los Angeles, Calif, 58-59; Santa Monica City Col, 63; Otis Art Inst, Los Angeles, Calif, 64-65. *Work:* Riverside Art Mus, Calif; Portland Mus Art; Garden Grove Artisans Guild; Kobayaashi Co, Tokyo, Japan; Lindora Med Clin, San Diego, Calif; and many others. *Exhib:* Environmental Exhib, Laguna Beach Mus Art, Calif, 65; Monothon, Riverside Art Mus, Calif, 86; Santa Monica City Col, Calif; Torrance Traditional Artist Group, Calif; Buena Park Open, Calif; Cypress Art League, Calif; Culver City Invitational, Calif; Allied Artists Am, NY; Otis Art Inst, Los Angeles, Calif; Mill House, Garden Grove, Calif; Claystone Studios, Perris, Calif. *Pos:* Dealer, Guest Fine Arts, 68-89; consult & appraiser, Int Soc Appraisers, 88-. *Bibliog:* Art World USA (film), Paramount W Production, 78-79. *Media:* Water Based, Collage. *Dealer:* Randy Holland 420131 Main St Temecula CA 92586. *Mailing Add:* 27289 Capalino Dr Sun City CA 92586

GUIDA, DOMINICK
PAINTER
b New York, NY, June 24, 46. *Study:* Calif Inst Arts, with Edward Reep & Emerson Woelffer, BFA, 73. *Work:* Chemical Bank & Goldman Sachs & Co, NY; Conn Bank & Trust Co, Norwalk; Continental Corp, Sascataway, NJ; Cologne Life Reinsurance Corp, Stamford, Conn; Hilton SW, Houston, Tex; Nissan Motor Corp, Gardina, Calif. *Comn:* Painting on wood relief structure, Edward Albee Found, NY, 78. *Exhib:* Biennial Exhib, Whitney Mus Am Art, NY, 75; New Spiritual Abstraction of the 1980's, Nora Haime Gallery, NY, 84; Painting & Sculpture Today 1984 (with catalog), Indianapolis Mus Art, Ind, 84; The Gang of 12 from NY in Italy (with catalog), Galleria Centro Mascarella, Bologna & Mus Civico, Siracusa, Italy, 86; Alumni Invitational Exhib, Calif Inst of Arts, Valencia, Calif, 88; Indianapolis Collects, Herron Art Gallery, Indianapolis, Ind, 90; Open Studio 402, Painting Space 122 Asn, PS 122, NY, 95, 97 & 98; Living with Art, Brenda Reinertson Gallery, Oakland, Calif, 98; 7th Ann Exhib, 98 & 63rd Ann Nat, 98, Cooperstown Art Asn. *Bibliog:* Amei Wallach (auth), Artworks of Albee's Barn, Newsday, Long Island, NY, 6/82. *Mem:* Painting Space 122 Inc; PS 122 Comm Ctr, NY (bd dir, 87-); Cooperstown Art Asn. *Media:* Oil, Watercolor. *Mailing Add:* PO Box 1441 New York NY 10009

GUILLOUME, (GUILLOUME PEREZ-ZAPATA)
PAINTER, PUBLISHER
b Medellin, Colombia, July 2, 57. *Study:* Belles Artes Inst, MA, 1981. *Work:* Biblioteca Publica Piloto, Medellin, Colombia. *Comn:* Yuldama historical, Yuldama Hotel, Santa Marta, Colombia, 1982; Ceipa Univ, Ceipa University, Medellin Colombia, 1985. *Exhib:* Miniature Show, Albuquerque Mus, Albuquerque, NMex, 2000-2006; Biennale Internationale 3rd, Fortazzo De Vasso, Florence, Italy, 2003; Contemporary Hispanic Market, Museo Cultural de Santa Fe, Santa Fe, NMex, 2005. *Teaching:* Sculpture, Bronze, Guilloume Studio Sandia Park, 2005-2006. *Awards:* First Pier 62-63 (painting), Latinoamerican Artist, Isis on First, Seattle, Wash, 2002; Latinoamerica (Can) 2nd Latinoamerican (Toranto), Fundarte, 2005; Industry Award, Sculptural Pursuit, The Complete Sculpture, 2006. *Bibliog:* featured in Sculpture Magazine. *Mem:* Santa Fe Soc of Artist, 1993-2006; NMex Art League, 1995; Sonoran Art League, Ariz, 1998. *Media:* Oil, Bronze Sculpure. *Publ:* Sculptures & Paintings, Guilloume, 2003. *Dealer:* Naked Horse Gallery 4151 N Marshall Way Suite B Scottsdale AZ. *Mailing Add:* 16 Dinos Rd Sandia Park NM 87047

GUILMAIN, JACQUES
HISTORIAN, PAINTER
b Brussels, Belg, Oct 15, 26; US citizen. *Study:* Queens Col, City Univ New York, BS, 48; Columbia Univ, MA, 52, univ fel, 57, PhD, 58, and with Meyer Schapiro. *Exhib:* NY Acad Design, 48; Am Watercolors, Drawings and Prints, NY Metrop Mus Art, 52; Univ Calif, Riverside, 59; Queens Col, 61; SUNY, Stony Brook, 69-2003; two-man show, Gallery North, LI, 69; and others. *Teaching:* Vis asst prof hist art, Stanford Univ, 58-59; vis asst prof, Univ Calif, Riverside, 59-60; instr, Queens Col, 60-63; from asst prof to prof emer, State Univ NY, Stony Brook, 63-, chmn art dept, 70-76; vis prof, Columbia Univ, 68 & 70. *Awards:* Am Philosophical Soc Grant, 60; State Univ NY Res Found Grant, 64-79; Nat Endowment Humanities, 81. *Mem:* Medieval Acad Am. *Media:* Collage, Mixed Media, Oil. *Res:* Early Medieval ornaments; Mozarabic manuscript illumination; Carolingian manuscript illumination; early Medieval metalwork. *Publ:* auth, Zoomorphic decoration and the problem of the sources of Mozarabic illumination, XXXV, 60, Illuminations of the Second Bible of Charles the Bald, XLI, 66 & The Geometry of the Cross-Carpet Pages in the Lindisfarne Gospels, LXII, 87, Speculum; Enigmatic beasts of the Lindau Gospels lower cover, Gesta, X, 71; On the chronological development and classification of decorated initials in Latin manuscripts of 10th century Spain, LXIII, 81, Bulletin, John Rylands Univ Libr, Manchester; and others. *Mailing Add:* PO Box 2363 Setauket NY 11733

GUILMET, GLENDA J
PAINTER, PHOTOGRAPHER
b Tacoma, Wash, Mar 28, 57. *Study:* Clover Park Vocational Tech Inst, Tacoma, Wash, (photog) - 1982-83; Univ Puget Sound, Tacoma, Wash, BA (bus admin), 81, BA (art), 1989. *Work:* Photog collection, Bibliotheque Nat de France, Puyallup Tribe Indians, Wash; wheelock art collection, Univ Puget Sound, Wash; art collection, Chief Leschi Schs; mixed metaphor-video collection, Seattle Art Mus. *Exhib:* The Glass People, Daybreak Star Arts Ctr, Seattle Wash, 1996-97; Retrospective in Paint: 1991-98, Galleria on Broadway, Tacoma, Wash, 1998; New Work, Daybreak Star Arts Ctr, Seattle, Wash, 1999; Womenscapes: Expressions of Femininity, Daybreak Star Art Gallery, Seattle, Wash, 2005. *Pos:* Photogr, Univ Puget Sound, Tacoma, Wash, 1977-79; art dir, Tacenda & Willo Trees Press, Eureka, Calif, 2004; chwn, Finance Standing Committee, Tacoma Arts Comn, Tacoma Arts Comn, 1990-91. *Teaching:* Instr, Tacoma Arts Com, 89. *Awards:* First Prize, Shadow Dance, Crosscurrents Arts Contest, 1988; Hedgebrook Invitatiional Residency, Hedgebrook Foun, 2000. *Mem:* Tacoma Arts Comn, Tacoma, Wash (1989-92). *Media:* Painting, Photography, Printmaking & Sculpture. *Mailing Add:* 652 Old Blyn Hwy Sequim WA 98382-9695

GULLY, ANTHONY LACY
HISTORIAN, ADMINISTRATOR
b Orange, Calif, Feb 28, 38. *Study:* Univ Calif, Riverside, BA; Univ Calif, Berkeley, MA; Stanford Univ, PhD; with Jean Boggs, Jean Bony, Walter Horn, Lorenz Eitner & Albert Elsen. *Teaching:* Instr 17th-18th century art hist, Pomona Col, Claremont, Calif, 65-66; asst prof 19th-20th century art hist, Calif State Univ, Los Angeles, 66-68; assoc prof 18th-19th century art hist, Ariz State Univ, Tempe, 72-83, asst dean col fine arts, 81-, chair grad humanities prog, 83-84; vis prof, Stanford Univ, 81. *Awards:* Nat Defense Educ Act Award, Stanford Univ, 68-71; Mabel McLeod Fel, Rowlandson Study, London, Stanford Univ, 71-72; Nat Endowment Humanities Award, Yale Univ, 76; and others. *Bibliog:* J Hayes (auth), Rowlandson, Phaidon Art Bks, 72; R Paulsen (auth), Rowlandson: New interpretation, Yale Univ, 72; R Wark (auth), Rowlandson drawings in Huntington Libr, 75. *Mem:* Col Art Asn; Mid-Am Col Art Asn; Rocky Mountain Conf on Brit Studies (pres, 78-79); Nat Conf Brit Studies; Pacific Conf on Brit Studies. *Res:* Nineteenth century British art; John Sell Cotman, 1782-1842. *Publ:* Auth, Book reviews on eighteenth century art and aesthetics, Current Bibliog: 18th Century, 76; auth, Mr B and the cherubim: William Blake's descriptive catalog, 78, An unpublished sketchbook by Rowlandson, 79 & Milton's unholy trinity, 81, Phoebus; auth, Source of Goya's May 3, 1808, In: Studies in Iconography, 83. *Mailing Add:* 2618 Country Club Way Tempe AZ 85282-2922

GUMMELT, SAMUEL
PAINTER
b Waco, Tex, Aug 28, 44. *Study:* NTex State Univ, BA, 68; Southern Methodist Univ, MFA, 71. *Work:* Dallas Mus Fine Arts; Am Tel & Tel, Chicago; Ft Worth Art Mus. *Exhib:* Proj South/Southwest, 71 & Focus: Sam Gummelt, 79, Ft Worth Art Mus; Interchange, Dallas Mus Fine Art, 72 & Walker Art Ctr, Minneapolis, 73; Exchange, Ft Worth Art Mus, 75 & San Francisco Mus Mod Art, 76; Recent Works on Paper by Contemp Am Artists, Madison Art Ctr, Wis, 77; Projects: Sam Gummelt, Art Mus STex, Corpus Christi, 78; Am Drawing in Black & White 1970-1980, Brooklyn Mus, NY, 80. *Awards:* Purchase Awards, 4th Ann Prints & Drawing Exhib, Ark Art Ctr, 70, 35th Tarrant Co Ann, Ft Worth Art Ctr, 73 & Tex Invitational, Beaumont Art Mus, 78; Nat Endowment Arts Fel, 82 & 85. *Bibliog:* Jan Butterfield (auth), The young Texans: The phenomenon of interstitial art on America's last frontier, Arts Mag, 73; Jozanne Rabyor (auth), article, Art in Am, 74; Susan Platt (auth), Reviews: Houston, Art Forum, 79. *Media:* Oil, Wax on Canvas. *Dealer:* Janie C Lee Gallery 1209 Berthea Houston TX 77006; Eugene Binder Gallery 2701 Canton Dallas TX 75226. *Mailing Add:* 5909 Palo Pinto Dallas TX 75206-6831

GUMMER, DON
SCULPTOR
b Louisville, Ky, Dec 12, 46. *Study:* John Herron Art Inst, Indianapolis, 64-66; Sch Mus Fine Arts, Boston, 66-70; Yale Univ Sch Fine Arts, New Haven, BFA, 71, MFA, 73. *Work:* Chase Manhattan Bank, Chemical Bank, Int Creative Mgt, McCrory Corp, Joseph E Seagram Co & The Equitable, NY; Evansville Mus Arts & Sci, Ind; Kitakyushu Int Ctr, Japan; La Mus, Humleback, Denmark; and others. *Comn:* Interpretations 79, comn by Castle Clinton/Manhattan Cult Coun, Battery Park, NY, 79; outdoor installations, Dag Hammerskjold Plaza, 80 & Joseph E Seagram & Sons, 82, NY. *Exhib:* One-man shows, Sperone Westwater Fischer, NY, 77, 79, 82, 84, 86, 88, 90 & 96, Dag Hammarskjold Plaza, NY, 80, Seagram Plaza, NY, 82, The Planes of Nature, Evansville Mus Arts & Sci, Ind, 87, Recent Sculpture, Daniel Weinberg Gallery, Santa Monica, 92, Kitakyushu Int Ctr, Japan, 93, New Bronze Sculpture, Fred Hoffman Fine Art, Calif, 94, Nations Bank Plaza, Charlotte, NC, 98, Salander-O'Reilly Galleries, NY, 99, 2000, Eckert Fine Arts, Naples, Fla, 2000; Eight Sculptors, Albright-Knox Art Gallery, Buffalo, 79; Instruction Drawings, The Gilbert & Lila Silverman Collection, Cranbrook Acad Art Mus, Mich, 81; New Visions, 81 & Sculpture on the Wall, 83-85, Aldrich Mus Contemp Art, Conn; 40th Ann Acad-Inst Purchase Exhib, Am Acad & Inst Arts & Letts, 88; Summer Sculpture Exhib, Sperone Westwater Gallery, NY, 90; Artist for Amnesty, Blum Helman Gallery & Germans van Eck Gallery, NY, 90; Recent Works, Embassy Suyites Hotel, NY, 90; Yale Collects Yale (with catalog) Yale Univ Art Gallery, New Haven, Conn, 93; and many others. *Awards:* Grant, Nat Endowment Arts, 76, Tiffany Found, 78 & Creative Artists Pub Serv Prog, 79. *Bibliog:* Peter Frank (auth), Don Gummer, Contemporary Constructivism in the West, LA Weekly, 4/1/94; Susan Kandel (auth), Los Angeles Times, 4/15/94; Lee Siegel (auth), Don Gummer at Sperone Westwater, Artnews, Vol 95, No 10, 11/96; and others. *Media:* Wood, Stone

GUMPEL, HUGH
PAINTER, INSTRUCTOR
b New York, NY, Feb 3, 26. *Study:* Columbia Univ; Art Students League; Grande Chaumiere, Paris, France. *Work:* Nat Acad Design, NY; Norfolk Mus, Va; Hagerstown Mus, Md; Univ Wash, Seattle; Art Inst Zanesville, Ohio. *Comn:* Mural, State of NY Pub Works Admin Bldg, 63. *Exhib:* Am Watercolor Soc Anns, 53-78; Nat Acad Anns, 60-94; Royal Soc Painters, London, Eng, 67; Mex Art Inst, Mexico City, 68; Art Mus, Ontario, Can, 72. *Teaching:* Instr painting, Nat Acad Sch Fine Arts, 59-94; instr watercolor, State Univ NY, Purchase, Westchester Art Workshop. *Awards:* Gold Medal of Honor, Am Watercolor Soc, 59; Willlam A Paton Prize, Nat Acad, 73 & 78. *Bibliog:* Norman Kent (ed), Seascapes & Landscapes in Watercolor, pp 97-102, NY, 56; The Ranger Fund, Am Artist, p 50, 10/58; Ralph Fabri (auth), 147th Ann Nat Acad Design, Today's Art, p 7, 12/72. *Mem:* Nat Acad; Am Watercolor Soc. *Media:* Watercolor, Acrylic. *Mailing Add:* 31 High St Apt B Camden ME 04843-1736

GUMPERT, GUNTHER
PAINTER
b Krefeld, Ger, Apr 17, 19; US citizen. *Study:* Sch Fine Arts Krefeld; Sch Fine Arts, Wuppertal. *Work:* Metrop Mus Art, NY; Denver Art Mus, Colo; Phillips Collection, Washington; Victoria & Albert Mus, London; Albertina, Vienna, Austria; and others. *Comn:* Mural, Inter-Am Develop Bank, Washington, 68; and others. *Exhib:* Kaiser-Wilhelm Mus, 48, 49 & 52; one-man shows, USA, Latin Am & Eur, 53-2002; Salon Realites Nouvelles, Paris, 58-60 & 62; Int Exhib Abstr Art, Pistoia, 61; Int Exhib Contemp Art, London, 62; Salon Mai, Paris, 62; European Acad Art, Trier, 2000. *Bibliog:* Jean Grenier (auth), Gumpert, Preuves, Paris, 60; Victor Summa (auth), Gumpert & The Evolution of His Art (film), Educ TV Asn, 63; Prof Willy Huppert (auth), Gunther Gumpert, Kunst-und Kunstgewerbe Verein, Pforzheim, 64; Wolfgang Henze (auth), Gunther Gumpert, Berbn, 2000; and others. *Media:* All. *Dealer:* Gregory Gallery 41 East 57th St New York NY 10022; Galerie Henze & Ketterer AG Kirchstrasse 26-CH 3114 Wichtrach/Bern Switz. *Mailing Add:* 3752 McKinley St NW Washington DC 20015

GUNASINGHE, SIRI
EDUCATOR, HISTORIAN
b Ruanwella, Sri Lanka, Feb 20, 25. *Study:* Univ Ceylon, BA, 48; Univ Paris, PhD, 55; Univ Sri Jayewardene Pura, Sri Lanka, D Litt, 94. *Teaching:* Instr sanskrit, Univ Ceylon, 48-70; prof, Univ Victoria, BC, 70-88, emer 88-. *Awards:* Sr Specialist, Univ Hawaii, 68; Fel, Can Coun Leave, 78; Smithsonian Travel, 87. *Res:* History of Buddhist and Hindu art in India, Sri Lanka and Southeast Asia. *Publ:* Auth, La Technique de la Peinture Indienne, Univ Press France, 56; Masks of Ceylon, Dept Cult Affairs, 63 & Album of Buddhist Paintings from Sri Lanka, Nat Mus, 78, Colombo. *Mailing Add:* 4110 Ebony Terr Victoria BC V8N 3Z3 Canada

GUND, AGNES & DANIEL SHAPIRO
COLLECTOR, ADMINISTRATOR, PATRON
b Cleveland, Ohio, Aug 13, 38. *Study:* Conn Col, BA, 60; Boston Univ Grad Sch, hist, 60-63; Harvard Univ, Fogg Mus, AM(art hist), 80. *Hon Degrees:* Four hon degrees From var US Col & Univs. *Pos:* Trustee, Cleveland Inst Art, 68-72, Hirshhorn Mus Wash, DC, 87-91, Brown Univ, Providence, RI, 89-, Andy Warhol Found, NY, 90-, J Paul Getty Trust, 94-; bd pres, Mus Mod Art, NY, 72, pres emeritus, currently; pres, Studio Sch, NY, 77-91,; bd trustees, Wexner Ctr Found, 97-; trustee, Brown Univ, Aaran Diamond AIDS Res Ctr, Inst Advanced Study, Princeton, NJ, J Paul Getty Trust, Malibu, Calif; mem mus coun, Cleveland Mus Art. *Awards:* Gov's Award, Gov Mario Cuomo, 88; Coll Art Asn, Art Table award for Distinguished Serv to Arts, 94; Nat Medal Arts, Pres William J Clinton, 97; Montblanc de la Culture award, 97; Nat Medal Arts, 97; Am Acad Arts & Letters Award, 98; Arts Educ award, Am for the Arts, 99; Centennial Medal, Harvard Univ Grad Sch Arts & Sci's, 2003; Evan Burger Donaldson Achievement award, Miss Porter's Sch, 2003; Named one of Top 200 Collectors, ARTnews Mag, 2004, 2006; recipient Women in the Arts award. *Mem:* Fel Am Acad Arts & Sci's; Studio in a Sch Asn, founder. *Collection:* Collection covers work produced from 1940-1992; Contemporary African, & Chinese Art. *Publ:* Contribr, Mary Miss Catalogue for Fogg Mus, Harvard, 80; The New Democracy, Blueprints to Change Washington, Citizens Transition Proj, 92. *Mailing Add:* Mus Mod Art 11 W 53rd St New York NY 10019

GUND, ANN
ART ASSOCIATION ADMINISTRATOR
Pos: Pres, Friends of Art and Preserv in Embassies; head Contemp Art Comt, Mus Fine Arts, Boston, trustee; trustee, Concord Acad; bd chairperson, Skowhegan Sch Painting and Sculpture. *Awards:* Named one of Top 200 Collectors, ARTnews Mag, 2006. *Media:* miscellaneous

GUND, GRAHAM
ARCHITECTUAL FIRM EXECUTIVE
Study: Kenyon Col, educ; RI Sch Design, post grad; Grad Sch Design, Harvard Univ, M (archit), M (archit in urban design). *Pos:* Pres, founder, GUND Partnership, Boston, 71-; design peer, Gen Serv Admin, Design Excellence Prog; trustee, Nat Bldg Mus, Nat Trust for Hist Preserv, Boston Mus Fine Arts. *Awards:* Named on of Top 200 Collectors, ARTnews Mag, 2006. *Media:* miscellaneous. *Mailing Add:* Gund Partnership 47 THorndike St Cambridge MA 02141

GUNDERMAN, KAREN M
CERAMIST
b New York, NY, Feb 15, 51. *Study:* Syracuse Univ, BFA, 73; Univ Mich, MFA, 75. *Work:* Norwest Bank, Milwaukee, Wis; Paragon Group, St Louis, Mo; Plaines Art Mus, Mourehead, Minn; Mansfield Art Ctr, Mansfield, Ohio; East Bank Athletic Club, Chicago, Ill. *Exhib:* Solo exhibs, List Art Ctr, Hamilton Col, Clinton, NY, 77, Lawrence Col, Appleton, Wis, 79, Sinclair Galleries, Coe Col, Cedar Rapids, Iowa, 79, Centro-Cult Peruano-Noretamericano, Lima, Peru, 86, Bradley Galleries, Milwaukee, Wis, 87, Esther Saks Gallery, Chicago, Ill, 88 & Munson Gallery, Santa Fe, NMex, 90; Wall Ceramics/Ceramic Walls, Tarble Arts Ctr, Eastern Ill Univ, 91; Two Hands/One Heart, Katie Gingrass Gallery, Milwaukee, Wis, 93; two-person exhibs, Univ Wis-Milwaukee Art Mus, 93 & Bergstrom-Mahler Mus, Neenah, Wis, 94; Under the Influence of Women, Northern Clay Ctr, St Paul, Minn, 94; and others. *Teaching:* Asst prof art, Col Wooster, 76-77; assoc prof art, Univ Wis-Milwaukee, 78-91, assoc chairperson, 90-94, prof art, 91-. *Awards:* Visual Artists Fel, Nat Endowment Arts, 88; Virginia R Groot Found Fel, 91 & 92; Milwaukee Co Visual Artist Fel, 92. *Bibliog:* Fellowship awards: five artists recognized for their work, Milwaukee Sentinel, 10/2/92; Valerie Vail (auth), UWM Faculty Show, Art Muscle Mag, 1/93. *Mem:* Nat Coun Educ Ceramic Arts; Col Art Asn; Ctr Latin Am, Univ Wis-Milwaukee; Nat Fulbright Alumni Asn. *Dealer:* Esther Saks Gallery 3920 N Lake Shore Dr Chicago IL 60613. *Mailing Add:* 11618 N Country Ln No 17W Mequon WI 53092

GUNDERSON, BARRY L
SCULPTOR
b Baird, Tex, Feb 9, 45. *Study:* Augsburg Col, Minneapolis, BA; Univ NDak, Grand Forks; Univ Colo, Boulder, MFA. *Comn:* Large outdoor sculptures, Downtown Plaza, Portsmouth, 79, EOTC, Pendleton, Ore, 86, Porirua, Wellington, New Zealand, 90 & Franklin Park Conservatory, Columbus, Ohio, 92; Ohio State Univ, Marion, 96; Ohio State Fair Grounds, 96. *Exhib:* 5 Ohio Sculptors, Contemp Arts Ctr, Cincinnati, 80; Sculpture Outside in Cleveland, Edgewater Part, Cleveland, 81; Ohio Sculptors II, Taft Mus, Cincinnati, 86; Art for Urban Gardens, Ohio Designer Craftsmen Gallery, Columbus, 89. *Teaching:* Prof sculpture, Kenyon Col, 74-. *Mem:* Col Art Asn. *Media:* Welded, Painted Aluminum. *Mailing Add:* 205 E Brooklyn St Gambier OH 43022

GUNDERSON, KAREN
PAINTER
b Racine, Wis, Aug 14, 43. *Study:* Wis State Univ, Whitewater, BEd, 66, Univ Iowa, Iowa City, MA & MFA, 68. *Work:* Wustum Art Mus, Racine & Milwaukee Art; Haggerty Mus, Milwaukee, Wis. *Comn:* Paintings, comn by Mr & Mrs Leonard Gordon, NY & Dr & Mrs Clinton Levin, New Bedford, Mass, 88; Our Saviors Lutheran Church, Racine, Wis, 95-96; paintings, comn by David & Blanca Goldman, NY; painting, comn by Ralph Acampora, NY. *Exhib:* Solo exhibs, Wustum Art Mus, Racine, 69 & 85, Wis & Cedar Rapids Art Ctr, Iowa, 69, Minneapolis Inst Art, Minn, 71 & Hopkins Hall Gallery, Ohio State Univ, Columbus, 72; Hebrew Union Col, NY, 2000; Col Staten Island, NY, 2000; Holocaust Mus, Houston, 2001; Cornell Col Art Gallery, MT Vernon, Iowa, 2002; Brattleboro Mus & Art Ctr, VT, 2002; Skilball Mus, Cinn, Ohio, 2002; Gov of the Ministry, Sophia bulgaria, 2003; Congregation Beth Shalomrodfezedek, Chester, Conn, 2003; Circulo De Bellas Artes, 2004; New Old Masters, Nat Mus, Gdansk, Poland. *Awards:* Distinguished Alumni Award, Univ Wis, Whitewater, 85; ED Found Grant, 94; Hall of Fame, Washington Park High Sch, Racine, Wis; Lorenzo Magnifico-2nd Place/Painting Florence Biennale, 2001. *Bibliog:* Carter Ratcliff (auth), Karen Gunderson (catalog), Perimeter Press, 85; Linell Smith (auth), Painting pictures in the clouds: Karen Gunderson puts life in cumulus, Baltimore Evening Sun, 87; Donald Kuspit (auth), catalog, 98; Donald Kuspit (auth), Black Paintings, 2004-; Mark Daniel Cohen At the Heart of Light, 2004; Allesandro Riker Interview with, Karen Gunderson, 2004. *Media:* All Media. *Dealer:* Michael Lord Gallery 420 E Wisconsin Ave Milwaukee WI 53202. *Mailing Add:* 26 Beaver St No 14 New York NY 10004

GUNN, ELLEN
PAINTER, PRINTMAKER
b Rockville Center, NY, Jan 8, 51. *Study:* Parsons Sch Design, BFA, 73; Sch Visual Arts, 74; Kala Inst, Berkeley, Calif, 80; Calif Col Arts & Crafts, studied with Charles Gill, 81-82. *Work:* San Francisco Mus Mod Art, Calif. *Comn:* Paintings, Inn Keeper Asn, San Francisco, 85; paintings & fabric design, Read House Hotel, Chattanooga, Tenn, 86 & Sheraton O'Hare, Chicago, Ill, 90; paintings & monotypes, Kaiser Hosp, Santa Rosa, Calif, 87; paintings & menu design, Phoenix Sheraton, 88, 89. *Exhib:* Art Expo, NY, 90-94. *Awards:* 1st Place, Sr Student Competition, Parsons Sch Design, 73; Dean's Hon List & Grad Cum Laude, Parsons Sch Design. *Media:* All. *Publ:* Auth, Good Housekeeping Mag, 73; Vogue Mag, 74; Fiber Arts Design Book II, Lark Books, 83; The Goodfellows Review of Crafts, 83; California Living, San Francisco Chronicle, 84. *Dealer:* Winn Art Group 6015 Sixth Ave South Seattle WA 98108. *Mailing Add:* 40 Lincoln Ave Piedmont CA 94611

GUNN, PAUL JAMES
PAINTER, EDUCATOR
b Guys Mills, Pa, June 21, 22. *Study:* Edinboro State Teachers Col, BS, 47; Calif Col Arts & Crafts, MFA, 48; wood block printing with Hideo Hagiwara, Tokyo, Japan, 61-62. *Work:* Portland Art Mus; Seattle Art Mus; Am Info Serv, Athens, Greece; Bibliot Nat, Paris, France; Victoria & Albert Mus, London, Eng. *Exhib:* Int Bordighera Biennial, Italy; Bay Printmakers Second Ann, Oakland Art Mus, Calif; Ann Northwest Artists, Seattle Art Mus; Western Artists Ann, Denver Art Mus; Ore Artists Ann, Portland Art Mus. *Pos:* Resident dir, Japan Studies Prog, Ore Study Ctr, Waseda Univ, Japan, 72-74 & 83-84. *Teaching:* Prof painting & printmaking, Ore State Univ, 48-88, chmn dept art, 64-72. *Media:* Oil. *Mailing Add:* 609 NW 32nd St Corvallis OR 97330-5024

GUNNING, SIMON BEN
PAINTER, DRAFTSMAN
b Sydney, Australia, July 13, 56. *Study:* Alexander McKee, Sydney; Victorian Col Art, Melbourne, Australia, 78. *Work:* New Orleans Mus Art; Ogden Mus Southern Art, New Orleans; Microsoft Art Collection, Redmond, Wash; ITT Sheraton, New Orleans; Whitney Nat Bank Collection. *Comn:* Landscape, First Bank and Trust, New Orleans, 89; painting, Morrison Productions, New Orleans, 92; landscape, Murrphy, Rodgers, Sloss & Uware, New Orleans, 98; landscape, Middleberg, Riddle & Giana, New Orleans, 99; landscape, New Orleans Board of Avation, 99. *Exhib:* Drawing 6, Univ New Orleans, 95; Contemp Art Center, New Orleans, 98; River Series, Galerie Simonne Stern, New Orleans, 98; Art at the Bank of 21st Century, South East Asia; Outward Bound: Am, traveling exhib, 99-2000; New Orleans: A Creative Odyssey, Int Cult Center, Wash DC, 99-2000. *Teaching:* Instr drawing, Univ New Orleans, 95-98. *Awards:* Division of the Arts, Baton Rouge Federal Govt, 99. *Bibliog:* Chris Waddington (auth), Of Time and the Rider, The Oxford Am Mag, 9/98; Linda Price (auth), Artist as Editor, Am Artists, 9/2000; Nick Marinello (auth), Haunted Wharves, La Cultural Vistas, winter 99-2000. *Media:* Oil, Ink. *Publ:* contribr, Paintings Pulse with a Neighborhood Rhythm, Times Picaywne, 94, The Traveling Collector, Art and Antiques, 97, New American Paintings No IV, Open Studio Press, 97, The Artist and the American Landscape, First Glance Books, 98 & The Ultimate New Orleans Tour Guide, Chronicle Books, 98. *Dealer:* Galerie Simonng Stern 518 Julia New Orleans LA 70117. *Mailing Add:* 716 Port St New Orleans LA 70117

GUNNING, TOM
HISTORIAN, EDUCATOR
Study: Dept Cinema Studies, NY Univ, Phd. *Teaching:* Prof art hist, Univ Chicago. *Awards:* Guggenheim fel, 98. *Res:* Cinema (International early, silent, American avant-garde); Hollywood film genres; film theory (narrative and classical); film and still photography; film historiography. *Publ:* Auth, DW Griffith and the Origins of American Narrative Film: The Early Years, Biograph Univ Ill Press, 91; The horror of opacity: The melodrama of sensation in the plays of Andre de Lorde, Melodrama - Stage, Picture, Screen, 94; Tracing the individual body aka photography, detectives, early cinema and the body of modernity, Cinema and the Invention of Modern Life, Univ Calif Press, 95; From Kaleidoscope to the X-ray: urban spectatorship, Poe, Benjamin and traffic is souls (1913), Wide Angle, Vol 19, No 4; An aesthetic of astonishment: Early film and the (In) Credulous Spectator, Viewing Positions, NB: Rutgers, 89; and over 100 others. *Mailing Add:* 5027 S Dorchester Chicago IL 60615

GUNTER, FRANK ELLIOTT
PAINTER, EDUCATOR
b Jasper, Ala, May 8, 34. *Study:* Univ Ala, BFA; Fla State Univ, MA. *Work:* Sheldon Swope Gallery, Terre Haute, Ind; Evansville Mus Arts & Sci & Mead Johnson Corp, Evansville, Ind; Ill State Mus, Springfield; Ind State Mus, Indianapolis; Birmingham Mus Art, Ala; Krannert Art Mus, Univ Ill, Champaign; Chase Manhattan Bank, Chicago; Ill Acad Mathematics & Science, Aurora. *Comn:* Painting, Rochester State Bank, Ill, 74; painting of facade, Bank of Ind, Merrillville, 75; Dental Col, Southern Ill Univ, Alton. *Exhib:* Cult Ctr for Am Embassy, Paris, 71; Mus Art, Besancon, France, 72; Am Libr, Brussels, Belg, 73; Maison Descartes, Amsterdam, 73; Varieties of Visual Reality, Northern Ariz State Univ, 75; Am Exhib, Krannert Art Mus, Univ Ill, Urbana, 77; Univ Wis, Madison, 84; Hanover Coll, Ind, 92; Rapp Gallery, Louisville, Ky, 2000. *Teaching:* Instr art, Birmingham Pub Schs, Ala, 56-58; asst prof art, Murray State Univ, 60-62; emer prof art, Univ Ill, Urbana-Champaign, 62-91. *Awards:* Second Award for Painting, Soc Four Arts, 73; Purchase Awards, Wabash Valley Ann, Terre Haute, 74 & Union League Club, Chicago, 74. *Bibliog:* Stephen Spector (auth), Super realists, Archit Dig, 11/12/74; G A Rodetis (auth), Varieties of visual reality, Northern Ariz Univ Art Gallery 1-3/75; Henry Adams (auth), A Tribute, Nelson Gallery, 84; Katherine Manthone (auth), The Other Shore: River Landscapes, 90; Eunice Agar (auth), Am Artists Mag, p 41-45, 8/92. *Mem:* Am Ceramics Circle. *Media:* Acrylic on Canvas. *Dealer:* Rapp Gallery Louisville KY. *Mailing Add:* 211 W Second St Madison IN 47250-3722

GURALNICK, JODY
PAINTER, COLLAGE ARTIST
b Boston, Mass. *Study:* Boston Mus Sch, 1971-72; St Martin's Sch Art, BA in Painting (with honors), 1975; Pratt Inst, Bklyn, MFA in Painting, 1978. *Work:* The Progressive Collection, Cleveland, Ohio; US West Corporate Collection, Denver. *Exhib:* Colorado Biennial (auth, catalog), Mus Contemp Art, Denver, 2000; Aspen Valley Biennial, Aspen Art Mus, Aspen, Colo, 2000. *Teaching:* prof mixed media painting, Colo Mountain Col, 95, 96; prof collage & painting, Anderson Ranch Art Center, 2002, 2004. *Awards:* Visual Arts fellowship, Colo Coun Arts, 1998. *Bibliog:* The collage life, Aspen Mag, 99; Look deep into her work, Aspen Times, 99. *Media:* Oil, Encaustic. *Publ:* Contribr, New American Paintings, The Open Studio Press, 99; contribr, Nine Aspen Artists, The Third Eye Press, 95; contribr, The Progressive Corp, Ann Report, 97; contribr, New Am Paintings, The Open Studio Press, 2001. *Dealer:* David Floria/David Floria Gallery Aspen Colo 81611. *Mailing Add:* PO Box 3004 Aspen CO 81612

GURBACS, JOHN JOSEPH
PAINTER, RESTORER
b Budapest, Hungary, Oct 31, 47; US citizen. *Study:* Miami-Dade Junior Col, AA, 68; Fla State Univ, BFA, 70; Univ SFla, 72-75, with Bruce March & Paul Sarkisian. *Work:* Fla State House of Reps & Fla Senate, Tallahassee; Univ Cent Fla, Orlando; Southern Bell, Jacksonville, Fla; Tampa Elec & Barnett Bank, Tampa. *Exhib:* Am Painting, Soc Four Arts, Palm Beach, Fla, 75; Critic's Choice, 80 & Jim Rosenquist Invitational, 82, Artist Alliance Gallery, Tampa; Mus Choice, Loch Haven Art Ctr, Orlando, 81; New Talent Exhib, Barbara Gillman Gallery, Miami, Fla, 82; Triennial & Gasparilla's Best, Tampa Mus Fla, 85; Four Painters, Fla Ctr Contemp Art, 87; Fantasy Landscapes, Tampa Mus W, 87; Southern Arts Fed/Nat Endowment Arts Regional Fel Awards Exhib, Atlanta Sch Art, 87 & Ruth Eckerd Hall, Clearwater, Fla, 88; Scarfone Gallery, Univ Tampa, 88. *Pos:* Self-employed designer & artist, specializing in wall design & lettering, 77-86; exhib asst, Tampa Mus, 81-82; proj painter, Tampa Theater Restoration Proj, 81-84. *Awards:* Merit Award, Gulf Coast Art Ctr, 78; Individual Artist Fel, Fla Arts Coun, 85; Regional Fel Award, Southern Arts Fedn & Nat Endowment Arts, 86. *Bibliog:* Joanne Rodriquez (auth), Critic's Choice Exhibition, Tampa Tribune, 80; Robert Martin (auth), John Gurbacs exhibition, Tampa Times, 81; Audrey Lawler (auth), Local residents receive state grants, Carrollwood News, 85. *Media:* Acrylic, Oil. *Dealer:* Joan Hodgell Gallery 46 S Palm Ave Sarasota FL 33577. *Mailing Add:* 304 W Kirby St Tampa FL 33604-4048

GURDJIAN, ANNETTE
PAINTER, PHOTOGRAPHER
b Providence, RI. *Study:* RISD, BFA, 73, MFA, 76. *Work:* Whitney Mus Am Art, NY; Mus Mod Art, NY; San Francisco Mus Mod Art; Chicago Art Inst; Seattle Art Mus. *Comn:* Mural, Bay Area Rapid Transit, Oakland, Calif, 81; 3 paintings, Venice Biennial, 90; paintings, comn by Madonna, Malibu, Calif, 91; 5 paintings, Univ Ore Law Libr, Eugene, 99. *Exhib:* Altered Surfaces, Los Angeles Co Mus, 89, Mus Mod Art, NY, 94; Venice Biennale, 90; Figurative Allegories, Portland Art Mus, 91; Oil and Silver, San Francisco Mus Mod Art, 94; Whitney Biennale, NY, 98; Am Artists, Fresno (Calif) Art Mus, 98; Boundless, Seattle Art Mus, 99. *Awards:* Painting Fel NEA, 84; Guggenheim Grant, Guggenheim Found, 91; Visual Arts Fel, Ore Arts Comn, 2000. *Media:* Oil and Photography Mixed. *Mailing Add:* 95 W 30th Ave Eugene OR 97405

GUREVICH, GRIGORY
SCULPTOR, PAINTER, GRAPHIC ARTIST, PRINTMAKER, INVENTOR
b Leningrad, St Petersburg, Russia, Dec 26, 37; US citizen. *Study:* Acad Fine & Indust Arts, Leningrad, St Petersburg, Russia, Masters, 61. *Work:* NY Pub Libr; Brooklyn Mus Libr; Rare Books Collection, Newark Libr Mus; Rare Books Libr, St Bonaventure Univ, NY; Mus Russ Contemp Art, Jersey City, NJ; Hermitage Mus Lib, St Petersburg; and others. *Comn:* Commuters (7 bronze sculptures), Penn Sta Newark, NJ Transit, 85; Kazuo Hashimoto (bronze bust), NJ Inst Technol, 96; Finn Caspepsen (bronze bust) Banks, NJ, 97. *Exhib:* Solo show, CASE Mus Russ Contemp Art, Jersey City, NJ 83; Plakat, Plakat Gallery, Copenhagen, 83; Graphicworks, Musee de L'Art Russe Contemporian, France, 85; Retrospective, St Bonaventure Univ, NY, 96; Ideas, Morris Mus, Morristown, NJ, 96; Crossroads, Seton Hall Univ, NJ, 97. *Collection Arranged:* Pen & Ink Drawing, Jeraldine R Dodge Foundation, 2004. *Pos:* founder, artistic dir, Arts on Hudson Art Program, Jersey City, 1998-. *Teaching:* Instr sculpture & drawing, Newark Sch Fine & Indust Arts, 82-97; prof sculpture & ceramics, St Johns Univ, Queens, NY, 94-97. *Awards:* Marian W Reitman Award, Arts Coun Essex Area, 90; Nat Award, Am Artists Prof League, 92; Artist of the Year, Hudson Co Artists, 95; Katherine D Miller Award, 98; 1st Place in Watercolor, 1st Place in Painting, Drawing, St Johns Church, 2000. *Bibliog:* Harold Marcus (auth), The Case Mus of Russian Contemporary Art in exile, Arts, 2/88; Amy Kellog (dir), News 12 New Jersey, 8/19/96; Gregory R Gregor (auth), Fine Art Professor is true Renaissance Man, St John's Today, 96; and articles in NY Times, Star Ledger, Jersey Journal & others. *Mem:* Am Artists Prof League Inc. *Media:* Pen & ink, watercolor, acrylic, pencil, bronze, oils, art books. *Collection:* Picasso, Utemaro, Chiparus. *Publ:* Articles in NY Times, Star Ledger, Herald Tribune Denmark, Izvestia, others. *Dealer:* Art South Inc 161 Leverington Ave Philadelphia PA 19127; Gen Serv Admin Pub Bldg Serv Washington DC 20405. *Mailing Add:* 282 Barrow St Jersey City NJ 07302

GURLIK, PHILIP JOHN
PAINTER, PRINTMAKER
b Beaver Dam, Wis, Sept 26, 58. *Study:* Univ Wis, Green Bay, 76-79; Milwaukee Area Col, 79-80, Excelsior Col, Albany, NY, BA (music & painting), 99. *Work:* Dwight Merrimon Davidson Collection, Elon Col, NC; SAP America, Houston; Interchem, Houston; Sheppard Pratt, Baltimore. *Comn:* Painting, SAP Am, 96; painting, Hilton Hotel, Baltimore, 2006. *Exhib:* Watercolor, Miss Mus Art, Jackson, 95; Stamford Mus, 95; Sam Houston Mem Mus, 95; Minot State Univ, 96; and many others. *Teaching:* artist in residence, Md Hall for Creative Arts, Annapolis. *Awards:* Best of Painting, North Light, 98. *Media:* Painting. *Interests:* sailing, music, literature. *Publ:* Auth, Selected Works, Tafford Publ, 96. *Mailing Add:* PO Box 4474 Annapolis MD 21403

GURNEY, GEORGE
CURATOR, HISTORIAN
b Sharon, Conn, Nov 26, 39. *Study:* Brown Univ, BA, 62; Univ Pa, MA, 65; Univ Del, PhD, 78. *Collection Arranged:* Nineteenth Century Sculpture (auth, catalog), Nat Gallery Art, 74; Sculpture and the Federal Triangle, Nat Collection Fine Arts, 79; Elizabeth Catlett, 90; Revisiting The White City: American Art at the 1893 World's Fair, 93; Man on Fire: Luis Jimenez, 94; Chaim Gross: A Celebration, 96; Lost and Found: Edmmia Lewis's Cleopatra, 96; George Catlin and his Indian Gallery, 2002. *Pos:* Guest cur, Nat Mus Am Art, Smithsonian Am Art Mus, Washington, DC, 77-82, assoc cur sculpture, 85-93, cur, 94-99, deputy chief cur, 99-. *Teaching:* Teaching asst art hist, Univ Pa, Philadelphia, 64-65; instr art hist, Univ Hartford, Conn, 65-66 & Sweet Briar Col, Va, 66-69. *Awards:* Nat Gallery Art Samuel H Kress Fel, 73-74; Nat Mus Am Art Smithsonian Res Fel, 74-75; Herbert Adams Memorial Medal, Nat Sculpture Soc, 87. *Mem:* Col Art Asn Am; Soc Archit Historians; Nat Sculpture Soc. *Res:* Nineteenth and twentieth century American sculpture; Archit Sculpture at World's Columbian Exposition, 1893. *Publ:* Contribr, Sculpture of a City: Philadelphia's Treasures in Bronze and Stone, Walker & Co, 74; Sculpture and the Federal Triangle, Nat Sculpture Rev, 79; Cast and Recast: The Sculpture of Frederic Remington, Smithsonian Press, 81; Sculpture and the Federal Triangle, Smithsonian Press, 85. *Mailing Add:* 2023 N Taylor St Arlington VA 22207-3121

GURNEY, JANICE SIGRID
CONCEPTUAL ARTIST, PHOTOGRAPHER
b Winnipeg, Man, Mar 5, 49. *Study:* Univ Man, BFA, 73. *Work:* Nat Gallery Can; Winnipeg Art Gallery, Man; Robert McLaughlin Gallery, Oshawa, Ont; Can Coun Art Bank, Ottawa, Ont; Labatt's Photog Collection, Toronto, Ont; Art Gallery Ont, Toronto. *Exhib:* For the Audience, Mount St Vincent Univ Art Gallery, Halifax, NS, 86; Name, 49th Parallel, NY, 89; Traveling Theory, Jordan Nat Art Gallery, Amman, 92; Sum over Histories (with catalog), Winnipeg Art Gallery, Man, 92, The Power Plant, Toronto, 93, Mackenzie Art Gallery, Regina, Sask, 93, London Regional Art Gallery, Ont, 94 & Glenbow Mus, Calgary, Alta, 94; McIntosh Gallery, London, Ont, 99. *Pos:* Mem bd dir, YYZ Artists' Outlet, Toronto, 82-89. *Teaching:* Toronto Sch Art, 97-. *Awards:* Can Coun B Grants, 91, 92, 94 & 99. *Bibliog:* Jo-anna Issak (auth), The Mothers of Invention, Hobart & William Smith Col, 89; Mark Cheetham (auth), Remembering Post-Modernism, Oxford Univ Press, 91. *Media:* Mixed Media. *Publ:* Auth, Moveable Wounds (An Essay in Composition), Art Metropole, 84; coauth, The interpretation of architecture, YYZ Toronto, 86; auth, The surface of behaviour, Photo Communique, 88; Mortality, the body, and death, Artviews Visual Arts, 89; The salvage paradigm, YYZ Toronto, 90. *Dealer:* Wynick Tuck Gallery 80 Spadina Ave Toronto Ont M5V 2J3 Canada. *Mailing Add:* 243 Macdonell Ave Unit 2 Toronto ON M6R 2A9 Canada

GURSKY, ANDREAS
PHOTOGRAPHER
b Leipzig, Ger, Jan 15, 55. *Study:* Folkwangschule (GHS), Essen, 78-81; Kunstakademie, Dusseldorf, 81-87; Studied with Bernd Becher (Meisterschuler), 85. *Exhib:* Qui, quoi, ou? Un regard sur l'art en Allemagne en 1992, Musee d'art Moderne de la Ville de Paris, 92; Mythos Rhein, Wilhelm-Hauck-Mus, Ludwigshafen, 92; Doubletake: Collective Memory & Current Art, Hayward Gallery, London, Eng, 92 & Kunsthalle, Vienna, 93; Distanz und Nahe, Nationalgalerie, Berlin, Ger, 93; Siemens Fotoprojekte 1987-1992, Neve Pinakothek, Munich, Sprengel Mus, Hanover, 93; La Ville: Intimite et Froideur, Galerie des Archives, Paris, 94; Vis-a-vis, Rhurlandmuseum, Essen; Summer Exhib, Matthew Marks Gallery, NY, 95; Prospect 96, Schirn Kunsthalle, Frankfurt, Ger, 96; solo exhibs, Victoria Miro, London, 96, Galerie Rudiger Schottle, Munich, Ger, 97, Galerie Mai 36, Zurich, 97, Javier Lopez, Madrid, Spain, 97, Matthew Marks Gallery, NY, 97, 99 & 2001, Kunstmuseum Wolfsburg, traveling exhib, 98 & Milwaukee Art Mus, traveling exhib, 98, Regen Projects,. Los Angeles, 99 & Matthew Marks Gallery, NY, 2001; Alpenblick, Kunsthalle Vienna, 97; Positionen kunstlerischer Photographie in Deutschland seit 1945, Berlinische Galerie, Martin-Gropius-Bau, Berlin, 97; Belladonna, ICA, London, 97; Young Ger Artists 2, Saatchi Gallery, London, 97; About Painting, Robert Miller Gallery, NY, 97; Michael Askin, Andreas Gursky and Fischli & Weiss, Andrea Rosen Gallery, NY, 97; Landschaften/Landscapes: Michael Bach, Andreas Gursky, Axel Hutte, Michael van Ofen, Andreas Schon, Kunstverein Fur due Rheinlande und Westfalen, Dusseldorf, 98; Carnegie Mus of Art, Pitts, 99; The Big Picture: Large-Format Photog, Middlebury Col Mus of Art, Vt, 99, Raume, Kunsthaus Bregenz, Austria, 99; Fotowerken, Van Abbemuseum Eindhoven, The Neth, 2000; Photog Now, Contemp Arts Ctr, New Orleans, 2000; Walker Evans & Co, Mus of Modern Art, NY, 2000, 01; Szenenwechsel XVIII, Mus fur Moderne Kunst, Franfurt, Ger, 2000; Landmark Pictures in Boston, Harvard Univ Art Mus, Mass, 2000; Ansicht-Aussicht-Einsicht, Mus Bochum, 2000; How You Look At It, Sprengel Mus, 2000. *Mailing Add:* c/o Matthew Marks Gallery 523 W 24th St New York NY 10011

GURSOY, AHMET
PAINTER
b Turkey, Mar 5, 29; US citizen. *Study:* Tech Univ Istanbul, Turkey, 47-52; Ill Inst Technol, 54-56; Art Students League, 58-63. *Work:* Chase Manhattan Bank; Cornell Univ; St Lawrence Univ; Grey Gallery, NY Univ; Ulrich Mus, Wichita, Kans. *Exhib:* Wells Col, Aurora, NY, 77; Niagara Arts Ctr, Niagara Falls, NY, 77; Mohawk Valley Community Col, Utica, NY, 77; Nassau Community Col, Garden City, NY, 77; Hyden Collection, Glen Falls, NY, 77; and many others. *Awards:* Painting Prize, 21st Ann New Eng Exhib, Silvermine, Conn, 70. *Bibliog:* Grace Glueck (auth), article, New York Times, 68; C Giuliano (auth), article, 68 & Gordon Brown (auth), article, 70, Arts Mag. *Mem:* Fedn Mod Painters & Sculptors (pres, 75-); Silvermine Guild Artists; Music for People (treas, 71-72). *Media:* Oil. *Publ:* Auth, Convergence of Engineering & Art, 70. *Mailing Add:* 490 Bellwood Ave Tarrytown NY 10591-1426

GUSELLA, ERNEST
VIDEO ARTIST
b Calgary, Alta, Can, Sept 13, 41. *Work:* Pompidou Ctr, Paris; Lenbachhaus, Munich; Mus Mod Art, NY; Nat Gallery Can; Kawaski Mus Art; and others. *Exhib:* Spiral Gallery, Tokyo, 87; Lewbachhaus, Munich, 90; Jamia Miuia Islamia, New Delhi, 93; Univ SFla, Tampa, 94. *Pos:* Dir, Digital DADA Inc. *Teaching:* Guest prof, State Univ NY, Buffalo, 84-87, Jamia Millia Islamia Uni, New Delhi, Univ Manipur, India; guest artist, Allgemeine Geweres Chule, Basel, 90 & Univ Appl Art, Vienna, 90; prof electronic images, Univ SFla, Tampa. *Awards:* Can Coun Grant, 85-86 & 90; Checkerboard Grant, 87; Fulbright Scholar, India, 93-94. *Bibliog:* The 2nd Link, Banff, 83; Dis/Patches: The Learning Channel, 84; Review, Port Washington News, 85. *Media:* Video, Performance. *Publ:* Contribr, Kunst Und Video Book, Dumont Buchverlag, Koln, 83; Clip, Klapp, Bum, Dumont-Koln, 86. *Dealer:* Scan Gallery Tokyo Japan; The Tape Connection Rome Italy

GUSSOW, ROY
SCULPTOR, ENVIRONMENTAL ARTIST
b Brooklyn, NY, Nov 12, 18. *Study:* With Archipenko, Chicago & Woodstock, NY, 46-47; Inst Design, Chicago, BS, 48, with Moholy-Nagy. *Work:* Whitney Mus Am Art, Mus Mod Art, Brooklyn Mus & Guggenheim Mus, NY; NC Mus Art, Raleigh. *Comn:* Stainless steel sculpture, Xerox Corp, Rochester, NY, 69; Stainless steel sculpture, NY Family Ctr Bldg, 72; sculpture, Combustion Engine Corp, Stamford, Conn, 76; sculpture, City Reading, Pa, 78; sculpture, City Harrisburg, Pa, 83; and others. *Exhib:* Sculpture 1951, Metrop Mus Art, NY, 51; Pa Acad, Philadelphia, 51-59; NC Artists, NC Mus Art, Raleigh, 52-61; Whitney Mus Am Art, 56 & 62-68; solo show, Borgenicht Gallery, 64, 71, 73, 77, 80 & 87; Nat Gold Medal Exhib Bldg Arts, Archit League, NY, 62 & 65. *Teaching:* Instr design & sculpture, Bradley Univ, 48-49 & Colorado Springs Fine Arts Ctr, Colo, 49-51; prof design & sculpture, Univ NC Sch Design, 51-62; adj prof sculpture, Pratt Inst Sch Archit, 62-68, Columbia Univ Sch Art, 81-85; vis critic, Grad Sch Art, Univ Pa, 91-92. *Awards:* Purchase Awards, Ford Found, 60 & 62; First Prize, New York Family Ct Sculpture Competition, 72; Grant, Pollock-Krasner Found Inc, 97-98. *Mem:* Sculptors Guild (bd dir, 67-, pres, 76-80); NY Artists Equity Asn (bd dir, 77-, vpres, 80-82 & pres, 85-87); Fine Arts Fedn, NY (bd dir, 87, vpres, 92-93, pres, 93-98, hon vpres, 98). *Media:* Stainless Steel, Bronze. *Dealer:* Neuhoff Gallery 41 E 57 St New York NY 10022. *Mailing Add:* 4040 24th St Long Island City NY 11101

GUSSOW, SUE FERGUSON
PAINTER, EDUCATOR
b Brooklyn, NY, Aug 2, 35. *Study:* Cooper Union, with Stefano Cusumano & Bob Gwathmey, dipl, 56; Columbia Univ, BS, 60; Tulane Univ, MFA, 64. *Work:* Dallas Mus Fine Arts; New Orleans Mus Art; Philadelphia Free Libr; The Frick Collection Archives, & The Cooper Hewitt Mus of the Smithsonian; and others. *Exhib:* Print Biennial, Brooklyn Mus, 64; Drawings in St Paul, Minn Mus Art, 71-72; Benton Gallery, Southampton, NY, 87; Ctr Contemp Art, East Hampton, NY, 88; Marcelle Fine Arts, Southampton, NY, 89 & 90; Palace of Journalists, St Petersburg, Russ, 92; Artists of the Springs Invitational, E Hampton, NY, 93-2004; 40 yr retrospective (with catalog), Houghton Gallery, Cooper Union, NY, 97; On the Books Guild Hall E Hampton NY, 2004. *Teaching:* Prof Emer, Sch of Archit, Cooper Union, 1970-2005; Vis Prof, The Frick Collection 2002-05. *Awards:* Purchase Prize, Drawings USA, Minn Mus Art, 66; Pamela Djerassi Vis Artist Grant, Stanford Univ, 82-83; One Woman Retrospective Award, Houghton Gallery, Cooper Union, NY, 97; and others. *Bibliog:* Ann Glenn Crowe (auth), A French Heritage, Art Week, 7/2/83; Paul Goldberger (auth), The NY Times (review p C11), 4/16/97; Zöe Ingalls (auth), The Chronicle of Higher Education (article p B11), 11/21/97. *Mem:* Fel of ARC Soc for Arts & Religion in Contemp Cult. *Media:* Oil, Pastel. *Res:* Receipient of Tides Foundation & Graham Foundation grants for research on relation of drawing & architectural thought. *Publ:* Ed, Trees, Cooper Union, 85; auth, Women Artist Newsletter Book Review II, III, IV, V, 94, 95 & 96; auth & illus, DRAW POKER, Cooper Union, NY, 97; Drawing Dimensions, frontispiece & illus, Cynthia Maris Dantzic, Prentis Hall, NJ, 98. *Mailing Add:* PO Box 1609 Amagansett NY 11930

GUSTAFSON, PIER
ASSEMBLAGE ARTIST
b Minneapolis, Minn, 56. *Study:* Gustavus Adolphus Col, BS, 78; Univ Wis, MFA (painting), 82. *Work:* Mus Fine Arts, Boston, Mass; Minneapolis Inst Art, Minneapolis, Minn; Bank Boston, Boston, Mass, Pfeizer Chemical, NY. *Exhib:* Solo exhibs, Paper Constructions, 84, Installation: Suite in Sonata Form, 85 & Drapery Studies, 88, Gallery NAGA, Boston, Mass, Carnegie Gallery, Univ Maine, Orono, Maine, 86, Univ Gallery, Clark Univ, Worcester, Mass, 88 & Clark Gallery, Lincoln, Mass, 92; Recent Painting & Sculpture 1944-1984, Mus Fine Arts, Boston, Mass, 85; 50th Anniversary, Inst Contemp Art, Boston, Mass, 86; Art on Paper, Weatherspoon Art Gallery, Univ NC, Greensboro, 91; The Object, Fitchburg Art Mus, Mass, 91; Mus Art, RI Sch Design, 92; Recent Sculpture, Gallery NAGA, Boston, 93; group exhibs, Mount Ida Col, Newtown, Mass, 2002, Gallery NAGA, Boston, Mass, 2002, DeCordova Mus, Lincoln, Mass, 2003. *Awards:* Mass Artists Fel, 83 & 86; Nat Endowment Arts Fel, 86. *Bibliog:* Nancy Stapen (auth), Pier Gustafson: recent constructions, Boston Globe, 11/19/92; Christine Temin (auth), Exhibits: suspending disbelief, Boston Globe, 11/19/92; Shawn Hill (auth), The work of Gustafson & Dowd is haunted - by missing persons, Bay Windows, 2/18/93. *Mailing Add:* c/o Gallery NAGA 67 Newbury St Boston MA 02116

GUSTIN, CHRISTOPHER
CERAMIST
b Chicago, Ill, Jan 22, 52. *Study:* Kansas City Art Inst, Mo, BFA (ceramics), 75; NY State Col Ceramics, Alfred, MFA (ceramics), 77. *Work:* Everson Mus Art, Syracuse, NY; Los Angeles Co Mus Art, Calif; RI Sch Design Art Mus, Providence; Victoria & Albert Mus, London, Eng; Ore State Univ, Corvallis; Kalamazoo Inst Arts, Mich; Rayovac Corp, Madison, Wis; Bank Boston, New Bedford, Conn. *Exhib:* Solo exhibs, Kalamazoo Inst Arts, Mich, 88, Miami Univ, Oxford, Ohio, 88, Garth Clark Gallery, NY, 88, 90 & 91, Dartmouth Gallery, Mass, 93, Manchester Craftsmen's Guild, Philadelphia, 94, Paul Melon Arts Ctr, Wallingford, Conn, 99, John Elder Gallery, NY, 99, 2003, Gallery Materia/tye Hand and Spirit, Scottsdale, Ariz, 99, Works Gallery, Philadelphia, PA, 2000 & Judy Ann Goldman Fine Arts, Boston, MA, 2002; A Madcap Teapot Party at the Renwick, Renwick Gallery, Nat Mus Am Art, 96; Myth, Memory, Madness, Judy Ann Goldman Fine Art, Boston, 96; Sculptural Ceramics in New Eng Today, Boston Anthenaeum, 96; Eighth Triennial, Fuller Mus Art, Brockton, Mass, 96; Soc Arts & Crafts Artists Award Exhib, Boston, 96; group exhibs, Int Teapot Exhib, Yinge Ceramics Mus, Taipei, Taiwan, 2002, The Yixing Effect, The Art Complex Mus, Duxbury, MA, 2001, Color/Fire: Defining Moments of Contemp Ceramics, 1950-2000, Los Angeles, Calif, 2000; and others. *Pos:* Pres, bd dir, Watershed Ctr Ceramic Arts, N Edgecomb, Maine, 87-90, adv bd, 90-96; bd dir, Studio Potter Mag, 98-. *Teaching:* Instr crafts, Parsons Sch Design, New York, 78-80; asst prof, Boston Univ, Mass, 80-85; assoc prof ceramics, Swain Sch Design, New Bedford, Mass, 85-88 & Col Visual & Performing Arts, Univ Mass, Dartmouth, N Dartmouth, 88-98; lectr, Centro de Arte e Comunicacao Visual, Lisbon, Portugal, 92; vis lectr, Ceramics Univ of Mass, Dartmouth, 99-2000; prof emeritus, Univ Mass, Dartmouth, 2003-. *Awards:* Purchase Awards, Everson Mus Art 87 & Southern Ill Univ Edwardsville, 88; Artists Award, Soc Arts & Crafts, Boston, 96; hon mention, Twelth Ann San Angelo Nat Ceramic Competition, San Angelo Mus Fine Arts, Tex, 98. *Bibliog:* Clay Today; Contemporary Ceramists and Their Work, Chronicle Bks, San Francisco, 90; Susan Peterson (auth), The Craft and Art of Clay, Prentice Hall, NJ, 91; Pat Doran (auth), Ceramicist Chris Gustin, Art New Eng, 4-5/94. *Dealer:* Works Gallery Philadelphia PA. *Mailing Add:* 231 Horseneck Rd South Dartmouth MA 02748

GUTHMAN, LEO S
COLLECTOR
b Chicago, Ill. *Mem:* Gov life mem Art Inst Chicago; Soc Contemp Art, Chicago (dir); Art Club Chicago; Nat Collectors Comt, Nat Gallery Art, DC; and others. *Collection:* Contemporary painting, especially by Americans; international sculpture

GUTIERREZ, YOLANDA
SCULPTOR
b Mexico City, Mex, Feb 10, 70. *Study:* Univ Nac Autonoma de Mex, licenciatura, 87-92. *Work:* Banco de la Repub Biblioteque Luis Angel Avango, Bogota, Colombia; Mus Univ Contemp de Arte de la Univ Nac Autonoma de Mex, Mexico City. *Comn:* Installation ecologique, Xochitla Res naturel, Tepotzotlan, Mex, 98. *Exhib:* Habana - Sao Paolo, Arte, 95; Fluctuations Fugitives, la ferme de Buisson, Nuisel, France, 96;

Tierra Livgen, Alvary Carmen T Carrillo Gil, Mexico City, 97; 5th Ann Biennal d'Estanbul, Turkey, 97; Mex ahova punto de patida, Ohio & PR, 97; La Covriente Installation, Culturgent, Lisbon, Port, 98. *Teaching:* Asst prof dons l'atelier d'experimentation insuelle II, Ecole Nat d'Arts Plastiques & de l'Univ Nac Autonoma de Mex, 92-95. *Mailing Add:* c/o Espace d'Art Yvonamor Palix 13 rue Keller F-75011 Paris France

GUTKIN, PETER
SCULPTOR, DESIGNER
b Brooklyn, NY, 44. *Study:* Tyler Sch Art, Temple Univ, BFA, 66; San Francisco Art Inst, MFA, 68. *Work:* Sheldon Mem Art Gallery, Lincoln, Nebr; Oakland Mus, Calif; NASA/Ames Res Ctr, Mountain View, Calif; Portland Mus Art, Ore; San Francisco Mus Mod Art; and others. *Comn:* NASA/Ames Res Ctr, 87. *Exhib:* one-man shows, San Francisco Mus Art, 72, San Francisco Art Inst, 84, Modernism 90, San Francisco & Jernigan Wicker, San Francisco, 95; Menace, Mus Contemp Art, Chicago, 75; Sculpture in Calif 75-80, San Diego Mus Art, Calif, 80; Am Pop Cult Today, Laforet Mus, Tokyo, Japan, 87; Celebrating Modern Art, The Anderson Collection, San Francisco Mus Mod Art, 2000; 25th Anniversary Exhib, San Francisco, Calif, 2004; and others. *Pos:* Pres, Peter Gutkin Furniture & Design Inc. *Teaching:* Instr, Aspen Sch Contemp Art, Colo, 66, Univ Calif, Berkeley, 72-74, San Francisco Art Inst, 78 & Calif Col Arts & Crafts, 82, 94, 97 & 99; instr, Calif Col Art, 1997. *Awards:* Nat Endowment Humanities & Art Award, 66; Purchase Prize, San Francisco Art Festival, 72; Nat Endowment Arts Fel, 82 & 84; Product Design Award, Resources Coun, 86. *Bibliog:* Article, Compressed constructions, spiderweb sculptures, Art News, 12/77; Howard Junker (auth), San Francisco, Peter Gutkin at 170 Capp St, Art Am, 5/80; Jerome Tarshis (auth), San Francisco, Peter Gutkin at the San Francisco Art Inst, Art in Am Mag, 10/84; Lois Wagner Green (auth), Site specific, Peter Gutkin takes a furniture commission full circle in residential designs for a San Francisco art patron, Interior Design Mag, 5/86. *Media:* Wood; Miscellaneous. *Interests:* Furniture. *Publ:* Thomas Albright (auth), Art in the San Francisco Bay Area, Chronicle Publ; Denise Domerque (auth), Artists Design Furniture, Abrams Publ. *Mailing Add:* 2250 Jerrold Ave Unit 13 San Francisco CA 94124

GUTMAN, BERTHA STEINHARDT
PAINTER, PROFESSOR
Study: Queens Col, City Univ NY, BA, 72; State Univ NY, Stony Brook, MFA, 91. *Work:* Artist's Space Slide Registry, Soho, NY; Jewish Fed, Oklahoma City. *Exhib:* 58th Ann Mid Yr Exhib, Butler Inst Am Art, Youngstown, Ohio, 94; Hoyt Nat Art Show, Hoyt Inst Fine Arts, New Castle, Pa, 94; Art Exhibit Celebrating Women Artists, Hutchins Gallery-Long Island Univ, Brookville, NY, 94; Tabletop Narratives, Bryant Lib Gallery, Roslyn, NY, 94; Art Asn Harrisburg, Pa, 96 & 98; Still Life Show, Islip Art Mus, NY, 96; Armory Art Ctr, West Palm Beach, 96; 42nd Ann Long Island Artists Exhib, Heckscher Mus Art, Huntington, NY, 97; Images 97, Hub Galleries, Pa State Univ, 97; The Time Machine, Anchorage Mus Hist & Art, Alaska, 97; Trial by Jury, City Without Walls Gallery, Newark, NJ, 97; Omni Gallery, Uniondale, NY, 99; Art-trium, Huntington, NY, 2001; The Banana Factory, Bethlehem, Pa, 2002. *Pos:* Mus shop mgr, Jewish Mus, NY, 73-77. *Teaching:* Suffolk Community Col, St Joseph's Col, Adelphi Univ, Empire State Col, Nassau Co Community Col; Delaware Co Community Col, Media, Pa. *Awards:* Special Opportunity Stipend, NY Found Arts, 92-94; Grumbacher Gold Medalion, Art Asn Harrisburg, 95; 12th Ann Nat Women Arts Exhib, Second Place in Art, Women Ctr, Archard Ridge Campus, Oakland Community Col, 98; Grumbacher Gold Medallion, Art Asn Harrisburg, 95. *Bibliog:* Eleanor Martin (auth), A doll's house, Times-Herald Rec 94; Table-Top Narratives at Bryant, Roslyn News, 94; Dina Roberts (auth), Metaphorical Table-Top Narratives, Manhattan Arts Int, 95. *Mem:* Nat Asn Women Artists; Col Art Asn; Asn Community Col Profs of Art and Art Hist. *Media:* Oil on Canvas or Linen. *Publ:* Auth, Your Living Art, McGraw Hil Col Div, 2001. *Dealer:* Gallery 84 Inc 50 W 57th St New York NY 10019. *Mailing Add:* 165 Somerset Dr Blue Bell PA 19422

GUTZEIT, FRED
PAINTER, EDUCATOR
b Cleveland, Ohio. *Study:* Yale Norfolk Summer Sch, 61; Cleveland Inst Art, Mary C Paige Traveling Scholar, 62; Hunter Col, MA, 79. *Work:* Aldrich Mus, Ridgefield, Conn; Alternative Mus, NY; Fashion Moda; Cleveland Art Asn; Chemical Bank, NY. *Exhib:* Biennial, Butler Inst Am Art, 65; Contemp Images in Watercolor, Akron Art Inst, 76; solo exhibs, NY State Artist Series, Herbert F Johnson Mus, Cornell Univ, 77 & Distinguished Alumnus, Cleveland Inst Art, 77; Personal Visions, Places/Spaces, Bronx Mus Arts, 78; May Show, Cleveland Mus Art, 82; A Look Back, A Look Forward, Aldrich Mus, 82. *Teaching:* Instr painting, Philadelphia Col Art, 79-82, Brooklyn Mus Art Sch, 81-84 & Cleveland Inst Art, Lacoste France, 84 & 85; vis assoc prof, Pratt Inst, 86-2000; Cleveland Inst Art, 95-97; adj, City Univ New York, 97-. *Awards:* Pollock-Krasner Found Grant, 99-2000, 2006-2007. *Bibliog:* Patricia Eakins (auth), Fred Gutzeit: An organic approach to images, Am Artist Mag, 10/75 & article, Arts Mag, 4/77; Pete Hamill (auth), Tools As Art, Hechinger Collection, Harry Abrams Publ, 95. *Media:* Acrylic, Watercolor; Inkjet Print. *Interests:* Photography. *Dealer:* Joe Amrhein Pierog Gallery Brooklyn NY; Richard Timperio Sideshow gallery Brooklyn NY. *Mailing Add:* 264 Bowery New York NY 10013

GUYTON, WADE
PAINTER
b Tennessee, 72. *Study:* Univ Tenn, BA, 90-95; Hunter Col, MFA, 96-98. *Exhib:* Exhib incl, Against the New Passeism; Understanding this is only the beginning, hope for the end; Build, Destroy, Do Nothing, Andrew Kreps Gallery, NY, 99, After the Diagram, White Box Gallery, 2000-2001, Retrofit, Lombard-Freid Fine Arts, 2001-02, X, Power House, Memphis, 2003, Elements of An Incomplete Map, Artists Space, NY, 2003, Whitney Biennial, Whitney Mus Am Art, 2004, Objects Are Much More Familiar, Power House, Memphis, 2004. *Mailing Add:* c/o Lombard Fried Fine Arts 531 W 26th St New York NY 10001

GUZAK, KAREN W
PAINTER, PRINTMAKER,PUBLIC ARTIST
b Cambridge, Mass, May 21, 39. *Study:* Univ Colo, BS (Boettcher Scholar), 61; Cornish Inst Arts, BFA, 76. *Work:* Brooklyn Mus, NY; Portland Art Mus, Ore; Whatcom Co Art Mus, Bellingham, Wash; NY Pub Libr Print Collection, NY; City of Seattle, Wash. *Comn:* design for sculpted elevator enclosure, Sea Tac Airport, Seattle, 94; balcony railing, King Co Coun Chambers, Seattle, Wash, 98; sculpture garden & wall murals, South Seattle Community Col Libr, 99-2000; landmark sculpture and gateways, Overlake Ctr, Sound Transit, 2002; plaza sculpture, Redmond Town Ctr, 2003. *Exhib:* 22nd Ann Print Show, Brooklyn Mus, NY, 81; Seattle Artists, San Francisco Mus Mod Art, Calif, 83; Laura Russo Gallery, Portland, Ore, 91 & 96; Foster White Gallery, Seattle, Wash, 91, 94, 96, 98 & 2000; Boston Printmakers, 43rd Print Exhib, De Cordova Mus, Mass, 91; Am Print Survey, Baylor Univ, 91; Forum: Art & Sch New Dimensions, Gutersloh, Ger, 94; 9th Nat Computer Art Invitational, Eastern Wash Univ, 96 & 99; Int Print Invitational, Portland Art Mus, 97; Int Exhib Electronic Prints, Arcade II, Univ Broghton, Eng, 97-98; Tacoma Art Mus, Wash, 2002; Ctr Contemp Art, Seattle, Wash, 2000; Edmonds Community Col, 2004. *Pos:* Art comnr, King Co Arts Comn, 81-86, Metro Transit Tunnel Art Comt, 85-91; developer, proj mgr & pres, Sunny Arms Artists' Coop, Seattle, Wash, 88-90; developer & proj mgr, Union Art Cooperative, 93-94; proj mgr, On the Bds Contemp Performance Ctr, 97-98. *Teaching:* Instr, Univ Ore Workshop, High Tech/Low Tech, 89. *Awards:* Merit Award, 17th Nat Print Completion, Schenectady Mus, 94. *Bibliog:* Frank Pepper (auth), Art of the Electronic Age, Abrahms Publ, 94; Justin Henderson (auth), The art of co-op living, Interiors Mag, 94; Lois Allan (auth), Contemporary Printmaking in the Northwest, Craftsman House Press, 62-65, 97; Northwest Originals: Washington Women and Their Art, Matria Media Press, 90. *Mem:* Ctr Contemp Art (bd dir, 87); Northwest Print Coun (bd dir, 84-88, hist design rev bd, 2000-); On the Boards (bd dir, 87-90); Artist Trust (bd dir, 94); Artist Trust (pres bd, 96-2000). *Media:* Painting, Prints, Public Art. *Specialty:* Davidson Galleries, Prints & Paintings. *Interests:* Yoga, Teaching Yoga. *Collection:* Brooklyn Mus, NYC Library, City of Seattle, Tacoma Art Mus, Portland Art Mus, Whation Cty, Art Mus, WA. *Publ:* Auth, Leonardo Between Geometry & Gesture, J Int Soc Arts, Sci & Technol, 19-22, Vol 30, No 1, 97; Chaos, Order and Computers, Contemp Impressions, Vol 7, 99; co-auth, website, www.angelarmsworks.com. *Dealer:* Davidson Galleries 313 Occidental Ave S Seattle WA 98104; Laura Russo Gallery 805 NW 21st Portland OR 97209. *Mailing Add:* 230 Ave B Snohomish WA 98290

GUZEVICH-SOMMERS, KRESZENZ (CYNTHIA)
PAINTER, INSTRUCTOR
b Munich, Ger, May 24, 23; US citizen. *Study:* Acad Art, Munich; also with Frank Gervasi, Paul Strisik, Louis Krupp, Helen Van Wyk, Ramon Froman & Ken Gore; Acad, Florence, Italy. *Work:* First Nat Bank, Las Cruces, NMex; Truth or Consequences Mus, NMex; Branif Airline Collection. *Exhib:* El Paso Mus Art Exhib, Tex; Grand Nat Exhib, NY; Southwest Intercult Exhib, El Paso; Artists Equity Show, Albuquerque, NMex; Truth or Consequences Hist Mus; NY Overseas Press Club, O'Brians Gallery, Scottsdale, Ariz; int Govt Sponsored shows, starting Venezuela, ending in Mex City. *Collection Arranged:* Portfolio in Nat Mus for Woman Artists in Wash, D.C,. *Teaching:* Instr painting, workshops in var states & pvt studio, 65-. *Awards:* Artist of Year & Best in Show Award, Black Range Artists, 68; Best in Show Award, NMex Art League, 69; Largest Exhib in NMex Award. *Mem:* Am Artists Prof League; El Paso Mus Art Asn; Artists Equity Asn; Accademia Italia Delle Arti e Del Lavoro. *Media:* Oil. *Interests:* Judging Int dog shows. *Mailing Add:* 1635 Country Club Cir Las Cruces NM 88001

GUZY, CAROL
PHOTOGRAPHER
b Bethleham, PA, Mar 7, 56. *Study:* Northampton Co Area Community Col, Pa, Assoc Degree in Nursing, 78; Art Inst Ft Lauderdale, AAS in Photog, 80. *Pos:* Staff photog, The Miami Herald, 80-88; Staff photog, The Wash Post, 88—. *Awards:* Pulitzer Prize in spot news photog, 86 & 95; Leica Excellence medal, 94; Pulitzer Prize in feature photog, 2000. *Mailing Add:* The Wash Post 1150 15th St Northwest Washington DC 20071-0002

GWATHMEY, CHARLES
ARCHITECT
b Charlotte, NC, June 19, 1938. *Study:* Univ Pa, student, 59; Yale Univ, M (archit), 62. *Pos:* Partner Gwathmey-Siegel and Assocs Architects, NY City, 68-; pres bd trustees Inst Archit and Urban Studies, NY City, 78. *Teaching:* Vis prof archit design Pratt Inst, Yale Univ, Princeton Univ, Harvard Univ, Columbia, Univ, Cooper Union, UCLA; William A Bernoudy resident-in-architecture Am Acad, 2005. *Awards:* William Wirt Winchester traveling fellow, 62-63; Fulbright Grantee France, 62-63; Yale Alumni Arts Award for Outstanding Achievement, 85; Lifetime Achievement Medal in Visual Arts, Guild Hall Acad, 88; Lifetime Achievement Award, NY State Soc Architects, 90. *Mem:* Fel, Am Inst Arch; Am Acad Arts and Lettres (Arnold Brunner Prize, 70); Nat Acad. *Mailing Add:* Gwathmey Siegel and Assoc Architects 475 10th Ave 3rd Floor New York NY 10018-1198

GXI
PAINTER, WRITER
b Cedar Creek Homestead, Ill. *Study:* Princeton Univ, BA, 69; NY Univ, MA, 92. *Comn:* Mural, State of Ill, 78. *Exhib:* Art Gallery Ont, Toronto, Canada, 74; Bronx Mus Arts, NY, 85; Insul Hombrick, Koln, Ger, 90; Henie Onstad Art Ctr, Oslo, Norway, 95. *Media:* Digital Painting. *Publ:* Artificial Evolution, Mass Inst Technol Press, 97. *Mailing Add:* 361 Canal St New York NY 10013

GYERMEK, STEPHEN A
EDUCATOR
b Budapest, Hungary, Nov 9, 30. *Study:* Rijks Akad voor Beeldende Kunsten, Amsterdam, Holland, with Heinrich Campendonk; Academia de Bellas Artes Madrid, Spain; Univ Okla. *Comn:* Murals, Convent at Madrid, Spain, 55 & US Embassy, Spain, 55; stained glass windows, St Gregory's Abbey, Shawnee, Okla & St Benedict Church, Ada, Okla. *Exhib:* Amsterdam, 52-53; Madrid, 54; Okla Art Ctr, 60. *Collection Arranged:* Archaeology, Europe, Near & Far East, Egypt; American Indians & Central & South American Ethnology; Paintings from the Italian Renaissance; 19th Century American Paintings; plus others. *Pos:* Dir, Gerrer Mus & Art Gallery, Shawnee, Okla, 57-62; actg dir, Stovall Mus Sci & Hist, Univ Okla, 62-65; dir, Pioneer Mus & Haggin Art Galleries, Stockton, Calif, 65-70. *Teaching:* Lectr painting methods & religious art; asst prof art hist & art, Univ Okla; instr art hist, San Joaquin Delta Col, 67-. *Awards:* Prizes & Van Alabbe Award, Amsterdam, Holland, 52. *Mailing Add:* Dept Art San Joaquin Delta Col 5151 Pacific Ave Stockton CA 95207-6370

GYRA, FRANCIS JOSEPH, JR
INSTRUCTOR, PAINTER
b Newport, RI, Feb 23, 14. *Study:* RI Sch Design, dipl, hon BFA, 90; Parsons Sch Design, Paris, cert advert illus & X Ital Res Sch; Brighton Col Arts & Crafts, Sussex, Eng; Froebel Inst, Roehampton, Eng; Univ Hawaii; McNeese State Col; Keene State Col, BS. *Hon Degrees:* Hon Degree, BFA, RI Sch of Design, 95. *Work:* Providence Art Mus, RI; Tenn Fine Arts Ctr, Nashville; Vanderbilt Iniv Mus, Art Dept. *Exhib:* Int Watercolor Exhib, Art Inst Chicago, 38 & 40; First Int Ann, Marietta Col, Ohio, 69; First Art Ann, Northern New Eng, Canaan, NH, 69; Stratton Arts Festival, Vt, 70; Eighth Exhib Vt Artists, Norwich Univ, 71. *Pos:* Chmn, Vt Educ Asn Prog, 52; adv art & art educ, Aquinas Jr Col, Nashville, 66-. *Teaching:* Supv, Woodstock Union & Dist Schs, Vt, 49-69; dir art workshops, Vt State Dept Educ, 54-70; art educator, Woodstock Sch Dist, 69-84; retired. *Awards:* Recognition Reward, Nat Endowment Arts, 80; Vt State Teacher of Yr, 83; New Eng Art Educ Conf Award, Vt, 83; Fel, Vt Acad Arts & Soc, 2004. *Mem:* Woodstock Design Review Bd; life fel Int Inst Arts & Lett. *Media:* Oil, Varnish. *Publ:* Coauth, Vermont Art Guide for the Classroom Teacher K-6, 69. *Mailing Add:* Six Linden Hill PO Box 540 Woodstock VT 05091

H

HAACK, CYNTHIA R
PAINTER, PRINTMAKER
b Eagle Bend, Minn. *Study:* St Cloud State Univ, Minn, AE, 53; Univ Wyo, Laramie, 54; Idaho State Col, Pocatello, 57-58. *Work:* Wachovia Bank; Bank of America; Glaxo Pharmaceuticals. *Exhib:* Invitational, Winston-Salem Arts & Sci Gallery, NC, 79; RSVP Ann Show, Pittsburgh, 86-88; NC Watercolor Soc, 90-99; Festival In The Park, Charlotte, NC, 92; and others; Charlotte/Mecklenburg Co Sr Games Exhib, 93-98. *Collection Arranged:* Wachovia Bank, NC; Glaxo; Burlington Bag & Baggage; Weaver, Bennett & Bland, Matthews, NC; Terry Edwards Assocs, Matthews, NC; Bank Am, Gastonia, NC; The Schiele Mus, Gastonia, NC. *Teaching:* Private lessons, 61-66; instr painting, Rawls Mus, Courtland, Va, 72-73. *Awards:* First place acrylic, Charlotte/Mecklenburg Co Sr Games Exhib, NC, 94 to 2004, Gold & Silver Medals acrylics, 2000-2006; First place, Guild of Charlotte Artists Winter Show, 02, First place Oils & Acrylics, Mooresville Art Guild, Fall Show, 04; and others. *Bibliog:* Staff, Southside scenes, Daily Press Newspaper, 73; Barclay Sheaks (auth), Landscape illusion, 73; Lynn Bonney (auth), Travels inspire art, Emporia Gazette, 81; Becker (auth), Haack donates painting for fundraiser, Independent News Herald, 93. *Mem:* Charlotte Art League; Guild Charlotte Artists; NC Watercolor Soc (signature mem); Mooresville Artists Guild; and others. *Media:* Acrylic. *Dealer:* Seaside gallery 2716 Virginia Dare trail South Nags Head NC 27959. *Mailing Add:* 9400 Marshbrooke Rd Charlotte NC 28105

HAACKE, HANS CHRISTOPH
SCULPTOR, CONCEPTUAL ARTIST
b Cologne, Ger, Aug 12, 36. *Study:* Staatl Werkakademie, Kassel, Ger, MFA; Atelier 17, Paris, with SW Hayter; Tyler Sch Art, Philadelphia; Hon DFA, Oberlin Col, 91. *Hon Degrees:* D, Bauhaus Univ, Weimer, Germany, 99. *Work:* Centre Georges Pompidou, Paris; Tate Gallery, London; Mod Museet, Stockholm; Art Gallery Ont, Toronto; Nat Gallery Can, Ottawa. *Comn:* courtyard, Reichstag Bldg, Berlin, Ger. *Exhib:* Documenta, Kassel, 72, 82 & 87; Venice Biennial, 76 & 78; Sydney Biennial, 84 & 90; solo exhibs, Victoria Micro Gallery, London, 87, John Weber Gallery, NY, 88, 90, 92 & 94, Mus Nat d'art Mod, Centre Georges Pompidou, Paris, 89, Venice Biennial, Ger Pavilion, 93; and others; Portikus, Frankfort, 00; Serpentine Gallery, London, 01; Generali Found, Fienna, 02. *Teaching:* Prof art emer, Cooper Union, 67-02; guest prof, Hochschule Bildende Kunste, Hamburg, Germany, 73, 94, Gesamthochschule Essen, 79; regents lectr, Univ Calif, Berkeley, 97. *Awards:* Guggenheim Fel, 73; Nat Endowment Arts Fel, 78; Golden Lion, Venice Biennale, 93. *Bibliog:* Jack Burnham (auth), Hans Haacke's cancelled show at the Guggenheim, Artforum, 5/71; Douglas Crimp, Yve-Alain Bois, Rosalind Krauss (interview), October, Vol 30, fall 84; Benjamin Buchlon (auth), Hans Haacke: memory and instrumental reason, Art Am, 2/88. *Media:* All. *Publ:* Auth, Working conditions, Artforum, summer 81; Museums, Managers of consciousness, Art in Am, 84; In the Vice, Art J, fall 91; coauth, Bodenlos, 93; Libre-Echange, 94. *Mailing Add:* Cooper Union Union Square New York NY 10003

HAAR, TOM
PHOTOGRAPHER, FILMAKER
b Tokyo, Japan, June 2, 41; US citizen. *Study:* San Francisco State Col, BA, 64; Univ Hawaii, MFA, 67; Alexei Bradovitch Design Lab, scholar, 68; Int Ctr Photog Advan Workshop, scholar, 75. *Work:* Hawaii State Found Cult & Arts, Contemp Mus. *Exhib:* solo exhibs, Green Collections Gallery, Tokyo, 80, Capen Gallery, State Univ NY, Buffalo, 81, Hamanoya Gallery, Tokyo, 81, Space Art Gallery, Seoul, Korea, 83, Amono Gallery Osaka, Japan, 83, Univ Tsukuba Gallery, Japan, 84 & Nagase Photo Salon, Tokyo, Japan, 86; Three Photographers: Tom Hoor, Lisa Kanemoto and Aaron Dygart, Honolulu Acad Arts, Graphic Gallery, 87; The Second Ann Flora Ho'omaluhia, Ho'omaluhia, Hawaii, 87; Koa Gallery, Kapiolani Community Col, 88; On/Off Paper - An Alumni Exhib, Univ Hawaii Art Gallery, 88; traveling exhibs, Artist of Hawaii, Honolulu Acad Arts, 88, Our Elders, Ourselves: Hawaii 1890-1990, funded by Hawaii Comt Humanities, 90, Budapest Art Gallery, Hungary, 91, Gallery Saka, Tokyo, Japan, 91 & Image XVIII, Amfac Plaza Exhib Rm, 92; and others. *Teaching:* Instr photog, Haystack Mountain Sch Crafts, Maine, 73 & 80 & Univ Hawaii, 74; vis prof photog, Seoul Inst Arts, Korea, 83 & Univ Tsukuba, Japan, 84-86; lectr photog, Kapiolani Community Col, Hawaii, 87-90. *Awards:* Grants, Japan Found & Ishibashi Found, 79, Univ Tsukuba Proj Grant, 84 & Asian Cult Coun Proj Grant, 85. *Publ:* Auth, Color Communication (film), Univ Hawaii, 67; asst dir, Artists of Hawaii (film), Honolulu, 9/75; producer & dir, Festival at Mizumi (film), Japan, 79; dir & camera, PLPL (film), Miami, 82; ed & chief planner, Photo Newsletter (article), Gallery Min, Tokyo, 86-87. *Mailing Add:* 1650 St Louis Dr Honolulu HI 96816-1923

HAAS, RICHARD JOHN
PRINTMAKER, MURALIST
b Spring Green, Wis, Aug 29, 36. *Study:* Univ Wis, Milwaukee, BA, 59; Univ Minn, MFA, 64. *Work:* Mus Mod Art, Metrop Mus Art & Whitney Mus Am Art, NY; Yale Univ Art Gallery, New Haven, Conn; Walker Art Ctr, Minneapolis; St Louis Mus Art, Mo; Brooklyn Mus Art, NY; Nat Acad Design, NY & Wash, DC; NY Hist Soc; Smithsonian Inst, Wash, DC. *Comn:* Pittsburgh Cult Trust; Gateway to the Waterfront, City of Yonkers, NY; Co Courthouse, Sarasota, Fla; Huntsville, Tex; Fed Courthouse, Beckley, W Va; Fed Courthouse, Kans City, Kans; Nashville Pub Libr, Nashville, Tenn, 2003; Hub Robeson Ctr, Pa State Univ, Pa, 2005. *Exhib:* Brooke Alexander Gallery, 72, 76, 80, 85 & 89; Galerie Biedermann, Munich, Ger, 78; solo exhibs, Michael Ingbar Gallery, NY, 2002, John Szoke Editions, NY, 2003, Elisabeth Michitsch, Vienna, Austria, 2005, David Findlay Jr. Gallery, 2006; group exhibs, Museum of the City of NY, 2002, Fabric Workshop & Mus, Philadelphia, Pa, 2003, Mary Ryan Gallery, NY, 2003, Lower Manhattan Cult Coun, NY, 2005, Frederick Baker Gallery, Chicago, Ill, 2005, Hudson River Mus, Yonkers, NY, 2006, Nat Acad Mus, NY, 2006. *Pos:* New York City Art Comn, 76-79; bd mem, Pub Art Fund, 80-88 & Preservation League, NY, 83-90, Skowhegan Sch Painting & Sculpture, Hudson River Mus; bd governors, Skowhegan Bd Art, 80-; bd trustees, Hudson River Mus, 89-; vpres, Nat Acad Arts, NY; pres, Abbey Mural Fund, Nat Acad, 99-. *Teaching:* Instr art, Univ Minn, 63-64; asst prof art, Mich State Univ, 64-68; instr printmaking, Bennington Col, 68-80; fac fine arts, Sch Visual Arts, 77-81. *Awards:* Doris C Freedman Award, 89; Alumni of Yr Award, Univ Wis, 91; MacDowel Fel, 2003; Jimmy Ernst Award, Am Acad Arts & Letters, 2005. *Bibliog:* David Dillon (auth), Creating a whole new building solely with paint, Architecture, 11/88; Paul Goldberger (auth), The healing murals of Richard Haas, New York Times, 1/10/89; Amalie R Rothschild (auth), Painting the Town - The Illusionistic Murals of Richard Haas (film), 90. *Mem:* Archit League; Century Asn; Nat Acad (bd dir, 92-). *Media:* Intaglio; Watercolor, oil, mixed media. *Interests:* films, travel. *Publ:* Auth, An Architecture of Illusion, Rizzoli Publ, New York, 81; The City As A Canvas, Prestel Publs; Catalogue Raisonne, The Prints of Richard Haas, John Szoke Editions, 2005. *Dealer:* Printworks Chicago IL; John Szoke Editions New York NY; David Findlay Jr Fine Arts NY. *Mailing Add:* 361 W 36th St No 5A New York NY 10018

HAATOUM HAMADY, WALTER SAMUEL
COLLAGE ARTIST
b Flint, Mich, Sept 13, 40. *Study:* Wayne State Univ, BFA, 64; Cranbrook Acad Art, MFA, 66; Wis Alumni Res Found Grants, 68-70, 73, 77-96. *Work:* Libr Congress; Lenin Libr, Moscow; Getty Ctr, Santa Monica, Calif; Victoria & Albert Mus, London; Whitney Mus Art, NY. *Exhib:* Americans in Print, Gutenberg Mus, Mainz, Ger, 89; Int Book Design Exhib, Leipzig, Ger, 89; Walter Hamady: 25 Yrs (catalog), Wustum Mus, Racine, 91; The Beauty in Breathing, Marvin Sackner Arch, Miami, 92; handmade books, Woodland Pattern Book Ctr, Milwaukee, 2000. *Pos:* Proprietor, The Perishable Press Limited, 64-. *Teaching:* Prof drawing, bk illus, collage & artists books, Univ Wis-Madison, 66-96, prof emer, 96-. *Awards:* John Simon Guggenheim Fel, 69; Nat Endowment Arts Grant, 76, 78, 80; Howard Found Fel, Brown Univ, Providence, RI, 77. *Bibliog:* Walter Hamady: Handmade Books, Collage and Sculpture (monogr with essays by Toby Olson & Buzz Spector), Wustum Mus Art, Racine, Wis, 91; Mary Lydon (auth), The book as trojan horse of art: Walter Hamady, perishable press limited and gabberjabbs 1-6, Visible Language, Vol 25, No 2/3, 92; Wisconsin book artists: Reading the fine print, Am Craft, 4-5/96; The Gift of Gabberjabb, Print Mag, 1/2/97. *Media:* Collage, Books. *Publ:* Auth, Objects in Transition: Contemporary Book Art (exhib catalog), Temari Center, Honolulu, 84; Two Decades of Hamady and The Perishable Press Ltd: An Anecdotally Annotated Check-list for an Exhibition at Gallery 210, Univ of Mo, 84; Designing Literature, printing and the DP of the U, Fine Print, Vol 14 No 3, 7/88; Travelling or Neopostmodrin Premortemism or Dieser Rasen ist Kein Hundeklo II or Interminable Gabberjabb Number Seven, Perishable Press Ltd, 96. *Mailing Add:* The Perishable Press Ltd 201 N Hay Hollow Mount Horeb WI 53572

HABENICHT, WENDA
SCULPTOR
b Elkhart, Ind, June 7, 56. *Study:* Beloit Col, Wis, BA, 74-79; NY Studio Sch Drawing, Painting & Sculpture, 79; Columbia Univ, NY, MFA, 81; Phi Beta Kappa. *Work:* Va Ctr Creative Arts, Sweet Briar; Long Island Univ, CW Post Campus, Brookville, NY. *Comn:* Site specific sculpture, Red River Revel Arts, Shreveport, La, 85; site specific sculpture, Oper Greenthumb, NY, 87; site specific sculpture, The Midwest Coast, Art & Agr, Caledonia, Wis, 82. *Exhib:* The Ways of Wood, Queens Col, NY, 84; Sculpture: The Language of Scale, Bruce Mus, Greenwich, Conn, 85; The Chair Fair, Int Design Ctr, Long Island, NY, 86; Outdoor Sculpture, Connemara Conserv Found, Allen Tex, 86; The Engaging Object, The Clocktower, Inst Arts & Urban Resources, NY, 86; 10th Ann Sculpture Exhib, Snug Harbor Cult Ctr, Staten Island, NY, 87; Artists Choose Artists, Socrates Sculpture Park, Long Island, 87; Dream Retreat-City of Tilted Towers, Toronto Sculpture Garden, Can, 89. *Bibliog:* Michael Benson (auth), City as sculpture garden, New York Times, 87; Tiffany Bell (auth), Insight on Site (exhib catalog), Hillwood Art Gallery, Long Island Univ, 88; Connie Hitzeroth (auth), Habenichts inviting retreat, Now, Toronto, 89. *Media:* Wood, Miscellaneous Media. *Mailing Add:* 293 Co Hwy 40 Worcester NY 12197-9735

HABER, IRA JOEL
SCULPTOR, WRITER
b Brooklyn, NY, Feb 24, 47. *Work:* NY Univ Art Collection; Nueu Gallerie, Ludwig Collection, Aachen, Ger; Guggenheim Mus, NY; Hirshhorn Mus, Washington, DC; Albright-Knox Art Gallery, Buffalo, NY. *Exhib:* Information, Mus Mod Art, NY, 70; Whitney Mus Ann Sculpture Exhib, NY, 70; three one-man shows, Fischbach Gallery, NY, 71-74; Whitney Mus Contemp Art Biennial, 73; retrospective, Kent State Univ Art Gallery, 77, State Univ NY, Stony Brook, 81 & Philadelphia Art Alliance, 84; Tableaux Constructions, Univ Calif, Santa Barbara, 77; Pam Adler Gallery, NY, 78-80 & 82; Eight Sculptors, Albright-Knox Art Gallery; 1979 Street Sights, Inst Contemp Art, Philadelphia, 80; 55 Mercer St Gallery, 91; Bldg References, Roseenwald Wolf Gallery, Phila, PA, 2005. *Teaching:* Instr sculpture, Fordham Univ, 71-74; assoc prof, State Univ NY Stony Brook, 81; vis lectr, Univ Calif, San Diego, 82-84, Ohio State Univ, Columbus, 84. *Awards:* Creative Artists Pub Serv Grant, 74-75 & 76-77; Nat Endowment Arts Fel, 74-75, 77-78 & 83-84; Pollack-Krasner Fel, 86; Pollock-Krasner Found Grant, 2001; Gottleib Found Grant, 2004. *Bibliog:* Corrinne Robins (auth), Ira Joel Haber, Arts Mag, 11/77; Robert Berlind (auth), Ira Joel Haber at Pam Adler, Art in Am, 12/79; April Kingsley (auth), article, 9/80, Alex Gildzen (auth), article, 5/82 & William Schwedler (auth), article, 4/83, Arts Mag. *Media:* Mixed. *Publ:* Auth, Radio City Music Hall, 69; Five stories of the Music Hall, St Marks Poetry Proj, 73; Some thoughts on camouflage by John Perreault, Serif-Lit Quart, Kent State Univ, 74; M E Thelen Gallery Piece, Tri-Quarterly, 75; Some reasons why I do what I do, Appearances, Vol 1, 77. *Mailing Add:* 311 85th St Apt 2R Brooklyn NY 11209-4658

HACK, PHILLIP S & PATRICIA Y
COLLECTORS
Mr Hack, b Ill, Dec 8, 16; Mrs Hack, b Los Angeles, Calif, Dec 21, 26. *Study:* Univ Ariz; Stanford Univ; Oxford Univ; Ariz State Univ; Wabash Col; Purdue Univ. *Collection:* Contemporary paintings, sculpture, prints and drawings. *Mailing Add:* 7370 E Krall St Scottsdale AZ 85250-4518

HACKENBROCH, YVONNE ALIX
CURATOR, WRITER
b Frankfurt, Ger, Apr 27, 1912; US citizen. *Study:* Univ Frankfurt, 32-33; Univ Rome, 33-34; Univ Munich, PhD(summa cum laude), 36. *Pos:* Asst dept Brit & medieval antiq, Brit Mus, London, 36-45; cur, Lee Fareham Collection, Univ Toronto, 45-49, Irwin Untermyer Collection & Western European Arts, Metrop Mus Art, 49-67. *Awards:* Ford Found Grant, 63; Fel Soc Antiquaries, London, 87; Verdienst Kreuz Am Bande, Ger, 88. *Mem:* Siever Soc, London. *Media:* Ren Jewellery. *Res:* Decorative arts. *Publ:* Auth, Renaissance Jewellery, London, 79; Reinhold Vasters Journal, Metrop Mus Art, New York, 86; Smalti E Gioielli dal XV al XIV secolo, Mostra Mus Naz Bargello, Florence, 86; Jewels of Anna Maria Luisa de Medici (exhib catalog), Museo degli Argenti, Florence, 89; Enseignes: Renaissance Hat Jewels, Florence, 96; The Collection of Irwin Untermyer, VII volumes, 1956-63; Renaissance Jewellery, London and Munich, 79; plus others. *Mailing Add:* Flat 4 31 Hyde Park Gardens London W 2ND England United Kingdom

HACKETT, DWIGHT VERNON
PUBLISHER, DIRECTOR
b Modesto, Calif, Mar 21, 45. *Study:* San Francisco Art Inst, Calif. *Pos:* Manager, bronze casting, Nambe Mills Inc, Santa Fe, NMex, 71-80; dir, Art Foundry Inc (d/b/a/ Art Foundry Editions), Santa Fe, NMex, 80-. *Media:* Cast Metal. *Mailing Add:* Art Foundry Inc PO Box 8107 Santa Fe NM 87504

HACKETT, MICKEY
PAINTER, EDUCATOR
b Louisville, Ky. *Study:* Univ Louisville, Univ Tex, 48. *Work:* Brown-Williamson Corp, Brown Forman Distilleries, Univ Louisville, Ky; Philip Morris Corp; Ala Power Co; and others. *Comn:* Convention cover, Ky Bankers Asn, 81, 83 & 85. *Exhib:* Ky W C Soc; Aqueous, Catherine Lorillard-Wolfe, Nat Arts Club, NY, 80-82; Patron's Gala, Okla; J B Speed Mus; Watermedia 83, Mont; Milford Fine Arts Ctr; and many others. *Pos:* Interior designer, George Fetter Co, Louisville, 65-69. *Teaching:* Instr watercolor tech, Jefferson Community Col, Univ Ky, 78-89, col seminars & workshops. *Awards:* Purchase Awards, Kent State Fair, 72-96, Ind Chautauqua Arts, 89, Bank One, Ohio, 90, Mont Miniature Art Soc, 89 & 90, Lincoln Ill Arts Festival, 90-2002 & Golden Armor Exhib, Ft Knox; Del, Ohio Art Fest, Awards, 90-96; Watercolor Award, Akron Arts Expos, 94, Best of Show, 96. *Bibliog:* Featured article, Ky Monthly Mag, 2/2003. *Mem:* Am Soc Artists; Ky Watercolor Soc (founding mem); Mini Art Societies, Fla, NJ & Mont; Nat Soc Painters, Sculptors & Gravers, Washington, DC; Nat Soc Painters in Casein & Acrylic, NY; Miniature Art Soc Fla; Miniature Art Soc NJ; Miniature Art Soc Mont; Whiskey Painters Am; and others. *Media:* Watercolor, Acrylic, 3-D kinetics. *Publ:* Limited Edition Prints & Posters, 92-2002; auth, Canines for Indyesbase, Ky Humane Soc; auth, Guide Dogs for Blind, Ky Humane Soc. *Mailing Add:* 1901 Woodfield Rd Louisville KY 40220

HACKLIN, ALLAN DAVE
PAINTER, SCULPTOR
b New York, NY, Feb 11, 43. *Study:* Pratt Inst. *Work:* Whitney Mus Am Art, NY; Dallas Mus Fine Arts; Allen Mus, Oberlin, Ohio; Mus Fine Arts, Houston; NC Mus Art; Aldrich Mus Am Art. *Exhib:* Whitney Mus Am Art, 67; Meredith Long Gallery, 86 & 87; solo exhibs, Meadows Mus 87 & MB Mod, NY, 97. *Pos:* Dir, Glassell Sch Art, Mus Fine Arts, Houston, 82-89 & LeRoy Neiman Ctr Print Studios, 96-. *Teaching:* Instr painting, Pratt Inst, 69-70; prof, Calif Inst Arts, 70-77, assoc dean, 76; vis prof, Cooper Union, 77-80; prof, RI Sch Design, 79-82, chmn, Painting Dept, 80-82; Meadows prof, Southern Methodist Univ, 87; chmn, Visual Arts Dept, Columbia Univ, 89-97; prof, Leroy Neiman Sch Art, 96. *Awards:* Nat Endowment Arts, 75, 80 & 84. *Publ:* Auth, article, Artforum, 67. *Mailing Add:* Sch of the Arts Columbia Univ 310 Dodge Hall MC 1806 116th St & Broadw New York NY 10027

HADFIELD, TED LEE
SCULPTOR
b Flint, Mich, May 8, 50. *Study:* Mott Community Col, AA, 72; Colo State Univ, BFA, 78; Cranbrook Acad Art, MFA, 80. *Work:* Mott Found, Flint, Mich; Colo State Univ Art Gallery; Ingles & Assoc Design Firm; Uniprop Corp; Ameritech, Detroit, Mich. *Comn:* Chair design, Artists Interpret Utility. *Exhib:* Cranbrook Ceramics 1950-1980, Cranbrook Mus, 83; solo exhibs, Fine Arts Gallery, Mott Community Col, 88, Feigenson/Preston Gallery, 90 & 93 & Lemberg Gallery, Birmingham, Mich, 96; New Work by Gallery Artists, Lemberg Gallery, 94; The Pleasure of Making, Detroit Artists Market, 94; Works for Young Collectors II, Lemberg Gallery, 94; Gallery Selections, Lemberg Gallery, 95; Works for Young Collectors III, Lemberg Gallery, 95; Prototypes, Paint Creek Ctr Arts, Rochester, Mich, 95. *Pos:* Co-owner, Artpack Servs Co Art Installations, 81-. *Awards:* Mich Coun Arts Grant, 84-85 & 88-89. *Bibliog:* Michigan artists, article in Detroit News, 7/81; Artists studio, Detroit Free Press, 8/86. *Media:* Mixed

HAESSLE, JEAN-MARIE GEORGES
PAINTER
b Alsace, France, Sept 12, 39. *Study:* Ecole Nat des Beaux Arts, Paris; Ecole de la Grande Chaumiere, Paris. *Work:* Albright-Knox Art Gallery, Buffalo, NY; Bibliot Nat, Paris, France; Nat Art Mus, China; Southern Ill Univ, Edwardsville. *Exhib:* Lucien Durand Galerie, Paris, 87-88; Salon de Montrouge, Paris, France, 88; Jade Galerie, Colmar, France, 89; Athisma Galerie Lyon, France, 91; Navara Gallery, NY, 92; and others. *Bibliog:* Laurie Anderson (auth), reviews in Art News, 72; April Kingsley (auth), New York newsletter, Art Int, 73; Vivian Raynor (auth), review in Art in Am, 74. *Media:* Acrylic, Oil. *Mailing Add:* 112 Spring St New York NY 10012

HAFFTKA, MICHAEL D
PAINTER
b New York, Dec 18, 53. *Work:* Mus Mod Art, Metrop Mus Art, NY; Carnegie Inst, Pittsburgh, Pa; San Francisco Mus Mod Art, Calif. *Bibliog:* Michael Brodsky (auth), Hafftka Selected Drawings, Guignol Books, 81; Sam Unter (auth), Hafftka-Paintings, DiLaurenti Publ, 91. *Media:* Acrylic, Oil. *Mailing Add:* c/o M H Co 32 Tiffany Pl Brooklyn NY 11231

HAFIF, MARCIA
PAINTER, EDUCATOR
b Pomona, Calif, Aug 15, 29. *Study:* Pomona Col, BA(art), 51; Claremont Grad Sch; Univ Calif, Irvine, MFA, 71. *Work:* Studio A, Otterndorf, Ger; Von Der Heydt-Mus, Wuppertal, Ger; Clemens-Sels Mus, Neuss, Ger; FRAC, Bourgogne, France; Mass Inst Technol; The Chase Manhattan Bank, NY; The Am Embassy, Tokyo, Japan; Kunsthaus Aarau, Switz; Kunstraum Alexander Buerkle, Freiburg, Ger; Mamco, Geneva, Switz. *Comn:* Ohio Red (clay mural), Wright State Univ, Ohio, 77; 3 paintings, Sheldon Solow, NY, 80. *Exhib:* Abstract Painting: 1960-69, PSI Mus, 83; La Couleur Seule: L'Experience Monochrome, Musee St Pierre, Lyon, France, 88 & Aargauer Kunsthaus, Aarau, Switz, 95; solo exhibs, Inventory PSI Mus, 90, Von Der Heydt Mus, Wuppertal, Ger, 94, Hans fur Konstruklir & Konkrete Kunst, Zurich (with catalog), 95; Red Colors, Kunsthalle, Winterthur Switz & Wamås, 92; Italian Paintings, Peintures 1962-68, Mus d' Art Moderne et Contemporain, Geneva, 1999; Italian Paintings: 1962-65 FRAC, Bourgogne, Dijon, France, 2000; Italian Paintings: 1961-69, Mus Modern and Contemp Art, Geneva, 2001; Enamel on Wood, Installation, Lenbachhaus, Munich, Ger, 2001; Virtuel/Reel, Escape d'Art Concrete, Mouans-Sartoux France, 2001; Mamco, Geneva, Switz, 2000. *Teaching:* Instr painting & color, Sch Visual Arts, New York, 74-76; instr, Sarah Lawrence Col, 78-80; vis asst prof, Hunter Col, 82 & 85-; vis artist, Univ Calif, Irvine, 83; adj assoc prof & coordr painting & drawing dept, New York Univ, 85-87; lectr, Princeton Univ, 89. *Awards:* Creative Artists Pub Serv Prog Grant, 76; Nat Endowment Arts, 80-81 & 90. *Bibliog:* Lilly Wei (ed), Talking abstract (interview), Art in Am, 7/87; Marcia Hafif: From the Inventory (exhib catalog), Kunsthalle Barmen, 94. *Media:* All Traditional Paint Media. *Publ:* Beginning Again, Art forum, 9/78; Getting on with painting, Art Am, 4/81; Plain painting, Artistes, Paris, 7/84; True Colors, Art in Am, 6/89. *Dealer:* Charlotte Jackson 200 W Marcy St Suite 101 Santa Fe NM 87501; Galerie Mark Muller Gessnerallee 36 CH-8001 Zurich Switz; Larry Becker Contemp Art, 43 N Second St, Phila, US; Galerie Rupert Walser, Fraunhoferstrasse, 19 D-80469 Munich, Ger; Galerie Hubert Winter, Breite Gasse, 17 A-1070 Vienna, Austria. *Mailing Add:* 112 Mercer St New York NY 10012

HAGAN, JAMES GARRISON
SCULPTOR, INSTRUCTOR
b Pittsburgh, Pa, July 11, 36. *Study:* Carnegie-Mellon Univ, BFA; Iowa State Univ; Univ Pittsburgh, MA. *Work:* Column 5, Nat Gallery Art, Washinton, DC; Column 8, Princeton Univ, NJ; Barrier, Newark Mus. *Exhib:* One-man show, Zabriskie Gallery, 75; Nine Sculptures, Nassau Co Mus, NY, 76; Wood Works, Wadsworth Atheneum, Hartford, Conn, 77; Wood, Nassau Co Mus, NY, 77. *Teaching:* Prof sculpture, Univ Va, Charlottesville, 63-. *Media:* Wood, Composites. *Dealer:* Zabriskie Gallery New York NY 10019

HAGE, RAYMOND JOSEPH
ART DEALER, LECTURER
b Huntington, WVa, Nov 28, 43. *Study:* Univ Ky; Marshall Univ, BBA, 66; Darden Grad Sch Bus Admin, Univ Va, TEP, 71. *Pos:* Pres, Raymond J Hage Inc, 84-. *Collection:* American & European prints. *Publ:* Printsource. *Mailing Add:* 2105 Wiltshire Blvd Huntington WV 25701-5344

HAGEMAN, CHARLES LEE
EDUCATOR, JEWELER
b Clay Center, Kans, June 22, 1935. *Study:* Univ Kans, BFA, 57, MFA, 67. *Work:* Ill State Univ, Visual Arts Ctr, Normal, Ill; Univ Mo, Columbia. *Comn:* Univ Mace, Pres Chain of Off & 6 Board of Regent's Medallions, comn by Pres of Northwest Mo State Univ, Maryville, 77. *Exhib:* Juried Craft Exhib, Ark Arts Ctr, Little Rock, 73 & JP Speed Art Mus, Louisville, Ky, 74; Invitational Craft Exhib, Albrecht Mus, St Joseph, Mo, 75; Prof Jewelry Exhib, Univ Mo, Columbia, 76; Mid-Am Metalcrafts, Kansas City Pub Libr, Mo, 77. *Collection Arranged:* Mo Craftsman Exhib, Olive DeLuce Gallery, Maryville, Mo, 73. *Teaching:* Assoc prof jewelry & metals & chmn dept art, Northwest Mo State Univ, Maryville, 67-, emer fac; instr summer jewelry workshop, NMex State Univ, Las Cruces, 74-. *Awards:* Best Metals, Designer-Craftsman Show, Kans, 67; Metals Award, Springfield Art Mus, 69; Best Metals, Mo Craftsman Exhib, 70. *Mem:* Am Craft Coun; Soc NAm Goldsmiths. *Media:* Pewter & Gold. *Mailing Add:* 722 W Second St Maryville MO 64468

HAGER, HELLMUT W
HISTORIAN
b Berlin, Ger, Mar 27, 26. *Study:* Univ Bonn, PhD, 59. *Collection Arranged:* Architectural Fantasy and Reality, Mus Art, Pa State Univ, 81-82. *Pos:* Asst to dir, Bibliot Hertziana, Rome, 59-63. *Teaching:* Prof art hist, Pa State Univ, 71-, dept head, 72-. *Awards:* Named Distinguished Professor, 90. *Mem:* Col Art Asn Am; Soc Archit Historians; Am Soc 18th Century Studies; Am Inst Archeol. *Res:* Baroque architecture in Italy and Germany. *Publ:* Auth, Filippo Juvarra e il concorso di modelli del 1715 bandito da Clemente XI per la nuova sacrestia di S Pietro, 70; coauth, Carlo Fontana: The Drawings at Windsor Castle, 77; editor (co-editor Susan S Munshower), Projects and Monuments in Period of Roman Baroque, Vol I, 84 & Light on the Eternal City-Observations and Discoveries in Art and Architecture of Rome, Vol II, In: Papers in Art History, Pennsylvania State Univ, 84 & 87. *Mailing Add:* 318 E Prospect Ave State College PA 16801-5449

HAGIN, NANCY
PAINTER
b Elizabeth, NJ, June 19, 40. *Study:* Carnegie-Mellon Univ; BFA, 62; Yale Univ, MFA, 64. *Work:* Mus Fine Arts, Boston, Mass; Butler Inst Am Art, Youngstown, Ohio; Utah Mus Fine Arts, Salt Lake City; New Britain Mus Am Art, Conn. *Exhib:* Group shows, Baltimore Mus Ann Exhib, 65-70, IFA Gallery, Washington, DC, 68-73, Allen Frumkin Gallery, NY, 71, Smithsonian Inst, Washington DC, 74, Indianapolis Mus Art, 76, Butler Inst, Ohio, 77, Lehigh University, Pa, 79, Nassau Co Mus Art, Roslyn, NY, 80, New Britain Mus Am Art, Conn, 82, Rahr-West Mus, Wis, 83, Fitchburg Art Mus, Mass, 84, William Sawyer Gallery, San Francisco, 85, C Grimaldis Gallery, Baltimore, 86, Fay Gold Gallery, Atlanta, 89, Nat Acad Design, NY, 89-90, Rice Univ, Tex, 93, NJ Ctr Visual Arts, 94, Lizan Tops Gallery, NY, 95, Am Acad of Arts & Letters, NY, 2001, Doran Gallery, Tulsa, 2002, 323 West Gallery, NY, 2003, DeCordova Mus & Sculpture Park, Mass, 2003-2004; One-woman shows, Alpha Gallery, Boston, 72, 76, 74, 79, 82, 85, 92, 95, 2000, Univ Md, 73, Terry Dintenfass Gallery, NY, 75, 78, Fischbach Gallery, NY, 81, 82, 85, 87, 89, 91, 93, 95, 98, 99, 2002 & 2004; Contemp Naturalism: Work of the 1970's, Nassau Co Mus, NY, 80; Eight Women-Still Life, New Britain Mus Am Art, Conn, 82; Plimpton Collection of Realistic Art, Rose Art Mus, Brandeis Univ, Mass, 82; Am Realism: 20th Century Drawings & Watercolors, Mus Mod Art, San Francisco, Calif, 85; Four Artists Collaborating, Tatistcheff Gallery, NY, 87. *Teaching:* Prof, Md Inst Col Art, Baltimore, 64-73; prof, Pratt Inst, New York City, 73-74, 85, RI Sch of Design, 74, Fashion Inst Tech, New York City, 74-, Cooper Union, 82-92, State Univ NY Purchase, 94, Univ Arts, Philadelphia, 99. *Awards:* Fulbright Grant, 66; Creative Artists Pub Serv Grant, 75; Nat Endowment Arts Grant, 82 & 91. *Bibliog:* Marjorie Miller (auth), rev, Arts Mag, 82; Elaine King (auth), Celebrations of the Familiar (exhib catalog), Carnegie-Mellon Univ, 82; Gerrit Henry (auth), Hagin (exhib catalog), Lafayette Col, 86; John Arthur (auth), Hagin Exhibition Announcement Essay, 89. *Mem:* MacDowell Art Colony (colonist bd, 85-88); Nat Acad, 92. *Media:* Acrylic, Watercolor. *Dealer:* Fischbach Gallery 24 W 57th St New York NY 10019; Alpha Gallery Boston MA. *Mailing Add:* c/o Fischback Gallery 210 11th Ave New York NY 10001

HAGMAN, JEAN CASSELS
MUSEUM DIRECTOR, ART HISTORIAN
b Des Moines, Iowa, Sept 17, 47. *Study:* Mich State Univ, BA, 69; Wayne State Univ, MA, Mus Mgt Inst, 90. *Collection Arranged:* Jordan Shepard, Stained Glass, 73, Samuel Kirk, Silver, 74, Navajo Rugs, 75 & Our Heritage in Weaving, 76, Grand Rapids Art Mus, Mich. *Pos:* Educ dir, Grand Rapids Art Mus, 70-78; Flint Inst Arts, Mich, 78-81; Philbrook Art Ctr, Tulsa, Okla, 81-84; independent consult, Tulsa, 84-87; dir, Mus Southwest, Midland, Tex, 87-. *Teaching:* Instr, Midland Col, 89. *Mem:* Am Asn Mus. *Res:* Mid 19th to early 20th century American art; Southwestern art; Museum education. *Publ:* Auth, Mus Volunteers; The Fourth Dimension, Mus Info Serv, 85; The Museum Trustee: An Orientation, Mus Info Serv, 85

HAHN, BETTY
PHOTOGRAPHER, EDUCATOR
b Chicago, Ill, Oct 11, 40. *Study:* Ind Univ, BA, 63, MFA, 66 with Henry Holmes Smith. *Work:* Mus Mod Art, NY; Smithsonian Inst; Nat Gallery Can, Ottawa; Art Inst Chicago; San Francisco Mus Mod Art; and others. *Exhib:* Festival du Photographie, Arles, France, 75; Am Family Portraits 1730-1976, Philadelphia Mus Art, 76; Nat Gallery Can, Ottawa, 80; Smithsonian Inst, 80 & 81; Ctr Creative Photog, 81; Int Mus Photog George Eastman House, 81; San Francisco Mus Mod Art, 81 & 85; Musee d'Art Moderne de la Ville de Paris, France, 81; Houston Ctr Photog, Tex, 82; Hong Kong Arts Ctr, 82; Amerika Haus, Hanover, Berlin, Frankfurt, Heidelburg, Koln & Munich, Ger, 85. *Collection Arranged:* Spanish Photography Today, Univ NMex, 85. *Pos:* Consult, NY Graphics Soc, Boston, Mass, & Visual Arts Referral Serv Creative Pub Serv, NY, 77; guest artist, Tamarind Inst, Albuquerque, NMex, 78; adv, Art Students Asn Gallery & Conceptions Southwest (mag), Univ NMex, 81; consult ed, Univ NMex Press, 84. *Teaching:* Asst prof photog, Rochester Inst of Technol, NY, 69-76; assoc prof photog, Univ NMex, 76-86; lectr, numerous univs; prof photog, Univ NMex, 86-. *Awards:* Creative Artists Pub Serv Prog Grant, New York State Coun, 75; Res Grant, Univ NMex, 77; Nat Endowment Arts Grants, 78 & 83; Polaroid Grant, 79 & 88. *Bibliog:* James N Miho (auth), More than real, Commun Arts, 72; R Sobieszek (auth), Photographer: Betty Hahn, Czech Photo, 74 & Russian Photo Rev, 74. *Mem:* Soc Photog Educ (bd dir, 80). *Publ:* Auth, Speaking with a Genuine Voice: Henry Holmes Smith, IMAGE Eastman House, 73; contribr of chap on Gum Bichromate Printing, In: Darkroom, Lustrum Press, New York, 77; ed, Contemporary Spanish Photography, Univ NMex Press, Albuquerque, 87. *Dealer:* Witkin Gallery 41 E 57th St New York NY 10022; Andrew Smith Gallery 76 E San Francisco Santa Fe NM 87501. *Mailing Add:* Univ NMex 1511 Kit Carson Ave SW Albuquerque NM 87104

HAHN, CHARLES
SCULPTOR
Study: Art Students League, NY; Naguib Sch Sculpture, Ind; Johnson Atelier & Technical Sch Sculpture, NJ. *Exhib:* Allied Artists of Am, NY, 98-2000; Audubon Artists, Inc, NY, 98-2000; Cape Cod Art Asn, Cape Cod, Mass, 98-2000; Am Artists Prof League, NY, 99-2000; Acad Artist Asn, Springfield, Mass, 99-2000; Hudson Valley Art Asn, NY, 2000; Springfield Art League, Springfield, Mass, 2000. *Awards:* First Place Award, Sculpture, New Eng Exhib, Cape Cod Art Asn, 98; Honor Award, Sculpture, Acad Artists Asn, 99; Greg Wyatt Award, Hudson Valley Art Asn, NY, 2000. *Mem:* Salmagundi Club, NY; Rockport Art Asn; North Shore Art Asn; Cape Cod Art Asn; Acad Artists Asn. *Dealer:* McDougall Fine Arts Gloucester MA; Saltbox Gallery Topsfield MA; Sculpture Showcase LTD New Hope PA; Swain Gallery NJ; State of the Arts Gallery Gloucester MA. *Mailing Add:* 241 Howard St Melrose MA 02176

HAHN, MAURICE & ROSLYN
DEALERS
US citizen. *Study:* Mr Hahn, Northwestern Univ, BS(bus); Mrs Hahn, Univ Pa, BA, grad studies in art hist; Temple Univ, Tyler Sch of Art. *Collection Arranged:* Benton Spruance, Retrospective, William Penn Mus, Harrisburg, Pa, 77; Benton Spruance Traveling Exhib, (coauth, catalog), with Dr Ricardo Viera, Lehigh Univ, 77-78, Alfred Bendiner, The Philadelphia Years, William Penn Mus, Harrisburg, 78; 17th, 18th and 19th Century Japanese Woodblock Prints, Longwood Gardens, Kennett Square, PA, 82. *Pos:* Dir, Hahn Gallery, Philadelphia. *Mem:* Philadelphia Print Club; Prints in Progress (Mrs Hahn, bd mem, 70-77); Philadelphia Art Dealers Asn, Friends of Artists Equity (Mrs Hahn, bd mem). *Mailing Add:* c/o The Hahn Gallery 8439 Germantown Ave Philadelphia PA 19118-3396

HAI CHANG, WILLOW HAI
DIRECTOR
b Wuxi, China. *Study:* Nanjing Univ, BA, 82; Nanjing Univ, MA, 84. *Exhib:* Author, Song of Life, Naples Mus of Art, 00; Author, Passion for the Mountains:17th Century Landscape Masterpieces from the Nanjing Mus, China Institute Gallery, 03. *Collection Arranged:* Curator, A Year of Good Fortune, 93; curator, Animals of the Chinese Zodiac, 95; curator, Calligraphy as Living Art, 96. *Pos:* curator, China Inst Gallery, 95-99; dir, China Inst Gallery, 2000-. *Teaching:* lectr, The Wharton Sch, Univ Pa, 92. *Interests:* Chinese art; Impressionism. *Mailing Add:* China Inst Gallery 125 E 65th St New York NY 10021

HALABY, SAMIA A
PAINTER, WRITER
b Jerusalem, Palestine, Dec 12, 36; US citizen. *Study:* Mich State Univ, with Abraham Rattner & Borris Margo, MA, 60; Ind Univ, with James McGarrell, MFA, 63. *Work:* Art Inst Chicago; Detroit Inst Art; Cincinnati Art Mus; Cleveland Mus Art; Guggenheim Mus; and others. *Comn:* Lithograph, Cleveland Mus Print Club, 74; stage set and costume design, Dance Company Perspective in Motion, Pace Univ, NY. *Exhib:* Solo exhibs, Phyllis Kind Gallery, Chicago, 71, 72, Yale Sch Art Gallery, New Haven, Conn, 72, Marilyn Pearl Gallery, NY, 78, Housatonic Mus, Bridgeport, Conn, 83, Tossan-Tossan Gallery, New York City, 83, 88, Darat Al-Funun, Amman, Jordan, 95, Galerie Atassi, Damascus, Galerie le Pont, Aleppo, 97, Agial Gallery, Beirut, Lebanon, 99, Sakakini Art Ctr, Ramallah, Palestine, 00, Skoto Gallery, NY, 00, Artim Gallery, Strasbourg, France, 01, Agaial Gallery, Beirut, 2004; Group exhibs, Yale Univ

Gallery, New Haven, Conn, 73, Guggenheim Mus, New York City, 75, Susan Caldwell Gallery, New York City, 77, Ind Univ Art Mus, 77, Univ Hawaii, 90-91, Sangre de Christo Arts Ctr, Pueblo, Colo, 91, Nat Mus of Women, Washington, DC, 94, Elizabeth Found, UN lobby, NYC, 99, Bradley Univ, Ill, 01, Musee du Chateau Dufresne, Montreal, 01, The Station, Houston, 03. *Collection Arranged:* Art Inst Chicago; Detroit Inst Art; Cincinnati Art Mus; Cleveland Mus Art; Guggenheim Mus; Nat Mus Women in the Arts, Washington, DC; Yale Univ Gallery; British Mus; Indianapolis Mus Art; Inst du Monde Arab, Paris; Sioux City Art Ctr; Alternative Mus, NY; Mead Art Mus, Amherst, Mass; and others. *Pos:* Artist-in-residence, Tamarind Lithography Workshop, 72; cur, Al Jisser Group, 2001-; guest cur, The Subject of Palestine, at DePaul Univ Mus, 2005. *Teaching:* teaching asst, Ind Univ, Bloomington, 62-63; instr, Univ Hawaii, Honolulu, 63-64; asst prof, Kansas City Art Inst, Mo, 64-66; vis lectr, Univ Hawaii, Honolulu, 66; asst prof, Univ Mich, Ann Arbor, 67-69; assoc prof, Ind Univ, Bloomington, 69-72; vis lectr, Yale Univ Sch Art, New Haven, Conn, 72-73, assoc prof, 73 76, adj assoc prof, 76-82; vis prof, Univ S Fla, 90; adj prof, Cooper Union for the Advancement of Sci and Art, NY, 89-91; vis artist, BeirZeit Univ, Palestine, 97. *Awards:* Creative Artists Pub Serv Prog Grant Painting, 79. *Bibliog:* Art and liberation: Samia Halaby speaks, Aurora, spring 82; Jonathan Goodman (auth), Samia Halaby Arts Mag, 5/88; Samia A Halaby (auth), Liberation Art of Palestine, HTTB Pub, 2003. *Mem:* Al Jisser Group. *Media:* Oil, Acrylic; Computer. *Res:* Liberation Art of Palestine. *Interests:* programming moving abstract images. *Collection:* paintings/drawings done by Palestinian Artists with focus on Libertarian Art. *Publ:* Nature, Reality & Abstract Picturing, Leonardo, 10/87; Pictures in Computer Medium, Proceedings, 9th Symp of Small Computers in the Arts, 89; On Art and Politics, Arab Studies Quart, spring/summer 89; Technology, Abstraction & Kinetic Painting, Papers of the 4th Int Symp Electronic Art, 93; Rhythms, The aesthetics of electronic painting, Papers of the 7th Int Symp Electronic Art, 96. *Dealer:* Agial Gallery Beirut Lebanon; Artim Gallery Stasbourg France. *Mailing Add:* 103 Franklin St New York NY 10013

HALAHMY, ODED
SCULPTOR
b Baghdad, Iraq, Oct 10, 38; US citizen. *Study:* Bat Yam Sch Fine Art, BA, 65; St Martin's Sch Fine Art, MA, 68. *Work:* Herbert Johnson Mus Art, Ithaca, NY; Soloman R Guggenheim Mus, NY; Hirshhorn Mus and Sculpture Garden, Washington, DC; Chase Manhattan Bank, NJ; Chicago Athenaeum, Chicago, Ill; Jerusalem Mus, Israel. *Comn:* Sukkah (abstract sculpture), Hebrew Union Col, Jerusalem, 79; Family (abstract sculpture), pvt comn, Palm Beach, Fla, 81; Blue Party (abstract sculpture), Aldrich Mus Contemp Art, Ridgefield, Conn, 82. *Exhib:* Montreal Mus Fine Art, 68; Tel Aviv Mus, 70; solo exhibs, Herbert Johnson Mus Art, Ithaca, NY, 74 & Aldrich Mus Contemp Art, Conn, 82-83; Am Int Sculpture Symp, NY, 74; Louis K Meisel Gallery, 88, 90, 91, 93 & 98; Yeshiva Univ Mus, 2003. *Teaching:* Instr art, Ont Col Art, Toronto, 69-70 & Parsons Sch Design, NY, 75-77; vis artist, Cooper Union Art Sch, 71, NY Univ, 71 & New Sch Social Res, 74, NY. *Awards:* Peter Samuel Found Fel, London, 67-68; Am-Israel Cult Found, NY, 75. *Bibliog:* Noel Frackman (auth), article, Arts Mag, 5/74; Gerrit Henry (auth), article, New York Times, 12/79; article, New York Times, 4/3/83. *Mem:* Am Int Sculpture Symp. *Media:* Bronze, Wood. *Publ:* Oded Halahmy in Retrospect: Sculpture from 1962-1997, NY, 97; Homeward: Sculpture of Oded Halahmy, published by Sunrarm Tagore Gallery, 2004; Homelands Baghdad-Jerusalem-NY, published by Yeshiva Univ Mus, 2003; The Common Ground: The Sculpture of Oded Halahmy, published by Sundaram Tagore Gallery, 2002; Oded Halahmy in Retrospect: Sculpture from 62-97, published by Louis K Meisel Gallery, 97. *Dealer:* Louis K Meisel Gallery 141 Prince St NYC 10012; Sundaram Tagore Gallery 137 Greene St NYC 10012; Remy Toledo Gallery 529 W 20th St NYC 10011. *Mailing Add:* c/o Louis K Meisel 141 Prince St New York NY 10012

HALASZ, PIRI
CRITIC, HISTORIAN
b New York, NY, Apr 5, 35. *Study:* Barnard Col, BA, 56; Columbia Univ, MA, 76, PhD, 82. *Collection Arranged:* The Expressionist Vision: A Central Theme in New York in the 1940s, Hillwood Art Gallery, C W Post Ctr, Long Island Univ, 83-84; A Year in the Life of Present Modernism, Gathering of the Tribes Gallery, NY, 97-98. *Pos:* Contrib ed, Time Mag, 63-69, writer art sect, 67-69; online columnist, From the Mayor's Doorstep, 96-. *Teaching:* Adj art hist, C W Post Ctr, Long Island Univ, 76-77, adj prof, 85-86, coordr art, Westchester Campus, 85-86; adj prof, Molloy Col, 85-86; asst prof, Bethany Col, WVa, 90-94. *Awards:* Fel, Va Ctr Creative Arts, 86, 89, 97-98, 2001 & 2005. *Mem:* Int Asn Art Critics. *Res:* Twentieth century European and American art, especially in New York in the 1940s. *Interests:* contemporary art. *Publ:* Auth, Growing up progressive, Virginia Quart Rev, 90; Abraham Rattner: rebel with a cause, Arch Am Art J, 92; Ella Blooms at the Gershwin, lingo 7, fall 97; online column rev & excerpts, Night, 97-99, NY Arts, 97-2005; Al loving (auth), Lighter Than Air, a Gathering of the Tribes (online), 11/2004; David Smith (auth), A Centennial, A Gathering of the Tribes (online), 4/2006. *Mailing Add:* 520 E 76th St Apt 3A New York NY 10121

HALBACH, DAVID ALLEN
PAINTER, HISTORIAN
b Santa Barbara, Calif, Jan 12, 31. *Study:* Chouinard Art Inst, cert grad; with Rex Brandt, Edward Reep & Robert Uecker. *Work:* Permanent Collection, Bank Calif, San Francisco, San Jose & Seattle, Wash, also Buffalo Bill Mus, Cody, Wyo; Favell Mus Western Art, Klamath Falls, Ore; Cowboy Artists Am Mus, Kerrville, Tex. *Exhib:* Cowboy Hall of Fame, Oklahoma City, 75-79 & 81; Western Heritage Show, Houston, Tex, 78-81, 83 & 84, European tour, 83-; Biltmore Celebrity Show, Los Angeles, Calif, 81-84; Governor's Invitational, Cheyenne, Wyo, 81-84; Cowboy Artists of Am, Phoenix Art Mus, Phoenix, Ariz. *Pos:* Illusr, US Navy, 52-54; Walt Disney Studio, Burbank, 54-55; illusr & art ed, Cannon Elec Co, Los Angeles, 55-59; art dir, Mowinckle Advert, Los Angeles, 59-63. *Teaching:* Art teacher (adult educ), San Gabriel, Whittier & Covina High Schs, Calif, 65-73. *Awards:* Silver Medalist, Nat Acad-Cowboy Hall of Fame, 75; Gold Medal, Water Solubles, Cowboy Artists Am Show, 88-91 & 96, Silver Medal 89, 93, 94, 97 & 98; First Place, Art Parks Region II, 89; Mus Western Heritage Award, 90. *Mem:* Cowboy Artists Am. *Media:* Watercolor. *Publ:* Illusr, Orange Co Illustrated, 75 & Southwest Art, 78 & 98; 1988 Cowboy Artists of America, Art W Mag, 11-12/88; contribr, film proj, Nat Geographic, 97; Am Artist Publ, Watercolor summer issue, 98; Western Art Masterpieces & The West: A Treasury of Arts Literature, Walkins & Walkins. *Dealer:* Claggett/Rey Gallery Vail, CO; Settler's West Tucson AZ. *Mailing Add:* PO Box 1207 Graeagle CA 96103-1207

HALBREICH, KATHY
MUSEUM DIRECTOR
b New York, NY, April 24, 49. *Study:* Bennington Col BA, 1971; Skowhegan Sch Painting and Sculpture, Postgrad, Maine, 1965; Am Univ, Postgrad, Mexico City, 1966. *Pos:* Adminr, spec prog Bennington (Vt) Col, 1975-76; dir, teaching seminar Asn Collegiate Sch Archit, Wash, 1977; vpres prog, trustee Artist Found, Boston, 1979-84; dir comt on visual arts Hayden Gellery, List Visual Arts Ctr, Mass Inst of Tech, Cambridge, Mass, 1976-86; ind Cur-consultant, 1986-88; Consultant St Louis Art Mus, Artists Space, New York City, Capp St Project, San Francisco, Mus Modern Art, New York City, Seattle Arts Comn, Southeastern Ctr for Contemp Art, Louis Comfort Tiffany Found, Beacon Cos, Frito-Lay Inc, New Eng General Services Admin Art-in-Archit Prog, Nat Endowment for Arts, VA Art-in-Archit Prog; trustee MA Coun on the arts and Humanities; advisor Pub Art Policy Project and Publ, Nat Endowment for Arts, 1987; mem nat comt Pub Art in Am, Conf, Philadelphia, 1987; cur, contemp art Mus Fine Arts, Boston, 1988-90; dir, Walker Art Ctr, Minneapolis, 1991-. *Publ:* Trustee Twin Cities Pub. TV, 1992. *Mailing Add:* Walker Art Ctr 1750 Hennepin Ave Minneapolis MN 55403-1138

HALBROOK, RITA ROBERTSHAW
PAPERMAKER, PAINTER
b Greenville, Miss, May 22, 30. *Study:* Miss Art Colony, with Ida Kohlmeyer, 77; Delta State Univ, BFA, 82. *Work:* Northern Electric Co, Laurel, Miss; Deposit Guaranty Nat Bank, Jackson, Miss; The Garnard Collection, Cleveland, Miss; Cottonlandia Mus, Greenwood, Miss; Catfish Capitol Mus, Belzoni, Miss. *Comn:* Vestments, All Saints Cath Church, Belzoni, Miss, 78; cast paper prints, Delta Processors, Indianola, Miss, 85; paper sculptures, Northeast Miss Med Ctr Women's Hosp, 86; cast paper, comn by Am Legislative Exchange Coun for Vpres Dan Quale; cast paper, Catfish Mus, Belzoni, 93; Risen Christ sculpture, St Therese Church, Jackson, 96. *Exhib:* Mid-South Exhib, 66 & 67 & Artist Registry Show, 70, Brooks Mem Mus; Miss Gallery, Miss Mus Art, Jackson, 80-81; Wall Series, Cottanlandia Mus, Greenwood, Miss & Meridian Mus Art, Miss, 83; Regional telecast, Miss Educ TV Studios; Nat League Am Pen Women Bienniel, Washington, DC, 88 & Cork Gallery, Belzoni, Miss; Miss Gov Mansion Invitational, 89-90; Miss Craftsmens Guild Invitational, 89; Lincoln Ctr, NY, 94; and others. *Teaching:* Instr workshop, Allison's Wells Sch Arts & Crafts, Canton, Miss. *Awards:* Best in Show, Miss Art Colony, Crosstie Festival, 71 & Cottonlandia Competition, 83 & 90; First & Second Award, Miss Art Colony, 85; Best in Show, Miss Pen Women Statewide Competition, 88 & 95. *Bibliog:* Porioer (auth), Mississippi Artists, Univ Southern Miss Press, 78; Louis Dollahide (auth), Of Arts and Artists, Univ Miss Press, 81. *Mem:* Miss Art Colony (mem bd dir, 80-88); Miss Delta Br, Nat Pen Women; Craftsmen's Guild Miss (bd dir, 92-93). *Media:* Mixed Acrylic; Handmade Paper. *Dealer:* Gulf South Gallery Acton Ave McComb MS 39648. *Mailing Add:* 501 Cohn St Belzoni MS 39038-3703

HALBROOKS, DARRYL WAYNE
PAINTER, PRINTMAKER
b Evansville, Ind, May 3, 48. *Study:* Univ Evansville, Ind; Murray State Univ, Ky; Southern Ill Univ. *Work:* Brooks Mem Art Gallery, Memphis, Tenn; Huntington Gallery, WVa; Evansville Mus Arts & Sci, Ind; Millikin Univ; Frito-Lay/The Blount Collection; and others. *Exhib:* Dulin Nat Print & Drawing Exhib, Dulin Gallery, Knoxville, Tenn, 76; Exhib 280, 78 & 79; Watercolor USA, 79; solo exhibs, Joy Horwich Gallery, Chicago, Ctr Arts, Kinston, NC & Brooks Mem Gallery, Memphis, Tenn; and others. *Teaching:* Prof painting, Eastern Ky Univ, Richmond, 72-94. *Awards:* Realism Show, Evansville, Ind, 90; Kinston Art Ctr, NC, 92; and others. *Bibliog:* Marion Garmel (auth), Works on Paper, Indianapolis News, 5/74; article, Arts Mag, 5/77; article, New Art Examiner, Chicago, 10/81; and others. *Media:* Acrylic; Eucaustic. *Dealer:* Joy Horwich Gallery 226 E Ontario Chicago 60611. *Mailing Add:* Art Dept 309-3109 Campbell Eastern KY Univ Richmond KY 40475

HALE, NATHAN CABOT
SCULPTOR, WRITER, PAINTER
b Los Angeles, Calif, July 5, 25. *Study:* Chouinard Art Inst, Los Angeles; Art Students League; Empire State Col, BS, 73; Union Grad Sch, PhD, 86. *Work:* Bronze madonna, St Anthony of Padua, East Northport, NY; bronze reliefs, Rose Asn Bldg, Bronx, NY; also in mus & pvt collections. *Exhib:* Many group & one-man shows since 1947. *Pos:* Dir, Ages Man Found, 68-, sculptor, Cycle Life Chapel Sculpture Proj, 68-; sr ed, Art/World, 1985-1989. *Teaching:* Mem fac, Pratt Inst, Brooklyn, 63-64; instr anat & drawing, Art Students League, 66-72, instr & lectr anat, 85-91. *Awards:* Gold Medal, Nat Acad Design; Recipient Purchase Award in sculpture, Los Angeles Co Mus, 55; Silver medal, Audubon Soc Sculpture, 72. *Mem:* Art Students League; Audubon Artists; Nat Acad; hon Fel Nat Sculpture Soc; Century Asn. *Publ:* Auth, Welded Sculpture, 69, Embrace of Life--the Sculpture of Gustav Vigelund, 70 & Abstraction in Art & Nature, 72; Birth of a Family, Doubleday, 79; also contribr to archit & art mags; auth, On the Perception of Human Form in Sculpture, White Whale Press, 2000. *Mailing Add:* 57 Sheffield Rd Amenia NY 12501

HALEGUA, ALFREDO
SCULPTOR
b Montevideo, Uruguay, May 4, 30; US citizen. *Study:* Sch Bldg Design, Montevideo, Uruguay, 47; Sch Plastic Arts, Montevideo, BFA, 50; MFA 52. *Work:* Nat Gallery Art, Washington, DC; Baltimore Mus Art, Md; Ringling Mus Art, Sarasota, Fla; Denver Art Mus, Colo; Daytona Beach Mus Arts & Sci, Fla; Artist Sculpture Park, Monumental Works, Miami Dade Col, Fla. *Comn:* Sculpture, 70 & 77, City of Baltimore, Md; Obelisk, City of Salisbury, Md, 70; sculpture, Dade Co, Miami, Fla, 82; Fountains, City of Charlotte, NC, 89. *Exhib:* One-man show: Baltimore Mus, Md, 63 & 68; Int Exhib Contemp Sculpture, Rodin Mus, Paris, France, 66; Halegua-Monumental Sculpture, Baltimore Mus Art, Md, 68; Contemp Am Artists, Baltimore Mus Art, Md, 70; Halegua-Recent Sculpture, Mint Mus Art, Charlotte, NC, 81; Int Biennial Contemp Art, Mus Contemp Art, Montevideo, Uruguay, 81; Five Int Artists in DC, Robert Brown Contemp Art, Washington, 82; Halegua-Pub Sculpture & Proj, Mus Mod Art Latin Am, Washington, DC, 88-89; Washington Int Sculpture Art in Atrium, Washington, DC, 90. *Teaching:* Prof sculpture, Am Univ, Washington, DC, 64-65. *Awards:* Gold & Silver Medal, Nat Salon Fine Arts, Montevideo, Uruguay, 58; Research grant traveling exhib, Govt Uruguay, 59. *Bibliog:* Paul Richard (auth), Mood of elegance in H's, Washington Post, 7/28/68; Doug Davis (auth), Washington Letter, Arts Mag, 12/69 & 1/70. *Mem:* Int Sculpture Ctr. *Media:* Metals. *Publ:* Auth, Style and Content in Modern & Contemporary Art, Fine Arts Soc, 58; The role of art criticism, El Bien Publico, 2/8/59; Current trends in American Art, 9/12/63 & Models for integration of Sculpture & Architecture, 7/15/68, El Dia; The Magic Line-The Drawings of Pedro Figari, Monumental Sculptures, 88. *Mailing Add:* 2601 30th St NW Washington DC 20008-2711

HALEMAN, LAURA RAND
SCULPTOR, CRAFTSMAN
b New York, NY, Mar 3, 46. *Study:* New York Univ, BS (summa cum laude), 68; Sch Visual Arts, Columbia Univ, 83; New Sch Social Res, 83; studio of Minoru Niizuma, 84. *Work:* Citibank Corp, NY; First Long Island Investors Corp, Jericho, NY; Sid Jacobson YMHA & YWHA, Roslyn, NY; Duralee Fabrics Corp, NY; All Co Abstract Corp, Carle Pl, NY; Nubest & Co, Manhasset, NY; Jackie Products Corp, San Juan, PR. *Comn:* Lawrence Jr High Sch Lobby, Cedarhurst, NY, 81; Long Island Hall of Fame: NY Islanders; Gen Aerospace Materials Corp, 88. *Exhib:* Nassau Co Mus Fine Art, Roslyn, 83, 84 & 91; Fine Arts Mus Long Island, 85 & 91; Heckscher Mus, Huntington, NY, 85; CAPA Rotational Arts Exhib, 85-; Lever House, NY, 86-92; Crystal Pavillion, NY, 88 & 92; Blue Hill Cult Ctr, 88 & 92; Elaine Benson, Bridgehampton, NY; Green St Gallery, NY; Strikoff Gallery, NY; LS Singer Gallery, Palm Springs, Calif. *Collection Arranged:* Four Women Artists, 84 & 19 Artists, 85, Great Neck Libr Gallery, Hempstead Harbor Artists Asn, NY. *Pos:* Dir & prin owner, The Sculpture Workshop, Brookville, NY, 80-; artist-in-residence, Lawrence Jr High Sch, 81. *Teaching:* Instr cult arts develop prog, Jericho Pub Sch, 82-83; lectr on the art of stone carving, Sculpture Asn Art Group, currently; instr sculpture seminars, Studio Tours Art Soc & Long Island Pub Sch Syst, currently. *Awards:* First Prize Sculpture, Suburban Art League; Hon Mention, Nassau Co Mus Fine Arts; Sculpture Award, Independent Art League Invitational Open; and others. *Mem:* Stone Sculpture Soc NY; Art Deco Soc NY (bd mem, 84); Hempstead Harbor Artists Asn (bd mem, 84-); Independent Art Soc; Huntington Twp Art League; Suburban Art League. *Media:* Sandstone, Marble. *Mailing Add:* 30 Ormond Pk Rd Brookville NY 11545

HALEVI, MARCUS
PHOTOGRAPHER
b Croton-on-Hudson, NY, Jan 17, 42. *Study:* Univ Mich, BArch, 65. *Work:* Peabody Mus, Salem, Mass; Anchorage Fine Arts Mus, Alaska; Photogr Arch, Harvard Univ, Cambridge, Mass; DeCordova Mus, Lincoln, Mass. *Exhib:* As Seen by Both Sides, Boston Univ Art Gallery, Mass, 91; Artists Confront Child Abuse, Howard Yezerski Gallery, Boston, Mass, 92; Pictures of the Year, Nat Press Club, Washington, 92; Living with the Memories, Cambridge Multi-Cult Arts Ctr, Mass, 95; one-person shows, Carpenter Ctr Arts, Harvard Univ, 95, Cambridge Multicultural Art Ctr, 99 & Schlesinger Libr, Radcliffe Col, 2001; DeCordova Mus, Lincoln, Mass, 98; 10 Cambodian Women, Radcliffe Col Gallery, Cambridge, Mass, 2001. *Awards:* Pulitzer Prize for Gen News, 88; Photog Grant, Nat Endowment for Arts, 92; New Eng Found Arts Grant, 97; Mass Cult Coun Grant, 97; Evelyn Nef Fel (MacDowell residency), 97-98; Leff Found Grant, 99. *Media:* Black & White Photography. *Publ:* Auth, Alaska Crude: Visions of the Last Frontier Photographs by Marcus Halevi, Little, Brown & Co, 77; Building a Tall Ship, Thorndike Press, 85; Bedlum: Romanian Insane Asylums, Palm Press, 2000. *Mailing Add:* 33 Cedar St Somerville MA 02143

HALEY, GAIL E
ILLUSTRATOR, COLLECTOR
b Charlotte, NC, Nov 4, 39. *Study:* Richmond Prof Inst Va, 59-60. *Work:* Kerlan Collection, Univ Minn, Minneapolis; DeGrummond Collection, Univ Southern Miss, Hattiesburg. *Teaching:* Instr writing & illus for children (artist-in-residence), Appalachian State Univ, 80-. *Awards:* Caldecott Medal Best Illus Children's Book USA, 71; Kate Greenaway Medal Best Illus Children's Book England, 76; Kodai Tosho Award, Japan Best Book, 80; The Kerlan Award, Univ of Minn, 89. *Bibliog:* David Considine (auth), Toys, technology & teaching, Top of the News, summer 85 & An integrated approach to visual literacy and children's books, Sch Libr J, 9/86; Susan Austin (auth), Author illustrator profile, Library Talk, 11-12/89. *Mem:* Puppeteers Am; Int Visual Literacy Asn. *Collection:* Antique and contemporary children's games, toys, books, dolls and puppets from Europe and the US. *Publ:* Of Mermaids, Myths and Meaning: A Sea Tale, The New Advocate, winter 90; Mountain Jack Tales, Dutton, 92; Imagine That Integrating Imagery Intov Instruction, 92; coauth, Dream Peddler, Libraries Unlimited, Dutton, 93; coauth, Visual Messages: Developing Critical Viewing and Thinking Skills Through Childrens Literature, Libraries Unlimited, 94. *Mailing Add:* PO Box 1023 Blowing Rock NC 28605

HALEY, PATIENCE
PAINTER, CONSERVATOR
b Boston, Mass. *Study:* Oberlin Col, AB. *Work:* Addison Gallery Am Art, Andover, Mass; Smith Col Mus Art, Northampton, Mass; Ctr Arts, Wesleyan Univ, Middletown, Conn; Mus Art Ogunquit, Maine; Mus of Art, Lehigh Univ, Pa. *Comn:* History of Manchester, Conn (mural), Manchester Savings Bank; restoration of Faulkner murals, Columbia Univ, NY. *Exhib:* One-woman shows, George Walter Vincent Smith Mus, Springfield, Mass, 60, DeCordova Mus, Lincoln, Mass, 57 & Radcliffe Inst, Cambridge, Mass, 71; New Eng Drawings, Lyman Allyn Mus, Conn, 57; Highlights of Am Hist, Addison Gallery, Andover, Mass, 58; Mainescapes, Women Artists, OMAH, O Gun Quit, Me. *Pos:* Asst painting conserv, Dept Painting Restoration, Boston Mus, Mass, 73-76. *Teaching:* Middlebury Col, 53; Art instr, Abbot Acad, Andover, Mass, 56-59. *Awards:* Painting Scholar, Bunting Inst, Radcliffe Col, 69-71; Three-time Painting Fel, Yaddo Found & Macdowell Found; Gold Medal, New Eng Watercolor Soc, 79. *Bibliog:* Edward Betts (auth), Master Class in Watercolor, Watson-Guptill Publ, 75. *Mem:* New Eng Watercolor Soc; Ogunquit Art Asn, Maine; Radcliffe Inst Fels, Inc. *Media:* Watercolor; Ink

HALEY, PRISCILLA J
PAINTER, PRINTMAKER
b Boston, Mass, June 22, 26. *Study:* Oberlin Col, Ohio, BA(fine arts), 48; Brooklyn Mus Art Sch, 52-53; with Kienbusch, Rogalski, 54. *Work:* Libr Congress, Washington, DC; Addison Gallery, Andover, Mass; Nat Acad Galleries, NY; Brooklyn Mus, NY; Philadelphia Mus Art, Pa. *Exhib:* Print Ann, Philadelphia Mus Art, Pa, 57; Print Show, Inst Contemp Art, Boston, Mass, 58; Print Ann, Libr Congress, Washington, DC, 60; Print Ann, Brooklyn Mus, NY, 60; Print Ann, Farnsworth Mus, Rockland, Maine, 63; Worcester Print Show, Worcester Art Mus, Mass, 64; New Eng Artists, DeCordova Mus, Lincoln, Mass, 65; Soc Am Graphic Artists Print Show, Kennedy Galleries, NY, 76; Isliptown Art Gallery, Islip, NY, 77. *Awards:* Tiffany Found Grant, 59; Graphics Award, Providence RI Art Asn, 79; First Prize Watercolor, Babylon Arts Coun, NY, 92. *Mem:* Soc Am Graphic Artists. *Media:* Watercolor; Etching, Intaglio. *Publ:* Contribr, The Print, Adele Lewis Publ, 59; illusr, The Island, P J Haley, 60. *Mailing Add:* 133 Livingston Ave Babylon NY 11702

HALEY, SALLY
PAINTER
b Bridgeport, Conn, June 29, 1908. *Study:* Yale Univ Sch Fine Arts, BFA, 31; studies with Prof Maxon, Munich, Ger, 33. *Work:* Portland Art Mus & City of Portland, Ore; State Ore & Willamette Univ, Salem; Univ Wash, Seattle; Fed Reserve Bank, San Francisco; AT&T, NY. *Comn:* US Post Office, Works Progress Admin, McConnelsville, Ohio, 39. *Exhib:* Solo exhibs, Portland Art Mus, 60 & 75, Fountain Gallery Art, Portland, 62, 72, 77, 80, 81, 84 & 85, Governor's Office, Ore State Capitol, 76, Bush Barn, Salem, Ore, 84 & Wentz Gallery, Pac Northwest Col Art, Portland, 84; San Francisco Mus Art, 49; Reality and Fantasy, 1900-1954, Walker Art Ctr, Minneapolis, 54; Women's Building, Los Angeles, Calif, 77; Hubbard Mus, Ruidoso Downs, NMex, 90 & 91; Laura Russo Gallery, Portland, Ore, 90, 93 & 94; retrospective, Marylhurst Col, 93. *Awards:* Gov Awards Poster, State of Ore, 82; Oregon Governors Award for Arts, 89; Women's Achievement Award for Artistic Excellence, YWCA, 88. *Bibliog:* Ellen Nichols (ed), Northwest Originals, InUNISON Publ, Portland, Ore, 89; Barbara Melosh (auth), Engendering Culture: Manhood and Womanhood in New Deal Public Art and Theatre, Smithsonian Inst Press, Washington, 91; Joan Jeffri (auth), The Artist Speaks-Discuss Their Experiences & Career, Greenwood Press, Westport, Conn, London, 93. *Mem:* Portland Art Mus. *Media:* Acrylic, Egg Tempera. *Dealer:* Laura Russo Gallery 805 NW 21st Portland OR

HALL, DOUGLAS E
VIDEO ARTIST, PHOTOGRAPHER
b Apr 25, 44. *Study:* Harvard Univ, BA(Anthropology), 66; Rinehart Sch Sculpture Md Inst Art, Baltimore, MFA, 69. *Work:* Whitney Mus Am Art & Mus Mod Art, NY; San Francisco Mus Mod Art; Mus Contemp Art Chicago; Ctr George Pompidou, Paris; and others. *Exhib:* One-person exhibs, Long Beach Mus Art, 76 & 80, San Francisco Mobius Video Festival, 76, 80 Langton Street, San Francisco, 83, Whitney Mus, NY, 84, Shoshana Wayne Gallery, Santa Monica, Calif, 92, Univ Art Mus, Berkeley, 93, Rena Bransten Gallery, San Francisco, 94, 95, 97, 98 & 2001, Kunstwerke, Berlin, 94, Feigen, New York City, 99, Galerie Micha Kapinos, Berlin, Ger, 99, Rena Bransten Gallery, San Francisco, 01, 03, Bellevue Art Mus, Wash, 01, VOX, Montréal, 02, Feigen Contemp, New York City, 03, and others; Two Channel Video, Whitney Mus Am Art, NY, 78; Space/Time/Sound-1970's: A Decade in the Bay Area (auth, catalog), San Francisco Mus Mod Art, 79; Reading Video, Mus Mod Art, NY, 82; Whitney Mus Biennal, NY, 83 & 85; Video: Recent Acquisitions, Mus Mod Art, NY, 84; Video from Vancouver to San Diego, Mus Mod Art, NY, 85; Bay Area Media & New Acquisitions, San Francisco Mus Mod Art, 90; Video: Two Decades, Mus Mod Art, NY, 92-93; System Aesthetics: Works from the Permanent Collection, San Francisco Mus Mod Art, 96; Discloations, Philadelphia Mus Art, 96; Vision Ruhr, Zeche Zollern II/IV, Dortmund, Ger, 2000; Photog Now, Contemp Arts Ctr, New Orleans, 2000; Paradise in Search of a Future, CEPA Gallery, Buffalo, NY, 2001; Beyond Boundaries, Ansel Adams Ctr for Photog, San Francisco, 2001; Between Earth and Heaven-New Classical Movements in the Art of Today, Mus of Modern Art, Ostend, Belgium, 2001; Depicting Absence/Implying Presence, San Jose Inst of Contemp Art, Calif, 2001; Sarah Meltzer Gallery, New York City, 02; Vedanta Gallery, Chicago, 02; Henry Art Gallery, Seattle, 02; Elias Fine Art, Boston, 02; Mus Mod Art, 02; and many others. *Collection Arranged:* Mus Mod Kunst, Vienna; Mus Mod Art; Long Beach Mus Art; Mus Contemp Art, Chicago; Brooklyn Mus Art; Kunsthaus Zurich; San Francisco Mus Mod Art; Univ Mus, Berkeley; Ctr George Pompidou, Paris; Berlinsche Galerie, Martin Gropius Bau. *Teaching:* prof, San

Francisco Art Inst, New Genres Dept, 81-, dept chair, 89-91; vis artist, Va Commonwealth Univ, Richmond, 78, San Francisco Art Inst, 79-80, Minneapolis Col Art & Design, 83, Art Inst Chicago, 87, 94, Univ Sao Paulo, Brazil, 90, Univ Windsor, Can, 94, Univ Ill, Carbondale, 96. *Awards:* Governor of Prefecture's Award, Protopia '81, Tokyo, Japan, 81; Award in Video Art, US Film & Video Festival, Park City, Utah, 82; Gilmore D Clarke & Michael Rapuano Rome Prize in Visual Arts, Am Acad, Rome, 95-96; fel, Calif Arts Coun, 92-93; Flintridge Found Award for Vis Artists, 99-00. *Bibliog:* James Scarborough (auth), The Perils of Belief, Art Week, Vol 22 No 11, 3/21/91; Roberta Smith (auth) In Installation Art, A Bit of the Spoiled Brat, NY Times Arts & Leisure Section, p 31, 1/3/93; Mary Hull Webster (auth), In Mr Wizard's Shadow: Doug Hall at UAM Berkeley, Artweek, Vol 24, No 10, p 4-5, 5/20/93. *Mem:* Calif Art Comn (panelist, 92); Nat Endowment for Arts (panelist, 89); Calif Arts Comn (panelist, 87); Bay Area Video Coalition (bd dir, 84-89); San Francisco Art Inst (bd trustees, 80-85, artists comt, 79-85). *Media:* Photography; Video Installation. *Publ:* Sally Jo Fijer (co-ed), Illuminating Video, An Essential Guide to Video Art, Alperture Bks, 90. *Dealer:* Rena Branstén Gallery 77 Geary St San Francisco CA 94108; Feigen Contemporary 535 W 20th St NY 10011. *Mailing Add:* 4131 23rd St San Francisco CA 94114

HALL, JOHN A
PAINTER, EDUCATOR

b Toronto, Ont, Oct 10, 14. *Study:* Ont Col Art. *Work:* Art Gallery Ont; Nat Gallery, Ottawa; Robert McLaughlin Gallery, Oshawa. *Comn:* Murals in porcelain enamel on steel panels, Delhi, Port Colborne & Simcoe, Ont & Expo '67, Montreal, Que. *Exhib:* Can Group Painters; Ont Soc Artists; Royal Can Acad; NY World's Fair, 39; Rio, 44 & 46; and others. *Teaching:* Instr, Art Gallery Toronto; instr painting, Ont Dept Educ, summer courses; assoc prof drawing & painting, Dept Archit, Univ Toronto, retired. *Awards:* Can Arts Coun Sr Artists' Award, 63. *Mem:* Hon mem Ont Asn Archit; Ont Soc Artists. *Media:* Oil, Watercolor

HALL, LEE
WRITER, PAINTER

b Lexington, NC, Dec 15, 34. *Study:* Univ NC, Greensboro, BFA; NY Univ, scholar, 65, AM & PhD; Warburg Inst, Univ London. *Hon Degrees:* Univ NC, Greenboro, DFA (hon), 66. *Work:* Hudson River Mus; Montclair Art Mus; Drew Univ, NJ; Greenville Mus, SC; Mattatuck Mus, Conn; RISD Mus, RI; Citicorp; and others. *Exhib:* One-woman shows, Ruth White Gallery, 68, Drew Univ, 74 & Betty Parsons Gallery, 75, 77, 78, 80 & 82; RI Sch Design, 75; Phoenix Gallery, Washington, DC, 83; Elliot Smith Gallery, St Louis. *Pos:* Chmn dept art, Drew Univ, Madison, NJ, 65-74; consult, Nat Endowment for Humanities, 69-75; dean visual arts, State Univ NY, Purchase, 74-75; pres, RI Sch Design, 75-83; sr vpres & dir, Acad Educ Develop, 84-92. *Awards:* Am Philos Soc Grant, 65 & 68; Arts & Letters Purchase Prize, 1980. *Bibliog:* Wallace Herndin Smith, Paintings, Univ of Washington, Press, 87; Abe Ajay Univ of Washington Press, 89; Betty Parsons Artist, Dealer, Collector, Abrams, 91; Common Threads; A Parade of AM Clothing, Bulfinch Little Brown, 92; Elaine and Bill; Portrait of a Marriage, Harper Collins, 93; Olmsten's Am, Bulfinch, Little Brown, 94; Athens; A Biography, 94. *Mem:* Addison Wesley. *Media:* Watercolor, Oil. *Res:* History and theory of symbolism in 19th and 20th century art; intellectual & cultural history. *Publ:* Auth, Elaine & Bill, Harper Collections; Betty Parson artists, Dealer Collection, Abrams; Wallace Herndon Smith Painting, Univ Wash Press; Abe Ajay, Univ Wash Press; Athena, A Biography, Addison Wellesley. *Mailing Add:* 14 Silverwood Terr South Hadley MA 01075

HALL, MICHAEL DAVID
SCULPTOR, EDUCATOR

b Upland, Calif, May 20, 41. *Study:* Western Wash State Col, 58-60; Univ NC, BA, 62; Univ Iowa, 62; Univ Wash, MFA(sculpture), 64. *Work:* Princeton Univ Art Mus, NJ; City of Grand Rapids, Mich; Detroit Inst Arts; J B Speed Art Mus, Louisville, Ky; Milwaukee Art Mus; and others. *Comn:* Sculpture, Warren Plaza, Detroit, 80, Galeria Center, Southfield, Mich, 88. *Exhib:* Whitney Mus Am Art Ann Sculpture Exhib, NY, 68 & 73; Am Sculpture, Sheldon Mem Art Gallery, Univ Nebr, Lincoln, 70; Hammarskjold Plaza, NY, 72; Sculpture Off the Pedestal, Grand Rapids, Mich, 73; Three Installations, Detroit Inst Arts, 77; Scale & Environment, Walker Art Ctr, Minneapolis, 77; Los Angeles Inst Contemp Art, 80; Nassau Co Mus, Roslyn, NY, 83; Socrates Sculpture Park, Long Island City, NY, 88; Detroit Inst Arts, 2001; Scarab Club, Detroit, 2004; and others. *Collection Arranged:* North by Midwest; The Painting of Charles Burchfield, Columbus Mus of Art Columbus, March-May, 97; Great Lakes Mus; American Scene Painting in the Upper Midwest 1910-1960, Flint Inst of Art, Flint MI, Nov -Dec 2003. *Pos:* Guest Cur, Columbus Mus of Art, Columbus Ohio, 96-97; 99-2000; 2003-2004. *Teaching:* Instr ceramics & sculpture, Univ Colo, Boulder, 65-66; assoc prof sculpture, Univ Ky, 66-70; resident sculptor, Cranbrook Acad Art, 70-90; Miami Univ, Ohio, 91. *Awards:* Guggenheim Found Fel, 73; Nat Endowment Art Fel, 74; Mich Coun for Arts Fel, 85, 88. *Bibliog:* Articles, Arts Mag, 11/77, 2/78 & 6/79. *Mem:* Int Sculpture Ctr; Intuit The Ctr for Intuitive and Outsider Art; The Scarab Club of Detroit. *Media:* Steel, Aluminum. *Res:* The paintings of Emerson Burkhart, 1905-1969 (monograph in process). *Collection:* America Folk Art; American Scene Paintings; Inuit Sculpture and Prints. *Publ:* Stereoscopic Perspective, UMI Rsch Press, Ann Arbor, 88; The Artist Outsider, Smithsonian Press, 94; The Paintings of Charles Burchfield: North by Midwest, Abrams, 97; Grandma Moses in the Twenty First Century, Art Services International, Alexandria, VA, 2001; Great Lakes Mus, Flint Inst of Art, Flint MI, 2003. *Dealer:* Hill Gallery, 407 W Brown St. Birmingham, MI, 48009. *Mailing Add:* 3417 Caniff Ave Hamtramck MI 48212

HALL, ROBERT L
MUSEOLOGIST, PAINTER

b Miami, Fla. *Study:* Fisk Univ, BS(art), 72; George Washington Univ, MAT(mus educ), 75. *Work:* Fisk Univ Mus Art; Carroll Reece Mus, ETenn State Univ. *Comn:* Mural, Miami-Dade Community Col, Cult Arts Ctr, Miami, 73. *Exhib:* Lowe Art Mus, Univ Miami, 70; Zale Mus, Bishop Col, Tex, 78; Black Artists South, Huntsville Mus Art, Ala, 79; Recent Works, Van Vechten Art Gallery, Fisk Univ, 82; Carroll Reece Mus, ETenn State Univ, 84. *Collection Arranged:* Lev Mills Prints (auth, catalog), 78; Betty Blayton (auth, catalog), 79; Recent Acquisitions (auth, catalog), Fisk Univ Mus Art, 80; Portraits by Carl Van Vechten Traveling Show (auth, catalog), 80; Anderson, Hyman and Wood (auth, catalog), 81; Gathered Visions, 92; In the Arms of the Elders, 2002; New Visions, 2003; On their Own, 2005. *Pos:* Cur collections & educ, Fisk Univ Mus Art, 73-84; educ dir, Anacostia Community Mus, Smithsonian Inst. *Teaching:* Instr, Fisk Univ, 76-79. *Bibliog:* 250 Yrs of Afro-American Art: An Annotated Biography, Lynn Moody (auth), TT Bowker, 81. *Mem:* Am Asn Mus; African Am Mus Asn; Commonwealth Asn Mus. *Media:* Acrylic, Oil. *Res:* African American public art in Washington DC. *Publ:* Gathered Visions: Selected Works by African American Women Artists, 92; New Visions, 2003; On Their Own, 2005. *Mailing Add:* Anacostia Community Mus Smithsonian Inst Educ Dept 1901 Fort Pl SE Washington DC 20020

HALL, SUSAN
PAINTER, CERAMIST

b Point Reyes Station, Calif, Mar 19, 43. *Study:* Calif Col Arts & Crafts, Oakland, 62-65; Univ Calif, Berkeley, MA, 67. *Work:* Whitney Mus, NY; Brooklyn Mus, NY; Carnegie Inst, Pittsburgh, Pa; San Francisco Mus Art; Nat Mus Women in the Arts, Washington; Hudson River Mus, Yonkers, NY; New Mus, NY. *Exhib:* San Francisco Mus Art Ann, 66; One-woman shows, San Francisco Mus Art, 67, Whitney Mus, 72, Nancy Hoffman Gallery, NY, 73 & 75, Hamilton Gallery, 78-79 & 81 & Dart Gellery, Chicago, 81; Twenty-six Contemp Women Artists, Aldrich Mus Contemp Art, Ridgefield, Conn, 71; Printmaking-the 70's into the 80's, Mus Fine Arts, Boston; Am Realism, San Francisco Mus Art, 85; Trabia Macafee, NY, 87-89; Milagros, San Antonio, 95; Brendan Walter, Los Angeles, 95; Univ Tex, San Antonio, 96; Jan Holloway Gallery, 97; San Francisco Mus Art Gallery; Gail Harvey Gallery, Los Angeles, 99; Frank Lloyd Wright Civic Ctr, San Rafael, 99; Jernigan Wicker Gallery, San Francisco, 99; Gail Harvey Gallery, 99-2001; Sandy Erickson, Gallery Healdsburg. *Teaching:* Instr, Univ Calif, Berkeley, 67-70, Sarah Lawrence Col, Bronxville, NY, 72-75 & Sch Visual Arts, 81-92; vis artist, Univ Tex, Austin, 93, Univ Tex, San Antonio, 95 & San Francisco Art Inst, 96. *Awards:* Nat Endowment Arts Award, 79 & 88; Krasner Pollock Found, 86; Adolph Gottlieb Found Grant, 95; Bd Dirs Award, Marin Arts Coun, 98. *Bibliog:* William Zimmer (auth), article, NY Times-Westchester, 4/84; John R Clarke (auth), Image, technique & spirituality in Susan Hall's new work, Arts Mag, 6/88; Christine Liotta (auth), Review Art News, 3/90; Susan Hall, Finding Her Center, Woman's Art Jour, spring/summer 2000; Painting Point Reyes, A Book of Susan Hall's Paintings, Green Bridge Press, 2002; John R Clarke (auth), Susan Hall and the discourse of landscape; Independent Journal, Rick Polito, Point Reyes Perspective; book of paintings from Home Before Dark Show, Tobys Gallery, Point Reyes Station, 2005. *Media:* Oil; Ceramics. *Mailing Add:* Box 1295 Point Reyes Station CA 94956

HALL, WILLIAM A
ARCHITECT

b 1923. *Study:* Univ Okla, BA; Mass Inst Tech, M (city planning). *Mem:* Fel, Am Inst Architects; Nat Acad. *Mailing Add:* William A Hall Partnership 42 East 21 St New York NY 10010

HALLAM, BEVERLY (LINNEY)
PAINTER, PHOTOGRAPHER

b Lynn, Mass, Nov 22, 23. *Study:* Mass Col Art, BSEd, 45; Cranbrook Acad Art, 48; Syracuse Univ, MFA, 51-53. *Work:* Fogg Art Mus, Harvard Univ; Addison Gallery Am Art; Corcoran Gallery, Washington, DC; Everson Mus, Syracuse, NY; Worcester Art Mus, Mass; Nat Mus Women Arts. *Exhib:* Bowdoin Col Mus Art, Maine, 75, 81, 84 & 92; solo exhibs, Midtown Payson Galleries, NY, 88 & 92, Francesca Anderson Galleries, Boston, 88, 03, Hobe Sound Galleries N, Portland, Maine, 88, Sheldon Swope Mus, Terre Haut, Ind, 90, Art Mus Southeast Tex, Beaumont, 90, Bergen Mus Art & Sci, Paramus, NJ, 90, Polk Mus Art, Lakeland, Fla, 91, World Expo-92, Seville, Spain; one-person retrospectives, Addison Gallery Am Art, 71, Traveling exhib, Evansville Mus Arts & Science, Ind, 90 & Farnsworth Art Mus, Maine, 98; Mass Col Art, 2000; Univ New Eng, 2000, 2005; Ogunquit Mus of Am Art, Maine, 2002, 03; Addison Gallery of Am Art, 03; Koussevitzky Art Gallery, Berkshire Comm Col, MA; Portlnd Mus Art, ME, 2004; Center for Maine Contemp Art, 2006; Blaine House, Gov Mansion, Maine, 2006. *Teaching:* Chmn art dept, Lasell Jr Col, 45-49; assoc prof painting & teacher educ, Mass Col Art, 49-62; lectr & demonstr, Use of Polyvinyl Acetate (Acrylic) as Painting Medium, throughout Eastern US, 52-. *Awards:* Blanche E Colman Found Award, 60; New Eng Watercolor Soc, 60, 62 & 64; Deborah Morton Award, Westbrook Col, Maine, 90; Artist Achievement Airbrush Award, Am Artist Mag, 93; Distinguished Alumni Award, Mass Col Art, 2000; Award for Achievement as a visual artist, Maine Col Art, 2001. *Bibliog:* John Whitney Payson (auth, catalog), Beverly Hallam: The Flower Paintings (video), Evansville Mus Arts & Sci, 90; Beverly Hallam (auth), Painting Acrylics with Airbrush, Watercolor 92, fall 92; Carl Little (auth), Paintings of New England, 96 & Beverly Hallam: An Odyssey in Art, 98, Whalesback Books; Pamela J. Belanger (auth), Maine in America, Am Art at the Farnsworth Art Mus, 2000; On Paper: Masterworks from the Addison Collection, Addison Gallery of Am Art, 2003. *Mem:* New England Watercolor Soc; Ogunquit Art Asn (pres, 64); Barn Gallery Asn (bd dir, 70-2003). *Media:* Acrylic & oil on Canvas, Pastel, Digital Prints. *Mailing Add:* Surf Point Studio 30 Surf Point Rd York ME 03909

HALLAM, JOHN S
HISTORIAN, ADMINISTRATOR
b Seattle, Wash, Oct 10, 47. *Study:* Seattle Univ, BA, 70; Univ Wash, MA, 74, PhD, 80. *Pos:* Chmn dept art, Pacific Lutheran Univ, 90-92. *Teaching:* Assoc prof art hist, Pacific Lutheran Univ, 90-92. *Mem:* Col Art Asn; Am Soc 18th Century Studies. *Res:* 18th & 19th century Europ & Am Art, urban, imagery, still-life, genre painting & sculpture. *Publ:* Auth, Charles Willson Peale and Hogart's Line of Beauty, Mag Antiques, 86; Meaning & Manner in Chardin's La bonne Education, Bulletin Mus Fine Art, Houston, 86; 18th Century American Townscape and the Face of Colonialism, Smithsonian Studies in Am Art, 91. *Mailing Add:* Pacific Lutheran University Dept of Art Ingram Hall Tacoma WA 98447

HALLENBECK, POMONA JUANITA
PAINTER, PRINTMAKER
b Roswell, NMex, Nov 12, 38. *Study:* Eastern NMex Univ, AA, 65; Sch Visual Arts; Pan Am Sch Art; Arts Students League; Studies with Mario Cooper, John Groth, David Stone Martin, Skip Lawrence, Christopher Schink, Frank Webb, Arne Westerman & Don Andrews. *Work:* Eastern NMex Univ, NMex Hist Soc Mus, Roswell, NMex; Union Theological Sem, Levi-Strauss Co, New York, NY; Rochester Mus Fine Art, NY; Blue Cross & Blue Shield, Tulsa, Okla; Ghost Ranch Conference Ctr, Santa Fe, NMex; Cotton, Inc, NY; Mountain Bell Tel & Tel Co, NMex; Jack Leib Filmakers, Chicago; Mus Fine Art, Galveston, Tex. *Comn:* Watercolor, Jack Tar Enterprises, Galveston, Tex, 65; banners & posters, UN Action Against Apartheid, NY, 74; fabric designs, Wamsutta, Huckapoo, Burlington & JC Penny, NY, 74; Cotton Inc, 86; Lady J Designs (painting on silk), 88, book covers for Wink Trilogy, Augsburg Fortress', Minneapolis, Minn, 92; Southwest Expressions, Chicago; Ghost Ranch & Friends (book cover), Santa Fe, NMex, 92. *Exhib:* Finishing Touches, Trunk Show, Roswell, MNex, 88; Compadre Conference, Ghost Ranch, NMex; Southwest Expressions, Chicago; St Edwards Univ, Austin, Tex, 94; Bitzer-Johnson Gallery, NMex, 96; Ausburg Press, 2001; Ghost Ranch, NMex, 2005-2006. *Pos:* Designer window decor, Highland Mall, Austin, Tex, 77; co-ordination, Ghost Ranch Calendar Project, Santa Fe, NMex, 92; art workshop coordr, Ghost Ranch, Abiquiu, NMex, 94-96. *Teaching:* Artist & teacher watercolor & papermaking, Austin Community Col & Roswell Mus, 85; developer of 3 yr academic course in watercolor for NMex Military Inst, '84, workshops (W/C, Papermaking, Wearable Art) Carrizo Art School Ruidoso, NMex, 86, 87 & 88; workshops, Ghost Ranch, NMex, 84-2001; instr, Elderhostel Progs, 86-99; artist-in-residence, Ghost Ranch, Santa Fe, 94-2001; instr, Laughing at the Sun Gallery, Austin, Tex, 98, Art After Sch, Bastrop, Tex, 98-2001, Univ Tex, Austin, 98-2001, Bastrop Continuing Edu, 98-2001, Herman Miller Group, 99-2001 & Austin Mus Laguna Art Sch, Tex, 2000-2006. *Awards:* Purchase Award, Am Artist Exhib, 75; Bronze Medallion, Prix d'Paris Exhib, Raymond Duncan Gallery, Paris, France, 81; Hon Mention, NMex Watercolor Soc, 97. *Bibliog:* NMex videos, silk printing & book covers for educational channels; Five Astonishing Women (video), Los Angeles, 96-97; Painting the Pecos, Persimmon Hill Mag, 98; Pomona, Video, 2004. *Mem:* Women in the Arts, Washington; Western Colo Watercolor Soc; Tex Watercolor Soc; AWS Asn; La Guna Gloria Mus, Austin, TX. *Media:* Watercolor; Fiberart, Silk. *Res:* The sites & colonization of Pecos River. *Interests:* jazz musicians. *Publ:* Illusr, Scott Foresman Math, Scott Foresman, 75; Charles Dickens' Anthology, Crown Publ, 76; illusr bk covers, Julian of Norwich, Nachman of Bratslav & Pseudo Dionysius, Paulist Press, 77; Naming the Powers, Unmasking the Powers Engaging the Powers, Augsburg Fortress, 93; The Human Being, 02; Enigma oth the Son of the Man, 02; My Turkish Sketchbook, 05. *Dealer:* Bitzere-Johnson Gallery Roswell NM; Artisans Austin Teeks Wimberly TX; Trading Post-Abiquiu, NM. *Mailing Add:* 130 Old Austin Tr Elgin TX 78621-5744

HALLER, DOUGLAS MARTIN
CURATOR, HISTORIAN
b Detroit, Mich, July 28, 51. *Study:* Wayne State Univ, BA, 73, MA, 82; Acad Cert Archivists, cert, 89-. *Collection Arranged:* Portals of the Past, Hist Photographs, 83; C Watkins Photographic Murals, Calif Photogr, 83; Seeing Is Believing (auth, catalog), CIGNA Mus, Philadelphia, 89, Univ Pa Mus, 90; Jean Pascal Sebah's Athens, Ottoman Photographs, 93. *Pos:* Co-own & consult, Hermes Antiques, Washington, 74-79; cur photographs, Calif Hist Soc Libr, San Francisco & Los Angeles, 82-86; suject specialist hist photographs, John F Kennedy Univ Ctr for Mus Studies, San Francisco, 83-84; mus archivist, Univ Pa, 86. *Teaching:* Instr Ancient hist, Wayne State Univ,79-82. *Mem:* Soc Am Archivists (pres visual mat sect, 81-, chair, 89-91); Am Asn Mus; Nat Endowment for Humanities; Delaware Valley Archivists Group; Photog Sesquicentennial Proj, Delaware Valley. *Res:* Photographs as historical documents; vintage photographic processes; biography of photographers; portrait and architectural photography. *Publ:* Auth, Watkins photography exhibit, 83, the California Historical Society's Arnold Genthe collection, 84, CHS Courier; coauth, Four pioneer photographers in California, Calif Hist Soc, 86; auth, The William Pepper bust and statue, Univ Pa Mus Newsletter, 87. *Mailing Add:* Univ Pa Mus 33rd & Spruce Sts Philadelphia PA 19104-6324

HALLEY, PETER
PAINTER
b New York, NY, Sept 24, 53. *Study:* Yale Univ, New Haven, Conn, BA; Univ New Orleans, MFA. *Work:* Guggenheim Mus, NY; Wright State Univ, Dayton; Carnegie Mus Art, Pittsburgh; San Francisco Mus Modern Art, Calif; Addison Gallery Am Art, Andover, Mass; Whitney Mus. *Comn:* Painting for bd rm, Chase Manhattan Bank, NY, 89. *Exhib:* Biennial, Whitney Mus, NY, 87; Viewpoints: Postwar painting & sculpture, Guggenheim Mus, NY, 88; Binational: Am Art of the late 80's, Mus Fine Arts, Boston, 88; Carnegie Int, Carnegie Mus Art, Pittsburgh, 88; Ten plus Ten: Contemp Soviet and Am Painters, Ft Worth Mus, Tex, 89; Abstraction in Question, Ringling Mus Art, Sarasota, Fla, 89; Projects & Portfolios, Brooklyn Mus, NY, 89; Word as Image: Am Art 1960-1990, Milwaukee, Wis, 90; Touring Europ Retrospective, Switz, France, Spain & Amsterdam, 91-92. *Teaching:* Instr painting & sculpture, Sch Visual Arts, NY, 89-. *Bibliog:* Mark Stevens (auth), Neo-Geo Art's Computer Hum, Newsweek, 11/87; Roberta Smith (auth), Minimalism's Slow Fire, New York Times, 12/89; Jeanne Siegel, Art Talk Da Capo Press, NY, 89. *Media:* Acrylic, Oil. *Publ:* Auth, Collected Essays 1981-1987, Bruno Bischofberger, 88. *Dealer:* Gagosian Gallery 136 Wooster St New York NY 10012. *Mailing Add:* 12 Harrison St New York NY 10013-2838

HALLIDAY, NANCY R
ILLUSTRATOR, INSTRUCTOR
b Chicago, Ill, Mar 30, 36. *Study:* Mich State Univ, East Lansing, 54-56 & 58-61; Art Sch Soc Arts & Crafts, Mich, 56-57; Univ Okla, Norman, BSc, 62; Northeastern Ill Univ, Chicago, MA, 88. *Work:* Fla State Mus, Gainesville; Hunt Inst Botanical Documentation, Pittsburgh, Pa; Visual Arts Gallery, Pensacola Jr Col, Fla. *Comn:* One hundred nine drawings for publs on lichens, Mason Hale, Smithsonian Inst, 67, 69; Watercolor poster, Rare Animal Relief Effort, Inc, NY, 81; nine stamp paintings, Nat Wildlife Fedn, Washington, 82, 83, 85, 89, 92; 12″x18″ illustrated interpretive sign at Morton Grove Prairie, Morton Grove, Ill, 95; two illus interpretive signs, Lincoln Park, Chicago, Ill, 2005; and others. *Exhib:* Perfectly Beautiful: Art in Science, Smithsonian Inst, 78; one-person show, Thomas Ctr for the Arts, Gainesville, Fla, 82; two-person show, Macon, Ga, 82; Wildlife in Art, Nat Wildlife Fedn, Vienna, Va, 83; Ann Bird Art Exhib, Leigh Yawkey Woodson Art Mus, Wausau, Wis, 83; Sixth Int Exhib Botanical Art & Illustration, Hunt Inst Botanical Doc, Pittsburgh, 88; Wildlife Art in Am, Bell Mus Natural Hist, Minneapolis, Minn, 94; Art of the Prairie, Chicago Botanic Garden, Glencoe, Ill, 95; Picturing Natural Hist, Smithsonian Inst, 96; Guild of Natural Sci Illusr Ann Mems Exhib, Evora, Portugal, 2000; and others. *Pos:* Lectr & asst exhib preparator, Mus Mich State Univ, East Lansing, 57-60; asst, Mus Northern Ariz, Flagstaff, summer 63; artist, Nat Mus Natural Hist, Smithsonian Inst, 66-70; illusr, dept natural sci, Fla State Mus, Gainesville, 73-81; artist-naturalist, Forest Preserve Dist Cook Co, Ill, 89-2003. *Teaching:* Instr, animal illus, Univ Fla, Gainesville, 77, 78 & 82, biology illus, Univ Ill, Chicago, 85-86, nature illus, Gov State Univ, University Park, Ill, 93-2000, botanical illus (certified prog), Morton Arboretum, Lisle, Ill, 93-; artist-in-education, Ryerson Conserv Area, Deerfield, Ill, 86; artist-in-residence, Rockford Art Mus, Ill, 91; plus many other lectures and workhops. *Awards:* First Prize Color Wildlife, Guild Natural Sci Illusr Show, Hunt Inst Botanical Doc, Pa, 79; Second Prize Watercolor, Wildlife Art Exhib, Nat Wildlife Fedn, Vienna, Va, 83; Cur Choice Mammalogy, Guild Nat Sci Illusr Show, Art Inst, Arizona-Sonora Desert Mus, Tuscon, AZ, 2005. *Bibliog:* Vera Norwood (auth), Made from this Earth: American Women & Nature, Univ NC Press, 93. *Mem:* Soc Animal Artists; Guild Natural Sci Illusr (historian, 95-); Nature Artists' Guild of Morton Arboretum; Am Soc Botanical Artists. *Media:* Watercolor; Pen & Ink, Pastel, Oil. *Res:* History of biological illustration. *Interests:* Bird-watching, bicycling, canoeing & hiking. *Publ:* Illusr, Behavioral ecology of the Yucatan jay, Wilson Bulletin, 76; auth, Bird illustration, In: Guild Handbook of Biological Illustration (ed, Elaine R S Hodges), second edition, John Wiley & Sons, Inc, 2003; cover illus (2), Natural Areas Jour, 96, 99; illusr, Mammals of North America, Princeton Univ Press, 2002; illusr, Atlas of Breeding Birds in Pa, Univ Pittsburgh Press, 92; and many other scientific journals. *Mailing Add:* 1156 Pine St Apt 4 Glenview IL 60025

HALLIGAN, ROGER PHILLIP
SCULPTOR, DESIGNER
b Troy, NY, Mar 18, 48. *Study:* Le Moyne Col, BA, 70; Univ Ga, Athens, MFA, 77. *Work:* Weatherspoon Gallery, Univ NC, Greensboro; NC Ctr Advancement of Teaching, Collowhee, NC; Inst Ecology, Univ Ga, Athens. *Comn:* Sculpture, Shelter Cove/Palmetto Dunes, Hilton Head, SC, 89; sculpture, NC Zoo, Asheboro, 97; sculpture, Triad Regional Farmers Market & State of NC, Greensboro, 98. *Exhib:* Ann Juried Exhib, SECCA, Winston-Salem, NC, 78; Mint Mus Biennial, 79; Zoo Artists, Fayetteville Mus Art, NC, 80; NC in NY, Nat Arts Club, NY, 93; two-person show, Artspace, Raleigh, NC, 96; Art for Arts Sake, Green Hill Ctr NC Art, Greensboro, 97; solo shows incl Lee Hansley Gallery, Raleigh, NC, 94, Paisley Pineapple, Greensboro, NC, 99, Hodges-Taylor Gallery and Nations Bank, 2000. *Pos:* Exhib designer, NC Zoological Park, 77-90; guest cur, Green Hill Ctr NC Art, 98; ptnr, Two Oaks Studio, 98-. *Awards:* Best in Show, Sculpture 79, Weatherspoon Gallery, 79; Artist-in-Residence, NC Zoological Park, 97. *Bibliog:* Chuck Twardy (auth), Loading upon art, Raleigh News & Observer, 94; Burton Wasserman (auth), Outdoor Sculpture, Art Matters, Philadelphia; Blue Greenberg (auth), Review, Durham Herald Sun, 96. *Mem:* Tri State Sculptors Educ Asn (pres, 92-97); Int Sculpture Ctr; Green Hill Ctr NC Art (bd dir, 93-98). *Media:* Steel, Concrete. *Specialty:* NC and SE contemp art. *Mailing Add:* 842 S Park St Asheboro NC 27203-6365

HALLMAN, GARY LEE
PHOTOGRAPHER
b St Paul, Minn, Aug 7, 40. *Study:* Univ Minn, Minneapolis, BA, 66, MFA, 71. *Work:* Mus Mod Art, NY; Int Mus Photog, Rochester; Nat Gallery Can, Toronto; Fogg Art Mus, Harvard Univ; Princeton Univ Art Mus. *Comn:* Photo murals, Dayton-Hudson Corp, Minneapolis, 70. *Exhib:* Gary Hallman and Jeff Murphy, Dept Art Gallery, Univ Northern Iowa, Cedar Falls; Special Collectors' Special Collections, Mus NMex, Santa Fe; solo exhibs, Hudson Valley Inst Art & Photog Resources, Peekskill, NY & Dept Art Hist & Design, Univ Notre Dame, Ind, 96; Trues and Trials Color Photog since 1975, Minneapolis Inst Arts, Minn, 96; Int Photog & Digital Image Exhib, Welligton B Gregg Gallery, ECarolina Univ, Greenville, NC, 97. *Teaching:* Vis artist, Southampton Col, summer 72 & 73; asst prof photog, Univ Minn, Minneapolis, 70-76, assoc prof photog, 76-; vis adj prof photog, RI Sch Design, 77; vis exchange prof, Univ NMex, Albuquerque, 84-85; vis assoc prof, Colo Col, Colorado Springs,

90. *Awards:* Bush Found Fel for Artists, 76; Fel, McKnight Found Photog, 82 & 90; Artist Assistance Fel Grant, Minn State Arts Bd, 96. *Bibliog:* E W Peterson (auth), The photography of Gary Hallman, Image, 9/75. *Mem:* Soc Photog Educ. *Dealer:* Hudson Center For the Arts and Photographic Resource Peekskill NY. *Mailing Add:* 5411 Zenith Ave S Edina MN 55410-2464

HALLMAN, TED, JR
DESIGNER, EDUCATOR
b Bucks Co, Pa, Dec 23, 33. *Study:* Tyler Sch, Temple Univ, Sen scholar, BFA & BSEd; Fontainebleau Fine Arts, Pew scholar, cert, with Jacques Villon; Cranbrook Acad Art, West scholar, MFA(painting) & MFA(textile design); Bundestextilschule, Austria, cert; Univ Calif, Berkeley, PhD(educ). *Work:* Chicago Art Inst; Victoria & Albert Mus, London; Metrop Mus Art, NY; Smithsonian Inst, Washington, DC; Mus Applied Arts, Helsinki; Can Mus of Civilization, Ottawa; Royal Ontario Mus, Toronto; Mus Fine Arts, Houston; Decorative Arts Mus, Montreal; Brooklyn Mus Art; Philadelphia Mus Art; State Mus Pa; Governor's Gallery, Santa Fe. *Comn:* Translucent tapestry (11'x 21'), Nieman Marcus, Dallas; Reredos (10'x 32'), St John's Church, Allentown, Pa; Garden Divider, Am Chem Soc, Washington; wall hangings (4 squares), Killenure Castle Co Tipperary, Ireland; woven hangings, Marshal Field, Chicago. *Exhib:* Am Wallhangings, Victoria & Albert Mus, London, 62; Three Centuries of Am Art, Philadelphia Mus Art, 76; The Art Fabric-Mainstream, Am Fedn Arts, 82; One-man shows, London Regional Art Gallery, Can, Fashion Inst Technol Gallery, NY, 83, Brooklyn Mus Art, 84, Gallery 21, Tokyo, Fuji Gallery, Osaka & Kyoto, Am Ctr, Kyoto, 85, Hamilton Art Gallery, Can, 86, Cambridge Gallery, Ont, 95 & Allentown Art Mus, Penn, 98, 2003; Fiber Revolution, Milwaukee Art Mus Invitational, 86; Talkative Textiles, Trans-Am Gallery, San Francisco, 93; Focus on Textiles, Chicago Art Inst, 94; Five Decades of Fiber Art, Am Craft Mus, NY, 95; Teachers, Mentors & Makers, Ont Craft Coun, Toronto, 96; and others. *Pos:* Consult, ILO Textiles, Jamaica, summer 68; textile designer, var co. *Teaching:* Instr, Haystack Sch, Maine, Penland Sch Crafts, summers 58-95 & Taos Inst Art, 98, 99, 2002; prof textiles & chmn dept, Moore Col Art, 65-70; assoc prof textile design, San Jose State Univ, 72-75; lectr & workshop leader, US, Can & Eng (incl San Antonio, Vancouver, Ottawa & Mich, 77-78); head textiles, Ont Col Art, Toronto, 79-99; guest lectr, World Craft Conf, Mex, 76, Northern NMex Community Col, summers 92-96, Tyler Sch Fine Art of Temple Univ, 2000-01, Textile Arts Alliance, Wheelwright Mus, Santa Fe, 2004. *Awards:* Tiffany Found Grant, 62; Textile Prize, Int Kunsthandwerk Expos, Stuttgart, 67; Fel Am Craft Coun, 88. *Bibliog:* Peggy Hobbs (auth), Surface Design J, 41-42, summer 98; Trebbe Johnson (auth), Art: Weaving the Path of the Soul, New Age Mag, 22, 5-6/98; Michael Barnett (auth), Ted Hall - Passionate Weaver of Light, Craft Arts Int, Australia, 98-99. *Mem:* Philadelphia Coun Prof Craftsmen; Ont Craft Coun; hon mem Zurich, Int Soc Arts & Lett; Nat Soc Lit & Arts. *Media:* Fibers, Pigment. *Dealer:* Bruce Hoffman Snyderman/Works Gallery, Philadelphia, PA; Helen Dentt Gallery, Philadelphia, PA. *Mailing Add:* PO Box 281 Lederach PA 19450

HALLMAN, TED See Hallman, Ted, Jr

HALLMARK, DONALD
MUSEUM DIRECTOR, LECTURER
b McPherson, Kans, Feb 16, 1945. *Study:* Univ Ill, BFA (art hist), 67; Univ Iowa, MA (art hist), 70; St Louis Univ, PhD, 80. *Collection Arranged:* Richard W Bock Sculpture Collection (with catalog), Greenville Col, 75; 1984 Nat Print Exhib, Springfield Art Asn; Frank Lloyd Wright Decorative Arts Collection, Dana House, 81-88, Post Restoration Reopening of the Collection, 90-2005. *Pos:* Cur & dir, Richard W Bock Sculpture Collection, Greenville Col, 72-81; supt, hist site, Dana House, Springfield, Ill, 81-; auth, SITE Brochures, 81-2001. *Teaching:* Assoc prof art & fine arts, Greenville Col, 70-81, chmn dept art, 75-81, prof, 81-; lectr, Springfield Art Asn, 81-, Sangamon State Univ, 82-90, Art Inst Chicago, High Mus, Atlanta, Ga, Gamble House, Pasadena, Calif, Currier Gallery, Manchester, NH & Oak Park, Frank Lloyd Wright Home & Studio Lecture Series Preserving Historic Interiors Conf, Jefferson City, Mo, Mus Nat Heritage, Lexington, Mass & Nat Bldg Mus, Washington, DC. *Awards:* Kress Found Res Grant, Univ Iowa, 69; Shell Found Fac Improv Grant, 72-73; Nat Endowment Arts & Am Asn Mus Cur Seminar Scholar, 75 & 80; Nat Trust Hon Award for Preservation of Dana House. *Bibliog:* WR Hasbrouck (auth), Editors note, Prairie Sch Rev, Vol VIII, No 1, 71; H Allen Brooks (auth), Prairie Sch, Univ Toronto, 72; Narcisco Menocal (auth), Taliesin--and Flower in the Crannied Wall, Taliesin Studies, Vol I, 74; D Hoffmann, Frank Lloyd Wright: Architecture & Nature, Dutton, 86. *Mem:* Frank Lloyd Wright Bldg Conservancy; Walter Burley Griffin Soc; Nat Trust Hist Preserv. *Res:* Late 19th and early 20th century sculpture and architecture with emphasis on the Chicago School, 1880-1915. *Collection:* Original Frank Lloyd Wright decorative art objects. *Publ:* Auth, Richard W Bock, Sculptor, Prairie Sch Rev, 71; Chicago's prairie sculptor, R W Bock, 82; The Studio Collaborations, Decorative Arts Soc Newslett, 12/88; illusr, Frank Lloyd Wright's Dana-Thomas House, Ill Hist J, summer 89, rev ed 92; Paul Ashbrook (exhib catalog), Springfield Art Asn, 90; auth, Frank Lloyd Wright: The Phoeniz Papers-The Natural Pattern of Structure, Vol II, Univ Arizona, 95. *Mailing Add:* 605 W Sheridan Rd Petersburg IL 62675

HALPERN, NORA R
DIRECTOR, CURATOR
b New York, NY, Dec 5, 60. *Study:* Helena Rubenstein Fel, Whitney Mus Am Art Independent Study Prog, 82; Univ Calif, Los Angeles, BFA, 83, MFA, 90. *Collection Arranged:* Frames of Reference, Whitney Mus, Downtown Branch, 82; Jeune Californie, Am Ctr, Paris, 86; Fauxto graphy, Art Ctr Col Design, 89; Dynaton, Before & Beyond, Lee Mullican, Gordon Onslow-Ford, Wolfgang Paalen, Pepperdine Univ, 92. *Pos:* Cur Collections, Frederick Weisman Co, Frederick R Weisman Art Found & F Weisman Personal Collection, Los Angeles, 83-90; dir, Frederick R Weisman Mus Art, Pepperdine Univ, Malibu, CA, 92-94; dir fine arts, Sotheby's, Los Angeles, 94. *Teaching:* Adj prof art hist, Pepperdine Univ, Malibu, CA, 92-94. *Mem:* Los Angeles Inst Contemp Art (bd mem 83-87); Art Table. *Publ:* Auth & ed, Frames of Reference, Whitney Mus, New York, 82; FR Weisman Found Art, Volume II, 85, Selections from FR Weisman Collection, 87, Art & Architecture & Society, Vols I & II, 90, Weisman Found; ed, Art Fairs: Plans and Process, 89; Conservation & Contemporary Art, 90; Support for The Arts in Unsupportive Times, 90; Dynaton, Before & Beyond: Lee Mullican, Gordon Onslow-Ford, Wolfgang Paalen, Pepperdine Univ, 92

HALPRIN, LAWRENCE
ARCHITECT
b NY City, Jul 1, 1916. *Study:* Cornell Univ, BS (plant scis), 39; Univ Wis, MS (plant scis), 41; Harvard Univ, B Landscape Archit, 42. *Comn:* prin works incl, Ghirardelli Sq, San Francisco, 62, Sea Ranch, Calif, 65, Nicolett Mall, Minneapolis, Old Orchard Shopping Ctr, Skokie, Ill, Lovejoy Fountain, 61, Pettigrove Park, Forecourt Fountain, Portland, Ore, Market St reconstruction, San Francisco, Seattle Freeway Park, Rochester Manhattan Park, Franklin Delano Roosevelt Mem, Wash, Levi Park and Plaza, San Francisco, Haas Promenade, Jerusalem, Bunker Hill Stairs, Central Libr, Hope St and Olympic Park, Los Angeles. *Pos:* Sr assoc, Thomas D Church & Assos, San Francisco, 46-49; principal, Lawrence Halprin & Assos, 49-76; co-founder, Round House, 76-78; founder, Lawrence Halprin Studios, 78-; dir, Halprin Summer Workshop, 66, 68. *Teaching:* lectr, Univ Calif-Berkeley, 60-65, Regents prof, 82-83. *Awards:* Named One of Leaders of Tomorrow, Time Mag, 53; Thomas Jefferson Award, in archit, 79; Richard J Neutra Award, for Excellence, 86; Nat Medal of Arts, 2002; Friedrich Ludwig von Sckell Golden Ring, 2002; Michaelangelo Award, 2005. *Mem:* Fel Am Soc Landscape Archits; Am Acad Arts and Scis, Sierra Club; Nat Acad. *Publ:* rev. ed, 72, Freeways, 66, NY, 68, The RSVP Cycles, 70, Lawrence Halprin Notebooks, 59-71, 72; co-auth: The Freeway in the City, 68, Taking Part: A Workshop Approach to Collective Creativity, 74, The Sketch Books of Lawrence Halprin, 81; filmmaker: Le Pink Grapefruit, Franklin Delano Roosevelt Memorial, How Sweet It Is!, Designing Environments for Everyone; auth: Cities, 63. *Mailing Add:* 1160 Battery St Ste 50 San Francisco CA 94111-1215

HAMANN, MARILYN D
EDUCATOR, PAINTER
b Los Angeles, Calif, Nov 24, 45. *Study:* Univ Calif, Berkeley, BA, 67, with Robert Hudson & Jim Melchert, MA, 70. *Work:* Univ Ky Art Mus, Lexington; Citizen's Fidelity Bank & Trust Co & Liberty Nat Bank, Louisville, Ky; Cincinnati Bell Info Systems; Cent Bank & Trust Co, Lexington; Brown & Williamson Tobacco Corp; Gatton Col Bus and Econ, Univ Ky. *Exhib:* Whitney Mus Am Art, NY, 73; JB Speed Art Mus, Louisville, Ky, 74, 77, 81, 82 & 89; New Orleans Mus Art, 75; Oakland Mus Art, Calif, 75; Archive Small Press & Communs Space, Antwerp, Belg, 82; Ky Arts & Crafts Fedn, 91 & 92; SC State Mus, 92; Mich Art Train, 93-94; Owensboro Mus Art, 96; and others; Mail Art Shows, Berlin-Zehlendorf Pub Libr, Ger, 2001; Jeju Cult & Art Found, Jeju City, S Korea, 2001; COSLART 03, Concejalia de Cultura, Madrid, Spain. *Teaching:* Assoc prof, Univ Ky, Lexington, 80-. *Awards:* Al Smith Fel, Ky Arts Coun, 86; Ky Found Women Grant, 87; Award of Merit, Huntington Mus Art, 88. *Bibliog:* Jacqueline Rapp (auth), article, New Art Examiner, 78; Guy Mendes (producer), Kentucky Now, Ky Educ Television, 79; New Art Examiner, 2/90. *Mem:* Asn Independent Video & Filmmakers; Ky Woodworkers Asn. *Media:* Mixed Media, Video, Sculpture. *Publ:* Int Soc Copier Artists Quart, Vol 1, No 1 & 3, New York, 82 & 83. *Mailing Add:* Univ Ky Dept Art 207 Fine Arts Bldg Lexington KY 40506-0022

HAMAR, DIANA KATHLEEN
PAINTER
b Toledo, Ore. *Study:* Inst Am Univs, Aix-En-Provence, France; Univ Wash, Seattle, BFA, 78, MFA, 85. *Work:* Alaska State Mus, Juneau; Univ Alaska Mus, Fairbanks; Alaska State Coun Arts; Anchorage Mus Hist & Art. *Exhib:* Solo exhibs, Anchorage Mus Hist & Art, 90, Alaska State Mus, Juneau, 91, Gallery Parsons Paris Sch Design, France, 92 & Visual Arts Ctr Alaska, Anchorage, 92; Juneau Artists, Peterhof Benois Mus, St Petersburg, Russia, 92; Int Gallery Contemp Art, Anchorage, Alaska, 93 & 96; Site 250 Gallery, Fairbanks, Alaska, 97; Juneau Arts & Humanities Coun Gallery, Juneau, Alaska, 97. *Awards:* Individual Artist Fel, Alaska State Coun Arts, 88; Visual Artist Fel Painting, Nat Endowment Arts, 91-92 & US/France Artist Exchange Residency, 92; Individual Artist Grant, Juneau Arts & Humanities Coun, 94. *Mem:* Juneau Arts & Humanities Coun. *Media:* Oil on Canvas, Oil on Collaged Paper. *Publ:* La Napoule Art Foundation Chronicle, Editions Du Cygne, Paris, 93; Alaska Artists, Univ Alaska, 97; 50 Alaska Artists, Alaska State Coun Arts & Nat Endowment Arts, 98. *Dealer:* Hirsch & Associates PO Box 898 Carmel Valley CA 93924

HAMBLEN, DR KAREN A
EDUCATOR, WRITER
Study: Univ Oregon, BS(art educ), 74, MS, 77, PhD, 81. *Pos:* Co-ed, Green Hills Press Publ, 75-81; ed reviewer, Bull Caucus on Social Theory & Art Educ, 85-86, assoc ed, 87-88; ed bd mem, Studies in Art Educ, 86-88, co-ed, 89-91, sr ed, 91-; contrib ed, Arts Educ Rev of Books, 87-; ed reviewer, J Social Theory & Art Educ, 89 & 90; vis scholar, Getty Educ Inst Arts, 96-97. *Teaching:* Vis asst prof, art educ dept, Univ Ore, 81-82; asst prof, art dept, Calif State Univ-Long Beach, 82-85; assoc prof, Sch Art, La State Univ, Baton Rouge, 85-88, dept curric & instr, 88-90, prof, 90-. *Awards:* Manuel Barkan Mem Award, Scholarly merit of published work, 85; Mary Rouse Mem Award, Women's Caucus of Nat Art Educ Asn, 87; June King McFee Award, 95; Getty Mus Visiting Scholar, 99-2000; Studies in Art Educ Leadership, 2000. *Mem:* Nat Art Educ Asn; Int Soc Educ Through Art; Am Educ Res Asn; Los Angeles Co Art Educ; Coun Policy Studies Art Educ. *Publ:* Auth, Research in art education as a form of educational consumer protection Vol 31, No 1, Studies Art Educ, 89; Local Art Knowledge, Australian Art Education, Vol 14, No 3, 22-29, 90; In

the quest for art criticism Equity: A tenative Model Vol 29, No 1, Visual Arts Res, 91; Neo-DBAE in the 90s Vol 10, No 1, J Arts & Learning Res, 92-93; Beyond the public face of policymaking Vol 92, No 3, Arts Educ Policy Rev, 95. *Mailing Add:* Dept Curric & Instr Peabody Hall La State Univ Baton Rouge LA 70803

HAMBRICK, LYNN C See Lukkas, Lynn C

HAMBURGER, SYDNEY K
SCULPTOR, CURATOR
b New York, NY, Feb 2, 35. *Study:* Hood Col, Frederick, Md, 52-54; Frieda Sohn, BMA, 63; Johns Hopkins Univ, Baltimore, Md, 64-65; Studied with Reuben Kramer, Baltimore, Md, 69-77; Towson State Univ, BS(sculpture), 72, MEd(art ed & sculpture), 73; Oxford Univ, Eng, 77. *Hon Degrees:* Hood Col, D, 93. *Work:* Acad Arts, Easton, Md; MacDowell Colony, Peterborough, NH; Borough of Manhattan Community Col, NY; Helen Wurlitzer Found, Taos, NMex; Chesapeake Col, Wye Mills, Md; and other pub & pvt collections. *Exhib:* Solo shows, Washington Co Mus Fine Arts, Hagerstown, Md, 87, Marymount Manhattan Col, NY, 87, Gallery 10, Ltd, Washington, DC, 90 & 98, 14 Sculptors Gallery, NY, 91, Artemisia Gallery, Chicago, 94 & Sculpture Invitational, Acad Arts, Easton, Md, 94, Denise Bibro Fine Art, 99, Chsterwood, Stockbridge, Mass, 2000, Grounds for Sculpture, Hamilton, NJ, 2000; Convergence VIII 95 & Convergence, 98, Roger Williams Park, Providence, RI; Sante Fe Comm Col, NMex, 98; Rio Ojo Caliente Proj, Rio Arriba Co, NMex, 98; Quietude Garden Gallery, E Brunswick, NJ, 98; Pier Walk 98 Maquette Exhib, Wood St Gallery, Chicago, 98; Landscape and Still Life in Medallic Sculpture, Medialia, NY, 98; China at the Crossroads, Inform, NY, 98; plus many others. *Pos:* Cur, Acad Arts, Easton, 82-85. *Teaching:* Grad asst, Towson State Univ, 72-73, adj fac, 73-79; pvt students, sculpture & ceramics, 73-77; instr, Jewish Community Ctr, Baltimore, 74-77 & Manpower Prog, 76-79; adj fac, Essex Community Col, Md, 77-78 & Anne Arundel Community Col, Arnold, Md, 78-81; vis artist, Md Inst Col Art, 86. *Awards:* Resident Fel, Wurlitzer Found, Taos, NMex, 91; Hood Col, Frederick, Md, 93; Outdoor Sculpture Award, Quietude Garden Gallery, E Brunswick, NJ, 94; and others. *Bibliog:* Arlene Raven (auth), Safe Spaces & Ritual Objects. *Mem:* Col Art Asn; Artist Equity Asn; Washington Sculptors Group; Womens Caucus Arts; Philadelphia Sculptors; NY Sculptors Guild. *Media:* Wood, Metal. *Dealer:* Denise Bibro Denise Bibro Fine Art 529 W 20th Street 4th Fl New York NY 10011

HAMER, CHARLES JAMES
PAINTER
b Elmira, NY, Jan 5, 31. *Study:* Rochester Inst Technol, with Ralph Avery & Hans Barschel, BS(art & design), 56. *Work:* Lake St Presby Church, Elmira, NY; also pvt collections. *Exhib:* Salmagundi Club Ann Non-Mem, NY, 79-81; 155th Ann, Nat Acad Design, NY, 80; Nat Arts Club Ann, NY, 80-81; Allied Artists Asn, World Trade Ctr, NY, 81; and others. *Awards:* 1st Prize Watercolor, US Postal Serv, New York, 78; and others. *Mem:* Nat Acad Design; Allied Artists Am Asn. *Media:* Watercolor. *Publ:* Illusr, Newsprint application of Webb offset colour, Penrose Ann, Hasting House, 59. *Mailing Add:* 133 E 35th St New York NY 10016

HAMILL, TIM J
PAINTER, PRINTMAKER
b Clinton, Iowa, Dec 2, 42. *Study:* Univ Wis, 60-62; L'Ecole Nat Superieure Beaux-Arts, Paris, 62-63, Boston Univ Sch Fine Arts, BFA, 65, MFA, 68; Akademie Bildenden Künste, Munich, 65-66. *Work:* Boston Mus Fine Arts, Boston Pub Libr, Mass; DeCordova Mus, Lincoln, Mass; Minn Mus Art, St Paul; Worcester Mus, Mass; and many others. *Comn:* 11 paintings & 2 prints, Royal Palace, Riyadh, Saudi Arabia, 80. *Exhib:* One-man exhibs, Brockton Art Ctr, Mass, 69, Milton Acad, Mass, 71-80 & Gallery Naga, Boston, 78-83 & 85; Boston Printmakers, Rose Art Mus, Waltham, Mass, 70 & 72; DeCordova Mus, Lincoln, Mass, 73, 77, 80 & 82; Photog in Printmaking, Boston Mus Fine Arts, Mass, 75; Artists in Residence, Inst Contemp Art, Boston, 75; Art Complex Mus, Duxbury, Mass, 76-81; and many others. *Pos:* Founding mem, Boston Visual Artists Union, 72-, mem exec bd, 72-75; exec bd, Boston Printmakers; owner & dir, Hamill Gallery African Art, Boston, 90-. *Teaching:* Instr painting & drawing, Boston Univ, 68-71 & Milton Acad, Mass, 71-81. *Mem:* Boston Printmakers. *Media:* Oil, Acrylic; Silkscreen, Lithography

HAMILTON, ANN KATHERINE
SCULPTOR
b Lima, Ohio, June 22, 56. *Study:* St Lawrence Univ, Canton, NY, 74-76; Univ Kans, BFA(textile design), 79; Yale Sch Art, MFA(sculpture), 85. *Hon Degrees:* Honorary Doctorate, RI Sch of Design, 2002. *Work:* Albright-Knox Gallery, Buffalo, NY; Brooklyn Mus of Art, NY; Solomon R Guggenheim Mus, NY; Metropolitan Mus of Art, NY; NY Pub Libr, NY; Whitney Mus of Am Art, NY; Oberlin Col, Ohio. *Comn:* Mess Hall, Headlands Ctr Arts, Sausalito, Calif, 89-90; pub libr, Arts Comn San Francisco, 90-93; Pittsburgh River Front Park, Pittsburgh Cult Trust, 94-; Pub Art on Campus, Univ of Minn, Molecular and Cellular Biology, 2001; Seattle Central Libr, City of Seattle, 2002. *Exhib:* The Earth Never Gets Flat, Whitney Mus Am Art, 87; solo exhibs, Stedelijk van Abbemuseum, Eindhoven, The Neth, 96, Contemp Arts Mus, Houston, 97, Musee d'Art Contemporain de Lyon, France, 97, Musee d'Art Contemporain de Montreal, Canada, 98, Miami Art Mus, Fla, 98, Aldrich Mus Contemp Art, Conn, 98 & Am Pavillion, Venice, Italy, 99, Irish Mus of Modern Art, 2002; Dirt & Domesticity: Construction of the Feminine, Whitney Mus Am Art, 92; Readymade Identities, Mus Mod Art, NY, 93; Outside the Frame: Performance and the Object, Cleveland Ctr Arts, 94; Parts, Manoa Art Gallery, Univ Hawaii, 94; About Place: Recent Art of the Americas, Art Inst Chicago, 95; Longing and Belonging: From the Faraway Nearby, Site Santa Fe, 95; Along the Frontier, State Russ Mus, 96; Jurassic Technologies Reverent, 10th Biennale of Sydney, Australia, 96; Artist Projects, PS1 Contemp Art Ctr, Long Island City, 97; Addressing the Century/100 Yrs of Art & Fashion, Hayward Gallery, London, 98; Art Today, Indianapolis Mus, Ind, 98; Then and Now and Later, Yale Univ Art Gallery, Conn, 98; etrenature, Found Cartier pour l'art contemporain, Paris, France, 98; The Second Look: Poetic Objects and Strategies of Seduction, Apex Art Curatorial Prog, NY, 99; Venice Bienniale, 99; The Picture is Still, Akeda Gallery, Japan, 2001; group exhibs, Self and Soul: The Archit of Intimacy, Asheville Art Mus, NC, 2003, Magic Makers, Des Moines Art Ctr, Iowa, 2003. *Teaching:* Asst prof, Univ Calif, Santa Barbara, 85-91; prof, Ohio State Univ, 2003-. *Awards:* Guggenheim Mem Fel, 89; MacArthur Fel, 93; NEA Visual Arts fel, 93; Larry Alrich Award, Larry Alrich Found, 98. *Bibliog:* Wade Saunders (auth), Making art making artists, Art in Am, 1/93; Faye Hirsch (auth), Art at the limit: Ann Hamilton's recent installations, Sculpture, 7/93; Joan Simon (auth), Temporal crossroads: An interview with Ann Hamilton, Kunst & Mus J, Vol 6, No 6, 95. *Dealer:* Sean Kelly 728 W 29th St New York NY 10011. *Mailing Add:* 64 Smith Pl Columbus OH 43201

HAMILTON, GEORGE EARL
PAINTER, EDUCATOR
b Pittsfield, Mass, Oct 10, 34. *Study:* Int Christian Univ, 56-58; with Dr Samine Tuyoda, Japan, 58-60. *Work:* Frye Art Mus, Seattle; Univ Wash; Kaiser Found & First Nat Bank, Portland, Ore; Royal Bank Can; Ore State Univ. *Exhib:* One-man shows, Am Watercolor Soc, NY, 75 & 76, North Western Watercolor Soc, Seattle, 75-79, Mus Art, Casper, Wyo, 76, Frye Art Mus, Seattle, 76 & 81, Portland Art Mus, 77 & Univ Mus Art, Eugene, Ore, 77-79. *Teaching:* Instr watercolor, Univ Wash, 76- & Univ Idaho, 79-81. *Awards:* Am Watercolor Soc Award, 76; Ore Agriculture Purchase Award; SE Washington Silver Medal; 1st, 2nd, & 3rd prize, Beverly Hills Affaire in Garoew; Award of Excellence, Saratoga Rotorary Show. *Mem:* Ore Watercolor Soc; Northwest Watercolor Soc. *Media:* Watercolor, Collage. *Mailing Add:* 8956 SW 9th Dr Portland OR 97219-4706

HAMILTON, JACQUELINE
CONSULTANT, LECTURER
b Tulsa, Okla, Mar 28, 42. *Study:* Tex Christian Univ, BA; Stockholm Univ, MA equivalent. *Comn:* Galleria III mural and frieze, Hines, Houston. *Collection Arranged:* Staubach Co, Houston; KPMG, Houston; Four Oaks Place, TIAA-CREF, Houston. *Teaching:* lectr creativity and cognition class, Univ Houston. *Bibliog:* Lessons in How to be a Corporate Collector, Art Business News, 85; Corporate Art Brings Elevated Perspective to World of Business, Houston Bus Jour, 3/96; Culture Scouts, Houston Press, 8/99. *Publ:* Monthly contributor to KPMG - Houston Corporate Newsletter, 2000-2001; contrib, What is an Art Consulant?, Fr Am Chamber of Commerce, winter 99-2000. *Mailing Add:* Box 1483 Houston TX 77251-1483

HAMILTON, JUAN
SCULPTOR
b Dallas, Tex, Dec 22, 45. *Study:* City Col New York; New York Univ; Hastings Col, Nebr, BA(art), 68; Claremont Grad Sch, MFA prog. *Work:* Metrop Mus Art, NY; Art Inst Chicago; Albright-Knox Art Gallery, Buffalo, NY; Mus Fine Arts, Mus NMex, Santa Fe; Jacksonville Art Mus, Fla. *Exhib:* Robert Miller Gallery, NY, 78, 81 & 83; Janie C Lee Gallery, Houston, Tex, 80; Janus Gallery, Los Angeles, Calif, 83; Mus NMex, Santa Fe, 83. *Collection Arranged:* Georgia O'Keeffe: A Portrait by Alfred Stieglitz (coauth, catalog), Metrop Mus Art, New York, 78; Alfred Stieglitz (coauth, catalog), Nat Gallery Art, Washington, DC, 83. *Awards:* Am Bk Award for Alfred Steiglitz: Photographs and Writings. *Bibliog:* Barbara Rose (auth), The Sculpture of Juan Hamilton, Arts Mag, 79; Robert Knafo (auth), Juan Hamilton at Robert Miller, Art in Am, 81; Barnaby Conrad III (auth), Rising stars, Horizon Mag, 82. *Mailing Add:* PO Box 70 Abiquiu NM 87510

HAMILTON, PATRICIA ROSE
DEALER
b Upper Darby, Pa, Oct 21, 48. *Study:* Temple Univ, BA, 70; Rutgers Univ, MA(art hist), 71. *Hon Degrees:* Harvard Bus Sch, 80. *Exhib:* Baldwin Gallery, Aspen; Nova Haine Gallery, NYC. *Collection Arranged:* Ten Americans, Masters of Watercolor (with catalogue), 74, Edward Hicks, A Gentle Spirit (with catalogue), 75 & Malta: A Totemic World, 75, Andrew Crispo Gallery; Outdoor Sculpture 1974 (with catalogue), Merriewold West Gallery, Far Hills, NJ, 74; Silver and Gold, Baldrun Gallery, Aspen, Colo, 00; Bronze Hamilton Galleyr, 82. *Pos:* Curatorial asst, Whitney Mus Am Art, NY, 71-73; sr ed, Art in Am, NY, 73-74; cur exhibs, Andrew Crispo Gallery, NY, 74-75; dir, Hamilton Gallery Contemp Art, 77-84, artist agent, 84-90; private dealer, 1990-. *Awards:* Honory degree, bus. *Bibliog:* Laura de Coppet & Alan Janes (auth), The Art Dealers, Clarkson N Potter Books, 84; David France (auth), Bag of Toys, Warner Books, 92; Eleanor Munro (auth), Art Table Changing the Equation, Art Table, 2005. *Mem:* ArTable, New York & Los Angeles (found mem, chap chair, So Calif), 2003-05. *Specialty:* 20th century art. *Interests:* Tennis, music, cooking. *Mailing Add:* 6753 Milner Rd Los Angeles CA 90068

HAMILTON, W PAUL C
EDUCATOR, HISTORIAN
b Toronto, Ont, Mar 13, 38. *Study:* Williams Col, BA, 59; Univ Toronto, MA, 64; Johns Hopkins Univ, PhD(Fel), 73. *Pos:* Coordr educ English, Educ Serv, Nat Gallery Can, Ottawa, 73-76. *Teaching:* Asst prof, Univ Sask, Saskatoon, 70-78, assoc prof, 78-84, head dept, 81-84, prof, 85-. *Awards:* Grant, Italian Govt, 65-66; Can Coun Doctoral Fel, 68-69; Soc Sci & Humanities Res Coun Can Grant, 87-89. *Publ:* Auth, Andrea del Minga's Assunta in S Felicita, Kunsthistorisches Inst, 70; coauth, Grandmaison, Henderson, Kenderdine, Univ Sask, 79; auth, Disegni di Bernardino Poccetti, Olschki, 80; The Palazzo dei Camerlenghi in Venice, J Soc Archit Historians, 83. *Mailing Add:* Dept Art & Art Hist Univ Sask 3 Campus Dr Saskatoon SK S7N 5A4 Canada

HAMLET, SUSAN H
EDUCATOR, JEWELER
b Evanston, Ill, 54. *Study:* Mount Holyoke Col, BA, 76; Sch Am Craftsmen, Rochester Inst Technol, MFA, 78. *Work:* AT&T Dallas; Ark Art Ctr, Little Rock; Mus Mod Art, Kyoto, Japan; State Arts Collection, Okla; Bank One Ctr, Cleveland, Ohio. *Exhib:* One-person shows, Helen Drutt Gallery, Philadelphia, 83-85, Fergus-Jean Gallery, Columbus, Ohio, 87; Craft Today USA, Paris, France, 89; Silver: New Forms & Expressions, Fortunoff, NY, 89 & 91; Jewelries/Epiphanies, Boston, Mass, 91; On Scale, Bennett Siegel Gallery, NY, 92; Jewelry From the Permanent Collection, Am Craft Mus, NY, 95; Nat Ornamental Metal Mus, Memphis, Tenn, 97; 50 Yrs of Studio Jewelry, Mobilia Gallery, Cambridge, Mass, 99; Attitude and Action: North Am Figurative Jewelry, Univ of Ctrl Eng, then to Dublin, Ireland, 2000. *Teaching:* Vis asst prof art, Okla State Univ, 79-80, asst prof, 81-86, assoc prof, 87-88; assoc prof metals, Swain Sch Design, 86-87; asst prof design, Southeastern Mass Univ, 88-92; assoc prof design, Univ Mass, Dartmouth, 92. *Awards:* Nat Endowment Arts, 79 & 88; Oreg Col of Art &B Craft Residency, 2000. *Mem:* Soc NAm Goldsmiths. *Mailing Add:* 34 Buttonwood St New Bedford MA 02740

HAMLETT, DALE EDWARD
PAINTER, EDUCATOR
b Memphis, Mo, Aug 15, 21. *Study:* Northeast Mo State Univ, BS(cum laude), 44; Am Acad Art, with William Mosby; Acad Appl Art, Chicago; Chicago Art Inst, with Charles Wilamoski; Univ NMex, with Ralph Douglass & Elaine de Kooning, MA (painting), 63; also with Robert Wood, Millard Sheets, George Post, Edgar Whitney, Morris Shubin, Charles Reid & Milford Zornes; studied with Getz, Robert Landry, Gerald Brommer, Frank Webb & Don Andrews. *Hon Degrees:* Distinguished Prof Art 2000. *Work:* Univ NMex; State Fair Mus, Albuquerque; NMex Inst Mining & Technol; Eastern NMex Univ; Geronimo Mus, NMex. *Comn:* Drawings of 18 founders of Sigma Tau Gamma, Warrensburg, Mo, 71; portrait for Omar Naimi, Portales, NMex, 88; protrait, comn by for Dr Edward L Miller, Portales NMex, 90; portraits for Jon Mullen & Richard Kilmer, 2006. *Exhib:* Gran Premio della Citta Eterna Palazzo delle Esposizioni, Rome, Italy, 73; 14th Ann Artists Salon, Nat Show, Okla Mus Art, Oklahoma City, 75; Tucson Mus Art, 77; Sun Carnival, El Paso Mus Art, Tex, 80; Western Fedn Watercolor Soc, San Diego, Calif, 90 & Houston, Tex, 95; exhib, Lubbock, Tex, 98, Albuquerque, NMex, 99, Houston, Tex, 99; Lubbock, Tex, 2005; Macy Ctr, Socorro, NMex, 2006. *Collection Arranged:* Clovis Community College, Clovis, NMex, 2004; Eastern NMex Univ, 2004. *Pos:* Package designer, Montgomery Ward & Co, Chicago, Ill, 47-51; commercial artist, Ward Hicks Advert Agency, Albuquerque, NMex, 51-64; artist-in-residence, NMex Inst Mining & Technol, Socorro, NMex, 64-69. *Teaching:* Instr art, NMex Inst Mining & Technol, 65-69, teaching drawing, painting, figure study & art hist; prof art, Eastern NMex Univ, Portales, 69-87, teaching painting, figure drawing, drawing, color & design. *Awards:* First in Watercolor, Int Exhib Painting, Val de Isere, France, 72; Second Award in Watercolor, Panama City Art Asn, Nat Show, Fla, 79; Purchase Prize, Cent States Exposition, Pratt, Kans, 80; Best of Show, Black Canyon Painters, Hotchkiss, Colo, 80; Best of Show Watercolor, Mus SW, Nat Show, Midland, Tex, 85; Award, 2nd NMex Watercolor Soc Show; First in Watercolor, 14th Ann Nat, La Junta, Colo, 82. *Bibliog:* Three Artists/Three Styles (painting demonstrations), KENW Educational Television, 84; Jean Burrough's (auth), article in one-man show, Portales News Tribune Newspaper, 12/84; Clovis News Jour, 2003. *Mem:* Signature mem NMex Watercolor Soc; NMex Art League; signature mem Western Fedn Soc; La Escalara Art Guild; Llano Estacado Art Asn; West Tex Watercolor Soc; and others. *Media:* Watercolor, Gouache. *Res:* Compiling information for a book amplifying upon the 140 points of interest on a 1909 map of Portales, NMex. *Specialty:* Watercolor, Hamlett Gallery. *Interests:* Painting watercolor (plein air) travel; Photog. *Collection:* Dale/Ware, Forrest Walker, Wayne Stratton, Jon Mullen, Richard Kilmer & David Cacy. *Publ:* Illusr, City of Portales-1909 Map, Roosevelt Co Hist Soc, NMex, 96. *Dealer:* Gallery 15 1500 Pile Clovis NMex. *Mailing Add:* 2104 S Ave H Portales NM 88130

HAMLIN, LOUISE
PAINTER, PRINTMAKER
b Litchfield, Conn, June 26, 49. *Study:* Univ Pa, BFA, 72; NY Studio Sch. *Work:* Walker Art Ctr; Univ Iowa; Swarthmore Col; Wellington Mgmt Co; Metro Transit Auth. *Exhib:* One-woman shows, Blue Mt Gallery, NY, 84, 86, 89 & 92; Carleton Col, 94; Blue Mass Gallery, 95; plus many others. *Teaching:* Assoc prof, Dartmouth Col, 90. *Awards:* Djerassi Found Residency Award, 88; Mellon Found Res Grant, 93; Vt Coun Arts Fel Award, 94. *Bibliog:* Greg Masters (auth), Louise Hamlin, Arts, summer 85; Painting on Location, American Artists, 10/88; Eric Holzman (auth), Louise Hamlin, Cover, 1/90. *Media:* Oil, Pastel; Etching, Monoprint. *Publ:* Auth of art reviews in Arts, 9/82, 3/85, 5/85, cover, 2/87, M/E/A/N/I/N/G, 5/89; Bringing the Baby, 15 Poems by various poets, Coffee House Press, Minneapolis. *Dealer:* Blue Mountain Gallery 121 Worcester St New York NY 10012. *Mailing Add:* Dept Studio Art Dartmouth Col Hinman Box 6081 Hanover NH 03755

HAMMER, ALFRED EMIL
PAINTER, EDUCATOR
b New Haven, Conn, Jan 11, 25. *Study:* RI Sch Design, BFA; Yale Univ, BFA & MFA; and with John R Frazier, Josef Albers, Willem DeKooning, Stuart Davis, Abraham Rattner, Alvin Lustig & John Howard Benson. *Work:* Aetna Insurance Corp, Conn; Agnes Gund Collection; govt Conn; Portland Art Mus; govt Manitoba, Can; Otis Elevator Corp, Conn; Risch Design Mus. *Exhib:* Boston Art Festival, Mass, 58; Newport Ann, RI, 59; Four Americans, La State Univ, 62; one-man shows, Melnychenko Gallery, Winnipeg, 80, Univ Man, Winnipeg, 80 & Greene Gallery, Conn, 84 & Univ Hartford, 92; and others. *Pos:* Mem bd dir, Hartford Arts Coun, 82-86. *Teaching:* Painting, drawing, design & calligraphy, RI Sch Design, 53-69, chmn div grad studies, 63-65; vis prof painting, Minneapolis Col Art, 67; Dean, Cleveland Inst Arts, 69-74; vis lectr design & painting, Case Western Reserve Univ, 70; dir & prof sch art, Univ Man, 74-81; dir, Pac Northwest Col Art, 81; dean & prof, Hartford Art Sch, Univ Hartford, 82-86. *Awards:* Wintonbury Art League Open, Watercolor, 87; Conn Watercolor Soc Award, 96; Watercolor Award, New Britian Mus Am Art, 98. *Media:* Oil, Watercolor. *Publ:* Auth, Prize Winning Painting Allied Pub, 60. *Dealer:* Greene Gallery Guilford Conn. *Mailing Add:* 55 Bolton St Hartford CT 06114-2606

HAMMER, ELIZABETH B
PAINTER, ASSEMBLAGE ARTIST
b Washington, DC. *Study:* Univ Kans, Lawrence; Nat Art Sch, Washington, DC; Univ Md, Col Park, BA (summa cum laude). *Work:* Am Album Vol II, Nat Mus Women Arts, Washington, DC. *Exhib:* Black Mountain Col, NY, 87; Nat Mus Women Arts, Wash, DC, 91; Montgomery Col, Rockville, Md, 91; NVCC, Fairfax, Va, 92 & 93; Paris, Deauville & Avignon, France; and others. *Pos:* Illustr & ed, US Govt, formerly; editor, Embassy News, Paris, formerly. *Teaching:* Instr art, Rabat Am Sch, Morocco. *Awards:* Phi Kappa Phi Art Award, 81; Finalist, 34th Grand Prix Int de Deauville, France, 83; Art Citation, Montgomery Co Delegate, 86; Diplome Official, Deauville, Avignon. *Bibliog:* Annuaire National Des Beaux-Arts, 91-92. *Mem:* Past Societaire, Salon des Artistes Independants, Paris; Nat Gavel Soc; Nat Hon Soc. *Media:* Acrylic. *Res:* Hist of Am Art Schs; Hist of Fr Art. *Mailing Add:* 2238 Rockingham Loop College Station TX 77845-4854

HAMMERBECK, WANDA LEE
PHOTOGRAPHER
b Lincoln, Nebr, Mar 24, 45. *Study:* Univ NC, Chapel Hill, BA, 67, MA, 71; San Francisco Art Inst, MFA, 77; Yale Univ, post grad. *Work:* Mus Mod Art, NY; Fogg Mus, Harvard Univ, Cambridge, Mass; Houston Mus Fine Arts; San Francisco Mus Mod Art; Oakland Mus; numerous pub & pvt collections. *Exhib:* Object Illusion & Reality, Calif State Univ, Fullerton, 79; Images Considered, Visual Studies Workshop, Rochester, NY, 80; In Color, Ten California Photographers, Oakland Mus, Calif, 83; Cleveland Inst Art, Ohio, 85; Western Space, Burden Gallery, NY, 85; Pomona Art Mus; Mus fotografi, Norway, 2003; Solo exhibs, San Francisco Mus Mod Art, 78, OK Harris, NY, 79, Schienbaum & Russek Gallery, Santa Fe, 86, Etherton Gallery, Tucson, 86, Fuller Art Mus, 2000; Palm Springs Mus, Calif, 2005; Autry Mus, 2006. *Teaching:* Lectr photog & issues in art; guest lectr Mills Col, 1985, Art Ctr, Col Design, Pasadena, 1992 & 1994. *Awards:* Nat Endowment Arts Photogr Fels, 79 & 80 & Serv to Field Award, 80; Guest artist, Ansel Adams Workshops, 86; Tiffany Fel; Haynes Fel, Huntington Libr, 2002. *Bibliog:* Article, Untitled, Friends of Photog; Aperature, Vol 150, Winter 98. *Mem:* Soc for Photog Educ; Friends of Photog. *Media:* Photography. *Res:* Haynes Fel, Huntington Library, Pasadena, CA. *Publ:* Contribr, Problematic Photography, 80, NFS Press; A River too Far, Univ Nev Press, 91; Arid Waters, Univ Nev Press, 92; Nature through her Eyes: Art & Literature by Women, Nature Co, 94; The Altered Landscape, 99; Aperture, vol 150

HAMMERMAN, PAT JO
PAINTER, PRINTMAKER
b New York, NY, Oct 15, 1952. *Study:* Queens Col, BA, 75; Hunter Col, MA, 78. *Work:* Grand Rapids Mus, Mich; Brooklyn Mus; Lockhaven Art Ctr, Orlando, Fla; Amarillo Art Ctr, Tex; Firehouse Gallery, Nassau Community Col, NY; Queens Mus, NY; Guild Hall Mus, East Hampton, NY; Publisher's Clearing House; Pannei Kerr Foster Internat; Peachtree Hotel, Atlanta, Ga; Mitsui Bank LA; Lockhaven Mus, Orlando, Fla; Coldwell Banker, NY. *Comn:* Mural, Queensborough Community Col, 70; three-panel mural, Panell, Kerr, Foster, NY, 83; Deloitte, Haskins & Sells, Princeton, NJ, 87; Four Seasons Hotel, Newport, Calif, 87; Bankers Trust, NY, 88; Orlando Magic Basketball Team Hdqrs; Hyatt Regency Hotel, Chicago. *Exhib:* Print Biennial, Brooklyn Mus, 81; Handmade Paper Books, Am Craft Mus, NY, 82; Int Impact, Kyoto Munic Mus, Japan, 82; New Am Graphics, Alaska State Mus, Juneau, 83; Queens Mus, Flushing, NY, 85; Am Prints, Cairo Mus, Egypt, 85; and others; Flushing Town Hall, NY. *Pos:* Pres, 10-20 Artspace, currently; pres, Realart Corp, currently. *Teaching:* Asst prof fine art, Queensborough Community Col, 80-. *Awards:* First Prizes, Firehouse Gallery, Nassau Community Col, 79, 26th Ann, Parrish Mus, 79. *Bibliog:* John Fremont (auth), Paperworks, Am Craft Mag, 8/82; Ronnie Cohen (auth), Papermaking, Art News, 10/83; Ronnie Cohen (auth), New editions, Art News, 10/84; Helen Harrison (auth), Paper: medium with a message, New York Times, 3/27/88. *Mem:* Col Art Asn; Manhattan Graphic Soc; Conn Graphic Art Soc. *Media:* Oil; All Media, etching, printing ink. *Res:* Etching; Acrylic, Oil. *Collection:* African art, German stamps, Zepplin postcards. *Dealer:* John Szoke 164 Mercer St New York NY 10012; Peter Rose Gallery 200 E 57th St New York City NY. *Mailing Add:* 20724 27th Ave Flushing NY 11360

HAMMERSLEY, FREDERICK
PAINTER
b Salt Lake City, Utah, Jan 5, 19. *Study:* Univ Idaho Southern Br, Pocatello, 36-38; Chouinard Art Sch, Los Angeles, 40-42 & 46-47; Ecole des Beaux Arts, Paris, France, 45; Jepson Art Inst, Los Angeles, 47-50. *Work:* Los Angeles Co Mus Art & La Jolla Art Mus; Butler Inst Am Art, Youngstown, Ohio; Corcoran Gallery Art; San Francisco Mus Mod Art; Oakland Art Mus, Calif; Univ Art Mus, Berkely, Calif; Univ Nebr, Lincoln; Univ NMex, Albuquerque; Mus NMex Albuquerque; Mus Fine Art, Santa Fe, NMex; Washington Post, Petersburg Press, London, Eng, US Navy. *Exhib:* Geometric Abstraction Am, Whitney Mus Am Art, NY, 62 & Snyder Fine Art, NY, 97; Responsive Eye, Mus Mod Art, NY, 65; One-man shows, Univ NMex, Albuquerque, 69 & 75, LA Louver Gallery, Venice, Calif, 78 & 81, Modernism Gallery, San Francisco, 87, 90 & 95 & Modernism, San Francisco, 95, LA Louver, Venice, Calif, 99 & 2002, TBA Exhib Space, Chicago, Ill, Richard Levy Gallery, Albuquerque,

NMex, Gary Snyder Fine Art, N, 2001, and many others; Drawings & Paintings, Then & Now, Owings-Dewey Fine Art, Santa Fe, NMex, 92; Computer Drawings & Prints, Richard Levy Gallery, 93; 4 Abstract Classicists, Modernism, San Francisco, Calif, 93; Lyric Geometry, Mulvane Art Mus, Washburn Univ, Topeka, Kans, 93; Still Working Underknown Artists in the Age of Am (65 & older), Corcoran Gallery Art, Washington, DC, 94, Chicago Cult Ctr, Ill, 94, New, Sch Social Res, NY, 94, Virginia Beach Ctr Arts, Va, 95, Fisher Gallery, Univ Southern Calif, Los Angeles, 95, Portland Art Mus, Ore, 96; Taos, Albuquerque, Santa Fe, Cedar Rapids Mus Art, Iowa, 98; Beau Monde: Toward a Redeemed Cosmopolitanism, curated by Dave Hickey, Site Santa Fe 4th Int Biennial, NMex, 2001; Chouinard: A Living Legacy, Krglak Gallery, Oceanside, Calif, Boehm Gallery, San Marcos, Calif, Oceanside Mus Art, Oceanside, Calif, 2001; group exhibs, Smithsonain Inst, alker Art Center, Dallas Mus Art, San Francisco Mus Mod Art, Houston Mus Art, and many others; and many others. *Pos:* Guest artist, Tamarind Inst, Albuquerque, NMex, 73, 88 & 91. *Teaching:* Instr, Jepson Art Sch, Los Angeles, 48-51; lectr painting, drawing & design, Pomona Col, 53-62; instr, Pasadena Art Mus, 56-61; instr painting, drawing & design, Chouinard Art Inst, 64-68; vis assoc prof painting & drawing, Univ NMex, 68-71. *Awards:* Purchase Awards for Painting, Butler Inst Am Art, 61 & Los Angeles All City Ann, 64-66; Guggenheim Fel Painting, 73-74; Nat Endowment Arts Award Painting, 75 & 77; Guest Artist, Tamarind Inst, Albuquerque, NMex, 88 & 91; NMex's Gov's Award for Excellence in the Arts, 2005. *Bibliog:* Jules Langsner (auth), Four abstract classicists, Los Angeles Co Mus Art, 59; Lawrence Alloway (auth), West Coast hard edge, Inst Contemp Art, London, 60; Michel Seuphor (auth), Abstract Painting, Abrams, 62; Sandy Ballatore (auth), The personal abstract language of Frederick Hammersley, Artspace, 11-12/89; Kathleen Shields (auth), Paintings from left field, Art in Am, 1/91; Jon Carver (auth), Organically Grown, The Magazine, 8/2001; and several others. *Media:* Oil. *Specialty:* modern art. *Interests:* painting, drawing, photography. *Publ:* Contribr, Classicism or hard-edge?, 60 & Los Angeles letter, 2/61, Art Int; auth, My first experience with computer drawings, 10/69 & My geometrical paintings, 4/70, Leonardo Mag; contribr & illus, Visual Art, Mathematics and Computers, Pergamon Press, 79; and several others. *Dealer:* Snyder Fine Arts 20 W 57th St New York NY 10019; La Louver Inc 45 N Venice Blvd, Venice, Calif, 90291; Richard Levy Gallery, 514 Central Ave SW, Albuquerque, 87102; Charlotte Jackson Fine Art 200 W Marcy St Ste 101 Santa Fe NMex 87501. *Mailing Add:* 608 Carlisle SE Albuquerque NM 87106

HAMMETT, POLLY HORTON
PAINTER, INSTRUCTOR

b Oklahoma City, Okla, Jan 31, 35. *Study:* Univ Okla, 48-50; Union Col, BA, 78; study with Richard V Goetz & Eugene Bavinger. *Work:* Albuquerque Mus Art; Houston Neurosensory Ctr; Women's Hosp-Houston; Houston Power & Lighting; Methodist Hosp, Houston, Tex; Hill Country Arts Found, Tex; Kerr Mus, Okla; II Houston Ctr, Tex; Hutchins Sealy Nat Bank, Galveston, Tex. *Exhib:* Am Watercolor Soc Ann, Nat Acad Galleries, 76, 77, 80 & 82; Watercolor, Southwest Two, Tucson Mus Art, 76 & 82; Nat Watercolor Soc 56th Ann, Laguna Beach Mus Art, Calif, 76; two-artist exhib, Foothills Art Ctr, Colo, 74-76; Western Fed Watercolor Socs, 81; Nat & Am Watercolor Soc Traveling Exhib, 82; Tweed Mus; Frye Mus; Univ Wisc; Williamette Univ; Stetson Univ; Foothills Art Ctr, Golden, Colo. *Pos:* Dir educ, Art League Houston, Tex, 86-88; gallery dir, Nine Fine Artisans, 79-82. *Teaching:* Lectr & instr watercolor sem, Okla Arts Coun, 73; instr painting workshops, Colo, Okla, Tex, Calif, Ark, Ariz, SC, NMex, NC, Utah, Va, La, Ga & Wash; Tex Inst Child Psychiat, Houston, 74 & 75 & Houston Univ, Sch Continuing Educ Drug Abuse Prog, 76-77; instr, Art League Houston 80-90 & Hill Country Arts Found, 83-84. *Awards:* Mus Purchase Award & Merit Award Watercolor, Southwest One, Albuquerque Art Mus, 76; First Award, Southwestern Watercolor Soc, Dallas, Tex, 81; Clara Stroud Mem Award, 127th Int Exhib, Am Watercolor Soc, 94. *Bibliog:* Lynn Haggard (auth), Artist's paintings test limits, Times Record News; Mimi Crossley (auth), Houston Post. *Mem:* Nat Watercolor Soc; Am Art Therapist Asn; Am Watercolor Soc; Art League Houston; Women's Caucus Art. *Media:* Mixed Water Media; Collage, Monoprint. *Publ:* Watercolor, SW Art, 94. *Mailing Add:* 375 N Post Oak Ln Houston TX 77024-5903

HAMMOCK, VIRGIL GENE
CRITIC, PAINTER

b Long Beach, Calif, Aug 5, 38; Can citizen. *Study:* San Francisco Art Inst, BFA, 65, with James Weeks; Ind Univ, MFA, 67, with James McGarrell. *Work:* Ind Univ, Bloomington; Univ Alta, Edmonton; Art Bank Collection, Can Coun, Ottawa, Ont; Univ Man, Winnipeg; Mt Allison Univ, Sackville; and others. *Exhib:* 84th Ann, San Francisco Mus Art, Calif, 65; Young Alta Painters, Alta Col Art, Calgary, 68; West-71, Edmonton Art Gallery, 71; one-man shows, Owens Art Gallery, Sackville, NB, 73 & Drawings, Dalhousie Art Gallery, Halifax, NS, 77; Olympic Exhib, Montreal, 75; two one-man shows, Struts Gallery, Sackville, NB, 85 & 87. *Pos:* Dir exhibs, Univ Alta, 68-70 & Univ Man 70-73; actg dir, Owens Art Gallery, Mt Allison Univ, 88-89; vchmn, NB Arts Bd, 97-. *Teaching:* Instr design & drawing, Univ Alta, Edmonton, 67-68, asst prof drawing & art hist, 68-70, assoc prof art criticism, Univ Man, Winnipeg, 70-75; prof fine art & head, Dept Fine Art, Mt Allison Univ, 75-93 & 93-99, prof fine art, 99-; adjudication comt, Can-US Fulbright Comt, 94-97. *Awards:* Phelan Award, Trustees James D Phelan Awards Lit & Art, 65. *Bibliog:* Cameron (auth), Virgil Hammock, la Nostalgie du Romantisme, Vie des Arts, summer 78; B Sanderson (auth), Virgil Hammock: Studio pictures, Arts Atlantic 31, spring/summer 88. *Media:* Oil, Pencil. *Res:* Contemporary Canadian painting. *Publ:* Contribr, An art critic visits the Soviet Union, Arts Atlantic 37, spring/summer 90; Juan Kiti, Epid Lier, 55-61, 95; Cesar Baillcux, 73 95, 69 & Guy van der Bulcke, 51-61, 97, Roularta Art Bks; Christian Silvain, Lannoo, Tielt, Belg, 223-239, 97; Paul Smolders (ed, Marcel von Jole), pp 50-60, Nu Blonde Sa, Wommelgem, Belg, 94; The 49th parallel: An opinion, No 28, Artpost, spring 88; Critical word about critical words about art, Arts Atlantic, No 35, fall 89; Take me out to the ballgame: Michael Snow's the audience, Art Post, 35-36, winter/spring 90. *Dealer:* Fog Forrest Gallery Sackville NB Can. *Mailing Add:* Fine Arts Dept Mt Allison Univ 53 York St Sackville NB E4L 1C9 Canada

HAMMOND, GALE THOMAS
PRINTMAKER, EDUCATOR

b Lumberton, NC, Sept 27, 39. *Study:* Chicago Acad Fine Arts, com art dipl; ECarolina Univ, 62-64, BS & MAEd; Univ NC, Greensboro; Atelier 17, Paris, with S W Hayter, 77. *Work:* Italian Embassy, Washington, DC; NC Mus Art, Raleigh; Del Mar Col, Corpus Christi; Univ NC Sch Pub Health, Chapel Hill; Frans Masereel Ctr, Belg; Metrop Mus Art. *Exhib:* Colorprint USA, Lubbock, Tex, 71-75; Boston Printmakers, Mass, 72-2006; Budapest Hungary Cartoon Festival, 90; Trento, Italy Humor Exhib, 92; Obra Grafica, Oviedes, Spain, 94 & 96; Int Cartoon Festival, Kyoto, Japan, 2000-05; Print Consotium, MO, 2005. *Pos:* Mem, SC Governors Award Prog, The Penland Sch. *Teaching:* Drawing & printmaking, Univ Ga, Athens, 70-; Western Carolina, Greensboro Col; prof emeritus, Univ Ga; instr, Univ Ga Cortona studies abroad & Avignon, France studies abroad. *Awards:* Etching Award, Southeastern Ctr Contem Art, NC, 68; Drawing Award, Ga Arts Comn, Atlanta, 71; Etching Award, Southeastern Printmakers; Sea Grant, Ossabaw Island Proj. *Mem:* Print Consortium; Boston Printmakers. *Media:* Etching, Multimedia, Watercolor. *Mailing Add:* 195 Gibbons Way Athens GA 30605

HAMMOND, HARMONY
PAINTER, SCULPTOR, CURATOR, WRITER

b Chicago, Ill, Feb 8, 44. *Study:* Univ Minn, BA, 67. *Work:* Chicago Art Inst, Chicago, Ill; Brooklyn Mus, NY; Wadsworth Atheneum, Hartford, Conn; Gen Mills Corp, Minn; Metrop Mus Art, Brooklyn Mus Art, NY; Walker Art Ctr; Denver Art Mus; Mus Fine Arts, Santa Fe, NMex; Phoenix Art Mus; Philip Morris Co, NY; Nat Mus Women in the Arts, Washington. *Comn:* Rendez-vous, Int Sculpture, Que, Can. *Exhib:* The Am Artist as Printmaker, Brooklyn Mus, 83; One-person shows, Wadsworth Atheneum, Hartford, Conn, 84, Jonson Gallery, Mus Univ, NMex, Albuquerque, 87, Trabia Macafee Gallery, NY, 88, Linda Durham Gallery, Santa Fe, NMex, 88, Etherton Stern Gallery, Tucson, 89 & 94, Ctr Contemp Art, Santa Fe, NMex, 92, Tucson Mus Art, 93, Univ Tex, El Paso, 95 Linda Durham, Santa Fe, 98, Joseph Gross Gallery, Tucson, 99, Joyce Goldstein Gallery, NY, 99; Sexual Politics, Hammer Mus, Univ Calif, Los Angeles, 96; Division of Labor: Womens Work in Contemp Art, Bronx Mus, NY & Los Angeles Co Mus, 95; In a Different Light, Mus Univ Calif, Berkeley, 95; 25 Yrs of Feminism, 25 Yrs of Women's Art, Douglass Col, Rutgers Univ, 96; Material Girls, Gallery 128, NY, 97; Troubling Customs, Ontario Col Art & Design & Boston Mus Sch, 98; Lost & Found, Smack Mellon, Brooklyn, 98; Out West, Plan & Evolving Arts, Santa Fe, 99; High Times, Hard Times: NY Painting 1965-75, Am Univ Mus, Washington, DC, 2006-07. *Teaching:* Visiting artist & lectr many places; prof, Univ Ariz, Tucson, 88-. *Awards:* Nat Endowment Arts, 79-80 & 83-84; John S Guggenheim Mem Found Fel, 91; Pollock Krasner Fel, 89-90; Rockefeller Found Ballagio Study Ctr Grant, 94; Adolph & Esther Gotlieb Found Fel, 95; Art Matters Fel, 96; Joan Mitchell Found Grant, 98; Andrea Frank Found Grant, 2000; Can Literary Award for Excellence, 2000. *Bibliog:* Lucy Lipard (auth), The Pink Glass Swan, New Press, 95; Laura Cottingham (auth), Sexual Politics, Univ Calif, Los Angeles, 96; Art J, winter 97; Women and Art: Contested Territory, Avery Press, 99; Passionate Pictures, James Saslow (auth), Viking Press, 99; Out West, Hammond, Plan B, 99; Malin Wilson-Powell (auth), Wounds that Never Heal, essay, 99; Paul Ivey (auth), The Meeting of Equals, Goldstein Gallery, 99; Robert Atkins (auth), Art in America, 2001. *Mem:* Col Art Asn; Gay & Lesbian Caucus Art; Int Asn Art Critics; Nat Writers Union. *Media:* Oil, Acrylic; Mixed Media. *Res:* Women, feminism, lesbian/gay/bisexual/queer art. *Publ:* Auth, A Space of Infinite & Pleasureable Possibilities: Lesbian Self-Representation in Contemp Art (Joanna Frueh, Cassandra Langer, Arlene Raven, Harper Collins eds), Feminist Art Criticism, 93; Voicing Todays Visions (Mara Witzling, ed), Universe Publ, 94; Against Cultural Erasure, Art Papers, 94; A Lesbian Show, In A Different Light, Dutton, 2/95; Reminiscences, Sniper's Nest: Art That Was Lived with Lug Lippard, Bard Col, 95; Art History, Art Jour, Winter 96; The Ups & Downs of Site Santa Fe, Sculpture Mag, Feb 96; Meetings with Agnes Martin, Agnes Martin: Works on Paper, Mus Fin Arts, Santa Fe, 98; Feminist Aract Art - A Political Viewpoint, Modern Art in the USA: Issues & Controversies of the 20th Century, Prentice Hall, 2000; Lesbian Art in America: A Contemporary History, Rizzoli, 2000

HAMMOND, JANE
PRINTMAKER, PAINTER

b Bridgeport, Conn, 1950. *Study:* Mt Holyoke Col, BA, 72; Ariz State Univ, 73-74; Univ Wis, Madison, MFA, 77. *Work:* Albright-Knox Art Gallery; Bibliotiec Nationale, Paris, France; Mus Arte Contemporaneo, Mexico City, Mexico; Mus Fine Arts, Boston; NY Pub Libr; Mus Mod Art, NY; Whitney Mus Am Art, NY; Art Inst Chicago; San Francisco Mus Mod Art; Met Mus Art; Mus Contemp Art, Chicago; Detroit Inst of Arts. *Exhib:* Invitational, Stux Gallery, NY, 87; solo exhibs, Nina Freudheim Gallery, Buffalo, NY, 87, Exit Art, NY, 89, Wetterling, Goteborg, Sweden, 90 & Cincinnati Art Mus, 93, Greg Kucera Gallery, Seattle, Wash, 2000, Galerie LeLong, NY, 2001, The Cleveland Ctr for Contemp Art, Ohio, 2001, traveling to Lemberg Gallery, Mich, 2001, Whitney Mus at Philip Morris, NY, 2002, Gallery at Dieu Donne Papermill, Inc, NY, 2002, Lemberg Gallery, Mich, 2003; Brooklyn Mus, NY, 89; Nat Art Libr, Victoria & Albert Mus, London, Eng, 80; Milwaukee Art Mus, Wis & traveling, 90; Zolla-Lieberman Gallery, Chicago, 90; Feigenson-Preston, Detroit, 91; fiction/non-fiction, NY, 91-93; Wetterling Gallery, Stockholm, 92; Transepoca Gallery, Milan, 92; Galerie Barbara Farber/Jurka, Amsterdam, The Neth, 98; Galeria Senda, Barcelona, Spain, 99; Greg Kucera Gallery, Seattle, 2000; Galerie

Lelong, NY, 2001; Cleveland Ctr for Contemp Art, 2001. *Teaching:* Md Inst Col Art, 80-90. *Awards:* Nat Endowment Arts, 89; Louis Comfort Tiffany Award, 89; Nat Endowment, Tiffany; CAPS, NY Found Arts. *Bibliog:* Elizabeth Hess (auth), Fly on the Wall, Village Voice, 2/90; Terry R Myers (auth), Review, Flash Art, summer 90; Ellen Handy (auth), The Pearls and the String, Jane Hammonds, Arts Mag, 47-51, 9/90; Judith Stein (auth), The Painted Word, Art in Am, 5/95; and others; Sue Scott (auth), Selective Visions, Art & Antiques, 11/95; William Corbett (auth), Queen Jane Approximately, Modern Painters, Summer 98. *Dealer:* Galerie Lelong 20 W 57th St 5th flr New York NY 10019. *Mailing Add:* 75 Grand St Apt 4E New York NY 10013

HAMMOND, LESLIE KING
HISTORIAN, WRITER
b Bronx, NY, Aug 4, 44. *Study:* Queens Col, with Louis Finkelstein, Herb Aach, Paul Frazer, Marvin Belick & Harold Bruder, BA, 69; Johns Hopkins Univ, MA, 73, PhD, 75. *Collection Arranged:* 3400 on State, Baltimore Mus Art, 73; Baltimore Black Arts Calendar Retrospect, 1973-1978, Morris Mechanic Gallery, 78; Montage of Dreams Deferred (auth, catalog), Baltimore Mus Art, 79-80; Three Episodes in Black American Art, Harmon Found, Bronx & Queens Mus, 80; Celebrations: Myth & Ritual in African-American Art (auth, catalog), Studio Mus Harlem, 82; Reconstructed Elements, Artscape, 83, Lyric Theatre, 83; The Intuitive Eye-The Art of Self Taught Baltimore Artists (auth, catalog), Md Art Place, 85; 18 Visions/Divisions, Eubie Blake Cult Ctr & Mus, 88; Art as a Verb-The Evolving Continum (coauth, catalog), Md Inst Col Art, 88; Black Printmakers and the WPA (auth, catalog), Lehman Gallery Art, Lehman College, Bronx, NY, 89; Hale Woodruff Biennial, Studio Mus Harlem, New York, 89 & 94; Masters, Mentors and Makers, (auth, catalog), Artscape, 93. *Pos:* Actg dir, Cult Arts, Youth in Action, Bedford, Stuyvesant, NY, 66; chmn art dept, Performing Art Workshops, Queens, NY, 67-69; guest cur & mem bd dir, Morris Mechanic Gallery, formerly; coordr, Philip Morris Scholar for Artists in Visual Arts, 85-, dean grad studies, 76-; trustee, Baltimore Mus Art, 81-87. *Teaching:* Lectr art hist, Md Inst Col Art, 73-, dean grad studies, 76-; doctoral supvr, Dept African Studies & Res, Howard Univ, 77-82; instr, Corcoran Sch Art, 82. *Awards:* New York City SEEK Grant, 66-69; Horizon Fel, 69-73; Kress Found Fel, 74; Mellon Grant, 87. *Mem:* Nat Conf Artists; Col Art Asn (secy, 91-94). *Res:* Ninteenth and twentieth century Afro-American art; African Art; women artists; self-taught artists. *Publ:* Auth, Art as A Web, Md Inst, Studio Mus Harlem & Met Life Gallery, 88; May Howard Jackson, Black Women in America, Carlson Pub Co, NY, 93; Masks and Mirrors-African Art, 1700-Present, Abbeville Press, 95; Introduction, Gumbo YaYa-A Biobibliography of Contemporary African American Women Artists, Midmarch Art Press, 95; Painting and Sculpture, Encylopedia of African American History and Culture, Columbia Univ, NY, 95. *Mailing Add:* Md Inst Col Art 1300 W Mount Royal Ave Baltimore MD 21217-4191

HAMMOND, MARY SAYER
EDUCATOR, PHOTOGRAPHER
b Bellingham, Wash, Oct 1, 46. *Study:* Univ Ga, BFA(art educ), 67, MFA(photo design), 77; Ohio State Univ, PhD(hist photo/art educ), 86. *Work:* Int Mus Photog at George Eastman House, Rochester, NY; Nat Gallery Art, Wash; Nat Mus Women Arts, Wash; Ctr Creative Photog, Tucson, Ariz; Corcoran Gallery Art, Wash. *Exhib:* Pinhole Images, Eleven Photographers, Va Mus Art, 82; Recent Acquisitions, Corcoran Gallery Art, 86 & 89; Through a Pinhole Darkly, Fine Arts Mus Long Island, 88; City on a Hill, Ga Mus Art, 89; Poetics of the Real Am Landscape Photog, Columbus Mus Art, 91; Global Focus: Women in Art, Nat Mus Women Art, Wash, 95; Three Rivers Arts Festival, Carnegie Mus Art, 95. *Pos:* Co dir, Saturday Prog, Univ Ga, 66-76; admin assoc art educ, Ohio State Univ, 78-79; artist-in-residence, Study Abroad Prog, Univ Ga, Cortona, Italy, 81-88; dir, MSH Photgraphics, 88-. *Teaching:* From asst to assoc prof art & Am studies, George Mason Univ, 80-95, prof, 95-98; instr photog, Lyndon House Art Ctr, 2000-04. *Awards:* Photog Fel, Nat Endowment Arts, 82-84; Travel Grant, Samuel H Kress Found, 86. *Bibliog:* Duke T Y Liao (auth), The Charm of Pinhole Photography, Chinese Photography 3, 91; Duke T Y Liao (auth), Light and Shade, Chinese Ann Photog, 93-94. *Mem:* Soc Photog Educ (bd dir, mid Atlantic region); Daguerreian Soc; Col Art Asn; Nat Art Educ Asn. *Media:* Platinum, Color. *Res:* Photography. *Publ:* Illusr, Pienza: The Creation of a Renaissance City, Cornell Univ, 87; Emphasis Art, Harper Collins, 93; coauth, The Picture Book: Art Source and Resource, Nat Art Educ Asn, 95. *Dealer:* Kathleen Ewing 1609 Connecticut Ave Washington DC 20009. *Mailing Add:* 165 Watson Dr Athens GA 30605-3737

HAMMOND, PHYLLIS BAKER
SCULPTOR
b Elizabeth, NJ, Apr 13, 30. *Study:* Sch Mus Fine Arts, Boston, Mass, 60; Kyoto City Col Fine Arts, Japan, 62; Tufts Univ, BS, 64. *Work:* Mem Hall Libr, Andover, Mass; Am Savings Bank, White Plains, NY; Schmeltzer, Aptaker & Shepard, Washington, DC; Conn State Univ, New Haven; Noyes Mus, Oceanville, NJ. *Comn:* Unitarian Fellowship, Mount Kisco, NY, 84; Guest Quarters Hotel, Bethesda, Md, 86; Center point, Fairoaks, Md, 87; William Shakespeare Award, Shakespeare Theater at the Folgers, Washington, DC, 87; Art in Public Places, Hartford, Conn, 90. *Exhib:* Clay Sculpture, Hudson River Mus, NY, 76; Art in Transition, Boston Mus, 77; Clay Sculpture, Pinder Gallery, NY, 86; Architectural Ceramics, Franz Badar Gallery, Washington, DC, 87; Clay Transformations, Rockland Ctr Arts Nyack, Flushing, NY, 87; Sculptures as Pub Art, Art Gallery, Washington, DC, 89; Contemp Sculpture, Chesterwood, Stockbridge, Mass, 89; New Bronzes, Elaine Benson Gallery, Bridehampton, NY, 89; Recent Sculpture, Greene St Gallery, NY, 90. *Collection Arranged:* Renaissance Festival, Westchester Coun Art, NY, 75 & 77. *Teaching:* Adj asst prof, Col New Rochelle Graduate Sch, 81; ceramic sculpture, Mendocino Art Ctr, Calif, 81, 82 & 86. *Awards:* Clarissa Bartlett Traveling Fel, Boston Mus, 60; Second Prize, Mamaroneck Artist Guild, 73; Grant for Apprentice, National Endowment Arts, 76. *Bibliog:* Patricia Malarcher (auth), Clay that qualifies as sculpture, New York Times, 4/7/85; Roslyn Tunis (auth), Ancient Inspiration/Contemporary Interpretation (catalog, rev), Robertson Ctr Arts Sci, 85; Lauretta Dimmick & Jonathan Fairbanks (coauths), Contemporary Sculpture at Chesterwood (catalog, rev), 89. *Mem:* Artist-Craftsman New York; Nat Coun Apprenticeship; Int Laison; Visual Arts Affiliates of Westchester (vpres, 79-81). *Media:* Clay, Bronze. *Dealer:* Kendell Gallery Wellfleet MA; Pindar 127 Greene St New York NY 10012. *Mailing Add:* 1108 Springs Fireplace Rd East Hampton NY 11937

HAMMONS, DAVID
MUSEUM DIRECTOR, SCULPTOR
b Springfield, Ill, 1943. *Study:* Los Angeles Trade Technical City Col, Calif, 64-65; Chouinard Art Inst, Los Angeles, 66-68; Otis Art Inst Parson's Sch Design, Los Angeles, 68-72. *Exhib:* Solo exhibs, The Window, New Mus Contemp Art, 80, Higher Goals, pub installation, Harlem, 82, Just Above Midtown, NY, 86, Exit Art, 89, Jack Tilton Gallery, 90, Ace Gallery, NY, 2002 & 2003; retrospective, Contemp Art, PS1, Long Island, 90 & ICA, Philadelphia & San Diego Mus Contemp Art, 91; Heimat, Wewerka & Weiss Galerie, Berlin, 91; Places with a Past, Spoleto Festival, Charleston, SC, 91; Dislocations, Mus Mod Art, NY, 91; Carnegie Int, Carnegie Inst, Pittsburgh, Pa, 92; Documenta, Kassel, Ger, 92; Whitney Biennial, Whitney Mus Am Art, NY, 97; Zwirner & Wirth Gallery, NY, 2006. *Awards:* Nat Endowment Arts Fel, NY State Coun Arts, 82; John Simon Guggenheim Mem Found, 83-84; DAAD, Berlin, 92. *Bibliog:* Maurice Berger (auth), Interview with David Hammons, Art in Am, 9/90; Michael Brenson (auth), New Curator at Modern Challenges Convention, 12/28/90 & Visual Arts Join Spoleto Festival USA, New York Times, 5/27/91; Dan Cameron (auth), Good-Bye to All That?, Art & Auction, 1/91. *Mailing Add:* c/o AC Hudgins 94 Grand Ave Englewood NJ 07631

HAMPSON, FERDINAND CHARLES
ART DEALER, CURATOR
b Detroit, Mich, June 26, 47. *Study:* Wayne State Univ, dipl, 71. *Collection Arranged:* Emergence Art in Glass (auth, catalog), Bowling Green Univ & Kent State Univ, 81-82; Glass: Artist and Influence Traveling Exhib (auth, catalog), 81-82; Kyohe: Fujita Blown Glass (auth, catalog), Leigh Yawkey Woodson Mus & Burgstrom Mus, 81-82; Four Artists Four Views (auth, catalog), Jesse Besser Mus, 82; The Fine Art of Contemporary American Glass (auth, catalog), Columbus Col Art & Design, 83; Contemp Czechoslovakian Glass Art (catalog), Boca Raton Mus Art, 85; Bildwerke in Glass 25 Jahre New Glass in Amerika (catalog), Hessisches Landesmuseum Darmstadt, 87; Cristalomancia Arte Contemporaneo en Vidrio (catalog), Museo Rufino Tamayo & Marco Museo de Arte Contemporaneo, Mex, 92; Glass: 1962 to 1992 and Beyond (catalog), Morris Mus, 92. *Pos:* Dir, Habatat Galleries, 71-. *Bibliog:* Mack Talaba (auth), Art craft--glass has come a long way, Artcraft, 8/80; Janet Koplos (auth), Habatat Gallery, Am Craft, 9/80; Maureen Michelson (auth), Inside Habatat, Glass Studio, 4/81. *Mem:* Glass Art Soc; Detroit Art Dealers Asn (vpres, 76, pres, 78-80); Am Craft Coun; Mich Glass Month (chmn, 80-83). *Res:* Written history of contemporary glass. *Specialty:* Contemporary glass art. *Publ:* Auth, article, Glass Art J, 81; auth, article, Nues Glas, Verlagsanstalt Handweek, 81; Glass: State of the Art, 84; Glass: State of the Art II, 87; The Annual Invitational Exhibition 1973-1992: A Tradition in the Evolution of Glass, 92. *Mailing Add:* 3072 Bloomfield Park Dr West Bloomfield MI 48323-3507

HAMPTON, AMBROSE GONZALES, JR
COLLECTOR
b Statesburg, SC, July 24, 26. *Pos:* Mem, SC State Mus Comn, 73-78; pres, Columbia Mus Art, 75-77 & mem acquisitions comt, 87-; mem collection comt, Gibbes Art Mus, Charleston, SC, 89. *Collection:* Chiefly contemporary oils, graphics and sculpture, with emphasis on South Carolina artists. *Mailing Add:* 937 Sugar Mill Rd Chapin SC 29036

HAMPTON, ANITA
PAINTER, EDUCATOR
Study: Saddleback Col, El Torro, Calif; Laguna Beach Sch Art, Calif; Ventura Col, Calif; Calif Polytechnic State Univ, San Luis Obispo, Calif; Cuesta Col, San Luis Obispo, Calif. *Work:* numerous pvt collections. *Comn:* Numerous pvt comns. *Exhib:* Ann Art Festival, San Juan Capistrano Mission, Calif Art Club, 97, 98, 99 & 2000, Gold Medal Show, 98, 99 & 2000; Oil Painters Am Nat Show, 98; Oil Painters Am Nat Show; San Luis Obispo Art Mus; R Weisman Mus Art, Pepperdine Univ; Carmel Ann Painting Festival. *Pos:* Dir & instr fine art, Cent Coast Studios, Morro Bay, Calif, 94 & 95; juror, Allied Arts Ann Exhib & Cuesta Col Ann Scholarship Show, Calif, 96. *Teaching:* Instr, Cuesta Col, San Luis Obispo, Calif, 94 & 95; instr painting workshops (traveling nat & internat), 95-; art instr, S Bay Community Ctr, Calif, 96-97. *Awards:* Ann Art Festival Award, Calif Art Club, 97 & 98, Gold Medal Show Award, 98; Ann Art Competition Finalist, Artist's Mag, 98. *Mem:* Oil Painters Am; Calif Art Club; Laguna Plein Air Painters Asn; Signature Member of Oil Paints Am;. *Media:* Oil. *Specialty:* California Plein Air, representational impressionist, tonalist in all subject matter. *Interests:* Fine art including portraits, landscapes, seascapes, cityscapes, florals and still-life. *Collection:* Joan Irvine Smith, Roy Rose Plein Air Art Collection 93424. *Publ:* Contribr, Jewel of the Mission Calendar, 98; Best of the West, SW Art Mag, 8/98; The Jewel of the Missions Mag, fall 98; LA Times Newspaper (Metro Sect), Los Angeles, Calif, 8/16/98. *Dealer:* Salibury Fine Art, 1250 San Luis Bay Dr Avila Valley. *Mailing Add:* PO Box 6134 Los Osos CA 93412

HAMPTON, GRACE
ADMINISTRATOR, CRAFTSMAN
b Courtland, Ala, Oct 23, 1937. *Study:* Art Inst Chicago & Univ Chicago, BAE, 61; Ill State Univ, MSEd, 68; Ariz State Univ, PhD(art educ), 76. *Exhib:* Arizona Women, Tucson Art Mus, 75; Second World Festival of Black and African Arts and Cult, Lagos, Nigeria, 77; Howard Univ, 93; Lockhaven Univ, 97; Cult Diversity Exhib, Pa

Coun on the Arts, 99 & 2000. *Collection Arranged:* Dimension and Directions: Black Artists of the South (auth, catalog), Miss Mus Art, Jackson, 80; Africa & the Diaspora: Personal Collections, Penn State, Altoona, 95. *Pos:* Asst dir expansion arts prog, Nat Endowment Arts, Washington, DC, 83-85; mem adv bd, Getty Inst for Educators on Visual Arts, 83-84, fac mem, 85-88; dir, Sch Visual Arts, Penn State Univ, vice provost, 89-95, Exec Asst Develop arts, 96. *Teaching:* Asst prof art educ, Univ Ore, Eugene, 76-78; fac mem art & chairperson dept, Jackson State Univ, 78-83; fac mem, Sch Visual Arts, Pa State Univ, 85-; head dept African and African Am Art, Pa State Univ. *Awards:* Nat Endowment Arts Expansion Arts Prog Fel, 78; Inst Educ Mgt, Harvard, 90. *Bibliog:* Linderman & Herberholz (auths), Developing Artistic and Perceptual Awareness, 74 & Herberholz (auth), Early Childhood Art, 74, W C Brown; Lanier (auth), Studio Potter, 82, The Art We See, 82 & The Visual Arts & The Elementary Child, 83. *Mem:* Nat Art Educ Asn; Nat Conf Artists; Col Art Asn; Pa Art Educ Soc (bd dir & futures Comt); African Studies Asn. *Media:* Copper. *Publ:* Auth, Hayden House Program: Community involvement in the arts, Sch Arts, 79; auth, book reviews for J Negro Hist & Studies Art Educ; The Arts Education and Popular Culture in West Africa and the United States, Soc STudy Educ Through Art, 2003. *Mailing Add:* 861 Oak Ridge Ave State College PA 16801-6902

HAMPTON, JOHN WADE
SCULPTOR, PAINTER
b Brooklyn, NY, 1918. *Work:* The Cow Punchers, Cowboy Hall Fame, Oklahoma City; Will Rogers, Will Rogers Mem Mus, Claremore, Okla; Race for the Wagon, Ronald Reagan Libr, Calif; CM Russell Mus; Phoenix Art Mus; Cowboy Artists of Am Mus, Kerrville, Tex. *Comn:* mural, Marriotts Camelback Inn, Paradise Valley Ariz, 64; mural, Northwestern Univ Libr, Flagstaff, Ariz; portrait, James Coleman, Scottsdale, Ariz. *Exhib:* Cowboy Hall of Fame, Oklahoma City; Mont Hist Soc; Phoenix Art Mus; Will Rogers Mem Mus, Claremore, Okla; Grand Palais, Paris, France; Cowboy Artists of Am Mus, Kerrville, Tex; and others; C M Russell Mus; US Govt Bldgs in Washington, DC. *Collection Arranged:* Cowboy Artists Am Mus, Kerrville, Tex. *Teaching:* Pvt individuals. *Awards:* First Prize, World Telegram Artist Contest, 35; Gold Medal/Sculpture, Cowboy Artist of Am Show, 77, 79, 80, 81 & Silver, 82. *Bibliog:* article in NY Times, 2/77; SH Mcgarry & JH Pontello (coauth), Cowboy Artists of America 25 Yearbook, Wouthwest Art, vol 20, no 5, 10/90; Jim Jennings (auth), From Corral Dust to Black Tie, Quarter Horse J, vol 43, no 3, 12/90; articles Los Angeles Times, 6/4/90; Art West, vol 11-12, 80, vol 5-6, 81. *Mem:* Founder Cowboy Artists Am. *Media:* Oil, Watercolor; Clay, Bronze. *Publ:* Illusr in Ariz Hwys, The Cowboy in Art, CA His Friends' Cookbook, Cowboy Artists of Am & Western Horseman & other mags & books. *Dealer:* Hampton Studios Ltd HC1 Box 955 Sonoita AZ 85637-9700; Big Horn Galleries 1167 Sheridan Ave Cody WY 82414. *Mailing Add:* Hampton Studios Ltd HC 1 Box 955 Sonoita AZ 85637-9700

HAMPTON, PHILLIP JEWEL
PAINTER, EDUCATOR
b Kansas City, Mo, Apr 23, 22. *Study:* Citrus Jr Col, Glendora, Calif; Kans State Univ; Drake Univ; Kansas City Art Inst, BFA, 51, MFA, 52; Univ Mo Kansas City. *Work:* Tuskegee Inst, Ala; Ga Southern Col, Statesboro, Ga; New Atlanta Life Bldg, Ga; Obata Design, St Louis, Mo; Governor's Mansion, Ill; Southern Ill Univ, Edwardsville; Liberty Nat Bank, Savannah, Ga; St Louis Mus Art, Mo. *Exhib:* Huntsville Mus, Ala, 74; JB Speed Mus, Louisville, Ky, 82; Evansville Mus, Ind, 88; retrospectives, King-Tisdell Cottage Found, Savannah, Ga, 95; solo exhibs, KFUO-FM Special, St Louis, Mo, 96, So Ill Univ, Edwardsville, 2000, Mayor's Office, Complex, St Louis, Mo, 2000, St Louis Mus, Mo, 2000, Sheldon Art Galleries, St Louis, Mo, 2005, Ethical Soc Gallery, 2006; Looking Back: Art in Savannah 1900-1960, Ga, 96. *Pos:* Co-cur, Collectors' Choices, African Art St Louis Artists Guild, Mo, 98. *Teaching:* Assoc prof art & dir, Savannah State Col, 52-69; assoc prof painting & design, Southern Ill Univ, Edwardsville, 69-78, prof, 78-92, emer prof, 92-. *Awards:* Dr Scheinfurth Purchase Award, Mitchell Mus, Mt Vernon, Ill, 85; Lida & Jay Herndon Smith Fund Prize, St Louis Artists' Guild, 88; Gov Award, Ill Purchase Award for exec mansion, 90. *Mem:* St Louis Artists Coalition; St Louis Artists Guild. *Media:* Acrylic, Watercolor. *Res:* Investigating synthetic media; water-media techniques; an essence of form. *Publ:* Auth & designer, 3rd World Drawings 1979 (catalog), Soc Ethnic & Spec Studies Exhib, Los Angeles, 79; and others. *Dealer:* Galerie Bonheur, St Louis, Mo. *Mailing Add:* 832 Holyoake Rd Edwardsville IL 62025

HAMWI, RICHARD ALEXANDER
PAINTER, EDUCATOR
b Brooklyn, NY, June 11, 47. *Study:* Queens Col, BA(cum laude); Univ NMex, MA; Univ Calif, MFA; Pa State Univ, PhD; also with William Dole, Leonard Lehrer, Harry Nadler, James Brooks, Louis Finkelstein & John Ferren. *Work:* Phillips Mus; Queens Col; Nat Mus Am Art; Vassar Col; Ark Art Ctr; Art Mus, Univ Ky. *Exhib:* Parsons-Dreyfuss Gallery, NY, 79; Staempfli Gallery, 81; Phillips Collection, Washington, 82; solo shows, Queens Col, 82, Mus Art, Pa State Univ, 82, Univ Indianapolis, Ind, 90 & Prince St Gallery, NY, 93; Mus Art, Univ Ky, 90; Art Gallery, Mansfield Univ, 97. *Teaching:* Asst, Univ NMex, 72-73, Univ Calif, 73-74; instr, Pa State Univ, 77-87; assoc prof, Cumberland Col, 87-95 & 95- & Mansfield Univ, 95-. *Awards:* Purchase Award, Ball State Univ, 79; Mem Award, Chautauqua Nat Exhib, 81; Yaddo Fel, 83; Djerassi Found Fel, 87. *Mem:* Col Art Asn Am; Nat Art Ed Assoc. *Media:* Ink, Watercolor. *Publ:* Thoughtnotes on the Teaching of Art, J Ky Art Educ Asn, 90; Collage with self prepared colored papers, Arts & Activities Mag, 10/96. *Dealer:* Prince St Gallery 121 Wooster St New York NY 10012. *Mailing Add:* Mansfield Univ Art Dept Mansfield PA 16933

HANAN, LAURA MOLEN
ARTIST
b Ft Monmouth, NJ, Jan 30 54. *Study:* U Calif, BS, 1978; Humboldt State U, BA, 1980; Northwest Col Art, AOS, 1992. *Exhib:* Group shows, Emerald City Fine Art Gallery, Seattle, 1996-1997; Nicholas Joseph Fine Art, NYC, 1997-1998; Hastings Ray Gallery, Southern Pines, NC, 1997-2000. *Collection Arranged:* Pierce Co Libr. *Awards:* First Place, Peninsula Art League, 1995, 2nd Place 1996, 3rd Place 1997; Peoples Choice Award, Peninsula Art League, 1997

HANCHEY, JANET L
PAINTER, GILDER
b Dry Creek, La, Oct 30, 56. *Study:* La State Univ, BFA, 78; Parsons Sch of Design, MFA, 81. *Comn:* Recreate 8 paintings (ceiling & murals), New Amsterdam Theatre; reverse gilded glass, Barney's New York; murals, New Amsterdam Theatre, NY, 94-95; Kirtlington Park & Landsdowne Rooms Restoration, Metrop Mus Art, NY, 95; Bradley Mus, Columbus, Ga; IBM Corp, Atlanta, Ga; Marriott Corp, Los Angeles, Calif. *Pos:* Pres/dir Farris Howell Inc (Women's Business Enterprise). *Teaching:* Lectr, Md Inst Col of Art, Baltimore, 88 & Parsons Sch Design, NY, 82-; tech advisor gilding, Studio Sch, NY; guest lectr, Fashinon Inst Technol, NY, 89. *Mem:* Nat Artists Club. *Media:* Oil Pigment, Dry Pastel-Goldleaf. *Dealer:* Farris Howell Inc. *Mailing Add:* 35 Wood Rd Sands Point NY 11050

HANCOCK, TRENTON DOYLE
PAINTER
b Okla City, 74. *Study:* assoc sci, Paris Jr Col, Tex, 94; Tex A&M Univ, Commerce, BFA, 97; Temple Univ Tyler Sch Art, Phila, MFA, 2000. *Exhib:* Group exhibs including Whitney Biennial, 2000, 2002, 5th Anniversary Exhbn, Dunn and Brown Contemp, Dallas, 2004, Political Nature, Whitney Mus Am Art, NY City, 2004-05, Color / Pattern / Grid, Austin Mus Art, Austin, Tex, 2005, Swarm, Fabric Workshop, Philadelphia, 2005, The Compulsive Line, Mus Modern Art, NY City, 2006, The 181st Annual: An Invitational Exhbn Contemp Am Art, Nat Acad Mus, NY City, 2006, A Brighter Day, James Cohan Gallery, NY City, 2006; solo exhibs including Off Colored, Gerald Peters Gallery, Dallas, 98, Wow Thats Me?, Dunn and Brown Contemp, Dallas, 2000, The Legend is in Trouble, James Cohan Gallery, NY City, 2001, The Life and Death of #1, Contemp Art Mus, Houston, Modern Art Mus Ft Worth, Tex Fine Arts Asn at The Jones Ctr Contemp Art, Austin, Tex, 2001, Dunn and Brown Contemp, Dallas, 2002, For a Floor of Flora, James Cohan Gallery, NY City, 2003, Mus Contemp Art, North Miami, Fla, 2003, It Came from the Studio Floor, Dunn and Brown Contemp, Dallas, 2003, Moments in Mound History, Cleveland Mus Art, 2003, St. Sesom and the Cult of Color, Dunn and Brown Contemporary, Dallas, 2005, In the Blestian Room, James Cohan Gallery, NY City, 2006. *Pos:* Core Artist in Residence, Mus Fine Arts Glassell Sch Art, Houston, 2002. *Awards:* Arch and Anne Giles Kimbrough award, Dallas Mus Art, 97; Skowhegan Camille Hanks Cosby fel for African-Am Artists, 97; Joan Mitchell Found grant, 99; Artadia Found award, 2003; Penny McCall Found award, 2004; SJ Wallace Truman Fund prize, 2006. *Mailing Add:* 2510 W Campbell St Paris TX 75460-1646

HAND, JOHN OLIVER
HISTORIAN, CURATOR
b New York, NY, Aug 17, 41. *Study:* Denison Univ, AB, 63; Univ Chicago, MA(art hist), 67; Princeton Univ, MFA(art hist), 71, PhD(art hist), 78. *Pos:* Docent, Nat Gallery Art, 65-69, cur, Northern Europ Painting, 73-84; cur, Northern Renaissance Painting, 84-. *Teaching:* Teacher art & art hist, Denison Univ, 63 & Princeton Univ, 71. *Awards:* Samuel H Kress Found Fel, 71-72; Belg Am Educ Found Fel, 72-73; Nat Gallery Art Cur Fel, 94-95 & 2000-01. *Mem:* Historians Netherlandish Art. *Res:* Northern Renaissance painting; 15th and 16th century Northern Renaissance painting; Joos Van Cleve. *Publ:* Joos Van Cleve: The Early & Mature Paintings, Princeton Univ, 78; co-auth, The Collections of the Nat Gallery of Art Systematic Catalog, Early Netherlandish Painting, Wash, 86; essay, The 16th Century and catalogue entries in The Age of Bruegel, Netherlandish Drawings of the 16th Century (catalog), Nat Gallery Art, Washington; The Pierpoint Morgan Libr, NY, 86-87; German Paintings of the Fifteenth through Seventeenth Centuries (catalog), Nat Gallery Art, Washington, 93; Joos Van Cleve: The Complete Paintings, Yale Univ, 2004; Nat Gallery of Art: Master Paintings from Collection, Wash, 2004. *Mailing Add:* Nat Gallery Art Landover MD 20785

HANDELL, ALBERT GEORGE
PAINTER
b Brooklyn, NY, Feb 13, 37. *Study:* Art Students League, New York; La Grande Chaumiere, Paris. *Work:* Bates Col; Brooklyn Mus Art, NY; Schenectady Mus Art, NY; Salt Lake City Mus Fine Arts; Art Students League. *Exhib:* One-man show Schenectady Art Mus NY, Berkshire Mus, Pittsfield MA; ACA Gallery, NY, 66 & Eileen Kuhlik Gallery, NY, 72; Harbor Gallery, Cold Spring Harbor, NY; Ventana Gallery, Santa Fe, NMex, 87-94; two-man show, Total Arts Gallery, Taos NMex, 89. *Teaching:* Instr, Albert Handell Nation-wide Painting Workshops, 84-. *Awards:* Ranger Fund Purchase Prize, Audubon Artist, 68; Elizabeth T Greenshields Mem Found, 72; Master Pastelist, 84, Pastel Hall of Fame, 87, Pastel Soc Am; Cash Award, Am Artist Mag, 94; Silver Medal, 2nd Ann Laguna Plein Air Invitational Painting Competition, Laguna Art Mus, Laguna Beach, Calif, 2000; Numerous Awards in pastels, 2000. *Bibliog:* Heather-Meredith-Owens (auth), The inner univers of Albert Handell, Am Artist Mag, 4/71; Joe Singer (auth), Pastel Portraits, Watson-Guptill; Leslie Trainer (auth), Pastel landscapes of Albert Handell, Am Artist Mag, 12/82; and others; Joy Murphy (auth), Albert Handell, Enraptured, Southwest Art Mag, 4/86; and others. *Mem:* Allied Artist Am; Salmagundi Club; Art Students League; Pastel Soc Am (Hall of Fame). *Media:* Pastels, Oil. *Publ:* Coauth (with Leslie Trainor Handell), Oil Painting Workshop, 80 & Pastel Painting Workshop, 81, Watson-Guptill; (with

Leslie Trainor Handell), Intuitive Composition, 89; A Creative Approach to Realistic Painting & Intuitive Light, 95, Watson-Guptill; coauth (with Anita Louise West), Painting the Landscape with Pastel, Watson Guptill Pub, 2000. *Dealer:* Connie Axton, The Ventana Gallery, Santa Fe NM. *Mailing Add:* 1109 Don Gasper Ave Santa Fe NM 87501

HANDLER, AUDREY
GLASS BLOWER, SCULPTOR
b Philadelphia, Pa, Dec 9, 34. *Study:* Tyler Sch Fine Arts, Temple Univ, Philadelphia, 52-54; Art Students League, New York, summer 55; Boston Univ Sch Fine & Appl Arts, BFA, 56, study with David Aronson; Univ Ill, Champaign, 62; sr res fel, Royal Col Art, London, Eng, 67-68; Univ Wis-Madison, MS, 67, MFA, 70, study with Harvey Littleton. *Work:* Corning Mus Glass, NY; Lannan Found, Palm Beach, Fla; Royal Col Art, London, Eng; Lobmeyr Mus, Vienna, Austria; Hastings Col Glass Collections, Nebr; Ronald Abramson Glass Collection, Washington, DC; and others. *Exhib:* Nat Collection Fine Art, Renwick Gallery, Smithsonian Inst, Washington, DC, 73; Am Glass Now, San Francisco Mus Art, Calif, 74; Toledo Mus, 79; Renwick Gallery, 80; Metrop Mus Art, 80-81; Calif Palace Legion Honor, 81; Victoria & Albert Mus, London, 81; Musee des Arts Decoratifs, Paris, & Japan, 82; Glasmuseum, Ebeltoft, 86; Hokkaido Mus Modern Art, Sapporo, Japan, 88; and others; Wisc Glass Masters, Fairfield Pub Gallery, Sturgeon Bay, 2000. *Teaching:* Instr glass, Royal Col Art, London, 68, Penland Sch Crafts, NC, 71-85, Hunterdon Art Ctr, Clinton, NJ, 72, Haystack Mountain Sch Crafts, Deer Isle, Maine, 73, Archie Bray Found, Helena, Mont, 75, Univ Wisc, 84, Os-Box, Saugatuck, Mich, 97; instr commercial art dept, Madison Area Tech Col, Wis, 73-. *Awards:* Juror's Awards, 46th & 59th Wis Designer Craftsmen Shows, Milwaukee, 66 & 71 & Madison Artists Exhib, Madison Art Ctr, Wis, 70; Master Craftsmen Apprenticeship Prog Grant, Nat Endowment Arts, 77-78 & 80-81. *Bibliog:* Paula Orth (auth), Blown Glass, Milwaukee Sentinel, 72; Terri Gabriell (auth), Instructor Makes, Hunterdon Co Dem, Flemington, NJ, 72; S K Oberbeck (auth), Glass menagerie, Newsweek, 4/73. *Mem:* Hon life mem, Glass Art Soc, Inc (mem bd, 76-78); Nat Coun on the Educ of Ceramic Arts; Am Crafts Coun; World Crafts Coun; Wis Designer Craftsmen Coun. *Media:* Blown Glass, Silver & Gold Figures. *Dealer:* Audrey Handler 7560 Marsh View Rd Verona WI 53593. *Mailing Add:* 105 S Rock Rd Madison WI 53705

HANDLER, JANET
SCULPTOR, PAINTER
Study: Fairleigh Dickinson Univ, BS (educ); Lehman Col, MA (educ); Art & Life Studio, NY; Art Students League, NY; self taught. *Comn:* Wood & stone sculptures (8), Dr Theodore Sewitch, New York. *Exhib:* Art & Life Studio, 75-80; Central Park Conservatory, 81; Art Students League, League Gallery, 86-; Agora Gallery Group Show, 98; Allied Artists Am, NY, 99, 2002 & 04; 61st Ann Exhib, Salmagundi Club, NY, 2003. *Collection Arranged:* Ms Esteele Futterman, NY; Mr Steven Mader, Vancouver, Can; Mr & Mrs Aaron Curler, Larchmont, NY; Mrs. Julia Levine, West Orange, NJ; Mr & Mrs Hal Ritter, Hilton Head, SC. *Pos:* Sculpture Dir, Audubon Artists of Am, 2004-. *Teaching:* teacher, currently. *Awards:* Hononable Mention, Arts Students League, 95, 2000-04; Merit Scholarship, Art Students League, 96-97; Group Show Award, Agora Gallery, 98; Cleo Hartwig Award, Audubon Artists Inc. *Mem:* Art Students League; Audubon Artists Inc Allied Artist Am (sculpture dir). *Media:* Stone and Wood. *Specialty:* Painting & sculpture. *Collection:* Wood & stone sculpture, Dr. Theodore Sewitch, Michael & Eileen Himmel. *Mailing Add:* 408 West 57th St Apt 10G New York NY 10019

HANES, JAMES (ALBERT)
PAINTER
b Louisville, Ky, Feb 5, 24. *Study:* Philadelphia Sch Indust Art; US Army Univ, France; Pa Acad Fine Arts; Barnes Found, Pa. *Work:* Pa Acad Fine Arts, Philadelphia; Univ Tampa, Fla; Yale Univ, New Haven, Conn; La Salle Col, Philadelphia; Nat Acad Design, NY. *Exhib:* Palazzo Venezia, Rome, Italy, 52; Palazzo Esposizione, Rome, 53; Nat Inst Arts & Lett, NY, 56; Univ Pittsburgh, 72; Peale House Galleries of Pa Acad Fine Arts, 79; Goldsmith Gallery, Memphis, Tenn, 80. *Pos:* Art ed, Four Quarters, 70-. *Teaching:* Instr painting, Pa Acad Fine Arts, 80-81; asst prof painting & artist in residence, La Salle Col, 65-92. *Awards:* Cresson, Thuron & Lambert Awards, Pa Acad Fine Arts, 49; Tiffany First Award, 50; Prix de Rome, Am Acad in Rome, 51-54. *Bibliog:* Valerio Mariani (auth), Un pittore Americano, Idea, 8/16/53. *Mem:* Am Acad in Rome; fel Pa Acad Fine Arts. *Media:* Oil. *Mailing Add:* 415 W Stafford St Philadelphia PA 19144-4407

HANKEY, ROBERT E
EDUCATOR, ADMINISTRATOR
b Fargo, NDak, June 24, 31. *Study:* Quincy Col, Ill, BA, 57; Cath Theological Union, Chicago, MA, 61; Cath Univ Am, BA(studio art), 61; Loyola Univ Chicago, MEd, 71. *Pos:* Ed & illusr, Troubadour Mag, Franciscan Press, 59-61; dean of students, Minneapolis Col Art & Design, 70-80; freelance designer, 80-84; dir, Minn Indian Consortium Higher Educ, 80-; acad dean, Col Assoc Arts, St Paul, 84-87, pres, 87-93; owner & pres, Rehco, Inc, 93-. *Teaching:* Prof art & design, Col Assoc Arts, 84-93. *Mem:* Nat Asn Schs of Art & Design; Minn Indian Consortium Higher Educ; Am Inst Graphic Arts; Int Coun Design Schs. *Res:* Computer art, electronic media and phenomenology. *Publ:* Auth, Cybernetics, Duns Scotus Philos Rev, 57; Art and Theology, Duns Scotus Theology Rev, 61; Phenomenon of Art, Corcoran Art Gallery, 71. *Mailing Add:* 4825 Washburn Ave S Minneapolis MN 55410-1851

HANKS, DAVID ALLEN
CURATOR, WRITER
b St Louis, Mo, Dec 13, 40. *Study:* Washington Univ, St Louis, AB & MA. *Collection Arranged:* American Art of the Colonies and Early Republic (auth, catalog), Art Inst Chicago, 71; The Arts and Crafts Movement in America, 1876-1916 (contribr, catalog), 73; The Decorative Designs of Frank Lloyd Wright, Renwick Gallery, Smithsonian Inst, 77-78; Innovative Furniture in America, Smithsonian Inst, 81. *Pos:* Asst cur, Art Inst Chicago, 69-74; cur, Philadelphia Mus Art, 74-77; guest cur, Smithsonian Inst, 77-81; owner & pres, David A Hanks & assocs, 81-; dir, Exhibs Int, 93-2000; curator, Liliane and David M. Stewart Program for Modern Design. *Mem:* Decorative Arts Chap Soc Archit Hist (pres, 74-77); Philadelphia Chap Victorian Soc (pres 75-77). *Res:* American furniture of the 19th and 20th century; International design, 20th century. *Publ:* Auth, Isaac E Scott: Reform Furniture in Chicago, Chicago Sch Archit Found, 74; coauth, Daniel Pabst, Philadelphia Mus Art, 77. *Mailing Add:* Montreal Mus Fine Arts PO Box 3000 Station H Montreal PQ H3G 2T9 Canada

HANKS, STEVE
PAINTER
b San Diego, Calif, Nov 24, 49. *Study:* Acad Art, San Francisco, 68; Calif Col Arts & Crafts, BA, 72. *Work:* Gilcrease Mus, Tulsa, Okla; Mus Fine Arts, NMex; Bennington Ctr Arts, Utah. *Exhib:* Solo exhibs, Estevan Gallery/Old Town, Albuquerque, NMex, 81, Hang-Up Shoppe Gallery, 82, Leslie Levy Gallery, Scottsdale, Ariz, 83 & 85-91, Tohn-Atin Gallery, Durango, Colo, 83, Albuquerque Country Club, 86, O'Brians Art Emporium, Scottsdale, Ariz, 92, E S Lawrence Gallery, Aspen, Colo, 92-98 & Gilcrease Mus, Tulsa, Okla, 98; Peppertree Ranch Invitational, Ynez, Calif, 86-98; Artists of Am, Denver Natural Hist, 94-98; Prix de West, Nat Cowboy Hall Fame, Oklahoma City, 94-98; 1998 Rendezvous, Gilcrease Mus, Tulsa, Okla, 98. *Pos:* Bd mem, Albuquerque Arts Coun, 95; coun mem, Norwest Bank Leadership Coun, 97. *Awards:* Gold Medal, Nat Watercolor Soc, 92, Prix de West, 95 & Arts for the Park, 94 & 95. *Bibliog:* Steve Hanks, SW Art, 2/86 & Art of Steve Hanks, 6/98; Featured Artists, American Artist Watercolors 92, fall 92. *Media:* Watercolor. *Publ:* Contribr, Poised Between Heartbeats, Hadley House, 95. *Dealer:* E S Lawrence Gallery Aspen CO. *Mailing Add:* 1290 Calle de Sandias NE Albuquerque NM 87111

HANLEY, JACK
PAINTER, GALLERY DIRECTOR
b New York, NY, Jan 8, 52. *Study:* State Univ NY, BFA, 74; Univ Calif, Berkeley, MA, 80, MFA, 82. *Work:* Prudential, NY; Michener, Austin, Tex; Mus Southern Tex, Corpus Christi. *Exhib:* Skowhegan, Leo Castelli Gallery, 85; Tex Artists, San Francisco Mus, San Francisco, 86; solo exhib, Ohio State Univ, Columbus, 86; Four Tex Painters, Hal Bromm Gallery, NY, 88; Tex Triennial (traveling exhib), Contemp Art Mus, Houston, Tex. *Pos:* Owner & cur, Trans-Avant Garde Gallery, 85-90, Jack Hanley Gallery, San Francisco, Calif, 90-. *Teaching:* Vis lectr fine arts, Princeton Univ; asst prof fine arts, Univ Tex, 84-90. *Awards:* Visual Artist Fel, Nat Endowment Arts, 87. *Mem:* Col Art Asn. *Media:* Acrylic. *Mailing Add:* c/o Jack Henley Gallery 395 Valencia St San Francisco CA 94103

HANNA, ANNETTE ADRIAN
PAINTER, INSTRUCTOR
b New York, NY. *Study:* Traphagen Inst Fashion Illus; Art Students League, studied with Greene, Sanden & Passantino, 79-80; pvt study with J H Sanden & Burton Silverman, 82-91; Centenary Col, BFA, Hackettstown, NJ, 97. *Work:* Am Broadcasting Co, NY; US Coast Guard, Washington, DC; Schering Plough Corp, Madison, NJ; Marsh Insurance, Morristown, NJ. *Comn:* portrait, Hilton Hotels, Parsippany, NJ, 82; portrait, Riker, Danzig, Scherer, Hyland, Morristown, NJ, 84; portrait, State Senator Ret, Convent Station, NJ, 86; portrait, Judge Court of Appeals, Ret, NY, 87; portrait, NJ State CofC, 98. *Exhib:* Grand Nat Am Artists Prof League, 81-98 & Nat Open Juried Ann, 90-2000, Salmagundi Club, NY; Hudson Valley Art Asn, Westchester Co Community Ctr, White Plains, NY, 88-90; Portraits of the Northeast, Creative Workshops, New Haven, Conn, 89; Art Showcase, Schering Plough Corp, Madison, NJ, 89; PSA Nat Arts Club, NY, 91-2006; Conn Pastel Soc, Paul Mellon Arts Ctr, Wallingford, Conn, 96-98; Morris Mus, Morristown, NJ, 2005; Northwest Pastel Soc, Seattle, Wash, 2005-06; Blackwell St Ctr Arts, members & NJ HS students, 1986-2006; Arts Coun Morris Area, April Arts Biannual, Madison, NJ, 1996-2003. *Pos:* Sem admin & adv coun, Nat Portrait Sems, NY, 80-83; bd mem, Morris Co Art Asn, Morristown, NJ, 84-86; bd mem & pres, Blackwell St Ctr Arts, Dover, NJ, 89-2004. *Teaching:* Fac mem, portrait, Nat Portrait Home Study, 85-87; painting, portrait, still life, landscape, oil & pastel, Morris Co Art Asn, Morristown, NJ, 89-; instr oil, pastel & portrait landscape, Int Workshops, Italy, Panama, 92 & Switzerland, 94 & Coupeville, Wash, 2004; fac mem, Morris Co Art Asn, Somerset Art Asn; fac mem, Visual Arts Ctr, Summit, NJ, 2006. *Awards:* Portrait & Figure Award, Am Art Prof League, NJ, 81, 82, 84-87, Medal of Honor, 2000; Gold Medal Pastel, Am Art Prof League, NY, 90; First Place, Am Soc Portrait Art, 98; others. *Bibliog:* Anne Corcoran (auth), Dover gallery, 8/91 & Janet Adamec (auth), Portrait artist, 3/92, Star Ledger, Newark, NJ; Ruth Faulkner (auth), Reflective Moments, Am Artist Mag, 9/99. *Mem:* Pastel So Am, NY; Hudson Valley Art Asn, NY; Am Artist Prof Leage NY & NJ; Arts Coun Morris Area, NJ (visual art chmn, 82 & 92); Morris Co Art Asn, Morristown, NJ (bd, 84-86 & 2004-06); Northwest Pastel Soc, Seattle, Wash, 2005-06. *Media:* Oil, Pastel. *Specialty:* Realism, landscape, still life, portrait. *Interests:* Hiking, reading. *Publ:* auth, How to Paint Portraits in Oil, Walt Foster Publ, Tustin, Calif, 94; contribr, Best of Pastel 2, Rockport Pub., 98. *Dealer:* Blackwell St Ctr Arts PO Box 808 Denville NJ 07834; Revelation Gallery Denville NJ; Burnt Mills Gallery Bedminster NJ; Studio Gallery Bernardsville NJ. *Mailing Add:* 6 Overlook Rd Boonton NJ 07005

HANNA, PAUL DEAN, JR
PAINTER, PRINTMAKER
b Alice, Tex. *Study:* Austin Col, BA; Chouinard Art Inst; Tex Christian Univ, MFA. *Work:* Tex Tech Mus, Lubbock; Pace Collection, San Antonio; Bell Reproduction Collection, Ft Worth; Lubbock Art Asn, Tex; First Nat Bank, Hobbs, NMex. *Comn:* Six glass engraved windows & four stained glass windows, Covenant Presbyterian

Church, Lubbock, Tex, 77-. *Exhib:* Two-man show, Witte Mus, San Antonio, 68; Northwest Printmakers' Int, Seattle & Portland, 69; Southwestern Exhib Painting & Sculpture, Dallas, 71; Printmaking Now, Nat Print Exhib, 73; Longview Painting Exhib, 74; Tex Tech Univ, Lubbock, 77, 87 & 88. *Pos:* Paul Hanna Speaker series (ann), Tex Asn Sch Art, 92-. *Teaching:* Emer prof painting & drawing, Tex Tech Univ, 69-. *Awards:* Eight State Painting & Sculpture Award, Okla Art Ctr, 66 & 80; Longview Painting Award, 74; Juror's Award, 23rd Ann, Okla Art Ctr, 80; Grant, Nat Endowment Arts, 82. *Bibliog:* Gene Mittler & James Howze (auths), Creating and Understanding Drawings, Glencoe Publ Co, 89. *Mem:* Tex Watercolor Soc; life mem Tex Asn Schs Art (past pres). *Media:* Acrylic, Oil; Woodcut, Silkscreen. *Mailing Add:* 2831 24th St Lubbock TX 79410-1635

HANNAH, DUNCAN RATHBUN
PAINTER
b Minneapolis, Minn, Aug 21, 52. *Study:* Minneapolis Col Art & Design, 70; Bard Col, 71-73; Parsons Sch Design, BFA, 75. *Work:* Repub Bank Houston; Chase Manhattan Bank, Chemical Bank, Metrop Mus Art, NY; Minneapolis Inst Art; Chicago Art Inst. *Exhib:* New Talent, Albright-Knox Mus, 81; Art Against AIDs, 87 & solo exhib, Phyllis Kind Gallery, NY, 88 & 89; solo exhibs, Jon Oulman Gallery, Minneapolis, Minn, 88, 90, 92 & 94 Charles Cowles Gallery, NY, 89 & 91, Tatistcheff & Co, NY & Los Angeles, Calif, 91 & David Beitzel Gallery, NY, 94; The Landscape in 20th Century Am Art, Metrop Mus Art, Philbrook Mus Art, Tulsa, Okla, Ctr Fine Arts, Miami, Fla, Joslyn Art Mus, Omaha, Nebr, Tampa Mus Art, Fla, Greenville Co Mus Art, SC, Madison Art Ctr, Wis, Grand Rapids Art Mus, Mich, 91-92; Art for Childrens Survival, Unicef, Sothebys, NY, 91; Tibor de Nagy Gallery, 95 & 97; John Oulman Gallery, Minneapolis, Minn, 96 & 98; Rebecca Ibel Gallery, Columbus, Ohio, 2000, 2002 & 2005; Charles More Gallery, Philadelphia, 2002; The Charlotte St Gallery, London, 2002; James Graham & Sons, NY, 2002, 2004 & 2005; Modernism, San Francisco, 2005; The Downtown Show, Grey Art Gallery, New York; The Andy Warhol Mus, Pittsburgh, Pa; The Austin Mus of Art, Tex. *Teaching:* Instr visual essay, Sch Visual Arts, New York, 89-91. *Bibliog:* The Figure in 20th Century American Art, Metrop Mus Art, 85; Barry Blinderman (interviewer), Duncan Hannah: Mythic Times, Univ Galleries Ill State Univ, 90; Robert Rosenblum (intro), The Landscape in Twentieth Century Art: Selections from the Metropolitan Museum Art, Rizzoli, NY. *Mem:* Century Asoc. *Media:* Oil on Canvas. *Mailing Add:* James Graham & Sons 1014 Madison Ave New York NY 10021

HANNAH, JOHN JUNIOR
PRINTMAKER, EDUCATOR
b Buffalo, NY, Mar 23, 23. *Study:* Univ Buffalo, BFA; Univ Ill, with Lee Chesney, MFA, 55; Albright Art Sch, with Letterio Calapai; Neth Royal Acad Painting & Sculpture, Fulbright grant, 60-61; Pratt Graphic Art Ctr, 67; also Birgit Skiold Workshop, London. *Work:* Northwest Printmakers, Seattle Mus Art, Wash; Okla Printmakers Collection, Oklahoma City; 3-M Collection, Tweed Gallery, Duluth, Minn; Bradley Univ Collection, Peoria, Ill; Joslyn Art Mus, Omaha, Nebr; and others. *Comn:* Tourist, Friends of Art, Kans State Univ, 67. *Exhib:* 1st Int Print Exhib, Hilo, Hawaii, 76; Three Decades of Am Printmaking, Brooklyn Mus, NY, 77; Nat Color Blend Print Exhib, Univ Miss, 77; 44th Ann Miniature Printers Sculptors & Gravers, Washington, DC, 77; Six Printmakers, Loyola Univ, Los Angeles, 77; and others. *Teaching:* Instr drawing, Ohio State Univ, Columbus, 56; assoc prof printmaking, Kans State Univ, Manhattan, 57-68; prof printmaking & drawing, Calif State Univ, Northridge, 69-. *Awards:* Calif Art Coun Artist Grant, 78. *Mem:* Los Angeles Printmaking Soc (bd mem, 70-); Artists Econ Action (bd mem, 73-74). *Media:* Etching, Serigraphy. *Publ:* Contribr, Etching, Van Nostrand, 73; American Printmakers, 74 & California Graphics, 74, Graphis Group Arcadia, 74. *Mailing Add:* 665 Haverford Ave Pacific Palisades CA 90272

HANNAY, JANNEKA (JANN)
PAINTER
b Orange, NJ, Aug 16, 33. *Study:* Miami Univ, Oxford, Ohio, BFA, 55; Kean Col, MA, 73; NJ Ctr Visual Arts, with Voy Fangor, 76-78; Art Students League, 80-81; Pratt Inst, MPS, NY, 89. *Work:* Shearing Plough Collection, Morristown, NJ; Schoor & De Palma Collection, NJ; Pub Serv Elec & Gas Collection. *Comn:* Four panel mural, Carrier, Belle Head, NJ. *Exhib:* Invitational, Lever House, NY, 80 & Kean Col, 81; NJ Ctr Visual Arts, 89, 98; Vorpal Gallery, 88, 91, 94, 96 & 1999-2000; Art Miami, 93. *Pos:* Vpres, Summit Art Ctr Mus, 72-74, trustee, 72-80; chmn art dept, Kent Place Sch, 75-83; cur, Teaching Gallery, 77-83; registered art therapist, Carrier Found, 86-2003. *Awards:* Best in Show, NJ Ctr Visual Arts. *Bibliog:* Diana Freedman (auth), article, Artspeak, 87; Dennis Wepman (auth), article in Sunspeak, 98; J Am Art Therapy, 99. *Mem:* Artists Equity, NY; Women's Caucus Art, NY. *Media:* Oil on Canvas, Monotypes. *Dealer:* Vorpal Gallery 411 Broadway New York NY 10012

HANNER, JEAN PATRICIA
PAINTER, MURALIST
b Toronto Ont, Can, July 19, 40. *Study:* Chaffey Jr Col, RN, AA, 1970; Cal Polly Pomona Calif (DA Pub Admin with Hons), BA, 1972. *Work:* Pat Hanner Art Gallery, Ont, Calif. *Comn:* Charcoal, pastel portrait, Sugar Ray Lennard, Ont, Calif, 1965; Boston Terrier Portrait, Dr & Mrs S Woolington, Pomona, Calif, 1968; Portrait, Mother of Sylvia Rosas, Riverside, Calif, 1975; Murals (many large), Lanterman Develop Ctr, Pomona, Calif, 1980-1983. *Pos:* Owner, Pat Hanner Art Gallery, 1995-2005; Pres, Hanner Gallery Inc, 2004-2005. *Media:* Miscellaneous. *Publ:* Auth, Ont City Sewer System, Ont City Libr, 1970; auth, Miracle in the Making, 1993. *Mailing Add:* 911 W Rosewood Ct Ontario CA 91762

HANNIBAL, JOSEPH HARRY
EDUCATOR, PAINTER
b Brooklyn, NY, May 4, 45. *Study:* Austin Peay State Univ, Clarksville, Tenn, BS, 68; Univ Tenn, Knoxville, MFA, 72. *Work:* Austin Peay State Univ; Univ Wis, Stout. *Exhib:* One-man show, 118 Gallery, Minneapolis, 80; Austin Peay State Univ, 81; Los Angeles City Col, 82; Ontario Mus Art & History, Calif, 83; Laguna Beach Sch Art, 83; Distinguished Artist Exhib, The Chancellary, Long Beach, Calif, 86; Spacex Gallery, Exeter, Eng, 97; Kellogg Art Gallery, Pomona, Calif, 98; others; Four Int Artists, Stoberihallen Mus, Denmark, 00; One-man show: Crossing, Gjethuset Mus, Denmark, 00. *Collection Arranged:* Co-cur, Crossings exhib, Gjethuset Mus, Denmark, 2000. *Pos:* Dir, Art Treasures of Italy, 93 & 98, Art Treasures of Europe, 94; guest cur, UK/LA Festival, 94; cur, The Brewery, Los Angeles, Calif, 94; installation coordr, Memories & Modernity, Venice Biennale, Venice, Italy, 96; Am organizer Ital Summer Fresco Proj, Ital Ministry Cult, Erasmas Europ Educ Agency & Exeter Univ, Eng. *Teaching:* Head, Printmaking Area, Dept Art, Univ Wis-Stout, Menomonie, 72-81; head lithography dept, Cent Col Art & Design, London, Eng, 75-76; chmn art dept, Calif State Polytech Univ, Pomona, 81-85, head painting & photog areas, 85-; Zenobia instr for New Urban Landscape, Venice, Italy, 95; Col Art & Design, Univ Plymouth, Exeter, Eng, 96-97. *Awards:* Gold Medal, Italy, 81; Purchase Award, 12th Nat Drawing Exhib, Minot, NDak, 82; Cash Award, Multicultural Art Inst, San Diego, 82. *Bibliog:* Frederiksvaerk Ugeblad Newspaper, Denmark, 5/3/2000. *Mem:* Col Art Asn; Los Angeles Printmaking Soc; Los Angeles Art Core. *Media:* Painting; Photography. *Dealer:* 118 Gallery 1007 Harmon Pl Minneapolis MN 55403. *Mailing Add:* Dept Art Calif State Polytech 3801 W Temple Ave Pomona CA 91768

HANNUM, GILLIAN GREENHILL
EDUCATOR, HISTORIAN
b Jan 16, 54. *Study:* Principla Col, BA, 76 (fine arts, highest honors); Pa State Univ, MA (art hist), 81, PhD (art hist), 86. *Collection Arranged:* Photography and Humor (with B & H Henisch & L Greenhill), Pattee Lib, Pa State Univ, 81, Univ Gallery, Calif State Univ, Chico, 81; Shadows and Reflections: Pictorial Photography by Wilbur Porterfield (auth, brochure & checklist), Palmer Mus Art, Pa State Univ, 99, Burchfield-Penney Art Ctr, Buffalo State Col, 2000. *Pos:* Peer reviewer, NEH Preservation and Access Grants, 94-; panelist, Ford Found Post-doct Fellowships for Minorities, 98; panelist, Heathcote Award, Cult Devel and Diversity Grants, Westchester Arts Coun, 93-94. *Teaching:* Part-time instr, Pa State Univ, 81-86; from asst prof art hist to prof & dept chair, Manhattanville Col, 87-. *Awards:* Mabel Axcy Dominick Award Outstanding Achievement in Art History, Principia Col, 76; Alumni Achievement Award, Col Arts and Srchit, Pa State Univ, 92; Teaching Excellence Award, Ind Col Fund NY, Inc, 96; Samuel H Kress Found Travel Grant. *Mem:* Fel Royal Photog Soc Gt Brit; Col Art Asn; Soc Photog Educators; Hist Photog Group; Phi Kappa Phi; Phi Alpha Eta; Int Ctr Photog; Hist Photog Group; Soc Photog Educators; Print Club NY. *Res:* Photographic history; emphasis on pictorialism 1890-1915. *Publ:* contribr, Diane Arbus & Robert Mapplethorpe, Encyl of World Biography, 20th Century Supplement, No 17, 92; contribr, 1902 Stieglitz organizes a group of American photographers as the Photo-Secession, Great Events from History II: Arts and Culture, Salem Press, Inc, 93; Laura Gilpin, Great Lives from History, American Women, Salem Press, Inc, 95; Aubrey Beardsley & Robert Mapplethorpe, Ready Reference: Censorship, Salem Press, Inc, 95; Frances Benjamin Johnston: Promoting Women Photographers, The Ladies Home J, Nineteenth Century, Vol 24, no 2, fall, 2004. *Mailing Add:* Manhattanville Col 2900 Purchase St Purchase NY 10577

HANNUM, TERENCE J
CRITIC, DIRECTOR
Study: NYU, projects in painting, 2000; Fla Southern Col, Lakeland, BA in religion/philosophy & Studio Art, 2001; Sch of Art Inst, Chicago, Post-Baccalaureate Cert in Painting & Studio Art, 2002; Sch of Art Inst, Chicago, MFA in painting and drawing, 2004. *Exhib:* one-man shows, New Work, Small Gallery, Lakeland, Fla, 2000, New Paintings, Liquid, Naples, Fla, 2001, Valentine's Day Peep Show, Hyde Park Fine Arts, Tampa, Fla, 2000, Sr Thesis Exhib, Melvin Gallery, Fla Southern Col, Lakeland, Fla, 2001, Identities and Autobiographies, VonLiebig Art Ctr, Naples, Fla, 2002, The Pick-Up, 1926, Chicago, Ill, 2002, Fac Biennial, VonLiebig Art Ctr, Naples, Fla, 2002, MFA Post-Baccalaureate Exhib, G2, Chicago, Ill, 2002, Brilliant, Zolla/Lieberman Gallery, 2003, Song Lyrics, So-and-So Gallery, 2003, ArtHotel 2003, Embassy Suites, 2003, Stray Show, Zeek & Neen/Municipal, 2003, Modest Contemp Art Projects. *Pos:* Graphic designer, Steppendwarf Theatre Comp, Lakeland, Fla, 2000; gallery asst, Harmon-Meeks Gallery, Naples, 2001; off asst, painting and drawing dept, 2003; dir, Panel-House.com, Chicago. *Teaching:* painting and drawing instr, The VonLiebig Art Ctr, 2002; teacher asst, for Anatomy II, painting and drawing dept Sch of Art Inst Chicago, 2003. *Mem:* Chicago Art Critics Assoc. *Publ:* Writer (articles) Regulator, F News, Bridge Online, (art reviews) panel-house.com. *Mailing Add:* c/o Panel-House Terence Hannum 1046 N Honore St 1F PO Box 220651 Chicago IL 60622

HANSELL, FREYA
PAINTER, EDUCATOR
b Detroit, Mich. *Study:* Wayne State Univ, BFA, 70; Northwestern Univ, MFA, 72; Sch Art Inst Chicago, 72-74. *Work:* Contemp Art Ctr, Hawaii; Mus Contemp Art, Chicago; Chase Manhattan, NY; Milwaukee Art Mus; Mus Mod Art, Franklin Furnace Arch, NY. *Exhib:* Solo exhibs, Artists Space, NY, 80, Marianne Deson Gallery, Chicago, 81, Pub Image Gallery, NY, 84, Piezo Electric Gallery, NY, 84, 86 (with catalog) & 87; A View of Nature, The Aldrich Mus, 86; The New Romantic Landscape, Whitney Mus Am Art, 87; Nocturnes, Whitney Mus Am Art, 89; Buried Alive, ES VanDam, NY, 94; The Office Project, World Communications Bldg, NY, 94; Reinventing the Emblem, Yale Univ Art Gallery, Conn, 95; installation, Drawing Ctr,

NY, 95; installation, Art Exchange, NY, 95. *Teaching:* Instr, Bard Col, 81-82; Parsons Sch Design, 85-90; Sch Visual Arts, 86-89; State Univ NY, Purchase, 91; instr painting, NY Univ, 93-. *Awards:* Nat Endowment Arts, 89-90; grant, NY State Coun Arts, 94; Greenwall Found Grant, 96. *Bibliog:* Michael Brenson (auth), 12/9/88 & Grace Glueck (auth), 9/10/89, NY Times; Art in America, 3/89. *Mem:* Women's Action Coalition (WAC). *Publ:* Auth, Beyond Boundaries, Van Der Marck, 87

HANSEN, FRANCES FRAKES
EDUCATOR, PAINTER
b Harrisburg, Mo. *Study:* Univ Denver, BFA; Art Inst Chicago; Univ Northern Colo, MA; Univ Southern Calif; Univ Denver; Ecoles Art Am, Fontainebleau, France. *Exhib:* Denver Art Mus, 45, 49, 50-60, 62 & 68; Joslyn Mus Biennial, Omaha, Nebr 46, 49, 50, 52, 53 & 67; Gilpin Co Ann, Central City, Colo, 48-51, 53-58, 60, 61, 69 & 72; William Rockhill Nelson Mus, Kansas City, Mo, 50; Mus NMex Ann Regional, Santa Fe, 57 & 59; Colorado Springs Fine Arts Ctr, 61; Colo State Univ Centennial Exhib, 70; Mex Consulate, Denver, 80; and others. *Pos:* Researcher & display designer, Am Indian, Denver Mus Natural Hist, 73-78, 90-; artist-mem ed bd & illusr, Denver Botanic Gardens, 77-93. *Teaching:* Prof art, Colo Women's Col, 45-73; lectr, Am Indian Art. *Awards:* Painting Prize for Oils, Canyon Pastoral, Colo State Fair Prof Show, 65; Colo Women's Col Faculty Res Grant, 69; Painting Prize for Acrylic, Lights, Univ Northern Colo Centennial Exhib, 70; and others. *Mem:* Delta Phi Delta (Art Inst Chicago Chap); Denver Art Mus; Nat Audubon Soc; and others. *Media:* Acrylic, Watercolor. *Res:* Indexing Bratley Collection of Photographs of American Indians for Denver Museum of Nature and Science; identification of objects in collection originally collected by Photographer Bratley - 1880's and 1890's. *Publ:* Auth, Native arts in America, US Cult Bull, 66; illusr, Song of the Ghost Trains, Denver Symphony Guild, 81

HANSEN, GAYLEN CAPENER
PAINTER, EDUCATOR
b Garland, Utah, Sept 21, 21. *Study:* Otis Art Inst, 39-40; Art Barn Sch Fine Arts, 40-44; Art Ctr, Sale Lake City, 40-44; Univ Utah, 43-44 & 45-46; Utah State Agricultural Col, BS, 52; Univ Southern Calif, Los Angeles, MFA, 53. *Work:* Wash State Univ, Pullman; Seattle Arts Comn; Utah State Permanent Collection, Salt Lake City. *Comn:* Painting on canvas, Art in Archit Prog, Moscow, Idaho, 80. *Exhib:* Solo exhibs, Monique Knowlton Gallery, NY, 80, 81 & 83, Boise Gallery Art, Idaho, 85, Galerie Redman, Berlin, Ger, 85, 87, 91, 93, Greg Kucera Gallery Art, Seattle, Wash, 87, Whatcom Mus Hist & Art, Bellingham, Calif, 88, Yellowstone Art Ctr, Billings, Mt, 88 & Arts Club Chicago, 90, Koplin Gallery, 92, 94, Linda Hodges Gallery, Seattle, 93, 95, 98, 99, 02, 04, LewAllen Contemp, Sante Fe, 2000, Palo Alto Center, Calif, 2003, AVC Gallery, NY, 2003; retrospectives, Seattle Art Mus, Wash & Univ Art Mus, Pullman, Wash, 85 & Mus Art, Pa State Univ, Portland Ctr Visual Arts, Ore & San Jose Mus Art, Calif, 86; 38th Corcoran Biennial Exhib Am Painting - 2nd Western States Exhib, Washington, DC, traveling, 83; 5 Amerikanische Kunstler, Galerie Redmann, Berlin, Ger, 84; Second Western Biennial, Brooklyn Mus, NY, 85; Beyond the Real, Prichard Art Gallery, Moscow, Idaho, 86; Folk Images: The Animal Kingdome, Hippodrome Gallery, Long Beach, Calif, 87; Masters of the Inalnd Northwest, Cheney Cowles Mus, Spokane, Wash, 88; Northwest x Southwest Exploring Painted Fictions, Palm Springs Desert Mus, Calif, 90; Northwest Tales: Contemp Narrative Painting, Anchorage Mus Art, Alaska, 91; Drawings II, Koplin Gallery, Santa Monica, Calif, 92; Microsoft Collects, Henry Art Gallery, Seattle, 93; Humor, Frumpkin/Adams Gallery, NY, 94; Interior Idioms, Seafirst Gallery, Seattle, 95; Falling Timber, Tacoma Art Mus, Washington, 96; Outward Bound, American Art at the Brink of the Twenty-First Century, Meridan Int Center, Washington, DC, 1999-2000; Bumerbiennale: Paintings 2000, Bumbershoot, Seattle, Washington, 2000; Seattle Perspective, Washington State Convention Center, Seattle, 2004. *Teaching:* Instr painting & drawing, Univ Tex, Austin, 47-52; prof art, Wash State Univ, Pullman, 57-84. *Awards:* Purchase Prize, Utah State Fair Exhib, 44; First Prize, Fifth Ann Oil Exhib, Woessner Gallery, Seattle, 58; Second Prize, Northwest Watercolor Ann, Seattle Art Mus, 60; Sambuca Romana Prize, The New Mus, NY, 84; Gov's Arts Award, Washington State, 89; Flintridge Found Award for Visual Arts, 2001. *Bibliog:* Lissa August (auth), Westtern Artists Strut Their Stuff, People Weekly, 3/83; Grace Glueck (auth), Two Biennials: One Looking East & the Other West, NY Times, 3/27/83; Matthew Kangas (auth), Little Romances/Little Fictions, Vanguard, 5/84; Dieterich Kinderman (auth), Don't Mistake Gaylen Hansen's Art for Primitive, Idaho Statesman, 5/85. *Media:* Oil on Canvas. *Mailing Add:* c/o Linda Hodges Gallery 316 First Ave S Seattle WA 98104

HANSEN, HAROLD (HARRY) JOHN
EDUCATOR, PAINTER
b Chicago, Ill, June 18, 42. *Study:* Univ Ill, BFA, 64; Univ Mich, MFA, 66. *Work:* SC State Art Collection; SC Florence Mus Art; Univ South; Univ Pac; Carroll Reese Mus, E Tenn State Univ. *Comn:* cover, SC, A History, USC Press, 98. *Exhib:* Drawings USA Traveling Show, 73; Potsdam Drawings, Univ NY Potsdam, 79. *Collection Arranged:* SC Collects Watercolors: SC State Mus, 97. *Pos:* Guest cur, SC State Mus, Columbia, 6-8/97. *Teaching:* Instr art, Kendall Sch Design, Grand Rapids, Mich, 66-69; asst prof art, Ferris State Col, Big Rapids, Mich, 69-70; from asst prof art to assoc prof, Univ SC, 70-86, chmn, Div Art Studio, 75-82, assoc head dept art, 75-90 & prof, 86-, assoc head, 95-. *Awards:* First Prize, Caroliniana Watercolor Competition, Columbia, SC, 81; Grand Prize, SC State Fair, Columbia, 87; First Prize, Florence Mus BB&T Art Exhib, Florence, SC, 96. *Mem:* SC Watercolor Soc (bd). *Media:* Encaustic, Watercolor. *Res:* Technical investigation of the encaustic to improve working characteristics and hardness. *Publ:* Auth, A method for modern encaustic painting, Southeastern Col Art Asn Rev, spring 76; The development of new vehicle recipies for encaustic paints, Leonardo, 77. *Dealer:* City ARt, 1224 Lincoln St, Columbia, SC, 29201. *Mailing Add:* Univ SC Dept Art Columbia SC 29208

HANSEN, JAMES LEE
SCULPTOR
b Tacoma, Wash, June 13, 25. *Study:* Portland Art Mus Sch. *Work:* Seattle Art Mus; Univ Ore Mus Art, Eugene; Civic Transit Mall, Portland, Ore; State Capitol, Salem, Ore, Fresno, Calif. *Comn:* The Shaman, State Capitol Campus, Olympia, Wash, 70; Crescent Probe, Civic Ctr Fountain, Salem, Ore, 78; Stempost, Stadium Plaza Wash State Univ, Pullman, 80; The Oasis, Bur Land Mgt Bldg, Medford, Ore, 80. *Exhib:* 71st Ann Painting & Sculpture exhib, San Francisco Mus Mod Art, 52; Whitney Mus Am Art Ann, 53; NW art Today, Seattle Worlds Fair, Wash, 62; one-man shows, Fountain Gallery, Portland, 69, 77, 81 & 84, Univ Ore Mus Art, Eugene, 70, Portland Art Mus, 71, Friedlander Gallery, Seattle, 73 & 77, Hodges/Banks Gallery, Seattle, Wash, 83 & 85 & Abante Fine Arts, Portland, Ore, 86, 88 & 92; Artists of Oregon (paintings & sculpture), Portland Art Mus, Ore, 71; Art of the Pacific Northwest from 1930s to present, Nat Col Fine Art, Smithsonian Inst, Washington, 74; Mayor's Invit Art Show, Salem Civic Ctr, Ore, 76; Spokane Sculpture Invit, Wash, 77; An Am Tradition: Abstraction, Henry Gallery, Seattle, Wash, 81 & 82. *Pos:* Founder & 1st pres, Alliance of NW Sculptors, 77-80. *Teaching:* Prof sculpture, Portland State Univ, 64-90, emer, 90. *Awards:* Nat Ann, Award for Huntress, 52; Am Trust Co Award, 56 & Award for Ritual, 60, San Francisco Art Mus; Norman Davis Award for Neo Shang, Seattle Art Mus, 58. *Bibliog:* William Davenport (auth), Art treasures in the West, Lane, 10/66; JA Schinneller (auth), Art/search & self discovery, Int Textbk, 12/67. *Mem:* Portland Art Mus. *Media:* Cast Bronze. *Publ:* New Totems & Old Gods, Surgo Publ, 90. *Dealer:* Bryan Ohno Gallery, 155 S Main St, Seattle, Wa, 98104. *Mailing Add:* Peter Burtlow Gallery 44 E Superior Chicago IL 60611

HANSEN, ROBERT
PAINTER, SCULPTOR
b Osceola, Nebr, Jan 1, 24. *Study:* Univ Nebr, AB, BFA, 48; Escuela Univ Bellas Artes, San Miguel Allende, Mex, MFA, 49; also with Alfredo Zalce, Morelia, Mex, 52-53. *Work:* Mus Mod Art & Whitney Mus Am Art, NY; Los Angeles Co Mus Art; San Diego Gallery Fine Arts; Long Beach Mus Art. *Exhib:* Numerous solo exhibs, 57-2006; Carnegie Int, Pittsburgh, Pa, 61 & 63; Painting USA: Figure, Mus Mod Art, NY, 62 & Tamarind: Homage to Lithography, 69; retrospectives, Long Beach Mus Art, Calif, 67 & Los Angeles Munic Gallery, 73; New Vein, organized & mounted in mus of nat capitols in Europe & SAm, Smithsonian Inst, 68-70. *Teaching:* Prof art, Occidental Col, 56-87, emer prof, 87-. *Awards:* Guggenheim Fel, 61; Fulbright Sr Grant, 61; Tamarind Fel, 65. *Media:* Lacquer. *Publ:* Auth, This curving world: Hyperbolic linear perspective, J Aesthetics & Art Criticism, winter 73; transl, Curvilinear Perspective, Flocon and Barre, Univ Calif Press, 87. *Mailing Add:* 1498 Santa Ynez Carpinteria CA 93013

HANSEN, SARAH EVELETH CAMPBELL
ART DEALER, GALLERY DIRECTOR
b Attleboro, Mass, June 15, 17. *Study:* Wellesley Col, BA, 39; Boston Univ, MA, 41. *Pos:* Dir, Sarah Eveleth Antiques, Washington, DC or Bethesda, Md, 69-; from co-dir to dir, The Glass Gallery, Bethesda, Md, 72-. *Mem:* Glass Art Soc. *Specialty:* Contemporary glass, including mixed media pieces, in which glass is being used as an art medium for individual expression. *Mailing Add:* The Glass Gallery Chevy Chase Pavilion Level 2 5335 Wisconsin Ave NW Washington DC 20015

HANSLEY, LEE
ART DEALER, CURATOR
b Roanoke Rapids, NC, Jan 11, 48. *Study:* Univ NC, Chapel Hill (art hist). *Collection Arranged:* Awards in the Visual Arts 1-5, 1981-86; The Art of New Orleans, SECCA, 1984; Edith London Retrospective (auth, catalog), Durham, NC, 1992; Silvia Heyden: A Culmination of Tapestry Weaving in NC, 1993; E C Langford: A Half-Century of Painting, Sculpture and Collage, 1995; The Chapel Hill School: A Shared Aesthetic, 1998. *Pos:* Assoc cur, SECCA, Winston-Salem, NC, 1980-86; indep cur, 1986-92; proprietor/dir, Lee Hansley Gallery, Raleigh, NC 1993-. *Specialty:* American contemporary art. *Mailing Add:* 225 Glenwood Ave Raleigh NC 27603-1404

HANSMAN, BOB
PAINTER, INSTRUCTOR
b St Louis, Mo, Oct 21, 47. *Study:* Univ Kans, BFA, 70. *Work:* Towers-Perrin, Kranston Industries. *Exhib:* Solo shows, St Louis Community Col, Forest Park, 88, MJF Arts Studio Gallery, 90, Univ City Pub Libr, 92 & 95 & Bonsack Gallery, 95; Componere Gallery, 90; Not Just an Art Director's Club, 90; Art St Louis Gallery, 91; Gallery Connection, 91; Artists Choose Artists Invitational, Art St Louis X, 95. *Pos:* dir, City Faces, St Louis Pub Housing. *Teaching:* Instr, Proj Artspark, Dept Parks & Recreation, 93, Arts Connection/City Faces, Ctr Contemp Arts, 94-, Children's Art Circuit, Juvenile Detention Prog, 95 & Washington Univ, St Louis. *Awards:* Bi-State Arts in Transit Proj Grant, 95, 96 & 97; Mo Arts Award, Mo Arts Coun, 97; Emerson Electric Excellence in Teaching Award, 2000. *Bibliog:* Reader's poll best local artist, Riverfront Times, 95; Coming Up Taller (feature in White House Report), 96; cover article, Art St Louis, winter 98. *Mem:* Focus St Louis; Paint Louis; Art St Louis; Omicron Delta Kappa. *Media:* Mixed Media. *Publ:* Awakenings, St Louis Past-Dispatch, 1/15/95; Spreading the Light: Meeting Society's Needs and Sharing its Responsibilities, Washington Univ Annual Report, 95; Remembering the Spirit of a Teen-Ager Who Died Too Soon, Chronicle of Higher Edn, 2-97; Bob Hasman and City Faces, Mo Arts Coun Artlogue, fall 98; Community Partnerships-Making Art Work Together, Arts in Transit, 99. *Dealer:* Duane Reed Gallery 1 N Taylor St Louis MO 63108. *Mailing Add:* Sch Archit Washington Univ-Campus Box 1079 1 Brookings Dr St Louis MO 63130-4899

HANSON, ANNELIES RUTH
CERAMIST, CRAFTSMAN
b Dresden, Ger, Aug 17, 27; US citizen. *Study:* RI Sch Design, BFA; Tex Woman's Univ, MA. *Exhib:* Seventh Int Exhib Ceramic Art, Smithsonian Inst, Washington, DC, 58; Ann Area Competition, Corcoran Gallery, Washington, DC, 59; 22nd Ceramic Nat Traveling Show, Everson Mus, Syracuse, 62 & 68; Am Craftsmen's Coun Exhib, Oakland, Calif, 63; Form and Quality, Int Exhib, Munich, Ger, 64-69. *Pos:* Designer & glaze analyst, Calif Art Tile Co, Richmond, 51-52; asst to dir, Gump's Gallery, San Francisco, 52-53 & Fine Art Gallery, Dallas, 64-66. *Teaching:* Instr ceramics, Md Art Inst, Baltimore, 57-59 & Southern Methodist Univ, 64-69; instr ceramics & sculpture, Mountain View Col, Tex, 70-74. *Awards:* Craft Horizons Award, Smithsonian Inst, 58; First Prize, Corcoran Gallery, 59; 16th Tex Crafts Exhib Top Award, Dallas Mus Fine Arts, 74; and others. *Bibliog:* Creation in Clay (film), KERA TV, 68. *Mem:* Tex Designer Craftsmen (secy, 71, vpres, 74-75); Dallas Craft Guild; World Crafts Coun; Am Craftsmen Coun

HANSON, JB
SCULPTOR, WEAVER
b Gadsden, Ala, Oct 23, 46. *Study:* Md Inst, Col Art, 72-76. *Work:* Univ Md, College Park; Washington Co Mus Fine Art; Cloisters Children's Mus, Baltimore; Centre Int de la Tapisserie Ancienne et Moderne, Lusanne, Switzerland. *Comn:* 6 banners depicting the History of the Govans Community, City Baltimore, Md, 79, tapestry for Medfield Recreation Ctr, 79; mural, Mallory Ctr, Inst Arts, Inc, 81. *Exhib:* Maryland Ann, Baltimore Mus Art, 72; Maryland Biennial, Baltimore Mus Art, 74; Miniatures, West Tex Mus Art, Lubbock, 76; 11th Int Sculpture Symp, Studio Gallery, Washington, DC, 80; Am Clay 1981, Meredith Contemp Art, Md, 81; Fine Art Auction Exhib, Metrop Mus, Fla, 81; Art of Ceramics, Atheneum Mus, Va, 81. *Awards:* Sculpture Award, Baltimore Mus Art, 74; Sculpture Award, Md Crafts Coun, 78. *Bibliog:* David Tannous (auth), Baltimore art scene, Smithsonian Assoc Mag, 79; Thomas Haulk (auth), reviews, Craft Horizon Mag, 79; Elisabeth Stevens (auth), Pots full of wit: sculptor shows he has a way with animals, Baltimore Sun, 80. *Mem:* Artist Equity Asn (pres, 80-81, nat ECoast vpres, 81-83); Md Crafts Coun (pres, 76). *Media:* Clay; Fibers. *Mailing Add:* 622 Homestead St Baltimore MD 21218-3556

HANSON, JO
SCULPTOR, ENVIRONMENTAL ARTIST
b Carbondale, Ill. *Study:* San Francisco State Univ, MA (sculpture), 73. *Work:* San Francisco Mus Mod Art; Mills Col, Oakland, Calif; Oakland Mus Art; Herbert F Johnson Mus, Cornell Univ; San Francisco Arts Com; San Francisco Fine Arts Mus. *Comn:* Installation, multi-media, 1st Int Conf Healthy Cities, San Francisco, 93; installation, sculptural, Dublin Civic Ctr, Dublin Fine Arts Found, Calif, 94. *Exhib:* Corcoran Gallery Art, DC, 74; San Francisco Mus Mod Art, 76 & Pa Acad Fine Arts, Philadelphia, 77; San Francisco Mus Mod Art & San Francisco City Hall, 80, Illegal Sights-Sites, Int Sculpture Conf, San Francisco, 82; Mus Contemp Art, Univ Sau Paulo, Brazil, 80; Pratt Manhattan Ctr Gallery, NY, 81; Chance and Change, A Century of the Avant-Garde, Auckland City Gallery, New Zealand, 85; Garbage Out Front, Municipal Art Soc, NY, 90; Watershed/Waterwebs, Euprat Mus, de Anza Col, Calif, 98; Fresno Mus Art, Fresno, Calif, 98; plus others. *Pos:* Art comnr, City of San Francisco, 83-89; adv artist-in-res prog, Sanitary Fill Co, San Francisco, 89-; co-cur, Living in Balance, San Francisco Int Airport, 93, Richmond Art Ctr, Richmond, Calif, 94 & Olive Hyde Art Gallery, Fremont, Calif, 99; co-cur, Dear Mother Earth, Frank lloyd Wright Civic Ctr, Marin Co, Calif, 98; advisor art and ecology, Earthlight Mag, 99-, Bioneers Conf, 99-. *Awards:* Citations, San Francisco Bd Supervisors, 80 & Mayor, 89; Outstanding Achievement in Visual Arts, Nat Women's Caucas Art, 97; Distinguished Woman Artist of Year, Fresno Art Mus, Calif, 98; Honor Award Bioneers Conf, 2000; Honor Award, Calif Lawyers for the Arts, 2004. *Bibliog:* Thelma R Newman (auth), Innovative Printmaking, Crown Publ Inc, NY, 77; Suzanne Lacy (auth), Mapping the Terrain: New Genre Public Art, Bay Press, Seattle, 95; Distinguished Woman Artist of the Year 1998 (catalog), Fresno Art Mus; Judy Malley (ed), Women, Art & Technology, MIT Pres, 2003. *Mem:* Women's Caucus Art; Col Art Asn; Pacific Rim Sculpture Group. *Media:* Mixed Media. *Publ:* Auth, Artists Taxes, the Hands on Guide, Vortex Press, San Francisco, 87; co-ed, Living in Balance (catalog), 93 & 94; The healing role of art, Eco-Psychology Newsletter, fall 96; Nature Speaks (catalog essay), Santa Clara Univ, Calif, 99; co-publ, Women Environmental Artists Directory, 96-; contributor, Women, Art & Technology, MIT Press, 2003. *Mailing Add:* 201 Buchanan San Francisco CA 94102

HANSON, JUDY (JUDY COOKE) See Cooke, Judy

HANSON, PHILIP HOLTON
PAINTER
b Chicago, Ill, Jan 8, 43. *Study:* Univ Chicago, BA, 65; Art Inst Chicago, MFA, 69. *Work:* Mus des 20 Jahrhunderts, Vienna, Austria; Mus Contemp Art, Chicago; Krannert Mus, Champaign, Ill. *Exhib:* Extraordinary Realities, Whitney Mus, 73; Madison Art Ctr, 77; Contemp Chicago Painters, Univ North Iowa Gallery Art, 78; Fabrications, Univ Miami, Lowe Art Mus, 80; Some Recent Art from Chicago, Ackland Art Mus, Univ NC, Chapel Hill, 80; Who Chicago, London, Edinburgh and traveling, 80; Six Chicago Artists, Pace Gallery, NY, 82; one-man show, Phyllis Kind Gallery, Chicago, 82, Hyde Park Art Ctr, 85. *Teaching:* Prof, Sch Art Inst Chicago, 72-. *Awards:* Casandra Grant, 73; Nat Endowment Arts Grant, 78 & 83. *Media:* Oil. *Mailing Add:* Sch Art Inst Chicago Columbus Dr & Jackson St Chicago IL 60603

HAOZOUS, BOB
SCULPTOR
b Los Angeles, Calif, Apr 1, 43. *Study:* Utah State Univ, 61-62; Calif Col Arts & Crafts, BFA, 71. *Work:* Albuquerque Mus, NMex; Heard Mus, Phoenix, Ariz; Joslyn Mus Art, Omaha, Nebr; Philbrook Art Ctr, Tulsa, Okla; Southwest Mus, Los Angeles; and others. *Comn:* Mahogany relief wall mural, Daybreak Star Art Ctr, Seattle, Wash, 78; ann award bronze, Busn Comt Arts, NY, 83; sculpture for permanent collection, Heard Mus, Phoenix, Ariz, 83; monumental outdoor sculpture, City of Philadelphia, 88; 5 paired monumental sculptures, City of Phoenix, Ariz, 90. *Exhib:* One-man shows, Taylor Mus, Colorado Springs, 87, Wheelwright Mus, Santa Fe, NMex, 88 & Dartmouth Col, Hanover, NH, 89; Muerte/Amor, UNAM, Galeria Aristos, Mexico City, Mex, 90; Recent Major Work, Nev State Mus, Las Vegas, 92; The Vanishing White Man, Scotsdale Ctr Arts, Ariz, 92. *Pos:* Artist-in-residence, Dartmouth Col, Hanover, NH, 89 & Frankfort, Ger. *Bibliog:* Rosalind Constable (auth), Six Artists, Horizon, 82; Lucy Lippard (auth), New Art in Multicultural America, Pantheon Bks, 90; Robin Cembalilst (auth), Pride & prejudice, Artnews, 92. *Media:* Steel. *Mailing Add:* c/o The Heard Mus 22 E Monte Vista Rd Phoenix AZ 85004-1480

HAPGOOD, SUSAN T
CURATOR, CRITIC
b Riverhead, NY, Oct 18, 57. *Study:* Univ Rochester, BA, 79; Inst Fine Arts, NY Univ, MA, 85. *Collection Arranged:* Recent Acquisitions, 85, Homage to Louise Nevelson (auth, brochure), 86 & The Early Years: Non-Objective Paintings from the Permanent Collection, (auth, brochure), 88, Guggenheim Mus; Flux Attitudes, Hallwalls, (auth, catalog), 91; New Mus Contemp Art, 92; Neo-Dada: Redefining Art (auth, catalog) 58-62, Equitable Gallery, New York, 95; Video Divertimenti, Camera Oscura, Tuscany, Ital, 99. *Pos:* Archivist, Sperone Westwater Gallery, New York, 79-82, asst to dir, formerly; coordr, Art Quest, New Mus Contemp Art, New York, 83-84; cur coordr, Solomon R Guggenheim Mus, New York, 85-89, cur asst, formerly; cur, Woodner Family Col, New York, 94-97; researcher, ada'web, NY, 97-98; Cur exhibs, Am Fedn Arts, New York, 99-2003; Dir exhibs, ICI, NY, 2003. *Teaching:* Instr art hist, Sch Visual Arts, 88. *Awards:* Fel, List Ctr Art & Politics, New Sch, N, 98-. *Mem:* Col Art Asn. *Res:* Contemporary art. *Publ:* Auth, Remaking Art History, 90 & Whitney Mus: How American Is It?, Art Am, 91; About Art Criticism, Acme Art J, 92; Fonts of Wisdom, Frieze Mag, 96; Doppelhelix: Kunst und Geld, Der Standard, 96. *Mailing Add:* 326 W 22nd St New York NY 10011

HARA, KEIKO
PAINTER, PRINTMAKER (INSTALLATION)
b Oct 1, 42; Japanese citizen. *Study:* Gendai Art Sch, (painting), Japan, 64; Oita Junior Art Col, (painting), Japan, 65; Miss State Univ Women, BFA(painting), 74; Univ Wis, Milwaukee, MA(printmaking), 75; Cranbrook Acad Art, MFA(printmaking), 76. *Work:* Tacoma Art Mus, Wash; Art Inst Chicago; Detroit Inst Art; Milwaukee Art Mus; Libr Congress, Capital Heights, Md. *Comn:* Lithography, Perimeter Gallery, Chicago, 82; Gates - outdoor installation, Whitman Col, 98; Invitational King Co Pub Art Comn, 2002; painting installation, Wash Public Art Com, 2006. *Exhib:* 30th Am Invitational & 20th Nat Print Show, Brooklyn Art Mus, NY, 76; Gallerie in Den Vierlander, Hamburg, Ger, 81; Charles A Wustum Mus, Rachine, Wis, 81; Tacoma Art Mus, Wash, 94; Mus Art, Univ Ore, Eugene, 95; NW Int Print Art Exhib, Portland Art Mus, Ore, 97; Square Painting/Plane Painting, COCA, Seattle, 97; Topophilia Sumida River, Elizabeth Leach Gallery, Portland, Ore, 97; Japanese/Am: The In Between, Art Gym, Marylhurst Col, Portland, Ore, 98; Perimeter Gallery, Chicago, 98; ColorPrint USA, Nat Invitational Print Portfolio Exhib, 50 US States, 98; P Richard Art Gallery, Univ of Idaho, 99; Perimeter Gallery, Chicago, Ill, 2000, 03; Foster/White Gallery, Seattle, Wash, 2000; Autzen Gallery, Portland State Univ, Ore, 2001; Lorinda Knight Gallery, Spokane, Wash, 2002, Keiko Hara works on paper 7 Canvas, Perimeter Gallery, NY; Keiko Hara painting & works on paper, 2003; Keiko Hara-Seasons, The Northwest Mus of Arts & Cult, Spokane, WA, 2004; Keiko Hara, Imbuning in Monet, Perimeter Gallery, Chicago, 2006. *Collection Arranged:* Northwest Art Mus, Wash; MIC Software Co, Wash; Portland Art Mus/Gilkey Ctr Graphic Arts, Ore; Art Inst of Chicago; Tacoma Art Mus, Wash; King Co Art Comn, Wash; Milwaukee Art Mus, Wis; Sony Co, Washington, DC; Detroit Inst of Art, Mich; IBM Corp, Chicago; Muskegon Mus Art, Mich; Charles A. Wustum Mus, Wis; The Council House-Johnson Wax Co, Wis; Oita Art Col Japan; AT & T Co, Chicago; Jundt Art Mus, Gonzaga Univ, Wash. *Teaching:* Instr printmaking, Carthage Col, 79-80 & Univ Wis, River Falls, 80-85; prof art, Whitman col, 85-2006. *Awards:* Artist Trust Fel, Wash, 94; Purchase Award, Portland Art Mus/Gilkey Ctr Graphic Arts, Ore, 97; The Pollock-Krasner Found Grant, New York, 2005. *Bibliog:* Lois Allen (auth), Contemporary Printmaking in the Northwest, Craftsman House, Australia, 97; Keiko Hara at the Perimeter Galler, Artnews; Critic's Choice/Chicago Reader, Fred Camper, 2003; Robert C Morgan (auth), Keiko Hara's Springtime, Shreds of Language. *Dealer:* Perimeter Gallery 750 N Orleans Chicago IL 60610; Lorinda Knight Gallery, Spokane, WA. *Mailing Add:* 336 N Division Walla Walla WA 99362

HARBUTT, CHARLES
PHOTOGRAPHER
b Camden, NJ, July 29, 35. *Study:* Marquette Univ, BS, 56. *Work:* Mus Mod Art, NY; Art Inst Chicago; Smithsonian Inst; Bibliotheque Nat, Paris; George Eastman House, Rochester, NY. *Teaching:* Vis artist photog, Art Inst Chicago, 75, RI Sch Design, 76 & Mass Inst Technol, 79; prof Parsons School Design. *Awards:* Best Photog Book, Arles Festival, 74. *Media:* Photography. *Dealer:* Laurence Miller Gallery 20 W 57th St New York NY 10019. *Mailing Add:* One Fifth Ave #16-G New York NY 10003-4312

HARCUS, PORTIA GWEN
DEALER, CONSULTANT
b Brockton, Mass. *Study:* Wheaton Col, BA. *Pos:* Dir, Harcus Krakow Gallery, 64-82; dir & pres, Harcus Gallery, 82-. *Mem:* Art Dealers Asn Am; Asn Int Photog Art Dealers; Art Table Inc; Confederation Int Negociants Oeuvres D'Art. *Specialty:* Contemporary painting, sculpture, grahics and major 20th century works. *Mailing Add:* 6 Melrose St Boston MA 02116-5510

HARDEN, MARVIN
PAINTER, EDUCATOR
b Austin, Tex. *Study:* Univ Calif, Los Angeles, BA(fine arts) & MA(creative painting); Los Angeles City Col. *Work:* Whitney Mus Am Art & Mus Mod Art, NY; Smithsonian Inst, Archives Am Art; NY Pub Libr Spencer Collection; Los Angeles Co Mus Art; Getty Ctr Arts & Humanities. *Comn:* lithograph, Neighbors of Watts, 82; lithograph, UCLA Friends Graphic Arts, 86. *Exhib:* Los Angeles Co Mus Art, 65, 68, 69, 74. 77, 95 & 96; Amory Ctr Arts, Pasadena, Calif, 94; Tel Aviv Mus Art, Israel, 98; solo exhibs, Rath Mus, Geneva, Switz, 71, Whitney Mus Am Art, 71, Irving Blum Gallery, Los Angeles, 72, Cororan Gallery, Los Angeles, 78, Newport Harbor Art Mus, 79 & Los Angeles Munic Art Gallery, 82, Ventura Col Art Gallery, 97, Louis Stern Fine Arts, Los Angeles, 99; Armory Ctr, Art Pasadena, 92, 94, 97 & 2005; Schneider Mus Art, Ashland, Ore, 2004; Luckman Fine Arts Complex, Los Angeles, Calif, 2004. *Pos:* Co-founder, Los Angeles Inst Contemp Art, 73, exhib comt mem, 73-74; bd dir, Images & Issues, 80-86; mem visual arts panel, Nat Endowment for Arts, 1985; chair peer rev bd for visual arts, Los Angeles Cult Affairs Dept, 1990. *Teaching:* Instr drawing, Univ Calif, Los Angeles, 64-68; instr drawing, Los Angeles Harbor Col, 65-68; prof painting & drawing, Calif State Univ, Northridge, 67-97, prof emer, 97-. *Awards:* Nat Endowment Arts Fel, 72; Awards in Visual Arts fellow, 1983; Distinguished Prof Award, Exceptional Merit Serv Award, Calif State Univ, Northridge, 1984. *Bibliog:* Karen Anne Mason (auth), African-Americna Artists of Los Angeles: Marvin Harden, Univ Calif Los Angeles, 1995; Marvin Harden Paintings and Drawings 1961-1981, Los Angeles Munic Art Gallery, 1982; William Wilson (auth), Soul shapes in an empty field, Los Angeles Times, 3/17/82. *Media:* Painting, Drawing. *Publ:* Marvin Harden (auth), natural selections, Lapis Press, 1991. *Dealer:* Cirrus Editions Ltd 542 S Alameda Los Angeles CA 90013 (prints only). *Mailing Add:* Inwardness Ranch PO Box 1793 Cambria CA 93428

HARDER, RODNEY
PAINTER
b OGallala, Nebr, Apr 24, 50. *Study:* Fresno Pac Col, Calif, BFA, 73; Calif State Univ, Fresno, MA, 75. *Work:* Citibank, NY; IBM, NY; Can Imperial Bank, NY; Baltimore City Health Dept, Md; Fresno Art Mus, Calif; many pvt collections throughout US. *Exhib:* Solo shows, Gallery 25, Fresno, Calif, 82, Fresno Art Mus, Calif, 83 & 89, Farleigh Dickinson Univ, Hackensack, NJ, 87 & Peoples Place Gallery, Intercourse, Pa, 88; Gallery M, Fresno, Calif, 91; Sweet Briar Col, Va, 91; Diverse Visions, Art Ctr Gallery, Del, 92; The Blanket Project, Art in Gen, NY, 93; and others. *Teaching:* Prof art, Fresno Pac Col, Calif, 74-83; art instr, Fresno Art Mus, Calif, 80-83 & Calif State Univ, Fresno, 81-83; art instr/coordr, Col Sch, NY, 84-; adj art instr, NY Sch Visual Arts, 86. *Awards:* Nat Endowment Arts Fel, painting, 90 & 91; Milton Avery Residency Grant, Yaddo, 94; Ragdale Artists Colony Residency, 98; and others. *Mailing Add:* 115 104th St Apt 56 New York NY 10025-4261

HARDER, ROLF PETER
GRAPHIC DESIGNER, PAINTER
b Hamburg, Ger, July 10, 29; Can citizen. *Study:* Hamburg Acad Fine Arts, 48-52. *Work:* Libr Congress, Washington, DC; AGI Archives, Poster Mus, Essen, Ger; Nat Archives Can; Univ Reading, England; Mus de la Publicite Palais du Louvre, Paris; German Design Coun, Frankfurt; Mus for Arts and Crafts, Hamburg, Ger; Die Neue Sammlung, State Mus for Applied Arts, Munich; Design Austria, Vienna; Univ NY Col at Frdonia, NY; Musée du Québec, Can; Université Du Québec Á Montréal, poster collection, Images of Peace, Can; Montreal Mus Fine Arts, Mus Modern Art, NY, NY & San Francisco, Calif. *Comn:* 70 postage stamps, Can Post; visual images (symbols), numerous corps and insts; publs, Can Gov Depts. *Exhib:* Design Collaborative Int Traveling Exhib, 70-72; Biennale of Graphic Design, Brno, 70, 74, 78, 80, 82, 84, 92, 94 & 96; Experimental Graphic Design, Venice Biennale, 72; group exhibs, Can, USA, Europe, South Am, Japan, Russia & Korea. *Pos:* pres, Rolf, Harder & Assoc, Inc. *Teaching:* Guest lectr, graphic design. *Awards:* Spec Prize, 4th Biennale Graphic Design, Brno, 70; Spec Prize, Int Poster Competition, Moscow, 87; World Logo Design Award, Brussels, 98; and over 100 nat & int design awards. *Bibliog:* Theodore Hilten (auth), Rolf Harder, 9/64 & Hans Kuh (auth), Design Collaborative, 9/70, Gebrauchsgraphic, Munich; Peter Bartl, Novum, Munich, 87; Rose Deneve, Print, New York, 90; Eberhard Hoelscher (auth), Gebrauchsgraphic, Munich, Feb 61; CA Magazine, CA, 62; Hans Neuberg (auth), Graphis, Switz #143, 69; Gloria Menard (auth), Contemporary Designers, St James Press, London, Chicago. *Mem:* Royal Can Acad Arts; Alliance Graphique Int; Am Inst Graphic Arts; Int Ctr Typographic Arts; fel Soc Graphic Designers Can. *Media:* Oil, Acrylic. *Interests:* Music, Reading. *Publ:* Auth, Introd, Can Sect, World History of the Poster, Paris; Introduction (Canada): Who's Who in Graphic Arts, Zurich, 83; co-publisher, Pitseolak:Pictures Out of My Life, 72, Arts of the Eskimo: Prints, 74. *Dealer:* Artothèque De Montréal Art Gallery, Enigma, Toronto. *Mailing Add:* 43 Lakeshore Rd Beaconfield PQ H9W 4H6 Canada

HARDING, ANN
PAINTER
b Minneapolis, Minn, Mar 16, 42. *Study:* Univ Minn, BA, 66; Univ Cincinnati, MFA, 71. *Work:* Lutheran Brotherhood, Minneapolis; Sterling Drug Corp, Philapelphia, Pa; Ochsner Med Found, New Orleans, La; Rhone-Poulenc Rorer Corp, Philadelphia, Pa; Mount Sinai Med Ctr, NY; Random House, NY; and others. *Exhib:* 20th Exhib Southwest Prints & Drawings, Dallas Mus Fine Arts, 75; one-person exhibs, Friends Gallery, Minneapolis Inst Fine Arts, 81, West Baton Rouge Mus, Port Allen, La, 83, Still-Zinsel Contemp Fine Art, New Orleans, La, 91 & Reece Galleries, NY, 2001, 2003 & 2006; Nat Ann Midyear Show, Butler Inst Am Art, 81 & 82; Biennial Piedmont Painting & Sculpture, Mint Mus, 81 & 83; La Women in Contemp Art Traveling Exhib Invitational, 83-84; Hoyt Nat Painting Show, Hoyt Inst Fine Art, 83 & 85; Tampa Triennial, Tampa Mus, Fla, 85; Nat Art Festival, Atlanta, 89; and others. *Teaching:* Instr painting & drawing, La State Univ, 73-76, from asst prof to prof, 76-93, emer prof, 93-. *Awards:* Purchase Award, 35th Ann, La State Art Exhib, 80; SECCA Artist Fel, 81; Visual Arts Fel, La State Arts Coun, 85. *Media:* Oil on Canvas, Oil on Paper. *Dealer:* Reece Galleries 24 W 57 St New York NY 10019. *Mailing Add:* 408-410 Northampton St Easton PA 18042-3516

HARDING, NOEL ROBERT
SCULPTOR, VIDEO ARTIST
b London, Eng, Dec 21, 45. *Work:* Art Gallery Ontario, Toronto, Ontario; Nat Gallery Can, Ottawa, Ontario; Mus Mod Art, NY; Windsor Art Gallery, Windsor, Ontario; City Amsterdam, Netherlands; Mus Sztuki Aktualnej, Krakow, Poland. *Exhib:* Minneapolis Col Art & Design & Walker Art Ctr, Minneapolis, Minn, 72; Art Gallery Ont (installation), Toronto, 74, 76 & 77; Nat Gallery of Can, 77; Projects, Mus Mod Art, NY, 78; Nat Gallery Can (installation), Ottawa, 78, 91 & 94; Video Viewpoints, Mus Mod Art, NY, 80; Musee d'Art Contemporain (installation), Montreal, 81; retrospective, Art Gallery, Ont, Toronto, 82; Video Art: a Hist, Mus Mod Art, NY, 83; solo exhibs: Mississauga Civic Ctr Art Gallery, Can, 90; Mus Sztuki Aktualnej, Galeria Potocko, Krakow, Poland, 91; Genereux Grunwald Gallery, Toronto, 92; The Power Plant, Ctr Contemp Art, Toronto, 92; Anti-Heroes (with catalog), Mucsarnok Palace of Exhibs, Budapest, Hungary, 93; Contemp Art Gallery, Vancouve, 93; Anti-Heroes, Nat Gallery Slovakia, Bratislava, 94; Archive Gallery, Toronto, Ont, Can, 97; Wittmann Lawrence Gallery, Vancouver, BC, Can, 99; Liget Gallery, Budapest, Hungary, 93; Arti et Amicitiae, Amsterdam, The Neth, 93; Kolekcja Artystow, BWA, Bialystok, Poland, 93; Distinguishing Features, MacDonald Stewart Art Ctr, Guelph, Can, 94; Distinguishing Features, Pleasure Dome, Toronto, 94; Contemp Art Gallery, Vancouver, 95; MacDonald Stewart Art Gallery, Guelph, Ont, 96; Vancouver Art Gallery, 97; and many other solo and group exhibs; Scenic Events on a Path of Upheaval, Mus Contemp Can Art, Toronto, 2003; Three Pieces for Circuits, Art Gallery Ontario (collection), Toronto, Ontario, 2004; In Service, Macdonald Strewart Art Center, Guelph, Ontario, 2005; Green Corridor, Windsor, Ontario, 2006. *Pos:* Pub lect, McMaster Univ, Dept Fine Arts, Hamilton, Ontario, 2003; consult, Toronto Zoo (Live Arts Festival), 2004. *Teaching:* Instr fine art video, Univ Guelph, 74-77; instr independent 74-77, instr independent study utilizing video, 72-76, instr sr independent study utilizing any/all of film slide & video, 76 & instr experiments in art performance, 77; instr creative film/video, Photo Electric Arts Dept, Ont Col Art, 77; instr creative film video, Univ Guelph & Ont Col Art, 77-; plus many lectr in Can & Europe; artist-in-residence art academies, Eng, Scotland, Norway, Finland, Poland & Holland; artist docent, AKT Media Dept, Enschede, Neth, currently; adj prof, Univ Windsor, 2004-2005. *Awards:* Can Coun Arts Grant, 76 & 78-79, Travel Grant, 77 & Proj Grant, 78; Ont Arts Coun Grant, 77 & 79. *Bibliog:* Richard Rhodes (auth), Noel Harding, Artforum, 1/87; Carl Loeffler (auth), Noel Harding, Toronto Mag, 3/87; Robin Laurence (auth), Come to dada, Weekend Sun, Vancouver, 1/8/94; Joan Murray (author), Canadian Art in the Twentieth Century, Dundurn Press, 99; Anne Newlands (auth), Canadian Art: From the Beginning to 2000, Firefly Books Ltd, 2000. *Mem:* Int Kunstler Gremium, Berlin, Ger. *Media:* Diverse Materials. *Publ:* Video Art Video, TV Ont, Can, 94. *Dealer:* Linda Genereux Gallery 21 Morrow Ave Toronto ON M6R 2H9; Installations/Sculpture: John Gibson Gallery 392 W Broadway New York NY 10012. *Mailing Add:* 2154 Dundas St W Unit 303 Toronto ON M6R 1X3 Canada

HARDING, TIM
DESIGNER
Study: Hamline Univ, BA(painting); Minn Col Art. *Work:* Minn Hist Soc. *Comn:* Hyatt Regency Hotels, Minneapolis & Los Angeles, 82. *Exhib:* Traju: Um Obecto De Arte?, Gulbenkian Mus, Lisbon, 90; solo exhibs, Ctr Tapestry Arts, NY, 91 & Art Complex Mus, Duxbury, Maine, 92; Studio Production, Am Craft Mag, NY, 92; Noeuds Et Filets: Liens Spirituels, African Touring Exhib, USIA, 93; 50 Yrs of Am Craft, Minn Mus Am Art, 93; and others. *Awards:* Arts Midwest Artist Fel Grant, 85; Visual Artist Fel, Nat Endowment Arts, 86. *Bibliog:* Linda Dyett (auth), article, Am Craft Mag, 10-11/83. *Media:* Art Garments. *Mailing Add:* c/o Art Resources Gallery 494 Jackson St Saint Paul MN 55101

HARDY, DAVID WHITTAKER, III
PAINTER, INSTRUCTOR
b Dallas, Tex, Oct 5, 29. *Study:* Austin Col; Southern Methodist Univ; Univ Colo; Laney Col; Am Acad; Art Students League; Sch Visual Art; Calif Col Arts & Crafts; and with Ramon Froman, William Mosby, Joseph Van Der Brock, Robert Beverly Hale & Frank Mason. *Work:* Hall of Justice, Hayward, Calif. *Comn:* Pvt collections in US & abroad. *Exhib:* One-man shows, North Park, Dallas, 64, Pantechnicon Gallery, San Francisco, 70, Arden Van Wijk Gallery, Saratoga, Calif, 84, Alma Gilbert Galleries Inc, Burlingame, Calif, 92 & The Parrish Connection, Venice, Fla, 92; Hemisfair Art, Witte Mem Mus, San Antonio, 68; Soc Western Artists, M H De Young Mus, San Francisco, 70; San Francisco Ann, 71; J J Brookings Gallery, San Francisco, 96; and others. *Pos:* Guest, Wurlitzer Found, Taos, NMex, 65; owner, 13th Street Crafts Garden, Oakland, 73-76; training prog, Fine Arts, Mus San Francisco, 82 & 86. *Teaching:* Pvt art classes, 60-; instr art, Mendocino Art Ctr, Calif, 73-74 & Calif Col Arts & Crafts, Oakland, 79-86; guest lectr, Univ Calif, Berkeley, 81, 82 & Docent training prog, Fine Arts Mus, San Francisco, 82, 86. *Bibliog:* Daniel M Mendelowitz & Duane A Wakeham (coauth), A Guide to Drawing, 5th ed, Holt, Rinehart & Winston Inc; The Best of Oil Painting, Rockport Publ, Mass, 96; The Best of Flower Painting, N Light Bks Cincinnati, Ohio & Cassell Publ, London, 97. *Mem:* Berkeley Art Festival Guild (pres, 72-77); Soc Western Artists; Lillian Paley Ctr Visual Arts (bd trustees, 74-78). *Media:* Oil, Pastel. *Res:* Old master Baroque painting techniques. *Specialty:* Still lifes & landscapes. *Collection:* Dow Chemical Co; Hayward (CA) Hall of Justice. *Publ:* American Artist Magazine; American Artist Drawing Magazine. *Dealer:* John Pence Gallery 750 Post St San Francisco CA 94109. *Mailing Add:* 4220 Balfour Ave Oakland CA 94610-1750

HARDY, (CLARION) DEWITT
PAINTER, INSTRUCTOR, PRINTMAKERS
b St Louis, Mo, June 25, 40. *Study:* Syracuse Univ, 58-62. *Work:* San Francisco Mus; Cleveland Mus Art; British Mus; Joseph Hirshorn Found; Butler Art Inst Am Art, Youngtown, Ohio. *Exhib:* One-man shows, Frank Rehn Gallery, NY, 66-71 & Robert Schoelkopf Gallery, NY, 81-83; Art on Paper, Weatherspoon Art Gallery, Univ NC, Greensboro, 81; Am Realism, San Francisco Mus Mod Art, 86; Portland Mus Biennial, 98; Wentworth Coolidge, Portsmouth, NH, 2000; McCandless-Epstein, Portland, Me, 02. *Collection Arranged:* Young American Draughtsmen, Mus Art Ogunquit, 69 & Heartwood Col Art. *Pos:* Assoc dir, Mus Art Ogunquit, 64-77. *Teaching:* Instr, Heartwood Col Art & NH Art Inst; instr, Sch at Mus of Fine Arts, Boston. *Awards:* First Prize for Drawing, Summit Art Ctr, NJ, 65; Purchase Award, Butler Inst Am Art, 69; Best in show, Kennebunk Yacht Show, Maine, 98; Best in Show, K'bunk Yacht, 2000; Patron's Prize, K'bunk Yacht, 02. *Bibliog:* The watercolor page: Dewitt Hardy, Am Artists, 11/81; American Realism, San Francisco Mus Mod Art; The Face of America, Arts Ctr Old Forge, NY, 95. *Mem:* Ogunquit Art Asn, Maine. *Media:* Watercolor, Drawing. *Dealer:* Mast Cove Gallery Rte 9 & Mast Cove Lane Kennebunkport ME; Serge Sorokko Gallery San Francisco CA; Jane Haslem Washington DC; Camden Falls Gallery Camden ME; June Fitzpatrick Gallery Portland ME. *Mailing Add:* 32 Tibbetts St South Berwick ME 03908

HARDY, HUGH
ARCHITECT
b Spain, Jul 26, 32. *Study:* Archit asst to Jo Mielziner, New York City, 58-62; founder Hugh Hardy & Assoc, 62-67; partner, owner Hardy Holzman Pfeiffer Assoc, New York City and LA, 67-; Designer: Orchestra Hall, Minneapolis, 74, Cooper-Hewitt Mus, New York City, 76, St Louis Art Mus, 77, The Joyce Theater, New York City, 82, Rizzoli Bookstore, New York City, New Victory Theater, 95, Bryant Park Restaurant, 95, Windows in the World, 96, New Amsterdam Theater, 97, US Customs and Immigration Ctr Rainbow Bridge, Niagara Falls, NY, 98, Radio City Music Hall, New York City, 99, Bridgemarket, New York City, 2000. *Work:* Designer: Orchestra Hall, Minneapolis, 74, Cooper-Hewitt Mus, New York City, 76, St Louis Art Mus, 77, The Joyce Theater, New York City, 82, Rizzoli Bookstore, New York City, New Victory Theater, 95, Bryant Park Restaurant, 95, Windows in the World, 96, New Amsterdam Theater, 97, US Customs and Immigration Ctr Rainbow Bridge, Niagara Falls, NY, 98, Radio City Music Hall, New York City, 99, Bridgemarket, New York City, 2000. *Pos:* Archit asst, to Jo Mielziner, New York City, 1958-62; found, Hugh Hardy & Assoc, 1962-67; partner and owner, Hardy Holzman Pfeiffer Assoc, New York City & Los Angeles, 1967-; chmn, Design Arts Adv. Panel Nat Endowment for the Arts, formerly. *Teaching:* Davenport vis prof, archit design Yale Univ, 1976; Saarinen vis prof, Yale Univ, 1987; consult, lectr, in field, currently. *Awards:* Recipient D'Amato prize Princeton Univ, 54, Brunner prize in archit Nat Inst Arts and Letters, 74, Benjamin West Clinedinst medal Artists' Fel Inc, 88. *Mem:* Fel, Am Inst of Archit (NY chap medal of honor 78, Archit Firm award 81, several honor awards); mem Archit League NY (vpres for archit 77-81, bd dir 87-), Nat Acad (associate), Am Acad Arts and Letters, Century Assoc; appointed to Nat Coun on the Arts by Pres of US, 92. *Mailing Add:* Hardy Holzman Pfeiffer Assoc 902 Broadway Fl 19 New York NY 10010-6082

HARDY, JOHN
PAINTER
b Tours, France; US citizen. *Study:* Ga State Univ, BFA, 69. *Work:* Brooklyn Mus, NY; Nat Mus Am Art & Art in Embassies, US State Dept, Washington, DC; Mint Mus, Charlotte, NC; High Mus Art, Atlanta, Ga; Greenville Co Mus, SC; Morris Mus, Augusta, Ga; Mus of Western Va, Roanoke; Hunter Mus of Am Art, Chattanoga, Tenn. *Comn:* Portrait Michael Sovern, pres, Col Univ NY, 79; portrait Judge Wilfred Feinberg, Col Univ NY, 88. *Exhib:* Brooklyn Mus, NY, 80; Hunter Mus Am Art, Chattanooga, Tenn, 83; Ratner Gallery, Chicago, 91; Michael Walls Gallery, NY, 93; J Gibson/Hemphill Fine Arts Gallery, Washington, 93; Hurlbutt Gallery, Greenwich, Conn, 94, Brenda Taylor Gallery, NY, 96; Morris Mus Art, Augusta, Ga, 99; Art in General, NY, 01; Lizan Tops Gallery, East Hampton, NY, 01; DFN Gallery, NY, 02, 03, 06; R2 Gallery, NY, 03; Portraits, Lizan Tops Gallery. Easthampton, NY, 02; Its up to you, New York, New York,Susan Coach House Gallery, Atlanta, Ga, 03. *Teaching:* Chmn visual arts, Sch Archit, Ga Tech, 69-75; vis artist painting, Rice Univ, Houston & La State Univ, Baton Rouge, 79; adj fac painting, NY Univ, 80-82; masters workshop, Huntington Mus, WVa; tchr St Ann's Sch, Brooklyn, NY, 94-02. *Awards:* Nat Endowment Arts Grant, Huntington Mus, WVa, 87; Pollock-Krasner Found Grant, 96-97. *Bibliog:* Ann Weinstein (auth), article, Roanoke Times & World News, 10/7/87; Carol Graham Beck (auth), article, Art Papers, 90; Alan G Artner (auth), rev, Chicago Tribune, 91; Robert Long (auth) Rev, East Hampton Star, NY, 01. *Media:* Oil, Watercolor. *Specialty:* Contemporary Realism. *Dealer:* DFN Gallery 176 Franklin St New York NY 10013. *Mailing Add:* DFN Gallery 176 Franklin St New York NY 10013

HARDY, ROBERT
EDUCATOR, CERAMIST
b Millville, NJ, Aug 2, 38. *Study:* Calif State Univ, Long Beach, BA, MA; Univ Calif, Irvine; Scripps Grad Sch, Claremont, Calif. *Comn:* Numerous comns for interior designers in bas-relief ceramic sculptures. *Exhib:* Los Angeles Mus Sci & Indust, 62; Craftsmen USA, Lytton Gallery, Los Angeles Co Art Mus, Los Angeles, 66; Mus Contemp Crafts, NY, 66 & Ravinia Festival, Chicago, 67; Saginaw Art Mus, Mich, 68; Grand Rapids Art Mus, Mich, 68; Columbia Mus Art, SC, 68; Laguna Mus Art, Calif, 74. *Collection Arranged:* Religious Expressions in Art, 75, National Basketry Exhibition, 76, California Indian Basketry: An Artistic Overview (ed, catalogue), 76, June Wayne: Weaver of Tapestries, Painter & Printmaker, 77 & Year of the Horse: 4676, 78, Fine Arts Gallery, Cypress Col. *Teaching:* Prof art hist/drawing design, Cypress Col, 68-96. *Awards:* Merit Award, Craftsmen USA, Lytton Gallery, 66. *Media:* Ceramics. *Publ:* Auth, Living with Art, study guide for Rita Gilbert, McGraw Hill, 96. *Mailing Add:* c/o Cypress Col Fine Arts Dept 9200 Valley View St Cypress CA 90630-5897

HARDY, SARALYN REECE
MUSEUM DIRECTOR
Study: Univ Kans, BA, 76; Univ Kans, MA in Am Studies, 94. *Pos:* Proj coordr, Helen Foresman Spencer Mus Art, Univ Kans, Lawrence, 77-79, dir, 2005—, Salina Art Ctr, Kans, 86—2002; dir mus and visual arts Nat Endowment for Arts, Wash, DC, 99—2002. *Awards:* Recipient Women of Achievement award, Salina YWCA, Kans Gov's Art Award, 95. *Mem:* Inst Mus and Libr Serv, Mus Trustee Asn, Am Asn Mus, Am Fedn of Arts Mus Dir, Getty Leadership Inst. *Mailing Add:* Spencer Mus Art Univ Kans 1301 Mississippi St Lawrence KS 66045-7500

HARDY, THOMAS (AUSTIN)
SCULPTOR
b Redmond, Ore, Nov 30, 21. *Study:* Ore State Univ, 38-40; Univ Ore, BA, 42, with Archipenko, summer 51, MFA, 52. *Work:* Whitney Mus Am Art, NY; Seattle Art Mus, Wash; San Francisco Mus Art; Neuberger Mus, NY; Portland Art Mus, Ore; Santa Barbara Mus Calif; Springfield, Mo; Univ Ore, Mus Art, Eugene, Ore; Univ Maine Art Mus, Orono, Maine; Univ Wyo Art Mus, Laramie, Wyo. *Comn:* Diving Birds, Fed Bldg, Juneau, Alaska, 64; Duck Fountain, Univ Ore, Eugene, 64; Flight, Dorothy Chandler Music Ctr, Los Angeles, Calif, 65; wall sculpture, State Dept Agr, Salem, Ore, 68; Bear, Univ Calif, Berkeley, 80; Presdl Seal, FD Roosevelt Meml, Washington, DC, 97. *Exhib:* 3rd Biennial, Sao Paulo, Brazil, 55; Am Watercolors, Drawings & Prints, Metrop Mus Art, 56; Mus Mod Art Sculpture Exhib, 63; Whitney Mus Am Art Sculpture Ann, 64; Exhib Cand Grants, Am Inst Arts & Lett, 68. *Pos:* Mem, Portland Art Mus & Friends Mus Art, Univ Ore; comnr, Metrop Arts Comn, 81-85 & Portland Rev Comn, 86. *Teaching:* Lectr, Univ Calif, Berkeley, 56-58; instr, Calif Sch Fine Arts, San Francisco, 56-58; assoc prof sculpture, Tulane Univ, La, 58-59; artist-in-residence, Reed Col, 60-61; vis prof sculpture, Univ Wyo, 75-76. *Awards:* Color Lithography Award, Soc Am Graphic Artists, 52; Seattle Art Mus Northwest Ann Sculpture Award, 55; Distinguished Serv Award, Univ Ore, 64; Ore State Gov Ann Art Award, 86; Webfoot Award, Univ Ore, 87. *Bibliog:* H Wurdemann (auth), Recent art of the West Coast, Art Am, 2/55; Metal sculptures by Tom Hardy, Am Artist, 4/55; L Jones (auth), Tom Hardy: Sculptor-craftsman, Creative Crafts, 7/62. *Media:* Welded Bronze, Aquatint. *Dealer:* Kraushaar Galleries 724 Fifth Ave New York NY 10019. *Mailing Add:* 1530 SW Harrison #203 Portland OR 97201

HARI, KENNETH
PAINTER, SCULPTOR
b Perth Amboy, NJ, Mar 31, 47. *Study:* Newark Sch Fine & Indust Arts, dipl, 66; Md Inst Art, BFA, 68; also with Leon Franks & John Delmonte, Yale Univ, New York Univ. *Work:* Mus Mod Art, Barcelona, Spain; Nat Portrait Galleries, London, Eng & Washington; Vatican, Rome, Italy; Gore Vidal; Paul Newman. *Comn:* Portraits, W H Auden & M Moore, NY, 69, Pablo Casals, comn by Mrs Pablo Casals, Vt, 70, Salvador Dali, NY, 72, Ernest Hemingway, Hemingway House, Cuba, Michael York, & Aaron Copland, 82; Paul Robeson, for Paul Robeson Ctr, Rutgers Univ, 79; Douglas Fairbanks Jr, Nat Portrait Gallery, London, Eng, 92; Nirvasha, 2006. *Exhib:* Union Col, 69; Monmouth Col, 70; Newark Mus, 71; Trenton State Mus, 72; Va Polytechnic Inst, 74; solo exhibs, Centenery Col, NJ & Tennessee Williams Portraits, Pargot Gallery, NJ, 91; Tenn State Mus. *Pos:* Dir, NJ Art Festival, 64-69. *Teaching:* Lectr, various Univs. *Awards:* Pulaski Award, Kusciuszko Found, 63; Felice Found Award, 69; Trenton State Mus Award, 72. *Bibliog:* Art in the Hamptons, 69 & feature story, 73, NY Times; M Lenson (auth), Portrait of Casals, Newark News, 71; D Brown (auth), Poetess an artist, Home News, 72. *Media:* Oil, Graphite, Sculpture, Lithographs. *Interests:* Creating important works of art. *Publ:* Illusr, Vermont, 72, Folk Singer, 72 & Time for Peace, 72, H S Graphics; Abraham, 74, Marcel Marceau, 75, The Prophet, 92 & 94, Beatrice, 92, Moses, 92, Harmony, 92 & Portrait of 5, 92; Portrait of Anna, 96 & Pablo Casals Poster, 96; Nirvasha, 2006; Billy Mills, 2006. *Dealer:* Eastman & John Watson Gallery. *Mailing Add:* 228 Sherman St Perth Amboy NJ 08861

HARJO, BENJAMIN, JR
PAINTER, PRINTMAKER
b Clovis, NMex, Sept 19, 45. *Study:* Inst Am Indian Arts, cert, 66; Okla State Univ, BFA, 74. *Work:* Inst Am Indian Arts, Santa Fe; McFarlin Libr Indian Collection, Univ Tulsa & Tulsa City Co Libr; US Embassy, Mogadiscio, Somalia; Mus Northern Ariz. *Exhib:* Young Am Indian Artist, Riverside Mus, NY, 65-66; Nat Indian Arts Exhib, Heard Mus, Phoenix, Ariz, 66; Philbrook 30th Ann Am Indian Arts Exhib, Tulsa, 75; Ann Competition, 5 Tribes Mus, Muskogee, Okla, 76 & 80; Southern Plains Indian Mus, Anadarko, Okla, 80; Trail of Tears Ann, Cherokee Mus, Tahlequah, Okla, 81; Native Am Ctr Living Arts, Niagara Falls, NY, 81; One man show Wheelwright Mus, Skylight Gallery, Wichita Art Mus, 91; Franco-Am Inst, Renne, France, 92; Nat Cowboy Hall of Fame, 2000. *Pos:* Cult recreational coordr, Tulsa Indian Youth Coun, 74-76. *Teaching:* Jr gallery instr Indian cult, Philbrook Art Ctr, Tulsa, 76-77. *Awards:* Grand award, 1st place painting & 2nd place graphics awards, Red Earth Festival; Best of division, 1st place painting-minature, 2nd place painting & 1st place graphics award, 67th ann Indian Market; 1st place painting, Masters Show, Five Tribes Mus, 88; First Place, 69 Ann Indian Market, Santa Fe, 90; Woody Crumbo Mem Award; Second Prize, Red Earth, 90; Best of Class, Fine Art, Ann Heard Mus Guild, Indian Fair, 96; Spirit of Oklahoma Award, Masters Show Five Civilized Tribes, 97; Best of Show Five Civilized Tribes Mus, Muskogee, Okla, 2000; plus others. *Bibliog:* Peggy

Ridgeway (auth), Benjamin Harjo Jr, Art Voice S, 81; Rennard Steickland (auth), Indians of Oklahoma, Okla Press, 81; Southwest Art Mag, 3/88; Southern Living Mag, 10/88. *Mem:* Master Artist Five Civilized Tribes, Muskogee, Okla. *Media:* Gouache, Acrylic; Etching, Woodblock. *Mailing Add:* 1516 Northwest 35th Oklahoma City OK 73118-3214

HARKEY, RONALD P See Rophar

HARKINS, DENNIS RICHTER
ADMINISTRATOR, PHOTOGRAPHER
b Nelsonville, Ohio, July 20, 50. *Study:* Ohio Univ, BFA, 72, MA(int affairs), 73. *Collection Arranged:* African Art (with catalog), Ohio Univ, Alden Libr, 73. *Pos:* Educ chmn, Prof Photogr Guild Fla, 78-79 & bd dir, 79. *Teaching:* Dir photog, Art Inst Ft Lauderdale, 74-81; vpres & dir educ, Art Inst Atlanta, 81-. *Awards:* Cert Prof Photogr, 79; Lecture Award, Fla Prof Photogr Conf. *Mem:* Prof Photogr Am; Kodak Educ Adv Coun, Nat. *Mailing Add:* 2931 Mabry Ln NE Atlanta GA 30319-2603

HARKINS, GEORGE C, JR
PAINTER
b Philadelphia, Pa, June 15, 1934. *Study:* Philadelphia Col Art, BFA, 56; Univ Ariz, MFA, 69. *Work:* Charleston Mus Fine Art, SC; Montgomery Mus Fine Art, Ala; Arnot Art Mus, Elmira, NY; Tucson Mus Art, Ariz. *Exhib:* Am Realism: 20th Century Watercolors & Drawings, San Francisco Mus Mod Art, 85; Watercolor USA, Monumental Image, Springfield Art Mus, Mo, 86; The Face of the Land, S Alleghenies Mus Art, Loretto, Pa, 88; Realism Today: Am Drawings from the Rita Rich Collection, Nat Acad Design, NY, 88; Watercolor: Contemp Currents, Riverside Art Mus, Calif, 89; Representing Representation II, Arnot Art Mus, Elmira, NY, 95. *Bibliog:* Alvin Martin (auth), American Realism: 20th Century Drawings & Watercolors, H N Abrams, 86; Steven Doherty (auth), George Harkins, Am Artist, 5/89; John Arthur (auth), Spirit of Place, Bullfinch Press, Little Brown Co, 89. *Media:* Watercolor, Oils, Pastels. *Dealer:* Jane Haslem Gallery 2025 Hillyer Pl NW Washington DC 20009. *Mailing Add:* 137 Duane St 5E New York NY 10013

HARKNESS, JOHN CHEESMAN
ARCHITECT
b NY City, Nov 30, 16. *Study:* Harvard Univ, BFA (cum laude), 38; Harvard Univ, BArch, MArch, 41; Phi Beta Kappa. *Pos:* Archit, Saarinen & Swanson, Birmingham, Mich, Harrison, Fouilhoux & Abramovitz, New York City, Skidmore, Owings & Merrill, New York City, prior to 45; Mem design fac, Harvard Grad. Sch Design, 46-50, mem vis comt; prin, The Archit Collab, Cambridge, Mass, 45-95, pres, 66-67, 77-84, bd dir, chmn bd, principals, 84-86; mem vis comt, RI Sch Design; mem, capitol area planning bd, Minn State. *Awards:* Recipient various competition & archit design awards incl 6 awards, Am Asn Sch Adminr, 60-67; William Ware Award, Boston Soc Archit honor award, 93. *Mem:* Fel Am Inst of Archit; Nat Acad, Boston Soc Archit (pres, formerly); Mass State Asn Archit (pres, formerly); Archit League NY, Harvard Grad Sch Design Alumni Asn (pres, formerly), Harvard Univ Alumni Asn (dir, formerly, 88). *Publ:* Auth: Encyl of Archit, 89. *Mailing Add:* Fletcher Harkness 46 Waltham St Boston MA 02118-2436

HARKNESS, MADDEN
PAINTER
b Montclair, NJ, July 21, 48. *Study:* Calif Col Arts Crafts, MFA, 85; Boston Mus Sch, Tufs Univ, BS, 72. *Work:* Everson Mus, Syracuse, NY; Fresno Art Mus, Calif. *Exhib:* One-man show, Forum 88, Hamburg, Ger, 88; On the Horizon: Emerging in California, Fresno Art Mus, Calif, 87; Figurative Dimensions, Univ Art Gallery, Calif State Univ, Dominquez Hills, Calif, 88; Madden Harkness, Southern Calif Art Inst, Laguna Beach, 89 & Pepperdine Univ (catalog), Malibu, Calif, 90; The Figure, Tatistcheff Gallery, Santa Monica, Calif, 91; Addictions (catalog), Santa Barbara Contemp Arts Forum, Calif, 91; and others. *Awards:* Purchase Award, Everson Mus, 88; Julia Morgan Mem, Riverside Art Mus, 87; vis artist, Am Acad in Rome, Italy, 90; Artist-in-Residence, Ragdale Found, 87. *Bibliog:* Colin Gardener (auth), The Galleries, Los Angeles Times, 12/18/87; Betth Ann Brown & Arlene Raven (auths), Exposures; Women and Their Art, 89; David Pagel (auth), When Reason Dreams-Madden, Harkness, Vol II, No 3, Visions, 88. *Media:* Mixed Media, Oil. *Dealer:* Jan Baum 170 S LaBrea Ave Los Angeles CA. *Mailing Add:* PMB 78-180 827 Union Pacific Blvd Laredo TX 78045-9452

HARLE, MATT
SCULPTOR
Exhib: Derek Eller Gallery, NY City, 98; Painting Pushed to Extremes, Worcester Art Mus, Mass, 2000; 181st Ann: An Invitational Exhib Contemp Art, 2006; Some Lions Do Walk, Some Lions Do Not Walk, Genovese/Sullivan Gallery, Boston, 2006. *Awards:* Guggenheim fellow, 99. *Mailing Add:* c/o Genovese/Sullivan Gallery 450 Harrison Ave Boston MA

HARLESS, CAROL P
SCULPTOR
b Atlanta, Ga. *Study:* Shorter Col, Rome, Ga, BA (biology) (cum laude); studied with Joan Danziger. *Work:* Study in Time, Sundail/Moultrie Mem, Erskine Col, SC; Grief, Inspired by Martha Graham's dance, Lamentation, Martha Graham Sch, NYC; Charles Wadsworth, Father of Am Chamber Music Movement, Wadsworth Hall, Newnan, Ga; Dancers, Entrance to corp off, HPG Inc, Newnan, Ga. *Exhib:* One-woman show, West Ga Col, Cashen Hall Gallery, 92, Shorter Col, Rome, Ga, 95; group exhib, Christmas Show, Reg Artists, Spruill Ctr Gallery, Atlanta, Ga, 93, Art in Motion, An Exhib Hon Athletic Excellence, Ga Tech, Atlanta, 94, Audubon Artists, 55th Ann Exhib, NY, 97, Sculpture Now-The Figure, Wash Sq, Wash, DC, 98, Southeastern Juried Exhib (12 states), Mobile Mus Art, 99, Eleventh Ann Summer Showcase, Thomasville Cult Ctr, Ga, 2000, Gala 2000, Brenau Univ Invitational, Gainsville, Ga, 2000; juried exhib: Going for the Gold, National Sculpture Soc, NY, 1996, Nat Sculpture Soc Sports, NY, 2002, Nat Sculpture Soc 70th Annual Awards Exhib, Brookgreen Gardens, SC & NY, 2003, Contemporary Realism 2005, Cavalier Galleries, NY, 2005. *Pos:* Comptroller, human res int consult firm, 68-93; owner, sculpting studio, 89-. *Awards:* Jurors Award, Savannah Nat, Ga, 92; Elliot Liskin Mem Award, Audobon Artists, 55th Annual Exhib, NY, 97; second place, ARmory Art Ctr, West Palm Beach, Fla, 99; Tallix Foundry, Nat Sculpture Soc, NY, 2003; Medal of Honor, Catharine Lorillard Wolfe Art Club Inc 107th Annual Exhib, NY, 2003; finalist 2nd Int ARC Salon Comp, Art Renewal Ctr, 2005. *Mem:* Audubon Artists Inc.; Catharine Lorillard Wolfe Art Club Inc. *Media:* Sculptor, Bronze, Terracotta. *Mailing Add:* PO Box 1903 Newnan GA 30264

HARLOW, ANN
MUSEUM DIRECTOR, CURATOR
b Glen Cove, NY, June 15, 51. *Study:* Stanford Univ, BA, 73; Univ Calif, Berkeley, MA, 77. *Collection Arranged:* William Keith Collection (150 paintings, 1867-1911 & catalog 1988), St Marys Col, 92-94. *Pos:* Cur asst, Oakland Mus, Calif, 77-78; asst dir, Mills Col Art Gallery, Oakland, Calif, 80-82; dir, Hearst Art Gallery, St Mary's Col, Moraga, Calif, 82. *Mem:* Asn Col & Univ Mus & Galleries (pres 88-90). *Publ:* Co-auth, The Color Woodcut in America, 1895-1945 (exhib catalog), 84; auth, The MA Circle: Budapest and Vienna, 1916-1925 (exhib catalog), 85; Bicoastal artists of the 1870s (exhib catalog), Art Calif, 7/92; William Keith, Am Art Review, 12/94. *Mailing Add:* St Mary's Col of Calif Hearst Art Gallery St Mary's Rd PO Box 5110 Moraga CA 94575

HARMAN, MARYANN WHITTEMORE
PAINTER
b Roanoke, Va, Sept 13, 35. *Study:* Univ Va, Mary Washington Col, BA; Va Polytech Inst & State Univ, MA. *Work:* Mint Mus, Charlotte, NC; Philip Morris Corp, Richmond, Va; Hunter Mus, Chattanooga, Tenn; Gen Motors, Detroit; Boston Mus Fine Arts; and others; General Electric; 3-M; VA Mus; Manufactuers Hanover Trust. *Exhib:* one-person shows, Andre Emmerich Gallery, NY, 76 & 78, Allen Rubiner Gallery, Detroit, 77, 79, 90 & 92, Meredith Long Gallery & NY, 80; Sandy Carson Gallery, Denver, 89-2006; Carson Gallery, Denver, Colo, 90-2005; Gallery One, Toronto, Can, 90-2006; Gallery K, Washington DC, 95-2000; Studios in the Sq, 2000-2006; Lee Hansley Gallery, Raleigh, 2001-2006; Andersen Gallery, Va Commonwealth Univ, 2004; and others. *Pos:* Artist-in-residence, Emma Lake Workshop, Univ Saskatechewan, Can. *Teaching:* Assoc prof painting & drawing, Va Polytech Inst & State Univ, 64-81, prof, 81-. *Awards:* Purchase Awards, Hunter Mus, 74; Cert of Distinction, Va Mus Fine Arts, 74 & 76; Purchase Award, Mint Mus, 83. *Bibliog:* Barclay Sheaks (auth), Painting Natural Environment, 74 & Painting with Oils, 77, Davis; Marsha Miro (auth), rev, Detroit Free Press, 12/78; Edgar Buonagurio (auth), rev, Arts Mag, 5/80, 81, 82 & 84; articles, Los Angeles Times & Hollywood Press, 86. *Mem:* Col Art Asn Am; Southeastern Col Art Asn; Va Mus Fine Arts; Am Fedn Arts. *Media:* Acrylic, Oil and Watercolor. *Mailing Add:* 1120 Nellies Cove Rd Blacksburg VA 24060

HARMON, BARBARA SAYRE
PAINTER, BOOK ARTIST
b Yerington, Nev, Aug 8, 27. *Study:* Bisttram Sch Fine Art, painting & drawing; etching with Lawton Parker; Black Mountain Col, bookbinding with Johanna Jalowitz. *Work:* Harwood Mus, Univ NMex; Stanford Univ Libr, Univ NMex; Univ NMex Libr; Taos Art Mus. *Comn:* Numerous private commissions for fantasy and portrait paintings; original graphics acquisition fund, Harwood Mus Art, Univ NMex, Taos, 2005; book art display, Black Mountain College Mus and Art Ctr, Ashville, NC, 2005. *Exhib:* Continuous exhibs in southwestern galleries since 1963. *Pos:* Owner & found of Children's Gallery Press; co-dir of Tarreon Gallery. *Bibliog:* Mary Carrol Nelson (auth), Barbara Harmon: magic & mastery, Am Artist Mag, 5/75; Kelly Malore Cribbs (auth), The tumpfee wood world of Barbara Harmon, Santa Fe Mag, 7/79; Tricia Hurst (auth), All things are possible, NMex Mag, 81. *Mem:* Harwood Mus Art Alliance, Univ NMex. *Media:* Watercolor; Original graphic mediums. *Res:* Extensive research in tech of lithography, monotype and dry point since 1948. *Specialty:* contemp art. *Interests:* evolution of unique printmaking methods, floral and still life studies, dancing and song writing. *Collection:* Ernest Blumenschein, Greer Garson, Carl Dentzel, Jan & Paul Johnson, Laurel & Michael Mason, CJ & Wilson Crawford. *Publ:* Auth & illusr, Tabbigail's Garden, 67, The Little People's Counting Book, 68, Monday's Mouse, 70, This Little Pixie, 69, The Tumpfee Wood Acorn Book, 77 & Thimbly Hill, 80, The Children's Gallery Press & The Baker Co. *Dealer:* The Torreon Gallery, Taos, NM, 87571. *Mailing Add:* 234 Las Cruces Rd 6584 NDCBU Taos NM 87571

HARMON, CLIFF FRANKLIN
PAINTER
b Los Angeles, Calif, June 26, 23. *Study:* Bisttram Sch Fine Art, Los Angeles, Calif & Taos, NMex, with Emil Bisttram, 46-48; Black Mountain Col, NC, with Joe Fiore, 49-50; Taos Valley Art Sch, with Louis Ribak, 50-52. *Work:* Mus NMex, Santa Fe; Okla Art Ctr, Oklahoma City; Mus of Taos Art, Harwood Found, Univ NMex; Mus of Taos Art, NMex. *Exhib:* NMex & Southwest Biennials, NMex Mus, 66, 70-72, Watercolor NMex, 74; 11th Midwest Biennial, Joslyn Art Mus, Omaha, Nebr, 70; 1st Four Corners Biennial, Phoenix Art Mus, Ariz, 71; Bertrand Russell Centenary Art Exhib, Rotunda Gallery, London, Eng, 72; 60 Yrs in Taos Tri-Exhibits: Taos Art Asn, Van Vechtan-Lineberry Mus Taos Art, Total Arts, 96, NMex. *Awards:* First Premium for Abstract Painting, NMex State Fair, 68; Hon Mention, NMex Mus & Phoenix Art

Mus, 71; 1st Place Blue Ribbon, Taos Art Asn, 94. *Mem:* Taos Art Asn (first vpres, 68-69, pres, 78-79). *Media:* Oil, Acrylic. *Specialty:* traditional & contemporary art. *Dealer:* The Total Arts Gallery Taos NM 87571; The Torreon Gallery Taos NM 87571. *Mailing Add:* 234 Las Cruces Rd 6584 NDCBU Taos NM 87571

HARMON, DAVID EDWARD
PAINTER, EDUCATOR
b St Louis, Mo, May 30, 53. *Study:* Webster Univ, St Louis, Mo, BFA, 77; Penn State Univ, MFA, 82. *Work:* Univ Mo, St Louis; Univ Southern Miss, Woods Gallery, Hattiesburg; Liverpool Inst Higher Ed, UK; Univ Scranton, Pa; River Park UMC, South Bend, Ind; Environ Labs, South Bend, Ind. *Comn:* Painting, Crane Sch Music, Potsdam, NY, 86-87. *Exhib:* 30th Ann Nat Draw/Print Show, Univ NDak, Grand Forks, 87; 49th Ann juried exhib, Munson-Williams-Proctor Inst, Utica, NY, 87; Christ Imagery in Contemp Art, Albany Inst Art/Hist, NY, 88; South Bend Reg Mus Art, Inc, 92-93; Solo exhib, US Air Force Acad, 97; Arte Sagrado Exhib, Concordia Univ, Austin, Tex, 98; West Valley Mus Art, Supvise, Ariz, 2001. *Pos:* Art dir, Bethel Col, 90-; ed bd mem, Collegiate Press, Alta Loma, Calif, 92; moderator panel discussion, Nat Coun Art Adminr Conf, Anchorage, Alaska, 96 & Mid Am Col Art Asn Conf, Lexington, Ky, 98, Louisville, Ky, 2000; vis artist, Mont Artist Refuge Basin, 99, Jentel, Wyom, 2003. *Teaching:* vis prof gallery art hist, Univ SMiss, 82-83; vis prof paint draw design, Univ Ariz, Tucson, 84-85; prof art paint draw design, State Univ NY, Potsdam, 85-89; vis prof, Keystone Jr Col, La Plume, Pa, 89-90; art dir & assoc prof art, Bethel Col, Mishawaka, Ind, 90-. *Awards:* Purchase Award, Mo Photog, Univ Mo, St Louis, 76 & 5th Miss Annual, Univ Miss, 83; First Place, Sacred Arts Nat Show, Wheaton Col, 90; Purchase Award, Midwest Mus Am Art, Elkhart, Ind, 2000. *Bibliog:* Blair Schiller (auth), Group shows explore reality and dreams, Art Speak, 12/89; Carol Kotlarczyk (auth), Artist brings out intensity in soft colors, Daily Herald, 9/7/91; Julie York Coppens (auth), Picture Perfect, South Bend Tribuen, 11/5/2000. *Mem:* Col Art Assoc, NY; Southeastern Col Art Asn; Mid Am Col Art Asn; Nat Coun Art Adminrs. *Media:* Oil, Acrylic; Pastel. *Publ:* Contribr, Contemp Southwest Art, Gibson Gallery, 88; illusr, The Insanity of Samuel Beckett's Art, Paint Brush Press, Parker, Colo, 98. *Dealer:* Griffin Gallery South Bend IN. *Mailing Add:* Bethel Col Art Dept 1001 W McKinley Ave Mishawaka IN 46545

HARMON, FOSTER
ART CONSULTANT
b Judsonia, Ark, Nov 5, 12. *Study:* Ind Univ; Ohio Univ; State Univ Iowa, BA, 35, MFA, 36, Ohio Univ, DFA(hon), 92. *Pos:* Pub relations dir, Ringling Mus Art, Sarasota, Fla, 58-59; dir, Oehlschlaeger Galleries, Sarasota, 61-70; bd trustees, Ringling Sch Art & Design; bd dir, Asolo State Theatre, Sarasota Players, Sarasota Opera Asn, Van Wezel Performing Arts Ctr Found & Kennedy Mus Am Art, Ohio Univ; founder & dir, Harmon Gallery, Naples, Fla, 64-78; owner-dir, Foster Harmon Galleries Am Art, Sarasota, Fla, 80-93; founder, Foster & Martha Hamm Am Arts Study Ctr & Arch, Ohio Univ, 95. *Teaching:* Instr drama & dir univ theatre prod, Ind Univ, Bloomington, 36-42. *Awards:* Award of Merit for Long Serv & Contrib to Art, Ohio Univ, 70; Formal Commendations for Contributions to the Arts, Fla Gov & Secy State, 94. *Bibliog:* Biographical film at Sarasota Libr. *Mem:* Am Fedn Arts; Fla Cult Action Alliance; Ringling Mus Art; Sarasota Art Asn (pres, 59-60); Fla Artists Group; Archives of Am Art, Smithsonian Assocs. *Specialty:* Paintings, drawings and sculpture by major American artists of the 20th century. *Collection:* American art. *Mailing Add:* 1255 N Gulstream Ave Apt 1104 Sarasota FL 34236

HARMON, PAUL
PAINTER, PRINTMAKER
b Nashville, Tenn, Jan 23, 1939. *Study:* Univ Tenn. *Work:* Principality of Monaco, Monte Carlo; Hotel de Ville, Caen, France; Tenn State Mus, Nashville; George Bush Presidential Libr & Mus; Tampa Mus Art, Fla; Vanderbilt Univ Fine Arts Ctr; Capital Cult Ctr, Tallahassee; Georgetown Univ Libr; others; numerous corp collections. *Comn:* Wall mural, Biological Therapy Inst, Franklin, Tenn, 87; three lobby paintings, Vanderbilt Henry Joyce Cancer Ctr, Nashville, 89; glass panels, Bridgestone/Firestone USA, Nashville, 90; An American Mosaic (6x12' painting), Philip Morris USA, NY, 91; 4x6' Painting, Tenn State Mus, Nashville, 94. *Exhib:* Eglise du St Sepulcre, Caen, France; Galerie Art Pub, Paris; Galerie Art-Expo, Paris; Galerie Sabala, Paris; XXIV Prix int d'art contemp de Monte-Carlo; Mus de Lons-le-Saunier, France; 67th salon de la Soc des Artiestes Bas-Normands, Caen; Galerie Deprez-Bellorget, Paris; Art Contemp, St Martin du Tertre, Val d'Oise, France; Michel Vockaer Gallery, Brussels; IV Bienal de Arte, Medellin, Columbia; Galerie JPF, Montpellier, France; Folon & Rigsby Gallery, Nashville; Tenn State Mus, Maj Retrospective, 1984; Cavaliero Fine Arts, NY; Carl Van Vechten Gallery, Fisk Univ, Nashville; Vanderbilt Univ Fine Arts Center, Nashville; Smithsonian Inst Nat Collection Fine Arts, Washington; Southern Lit Festival, Nashville; Madison Art Directions Gallery, NY; Cheekwood Find Arts Center, Nashville; Windsors Gallery, Miami; Zeitgeist Gallery, Nashville; Parthenon, East Gallery, Nashville; GMB Galerie Int, Royal Oaks, Mich; Laura Pollack Gallery, San Diego; Aronson/Healey Gallery, Atlanta; Phoenix Fine Arts, Md; Studio/L'Atelier, Nashville; Phoenix II Gallery, Washington; Malton Gallery, Cincinnati; South Wharf Gallery, Nantucket; Zantman Art Galleries, Palm Desert; Sande Webster Gallery, Phila; Edith Caldwell Gallery, San Francisco; Nashville Int Airport. *Awards:* Prix Ville de Monaco, Monte Carlo, 90; Prix Soc EJA, Monte Carlo, 90; Commemorative Medal, St Martin Tertre, 90. *Bibliog:* Ganne Heinitsh (auth), Paul Harmon (exhib catalog), 88; Monique Vacarisas (auth), L'Oil Mag, Paris; Marilyn Mars, former cur contemp art Tampa Mus Art; Georganne Harmon (auth), poet; Solange Yver de la Vigne-Bernard (critic), Paris. *Media:* Oils on Canvas. *Publ:* Coauth, La Voyage, the Electronic Coffee Table Art Book (CD-rom & internet site), Bookpage Inc, 95; Dante's Stones, 2000; Paul Harmon, exhib catalog. *Mailing Add:* 1304 Wilson Pike Brentwood TN 37027-6731

HARNETT, LILA
COLLECTOR
Study: Brooklyn Col, BA; New Sch Social Res; Phi Beta Kappa. *Pos:* Publ, Bus Atomics Report, 53-63; cult reporter, NY State newspapers, 64-74; fine arts ed, Cue Mag, 75-80; Phoenix Home & Garden, 80-88, assoc publ, 88-, ed, 95-98; publ, Scottsdale Scene, 92-98. *Mem:* founder Art Table Inc. *Collection:* Works by Burchfield, Hopper, Marsh, Warhol, Anuszkiewcz, Tooker, Pearlstein, Lamis, Fletcher Benton, Audobon, Catlin, Beal & Birmelin, Allan Houser, Fritz Scholder, and Dennis Numkena. *Mailing Add:* 4523 E Clearwater Pkwy Paradise Valley AZ 85253

HARNICK, SYLVIA
PAINTER
b New York, NY. *Study:* Brooklyn Col, BA, 54; C W Post with Robert Yasuda, 87-89. *Work:* Fine Arts Mus Long Island, Hempstead, NY; Queensborough Community Col Art Gallery, Bayside, NY; Islip Art Mus, E Islip, NY. *Exhib:* Art of the Northeast USA, Silvermine Guild Arts, New Canaan, Conn, 90; Nat Drawing Asn, SW Tex State Univ, San Marcos, Tex, 94; 12″ X 12″ (X 12″), Islip Art Mus, East Islip, NY, 94; Drawing, Rathbone Gallery, Sage Jr Col, Albany, NY, 96; Layers: Mining the Unconscious, Western NMex Univ, 96; Photoesque, Anthony Giordano Gallery, Dowling Col, Oakdale, NY, 97; Artas Spectale, Katonah Mus Art, NY, 98; Long Island Artists: Focus on Materials, Univ Art Gallery, State Univ NY, Stony Brook, 98; A Survey of Contemp Art, NY State Biennial, NY State Mus, Albany, 98; Personal Archeologics, Bryant Libr, Hecksher Mus Art, Roslyn, NY, 98; and others; NJ Ctr for Visual Arts, Summit, 99; Faber Birren Nat, Stanford, Conn, 99; Parrish Art Mus, Southampton, NY, 99; Katonah Mus, Breaking the Rules, 01; Lamar Univ, Dishman Art Gallery, Beaumont, Tex, 2002; Nat Small Work, Scholarie Co, Cobleskill, NY, 2002; Gallery North, Setauket, NY, 2003; Painting Ctr, Solto, New York City, Big Abstract Show, 2003; Poughkeepsie Art Mus Point of View, 2004; Celebrating Color/Alpan Gallery, Huntington, NY, 2003, 2004; Summer Sch Mus, Biennial NLAPW, Washington DC, 2004. *Awards:* Best in Show, Earthly Visions, Nassau Co Mus Art, 92; Finalist, Grumbacher Hall Fame Award, 96; Liquetex Art Award Excellence, Nat League Am Pen Women; Dir's Award-Nat'l Smallwork's Schlorie, Cobleskill, NY, 2002; S Magnet Knapp Award, NAWA, 2002; and others. *Bibliog:* Helen Harrison (auth), Turning photographs into the metaphorical, New York Times, 11/9/97; D Dominick Lombardi (auth), Not in New York, The Record Rev, 12/5/97; William Zimmer (auth), Innovative use of materical, New York Times, 3/1/98; Helen Harrison (auth), Layers of Intention, NY Times, 5/26/02; Helen Harrison (auth), Winter Selections, NY Times, 1/19/03; Helen Harrison-Acelebration of the Outdoors & Its Colors, 1/23/2005. *Mem:* Nat Asn Women Artists (mem jury, 92-97); Nat League Am Pen Women; Long Island Network Women Artists; Soc Layerists Multi-Media. *Media:* Acrylic, Mixed Media. *Specialty:* Abstract Work. *Collection:* Islipart Mus, East Islip, NY, (Famil), Hempstead, NY, Qccart Gallery, Queensborough Community College, Bayside, NY. *Dealer:* Nese Alplan Karakaplan 2 W Carver St Huntington NY 11743. *Mailing Add:* Four Parkside Dr Great Neck NY 11021

HAROLD-STEINHAUSER, JUDITH
PHOTOGRAPHER, EDUCATOR
b Niagara Falls, NY, Dec 19, 41. *Study:* SUNY Col, Buffalo, BS, 63; Inst Design, IIT Chicago, with Aaron Siskind, MS, 67. *Work:* Smithsonian Ist; Philadelphia Mus Art; Nat Gallery Can, Ottawa; Ctr for Photog, Woodstock, NY; SUNY at Potsdam. *Exhib:* Nude Outside the Studio, Philadelphia Art Alliance, 95; Artist-in-the-Studio, Philadelphia City Hall, 2000; Am Identity, SUNY Potsdam, 2000; About Face, Delaware Ctr Contemp Art, Wilmington, 2000; Prints from PMA Collections, Philadelphia Mus Art, 2000. *Teaching:* photog, Moore Col Art & Design, Philadelphia, 76-. *Awards:* Nat Endowment for Arts, 73; Pa Arts Coun Grant, 92, 99. *Publ:* Coauth, History of Women Photographers, Abbeville Press, 94; Coauth, Exploring Color Photography, Brown & Benchmark, 97; Coauth, Center for Photography Quarterly, Ctr for Photog, 98; Coauth, Black and White Photography: A Manifest Vision, Rockport Press, 2000. *Dealer:* Schneider Gallery West Superior Chicago IL 60610

HAROOTUNIAN, CLAIRE M
SCULPTOR, EDUCATOR
b Philadelphia, Pa, Feb 7, 30. *Study:* Univ Pa, BA, 52; Univ Del, MEd, 64; Syracuse Univ, MFA (sculpture), 79. *Work:* Munson-Williams Proctor Inst, Utica, NY; Cazenovia Col, NY; Va Ctr Creative Arts, Sweetbriar; Everson Mus Art, Syracuse, NY. *Exhib:* Solo exhibs, Everson Mus, Syracuse, NY, 83 & Ben Mangel Gallery, Philadelphia, 84; Ransburg Art Gallery, Indianapolis, Ind, 84; Arco Art Fair, Madrid, 92; Fundacion Centro Civico, Guayaquil, Ecuador, 94; Int Sculpture Exhib, Technikon, Pretoria, S Africa, 96. *Teaching:* Instr sculpture, Everson Mus Art, Syracuse, 79-80; adj prof sculpture, Syracuse Univ, 80-94. *Awards:* Fel, Va Ctr Creative Arts, 83-85 & 88; Yaddo Fel, Saratoga Springs, NY, 83; Fel, Int Workshop, San Pere, Barcelona, Spain, 88. *Media:* Cast Metal, Forged Metal. *Mailing Add:* 602 Jamesville Ave Syracuse NY 13210

HAROUTUNIAN, JOSEPH HALSEY
PAINTER
b Chicago, Ill, Sept 22, 44. *Study:* Lawrence Univ, BA, 67; Art Inst Chicago, with Paul Wieghardt, 68-69. *Work:* Portland Mus Art, Maine; Univ Maine Art Mus, Orono; Visual Arts Ctr, Mass Inst Technol; Bates Col Art & Mus, Lewiston, Maine; Univ Maine; and others. *Exhib:* Life Is the Secret, Univ Maine Art Mus, Orono, 74; 59 Faces of Cadillac Mountain, Univ Maine Art Mus, Orono, 79; Effects of Time, Frank Bustamante Gallery, NY, 90; Art in the Embassies, US Embassy, Bogota, Colombia, 94; Col Atlantic, 96; Univ Maine, Machias, 98; Asian Identities, East & West (traveling show), Hammond Mus, NY & Robert Ferot Ctr, Ga Inst Technol, 98; Frequencies of Nature (traveling show), Fernbenk Mus, Atlanta & Tallahassee Mus

Hist & Natural Sci, Fla. *Awards:* Purchase Award, Hassam & Speicher Fund Exhib, Am Acad & Inst, 80. *Bibliog:* Robert Taylor (auth), Review, Art Gallery Mag, 2/71; Jill Janows (auth), 2 artists explore fantasy, Boston Globe, 9/14/79; Michael Kimmelman (auth), Review, NY Times, 5/12/89. *Media:* Oil. *Dealer:* Frick Gallery 139 High St Belfast ME 04915; Creiger Dane Gallery 36 Newbury St Boston 02116. *Mailing Add:* Rogers Point Rd Steuben ME 04680

HARPER, GREGORY FRANKLIN
DIRECTOR, CURATOR
b Covington, Ky, May 7, 54. *Study:* Northern Ky Univ, BA(art hist), 76; Univ Cincinnati, MA(art hist). *Work:* Behringer-Crawford Mus, Covington, Ky; Contemp Arts Ctr, Cincinnati, Ohio; Cincinnati Pub Schs, Ohio; Cape Mus Fine Arts, Dennis, Mass. *Collection Arranged:* Harlan Hubbard: A River Way of Life (auth, catalog), 86; Frank Duveneck; Dreaming Before Nature: Non Objective, 93; Permanent Collection, Cape Mus Art, 93. *Pos:* Exec dir, Behringer-Crawford Mus, Covington, Ky, 79-92; exec dir & cur, Cape Mus Fine Arts, Mass, 93-. *Teaching:* Adj prof art hist, Thomas More Col, Crestview Hills, Ky, 89-91. *Awards:* Citizen of the Year, N Ky CofC, 89; Outstanding Alumnus, N Ky Univ, 92; Service Above Self, Hyannis Rotary, 97. *Res:* American decorative arts; American art; performance art; Red grooms; Franz Kline. *Publ:* Auth, River Heritage Week, Classroom Celebration (exhib catalog), Behringer-Crawford Mus, 87. *Mailing Add:* 151 W 7th St Apt 405 Cincinnati OH 45202-2355

HARPER, MICHAELE ANN
PAINTER
b Port Clinton, Ohio, Jan 20, 43. *Study:* Jefferson Community Col, Ky, AS(com art), 76; Western Ky Univ, Bowling Green, BFA(magna cum laude), 85. *Comn:* Paintings, Hotel Lutetia, Paris, France; paintings, Opera Cadet Hotel, Paris, France; painting, comn by pvt parties, Highland Park, Tex. *Exhib:* Selected Students Show, Western Ky Univ, Bowling Green, 81; 8 States Ann: Painting, Speed Art Mus, Ky, 82; The Laurel Art Guild Art Show, Montpelier Art Ctr, Md, 89 & 92; All Media Mem Show, Art League Gallery, Torpedo Factory, 89; Paint the Town Pink, Washington Post, DC, 90; United Cerebal Palsy Metro Dallas, Tex; Laurel Art Guild Mem Show, Slayton House Gallery, Md, 91; Art in the Metroplex, Tex Christian Univ & Templeton Art Ctr, Ft Worth, 93; The Art of Penwomen, Gallery 10, Ft Worth, 95; Landscapes: Real and Imagined, La Salle Gallery, Tex, 95; Women of Worth, Ft Worth, 95, 96 & 97; Southwestern Watercolor Soc Ann Mem Exhib, Dallas, 96, 97 & 2000; Dallas Visual Art Ctr Mem Exhib, Tex, 97, 98, 99, 2000; Four Artists Alumni, Western Ky Univ, Bowling Green, 97; The Art Annex, Coppell, Tex, 2004; Woodbine Furniture Company, Keller, Tex, 2004; The Gardens Restaurant, Ft Worth Botanical Gardens, Ft Worth, Tex, 2004; Creative Arts Sudio & Gallery, Colleyville, Tex, Feb, 2005; Langdon Ctr of Taleton State Univ, Granbury, Tex, June, 2005; Coastal Frame & Gallery, Rehoboth, Del, 2006. *Pos:* Pres, Laurel Art Guild, Md, 91-92; dir, owner & cur, Yellow House Gallery, Ft Worth, Tex, 96-2001; juror various art festivals and shows, 82-. *Teaching:* Instr com art, Jefferson Community Col, Louisville, Ky, 78-80; instr continuing educ, Anne Arundel Col, Md, 92-93; pvt instr The Gallery, 94-; Instructor FW Woman's Club Art Department Fort Worth, 2001-Present. *Awards:* Equal Award, Torpedo Factory Art League, Alexandria, Va, 91, 92; First Place, SWA Nat Juried Show, Ft Worth, Tex, 99; Winsor Newton Award, SWS 37th Ann Mem Juried Show, Dallas, Tex; plus others. *Bibliog:* Panorama Am Published by Estel Arts & Communications Centre, Columbia, Maryland; Interviewed for Art and Culture Article, Spring, 1999; Alumni Published by Western Kentucky Univ, Bowling Green, Kentucky: Interview for Article, Fall 2000; Biographical Enclopedia of American Painters, Sculpors & Engravers of the US-Colonial to 2002, Published by Dealers Choice Books Inc., Land O' Lakes, FL, 2002. *Mem:* SW Watercolor Soc, Dallas; SWA, Fort Worth; Signature Member. *Media:* Paper & Canvas, Mixed Media. *Specialty:* Original work in a Variety of Mediums by Artists in England, France, Argehtina & US. *Interests:* Travel and Art

HARPER, WILLIAM
JEWELER
b Bucyrus, Ohio, June 17, 44. *Study:* Western Reserve Univ, BS, 66, MS, 67; Cleveland Inst Art, cert, 67. *Work:* Philadelphia Mus Art, Pa; Renwick Gallery Smithsonian Inst, Washington, DC; Victoria & Albert Mus, Eng; and others; Metrolitan Mus Art, NY. *Comn:* Collar and Jewel of Office of the President, Yale Univ, 82. *Exhib:* Ear Follies, Peter Joseph Gallery, NY; William Harper: Recent Works in Enamel, Renwick Gallery, Smithsonian Inst, 77; Craft Art & Religion, Vatican Mus, 78; one-man show, Kennedy Galleries, NY, 81 & 82, Ruth Siegel Ltd, NY, 87; Masterworks of Am Jewelry, Victoria & Albert Mus, London, 85; The Eloquent Object, Philbrook Mus, Tulsa & traveling, 87-89; William Harper: Artist As Alchemist, Orlando Mus Art & Traveling, 89-91; Jasper's Variations (auth, catalog essay), Faberge's Seeds, Peter Joseph Gallery, 94; Books, Boxes and Jewels, Newark Mus, NJ, 2001; Experiment Schmuck, Pforiheim, Ger, 2003. *Teaching:* Vis artist enamels, Kent State Univ, 70-73; from assoc prof to dist research prof metals & enamels, Fla State Univ, 73-91; vis prof, Parsons Sch Design, New York, 79 & Cleveland Inst Art, 84-85. *Awards:* Fla Artist Fel, 80-81 & 85-86; Individual Artists Grant, Nat Endowment Arts, 90-91; fel, Am Craft Coun, 98. *Bibliog:* Self Portrait: Sacred & Profane, Franklin Parrasch Gallery; Michael W Monroe (auth), Volumes of Souls, Kennedy Galleries, NY, 98; Toni Greenbaum (auth), The Barbarian's Trapeze and other Jewels, Primavera Gallery, NY, 98. *Media:* Coisonne Enamel, Gold. *Publ:* Contribr, The Art of Cloisonne, Lowe Art Mus, Coral Gables, Fla, 72; auth, Step by Step Enameling, Western, 73; The magic of cloisonne: William Harper, Craft Horizons, 6/77

HARRELL, MARGARET ANN
PHOTOGRAPHER
b Greenville, NC, 40. *Study:* Duke Univ, BA(hist) (magna cum laude), 62; Columbia Univ, MA(contemp brit & am lit), 64; Univ NC, 76; Carl Jung Inst, Zurich, Switz, 87; Inst Human Devel, Ghent, 92; Studies at Tobias Sch Art, summer 93. *Exhib:* solo show, The Sun in Profile: So Bright It's Dark, Sibiu, Romania, 2005. *Pos:* ed, 68-; asst, to psychologist, dream res, 83-84; co-organizer, US & Indian workshops & lectrs, Belgium, 93-; int ed coordr, Mus Exhib on Life of Jan Mensaert, 95-2001; solo photography exhib, The Sun in Profile, 2005. *Teaching:* instr, dance 69; guest lectr, Sibiu Univ, 95; pvt teacher, LuminEssence, Awakening Your Light Body, 2002-, Radiance: Self Exciting, 2004-. *Awards:* Fel MacDowell Colony, 69, 70 & 73; Hon Writer in Res, C Peter McGrath Ctr, Lucian Blaga Univ, Romania, 2005. *Mem:* Publ Marketing Asn; Am Soc for Psychical Res; Romanian Cure Hist Archeological Soc (hon mem); Kayumari, various wildlife orgns; NC Writers Network. *Media:* photography. *Res:* Effects of direct & other sunlight in photography. *Interests:* T'ai chi, energy studies, art & computers. *Publ:* Auth: Marking Time with Faulkner: A Study of the Symbolic Importance of the Mark and of Related Actions, 1999, Love in Transition: Vol. I: Voyage of Ulysses: Letters to Penelope, 96, Vol. II: Voyage of Ulysses: Letters to Penelope, 96, Vol. III: The Christ State, 96, Vol. IV: The Bedtime Tales of Jesus, 98, Space Encounters: Chunking Down the 21st Century (Love in Transition Vol. Virgin Islands), 2002, Space Encounters II: Chunking Down the 21st Century (Love in Transition Vol. VII), 2002, Space Encounters III: Inserting Consciousness into Collisions (Love in Transition Vol. VIII), 2003, Toward a Philosophy of Perception: The Magnitude of Human Potential: Cloud Optics, 2005; author numerous poems; international editing coordinator Life, Page One (museum e-book and 2 music CD-roms), 2001; contribr, articles to prof jour; auth, numerous poems. *Mailing Add:* 5048 Amber Clay Lane Raleigh NC 27612

HARRIES, MAGS (MARGARET) L
SCULPTOR, EDUCATOR
b Barry, SWales, Gt Brit, April 6, 45. *Study:* Leicester Col Art & Design, England, dipl, 67; Univ Southern Ill, MFA, 70. *Hon Degrees:* Doc Fine Arts, Regis Col, MA, 98. *Work:* Boston Mus Fine Arts; Univ Southern Ill; Nat Mus Wales; Rose Art Mus, Brandeis Univ, Waltham, Mass; Waterworks, Phoenix, Ariz, 2003. *Comn:* 19 Sculptures, Wall Cycle to Ocotillo, City of Phoenix, Ariz, 91; floor, City of the Falls, Commonwealth Convention Ctr, Louisville, Ky, 2000; water works, Drawn Water, City of Cambridge, Mass, 2000; installations, Nat Park Svc, Bronx River, NY, 98-99, Regis Col, Western Mass, 99, Nat Park Svc, Merrimac River, Lawrence, Mass, 99-2000, many others; Connections, Central Conn State Univ; Benefit of Mr Kite, San Diego, Calif, 2004; Park, Terra Fugit, Miramar, Fla, 2005. *Exhib:* solo exhib, DeCordova Mus, Lincoln, Mass, 82, Lucid Moment, Regis Col, Weston, Mass, 99; Border Gardens Installation, San Diego Mus Contemp Art, La Jolla, Calif, 90; Changing Places, Cardiff Bay Art Trust, Wales, 97; Knowing Limits (traveling show), Pratt Inst & Nat Park Svc, 2000; Projections through Glass, NAO Project Gallery, Boston, MA, 2003; Reaching Water, CAC Gallery, Cambridge, MA, 2004; and others. *Teaching:* Fac sculpture, Sch Mus Fine Arts, Boston, 78-. *Awards:* Govs Design Award, Mass, 86; Artist Educ Award, Boston Mayor's Off, 92; Top Honor Award for design collab, Boston Soc Architects, 93; Idiv Artist Grant, Mass Cult Council, 2003; Valley Forward Presidential Award, top award for Water Works, Ariz. *Bibliog:* Creating a 'there, there', Landscape Architecture, 2002; Drawn Water, Sculpture Mag, 2002; Waterworks Arizona Falls, Sculoture Mag, Feb 2004; Uncovered Landscape, Landscape Architecture, Feb 2005; Sculpture Mag, 10/2005; Landmarks-5 Projects that Left a Mark on the 70's, Architecture Boston, 7/2006. *Mailing Add:* 34 Porter Rd Cambridge MA 02140

HARRINGTON, CHESTEE MARIE
PAINTER, SCULPTOR, PRINTMAKER
b New Iberia, La, Dec 5, 41. *Study:* Art Students League, New York, with Sidney Simon & Michael Pelletieri, 84; Woodstock Sch Art, with Richard McDaniel, 85; Shidon, Bronze Foundry, with Tommy Hicks, 86. *Work:* Art Ctr SW La, Lafayette, La; Mc Ilhenny Collection, La State Univ, Baton Rouge; La State Mus, New Orleans; Hist New Orleans Collection, La; Inst Applied Ontology, Atlanta, Ga. *Comn:* Bronze bust, Bouliguy Plaza, New Iberia, La, 76; wood Polychromatic bas relief, St Landry Bank, Opelousas, La, 81; Lead Relic Tricentennial, Dept Cult, Baton Rouge La, 83; Womans Hosp Wood Polychromatic bas relief, Baton Rouge, La, 87; mural, wood polychromatic bas relief, Cameron State Bank, Sulphur, La, 89. *Exhib:* One-woman shows, Art Ctr SW La, Lafayette, La, 68-75, Masur Mus, Monroe, La, 76, Zigler Mus, Jennings, La, 77 & Meet the Artist, McNeese State Univ, Lake Charles, La, 84, Sans Souci Gallery, Lafayette, La, 97, Mus Gulf Coast, Port Arthur, Tex, 99, Jean Lafitte Nat Historic Park, Lafayette, La, 99, Shadows on the Teche, Nat Trust: L'Espirit de a Louisiane, New Iberia, La, 2003, Corcoran Gallery, DC, 2003, Cigar Factory Red Room, Charleston, SC, 2005; group shows, French Louisiana Bicentennial, Fr Radio Network, Paris, Fr, 75 & Legacy in Progress, La State Univ, Alexandria, La, 85; Tricentennial Celebration, La State Mus, New Orleans, La, 84; We're Saving a Place for You, Shadows on the Teche, Nat Trust. *Collection Arranged:* The White House, Washington, DC; Mus Moncton, New Brunswick, Can; Sunrise Ranch, Loveland, Colo; McIlhenny Collection, La State Univ, Baton Rouge; Touro Hosp, New Orleans. *Teaching:* Instr, basic drawing, Iberia Parish Park Serv, 66-68. *Awards:* Grammy Nominee for L'Esprit de la Louisiana (cajun music cd), 2000. *Bibliog:* Morris Raphael (auth) Battle in the Bayou Country, Harlo Press, 75; Kenneth Nahan (auth) Chestee Harrington Biog, Nahan Galleries, 75; Cristy Viviano (auth), L'Esprit de la Louisiana, & E'Samtele Louisiana, 99, Tree House Press. *Mem:* Nat Artist Equity. *Media:* Wood, Polychromatic Bas Relief. *Interests:* moments of spiritual expressionism set in the multicultural south Louisiana environment. *Publ:* Illusr, Battle in the Bayou Country,

Harlo Press, 75; So you want to invest in art, Baton Rouge Mag, 82; auth, The Advocate, Baton Rouge, 71, 80, 82, 83, 99; auth, The Daily Advertiser, Lafayette, La, 69, 75, 87, 99; auth, Beaumont Enterprise, Tex, 99; auth, Charleston City Paper, SC, 1/12/2005; auth, The Independent, Lafayette, La, 11/5/2003. *Dealer:* Chestee Harrington Gallery New Iberia LA 70560

HARRINGTON, LAMAR
CURATOR, DIRECTOR
b Iowa, Nov 2, 17. *Study:* Iowa State Col, 35-36; Cornish Sch Fine Arts, Seattle, 45-50; Univ Wash, BA, 79. *Collection Arranged:* Art and Machines: Light, Motion and Sound, 69; Claes Oldenburg Icebag, 71; More Art for Public Places, 71; New Works from the Walker, 71; Kenneth Callahan: A Universal Voyage, 73; Adventures in Photography, 75; Arch of Northwest Art, Univ Wash, 75-77; Another Side to Art: Ceramic Sculpture in the Northwest, 79; Washington Craft Forms: Creators and Collectors, 82; Historical Survey of Crafts in the Northwest, 83; Wyoming Arts Coun, Third Wyoming Biennial, 88-89; Frank Lloyd Wright: In the Realm of Ideas, nat traveling exhib, 89 & James W Washington Jr: The Spirit in the Stone, 89 & Eternal Laughter: A 60-Year Retrospective by George Tsutakawa, 90, Bellevue Art Mus; The History of 20th Century American Craft (contribr, catalog), Am Craft Mus, 96. *Pos:* Staff mem, Henry Gallery, Univ Wash, 56-75, assoc dir, 72-75; panel mem visual arts, Nat Endowment for the Arts, 76-78; bd trustees, Pilchuck Glass Sch, Seattle, Wash, 81-87, int coun, 87-92 & adv coun, 92-95; dir & chief cur, Bellevue Art Mus, Bellevue, Wash, 85-90; cur, Univ House, Wallingford, Seattle, Wash, 96-. *Awards:* Community Serv Award, Am Inst Interior Designers, 90; Pyramid Award, Corp Coun Arts, 90; Estab of LaMar Harrington Endowment, Bellevue Art Mus, 91. *Mem:* Western Asn Art Mus (bd trustees, vpres, 73, pres, 74 & 75); hon mem Am Inst Architects; Pac Northwest Arts & Crafts Asn (life mem bd trustees, pres, 57 & 58); Pottery NW (bd trustees, vpres, 76 & 77). *Publ:* Contribr, 74th Western Annual (exhib catalog), Denver Art Mus, 73; auth, Ceramics in the Pacific Northwest: A History, Univ Wash Press, 79; Washington Craft Forms: An Historical Perspective, State Capitol Mus, Olympia, Wash, 82; The making of a modernist metalworker, J Archives Am Art, 10/83; Robert Sperry, the Growing of a Taproot, Bellevue Art Mus, 85

HARRINGTON, WILLIAM CHARLES
SCULPTOR
b Chicago, Ill, 42. *Study:* Univ Ill, Champaign-Urbana, with Roger Majorowicz & Frank & Julio Gallo, BFA; Univ Hartford Art Sch with Ted Behl & Lloyd Glasson, MFA. *Work:* Nat Archives, Washington, DC. *Comn:* 15 ft concrete & steel, Cabot, Cabot & Forbes, Seattle, Wash, 75; 4 ft wood relief, Amalgamated Spirits & Provisions, Ames, Iowa, 75 & Cedar Rapids, Iowa, 76; carved compos, Cabot, Cabot & Forbes, Bellevue, Wash, 84; Top Walk (mixed media), Arlington, Va. *Exhib:* Fuel for Thought, Attleboro Mus, Mass, 96; Burlington Sculpture Garden Exhib, Pemberton, NJ, 91-97; Environmental Arts Inc, Fuller Mus, Brockton, Mass, 97; Mass: Outdoor Sculpture, Green Hill Ctr NC Arts, Greensboro, 97, 98, 99; Rcd, Cambridge Art Asn, Mass, 00; Sculpture at New Horizons, Salisbury, Conn, 00, 01, 02; Salmagundi V, Rocky Mount, NC, 01-02; Lucia and Me, Warwick Mus Art, RI, 02; Art Inst Boston, 02; Earthworks, NC Zoological Park, Ashboro, 02-03; Five Vets, Randolph Art Ctr, Ashboro, NC, 02; Summer Exhib, Grounds for Sculpture, Hamilton, NJ, 02; Sculpture Mile, Madison, Conn, 2003-06; Burlington Co Col, Pemberton, NJ, 2003-04, 04-05; 8th Int Shoebox Sculpture, Hawaii, Taiwan, Guam, mainland US, 2003-05; Salmagundi IX, Rocky Mt, NC, 2005-06; Salmagundi X, Rocky Mt, NC, 2006-07; Sculpture Mile, Middletown, CT, 2005-07; and many others. *Collection Arranged:* NC Zoological Park, Asheboro, NC; State of Hawaii Found on Cult and the Arts. *Pos:* Workshop asst, George Rickey, East Chatham, NY, 65; mem, Combat Artists Team VII, Vietnam/Hawaii, 68-69. *Teaching:* Asst prof sculpture & drawing, Ind State Univ, Terre Haute, 70-72; asst prof sculpture, Iowa State Univ, 74-78; creative consult, Babson Co, Babson Park, Mass, 96-99. *Mem:* Tri-State Sculptors Guild. *Media:* Carved Wood, Collage, Mixed Media. *Publ:* Contribr, Collage Art, JL Alkinson Quarry Press, 96; Art of War: Eyewitness US Combat from the Revolution through the 20th Century, H Avery Chenoweth Friedman Publishing Group Inc, 02. *Mailing Add:* 120 Goulding St Holliston MA 01746

HARRIS, ALFRED PETER
PAINTER, ADMINISTRATOR
b Toronto, Ont, Apr 4, 32. *Study:* Ont Col Art, Toronto, hon dipl; Brock Univ, St Catharines, Ont, LLD, 85. *Work:* Sir George Williams Univ, Montreal; Bronfman Collection, Montreal Mus Fine Art; Brascan Collection, Toronto; Can Coun Art Bank; Northern & Cent Gas Co. *Exhib:* Mem Gallery, Albright-Knox Gallery, Buffalo, 62; four man exhib, London Pub Libr & Art Mus, 63-65; two-man exhibs, Dorothy Cameron Gallery, 64-65; two-man show, Roberts Gallery, Toronto, 70; Ann Exhib Contemp Can Art, Hamilton, 70-72. *Collection Arranged:* J W Morrice, J Chambers Retrospective & William Kurelec Retrospective, 66; Baker, Boyle & Hollenback, 67; John Newman, 68; Soul of Niagara, 69; John Boyle, Ed Fantinel, 70; Harvey Breverman & Niagara Now, 71. *Pos:* Dir, Rodman Hall Arts Ctr, 59-; pres, Ont Asn Art Galleries, 70-71. *Teaching:* Art instr, Ont Col Art, 59-60; instr gen art, Ridley Col, St Catharines, 63-65; spec lectr mod art, Brock Univ, 66. *Bibliog:* Harry Malcomson (auth), Artist, Toronto Life, 69. *Mem:* Can Soc Graphic Art; Ont Soc Artists; Ont Arts Coun. *Media:* Oil. *Publ:* Contribr, Nude in Canadian Art, 72. *Dealer:* Roberts Gallery 641 Yonge St Toronto ON Can

HARRIS, ANN SUTHERLAND
HISTORIAN, ADMINISTRATOR
b Cambridge, Eng, Nov 4, 37. *Study:* Courtauld Inst Art, Univ London, BA(hon, first class), 61, PhD, 65. *Collection Arranged:* Women Artist 1550-1950 (coauth, catalog), Los Angeles Co Mus Art, Los Angeles, 76-77; Univ Art Mus, Univ Tex, Austin, 77; Mus Art, Carnegie Inst Int, Pittsburgh, 77; Brooklyn Mus, 77. *Pos:* Chmn acad affairs, Metrop Mus Art, NY, 77-80. *Teaching:* Asst prof art hist & archeol, Columbia Univ, 66-71; vis lectr, Yale Univ, 72-73; asst prof art hist, Hunter Col, NY, 71-73; assoc prof, State Univ NY, Albany, 73-77; vis assoc prof, Inst Fine Arts, NY Univ, 74-75; adj prof, Juilliard Sch, 78-; Mellon prof, Univ Pittsburgh, spring 84 & prof art hist, 84-. *Awards:* Woman of Year, Mademoiselle Mag, 77. *Mem:* Col Art Asn Am (mem bd dir, 75-79); Women's Caucus for Art (pres & founder mem, 71-74, mem exec adv bd, 74-80). *Res:* Italian and French, 16th & 17th century painting and drawing; contemporary women artists. *Publ:* Coauth, Die Zeichnungen von Andrea Sacchi & Carlo Maratta, Kataloge des Kunstmuseums, Düsseldorf, III, Düsseldorf, 67; ed, Selected Drawings of Gian Lorenzo Bernini, Dover Publ, 77; auth, Andrea Sacchi, Complete Edition of the Paintings, Phaidon, Oxford, 77; Coauth, The Collections of the Detroit Institute of Arts: Italian, French and English Drawings and Watercolors, 92; Coauth, The Katalan Collection of Italian Drawings, (exhib catalog), 95-96, plus other catalogs; contributor articles to The Burlington Mag, Art Bulletin between 1964 and 1989; contributor to several volumes of Master Drawings between 1968 and 2001. *Mailing Add:* Dept History Art and Architectures c/o Univ Pittsburgh Pittsburgh PA 15260

HARRIS, CAROLYN
PAINTER
b Wilmington, NC, Jul 16, 37. *Study:* Univ NC, Greensboro, BFA (painting), 59; New York Univ, MA (art educ), 61. *Work:* Cape Ann Hist Asn, Gloucester, Mass; Erie Art Ctr, Pa; NC State Univ, Raleigh; Scott Mem Study Collection, Bryn Mawr Col, Pa. *Exhib:* Art from the Fifties, Woman's College of the Univ of NC, 1950-1963, Marita Gilliam Gallery, Raleigh, NC, 94; Women in The Visual Arts, Hollins Col, Roanoke, Va, 96; Art and Friendship, II: Selections from the Nell Blaine Collection, Tibor de Nagy Gallery, NY, 98; Kinds of Drawings, Western Carolina Univ, Cullowhee, NC, 99; Zeuxis: A Movable Feast, Westbeth Gallery, NY, 2003; Watercolor, Kouros gallery, NY and Schweinfurth Memorial Art Ctr, Auburn, NY, 2003; Alice Ehrlich & Her Students, Lee Hansley Gallery, Raleigh, NC, 2003; Watercurrents: 12 Artists Working in Watercolor, Kouros Gallery, NY, 2004; Carolyn Harris, Paintings and Works on Paper, solo exhib, Tibor de Nagy Gallery, NY, 2004-05; Watercurrents, Kouros Gallery, NY, 2005. *Pos:* Asst to Alfred H Barr Jr & Dorothy C Miller, Mus Collections, Mus Mod Art, New York, 61; asst to adminr & asst mgr bookshop, San Francisco Mus Mod Art, 62-65. *Awards:* Second Purchase Prize, Int Drawing Competition, State Univ NY, Potsdam, 60; grant, Creative Artists Pub Serv Prog, NY, 74; Benjamin Altman (Landscape) Prize, 159th Ann Exhib, Nat Acad Design, 84. *Bibliog:* Cape Ann Hist Asn Bull, Vol 13, No 2, 4-6/93; Blue Greenberg (auth), Women artists show skills, Herald-Sun, Durham, NC, 8/7/94; Hilton Kramer (auth), Carolyn Harris Solos, Capturing Cape Ann in Inspired Landscape, New York Observer, 1/10/2005; Molly Hutton (auth), Carolyn Harris: Drawing in Paint, Gettyburg Rev, 2006. *Mem:* New York Artists Equity Asn. *Media:* Oil, Watercolor. *Publ:* Illusr, Parker Hodges, Heart of a Plum/Heart of an Owl, Conahan Press, San Francisco, 65; John Heath-Stubbs, Four Poems in Measure, Helikon Press, New York, 73. *Dealer:* Tibor de Nagy Gallery 724 Fifth Ave New York 10019. *Mailing Add:* 210 Riverside Dr Apt 8A New York NY 10025

HARRIS, CHARNEY ANITA
PAINTER, SCULPTOR
b Chicago, Ill. *Study:* Univ Arts, Philadelphia; Philadelphia Mus Art, 64-68; New Sch Social Res, 70-73. *Work:* Philadelphia Mus Art; Allentown Art Mus, Pa; Hobson Pitman Mus House, Bryn Maur, Pa; First Ronald McDonald House. *Comn:* Universal Domain, Hudson River Mus, Yonkers, NY, 85 & Moore Col Art, Philadelphia, 86; Ja,es A Michener Art Mus, Pa, 97; Millicent Roger Mus, Taos, NMex, 96. *Exhib:* a j Wood Galleries, Philadelphia, 79, 80; Mangel Galleriy, Philadelphia, 82, 91; Mangel Gallery, 85, 90, 92-95, 98-2000, 02-06; Artists Xmas Show, Cleveland Ctr Contemp Art, 86; Millicent Roger Mus, Taos, NMex, 96; James Michener Art Mus, Doylestown, Pa, 97; One woman show James A Michener Art Mus, 98. *Awards:* Painting Prize, New York Sch Social Res, 70; Painting Prize, Pa Acad Fine Arts. *Bibliog:* Victoria Donohoe (auth), article, Philadelphia Inquirer, 82 & 88; article in the Washington Post, 84; Aimee Young Jackson (auth), article in Kalliope, 89, 93 & 94. *Mem:* Artists Equity Asn Inc; Am Fedn Arts. *Media:* Oil; Wood. *Publ:* Contribr, Bucks County & Country Living, 96; Art Matter, 98. *Dealer:* Mangel Gallery 1714 Rittenhouse Sq Philadelphia PA 19103. *Mailing Add:* 2 Sunnyside Ln Yardley PA 19067

HARRIS, CONLEY
PAINTER, PRINTMAKER
b Kans, July 7, 43. *Study:* Univ Kans, BFA, 65; Univ Wis, MFA, 68. *Work:* Fogg Art Mus, Harvard Univ, Cambridge, Mass; Boston Mus Fine Art; Wichita Art Mus, Kans; Citi-Corp Bank & Rockefeller Financial Serv, NY; Fed Reserve Bank, Chicago; De Cordova & Dana Mus, Lincoln, Mass; Portland Mus Art, Portland, ME; CitiBank, NY; Fidelity Management & Research, Boston, Mass; Met Life Insurance, NY; Mass Financial Services Co, Boston, Mass; Federal Reserve Bank, Chicago, Ill; John Hancock Insurance, Int Div, Boston, Mass; pvt collections of Mary Darmstaetter, Yasuko & Dr. John Bush, Gerard Evers, Fredricka Merck, Rita Fraad, Barbara & Steve Grossman and many others. *Comn:* Oil painting, Chubb Insurance Co, 85; Oil painting, Gannett Co, 87; pastel drawings, Fidelity Mgt & Res, 94; Harvard Univ, 98; oil paintings, comn by Eaton Vance Mana, Boston, 2000; Gannett Co Inc, Rosslyn, Va. *Exhib:* Made in Boston, Fogg Art Mus, Harvard Univ, Cambridge, Mass, 80; Am Drawings, Smithsonian tour, 83-85; Figuration on Paper, Boston Mus Fine Arts, 83; one-person shows, Barridoff Galleries, Portland, Maine, 83, Thomas Segal Gallery, Boston, Mass, 85 & DeCordova Mus, Lincoln, 85, Pursuing Beauty and Light, David Findlay Jr Fine Art, NY, 2001, Silas Kenoyn Gallery, Provincetown, MA, 2001-2002; New Prints, EES Studio, Estampe du Rhin, Strasbourg, France, 90; Barbara Greene Gallery, Miami, Fla, 91; Gallery Viva, Kawasaki, Japan, 94; Andrea Marquit Fine Art,

Boston, 95 & 97; David Findlay Jr Fine Art, NY, 98; Bradford Campbell Gallery, San Francisco, 2000; New Landscapes, Art Life Mitsuhashi Gallery, Kyoto, Japan, 2001; The Landscape, Virginia Lynch Gallery, Tiverton, RI, 2002; Intimate Views, Silas-Kenyon Gallery, Provincetown, Mass, 2002 & 2005; Hindu Dieties, Haughton Asia Art Fair, Theresa McCullough Ltd, NY, 2003; Hindu Tableaux, Bernard Toale Gallery, Boston, MA, 2003; Paintings, Drawings, Judith Dowling Asian Art, Boston, MA, 2004. *Teaching:* Vis artist drawing, Boston Univ, Mass, 69-70; assoc prof drawing & painting, Univ NH, Durham, 70-88; Art New England Workshops, Bennington Col, 84, 85, 87, 88 & 90. *Awards:* Wurlitzer Found Residence Grant, Taos, NMex, 75; Purchase Prize, Am Drawing, Portsmouth, Va, 76; Mass Artist Found Fel, 86. *Bibliog:* Nancy Stapen (auth), rev, Art News Mag, 11/95; John Arthur (auth), New England Landscape Painting, Art New Eng, 6/97; Cate McQuaid (auth), Toying with Reality Rev, Art New Eng, 11/97. *Media:* Oil, Watercolor; Monotype. *Dealer:* Victoria Munroe Fine Art Boston Mass. *Mailing Add:* 1140 Washington St Boston MA 02118

HARRIS, DAVID JACK
PAINTER, MURALIST

b San Mateo, Calif, Jan 6, 48. *Study:* San Francisco State Univ, BA, 72, MA, 75. *Work:* San Francisco State Univ, Bain & Co, Pacific Bell & Int Red Cross, San Francisco; Stanford Univ, Palo Alto, Calif; Litton Industs, Mountain View, Calif; N Cent Wash Mus, Wenatchee, Wash; Maturugo Mus, Ridgecrest, Calif. *Comn:* Lawry's, Beverly Hills, Calif; Sheraton Grande, Los Angeles; Royal Family, Saudia Arabia; Uoysys Corp, Fremont, Calif; Spieker Partners, Pleasanton, Calif; and others. *Exhib:* Fine Arts Mus, San Francisco, 68-70; San Mateo Co Mus, Calif, 70; California Artists, Palace Fine Arts, San Francisco, 75; solo exhib, Hewlett Packard Gallery, Palo Alto, Calif, 86, California Concepts, N Cent Wash Mus, Wash, Coastal Arts League Mus, San Mateo, Calif, 88 & Matur Augo Mus, Ridgecrest, 92. *Pos:* Dir, Galerie de Tours, San Francisco, 71-72; pres, 1870 Gallery & Studio, Belmont, Calif, 86-87; UP Coastal Arts League Mus, 90-. *Teaching:* Instr painting & art hist, Chabot Col, Hayward, Calif, 76-81. *Awards:* Best of Show, Univ Santa Clara, Calif, 75; First Place, Bay Area Artists Group, San Francisco Co, 78; First Place, San Mateo Co Artist Show, 80. *Bibliog:* Mary Helen McAllister (auth), David Harris, N Co Publ, 84; Mark Stevens (auth), David Harris: A World in Motion, Valley Mag, San Clemente, Calif, 89; Spectacular Houses of California; Finest Designers in California. *Mem:* Int Soc Interior Designers; 1870 Gallery & Studios; Coastal Arts League, San Mateo, Calif; Col Art Asn. *Media:* Oil, Acrylic. *Specialty:* Abstract Acrylies. *Interests:* hiking, camping, travel. *Publ:* Auth, California Concepts brochure, N Cent Wash Mus Publ. *Dealer:* A Gallery 73-580 El Paseo Palm Desert CA 92260. *Mailing Add:* 485 Miramar Half Moon Bay CA 94019

HARRIS, ELLEN SCHWARTZ
ADMINISTRATOR, MUSEOLOGIST

b Washington, DC, Nov 3, 49. *Study:* Yale Univ, BA(A Conger Goodyear Award & Marshall-Allison Fel), 71; Inst Fine Arts, NY Univ, MA (art hist), 79; Yale Sch Mgmt, MPPM, 86. *Collection Arranged:* Images of Experience (auth, catalog), 82, The Art of Notation (auth, catalog), 82, Partitions, 82, The Destroyed Print (auth, catalog), 82, Exceptions, 83, Bridges (auth, catalog), 83, Contemporary Third World Architecture (auth, catalog), 83 & Beauties & Beasts, 84, Dottie Attie, 92, Robert Kushner, 93, Passionate Pursuits, 96, Janet T Pickett, 97, Pratt Inst; and others. *Pos:* Paris corresp, Art Int Mag, Lugano, Switz, 71-72; admin asst, Hirshhorn Mus & Sculpture Garden, 76; ed, Harry N Abrams, New York, 76-79; contrib ed, Art News Mag, New York, 77-86; dir exhibs, Pratt Inst, Manhattan & Brooklyn, 79-84; chmn bd trustees, Rotunda Gallery, Brooklyn Borough Hall, 81-84; treas, Franklin Furnace, 87-; deputy dir finance & auxiliary activities, Mus Mod Art, New York, 89-92; dir, Montclair Art Mus, 92-; trustee, Art Table, 92-94, NJ Asn Mus, 92-95 & Art Pride, 93-. *Teaching:* Vis asst prof, Pratt Inst, 81-84. *Mem:* Am Asn Mus; Asn Art Mus Dirs (chair, Women's Caucus, 93-); Art Table (trustee). *Publ:* Ed, The Mechanism of Meaning (Arakawa/Gins), Harry N Abrams, 79; auth, Vito Acconci, 81, Artists the critics are watching, 81, At the Whitney and the Guggenheim: No surprises, 81, Dennis Oppenheim, 82 & others, Art News; contribr, Art Int, Art in Am & The Village Voice; contrib ed, Art News; ed, various art books, Hary N Abrams, Inc. *Mailing Add:* c/o Montclair Mus Three S Mountain Ave Montclair NJ 07042

HARRIS, GLORIANE
PAINTER, EDUCATOR

b Santa Monica, Calif, Jan 7, 47. *Study:* Art Ctr Col Design, Los Angeles, 64; Univ Southern Calif, 64-66; El Camino Col, 65; Los Angeles City Col, 66; Otis Art Inst of Los Angeles Co, 66, BFA, MFA(fel), 70; Los Angeles Trade Tech Col, 78. *Exhib:* New Talent, New Work, Los Angeles Co Mus Art, Calif, 71; Video Los Angeles, Palais de Beaux Artes, Brussels, Belg, 77; Painting Show, Mount San Antonio Col, Walnut, Calif, 78; Painting, Newport Harbor Art Mus, Calif, 79; Hang Eight: Artists from Southern California (with catalog), Foundations Gallery, NY, 82; Self-Portrait Invitational, Am Gallery, Los Angeles, 82; solo exhibs, Sea Sections, AAA/Michael Salerno Gallery, 84, Metro Rail Transit Consult Visual Arts, Los Angeles, 84 & Culver Nat Bank, Culver City, Calif, 84-85; Fac Exhib, El Camino Col Gallery, Torrance, Calif, 93 & 94. *Pos:* Co-organizer, Experiments in Art & Technol, 68-71; co-organizer & founding mem, Los Angeles Inst Contemp Art, 73-75; tech asst, Documenta, Kassel, Ger, 77; art dir, Vintage Image, 81-83; freelance production graphic artist & photo retoucher, 83-; graphic artist, Mark Taper Forum, 84-85; art dir, Lone Eagle Publ, 85-; asst art dir, Bon Appetit Mag, Knapp Commun Corp, 85-90. *Teaching:* Lectr painting, drawing & design, Cerritos Col, Calif, 70-72; lectr painting & drawing, W Los Angeles Col, Culver City, Calif, 71-74; lectr design & drawing, El Camino Col, Torrance, Calif, 74-78; lectr photo retouching, Otis Art Inst of Parsons, Los Angeles, Calif, 80-81; lectr drawing art history, El Camino Col, Torrance, Calif, 91-. *Bibliog:* William Wilson (auth), article in Los Angeles Times, 6/14/74; Ronald Steen (auth), Gloriane Harris and Steven Semeyer, Artweek, 9/27/75; Peter Frank (auth), Unslick in Los Angeles, Art in Am, 9-10/78; Juri Koll (dir), Oil and Water--A Portrait of Gloriane Harris (film), 83. *Mem:* Artists Equity. *Media:* Oil, Watercolor. *Publ:* Brain Child Mag, Los Angeles, Calif

HARRIS, LILY MARJORIE
ART DEALER, ADMINISTRATOR

b Rochester, NY, Nov 12, 56. *Study:* Syracuse Univ, BFA(textile design), 78; Victoria & Albert Mus, London, 78; Rochester Inst Technol, MS, 81. *Pos:* Restorer, Metrop Mus Art, New York, 78-79; colorist, Thomas Strahan Co, Chelsea, Mass, 79; asst dir, George Frederic Gallery, Rochester, NY, 82-83; admin asst, Thomas Burke Woodworkers, Rochester, NY, 84-85; dir-owner, Galerie Oboussier, Nantucket, Mass, 84-86; asst dir, Main St Gallery, Nantucket, 86-92, decorative painter, 92-. *Teaching:* Instr, Mem Art Gallery, Rochester, 80; workshop instr, Nantucket Island Sch Design & Arts, 81. *Mem:* Am Asn Mus. *Specialty:* Contemporary art, fine crafts, and photography. *Mailing Add:* 7 1/2 Back St Nantucket MA 02554

HARRIS, PAUL
SCULPTOR

b Orlando, Fla, Nov 5, 25. *Study:* With Joy Winslow, Orlando; Univ NMex; New Sch Social Res, with Johannes Molzahn; Hans Hofmann Sch. *Work:* Los Angeles Co Mus Art; Mus Mod Art, NY; San Francisco Mus Mod Art; Neue Galerie der Stadt Aachen; Univ Art Mus, Berkeley; Cath Univ Chile; and many others. *Exhib:* Sculpture USA, 59 & Hans Hofmann & His Students, 64-65, Mus Mod Art, NY, 58, 63; Sculpture of the Sixties, Los Angeles Co Mus & Sao Paulo Biennial, 67; Crocker Art Gallery Asn, Sacramento, 68; Soft Art, NJ Mus, 69; New Vein Show, Vienna, Cologne, Belgrade, Baden-Baden, Geneva, Brussels & Milan, 69-70; solo exhibs, San Francisco Mus Art, 72, Univ Calif, Santa Barbara, 72, Univ NMex, 73, Ark Art Ctr, Little Rock, 74 & Galerie Redmann, Berlin, 90, 91 & 92; Iannetti-Lanzone, San Francisco, 89; C Grimaldis, Baltimore, 89; Fresno Mus Art, 99; The Col of Marin Gallery, Kentfield, Calif, 2000. *Pos:* founder, Wrongree Press, 73. *Teaching:* Instr art, Univ NMex, Knox Col, BWI, State Univ NY, New Paltz, San Francisco Inst Art, Universidad Catholica de Chile, NY Univ & Univ Calif, Berkeley; prof art, Calif Col Arts & Crafts, retired; vis critic, lectr, USFS Ctrs, Valparaiso and Concepcion, Chile, 62, Rinehart Sch Sculpture, Spring 81, Md Inst Art, (9 times), 63-86, Univ Oreg, Eugene, 68, Newark State Univ, NJ, 70, Mont State Univ, Bozeman, 70, 74, State Univ NMex, Las Cruces, 71, Montclair Col, 77, Phila Col Art, 77, RI Sch Design, 77, Univ Ariz, Tucson, 86. *Awards:* Neallie Sullivan Award, 67; Tamarind Fel, 69-70; Resident MacDowell Colony, 77; Longview Found Grant, 78; Guggenheim Fel, 79; artist-in-residence, Rinehart Sch Sculpture, Md Inst Art, 81, Univ Ariz, Tucson, 86; Lebovitz Fund Grant, 78. *Bibliog:* Paul Harris (auth), Pas D'Une Bolinas, Ca, Wrongtree Press, 82; Thomas Albright (auth), Art in the San Francisco Bay Area 1945-1980, Univ Calif Press, Berkeley, 85; Bill Berkson (auth), Paul Harris, Works in Bronze, Iannetti-Lanzone Gallery, 89. *Media:* Bronze. *Publ:* Contribr, Art News & Art in Am; illusr, Dorothy Schmidt's Torso, 74 & Pas d' Une, 79; Phases of The Moon, Wrongtree Press, 95; design of book Motives and Cues, Marguerite Harris (auth), 93; lithographs, Paradise: Variations, 96; drawings, Paul Harris, 98; Paul Harris, Fifty Years, Univ Wash Press, 99. *Mailing Add:* Box 930 Bolinas CA 94924

HARRIS, PAUL ROGERS
PHOTOGRAPHER, CURATOR

b Dallas, Tex, Jan 2, 33. *Study:* Univ NTex, BA, 54, MA, 56; NY Univ, 65-67; Inst Arts Admin, Harvard Univ, cert, 78. *Exhib:* 50 Yrs in Art, Mt View Col, Dallas, Tex. *Collection Arranged:* Emerging Texas Photographers (with catalog), 80; Inaugural Exhibition, Gateway Gallery, Dallas Mus Fine Art, 84; Handmade in Texas, Craft Guild Dallas, 87; City Life: Views of the City, Zoomorphism: Animals in Art & A Decade of Dallas Crafts, 1949-1959, 88; Houses of God: Charles De Bus, 89; Texas Printmakers: 1940-1965, Meadows Mus Southern Methodist Univ, 90; Mystery and Intrigue, Peregrine Gallery, Dallas, 91; Metal and Mettle: Art and Spirit, Ida Green Gallery, Austin Col, Sherman, Tex, 92; Landscape Remembered: Paintings by Mary Vernon, Wichita Falls Mus & Art Ctr, Tex, 93; Point of No Return, 94; A Point of View: Texas Women Painters, 1900-1960, El Paso Mus Art, Tex, 96; Breaking Into the Mainstream: Texas African-American Artists, Irving Arts Ctr, Tex, 96; Portraits & Self-Portraits: Fact or Fiction, Brazos Gallery, Richland Col, Dallas, 96. *Pos:* Coordr educ servs, Mus Mod Art, New York, 65-70; dir, Art Ctr, Waco, Tex, 74-86; chmn visual arts & archit adv panel, Tex Comn on Arts, 80-83; bd dir, Tex Arts Alliance, 80-86; exec dir, Craft Guild Dallas, 86-88; mem, Arts Adv Comt, African-Am Mus, Dallas, 90-. *Teaching:* Supvr art, Children's House, Dallas Mus Contemp Arts, Tex, 60-65; head dept art educ, Southern Methodist Univ, Dallas, Tex, 70-74; instr art, El Centro Col, Dallas, 92-95, Navarro Col, Corsicana, Tex, 92-95 & Mt View Col, 95-. *Awards:* Alumni Hon, NTex State Univ, 85; Twentieth Anniversary Celebration, Art Ctr, Waco, 92; Legend Award, Prof Dallas Ctr for Contemporary Art, 02; Scholorship named PRH for Art Student at Univ, 04, 05. *Bibliog:* Janet Kutner (auth), Texas small museums discovering each other, Art News, 2/77; Charlotte Moser (auth), Texas museums: Gambling for big change, Art News, 12/79; Janet Kutner (auth), A celebration of city life, Dallas Morning News. *Mem:* Tex Asn Schs Art; Dallas Visual Arts Ctr; McKinney Ave Contemp; Dallas Mus Art. *Media:* Digital Imaging. *Interests:* photography, contemporary art, fold art. *Publ:* Auth, Gillian Bradshaw-Smith: Soft Sculptures & Drawings, 76, Richard Hunt: Sculpture, Drawings, Prints, 78, Pedro Friedeberg, 78 & many others. *Mailing Add:* 7211 Concord Ave Dallas TX 75235-4414

HARRIS, ROBERT GEORGE
PAINTER, ILLUSTRATOR
b Kansas City, Mo, Sept 9, 11. *Study:* Kansas City Art Inst, with Monte Crews; Grand Cent Sch Art, with Harvey Dunn; Art Students League, with George Bridgeman. *Work:* Portraits, Phoenix Jr Col, Dept of Justice, Washington, DC, Seabury Western Theol Sem, Chicago, Ill, Wabash Col, Crawfordsville, Ind & Franciscan Renewal Ctr, Scottsdale, Ariz; also in many pvt collections in US. *Exhib:* Soc Illusr; Art Dirs Club, 43-46; New Rochelle Art Asn, 49; Westport Artists, 50; one-man show of portraits, Phoenix Art Mus, 62. *Mem:* Soc Illusr; Phoenix Fine Art Asn; Phoenix Art Mus. *Media:* Oil. *Publ:* Illusr, McCall's, 39-60, Sat Eve Post, 39-61, Good Housekeeping, 40-60, Ladies' Home J, 40-61 & other nat mags. *Mailing Add:* PO Box 1124 Carefree AZ 85377

HARRIS, RONNA S
PAINTER, EDUCATOR
b Los Angeles, Calif, July 25, 52. *Study:* San Francisco Art Inst, 73; Calif State Univ, Northridge, BA, 74; Univ Calif, Santa Barbara, MFA, 77. *Work:* Jacksonville Art Mus; White House Visitor Center. *Exhib:* Birmingham Biennial, Birmingham Art Mus, Ala, 87; Fla Artists, Jacksonville Art Mus, 87; Magic Realism, Vero Beach Ctr Arts, Fla, 88; Women Artists, Metrop Mus & Art Ctr, Coral Gables, Fla, 88; Still, Zinsel, 90, 92, 94, 96, 99, 2003, 2005; Impostorphobia, Contemp Art Ctr, New Orleans, 92; Contemp Work, Pensacola Art Mus, Fla, 93; Univ Western Ala, 2003; Palma Gallery, New Orleans, 2005; Northwestern State Univ, Natchitoches, La, 2006; Appalachian State Univ, Turchin Ctr for the Arts, Boone, NC, 2006. *Collection Arranged:* Jacksonville Art Mus, Fla; Claiborne Collection, Baton Rouge, La; White House Hist Asoc, Washington DC; Huntsville Art Mus, Ala; Birmingham Art Mus, Ala; Morris Art Mus, Ga. *Pos:* Scenic artist, Universal, Disney, NBC & ABC, Los Angeles, Calif, 79-85. *Teaching:* Instr painting & drawing, Humboldt State Univ, Calif, 77-78; asst prof figure drawing, Univ Miami, Fla, 85-89; assoc prof painting & drawing, Tulane Univ, New Orleans, 89-. *Awards:* Purchase Award, Fla Artists, Jacksonville Art Mus, 87; Max Orovitz Res Grant, Lowe Art Mus, Univ Miami, 88; Fel Grant, Newcomb Col, 90 & 93. *Bibliog:* Heidi Schiff Tuby (auth), In Sharp Focus, Boca Raton, 88; WCA Miami Chap, The Way of the Woman Artist (film), Dade Co Television, Channel 1, 89; New American Paintings, Southern Edition, Open Studio Press, 95. *Mem:* Col Art Asn. *Media:* Oil, Pastel. *Specialty:* Palma Gallery, New Orleans, La. *Dealer:* Palma Gallery 328 Howard St New Orleans LA 70112. *Mailing Add:* 4111 Vincennes Pl New Orleans LA 70125

HARRIS, WILLIAM WADSWORTH, II
PAINTER, COLLAGE ARTIST
b Hamden, Conn, 1927. *Study:* Yale Univ, BA; Univ Mich, MA; also with Richard Wilt, Deane Keller & Jerry Farnsworth. *Work:* Galerie Moos, Geneva, Switz; Toledo Mus Fine Arts, Ohio; Yale Univ Collection; Mattatuck Mus Arts & City Nat Bank, Waterbury, Conn; Northwestern Conn Col, Winsted; and in pvt collections in Europe, Mid East & US. *Exhib:* Ringling Mus Art, Sarasota, Fla, 61; Galerie Georges Moos, Geneva, Switz, 64-69; Hub Gallery, Pa State Univ, State Col, 73; Conn Soc Fine Arts, Wadsworth Atheneum, Hartford, 74; Am Painters in Paris Exhib, France, 75-76; Berkshire Mus Fine Arts, Pittsfield, Mass, 77; Munson Gallery, New Haven, Conn, 80-83; one-man exhib, Scranton Mem, Madison, Conn, 97; Wall St Gallery, Madison, Conn, 2001-03. *Awards:* Top Awards, Waterbury Arts Festival, Conn, 67 & 68; Winsted Award, 75 & Top Purchase Award, 79, Northwest Conn Art Asn; New Brit Mus Am Top Award, 97. *Bibliog:* Prize Winning Art, Bk 7, Allied Publ, 67. *Mem:* New Haven Paint & Clay Club (bd dir, 67-69); New Haven Festival Arts (bd dir, 71-73); Conn Acad Fine Arts. *Media:* Oil on Canvas, Collage in Mixed Media. *Mailing Add:* 156 Chestnut Hill Rd Killingworth CT 06419-1353

HARRISON, ALICE
PAINTER, COLLAGE ARTIST
Study: Art Students League; Cornell Univ; NY Univ. *Work:* Johnson & Johnson Corp, NJ; Noyes Mus, NJ; Int Mus Collage, Mex; Art Colle, France. *Exhib:* Paterson Mus, NJ, 95; Jersey City Mus, NJ, 96; Bergen Mus, Paramus, NJ, 98. *Teaching:* instr, collage, home studio, currently. *Awards:* Skylands Select, NJ, 2002; Celebration Landscape, MD, 2003; NAWA Annual, NY, 2004. *Mem:* NAWA; SLMM; ISEA; Salute to Women in Arts; Painting, Printmaking, Watercolor Affiliates, NJ. *Media:* Mixed media, paint & collage. *Publ:* Contribr, Art of Layering: Making Connections, SLMM, 2003; Am Art Collector, Alcove Books, 2004

HARRISON, CAROL LOVE
PHOTOGRAPHER
b Washington, DC, 50. *Study:* Georgetown Univ Sch For Serv, BSFS, 73; Univ Md, MFA, 83. *Hon Degrees:* Georgetown Univ, Hon BSFS, 1973. *Comn:* Color Photographs, Nat Strategy Info Ctr, Wash, 2002-2004; Georgetown B&W Photographs, Swidler and Berlin, Wash, 85; 350 Yrs of Art and Archit, The Art Gallery, Univ Md, 85. *Exhib:* The Beijing Exchange Exhib, The Cult Palace, Beijing, 86; Snapshot, The Contemp Mus, Baltimore, 99-03; Moca DC's Ann Show, Mus of Contemp Art, Washington, 2000-02; The Pursuit of Excellence, Southeast Exhbn at Cen Gallery, NC, 87; Kathleen Ewing Gallery, 2005. *Collection Arranged:* Nat Gallery of Art, Washington, DC; Corcoran Gallery of Art, Washington; Va Mus of Fine Arts, Richmond, Va; US Holocaust Mus Portraits of Jan Karski, Washington. *Teaching:* teacher artist workshop prog, The Va Mus of Fine Arts, 88-89; advanced portraiture lectr, No Va CC, Alexandria, Va, 90; artist Fairfax Co Coun of the Arts, Mobil Oil Corp, 90, 92; instr, The Bullis Sch, 2005-2006. *Awards:* Excellence in Photography, The Nex Juried Show, Va Mus of fine Arts, 83-85; Honorarium, Calliope, Fla Dept Cultural Affairs, 98; Juried Photography Exhibit Award, Westmoreland Art Nats, 98. *Bibliog:* C-Dezinformatsia: Active Measures in Soviet Strategy, Pergamon, 84; C-The Photo Review, Nat Photographic Com, Brasseys, 86; C-The Washington Rev, 80-90; C-The Antietam Rev; C-The Washingtonian. *Mem:* Nat Mus of Women in the Arts. *Specialty:* Fine Art Photog. *Mailing Add:* 666 Live Oak Dr McLean VA 22101-1569

HARRISON, CAROLE
SCULPTOR
b Chicago, Ill, Oct 30, 33. *Study:* Cranbrook Acad Art, BFA, 55, MFA, 56; Cent Sch Art, London, with Robert Adams, Fulbright Scholar, 58. *Work:* Springfield Mus Art, Ill; Kalamazoo Inst Art; Cranbrook Mus Art; Fine Arts Complex, Western Mich Univ; Nat Mus Women Arts, Washington, DC. *Comn:* Unity and Growth (brass & copper), City Oak Park, Ill, 66; Seated Figure (cast brass), Kalamazoo Art Inst, 69; Fountain (welded brass); Three Figures (welded brass), 72 & Motif (welded brass & copper), Western Mich Univ, 82; Friends Meet (welded brass), Cottey Coll, Nevada, Mo, 84. *Exhib:* Second Biennial Am Painting & Sculpture, Detroit Art Inst & Pa Acad Fine Arts, 59; New Horizons in Sculpture, McCormick Pl, Chicago, 61; Painting & Sculpture Today, Herron Mus Art, Indianapolis, 67; solo exhib, Women & Landscape, Kalamazoo Inst Arts, 76; Nat Acad Design Exhib,NY, 82 & 92; Sculpture Ctr, NY, 85. *Teaching:* Assoc prof sculpture, Western Mich Univ, 60-74 & State Univ NY, Fredonia, 75-78. *Awards:* Tiffany Found Fel, 60; First Prize, New Horizons in Sculpture, McCormick Pl, Chicago, 61; 161st Ann Artists Fund Prize, Nat Acad of Design, 86; Fulbright fellow, Eng, 57. *Bibliog:* Cesta Peekstok (producer), Art and Architecture in Kalamazoo (video), Western Mich Univ, 76; Marcia Wood (auth), Sculpture, Carole Harrison, Kalamazoo Col, 77; Cesta Peekstok (producer), Art is All Around Us (video), Western Mich Univ, 80; Fay L. Hendry (auth), Outdoor Sculpture in Kalamazo, 80; Virginia N Jones (auth), Contemporary American Women Sculptors, Oryx Press, 86. *Mem:* New York Artists Equity; Nat Asn Women Artists; Sculptors Guild. *Media:* Metal, Wood. *Publ:* Auth, Building three figures, Western Mich Univ Press, 73. *Dealer:* Water Street Gallery Saugatuck MI 49453. *Mailing Add:* Box 19555 Kalamazoo MI 49019

HARRISON, HELEN AMY
MUSEUM DIRECTOR, CRITIC
b New York, NY, Dec 4, 43. *Study:* Adelphi Univ, Garden City, NY, AB(art), 65; Brooklyn Mus Art Sch, Max Beckmann Mem scholar in sculpture, 65-66; Hornsey Col Art, London, Eng, 66-67; Case Western Reserve Univ, Cleveland, MA(art hist), 75. *Collection Arranged:* Seven American Women: The Depression Decade (co auth, catalog), 76; David Burliuk: Years of Transition, 1910-1931 (auth, catalog), 78; Dawn of a New Day: the 1939/40 New York World's Fair (auth, catalog), 80; Larry Rivers: Performing for the Family (auth, catalog), 83; Jimmy Ernst: A Survey, 1942-1983, 85; Crosscurrents: East Hampton and Provincetown (coauth, catalog), 86; Ibram Lassaw: A Retrospective Survey, 1929-1988 (auth, catalog), 88; En Plein Air (coauth, catalog), 89; East Hampton Avant-Garde (auth, catalog), 90; Alfonso Ossorio: The Victorias Drawings, 1950, 91; Betty Parsons: Paintings on Paper, 92; The Abstract Spirit: John Ferren, 93; Jackson Pollock: The New-Found Screen Prints, 95; Lee Krasner Drawings, 95; New Possibilities 1947/1997, 97; Photographs by Martha Holmes, 98; NOT Pollock/NOT Krasner, 00; others. *Pos:* Cur, Parrish Art Mus, Southampton, NY, 77-78 & Guild Hall Mus, East Hampton, NY 82-90; art critic, NY Times, Long Island Weekly, 78-; guest cur, Queens Mus, Flushing, NY, 79-81; exec dir, Pub Art Preserv Comt, 80-82; dir, Pollock-Krasner House Study Ctr, East Hampton, NY, 90-. *Teaching:* Instr, Sch Visual Arts, 85 & 86 & State Univ NY, Stony Brook, 92 & 94. *Awards:* Acad of Distinction, Adelphi Univ Alumni Asn, 86; Media Awards, Press Club of Long Island, 86, 87. *Mem:* Int Asn Art Critics, Am Section; Am Studies Asn. *Res:* Federal art patronage projects of the New Deal era, especially mural painting; the 1939/40 New York World's Fair; contemporary American Art. *Publ:* contribr, The Figurative Fifties (exhib catalog), Newport Harbor Art Mus, 88; Remembering the future, Queens Mus, Rizzoli, 89; The American Art Book, Phaidon, 99; Such Desperate Joy: Imagining Jackson Pollock, Thunder's Mouth Press, 00. *Mailing Add:* 760 E Hampton Tpke Sag Harbor NY 11963-4230

HARRISON, HELEN MAYER (MRS NEWTON HARRISON)
ENVIRONMENTAL ARTIST, CONCEPTUAL ARTIST
b New York, NY. *Study:* Queens Col, BA; Cornell Univ; NY Univ, MA, 53. *Work:* Brooklyn Mus; Mus Mod Art, NY; Chase Manhattan Bank; Metromedia Inc; Washington Univ Gallery Art, St Louis; and others. *Comn:* Pasadena Parts 1 & 2, Pasadena Civic & Art Orgn; Yarkon River, Tel Aviv Found, Israel; Intersection: Pico-Seagate, Santa Monica, Calif; San Diego Landfill, Calif; Disappearing Path, Newport, Calif. *Exhib:* Mus Revolution, Zagreb, 90; Nagoya Bienale, Japan, 91; group exhib, Imperiled Shores, The Baxter Gallery, Portland Sch of Art, Portland, ME, 92; The Serpentine Lattice (with catalog), Douglas F Cooley Mem Art Gallery, Reed Col, Portland, Ore & Ronald Feldman Fine Arts, NY, 93; group traveling exhib, Generations of Mentors, Nat Mus of Women in the Arts, Washington, DC, 94; Fragmentation and Unity: Der Einzugsgebietmeister, Gallery, Bauhaus Dessau, Ger, 94; Green Heart Vision (with Harrison Studio), Kunstmuseum Bonn, Bonn, Ger, 97. *Pos:* Consult, Presidential Task Force on Educ, Nat Endowment Arts, 79; mem, Pub Art Adv Bd, San Diego, 83-88. *Teaching:* Prof visual arts, Univ Calif, San Diego, 81-, chmn visual arts dept, 83. *Awards:* DAAD Fel, Berlin, 88 & 89; 2nd Prize, Nagoyo Bienale, 91; Vesta Award, Women's Bldg, La, 89; and others; . *Bibliog:* Robin Cembalest (auth), Ecological Art Explosion, Art News, Vol 90, No 6, 91; Arlene Raven (auth), Main Stream, Village Voice, 4/9/91; Craig Adcock (auth), Conversational drift: Helen Mayer Harrison & Newton Harrison, Art J, Vol 51, No 2, 92; and others. *Media:* Mixed. *Publ:* Illusr, One full work and part of another, 12/77-1/78 & Great Lakes Meditations, summer 79, New Wilderness Lett, NY; auth,

The Book of the Grab, In: Dialogue, Discourse, Research, Santa Barbara Mus Art, 79; The Book of the Seven Lagoons, Limited Eds Artists Bk, 85; A Lattice or a Serpentine, Seattle Arts Lett, 92; cover illusr, Leonardo 26, 93. *Dealer:* Ronald Feldman Fine Arts 31 Mercer St New York NY 10013. *Mailing Add:* 415 Linden St Santa Cruz CA 95062-1023

HARRISON, JAN
PAINTER, SCULPTOR
Work: Samuel Dorsky Mus Art, New Paltz, NY; Cincinnati Art Mus; Wexner Ctr for Visual Arts, Ohio State Univ, Columbus; Arco Ctr for Visual Arts, Los Angeles, Calif; Women's Studio Workshop, Rosendale, NY. *Comn:* Divining House (structure), Contemp Arts Ctr, Fed Res Plaza, Cincinnati, 86. *Exhib:* Chaosmos, Kleinert/James Arts Ctr, Woodstock, NY, 2001; Making Their Mark, Cincinnati Art Mus, 2003; Ideas Into Objects: Reinterpreting the Notebooks of Leonard da Vinci, Alice F and Harris K West Art Gallery, Aronoff Ctr for Arts, Cincinnati, 2005; Encaustic Works: 2005, Samuel Dorsky Mus, New Paltz, NY, 2005; solo exhib, Sentient Animals, Gallery at R & F, Kingston, NY, 2005; and others. *Pos:* mem artists adv com, Contemp Arts Ctr, Cincinnati, 87-88; panelist, Ohio Arts Coun, Columbus, 91, Dutchess Co Arts Coun, NY State Coun on Arts, 97-98; membership dir, Women's Studies Workshop, 92-93. *Teaching:* vis asst prof painting, Antioch Col, Yellow Springs, Ohio, 86-87; adj lectr painting, Marist Col, Poughkeepsie, NY, 99-05. *Awards:* Ohio Arts Coun New Works Grant, 86; Summerfair Aid to Individual Artist Grant, 99; Purchase Award, Cincinnati Graphic Ars Forum, 89. *Bibliog:* Steven Kolpan (auth), Woodstock Times, 5/25/92; Linda Weintraub (auth), In the Making: Creative Options for Contemporary Art, Art Pub, 2003; Paul Smart (auth), Painting In The Language of Animals, Ulster Pub, 11/17/2005. *Mem:* Women's Studio Workshop; Arts Soc Kingston. *Media:* All Media. *Publ:* The Definitive American Contemporary Quilt, 90; Animal, Anima, Animus, Pori Contem Art Mus Pub, 98; Encaustic Works. *Mailing Add:* 34 Hunter St Kingston NY 12401-6022

HARRISON, JIMMIE
JEWELER, CRAFTSMAN
b Shiprock, NMex, Feb 4, 52. *Study:* Univ NMex, 71-73; Acad Arts, Paris, France, 76. *Work:* Heard Mus, Phoenix, Ariz; Wheelwright Mus, Santa Fe, NMex; Northern Ariz Mus, Flagstaff; Squash Blossoms, Vail, Colo. *Comn:* Gold buckle, watchband & bolo tie, Toh-Atin Gallery, Durango, Colo, 84. *Exhib:* All Navajo Show, Northern Ariz Mus, Flagstaff, 81, 87 & 88; Santa Fe Indian Market, NMex, 84, 85, 87 & 88; Indian Arts & Crafts Asn, Denver, Colo, 84 & 88; Gallup Ceremonials, Red Rock State Park, Gallup, NMex, 87 & 88; Northern Pueblo Show, San Idelfonso, NMex, 88; Heard Mus, Phoenix, Ariz, 88; Palm Springs Indian Art Show, Palm Springs, Calif, 88; Gallery of Functional Art, Santa Monica, Calif, 88. *Awards:* Best of Show, All Navajo Show, Northern Ariz Mus, 81; Best of Show, Navajo Nation Fair, 81; Best in Class & Design, Northern Pueblo Show. *Bibliog:* Article, Aspen Times, 2/84; Off hours, Farmington Daily Times, Farmington, NMex, 4/86. *Mem:* Indian Arts & Crafts Asn; Am Crafts Coun & Enterprises. *Media:* Gold, Silver. *Dealer:* Christophers Enterprises PO Box 25621 Albuquerque NM 87125; Packards 61 Old Santa Fe Trail Santa Fe NM 87501. *Mailing Add:* c/o Dewey Galleries 53 Old Santa Fe Tr No 2 Santa Fe NM 87501-2009

HARRISON, MYRNA J
PAINTER, INSTRUCTOR
b Hollywood, Calif, Jan 31, 32. *Study:* Hans Hofmann Sch Fine Art, NYC & Provincetown, Mass, 1953-57; NY Univ, NYC, with Philip Guston, BA, MA, 1959-60; Univ Calif, Berkeley, 1960-64. *Work:* Brandeis Univ Rose Art Mus, Waltham, Mass; Cape Cod Mus Art, Dennis, Mass; Provincetown Art Assoc & Mus, Mass. *Comn:* Triptych of Boulder Mountains, Idaho, Elmer Johnson, Chicago Ill, 2003. *Exhib:* Juried Group Shows, Provincetown Art Assoc & Mus, Mass, 1952-57; Int Watercolor Show, Brooklyn Art Mus, NY, 1953; Juried Group Shows, Cape Cod Mus Art, Dennis, Mass, 1954-56; Juried Group Shows, Staten Island Mus, NY, 1955-57; Raft - A Grand Canyon Landscape Exhib, Scottsdale Mus Contemp Art, Ariz, 1983. *Pos:* dean, San Jose City Col, Calif, 76-80; pres, Rio Salado Col, Phoenix, Ariz, 80-85; pres, Gateway Col, Phoenix, Ariz, 85-87; pres, Phoenix Col, Phoenix, Ariz, 87-92; interm dir, Desert Caballeros Western Mus, Wickenburg, Ariz, 1996-97. *Teaching:* vis art painting, Vermont Studio Ctr, Johnson, 2004 & 2005. *Bibliog:* Betsy Dillard Stroud, Abstract Art and the Gleb J Fracks Factor, Int Artist, Oct/Nov 1988; Open Portfolio: Myrna Harrison, Sedona Monthly, 9/2005; 2006 Art/Architecture Tour, Sedona Monthly, 5/2006. *Mem:* Asian Arts Council Phoenix Art Mus, Ariz (bd mem 2006-09); Desert Caballeros Western Mus, Wickenburg, Ariz (bd mem 1997-2001); Scottsdale Mus Contemp Art, Ariz; Provincetown Art Assoc & Mus, Mass; Nat Mus Women in Arts, Wash, DC. *Media:* All Media. *Publ:* auth, William Freed: A Disciplined Passion for Art, William Freed Catalog, 2003. *Dealer:* Acme Fine Art and Design 38 Newbury St Boston MA 02116; Beauregard Fine Art 109 E River Rd Rumson NJ 07760; Gold Nugget Art Gallery PO Box 359 Wickenburg AZ 85359; James Ratliff Gallery 431 Hwy 179 Sedona, AZ 86336. *Mailing Add:* PO Box 3139 Wickenburg AZ 85358

HARRISON, NEWTON A
ENVIRONMENTAL ARTIST, CONCEPTUAL ARTIST
b New York, NY, Oct 20, 32. *Study:* Yale Univ Sch Art & Archit, BFA & MFA; Pa Acad Fine Arts, cert. *Work:* Los Angeles Co Mus, Calif; Brooklyn Mus & Mus Mod Art, NY; Mus Photog Art, San Diego, Calif; Washington Univ Gallery Art, St Louis; and others. *Comn:* Baltimore Promenade, Md Inst, 81; Pasadena Parts 1 & 2, Pasadena Civic & Art Orgns; Santa Barbara Sites, City of Santa Barbara: The Yarkon River, Tel Aviv Found, Israel; Intersection: Pico-Seagate, Santa Monica, Calif; Disappearing Path, Newport, Calif; San Diego Landfill, Calif. *Pos:* Chmn Policy Panel, Nat Endowment Arts, Vis Arts Sect, 77-79; founding mem, Stewart Found Sculpture Gardens, 82-87. *Teaching:* Asst prof art, Univ NMex, 65-67; assoc prof art, Univ Calif, San Diego, 67-77, prof & chmn dept, 73-76, prof, 75-. *Awards:* Nat Endowment Arts Grant, 75; DAAD Fel, Berlin, 88& 89; 2nd Prize, Nagoya Bienal, 91; and others. *Bibliog:* Madeleine Burnside (auth), Helen Mayer Harrison and Newton Harrison, NY Rev Arts News, 4/78; Kim Levin (auth), Helen and Newton Harrison: New grounds for art, Vol 52, No 6 & Peter Selz (auth), Helen and Newton Harrison: Art as survival instructions, Vol 52, No 6, Arts Mag; and others. *Publ:* Illusr, San Diego as the center of the world, Los Angeles Inst Contemp Art J, 2/75; illusr, One full work and part of another, 12/77-1/78 & Great Lakes meditations, summer 79, New Wilderness Lett, NY; auth, The book of the crab, In: Dialogue, Discourse, Research, Santa Barbara Mus Art, 79; The Book of Seven Lagoons, limited edition artists book, 85; A Lattice or a Serpentine, Seattle Arts Comn Lett, 92. *Dealer:* Ronald Feldman Fine Arts 31 Mercer St New York NY 10013. *Mailing Add:* 415 Linden St Santa Cruz CA 95062-1023

HARRISON, RACHEL
ARTIST
b NY City, 66. *Exhib:* One-woman shows, Posh Floored as Ali G Tackles Beck, Galerie Arndt & Partner, 2004, Brides & Bases, Oakville Galleries, Can, 2002, Look of Dress-Separates, Greene Naftali Gallery, New York City, 97, Should Home Windows, Arena Gallery, Brooklyn, 96; group shows at Dreams & Conflicts: Dictatorship of Viewer, La Biennale di Venezia, Venice, 2003, Experimenters, Lombard-Freid Fine Arts, New York City, 97, Rachel Harrison & Michael Lazarus, Feature, New York City, 96, Space, Mind, Place, Andrea Rosen Gallery, NY, 96, Summer Exhib, Greene Naftali Gallery, NY, 96, Sex, Drugs & Explosives, New London Art Forms, London, 96, Sculpture Incorporating Photog, Feature Gallery, NY, 96, Post Hoc, Stark Gallery, NY, 96; Facing the Millennium: The Song Remains the Same, Arlington Mus, Tex, 96, Oy, 121 Greene St, NY, High Anxiety, 66 Crosby, NY, 95, Looky Loo, Sculpture Ctr, NY, 5, Dark Room, Stark Gallery, NY, 95, Unsuccess, 479 Broome St, NY, 94, Tight, Tannery Gallery, London, 94, Dirty, John Good Gallery, NY, 94, I Could Do That, 109 Spring St, NY, 94; Poverty Pop: Aesthetics of Necessity, Exit Art, NY, 93, Resurrections, William Benton Mus Art, Univ Conn, 93, Benefits for Four Walls Gallery, David Zwirner Gallery, NY, 93, Shooting Blanks, 81 Greene St, NY, 93; Subtlety of Subversion, Continuity of Intervention, Exit Art, NY, 1993, Simply Made in Am, Aldrich Mus Contemp Art, 1993, I Was Born Like This, Mulberry St Gallery, NY, 1993, Morality Cafe, Postmasters Gallery, NY, 1993, Unlearning, 142 Greene St, NY, 1991, Open Bar, Flamingo East, NY, 1991. *Mailing Add:* c/o Greene Naftali Gallery 526 W 26th St New York NY 10001

HARRISON, TONY
PAINTER, EDUCATOR
b Eng, Aug 18, 31; US citizen. *Study:* Northern Polytech Eng; Chelsea Sch Art, London; Cent Sch Arts & Crafts, London. *Work:* Aldrich Mus Contemp Art, Ridgefield, Conn; Achenbach Found, Calif Palace Legion Hon, San Francisco; Arts Coun Gt Brit, London; Royal Collection, Stockholm, Sweden; Nat Gallery S Australia; and many others. *Exhib:* One-man shows, San Francisco Mus Art, 64, Bertha Shaefer Gallery, NY, 68-69, 72 & 74 & Soho Ctr Visual Artists, NY, 77; Third Int Biennial Print Exhib, Taiwan, 87; Nat Inst Arts & Lett, NY, 73; Wood, Anita Shapolsky Gallery, NY, 90; and others. *Pos:* Printmaking Workshop, NY, 74-75. *Teaching:* Instr drawing & printmaking, Columbia Univ, 71-94; sr lectr painting, NY Univ, 72. *Awards:* Nat Endowment Arts Grant, 75; Creative Artists Pub Serv Grant, 76; Fel, NJ State Coun Arts, 87. *Bibliog:* Robert Erskine (producer), Artists proof (film), St Georges Gallery, 57; Collectors Choice, produced on ITV, London, 62. *Media:* Acrylic, Mezzotint. *Mailing Add:* 106 Hopkins Ave Jersey City NJ 07306

HARROFF, WILLIAM CHARLES BRENT
CONCEPTUAL ARTIST, ILLUSTRATOR
b Elkhart, Ind, Nov 20, 53. *Study:* Purdue Univ, BA, 78; Ind Univ, MLS, 81; ISBK, Salzburg, Austria, under Luis Murschetz, dipl, 83. *Work:* Franklin Furnace, NY Pub Libr, NY; Victoria & Albert Mus, London, Eng; Artpool, Budapest, Hungary; Lovejoy Libr, Southern Ill Univ, Edwardsville, Ill. *Comn:* Electronic Designs, Ill OCLC Users Group, 2001; Electronic Designs, Lewis & Clark Libr System, 2002. *Exhib:* Group 90, Vasarely Mus, Budapest, Hungary, 91; Artists Book Works, Ill Art Gallery, Chicago, 93; Artists' Books & Art, Pratt Manhattan Gallery, NY, 93; one-man show, New Harmony Gallery Contemp Art, Ind, 97, William Harroff: Pictures & Books, Books & Pictures, Arts Iowa City, 2000, Ebooks, McKendree Col, Lebanon, Ill, 2001; Third Int Artists' Book Exhib, King St Stephen Mus, Oskola,Hungary; Second Int Artists' Book Triennial Vilnius 00, Contemp Art Ctr, Akademija Gallery, Vilnius, Lithuania; Imagining the Book, Bibliotheca Alexandrina, Alexandria, Egypt, 2002; Future of the Book, Cairns Convention Centre, Cairns, Australia, 2003; Exlibris in Chengdu, Sichuan Exlibris Asn, Sichuan, China, 2003; The Spines that Bind, Buddy Holly Mus, Lubbock, Tex, 2003; Sea Words, Wexford Arts Centre, Wexford, Ireland, 2003; Mobilivre, Bookmobile Project, Traveling Exhib, Eastern Can & Northeast US, 2004; Readers Art 5, Susan Hensel Gallery, Minneapolis, Minn, 2005. *Pos:* Staff writer & illusr, Art St Louis, 86-91; mem bd dir, Madison Co Arts Coun, Edwardsville, Ill, 86-91, St Louis Volunteer Lawyers & Accountants for Arts, 91-; assoc ed, Int Journal of the Book, 2004-. *Teaching:* Librn archit, Okla State Univ, 81-84; artist illus, ISBK, Salzburg, Austria, 84-85; vis artist, Madison Co Arts Coun, Edwardsville, Ill, 85-90 & Fine Arts Inst, Wash Univ, St Louis, 95; librn, McKendree Col, Lebanon, Ill, 97-. *Awards:* Art Matters Inc Fel, 92; Regional Artists Proj Grant, Nat Endowment Arts, 93; Arts Midwest Nat Endowment Arts Fel, 95; First Prize Postcard Art Competition/Exhib '99, Wauconda, Ill, 99; First Prize Scrolling the Page Competition, Am Print Alliance, Peachtree City, Ga, 99; Ill First Grant, E-T Tech Fund, 2000; Ill First Grant, E-T Tech Fund, 2000 & 2002; Planting the Seed Grant, LCLS/LSTA, 2001; First Prize, P22 Fonts in Use, 2002; Int Artist Travel Award, Ill Arts Coun, 2003; Technos Int Award, Tanaka Ikueikai Educ Trust, Tokyo, Japan,

2006; Japan found Grant, Arts & Cult, 2006. *Bibliog:* USA/USSR Calligraphia, Int Typeface Corp, 91; Bess Liebenson (auth), What is a book, NY Times, 6/5/94; Bess Liebenson (auth), On Beyond the Book, Forum For Contemporary Art, 95; In a snowglobe, Contemporary Impressions, Fall, 2000; Martha Hellion (auth), Artist's Books: Ulises Carrion. D.A.P., 2003. *Mem:* Chicago Artists' Coalition; Ctr Book Arts; Art St Louis; Minn Ctr Book Arts. *Media:* Book Art. *Res:* Electronic Books and Literacy. *Interests:* Book Art; Digital Art; Conceptual Art. *Publ:* Auth, Ill artists overcoming disabilities, Chicago Artists Coalition, 93; auth & illusr, Artists overcoming disabilities, Chicago Artists' News, 9/92; Artists overcoming disabilities, Art Papers, 3/93; Dealing with disabilities, Art Calendar, 2/94; contribr with Charlotte Johnson, (r)Evolutionary (e) Books Website, McKendree Col, 2000-2003; auth, A Road Less Traveled, Afterimage, 11, 11-12/2001,; co-auth with Charlotte Johnson, (r)Evolutionary (e)Books, William Harroff Studios & Shypoke Press, 2002; co-auth, (r)EVOLUTIONARY (b)OOKS Model, Intl Journal of the Book, 2004. *Dealer:* Towata Gallery PO Box 675 206 W Third Alton IL 62002. *Mailing Add:* 453 Cass Ave Edwardsville IL 62025

HARROUN, DOROTHY SUMNER
PAINTER, GRAPHIC ARTIST
b El Paso, Tex, Nov 29, 35. *Study:* With Roderick Mead, 44-53; Univ NMex, BFA; Univ Paris, France(Fulbright Scholar), 57; Univ Colo, MFA, 60; with Peter Hurd, 63. *Work:* Univ Colo Fine Arts Mus, Boulder; Mus Fine Arts, Carlsbad, NMex; Nat Conf Women (albums), Nat Mus Women in Arts, Washington, DC; NMex State Capitol; Nat Mus of Women in the Arts. *Comn:* Mural of Sandia Mountains, comn by Jon ver Ploegh, Albuquerque, 77. *Exhib:* solo shows, Gondolier Gallery, Boulder, Colo, 61, Art Mus, Coos Bay, Ore, 80; El Paso Mus Art, El Paso, Tex, 87; New Eng Fine Art Asn, Nat Juried Show, Boston, Mass, 93; Juried Show, Carlsbad Mus Art, 2004. *Pos:* Art dir, Wood-Reich Advert Agency, Boulder, Colo, 60-61. *Teaching:* Instr, Univ Colo, 61-62, San Francisco State Col, 63-65, Art Ctr Sch, Albuquerque, 75-79, Sanado Group, Sandia Base, Albuquerque, 78-80 & Univ NMex, 80-81. *Awards:* First Place Painting, Ouray Nat Show, Colo, 78; First Prize Watercolor, Carlsbad Area Art Asn, Carlsbad Fine Arts Mus, 80 & Black Canyon Nat Art Show, Hotchkiss, Colo, 80; Lobo Award of Distinction, Univ NMex, 2000. *Mem:* Nat League Am Penwomen (pres Albuquerque branch, 82-84); Signature mem, NMex Watercolor Soc (pres 85-86); Artists Equity Asn (pres Albuquerque chap & mem nat bd, 77-79); Albuquerque United Artists (mem bd, 78-80); Am Asn Univ Women (State Cult chmn, 80-84); Univ NMex Fine Arts Alumi Bd (pres, 89-91). *Media:* Tempera, Watercolor; Oil, Pen & Ink. *Publ:* Auth & illusr, Take Time to Play and Listen, Chapman Press, 63; auth & illusr, Phun-y Physics, Living Vine Press, 75; illusr, Mini Walks on the Mesa, 89. *Dealer:* Geri McGary Expressions in Fine Art Gallery Sant Fe NM. *Mailing Add:* 1365 Thunder Ridge Santa Fe NM 87501

HARSHFIELD, NEIL ALAN
SCULPTOR, EDUCATOR
b Washington, DC, Aug 4, 62. *Study:* George Mason Univ, BA, 88; Tyler Sch Art, Temple Univ, with Jon Clark, 90 92; Tulane Univ, MFA, 95. *Work:* George Mason Univ, Fairfax, Va; Tulane Univ Law Sch, New Orleans; Sins of Ambivalence, Contemp Art Ctr, New Orleans, 2000. *Comn:* Reception desk, Emeril's Restaurant, New Orleans, 95. *Exhib:* Louisiana Sculpture Biennial, Southeastern La Univ, Hammond, 96; Entergy Louisiana Open Exhib, Contemp Art Ctr, New Orleans, 97; Five Young Artists, Art League Houston, Tex, 98. *Pos:* Hotshop coordr/technician, Tulane Univ, 94-98; gallery preparator, Woldenberg Art Ctr, New Orleans, 96-; Gallery preparator, Arthur Roger Gallery, New Orleans, 99-; instr glass/sculpture, Tulane Univ, 99-. *Teaching:* Instr glass/sculpture, Tulane Univ, 94-98; instr art, Urban Arts Training Prog, New Orleans, 97; instr sculpture, Loyola Univ, New Orleans, 98-. *Awards:* Outstanding Sculpture Award, Int Sculpture Ctr, 95. *Bibliog:* Ileana Marcalesco (auth), Houston/Neil Harshfield, Sculpture Mag, 11/96, Glass Mag, fall 98; Lake Douglass (auth), New Orleans Glass, Glass Mag, summer 97; Michael Plante (auth), Houston/Neil Harshfield, Art Am Mag, 12/98. *Mem:* Glass Art Soc; Int Sculpture Ctr. *Media:* Glass. *Dealer:* James Gallery 307 Sul Ross Houston TX 77006; Still/Zinsel Gallery 328 Julia St New Orleans LA 70130

HART, ALLEN M
PAINTER, ADMINISTRATOR
b New York, NY, June 12, 25. *Study:* Art Students League, with Anne Goldthwaite, Frank Vincent Dumond & Jean Liberte; Brooklyn Mus Art Sch, with Vincent Candell; Morelia, Mex with Alfredo Zalce. *Work:* Butler Inst Am Art, Youngstown, Ohio; Univ Mass, Amherst; Slater Mem Mus, Norwalk, Conn; Children's Aid Soc, NY; Union Am Hebrew Congregations. *Exhib.* Cober Gallery, 66-70; solo shows, Visual Arts Ctr, 70, Boiborik Gallery, 76, NJ Cult Arts Ctr, 78, Broome Street Gallery, 92; Joseph & Betty Harlem Gallery; Lerner Heller Gallery, 73; Visual Arts Ctr, 74-90; Flat Rockbrook's Wildlife Exhib, 92; Multimedia Arts Gallery, 92; S Presb Church Gallery, 98; Arrowwood Conv Ctr, 98; Art Int, Javits Ctr, 98; Works on Paper Exhib, Park Ave Armory, 98; Westchester Arts Coun Gala, 99-2000; Am Festival Art, Sulmona, Italy, 2000; Collectors Exhib, Rockland Ctr Arts, Nyack, NY, 2000; retrospective Atelier A/E, NY, 2000; Hudson Rivergal Conservators, 2001; Westchester Community Col, Valhalla, NY, 2002; Rockland Ctr Arts, Nyack, NY, 2003; Nat Arts Club, New York City, 2004; Upstream Gallery, NY, 98-2005; Butler Hall Gallery, Fordham Univ, 2005; Upstream Gallery, 2006. *Teaching:* Instr painting, Samuel Field YMHA & YWHA, Little Neck, NY, 62-68; dir painting, Visual Arts Ctr, 68-92, adminr, 92-; dean visual arts, Union Am Hebrew Congregations, 70-85, resident artist, 72-; art consult, Bd Coop Educ Serv, 71-; art consult, Children's Aid Soc, NY, painting instr adult dept. *Awards:* Merit Scholarship, Brooklyn Mus Art Sch; Hammond Mus Award, Westchester, NY, 2002. *Bibliog:* New York illustrated, NBC-TV, 70; illustrator, Allen M Hart, In Retrospect, 1965-1999, Rattapallax Pubs; video documentary with CD-ROM, Life and Works of Allen M Hart. *Mem:* Life mem Art Students League; Artists Equity Asn; Katonah Art Mus Asn; Gallery on the Hudson; Rivertown Arts Coun; Westchester Arts Coun. *Media:* Oil, Mixed Media. *Interests:* art, art history, historical research. *Publ:* Auth, articles, Lower Manhattan Twp, 2/20/71 & Herald, 5/1/71. *Dealer:* Atelier Gallery NY. *Mailing Add:* 105 Beacon Hill Dr Dobbs Ferry NY 10522

HART, JOHN LEWIS
CARTOONIST
b Endicott, NY, Feb 18, 31. *Pos:* Comic strip BC nat syndicated, 58- & The Wizard of Id, 64-. *Awards:* Outstanding Cartoonist of Year, 68; Yellow Kid Award, Int Cong Comics for Best Cartoonist, Lucca, Italy; France's Highest Award Best Cartoonist of Year, 71. *Mem:* Nat Comics Coun; Nat Cartoonists Soc. *Publ:* The Peasants are Revolting, Remember the Golden Rule & There's a Fly in my Swill; The Wonderous Wizard of Id; The Wizard's Back; plus others. *Mailing Add:* c/o Creators Syndicate 5777 W Century Blvd Suite 700 Los Angeles CA 90045-5600

HART, ROBERT GORDON
ADMINISTRATOR
b San Francisco, Calif, Dec 28, 21. *Pos:* Ed, Brooklyn Mus, NY, 59-61; gen mgr, Indian Arts & Crafts Bd, US Dept Interior, 61-93; chmn, Fed Interagency Crafts Comt, 74-93; pres, The Crafts Report Educ Fund, 90; retired. *Mem:* Am Asn of Mus; Conseil Int des Musees; Foxfire Nat Bd; Am Crafts Coun; World Crafts Coun

HARTAL, PAUL
PAINTER, WRITER
b Szeged, Hungary, Apr 25, 36; Can citizen. *Study:* Hebrew Univ Jerusalem, BA, 64, dipl, 66; Concordia Univ, Montreal, MA, 77; Univ Delle Arti, Salsomaggiore, Italy, Hon Dipl, 82; Columbia Pacific Univ, San Rafael, Calif, PhD, 86. *Work:* Mus Fine Arts, Montreal; Nat Gallery, Ottawa; Guggenheim Mus; Israel Mus, Jerusalem; Galleria Naz Arte, Rome; Musee du Quebec; Seoul Int Fine Art Ctr, Korea. *Comn:* Olympic Project (graphs), Seoul, Korea, 86; Pour Une Pedagogie Interactive by Jean Marc Denomme et Madeleine Roy (bk cover painting); Einstein Mind & Matter (frontis piece), comn by Clifford Pickover, Strange Brains and Genius, Plenum, NY, 98; Danilo Carrer Mus, Milano, Italy, 2000; Dr Patch Adams, MD, Gesundheit Inst, Arlington, 2000. *Exhib:* Spaceweek Int Art Exhib, Invitational Juried, Houston, Tex, 94; Centro Civico Social, Alcorcon Int Invitational, Madrid, Spain, 94; Galleria Communale d'Arte Mod, Italy, 94; Intercommunication Ctr, Tokyo: CD-Rom, 94; one-man show, Tribute to Paul Hartal's Works, Munic Libr, Saint-Laurent, Que, Can, 94, Contemp Art Gallery, Gudapest, 2000, Galerie Alef, Montreal, 99; Musee de la Poste, Paris, 94; Art Electrografica, Palazzo Gambacorti, Pisa, 95; Univ Calif, Berkeley, 95; Seoul Int Fine Art Ctr, Icepco Plaza Gallery, 95; Galerie Michel-Ange, Montreal, Can, 97; Dansung Gallery, Seoul, Korea, 98; Adell McMillan Gallery, Univ Oreg, Eugene, 2000; Hanseo Univ Art Mus, Seoul, 2004; Chateau Ramezey Mus, Montreal, 2005. *Collection Arranged:* Natl Gallery of Canada, Ottawa; Hanseo Univ Art Mus, Seoul. *Pos:* Dir, Ctr Art, Sci & Technol, 87-; consult, McGill's Teacher Training Prog, currently; proj dir, Shivagi Univ, India, currently; anthrop consult, Karnatak Univ, India, currently. *Teaching:* Lectr, McGill Univ, Montreal, Canada; Lectr, Univ Oregon, Eugene, OR. *Awards:* Selected Olympic Artist, Seoul, Korea, 88; Int Poetry Hall Fame, Nat Libr Poetry, Owings Mills, Md; Ed Choice Award, Judith Grant, NY; and others. *Bibliog:* Barbara Costa (auth), Dall aeropittura futurista alla Space Art, Epiphaneia, Italy, 38-42, 3/97; Paul Hartal's Exhibition, The Seoul Daily, 5/22/98; Kim Edward (auth), East Meets West in Joint Exhibit, The Korea Herald, Seoul, 5/23/98; and many others. *Mem:* Int Soc Artists; Graphic Soc; Les Surindependants, Paris; founding mem Lyrical Conceptualist Soc (dir, 77-); Orbiting Unification Ring Satellite Project, Switz. *Media:* Acrylic & Oil, Watercolor, Collage, Drawings. *Res:* Interdisciplinary aspects of the relationships of art & space exploration; art & mathematics. *Publ:* Auth, To Humanize the World, YLEM, Orinda, Calif, 9/94; Abstract Art is Like Math, Montreal Gazette, 5/19/94 reproductions), Orbiter Mag, 1-2/95; Manifesto on Lyrical Conceptualism, 95; Rendering Science More Scientific through Art, Lo Straniero, Italy, 95; auth & illusr, The Kidnapping of the Painter Miro, or the Butterfly Kite, Elore Publ, 97; contribr, Visions (poems on audio cassette), Nat Libr Poetry, Owings Mills, Md, 98; The Brush and the Compass, Univ Press Am, 88; Homage to a blue planet: aeronautical and astronomical art works, Leonardo, Vol 25, No 2, 92; Love Poems, Montreal: Editions La Galerie Fokus, Seoul: Hanseo Univ, 2004; The Songs of the Double Helix: The Symmetry and Lyrical Conceptualism, I hargittai & T Laurent Eds, Symmetry, London, 2000; Cesarean Section, Poetry Canada, Summer, 2004. *Dealer:* Michel Ange Gallery Montreal Can. *Mailing Add:* 2360 Valade Montreal PQ H4M 1N1 Canada

HARTE, JOHN
PAINTER, MISC MEDIA
b Omaha, Nebr, June 11, 27. *Study:* Univ Wyo, Laramie, BA, 55; Chicago Art Inst; Univ Calif, Berkeley, study with Glen Wessels; Calif Col Arts & Crafts, Oakland; Univ Ariz, Tucson. *Work:* Grand Canyon Nat Park, Ariz; Oakland Mus, Calif; Palm Springs Desert Mus, Calif; Chevron Corp, Richmond, Calif; State of Fla Pub Art, Tallahassee, Fla; Archeol Conserv, Albuquerque, NMex. *Comn:* painting, Geraldine C M Livingston Found, Greenville, Fla. *Exhib:* Univ Calif, Morgan Hall, Berkeley, Calif, 65; Frank Lloyd Wright Marin Co Civic Ctr, San Rafael, Calif, 77; Grand Canyon Nat Park, 84; Mesa Verde Nat Park, Chapin Mesa Mus, Colo, 86; Chevron Corp, San Francisco, Calif & Richmond, Calif, 88; Gov's Gallery, State Capitol, Tallahassee, Fla, 99; Lemoyne Art Found, Hoover Gallery, Tallahassee, Fla, 01. *Awards:* Gold Star, Marin Soc Artists, Ross, Calif, 71; Gold Ribbon, Chevron USA, San Francisco, 77; Hon Mention, Renaissance Vinoy Hotel Anniversary, 02; Hon Mention, The Arts Ctr, St Petersburg, Fla, 02. *Mem:* Mus Fine Arts, St Petersburg, Fla; Arts Ctr, St Petersburg, Fla. *Media:* Watercolor, Miscellaneous Media. *Interests:* Botanical, Landscape, Archit subjects. *Collection:* Pfizer Inc, NYC; Palm Springs

Desert Mus, Palm Springs; Oakland Mus, Calif, Lemoyne Art Tallahassee, Fla. *Publ:* Contrib, Calif Art Rev, 89 & 91; Contrib, The New St Pete News, 02. *Dealer:* Red Cloud Indian Arts 208 Beach Dr St Peterburg FL; Palmavene Gallery 45 S Palm Ave Sarasota Fla; Soho Myriad Gallery 1250B Menlo Dr Atlanta Ga. *Mailing Add:* PO Box 1523 Saint Petersburg FL 33731-1523

HARTER, JOHN BURTON
CURATOR, PAINTER
b Jackson, Miss, Oct 7, 40. *Study:* Hanover Col, Univ Louisville, BA(art hist); Univ Vienna; Univ Pa; grad archaeol, Hebrew Univ, Jerusalem; La State Univ, MA(studio art); Williamsburg Seminar. *Exhib:* Group show, Leslie-Lehman Gallery, NY, 2000. *Collection Arranged:* Louisiana Folk Art, 75, Louisiana Portrait Gallery (coauth, catalog), 77 & Louisiana Landscape, 81, La State Mus. *Pos:* Cur paintings & graphics, La State Mus, 67-86, dir collections, 86-91. *Mem:* Am Asn Mus. *Media:* Oil, Acrylic. *Publ:* Encounters, GMP Publ (in prep)

HARTFORD, JANE DAVIS
TEXTILE ARTIST, CRAFTSMAN
b Erick, Okla, Aug 21, 27. *Study:* Univ Okla, Norman, BFA, 49; Univ Louisville, Ky, MA, 60; Parson's Sch Design; Univ Ill, art hist; Univ Hawaii, graphics with Jean Charlot; weaving with Lou Tate, Theo Moorman, Sallie O'Sullivan, Irene Waller, Mary Jane Leland & Jon Eric Riis. *Comn:* Ceremonial basket, Mrs LeRoy W Horne, Tulsa, Okla, 78; tapestry, Mr & Mrs Leonard Good, Chickasha, Okla, 82; eucharistic vestments, Zion Lutheran Church, Salt Lake City, Utah, 86 & 89. *Exhib:* Liturgical Weaving Convergence, Toronto, Can, 86; Conference of S Calif Handweavers, Riverside, 91; Fabrics of Faith, Nat Cathedral, Washington, DC, 92; Fiber 7 Textile Exhib, Univ Wis, 95; Fiber Arts Fiesta, Albuquerue, NMex, 97; solo exhib, Univ Okla, 98. *Pos:* Bd dir, Handweavers Guild Am Inc, 80-88, pres, 83-85, chmn bd, 85-88; bd dir, Intermountain Weavers Conf, 79-83. *Teaching:* Utah Handweavers Conf, Logan, 82; Midwest Weavers Conf, Denver, Colo, 86; Conference S Calif Handweavers, Riverside, Calif, 91. *Awards:* Merit Award, Southwest Crafts Biennial, NMex Art Mus, 75; Fiber Award, Utah Arts Coun Exhib, 80; Cash Award, Intermountain Weavers Conf Exhib, 83; First Prize (cash award), Containers, Branigan Cult Ctr, Las Cruces, NMex, 90; HGA Award, Las Tejedoras Guild Exhibit, Fuller Lodge Art Ctr, Los Alamos, NMex, 91. *Mem:* Hon life mem, M M Atwater Weavers Guild (pres, 74-75); Cross Country Weavers; Las Tejedoras de Santa Fe y Los Alamos, NMex (vpres 90-92); Midwest Weavers Conf. *Media:* Handweaving, Surface Design. *Publ:* Auth, Fashion Ballet, winter 74, auth, Sheep to shawl, spring 77, & coauth, Flight into fantasy, fall, 80, Shuttle, Spindle & Dyepot; contribr, Weaving for Worship, Robin & Russ Handweavers Inc, McMinneville, Ore, 98. *Mailing Add:* 500 Bishops Lodge Rd Santa Fe NM 87501

HARTIGAN, GRACE
PAINTER
b Newark, NJ, Mar 28, 22. *Study:* Pvt art classes with Isaac Lane Mus. *Hon Degrees:* Md Inst Art, Baltimore, DFA; Goucher Col, DFA; Towson State Univ, DFA; Lafayette Col, DFA; Moore Col, Philadelphia, DFA. *Work:* Whitney Mus Am Art & Metrop Mus Art, NY; Walker Art Ctr, Minneapolis, Minn; Art Inst Chicago, Ill; Albright-Knox Art Gallery, Buffalo, NY; plus many others. *Exhib:* Am Vanguard, US Info Agency, Austria, Eng, Ger & Yugoslavia, 61-62; Martha Jackson Gallery, 62-70; A Decade of New Talent, Am Fedn Arts Exhib, 64-65; solo exhibs, Univ Chicago, 67 & Gertrude Kasle Gallery, Detroit, 68; Gruenebaum Gallery, NY, 84 & 86; Grimalis Gallery, 93, 98 & 2000; ACA Gallery, NY, 94; and others. *Pos:* dir, Hoffengerber Grad Sch Painting. *Teaching:* Dir, Hoffberger Md Inst Grad Sch Painting, 65-82. *Awards:* Lifetime Achievement Award, Neuberger Mus. *Bibliog:* Dr Robert Mattison (auth), Grace Hartigan, A Painters World (monogr), Hudson Hills Press. *Media:* Oil, Watercolor. *Dealer:* ACA Galleries 529 W 20th St New York, NY 10011

HARTIGAN, LYNDA ROSCOE
CURATOR, HISTORIAN
b Scranton, Pa, Aug 26, 50. *Study:* Bucknell Univ, Lewisburg, Pa, BA(art hist, cum laude), 72; George Washington Univ, DC, MA(art hist), 75. *Collection Arranged:* James Hampton: The Throne of the Third Heaven for Naives and Visionaries (contribr, catalog), Walker Art Ctr, 74; Joseph Cornell: An Exploration of Sources, 82 & Sharing Traditions: Five Black Artists in 19th Century Am (auth, catalog), 85-, Nat Mus Am Art. *Pos:* Curatorial asst, 20th Century Painting & Sculpture Dept, Nat Mus Am Art, Smithsonian Inst, Washington, DC, 74-76, asst cur, 76-86, cur, Joseph Cornell Study Ctr, 78-; assoc curator, 86-. *Teaching:* Vis art critic, Md Inst, Col Art, Baltimore, 85. *Awards:* Grad internship, Nat Collection Fine Arts, Smithsonian Inst, DC, 73-74; Nat Endowment Humanities Res Grant, 76-78; Smithsonian Inst Scholarly Studies & Special Exhib Grants, 86-89. *Bibliog:* Peggy Thomson (auth), Museum People, Prentice-Hall, 77. *Mem:* Col Art Asn; Art Table; Am Folklore Soc. *Res:* 20th century American art, especially sculpture 1930s to present, with major research conducted on Joseph Cornell; American folk art; Afro-American art. *Publ:* Contribr, Joseph Cornell: A Biography (monograph), Mus Mod Art, New York, 80; Yuri Schwebler: His Art and the Studio (exhib catalog), Hudson River Mus, Yonkers, NY, 81; Sited Toward the Future: Proposals for Public Sculpture (exhib catalog), Arlington Arts Ctr, Va, 84; auth, Made with Passion: Hemphill Folk Art Collection, Smithsonian Inst Press, 90. *Mailing Add:* Nat Mus Am Art Smithsonian Eighth & G Sts NW Washington DC 20560

HARTLEY, KATHERINE ANN
PAINTER, INSTRUCTOR
b Chatham, MA Jan 11, 59. *Study:* Scottsdale Community Col, 1987; Private instr, John Court, 1988-1989; Art Students League, David Leffel, NYC, 1990-1992. *Work:* Cape Cod Mus of Art, Dennis, Mass; Oyster Harbor Country Club, Osterville, Mass. *Comn:* still life painting, comn by Don Shellenberger, Brewster, Mass, 2000; still life paintings (3), comn by Gloria & Victor Leon, Orleans, Mass, 2001-2003; still live painting, comn by John Murphy, Orleans, Mass, 2005; still life painting, comn by Bob & Marion Howard, Orleans, Mass, 2005. *Exhib:* Fanellis Show, OK Harris, NYC, 1998; Women Creating, Cahoon Mus, Dennis, Mass, 1998; Mystic Art Asn, Mystic, Conn, 2003; Of Time & Light, Cape Cod Mus of Art, Dennis, Mass, 2005. *Teaching:* Instr oil painting, Cape Cod Mus of Art, 2006-. *Awards:* Silver Medal of Honor, Allied Artists, 1995; Augie Napoli Award, Salmagundi, 1996; Len G Everett Mem, Allied Artists, 2003. *Bibliog:* Kevin Mullany (auth), Katherine Ann Hartley, Province Town Banner, 2001; Beth Seiser (auth), Katherine Ann Hartley, Cape Arts Review, 2005; Lynne Moss Perricelli (auth), Focus on Painting, Am Artist, 2006. *Mem:* Allied Artists of Am; Oil Painters of Am; Art Students League (lifetime mem); Cape Cod Mus of Art (contrib mem). *Media:* Oil. *Dealer:* David Findlay Galleries 984 Madison Ave NYC 10021; Kiley Court Gallery 445 Commerical St Province Town MA 02657; Hearle Gallery 488 Main St Chatham MA 02633. *Mailing Add:* 445 Commercial St Provincetown MA 02657

HARTLEY, PAUL JEROME
PAINTER, EDUCATOR
b Charlotte, NC, Dec 30, 43. *Study:* NTex State Univ, BA; ECarolina Univ, MFA. *Work:* Glaxo Welcome, Inc; Southeastern Ctr Contemp Art; Rausch Indust Collection; NC Art Soc, Raleigh; Greenville Mus Art. *Teaching:* Prof, ECarolina Univ, 75-. *Media:* All. *Dealer:* Lee Hansley Gallery Raleigh NC. *Mailing Add:* Sch Art E Carolina Univ Greenville NC 27834

HARTMAN, JOANNE A
PAINTER, EDUCATOR
b Brooklyn, NY, Nov 15, 31. *Study:* Brooklyn Col, City Univ New York, BA, 52; Queens Col, City Univ New York, MFA, 75. *Exhib:* Solo exhibs, Ingber Gallery, NY, 81 & Nassau Co Mus Fine Arts, Roslyn, NY, 88; 55 Mercer, NY, 87; June Kelly Gallery, NY, 87; Fed Hall, NY, 90; Islip Art Mus, NY, 90; Gallery North, Setauket, NY, 91. *Teaching:* Adj assoc prof art, Suffolk Community Col, Selden, NY, 75- & NY Inst Technol, Westbury, NY, 82-. *Awards:* Va Ctr Creative Arts, 87-88 & 90; Ragdale Found, 89. *Bibliog:* Phyllis Braff (auth), Diverse paths at Nassau Museum, NY Times, 1/88; Karin Lipson (auth), Visual and mental images, Newsday, 1/88; Betty Booker (auth), Colony gives artists time for creativity, Richmond Times Dispatch, 7/88. *Mem:* Col Art Asn; Nat Drawing Asn. *Media:* Acrylic, Mixed Media. *Dealer:* June Kelly 591 Broadway New York NY 10012. *Mailing Add:* 526 W 26th St Rm 612 New York NY 10001

HARTMAN, ROBERT LEROY
PHOTOGRAPHER, EDUCATOR
b Sharon, Pa, Dec 17, 26. *Study:* Univ Ariz, BFA & MA; Colo Springs Fine Arts Ctr, with Vaclav Vytlacil & Emerson Woelffer; Brooklyn Mus Art Sch. *Work:* Nat Collection Fine Arts, Smithsonian Inst, Washington, DC; Colo Springs Fine Arts Ctr; Oakland Mus Art, Calif; Henry Gallery, Univ Wash; Princeton Art Mus; Photo Mus, Osaka, Japan. *Exhib:* Santa Barbara Mus Art, 73; Whitney Mus Biennial, NY, 73; photog, San Jose Mus Art, 83; Bluxome Gallery, San Francisco, 84 & 86; Univ Art Mus, Berkeley, 86, 90; Triangle Gallery, San Francisco, 92, 93, 95 & 97, 99-02; Oakland Mus, Solo Flights, 02; Viewpoint Photog Art Ctr, Sacramento, 2006; and others. *Teaching:* Instr art, Tex Technol Col, 55-58; asst prof, Univ Nev, Reno, 58-61; from assoc prof to prof art, Univ Calif, Berkeley, 61-91, prof emer, 91-. *Awards:* Emanuel Walter Fund First Prize, 85th Ann San Francisco Art Inst, 67; Hon mention, 4th Int Young Artists Exhib Am-Japan, 67; Award, Snap! Photography '85, San Francisco Arts Comn Gallery. *Bibliog:* Peter Nabokov (auth), Flight patterns--photographs by Robert Hartman, Camera Arts, 1/83; Philip Morsberger (auth), Solo Flights - The Aerial Photog of Robert Hartman, Oakland Mus Exhib (catalog), 2002. *Media:* Photography, Oil. *Dealer:* Triangle Gallery 47 Kearny St San Francisco CA 94108. *Mailing Add:* 1265 Mountain Blvd Oakland CA 94611

HARTMAN, ROSE
PHOTOGRAPHER, EDITOR
b May 16, 37. *Study:* Studied at City Univ NY. *Exhib:* The Cream of the Crop, Mus City NY, 94; The Warhol Look, Whitney Mus Am Art, NY, 97; DFN Gallery, NY, 2000; Artmosphere Gallery, NY, 2000; Eqizios Project, NY, 2000; Disco: A Decade of Saturday Nights, Experience Music Proj, 02; Performing Arts, Lincoln Ctr, 05. *Collection Arranged:* Peterson Mus, Paterson, NJ. *Mem:* Prof Women Photogrs, Ny. *Interests:* International Travel, biking. *Collection:* Newark Museum, Whitney Museum, Jerry Hall Museum. *Publ:* Auth & photogr, Birds of Paradise-An Intimate View of the NY Fashion World, Delacorte Press, 80; contribr, True colors: the real life of the art world (photog), Atlantic Monthly, 96; Basquiat, Viking, 98; Trust No One, St Martin's Press; auth, Anna Wintour, Front Row, St. Martin's Press, 2005. *Mailing Add:* 88 Charles St New York NY 10014

HARTSHORN, WILLIS E
DIRECTOR, PHOTOGRAPHER
b Fairfield, Conn, Sept 9, 50. *Study:* Univ Rochester, NY, BA, 73; Pratt Inst, Brooklyn, NY, 75; Visual Studies Workshop, Rochester, NY, MFA, 81. *Work:* Visual Studies Workshop Arch, Rochester, NY. *Exhib:* Contemp Still Life Photog Traveling Exhib, 82-84; one-man show, Mass Inst Technol, 83; Washington Projects Arts, Washington, DC, 83; The Bond Gallery, NY, 86; Lieberman & Saul Gallery, NY, 88; White Columns, NY, 88; and others. *Pos:* Assoc dir exhibs, Int Ctr Photog, 82-85, dir, 86-89, deputy dir progs, 90, exec dir, 94-. *Teaching:* Instr photog, Int Ctr Photog, New York, 79-90; teaching asst photog, Sch Visual Arts, New York, 79; instr, Univ Rochester, NY, 73-74. *Awards:* Resource Access Develop Proj, State Univ NY, 79; Materials Grant, Polaroid Corp, 79; Major Fel in Photog, Nat Endowment Arts, 81 & 86. *Mem:* Asn Art Mus; Col Art Asn. *Media:* Black & White. *Publ:* Auth, Printletter, Zurich, Switz, 80; coauth (with John Esten), Man Ray/Bazaar Years, Rizzoli, NY, 88; auth, Man Ray: Fashion, ICP, New York, 90; coauth, Czech Modernism, Mus Fine Arts, Houston, 90. *Mailing Add:* 98 Luquer St Brooklyn NY 11231

HARTWIG, HEINIE
PAINTER - ACRYLIC, OIL, INSTRUCTOR
b Santa Clara Co, Calif, Feb 3, 39. *Study:* Self taught. *Work:* Monterey Inst Foreign Studies, Calif; Brigham Young Univ, Provo, Utah; Mills Col, Oakland, Calif; Robert Louis Stevenson Sch, Monterey, Calif. *Pos:* pres, Grovland Art Asn Calif, 2005. *Teaching:* Instr art, pvt studio. *Awards:* First Place, Triton Mus, Santa Clara, Calif, 71; First Place Oil, First Place Popular & Best of Show, Twain Harte Art Show, 81; Best of Show, Grand Nat 2000 Celebration of Western Art, San Francisco Cow Palace, Second place, 2003. *Media:* Oil. *Mailing Add:* PO Box 976 Soulsbyville CA 95372

HARTZ, JILL
MUSEUM DIRECTOR, CURATOR
b Montreal, Quebec, Can, Jul 25, 50. *Study:* Oberlin Univ, Undergrad study, 1971; Univ St Andrews, Scotland, MA in Eng Lang and Lit with honors, 1973; Student, Cornell Univ, 1994. *Collection Arranged:* Karen Shea: Oddyssey, Univ Va Art Mus, 2004; Mi Cuerpo Mi País: Cuban Art Today, Univ Va Art Mus, 2005. *Pos:* Mgr, Tompkins Co Arts Coun, Ithaca, 1981-82, Grapevine Graphics, Ithaca, 1982-83; co-editor, Grapevine Weekly Mag, 1983-84, Living Publ, Ithaca, 1984-86; coordr, exhib, asst to dir, Herbert F Johnson Mus of Art, Cornell Univ, 1976-81, dir, pub relations and publ, 1986-93; asst to chair, dept of art Cornell Univ, 1993-94; coordr, pub relations and spec programs Coun for the Arts, Cornell Univ, 1993-94; dir communs Arts & Scis. Devel. Office, Univ Va, Charlottesville, 1994-97; interim dir, Univ Va Mus Art (Bayly Art Mus), 1997, dir, 1997-; Co-cur, Agnes Denes exhib, 1991-92, editor monograph; co-found, partner LunaMedia pub relations co, Ithaca, 1993-94. *Awards:* Am Asn Mus Peer Reviewer Award, 2005. *Mem:* Am Asn Mus, Nat Cult Alliance; Va Asn Mus. *Res:* Mus Schs; Cuban Contemp Art. *Specialty:* Univ Mus, more than 10,500 works in a range of media, representing world cultures from ancient times to present. *Publ:* ed, Siting Jefferson: Contemporary Artists Interpret Thomas Jefferson's Legacy, Univ Va Press, 2003; In Pursuit of Art, The Museum: Conditions and SPeces, Selections from the University of Virginia Art Museum, Univ Va Art Mus, 2004; Infuse Your Museum with Passion, Vision, and a Business Sense, The Business of Museums, A Behind the Scenes Look at Curatorship, Management Strategies and Critical Components for Sucess, Aspatore Books, 2004; Mi Cuerpo, Mi País:Cuban Art Today, Univ Va Art Mus, 2005; A Jeffersonian Ideal, A Jeffersonian Ideal: Selections from the Dr and Mrs Henry C Landon III Collection of American Fine and Decorative Arts, Univ Va Art Mus, 2005. *Mailing Add:* Univ Va Mus Art 155 Rugby Rd Charlottesville VA 22903

HARVEST, JUDITH R
CONCEPTUAL ARTIST, PAINTER
b Miami, Fla. *Study:* Barry Univ, Miami, Fla, BFA(cum laude), 73; Tyler Sch Art, Temple Univ, Rome, Italy, 73; NY Studio Sch, with Robert Storr, Ross Bleckner & Peter Agostini, 85; Sch Visual Arts, Urbino, Italy, with Enzo Cucchi & Kounellis, MFA, 87. *Work:* Aldrich Mus Contemp Art, Ridgefield, Conn; Art Forum, Galerie Thomas, Munich, Ger. *Comn:* Campbell Soup Painting, comn by Dorrance Family, Paradise Valley, Ariz, 92. *Exhib:* Recent Acquisitions, Aldrich Mus Contemp Art, Ridgefield, Conn, 88; Judith's Harvest, Artforum, Galerie Thomas, Munich, Ger, 88; Il Soffio Di Eolo, Isole Eolie, Salina, Sicily, 90; Small Works, 80 Wash Square East, NY, 91; Art from Italy, Harvest, Pistoietto, Paladino and Baj, Greene Gallery, Bal Harbour, Fla, 91; Modern Times Through the Concerned Eye, Katonah Mus, NY, 92; National Showcase Exhib, Alternative Mus, NY, 92. *Awards:* Honorable Mention, Small Works, NY, Brooke Alexander, 91. *Bibliog:* Andrea Pagnes (auth), Judith Harvest, Veranda del Arsenale, Venice, Flash Art, summer 90; Stuart Morgan (ed), Judith Harvest 1990, Artscribe, 5/90; Isa Vercelloni (ed), The seasons of Judith, Casa Vogue, 10/90. *Media:* Oil on Linen, Motorized Sculptures. *Publ:* Auth, Il Soffo Di Eolo, Mazzotta, Milano, 90; Where have all the suicides gone?, Pig Mag, Erik Oppenhiem, 92; auth & illusr, Safe Art, Spark, Romar & Melamio's Sch Bayonne, 92. *Dealer:* Bugno & Samueli Campo San Fantin 1966/A Venice Italy 30124. *Mailing Add:* 105 Duane St New York NY 10007-3601

HARVEY, ANDRE
SCULPTOR
b Hollywood, Fla, Oct 9, 41. *Study:* Univ Va, BA; with Michael Anasse, Valauris, France. *Work:* Del Art Mus, Wilmington; Hunter Mus, Chattanooga; Greenville Mus Art, SC; Brandywine River Mus, Chadds Ford, Pa; Ark Art Ctr. *Comn:* Sculpture, De Bartolo Corp, Youngstown, Ohio, 89 & 90; Frederik Meijer Gardens, Grand Rapids, Mich, 95; Botanic Garden Ctr & Conserv, Ft Worth, Tex, 98. *Exhib:* Hunter Mus, Chattanooga, Tenn, 77; Nat Sculpture Soc, 81-2005; Brandywine River Mus, Chadds Ford, Pa, 91 & 2005; Nat Sculpture Soc, Palazzo Mediceo, Seravezza, Italy, 94; Longwood Gardens, Kennett Sq, Pa, 96; and others. *Awards:* Joel Meissner Award, 80, Nat Sculpture Soc & Tallix Foundry Award, 89. *Bibliog:* Susan Stiles Dowell (auth), Pure Brandywine, Southern Accents, Mar/Apr, 93; Edgeworth & Zeidner (auth), Brandywine, 3/95; Arthur Williams (auth), Sculpture, 95; Arthur Williams (auth), Beginning Sculpture, 2005, The Sculpture Ref, 2005; and others. *Mem:* Fel Nat Sculpture Soc; Artists Equity; Int Sculpture Ctr. *Media:* Metal, Cast, Precious, Stone, Miscellaneous Media. *Dealer:* Gerald Peters Gallery 1011 Paseo De Peralta Santa Fe NM 87501. *Mailing Add:* PO Box 8 Rockland DE 19732

HARVEY, DERMOT
KINETIC ARTIST, SCULPTOR
b Amersham, Eng, June 26, 41. *Study:* Univ Dublin, Trinity Col, MA; Univ London, MPhil. *Work:* Okla Art Ctr. *Comn:* Muse Aurora (liquid projections exhib operated by viewer), Brooklyn Children's Mus, 70; portable, multi-image aurora, Okla Art Ctr, 73; liquid projection exhib, Arnot Mus, Elmira, NY, 75; portable muse aurora, Continuum Mus, Ft Lauderdale, Fla, 76. *Exhib:* 24 Hour Technicolor Dream, Alexandra Palace, London, 67; Alliance of Light Artists, Fillmore East, NY, 69; Liquid Projections, Montreux Television Festival, Switz, 69; Projected Environments, NY Avant Garde Festival, 72, 74 & 75; Light Works, Intermedia Found, Garnerville, NY, 75. *Pos:* Dir theater of light prog, Intermedia Found, 74-; spec effects lighting for revue, Hot Stuff, Wailea Town Ctr, Maui, Hawaii, 80. *Teaching:* Instr kinetic & light art, Rockland Community Col, Suffern, NY, 75-77. *Awards:* Creative Artists Pub Serv Grant, NY Cult Coun, 71. *Bibliog:* Martha Geacintov (auth), He practices his art in the light side, 3/5/74 & Michael Hitzig (auth), Theater of light, 5/4/75, Journal News; Carol Lawson (auth), Film night with a Gothic twist, NY Times, 6/18/76. *Mailing Add:* 17 Church St Garnerville NY 10923

HARVEY, DONALD
PAINTER, PRINTMAKER
b Walthamstow, Eng, June 14, 30; Can citizen. *Study:* West Sussex Col Art, nat dipl painting; Brighton Col Art Eng, art teachers dipl. *Work:* Montreal Mus Fine Arts; Charlottetown Confedn Gallery, PEI; Seattle Art Mus, Wash; Albright-Knox Mus, Buffalo, NY; Saskatdrewan Arts Bd; and others. *Comn:* Large mural, BC Provincial Govt, Nelson, BC, 75. *Exhib:* Brit Print Biennial, Bradford, Eng, 68; Int Print Exhib, Seattle, 69; Art Gallery Greater Victoria, 79; Kyles Art Gallery, Victoria, 80; Can Nat Exhib, Toronto, 80; and others. *Teaching:* Prof painting, Univ Victoria, 61-94, emer prof, 94-. *Awards:* Sadie & Samuel Bronfmann Purchase Prize, Montreal Mus, 63; First Prize, Vancouver Island Show, Art Gallery Gt Victoria, 64-66 & 69; First Prize, Exhib Can Art, Vancouver Art Gallery, 64. *Bibliog:* Tony Emery (auth), Canadian art today, Artscanada, 65. *Mem:* Royal Can Acad Arts. *Dealer:* Paul Kuhn Fine Arts Gallery Calgary AB Canada; Fran Willis Store St Victoria BC Canada. *Mailing Add:* 1025 Joan Crescent Victoria BC V8S 3L3 Canada

HARVEY, DONALD GENE
SCULPTOR, INSTRUCTOR
b Louisville, Ky, June 25, 47. *Study:* Dixie Col, 65; Utah State Univ, BFA, 69; Univ Hawaii, MFA, 71. *Work:* Honolulu Acad Arts, Hawaii; State Found Cult & Arts, Honolulu; Utah State Univ; Honolulu Community Col; Honolulu Int Airport; and others. *Exhib:* Hawaii Craftsman, 69-70; Artist of Hawaii, 70; Easter Art Festival, Honolulu, 70-71; one-man show, Contemp Art Ctr Pac, 72; Artist Hawaii, Honolulu Acad Arts, 83. *Teaching:* Lectr art, Univ Hawaii, 70-71; instr art, Kamehameha High Sch, 71-. *Awards:* Honolulu Acad Arts Purchase Award, 70; Purchase Award, Contemp Art Ctr, Hawaii, 78; Juror's Award of Excellence, Easter Art Festival, 79. *Bibliog:* Nicholas Roukes (auth), Masters of Wood Sculpture, Watson-Guptill. *Mem:* Hawaii Painters & Sculptors League; Nat Art Educ Asn. *Media:* Mixed Media. *Mailing Add:* 204 W Coshocton St Johnstown OH 43031-1111

HARVEY, PETER FRANCIS
PAINTER, DESIGNER
b Quiriqua, Guatemala, Jan 2, 1933; US citizen. *Study:* Univ Miami, Fla, BA, 55; studied at Art Students League NY. *Comn:* Original ballet design for Anthony Tudor, Metropolitan Opera Co, NY, 64; 3 act ballet design for George Balanchine's "Jewels", Linc Kirstein & New York City Ballet, 67; full length ballet design for "A Midsummer Night's Dream", George Balanchine & Zurich Opera, Switz, 78; 4 Balanchine ballets for tv, WNET-PBS, NY, 79; oil portrait for libr benefactor, Millis, Mass, 94; Re-design of Balanchine's "Jewels," New York City Ballet, 2004. *Exhib:* Tops in NY - 10 Designers, Melvin Gallery, Fla Southern col, Lakeland, 72; one-man shows, Southern-Newman Gallery, Gaylordsville, Conn, 78, The Unknown Remembered, Nicholas Davies & Co, NY, 96; Water Color Today, Creative Arts Workshop, New Haven, Conn, 92; group exhib, John Martin Gallery, London, Eng, 94; Family Values, White Columns, NY, 97; Art Group Pride, Vincent Louis Gallery, NY, 98; Working for Balanchine, Gotham Book Mart Gallery, NY, 98; Dance for a City, NY Hist Soc, 99; Other Rooms: Paintings of Interiors, Hudson Guild Gallery, NY, 2005; one man show, Text/Eros, Riskpress Gallery, Los Angeles, Calif, 2006. *Collection Arranged:* Lincoln Ctr Libr Performing Arts, NY. *Teaching:* Instr theatre design, Pratt Inst, 70-87. *Awards:* Los Angeles Drama Critics Award for Best Set Design of Yr, 69; Excellence in Scenic Design, Soc Educ Television Asn, 78. *Bibliog:* Lynn Pecktal (auth), Designing & Painting for the Theatre, Holt-Rinehart & Winston, 75; Lynn Pecktal (auth), Drawing for the Theatre, McGraw-Hill, 95; Laurie Fitzpatrick (auth), History at ground zero-paintings by Peter Harvey, Art & Understanding, Vol 5, No 5, 7/96; David Leddick (auth), Male Nude Now, Universe Publ, 2001. *Mem:* RI Watercolor Soc; Salmagundi Club; United Scenic Artists. *Media:* Oil, Watercolor. *Publ:* auth, Design journals of Peter Harvey - working for Balanchine, Dance Chronicle, Vol 20, No2, Mercel Dekker, Inc, New York, 97, Vol 20, No 3, 97 & Vol 21, No 1, 98; David Leddick (auth), Male Nude Now, Universe Publ, 2001; Reed Massengill (auth), Text/Eros (catalog), 2006. *Mailing Add:* 96 Perry St New York NY 10014

HASEGAWA, NORIKO
PAINTER
b Toyama Prefecture, Japan; US citizen. *Study:* Toyama Univ, Japan, BS(pharmacy), 56 & PhD(pharmacy), 71; private intsr Ikebana, MA(design), 65. *Work:* Nat Mus Women Art, Washington, DC; San Francisco Art Comn, Calif; Toyama Med & Pharm Univ, Japan; Nat Asn Women Artist Permanent Collection at Rutgers, J V Zimmerli Mus Art, NJ; State Univ NY, Plattsburgh Art Mus; Calif Palace of Legion of Honor. *Comn:* Painting of Koi, Redwood City Pub Libr, Calif, 88. *Exhib:* Plattsburgh State Art Mus, 84; Nat Exhib, Nat Watercolor Soc, 87, 90, 94-96, 2002; France Japan Exhib, Grand Palais, Paris, Tokyo Metrop Mus Art & Osaka City Mus Art, Japan, 93-94 & 94-95; Butler Inst Am Arts, Youngstown, Ohio, 99-04; Around the House, Stanford Fac Club, Calif, 2000; Chatahoochee Valley Art Mus, 2001; Biennial Watercolor Exhib, 2001-2004; Quicksilver Mine Co, 2004; Biennial, Sonoma Valley Art Mus, Calif, 2005; LELA Internat, Museo de Arte Contemporaneo, Ensenada, Mex, 2005. *Awards:* Gold Medal Audubon Artists Ann Exhib, 98; Purchase Award, Springfield Art Mus, 2000; Purchase Award, Chattahoochee Valley Art Mus, 2000;

Merit Award, La Grange Nat Biennial, Ga, 2000. *Bibliog:* John Schwartz (auth), East meets west, Am Artists Mag, Spring, 90; Extended Education Catalog, Sonoma State Univ, fall 94; Ginny Blair (auth), Color Blue, Am Artists Mag, spring 95. *Mem:* Signature mem Nat Watercolor Soc; Nat Asn Women Artists; Allied Artists Am; Rocky Mountain Nat Watermedia Soc; Watercolor USA Honor Soc. *Media:* Watercolor. *Publ:* Less is more, Artists Mag, 12/99; contribr, The Best of Watercolor, Rockport Publs, 95, 97 & 99,. *Dealer:* Ren Brown Collection Gallery 1781 Hwy 1 Bodega Bay CA 94923; Quicksilver Mine co Forestville CA; A Street Gallery Santa Rosa CA. *Mailing Add:* 3105 Burkhart Ln Sebastopol CA 95472

HASELTINE, JAMES LEWIS
PRINTMAKER, PAINTER, CONSULTANT
b Portland, Ore, Nov 7, 24. *Study:* Portland Mus Art Sch, Ore, 47 & 49; Art Inst Chicago, 47-48; Brooklyn Mus Sch, 50-51. *Work:* Portland Art Mus, Ore; Oakland Art Mus, Calif; Mus Art, Univ Ore; Fine Art Mus, Univ Utah; Tacoma Art Mus; Hallie Ford Mus of Art, Willamette Univ, Salem, Oreg. *Exhib:* Libr Cong, Washington, 51; Brooklyn Mus, NY, 51-52; Portland Art Mus, Ore, 51-58; Seattle Art Mus, Wash, 52, 53, 57 & 59; San Francisco Mus Art, Calif, 53-54; Phillips Gallery, Salt Lake City, Utah, 79 & 84; Evergreen State Col, 82; Childhood's End Gallery, Olympia, Wash, 84, 88, 93, 95 & 00; White Sturgeon Gallery, Vancouver WA, 2002. *Pos:* Dir, Salt Lake Art Ctr, Utah, 61-67; exec dir, Wash State Arts Comn, Olympia, 67-80. *Teaching:* Vis lectr art hist, Univ Utah, 64-65. *Awards:* Purchase Prize, Portland Art Mus, 53; Best Monogr, Mormon Hist Asn, 65. *Mem:* Western Asn Art Mus (pres, 64-66); Brit Am Arts Asn (bd mem, 80-83); Nat Assembly State & Prov Arts Agencies (exec comt, 68-70); Nat Endowment Arts (mus panel, 70-72 & visual arts policy panel, 77-79). *Media:* Oil; Woodcut, Drawing. *Publ:* Auth, 100 Years of Utah Painting, 65; contribr, Mus News, 65; Utah Hist Quart, Dialogue & American West, 66; Don Olsen (monogr), Salt Lake Art Ctr, Utah, 84; Francis Zimbeaux (Monogr), Salt Lake Art Ctr, Utah, 90. *Dealer:* Childhood's End Gallery 222 West 4th Ave Olympia WA 98501. *Mailing Add:* 3820 Sunset Beach Dr NW Olympia WA 98502

HASEN, BURT STANLEY
PAINTER, PRINTMAKER
b New York, NY, Dec 19, 21. *Study:* Art Students League, 40, 42 & 46, with Morris Kantor, George Bridgeman, Frank Vincent Dumond & Will Barnet; Hans Hofmann Sch Fine Arts, 47-48; Acad Grande Chaumiere, Paris, 48-50; Acad Belle Arti, Rome, 59-60. *Work:* Walker Art Ctr, Minneapolis; Princeton Univ; Ciba-Geigy Collection; CCNY, NY; Brooklyn Mus, NY; and others. *Comn:* Mural, YMHA & YWHA, Bronx, NY, 47. *Exhib:* Gallery 1100, Buffalo, NY, 93; Staller Ctr Arts, State Univ, Stony Brook, NY, 95; Hamilton Col, Clinton, NY, 96; Nat Acad Design Mus, NY, 97, 99 & 2001; Islip Art Mus, Islip, NY, 2003; One-man shows, T'Pandje Gallerie, Belg, 81, Anita Shapolsky Gallery, 87, 92, 94, Gallery 1100-Niagara, Buffalo, 1993, Staller Ctr for Arts, State Univ of NY, Stony Brook, 95, Hamilton Col, Clinton, NY, 1996, Hugode Pagano Gallery, New York City, 1997, Nat Jewish Mus, Wash DC, 97, Islip Art Mus, NY, 2003; Group shows, Mus Modern Art, Paris, 51, Whitney Mus Am Art, New York City, 64, Corcoran Gallery Art, Wash, 59, Kresge Art Ctr, Univ South Berlin Acad Arts, 56, WG Picker Gallery, 69, Colgate Univ, Hamilton, NY, 69, Mus Modern Art, New York City, 66, Metrop Mus Art, New York City, 52, Worcester (Mass) Art Mus, 68, Walker Art Ctr, Minneapolis, 66, Brooklyn Mus, 54, Artist Choice Mus, New York City, Nat Acad of Design, New York City, 85, Anita Shapolsky Gallery, 89, 90, 92, 2000, Neo Persona Gallery, 89, 90, Rider Col, 92, Albright-Knox Mus, 92, Islip Art Mus, 92, Cleveland Inst Art, 93, Swiss Cultural Inst, 93, David Anderson Gallery, Buffalo, 93, Henry St Settlement, New York City, 93, Sordoni Art Gallery, Wilkes-Barre, Pa, 94, Nat Acad, 95, 96, 97, 99, 2000, 01, 03, Alysia Duckler Gallery, Portland, 96, Pagano Gallery, New York City, 97, 98, Sheldon Mem Art Gallery, Univ Nebr, Lincoln, 03, Denise Bibro Gallery, NY, 04, Lohin Gedulo Gallery, NY, 04. *Teaching:* Prof painting & drawing, Sch Visual Arts, 53-2000, ret, 2000; vis prof painting, Col Art & Design, Minneapolis, 66, Am Sch Tangiers, Morrocco, 80. *Awards:* NY Found Arts, 90; Krasner Pollack Fel, 95; Nat Acad Design Mus, 2001. *Bibliog:* Christopher Youngs, Reconnaissance: An Overview of Burt Hasen's Recent Paintings (brochure essay), Stonybook, 95; Lise Holst (auth), Aerial Prospectives, Paintings by Burt Hasen 'Flyer' for Emerson Gallery, Hamilton, Col, Clinton, NY, 9/96; Grace Glueck (auth), NY Times Review, Hugo de Pagano Gallery, NY, 10/17/97. *Mem:* Nat Acad, NY; Fubright Alumni Asn; NY Artists Equity. *Media:* Oil, Acrylic. *Publ:* Illusr, Contes del'Inattendu, 59, De la Terre a la Lune, 61, Voltaire, 61, Moliere, 61, Lavoisier, Fourier, Faraday, 85 & Beyond the "Furies" by Paul Oppenheimer, 85. *Dealer:* Susan Teller Gallery 568 Broadway New York NY 10012

HASHIMOTO, KELLY ANN
CONCEPTUAL ARTIST, VIDEO ARTIST
b Chicago, Sept 22, 60. *Study:* Fullerton Col, AA(studio & art hist), 84; Univ Calif, Los Angeles, BA(studio & art hist), 88; Calif Inst Arts, Valencia, MFA(photog & critical theory), 91; Deutscher Akad Austausch Dienst Stipendium, Hochsch Bildende Kunst, Hamburg, independent art/res proj, 91. *Work:* pvt collections in Boston, Los Angeles, NY, Ger & Switz. *Exhib:* SITE/Seeing: Travel & Tourism in Contemp Art (exhib catalog), Whitney Mus Am Art, 91; Joint Ventures, Basilico Fine Arts, NY, 96; Spec/OK, allgirls galerie, Berlin, Ger, 96; Buck Stop: Pro-Vanities in the Bathroom, 71 Spot, NY, 96; Catalogue of Knowledge: Los Angeles Co Mus Art Libr Renovated, Blast/X-Art Found, NY, 96; Babes in Toyland (working title), NY, 97. *Pos:* Staff photogr, Hornet, Fullerton Col, 83; archit photog, Barry Schweiger, 84; corp photog, Cushman-Wakefield, Bunker Hill, 85; admin asst & media & performing arts cur, Mus Contemp Art, Los Angeles, 88; libr asst, Los Angeles Co Mus Art, 90; admin asst, Richard Meier & Partners, Architects, NY, 93; freelance computer, Pat Hearn Gallery, FlashArt Mag & Gale Elston, Esq, 96. *Teaching:* vis artist & lectr, Univ S Fla, Tampa, 96. *Bibliog:* Hair-hanging was research for senior's thesis, Daily Bruin, 5/19/88; David Mori (auth), Act examines personal/political, High Performance, fall 88; Brigitte Werneberg (auth), Entschieden gewitzt: Kunst in Berlin jetzt, die tageszeitung, 7/13-14/96. *Mem:* Col Art Asn. *Media:* Performance; Photography, Video. *Publ:* Auth, Special/OK, Art Link (website), 96; Art and architecture (in prep), Flash Arts, 97. *Mailing Add:* 501 Silver Canyon Wy Brea CA 92821

HASKELL, BARBARA
CURATOR
b San Diego, Calif, Nov 13, 46. *Study:* Univ Calif, Los Angeles, BA(philos & art hist), 69. *Exhib:* Retrospective (auth, catalog): Whitney Biennial, 77, 79, 81, 83, & 85; Marsden Hartley, 80; Milton Avery, 82; Ralston Crawford, 85; Charles Demuth, 87; Donald Jud, 88; Burgoyne Diller, 90; Agnes Martin, 93, traveling, 93-94; Joseph Stella, 94; The American Century: Art and Culture 1900-1950, 99; Edward Steichen, 2000; Elie Nadelman: Sculptor of Modern Life, 2003 & Oscar Bluemner: A Passion for Color, 2005. *Pos:* Asst registrar, Pasadena Mus Mod Art, 69, from asst cur to cur painting & sculpture, 70-73, dir exhib & collections, 74; cur, San Francisco Mus Art, 74; cur painting & sculpture, Whitney Mus Am Art, New York, 75-; panel mem, Nat Endowment Arts, Art Comn of City of New York; adv bd, Edith C Blum Art Inst, Bard Col; past adv bd, Int Mus Photog at George Eastman House. *Awards:* Woman of the Year, Mademoiselle Award, 73; Leadership Among Professional Women, Los Angeles Soroptimist, 73. *Publ:* New Masters-Bryan Hunt (exhib), Amerika Haus, Berlin, 83; Bryan Hunt: Sculpturen und Zeichnugen (exhib catalog), Knoedler Gallery, Zurich, 85; Georgia O'Keefe, Works on Paper-A Critical Essay (exhib catalog), Mus Fine Arts, Mus NMex, Santa Fe, Mus NMex Press, 85; Transcendental Realism in the Steiglitz Circle (exhib catalog), The Expressionistic Landscape, Birmingham Mus Art, 87; Yoko Ono: Arias & Objects, Peregrine Smith Books, Salt Lake City, 91; and others. *Mailing Add:* Whitney Mus Am Art 945 Madison Ave New York NY 10021

HASKELL, JANE
ENVIRONMENTAL ARTIST, PAINTER
b Cedarhurst, NY, Nov 24, 23. *Study:* Skidmore Col, Saratoga Springs, NY, BS, 44; Univ Pittsburgh, Pa, MA, 61. *Work:* Carnegie Mus Art, Pittsburgh; Mead Art Mus, Amherst, Mass; Milwaukee Art Mus, Wis; Mus Neon Art, Los Angeles; Westmoreland Co Mus Art, Greensburg, Pa. *Comn:* Tree of Knowledge (neon 12' x 18'), William Pitt Student Union, Univ Pittsburgh, 87; Windows of Light (neon), Massport, Boston, Mass, 90; Let the Waters Teem with Living Creatures and Let Birds Fly Above the Earth, Genesis (fiberoptic light installation), Ft Lauderdale Airport, Fla, 94; Leaves of Light (stairwell-painted panels with fiberoptics), Pressure Chem Inc, Pittsburgh, 95; Neon installation, Pittsburgh Ctr Arts, 97. *Exhib:* One-woman shows, Color & Light Environment, Allegheny Col, Meadville, Pa, 85, Drawings & Neon Constructions, Assoc Artists Pittsburgh Ctr Arts, Pa, 87, Construction with Light & Installation with Light, AIR Gallery, NY, 88, 90 & 92, Window Series, Concept Art Gallery, Pittsburgh, 91, Vinyard Studio Gallery, 94 & Westmorland Mus Am Art, 96; St Petersburg Bienniale, Neon Installation, Russ, 96; To the Edge of Time: A Two Decade Retrospective, Jewish Community Ctr Asn, Pittsburgh, 97; Drawings in Light, Asn Artists Pittsburgh Gallery, 98; Light Installation, Pittsburgh Biennial, Ctr for the Arts, 2000; Gestures, An Exhibition of Small Site-Specific Work, Mattress Factory, Pittsurgh, Pa, 2002; The Bells of Amherst, Contemp Women Artists in the Collections of the Mead Art Mus and the Univ Gallery, Univ of Amherst, MA, 2002; Panopticon, an Art Spectacular, Carnegie mus of Art, Pittsburgh, Pa, 2002; Light and Glass, Challange Exhib, Gallery 707, Pittsburgh, Pa, 2005; 2006 Artist of the Year, Pittsburgh Ctr for the Arts, Pittsburgh, Pa; and others. *Pos:* Bd trustees, Pittsburgh Ctr Arts, 91-94; bd trustees, Carnegie Mus of Art, 99-. *Teaching:* Instr art hist, Duquesne Univ, Pittsburgh, Pa, 68-78; Symp on Light, Pittsburgh Ctr for the Arts, Pittsburgh, Pa, 2006. *Awards:* AAP Juror's Award, Assoc Artists Pittsburgh, Susan & Morton Gurrentz, 82; Jury Award, Soc Sculptors, Pittsburgh, Pa, 95; Award of Distinction, Art for AIDS, Persad Ctr, Pittsburgh, 95; Juror's Award, Soc Sculptor's Ann Exhib, 97; Juror's Award, Assoc Artist Pittsburgh, Red Exhib, Red Alert, Pittsburgh, Pa, 2006. *Bibliog:* Vilma Barr (auth), Best of Neon, Allworth Press/Rockport Pubs, 92; Marty Carlock (auth), Guide to Public Art in Greater Boston, revised ed, Harvard Common Press, 93; Abigal Pesta (auth), Electric art, Jane Haskell's neon creations: Changing colors, changing moods, Lighting Dimensions Mag, 4/94. *Mem:* Soc Sculptors; Asn Artists Pittsburgh; Pittsburgh Ctr Arts; Carnegie Mus Art. *Media:* Neon, Fiber Optics, Flourescent Light, Black Light. *Dealer:* Concept Art Gallery, 10315 Braddock Ave, Pittsburgh, PA 15218. *Mailing Add:* The Park Mansions Apt 6AD 5023 Frew St Pittsburgh PA 15213

HASKIN, DONALD MARCUS
EDUCATOR, SCULPTOR
b St Paul, Minn, July 28, 20. *Study:* Univ Minn, study with Tovish, BA; Cranbrook Acad Art, MFA. *Comn:* Bronze figure & stainless steel fountain, 72, City Tucson; sculpture, Univ Ariz, 73; portrait, Tucson Boys Choir; portrait, McKale Ctr, Univ Ariz. *Exhib:* Contemp Crafts Mus, NY, 61; San Francisco Mus Art, 62; Preview '65, Alamo Gallery, Benicia, Calif, 65; Southwestern Invitational, Yuma Art Asn, 72-75; Tucson Mus Art, 75. *Teaching:* Lectr sculpture, Univ Calif, Berkeley, 63-65; prof sculpture, Univ Ariz, Tucson, 65-82, prof emer, 82; retired. *Awards:* First Prize, Minn State Fair, 58; Purchase Award, City of Benicia, 65; Purchase Prize Award, Yuma Art Asn, 72. *Media:* Metal, Cast

HASLEM, JANE N
DEALER
b Knoxville, Tenn, Dec 26, 34. *Study:* DePauw Univ, BA; Ind State Univ; Grad Studies Art Hist, Univ Md, 90-93. *Work:* Var Nat & Int collections. *Pos:* Dir, Jane Haslem Gallery, Chapel Hill, NC, 60-65, Madison, Wis, 65-71 & Washington, 69-71. *Teaching:* Instr art, Mecklenburg Co, NC, 58-59; resident assoc prog, Smithsonian Inst. *Mem:* Washington Print Club (bd adv); Art Dealers Asn Greater Washington

(found mem & bd dir, 81-93 & 97, secy, 91-93, treas 84-89, pres 97-2001); founding mem Int Fine Print Dealers Asn, NY; Arttable NY; Print Club NY. *Specialty:* Contemporary American paintings, prints and works on paper; publisher of art catalogues and CD presentations; internet exhibs. *Publ:* Selected publ, Jane Haslem Gallery Newsletter, 72-; auth, American Drawings/Realism Idealism, 86; David Hollowell, 86; Larry Day Paintings: 1958-1988, 88; Gabor Peterdi: Pacific and Other Recent Works, 90. *Mailing Add:* 2025 Hillyer Pl NW Washington DC 20009

HASSANAL BOLKIAH, HIS MAJESTY MUTZZADDIN WADDAULAH
COLLECTOR
b Darussalam, Brunei, July 15, 46. *Study:* Student Victoria Inst, Kuala LUmpar, Malaysia, 61-63, Royal Military Acad, Sandhurst, England, 63-67. *Pos:* Appointed crown prince and heir apparent for State of Brunei, 61; Ruler of state, sultan, 67-, prime minister, 84-, minister fin and home affairs, 84-86, minister of defense, 86-. *Awards:* Named One of Top 200 Collectors, ARTnews Magazine, 2004, 2005, 2006. *Collection:* Impressionism and Islamic art. *Mailing Add:* Office of HM The Sultan Bandar Seri Begawan 01000 Brunei Darussalam

HASSINGER, MAREN J
SCULPTOR
b Los Angeles, Calif, 1947. *Study:* Bennington Col, Vt, BA, 69; Univ Calif, Los Angeles, MFA, 73. *Work:* Calif Afro-Am Mus, Los Angeles; Univ Gallery, Calif State Univ, Long Beach; Greater Pittsburgh Int Airport, Pa; Seattle Transit Authority, Wash; Studio Mus, Harlem, New York. *Exhib:* Solo shows, Focus: Environment, Maren Hassinger, Art Gallery, Calif State Univ, Northridge, 85, Blanket of Branches & Dancing Branches, Contemp Arts Forum & Alice Keck Park, Santa Barbara, Calif, 86, Field, SoHo 20 Gallery, NY, 89, Gracie Mansion Gallery, NY, 91, Bushes, Fine Arts Gallery, LIU/Southhampton Campus, NY, 92, Memory, Benton Gallery, Southampton, NY, 93 & Treachery and Consolation, Trans-Hudson Gallery, Jersey City, NJ, 96; Benton Gallery, Southampton, NY, 92 & 93; Trans Hudson Gallery, Jersey City, NJ, 93 & 94; Black Prints, Elsa Mott Ives Gallery, NY, 94; Peg Alston Fine Arts, NY, 94; Sightings, Parrish Art Mus, Southampton, NY, 94; 27th Ann Artists of the Springs Invitational Exhib, Ashawgh Hall, East Hampton, NY, 94; Univ Art Gallery, Staller Ctr Arts, State Univ NY, Stony Brook, 94 & 97; African-Am Women Prints, Printed Image Galleries, Firehouse Art Ctr, Philadelphia, Pa, 94; Inspried by Nature, Neuberger Mus Art, Purchase, NY, 94; Robert Blackburn: Inspriation and Innovation in Am Printmaking, Kenkeleba Gallery, NY, 94; Listening to the Earth: Artists and the Environment, Emerson Art Gallery, Hamilton Col, Clinton, NY, 95; Black Pearls: Treasures of African-Am Women Artists, Cirque Gallery, NY, 95; Required Nuance: Three Contemp Sculptors, Studio Mus Harlem, NY, 95; Whisper, Stomp,Shout A Salute to African-Am Performance Art, Colo Springs Fine Arts Ctr, 96; 4 Who Teach, Omni Gallery, Uniondale, NY, 96; First Lady's Sculpture Garden, White House, Washington, DC, 96; Eight by Eight, Heckscher Mus Art, Huntington, NY, 97; Decker Gallery, Station Bldg & Meyerhoff Gallery, Fox Bldg, Md Inst Col Art, 97; Los Angeles Mus Contemp Art, 98; And many others. *Pos:* Dir, Rinehart Sch Grad Sculpture, Md Inst, Col Art, 97. *Teaching:* Instr, Calif State Univ, Long Beach, 73-74, Los Angeles, 74-76 & 79, Barnsdall Jr Art Ctr, Los Angeles, 75-77, Los Angeles Co Mus Art, 77 & 78, Otis/Parsons Inst, Los Angeles, 80 & 81, Pasadena Art Workshops, 81, Univ Calif Extension, 83-84, Parsons Art Inst, 85 & Arts Partners, Studio Sch Asn, 85-88; adj prof art, Hunter Col, NY, 88-91 & Sch Visual Art, NY, 90; assoc adj prof art, Long Island Univ, Southampton, NY, 92; lectr, Art Dept, State Univ NY, Stony Brook, 92-97. *Awards:* Artists Fel, 80 & Nat Endowment Arts, 97; Grant, Joan Mitchell Found, 96; Artists' Grant, Anonymous Was a Woman, New York, 97. *Bibliog:* Judith H Dobrzynski (auth), Anonymous gifts, So women artists won't be, NY Times, 10/12/97; Arlene Raven (auth), New York Story, Sculpture Mag, 1/98; Sharon F Patton (auth), African-Am Art, Oxford Univ Press, 98. *Mailing Add:* 723 Colorado Ave Baltimore MD 21210

HASSRICK, PETER H
MUSEUM DIRECTOR, HISTORIAN
b Philadelphia, Pa, Apr 27, 41. *Study:* Univ Colo, BA(hist & classics); Harvard Univ(classics); Univ Denver, MA(art hist). *Collection Arranged:* Albert Bierstadt, 72, Frederic Remington (auth, catalog), 73 & Peter Rindisbacher, 70, Amon Carter Mus, Ft Worth, Tex; The Rocky Mountains (auth, catalog), Buffalo Bill Hist Ctr, Cody, Wyo, 83; Treasures of the Old Wes (auth, catalog), 84; Am Frontier Life, 87; Frederic Remington: The Masterworks, 88; In Search of Frederic Remington (auth, catalog), 96; The American West (auth, catalog), 99; Remington, Russel and the Language of Western Art, 2000; The Unending Frontier, 2000. *Pos:* Cur collections, Amon Carter Mus, Ft Worth, Tex, 69-75; dir, Buffalo Bill Hist Ctr, Cody, Wyo, 76-96 & Georgia O'Keffe Mus, Santa Fe, NMex, 96-97. *Teaching:* Adj prof hist, Univ Wyo, Laramie, 80-; Charles M Russell prof Art Hist, Univ Okla. *Mem:* Wyo Coun on the Arts (vchmn, 76-85); Nat Endowment Arts Mus (oversight panel, 91-). *Res:* Nineteenth and early twentieth century artists of the American West. *Publ:* Auth, Drawings of the North American Indian, Doubleday, 84; coauth, American Frontier Life, Abbeyville, 87; Frederic Remington: The Masterworks, Harry N Abrams Inc, 88; auth, Charles M Russell, Harry N Abrams, Inc, 89; coauth (with Melissa Webster), Frederic Remmington: A Catalogue Raisonne, 96

HASTENTEUFEL, DIETER
SCULPTOR, PAINTER
b Basel, Switz, 1939; Can citizen. *Study:* Sch Applied Arts, Gelsenkirchen, Ger, 58-60; Werkkunstschule, Krefeld, 61; Werkkunstschule, Wuerzburg, 64; Acad Fine Art, Stuttgart, Ger, dipl, 68. *Work:* Art Gallery Ont; Art Gallery Hamilton; Art Gallery Peterborough, Ont; Sculpture Park, Liberty Hill, Tex; Can Coun Art Bank. *Comn:* Many pvt commissions. *Exhib:* Solo exhibs, Art Gallery Windsor, 83, Burlington Cult Ctr, 83, Kitchener-Waterloo Art Gallery, 83, New Art Gallery Toronto, 85, Ed Video Media Arts, Guelph, 91, White Water Gallery, North Bay, 91 & Koffler Gallery, Toronto, Ont, 92; Hamilton Art Gallery, Ont, 82; Art Gallery Ont, 85; Cold City Gallery, Toronto, Ont, 87; Workscene Gallery, Toronto, Ont, 92; and others. *Teaching:* Sheridan Col, Brampton, 72 Dundas Valley Sch Art, 72-80, Manitou-Wabing Sports & Art Ctr, Parry Sound, 81-92, Mohawk Col, Hamilton & George Brown Col, Toronto; vis artist in numerous schs. *Awards:* Grants, Can Coun, 76, 79, 82 90-91, Ont Art coun, 76-78, 80-82, 85, 90 & 92, CAIS, 83-92. *Bibliog:* Joy Ilakanson Colby (auth), article, Detroit News, 4/24/83; John Bentley Mays (auth), The Globe & Mail, 12/85; Kate Taylor (auth), Art About, Globe & Mail, Can, 5/15/92

HASTINGS, JACK BYRON
SCULPTOR
b Kennett, Mo, Nov 16, 25. *Study:* La State Univ, 1946-47 & 1949-50; Escuela Pintura & Escultura, Mexico City, 1951. *Comn:* Playground Percussion sculptures (bronze), NY Dept Educ, Harlem Elem Sch, 1960; public seating & plant containers (carved cement), Ariz Sonora Desert Mus, Tucson, 1970; Homage to Calder (painted metal mobile), Tenn Valley Authority Hqrs, Chatanooga, Tenn, 1982; Environmental Garden (carved cement sculptures), Tenn Dept Tourism, 1-75 Welcome Ctr/Tenn Arts Commn, 1984; Dancing on Air (2 painted metal mobiles), Metro Nashville Airport Authority, 2000. *Exhib:* One-man shows, Work on Jack Hastings, New Orleans Mus, 1954 & Art for the Garden, Am Craft Gallery, Cleveland, 1989; Now in New Orleans, Riverside Mus, NY, 1955; Orleans Gallery Founders, NO Historic Collection Gallery, New Orleans, 1982; Sculpture Invitational, Radford Univ, Radford, Va, 1988; Seven Sculptors, Zimmerman Saturn Gallery, Nashville, 1989; solo show, Barone Galley, New York City, 1959. *Collection Arranged:* New Orleans Historic Collection; The Children's Mus; Tenn State Mus, Nashville. *Awards:* Purchase Awards, New Orleans Mus of Art, Tenn Crafts Fair & Rutherford Bicentennial Exhib. *Bibliog:* Archit Record; Interiors; ARTNews; Crafts Horizons; Arts and Archit; Sunset; Nashville!. *Media:* Metal, Cast, Welded, Fabricated. *Publ:* Auth, The Illuminated History of Darkness, Cosmic Aye Press, 2000. *Mailing Add:* 464 Wildwood Lane Sewanee TN 37375

HATCH, CONNIE
PHOTOGRAPHER, EDUCATOR
b Muskogee, Okla, Apr 12, 51. *Study:* Univ Tex Austin, BFA, 73; San Francisco Art Inst, MFA, 79. *Comn:* Art in the Urban Landscape, Capp St Proj & The Wallace Alexander Gerbode Found, San Francisco, 95. *Exhib:* Who Counts?, Randolph St Gallery, Chicago, Ill, 90; Spectacular Women, Film Cities, St Paul, Minn, 90; After the Fact, Mills Col Art Gallery, Oakland, Calif, 90; Picture Plane to Object, Brea Cult Ctr, Calif, 91; In and Around: Selections From the Permanent Collection, Univ Art Mus, State Univ NY, Binghampton, 91; Sightlines, Newport Harbor Art Mus, Calif, 91; Navigational Crossroads, Capp St Proj, San Francisco, 95-96; Gallery, NY, 92; (Original Accounts) of the Lone Woman of San Nicolas, 18 Street Complex, Santa Monica, Calif, 98; Fin de Siecle Terrain Gallery, San Francisco, 99. *Teaching:* Fac, Calif Inst Arts, Valencia, 83-2003; vis lectr photog, Univ Calif, Los Angeles, 91-92. *Awards:* Charlene Engelhard Found Award, 88; Visual Artists' Fel, New Genre, Nat Endowment Arts, 91; Comn Award, Wallace Alexander Gerbode Found, 95. *Bibliog:* David Trend (auth), Connie Hatch at Mills Col, Art Am, 5/91; H Pakasaar, Brian Wallis, William Wood (auths), Camera Lucida: What is not Seen, Camera Lucida, Banff Centre, Alta, Can, 91; Daniel Veneciano (auth), Power rips, Artweek, 12/26/91. *Media:* Photography, New Genre. *Publ:* The DeSublimation of Romance: Consider the Difference, Spec Issue Sexuality, Wedge, winter 84; Serving the Status-Quo, Blasted Allegories: An Anthology of Writings by Contemp Artists, 87; Small Miracle, red, New Langton Arts. The First 15 Years, San Francisco, 90; After the Fact, Exposure, Boulder, Colo, 90; The De Sublimation of Romance (exerpts), Reframings: New American Feminist Photographies, Temple Univ Press, 95. *Mailing Add:* c/o Calif Inst Arts 24700 McBean Pkwy Valencia CA 91355

HATCH, (MR & MRS) MARSHALL
COLLECTORS
Mr Hatch, b Seattle, Wash, Aug 26, 18; Mrs Hatch, b Seattle, Wash, July 7, 18. *Study:* Mr & Mrs Hatch, Univ Wash. *Pos:* Mr Hatch, pres, Seattle Art Mus, formerly. *Collection:* Morris Graves, Mark Tobey, other Northwest artists, The Eight (Ashcan Group), Mexican paintings and ethnic art. *Mailing Add:* 1301 Spring St No 19 G & J Seattle WA 98104-3533

HATCH, MARY
PAINTER
b Saginaw, Mich, Dec 12, 35. *Study:* Skidmore Col, 51-53; Western Mich Univ, MA(painting), 72; studied with Harvey Breverman, 74-77. *Work:* St Johns Univ, NY; Southwestern Mich Col, Kalamazoo Inst Arts, Mich, Art Ctr Battle Creek, Mich; Upjohn Co; Mich Comn Art in Pub Places. *Exhib:* One-person exhibs, CPL Cult Ctr, Chicago, 82 & Gilman-Gruen Galleries, Chicago, 96, 2000; New Talent--New Visions, Zolla/Lieberman Gallery, Chicago, 83; Kouroi & Korai, Kouros Gallery, NY, 84; Constructing A Modern World, Mich Coun Arts, Detroit, 90; West, Art & the Law, 20th Ann Exhib, Nev Mus Art & Springfield Mus Art, Ohio, 95; Death Matters, Urban Inst Contemp Art, Grand Rapids, Mich. *Awards:* Susan Kahn Prize, 83 & Charles Horman Mem Award, 85, Nat Asn Women Artists; Mich Coun Arts Grant, 85-86 & 88-89. *Bibliog:* Ben Mitchell (auth), To Get Hold of the Invisible, Passages North, Winter 87; Western Michigan Presents, Western Mich Univ, Vol 3, No 3; Effie Mihopoulos (auth), Silent Messages, Reader, Chicago, 92. *Mem:* Chicago Artists Coalition. *Media:* Oil. *Mailing Add:* 6917 Willson Dr Kalamazoo MI 49009

HATCH, W A S
PAINTER, EDUCATOR
b Bridgeport, Conn, Mar 19, 48. *Study:* Syracuse Univ, BFA, 70; Pratt Inst, MFA, 72. *Work:* City Col NY; Kemper Collection, Chicago, Ill; US Info Agency Embassy Collection; Univ Leeds; San Diego Mus; and others. *Comn:* Spec ed prints, Pratt Graphic Ctr, NY, 73. *Exhib:* Brooklyn Mus 19th Nat Print Exhib, 74-75; 5th Int

Drawing Show, Mus Mod Art, Riejka, Yugoslavia, 76; World Print Competition, 77; Am Printmakers, Venice, 77; Sande Webster Gallery, Philadelphia, Pa, 75, 77 & 84; New Talent in Printmaking Show, Assoc Am Artists, NY, 77; 6th Brit Int Print Biennale, 79; Handmade Paper, Silver Cloud Gallery, Chicago, 81; Delaware Art Mus, 85 & 91; one-person show, Carspecken-Scott Gallery, Wilmington, Del, 99, Station Gallery, Greenville, Del, 92, Blue Streak Gallery, Wilmington, Del, 99; and many others. *Pos:* Cur, The Making of Print, DCCA, Del, 90. *Teaching:* Asst prof printmaking, Bradley Univ, 73-79; instr drawing, Columbia Col, 79-80; adj prof, Widener Univ, 82-; instr watercolor, Del Art Mus, 82-. *Awards:* Purchase Award, Los Angeles 2nd Nat Print Exhib, 74; Merit Award, Boston Printmakers 26th Ann Exhib, 74; Purchase Award, Eastern Regional Drawing Exhib, 83. *Bibliog:* The European Graphic Biennale, Print Rev, 77. *Mem:* Del Ctr Contemp Arts (vpres, 82-83). *Media:* Intaglio, Watercolor. *Dealer:* Ellen Bartholmus Blue Streak Gallery 1721 Delaware Ave Wilmington DE 19806. *Mailing Add:* 2100 Kentmere Pkwy Wilmington DE 19806-2016

HATCHER, (L) BROWER
SCULPTOR
b Sept, 42. *Study:* Vanderbilt Univ, Nashville, Tenn, 61-63; Pratt Inst, Brooklyn, NY, BA(indust design), 67; St Martins Sch Art, grad studies sculpture, London, Eng, 67-69. *Hon Degrees:* State Univ of NY, PhD, 97. *Work:* Adirondack Guide Monument, NY State Coun Arts, Lake George, 84. *Comn:* Thomas Jefferson Park, Dept Cult Affairs, NY, 93; Brigham Young Univ Arts Mus; Provo, Utah, 94; Columbus State Community Col; Ohio State Art Coun, Columbus, 99; Radial Light, Fidelity Investments, Smithfield, RI, 2000; Brainstorm, ADC Telcom, Mimmeapolis, 2001; Passage, Columbus State Community Col, 2001; Starman Tapestry, Wills Eye Hosp, Phildelphia, 2002; Cultural Tapestry, Dist 3 Police Station, Denver, 2002; Weaving Waters, Glendale Adult Center, Ariz, 2002; and others. *Exhib:* Solo shows, State Univ NY Grad Ctr, 75, Diane Brown Gallery, 82 & 87, Meyers Fine Arts Ctr, State Univ NY, Plattsburg, 80, Vaughn & Vaughn, Minneapolis, Minn, 89, Ctr Int Contemp Art, NY, 91, Paul Cava Gallery, Philadelphia, Pa, 91, Heath Gallery, Atlanta, Ga, 92 & Eve Mannes Gallery, Atlanta, Ga, 92; Sculpture Inside Outside, Walker Art Ctr, Minn, 88-89; Houston Mus Fine Arts, Tex, 89; Sculpture Commerce Square, IBM Ctr, Philadelphia, Pa, 90; Roanoke Mus Fine Arts, Va, 90; Gateway Ctr, Prudential Art Prog, Newark, NJ, 90; Paul Cava Gallery, Philadelphia, Pa, 90; Nancy Drysdale, Washington, DC, 92; Carolyn Ruff, Minneapolis, Minn, 96; Bard Col, Annondale-on-Hudson, NY, 98; Laumeier Sculpture Park, St Louis, 2000; Grounds for Sculpture, Hamilton, NJ, 2000; and others. *Teaching:* Sculpture, St Martins Sch Art, London, Eng, 69-72; vis artist & lectrs, many col & univs, 70-91, including Walker Art Ctr, 89 & RI Sch Design, Providence, 91; fac sculpture, Bennington Col Art, 72-85; distinguished vis prof, State Univ NY, Plattsburg, 88-89. *Awards:* Nat Endowment Arts Fels, 74, 80 & 90; Guggenheim Fel, 85; NY Found Arts Fel, 91; Honeywell Environ Excellence Award, 93. *Bibliog:* Irving Sandler (auth), Brower Hatcher Structures (catalog), Ctr Int Contemp Art, NY, 91; Carol Vogel (auth), The art market, NY Times, 2/14/92; Janet Wilson (auth), Sculpture of new dimensions, Washington Post, 2/22/92. *Dealer:* Heath Gallery Inc 57 26th St Atlanta GA 30305

HATCHETT, DUAYNE
SCULPTOR, PAINTER
b Shawnee, Okla, May 12, 25. *Study:* Univ Mo; Univ Okla, BFA & MFA. *Work:* Whitney Mus Am Art; Rochester Mem Mus, NY; Ft Worth Art Mus, Tex; Carnegie Inst, Pittsburgh, Pa; Albright-Knox Gallery, Buffalo, NY; Pittsburgh Univ, Pa; many others. *Comn:* Whitney Mus Am Art, 1967; Nat Endowment Arts, Downtown Riverfront Park, Flint, Mich, 1978-79; GSA Fed Bldg, Rochester, NY, 1978; Ashford Hollow (NY) Sculpture Park, 1986; other pub and private comns. *Exhib:* Solo exhibs, Rockefeller Art Ctr, Fredonia, NY, 82, Kirkpatrick Ctr, Okla City, 87, Chautauqua Art Asn Galleries, NY, 87 & Concept Gallery, Pittsburgh, Pa, 90, Dunkirk Art Center, NY, 1991, Alexandre Hogue Gallery, Tulsa Univ, 1992, Daemen Col, Buffalo, 1993; Pub Works, Smithsonian Gallery, Washington, 80; Sculptors Drawings: 1910-1980, 81 & The Sculptor as Draftman, 83, Whitney Mus Art NY; Outside New York City: From Drawings to Sculpture, Syracuse Univ, NY, 82; The Wayward Muse, 87, & Western NY Invitational, Albright Knox Art Gallery, Buffalo, NY, 89; The Eloquent Object, traveling show, 87-89; Big Orbit Gallery, Buffalo, 1991; Hallwalls Gallery, Buffalo, 1992; Anderson Gallery, Buffalo, 1993, 94. *Pos:* Comt chmn, Coun for Int Exchange of Scholars, Washington. *Teaching:* Assoc prof sculpture, Ohio State Univ, 64-68; prof art, State Univ NY Buffalo, 68-92, ret. *Mem:* Nat Sculpture Soc. *Media:* Sculpture/Metal, Printmaking. *Mailing Add:* 18 Essex St Buffalo NY 14213

HATFIELD, DAVID UNDERHILL
PAINTER
b Plainfield, NJ, July 16, 40. *Study:* Miami Univ, BFA, 62; Sch Visual Arts, 63; Art Students League, 64. *Work:* Southern Vt Art Ctr; West Point Mil Acad; Fed Court House, White Plains, NY. *Exhib:* Nat Acad Design Ann, NY, 70, 73, 84 & 94; Nat Arts Club Ann, NY, 69-72, 75 & 76; Am Artists Prof League Grand Nat, NY, 71-77; One man shows, Nat Arts Club, 76, Christopher Gallery, NY, 81 & Southern Vt Art Ctr, 86, 91, 93, 96 & 04. *Awards:* Wm Meyerowitz Award, Rockport Art Asn, 90; Robert Nally Award, Rockport Art Asn, 91 & Portrait Award, 98; W M Meyerowitz Mem Award, North Shore Arts Asn, 96 & Gorton's of Gloucester Award, 98; Rockport Art Assoc, Silver Metal, 98, Paul Strisik Gold Metal, 00, Amee B Davis Award, 04, Dr Henry Kaplan Mem Award; and others. *Bibliog:* C Movalli (auth), article, Am Artist Mag, 12/81. *Mem:* North Shore Arts Asn; Allied Artists Am; Rockport Art Asn; Southern Vt Artists Inc; and others. *Media:* Oil. *Publ:* Cover painting, Prevention Mag, 1/82. *Dealer:* J R Leigh Gallery PO Box 70116 Tuscaloosa, AL 35407; State of the Art Gallery 4 Wonson St Gloucester MA 01930; Lily Pad Gallery 1 Bay St Watch Hill RI 02891. *Mailing Add:* 9 River St Hoosick Falls NY 12090

HATFIELD, DONALD GENE
PAINTER, EDUCATOR
b Detroit, Mich, May 23, 32. *Study:* Northwestern Mich Col, AA; Mich State Univ, BA & MA; Univ Wis, MFA; Studied with Abraham Rattner, Warrington Colescott & Robert Grilley. *Work:* Jacksonville State Univ, Ala; Tuskegee Inst, Ala; Brandt Corp, New Orleans; South Cent Bell, Birmingham; Southern Servs, Birmingham; Montgomery Mus Art, Ala; and others. *Exhib:* solo shows, La Crosse State Col Mus, QI, 63, Birmingham Southern Col Gallery, Ala, 70; 48th-50th Ann Exhib Wisc Art, Milwaukee Art Ctr, 62-64; 59th Ann Jury Exhib, Birmingham Mus Art, Ala, 67; Ann Mus Gallery Exhib, Mus Arts & Science, Macon, Ga, 68; Ala Watercolor Soc Show, Birmingham Mus Art, Ala, 68; 30th Ann Nat Competition, Ala Watercolor Soc, Birmingham Mus Art, Ala, 69; Ala Art League, Montgomery, 81; Columbia Col, Mo, 83; Del Mar Col, 83; Ala Works on Paper, Auburn, Ala, 83; Competition for Spoleto, Marble Arch Gallery, Charleston, SC, 83; 17th Ann Nat Drawing & Small Sculpture Show, Del Mar Col, Corpus Christi, Tex, 83. *Teaching:* Elem art supvr, Auburndale Elem Sch Syst, Wis; instr jr & sr high art classes, Auburndale High Sch, 62-64; Instr, Auburn Univ, 64-94; asst prof art, Auburn Univ, 64-71, assoc prof art, 71-81, prof art, 81-94, student academic adv, 90-94, prof emer, 94; part time instr hist archit & art, Tuskegee Inst, 68-69. *Awards:* Purchase Award, 49th Ann Exhib Wisc Art, Milwaukee, 62; Purchase Award, Opelika Arts Festival, Opelika Arts Asn, Ala, 71-72; Purchase Award, 5th Ann Miniworks Exhib, Jacksonville State Univ, Jacksonville, Ala, 83; plus many others. *Bibliog:* La Revue Moderne des Art de la Vie, Paris, Francem 64; Ernest Kay (ed)Dictionary of Intl Biography, Vol 6 IX, Melrose Press Ltd, Cambridge, England 72-73; Les Krantz (auth), The New York Art Review, an Illustrated Survey of the City's Mus, Galleries & Leading Artists, Americas References, Inc, Chicago, IL. 88. *Mem:* Ala Art League (first vpres, 69-70, pres, 70-72); Opelika Arts Asn (bd trustees, 71-73). *Media:* Watercolor. *Mailing Add:* 550 Forest Park Cir Auburn AL 36830

HATGIL , PAUL
EDUCATOR, PAINTER
b Manchester, NH, Feb 18, 21. *Study:* Harvard U, summer 50; Mass Col Art, BFA, 50; Columbia Univ, MFA, 51. *Work:* Fed Aviation Agency, Balboa, CZ; Litton Industs; Ft Worth Nat Bank; Mitchell Energy Corp; Tandy Corp; Univ Tex, Performing Arts Ctr, Austin. *Comn:* St Paul's Lutheran Church, Austin, Tex; Univ Tex Bus & Admin Bldg, Austin; Our Saviour's Lutheran Church, Victoria, Tex; Design Assocs Bldg, Dallas, Tex; Rio Bldg, Austin; plus others. *Exhib:* 4th-6th Int Invitational, Smithsonian Inst, Washington, DC; Int Invitational, Gulf-Caribbean Exhib, Houston, Tex; Philbrook Art Ctr Int, Tulsa, Okla; US World's Fair Pavilion, NY; Hemisphere 1969, Tex Pavilion, San Antonio, Tex; US Senate, St Petersburg, Jacksonville & Fla Mus; solo shows, Sunset Galleries, Austin, Tex, 91, Univ Tex 54th Ann Art Faculty Exhib, 91, Baylor Univ Mus Fine Arts, Waco, Tex, numerous others. *Teaching:* Instr, Columbia Univ; instr, San Antonio Art Inst; instr, Tex Fine Arts Asn, Austin; prof art, Univ Tex, Austin, 51-86, prof emer, 86. *Awards:* Univ Tex Res Inst Grants, 64 & 65. *Mem:* Am Craftsmen Coun; Col Art Asn Am; Nat Educ Foundation. *Media:* Encaustic Painting. *Publ:* Auth, articles in, Ceramic Monthly, Sch Arts, Tex Trends Art Educ, La Rev Mod, Ceramic Age & Hellenic Chronicle. *Mailing Add:* 2203 Onion Creek Pkwy Unit 7 Austin TX 78747

HATKE, WALTER JOSEPH
PAINTER, EDUCATOR
b Topeka, Kans, Jan 11, 48. *Study:* Great Lakes Col Assoc Arts Prog, NY; 1st painting asst to Jack Beal, 69 & 72-73; DePauw Univ, BA, 71; asst to Alexander Calder, 74-76; Univ Iowa, Iowa City, MA, 81, MFA, 82. *Comn:* Mobile sets, Nat Tribute to Alexander Calder, Socrate NY, 77; Oil on Linen Portraits, (innovators: H Ford, T Edison, R Hull), Wilkes Univ, Wilkes Barre, Pa. *Exhib:* Solo exhibs, Swathmore Col, 84, DePauw Univ, 86, Robert Schoelkopf Gallery, NY, 77, 80, 83, 89 & Babcock Galleries, NY, 92 & 93; group exhibs, Am Realism traveling exhib, San Francisco Mus Mod Art, 86-87, Narrative Paintings & Sculpture, Nassau Co Mus Art, NY, 91, New Horizons in Am Realism, Flint Inst Arts, Mich, travel 91-92, Major Works, John Pence Gallery, San Francisco, 92 & The Artist as Native, traveling, 93-94; Am Drawings, Nat Acad of Design, NY, Travel 87-88; Gerald Peters Galleries, Santa Fe, 2002, NY, 2004; Disegno Nat Acad Design, NY, 2005. *Collection Arranged:* 1992 Mohawk (juror), Hudson Art Exhib, Albany Inst Art, Schenectady Mus & Planetarium, Univ Art Mus, State Univ NY-Albany. *Pos:* Asst to dir, Perls Galleries, New York, 73-77; vis artist/critic/lectr, Am Univ, Washington, DC, Dartmouth Col, Hanover, NH, Kansas City Art Inst, Smith Col, Northampton, Mass, Swarthmore Col, Pa; Yale Univ, New Haven, Conn. *Teaching:* Asst prof, Pa State Univ, 82-86; prof Fine Arts, Union Col, Schenectady, NY, 87-. *Awards:* Ingram Merrill Grant, 81; Nat Endowment Arts Fel, 85; Pa State Univ Res Initiation Grant, 85; Union Col Humanities Develop Grants, 87-2005; Painting Award, Am Acad Arts & Letters, 1990. *Bibliog:* John Russell (auth), The many faces of naturalism, New York Times, 8/11/80; John Arthur (auth), The Spirit of Place, Little Brown, 89; Alan Gussow (auth), The Artist as Native, Pomegranate, 93. *Mem:* Nat Acad, NYC. *Media:* Oil, Watercolor. *Specialty:* Am painting & Sculpture, 19th-21st century. *Interests:* Fishing, hiking, boating. *Publ:* Jordan Smith (auth), Upstate Diary, Gerald Peters Gallery. *Dealer:* Gerald Peters Galleries 24 E 78 NYC 10021 & 1011 Paseo de Peralto Santa Fe NM. *Mailing Add:* 1513 Lenox Rd Schenectady NY 12308-2005

HATTEN, THOMAS M See Kocot & Hatton

HATTON, JULIAN BURROUGHS, III
PAINTER
b Grand Haven, Mich, Dec 19, 56. *Study:* Harvard Col, BA, 79; NY Studio Sch Painting, Drawing & Sculpture, 80-82. *Work:* Hijirzaka Collection, Tokyo, Japan; IBJ Schroder Bank & Trust Co, NY; Brook Partners, Dallas. *Exhib:* Western Mich Collects, Hackley Mus Art, Muskegon, Mich, 86; one person exhibs, Conn Gallery,

Marlborough, 88, Elizabeth Harris Gallery, NY, 94, 96, 99, 2001 & 02, List Gallery, Swarthmore Col, Pa, 95 & Kara Wharton & Wharton Ltd, Dallas, 97; Elizabeth Harris Gallery, NY, 93, 97; R B Stevenson Gallery, Calif, 95 & 97; Am Painters and French Sculptors, Mus at Rochefort-en-Terre, France, 95; Field of Vision, Kendall Art & Design, NY, 97; Winter Group Show, R B Stevenson Gallery, La Jolla, Calif, 97; Elizabeth Harris Gallery, NY, 2006. *Pos:* Partner, Hatton-Berry Decorative Painting, 90-. *Awards:* Residency Fel, MacDowell Art Colony, fall 92; Visual Artists Grant in Painting, Nat Endowment Arts, 93-94; NY Found Arts Fel Painting, 98. *Bibliog:* Jude Schwendenwien (auth), Four views that connect, Hartford Courant, 8/2/93; Robert Edelman (auth), Landscape: seen & remembered, Orgn Independent Artists, 10/94; Jonathan Shimony (auth), New York art scene now, Art Vision Mag, Tokyo, autumn 94; David Ebony (auth), Review, Art in Am, 2/95. *Media:* Oil Paint. *Dealer:* Elizabeth Harris Gallery 529 W 20th St #6E New York NY 10011. *Mailing Add:* 489 Broome St New York NY 10013

HATTON AND KOCOT, MARCIA X See Kocot & Hatton

HAUER, ERWIN FRANZ
SCULPTOR, EDUCATOR
b Vienna, Austria, Jan 18, 26; citizen: Austria. *Study:* Acad Appl Arts, Vienna, Austria, dipl, 47-54; post grad studies with Marino Marini, Acad di Brera, Milan, Italy; with Gilbert Franklin, RI Sch Design; (US Dept State Fulbright travel grant), 55 & with Josef Albers, Yale Univ, 56-57. *Hon Degrees:* Yale Univ, Hon MFA, 87. *Work:* Chicago Art Inst; Kunsthaus, Basel, Switz; Wadsworth Atheneum, Hartford, Conn; Chase Manhattan Bank, NY; Benson Sculpture Park, Loveland, Colo, Brooklyn Mus Art, NY. *Comn:* Trellis wall, Nat Race Track, Caracas, Venezuela, 58; room divider, Showroom Knoll Int, Mex, 61; ceiling treatment, Imperial Can Bank Com, Montreal, Que, 63; wall treatment, Coca Cola Bldg, NY Worlds Fair, 64; E Pluribus Unum (sculpture), Super Ct Bldg, New London, Conn, 86. *Exhib:* One-man shows, Old Dominion Col, Norfolk, Va, 64, Am Mex Inst Cult Relations, Mexico City, 63, Yale Univ, 64, 65, Dartmouth Col, Hanover, NH, 76, Sindin Galleries, New York City, 77, Mid Hudson Arts and Sci Ctr, Poughkeepsie, NY, 81, Smithsonian Inst, 81, Univ Conn, Storrs, 81, Hartford Childrens Mus, 82, 1708 E Main St, Richmond, Va, 83, Nat Soaring Mus, Elmira, NY, 84; group shows, Vienna, Rome, Italy, Boston, Cleveland, Ann Arbor, Hartford, Manchester, NH, Yale Univ, Galerie Chalette, New York City, 61, 68, Sculptors Guild, New York City, 83, 84, Silvermine Collection, Westport, Conn, 84, Silo Gallery, New Milford, Conn, 84, Arrowwood, Purchase, NY; Reflections of the Inner Light, Lyman Allyn Mus, New London, Conn, 93; Vital Forms, Brooklyn Mus of Art, NY, 2001; San Diego Mus Art, 2002; Frist Ctr for Visual Arts, Nashville, 2002. *Teaching:* Prof sculptor, Yale Univ, New Haven, Conn, 57-60 & 63-90; artist in residence, Dartmouth Col, Hanover, NH, 76; vis critic sculpture, Univ Pa, 79-80. *Awards:* Ann Award, Indust Designers Inst Chicago, 59. *Bibliog:* Horacio Flores Sanchez (auth), La Escultura en la Construccion, Arquitectura, Mex, 9/57; Wilhelm Mrazek (auth), Modernes Mass & Gitterwerk, Alte und Moderne Kunst, Austria, 6/61; Karen O'Brien (auth), A Blurring of boundaries, Yale Scientific, 89. *Mem:* Sculptors Guild, NY; Int Soc Interdisciplinary Study Symmetry, Budapest, Hungary; Nat Acad, NY. *Media:* Plastic, Metal. *Publ:* Contribr, Olgyay and Olgyay: Solar Control & Shading Devices, Princeton Univ Press, 57; George Rickey: Constructivism Origins & Evolution, 68 & Jack Burnham: Beyond Modern Sculpture, 68, George Braziller; Senechal and Fleck: Shaping Space, A Polyhedral Approach, Birkhauser, 86; Zelanski and Fisher: Shaping Space, Harcourt, Brace, 87; auth, Princeton Architectural Press, NY, 2004. *Mailing Add:* 303 Wooding Hill Rd Bethany CT 06524

HAUFT, AMY
SCULPTOR
b Cincinnati, Ohio. *Study:* Univ Calif, Santa Cruz, BA, 80; Skowhegan Sch Painting & Sculpture, 81; Art Inst, Chicago, MFA, 83. *Comn:* Outdoor installation, Art Awareness, Lexington, NY, 87; outdoor installation, Art Park, Lewiston, NY, 88; outdoor installation, Pub Art Fund, Cadman Plaza Park, Brooklyn, NY, 93. *Exhib:* Working in Brooklyn-Installations, Brooklyn Mus, NY, 90; Int Artists' Mus, Lodz, Poland, 93; Disaster Plans: NY, Andrea Rosen Gallery, NY, 93; Counting To Infinity, Lipton & Owens Co, NY, 94; The Unreliable Narrator, Neuberger Mus, Purchase, NY, 95; Drawn & Quartered, Katonah Mus, NY, 96; If This Is True-Version 2, Derek Eller Gallery, NY, 98; Period Room: A Project By Amy Hauft (with catalog), Beaver Col Art Gallery, Glenside, Pa, 98; Working Knowledge, Am Acad, Rome, Italy, 99; When I say Marco You say Polo, Cooper Union, NY, 99; Spray Skirt in a folding field, Art Container project, NY, 2001, 2003; Biennial Exhib of Pub art, Neuberger Mus, Purchase NY, 2003. *Teaching:* Vis instr installation sculpture, Cal Arts, Los Angeles, 88; vis lectr sculpture, Princeton Univ, 89; Tyler sch Art, Philadelphia, 89-2004; Chair & prof, VA Common Wealth Univ, Richmond, 2004. *Awards:* Residency, Civitella Ranieri Found Fel, Italy, 95; Grant, NY Found Arts, 95; Philadelphia Exhibs Initiatives/PEW Charitable Trusts, 98; St Gaudens Memorial Fel, 99; NY Found Arts, 2002; and others. *Bibliog:* Charlotta Kotik (ed), Working in Brooklyn- Installations (exhib catalog), Brooklyn Mus, 90; Connie Butler (auth), Terrible Beauty & Enormity Space, Art & Text, 93; Eileen Neff (auth), Amy Hauft at Beaver College Art Gallery, Artforum,98; Richard Torchia (ed), Period Room; Projects by Amy Hauft (exhib catalog), Beaver Gallery, 99. *Media:* Installation Sculpture

HAUGHEY, JAMES M
PAINTER, CALLIGRAPHER
b Courtland, Kans, July 8, 14. *Study:* Univ Kans Sch Fine Art, 32-34; with Leroy Greene, 43-53. *Work:* Mont Inst Arts Permanent Collection & Yellowstone Art Mus, Billings, Mont; Mont Hist Soc Mus, Helena. *Exhib:* Am Watercolor Soc Ann Exhib, Nat Acad Galleries, NY, 61-80; Allied Artists Am, 63; Am Artists Prof League, various galleries, NY, 71-82; Rocky Mountain Watercolor Painters, 13 western states, 75; retrospective, Yellowstone Art Ctr, 80 & Watercolor West, 85. *Pos:* Pres, Yellowstone Art Ctr Found, 64-65 & Mont Inst Arts Found, 65-66. *Awards:* First Award Watercolor, Hockaday Ctr Arts, 73; Coun Am Artists Socs Award, Am Artists Prof League, 81; Governor's Award for Arts, 81. *Bibliog:* Dale A Burk (auth), The Element of Chance: James Haughey, New Interpretations, Western Life Publ, 69; Jeanne Rhodes (auth), James Haughey, The Arts in Mont, Mont Press Publ Co, 77; Weldon Blake (auth), James Haughey, Acrylic Watercolor Painting, Watson-Guptill. *Mem:* Am Watercolor Soc (vpres, 78-81); fel Am Artists Prof League; hon mem Kans Watercolor Soc; life mem Northwest Watercolor Soc; hon mem Mont Watercolor Soc; and others; Stillwater Soc. *Media:* Watercolor, Oil. *Publ:* Auth, Calligraphy: The gracile art, 67 & The arts in our society, 73, Mont Arts, Mont Inst Arts; The watercolor page, Am Artist, 80; The arts and the lawyer, Kansas Law Review, 81. *Mailing Add:* Crowley Haughey Hanson Toole & Dietrich TransWestern Plaza II 490 N 31 St Ste 500 Billings MT 59101-1256

HAUPTMAN, SUSAN
ILLUSTRATOR
b Detroit, Mich, 47. *Study:* Carnegie Inst Technol, Pittsburgh, Pa, 65-66; Univ Mich, Ann Arbor, BFA, 67-68; Wayne State Univ, Detroit, Mich, MFA, 69-70. *Work:* Corcoran Gallery Art, Washington, DC; Detroit Inst Art; Minn Mus Art, St Paul; Metrop Mus Art, NY; Oakland Mus, Calif; and others. *Exhib:* Drawing USA, Minn Mus Art, St Paul, 71, 73 & 75; 19th Drawing & Sculpture Exhib, Ball State Univ, Muncie, Ind, 73; solo exhibs, Jeremy Stone Gallery, San Francisco, 84, 89, Allan Stone Gallery, NY, 84, 88, Corcoran Gallery Art, Washington, DC, 90, Tatistcheff Gallery, Santa Monica, Calif, 92, Norton Gallery Art, West Palm Beach, Fla, 92, Tatistcheff & Co, NY, 93, Campbell-Thiebaud Gallery, San Francisco, 93, Tatistcheff/Rogers Gallery, Santa Monica, Calif, 96, Tatistcheff Gallery, NY, 96, Forum Gallery, NY, 99, 02, Ga Mus Art, Athens, 2000, Huntington Mus Art, WVa, 2000; Under the Influence: Mentors/Teachers/Colleagues, Tatistcheff Gallery, Santa Monica, Calif, 92; (Basically) Black & White, Riverside Art Mus, Calif, 92; The Female Nude in Western Art, Ind Univ Art Mus, Bloomington, 92; Nat Drawing Invitational, Ark Art Ctr, Little Rock, 94; Contemp Still Life, Contemp Art Ctr Va, Va Beach, 99; New Visions by Nine Contemp Women, Forum Gallery, NY, 99; Nude + Narrative, PPOW, New York City, 2000; Drawings, McNeese State Univ, Lake Charles, La, 01; Magic Vision, Ark Arts Ctr, Little Rock, 01-02; Dog Days of Summer, Savannah Col Art Design, Ga, 02; A Decade of Am Contemp Figurative Drawing, Frye Art Mus, Seattle, 02; New Generation of Magic Realists, Sangre de Cristo Art Ctr, Pueblo, Colo, 03; Transforming the Commonplace, Susquehanna Art Mus, Harrisburg, Pa, 03; Modern and Contemp Portraits curated by Townsend Wolfe, Forum Gallery, NY, 03; and others. *Collection Arranged:* Drawing USA, Minn Mus Art, St Paul, 71, 73 & 75; 19th Drawing & Sculpture Exhib, Ball State Univ, Muncie, Ind, 73; solo exhibs, Jeremy Stone Gallery, San Francisco, 84 & 89, Allan Stone Gallery, NY, 84 & 88, Corcoran Gallery Art, Washington, DC, 90, Tatistcheff Gallery, Santa Monica, Calif, 92, Norton Gallery Art, West Palm Beach, Fla, 92, Tatistcheff & Co, NY, 93 & Campbell-Thiebaud Gallery, San Francisco, 93, Tatistcheff/Rogers Gallery, Santa Monica, Calif, 96, Tatistcheff Gallery, NY, 96, Forum Gallery, NY, 99, Ga Mus Art, Athens, 2000, Huntington Mus Art, WVa, 2000; Under the Influence: Mentors/Teachers/Colleagues, Tatistcheff Gallery, Santa Monica, Calif, 92; (Basically) Black & White, Riverside Art Mus, Calif, 92; The Female Nude in Western Art, Ind Univ Art Mus, Bloomington, 92; Nat Drawing Invitational, Ark Art Ctr, Little Rock, 94. *Pos:* vis artist, St Lawrence Univ, Canton, NY, 74, Univ Calif, Davis, 85, Wayne State Univ, Detroit, Mich, 90, San Francisco Art Inst, 90, Anderson Ranch, Aspen, Colo, 95, Univ Calif, Santa Barbara, 96, Oreg Sch Arts and Crafts, 96, Harvard Univ, Cambridge, Mass, 97, 00-02. *Teaching:* instr, Univ Pittsburgh, Pa, 72-74; asst prof, Skidmore Univ, Saratoga Springs, NY, 74-78; Lamar Dodd prof chair, Univ Ga, Athens, 97-00. *Awards:* Nat Endowment Arts Fel Drawing, 85, 91; Art Matters Inc Grant, 89, 95; Visual Artist Fel, Calif Arts Coun, 90; Adolph and Esther Gottlieb Found Grant, 96; Elizabeth Found for the Arts Grant, 96; Pollock-Krasner Found Grant, 02. *Bibliog:* Jan Sjostrom (auth), Inner limits, Palm Beach Daily News, 5/4/92; Gary Schwan (auth), Art review, Palm Beach Post, 5/8/92; Helen L Kohen (auth), Art review, Miami Herald, 5/10/92. *Dealer:* Forum Gallery 745 Fifth Ave New York NY 10151. *Mailing Add:* 262 Mott St #324 New York NY 10012

HAUSEY, ROBERT MICHAEL
PAINTER
b Baton Rouge, La, Nov 25, 49. *Study:* La State Univ, BFA, 71; Univ Pa, MFA, 74; Skowhegan Sch Painting & Sculpture, 75. *Work:* La State Univ & City Nat Bank, Baton Rouge; West Baton Rouge Art Mus, Port Allen, La; Louisiana Nat Bank, Baton Rouge. *Exhib:* Robert Hausey & Chris Guarusco, Galerie Simonne Stern, New Orleans, La, 87; Landscape, Seascape, Cityscape, Contemp Art Ctr, New Orleans, 86; Southern Discomfort, Mint Mus, Charlotte, NC, 86; Southern Exposure, Alternative Mus, NY, 86; New Orleans Acad Art miniatures, 89; Cult Activities Ctr, Temple, Tex, 90; one-person shows, Arthur Roger Gallery, New Orleans, 91, Sylvia Schmidt Gallery, New Orleans, 92 & 94, Zigler Mus, Jennings, La, 92 & Cason Gallery, Baton Rouge, 93; and others. *Teaching:* Instr painting, Univ Tex, San Antonio, 76 & Sam Houston State Univ, 76-77; assoc prof, La State Univ, 77-90, prof, 90-; vis prof, Ohio Univ, 91. *Awards:* Merit Award, Birmingham Biennial, Birmingham Mus, 81; Jean Despuljols Award, Meadows Mus Biennial, 82; Nat Endowment Arts-Southeasten Ctr Contemp Arts Fel, 83-84. *Media:* Oil on Canvas, Watercolor. *Dealer:* Simms Fine Art 827 Girod St New Orleans La 70113. *Mailing Add:* 9498 Hooper Rd Baton Rouge LA 70818

HAUSMAN, FRED S
SCULPTOR, DESIGNER
b Bingen on Rhine, Ger, Apr 27, 21; US citizen. *Study:* Pratt Inst; New Sch Social Res, with Stuart Davis. *Work:* Emily Lowe Collection, Univ Miami; Mus Mod Art, Bogota, Colombia; Evansville Mus; Rutgers Univ; Fordham Univ. *Exhib:* NY Univ, 66; Contemp Art USA, Norfolk Mus, 67; Columbia Univ, 68; Black & White Show, Smithsonian Inst, 69-70; 2nd Biennial, Medellin, Colombia, 70. *Media:* Acrylic. *Dealer:* Bodley Gallery 1063 Madison Ave New York NY 10028. *Mailing Add:* 100 Pembroke Dr Stamford CT 06903-4214

HAUSMAN, JEROME JOSEPH
EDUCATOR
b New York, NY, May 4, 25. *Study:* Pratt Inst, 42-43; Cornell Univ, AB, 46; Columbia Univ, 47-48; Art Students League, 48; NY Univ, MA, 51, EdD, 54. *Pos:* Mem arts & humanities panel, US Off Educ, 64-70; ed bd, J Aesthetic Educ, 68-80; consult, John D Rockefeller III Fund, 69-75; pres, Minn Alliance Arts Educ, 77-79; bd dir, Arts, Educ & Americans, 79; bd trustees, Minn Mus Art, 79-82, Ragdale Found, 87- & Evanston Art Ctr, 93-2002; bd trustees, Chicago Artists Coalition, 2004-; bd trustees, Art Encounter, Evanston, Ill, 2005-. *Teaching:* Instr art, Elizabeth Pub Schs, NJ, 49-53; assoc prof, Sch Fine & Appl Arts, Ohio State Univ, 53-68, actg dir, 58-59, dir, 59-68; vis lectr, Sch Art, Syracuse Univ, 57; vis prof art educ, Pa State Univ, 58; prof div creative arts, NY Univ, 68-75; pres & prof, Minneapolis Col Art & Design, 75-82; acad vpres, Mass Col Art, 82-85, prof art, 82-85; dir, Ctr Curric Planning & Evaluation, Urban Gateways, Chicago, 86-95; vis prof, Dept Art, Univ Wis, Milwaukee, Art Inst Chicago & Northern Ill Univ. *Awards:* Art Educator Award, Nat Art Educ Asn, 86. *Mem:* Distinguished fel Nat Art Educ Asn, 84-; Nat Comn Art Educ (chmn); Am Soc Aesthetics; Western Arts Asn; Inst Study Art Educ. *Publ:* Ed, Research in Art Education (yearbk), Nat Art Educ Asn, 59; contribr, articles in prof journals; ed, Arts and the Schools, McGraw-Hill, 80; Art Education J Nat Art Educ Asn, 89. *Mailing Add:* 1501 Hinman Apt 4A Evanston IL 60201

HAUSRATH, JOAN W
PRINTMAKER, WEAVER
b Detroit, Mich, May 29, 42. *Study:* Bowling Green State Univ, Ohio, BS(educ), 64, MFA(printmaking), 66; Ohio State Univ, MA(art hist), 70. *Work:* Teradyne Inc, Nashua, NH; Nat Fire Prevention Agency, Quincy, Mass; Bowling Green State Univ, Ohio; Iceland Air, Reykjavik; Pub Libr, Plymouth, Mass. *Comn:* Fiber panel, Spaulding & Slye, Burlington, Mass; Sheraton Hotel, Tulsa, Okla; Magner-Harris, Atlanta, Ga. *Exhib:* Marietta Col Craft Nat, GM Hermann Art Ctr, Ohio, 80 & 81; solo exhibs, Signature Gallery, Boston, 82, Bridgewater State Col, 89 & 97; Am Crafts in Iceland, Kjarvalsstadir Mus, Reykjavik, 83. *Collection Arranged:* New Eng Fiber Arts, Newport Mus, RI, 85; Fiber, Atlanta Financial Ctr, 87; Monotype Guild New Eng, Fed Reserve Bank, Boston, 98. *Teaching:* Instr art hist, Ohio State Univ, Columbus, 70-71; prof art, Bridgewater State Col, Mass, 71-; craft instr weaving, Summer Workshops, Eastern Conn State Col, Willimantic, 79-81. *Awards:* Mass Artists Found Fel Crafts, 83; Bridgewater State Col CART Grant, 95 & 98. *Bibliog:* Roger Dunn (auth), The Ikats of Joan Hausrath, a painterly approach to weaving, Fiberarts Mag, 11-12/81. *Mem:* Monotype Guild New Eng; Boston Weavers' Guild. *Media:* Ikat, Monotypes. *Mailing Add:* Bridgewater State Col Dept Art Bridgewater MA 02325

HAUT, CLAIRE (JOAN)
PAINTER, GRAPHIC ARTIST
Study: Augustana Col; Am Acad Art, Chicago; Sch Design, Chicago, Lazlo Moholy-Nagy scholarship; Inst Design; also with Hin Bredendieck, John Kearney & Gyorgy Kepes. *Work:* Libr Cong, Washington, DC. *Comn:* Screen, woven and printed drapes, rug and upholstery, Teachers Rm & Home Econ Rm, Saarinens Crow Island Sch, Winnetka, Ill, 40; libr traveling display throughout S & Cent Am, Am Libr Asn, 40; and pvt comn. *Exhib:* One-man shows, Jonson Gallery, Univ NMex, 79, Artichoke Gallery, 80 & Balloon People, Go-Shoppe, 80 & 81, Albuquerque; Traveling Exhib, Works Progress Admin Crafts, Chicago Art Inst, Mus Mod Art, NY, Corcoran Mus, San Francisco Mus, Carnegie Inst, Mus St Louis & Toledo Mus; Contemp NMex Fine Art Invitational, Sweeney Ctr & Santa Fe Festival of Arts, 79; 18th Ann Nat Artists Salon, Okla Mus Art, 79; 20th Nat Sun Carnival Exhib, El Paso Mus, 78-79; Carlsbad Fine Arts Mus, NMex, 82; Fiesta Encantada Exhib, Albuquerque Mus, 82; Watercolor & Area Show, Albuquerque, 82; and others. *Pos:* Artist-designer, Experimental Design Workshop, Ill Art Project, Chicago, 39-42; art ed, Cudahy Packing Co, Chicago, 43-45; illusr, Sandia Labs, Albuquerque, 58-74. *Awards:* Pop Art Exhib First Prize, NMex Art League, 64; First Prize for Graphics, NMex State Fair Prof Artists Exhib, 67; First Purchase Prize for Crafts & Sculpture, Llano Estacado, 71; and others. *Mem:* Artists Equity (secy-treas, 73 & pres, 76, Albuquerque Chap); Albuquerque Designer Craftsmen; Nat League Am Pen Women (pres, Manzanita Br, 70-72, state chmn, Biennial Exhib, 75-76); NMex Art League. *Media:* Acrylic, Watercolor

HAVEL, JOSEPH G
SCULPTOR
b Minneapolis, Minn, Aug 20, 54. *Study:* Univ Minn, BFA, 76; Pa State Univ, MFA, 79. *Work:* Mus Fine Art, Houston; Dallas Mus Art; The Barrett Collection, Dallas. *Exhib:* Solo exhibs, A Century of Texas, Sculpture, Huntington Gallery, Austin, 89, Barry Whistler Gallery, Dallas, Tex, 91, Davis/McClain Gallery, Houston, Tex, 92, Linda Farris Gallery, Seattle, Wash, 92. *Teaching:* Assoc dir, Glassell Sch Art, Houston. *Awards:* Nat Endowment Visual Arts Fel, 86; Otis & Velma Dozier Travel Grant, Dallas Mus Art, 91. *Bibliog:* Joan Davidow (auth), Balancing act, Detour Mag, 3/90; Elizabeth McBride (auth), Multiples, Art News, 5/90; Don Bacigulup (auth), Houston Contemp Mag, 9/89; Susan Chadwick (auth), Sculpting with poetic license, Houston Post, 7/89; Patricia Johnson (auth), Introductions gains strength, Houston Post, 7/89. *Media:* Miscellaneous. *Mailing Add:* 515 W 18th St Houston TX 77008-3607

HAVELOCK, CHRISTINE MITCHELL
HISTORIAN, EDUCATOR
b Cochrane, Ont, June 2, 24; US citizen. *Study:* Univ Toronto, AB; Radcliffe Col, AM; Harvard Univ, PhD(Charles Eliot Norton Fel, Am Asn Univ Women Fel), 58. *Pos:* Chairperson art, M C Mellon, 85-90. *Teaching:* Prof art hist, Vassar Col, 53-90, cur classical collection, formerly. *Awards:* Radcliffe Grad Medal, 87; Fel, Col Teachers, Nat Endowment Humanities, 86. *Res:* Greek sculpture of Hellenistic period. *Publ:* Auth, Hellenistic Art, W W Norton, rev ed 81; The Aphrodite of Knidos and Her Successors: A Historical Review of the Female Nude in Greek Art, 95. *Mailing Add:* 1010 Waltham St Lexington MA 02421

HAVENS, JAN
SCULPTOR, PRINTMAKER
b Norfolk, Va. *Study:* Atlantic Christian Col, BS, 70; Peabody Col, Vanderbilt Univ, Nashville, Tenn, MA, 73. *Work:* Tenn Botanical Garden & Fine Arts Ctr, Nashville; Dirkson Senate Office Bldg, Washington, DC; Appalachian Cult Ctr, Boone, NC; Radio City Music Hall Golden Jubilee, NY; Hanes Collection, Winston-Salem, NC. *Comn:* Sculpture, Radio City Music Hall, NY, comn by, Governor Alexander, Nashville, Tenn, 81. *Exhib:* Solo exhibs, Cheekwood Botanical Gardens, Nashville, 80, Tenn Botanical Garden & Fine Art Ctr, Nashville, 81, Southeast Ctr Contemp Art, Winston-Salem, NC, 83 & Zimmerman/Saturn Gallery, Nashville, Tenn, 91; The Animal Image: Contemp Objects and the Beast, Renwick Gallery, Smithsonian Inst, Washington, DC, 81; Images of Faith III, Blue Spiral Gallery, Ashville, NC, 93; Printmaking: Image and Technique, AVA Gallery, Chattanooga, Tenn, 98; Best of Tennessee Crafts, TACA Biennial, Nashville, Tenn, 98; Power of Excellence, Southeastern Ctr Contemp Art, NC, 2004. *Bibliog:* Virginia Watson-Jones (auth), Contemporary American Women Sculptors, Oryx Press, 86; The Crafts Report, 1/87; Cecelia Tichi (auth), Electronic Hearth: Creating an American Television Culture, Oxford Univ Press, 91. *Mem:* Kent Guild Artists & Craftsmen; Tenn Artist-Craftsmen's Asn; Southern Highland Guild; Piedmont Craftsmen; Carolina Designer Craftsmen. *Media:* Clay; Etching. *Mailing Add:* 1121 Graybar Ln Nashville TN 37204

HAVERTY, GRACE
PAINTER
b Brooklyn, NY. *Study:* Am Acad Art, Chicago; Col Du Page, Glen Ellen, Ill, 70-89. *Work:* Du Page Libr System, Geneva, Ill; Sandburg Sch, Wheaton, Ill. *Exhib:* Catherine Lorillard Art Club 101st Ann Exhib, 97; Arizona Watercolor Soc, 2000; Ariz Watercolor Asn Mem Exhib, 2002-03; Western Fed Watercolors 27th Ann Exhib, 2002; Ariz Aqueous XVIII Nat Exhib, 2003-05; Rocky Mt Nat Watermedia Exhib, Golden Colo, 2004; Transparent Watercolor Soc Am, 96, 2003-2004. *Teaching:* Watercolor, Pastel & Sketching. *Awards:* Pastel Soc Am Award, NY, 88, 93, 95, 96 & 2000; Honorable Mention, Int Asn Pastel Soc, Santa Fe, 2001; Best of Show, Honorable Mention, Ariz Watercolor Asn, 2004; Best of Show, Contemp Watercolor Asn, 2006. *Bibliog:* O'Toole & Triner (auths), Profile of an Artist, DuPage Arts Life, Ill Benedictine Col, 92. *Mem:* Ariz Watercolor Asn; signature mem Midwest Pastel Soc; master pastelist and signature mem, Pastel Soc Am; signature mem, Transparent Watercolor Soc Am, Ariz Watercolor Asn; Knicbocker Artists. *Media:* Pastel, Watercolor, Oil. *Publ:* The Best of Pastel 2, Rockport Publ; The Best of Watercolor, Vol 3, Rockport Publ; Pushing the Limits of Pastels, Artist Mag, 10/2000; Pastel Artists Int Mag, 11/2000; Pushing the Limits of Pastel, Artist's Amg, 10/2000; 100 Ways to Paint Still Life, Artist Publ, 11/2000 & 1/2001; Sketches of LIfe, Artist's Sketchbook, fall 2001; Uninhibited Watercolors, Watercolor Mag, summer 2006. *Mailing Add:* 11795 N 95th St Scottsdale AZ 85260

HAWKES, ELIZABETH H
CURATOR, CONSULTANT
b Wilmington, Del, Aug 12, 43. *Study:* Mary Washington Col, BA, 65; Univ Del, MA, 69. *Collection Arranged:* American Painting and Sculpture (auth, catalog), 75; Bertha Corson Day Bates (auth, catalog), 78; City Life Illustrated (auth, catalog), 80; New York: New Work (auth, catalog), 86; Howard Pyle: The Artist & His Legacy (contribr, catalog), 87; John Sloan: Spectator of Life (coauth, catalog), 88. *Pos:* Asst cur, Del Art Mus, 69-79, cur, John Sloan Collection, 77-90, actg cur mus, 80-81, assoc cur, 81-90, independent cur, 90-. *Mem:* Asn Am Mus. *Publ:* John Sloan's Illustrations, 92, Del Art Mus & John Sloan's Newspaper Career, Proceedings of the Am Antiquarian Soc, 95; contrib, Vision of Adventure: NC Wyeth and the Brandy Wine, artists, 2000; contrib, John W McCor, American Painter, 2001; contrib, The Sewell C Biggs Collection of American Art, 2002. *Mailing Add:* 715 N Creek Rd West Chester PA 19380

HAWKINS, MARGARET
CRITIC, EDUCATOR. WRITER
Teaching: Teacher, Sch of the Art Instit, Chicago. *Mem:* Chicago Art Critics Asn. *Publ:* Contribr weekly column in the Chicago Sun Times; Chicago Corr, ARTnews; contribr articles to a number of other nat and local art publ. *Mailing Add:* 1835 Old Briar Rd Highland Park IL 60035

HAWKINS, MYRTLE H
PAINTER, WRITER
b Merrit, BC. *Study:* Harnell Col, AA; San Jose State Univ; Univ Calif; WValley Col; also with Marshall Merrit, Maynard Stewart & Thomas Leighton. *Work:* Nat Easter Seal Soc, Chicago. *Comn:* Portrait, Rev John Foster, First Congregational Church, San Jose, Calif, 70; portrait, Rose Shenson, Triton Mus, Santa Clara, Calif, 71. *Exhib:* De

Saisset Gallery, Santa Clara, 68; Hartnell Col, 69; one-man shows, Triton Mus Art, 71 & Rosicrucian Mus Art, San Jose, 73 & 77; Am Artist Prof League Nat Exhib, Lever House, NY, 71. *Pos:* Judge & juror of many art shows. *Teaching:* Instr painting, Calif State Dept Vocational Rehab, San Jose & Palo Alto, 69-71; also pvt painting lessons. *Awards:* First Place, Nat Easter Seal Soc, Chicago, 65; Gold Seal Award, de Saisset Art Gallery, 66; Best of Show, St Mark's Art Ann, Santa Clara, 68. *Bibliog:* Article, Rosicrucian Digest, 11/73; article, Grit, 8/28/77; Directory of American Portrait Artists, 8/85; Little Known Women: Twenty Extraordinary Achievers, 10/87. *Mem:* Encaustics Network Unlimited; Gualala Art Asn; Triton Mus Art. *Media:* Pastel, Oil. *Publ:* Illusr, The Adventures of Mimi, Books I & II, 66; auth, Art as Therapy, Recreation and Rehabilitation for the Handicapped, 74. *Mailing Add:* 646 Bucher Ave Santa Clara CA 95051

HAWKINS, THOMAS WILSON, JR
PAINTER, INSTRUCTOR
b Los Angeles, Calif, 41. *Study:* Pasadena City Col, AA, Calif State Univ, Long Beach, BA(design) & MA(drawing, painting); Calif State Univ, Los Angeles, art hist, design & ceramics. *Work:* Overholt & Overholt Law Off, Los Angeles; Home Savings & Loan Art Collection; Dr Clinton Roath, Diana Roath Collection; Roath Collection. *Exhib:* Southern Calif Expos, Del Mar, 67-77; Inland Exhibs, 68-77; Butler Inst Am Art, Youngstown, Ohio, 70; DaVinci Open Art Competition, NY, 70; Bertrand Russell Centenary Art Exhib, London & Nottingham, Eng, 73; and others. *Teaching:* Instr drawing & design & introd to art, painting, Rio Hondo Community Col, Whittier, Calif, 67-; instr art, drawing & art hist, Long Beach City Col, 67-72; instr painting, Golden West Col, Huntington Beach, Calif, 72-78; Rio Hondo Col, currently, printing art 135, 136, 235, 236, col art courses; instr painting (part-time), Tencoed, 1974, CSC, 1979. *Awards:* Best Painting, Art in All Media, Southern Calif Expos, 67, Third Prize, 70; Second Award, Inland Exhib, San Bernardino Art Asn, 71 & 73; Purchase Award 25th All City Los Angeles Art, Barnsdall, 77; Whittier Art Asn, 2006. *Mem:* Whittier Art Asn; Nat Educ Asn; Calif Teachers Asn. *Media:* Oil. *Res:* Florence, Italy, Alaska. *Interests:* Painting backyard, landscape, still-life. *Collection:* Dr Clinton Roath Art. *Publ:* Lecture Outline Notes for Art 101, LCC 93, TX3-611-938, edits 2 & 3. *Mailing Add:* 414 Fairview Ave Arcadia CA 91007

HAWKINSON, TIM
SCULPTOR
b San Francisco, Calif, 60. *Study:* San Jose State Univ; Univ Calif, Los Angeles, MFA, 89. *Work:* Egg, 97; Bird, 97; Shatter, 98; Aerial Mobile, 98; Pentecost, 99; Bear, Univ Calif, San Diego, Stuart Collection, 2005; Uberorgan, Mass Mus Contemp Art. *Exhib:* Venice Biennale, 99; Mass Mus Contemp Art, 2000; Power Plant, Toronto, Can, 2000; Whitney Biennial, 2002; Corcoran Biennial, Washington, DC, 2003; Akira Ikeda Gallery, Japan; Serpentine Gallery, London; Cartier Found, Paris. *Mailing Add:* c/o Stuart Collection 0010 U Calif San Diego 9500 Gilman Dr La Jolla CA 92093-0010

HAWLEY, ANNE
MUSEUM DIRECTOR
b Iowa City, Iowa, Nov 3, 43. *Study:* Univ Iowa, BA, 66; George Washington Univ, MA, 69; Sr Exec Prog, Kennedy Sch Govt; Lesley Col, DLett, 87, Babson Col, 90; Williams Col, LHD, 89. *Pos:* Exec dir, Cult Educ Collab, 74-77 & Mass Coun Arts/Humanities, 77-89; dir, Isabella Stewart Gardener Mus, 89-. *Awards:* Lyman-Ziegler Award; Polaroid Travel Grant; Fullbright Fel. *Mem:* Am Asn Mod Dirs; Mass Hist Soc; Saturday Club; Save Venice; Inst Contemp Arts (bd overseers). *Publ:* Contribr, Economics of Art Museums, 91. *Mailing Add:* Isabella Stewart Gardner Mus 2 Palace Rd Boston MA 02115-5807

HAXTON, DAVID
PHOTOGRAPHER, FILMMAKER
b Indianapolis, Ind, Jan 6, 43. *Study:* Univ SFla, BA, 65; Univ Mich, MFA, 67. *Exhib:* Two-person show, Whitney Mus Am Art, NY, 78 & Biennial Exhib, 79; Cineprobe, Mus Mod Art, NY, 78; Photog in the 70's, Art Inst Chicago, 79; one-man show, Sonnabend Gallery, NY, 79 & 83; Whitney Biennial Exhib, 79, 86; Recent Color, San Francisco Mus Art, 83; This Is Not A Photograph, Ringling Mus, Sarasota, Fla, 88; Siggraph Electronic Theater, Chicago, Ill, 92; Cimemateque Francaise, Un Cabinet D'Amateurs, Paris, France, 95; Ikon Gallery, 2001; Siggraph Art Show, Los Angeles, 2001; True Fictions, Kunstverein Dresden, Ger, 2002; Stadtische Galerie Erlangen, Ger, 2003; Constructed Realitites, Orlando Mus Art, 2003; True Fictions, Stadtmus, Hofheim a, Taunus, Ger, 2004. *Collection Arranged:* Whitney Mus Am Art, Mus Mod Art, NY; Denver Mus Art; Albright-Knox Gallery, Buffalo, NY; Australian Mus Art; Univ SFla Art Mus, Tampa. *Teaching:* Instr art, San Diego State Univ, 69-72; computer graphics, William Paterson Col, Wayne, NJ, formerly; prof art, Univ Cent Fla, 95-. *Awards:* Caps grant for filmmaking, NY State Coun for the Arts, 77-78; fel in film, Nat Endowment for the Arts, 78-79; fel in photog, NEA, 79-80. *Bibliog:* David Shapiro (auth), Inner city, Camera Arts, 1-2/82; Gene Markowski (auth), The Art of Photography, Prentice Hall, 84, Art and Photography, David Campany, 2003; Gary Kolb (auth), Photographing in the Studio, Brown & Bengamark, 93. *Media:* Photographs. *Dealer:* Cinedoc Paris 18 Rue Montmartre 75001 Paris France. *Mailing Add:* 2036 Sharon Rd Winter Park FL 32789-1517

HAY, A JOHN
HISTORIAN, EDUCATOR
b Penang, Malaysia, May 9, 38; Brit citizen. *Study:* Exeter Col, Oxford Univ, BA, 61; Princeton Univ, PhD, 78. *Teaching:* Asst prof Asian art hist, Univ Denver, 76-77; from asst prof Chinese art hist to assoc prof, Harvard Univ, 77-84; assoc prof, Inst Fine Arts, NY Univ, 84-. *Res:* Chinese art, especially painting. *Publ:* Auth, The human body as a microcosmic source of macrocosmic values in calligraphy, Bush, Theories of Arts in China, 83; Values and history of Chinese painting I and II, RES 6, 83-84; Surface and the Chinese painter, Archives of Asian Art, 85; Kernels of Energy, Bones of Earth: The Rock in Chinese Art, China Inst, NY, 85. *Mailing Add:* Inst Fine Arts New York Univ One E 78th St New York NY 10021-0178

HAY, ALEX
PAINTER, SCULPTOR
b Fla, 30. *Work:* Whitney Biennial, Whitney Mus Am Art, 2004. *Exhib:* Exhibs incl Work From the 60's, Peter Freeman, New York City, 2002. *Pos:* Retired from art world, 69; artist, 2003-. *Mailing Add:* c/o Whitney Mus Am Art 945 Madison Ave New York NY 10021

HAY, (GEORGE) AUSTIN
PAINTER, FILMMAKER
b Johnstown, Pa, Dec 25, 1915. *Study:* Pa Acad Fine Arts; Art Students League; Nat Acad; Univ Rochester; Univ Pittsburgh, BS & MLitt; Columbia Univ, MA; also with Robert Brackman & Dong Kingman. *Work:* Pub Libr, Metrop Mus Art, NY; Dept Army; Libr Cong, Washington, DC; NY Pub Libr; numerous pvt collections. *Exhib:* Carnegie Inst, Pittsburgh, 72; Duncan Galleries, NY, 73; Manufacturers Hanover Trust, 73; Bicentennial Exhib of Am Painters in Paris, 76; Watergate Gallery, Washington, DC, 81; Salon des Nations, Paris, 83. *Pos:* multimedia specialist, US Govt, 55-. *Awards:* Documentary Award, Int Film Festival, Zagreb, Yugoslavia, 75; Academy Gold Medal, Accademia Italia, 80; Pictorial Award, Smithsonian Inst, 82. *Bibliog:* subject, Speak for Yourself (film), 90. *Mem:* Am Artists Prof League; Allied Artists Am; Nat Soc Arts & Lett; Nat Acad Television Arts & Sci; Washington Film Coun. *Media:* Oil, Miscellaneous Media. *Res:* The life & work of American artists William Merritt Chase & Robert Henri. *Publ:* Auth & illusr, Seven Hops to Australia, 45; Life About the Universe (television prog), Nat Coun of Churches, 65; The Performing Arts Experience, 69; auth & dir, Visit to the Museum of Modern Art (film), 72; dir, Highways of History (film depicting 100 oil paintings), 76. *Dealer:* Arts Club Galleries 2017 Eye St NW Washington DC 20006. *Mailing Add:* 2022 Columbia Rd NW Washington DC 20009-1314

HAY, DICK
SCULPTOR, EDUCATOR
b Cincinnati, Ohio, Nov 19, 42. *Study:* Ohio Univ, BFA; NY State Col Ceramics, Alfred Univ, MFA. *Work:* Butler Inst Am Art, Youngstown, Ohio; Latvia Art Mus, Riga; Sea of Japan, Kanazawa-shi, Japan; Pushkin Mus, Moscow; Won-Kwang Univ, Chun-Bok, Korea. *Exhib:* Contemp Ceramic Sculpture, Univ NC, Chapel Hill, 77; Nat Clay, Univ Hartford, Conn, 81; The Art of Ceramics, Paducah Gallery, Ky, 89; Maj Artists, Ctr for Arts, Phoenix, Ariz, 91; Am Exhib, Latvia Art Mus, Riga, 91; Int Invitational Exhib, Seoul, Korea, 95; and over 250 others. *Teaching:* Prof art/ceramics, Ind State Univ, Terre Haute, 66-; guest lectr, Sheridan Col Appl Arts, Toronto, Ont, 74, La State Univ, 76, Univ Miami, 76, Col Santa Fe, 77, Princeton Univ, 79, Ga State Univ, 83, NDak State Univ, 85, Alfred Univ, 86 & Buffalo State Univ, 90, Dzintari Inst Art, Jurmala, Latvia, 91, Muju Int Art Symposium, Korea, 95 and over 230 others. *Awards:* Nat Coun Educ Ceramic Arts Fel; Distinguished Teaching Award, Ind State Univ; Lifetime Achievement Award, Nat Council Educ Ceramic Arts. *Mem:* Nat Coun Educ Ceramic Arts (pres, 78-80). *Media:* Clay. *Dealer:* Martha Schneider Gallery Inc Chicago IL; Signature Gallery Boston MA. *Mailing Add:* 2108 W 340 Brazil IN 47834

HAY, IKE
SCULPTOR, EDUCATOR
b Atlanta, Ga, Apr 28, 44. *Study:* Univ Ga, BFA & MFA. *Work:* Indianapolis Mus Art; New Orleans Mus Art; Mint Mus Art, Charlotte, NC; Chancellor's off, Pa Univ System, Harrisburg; State Mus Pa, Harrisburg; and others. *Comn:* Hines Industrial Develop Corp, Tulsa, 83; Reading Redevlopment Authority Ctr Park Place, Reading, Pa, 86; Harrisburg/Dauphin Co, 86; Rouse & Assoc, Univ Place, Tampa, Fla, 88; Environ Compliance Servs Corp, Exton, Pa, 92. *Exhib:* High Mus Art, 69; one-man shows, New Orleans Mus Art, 69 & Franklin & Marshall Col, 81; Nat Sculpture 73 traveling show, 73; Pa State Mus, Harrisburg, Pa, 79; PSEA, State Mus Pa, 84; Invitational, Messah Col, Grantham, Pa, currently. *Pos:* Nat Endowment artist-in-residence, Decatur, 74-75. *Teaching:* Asst prof sculpture, Purdue Univ, West Lafayette, 69-74; asst prof sculpture, Millersville Univ, Pa, 75-81, assoc prof, 81-95, prof, 95-. *Awards:* Rosenblatt Scholarship, Univ Ga, 68; Grant in Aid, Arts Festival Atlanta, 68; Fac Grant, Purdue Univ, 70. *Bibliog:* John Spofforth (auth), The Ike Hay workshop, Ala-Arts, Ala State Arts Coun, 74. *Mem:* Am Asn Univ Prof; Napoleonic Soc Am (bd mem, currently); fel Int Napoleonic Soc. *Media:* Steel, Bronze. *Mailing Add:* 3200 Blue Rock Rd Lancaster PA 17603-9451

HAYES, CAROLYN HENDRICK
PAINTER, SCULPTOR
b Green Valley, Ill, Nov 25, 25. *Study:* MacMurray Col, Jacksonville, Ill, AB (painting), 47; Univ Iowa, 48; Colo Springs Sch Fine Arts, 48; Univ Colo, studied with James Guy, Ricardo Martinez, James Pinto, Clifford Still, Richard Diebenkorn & Joan Brown, 56, 60 & 64; Univ Ill, 56; Cranbrook Acad Art, 60; Instituto Allende, San Miguel Allende, Mex, MFA (painting), 68. *Work:* Ill State Mus, Springfield; Yugoslavian Mus Solidarity, Montenegro; Peruvian Mus Collection, Lima; Instituto Mexicanonorteamericano, Mex; Galeria Libertad, Quertaro, Mex. *Comn:* Sagrado Corazon de Jesus (drawing), Munic Govt, San Miguel, Mex, 92. *Exhib:* Six States Exhibit, Joselyn Mem Art Mus, Omaha, Nebr, 48; Northen Miss Arts Exhibit, Ill State Mus, Springfield, 60, 61, 81; Northern Mirrijoyi Exhib, Springfield, IN, 60,61,66,68,71; Peoria Area Art Show, Peoria Art Mus, Ill, 66; Mac Allen Art Mus, 81; Havana Gallery, Cuba, 96; one-woman show, IL State Mus, 74-75, Una Danza de Colores Geom, Museo de Universidad de Puebla, Mex, 83-84, Fiesta de Colores

Geometrico, Diego Rivera Mus, Gto, Mex, 83, Humanidad del Arte Moderno, Casa de La Cultura, San Luis Potosi, Mex, 97, Technica Mixta, Instituto Nat Bellas Artes, San Miguel Allende, Mex, 99, Casa Diana Exhib, San Miguel Allende, Mex 2003, Kunsthaus Exhib, 2005, Ra Luz Sala de Arte, Mex, 2006. *Pos:* head art dept, Ill State Lib, Springfield, 56-60; head art, music & drama, Flint Pub Libr, Mich, 61-63. *Teaching:* instr art, Peoria Pub Schs, Ill, 51-52. *Awards:* Instituto Allende Award for contribution to art, 2001. *Bibliog:* Robert Evans (auth), Carolyn Hayes, State IL, 74: Robert Somerlott (auth), Art of Carolyn Hayes, Inst Allende, 97; Ana Quiroz (auth), Carolyn Hayes-Culturas Cruzadas, Kuns thaus Publ Mex, 2000. *Media:* Acrylic, Sand; Wood, Plastic. *Interests:* write poetry, Travel, photogr, ballet, film, theater, latin music. *Publ:* Picasso and the library, 58; Experiment with art, 59, IL Librs; Ink Drawings, 94, Illustrations of my original paintings, 98 & illustration of my original painting and poem, 2000, O'Zone. *Dealer:* San Francisco 11 Apartado 552 San Miguel Allende Guanajuato Mex 37700. *Mailing Add:* Apartado 678 San Miguel Allende Guanajuato Mexico 37700

HAYES, DAVID VINCENT
SCULPTOR
b Hartford, Conn, Mar 15, 31. *Study:* Univ Notre Dame, AB; Ind Univ, sculpture with David Smith, MFA. *Work:* Mus Mod Art, Brooklyn Mus, Guggenheim Mus, NY; Mus Arts Decoratif, Paris; Mus Fine Arts, Houston. *Comn:* Ceramics, walls, De Porceleyne Fles, Delft, Holland, 67, Lee Kolker, Stanfordville, NY, 70 & Elmira Col, 71, mural, Great Southwest Corp, Atlanta, Ga, 68 & relief, comn by David Anderson, Ardsley, NY, 69. *Exhib:* Salon Mai, Mus Art Mod, Paris, 66; Jewelry 71, Art Gallery Ont, 71; State Univ NY, Albany, 78, Dartmouth Col, NH, 78, Amherst Col, Mass, 79, Nassau Co Mus, Port Washington, NY, 79 & Univ Conn, Storrs, 79; and others. *Teaching:* Vis artist, Carpenter Art Ctr, Harvard Univ, 72. *Awards:* Fulbright Res Grant, 61; Guggenheim Found Fel, 61; Nat Inst Arts & Lett Award, 64. *Media:* Metal, Ceramics. *Mailing Add:* PO Box 509 Coventry CT 06238

HAYES, GERALD
PAINTER, PHOTOGRAPHER
b Los Angeles, Calif, Apr 9, 40. *Study:* Auburn Univ, BVA, 62; Univ Ill, MFA, 66. *Work:* Art Ctr Am, Englishtown, NJ; AT&T, Liberty Corner, NJ; Huntsville Mus Art, Ala; Mobile Mus Art, Ala; Stockton State Col, Pomona, NJ; Addison Gallery of Art, Phillips Acad, Andover, MA. *Exhib:* Elements of Art, Mus Fine Art, Boston, 71; Tondos & Squares; Newcastle Salutes NY, Polytech Art Gallery, Eng, 83; Small Scale Abstraction, Grace Borgenicht Gallery, 86; Impact, Fine Arts Mus S Mobile, Ala, 95; Photographism in Painting, Pratt Manhattan Gallery, NY, 96; solo exhibs, Harm Bouckaert Gallery, NY, 82, Calkins Gallery, Hofstra Univ, NY, 90, Stockton State Col, Pomona, NJ, 90, Drawings after the Arcade, Southern Cross Univ Art Mus, Lismore, NSW, Australia, 96 & Southern Queensland Mus, 97, Abstraction INDEX, Condesco/Lawler Gallery, NY, 97, Signature Painting, Gallery Korea, NY, 98, Reconstructing Abstraction, Mitchell Algus Gallery, NY, 2000. *Teaching:* Prof grad art, Pratt Inst, 71-83, chmn painting & drawing, 83-85, asst chmn fine arts, 92-; vis prof painting, Parsons Sch Design, 81-83; prof, asst chmn fine arts, Pratt Inst, 92-. *Awards:* Pollock-Krasner Found Grant, 2002. *Bibliog:* Virginia Gunter (auth), Gerald Hayes: The Creativity of the Psychological Eye, Artforum, 5/73; Robert Pincus-Witten (auth), Entries: Styles of Artists and Critics, Arts Mag, 11/79; Mario Naves (auth), Studio View, New Art Examiner, summer 93; Saul Ostrow (auth), Gerald Hayes, Tema Celeste Art Review, 6/93. *Mem:* Col Art Asn, NY. *Dealer:* Mitchell Algus Gallery. *Mailing Add:* PO Box 305 Swampscott MA 01907-3305

HAYES, LAURA M
DEALER, HISTORIAN
b Birmingham, Ala, Nov 28, 27. *Study:* Univ Wyo. *Pos:* Head photog section, Wyo State Art Gallery, 65-74, art registrar, 67-71, curator art, 71-79; owner, Wild Goose Gallery, Cheyenne, Wyo. *Mem:* Wyo Press Women; Nat Fedn Press Women; and others. *Media:* Watercolor. *Specialty:* Original Works of Art & Limited Edition prints, work for collectors

HAYES, RANDY (RANDOLPH) ALAN
PAINTER
b Jackson, Miss, June 11, 44. *Study:* Rhodes Col, Memphis, Tenn, 62-65; Memphis Col Arts Acad Arts, BFA(Ford Found Grant), 68; Univ Ore, Eugene, 68. *Work:* Laguna Beach Mus Art, Calif; Seattle Art Mus; City Seattle One Percent for Art; Wash State One Percent for Art, Olympia; Mississippi Mus Arts; Microsoft Corp, Redmond, Wash. *Comn:* Murals, Seattle Ctr, 83 & State of Wash, Monroe, 83; Port Seattle Hqs, Wash, 92. *Exhib:* Outside NY: Seattle, The New Mus, NY, 83 & Seattle Art Mus, 83; solo exhib, Linda Farris Gallery, Seattle, 84; Setting the Stage, Los Angeles Co Mus Art; Scapes, Univ Calif Art Mus, Santa Barbara; Linda Farris Gallery, Seattle, Wash, 86; Cheney Cowles Mus, Spokane, Wash, 92; G Gibson Gallery, Seattle, 94; Comus Gallery, Portland, 94. *Awards:* WGBH New TV Workshop Grant, Boston, 75; Visual Arts Award, Mississippi Inst Arts & Letters, Jackson, 90. *Bibliog:* Regina Hackett (auth), Seattle artists come home in New York show, Seattle Post-Intelligencer, 10/20/83; Lynn Smallwood (auth), Seattle art from New York City, The Weekly, 10/26/83; Bruce Guenther (auth), 50 Northwest Artists, Chronicle Bks, 83; Lynn Smallwood (auth), Randy Hayes, Art News, 5/1/86; Bill Berkson (auth), Report From Seattle, Art in Am, 86. *Media:* Pastels, Oils. *Mailing Add:* 5810 Cowen Place Apt 306 Seattle WA 98105

HAYES, TUA
PAINTER
b Anniston, Ala. *Study:* Converse Col, BA; Columbia Univ Teacher's Col; also with Henry Lee McFee. *Work:* Del Art Mus, Wilmington; Wilmington Trust Co; Univ Del; Blount Collection; Converse Col, Spartanburg, SC; and others. *Exhib:* Philadelphia Pro-Show, Pa, 67; Nat Acad Design, NY, 70; Baltimore Mus Regional Show, Md; Am Drawings 1976, Portsmouth, Va; Distinguished Mid-Atlantic Artists, Univ Del, 80; Del Ctr Contmep Art, 83; and other group and one-man shows. *Awards:* First Prize for Drawing, Del Art Mus, 67; Second Prize, Asn Community Art Ctrs, Philadelphia, 82; First Prize, Hercules Expo, 82. *Mem:* Philadelphia Art Alliance; Studio Group, Inc (pres, 54-56); Del Art Mus (bd dir, 62-80); Hilton Head Art League; Delaware Ctr Contemp Arts. *Media:* Oil, Watercolor. *Dealer:* Red Piano Art Gallery 220 Cordillo Pkwy Hilton Head Island SC 29928. *Mailing Add:* c/o Carspecken-Scott Gallery 1707 N Lincoln St Wilmington DE 19806-2390

HAYNES, DAVID
HISTORIAN, CONSULTANT
b Washington, DC, Jan 13, 42. *Study:* Univ Tex Austin, BJ, 63, BA, 64 & MA, 69. *Mem:* Daguerreian Soc. *Res:* 19th century Texas photography and photographers. *Publ:* Auth, Descriptive catalog of filmic items in Gernsheim Collection, Performing Arts Res, 75; Conservation of historic photographs, Proc Mt Plains Mus, 79; Where did you find that one?, Photogrs, 91; Catching Shadows: Directory of 19th Century Texas Photography, Tex State Hist Asn, 93; Photography, New Handbk Tex, 96. *Mailing Add:* 1810 W Mulberry San Antonio TX 78201

HAYNES, DOUGLAS H
PAINTER, EDUCATOR
b Regina, Sask, Jan 1, 36. *Study:* Provincial Inst Technol & Art, Calgary, Alta, with R Spickett; Royal Acad Fine & Appl Arts, The Hague, Holland. *Work:* Edmonton Art Gallery, Alta; Confederation Art Gallery, Charlottetown, PEI; London Pub Mus & Art Gallery, Ont; Univ Calgary, Alta. *Comn:* Edmonton City Hall. *Exhib:* Fifth Biennial Exhib Can Art, London, Eng & Ottawa, Can, 63 & Sixth Biennial Exhib, Ottawa, 65; All Alberta '70, Edmonton, 70; West '71 Exhib, Edmonton, 71; Royal Can Acad Arts 91st Ann, Montreal, 71; Nat Can Touring Exhib, 91-92. *Pos:* Art adv, Govt Alta, 67-70. *Teaching:* From assoc prof to prof art & design & chair dept, Univ Alta, 70-. *Awards:* Govt of Neth Scholar, 60; All Alta First Prize, Jacox Gallery, 65; Can Coun Sr Award, Can Govt, 67. *Bibliog:* N Yates (auth), Three from Edmonton, Arts Can, 10/69; K Wilkin (auth), Western Canada, a survey, Art in Am, 5-6/72. *Mem:* Assoc Royal Can Acad Arts; Univ Art Asn Can. *Media:* Acrylic, Mixed. *Dealer:* Kathleen Laverty Gallery Edmonton AB Canada. *Mailing Add:* 14312 Ravine Dr Edmonton AB T5M 3M3 Canada

HAYNES, NANCY
PAINTER
b Conn, 47. *Work:* Brooklyn Mus, NY; Hood Mus, Dartmouth, NH; Denver Art Mus; Met Mus Art, NY; Nat Gallery Art, Washington, DC; Gemeentemus, The Hague, Neth; Fogg Art Mus, Cambridge, Mass; Whitney Mus Am Art; Mus. Fine Arts, Houston; Albertina Mus, Vienna. *Exhib:* Solo exhibs, PS 1 Project Room, Long Island City, NY, 84, Haags Gemeentermseum, The Hague, The Neth, 85, Plus-Kern Gallery, Brussels, Belg, 85, John Gibson Gallery, NY, 85 & 86, Julian Pretto, NY, 87, John Good Gallery, NY, 89, 90, 91, 92 & 93, Monoprints, Pamela Auchincloss, NY, 90, Chrysler Mus Art, Norfolk, Va, 92, Lawing Gallery, Houston, 98, Galerie Van Bartha, Basel, Switz, 98, Stark Gallery, NY, 2000, Galerie Hubert Winter, Vienna, 2001; Singular & Plural, Recent Acquisitions, Drawings & Prints 1945-1991, Mus Fine Arts, Houston, 92; Summer Group Exhib & Single Frame, John Good Gallery, NY, 93; Some Like it Cool, Barbara Karakow Gallery, Boston, 94; Prints of Darkness, Fogg Art Mus, Mass, 94; Visiting Artistry, Carpenter Ctr Visual Arts, Harvard Univ, Mass, 94; Fall Group Exhib, John Good Gallery, NY, 94; Contemp Abstract Painting, Grant Gallery, Denver, & Tavelli Gallery, Aspen, 94. *Teaching:* Adj Lectr, Hunter Col, NY, 86-89; vis lectr, Brandeis Univ, Waltham, Mass, 88-89; lectr, Carpenter Ctr, Harvard Univ, 92. *Awards:* Fel, Nat Endowment Arts, 87 & 90; New York Found Arts, 87. *Bibliog:* Ellen Handy (auth), Nancy Haynes: New York in Review, Arts Mag, 1/92; Barbara MacAdam (auth), Nancy Haynes, Artnews, 1/94; Ann Wilson Loyd (auth), Nancy Haynes, Art in Am, 5/94; Barbara MacAdam (auth) Something to Grow on, Artnews, 9; Lilly Wei (auth) Nancy Haynes at Stark Gallery, Artnew, 2000

HAYNES, R (RICHARD) THOMAS
PAINTER, ILLUSTRATOR
b Rome, Ga, Feb 17, 34. *Study:* Auburn Univ, BS, 56; painting with James Harmon, 60; watercolor with Zoltan Szabo, 75. *Work:* Univ Pac, Stockton, Calif; Colby Col, Waterville, Maine; Mo Hist Soc Print Collection, St Louis. *Exhib:* NMex Int, Portales, 76; St Louis Artists Guild, Webster Groves, 77; Southern Watercolor Soc, Columbus Art Mus, Ga, 78; Pittsburgh Aqueous 78, Pa; Ark Wildlife Fedn, Pine Bluff, 78 & 79; and others. *Awards:* First Place, St Louis Co Div Parks, 75; Second Place, NMex Int, 76. *Bibliog:* Member of the issue, North Light Mag, 81. *Mem:* Southern Watercolor Soc; Acad Professional Artists. *Media:* Egg Tempera, Watercolor. *Dealer:* Aldridge Fine Arts I & II 104 Romero NW Albuquerque NM 87104. *Mailing Add:* 206 Thiebes Rd Labadie MO 63055

HAYNIE, RON
PAINTER, EUDUCATOR
b Farmville, Va, Dec 31, 45. *Study:* Am Univ, BA, 68, MFA, 69. *Work:* George Mason Univ, Fairfax, Va; Watkins Collection, Am Univ, Washington, DC; Northern Va Community Col, Annandale, Va; WVa Wesleyan Col, Buckhannon; Rehoboth Art League, Del. *Exhib:* 19th Area Exhib, Corcoran Gallery Art, Washington, DC, 74; Areawide Juried Exhib, Arlington Arts Ctr, Va, 85; New on View, Strathmore Hall Arts Ctr, Rockville, Md, 88; I Am: Self Portraits, Dundalk Community Col, Baltimore, Md, 90; Past as Prologue, Greater Reston Arts Ctr, Va, 91. *Pos:* Dir, Watkins Collection, Am Univ, Washington, DC, 90-. *Teaching:* Instr painting & drawing, Dumbarton Col, Washington, DC, 69-73; instr painting & drawing, Trinity Col, Washington, DC, 74- 77; assoc prof painting & drawing, Am Univ, Washington, DC, 80-. *Awards:* Purchase Award, 1975 Area Exhib, Fairfax Coun Arts, 75. *Bibliog:*

Joanne Lewis (auth), Reviews column, Wash Post, 87; Marci Nadler (auth), From the beach series, Eye Wash, 91; Roberta Morgan (auth), Two solitary visions, Rockville Gazette, Md, 91. *Mem:* Wash Proj Arts; Arlington Arts Ctr; Phillips Collection; Coalition Wash Artists. *Media:* Acrylics. *Mailing Add:* 4811 Hutchins Place NW Washington DC 20007-1529

HAYWARD, JAMES
PAINTER
b San Francisco, Calif, Sept 22, 43. *Study:* San Diego State Univ, BA; Univ Calif, Los Angeles; Univ Wash, Seattle, MFA. *Work:* Los Angeles Co Mus Art; San Francisco Mus Mod Art; Cleveland Mus Fine Art, Ohio; Mus of Contemp Art, Calif; Laguna Beach Mus of Art, Calif. *Exhib:* New Abstract Painting in Los Angeles, Los Angeles Co Mus Art, 76; Los Angeles Inst Contemp Art, 79; solo shows, Modernism, San Francisco, Calif, 80, 82, 84, 87, 89, 93 & 95, Ace Contemp Exhibs, 87, 88, 90-93, M-13, NY, 89, Genovese Gallery, Boston, 93, New Image Art, Los Angeles, 98, Chac-mool, Los Angeles, 98 & Sala Diaz, San Antonio, Tex, 98, Modernism, the Ital Paintings, San Francisco, Calif, 2000, Chac-mool, Recent Work, Los Angeles, Calif, 2001; Young Talent 1963-1983 (with catalog), Los Angeles Co Mus Art, 83; Changing Trends--Content & Style, Laguna Beach Mus Art, 82 & Los Angeles Inst Contemp Art, 83; 50th Anniversary Show, San Francisco Mus Mod Art, 84; Rosamund Felsen Gallery, Los Angeles, 86; Contemp Southern Calif Painting, Taipei Fine Arts Mus, 87; Paint-Film, Bess Cutler Gallery, NY, 87; Affinities, April Sgro-Riddle Gallery, Los Angeles, 88; Works on Paper, Modernism, San Francisco, 88; Awards in the Visual Arts 10, Hirshhorn Mus, Washington, DC, 91; Artificial Paradise, Burnett Miller Gallery, Los Angeles, 93; Let's Get Physical, Blum Helman Gallery, NY, 93; In Plain Sight: Abstract Painting in Los Angeles (with catalog), Blue Star Art Space, San Antonio, Tex, 94-95; Plane/Structures (with catalog), Otis Gallery, Otis Col Art & Design, Los Angeles, 94-95; Starting with McLaughlin, Patricia Faure Gallery, Santa Monica, 98; and others. *Teaching:* Instr, Col Creative Studies, Univ Calif, Santa Barbara, 76-78 & 83-85, Calif State Univ, Bakersfield, 79, Univ Calif, Berkeley, 83, Univ Southern Calif, Los Angeles, 87, 92-95, Art Ctr, Calif, 94-; vis artist, Minneapolis Col Art & Design, Minn, 80-81; guest artist, Univ Tex, San Antonio, 97. *Awards:* Guggenheim Fel, 83-84; Nat Endowment Arts Visual Arts Fel, 93; Pollock-Krasner Found Grant Painting, 96. *Bibliog:* Jeremy Gilbert-Rolfe (auth), Abstract painting and the historical object: considerations on the new paintings of James Hayward, Arts, 4/87; Buzz Spector (auth), James Hayward: The Space Behind the Gesture, Visions (cover), spring 89. *Media:* Acrylic, Oil. *Dealer:* Modernism 685 Market St San Francisco CA 94105; M13 72 Greene St New York NY 10012; Ace Gallery, 5514 Wilshire Blvd, LA 90036. *Mailing Add:* 12241 Broadway Rd Moorpark CA 93021-9799

HAZLEHURST, FRANKLIN HAMILTON
HISTORIAN, EDUCATOR
b Spartanburg, SC, Nov 6, 25. *Study:* Princeton Univ, BA, 49, MFA, 52, PhD, 56. *Teaching:* Instr art hist, Princeton Univ, 54-56; lectr art hist, Frick Collection, New York, 56-57; from asst to assoc prof, Univ Ga, 57-63; prof & chmn dept fine arts, Vanderbilt Univ, 67-91; prof fine arts, emeritus, 1995. *Awards:* Fulbright Fel, 53-54; Am Coun Learned Soc Grant in Aid, 67; Madison Sarratt Prize, Vanderbilt Univ, 70; Alice Davis Hitchcock Award, Soc Archit Hist, 82; Officie de l'ordre des arts et des leffres, Paris, 2006. *Mem:* Am Archaeol Soc; Col Art Asn Am; Southeastern Col Art Asn (pres, 73-74); French Soc Hist Art; Soc Archit Historians. *Res:* Seventeenth and 18th century French art, especially landscape architecture. *Publ:* Auth, Artistic origins of David's oath of the Horatii, Art Bulletin, 60; auth, Jacques Boyceau and the French Formal Garden, 66; auth, Additional sources for the Medici Cycle, Bulletin Musees Royal Beaux Arts Belg, 67; ed, French Formal Garden, Third Colloquium Landscape Archit, Dumbarton Oaks, 74; auth, Gardens of Illusion: The Genius of Andre Le Nostre, 80; and others; Le jardins d'illusion, Le genia d'Anchre Le Nostre, 2005. *Mailing Add:* 2104 Golf Club Ln Nashville TN 37215

HAZLEWOOD, CARL E
CURATOR, PAINTER
b Georgetown, Guyana, SAm, Apr 28, 50; US citizen. *Study:* Brooklyn Mus Sch (scholarship), 71 & 73-74; Skowhegan Sch Painting & Sculpture (scholarship), 73; Pratt Inst, New York, BFA(with honors), 75; Hunter Col City Univ New York, MA, 77. *Work:* Dept of the Treasury, State NJ, Trenton; Nat Collection Fine Arts, Georgetown, Guyana; Booker Brothers & McConnel & Co Ltd, London, Eng; State Legislative Bldgs, Albany, NY; Borough Manhattan Community Col, City Univ NY. *Comn:* Many portraits in Am & abroad, 67-72. *Exhib:* Vital Abstractions, William Carlos Williams Ctr Arts, Rutherford, NJ, 87; Four Artists, Newark Mus, NJ, 90; Monochrome, Inst Contemp Art, Clocktower Gallery, NY, 90; Generated Realities, Middleton-McMillan Gallery, Charlotte, NC, 91; Drawings from Beginning to End, Ben Shahn Galleries, William Paterson Col, Wayne, NJ, 92; Curators as Artists/Artists as Curators, Bergen Mus Art, NJ, 95; Nat Gallery Art, Smithsonian Inst, Washington, DC, 96-97; Castellani Art Mus, Niagara Univ, NY, 96-97; Recent Aquisitions, Georgetown, Guyana, 96-97. *Collection Arranged:* Revelations (paintings; auth, catalog), Hallwalls, NY, 87; Nexus, Transformation/Transfiguration (auth, catalog), PS 122, 3 Artists of Diverse Cultures, 89; Environmental Explorations (auth, catalog), Three Part Ser, 90-91; Selections (auth, catalog), NY & NJ Artists, Multi Media Work, 90; Essential Structures (auth, catalog), 3 Installations, NJ, 92; Current Identities: Recent Painting in the United States (auth, catalog), IV Int Bienal de Pintura, Cuenca, Ecuador, 94; Required Nuance (sculpture; auth), Studio Mus, Harlem, 95. *Pos:* Cur, Hazlewood Fine Art, Brooklyn, NY, 77-; co-founder & artistic dir, Aljira, Ctr Contemp Art, Newark, NJ, 84-; auth & ed, Nka J Contemp African Art, Cornell Univ, 94-. *Teaching:* Instr painting, Newark Mus Art, NJ, 91; adj prof art hist, Jersey City State Col, NJ, 91-. *Awards:* Edward Arthur Mellinger Found Scholar; Max Beckmann Int Award for Advanced Study; Anco-wood Found Award/Rosalie Retrash Schmidt Mem Award Exhib Grants-Artist Space. *Bibliog:* Joseph E Young (coauth with Barbara Cortright), Phoenix letter, Artspace Mag, 8/86; Vivian Raynor (auth), Art: Drawing from beginning to end, NY Sunday Times, 4/92; Who's Who in the East, Silver Anniversary 25th ed, Marquis Who's Who in Am, 95-96. *Mem:* Newark Arts Coun; Nat Asn Artists Orgn; NY State Arts Coun Visual Arts Panel. *Media:* Multi Media. *Publ:* Auth, Newark Boasts Long History of Public Art, Newark Arts Coun, 88; illusr (cover), The Signal Network Int Lit, Art Ideas, Signal, 89; auth, In Marble Hill: Peter Spaans, The Art of Peter Spaans, Under Construction Art Proj Ltd, Amsterdam, Neth, 93; Interior lif contests, conservatism, Flash Art Int, Rome, 11-12/97; Art by African Americans in the Collection of the New Jersey State Museum (catalog), NJ State Mus, 98. *Mailing Add:* Hazlewood Fine Art 499 Lincoln Pl No 4N Brooklyn NY 11238

HEAD, GEORGE BRUCE
PAINTER, DESIGNER
b St Boniface, Man, Feb 14, 31. *Study:* Univ Man, Dipl(fine art), 53. *Work:* Nat Gallery Can; Pub Libr, Art Mus, London; Montreal Mus Art; Can Coun Art Bank. *Comn:* Oil on panels, Manitoba Teachers Col, 59; main wall, Woodsworth Bldg, Mb Gov, 76; cast concrete sculpture, City of Winnipeg Underground Concourse, 78; portage and main concourse, City of Winnipeg, 80; mural, Woodsworth Bldg, Manitoba Govt. *Exhib:* Nat Gallery, Australian Art Tour, 67-68; Tenth Winnipeg Art Gallery Biennial, 70; Montreal Spring Exhib; Nat Gallery Can Biennial; one-man show, Winnipeg Art Gallery, 73, Univ Winnipeg, 88 & Univ Manitoba, 89; Ostrava Czech Republic, Amsterdam, 2000; group exhib, Brian Melnychenko Gallery, 80. *Awards:* Purchase Prizes, Winnipeg Show, Winnipeg Art Gallery & 20th Western Ont Exhib; Benson & Hedges Art Wall Design Award, 72. *Bibliog:* H Ochi (auth), article, Ideas Mag, Japan; W Hertig (auth), Graphics Annual, Graphic Press; article, Art Director Ann; and others. *Mem:* Royal Can Acad. *Media:* Acrylic; Concrete Sculpture. *Mailing Add:* 19 Woodlawn Ave Winnipeg MB R2M 2P3 Canada

HEAD, ROBERT WILLIAM
PAINTER, EDUCATOR
b Springfield, Ill, Aug 6, 41. *Study:* MacMurray Col, BA(art educ), 63, with Sidman & Foresterling; Kent State Univ, MFA, 65, with Shock, Morrow & Petersham, Colo Outward Bound Sch, 71. *Hon Degrees:* DHL, MacMurray Col, 95. *Work:* JB Speed Art Mus, Louisville, Ky; Mint Mus, Charlotte, NC; Del Mar Col, Corpus Christi, Tex; MacMurray Col, Jacksonville, Ill; Massillon Mus, Ohio. *Exhib:* Ball State Univ Nat Drawing Show, Muncie, Ind; Bucknell Nat Drawing Exhib, Lewisburg, Pa; Mainstreams Int Painting Exhib, Marietta, Ohio; Brooks Mem Gallery Show, Memphis, Tenn; Weatherspoon Ann Drawing Exhib, Univ NC; solo shows, JB Speed Mus, Louisville, Ky, Univ Mass, Amhurst, Yeiser Art Ctr, Paducah, Ky, Capitol Arts Ctr,& Western Ky Univ, Bowling Green, Ky, Sangamon State Univ, Springfield, Ill, Concord Col, Athens, WVa, Doane Col, Crete, Nebr, Cocino Arts Ctr, Flagstaff, Ariz; The Parthenon, Bd Parks & Recreation, Nashville, Tenn; Louisville Vis Arts Asn, Ky. *Teaching:* Prof emer drawing & painting, Murray State Univ, 65-; assoc prof drawing & introd art, World Campus Afloat, Chapman Col, spring 70 & 72; vis prof, Univ Alaska, Fairbanks, fall 86. *Awards:* Merit Award for Excellence in Teaching, Murray State Univ, 70; Purchase Award, Mid-States Exhib, Evansville Mus; Distinguished Prof, Murray State Univ. *Mem:* Wilderness Soc; Ky Ornith Soc. *Media:* Paint. *Mailing Add:* 2438 Univ Station Murray KY 42071

HEADLEY, DAVID ALLEN
PAINTER
b Washington, Pa, Dec 11, 46. *Study:* Washington & Jefferson Col, BA, 68. *Work:* Corcoran Gallery Am Art, Washington, DC. *Exhib:* Eastern Mich Univ, Ypsilanti, Mich, 67; Butler Inst Art, Youngstown, Ohio, 67 & 68; Detroit Inst Art, 72; Corcoran Gallery, Washington, DC, 76 & 77; Health, Educ & Welfare Bldg, Washington, DC, 79-80; Manhattan Ctr Gallery, NY, 83; Pratt Inst Gallery, NY, 83; and others. *Awards:* First Prizes, Washington & Jefferson Arts Festival, 65 & 66 & Morgantown Art Asn, WVa, 66 & 67. *Bibliog:* John Deckert (auth), David Headley, Arts Mag, 9/81. *Mailing Add:* c/o Tepper Takayama Fine Arts 20 Park Plaza Suite 600 Boston MA 02116

HEALY, ANNE LAURA
SCULPTOR, EDUCATOR
b New York, NY, Oct 1, 39. *Study:* Queens Col, New York, BA, 62. *Work:* Chemical Bank, NY; NY Cult Ctr; Allen Art Mus, Oberlin, Ohio; City Univ Grad Ctr, NY; Mich State Univ, East Lansing; and others. *Comn:* Washington State, 85; City of Oakland, 85; Stanford Univ, 90-91; Art Inst Southern Calif, 89; State Wash, 85 & 95. *Exhib:* Individual exhibs, AIR Gallery, NY, 72, 74, 78, 81 & 83, Matrix Gallery, Sacramento, Calif, 82, Pub Art Fund, NY, 83, Douglas Col, Rutgers Univ, New Brunswick, NJ, 84, Festival Lake, Oakland, Calif, 85 & San Francisco Mus Mod Art Artists Gallery, 88; Mus Contemp Crafts, NY, 72; Sculpture Outdoors, Nassau Co Mus Fine Arts, Roslyn, NY, 75; Int Women's Yr, Bronx Mus, NY, 75; South East Tex Mus, Corpus Christi, 77, Baruch Col, NY, 78, Candidates for Grants, Am Acad & Inst of Arts & Lett, 79 & Hofstra Univ, Hempstead, NY, 80; New Directions in Drawing, 1950-80; A Women's Place, Kingsborough Community Col, Brooklyn, NY, 82; KQED Art Auction Invitational, Fuller-Golden Gallery, San Francisco, Calif, 85; Am Heart, San Francisco Art Inst, Calif, 86; Terrain Gallery, San Francisco, 98; AIR Gallery, NY, 2006. *Pos:* Bd mem, bd dir & head curatorial comt, San Francisco Arts Comm Gallery, Calif, 85-89; bd trustees, San Francisco Art Inst, Calif, 85-88; art comnr for Sculpture City of San Francisco, head, visual art comt, mem, civil design comt, 89-; pres, San Francisco Art Comn, 92-96. *Teaching:* Instr sculpture, St Ann's Sch, Brooklyn; vis artist, Mich State Univ, East Lansing, 73 & Broward Col, Ft Lauderdale, Fla, 76; vis artist-in-residence, Univ Cincinnati, 76; adj asst prof, Baruch Col, City Univ New York, 76-; guest lectr, Sch Visual Arts, New York, 77, Bard Col & Univ Iowa, 78 & Univ Northern Iowa, 79; vis prof sculpture, Univ Iowa, Iowa City, 79; asst prof, Univ

Calif, Berkeley, 81-85, assoc prof, 85-93, chair art dept, 90-94, prof, 93-. *Awards:* Award for Sculpture, Asn Am Univ Women, 76-77; Am Acad & Inst Arts & Lett, 79-80; Macdowell Colony, 80. *Bibliog:* Ellen Lubbell (auth), Healy's double header, Soho Weekly News, 10/18/78; Corinne Robins (auth), Anne Healy: Ten years of temporal sculpture, Arts, 10/78; The great goddess, Heresies 5th Issue, spring 78. *Mem:* Col Art Asn; Women's Caucus Art Asn. *Media:* Sculpture, Drawing. *Res:* public art, sculpture. *Specialty:* contemporary art. *Interests:* film, photography, popular culture, feminist theory, theatre. *Dealer:* Terrain Gallery 165 Jessie St San Francisco CA 94102. *Mailing Add:* 1825 Harmon St Berkeley CA 94703

HEALY, DEBORAH ANN
ILLUSTRATOR, EDUCATOR

b Newark, NJ. *Study:* Col New Rochelle, BA; Montclair State Univ, MA, 76; Syracuse Univ, with Isadore Selzer, James McMullen, Doug Johnson & others, MFA, 79. *Work:* Danish Pub Television; Swedish Pub Television; Italian Pub Television; Vanderbilt Univ; Forbes Mag; Johnson & Johnson. *Comn:* Films, animated Women, 80, Owl & Pussycat, Little Birds, 81 & Three Love Poems; paintings & illus for Harper & Row, Doubleday, Glazen Advert, Douglas Group, Monsanto, Donald Sacks, Inc, United Nations, Yankee, New Eng, Living, Simon & Schuster, Bantam, New Am Libr, Philadelphia Mag, Enquirer & others. *Exhib:* Film Festival, Morris Mus Arts & Sci, Morristown, NJ, 76; Artist in Am Series, Fairleigh Dickenson Col, Madison, NJ, 76; Annecy Int Film Festival, Paris, France, 77; Zagreb Int Animation Festival, Yugoslavia, 78; Sinking Creek Winners' Invitational, Chicago Art Inst, 78; Invitational, Montclair Art Mus, NJ, 79; Painting Exhib, Soc Illus, 85 & 95; paintings of Turkey in Pentagon, Airforce Artist, 89; Earth Island proj, UN, 90. *Teaching:* Prof visual communications, Moore Col Art, Philadelphia, Pa, 86-; lectr, Parsons Sch Design, 82- & Kean Col, 85; hist illusr, Rochester Inst Technol & Second Ann Graphic Design Symposium. *Awards:* First Prize-Best in Show, Stockton State Spring Film Festival, NJ, 78; Nat Mag Nomination, Philadelphia Mag, 88; Film Grant, NJ State Coun Arts, 81-82 & 85-86; and others. *Bibliog:* Interview, Edison Black Maria Film Fest, NJ Independent Filmmakers, NJ Cablevision, 5/29 & 6/15/85. *Mem:* Art Dirs Club NJ; Col Art Asn; Graphic Artists Guild; Soc Illustrators; Soc Childrens Book Writers & Illus. *Media:* Oil & Watercolor. *Publ:* Illusr, Elizabeth and The Water Troll, The Little Old Man and His Dream, Waiting For You, Desserts, Harper & Row, 87-89; Branta, Simon Schuster, 94; The Gift of the Fawn, 95. *Dealer:* Clapp & Tuttle Gallery CT. *Mailing Add:* Comm Arts Moore Col Art 1920 Race St Philadelphia PA 19103

HEALY, JULIA SCHMITT
PAINTER, EDUCATOR

b Elmhurst, Ill, Mar 28, 47. *Study:* Univ Chicago, 66-70; Yale Univ Summer Sch, 69, with Mel Bochner, Bob Mangold & Bob Moskowitz; Art Inst Chicago, BFA, 70, MFA, 72. *Work:* Can Coun Art Bank, Ottawa, Ont; NS Art Bank, Halifax; Confederation Art Gallery, Charlottetown, PEI; Mount St Vincent Univ Art Gallery, Halifax; Dept Educ, Prov of NS, Halifax; Staten Island Mus; Roger Brown Collection; pvt collections of Don Baum, John Perreault, Jeff Weinstein, Dennis Adrian, Charles Riley and others. *Comn:* Halifax Diary (print), Dept Pub Works, NS, 75; Staten Island Children's Mus, 89-91; Cowparade, 2000; Dolphin Sitings, 2005. *Exhib:* Art Inst Chicago, 72 & 76; solo exhibs, Owens Art Gallery, Mt Allison Univ, Sackville, NB, 77 & Susan Whitney Gallery, Regina, Sask, 81 & 83; Atlantic J (traveling exhib), Nat Gallery Can, 76-77; Artists Space, 89, 90 & 91; Guggenheim Soho, 94; Soho 20, 96; ArtLab, 96; Soho 20 Chelsea, Phyllis Kind Gallery; Chrystie Street Studios, 2003-2006; Sch Art Inst Chicago, 2005; Pleiades Gallery, NY, 2006; Oxbow, Saugetuc, Mich, 2006. *Collection Arranged:* Intercourse (co-cur with Ray Johnson), Wabash Transit Gallery, Chicago, 71; Grassroots-Nova Scotian Folk Art, Eye Level Gallery, Halifax, 75. *Pos:* Dir, Eye Level Gallery, 75-76; dir related arts, West Hempstead Schs, NY, 2005-. *Teaching:* Instr painting & drawing, Sch Art Inst Chicago, 71-72; instr visual art, Ocean Co Col, Toms River, NJ, 79-82; asst prof, Pratt Inst, Brooklyn, NY, 91-94, dir, Saturday Sch, 92-94; Howell Road Sch, Valley Stream, NY, 94-2005; CUNY, 98-. *Awards:* Can Coun Arts grant, 76-77 & 77-78; Purchase Award, Staten Island Mus, 86; Staten Island Coun Arts Grant, 87 & 91; Distinguished Alumni, SAIC. *Bibliog:* Ron Shuebrook (auth), The Atlantic Provinces: Letter, Artscanada, 3/75; Marilyn Smith (auth), Some Nova Scotian Women Artists, 12/75 & Ron Shuebrook (auth), Some Major Nova Scotian Painters, 10-11/76, Art Mag; Vivian Raynor (auth), Eccentric vision, Humorous touches, NY Times, 8/27/89; John Perreault (auth), Dispatches from the Front, 89, Artmakers Staten Island Advance, 90-. *Mem:* Col Art Asn; Found Commun Artists; Chancellors Art Adv Bd, 91-95. *Media:* Mixed Media. *Res:* Motivation in Art Education. *Specialty:* Canadian Art, folk art, contemporary art. *Interests:* Opera. *Publ:* Ed, Recent Work: Julia Schmitt Healy, Dalhousie Art Gallery, 76; illusr, What Kids Like to Do, 94; Artmakers Activity Book, 95; doodlelines, 95. *Dealer:* Susan Whitney Gallery 2220 Lorne St Regina SK Can. *Mailing Add:* 63 E 9th St 14R New York NY 10003

HEARN, M F (MILLARD FILLMORE), JR
ADMINISTRATOR, HISTORIAN

b Lincoln, Ala, Aug 18, 38. *Study:* Auburn Univ, Ala, BA, 60; Ind Univ, MA(hist), 64, MA(art hist), 66, PhD, 69; Univ Calif, Berkeley, study with Jean Bony, 65-66; Courtauld Inst Art, 66-67. *Pos:* bd dir, Int Center Medieval Art, 85-88; academic dean, Semester at Sea, 98, 2001 & 2006; bd dir, Pittsburgh Chamber Music Soc, 2001-. *Teaching:* From instr to prof medieval & mod archit, Univ Pittsburgh, 67-2006, actg chmn fine arts dept, 73-74, chmn, 74-78, dir archit studies prog, 81-2006; vis prof, Carnegie Mellon Univ, 79. *Awards:* Grant, Nat Endowment Humanities Summer Inst, 84; Grant, Nat Endowment Humanities Summer Stipend, 90; Grant, CASVA, Paul Mellon Vis Senior Fel, 92. *Mem:* Soc Archit Historians; Int Ctr Medieval Art; Brit Archeol Asn. *Res:* Twelfth-century architecture of England and Northern France; Romanesque sculpture; theory of architecture. *Publ:* Auth, The Rectangular Ambulatory in English Medieval Architecture, J Soc Archit Historians, Vol 30, 71; Romanesque Sculpture: The Revival of Momental Stone Sculpture in the Eleventh and Twelfth Centuries, Ithaca and Oxford, 81; Ripon Minster: The Beginning of the Gothic Style in Northern England, Philadelphia, 83; The Architectural Theory of Viollet-le-Duc: Readings and commentary, Cambridge, Mass, 90; Canterbury Cathedral and the Cult of Becket, Art Bull, Vol 76, 94; Ideas that Shaped Buildings, Cambridge, Mass, 03, Spanish & Chinese transl, 2006. *Mailing Add:* Univ Pittsburgh 104 Frick Fine Arts Bldg Pittsburgh PA 15260

HEARTNEY, ELEANOR
CRITIC, CURATOR

b Des Moines, Iowa, Aug 5, 54. *Study:* Univ Chicago, BA, 76, MA, 80. *Pos:* Ind art critic, New York City, 1982-; contribr ed, Art Am, New Art Examiner, Artpress, 86-; Ed assoc, Art News, 86-93; cur, Pub Interventions, ICA Boston, 94; vis cur, Inst Contemp Art, Boston, 1994; critic in residence, Univ NMex, 95; panelist, vis critic, lectr for various nat and int organizations. *Teaching:* Art in Am, New York City, 1989-; Critic, in residence Sculpture Mag, wash, 1989-90; vis lectr, Univ New Mex, Albuquerque, 1995-96. *Awards:* Frank Jewitt Mather Award for Distinguished Art Criticism, 92; NY Found Arts Grant, 93; Am Crafts Coun Grant, 95. *Mem:* Int Asn Art Critics; Etant Donnes. *Publ:* Auth, A necessary transgression: pornography & postmodernism, New Art Examiner, 11/88; The whole earth show part II, Art Am, 7/89; Social Responsibility in Censorship, In: Culture Wars, Richard Bolton, ed, New Press, 92; New World Order, In: Beyond PC: Toward a Politics of Understanding, Pat Aufterheide, ed, Graywolf Press, 92; Eco-poetry, Eco-politics, Inc: But is it Art?, Nina Felshin, ed, Bay Press, Seattle, 94; Critical Condition: American Art at the Crossroads, Cambridge Univ Press, 97. *Mailing Add:* Am Chpt Internat Art Critics 105 Duane St Apt 40E New York NY 10007-3612

HEATH, DAVE (DAVID) MARTIN HEATH
PHOTOGRAPHER

b Philadelphia, Pa, June 27, 31. *Study:* Philadelphia Col Art, 54-55; New Sch, with W Eugene Smith, 59 & 61. *Work:* Nat Gallery Can, Ottawa; CMCP, Ottawa; Mus Mod Art, NY; Int Mus Photog, George Eastman House, Rochester, NY; Minneapolis Inst Art; Can Mus of Contemp photog, others; Hallmark Collection, Kansas City, MO. *Comn:* Collab with Robert Frank, Robert Heinecken & John Wood, William Johnson & Susan Cohen (dir), 83-85. *Exhib:* A Dialogue with Solitude, Eastman House, Rochester & Art Inst Chicago, 64 & Minneapolis Art Inst, 94; Nat Gallery Can, 67, 74 & 81; Photog in Am, Whitney Mus Art, NY, 74; Mirrors & Windows: Am Photog since 1960, Mus Mod Art, NY, 78; Songs of Innocence, Harbourfront Gallery, Toronto, 81; Le plaisir de voir, la passion du regard, Light Impressions Spectrum Gallery, Rochester, 88; Lesley Walker, a collaborative portrayal, Artscourt, Ottawa, 89; ADWS (master set & layout maquette), Simon Lowinsky, NY, 97; Howard Greenberg, NY, 2001; group show, The Street, Can Mus Contemp Photog, 2006; plus others. *Pos:* Artist in residence, Univ Minn, Minneapolis, 65 & Int Ctr Photog, NY, 78. *Teaching:* Instr photog, Sch Dayton Art Inst, 65-67; asst prof photog, Moore Col Art, Philadelphia, 67-70; prof photog, Ryerson Polytech Univ 70-96; adj fac, Visual Studies Workshop, 76-77. *Awards:* Guggenheim Found Fel, 63 & 64. *Bibliog:* Charles Hagen (auth), Le grand ALBUM ordinaire, Afterimage Visual Studies Workshop, 2/74; James Borcoman (auth), David Heath: a dialogue with solitude, J 34, Nat Gallery of Can, 10/79; Michael Torosian (auth & ed), David Heath, Extempore, Reflections on Art & Personal History, Lumiere Press, Toronto, 88, 2004; Michael Torosian (auth & ed), Korea, Photographs 1953-1954, Fiftieth Anniversary Portfolio, Lumiere Press, Toronto, 2004. *Media:* Chromogenic Print, Journals, Digital Color. *Publ:* Auth, A Dialogue with Solitude, Community Press, 65, 2nd edit, Lumiere Press, 2000; contribr, Photography in the 20th Century, 67; Photography in America, 75; Mirrors and Windows, 78; Magicians of Light, 80; Wonderland, 99; Dave Heath's Art Show, Anonymous Press, Toronto, 2006. *Dealer:* Steven Bulger Gallery 700 Queen St East Toronto Ontario Canada M6J; Howard Greenberg, 4 E 57th, Ste 1406 NYC 10022. *Mailing Add:* 120 Wolfrey Ave Toronto ON M4K 1L3 Canada

HEATH, DAVID C
DEALER

b Atlanta, Ga, June 6, 40. *Study:* Vanderbilt Univ; Univ Vienna; Columbia Univ. *Pos:* Pres, Heath Gallery, DC Heath & Assoc & Adv on Int Sculpture Inc, currently. *Specialty:* 20th century American & large scale sculpture. *Mailing Add:* c/o Gallery Revel 416 E Paces Ferry Rd NE Atlanta GA 30305

HEATH, DAVID MARTIN See Heath, Dave (David) Martin Heath

HEATH, SAMUEL K
MUSEUM DIRECTOR

b Exeter, NH, Sept 10, 54. *Study:* Yale Univ, BA(art hist), 76; Columbia Univ, Dept Art Hist, MA, 83, MPhilos, 84. *Pos:* Staff lectr, Nat Gallery Art, Washington, DC, 76-78; curatorial intern, Boston Mus Fine Arts, 80-81; proj dir inventory & catalog colonial paintings, Cuzco, Peru, Int Found Art Res, NY, 83-85; lectr spec exhibs, Dept Pub Progs, Metrop Mus Art, 83-90; prog specialist Spain & Latin Am, World Monument Fund, NY, 88-90; cur Span art, Meadows Mus, Southern Methodist Univ, Dallas, Tex, 90-92, dir, 92-; dir, Lamont Gallery, Phillips Exeter Acad, 97-. *Teaching:* Instr art hist, Phillips Exeter Acad, NH, summers 76-79, Sch Visual Arts, NY, 85 & Southern Methodist Univ, Dallas, Tex, 90-. *Awards:* Columbia Univ Pres Fel, 79-80 & Univ Fel, 80-81; Samuel H Cress Found Res Fel, 85; Chester Dale Fel, Metrop Mus Art, 86-87. *Mem:* Int Coun Mus; Am Asn Mus; Col Art Asn; Art Mus Asn; Asn Art Mus Dirs; and others. *Publ:* Auth, Spanish Polychrome Sculpture 1500-1800 in United States Collections (catalog), Spanish Inst New York, 92. *Mailing Add:* c/o Lamont Gallery 20 Main St Exeter NH 03833

HEATON, JANET N
PAINTER, GALLERY DIRECTOR
b Miami, Fla, May 27, 36. *Study:* Fla State Univ. *Work:* State House, Nairobi, Kenya; Leigh Yawkey Woodson Art Mus, Wausau, Wis. *Comn:* PGA National, Palm Beach Gardens, Fla. *Exhib:* Birds in Art, 88, 91 & 92 & Wildlife the Artists View, 89, Leigh Yawkey Woodson Art Mus, Wausau, Wis; SAA Ann Exhib, Witte Mus, San Antonio, 92; Birds In Art, Travel Exhib, Am Mus Natural Hist, NY, 92; Art & The Animal, SAA Va Mus Natural Hist, Martinsville, 92; Birds In Art Travel Exhib, The Ward Mus of Wildfowl Art, Salisbury, Md, 92; SAA '93, traveling exhib. *Awards:* Winslow Homer Award & Liquitex Award, Fla Watercolor Soc, 90; Merit Award, Fla Watercolor Soc, 92. *Mem:* Signature Mem Soc Animal Artists; Signature Mem Pastel Soc Am; Signature Mem Fla Watercolor Soc; Catharine Lorillard Wolfe Art Club Inc; Outdoor Writers Asn Am. *Media:* Pastel, Watercolor. *Publ:* Contribr, Wildlife Art, The Female Perspective, Sports Afield, 86; A Painting Safari Through Southern Africa, Am Artist, 88; Artists of Florida, Mountain Products of Tex, Vol II, 90-92; African Wildlife In Art, Clive Holloway Bks, London, Eng, 91; The Killers of Old Africa, Outdoor Life, 91. *Dealer:* J N Bartfield Gallery 30 W 57th St New York NY 10019

HEBALD, MILTON ELTING
SCULPTOR, PRINTMAKER
b New York, NY, May 24, 17. *Study:* Art Students League, with Ann Goldwaithe, 27-28; Master Inst United Arts, 31-34; Beaux-Arts Inst Design, 32-35; Nat Acad Design, 32-33. *Work:* Whitney Mus Am Art; Philadelphia Mus Art; Tel-Aviv Mus, Israel; HF Johnson Mus Art, Cornell Univ; Joyce Mus, Dublin, Ireland. *Comn:* Bronze frieze, Pan-Am Terminal, Kennedy Airport, NY; James Joyce Monument, Zurich, Switz, 66; Tempest Group Bronze, Cent Park, NY, 72; Bronze Olympiads (2), YMCA, Los Angeles, 86; Bronze frieze, 220 Foot long double sided Zodiac Screen; Romeo & Juliet Central Park. *Exhib:* Nordess Gallery, NY, 60-72; Va Mus Fine Arts, 67; Solo exhibs, Yares Gallery, Scottsdale, Ariz, 76-78, Harmon Meek Gallery, Naples, Fla, 78-94, Randall Galleries, NY, 78, Byck Gallery, Louisville, Ky, 78 & Cheekwood, Nashville, Tenn, 78; and others. *Collection Arranged:* Univ Ariz, Tucson; Ark Art Ctr, Little Rock; Israeli Mus Art, Tel Aviv, Israel; Herbert F Johnson Mus Art, Cornell Univ, Ithaca, NY; Whitney Mus Am Art, NYC. *Teaching:* Instr, Brooklyn Mus Sch Art, 46-51, Cooper Union, 46-53, Univ Minn, 49, Skowegan Sch Painting & Sculpture, 50-52 & Long Beach State Univ, Calif, 68. *Awards:* Second Prize, Pa Acad Fine Arts, 51; First Prize New York City Dept Pub Works, E Bronx TB Hosp, 52; Prix de Rome, 55-58; and others. *Bibliog:* Martha C Cheney (auth), Modern Art in America, McGraw-Hill, 39; C Ludwig Brumme (auth), Contemporary American Sculpture, Crown, 48; Frank Getlein (auth), Milton Hebald, Viking, 71. *Mem:* Fel Am Acad in Rome; Asn Am Group; Cosmos Club, Washington, DC. *Media:* Bronze, Wood, Terra Cotta, Lithography. *Interests:* Collector of old master drawings. *Publ:* Illusr, An Alphabestiary, Ciardi Lithograph 34, Touchstone Press, Lippincott Co, NY, 66; Sounds & Shapes, Univ Soc, 70. *Dealer:* William Meek Harmon-Meek Gallery 1258 Third St S Naples FL 33940; Worthmore Galleries 5723 Magazine St New Orleans LA 70115; Shidoni Foundry Galleries 1508 Bishops Lodge Rd Tesuque New Mexico 87574. *Mailing Add:* 613 Avenida Colima Santa Fe NM 87507

HECHT, IRENE
PAINTER
b New York, NY, Dec, 1, 49. *Study:* Case Western Reserve Univ, BA, 71; Art Student League with Everett Raymond Kinstler, Burt Silverman & Aaron Shikler & David Levine. *Work:* Portraits of Isaac Stern, Martin Bookspan & Zubin Mehta, Nat Arts Club, Prof Eugene P Wigner, Princeton Univ; Lotos Club: Kathleen Battle, Bill Bradley; Itzak Perlman, Emanuel AX; Robert Morganthau, David Rockefeller. *Comn:* Portraits, Louis Nizer, 82, Arthur Krim, 83 & Charles Scribner IV, 86, NY; portrait, Nobel Laureate Nuclear Physicist Prof Eugene P Wigner; portrait, Marjorie Wynn, Beinecke Rare Books & Manuscript Libr, Yale Univ. *Exhib:* First Street Gallery; Audubon Artists; Am Acad Eguine Art. *Pos:* Portrait Painter. *Teaching:* Instr portrait painting, Delaware Art Mus, 84-87; instr, Figure Painting Workshop, Nat Acad Design, 93-96. *Awards:* Betty Salzmann Award, 80; House of Heydenryk Award, 88; Bruce Stevenson Mem Award, 91 & 92, Exhi Comt Award, Nat Arts Club, 93; President's Award, 2000. *Mem:* Nat Arts Club; Artists Fel; Lotos Club. *Media:* Oil. *Collection:* New York Univ; Princeton Univ; National Arts Club; Lotos Club; David Rockefeller; Aaron Shikler, etc. *Publ:* painting in Allure Mag, 93. *Mailing Add:* 15 W 67th St New York NY 10023

HECKERT, MATTHEW
SCULPTOR
b Kent Co, RI. *Study:* San Francisco Art Inst, BFA, 79; self taught. *Exhib:* solo exhib, Whitney Mus Am Art, New York City, Newhouse Ctr Contemp Art, Snug Harbor Cult Ctr, NY, Spaces Gallery, Cleveland, Ohio, Yerba Buena Ctr for Arts, San Francisco, Calif, 99. *Teaching:* instr, sound art, San Francisco Art Inst, Calif, formerly; instr, teaching sculpture, San Francisco State Univ, 2001-. *Awards:* Golden Reel Award, best soundtrack, Motion Picture Sound Ed, 88; fel, Nat Endowment for Arts, 91; Honorable Mention, Prix Arts Electronica, 96. *Media:* digital. *Specialty:* Sound producing mechanical sculptures, perfromance installations. *Mailing Add:* 2245 Quesada Ave San Francisco CA 94124

HEDBERG, GREGORY SCOTT
ART DEALER, GALLERY DIRECTOR
b Minneapolis, Minn, May 2, 46. *Study:* Princeton Univ, BA, 68; Inst Fine Arts, NY Univ, MA, 71, PhD, 80. *Collection Arranged:* Picasso, Braque, Leger (coauth, catalog), 75; Charles Biederman: A Retrospective (auth, catalog), 76; Millet's Gleaners (auth, catalog), 78, Victorian High Renaissance (auth, catalog), Manchester City Art Galleries, Minneapolis Inst Arts & Brooklyn Mus, 78-79; Leger's Le Grand Dejeuner (auth, catalog), 80; German Realism of the Twenties: The Artist as Social Critic (auth, catalog), Minneapolis & Chicago, 80; The Tremaine Collection (auth, catalog), Hartford, 84; J Pierpont Morgan, Collector (coauth, catalog), travelling exhib, 87; Soviet Art from the Academy, NY Acad Art, 88. *Pos:* Lectr, Frick Collection, NY, 71-74; cur paintings, Minneapolis Inst Arts, 74-81; chief cur, 81-86, asst dir, 86-87, Wadsworth Atheneum, Hartford, Conn; dir, NY Acad Art, 87-92; dir European art, Hirschl & Adler Gallery, NY. *Res:* Fifteenth century painting in Rome. *Publ:* Auth, The Farnese Courtyard Windows and the Porta Pia: Michelangelo's creative process, Marsyas, 71; auth, The Jerome Hill bequest: Delacroix's Fanatics of Tangiers and Corot's Silenus, 76 & In favor of Nicola di Maestro Antonio d'Ancona, 77, Minneapolis Inst Arts Bulletin. *Mailing Add:* 336 E 69th St New York NY 10021

HEDDEN-SELLMAN, ZELDA
PAINTER, INSTRUCTOR
b Farmington, Ill. *Study:* Bradley Univ, BS & MA; Ohio Univ; Harvard Univ; Western Reserve Univ; also with Ben Shahn, Arnold Blanch & Gladys Rockmore Davis. *Work:* Bertrand Russell Found, Nottingham, Eng; Ill Cent Col Permanent Collection. *Exhib:* one-woman show, Western Ill Univ, 79 & 81; Embassy Suites, Denver, 94; David Macc Gallery, Ill, 95; Watercolor USA, 95; Ill Cent Col, 97. *Pos:* Dir, Peoria Art Ctr Sch, 54-56. *Teaching:* Instr art, Ind State Univ, Terre Haute, 53-54; instr art, Spoon River Col, 66-74; instr art, Ill Cent Col, Peoria, 69-71 & 88-; instr, Bradley Univ, 76-86. *Awards:* Cent Ill Artists Award. *Mem:* Peoria Art Guild. *Media:* Acrylic, Watercolor. *Publ:* Auth, Treasures in the Snow, 64. *Mailing Add:* 307 Timberland Metamora IL 61548-9104

HEDMAN, TERI JO
PRINTMAKER, PAINTER
b St Paul, Minn, Oct 10, 44. *Study:* Univ Minn, BS(design); also with Paul Hapke, Toshi Yoshido, Pat Austin & Marge Horton. *Exhib:* All Alaska Exhib, 72, 74, 75 & 78; one-man show, Univ Minn, 67 & Artique Ltd, 73-80. *Pos:* Designer-draftsman, Minneapolis Housing Authority, 68-70; interior designer, Tiptons Interiors, Anchorage, 70-71. *Teaching:* Traveling instr printmaking, Naknek, Bethel & Nome, Alaska, 73. *Awards:* Print Award, All Alaska Juried Exhib, 78; Purchase Award, State Art Bank, State Print Competition, 79. *Mem:* Alaska Artists Guild (prof chmn, 72, funding chmn, 73, vpres, 74, pres, 75, mem bd, 76, vpres, 80); Anchorage Arts Coun (visual arts adv comt, 75). *Mailing Add:* 2219 St Elias Dr Anchorage AK 99501

HEDREEN, BETTY
COLLECTOR
Awards: Named to Top 200 Collectors, ARTnews Mag, 2006. *Mailing Add:* 836 36th Ave E Apt 19I Seattle WA 98112

HEDREEN, RICHARD
Study: Univ Wash, (civil eng), 57. *Pos:* Chief Exec Officer, pres, founder, RC Hedreen Co, 65-. *Awards:* Named to Top 200 Collectors, ARTnews Mag, 2006. *Mailing Add:* 836 36th Ave E Apt 19I Seattle WA 98112

HEDSTROM, ANA LISA
CRAFTSMAN
b Ind. *Study:* Mills Col, BA, 65; Kyota Art Col, Japan, 66-67. *Comn:* Miniature hangings, US Govt Bldg, ICS, Islambad, Pakistan. *Exhib:* Renwick Gallery, Smithsonian Inst, Washington, DC, 78; Metrop Mus Philippines, Manila, Philippines, 80; Am Craft Mus, NY, 83-84, int tour, 84-85; Brit Crafts Ctr, London, Eng, 85. *Awards:* Nat Endowment Arts, 82. *Mailing Add:* c/o Julie: Artisans' Gallery 762 Madison Ave New York NY 10021

HEEKS, WILLY
PAINTER
b Providence, RI, Apr 28, 51. *Study:* Univ RI, BFA, 73; Whitney Mus Am Art Independent Study Prog, 73; Tyler Sch Art Grad Prog, 76; RI Col, Hon Dr Fine Arts, 95. *Work:* Brooklyn Mus Art; Corcoran Gallery Art, Washington; Mus Fine Arts, Boston, Mass; Mus Mod Art, NY; Mus Mod Art, San Francisco; and others. *Exhib:* one-man shows, David Beitzel Gallery, NY, 87-90, 92, 94 & 96, Nielsen Gallery, Boston, 92 & 96, Larry Becker Contemp Art, Philadelphia, 92 & 97, Soma Gallery, LaJolla, Calif, 93, 95, 97 & 2000, Nancy Drysdale Gallery, Washington, 94, Mark Moore Gallery, 95 & 97 & Stephen Wirtz Gallery, San Francisco, 97, David Beitzel Gallery, NY, 99 & 2000, Salve Regina Univ, Newport, RI, 01; The Unique Print, Boston Mus Fine Arts, 90; 42nd Biennial Contemp Am Painting, Corcoran Gallery Art, Washington, 91; Vital Forces: Nature in Contemp Abstr, Hecksher Mus, Huntington, NY, 91; Organic Abstr, Nelson Atkins Mus Art, Kansas City, Mo, 91; Smith Col Mus Art, 94; New Acquisition, Mus Art, RI Sch Design, Providence, 95; Newance, Stephen Wirtz Gallery, San Francisco, 96; The Forty-Fifth Biennial: The Corcoran Collects, 1907-1998 (with catalog), Corcoran Gallery Art, Washington, DC, 98; Cleveland Collects Contemp Art (with catalog), Cleveland Mus Art, Ohio, 99; Six Painters, Sonoma State Univ Art Gallery, Rohnert Park, Calif, 2000; Layering, Elizabeth Leach Gallery, Portland, Ore, 01. *Teaching:* Grad Prog, Vermont Col, 96. *Awards:* Artists Fel, Nat Endowment Arts, 78, 87 & 89; Painting Award, Am Acad & Inst Arts & Letts, 89; Pollock-Krasner Found Grant, 97. *Bibliog:* Edith Newhall (auth), Fall preview-galleries, NY Mag, Sept 20, 99; Mario Naves (auth), Beauty is back? Willy Heeks' tender, sensuous pictures, The NY Observer, Sept 27, 99; Ann Landi (auth), New York: Reviews, Willy Heeks at David Beitzel Gallery, ARTnews, 12/99. *Dealer:* David Beitzel Gallery 102 Prince St New York NY 10012; Nielsen Gallery 179 Newberry St Boston MA 02116

HEFFERNAN, JULIE
PAINTER
b Peoria, Ill, 56. *Study:* Univ Calif, Santa Cruz, BFA(high hons, painting & printmaking), 81; Yale Sch Art, New Haven, Conn, MFA(painting), 85; Goethe Inst, Regensburg, Ger, 86; Alliance Française, 87. *Work:* The Palmer Mus Art, Pa; Columbia Mus Art, SC; Norton Mus Art, West Palm Beach, Fla; Knoxville Mus Art,

Tenn; The Prudential Corp, NJ; Wake Forest Univ, NC; The Progressive Corp, Ohio; Weatherspoon Art Mus, NC. *Exhib:* The Enduring Figure in Contemp Art, Norton Mus Art, West Palm Beach, Fla, 2000; Am Art Today: Fantasies and Curiosities, The Art Mus at Fla Int Univ, Miami, 2000; Littlejohn Contemp, NY, 2000; Pixeria Witcheria, Univ Galleries Ill State Univ, Normal, 01; Herter Art Gallery, Univ Mass, 03, Peter Miller Gallery, Il, 98, 01. *Teaching:* Instr drawing, Santa Cruz Art Ctr, Calif, 81; grad asst, Yale Col, New Haven, Conn, fall 84; vis asst prof fine arts, Univ Ind, Bloomington, 92 & dir Florence Italy & Abroad Drawing Prog, 92; vis asst prof fine arts, Univ NC, Greensboro, 92-93; asst prof fine arts, Pa State Univ, University Park, 94-98; vis artist, Univ Ariz, Tempe, fall 96 & Boston Mus Sch, fall 96; asst prof fine arts, Montclair Univ, NJ, 98-. *Awards:* Inst Res Grant & Col Fac Res Grant, Pa State Univ, 95; Individual Artist's Grant, Nat Endowment Arts, 95 & NY Found Arts, 96; Lila Acheson Wallace Reader's Digest, Artists at Giverny Prog, individual artists grant & residency, France, 97. *Bibliog:* Grace Glueck (auth) rev, Rich Mix of Styles and Stimulations Under One Roof, The New York Times, 2/2000; Edward Gomez (auth), Florida: Where Exuberant Dreams Often Sink Out of Sight, The New York Times, 4/01; Joel Silverstein (auth), Conversation with Julie Heffernan, NY Arts, 4/01. *Publ:* James Elkins (auth), Strange Stories, and The Balm (exhib catalog essay), 01; Mario Naves (auth) rev, Even the Intricacies are Self-conscious, The New York Observer, 4/01. *Dealer:* Littlejohn contemporary, 41 E 57 St, New York, 100022. *Mailing Add:* c/o Littlejohn Contemporary 41 E 57th St New York NY 10022

HEFLIN, TOM PAT
PAINTER, DESIGNER
b Monticello, Ark, July 18, 35. *Study:* Northeast La State Col; Chicago Art Inst. *Work:* Ill State Libr, Springfield; Blue Cross & Blue Shield Hq, Chicago; Sundstrand Corp, Rockford, Ill; Clarcor Co, Rockford, Ill; Rockford Art Mus. *Comn:* Winter Fields (painting), State Ill, Ill State Libr; Clarcor Corp, 97; Alpine Bank, 98; St Anthony Hosp, 92. *Exhib:* Butler Inst Am Art, Youngstown, Ohio, 73; New Horizons in Art, Chicago, 75; Am Watercolor Soc, NY, 75; Arts for the Parks, Jackson Hole, Wyo; Allied Artist Am, NY. *Collection Arranged:* Rockford Art Mus; Blue Cross Blue Shield, Chicago, IL; Maietta Oil, Chicago, IL; Harry Stonecipher, CEO Boeing Airtcraft; and many others. *Teaching:* Instr painting, Burpee Art Mus, 69-71 & Rock Valley Col, 70-. *Awards:* First Prize Medal, Nat Soc Painters Casein & Acrylic; First Prize, Ark Nationwide Bicentennial Medal Design, Franklin Mint; First Prize in Painting, Mainstreams 72, Ohio; Historical Medal Award, Arts for the Parks, Jacksonhole, WY, 2003. *Bibliog:* Articles in Famous Artists Mag, 70 & Contemp Western Artists, Southwest Art Publ, 82. *Mem:* Nat Soc Painters in Casein & Acrylic; Rockford Art Asn; Fishy Whale Litho Workshop, Milwaukee. *Media:* Oil, Acrylic. *Collection:* Ill State Libr, Rockford Art Mus, Freeport Art Mus. *Publ:* Auth, Quiet Places, 77; The Art of Heflin (video), 89; illusr, The First Forest, 90; Roots & Wings, The Art of Tom Heflin, 97. *Dealer:* Heflin Gallery Rockford IL. *Mailing Add:* 1162 S Weldon Rd Rockford IL 61102

HEFNER, HARRY SIMON
PAINTER, EDUCATOR
b Kalamazoo, Mich, Nov 20, 11. *Study:* Western Mich Univ, BA, 36; Columbia Univ, MA, 39. *Work:* Kalamazoo Col; South Bend Art Ctr; Albion Col; Western Mich Univ. *Exhib:* Detroit Inst Arts, 63-64; Kalamazoo Inst Arts, 63-66; Grand Rapids Inst Arts, Mich, 64-65; South Bend Inst Arts, Ind, 64-66; Battle Creek Inst Arts, 66; plus others. *Teaching:* Instr, Muskegon Pub Schs, Mich, 37-38, Cranbrook Boys Sch, summers 37-39 & Skidmore Col, 39; mem fac, Western Mich Univ, 40-77, prof watercolor & design, 56-77, head dept art, 63-66, emer prof, 77-; teacher, Harvard Univ, summer 41 & Univ Vt, summers 54-56; retired. *Media:* Watercolor. *Mailing Add:* 1700 Bronson Way No 147 Kalamazoo MI 49009-1095

HEGINBOTHAM, JAN STURZA
SCULPTOR
b New York, NY, Dec 8, 54. *Study:* Univ Md, BA, 75; pvt study with Boris Blai, Philadelphia, 76-78; Am Univ, Washington, DC, with Mark Oxman & Stanley Lewis, MFA(sculpture, fel), 92. *Comn:* Spirit (bronze sculpture), Montgomery Co Pub Sch, Burtonsville, Md, 88. *Exhib:* Allied Artist Am Ann, NY, 82, 86, 88, 89; Cannon Rotunda, US Cong, Washington, DC, 85; one-man show, Holy Family Col, Pa, 85; two-person show, Staunton Fine Arts Mus, Va, 89; The Nude, Loudon House Gallery, Ky & Perry House Gallery, Va, 97; Raab Gallery, Philadelphia, Pa, 99; Art Inst & Gallery, Salisbury, Md, 99; nat Small Sculpture Exhib, Httiesburg, Miss, 2000; Washington Square, DC, 2000; Craig Flinner Cantapery Gallery, Baltimore Md, 2001-2004; Nathen D Rosen Mus, Boca Raton, Fla, 2002 & 2004; Wash County Mus Fine Arts, Hagerstown, Md, 2003-2004; one-man show, Glenview Mansion Gallery, Rockville Civic Ctr, Md, 2004; Palm Springs Desert Mus, Calif, 2005; Attleboro Mus, Mass, 2005; Owensboro Mus, Ky, 2005. *Pos:* Sculptor's asst, Barry Johnston, Washington, DC, 81 & Raymond Kaskey, Md, 92; drawing group coordr, Arlington Arts Ctr, Va, 86-90. *Teaching:* Asst sculpture, Am Univ, Washington, DC, 90-92. *Awards:* Mayor Marion Barry Cert Award, City Hall, 81; Orion Nova, Mem & Assocs Award, Allied Artists Am, NY, 82 & 86; Award, Washington Co Mus Fine Art, Hagerstown, MD, 2003-2004. *Bibliog:* David Scott (auth), The Daily Times, Salisbury, Md, 3/99; Alice Ross (auth), Elan Magazine, Great Falls, Va 11/01. *Mem:* Washington Sculptors Group, Washington, DC. *Media:* Plastilene Clay, Bronze

HEIDEL, THERESA TROISE
PAINTER, INSTRUCTOR
b Teaneck, NJ, Aug 16 50. *Study:* St Peter's Col, BA; Accademia delle Belli Arti (post grad work), Florence, Italy; Ridgewood Art Inst, NJ. *Comn:* Homeland, Barbara Havenick, Bolton Landing, NY; Elberon Beach Club, Long Branch, NJ; Robin and Ivor Braka, Deal, NJ; Chateau Hotel, Spring Lake, NJ. *Exhib:* Solo exhibs, St Peter's Col, Jersey City, NJ, Fort Lee Libr, Fort Lee, NJ, Oceanside Gallery, Belmar, NJ, Lakeshore Gallery, Bolton Landing, NY; group exhibs, Talent, Allan Stone Gallery, NY; Audubon Artists Ann Nat Juried & Ann Non Mems Juried Art exhib, Salmagundi Club, NY; Watercolors of the Garden State, Monmouth Mus, Lincroft, NJ, Ridgewood Art Inst, NJ, New American Gallery, Princeton, NJ; NJ ann juried watercolor exhib, NJ Watercolor Soc, 2005, 06. *Collection Arranged:* Latham & Watkins Law Int Law Firm, Newark, NJ; Holy Name Hos, Teaneck, NJ; Jersey Shore Med Ctr, Neptune, NJ; Salvation Army, Asbury Park, NJ; Ocean Grove Hist Soc, Ocean Grove, NJ. *Teaching:* pvt instr. *Awards:* Catharine Lorillard Wolfe Art Club Award, Ridgewood Art Inst 17th Regional Open Juried Show, Ridgewood, NJ; Pennell Memorial Award, Kent Art Asn, Kent, Conn; Marie La Greca Award, Hudson Valley Art Asn. Ann, 2005. *Bibliog:* Beatrice Goodrich (auth), Happy Hollow Books I, II & III, Windswept House, Mt Desert, Maine, 1987; Marie Maber (auth), The Many Faces of Asbury Park, Asbury Park Press, 2004; Louise Hafesh (auth), Splashes of Color, 201 Mag, N Jersey Media Group Inc, W Paterson, NJ, 2005. *Mem:* Catherine Lorillard Wolfe Art Club; NJ Watercolor Soc; Kent Art Asn. *Media:* Watercolor. *Publ:* Integrating Studio Work & Outdoor Painting, Am Artist Mag, 1989; Ad Book J, Monmouth Co Cancer Soc, 1994; Jersey Shore Guide Book, Jersey Shore Vacation Guide, Jersey Shore Home & Garden, Jersey Shore Publs, Bayhead, NJ, 1995-. *Dealer:* Lakestore Gallery of Bolton Landing 4985 Lakeshore Dr (Rte 9 & Sagamore Rd) Bolton Landing, NY 12814; New Am Gallery Princeton Junction NJ. *Mailing Add:* 333 Main St Ridgefield Park NJ 07660

HEIFERMAN, MARVIN
CURATOR, WRITER, PUBLISHER
b New York, NY, 48. *Study:* Brooklyn Col, BA, 68; Columbia Univ: Sch Arts, Film Div; Sch Visual Arts, New York; Brooklyn Mus Art Sch. *Collection Arranged:* To the Rescue: Eight Artists in Am Archive Int Ctr of Photography, Miami Art Mus, Jewish Mus, San Francisco, Contemporary Art Mus, Houston, 1999-2000; Fame After Photography, Mus Modern Art, NY, 1999; Paradise Now: Picturing the Genetic Revolution, Exit Art, Tang Teaching Mus & Art Gallery, 2000-; Genomic Issue(s): Art & Science, Art Gallery of the Graduate Center, City Univ NY, 2003; John Waters' Change of Life, New Mus, NY, 2004; Photo Mus Winter Thur, Switzerland, 2004; Orange Co Mus Art, Calif, 2004; City Art: NY's Percent for Art Prog, Ctr for Archit, NY City, 2005. *Pos:* Asst dir, Light Gallery, NY, 72-74; dir photog, Castelli Graphics, NY, 75-82; founder, ptnr, Lookout, NY, 1991-2003; creative cons, Smithsonian Photography Initiative, Smithsonian Inst, 2005-. *Teaching:* MFA prog photogand related media, Sch Visual Arts, 91-; instr, ICP & BARD Col Prog in advan photographic studies, 2004-. *Publ:* Growing Up with Dick and Jane: Learning and Living the American Dream, Collins, 1996; To the Rescue: Eight Artists in An Archive, 99; Paradise Now: Picturing the Genetic Revolution, Tang/DAP, 2002; John Waters: Change of Life, Abrams, 2004; City Art: New York City's Percent for Art Program, Merrell, 2005. *Mailing Add:* 1024 Ave Americas New York NY 10018-5415

HEIMDAL, GEORG
PAINTER, INSTRUCTOR
b Pocatello, Idaho, Aug 6, 43. *Study:* San Francisco State Univ, BA, 66; Univ Calif Davis, MA, 68; Claremont Grad Sch, res fel, 78-79; Wash State Univ, MFA, 80. *Work:* Eastern Wash State Hist Soc, Spokane; Ohio State Univ, Columbus Mus Art, Huntington Bank, Columbus, Ohio; McDonald's Corp, Dayton, & Westerville, Ohio. *Exhib:* Nat Drawing Ann, San Francisco Mus Art, 70; Northwest Ann, Seattle Mus Art, 75; solo exhibs, Wash State Univ, 80, Traver-Sutton Gallery, 82, Hank Baum Gallery, San Francisco, 80, 81, 83 & 85, Belmont Gallery, Columbus, Ohio, 86, Ala State Univ, Montgomery, 87, Ind State Univ, Terre Haute, 88 & Roberta Kuhn Gallery, Columbus, Ohio, 89. *Pos:* Dir studio humanities, Ohio State Univ, Columbus, 80-89, chmn grad studies, 89-90. *Teaching:* Instr drawing, Spokane Falls Community Col, Wash, 69-80; assoc prof, Ohio State Univ, Columbus, 80-. *Awards:* Painting Award, Spokane Ann, Fremont Lane S, 73; Purchase Award, Columbus Mus Art, 85; Nat Endowment Humanities/Mellon Found Grant, 79; GCAC Individual Artists Fel, 87. *Bibliog:* Allegra Berrian (auth), Bringing art to life, Spokesman-Rev, 74; Ron Glowan (auth), Painters from the other side, Artweek, 77; Terry Barrett (auth), Trouble in the house, Columbus Art, 84; Jeanne Fryer Kohles (auth), Georg Heimdal, New Art Examiner, 3/89; Terry Barrett (auth), New Works, New Directions, Dialogue Mag, 89. *Media:* Multi. *Publ:* Auth, New Generation Drawings (exhib catalog), 74 & Northwest Eccentric Art (exhib catalog), 76, Eastern Wash Hist Soc; Reflections on a decade, Dialogue Mag, 11/88

HEIN, JOHN
CRAFTSMAN
b Albany, NY, July 21, 55. *Study:* Temple Univ, Philadelphia, AB, 77. *Work:* Zimmerli Art Mus, New Brunswick, NJ; Mt Holyoke Col, South Hadley, Mass; Newark Mus, NJ; Keuka Col, Keuka Park, NY. *Exhib:* NJ Arts Ann: Crafts, NJ State Mus, Trenton, 86, 92 & 96, Noyes Mus Art, Oceanville, NJ, 88, 90 & 98 & Morris Mus, 91 & 97; Am Craft at the Armory, Seventh Regiment Armory, NY, 90; one-man shows, Newark Mus, NJ, 92, Meredeth Gallery, Baltimore, Md, 93 & The Finer Side, Salisbury, Md, 93; Contemp Furniture Makers of the Am Northeast, Gallery at Bristol-Myers Squibb, Princeton, NJ, 91; Meredith Gallery, Baltimore, Md, 91, 92, 93, 95-97; and others. *Collection Arranged:* Out of the Woodwork, Holman Hall Gallery, Trenton State Col, Trenton, NJ. *Pos:* Advisor - The Forest Refined, Trenton City Mus, NJ; grant rev panelist & on-site arts evaluator, NJ State Coun Arts, 98. *Teaching:* Lectr, Works in Wood, NJ Designer Craftsmen Gallery, New Brunswick, 89, Cent Jersey Woodworker's Asn, 97. *Awards:* NJ State Coun Arts Individual Fel, 88; Nat Endowment Arts Visual Artists Fel, 90; NICHE Award Winner, wood, functional category, NICHE Mag, Baltimore, Md, 92, Wood one-of-a kind, 93 & 96 & Wood traditionally joined, 99 & 2000. *Bibliog:* Am Style, Baltimore, Md, summer 95 & 9/99; Art & Antiques, Studio Session, 4/2000; NY Times, 10/1/2000; many others. *Mem:* Am Craft Coun; Am Soc Furniture Artists; The Furniture Soc; Arts Wire; Nat Asn Independent Artists. *Media:* Wood. *Mailing Add:* 105 Featherbed Ln Hopewell NJ 08525

HEIN, MAX
GRAPHIC ARTIST, EDUCATOR
b Lincoln, Nebr, Dec 27, 43. *Study:* San Diego State Univ, AB, 66; Univ Calif, Los Angeles, MA, 68, MFA, 69. *Work:* Int Mus Photog, George Eastman House, Rochester, NY; Frederick S Wight Galleries, Univ Calif, Los Angeles; Newport Harbor Mus Art, Calif; Bradford City Art Gallery, Yorkshire, Eng; DeAnza Col Art Gallery, Calif; plus others. *Exhib:* Four Printmakers: Benson, Foote, Hein & Quandt, San Francisco Mus Art, 71; 3rd Brit Int Print Bienniale, Bradford City Art Gallery, Yorkshire, Eng, 72; Recent Photog, NS Col Art & Design, Halifax, 72; San Francisco Bay Area Printmakers, Cincinnati Art Mus, Ohio, 73; 8th Nat Print & Drawing Competition, Dulin Gallery Art, Knoxville, Tenn, 74-75; Smithsonian Traveling Exhib, Nat Collection Fine Art, Washington DC. *Teaching:* Instr silkscreen printmaking, Univ Calif, Los Angeles Exten, 68-69; instr art, Santa Rose Jr Col, Calif, 69-; vis artist silkscreen printmaking, Visual Studies Workshop, Rochester, NY, summer 75. *Awards:* Guest Ed Award, 6th Ann Los Angeles Printmaking Soc Exhib, 69; Purchase Award, 3rd Brit Int Print Biennale, 72 & Bay Area Print Exhib, DeAnza Col Gallery, 75. *Bibliog:* Alfred Frankenstein (auth), Photo image in printmaking, San Francisco Chronicle, 11/71; Carole Schuck (auth), Max Hein prints, 9/72 & Gerry Payne (auth), Geometric dynamics, 11/75, Art Week. *Media:* Painting, Mixed Media. *Publ:* Illusr, Half a Century, Nat Football League, 70. *Mailing Add:* Dept Art Santa Rosa Jr Col 1501 Mendocino Ave Santa Rosa CA 95401

HEINE-BAUX, MANFRED
PAINTER, PRINTMAKER
b Munich, Ger, Dec 24, 40, nat Canadian. *Study:* Acad Fine Arts, Munich, MFA, PhD(art hist), 64. *Work:* Mercedes-Benz, Stuttgart, Ger; BMW Munich, Toronto; Haus der Kunst Mus, Munich; Univ Toronto; Univ Kyoto. *Comn:* Portrait, King Faisal, Saudi Arabia, 74; Siemens Calendar, 92. *Exhib:* Thompson Gallery, NY, 74; Living Arts Biennale, Johannesburg, S Africa, 76; Le Grand Palais, Paris, 77; RUF Gallery (with Chagall & Dali), Munich, 83; Art Guild of Can, 84-; solo exhibs, Carimor Gallery, NY, 85 & 86; retrospective, BMW Gallery, Toronto, 89. *Teaching:* Asst prof, Acad Fine Arts, Munich, 64-66. *Awards:* First Place Painting, Living Arts Biennale, Johannsburg, SA; First Place Etching, Living Arts Biennale; Best Show, Ann Arbor, 92. *Bibliog:* Lifestyles, Spring 87; Guide Vallèe II & III; Arts on View: Heine Baux (film). *Mem:* Soc Can Artists; Am Soc Artists. *Media:* Acrylic; Aquatint-etchings, Serigraphs. *Dealer:* Art Guild of Canada 641 Queenston Rd Cambridge ON N3H 3K2. *Mailing Add:* 641 Queenston Rd Cambridge ON N3H 3K2 Canada

HEINEMANN, PETER
PAINTER, INSTRUCTOR, EDUCATOR
b Denver, Colo, Apr 22, 31. *Study:* Black Mountain Col, 1 yr, with Joseph Albers, 48-49. *Comn:* Multi-figure oil mural, NY Coun Arts, 71-72. *Exhib:* Nat Inst Arts & Lett, NY, 60, 61 & biennially 70, 71 & 72; Heckscher Mus, Huntington, NY, 79; Nat Acad Design, 81 & 82; Gallery 120, NY, 83; Visual Arts Mus, 83; Schlesinger Boisante Gallery, NY, 85, 87, 89, 92 & 94. *Teaching:* Instr painting & drawing, Sch Visual Arts, NY, 60-, Studio Sch, NY, 83-84. *Awards:* Creative Artists Pub Serv Grants, 71-72, 74-75 & 77-78; Childe Hassam Purchase Award, 72; Nat Endowment Arts, 83-84; NY Found Arts Grant, 86. *Mem:* Nat Acad. *Media:* Oil. *Mailing Add:* Sch Visual Arts 209 E 23rd St New York NY 10010-3994

HEINICKE, JANET L HART
PAINTER, EDUCATOR
b Richmond, Ind. *Study:* Wittenberg Univ, BS(art educ, cum laude), 52; Univ Wis-Madison, MS(art educ), 56, study with Colescott & Meeker; Northern Ill Univ, EdD, 76, MFA(painting), 77, Syracuse Univ, 92. *Work:* Richmond Art Asn, Ind; Kankakee Community Col, Ill; Simpson Col, Indianola, Iowa; Wausau Medical Group, Wis; Iowa Lakes Community Col, Estherville, Iowa; We-toast Corp, Chicago, Ill; Artists of Iowa Collection, Nat Bank Waterloo; Hy Vee Corp, Des Moines, Iowa; Caterpillar Corp, Peoria, Ill; Farm Services Corp, Blooming, Ill. *Comn:* Painting, Caterpillar Corp, Peoria, Ill, 80. *Exhib:* Solo exhibs, Western Ill Univ, Macomb, 83 & Cedar Rapids Mus Art, Iowa, 84, Small Surprises, Kirkwood Community Col, 2005; Stavropol City Mus, Stavropol Krai, Russia, 92; State Mus, Cherkassy Oblast, Ukraine, 98; Woodland Scenes, Kirkwood Community Col, 2000; Ariz Aquons, Tubac Ctr for the Arts, 03; Ia Watercolor Traveling Exhib 2004-2005; Nat Exhib of Sacred Art, First Methodist Church, Evanston, Ill, 2004; Watercolor Nat Show, Norris Ctr, St Charles, Ill, 2005. *Pos:* Art dept prog coordr, Kankakee Community Col, Ill, 77-81; guest lectr, Univ Dar es Salaan Tanzania, E Africa. *Teaching:* Asst prof art, Judson Col, Elgin, Ill, 69-74; chmn art dept, Simpson Col, Indianola, Iowa, 81-2001, prof & chmn fine arts div, prof emeritus, 01-; educ consult, Univ Latvia, Riga, 93; vis scholar, Fukuoka Jo Gakin, Japan, 93; vis lectr, Univ Phillipines, Cebu, 95, Univ Cantho, Cantho Province, Vietnam, 95, Cherkassy, Ukraine, 98; teacher, relief printmaking, Japanese paper, Malaysian silk batik, Des Moines Art Center, educ progr,. *Awards:* Best in Show, Landscape Painters Midwest, Tower Park Gallery, Peoria, Ill, 79; Research Award, Simpson Col, 94, Governors Award, 95 & Fac Serv Award, 94; Merit Award, Iowa State Fair, 97; Merit Award, Bismarck Art Asn, 01; Alumni Award, Wittenberg Univ, 02; Alumni Award, Col of Educ, Northern Ill Univ, 03; Fourth Place Prize, Iowa Watercolor Asn Ann Show. *Mem:* Iowa Arts Coun; Ill Arts Coun; Col Art Asn; Chicago Artists Coalition; Nat Coun Art Adminrs; Christians in Visual Art. *Media:* Acrylic, Watercolor, Mixed Media, Monoprint, Collagraph. *Publ:* Iowa Women Artists, Oral Hist Project, 2000; reviewer, Choice, Am Libr Asn. *Mailing Add:* 1302 W Boston Ave Indianola IA 50125

HEINTZ, FLORENT
APPRAISER
Study: Harvard Univ, ThM, 93, PhD, 99. *Pos:* Keeper of Coins, Harvard Univ Art Mus; cur asst, Worcester Art Mus, Mass; antiquities specialist to asst vice-pres Sotheby's, NYC, 2001-. *Awards:* Named Dunbarton Oaks Junior Fel, Harvard Univ, 98-99. *Publ:* Auth, Agnostic Magic in the Late Antique Circus, 99. *Mailing Add:* Sotheby's NY 1334 York Ave New York NY 10021

HEINZ, SUSAN
ADMINISTRATOR
Study: Brown Univ, BA; Harvard Univ, MA; Univ Calif, Los Angeles, MA(film hist & criticism); Phi Beta Kappa. *Pos:* Educ coordr, Jr Arts Ctr, Los Angeles Munic Arts Dept, 68-73; mem, Los Angeles Munic Arts Comn, 73-78; exec dir, Palos Verdes Art Ctr & Mus, Rancho Palos Verdes, 74-78; mem, Mayor's Citizen's Adv Comt Arts, Los Angeles; dir, Corp Progs, Asia Soc, New York, 78-, vpres, 95-97; consultant on Asian affairs, currently. *Awards:* Am Film Inst Scholar, 72-73; Smithsonian Inst Grant (res in India), 74. *Mem:* Cosmopolitan Club, NY. *Mailing Add:* 315 E 68th St New York NY 10021-5692

HEINZEN, MARYANN
PAINTER, ASSEMBLAGE ARTIST
b Bronx, NY, July 30, 52. *Study:* Art Students League, 86, with Mario Cooper & Joseph Rossi; Nat Art League, Douglaston, NY, with Ed Whitney, Pvt instr, 6 yrs with Yukio Tashiro. *Work:* DuPont Pharmaceuticals, Endo Bldg, Garden City, NY. *Exhib:* Salmagundi Club Exhib, NY, 83, 88 & 91; Nat Arts Club Exhib, NY, 88; Nassau Co Mus Art, Vaali, 88 & Artists at Work, 91, The Expert Eye, Wunsch Gallery, Coun Arts, Long Island, 90; solo shows, James Beard House, Greenhouse Gallery, NY, 93-94 & 97-98 & Natural Eclectic, NYack, NY, 98. *Pos:* Pres, Nat Art League, Douglaston, NY, 90-92, vpres, 92-; demonstr, Nat Art League, Floral Park, Flushing Art League, NY & Tri Co Artists. *Teaching:* Teacher watercolor, formerly; artist in residence, Freeport Coun Arts, Chelsea Ctr, E Norwich, 93-94; instr watercolor, Nat Art League, Douglaston, 91-92. *Awards:* Award of Excellence, Tri Co Exhib, Tri Co Art League, 90 & 94; First Prize, Rockville Ctr Guild Arts, 90; Award of Excellence, Indep Art Soc, Long Island, 90; Best in Show, North by South Exhib, Nassau Co Mus Art, 93; Gene Alden Walker Award, Nat Asn Women Artist, NY, 74; and others. *Mem:* Nat Asn Women Artists; Coast Guard Artists (mem chmn 88-90, pres 90-92 & vpres, 92-); Nat Art League. *Media:* Watercolor. *Publ:* Contribr, The Artists Guide to Showing & Selling Your Work, North Lights Books, 89; summer & fall issues of continuing educ, Queensboro Community Col Catalog; Queens Borough Community Col, 92. *Dealer:* Chandler-Edwards Gallery Port Washington NY; Owl 57 Gallery Woodmere NY. *Mailing Add:* 208 Waters Edge Valley Cottage NY 10989

HEIPP, RICHARD CHRISTIAN
PAINTER, INSTRUCTOR
b Cleveland, Ohio, June 23, 52. *Study:* Ceveland Inst Art, BFA(Agnes Gund Scholar), 76; Univ Wash, Seattle, MFA, 79. *Work:* Seattle Art Mus, Seattle, Wash; Jacksonville Art Mus, Jacksonville, Fla; Art in State Bldgs, State Fla; Shriners Children's Hosp, Tampa, Fl; Miami Univ, Oxford, Ohio; Albion Col, Mich; Polk Mus, Lakeland FL; Collection in Perspective, Tampa Mus Art, 2001. *Comn:* Paintings, Citrus Res Ctr, Lake Alfred, Fla, 87; State Fire Col, Art in State Bldg Prog, Marion Co, Fla, 89, Hurston Regional Serv Ctr, Orlando, Fla, 90; Student Recreation Ctr, Fla State Univ, Tallahassee, 91; Jacksonville Mus Modern Art, 2000; IFAS Cent Fla Res & Educ Center, 2001; Col of Journalism, Univ Fla, Gainesville, 02; N Ft Lauderdale Pub Libr, Broward Co, Fl, 03. *Exhib:* One-person exhibs, Seattle Pac Univ, Wash, 80, Huntingdon Col, Montgomery, Ala, 83, Ctr Contemp Art, Univ Ky, Lexington, 84, The Barn Gallery, Middle Tenn State Univ, Murfreesboro, 87, Fine Art Gallery, Stetson Univ, Deland, Fla, 92, Savannah Col Art & Design, Savanna, Ga, 92, Low Gallery, Atlanta, 96; May Show, Cleveland Mus Art, Ohio, 75-77; Fla Creates, Jacksonville Art Mus, 87; All Fla Bi-Annual, Polk Mus Art, Lakeland, Fla, 89; All Fla Exhib, Boca Raton Mus Art, Fla, 91; Group exhib: Fla Fellowship Exhib, Univ W Fla, Pensacola, 99, 50th Ann All Fla Invitational, Boca Raton Mus Art, 03, Richard Heipp, 2 works, Galleria Exhib, Harn Mus Art, Gainesville, 02-03. *Collection Arranged:* Ala Power and Light, Birmingham, Albion Col Collection, Mich, City of Seattle, Harn Mus Art, Gainesville, Fl, Miami Univ Collection, Oxford, Ohio, Seattle Art Mus, Shirner's Children's Hosp, Tampa, Univ Fla, Gainesville. *Teaching:* Vis instr drawing, Univ Puget Sound, 79-80; assoc prof painting, Univ Fla, Gainesville, 80-95; prof painting, Univ Fla, Gainesville, 95-. *Awards:* Ford Found Travel Grant, Univ Wash, 79; Fla Individual Artist Fel, State of Fla, 83, 89 & 97-98; Res Develop Award, DSR, Univ Fla, 82, 87 & 92; Prof (Res Found) Coll Fine Art, Univ Fla, 99-2001; Southern Arts Fedn Endowment of Arts in Painting, 96-97; Scholarship Enhancement Award, Univ Fla, 01-03; Fla Individual Artist Fel, State of Fla, 02-03. *Media:* Airbrush, Mixed. *Mailing Add:* 1500 NW 35th Terr Gainesville FL 32605-4832

HEISE, MYRON ROBERT
PAINTER
b Bancroft, Nebr, June 30, 34. *Study:* Univ Omaha; Art Students League; Pratt Ctr Contemp Printmaking, New York; Acad Fine Arts, Florence, Italy; also with Arthur Lee, Robert Brackman, Marshall Glaisier & Frank Mason. *Work:* Mus City NY, NYNEX Corp & Peat, Marwick Main & Co, NY; Creighton Univ, Omaha, Nebr; John G Neihardt Found, Bancroft, Nebr; Sheldon Art Mus, Lincoln, Nebr; Mus Nebr Art, Kearny. *Comn:* Mural, Manhattan Lab Mus,80; two murals, NYNEX Corp, NY, 84; two murals, Realex Corp, NY, 99. *Exhib:* One-man exhibs, Capricorn Gallery, Bethesda, Md, 80, Wayne State Col, Nebr, 81, Norfolk Arts Ctr, Nebr, 81, Neihart Ctr, Bancroft, Nebr, 81-82 & 94-96, Creighton Univ, Omaha, Nebr, 85, Dana Col, Blair, Nebr, 86 & Noho Gallery, NY, 89; Street Painters, Lincoln Ctr Cork Gallery, NY, 84-96; Artists Choice, The First Eight Yrs, Artist's Choice Mus, NY, 84; Street

Painters, Summit Art Ctr, NJ, 84; Street Painters, NY Inst Technol, 85; New York City Works, 1 Penn Plaza, 88; FDR Gallery, NY, 94; Gallery 72, Omaha, Nebr, 94-96; and many others. *Pos:* Assoc art ed, Time Capsule Mag, currently. *Teaching:* Teacher painting & drawing, New Sch Social Res, 77-78, Educ Alliance Art Sch, 78-84 & Sch Body-Mind Centering, 78-83; numerous workshops 81, 82 & 89. *Awards:* Nat Endowment artist-in-residence Grant, St Mary's Creative Arts Forum, 80; artist-in-residence, Neihardt Found, Bancroft, Nebr, 81-94; and others. *Bibliog:* Judy Johnson (auth), The New York street painter who also does Main Street, Mag Midlands, 10/83; article, Myron Heise does demonstration painting, Norfolk News, 8/85; article, Myron Heise celebrates hometown, Sioux City J, 8/85; Night visions of Myron Heise, Art World, 5/89; Artist and Critic, Channel C, Cable TV, New York, 4/89. *Mem:* Alliance Figurative Artists (founding mem, 69-, chmn, 76-78); Artists Equity, NY; Fedn Mod Painters & Sculptors, NY. *Media:* Oil, Etching. *Publ:* Auth, Introducing the street painters, Time Capsule, fall 81; and others. *Dealer:* Gallery 72 Omaha NE

HEISKELL, DIANA
PAINTER
b Paris, France; US citizen. *Work:* Santa Barbara Mus Art, Calif; Slater Mus, Norwich, Conn; S Vermont Art Ctr, Manchester. *Exhib:* Whitney Mus Am Art Ann, 2 yrs; Chicago Art Inst; Boston Arts Festival; De Cordova & Dana Mus, Lincoln, Mass; Southern Vt Art Ctr, Manchester; and others. *Awards:* Hon Mention, Berkshire Art Asn; Grumbacher Prize, Southern Vt Art Ctr. *Mem:* Southern Vt Art Asn (trustee); Berkshire Art Asn. *Media:* Oil, Watercolor. *Mailing Add:* RFD 4 Box 375 Brattleboro VT 05301

HEIZER, MICHAEL
ENVIRONMENTAL ARTIST, SCULPTOR
b Berkeley, Calif, Nov 4, 1944. *Study:* San Francisco Art Inst, 63-64. *Work:* Mus Contemp Art, Los Angeles; Metrop Mus, NY; Detroit Inst Arts, Mich; Rijksmuseum Krôller-Mûller, Otterlo, Holland; Kunsthalle, Berne, Switz. *Comn:* This Equals That (outdoor sculpture), Capital Plaza, Lansing, Mich, 77-80; Platform, Oakland Mus, Calif, 80; Levitated Mass, IBM Corp, NY, 82; North, East, South, West, Rockerfeller Develop Corp, Los Angeles, Calif, 82; Effigy Tumuli (sculpture), Ottawa Silica Found, 85. *Exhib:* Currents 7, St Louis Art Mus, Mo, 80; The Americans: The Landscape, Contemp Arts Mus, Houston, Tex, 81; 20 Am Artists: Sculpture 1982, San Francisco Mus Mod Art, Calif, 82; Geometric Extraction, Mus Contemp Art, Los Angeles, Calif, 84; Dragged Mass Geometric, Whitney Mus Am Art, NY, 85; Art Before Life, Ace Gallery, 94; Works: 1972-76, Galerie Frank + Schulte, Berlin, Germany; Negative - Positive +, Fondazione Prada, Milan, Italy, 96; Hard Edge Ejecta, Knoedler & Co, NY, 98; PaceWildenstein, NY, 2006. *Bibliog:* Ellen Joosten & Feliz Zdenek (coauths), Michael Heizer Mus Folkwang & Rijksmuseum Keoller-Muller, 79; Julia Brown (ed), Michael Heizer sculpture in reverse, Mus Contemp Art, Los Angeles, 84; David Bourdon (auth), Working with earth Michael Heizer makes art big as all outdoors, Smithsonian, Vol 17, No 1 pg 68-74 & 76-77, 4/86. *Media:* Earthworks. *Mailing Add:* c/o Knoedler & Co 19 E 70th St New York NY 10021

HELD, (JOHN) JONATHAN, JR
MAIL ARTIST, WRITER
b New York, NY, Apr 2, 47. *Study:* Utica Col, Syracuse Univ, BA, 69, Sch Info Sci, MLS, 71; Studied with Prof Emer Antje Lemke. *Work:* Jean Brown Collection, Getty Ctr Humanities, Santa Monica, Calif; Mus Mod Art Libr, NY; papers, Arch Am Art, Smithsonian Inst; Musee de la Paste, Paris, France, Mayakovsky Mus, Moscow Russia. *Comn:* Stanley Marsh III, Amarillo, Tex; Am Philatelic Soc, 2002. *Exhib:* Stampworks, Stempelplaats Gallery, Amsterdam, The Neth, 76; Timbres d'Artistes, Mus de la Poste, Paris, France, 93; Networker Stamp Portfolio, National Acad of Art, Prague, Czech Republic, 94; 1st Int Post-Futurist Exhib, Mayakovsky Mus, 2003; Post-Modern Perforations, Cult Centre Buz, Minden, Ger, 2004. *Collection Arranged:* Mail Art About Mail Art, Richland Col, 82; Int Mail Art, Nat Mus Beaux Arts, Havana, Cuba, 95; Faux Post, Various Venues, Visual Arts Resources, Portland, Ore, 95-98; Bay Area Dada, San Francisco Pub Libr, San Francisco, Calif, 98; Printed Matter, New York, 99; Peace Island, Jeju Island, South Korea, 2001. *Pos:* Video librn, Mid-York Libr System, Utica, NY, 76-81; art librn, Dallas Pub Libr, 81-95; Stamp Art Gallery, San Francisco, Calif, 95-97; dir, Modern Realism Gallery, San Francisco, 97-. *Awards:* Can Coun Arts, Que Networker Congress, 94; Artpool Art Res Ctr, Budapest, Hungary, 94. *Bibliog:* Clive Phillpot (auth), Mail art review, Art Libr. J, 92; V Vale (auth), Zines Vol 2, RE/Search, San Francisco, CA, 97; Vittore Baroni (auth), Arte Postale; Guida al Network della Corrispondenza Creativa, AAA Edizioni, Bertiolo, Italy, 98; Saper, Craig, Networkd Art, Univ of Minn, Press, 2001. *Media:* Mail Art, Rubber Stamps, Artist Postage Stamps. *Res:* history of 20th century avant-gardes; Russian modernism, dada, fluxus, mail art. *Specialty:* Relies and Documents of the 20th Century Avant-Garde. *Interests:* Mail art, Artistamps. *Publ:* Contribr, Dictionary of Art, Grove, 96: (auth) Mail Art; An Annotated Bibliog, Scarecrow Press, 91; Rubber Stamp Art, AAA Edizioni, Betiolo, Italy, 99; Ray Johnson (auth), A Living Thing In Flight; Collection and Preparing Contemporary Avant-Garde Materials for an Archive, Archives Am Art Jour, 2000; At a Distance, MIT Press, 2005. *Dealer:* Mod Realism Gallery 263 8th Ave San Francisco CA 94118. *Mailing Add:* PO Box 410837 San Francisco CA 94141

HELDER, DAVID ERNEST
PAINTER, SCULPTOR
b Seattle, Wash, Feb 4, 1947. *Study:* Calif Col Arts & Crafts, BA, 69, MFA, 71; Stanford Univ, MA, 75. *Work:* Oakland Mus, Calif. *Exhib:* Galex 23 Nat Juried Exhib, Galesburg Civic Art Ctr, Ill, 89; The Surrealist Salon, RayKo Ctr, San Francisco, 91; The Summer Salon, Helio Gallery, NY, 91; Macro/micro Int Exhib, Helio Gallery, NY, 91; and others. *Pos:* Aesthetic ed consult, Isaacson Inst, Berkeley, Calif, 72-74 & Univ Minneapolis, 88-; Aesthetic Ed Consult, Univ of Minneapolis,88-. *Awards:* Westmorland Award, 88; Cert of Excellence Int Art Comp, Westmorland Art and Heritage Festival, 88. *Bibliog:* Charles Shere (auth), Mind in the matter, Oakland Tribune, 5/74; Bob Harrison (auth), Artist makes it easy to see, San Francisco Visitors News, 2/81; Diane L Saiget (auth), David Helder's magic doors, City Arts, 2/81. *Media:* Acrylic, Oil; All Media. *Dealer:* Michael Bell 140 Page St No 1 San Francisco Calif 94102. *Mailing Add:* 636 Stanyan St San Francisco CA 94117-1807

HELDT, CARL RANDALL
EDUCATOR, PAINTER
b Stanford, Ill, Sept 8, 25. *Study:* Wittenburg Col, Springfield, Ohio, 43-44; Univ Ill, Urbana, BFA, 53; Ariz State Univ, Tempe, 60-61. *Work:* Fennemore Craig Law Firm, Phoenix; Hallmark Cards, Kansas City; Phoenix Col, Phoenix; Univ Ariz, Tucson. *Comn:* Murals, Kahler Hotel, Rochester, Minn, 54; watercolors, Ford Motor Co, Deerborn, Mich, 63; cards, toys & crafts, Hallmark Cards, Kansas City, 68-73; Baptismal Font, Fountain of Life Lutheran Church, Tucson; stained glass, Ascension Luthern Church, Tucson. *Exhib:* Southwestern Invitational, Yuma Art Ctr, Ariz, 67-75; Cedar City Invitational, Utah, 67-76; 4 Corners Biennial, Phoenix Mus, Ariz, 71; 22nd Ann NY Soc Illustrators; solo, Univ Ill, Urbana; plus others. *Pos:* Med illusr, Univ Ill, Urbana, 49-53; art dir, Our Wonderful Encycl, Champaign, Ill, 53-55; artist-in-residence, Hallmark Cards, Kansas City; bd dir, Waste Management Symp, Tucson, 93. *Teaching:* Instr graphic design, Univ Ill, Urbana, 55-60; prof graphic design, Univ Ariz, 61-90. *Awards:* Phoenix Art Dirs Club, 68; Purchase Award, Cedar City Invitational; Col Southwestern Utah, 75. *Media:* Oil, Acrylic. *Publ:* Illusr, New York Times, 62; illusr, Ford Times Mag, 63; contribr, Arizona Alumnus Mag, Univ Ariz, 79; Arizona Review Mag, 80; Arizona Highways, 85; Nuclear Tech, 90. *Dealer:* Details & Green Shoelaces 2990 N Swan Tucson AZ 85712. *Mailing Add:* 4560 N Via Sinuosa Tucson AZ 85745-9764

HELFAND, FERN M
PHOTOGRAPHER, DIGITAL ARTIST
b Toronto, Ont. *Study:* York Univ, Toronto, BA(studio art, honours), 74; Univ Fla, with Jerry Uelsmann, MFA, 80; Sheridan Col, cert(computer graphics), 94. *Work:* Can Coun Art Bank, Can Mus Contemp Photog, Dept External Affaires Can, Ottawa, Ont; McIntosh Gallery, Univ Western Ont, London, Ont; Nat Gallery Malaysia, Kuala Lumpur; London Life Insurance; London Regional Art & Hist Mus. *Exhib:* London/Havana Exchange, Casa de las Americas, Cuba, 88; Arts & The Social Context, Nat Gallery Malaysia, Kuala Lumpur, 91; Women & Creativity, Nat Gallery Malaysia, Kuala Lumpur, 92; solo exhib, London Regional Art Gallery & Mus, London, Ont, 94-95 & McIntosh Gallery, Univ Western Ontario, London, Ont, 99; Niagara, Art Gallery Windsor, Ont, 2000; Photo Gallery, Harbourfront, Toronto, 2003; Kelowna Art Gallery & Kelowna Mus, 2005; Kaunas Photo Days '06, Kaunas, Lithuania, 2006. *Collection Arranged:* Work of Art & Scholar (with catalog), Fac Show, Univ Western Ont, 85; Beyond the Document, Forest City Gallery, London, Ont, 89; Bengawan Solo Sekali Sekala (Penang artists), Maybank Gallery & Univ Kebangsaan, Kuala Lumpur, 92; Valley 2000, Kelowna Art Gallery & Kelowna Mus, 2002. *Pos:* Bd mem, Forest City Gallery, Sunfest Int Music & Arts Festival & pres, Alternator Gallery, Kelowna, Can; pub art com, City of Kelowna. *Teaching:* Asst prof photog, Univ Western Ont, 82-89; vis prof, Univ Sci Malaysia, 89-92; vis lectr, Ont Col Art, 94-95; assoc prof, Okanagan Univ, 98-05; assoc prof, Univ of British Columbia, Okanagan, 2005-. *Awards:* Can Coun B Grant, 83; First Place, Nat Gallery Malaysia, 91; Millennium grant, Govt Can, 2000. *Bibliog:* Rodney Gilchrist (auth), The transcendetal tourist, Photo Life, 7/89; James Patton (auth), Fern Helfand, Another Time, Another Place, London Regional Art Gallery Mus, 12/94; Catherine Elliot Shaw (auth, editor), Fabricated Communities, McKintosh Gallery, 2000; Dr Robert Belton (autho), Sites of Resistance, Canadian Visual Culture, 2001; Artspots CBS Television & Website, 2002. *Mem:* Int Vis Sociology Asn. *Media:* Digital Imaging, Photography. *Res:* Visual sociology; tourism; fabricated communities. *Mailing Add:* Univ of British Columbia Okanagan 3333 Univ Way Kelowna BC V1V 7766 Canada

HELGESON, PHILLIP LAWRENCE
PAINTER, ILLUSTRATOR, GRAPHIC ARTIST
b Albuquerque, NMex, June 11, 60. *Study:* Cincinnati Art Acad, BFA, 60, studied with Stuart Goldman, Anne Miotke, Constance McClure, Cole Corathers, Michael Scott & Robert Fabe. *Work:* Clossons Art Gallery, Cincinnati Art Club & Lexington Art Works Expo, Cincinnati, Ohio; Janet Gamin, 97; Tina Montano, 97; Jennie Heine, 97. *Comn:* Marathon mural, comn by Mark Mandefield, Helgeson, Cincinnati, 83; portrait, comn by Vicky Elsbrock, Cincinnati, 87; Indian painting, comn by Donald Helgeson, Ocean Springs, Miss, 89; Garden portrait, Clossons Art Gallery, Cincinnati, 98; 40th Anniversary Poster, Moeller High Sch (finalist), Bill Long, Cincinnati, 98. *Exhib:* Art Acad Show, Cincinnati Art Mus, 84; Art Acad Sr Show, Art Acad Cincinnati, 84; Members Show, Cincinnati Art Club, 97; Clossons Art Gallery, Cincinnati, 97 & 99; Clossons Say It With Flowers Exhib, Cincinnati, 97-98; Viewpoint Exhib, 98; Cinergy Art Exhib, 98; Montgomery Art Show. *Pos:* chief creative officer, T-Shirt Co, Cincinnati, Ohio, 88-. *Awards:* Scholarship painting, Acad Cincinnati, 83. *Bibliog:* Art exhibitions, City Beat, 97; Gallery News, Clossons, 97; City Beat, 2/16/2005. *Mem:* Art Acad Alumni Asn; Taos Art Asn; Cape Ann Art Asn; Ohio Watercolor Soc; Cincinnati Art Club; Am Impressionists Soc. *Media:* Oil, Watercolor; Gouache. *Specialty:* Impressionism. *Collection:* Artists from Golden Age of Cincinnati including Constance McClure, Charles Kaelin, Carl and Carolyn Zimmerman, Robert Fabe and John Weis; Reginald Grooms. *Dealer:* Clossons-Marie Rigney 10100 Montgomery Rd Cincinnati OH 45242-5324. *Mailing Add:* 12009 Stillwood Dr Cincinnati OH 45249

HELIOFF, ANNE GRAILE (MRS BENJAMIN HIRSCHBERG)
PAINTER, COLLAGE ARTIST
b Liverpool, Eng; US citizen. *Study:* Art Students League; Homer Boss & Kuniyoshi; Hans Hofmann Sch. *Work:* Archives Am Art; Smithsonian Mus; Whatcom Mus; Woodstock NY Hist Soc. *Exhib:* Paintings of the Yr, 46, Pepsi Cola Nat; Pa Acad Fine Arts, Philadelphia; Dedication Exhibition, Nat Gallery Art, Washington, DC; Art USA Traveling Exhib; Am Exhib, Palazzo Uecchio, Florence, Italy & Mus Naples, Italy, 72; Bicentennial Expo Six Am Painters, Annemasse & Cluses, France; Philadelphia Mus; Berkshire Mus; solo exhibs, Capricorn Gallery, 64, 66, 69 & Phoenix Gallery, NY, 71, 73, 76, 82, 83 & 85; Woodstock Artists Asn, 88; Milch Gallery, NY; Albany Mus Art & Sci. *Pos:* Mem, US Deleg to 5th Cong, Int Asn Artists, Tokyo, 66; dir exhib, Dedication New York City Lighthouse, Tricentennial; 50 Years of Woodstock Art, YMHA Series, Kaufmann, NY. *Teaching:* Lectr, Y Kuniyoshi Summer Sch, Woodstock, NY, 42-44. *Awards:* Silver Medal, Albany NY Mus Art & Sci; Oil Awards, Am Soc Contemp Artists, Riverside Mus, 62 & Berkshire Mus; Three Cert of Merit, Am Soc Contemp Artists, 70; and others. *Bibliog:* C Offin (auth) article, Pictures exhib, 11/76; N Frachtman (auth) article, Arts Mag, 1/77; William Pellicone, 82 & Palmer Poroner, Artspeak, 85; Gordon Brown, Arts, 82; Dorothy Hall, Park East, 85; and others. *Mem:* Am Soc Contemp Artists; NY Soc Women Artists; life mem Woodstock Artists Asn. *Media:* Acrylic, Oil

HELLER, BEN
DEALER, COLLECTOR
b New York, NY, Oct 16, 25. *Study:* Bard Col, BA. *Pos:* Benefactor, Metrop Mus Art, NY; past trustee or bd mem, Int Coun of Mus Mod Art, Friends of Whitney Mus Am Art & Jewish Mus. *Collection.* Contemporary American painting and ancient Asian art, Eastern and primitive arts. *Mailing Add:* 14 Webber Rd Sharon CT 06069

HELLER, DOROTHY
PAINTER
b New York, NY. *Study:* With Hans Hofmann. *Work:* Metrop Mus Art, NY; Univ Calif Art Mus, Berkeley; Smithsonian Inst-Archives; Wadsworth Atheneum, Hartford, Conn; Allen Mem Art Mus, Oberlin, Ohio; Johnson Mus at Cornell Univ, Ithaca, NY; and others. *Exhib:* Solo exhibs, Poindexter Gallery, NY, 56-57, Easthampton Gallery, NY, 63, Betty Parsons Gallery, NY, 72, 76 & 78, Libr, NJ, 75, Cathedral St John Divine, NY, 76, Univ Pa, Philadelphia, 76 & St Pete's Church, NY, 79; Whitney Mus Ann, NY, 57; Carnegie Int, Pittsburgh, 59; Mus Mod Art Traveling Show, 63; Wadsworth Atheneum, Hartford, Conn, 64; Betty Parsons Gallery, NY, 72-91; Albright-Knox Gallery, Buffalo, NY, 74; Univ Calif Art Mus, Berkeley, 74; Otis Art Inst, Los Angeles, 79; Metrop Mus Art, NY, 79; Brooklyn Col Art Gallery, NY, 90; and others. *Awards:* Int Women's Year Award, 76. *Bibliog:* Simone Auger (auth), La Presse, Montreal, Can, 63; Diana Loercher (auth), Christian Sci Monitor, 10/22/76; Theodore Wolff (auth), Christian Sci Monitor, 5/22/79. *Media:* Acrylic on Paper & Canvas. *Mailing Add:* 8 W 13th St New York NY 10011

HELLER, GOLDIE (MRS EDWARD W GREENBERG)
COLLECTOR, CONSULTANT
b Salem, Mass. *Study:* Mass Col Art. *Exhib:* Andy Warhol Gold Shoe, Andy Warhol: A Retrospective, 89. *Pos:* Art dir, vpres. *Mem:* Mus Mod Art; Metrop Mus Art. *Collection:* Braque, Roualt, Henry Botkin, Ralph Rosenborg, Byron Browne, Noel Rockmore, Andy Warhol, Francisco Larez, Jose de Creeft, John Ross, June Rogoff, Joseph Bolegard, Clare Romano, Erwin Wending, William Seidel, and others

HELLER, REINHOLD AUGUST
HISTORIAN
b Fulda, Ger, July 22, 1940; US citizen. *Study:* St Joseph's Col, Philadelphia, BS, 63; Ind Univ, Bloomington, MA, 66, PhD, 68, with Albert Elsen, John Jacobus & Sven Loevgren. *Pos:* Guest cur, Nat Gallery, Washington, DC, 78-79. *Teaching:* Prof art hist, Univ Pittsburgh, 68-78 & Univ Chicago, 78-. *Awards:* Foreign Area Prog Fel, 66-68; Guggenheim Found Fel, 73-74; d'Harnoncourt Fel, Mus Mod Art, New York, 70. *Mem:* Col Art Asn; Ger Studies Asn; Historians of Ger & Cent Europ Art. *Res:* Art criticism; Symbolism; Expressionism; German Romanticism; German art of the 1920's. *Publ:* Auth, Art of Wilhelm Lehmbruck, Nat Gallery, Washington, DC, 72; Hildegard Auer: A Yearning for Art, Belserverlag, 87; Brücke: German Expressionist prints in the Granvil and Marcia Specks Collection, Block Gallery, Northwestern Univ, Evanston, Ill, 88; Art in Germany 1909-1936: From Expressionism to Resistance, The Marvin and Janet Fishman Collection, Prestel-Verlag, 90; Toulouse-Lautrec: The Soul of Montmartre, Prestel-Lerlag, 97 & Gabriele Munter: The Years of Expressionism, 97. *Mailing Add:* 1325 Linden Rd Homewood IL 60430

HELLER, SUSANNA
PAINTER, INSTRUCTOR
b New York, NY, 1956. *Study:* Nova Scotia Col Art & Design, BFA, 74-77. *Work:* Art Gallery of Ontario; Concordia Univ, Montreal; Canadian Art Bank, Ottawa; TD Waterhouse Corp; Air Canada Corp. *Exhib:* Mus London, Can, Concordia Univ Gallery, Mocca-Contemp Art, Toronto, Shangha Art Mus, China, Nova Scotia Mus Art; Olga Korper Gallery, Toronto, Luise Ross Gallery, NY, Galerie Paul Andresse, Amsterdam, AIR Gallery, NY, Tibor de Nagy Gallery, NY. *Teaching:* lectr, painting & drawing, Purchase Col, The New Sch, Bennington Col, Yale Univ, Nova Scotia Col Art. *Awards:* The Nat Endowment for the Canada Council; John Simon Guggenheim Mem Found Fel, 88. *Bibliog:* John Clark (auth), No Apologies, Vanguard, Vancouver, 2-3/89; Robert Berlind (auth), review, Art in Am, 2/89; Ken Johnson (auth), The New York Times, review, 1998; March Gregoroff (auth), Flash Art, review, 2002; Gary Michael Dault (auth), The Globe & Mail, Toronto, review, 2002. *Mem:* Col Art Asn. *Media:* Acrylic, Oil. Mixed Media. *Specialty:* Fine Arts. *Publ:* auth, From Here, catalogue, Mus London, color & 3 essays, 2002. *Mailing Add:* 233 N Henry Brooklyn NY 11222-3645

HELSELL, CHARLES PAUL
CURATOR
b Ft Dodge, Iowa, Nov 13, 40. *Study:* Mont State Univ, BS, 63. *Collection Arranged:* Hylton A Thomas Collection (paintings, drawings & prints; auth, catalog), Univ Minn Art Mus, 70; Mr Possum and Friends: Prints by Malcolm Myers (auth, catalog), 82; Women in Print: Prints from 3M by Contemporary Women Printmakers (auth, catalog), 3M, 95 & Made in Minnesota I: Art at 3M by Artists Born Before 1930, 97; Country Life, City Life: Prints from the Harold D Peterson Collection (auth, catalog), 96. *Pos:* Asst cur, Dept Prints, Minneapolis Inst Arts, 66-69; cur, Weisman Art Mus (formerly Univ Art Mus), Minneapolis, 69-84; cur art collection, 3M, 84-99; dir Blanden Meml Art Mus, Fort Dodga, Iowa, 2000. *Mem:* Col Art Asn; Print Coun Am. *Mailing Add:* Blanden Mem Art Mus 919 Third Ave South Fort Dodge IA 50501-4723

HELZER, RICHARD BRIAN
METALSMITH, SCULPTOR
b Hastings, Nebr, Aug 27, 43. *Study:* Kearney State Col, Nebr, BA, 65; Univ Kans, MFA, 69. *Work:* C M Russell Mus, Great Falls, Mont; Rocky Mountain Col Libr, Billings, Mont. *Comn:* Altar serv, St Elizabeth's Episcopal Church, Nebr, 69 & Hope Lutheran Church, Kans, 70; alter cross, Univ Kans Chapel, Lawrence, 70 & Sacred Heart Cath Church, Butte, Mont, 86. *Exhib:* Hist of Gold & Silversmithing in Am, Lowe Art Mus, Univ Miami, Coral Gables, Fla, 75; NW Invitational Silversmiths, Seattle Art Mus, Wash, 76; US Off Info Goldsmiths Exhib, Melbourne, Australia, 76; 3rd Profile of US Jewelry, Tex Tech Univ, Lubbock, 77; Metal-non Metal, Synopsis Gallery, Chicago, 80; North Am Goldsmiths European Exhib (traveling); San Francisco Mus Mod Art, 89; Art Equinox Exhib, Paris Gibson Mus Art, Great Falls Mont, 92; Ana 22, Holter Mus, Helena, Mont, 93; and others. *Pos:* Guest cur, Metalsmithing Invitational, Yellowstone Art Ctr, Billings, Mont, 81; vis artist, E Carolina Univ, 89, Arrowmont Sch, Tenn, 88, Penland Sch, NC, 92. *Teaching:* Teaching asst, Univ Kans, Lawrence, 68-69; asst prof art, Mont State Univ, Bozeman, 70-74, assoc prof, 75-80, prof, 80-, dir sch art, 95-. *Awards:* Nat Endowment Arts Fel, 76 & 78; Best of Show, Art Equinox Exhib, Paris Gibson Mus Art, 92; Best of Show, Ana 22, Holter Mus, 93; Westerm States Fel, 79. *Bibliog:* Jewelry Making, Bovin Publ, 80; Oppi Untracht (auth), Jewelry Concepts & Technology, Doubleday & Co; Alice Sprintzen (auth), Jewelry: Basic Techniques & Design, Chilton. *Mem:* Soc NAm Goldsmiths; Am Crafts Coun. *Media:* Multi-Metals, Wood. *Dealer:* Gallatin River Gallery Big Sky Mont; Wood Street Gallery Chicago Ill. *Mailing Add:* 52 Hitching Post Rd Bozeman MT 59715

HEMBREY, SHEA
PAINTER
b Newport, Ark, Aug 21, 74. *Study:* Lyon Col, BA, 96; Univ Canterbury, COP, 98; Ark State Univ, MA, 99. *Work:* Ark State Capitol, Little Rock; Lyon Col, Batesville, Ark; Ark State Univ, Jonesboro. *Exhib:* Guaranteed Fresh: Still Life Today, Invitational, Davidson Galleries, Seattle, Wash, 2003; Summer in the City, J Cacciola Gallery, NY, 2003; Ark Arts Coun Fellows Exhib, Criswell, Hembrey, McCann & Musgnug, Univ Ark Gallery, Little Rock, 2003; Offerings: Shea Hembrey Paintings, David Lusk Gallery, Memphis, Tenn, 2003; Ark State Senate Chambers, Little Rock, 2003; USArtists Am Fine Art Show, Philadelphia, Pa, 2003; Holiday, David Lusk Gallery, Memphis, Tenn, 2004; Wallflowers, Bradbury Gallery, Ark State Univ, 2004; Celebrating Art, The Anderson Ctr, Red Wing, Minn, 2004; Art at Steepletop, Millay Colony for the Arts, Austerlitz, NY, 2004; Bound-Paintings by Shea Hembrey, Helen Day Art Ctr, Stowe, Vt, 2005; New Works, The Anderson Ctr, Red Wing, Minn, 2005; Gags, Tjaden Gallery, Cornell Univ, Ithaca Univ, NY, 2005; Mind the Gap, Tjaden Gallery, Cornell Univ, Ithaca, NY, 2006; Four Walls, Hartell Gallery, Cornell Univ, Ithaca, NY, 2006; Ark Artists, Cox Gallery, Little Rock Public Libr, 2006. *Awards:* Artist Fel Grant, Ark Arts Coun, 2003; Ucross Found Residency, 2004; Caldera Residency, 2005; Weir Farm Residency, 2005; Patterson Decade Award, Lyon Col, 2006. *Media:* Acrylic on Board. *Interests:* Anthropology, folk wisdom, ornithology. *Collection:* Mus quality mezzotint collection with prints by 40 int artists. *Dealer:* David Lusk Gallery, 4540 Poplar Ave, Memphis, TN, 38117. *Mailing Add:* 610 Jackson 63 Newport AR 72112

HEMMERDINGER, WILLIAM JOHN, III
PAINTER, CRITIC
b Burbank, Calif, July 7, 1951. *Study:* Col Desert, Calif, AA, 72; Univ Calif, Riverside, BA, 73; Claremont Grad Sch, MFA, 75, PhD, 79. *Work:* Smithsonian Inst; Tate Gallery, London; Barbara Hepworth Mus, Cornwall, Eng; Fed Reserve Bank, San Francisco; Mus Contemp Art, Los Angeles; Mobil Oil Corp, NY. *Comn:* A Vintage Foyer, comn by the MacDonalds, Indian Wells, Calif, 98; A Shellfisherman's Temple (mixed media sculpture), comn by the McCartys, Osterville, Mass, 97; California Stories, comn by the Nortons, Indian Wells, Calif, 97; California Paintings, Le Merigot Hotel, Santa Monica, Calif, 98; and others; Plaza Hotel Murals, NY. *Exhib:* Solo exhibs, Cirrus Eds, Ltd, Los Angeles, 82, 84, Brand Libr Art Ctr, Glendale, Calif, 90 & Old Selectmens Building Gallery, Barnstable, Mass, 96-99; Olympic Arts Festivals, Los Angeles, Calif & Seoul, Korea; Act IV: Mixed Media, Los Angeles Co Mus Art; Ten Contemp Watercolor Painters, Scripps Col, Claremont, Calif, 87; Boyusan Citizen's Hall, Pusan, Korea, 87; Lalit Kala Acad, Nat Gallery Art, New Delhi, 96; Cahoon Mus Am Art, Cotuit, Mass, 97; Lantern of the East, Pyong-Taek Municipal Mus, Pyong-Taeki, Korea, 98; Nat Acad Design, NY, 71; Am Watercolor Soc, NY, 71; Los Angeles Co Mus Art, 77; Mus Mod Art, Seoul, Korea, 89; Fukuoka Prefecture Mus, Japan, 2000; Int Contemp Art Fairs, London, NY, Chicago, Basel, 72-2000; Otto Galerie, Munich, Ger, 2001; Kitakyushu Mus of Art, Kyushu, Japan, 2001; Double Vision Gallery, Los Angeles, Calif, 2002. *Pos:* Cur, Mus Photog, Univ Calif, Riverside, 73-74; Hemmerdinger Fine Art & Appraisal, Palm Desert, Calif, 84-2002. *Teaching:* Col Desert, Calif, 74-84, Calif State Univ, Long Beach, 79-80, Otis Art Inst, Parsons Sch Design, Los Angeles, 79-81, Univ Calif, Riverside, 82-83,

Calif Inst Arts, Valencia, Calif, 88 & Pomona Col, Claremont, Calif, 90-94; Boston Archit Center, MA, 2002-. *Awards:* Award for Drawing, Nat Watercolor Soc, 74; Nat Watercolor Soc, 79. *Bibliog:* Michael Zakian, PhD (auth), William Hemmerdinger: Paintings, Old Selectmen's Bldg Gallery; Katherine Holland (auth), The Art Collection, Fed Reserve Bank, San Francisco; Robert Perine (auth), The California Romantics, Artras Press. *Media:* Mixed Media Painting & Sculpture. *Res:* Appraisals; archives profiling Am artists of Southern Calif. *Publ:* Auth, Lowell Nesbitt (exhib catalog), Louis Newman Galleries, Los Angeles, 87; Matsumi Kanemitsu (exhib catalog), Japanese Am Community Cult Ctr, Los Angeles, 88; Katherine Chang-Liu (exhib catalog), Louis Newman Galleries, Beverly Hills, 88; Chinese Artists (exhib catalog), Macao Mus, 93; Bong Tae Kim: Thirty Years of Printmaking, Song Bong Ku Press, Seoul, Korea, 94. *Dealer:* Ming Fei Gao Double Vision Gallery Los Angeles CA. *Mailing Add:* Boston Archit Center 320 Newbury St Boston MA 02115

HENDERSHOT, J L
PRINTMAKER, EDUCATOR
b Cleveland, Ohio, Nov 3, 41. *Study:* Cleveland Inst Art, with H C Cassill, Louis Bosa & Julian Stanczak; Syracuse Univ, NY, with George Vander Sluis & Donald Cortesse. *Work:* Rochester Mus Art, NY; Pennell Fund, Libr Cong. *Comn:* Drawing, Alumni Asn, St John's Univ, Collegeville, Minn, 73; drawing for gift, Spira Dance Co, Portland, Ore, 74; print, St Cloud State Col, 75; 50th Anniversary lithographs (50 ed), Minn Mus; lithographs ed, Asn Am Artist. *Exhib:* One-man shows, RI Sch Design, Providence, 75, Assoc Am Artists Gallery, NY, 76, Red River Art Ctr Mus, Moorehead, Minn, 76 & Uptown Gallery, NY, 77; 7th Nat Biennial Drawing US Show, St Paul, Minn, 75; and others. *Pos:* Art gallery dir, St John's Univ, 75-. *Teaching:* Asst instr drawing & printmaking, Syracuse Univ, 68-70; asst prof drawing & printmaking, St John's Univ, 71-. *Awards:* Philadelphia Print Club Purchase Award, Philadelphia Mus Art, 68; Univ NDak Purchase Award, 15th Nat Print & Drawing Exhib, 72; Minn Mus Art Purchase Award, 7th Nat Biennial Drawing US Show, 75. *Mem:* Graphic Soc, Hollis, NH; Boston Printmakers; Pratt Graphics Print Club, NY. *Media:* Intaglio, Lithography. *Mailing Add:* 169 Riverside Dr NE Saint Cloud MN 56304-0437

HENDERSHOT, RAY
PAINTER
b Bangor, Pa, May 26, 31. *Study:* Self taught. *Exhib:* Arts for the Parks Top 100, Nat Parks Acad of the Arts, Jackson Hole, 1993; Nat Watercolor Soc, Brea Civic & Cultural Ctr, Calif, 1999; Pa Watercolor Soc, Behrman Gallery, Ursinus, Collegeville, Pa, 2003; Phila Watercolor Soc, Behrman Gallery, Ursinus, Collegeville, Pa, 2006; Am Watercolor Soc, Salmagundi Club, New York City, 2006. *Awards:* Barse Miller Mem, Am Watercolor Soc, Barse Miller Estate, 2000; PWCS Award for Excellence, Phila Watercolor Soc, 2006; Anne Williams Glushien, Am Watercolor Soc, 2006. *Bibliog:* Stephen Doherty (auth), Textures to Simulate Memories, Am Artist, 2001; Guan Weixing (auth), Ray Hendershot, Chinese Watercolor, 2003; Tom Zeit (auth), Artist's, Recycling For, Artist's Sketchbook, 2004. *Mem:* Signature mem, Am Watercolor Soc; signature mem, Nat Watercolor Soc; signature mem & Sylvan Grouse Recipient, Pa Watercolor Soc; signature mem & Crest Medal Recipient, Phila Watercolor Soc; Int Soc of Acrylic Painters. *Publ:* auth, Blizzard of '93, Palette Talk/Grumbacher, 1994; auth, Texture Techniques for Winning Watercolors, My Own Book/North Light, 1999; auth, Growing Old, Artist's Mag/North Light, 2003. *Mailing Add:* 1007 Lakeview Terr Pennsburg PA 18073

HENDERSON, LINDA DALRYMPLE
HISTORIAN, EDUCATOR
b Warren, Pa. *Study:* Dickinson Col, BA, 69; Yale Univ, MA, 72, PhD, 75. *Pos:* assoc cur mod art, Mus Fine Arts, Houston, 74-76, cur, 76-77. *Teaching:* asst prof, Univ Tex, Austin, 78-84, assoc prof, 84-91, prof, 91-, centennial prof art hist. *Awards:* Vasari Award, Dallas Mus Art, 85; Guggenheim Fel, 88-89; Robert W Hamilton Author Award, 99. *Mem:* Col Art Asn; Modernist Studies Asn; Soc for Sci, Lit & the Arts; Int Soc for Arts, Sci and technol. *Res:* Twentieth century European and American art, including its interaction with geometry, science and technology, and mysticism/occultism. *Publ:* The Fourth Dimension and Non-Euclidean Geometry in Mod Art, Princeton Univ Press, 83, MIT Press, 2006-; auth, Mysticism as 'the tie that binds': the case of Edward Carpenter and modernism, Art J, 87; X-rays and the quest for invisible reality in the art of Kupka, Duchamp and the cubists, Art J, 88; Duchamp in Context: Science and Technology in the Large Glass and Related Works, Princeton Univ Press, 98; co ed, From Energy to Information: Representation in Science and Technology, Art, and Literature, Stanford Univ Press, 2002; The Large Glass seen anew: reflections of contemp science and tech in Marcel Duchamp's Hilarious Picture, Leonardo, 99; Ed's introd; Writing modern art & sci-an overview, Sci in Context, Cubism, Futurism & Exeter Physics in the Early 20th Century, 2004; Four Dimensional Space or Space Time: The Emergence of the Cubism Relativity Myth in NY in the 1940's, in The Visual Mind II, ed Michele Emmer, MIT Press, 2005. *Mailing Add:* Univ Tex Dept Art & Art Hist Austin TX 78712

HENDERSON, MIKE
PAINTER, FILMMAKER
Study: San Francisco Art Inst, BFA, 69, MFA, 70. *Work:* Crocker Art Mus, Sacramento; Honolulu Acad Arts; Oakland Mus; San Francisco Mus Mod Art. *Exhib:* San Francisco Mus Mod Art, 74 & 78; Whitney Mus, NY, 70 & 71; Honolulu Acad Arts, 78; solo exhibs, Walter/McBean Gallery, San Francisco, Calif, 90, Haines Gallery, San Francisco, Calif, 91, 92, 94, 99, 2002, Calif Mus Art Luther Burbank Ctr, Santa Rosa, Calif, 96 & San Marco Gallery Dominican Col, San Rafael, Calif, 96, Triton Mus, Calif, 2003; Oakland Artists '90, Oakland Mus, Calif, 90; From the Studio: Recent Paintings & Sculpture by 20 California Artists, Oakland Art Mus, Calif, 92; Selections from the Rene & Veronica di Rosa Collection, Oakland Mus, Calif, 94; Triton Mus Art, Santa Clara, Calif, 97; Beyond Color, CN Gorman Mus, Univ Calif, Davis, 97; The Painters Craft, Reese Bullen Gallery, Humbolt State Univ, Arcata, Calif, 97; What Is Art For?, Oakland Mus Calif, 99; Music in My Soul, Portsmouth Mus, Virginia, 01; and others. *Teaching:* Instr art, Univ Calif, Davis, 70-. *Awards:* Guggenheim Fel, 73; Nat Endowment Arts, 78 & 89; Adeline Kent Award, 90; Distinguished Alumni Award, San Francisco Art Inst, 90. *Bibliog:* Peter Frank (auth), Four & Four, Prism-Arts of Pacific, 6/95; Gretchen Giles (auth), Paint it Black, Sonoma Co Independent, 5/96; Kenneth Baker (auth), Substance with Style, 8/96, Celebrating Art's Generations, 9/96, Painter with Open Heart, 7/99, San Francisco Chronicle; and others. *Mailing Add:* c/o Haines Gallery 49 Geary St San Francisco CA 94108

HENDERSON, ROBBIN LEGERE
PAINTER, CURATOR
b Stockton, Calif, April 19, 1942. *Study:* Reed Col, 59-61; Univ Calif, Berkeley, BA, 63; San Francisco Art Inst, 68-70. *Exhib:* Solo exhibs, Mills Col Gallery, 76, Floating Mus, 77, Southern Exposure Gallery, San Francisco, 78 & 85, Intersection Gallery, San Francisco, 82 & Berkeley Store Gallery, 94; Art for Giving & Collecting, 78, San Francisco Mus Mod Art; San Francisco Exchange Show, Fashion Moda, NY, 82; San Francisco Art Inst Ann, 84; Alternative Mus, 84; Mission Cult Ctr, 85; Southern Exposure, 94; Intersection Gallery, 95. *Collection Arranged:* Alice Neel, Paintings from 1920-1974, Am Can Gallery, 74; Ethnic Notions: Black Images in the White Mind, 82 & Mothers Gifts to their Children, 84, (with catalogs), Berkeley Art Ctr; Beyond 1992, 92; 10x10: Ten Women Ten Prints, 95; Bodies & Souls, 94. *Pos:* Dir, Southern Exposure Gallery, San Francisco, 74-77; cur, Intersection Gallery, San Francisco, 77-79; cur & exec dir, Berkeley Art Ctr, 79-85 & 91-; artist-in-residence, Calif Arts Coun, 83-86. *Bibliog:* Robert MacDonald (auth), Images of women, Artweek, 4/79; Charles Shere (auth), article, Oakland Tribune, 8/30/82; Artweek, 7/94. *Mem:* Non-Profit Gallery Asn (pres); AFA. *Media:* Oil on Canvas, Mixed Media. *Mailing Add:* Berkeley Art Ctr 1275 Walnut St Berkeley CA 94709-1406

HENDERSON, VICTOR
PAINTER, MURALIST
b Cuyahoga Falls, Ohio, Nov 30, 39. *Study:* San Francisco State Col, BA, 63. *Work:* Newport Harbor Mus, Newport Beach, Calif; Chicago Art Inst; M H De Young Mem Mus, San Francisco; Los Angeles Co Mus. *Comn:* Beverly Hills Sidhartha, Michael Huit, Los Angeles, 69-70; Venice in the Snow, Jerry Rosen, Los Angeles, 70; Isle of Calif, Jordy Hormel, Los Angeles, 70-72; Hippy Knowhow, French Govt, Paris, 71; Ghost Town, Ed Janss, Thousand Oaks, Calif, 72-73 (all the above murals were executed under the name Los Angeles Fine Arts Squad); Breakers Mural, comn by Arco Co, Santa Barbara, Calif, 78-79; City of Los Angeles, Calif, 95; City of Montebello, 98; City of Santa Fe Springs, 99. *Exhib:* LA Eight, Los Angeles Co Mus Art, Calif, 76; 100-plus, Los Angeles Inst Contemp Art, 77; Illusion & Reality, Australian Nat Gallery, Canbera, and six other Australian galleries & mus, 77; Victor Henderson Takes a Walk, Newport Harbour Art Mus, 78; one-person shows, Ulrike Cantor Gallery, Los Angeles, 81 & 83 & Los Angeles Co Mus, Calif, 83; Artists Space, NY, 83; and others. *Pos:* Co-founder, Los Angeles Fine Art Squad, Calif, 69-73. *Teaching:* Lectr drawing, Univ Calif, Los Angeles, 75-77; Otis Art Inst, Los Angeles, 80-83 & Univ Calif, Irvine, 84-85. *Awards:* Nat Endowment Arts Painting Fel, 83-84. *Bibliog:* T H Garver (auth), Artforum, Vol 9, 71; Peter Plagens (auth), Sunshine Muse, Praeger, NY, 73; Eva Cookcroft (auth), Towards a People Art, E P Dutton & Co, NY, 76; Volger Barthelmeh (auth), Street Murals, Alfred A Knopt, 82; Edward Lucie-Smith (auth), American Art Now, William Marrow, 85. *Publ:* Auth, Mega Murals & Big Art, Running Press, Philadelphia, 77. *Mailing Add:* 474 Lewis St Los Angeles CA 90042

HENDON, CHAM
PAINTER
b Birmingham, Ala, Sept 14, 36. *Study:* Art Inst Chicago, BFA, 63; Univ NMex, MA, 65; Univ Wis, MFA, 77. *Work:* Metrop Mus Art, NY; Mus of City NY; Neuberger Mus Art, Purchase, NY; New Mus Contemp Art, NY; Birmingham Mus Art, Ala. *Exhib:* Bad Painting, New Mus, NY; Painting & Sculpture Today, Indianapolis Mus, Ind; Dialoghi Nell Arti, Palazzo Ducale, Gubio, Italy, 85; Nueva Pintura Narrativa, El Museo Rufino Tamayo, Mexico City, 85; Painting: The 1980's, Ringling Mus Art, Sarasota, Fla, 91. *Pos:* dir, Madison Art Center, Wis, 67-76. *Media:* All Media. *Mailing Add:* 3619 Midvale Ave Oakland CA 94602

HENDRICKS, BARKLEY LEONNARD
PAINTER
b Philadelphia, Pa, Apr 16, 45. *Study:* Pa Acad Fine Arts, 63-67, William Cresson European Traveling scholar, 66; Yale Univ Sch Fine Art, 70-72. *Work:* Philadelphia Mus Art; Pa Acad Fine Arts, Philadelphia; Cornell Univ; Wichita State Univ, Kans; Nat Gallery, Washington, DC. *Exhib:* Fel Exhib, Pa Acad Fine Arts, 67-72; Nat Acad Design Ann, NY, 70-71 & 74-75; Contemp Black Artists, Whitney Mus Am Art, NY, 71; Childe Hassam Fund Exhib, Am Acad Arts & Lett, 71 & 75; Nat Inst Arts & Lett Ann, 71-72. *Teaching:* Instr painting & drawing, Pa Acad Fine Arts, 71-72; asst in painting, Yale Univ, 71-72; asst prof painting & drawing, Conn Col, 72-81, prof, 81-88. *Awards:* Julius Hallgarten Second Prize, Nat Acad Design, 71; Richard & Hilda Rosenthal Award, Nat Inst Arts & Lett, 72. *Media:* Oil, Acrylic. *Mailing Add:* 22 Addison St Conn Col 270 Monegan Ave New London CT 06320-5309

HENDRICKS, DAVID CHARLES
PAINTER, VISUAL ARTIST
b Hammond, Ind, Mar 25, 48. *Study:* Skowhegan Summer Sch Painting & Sculpture, Maine, 69, Univ Ill, BFA, 70; Ox-Bow Summer Sch Painting, Saugatuck, Mich, 70. *Work:* Brooklyn Mus, NYNEX & Reader's Digest, NY; Hirshhorn Mus & Sculpture Garden, Washington, DC; NC Nat Bank; AT&T; Haynes & Boone, Dallas, Tex; Nat

Health Insurance Underwriters, Dallas, Tex; and others. *Exhib:* One-man shows, Monique Knowlton Gallery, 77, Fischbach Gallery, NY, 84, 87, 88 & 90, Keene State Col, NH, 89; Davidson Nat Print and Drawing Show, Davidson Col, NC, 76; Childe Hassam Foundation Show, Am Acad & Lett, NY, 76; Queensboro Community Col, Bayside, NY, 77; Wave Hill Ctr for Environ Studies, Riverdale, NY, 79; Portsmouth Community Arts Ctr, Va, 82; Greenville Co Mus Art, SC, 85; William Sawyer Gallery, San Francisco, Calif, 85; traveling exhib, San Francisco Mus Mod Art, De Cordova & Dana Mus & Park, Lincoln, Mass, Archer M Huntington Art Gallery, Austin Tex, Mary & Leigh Block Gallery, Evanston, Ill, Arkon Art Mus, Ohio, Madison Art Ctr, Wis; 50th Nat Midyear exhib, Butler Inst Am Art, Ohio, 86; Face of the Land, Southern Alleghenies Mus Art, Loretto, Pa, 88; Art on Paper 1988, Weatherspoon Art Gallery, 88; Drawn from Life: Contemp Interpretive Landscape, Sewall Art Gallery, Tex, 88; Utopian Visions, Art Adv Serv Mus Mod Art, NY, 88; Water, Pfizer Inc, Art Adv Service Mus of Mod Art, 89. *Awards:* Mary C McLellan Scholar, 70; MacDowell Colony Fel, Peterborough, NH, 71, 72, 74, 75, 79, 80, 83, 85 & 86; Fel, Ossabow Island Proj Found, Ga, 76; Davidson Nat Print & Drawing Show Purchase Award, Davidson Col, NC, 76; Fel, Yaddo Corp, Saratoga Springs, NY, 77, 81 & 82; Nat Endowment for the Arts, Visual Arts Fel, 77 & 80. *Bibliog:* John Russell (auth), Invigorating breezes of the fall season, NY Times, Arts & Leisure, 10/2/76; Lenore Malen (auth), David Henricks, Arts Mag, 2/77. *Media:* Pencil, Graphite; Oil. *Dealer:* Fischbach Gallery 24 W 57th St New York NY 10019. *Mailing Add:* 652 Broadway No 7F New York NY 10012-2316

HENDRICKS, EDWARD LEE
SCULPTOR, KINETIC ARTIST
b Charleston, WVa, Nov 9, 52. *Study:* Birmingham Southern Col, BFA, 74; Univ NC, Chapel Hill, MFA, 76. *Work:* Hunter Mus Art, Chattanooga, Tenn; Mint Mus Art, Charlotte, NC; New Orleans Mus Art; Phoenix Art Mus, Ariz; Birmingham Mus Art, Ala. *Comn:* Sculpture, Birmingham Bd Educ, 76; sculpture, Birmingham Realty Co, 85; sculpture, Birmingham Mus Art, 86; sculpture, Am Republic Insurance, Des Moines, 86; sculpture, Datran Ctr, Coral Gables, Fla; sculpture, Turco Develop Co, St Louis, 89. *Exhib:* One-man shows, Southeastern Ctr Contemp Art, 80, 84, Alexander F Milliken Inc, NY, 80, 82, 84 & 89, Montgomery Mus Fine Arts, Ala, 81, Osuma Gallery, Washington, DC, 81 & 83, O K Harris West, Scottsdale, Ariz, 81, 83 & 84, Birmingham Mus Art, 81 &84, Hunter Mus Art, 82, Eric Makler Gallery, Philadelphia, 82 & 83 & Davis McClain Gallery, Houston, 85, 87 & Ardew Gallery, Boston, 87; Elaine Horwitch, Palm Spring, Calif, 88 & 90. *Awards:* Second Award, Nat Sculpture, 75; Juror's Award, Birmingham Art Asn, 79; Southeast Artists Fel, Southeastern Ctr Contemp Art, 83. *Bibliog:* Bob Yoskowitz (auth), articles, Arts Mag, 80 & 81; Carol Donnel-Kotrozo (auth), article, Art Express, 82; Vivien Raynor (rev), article, NY Times, 10/5/84. *Media:* Metal. *Dealer:* Alexander F Milliken Inc 98 Prince St New York NY 10012. *Mailing Add:* c/o McClain Gallery 2242 Richmond Houston TX 77098

HENDRICKS, GEOFFREY
PAINTER, ENVIRONMENTAL ARTIST
b Littleton, NH, July 30, 31. *Study:* Amherst Col, BA, 53; Norfolk Art Sch, Yale Univ, scholar, summer 53; Cooper Union Art Sch, 53-56; Columbia Univ, MA, 62. *Work:* Mus Mod Kunst, Vienna, Austria; Wilhelm Lehbruck Mus, Duisburg, Ger; Mus Mod Art, NY; Staatsgalerie, Stuttgart, Ger; Nordjyllands Kunstmuseum, Aalborg, Denmark; and others. *Exhib:* Silverman Collection, Cranbrook Art Mus, Bloomfield Hills, Mich, 81; Fluxus (catalog, ed by Jon Hendricks & Clive Phillpot), Mus Mod Art, NY, 88; In the Spirit of Fluxus, Walker Art Ctr, Minneapolis, Minn, 93 & Whitney Mus Am Art, NY, 93; The Living Art Mus, Reykjavik, Iceland, 84; Galerie Baecker, Cologne, Ger, 86; Himmels Aquarelle, Rupertinum, Salzburg, Austria, 92; Day into Night, Kunsthallen Brandts Kloedelfabrick, Odense, Denmark, 93, Kjarvalsstadir, Munic Art Mus, Reykjavik, Iceland, 94, Porin Taidemuseo, Pori, finland, 94, Henie-Onstad Kunstsenter, Hovikodden, Oslo, Norway, 94; solo-exhibs, Ctr Contemp Art, Ujazdowski Castle, Warsaw, Poland, 94; and many other group & one-man shows. *Teaching:* Asst instr, Art Dept, State Univ NJ, Rutgers, Douglass Col, 56-58, instr, 58-61, asst prof, 61-67, assoc prof, Visual Arts Dept, Mason Gross Sch Arts, 67-80, prof, 80-; instr art, New York Fine Arts Winter Term Prog of Earlham Col, Richmondd, Ind, 65-69. *Awards:* Fel, Nat Endowment Arts, 76 & 77; Deutscher Akad Austauschdienst, Berlin Artist Prog, 83; Barkenhoff Stiftung, Found Fel, Worpswede, Ger, 85-86. *Bibliog:* Marianne Beck & Robert Rosenblum (auths), Night into Day (catalog), interview with Cars Movin for traveling retrospective exhib, 93 & 94; Jill Johnston (auth), Secret Lives in Art, 94; Henry Martin (auth), Anatomy of the Sky (catalog), 95; and others. *Mem:* Col Art Asn Am; Am Asn Univ Prof; Fluxus. *Media:* Acrylic, Intermedia. *Publ:* Auth, Between Two Points/Fra Due Poli, Edizioni Pari & Dispari, Reggio Emila, Italy, 75; La Capra, Edizioni Morra, Napoli, 79; Sky Anatomy, Rainer Verlag, Berlin, 84; 100 skies, Barkenhoff Found, Worpswede, Ger, 87; 100 Skies, Money for Food Press, New York, 93. *Dealer:* Galerie Baecker Zeughausstrasse 13 Cologne Ger Koln 1 WGer. *Mailing Add:* 486 Greenwich St New York NY 10013-1313

HENDRICKS, JAMES (POWELL)
SCULPTOR, PAINTER
b Little Rock, Ark, Aug 7, 38. *Study:* Univ Ark, Fayetteville, BA, 63; Univ Iowa, MFA, 64. *Work:* Mus Fine Arts, Springfield, Mass; Smithsonian Inst, Washington; Ark Arts Ctr, Little Rock; Hudson River Mus, Yonkers, NY; Mus Fine Arts, Boston. *Comn:* Painting, Apollo 14 Launch, Nat Gallery Art & NASA, 71; painting (cover), Time Mag, 8/9/71. *Exhib:* One-man shows, Smithsonian Inst Nat Air & Space Mus, 69, Hudson River Mus, Yonkers, 70; Helen Shlien Gallery, Boston, 80, 82 & 84; IV Int Bien de Arte Medellin, Colombia, SAm, 81; Tyler Art Gallery, 83; Portland Sch Art & Baxter Gallery, 85; Mus Fine Arts, Springfield, Mass, 86; Space Art Gallery, Seoul, Korea, 86; Slater-Price Fine Arts, NY, 89 & 90; Works on Paper (traveling exhib), Umetnicka Galerija, Prilep, Daut Pastin Aman, Skopje, Bitola & Repub Macedonia; Westwood Gallery, NY, 96, 2001. *Collection Arranged:* Assemblage/Collage: Works by 24 Artists & Poets, Seoul Inst of the Arts, Korea, 88. *Pos:* Vis artist, Portland Sch Art, ME, 85 & Seoul Inst Arts, Korea, 86. *Teaching:* Grad instr drawing, State Univ Iowa, 63-64; instr art, Mt Holyoke Col, 64-65; from asst prof to assoc prof painting & drawing, Univ Mass, Amherst, 72-79, dir grad progs in art, 72-, prof art, 79-. *Awards:* Painting Awards, Soc Four Arts, 68 & Silvermine Guild Artists, 69; Ark Traveler Award, 71. *Bibliog:* Robert Ackermann (auth), article, Arts Mag, 9-10/74 & Art in Am, 3-4/76; Nancy Stapen (auth), article, Artforum, 1/83; and others. *Media:* Acrylic, Wood; Bronze, Mixed Media. *Publ:* Illusr cover, Time, 71. *Dealer:* Westwood Gallery New York NY. *Mailing Add:* Univ Mass Dept Art Amherst MA 01003

HENDRIX, CONNIE SANDAGE MANUS
PAINTER, INSTRUCTOR
b Mt Ayr, Iowa, May 30, 42. *Study:* Drake Univ, Des Moines, BFA, 64; Memphis State Univ; special study with Jason Williamson, Irving Shapiro, Murray Wentworth, Lee Weiss, Ed Betz & Charles Reid. *Work:* Foothills Art Ctr, Golden, Colo; Ponca City Fine Arts Ctr, Okla; Tenn Arts Comn, State of Tenn, Nashville; State of Iowa, Wallace Agriculture Bldg, Des Moines; Nat Bank Commerce, Memphis, Tenn. *Comn:* Six watercolors of vegetables (with Julie Wells), United Foods, Bells, Tenn, 76; three watercolors of Olympics for limited ed wall covering (with Tom Welsh), Welsh Forest Products, Memphis, Tenn, 79-80; three watercolors for poster, Opera memphis, Tenn, 88. *Exhib:* Rocky Mountain Nat Watermedia Exhib; Southern Watercolor Soc, NTex State Univ Art Gallery, Denton; Georgia Watercolor Soc; Columbus Mus Arts & Sci & Checkwood Fine Arts Ctr, Nashville, Tenn, 76-79; Allied Artists Am Ann Exhib, Nat Arts Club, NY, 81. *Collection Arranged:* Nat Bank Commerce (auth, catalog), Commerce Sq Invitational, Memphis, Tenn, 73; Bicentennial Salute to Memphis, Nat Bank Commerce Salutes, 76. *Pos:* Artist, Look Mag, Des Moines, Iowa, 60-64; sr art dir, Ward Archer & Assocs Advert, Memphis, 69-79; creative dir, designer & illusr, Connie Hendrix & Assocs, Memphis, 79-. *Teaching:* Memphis City Sch System, Tenn, 66-69; instr watercolor, Univ Tenn Student Alumni Educ Ctr, Adult Educ Prog, 73-; Memphis State Univ Continuing Educ, 75-; and various workshops in midsouth area. *Awards:* First Place Purchase Award, 11th Tenn All-State, First Am Nat Bank, 71; Top Cash Award, Watercolor Div, 8th Cent South Art Exhib, Commerce Union Bank, 73; Nat Bank of Commerce Award, Tenn Watercolor Soc Ann, 73, 74, 76, 78, 81, 83 & 87. *Mem:* Tenn Watercolor Soc (regional dir, 71-73, corresp secy, 72, vpres, 74 & pres, 75-76); assoc mem Am Watercolor Soc; assoc mem Allied Artists Am; Art Dirs' Club Memphis (secy, 70 & 71, vpres, 72 & pres, 73); charter mem Memphis Watercolor Soc; Memphis Soc Visual Commun; charter mem Southern Watercolor Soc (secy, 75-76); Memphis Ad Fed (dir, 89, 90, 91 & 92). *Media:* Watercolor. *Publ:* Auth, article, Northlight Mag, 5-6/75; Bicentennial Salute to Memphis (film), Cablecom/Educ TV, 76; Watercolor, winter issue, 96. *Dealer:* Elkanah Gallery Jackson TN; Classic Antiquities Ltd Gallery Los Angeles CA

HENES, DONNA
ENVIRONMENTAL ARTIST, SCULPTOR
b Cleveland, Ohio, Sept 19, 45. *Study:* Ohio State Univ; City Col New York, BS, 70, MS, 72. *Comn:* Pub participatory event, Bicentennial Comn, NY, 76; Vernal Equinox Celebration, Port Authority NY & NJ, 80-90; web installation, Indianapolis Mus, 83; installation, Maine Monument, New York Cult Affairs Dept, 83; seasonal pub celebrations, Lower Manhattan Cult Coun, 83; Olympic Ticker Tape Parade, New York City Mayor's Off, 84; Holiday Lighting Installation, Rosendale, NY, 86 & 87, Bay Shore, NY, 88; Vernal Equinox Celebration, Battery Park City Authority, 91-94. *Exhib:* Women in Am Archit, Brooklyn Mus & traveling, 77; Hilosphia, Spain, 82; Sculpture Tricentennial, Philadelphia Arts Alliance, 82; solo shows, Wash Proj Arts, 82 & Indianapolis Mus Art, 83; At Home, Newport Harbor Mus, Calif, 83; Artist Books Biennial, Ctr Arte & Communicacion, Buenos Aires, 83; Latitudes of Time, New York City Gallery, 85; Streets, Gardens & Altars, Cent Hall Gallery, 86; Public Visions-Public Monuments, Soho 20 Gallery, 86; Ritual in the 20 Century, Islip Mus Art, 87; The Meeting of the Holy Pictures, Panstwowe Mus Ethograficzne, Warsaw, Poland, 91; Completing the Circle, Minn Ctr Bk Art & Nat Tour, 92-93, Images of 9/11, The Prints and Photographs, Div of Libr Congress, Washington, 2003; Salute to the Sun, Socrates Sculpture Park, NY, 2004; Vlepo Gallery, Staten Island, NY, 2004; WACK! Art & the Feminist Revolution, Mus Contemp Art, Los Angeles, Calif, 2006. *Pos:* Writer, celestially auspicious occasions, nationally syndicated column, currently. *Teaching:* Minneapolis Col Art & Design, 87 & 89; Pratt Inst, 91; Cooper Union, 92; Parsons, 99. *Awards:* Fel, Nat Endowment Arts, 83 & 84; NY Found Arts Fel, 86 & 90. *Bibliog:* Lucy Lippard (auth), Overlay, Pantheon Books, 82; Eggs on end, New Yorker, 83; Moira Roth (auth), The Amazing Decade, Astro Art, 83; Artists' Books: A Critical Anthology, Visual Studies Workshop, 85; Annie Gottlieb (auth), Do You Believe in Magic?, 87; Encyclodpedia of Women & World Religion, 98; Kay Turner (auth), Beautiful Necessity, 99; Brigitta, Johnsdattir (ed), The World Healing Book, 2002; Oberon & Morning Glory Zell, Raven leant(ed), Creating circles & Ceremonies, 2006; Cristina Biaggi (ed), The Rule of Mors, 2006; Barbara Love (ed), Feminists who changed Am, 1963-1975 & 2006; Sayne work (auth), Radical gestures, 2006. *Mem:* Founding mem Ctr Celebration (bd dir, 80-); Soc Women Geographers; Women's wellness society. *Media:* Ritual Celebration, Environmental Transformation. *Res:* Ongoing Independent Studies in Astronomy, Anthropology, Folklore, Mythology, Travel. *Publ:* Contribr, The Politics of Women's Spirituality, Doubleday, 81; auth, Dressing Our Wounds in Warm Clothes, Astro Artz, 82; ed, Celebration News, 86; auth, Celestially Auspicious Occasions, Putnam-Berkley, 96; Reverence to Her, Part I, Mythology, Matriarchy & Me (CD), 10 Productions, 98; auth, Moon Watcher's Companion, Galison Press, 2002; ed, Serenity Young; The Moon Watchers Companion, Marlowe & Co Pub, 2004; The Queen of My Self, Monarch Press, 2005; United press int, weekly colomnist gov UPI, Religion & Spirituality forum. *Mailing Add:* PO Box 380403 Brooklyn NY 11238-0403

HENKLE, JAMES LEE
SCULPTOR, DESIGNER
b Cedar Rapids, Iowa, Mar 13, 27. *Study:* Univ Nebr, BA; Pratt Inst, cert(indust design). *Work:* Univ Okla Art Mus, Norman; Okla State Art Collection, Okla Arts & Humanities Coun, Okalahoma City; Ark Art Ctr, Little Rock. *Comn:* Sculpture mural, Numerical Anal Res Ctr, Norman, 63 & Tulsa Pub Libr, Tulsa Hist Soc, Okla, 65; sculpture, Norman Pub Libr, 75th Anniversary Comt, 66; wall sculpture, Dale Hall, Univ Okla; communion table, First Presby Church, Norman, 88; Furniture Designs, Mabee-Gerrer Mus Art, Shawnee Okla, 90. *Exhib:* Eight State Art Exhib, Oklahoma City Art Ctr, 61; one-man sculpture exhib, Univ Okla Mus Art, 68 & Philbrook Art Ctr, Tulsa, 70; Okla State Univ, 79; Okla Designer Craftsman Exhibs, 76-81; Vision Makers, Kilpatrick Ctr, Oklahoma City, 88; Philbrook Art Ctr, Tulsa, Okla, 88. *Pos:* Designer, Dave Chapman Design Firm, 52-53. *Teaching:* Prof art, Univ Okla, 53-; prof art, emer, 90. *Awards:* Purchase Prize Sculpture, Okla Art Ctr, 65; Purchase Prize Painting, Springfield Art Mus; Purchase Award Crafts, Eighth Ann Print, Drawing & Crafts Exhib, Ark Arts Ctr, 75. *Mem:* Okla City Art Mus; Firehouse Art Ctr; Univ Okla Art Mus. *Media:* Wood; Acrylic Paint. *Publ:* Contribr, Fine Woodworking Biennial Design Book (Vol 1, 2, 3 & 4), Taunton Press. *Mailing Add:* 2719 Hollywood Ave Norman OK 73072

HENNESSEY, WILLIAM JOHN
MUSEUM DIRECTOR
b Summit, NJ, July 15, 48. *Study:* Wesleyan Univ, BA, 70; Ford Found fel, Worcester Art Mus, 71-73; Columbia Univ, PhD, 78. *Collection Arranged:* The American Portrait: From Stuart to Sargent (auth, catalog), Worcester Art Mus, 73; Artists Look at Art (auth, catalog), 78 & Permanent Collection, 78, Spencer Art Mus, Univ Kans; Hudson Valley People, Vassar Col Art Gallery, 82; Russel Wright: American Designer, Gallery Asn NY State & MIT Press, 83; Thomas S Noble, Univ Ky Art Mus, 88; Havemeyer Tiffany Collection, Univ Mich, 92; From Ansel Adams to Andy Warhol, Univ Mich, 94. *Pos:* Res assoc, Solomon R Guggenheim Mus, 73-74; cur, Spencer Art Mus, Univ Kans, 75-79; dir, Vassar Col Art Gallery, 79-82, Univ Ky Art Mus, 82-90, Univ Mich Mus Art, 90-97 & Chrysl. *Teaching:* Instr, Brooklyn Col & Sch Visual Arts, 73-75; asst prof, Univ Kans, 75-79 & Vassar Col, 79-82; adj prof art, Univ Ky, 82-90; assoc prof, Univ Mich, 90-97. *Mem:* Col Art Asn; Soc Archit Historians; Asn Art Mus Dirs. *Res:* 19th & 20th Century architecture & design. *Publ:* Auth, A Handbook of the Worcester Art Museum, 73; Friedrich Overbeck's Drawing of Elijah, Regist Spencer Mus, spring 77; Frank Lloyd Wright and the design of the Guggenheim Museum, Arts Mag, 4/78; series of 24 articles for the World Book Encyclopedia; Michelangelo & the Art of Automobile Design, 93. *Mailing Add:* Chrysler Mus Art 245 W Olney Rd Norfolk VA 23510

HENNESY, GERALD CRAFT
PAINTER
b Washington, DC, June 11, 21. *Study:* Corcoran Sch Art; George Washington Univ; Am Univ; Univ Md; also with C Gordon Harris. *Work:* Nat Hq Am Legion & Nat Hq Daughters Am Revolution, Wash; Md State Exec Mansion, Annapolis; US House Rep Off Bldg, Wash; Hq FDIC, Washington, DC. *Comn:* Paintings, Gibson Bldg, Fairfax, Va, 74, United Va Bank, Richmond, 75, Hq Blue Cross & Blue Shield Asn, 82 & Nat Hq Fed Deposit Insurance Corp, 83, Washington. *Exhib:* Baltimore Mus Art Regional, 63; NY World's Fair, 65; one-man show, Pla Gallery, McClean, Va, 67; Allied Artists of Am, NY, 75 & 76; Venable Nestage Galleries, Wash, 93; Marin-Price Galleries, Chevy Chase, MD, 95-96, 2000, 02, 04 & 06; Prince Royal Gallery, Alexandria, Va, 99, 2003 & 05. *Pos:* Advert artist, Washington Times Herald, Washington, 41-42. *Awards:* First Prize, Gilham Show, 66; Lorbmer Award, Salmagundi Club, 94; Wright Award, Hudson Valley Art Asn, 2004; Loughlin Award, 2005. *Mem:* Wash Soc Landscape Painters (treas, 73-77, 87-89); Hudson Valley Art Asn. *Media:* Oil, Watercolor. *Dealer:* Marin-Price Gallery, 7022 Wisconsin Ave, Chevy Chase, Md, 20815. *Mailing Add:* 6811 White Rock Rd Clifton VA 20124

HENRICKSON, PAUL ROBERT
PAINTER, WRITER
b Boston, Mass. *Study:* RI Sch Design, BFA; Univ Mass, ME; Univ Minn, PhD; Clark Univ; Statens Kunst Akademiet, Oslo; Statens Kunst Industriskole, Oslo. *Work:* Mus of NMex, Santa Fe; Statens Kunst Industriskole; Mus Fine Arts, Santa Fe. *Comn:* Crash (canvas panel), in pvt collection, NDak; four part canvas panel, pvt collection, NY. *Exhib:* One-man exhibs, Am & Mex Mus. *Pos:* Exec dir, Insular Arts Coun, Gov Guam, 65-68; free lance art critic, Santa Fe Reporter, NMex & Art Voices/South, Palm Beach, Fla; producer, Santa Fe Int Scandinavian Film Festival, 84. *Teaching:* Prof & head div fine arts, Univ Gaum, 64-68; prof res art, Univ Northern Iowa, 68-72. *Res:* Psychology of art. *Publ:* Auth, Two Primitive Micronesian Art Forms, 68; Lying, Dogmatic and Creative Persons, 70; The Perceptive and Silenced Minorities, 72; Georgia on his mind, Santa Fe Reporter, 75; The Word for Cross is Cryptic, 77

HENRY, DALE
PAINTER
b Anniston, AL, Feb 8, 1931. *Comn:* The Clocktower, Inst for Art and Urban Resources, NY, 75; Room Installation, Inst Art and Urban Resources, Long Island City, NY, 76; Ben Shahn Gallery, William Paterson Coll, Wayne, NJ, 80; Works and Projects of the 70s, USIA World Traveling Exhbn, Washington, 77-80; Builtworks, Sarah Lawrence Coll, Yonkers, NY, 85. *Exhib:* solo exhibs, Gallery Nine, Berkeley, Calif, 61, Legion of Honor, San Francisco, 61, Esther Robles Gallery, Los Angeles, 65, Mills Col Art Gallery, Oakland, Calif, 68, Fischbach Gallery, NY, 71, John Weber Gallery, NY, 72, 73, 76, 77, 79, Galleria Toselli, Milan, 72, Hal Bromm Gallery, NY, 78, William Paterson Col, Ben Shahn Gallery, Wayne, NJ, 80, Sarah Lawrence Col, Yonkers, NY, 85; Calif Palace Legion of Honor, San Francisco, 60, 61, 62, 63, 64, Esther Robles Gallery, 65, Inst for Art & Urban Resources, Long Island City, NY, 76; Basel Art Fair, Switz, 76; Moore Col Art, Philadelphia, 77; Grommet Gallery, NY, 82; and others. *Collection Arranged:* Legion of Honor Mus, San Francisco; Mills Coll Art Gallery, Oakland, Calif; Albert A List Found, Vera List collection, NY; Brutten-Herrick Collection, Philadelphia; Elise Haas Found, San Francisco,; Marconi, Milan. *Teaching:* Instr fine arts, Sch of Visual Arts, NY, 70-86. *Awards:* Award Nat Endowment Arts, 82; award, CAPS, NY, 81. *Bibliog:* (auth) John H.I. Baur, The New Landscape, Art in Am, Summer 63; (auth) Nancy Foote, Apotheosis of the Crummy Space, ArtForum, Oct 76; (auth) Marcia Hafif, Beginning Agin, ArtForum, Sept 78; (auth) Marcia Hafif, Getting on with Painting, Art in America, 4/1981; (auth) Peter Bellamy, The Artist Project, 91. *Publ:* photo, Primer Sets of a Revealingly Graphic Personal History of Western Painting Using the Complete and Basic Iambus Throughout, Flash Art, 1/1973. *Mailing Add:* 243 Ampthill Rd Cartersville VA 23027

HENRY, DAVID EUGENE
PAINTER, SCULPTOR
b Rome, Ga, Dec 10, 46. *Study:* Ga Tech, BA(archit), 69; Ga State Univ, MVA(visual arts), 72; Art Students' League NY; studied under Philip Pearlstein, 96. *Work:* Albany Mus Art, Ga; Olgethorpe Univ Mus, Atlanta; Morris Mus Art, Augusta, Ga; Ga Mus of Art, Athens; La State Mus, New Orleans; Edisto island Mus, Edisto Island, SC; Indianapolis Mus Art; MC Carlos Mus, Atlanta; Marietta-Cobb Mus Art, Ga. *Comn:* Murals, Ga Tech Univ, 72; mural, Atlanta Area Tech Sch, 72; mural, Bayfront Mcpl Civic Ctr, St Petersburg, Fla. *Exhib:* 23rd Southeastern Exhib, High Mus Art, Atlanta, Ga, 69; drawing exhib, Montgomery Mus Art, Ala; Ga Artists Exhib II, High Mus Art, 72; Ninth Piedmont Graphics Exhib, Mint Mus Art; Third Greater New Orleans Nat Exhib; 54th Nat Painting Exhib, Ogunquit Art Ctr, Ogunquit, Maine; 3rd Biennial Tweed Mus Exhib; 16th All Am Exhib, Barnegat Light; Heroes to Dudes, Ga Mus Art, 2003; Travelers in Foreign Land, MC Carlos Mus, 2003. *Teaching:* Teacher painting, Eckerd Col, St Petersburg, Fla, 76-77; teacher drawing, Am Col Applied Arts, Atlanta, Ga, 96-; Am Intercontinental Univ, 98; tchr painting, Gov's Honor Program, Wesleyan Col, 74. *Awards:* Purchase Award, Piedmont Exhib, NC Nat Bank, 72; First Prize in Painting, Arts Festival Atlanta, 75; Mural Design Comptition, Nat Endowment Arts, St Petersburg, Fla, 77. *Mem:* Salmagundi Club; Allied Artists of Am; Nat Soc Artist; Am Soc Classical Realism; Am Artists Prof League; and others. *Media:* Paint, Charcoal, Bronze. *Mailing Add:* 130 26th St NW No 105 Atlanta GA 30309

HENRY, FREDRICK B
PATRON
Pos: Pres Bohen Found, 84-; bd mem, Am Ctr, Paris, 91; bd trustee, Solomon R Guggenheim Mus, 2002-; bd dir, Georges Pompidou Art & Cult Found, Paris & Houston, Aspen Valley Community Found, Aspen, Colo, Brooklyn Acad Music, Des Moines Art Ctr, Iowa, Dia Ctr for Arts, New York City, Pub Agenda Found, New York City, Whitney Mus Am Art, New York City; chmn, Am Ctr Found. *Mailing Add:* Bohen Found 415 W 13th St New York NY 10014

HENRY, JEAN
PAINTER, INSTRUCTOR
b San Francisco, Calif. *Study:* Art Acad, Amsterdam, Holland; Am Univ Berlin; Md Inst, Baltimore; Western Reserve Univ. *Exhib:* Soc Western Artists, De Young Mus, 68; De Saisset Gallery, Santa Clara, Calif, 69; one-man show, Triton Mus Art, 70; Marin Art & Garden Show, 71; Rosicrucian Mus Invitational Show, 71; impressionist painting at semi-ann exhibs, Vel Oyana Gallery, Tokyo, Japan & Nihon Gallery, Nagoya, Japan; and others. *Pos:* Jean Henry Sch Art, San Francisco, currently. *Teaching:* Instr portrait painting, Md Inst, Johns Hopkins Univ, 58-60; owner & instr painting, Jean Henry Sch Art, San Francisco, 69-. *Awards:* First Award, De Young Mus, 68; First Award, Antioch Outdoor Festival, 69; First Award for Portrait, De Saisset Gallery Ann, 70. *Mem:* Soc Western Artists. *Media:* Oil, Acrylic. *Specialty:* impressionism. *Dealer:* Galleria Luna Half Moon Bay, Calif. *Mailing Add:* Jean Henry Sch Arts 2636 Ocean Ave San Francisco CA 94132-1616

HENRY, JEAN
MUSEUM DIRECTOR, CURATOR
Study: Fla Atlantic Univ, BA, 71; Univ Miami, MA, 73; Fla State Univ, PhD(hist & criticism of art), 78; Mellon Post-Doctoral Fel, Yale Univ, 82-83; Western New Eng Inst Psychoanalysis, 82-83, Bryn Mawr Col, MSS, 92. *Collection Arranged:* Drexel's Great Sch of Am Illus (ed, catalog), 84-85; Frank E Schoonover at Drexel: Illus and the Am Tradition 1892-1903 (co-ed, catalog), 86; Nat Sculpture Soc Celebrates the Figure (ed, catalog), 87; Paintings of Gershon Benjamin, 96. *Pos:* Dir & cur, Drexel Univ Art Mus, 83-92; exec bd, Mus Coun of Philadelphia and the Del Valley, 85-87; guest cur, Nat Sculpture Soc, 87; Dep Dir, Smithsonian Inst, 93, 94. *Teaching:* Instr, Hamilton Col, 75-76; asst prof, Univ Maine, 76-79; assoc prof & chair, dept art, Univ New Haven, 79-83; adj assoc prof, Drexel Univ, 83-92. *Awards:* Col Art Asn travel grant, 79. *Mem:* Col Art Asn; Soc Archit Historians; Am Asn Mus. *Publ:* essay in John Frazee, Sculptor (exhib catalog), Smithsonian Nat Portrait Gallery, 86; auth, Sculpture Entries Since 1970 (exhib catalog), Pa Acad Fine Arts, 90

HENRY, JOHN RAYMOND
SCULPTOR
b Lexington, Ky, Aug 11, 43. *Study:* Univ Ky; Univ Wash; Univ Chicago; Art Inst Chicago, BFA; Edward L Reyerson fel, 69; Univ Ky, Hon Dr Art, 96. *Hon Degrees:* D Arts, Univ Ky, 96. *Work:* British Mus; Smithsonian Inst, Washington, DC; Dade Co Art in Pub Places, Miami, Fla; Dallas Mus Art, Tex; Hunter Mus Art, Chattanooga, Tenn. *Comn:* Illinois Landscape (sculpture), Nat Endowment Arts, Works of Art Pub Places, Nathan Manilow Sculpture Park, Govs State Univ, Univ Park, Ill, 74; Bridgeport (sculpture), State Ill, 82; Anchorage (sculpture), Anchorage Int Airport, Alaska, 85; Alachua (sculpture), Fla Art State Bldgs, Fla Arts Coun, Univ Fla, Gainesville; Dance of the Sun (sculpture), Sonje Mus Contemp Art, Kyongju City,

Korea, 91. *Exhib:* Art Inst Chicago, 68; one man shows, Ill State Mus, Springfield, 73, Riverside Park, NY, 75; Retrospectives, Evolution in Scale, 88-89, Art Mus STex, Corpus Christi, Mus Art, Ft Lauderdale, Mus Fine Arts, St Petersburg, Fla, Hunter Mus Art, Chattanooga, Tenn & Ctr for the Arts, Vero Beach, Fla, 91; FIAC, Paris, France, 93; Seo Hwa Gallery, Seoul, Korea, 93; MANIF-Seoul, Korea, 96; Art in Chicago 1945-1995, Mus Contemp Art, Chicago, 96; and many others. *Pos:* Bd trustees, Nat Found Advancement Arts, 91-, Int Sculpture Ctr, 96-, chmn bd trustees. *Teaching:* Vis prof, Univ Iowa, 69; artist in residence, Univ Wis-Green Bay, 69-70; vis prof, Univ Chicago, 70-71; vis lectr, Art Inst Chicago, 78. *Awards:* Edward L Ryerson Fel, Art Inst Chicago, 69; Individual Artists Grant, Nat Endowment Arts, 75. *Bibliog:* James L Reidy (auth), Chicago Sculpture, Univ Ill Press, Urbana, Chicago, London, 81; Claudia Sabin & Philip Yenawine (auths), Evolution in scale: The Sculpture of John Henry 1967-1988, Design Found, Chicago, Ill, 88; Victoria Lightman (auth), John Henry: Defying Gravity, Seoul, 93. *Mem:* Int Sculpture Ctr, Hamilton, NJ; Chicago Artists Coalition; Nat Found Advancement Arts, Miami, Fla; hon life mem Southeast Sculpture Asn. *Media:* Metal, Stone. *Dealer:* T Curtsnoc Fine Art 1100 E 16th St, Chattanooga, Tenn, 37408. *Mailing Add:* 7809 Joyce Dr Louisville KY 40219-4131

HENRY, ROBERT
PAINTER, EDUCATOR
b Brooklyn, NY, Aug 3, 33. *Study:* Hans Hofmann Sch Fine Art, New York & Provincetown, Mass; Brooklyn Col, with Ad Reinhardt & Kurt Seligmann, BA. *Work:* Neuberger Mus, Purchase, NY; Tucson Mus, Ariz; Provincetown Art Asn, Mass; Columbia Univ, NY; Cape Code Mus, Dennis, Mass. *Exhib:* One-man shows, Green Mountain Gallery & Ingber Gallery, NY; Contemp Figurative Painting, Suffolk Co Mus, Stony Brook, NY, 71; Hudson River Mus, Yonkers, NY, 71; Berta Walker Gallery, Provincetown, Mass, 91, 92, 94, 96, 98, 99 & 2000. *Teaching:* From asst prof to emer prof, Brooklyn Col, 60-. *Bibliog:* L Campbell (auth), Stop, look & look & look, Art News, 2/72; April Kingsley (auth), The interiorized image, Soho Weekly News, 2/5/76; Susan Koslow (auth), Robert Henry, Arts, 80. *Mem:* Provincetown Art Asn & Mus; NY Artists Equity Asn; Tru So Center for the Arts. *Media:* Oil, Watercolor. *Publ:* Auth, Horizontally oriented rotating kinetic painting, Leonardo, 69; contbr Hofmann, Farnham Emily, 67-75. *Dealer:* Berta Walker Gallery 208 Bradford St Provincetown MA 02657. *Mailing Add:* c/o Berta Walker Gallery 208 Bradford St Box 261 Provincetown MA 02657

HENRY, SARA CORRINGTON
HISTORIAN, CRITIC
b Teaneck, NJ, Sept 24, 42. *Study:* Denison Univ, BFA; NY Univ, with Robert Goldwater, BA(art hist); Univ Calif, Berkeley, with Peter Selz & Herschel B Chipp, PhD. *Teaching:* Lectr art hist, Goucher Col, Towson, Md, 70-71; vis instr, Ohio State Univ, Columbus, 71-72; instr, Carnegie-Mellon Univ, Pittsburgh, 73-76; assoc prof, Drew Univ, 76-. *Mem:* Col Art Asn; Women's Caucus for Art. *Res:* Paul Klee; abstract expressionism; contemporary art. *Publ:* Contribr, New Catholic Encyclopedia, McGraw-Hill, 66; Selection 1968, Univ Art Mus, Univ Calif, Berkeley, 68-69; coauth, The Political Art of Duncan MacPherson, Can Dimension, 3-4/70; auth, Form-creating energies: Paul Klee & physics, Arts Mag, 9/77; Klee's Kleinwelt & creation, Print Rev, fall 77. *Mailing Add:* BC Drew Univ Dept Art 36 Madison Ave Madison NJ 07940

HENSELMANN, CASPAR
SCULPTOR, ILLUSTRATOR
b Mannheim, Ger, US citizen, 33. *Study:* Univ Ill Col Med, dipl Med-Art, 1955; Art Inst Chicago, BFA, 1956; Northwestern Univ, 1950-52; Columbia Univ, 1961-62. *Work:* Lehmbruck Mus, Duisburg, Ger; Kunsthalle Bremen, Ger; Ritterhaus Mus, Offenburg, Ger; Technicon Corp, Tarrytown, NY; Lindenau Mus, Altenburg; Villa Haiss Mus, Zell AH, Ger. *Comn:* Glass lobby piece (oil, air), Marshall-Ilsley Bank, Milwaukee, 71; Union Bank Switzerland, NY, 83; SMS Eng, Pittsburg, Pa, 89; Deutsche Bank, NY, 90; Bank Julius Bear, NY, 92; Swiss Paraplegic Ctr, Nottwil, Switzerland; Deutsche Bank, NY; SMS Engineering, Pittsburgh; F Scheidt Collection, Essen Kettwig, Ger; Mannesman Int, Dusseldorf, Ger; Marshall-Isley Bank, Milw; Southridge Shopping Center, Milw. *Exhib:* solo exhib Dorothea Van Der Koelen, Mainz, Ger, 1989, Sandra Gering Gallery, 1989, Kunstverein Bielefeld Mus, Waldhof, Ger, 1991, Stadt Gallery, Lahr, Ger, 1993, Bill Bace Gallery, NY, 1992, 1995, Offenburg Mus, Ger, 1994, Walter Bischoff Gallery, Berlin, Stuttgart, 1986, 1990, 1994, 1997, Lindenau Mus, Altenburg, Ger, 1997, Kingsborough Community Col, Brooklyn, 1997, Robert Pardo Gallery, NY, 1999, Neuberger Mus, Purchase, NY, 1999, others; Nanjing Art Col, China, 1997; Wilhelm Lehmbruck Mus, Duisburg, Ger, 1999; Robert Pardo Gallery, NY, 1999, 2002 & 2004; Pardo-Lattuada Gallery, Milan, 2001; Chelsea Studio Gallery, NY, 2002; Woodster Arts Space, 2003-05. *Pos:* freelance pharmaceutical/surgical illustrator, 3-D models, 1968-; art dir, Aron & Falcone Advert, Chatham, NJ, 1972-73; ptnr, Johnson Med Illustration Studio, New York, 1962-68; fel, WB Saunders Publ Co, Phila, 1956. *Teaching:* Instr, St Cloud State Col, 75; asst prof, C W Post Ctr, Long Island Univ, 1976-77, Univ NC, Chapel Hill, 1983, Hofstra Univ, Hempstead, NY, 1987-88; lectr, critic, Columbia Univ Grad Sch Architecture, 1994; assoc prof, LI Univ, Brooklyn, 1996-; vis artist, Memphis Acad Arts, 2002. *Awards:* Ford Found Artist in Residence, Am Fedn Arts, 1965; Nat Endowment Arts Award, 79, Grant, 1984; Gottlieb Award, 2003. *Bibliog:* Articles in: The Village Voice, 74 & 79 & The Soho News, 76, 77, 78 & 79. *Specialty:* Contemporary Art, Robert Prado Artefact, NY. *Publ:* Ambulatory Surgery of the Hernia, E Trabucco, Piccoli Press, Padua, Italy; Anatomy, Gardner, Gray O'Rahilly, WB Saunders Co, Phila; Atlas of Biliary Tract Surgery, F Glenn, Macmillan Publ Co; Atlas of Hernia Surgery, G Wantz, Raven Press; Knee Arthroplasty, ed: Paul A Lotke, Raven Press; Master Techniques in Orthopedic Surgery; Office Hernioplasty & the Trabucco Repair, Trabucco Ann Ital Chir, 1994; Atlas of Operative Strategy in General Surgery, Jameson Chassen, Springer-Verlag, NY. *Mailing Add:* 21 Bond St New York NY 10012

HENSLEY, JACKSON MOREY
PAINTER
b Portales, NMex, Sept 6, 1940. *Study:* Nat Acad Design, 59-61. *Work:* Arabian Horse Trust Mus, Denver, Colo; Los Angeles Natural Hist Mus, Calif; Leanin Tree Mus, Boulder, Colo, Taos Art Mus; Taos Art Mus, NMex; and others. *Exhib:* Nat Acad Fine Arts, NY; Nat Arts Club; Salmagundi Club, NY; over 200 other exhibits; One-man exihibs incl, Knickerbocker Artist Exhib, Stamford Mus, Conn, Jones Gallery, La Jolla, Calif, Farleigh Dickerson Traveling Exhib Burr Galleries, Denver. *Collection Arranged:* Madewood Plantation House Mus, New Orleans, Arabian Horse Trust Mus, Denver, Southside Bank Collection, Tyler, Tex, Highlands Univ Collection, Fire House Collection, Taos, NMex. *Awards:* Dr Ralph Weiler Award, Nat Acad, 60; Arthur T Hill Mem, Salmagundi Club, New York, 63; Mary Hingman Carter Award, Nat Arts Club, 63. *Bibliog:* Peggy & Harold Samuels (auth), Contemporary Western Artist, 82. *Media:* Watercolor, Oil. *Publ:* Illusr, Rockies Mag & Landscape Printers Am. *Dealer:* Reflection Gallery 201 Canyon Rd Santa Fe NM; Thompson Gallery New York NY. *Mailing Add:* 311 Paseo Del Pueblo Norte Taos NM 87571-5905

HEPPER, CAROL
SCULPTOR
b McLaughlin, SDak, Oct 23, 53. *Study:* SDak State Univ, Brookings, BS, 75. *Work:* Mus Mod Art, Metrop Mus, Solomon R Guggenheim Mus & Dannheisser Found, NY; Portland Art Mus, Ore; Walker Art Ctr, Minneapolis, Minn; Newark Mus, NJ; Detroit Inst Arts, Mich; and many others. *Exhib:* Material Matters, Permanent Collection Sculpture, Walker Art Ctr, Minneapolis, Minn, 80; New Perspectives in Am Art (with catalog), Guggenheim Mus, 83; Am: Art and the West (with catalog), Art Gallery of Western Australia, Perth, 86 & Art Gallery of New South Wales, Sidney, 87; solo exhibs, Worchester Art Mus (catalog), Mass, 92, Orlando Mus Art (catalog), Fla, 94; Innovations in Sculpture, 1985-1988, Aldrich Mus Art, Ridgefield, Conn, 88; 100 Drawings by Women, Hillwood Art Gallery, Long Island Univ, 89; Material Identity: Sculpture between Nature & Cult, Portland Art Mus, 93; Fabricated Nature, Boise Art Mus, Idaho, 94. *Collection Arranged:* Portland Art Mus, Portland, OR. *Pos:* Lectr, Princeton Univ. *Teaching:* Instr drawing, Standing Rock Sioux Indian Community Col, Ft Yates, NDak, 80-82 & Sch Visual Arts, NY, 84; vis fac sculpture, Md Art Inst, Baltimore, & RI Sch Design, 88, State Univ NY, Purchase, 89 & Princeton Univ, NJ, 90; Harvard Univ, 2000. *Awards:* Louis Comfort tiffany, 84; NY Found, 89; Nat Endowment Arts, 90; and others. *Bibliog:* Cynthia Nadelman (auth), New American sculpture, 1/84 & Gabo's Progeny, 12/87, Art News; Michael Brenson (auth), Sculpture breaks the mold of minimalism, NY Times, 11/23/86; Diane Waldman (auth), Emerging artists 1978-86: Selections from the Exxon Series & Deborah Pearlburg (auth), New York: Day by day, 9/88, Art News. *Media:* All. *Mailing Add:* 9 E Broadway New York NY 10038

HERA
SCULPTOR, ENVIRONMENTAL ARTIST
b New Orleans, La, Sept 28, 40. *Study:* Mt Holyoke Col; Sch Art Inst Chicago; Univ Dallas, Tex, BA, 70; Southern Methodist Univ, MFA, 74. *Work:* In Collections of: Okla Arts Ctr, Oklahoma City; Longview Mus, Tex; Rose Art Mus, Brandeis Univ, Waltham, Mass; Mount Holyoke Col Art Mus; Tampa Mus Art; Texas Instruments, New Orleans Mus. *Comn:* Snail Shell Maze, Boxford MA, 1979, Storm Flower Univ New Orleans, 1980, Floribunda, Queen, NY, 1980 Spirit House, Laumeier Sculpture Park, St Louis, Mo, 86; Singing Rock Sitting Place, Arboretum, Fairmont Park, Philadelphia, 88; Orbital Connector, Gov Smith Houses, Manhattan, 89; Tower as Inland Lighthouse, Marion St Transit Pkwy, Tampa, Fla, 90; Community Based Design Pilot, Philadelphia Art Comn, 91-92. *Exhib:* One-woman shows, Lifeways, Inst Contemp Art, Boston, 76, Butcher Shop, Brooks Jackson Gallery Iolas, NY, 79; Family Room, Contemp Art Ctr, New Orleans, La & Nexus Gallery, Philadelphia, 81; Dream Feast, Alternative Mus, NY, 81; Niagara-Knossos-Carranza Connector, Artpark, 82. *Pos:* Procession designer, First Night, Inc, Boston, 77-78; consult, Women's Slide Arch, Schlesinger Libr Hist Women Am, Radcliffe Col, 77-80; vis artist, Sch Mus Fine Arts, Boston, 78; artist-in-residence, Palisades Interstate Park Com, Bear Mountain, NY, 81; major proj artist, Artpark, 82; vis artist, Gerrit Rietveld Acad, Amsterdam, 85; design team, Marion St Transit Pkwy, Tampa, Fla, 88. *Teaching:* Artist-in-residence painting, drawing & sculpture, Fed Correctional Inst, Nat Endowment Arts Pilot Prog, Tallahassee, Fla, 75-76; instr, Framingham State Col, Mass, 77-78, & Cooper Union, 91-92; lectr, State Univ NY, New Paltz, 96. *Awards:* America the Beautiful Fund, 82, Glickenhaus Found 82, NY State Council on the Arts, 83, Committee for Visual Arts, 83, Dept Cult Affairs NY Award, 83 & 87; NY State Coun Arts Award, 83; Unity Day Citation from David Dinkins, NY, 88; Thanks to be to Grandmother Winifred Found, 95. *Bibliog:* Lucy Lippard (auth), Overlay, Pantheon, 83:; Placemakers II, Fleming & Von TsCharner, Hastings House, 87; George McCue (auth), Sculpture St. Louis Hudson Hills Press, NY 88; Marinna Harrison & Lucy Rosenfeld (auths), Artwalks in New York, Michael Kesend Publ, NY, 94; Artonsite Harrison & Rosefeld Kensend Pub 94; In the Footsteps of the Goddess Biaggi: Kit, 2000; Detours Peonides: 10LKOS, Athens GR, 2000. *Mem:* Col Art Asn; Women's Caucus Art; Woodstock Guild. *Media:* Steel, Wood; Plants, Fabric, Fiberglass. *Interests:* Sailing, X-C Skiing, Hiking, Travel, Languages, Poetry. *Publ:* The Tent Book, Hatton Houchton Mifflin, 79; Overlay, Lucy Lippard, Pantheon, 83; Sculpture City: St Louis, McCue, Finn & Binder Hills Press, NY, 88; Art Walks Harrison & Rosenfeld Pub, 94; Sculpture Parks & Gardens, Mc Carthy & Epstein; Kensend Pub, 96. *Mailing Add:* 145 Cold Brook Rd Bearsville NY 12409

HERARD, MARVIN T
SCULPTOR, EDUCATOR
b Puyallup, Wash, July 4, 29. *Study:* Burnley Sch Art, Seattle; Seattle Univ; Univ Wash, BA; Cranbrook Acad Art, MFA; Acad Fine Arts, Florence, Italy; Fonderia Artistica Florentina, Italy. *Comn:* Sculpture, Renton Pub Libr; Lemieux Libr, Seattle Univ. *Exhib:* Palazzo Venezia, Rome, 62; Seattle Art Mus, 65-67; Gov Exhib, State

Capitol Mus, 67-69; Henry Gallery, Univ Wash, 68; Cheney Cowles Mus, Spokane, Wash, 69; and others. *Teaching:* Instr, Seattle Pub Schs, 56-58; teaching fel sculpture, Cranbrook Acad Arts, 59-60; from assoc prof to prof art & chmn fine arts dept, Seattle Univ, 60-94; instr painting, Pius XII Inst Art, Florence, Italy, 62. *Awards:* Am Craftsmen Award, Henry Gallery, 61 & 65; Spokane Pac Northwest Exhib, 63, 64 & 66; Seattle Art Mus, 65; and others. *Mem:* Nat Art Educ Asn; Am Asn Univ Prof. *Mailing Add:* 1131 23rd Ave E Seattle WA 98112

HERBERT, APRIL H
SCULPTOR
b New York, NY, Apr 30, 34. *Study:* Empire State Col, State Univ New York, BA, 67; welding workshop with Jean Woodham, 83. *Comn:* Steel sculptures & jewelry, pvt collectors, NY & Conn, 86-89. *Exhib:* In Celebration, A Room of One's Own, Somerstown Gallery, NY, 85-89; 39th, 43rd & 44th Art of the Northeast, Silvermine Guild, Conn, 88 & 92; Ridgefield Guild of Artists, Conn, 89-91 & 94-96; Faber-Birren Color Show, Stamford Mus & Nature Ctr, Conn, 90 & 94; Modern Times through the Concerned Eye, Katonah Mus Art, 92; On & Off The Wall, Stamford Art Asn, 97; New Art Ann, Stamford Mus, Conn, 99; Spectrum 99, New Canaan, Conn. *Awards:* Silvermine second prize, Amidar Award, Silvermine Guild Art, Conn, 88; Fred Kraus Mem Award, Stamford Art Asn, 90, 1st Prize Sculpture, 97; 1st Prize Sculpture, Art Show, Bedford, 96. *Mem:* Katonah Mus Artists Asn; Stamford Art Asn (bd dir, 87-90); Ridgefield Guild Artists; Pound Ridge Art Guild. *Media:* Welded Steel. *Publ:* Auth, The Tailgate Cookbook, Funk & Wagnalls, 69. *Dealer:* Leander Pope The Schoolhouse Owens Rd Croton Falls NY 10519. *Mailing Add:* 254 Salem Rd Pound Ridge NY 10576

HERBERT, FRANK LEONARD
PAINTER, EDUCATOR
b New Orleans, La, Apr 27, 56. *Study:* La Tech Univ, BFA (Rome Studies Fel), 78; Colo State Univ, MFA, 82. *Work:* Peat, Marwick, Mitchell & Co, Denver; Rapid Transit of Denver, Colo; East Carolina Univ, Greenville; Poudre Valley Reg Hosp, Ft Collins, Colo; Colo State Univ, Ft Collins. *Exhib:* New Am Talent, Laguna Gloria Art Mus, Austin, 93; Miss Gallery, Bay St Louis, Mo, 95; 39th Ann Invitational, Longview Mus Fine Arts, 98; The Song of Images, Acad Fine Arts, Hoshiarpur, India; Indian Acad of Fine Arts, Amritsar, India, 99; A Backward Glance, Tower Gallery, Shreveport Regional Arts Coun, Shreveport, La, 99; The Secret Garden, Fine Arts Ctr, Kingwood Col, Kingwood, Tex, 99; East Tex Regional Exhib, Longview Mus Fine Arts, 2004; Paris Junior Col, Paris, Tex, 2005; Temple Col, Temple, Tex, 2006. *Pos:* Bd dir, Tex Asn Sch Arts, 89-92. *Teaching:* Instr art, Kilgore Col, Tex, 84-86, lead instr, 86-93, chmn visual arts, 93-97, coord visual arts, theater, commun, 97-. *Awards:* Visual Arts Fel, Mid-Am Arts Alliance, Nat Endowment Arts, 90; Nat Endowment Arts Fels Elec Database, Nat Mus Am Art, Washington, 96. *Mem:* Tex Asn Sch Arts (pres elect, 92-94, pres, 94-96); Col Art Asn; Nat Asn Sch Art & Design. *Media:* All Media. *Publ:* Contribr, Poudre Mag, 82-83. *Dealer:* Art Dept Kilgore Col 1100 Broadway Kilgore TX 75662. *Mailing Add:* 608 E Melton Longview TX 75602-1806

HERBERT, JAMES ARTHUR
PAINTER, FILMMAKER
b Boston, Mass, Feb 13, 38. *Study:* Dartmouth Col, AB(art hist, magna cum laude); Univ Colo, MFA; also with Clyfford Still, Kenzo Okada & Stan Brakhage. *Work:* Whitney Mus Am Art, NY; Mus Mod Art, NY; Walker Art Ctr; Royal Film Arch Belgium; Centre Beaubourg, Paris, France; and others. *Comn:* Film, Libr Congress, 83; Kennedy Ctr, 84. *Exhib:* Hradiste Film Festival, Czech Repub, 94; 100 Yrs Cinema, Paris, 95; Mus Mod Art, Barcelona, 98; New Harvest Film Festival, Leuveen, Bel, 98; Oberhausen Film Festival, 99; Retrospective, Atlanta Contemp Art Ctr, 2000; Premiers, Mus of Modern Art, 2005; London Film Festival, British Film Inst, 2005. *Teaching:* Resident artist, Yale Summer Sch Art & Music, Norfolk, Conn, 65; prof painting, Univ Ga, 62-2006, Res prof, 92-2006; Distinguised Res Prof Emeritus, Univ Ga, 2006. *Awards:* Guggenheim Mem Found Fel, 71 & 89; Nat Endowment Arts Grant, 75, 78, 81 & 82; Louis Comfort Tiffany Found Award, 80; Awards in the Visual Arts 7, Rockefeller Found, 88; Adolph & Esther Gottlieb Found, 92; Rockefeller Found, 93. *Bibliog:* Roger Greenspun (auth), Quick-who are David Rimmer & James Herbert?, NY Times Sunday Ed, 10/8/72; Larry Kardish (auth), Of Light and Texture, Andrew Noren/James Herbert, Mus Mod Art, 81; Larry Kardish (auth), Afterimages, Ga Rev, spring 89; Stephen Holden (auth), Taking Liberties with the World, NY Times, 10/5/92; Donald Kuspit (auth), James Herbert, Demonic Painter, Atlanta Contemp Art Ctr, 2000. *Publ:* Stills, Photographs by James Herbert, Twelvetrees Press, Santa Fe, NMex, 92. *Dealer:* Sandler Hudson Gallery 1831 Peachtree Rd Atlanta GA 30309. *Mailing Add:* 243 Dearing St Athens GA 30605

HERBERT, PINKNEY
PAINTER, EDUCATOR
b Charlotte, NC, April 23, 54. *Study:* Memphis Col Art, 75-76; Rhodes Col Art, BA, 77; Univ Memphis, MFA, 82. *Work:* NYNEX Corp, White Plains, NY; Prudential-Bach, NY; Arthur Anderson Assoc, Chicago, Ill; Ark Art Ctr Found, Little Rock; Tenn State Mus, Nashville; and others. *Comn:* Wolfchase Galleria, Memphis, 96; vestibule floor, Public Libr Bldg, Memphis, 98. *Exhib:* one-man shows, City Gallery Contemp Art, Raleigh, NC, 92, Robinson/Willis Gallery, Nashville, Tenn, 92, Austin Peay Univ, Clarksville, Tenn, 93, Galerie Pelin, Helsinki, Finland, 93, Sandler Hudson Gallery, Atlanta, Ga, 94 & 96, Murray State Univ, Ky, 96 & Ledbetter Lusk Gallery, Memphis, 96, Gallery WDO, Charlotte, NC, 97, Ledbetter Lusk, Ledbetter Lusk Gallery, Memphis, 98, Nashville Int Airport, Tenn, 99, Ark State Univ, 00, David Lusk, Memphis, 01, Medallion Gallery, New Orleans, 01; Twelve in Tenn, Tenn State Mus, Nashville, 94; Triennial, New Orleans Mus Art, La, 95; The Blind Man and the Elephant, (traveling) Free Libr of Philadelphia, Chicago, Tucson, Ariz, Palo Alto, Calif, Savannah, Ga, Augusta, Ga, San Juan, PR & Memphis, Tenn, 98; Price is Right, Ledbetter Lusk Gallery, Memphis, 99; MAX 99, Univ of Memphis Art Mus, 99; Outward Bound: Am Art on the Brink of the 21st Century (traveling), Hanoi Mus of Fine Arts, Vietnam, Painting Inst, Shanghai, China, Hall of Ancestors, Beijing, China, Jakarta Arts Ctr, Indonesia & Singapore Mus of Art, 1999-2000; The Price is Right 2, Once is Never Enough, David Lusk Gallery, Memphis, 2000; 43rd Ann Delta Exhib, Ark Arts Ctr, Little Rock, 2000; Cheekwood Mus Art, Nashville, 02; and others. *Collection Arranged:* Ark Arts Ctr, Little Rock; Landers & Assocs, Memphis; Arthur Anderson Assocs, Chicago; First Tenn Bank, Memphis; New Orleans Mus Art; NYU; Pfizer, Memphis; Prudential Life Insurance Co, Newark, NJ; Tenn State Mus, Nashville; Wolfchase Galleria, Memphis. *Pos:* Artist-in-residence, NC Arts Coun, 82-83; founder & dir, Marshall Arts, 92-; grad sch coordr, Memphis Col Art, 94-; artist-in-residence, Penland Sch Crafts, (summer) 95 & 97. *Teaching:* Instr art dept, Memphis State Univ, 89-91; vis artist, Univ Tenn, Knoxville, 92, Art Inst Lahti, Finland, 93, Acad Fine Arts, Helsinki, Finland, 93; guest teacher, lectr, Harwood Art Ctr, Albuquerque, 98. *Awards:* Nat Endowment Arts Fel, 87; Va Ctr Creative Arts Fel, Sweet Briar, 90 & 91; Art Fel, Tenn Arts Comn, 91; USIA-Arts Am Artist/Teaching Fel, Helsinki, Finland & Budapest, Hungary, 93; Va Ctr for Creative Arts Fel, 95. *Bibliog:* Jerry Cullum (auth), Bold Strokes Distinguish Herbert's Work, Atlanta Jour Constitution, 3/18/94; Donald La Badie (auth), Abstraction Links Works by Herbert & Miller, Memphis Com Appeal, 1/26/94; Marian McLellan (auth), New Orleans Art Review, 10-11/96; Glenna Park (auth), Irony of life assumes guise of art, Commercial Appeal, 6/26/99; Melody Barnett (auth), MAX:99 A mix of some highs, some lows, Dateline Memphis, 6/24-30/99; Jean Robertson & Craig MacDaniel (coauth), Painting as a Language: Material, Technique, Form, Content, Harcourt Brace, 2000. *Mem:* Col Art Asn. *Media:* Oil, Drawing. *Dealer:* David Lusk Gallery 4540 Poplar Memphis, TN 38117. *Mailing Add:* c/o Marshall Arts Studio 639 Marshall St Memphis TN 38103

HERBERT, ROBERT L
HISTORIAN, EDUCATOR
b Worcester, Mass, Apr 21, 29. *Study:* Wesleyan Univ, Middletown, Conn, BA, 51; Inst Art & Archeol & Ecole du Louvre, Paris, Fulbright Scholar, 51-52; Yale Univ, MA, 54, PhD, 57; Am Coun Learned Soc Grant, 60; Morse fel, London, 60-61; sr fac fel, Paris, 68-69; Guggenheim fel, Paris & New Haven, Conn, 71-72. *Pos:* Chmn, Sessions Mod Art, Col Art Asn, 65, 71, 81 & 85. *Teaching:* Asst instr hist of art, Yale Univ, 54-55, actg instr, 55-56, instr & mem comt hist, arts & lett, 56-60, from asst prof to prof hist art, 60-74, Robert Lehman prof hist of art, 74-, dir undergrad studies, 62-64, actg chmn, 65-66, chmn, 66-68; Slade prof, Oxford Univ, 78; prof art, Mount Holyoke Col, 90-97. *Awards:* Distinguished Teaching of Art Hist Award, Col Art Asn, 82; Rockerfeller Found Humanities Fel, 86; elected mem Am Philos Soc, 93. *Bibliog:* Impressionism, originality, and laissez-faire, Radical Hist Rev 38, spring 87. *Mem:* Ordre Arts Lettres (chevalier, 76, officer, 90). *Res:* 19th and 20th century French art. *Publ:* Contrib, French Cities in the Nineteenth Century, Hutchinson, London, 82; auth, Impressionism: Art, and Partisan Soc, New Haven and London, Yale Univ Press, 88; auth, Léger, the Renaissance, and "Primitivism", Mélanges Michel Laclotte, Paris, 94; Auth, Peasants and "Primitivism", French Prints from Millet to Gauguin (exhib catalog), Mt Holyoke Col Art Mus, Mus Art RI Sch Design & Smart Mus Art, Univ Chicago, 95-96; auth, From Miller to Leger, Essays in Soc Art History, New Haven and London, Yale Univ Press, 2002. *Mailing Add:* 26 Ashfield Ln South Hadley MA 01075-1341

HERBERT CONSTRANSITCH, PHYLLIS
SCULPTOR, EDUCATOR
b Houma, La, Sept 29, 63. *Study:* Nicholls State Univ, BFA, 86; Studies in Cortona, Italy, 89; Univ Ga, MFA, 90. *Exhib:* Mostra, Pallazzo Casalli, Cortona, Italy, 89; All That Remains, Charleston City Gallery, Piccolo Spoleto Festival, Charleston, SC, 93; KY/SCnyc, The Nat Arts Club, NY, 96; Wide-Open Canvas, Connemara Conservancy, Dallas, 97; Mayfair: Festival of Arts, Allentown City Park, Pa, 97; Maovani Prostoru, Klatovy-Klanova Mus, Czech Republic, 98; ESP 98 Invitational, Franconia Sculpture Park, Shafer, Minn, 98; 99 Colorado Vision Awards, Western Colo Ctr for Arts, Grand Junction, 99. *Teaching:* instr sculpture, Cen Piedmont Community Col, Charlotte, NC, 90-92; adj prof sculpture, Col Charleston, SC, 92-96; asst prof sculpture, Met State Coll Denver, 97-. *Awards:* Alternate Visions Award, Alternate Roots, Atlanta, 93; SC Visual Arts Fel, SC Arts Comn, 95; Colorado Vision Award, Colo Coun Arts, 99. *Mem:* Internat Sculpture Ctr; Col Art Asn. *Media:* Mixed Media. *Mailing Add:* 1045 Dudley St Denver CO 80215

HERFIELD, PHYLLIS
PAINTER
b Dec 6, 47. *Study:* Art Students League, 65; Tyler Sch Art, Rome, 67-68; Temple Univ, BFA, 69; Nat Acad Design, 79-80. *Work:* Brooklyn Acad Music; Metrop Mus Art; Ft Lauderdale Mus; Cincinatti Mus; Nat Portrait Gallery; Hunter Col; Univ of Indianapolis; Montefiore Medical Ctr; Mount Union Col; Portland Art Mus; Yale Univ Art Gallery. *Comn:* Prints: Orion Gallery; portraits: Salander O'Reilly Galleries, Portraits Inc. *Exhib:* Mus Mod Art, Paris, 75; Butler Inst, Youngstown, Ohio, 85; Solander O' Reilly, NY, 85; OK Harris Works of Art, NY, 90; Helander Gallery, Palm Beach, 91; Vered Gallery, East Hampton, NY, 93; Gallery Henoch, NY, 94; Foster Goldstrom, NY, 94; Steibel Modern, NY, 94; Nat Portrait Gallery, Washington, 96; Lizan-Tops, East Hampton, NY, 96; Maymount Manhattan Col Gallery, NY, 99; Portland Art Mus, 2002; Armory Art Ctr, W Palm Beach, 2005. *Awards:* Julius Hallgarten Prize, Nat Acad Design, 81. *Bibliog:* Reviews, Print Collectors Newslett, 5-6/77 & 5-6/78; Hilton Kramer (auth), rev, NY Times, 3/5/81; article, Christian Sci Monitor, 3/81; Valentin Tatransky (auth), article, Arts Mag, 10/85; Diversions, 2/89 & Femme Mag, 1/89. *Media:* Oil. *Publ:* Illusr, NY Times, Esquire, Psychology Today; Criticism, New York Reviews of Art; and many others. *Dealer:* Salander-O'Reilly Gallery 20 E 79th St New York NY 10021; Portrait Inc 985 Park Ave New York NY 10028. *Mailing Add:* 172 E 90th St New York NY 10128-2619

HERIC, JOHN F
SCULPTOR
b Reno, Nev, Feb 28, 42. *Study:* Ariz State Univ, with Ben Goo, BFA, 63; Southern Ill Univ, Carbondale, with Milt Sullivan, MFA, 65. *Work:* Scottsdale Ctr Arts; Northern Ill Univ; Ariz State Univ Mus Art; Tucson Mus Art; Univ Ariz Mus Art. *Comn:* Steel sculpture, Ridgewood High Sch, 64; courtyard, Sopori Sch, Sahaurita Sch Dist, Ariz, 71; Downtown Develop Corp, Tucson, Ariz; The Bohm Co, Tucson, Ariz; City of Phoenix; City of Tucson. *Exhib:* St Paul Mus Art, Minn, 65; one-man shows, Univ Wis-Milwaukee, 66, Grossmont Col, 69 & Elaine Horwitch Gallery, Scottsdale, 74; Southwestern Invitational, Yuma, Ariz, 69-74; Romanek Sculpture Park, Chicago, Ill; Sculpture at the Crossroads, Indianapolis, Ind; Construct Gallery, Chicago, Ill; Univ NDak, Grand Forks; Ariz State Univ, Tempe; Tucson Mus Art, Ariz; Grossmont Col, El Cajon, Calif; Pac Lutheran Univ, Tacoma, Wash. *Pos:* Vis artist, Grossmont Col, 74-75. *Teaching:* Instr sculpture, Wis State Univ-Platteville, 65-67; vis lectr sculpture, Ariz State Univ, 67-69; from lectr sculpture to assoc prof art, Univ Ariz, 69-; Southern Ill Univ, Carbondale. *Awards:* Best of Show, Ariz Designer Craftsmen, 68; First Award Sculpture, Ariz Ann, 68; Purchase Award, Southwestern Invitational, 71, 72 & 74. *Media:* Stone, Plastics. *Dealer:* Elaine Horwitch Gallery 4200 N Marshall Way Scottsdale AZ 85251. *Mailing Add:* Univ Ariz Dept Art Tucson AZ 85721

HERMAN, ALAN DAVID
DESIGNER, GRAPHIC ARTIST
b Kew Gardens, NY, Mar 8, 47. *Study:* Pratt Inst Sch Art & Design, Ida D Haskell scholarship & BFA(cum laude), 69. *Comn:* Consumer advert promotion, Carrier Air Conditioning Co, Southern Calif, 73-; med insurance commun & marketing prog, Johnson & Higgins, Los Angeles, 76-; international design programs, Xerox Corp, 80-; product launches int corps, Dupont, Mitsubishi, Kinemetrics & Nat Peripherals; exterior bus graphics system, City of Los Angeles. *Exhib:* 1972 Exhib of Best Advertising & Editorial Art in the West, 72; IAM Graphics Exhib, NY, 74; Indust Graphics Int, San Jose, Calif, 77; AIGA Packaging Exhib, Chicago, 80; Creativity 80 Show, NY. *Pos:* Pres & creative dir, Alan Herman & Assoc, Inc, Los Angeles, 70-. *Awards:* Top Package of the Yr, Print Mag, 76; IGI Distinctive Merit, 77; AIGA Graphic Design USA Award, 79. *Mem:* Art Dir Club Los Angeles; Los Angeles Co Mus Art. *Mailing Add:* c/o Alan Herman & Assoc 3280 E Foothill Suite 270 Pasadena CA 91107-3103

HERMAN, DAVID H
PAINTER
b Brooklyn, NY, Apr 28, 40. *Study:* NY Univ, BS, 61; Art Students League NY, with Rudolf Baranik, Brooklyn Col, MA, 70. *Work:* Sch for Strings, New York City; East Meadow Jewish Center, NY. *Comn:* mural, Elmont Mem High Sch, NY, 94. *Exhib:* Int Small Works Exhib, Amos Eno Gallery, New York City, 98; Denise Bibro Gallery, New York City, 99 & 2003; Am Drawing Biennial, Muscarelle Mus Art, Williamsburgh, Va, 2000; Albright-Knox Gallery, Buffalo, NY, 2000-2001 & 2002-2003; Exposed, Fairleigh Dickinson Univ, Fair Lawn, NJ, 2001; Denis Bibro Gallery, New York City, Champions of Modernism Ill, 2004; Mills Pond House, St James NY, 2004; Denise Bibro Fine Art, New York City, 2006. *Teaching:* dir orchestral music, Elmont Mem High Sch, NY, 64-94; founding mem, Rudolf Baranik Ongoing Art Sem, 96-98. *Awards:* First Place, Jewish Arts Festival, 99; Honorary Award, Am Drawing Biennial 7, 2000; Expo XX, BJ Spoke Gallery, Huntington, NY, 2001. *Bibliog:* Using Recent Events as a Theme for Social Commentary, NY Times, 6/10/1994; Turning Photographs into the Metaphorical, NY Times, 11/9/1997; Donald Kuspit (auth), Exposed, Denise Bibro, 2000; Helen Harrison (auth), Photographs that Comment on the Subject, NY Times, 2/2004; Divided by Beliefs, but United in Abstraction, 3/18/2001. *Mem:* Appraisers Asn Am; NY Artists Equity. *Media:* Acrylic. *Interests:* Contemporary Art. *Dealer:* Denise Bibro Fine Art, NYC; Nexus Gallery, NYC. *Mailing Add:* 1511 Dieman Ln East Meadow NY 11554

HERMAN, LLOYD ELDRED
MUSEUM DIRECTOR
b Corvallis, Ore, Mar 19, 36. *Study:* Ore State Univ, 54-56; Univ Ore, 58-59; Am Univ, Washington, DC, BA(lib arts), 59-60. *Pos:* Prog mgr, Off Dir-Gen Mus, Smithsonian Inst, 66-71; dir, Renwick Gallery, 71-86; cur, mus consult, auth, Am craft & design topics, 86-; consult dir, Cartwright Gallery, Vancouver, BC, Can, 88-90, curatorial consult, 90-92; act cur, Can Craft Mus, Vancouver, BC, 92-; actg sr cur, Int Glass Mus, Tacoma, Wash, 98-99. *Awards:* Potomac Chap Am Soc Interior Designers Award, 79; Decoration, Order of Leopold II King of Belgians, 79; Decoration, Order of Danebrog, Chevalier, Queen of Denmark, 82. *Mem:* Hon fel Am Craft Coun; Bellingham Munic Arts Comn (chmn, 95). *Interests:* Twentieth century crafts and industrial design. *Publ:* Auth, Brilliant Stories: American Narrative Jewelry, US Info Agency, 92; Clearly Art: Pilchucks Glass Legacy, Whatcom Mus Hist & Art, Bellingham, Wash, 92; coauth, Tales & Traditions: Storytelling in Twentieth Century American Craft (with Matthew Kangas), Craft Alliance, St Louis, 93; The collectors Eye, Koffler Gallery, Toronto, 94; Trashformations: Recycled Materials in Contemporary American Art & Design, Whatcom Mus His & Art, Bellingham, Wash, 98; co-auth (with Andre Codrescu), Thomas Mann, Metal Artist, Guild Publs, Madison, Wis, 2001

HERMAN, ROGER
PAINTER, PRINTMAKER
b Saarbruchen, Saarland, Nov 21, 47, Ger citizen. *Study:* Kunstakademie Karlsruhe, MFA, 79. *Work:* Walker Art Ctr, Minneapolis; Los Angeles Co Mus, Calif; San Francisco Mus Art; Denver Art Mus; Newport Harbor Art Mus. *Exhib:* One-man show, La Jolla Mus, 83; III Bienale, San Francisco Mus, 84; Painters Who Print, Walker Art Ctr, Minneapolis, 84; Inst for Contemp Art, Philadelphia, 84; Larry Gagosian Gallery, Los Angeles, 85, 86. *Awards:* New Talent Award, Los Angeles Co Mus, 83; Nat Endowment Art, 83 & 89. *Media:* All; Woodcuts. *Dealer:* Ace Gallery 5514 Wilshire Blvd Los Angeles CA. *Mailing Add:* 729 Academy Rd Los Angeles CA 90012-1004

HERMANN, MILDRED L
COLLAGE ARTIST, PAINTER
b Brooklyn, NY, Mar 8, 1920. *Study:* Artists in Am Sch Painting, with Leo Manso, Jerry Okimoto & Kim Chung, 68-74. *Work:* Norton Gallery & Mus, West Palm Beach, Fla; Fine Arts Mus Long Island, Hempstead, NY; The Bond Buyer, NY; YMCA, NY; Albright-Knox Gallery, Buffalo, NY. *Exhib:* Childe Hassam Purchase Fund Exhib, Am Acad & Inst Arts & Lett, NY, 78; Collage and Assemblage, Miss Mus Art, Jackson, 81 & Tampa Mus, Fla, 82; 36th Art Northeast USA, Silvermine Guild Artists, New Canaan, Conn, 85; Butler Inst Am Art, Youngstown, Ohio, 86; Sixth Juried Show, Fine Arts Mus Long Island, 85; Tex Fine Arts Asn, Austin, Tex; Gloria Laguna Mus. *Pos:* Juror, Works on Canvas, Nat Asn women Artists, NY, 84-86. *Awards:* Juror's Choice Award, Tex Fine Arts Asn, Austin, 89; First Prize, Prof Artists Guild; Childe Hassam Purchase Award Am Acad Arts and Letters, NY, 80. *Mem:* Nat Asn Women Artists; Audubon Artists; Artists Guild, Norton Gallery & Sch Art; Prof Artists Guild, Boca Raton Mus, Fla. *Media:* Collage, Acrylic, Oil, Mixed Media, Miscellaneous Media. *Publ:* Col & Assemblage, Miss Mus Art, catalogue no 41, 81; NY, Tex, CA: New Art Catalog, Tex Fine Arts Asn 89, 10; Who's Who in Am Art, 26th Ed, NJ; Contemporary Women Artists, St James Press, Mich, 1999. *Dealer:* Denise Bibro Fine Art 529 W 20th St No 4W NY 10011; Denise Bibro Fine Art. *Mailing Add:* 55 Salem Rd Roslyn Heights NY 11577

HERMS, GEORGE
SCULPTOR, PAINTER
b Woodland, Calif, 1935. *Work:* Portals to Poetry, Citicorps Plaza, Los Angeles; Moon Dial, Beverly Hills, Calif; Clock Tower Monument to Unknown, MacArthur Park Pub Art Prog, Los Angeles. *Exhib:* The Art of Assemblage (with catalog), Mus Mod Art, NY, 61; Whitney Mus Am Art, NY, 62 & 90; Mixed Media, Rental Gallery, Los Angeles Co Mus Art, 74; 3 Los Angeles Sculptors, Los Angeles Inst Contemp Art, Calif, 75; Assemblage, Los Angeles Inst Contemp Art, Calif, 75; Painting and Sculpture in California: The Modern Era (with catalog), San Francisco Mus Mod Art, 76, 77; Los Angeles Inst Contemp Art, 78; Sculpture in California, 1975-80 (with catalog), San Diego Mus Art, Calif, 809; Ann Exhib (with catalog), Am Acad Rome, Italy, 83; Collage, The Americans (with catalog), Mus Fine Arts, Houston, Tex, 83; Gala, Gala, Mus Contemp Art, Los Angeles, 85; Recent Acquisitions, Los Angeles Co Mus Art, Calif, 87; Loans from the Norton Simon Collection, Los Angeles Co Mus Art, Calif, 88; Art for Milk, Armand Hammer Mus Art, Los Angeles, Calif, 91; The Elegant, Irreverent & Obsessive: Drawing in Southern California, Calif State Univ, Fullerton, 93; Old Glory: The Am Flag in Contemp Art (with catalog), Cleveland Mus Arts, Ohio, 94; World in a Box (with catalog), S Bank Ctr, London, Eng, 94; solo exhibs, Kohn Turner Gallery, Los Angeles, Calif, 94, Fred Spratt, San Jose, Calif, 94, Riverside Art Mus, Calif, 95, Jack Rutberg, Los Angeles, Calif, 95, Tony Shafrazi Gallery, NY, 95, Katharine Clarke Gallery, Los Angeles, Calif, 96 & La Mus Mod Art, Denmark, 97; Beat Cult and the New Am, Whitney Mus Am Art, NY, 95; Gallery 258, Los Angeles, Calif, 95; From Behind the Orange Curtain (with catalog), Muckenthaler Cult Ctr, Fullerton, Calif, 95; Works Saluting San Francisco 1962-1996, Catharine Clark Gallery, San Francisco, 96, Bed of Roses., 2001; Crossings, Fred Spratt Gallery, San Jose, 96, Poet Heroes of My Youth, 99; Office of the Future, Robert Berman Gallery, Santa Monica, 98; Fifty Years of Assemblage, Seraphin Gallery, Phila, 2002; Hot Set, Santa Monica Mus Art, Calif, 2005; Pandoras Box: The Sculpture of George Herms, Crocker Art Mus, Calif, 2005; Retrospective, Tobey C Moss Gallery, Calif, 2005; Lost but Found: Assemblage, Collage and Sculpture, Norton Simon Mus, Pasadena, 2005. *Awards:* Nat Endowment Arts Individual Fel, 68, 77 & 84; John Simon Guggenheim Fel Sculpture, 83-84; Working Grant, Pollock-Krasner Found, 87

HERNANDEZ, ANTHONY LOUIS
PHOTOGRAPHER
b Los Angeles, Calif, July 7, 47. *Study:* E Los Angeles Col, 66-70; Ctr Eye, Aspen, Colo, 69; Studied with Lee Friedlander. *Work:* Univ Calif, Davis; Mus Mod Art, NY; Bibliot Nat, Paris, France; Int Mus Photog, George Eastman House, Rochester, NY; Corocoran Gallery Art, Washington, DC. *Comn:* Photographs, Corcoran Gallery Art, Washington, DC, 76. *Exhib:* One-man shows, Corcoran Gallery Art, Washington, DC, 76, Orange Coast Col, Costa Mesa, Calif, 78, Univ Calif, Santa Barbara, 79, Calif Mus Photog, Riverside, 82, Susan Spiritus Gallery, Newport Beach, Calif, 84, Northlight Gallery, Ariz State Univ, 85, Opsis Found, NY, 90, Turner/Krull Gallery, Los Angeles, 91 & 93, Sprengel Mus, Hanover, Ger, 95, Mus l'Elysee, Switz, 96, Centre Nat Photog, Paris, France, 97, Galerie POLARIS, Paris, France, 97, 99 & 2001, Calif Col Arts and Crafts, Oakland, 2001, Pictures for Los Angeles, Grant Selwyn Fine Art, 2003; Photog and the City, Seattle Art Mus, 1980; Facets of the Collection: Urban Am, San Francisco Mus Modern Art, Calif, 82; Slices of Times: Calif Landscapes, 1860-1880, 1960-1980, Oakland Mus, Calif, 82; Exposed and Developed: Am Photog in the 1970's, Nat Mus Am Art, Washington, DC, 84; Recent Acquisitions, Oakland Mus, Calif, 87; Landscape Photographs from the Permanent Collection, Corcoran Gallery Art, Washington, DC, 88; Picturing California, Oakland Mus, Calif, 89; Between Home and Heaven: Contemp Am Landscape Photog, New Orleans Mus Art, La, 92; Wasteland: Landscape Form Now On, Fotografie Biennale III, Rotterdam, The Netherlands, 93; Crossing the Frontiers: Photographs of the Developing West, 1849 to the Present, San Francisco Mus Modern Art, Calif, 96; TRASH: When Waste Materials Become Art, Mus d'Arte Mod Contemporania Trento e Rovereto, Italy, 97; Hasselblad Center, Goteberg, Sweden, 99; Identification of a Landscape, Venezie-Marghera, Venice, Italy, 2000; Documents and Beyond, Reina

Sofia Mus, Madrid, Spain, 2001; Made in Calif, 1900-2000, Los Angeles Co Mus Art, Calif, 2001; Calif Invitational, Ansel Adams Ctr Photog, San Francisco, Calif, 2001. *Awards:* Ferguston Grant, Friends Photog, Carmel, Calif, 72; Nat Endowment Arts Photog Fel, 75 & 78; Rome Prize, Am Acad, Rome, 98-99. *Bibliog:* Photography view: between home and heaven, contemporary American photography, NY Times, 6/4/92; A Gueze (auth), Wasteland, Blauwe Kamer, 9/92; Peter Kosenko (auth), No one home: Anthony Hernandez at Turner/Krull Gallery, 4/22/93; Ann Walters (auth), Fotografie Biennale Rotterdam III, Art Press, 11/94; K McKenna (auth), A career begins to click, LA Times, Calendar, 10/29/95; David Pagel (auth), Nature's beauty, LA Times, 11/9/96; David Pagel (auth), LA Times, Calendar, 6/20/97; Claudine Ise (auth), Photos from a very unpleasant decade, 9/18/98; Ralph Rugoff (auth), Familiar haunts: the photography of Anthony Hernandez, Artforum, 11/2000. *Dealer:* Grant Selwyn Fine Arts Los Angeles CA. *Mailing Add:* 255 1/2 S Carrondelet Ave Los Angeles CA 90057-2065

HERNANDEZ, JO FARB
MUSEUM DIRECTOR, CURATOR

b Chicago, Ill, Nov 20, 52. *Study:* Univ Wis-Madison, BA, 74; Univ Calif, Los Angeles, MA, 75; Univ Calif, Berkeley; Mus Mgt Inst, cert, 81. *Collection Arranged:* Jewish Marriage Contracts, 83; Harriete Estel Berman: A Family of Appliances You Can Believe In (auth, catalog), 83; New Work/New Looks, 83; Day of the Dead: Tradition and Change in Contemporary Mexico (coauth, catalog), 81; Crime and Punishment: Reflections of Violence in Contemporary Art (auth, catalog), 84; Henrietta Shore: Retrospective (ed, catalog), 85; The Monterey Photog tradition: The Weston Years (ed, catalog), 85; Adat: Tribal Imagery/Ancestral Law, 86; The Artist and Myth (auth, brochure), 87; The Art of Eating, 88; Colors & Impressions: The Early Work of E Charlton Fortune (ed, catalog), 89; Lorser Feitelson: Exploration of the Figure, 1919-1929 (auth, brochure), 90; Chipping Away at the Layers: The Puzzle of Tramp Art, 91; The Quiet Eye: Pottery of Shoji Hamada & Bernard Leach (ed, catalog), 91; Painted Tintypes, 92; Julius Hatofsky: Against the Grain, 93; Jeannette Maxfield Lewis: A Centennial Celebration (auth catalog), 94; Sam Colburn: Creating a Style/The Early Years, (co-auth, catalog), 94; Jeremy Anderson: The Critical Link/A Quiet Revolution (auth catalog), 95; AG Rizzoli: Architect of Magnificent Visions (auth, bk), 97; Misch Kohn: Six Decades/Beyond the Tradition, (auth, bk), 98; Paul Pratchenko: Metarealistic Paintings, 2001; Diana Bates: Sculpture, 2002; Irvin Tepper: When Cups Speak (coauth, bk), 2002; Sam Richardson: Shaping Space (coauth, catalog), 2002; Jennifer & Kevin McCoy: Stardust, 2003; Marc D'Estout: Domestic Objects (coauth, catalog), 2003; Contmp Cuban Art and the Art of Survival, 2003; James Surls: From the Garden, 2003; Misch Kohn: A Life in Prints, 2004; Machiko Agano/Masako Takahashi, 2004; Peter Shire, Go Beyond the Ordinary (coauth, catalog), 2004; Nunca Mas/Never Again, 2004; Forms of Tradition in Contemporary Spain (coauth, book), 2005; Ron Nagle, 2005; Nic Nicosia: Making Pictures, 2006; Oliver Jackson: Drawing/the Incised Line, 2006; Marko Peljhan: Spectral System, 2006; Charles Krafft, Ceramic Sabotage, 2006. *Pos:* Curatorial asst, Mus Cult Hist, Los Angeles, 74-75; guest cur & lectr, various mus & univs, 75-; cur/educ asst, Dallas Mus Fine Arts, 76-77; dir & chief cur, Triton Mus Art, Santa Clara, Calif, 77-85 & Monterey Peninsula Mus Art, 85-93; consulting cur, Monterey Peninsula Mus Art, Calif, 93-2000; prin, Curatorial & Mgt Serv, 93-; dir, San Jose State Univ Gallery, Calif, 2000-. *Teaching:* Adj prof, ETex State Univ, 77, John F Kennedy Univ, 78, Univ Calif, Santa Cruz, 99-2000, San Jose State Univ, 2000-. *Awards:* Ralph C Altman Award, UCLA, Calif, 75; Rockefeller Fel, Dallas Mus Fine Arts, 76-77; Leader of the Decade-Arts, Leadership Monterey Peninsula, 92; Golden Eagle Award, Cinematographic, 92; Tech Asst Grant, Alliance Calif Traditional Arts, 2002; CSU Reseach Grants, Lottery Awards & Dean's Awards. San Jose State Univ, 2000-2006. *Mem:* Calif Asn Mus (bd dir, 85-, vpres, 87-91, pres, 91-92); Western Mus Conf (bd dir, 89-91, exec comt, 89-91, prog chmn, 90); Am Folklore Soc; Am Asn Mus; Alliance Calif Traditional Arts (exec bd); Friends of Fred Smith (nat adv bd) (int ed bd) Raw Vision mag; Bd Dirs, Spaces (Saving & Preserving Arts & Cultural Enviroments). *Res:* Spanish traditional/folk arts, outsider arts, art environments, contemporary art. *Publ:* auth, Jeremy Anderson: The Critical Link/A Quiet Revolution, 95; AG Rizzoli: Architect of Magnificent Visions, 97; auth, Misch Kohn: Beyond the Tradition, 98; Mel Ramos: The Galatea Series, 2000; coauth, Fire & Flux: The Art of Charles Strong; Irvin Tepper: When Cups Speak: Life with the Cup, 2002; Sam Richardson: Color of Space, 2002; Marc D'Estout Domestic Objects, 2003; Peter Shire: Go Beyond the Ordinary, 2004; Forms of Tradition in Contemp Spain, 2005; and many others. *Mailing Add:* 345 White Rd Watsonville CA 95076

HERNANDEZ, SAM (SAMUEL) RUDOLPH
SCULPTOR, EDUCATOR

b Hayward, Calif, Jan 23, 48. *Study:* Calif State Univ, Hayward, BA, 70; Ariz State Univ, 73; Univ Wis-Madison, MFA, 74. *Hon Degrees:* Univ Sonora, Hermosillo, Mex, diploma. *Work:* Yale Univ Art Gallery; Stanford Univ Arts Ctr; Oakland Mus, Calif; Arco Collection, Los Angles, Calif; City of San Jose Publ Art Prog; Contemp Mus, Honolulu; Mex Mus, San Francisco; Mus of Contemp Art Skopje, Macedonia; New Orleans Mus of Art. *Comn:* Monterey Co agricultural Commission, 95; Santa Lucia Preserve, Carmel Valley, Calif, 96; Pvt residences, Calif, 2004. *Exhib:* San Francisco Mus Mod Art, 79-80; Elvehjem Mus Art, Madison, Wis, 80; Crocker Art Mus, Sacramento, Calif, 84 & 2002; San Jose Mus Art, 84, 86 & 94; Monterey Pennisula Mus Art, Calif, 85; Contemp Art Ctr, Cinn, 86; Mex Mus, 86; Am Craft Mus, NY, 86; Philbrook Mus Art, Tulsa, 87; College Arts & Crafts, Oakland, Calif, 89, Univ Calif, Davis, 90, Oakland Mus, 92, Palm Springs Desert Mus, 93, Honolulu Acad Arts, 94, Redding Mus, 95, Univ Ore Mus, 95 & Calif Mus Art, 95; Calif State Univ, Sacramento, 99; Southwest Sch Art & Craft, San Antonio, Tex, 2000; Magdalena Baxeras Gallery, Barcelona, 2001; Univ Paris, Sorborne, 2003; Wiegand Gallery, Notre Dame de Namur Univ, 2005; and many others. *Collection Arranged:* The Day of the Dead: Tradition and Change in Contemporary Mexico (coauth, catalog), Triton Mus Art, 79; Columbus: The Good, The Bad & The Ugly, Univ Santa Clara, 92. *Pos:* Mem adv bd, Triton Mus Art, 81-85; adv bd, Djerassi Found, 95-96; artists' residency adv bd, Montalvo Ctr for Arts, 98-99; Art in Publ Places Commissioner, City of San Jose, 90-93. *Teaching:* Instr sculpture, E Tex State Univ, Commerce, 74-77; asst prof, Univ Santa Clara, Calif, 77-83, chmn art dept, 80-86, assoc prof sculpture, 83-96, prof, 96-; vis prof sculpture, Univ Wis-Madison, summer 80, Honolulu Acad Arts, 92, Anderson Ranch, 94, 95, 2001, 2005 & Haystack Mountain Sch, 94; vis lectr Calif State Univ, Sacramento, 99. *Awards:* San Francisco Found Phelan Award, 79; Fel, Cult Coun Santa Clara Co, 83; Nat Endowment Arts Fel, 84; Sr Fulbright Scholar, 86; Individual Artist Grant, Nat Endowment Arts, 89; Santa Clara Univ Dean's Fund Grant, President's Fun Grants, Curriculum Develop Grant, Thomas Terry Grant, Ctr for Multicultural Leaning Grant, 80-2005. *Bibliog:* Henry Hopkins (auth), Sam Hernandez, 88; L Price Amerson (auth), Sam Hernandez, 89; Bruce Guenther (auth), Sam Hernandez: Abstract Imagist, 93; Elizabeth Adan (auth), 100 Meditations, 2002; Frank Cebulski (auth), Sam Hernandez, 2005. *Mem:* Col Art Asn; Int Sculpture Asn; Nat Coun Educ Ceramic Arts; Calif Folklore Soc. *Media:* Wood, Bronze. *Res:* Spanish Traditional Arts & Performance events. *Publ:* Co-Auth, Day of the Dead: Tradition and Change in Contemporary Mexico, Triton Mus Art, 79; co-auth, Mexican Indian Dance Masks, Triton Mus Art, 82; A Conversation with Dr Jake (video), 94; videographer, Forms of Tradition in Contemporary Spain, 2006. *Mailing Add:* 345 White Rd Watsonville CA 95076

HERO, PETER DECOURCY
ADMINISTRATOR, HISTORIAN

b Washington, DC, Sept 10, 42. *Study:* Williams Col, Williamstown, Mass, with George Heard Hamilton & Whitney Stoddard, BA, 64, MA(art hist), 75; Stanford Univ, Calif, MBA, 66. *Hon Degrees:* Doc Laws, Maine Col of Art. *Collection Arranged:* The Elegant Academics (contribr, catalog), Clark Art Inst, Williamstown, Mass & Wadsworth Atheneum, Hartford, Conn, 75; Folk Art of the Oregon Country, Univ Ore Art Mus, Ore Hist Soc, Renwick Gallery, 80; On-Site New England, Public Art in Perspective (curator), traveling exhib, open at Bank of Boston, 89. *Pos:* Exec dir, Ore Arts Comn, 75-85; pres, Portland Sch of Art, Maine, 85-89; pres, Community Foundation Silicon Valley, San Jose, Calif, 89; mem, Nat Council on Arts, 91-96; mem, Nat Mus Serv Bd, 2003-. *Teaching:* Arts adminr, Lewis & Clark Col, Portland State Univ Grad MPA Prog, 82-86. *Awards:* Kress Found Fel, 6/75. *Bibliog:* The Man Who Sold SIlicon Valley on Giving, Fortune Magazine, Dec 2000. *Mem:* Western States Arts Found (bd chmn, 83-85); Art Mus Asn (bd dir, 79-81); Nat Assembly State Arts Agencies (bd dir, 77-81, chmn bd, 79-81); Nat Endowment Arts; Maine Independent Col Asn (bd dir, 86-); Art Col Exchange (chmn bd, 88-89); Arts Council Silicon Valley, 89-93; Found for a Civil Soc (dir bd, 97-); Am Indian Found (bd dir, 2001-); Pub Broadcasting Serv (mem, 02-). *Res:* Influence of Japanese prints upon evolution of perspective and space in Edgar Degas' work; cultural economics and public policy in the arts; non-profit organization management; public and private partnerships to promote cultural development. *Interests:* Community foundation development and education; cultural characteristics of philanthropy. *Publ:* Contribr, New legislation can integrate art and architecture, Western States Arts Found, 76; Marketing the arts, Study Ctr Cult Policy & Arts, Univ Calif, Los Angeles Grad Sch Mgt, 78; Cultural Development with Non-appropriated Funds, Assoc for Cult Econ, Akron, Ohio, 86; Des Modes de Financement Culturel public, French Ministry of Culture, Paris, 88; Community Foundation and Cultural Pluralism, J of Cult Econ, Akron, Ohio, 90; (auth) Venture Philanthropy: Emerging Patters of a New Cultural Dynamic, Univ Indiana Press, 2001. *Mailing Add:* 1321 University Ave Palo Alto CA 94301-2243

HERR, RICHARD JOSEPH
SCULPTOR, INSTRUCTOR

b Sheboygan, Wis, Jan 17, 37. *Study:* Layton Sch Art, Milwaukee; Marquette Univ; Univ Wis-Milwaukee; also with Oscar Binder, Stuttgart, Ger. *Work:* Borg-Warner Collection, Chicago; Univ Wis-LaCrosse; Univ Wis-Parkside, Kenosha; Prairie Sch, Racine, Wis. *Comn:* Relief sculpture, Northern Precision Casting, Lake Geneva, Wis, 73; door, Nafziger & Assocs, Lake Geneva, 79; door and relief, Petroskie Design, Lake Geneva, 80; door, Elaine Burnell, Santa Barbara, Calif, 86. *Exhib:* Critic's Choice Show, Chicago Art Inst, 72; one-man shows, Wustum Mus, Racine, 73 & Ozaukee Art Ctr, Cedarburg, Wis, 78; First Chicago Sculpture Invitational, Fed Bldg, 74; Milwaukee Art Ctr, 77; Art Milwaukee Invitational, Pfister Hotel, 95. *Collection Arranged:* Univ Wis, Parkside, Kenosha, Wis; Univ Wis, La Crosse; Saint Mary's Sch, Milwaukee, Wis; the Prairie Sch, Borg-Warner Corp, Chicago. *Pos:* Owner-dir, Art Independent Gallery, Lake Geneva, 68-; Johnson Wax Found grant sculptor in residence, Prairie Sch, 70-71; bd dir, Wis Art Edn Asn, 74-75; bd dir, Visual Art in Pub Places, Santa Barbara, 83-85; exec bd, Art Affils, Univ Calif, Santa Barbara, 87. *Teaching:* Instr art & chmn dept, Col Racine, 71-72; instr art, Prairie Sch, 71-; instr 3-D design, Univ Wis-Parkside, 73-74. *Awards:* Award for Sculpture, Va Beach Invitational, 71; Chicago Tribune Duo Critic's Award, Chicago Art Inst, 72; Award for Sculpture, Old Orchard Invitational, Chicago, 73. *Bibliog:* (auth) Karen Tancil, Art is Herr Apparent, Racine Sunday Bulletin, Mar 69; (auth) Michael Kirkhorn, Cryptic Metal Sculptures, Milwaukee Journal, Oct 68; (auth) Laura Watters, Aluminum Sculptures Reveal Herr's Artistic Philosophy, View of Technology, The Northern Star, Nov 72. *Mem:* Southern Asn Sculptors; Am Int Sculptors; Wis Art Educ Asn (bd mem). *Media:* Aluminum, Resin. *Publ:* contribr, Sculpture Casting, 72, Collage and Assemblage, 73 & Soft Sculpture and Related Soft Art, 75, Crown; contribr, Playboy, 74; contribr, Soft Sculpture and Related Soft art, Crown, 75; contribr, Racine Journel Times, Racine Journel, 81. *Dealer:* Boston Corp Art, 27 Drydock Ave, Boston, MA 02210; Ellen Wallace Art Cons, Inc, 593 Cherokee Rd, Highland Park, IL 60035. *Mailing Add:* W5284 Wisconsin Dr Elkhorn WI 53121

HERRERA, ARTURO
COLLAGE ARTIST
b Caracas, Venezuela, 59. *Study:* Univ Tulsa, BFA, 82; Univ Ill, Chicago, MFA, 92. *Exhib:* One-man shows include MWMWM Gallery, Chicago, 93, 94, Ctr Contemp Arts, Santa Fe, 93, Randolph St Gallery, Chicago, 95, Hermetic Gallery, Milwaukee, 95, Mus Contemp Arts, Chicago, 95, Revolution Gallery, Ferndale, Michigan, 96, Univ Club, Chicago, 96, Gahlberg Gallery Col DuPage, Glen Ellyn, 96, Brent Sikkema/Wooster Garden, NY City, 98, Renaissance Soc Univ Chicago, 98, Worcester Art Mus, Massachusetts, 98, Art Inst Chicago, 98, Dia Ctr Arts, 98; exhibited in group shows including Gallery 400, Chicago, 92, Nomadic Site, Los Angeles, 92, Klein Art Works, 93, Sch Art and Design Univ Chicago, 94, Sotheby's Inc, Chicago, 94, Drawing Ctr, NY City, 94, Layton Gallery Milwaukee Inst Art and Design, 94, Feature, NY City, 94, 95, PS 122, 94, Ten in One Gallery, Chicago, 94, LACE, Los Angeles, 95, 213 Inst Pl, Chicago, 95, TBA Exhbn Space, 95, Chicago Cultural Ctr, 96, NIU Gallery, Chicago, 96, Randolph St Gallery, 96, Thread Waxing Space, NY, 96, Stephen Friedman Gallery, London, 98, Brent Sikkema, NY City, 99, Whitney Biennial, 2002, Perforations, McKenzie Fine Art Inc, NY City, 2003, MoMa at El Museo, El Museo del Barrio, NY City, 2004; Gallery 312, Chicago, 96; Prep, Gallery 16, San Francisco, 97; Twister, Real Art Ways, Conn, 97. *Pos:* Resident, ArtPace, San Antonio, 99-. *Awards:* Marie Walsh Sharpe Art Found Fel, NY, 97; Louis Comfort Tiffany Found Award, NY, 97; Pollack-Krasner Found Grant, NY, 98; YADDO fel, Saratoga Springs, NY, 2002, DAAD fel, Berlin, 2003, John Simon Guggenheim Mem Found Fel, 2005. *Bibliog:* Cara Glatt (auth), Intriguing again, Hyde Park Herald, 1/28/98; Fred Camper (auth), Arturo Herrera at the Renaissance Society and Wooster Gardens, Art Press, 4/98; Jan Estap (auth), Arturo Herrera, New Art Examiner, 3/98. *Mailing Add:* c/o Sikkema, Jenkins & Co 530 W 22nd St New York NY 10011-1108

HERRERA, CARMEN
PAINTER
b Havana, Cuba, May 31, 15; US citizen. *Study:* Studio Federico Edelman, Havana; Marymount Col; Paris, France; Sch Archit, Havana; Art Students League. *Work:* Havana Mus; Cintas Collection; Jersey City Mus, NJ; Mus Del Barrio, NY; Housatonic Mus Art, Conn. *Exhib:* Art Cubain Contemporain, Mus Mod Art, Paris, 51; Ctr Interam Rels, 68 & 75; Inst Int Educ, 80-81; Buecker & Harpsichords, 81; solo exhibs, Rastovski Gallery, NY, 87 & 88; Outside Cuba, Jane Vorheeszimerli Art Mus, Rutgers, State Univ NJ, 87; Duo Geo; Two Geometric Artists, Carmen Herrera & Ernesto Briel, Jadite Galleries, NY, 92. *Collection Arranged:* Rusk Inst; Cintas Found Collection; Ella Cisneros; Carnen Ana Unaue; Viola McCausland; Mus Modern Art, NYC; Tatemodern, London. *Awards:* Cintas Found Fel, 66 & 68; Creative Artists Pub Serv, 77-78. *Bibliog:* Don Bacigalupi (auth), Contemporanea, 6/89; Holland Cotter (auth), NY Times, 7/24/98 & 2004; Edward J Sullivan (auth, catalog), Concrete Realities, 4/14/04; Grace Glueck (auth), NY Times, 2005. *Mem:* Int Art Relations. *Dealer:* Latin Collector Gallery 44 W 77the St 13th Floor New York NY 10036. *Mailing Add:* 37 E 19th St New York NY 10003

HERRIDGE, ELIZABETH
DIRECTOR
Pos: Managing dir, Guggenheim Hermitage Mus, Las Vegas, 2003-. *Mailing Add:* c/o Guggenheim Hermitage Mus 3355 Las Vegas Blvd S Las Vegas NV 89109

HERRING, JAN (JANET) MANTEL
PAINTER, WRITER
b Havre, Mont, May 17, 23. *Study:* Northern State Teachers Col; also painting with Frederic Taubes. *Work:* Grumbacher Collection, NY; Lubbock Art Ctr, Tex; Univ Idaho, Pocatello; Roswell Mus, NMex. *Exhib:* One-woman shows, El Paso Mus Art, Santa Fe Mus Art, Tulsa Art Ctr, Roswell Mus & Brigham Young Univ. *Teaching:* Pvt instr. *Bibliog:* F Taubes (auth), article, Am Artist Mag, 55; articles, La Rev Mod, 61 & House Beautiful, 64. *Publ:* Auth, The Painters Composition Handbook, 71 & The Painter's Complete Portrait and Figure Handbook, 77, Poor-Henry Publ Co. *Mailing Add:* 270 Wedgewood Dr Montgomery TX 77356-8348

HERRING, OLIVER
PAINTER
b Heidelberg, Ger, 64. *Study:* Ruskin Sch Drawing & Fine Art, Univ Oxford, Eng, BFA, 88; Hunter Col, NY, MFA, 91. *Exhib:* Dennison Collection, Morris Mus, Morristown, NJ, 93; Ciphers of Identity (with catalog), Univ Md Art Gallery, Baltimore & Ronald Feldman Fine Arts, NY, 93-96; Empty Dress: Clothing as a Surrogate in Recent Art (with catalog), Neuberger Mus, State Univ NY, 93-96; Guys Who Sew (with catalog), Univ Calif Art Mus, 94; Athena and Arachne (with catalog), Apex Art, NY, 94; Div Labor: Women's Work in Contemp Art (with catalog), Mus Contemp Art, Los Angeles, 95; Human/Nature, New Mus Contemp Art, NY, 95; Thread Bare, SE Ctr Contemp Art, Winston-Salem, NC, 95; A Labor of Love, New Mus Contemp Art, NY, 96; Time Wise, Swiss Inst, NY, 96; Shirts and Skins -- Absence/Presence in Contemp Art, Contemp Mus, Honolulu, Hawaii, 96; Projects 53, Mus Mod Art, NY, 96; One Day (a performance), Solomon R Guggenheim Mus, NY, 96; one-man shows, Manfred Baumgartner Gallery, Washington, DC, 96, Camden Art Ctr, London, Newlyn Art Gallery, Penzance, Eng & Max Protetch Gallery, NY, 97, Ace Galleries, Los Angeles, 99, Max Protetch Gallery, NY, 99, 02, Cleveland Ctr for Contemp Art, 01, Inst Vis Arts, Milwaukee, 01, Herbert F Johnson Mus Art, Cornell Univ, Ithaca, NY, 01, Landmark Gallery, Tex Tech Univ, Lubbock, 01, Rhodes & Mann, London, 02; Anne Agee, Oliver Herring, Kara Walker, Univ Mich Sch Art & Design, Ann Arbor, 97; Art/Fashion (with catalog), Solomon R Guggenheim Mus, NY, 97; group exhibs, Collectors' Choice, Exit Art, New York City, 00, Let's Get to Work, Susquehanna Art Mus, Harrisburg, Pa, 01, Galleria d'Arte Moderna, Bologna, Italy, 02. *Awards:* Mass Arts Lottery Grant, 89; NY Found Arts Grant, 95; Joan Mitchell Found Grant, 99. *Bibliog:* Leslie Camhi (auth), Sewing Circle, Village Voice, 2/6/96; Bill Arning (auth), Projects: Oliver Herring/Leonilson, Time Out NY, 2/14-21/96; Eva Karcher (auth), Kunste & Mode-Flirt, Ger Elle, 62-66, 1/97. *Mailing Add:* c/o Max Protetch Gallery 511 W 22nd St New York NY 10011

HERRING, WILLIAM ARTHUR
PAINTER
b El Paso, Tex, Feb 18, 48. *Study:* Tex A&M Univ, BA, 71; spec studies with Jan Herring, 72-82 & Charles Reid, 80-83. *Work:* San Angelo Mus Fine Art, Tex; El Paso Mus Fine Art, Tex; Tex A&M Univ, College Station; Eastern NMex Univ, Portales; US Air Defense Mus, Fort Bliss, Tex; Univ Science & Arts Oklahoma, Tulsa; US Dept Interior Nat Park Serv, Chamizal Nat Mem, El Paso, Tex. *Comn:* Watercolor, horse racing, Ruidoso Racetrack Jockey Club, NMex, 87; watercolor, dancer, viva El Paso Production Co, 90; rodeo drawing, Coors World Finals Rodeo, El Paso, Tex, 90; watercolor, prints of three cultures, El Paso Legislative Days, 90; pastel landscape, El Paso Symphony Orchestra, 91. *Exhib:* Solo exhib, Centenial Mus, El Paso, Tex, 86; 75th Allied Artists of Am, Nat Arts Club, NY, 88; Borderlands Exhib, Americana Mus, El Paso, Tex, 89; 1992 Knickerbocker Artists, Salmagundi Club, NY, 92; Sierra Med Ctr 25th Exhib, El Paso Mus Art, 92; One-man show, When Fun Takes Over, Chamizal Nat Mem, El Paso, Tex, 2002; and others. *Pos:* Found, Master Class Workshops, Cloudcroftm NMex, 91-. *Teaching:* Guest instr, fashion illustrator, Parsons Sch Design, NY, 91. *Awards:* William Hollingsworth Award, Miss Watercolor Soc Exhib, 87; Gold Medal for Watercolor, El Paso Mus Art, Melvin Simon & Assocs, 88; Bd Dirs Award, Pastel Soc Am, NY, 90. *Bibliog:* William Herring, artist, Santa Fean Mag, 5/87; Museum shows off top paintings, Accent Mag, El Paso Herald Post, 6/87; Cover artist, Southwest Guide Mag, 4/88; Herring of Many Colors, Wash Times, 4/9/94. *Mem:* Knickerbocker Artists, NY (pres, emeritus); Pastel Soc Am, NY; Am Artists Prof League, NY; Acad Artists Am, Mass; Blackhat Soc. *Media:* Pastel, Watercolor, Acrylic, Oil. *Interests:* Karate, Gongoristic Aphorisms. *Collection:* Former President, Ronald Reagan, Peter Coors, Goldie Hawn. *Publ:* Auth, The Wonderful Madness of Becoming a Horse of a Different Color, Red Tree Publ Co; features in SW Art Mag, 4/94 & Am Artist Mag, 3/97; featured in Lambs Among Wolves, Bob Briner (auth), 1996. *Dealer:* Home Studio 340 Higley Cir Horizon TX 79928. *Mailing Add:* Box 223 Clint TX 79836

HERRITT, LINDA S
SCULPTOR
b Columbus, Ohio, June 20, 50. *Study:* Ohio State Univ, BFA, 78; Univ Mont, MFA, 80. *Work:* Univ Mont; Boulder Mus Contemp Art. *Exhib:* Decor/Decorum, Art Inst, San Francisco, Calif, 90; Washington Proj Art, Washington, Dc, 91; Return of the Cadavre Exquis, The Drawing Ctr, NY, 93; Barcelona Proj FAD, Spain, 93; Mexico City, Mex 95; solo show, Pierogi 2000, Brooklyn, NY, 98 & Galeria Nina Menocal, Mex City, 98. *Teaching:* Instr, Univ Maine, 80-82; assoc prof art, Univ Colo, 82-. *Awards:* Sculpture Fel, Nat Endowment Arts, 90; Colo Coun Fel, 93 & 96; Rockefeller/Forica US Mex Fund Cult, 98. *Bibliog:* Glen Helfand (auth), rev, Artweek, 8/16/90; Kathleen Mendus Dlugos (auth), New Art Examiner, 5/93; Ruth Noak (auth), Before Information, Vienna, Austria, 96. *Mem:* Col Art Asn; Women's Caucus Art. *Mailing Add:* 210 Varet St Apt 404B Brooklyn NY 11206

HERRMANN, JOHN J, JR
CURATOR
b Chicago, Ill, Mar 16, 37. *Study:* Yale Col, BA, 59; Inst Fine Arts, NY Univ, MA, 64, PhD, 73. *Collection Arranged:* coauth, catalog, Pompeii AD 70, 1978; auth, Roman and Classical and Hellenistic Greek Galleries, 1979; auth,The Excavations of Assos Revisited, 1979; coauth, catalog, The Search for Alexander, 1981; auth, catalog, The Gods Delight, 1988; auth, Human Figure in Early Greek Art, 1988; auth, Bronze Age Gallery, 1994; auth, catalog, In the Shadow of the Acropolis: Popular and Private Art from 4th Century Athens, 1984; auth, Ancient Gold, Wealth of the Thracians, 1998; coauth, catalog, Light From the Age of Augustine, 2002. *Pos:* Fel, Comt Rescue of Italian Art, 69-70; asst cur, Mus Fine Arts, Boston, 76-85, assoc cur, 85-96, cur 96-, John F Cogan Jr and Mary L Cornille cur. *Teaching:* instr, Am Univ, Rome, Italy, 74-75, Ctr Materials Res Archeol, Mass Inst Technol, 97-2003. *Mem:* Archeol Inst Am; Asn Study Marble & other Stones In Antiquity; Inst Nautical Archeol. *Publ:* Auth, Ionic Capital in Late Antique Rome, Rome, 88; Rearranged Hair, J Mus Fine Arts, Boston, 91; Carrieres et Sculpture en Marbre a L'epogue Romaine et Tardive, Dossiers d'archeologie, 92; A Passion for Antiquities, J Paul Getty Mus, 94; Exportation of Dolomitic Marble from Thasos, 95 & Futher research on Boston three-sided releif, 96, Study of Marble and Other Stones; Egyptian Demeter, Jahrbuch German Archeol Inst, 99; editor, auth, Asmosia 5: Interdisciplinary Studies on Ancient Stone, 2002. *Mailing Add:* c/o Mus Fine Arts Boston 465 Huntington Ave Boston MA 02115

HERSCH, GLORIA GOLDSMITH
PAINTER, LECTURER
b New York, NY, Jan 5, 28. *Study:* Community Col Allegheny County; Westmoreland County Community Col; Penn State Univ. *Work:* Hoyt Inst Fine Arts, New Castle, Pa; Monroeville Pa Pub Libr; Export Volunteer Fire Hall, Export, Pa; HJ Heinz Co, World Headquarters, Pittsburgh, Pa; Greater Latrobe, Pa School District Art Coll of 200 Works Started in 1936. *Comn:* portrait, John Minadeo Public Sch, Pittsburgh, Pa, 92; painting, comn by Dr & Mrs Charles Einolf, Mitchellville, MD, 98; portrait, comn by Dr & Mrs Bruce Malen, Monroe, NY, 99 & 2001; portrait, comn by Mr & Mrs Dennis Malen, Jericho, NY, 99 & 2003; portrait, comn by Mr & Mrs Paul Wursch, Erie, Pa, 99; portrait, comn by Ms Kathy Rogers, 2005. *Exhib:* Triennial VI, S Alleghenies Mus Art, Loretto, Pa, 96; Westmoreland Art Nat, Greensburg, Pa, 96-98, 2001-2003 & 2005-2006; SW Pa Art Exhib, Westmoreland Mus Am Art, Greensburg, Pa, 96, 2001 & 2006; 62nd Nat Midyear, Butler Inst Am Art, Youngstown, Ohio, 98; Southern

Alleghenies Mus Art, Ligioneer, Pa, 98; Southwestern Pa Regional, Saint Vincent Gallery, Latrobe, Pa, 99; PSA's First Biannual, Butler Inst Am Art, Salem, Ohio, 99; Central Pa Robeson Art Gallery, State Col, Pa, 2000-2005; Hoyt Inst Fine Arts, New Castle, Pa, 2000 & 2001; Harlan Gallery, Seton Hill, Greensburg, Pa, 2001 & 2005; Hudson Valley Asn 73rd Ann, Hastings-on-Hudson, NY, 2004; one person shows, Gallery Space, Monroeville, Pa, 97 & 2005, Hoyt Inst Fine Arts, New Castle, Pa, 2001, Penn State Univ, New Kensington, Pa, 2002 & Maggie L Gallery, Murrysville, Pa, 2003. *Pos:* senior advert & marketing specialist, Pittsburgh-Corning Corp, Pa, 75-91. *Awards:* Merit, Hoyt Inst Fine Arts, 2001; Best of Show, Somerset Co Ann, 2002; Best of Show, Westmoreland Co Arts & Heritage Festival, 2003; Best of Show, Cranberry Township Festival, 2003; Best of Show, McKeesport, Pa, 2005-2006; Over 200 awards recieved since entering competition in 1991. *Bibliog:* An Artist's Life, Pittsburgh Post-Gazette, 7/21/96 & 6/29/05; Artist Paint Realism, Tribune-Review, 6/27/97 & 9/22/01; The Write Side, Penn State Univ, spring 98 & 99; Gateway Star, 1/10/2001; Pittsburgh Area Gateway Press, 1/10/01 & 8/27/03; Mckeesport Daily News, 5/21/01; Jewish Chronicle, 2/27/03; Pittsburgh City Paper, 1/1/03; Penn Franklin News, 1/13/03; Monroeville, PA TV Station, 1997 & 2004. *Mem:* Pittsburgh Soc Artists (prog chair, 2002-2006); East Suburban Artists League; Penn Art Asn; Assoc Artists of Pitt; Hoyt Artists Asn. *Media:* Acrylic. *Mailing Add:* 2362 Adams Court Export PA 15632-9040

HERSCH, JEFF
PHOTOGRAPHER
b Gary, IN, Sept 25, 47. *Study:* Art Inst of Chicago, 63; Ind Univ, BA, 70. *Comn:* Calendar, Mountain Inst, Franklin, W Va, 99. *Exhib:* Portrait of Nepal, Foothills Art Center, Colo, 94; Gallery Soap, Japan, 99; Christmas Show, Arvada Ctr for Arts, Colo, 99; Colo Coun Expo, Republic Plaza, 02. *Collection Arranged:* Smithsonian Inst, Washington DC; Mus of Art, Denver. *Awards:* Anderson Ranch Fel, Anderson Ranch, 98, 00; Colo Coun of Arts Fel, State of Colo, 02. *Publ:* Photographers Forum, Serbin, 96; Travelers Tales Nepal, O'Reilly, 98. *Mailing Add:* Carson Masuoka Gallery 760 Santa Fe Dr Denver CO 80204

HERSCHLER, DAVID ELIJAH
SCULPTOR, PAINTER
b Brooklyn, NY, Mar 1, 40. *Study:* Acad Belli Arte, Perugia, Italy, 60; Univ Rome, 60; Cornell Univ, BArch, 62; Claremont Grad Sch, MFA, 67. *Work:* Joseph H Hirshhorn Found, Washington; La Jolla Mus Art, Calif; Storm King Art Ctr, Mountainville, NY; Palm Springs Mus, Calif; Israel Mus, Jerusalem; Hartford Life Insurance; Daimler-Benz Corp; General Motors; Mercedez-Benz; NASA; Allegheny Teledyne. *Comn:* Sculptures, comn by Mr & Mrs NS Walbridge, La Jolla, 70, Sigmund Edelstone, Chicago, 71, Mr & Mrs JW Constance, Santa Barbara, 72, Mr & Mrs Marvin Smalley, Beverly Hills, 72 & Storm King Art Ctr, 72. *Exhib:* One-man shows, La Jolla Mus, 72, Santa Barbara Mus, 74, Palm Springs Mus, 77, Aspen Inst, 85, NASA-Kennedy Space Ctr, 86 & Westment Col, 90, Pac Asian Art Mus, 97. *Awards:* United States Info Serv Golden Eagle Award; Kurt Diebus Trophy Award; Setp Trophy Award. *Media:* Stainless Steel, Gold. *Mailing Add:* c/o New Horizon Gallery PO Box 5859 Santa Barbara CA 93150-5859

HERSEY, GEORGE LEONARD
HISTORIAN
b Cambridge, Mass, Aug 30, 27. *Study:* Harvard Univ, BA, 51; Yale Univ, MFA, 54, MA, 61, PhD, 64; Fulbright scholar & Am Philos Soc fel, Italy, 62; Tatti, Florence, 80; Am Acad Rome, 94. *Pos:* Co-ed, Architectura, 71-; ed, Yale Publ in Hist of Art, 74-95; mem, Conn State Comn Capitol Restoration, 77-79. *Teaching:* Instr art, Bucknell Univ, Lewisburg, Pa, 54-55, asst prof, 54-59, actg chmn dept, 58-59; instr hist art, Yale Univ, New Haven, Conn, 63-65, asst prof 65-68, assoc prof, 68-74, prof, 74-98, prof emer, 98-. *Awards:* Morse Fel, 66; Schepp Fel & Vogelstein Fel, Florence, Italy, 72 & 80. *Mem:* Soc Archit Historians (dir, 71-73); Renaissance Soc Am; Col Art Asn. *Res:* Renaissance and Baroque. *Publ:* Auth, Possible Palladian Villas (with Richard Freedman), 92; High Renaissance Art in St Peter's & the Vatican, 93; The Evolution of Allure: Art and Sexual Selections from the Medici Venus to the Incredible Hulk, 94; The Monumental Impulse: Architecture's Biological Roots, 99; Architecture and Geometry in the Age of the Baroque, 2001; Falling in Love with Statues: Art and Artificial Life from Prehistory to the Present, Univ Chicago Press, 03; Ruins: The beauties of Devastation (1200BC-2001AD). *Mailing Add:* 167 Linden St New Haven CT 06511

HERSHEY, NONA
PRINTMAKER, PAINTER
b New York, NY, 46. *Study:* Tyler Sch Art in Rome, BFA, 67, MFA, 69; Instituto Statale d'Arte di Urbino, dipl, 79; Yoshida Hanga Acad, Tokyo, 91. *Work:* Libr Congress, Washington, DC; Metrop Mus Art, NY; Minn Mus Am Art, St Paul; Pa Acad Fine Arts, Philadelphia; Fogg Art Mus, Harvard Univ, Cambridge. *Exhib:* group exhibs incl, Smithsonian Inst, Wash, 73, Honolulu Acad Arts, 73, USIS, Rome, 73, Jane Haslem Gallery, 74, 75, Mus Fine Arts, Boston, 75, Garden Gallery Modern Art, Raleigh, NC, 75, Metrop Mus, Fla, 77, USIS, Bucharest, Hungary, 78, Am Acad, Rome, 78, Laboratorio Artivisive, 81, 92, Rassegna di Grafica Contemporanea, Casalpusterlungo, Italy, 82; Clark Gallery, Lincoln, Mass, 83, Mary Ryan Gallery, 83-86, 88, 91, 92, Noyes Mus, NJ, 84, Galleria Il Ponte, 84, Dolan/Maxwell Gallery, 85, Calcografia Nazionale, Rome, 86, Palazzo Ducale, Pesaro, Italy, 86, Brooklyn Mus, 86, Walker Art Center, Minneapolis, 86, Garton & Cooke Gallery, London, 87, Istituto per la Grafica, Latina, Italy, 87, Premio Sassoferrato, Italy, 87, Premio Int Biella per l'Incisione, Italy, 87, Pa Acad Fine Arts, Philadelphia, 87, Premio Internazionale d'Arte Contemporanea, Campobello di Mazara, Italy, 88, Greenville Mus Fine Arts, NC, Taipei Fine Art Mus, 88, Dedalos Gallery, San Severo, Italy, 90, Gallery Kabutoya, Tokyo, 91, Art Multiple, Dusseldorf, Ger, 92, GW Einstein Gallery, NY City, 93; New Talent in Printmaking, Asn Am Artists, NY, 75; one-woman show, Galleria Il Ponte, Rome, 82, 85 & 90, Mary Ryan Gallery, NY, 83 & 87, Miller Block Gallery, Boston, 95, 99, 2002, 2004; Great Am Prints, Dolan-Maxwell Gallery, Philadelphia, 85; 24th Nat Exhib, Brooklyn Mus, NY, 86; 12th Int Print Biennial, Krakow, Yugoslavia, 88. *Pos:* over 35 int pub & corp collections. *Teaching:* Asst prof printmaking, Temple Abroad, Rome, Italy, 79-90; assoc prof, Temple Univ Japan, Tokyo, 90-91; prof, Mass Col Art, Boston, Mass, 93-. *Awards:* Award, MacDowell Colony, Peterborough, NH, 89 & 93; Award, Ballinglen Arts Found, Ireland, 2001; grant, Mass Cult Council, 2004; and others. *Bibliog:* Marisa Volpi Orlandini (auth), Nona Hershey, Artisti Contemporanei, Interviste, 85; Ellen Lask (auth), Nona Hershey (exhib catalogue), Palazzo-Sormani, Milan, Italy, 92; New Am Paintings, Open Studio Press, 2004. *Mem:* Boston Printmakers; Printmaking Coun NJ; Nat Acad; Soc Am Graphic Artists. *Media:* All Media. *Dealer:* Miller Block Gallery 14 Newbury St Boston MA 02116; Dolan/Maxwell Inc 2046 Rittenhouse Sq, Philadelphia, PA, 19103

HERTZ, RICHARD A
EDUCATOR, CRITIC
b La Crosse, Wis, Aug 19, 40. *Study:* Univ Calif, Los Angeles, BA, 62; Univ Calif, Santa Barbara, MA, 64; Univ Pittsburgh, PhD, 67. *Teaching:* Asst prof philos, Calif Inst Technol, 68-74; instr art theory, Calif Inst Arts, 74-79; chmn acad studies & grad prog, Art Ctr Col Design, 79-. *Mem:* Col Art Asn, Mus Contemp Art, Los Angeles. *Res:* Twentieth century art theory and criticism. *Publ:* Auth, Philosophical foundations of modern art, Brit J Aesthet, summer 78; ed, J Los Angeles Inst Contemp Art, summer 82; auth, A critique of authoritarian rhetoric, Real Life Mag, summer 82; ed, Theories of Contemporary Art, Prentice-Hall, 85, 2nd ed, 93-; ed, with Norman Klein, Twentieth Century Art Theory: Urbanism, Politics and Mass Culture, Prentice-Hall, 90. *Mailing Add:* Art Ctr Col Design 1700 Lida St PO Box 7197 Pasadena CA 91103-1999

HERTZLIEB, GREGG
DIRECTOR
b Hammond, Ind, 65. *Study:* Art Inst Chicago, BFA, 87; Art Inst Chicago, MFA, 89; Univ Ill, MEd, 91. *Collection Arranged:* Brauer Mus of Art, Konrad Juestel Retrospective, 01. *Pos:* art editor, The Cresset, Valparaiso, Ind, 02-. *Teaching:* adj instr, Valparaiso Univ, 02-. *Mem:* AAM; CAA; AFA; AMM; MRC. *Dealer:* Uncle Freddy's Gallery, Hammond, Ind, 46320. *Mailing Add:* Valparaiso Univ Brauer Mus Art Center for Arts Valparaiso IN 46383

HERTZMAN, GAY MAHAFFY
ADMINISTRATOR, HISTORIAN
b West Liberty, Iowa, Jan 22, 31. *Study:* Univ Iowa, Iowa City, BA, 60; Univ NC, Chapel Hill, MS(libr sci), 65, MA(art hist), 69. *Pos:* Registr-librn, NC Mus Art, Raleigh, 61-64; actg cur, Wm Hayes Ackland Art Ctr, Univ NC, Chapel Hill, 67-69; asst cur & cur European painting, NC Mus Art, 71-75, head collections res & publ, 75-79, chief cur, 80-81, asst dir, 81-. *Res:* Western European art. *Mailing Add:* 6308 Lakeway Dr Raleigh NC 27612-6527

HERZBERG, THOMAS
ILLUSTRATOR
b Chicago, Ill. *Study:* Northeastern Ill Univ, BA, 75; Art Inst Chicago, 76-77; Northern Ill Univ, MFA, 79. *Work:* Van Straaten Gallery, Chicago; De Cordova Mus, Lincoln, Mass; Terrance Gallery, Palenville, NY; Metrop Mus & Art Ctr, Coral Gables, Fla; Silvermine Guild Artists. *Exhib:* Chicago and Vicinity Show, Art Inst Chicago, 78 & 84; Boston Printmakers, De Cordova Mus, Lincoln, Mass, 78, 79 & 82; 13th Nat Print Exhib, Silvermine Guild Artists, New Canaan, Conn, 80; Mus Publs Competition, Am Asn Mus, 90; Ann Awards Competition, Soc Newspaper Design, 91; Excellence in Graphics, Am Soc Bus Press Eds, 92; Creativity 1993, Art Direction Mag, 93; Print's Regional Design Ann, 94, 96 & 97; 28th, 39th & 41st Ann Exhib, Soc Illusrs, NY. *Pos:* Illusr, Chicago Mag, Advertising Age, Playboy Mag, World Bk, Am Bar Asn, Chicago Tribune, Washington Post, Lincoln Park Zoo, Art Inst Chicago, Goodman Theater, Am Med Asn. *Teaching:* instr, Am Acad Art, Chicago, Ill, 2001-, chair fine art dept; Instr photog, Oak Park River Forest High Sch, 76-77; asst printmaking, Northern Ill Univ, 78-79, instr, 81-82. *Awards:* 3 Certs Distinction, Creativity Show, Art Direction Mag, 93; Cert Design Excellence, Print's Regional Design Ann, Print Mag, 94 & 96. *Bibliog:* Best of Newspaper Design, 7th, 10th, 12th & 13th eds; Illusr, No 28, 39, 41. *Mem:* Air Force Art Prog. *Media:* Pen & Ink; Watercolor. *Mailing Add:* 4128 W Eddy St Chicago IL 60641

HERZOG, PRISCILLA JENNE
PAINTER, INSTRUCTOR
b Minneapolis, Minn, Aug 21, 22. *Study:* Minneapolis Sch Art, BFA, 51; Art Students League NY; Sch Art Inst Chicago, Studied with B J O Nordfeldt, Will Barnet, Howard Cook, Frances C Greenman & Gustav Krollman. *Work:* Archer Daniels Midland Inc, Univ Minn, St Paul; Booz-Allen Inc, Chicago, Ill; Noyes Found Inc, Leader & Berkon Inc, NY. *Comn:* Portrait, comn by Carol Atwood; family portrait, comn by Gen John Morgan; family portrait, comn by Lawrence Reed; portrait, comn by Kalfayan family; portrait, comn by Prof Mark Rislav. *Exhib:* Solo-exhibs, Minneapolis Sch Art, 49 & Univ Minn, St Paul, 58; Bronx Artists 80's, Bronx Mus Art, NY, 80; Federation of Modern Painters & Sculptures, Fordham Univ, NY, 80 & 94; exhib & forum, Am Soc Fine Arts, Art Students League, NY, 89; 167th Ann, Nat Acad Design, NY, 92; Six Painters, Nicholas Alexander Gallery, NY, 95; Studio Safari Tour, Univ NMex Col Fine Arts, Alumni Chapter, 98. *Teaching:* Instr painting & drawing, Minneapolis Sch Art, 43-47; instr gallery club, Minneapolis Inst Art, 50-56; instr color & design, Univ Minn, St Paul, 57-58; instr watercolor, painting & drawing, New Sch Social Res, 92-93; instr drawing & watercolor, Vista Grande, Sandia Park, NMex, 98. *Awards:* 1st Prize Watercolor, Twin City Ann, Minneapolis Inst Art, 46 & 48; Winsor & Newton

Award, Nat Arts Club, NY, 85 & 94; Jody Starr Leibovitz Mem Award, 87. *Bibliog:* Panorama of America unveiled in RCS show, Riverdale Press, NY, 11/70; Refreshing watercolors at River Gallery, Irvington, NY, Gannett Westchester Newspapers, 3/82. *Mem:* Fedn Mod Painters & Sculptors (vpres, 83-); Aubudon Artists (asst corresp secy, 88-89); life mem Art Students League, NY; Artists Equity Asn, NY. *Media:* Oil, Watercolor. *Specialty:* fine arts, crafts. *Publ:* Illusr, Gopher Historian, Minn Hist Soc; contribr, Nordfeldt the Painter, Univ NMex Press, 72. *Dealer:* The Johnsons of Madrid, 2843 Hwy 14, Madrid, NMex, 87010. *Mailing Add:* 8243 E Big Dry Creek Dr Centennial CO 80112

HESS, DONALD MARC
COLLECTOR
b Bern, Switz, Aug 3, 36. *Study:* Ecole Superieure De Commerce, Neuchatel Univ; Brewmaster, Doemens, Munich, 57. *Pos:* Pres, Steinholzli Brewery, Bern, 57-68; chmn, Hess Holding, 68-; Co-founder, Kunst Heute Found, Bern, 82; pres, mem exec comt, Int Green Cross Switz, 94-96; Chmn, Valser Mineral Water, Ltd, Vals, CH, Hess Ltd, Bern, Blue Lake, Ltd, Blausee, CH, Hess Int, VV, Rotterdam, The Neth; Chief Exec Officer, The Hess Collection Winery, Napa, Calif; bd dir, Kambly Bisquits, Ltd, Trubschachen, CH, 88-, Hess Art Collection Ltd, Bern, CH, 98-; founder, Hess Collection Contemp Art Mus, Napa, Calif, 89-, Hess Collection Art Exhib Space at Vinopolis-City of Wine, 1 Bank End, London, 99-. *Awards:* Named one of Top 200 Collectors, ARTnews Mag, 2004-06. *Mem:* Founder & hon chmn, Hess Group Ltd. *Interests:* Contemporary Art, Wine, Tennis. *Collection:* Contemporary art. *Publ:* Ed, Hess Collection, 89 (named one of best books in Switz, 89), Hess Collection New Works, 98, Franz Gertsch, Hess Collection, 99, Georg Baselitz, Works from the Hess Collection, 2003. *Mailing Add:* Roserswyl Bolligen CH 3065 Switzerland

HESS, F SCOTT
PAINTER, INSTRUCTOR
b Baltimore, Md, 55. *Study:* Univ Wis, Madison, BSA, 77; Acad Fine Arts, Vienna, Austria, 79-83. *Work:* Oakland Mus, Calif; Smithsonian Inst, Washington, DC; Univ Wis, Madison; Los Angeles Co Mus Art, Orange Co Mus, Calif; Prudential Insurance Co Am, Newark, NJ; Norton Family Found, Santa Monica, Calif; Kinsey Inst of Sex Res, Bloomington, Ind; Oesterreiches Tabakmuseum, Vienna, Australia. *Exhib:* One-person exhibs, Ovsey Gallery, Los Angeles, 94, Art Inst Southern Calif, 96, Mount San Antonio Col, Walnut, Calif, 97, Hackett-Freedman Gallery, San Francisco, Calif, 99, 2002, Orange Co Mus Art, Calif, 01; Figures, Frye Art Mus, Seattle, Wash, 2000; Pvt to Pub: Gift to the Boise Art Mus from Eileen and Peter Norton, Boise Art Mus, Idaho, 2000; Representing Los Angeles: Pictorial Currents in Contemp Southern Calif Art, Frye Art Mus, Seattle, Wash, 2000-01; The Importance of Being Earnest, Occidental Col, Los Angeles, Calif, 2001; Storytellers: The Figure in Time and Place, Fine Arts Gallery, San Francisco State Univ, Calif, 2001; and others. *Teaching:* Instr, Art Ctr Col Design, Pasadena, 95-; instr, Univ Southern Calif, Los Angeles, 95-96. *Awards:* Getty Fel Award, 91; Nat Endowment Arts Award, 91; Faculty Enrichment Grant, Art Ctr Col of Design, Pasadena, Calif, 99. *Bibliog:* Michael Duncan (auth), F. Scott Hess: The Passing Hours, Hackett-Freedman Gallery (exhib catalog), San Francisco, 99; Color Reproduction, Harper's Mag, 4/2000; Gordon L Fuglie (auth), Realism Today: Representing L.A., Southwest Art, 1/01. *Mem:* The Drawing Group. *Dealer:* Hackett/Freedman Gallery 250 Sutter St San Francisco CA 94108. *Mailing Add:* 1830 Lake Shore Ave Los Angeles CA 90026

HESS, STANLEY WILLIAM
CURATOR, LIBRARIAN
b Bremerton, Wash. *Study:* Olympic Community Col, 58-60; Univ Wash, BA, 64 & grad work, 67-71; Case Western Reserve Univ, MSLS, 76. *Exhib:* Aurora Valentinetti, Holiday Exhibit, 2003-2004; Gift of Puppets: Bridging Oceans and Borders to Bring Understanding and Knowledge of the History and Cult of China, Through Art of Puppets to Young People, WA, 2004 & 2005; The World of Childhood, Books and Puppetry, 2005; All Creatures Great & Small, 2005; Nutcrackers & Pop-up Books, 2005; Punch & Judy, 2006; Everyman & Friends, 2006; Special Exhib featuring Aurora Valentinetti Puppet Mus & Evergreen Children's Theatre, Olympia, Wash, 2005. *Pos:* Supvr, Photog & Slide Libr, Seattle Art Mus, Wash, 64-73; assoc librn photographs & slides, Cleveland Mus Art, 73-80; head librn, Spencer Art Reference Libr, Nelson-Atkins Mus Art, Kansas City, 80-91; consult & librn, 92-; bd dir, Evergreen Children's Theater, 97-, cur puppet mus, 98-. *Awards:* Pi Beta Mus, 76. *Mem:* Art Libr Soc NAm, (Central Plains, secy-treas, 86-87, vchmn-chmn, 90-91 & Northwest Chap, 92-); Spec Libr Asn (picture div, pres elect & pres, 78-79); Kansas City Metrop Libr Network (mem, 80-91, secy, 85-86); Kitsap Hist Soc (bd dir, 96-97). *Res:* American arts & crafts silver; life & work of Clara Barck Welles; production of the Kalo shop of Chicago and New York; Am & int puppet collections of Aurora Valentinetti Puppet Mus, Bremerton, Wash, & Collection, Seattle, Wash; and Marshall Campbell Collection, Palm Springs, Calif. *Interests:* Publishing, lecturing and teaching about the visual resources in the fine arts, information resources. *Publ:* Auth, Annotated Bibliography of Slide Library Literature, Sch Info Studies, Syracuse Univ, 2/78; coauth, with A Hoffberg, et al, Directory of Art Libraries, Neal-Schuman Publ, 5/78; contribr, Picture Librarianship, Libr Asn, London, 81; and others. *Mailing Add:* 14841 Olympic View Loop Rd NW Silverdale WA 98383

HESSEL, MARIELUISE
COLLECTOR
b Germany. *Awards:* One of 200 Top Collectors, ARTnews, 2003-06. *Collection:* Over fifteen hundred late 20th century artworks on permanent loan to the Center for Curatorial Studies at Bard College in New York. *Mailing Add:* 65 Avalanche Canyon Dr Jackson WY 83001-9009

HESTON, JOAN
PAINTER, INSTRUCTOR
b Hartford, Conn. *Study:* Pratt Inst, three yr cert; Art Students League, with Robert Brackman; Stamford Mus, 73; Silvermine Guild Art, 73-74; Studio II, 75-76; with Charles Reid, 76-78. *Exhib:* Nat Acad Design, NY; Am Watercolor Soc Traveling Exhib; Nat Acad Arts & Lett, NY; Wadsworth Atheneum, Hartford, Conn; Frye Mus, Seattle, Wash; Tweed Mus, Duluth, Minn; Salmagundi Club, NY; Loveland Mus, Colo; Stamford Mus, Conn; Grants Pass Mus, Ore; and many others; Fairfield Univ Art Gallery, Conn. *Teaching:* Instr oils & watercolor, Silvermine Guild of Arts, 86-; Int workshops, The Oil Painters Solution Bk, 90. *Awards:* Gold Medal, Catharine Lorillard Wolfe Art Club, 81 & 83; Silver Medal, Allied Artists Am, 85 & Knickerbocker Artists, 86; and many others; B Stevenson Portrait award, Nat Arts Club. *Bibliog:* Jolene Goldenthal (auth), Show at Atheneum, The Hartford Courant, 6/29/75; Muriel Brooks (auth), Art scene, New York Sunday News, 12/26/76; Public interest, Channel 13, 12/81 & 12/82; Letter from the editor, Artist's Mag, 9/85. *Mem:* Allied Artists Am (pres, 84 & hon lifetime pres); Silvermine Guild; Audubon Artists; Nat Arts Club; Catharine Lorillard Wolfe Art Club (mem, bd dir,82); Conn Acad Fine Arts. *Media:* Oil, Watercolor. *Publ:* Contribr, Painting Flowers in Watercolor, 80, Light: How to See It, How to Paint It, 88, The Watercolor Painter Solution Book, 88 & Tonal Values, 88, North Light Bks; auth, Concept and design in oil painting, Artist Mag, 9/85; The Oil Painters Solution Book. *Mailing Add:* 29 Hemlock Dr Stamford CT 06902

HEUSSER, ELEANORE ELIZABETH HEUSSER FERHOLT
PAINTER
b North Haledon, NJ. *Study:* Cooper Union, dipl; Columbia Univ Sch Painting & Sculpture, fel, 45-46; Innsbruck Univ, Fulbright Fel, 52-55; Montclair State Univ (fine arts, printmaking), 91-2003. *Work:* Newark Mus; Lending Libr Mus Mod Art, NYk. *Exhib:* Kunsthistorisches Inst, Innsbruck, Austria, 54; Konzerthaus Gallery, Vienna, Austria, 54; Fulbright Grantees Show, Duveen-Graham Gallery & mus throughout US, 57-58; Pa Acad Fine Arts Ann, Philadelphia, 59 & 65; NJ Artists Biennial, NJ State Mus, Trenton, 72 & 79. *Pos:* Juror, Fulbright Painting Fel, 85-87; juror, Fulbright Collaborative Res Grant, 87. *Teaching:* Instr fundamentals art, Columbia Univ Sch Painting & Sculpture, 46-52; instr drawing, City Col New York, 60-62; pvt instr painting, New York, 60-72 & North Haledon, NJ, 72-. *Awards:* Pvt Grant Study in Mex, provided by George Grebe, 43. *Bibliog:* M Finkelstein (auth), Artist in the Alps, Inst Int Educ News Bull, 6/55; article, Revue Mod, 10/72. *Media:* Ink, Oil, Etching. *Mailing Add:* 60 Roosevelt Ave North Haledon NJ 07508

HEWITT, DUNCAN ADAMS
SCULPTOR, EDUCATOR
b New York, NY, April 5, 49. *Study:* Colby Col, BA, 71; Univ Pa, MFA, 75. *Comn:* Bronze, stone & earthwork installation, Univ Maine, Augusta; installation, Bonney Eagle Middle Sch, Standish, Maine. *Exhib:* Philadelphia Mus Art, 72; Inst Contemp Art, Philadelphia, 73-75; Payson Gallery Art, Portland, Maine, 81; Maine Artists Invitational, Bowdoin Col Mus Art, 83; one-person exhib, Baxter Gallery, Portland Sch Art, Maine, 85; Perspectives, three-person show, Portland Mus Art, 89; Contemp Sculpture at Chesterwood, Stockbridge, Mass, 91; Barrows Rotunda, Dartmouth Col, 94. *Teaching:* Asst prof art, Univ Southern Maine, 76-92, assoc prof, 82-, chairperson dept, 82-; vis artist, Colby Col, fall 82 & Portland Sch Art, spring 83, chairperson, spring 92. *Mem:* Visual Arts Panel; Maine State Comn Arts & Humanities. *Media:* Steel, Wood. *Mailing Add:* Pleasant Hill Rd Hollis Center ME 04042

HEYMAN, IRA MICHAEL
ADMINISTRATOR, EDUCATOR
b New York, NY, May 30, 30. *Study:* Dartmouth Col, AB(govt), 51; Yale Law Sch, JD, 56. *Pos:* Secy, Smithsonian Inst, 1994-2000. *Teaching:* Prof law, Univ Calif, Berkeley, 61-96

HEYMAN, LAWRENCE MURRAY
PAINTER, PRINTMAKER
b Washington, DC. *Study:* Tyler Sch Fine Arts, Temple Univ, BFA, 54, BS (educ), 55; Atelier 17, Paris, experimental printmaking with SW Hayter, 60-63, 69-70; Am Univ, MFA, 72. *Work:* Brooklyn Mus; Biblio Nat, Paris, France; Brooks Mem Mus, Memphis, Tenn; Portland Art Mus, Ore; Free Libr Philadelphia; Mus City NY. *Comn:* Print eds, Asn Am Artists, NY, 64, 68 & 69 & Antares Eds d'Art, Paris, France, 70, 71 & 72; cover painting for History of American West, US Info Agency, for Vent d'Ouest Book Collection, Paris, France, 65; prints, Judith Selkowitz Fine Arts, NY, 78; oil painting, Providence Art Club, 97. *Exhib:* Northwest Printmakers Int, Seattle Mus Fine Arts, 62-65; Audubon Artists Ann, Nat Acad Design, NY, 76; Realites Nouvelles, Parc Floral, Paris, 76 & 78; Le Trait, Cite des Arts, Paris, 77; World Print Competition '77, San Francisco Art Mus, 77; Atelier 17 Retrospective, Brooklyn Art Mus, 77-78 & Elvehjem Art Ctr, Minn, 77-78; L'Estampe Aujourd hui 73/78, Biblio Nat, Paris, 79; solo exhibs, Mus City NY, 84, Nat Inst Health, Bethesda, Maryland, 89-90; The Capital Image Today, Plum Gallery, Kensington, Md, 85 & 89; New Eng Artists, Newport Art Mus, Newport, RI, 88; Galerie Foret-Verte, Paris, 2004. *Pos:* Critic/evaluator printmaking books, Choice Mag, Middletown, Conn, 77-79. *Teaching:* Instr printmaking, RI Sch Design, 67-69, asst prof, 72-79 & dir print prog, 76-79; lectr printmaking, Am Univ, Washington, DC, 71-72. *Awards:* Purchase Award, Le Trait, Biblio Nat, Paris, 77; Nominated & Finalist Nat Art Medal, Nat Endowment Arts, 87; Finalist, Nat Portrait Painting Competition, Artists Mag, 89. *Bibliog:* Dale Jacquette (auth), Lawrence Heyman's paintings of street life, RI Rev, 1/81; Jo Ann Lewis (auth), Heyman paintings at Plum, Wash Post, 10/86; Les Krantz (auth), Artist Profile: Lawrence Heyman, NY Art Rev, 3rd ed, 88. *Media:* Oils, Watercolor; Intaglio. *Publ:* Auth, Painting the Town City Scapes of New York, Yale Univ Press, 2000; Painting and Essay, Times Square Feature; auth, Painting the Town, Cityscapes of New York, Paintings from the Mus of the City of New York, Yale Univ Press, 2000. *Dealer:* Whitegate Representation. *Mailing Add:* 71 Faunce Dr Providence RI 02906

HEYMAN, RONNIE FEUERSTEIN
COLLECTOR
b New York, NY, 48. *Study:* Harvard Univ, BA, 69; Yale Univ, JD, 73. *Pos:* Estab, The Heyman Chair in Legal Ethics Yale Law Sch; The Samuel and Ronnie Heyman Ctr for Ethics, Pub. Policy and the Prof Duke Univ; The Samuel & Ronnie Heyman Ctr on Corp Governance Yeshiva Univ, bd trustees, bd dir Benjamin N Cardozo Sch Law; trustee Barnard Col; exec comt int dirs' coun Guggenheim Mus; collectors' comt Nat Gallery, Wash, currently; Atty & principal, Heyman Properties, Westport, Conn, currently. *Awards:* Named one of Top 200 Collectors, ARTnews Mag, 2000-06. *Mem:* Bar: Conn 73. *Collection:* Modern & Contemporary art, especially Miro, Meger, Gorky, Giacometti & Dubuffet. *Mailing Add:* Heyman Properties 333 Post Rd W Westport CT 06880

HEYMAN, SAMUEL J
COLLECTOR
b New York, NY, Mar 1, 39. *Study:* Yale Univ, BS(magna cum laude), 60; Harvard Univ, LLB, 63. *Pos:* Chief Exec Officer, Heyman Properties, Westport, 68-; chmn, G-I Holdings Inc, (formerly GAF Corp), Wayne, NJ, 83-, Int Specialty Products Inc, Wayne, 91-, Chief Exec Officer, 91-99; founder & chmn Partnership, for Pub Serv Wash, 2001-; Hon dir, Benjamin N Cardozo Sch Law Yeshiva Univ, estab The Samuel & Ronnie Heyman Ctr on Corp Governanance; bd visitors, Terry Sanford Inst Pub Policy Duke Univ, estab The Samuel and Ronnie Heyman Ctr for Ethics, Pub Policy and the Professions; dean's adv bd, Harvard Law; established The Heyman Chair in Legal Ethics Yale Law Sch. *Awards:* Named one of Top 200 Collectors, ARTnews Mag, 2000-06. *Collection:* Modern art, including de Kooning, Picasso and Pollock; Modern & Contemporary Art, especially Miró, Léger, Gorky, Giacometti, and Dubuffet. *Mailing Add:* Int Specialty Products Inc 1361 Alps Rd Wayne NJ 07470

HEYMAN, STEVEN
PAINTER
b Los Angeles, Calif, Sept 22, 52. *Study:* Univ Calif, Los Angeles, BA, 76; Art Inst Chicago, MFA, 80. *Work:* Mus Contemp Art, McArthur Found, Chicago; Coca-Cola Corp; Prudential Insurance Co Am, Newark, NJ; Rockford Art Mus, Ill; also many private collections. *Exhib:* Painting and Sculpture of 1980-82: Fellowship Winners, Art Inst Chicago, 83; Chicago: Some Other Traditions, Madison Art Ctr, Wis (toured US & Can), 83-86; solo exhibs, Fay Gold Gallery, Atlanta, 89, Galerie Rohrbach, Obernburg, Ger, 90, Lichthof Gallery, State Acad Pictorial Art, Karlsruhe, Ger, 92; Lichthot Gallery, Karlsruhe, Ger, 92; Klein Artworks, 93; Chicago Cult Ctr, 94-95; Evanston Art Ctr, 95. *Pos:* Illus, Passover Haggadah for the Pardes Rimonim Press, Woodmere, New York, 88-89; co-cur, Goethe Inst, Chicago, 92. *Awards:* Fel, Nat Endowment Arts, 87; John Quincy Adams Fel, 80; Chicago Artists Int Prog Grant, Chicago Cult Ctr, 95-96. *Bibliog:* Micheel Bonesteel (auth), Chicago, Art Am, 6/89; articles, Chicago Tribune, 1/22/87, 2/22/89. *Dealer:* Zolla/Lieberman Gallery Inc 230 West Huron Chicago Ill 60610. *Mailing Add:* 1452 W Chicago Ave Chicago IL 60622

HIBBS, BARBARA J E
PAINTER, INSTRUCTOR
b New York, NY. *Study:* With A Haff; Art Student's League, with Sydney Dickinson, Dan Greene & Mario Cooper. *Work:* Wall Street Transcript & Ackerman Realty Co, NY. *Exhib:* Allied Artists Am, Nat Acad/Nat Arts Club, NY; Salmagundi Club Ann, NY; Knickerbocker Artists, Nat Arts Club/Salmagundi, NY; Hermitage Found Mus, Norfolk, Va, 83; Hammond Mus, 95; Lever House; Xian Acad Fine Arts, Nanking, China; Butler Mus & John Brown Univ, 2005-2006. *Teaching:* Pastel painting, Pastel Soc Am, Nat Arts Club, 82-83. *Awards:* Gold Medal Hon, Wall Street Transcript; Purchase Award, Pastel Soc Am, 96 & MH Hurliman-Armstrong Award, 97, 98; Pastel Soc Award for Pastel, Allied Artists, 97; Pastel Soc Purchase Award, 2003; Audubon Artist Silver Medal, 2004; Allied Artists Silver Medal, 2005. *Mem:* Pastel Soc Am (recording secy, 81-); Allied Artists Am (dir watercolor 91-); Knickerbocker Artists; C L Wolfe Art Asn; life mem Art Student's League NY. *Media:* Pastel, Watercolor. *Publ:* Bets of Pastels II, Rockport Publ. *Mailing Add:* 23 E 81st St New York NY 10028

HIBEL, EDNA
PAINTER, PRINTMAKER
b Boston, Mass, Jan 13, 17. *Study:* With Gregory Michaels, 30-34; Boston Mus Sch Fine Arts, Cert, 35-39; with Elliott O'Hara Watercolor Sch, 36-37. *Hon Degrees:* United Nats Univ for Peace, Hon Dr Art, 88; Mt St Mary's Col, LHD, 88; Eureka Col, LHD, 95; Providence Col, 96; Northwood Univ, 97; Simmons Col, 2005. *Work:* Mus Fine Arts, Boston; Detroit Art Inst; Milwaukee Art Mus; Phoenix Art Mus; Russian Acad Art, St Petersburg; Lomonosov Porcelain Mus, Russ Acad Art, St Petersburg, Russ; Harvard Univ; UN Hq, NY; and others. *Comn:* Hello Dolly, comn by Ginger Rogers, Palm Springs, Calif, 67; Prince of Peace, 85, Holy Family, 86, Soc Little Flower, Darien, Ill; Our Mother Before Us, Found US Nat Archs, Washington, 95; The Most Reverend Robert F Mulvee, Catholic Charities, Providence, RI, 96. *Exhib:* One-woman shows, Nat Mus Fine Arts, Rio de Janeiro, Brazil, 76, Hebrew Univ Mus, Jerusalem, 83, China Nat Art Gallery, Beijing, 86; Celebration of Life, Nat Mus Costa Rica, 88; Peace Through Wisdom, Dubrovnik Mus, Yugoslavia, 88; A Golden Bridge, Nat Mus Women Arts, Washington, 89, Soviet Union Acad Art Mus, Leningrad, 90; Grenchen Mus Art, Switz, 92; Lyme Acad Fine Arts, Conn, 94; Mitsukoshi Fine Art Gallery, Tokyo, 95. *Pos:* Founder, Boston Art Festival, 54; Art Dir, Edna Hibel Gallery, Boston & Palm Beach, Fla, 60-; cur, Hibel Mus Art, 77-. *Teaching:* Watercolor, Elliott O'Hara Watercolor Sch, 37; pvt lessons, oil painting, 57-58. *Awards:* Medal Hon, The late Belgian King Baudouin, Brussels, 83; Medal Hon & Citation, Pope John Paul II, Vatican, 85; Leonardo da Vinci World Award of Arts, World Cultural Council, Utrecht, 2001; Lifetime Achievement Award, Women in Visual Arts, 2001. *Bibliog:* Kay Pedrik (auth), Edna Hibel: An Album and Biography, Tradition Inks, 85; Hibel's Russian Palette (film), Hibel Mus Art, 91; Olga Cossi (auth), Edna Hibel: Her Life and Art, Discovery Enterprises, 94; Shawn McAllister (auth), The Life & Art of Edna Hibel, Star Group International, West Palm Beach, Fla; Millie Brawn (auth), Edna Hibel: An Artist's Story of Love & Compassion, Pelican Publ Co, New Orleans, LA. *Media:* Oil; Stone, Lithography, Serigraphy, Etching. *Interests:* Tennis, gardening, reading. *Publ:* Auth, Paintings of Edna Hibel, JAR Publ, 74, Progressions of a Lithograph, 77, coauth, The Sundial Ticking, 78, Fay Burg's Lake Kezar Cookbook with a Gallery of Paintings by Edna Hibel; auth, Hibel Mus Art Datebook, Hibel Mus Art, 81; auth, Stories that Warm the Heart, Hibel Mus Art, 96. *Dealer:* Edna Hibel Corp 1910 7th Ave N Lake Worth Fla 33461. *Mailing Add:* c/o Edna Hibel Corp 1910 7th Ave N Lake Worth FL 33461

HICKMAN, PATRICIA
CRAFTSMAN
Study: Univ Colo, Boulder, BA, 62; Univ Calif, Berkeley, MA(design/textiles), 77. *Work:* Renwick Gallery, Smithsonian Inst, Washington, DC; Oakland Mus, Calif; Erie Art Mus, Pa; Am Craft Mus, NY; Honolulu Acad Art & Contemp Mus. *Comn:* Nets of Makali'i Nets of Pleiades (entrance gates), Maui Arts & Cult Ctr, Kahului, 91-94; cast bronze panel, Gertrud Parker Sculpture Garden, Tiburon, Calif, 2000. *Exhib:* K18-Stoffwechsel Projektgruppe Textilforum, Kassel, Ger, 82; Knots & Nets: Spiritual Connections, Arts Am Prog, US Info Agency Tour in Africa, 92-94; one-person exhibs, Structure & Skin, Commons Gallery, Art Dept, Univ Hawaii, Manoa, 91, Before and After: Liminal Space, Contemp Mus, Honolulu, 95-96, Afterthoughts: New Work, Banaker Gallery, San Francisco, 96 & Through the Gates, San Francisco Craft & Folk Art Mus, 98-99, Honolulu Acad Arts, 99; 12th Biennale Int de la Tapisserie, Lausanne, Switz; two person exhibs, Miller/Brown Gallery, San Francisco, 83 & 86, San Francisco Craft & Folk Art mus, 84, The Woman's Bldg, Los Angeles, 86, Philharmonie Gallery, Liege, Belgium (with catalogue), 86, Richmond Art Ctr, 87, Sybaris Gallery, Royal Oak, Mich, 97; int exhibs 99 Miniattextil Como, Italy, Skin, Gallery B, Univ Tasmania, Launceston, Australia, 99, Sculpture by the Sea, Bond 1999, Sydney, Australia, Miniatures: 2000, Mus Art & Design, Helsinki, Finland, Kazuma Int Gallery, Maui Arts & Cult Ctr, 98, Acad Art Ctr Linekona, Honolulu, 2000, Snyderman/Works Galleries, Philadelphia, 2000, Iolani Gallery, Windward Community Col, Kaneohe, Hawaii, 2000, del Mano Gallery, Los Angeles, 2001, Textile Ctr Minn, Minneapolis Col Art & Design, 2001. *Collection Arranged:* Renwick Gallery, Smithsonian Instn, Washington, Pierre Pauli Found, Lausanne, Switzerland, Savaria Mus, Szombathely, Hungary, Wadsworth Atheneum, Hartford, Conn, Matthews Ctr, Ariz State Univ, Tempe, Oakland Mus, Erie Art Mus, Pa, Neutrogena Corp, Los Angeles, El Canelo De Nos Ctr, San Bernardo, Chile, Arrowmont Sch, Gatlinburg, Tenn, Ark Arts Ctr, Little Rock, Am Craft Mus, NYC, Honolulu Acad Arts, State Found Culture and Arts, Honolulu, Contemporary Mus, Honolulu, Longhouse Collection, East Hampton, NY. *Pos:* juror Textile Ctr Minn, Mpls, 2001. *Teaching:* teacher textile and fiber programs Univ Calif, Berkeley & Davis; San Francisco State Univ; M H deYoung Mus Art Sch; JFK Univ, San Francisco; Pacific Basin Sch Textile Arts, Berkeley; Calif Col Arts & Crafts, Oakland; prof, head fiber program, art dept, chair grad study in art, Univ Hawaii, Manoa, Honolulu; guest artist Can Arts Coun Grants: Banff Sch Art, Nova Scotia Col Art & Design; panelist 2000 Invitational Visual Arts Fellowship Rev, State Found Culture & Arts, Hawaii, 2000; Col of Marin, Calif, 98; San Francisco Loom & Shuttle Guild, 98; Univ Wis, Madison, 99; Nat Art Sch, Sydney, Australia, 99; Univ Calif, Davis, 2001; workshops at Univ Alaska, Fairbanks, 98, Split Rock Arts Program, Duluth, Minn, 2001, Textile Ctr Minn, St Paul, 2001. *Awards:* Individual Artist's Grant, Nat Endowment Arts, 86-87 & 94-95; Individual Artist Visual Arts Fel, Hawaii State Found Cult & Arts, 98; Faculty Trafel Grant to Sydney Australia, Univ Hawaii Research Coun, 99. *Bibliog:* exhib catalogues A Basketmaker's Legacy, Joanne Segal Brandford 1933-1994, 95, Collective Visions 1967-1997, State Found on Culture and the Arts, A Report, Through the Gates: Recent Work by Pat Hickman, San Francisco Craft and Folk Art Mus, 98, Surface-Strength-Structure: Pertaining to Line, Snyderman/Works Galleries, 2000, Miniatures 2000, Helen Drutt: Philadelphia, Artprint, Contemporary Textile Art: Collection of the Pierre Pauli Association, Benteli Pubs, 2000. *Mem:* Textile Soc Am (artist rep 94-); Asn for Promotion Pacific island Art. *Publ:* Coauth, Special Issue: Collaboration, Fiberarts Mag, 22-25, 9-10/85; auth, Lillian Elliot: Artist and Teacher, San Francisco Craft & Folk Art Mus, Vol 10, No 3, 92; contribr, More Random Thoughts About Baskets, Grace Hudson Mus, Ukiah, Calif, 95; Eventails catalogue, Philharmonie Gallery, Liege, 91-93; Arts in Embassies Program collection of fiber art, US Ambassador in Warsaw, Poland, 91-93; Contemporary Textile Art, Collection of Pierre Pauli Asn, Musee Arlaud, Lausanne, Switzerland, 2000; Auth, Baskets: Tradition and Beyond, Guild Pubs, 2000; The Visible Self, Global Perspectives on Dress, Culture and Society, 2d edit, 2000; contbr articles to profl publs; videotape The Gates, Maui Arts & Cultural Ctr, 97. *Mailing Add:* 426 Ulupaina St Apt D Kailua HI 96734-2467

HICKMAN, PAUL ADDISON
EDUCATOR, SLIDE CURATOR
b Iowa City, Iowa, May 24, 50. *Study:* Col Liberal Arts, 71-72; Univ Ill, Urbana-Champaign, BA, 73; Columbia Col, Chicago, BA, 75; Princeton Univ, 77; Ariz State Univ, Tempe, MA(art hist), 79; Univ NMex, Albuquerque, with Beaumont Newhall, Thomas F Barrow & Bill Jay, PhD(art hist), 87. *Work:* Mus Contemp Photog, Chicago, Ill; Chicago Hist & Archit Landmarks, Ill. *Exhib:* Group Exhib, Mus Contemp Photog, Chicago, 74-75, Mont State Univ, Boseman, 76, Phoenix Art Mus, Ariz, 76, Northlight Gallery, Tempe, 76; one-man shows, Ark State Univ, 90, Books & Books, Coral Gables, Fla, 91. *Collection Arranged:* Early Photographs of the Southwest, 76; William J Lucas: documentary photographs taken alongside Route 66, 86; West of Eden: Conceived, organized, prepared & installed, 89; Solicit, select, publicize & install seven exhibs per year in univ res libr, 89-92. *Pos:* Slide cur, Ark State Univ, 92-96 & slide librn, 96-. *Teaching:* Asst, Art Hist Survey, Ariz State Univ, 75-76; assoc photog hist, Univ NMex, Albuquerque, 78-81; instr, Col Santa Fe, NMex, 88; asst prof art hist, Ark State Univ, 89-. *Mem:* Col Art Asn; Visual Resources

Asn; Soc Photog Educ; Friends Photog; Nat Stereoscopic Asn. *Media:* Photography. *Collection:* Niagara Falls, Trans-Mississippi West, California, Yosemite, Big Trees & Sierra Nevada, Carleton E Watkins, John James Reilly, Martin Mason Hazeltine, George Fiske. *Publ:* Coauth, George Fiske, Yosemite Photographer, Northland Press, 80; auth, Art, Information and Evidence: Early Landscape Photographs of the Yosemite Region, Exposure, 84; John James Reilly, 1838-1894, Univ Microfilms Int, 88; Martin Mason Hazeltine, 1827-1903: A Chronology, Stereo World, 94; Carleton E Watkins in Yosemite Valley, 1861-1866, Hist Photog, 96; Genesis and Revelation: Geologic Theory and Photographic Practice in Yosemite Valley, 1859-1900, Architecture of Chicago Gold Coast, 1880-1920; John James Reilly: catolog, three articles, Old Series (1867-75) & Views (1865-70), New Series (1879-86) & Views (1870-86), Additions to Chronology (1864-76) and Old & New Series Titles & Views (1865-86), Stereo World, 2006. *Mailing Add:* Ark State Univ PO Box 2764 State University AR 72467

HIDE, PETER NICHOLAS
SCULPTOR, EDUCATOR
b Carshalton, Surrey, Eng, Dec 15, 44. *Study:* Croydon Col Art, 61-64; St Martin's Sch Art, 64-67. *Work:* Tate Gallery, London, Eng; Mus Fine Art, Boston; Univ Calif; Arts Coun Gt Brit, London; Can Coun Art Bank, Ottawa; City of Barcelona; Univ Alta; Sculpture at Goodwood, Sculpture Park, Sussex, UK, 2000. *Comn:* Sculpture for travelling show, Arts Coun Gt Brit, 69; Sculpture, cast iron & concrete, Peter Stuyvesant Found, Southampton, Eng, 72; steel sculptures, Commonwealth Games Comt, Edmonton, Alta, 78 & City of Red Deer, Alta, 81; Stainless steel sculpture, Campeaux Corp, Edmonton, 84; The Winspear Centre for Performing Arts, Edmo, 97. *Exhib:* The Condition of Sculpture, Hayward Gallery, London, Eng, 75; Silver Jubilee Exhib, Battersea Park, London, 76; solo exhibs, Serpentine Gallery, London, 76, Sculpture Made in USA, Clayworks Gallery, NY, 84, Peter Hide in Canada, Edmonton Art Gallery, Alta, 86, Recent Sculptures, Mira Godard Gallery, Toronto, 88 & Andre Emmerich Gallery, NY, 90; Peter Hide in Context, 25 yr Retrospective, Edmonton Art Gallery. *Pos:* Artist/advisor, Triangle Workshop, NY & Hardingham Sculpture Works; President Edmonton Cont Art Soc. *Teaching:* Lectr sculpture, Norwich Sch Art, Norfolk, Eng, 68-74; lectr, St Martins Sch Art, London, 71-78; prof, Univ Alta, Edmonton, 77-. *Awards:* Canada Coun A Grant, 92. *Bibliog:* Terry Fenton (auth), Peter Hide & the monolith, Vanguard Mag & Peter Hide in Canada (catalog), Edmonton Art Gallery, 86; Peter Hide in Context (Catalog) Edmonton Art Gallery. *Mem:* Edmonton Contemp Art Soc (ECAS). *Media:* Steel. *Dealer:* Scott Gallery 12323 104 Ave, Edmonton; Andre Emmerich Gallery 41 E 57th St New York NY 10022. *Mailing Add:* Dept Art & Design Univ Alberta Edmonton AB T6G 2C9 Canada

HIGBY, (DONALD) WAYNE
PAINTER, SCULPTOR
b Colorado Springs, Colo, May 12, 43. *Study:* Univ Colo, BFA, 66; Univ Mich, MFA, 68. *Work:* Philadelphia Mus Art; Am Craft Mus, Brooklyn Mus, Metrop Mus Art, Mus Contemp Crafts, NY; Minneapolis Mus Art, Wis; Everson Mus Art, Syracuse; Everlon Mus Art; Mus Fine Arts, Boston; Nat Mus Art, Toyko; Renwick Gallery, Smithsonian, Washington, DC; Los Angeles Co Mus Art; and others. *Comn:* Arrow Int, Reading, Pa, 95; Miller Performing Arts Bldg, Alfred, 2006. *Exhib:* One-man shows, Joslyn Art Mus, 69, Mus Contemp Crafts, 73, Helen Drutt Gallery, NY, 88 & 90 China, 85; The Eloquent Object, Philbrook Mus Art, Tulsa, Okla, 87; Power over the City: Am Studio Potters, Detroit Inst Arts, Mich, 88; East-West Contemp Ceramics Exhib, Seoul Olympic Arts Festival, South Korea, 88; Power Over the Clay: Am Studio Potters, Detroit Inst Arts, Mich, 88; Everson Mus Art, Syracuse, NY, 89; Am Craft Mus, NY, 90; Kanazawa Ishibtawa Pref, Japan, 91; Mus Mod Art, Tokyo, Japan, 93; Ark Art Ctr, Little Rock, 94; Krannert Art Mus, Champaign, Ill, 94; Clay into Art, MET Mus Art, NY, 98 & Los Angeles Co Mus Art, 2000. *Pos:* Chmn, Div Ceramic Art, NY State Col Ceramics, Alfred Univ, 84-91; adv, Task Force Individual Artist, NY State Coun Arts, 80-82; bd dir, Haystack Mountain Sch Crafts, Deer Isle, Maine, 83-; adv, Nat Endowment Arts, 89-91; council of dir, Int Acad of Ceramics, 99-. *Teaching:* Asst prof ceramic art, RI Sch Design, 70-73; prof ceramic art, NY State Col Ceramics, Alfred Univ, 73-; hon prof art, Jingdezhen Ceramic Inst, Repub China, 94-, Shanghai Univ, 2000-. *Awards:* Nat Endowment Arts Fels, 73-74, 77-78 & 88-89; Individual Artist Grant, NY Found Arts, 85 & 89; Col Fels, Am Craft Coun, 95; Am Craft Visionary Award, Am Craft Mus, 95; Honorary Prof Jingdezhen Ceramics Inst; Honorary Prof Shanghai Univ; Dist Edu Award, Bd of the Renwick, Smithsonian Inst, 2002; Master of the Media Bd of the Renwick Smithsonian Inst, Nat Gallery of Am Art; Honorary Citizen of Jingdezhen, PR China May, 2004; Honor of the council, NCECA (Nat Council of Educ in Ceramic Art), 2005. *Bibliog:* The Eloquent Object, Philbrook Mus Art, Univ Wash Press, 87; Ceramics Monthly, 12/87; Robert Tuner (auth), feature article, Ceramic Art & Perception, 91; Kenneth Trapp (auth), Skilled Work, Renwick Gallery, Smithsonian, 98; Timothy Burgard (auth), Art of Craft, Fine Arts Mus of San Francisco, 99. *Mem:* Fel Am Crafts Coun; Empire State Craftsmen; NCECA; Haystack Mont Sch of Crafts, (honorary bd mem), Bd Mem Art Gallery, Rochester, NY. *Media:* Clay, Glaze, Fire. *Publ:* Contribr, Craft Horizons, ed by Rose Slivka, Am Crafts Coun, 70; Creative Landscape Containers, by Jane Holtz Kay, Christian Sci Monitor, 73; High Crafts (collecting boom), by Monica Meenan, Town & Country, 77; Ceramic Art, Comment and Review, 78 & Century of Ceramics in The United States, 79, by Garth Clark, E P Dutton; Handmade In America, B Dramoustein, 86 & 95; The New Ceramics, P Dormer, Thames + Itedson, 86 & 94. *Dealer:* Helen Drutt Gallery Philadelphia PA 19106. *Mailing Add:* 1842 Route 244 Alfred Station NY 14803

HIGGINS, BRIAN ALTON
PAINTER
b Brookline, Mass. *Study:* Motion Picture Sch, Fort Monmouth, NJ; Emerson Col; Mus Fine Arts, Boston, Mass. *Work:* Va Mus Art; Boyle Co Sch Sys, Constitution Sq, Danville, Ky. *Exhib:* Nat Art Club, New York City; Salmagundi Club, New York City; Pastel Soc Am, New York City; Lyme Art Ctr, Conn; San Diego Art Inst, Calif; Red River Valley Mus, Tex; Mass Gen Hosp, Mass; Danforth Mus Art, Mass. *Collection Arranged:* Boyle Co Sch Sys, Constitution Sq, Danville, Ky. *Pos:* chmn bd, Cent Mass Symphony Orch. *Awards:* Perkins-Elmer award, Silvermine Art Guild, Conn, 99; Purchase award, Gallery Constitution Sq, Danville, Ky, 00; Grumbacher Gold Medal, Cooperstown, NY Art Ctr, 03. *Bibliog:* Robt Moler, Ky Sunday Advocate, 01; N. Basbanes, Among the Gently Mad, Henry Holt Pub, 02; Nancy Sheehan (auth), Arts Watch, Sunday Telegram, Worcester, Mass. *Mem:* Degas Pastel Soc; United Pastelists of Am; Conn Acad Fine Arts; Pastel Soc Am; Acad Artists' Asn. *Media:* Pastels. *Publ:* William Zimmer, Art of the Week, NY Sunday Times, 99; Nancy Chapman, Featured Artist, Pastelink Monthly, 01; art book reviews, Worcester Sunday Telegram, Mass. *Dealer:* The Edgington Collection of American Art, Ridge Rd, West Brookfield, MA, 01585; Caladan Galllery Peabody Mass 01915. *Mailing Add:* PO Box 1011 West Brookfield MA 01585

HIGGINS, (GEORGE) EDWARD
SCULPTOR
b Gaffney, SC, Nov 13, 30. *Study:* Univ NC, BA, 54. *Work:* Mus Mod Art, Guggenheim Mus, Whitney Mus Am Art, NY; Albright-Knox Art Gallery, Buffalo, NY; Dallas Mus Fine Arts; and others. *Comn:* Sculpture, Cameron Bldg, NY, 62 & NY State Theatre, Lincoln Ctr for Performing Arts, NY, 64. *Exhib:* NY World's Fair, 64-65; Contemp Am Sculpture, Selection 1, Whitney Mus Am Art, 66; Flint Inst Art, Mich, 66; Documenta IV, Kassel, Ger, 68; Duke Univ, 69. *Teaching:* Instr sculpture, Parsons Sch Design, 61-62; Philadelphia Mus Sch, 63; Cornell Univ, 67; Univ Wis, 68; Univ Ky, 70. *Awards:* Louis C Tiffany Grant, 62; Purchase Prize, Flint Inst Art, 66. *Bibliog:* Harriet Janis & Rubi Blesh (auth), Collage: Personalities--Concepts--Techniques, Chilton, 62; Sam Hunter (ed), New Art Around the World: Painting & Sculpture, Abrams, 66; Eduard Trier (auth), Form & Space: Sculpture in the 20th Century, Praeger, 68. *Media:* All. *Mailing Add:* 2655 Henley Rd Sanford NC 27330

HIGGINS, EDWARD FERDINAND III See Doo Da Post, Edward Ferdinand Higgins III

HIGGINS, EDWARD KOELLING
CERAMIST, JEWELER
b Milwaukee, Wis, Apr 30, 26. *Study:* Univ Wis, Milwaukee, BS(art educ), MS(ceramics); Univ Wis-La Crosse; Northwestern Univ. *Work:* Mus of Contemp Crafts, NY; Theo Portney Gallery, NY; many pvt collections. *Exhib:* Mississippi River Art Festival, Jackson, Miss, 67-; Southern Tier Art & Craft Exhib, Corning Mus, NY, 69-; Crafts-1970, Inst of Contemp Art, Boston, 70; Appalachian Corridors Exhib, Charleston Art Gallery, WVa, 70-; Harrisburg Festival of the Arts, Harrisburg Art Gallery, Pa, 70; Cooperstown NY Festival of the Arts, 70. *Collection Arranged:* Fantasy in Silver, Akron Art Inst, Ohio; Jewelers, USA, Calif State Col at Fullerton; Am Evolution in Art, Chambers Gallery, Pa State Univ; Box Exhib, Kohler Art Ctr; Celebration 20, Mus of Contemp Crafts, NY; Forms in Metal, Montgomery Mus of Fine Arts, Fine Arts Mus at Mobile, Ala, Philbrook Art Ctr, Tulsa, Okla, Va Mus of Fine Arts, Richmond & Huntsville Mus of Art, Ala; 100 Artists Celebrate 200 Yrs, Fairtree Gallery, NY; Xerox-Fun & Fantasy Exhib, Xerox Hall, Rochester, NY. *Teaching:* Asst prof jewelry, Mansfield State Col, Pa, 69-70; assoc prof jewelry, ceramics & photog, Mercyhurst Col, 71-82. *Awards:* Sculpture Award & Merit Award for Metal, Mississippi River Art Festival, Jackson Art Gallery; Silver Award, Appalachian Corridors Exhib, Charlestown Art Gallery. *Bibliog:* Dona Meilach (auth), Box Art Assemblages, Crown, 76; Jewelry: The Fine Art of Adornment Fabrication Method & Jewelry: The Fine Art of Adornment Casting Method (filmstrips), Warner Educ Productions; Casting, Bovin Publ. *Media:* Silver, Clay, Wood. *Interests:* Wood Sculpture. *Publ:* Contribr, Body Jewelry, Regnery, 73; contribr, Box Art Assemblages, 76 & Career Opportunities in Crafts, 77, Crown. *Dealer:* Somerhill Gallery, Chapel Hill, NC. *Mailing Add:* 166 Wintersage Pittsboro NC 27312-8553

HIGGINS, LARKIN MAUREEN
CONCEPTUAL ARTIST, EDUCATOR
b Santa Monica, Calif. *Study:* Calif State Univ, Long Beach, BA, 76; Calif State Univ, Fullerton, MA, 83; Otis Col Art & Design, MFA, 95. *Work:* Grunwald Col, Armand Hammer Mus, Los Angeles; Erie Art Mus, Erie, Pa; Calif Mus Photography, Riverside; Laguna Beach Mus Art, Calif; Calif Univ Nebr Art Galleries, Lincoln. *Comn:* Wall installation, Nicki Huggins/Scott Sternberg, Topanga, Calif, 97; Artist Book, Los Angeles Poetry Festival, Calif, 99. *Exhib:* Contacts, Western Heritage Mus, Omaha, Nebr, 80; Photonational, traveling exhib, Erie Art Mus, Pa, 84; Solo exhib, Couples, Harvard Univ, Visual & Environ, Cambridge, Mass, 85, Book /Object, Dickson Art Ctr, Art Libr, Univ Calif, Los Angeles, 89; Bare Facts, Sly Humor, Irvine Fine Arts Ctr, Calif, 88; Words & Windows, Sam Francis Gallery, Santa Monica, Calif, 94; Before/Now, Artworks/Bookarts, Santa Monica, Calif, 98; Artists & Writers Simpatico, dA Ctr for the Arts, Pomona, Calif, 2000. *Collection Arranged:* Tonal Persuasions, Kwan Fong Gallery Art, 99. *Pos:* bd dir, Westwood Ctr of Arts, 79-81; chmn, lectr comt, Los Angeles Ctr for Photographic Studies, 83; Artist in Residence, Dorland Mountain Arts Colony, Temecula, Calif, 2000, 2001, 2002; chmn, art dept, Calif Lutheran Univ, 2004-2005. *Teaching:* Assoc Prof Art, painting & drawing, Calif Lutheran Univ, 94-2001, prof art, painting & drawing, interdisciplinary art, 2001-. *Awards:* Cash Award, ASA Southwest Reg Show, ASA Gallery, Univ NMex, 82; Purchase Award, Photonational, Erie Art Mus, 84; Fac Develop Grant, Hewlett Found,

1987, 1999, 2004, 2006. *Bibliog:* Peter Frank, Stick-To-It-Iveness, LA Weekly, 88; Leah Ollman, A Wry Look at Life, Artweek, 88; Jessica Bethoney, A Primer in Colorful Expressions, The Boston Globe, 81. *Mem:* Coll Art Asn; Beyond Baroque Found. *Media:* Inter-Disciplinary. *Res:* shared intersection of text and visual image. *Publ:* Real Couples, U-Turn, 85; Once Upon a Moment, Women's Graphic Center, 89; A Bibliophile's Rebellion: A Mixed Media Essay, Genre 14: Flux, 92. *Mailing Add:* PO Box 341751 Los Angeles CA 90034-8751

HIGGINS, MARYLOU
CERAMIST, PAINTER
b Milwaukee, Wis, June 27, 26. *Study:* Univ Wis-Milwaukee, BS(art educ), MS(weaving). *Work:* Mint Mus, Charlotte, NC; Newark Mus, NJ; Northern Telecom Res, Glaxco Res, Triangle Park, NC; High Mus, Atlanta, Ga; Fayetteville Mus Art, Fayettville, NC; and others. *Comn:* 10 stoneware goblets, comn by Ctr Women Policy Studies to be given to recipients of Wise Women Awards, Washington, DC. *Exhib:* One-woman shows, Sol Del Rio, San Antonio, Tex, 77-80, Shelia Nussbaum Gallery, NJ, 85, 88, 93 & 95, Somerhill Gallery, Chapel Hill, NC, 91, 94, 97, 2000 & 04, NC Pottery Ctr, Seagrove, 2006-06; Nothern Telecom Juried Sculpture, Ceramic, NC, 85-88; Biennial '88 Ceramics, Mint Mus, Charlotte, NC; Auction Benefit, Bewitched by Craft, Am Craft Mus, NY 88 & 89; North Carolina Clay, invitational, Visual Arts Ctr, NC State Univ, Raleigh, 92; Feats of Clay VII, Lincoln, Calif, 94; Fanciful & Functional: Art Furniture, Hickory Mus, Hickory, NC; Interiors Invitational, Blue Spiral 1, Asheville, NC, 2000, 04; plus others. *Teaching:* Instr art educ & fiber & fabrics, Mansfield State Col, 69-71; asst prof ceramics, fiber & fabrics & art educ, Mercyhurst Col, 71-74. *Awards:* Purchase Award, 4th Ann Exhib NC Sculpture, Northern Telecom, 85; Mint Mus Biennial Purchase Award, Sculptural Vessel, Charlotte, NC, 88; Merit Award, Feats of Clay VII, Lincoln, Calif, 94; and others. *Bibliog:* Nancy Tilly (auth), Carolina original, NC Homes & Gardens, 12/90; Harriet Gamble (auth), Mary Lou Higgins, Arts & Activities, 92; Marylou Higgins (auth) A Show Story, Pottery Making Illustrated, Winter 98. *Mem:* Am Craft Council. *Media:* Clay, Graphite. *Publ:* Contribr, Basketry, 44, A New Look at Crochet, 75 & Wearable Crafts, 76, Crown; Inventive Fiber Crafts, Prentice-Hall, 77; Career Opportunities in Crafts, Crown, 77; The Jeweler's Art - A Multimedia Approach, Davis, 94; Handbuilt Ceramics, Lark Books, 97; The Clay Lover's Guide to Making Molds, Lark Books, 98; The Ceramic Design Book, Lark Books, 98; Surface Decoration, Lark Books, 99; 500 Figures in Clay, Larkbooks, 2004. *Dealer:* Somerhill Gallery 3 Eastgate E Franlin St Chapel Hill NC 27514. *Mailing Add:* 166 Fearrington Post Pittsboro NC 27312

HIGH, KATHRYN
PAINTER, WRITER
Study: Colgate Univ, BA, 77; State Univ NY, Buffalo, MA(arts & humanities), 81. *Exhib:* Not So Ancient Hist, Women & Medicine/Voices in My Head, Mus Mod Art, NY, 90; Underexposed: Temple of the Fetus, Women & Medicine/Voices in My Head (video), Mus Mod Art, NY, 93; Art in General, NY, 95; Images Film/Video Festival, Toronto, 95; L'Oggetto/Arte e Video Negli Stati Uniti, Mus Laboratorio Di Arte Contemporanea, Rome, Italy, 95 & Mus Mod Art, NY, 96; Topographies, Vancouver Art Gallery, BC, 95. *Pos:* Panelist & juror, Media Bur, 87, NY Found Arts, 88, Boston Film & Video Festival, 91, Nat Endowment Arts/Media Arts, 91, Conn Arts Coun, 92, UFVA Student Festival, 93-94, Pew Fel, 94 & Balck Maria Film/Video Festival, 96; ed & publ, FELIX, J Media Arts & Communications, 89-; co-cur, Landscapes Prog, Robert Flaherty Film Seminar, Int Film Seminars, NY, summer 96; cur, Reel New York, series of independent film/video, WNET & PBS, NY, 96-97. *Teaching:* Lectr, Film/Video Dept, Sch Visual Arts, NY, 88-92, Dept Computer Graphics, Pratt Inst, Brooklyn, spring 93, video production/theory classes, Vis Arts Prog, Princeton Univ, NJ, spring 95, 96 & 97 & NY Univ, fall 96. *Awards:* Fels Nat Endowment Arts, 89 & 95; Fel, Art Matters Inc, 95; Award for The 23 Songs of the Chromosomes, Jerome Found, 95. *Mem:* NY Found Arts; Lyn Blumenthal Found; Int Film Seminars; Standby Prog Inc. *Publ:* Auth, Finding One's Voice: Releasing the Other Into American Media (exhib catalog), Nat Ctr Video & New Media Art, London, 91; Wide Angle, Robert Flaherty Seminar issue, 95; Hallwalls Twenty Years, Hallwalls Gallery Publ, 95; 23 Questions, in Gender and Technology, Routledge, 96; (A few) statistics on the (possible) meaning of an encounter with (some) (middle-class) academic women, In: Mixed genres issue, Chains, spring 96. *Mailing Add:* 138 Baltic St No 4C Brooklyn NY 11201

HIGH, STEVEN S
MUSEUM DIRECTOR, CURATOR
b Twin Falls, Idaho, June 17, 56. *Study:* Univ Utah, Salt Lake City, 74-76; Antioch Col, Yellow Springs, Ohio, BA, 79; Williams Col, Williamstown, Mass, MA, 85; Va Commonwealth Univ, Richmond, MBA, 95. *Collection Arranged:* Young German Painters, 86; Antoni Tapies: Graphic Work, 88; Abstraction Contemporary Photography, 89; Nightmare Works: Tibor Hajas (auth, catalog), Anderson Gallery, 90; Alfredo Jaar: Geography-War, 91; Anonymity & Identity (auth, catalog), 93; Repicturing Abstraction (auth, catalog), 94; The Rights of Science (auth, catalog), 97. *Pos:* Researcher, San Francisco Mus Mod Art, Calif, 79-80; preparator/asst cur, MIT Mus, Cambridge, Mass, 80-82; dir, Baxter Gallery, Portland Sch Art, Maine, 85-88 & Anderson Gallery, Va Commonwealth Univ, Richmond 88-96; exec dir, Nev Mus Art, 96-. *Teaching:* Instr art hist, Portland Sch Art, Maine 85-88; asst prof art, Va Commonwealth Univ, Richmond, 88-94, assoc prof, 95-96. *Mem:* Am Asn Mus (bd 2006); Nev Mus Asn (pres, 2002-2004); Western Mus Asn (bd 2004); Richmond Arts Coun (bd mem, 89-96). *Publ:* Auth, Antoni Tapies: Graphic Work 1947-1987, Baxter Gallery, Portland, Maine, 88; Young German painters, Art Criticism, spring, 88; contribr, Clemens Weiss: Towards Knowledge, Neurer Achener Kunstverein, 90; Alfredo Jaar: Geography equals War, Va Mus & Anderson Gallery, 91; New Art from an Ancient Land, 96. *Mailing Add:* Nevada Mus 160 W Liberty St Reno NV 89501

HIGH, TIMOTHY GRIFFIN
PRINTMAKER, SCULPTOR
b Memphis, Tenn, Mar 10, 49. *Study:* Tex Tech Univ, BFA(printmaking & drawing), 73; Univ Wis-Madison, MA(printmaking), 75, MFA(printmaking & art hist), 76. *Work:* Chicago Art Inst; Grunwald Ctr Graphic Arts, Univ Calif, Los Angeles; Brooklyn Mus Fine Art, NY; Jack S Blanton Art Mus, Univ Tex, Austin; Milwaukee Art Mus, Wis; Boston Mus Fine Art; Fogg Mus, Harvard Univ; Metrop Mus Fine Art, NY. *Comn:* Point of Departure (portfolio), Univ Wis, 84; Colorprint USA (portfolio), Tex Tech Univ, 98; Tex Comn for the Arts, 2000; Tex Prints, 2001. *Exhib:* Seventh & Eighth Brit Biennale, 79 & 82; Metrop Ctr Visual Arts, Denver, Colo, 91; Creative Spirit I & II, Austin, Tex, 92 & 93; solo exhibs, Amarillo Art Mus, Tex, 93 & Flatbed Press & Gallery, Austin, Tex, 96; Veiled Images, Art Mus S Tex, Corpus Christi, Tex, 94; Nat Screenprinters Invitational, Mus Sch, Boston, Mass, 94; and others. *Collection Arranged:* Metropolitan Mus of Art, NY; Chicago Art Inst; Library of Congress; Fogg; Art Mus, Cambridge, MA; Boston Mus of Art; Houston Mus of Art. *Pos:* Studio Art, Univ Tex, Austin, 76-. *Teaching:* Instr art, Univ Tex, Austin, 76, assoc prof serigraphy-printmaking, papermaking, drawing & design, 82-. *Awards:* Juror's Purchase Awards, 5th Int Nat Media Exhib, Dickerson, NDak, 75, Boston Print, De Cordova Mus; Nat Endowment Arts fel, 89; Longview Art Mus Best of Show, 35th Ann Invitational Art Exhib, 94. *Bibliog:* EC Cunningham (auth), Printmaking: A Primary Form of Expression, 92; EC Cunningham (auth), Printmaking: A Primary Form of Art, 92; Glenn R Brown (auth), rev, Art Papers, 93 & 94; Steven T Zevitas (auth), New American Painting, Open Studio Press, 97. *Mem:* Boston Printmakers; Southern Graphics Coun; Tex Fine Arts Asn; Austin Christian Arts Fel (pres, 94-96); Christians in Visual Arts Asn. *Media:* Prismacolor, Enamel Drawing; Serigraphy, Papermaking. *Publ:* Contribr, New American Graphics--1975, Univ Wis-Madison, 75; Terrence Greider (auth), Artist & Audience, 90. *Dealer:* Adair Margo Gallery 415 E Yandell El Paso TX 79902. *Mailing Add:* Univ Tex Dept Art Austin TX 78712

HIGHSTEIN, JENE
SCULPTOR
b Baltimore, Md, 42. *Study:* Univ Md, BA, 63; Univ Chicago, 63-65; New York Studio Sch, 66; Royal Acad Sch, London, dipl, 70. *Work:* Victoria & Albert Mus, London; Mus Contemp Art, Chicago; Los Angeles Co Mus Art; Rose Art Mus, Brandeis Univ, Mass; Guggenheim Mus, Mus Mod Art, NY; Balt Mus Art; Walker Arts Center; and many others. *Comn:* Granite carvings, General Mills Corp, 89; granite carvings, Walker Arts Ctr, 89; concrete sculptures and Park, Rutgers Univ, 90; concrete sculpture, Laumier Sculpture Park, St Louis, Mo, 91; granite carving, Carnegie Bank, Stockholm, 98; Tower, Fountain and Park, Stone, Houston, TX, 2005. *Exhib:* One-man exhibs, Univ Art Mus, Berkeley, Calif, 79, Renaissance Soc, Univ Chicago, 80, Ugo Ferranti Gallery, Rome, Italy, 81, Oscarsson Hood Gallery, NY, 82, Miami-Dade Community Col, 83, Anders Tornberg Gallery, Lund, Sweden, 84, Mattress Factory, Pittsburgh, 85 & Flow Ace Gallery, Los Angeles, 86; An Int Survey of Recent Painting and Sculpture, Mus Mod Art, NY, 84; Ace Gallery, NY, 96; Art Space Seoul, 96; Stark Gallery, NY, 97; Anders Tornberg Gallery, Lowd, Sweden, 98; Todd Gallery, London, 98; Grant Selwyn Gallery, Los Angeles, Calif, 2000; Bilboa Guggenheim, Bilboa, 2000; Grant Selwyn, NY, 2001; Art Mus Memphis, Tenn, 2001; Tex Gallery, Houston, 2002; Anthony Grant Fine Art, NY, 2004. *Teaching:* Instr, Sch Visual Arts, 73, Parsons Sch Design, 83 & New York Univ, 84-85, NY; vis artist, Yale Univ, 74-75, C W Post Col, Old Westbury, NY, 75 & 79, Emily Carr Col, Vancouver, BC, 80, Rutgers Univ, Camden, NJ, 82 & Miami-Dade Community Col, Fla, 83; artist-in-residence, Sarah Lawrence Col, Bronxville, NY, 76; vis lectr, Harvard Univ, 96; vis distinguished prof, Southern Methodist Univ, Dallas, 98. *Awards:* Sculpture Awards, Creative Artists Pub Serv Prog, 79 & Nat Endowment Arts, 84 & 94; Guggenheim Fel, 85; St Gauden's Mem Prize, 92. *Bibliog:* Linda Forshey (auth), Jene Highstein, La Jolla Mus, Calif, 87; Jean Feinberg (auth), Jene Highstein at Wave Hill, Wave Hill, 89; Jene Highstein (auth), Gallery/Landscape Santa Barbara, Contemp Arts Forum, 91; Thomas McEvilley (auth), New Sculpture, Anthony Grant Inc, 2004; Lily Wei (auth), Madison Square Art, 2006, Jene Highstein, 2006. *Media:* All Media. *Mailing Add:* 515 W 36th St New York NY 10018

HIGHTOWER, JOHN B
ADMINISTRATOR, MUSEUM DIRECTOR
b Atlanta, Ga, May 23, 33. *Study:* Yale Univ, BA, 55; Calif Col Arts & Crafts, hon DFA, 75. *Pos:* Asst to pub, Am Heritage Publ Co, 61-63; exec asst, NY State Coun on the Arts, 63-64, exec dir, 64-70, mem, 70-76; cult adv, Rockefeller Mission to Latin Am, 69; Am rep, United Nations Educ, Sci & Cult Orgn Conf on Performing Arts, Canberra, Australia, 69; dir, Mus Mod Art, NY, 70-72; pres, Assoc Councils of the Arts, 72-74 & S St Seaport, 77-83; founder & chmn, Advocates for the Arts, 74-77; The Maritime Ctr, 83-84, exec dir, 84-89; dir planning & develop for arts, Univ Va, 89-93; pres & chief exec officer, Mariners Mus, 93-. *Teaching:* Instr arts mgt, Wharton Sch of Bus, New Sch, Yale Grad Sch Drama, 75-77. *Awards:* NY State Award, 70. *Mem:* Buffalo Acad Fine Arts; Century Asn, 1805 Club, London; and others. *Mailing Add:* 101 Museum Ave Newport News VA 23606

HIGHWATER, JAMAKE
CRITIC, LECTURER
Study: Spec study in comparative lit, music, dance, cult anthrop & art hist; Minn Col Art & Design, Hon DFA, 86. *Pos:* Consult, Task Panel on the Individual Artist & Lit Panel, NY State Coun Arts, 75-80; mem art task panel, Pres Carter's Comn on Mental Health, 77-79; pres cult coun, Am Indian Community House, NY, 77-79; nominator, Awards in the Visual Arts, WNET-NY, 80-84; writer & narrator, Native Americans (8 part series), The Primal Mind & Native Land, PBS; moderator, Aspen Inst Seminar, Indian Am: Past, Present and Future, 81-84; exec bd, PEN, Am Ctr, 83-85; art critic, Christian Science Monitor, 88-91; panelist, PEW Charitable Trusts Art Awards, 93-. *Teaching:* Lectr for Speakers Bur, Washington; appointed lectr, NY Univ, Continuing

Educ, 76-80; adj asst prof, Grad Sch Archit, Columbia Univ, 84-85; gen dir, Native Arts Festival, Houston, 86 & Festival Mythos, Philadelphia, 91; nat adv comt, Pew Fels Arts, 90-92; bd, Am Poetry Ctr, 91, lectr, Exten Performing Art Prog, Univ Calif, Los Angeles, 98-. *Awards:* Best Film, Nat Educ Film Festival, 86; Japanese Libr Asn Commendation, 89; ACE Award for best cable television educ mini-series, 90. *Mem:* Author's Guild; Dramatists Guild; PEN Int. *Res:* Concerned with all aspects of art, crafts and culture. *Publ:* Writer, host & co-producer, The Primal Mind (doc film), PBS, 84; Native Land (doc film), PBS, 86; auth, Shadow Show: An Autobiographical Insinuation, Van der Marck, 86; Language of vision, Grove Press, 94; Dance: Rituals of Experience, Oxford, 96; and others

HIJAR, ALBERTO SERANO
CRITIC, EDUCATOR
b DF Mex, Dec 7, 35. *Study:* Univ Nac Autonoma de Mex de Filosofia, Maestro, 74; Diplomados Ministeris de Cultura, Nicaragua Univ, 82 & 98; Acad de Cienciar de Cuba, Medalla 30 aniversaio. *Work:* Mus estudeo Diego Rivera, Mex; Mus de Arte Mod, Mex; Fundacion Maria y Pablo O'Higgins, Mex; Inst Colimeuse de Cultra, Colima, Mex; Secretaria de Relacionale Exterior, Mex. *Collection Arranged:* Diego Rivera Centenial, Cuba, 89; Influencias Mutuar, San Antonio, Tex, 92; Alfredo Zulce Homenaje, Mex, 93; Adolfo Mexiac, Libertad de expresiorio, Dist Fed, Mex, 98. *Pos:* Vincular, articular, fusionar, Taller de Arte e Ideologia, Mex-Italia, 74-98; Arte y luchar populars, Diplomador en Aguascalientes y el Dist Fed, Mus de Arte Contemp, Centro Nac Artes, 96-98. *Teaching:* Estetica contemp, Univ Nac Mex, Fac Filusofia, Dist Fed, Mex, 61-90; teoria de la ideologia contemp, Esc Nac Antropologia, Dist Fed, Mex, 68-97; Arte mod America, Esc de Restauracion y Causervacion, Dist Fed, 70-80. *Bibliog:* Esther Civret (auth), Teoria y muralismo, Univ Aut Metrop, 84; Alicia Azuela (auth), Diego Rivera en Detroit, Inst Inv Esteticas, Univ Nac Autonoma Mex, 85; Raquel Bolauos (auth), Armar la nacion, Taller de Arte Ideologia, 98. *Mem:* Comt Mexicano de Hist de Art; Found Maria y Pablo O'Higgins; Taller de Arte e Ideologia; Proyecto Archiopielago, Baja, Calif. *Publ:* Coauth, Alfonso Michel, Inst Colimeuse de Cult, 97; Siqueiros Iconografia, Inst Nac de Bellas Artes, 97; Auth, Introducion al Neoliberalismo, Taller Art e Ideologia, 98; Adolfo Mexiac, libertad de expresior, Inst Nac de Bellas Artes, 98; coauth, Armar la nacion, Taller Art e Ideologia, 98. *Mailing Add:* Tezoquiqa 46 14090 DF Distrito Federal Mexico

HILD, NANCY
PAINTER
b Cincinnati, Ohio, Apr 7, 48. *Study:* Ind Univ, BFA, 70, MFA, 76. *Work:* Ind Standard Oil, Chicago; Sandoz Corp, Des Plaines, Ill; Tri-Star Med Serv, Houston; Ind Univ Fine Arts Dept, Bloomington. *Exhib:* Artists of Chicago & Vicinity, Art Inst Chicago, 77 & 81; John Yau Selects Portraits, Urban Inst Contemp Art, Grand Rapids, Mich, 89; Face to Face, Chicago Cult Ctr, Ill, 92; Latina/Americana: Fertile Ground, La Sala De Exposiciones, Cali, Columbia, 93; Pets: Artists & An Am Obsession, Charles A Wustum Mus Fine Arts, Racine, Wis, 93; Artemisia at Transmission, Transmission Gallery, Glasglow, Scotland, 94; Nancy Hild with Silvia Malagrino (with catalog), Catalyst Gallery, Belfast, Northern Ireland, 96; Sesquicentennial Celebration Faculty Exhib, Elvehjem Mus Art, Madison, Wisc, 98; The Nat Mus Women in the Arts, Ill Women Artists: The New Millennium, Washington and The Ill State Mus, Springfield, 2000; The Chicago Cult Ctr, 2001; Shanghai in the Eyes of World Artists, China, 2002; Casa de la Cultura Oaxaquena, Mexico, 2003; Gescheidle Gallery, 2005; Lidxi Guendabiaani Casa De La Cultura, Juchitán, Mex, 2005; Womanmade Gallery, Chicago, 2006. *Collection Arranged:* Mothers & Daughters, Julius Tobias, Artemisia Gallery, Chicago, 91-92; Jack and Jill, Womanmade Gallery, Chicago, 94. *Pos:* Vpres & grant dir, Artemisia Gallery, Chicago, 90-92. *Teaching:* Lectr & prof painting, Univ Wis, Madison, 98. *Awards:* Munic Art League Prize, Artists Chicago & Vicinity, Art Inst Chicago, 81; Arts Midwest General Support Award, Nat Endowment Arts, 91; Chicago Arts Int Award, Catalyst Art Belfast, 96. *Bibliog:* M Therese Southgate MD (auth), Nancy Hild, the cover, Jour Am Med Asn, 9/26/90; Janina Ciezadlo (auth), Nancy Hild: New signs of the feminine, Chicago Reader, 10/9/94; Ken Indermark (auth), Nancy Hild, Home Brew Video, Harold Washington Libr, 96; Ivy Sundell (auth), Living Artists, 2005; Gedardo Valdivieso Parada (auth), Nancy Hild Y Manuel Cabrera Aquí y Allá, Tiempo del Istmo, 5/20/2005. *Mem:* Nat Womens Caucus Arts; Chicago Artists' Coalition. *Media:* Acrylic. *Dealer:* Gescheidle Gallery 300 W Superior, Chicago, IL 60610. *Mailing Add:* 1834 W North Ave Chicago IL 60622-1312

HILDEBRAND, JUNE MARIANNE
PRINTMAKER, ILLUSTRATOR
b Eureka, Calif, Nov 2, 30. *Study:* Calif Col Arts & Crafts; Art Students League, scholar; Queens Col, BFA; Hochschule Bildende Kunste Berlin; Hunter Col, MA; Pratt Graphic Ctr. *Work:* Philadelphia Mus Art, Pa; Univ Wis-Madison; NY Pub Libr; Everson Mus Art; Univ Minn; Hunt Inst, Carnegie Mellon Univ. *Exhib:* Pratt Int Miniature Print Exhib, 66 & 68; Oneonta State Univ, 67; Montclair State Col, 68; Gotham Bk Mart, NY, 69; Pratt Inst, 79; and others. *Media:* Linoleum, Silkscreen. *Publ:* Illusr, Eight Poems by Michael Benedikt, Assoc Am Artists, 65; contribr, graphics, Artists Proof Mag, 66 & 67; Wild Fruits and Flowers, 80 & A Book of Flowers, 82, Claremount Press; Four Poems by Kirby Congdon, Ctr Book Arts, 86. *Mailing Add:* 229 E 12th St Apt 2 New York NY 10003

HILDRETH, JOSEPH ALAN
PRINTMAKER, PAINTER
b Bowling Green, Ky, Sept 2, 47. *Study:* Western Ky Univ, BFA, 69; Pratt Inst, with Walter Rogalski, MFA, 71. *Work:* Mint Mus, Charlotte, NC; Eric Fine Arts Ctr, Pa; State Univ NY Col, Potsdam. *Exhib:* Eight Upstate, Artists' Space Gallery, NY, 74; Nat Print Exhib, Second St Gallery, Charlottesville, Va, 76; 16th Bradley Nat Print Exhib, Bradley Univ, Peoria, Ill, 77; NY Landscape, Plaza Gallery, Albany, 81; 11th Nat Print & Drawing Exhib, Minot State Col, NDak, 82; and many others. *Pos:* Chmn art dept, State Univ NY, Potsdam, 86-94, prof printmaking, 94-. *Teaching:* Assoc prof printmaking, State Univ NY Col Potsdam, 71-. *Awards:* Carnegie Found Grant, 81; NY State Coun Arts Grant, 82. *Media:* Mixed. *Publ:* Auth, Contemporary Realism (catalog essay), 82. *Mailing Add:* Pierpoint Ave Dept Art State Univ Potsdam Potsdam NY 13676

HILL, CHARLES CHRISTOPHER
COLLAGE ARTIST, PAINTER
b Greensburg, Pa, Mar 4, 1948. *Study:* E Los Angeles Col, AA(art), 68; Univ Calif, Irvine, BA, 70, MFA 73. *Work:* Gugenheim Mus, NY,; Metrop Mus Art, NY; Mus Nat d'Art Moderne, Ctr George Pompidou, Paris; Los Angeles Co Mus Art, Calif; Honolulu Acad Art, Hawaii. *Comn:* Painting, Northrup, El Segundo, Calif, 80; Drawings, Hilton Hotels, Narita, Japan 87. *Exhib:* Market St Prog, Oakland Mus Art, Calif 73; Los Angeles Artists, Mus Mod Art, NY, 76; Eighth Int Painting Festival, Cagnessur Mer, France, 77; Matter-Meaning-Memory, Honolulu Acad Art, Hawaii, 80; One-person exhibs, Cirrus Gallery, Los Angeles, 80, 82-84 & 87-88, Simon Lowinsky Gallery, San Francisco, 81, Galerie Maurer, Zurich, 81 & 82, Baudoin Lebon, Paris, 82 & 85, Van Straaten Gallery, Chicago, 83, DBR Gallery, Cleveland, 84, Galleria del Cavallino, Venice, 85 & Ctr d'Action Culturelle de St-Brieuc, France, 87. *Teaching:* Vis instr, Art Ctr Col Design, 78-79; Univ Calif, Los Angeles, 80-81. *Awards:* Young Talent Award, Los Angeles Co Mus Art, 76; Grant, Slides, Nat Endowment Arts, 76; Special Mention, Modern Trends, City of Cagnes sur Mer, France, 76. *Bibliog:* Deborah Irmas (auth), Charles Hill, Carte d'Arte, Messina, Italy, 11/87; Gilbert Lascault (auth), Le Bamboo, Bambouserie de Prafrance, 8/88; Constance Glenn (auth), New Venice vernacular, Angeles Mag, 11/88. *Media:* Watercolor & Paper. *Dealer:* Cirrus Gallery 520 S Alameda Los Angeles CA 90291. *Mailing Add:* 1158 Palms Blvd Venice CA 90291-3525

HILL, DANIEL G
PAINTER
b Providence, RI, Apr 6, 56. *Study:* Brown Univ, Providence, RI, BA, 79; Hunter Col, City Univ New York, MFA, 85. *Work:* Prudential Insurance Co Am; Parasol Press, Ltd; and other pvt collections. *Exhib:* Solo exhibs, Thomas Hunter Gallery, NY, 84 & Koussevitzky Gallery, Berkshire Community Col, Pittsfield, Mass, 88; Small Works V, Parsons Sch Design, NY, 96; Art Walk NY, Puck Bldg, NY, 96; Small Works Benefit, PS 122 Gallery, NY, 96; 1: One, Herter Art Gallery, Univ Mass, 97. *Teaching:* Asst prof art, Col Holy Cross, Worcester, Mass, 85-87; lectr visual arts, Princeton Univ, 90; adj lectr, Hunter Col, New York, 87-91, adj asst prof, 91-; adj fac, Parsons Sch Design, 95-. *Awards:* Batchelor (Ford) Summer Fac Fel, Col Holy Cross, Worcester, Mass, 86; Artist Grant, Artists Space, New York, 90; Fel, Nat Endowment Arts, 93-94. *Mailing Add:* 219 E Second St No 2D New York NY 10009

HILL, DRAPER
EDITORIAL CARTOONIST, HISTORIAN
b Boston, Mass, July 1, 35. *Study:* Harvard Col, BA(magna cum laude), 57; Slade Sch Fine Arts, London, Eng, 60-63. *Work:* Wiggin Gallery, Boston Pub Libr; Univ Va; Lyndon B Johnson Libr, Austin; Nat Gallery Can, Ottawa; Detroit Inst Arts. *Exhib:* Int Salon de Caricature, Montreal, PQ, 66-86; Image of Am in Caricature and Cartoon, Amon Carter Mus, Ft Worth, 75; Am Presidency in Political Cartoons, Univ Art Mus, Berkeley, 75-76; retrospective, Political Asylum, Art Gallery of Windsor, Ontario, Can, 85-86; A Brush with Satire, Detroit Hist Mus, 96; and others. *Collection Arranged:* Cartoon and Caricature from Hogarth to Hoffnung, 62 & James Gillray 1756-1815, 67, Arts Coun Gt Brit; exhib on hist caricature, Boston Pub Libr, 64, 66 & 70. *Pos:* Ed cartoonist, Worcester Telegram, Mass, 64-71, Com Appeal, Memphis, Tenn, 71-76 & Detroit News, 76-; contrib ed, Eighteenth Century Life, Williamsburg, Va, 80-88; ed bd mem, Inks Cartoon & Comic Art Studios, Columbus, Ohio, 93-. *Teaching:* Instr life drawing, Sch Worcester Art Mus, 67-71; lectr, Amon Carter Mus, Ft Worth, Tex, 75 & Yale Ctr for British Art, New Haven, Conn, 84. *Awards:* Guggenheim Fel, 83-84; Thomas Nast Prize, Landau, Ger, 90. *Bibliog:* Lydel Sims (auth), article, Cartoonist Profiles, 3/75; Guy Northrop (auth), The Editorial Art of Draper Hill, Brooks Gallery, Memphis, 75; Alan Westin (auth), Getting Angry Six Times a Week, Beacon Press, Boston, 79. *Mem:* Asn Am Ed Cartoonists (vpres & dir, 70-75, pres, 75-76). *Collection:* Caricature and cartooning, with particular emphasis on eighteenth and nineteenth century English satire. *Publ:* Illingworth on Target, 70; co-illusr, The Decline and Fall of the Gibbon, 74; auth, The Satirical Etchings of James Gillray, 76; three collections of cartoons about Detroit's Mayor Coleman Young, 77, 82 & 86; auth, Cartoons and Caricatures, Vol III, Time-Life Encycl of Collectibles, 78; and others. *Mailing Add:* c/o Detroit News 615 W Lafayette Blvd Detroit MI 48226

HILL, ED(WARD) J See Manual, Ed Hill & Suzanne Bloom

HILL, GARY
VIDEO ARTIST
b Santa Monica, Calif, Apr 4, 51. *Study:* Art Students League, Woodstock, 69. *Comn:* Video installation, Musee Nat d' Art Moderne, Centre Georges Pompidou, Paris, 88. *Exhib:* Solo exhibs, Mus Mod Art, NY, 80 & 90, Whitney Mus Am Art, NY, 83, Galerie des Archives, Paris, 90 & 91, Watari Mus Contemp Art, Tokyo, Japan, 92, Mus Mod Art, Oxford, Eng, 93, Mus Contemp Art, Los Angeles, 94, Mus Contemp Art, Chicago, 94, Inst Contemp Art, Philadelphia, 96, Whitney Mus Art, NY, 98-99, Language Willing, Boise Art Mus, Ariz State Univ Art Mus, Northwest Mus of Art and Cult, Art Gallery of Nova scotia, Can, Salt Lake Art Ctr, 2002-, Kunstmuseum Wolfsburg, Germ, 2002 & 03; retrospectives, Am Ctr, Paris, 83, Whitney Mus Am Art, NY, 86, St Gervais, Geneva, 2nd Seminar on Int Video, 87, ELAC Art Contemporain, Lyon, France, 88; Biennial Exhibition, Whitney Mus Am Art, 91 & 93; Light Into Art,

Contemp Arts Ctr, Cincinnati, Ohio, 94; Facts and Figures, Lannan Found, Los Angeles, 94; Multiplas Dimensoes, Centro Cultural de Belem, Lisbon, Portugal, 94; Beeld, Mus van Hedendaagse Kunst, Ghent, Belg, 94; Video Spaces, Mus Mod Art, NY, 95; Being and Time: The Emergence of Video Projection, Albright-Knox Art Gallery, Buffalo, 96; MOMA 2000, Mus of Modern Art, NY, 99-2000; Seeing Time: Selections from the Pamela and Richard Kramlich Collection of Media Art, San Francisco Mus of Art, 99-2000; The Am Century: Art & Cult Part II 1950-2000, Whitney Mus of Am Art, NY, 99-2000; Between Cinema and a Hard Place, Tate Modern, London, 2000; 46th Biennial Exhib: Media/Metaphor, The Corcoran Gallery of Art, Washington, 2000-01; and many others. *Pos:* Founder & dir, Open Studio Video, Tarrytown, NY, 77-79; artist-in-residence, Experimental Television Ctr, Binghamton, NY, 75-77, Portable Channel, Rochester, NY, 78, Sony Corp, Hon Atsugi, Japan, 85, Chicago Art Inst, 86, Calif Inst Arts, Valencia, 87 & Hopital Ephemere, Paris, 91, Capp St Project, San Francisco, 98. *Teaching:* Vis assoc prof, Ctr Media, State Univ NY, Buffalo, 79-80; vis prof art, Bard Col, Annandale-on-Hudson, NY, 83; art fac, Cornish Col Arts, Seattle, Wash, 85-92. *Awards:* First Prize, Int Asn Art Critics (AICA), 95; Artist Award for Distinguished Body of Work, Col Art Asn, NY, 96; MacArthur Found Fel, 98; Joseph H Hazen Rome Prize Fel, Am Acad in Rome, 2000-01; Kurt Schwitters Award, 2000; Joseph H Hazen Rome Prize Fel, Am Acad, Rome, 2000 & 01, Skowhegan Medal for Video Installation, 2003, Artist Trust, wash State Art Comn Fel, 2003. *Bibliog:* Ruth Barter (auth), Doubletake, Art Monthly, 4/92; Bruce Barcott (auth), Gary Hill, New Art Examiner, 5/93; Deloris Tarzan Ament, Artist uses videos to tease viewers, Seattle Times, 2/22/93. *Publ:* Auth, Primarily Speaking, 1981-83, Whitney Mus Am Art, 83; Primarily Speaking, Communications, 88; And if the Right Hand did not Know What the Left Hand is Doing, Illuminating Video, 90; Unspeakable Images, Camera Obscura, 91. *Mailing Add:* c/o Donald Young Gallery 933 W Washington Blvd Chicago IL 60607

HILL, JAMES BERRY
DEALER
b New York, NY, June 24, 45. *Study:* Cornell Univ, AB, 67. *Collection Arranged:* Coggins Collection, Selections from the Robert P Coggins Collection of American Painting, 76. *Pos:* Co-dir, Berry-Hill Galleries, Inc, 67-. *Awards:* Presidential Appointment (2 terms), Cult Property Adv Comt, Washington, DC. *Mem:* Nat Arts Club; Appraisers Asn Am; Artists Fel; Art Dealers Asn Am. *Specialty:* American art of the nineteenth and early twentieth century; China trade paintings. *Mailing Add:* Berry-Hill Galleries 11 E 70th St New York NY 10021

HILL, J(AMES) TOMILSON
COLLECTOR
b Westbury, New York, May 24, 48. *Study:* Harvard College, BA, 70; Harvard Bus Sch, MBA, 73. *Pos:* Vpres, mergers and acquisitions 1st Boston Corp, New York City, 73-79; sr Vpres, Smith Barney, Harris Upham & Co Inc, 79-82; managing dir, dir mergers and acquisitions, co-head investment banking div. Shearson Lehman Brothers Inc, 82-90; vchmn, co-chief exec officer Lehman Brothers, 90-93; also bd dir Shearson Lehman Brothers Holdings, Inc, co-pres, co-chief operating officer, 93; co-chief exec officer Lehman Brothers, 93, Shearson Lehman Brothers, 93, SLB Asset Mgt, 93; vchmn, mem investment and mgt comt Blackstone Group, New York City, 93-; pres, Chief Exec Officer, Blackstone Alternative Asset Mgt, 95-; bd dirs, Allied Waste. *Awards:* Named one of 200 Top Collectors, ARTnews magazine, 2003-06. *Mem:* Council Foreign Relations (chmn investment subcom of financial and budget committee), Piping Rock Club, Meadow Brook Club, Links Club, River Club, Knickerbocker Club. *Collection:* Postwar A. & European Art. *Publ:* Contribr articles to prof publs. *Mailing Add:* Blackstone Group 345 Park Ave Ste New York NY 10154-0004

HILL, JANINE
COLLECTOR
Pos: Assoc Sullivan & Cromwell; vpres corp financial dept, Salomon Brothers; asst treas, Time Inc; deputy dir studies admin, Coun For Relations, New York City; bd advs, Duke Univ Nasher Mus Art; mem bd Am friends, Louvre. *Awards:* Named one of Top 200 Collectors, ARTnews mag, 2003-06. *Mailing Add:* Coun For Relations Harold Pratt House 58 E 68th St New York NY 10021

HILL, JOHN CONNER
ART DEALER, DESIGNER
b Philadelphia, Pa, Feb 17, 45. *Study:* Pratt Inst, BID, 68; Cosanti Found, Paradise Valley, Ariz, with Paolo Soleri, 72-76. *Exhib:* Ariz Photog Biennial, Phoenix Art Mus, 69; Southwest Biennial, Int Folk Art Mus, Santa Fe, NMex, 70, NMex Biennial, 71; Tucson Festival Crafts Exhib, Tucson Mus, Ariz, 77; Ariz Textile Exhib, Matthews Ctr, Ariz State Univ, Tempe, 77. *Pos:* Bronze sculpture casting, Cosanti Found, 74-76; publ-owner, Kokopelli Press, Phoenix, 76-90; Gallery owner, Scottsdale, 89-; adv bd mem, Ariz State Univ Art Mus. *Teaching:* Instr art, Rough Rock Demonstration Sch, Navajo Nation, Ariz, 68-70. *Awards:* Third Award, Ariz Textile Exhib, Scottsdale Ctr for the Arts, 76. *Mem:* Charter mem Antique Tribal Art Dealers Asn. *Specialty:* Early American Indian art, American folk art. *Dealer:* John C Hill Antique Indian Art Gallery 6962 First Ave Scottsdale AZ 85251. *Mailing Add:* 6962 E First Ave Scottsdale AZ 85251

HILL, MEGAN LLOYD See Romero, Megan H

HILL, PETER
PAINTER, EDUCATOR
b Detroit, Mich, Nov 29, 33. *Study:* Albion Col, AB, 56; Cranbrook Acad Art, Bloomfield Hills, Mich, MFA, 58. *Work:* Joslyn Art Mus, Omaha, Nebr; Sheldon Mem Gallery, Lincoln, Nebr; Springfield Art Mus, Mo; Sioux City Art Ctr, Iowa; Spiva Art Gallery, Joplin, Mo. *Exhib:* Springfield Art Mus Ann, Mo, 70 & 74; Midwest Biennial, Joslyn Art Mus, 72, 74, 78, 82 & 84; Colo-Nebr Exchange Exhib, Denver, 73; one-man show, Sheldon Mem Art Gallery, Lincoln, Nebr, 78; Am Art, Pillsbury Co, Minneapolis, 81; Watercolor Now, Springfield Art Mus, Mo, 87; and others. *Teaching:* From instr to chmn dept, Univ Nebr, Omaha, 58-99. *Awards:* Ann Exhib Purchase Awards, Springfield Art Mus, 63 & 74; Best Painting, Joslyn Mus, 78 & 82; Purchase Award, Nat Competitive Exhib, Peru State Col, Nebr, 89. *Mem:* Watercolor USA Honor Soc. *Media:* Acrylic, Oil, Watercolor. *Dealer:* Adam Whitney Gallery Omaha NE 68102; Haydon Art Gallery Lincoln NE 68508. *Mailing Add:* 11734 Shirley St Omaha NE 68144-2914

HILL, ROBYN LESLEY
PAINTER, DESIGNER
b Sydney, New South Wales, Australia, Apr 28, 42. *Study:* Nat Art Sch, Sydney, Australia, ASTC, 62; studied with Edward Betts, Nita Engle & Fred Leach in USA. *Work:* Key West Mus, Fla; Springfield Mus Art, Utah; Palm Springs Desert Mus, Calif; Nat Arts Club, NY; Canton Art Inst, Ohio; Massillon Mus Invitational, Ohio. *Exhib:* Am Watercolor Soc Traveling Exhib, Salmagundi Club, NY; Nat Watercolor Soc Traveling Exhib, Palm Springs Desert Mus, Calif; Catherine Lorillard Wolfe Nat Exhib, Nat Arts Club, NY; Watercolor USA, Springfield Art Mus, Mo; solo exhib, Moments in Nature, Wagner Gallery, Sydney, Australia; Massilon Mus Invitational, Ohio, 87; Adirondacks Nat Show, NY. *Pos:* Art dir, Am Greetings, (1st woman in marketing) Cleveland; sr prog dir, Those Characters from Cleveland, Ohio. *Teaching:* Art mistress, Sydney Church of Eng Girls Grammar Sch, Redlands, Sydney, Australia, 62-65. *Awards:* Humana Award, Blue Grass Biennial, Humana Inc; Southern Ohio Bank Award, Ohio Watercolor Soc; Springfield Art Mus Award, Watercolor USA. *Mem:* Watercolor USA; Nat Watercolor Soc; Ohio Watercolor Soc; N Coast Collage Soc; Nat Mus Women in Arts. *Media:* Watercolor, Watermedia. *Publ:* contribr, The Best of Flower Painting, N Light Bks; article, Palette Talk, No 75 Grumbacher; Artists directory, Portfolio 83, Cleveland, Ohio. *Dealer:* A Gallery West 20370 Center Ridge Rd Rocky River OH 44116. *Mailing Add:* 27004 Lakeshore Blvd Euclid OH 44132-1242

HILLER, BETTY R
CONSULTANT, APPRAISER
b El Paso, Tex, Sept 25, 25. *Study:* Univ Tex, El Paso; Univ NMex; Univ Southern Calif, BFA, 45; Univ Nebr, Omaha; Creighton Univ. *Collection Arranged:* Arthur Andersen Co, Omaha, Nebr; Brody Col African Art, Univ Nebr, Omaha, 73; Robert Nelson Prints; Warrington Colescott Prints, 70's; and others. *Pos:* Ed arts, Spectrum Page, Sun Newspaper, 68-69; gallery dir, Creighton Univ, Omaha, 68-70; original developer, Children's Mus of Omaha, 75, first mus pres, 77-78; gallery dir, Univ Nebr, Omaha, 76; dir & mgr gallery, Univ Nebr, Omaha, 76-78. *Awards:* Special Achievement Award, Am Soc Appraisers, 93. *Bibliog:* Beth Weiver (auth), Rancho Bernardo J; Jimmy Thornton (auth), San Diego Union; Bernardo News, 93. *Mem:* Am Soc Appraisers (sr mem). *Interests:* 19th, 20th Century Am and European Art; Art travel and art appraising. *Collection:* Pre Columbian, Contemp and Mod Am and European. *Mailing Add:* 3634 Seventh Ave 4A San Diego CA 92103

HILLER, SUSAN
CONCEPTUAL ARTIST
b Tallahassee, FL, Mar 7, 40. *Study:* Smith Col, BA, 1961; Tulane Univ, MA, 1965; Dartington Col Arts, Eng, Hon Fel, 1998. *Exhib:* Solo shows in London, Toronto, Zurich, Warsaw, NY & Paris; retrospective survey exhib, Inst Contemp Art, London, 86 & Tate Gallery, Liverpool, 96; Rites of Passage, Tate Gallery, London, 95; Sydney Biennale, 96; Now/Here, La Mus, Humbleback, 97; Out of Actions, Mus Contemp Art, Los Angeles, 98; The Muse is the Mus, Mus Mod Art, NY, 99. *Teaching:* Slade Sch Art, London, 82-90; prof fine art, Sch Art & Design, Univ Ulster, Belfast, 91-97; vis prof, Univ Calif, Los Angeles, currently; prof contemp art, Univ Newcastle, 1998-2004. *Awards:* Gulbenkenian Found Visual Artist's Award, 76 & 77; Nat Endowment Arts, 82; Guggenheim Fel, 98. *Mailing Add:* 83 Loudon Rd London NW8 0DL England United Kingdom

HILLIS, RICHARD K
PAINTER, PRINTMAKER
b Cincinnati, Ohio, Oct 3, 36. *Study:* Ohio Univ, BFA, 60, MFA, 62, Carnegie Mellon Univ, DA (Dr Arts), 73, San Francisco Art Inst, 81-83; Burne Hogart Anat Workshop, 93; Burt Silverman Master Class, 94; Portrait Inst Am, New York, 96; David Leffel Master Class, 99; Raymond Kinstler Master Class, 2002. *Work:* Muscarelle Mus Art, Col William & Mary, Williamsburg, Va; Hoyt Inst Fine Arts, New Castle, Pa; Ark Art Ctr, Little Rock; Glendale Publ Libr, Ariz; Southwest Airlines; Gammage & Burnham Law Firm, Phoenix, Ariz. *Comn:* comn numerous portraits. *Exhib:* 49th Ann Midyear Exhib, Butler Inst Am Art, Youngstown, Ohio, 84; Art USA Exhib, Western Colo Ctr Arts, Grand Junction, 86; 64th April Salon, Springville Art Mus, Utah, 88; Am Drawing Biennial, Muscarelle Mus Art, Va, 88; Los Angeles Nat Watercolor Exhib, 91; 35th Chataqua Nat, 92; West Valley Art Mus, Sun City, Ariz, 99; Phoenix Col, 2000; and others. *Pos:* founder, chair Peoria Arts Comn, 90. *Teaching:* Asst prof art, Kent State Univ, Ohio, 69-73; assoc prof, Tex Tech Univ, Lubbock, 73-74; prof, Glendale Col, Ariz, 82-2003, prof emeritus, 2003-. *Awards:* Cash Award 11th Ann Nat Realist Exhib, 99; Best of Show 37th Ann Glendale Art Exhib, 2000; First Prize Best of Show, Ariz State Fair Art Exhiv, 2002; Best of Show, Ariz State Fair, 03; Best of Show, Peoria Art Exhib, 05. *Mem:* Col Art Asn Am; Am Asn Univ Professors. *Media:* Oil. *Interests:* etching & tennis. *Publ:* Auth, Line Shape & Contrast, Sch Arts Mag, 88; Hooked on Colored Pencils, Sch Arts, 91; Drawing on Gray Toned Paper, Sch Arts, 95; Shape Self Esteem & the Self Portrait, Sch Arts, 96; Accountability in Art, Sch Arts, 98; A Simple Motif for Exploration of Line, Weight & Value, Sch Arts, 01; Best of Sketching & Drwaing, 98. *Mailing Add:* 6741 W Cholla Peoria AZ 85345

HILLMAN, ARTHUR STANLEY
GRAPHIC ARTIST, EDUCATOR
b Brooklyn, NY, Feb 21, 45. *Study:* Philadelphia Col Art, with Jerome Kaplan & Benton Spruance, BFA; Univ Mass, Amherst, MFA. *Work:* Libr Congress, Washington, DC; Northern Ill Univ. *Exhib:* Prize Winning Am Prints, 69 & 4th Int Miniature Print Exhib, 71, Pratt Graphics Ctr, NY; one-man shows, Philadelphia Art Alliance, 70, Alfred Univ, Suny, 77, Simon's Rock Col, 83, 84, 90, 02, 93, 95, 97, 2000, 02 & 05; Williams Col Mus Art, 76; 29th Nat Print Exhib, Hunterdon Art Ctr, NJ, 85; 16th Nat Works on Paper, Minot State Col, NDak, 86; Northern Nat, Nicolet Col, 89; group shows incl: Welles Gallery, 94, Spazi Contemp Art, 94 & 96, Berkshire Community Col, 97, Albany Ctr Galleries, 99, The Berkshire Mus, 2005. *Teaching:* Instr & asst prof printmaking & chmn dept, Mass Col Art, Boston, 68-74; prof printmaking, design & photog, Simon's Rock Col, Great Barrington, Mass, 74-, chmn arts div, 81-84 & 89-92, chmn visual arts prog, 87-89. *Awards:* Univ Mass Fel, 67; Pennell Fund Purchase Award, Libr Cong, 69; Northern Ill Univ Purchase Award, 70. *Mem:* Col Art Asn Am; Philadelphia Print Club; Photog Resource Ctr, Boston Univ. *Media:* Digital photography. *Collection:* Work in collections of library of congress; Northern Illinois Univ; Philadelphia Col Art; Simmons Col, Boston Mass; Stanislaus State Col, Turlock, Calif

HILLS, PATRICIA
HISTORIAN, CURATOR
b Baraboo, Wis, Jan 31, 36. *Study:* Stanford Univ, BA, 57; Hunter Col, City Univ New York, MA, 68; NY Univ Inst Fine Arts, PhD, 73. *Collection Arranged:* Eastman Johnson (auth, catalog), Clarkson-Potter, 72; The American Frontier: Images and Myths (auth, catalog), 73, Turn-of-the-Century America: Paintings, Graphics, Photographs (auth, catalog), 77 & The Figurative Tradition and the Whitney Museum (coauth, catalog), 80, Whitney Mus Am Art; The Painter's America: Rural and Urban Life, 1810-1910 (auth, catalog), Praeger, 74; John Singer Sargent (cur, auth, catalog), Abrams, 86; Social Concern and Urban Realism: American Painting of the 1930s (auth catalog), Boston Univ Art Gallery, 83; Eastman Johnson: Painting America (co-auth, catalog), Rizzoli, 99; Syncopated Rhythms: 20th Century African Am Art from the George & Joyce Wein Collection, Boston Univ Art Gallery, 2005. *Pos:* Assoc cur, Whitney Mus Am Art, 72-74, adj cur, 74-87; Dir, Boston Univ Art Gallery, 80-89. *Teaching:* Assoc prof, York Col, City Univ New York, 74-78; assoc prof Am painting, Boston Univ, 78-88, prof, 88-. *Awards:* Fel, Guggenheim, 82 & Nat Endowment Humanities, 95; Mid-Career Award, Women's Caucus for Art, 87; W E B DuBois Inst, Harvard Univ, 91-92 & 2006-07; Fel, Gilder Lehrman Inst of Am Hist, 2005; Fel, Smithsonian Am Art Mus, 2005-06; Fel, Georgia O'Keeffe Mus Research Ctr, 2006. *Mem:* Col Art Asn; Women's Caucus for Art; Am Studies Asn; AAM. *Res:* American painting from Civil War to present, particularly figurative painting; art & politics; African-American art. *Publ:* Alice Neel, Abrams, 83; Stuart Davis, Abrams, 95; Modern Art in the USA: Issues and Controversies of the 20th Century, Prentice Hall, 2001; May Stevens, Pomegranate, 2005. *Mailing Add:* Dept Art Hist Boston Univ 725 Commonwealth Ave Boston MA 02215

HILLSMITH, FANNIE
PAINTER - ACYLIC, OIL
b Boston, Mass, Mar 13, 11. *Study:* Boston Mus Fine Arts Sch; Art Students League, with Alexander Brook, Kuniyoshi, Zorach & Sloan; Atelier 17, with Stanley Hayter. *Work:* Mus Mod Art, NY; Boston Mus Fine Arts; Currier Gallery Art, Manchester, NH; Fogg Mus Art, Cambridge, Mass; Metrop Mus Art, NY; and others. *Exhib:* Boston Arts Festival, 50-54 & 56-61; Cornell Univ, 64; one-man retrospective, Brockton Mus, Mass, 71, Bristol Mus, RI, 72 & Currier Gallery Art, Manchester, 87; Brattleboro Mus, 74; group show, Am Cubism, Sidney Deutsch Gallery, NY, 92; Susan Teller Gallery, NY, 94, 97, 2001 & 2003. *Teaching:* Vis critic, Black Mountain Col, 45 & Cornell Univ, 63-64. *Awards:* Alumni Traveling Scholar, Boston Mus Fine Arts Sch, 58; Tour Gallery Award, 64; Berkshire Mus Award, 64; and others. *Mem:* Artists Equity. *Publ:* Auth & illusr, The Ups and Downs of Needlepoint, Barnes, 76; two children's books. *Dealer:* Susan Taller Gallery 568 Broadway Rm 405A NY NY 10012

HILSON, DOUGLAS
PAINTER, EDUCATOR
b Flint, Mich, Dec 7, 41. *Study:* Cranbrook Acad Art, Bloomfield Hills, Mich, BFA; Univ Wash, MFA. *Work:* Indianapolis Mus Art; Ill Art Mus, Springfield, DeWaters Art Inst, Flint, Mich; Decatur Art Mus, Ill; Western Mich Univ Art Mus, Kalamazoo. *Comn:* 5 works reproduced for 298 rooms for Charles Hotel, Cambridge, Mass, 2006. *Exhib:* One-person shows, Bernice Steinbaum Gallery, NY, 83 & 85, Donahue/Sosinski Gallery, NY, 99, 206 drawings, Del Art Ctr, NY, 2005; New Still Life, Borgenicht Gallery, NY, 90; Artist's Space, New York City, 92-; Rosenberg Gallery, Hempstead, NY, 96; 10 Yr Retrospective, Bradford Col, Mass, 97-98. *Pos:* Chair, Dept Fine Arts, Art Hist, & Grad Humanities, Hofstra Univ, Hempstead, NY. *Teaching:* Prof painting & dir grad painting prog, Univ Ill, Champaign, 65-; vis prof, Pratt Inst, 81-; prof art, Hofstra Univ, 86-. *Awards:* First Prize, Nat Works Art on Paper, 76; Purchase Award, 29th Ill Invitational, Ill Art Mus Permanent Collection, 76; Ctr Advanced Study, 73-74. *Bibliog:* Peter Plagens (auth), catalog essay. *Media:* Oil, Acrylic. *Mailing Add:* 77 Pearl St Apt 2A New York NY 10004-2613

HILTON, ALISON
HISTORIAN, EDUCATOR
b Cedar Rapids, Iowa, Aug 2, 47. *Study:* Vassar Col, BA, 70; Columbia Univ, MA, 72, PhD, 79. *Pos:* chair, Dept of Art, Music & Theater, Georgetown Univ, Washington DC, 84-86, 00-. *Teaching:* vis asst prof art hist, Ind Univ, Bloomington, 76-79; asst to assoc prof art hist, Wayne State, Detroit, Mich, 79-83; Wright Family Distinguished prof art hist, Georgetown Univ, Washington, DC, 83-00. *Awards:* Woodrow Wilson Fel, 70; Int Res & Exchange Fel, 74-75, 82 & 93. *Mem:* Col Art Asn (bd dir, 2000-02); Soc Historians of Russ & E Europ Art (bd mem, 99-02); Am Asn for Advan of Slavic Studies; Assoc Hist of 19th Century Art. *Res:* Russian & Soviet Art; 19th - 20th century European & American art history. *Publ:* contribr, New Art from the Soviet Union, Acropolis, 78; auth & ed, Emile Zola and the Arts, Georgetown Univ Press, 86; auth, The Exhibition of Experiment, Art Bulletin, 88, Kazimir Mazevich, Rizzoli, 92 & Russian Folk Art, Ind Univ Press, 95. *Mailing Add:* Dept of Art Music and Theater Georgetown Univ Washington DC 20057

HILTY, THOMAS R
GRAPHIC ARTIST, PAINTER
b Gary, Ind, May 29, 43. *Study:* Ind Univ; Western State Col, Colo, BFA, 65; Univ NMex; Bowling Green State Univ, MFA, 68. *Work:* Dayton Art Inst, Ohio; Toledo Mus Art, Ohio; Omni Marketing Inc, Chicago; IBM Corp; Toledo Trust Corp. *Comn:* Frames of Reference, Boston New TV Wrokshop, 79-80; Musical Arts Ctr, Bowling Green State Univ, 80; J Barrett Galleries, Toledo, 82; R Valicenti Design, Chicago, 83; Riverside Hosp, Toledo, 86. *Exhib:* Ankrum Gallery, Los Angeles, 83; US Nat Fine Arts Competition & Int Exhib, 84; 20th Cent Am Drawing, Chicago, 84; Rosenthal Gallery, Chicago, 84 & 86; and others. *Pos:* Dir, Sch Art, Bowling Green State Univ, 86-94; bd dir, Nat Asn Schs Art & Design, 93-95 & Studio Art Ctrs Int, 93-. *Teaching:* Prof art, drawing & painting, Bowling Green State Univ, 68-. *Awards:* Purchase Awards, All Ohio Exhib, Ohio Arts Coun, 72, All Ohio Exhib, Dayton Art Inst, 76, 80 & 81 & Toledo Area Artists Exhib, Toledo Mus, 80, 81, 82, 84 & 85. *Bibliog:* Louise Bruner (auth), Thomas Hilty, Am Artist, 80. *Mem:* Nat Asn Schs Art & Design. *Media:* Graphite, Charcoal; Pastels, Conte. *Publ:* Auth, article, Art News, 6/83. *Dealer:* Miller Gallery 2715 Erie Ave Cincinnati OH; Robert L Kidd Assoc Inc 107 Townsend St Birmingham MI 48011. *Mailing Add:* 21 Parkwood Dr Bowling Green OH 43402-3644

HIMMELFARB, JOHN DAVID
PAINTER, GRAPHIC ARTIST
b Chicago, Ill, June 3, 46. *Study:* Harvard Univ, BA, 68, MAT, 70. *Work:* Art Inst Chicago; Nat Mus Am Art, Smithsonian Inst, Washington, DC; Musee Nat d'Art Moderne Centre George Pompidou, Paris, France; The British Mus, London; Brooklyn Mus. *Comn:* Ceramic tile mural, Omaha Pub Schs, Nebr, 92, Univ of Nebr, Lincoln, 2003; Ceramic Tile Mural Chicago Transit, Author, 2004; Painting Delta Airlines Terminal Logan Boston, 2005. *Exhib:* Am Drawings in Black and White: 1970-1980, 80, Monumental Drawings: 20 Contemp Americans, 86, Brooklyn Mus, NY; Works on Paper, 78, Prizewinners Revisited, 79, Prints and Multiples, 81, 81st Chicago and Vicinity Show, 85, Art Inst Chicago; Large Drawings & Objects, Ark Art Ctr, 96; Jean Albano Gallery, Chicago, 96, 98 & 2000, 2002, 2005; Second Sight: Printmaking in Chicago 1935-95, Block Gallery, Northwestern Univ, Evanston, Ill, 96; Cultured Pearl, Metrop Mus Seoul, Korea, 96; and others; solo exhib, Kalamazoo Inst Arts, 89, Huntington Mus Art, WVa, 90, Chicago Cult Ctr, Ill, 96, Ctr for Contemp Art (COLA), 2001. *Pos:* Artist. *Teaching:* Vis artist, New Master Workshop, Huntington, Mus Art, WVa, 90, Miami Univ, Oxford, Ohio, 90, Kalamazoo Inst Art, 90 & Indiana Univ, Northwest, Gary, 92. *Awards:* Nat Endowment Arts, 82 & 85; Chicago Artist Abroad, 89; Ill Arts Coun, 86, 2003; Pollock, Krasner, 86, 2002. *Bibliog:* Alan Artner (auth), Galleries, Chicago Tribune, 1/25/96; Barbara Buchholz (auth), Gallery Scene, Chicago Tribune, 1/23/96 & 9/27/96; John Brunetti (auth), John Himmelfarb at Jean Albano Gallery (rev), New Art Examiner, 1/97; Alan Artiner (auth) Galleries, Chicago Tribune 2/25/2005; Art Galleries Art Scene John Himmel Farbic, One Man reanaissance (auth) Lisa Stein Chicago Tribune, 3/11/2005. *Mem:* Chicago Artist Coalition; Arts Club Chicago. *Media:* Acrylic. *Publ:* The Prints of John Himmelfarb, Hudson Hills Press, 2006. *Dealer:* Gallery 72 2709 Leavenworth Omaha NE 68105; William Havv Gallery, 1040 Cherokee St, Denver, Colo; Phyllis Stigliano Gallery 62 8th Ave, Brooklyn, NY, 11217. *Mailing Add:* 2400 S Oakley 2R Chicago IL 60608

HINDES, CHUCK (CHARLES) AUSTIN
CERAMIST, EDUCATOR
b Muskegon, Mich, May 30, 42. *Study:* Univ Ill, Urbana-Champaign, BFA(crafts), 66; RI Sch Design, MFA(ceramics), 68. *Work:* St Louis Mus Art; Everson Mus Art. *Exhib:* Teapots, De Pauw Univ, Greencastle, Ind, 91; Redefining Clay, St Louis, Mo, 91; Contemp Views: Teapots, Pro-Art Gallery, St Louis, Mo, 92; Teapot Exhibition, Octagon Art Ctr, Ames, 92; One on One, group exhib, Northwest Craft Ctr, Seattle, Wash, 92; and others. *Teaching:* Instr ceramics, Univ Fla, Gainesville, 69-72; adj prof, RI Sch Design, 72-73; from asst prof to prof, Univ Iowa, Iowa City, 73-. *Awards:* Purchase Award, Nat Exhib Ceramic Sculpture & Jewelry, Brigham Young Univ, 76; First Prize Ceramics, 32nd Ann Iowa Artists Exhib, Des Moines Art Ctr, 80; Hon Mention Int Ceramics Festival, Mino, Japan; Hon Mention, The Dripless Spout: Innovative Teapots, Arrowmont Sch, 88. *Mem:* Nat Coun Educ Ceramic Arts. *Publ:* Auth, Saggar firing, Studio Potter, 79. *Mailing Add:* 728 Fairchild St Iowa City IA 52245-2830

HINES, JESSICA
PHOTOGRAPHER
b St Louis, Mo, Nov 4, 58. *Study:* Washington Univ, St Louis, BFA(photog), 82; Univ Ill, Champaign-Urbana, MFA(photog), 84. *Work:* Erie Art Mus, Pa; State of Ga; numerous pvt collections. *Exhib:* Solo exhib, Women's Studio Workshop-Ctr Visual Arts, NY, 86, Ark State Univ Gallery, Jonesboro, 88, Exhib A Gallery, Savannah Sch Art & Design, Ga, 89, Ga Coun Arts, Carriage Works Gallery, Atlanta, 93, Hollins Col, Roanoke, Va, 95, Lamar Dodd Gallery, Univ Ga, Athens, 96 & Sch Art & Archit, La Tech Univ, Rustin, 97; Artists in Georgia, Nexus Contemp Art Ctr, Winston-Salem, NC, 88; National Exposures '90: A National Exhibition of Photog, Winston-Salem, NC, 90; Photonominal '91 (auth catalog), Forum Gallery, Jamestown Community Col,

NY, 91; Women Viewing Women, Rockford Col, Ill, 91; New Visions Gallery Contemp Art, Atlanta, Ga, 92; Crealde Sch Art Invitational, Winter Park, Fla, 94; Georgia State Capitol: Selections from the State Art Collections, Governor's Off, Atlanta, 94; At Issue: Our Environment, An Exhib of Contemp Landscapes, San Giuseppe Art Gallery, Col Mount St Joseph, Cincinnati, 95; SE Art Exhib, Savannah, Ga, 95; Toledo Friends Photog Nat Photo Exhib, Ctr Visual Arts, Univ Toledo, 95; One Light, Three Visions, Rocky Mt Ctr Arts, Wilson, NC, 96; Art & Science: A National Exhibition of Artworks Inspired by the Sciences, Mariobe Gallery, NJ, 97; Derivatives of the Landscape, Athena Gallery, Savannah, Ga, 98; Photog, A Multi Vision Art, Assoc Artists, Sawtooth Ctr, Winston-Salem, NC, 99; Photon Rangers, Eight Southeastern Photographers, Art Coun Wilson, NC, 99. *Teaching:* Instr photog, Univ Ill, Champaign-Urbana, 83-84; prof art, Ga Southern Univ, 84-. *Awards:* Alternative Media Excellence Award, Nat Exposures '90, Sawtooth Galleries, Asn Artists, Winston-Salem, NC, 90; Individual Artist's Grant, Spirit of Place, Ga Coun Arts, 92; Am Coun Grant, Universidade Federal de Pernambuco, Brazil, 97. *Mem:* Soc Photog Educ; Col Art Asn. *Mailing Add:* 108 Nottingham Tr Statesboro GA 30458-4265

HINKHOUSE, FOREST MELICK
WRITER, CONSULTANT
b West Liberty, Iowa, July 7, 25. *Study:* Coe Col, AB; Univ Mex; Fogg Art Mus, Harvard Univ; NY Univ Inst Fine Arts, MA; Univ Madrid, PhD; Eureka Col, DHL, 83. *Collection Arranged:* Industrial Gouaches of John Hultberg, 57; Paintings & Portraits by Frank Mason, 58; Contemporary Arizona Painting, 58; Festival of Arts, 58; One Hundred Years of French Painting 1860-1960, 61; English Landscape Painting, 61. *Pos:* Pub relations, Int House Asn, NY; art critic, Buffalo Eve News, Ariz Repub & Phoenix Gazette; founding dir, Phoenix Art Mus & Phoenix Fine Arts Asn, 57-67; co-founder, Hinkhouse Gallery, Coe Col, 65; consult & adv, Phoenix Art Mus, 67-; consult, Calif Art Comn, 68-; co-founder, Hinkhouse Collection, Melick Libr, Eureka Col, 69; mem bd trustees, Coe Col, Cedar Rapids, Iowa; founder, Hinkhouse Gallery Art, Stephens Col, Columbia, Mo; founder, Forest Melick Hinkhouse Collection, Lakeview Mus Arts & Sci, Peoria, 86. *Teaching:* Asst prof art, Albright Art Sch, Univ Buffalo, 56-57 & chmn hist art dept; guest lectr, Prudential Lines, 77. *Mem:* Claustro Extraordinario, Madrid; Col Art Asn Am; Am Asn Mus. *Publ:* Auth, Catalogue of the Collections of the Phoenix Art Museum; contribr, articles in Oregonian, 75-

HINMAN, CHARLES B
PAINTER, EDUCATOR
b Syracuse, NY, Dec 29, 32. *Study:* Syracuse Univ, BFA, 55; Art Students League, with Morris Kantor. *Work:* Mus Mod Art, NY; Whitney Mus Am Art, NY; Los Angeles Co Mus; Hirshhorn Mus, Smithsonian Inst, Washington; Mus Mod Art, Nagaoka, Japan; Louisiana Mus, Humlebaek, Denmark; Musee' des Beaux Arts de l'Ontario, Toronto, Ontario, Can; Detroit Inst Art, Mich; Chase Manhattan Bank, NY; The Rockefeller Collection, NY; Tel Aviv Mus, Israel; Shearson Co, NY; Denver Mus, Co; and others. *Comn:* Red Vista, 3-D painting, Continental Group, Stamford, Conn, 81; Excelsior, 3-D painting, Southeast Bank, Miami, Fla, 83; Adretto, 3-D painting, Europ Am Bank, Huntington, NY, 85; Aviary, suspended 3-D painting, Greenway Plaza, Hempstead, NY, 86; Zephyr, stainless steel sculpture, Burton Resnick, NY, 87. *Exhib:* Smithsonian Inst, Washington, 68; Solo exhibs, Richard Feigen Gallery, NY, 64 & 66, Chicago, 66, Irving Galleries, Milwaukee, 77, Palm Beach, 77-87, Donald Morris Gallery, Birmingham, Mich, 79, Douglas Drake Gallery, NY, 90-94; Honolulu Acad Arts, Hawaii, 68; Mus Mod Art, NY, 69; Whitney Mus Am Art, NY, 69; Aldrich Mus Contemp Art, Ridgefield, Conn, 71, 75 & 77; Mus Art, Ft Lauderdale, Fla, 80-81; Hickory Mus, NC, 90-92; Douglas Drake Gallery, NY, 90-94; Ga Mus Art, 94; Bergen Co Mus, NJ, 97; Boca Raton Mus Art, Fla, 2001; Butler Inst Am Art, Youngstown, OH, 2006. *Pos:* Artist-in-residence, Aspen Inst, Colo, 66. *Teaching:* Instr painting, Cornell Univ, New York, 67-68, Syracuse Univ, 71, Pratt Inst, Brooklyn, 75, Sch Visual Arts, New York, 76, Cooper Union, New York, currently; vis prof, Princeton Univ, NJ, 94 & 96; Lamar Dodd Distinguished prof art, Univ Ga, Athens, Ga, 91-94; Art Students League, NY, 95-. *Awards:* Int Prize Exhib, Torcuato di Tella, Buenos Aires, 57; First Prize, Mus Contemp Art, Nagoaka, Japan, 65; Grant, Nat Endowment Arts, 80; Adolph & Esther Gottlieb Found Grant, 96; and others. *Bibliog:* Richard Pincus-Whitten (auth), Exhibition at Feigen, Art Forum, 3/96; Henry Geldzahler (auth), Charles Hinman, Metrop Mus Art Mag, 70; Donald Kuspit (auth), The Cunning of Unreason: Charles Hinman's Absurdist Constructions, Idiosyncratic Identities, Cambridge Univ Press, 96; Carter Ratcliff (auth), Robert Morgan (auth), Meteorshowers, Boca Raton Mus Catalog, 2001; Claudine Humblet (auth), La Nouvelle Abstraction Americaine, 2005. *Mem:* Col Art Asn; Am Abstr Artists. *Media:* Acrylic, Pigment on Fabric; Wood. *Res:* Three Dimensional Painting. *Dealer:* Studio 231 Bowery NY 10002. *Mailing Add:* 231 Bowery New York NY 10002

HINSON, TOM EVERETT
CURATOR, HISTORIAN
b Henderson, Tex, Oct 25, 44. *Study:* Univ Tex, Austin, BA(art hist), BS(archit studies); Case Western Reserve Univ, Cleveland, Ohio, MA(art hist). *Pos:* Mus fel, Toledo Mus Art, Ohio, 70-71; asst cur, Dept Mod Art, Cleveland Mus Art, Ohio, 73-77, assoc cur, 78-81, cur contemp art, 82- & cur contemp art & photog, 96-. *Mem:* Am Asn Mus. *Res:* Contemporary and modern art; 19th and 20th century photography; 20th century architecture. *Publ:* Contribr exhib catalogs, Cleveland Mus Art, 91-98. *Mailing Add:* c/o Cleveland Mus of Art 11150 E Blvd Cleveland OH 44106

HIRONDELLE, ANNE E
CERAMIST
Study: Univ Puget Sound, BA, 66; Stanford Univ, MA, 67; Factory Visual Art, Ceramics Prog, Seattle, 73-74; Univ Wash, BFA prog, 74-76. *Work:* Am Craft Mus, NY; Howard & Gwen Laurie Smith Collection, Los Angeles Co Mus Art; Newark Mus, NJ; The White House, Washington; Ariz State Univ, Art Mus, Tempe; Stanford Univ Mus, Calif; and others. *Exhib:* One person exhibs, Garth Clark Gallery, Los Angeles, 87, 89, 90, 93, 95, Foster/White Gallery, Seattle, 89, 92, 94, 97 & 99, Joanne Rap Gallery/The Hand & the Spirit, Ariz, 91, 93, 96, Garth Clark Gallery, NY, 92, 94, Frank Lloyd Gallery, Santa Monica, 98, Edward Cain Galleries, Wash, 98 & Nancy Margolis Gallery, NY, 2000; Artfair Seattle, 94; Cups 1994, Artworks Gallery, Seattle, 94; Night of One Thousand and One Cups, Garth Clark & Mary Ryan Galleries, NY, 94; Dialogues: On and Off the Wall, Schmidt-Bingham Gallery, NY, 94; The White House Collection of Am Crafts, Colby Col Mus Art, Waterville, Mass, 97, Tampa Mus Art, Fla, 97, Del Art Mus, Wilmington, 97; Fabulous Fifty: Ceramic Cups by 50 NW Artists, Bainbridge Arts & Crafts, Bainbridge, Wash, 98; Artists Trust 11th Ann Art Auction, Seattle Ctr, Seattle, Wash, 98; San Francisco Craft and Folk Art Mus Ann Benefit Auction, San Francisco, 98; Artists and Collectors, Edward Cain Galleries, Port Townsend, Wash, 98; 6th Ann Teapot Exhib, Craft Alliance, St Louis, Mo, 98; About Drawing, Edward Cain Galleries, Port Townsend, Wash, 98; At Home with Crafts, James Renwick Alliance Benefit Auction, Nat Mus Am Art, Washington, DC, 98; The Sea, Edward Cain Galleries, Port Townsend, Wash, 98; Connections, Mobilia Gallery, Cambirdge, Mass, 98; Gallery Roster: July/Clay, Joanne Rapp Gallery, Scottsdale, Ariz, 98; Group Show: Gallery Artists, Frank Lloyd Gallery, Santa Monica, Calif, 98; and others. *Pos:* Var workshops, lect & artist-in-residences, 78-92; symposium participant, White House Collection Am Crafts, Los Angeles Co Mus Art, 96; juror, Bunnell St Gallery, Homer, Alaska, 96. *Teaching:* workshop lectr, Seward Park Art Studio, Seattle, Wash, 88, 90 & 2000, Ariz State Univ, Tempe, 91, 96 & 99, Arrowmont Sch Arts & Crafts, Gatlinburg, Tenn, 93, 96 & 2001, Mesa Community Col, Ariz, 96 & 99, Wagner Potters Asn, Southern Ill Univ, Edwardsville, 97 & Haystack Mountain Sch Crafts, Deer Isle, Maine, 2000, many others. *Awards:* Visual Arts Fel, Nat Endowment Arts, 88; $1000 First Place Award, Cedar Creek Nat Teapot Show, 89; First Place Award, Women in Washington: The First Century, 89. *Bibliog:* Anne Hirondelle, Ceramics Monthly, 3/93; Gretchen Adkins (auth), The Aquaria of Anne Hirondelle, Ceramics: Art & Perception, 31, 44-46, 98; Robin Horn (auth), Living with Form: The Horn Collection of Contemporary Crafts, Bradley Publ, 99; and others. *Publ:* Gallery, American Craft, Vol 57, No 4, 70, 8-9/97; Auth, Edward J Sozanski, Art Critic, The Philadelphia Inquirer, 40, 6/20/97; Anne Hirondelle, Nouvel Objet III: Artists in the World, Design House Publ, Seoul, Korea, 76-79 & 97; Auth, Gretchen Adkins, The Aquaria of Anne Hirondelle, Ceramics: Art and Perception, No 31, 44-46, 98; Auth, Peter Lane, Ceramic Form: Design and Decoration, Rizzoli Intl Publ, New York, 98. *Mailing Add:* 2255 Haines St Port Townsend WA 98368-7820

HIRSCH, FAYE
EDITOR
Pos: Ed, Print Collectors Newsletter; founding ed, Art on Paper; sr ed, Art in America, NYC. *Mailing Add:* Art in America Brant Art Publications 575 Broadway New York NY 10012

HIRSCH, GILAH YELIN
PAINTER, WRITER
b Montreal, Que, Aug 24, 44. *Study:* McGill Univ; Hebrew Univ; Sir George Williams Univ; Boston Univ; San Francisco State Univ; Univ Calif, Berkeley, BA, 67; Univ Calif, Los Angeles, MFA, 70. *Work:* Security Pac Banks, Calif State Univ & Greenberg & Glusken, Los Angeles; City of Santa Monica Art Bank, Calif; Nat Endowment Arts, Washington; Charles Wustum Mus Fine Arts, Racine, Wis; Tyrone Guthrie Ctr, Annamagkerrig, Ireland. *Exhib:* Whitney Mus Am Art, NY, 72; Santa Monica Libr, 94; Walton Art Ctr, Fayetteville, Ark, 94; Univ Judaism, La, 95; Barnsdall Munic Gallery, Los Angeles, 95; Irvine Fine Arts Ctr, 96; Claremont Sch Theology, Kresge Chapel, 97. *Collection Arranged:* Metamagic (auth, catalog), Calif State Univ, Dominguez Hills, 78. *Pos:* chair art dept, Calif State Univ, Dominguez Hills. *Teaching:* Prof art, Calif State Univ, Dominguez Hills, 73-; fac tutors, Int Col, 80-. *Awards:* Award, Banff Ctr for the Arts, 85; Nat Endowment Arts Fel, 85; Rockefeller Bellagio Grant, Italy, 92; and others. *Bibliog:* Articles in over 100 international newspapers, journals & magazines. *Mem:* Artists Equity. *Media:* Oil, Acrylic. *Publ:* Auth, Joan of art seminars, Artweek, 72; Emily Carr, Feminist Art J, 76; The Pararational, Visionary and Mystical Pespective, Calif State Univ, Dominguez Hills, 77; Emily Carr, Women's Studies, 78; Persistence of time and memory: The art of Ruth Weisberg, Womans Art J, winter 85; The illusion of potential: The delusion of the creative person in relationships, The Quest, autumn 92; Bringing the Himalayas Home, Saliman Mag, 99; Art & Healing, 99. *Mailing Add:* Dept Art Calif State Univ Dominguez Hills 1000 E Victoria Ave Carson CA 90747

HIRSCHFIELD, JIM
SCULPTOR
b Pittsburgh, Pa, Mar 7, 51. *Study:* Carnegie-Mellon Univ, Pittsburgh, studied hist fine arts, 69-70 & 72-73; Kans City Art Inst, Mo, BFA, 73-76; Univ Ore, Eugene, MFA, 76-78. *Work:* Meditation Room, Doernbecher Children's Hosp, Portland, Ore; Sculpture installation, City Atlanta Detention Ctr, Ga; NC Zoological Park, Asheboro; Horizon Jr High Sch, Spokane, Wash; Snohomish High Sch, Wash. *Comn:* Int Sculpture Conf, Lake Merrit-Bart Station, Oakland, Calif, 83; Connomara Found, Dallas, Tex, 86; Duke Med Ctr, Durham, NC, 89, 90, 93 & 95; Pub Art Works, San Rafael, Calif, 91 & 97; S Reg Libr, Charlotte, NC, 98; Paseo del Norte Road Extension, Albuquerque, NMex, 2004; Houston Airport, Houston, Tex, 2000; Anchorage Jail, Anchorage, Ark; Fla Atlantic Univ, Boca Raton, Fla, 99; NC Sch Arts, Winston-Salem, NC, 97. *Exhib:* Solo exhibs, Mattress Factory, Pittsburgh, Pa, 85,

Seattle Art Mus, 89, Nexus Contemp Art Ctr, Atlanta, Ga, 91, Walker's Point Ctr Arts, Milwaukee, Wis, 92, Kala Inst, Berkeley, Calif, 92, Acme Arts, Columbus, Ohio, 94, Spaces, Cleveland, Ohio, 94, Asheville Art Mus, NC, 94 & Southeastern Ctr Contemp Art, Winston-Salem, NC, 94; Ackland Art Mus, Chapel Hill, NC, 92; Fayerweather Gallery, Univ Va, 92; Duke Univ, Durham, NC, 94; Snug Harbor Cult Ctr, NY, 94; and others. *Pos:* Vis artist, Univ Wash, Seattle, 84; consult, Pub Art Plan, Seattle Arts Comn, 82-84 & Kingdom Art Plan, King Co Arts Comn, Seattle, Wash, 88-89; bd mem, Ctr Contemp Art, Seattle, Wash, 84-88; pub arts comnr, Chapel Hill Arts Comn, NC, 94-97. *Teaching:* Vis lectr, Univ Ore, Eugene, 78 & Ohio State Univ, Columbus, 87; instr, Factory Visual Art, Seattle, Wash, 79-80; vis asst prof, Univ Nev, Reno, 86; prof & asst chmn studio art/dir grad studies, Univ NC, Chapel Hill, 88-. *Awards:* Phillip & Ruth Hettleman Prize for Artistic Excellence, Fel, 93; Cult Olympiad Regional Designation Award Arts, 94; Proj Grant, 95 & Artist Fel, 96, NC Arts Coun. *Bibliog:* Tom Patterson (auth), Time is Running Out to Observe Hirschfield Work, Winston-Salem J, 9/25/94; Connie Bostic (auth), Jim Hirschfield, Asheville Art Mus, Artpapers, 11-12/94; Keith Ervin (auth), Bellevue, is it you?, Seattle Times, 5/20/96. *Publ:* Artwork/Network, Seattle Arts Comn, 84; Coauth, Public Art Master Plan for the Kingdome, Seattle, 88; plus many others. *Mailing Add:* 312 Ridgecrest Dr Chapel Hill NC 27514

HIRSH, ANNETTE MARIE
SILVERSMITH, GOLDSMITH
b Milwaukee, Wis, Oct 20, 21. *Study:* Milwaukee State Teachers Col, 39-41; Milwaukee Area Tech Col, 53-57;. *Work:* Milwaukee Art Mus, Baron Mus Judaica, Milwaukee, Wis; Madagascar Nat Mus; Israeli Embassy, Washington, DC. *Comn:* Silver spice-box, North Shore Congregation Israel, Glencoe, Ill, 70; silver kiddush cup, Shalom Temple, Sun City, Ariz, 76; silver rimonim & torah pointer, Congregation Emanuel, Chicago, Ill, 81; breast-plate (silver & semi-precious stones), Sinai Temple, Champaign, Ill, 85; Holocaust Mem (brass & wood), Milwaukee Jewish Home, 90. *Exhib:* Biennial Painting & Sculpture, Walker Art Inst, Minneapolis, Minn, 47; Small Sculpture, Ball State Col, Muncie, Ind, 65, 67 & 68; Religious Art, Cranbrook Acad, Bloomfield Hills, Mich, 66; Mississippi River Craft Show, Brooks Mem Art Gallery, Memphis, Tenn, 69; Chicago and Vicinity Biennial, Chicago Art Inst, 77; Chicago Area Jewish Artists, Spertus Mus, Chicago, 85; Contemp Artifacts, Nat Mus Am Jewish Hist, 87, 88, 89, 90, 91, 92 & 93. *Collection Arranged:* Old Testament, 72 & Exodus, 74, Milwaukee Jewish Community Ctr; Jewish Scriptures, Congregation EmanuEl, Milwaukee, 94. *Pos:* Illusr, Boston Store, Milwaukee, Wis, 42-44 & Goldblatt's Dept Store, Chicago, Ill, 44-46; mus chmn & cur, Baron Judaica Mus, Milwaukee, 70-. *Teaching:* Teacher drawing & watercolor, Milwaukee Area Tech Col, Wis, 68-2001. *Awards:* Purchase Award, Wis Designer Crafts Exhib, Milwaukee Art Mus, 64; Sculpture Award, Wright Art Ctr, Beloit, Wis, 66; Purchase Award, Mizel Mus Judaica, Denver, Colo, 86; First Prize, Judaica, Dallas, 2006; others. *Bibliog:* Bob Orvis (auth), Point of view, Milwaukee Mag, 2/78; James Auer (auth), Hebrew imagery, an updating, Milwaukee J, 4/5/81; Rachel Heimovics (auth), The Chicago Jewish Source Book, 81; James Auer (auth), Dual Show, Milwaukee J, 11/19/89; James Auer (auth), Judaica, 3/15/00. *Mem:* Wis Designer Crafts Coun (treas, 60-66, historian, 90-2005); Soc NAm Goldsmiths. *Media:* Metal Jewelry; Small Sculpture, Judaica Objects. *Collection:* Synagogues in Wisconsin, Illinois, Arizona, Michigan, Connecticut, Israeli Embassy (Washington, D.C.), etc. *Mailing Add:* 4124 N Ardmore Ave Milwaukee WI 53211

HIRSHFIELD, PEARL
PAINTER, SCULPTOR
Study: Sch of Art Inst, Chicago, BA, 79; Northwestern Univ, Columbia Col. *Work:* Peace Mus, Chicago, Ill; many pvt collections; Joan Flasch Artists Bk Collection, Flaxman Libr, Sch Art Inst, Chicago. *Exhib:* Aurora Univ, Ill, 94; Minn Mus Am Art, 95; solo show, Univ Wis, River Falls, 95; Columbus Mus Art, Ohio, 95; Finegood Art Gallery, Los Angeles, 96; Nat Mus Women in Arts, Washington, DC, 96; Orange Co Ctr Contemp Arts, Santa Ana, Calif, 96; Finegood Art Gallery, West Hills, Calif, 96; Blaffer Gallery, Houston, Tex, 97; Aurora Pub Art Comn, Ill, 97; Found Auschwitz, Brussels, Belgium, 97; Knoxville Mus Art, Tenn, 98; Northern Ill Art Mus, Chicago, 98; Tampa Bay Holocaust Mus, St Petersberg, Fla, 98; NJ State Mus, Trenton, 99; Okla City Art Mus, 99; Nat Mus of Women in the Arts, Washington, DC, 99; Telfair Mus, Savannah, Ga, 99; DeCordova Art Mus, Boston, 2000; Huntsville Mus Art, Ala, 2000; Tucson Art Mus, Ariz, 2000; Frye Mus, Seattle, Wash, 2001. *Pos:* Film coordr, Peace Productions, Inc, 83; art adv & consult, Gallery Workshop, Evanston, Ill. *Awards:* Visual Arts Award, Ill Arts Coun, 83 & 84 & 93, fellowship 86; Citizens Alert Bill of Rights Award for Visual Arts, 91; Visual Arts Award, Task Force Against Police Brutality Orgn, 93; Puffin Found Grant, 96; Best Three-Dimensional Art Award, 22nd Annual Baer Competition, 98. *Bibliog:* Matthew Baigell (pub), Jewish American Artists and the Holocaust, Rutgers Univ Press, 56, 90-91, fig 27, 97; Pub, Art After Auschwitz: The other side of memory, Response, A Contemporary Jewish Review (article), 30th Anniv Issue, 167, fig 172, 97; Kennan Heise (pub), Chaos Creativity and culture: A Sampling of Chicago inthe 20th Century, Gibbs Smith/Peregrine Smith, 168-170, 98; Daniel Weyssow & Yannis Thanassekos, The Memory of Auschwitz in Contemporary Art, Foundation Auschwitz Publ, Brussels, Belgium, 98; Stephen C. Feinstein, Reclaiming Memory; American Representations of the Holocaust, Memory and Re-memory: American Installation Artand Holocaust Imagery, Pirjo Ahokas & Maxine Chard-Hutchinson, Univ Turku (publ), Finland, 98. *Mem:* Nat Women's Caucus Art; Chicago Artists Coalition; Nat Mus Women Arts, Washington, DC. *Media:* All Media. *Publ:* Auth, Limited Edition Portfolio of 13 Major Artists, Ctr Constitutional Rights, New York, 72; Conspiracy, The Artist as Witness, Godine Press; Sculptural Constructions Involving Water Dynamics, Leonardo, Pergamon Press, Vol 18, Issue 3; Hedwig Brenner, Judische Frauen in der bildenden Kunst 11, German Text, Konstanz, Germany, 2004. *Mailing Add:* 1333 Ridge Ave Evanston IL 60201

HITCH, JEAN LEASON
PAINTER
b Sydney, Australia, Oct 18, 18; US citizen. *Study:* Melbourne Tech Art Training Sch, Australia; Leason Sch Painting; Wayman Adams Sch Painting, Adirondacks, NY. *Work:* Dr Hall, Cape Cod Community Col; Co Sheriff Gerry Bowes, Barnstable Co Ct House, Cape Cod; Dr Irving Bartlett, Cape Cod Community Col, 92; Mass Maritime Acad. *Comn:* Buccaneer, Mass Maritime Acad, 82. *Exhib:* Allied Artists Am, Am Artist Prof League & Catharine Lorillard Wolfe Art Club, NY; Hudson Valley Art Asn, White Plains, NY; Audubon Artists, NY; Nat Acad, NY; Newton Galleries; Salamagundi Club; Nat Arts Club; Richmond Co Country Club; Burr Galleries. *Pos:* Art cur, Staten Island Inst Arts & Sci, 45-51; former dir & owner, Dennis Common Fine Art Gallery. *Awards:* Anna Hyatt Huntington Horse-Head Award, 72; Am Arts Coun Award; Margaret Dole Portrait Award, 91. *Mem:* Cape Cod Art Asn (instr painting, formerly); Allied Artists Am (hon mem); Catharine Lorillard Wolfe Art Club; Am Artist Prof League (hon mem); Copley Arts Soc, Boston. *Media:* Oil. *Mailing Add:* 51 Gordon Ln Yarmouth Port MA 02675

HITCHCOCK, HOWARD GILBERT
EDUCATOR, SCULPTOR
b Ava, Mo, Aug 20, 27. *Study:* Col Puget Sound, BA, 50; Univ Wash, with Glen Alps, Everett DuPen & Alexander Archipenko, MFA, 53; Brooklyn Mus Art Sch, fall 62; Teachers Col, Columbia Univ, EdD, 63. *Work:* JB Speed Mus, Louisville, Ky; Mus de la Acuarela Mus, Coyoacan, Mex; First Repub Bank Ore, Portland, Ore; Casa Museo Vladimir Cora, Acaponeta, Nayarit, Mex. *Comn:* Altar cross & candelabra, Los Altos United Methodist Church, Long Beach, Calif, 65; sculpture, Am Cancer Soc, Long Beach, Calif, 86; sculpture, comn by Jack Dameron family, Long Beach, Calif, 93; relief sculpture comn by Richard and Karen Clements, Long Beach, Calif, 98. *Exhib:* Solo shows, Gallery West, Portland, Ore, 77 & 83, Allied Arts Gallery, Huntington Beach, Calif, 83, Civic Ctr, Anjo, Japan, 89, Heaton House Gallery, Edmonds, Wash, Magnolia Fine Arts Gallery, Seattle, Wash, 94 & Anderson Gallery, Sunset Beach, Calif, 96, 98, 99, 00; Five Calif Artists, Mus de la Acuarela Mexicana, Coyoacan, Mex, 93; Sculpture '93, City Brea Gallery, Brea, Calif, 93; First Int Watercolor Biennial, Mus dela Acuarela Mexicana, Coyoacan, Mex, 94; All Calif: All Media, Downey Mus of Art, Calif, 96; So Calif Open Juried Exhbn, Laguna Art Mus, Laguna Beach, Calif, 97. *Pos:* Chmn, Dept Art, Calif State Univ, Long Beach, 76-82; mem, Comn Accreditation, Nat Asn Sch Art & Design, Reston, Va, 81-83. *Teaching:* Instr art, Sue Bennett Col, London, Ky, 53-54; asst prof, Union Col, Barbourville, Ky, 54-57; from assoc prof to prof art educ & sculpture, Calif State Univ, Long Beach, Calif, 58-90. *Awards:* JB Speed Mus Blue Boar Ceramic Sculpture Purchase Prize, 27th Ky & Southern Ind Exhib Art, 54; Outstanding Artist Award, City Huntington Beach, 87; First Prize, Automobile in Art, Long Beach Arts, 96. *Bibliog:* Shirle Gottlieb (auth), Beauty in bronze: The evolution of a sculptor's technique, Long Beach Press-Telegram, 11/1/83. *Mem:* Int Sculpture Ctr; Am Craft Coun; Los Angeles Co Mus Art; Long Beach Mus Art. *Media:* Cast Metal; Watercolor. *Publ:* Auth, Out of the Fiery Furnace: Casting Sculpture from Ceramic Shell Molds, William Kaufmann, Inc, 85. *Dealer:* Anderson Gallery 16812 Pacific Coast Hwy Sunset Beach CA 90742. *Mailing Add:* 17161 Friml Ln Huntington Beach CA 92649-4510

HITE, JESSIE OTTO
MUSEUM DIRECTOR
b Apr 4, 47; US citizen. *Study:* Univ Tex, Austin, BS, 69, MA, 81. *Pos:* Asst cur, Archer M Huntington Art Gallery, Univ Tex, Austin, asst dir pub affairs, 84-91, acting dir, 91-93, dir, 93-. *Mem:* Am Asn Mus; Asn Art Mus Dirs. *Mailing Add:* c/o Univ Tex at Austin Archer M Huntington Art Gallery Austin TX 78712

HITNER, CHUCK
PAINTER, EDUCATOR
b Nashville, Tenn, Sept 10, 43. *Study:* Mid Tenn State Univ, with David LeDoux, BS(art), 67; Southern Ill Univ, Carbondale, MFA(painting & drawing), 68. *Work:* Chrysler Mus, Norfolk, Va; Southern Ill Univ, Carbondale; Allersmaborg, Ezinge, Neth; Tucson Mus Art, Ariz. *Exhib:* Calif State Poly-Tech Univ, Pomona, Calif, 81; Triton Mus Art, Santa Clara, Calif, 84; Mus Art, Univ Ariz, Tucson, 87; Univ Ctr Gallery, Univ Mont, Missoula, 88; Traditions 3 Thousand Gallery, NY, 88; Pentonville Gallery, London, Eng, 88; Allersmaborg, Ezinge (Gr), The Neth, 88; Roland Gibson Gallery, State Univ NY, Potsdam, 88; Selections 45, Drawing Ctr, NY, 89. *Teaching:* Asst prof painting & drawing, Eastern Ky Univ, 69-72; assoc prof painting & drawing, Univ Ariz, 72-82, prof, 82-; prof, Univ Ariz, Tucson, 82-. *Bibliog:* Donald Kuspit, Chuck Hitner: Recent Work (catalog), Mus Art, Univ Ariz, Tuscon, Ariz, 87; Robert Quinn, Frantic images from a calm hand, Artspace Mag, 85; Marcia Tucker, 20 Arizona artists (catalog), Phoenix Art Mus, 78. *Media:* Drawing, Painting. *Mailing Add:* 3839 E Calle Ensenada Tucson AZ 85716-5127

HIXON, KAREN J
PATRON
Pos: Supporter of numerous environ orgn's; bd trustees, Amon Carter Mus, Ft Worth. *Awards:* Named a Texas Legend of Conserv, Nat Fish & Wildlife Found, 2004. *Mailing Add:* Amon Carter Mus 3501 Camp Bowie Blvd Fort Worth TX 76107-2695

HIXSON, KATHRYN
CRITIC
Study: Studio grad, Sch of Art Inst, Chicago. *Teaching:* Cur, contemp art; teacher, contemp art and conceptual art theory, dept art criticism, hist & theory Sch of the Art Inst Chicago. *Mem:* Chicago Art Critics Asn. *Publ:* Writer, art criticism, Chicago, 85—, New Art Examiner, Arts Mag, NY, Flash Art, Milan, Italy, writer (of catalogue essays for galleries and mus), former editor New Art Examiner. *Mailing Add:* 900 Grove St Evanston IL 60201

HLAVINA, RASTISLAV
SCULPTOR, WRITER

b Topolcany, Slovakia, June 5, 43; Can citizen. *Study:* Art Col, Bratislava, with A Drexler & L Korkos, dipl(sculpture), 62; Nat Conserv & Restoration Inst, Pelhrimov, with Vaclav Vanek, 66; Cult DFA, W Univ Ariz, 88. *Work:* Hakone Open-Air Mus; Utsukushi-Ga-Hara Open-Air Mus; Slovak Nat Gallery; City of Fukuoka; pvt collections in Can, Czech Repu, France, Russia, Slovak Rep, US. *Comn:* Restorations: Altarpiece Dobra Voda, 64-65, Loreta, Royal Summer Palace, Prague, 65 & Monastery Libr Cistercian Abbey, Vyssi Brod, 65-66, Nat Heritage Inst, Prague; sculpture, Melody, Prov Gov, Japan, 88. *Exhib:* Look, Pub Art Gallery Sarnia, Ont, 82; Synthesis: Idea and Form, Multicult Mus & Gallery, Toronto, 82; New Artists, NY, 82; Artists of Czechoslovak Origin, Univ Pittsburgh, 82; CKOC Arts Hamilton, Art Gallery Hamilton, 82-83; Int Juried Art Competition/Exhib, by IJAC, NY, 85; First & Second Rodin Grand Prize Exhib, Hakone Open-Air Mus, 86-88; A Praise of Small Format in Contemp Art, Paris, 2000. *Pos:* Conservator & restorer fine arts, Nat Conserv & Restoration Inst Fine Arts, Pelhrimov, Czech, 64-66; art dir, MIER Nat Enterprise, Topolcany, Slovakia, 67-68. *Awards:* Merit Distinction, Expo Brno, 67; Award, Outstanding Achievement in Sculpture, IJAC, New York, 85; Superior Prize, 1st Rodin Grand Prize Exhib, Hakone Open-Air Mus, 86; Superior Prize, 2nd Rodin Grand Prize Exhib, Hakone Open-Air Mus, 88. *Bibliog:* Jenny Bergin (auth), Sculptor takes your all, Ottawa Citizen, 10/28/72; Nancy Baele (auth), Perseverance pays off, Citizen, 11/26/81; Margarat Virany (auth), Aylmer sculptor starts art movement, Aylmer Bulletin, 12/17/81; Celina Bell (auth), Area artists to exhibit with best in New York, Citizen, 8/23/85. *Media:* All. *Res:* From multiple sculpture (1969) to multiple thought & understanding; art & the emergence of a new comprehension of reality; global interpretation; art as an introductory element & an educational tool in the process of development of our society. *Publ:* Auth, Legacy of Vinland: The Multiple Sculpture, pvt publ, 81; Introduction, Multiple Sculpture and the Multiple Art, ABIRA Digest, Spring, 88; Collection of postal cards Les Artistes et Matres du XXe siecle (Artists & Masters of XXth Century), Inclusion in The Golden Book for Art Collectors and Art Lovers, Arts et Images du Monde, Paris, France; Le Grand Livre d'Art des Salons et Biennales De France et de leurs Exposants, Editions Pergame, Geneve, 94; Europ'ART, Genève, 2005. *Dealer:* Passage de l'Art. *Mailing Add:* 1769 Rte 148 Luskville PQ J0X 2G0 Canada

HO, FRANCIS T
PHOTOGRAPHER, EDUCATOR

b Honolulu, Hawaii, Aug 29, 38. *Study:* Yale Univ, BFA, 61; Rochester Inst Technol, MFA, 67. *Work:* Nikon Camera Co, NY; Canon Photo Gallery, Amsterdam; Photo Gallery Int, Tokyo; Silver Image Gallery, Seattle. *Comn:* Photograph, Seattle Arts Comn, 83. *Exhib:* Focus Gallery, San Francisco, 73; A Temporary Possession: The Human Image in 20th Century Photog, Wash State Univ Mus Art, 76; solo exhibs, Canon Photo Gallery, Amsterdam, 77 & Photo Gallery Int, Tokyo, 80; Fantastic Photog in the USA, Mus Fundacio Miro, Barcelona, 78, Hall Palais Beaux Arts, Brussels, 78 & Mus Mod Art, Mexico City, 79. *Teaching:* Prof photog & graphic design, Wash State Univ, 67-; exchange prof graphic design, Nihon Univ, Tokyo, 79-80. *Awards:* Cert Excellence, Exhib Communication Graphics, Am Inst Graphic Arts, 74-75; Merit Award, The One Show, New York Art Dirs Club, 75; Award Excellence, 16th Ann Exhib, Communication Arts Mag, 75. *Bibliog:* Drukkerij Rosbeek (auth), Hose Valley, Hoensbroek, Neth, 76; Attilio Columbo (auth), Fantastic Photographs, Random House & Gordon Frazer, 79; Yaomi Yoshikawa (auth), article, Commercial Photo, Japan, 80; Tokumi Sawamoto (auth), article, Camera Mainichi, Tokyo, 2/80. *Mem:* Friends Photog. *Mailing Add:* 7103 NE 136th St Kirkland WA 98034-5009

HOADLEY, THOMAS A
CERAMIST

b North Adams, Mass, July 19, 49. *Study:* Skowhegan Sch Painting & Sculpture, Maine, 70; Amherst Col, Mass, BA(cum laude), 71; Apprentice to Malcolm Wright, Marlboro, Vt, 74; Ill State Univ, Normal, MS(ceramics), 77. *Work:* The White House, MCI Collection, Nat Mus Am Art & Renwick Gallery, Smithsonian Inst, Washington; Philadelphia Mus Art; Los Angeles Co Mus Art; Univ Iowa Mus Art. *Exhib:* One-man shows, Jackie Chalkley Gallery, Washington, DC, 81 & 83, Clay Pot, Brooklyn, 82, 83 & 84, Venture Gallery, Lathrup Village, Mich, 83 & 85, Elaine Potter Gallery, San Francisco, Calif & Swan Gallery, Philadlephia, Pa, 84, Lawrence Gallery, Portland, Ore, 87 & Mendelson Gallery, Washington Depot, Conn, 88 & 91; Art that Works: Decorative Arts of the Eighties, Crafted in Am, Mint Mus Art, Charlotte, NC, 90; Am Crafts: The Nation's Collection, Renwick Gallery, Washington, 92; Group Clay Show, Mendelson Gallery, Washington Depot, Conn, 93; White House Collection of Am Crafts, Nat Mus Am Art, Washington, 95-99; Int Ceramic Festival, Mino, Japan, 95; Fletcher Challenge, Oakland, NZ, 98. *Awards:* Award Excellence, Wash Craft Show, 89; Visual Artists Fel, Nat Endowment Arts, 90 & 92; Bronze Award, Int Ceramic Festival, Mino, Japan, 95. *Bibliog:* Tony Birkes (auth), The Complete Potter's Companion, Conran Octopus Ltd, London, 93; Caroline Whyman (auth), The Complete Potter: Porcelain, Univ Philadelphia Press, 94; Peter Lane (auth), Contemporary Porcelain, Rizzoli, NY, 94. *Dealer:* Hoadley Gallery Lennox MA. *Mailing Add:* PO Box 372 Lanesborough MA 01237

HOARE, TYLER JAMES
SCULPTOR, PRINTMAKER

b Joplin, Mo, June 5, 40. *Study:* Univ Colo, 59; Sculpture Ctr, New York, 60; Univ Kans, BFA, 63; Calif Col Arts & Crafts, Oakland, 66;. *Work:* US Info Agency, Washington, DC; State Univ NY Albany; Oakland Mus, Calif; Calif Col Arts & Crafts; and many pvt collections. *Exhib:* One-man shows, John Bolles Gallery, San Francisco, Calif, 69, 71, 74, Camberwell Sch Art, London, 71, Cent Sch Art & Design, London, 74, Purdue Univ, Gallery 1, West Lafayette, Ind, 76, Geotrope Gallery, Berkeley, Calif, 81, Studio Nine, Benicia, Calif, 82, Oakland Art Asn Gallery, Calif, 86, Costal Art League Mus, Half Moon Bay, Calif, 89, George A Spiva Art Ctr, Joplin, Mo, 97, Epperson Gallery, Crockett, Calif, 98; 22nd Nat Print Exhib, Libr Cong, Washington, DC, 71; Xerographic Art, Xerox Corp, NY; Int Mail Art, Guanajuato, Mex, 81; The Centre Documentazione Organizzazione, Parma, Italy, 82; Works by California Cookbook Artists, San Francisco Mus Mod Art, 82 & Artists, in the Spotlight, 84; Whitney Mus Am Art Libr, 83; Gracie Mansion Gallery, NY, 83; Contemp Surrealism Slide Lect, San Francisco Art Inst, Calif, 84; San Francisco Mus Mod Art, Rental Gallery, 85; San Francisco Arts Comn Festival, 86; Calif Mus Photog, Riverside, Calif, 84, 86, 87, 88, 89, 90; Cleveland Inst Art, 89; Ore State Univ, Corvallis, 90; Gallery One, Point Reyes, Calif, 90; Contemp Art Gallery, Aono, Japan, 91; Univ Tex, Dallas, 93; Gallery Without Walls, Australia, 94; Mus Mod Art, 96; Epperson Gallery, Crockett, Calif, 98, 99, 00, 01, 02, 06; and many others. *Collection Arranged:* US Info Agency, Washington, DC; SUNY at Albany; Oakland Mus, Calif; Harvard Univ, Cambridge, Mass. *Pos:* guest cur, Magic Machine, Ctr Gallery, Univ Calif, San Francisco, 73, The Trading Company, 74, 88, Ctr Visual Arts Catalog, Oakland, 82. *Teaching:* guest lectr, San Francisco Art Inst, 72, San Francisco State Univ, 72-75, Oakland Mus, Calif, 74, Calif State Univ, Hayward, 74 & 79, Col of San Mateo, 75, Mo Southern State Col, 79, Univ Wyo, Laramie, 79, Colo State Univ, 79, Solano Community, Suisun City, Calif, 83, Calif Col Arts & Crafts, 84; instr, Univ Calif, Berkeley, 73-74. *Awards:* 2nd Ann Graphic Exhib, Olive Hyde Art Ctr, 72; Focuserie Award, Nat Photog Exhib, Erie, Pa, 74; Master of Painting Honoris Causa, Accademia Italia; plus many others. *Bibliog:* Thelma Newman (auth), Innovative Printmaking, Crown Publ, Inc, NY; article, Spotlight on Sculpture, Tyler James Hoare, Ctr Visual Arts, 82; Nicholas Roukes (auth), Art Synectics, Juniro Arts Publ, Calgary, 84; and many others. *Mem:* Nat Soc Lit & Arts; Metal Arts Guild, San Francisco; Richmond Art Ctr, Calif; Pro Arts, Oakland, Calif; LA Print Soc; Oakland Mus Asn; San Francisco Art Inst; San Francisco Mus Art; Ctr for Vis Arts, Oakland, Calif; Pro Arts, Oakland, Calif. *Media:* Wood, Metal. *Publ:* Megan Greenwell (auth), Albany Sculptor Brings Art Back to East Bay Shoreline, Berkeley Daily Planet, 7/18/2003; Matthew Artz (auth), Art at Sea: Berkeley artist still building relics along East Bay coast, Berkeley Daily, 10/9/2006. *Dealer:* Epperson Gallery 1400 Pomona St Crocket Calif. *Mailing Add:* 30 Menlo Pl Berkeley CA 94707

HOBBS, FRANK I, JR
PAINTER, INSTRUCTOR

b Lynchburg, Va, Dec 3, 57. *Study:* Art Inst Pittsburgh, 75; Va Polytech Inst/State Univ, BA, 80; Am Univ MFA (painting), 84. *Work:* Univ Va Hosp, Charlottesville; Med Col of Va, Richmond; Lynchburg Col, Va; Va Polytech Inst & State Univ, Blacksburg; Mary Baldwin Coll, Staunton, Va. *Exhib:* Contemp Realism, Gallery Alexy, Philadelphia, 96; Small Figurative Works, Armory Art Ctr, Palm Beach, Fla, 96; The Virginia Landscape: A Cult History, Va Hist Soc, Richmond, 2000, Mus Western Va, 2000; Transitions: Narratives of Change, Danville Mus Art, Va, 2000; Commerce Sch Gallery, Lexington, Va, 2001; College of William and Mary, Andrews Art Gallery, Williamsburg, Va, 2002. *Pos:* Founder, pres, isntr Beverly Street Studio Sch, Staunton, Va, 92-. *Teaching:* Asst prof painting/drawing, Mary Baldwin Col, Staunton, Va, 87-91; asst prof printmaking/drawing, Randolph Macon Womans Col, Lynchburg, Va, 92-94; asst prof drawing, Washington & Lee Univ, Lexington, Va, 97; adj asst prof art, Va Military Inst, Lexington, Va, 96-. *Awards:* Va Mus Fine Art Fel, 82; Fel Works on Paper, NEA/Mid Atlantic Arts Found, 96; Fel in Painting, Va Comn for the Arts, 2000. *Bibliog:* Mearne Pardee (auth), Virginia Realism, Second Street Gallery,94; James Kelly-William Rasmussen (co-auths) The Virginia Landscape: A Cultural History, 2000. *Mem:* Col Art Asn. *Media:* Painting, Drawing, Printmaking. *Dealer:* Reynolds Gallery 1514 W Main St Richmond Va 23220. *Mailing Add:* c/o Hodges-Taylor Gallery Transamerica Square 401 N Tryon St Charlotte NC 28202

HOBBS, FREDRIC
SCULPTOR, FILMMAKER

b Philadelphia, Pa, Dec 30, 31. *Study:* Cornell Univ, BA; Acad San Fernando Bellas Artes, Madrid, Spain. *Work:* Mus Mod Art, NY; Metrop Mus Art, NY; Finch Col Mus, NY; San Francisco Mus Mod Art, San Francisco Fine Arts Mus; Oakland Mus Art; Sierra Nevada Mus Art; Johnson Mus, Cornell Univ; and many others. *Comn:* Nev Art Eco Demonstration Proj; Penn treaty Park Place, Phila. *Exhib:* Biennial Exhib Am Art, Pa Acad Fine Arts, Philadelphia, 64; Nat Fine Arts Collection, Smithsonian Inst, Washington, DC, 64; The Highway Traveling Exhib, Inst Contemp Art, Philadelphia, 70; one-man shows, Calif Palace Legion of Honor, San Francisco & Mus Sci & Indust, Los Angeles, 76; San Francisco Mus of Mod Art, 80; Sierra Nev Mus, 84; and many others. *Pos:* Exec producer, Madison Hobbs Studio, KRCB TV. *Teaching:* various schs and cols, 56-64. *Bibliog:* John W McCoubrey (auth), Art & the road, Highway, 70; Thomas Albright (auth), Visuals, Rolling Stone Mag, 71; Subject in Printmedia, NY & Calif. *Media:* Steel Supported Fiberglass, Acrylic. *Publ:* Coauth, The Richest Place on Earth, Houghton-Mifflin, 78; auth, Eat your house: ART ECO guide to self sufficiency, Mayfield, 80; feature articles, City Mag, San Francisco Mag & San Francisco Examiner; writer, dir & producer, feature films & TV-Expo short features; Taiwain, The Other China (PBS mini-series), 80-90; auth, The Spirit of the Monterey Coast, Tioga Pub Co, 90; Faqfuture (multi-media PBS programs), 96-. *Dealer:* Ebert Gallery 49 Geary St San Francisco CA 94108

HOBBS, GERALD S
DEALER, PUBLISHER

b New York, NY, Nov 5, 41. *Pos:* Publ, Am Artist Mag, 73, The Artist Mag, 76, Art & Antiques: The Am Mag for Connoisseurs & Collectors, 78-, Interiors Mag, 78, Residential Interiors Mag, 78 & Int Soc Artists. *Mem:* Nat Arts Club; Salmagundi Club; Nat Art Material Trade Asn; Artists' Fel. *Specialty:* Publisher of The American Artist Collection (unlimited edition prints). *Mailing Add:* 29 E 64th St Apt 8D New York NY 10021

HOBBS, JACK ARTHUR
EDUCATOR, WRITER
b Lincoln, Nebr, Dec 26, 30. *Study:* Univ Iowa, BA, 52, MA, 56, PhD, 71. *Exhib:* 14th & 17th Nat Exhibs Prints, Libr Cong, Washington, 56 & 59 & Invitational Traveling Show, 59-61; Art in the Embassies Prog, Dept State, Washington, 69. *Pos:* Publ ed, Studies in Art Educ, 85-87; Ed Bd, Studies in Art Educ, 89-93. *Teaching:* Emer prof art appreciation & art educ, Ill State Univ, 70-94. *Bibliog:* Robert Hiedemann (auth), bk rev, Art Educ J, Vol 29, 1/76; Howard Conant (auth), bk rev, Leonardo, spring 77; Georgia C Collins (auth), bk rev, Studies in Art Educ, Vol 27, 3/86. *Mem:* Nat Art Educ Asn. *Publ:* Auth, Art in Context, Harcourt Brace Jovanovich, 75, 2nd ed, 80, 3rd ed, 85 & 4th ed, 91; Arts, Civilization and Ideas, Prentice-Hall, 89, 2nd ed, 92; The Visual Experience, Davis Publ, Inc, 90, 2nd ed, 95 & 3rd ed, 2005; Arts in Civilization: Prehistoric culture to the twentieth century, Bloomsbury Books, London, 92; Teaching Children Art, Prentice-Hall, 97; (reissue) Waveland Press Inc, 2006. *Mailing Add:* 103 S Williamburg Dr Bloomington IL 61704

HOBBS, ROBERT CARLETON
MUSEUM DIRECTOR, HISTORIAN
b Brookings, SDak, Dec 6, 46. *Study:* Univ Tenn, Knoxville, BA, 69; Nat Defense Educ Act grant fel, 71-74; Samual H Kress fel, 74-75; Helena Rubinstein fel, 75; Univ NC, Chapel Hill, PhD, 75. *Pos:* Cur, Mint Mus Art, 69-71; adj cur, Cornell Univ, Herbert F Johnson Mus, 76-; sr cur & chmn curatorial div, Tehran Mus Contemp Art, 78; dir, Univ Iowa Mus Art, formerly. *Teaching:* Lectr mod art, Yale Univ, 75-76; assoc prof mod art, Cornell Univ, Ithaca, NY, 76-83. *Mem:* Am Asn Mus; Col Art Asn; Int Asn Art Critics. *Res:* Currently under contract to edit writings of Robert Motherwell for documents of 20th century art series. *Publ:* Auth, Elliott Daingerfield Retrospective Catalogue, Mint Mus, 71; coauth, Abstract Expressionism: The Formative Years, Whitney Mus & Cornell Univ Press, 78; auth, Robert Motherwell, Stadtische Kunsthalle, Dusseldorf, 76; auth, Michelle Stuart, Comt Visual Arts, MIT, 77; Auth, Robert Smithson: Sculpture, Col Art J, fall 82; auth, Tony Smith, Pace Gallery, 83; and others. *Mailing Add:* 2221 Grove Ave Richmond VA 23220-4438

HOBBS, ROBERT DEAN
PRINTMAKER, CONSULTANT
b Merkel, Tex, Apr 21, 28. *Study:* WTex State Univ, Canyon, with Emillio Caballero, BA; Northern Colo State Univ, Greeley, with Richard Ellinger, MA; Pa State Univ, State Col, with Will Barnett, DEd. *Work:* WTex State Univ, Canyon; Colo State Col, Greeley; Viktor Lowenfiel Mem Collection, Pa State Univ, State Col; Smithsonian Inst, Washington, DC. *Exhib:* Solo exhibs, John Sloan Gallery, Lock Haven State Col, Pa, 78 & 80, Nat Art Educ Bldg, Reston, Va, 78, West Broadway Gallery, NY, 80 & Haas Gallery, Bloomsburg State Col, Pa, 81. *Pos:* Art Consulant, 88 to present. *Teaching:* Art teacher in pub sch, Midland, Tex, 54-58; instr art, WTex State Univ, 58-63, assoc prof, 67-71; grad asst, Pa State Univ, 65-67; prof art & chmn art dept, Clarion Univ Pa, 71-88; retired, summer 88. *Mem:* Nat Art Educ Asn; Pa Art Teacher Asn, Harrisburg; Asso of Penn State Col & Univ Faculties, Harrisburg, PA. *Media:* Serigraphy, Silkscreen. *Publ:* Effect of Variation of Stimulus Set and the Sequence of Two Media on the Drawings and Prints of Classified College Subjects, Penn State Univ, 68. *Dealer:* West Broadway Gallery 431 West Broadway New York NY 10012. *Mailing Add:* 8005 Classic Ave NE Albuquerque NM 87109

HOBGOOD, E WADE
ADMINISTRATOR, EDUCATOR
b Wilson, NC, June 28, 53. *Study:* ECarolina Univ, Greenville, NC, BFA, 75, MFA, 77, Am Inst Philantrophic Studies, Cert Planned Giving, 95, Harvard Univ, Inst Educ Mgt, 97. *Work:* RJ Reynolds, Winston-Salem, NC; Orthopedic Hosp, Charlotte, NC; Gov's Off, Little Rock, Ark; ECarolina Univ, Greenville, NC; Winthrop Univ, Rock Hill, NC. *Exhib:* NCarolina Photogrs Invitational, High Point Mus Art, NC, 80; Western Carolina Univ Invitational, Black Mountain, NC, 81; solo exhib, Limestone Col, Gaffney, SC, 85; Southern Vision's, traveling exhib, 87; Art Fac Exhib, Stephen F Austin State Univ, Nacogdoches, Tex, 92; and others. *Pos:* Chmn dept art & design, Winthrop Univ, Rock Hill, SC, 84-89; bd dir, Graphic Design Educ Asn Inc, 86-90; proj dir, Arts in Basic Curriculum, Nat Endowment Arts, 87-92; sr evaluator, Nat Asn Schs Art & Design, 87-; assoc dean, Col Visual & Performing Arts, Winthrop Univ, 88-92; dean, Col Fine Arts, Stephen F Austin State Univ, Nacogdoches, Tex, 92-93; field reader, US Dept Educ, 92-; dean, Col Arts, Calif State Univ, Long Beach, 1993-2000; chancellor, NC Sch Arts, 2000-2005. *Teaching:* Asst prof design & photog, Ark State Univ, Jonesboro, 77-78; asst to assoc prof, Western Carolina Univ, 78-84; prof, Univ NC, Asheville, 2006-. *Awards:* Higher Educ Art Educator of Yr, SC Art Educ Asn, 89; Art Educator of Yr, SC Art Educ Asn, 90; Fel Japanese Studies, Grants Sashakawa/Nippan Found, 98. *Mem:* Graphic Design Educ Asn Inc (treas, 86-90); Bd dirs, Int Coun Fine Arts Deans, 98-; Fine Arts Affil

HOCHFIELD, SYLVIA
EDITOR
Pos: Assoc Ed, ARTnews Mag, NYC. *Publ:* Auth, Beautiful Loot: Soviet Pluder of Europe's Art Treasures, 95; auth, Stolen Treasure: The hunt for the World's Lost Masterpieces, 95. *Mailing Add:* ARTnews Magazine 48 W 38th St New York NY 10018

HOCHHAUSER, MARILYN HELSENROTT
PAINTER, EDUCATOR
b Chicago, Ill, April 18, 28. *Study:* C W Post Ctr, Long Island Univ, BA(art educ; magna cum laude), 73, MA(painting; scholar), 75; New York Univ, Mus Studies, 86-88. *Work:* Language Plus, Alma, Que; Ore Art Inst, Portland; Elings Park, Santa Barbara, Calif. *Exhib:* Muscarelle Mus Art, 88; Col William & Mary, Williamsburg, VA, 88; Sculpture & Abstract, San Francisco State Univ, 90; Columbia Col, Mo, 91; Perth Galleries, Australia, 92; and others; The Hall of AWA Int Paper Art, Japan, 93; Contemp Art Forum, 94, Korean Cult Ctr, Los Angeles, 96; Westmount Col, Calif, 97, Univ Minn, 98; Santa Barbara City Col, 99, West Coast Paper Co, 99; Maryland Fed Art, 2000; Fresno Mus, Fresno, Calif, 2004; Westmount Col, Montecito, Calif, 2005; Elings Park Found, Santa Barbara, Calif, 2006. *Collection Arranged:* Oregon Art Inst. *Pos:* Prof Art, Trenton State Col, 80-85. *Teaching:* Art Lectr, Adult Educ, Roslyn & Merrick, NY, 71-79; prof, Trenton State Col, 80-85; instr, Santa Barbara Mus Art, 89-90 & City Col Art, 90. *Bibliog:* Lelac-Jean Papier (auth), article, Alma, PQ Canada, 2/82; C Laforge (auth), New York Daily News, 9/83; Joan Shepard (auth), article New York Post, 9/83. *Mem:* Women in Arts. *Res:* Japanese Paper Making. *Mailing Add:* 5041 Via Lara Ln Santa Barbara CA 93111

HOCHMAN, KITTY
PRINTMAKER
b Brooklyn, NY. *Study:* Hans Hofmann Sch Painting with E Eisgraw, 75; Art Am Sch with Nicholas Carone, 80; printmaking with Ruth Leaf Atelier, 80-. *Work:* Orion Pictures & Dupont, NY; Sandos Pharmaceutical, Int Serv Systems & Clairol, NJ; Jane Voorhees Zimmerli Art Mus, Rutgers, NJ; Merrill Lynch; Philip Morris. *Exhib:* 8th Int Miniatures, Pratt Graphic Ctr, NY, 85; Soc Am Graphic Artists, NY, 85; Int Miniature, Space Gallery, Seoul, Korea, 85; Karagawa Kennin Hall, Yokahamo, Japan, 94; Solo exhib, Port Washington Libr, 94-95; Shelter Rock Gallery, NY, 95; Hudson River Mus, NY; Zhejian Acad Fine Arts, Haugzhou, China; Chiba Shimin Gallery, Inage, Japan. *Pos:* Dir, Prints Etc, NY, 87-. *Teaching:* Instr, Clearview Community Coun, 70-75, pvt lessons, 80 ; adult educ, Forest Hills High Sch, NY. *Awards:* Janet Turner Graphic Award, 84; Carvel Printing Spec Award, Nassau Co Mus, 88; Printing Special Award, Nassau Mus, 88; Medal of Honor, Nat Asn Women Artists, 96. *Bibliog:* Phyllis Braff (critic), NY Times, 83; Helen Harrison (critic), NY Times, 83; Malcolm Preston (critic), NY Newsday, 84. *Mem:* Nat Asn Women Artists (juror, 88-90); NY Artists Equity; Audubon Artists; Philadelphia Print Club; Soc Am Graphic Artists. *Media:* Etching, Monoprint. *Publ:* Contribr, Space, art architecture and environment, Korean Publ, 82; Brides Mag, 83; Monotypes, New York Newsday, 83; Graphics everywhere, NY Times, 84; Works on paper, NY Times, 85. *Dealer:* G J Cloninger & Co 39 E Hanover Ave Morris Plains NJ 07950; Skidmore Assoc 645 Snowden Lane Princeton NJ 08540

HOCHSTETLER, T MAX
PAINTER, EDUCATOR
b Terre Haute, Ind, May 13, 41. *Study:* Univ Evansville, BA, 64; Southern Ill Univ, MFA, 67. *Work:* Owensboro Art Mus; Tenn State Mus & Cheekwood Fine Arts Ctr, Nashville; Evansville Mus Arts & Sci; Tenn Valley Authority. *Comn:* Nashville murals, 76-77 & Centennial murals, 80-81, Opryland Hotel, Nashville; Cheatham Co Paintings, Dominion Bank of Ashland City, Tenn, 82; Public Square Clarksville (mural); First Am Bank, Clarksville, Tenn, 83; Hist Broadcasting mural, the Nashville Network (TNN), Nashville, 85; decade mural, TNN, Nashville, 94. *Exhib:* Ind Artists Exhib, Evansville Mus, 75; Tenn Bicentennial Exhib, State Mus, Nashville, 76; Mid-Am Art Exhib, Owensboro Mus Art, Ky, 79; Tenn Artists, Doyle Fine Arts Ctr, Western Ky Univ, Bowling Green, 79; Choice Painting Invitational, Ctr Contemp Art, Univ Ky, 82; Ten in Tennessee, Dulin Gallery Art, Knoxville, 86. *Teaching:* Prof painting & drawing, Austin Peay State Univ, 67-99, emer prof art and artist-in-residence, 99-. *Awards:* Second Place Award, City of Owensboro, 74; Patrons Purchase Award, Evansville Mus, 75; Mus Purchase Award, Owensboro Mus, 79. *Mem:* Tenn Watercolor Soc; Col Art Asn; Southeastern Col Art Asn. *Media:* Acrylic, Watercolor. *Mailing Add:* Austin Peay State Univ Clarksville TN 37044

HOCKNEY, DAVID
DESIGNER, PHOTOGRAPHER
b Bradford, Yorkshire, Eng, July 9, 37. *Study:* Bradford Col Art, 57; Royal Col Art, 62, hon doctor Univ Aberdeen, 88. *Work:* Mus Contemp Art, Los Angeles, 2001, Kunst-Und Ausstellung Halle, Bonn, 2001, Louisiana Mus Mod Art, Copenhagen, 2001, Whitney Biennial, NY, 2004. *Exhib:* One-man shows, Kasmin Gallery, 63-89, Mus Mod Art, NY, 64, Stedelijk Mus, Amsterdam, The Neth, 66, Metrop Mus Art, 88, Tate Gallery, London, 88, Royal Acad Arts, London, 95, 99 & 2004; exhib Great Graphics, Karen McCready Fine Art, New York City, 98, Drawings, Jason McCoy Gallery, NY Univ, 97-98, Contemp Master Prints, Jim Kempner Fine Art, NY Univ, 97-98, Male, Wessel & O'Connor Gallery, New York City, 97-98, Cityscape/Landscape, Karen McCready Fine Art, New York City, 98-99, Looking West, CollectFineArt.com, Venice, Calif, 99-2000, Evidence of Love, Romance, Desire & Fantasy, Jack Rutberg Fine Arts, Los Angeles, 2000-01; Centre Georges Pompidou, Paris, 99; Musee Piccasso, Paris, 99; pub collections Nat Gallery Victoria, Melbourne, Australia, Richard Gray Gallery, NY Univ, Tate Gallery, London, Town Linz Gallery/Wolfgang Gurlitt, Linz, Patrick & Beatrice Haggerty Mus, Milwaukee, Mus Modern Art, Stockholm, Scotland Nat Gallery Modern Art, Edinburgh, Mulvane Art Mus, Topeka, Kan, Art Inst Chicago, Wallrof Richartz Mus, Cologne, Ger, Phillips Collection, Washington, DC, Nat Portrait Gallery, Smithsonian Institution, Washington, DC, Hirshhorn Mus & Sculpture Garden, Smithsonian Instn, Washington, DC, Oakland Mus, Sheffield Art Galleries G & Mappin, Southampton Art Gallery, Mus of 20th Century, Vienna, Austria, Nat Gallery Australia, Canberra. *Pos:* Lectr, Univ Iowa, 64, Univ Colo, 65, Univ Calif-Los Angeles, 66, Univ Calif-Berkeley, 67; designer, sets for Magic Flute, 78, Parade Triple Bill, Stravinsky Triple Bill, Metrop Opera House, 80-81, and others. *Awards:* Guiness Award & First Prize for etching, 61; Gold Medal, Royal Col Art, 62; 1st prize John Moores Exhib Liverpool, Eng, 67; Ger award of Excellence 83; Kodak Photog Book Award for Cameraworks, 84; 1st prize Int Ctr of Photog, NY, 85; Praemium Imperiale Japan Art Asn, 89; 5th Ann Gov Calif Visual Arts award, 94; named Companion of Hon, Her Majesty, the Queen of Eng, 97; Charles Wollaston award Royal Acad Arts London, 99. *Bibliog:* Portrait of David Hockney, Peter Webb, 88, Kenneth Silver, David Hockney,

Rizzoli Internat Publs, 94, David Hockney, Paula Melia, Manchester Univ Press, 95, David Hockney, Marco Livingstone, Thames & Hudson, 96, Hockney on Art: Conversations with Paul Joyce, Paul Joyce, Little Brown, 99, Hockney Paints the Stage, Martin Friedman, Thames & Hudson, 83, supplement, 85, David Hockney, Penelope Curtis, Tate Gallery Pub, 93, David Hockney, Peter Clothier, Abbeville Press, 95, Outstanding Lives: Profiles of Lesbians and Gay Men, Michael Bronski, 96. *Publ:* Illusr, Six Fairy Tales of the Brothers Grimm, 69; The Blue Guitar, 77; Hockney's Alphabet, 91; Hockney's Portraits and People, 2003, Hockney's Pictures, 2004, Dog Days, 2006. *Mailing Add:* 7508 Santa Monica Blvd Los Angeles CA 90046-6407

HODES, BARNEY
SCULPTOR
b Mar 11, 43. *Study:* Columbia Col, AB, 64; Brooklyn Mus Art Sch, 64-66; Univ NC, MFA, 68. *Work:* Art Students League. *Exhib:* NC Mus Art; Brooklyn Mus, Brooklyn Mus Art Sch; one-man show, Weatherspoon Gallery, Suffolk Co Community Col, 2000; Artists & Friends, First St Gallery, 81; Numeroff Gallery; The Human Presence, First Street Gallery, 95; Denise Bibro Gallery, 99. *Pos:* Co-dir, NY Acad Art, formerly. *Teaching:* Lectr, Fairleigh Dickinson Univ, Teaneck, NJ, 70-72; instr, Brooklyn Mus Sch Art, 70-81, Brooklyn Col, 73-76; assoc prof, St John's Univ, 77-83, NY Acad Art, 83-86, New Brooklyn Sch Life Drawing, Painting & Sculpture, 80-83 & Art Students League, 86-; instr sculpture, Nat Acad Design, 2000-. *Awards:* Art Students League Award. *Media:* Bronze. *Interests:* portraits & nudes. *Publ:* auth, Linea, 98, 99, 2000. *Mailing Add:* Art Students League 215 W 57th St New York NY 10019

HODES, SUZANNE
PAINTER, PRINTMAKER
b New York, NY. *Study:* Radcliffe Col, Brandeis Univ, BA(fine arts, magna cum laude), 60; Columbia Univ, MFA, 62; studied with Oskar Kokoschka, Salzburg, Austria, & George Grosz, Maine. *Work:* Fogg Art Mus, Cambridge, Mass; De Cordova Mus, Lincoln, Mass; Print & Drawing Collection, Boston Pub Libr, Mass; Rockefeller Univ, NY; Casali Inst, Jerusalem. *Comn:* Lithograph, Physicians Social Responsibility, Cambridge, Mass, 84; landscape painting, New Eng Life Co, Burlington, Mass, 85; Portrait of Judge Doyle, Middlesex Bar Asn, Waltham, Mass, 93. *Exhib:* Figure & Landscape, De Cordova Mus, Lincoln, Mass, 88; Tenth Sept Competition, Alexandria Mus Art, La, 91; solo exhib City Reflections, (with catalog) Bunting Inst Radcliffe Col, Cambridge, Mass, 1996, NY Reflections, Joan Whalen Gallery, NY, 2002-2003, People and Places, paintings, drawings & monotypes, Schlesinger Libr at Radcliffe, 2002-2003; "One of a kind" Monotype Exhib, Sigma Gallery, NY, 91; solo show, paintings, Reflections, Artana Gallery, Brookline, Mass, 04; 4 person show, Rotenberg Gallery, 04. *Pos:* Co-founder, Artists for Survival, 82-92; pres, Artists West Studios, 85-89; teacher, mem, Mayor's Cult Comn, Waltham, Mass, 87-90. *Teaching:* painting, Cambridge Ctr Adult Educ, 72-74 & Sr Citizen Prog, Waltham, Mass, 90-93; painting, Lesley Univ Seminars. *Awards:* Grumbacher Award, Audubon Artists Exhib, 63; Fulbright Fel, Fulbright Comn, 63-64; Bunting Inst Fel, 70-72. *Bibliog:* W Zimmer (auth), Review of one of a kind monotypes, New York Times, 7/29/90; Suzanne Hodes '60: Something of the spirit, Brandeis Review, spring 91; C Temin (auth), Review of creativity & spirituality, Boston Globe, 1/5/94. *Mem:* Boston Printmakers (artist mem, 86-94); Monotype Guild New Eng; Copley Soc & Copley Master; Soc Bunting Inst Fel; Women's Caucus for Art. *Media:* Oil, Mixed Media; Monotype. *Collection:* Fidelity Investment, Wempe Jewelers, Yawkey Ctr, Cabot Corp, Bank of Am. *Publ:* Contribr (with Julia Ayres), Monotype Techniques, Watson Guptil, 91; Printmaking Techniques, Watson Guptil, 93; New American Paintings, Open Studios Press, 93; Suzanne Hodes' New York: Expressionism Redefined, exhib catalog, 1999; contrib, Boston Modern, Judith Bookbinder (auth), 2005. *Dealer:* Artana Gallery Coolidge Corner Brookline MA; ART 3 Gallery, Manchester, NH; The Art Exchange, Columbus, OH. *Mailing Add:* 35 Riverside Dr Waltham MA 02154

HODGE, DOROTHY (SCOTTIE) W
GALLERY DIRECTOR, ASSEMBLAGE ARTIST
b Darlington, SC, Oct 21, 40. *Study:* Winthrop Col, Rock Hill, SC, BA, 62; Furman Univ, Greenville, SC, MA, 73; Greenville Co Mus Art Sch, 74-75. *Work:* Garfield Inc, Greenville, SC; Greenville Hosp System, SC. *Exhib:* Charlotte Open Exhib, NC, 80 & 81; Tempo Gallery, SC, 80, 83 & 93; Curs Choice Exhib, Greenville Mus, SC, 81; Francis Marion Col, SC, 83. *Pos:* Founder & dir, Tempo Gallery, Greenville, SC, 75-; co-founder, SC Watercolor Soc, 77; pres, Greenville Artists Guild, 78-79; founding bd mem, Upstate Visual Arts, Greenville, SC, 90-; event chair, Art in the Park, Greenville, SC, 93-; artistic dir, Upstate Visual Arts, Greenville, SC, 98-. *Teaching:* Lectr, Prof Presentation of Art Works on Paper, Art-Gallery Relationships & Selecting Original Art for Home Interiors. *Awards:* Curators Choice Award, Greenville Mus, SC, 80; Special Recognition Award, SC Watercolor Soc, 88; Heart in the Arts Award, Greenville Metrop Arts Coun, Greenville, SC, 93. *Bibliog:* Article, in: The Greenville Woman Mag, 3/86. *Mem:* SC Watercolor Soc (bd mem, 81-87 & 91-); Upstate Visual Arts, Greenville, SC (founding bd mem, 90); Greenville Art Asn (bd mem, 78-79); co-founder SC Watercolor Soc; Greenville Metrop Arts Coun. *Specialty:* Original artworks by local, regional artists only. *Publ:* Auth, How to Mat and Frame Your Art Works on Paper, 85, rev 92; article, Don't Kill the Artists' Market, SC Watercolor Soc, 2/92; article, Shipping Artwork to Juried Shows, SC Watercolor Soc, 6/92; Carrie Brown, visual artist: mature & still maturing, Artscene Mag, spring 93; Aqua-media coming of age, Artscene Mag, 93. *Mailing Add:* c/o Tempo Gallery 125 W Stone Ave Greenville SC 29609

HODGE, R GAREY
PAINTER
b Moweaqua, Ill, July 27, 37. *Study:* Eastern Ill Univ, BS, 61, MA(painting), 73; Harvard Univ Summer Sch, with William Georgenes. *Exhib:* Tri-State Exhib, Evansville Mus, Ind, 59; Miss Valley Exhib, Ill State Mus, Springfield, 64; Ill Bell Tel Exhib, Chicago, 67; River Roads Exhib, St Louis, 69, 70 & 72; 5th Int Biennial Sport Fine Arts, La Pinacoteca, Barcelona, Spain, 75; Western Ill Univ, 78. *Teaching:* Instr painting, graphics & design, Springfield High Sch, formerly. *Awards:* Runner Up, New York World's Fair Sculpture Design, Int Fair Consults, 63; Second in Painting, Northside Art Asn, St Louis, 69; Grand Prize, US Hockey Hall of Fame, 76. *Mem:* League Fine Arts, Brandon, Fla; Ill State Mus Soc; Springfield Art Asn. *Media:* Acrylic, Watercolor. *Mailing Add:* 2413 Raleigh Rd Springfield IL 62704-6111

HODGELL, ROBERT OVERMAN
PRINTMAKER, SCULPTOR
b Mankato, Kans, July 14, 22. *Study:* Univ Wis, BS & MA; Dartmouth Col; Univ Iowa; Univ Ill; Univ Michoacana, Mex; also with John Steuart Curry. *Work:* Joslyn Art Mus; Dartmouth Col; Libr Cong, Washington; Ringling Mus Art, Sarasota, Fla; Metrop Mus Art; and others. *Pos:* Asst art dir & illus, Our Wonderful World, Champaign, Ill, 53-56; art dir, ed & commun serv, Exten Div, Univ Wis-Madison, 57-59; bk illusr for UNESCO in Pakistan, 60; co-owner, Joan Hodgell Gallery, Sarasota, Fla, 77-88. *Teaching:* Artist in residence & instr, Des Moines Art Ctr, 49-53; assoc prof art, Eckerd Col, 61-67, artist in residence, 67-77, adj art instr, 81-; instr, Ringling Sch of Art, 77-; art instr, New Col, Univ SFla, Sarasota, 80. *Awards:* Artist of the Year, Pinellas Co, Fla Art Coun, 91-92; Artist of the Year, Sarasota Visual Arts Ctr, 96-97. *Mem:* Nat Acad Design. *Media:* Lino-Cut. *Mailing Add:* 6418 Lincoln Rd Bradenton FL 34203-9729

HODGES, JIM
PAINTER
b Spokane, Wash, 57. *Study:* Ft Wright Col, Wash, BFA, 80; Pratt Inst, MFA, 86. *Exhib:* One-man shows, A Diary of Flowers, CR Gallery, NY, 94, States, Fabric Workshop & Mus, Philadelphia, 96, yes, Marc Foxx, Santa Monica, Ca, 96, Every Way, Mus Contemp Art, Chicago, 99, This and This, CR Gallery, NY, 2002, Colorsound, Addison Gallery Am Art, Phillips Acad, Mass, 2003, Returning, Art Pace, San Antonio, 2003, Don't be Afraid, Worcester Art Mus, Mass, 2004, Heaven & Earth, Centro Galego de Arte Contemporanea, Santiago de Compostello, Spain, 2005; group shows at Selections From The Artists File, Artists Space, NY, 88, Partnership for the Homeless with AIDS, Christie's, NY, 90, Our Perfect World, Grey Art Gallery, NY, 93, Ethereal Materialism, Apex Art, NY, 94, It's How You Play the Game, Exit Art/The First World, NY, 94, New Works, Feigen Gallery, Chicago, 95, Poetics of Obsession, Linda Kirkland Gallery, NY, 97, Age of Influence: Reflections in the Mirror of Am Cult, Mus Contemp Art, Chicago, 2000, Gardens of Pleasure, John Michael Kohler Arts Ctr, Sheboygan, Wis, 2000; CAMERA WORKS: The Photog Impulse in Contemp Art, Boesky Gallery, NY, 2001, Life Death Love Hate Pleasure Pain, Mus Contemp Art, Chicago, 2002, In Full View, Andrea Rosen Gallery, NY, 2003, Treble, Sculpture Ctr, Long Island City, NY, 2004, Whitney Biennial, Whitney Mus Am Art, 2004, Visual Music: 1905-2005, Mus Contemp Art, Los Angeles, 2005, Landscape Confection, Wexner Ctr Arts, Columbus, Ohio, 2005. *Awards:* Recipient, Mid Atlantic Arts Found, Nat Educ Asn, 92, Albert Ucross Prize, 2001; Reg Fel, Paper & Works on Paper, 92; grantee Louis Comfort Tiffany Found, 95. *Mailing Add:* c/o CR Gallery 535 W 22nd St 3rd fl New York NY 10011

HODGKINS, ROSALIND SELMA
PAINTER
b Farmington, Maine, May 25, 42. *Study:* Univ SFla; Pratt Inst, BFA; Art Students League. *Work:* Southern Ill Univ, Carbondale; Bronx Mus Fine Arts, NY; Hewitt Sch, NY; Prudential Insurance Co. *Exhib:* One-woman shows, Warren Benedek Gallery, NY 72 & 73 & James Yu Gallery, NY, 76; Kensington Arts Asn, Toronto, Ont, 75; PS 1 Pattern Painting Show, NY, 77; O1A Art in Pub Places Show, NY, 77; Soho Ctr Visual Arts Show, NY, 81; 55 Mercer Gallery, NY, 86. *Awards:* MacDowell Colony Fel, 77-78. *Media:* Oil. *Mailing Add:* PO Box 362 Otisville NY 10963-0362

HODLEY, JANE See Dixon, Jenny (Jane) Hodley

HOFER, EVELYN
PHOTOGRAPHER
b Marburg, Ger; Brit citizen. *Study:* Switz. *Work:* Metrop Mus Art, NY; Smith Col Mus Art, Northampton, Mass; Univ Colo Libr, Boulder. *Exhib:* Manhattan Now, NY Hist Soc, 74; Witkin Gallery, 77, 83, 87, 89 & 94; Musee Elyse, Lausanne, Swit, 95. *Media:* Four by Five Camera. *Publ:* Coauth, The Stones of Florence, 59, London Perceived, 63, The Presence of Spain, 64 & New York Proclaimed, 65, Harcourt, Brace, Jovanovich; Dublin, A Portrait, Harper & Row, 67; Emerson in Italy, Henry Holt, 87. *Dealer:* Witkin Gallery 415 West Broadway New York NY 10012. *Mailing Add:* 55 Bethune St New York NY 10014

HOFER, INGRID (INGEBORG)
PAINTER, INSTRUCTOR
b New York, NY. *Study:* Meisterschule Fuer Mode, Hamburg, Ger, BA, 1948; Univ Hamburg; Traphagen Sch Design, New York, 1951; with A Odefey, Goettingen, Ger, Albert Bross, Jr, John R Grabach, Adolf Konrad & Nicholas Reale, Alex Powers; Kathrine Chang Liu, master classes with Prof Glenn Bradshaw, 1998. *Work:* Fairleigh Dickinson Univ, NJ; Good Shepherd Hosp, Ill; Lumus Co, NJ; Dana Corp, Ohio; Piedmont Tech Col, SC. *Comn:* Many pvt comns in Ger, Switz, Sweden & US, 56-. *Exhib:* Tweed Mus; Union League, Chicago, 81; Women Alive, Toledo, Ohio, 86, 87 & 89; Winter Sojourn, Edison Plaza, Toledo, 87; Collectors Corner, Toledo Mus,

89-93 & 98-; Women on Paper, Anderson, SC, 96; Arnold Gallery, Aiken, SC, 97-98; Aiken Ctr for the Arts, SC, 2000; one-woman show, Channing Gallery, Toledo, Ohio, Covenant Club Gallery, Chicago, Ill, Coach House Gallery, Detroit, Mich, Lyle Studio, Augusta, Ga, Studio Four, Roseland, NJ, Arnold Gallery, Aiken, SC; USAA Etherredge Art Gallery, 2002-2003. *Teaching:* Instr mixed media, Acad Artists, Trailside Mus, Mountainside, NJ, 1968-70; instr, Grosse Pointe War Mem, Mich, 1974-78, Country Side Art Ctr, Arlington Heights, Ill, 1981-83, Toledo Artists Club, 1983-93, Lourdes Col, Sylvania, Ohio, 1988-93, McCormic Arts Coun, SC, 1993-; instr, Toledo Arts Club 81-93; instr, Lourdes Collage, 90; instr, McCormack Arts Council, 94; art instr (retired). *Awards:* Am Watercolor Soc Traveling Show Award, 1973; Purchase Award, Union League, Ill, 1981; Nat Award, Ga Watercolor Soc, 1994, 1996-2000. *Mem:* Fel Am Artists Prof League; Catharine Lorillard Wolfe Art Club; SC Watercolor Soc; NJ Watercolor Soc; assoc Am Watercolor Soc; Ga Watercolor Soc. *Media:* Watercolor, Mixed Media. *Specialty:* Visual arts, paintings. *Interests:* Watercolor, pastel, acrylic, mixed media, abstract. *Dealer:* The Arnold Gallery Aiken SC 29801; Rabbet Gallery NJ; Cameo Art Gallery, Columbia, SC, Am Gallery, Sylvania, OH; Art on Board, Augusta, GA. *Mailing Add:* 209 Old Ferry Rd McCormick SC 29835

HOFF, MARGO
PAINTER, COLLAGE ARTIST
b Tulsa, Okla. *Study:* Tulsa Univ; Art Inst Chicago; Pratt Graphics Ctr; St Marys Col, Notre Dame, hon DFA, 69; Drew Univ, hon DFA, 86. *Work:* Whitney Mus Am Art, NY; Brooklyn Mus, NY; Art Inst Chicago; Krannert Mus, Univ Ill; Rosenwald Found Collection; Metrop Mus, NY, 82-86. *Comn:* Wall design, Home Fed Bank, Chicago, 66; Mirror to Man (mural), Mayo Clinic, Rochester, Minn, 68; stage set & costumes for Murray Louis Dance Co, 69; portrait of S Madeleva, St Marys Col, Notre Dame, 70; two murals, New Govt Bldg, Plattsburgh, NY, 77-79; Wall Hanging: Peat, Marwick, Mitchel, Washington, DC. *Exhib:* One-man shows, Banfer Gallery, NY, 64, 66 & 68, Fairweather Hardin Gallery, 64-79, 81, 83, 86, Bednarz Gallery, Los Angeles, 67 & Babcock Gallery, NY, 74; Hadler Rodriguez Galleries, 78 & 79; Betty Parsons Gallery, NY, 81-82. *Teaching:* Teaching Grant, Duke Foun, Am Univ, Beirut, 56-57; artist in residence, Univ Southern Ill, 66-67; artist in residence, St Marys Col, Notre Dame, 69-70, 78, 82, & 84; teaching grant, Goretti Sch, Fort Portal, Uganda, E Africa, 71; Col St Maria, Sao Paulo, Brasil; AIR, Rhode Island Sch Design, 80. *Publ:* Illusr, Christmas House, Coachhouse, 65; illusr, 4 Seasons & 5 Senses, 66 & Christmas Cupboard, 67, Funk & Wagnall. *Mailing Add:* 114 W 14th St New York NY 10011-7304

HOFFBERG, JUDITH A
PUBLISHER, CURATOR
b Hartford, Conn, May 19, 34. *Study:* Univ Calif, Los Angeles, BA, MA & MLS; Ital Govt grant, study of Leonardo da Vinci. *Pos:* Dir, Umbrella Assoc, 78-; bd dir, Franklin Furnace, 76-77; exec dir, Assoc Councils of the Arts, 78-79; cur, Umbrella Show, Univ Calif, Riverside, 79; co-cur, Traction Gallery, Los Angeles, 81; cur, Editions & Additions, Int Bookworks, IDEA, Northlight Gallery, Tempe, Ariz, 85, traveled to Sacramento & Univ Calif, Riverside, 86; cur, Undercover: The Book as Format, Fresno, 87; cur, Art from the Page: Bookworks, Salem, Ore, Salem Art Asn, traveled to Tex Women's Univ, Denton, 87; cur, a Book of His Own: Men's Visual Diaries, Woodland Pattern, Milwaukee, Wis, 87 & Univ Calif Los Angeles Art Libr, 90; A Book in Hand, Arvada Ctr for Arts, Colo, 89; Books from the Edge of the Pacific, Univ Calif, Santa Barbara, 90-91; Boundless Vision: Contemp Bookworks, San Antonio Art Inst, 91; Ringling Sch Art Gallery, Sarasota, 92,; cur, Cross Currents, Calif State Univ, Hayward, 92, Freedom: Int Mail Art Show, Armory for Arts, Pasadena, 92, The Amazing Decade: Women & Performance Art in America, 1970-1980, Santa Monica, 93 & Ore Sch Arts & Crafts, Portland, 93; co-cur, Multiple World, Atlanta Col Art, 94, Barbara Turner Smith: Who are we?, Hirokozu Kosaka: Woman with Mole, Santa Monica, 94, Journey/Journals: Elsa Flores & Gronk, Santa Monica, 94, The Reading Room of Madam X, Santa Monica, 97, Boundless: Liberating the Book Form, San Francisco, 98, Women of the Book: Jewish Artists, Jewish Friends, 97-2002 & 6 Degrees: Art in the Libr, Los Angeles, 2001. *Teaching:* Lectr on artist's books worldwide; lectr, Univ Calif, Santa Barbara, 90. *Awards:* British Coun grant, 83; Fulbright Grant, New Zealand, 84; Fluxus Res Fel, Sonja Henie & Onstad Fdn, Oslo, Norway. *Mem:* Int Platform Soc; Soc Archit Historians (mem bd dir, 79-82); Col Art Asn; Honorary life mem Art Libr Soc of NAm, Art Libr Soc of United Kingdom; Int Asn of Art Critics, Am Sect. *Publ:* Auth, Introductions to various books in field of book arts, Correspondence Art; The medium is the message, Press/Art, Long Beach Pres-Telegram, 4/23/87; Sandra Schwimmer: Bookworks (exhib catalog), Riverside Art Mus, 87; interview: Piotr Rypson, Warsaw in High Performance, 10/88; review, Edie Danieli Ellis at Orlando Gallery, Artscene, 1/90; publ, Robert C Morgan (auth), Commentor's on the New Media Arts, 92; Buzz Spector (auth), The Book Makers Desire: Writings on the Art of the Book, 95; auth, Umbrella: The Anthology, Umbrella Ed, 2000 & Women of the Book: Jewish Artists, Jewish Themes (exhib catalog), Boca Raton, Fla, 2001; Articles in ArtScene, 95-. *Mailing Add:* PO Box 3640 Santa Monica CA 90408

HOFFELD, JEFFREY M
ART DEALER
b Brooklyn, NY, Dec 3, 45. *Study:* Brooklyn Col, BA, 66; Columbia Univ, MPhil, 73; New York Univ, MA, 86. *Pos:* Asst cur, Medieval art & The Cloisters, Metrop Mus Art, New York, 67-73; dir, Neuberger Mus, State Univ NY, Purchase, 74-77; vpres & partner, Pace Gallery, New York, 78-83; pres, Jeffrey Hoffeld & Co, Inc, 83-; sr vpres, Hir Sch & Adley Galleries, New York, 86-87. *Teaching:* Asst prof art, Brooklyn Col, NY, 68-73, State Univ NY, Purchase, 73-77; assoc prof english, New York Univ, 86. *Awards.* Nat Endowment Arts Grant, 75-76. *Res:* Medieval and contemporary art. *Specialty:* European and American 20th century art. *Publ:* Coauth, The Cloisters Apocalypse, Metrop Mus Art, New York, 70; Picasso: The Late Drawings, New York, 88

HOFFMAN, ELAINE JANET
PAINTER, LECTURER
b Oak Park, Ill. *Study:* Averett Col; Portland Art Mus; Northwest Watercolor Sch, with Irving Shapiro; Maryhurst Educ Ctr, BA, 78; also with Charles Mulvey, Perry Acker, George Hamilton, Phil Austin, Nita Engel, 95 & Tom Sqouros, 95. *Work:* US Interstate Bank; Boise Cascade Paper Co; Payless Drug Store; Beloit Corp; Willamette Indust. *Exhib:* Am Artists Prof League, NY, 71; Prof Ore Artists Invitational, Coos Bay, Ore, 72-74; George Fox Col Invitational Newberg, Ore, 72-75; one-man shows, Courtyard Gallery, 79, Art Adventures, 80-81, Hoffman Studios, Portland, 84-90 & Coos Bay Art Mus, Ore, 94; juried shows, Ore Watercolor Soc, 92-98; State Capitol Gallery, Salem, Ore, 98-2000; Heritage House, Lake Oswego, 2003. *Pos:* Bd dir, Lake Oswego Art Guild, Ore, 65-68; pres, Lake Area Artist, 67-69, 81 & Lake Oswego Art Develop, 89. *Teaching:* Pvt classes in watercolor landscapes, 65-81; instr, Portland Community Col, 75-81. *Awards:* First Award, Lake Oswego Art Festival, Ore, 78 & 82; Best of Show, Ciackahas Fair, 91; Watercolor Soc Ore Award, 92-94. *Mem:* Fel Am Artists Prof League; Ore Watercolor Soc; Lake Area Artists (pres, 67-68, 71-72 & 75-76); Watercolor Critique Group, Ore Art Inst; Colored Pencil Soc Am (vp dist chap 201, 2000-01). *Media:* Watercolor. *Publ:* Illusr 4 paintings, Willamette Savings & Loan Calendar, 88; The Oregonian, Portland; The Review, Lake Oswego, Ore; Portland Open Studio Calendar, 2000. *Dealer:* Hoffman Studios Lake Oswego. *Mailing Add:* 16695 Glenwood Ct Lake Oswego OR 97034

HOFFMAN, ERIC
PAINTER, PRINTMAKER
b Santa Cruz, Calif, July 16, 52. *Study:* Cabrillo Col, Aptos, Calif, AA, 72, San Jose State Univ, BA, (painting), 75, & MFA (painting), 78. *Work:* Am Express; Monterey Peninsula Mus Art, Calif; San Jose Mus Art; E F Hutton, NY; Bumper Develop Corp, Ltd, Calgary; Price-Waterhouse; Merril, Skidmore, Owens, NY. *Comn:* Large scale 2-part panel painting, Bumper Develop Corp Ltd, Calgary, Alta, 81; 2-part panel painting, Juan Montoya Design, NY, 83; 3-part enviro piece, Emerald Fund, San Francisco, Calif, 84; 3-part panel, Battenberg, Fillhardt & Wright, San Jose, Calif, 84; series of 28 monogotypes, Arts Coun, Santa Clara Co, 86. *Exhib:* Oakland Mus, Calif, 81; Chain Reaction, San Francisco Arts Comt, Calif, 85; Scratching the Surface, San Jose Mus Art, Calif, 85; San Jose Inst Contemp Art, Calif, 86; Metrop Mus Art, Miami, Fla, 86; Miller-Brown Gallery, San Francisco, 86; Expressive Surfaces, Beverly Gordon Gallery, Dallas, Tex, 88; Twining Gallery, NY, 88; Maison du Cult, Grenoble, France, 88. *Pos:* Asst preparator, San Jose Mus Art, Calif, 76-79. *Teaching:* Guest lectr expressive drawing, Calif Polytech Univ; grad seminar ceramics & pictorial arts, San Jose State Unvi, 85; instr, color-design, Cabrillo Col. *Awards:* Du Credit Commercial de France Award, 85; Du Ministere de al Culture, Paris, France, 85; De la Villa de Granonle, France, 85. *Bibliog:* Article, Arts Mag, 82; Sally Robertson (auth), Art in San Jose, Art Week, 76; Catalog, E F Hutton Collection, 86. *Mem:* San Jose Inst Contemp Art. *Media:* Miscellaneous. *Dealer:* Twining Gallery 568 Broadway Suite 107 New York NY 10012; Katia LaCoste Gallery 227 N First St San Jose CA 95062. *Mailing Add:* c/o Frederick Spratt Gallery 920 S First St San Jose CA 95110-3125

HOFFMAN, HELEN BACON
PAINTER
b San Antonio, Tex, July 14, 30. *Study:* Ogontz Col, Philadelphia; Parsons Sch Design. *Work:* NAm-Mex Inst Cult Relations, Mexico City, Mex; Wichita Art Asn, Kans. *Exhib:* One-man shows, North Star Gallery, San Antonio, Tex, 66-80, Grand Cent Art Galleries, NY, 69-80 & Veerhoff Galleries, Washington, DC, 64, 74 & 78; Musselman River Walk Gallery, San Antonio, 81 & 82 & Houston, 82 & 83. *Awards:* First Place Award, Catherine Lorillard Wolfe Art Club Show, 73; First Place Painting, Salmagundi Club, 74; Kalikow Award Excellence, Pastel Soc Am, 82. *Mem:* Artists Equity Asn; Soc Washington Artists; Pastel Soc Am; Nat Arts Club; Catherine Lorillard Wolfe Art Club; and others. *Media:* Pastel, Oil. *Dealer:* Veerhoff Galleries 1604 17th St NW Washington DC 20009; Grand Central Art Galleries 24 W 57th St New York NY 10019

HOFFMAN, MANDY LIPPMAN
CONSULTANT, WRITER
b Baltimore, Md, Sept 23, 56. *Study:* George Washington Univ, BA, 78; Parson's Sch Design, AAS, 81. *Collection Arranged:* Baltimore Off of KPMG/Peat Marwick (law off of Melnicove, Weiner, Smouse & Garbis); Artist Designed Furniture, Norton Gallery Art, W Palm Beach, Fla, 86. *Pos:* Dir, Meredith Gallery, Baltimore, Md, 81-87; self-employed consultant, 88-; bd mem, James Renwick Alliance, 90. *Teaching:* Instr, Md Inst Art, Baltimore, 83, Visit the Artist, Jewish Community Ctr, Washington, DC, 89 & Contemp Art in Washington, Smithsonian, 90. *Mem:* James Renwick Alliance. *Collection:* Contemporary American crafts, prints and paintings (1970 to present). *Publ:* Auth, The new art furniture: Functional creativity, Home Mag, 11/90. *Mailing Add:* 6605 Paxton Rd Rockville MD 20852

HOFFMAN, MARGUERITE STEED
COLLECTOR
Pos: dir, Gerald Peters Gallery, formerly; bd trustees, Dallas Mus Art, 99-, chmn bd; With, Dallas Mus Art, currently; bd dir, Tex Freedom Network, currently; mem coun, Dallas Women's Found, currently. *Awards:* Named one of Top 200 Collectors, ARTnews Mag, 2003-06; donated contemp art collection and $20 million endowment Dallas Mus Art, 2005. *Collection:* Postwar American and European Art; Chinese monochromes. *Mailing Add:* Dallas Mus Art 1717 N Harwood Dallas TX 75201

HOFFMAN, MARILYN FRIEDMAN
DIRECTOR
b Jan 27, 46. *Study:* Brown Univ, Providence, RI, BA(hon; art hist), 67, MA(art hist), 71; Montserrat Col Art, Beverly, Mass, Hon Dr fine arts, 96. *Pos:* Cur asst, Educ Dept, Mus Art, RI Sch Design, 67-68; gallery asst, Adelson Galleries, Inc, Boston, 68-69 & 70-71; grad asst, Educ Dept, Metrop Mus Art, New York, 69; adj lectr, Dept Pub

Educ, Mus Fine Arts, Boston, 70-71; cur, Brockton Art Mus-Fuller Mem, Mass, 71-73, actg dir, 73-74, dir, 74-84; cur, Currier Gallery Art, Manchester, NH, 84-88, dir, 88-; chair, NH Large Cult Orgn, 91; bd mem, Arts 1000, 94. *Teaching:* Teaching asst, Brown Univ, 69-70. *Mem:* Am Asn Mus; Col Art Asn Am; New Eng Mus Asn (secy, treas); NH Large Cult Orgn; Arts 1000. *Publ:* Auth, Pssst, Airbrush Painting (catalog), 72, The Good Things in Life/19th Century American Still Life (catalog), 73 & Unstretched Paintings (catalog), 73, Brockton Art Ctr-Fuller Mem; Museum Loans at Brockton, Art J, Vol 32, 73. *Mailing Add:* 45 Hardy Rd Londonderry NH 03053-2872

HOFFMAN, MARTIN
PAINTER, ILLUSTRATOR
b St Augustine, Fla, Nov 1, 35. *Study:* Univ Miami, 55; Fla State Univ, 56. *Work:* Miami Mus Mod Art; Va Mus Fine Arts, Richmond; Indianapolis Mus Art; JB Speed Mus, Louisville, Ky; Norton Gallery of Art, West Palm Beach, Fla. *Comn:* numerous paintings & illus, Playboy Mag, 66-05; Basile, Milan, 80-82; NASA Space Shuttle Program, 82-92; Hakehodo Agency, Tokyo, 85; Toyo Cinema, Japan, 86. *Exhib:* Air & Space Mus, Smithsonian Inst, 82-83; Johnson Space Ctr, Univ Houston, 83; The Educated Eye, State Mus, Albany, NY, 84; The Epic New York Paintings, Stetson Univ, 90; Intimate Works, R Thames Fine Art, Ormond, Fla, 91; The Realist Painting, Ormond Mem Mus, 91; Ok Harris Works of Art, New York City, 72-75. *Collection Arranged:* Joan & Roland Des Combes, Windermere, Fla; Mary T & James Zaengle, Cooperstown, NY. *Pos:* Art dir, munerous Miami advert agencies, 57-70; designer-illusr, Graphic Arts, Inc, 60-70. *Teaching:* Instr grad painting & drawing, Univ Miami, 69-71 & Casements Cult Ctr, 91-92. *Awards:* Art Dir Awards, Miami Art Dirs Club, 59-70; Illus Awards, Chicago Advert Club, 71-79; Elegance for the Eighties, Best Serv Illusr, Playboy, 79; and others. *Bibliog:* Griffin Smith (auth), article, Tropic Mag, 9/71; article, Illus Japan, No 18, 10/82; Diane Copelon (auth), article, Ormond Beach Observer, 8/26/90; John Wirt (auth), article, Daytona Beach News-J, 5/26/91; Chuck Twardy (auth), article, Orlando Sentinel, 6/2/91. *Media:* Acrylic, Oil, Watercolor. *Res:* Classical painting methods, Pompeii, Herculaneum, Autobiographies. *Interests:* Asian and Western philosophy; Modern music. *Collection:* Numerous private collections. *Publ:* Illusr, Playboy, 67-2005, Italian, Spanish, Japanese edits Playboy, 67-2000; Art Direction, 4/72; NY Times & Artforum, 74; Fortune, 74; illustr Rolling Stone, 73, Record World Cover, 80, and others. *Dealer:* OK Harris Gallery 383 W Broadway New York NY 10012; Advert Rep: Frank & Jeff Lavaty 50 E 50th St New York NY 10022. *Mailing Add:* 1840 Waterford Dr #2 Vero Beach FL 32966-8039

HOFFMAN, MICHAEL E
EDITOR, CURATOR
b New York, NY, July 5, 42. *Study:* St Lawrence Univ, BA, 64; also adv studies with Minor White, Mass Inst Technol. *Collection Arranged:* Paul Strand: Retrospective, Clarence John Laughlin: The Personal Eye & French Primitive Photography, Philadelphia Mus Art; August Sander: Photographs of an Epoch; The Face of China; Tibet: The Sacred Realm; Minor White: Retrospective; 40 exhibs at Philadelphia Mus Art, with many traveling in US, Canada & abroad, 69-. *Pos:* Ed & publ, exec dir, Aperture Found Inc, 64-; exec dir, cur, Alfred Stieglitz Ctr, Philadelphia Mus Art, 69-. *Awards:* Pi Delta Epsilon. *Mem:* Soc Photog Educ. *Publ:* Editor of over 350 publications in fine arts & photog, 64-. *Mailing Add:* RD 2 Box 85 Pine Plains NY 12567

HOFFMAN, NANCY
DEALER
b New York, NY, Feb 23, 44. *Study:* Wellesley Col, 62-64; Barnard Col, Columbia Univ, BA(art hist), 66. *Pos:* Asst registrar, Asia House Gallery, New York, 64-69; dir, French & Co Contemp Gallery, New York, 69-72 & Nancy Hoffman Gallery, New York, 72-. *Mem:* Art Dealers Asn Am. *Specialty:* Contemporary art: paintings, drawings, sculpture and graphics. *Mailing Add:* Nancy Hoffman Gallery 429 W Broadway New York NY 10012

HOFFMAN, NEIL JAMES
ADMINISTRATOR, EDUCATOR
b Buffalo, NY, Sept 2, 38. *Study:* State Univ NY Buffalo, BS, 60, MS, 67. *Pos:* Dir, Prog Artisanry, Boston Univ, 74-79; dean & chief admin officer, Otis Art Inst Parsons Sch Design, 79-83; pres, Sch Art Inst Chicago, 83-85, Calif Col Arts & Crafts, 85-93 & Otis Col Art & Design, 93-. *Teaching:* Art & chmn unified art dept, Grand Island Pub Schs, NY, 61-68; assoc prof design & art educ & assoc dean col fine & appl arts, Rochester Inst Technol, 68-74. *Mailing Add:* 9045 Lincoln Blvd Los Angeles CA 90045

HOFFMAN, WILLIAM A
CERAMIST, SCULPTOR
b Roswell, NMex, May 4, 20. *Study:* Eastern NMex Univ, Portales, AA, 40; Art Inst Chicago, BAE, 49, MAE, 50; Univ Southern Calif, Los Angeles, 51; State Univ NY, Col Ceramics, Alfred, MFA, 53. *Work:* Roswell Mus, NMex; St Mary's Col, South Bend, Ind; Kessel Ceramic Collection, Whitewater, Wis; and many pvt collections. *Exhib:* One-man shows, St Mary's Col, South Bend, Ind, 69, Lewis Towers Galleries, Loyola Univ, Chicago, 73, Triton Col, River Grove, Ill, 74, Pot Shop, Evanston, Ill, 75, Nina Owen Gallery, 86, Marmion Univ, Aurora, Ill, 88 & 89 & Valparaiso Univ, Ind, 89; Union Gallery, Mankato State Univ, Minn, 78; Fairweather-Hardin Gallery, 81, 84 & 87; Arts Club Chicago, 85, 87, 89, 91, 94 & 98; Univ Wis, Whitewater, 86; and other one-man shows. *Collection Arranged:* Japanese Prints Exhib, Northwestern State Col, Natchitoches, La, 50; Tower League of Young Adults Exhib, New York, 55. *Teaching:* Instr design, ceramics & figure drawing, La State Univ, Baton Rouge, 57-58; asst prof design, pottery & sculpture, Art Inst Chicago, 58-70; adj prof pottery, Loyola Univ, Chicago, 70-83. *Bibliog:* Joshua Kind (auth), rev, New Art Examiner; American Artists, 85 & 90, NY Art Review, 87, Chicago Artists, 89, Les Krantz; Chicago Art Rev, 89. *Mem:* Am Crafts Coun, NY; Chicago Artists Coalition; Arts Club Chicago. *Media:* Clay. *Mailing Add:* 1925 N Hudson Chicago IL 60614

HOFFMAN, WILLIAM MCKINLEY, JR
PAINTER, EDUCATOR
b Blairsville, Pa, Jan 25, 34. *Study:* Pa Acad Fine Arts & Univ Pa, BFA, 62; Tyler Sch Art, Temple Univ, MFA, 67. *Work:* NJ State Mus, Trenton; Stedman Art Gallery, Rutgers Univ, Camden, NJ; Camden Co Cult & Heritage, NJ; Thomas Jefferson Univ, Philadelphia; City Camden, NJ; Woodmere Art Mus, Philadelphia. *Comn:* Portrait paintings, Sch of Law, Rutgers, Camden, 86 & 88; landscape painting, Marriott Corp, 87; cityscape, Copper Hosp Univ Med Ctr, 92; Latrobe Trinity Lutheran Church, 02. *Exhib:* Eastern Regional Drawing Soc Show, Philadelphia Mus Art, 65; 55th Ann, Allied Artists Am, Nat Acad Design, NY, 68; 164th Ann, Pa Acad Fine Arts, Philadelphia, 69; 34th & 35th Ann, Butler Institute Am Art, Youngstown, Ohio, 69 & 70; Earth Art 1 & 2, Philadelphia Civic Ctr Mus, 73 & 79; Art from NJ IX & X, 74 & 75 & Visual Arts Fel Winners Exhib, 80, NJ State Mus, Trenton; Peale House Gallery, Pa Acad Fine Arts, Philadelphia, 83; retrospective (with catalog), Stedman Gallery, Rutgers Univ, Camden, 91; St Martin-in-the-Fields Gallery, London, Eng, 94; St Vincent Col, Latrobe, Pa, 2001. *Teaching:* Instr to prof, Rutgers Univ, Camden Col Arts & Sci, NJ, 67-, chmn, Dept Art, 67-76, 79-82 & 92-95, prof emeritus, 2000; Adjuct Prof- St Vincent College. *Awards:* Purchase Award, Earth Art 3, Touche, Ross & Co, Philadelphia, 79; Artists Fel, NJ State Coun Arts, 80 & 84; Purchase Award, City of Camden, NJ, 88; and others. *Bibliog:* Piri Halasz (auth), State artists display skills, New York Times, 7/6/75; Robert Baxter (auth), Romantic realist, Courier Post, NJ, 10/30/81; Judy Baeher (auth), Preserving Camden's history on canvas, Philadelphia Inquirer, 4/7/91; Marjorie Wertz (auth), Pa has a Friend in Uruguay, Greenburg Tribune-Review, 6/2/2002. *Mem:* Artists Equity Asn; fel Pa Acad Fine Arts; Col Art Asn. *Media:* Oil, Casein. *Mailing Add:* 110 Beech Dr Ligonier PA 15658

HOFMANN, DOUGLAS WILLIAM
PAINTER, PRINTMAKER
b Baltimore, Md, Feb 13, 45. *Study:* Md Inst Col Art, BFA(cum laude), studied with Joseph Sheppard, 64-68. *Work:* Del Art Mus, Wilmington; Joslyn Art Mus, Omaha; Marquette Univ Fine Art Collection, Milwaukee; Nat Mem Mus & Archives, Washington, DC; Nassau Co Mus, NY. *Comn:* Painted stained glass panels, Baltimore City Schs, Md, 70. *Exhib:* Peale Mus, Baltimore, 70; Md Biennial, Baltimore Mus Art, 71 & 73; Realism in Maryland, Washington Co Mus, Hagerstown, Md, 72; Allied Artists Am, 74 & Audubon Artists Ann, 76, Nat Acad, NY; Ann Mid-Yr Exhib, Butler Inst, Youngstowm, Ohio, 74-75; Cherry Creek Gallery, Denver, 78; one-man show, Jack Gallery, NY, 79, 81, 84 & 89; 30th Nat Print Exhib, Hunterdon Art Ctr, Clinton, NJ, 86; Nat Acad Design, NY, 87; Halcyon Gallery, London, 94. *Teaching:* Instr painting, Md Inst, Baltimore, 74-75. *Awards:* Best Traditional Painting, Md Biennial, Baltimore Mus, 71; Award, Soc Am Graphic Artists, New York, 87; Award, Salmagundi Club, New York, 88. *Bibliog:* Jack Solomon (auth), Douglas Hofmann, Circle Fine Art Corp, 81; Will Grant (auth), Old and established, Artspeak, 6/2/81; Jerry Tallmer (auth), Mr Vermeer say hello to this here Mr Hofmann, New York Post, 10/31/81. *Media:* Oil; Lithography. *Publ:* Auth, A Retrospective Exhibition 1978-1989, Circle Fine Art Corp, New York, 89; Tales of Hofmann, Dance Pages Mag, 94. *Dealer:* Washington Green 59/60 The Pallasades B24XJ Birmingham England; Halcyon Gallery London. *Mailing Add:* 15 W Mt Vernon Pl Baltimore MD 21201-5108

HOFMANN, KAY
SCULPTOR
b Green Bay, Wis, Dec 3, 32. *Study:* Art Inst Chicago(Ryerson Fel), grad, 55; studied at Acad de Grande Chaumiere, Paris, with Ossip Zadkine, 55-56. *Work:* Borg Warner, Chicago. *Comn:* Marble sculpture, Continental Plaza Hotel, Chicago, 70; two wood carvings, comn by Hugh Hefner, Los Angeles, 77; marble portrait, Gonstead Med Ctr, Mt Horeb, Wis, 81; alabaster sculpture, Arthur Anderson Assocs, Chicago, 84-90. *Exhib:* Solo exhibs, Art Inst Chicago, 78 & Rahr-West Mus, Manitowoc, Ill, 85; 30th Illinois Invitational, Ill State Mus, Springfield, 78; 37th & 40th Indiana Salon Shows, Northern Ind Arts Assoc, Munster, Ind, 79 & 83; Lakeview Mus, Peoria, Ill, 79; Foothills Art Ctr, Golden, Colo, 83. *Teaching:* Instr sculpture, N Shore Art League, Winnetka, Ill, 58-83; instr stone carving, Suburban Fine Arts Ctr, Highland Park, Ill, 59-90 & Blackhawk Mountain Sch Art, Colo, summers 83-90. *Awards:* Best of Show, 29th Ann Open Spectrum, Libertyville Art Ctr, 83 & Arthur Baer Competition, 85. *Bibliog:* Elaine Snyderman (producer), Viewpoints/Kay Hofmann, Cable TV, 86; Michael Bonesteel (auth), Caught in the Coils, Pioneer Press, 86; Arthur Williams (auth), Sculpture: Technique, Form, Content, 89. *Mem:* N Shore Art League; Suburban Fine Arts Ctr; Nat Wildlife Fedn; World Wildlife Fund; Sierra Club. *Media:* Stone, Wood. *Interests:* Collectible dolls and toys; wildlife. *Mailing Add:* 3140 N 77th Ave Elmwood Park IL 60707

HOGAN, FELICITY
MUSEUM DIRECTOR
b England. *Work:* Mus Contemp Art, 1997-. *Exhib:* Clark & Hogan; Paintings & Collab, Barry Gallery, 2002—03; Clark in Context: Day of the Revolutionary, 2003. *Pos:* Co-Dir, Mus Contemp Art, Wash, 96-. *Mailing Add:* Mus Contemp Art 1054 31st St Washington DC 20007

HOGBIN, STEPHEN
SCULPTOR
b Tolworth Surrey, United Kingdom. *Study:* Kingston Col Art, United Kingdom, NDD; Royal Col Art, United Kingdom, Des RCA. *Work:* Art Bank Can Coun, Ottawa, Ont; Australia Coun, Sydney; Ariz State Univ Art Mus; Can Mus Civilization, Ottawa; Yale Univ Gallery; Tom Thomson Mem Art Gallery, Ont; Los Angeles Co Mus; and others. *Comn:* Sculpture, Melbourne State Col, Australia; entrance & screen, Metrop Toronto Libr Can, 77 & 89; murals, Queens Park, 80 & CIL Inc, Toronto, 81; installation, Cambridge Gallery, Ont; City of Owensound, Ont. *Exhib:* Chairs, Art

Gallery Ont, Toronto, 75; Art of Woodturning, Am Craft Mus, NY, 83; Painted Reliefs Traveling Exhib (catalog), 89; Re; Turning (catalog), 90, John B Aird Gallery, Toronto; McMaster Univ, Hamilton, 92; Progress of Walking: The Body in Pub Art, Can Ctr Arts at Owen Sound, 92; and others. *Collection Arranged:* Political Landscapes: Sacred and Secular Sites, Tom Thomson Gallery, 91; Curators Focus: Turning in Context, W Turning Ctr, 97; Wood: An Aesthetic and Social Ecology, Tom Thomson Gallery, 98; Fragments, Cafe Gallery Projects, London, Tom Thomson Gallery. *Pos:* Artist-in-residence, Melbourne State Col, Australia Coun, 75-76, Haystack Mountain Sch Crafts, 96, Australian Nat Univ, 02, Univ of the Arts, Philadelphia, 02. *Teaching:* Col Educ, Univ Toronto, 71-72; instr sculpture, Georgian Col, Barrie, Ont, 85-87; lectures & workshops, Royal Col Art, UK, RI Sch Design, USA, Melbourne State Col, Australia, Forestech Australia, 99; and others. *Awards:* Award, Ontario Arts Coun, 99, Can Coun, 02, Royal Col Art; and others. *Bibliog:* D L McKinley (auth), The forms of Stephen Hogbin, Craft Horizons, 4/74; Jeanne Parkin (auth), Art in Architecture, 82; Helen Duffy (auth), Stephen Hogbin, Ont Craft, spring 84; Edward Cooke (auth), The makers hand, Wood Turning in NAm, 03. *Mem:* Royal Can Acad. *Media:* Wood. *Res:* investigation of fragmentation. *Publ:* Auth, Turning full circle, Fine Woodworking, 79; Wood Turning, Van Nostrand Reinhold, 80; Curator's Focus, Wood Turning Ctr, 97; Wood: An Aesthetic and Social Ecology, Tom Thomson Gallery, 98; Appearance & Reality, 00. *Dealer:* Prime Gallery 52 McCaul St Toronto M5T 1V9 Canada. *Mailing Add:* RR 2 Wiarton ON N0H 2T0 Canada

HOGE, ROBERT WILSON
CURATOR, EDUCATOR
b Wilmington, Del, Apr 5, 47. *Study:* Univ Colo, BA (anthrop), 69; Univ Chicago, 69-70; Univ Colo, Teacher cert, 73. *Collection Arranged:* Thematic Exhibitions in Art & Sci, Sanford Mus & Planetarium, 76-81; Exhibits of Coins, Paper Money, Tokens & Medals, Mus Am Numismatic Asn, 81-98; Two Bits: the Quarter Dollar in American History; ANA Museum: Recent Acquisitions; Money of Vermont; ANA Hall of Fame, Mus Am Numismatic Asn, 99; A Salute to the Dollar, Mus Am Numismatic Asn, 99; The 1943 Copper Cent, Mus Am Numismatic Asn, 99; Balkan Bonanza, Roman Provincial Coins in the ANA Museum, Mus Am Numismatic Asn, 99; Holiday Numismatics, Mus Am Numismatic Asn, 99; Let Us Show You the Money?, Mus Am Numismatic Asn, 2000; The Wonderful World of Money: Coming to 'Terms' with Numismatics, Mus Am Numismatic Asn, 2000; Coinage of the Romans: Selected Themes, Mus Am Numismatic Asn, 2000; Numismatic Technology, Mus Am Numismatic Asn, 2000; Platinum: a Metal with a Message, Mus Am Numismatic Asn, 2000. *Pos:* dir, Sanford Mus and Planetarium, 76-81; cur, Mus Am Numismatic Asn, 81-; mgr, Am Numismatic Asn Authentication Bur, 90-; prog partic, Int Partnerships among Mus, Am Asn Mus & Int Coun Mus, 90; cons, Native Am Rights Fund/Pawnee Indians repatriation Mus Nebr Hist, Nebr Hist Soc, Lincoln, 90, Joslyn Art Mus, Omaha, Nebr, 91 & Art and Architecture Thesaurus, Getty Art Hist Info Prog, Williamstown, Mass, 91. *Teaching:* tchr, Boulder Valley Sch Sys, Colo, 73-75; instr anthrop, Buena Vista Col, Storm Lake, Iowa, 76; sem instr, Colo Col, Colorado Springs, 83-. *Awards:* Outstanding Young Men of Am, 81. *Mem:* Am Numismatic Soc; Int Coun Mus; Colo-Wyo Asn Mus; Am Asn Mus; Mountain Plains Mus Asn; Royal Numismatic Soc. *Res:* American archaeology, historical studies; Old World archaeology; numismatics. *Publ:* Ed, Northwest Chapter Newsletter, Iowa Archaeol Soc, Sanford Mus; Museum, Column, The Numismatist, 83-; auth, Crack-up! Notes on a Vietnamese Issue, Asia Numismatics, No 1, 2000; Chinese numistmatics in American museums, ICOMON: Int Com Money and Banking Mus, 2000; ed, contribr, reviewer, Oxford English Dictionary, New Am edit, 2001. *Mailing Add:* Am Numismatic Asn 818 N Cascade Ave Colorado Springs CO 80903

HOGLE, ANN MEILSTRUP
PAINTER
b San Francisco, Calif, Sept 23, 27. *Study:* Univ Ore; Portland Mus Sch; Calif Col Arts & Crafts, BFA, MFA, 79. *Work:* Neuberger Collection, NY; Kemper Group, Long Grove, Ill; St Francis Mem Hosp & Security Pac Bank, San Francisco; Int Bus Machines; Merril Lynch; and others. *Comn:* Triptych, Menlo Park Pub Libr, Calif. *Exhib:* Artists of Oregon, Portland Mus, 63 & 70; Phelan Awards, Calif Palace Legion Hon, San Francisco, 65; solo exhibs, William Sawy Gallery, San Francisco, 88, 90 & 93, Butters Gallery, Portland, Ore, 93, Bolinas Mus, Calif, 98, Smith Andersen Gallery, Palo Alto, Calif, 98, Fresno Art Mus, Calif, 98, de Saisset Mus, Santa Clara Univ, Calif, 98 & Commonweal, Bolinas, 99; Syntex, Palo Alto, 89; group exhib, Monterey Mus, Calif, 93, Bolinas Mus, Calif, 94. *Bibliog:* Peninsula painter brings Bay Area's terrain to life, San Jose Mercury News, 5/31/98; Ann Hogle at the De Saisset Museum, Artweek, 7-8/98; Artist paints her life's story one brushstroke at a time, San Jose Mercury News, 9/20/98. *Media:* Oil. *Dealer:* Paragone Gallery Los Angeles CA; John Natsoulas Gallery Davis CA. *Mailing Add:* 45 Upper Lake Rd Woodside CA 94062-2634

HOI, SAMUEL CHUEN-TSUNG
EDUCATOR, ADMINISTRATOR
b Hong Kong, Mar 25, 58; US citizen. *Study:* Columbia Col, NY, AB, 80; Columbia Sch Law, NY, JD, 83; Parsons Sch Design, NY, AAS, 86. *Pos:* Dir, AAS degree prog, Parsons Sch Design, NY 87-88; dir, Parsons Sch Design, Paris, 88-91; dean, Corcoran Sch Art, Wash, DC 91-2000; pres, Otis Coll Art & design, LA, 2000-. *Mem:* Asn Independent Sch Art & Design; Nat Asn Sch Art & Design; Partnership Community Health. *Mailing Add:* Otis Coll Art & Design Off of the Pres 9045 Lincoln Blvd Los Angeles CA 90045

HOIE, CLAUS
PAINTER
b Stavanger, Norway, Nov 3, 11; US citizen. *Study:* Pratt Inst; Art Students League; Ecole Beaux Arts, Paris. *Work:* Brooklyn Mus, NY; Norfolk Mus, Va; Butler Inst Am Art, Youngstown, Ohio; Okla Mus Art; Guild Hall Mus, East Hampton, NY; South St Seaport Mus, NY. *Exhib:* Am Watercolor Soc Ann, NY, 60-94; Brooklyn Mus Watercolor Biennial, 63; Mus Watercolor Painting, Mexico City, Mex, 68 & 89; Pa Acad Fine Arts Ann, 69; Childe Hassam Award Exhib, Nat Inst Arts & Lett, 73; one-man shows, Akershus Castle Mus, Oslo, Norway, 82, South St Seaport Mus, NY, 92, Mystic Seaport Mus, 94 & 98, Nordic Heritage Mus, Seattle, 98; Retrospective, Watercolors, and Drawings, 43-2003; Guild Hall Mus, East Hampton, NY, Nov 13, 2004- Jan 9, 2005; and many others. *Awards:* Award for Painting, Am Acad Arts & Lett, 75; Award of Merit, Nat Acad Design, 81 & Obrig Prize, 85; Marine Environmental Wildlife Award, Mystic Seaport Mus Int, 98, 2002. *Mem:* Nat Acad (coun mem); Am Watercolor Soc (vpres, 60-62); Nat Arts Club, Audubon Soc. *Media:* Watercolor, Graphics. *Publ:* Auth, Technique of watercolor, Am Artist Mag, 57; My views on watercolor painting, North Light Mag, 70; The Log of the Whaler Helena, Two Bytes Publ Ltd, 94. *Mailing Add:* Hook Pond Ln PO Box 1323 East Hampton NY 11937

HOLABIRD, JEAN
PAINTER, PRINTMAKER
b Boston, Mass. *Study:* Art Students League, New York, 65-69; Inst Allende, Mexico, summers 65-69; Bennington Col, Vt, BA, 69. *Work:* Prudential Life Insurance Co, Newark, NJ; First Nat City Bank, Chicago; Staatmuseum, West Berlin, Ger; Ragdale Found, Lake Forest, Ill; Metrop Mus Art, NY. *Comn:* Drawings, Bennington Rev, Vt, 69-70; cover illus, World Mag, NY, 80; cover, Hanging Loose Mag, NY, 81; and others. *Exhib:* Camden Coun Arts, London, Eng, 73; Two Painters, Saray Y Rentschler Gallery, NY, 78; one-woman show, Nathan A Bernstein Ltd, NY, 80; Hand-colored Etchings, Sarah Y Rentschler Gallery, NY, 82; Usdan Gallery, Vt, 84; Neo Persona, NY, 88, 90 & 91; Keyes Gallery, Sag Harbor, NY, 99 & 2000. *Teaching:* Instr painting, Inst Allende, San Miguel Allende, Mexico, summer 68; guest lectr, Parsons Sch Design, Pratt Inst, Cooper Union, New York, 75 & Sch Visual Arts, 79; artist-in-residence, Ragdale Found, 81. *Awards:* Cert Merit, Vt Coun Arts, 69; and others. *Bibliog:* Palmer Hasty (auth), A collaboration, Villager, 3/82; Bob Mahoney (auth), Arts Mag, 5/88; Greg Masters (auth), Interview Cover Mag, 5/91. *Mem:* Artists Equity Asn. *Media:* Watercolor, Oil. *Publ:* Auth, Out of the Runs - A New York Record, Gingko Press, 2002. *Mailing Add:* 81 Warren St New York NY 10007

HOLBROOK, PETER GREENE
PAINTER, PRINTMAKER
b New York, NY, Apr 13, 40. *Study:* Dartmouth Col, BA(Marcus Heiman Award), 61; Brooklyn Mus, with Reuben Tam, cert(Beckman Fel), 63. *Work:* Nat Collection Fine Arts, Washington; Brooklyn Mus, NY; Art Inst Chicago; Springfield Art Mus, Mo; Tucson Mus Art, Ariz; Oakland Mus Art, Calif. *Comn:* Gen Serv Admin (painting), Fed Courthouse, Sacramento, Calif, 98. *Exhib:* Chicago and Vicinity, Art Inst Chicago, 65 & 67-69; solo exhib, Indianapolis Mus Art, 70, Peter Holbrook: Paintings (with catalog), Mesa SW Mus, Ariz, 96, N Ill Univ Art Mus, DeKalb, 97 & Springfield Art Mus, 97; Koffler Fund Collection, Smithsonian Inst, 79; Davidson Collection, Pa Acad Fine Arts, Philadelphia, 82; Green Woods and Crystal Waters, Phil Brook Mus Art, Tulsa, 99; Ten Painters, Morris Graves Mus Art, Eureka, Calif, 2000; Images of Water, Eureka City Hall, 2000; Magnifying the Mark, Morris Graves Mus Art, 2002; Landscape Interpretations, Grace Hudson Mus, Ukiah, Calif, 2005. *Teaching:* Lectr painting, Univ Ill, Chicago Circle, 68-70 & Calif State Univ, Hayward, 70-71. *Awards:* Wild, Bartels & Clark Prizes, Chicago and Vicinity, Art Inst Chicago, 65, 67 & 68; Walter H Stevens Award, Watercolor USA, Springfield Art Mus, 81; Raffael Prize for Watercolor, Humboldt Cult Ctr, Eureka, Calif, 81. *Bibliog:* William Struve (auth), An American Landscape Collection, Zurick Kemper Dist Inc, Chicago, Ill, 97; Joni Louise Kinsey (auth), Majesty of the Grand Canyon: 150 Years in Art, First Glance Books, Cobb, Calif, 98; Katharine Kia Tehranian (auth), The Aesthetics of Presence: The Landscape Paintings of Peter Holbrook, Prospects: An Ann Am Cult Studies, Cambridge Univ Press, Mass, 99; and others. *Media:* Oil. *Publ:* Auth, article, 11/67 & The Chicago saga of Carolee Schneemann, 3/68, Art Scene Mag. *Dealer:* The Charlene Cody Gallery Sante Fe NMex; Leslie Levy Gallery Scottsdale AZ. *Mailing Add:* 5719 Briceland-Thorn Rd Redway CA 95560

HOLCOMB, GRANT
MUSEUM DIRECTOR, EDUCATOR
b San Bernardino, Calif, Sept 30, 44. *Study:* Univ Calif, Los Angeles, AB, 67; Univ Del, MA, PhD, 72. *Awards:* Kress fel, Nat Gallery Art, 71; Am Coun 7 Learned societies, 79; NEA, 99; NY State Coun of the Arts, 00. *Mem:* Asn Art Mus Dirs; Asn Art Mus; Col Art Asn. *Publ:* Auth, The Forgotton Legacy of Jerome Myers, Am Art J, 5/77; John Sloan in Santa Fe, Am Art J, 5/78; John Sloan, The Gloucester Years, Mus Fine Arts, Springfield, 80; John Sloan, The Wake of the Ferry, Timken Art Gallery, 84; Joyce Treiman, Friends & Strangers, Univ Southern Calif, 88. *Mailing Add:* c/o Memorial Art Gallery 500 University Ave Rochester NY 14607

HOLDEMAN, JOSHUA
COLLECTOR, APPRAISER
Study: Bates Col, ME, BA & MA. *Pos:* Dept head, Photogrpahy Dept, Phillips de Pury & Luxembourg; photogrpah expert, Robert Miller Art Gallery. *Mailing Add:* Christie's 20 Rockafeller Plz New York NY 10020

HOLDEN, DONALD
PAINTER, WRITER
b Los Angeles, Calif, Apr 22, 31. *Study:* Parsons Sch Design, New York, 46-47; Art Students League, 48; Columbia Univ, BA, 51; Ohio State Univ, MA, 52; Maine Col Art, LLD, 86. *Hon Degrees:* Maine Col Art, hon LLD, 86. *Work:* Corcoran Gallery; Fine Arts Mus San Francisco; Metrop Mus Art; Victoria & Albert Mus; Nat Gallery

Art; Philadelphia Mus Art; British Mus; New Britain Mus Am Art; Phillips collection; Nat Acad; Yale Univ Art Gallery; Smithsonian Am Art Mus; and others. *Exhib:* solo exhibs, Manhattanville Col, 83, Century Asn, 84, 02, Susan Conway Gallery, 90, 92, 99, Campbell-Thiebaud Gallery, 93, Hudson River Gallery, 98, 00, Curwen Gallery, 99, Butler Inst Am Art, 99; Portland Mus of Art, Maine, 2004; Springfield Art Mus, MO, 2004; Round Top Arts Ctr, 2004; White Gallery, 2004; numerous group & one-man exhibs, incl retrospective watercolor exhib at Butler Inst Am Art, Youngstown, Ohio, 99. *Pos:* dir, pr & personnel, Henry Dreyfuss Assocs, NY, 56-60; assoc mgr pr, Metrop Mus Art, NY, 60-61; art consult, Fortune Mag, 62; ed dir, Watson-Guptill Publ, 63-79, ed consult, 79-88; ed dir, Am Artist Mag, 71-75. *Teaching:* Instr painting & drawing, Scottsdale Artists Sch, Ariz, 85-92. *Awards:* Florsheim Art Fund Grant, 99; Adolph and Clara Obrig Prize, Nat Acad Design, 2001; Century Medal, 2005; Jo Ann Leiser Mem Award, Salmagundi Club, 2005. *Bibliog:* M Stephen Doherty (auth), Donald Holden, Am Artist Mag, 4/89; Richard J Boyle (auth), Donald Holden Watercolors, 04. *Mem:* Nat Art Educ Asn; New York Artists Equity Asn; Nat Acad; Century Asn. *Media:* Aquamedia, Drawing. *Publ:* auth, Creative Color for the Oil Painter, 83; auth, The Complete Acrylic Painting Book, 89, Oil Painting Book, 89, Watercolor Book, 89; auth, Painting from Nature in the Studio, Watercolor 93, Fall 93; auth, Donald Holden Watercolors, Butler Inst Am Art (exhib catalog), 99. *Dealer:* Pucker Gallery 171 Newbury St Boston MA 02116; Stremmel Gallery 1400 S Virginia St Reno NV 89502; Davidson Galleries 313 Occidental Ave S Seattle WA 98104; White Gallery 342 Main St Lakeville CT 06039

HOLDEN, MICHAEL B
PAINTER, SCULPTOR
b San Francisco, Calif, Dec 30, 69. *Study:* Univ Calif, Santa Cruz, BA, 93; Boston Univ, MFA, 96; Santa Rosa Jr Col, AA (lib arts), 91. *Exhib:* Small Works Show, Sonoma Mus Visual Art, Santa Rosa, Calif, 94; solo show, Cobra Valley Ctr for the Arts, Globe, Ariz, 2001, Agilent Technols, Palo Alto, Calif & Sherman Gallery, Boston Univ, Boston, 2002. *Teaching:* adj drawing prof, Santa Rosa Jr Col; teaching asst beginning non-major drawing & advanced drawing, 95-96; adj drawing instr, Santa Rosa Jr Col, 2002; guest lectr, Santa Rosa Campus, Santa Rosa Jr Col, Boston Univ, Grad Art Dept, 2002. *Awards:* Fel, Vt Studio Ctr, 96 & grant, 2000; Fel, John Simon Guggenheim Mem Found, 2000; Fel, Vermont Studo Center, 96; Grant, Vermont Studio Center, 2000; Painting Fel, John Simon Guggenheim Mem Found, 2000. *Bibliog:* Tanya Schevitz (auth), Guggenheim felllowships awarded to 14 in Bay Area, San Francisco Chronicle, 4/12/2000; Taylor McNeil (auth), Abstract in Arizona, Bostonia, Number 2, summer 2001. *Mem:* Col Art Asn. *Media:* Oil. *Res:* petroglyphs, pottery chards & archit vestiges of two unchartered Hohokam citiesin Ariz wilderness. *Interests:* Painting in Johnson, Vermont, Italy, France, Switz & Eng. *Dealer:* Ebert Gallery 49 Geary St San Francisco CA 94108. *Mailing Add:* 197 Clifton Place Brookyn NY 11215

HOLDER, KENNETH ALLEN
PAINTER, EDUCATOR
b Heald, Tex, Sept 11, 36. *Study:* Tex Christian Univ, BFA(com art), 59; Art Inst Chicago, MFA(painting), 65. *Work:* Ill State Mus, Springfield; Cultural Activities Ctr, Temple, Tex; Ratir/West Mus, Manitowoc, Wis; Mazur Mus, Monroe, La; Univ Chicago, Ill. *Comn:* Fresno City Col, Calif, 73; Va Commonwealth Univ, 73; Cent Mich Univ, 75; all in collab with Harold Gregor. *Exhib:* Watercolor USA, Springfield, Mo, 77, 80, 81, 82, 85, 87 & 88; Chicago Vicinity Show, Art Inst Chicago, 73; The Chicago Connection, Crocker Gallery, Sacramento, Calif; one-man shows, Nancy Lurie Gallery, Chicago, 75 & Zolla/Lieberman Gallery, Chicago, 82 & Conduit Gallery, Dallas, 85, 87 & 90. *Teaching:* Asst prof drawing & painting, Western Ill Univ, 65-69; prof drawing & painting, Ill State Univ, 69-. *Awards:* NEA Artist Fel, 87. *Bibliog:* Henry Glover (auth), Artist (video), Ill State Univ, 72; "Ken Holder's Autobiographical Art," American Artist, 9/86. *Mem:* Charter mem, Watercolor USA Honor Soc. *Media:* Acrylic; Mixed Media. *Publ:* Ken Holder (auth, catalog for one-man, travelling show), 84-85

HOLDER, TOM
PAINTER
b Kansas City, Mo, Jan 21, 40. *Study:* San Diego State Univ, BA; Univ Wash, MFA. *Work:* Metromedia Collection, Los Angeles; ITT, Los Angeles, Calif; San Diego Fine Arts Gallery, Calif; Valley Bank, Las Vegas & Reno, Nev; Las Vegas Art Mus, Nev. *Comn:* Mural, Seattle-Tacoma Int Airport, 73; exterior wall mural, Seattle Steam Corp Plant, Seattle Arts Comn, 75; exterior wall mural, CETA Bldg, Las Vegas, Nev, 79; painting, State Capitol Bldg, Nev, 81. *Exhib:* Univ Mass, Amherst, 91; Pensacola Art Mus, Fla, 91; Brenau Col, Gainesville, Ga, 91; Brendan Walter Gallery, Santa Monica, Calif, 92; Northern Ariz Univ Art Mus, Flagstaff, 92. *Pos:* Founding dir, Nev Inst Contemp Art, 85-91. *Teaching:* Instr painting, Univ Wash, 67-69; prof painting, Univ Nev, Las Vegas, 71-. *Awards:* Charles Vanda Award for Creative Excellence, 92; Visual Arts Fel, Nev State Coun of the Arts, 92-93. *Bibliog:* James P Rupp (auth), Art in Seattle's public places, Univ of Wash Press, Seattle, 92. *Dealer:* William Traver Gallery 110 Union St Seattle WA 98101; Brendan Walter Gallery 1001 Colorado Ave Santa Monica CA 90401. *Mailing Add:* 740 N Magic Way Henderson NV 89015-4709

HOLEN, NORMAN DEAN
SCULPTOR, EDUCATOR
b Cavalier, NDak, Sept 16, 37. *Study:* Concordia Col, BA, 59; State Univ Iowa, MFA, 62; Univ Minn, Minneapolis, 72. *Work:* 3M Co, Minneapolis, Minn; Univ Lutheran Church of Hope, Minneapolis; Augsburg Col, Minneapolis; Civic Plaza, Richfield, Minn; and others. *Comn:* Brazed steel bas relief, Luther Theological Seminary, St Paul, Minn, 77; half life size terra cotta figures, Vinge Lutheran Church, Wilmar, Minn, 80; brazed steel sculpture & baptismal font, St Paul, Minn, 86; stainless steel abstract piece, Augsburg Col, Minneapolis, Minn, 89; stainless steel sculpture, Kirchbak Gardens, Richfield, Minn, 2000. *Exhib:* One-man show, Minneapolis Inst Art, 68; Nat Gallery, Washington, DC, 69; Nat Sculpture Soc, 77, 80-86; Allied Artists Am, NY, 80, 82, 83 & 85; Port of Hist Mus, Philadelphia, Penn, 87. *Teaching:* Prof art, drawing, sculpture & ceramics, Augsburg Col, 64-2002. *Awards:* Rachel Leah Armour Award, 80 & 82 & In Memorium Award, 83, Allied Artists Am; Bronze Medal, 80 & Joel Meisner Award, 83, Nat Sculpture Soc; Alumni Achievement Award, Concordia Col, Moorhead, Minn, 85. *Bibliog:* Sculptor likes 'em ample, Chicago Sun-Times, 6/25/89; Paul Levy (auth), Extending the left foot: Augsburg College's Norman Holen makes devices to help his students produce art, Star Tribune Mag First Sunday, 10/7/90; Sheldon Green (ed), Instinctive ingenuity, NDak Horizons, spring 93. *Mem:* Allied Artists Am; Nat Sculpture Soc; Minn Sculptors Soc. *Media:* Stoneware, bronze & welded steel. *Interests:* Making tools and sprints for physically challenged art students; playing classical guitar music. *Publ:* Auth, Setting up a studio, Int Sculpture Mag, 9/85; Expressing the human form in terra cotta, 11/86, Drawing nature close up, 5/95, Am Artist; Sculpting made simple, Artist's Mag, 9/96; Ceramic figures made from molds, Clay times, 3/2003. *Mailing Add:* 7332 12th Ave S Minneapolis MN 55423

HOLL, STEVEN MYRON
ARCHITECT
b Bremerton, Washington, Dec 9, 47. *Study:* Univ Washington, BA, 71; postgrad in Rome and London. *Comn:* Loisium Visitors' Ctr, Langenlois, Austria, 2003 (NY Am Inst Architects Project Award); Simmons Hall, Mass Inst Technology (Award for Design Excellence, Am Inst Architects, 2003). *Exhib:* Whitney Mus Am Art, 84, 85; Facade Gallery, 84; Architecture in Transition, Berlin, Ger, 84; VII Triennale Milan, 87; John Nicols Gallery, NY City, 87; GA Gallery, Toyko, 87, 82, 97, 99; Mus Modern Art, NY City, 87, 99, 200; Aedes Gallery, Berlin, 89; Venice Biennial, Italy, 91, 2002; Walker Art Ctr, 91; Henry Art Gallery, Seattle, 91; Canadian Ctr Architecture, Montreal, 92; Ctr de Cultura Contemporania de Barcelona, 96; Mus Contemp Art, Los Angeles, 98; Mus Modern Art, San Francisco, 99; Cooper Hewitt Mus, NY, 2000; Max Protetch Gallery, Parallax, NY, 2000, 2002; Van Allen Inst, NY, 2001; Am Acad Rome, 2001; Nat Bldg Mus, Washington, DC, 2002; Basilica Palladiana di Vicenza, Italy, 2002; Arkiteckturmuseet, Stockholm, 2003; Nat Acad Mus, NY City, 2006. *Pos:* Individual practice architecture, San Francisco, 74-76, NY City, 77-. *Teaching:* Architect, tchr archit design, Univ Washington, Seattle, 79; prof grad sch architecture, Columbia Univ, 81-. *Awards:* Nat Endowment Arts Award, 82; Progressive Archit Award,78, 82, 84, 86-87, 90; Am Inst Architects Award, 85-86, 89-90; Arnold W Brunner Prize in Architecture, Am Acad and Inst Arts and Letters, 90; Cooper Hewitt Nat Design Award in Architecture, Smithsonian Inst, 2002; named America's Best Architect, Time Magazine, 2001; Fellow in Architecture, NY State Council Arts, 79; Nat Endowment Arts Grant. *Mem:* NCARB; Am Inst Architects; Am Asn Mus; Hon Whitney Cir; Alvar Aalto Found. *Publ:* Auth, The Alphabetical City, 80; auth, Urban and Rural House Types in North America, 83; auth, Within the City, 88; auth, Anchoring, 89. *Mailing Add:* Steven Holl Architects 11th Floor 450 W 31st St New York NY 10001

HOLLADAY, HARLAN H
HISTORIAN, PAINTER
b Greenville, Mo, Dec 10, 25. *Study:* SE Mo State Col, BS(educ); Wash Univ, St Louis Mo; State Univ Iowa, MA; Cornell Univ, PhD. *Work:* Munson-Williams Proctor Inst, Utica, NY; St Lawrence Univ Collection, Canton, NY; Des Moines Art Ctr, Iowa; SE Mo State Univ Collection; Springfield Art Mus, Mo. *Exhib:* Corcoran Gallery Art Biennial, Washington, 51; Whitney Mus Am Art, NY, 52; Pa Acad Fine Arts, Philadelphia, 52, 53 & 59; 61st Nat Watercolor Ann, Washington, 58; and others. *Teaching:* Art teacher, Poplar Bluff Pub Schs, Mo, 51-53 & Des Moines, Iowa, 53-55; from instr to asst prof drawing & painting, Univ Nev, Reno, 55-58; asst prof to prof fine arts, St Lawrence Univ, 61-91, head dept, 65-71, LM&GL Flint prof, 67-91, prof emer, 91; prof art & artist-in-residence, Am Col Switz, 68-69. *Awards:* Hon Mention, 61st Nat Watercolor Ann, Washington, 58; Reynolds Awards, Cooperstown Art Asn, 67; First Prize Painting, NY State Fair, Syracuse, 74; plus others. *Mem:* Col Art Asn Am; Soc Archit Historians; St Lawrence Co Hist Asn. *Media:* Oil, Acrylic. *Res:* 15th century art, especially Italian painters; mosaics & studies related to Venice. *Publ:* Auth, Art in the liberal arts curriculum, 64 & auth, The value of a teaching collection, 70, St Lawrence Bull; auth, Catalogue for the McGinnis Collection, St Lawrence Univ, 70. *Mailing Add:* 2521 Greenway Dr Cape Girardeau MO 63701

HOLLADAY, WILHELMINA COLE
COLLECTOR, PATRON
b Elmira, NY. *Study:* Elmira Col, BA, 44; Univ Paris; Univ Va; Dr Humanities Moore Col Art, Dr, 88. *Pos:* Dir, Holladay Corp, Interior Design, Washington DC, 72-84; pres, The Holladay Found, Washington DC, 80-84; chmn bd, Nat Mus Women in the Arts, 81-. *Awards:* Induction, Nat Women's Hall Fame, 96; Gold Medal Honor Award, Nat Inst Social Scis, 2000; Nat Women in Arts Award, Phoenix Art Mus League, 2003; Visionary Woman award, Moore Coll. Art & Design, 2005. *Mem:* Corcoran Gallery, Washington DC (trustee); Am Asn Mus; Am Federation Art; Mus Mod Art; Women's Caucus Art; Nat Women's Economic Alliance (bd). *Interests:* Contribution of women to history through art from Renaissance to present. *Collection:* Women's art from the Renaissance to contemporary period. *Mailing Add:* 3215 NW R St Washington DC 20007

HOLLAND, DIANE LEE
COLLAGE ARTIST, CONCEPTUAL ARTIST
b Los Angeles, Calif. *Study:* Immaculate Heart Col, BA(with honors), 80; Otis/Parsons Col, MFA, 84. *Work:* Long Beach Mus Art video collection; Cabinet des Estampes, Bibliotheque Nationale de France. *Exhib:* Los Angeles Juried Exhib, Jr Arts Ctr, Barnsdall Art Park, 93; Women at Work, Roger Smith Gallery, NY, 93; Six Artists

Tackle the Machine, Carnegie Art Mus, Calif, 94; Pasted Papers: Collage & the 20th Century, Lewis Stern Gallery, 95; solo exhib, Kantor Gallery, Calif, 95 & Writer's Guild Am/West, Bev Hills, 96; Livres d'artiste/Estampes Numeriques, Galerie Toner, Sens, France. *Pos:* Cur, Insomnia Cafe, Los Angeles, 93. *Awards:* Hon Men, Found Objects, Long Beach Arts, 94; Hon Men, 91st Nat Open, Long Beach Arts, 95; Hon Men, ARTernatives 97, San Wish Obispo, 97. *Bibliog:* Judith Hoffberg (auth), The Sticking Place, Rev, Visions, Fall 93; Josef Woodard (auth), Laser print exhibition proves, Los Angeles Times, 3/10/94; Ruth Weisberg (auth), Transculturations, Visions, Winter 94. *Media:* Electrotransfer, Assemblage; Collage, Performance. *Publ:* contribr, Family Album, Calif State Univ, Fullerton Gallery, 94; auth, Significant Mothers, Visions Art Quarterly, 95; coauth, Amari Marbu (artist's bk), 97; cover, Strindberg and Photography, 2000. *Dealer:* Kantor Gallery 8642 Melrose Ave West Hollywood CA 90069. *Mailing Add:* PO Box 16505 Beverly Hills CA 90209

HOLLAND, HILLMAN RANDALL
ART DEALER
b Athens, Ala, Apr 17, 50. *Study:* Auburn Univ, BA, 73; Ga State Univ, BS, 75; Atlanta Law Sch, JD, 76; Parsons in Paris, cert, 80; Attingham Summer Sch, Eng, cert, 82; Winterthur Summer Inst, Del, cert, 83. *Pos:* Dir, Hillman Holland Gallery, 83-; Trustee, Atlanta Col Art; Trustee Nexus Contemp Arts Ctr; & Trustee Decorative Arts, High Mus Art, Atlanta. *Specialty:* International avant-garde art, Arnulf Rainer, Milan Kunc, Tishan Hsu, Barbara Kruger, Tim Head, Pat Courtney, Thomas Nozowski, Francesco Clemente & Mimmo Paladino. *Mailing Add:* 2575 Peachtree Rd NE Atlanta GA 30305-3694

HOLLAND, JULIET
PAINTER
b Buffalo, NY. *Study:* NY Univ; Harvard Univ, Cambridge, Mass; New Eng Sch Art, Boston, Mass. *Work:* Reading Pub Mus, Pa; Univ Iowa Mus Art, Iowa City; Housatonic Mus Art, Bridgeport, Conn; San Antonio Mus Mod Art, Tex; Stamford Mus, Conn. *Comn:* Fragmented Tablets, MBIA, Armonk, NY; Twelve Fragments, General Electric, Stamford, Conn; Blue Elements, Loctite Corp, Hartford, Conn; Ancient Sources, comn by Dr Michael Albom, NY; Elements, R R Donnelley & Sons, NY. *Exhib:* Mixed Media, Albright-Knox Mus Gallery, Buffalo, NY, 85; The Nature of Our Collection, Stamford Mus, Conn, 92; Earth, Matter & Spirit, Gallery Poem, Tokyo, Japan, 92-97; Recent Work, Reece Gallery, NY, 95; Earth, Man & Spirit, Sun Cities Art Mus, Ariz, 95; Bridge, Sakai City Mus, Japan, 98; Elusive Traces, Univ RI Art Gallery, Kingston, 98; Matter of Abstraction, Cortland Jessup Gallery, NY, 98; Housatonic Mus Art, 2000; Sakai City Mus, Japan, 2001, 02; CJG Project Int, Gallery Poem, Tokyo, 2002; CJG Projects Int, Gallery 141, Nagoya, Japan, 2003; Gallery Marya, Osaka, Japan, 2004; Gallery LL, Kobe, Japan, 2004; Cella Surland, Fairfield, CT, 2004; Hammond Mus, North Salem, NY, 2004. *Collection Arranged:* Sakai City Municpal Art Collection, Sakai City, Japan; Pepsico Corp., Purchase, NY; IBM Corp., Atlanta GA; Citibank, New York, NY. *Pos:* Instr painting, Stamford Mus. *Bibliog:* Dr Robert P Metzger (auth), Juliet Holland, Provincetown Arts, 95; Anthony Crisafulli (auth), Juliet Holland Rev, Cover-Arts NY, 95; Mark Daniel Cohen (auth), Juliet Holland-Matter of Abstraction, Rev NY, 97; John Gimour, Author & Professor of Philosophy, 2005. *Mem:* Artist Equity; Int Friends Transformative Art; Silvermine Artist Guild; Women's Caucus Arts. *Media:* acrylic, oil; all media. *Dealer:* Cortland Jessup Gallery 670 Broadway No 505 New York NY 10012. *Mailing Add:* 640 Broadway No 4RW New York NY 10012

HOLLAND, TOM
PAINTER
b Seattle, Wash, 36. *Study:* Willamette Univ, 54-56; Univ Calif, Santa Barbara & Berkeley, 57-59. *Work:* Whitney Mus Am Art, Mus Mod Art & Guggenheim Mus, NY; St Louis City Mus; San Francisco Mus Art; Los Angeles Co Mus, Calif; Art Inst Chicago; plus many others. *Exhib:* Kid Stuff, Albright-Knox Art Gallery, Buffalo, NY, 71, Working in Calif, 72; New Options in Painting, Walker Art Ctr, Minneapolis, 72; California Prints, Mus Mod Art, NY, 72; Calif Printmakers, Whitney Mus Am Art, 73, New Aquisitions, 78; Corcoran Biennial, Washington, DC, 75; One-man shows, San Francisco Art Inst, 79, Blum-Helman Gallery, NY, 79 & Watson-De Nagy, Houston, 79; Felicity Samuel Gallery, London, 80; James Corcoran Gallery, Los Angeles, Calif, 80, 82 & 84-88; Charles Cowles Gallery, NY, 81-86, 88-90 & 93-2000; Berggruen Gallery, San Francisco, 87-89, 91-93 & 96-98. *Teaching:* Instr art, San Francisco Art Inst, 61-68 & 72-80, Univ Calif, Los Angeles, 68-69, Berkeley, 78-79 & Cornish Inst, Seattle, 78. *Awards:* Fulbright Grant, Santiago, Chile, 59-60; Nat Endowment Arts Sculpture Grant, 75-76; Guggenheim Fel, 79. *Media:* All. *Dealer:* John Berggruen Gallery 228 Grant Ave San Francisco CA 94108; Charles Cowles Gallery 420 W Broadway New York NY 10012; Imago Gallery 45-450 Highway 74 Palm Desert CA 92260. *Mailing Add:* 28 Roble Rd Berkeley CA 94705

HOLLANDER, ROZ
PAINTING
Study: Parson's Sch Design, BFA, 56; NJ Ctr Visual Arts; Columbia Univ Sch Gen Studies, NY; studied with David Finkbeiner, Jacqueline Chesley, Joe Hing Lowe, Sally Strand & Wolf Kahn. *Exhib:* solo exhib, Bergen Mus Art & Sci, Paramus, NJ, Peck Sch, Morristown, NJ, Drue Chryst Gallery, Sparta, NJ, Merrill Lynch Nat Hq, Princeton, NJ, Thompson Park Gallery, Lincroft, NJ, Art Alliance, Red Bank, NJ, Blair Acad, Blairstown, NJ; group exhib, Lever House, Pastel Soc Am, NY, Bergen Mus Art & Sci, Paramus, NJ, Monmouth Art Alliance, NJ, Ben Shahn Galleries at William Pateson Col, NJ, Berl, NJ, John Pence Gallery, San Francisco, Calif. *Collection Arranged:* Johnson & Johnson Pharmaceutical Co, Hq, NJ; Brinker Int, Dallas, Tex; Schering-Plough, NJ; Blair Acad, NJ; Ciba-Geigy, NJ. *Awards:* First Place in Pastels, The Artist Mag, 94, finalist, 99; Gold medal, Bronze Award, Horsehead, Catherine Lorillard Wolfe Art Club, NY; 3rd place Award, The Pastel J, 2000; Pastel Soc Am (PSA), inducted mem Master Pastelist. *Publ:* auth, Artists Mag, 94; auth, Pastel Highlights, 96; auth, The Best of Pastel I, Rockport Publ, Inc, 96; The Best of Pastel II. *Mailing Add:* 5 Dogwood Dr Newton NJ 07860

HOLLEN-BOLMGREN, DONNA
PAINTER, PAPERMAKER
b Willmar, Minn, May 28, 35. *Study:* Univ Minn, BS(art educ), 57; Univ Pittsburgh, 58; Carnegie-Mellon Univ, 59. *Work:* Blount Inc; Westinghouse; Alcoa; McDonalds; Zanesville Art Ctr, Ohio; many corp & pvt collections. *Comn:* Vista Int Hotel, Pittsburgh. *Exhib:* Gallery Upstairs, Pittsburgh Ctr for Arts, 70, 76 & 82; William Penn Mus, Harrisburg, Pa, 71-73; Ogleby Mus, Wheeling, WVa, 72; Butler Inst Am Art Mid-Year Nat, Ohio, 73 & 81; 10 year retrospective, Allegheny Co Courthouse Gallerie, 85; Chatauqua Nat Painting, Gallery 6, 89; and others. *Teaching:* Instr design, Pittsburgh Ctr for Arts, 70-, instr painting & papermaking, 73-. *Awards:* Excellence in Contemp Art, William Penn Mus; Assoc Artist, Pittsburgh, Carnegie Mus Art, 87; Frank Ross Award, Pittsburgh Craftsmen's Guild, 91-92; and others. *Mem:* Assoc Artists of Pittsburgh (pres, 74-); Craftsmen's Guild; Artists Equity; Int Asn Papermakers & Artists; Friends of Dard Hunter Mus. *Media:* Pure Pigment; Handmade Paper Pulp. *Dealer:* Gallery G 211 Ninth St Pittsburgh PA 15222; Artsouth Philadelphia PA. *Mailing Add:* 5703 Kentucky Ave Pittsburgh PA 15232

HOLLERBACH, SERGE
PAINTER, INSTRUCTOR
b Pushkin, Russia, Nov 1, 23; US citizen. *Study:* Acad Fine Arts, Munich, Ger, 46-49; Art Students League, with Ernst Fiene, 50; Am Art Sch, with Gordon Samstag, 51. *Work:* St Paul Gallery Art, Minn; Bridgeport Mus Art, Sci & Indust, Conn; Ga Mus Art, Athens; Seton Hall Univ Art Gallery; Russian Mus, St Petersburg, Russia. *Exhib:* Am Watercolor Soc Ann Exhib; Nat Acad Design Ann Exhib; Drawings USA, St Paul, Minn; 200 Yrs of Watercolor Painting in Am, Metrop Mus Art, NY; Am Acad Arts & Lett, NY. *Teaching:* Various painting workshops across America. *Awards:* Gold Medal, Allied Artists Am, 85, 87; Gold Medal, Am Watercolor Soc, 83; Silver Medal, Am Watercolor Soc, 89, 90, 95. *Bibliog:* Aleksis Rannit (auth), Arts Mag, 1/81; Scott Elliot (auth), Portrait of an artist, Artists' Mag, 6/86. *Mem:* Am Watercolor Soc (vpres, 79); Audubon Artists; Allied Artists; Nat Acad. *Media:* Acrylic, Watercolor. *Publ:* Auth, Composing in Acrylics, Watson-Guptill Publ, 88; sketches in pen & ink & watercolor, The Beach (exhib catalog), Newman & Saunders Galleries, Albatross Publ, Paris. *Dealer:* Newman & Saunders Galleries Wayne PA. *Mailing Add:* 304 W 75th St New York NY 10023

HOLLINGER, MORTON
PAINTER
b Port Chester, NY. *Study:* Syracuse Univ, BA, 49; studied with Louis Di Valentin, 1950; Studied oboe with Wm Arrowsmith, princ oboeist with Metropolitan Opera. *Exhib:* Regional Competition, West Chester Co Ctr, White Plains, NY, 58, won first prize oils (475 entries); Award Winners Show, Stamford Mus, Conn, 68; Group Show, Stamford Mus, Conn, 91-95; Soto Gallery, Boston, Mass, 2004. *Awards:* Cash Award, Westchester Co Ctr Regional Competition, 58; first prize, (475 entries) Westchester Arts Crafts Guild, Westchester Co Ctr, White Plains, NY, 58; Stamford Mus, Conn, 68; Windsor & Newton Award, Stamford Mus, Conn, 91. *Bibliog:* William Zimmer (auth), A show that's refined and raucous, NY Times, 4/93; Vivien Raynor (auth), Familiar names at the Conn art show, NY Times, 4/94; Among a judge's choices, NY Times, 4/95. *Mem:* Stamford Art Asn, Conn. *Media:* Oil. *Interests:* music. *Publ:* Illusr, Paintings of Morton Hollinger, S H Pierce & Co, Cambridge, Mass, 98. *Mailing Add:* 11 Ledge Ter Stamford CT 06905

HOLLINGSWORTH, ALVIN CARL
PAINTER, INSTRUCTOR
b New York, NY, Feb 25, 30. *Study:* City Univ New York, BA, 56, MA, 59; Art Students League, with Kunioshi, Ralph Fabri & Dr Bernard Myers, 50-52. *Work:* Chase Manhattan Bank, NY; Brooklyn Mus Permanent Collection, NY; IBM Collection, White Plains, NY; Williams Col Art Collection; Johnson Publ Permanent Art Collection, Chicago; plus others. *Comn:* Don Quixote limited ed lithographs, Orig Lithographs Inc, 67; Don Quixote murals, Don Quixote Apts, Bronx, NY, 69; mural, Rutgers Univ, New Brunswick, NJ, 70. *Exhib:* Emily Lowe Award Exhib, 63; Traveling Exhib Black Painters Am, Univ Calif, Los Angeles, 66; 15 New Voices, Hallmark Gallery, NY & traveling, 69; Am Black Painters, Whitney Mus Am Art, NY, 71; One-person shows, The Women, Interfaith Coun of Churches, 78, Reflections of the Prophet, Pa State Univ, 78 & others. *Pos:* Consult art & art coordr, Harlem Freedom Sch, Off Econ Opportunity, 66-67; dir, Lincoln Inst Gallery, Lincoln Inst Psycho-Ther, 66-68; supvr art, Proj Turn-On, New York, 68-69. *Teaching:* Instr graphics, High Sch Art & Design, 61-70; instr painting, Art Students League, 69-75; asst prof painting, Hostos Community Col, 71-77, assoc prof, 77-, prof visual & performing arts, currently. *Awards:* Emily Lowe Art Competition Award, 63; Whitney Found Award, 64; Award of Distinction, Smith Mason Gallery, 71. *Bibliog:* Cedric Dover (auth), American Negro Art, 61; Samella Lewis (auth), Black Artist on Art, pvt publ, 71. *Media:* Acrylic, Collage. *Res:* Aesthetic use of fluorescent materials in the fine arts. *Publ:* Auth & illusr, I'd like the Goo-gen-heim, Regnery, 69; coauth, Art of Acrylic Painting, Grumbacher, 69; illusr, The Sniper, McGraw, 69; illusr, Black Out Loud, Macmillan, 70; illusr, Journey, Scholastic, 70. *Dealer:* Lee Nordness Gallery 252 W 38th St New York NY 10021; Harbor Gallery 43 Main St Cold Spring Harbor NY 11724. *Mailing Add:* 12 Edgewood Ave Hastings-on-Hudson NY 10706-2024

HOLLIS, DOUGLAS
SCULPTOR
b Ann Arbor, Mich, Apr 21, 48. *Study:* Univ Mich, BFA, 70. *Work:* Nat Oceanic & Atmospheric Admin, Seattle, Wash; San Francisco Exploratorium, Calif; US Geological Survey, Menlo Park, Calif. *Comn:* Rain Column, Rincon Ctr, San Francisco, Calif; Univ S Fla, Tampa, 98; San Jose, Repertory Theatre, Calif, 98. *Exhib:* Listening Vessels, Univ NC, Raleigh. *Teaching:* Instr, Harvard Sch Design, 98-. *Awards:* Art Fel, Nat Endowment Arts, 80 & 86; Art Fel, Calif Arts Coun, 87; GFA Design Award, 96. *Mailing Add:* 136 Ripley St San Francisco CA 94110

HOLLISTER, VALERIE (DUTTON)
PAINTER
b Oakland, Calif, Dec 29, 39. *Study:* Stanford Univ, AB, 61 & MA, 64 San Francisco Art Inst, 63; Col Art Study Abroad, Paris, 64-65. *Work:* Stanford Univ Mus; Madison Art Ctr, Wis; Williams Col; Woodrow Wilson Sch-Princeton Univ; Russell Sage Found, NY. *Comn:* Winter Light (outdoor mural), Swarthmore Col, 88. *Exhib:* Biennial Contemp Am Painting & Area Show, Corcoran Gallery Art, Washington, DC, 67; Whitney Mus Ann Contemp Am Painting, 67-68; one-woman shows, Jefferson Place Gallery, Washington, 66, 68, 69, 72, Madison Art Ctr, Wis, 68, Swarthmore Col, Pa, 72, 77, 82 & 90, 2004; Westbroadway Gallery, NY, 73 & Selected Paintings Since 1965, Washington Proj for the Arts, Wash, DC, 78; Widener Univ Art Mus, Chester, Pa, 93; and other one-woman & group shows. *Awards:* Artist residency Yaddo Corp, 2000. *Media:* Painting. *Publ:* Coauth, Toward A History of Women's Traditional Arts, Heresies, winter 78; Auth, Seven Computer Landscapes, Occasional Works, Woodside, Calif, 93. *Mailing Add:* P O Box 25 Swarthmore PA 19081

HOLM, BILL
HISTORIAN, PAINTER
b Roundup, Mont. *Study:* Univ Wash, BA, 49, MFA, 51. *Work:* Alaska State Mus; Can Mus Civilization. *Exhib:* Burke Mus, 92. *Collection Arranged:* Arts of the Raven (with Doris Shadbolt, Bill Reid & Wilson Duff), Vancouver Art Gallery, 67; Crooked Beak of Heaven, Henry Art Gallery, Univ Wash, Seattle; Smoky-Top (auth, catalog), Pac Sci Ctr, 83; The Box of Daylight (auth, catalog), Seattle Art Mus, 83; Crossroads of Continents, Smithsonian Inst, 88. *Pos:* Cur, Northwest Coast Indian art, Thomas Burke Mem Wash State Mus, Univ Wash, Seattle, 68-85, cur emer, 85-. *Teaching:* Prof Northwest Coast Indian art, Univ Wash, Seattle, 68-85, Prof emer, 85-. *Awards:* Governor's Art Award, 76; Governor's Writers Award, 66, 77 & 81; Honor Award, Native Am Art Studies Asn, 91. *Bibliog:* Sun Dogs and Eagle Down: The Indian Paintings of Bill Holm, Univ Wash Press, 2000. *Mem:* Native Am Art Studies Asn. *Media:* Acrylic. *Res:* All aspects of Northwest Coast Indian art, with concentration on form and style and relation to ceremonialism. *Publ:* Auth, Northwest Coast Indian Art: An Analysis of Form, 65; auth, Crooked Beak of Heaven, 72, Univ Wash Press; coauth (with Bill Reid), Indian Art of the Northwest Coast, Univ Wash Press, 76; The Art and Times of Willie Seaweed, Univ Wash Press, 83; auth, Spirit and Ancestor, Univ Wash Press, 87. *Mailing Add:* 1027 NW 190th St Shoreline WA 98177

HOLM, MILTON W
PAINTER
b Rochester, NY. *Study:* With Edward S Siebert, Rochester. *Work:* Mem Art Gallery, Rochester, NY; Rochester Inst Technol; Univ Rochester; Greenville Pub Libr, SC. *Exhib:* Mem Art Gallery, Rochester, NY, 24-82; Nat Acad Design Ann, NY, 35-73; Allied Artists Am, NY, 38-71 & 77; Currier Art Gallery, Manchester, NH, 40; Cincinnati Art Gallery, 45. *Awards:* Ranger Purchase Award, Nat Acad Design, 40; James Hogarth Dennis Award, Mem Art Gallery, 58-62; Rochester Art Club Award, 69-82. *Bibliog:* C Movalli (auth), article, Am Artist, 11/78. *Mem:* Allied Artists Am; Rochester Art Club (pres, 57-59); Genesee Group (pres); Rockport Art Asn, Mass. *Media:* Oil. *Dealer:* Oxford Gallery 267 Oxford St Rochester NY 14607. *Mailing Add:* 4168 Pepper Ave Yorba Linda CA 92886

HOLMAN, ARTHUR (STEARNS)
PAINTER
b Bartlesville, Okla, Oct 25, 26. *Study:* Univ NMex, BFA, 51; Hans Hofmann Sch Art, Provincetown, Mass, 51; Calif Sch Fine Arts, San Francisco, 53. *Work:* San Francisco Mus Art; Oakland Mus, Calif; Achenbach Collection, Fine Arts Mus San Francisco; Stanford Univ; Mills Col; Eureka Col, Ill; Di Rosa Art Preserve, Napa, Calif. *Exhib:* One-man shows, Esther Robles Gallery, Los Angeles, 60, M H De Young Mem Mus, San Francisco, 63, San Francisco Mus Mod Art, 63, Gumps Gallery, San Francisco, 64, 65, 66, 69 & 87, Marin Civic Ctr Gallery, 70 & 95, William Sawyer Gallery, San Francisco, 71, 73, 74 & 76, David Cole Gallery, Inverness, Calif, 80 & Braunstein/Quay Gallery, San Francisco, 92, Art Foundry Gallery, Sacramento, Calif, 2003; Bay Area Regionalists, Hall of Flowers, San Francisco, 85 & 86; 20th Century Landscape Drawings, De Young Mus, San Francisco, 89; Jan Holloway Gallery, San Francisco, 89; Bolinas Mus, 97; San Francisco Art Inst, 2001; Marin Civic Ctr, 2005. *Awards:* Purchase Award, Invitational Show, Stanford Univ, 62; Pub Vote Prize, Bay Area Art, First Savings Bank of San Francisco, 64. *Media:* Oil. *Mailing Add:* Box 72 Lagunitas CA 94938

HOLMES, DAVID VALENTINE
SCULPTOR, PAINTER
b Newark, NY, Nov 27, 45. *Study:* Temple Abroad Tyler Sch, Rome, Italy, 66-67; Tyler Sch Art, Temple Univ, Philadelphia, Pa, BFA(cum laude), 68; Univ Wis, Madison, MFA, 72. *Work:* Milwaukee Art Mus, Wis; Kohler Arts Ctr, Sheboygan, Wis; Madison Art Ctr, Wis; Kent State Univ. *Comn:* Murals, Racine, Kenosha & Madison Pub Schs, Wis. *Exhib:* Chicago & Vicinity, Chicago Art Inst, Ill, 75; one-man shows, Madison Art Ctr, Kohler Arts Ctr, Wis, 72 & 77 & Ringling Sch Art, 91; Harmonious Craft, Am Craft Mus, NY & Renwick Gallery, Smithsonian Inst, Washington, DC, 79; two-artist exhib, Milwaukee Art Mus, Wis, 80; Animal Images, Renwick Gallery, Smithsonian, Washington, DC, 81; Renwick Souvenir Show, Smithsonian Inst, 82; Traveling one-man show, Ind State Univ, Kent State Univ & Northwestern Univ, 83; Midwest Int Exhib, Cent Mo State & Maastricht, The Neth, 87; Alchemic Emporium (traveling exhib), Swope Art Mus, Terre Haute, Ind; MacNider Mus, Mason City, Iowa; Fed Reserve Bank, Kansas City, Mo; Southeast Ark Arts Ctr, Pine Bluff, Ark, Edison Community Col, Ft Meyers, Fla, Bergstrom-Mahler Mus, Neenph, Wis, Muscatine Art Ctr, Muscatine, Iowa, 91-93; Col Lake Co, Grays Lake, Ill, 96. *Teaching:* Resident artist, Madison Pub Schools, Wis, 72-74; asst prof drawing & design, Univ Wis, Milwaukee, 74-76; prof drawing & design, Univ Wis-Parkside, Kenosha, 77-. *Awards:* Nat Endowment Arts Fel, US Government, 76-77. *Media:* Wood; Acrylic. *Mailing Add:* 2915 Washington Ave Racine WI 53405-5004

HOLMES, LARRY W
PAINTER, EDUCATOR
b Kansas City, Kans, Nov 12, 42. *Study:* Pittsburg State Univ, Kans, BFA, 64, MS, 65; Cranbrook Acad Art, with George Ortman, MFA, 73. *Work:* Cranbrook Acad Art, Bloomfield Hills, Mich; Pittsburg State Univ, Kans; City of Newark, Del; City of Parsons, Kans; St Lawrence Univ, Canton, NY; Hoyt Inst Fine Arts, New Castle, PA. *Exhib:* Solo exhibs, Del Art Mus, Wilmington, 84, Greenville Mus Art, NC, 87, Littlejohn-Smith Gallery, NY, 88, Littlejohn-Sternau Gallery, NY, 94, Hoyt Inst Fine Arts, New Castle, Pa, 96, Jack Meier Gallery, Houston, Tex, 96 & 98; Dog Days of August, Littlejohn-Smith Gallery, NY, 86; The Nature of the Beast, Hudson River Mus, NY, 89; A XX Century Bestiary, Renee Fotouhi Fine Art, NY, 90; Pastels: Big and Otherwise, Asheville Mus Art, NC, 92; 40 Yr Retrospective at the Univ of Del, Newark, DE, 04; solo exhib, Delawaer Ctr for the Contemp Art, Wilmington, DE, 05. *Teaching:* Prof painting, Univ Del, Newark, 73, chmn dept art, 82-92, retired. *Awards:* Yaddo Fel, Yaddo Corp, Saratoga Springs, NY, 80; Outstanding Teacher Award, Col of Arts and Science, 2003. *Bibliog:* Ann Jarmusch (auth), Larry Holmes at Arch St Gallery, Art News, summer 79; Carrie de Santis Tull (auth), Larry Holmes at Delaware Art Mus, New Art Examiner, 1/85; Victoria Donohue (auth), Larry Holmes at Rosenfeld, Philadelphia Inquirer, 6/21/86; Frank Thomson (auth), Catalogue for Pastels: Big and Otherwise, Asheville Mus Art; Janis Tomlinson (auth), Catalogue for 40 Yr Retrospective at the Univ of Delaware. *Mem:* Col Art Asn. *Media:* Pastel, Oil. *Dealer:* Jack Meier Gallery 2310 Bissonet Houston TX 77005. *Mailing Add:* 141Rocky Glen Rd Oxford PA 19363

HOLMES, WENDY (DIANA) H NOYES
PHOTOGRAPHER
b New York, NY, Oct 21, 46. *Study:* Mass Inst Technol. *Work:* Bibliot Nat, Paris; NJ State Mus, Trenton; Addison Gallery Art, Andover, Mass; Vassar Gallery, Poughkeepsie, NY; Toledo Mus of Art, Ohio; State Univ Art Mus, New Paltz. *Exhib:* Peters Valley Exhib, Newark Mus, NJ, 80; NJ State Mus, Trenton, 80 & 86; Upstate Exhib, NY State Mus, Albany, 82; Paul Mellon Arts Ctr, Wallingford, Conn, 82; Catskill Ctr Photog, Woodstock, NY, 84 & 86. *Collection Arranged:* Seven Photographers: The Delaware Valley (auth, catalog), Peters Valley, NJ, NJ State Mus & Nexus, Atlanta, Ga, 76-78. *Pos:* Staff photogr, Wave Hill Environ Ctr, Bronx, NY, 70-73. *Teaching:* Instr photog, Peters Valley Photog Workshop, Layton, NJ, 75-83, Int Ctr Photog, New York, 79-81 & Catskill Ctr Photog, Woodstock, NY, 86. *Awards:* Survey Grant for Seven Photographers Exhib, Nat Endowment Arts, 76; Fel, NJ State Coun Arts, 79; Photogr Fund Award, Catskill Ctr Photog, 84. *Bibliog:* Article, New York Times, 7/22/79. *Publ:* Auth & illusr, Hudson City: The Living River, Wave Hill Ctr, 72; coauth, Brother Can You Spare a Dime, Paddington Press, 75. *Mailing Add:* 73 Everette Ave Providence RI 02906-4206

HOLMES, WILLARD
MUSEUM DIRECTOR
b Saskatoon, Saskatchewan, Can, 49. *Study:* Univ British Columiba, Grad in art hist, 1972. *Pos:* With Fine Arts Gallery, Univ British Columbia; head of exhib Nat Gallery of Can; cur Vancouver Art Gallery; dir, Pender St Gallery, from 1975; chief cur, dir, Charles Scott Gallery, head cur studies prog Emily Carr Col, 1976-87; chief cur, interim dir, then dir, Vancouver Art Gallery, 1987-93; deputy dir, Chief Exec Officer, Whitney Mus Am Art, New York City, 1994-2003; dir Wadsworth Atheneum Mus Art, Hartford, Conn, 2003-. *Mailing Add:* Wadsworth Atheneum Mus Art 600 Main St Hartford CT 06103

HOLO, SELMA R
MUSEOLOGIST, MUSEUM DIRECTOR
b Chicago, Ill, May 21, 43. *Study:* Northwestern Univ, BA, 65; Hunter Col, City Univ NY, MA, 72; Univ Calif, Santa Barbara, PhD, 80. *Work:* Norton Simon Mus, Pasadena, Calif; Getty Mus, Malibu, Calif; Fisher Gallery, Univ Southern Calif, Los Angeles; Milwaukee Art Mus. *Pos:* Cur acquisitions, Norton Simon Mus, 77-81; dir, Fisher Gallery, Univ Southern Calif, 81-. *Teaching:* Instr art hist, Art Ctr Col Design, Pasadena, 73-77. *Awards:* La Napoule Distinguished Scholar Fel, 88; Tokyo Fuji Mus Fine Arts Award, 90. *Bibliog:* Eric Young (auth), Los Disparates, Burlington Mag, 2/77; various reviews in Los Angeles newspapers. *Mem:* Am Asn Mus; Col Art Asn; Int Coun Mus. *Res:* Goya. *Publ:* Auth, Despreciar los Insultos: A New Goya Acquisition, 83 & An Unsuspected Poseur in a Goya Drawing, 85, J Paul Getty Mus J; Joseph Alsop's The rare art traditions, Art News, 83; Training Future Curators to buy Art, Mus Studies J, 85; Interns Ins & Outs, Mus News, 89. *Mailing Add:* c/o Fischer Gallery Univ of South Calif Univ Park 823 Exposition Blvd Los Angeles CA 90089-0292

HOLOUN, HAROLD DEAN
PAINTER, SCULPTOR
b Ord, Nebr, Oct 16, 39. *Study:* Hastings Col, Nebr, BA, 61; Univ Wyo, Laramie, MA, 62. *Work:* Sheldon Mem Gallery, Univ Nebr, Lincoln; Nebr Art, Kearney; Nebr Wesleyan Univ, Lincoln. *Comn:* Portrait, Baker Univ, Baldwin, Kans, 75; two portraits, Liberty Glass Corp, Sapulpa, Okla, 79; painting-sculpture, City of Grand Island, Nebr, 81. *Exhib:* Painting-Sculpture Today, Indianapolis Mus Art, Ind, 78; Visions 81, Mid-Am Arts Alliance Touring Exhib, Kansas City, 80-81; Sheldon Mem Gallery, Lincoln, Nebr, 81; Art and Artists in Nebraska, Sheldon Mem Gallery, Lincoln, Nebr, 82; Twelve Midwest Realists, Sioux City Art Ctr, Iowa, 82; Reflectons Exhib, Elder Gallery, Lincoln, Nebr, 83; MJF Gallenigi, Kansas City, Mo, 85. *Awards:* Juror's Award, Reflections Exhib, Elder Gallery, 83. *Media:* Oil, Alkyd; Bronze, Photography. *Dealer:* Pickaro Galleries Inc 7108 N Western Oklahoma City OK 73116. *Mailing Add:* 812 Moore Dr Bellevue NE 68005-4436

HOLOWNIA, THADDEUS J
PHOTOGRAPHER, EDUCATOR
b Bury St Edmunds, Eng; Can citizen. *Study:* Univ Windsor, BA. *Work:* Nat Gallery Can; Mus Fine Arts Houston; Can Mus Contemp Photog, Ottawa; Can Coun Art Bank, Ottawa; Am Inst Graphic Arts, NY. *Comn:* Large Aeolian Piano (sound sculpture), with Gordon Monahan, Sound Symp, St John's, Nfld, 88; on-site photog, Can Mus Contemp Photog, Ottawa, 90; Landscapes in Times; Twelve Artists Reflects on the Nature of Canada (landscape photographes) The Nature Conservancy of Canada, Ottawa, 2005. *Exhib:* Dykelands, Art Gallery Hamilton, Ont, 86; Beau, Can Mus Contemp Photog, Ottawa, 92; The Landscape: Eight Canadian Photographers (with catalog), McMichael Gallery, Kleinberg, Ont, 92; 150 Yrs of Children in Photog, Winnipeg Art Gallery, Manitoba, 92; Sable Island: An Elemental Landscape (with catalog), Art Gallery NS, Halifax, 96; Extended Vision; The Photog of Thaddeus Holowina, 75-97; (with catalogue) The Canadian Mus of Contemp Photog, Ottawa, 98; Owens Art Gallery, Sackville, 99, Saint Mary's Univ Art Gallery, Halifax; Beaverbrook Art Gallery, Frederiction, 2000; Mc Michael Gallery, Kleinberg; Centro de la Imagen, Mexico City, 2002; Monet's Legacy; Series-Order and Obsession, Hamburger Kunsthalle, Hamburg, 2001; Anatomay of a pipeline, Owens Art Gallery, Sackville, 2003; 24 Studies for Henry David Thoreau, Tsongas Gallery at Walden Pond, Concord; Broken Ground; Canadian photographs from the New World, Martin-Gropius-Bau, Berlin; Exhib A Newfoundland and Labrador Project, The Rooms, The Art Gallery of New foundlands and Labrador, St, John's 2006. *Pos:* Prof Head of Dept, of Fine Arts, Mount Allison Univ, Sackville, NB. *Teaching:* Prof fine arts, Mt Allison Univ, 77-. *Awards:* AIGA Book Show, 50 Best Books 89 Graphic Design USA, Am Inst of Graphic Arts Book Show NY, Award of Excellence for Dykelands, 89; AIGA Book Show 50 Best Books, 99 Graphic Design USA, Am Inst of Graphic Art Books Show NY, Award of Excellence for extended Vision, 99; Fulbright Fel, Fulbright Found, 2001; Strathbutler Award, the Shelia Hugh McKay Found, 2003. *Bibliog:* Robert Tombs, The Newfoundland Project, Thaddeus Holownia's Coney Island of the Mind, Art Atlantic, Summer 2002, vol #72; Robert Enright, The Landscape of Thaddeus Holownia, Border Crossing # 84, 2002; Sarah Milroy, Tangled up with Walden, The Globe and Mail, Nov, 22, 2004. *Mem:* Royal Canadian Acad; N Am Nature Photography Asn. *Media:* Photography. *Publ:* Ironworks, Anchorage Press, 96; Extended Vision; The Photography of Thaddeus Holownia, 75-97, The Canadian Mus of Contemporary Photography, 98, Ova Aves, Anchorage Press, 2003; Arborealis, Ancorage Press, 2005. *Dealer:* Jane Corkin Gallery 179 John St Toronto Ont Can; Corkin Shopland Gallery, 55 Mill St, Bldg 61, Toronto, Ontario, M5A 3C4, Canada 416-979-1980; Hollinger Collins Contemporary Art, 4928 Sherbrooke Ouest, Montreal. Quebec, H3Z 1H3 Canada. *Mailing Add:* 440 Jolicure Rd Jolicure NB E4L 2S4 Canada

HOLSTAD, CHRISTIAN
ARTIST
b Anaheim, Calif, 1972. *Study:* Kans City Art Inst, BFA, 94. *Exhib:* One-man shows incl Sand Day: A Show of Artifacts, Absentia Art Gallery, Williamsburg, NY, 2002, Chris Verene The Self-Esteem Salon: The Baptism Series, Deitch Projects, NY, 2003, Life is a Gift, Daniel Reich Gallery, 2002, Sonnenaufgang, Aurel Scheibler Gallery, Ger, 2003, Sonnenuntergang, Daniel Schmidt Gallery, Ger, 2003, The Birth of Princess Middlefinger, Prague Biennial, 2003, The Housekeepers, Daniel Reich Gallery, NY, 2003, Am Express, Galeria Massimo de Carlo, Milan, Italy, 2004, Moving toward the Light, Daniel Reich Gallery, 2004, Innocent Killers, P S 1 Contemp Art Ctr, Queens, NY, 2004, Gaity; Discovering the Lost Art, Kunsthalle, Zurich, Switz, 2004; exhib in group shows at Midwest Bound, Chorus Gallery, Minneapolis, 95, Sauna Hut Available, 96, Cult of Claude, Here Arts Gallery, NY, 97, Fleshy Juggler, Brownies, NY, 98, Car Show, Reported Injuries Art Space, Brooklyn, 99, Slide Show, John Michael Kohler Art Ctr, Sheboygan, Wis, 2000, Zeek Sheck Collaboration, Knitting Factory, NY, 2001, Bathroom Group Show, Daniel Reich Gallery, NY, 2002, Now Playing, D'amelio Terras, NY, 2003, Calif Earthquakes, Daniel Reich Gallery, NY, 2004, Whitney Biennial, Whitney Mus Am Art, 2004. *Mailing Add:* c/o Daniel Reich Gallery 537 A West 23 St New York NY 10011

HOLSTE, THOMAS JAMES
PAINTER, EDUCATOR
b Evanston, Ill, Jan 12, 43. *Study:* Calif State Univ, Fullerton, study with Vic Smith, BA, 67, MA, 68; Claremont Grad Sch, study with Guy Williams & Mowry Baden, MFA, 70. *Work:* La Jolla Mus Contemp Art, Calif; Chase Manhattan Bank, NY; Solomon R Guggenheim Mus, NY; Security Pac Nat Bank; Int Tel & Tel, NY. *Exhib:* The Market St Prog, Los Angeles Co Mus Art, Los Angeles, 72; One-man show, Newspace Gallery, Los Angeles, 73-88; Aber, Buchanan, Holste, Newport Harbor Art Mus, Newport Beach, Calif, 76; Mind Set: An Ongoing Involvement with the Rational Tradition, John Weber Gallery, NY, 79; Four Artists, Otis Art Inst Parsons Sch Design, Los Angeles, 79; Emergent Americans, Guggenheim Mus, NY, 81; Alice Aycock, Tom Holste, Michael Singer, Fort Worth Art Mus, Tex, 81; Concepts in Construction: 1910-1980 Traveling Exhib, 83-; and others. *Teaching:* Prof painting, Calif State Univ, Fullerton, 69-. *Awards:* Individual Artists Fel Grant, Nat Endowment Arts, 80. *Bibliog:* Peter Frank (auth), Review--Tom Holste, Artforum, 2/78 & Unslick in LA, Art Am, 9-10/78. *Media:* Mixed. *Mailing Add:* 17201 Harding Cyn Rd Modjeska Silverado CA 92676-9801

HOLT, DAVID JOHN
PAINTER, EDUCATOR
b Salt Lake City, Utah, July 16, 54. *Study:* Academia delle Belle Arti, Florence, Italy, dipl in painting, 78; Univ Utah, BFA, 80; Am Univ, MFA, 84. *Work:* Watkins Mem Collection, Am Univ, Washington, DC; Montgomery Co Collection Contemp Art, Bethesda, Md. *Exhib:* Approaching the Figure, Georgetown Univ, Washington, DC, 90; 72nd National Exhibition, GWV Smith Art Mus, Springfield, Mass, 91; Small Immeusities, The Paintings Ctr, NY, 03; Bowery Gallery, NY, 95, 03-05; Ceres Gallery, NY, 96; one-man show, Albertus Magnus Col, New Haven, Conn, 87, Erector Sq Gallery, New Haven, Conn, 87, Butler Gallery, Marymount Col, Tarrytown, NY, 88, 2002, Dudley House, Harvard Univ, Cambridge, Mass, 91, Atlantic Gallery, NY, 92, John Lyman Center, Southern Conn State Univ, New Haven, 93 & Courtyard Gallery, Wash Studio Sch, DC, 86, 86, 89, 90, 94 & 98, Bowery Gallery, 04; District Visions, Diverse Pursuits, Col of William and Mary, Williamsburg, Va, 2001. *Pos:* chmn dept art, Marymount Col of Fordham Univ, Tarrytown, NY, 94-. *Teaching:* assoc prof art, Marymount Col of Fordham Univ, Tarrytown, NY, 93-98, prof art, 98-. *Awards:* Painting Grant, Ludwig Vogelstein Found, 87. *Bibliog:* Anne Behrens (auth), The eyes have it, The Washington Post, Virginia Weekly, 4/26/84; Mark St John Erickson (auth), Visual orchestration, The Virginia Gazette, 3/20/85; Mary Jane Pagan (auth), Approaching the figure, Georgetown Univ, 90. *Mem:* Col Art Asn; Founds in Art: Theory & Educ. *Media:* Oil. *Dealer:* Bowery Gallery 530 W 25th St 4th Fl NY NY 10011. *Mailing Add:* Marymount Col Fordham Univ Dept Art 100 Marymount Ave Tarrytown NY 10591

HOLT, MARTHA A
CERAMIST, SCULPTOR
b Chatham, NJ, Apr, 15, 45. *Study:* Univ Miami, Fla, BS, 67; Norfolk Mus Sch, 67-68; Penland Sch Crafts, 68-69; Cranbrook Acad Art, MFA, 71. *Work:* Ga Power & Light Co, Atlanta; Peat Marwick Co, Pittsburgh, Pa; W Forest High Sch, Tionesta, Pa; Erie Art Mus, Pa. *Exhib:* Solo exhibs, Portnoy Gallery, NY, 77, 79, 80 & 82, Erie Art Mus, Pa, 83, Pittsburgh Ctr Arts, Pa, 83 & Belk Art Gallery, W Carolina Univ, NC, 85, Lill Street Gallery, Chicago, 86 & The Clay Place, Pittsburgh, 87 & 89, Canton Art Inst, 89. *Pos:* Dir, Allegheny Col Galleries, 76-83. *Teaching:* Instr ceramics, Penland Sch Crafts, 86, 87, 89 & 91; conducts workshops nationally. *Awards:* Visual Arts Fel Grants, Pa Coun Arts, 80 & 86; Vis Artist, Penland Sch, 87-88. *Bibliog:* Susan Wechsler (auth), Low-Fire Ceramics, Watson Guptill, 81; Charlotte Speight(auth), Ceramic Sculpture, Harper & Row, 83; Richard Zakin (auth), Ceramics, Mastering the Craft, Chilton Bk Co, 90. *Mem:* Int Sculpture Ctr; Artists Equity Asn. *Media:* Clay. *Publ:* Coauth, New Relationships, private publ, 80. *Dealer:* The Clay Place 5416 Walnut St Pittsburgh PA 15232

HOLT, NANCY LOUISE
SCULPTOR, FILMMAKER
b Worcester, Mass, Apr 5, 38. *Study:* Tufts Univ, BS, 56-60. *Comn:* Landscape Sculptures, Art park, Lewiston, NY, 74, Western Wash Univ, 78, Wellesley Col, Mass, 80, Miami Univ, Ohio, 80, Laguna Gloria Art Mus, Austin, 81, Arlington Co, Va & Gallaudet Col, Washington, DC, 84; Southern Conn Univ, New Haven, 85; Solar Rotary, Univ SFla, Tampa, 93-. *Exhib:* Solo-exhibs, LoGuidice Gallery, NY, 73, Bykert Gallery, NY, 74, Whitney Mus, NY, 77, John Weber Gallery, NY, 79, 82, 84, 86 & 93 & Flow Ace Gallery, Los Angeles, 85; New Am Filmaker's Series, Whitney Mus Am Art, NY, 75 & 77; Whitney Biennial (with catalog), Whitney Mus Am Art, 77, 79 & 81; Artists' Gardens and Parks, Hayden Gallery, Mass Inst Technol, 81; Artist as Social Designer, Los Angeles Co Mus, Calif, 85; Consumer Tools: Personal Visions, Mus Mod Art, NY, 91; Making Their Mark, Cincinnati Art Mus, New Orleans Mus Art, Denver Art Mus, Pa Acad Fine Arts, 89; Fragile Ecologies: Artists' Interpretations & Solutions, Queens Mus, Flushing, NY, Smithsonian Inst Traveling Exhibs, 91; The Lure of the Local, CU Art Galleries, Univ Colo, Boulder, 94; Differentes Natures, Art Defense (catalog), EPAD, Paris, 93; Mapping, Mus Mod Art, NY, 94; City Site Sculpture, Toronto, 82. *Awards:* Creative Artists Pub Serv Grant, 75 & 78; Nat Endowment Arts Fels, 75, 78, 85 & 88; Guggenheim Fel, 78. *Bibliog:* Monroe Denton (auth), Nancy Holt: Sculpting the Elements, Vol 1, No 1, Pub Art Rev, Winter/Spring 89; Barbara C Matilsky (auth), Nancy Holt: Reconnecting to the Stars Fragile Ecologies, Rizzoli, NY, 92; Gilles A Tiberghien (auth), Land Art, Ed Carre, Paris, 93. *Publ:* Auth, Sun tunnels, Artforum, 4/77; Stone enclosure: Rock rings, Arts, 6/79; Ransacked, Printed Matter, 80; Time Outs, Visual Studies Workshop Press, 85; Ecological Aspects of My Work (catalog), Gail Gelburd Creative Projs, New York, 93

HOLTON, WILLIAM
PAINTER, PRINTMAKER
b Knoxville, Tenn, 66. *Study:* Univ Ariz, Tucson, 87-88; Atlanta Col Art, BFA(painting & Printmaking), 91. *Exhib:* Anthony Ardavin Gallery, Atlanta, Ga, 93, 94, 95, 96, 97 & 99; Alumni Exhib, Atlanta Col Art, Atlanta, Ga, 93; Artcare, Atlanta, Ga, 93, 94 & 95; The November Show, Atlanta, Ga, 93; solo exhibs, Anthony Ardavin Gallery, Atlanta, Ga, 93 & TVUUC Gallery, Knoxville, Tenn, 99; Southeastern Ctr Contemp Art, Winston-Salem, NC, 97; Zoe Gallery, Louisville, Ky, 98 & 99. *Pos:* Intern, Rolling Stone Press, Atlanta, Ga, 89; Atlanta Arts Festival, Atlanta, Ga, 91. *Awards:* Merit Award, Magic City Arts Festival, Birmingham, Ala, 91; Best of Show, Artfest, Mod & Contemp Art, High Mus Art, Atlanta, Ga, 94; Southern Arts Fedn Visual Arts Fel, Nat Endowment Arts, 96. *Bibliog:* Critics notebook-William Holton, Atlanta J-Constitution, 1/29/96

HOLTZ, ITSHAK JACK
PAINTER, PRINTMAKER
b Skernewiz, Poland, Dec 14, 1925; US citizen. *Study:* Bezalel Acad Art, Jerusalem; Art Students League; Nat Acad Design, NY. *Exhib:* Karlebach Gallery, Fair Lawn, NJ, 65-85; Audubon Artists of NY, 66; Tyringham Galleries, Mass, 66-86; Allied Artists Am, NY, 72; Nat Acad Design, 77; Yeshiva Univ Mus, NY, 83 & 92; Jewish Community Ctr on the Palisades, 90; YMWA, Washington Township, NJ, 91. *Awards:* Gold Medal, Academia Italia, 83; Bd Dir Award, NY Art's Interaction, 89-90. *Bibliog:* Articles in Art Rev Mag, 5/66 & La Rev Mod, 6/66. *Mem:* Art Students League; Academia Italia delle Arti; Artists Equity Asn NY. *Media:* Oil, Felt Pen & Ink; Lithography. *Mailing Add:* 118 E 28th St New York NY 10016

HOLVERSON, JOHN
CURATOR, MUSEUM DIRECTOR, ART DEALER
b Marshfield, Wis, June 14, 46. *Study:* Univ Iowa, 65-66; MacMurray Col, Jacksonville, Ill, BA, 67; Univ Iowa, Iowa City, MA, 71; Attingham Summer Sch, 82. *Collection Arranged:* Images of Women Photog Exhib (auth, catalog), 77; The Revolutionary McLellans, 77; Miss Mary Cassatt: Impressionist from Pennsylvania, 79; James Brooks: Paintings and Works on Paper 1946-1982, 83; Winslow Homer: The Charles Shipman Payson Collection, 83; Maine Light: Temperas by Andrew Wyeth, 83; Gaston Lachaise: Sculpture & Drawings (auth, catalog), 84; Jamie Wyeth: An American View, 84; 1985 Maine Biennial; John Marin in Maine, 85. *Pos:* Summer intern, Art Inst Chicago, 68-69; grad asst, Mus Art, Univ Iowa, 68-69, head grad asst, 69-70; cur, Portland Mus Art, Maine, 70-73, cur collections, 73-81, actg dir, 73-75, dir, 75-87; consult; founder, J H Holverson Co, Portland, 87-; dir, Jones Mus of Glass & Ceramics, Sebago, Maine, currently. *Teaching:* Asst dept art, MacMurray Col, Jacksonville, Ill, 63-67; grad asst, Univ Iowa Mus Art, 68-69, head grad asst, 69-70; Mus Collab Mgt Inst Cult Inst, Arden House Columbia Univ Grad Sch Bus, 82, vis fac mem, 83; sponsored & collaborated with Maine Hist Preserv Comn on The Portland Glass Company: Background Research & Survey Plan, 86; scholar, Paul Getty Trust & Art Mus Asn, Mus Mgt Inst, 87; instr community progs, Univ Southern Maine, 90-91; invited participant New Art Mus Construction in the 1980's, Nat Gallery Art, Inst Advan Studies. *Awards:* Excellence Award, Am Inst Architects, 85. *Mem:* Am Asn Mus; Asn Art Mus Dirs; Archives Am Art; Col Art Asn. *Specialty:* fine arts, sculpture, works on paper, antiques, decorative arts, Native American rugs, pottery, jewelry. *Publ:* Auth, Rene Dubois and the cathedrals of the future, Greater Portland Landmarks Observer, fall 73; Fire buckets and bags in Portland, 1783, Antiques, 3/74. *Mailing Add:* 292 Spring St Portland ME 04102

HOLVEY, SAMUEL BOYER
SCULPTOR, DESIGNER
b Wilkes Barre, Pa, July 20, 35. *Study:* Syracuse Univ, BFA, 57; Am Univ, MA, 69. *Comn:* Bas-relief mural, Wyo Valley Country Club, Wilkes Barre, 62. *Exhib:* Corcoran Gallery Area Show, Washington, 68; Greater Wash Area Show, 72; 2nd Ann Wash Area Sculpture Show, 74; The Am Genius, Corcoran Gallery, 76. *Pos:* Designer, William Fertig Interiors, Kingston, Pa, 57-58, 63-64; art dir, WFM-TV, Eatontown, NJ, 60-61; designer display exhibs, The Displayers Inc, NY World's Fair Pavilions, 61-63; designer, Robert Kayton Assocs, NY, 62; pres, Holvey Assoc Inc, 87-97. *Teaching:* asst prof design, Univ Md, College Park, 67-78; Assoc prof graphic design, Corcoran Sch Art, Washington, 78-93. *Mem:* Art Dirs Club Metrop Washington; Graphic Design Educators Asn. *Media:* Metal Direct Construction, Lumia. *Mailing Add:* 20765 Parkside Cir Sterling VA 20165-3516

HOLZER, JENNY
CONCEPTUAL ARTIST
b Gallipolis, Ohio, July 29, 50. *Study:* Ohio Univ, BFA, 72; RI Sch Design, MFA, 77; Whitney Mus Independent Study Prog, fel, 77. *Work:* Van Abbe Mus, Eindhoven, Neth; Mus Contemp Art, Chicago; Tate Gallery, London; Mus Mod Art Lending Serv, NY. *Comn:* Project Grand Central, Remy Martin, NY, 80; posters, Nouveau Mus, Lyon, France, 82; sign, City Amsterdam, 82; spectacolor board, Pub Art Fund, NY, 82; Urban Art Works Proj, City Seattle, 83; Green Table (granite table with benches, 20 x 6 feet), Univ Calif, San Diego, 93. *Exhib:* 74th Am Show, Art Inst Chicago, 82; 1983 Biennial Exhib (catalog), Whitney Mus Am Art, NY, 83; The Human Condition Biennial III (catalog), San Francisco Mus Art, 84; Mus d'Art Mod, Paris, 84; 1985 Biennial Exhib (catalog), Whitney Mus Am Art, NY, 85; Currents 7: Words in Action, Milwaukee Art Ctr, 85; Dissent: The Issue of Modern Art in Boston, The Expressionist Challenge (catalog), Inst Contemp Art, Boston, 85; Musee d'Art Contemporain de Montreal, 85; In Other Words (catalog), Corcoran Gallery Art, Washington, DC, 86; Committed to Print: An Exhib of Recent Am Printed Art with Social and Political Themes (catalog) Mus Mod Art, NY, 88; 1988: The World of Art Today, Milwaukee Art Mus, 88; Modes of Address: Language in Art Since 1960, Whitney Mus Am Art Downtown Fed Plaza, NY, 88; Image World-Art & Media Cult (catalog), Whitney Mus Am Art, 89; Affinities--The Gerald S Elliot Collection (catalog), Art Inst Chicago, 90; Language in Art, Aldrich Mus Contemp Art; High & Low: Modern Art & Popular Cult, Mus Mod Art, NY, 90; solo-exhibs, Seattle Art Mus, 84, Cranbrook Mus, 84, Dallas Mus Art, 84-93, Brooklyn Mus, 88, Solomon R Guggenheim Mus, 89, Walker Art Gallery, 91, Albright-Knox Art Gallery, 91; Am Art in the 20th Century Traveling Show (catalog), Royal Acad Arts, London, 93; The Language of Art, Kunsthalle, Vienna, 93; Don't Ask, Don't Tell, Don't Pursue, Fairfield Univ, Conn, 93; Virtual Reality: An Emerging Medium, Guggenheim Mus, 93; Translucent Writings, Neuberger Mus Art, NY, 94. *Awards:* Blair Award, 79th Americans Show, Art Inst Chicago, 82; Gold Medal Award for title & edition design, Art Dir Club, Ger, 93. *Bibliog:* Time Span (portfolio), Fundacio Caixa de Pensions, Barcelona, 90; Hiroko Tanaka (auth), Art is Beautiful: Interviews with New York Artists, Kawade Shobo Shinsha, Tokyo, 90, 98-115; Susan R Suleiman (auth), Subversive Intent: Sender, Politics and the Avant-Garde, Howard Univ Press, Cambridge, 90. *Mem:* Collaborative Proj, NY. *Media:* Multi-Media. *Publ:* Coauth, Position papers, Art Forum, 80; contribr, Hotel, 80 & coauth, Eating Through Living, 81, Tanam Press; coauth, Eating Friends, Top Stories, 81; auth, Truisms and Essays, Press NS Col Art & Design, 83. *Mailing Add:* 80 Hewitt Rd Hoosick Falls NY 12090

HOLZMAN, ERIC
PAINTER
b Bronx, NY, Nov 4, 49. *Study:* Tyler Sch Art, BFA, 71; Yale Univ, MFA, 73. *Work:* Exxon; plus many pvt collections. *Exhib:* Solo-exhibs, KNE Gallery, NY, 93, Jason McCoy, NY, 96, Mercury Gallery, Boston, 96 & Rice Pollack Gallery, Provincetown, Mass, 96, Jason McCoy, 00; Dan Beckerman, Redlands, Calif, 94; Nichola Davies Gallery, NY, 95; Johan Westerbury Gallery, Vt, 96; Still Life, Boston Globe, 96; and others. *Teaching:* Vis critic & lectr, Pace Col, 90; vis artists, Md Inst, 91, Boston Univ, 91-93, Knox Col, 92-93 & Dartmouth, 92-93; instr painting & drawing, NY Studio Sch, 93-; fac NY Studio Sch, 96; instr, Pratt Inst, 95 & NY Acad, 95, Bard, 97. *Awards:* Nat Endowment Arts Grant, 89; Guggenheim Found Grant, 91; Louis Comfort Tiffany Found Grant, 98. *Publ:* NY Observer, 6/01. *Dealer:* Jason McCoy Inc 41 E 57th St New York NY 10022. *Mailing Add:* 121 Wooster New York NY 10012

HOM, MEI-LING
SCULPTOR
b New Haven, Conn, 1951. *Study:* Kirkland Col, BA, 73; NY State Col Ceramics Alfred Univ, MFA, 87. *Comn:* ChinaWedge, Philadelphia Conv Ctr, 94; Moss Ghosts, pvt comn by Marsha & Jim Moss, 2000. *Exhib:* Challenge Exhib, Fleischer Art Mem, Philadelphia, 91; Thai Space, Silpakorn Univ Gallery, Bangkok, Thailand, 93; Offering, Alternative Mus, NY, 96; 20 Philadelphia Artists, Philadelphia Mus Art, 98; Biennial Exhib of Pub Art, Neuberger Mus of Art, Purchase, NY, 2001; solo exhib, Fleisher-Olman Gallery, Philadelphia, PA, 2004; Matchmaking at Suzhou Creek, East Link Gallery, Shanghai, China, 2004; Chinatown Influx, Asian Arts Initiative, Philadelphia, Pa, 2005; solo exhib, Mercer Gallery, Rochester, NY, 2005; Mid Career Show, Asian Am Arts Ctr, NY, 2005; solo exhib, Koppelman Gallery, Tufts Univ, Boston, Mass, 2005; Perpectives at the Sacker Pavillion, Smithsonian Inst, Washington, DC, 2005. *Teaching:* Asst prof art, Community Col Philadelphia, 83-2003. *Awards:* NEA Fel, Visual Arts, 1994; Creative Artists Exchange Fel, US, Japan, 96; Excellence Grant, The Leeway Found, 99; Visual Artist Grant, Joan Mitchell Found, 2005; Fulbright Res Grant to Korea, 2006. *Mem:* Asian Am Arts Alliance (NY chap); Ctr for Book Arts (NY chap); Int Sculpture Ctr (DC chap); Women's Studio Workshop (NY chap); Headlands Ctr Arts, Marin Co, Calif, (artist mem). *Media:* Porcelain, Styrene, Limestone, Wire Netting. *Dealer:* John Olman, Fleisher-Olman Gallery, 1616 Walnut St, Philadelphia, PA. *Mailing Add:* 2306 Fitzwater St Philadelphia PA 19146

HOMER, WILLIAM INNES
HISTORIAN, EDUCATOR
b Merion, Pa, Nov 8, 29. *Study:* Princeton Univ, BA; Harvard Univ, MA & PhD. *Pos:* Cur, Mus Am Art, Ogunquit, Maine, 55-58; actg asst dir, Princeton Univ Art Mus, 56-57. *Teaching:* Asst prof art & archaeol, Princeton Univ, 61-64; assoc prof art hist, Cornell Univ, 64-66; prof art hist, Univ Del, 66-99, chmn art hist dept, 66-81, 86-93. *Awards:* Am Coun Learned Soc Fel, 64-65; Guggenheim Fel, 72-73; Nat Endowment Humanities Fel, 80-81. *Mem:* Col Art Asn; Royal Photog Soc; Royal Soc Arts; Nat Arts Club; Cosmos Club. *Publ:* Alfred Stieglitz & the American Avant-Garde, 77; Alfred Stieglitz & the Photo-Secession, 83; coauth, Albert Pinkham Ryder: Painter of Dreams, 89; auth, Thomas Eakins: His Life and Art, 92; The Language of Contemporary Criticism Clarified, 99; Stieglitz and the Photo-Scecession, 1902, 02. *Mailing Add:* PO Box 4195 Wilmington DE 19807-0195

HOMITZKY, PETER
PAINTER
b Berlin, Ger, Dec 7, 42; US citizen. *Study:* Art Students League, with F Reilly, J Leberte, J Hirsh, 59-63; San Francisco Art Inst, 65-66. *Work:* Wichita Mus Art, Kans; San Francisco Mus Art; Prudential Ins Co, Newark, NJ; Newark Mus, NJ; NJ State Mus, Trenton, NJ; Rutgers Univ; Jane Voorhees Zimmerli Mus. *Exhib:* One-man shows, Roko Gallery, NY, 74 & State Mus, Trenton, NJ, 77; Alonzo Galleries, NY, 76-77; Educ Testing Serv, Princeton, NJ, 82; Sid Deutsch Galley, NY, 83; Jersey City Mus, 84; Robeson Gallery, Rutgers Univ, Newark, 84; Frank Caro Gallery, NY, 89; Art Awareness, Lexington, NY, 89. *Teaching:* Instr painting, Art Students League, New York, currently. *Awards:* Purchase Awards, First NJ Biannual, Newark Mus, 77 & NJ State Mus; Aidekman Found, Newark Mus, 78; Harry Devlin Visual Arts Award, NJ State Coun Arts, 81 & 82; NJSCA Fel, 82. *Bibliog:* Diane Cochrane (auth), Industrial American landscapes of Peter Homitzky, Am Artist, 5/74; Susan Myer (ed), 20 Landscape Painters, Watson-Guptill, 77; Hilton Kramer (auth), article, New York Times, 12/9/77. *Media:* Oil, Pastel. *Dealer:* Frank Caro Gallery 41 E 57th St New York NY. *Mailing Add:* 227 Grand St Hoboken NJ 07030-2511

HOMMA, KAZUFUMI
PAINTER
b Matudo-City, Japan, Apr 21, 43. *Study:* Tokyo Contemp Art Sch, 66-68; Brooklyn Mus Art Sch, 68-71. *Work:* Chase Bank Int & Home Insurance, New York, NY. *Comn:* Acrylic on canvas, Repub Bank, Houston, Tex. *Exhib:* Surugadi Gallery, Tokyo, Japan, 68; Brooklyn Mus Community Gallery, NY, 75; Brooklyn '81, Brooklyn Mus, 81; one-man shows, Limbo Lounge, 84 & Hal Bromm Gallery, 84 & 88, NY. *Collection Arranged:* Mixed Bag (auth, catalog), Alternative Mus, 82. *Media:* Acrylic. *Dealer:* Hal Bromm Gallery 90 W Broadway New York NY 10007. *Mailing Add:* 437 16th St No 4L Brooklyn NY 11215-5822

HONIG, ELEANOR D
PAINTER, PRINTMAKER
b New York, NY. *Study:* Fashion Inst Technol & Design, NY, Apparel Design Prof Fashion Degree; Queens Col, NY, BA, 67; CW Post Univ, Greenvale, NY, MA, 72. *Work:* Islip Art Mus, Long Island, NY; Jane Voorhees Zimmerli Art Mus, Rutgers Univ, NJ. *Comn:* Mural, Boces Cult Arts, Syosset, NY, 79. *Exhib:* solo exhib, Gallery at Bryan Libr, Roslyn, NY, 94; Nat Asn Women Artists Traveling Exhib, Purdue Univ, Ind, 98-99; For Pastels Only, Nat Arts Club Gallery, NY; Islip Mus, East Islip, NY, 99; Okn Gallery, Uniondale, NY, 00. *Pos:* Artist-in-residence, Boces Cult Arts, Syosset, NY, 79-81; package designer, Cher-Ami Natural Sweet Treats, NY, 79-84; fashion designer, clothing indust & freelance, NY. *Teaching:* Secondary supervisor art, Oyster Bay-East Norwich Cent Schs, Oyster Bay, NY, 67-79; artist-vis instr, Boces Cult Arts Ctr, Syosset, NY, 79-81; adj prof, Art Dept, Nassau Community Col, Garden City, NY, 80-. *Awards:* First Prize, Parish Art Mu, South Hampton, NY, 92; Medal Honor & Elizabeth Stanton Blake Award Excellence, Nat Asn Women Artists Exhib, NY, 91, M de Sola Mendes Award, 94; Printmaking Award, NAWA, 99. *Bibliog:* Eleanor Honig - Lecture Biography, Art a la Carte, Heckscher Mus, 84 & 87 & Lecture Biography, Aspect Int Language Sch, C W Post Col, NY, 91; Elizabeth Wix (auth), Five artists discover the inner eye, Newsday, NY, 10/23/92; Helen Harrison (art review), 20th Century Traditions, NY Times, 1/2/00. *Mem:* Nat Asn Women Artists, NY (exec bd, 86-92); Pastel Soc Am, NY; Hempstead Harbor Artists Asn, Glen Cove, NY (exec bd & vpres, 82-92); Nat Drawing Asn. *Media:* Mixed. *Mailing Add:* 25 Hightop Ln Jericho NY 11753

HONJO, MASAKO
PAINTER
b Gi Fu Pref, Japan, May 3, 48. *Study:* Art Student League, 82. *Exhib:* Nat Asn Women Artists Traveling Painting Exhib USA, Monmouth Mus, NJ, 87, Hiddenite Art Mus, NC, 88 & Nicolaysen Art Mus, Casper, Wyo, 88; 100 Yrs/100 Works, Nat Asn Women Artists, Islip Mus, East Islip, NY, 89, Fine Art Mus of the S, Mobile, Ala, 89, Chattanooga Regional Hist Mus, Tenn, 89, Longview Mus Art, Tex, 89 & Kirkpatrick Art Ctr, Oklahoma City, 90. *Awards:* Zluta & Joseph Akston Found Award, 88. *Bibliog:* David Howard (auth), David Howard art seen, Visual Studies, 90. *Mem:* Nat Asn Women Artists (oil juror, 88-89); Hudson River Contemp Artists; Am Soc Contemp Artists. *Media:* Oil. *Dealer:* 55 Mercer Gallery 55 Mercer St New York NY 10013. *Mailing Add:* 176 Silver Hollow Rd Chichester NY 12416-5113

HOOD, GRAHAM STANLEY
MUSEUM DIRECTOR, WRITER
b Stratford-on-Avon, Eng, Nov 6, 36; US citizen. *Study:* Keble Col, Oxford Univ, MA(mod hist); Courtauld Inst Art, London Univ. *Work:* Detroit Inst Art; Colonial Williamsburg Found, Va. *Pos:* Cur Europ decorative arts, Wadsworth Atheneum, Hartford, Conn, 61-64; assoc cur, Garvan Collection, Yale Univ Art Gallery, New Haven, 64-68; cur Am art, Detroit Inst Art, 68-71; vpres, Carlisle H Humelsine & cur, Colonial Williamsburg Found, 71. *Teaching:* Adj prof hist art, Wayne State Univ; lectr hist art, Col William & Mary, Williamsburg, Va, 74-. *Mem:* Asn Art Mus Dirs; Am Antiquarian Soc. *Publ:* Auth, American Silver, a History of Style, 1650-1900, Praeger Publ, 71; coauth, The Garvan Collection of American Silver at Yale, Yale Univ Art Gallery, 71; auth, Bonnin and Morris of Philadelphia: The First American Porcelain Factory, Univ NC Press, 72; co-auth, The Williamsburg Collection of Antique Furnishings, 73 & auth, Charles Bridges and William Dering: Two Virginia Painters, 1735-1750, 78, Colonial Williamsburg Found; The Governor's Palace in Williamsburg: A Cultural Study, Colonial Williamsburg Found & Univ NC Press, 91. *Mailing Add:* Colonial Williamsburg Found Williamsburg VA 23185

HOOD, MARY BRYAN
MUSEUM DIRECTOR, ADMINISTRATOR, PAINTER
b Central City, Ky, July 5, 38. *Study:* Ky Wesleyan Col, dipl(theatre), 60, dipl(art & art hist), 74. *Collection Arranged:* The American Artist Looks at the American Soldier: 1915-1975, 80; The Kentucky Tradition in American Landscape Painting (coauth, catalog), 83; Kentucky Expatriates: In Major American Museum Collections (ed, catalog), 84; The Art of the Native American: The Southwest 19th Century to the Present (auth, catalog), 85; Christianity and the Visual Arts: Kentucky Collections (ed, catalog), 86; The Kentuckians (ed, catalog), 87; The Experienced Eye (auth, catalog), 88; Contemplating the American Watercolor: The Transco Collection (auth, catalog), 89; Kentucky Spirit: The Naive Tradition (auth, catalog), 91; Art of Africa: Before it was Art it was Life, 95; Dreamtime: Art of the First Australians, 96; The Legacy of Spanish Colonial America, 98; Glorious Glass: Late 20th Century Studio Art Glass, 97; Navajo Folk Art: The Rosenak Collection, 99; Kentucky Womens artists: 1850-00, co-curator. *Pos:* Exec dir, Owensboro Arts Comn, Ky, 73-77; founding dir, Owensboro Mus Fine Art, Ky, 77-; pres Owensboro Mus Fine Art Found, Inc, 95-. *Mem:* Ky Arts Comn (mem bd, 77-78); Am Asn Mus; Ky Citizens for the Arts (exec bd, 84-); Ky Bicentennial Steering Comt (mem, 90-92); Year of American Craft (Ky comt, 91-93); Ky Asn Mus (pres 83); Owenboro Pub Art Comn chmn, 2003-. *Res:* Am art with emphasis on art and artists with Ky connections & Southeastern Folk Art. *Mailing Add:* 432 Maple Ave Owensboro KY 42301

HOOD, WALTER KELLY
HISTORIAN, PAINTER
b Catawba Co, NC. *Study:* Antioch Col, 48-49; Pa Acad Fine Arts, 49-53; Am Acad Rome, 53-55; Univ Pa, BFA, 57; Univ Hawaii, MFA, 61; Northwestern Univ, PhD(art hist), 66; mural studies with George Harding & Jean Charlot. *Work:* Pa Acad Fine Arts, Philadelphia; Fred T Foard Sch, Vale, NC; Corriher-Linn-Black Libr, Salisbury, NC. *Comn:* Six egg tempera murals, Christ's Life, Death & Resurrection, St Peter's Episcopal Church, Glenside, Pa, 57-58; three frescoes, Bd Regist for Engrs, Architects & Land Surveyors, Honolulu, 61; egg tempera mural, Chapel Hill, NC, residence, 87; egg tempera mural, Hist of Rowan Co, Salisbury Mall, NC, 90. *Exhib:* III Mostra de Pittura Americana, Bordighera, Italy, 55; One-man exhib of mural designs, Archit League NY, 56; 152nd Ann Exhib, Pa Acad Fine Arts, 57; 1974 Grand Nat Exhib, Am Artists Prof League, Lever House, NY, 74. *Teaching:* prof art, chmn art dept, Catawba Col, Salisbury, NC, 71-90, prof emeritus, Catawba Col. *Awards:* Cresson European Traveling Award, Pa Acad Fine Arts, 52 & Schiedt Foreign Traveling Award, 53; Abbey Mural Fel, Am Acad Rome, 53-54. *Bibliog:* Frederick Williams (auth), To the Glory of God: Glimpse of a Man (biog film), 70. *Mem:* Nat Soc Mural Painters; fel Am Acad Rome. *Media:* Fresco, Egg Tempera. *Res:* Definitive study of the art life of George Harding. *Publ:* Auth, Fire and Autumn Frost, 92; Flake and Petal White, 93; Dust and Drops of Dew, 94; Petals On a Rainy Path, 95; Clouds Beyond a Valley, 96 & Fall Diminuendo, 97, pvt publ; Days of Powdered Vapor, 98; Cold and Springtide Sun, 99; Winter in Declension, 2000; Leaves of Weathered Gold, 2001; Snow and Days of Lent, 2002. *Mailing Add:* 2508 W Innes St Salisbury NC 28144

HOOKS, EARL J
EDUCATOR, SCULPTOR
b Baltimore, Md, Aug 2, 27. *Study:* Howard Univ, BAE; Cath Univ; Rochester Inst of Technol, NY, cert. *Work:* DePauw Univ, Greencastle, Ind; Harmon Found, NY; City of Gary, Ind; State of Tenn Arts Comn. *Comn:* Ceramic sculpture, State Gift to Gov Ray Blanton, Tanzania, 77. *Exhib:* Howard Univ Invitational, 61; 21st Syracuse Biennial Traveling Exhib, Smithsonian Inst, 61-62; Int Minerals & Chemicals, Skokie, Ill, 66; three-man show, Art Inst Chicago, 67; Ball State Mus, Muncie, Ind, 69; Two Centuries of Black Am Art, Los Angeles Co Mus Art, 76; Dallas Mus Fine Arts, 77; High Mus, Atlanta, 77; Brooklyn Mus, 77. *Teaching:* Instr ceramics & drawing, Shaw Univ, Raleigh, NC, 53-54; instr & art consult, Gary Pub Schs, Ind, 59-68; instr ceramics & drawing, Ind Univ, Gary, 64-67; assoc prof sculpture & ceramics & chmn dept art, Fisk Univ, 68-. *Awards:* Second Prize, Arts & Crafts, John Herron Art Sch, 59; Purchase Prize, Dedication of Art Bldg, Howard Univ, 60; Cert of Honor, Int Festival of Lagos, Nigerian Govt, 77. *Bibliog:* Cedric Dover (auth), American Negro Art, 60; Elton Fax (auth), Seventeen Black Artists, Dodd-Mead, 71; 00025744xxxauth), The Rites of Color and Form, Fisk Univ, 74. *Media:* Ceramics. *Publ:* Coauth, Extended Services in Museum Science Training, 72 & Ben Jones (catalog), 77, Fisk Univ. *Mailing Add:* 2733 Buena Vista Pike Nashville TN 37218-2329

HOOKS, GERI
DEALER, COLLECTOR
b Houston, Tex, Apr 24, 35. *Study:* Stephens Col, AA, 53; Tex Univ, 53-54. *Pos:* Pres/dir, Hooks-Epstein Galleries Inc, currently. *Mem:* Houston Art Dealers Asn (founder). *Specialty:* Late 19th century and 20th century representational American, European and Latin paintings, sculpture and works on paper. *Collection:* Sculpture and works on paper of 20th century American and European Masters. *Mailing Add:* 4703 Yoakum Blvd Houston TX 77006

HOOPER, JACK MEREDITH
PAINTER, PRINTMAKER
b Los Angeles, Calif, Aug 26, 28. *Study:* Los Angeles City Col, AA(art), 51; Col Am, Mexico City, asst to Siqueiros, BA(art; cum laude), 52; Acad Julian, Paris, with Chaplin Midi & Pierre Jerome, 54; Univ Calif, Los Angeles, MA(art), 56. *Work:* Lannan Found, Fla; Stanford Univ Mus; Long Beach Mus; Univ Calif, Los Angeles & Santa Cruz. *Exhib:* The Artist's Environment--The West Coast, Oakland Art Mus, Amon Carter Mus, Ft Worth & Univ Calif, Los Angeles Galleries, 62; Fifty Calif Artists, Whitney Mus Am Art, Albright Art Gallery & Walker Art Ctr, 62-63; Art Across Am, San Francisco Mus Mod Art & Knoedlers Galleries, NY, 65-66; retrospective, Smith & Cowell Gallery, Santa Cruz & Univ Santa Cruz, 75; Sixth Hawaii Nat Print Exhib, Honolulu Acad Art, 82. *Pos:* Dir, Sculptural Walls, Los Angeles, 62-66. *Teaching:* Asst prof art, Univ Calif, Los Angeles, 57-62; vis prof, Univ Colo, Boulder, 62; prof, chmn dept & dir art galleries, Mt St Marys Col, 63-69; prof, Univ Calif, Santa Cruz, 76. *Awards:* New Talent in America--Top 100 in Nation, Art in Am, 57; Los Angeles Ann Award Painting, 59; Purchase Award, Long Beach Mus Art, 65. *Bibliog:* Jack Hooper, Univ Calif, Santa Cruz, 75. *Mem:* World Print Coun. *Mailing Add:* c/o LaGuna De Sta Maria Oro Nayarit 63830 Mexico

HOOPER, JACK MEREDITH
SCULPTOR
b Los Angeles, Calif, Aug 26, 28. *Study:* Miami Univ, Oxford, Ohio, BA(archit), 66; RI Sch Design, MFA(sculpture), 68. *Work:* Oakland Mus Art, Calif; Evansville Mus Arts & Sci, Ind; Atlantic Richfield Collection, Los Angeles; Embarcadero Ctr, San Francisco; Vassar Col; and others. *Comn:* Monumental sculpture, Provincial Govt Man, Thompson, 77; large-scale sculpture, First Nat Bank, Erie, Pa, 80; monumental sculpture, Cincinnati Zoological Soc; Univ Maine, Augusta; interior sculpture, Federal Industries, Winnipeg, Man; monumental sculpture, Grupo Villacero, Monterey, Mex; exterior fountain, Plymouth Congregational Church, Minneapolis, Minn. *Exhib:* Annual Contemp Sculpture, Whitney Mus Am Art, 68; Structured Art, DeCordova Mus, Lincoln, Mass, 69; Sculpture on the Prairies, Winnipeg Art Gallery, Man, 77; 25th Ann, Longview Mus, Tex, 83; Int Art Expos, Navy Pier, Chicago, 83; Fifth Tex Sculpture Symp, Dallas, 85; Melnychenko Gallery, Winnipeg, 90; Gallery Artists, Flanders Contemp Art, Minneapolis, 92-96; solo show, Instituto Mexicano Norte Americano, Monterrey, Mex, 93, The Phipps Ctr for the Arts, Hudson, Wis, 99, Universidad Nacional Autonoma de Mexico, San Antonio, 2000; Drexel Gallery, Monterrey, Mex, 93; Faculty Show, Minn Col Art & Design, 98, 2000; The Iron Circus, Univ of Minn Sculpture Dept Invitational, 99; City of Palm Desert Art in Pub Places 99/2000 El Paseo Exhibition; Niemi Fine Arts at SOFA, Chicago, 99; Pierwalk, Navy Pier, Chicago, 2000, 2001; HIP 2000 Cast Metal Invitational, Univ Minn, Morris; Koechel Peterson Gallery, Mpls, 2001. *Pos:* Vis artist, Mexican State of Nuevo Leon & Grupo Villacero, Monterrey, Mex, 93. *Teaching:* Instr 3-D design,

Atlanta Sch Art, 70-71; chmn sculpture dept, Univ Man, Winnipeg, 75-79; asst prof, Univ Tex, San Antonio, 81-88; prof, Minneapolis Col Art & Design, 88-; vis artist bronze casting, Univ Maine, Augusta, summer 90. *Awards:* Olivetti Award Sculpture, 23rd Ann New England Exhib, 72; Judge's Award, Drawing & Small Sculpture, Galveston Art Ctr, 81; First Prize, Expos Plaza Sculpture Competition, 4-M Properties, 81; Man Arts Coun Grant, Pub Sculpture, 76, Serigraph, 79; Can Coun Grant, 78; Connemara Found Grant, Dallas, 84; Villacero Corp Artist-in-Residence Sabbatical Grant, Monterrey, Mex, 93-94. *Mem:* Am Watercolor Soc; Am Welding Soc. *Media:* Metal, Multi-Media. *Mailing Add:* 2226 27th Ave S Minneapolis MN 55406

HOOPER, ROBERT T
PAINTER, INSTRUCTOR
b Detroit, Mich. *Study:* Yale U; Pratt Inst. *Work:* Rose Art Mus, Boston. *Teaching:* instr Univ Chicago. *Awards:* Rome Prize, 79; Pollock/Krasner Award, 95; Guggenheim Award, 99. *Mailing Add:* 21287 W Cliffside Dr Kildeer IL 60047

HOOVER, FRANCIS LOUIS
COLLECTOR, JEWELER
b Sherman, Tex, Mar 12, 13. *Study:* NTex State Univ, BS, 33; Columbia Univ, MA, 35; Art Students League, 40-41; New Sch Social Res, 40-41; NY Univ, DEd, 41. *Exhib:* Biennial exhibs, Am Child Art, 55, 57, 59 & 61. *Pos:* Dir, LaSalle Art Gallery 33-36 & Fairway Gallery, 62-67; ed, Arts & Activities Mag, 52-67; bd dir, Art Educ Found, 56-66; pres, Quadradic Soc, 90-91. *Teaching:* Art dir, Carden Pvt Sch, New York, 34-36; asst prof art, NTex State Univ, 36-40 & Eastern Ill State Univ, 41-44; distinguished prof art & chmn dept, Ill State Univ, 44-73, dir, Univ Mus, 72-73. *Awards:* Merit Award Ed Excellence, Indust Mkt 6th Ann, 54; Distinguished Fel, Nat Art Educ Asn, 86. *Mem:* Appraisers Asn Am; Am Soc Appraisers; Int Platform Asn; Art Educ Found; Delta Phi Delta. *Media:* Gold, Gems. *Collection:* Art of the Cuna Indians; pre-Columbian ceramics and jade; primitive arts of Africa and Oceania; folk arts of Middle America; works are in permanent collections of Philadelphia Museum of Art, Cleveland Museum of Art, Art Institute of Chicago, Field Museum of Natural History, Harvard Univ, Peabody Museum, Smithsonian Inst and others. *Publ:* Auth, Guide for Teaching Art Activities in the Classroom, 56; Art Activities for the Very Young, 62; Young Printmakers I, 63 & II, 64; Young Sculptures, 67; African Art, 74

HOOVER, GEORGE SCHWEKE
ARCHITECT
b Chicago, Jul 1, 35. *Study:* Cornell Univ, BArch, 58. *Collection Arranged:* Principal works incl: Douglas Co Admin Bldg, Light of the World Catholic Church, Univ Colo Bldg, Denver, Denver Diagnostic & Reception Ctr, Labs for Atmospheric & Space Physics, Univ Colo, Boulder, Colorado Academy Master Plan, Univ Ariz Engineering Complex Master Plan, Multipurpose Arena, Nat Western Stockshow, Nat Wild Animal Research Center, Colo State Univ Conference Ctr, Storage Tech. Corp, Aerospace & Mechanical Engineering Bldg Univ Ariz, Environ & Natural Resources Building Univ Ariz, Master Plan Cummins Power Generation Group Hdqs., Fridley, Minn, Master Plan Fleetguard and Manufacturing Plant, Cookeville, Tenn; finalist Denver Cen. Libr. Competition, 91; exhib Gund Hall Gallery, Grad. Sch Design, Harvard Univ, 86; mem ed bd Avant Garde. *Pos:* Draftsman, Holabird Root and Burgee, Chicago, 57; Designer, James Sudler Assoc, Denver, 61-62; archit, Ream, Quinn Assoc, 62-65, Muchow Assoc, Denver, 65-76; principal, Hoover Berg Desmond, 76—. *Teaching:* Tenured prof, archit Univ Colo Col Archit & Planning, chmn dept archit, 97-; vis lectr Univ NMex, Okla State Univ, Harvard Univ, Miami Univ, currently. *Awards:* named Outstanding Young Archit, Archit Record, 74; Honor award Interfaith Forum on Religion, Art, and Archit, 86; Tau Sigma Delta medal, 91. *Mem:* Fel Am Inst of Archit (steering comt, Pittsburgh Corning award 89, Nat Honor award 75, 83, 90, Firm of Yr award Colo chap 91, Regional Firm of Yr award 92, Archit of Yr award Colo chap 95); Nat Acad; Nat Comt Design (steering comt, chmn awards task group, 89-92); Nat Comt Archit Educ (steering comt 90-92). *Mailing Add:* Art Hoover Desmond Archit 1645 Grant St Denver CO 80203-1601

HOOVER, JOHN JAY
SCULPTOR
b Cordova, Alaska, Oct 13, 1919. *Study:* Derbyshire Sch of Fine Arts, Seattle, Wash. *Work:* Bur Indian Affairs, Washington, DC; Seattle Art Mus, Wash; Gulf Paper Co; Heard Mus, Phoenix, Ariz; King Co & Seattle Art Comn. *Comn:* Mural, Tyonek Tribe, Anchorage, Alaska, 64; mobile, James Bialac, Ariz, 76; mural, City Light Co, Seattle, 77. *Exhib:* Sculpture I & Sculpture II, Heard Mus, Phoenix, Ariz, 73 & 74; one-man shows, Whatcom Co Mus, Bellingham, Wash & Mus of Plains Indians, Browning, Mont, 75; Sculpture Invitational, Heard Mus, Phoenix, Ariz, 77. *Teaching:* Artist-in-residence sculpture, Inst of Am Indian Art, Santa Fe, NMex, 72 & DOD Sch Syst, Japan, Taiwan & the Philippines, 74; instr, Northern Ariz Univ, Flagstaff, 79. *Awards:* First Prize/Sculpture, Cent Wash State Col, 73, Philbrook Art Ctr, Tulsa, Okla, 74 & Heard Mus, Phoenix, Ariz, 75. *Media:* Wood, Cast Metal. *Publ:* This Song Remers Jane B Katz, HM Co; Aleut & Eskimo Art, Dorothy J Ray, Washington; Aleut Art, Lydia T Black & Aleutian/Pribilof; Sweet Grass Lives On Highwater, Lippincott & Crowell. *Dealer:* Gallery Wall Santa Fe NM & Phoenix AZ; Stonington Gallery 2030 First Ave Seattle WA. *Mailing Add:* E 841 W Stadium Beach Dr Grapeview WA 98546

HOPKINS, B(ERNICE) ELIZABETH
PAINTER, SCULPTOR
b Marinette, Wis, Mar 7, 26. *Study:* Maryville Col, Tenn. *Work:* Edna Carston Gallery, Univ Wis, Stevens Point; Visual Arts Ctr NW Fla, Panama City; City of Tallahassee, Fla. *Exhib:* Pastel Soc Am, Nat Arts Club, NY, 84 & 87, Hermitage Mus, Norfolk, Va 84, Monmouth Mus, Lincraft, NJ, 85 & Harmon Meek Gallery, Naples, Fla, 91-92; Degas Pastel Soc, World Trade Bldg Gallery, New Orleans, La, 87; Societe des Pastellists de France, Lille, France, 88; Pastel Soc West Coast, Sacramento Fine Arts Ctr, Carmichael, Calif, 88. *Awards:* Still Life, Pastel Soc Am, Philip M Lahn, 84; Still Life, Pastel Soc Am, David Rosenthal, 87; Still Life, Pastel Soc Am, Morilla-Conson-Talens, 89; Master Pastelist Status, Pastel Soc Am, NY, 88; Best of Show, Bay Ann Exhib, Visual Arts Ctr, 99. *Bibliog:* Best of Pastel, Rockport Publ, 93. *Mem:* Pastel Soc Am; signature mem Pastel Soc N Fla; Visual Arts Ctr NW Fla (secy, 86-88). *Media:* Pastel. *Publ:* Auth, The Best of Pastel, Quarry Books. *Dealer:* The Gallery of Art 36 Beach Dr W Panama City FL 32401; LeMoyne Art Found Inc 125 N Gadsden St Tallahassee FL 32301. *Mailing Add:* 3280 Hillside Dr Apt 114 Delafield WI 53818-2183

HOPKINS, BUDD
PAINTER, SCULPTOR
b Wheeling, WVa, June 15, 31. *Study:* Oberlin Col, BA, 53; Columbia Univ, with Meyer Schapiro, 53-54. *Work:* Brooklyn Mus, NY; Whitney Mus Am Art, Guggenheim Mus Art, Metrop Mus Art, Mus Mod Art, NY; San Francisco Mus Art; Corcoran Gallery Art, Washington, DC; Williams Col Mus; Hirshhorn Mus & Sculpture Garden; Carnegie-Mellon Art Mus, Pittsburgh, Pa; Mass Inst Technol; Allen Mem Art mus; Boston Mus Fine Art; Met Mus; Mus Modern Art; plus others. *Comn:* Oil painting, WVa State Humanities Coun, 72. *Exhib:* Solo exhibs, Poindexter Galerie, NY, 56-63, 66, 67 & 71, Galerie Liatowitsch, Basel, Switz, 74, Long Point Gallery, Provincetown, Mass, 82, 85 & 91, 93, 97, Jan Cicero Gallery, Chicago, 85, Marilyn Pearl Gallery (with catalog), NY, 85 & 88, Drew Univ, Oakland, NJ, 90 & Long Point Gallery, Provincetown, Mass, 94 & 97; Two Decades of Am Painting, Solomon R Guggenheim Mus, NY, 75; Recent Acquisitions, Solomon R Guggenheim Mus, 87; Postwar Geometrical Painting, Marilyn Pearl Gallery, 91; Corporations Collection, Morris Mus, NJ, 91; Am Abstract Artists, Valletta, Malta & Ottawa Mus, Can, 91; Gallery Group, Longpoint Gallery, Provincetown, 92 & 94; Drew Univ, 90; and others. *Teaching:* Docent, Mus Mod Art, summers 55-56; docent, Whitney Mus Am Art, 57-60; instr, Pratt Inst, Provincetown, summer 75; instr, RI Sch Design, Provincetown, summer 75. *Awards:* Guggenheim Fel, 75; Nat Endowment Arts Award, 79; Spec Project Grant, NY State Coun Arts, 82; Named to Wheeling, WVa Hall of Fame, 92. *Bibliog:* Brian O'Doherty (auth), Budd Hopkins, master of a movement manque, Object & Idea, 67; April Kingsley (auth), Energy and order--the paintings of Budd Hopkins, Art Int, 4/73; Peter Frank (auth), Budd Hopkins: The works on paper, Kresge Art Ctr Bull, 4/74; Carter Ratcliffe (auth), The distractions of theme, Art in Am, 9-10/78; Robert Motherwell (auth), catalogue, Marilyn Pearl Gallery, 88. *Mem:* Provincetown Art Asn (hon vpres, 68-70 & 77-79); Am Abstract Artists, 85-; Fel: Nat Educ Asn, 1976, John Simon Guggenheim, 1976; Am Abstract Artists, Provincetown Art Asn & Mus, Nat Acad. *Media:* Acrylic, Oil; Wood. *Publ:* Auth, First person singular, Art Gallery Mag, 4/72; Budd Hopkins on Budd Hopkins, Art in Am, 7-8/73; contribr, Roundtable on painting, 9/75, Richard Diebenkorn & Franz Kline, 79, Artforum; auth, de Kooning's Drawings, Drawing, 3-4/84; The collages of Fritz Bultman, Provincetown Arts, 6/86; and others; Modernism & The Coll Esthetic, New Eng Rev, Spring 97. *Dealer:* Longpoint Gallery Provincetown. *Mailing Add:* Intruders Foundation PO Box 30233 New York NY 10011

HOPKINS, HENRY TYLER
MUSEUM DIRECTOR, EDUCATOR
b Idaho Falls, Idaho, Aug 14, 28. *Study:* Art Inst Chicago, BAE & MAE; Univ Calif, Los Angeles; Calif Col Arts & Crafts, Hon PhD, 84; San Francisco Art Inst, Hon PhD, 86. *Exhib:* One-person show, Off Main Gallery, Los Angeles, 2001, 2003; Drawings, Louis Stern Gallery, Los Angeles, 2006. *Collection Arranged:* 30 California Artists, 61; Reuben Nakian, 62; Josef Albers: White Line Squares (with catalog), 66; Robert Rauschenberg: Selections, 69; Milton Resnick: Large Paintings (with catalog), 71; Irwin-Wheeler, 72; Joe Goode: Work Until Now (with catalog), 73; Clyfford Still (with catalog), 75; Painting & Sculpture in California: The Modern Era (with catalog), 76; Philip Guston (with catalog), 80; Expressionism & German Intuition, 83; The Human Condition, 84; Lita Albuquerque, 89. *Pos:* Head educ, Los Angeles Co Mus Art, Los Angeles, 61-65, cur exhib, 65-68; dir, Ft Worth Art Mus, Tex, 68-74, San Francisco Mus Mod Art, 74-86 & Frederick R Weisman Found, 86-91; chmn art dept, Univ Calif, Los Angeles, 91-95, dir, Armand Hammer Mus Art & Cult Ctr, 94-99. *Teaching:* Instr art hist & theory, Univ Calif, Los Angeles Exten, 58-68; instr art hist, Tex Christian Univ, 68-73; vis prof, Univ Calif, Los Angeles, 90 & prof, 91, 98-; prof emeritus, UCLA, 2002. *Awards:* Order of Leopold II, Knight. *Bibliog:* Henry T Hopkins: A Life in Art, Two Vol Oral Hist, Univ Calif, Los Angeles, 98. *Mem:* Nat Endowment Arts (chmn mus policy panel, 79-83); Nat Endowment Humanities (panelist, 76-77); Art Mus Asn Am (trustee, 75-77, pres, 78); Asn Art Mus Dir (vpres, 84, pres, 85); Int Exhibs Comt. *Res:* Twentieth century art of California; modern art. *Publ:* Contribr, Art in Am, Art News & Artforum Mag, 61-75; auth, Modern & contemporary art, Art News; Clyfford Still, 76, Fifty California Artists, 84, California Painters, 89; archives at Getty Res Ctr, Los Angeles, 2005. *Mailing Add:* 939 1/2 Hilgard Ave Los Angeles CA 90024

HOPKINS, KENNETH R
MUSEUM DIRECTOR, RESTORER
b Springfield, Mass, Aug 24, 22. *Study:* Pratt Inst; Univ Vt; Parsons Sch of Design; NY Univ, BS; Univ Wis, MS. *Pos:* Art dir, Univ Wis, Madison, 48-50; cur exhib, State Hist Soc Wis, Madison, 50-52; art dir, Old Sturbridge Village, Mass, 52-56; cur, Buffalo & Erie Co Hist Co, Buffalo, NY, 56-60; hist preservationist, Bethelehm Steel Co, Pa, 60-62; dir, Explorers Hall, Nat Geog Soc, Washington, DC, 62-65; dir, State Capitol Mus, 65-82; retired; woodcarver and restorer, currently. *Mailing Add:* 3001 Monte Vista SE Olympia WA 98501

HOPKINS, TERRI
CURATOR, ADMINISTRATOR
b Tenn, 1949. *Study:* Oberlin Col, BA(art hist), 71; Univ Chicago, MA(art hist), 72. *Collection Arranged:* Approximately 60 exhibs, 80-. *Pos:* Dir art gym, Marylhurst Col, 80-. *Teaching:* Marylhurst Col. *Publ:* Auth, Paul Sutinen: Five Works 1982-1987, 87, Barbara Thomas: Paintings, 89, Fernanda D'Agostino: Offering, 89, Barbara Fealy's Gardens, 90 & Unabandoned Abstraction, 91, Marylhurst Col; Sally Haley: A Lifetime of Painting, 93; Representing the object, 94. *Mailing Add:* Marylhurst Col Gallery of Art PO Box 261 Marylhurst OR 97036-0261

HOPPER, DENNIS
PHOTOGRAPHER
b Dodge City, Kans, 1936. *Exhib:* Primus/Stuart Gallery, Los Angeles, 63; Calif Now, Robert Fraser Gallery, London, Eng, 65; Pasadena Art Mus, Calif, 67; Corcoran Gallery Art, Washington, DC, 71; AIACE Torino, Italy, 88; Kunsthalle Basel, Switz, 88; Hoffman Borman Gallery, Santa Monica, Calif, 87; Graham Parson Gallery, London, Eng, 84; LA Louver, Venice, Calif, 89; Davis/McClain, Houston, Tex, 90; Kiyomuizu Temple, Kyoto, Japan, 90 & 94; Parco Gallery, Tokyo, Japan, 90 & 94; Proof: Los Angeles Art and the Photog 1960-1980 (with catalog), Laguna Mus Art, Calif, 92; Photographs and Paintings, 1961-1993, Galerie Thaddeus Ropac, Paris, France, 92 & Speilraum fur Kunst, Furth, Ger, 92; New Work, Sena Galleries, Santa Fe, NMex, 92; Dennis Hopper: Fotos und Gemalde, Aktionsforum City-Ctr Furth, Ger, 92; James Corcoran Gallery, Santa Monica, Calif, 92; Dennis Hopper and Ed Ruscha, Tony Shafrazi Gallery, NY, 92; Bad Heat: Photographs and Paintings, 1961-1993 (with catalog), Fronto Colom, Univ Pompeu Fabra, Barcelona, Spain, 93; Photog Resource Ctr, Boston, Mass, 94; Photographs 1961-1967, Karolinum, Prague, Czech Repub, 95; Beat Cult and the New Am: 1950-1965 (with catalog), Whitney Mus Am Art, NY, 95; George Herm, From There and Then to Here and Now, with a little Help From His Friends, Wallace Berman, Bruce Connor & Dennis Hopper, Tony Shafrazi Gallery, NY, 95; Whitney Mus Am Art Biennial, NY, 95; Halls of Mirrors: Art and Film Since 1945, Mus Contemp Art, Los Angeles, Calif, 96; Tony Shafrazi Gallery, NY, 96; Ochi Gallery, Kethum, Idaho, 96. *Bibliog:* Dennis Hopper lit sur les murs, La Liberation, 9/23/92; Dennis Hopper: James Dean m'a pousse a faire de la photo, Le Figaro, 9/24/92; Ann Hindry (auth), Cinema and art, Galeries Mag, 10-11/92. *Publ:* Coauth, Hopper, Dennis: A Tourist, File Inc, Kyoto, Japan, 94. *Mailing Add:* c/o Creative Artists Agency 9830 Wilshire Blvd Beverly Hills CA 90212

HOPPER, FRANK J
PAINTER, MURALIST
b Evansville, Ind, Oct 15, 24. *Study:* Ind Univ, BFA; Art Inst Chicago; Am Acad Art, Chicago. *Work:* Famous Am Series, Historic Mus, Washington, DC. *Comn:* mag covers, Yachting; portraits, Pres Nixon & Pres Reagan & two for Pres Bush, presidential libr; The Story of Israel, Technion; 200 paintings, Archdiocese of Chicago, 67; mural & 14 stations of the cross, St Mary Star of the Sea Catholic Church, Longboat Key, Fla, 78; mural, St Peter & Paul, Bradenton, Fla, 89. *Teaching:* Instr, Art Inst & Am Acad, formerly; lectures worldwide. *Awards:* Gold Medal, Accademia Italia; Posey Found Scholarship evaluations. *Bibliog:* Time study of mural production (film), NBC doc. *Mem:* Am Portrait Soc; Artist Watercolor Soc; Int Soc Marine Painters; Artist Guild, Chicago; Mensa, Chevaliers du Tastevin; Accademia Italia. *Media:* Acrylic, Oil. *Publ:* Illusr, co-auth, ed or contribr to various publ including Chicago publs & newspapers, Western Publ Co, Chicago Tribune, Art Inst Chicago, books for Chicago Area Sch TV, Yachting Mag & Extension Mag

HOPPER INC See Hopper, Frank J

HORMAN, ELIZABETH
PAINTER, MURALIST
b New York, NY, Dec 30, 04. *Study:* Barnard Col, BA, 26; Columbia Col; Art Students League, 26-33; studies with George Grosz, Homer Boss, Bernard Klonis Soyer & Harvey Dunn. *Work:* Tennacre Found, Princeton, Pa; High Ridge, House Collection, NY; Hebrew Home for the Aged, NY; Mellon Found, NY. *Comn:* India House (mural), 55, Wagner Col (mural), 58, comn by Robert Collins, NY; Hotel-Chicago (mural), 57, Hotel-Philadelphia (mural), 60, Blackstone; Dakota, NY (mural), 70. *Exhib:* Ann Nat Asn Women Artists Show, NY, 48-94; Barthelet Gallery Invitational, NY, 81; Interchurch Gallery Invitational, NY, 84; Manchester Southern Vt Art Ctr Invitational; 8-10 one man shows, Barbizon Gallery, Frisch Gallery. *Awards:* Medal of Honor, Nat Asn Women Artists, 84. *Mem:* Nat Asn Women Artists (pres, formerly); Fine Arts Fedn, NY. *Media:* Oil. *Publ:* Illustr, Math-Reading for Grade Schs, Grinn & Co, 42-48; New York University Children's Book, NY Univ Hosp, 82

HORMUTH, JO
SCULPTOR, PRINTMAKER
b Grand Rapids, Mich, 1955. *Study:* Slade Sch Art, London, 78; Grand Valley State Col, Allendale, Mich, BFA, 81; Art Inst Chicago, MFA, 83. *Work:* Art Inst Chicago; Cranbrook Acad Art; MacArthur Found. *Exhib:* Group Show, Sch Gallery, Art Inst Chicago, 85; What Price Beauty; Looking at Labor, Randolph St Gallery, Chicago, 91; Home Sweet Home, Columbia Col Art Gallery, Chicago, 92; Buy/Low, Prairie Ave Gallery, Chicago, 91; Valentine's Day Auction, NAME Gallery, Chicago, 92; Forecast, Zolla/Lieberman Gallery, Chicago, 92. *Bibliog:* Carol Vogel (auth), Visions of Home Sweet Home, NY Times, 2/14/91; Alan Artner (auth), Installations: Things to Catch the Eye and Ear, Chicago Tribune, 7/24/92; Mandy Morrison (auth), The Harder They Drum, The Reader, 8/14/92. *Media:* Mixed. *Mailing Add:* 1742 W Haddon Chicago IL 60622-3222

HORN, ALAN F.
COLLECTOR
Study: Harvard Univ, MBA with distinction. *Pos:* With Proctor & Gamble, Tandem Productions, TAT Commun, Embassy Commun, 73-86; pres, Chief Operating Officer, 20th Century Fox Film Corp, 86-87; co-founder, chmn, Chief Exec Officer, Castle Rock Entertainment, Beverly Hills, 87-99; pres, Chief Operating Officer, Warner Brothers Entertainment, Burbank, Calif, 99-; bd dirs, Univision Commun, Natural Resources Defense Coun; vice chmn, bd trustees, Autry Mus Western Heritage; mem bd assocs, Harvard Bus Sch; founding mem, bd dirs, Environ Media Asn. *Awards:* Named one of 50 Most Powerful People in Hollywood, Premiere mag, 2004-06, Top 200 Collectors, ARTnews mag, 2006. *Mem:* Hollywood Radio and TV Soc; Am Film Inst; Acad TV Arts and Scis; Acad Motion Picture Arts and Scis. *Mailing Add:* Warner Brothers 4000 Warner Blvd Burbank CA 91522-0002

HORN, BRUCE
PAINTER, EDUCATOR
b Circleville, Ohio, June 30, 46. *Study:* Miami Univ, BFA, 68; Ohio State Univ, MFA, 70; Arnot Mus, New York with Clyde Aspevig; Fechin Inst, NMex with Gregg Kreutz. *Work:* Trenton State Col, NJ; Tyler Sch Art, Philadelphia; Nat Gallery Art, Washington; Honolulu Acad Arts, Hawaii; and others. *Exhib:* Sixteenth Nat Exhib, New Orleans Art Asn, La, 95 & 97; Grand Exhib, Akron Soc Artists, Ohio, 95; solo exhib, Prescott Fine Art Asn Gallery, Ariz, 96; Nat Realism Exhib, Parkersburg, WVa, 98; Art Colo Plateau, Aspen Fine Arts Gallery, Flagstaff, Ariz, 99 & 2000; retrospective, Northern Ariz Univ, 2001; Oil Painters of Am, Western Region Exhib; Waterhouse Gallery, Santa Barbara, Calif, 2003; Nat Fine Art Exhib; Morro Bay Art Asn, Calif, 2005; solo exhib, Paris & Normandy, Hudgens Gallery Fine Art, Flagstaff, Ariz, 2006. *Pos:* Package designer, Diamond Nat Paper Co, Middletown, Ohio, 68; art dir, Eighth Ann Flagstaff Summer Festival, Ariz, 74. *Teaching:* Prof painting, Blackburn Col, Carlinville, Ill, 70-72 & Northern Ariz Univ, 72-99, prof emeritus. *Awards:* Purchase Award, Int Exhib Prints, Wesleyan Col, Macon, 83; Gold Medallion Award, Nat Printing Exhib, NMex Art League, 95; Bronze Award, Int Film Festival, Houston, 99i. *Mem:* assoc Oil Painters Am; Calif Art Club; Artists' Coalition Flagstaff. *Media:* Oil, Miscellaneous Media. *Publ:* No Ariz Mountain Living Mag. *Dealer:* Tanglewood Fine Art 114 S San Francisco St Flagstaff AZ 86001. *Mailing Add:* 2197 Twisted Limb Way Flagstaff AZ 86004

HORN, CINDY HARRELL
COLLECTOR
b Durham, NC. *Pos:* Model, actress, 75-88; mem, Nat Educ Adv Coun, 91; founding trustee, Heal the Bay, Archer Sch Girls; bd mem, Coalition for Clean Air, Tree People, Natural Step, Bay Keeper, Center Environ Educ, Univ Calif Los Angeles Sch Pub Health; mem painting conservatory coun, J Paul Getty Mus. *Awards:* Named one of Top 200 Collectors, ARTnews mag, 2006. *Mem:* Environ Media Asn (co-founder, bd mem). *Mailing Add:* Environ Media Asn 10780 Santa Monica Blvd Suite 210 Los Angeles CA 90025

HORN, ROBERT NELSON
PAINTER, DESIGNER
b Alton, Ill, Oct 02, 47. *Study:* Southern Ill Univ, Carbondale, BA, 69; Art Inst Chicago, independent study art hist, 71; studied in Amsterdam, 85-91. *Work:* Mitchell Gallery, Southern Ill Univ, Carbondale; Moss Thorns Gallery Art, Fort Hays State Univ, Kans. *Comn:* Sculpture of Edgar Miller, Carl St Studios, Chicago, 89; Markmamolen oil portrait, Chicago, 96; Dual portrait, John Montague, 97. *Exhib:* Hoyt Nat Drawing & Painting Show, Hoyt Inst Fine Arts, New Castle, Pa, 89; 22nd Bradley Nat, Bradley Univ, Peoria, Ill, 89; Artists View the Human Form Int Competition, Clary-Miner Gallery, Buffalo, NY, 89; Chicago Show, Art Inst & Mus Contemp Art, Chicago, Ill, 90; solo exhib, Harper Col, Palatine, Ill, 94, Southeastern State Col, Ill, 99 & Sarah Walker Gallery, Castletownbere, Ireland, 2000; Beara Arts, Castletownbere, Cork, Ireland, 1995-2000. *Pos:* artist-in-residence, Wells St Studios, Chicago, 71-; Dir, NAB Gallery, Chicago, 74-, inst drawing workshops, 85-; artist-in-residence, Carl St Studios, Chicago, 86-. *Teaching:* Allihies Lang & Arts Ctr, Cork, Ireland, 93-; Sch Art Inst Chicago, Ill, 97-2003; Lill St Art Ctr, Chicago, Ill, 98-2003; Evanston Art Ctr, Ill, 2000-2003. *Awards:* Palmer Prize, Art Inst Chicago, 90; Chicago Off Fine Arts Grants, 89, 91 & 93; Finalist, Nat Portrait Competition, Artist Mag, 89 & 91. *Bibliog:* Joshua Kind (auth), Six Artists, New Art Examiner, 82; Home design, NY Times Mag, 10/93. *Media:* Oil

HORN, RONI
SCULPTOR
b New York, NY, 55. *Study:* RI Sch Design, BFA, 75; Yale Univ Sch Art, MFA, 78. *Work:* Toledo Mus Art, Toledo, Ohio; Harfa, Chinati Found, Presidio Co, Tex. *Comn:* Collection of Eric Mosel, comn by Doln Mühle. *Exhib:* Solo shows include Fotomuseum Winterthur, Switz, 97, Patrick Painter Gallery, Los Angeles, 98, Gallery Xavier Hufkens, Brussels, 98, Jabloonka Galerie, Cologne, 98 & 99, Mus fur Gegenwartskunst, Basel, 98 & De Pont Found Contemp Art, Tilburg, The Neth, 98, Matthew Marks Gallery, NY, 99, 2002, Musee d' Art Moderne de la Ville de Paris, 99, CAPC Musee d' Art Contemporain, Bordeaux, 99, Whitney Mus of Am Art, NY, 2000, Timothy Taylor Gallery, London, 2000 & Gastello di Rivoli, Torino, 2000, Dia Ctr for the Arts, NY, 2002; group shows include Kunstforum Lenbachaus State Mus, Munich, Ger 83; Glyptothek Mus, Munich, Ger 83; Neuberger Mus, State Univ NY, Purchase, 86; Similia/Dissimilia, Castelli Gallery, NY & Kunstalle, Dusseldorf, Ger, 87; Detroit Inst Arts, Mich, 88; Whitney Biennial, Whitney Mus Am Art, 91, 2004; Sleight of Mind/The Angle of a Landscape, Ctr Curatorial Studies Mus, Bard Col, Annandale-On-Hudson, NY, 97; Galerie Nacht St Stephan, Vienna, 97; Density of the Unimaginable Mus, Centre d'Art Contemporain du Domaine de Kerguehennec, Bignan, France, 97; Maverick, Matthew Marks Gallery, NY, 98; Pi, Sydney Biennale,

98; Travel & Leisure, Paula Cooper Gallery, NY, 98; Surrogate: The Figure in Contemp Sculpture and Photog, Henry Art Gallery, Univ Wash, Seattle, 98; View 2, Mary Boone Gallery, NY, 98; 00, Barbara Gladstone Gallery, NY, 2001; Xavier Hufkens, Brussels, 2001; The Photographers' Gallery, London, 2001; Silent Poetry, Timothy Taylor Gallery, London, 2002. *Awards:* Nat Endowment Arts Fel, 84, 86 & 90; Guggenheim Fel, 90; Alpert Award in the Arts, 98. *Bibliog:* Sue Scott (auth), The Edward R Broida Collection, Orlando Mus Art, Fla, 98; Monique Beudert (auth), Contemporary Art: The Janet Wolfson de Botton Gift, Taft Gallery Publ, London, 98; Jill Connor (auth), Roni Horn: Earth's grow thick, Art Papers, 5-6/98. *Mailing Add:* c/o Matthew Marks Gallery 523 W 24th St New York NY 10011

HORNADAY, RICHARD HOYT
PAINTER, EDUCATOR
b Joplin, Mo, Aug 15, 27. *Study:* Iowa State Univ, BFA, 1950; MFA, Art Inst Chicago, 1952. *Work:* Iowa State Univ Collection, Iowa City; Turner Print Gallery & Kendall Hall Permanent coll, Calif State Univ, Chico; Shasta Col Collection, Redding, Calif. *Exhib:* Ruthermore Gallery, San Francisco, 58-68; Recent Painting, USA, The Figure (with catalog), Mus Mod Art, NY, 65; 23rd Am Drawing Biennial, Norfolk Mus, Va, 69; Nat Small Painting Exhib, Univ of the Pac, Stockton, Calif, 70; Fifty Yrs of Crocker-Kingsley (with catalog), Crocker Art Gallery, Sacramento, 75; Nat Drawing & Painting Exhib, Southeastern Mass Univ, 81; 30-Year Retrospective Survey (with catalog), Redding Mus & Art Ctr, Calif, 83; relief print, Manhattan Kans Nat, 84; Watercolor Gallery, Berkeley, Calif, 85; Rosicrucian Egyptian Mus, Iman, 86; Brand XVIII-XIX, Brand Libr Art Galleries, Glendale, Calif, 88-89; Blue Heron Fine Arts, Chico, Calif, 90; Himovitz Pavilions Gallery, Sacramento, 92; Nat Watercolor exhib, Concold, Calif, 96; Aqueous XI nat, Tubac, AZ, 97; Watercolor USA, Springfield, Mo, 98. *Pos:* Grad adv, Calif State Univ, Chico, 68-72, prof grad studies, 68, chmn dept art, 72-80, prof emer, 88. *Teaching:* Instr drawing & painting, Shasta Col, 56-63; prof drawing & painting, Calif State Univ, Chico, 81-. *Awards:* Kingsley, Crocker Mus, Sacramento, Calif, 55 & 56; Am Fed Art, Redding Calif Mus, 57. *Bibliog:* Alfred Frankenstein (auth), Ruthermore Gallery--Richard Hornaday, San Francisco Chronicle, 62; Calif Art Review, Am References, Chicago, 89; Robert Spear (auth), A certain joy, Hornaday & Hornaday, Vagabond Rose gallery, Chico, Calif. *Media:* Oil, Acrylic, Mixed Watercolor, Graphite, Conte Crayon. *Publ:* A Retrospective Sruvey (catalog), Redding Art Mus, Redding, Calif, 83; Recent Painting, USA, The Figure, Mus Mod Art, New York City, 65; 50 yrs of Crocker-Kingsley, Crocker Art Gallery, Sacramento, Calif, 75. *Dealer:* Vagabond Rose Gallery 236 Main St Chico CA 95928. *Mailing Add:* PO Box 7652 Chico CA 95927

HORNE, RALPH ALBERT
PAINTER, WRITER
b Haverhill, Mass. *Study:* Sch Mus Fine Arts, Boston, cert; San Francisco Art Inst; Univ Ariz, Florence, Italy; MIT, Cambridge, Mass, BS; Boston U, MA; U Vt, MS; Columbia U, PhD; Law Sch, Suffolk U, JD. *Work:* John D Merriam Collection, Boston Pub Libr. *Exhib:* Boston Pub Libr; San Francisco Art Inst; Currier Gallery, Manchester, NH. *Mem:* Boston Mus Fine Arts. *Media:* Mixed Watercolor & Poster Paint on Masonite Panels. *Res:* 19th century American art; antiques and architecture. *Interests:* restoration & furnishing of 18th and 19th century houses. *Collection:* 19th century Am Houses, art, antiques. *Publ:* Articles in Victorian Homes, 91 & 94. *Mailing Add:* 9 Wellington St Boston MA 02118

HORNSCHEMEIER, PAUL
GRAPHIC NOVELIST
b Cincinnati. *Study:* Ohio State Univ, BS (philosophy and cognitive psychology). *Work:* Creator, (comic series) Sequential, 1999-2002; (graphic novels) Mother Come Home, 2003, The Collected Sequential, 2004, The Three Paradoxes, 2005; contribr to MOME mag. *Mailing Add:* c/o Fantagraphics Books 7563 Lake City Way NE Seattle WA 98115

HOROWITZ, DIANA
PAINTER
b New York, NY, 58. *Study:* Rome prog, State Univ NY, Purchase, BFA, 80; Tyler Sch Art, Philadelphia, MFA, 84; Brooklyn Col, MFA, 87. *Work:* Hunter Mus Am Art; Sheldon Swope Art Mus, Terre Haute, Ind; Bellevue Hosp, NY; Brooklyn Union Gas Co, NY. *Exhib:* 25 Yrs of Visual Arts, Neuberger Mus, Purchase, NY; Work by Newly Elected Mems, Am Acad Arts & Letters, NY; Artists Select Artists, Trenton City Mus, NJ; Landscape Painting 1960-1990, Gibbes Mus Art, Charleston, SC; NY Acad Art, NY. *Awards:* Ingram Meml Found Grant, 88; Pollock-Krasner Grant, 89 & 93; Rosenthal Found Award, Am Acad Arts & Letters, NY, 96. *Bibliog:* John Hollander (auth), Italian Tradition in American Art (exhib catalog), Gibbes Mus Art, Charleston, SC, 90; Lois Martin (auth), Classical landscapes, Am Artist, 94; Laurie S Hurwitz (auth), Oil highlights: Landscapes, Am Artist, 95. *Mem:* Nat Acad. *Media:* Oil, Canvas. *Mailing Add:* c/o Hackett-Freedman Gallery 250 Sutter St No 4 San Francisco CA 94108-4451

HOROWITZ, (MR & MRS) RAYMOND J
COLLECTORS
Study: Mr Horowitz, Columbia Univ, AB, 36 & LLB, 39; Mrs Horowitz, NY Univ, AB, 36; Columbia Univ, MA, 37. *Bibliog:* John K Howat & Dianne H Pilgrim (auth), American Impressionist and Realist Paintings and Drawings from the Collection of Mr and Mrs Raymond J Horowitz, Metrop Mus Art, 4-6/73. *Collection:* American turn of the century Realist and Impressionist paintings, watercolors and drawings. *Mailing Add:* 930 Fifth Ave New York NY 10021-2651

HORRELL, JEFFREY L
LIBRARIAN
b Carbondale, Ill, Sept 19, 52. *Study:* Miami Univ, Oxford, Ohio, BA, 75; Univ Mich, AMLS, 76, MA(art hist), 78; Syracuse Univ, MPhil, 95, PhD, 95. *Pos:* Archivist, Mus Art, Univ Mich, 76-78; libr internship, Nat Gallery Art, Wash, DC, 77; asst art librn, Art & Arch, Libr, Univ Mich, 78-80; art librn, Sherman Art Libr, Dartmouth Col, 80-86; asst librn, Personnel, Budget & Planning, Syracuse Univ Libr, NY, 86-92; librn, Fine Arts Libr, Harvard Univ, 92-97; assoc libr, Harvard Col for Collections, 98-2005; dean libr, Dartmouth Col, 2005. *Awards:* Coun Libr Resources Acad Libr Mgt Intern, 86-87. *Mem:* Art Libr Soc NAm (treas, 82-84, vpres & pres elect, 86-88); Col Art Asn; Am Libr Asn; The Grolier Club. *Res:* Development of automated database on art works produced in Florence and Siena in the 13th and 14th centuries. *Interests:* Art documentation and access. *Publ:* Auth, The picturesque: Literature of the English landscape garden, Dartmouth Col Libr Bull, 83; contribr, Treasures of the Hood Museum of Art, Hudson Hills Press, 85; Second international conference on automatic processing of art history and data documents, Art Doc, 85; Seneca Ray Stoddard: Transforming The Adirondack Wilderness in Text and Image, Syracuse Univ Press, 99. *Mailing Add:* 5 Hathoin's Hell Woodstock VT 05091

HORSFIELD, CRAIGIE
ARTIST
b Cambridge, Eng, 1949. *Work:* A Dialogue about Recent Am. & European Photog in Art, Mus Contemp Art, LA, 1991; Carnegie Mus, Pittsburgh, 1994; Carnegie Int, Carnegie Mus, Pittsburgh, 1995. *Exhib:* Another Objectivity, Inst Contemp Arts, London, 88; Blasphemies, ecstasies, cries, The Serpentine Gallery, London, 89; Ydesssa Hendeles Found, Toronto, Can, 90; Frith Street Gallery, Eng, 90 & 2003; Monica De Cardenas, Milan, Italy, 98; El Hierro Conversation, Soundwork 4.1, Documenta 11, Kassel, Ger, 2002; El Hierro Project, El Hiero, Canary Islands, Spain, 2001—05. *Publ:* co-auth: The Lectures, 1992, 1993, Amnesia. Collaboration & Responsibility, 1997, Craigie Horsfield Im Gresprach/Conversation, 1999, Mus Conversations, 2002, Table book, 2002, El Hierro Conversation, 2003, What Film May Be, 2003—04, and others. *Mailing Add:* c/o Barbara Gladstone Gallery 515 W 24th St New York NY 10011

HORT, MICHAEL
COLLECTOR
Pos: Founder Rema Hort Mann Found, New York City, 1995-. *Awards:* Named one of Top 200 Collectors, ARTnews magazine, 2003-06. *Collection:* Contemporary art. *Mailing Add:* Rema Hort Mann Found 153 Hudson St New York NY 10013

HORT, SUSAN
COLLECTOR
Pos: Founder, Rema Hort Mann Found, New York City, 95-. *Awards:* Named one of Top 200 Collectors, ARTnews mag, 2003-06. *Collection:* Contemporary art. *Mailing Add:* Rema Hort Mann Found 153 Hudson St New York NY 10013

HORVAT, OLGA
PAINTER, COLLAGE ARTIST
b Yugoslavia. *Study:* Studied with Cambridge & Ely Brass Rubbing Ctr, England, Cert, 78; Faculty Arts, Zagreb Univ, Croatia, BA, 87; Fashion Inst Tech, NYC, MA, 91. *Work:* San Francisco Folk Art Mus, Calif; Los Angeles Folk Art Mus, Calif; Renwick Gallery of Nat Mus Am Art, Washington, DC; CASE Mus, Jersey City, NJ; The Mus New Art, Detroit, Mich. *Comn:* fabric constructions, Walt Disney World Co, Orlando, Fla, 95; wall hanging, Mr & Mrs Walters, Los Angeles, Calif, 96; fabric constructions, D & D Building, NY, 97; mixed media (silk & paper), Gemelli at the World Trade Ctr, NY, 99; custom portraits, Mr & Mrs Tomson, Chicago, Ill, 2000. *Exhib:* Cooks Third Voyage, Acquario Di Genova Area, Genova, Italy, 90; Magies, Gallerie Vanuxem, Paris, France, 92; Artist Friends of Ceres, Ceres Gallery, NY, 98; Plan for Peace, Times Square Gallery, NY, 99; Novoye, CASE Mus, Jersey City, NJ, 99; A Salute to Hispanic Herigage, Borough Presidents Gallery, NY, 2000; Colored Artworks, Queens Mus Art, NY, 2000; Expressions, Khan Mus, Ashkelon, Israel, 2000. *Pos:* curator asst, The Met Mus Art, 90-91; rsch asst, AD Lederman Fine Art Gallery, 91-92; art dir, Absolute Image, Inc, 94-98; Asst to Pres Basically Kids, 98-2001; Dir, Olga Horvat Art, 2001-present. *Awards:* cert excellence Plan for Peace, NY Times, 99; Twentieth Century Achievement Award, Am Biographical Inst, 99; Accademia Internazionale Greci-Marino, Italy, 2000. *Bibliog:* videocassette, Olga Horvat Collection, Absolute Image, Inc, New York, 96; Jeremy Sedley (auth), Newart International, Art Press, Woodstock, NY, 98; Marilyn Wachtel (auth), Olga Horvat's Post-Pop Celebrity Puzzles, Gallery & Studio, 99; Roberto Puviani (auth), Dizionario Enciclopedico Internazionale D'Arte Contemporane, Case Editrice Alba, Ferrara, Italy, 99; Renee Phillips (auth), A Salute to Ashekelon, Manhattan Arts Internat, 2000. *Mem:* Nat Mus Women in Arts; NY Artists Equity Asn; Queens Mus Art; Nurture Art; Collage Assemblage Soc. *Media:* Mixed Media, Oil, Digital Art. *Interests:* Tennis, Aerobics, Travel. *Mailing Add:* 457 W 57th St Ste 1704 New York NY 10019

HORVAY, MARTHA J
PAINTER, ENVIRONMENTAL ARTIST
b Schenectady, NY, Jan 7, 49. *Study:* Univ Mich, Ann Arbor, BS(design), 71, Univ Louisville, MA, 74, Temple Univ, Tyler Sch Art, MFA, 80. *Work:* Sheldon Memorial Gallery Art & Sculpture Garden, Lincoln, Nebr; Hastings Col, Nebr; Del Mar Col, Corpus Christi, Tex; Mus Nebr Art, Kearney. *Comn:* 2 paintings, Bessey Hall, Univ Nebr, Lincoln; 1percent-for-Art, Nebr, pub outdoor sculpture, Univ Nebr-Lincoln. *Exhib:* 34th Small Drawing & Sculpture, Ball State Univ, Muncie, Ind, 88; 2-person exhib, Quincy Col Art Gallery, Ill, 89; 33rd Chautauqua Nat, Chautauqua Art Asn Gallery, NY, 90; Midlands Invitational 1990, Joslyn Art Mus, Omaha, Nebr; New Am Talent, Laguna Gloria Art Mus, Austin, Tex; solo shows, A Personal Geometry,

Sheldon Mem Gallery Art, Lincoln, Nebr, 92 & Haydon Gallery, Lincoln, Nebr, 95; Morehead State Univ, Ky, 98. *Collection Arranged:* Bemis Center for Contemporary Art, 2004; AIR Gallery, 2004. *Teaching:* Vis asst prof drawing found, Univ Tex San Antonio, 81-82; temporary instr drawing design, Kans State Univ, Manhattan, Kans, 82-83; prof drawing & painting, Univ Nebr, Lincoln, 83-2000, sr lectr (part time). *Awards:* Juror's Award, 49th Ann Competition, Sioux City Art Ctr, Iowa, 90; Artist's Fel Award, Nebr Arts Coun, 91 & 98; Individual Artist's Fel Award, Mid-Am Arts Alliance, 92. *Bibliog:* Kyle MacMillan (auth), Unusual work explores space, volume, time, Omaha World-Herald, 7/24/91; Daphne Anderson Deeds (auth), A Personal Geometry, Sheldon Memorial Gallery Art, 92; Joel Geyer (producer), Is It Art? (film), Nebr Educ TV, fall 92; Kent Wolgart, Art Papers, Jan. 2004. *Media:* Acrylic. *Specialty:* Regional Contemporary Art. *Publ:* New American Paintings, 10/98. *Dealer:* Haydon Gallery 335 N 8th St Lincoln NE 68508; www.guild.com on line gallery; Modern Arts Midwest, 800 P St, Lincoln, NE 68508. *Mailing Add:* 4433 Pawnee St Lincoln NE 68506

HORVITZ, SUZANNE REESE
PAINTER, SCULPTOR

b Philadelphia, Pa. *Study:* Philadelphia Col Art, BFA, MA, 72; Columbia Univ, doctorate, 77. *Work:* Corning Mus Glass, Corning, NY; Musee d'Art Contemporain, Chamaliéres, France; Fyns Kunstmuseum, Odense, Denmark; Mus Am Glass, Millville, NJ; Glasmuseum, Ebeltoft, Denmark. *Comn:* Wallwork, Legent Corp, 94. *Exhib:* Solo exhibs, Harbiye Sanat Galerisi, Istanbul, Turkey, 85, Utah Mus Fine Arts, Salt Lake City, 87, Mus Greater Victoria, BC, Can, 90, Musee d'Art, Contemporain, Chamaliéres, France, 91, Centro de Arte Moderna, Portugal, 91, Fyns Kunst Mus, Odense, Denmark, 91, Centre d'Art Contemporain, Niort, France, 91, Mangel Gallery, Philadelphia, Pa, 93 & Kunstzaal Marktzeventien, Enschede, The Neth, 94. *Pos:* Exec Dir, Found Today's Art/Nexus, Philadelphia, 75-. *Teaching:* instr, Pa Acad Fine Arts, 80-81. *Awards:* Masterworks Fel, Creative Glass Ctr Am, 90; Visual Arts Fel, Mid Atlantic States, 92; Grant, Pa Coun Arts, 93. *Bibliog:* E F Sanguinetti & Thomas V Southam (auths), Suzanne Reese Horvitz, Utah Museum of Arts, 87; Corrine Robbins (auth), Arts Mag, 11/88; Otis Larren (auth), Suzanne Horvitz, Glass Mag, 90. *Mem:* Philadelphia Art Alliance (vpres, 79-); Artists Equity Asn; Women's Caucus Arts. *Media:* Acrylic, Oil; Metal, Glass. *Publ:* Auth, Rope Trick, 80; Thou Hast Ravished My Heart, 81; Sick of Love, Synapse Press, 81; coauth, Vampyr, Synapse Press, 85; Tender Tearful Places, VSW Press, 92. *Dealer:* Mangel Gallery 1714 Rittenhouse Sq Philadelphia PA 19103; Galerie Tower 33 rue du Fauburg Poissonniére 75009 Paris France. *Mailing Add:* 2310 Perot St Philadelphia PA 19130-2526

HORWITZ, CHANNA
CONCEPTUAL ARTIST, PAINTER

b Los Angeles, Calif, May 21, 32. *Study:* Art Ctr Sch Design, 50-52; Calif State Univ, Northridge, 60-63; Calif Inst Arts, BFA, 72. *Work:* Nat Gallery Art, Washington; Los Angeles Co Mus Art, Grunwald Ctr Graphic Arts, Univ Calif & Armand Hammer Mus Art, Los Angeles; Hartford Atheneum, Conn; Neuberg Mus, State Univ New York, Purchase; Pardo Lattuada Gallery, 00. *Comn:* Volt Industs, Orange Co, Calif; Ramada Renesaunce Hotel, Long Beach, Calif; Grand Champion Hotel, Indian Well, Calif. *Exhib:* Los Angeles Co Mus Art, 73; Musical Drawings, PSI, Brooklyn, NY, 79; Los Angeles Munic Art Gallery, 88; Drawing in Southern Calif, 93; Armand Hammer Mus Art, Univ Calif Los Angeles, 94; Sonakinatography: Sound & Motion Notations (with catalog), Los Angeles Munic Art Gallery, 96; Beyond Geometry 1940-1970, Los Angeles County Mus Art, 2004; Language Series (with catalogue), Solway Jones Gallery, Los Angeles, 2005. *Awards:* James D Phelan Award, 63; Winner's Circle, Los Angeles, Calif, 65; Artist Fel, Nat Endowment Arts, 78. *Mem:* Los Angeles Artists Equity Asn. *Media:* Acrylic, Oil. *Publ:* Auth, My statement, 76; auth, Sun & Moon A Quarterly Statement by Artist, Howard Fox, 76; auth, Channa Horwitz, Full Circle 1964-2005 (catalogue). *Dealer:* Solway Jones Gallery 5377 Wilshire Blvd Los Angeles Calif 90036. *Mailing Add:* 1742 S Barrington #4 Los Angeles CA 90025

HOSTETLER, DAVID L
SCULPTOR

b Massillon, Ohio, Dec 27, 26. *Study:* Indiana Univ, BA; Ohio Univ, MA. *Work:* Mus Fine Arts, Boston; Columbus Mus Fine Arts, Ohio; Speed Mus, Louisville, Ky; Butler Art Inst, Youngstown, Ohio; Trump Int Hotel & Tower, NY. *Comn:* Semaphore Woman, Philharmonic Ctr Arts, Naples, Fla, 94; Standing Woman, Ohio Univ, 95; Cape Lady, comn by Tom Kershaw, Beacon Hill, Boston, 97; The Duo, Trump Int, NY, 97; Summertime, Grounds for Sculpture, Hamilton, NJ, 98; DeCordava Mus and Sculpture Park, Lincoln, Mass. *Exhib:* Columbus Collects, Columbus Mus Art, Ohio, 93; Hostetler Major Woods, Parkersburg Art Ctr, WVa, 97; 7 World Trade Ctr, NY, 2000; Univ Hartford, Conn, 2003; City of Stamford, 2003; DeCordava Mus, 2003; Grounds for Sculpture, 2005; Sculpture Ctr, 2005. *Teaching:* Prof art sculpture, Ohio Univ, 48-85. *Awards:* Prof Year, 79 & 80; Ohioanna Career Medal Lifetime Achievement, 89. *Bibliog:* Roulker (auth), Masters of Wood Sculpture, 80; Hostetler, Four Decades (film), PBS TV, 88; Dick Wooten (auth), Hostetler the Carver, Ohio Univ Press, 92. *Media:* Wood. *Mailing Add:* PO Box 989 Athens OH 45701

HOTCHNER, HOLLY
MUSEUM DIRECTOR, CONSERVATOR, CURATOR

b New York, NY. *Study:* Trinity Col, Hartford, Conn, BA(art hist & studio art), 73; Inst Fine Arts, NY Univ, MA(art hist), 82; Mus Management Inst, Univ Calif, Berkeley, 92; Phi Beta Kappa, 73. *Pos:* Collections & exhib cataloguer, Mus Mod Art, NY, 73-76; intern, paintings conserv, Hirshorn Mus, Washington, DC, 80 & Tate Gallery, London, Eng, 80-81; chief conserv, NY Hist Soc, 84-88 & dir, 84-95; pres, Holly Hotchner Mus Arts & Design (foormerly Holly Hotchner Fine Arts Mgt), NY, 95-96; dir, Am Craft Mus, NY, 96-. *Awards:* Conserv Internship Grant, Nat Mus Arts, 82-83; Travel Grant studies in conserv & Sherman Fairchild Conserv Fel, Metrop Mus Art, New York, 83-84; Samuel H Kress Found Grant, 83-84. *Mem:* Elected mem Art Table; Am Asn Mus; NY Landmarks Conserv (bd trustees, 96-05); Fel, Am Inst Conserv; Fel, Int Inst Conserv. *Publ:* Auth, John James Audubon: The Watercolors for the Birds of America, Random House, New York, 93; Forty Years, Anniversary Issue, Am Craft Mus, New york, 96, Beatrice Wood: A Centennial Tribute, 97 & Four Acts in Glass: Installations by Chihuly, Morris, Powers, ad Vallien, 98; contribr, Institutional Trauma: Major Change in Museums and Its Effect on staff, Am Asn Mus, Washington, DC, 97. *Mailing Add:* Mus Arts & Design 40 W 53rd St New York NY 10019

HOTVEDT, KRIS J
PRINTMAKER, PAINTER

b Wautoma, Wis, 1943. *Study:* Layton Sch Art, Milwaukee, Wis, 61-64; San Francisco Art Inst, BFA, 65; Inst Allende, Mex, with D Kortlang, MFA, 67. *Work:* Mus NMex; Univ Sonora, Mex; Huntington Art Alliance, Calif; Ariz State Univ Mem Union Collection; Westat Inc, Rockville, Md; Farmers & Merchants Bank, Menomonee Falls, Wis; St Vincent's Hosp, Santa Fe. *Comn:* Scand Film Festival Poster, Santa Fe, 84; doors & wall murals, Hogan In The Hilton, Sante Fe, 94; Rocky Mountain Biannhormoca, Ft Collins, 2004. *Exhib:* One-woman exhib, Ore Univ Mus, 74-76; La Bodega, Santa Fe, 83; Lincoln Ctr, Ft Collins, Colo, 85; Waxlander Gallery, Santa Fe, 86 & 89; City Gallery, Sacramento, Calif, 86; Euro Am Gallery, Santa Fe, 92; Bardean Gallery, Albuquerque, 94; Galeria Vivencia, Arta, Majorca, Spain, 98; and others; Women Artists in the Land of Enchanment, Lew Allen Gallery, Sante Fe, 99; i Magnifico, Albuquerque Mus, 99; Moxley Ross Naranjo, Sante Fe, 99; Eldridge McCarthy Fine Art, Sante Fe, 2000; Magnifico, Albuquerque Mus, 2002; Traces of the Journey, Women in The Arts, Albuquerque, 2003; retrospective, Woodcuts, Blaire Carnahan Gallery, Santa Fe, 2003. *Pos:* Art ed, Pembroke Mag, 72-. *Teaching:* Instr painting & printmaking, Pembroke State Univ, 67-69; art instr, St Johns Col, NMex, 69-80; continuing educ, Santa Fe Community Col, 92-2000; Ghost Ranch, Abiquiu, NMex, 97-99; Santa Fe Community Col, 98-2000; workshop, Prescott Col, Ariz, 98. *Awards:* NMex Arts Comn Grant, Art in Pub Places, 77-78. *Bibliog:* Article, Art Voices South, 7-8/80. *Mem:* Nat Mus Women in Arts. *Media:* Woodcut; Mixed Media. *Publ:* Illusr, Fry Breads, Feast Days and Sheeps, 87 & Pueblo and Navajo Life Today, 94, Sunstone Press; cover painting, El Norte Cookbook, Redcrane, 94; illus, Little Juan Learns a Lesson, 97 & bk cover, Spanish Riddles and Colcha Designs, 97, Sunstone Press; bk cover, Of Memory and Desire, Univ La Press; illsu, The Little Ghost who Wouldn't go Away, LaConquistadora Sunstone, 2000, Angel on Daniels Shoulder, Manuel. *Dealer:* Jospeh Gierek Gallery, Tulsa Oka; Mese Arts, Birmingham MI; Ernesto Mayans Gallery Santa Fe NM; Blair Carnahan FGine Arts, Santa Fe NM; Mesa Arts Birmingham MI; Hand Arts Truchas NM; Hopkins Fine Arts, Scottsdale AZ. *Mailing Add:* PO Box 1543 Pena Blanca NM 87041

HOTZ, THEO
COLLECTOR

b Aug 2, 28. *Exhib:* Swiss Post Off and Telecom Bldg, ABB Power Generation Hdqs, Baden, Switz, EMPA Nat Material Testing Inst, St Gallen (European Solar Prize for best integrated buildings, 96), Municipal Works Bldg, Winterthur, addition to Basel Trade Fair complex. *Awards:* Recipient RS Reynolds Memorial Award, Am Inst of Architects, 88; Named one of Top 200 Collectors, ARTnews magazine, 2004. *Collection:* contemporary art. *Mailing Add:* Theo Hotz AG Architekten & Planer Münchhaldenstrasse 21 Posttach Zürich 8034 Swaziland

HOUGH, JENNINE
PAINTER

b Charlotte, NC, Mar 17, 48. *Study:* Univ NC, Chapel Hill, BA, 70; Univ NC, Greensboro, MFA with cert, 73; Skowhegan Sch Painting & Sculpture, Maine, summer 74. *Work:* High Mus Art & Ga Arts Coun, Atlanta; Columbus Mus Art, Ga; Miss Mus Art, Jackson; Gibbes Art Mus, Charleston, SC; State of Ga, Fine Arts Mus, South Mobile, Ala; and others. *Comn:* Dekalb Co Libr Syst, Dunwooday, Ga, 91; Ducks Unlimited, 96; IAHI, 96. *Exhib:* One-woman shows, Columbus Mus Fine Arts, Ga, 77, Monique Knowlton, NY, 82, Trinity Gallery, Atlanta, 90, 91 & 92, Jane Haslem Gallery, Washington, 91 & 93, Marita Gilliam Gallery, Raleigh, 91; Fernbank Mus Natural Hist, Atlanta, 94; Ghost Ranch Mus, Abiquiu, NMex, 94; Contemp Southwest Galleries, Santa Fe, 98; Vectr in Aspen, 2001; Aspen Chapel Gallery, 2002-05; Aspen Art Mus Ann, 2001, 2003, 2005-2006; Moca-Ga Atlanta, 2004. *Teaching:* Eve prog, Emory Univ, 79-84; Atlanta Col Art, 86-87. *Awards:* Nat Endowment Arts & Southeastern Ctr Contemp Arts Fel Grant, 80; Archives Nat Mus Women Arts, 90; Art in Embassy Prog, US State Dept, Barbados, 94-96. *Bibliog:* Southern Realism, Art in Am, 12/80; Articles in Am Artist, 85, 91 & 95; Southern Accents, Honoring American Artists, 87, 95. *Mem:* Nat Asn Women Artists, NY. *Media:* Oil; Watercolor. *Interests:* Piano, gardening, reading, running and my animals. *Mailing Add:* 421 W Hallam St Aspen CO 81611

HOUGH, WINSTON
PAINTER, DRAFTSMAN

b Hartford, Mich, July 12, 28. *Study:* Art Inst Chicago, BFA, 53; Northeastern Ill Univ, MA, 71. *Comn:* 14 Watercolors Midwest Stock Exchange Serv Corp, 1967. *Exhib:* Exhib Momentum Midcontinental, Chicago, Ill, 53; Chicago Artist, Art Inst Chicago, Ill, 55; Richmond Artist, Valentine Mus, Va, 57-59; Virginia Artist, Chrysler Mus, Norfolk, 57-60 & Va Mus Art, 58; Winston-Salem Gallery Fine Art Semiannual, NC, 57-68; Seven Arts Ann, Palm Beach, Fla, 65 & 73; solo exhib, Paul Theobald Book Store Gallery, 78, Queen Gallery, Chicago, 84, Concordia Col Fergeson Gallery, River Forest, Ill, 87, Beverly Arts Ctr Pillsbury Concouse Gallery, Chicago, 88, Artreach Gallery, Columbus, Ohio, 90. *Teaching:* Asst prof, Va Commonwealth Univ, Richmond, 56-62; lectr art, Univ Ill, Chicago, 64-65. *Awards:* Huntington Hartford Fel, 58; Best Painting, Birmingham Mus, 58; Cert of Award, Rockport Publ, 98.

Bibliog: Leslie Judd Ahlander (auth), New Painter, Washington Post, 61. *Mem:* Chicago Artist Coalition. *Media:* Oil, Watercolor. *Publ:* Illusr, Best of Oils, Best of Acrylics & Portrait Inspirations, Rockport Publ, 97-98; illusr, Watercolor Expressions Selected by B L Schlemm, 00. *Dealer:* www.caconline.org/cacartists/houghw/houghw; www.artworkonview.com; www.artworldchicago.com. *Mailing Add:* 937 Echo Ln Glenview IL 60025

HOUGHTON, BARBARA JEAN
PHOTOGRAPHER, VIDEO ARTIST
b Chicago, Ill, Nov 2, 47. *Study:* Univ Ill, Chicago, BA(art), 71; Sch Art Inst Chicago, MFA(photog), 73, also grad study with Shigeko Kubota. *Work:* Art Inst Chicago; Atlantic Richfield Corp, Denver & Houston; Chase Manhattan Bank, NY; Am Oil Co, Denver; Ctr Creative Photog, Univ Ariz, Tucson. *Exhib:* 74th Chicago & Vicinity Show, Art Inst Chicago, 73; Lensless Photog, Franklin Inst, Philadelphia, 82; Colo; State of the Arts, Denver Art Mus, 82; New Epiphanies, Ohio Found Arts & traveling, 83; Unsportsmanlike Conduct, Sebastian-Moore Gallery, Denver & Univ Conn, 83 & 84; Photograms, John Michael Kohler Art Ctr, Sheboygan, Wis, 85; The Art of Tattoo, City of Denver, 85; I Always Cheat at Croquet, Ctr Idea Art, Denver, 86. *Teaching:* Prof art & photog, Metrop State Col, Denver, 74-92 & Northern Ky Univ, 92-. *Awards:* Nat Endowment Arts Photog Grant, 78; Grant, Mayor's Comn Cult Affairs, City of Denver, 85; Interdisciplinary Grant, Nat Endowment Arts/Rockefeller Found, 86. *Bibliog:* Andy Grundberg (auth), From this land, Mod Photog, 6/79; William Peterson (auth), 4/81 & Jane Fudge (auth), summer 84, Photography Notes, Artspace. *Mem:* Col Art Asn; Soc Photog Educ. *Mailing Add:* Fine Arts Dept Rm 312 Northern Ky Univ Highland Heights KY 41099

HOUK, PAMELA P
CURATOR
b Dayton, Ohio, Jan 8, 35. *Study:* Skowhegan Sch Painting & Sculpture, Maine, 54; Sch Dayton Art Inst, Ohio, 55-65; Cincinnati Art Acad, Ohio, 61-63; Wright State Univ, Dayton, Ohio, BS, 71, MA, 81. *Work:* Bradford Col, Haverhill, Mass; Cincinnati Mus Art, Ohio. *Collection Arranged:* Bookforms (auth, catalog), Artists' Books, 78; Patterns Plus (auth, catalog), Patterns and Systems, 79; Japanese House (auth, catalog), Household Objects of Edo Period, 79; Woodworks II: Folk Traditions in Ohio and Kentucky (auth, catalog), 81; Cloth Forms (auth, catalog), Fabric Constructions, 82; Inside Self, Someone Else (auth, catalog), The Alter Ego as Self Portrait, 83; Lines of Art Nouveau (auth, catalog), Aspects and Sources of International Art Nouveau Movement, 83-84; Ink Under Pressure (auth, catalog), 84; Clay (auth, catalog), 85; Thomas Macaulay: Sculptural Views on Perceptual Ambiguity, 1968-1986 (coauth, catalog), Dayton Art Inst, Ohio, 86; Art for the Public: New Collaborations (coauth, catalogue), 88; Art that Flies (book, coauth), Sky Art, 90; Fit to Print, Basic Printmaking Processes in 500 years of Master Prints, 92; Inside Japanese Space, Japanese Aesthetic Concepts Related to Space, 93; Making Faces, 93-94; Starting with Art (introd to looking at art), 94-95; Stories in Art (introd for families to the exhib, Botticelli to Tiepolo), 95-96; Art Zoo, 97-98; Color Connections, 99-. *Pos:* Dir, Living Arts Ctr Gallery, Dayton, Ohio, 72-76; cur, Experiencenter Gallery, Dayton Art Inst, Ohio, 76-. *Awards:* Governors Award for Excellence in Art Educ, Ohio, 93. *Mem:* Am Asn Mus. *Mailing Add:* Dayton Art Inst 456 Belmonte Park N Dayton OH 45405-4700

HOULE, ROBERT JAMES
PAINTER, CONSULTANT
b St Boniface, Man, Mar 28, 47. *Study:* Univ Man, Winnipeg, BA(art hist), 72; Int Summer Acad Fine Arts, Salzburg, Austria, 72; McGill Univ, Montreal, BEd(art), 75. *Work:* Art Gallery of Ontario, Toronto; Heard Mus, Phoenix; Mus Contemp Art, Sydney; Nat Gallery Can, Ottawa. *Comn:* Mural, McGill Univ, Montreal, 73; poster, Assembly First Nations, Ottawa, 81; Gambling Sticks, Sculpture, The Forks, Winnipeg Art Gallery, 99. *Exhib:* Works on Paper, Galerie Sarah McCutcheon, Montreal, 81; New Work by a New Generation, Norman Mackenzie Art Gallery, Regina, Sask, 82; New Growth from Ancestral Roots, Koffler Gallery, Toronto, 83; Contemp Native Am Art, Okla State Univ, Stillwater, 83; Innovations: New Expressions in Native Am Painting, Heard Mus, Phoenix, 83. *Collection Arranged:* New Work by a New Generation, 82. *Pos:* Cur contemp Indian art, Nat Mus Man, Ottawa, 77-80; art consult, Indian & Northern Affairs, Ottawa, 80-81 & Assembly First Nations, Regina, Sask, 82; Cons Contemp First Nations art holding: McMichael Can Collection, 85. *Teaching:* Specialist art, James Lyng High Sch, Montreal, 74 & Verdun Cath High Sch, Montreal, 75-76; Ontario Col Art & Design, 90-03. *Bibliog:* Carol Phillips (auth), New Work by a New Generation, Artscanada, 11/82; Nancy Baele (auth), Indian adds to Mondrian, Ottawa Citizen, 6/4/83. *Mem:* Royal Can Acad. *Media:* Acrylic, Watercolour. *Res:* Contemporary native art in Canada. *Publ:* Auth, Search for identity, Tawow, Vol 1, No 3, 70; auth, Alex Janvier: 20th century native symbols and images, 78 & Odjig: An artist's transition, 78, Native Perspective; auth, A firm statement on the demoralization of Indian people, Gazette, 79; Dibaajimowin/Storytelling, The Art of Bonnie Devine, Algoma Gallery, Sault Ste Marie, 03. *Dealer:* Goodwater Gallery, 800 Dundas St W, Toronto. *Mailing Add:* 387 Ontario St Toronto ON M5A 2V8 Canada

HOURIAN, MOHAMMAD
PAINTER, ART DEALER
b Hamedan, Iran, 1955. *Study:* Apprentice with Haj Hosen-Esalmiyan, 67-77; Univ Tehran, BA(art), 77. *Work:* Swanson Fine Arts Gallery, Tate Gallery, San Francisco, Calif; Galerie Rivolta, Lausanne, Switz; Roma Gallery, Rome, Italy; Sweden Helsingborg, Lajos Flesser Gallery, 98. *Comn:* 3 paintings, comn by Charlotte Tilton, Beverly Hills, Calif, 85; painting, comn by Geoffrey Watson, Oakland, Calif, 89. *Exhib:* Persian Art, Fine Arts Mus, Tehran, 75; Persian Art, Mus Fine Arts, Brussels, 76; Persian Art, Fine Arts Mus, Tokyo, Japan, 85; Persian Art, Antiques Gallery, San Francisco, 92, Tresidder Union, Stanford Univ, Palo Alto, 97, Vorpal Gallery, San Francisco, 2000, Int Artexpo, NY, 2006. *Collection Arranged:* Persian Art, Noori Gallery, 90; Persian Art, Swanson Fine Arts, 92. *Teaching:* Prof art, Univ Tehran, Iran, 78 & Univ Calif, Berkeley, 87. *Awards:* Gold Medal, Int Tehran Exhib, 75; First Prize, Tehran Painters Exhib, 76. *Media:* Watercolor, Gold Base Acrylic. *Collection:* Persian miniature art. *Publ:* Auth,Dreams of Realty in Perian Art, 90. *Dealer:* Nat Art Gallery Tokyo Japan. *Mailing Add:* 1843 Union St San Francisco CA 94123

HOURIHAN, DOROTHY DIERKS
PAINTER, EDUCATOR
b Columbus, Ga, Aug, 19, 1935. *Study:* Gulf Park Col, Miss, AA, 55, Univ Colo, with Mark Rothko, BFA, 57; Columbia Univ, Teachers Col, MA, 60 Ed D, 84. *Work:* Montclair Art Mus, NJ; Columbus Mus, Ga; Hebrew Home for the Aged, Riverdale, NJ; NJ City Univ; Noyes Mus, Oceanville, NJ; NJ Center Visual Arts; Albrecht Art Mus, St. Joseph, Mo; Springfield Art Mus, Mo. *Comn:* comn by Mr & Mrs Leonard Block, NY. *Exhib:* 1st Ann Opening Show, Birmingham Mus, 59; St Louis Art Mus, Mo, 61; Mussavi, NY, 88; Nabisco Gallery, 88; Columbus Mus (group), Ga, 90; Korean Cult Ctr, NY, 90 & 96; KL Fine Arts, Chicago, 99; solo shows, Viridian Gallery, NY, 87, 89, 92 & 95, Montclair Mus, NJ, 89, Courtney Gallery, NJ City Univ, 98, Pen & Brush Club, NY, 98, 2000. *Pos:* Bd dir, Nat Asn Schs Art & Design, 86-92; cur, Lever House Group Show, NY, 92; adv coun, Hudson Repertory Dance Theatre; bd trustees, Thomas A Edison Film Consortium. *Teaching:* Prof painting, NJ City Univ, 62-94, chmn dept art, 82-91, prof emeritus, fine arts, 95-; dean, Sch Arts & Scis, 91-94; ret, 94. *Awards:* Second Prize Watercolor, 12th Ann Juried Exhib, Summit Art Ctr, NJ, 76; Cert Appreciation, Jersey City Cult Arts Comn, 85. *Mem:* Hudson Co Cult & Heritage Coun (adv coun, 84-85); Nat Asn Sch Art & Design (bd dir, 85-); Hudson Repertory Dance Theatre (adv bd, 85-); Pen & Brush Club; Veridian Gallery, New York City. *Media:* Oil, Mixed Media. *Dealer:* Pen & Brush Inc NYC. *Mailing Add:* 257 Kerrs Corner Rd Blairstown NJ 07825

HOUSE, SUDA KAY
PHOTOGRAPHER, VIDEO ARTIST
b Du Quoin, Ill, Jan 31, 51. *Study:* Univ Southern Calif, BFA, 73; Calif State Univ, Fullerton, MA, 76. *Work:* Polaroid Corp, Boston; Los Angeles Co Mus Art; Mus Photog Arts, San Diego; Creative Ctr Photog, Univ Ariz; Minneapolis Inst Arts. *Exhib:* Attitudes: Photog in the 1970s, Santa Barbara Mus Art, 79; Uniquely Photog, Honolulu Acad Art, 79; Electro Works, George Eastman House, Rochester, NY, 81; Photographer as Printmaker, Arts Coun Gt Brit, London, 82; Eight from San Diego, San Diego Mus Art, 82; Polaroid: The Big Picture, Mus Photog Arts, San Diego, 83. *Teaching:* Guest instr photog, Univ Calif, Los Angeles Exten, 77; instr, East Los Angeles Col, 78-79; prof, Grossmont Col, 79-. *Awards:* Nat Endowment Arts Emerging Photogr Fel, 80. *Mem:* Los Angeles Ctr Photog Studies (trustee, 74-81, pres, 75-78); Soc Photog Educ (chmn western region, 81-82). *Publ:* Auth, Artistic photographic processes, Amphoto, 81. *Mailing Add:* Dept Commun Arts & Sci Grossmont Col 8800 Grossmont College Dr El Cajon CA 92020-1798

HOUSER, CAROLINE MAE
HISTORIAN
b Walla Walla, Wash. *Study:* Mills Col, BA; San Francisco Art Inst; Harvard Univ, AM, PhD; Am Sch Classical Studies, Athens, Greece. *Teaching:* Asst prof art hist, Univ Tex, Austin, 75-78; Mellon Fel art hist, Harvard Univ, Cambridge, Mass, 78-79; asst prof art hist, Smith Col, Mass, 79-. *Awards:* Andrew W Mellon Fel. *Mem:* Archaeol Inst of Am; Col Art Asn; Am Sch Classical Studies (managing comt). *Res:* Greek sculpture, especially monumental work in bronze. *Publ:* Auth, Is it from the Parthenon, Am J Archaeol, 72; auth, Dionysos and his circle, 79; auth, The Riace Marina bronze statues, classical or classicizing?, Source, 82; auth, Greek Monumental Bronze Sculpture, Vendome, 83. *Mailing Add:* 50 Strawberry Hill St Florence MA 01062-1339

HOUSER, JIM
PAINTER, EDUCATOR
b Dade City, Fla, Nov 12, 28. *Study:* Ringling Sch Art, BS, 49; Fla Southern Col, BFA, 51; Art Inst Chicago, postgraduate, 52; Univ Fla, MFA, 53. *Work:* Univ Notre Dame; Cornell Univ; NY Univ; Soc Four Arts Collection, Palm Beach, Fla; Syracuse Univ Art Collection; and others. *Exhib:* One-man shows, Grand Cent Mod, NY, 66-, Lehigh Univ, Bethlehem, 68, Gallery Camino Real, Boca Raton, Fla, 72-89, 99, 03 & 05, Brevard Community Col, Cocoa, Fla, 73, Valencia Community Col, Orlando, Fla, 74, David Findlay Galleries, New York City, 76, 78, 81, 83, Northwood Inst, 86, Palm Beach Community Col, 88, and others; Mainstreams USA, Ohio, 68; David Findlay Galleries, NY, 76-84; Yellow Banks 50th Art Exhib, Owensboro, Ky, 89; Ft Lauderdale Mus Art Invitational Exhib, 91; Group shows, Dept State Spec Exhib, Wash, 67, Major Fla Artist Invitational Exhib, Sarasota, Fla, 81-92, North Miami Mus and Art Center, North Miami, Fla, 85, Men's Art Northwood Univ, West Palm Beach, Fla, 94, Festival Int Peinture, Cagnes-sur-Mer, France, 2001; Permanent collection Boca Raton Mus Art. *Collection Arranged:* Notre Dame Univ; Cornell Univ; NY Univ. *Pos:* Artist, Norte Dame Univ, 1970; artist, Cornell Univ, NY Univ, 1971; judge local and nat art competitions; lectr in field. *Teaching:* Sr. Instr Art, Ky Wesleyan Col, Owensboro, 54-60, fine arts chm, 58-60, art chmn, 64-70, dir art gallery, 74-91; instr painting, Palm Beach Jr Col, 60-92, gallery dir, 74-90. *Awards:* Akston Award, Soc Four Arts, 77; Merit Award, 16th Hortt Competition, Ft Lauderdale Mus Arts, 74; Philip Hulitar Award, 82; Atwater/Kent Award, Soc of the Four Arts, 77, 89; Four Arts Award, Soc of the Four Arts, West Palm Beach, 92, 93; established Connie and Jim Houser Award for the Contemporary Exhib Soc of the Four Arts, 96-. *Bibliog:* Article, Arts Mag, 81. *Mem:* Soc of the Four Arts (Certificate of Appreciation 1996, 10 other awards). *Media:* Acrylic. *Publ:* Auth, Color for the Artist, Palm Beach Jr Col, 75; Perspective, video, Palm Beach Jr Col, 86; Perspective Drawing, video, Palm Beach Jr Col, 90. *Dealer:* Gallery Camino Real 608 Banyon Trail Boca Raton Fla 33431. *Mailing Add:* 8338 SE Coconut St Hobe Sound FL 33455-2911

HOUSEWRIGHT, ARTEMIS SKEVAKIS JEGART
PAINTER, SCULPTOR
b Tampa, Fla. *Study:* Fla State Univ, Tallahassee, BA, 49, MA, 52; study with Edmund Lewandowski & Karl Zerbe. *Work:* Tallahassee Democrat Bldg, Fla; Gulf Life Insurance Bldg, Jacksonville, Fla; Washington Federal Bldg, Hollywood, Fla; Tallahassee Community Col, Admin Bldg, Fla; Student Union Bldg, La State Univ, Baton Rouge. *Comn:* Cement & Shell Mosaics, Phipps family mansion, Old Westbury Gardens, Old Westbury, Long Island, NY, 1969; Shell mosaic wall sculpture & 3 rug hangings, Wash Fed Bank, Hollywood, Fla, 77; oil painted murals done in private residences throughout the US, 85, 88, 89, 95 & 96; cement/shell mosaic panels, 2nd Nat Bank, Washington, 88; mural & archit decor, Ceresville Mansion, Md, 90; oil mural, Fla State Univ, Tallahassee, 2000. *Exhib:* One-person shows, 30 exhibs in galleries in Fla, Va, Ga & NY, 53-72, Cosmos Club, Washington, DC, 81, 97, Points of the Compass, Fla State Univ, Fine Arts Mus, 98, Retrospective Painting exhib, Vero Beach Mus Art, 2003, Painting exhib, Claude Pepper Foundation Gallery, Tallahassee, Fla, 2003; 21st Ann Mid-Year Show, Butler Inst Am Art, Youngstown, Ohio, 56, 57 & 60; two-person exhib, Jacksonville Mus Art, Fla, 58, Fla State Art Gallery, Tallahassee, 59; Invitational Paul Miller exhib, Jacksonville Art Mus, 61; 66 Artists of the Southeast, Delgado Mus, New Orleans, La, 66; Watergate Gallery, Washington, DC, 72. *Awards:* 1st Prize, Purchase Award, Soc Four-Arts, Palm Beach, Fla, 55, 56 & 57; 1st Prize, Purchase Award, Tampa Art Inst, 57; 1st Prize, Purchase Award, Mississippi Art Asn, 57. *Mem:* Artists Equity. *Media:* Oil; Cement & Shell Mosaic. *Interests:* design; architecture. *Publ:* Contrib, Washington Star (newspaper mag), 76, Baltimore Sun (newspaper mag), 77, Golden Eye (bk), 83, Interior Design (trade mag), Washington Home & Garden (mag), 90, House & Garden (mag), 92, The Grove (bk), 98, Coast to Coast (bk), 99 & Frederick Mag, 7 & 10/99; Cover art (book) Voices, 150 Yr Informal History of Florida State University, 2002; Hugh Sidey's Color prints of Greenwood, Iowa, paintings for historic preservation, 2003. *Mailing Add:* 9 Vista Estrella S Santa Fe NM 87540-9631

HOUSMAN, RUSSELL F
PAINTER, EDUCATOR
b Buffalo, NY, Jan 13, 28. *Study:* Albright Art Sch, Buffalo, dipl; State Univ NY Col Buffalo, BS; NY Univ, MA & PhD; also with Hale Woodruff & Revington Arthur. *Work:* Anderson Col, SC; Butler Inst Am Art; Chautauqua Ctr Visual Arts, NY; Dayton Art Inst, Ohio; Sivermine Guild Arts Ctr, Conn; and others. *Comn:* Mural, USA, Kans Munic Auditorium, 52; painting, L Goodyear Collection, 57; Discovery Ctr, Human Resources Ctr, 72. *Exhib:* Solo exhib, Wellons Gallery, NY, McFall Gallery, NY, Silvermine Guild Arts Ctr, New Canaan, Conn, Albany Inst Hist & Art, Country Art Gallery, Locust Valley, NY, Nassau Community Col, NY, Southern Vt Art Ctr, Chaffee Art Ctr; retrospective, Albany Inst Hist & Arts, Nassau Co Mus & Nassau Community Col; Willard Gallery; Nordness Gallery; Kornblee Gallery; Arms & Armor, Civil War Cent, Decatur City Art Ctr; Images & Industry Exhib & Conf, Milliken Univ. *Pos:* Dir, Decatur City Art Ctr, 59-61 & Art Sch Adventure, Long Trail Sch, Dorset, Vt, 94-; art consult, Human Resources Ctr, Albertson, NY, Aging in Am & Nat Ctr Disability Serv Others; founder & dir, Firehouse Gallery, Nassau Community Col, 63-70. *Teaching:* chair art, Hofstra, 53-56; Prof art, Adelphi Univ, 56-59; prof art & chmn dept, Milliken Univ, 59-61; prof art, Nassau Community Col, emer prof. *Awards:* Purchase Award, State Univ NY, 68; Prizes, Silvermine Art Guild & Chautauqua Art Ctr; Nat Endowment Arts; NY State Coun Arts; Grand Concourse, Albany, NY. *Bibliog:* Viscardi (auth), The School, Eriksson, 64; 21 Paint in Hyplar, Grumbacher, 68; Watson (auth), The Senseous Carrot-The Artist as a Cook, Country Art Gallery, 72. *Mem:* Am Fedn Art; Silvermine Art Guild; NY State Art Teachers (ed, 69); Long Island Art Teachers; Phi Delta Kappa. *Publ:* Auth, Psychological Warfare Capabilities & Vulnerabilities as Found in Soviet Art, 54; The Design of an Art Room, 55; Utilization of Artist Personnel in Psychological Warfare, 63; Telephone Assisted Teaching Devices, 69; Core Humanities Curriculum for Disabled Children, 70. *Dealer:* Country Art Gallery Locust Valley NY; Beside Myself Gallery Manchester VT. *Mailing Add:* 38 McKee Rd Arlington VT 05250

HOUSTON, BRUCE
SCULPTOR, ASSEMBLAGE ARTIST
b Iowa City, Iowa, Jan 23, 37. *Study:* Univ Nebr, Lincoln, BA, 59; Art Ctr Col Design, Los Angeles, 61-62; Univ Calif Los Angeles, MA(graphic design), 65; Univ Iowa, MFA(painting), 74. *Work:* Univ Art Mus, Albuquerque. *Comn:* Outdoor sculpture, Progressive Corp, Cleveland, Ohio. *Exhib:* Des Moines Art Ctr, 87; Lost & Found in Calif Four Decades of Assemblage Art, James Corcoran Gallery, Santa Monica, Calif, 88; Forty Yrs of Calif Assemblage, Frederick Wight Gallery, UCLA, Los Angeles, San Jose Mus Art, Fresco Art Mus & Joslyn Art Mus, Omaha, Nebr, 89; Calif Surrealism, Bronx River Art Gallery, Bronx, NY, 89; solo shows, Chrysler Mus, Norfolk, Va, 91, Palm Springs Desert Mus, Calif, 92, Lamont Gallery Phillips Exeter Acad, NH; plus many others. *Teaching:* Slide lectr in many cols & univs throughout Calif, 79-. *Awards:* Best in Show, Davenport Art Mus, 72. *Bibliog:* Suzanne Muchnic (auth), Bruce Houston assemblages, Art Voices S, 1/80. *Dealer:* Allan Stone Galleries 113 E 90th St New York NY; Jan Baum Galleries 170 LaBrea Los Angeles CA; Imago Galleries 45-450 Hwy 74 Palm Desert CA 92260

HOUSTON, JOHN STEWART See Stewart, John Stewart Houston

HOVING, THOMAS
CONSULTANT
b New York, NY, Jan 15, 1931. *Study:* Princeton Univ, BA(summa cum laude), 53, Grad Sch Art & Archaeol (Nat Coun Humanities Fel), 55, Grad Sch Fine Arts, MFA(Kienbusch & Haring Fel), 58, PhD(art hist), 59; five honorary doctorates. *Hon Degrees:* Hofstra Univ, LHD, 66; Pratt Inst, LLD, 67; Princeton Univ, HHD, 68; NY Univ, DFA, 68; Middlebury Col, LittD, 68. *Collection Arranged:* Initiated and developed series of art exchanges between museums of France, Soviet Union and the US; arranged Tutankhamun Tour of US, 76-79. *Pos:* Curatorial asst, Dept Medieval Art & The Cloisters, Metrop Mus Art, 59-60, asst cur, 60-63, assoc cur, 63-65, cur, 65-66, dir, 67-77; admin, Recreation & Cult Affairs, NY, 66-67; commr parks & adminr, Recreation & Cult Affairs, New York City, 66-67; corr & arts editor, ABC News 20/20, 78-84; ed-in-chief, Connoisseur Mag, 81-91; pres, Hoving Assoc Inc, currently. *Awards:* Chevalier De La Legion d'Honneur, 70; Woodrow Wilson Award, Princeton Univ, 77; Order of Distinguished Serv, Egypt, 79. *Mem:* Int Ctr Medieval Art (mem bd dir). *Publ:* Auth, Andrew Wyeth, Autobiography, Bulfinch Press, 95; False Impressions, The Search for Big Time Art Fakes, Simon & Schuster Inc, 96; Greatest Works of Art in Western Civilization, Artisan, 97; Art for Dummies, IDG, 99; The Art of Nan Namingha, Abrams, 2000. *Mailing Add:* 150 E 73rd St Apt 2C New York NY 10021

HOVSEPIAN, LEON
PAINTER, DESIGNER
b Bloomsburg, Pa, Nov 20, 15. *Study:* Worcester Art Mus Sch, cert; Yale Univ, Alice Kimball traveling fel, BFA, 42; Fogg Mus. *Work:* Worcester Art Mus, Mass; Fitchburg Art Mus, Mass; Fine Arts Collection, Washington; Springfield Mus, Mass; Mus Mod Art, Yerevan, Armenia, USSR. *Comn:* Mosaics, Oblate Fathers Retreat House, Willimantic, 61; stained glass, Holy Cross Col, Worcester, 65; portraits, Leiceister Jr Col, Mass, 68-69; fresco mural, Church of the Annunciation, Washington, 74; portrait, Judge Morris N Gould, Worcester, Mass; design of Archeveque Chapel, Papeet, Tahiti, 83; resurrection mural, St Joseph's Cemetery, Chelmsford, Mass, 84; and others. *Exhib:* Art Inst Chicago, 41; Albright Art Gallery, 46; Nat Gallery Art, 47; RI Sch Design, 48; Worcester Art Mus Am Biennial, 48; By the People For the People--New Eng, De Cordova Mus, Lincoln, Mass, 77; one-man exhib, Armenian Libr & Mus Am Inc, Watertown, Mass, 91; traveling exhib, Looking past the painting--Underlying Structure, Fitchburg Art Mus, Mass, 92-93. *Collection Arranged:* ARTSworcester, Aurora Gallery, Worcester, Mass; Worcester Pub Lib. *Pos:* Dir, Boylston Summer Art Sch, Mass, 41-; fac, Clark Univ Sch Worcester Art Mus, formerly. *Teaching:* Instr art, Bancroft Sch, 36-38; prof, Woman's Col, New Haven, 38-40; instr, Worcester Art Mus Sch, 40-, instr, Pub Educ Div, 41-56. *Awards:* St Wulstan Soc Art Award, 38-40; Painting Prize, Fitchburg Art Mus; Ford Found Grant to exhib in Armenia, USSR. *Bibliog:* Adlow (auth), Stuart Gallery, Christian Sci Monitor, 46; Sandrof (auth), Artist in his studio, Feature Parade, 53; Browne (auth), Leon Hovsepian, Art News, 11/66. *Mem:* Bohemians Inc; elected mem Pi Alpha, Yale Univ. *Publ:* Illusr, Worcester Federal, Past--Present--Future, 52; illusr, Androck, 58. *Dealer:* Triart Studios 96 Squantum St Worcester MA 01606. *Mailing Add:* 96 Squantum St Worcester MA 01606

HOWARD, (HELEN) BARBARA
PAINTER, PRINTMAKER
b Long Branch, Ont, Mar 10, 26. *Study:* Western Tech & Commun Sch, Toronto; Ont Col Art, Toronto, AOCA, 51; St Martins Sch Art, London, 54. *Work:* Nat Gallery Can; Art Gallery Ont; Brit Mus, London; Bodleian Libr, Oxford, England; Libr Cong; Nat Libr of Can. *Exhib:* Can Soc Graphic Arts, 58-60 & 63; Can Watercolours, Drawings and Prints, Nat Gallery, Can, 66; solo-exhib, Wells Gallery, Ottawa, 66, 82 & 84 & Prince Arthur Galleries, Toronto, 80 & 82, O'Keefe Ctr, Toronto, 86; Douglas Duncan Collection, Windsor, London, Hamilton, 67; Drawings and Sculpture, Art Gallery, Ont, 76; Lt Govs Exhib, Queens Park, Toronto, Can, 1999-2000; plus others. *Bibliog:* Profile of Barbara Howard, City & Country Home, Toronto, 4/84 & Equinox Mag, 87; Endgrain: Contemporary Wood Engraving in North America, Barbarian Press, British Columbia, 95; DA44, A Journal of the Printing Arts, Porcupines Quill, 99. *Mem:* Royal Can Acad Arts (mem coun, 80-82); hon life mem Art Gallery of Ont; Arts and Letters Club of Toronto. *Media:* Oil; Wood Engraving, Black and White Graphic. *Publ:* Illusr, Turns and Other Poems, Anson-Cartwright Ed, 75; The Promise of Light, Anson-Cartwright Ed, 80; Selected Poems: Exile Ed, 84; illusr, Man in Love, Porcupine's Quill, Inc, 85; Hiram and Jenny, Porcupine's Quill, Inc, 88. *Dealer:* Contemp Fine Arts Serv Inc 413 Dundas St E Toronto ON M5A 2A9. *Mailing Add:* 226 Roslin Ave Toronto ON M4N 1Z6 Canada

HOWARD, DAN F
PAINTER, EDUCATOR
b Iowa City, Iowa. *Study:* Univ Iowa, BA, 53, MFA, 58. *Work:* Joe & Emily Lowe Art Mus, Miami, Fla; Chautauqua Inst, NY; Sheldon Mem Art Gallery, Univ Nebr, Lincoln; Smithsonian Nat Mus Am Art, Washington, DC; Joslyn Art Mus, Omaha, Nebr; Hallmark Coll, Kansas City, Mo; Mus Nebraska Art, Kearny, NE; and many others. *Exhib:* Contemp Am Painting Exhib, Soc Fine Arts, Palm Beach, Fla, 79, 83, 84, 85, 86, 89, 96; Butler Midyear Show, Butler Inst Am Art, Youngstown, Ohio, 66, 83, 84, 89, 93; traveling retrospective, 83-84; solo exhibs, Wichita Art Asn Galleries, Kans, 88, New Gallery, Houston, Tex, 89 & 93; Joy Horwich Gallery, Chicago, Ill, 90 & Vorpal Gallery, NY, 91; West/Art & Law Touring Exhib, 93-94; group exhibs, 90, 92, 93 & 94; Univ Northern Iowa, Cedar Falls, 94; Soliloguium, Mus Nebr Art, Kearney, 2004-05; and others. *Teaching:* From instr to assoc prof painting & drawing, Ark State Univ, 58-71, chmn div art, 65-71, dir art gallery, 67-71; prof painting & drawing & head dept art, Kans State Univ, 71-74; prof art, Univ Nebr, Lincoln, 74-96, chmn dept, 74-83, prof emer, 96-. *Awards:* Butler Institute Top Award, Nat Midyear Show, Youngstown, Ohio, 84; Hulitar Prize, Contemporary Am Painting Exhib, Palm Beach, Fla, 97; artist fel, Nebr Arts Coun, 95; and over 100 other prizes, awards and honors. *Bibliog:* In View of the Law, West Publishing Co, St Paul, Minn, 79; Dan Howard: A Retrospective: A Selection of Paintings from 1968-1982, Blanden Mem Art Mus/Sioux City Art Ctr; Christin J. Mamiya (auth), Valedictory Exhib Tribute, 97. *Mem:* Col Art Asn Am; Mid-Am Col Art Asn (vpres, 75, pres, 76, bd dir, 75-79); Nebr Art Asn (bd trustees, 74-83). *Media:* Oil Painting, Drawing. *Dealer:* Kiechel Fine Art 5733 S 34th St Lincoln NE 68516. *Mailing Add:* 2110 Heritage Pines Ct Lincoln NE 68506-2866

HOWARD, DAVID
PHOTOGRAPHER, FILMMAKER
b Brooklyn, NY. *Study:* Ohio Univ, 69-71; San Francisco Art Inst, MFA, 74; addn study with Ansel Adams, Duane Michaels, Jerry Uelsmann, Ralph Gibson, Robert Heineken, Arron Siskin & Robert Frank. *Work:* Mus Mod Art, Whitney Mus Am Art & Am Mus Nat Hist Spec Collections, NY; San Francisco Mus Mod Art; Oakland Mus, Calif; Mus Fine Arts Houston; Hirshorn Mus, Smithsonian Inst, Washington, DC; pvt collections include Mr and Mrs James Conlon, Los Angeles, Jane Roth, NY, Alex Arthur, San Francisco, Dr and Mrs Richard Stumple, San Francisco, Yoko Asano, Nagoya, Japan, Toshinori Fukrda, Tokyo, Japan, Mr and Mrs Robert Bane, Los Angeles, many others. *Exhib:* Calif Palace Legion Honor; Oakland Mus; MH de Young Mem Mus, 74; Whitney Mus Am Art; solo exhibs, Third Eye Gallery, NY, 86, Marc Richards Gallery, Los Angeles, 87, EZTV, Los Angeles, 87 & 88, G Ray Hawkins Gallery, Los Angeles, 88, Philadelphia Mus Art, 90 & Hirshhorn Mus, Smithsonian Inst, 90; Hadley Martin Gallery, San Francisco, 87; San Francisco Pub Libr System, 87; Calif State Univ, Northridge, 88; Fine Arts Mus Long Island, NY, 89; Chandler Gallery, Seattle, 91. *Collection Arranged:* 9th Century Landscapes; The Last Filipino; Head Hunters; The Figure; 64 Video Tapes about Art; The 60's; Nepal: Everest to the Sacred Hindu Shrines; Photographic Abstraction; Filipino Tribal Artifacts; English Engravings From 1877; Palawan: The Final Filipino Frontier; The Renaissance; Land Sea and Sky; The Yoruba: An Africa's Tribe's Bead Work; Antique Cameras and Photographs; Mexico: The Noble Nation; Monastery and Tribal Budhism; African Art; Catholic Icons and Art; Relics of the Reborn: Sacred Skulls; Pop Art and Beyond; Photographic Sculpture; Rural America; European Architecture; Theme Variations; Naga Artifacts and Historical Photographs; Sacred Journey: The Ganges to the Himalayas. *Pos:* Vis artist art hist, San Francisco City Col, 73; dir photog, San Francisco Ctr Visual Studies, 74-, photog instr, 73-78; dir, Art Seen (wkly cable series), San Francisco, 87-; Art Seen, New York, 89-. *Teaching:* Vis instr, City Col San Francisco; grad instr, San Francisco Art Inst. *Awards:* Black Star Syndicated Photogr, Photog Agency, NY; Purchase Award, 27th San Francisco Art Festival, City of San Francisco, 73. *Bibliog:* Flashart, 12/89; Soma Mag, No 18, 92; Art Calendar Mag, 2/95. *Media:* Photography; Video. *Publ:* The World of Tribal Art, 4/98; Filipinas Mag, 4/98; Broadcast, KMTP-32, San Francisco, 3/94; numerous TV broadcasts & weekly TV series, Art Seen; produced & directed numerous videos & films; auth, The Last Filipino, Head Hunters, 2001; Sacred Journey, The Ganges to the Himalayas, 2004. *Dealer:* Scott Nichols Gallery San Francisco CA. *Mailing Add:* c/o Visual Studies 49 Rivoli St San Francisco CA 94117

HOWARD, LINDA
SCULPTOR
b Evanston, Ill, Oct, 22, 34. *Study:* Univ Colo; Northwestern Univ; Chicago Art Inst, 53-55; Univ Denver, BA, 57; Hunter Col, New York, MA, 71; City Col New York, archit, 82. *Work:* K & B Plaza, Virlane Found, New Orleans, La; Allstate Insurance Corp, Bush Corporate Ctr, Columbus, Ohio; Zig-Zag, Col City Tampa, Fla Council, Spain, 82. *Comn:* Space Wave (aluminum), Barclays Bank, Miami, 90; Up/Over Around (5' x 15' x 8' aluminum), Tropicanna Corp, Bradenton, Fla, 90; Wall Wave (12' x 6' x 6' aluminum), Gen Servs, Miami, Fla, 91; Archway (12' x 18' x 9' aluminum), Fla Int Univ, Miami, 91; Centerpeace (aluminum), Bradley Univ, Peoria, Ill, 91. *Exhib:* One-woman exhibs, Silvermine Guild, Conn, 71 Sculpture Now Gallery, NY, 75 & 78, Northwestern Univ, Evanston, Ill, 78, Construct Gallery, Chicago, Ill, 80, Max Hutchinson Gallery, Houston, Tex, 80 & NY, 81, Heath Gallery, Atlanta, Ga, 88 & Mus Art, Ft Lauderdale, Fla, 93; New Reflections, Aldrich Mus, Ridgefield, Conn, 73; Penthouse Show, Mus Mod Art, NY; 100 Yrs, 100 Artists, Chicago Art Inst, 80; Sculpture, The Language of Scale, Bruce Mus, Greenwich, Conn, 85; Am Women, Am Art, Stamford Mus, Conn, 85; Park Sculpture, Whitney Mus, 86 & Stamford Mus, Conn, 86 & 87; Contemp Sculpture, Univ Fla, Gainesville, 87; Artpark, Art Mus, Fla Int Univ, Miami; Paris Art Int, France, 82; Sculpture, The Language of Scale, Bruce Mus, Greenwich, Conn, 85; Am Women, Am Art, Stamford Mus & Nature Ctr, Stamford, Conn, 85; Continuity and Change, The Gallery, Ringling Art Sch, Sarasota, Fla; Sculpture Fields, Kenosa Lake, NY; Contemp Sculpture from Fla Collections, Univ Gallery, Univ Fla, Gainesville, 87. *Pos:* Vis artist, Alfred Univ, NY, Bennett Col, Milbrook, NY & Colgate Univ, Hamilton, NY, 73, Potsdam State Univ, NY, 75, San Jose State Univ, Calif & Northwestern Univ, Evanston, Ill, 78; designer-model studio, Skidmore, Owings & Merrill Archits, NY, 84-85; vis artist master print prog & sculpturc, Bradley Univ, Peoria, Ill, 91. *Teaching:* Asst prof sculpture, Hunter Col, NY, 69-72 & Lehman Col, NY, 73-76; assoc prof, NY Univ, 76-77 & Hunter Col, 77-82; adj assoc prof, Univ S Fla, Tampa, 85; adj prof, Manatee Community Col, Bradenton, Fla, 89. *Awards:* NJ Cult Coun; City Univ New York Fac Res Grant, 74 & 75; Creative Artists Pub Serv Grant, NY State, 75. *Bibliog:* Doc films, Linda Howard, Sculpture, 76, Constructions Sculpture, 76 & 500 Mile Sculpture Garden, 76, Nebr Educ TV; and others. *Dealer:* David Heath Atlanta GA; Barbara Gilman Miami FL. *Mailing Add:* 330 60th St W Bradenton FL 34209

HOWARD, MILDRED
SCULPTOR
b San Francisco, Calif, 45. *Study:* Col Alameda, AA & cert(fashion arts), 77; John F Kennedy Univ, MFA (fiberworks), 85. *Work:* Oakland Mus, Calif; Wadsworth Athaneum, Hartford, Conn; Rene & Veronica di Rosa Found, Napa, Calif; Rena Bransten, San Francisco, Calif; Miami Dade Public Libr, Miami, Fla; Oakland Mus, Oakland, Calif; Rene de Rosa Art Preserve, Napa, Calif; San Francisco Int Airport, San Francisco, Calif; Wadsworth Athenaeum, Hartford, Conn. *Comn:* Pub art, San Francisco Art Comn, 90; ten works, Wash State Arts Comn, 91. *Exhib:* Solo exhibs, This Time, Dade Co Libr, Miami, 85, Transparent Views, Calif State Univ, Hayward, 87, Memory Garden, Headlands Ctr Arts, Sausalito, Calif, 91, Gallery Paule Anglim, San Francisco, 93, Nina Nielsen Gallery, Boston, 94, San Jose Mus Art, Calif, 94, Hammonds House Galleries, Atlanta, 94, Gallery Troupe Gallery, San Diego, Calif, 97, Porter Troupe Gallery, San Diego, 97; Living in Balance Traveling Exhib, Richmond Art Ctr, Calif, Mus Art, Univ Calif, Berkeley, Sci & Cult at Blackhawk, Danville, 94; Transparency and Metaphor, Calif Crafts Mus, San Francisco, 94; Breaking Traditions, Mus at Blackhawk, Danville, 94; Sharing the Dream (auth, catalog), Hampton Univ Mus, Va, 94; Contemp Collage/Assemblage, Jewett Hall Gallery, Univ Maine, Augusta, 94; 20th Anniversary Exhib, Oakland Mus, Calif, 94; Am Color, Louis Stern Fine Arts, Los Angeles, 95; group exhibs, Invitational, Portraits, Nielsen Galery, Boston, MA, 98, Boston Int Fine Art Show, Boston, MA, 99; Retrospective (with catalog), Mildred Howard: In the Line of Fire, The City Gallery, Leicester, Eng, Univ Bradford, Eng, 99. *Awards:* Fel in sculpture, Nat Endwoment for the Arts, 94-95; Rockefeller Found Grant, San Francisco Pub Art Comn at San Francisco Airport, San Francisco, 96, Calif Bellagio Center, Bellagio, Italy, 96. *Bibliog:* Sarnella Lewis (auth), Celebrations: Sights and Sounds of Being, Fisher Gallery, Univ Southern Calif, 90; Lizzetta La Falle-Collins (auth), Emerging Artists: New Expressions, Calif Afro-Am Mus, Los Angeles, 90; New World Dis(Order), Northern Calif Coun, 93; Christine Temin (auth), Art in the Frame of History, The Boston Globe, Friday, 98; Freedom Ring, Art New England, 98, 99, others. *Dealer:* Nielsen Gallery, 179 Newbury St, Boston 02116. *Mailing Add:* c/o Nielsen Gallery 179 Newbury St Boston MA 02116

HOWARTH, SHIRLEY REIFF
PUBLISHER, HISTORIAN
b Ft Benning, Ga, Oct 1, 44. *Study:* Dickinson Col, Carlisle, Pa, BA (art hist); Pa State Univ, Univ Park, MA (art hist). *Collection Arranged:* Recent Sculpture: Steven Urry, Hackley Art Mus, Muskegon, Mich, 76; C Paul Jennewein (auth, catalog), Tampa Mus, Fla. *Pos:* Asst cur, William Penn Mem Mus, Harrisburg, Pa, 69-74, cur prints, Pa Collection Fine Arts, 74-75; dir, Hackley Art Mus, Muskegon, Mich, 75-79; dir, Tampa Mus, Fla, 79-80; publ, dir & ed, Int Art Alliance, Largo, Fla, 80-; dir & ed, Humanities Exchange, Largo Fl, 80-; publ & ed, Artworld Europe, 90-; publ & ed, Art Brief, 96-. *Teaching:* Adj prof, St Leo Col, Fla, 80-87. *Mem:* Am Asn Mus; Col Art Asn; Int Coun Mus; Int Comt Exhib Exchange (secy, 89-98). *Res:* Primarily in fields of Medieval and Northern Renaissance art; history of photography, contemporary arts & architecture. *Publ:* Auth, Marcel Breuer: Concrete and The Cross, Hackley Art Mus, 79; C Paul Jennewein, Tampa Mus, 80; European Paintings, Muskegon Mus Art, 81; ed, Int Directory of Corporate Art Collections, Artnews & Int Art Alliance, 82, 83, 84, 86, 88, 90, 93, 96 & 2000; Guide to organizers of Travelling Exhibitions, Humanities Exchange, 92, 94, 96, 97, 98 & 2000

HOWAT, JOHN KEITH
CURATOR, HISTORIAN
b Denver, Colo, Apr 12, 37. *Study:* Harvard Univ, BA, 59, MA, 62. *Collection Arranged:* David Smith, Hyde Collection, 64; John F Kensett (with catalog), Am Fedn Art, 68; 19th Century America: Paintings & Sculpture (with catalog), 70, American Paintings & Sculpture, 71, Heritage of American Art: Paintings from the Collection, 75 & A Bicentennial Treasury: American Masterpieces from the Metropolitan, 76, Am Wing, Metrop Mus Art, 80; John Frederick Kensett (with catalog), 85; American Paradise: The World of the Hudson River School (with catalog), 87; Art and The Empire City: New York, 1825-1861 (with catalog), 2000. *Pos:* Cur, Hyde Collection, 62-64; asst cur Am painting, Metrop Mus Art, 67-68, assoc cur, 68-70, cur Am painting & sculpture, 70-81, chmn, Dept Am Art, 81. *Awards:* Ford Found Fel, 65; Chester Dale Fel, Metrop Mus Art, 65-67; Lawrence A Fleischman Award for scholarly excellence in the field Am art hist, Archives Am Art, Smithsonian Inst, 2000. *Mem:* Arch Am Art. *Res:* American paintings of 18th and 19th centuries, especially the Hudson River School. *Publ:* Auth, Hudson River & Its Painters, 72. *Mailing Add:* Dept Am Art Metrop Mus Art New York NY 10028

HOWE, NANCY
PAINTER
b Summit, NJ, Nov 17, 50. *Study:* Middlebury Col, Vt, AB, 1973. *Work:* Nat Mus Wildlife Art, Jackson Hole, Wyo; Leigh Yawkey Woodson Art Mus, Wausau, Wis; Ella Carothers Dunnegan Gal of Art, Bolivar, Mo; R W Norton Art Gal, Shreveport, La. *Exhib:* Birds in Art, Woodson Art Mus, Wausau, Wis, 1991-2006; Art and the Animal, Soc of Animal Artists, varied venues, 1993-2006; Artists of Am, Colo Hist Mus, Denver, Colo, 1994-2000; Great Am Artists, Cin, Ohio, 1996-2003; Wildlife Art for a New Century, Nat Mus Wildlife, Jackson, Wyo, 2000 & 2005; Int Masters of Fine Art, Int Mus of Contemp, San Antonio, TX, 2001-05; Oil Painters of Am Nat Juried Exhib, varied venues and locations, 2002-05. *Pos:* Vpres bd nominating comt, Am Acad Women Artists, 1998-. *Awards:* Int Masters Award, Int Mus Contemporary Masters of Fine Art, 2001; Grand Prize Am Nat Award of Excellence, 12th Ann Nat Exhib, Oil Painters of Am, 2003; Master Wildlife Artist, Birds in Art, Woodson Art Mus, 2005. *Bibliog:* Gussy Fauntleroy (auth), Renaissance Woman, Southwest Art Mag, 6/2003; Ken Stroud (ed), The Art of Nancy Howe, Wildscape: A Journal of Wildlife Art & Conserv, 6/2003; Kim Kiser (auth), The Sky's The Limit, Wildlife Art Mag, Jan-Feb, 2004. *Mem:* Soc Animal Artists; Am Acad of Women Artists (bd mem 2000-06 & Vpres currently); Oil Painters of Am. *Media:* Oil. *Publ:* Ill, Working with Your Woodland, Beattie Thompson Levine, 1983; contribr, The Best of Wildlife Art (1&2), 1997 & 1999 & Art from the Parks, 2000, North Light Books; contribr, Wildlife Art, Rockport Publ, 1999; contribr, Wildlife Art: Sixty Contemp Masters and their Work, Portfolio Press, 2001. *Mailing Add:* 3916 Mad Tom Rd East Dorset VT 05253

HOWE, NELSON S
DESIGNER, ASSEMBLAGE ARTIST
b Lansing, Mich, Nov 5, 35. *Study:* Univ Mich, BA, 57, MA, 61. *Work:* New Orleans Mus Fine Arts, La; Libr Collections, Mus Mod Art, NYC Pub Libr, Finch Col Mus Art & Chase Manhattan Bank Collection, NY; Univ Calif, Berkeley; and others. *Comn:* Wall I (fabric wall), comn by Mr & Mrs Keith Waldrop, Providence, RI, 68; Fur Music (installation unit), Mus Contemp Crafts, NY, 71; Fur Score (fur wall), New

Orleans Mus Fine Arts, 72. *Exhib:* One-man show, Little Gallery, Minneapolis Inst Art, Minn, 67; Fur & Feathers Show, Mus Contemp Crafts, 71; Experimental Sound, ICES Festival, London, Eng, 72; Mus Mod Art, NY; and other group & one-man shows. *Pos:* Pres & founding artist mem, bd dir, Participation Proj Found, 73-. *Teaching:* Adj instr, Parsons Sch Design, NY, 67-68; instr, NJIT, Newark, NJ, 67-74. *Awards:* 50 Best Books of the Yr Award, Am Inst Graphic Arts, 69; Intermedia Found Grant for Lab Serv, 72. *Bibliog:* Rose De Neve (auth), Art - notation - art, Print Mag, Vol 25, No 1; Source: Music Avant Garde, No 9, 72; and others. *Mem:* Nat Expressive Therapy Asoc; Nat Inst Expressive Therapy. *Publ:* Illusr, To the Sincere Reader, 68 & Body Image, 70 & co-auth, Job Art, 71, Wittenborn; illusr & auth, Daily translating systems, Circle Press (London), 71; contribr, Harpers' Mag Wraparound Sect, 5/73; and others. *Mailing Add:* 637 Carlton Ave Brooklyn NY 11238-3809

HOWELL, GEORGE
CRITIC
Pos: Writer, Wash, DC and Baltimore area art scene Art Papers, Atlanta, 94-; documentation production specialist, 2000-. *Mailing Add:* Art Papers PO Box 5748 Atlanta GA 31107

HOWELL, JAMES
PAINTER, ARCHITECT
b Kansas City, Mo, Nov 17, 35. *Study:* Univ Washington, Seattle, 74; Stanford Univ, BA, 57, BArch, 61; Nelson Art Inst, Kansas City, 76. *Work:* Pay & Save Corp, Seattle. *Exhib:* Butler Art Inst Ann, 69; Seattle Art Mus Northwest Ann, 70; Frye Art Mus Ann, Seattle, 70; Oklahoma Art Inst Ann, 71; Seattle Art Mus Rental Galllery, 73; solo exhibs, Gumps Gallery, 82, Wagner Gallery, 90, Windows Art Gallery, 92, Henry Art Gallery, 93, Univ Washington, 93, Charlotte Jackson Fine Art, 95, Sharon Traux Fine Art, 95; New Works, Henry Art Gallery, Univ Wash, Seattle, 93; and many others. *Awards:* Art Prize, Hill Sch, 53; Humanities Prize for the Arts, Stanford Univ, 61. *Bibliog:* Richard Campbell (auth), Jim Howells Good Cheer, Seattle Post Intelligencer, 10/6/74; Regina Hackett (auth), James Howell Paints on the Outer Edge of Abstraction, Seattle Post Intelligencer, 6/9/92; Lis Bensly (auth), Subtle Spaces Midway between Light, Dark, Santa Fe New Mexican, 11/10/95. *Media:* Painting, acrylic. *Publ:* Auth, James Howell Series, Sharon Truax, 95; James Howell Gradient Intervals, Gerngrosse Co, 95. *Dealer:* Charlotte Jackson Fine Art 123 E Marcy St Suite 108 Santa Fe NM 87501. *Mailing Add:* 140 Perry St 2nd Fl No 5 New York NY 10014-2364

HOWELL-COON, ELIZABETH (MITCH)
PAINTER
b Hartselle, Ala, Feb 27, 32. *Study:* Birmingham Southern Col, BA; also with Edgar Whitney, Zoltan Szabo & Charles Reid; NALL, Venice, France. *Work:* Birmingham Mus Art, Ala; Montclaire Gallery, Birmingham; Firt Nat Bank, Decatur, Ala; Southtrust Bank of Hartselle, Ala; Parkway Med Ctr, Decatur, Ala. *Comn:* Illus & cover for cook bk, Decatur Jr Serv League, Inc, 72; portraits of vpres Dan Quayle & Gov Guy Hunt by USX; Crew of Challenger, NASA Atronauts. *Exhib:* Williamsburg Art Exhib, Va, 70; Charleston Art Exhib, SC, 70; Int Platform Asn Art Exhib, Washington, 71; Ala Watercolor Soc Nat Exhib, 80; Solo Exhib, Kennedy Douglas Ctr Arts, Florence, Ala, 98. *Pos:* Dept head, Hubert Mitchell Industs, Inc, Hartselle, 49-55; owner, Howell-Baxter Gallery, Hartselle, Ala, 83- & Mitch Howell Studio, 96-. *Teaching:* Head dept fine art, Morgan Co High Sch, 64-66. *Awards:* Hannah Elliott Award, Lovemans, Birmingham, 69; Medwise Best of Show, Univ Ala, Birmingham, 98. *Bibliog:* France-Amerique, Courrier Etats-Unis, New York, 69; Huida G Lawrence (auth), article, Park East News, New York, 69; article, Aufbau, New York, 69. *Mem:* Life mem Kappa Pi (pres col chap, 53-54); founding mem Decatur Arts Coun; Decatur Art Guild (founder, actg pres, publ chmn & vpres, 67-); Ala Watercolor Soc. *Media:* Watercolor. *Specialty:* Watercolor portraits. *Interests:* travel, music. *Publ:* Illusr, Emmanuel-God With Us, 67 & Cotton Country Cooking, 72; When the Knead Rises, 93; auth & illusr, Paint a Prayer; Southern Scrumptious. *Dealer:* Mitch Howell Studio 805 Barkley St SW St Hartselle AL 35640; Emporium at Hickory Crossing 200 Railroad St SW Hartselle AL 35640. *Mailing Add:* 805 Barkley St SW Hartselle AL 35640

HOWER, ROBERT K
PHOTOGRAPHER
b Boston, Mass, Jan 9, 47. *Study:* Middlebury Col, BA(Am lit), 64; studied with Len Gittleman, Harvard; studied with Minor White, Mass Inst Technol. *Work:* Mus Fine Arts, Boston; Mus Mod Art, NY; ICP Midtown, NY; JB Speed Mus, Louisville, Ky. *Comn:* Photog, Polaroid, New Orleans, 80; photog, Flat Iron Bldg, pvt comn, NY, 83; photog oil indust, Polaroid, Houston, 81. *Exhib:* Mus Fine Arts, Boston, 74; JB Speed Art Mus, Louisville, 76; Minn Mus Art, St Paul, 79; Nat Mus Am Art, St Paul, 85; Everson Mus Art, Syracuse, 85; Images, Cincinnati, 86; Zephyr Gallery, Louisville, 89; one-man shows, Robert B Menschel Gallery, 87, OK Harris Mus, 89, JB Speed Art Mus, 89, Cheekwood Fine Arts Ctr, 91, Photog Archives, 92, Galerie Hertz, 92 & 95. *Pos:* Co-founder, Quadrant, Jeffersonville, Ind, 86-. *Teaching:* Photog, Wright State Univ, 74-78. *Awards:* Residency, Light Work, Syracuse, NY, 81; Ohio Arts Coun Individual Artist's Fel, 83 & 85; Nat Endowment Arts Individual Artist's Grant, 90-91. *Bibliog:* Stern Mag, 3/86; Ohio Mag, 1/87, 2/87, 11/87, 1/88 & 11/90; Am Photogr, 10/89. *Publ:* Auth, Photography Year 1981, Time-Life, 81; Exposed & Developed, Smithsonian Inst Press, 84; many articles in, Bus Week, Fortune Mag, Stern, 86, Ohio Mag, 87, 88 & 90 & Am Photog, 89. *Mailing Add:* 2119 Highland Ave Louisville KY 40204

HOWES, ROYCE BUCKNAM
PAINTER
b Mt Clemens, Mich, Sep 20, 50. *Study:* RI Sch of Design, BFA, 73; Skowhegan Sch of Painting & Sculpture, 74; Tyler Sch Art, MFA, 77. *Work:* Metrop Mus Art, NY; Univ Tenn, Knoxville; Kans State Univ, Manhattan. *Bibliog:* Wayne Toepp (auth), The Image Combines of Royce Howes, Arts Mag, 1/88. *Media:* Oil. *Dealer:* Grace Borgenicht Gallery 724 Fifth Ave New York NY. *Mailing Add:* 5 Fourth St Apt 10 Brooklyn NY 11231-4558

HOWETT, JOHN
HISTORIAN, CRITIC
b Kokomo, Ind, Aug 7, 26. *Study:* John Herron Inst, BFA; Univ Chicago, MA, 62, PhD, 68. *Collection Arranged:* Kress Study Collection Notre Dame (auth, catalog), 62; Renaissance Illuminations (auth, catalog), High Mus Art, Atlanta, 74; Twelve in Atlanta (auth, catalog), 79. *Teaching:* Asst prof & cur collections, Univ Notre Dame, 61-66; assoc prof Renaissance & mod art, Emory Univ, 66-80, prof, 80-96, chair dept hist art, 73-96; prof, Art & Hist, Emer, currently. *Awards:* Emory Teaching Award, 82; Emory Alumni award of distinction, 2002. *Mem:* Col Art Asn; Southeastern Art Conf. *Res:* Italian and Northern Renaissance painting and sculpture; contemporary art and culture. *Interests:* Art and Hist. *Publ:* Auth, Two panels by the master of the St George Codex in the Cloisters, Metrop Mus J, Vol 11, 85-102; Boondocks Bohemias: A case for the regional avant-garde, Contemp Art/SE, Vol 1, 77; coauth, Martin Emanuel, High Mus Art, 80; Carl Andre, Heath Gallery Art, 83; Woodcuts by Albrecht Durer, Emory Univ Mus, 86. *Mailing Add:* 1636 Ridgewood Dr NE Atlanta GA 30307

HOWLAND, RICHARD HUBBARD
ARCHITECTURAL HISTORIAN
b Providence, RI, Aug 23, 1910. *Study:* Brown Univ, AB, 31; Harvard Univ, AM, 33; Johns Hopkins Univ, PhD, 46; Brown Univ, Hon DArts, 62. *Pos:* Fel Agora Athens, Greece, 36-38; chief pictorial rec sect, OSS, 43-44; pres, Nat Trust Hist Preserv, 56-60; chmn dept civil hist, Smithsonian Inst, 60-67, spec asst to secy, 68-85; founding mem, Am Comt Int Comn Hist Sites & Monuments; trustee, Sotterley Fund & Evergreen Found. *Teaching:* Instr, Wellesley Col, 39-42; organizer dept hist art, Johns Hopkins Univ, 47, chmn dept, 47-56. *Awards:* Athenaeum of Philadelphia Fel; Royal Soc of Arts Fel, London. *Mem:* Fel US Int Coun Monuments & Sites; Soc Archit Historians; Irish Georgian Soc (trustee); Archaeol Inst Am; Am Sch Classical Studies, Athens (trustee). *Publ:* Coauth, Architecture of Baltimore, 54; auth, Greek Lamps & Their Survivals, 58 & 66. *Mailing Add:* 3900 Cathedral Ave NW Washington DC 20016-5201

HOWLETT, D(ONALD) ROGER
ART DEALER, HISTORIAN
b Syracuse, NY, 45. *Study:* Hamilton Col, NY, BA, 66; State Univ NY, Cooperstown, grad prog, MA, 67; Yale Univ, PhD prog, art hist. *Exhib:* D Roger Howlett: Watercolors, Monotypes, Oil Paintings, St Botolph Club, Boston, 3/27/2006-5/8/2006. *Collection Arranged:* George Luks (auth, catalog), 73-74 & Molly Luce: Eight Decades of the American Scene (auth, catalog), 83, Childs Gallery, Boston. *Pos:* Vpres, Childs Gallery, Boston, 73-83, pres, Childs Gallery, NY, 83-91, Boston, 83-. *Mem:* Antiquarian Booksellers Asn Am; Internat Fine Print Dealers Asn; Emerson Gallery, Hamilton Col, NY (bd adv, currently); Lyme Acad Fine Arts (trustee, 93-2002); New England String Ensemble (dir, vpres, 2004-05, pres, 2005-); Boston Athenaeum (proprietor); Harvard Musical Asn; St Botolph Club. *Media:* Watercolor. *Res:* 19th and 20th century American artists, including Molly Luce, I M Gaugengigl, Laura Hills, Donald De Lue and George Luks. *Specialty:* American and European paintings, prints and drawings, 16th to mid 20th centuries; 19th and 20th century realist sculpture; Japanese prints and China Trade paintings. *Publ:* The Sculpture of Donald De Lue: Gods, Prophets, and Heroes, David R Godine, 90; American Figurative Sculpture of the Thirties: A Rebirth in Bronze, The Journal of Decorative and Propaganda Arts, No 16, 90; William Partridge Burpee: American Marine Impressionist, Northeastern Univ Press, 91; The Lynn Beach Painters, Lynn Hist Soc, 98; Gertrude Beals Bourne: Artist in Brahmin Boston, Northeastern Univ Press, 2004. *Mailing Add:* Childs Gallery 169 Newbury St Boston MA 02116-2895

HOWLETT, RAY
PAINTER
b Lincoln, Nebr, Aug 6, 40. *Study:* Univ of Nebr, BFA, 1963. *Work:* Frederick R Weisman Art Found, Los Angeles, Calif; Mus of Science, Boston, Mass; Mus of Neon Art, Los Angeles, Calif; Midwest Mus of Am Art, Elkhart, Indiana; West Valley Art Mus, Surprise, Ariz. *Comn:* Electric Light & Glass, Zerox Corp, Webster, NY, 2005; Electric Light & Glass, UDS Uniphase, Santa Rosa, Calif, 1980. *Exhib:* Dichroism in Light, Midwest Mus of Am Art, Elkhart, Ind, 2001; Ray Howlett, Light, Masur Art Mus, Dothan, Ala, 2002; Dichroil Color, Electric Light, Blanden Mem Art Mus, Ft Dodge IA, 2003; Glass Sculpture, Nat Liberty Mus, Philadelphia, Pa, 2004. *Bibliog:* Space-Age Artwork, Lincoln J Star, 8/23/1996; Light as a Plaything, NY Times, 2/14/1999; Inner Light, So Bend Tribune, 8/1/2001. *Media:* Misc Media. *Mailing Add:* 4230 W St Lincoln NE 68503

HOWZE, JAMES DEAN
DRAFTSMAN, WRITER, ASSEMBLAGE ARTIST
b Lubbock, Tex, Apr 8, 30. *Study:* Austin Col, BA; Art Ctr Col Design; Univ Mich, MS. *Work:* Del Mar Col, Corpus Christi; Hobbs Pub Schs, NMex; San Antonio Col; San Diego State Univ, Calif; Trenton State Col, NJ. *Exhib:* Two Smithsonian Inst Traveling Exhibs, US & Can, 79-82; Am Drawing II & III, Portsmouth, Va, 79 & 81; Nat Small Works Exhib, Schoharie Co, NY, 83; Toys Designed by Artists, 12th Ann Exhib, Ark Arts Ctr, Little Rock, 84; Nat Drawing Asn, Hermitage Found Mus, Norfolk, 88, CW Post Ctr, Long Island Univ, NY, 89 & Md Inst Col Art, Baltimore,

92; Nat Drawing Asn (various venues), Trenton State Col; Col et al, Fine Arts Festival Gallery, Lubbock Arts Alliance, 2003 & 04. *Pos:* Prof Emer, col Fine Arts, Tex Tech Univ, currently. *Teaching:* Assoc prof, Dept Archit & Allied Arts, Tex Tech Univ, 58-68, prof studio art, Dept Art, 68-92, dir core curric, 79-87, assoc chmn, 88-91. *Awards:* Cash Awards, Nat Drawing & Small Sculpture Exhib, Del Mar Col, 70, 74, 78 & 81; Best in Exhib, Nat Mensa Mem Exhib, 71; Nat Digital Art Exhib, E Tenn State Univ, 97; and others. *Mem:* Hon mem Dallas-Ft Worth Soc Visual Commun; Lubbock Arts Alliance Asn; Tex Asn Schs Art. *Media:* Charcoal Pencil; Mixed Media, Assemblage. *Interests:* Choral music, poetry writing; Firearms (post 1873). *Publ:* Contribr, cartoons & humorous verse, Sports Car Graphic, 65-66; poet & illusr, Images from the High Plains, Staked Plains Press, Canyon, Tex, 79; drawing, Cheatham, Cheatham & Haler, Design Concepts and Applications, Prentice Hall, p 86, 83; drawing, Frank M Young, Visual Studies, Prentice-Hall, p 86, 85; auth & illusr, Creating and Understanding Drawings, Mittler & Howze, Glencoe, 89. 94, 2001 & 2005. *Mailing Add:* 2503 45th St Lubbock TX 79413

HOY, HAROLD H
SCULPTOR

b Spokane, Wash, May 16, 41. *Study:* Central Wash Univ, BA, 65; Univ Oregon, MFA(painting), 67, MFA(sculpture), 69. *Exhib:* Solo exhibs: Univ Oregon Art Mus, Eugene, 79, William Sawyer Gallery, San Francisco, Calif, 79, Blackfish Gallery, Portland, Ore, 81 & Univ Northern Iowa, Cedar-Falls, 89; The Animal Image, Smithsonian Mus, Washington, DC, 81; Animals, Celebration, Communion, San Jose Mus, Calif, 81; Oregon Biennial Exhib, Portland Art Mus, Ore, 81; Quartersaw Gallery, Portland, Ore, 91, 93 & 95. *Pos:* Gallery Dir, Lane Community Col, 70-. *Teaching:* Instr art, Lane Community Col, 70-. *Awards:* Fel Oregon Arts Comn, 71 & 77. *Bibliog:* Jean Cutler (auth), Sculpture of the Pacific Northwest: A Photographic Essay, Univ Ore Press; Thelma R Newman (auth), Encyclopedia of Woodworking, Crown Publ; 2nd Biennial Book, Fine Woodworking Mag. *Mem:* Col Art Asn. *Media:* Sculptor. *Dealer:* Quartersaw Gallery 528 NW 12th Ave Portland OR; Linda Cannon Gallery 520 Second Ave Seattle WA. *Mailing Add:* Lane Community College Art Gallery 4000 E 30th Ave Eugene OR 97405

HOYT, ELLEN
ASSEMBLAGE ARTIST, LECTURER

b Brooklyn, NY, Nov 8, 33. *Study:* Pratt Inst, 53; Brooklyn Mus & Mus Nat Hist, 65-75 & 83; with Ed Whitney, Frank Webb, Jankowski DeStefano & Ernest Chrichlow. *Work:* Gateway Nat Recreation Area, NY; Austrian Lender Bank; Stuhr Mus Prarie, NB; Griplock Corp; Health Hosp Corp, NY. *Comn:* Painting, Sierra Club for Gateway Nat Park, NY, 82; British Consulate Gen, 92. *Exhib:* Lever House, NY, 85; Fed Bldg NY, 89; Pam Am Bldg, NY, 91; Metrotech, Brooklyn, 92; Cornell Med Ctr Libr, NY, 97; Dag Hammer Kjold Tower Condo Gallery, 98; Adlephi Univ Gallery, 98. *Pos:* Instr, consult auth & juror, Nat Contemp Expos Artists Archievement, Fed Bldg, NYC, 87; Dir, art, Salt Marsh Nature Ctr, currently. *Teaching:* Instr art, Kingsway Acad, 70-75, Studio Dragonette, 77-80 & Unger Studios, 83-90; Hemlock Farms Art Soc, 88-92; Brand Studio, 91-93; Sierra Art Club Inst, 93-98; Watercolor Art Soc, 94-. *Awards:* Best in Show, Brooklyn Mus, 80; Travel Award, Washington Sq Outdoor Art Exhib, 81; Pilots Club Award, 83, 4th prize 87 & Landscape Award, 90. *Bibliog:* Emanuel Stromm (auth), Profile of an artist, Courier, 82; Eve Wilen (auth), New Exciting Approach, NY Artists Equity, 82. *Mem:* Artists Equity, NY; Visual Individualist; Brooklyn Watercolor Soc (secy, 79-86); Am Artist Prof League; Assoc Am Watercolor Soc. *Media:* Watercolor. *Specialty:* White Silo Gallery; Metropolitan Transit Authority Gallery, NY. *Interests:* Hiking, reading & people. *Publ:* Auth, Flare Printing, 75; Mariner, Flare Printing, 75; Never on Sunday Cookbook, Peerless Press, 70; NY Art Review, 88, 89; Sierra Club Periodical, 88-92. *Mailing Add:* 1551 E 29th St Brooklyn NY 11229

HSIAO, CHIN
PAINTER, SCULPTOR

b Shanghai, China, 1935. *Study:* Taipei Normal Col, BA; with Li Chun-Sen, Taipei, Taiwan. *Work:* Mus Mod Art & Metrop Mus Art, NY; Nat Gallery Mod Art, Rome, Italy; Philadelphia Mus Art; Detroit Inst Art; Mus de Arte Mod, Barcelona; Art Gallery Ont; Taiwan Mus Art, Taichung. *Comn:* Mural, Mr S Marchetta, Messina, Sicily, 71. *Exhib:* Carnegie Inst, Pittsburgh, 61; Int Malerei 1960/61, W Eschenbach, 61; Art Contemporain, Grand Palais, Paris, 63; 7th Biennial, Sao Paulo, Brazil, 63; 4th Salon Galeries-Pilotes, Lausanne, Switz & Paris, 70; Quadriennale Naz di Roma, 77. *Collection Arranged:* more than 40 internat mus worldwide. *Pos:* Prof artistic anat, Urbino Fine Arts Acad, Italy, 83-84; prof decoration, Turin Fine Arts Acad, Italy, 84-85; prof printmaking, Milan Fine Arts Acad, Italy, 85-96; prof creative art, Nat Taiwan Arts Col, 96-97. *Teaching:* Instr art, Southampton Col, Long Island Univ, 69; prof visual commun, Inst Europ Design, Milan, Italy, 71-72; vis artist, La State Univ, Baton Rouge, 72-. *Awards:* City of Capo d'Orlando, Italy Prize, 70; Gold Medal, Norwey Print Biennial, 84; First achievement Award Contemp Painting, Li Chun-Shen Found, Taipei, 89; Award for Nat Vis Prize from Taiwan Nat Art, 2002; Decorated by Italian Presidency, the Order of Knight of Italian Solidarity Star, 2005. *Bibliog:* W Schonenberger (auth), Hsiao, Prearo, 72; La Via Di Hsiao, Nuova Foglio, 78, Hsiao, Vanessa, 79; Hsiao Chin, Monography, Mazzotta ed, Milan, 88; and others. *Media:* Acrylic, Ink; Ceramic. *Res:* Spirituality in art. *Publ:* Retrospective, print portfolio, Milan, 63; Oh Che Vertigine, poems & prints, Milan, 66; Un processo di penetrazione, lithograph collection, Milan, 72; Ch'an, prints portfolio, Milan, 77. *Dealer:* Giorgio Marconi 15 Via Tadino Milan Italy; Lin/Keng Gallery, Taipei. *Mailing Add:* Via G Modena 35 Milan 20129 Italy

HU, CHI CHUNG
PAINTER

b Chekiang, China, Jan 27, 27. *Study:* Self-taught. *Exhib:* Bienal Sao Paulo, Mus Art Modern, Brazil, 59, 61, 63 & 67; Fifth Moon Group Exhib, Honolulu Acad Arts, 71, Taft Mus, Cincinnati, 71 & Arts Club Chicago, 74; Contemp Chinese Paintings & Prints, Denver Art Mus, 73; Pittsburgh Int Exhib, Mus Art, Carnegie Inst, Pa, 67; Now Current Show, Smithsonian Inst, Washington, 68; Sangre de Cristo Arts & Conf Ctr, Pueblo, Colo, 83; one-man shows, Fine Arts Gallery, San Diego, 73, Nat Mus Hist, Taipei, Taiwan, 86, Ming Ren Art Gallery, Taiwan, 89, Gauguin Gallery, Taiwan, 90 & Contemp Gallery, Taiwan; and others. *Bibliog:* The Imagery of Hu, Chi-Chung, Heritage Press, 62; Hu, Paintings by the Contemporary Artist, Nat Taiwan Arts Ctr, 67; Five Chinese Artists, Nat Mus Hist, 70. *Media:* Oil. *Dealer:* Zantman Art Gallery Box 5818 Carmel CA 93921

HU, MARY LEE
GOLDSMITH, EDUCATOR

b Lakewood, Ohio, Apr 13, 43. *Study:* Miami Univ, Oxford, Ohio, 61-63; Sch for Am Craftsmen, Rochester Inst Technol, with Hans Christensen; Cranbrook Acad Art, Bloomfield Hills, Mich, BFA, 65, with Richard Thomas; Southern Ill Univ, MFA, 67, with Brent Kington. *Work:* Mus Contemp Crafts, NY; Renwick Gallery, Washington; Yale Univ Art Gallery, New Haven, Conn; Art Inst Chicago; Victoria & Albert Mus, London; Mus Fine Arts, Boston; Tacoma Art Mus, Wash. *Exhib:* 4th Int Jewelry Art Exhib, Mikimoto, Tokyo, 79; Goldsmith '78, Schmuck Mus, Pfortzheim, Ger & touring 8 Europ countries, 79-80; Silver in Am Life, Carnegie Inst, Pittsburgh & touring US, 79-81; Good as Gold, Renwick Gallery & touring US & S Am, 81-84; Jewelry USA, Am Craft Mus, NY & touring US, 84-85; Am Jewelry Now, Am Craft Mus & touring Asia, 85-87; Craft Today: Poetry of the Physical, touring US, 86-88; Korean Am Contemp Metalwork Exhib, Seoul, Korea, 88; Craft Today USA, Touring Europe, 89-92; 6 NW Jewelers, Seattle Art Mus, 93; and many others. *Teaching:* Vis artist metalsmithing, Univ Iowa, Iowa City, fall 75; lectr, Univ Wis, Madison, 76-77; asst prof, Mich State Univ, East Lansing, 77-80; assoc prof metal design, Univ Wash, Seattle, 80-85, prof, 85-2006. *Awards:* Nat Endowment Arts Craftmen's Fel, 76, 84 & 92; Alumni Achievement Award, Southern Ill Univ, Carbondale, 88; Master of the Medium Award, James Renwick Alliance, Washington, DC, 98; Flintridge Found Award for Vis Arts, 2001-02; Univ Wash Peterson Fel, 2002. *Bibliog:* Carolyn Benesh (auth), Mary Lee Hu, Ornament, spring 83; Karen Du Priest (auth), Craft into art: Mary Lee Hu takes gold & silver jewelry in a new direction, Connoisseur, 10/86; Annette Mahler (auth), Mary Lee Hu: The purpose and persistence of wire, Metalsmith, winter 89. *Mem:* Soc North Am Goldsmiths (vpres, 76-77, pres, 77-80); Fel Am Crafts Coun (craftsman trustee, 80-84); Northwest Designer Craftsmen; Seattle Metals Guild. *Media:* Silver, Gold Wire. *Res:* history of body adornment. *Publ:* Contribr, Body Jewelry--International Perspectives, Henry Regnery, 73; Wire Art, Crown, 75; Jewelry Concepts & Technology, Doubleday, 82; Artists at Work, Alaska NW Bks, 90; Contemporary American Jewelry Design, Van Nostrand Reinhold, 91; Textile Techniques in Metal, Altahont Press, rev ed, 96. *Dealer:* Facere Jewelry Art Seattle WA; Mobilia Gallery, Cambridge MA,. *Mailing Add:* PO Box 16508 Seattle WA 98116-0508

HUANG, FRANK C
COLLECTOR

b Nov, 49. *Study:* Pysics, Nat Taiwan Univ, BA; 71; PhD, Mount Sinai Sch Medicine, New York City, 78. *Pos:* Founder, UMAX Data Systs Inc, 87-, chmn, currently; founder, Powerchip Semiconductor Corp (PSC), 94-, chmn, currently; chmn, Taiwan Semiconductor Industry Asn; pres, Taipei Computer Asn. *Awards:* Named one of Top 200 Collectors, ARTnews Mag, 2004. *Collection:* Chinese porcelain, Impressionist and modern paintings. *Mailing Add:* UMAX Data Systems Inc 8F 68 Sec 3 Nanking E Rd Taipei Taiwan

HUBBARD, JOHN
PAINTER

b Ridgefield, Conn, Feb 26, 31. *Study:* Harvard Univ, Cambridge, Mass, AB, 53; Art Students League, New York, study with Morris Kantor, 56-58; study painting with Hans Hofmann, Provincetown, Mass. *Work:* Tate Gallery, London, England; Scottish Nat Gallery Mod Art, Edinburgh; Arts Coun Great Brit, London; Arts Coun Northern Ireland, Belfast; Australian Nat Gallery, Melbourne; and others; Penna Acad Fine Arts; Phila Mus Art. *Comn:* Midsummer, 83 & Sylvia, 85, Royal Opera House, Covent Garden, London; Wadderdon Manor, UK, 99; Said Business Sch, Oxford, 2005. *Exhib:* Brit Colour (SAm tour), Brit Coun, 78-79; one-man shows, Fischer Fine Art, London, 79, 81, 88, 91 & Warwick Arts Trust, London, 81; Mus Mod Art, Oxford, 85; Yale Ctr Brit Art, 86; Purdy Hicks Gallery, London, 94 & 96; Scottish Paintings, UK Tour, 96; Marlborough Fine Art, 2000 & 2004. *Pos:* Mem, Coun Mgt, SPACE/AIR, London, 71-75; collabr, Mark Rothko Mem Portfolio, London, 73; chmn, Art Panel, Southwest Arts, Exeter, Devon, 73-75; mem, Arts Panel, Arts Coun Great Brit, London, 73-78; consult, J Sainsbury Ltd, 79-81; adv, Tate Gallery, St Ives, 93-98. *Teaching:* Vis painting instr, Camberwell Sch Art, London, 63-65. *Awards:* Jerwood Prize, 96. *Bibliog:* Hubbard's Search, Art Int, 78-79; article, Times, London, 2/81; Jeff Dunlop (dir), film, London Weekend Television, 3/81; Journey of John Hubburd, Douglas Hall, 96. *Publ:* Portrait of New Harmony, 89. *Dealer:* Marlborough Fine Art 6 Albemarle St London WIX. *Mailing Add:* Chilcombe Chilcombe NR Bridport Dorset DT6 4PN Britain United Kingdom

HUBBARD, TERESA
FILMMAKER

b Dublin, Ireland, 65. *Study:* Univ Tex, Austin, BFA; attended, Skowhegan Sch Painting & Sculpture, 87; Yale Univ, MFA (sculpture), 88; Nova Scotia Col Art & Design, Halifax, MFA, 92. *Work:* Columbus Mus Art, OH; Neues Mus, Nuremberg, Ger; Ulrich Mus Art, Wichita, Kans; Yokohama Mus Art, Japan; and numerous other works. *Exhib:* solo shows, Slow Place, Mus Fur Gegenwartskunst Basel, 97; Stripping, Kunstlerhaus Bethanien, Berlin, 98; Gregor's Room, Gallery Bob van Orsouw, Zurich, 99; Motion Pictures, Gallery Barbara Thumm, Berlin, 99; County Line Road, 2003; Arsenal, Bonakdar Jancou Gallery, NY, 2000; Tanya Bonakdar Gallery, NY, 2002; ArtPace Found Contemp Art, San Antonio, Tex, 2002; Single Wide, Whitney Mus Am Art, NY, 2004; Editing the Dark, Kemper Mus Contemp Art, Kansas City, 2005; Little Pictures at Mrs Owens House, Centro Galego de Artr Contemporanea, Santiago de Compostela, 2005; House with Pool, Miami Art Mus, 2006; Galerie Barbara Thumm, Berlin, 2006; group shows, Nonchalance Revisited, Akademie der Kunste, Berlin, 98; Solitude in Budapest, Kunsthalle, Budapest, 99; Every Time, La Biennale de Montreal, 2000; New Work, Tanya Bonakdar Gallery, NY, 2001; Out of Place: Contemp Art & The Architectural Uncanny, Mus Contemp Art, Chicago, 2002; Adolescence, Reina Sofia Mus, Madrid, 2003; Eight, Centre Culturel Suisse, Paris, 2004; Swiss Experimental Film, Image Forum, Tokyo, 2005; Roaming Memories, Ludwig Forum, Aachen, 2005; Melancholy, Nationalgalerie, Berlin, 2006; Picture Ballot, Kunsthaus, Zurich, 2006; Raised by Wolves, Art Gallery Western Australia, Perth, 2006. *Teaching:* lectr various univs & insts, 92-; prof, dept Art & Art History, Univ Tex, Austin, 2000-; core fac mem, Milton Avery Grad Sch Arts, Bard Col, NY, 2004-. *Bibliog:* Dora Imhof (auth), Teresa Hubbard & Alexander Birchler, House with Pool, Kunstforum, Vol 161, 3-4/2004, 504-505; Amoreen Armetta (auth), Teresa Hubbard/Alexander Birchler, Flash Art, 1/2005, 69; Rene Morales (auth), Teresa Hubbard & Alexander Birchler, MAM Portrait: Miami Art Mus, Miami, 7-9/2006, 6; and many others. *Mailing Add:* c/o Tanya Bonakdar Gallery 521 W 21st St New York NY 10011

HUBERT, ANNE M
CURATOR, COLLECTOR
Study: Boston Mus Fine Art, spec studies, with Claude Croney & King Coffin. *Exhib:* James Fitzgerald 1898-1971, Hopkins Ctr, Dartmouth Col, Hanover, NJ, 75, Mead Gallery, Amherst Col, Mass, 76, Ctr Visual Arts, Antioch Col, Columbia, Md, 77, Danforth Mus, Framingham, Mass, 77, Monterey Peninsula Mus Art, Calif, 79 & 85, Mass Col Art, Boston, 80, Farnsworth Mus, Rockland, Maine, 84, DeCordova Mus, Lincoln, Mass, 85, Portland Mus Art, Maine, 92 & Plattsburgh Art Mus, NY, 92; Mass Col Art, Boston, 97; St Botolph Club, Boston, Mass, 97; Susquehanna Univ, Selens Grove, Pa, 97. *Pos:* Cur, James Fitzgerald Collection, James Fitzgerald Mem Studio, Monhegan, Maine, 71-. *Mem:* Hon charter mem Steinbeck Ctr Found; Portland Mus Art; Boston Mus Fine Arts; Farnsworth Libr & Art Mus. *Collection:* Twentieth century watercolors, oils and prints. *Publ:* Auth, Legacy of beauty, Kent Collector, 76; auth, Recollections of the Artist, Fitzgerald Mem Studio, 77. *Mailing Add:* PO Box 1813 Windermere FL 34786-1813

HUBSCHMITT, WILLIAM E
EDUCATOR, ADMINISTRATOR
b NJ, May 23, 49. *Study:* Sate Univ NY, Binghamton, PhD, 84. *Exhib:* Nat Computer Art Invitational, Univ Wash, Spokane, 90; William Hubschmitt Recent Work, Canovassio, Rome, Italy, 94; Figure Painting Digital Works, Mus Hartwick, Oneonta, NY, 95; S Ill Nat, Mitchell Art Mus, Mt Vernon, 97. *Teaching:* State Univ NY, Oneonta, 82-96; chmn & asst prof art hist & computer art, E Ill Univ, Charleston, 96-. *Awards:* Best in Media, S Ill Nat, Mitchell Art Mus, 95. *Media:* Computer art. *Res:* Dutcy Baroque - genre and artist in studio images. *Publ:* Auth, Distorted View of Delft, Apocrypha, Binghamton Univ Press, fall 80; Intro to Andrea Modica (exhib catalog), Miami-Dade Community Col Art Mus, 89; Art History and the Computer in Liberal Arts Environment, Univ Vt, 92; Figure Painting Works by Bill Hubschmitt (CD Rom), Hartwick Col, 95. *Mailing Add:* 819 Jackson Charleston IL 61920

HUCHTHAUSEN, DAVID RICHARD
SCULPTOR, EDUCATOR
b Wisconsin Rapids, Wis, 51. *Study:* Univ Wis, BS, study with Harvey K Littleton; Ill State Univ, MFA, study with Joel Philip Myers; Vienna Univ of Applied Arts (Fulbright scholar). *Work:* Hokkaido Mus Art, Saporro, Japan; Smithsonian Inst; Metrop Mus Art, NY; Musee du Verre, Liege, Belg; Art Mus, Dusseldorf, Ger; Mus Fine Arts, Lausanne, Switz; Corning Mus of Glass, NY; High Mus Art, Atlanta; Los Angeles Co Mus Art; and many others. *Comn:* Sculpture, Hospital Corp Am, 85. *Exhib:* Lake Superior Int Crafts Exhib, Tweed Mus Art, Duluth, Minn, 75-77; New Glass, Corning Mus Traveling Exhib, 79-81; Huntsville Mus, Ala, 81; solo exhibs, Habatat Galleries, 75-94, St Louis Art Mus, Missouri, 85 & Mus Contemp Photogr, Chicago, 85; Corning Mus, NY, 90; Naples Mus Art, Fla, 93; Tamayo Mus Art, Monteray, Mex, 93; Mus of the South, Ala, 93; Toledo Mus Art, Ohio, 93; Birmingham Mus Art, Ala, 94; and others. *Pos:* Consult, Woodson Art Mus, Wausau, Wis, 77-; vis artist, J & L Lobmeyr, Vienna, 77-78; design dir, Milropa Studios, New York, 79-80. *Teaching:* Instr glass, Ill State Univ, Normal, 76-77; lectr glass, Royal Col Art, London, 78; assoc prof, Tenn Tech Univ, 80-90. *Awards:* Newberry Award, Univ Wis, 73; Elizabeth Stein Fel, Ill State Univ, 76; Nat Endowment Arts Grant, 82. *Bibliog:* Cover article, Neues Glas, Eng/Ger ed, 9/83; Sidney Goldstein (auth), Huchthausen, solo exhib catalog, St Louis Mus Art, 84; Robert Silverman (auth), cover article, Am Craft, 9/87. *Mem:* Am Craft Coun; Glass Art Soc. *Media:* Glass, Light. *Publ:* Auth, Americans in Glass, Marathon Press, 81 & 84. *Dealer:* Leo Kaplan Mod 965 Madison Ave New York NY 90021. *Mailing Add:* 3911 Airport Way S Seattle WA 98108

HUDDY, MARGARET TERESA
PAINTER, PHOTOGRAPHER, ILLUSTRATOR, WRITER
b Philadelphia, Pa, July 4, 39. *Study:* Moore Col Art, Philadelphia, Pa, 57-59; Monterey Peninsula Col, Monterey, Calif, 64-66. *Work:* Supreme Court US, Washington; US Dept State, US Embassy, Botswana, Africa; Texaco, Inc, Harrison, NY; Am Dental Asn, Washington; Marriott Corp, Washington. *Comn:* The Evening Parade (painting), USMC, 83; paintings-5 DC monuments, Am Security Bank, Washington, 88; Farragut Square (painting), Palmer Nat Bank, Washington, 89; The Supreme Court (painting), Supreme Court Hist Soc, Washington, 92; The Capitol (painting), Allied Capital Corp, Washington, 93. *Exhib:* Nat Midyear Exhib, Butler Inst Am Art, Youngstown, Ohio, 85; Nat Watercolor Soc, Brea Cult Ctr, Calif, 93; Irene Leach Mem Exhib, Chrysler Mus, Norfolk, Va, 94; Am Watercolor Soc, Salmagundi Club, NY, 94; Okla Watercolor Soc, Kirkpatrick Ctr Mus, Oklahoma City, Okla, 94; solo-exhibs, Carnegie Mus Art, Oxnard, Calif, 96, Walter Wickiser Gallery, NY, 96 & Ellen Noel Mus, Odessa, Tex, 97; Butler Inst Am Art, Youngstown Ohio, 99, 2000; Watercolor USA, Springfield Art Mus, Mo, 2000; Foxhall Gallery, 2002, 03; Butler Inst of Am Art, Youngstown, Ohio, 2001, 06. *Collection Arranged:* Nat Park Serv; Carnegie Mus of Art; Supreme Court of US; Nat Cathedral, Washington, DC. *Pos:* residency, Dinan, France, 2006. *Teaching:* Elem art teacher, Marymount Jr Sch, Arlington, Va, 69-76; art teacher adult educ, Coastal Carolina Community Col, 78-80, Fairfax Co Pub Sch, 80-85, Art League Sch, Alexandria, Va, 92-; Art League Sch, Alexandria, Va, 92-; prof watercolor Corcoran Col Art and Design, Washington, DC, 98-. *Awards:* Award of Excellence, La Watercolor Soc, 89; Aaron Bros-Strathmore Excellence Award, Nat Watercolor Soc, 91; CFS Medal, Am Watercolor Soc, 94; Open Exhib Award, Annandale, Va, 98; Southern Watercolor Soc Award, 99; Va Watercolor Soc, 2002; Watercolor USA, 2003; Nat Watercolor Soc, 2004. *Bibliog:* Ginny Baier (auth), The Color Red, Watercolor/94, Am Artist, 94; Best of Watercolor, Rockport Publ, 95; Ginny Baier (auth), The Color White, Watercolor/95, Am Artist, fall 95. *Mem:* signature mem Nat Watercolor Soc; signature mem Am Watercolor Soc; signature mem Pa Watercolor Soc; Watercolor USA Hon Soc. *Media:* Watercolor. *Specialty:* Foxhall Gallery - Realism. *Publ:* auth, The Color of Light, Watercolor Magic/Artist's Mag, winter 97; auth, Sharing the Joy, Watercolor Magic, 2002; Ship to Shore, Artist's Sketchbook, 2002; Exaggerate Reality, Artists Mag, 2003; auth, Secrets to Plein Air Painting, Artists Mag, 9-2006. *Dealer:* Foxhall Galler, Washington, DC. *Mailing Add:* 105 N Union St No 203 Alexandria VA 22314

HUDSON, EDWARD RANDALL
PATRON
b Ft Worth, Tex, July 24, 1934. *Study:* Univ Tex, BA, 1955; Harvard Univ, JD, 1958; Phi Beta Kappa. *Pos:* Owner, oil producer, Hudson Oil, Ft Worth; vchmn, cult property comt, US Info Agency; bd dir, Kimbell Art Found, Aspen Ctr Physics; sect bd dir, Burnett Found; chmn, bd dir, Modern Art Mus Ft Worth, formerly; nat comt, founding co-chmn bd dir, Aspen Art Mus. *Mem:* River Crest Country Club; Ft Worth Club; Order of the Alamo. *Mailing Add:* 55 Westover Terrace Fort Worth TX 76107-3106

HUDSON, GARY
PAINTER
b Auburn, NY, Jan 21, 36. *Study:* Studied in Grand Chaumier, Paris, 59; Yale Univ, BFA, 66; Yale Sch Art &Archit, MFA, 66. *Work:* Whitney Mus Am Art, New York; San Diego Mus Fine Arts, Calif; Worcester Mus, Mass; Co Mus Art, Greenville, SC. *Exhib:* One-man shows, La Jolla Art Mus, Calif, 69, San Diego Mus Fine Arts, 72; Lyrical Abstraction, Philadelphia Mus, Phoenix Mus, Whitney Mus Am Art, 70-71; Structure of Color, Whitney Mus Am Art, 71; Spray Exhibition, Santa Barbara Mus, Calif, 71; Kolner Kunstmarkt '71, Kolner, Ger, 71; 34th Corcoran Biennial, Corcoran Fine Arts Mus, Washington, 75; Select Exhib CAPS Artists, Rockefeller Plaza Mus, Albany, NY, 81. *Pos:* vis artist, Boston Univ Grad Sch Painting, 2000. *Teaching:* Asst prof studio art, Univ Calif, La Jolla, 71-73; asst prof, Yale Sch Art & Archit, 75-76; vis artist, Victoria & Albert Sch Art, Melbourne, Australia, 83. *Awards:* NY State Grant Artists, 78; Pres Rsch Grant, Univ Calif, 72. *Bibliog:* Douglas Davis (auth), New color painters, Newsweek, 5/70; Peter Scheldahl (auth), Gary Hudson, NY Times Sunday, 12/71; Frank Bowling (auth), Revisionism, Arts Mag, 2/72. *Media:* Oil, Acrylic on Canvas

HUDSON, JON BARLOW
SCULPTOR, ENVIRONMENTAL ARTIST
b Billings, Mont, Dec 17, 45. *Study:* Calif Inst Arts, with Allen Kaprow, Paul Brach, Lloyd Hamroll & Judy Chicago, BFA, 71, MFA, 72; Stuttgart State Art Acad, West Germany, with Rudolph Hoflehner, 69; Dayton Art Inst, with Charles Ginnever, Bob Koepnick, Ann Tabatchnick & Kimber Smith, BFA, 75. *Work:* Eupopos Parkas; Vilniaus, Lithuania; City of Brisbane, Australia; Benburb Heritage Park, Co Armagh, Northern, Ireland; Sculpture Park, Dunaujvaros, Hungary; Green Co Pub Libr, Yellow Springs, Ohio. *Comn:* Sublime Portal: Pi (sculpture), Mulia Tower, Jakarta, Indonesia, 91; Rivers of Time Sculpture, Royal Abjar Hotel, Dunbai, United Arib Emerites, 92; Oh, Peace Wall & Gate, Lion & Lamb Peace Arts Ctr, Bluffton Col, Ohio, 97; Ts'ung Tube XXVII, Lapidea Naturstein, Mayen, Ger, 97; Caduceus Fountain, Med Col, Ohio, Toledo, 98; and many others. *Exhib:* Group show, Univ Dayton, 94; Westward Ho, Nat Sculpture Soc, NY, 95; Herndon Gallery, Antioch Univ, 95 & 96; NAm Sculpture, Foothills Art Ctr, Colo, 96; Gremillion & Co Gallery Artists Furniture, Houston, Tex, 96. *Teaching:* Vis sculptor, Stephens Col, Columbia, Mo, 75-76; adj instr sculpture, Wright State Univ, Dayton, Ohio, 75-77; asst prof sculpture, Antioch Univ, Yellow Springs, Ohio, 80. *Awards:* Projs Grant, 78 & Prof Develop Award, 85 & 94, Ohio Arts Coun; Lusk Mem Fel, IIE, Italy, 82-83; Ludwig Vogelstein Found Grant, 96. *Bibliog:* Johan DeRoey (auth), Geometry of mysticism, KNACK, Brussels, Belgium, 2/80; B Lealman & E Robinson (auths), Exploration into Experience, Knowing and Unknowing, Manchester Col, 81; Baile Oakes (auth), Sculpture expo in Australia, Sculpture, 5-6/89. *Mem:* Int Sculpture Ctr, Washington, DC; Royal Soc Brit Sculptors Int; Sculptor's Soc Ireland. *Media:* All. *Publ:* Auth, Pluralistic Vocabulary of Spiritual Unity, Studia Mystica, Calif State Univ, Sacramento, 80. *Mailing Add:* 325 N Walnut PO Box 710 Yellow Springs OH 45387

HUDSON, ROBERT H
PAINTER, SCULPTOR
b Salt Lake City, Utah, Sept 8, 38. *Study:* San Francisco Art Inst, BFA, 62, MFA, 63. *Work:* Los Angeles Co Mus; San Francisco Mus Art; Mus Mod Art Boston & Whitney Mus, NY; Mus Fine Arts, Boston; Chicago Art Inst; and others. *Comn:* Fed Bldg, Anchorage, Alaska. *Exhib:* Five Whitney Mus Am Art Ann, NY, 64-72; Los Angeles Co Mus Art, 67; Philadelphia Mus Art, 67; Art Inst Chicago, 67; Walker Art Ctr, Minneapolis, 69; Retrospective, Moore Col of Art, 77; solo exhibs, Allan Frumkin Gallery, NY, 78, 81, 84 & 86, Hansen Fuller Gallery, San Francisco, Calif, 79 & 82, Morgan Gallery, Shawnee Mission, Kans, 83 & 96, A Survey, San Francisco Mus Mod Art, Albright Knox Art Gallery, Buffalo, NY, Art Mus Fla Int Univ, Miami, Laguna Beach Mus Art (with catalog), Calif, 85-86, Dorothy Goldeen Gallery, Santa Monica, Calif, 87 & 89, Fresno Art Mus, Calif, 89-90, John Berggruen Gallery, San Francisco, Calif, 91 & 94, Struve Gallery, Chicago, Ill, 95 & Nancy Margolis Gallery, NY, 98; Collaborations: William Allan, Robert Hudson, William Wiley, Palm Spring Desert Mus, Palm Springs, Calif, Art Mus Fla Int Univ, Miami, 98, Wash State Univ Mus Art, Pullman & Scottsdale Mus Art, Ariz, 99; Wild Things: Artists' Views of the Animal World, John Berggruen Gallery, San Francisco, Calif, 98. *Teaching:* Instr, San Francisco Art Inst, 64-65, chmn, Sculpture & Ceramic Dept, 65-66 & asst prof art, 76-78; asst prof art, Univ Calif, Berkeley, 66-73. *Awards:* Purchase Prize, San Jose State Col, 64; Nealie Sullivan Award, San Francisco, 65; Guggenheim Found Fel, 76; plus others. *Bibliog:* Peter Selz (auth), Funk, Univ Calif, 67; Maurice Tuchman (auth), American Sculpture of the Sixties, Los Angeles Co Mus Art, 67; Graham Beal (auth), Robert Hudson, A Survey, San Francisco Mus Mod Art, 85. *Dealer:* John Berggruen Gallery 228 Grant Ave San Francisco CA; Dorothy Golldeen Gallery Santa Monica CA. *Mailing Add:* 392 Eucalyptus Cotati CA 94931

HUEMER, CHRISTINA GERTRUDE
LIBRARIAN
b Orange, NJ, May 24, 47. *Study:* Mt Holyoke Col, BA, 69; Columbia Univ, MS, 70; Cornell Univ, MA, 75. *Pos:* Asst art librn, Cornell Univ, Ithaca, NY, 70-75; indexer, Art Index, H W Wilson Co, Bronx, NY, 75-76; art librn, Oberlin Col, 76-80; deputy librn, Avery Library, Columbia Univ, 80-85; librn, ICCROM, 85-87 & Am Acad Rome, 92-; ed, RILA/BHA, 88-92. *Teaching:* Instr, Sch Libr Serv, Columbia Univ, New York, 83. *Mailing Add:* 9920 Diamond Reef Way Las Vegas NV 89117-0906

HUERTA, BENITO
PAINTER, CURATOR
b Corpus Christi, Tex, Apr 30, 52. *Study:* Univ Houston, BFA, 75; NMex State Univ, MA, 78. *Work:* Mus Fine Arts, Houston; Menil Collection, Houston; El Paso Mus; Ariz State Univ Art Mus; Weatherspoon Art Gallery Univ NC. *Comn:* design (with Ray de la Reza), Metro Transit Authority, Houston, 95-; sculpture, San Antonio, Tex, 97-; design, Dallas Area Rapid Transit, 98-. *Exhib:* Attempted, Not Known, Nez Son-Atkins Mus, Ky, San Jose (Calif) Mus Art, Univ North Tex, Denton, Contemp Arts Mus, Houston, 91-93; Out Of This World, Contemp Arts Mus, Houston, 94; To Transcend, Tonegate and To Preserve, Ariz State Univ Art Mus, Tempe, 94; The Figure In The New Millenium, Art Mus South Tex, Corpus Christi, 94; Highlights from Permanent Collection, El Paso Mus Art, 2000; Fire and Earth, San Antonio Mus Art, 2000. *Collection Arranged:* Working Class Heroes, 97-2000; Inescapable Histories, 97-99; Cultura de Southern Tex, 98; Stories Your Mother Never Told You, 2000-. *Teaching:* vis artist, East Carolina Univ, Greenville, NC, 90-91; vis artist, Univ NC, Greensboro, 95; asst prof, Univ Tex, Arlington, 97-. *Bibliog:* Charles Dee Mitchen (auth), Art In America, 10/97; Janey Tyson (auth), 10 Artists on the Brink of Big Time, 98; J Claire Van Ryzin (auth), Patterned Out of Order-Chaos, Austin Am State, 3/2000. *Mem:* Ft Worth Art Dealers Asn. *Publ:* coauth, American Images: The SBL Collection, Abrams, 96; auth, A Place for All People, MFAH, 96; coauth, 5000 Artist Return To Artist Space: 25 yrs., Artist Space, 98; auth, Texas: 150 Works From Museum of Fine Arts, Hoolton Abrams, 2000; coauth, Comtemporary Chicana & Chicano Art, Bilingual Press, 2000. *Dealer:* Berman Gallery-Austin; Parchman-Stremmer Gallery, San Antonio. *Mailing Add:* 1128 W Park Row Dr Arlington TX 76013

HUETER, JAMES WARREN
SCULPTOR, PAINTER
b San Francisco, Calif, 1925. *Study:* Pomona Col, BA; Claremont Grad Sch, MFA, with Henry Lee McFee, Albert Stewart & Millard Sheets. *Work:* Scripps Col, Claremont, Calif; Univ Calif, Davis, Calif; Long Beach State Col; Pomona Col, Claremont, Calif; Security Pacific Nat Bank, Los Angeles, Calif; Carnation Co, Calif. *Exhib:* Artists Los Angeles & Vicinity, Los Angeles Co Mus, 52 & 54-59; Denver Mus Art Ann, 54 & 59; Butler Inst Am Art Midyear Ann, 55, 57-59 & 62; Long Beach Mus Art Drawing Exhib, 60; Southern Calif 100, Laguna Beach Mus, 77; one-man shows, Pasadena Art Mus, 55 & Mt San Antonio Col, Walnut, Calif, 77; 38th Corcoran Biennial Am Painting, Washington, DC, 83; Univ Calif, Davis, Calif, 86; Univ Calif, Santa Cruz, Calif, 95. *Teaching:* Instr sculpture, Pomona Col, 59-60; instr drawing, Claremont Grad Sch, summer 63; lectr art, Pitzer Col, 72. *Awards:* First Prize for Sculpture, Los Angeles Co Mus, 55; First Prize for Painting, Frye Mus, Seattle, 57; Nat Design Award Drawing, Boulder Ctr Visual Arts, Colo, 82. *Bibliog:* A Segunda (auth), Reviews, Vol 1, No 8 & Delores Yonker (auth), James Hueter, Vol 2, No 2, Artforum; Fidel Danieli (auth), Rev, Artscene, 86. *Media:* Wood, Oil. *Dealer:* Tobey C Moss Gallery 7321 Beverly Blvd Los Angeles CA 90036. *Mailing Add:* 190 E Radcliffe Dr Claremont CA 91711

HUFF, LAURA WEAVER
PRINTMAKER, INSTRUCTOR
b Mt Vernon, NY, Dec 24, 30. *Study:* Syracuse Univ, NY; Univ Del, Newark, BA, 64; painting with James Twitty, Corcoran Sch Art, 65-67; George Wash Univ, Washington, MFA, 68. *Work:* Libr Cong Collection of Fine Prints; Am Embassy, Jakarta, Indonesia; Corcoran Gallery Art, Washington; Nat Mus, Women in Arts, Washington; Nat Mus Am Hist, Graphic Arts, Smithsonian Inst, Washington. *Comn:* 200 silkscreen posters, Amelia Earhart's Lockheed Vega, 85, comn by Carol Heiderman; 200 posters, The Tin Goose, Nostalgic Aviator, Alexandria, Va, 87. *Exhib:* One-person shows, Wash Printmakers Gallery, 86 & 89, Am Asn Advan Sci, Washington, 86 & 89, River Road Unitarian Church, Bethesda, Md, 92, 95 & 99; As Time Goes By, Columbia Art Ctr, Md, 94; Wash Area Printmakers, Nat Mus Women Arts, Washington, 96; Keystones & Cornerstones, Touchstone Gallery, Washington, 96; plus many others; Spring Open, Rock Creek Gallery, Washington, DC, 98. *Pos:* Illusr, Project LIFE, Washington, 71-73; graphics specialist, Hazeltine Corp, McLean, Va, 79-80. *Teaching:* Lectr painting, Howard Community Col, Columbia, Md, 70-71; instr screen printing, Graphics Workshop, Glen Echo Park, Md, 74-76, Chautaqua artist/instr, 91-92; lectr screen printing, NVa Community Col, Alexandria, 76; instr screen printing, Art League Sch, Alexandria, 85; drawing & painting for sr adults continuing educ, Montgomery Col, Germantown, Md, 89-91, instr drawing 1, 93-95, art appreciation, 94 & 95, color, 96 & 97; art teacher, Arts for the Aging, Bethesda, Md, 89- & D C Coalition for Homeless, 98; Am art slide/lectures for three senior cens through Arts Coun Montgomery Co grants, 95, 96 & 98. *Awards:* Juror's Choice Award, Spring Open, Rockcreek Gallery, Washington, DC, 98. *Bibliog:* Colleen Caprara, (auth), Laura Huff-Designing with Nature's Beauty, World & I 6/86; JoAnn Goslin (auth), Making a Mark in Silkscreens, Potomac Life, 9/90. *Mem:* Washington Print Club; Art League, Alexandria, Va; Md Printmakers. *Media:* Screenprinting, Miscellaneous Media. *Publ:* Illusr, Copycat Sam, Human Sci Press, New York, 82. *Mailing Add:* 11636 Brandy Hall Ln Gaithersburg MD 20878

HUFF, ROBERT
SCULPTOR, PAINTER
b Kalamazoo, Mich, Jan 4, 45. *Study:* Univ SFla, BA, 66, MFA, 68. *Work:* Ringling Mus Art, Sarasota, Fla; Mus Art, Ft Lauderdale, Fla; Erie Art Ctr, Pa. *Comn:* Sculptures, Dade Co Art in Pub Places, Miami, 77, 81 & 95; paintings, Broward Co Art in Pub Places, 91; paintings, Palm Beach Art in PubPlaces, 92. *Exhib:* Chicago Int Art Expos, Lakeside Gallery, Ill, 91 & 92; SFla Invitational: George Bolge Selects, Mus Art, Ft Lauderdale, 91; Chicago Int New Art Forms Expos, Lakeside Gallery, Ill, 91; 41st Ann All Fla Juried Exhib, Boca Mus, Boca Raton, 92; Sculpture for Sculptors, New Gallery, Univ Miami, Fla, 92; and others. *Teaching:* Prof sculpture, Miami Dade Community Col, 68-, chmn dept, 78-2005; vis artist, Soviet Artists Union & Lakeside Studios, USSR, 89; vis artist sculpture, Univ Miami, 90. *Awards:* Fla Fine Arts Fel, Fla Arts Coun, 78 & 80; Channel 2 Juried Exhib Award, Miami, Fla, 80; Honorable Mention, Fla Nat, Fla State Univ, 88. *Bibliog:* Robert Sindelir (auth), Art corner, Ideas, 78; Elisa Turner (auth), Artists the critics are watching, Art News, 86; Leslie Judd Ahlander (auth), Miami art scene, Miami News, 87. *Mem:* Int Sculpture Ctr. *Media:* Miscellaneous Media. *Dealer:* Bernice Sfeinbaum Gallery. *Mailing Add:* 7231 SW 61st St Miami FL 33143

HUFFINGTON, ANITA
SCULPTOR, DRAFTSMAN
b Baltimore, Md, Dec 25, 34. *Study:* Univ NC; Bennington Col; Univ S Fla; City Col, NY, BA, FMA. *Exhib:* Solo shows, City Univ NY Grad Ctr, 75, Univ Ark, Fayetteville, 82, Valley House Gallery, Dallas, Tex, 86, Benton Gallery, Southampton, NY, 89, Art Arts Ctr, Little Rock, 90, O'Hara Gallery, NY, 94, 96 & 99, Univ Cent Ark, Convay, 97 & Triangle Gallery, San Francisco, Calif, 98; Int Women's Art Festival, NY, 76; NW Art Artists Exhib, Univ Art, Fayetteville, 78; Delta Art Exhib, Art Arts Ctr, Little Rock, 79-81; Territorial Restoration Gallery, Little Rock, Ark, 81; Harris Gallery, Houston, Tex, 81-83; Great Garden Sculpture Show, Scuptural Arts Mus, Atlanta, Ga, 82; Third Ann Inviational, Benton Gallery, Southampton, NY, 88; M A Doran Gallery, Tulsa, Okla, 88-92; A Select Gathering, Kornbluth Gallery, Fair Lawn, NJ, 88-92; The Art Show, 7th Regiment Armory, Vallery House Gallery, NY, 89-95; Fort Smith Art Ctr Benefit, Ark, 90; Salon De Mars, Champ de Mars, Paris, France, 92; US Artists, Pa Acad, Valley House Gallery, Philadelphia, 92-98; ARTexas, Dallas Convention Ctr, Valley House Gallery, Tex, 93-94; 40th Ann Exhib, Valley House Gallery, Dallas, Tex, 94; Introductions VI, Lisa Kurts Gallery, Memphis, Tenn, 95; Triangle Gallery, San Francisco, Calif, 96; Am Acad Invitational Exhib Painting & Sculpture, Am Acad Arts & Letts, NY, 97; Body and Soul: Contemp Southern Figures, Mobile Mus Art, Ala & Cummer Mus Art & Gardens, Jacksonville, Fla, 98; The Figure in 20th Century Sculpture, Two Sculptors Inc, NY, 98; plus many others; Dixon Gallery and Gardens, Memphis, Tenn, 2002; plus many others. *Awards:* Fel, Ark Arts Coun, 92; La Napoule Art Found Residency, France, 96; Jimmy Ernst Award Art, Am Acad Arts & Letts, NY, 97. *Bibliog:* Amei Wallach (auth), A fair of the best in gallery art, NY Newsday, 2/26/93; Holland Carter (auth), Art in review: critic's choice, NY Times, 3/22/96; Mark Daniel Cohen (auth), The figure in 20th century art, rev, Critical State of Visual Art New York, 3/15/98; Lynn Fisher (auth), Ozark inspiration, Ark Democrat-Gazette, Little Rock, 6/23/98; Susan Marquez (auth), Anita Huffington at Triangle Gallery, World Sculpture News, Vol 5, winter 99; plus others. *Media:* Clay, Stone. *Dealer:* Lisa Kurtz Gallery 166 S White Slatron Rd Memphis TN 38117; Valley House Gallery 6616 Spring Valley Rd Dallas TX 75254. *Mailing Add:* c/o O'Hara Gallery 41 E 57th St Suite 1302 New York NY 10022

HUGGINS, VICTOR, JR
PAINTER, PRINTMAKER
b Durham, NC, July 23, 36. *Study:* Univ NC, Chapel Hill, AB & MA. *Work:* Ackland Art Ctr, Univ NC, Chapel Hill; B Carroll Reece Mus, ETenn State Univ; Brooks Mem Gallery Art, Memphis, Tenn; Vanderbilt Univ; Weatherspoon Art Gallery, Univ NC, Greensboro. *Comn:* Mural, Colonial Williamsburg Found, Durham, NC, 84. *Exhib:* One-man shows, Jane Haslem Gallery, Washington, DC, 71, 20th Century Gallery, Williamsburg, Va, 71, B Carroll Reece Mus, Johnson City, Tenn, 72 & Somerhill Gallery, Durham, NC, 85; group show, Nat Mus Am Art, Washington, DC, 81.

Teaching: Asst prof art, Vanderbilt Univ, 68-69; prof, Va Polytech Inst & State Univ, currently. *Awards:* First Purchase Awards, NC Nat Bank, 67, Springs Art Contest, Springs Mills, 67 & Ann Southern Contemp Painting Exhib, 68. *Media:* Acrylic. *Mailing Add:* c/o Somerhill Gallery 1800 E Franklin St Chapel Hill NC 27514-5852

HUGHES, BEVERLY
DESIGNER, WEAVER
b Belcrossing, NC, Feb 24, 49. *Study:* Barn Studio, Millville, NJ, studied with Pat Witt, 71-74; Acad Fine Arts, studied with Morris Blackburn, 74; Moore Col Art, Philadelphia, Pa, BFA, 76, Moore Col Art, Art Ed Cert, 90. *Work:* Fidelity Bank, Philadelphia, Pa; Afro-Am Cult Mus, woven mask, permanent collection, 89; Arco Chemical Corp, raffia mask, permanent collection, 91; United Bank, Philadelphia, Pa; Franklinia postcard, Bartram Garden Tencentennial Celebration, 99. *Comn:* rose illus, comn by West Philadelphia Cult Alliance for Paul Robeson House; Blue Delphiniums illus, pvt comn in Paris, 99. *Exhib:* botanical postcards, Philadelphia Flower Show, 98. *Pos:* Owner-designer, Winterwood Designs, Philadelphia, Pa, 85-; team mem, West Philadelphia High Sch Coun, 95-96; mem adv comt, Community Col Philadelphia, Western Region, 95-97; invited artist, mask making worshop, Children's Inaugural Salute, State Mus, Harrisburg, Pa for Gov Tom Ridge, 95. *Teaching:* Instr art textiles, Moore Col Art, Philadelphia, Pa, 76; art teacher, Philadelphia Sch Dist, 86-91; Moore Col Art Saturday classes, Philadelphia, Pa, 90; botanical illus teacher, Univ City Arts League, 2000. *Awards:* First Prize, Expressions 80, Afro Am Cult Mus, 80; Outstanding Achievement Award, Fabric Workshop at Long Beach Island Found Arts & Scis, Loveladies, NJ, 94. *Bibliog:* Edward J Sozanski, rev masks, Philadelphia Inquirer, 9/9/91; appeared in Int Hair, 3/95. *Mem:* Philadelphia Soc Botanical Illusrs. *Media:* Colored Pencil, Ink. *Publ:* creator, off t-shirt for 2001 Philadelphia Flower Show, Pa Horticultural Soc. *Mailing Add:* 4832 Sansom St Philadelphia PA 19139

HUGHES, EDWARD JOHN
PAINTER
b North Vancouver, BC, Feb 17, 1913. *Study:* Vancouver Sch Art. *Hon Degrees:* Emily Carr Inst, DLitt, Vancouver, BC, 97; Malaspina Col Univ, DLitt, Nanaimo, BC, 2000. *Work:* Nat Gallery Can, Ottawa; Art Gallery Ont, Toronto; Vancouver Art Gallery; Montreal Mus Fine Art; Gtr Victoria Art Gallery; Nat War Mus, Ottawa. *Comn:* murals, San Francisco Golden Gate Exposition, 39; murals, Can Pacific RR Dome, 54. *Exhib:* Retrospective, Vancouver Art Gallery, 67 & Surrey Art Gallery, 83; Art Gallery of Greater Victoria, 83; Edmonton Art Gallery, 83; Nat Gallery Can, 83; Glenbow Mus Calgary, 83; and others. *Pos:* War artist, Can Army, 40-42, off war artist, 42-46. *Teaching:* prof fine art, Univ Victoria, 95-. *Awards:* Emily Carr Scholar, Lawren Harris, 47; Can Coun Fels & Awards, 58, 63 & 67, Short Term Grant, 70. *Bibliog:* Doris Shadbolt (auth), E J Hughes, Can Art Mag, spring 53; Anthony Robertson (auth), E J Hughes, Vanguard Mag, 12/81; Patricia Salmon & Leslie Black (auths), E J Hughes, Raincoast Chronicles Mag, 10/83. *Mem:* Royal Can Acad Art. *Media:* Acrylic, Oil. *Dealer:* Mr Michel Moreault Gallery 709-1545 Dr Fenfield Montreal PQ H3G 1C7. *Mailing Add:* 2449 Heather St Duncan BC V9L 2Z6 Canada

HUGHES, PAUL LUCIEN
DEALER, CONSULTANT
b New York, NY, Apr 8, 38. *Study:* NY Univ, BA, 67; Sch Visual Art, 68-69. *Exhib:* State Wyo Fel, 88. *Collection Arranged:* Harry Bertoia Retrospective (guest cur), Colorado Springs Fine Arts Mus, 80; Vance Kirkland retrospective, 28-81; George Rickey, 84, 87 & 90. *Pos:* Dir, Inkfish Gallery, Denver. *Mem:* Alliance for Contemp Art; DADA. *Specialty:* Contemporary abstract art. *Collection:* Bertoia, Anuszkiewicz, Henry Moore, Herbert Bayer, Vance Kirkland, Dave Yust, George Rickey, Philip Tsiaras, Italo Scanga, Werner Drewes and many others. *Mailing Add:* c/o Inkfish Gallery 1672 S Lansing St Aurora CO 80012

HUGHES, ROBERT S F
CRITIC, LECTURER
b Sydney, Australia, July 28, 38. *Study:* St Ignatius Col; Sydney Univ, studies in art & archit. *Pos:* Contribr, The Observer, The Spectator, The Sunday Times, The Daily Telegraph & Encounter, in Eng, The Nation & The Sunday Mirror, in Australia, formerly; contribr, The New York Rev of Bks & The New Repub, currently; art critic & sr writer, Time Mag, 70-. *Awards:* Frank Jewett Mather Award, Col Art Asn Am, 82 & 85; W H Smith Lit Award, 87; Duff Cooper Prize, 87; Golden Plate Award, Am Acad Achievement, 88. *Mem:* Am Acad Arts & Sci. *Publ:* Auth, The Fatal Shore, 87; Nothing, if not critical, Knopf, 90; Frank Auerback (monogr), 90; Barcelona, 92; Culture of Complaint, 93; (auth), American Visions-The Epic History of Art in America, Alfred A Knopf, 97. *Mailing Add:* c/o Time & Life Bldg Rockefeller Ctr New York NY 10020

HUGHES, SIOCHAN I
SCULPTOR, PHOTOGRAPHER
b Dublin, Ireland, Mar 1, 61; US citizen. *Study:* Parsons Sch Design, New York, BFA, 83; Cleveland Inst Art, 87-88; Hunter Col MFA(sculpture), 92; Hochschule der Künst, Berlin, Fulbright to study with prof Dieter Appelt, 93-95. *Exhib:* Three Rivers Arts Festival, Carnegie Mus Art, 93; Fulbright Berlin Seminar Week, Amerika Haus Libr, 94; Am is on Your Side, Amerika Haus, 94; one-person show, Roloff Momin, Berlin, 95; and many others. *Awards:* Madeline Sadin Award, Greewich House Pottery, 81; William Graf Travel Grant, Hunter Col, 90. *Bibliog:* Roberta Smith (auth), Art in Review, Casual Ceremony, New York Times, 1/3/92; Gretchen Faust (auth), New York in Review, Arts Mag, 3/92; Anja Oberhardt (auth), Kunst aus dem Waggon ein Wunder auf Schienen, Die Welt, 1/20/94. *Mem:* Col Art Asn. *Media:* Sculpture Media, Photography; Photography, Digital Art. *Mailing Add:* 61 Yantecaw Ave Bloomfield NJ 07003-2834

HUGHTO, DARRYL LEO
PAINTER
b Watertown, NY, June 10, 43. *Study:* State Univ NY, Col Buffalo, BS(art educ), 65; Cranbrook Acad Art, MFA(painting), 69. *Work:* Edmonton Art Gallery, Alta; Everson Mus Art; Boston Mus Fine Arts; Mus Fine Arts, Houston; Guggenheim Mus; Abbeyville Press, Westchester, NY; Mus Contemp Art, Houston, Tex. *Comn:* Mural (acrylic on canvas), Charlestown Savings Bank, Boston, 77. *Exhib:* One-man shows, Gallery 99, Bay Harbor Island, Fla, 80, 81, 86 & 87, Salander-O'Reilly Galleries, NY, 81, 82, 83, 84, 86, 89 & 91, Gallery One, Toronto, 81, 83, 88 & 91, Stein Bartlow Gallery, Chicago, 92, Galerie Elca London, Montreal, 86, 87, 89 & 93, CS Schulte Galleries, NJ, 93, 95, 97 & 98 & Rome Art & Community Ctr, NY, 95; Corcoran Gallery, 77; New Abstract Art, Edmonton Art Gallery, Alta, 77; Theodoran Award Show, Guggenheim Mus, 77; 20th Century Painting & Sculpture, Metrop Mus Art, NY, 79; Gallery 99, Miami, Fla, 81-; Gallery One, Toronto, Ont, 81-; Meredith Long, Houston, Tex, 78-; 871 Fine Arts, San Francisco, Calif, 86-; Salander-O'Reilly Galleries, NY, 90; The Artist at Ringside, Butler Inst Art, Ohio & Nat Art Mus Sport, Ind, 92; Important Works by Modern Masters, CS Schulte Galleries, NJ, 93; New Landscape Paintings, CS Schulte Galleries, NJ, 96; Landscapes from the Permanent Collection, Mendell Art Gallery, Sask, 96; Painters on Site, Mendell Art Gallery, Sask, 96; and others. *Teaching:* Teaching asst painting, Cranbrook Acad Art, 68-69; asst prof, Syracuse Univ, 71-79; artist-in-residence, Va Polytech Inst, Blacksburg, 84; vis artist, Western Mich Univ, Kalamazoo, Mich, 85. *Awards:* Theodoran Award, Guggenheim Found, 77; Humanities Award, Nat Endowment Arts, 83 & 84. *Bibliog:* Ken Carpenter (auth), Third generation abstraction: Darryl Hughto, Arts Mag, 2/75; Kenworth Moffett (auth), The New Generation, Rhineburgh Press, 80; Stephan Pentak (auth), Darryl Hughto, Arts Mag, 5/81; Karen Wilkin (auth), At the Galleries, Partisan Review, 89. *Mem:* Visual Artists & Galleries Asn Inc. *Media:* Acrylic on Canvas. *Dealer:* CS Schulte Galleries 340 Millburn Ave NJ 07041; Gallery One 121 Scollard St Toronto Ont M5R 1G4. *Mailing Add:* 8076 N Main St Rd Canastota NY 13032

HUGHTO, MARGIE A
CERAMIST, CURATOR
b Endicott, NY, March 29, 44. *Study:* State Univ NY, Buffalo, BS(art educ), 65; Cranbrook Acad Art, Bloomfield Hills, Mich, MFA(ceramics), 71; with Richard DeVore. *Work:* Boston Mus Fine Arts, Mass; Albright-Knox Art Gallery, Buffalo, NY; Everson Mus Art, Syracuse, NY; Cranbrook Acad Art Mus, Bloomfield Hills, Mich. *Comn:* Ceramic wall pieces, Marina Casino, NJ, 80; ceramic wall pieces, United Energy Resources, Houston, Tex, 81; ceramic wall pieces, Presbyterian Hospital, Philadelphia, Pa, 81. *Exhib:* Language of Clay, Birchfield Ctr, Buffalo, NY, 79-80; Century of Ceramics US, Everson Mus Art, Syracuse, NY, 79-81; Women Artists, Suzanne Brown Gallery, Scottsdale, Ariz, 80; Scripps Invitational, Scripps Col Mus, Claremont, Calif, 81. *Collection Arranged:* New Works in Clay by Contemp Painters & Sculptors (auth, catalog), Am Ceramics, 76, 78 & 81; A Century of Ceramics in the US 1878-1978 (auth, catalog), Am Ceramics, 78. *Pos:* Cur of Ceramics, Everson Mus Art, Syracuse, NY, 73-81; dir, Syracuse Clay Institute, NY, 75-81. *Teaching:* Prof ceramics, Syracuse Univ Sch Art, NY, 71-81. *Bibliog:* Sherry Chayat (auth), The Ceramic Fans of Margie Hughto, Ceramics Monthly, 5/80; Earth, Fire & Water (film), Philip Morris Corporation, 78. *Mem:* Inst Ceramic History. *Media:* Ceramic, Handmade Cotton Paper Pulp. *Res:* Contemporary American ceramics. *Mailing Add:* 6970 Henderson Rd Jamesville NY 13078

HUGO, JOAN (DOWEY)
CRITIC, ADMINISTRATOR
b Weehawken, NJ, Jan 12, 30. *Study:* Simmons Col, Boston, MA BLS, studied performance with Rachel Rosenthal, 80-81 & Rudy Perez, 81-82. *Collection Arranged:* Artwords & Bookworks Traveling Exhib, Los Angeles Inst Contemp Arts, Calif, 78; Letterforms; When Beauty is Enough A Women's Bldg, Los Angeles, Calif. *Pos:* Cataloger, Brooklyn Mus Libr, 52-53; librn, Am Libr Paris, Left Bank Br, 53-54; art librn, Otis Art Inst Los Angeles Co, 57-80; Southern Calif ed, Artweek, 79-90; Calif ed, New Art Examiner, 90-94; asst to provost, Calif Inst Arts (Valencia, Calif), 90-01; cur, Santa Barbara Contemp Arts, Calif, 93, Korean Cult Center, 93, Los Angeles Artists Korean Descent, Cerritos, Calif, 95 & Calif Arts Students and Alumnae, 99. *Teaching:* Instr artist & the book, Otis Art Inst, 77-80, mod art hist, 80-90; instr, Univ Calif, Los Angeles Extension, 82-90 Modernism & Spirituality; History & Theory of Criticism; Guest critic: Claremont Graduate School. *Awards:* Vesta Award, 90 for journalism; Lifetime Achievement Award, Artcore, 2001. *Mem:* Col Art Asn; Art Table; Asn Internationale des Critiques d'Art; Los Angeles Contemp Exhibs (bd mem) 79-83; Woman's Bldg, 85-88; Asn Internat des Critiques d' Art. *Res:* History of artists' books; history of visual communications; contemporary American & European artists, history of performance; public art. *Interests:* Contemporary art, especially the relationships between the arts and social history; the concept of future and the arts; history of performance. *Publ:* Contrib ed, Artweek, Art Issues & Artspace; contribr, spec issue on artists' bks, Dumb Ox, 77; ed, Artwords & Bookworks: A Set of Artists' Postcards, 77. *Mailing Add:* 3400 Ben Lomond Pl Apt 109 Los Angeles CA 90027

HUGUNIN, JAMES RICHARD
CRITIC
b Milwaukee, Wis, June 20, 47. *Study:* Art Ctr Col Design, Los Angeles, 71; Calif State Univ, Northridge, BA, 73; Univ Calif, Los Angeles, MFA, 75. *Work:* Santa Barbara Mus Art; Grunewald Print collection, Univ Calif, Los Angeles; Shaker Seed House, Tyringham, Mass. *Exhib:* Language & Image, Santa Barbara Mus Art, 77; Narrative Art: 1967-1976, Contemp Arts Mus, Houston, 77; Book Exhib, Art Ctr, Sonja Henie--Neils Onstand Found, Hovikodden, Norway, 78; Los Angeles Invitational, Fisher Gallery, Univ Southern Calif, 79; Object, Illusion & Reality, Muckenthaler Gallery, Calif State Univ, Fullerton, 79; Kunstenaarsboeken, Stedelijk

Mus, Schiedam, The Neth, 81. *Pos:* Founder, ed & publ, Dumb Ox & U-Turn Art Mags, 76-80 & 82-; contrib ed, Obscura Mag, 79-82; Midwest ed, New Art Examiner, 89-90. *Teaching:* Prof art, Calif Lutheran Col, 77-85; lectr, Chaffey Col, 82, Art Ctr Col Design, 83, Calif Inst Arts, 85 & Sch Art Inst Chicago, 85-86; vis prof, Art Inst Chicago, 85-; sr lectr, Roosevelt Univ, Chicago, 89-. *Awards:* First Place, Calif Col Photog Exhib, Calif State Univ, Northridge, 74; Purchase Award, Light II, Calif State Univ, Humbolt, 76; David & Reva Logan Grant New Critical Writing, 83. *Bibliog:* Howardina Pindell (auth), article, Print Collectors Newsletter, 9-10/77; Marcia Corbino (auth), Contemporary art criticism, Am Art, 10/83. *Mem:* Int Art Critics Asn. *Publ:* Auth, Apocryphal conversations, Afterimage, 6/81; Photography: A bourgeois success story, J Los Angeles Inst Contemp Art, 5-6/82; Joe Deal's Optical Democracy, Reading into Photography, Univ NMex, 82; Meditations on an Uranian Easter egg, Vies, Photog Resource Ctr, 83. *Mailing Add:* 454 Iowa St Oak Park IL 60302-2268

HUI, PAT
PAINTER

b Hong Kong, Aug 25, 43; US citizen. *Study:* Study of Chinese ink painting with Lui Shou-Kwan, 61-64; Univ Hong Kong, BA, 67; Univ Minn, 67-71. *Work:* McDonald Corp, Hong Kong Landmark Ctr. *Exhib:* Shadow of Poetry, Honeywell Corp Gallery, Minneapolis, Minn, 85; Poetic Vision, Alisan Fine Arts, Hong Kong, 87; Lesch Gallery, Minneapolis, 88; Asian Fine Arts, Minneapolis, 89; Alisan Fine Arts, Hong Kong, 93, 2005. *Collection Arranged:* Lui Shou-Kwan, 1919-1975, Gallery 80's, Toronto, 80; Nine Chinese Artists, Honeywell Corp Gallery, Minneapolis, Minn, 82; New Visions in Chinese Painting, 84 & Painting, Poetry & Calligraphy, 85, Hui Arts, Minneapolis, Minn. *Pos:* Cur, Gallery 80's, Toronto, 80; dir, Hui Arts, Minneapolis, 82-; steering comt, Asian Art Coun, Minneapolis Inst Arts, 83-2005. *Bibliog:* Laura Weber (auth), Hui Arts, Minnesota Design, 5/83; Mark Stanley (producer), Pat Hui, Video, 5/85; Wilma Wenick (auth), Shadow of poetry, Artnews, Minneapolis, 5/85. *Mem:* Art Dealers Asn Twin Cities (vpres, 83-85, treas, 85); Minneapolis Inst Arts; Am Art Coun; Walker Art Ctr. *Media:* Watercolor, Ink on Paper and Silk. *Specialty:* Contemporary Chinese artists in all media. *Publ:* Auth, Alisan Fine Art Ltd, Hong Kong, 93; auth, The Poetic Visions, 2005. *Dealer:* Alisan Fine Arts Hong Kong. *Mailing Add:* Hui Gallery 1225 LaSalle Ave Minneapolis MN 55440

HULICK, DIANA EMERY
SCULPTOR, PHOTOGRAPHER

b Boston, Mass, 50. *Study:* Bryn Mawr, AB, 71; Ohio Univ, MFA, 73; Princeton Univ, MFA, 78, PhD (McCormick Fel), 84. *Work:* Carleton Col; Stephens Col; Ohio Univ; Photoworks, Boston; Graphic Arts Collection, Princeton Univ. *Comn:* Advent Wreath, 2000, Stations of Cross, 2004, Grail Fountain, 2005, Trinity Cath, Phoenix, 2005; metal sculpture, Burning Bush, St Barnabas in the Desert; Jerusaleum Cross, All Saints, Phoenix, Ariz, 2004; Cathedral Ctr Arts. *Exhib:* Smithsonian Inst, Washington, DC, 73; Kansas City Art Inst, 76; New Photogs, 76; RI Sch Design, 79; Cathedral Ctr Arts, Phoenix, Ariz, 2004. *Collection Arranged:* Waldo Pierce: A New Assessment (auth, catalog), 84; Sabbathday Lake Shakers, Exhib Time & Eternity (with catalog), 85; Through Their Own Eyes, The Personal Portfolios of Edward Weston and Ansel Adams (with catalog); Stephens Col, Mo; Smithsonian Instn; Princeton Univ. *Pos:* Modernist & gallery dir, Univ Denver, 82-83; dir & cur, Univ Maine, Orono, 83-86; adjudicator, Nat Found Advan Arts, Fla, 83-87; co-ed, Photography as Document: Shaker Spirituality and the Modern Age, Vol 11, NMex Studies Fine Arts, 87; Int adv bd, History of Photography (an int quarterly). *Teaching:* Asst prof art hist, Univ Maine, 83-86 & Univ NMex, 85; asst prof photohist, theory & criticism, Ohio State Univ, 86-88; asst prof art, Ariz State Univ, 88-95. *Awards:* Woodrow Wilson Res Grant Women's Studies, 80; Dayton Hudson Distinguished Vis Artists Carleton Col, 80. *Mem:* Evidence Photographer's Intl Coun; Artist-Blacksmith Asn of North Am. *Media:* Photography, Mild steel. *Res:* Shaker photography; Diane Arbus, minority and women photographers. *Publ:* The Transcendental Machine? A Comparison of Digital Photography and Ninettenth Century Theories of Photographic Representation Leonardo, a refereed international quarterly, Vol 23, No 3, pp 419-425, summer 90; Continuity and Revolution: The Work of Ansel Adams and Edward Weston, Through Their Own Eyes: The Personal Portfolios of Edward Weston and Ansel Adams, pp 22-23, Univ Wash, Seattle, 91; From Prohibition to Acceptance: Shakers and Photography in the Nineteenth and Twentieth Centuries, Visual Resources, vol VIII, pp 81-103, fall 91; George Platt Lynes: The Portrait Series of Thomas Mann, History of Photography, an international quarterly, Vol 15, No 2, pp 211-221, fall 91; co-auth, Photography, 1900 to the Present (with J Marshall), Prentice Hall, 98. *Mailing Add:* 805 N Robson Mesa AZ 85201

HULINGS, CLARK
PAINTER, ILLUSTRATOR

b Brewster, Fla, 22. *Study:* Harverford Col, PA, BA; Art Students League, NY, 46-50; studied with Sigismund Ivanowski, Frank Reilly & George Bridgman. *Work:* Mus Wesern Art, Denver, Colo; Nat Cowboy & Western Heritage Mus, Okla City; Tucson Mus Art, Ariz; Wright Mus Art, Beloit, Wis. *Exhib:* Nat Acad Western Art; Allied Artists Am, Denver, 90-95; Solo exhib, Nat Cowboy & Western Heritage Mus, Mus of Soutwest, Midland, Tex, Grand Central Galleries, NY, 62, Nedra Matteucci Gallery, Santa Fe, NMex, 98. *Awards:* Prix de West, 3 Gold Medals, 1 Silver Medal, Nat Acad Western Art; Gold Medal, Allied Artists Am. *Mem:* Allied Artists Am; Nat Acad Wetern Art; Soc Illustrators. *Media:* Oil. *Specialty:* Rural and Village landscapes, still lifes & market scenes. *Mailing Add:* 1012 Placita Don Andreas Santa Fe NM 87501

HULL, CATHY
ILLUSTRATOR, CONCEPTUAL ARTIST

b New York, Nov 4, 46. *Study:* Conn Col, New London, BA, 68; Sch Visual Arts, New York, cert, 70. *Work:* Fourth World Cartoon Gallery, Skopje, Yugoslavia; Collection of Caricatures and Cartoons, Basel, Switz; The Sixth World Cartoon Gallery, Skopje, Int Cartoon Exhib, Istanbul, Mus of Caricatures of Cartoons, Basel, Switzerland. *Exhib:* Seventeenth Nat Print Exhib, Brooklyn Mus, 70; Soc Illusrs Ann, NY Times Show, 73; one-woman show, 6th World Cartoon Gallery, Skorje, Yugoslavia, 74; Mus De Beaubourg, Paris, France, 77; Women in Design, Pac Design Ctr, Los Angeles, 80; Women in Design Int Ariz, Scottsdale Ctr Arts, 81; Contemp Graphics, Design & Illus, The Md Inst, Baltimore, 81; Collection of Caricatures & Cartoons Show, Basel, Switz, 80, 82, 90; Contemp Design & Illus Show, Butler Inst Am Art, Youngstown, Ohio, 83; Quebec City Exhib, 85; Bienniale of Humor, Fredikstad, Norway, 87; 6th Int Cartoon Competition, Istanbul, Turkey, 88, Soc Illusrs Ann, 93, Smithtown Twp Arts Counc, 95. *Pos:* Freelance illusr, 71-. *Teaching:* Instr, illus & portfolio, Sch Visual Arts, NY, 83-94 & Parsons Sch Design, 94-97. *Awards:* Certificate of Excellence, Am Inst Graphic Arts Inside Show, 71; Silver Award & 2 Certificates of Merit, Soc Publ Designers, 74; Fifty Best Books of the Year Award, 74; Award of Excellence, Soc Newspaper Design, 84 & 85. *Mem:* Exec Bd of (the friends of Art & Design) FAD 2002-. *Media:* Computer. *Collection:* Karikahr of Cartoon Mus Basel. *Publ:* Contribr & illusr, Graphis #164, 72-73; Print, 5-6/77; Art Direction, 5/77; Nebelspalter, 75-83; V & K, 86. *Mailing Add:* 180 E 79th St Apt 7F New York NY 10021

HULL, GREGORY STEWART
PAINTER

b Okmulgee, Okla, Sept 2, 50. *Study:* Univ Utah, BFA, 73, MFA, 77, studied with Alvin Gittins. *Work:* State Utah Inst Fine Arts, Salt Lake City; Butler Inst Am Art, Youngstown, Ohio. *Comn:* Westin Kierland Resort and Spa, Scottsdale, Ariz; Montage Resort & Spa, Laguna Beach, Calif; Patricia Hearst (portrait), John Mellencamp (portrait), Indiana Co, Pa Judges (portrait), 74-. *Exhib:* 7th Intermountain Biennial, Salt Lake Art Ctr, Utah, 75; 52nd Ann, Springville Mus Art, Utah, 76; Utah Mus Fine Arts, Salt Lake City, 76; Munic Art Gallery, Los Angeles, 78; Butler Inst Am Art, Youngstown, Ohio, 81; 64th Ann, Springville Mus Art, Utah, 88; East Coast Ideals, West Coast Concepts, Carnegie Art Mus, Oxnard, Calif, 98; PAPA Plein Air Show 99, 2000. *Teaching:* Sedona Art Center, 2000; Univ Utah Teaching Asst, 75-77. *Awards:* Best Show-Purchase, Utah Painting & Sculpture, 76; 1st Prize, Davis Co Art Ctr, Utah, 76; Am Artists' Golden Anniv Nat Art Competition Winner, 87; Best of Show, Members Exhibit, Sedona Arts Center, 99; 1st Place, Members art Exhibit, 2000; 2nd Place, Crystal Cove Alliance, 2004; Honorarium, Tucson Plein Air, 2005. *Bibliog:* M Stephen Doherty (auth), Closing in on a Strong Painting, Am Artist, 7/98; Lynn Pyne (auth), An Eclectic Approach, Southwest Art, 5/99; Kathleen Bryant (auth), Into the Heart of the Grand Canyon, Am Artist, 12/2000; The Grand Adventure, Art of the West, 11-12/2000; Lynn Pyne Davis (auth), Arizona Regionalists, Southwest Art, 9/2002. *Mem:* California Art Club; Metro Opera Guild. *Media:* Oil. *Publ:* Enchanted Isle by Sapap, 2003; From Sea to Shining Sea: A Reflection of America, Haggin Museum. *Dealer:* John Pence Gallery 750 Post St San Francisco Calif 94109; Medicine Man Gallery 7000 Tanque Verde Rd Tucson Ariz 85715; Redfern Gallery 1540 S Coast Hwy Laguna Beach Calif 92651. *Mailing Add:* 3665 Zia Dr Sedona AZ 86336

HULL, JOHN
PAINTER

b New Haven, Conn, Feb 14, 52. *Study:* Yale Univ, BA, 77; Univ Ill, MFA, 81. *Work:* Metrop Mus Art; Yale Univ Art Gallery; New Mus Contemp Art; Israel Mus, Jerusalem; Greenville Co Art Mus, SC; Yellowstone Art Mus, Billings, Mont; Denver Art Mus, Colo. *Exhib:* Metrop Mus Art, NY, 88; Nat Gallery, NZ, Wellington & Art Gallery Western Australia, Perth, 89; one-man show, (auth, catalog), JB Speed Art Mus, 90, Yellowstone Art Ctr, Billings, Mont, 92, Grace Borgenicht Gallery, New York, 92 & 94, Jonson Gallery, Univ NMex, Albuquerque, 93, Kohn Turner Gallery, Los Angeles, 95 & Tatistcheff & Co Inc, NY, 96 & 99; Butler Mus Am Art, 92; Richard Bosman and John Hull, ART Resources, NY, 98; Selections from permanent collection, Yellowstone Mus, billings, Mont, 98; Art of the Am West, Denver Art Mus, Colo, 99; Ron Judisg Fine Arts, Denver, Colo, 99 & 2002; Tatistcheff & Company, Inc, NY, 99 & 2001; Arvada Ctr Arts and Humanities, Nevada, 99; The Figure: Another Side of Modernism (auth, catalog), New House Ctr Contemp Art, Snug Harbor, NY, 2000; Crowded Prairie, Nicolaysen Art Mus, Casper, Wyo, 2000; (auth, catalog), Roseberg Gallery, Goucher Col, Baltimore, Md, 2001; Edwin A Ulrich Mus, Wichita State Univ, Kans, 2001; Ctr Contemp Art, Univ Colo, Colorado Springs, Colo, 2002; Mus Contemp Art Boulder, Boulder, Colo, 2003; E J Bellocq Gallery, La tech Univ, Ruston, La, 2004; Nicolaysen Art Mus, Casper, Wyo, 2005. *Teaching:* Assoc prof painting, Yale Univ Sch Art, New Haven, Conn, 88-97; prof painting, Univ Colo, Denver, 98-. *Awards:* Fel, Nat Endowment Arts, 82-86 & 87; Achievement Award for Acrylic, Am Artist, 95; Thomas Benedict Clark Prize, Nat Acad Design, 2004. *Bibliog:* Pictures from Sonny's place (catalog for exhib) by Annie Proulx, Ucross Found & Univ Wyo Art Gallery; Marcia Tucker (auth), Outpost of Progress: The Paintings of John Hull (catalog for exhib), New Mus Contemp Art, NY, 85; Lance Esplund (auth), John Hull at Tatistcheff, Art in America, 12/99; Alexi Worth (auth), The New Yorker, 4/20/2001. *Publ:* The 179th Annual: An Inventational Exhib of Contemp Am Art, Nat Acad Design, NY, 2004; Auth, A Creative Legacy, A History of the National Endowment for the Arts Visual Artists Fel Program, Harry N. Abrams, NY, 2002; auth, Baseball: The National Pastime in Art and Literature, edited by David Colbert, Time Life Books, NY, 2000. *Dealer:* Plus Gallery 2350 Lawrence St Denver CO 80205. *Mailing Add:* 7546 E Davies Ct Englewood CO 80112

HULL, MARGARIDA KENDALL
EDUCATOR, PAINTER

b Lisbon, Portugal. *Study:* student, history & philosophy, Univ Lisbon; Corcoran Sch Art, BFA, 73; Cath Univ, MFA, 82. *Work:* Art Inst Chicago; Gulbenkian Mus Contemp Art, Lisbon, Portugal. *Exhib:* Osuna Gallery, Wash, DC, 83; Gulbenkian Found, 84; Baltimore, Chicago, NY, Philadelphia, Glallery K, Dupont Cir. *Teaching:* vis prof, studio art,Towson State Univ, 86; asst prof, studio art, George Mason Univ, 87, assoc prof, 94-2000-. *Mailing Add:* George Mason Univ Art Dept 4400 Univ Dr Fairfax VA 22030-4444

HULL, RICHARD
PAINTER
b Oklahoma City, Okla. *Study:* Skowhegan Sch Painting & Sculpture, 76; Kansas City Art Inst, BFA, 77; Art Inst Chicago, MFA, 79. *Work:* Smithsonian Inst; Art Inst Chicago & Mus Contemp Art, Chicago; Milwaukee Art Mus; Chase Manhattan Bank, NY. *Exhib:* Prints & Multiples, Art Inst Chicago & Smithsonian Inst, 81 & 83; Painting & Sculpture Today, Indianapolis Mus Art, 82; Skowhegan Alumni Exhib, Leo Castelli Gallery, NY, 86; Recent Acquisitions, Milwaukee Art Mus, 89; Am Art since WWII, Art Inst Chicago, 89 & Landfall Press Show, 95; Art in Chicago, Mus Contemp Art, Chicago, 96-97. *Bibliog:* James Yood (auth), Richard Hull, Artforum, 91; Richard Vine (auth), Where the wild things were, Art in Am, 97; Dennis Adrian (auth), Richard Hull, Bradley Univ, 98. *Media:* Oil on Linen. *Dealer:* Carrie Secrist

HULL, SHAYNE L
INSTRUCTOR, PAINTER
b Davenport, Iowa, Nov 16, 60. *Study:* Wichita State Univ, 79-82; Corpus Christi State Univ, BFA, 85; Col Art, Md Inst, MFA, 94. *Comn:* mural, Calif Community Center, Louisville, Ky, 96; portrait, Al & Mary Shands III, Crestwood, Ky, 99. *Exhib:* Works by Shayne Hull, Capitol Gallery, Landover, Md, 95; Paintings by Shane Hull, The Carnegie Ctr for Arts, Covington, Ky, 96; New Works by Shayne Hull, Floyd Co Mus, New Albany, Ind, 97; Works by Shayne Hull, Ashland Art Gallery, Ky, 99; Ky Visions 2000, Ky Arts Coun, Frankfurt, 2000; Mt Royal Sch Art The First 25 Yrs, Decker Hall Md Inst, Baltimore, 2000. *Teaching:* dir educ, instr, Ky Art & Craft Found, Louisville, 95-, Jefferson Community Coll, Louisville, 97-. *Awards:* Merit Award, Kunst In Der Stadt, 1998; Al Smith fellow Ky Arts Coun, 1998; Individual Artist grant Ky Arts Coun, 2000. *Bibliog:* New American Paintings, Open Studios Press, 97; Julie Ball (auth), Shayne's World-Dialogue: Voicing The Arts, 2000; Bruce Nixon (Auth), Shayne Hull At Galerie Hertz, Louisville Eccentric Observer, 2000. *Mem:* Nat Polymer Clay Guild; Artcentric; Louisville Visual Art Asn; Sister Cities of Louisville Int Arts Program (chair Mainz art comt). *Media:* Oil. *Dealer:* Galery Hertz 327 E Market Louisville KY 40202

HUMMEL, CHARLES FREDERICK
ADMINISTRATOR
b Brooklyn, NY, Sept 16, 32. *Study:* City Col New York, BA(magna cum laude), 53; Univ Del, MA, 55; Mus Mgmt Inst, Univ Calif, 85. *Collection Arranged:* Philadelphia Reviewed, 61; Rugs from the Orient, 64; The Pennsylania Germans, 82-84; North American Wood Turning Since 1930, 2001-02. *Pos:* Curatorial asst, H F du Pont Winterthur Mus, Del, 55-58, asst cur, 58-60, assoc cur, 60-67, cur, 67-79, deputy dir for collections, 79-89, deputy dir mus & libr dept, 89-91 (retired). *Teaching:* Adj assoc prof art hist, Univ Del, 64-93, adj prof, 93-. *Awards:* Winterthur Fel, 53-55; Katherine Coffey Award, Mid-Atlantic Asn Mus, 89; Winterthur Cur Emer, 91; Charles F Hummel internship, The Chipstone Found. *Mem:* Int Rug Soc (dir, 71); Am Asn Mus (secy, 88-90); Chipstone Found (trustee, 1991-); Philadelphia Soc for Preservation of Landmarks (trustee, 1993-1999); Wood Turning Center Philadelphia (trustee, 1993-1999, 2001-2006); Strawbery Banke Mus (advisory committee, 1997-2002, 2004); Am Inst Conserv Hist & Artistic Objects; Nat Inst Conserv Cult Property. *Res:* Pocket watch ownership, L.I. and Conn., 1762-1827. *Publ:* Auth, With Hammer in Hand, Univ Press Va, 68, 73, 77 & 83; contribr, Furniture to 1790, Britannica Encycl of Am Art, Encycl Brit Inc, 73; auth, A Winterthur Guide to American Chippendale Furniture: Middle Atlantic & Southern Colonies, Crown/Rutledge, 76; Floor coverings in 18th century America, Irene Emery Textile Roundtable 1975, Textile Mus, 77; coauth, The Pennsylvania Germans: A Celebration of Their Arts, Philadelphia Mus Art, 82. *Mailing Add:* Berkshire 1112 Braken Ave Wilmington DE 19808

HUMPHREY, DAVID AIKEN
PAINTER, PRINTMAKER
b Augsburg, Ger, Aug 30, 55; US citizen. *Study:* New York Studio Sch, 76-77; Md Inst Col Art, BFA, 77; New York Univ, MA, 80. *Work:* Seattle Mus, Wash; Carnegie Inst, Pittsburgh, Pa; Metrop Mus Art, Brooklyn Mus & New York Pub Libr, NY; Walker Art Ctr, Minneapolis, Minn; Mus Fine Art, Boston. *Exhib:* Solo exhibs, Patricia Shea Gallery, Santa Monica, 92, Contemp Arts Ctr, Cincinnati, Ohio, 95, The Woodstreet Galleries, Pittsburgh, Pa, 96, Nancy Solomon Gallery, Atlanta, Ga, 96, I Space, Univ Ill, Chicago, 96, Deven Golden Fine Art, NY, 97 & Zolla/Lieberman Gallery, Chicago, 98, Holiday Melt, Saks Fifth Ave Project Art, Palm Beach, Fla, 2002, Holiday Melt, Solomon Projects, Atlanta, Ga, 2002, Both Less and More, Sculpture and Piantings, A Project Exhib, Littlejohn Contemp, NY, 2002; Pub and Pvt: Am Prints Today, Brooklyn Mus Art, NY, 86; Art on Paper, Weatherspoon Art Gallery, Univ NC, Greensboro, 95; Alternation, K&E Gallery, NY, 96; Face, One Great Jones, NY, 96; Thing, Deven Golden, NY, 96; Shag: Team Paintings by Sillman, Humphrey and Greene, Postmasters, NY, 97; Jeremy Adams: New Paintings, TZART & Co, NY, 97; Sculpture, McKee Gallery, NY, 98; Peep Show, Wise Ross Gallery, NY, 98; group exhibs, Fhuh, Fishtank Gallery, NY, 2001, Someone Must Have Been Telling Lies, Forde Gallery, Geneva Switz, 2002, New Prints, McKee Gallery, NY, 2003. *Teaching:* Instr drawing, Cooper Union, 85. *Awards:* Creative Artist Pub Serv Grant, NY, 79-80; NY State Coun Arts Award, 85; Nat Endowment Arts, 87 & 95. *Bibliog:* Owen Findsen (auth), Mysterious narratives enter new art dimension, Cincinnati Enquirer, 4/11/95; Eva Heisler (auth), Computer gargoyles, Dialogue, 9-10/95; David Carrier (auth), Pittsburgh-David Humphrey, ArtForum, 4/96. *Media:* Oil on Canvas. *Publ:* Auth, The abject romance of low resolution, Lusitania, Vol 1, No 4, 93; 1992: Selected photographs from the files of the Associated Press, 3-4/93, Lisa Hein, Tom Friedman, and Robert Gober, 5-6/93, Margaret Curtis, Drew Beattie and Daniel Davidson, 9-10/93, Art Issues; David Shirley, Option Mag, 10/93; coauth, Telepathy, 93; auth, New York fax, Art Issues, 11-12/95

HUMPHREY, JUDY LUCILLE
GRAPHIC ARTIST, PRINTMAKER
b Columbia, SC, April 6, 1949. *Study:* Univ Ga, BFA(art educ), 71, MFA(printmaking), 73. *Work:* Tenn Valley Authority Art-in-Archit, Shiloh, & Knoxville, Tenn; E Tenn State Univ, Johnson City; McDonalds Corp Hqs, Chicago, Ill; Williams House Collection, Winston-Salem, NC; Contemp Drawing Collection, Trenton State Collection, Queens Col Gallery, Bayside, NY. *Exhib:* Hoyt National New Castle, PA, 92; Northern Nat, Nicolet Gallery, Rhinelter, WI, 93,94; Print Club Int, Philadelphia, PA, 93; Boston Printmakers 44th Print Exhib, Boston, MA, 93; Paper in Porticulor, Columbia, MI, America's 2000 Int, Minot, ND, 93; Art on Paper Gallery on Circle, MD, 93; Prints and Paper, San Diego Art Inst Mus, San Diego, Calif, 93; 6th Print Ann, New World Sch Gallery, Miami, Fla, 94; All Am Print Comp Mory Moody Gallery, Canyon Tex, 94; 5th Ark Biennal Art & Sci Ctr, Pine Bluff, Ark, 94; Priva Gross Int, Qcc Gallery, Bayside NY, 94; 44th Ann Exhib of Contemp Realism; Church Gallery, Springfield, MA, 94; All Am Print Comp Univ Gallery, Canyon, Tex, 94; 18th Art on Paper; Gallery on Circle Innopolis, MD, 94; Printmakers Renaissance II Rolling Stone Press, Atlanta GA, 95; Stockton National VIII, Haggin Mus, Stockton CA, 95; Artistic Impression of the Environment Dept of Interior Mus, Washington, DC, 96; Stockton National IX Haggin Mus, Stockton, Calif, 96; Border Biennal, Mus of York, Rock Hill, SC, 98; 18th Nat Print Ex Artistic Gallery, Fort Loayne, in 98; On/Off Paper EX, Green Hall Gallery, Murfresboro, NC, 99; Celebrating Legacy of Romare Bearden, McColl Center, Charlotte, NC, 2002; Southern Printmaking Biennal, Holg Gallery, Dattonega, GA, 2002. *Teaching:* Prof 2D design, printmaking & photog, Appalachian State Univ, 73-. *Awards:* Purchase Award, 9th Ann Henley Southeastern Spectrum, NC, 90; Merit Award, 72nd Nat Exhib, 91; Purchase Award, 33rd NDak Print & Drawing Ann, 91; Regional Artist Project Grant From NC Art Council, 2000; URC Grant, Crotis Williams Graduate Sch and Univ Research Council, ASU, Boone NC, 2000; Univ of NC of Governor's Excellence in Teaching Award, 2002. *Mem:* Southern Graphics Coun; NC Print & Drawing Soc; Col Art Assoc, Southeastern Col Art Assoc. *Media:* Pencil, Gouache; Etching, Mixed Media Collage, Refief, MonoType, Polaroid Transfers, PineHole Photography. *Mailing Add:* Appalachian State Univ Dept Art Boone NC 28608

HUMPHREY, NENE
SCULPTOR, INSTRUCTOR
b Portage, Wis, Mar 18, 47. *Study:* St Mary's Col, Notre Dame, Ind, BFA, 69; Goddard Col, Boston, MA, 72; York Univ, Toronto, Can, MFA, 78. *Work:* York Univ, Toronto, Ont; Hofstra Univ; Best Products, Va; High Mus Art, Atlanta, Ga; Smithsonian, Washington, DC. *Comn:* Enclosed Garden-Landscape (sculpture), Artpark, Lewiston, NY, 80; Meadow Passage-Forest House (sculpture), Morris Mus, Morristown, NJ, 81; Roadrise-Resting Space, Creative Time, NY, 83; Atlanta Road, Atlanta Arts Festival; Passages (sculpture), St Mary's Col, Notre Dame, Ind. *Exhib:* Lines of Vision: Drawings by Contemp Women, Hillwood Gallery & Blum Helman Warehouse, NY; Threadwaxing Space, NY; Boise Art Mus, Idaho; High Mus, Atlanta, Ga; Sculpture 94, SC State Mus, Columbia; Sandler Hudson Gallery, Atlanta, Ga; Univ Colo; Katonah Mus, 99; Hecksler Mus, 99. *Pos:* Consult, Art in Pub Places, Seattle Arts Commission, 81-; adv panel, Recontres Choregraphiques Int/Danspace, NY, 97. *Teaching:* Vis artist, Nova Scotia Col Art & Design, 82, Parsons Sch Art, NY & Princeton Univ, 98, RI Sch Design. *Awards:* Macdowell Fel, Macdowell Colony, 78; Nat Endowment Arts Grant, 83; Rockefeller Artist Fel, Bellagio, Italy, 87; Anonymous Was A Woman Award, 98. *Bibliog:* Cynthia Nadelman (auth), Recent Drawings by Sculptors: A Common Language, Drawing, 7/94 & 8/94; Susan Hapgood (auth), Feminine Strategies, Object Lessons, Feminine dialogues with the surreal, Mass Col Art, 95; Susan Krane (auth), Nene Humphrey, A Wild Patience, Univ Colo, 98. *Mem:* Col Art Asn; fel mem MacDowell Colony. *Publ:* Illusr & contribr, Three stories, Criss-Cross Communications Mag, Colo, 81; Lines of Vision: Drawings by Contemporaves Women, Hudson Hills Press, NY, 89. *Mailing Add:* 325 W 37th St New York NY 10008

HUNG, CHIN-CHENG
CALLIGRAPHER, PAINTER
Study: Nat Military Inst; Fu Hsing Kang Col; Savannah Col Art & Design, MFA, 77. *Comn:* Many pvt collections. *Exhib:* numerous group and solo exhib's. *Pos:* Off, Rep China Army, Taiwan, formerly. *Teaching:* instr, Found Studies, 99-. *Awards:* numerous juried awards. *Media:* Paints, Oils and Pastels. *Mailing Add:* 14 Steeple Run Way Savannah GA 31405

HUNGERFORD, CONSTANCE CAIN
EDUCATOR, HISTORIAN
b Chicago, Ill, Apr 26, 48. *Study:* Wellesley Col, BA, 70; Univ Calif, Berkeley, MA, 72, PhD, 77. *Teaching:* From instr to prof hist art, Swarthmore Col, Pa, 75-, chmn dept art, 81-87. *Awards:* Am Coun Learned Soc, 78; Am Philos Soc, 80; Am Asn Univ Women, 82-83; NEH, 92-93. *Mem:* Col Art Asn. *Res:* Nineteenth century French painting, specifically Ernest Meissonier (1815-1891). *Publ:* Auth, Meissonier's Souvenir de Guerre Civile, Art Bulletin, 79; Meissonier's first military paintings, Parts I & II, Arts Mag, 80; Meissonier and the founding of the Societe Nationale des Beaux Arts, Art Journal, 89; Meissonier's Siege de Paris & Ruines des Tuileries, Gazette des Beaux-Arts, 90; Ernest Meissonier Rétrospective, Musée des Beaux Arts, Lyons, 93. *Mailing Add:* Swarthmore Col Dept Art Swarthmore PA 19081

HUNKLER, DENNIS
PAINTER, DRAFTSMAN
b Oakland, Calif, Mar 3, 43. *Study:* New Sch Art, Toronto, 65-69; studio asst to Jack Bush, Toronto, 69-70; San Francisco Art Inst, BFA, 72. *Work:* Oakland Mus, Calif; Mus de Arte Contemp Int, Salvador, Bahia, Brazil. *Comn:* Walks, US of A (set design), Jane Brown & Co. *Exhib:* Origins - Past and Future, Art Dialogue Gallery,

Toronto, 90; Telic IV, Art Res Ctr, Kansas City, Mo, 91; Bohmische Dorfer, Mus Osdeutsche Galerie, Regensburg, 91; Okresni Vlastivedne Mus, Krumau, CSFR, 92; Adalbert Stifter Verin, Munich, 92; Blind Mirror, Newman Gallery, Toronto, 96; Abstract Reality, Simcoe Gallery, 99; plus others. *Pos:* Asst dir, Artists Resource Ctr, Oakland, Calif, 73; mem adv comt, Jane Brown Found Dance & Related Studies, Oakland, 79-. *Teaching:* Instr figure drawing, Cent Tech Sch, Toronto, 88-89. *Bibliog:* Alexander Fried (auth), The fantasy of three artists, San Francisco Examiner, 12/6/74; Thomas Albright (auth), Unique visions of nature, San Francisco Chronicle, 12/11/74; RF Stepan (auth), Dennis Hunkler's private world, Artweek, Vol 6, No 26. *Media:* Acrylic on Canvas; Pen and Ink. *Publ:* IXTUS: Poesia La Visibilidad de Lo Invisible, 2004; Numero 44, Mex, Illus. *Dealer:* Gallery Sunami 2387 Weston Rd Toronto ON M9N 1Z8. *Mailing Add:* 1080 Kingston Rd Apt #409 Toronto ON M1N 1N5 Canada

HUNT, BRYAN
SCULPTOR, PAINTER
b Terre Haute, Ind, June 7, 47. *Study:* Otis Art Inst, Los Angeles, BFA, 71; independent study, Whitney Mus Am Art, 72. *Work:* Metrop Mus Art, Solomon R Guggenheim Mus, Mus Mod Art & Whitney Mus Am Art, NY; Albright-Knox Art Gallery, Buffalo, NY; Dallas Mus Art, Tex; San Francisco Mus Mod Art; High Mus, Atlanta, Ga; Art Inst Chicago; Fogg Art Mus, Cambridge, Mass; and others. *Exhib:* Solo exhibs, Orlando Mus Art, Fla, 92, Tavelli Gallery, Aspen, Colo, 93, Laura Carpenter Fine Art, Santa Fe, NMex, 94, Gagosian Gallery, NY, 95, Locks Gallery, Philadelphia, 95, Galerie Francoise esf, Brooklandville, Md & Harley Baldwin Gallery, Aspen, Colo, 96; Solomon R Guggenheim Mus, NY, 78, 82, 88 & 89; Whitney Mus Am Art, NY, 79, 81, 82, 83, 85, 88 & 90; Mus Mod Art, NY, 79, 80, 82, 84 & 86; Hayden Gallery, Mass Inst Technol, Cambridge, 79, 82 & 85; San Francisco Mus Mod Art, Calif, 80 & 83; Art Inst Chicago, Ill, 82; Newport Harbor Art Mus, Newport Beach, Calif, traveling, 82; Houston Mus Fine Arts, Tex, 83; Inst Contemp Art, Boston, Mass, 83; Seattle Art Mus, Wash, 84; Brooklyn Mus, NY, 85, 86 & 93; Aldrich Mus Contemp Art, Ridgefield, Conn, 85, 89 & 92; Albright-Knox Art Gallery, Buffalo, NY, 86 & 87; Mus Contemp Art, Los Angeles, Calif, 86; St Louis Art Mus, Mo, 87; Sightings, Parrish Art Mus, Southampton, NY, 94; Twentieth Century Am Sculpture at the White House, The White House, Washington, DC, 94; Dennis Ochi Fine Art Serv, Ketchem, Idaho, 94; Inside Outside, From Sculpture to Photog, Lawrence Miller Gallery, NY, 95; Going for Baroque, Walters Art Gallery, Baltimore, Md, 95; Drawings from the Collection of Agnes Gund, Century Asn, NY, 95; and others. *Awards:* Grand Prize, Int Seoul Art Festival, Nat Mus Contemp Art, 90. *Bibliog:* Phyllis Tuchman (auth), Bryan Hunt Twenty Years (exhib catalog), Locks Gallery, Philadelphia, 95; John Dorsey (auth), The slightest touch is quite enough, Sun Baltimore, 2/27/96; Eric Gibson (auth), Bryan Hunt, Philadelphia Locks Gallery, Art News, 3/96; Carrie Click (auth), Bryan Hunt brings his art to Baldwin Gallery, Aspen Times, 7/96. *Media:* Construction, Bronze. *Publ:* Auth, Conversations with Nature, Mus Mod Art, New York, 82; Drawings & Fragments of Sculpture, Kyoto Sowin Int, Japan, 89. *Mailing Add:* 9 White St New York NY 10013

HUNT, COURTENAY
PAINTER, INSTRUCTOR
b Jacksonville, Fla, Sept 17, 17. *Study:* Ringling Sch Art, Studies with Jerry Farnsworth. *Work:* Univ Fla; Independent Life Insurance; Circuit Court, Jacksonville, Fla; Jacksonville Univ; Shrine Mus, Washington, DC. *Exhib:* Allied Artists Am; Sarasota Art Asn, Fla; Audubon Artists Am; Soc Four Arts, Palm Beach, Fla; Fla Artist Group Inc, Norton Gallery, Palm Beach; St Augustine Art Asn; Cummer Gallery, Jacksonville, Fla. *Teaching:* Instr, Jacksonville Art Mus & Jacksonville Jr Col & Cummer Art, Jacksonville, Fla, currently. *Awards:* St Augustine Awards, SFla Univ. *Mem:* St Augustine Art Asn. *Media:* Oil, Pastel. *Interests:* piloting aircraft. *Publ:* Artist of Fla, 90; American Art Review. *Mailing Add:* 2248 Carnes St Orange Park FL 32073-5418

HUNT, DAVID CURTIS
MUSEUM DIRECTOR, CURATOR
b Oswego, Kans, Dec 7, 35. *Study:* Univ Tulsa, BA(com design), 58, with Alexandre Hogue, MA(art hist), 68;. *Exhib:* Okla Artists Ann, Philbrook Art Ctr, Tulsa, 62-65; Legacy of the West, Joslyn Art Mus, Omaha, Nebr, 82. *Collection Arranged:* Currier & Ives' America: The Conagra Collection, Permanent installation for Conagra Inc, Omaha, Nebr, 91; Views of a Vanishing Frontier, Bodmer Exhib, InterNorth Art Found, Omaha, Nebr, 95. *Pos:* Ed, Am Scene Quart, Gilcrease Mus, 65-72, cur art, Gilcrease Inst, Tulsa, Okla, 67-72; cur collections, Stark Mus, Orange, Tex, 72-76, chief cur, 96 & 97-, dir, 98-2000; dir, Missoula Mus of the Arts, Mont, 77-80; cur art, Ctr Western Studies, Joslyn Art Mus, Omaha, 80-95. *Teaching:* Instr mus practices, Univ Tulsa, 70-72. *Awards:* Wrangler Award, Nat Cowboy Hall of Fame & Western Hertiage Ctr, 72; George Wittenborn Mem Award, Art Libr NAm, 85; Silver Medal, Int Bk Exhib, Leipzig, Ger, 89; Okla Bk Award, Okla Libr Asn, 89. *Mem:* Am Asn Mus. *Res:* 19th & 20th century American western artists and works. *Publ:* Coauth, The West as Romantic Horizon, Joslyn Art Mus & Univ Nebr Press, 81; auth, Guide to Oklahoma Mus, Univ Okla Press, 81; Legacy of the West, Joslyn Art Mus and Univ Nebr Press, 82; coauth, Karl Bodmer's America, Univ Nebr Press, 84; auth, The Lithographs of Charles Banks Wilson, Univ Okla Press, 89; Bodmer's America: The Aquatint Atlas, Alecto Hist Ed, London, 91; coauth, Tribes of the Buffalo: A Swiss Artist on the American Frontier, Cleveland Mus Natural Hist, 94; others. *Mailing Add:* c/o Stark Mus Art PO Box 1897 Orange TX 77630

HUNT, RICHARD HOWARD
SCULPTOR
b Chicago, Ill, Sept 12, 35. *Study:* Art Inst Chicago, BAE, 57. *Hon Degrees:* numerous hon degrees from US cols & univs. *Work:* Mus Mod Art, Metrop Mus Art & Whitney Mus Am Art, NY; Cleveland Mus Art, Ohio; Art Inst Chicago; Hirshhorn Mus; Mus 20th Century, Vienna, Austria; Nat Mus Art, Wash; Albright-Knox Gallery, Buffalo, NY. *Comn:* A Bridge Across and Beyond (welded bronze), Howard Univ, 78; Build-Grow (welded stainless steel), York Col, Queens, NY, 86; Freedman's Column (welded bronze), Howard Univ, Wash; Spatial Interactions (welded bronze), Hunter Mus Art, Chattanooga, Tenn, 91; Build-Grow, Growth Columns, Branching Column and Crane Column (welded bronze), Edward Bennett Williams Bldg, Wash, 92. *Exhib:* Retrospective, Mus Mod Art, NY, 71 & Chicago Art Inst, 71; solo exhibs, Milwaukee Art Ctr, 67, Mus Mod Art, NY, 71, Art Inst Chicago, 71, Okla Art Ctr, 73, Century City, Los Angeles, 87, Mus African Am Art, 87-88 & Kalamazoo Inst Art, 90; Gwenda Jay Gallery, Chicago, Ill, 91; Louis Newman Gallery, Los Angeles, Calif, 91; Shiduni Gallery, Santa Fe, NMex, 92; Woolot Gallery, Sheboygan, Wis, 94. *Pos:* Mem, bd gov, Sch Art Inst, Chicago, 85-91. *Teaching:* Asst prof, Sch Art Inst Chicago, 60-62, Univ Ill, 61-63; vis artist, Yale Univ, 64, Northwestern Univ, 68-69 & Washington Univ, 77-78; artist-in-residence, Eastern Mich Univ, Ypsilanti, 88 & Harvard Univ, 89-90. *Awards:* Guggenheim Fel, 62-63; Tamarind Artist Fel, Ford Found, 65; Am Acad Arts & Letts Award, 98. *Mem:* Am Coun Arts (bd dir, 74-); Col Art Asn Am (bd dir, 72-76); Am Acad Rome (bd trustees, 80-82); Nat Acad. *Media:* Welded Metal, Cast Metal. *Dealer:* Worthington Gallery. *Mailing Add:* 379 W Broadway New York NY 10012-5121

HUNTER, DEBORA
PHOTOGRAPHER, EDUCATOR
b Chicago, Ill, June 16, 50. *Study:* Northwestern Univ, BA, 72; RI Sch Design, MFA(photog), 76. *Work:* Yale Univ Art Mus; Wesleyan Univ Art Mus; Dallas Mus Art; RI Sch Design, Providence; Amon Carter Mus Art; Houston Mus Fine Art. *Exhib:* Dallas Mus Fine Arts, 79; The New Season, Witkin Gallery, NY; Second Sight, Carpenter Ctr Arts, Harvard, 81; Invisible Light Traveling Exhib, Smithsonian Inst, 80; one-person shows, Delahunty Gallery, Dallas, 80, The Light Factory, Charlotte, NC, 81, Int Mus Photog, 80, Meadows Mus, Southern Methodist Univ, 89 & Emporia State Univ, 89; Directions 1981, Hirshhorn Mus, 81; Mus Contemp Photog, Chicago, 85; Trains & Boats & Planes, Witkin Gallery, NY, 88; Portrayal, Bridge Ctr Contemp Art, El Paso, Tex, 89; two person show, Sitting Pretty, Art Inst Chicago, 92. *Teaching:* Instr, Swain Sch Design, New Bedford, Mass, 75-76; assoc prof photog, Southern Methodist Univ, Dallas, 76-; vis assoc prof Sch Art Inst Chicago, 84-85. *Awards:* Boston Ctr for the Arts Award, Photovisions, 75; First Prize in Photog, Tarrant Co Ann, Ft Worth Art Mus, 76; Mid Am Arts Alliance, NEA, 87. *Bibliog:* Lucy Lippard (auth), From the Center: Feminist Essays on Women's Art, Dutton, 76; David Dillon (auth), From the lighthouse, D Mag, Dallas, 78; article, Artforum, 4/81; article, Chicago Tribune, 12/6/85; article, Dallas Life Mag, Dallas Morning News, 11/5/89; article, Photo J Asahi Camera (Japanese), 8/90. *Media:* Black & White, Color. *Publ:* Contribr, Camera, 8-9/75; Women See Women, Crowell, 76; A Ten Year Salute, Addison House, 79; Popular Photog, 8/80. *Dealer:* Witkin Gallery 41 E 57th St New York NY 10022. *Mailing Add:* Dept Art Southern Methodist Univ Dallas TX 75275

HUNTER, JOHN H
PAINTER, PRINTMAKER
b Pa, Sept 26, 34. *Study:* Pomona Col, BA, 56; Claremont Grad Sch, MFA, 58. *Work:* Mus Mod Art, NY; Los Angeles Co Mus; Pasadena Art Mus, Calif; Amon-Carter Mus, Ft Worth, Tex; Nat Gallery Art, Washington, DC; and others. *Comn:* Poster for Tamarind Exhib, Mus Mod Art, Tamarind Lithography Workshop, Los Angeles, 69. *Exhib:* Western Painters Under 35, Univ Calif, Los Angeles, 58; Fulbright Artists Show, US Info Serv, Florence, Italy, 65; Cannes Film Festival, 66; Painters Behind Painters, Calif Palace of Legion of Honor, San Francisco, 67; Drawings, Ft Worth Art Ctr Mus, 69; Decade of Accomplishment, Ill Bell Tel Co, Chicago, 70. *Teaching:* Instr fine art, Ohio State Univ, 60-63; guest artist, Ind Univ, Bloomington, summer 63; prof art, Calif State Univ, San Jose, 65-; guest artist, Tamarind Lithography Workshop, 69 & Lakeside Studios, 79. *Awards:* Fulbright Fel Painting, Florence, 63-64, Renewal Grantee, 64-65. *Bibliog:* Peter Plagens (auth), Possibilities of drawing, Artforum, 10/69; articles, New York Times, Los Angeles Times, Rome Daily Am, Art News & others. *Mem:* Artists Equity Asn. *Media:* Multimedia. *Mailing Add:* 1621 Mable Ave Modesto CA 95355-1240

HUNTER, LEONARD LEGRANDE, III
SCULPTOR, EDUCATOR
b Washington, DC, July 3, 40. *Study:* Univ Miami, BA; Grad Sch Archit, Univ Pa; Univ Calif, Berkeley, MFA. *Work:* Hopkins Ctr, Dartmouth Col; The City of San Francisco; Headland Ctr Arts; The City of Busan, Korea. *Comn:* Environmental outdoor hydraulic-kinetic sculpture, Crossroads Plaza, Lexington, Ky, 74. *Exhib:* One-man show, Univ Art Mus, Berkeley, 72; Biennial, New Orleans Mus Art, 73; Annual, Whitney Mus Am Art, 75; Film Festival of the Americas, Virgin Islands, 77; Busan Biennale, Korea; and others. *Pos:* Asst dir, Visual Arts Prog, Nat Endowment Arts, 80-83, acting dir, 81-82. *Teaching:* Assoc prof art, Univ Ky, 72-80, chmn dept art, 78-80; prof art, San Francisco State Univ, 83-. *Awards:* Teaching Fel, Univ Ky, 73-74; Golden Venus Medallion, Film Festival of the Americas, 77; and others. *Media:* Stainless Steel. *Res:* Public art & community research. *Interests:* Public art & architecturally-scaled sculpture. *Mailing Add:* San Francisco State Univ Dept Art 1600 Holloway Ave San Francisco CA 94132

HUNTER, PAUL
PAINTER, SCULPTOR
b Paris, France; US citizen. *Study:* Laval Univ, Quebec City, BA (vis arts), 1977; Concordia Univ, Montreal, MFA, 1979. *Work:* Coca-Cola Co, Atlanta, Ga; Quebec Mus; Refco Group Ltd, Chicago, Ill; Lighting Asn Inc; March & McClennan, Boston, Mass; Bessemer Trust Co, Los Angeles, Calif; Nationsbank, bd rm, Miami, Fla; Alston & Bird LLP, lobby & conf room, NY; Reliance Int, NY; Art Mus Princeton, NJ; Arthur Anderson & Co, NY; and others. *Comn:* Mural, St Francis Hosp, Quebec City, 1988; murals, Madeleine Islands Hosp, PQ, 1992; McKinsey and Co, Miami,

Fla, 1998. *Exhib:* Les Temps Chauds, Montreal Mus Contemp Art, traveled, France & Belg, 88; Tribute to Tibor de Nagy, Butler Inst Am Art, Youngstown, Ohio, 89; Miniature Environments, Whitney Mus Art at Philip Morris, NY, 89; Harmond & Discord: Am Landscape Painting Today, Va Mus Fine Arts, Richmond, 90; Paul Hunter in Perspective, Musee du Que, Can; Solo Exhib: Selected Paintings, Byron Roche Gallery, Chicago, 2005, Gotik, Matermushaus XX, World Youth Day, Cologne, 2005, Nucturnes Series, Byron Roche Gallery, 2005, Variations on a Theme, Pan Am Gallery, DAllas, 2005, Life Paintings, 150 E 4nd St, New York City, 2006, Works on Paper, Andrea Horstmann-Osterich, Cologne, 2006 and others; All Than Glitters, Islip Art Mus, NY, 2003; Small Treasures, A&C Fine Art, East Greenwich, RI, 2003; Chicago Art Fair, 2004; Landscape Abstracts, Allen Sheppard Gallery, New York City, 2004; Works on Paper, Andrea Horstmann-Osterich, Cologne, 2006; and others. *Collection Arranged:* The Art Mus of Princeton Univ, Princeton, NJ; The Butler Inst, of American Art, Youngtown, OH; Montreal Mus of Fine Art, Montreal, QC; Quebec Mus, Quebec, QC. *Awards:* Can Coun grant, 1986-1988, 1991; Pollock-Krasner Found Award, 87; Quebec Govt artists fel, 1984, 1988, 1991; Nat Studio Program, Inst Art & Urban Resources, 1985. *Bibliog:* Jurgen Kisters, J Deutsch-Kanadischen Gesellschaft, 3/2005 & Kolner Stadt-Anzeiger, 8/23/2005; Michel Bois (auth), Le Soleil, 10/23/2005; and others. *Media:* Mixed Media on Gold on Canvas. *Publ:* Auth, Les Temps Chauds (exhib catalog), Montreal Mus Contemp Art, 88; Drawn from Life: Contemporary Interpretive Landscape (exhib catalog), Sewell Art Gallery, Rice Univ, Houston, Tex, 88; Paul Hunter in Perspective (exhib, catalog), Musee du Que, Can, 90; All That Glitters, Karen Shaw, Islip Art Mus, Islip, NY, 2004. *Dealer:* Byron Roche Gallery, Chicago IL. *Mailing Add:* 550 Riverside Dr New York NY 10027

HUNTER, ROBERT DOUGLAS
PAINTER, INSTRUCTOR
b Boston, Mass, Mar 17, 28. *Study:* Cape Sch Art, Provincetown, Mass, with Henry Hensche; Vesper George Sch Art, Boston; also with R H Ives Gammell, Boston. *Work:* Northeastern Univ, Boston; Tufts Univ; Boston Univ Med Ctr; Mass Inst Technol; Harvard Univ. *Comn:* Epiphany mural, Church St Mary of the Harbor, Provincetown, 56; altar frontal, Emmanuel Church, West Roxbury, Mass, 62. *Exhib:* Acad Artists Show, Springfield, Mass, 61; Am Artist Prof League Show, NY, 66, 67 & 70; New Eng Artists Exhib, Boston, 70 & 74. *Teaching:* Instr fine arts, Vesper George Sch Art, 55-83 & Worchester Art Mus, 70-79. *Awards:* 15 Richard Mitton Gold Medals, New Eng Artists Exhib, 54-70; Newington Prize, 66 & 67, Am Artists Prof League; Frederick Thompson Found Award, 76. *Bibliog:* Richard Goetz (auth), Sight sized method, Am Artist, 70; Edward Fett (auth), Robert Douglas Hunter The Boston School Tradition, Am Artist, 90. *Mem:* Am Artists Prof League (dir, 60-70); Guild Boston Artists (vpres, 68-73, pres, 73-78); Acad Artists Asn; Copley Soc Boston. *Media:* Oil. *Dealer:* Tree's Place Gallery Orleans Mass; J Todd Gallery Wellesley Mass. *Mailing Add:* 492 Lincoln Rd Walpole MA 02081

HUNTER, ROBERT HOWARD
PAINTER
b Auburn, Wash, May 17, 29. *Study:* Ore State Univ, 47-49; Univ Ore, BS & MFA, 49-53; Univ SC, 55-56. *Work:* Greenville Co Mus Art, SC; SC State Mus; Pepsico Corp, Purchase, NY; IBM Charlotte, NC; MCI Corp, Rye, NY; Springs Mills, Inc, NY; Wachovia Bank, Charlotte, NC. *Exhib:* 159th Ann Painters & Sculptors, Philadelphia, 64; 7th Nat Show Art, Brockton, Mass, 64; Art on Paper, Weatherspoon Art Gallery, NC, 65; one-man show, Ackland Art Ctr, Univ NC, Chapel Hill, 68; 16th Ann Drawing & Small Sculpture Show, Ball State Univ, 70; one-man retrospective (with catalog), SC State Mus, Columbia, 92. *Pos:* Gallery dir, Rudolph Lee Gallery, Clemson Univ, 58-68; Ford Found fel, Univ NC, Chapel Hill, 66-67. *Teaching:* Instr figure drawing, Univ Ore, 52-53; prof printmaking, painting & basic design, Clemson Univ, 56-92, head dept visual arts 67-71, prof art, 68-92; prof emer, visual arts, 1992. *Awards:* Guild of SC Artists Awards, 56-63; Springs Art Contest, SC, 61 & 77; 8th Ann Painting of Yr, Atlanta Art Asn, 62. *Media:* Painting, Watercolor. *Publ:* Auth, Twenty Lithographs by Robert Hunter, 61; The Shape of R Hunter, 66; illusr, The Binnacle, R Peterson, 67; contribr, Contemporary Artists of South Carolina, 70; auth Robert Hunter, SC TV, 92; Hunter, Alaska, 2000; Robert Hunter (promotional video), Hunter Art Studio, 2001; Hunter, 2003. *Dealer:* Hunter Art Studio 750 Broadway Skagway AK 99840

HUNTER, SAM
HISTORIAN
b Springfield, Mass, Jan 5, 23. *Study:* Williams Col, AB; Univ Florence, cert; Breva Acad Fine Arts, Milan, Italy, hon degree, 93. *Exhib:* A View from the Sixties: Selections from the Leo Castelli collection and the Michael and Ileana Sonnabend collection (exhib & catalog), Guild Hall Art Mus, EHampton, NY, 91; The NY Sch, Arte Americana, 1930-1970, Il Lingotto Mus, Torin, Italy, 92; Against All Odds & An Am Master: Jason Pollock Paintings, Prints & Drawings, Ueno Royal Mus, Tokyo, 94. *Collection Arranged:* Many exhibs at Mus Mod Art, New York, Minneapolis Inst Arts, Rose Art Mus, Jewish Mus, New York & Princeton Art Mus; American Art from the Commodities Collection (catalog), circulating exhib to six Am Mus, 81-82; Aspects of Post-Modernism: Decorative and New Image Art, ER Squibb & Sons Art Galleries, Princeton, NJ, 81; Richard Pousette - Dart, Karel Appel Retrospectives, 86; Mus Art, Ft Lauderdale, Fla, 86-89. *Pos:* Art critic, NY Times, 47-49; ed, Harry N Abrams Inc, NY, 52-53, consult ed, 68-, vpres & ed-in-chief, 71-72; cur, Mus Mod Art, 56-58; dir, Minneapolis Inst Art, 58-60, Rose Art Mus, Brandeis Univ, 60-65 & Jewish Mus, 65-68; fac cur mod art, Princeton Art Mus, 69-; consult, Commodities Corp, Princeton, NJ, 80-; consult & guest cur, Mus Art, Fort Lauderdale, Fla, 85-87; adv, Mus Mod & Contemp Art, Nice, France, 87-89 & M Knoedler & Co, New York, 89-92; adv, Fujisankei Mus Japan, 92-, Very Special Arts, Kennedy Ctr, Washington, DC, 93-; int jury, Fujisankei Biennale, 93, 95. *Teaching:* instr, Harvard Univ, Univ Calif, Los Angeles, Barnard Col, Columbia Univ & Cornell Univ, formerly; asst prof, Univ Calif, Los Angeles, 55-57; assoc prof art hist, Brandeis Univ, 63-65; prof art hist, Princeton Univ, 69-91, emer prof, 91-98; Robert Sterling Clark vis prof, Williams Col, 76. *Awards:* Hubbard Hutchinson Fel Critical Studies, Williams Col, 49-52; Guggenheim Fel, 70-71. *Mem:* Col Art Asn Am. *Publ:* Auth, Marino Marini, Harry N Abrams Inc, New York & Fabbri Ed, Milan, 92; Gaston Lachaise, Abbeville Press, 93; Figure & Form: Present, Past & Personal: The Collection of Dr Frank Purnell & Dr Mel Blake, Millwood Publ, New York, 94; Arnaldo Pomodoro, Rizzoli, New York & Fabbri Ed, Milan, 95; Tom Wesselmann, Rizzoli, New York, 95; Modern Art: Painting, Sculpture Architecture, Harry N. Abrams, Inc, four edits; Robert Rauschenberg, Rizzoli, NY, 99; plus others. *Mailing Add:* 57 Sycamore Ln Skillman NJ 08558-9648

HUNTER-STIEBEL, PENELOPE HUNTER STIEBEL
CURATOR
b Washington, DC. *Study:* Barnard Col, BA; Inst Fine Art, NY Univ, MA. *Collection Arranged:* Twentieth Century Decorative Arts Gallery, 71-74 & 78-83; The Grand Gallery Int Exhib (ed, catalog), 74; New Glass Exhib, Metrop Mus Art, 80; The Fine Art of the Furniture Maker (coauth, catalog), Mem Art Gallery, Rochester, 81; Elements of Style: The Art of the Bronze Mount in the 18th and 19th Century France (auth, catalog), 84, A Bronze Bestiary (auth, catalog), 85 & Menuiserie, the Carved Wood Furniture of 18th Century France, 86, Chez Elle, Chez Lui, At Home in 18th Century France (auth, catalog), 87, Rosenberg & Stiebel Inc; Louis XV & Madame De Pompadour: A Love Affair with Style (auth, catalog), Dixon Gallery, Memphis, Rosenberg & Stiebel; William Beckman: Dossier of a Classical Woman (auth, catalog), Stiebel Mod, Ind Univ Art Mus, 91; Stroganoff the Palace & Collections of a Russian Noble Family (ed, catalog), Portland Art Mus, Oreg, 2000. *Pos:* Asst cur, Metrop Mus Art, 75-80, assoc cur, 80-83; contrib cur, Philbrook Art Ctr, Tulsa, 82-87; guest cur, Detroit Inst Arts, 83-85; principal, Rosenberg & Steibel Inc, 86-2000; adv coun, Grad Prog, Fashion Inst Technol, currently; consult cur European art, Portland Art Mus, 2000-. *Res:* Sixteenth through twentieth century decorative arts. *Publ:* Auth, Gustav Serrurier-Bovy, a forgotten master of Art Nouveau, Connoisseur, 11/82; The transcendent materialism of Albert Paley, Mus Fine Arts, Springfield, Mass, 85; Four masters of art deco, Antiques, 8/85; French Furniture of the Eighteenth Century by Pierre Verlet, Univ Press Va, 91; Art collecting, Encyclopedia Americana, 96; and others. *Mailing Add:* 252 E 68th St New York NY 10021

HUNTINGTON, JIM
SCULPTOR
b Elkhart, Ind, Jan 13, 41. *Study:* Ind Univ, Bloomington, 58-59; El Camino Col, 59-60. *Work:* Addison Gallery Am Art, Andover, Mass; Oakland Mus, Calif; Whitney Mus Am Art, Chase Manhattan Bank, Madison Square Garden Corp & Storm King Art Ctr, NY; Aerobay Off Ctr, Burlingame, Calif; and others. *Comn:* Taubman Co, Stoneridge Ctr, Pleasanton, Calif, 80; Henry Segerstrom, South Coast Plaza, Costa Mesa, Calif, 81; Hahn Co, Santa Rosa, Calif, 82; Insurance Co NAm, Wilmington, Del, 82; IBM, San Jose, 84. *Exhib:* Selections 1964, Inst Contemp Art, Boston, 64; Art Across Am, Inst Contemp Art, Boston, 65; Biennial, Corcoran Gallery, Washington, 65 & 67; Art for Embassies, Inst Contemp Art, Boston, 66; Ann, Whitney Mus Am Art, NY, 68 & 69; one-man shows, Hayden Gallery, Mass Inst Technol, 68, David McKee Gallery, NY, 75, 76 & 80, Leah Levy Gallery, San Francisco, 82, Gallery Paule Anglim, San Francisco, 85, RC Erpt Gallery, NY, Stephen Wirtz Gallery, San Francisco, 88, 89, 91 & 92 & Putter/Pence Gallery, Los Angeles, 88; Bay Area Sculpture: Metal, Stone and Wood, Palo Alto Cult Ctr, Calif, 88; Traveling Exhib, Sightings: Drawing with Color, NY, Spain & Portugal, 88; Wood, Metal Stone, Andre Zarre Gallery, NY, 89; Sculptural Intimacies: Recent Small-Scale Work (with catalog) Security Pac Gallery, Los Angeles, 89; and others. *Teaching:* Instr art, Cooper Union, NY, 68, Hunter Col, NY, 70-72, Lehman Col, NY, 70-76 & Princeton Univ, NJ, 78. *Awards:* Grand Prize Award, Sheraton-Boston Competition & Blanche Colman Award, Boston, 65; Nat Endowment Arts Fel, 80-81 & 84-85; Pollock-Krasner Found Grant, 86; Adolph & Esther Gottlieb Found Grant, 86. *Bibliog:* Kenneth Baker (auth), San Francisco Chronicle, 72, 88, 91 & 92; Steven Appleton (auth), A Visual Conspiracy, Artweek, 12/28/89; Susan Geer, Los Angeles Times, 11/25/88. *Media:* Stone, Cast Iron. *Mailing Add:* c/o Stephen Wirtz Gallery 49 Geary St San Francisco CA 94108

HUNTOON, ABBY E
SCULPTOR, CRAFTSMAN
b Providence, RI, Sept 8, 51. *Study:* Boston Univ, MFA(ceramics), 83. *Work:* Index Group Inc & Putnam, Hayes, Bartlett Inc Cambridge, Mass; Standish, Ayer & Wood, Boston, Mass. *Comn:* Wallhanging, Mast Landing Elem Sch, Freeport, Maine, 92; wall hanging, Woodside Elem Sch, Topsham, Maine, 93; Wall Hanging, Pitston Elem Sch, Pitston, Maine, 94. *Exhib:* Everson Mus, Syracuse, NY, 87-89; Tenth Ann Exhib, Maine Coast Artist, Rockport, 89; 46th Ceramics Ann, Lang Art Scripts Col, Claremont, Calif, 90; one-woman show, Frick Gallery, Belfast, Maine, 90; Frick Gallery, Belfast, Maine, 92; Lakes Gallery, Casco, Maine, 94; and others. *Awards:* Merit Award, Biennial Exhib Maine Crafts, 86; Nat Endowment Arts Visual Artists Grant, 88. *Bibliog:* articles in various mags incl Ceramics Monthly, Am Craft, Portland Mag, Greater Portland Mag, 86-90. *Mem:* Maine Art Comn. *Publ:* Auth, The Best of Pottery, 96. *Mailing Add:* 170 Harriet St Portland ME 04106

HUOT, ROBERT
PAINTER, FILMMAKER
b Staten Island, NY, Sept 16, 35. *Study:* Wagner Col, Staten Island, 53-57, BSc, 57; Hunter Col, grad art, New York, 61-62. *Work:* Frank Stella, NY; Paula Cooper, NY; William Rubin Collection, NY; Doberman Collection, Munster, Ger; Mus of Mod Art, NY. *Exhib:* Systematic Painting, Guggenheim Mus, NY, 66; The Art of the Real Traveling Exhib, 68 & Recent Acquisitions, 78, Mus Mod Art, NY; Whitney Painting Ann, Whitney Mus, NY, 67 & 69; New Art USA, Mod Mus of Art, Minchem, WGer,

68; Seattle Art Mus, Wash, 69; Modular Painting, Albright-Knox Gallery, Buffalo, NY, 70; one-man shows, Paula Cooper Gallery, NY, 69-74, Millennium, NY, 75 & 79 & State Univ of NY, Albany, 76; Utica Col, 79-80; Hetzler Galerie, WGer, 80-81. *Pos:* Pigment chemist, Sun Chemical Co, Staten Island, 57-58 & 60-62; plant mgr, Neti Art Color, New York, 62-63. *Teaching:* Assoc prof painting, drawing & filmmaking, Hunter Col, New York, 63-81. *Awards:* Nat Coun Arts Grant, New York, 66 & with Twyla Tharp Dance Co, 77. *Bibliog:* S MacDonald (auth), article, 4/79 & An interview with Robert Huot, 2/80, Afterimage. *Media:* Unstretched Canvas; Film. *Dealer:* Filmmakers Coop 175 Lexington Ave New York NY 10016; Max Hetzler Stuttgart WGer. *Mailing Add:* Spurr St RD 1 Box 41 New Berlin NY 13411

HUPP, FREDERICK DUIS
PAINTER, EDUCATOR
b Streator, Ill, Dec 21, 38. *Study:* Univ Ariz, BFA, 62, MFA, 66. *Work:* Tucson Mus Art, Ariz. *Exhib:* Univ Man, Winnipeg, 76; SW Biennial, Mus NMex, Santa Fe, 76; Eight State West Biennial, Grand Junction, Colo, 76; Four Corners Biennial, Phoenix, Ariz, 77; Univ Ariz Art Mus, Tucson, 79; and others. *Pos:* Cur, Univ Ariz Art Mus, 60-61 & Mus Fine Arts, Santa Fe, 62; instr, Fenster Ranch Sch, Tucson, 64-65. *Teaching:* Instr design, Univ Ariz, 68-79; asst prof drawing & painting, Tucson Mus Sch, 68-80, dir educ, 68-70; instr design & drawing, Pima Col, Tucson, 77-. *Awards:* Eight West State Biennial Cash Award, Grand Junction, Colo, 74; Four Corners Biennial Cash Award, Phoenix, Ariz, 75; Cash Award, Cedar City Nat, Utah, 76. *Media:* Acrylic, Mixed. *Mailing Add:* 7 N Tucson Terr Tucson AZ 85745

HUREWITZ, FLORENCE K
PAINTER, EDUCATOR
b Passaic, NJ. *Study:* Cooper Union Sch Art & Archit, BFA, 76; Art Students League; Am Art Sch. *Work:* Bergen Community Mus, Paramus, NJ. *Exhib:* Biannual Show, NJ State Mus, Trenton, NJ; Invitational for Prize Winners, Jersey City Mus, NJ; Am Drawing Biennial, Norfolk Mus Art, Va; Nat Asn Women Artists Travel Oil Show, Pallazzo Vechio, Florence, Italy; Audubon Artists, Nat Acad, NY. *Pos:* Designer stained glass, Rambusch & Co, NY; asst exhib cur, Cooper Union Mus. *Teaching:* Inst fine art painting, Bergen Community Col, Paramus, NJ, 73-85; Art Ctr of N NJ, New Milford, 85-. *Awards:* Medal of Honor, Nat Asn Women Artists, 75; Medal of Honor, Nat Asn Women Artists, 86; Jersey City Mus Medal, Painters & Sculptors Soc. *Bibliog:* David Spengler (auth), Woman as an Artist, Bergen Record, 74; Kathy Damecker (auth), Studio Visit--F Hurewitz, Cablevision, NJ, 82; Eileen Watkins (auth), Woman on the Verge, Star Ledger, Newark, 89. *Mem:* Col Art Asn; Nat Asn Women Artists; Womans Caucus for Arts; Artist's Equity of New York. *Media:* Oil. *Dealer:* Kornbluth Gallery Fairlawn Ave Fairlawn NJ 07410. *Mailing Add:* 0-95 Midland Ave Fair Lawn NJ 07410

HURLEY, DENZIL H
PAINTER, PRINTMAKER
b Barbados, West Indies, Jan 16, 49. *Study:* Portland Mus Art Sch, BFA, 75; Yale Univ, MFA, 79. *Work:* Metrop Mus Art & Brooklyn Mus Art, NY; San Francisco Mus Mod Art, Calif; Portland Art Mus, Ore; Libr Congr, Washington. *Comn:* Murals, 76 & 77, prints, 76, City of Portland, Ore. *Exhib:* Oregon Print Ann, Portland Art Mus, 75; 21st Print Biannual, 78-79, 22nd Print Biannual, 81-82, Brooklyn Mus, NY; New Geometry, Del Ctr for Contemp Art, 89; Minimalism, Its Affinities & Aftermath, Seattle Art Mus, 96; Abstract Painting, Ctr Contemp Art, Seattle, Wash, 97; Am Acad Arts & Letts, NY; Ctr Contemp Art, Seattle, Wash, 97; Edward Broida Col, 98; Holland Gallery, Southern Methodist Univ, 98. *Teaching:* Lectr printmaking, Yale Sch Art, 79-83; asst prof painting, Scripts Col & Claremont Grad Sch, 84-86; from asst to assoc prof, Hampshire Col, 86-94; prof painting, Sch Art, Univ Wash, Seattle, 94-. *Awards:* Guggenheim Fel, 80; Pollock-Krasner Found Grant, 89; Nat Endowment Arts Fel, 89, 93 & 94. *Bibliog:* Colin Gardner (auth), article, Los Angeles Times, 7/25/86. *Mem:* Col Art Asn. *Media:* Oil; Etching. *Publ:* Contribr, Perspecta 19, MIT Press, 82. *Dealer:* Burnett Miller Gallery 964 N LaBrea Los Angeles CA. *Mailing Add:* Univ of Washington 336 Art Bldg Seattle WA 98104

HURLEY, WILSON
PAINTER
b Tulsa, Okla, Apr 11, 24. *Study:* US Mil Acad, BS, 45; George Washington Univ Law Sch, LLB, 51. *Work:* US Air Force Mus, Wright-Patterson AFB, Ohio; Buffalo Bill Hist Ctr, Cody, Wyo; Nat Cowboy Hall Fame, Okla City; Gilcrease Mus, Tulsa, Okla; Eiteljurg Mus, Indianapolis, Ind. *Comn:* Mural (triptych), Metrop Libr, Midwest City, Okla; Albuquerque (diptych), Int Airport; murals, Nat Cowboy Hall of Fame, Oklahoma City, Okla. *Exhib:* Nat Acad Western Art, Oklahoma City, 73-88; solo exhibs, Nat Cowboy Hall Fame, 77 & Thomas Gilcrease Mus, Tulsa, 83; solo: retrospective Albuquerque Mus Art & Whitney Mus Western Art, Cody, Wyo, 85; Artists of Am, Denver, 81-88. *Teaching:* Scottsdale Artists Sch, 84 & 87. *Awards:* Silver Medal, 73 & 80 & Gold Medal, 77, 78 & 84, Nat Acad Western Art; Prix de West, Nat Acad Western Art, 84. *Bibliog:* Lowell Press, 77; Gilcrease Mag Am Hist & Art, Vol 5, No 2, 83; A retrospective exhib, Lowell Press, 85. *Media:* Oil. *Publ:* Illusr, Without Noise of Arms, Briggs, Northland, 75. *Dealer:* Altermann & Morris Galleries Dallax TX; Nedra Matteucci Galleries Santa Fe NM. *Mailing Add:* 237 Spring Creek Ct NE Albuquerque NM 87122

HURLSTONE, ROBERT WILLIAM
GLASS ARTIST, EDUCATOR
b Chicago, Ill, June 3, 52. *Study:* Ill State Univ, BS, 74; Southern Ill Univ, MFA, 78. *Work:* Corning Mus Glass, NY; Am Crafts Mus, NY; Rahr-West Mus & Civic Ctr, Manitowoc, Wis; Ind Univ Art Mus, Bloomington. *Exhib:* New Glass Traveling Exhib, 78-; Art for Use, Olympics Exhib, Lake Placid & Am Crafts Mus, NY, 80; Small group, Sales Gallery Show, Smithsonian Inst, Washington DC, 80; Ohio Glass Artists, Massillon Mus, Ohio, 80; one-man show, New Works, Habatat Gallery, Mich, 81; Am Glass Now, III, touring Japan, 81-. *Teaching:* Asst prof glass, 3-D design, Bowling Green State Univ, 78-. *Awards:* Mus Dirs Award, Evansville Mus, 77; Third Place Award, Toledo Mus, 81. *Bibliog:* Terri Sharp (auth), Artist profile, Art Craft Mag; Portfolio Section, Am Craft Mag; Photograph of work, Village Voice. *Mem:* Glass Art Soc; Ohio Designer Craftman. *Media:* Glass. *Mailing Add:* 1771 Kettle Run Ct Perrysburg OH 43551-5414

HURSON, MICHAEL
DRAFTSMAN, PAINTER
b Youngstown, Ohio, 1941. *Study:* Art Inst Chicago, BFA, 63; Oxbow Summer Sch Painting, Saugatuck, Mich, 60 & 61; Yale Univ, Norfolk, Conn, 62. *Work:* Art Inst Chicago; Guggenheim Mus, Whitney Mus Am Art & Metrop Mus Art, NY; Nat Gallery Australia, Canberra. *Exhib:* Chicago & Vicinity, Art Inst Chicago, 61, 63, 64 & 73, Small Scale in Contemp Art, Soc for Contemp Art, 75 & Drawings of the 70's, 77; one-man shows, Mus Contemp Art, Chicago, 72, Mus Mod Art, NY, 74, Daniel Weinberg Gallery, San Francisco, 80 & 83, Paula Cooper Gallery, NY, 82, 85-87, 89, 91 & 94, Inst Art & Urban Resources, NY, 84, Heath Gallery, Atlanta, Ga, 86 & 93, Joe Fawbush Editions, NY, 87, Works by Michael Hurson, Mus Contemp Art, San Diego, Calif, 96; Recent Acquisitions, Metrop Mus Art, NY, 74 & 20th Century Recent Acquisitions, 79; The Small Scale in Contemp Art, Soc Contemp Art, Art Inst Chicago, 75; Nine Artists: Theodoron Awards, SR Guggenheim Mus, NY, 77; Drawings of the Seventies, Soc Contemp Art, Art Inst Chicago, 77; Am Art Since 1950, Whitney Mus Am Art, NY, 78, All About Art, 78, New Image Painting, 78, Archit Analogues, 78 & Artists by Artists, 79; Summer Light, Mus Mod Art, NY, 81; New Dimensions in Drawing, Aldrich Mus, 81, Made in New York, City Gallery, NY, 82; Spectrum: Drawn Out, Corcoran Gallery Art, Washington, 86; Drawing New Conclusions, Art Inst Chicago, 92; Medium Rare, Nat Arts Club, NY, 95; Epitaphs, Edward Thorp Gallery, NY, 96; Works on Paper, Andre Zarre Gallery, NY, 96; Selected Am Drawings - 1945-1995, Noyes Mus, Oceanville, NJ, 96; Pet Shop: Artists Look at Animals, Nicholas Davies Gallery, NY, 98; and others. *Awards:* Nat Endowment Arts Grant, 74-75; Theodoron Award, Guggenheim Mus, 77; Vaklova Purchase Award, Mus Contemp Art, Chicago, 80. *Bibliog:* Edward L Saxe (auth), On the margin of society, Am Artists, 9/81; Prudence Carlson (auth), Arch Limner: Michael Hurson, Art in Am, summer 82; Irving Sandler (auth), Art of the postmodern era: From the late 1960's to the Early 1990s, Harper Collins, New York, 96. *Mailing Add:* c/o Paula Cooper Gallery 534 W 21st St New York NY 10011

HURST, ROBERT JAY
PATRON
b New York, NY, Nov 5, 45. *Study:* Clark Univ, BA, 66; Admin, Univ Pa, Master in govt, 68; Univ Pa, Pub Fin fel, 69. *Pos:* Fac, investment banking div Merrill Lynch, Pierce, Fenner & Smith, Inc, New York City, 69-74; vpres, 74, Goldman, Sachs & Co, New York City, 74-80, general partner, 80-2000, mem mgt comt, 90-2000, co-head investment banking div, 90-96, head investment banking div, 96-99, mem exec comt, 95-2000, vchmn, 99-2000; chmn, Jewish Mus, 97-2002; trustee, Whitney Mus Am Art, 98-, pres, 2002-; Chief Exec Officer, 9/11 United Servs Group, 2001-; trustee coun, Nat Found for Teaching Entrepreneurship, bd dir, currently; mem bd overseers, Wharton Sch, Univ Pa, coun on foreign relations, comt for economic develop; bd trustees, Manhattan Inst; trustee coun Nat, Gallery Art; trustee Committee Economic Develop, Central Park Conservancy; bd dir, Air Clic Inc, New York City 2012, IDB Holding Ltd, Constellation Energy Group, VF Corp. *Awards:* Recipient Louis Marshall Award, Jewish Theological Soc, 2000. *Mem:* Maroon Creek Club (Aspen), Atlantic Golf Club (Bridgehampton), Univ Club. *Mailing Add:* c/o Whitney Mus Am Art 945 Madison Ave New York NY 10021

HURT, SUSANNE M
PAINTER
b New York, NY. *Study:* Duke Univ; Art Students League, with Frank V Dumond & Kenneth Hayes Miller; Corcoran Sch Art; also with Wayman Adams & A Ginsburg. *Work:* In pvt collections. *Comn:* Portrait, Harold Weill, Weill-Traeger Clinic, NY Hosp, 81; portrait, Col Herbert Nash Dillard, Va Mil Inst Libr, 86; portrait, Claudia Haines Marsh, Pub Welfare Found Inc, Washington, DC, 92; Sara Agnes Rice Pryor, DAR Mem Hall, Washington, DC, 95. *Exhib:* One-man show, Grist Mill Gallery, Chester, Vt, 76; Cayuga Mus, Auburn, NY, 71; Mus Fine Arts, Springfield, Mass; Hammond Mus, North Salem, NY; Nat Arts Club; Salmagundi Club; and others. *Pos:* secretary, Am Artist Prof League. *Teaching:* Pvt classes & demonstrations. *Awards:* 1st prize, Anna Hyatt Huntington Painting Award, 70; Grand Prize, Dept Parks & Recreation, New York, 78; Katherine A Lovell Mem Award, 81; and others; Helen DeCozen Award for Floral, 2003. *Mem:* Catharine Lorillard Wolfe Art Club (corresp secy, 71-74); Am Artists Prof League (secy, 87-); Hudson Valley Art Asn; Royal Soc Arts; Nat League Am Pen Women. *Media:* Oil. *Interests:* Portraits, Still Life, Florals. *Mailing Add:* 299 Riverside Dr New York NY 10025

HURTIG, MARTIN RUSSELL
PAINTER, SCULPTOR
b Chicago, Ill, Aug 11, 29. *Study:* Inst Design Chicago, BS, 52, MS, 57; Atelier 17, Paris, 55. *Work:* Bibliot Nat, Paris; Philadelphia Free Libr; Carroll Reese Mus, Johnson City, Tenn; Honolulu Acad Art; Mus Contemp Art, Chicago. *Comn:* Stained glass windows & mural wall, Union Church, Lake Bluff, Ill, 63; outdoor court sculpture, Waukegan Pub Libr, Ill, 64; lobby relief sculpture, Midwest Iron Works, Chicago, 67. *Exhib:* Nat Print Exhib, Brooklyn Mus, 58 & 68; one-man shows, Flint Inst Arts, 61 & 68, Alonzo Gallery, 66 & 67 & Ecole Spec Archit, Paris, 69; 6th Am Artists Traveling Show, Paris & 12 French cities, 69-70; Jan Cicero Gallery, Chicago, 80, 81 & 83; Mus Mod Art, Paris, 85; Osaka Triennale, Japan, 90; Chicago/Paris Abstract Affinities, Ukranian Mus Mod Art, Chicago, 95; Koehline Gallery,

Desplaines, IL, 2000; Bradley Univ, Peoria, IL, 2001. *Teaching:* Asst prof drawing & design, Mich State Univ, 57-62; prof painting, Univ Ill, Chicago, 62-; dir, Sch Art & Design, Univ Ill, Chicago, 82-88, prof painting, 88-91, ret, 91. *Awards:* Purchase Awards, Carroll Reese Mus, 67 & Honolulu Acad Arts, 71. *Bibliog:* F Schulze (auth), Art news in Chicago, Art News, 11/71; A Goldin (auth), Vitality vs greasy kids stuff, Art Gallery Mag, 4/72; D Guthrie & J Allen (auth), Waging polemical warfare, Chicago Tribune, 4/30/72; Charles Fambro (auth), exhibition review, New Art Examiner, 5/90. *Dealer:* Robert Henry Adams Fine Art, 715 N. Franklin, Chicago, IL 60610. *Mailing Add:* 1727 Wesley St Evanston IL 60201

HURTUBISE, JACQUES
PAINTER
b Montreal, Que, Feb 28, 39. *Study:* Beaux Art Sch, Montreal, BFA, 60. *Work:* Mass Inst Technol; Peter Stuyvesant Art Found, Amsterdam; Galerie Nat Can, Ont; Art Gallery Ont, Toronto; Vancouver Art Gallery; and others. *Comn:* Murals, Ottawa Univ, 69, Place Radio Can, Montreal, 72 & Ministry of Defense, Ottawa, 72. *Exhib:* 300 Yrs of Canadian Art, Nat Gallery Can, Ottawa, 67; Art d'Aujourd'Hui, Paris, Rome, Lausanne, Brussels, 68; Seven Montreal Artists, Mass Inst Technol, Cambridge, Gallery Mod Art, Washington & Stratford Festival, Ont, 68; Grand Formats, Musée d'Art Contemporain, Montreal, 70; Birmingham Festival of the Arts, Ala, 79; Mem Univ Art Gallery, St John's, Nfld, 85; Art Gallery, Acadia Univ, Wolfville, NS, 86; Art Gallery NS, Halifax, 86; Beaverbrook Art Gallery, Fredericton, NB, 86; Galerie Restigouche, Campbelton, NB, 87; Confederation Ctr Art Gallery & Mus, Charlottetown, Pei, 87; plus many other one-man & group exhibs. *Pos:* Artist-in-residence, Dartmouth Col, 67. *Awards:* Max Beckmann Scholar, 60; First Prize, Concours Artistique Que, Que Govt, 65; Prize, Expos Hadassah, 68; and others. *Bibliog:* Laurent Lamy (auth), Hurtubise, Lidec, 71. *Mem:* Royal Can Acad Art. *Media:* All. *Mailing Add:* RR 1 Marjaree Harbor Cape Breton NS B0E 2B0 Canada

HURWITZ, ADAM
Study: Boston Univ, BFA, 89; Yale Sch Art, MFA, 94. *Exhib:* Solo shows at Debs and Co, NY, 2002, Michael Steinberg Fine Art, NY, 2004; group shows at Domestic Bliss/Cloning, DNA Gallery, Provincetown, Mass, 97; Diverse Works/Urban Configuration, Starwoos Urban, Washington, DC, 98; Exit Art, NY, 99; The Road Show, DFN Gallery, NY, 99; Distilled Life, Bard Col, Annadale-on-Hudson, NY, 99; Outer Boroughs, White Columns, NY, 99; Night Vision, 2003; Flat File, Bellwether Gallery, Brooklyn, NY, 2000; Violent Beauty, Debs and Co, NY, 2001. *Pos:* Art dir, designer, Fence Magazine, formerly. *Awards:* Joan Mitchell Found Award, 99. *Mailing Add:* c/o Michael Steinberg Fine Art 526 West 26th St #215 New York NY 10001

HURWITZ, MICHAEL H
CRAFTSMAN, MOSAIC ARTIST
b Miami, Fla, Feb 26, 1955. *Study:* Mass Col Art, 74-75; Boston Univ, BFA, 79; studied with Kenkichi Kuroda, Kyoto, Japan, 90-91. *Work:* Gallery Am Art Renwick Smithsonian, Washington, DC; Mus Fine Arts, Boston, Mass; Mus RI Sch Design, Providence; Art Gallery Yale Univ, New Haven, Conn; Altos De Chavon Found, NY. *Exhib:* New Am Furniture, Mus Fine Arts, Boston, 89 & Oakland Mus Art, Calif, 90; solo exhibs, Pritam & Eames Gallery, East Hampton, NY, 89 & Peter Joseph Gallery, NY, 92; Child's Play, Mem Art Gallery, Rochester, NY, 94; Living, Peter Joseph Gallery, NY, 94; A Good Cup of Coffee & other Antidotes for Modern Day Living, Peter Joseph Gallery, NY, 94; Peter Joseph Gallery, NY, 96; John Elder Gallery, NY, 98; and others. *Teaching:* Slide lectr, various Univs, schs & mus, 83-94; assoc prof & prog head furniture, Univ Arts, Philadelphia, 85-90; instr, Haystack Mountian Sch Crafts, Deer Isle, Maine, 94. *Awards:* Visual Arts Fel, 90 & 92, Nat Endowment Arts, 88, 90, & 92; Grand Prize, Am Craft Awards, Krauss Sikes Publ Co, 90; Japan Found Fel, 96; Pew Fel for Arts, 99. *Bibliog:* B Steinbaum (auth), The Rocker, An American Design Tradition, New York, 92; Now That's Rockin, Am Woodworker, 11-12/93; Peter Joseph & Emma Cobb (auths), Masterworks Two, Peter Joseph Gallery, New York, 94. *Media:* Furniture Maker, Wood and Other Natural Materials. *Mailing Add:* 16 S 3rd St Philadelphia PA 19156

HURWITZ, SIDNEY J
PAINTER, PRINTMAKER
b Worcester, Mass, Aug 22, 32. *Study:* Sch Worcester Art Mus; Brandeis Univ, BA; Boston Univ, MFA; Stuttgart Acad Art, Ger; Skohegan Sch, Maine. *Work:* Libr Cong, Washington, DC; Mus Mod Art, NY; Mus Fine Arts, Boston; Minneapolis Mus, Minn; Victoria & Albert Mus, London; Worcester Art Mus. *Comn:* Mosaic mural, Skowhegan Sch Art, Maine, 64; ed of woodcuts, Wellesley Col, Mass, 67; six paintings of London, Japan Int Bank, London, 73; ten etchings, Bldg Design & Construction Mag, Chicago. *Exhib:* Am Drawing, Mus Mod Art, NY, 56; Print Biennial, Libr Cong, Wash, DC, 62; Pa Acad, Philadelphia, 64; New Eng Artists, Boston, 71; Martin Sumers Gallery, NY; Mary Ryan Gallery, NY; British Int Print Biennale. *Teaching:* Prof art, Boston Univ, 62-99, prof emer, currently; prof, Wellesley Col, Brandeis Univ, Amherst Col. *Awards:* Louis Comfort Tiffany Award, 66; Artist Award, Am Inst Arts & Lett, 69; Mass Found Arts Fel, 76. *Mem:* Col Art Asn Am; Boston Printmakers Soc; Nat Acad. *Media:* Painting, Printmaking. *Publ:* Auth, Etchings of Sigmund Abeles, 66 & My woodcut technique, 67, Am Artist; Etchings, Scarecrow Press, 85. *Dealer:* Audrey Pepper Gallery 38 Newbury St Boston MA 02216. *Mailing Add:* 175 Parker St Newton MA 02459

HUSEBOE, ARTHUR ROBERT
WRITER, COLLECTOR
b Sioux Falls, SDak, Oct 6, 31. *Study:* Augustana Col, BA, 53; Univ SDak, MA(summa cum laude), 56; Ind Univ, PhD(summa cum laude), 63. *Work:* Ctr Western Studies, Augustana Col, Sioux Falls, SDak. *Comn:* An Illustrated History of Le Avls in South Dakota, 89. *Pos:* Bd dir, SDak Symphony Orchestra, 66-. *Teaching:* Prof lit, Augustana Col, 61-, creative writing, 80-. *Awards:* SDak Gov Award for Support of Arts, Gov George Mickelson, 89. *Mem:* SDak Symphony Orchestra (pres, 71-75); Western Lit Asn (pres, 76-77). *Res:* Western American literature; the visual, lit and performing arts of South Dakota and the region; Sioux Indian art. *Collection:* Originals of Harvey Dunn, Salvidor Dali, Oscar Howe, Arthur Amiotte, Carl Grupp and Palmer Eide. *Publ:* Auth, An Illustrated History of the Arts in South Dakota, Ctr Western Studies, 89; ed, Yanktonai Sioux Water Colors, 93, Display of Plains Indian Artifacts, 94, Ctr Western Studies. *Mailing Add:* 813 E 38th St Sioux Falls SD 57105

HUSHLAK, GERALD
COMPUTER ARTIST, PAINTER
b Edmonton, Alta, Feb 15, 45. *Study:* Univ Alta; Univ Calgary, Alta; Univ Calif; Royal Col Art, London, Eng, MARCA. *Work:* Can Coun Art Bank, Ottawa, Ont; San Francisco Mus Mod Art, Calif; Vancouver Art Gallery, BC; Smithsonian Inst, Washington, DC; Alta Art Found. *Exhib:* Glenbow Mus, Calgary; Mendel Mus, Sask; Art Gallery Greater Victoria, BC; York Univ Art Gallery, Toronto; Mus Art Mod, Paris; and others. *Teaching:* Assoc prof painting, Univ Calgary, Alta, 75-. *Awards:* Purchase Award, World Print Competition, San Francisco Mus Mod Art, 77. *Bibliog:* Articles, Vanguard Mag, 80, Arts Can, 80, Art Mag & Artweek, 80. *Mem:* Royal Can Acad; Royal Can Acad Art. *Media:* Computers; Acrylic. *Mailing Add:* Dept of Art Univ Calgary 2500 University Dr NW Calgary AB T2N 1N4 Canada

HUSSONG, RANDY
SCULPTOR, PRINTMAKER
b Redwood City, Calif, 55. *Study:* Univ Calif, Berkeley, BA, MFA, 76-80; studied with Jim Melchert. *Work:* Mus Modern Art, San Francisco, Calif; Di Rosa Art Preserve, Napa, Calif; Oakland Mus, Calif; CA Progressive Insurance, Chicago, Ill. *Exhib:* Los Angeles Co Mus of Art, 2000; Mus Art & Hist, Santa Cruz, Calif; Milwaukee Art Mus; traveling exhib, Japan, 98-2000; Solo exhib, Gallery Paule Anglim, San Francisco, Calif, Mincher/Wilcox Gallery, San Francisco, Calif, Inst Contemp Art, San Jose, New Langton Arts. *Teaching:* instr, sculpture, printmaking, Univ Calif, Berkeley, 94-2001. *Mem:* San Francisco Art Inst, Calif. *Media:* Metal, auto parts, woodcuts, blown glass. *Specialty:* Political themes, abstract sculptures, wall constructions. *Mailing Add:* 1333 Sylvaner Ave Saint Helena CA 94574

HUSTON, PERRY CLARK
CONSERVATOR
b Mo, Jan 4, 33. *Study:* Univ Mo, AB, 55, Medical Sch, 55-57; Nelson Art Gallery, with James Roth, 63-70; special study with Sheldon & Caroline Keck, 68. *Pos:* Assoc conservator, Nelson Art Gallery, 66-70; chief conservator, Kimbell Art Mus, 71-. *Teaching:* Supervisor internships, Conserv Grad Progs, Cooperstown & Oberlin Grad Conserv Progs, 72-, teaching consult, 75-77. *Mem:* Fel Am Inst for Conserv Hist & Artistic Works (vpres, 78-79, pres, 80-). *Mailing Add:* 324 N Bailey Ave Ft Worth TX 76107-1003

HUTCHENS, JAMES WILLIAM
ADMINISTRATOR, EDUCATOR
b High Point, NC, Oct 3, 47. *Study:* Western Carolina Univ, BA, 70; Ga State Univ, MVA, 75; Fla State Univ, PhD, 79. *Teaching:* Prof art educ, Ohio State Univ, Columbus, 79-88, assoc dean, Col Arts, 88-92; prof & chair, Dept Art, Appalachian State Univ, Boone, NC, 92-. *Mem:* Coun Policy Studies Art Educ (exec secy); Nat Coun Art Adminrs; Nat Art Educ Asn. *Res:* Art education; art administration. *Publ:* Coauth, Disciplinary & institutional bases for arts research, Design Arts Educ, 88; Preparing arts administrators of the future, Design Arts Educ, 89; auth, Civilization and arts education, J Aesthetic Educ, 89; contribr, Future of the Arts: Public Policy & Arts Research, Praeger, 90. *Mailing Add:* Appalachian State Univ Dept Art 233 Wey Hall Boone NC 28608

HUTCHINS, ROBIN
ART DEALER, GALLERY DIRECTOR
b Newark, NJ, May 26, 38. *Study:* Nat Art Acad, Washington, DC, BFA, 59; Kean Col, Union, NJ, MA, 73. *Teaching:* Lectr, Montclair Hist Soc, NJ, 91; lectr computer art, Fedn, Artists, NJ, 91. *Awards:* ASID Presidential Citation, 90; Daily Point of Lite Presidential Award, AIDS Resource Found, White House, 91. *Mem:* Burgdorf Cult Comn (bd mem, 90-); Maplewood Cult Comn (co-chmn, 88-); Fed Artists NJ; Newark Mus Ballentine House Restoration Comt. *Specialty:* Contemporary American Art. *Mailing Add:* 2719 Bright Star Pl Las Cruces NM 88011

HUTCHINSON, JANET L
COLLECTOR, CURATOR
b Washington, DC, May 2, 17. *Collection Arranged:* Diana Kan, Marc Mellon, Walt Kuhn, Samuel Margolies, Carol Sadowski, Rose W Traines, Carmen Z Simpkins, Nina Buxton, and many others. *Pos:* Owner-dir, Broadlawn Gallery, Camden, Maine, 57-64; cur, Old Merchant's House, New York, 61-62; dir emer, Hist Soc Martin Co, Elliott Mus & House of Refuge Mus, Hutchinson Island, Fla, 65-92. *Awards:* Woman of Yr, AAUW, Martin Co, 75; Martin Co Citation; Bicentennial Award, Martin Co. *Mem:* Salmagundi Club, Nat Arts Club, NY; Hist Soc Martin Co (dir emeritus, dir Elliott Mus, Elliott Mus Art Gallery, Gilber's Bar House of Refuge); Nat Arts Club; DAR (Halpatiokee chpt). *Interests:* Arranging Exhibits. *Publ:* History of Martin County, 75. *Mailing Add:* 1023 NW Spruce Ridge Dr Stuart FL 34994

HUTCHINSON, PETER ARTHUR
CONCEPTUAL ARTIST, ENVIRONMENTAL ARTIST
b London, Eng, Mar 4, 32. *Study:* Univ Ill, BFA, 60. *Work:* Mus Mod Art, NY; Mus Pompidou, Paris, France; Frac Limousin, France, 2006. *Comn:* Only in America, Sculpture, Philadelphia, 87; sculpture Basel Art Fair, Switzerland, 2000. *Exhib:* Images: 2 Ocean Projects, 69 & Information, 70, Mus Mod Art; Nature & Art, Krefeld

Mus, Haus Lange, Ger, 72; Stedelijk Mus, Amsterdam, 74; Venice Biennale, Am Pavilion, 79; John Mayor Gallery, London,Eng, 93; Holly Solomon Gallery, 91 & 94; Galerie Gaillard, Paris, 1999; Galerie Bugdahn und Kaimer, 2000, 2005; Galerie Blancpain/Stepczynski, Geneva, 2001, 2004; Frac Limousin, France, 2006; and others. *Teaching:* Instr, Sch Visual Arts, New York, NY, 77. *Awards:* A & E Gottlieb Found, 87; Nat Endowment Arts Individual Artist Award, 74; Krasner-Pollack Grant, 89. *Bibliog:* Scheldahl (auth), Breadworks as earth works, NY Times, 69; Back to nature, Time, 6/70; Carter Ratcliff, Peter Hutchinson, Art in Am, 12/02. *Mem:* Am Rock Garden Soc. *Media:* Mixed Media; Photograph collage. *Specialty:* Art. *Interests:* Hist, botany, horticulture, chess and bridge. *Collection:* MOMA, NYC, Pompidou, Paris, Arp Mus, Ger. *Publ:* Auth, Earth in upheaval, Arts, 68; Science fiction: an aesthetic for science, Art Int, 68; Is there life on earth, 68 & Foraging: being an account of a hike through the snow-mass wilderness as a work of art, 72, Art Am; Alphabet Cottage Book, OONA Press, Ger, 80; Dissolving Clouds, Provincetown Arts Press, 94; Undersea Sculpture, 2d edit, 02; auth, Thrown Rope, Sport Mag & Princeton Archit Press, 2006. *Dealer:* Galerie Bugdahn, Kaimer Germany; Blancpain/Stepczynski, Geneva; Fredericke Taylor Gallery NYC; Volume Gallery NYC; Mayor Gallery London. *Mailing Add:* 10 Holway Ave Provincetown MA 02657

HUTCHISON, JANE CAMPBELL
EDUCATOR, HISTORIAN
b Washington, DC, July 20, 32. *Study:* Western Md Col, BA(cum laude), 54; Oberlin Col, With Wolfgang Stechow, MA, 58; Kunsthist Inst, Utrecht, with J G van Gelder, 60-61; Univ Wis, with James S Watrous, PhD, 64. *Work:* Pennell Collection, Libr Cong, Washington, DC. *Exhib:* US Nat Printmakers, Libr Cong, 56. *Collection Arranged:* Dutch & Flemish Paintings from Private Collections, 74 & Graphic Art in the Age of Martin Luther, 83, Elvehjem Mus, Univ Wis, Madison. *Pos:* Libr asst, Toledo Mus Art, Ohio, 58-59; consult to Rijksprentenkabinet, Amsterdam & Stadelsches Kunstinstitut, Frankfurt, 85; consult, Cincinnati Art Mus, 91-92. *Teaching:* Instr art hist, Univ Wis, Madison, 63-64, from asst prof to assoc prof, 64-75, prof, 75- & dept chmn, 77-80 & 92; vis asst prof, Tyler Sch Art, Temple Univ, summer 67. *Awards:* Fulbright Fel, 60-61; Nat Endowment Humanities Grant, 83; Am Coun Learned Soc Grant, 84; Deutscher Akademischer Austauschdienst (DAAD), 89. *Mem:* Col Art Asn; Medieval Acad Am; Midwest Art Hist Soc (secy-treas 81-83, pres 83-); Historians Netherlandish Art (treas, 94-98); Am Asn Mus; Print Coun Am; St Andrew's Soc Madison (pres 1995-); Univ Club (bd dirs). *Res:* Late fifteenth and early sixteenth century Dutch and German engravings. *Publ:* Ed, Early German Artists: The Illustrated Bartsch, Plate, Vols 8 & 9, Commentary, Vol 9, Part II & Vol 8, Part I, Abaris, 80, 81, 91 & 96; auth, Albrecht Duer: A Biography, Princeton Univ Press, 90; Six Centuries of Master Prints: Treasures of the Herbert Greer French Collection, Cincinnati Art Mus, 93; Schongauer Copies and Forgeries, In: Colloque Internationale Schongauer, Mus d'Unterlinden, 94; Campas Verlag, Ger ed, Frankfurt Am Main, 94; auth, Albrecht Duer: A Guide to Research, Taylor & Francis, NY/London, 2000. *Mailing Add:* Univ Wis Dept Art Hist 800 University Ave Madison WI 53706

HUTT, LEE
SCULPTOR, PHOTOGRAPHER
b New York, NY. *Study:* Columbia Univ, MS; New Sch; Univ Lourain, Belg, Art Cert. *Exhib:* Ann Exhib, Nat Sculpture Soc, NY, 1996-2002, 2005; Contemp Sculpture, Chesterwood Nat Trust, Lennox, Mass, 1997, 2000; Ann Exhib, Allied Artists of Am, NY, 1998-2006; Ann Exhib, Pen & Brush, NY, 1999-2005; Ann Exhib, Brookgreen Gardens, SC, 2000-2002; Changing the Am Landscape thru Sculpture, Ind Univ, South Bend, Ind, 2003. *Pos:* Sculpture chair, Allied Artists of Am, NY, 2005-. *Awards:* Ann Award Show, Nat Sculpture Soc, 1996, 2000; Pen & Brush, Ann Exhib, Pen & Brush, 1999, 2000, 2001; Medal of Honor, Ann Exhib, Catharine Lorillard Wolfe, 2000. *Mem:* Nat Sculptor Soc; Catharine Lorillard Wolfe Club; Allied Artist Am (sculpture chair), 2005-; Pen & Brush Inc; Acad Artists Asn; Audubon Artists Inc. *Media:* Clay, Bronze and Plaster. *Mailing Add:* 106 Woodbridge St South Hadley MA 01075

HUXTABLE, ADA LOUISE
CRITIC, HISTORIAN
b New York, NY. *Study:* Hunter Col, AB(magna cum laude); NY Univ; Nine Hon doctorates. *Pos:* Asst cur archit & design, Mus Mod Art, New York, 46-50; contrib ed, Progressive Archit Art in Am, 50-63; archit critic, New York Times, 63-83, mem ed bd, 73-82. *Awards:* Elsie de Wolfe Award, Am Inst Interior Designers, 69; Pulitzer Prize for Distinguished Criticism, 70; Nat Arts Club Lit Award, 71; Macarthur Fel, 82; and others. *Mem:* Am Soc Archit Historians. *Publ:* Auth, Pier Luigi Nervi, Braziller, 60; Classic New York, 64; Will They Ever Finish Bruckner Boulevard?, Macmillan, 70; Kicked A Building Lately?, 76. *Mailing Add:* 969 Park Ave New York NY 10028

HYAMS, HARRIET
STAINED GLASS ARTIST, SCULPTOR
b Jersey City, NJ, 1929. *Study:* Rutgers Univ, BA, 50; Columbia Univ, MA, 72; with Zorach, J Hovannes, Marshall Glasier, Lorrie Goulet. *Work:* Delta Dental Health Plan of NJ; Columbia Univ. *Comn:* SW Ohio Senior Citizens Inc, Springdale, Ohio, 77; stained glass windows, New Dorp High Sch, Staten Island, NY, 82; stained glass windows, St Vartanantz Church, Ridgefield, NJ, 83; stained glass wall, Harcourt Brace Jovanovich, Orlando, Fla, 84; stained glass skylight for sailing yacht, pvt comn, 91; stained glass windows for Jewish Cadet Chapel, West Point, NY, 98; stained glass windows, Dominican Congregation of Our Lady of the Rosary, Sparkill, NY, 2001; etched folding doors for Trinity Luthern Church, Tenafly, NJ, 2003; stained glass windows for Jersey City Med Ctr (Wilzig Hosp), 2004. *Exhib:* Stained Glass Int, NY, 82; Glass Am, NY, 84; one-person show, Harriet Hyams: Stained Glass and Sculpture, Rockland Ctr Arts, Nyack, NY, 88; Montclair Art Mus; Newark Art Mus; welded sculpture & stained glass, Blue Hill Cult Ctr, Pearl River, NY, 2005-06. *Pos:* Co-cur, Catherine Konner Sculpture Park Rockland Ctr for the Arts, Nyack, NY, 2005-06. *Teaching:* Instr stained glass, Columbia Univ, 72-74. *Awards:* Purchase Award, Columbia Univ, Arthur Wesley Dow Award, 1972; Compendium 1976, Corning Mus, 1976; Bene Awards, Ministry & Liturgy Mag; Bene Awards, Ministry & Liturgy Mag, 2002. *Bibliog:* Yehuda Yaniv (auth), Film on Stained Glass, Ed Devel Corp, 72; Richard Avidon (auth), Harriet Hyams, Bergdorf Goodman, Glass Arts Mag, 76; Richard Hoover (auth), Dancing on the ceiling, Stained Glass Quart, fall 92. *Mem:* Stained Glass Asn Am; UAHC Accredited List of Synagogue Artists & Craftsmen; Interfaith Forum on Relig, Art and Archit, Affiliate of AIA. *Media:* Stained Glass. *Publ:* Art in Architecture, Glass Mag, 1/78; Auth, A sculptor turns to stained glass, Stained Glass, 82; The Chairman's Office, 85-86; From Gallery to Gallery, Stained Glass Quart, summer 89; front cover Blue Lioness (by Betty S FLowers), 2002; front cover, Extending the Shade (by Betty S Flowers), 1990; Stained Glass Quar, fall 1992, winter 1993, spring, 2003, fall, 2006; Women working in glass by Lucartha Kohler, 2003. *Mailing Add:* PO Box 178 Palisades NY 10964

HYDE, SCOTT
PHOTOGRAPHER, PRINTMAKER
b Montevideo, Minn, Oct 10, 26. *Study:* Art Ctr Sch, Los Angeles; Columbia Univ, with Ralph Mayer; Art Students League. *Work:* Mus Mod Art, Metrop Mus Art, Int Ctr Photog, NY; Int Mus Photog, Rochester, NY; Bibliot Nat, Paris. *Exhib:* Synthetic Color, Southern Ill Univ, Carbondale, 74; Mirrors & Windows: Am Photog Since 1960, 78; Master Photogrs Focus Gallery, San Francisco, 81; Off the Press, Col Art Gallery, State Univ NY, New Paltz, 84; City Light, Int Ctr Photog, 86; The Sense of Abstraction, Mus Mod Art, 60; Photog in the 20th Century, Nat Gallery, Canada, 67; Silver and Silk Photog Silk Screen Prints, Smithsonian Inst, 75; plus others. *Teaching:* Adj prof photog, Cooper Union, 68-70, New York Univ Exten, 71-72 & Manhattanville Col, 72-75. *Awards:* Guggenheim Fel, 65; Creative Artists Pub Serv Prog Grants, 72 & 75. *Bibliog:* Syl Labrot (auth), Scott Hyde photographs, Aperture, 70; Thomas Dugan (auth), Photography between covers, Light Impressions, 75; Naomi Rosenblum (auth), A World History of Photography, 84. *Mem:* Soc Photographic Edn. *Media:* Offset Lithography. *Publ:* CAPS Book, 75; Auth, Dust Map, 79; auth, The Real Great Society Album, 79. *Mailing Add:* 7411 Dreyfuss Dr Amarillo TX 79121-1411

HYLAND, DOUGLAS K S
MUSEUM DIRECTOR
b Salem, Mass, Oct 7, 49. *Study:* Univ Pa, BA, 70; Univ Del, MA, 76, PhD, 80. *Pos:* Cur painting & sculpture, Spencer Mus Art, Univ Kans, 79-82; dir, Memphis Brooks Mus Art, 82-84; dir, Birmingham Mus Art, 84-91, San Antonio Mus Art, 92-. *Teaching:* Asst prof art hist, Univ Kans, 79-82; vis prof, Southwestern Univ, Memphis, 83-84 & Univ Ala, 84-. *Awards:* Fels, Kress Found, 78 & Smithsonian Inst, 78-79 & 92; Chevalier Des Arts Et Lettres, 90. *Mem:* Col Art Asn; Asn Art Mus; Am Asn Mus Dirs. *Res:* American and European painting and sculpture of the 19th and 20th centuries. *Publ:* Lorenzo Bartolint & American Sculptors, 86; Birmingham Photography Proj, 88; Anders Zorn, 89; Kelley Collection of African American Art, 94; 500 Years of French Art, 95; and others. *Mailing Add:* 200 W Jones Ave San Antonio TX 78215

HYMAN, ISABELLE
HISTORIAN, EDUCATOR
b New York, NY, Apr 19, 30. *Study:* Vassar Col, BA, 51; Columbia Univ, MA, 55; Inst Fine Arts, NY Univ, MA, 66, PhD, 68. *Teaching:* From instr to assoc prof, NY Univ, 63-79, prof hist art, 79-. *Awards:* Fel, Villa I Tatti, Florence, 72-73; John Simon Guggenheim Mem Found Fel, 88-89; Fel, Graham Found Advanced Studies Fine Arts, 88-89. *Mem:* Col Art Asn (bd dir, 82-86); Soc Archit Historians (bd dir, 93-); Renaissance Soc Am. *Res:* Art and architecture in Renaissance Florence; archit of Marcel Breuer. *Publ:* Ed, Brunelleschi in Perspective, Prentice-Hall, 74; auth, Fifteenth Century Florentine Studies, Garland, 77; articles relating to Italian Renaissance art and the architecture of Marcel Breuer in scholarly journals; coauth, Architecture: From Pre-History to Post Modernism, Harry N Abrams Inc, 86. *Mailing Add:* Fine Arts Dept 303 Main Bldg NY Univ New York NY 10003

HYMAN, LINDA
ART DEALER, HISTORIAN
b Buffalo, NY, May 11, 40. *Study:* Vassar Col, 58-60; Columbia Univ, with Barbara Novak, BA, 61, MA, 63; City Univ New York Grad Ctr, with Milton Brown, PhD, 78. *Collection Arranged:* New York Crystal Palace, City Univ NY Grad Ctr, 74; Gertrude Greene (auth, catalog), 81, Ernest Fiene (auth, catalog), 81 & Social Art in America 1930-1945 (auth, catalog), 81, ACA Galleries, NY; Arthur Lindberg (auth, catalog), 87 & Oscar Bluemner (auth, catalog), 88, Linda Hyman Fine Arts, NY. *Pos:* Historian, Metrop Mus Mod Art, 67-71; staff, ACA Galleries, 78-82; pvt art dealer & consult, 82-. *Teaching:* Asst prof art hist, City Univ New York, Richmond Col, Staten Island, 73-76, Emory Univ, Atlanta, Ga, 76-78. *Specialty:* American and European art, 20th century. *Publ:* Auth, Winslow Homer: America's Old Master, Doubleday, 73; Hiram Powers' Greek slave: High art as popular culture, Art J, 75; American Modernist Landscapes: The Spirit of Cezanne, Linda Hyman Fine Arts, 89

HYSON, JEAN
PAINTER
b Alvarado, Tex, Mar 4, 31. *Study:* NY Univ with William Baziotes, 52; Art Students League with Yasuo Kuniyoshi, George Grosz & Harry Sternberg, 52-56. *Work:* Walter Barriese Collection, Metromedia, NY; Oakland Art Mus, Calif; Int Banking Ctr, Sutro, Madison, Pillsbury, Levi-Strauss, City of San Francisco, Bill Graham & Pac Bell, San Francisco, Calif; Santa Barbara Mus, Calif; Container Corp Am, Chicago. *Exhib:*

One-person shows, San Francisco Mus Art, 67, Calif Palace of the Legion of Honor, 69, William Sawyer Gallery, San Francisco, 72, Richmond Art Mus, Calif, 77, Calif Med Asn, 87 & Nat Small Painting Exhib, Boise State Univ, Idaho, 91; Fine Arts Contemp Exhib, Northern Ill Univ, 69; California Artists, Western Art Mus Asn, 70 & 92; Mus Mod Art Rental & Sales Gallery, NY, 71; Collectors Gallery, Oakland Mus, 86. *Teaching:* Instr & Artist in Res, Mex Exten, Calif Col Arts & Crafts, Critiques & Painting, Oakland, 70-74. *Awards:* Adolph & Esther Gottlieb Found Grant, 91; Pollock-Krasner Found Grant, 96. *Mem:* Artists Equity Asn, Washington, DC; Mechanics Inst San Francisco; San Francisco Women Artists. *Media:* Oil, Acrylic, Watercolor. *Specialty:* To provide juried shows. Non-profit gallery. *Interests:* Chess, volunteering, special events, San Fransisco Symphony. *Dealer:* SFWA Gallery, San Francisco, Calif. *Mailing Add:* 950 Franklin No 56 San Francisco CA 94109

I

IANNETTI, PASQUALE FRANCESCO PAOLO
ART DEALER, COLLECTOR
b Florence, Italy, Apr 10, 40; US citizen. *Study:* Univ Florence; Acad di Belle Arti, Florence; Univ Minn, Minneapolis. *Pos:* Pres, Pasquale Iannetti Inc Galleries, San Francisco. *Teaching:* Lectr fine prints, Col Marin, Kentfield & Univ Calif, Davis. *Mem:* Int Soc Appraisers; Graphic Art Coun, Los Angeles Co Mus & Achenbach Found, San Francisco; Museo Italo Americano, San Francisco. *Specialty:* Fine original prints, drawings and other unique works form the sixteenth century through the twentieth century. *Collection:* Contemporary prints, drawings and paintings; Pre-Columbian and African art; antiquities. *Mailing Add:* 522 Sutter St San Francisco CA 94102-1102

IANNONE, DOROTHY
PAINTER, WRITER
b Boston, Mass, Aug 9, 33. *Study:* Boston Univ BA(phi beta kappa), 57; Brandeis Univ, studied literature & criticism with J V Cunningham, Phillip Rahv & Irving Howe, 58. *Work:* Nat Mus Women Arts, Washington; Mus Drawings & Prints (Kupferstichkabinet), Berlin, Ger; Ludwig Mus Collection, Aachen, Ger; Mus Mod Art, Saint-Etienne, France; Kunst Mus, Basel, Switz. *Exhib:* Boxes (Boites), Mus Mod Art, Paris, France, 76; Daily Bul, Fondation Maeght-St Paul De Vence, Mus Mod Art, Paris, France, 76; Dorothy Iannone, Ludwig Mus (Neue Galerie Stadt Aachen), Ger, 80; Listening with the Eyes, Mus Mod Art, Paris, France, 80; Artists' Books, Centre Pompidou (Beaubourg), Paris, France, 85; The Caravan Passes And, Mus Mod & Contemp Art, Nice, France, 91; one-woman show, New Soc Fine Arts (NGBK), Berlin, 97 & Mus Mod Art, Arnhem, The Neth, 98; Sprengel Mus (w Dieter Roth), Hanover, Ger, 2005; Whitney Biennial, Whitney Mus. Art, NYC, 2006. *Pos:* guest artist, Rijs Acad, Amsterdam, 82 & 84, Jan Van Eyck Acad, Maastricht, Holland, 82 & 83 & Enschede Acad, Holland, 83. *Teaching:* instr open workshop, Col Art, West Berlin, 77 & 79. *Awards:* Berlin Artists' Prog (Deutscher Akademischer Austauschdienst), 76; Art Found Bonn Grant, 88; Women Artists Prog, Berlin Senate, Ger, 94. *Bibliog:* Barbara Wien (auth), John Lennon & Cleopatra, Tip, Berlin, 6/89; Ulrike Abel (auth), Love is Forever Isn't it, Berlin, 97; Annette Tietenberg (auth), Can Painting Really be a Sin?, Frankfurter Allgemeine, 6/97; Dieter Roth & Dorothy Iannone, Spengel Museum, Hanover, 2005. *Mem:* Phi Beta Kappa. *Media:* Acrylic, Gouache. *Publ:* auth, Story of Bern, Dieter Rot, Dusseldorf, 70; The Berlin Beauties, Mary Dorothy Verlag, Berlin, 78; The Whip, Rainer Verlag, Berlin, 80; Censorship & the Impressible Drive toward Love and Divinity, Ars Viva, Berlin, 82; 720 Courting Ajaxander, Haus am Lutzow Platz, Berlin 93; Dieter & Dorothy, Bilger Verlag, Zurich, 2001. *Dealer.* Andy Jullien Gallery Rami Strasse 18 8001 Zurich Switzerland. *Mailing Add:* Olivaer Platz 16 Berlin 10707 Germany

ICAHN, CARL CELIAN
COLLECTOR
b Queens, NY, 36. *Study:* Philosophy, Princeton Univ, 57, BA; Postgrad, NYU Sch Medicine. *Pos:* Apprentice broker Dreyfus Corp, New York City, 1960-63; options manager Tessel, Patrick & Co, 1963-64, Gruntal & Co, 1964-68; chmn, pres, Icahn & Co, New York City, 1968-; chmn, dir, Starfire Holding Corp (formerly Icahn Holding), 84-; chmn, ACF Industries Inc, St Charles, Mo, 84-, also bd dir; chmn bd dir, pres, Chief Exec Officer, Trans World Airlines Inc, New York City, 85-93; chmn bd, Am Real Estate Partners, 90-, Am Property Investors Inc, 90-, Am Railcar Industries, 94-; pres, dir, Stratosphere Corp, 98-2004; chmn bd, GB Holdings, 2000-, XO Communications, 2003-; dir, Cadus Pharmaceutical Corp, 1993-. *Awards:* Named one of Top 200 Collectors, ARTnews magazine, 2004. *Collection:* Old Masters and Impressionist art. *Mailing Add:* Icahn and Co 82 Beaver St New York NY 10005

IDA, SHOICHI
PAINTER, PRINTMAKER
b Kyoto, Japan, Sept 13, 41. *Study:* Kyoto Munic Univ Art, BFA(oil painting), 65. *Work:* Nat Mus Mod Art Tokyo, Japan; Mus Mod Art, NY; Mus Cincinnati, Ohio; Mus Mod Art, Chicago; Mus Mod Art, San Francisco. *Exhib:* Ten Selected Artists, Mus Mod Art, Chicago, 80; Japanese Prints of the 20th Century, Portland Mus Art & St Louis Mus, Ore, 83; 25th Anniversary Show for Crown Point Press, Mus Mod Art, NY, 87; Contemp Art Fair, Los Angeles, 88; retrospective exhibs, Mus Portland, Ore, 89 & Art Mus Cincinnati, Ohio, 90. *Media:* Multi Media. *Mailing Add:* c/o Irene Drori 138 N Orange Dr Los Angeles CA 90036-3015

IGO, PETER ALEXANDER
PRINTMAKER, PAINTER
b Riverhead, NY, Jan 9, 56. *Study:* Colo Rocky Mountain Sch, Carbondale, 71-74; apprentice to Thomas Benton, printmaker, Aspen, Colo, 74; Univ Calif Los Angeles, 75; Univ NMex, 76-78; Univ Calif, Berkeley, 79; Belles Artes Nat Fine Arts Sch Mex, lithography with Ralph Bishop, 86; studied non-silver photog with Debra Flynn, 88; Indian Arts Mus NMex, Japanese rice paper making with Suki Hughes, 89. *Work:* Mus NMex, Sch Am Res & Sen Jeff Bingaman, Santa Fe, NMex; Maxwell Mus Anthrop, Univ NMex, Mountain States Insurance Co & Prudential Bache, Albuquerque, NMex; Sen Jeff Bingamann & World Bank, Washington; Verde Valley Sch, Sedona, Ariz; First Nat Bank & Mission Insurance, Phoenix, Ariz. *Comn:* Paper cast petroglyph, E F Hutton, Santa Fe, NMex, 85; paper cast petroglyph, Hilton Hotel, 85 & Quail Run Develop, Santa Fe, 88. *Exhib:* One-man Shows, Primitive i gallery, Chicago, 79, Sch Am Res, Santa Fe, 84, Bank Santa Fe, 84, St Johns Col, 86; Govs Gallery, NMex, 89; Best of the Southwest, Dallas, 91; Am Wildlands: An Artistic Inspiration, Santa Fe, 94; El Dorado Arts Show, Santuario de Guadalupe, Santa Fe, 95. *Pos:* Master serigraph printer, ltd eds, 87-96. *Teaching:* Part time instr, screen printing, Verde Valley Sch, Sedona, Ariz, 80-82 & 84. *Media:* Acrylic on Paper & Canvas, Serigraphy. *Mailing Add:* 19 Cerrado Loop Santa Fe NM 87505-8249

IHARA, MICHIO
SCULPTOR
b Paris, France, Nov 17, 28; US citizen. *Study:* Tokyo Univ Fine Arts, BFA, 53; Mass Inst Technol, Fulbright Fel; also with Gyorgy Kepes, 61. *Work:* Wind, Wind, Wind, Kanagawa Mus Mod Art, Kamakura, Japan. *Comn:* Metal screen, Rockefeller Ctr, 78; suspended sculpture, Neiman-Marcus, Beverly Hills, 79, Pavilion Hotel, Singapore, 82, AT&T Long Lines, Atlanta, 82 & Marriott Hotel, NY, 85; plaza sculpture, New World Ctr, Hong Kong, 82; wall sculpture, Harvard Univ, Mass, 86; Tokyo City Hall, 91; and others. *Exhib:* Selection 64, Inst Contemp Art, Boston, 64 & Boston Celebrations, 75; Trends Contemp Art, Kyoto Mus Mod Art, 68; Ann Exhib, Nat Inst Arts & Lett & Am Acad Arts & Lett, 73; Japanese Artists in Am, Tokyo Mus Mod Art & Kyoto Mus Mod Art, 73-74; one-man show, Staempfli Gallery, NY, 77, 80 & 84. *Pos:* Fel, Ctr Advan Visual Studies, Mass Inst Technol, 70-75. *Teaching:* Instr basic design, Musashino Fine Arts Univ, Tokyo, 66-68. *Awards:* Graham Found Fel, 64; Ann Award, Am Acad Arts & Lett & Nat Inst Arts & Lett, 73; First Prize, Fitchburg Libr Art Competition, Mass Coun Arts & Humanities, 74; others. *Mem:* Japanese Artists Asn. *Media:* Stainless Steel, Brass. *Mailing Add:* 63 Wood St Concord MA 01742

IIMURA, TAKAHIKO
FILMMAKER, VIDEO ARTIST
b Tokyo, Japan, Feb 20, 37. *Study:* Keio Univ, Tokyo, BA(political sci), 59. *Work:* Anthology Film Arch, Metrop Mus Art & Whitney Mus Art, NY; Centre Beaubourg des Art Plastiques, Paris; Royal Film Arch, Brussels, Belg; Neuer Berliner Kunstverein, Berlin. *Comn:* Film/video, Metrop Mus Prog for Art on Film, NY, 89. *Exhib:* Japanese Experimental Films, Mus Mod Art, NY, 66; one-man shows, Mus Mod Art, NY, 75, Whitney Mus Am Art, 79, Millennium, NY, 92, Mus Sound & Image, Sao Paulo, Ariz State Univ, 92, Electronic Cafe, Santa Monica, 93, Mint Mus Art, Charlotte, NC, 94, Tokyo Metrop Mus Photog, 95, Japan Cult Ctr, Rome, 97, Lux Ctr, London, 98 & Filmmuseum, Munich, 98; Pandemonium Festival, ICA, London, 96; New Zealand Film Festivals, Auckland, 98; Int Kurzfilmtage, Oberhausen, 98; Videonale, Bonn, 98. *Teaching:* Vis tutor film, Schiller Col, Berlin, 73, Univ Minn 75-76; vis asst prof film, Kent State Univ, 76; State Univ NY, Binghampton, 78; vis prof, Osaka Univ Arts, Osaka, 85-92; prof, Nagoya Zokei Univ Arts & Design, 92-2000 & Tokyo Poly Univ, 2000-. *Awards:* Japan Found Fel, Tokyo, 82, 85, 89, 90 & 92; Gt Brit-Sasakawa Found Fel, Tokyo, 98; Japan Art Funds Fel, Tokyo, 94, 97 & 98. *Bibliog:* Carl Eugene Loeffler (auth), Media World of Takahiko Iimura II, Kirin Plaza Osaka, 93; Bruno Di Marino (auth), From Time to See You, Takahiko Iimura, Istituto Giapponese di Cultura, Diagonale, 97; Makolm Le Graice (auth), Takahiko Iimura at the Lux, 98. *Mem:* Filmmakers Coop, NY; Japan Soc Image Sci, Tokyo; London Film Makers Coop. *Media:* Film, video. *Publ:* Auth, Eizo Jikken No Tameni (For Visual Experimentation), Seido Sha, Tokyo, 86; Film and Video of Takahiko Iimura, Anthology Film Arch, New York, 90; CD-ROM: Eizo Jikken No Temeni (For Visual Experimentation), Euphonic, 97; CD-ROM: Observer/Observed, Banff Art Ctr & Euphonic, 98. *Mailing Add:* 115 E 9th St No 18H New York NY 10003

IKEDA, YOSHIRO
CERAMIST, EDUCATOR
b Kushikino-City, Kagoshima, Japan, Apr 10, 47; US citizen. *Study:* Portland State Univ, Ore, BS(painting & drawing), 70; Kyoto City Univ Fine Art, Japan, cert, 73; Univ Calif, Santa Barbara, MFA, 77. *Work:* Japanese Govt Ministry Educ, Tokyo; Kyoto City Univ Fine Art, Japan; Utah State Univ, Logan; Calif Polytech State Univ, San Luis Obispo; Topeka Pub Libr, Kans; & others. *Exhib:* El Paso Mus, Tex, 79; Foothills Art Ctr, Denver, 79; Cooperstown Art Asn, NY, 81; Purdue Univ Gallery, West Lafayette, Ind, 81; War Mem Mus, Aukland, NZ, 81; Wichita Mus, Kans, 81; Jinro Int Ceramics Art, Korea; The Fletcher Brown Build Int Pottery Show, 87, 88, 92 & 95. *Teaching:* Instr ceramics, Utah State Univ, 73-74 & Ventura Col, 77-78; asst prof ceramics, Kans State Univ, 78-, area head, 81-, prof ceramics, 89. *Awards:* First Place Award, Austin Art Asn, 78; Juror's Award, Calif Polytech State Univ, 78; Merit Award, Fletcher Brownbuilt Pottery Guild, 81. *Mem:* Nat Coun Educ Ceramic Arts; Kans Artist Craftsman Asn; Kans Designer Craftsman Asn. *Media:* Clay. *Publ:* Auth, Asymmetrical thrown form, Ceramic Monthly, 6/78. *Dealer:* Marcia Rodell Gallery 11714 San Vicente Blvd Los Angeles CA 90049. *Mailing Add:* 808 Wildcat Ridge Manhattan KS 66502

ILES, CHRISSIE
CURATOR
Study: Bristol Univ, BA; City Univ, London, grad studies. *Collection Arranged:* Co-cur, Whitney Biennial, 2004 & 2006; co-cur (with Eric de Bruyn), Flashing into the Shadows - The Artist's Film after Pop and Minimalism 1966-1976; cur, Scream and Scream Again: Film in Art; Signs of the Times: Film, Viedo and Slide Installations in Britain in the 1980s; Into the Light: The Projected Image in American

Art 1964-1977, NY, 2002 (best exhib in NY City, Int Asn Art Critics); Jack Goldstein - Films and Performance; The Originof the Night (Lothar Baumgarten); 31 (Lorna Simpson); Blind Side (Liisa Roberts); Ana Mendieta: Earth Body; War! Protest in America 1965-2004; James Lee Byars: The Perfect Silence. *Pos:* Head of exhibs, Mus Modern Art, Oxford, Eng, 1988-97; cur, Whitney Mus Am Art, NY, 1997-; mem adv comt, NY State Council on Arts. *Teaching:* Adj prof, Columbia Univ; faculty mem, Ctr for Curatorial Studies, Bard Col; external examiner, Goldsmith's Col, London. *Mailing Add:* Whitney Museum of American Art 945 Madison Ave New York NY 10021

IMANA, JORGE GARRON
PAINTER, MURALIST
b Sucre, Bolivia, Sept 20, 30; US citizen. *Study:* Univ San Francisco Xavier, Sucre, MA; Academia de Bellas Artes. *Work:* Nat Mus, La Paz, Bolivia; Univ San Francisco Xavier Mus, Sucre; Nat Mus, Bogota, Colombia; Casa de la Cult, Quito, Ecuador; Bolivian Embassy, Moscow & Washington DC. *Comn:* Hist mural, Bolivian Govt, Junin Col, Sucre, 58; History of Education in Bolivia (mural), comn by Bolivian Govt, Padilla Col, Sucre, 59; Social History in Peru (mural), Constructors Union, Lima, Peru, 61; Ciudad de Dios Sch (mural), comn by students' parents, Lima, 62. *Exhib:* Nat Salon, La Paz, 62; Latin Am Show, Fine Arts Gallery, San Diego, 64; Bolivian Paintings, Mus of Mod Art, Paris, France, 73 & Nat Gallery, Warsaw, Poland, 75; House of Friendship of the Peoples, Moscow, 75; Gallery IDB, Washington, DC, 76; plus 102 one-man shows. *Teaching:* Prof drawing, Univ San Francisco Xavier, Sucre, 54-60; prof drawing & watercolor, Nat Acad, La Paz, 60-62; dir art dept, Inst Normal Superior, La Paz, 60-62. *Awards:* Nat Award, Nat Show, La Paz, Bolivian Govt, 62; Watercolor Award, Nat Watercolor Show, Lima, Peru, Watercolor Soc, 62; Purchase Awards Oil & Watercolor, Ann Show, San Diego Art Inst, 64. *Mem:* La Jolla Art Asn; San Diego Art Inst; Accademia Italia delle Artie del Lavoro. *Mailing Add:* 2510 Torrey Pine Rd Apt 212 La Jolla CA 92037-3450

IMBER, JONATHAN
PAINTER, PRINTMAKER
b Baldwin, NY, 50. *Study:* Cornell Univ, BFA, 72; Boston Univ, MFA, 77. *Work:* Boston Mus Fine Arts; Fogg Art Mus, Cambridge, Mass; Rose Art Mus, Waltham, Mass; Currier Gallery Am Art, Manchester, NH; Broida Trust, Los Angeles, Calif; Farnsworth Mus, Rockland, Maine; US State Dept. *Exhib:* Fresh Images, Rose Art Mus, 78; Boston Now, Inst Contemp Art, Boston, 82 & 83; The Figure Again, Currier Gallery Art, Manchester, NH, 84; Awards in the Visual Arts, Albright Knox Gallery, Buffalo, NY, 85; Expressionism in Boston, 1945-1985, DeCordova Mus, Lincoln, Mass, 86; Jewish Themes-Am Contemp Artists, Jewish Mus, NY, 86; New Eng NOW, DeCordova Mus, Lincoln, Mass, 87-89; solo show, Survey of Paintings, Fitchburg Art Mus, Mass, 90; Retrospective of Paintings 1978-1998, Boston Univ, 1999; 20-yr Retrospective, Main Coast Artists, Rockport, Maine, 2000; Portland Mus of Art Biennial, Maine, 2003. *Teaching:* Vis artist, Harvard Univ; Grad Sch, Sch Visual Arts, NY; Boston Mus Sch; Mass Col Art; vis artist, RI Sch Design; instr, Vt Studio Ctr. *Awards:* Engelhard Award, 85; Mass Artists Fel, 85; Nat Endowment, 87; AVA, 1984; Distinguised Alumni Award, Boston Univ, 2004. *Bibliog:* Lois Tarlow (auth), Jon Imber: Painter, Art New Eng, 81; Pam Allara (auth), Issues: new allegory, Art News, 82; Nancy Stapen (auth), Jon Imber, Artforum, 86; William Corbett (auth), Jon Imber, Arts Mag, 5/89; William Leites (auth), Jon Imber, Art in Am, 12/89; John Arthur (auth) Spirit of Place, 89; John Driscoll, The Artist and the American Landscape, 1998; Carl Little, Art of the Maine Islands, 1997; John Stomburg, Jon Imber: World as Mirror, 1999; John Arthur (auth) Green Woods & Crystal Waters, 1999. *Media:* Oil; All. *Mailing Add:* c/o Nielson Gallery 179 Newbury St Boston MA 02116

IMES, BIRNEY
PHOTOGRAPHER
b Columbus, Miss, Aug 21, 51. *Work:* Bibliotheque Nat, Paris, France; San Francisco Mus Art, Calif; Mus Mod Art & Metrop Mus Art, NY; Art Inst Chicago, Ill; plus many more. *Exhib:* solo exhibs, Southern Arts Fedn, 89-91, Juke Joints of the Mississippi Delta, Old Capitol Mus, Jackson, 89, Mississippi: A Lande Apart, Edison Community Col, Ft Myers, Fla, 90, Jackson Fine Art, Atlanta, 91, Benteler-Morgan Gallery, Houston, 92, The Whispering Pines, The Tartt Gallery, Washington, DC, 92 & Gallery for Contemp Photog, Santa Monica, Calif, 94; Recent Acquisitions, Mus Mod Art, NY, 87; Road and Roadside: Am Photographs 1930-1986, Art Inst Chicago, 87; Real Faces, Whitney Mus Am Art, 88; New Southern Photog: Between Myth & Reality, Burden Gallery, Aperture Found, NY, 89; True Grit, Tartt Gallery, Washington, DC, 91; New Orleans Triennial, New Orleans Mus, 92; Montgomery Biennial, Montgomery Mus Art, 92; Picture Relations: Photog Essays from the South, Ctr for Creative Photog & The Birmingham Mus Art, 92 & 93; and many others. *Awards:* Individual Artist Fels, Nat Endowment Arts, 84 & 88; Photography Award, Miss Inst Arts & Lett, 87 & 91. *Publ:* Auth, New Southern Photography: Between Myth and Reality, Aperture, 89; Close to Home: Seven Documentary Photographers, The Friends of Photog, 89; Juke Joint: Photographs by Birney Imes, Univ Press Miss, 90; Partial to Home Photographs by Birney Imes, Smithsonian Press, 94; Whispering Pines, Univ Press of Miss, 94. *Dealer:* Gallery Fine Photography 313 Royal St New Orleans LA 70130; 20th Century Photography Ltd 305 E 63rd New York NY 10021. *Mailing Add:* 802 Third Ave S Columbus MS 39701

IMLAH, RACHEL CRAWFORD
PAINTER, PHOTOGRAPHER
b Asheville, NC, Dec 7, 40. *Study:* Univ Tex scholar, El Paso, 57-58; Acad Fine Arts scholar, Naples, Italy, 58-59; Furman Univ, Greenville, SC, BA, 62. *Work:* Acad Fine Arts, Naples, Italy; Columbia Mus Art, SC; Thompson Gallery Permanent Collection, Furman Univ, Greenville, SC; and others. *Comn:* Nat advert poster, World Book Encyl, El Paso, Tex, 57; socio-political cartoonist, Univ Tex, El Paso, 57-58, Furman Univ, Greenville, SC, 60-62, World Bank, Washington, DC, 74-78. *Exhib:* Carolina's Fourth Col Art Ann, Columbia Mus Art, SC, 62; Jeddah Fine Arts Soc Third Ann Int Exhib, Jeddah Dome, Saudi Arabia, 79; solo exhibs, Buttonwood Tree, Middletown, Conn, 93, Brownsboro Gallery, Louisville, 96, Galleria Palacio, El Paso, 97 Art Int Asheville, NC, 97; and other group shows. *Collection Arranged:* First Ann Saudi Arabian Beaux Arts Exhib, Kings Pavilion, Yanbu, Saudi Arabia, 82. *Pos:* Cartoon ed, Univ Tex, El Paso, 57-58, Furman Univ, Greenville, SC, 60-62; tech illusr, WR Grace & Co, Greenville, SC, 62-63; ed consultant, Washington, DC, 71-78. *Teaching:* Instr oil painting, US Army, Ft Bliss, Tex, 57 & pvt individuals, New Orleans, Washington & Saudi Arabia, 64-82. *Bibliog:* Anonymous (auth), Maturity in Exhibit at Furman, Greenville Piedmont, 5/8/62; Jim Landers (auth), Pristine pictures at an exhibition, Arab News, 4/9/79 & 4/11/79; Julie Lynch (auth), Artist helps out, Middletown Press, 6/18/93. *Media:* Oil on linen. *Publ:* Auth, Guide to Research, Washington Sch Secys, 72; ed, The Design of Rural Development, World Bank, 75; Turkey: Prospects & Problems of an Expanding Economy, World Bank, 75; Korea: Problems & Issues in a Rapidly Growing Economy, World Bank, 76; Mexico: Tourism, World Bank, 78; Best of Floral Painting, North Sight Books, 1999. *Mailing Add:* 199 Markham St Middletown CT 06457

IMMONEN, GERALD
PAINTER
b Detroit, Mich, 36. *Study:* Cooper Union Art Sch, cert, 58; Yale Univ, New Haven, BFA, 60, MFA, 62. *Work:* Memphis Brooks Mus Art; Metrop Mus Art, NY; Herbert F Johnson Mus Art, Cornell Univ, Ithaca, NY; Mus Art, Rhode Island Sch Design, Providence; Suomi Col, Hancock, Mich. *Exhib:* Prelude to Discoveries and Disclosures, George Ciscle Gallery, Baltimore, Md, 85; Rhode Island Sch Design: Selected Faculty, George Ciscle Gallery, 86; Gerald Immonen: Paintings, Acme Art, San Francico, 87; New Works by Gallery Artists, Charles Cowles Gallery, 87-88; solo exhib, Sixth Ann Suomi Col Contemp Finnish-Am Artist's Exhib, Finnish-Am Heritage Ctr, Hancock, Mich, 96, Taichung Municipal Cult Ctr, Taichung, Taiwan, 8/98, G Watson Gallery, Stonington, Maine, 2005; and others. *Teaching:* Prof, RI Sch Design, Providence, currently. *Awards:* Alice Kimball English Fel, Yale Univ, 60; John F Frazier Award for Excellence in Teaching, RI Sch Design, 90. *Bibliog:* Kenneth Baker (auth), Art in America-March 1985, Chronicle, 10/28/87. *Mailing Add:* 19 Creighton St Providence RI 02906

IMPIGLIA, GIANCARLO
PAINTER, SCULPTOR
b Rome, Italy, Mar 9, 40; US citizen. *Study:* Tech Sch Photog, Rome; Artistic Lyceum, Rome; Acad Fine Arts, Rome. *Work:* Jane Voorhees Zimmerli Art Mus, New Brunswick, NJ; Snite Mus Art, Notre Dame, Ind; Mus City New York. *Comn:* Five panel mural, Am Insurance Bldg, NY, 75-76; mural, 57th Street Playhouse, NY; two panel mural, Fortunoff Co, NY, 79; five panel mural, Cafe Soc, NY, 87; three murals, Queen Elizabeth 2, 94. *Exhib:* Solo exhibs, Rizzoli Gallery, NY & Chicago, 81 & 82, Alex Rosenberg Gallery, NY, 84, Carolyn Hill Gallery, NY, 85, Long Island Focus on Art Show, Old Westbury, NY, 89, RVS Fine Art, Southampton, 89, 9th Ann Philadelphia Art Show, Philadelphia, 89, Uptown Gallery, NY, 90, Robert Mondavi Winery, Oakville, Calif, 90, Hansen Galleries, NY, 91 & 92, Ministero per i Beni Culturali e Ambientali, Rome, 92, Deco Gallery, Wash, DC, 92, Gallery 13, Palm Beach, Fla, 93 & Laura Paul Gallery, Cincinnati, Ohio, 94; Elaine Benson Gallery, Bridgehampton, NY, 94 & 95; Artexpo, Jacob Javitz Conv Ctr, NY, 94; Wilfredo Lam Ctr, Havana, Cuba, 95; Bruce R Lewin Gallery, NY, 95. *Teaching:* Instr, studio seminars. *Awards:* Philadelphia Bowl, 86; Black Tie Award, Am Formal Wear, Inc, 86. *Bibliog:* Ronnie Cohen (auth), Giancarlo Impiglia, Art News, 9/84; Laurel Graeber (auth), The Patron Saint of the Formal Wear Industry, Daily News Record, 9/86; The Art of Giancarlo Impiglia, Rizzoli Int Publ Inc. *Media:* Oil, Acrylic; Wood. *Dealer:* Elaine Benson Gallery Bridgehampton NY; Claudia Carr Gallery New York NY. *Mailing Add:* 182 Grand St New York NY 10013

INCANDELA, GERALD JEAN-MARIE
PHOTOGRAPHER, MURALIST
b Tunis, Tunisia, Feb 19, 1952; French citizen. *Study:* Univ Paris, Nanterre, France, 70-72. *Work:* Getty Mus, Malibu, Calif; Metrop Mus Art & Mus Mod Art, NY; Albright-Knox Mus, Buffalo, NY; Mus Fine Arts, Houston, Tex; Philadelphia Mus Art, Pa. *Comn:* Bronx Zoo Animals, comn by Robert Woolcy, NY, 78; View of Central Park, Mus of Mod Art, NY, 79; murals of puppies & penguins, Thermo Electric Co, NJ, 80; paintings, Archer Daniel Midland Co, 83. *Exhib:* Solo exhib, The Kitchen, NY, 81; Corcoran Gallery, Washington, DC, 78; Photo Start, Bronx Mus, NY, 82; Counterpart, Metrop Mus Art, NY & traveling, 82; How to Draw What to Draw, Parrish Art Mus, Southampton, NY, 82; Still Modern After All These Years, Chrysler Mus, Norfolk, Va, 82; Drawing Ctr, NY & traveling, 82; Mus Modern Art, NY, 83; Mus Modern Art, Oxford, Eng, 86; J Paul Getty Mus, Santa Monica, 98 & Malibu, Calif; Gallerie Beyeler, Basel, Switz, 2002; Metrop Mus Art, New York; Albright-Knox Mus, Buffalo, NY; Phila Mus; Mus Fine Arts, Houston, Tex; Chase Manhattan Bank, NY; Johnson Wax, Racine, Wis; First Bank, Minn. *Bibliog:* Deborah C Phillips (auth), Gerald Incandela photo images, Print Collector's Newslett, 79; Klaus Kertess (auth), Developing an image, Artforum Mag, 81; Pepe Karmel (auth), Photography: Urban disjunctions, Art in Am, 82. *Collection:* Estee Lauder Corp, New York. *Publ:* Coauth with Brad Gooch, Pictures-Story, Oakhurst, 81; coauth with Derek Jarman, Caravaggio, Thames & Hudson, 87. *Mailing Add:* 88 Lexington Ave New York NY 10016

INDICK, JANET
SCULPTOR
b Bronx, NY, Mar 3, 32. *Study:* Hunter Col, with Robert Motherwell & Dong Kingman, BA(art), 53; The New Sch, with Gregorio Prestopino & Richard Pousette-Dart, 61. *Work:* Nat Asn Women Artists Collection, Jane Voorhees Zimmerli Art Mus, Rutgers Univ, New Brunswick, NJ; Bergen Mus Art, Paramus, NJ; Towers

Perin Corp, New York, NY; Amp Corp, Lancaster, Pa; Myron Manufacturing Corp, Maywood, NJ; and numerous others. *Comn:* Steel sculpture, The Jewish Ctr, Teaneck, NJ, 74; steel menorah, Franklin Lakes Pub Sch, NJ, 80; bronze wall sculpture, 81 & sanctuary & wall, wood menorah, 83, Temple Beth Rishon, Wycoff, NJ; sculpture, Temple Sharey Tefilo Israel, South Orange, NJ, 93; outdoor Holocaust steel sculpture, North Shore Synagogue, Syosset, NY, 93. *Exhib:* Morris Mus, NJ, 84; Interplay, Summit Art Ctr Invitational, NJ, 86; solo shows, Edward Williams Gallery, Fairleigh Dickinson Univ, NJ, 86, Bergen Mus, Paramus, NJ, 94, Kerygma Gallery, Ridgewood, NJ, 99, Interchurch Ctr Gallery, NY, 99 & Boathouse Gallery, NY, 99, Broadfoot & Broadfoot, Boonton, NJ, 2000-01, Atrium Gallery, JCC, Washington Township, NJ, 02, Johnson & Johnson Corp, New Brunswick, NJ, 03; traveling exhibs, US mus organized by Nat Asn Women Artists, 100 Yrs/100 Works, USA, 89-90, Sculpture Show, India, 89-90 & Art Exhib, Athens, Greece, 96; traveling painting show, US, 98-99; solo exhibs, Yeshiva Univ Mus, New York City, 2004. *Collection Arranged:* Art Explores Jewish Themes, N.A.W.A. Gallery, New York, NY, 2004. *Awards:* Nat Endowment Arts Fel Grant, 81; Manhattan Arts Int Award, 2000; Harriet Frismuth Bronze Sculpture Award, Catherine Lorilland Wolfe Art Club, 2000; Nat Asn Women Artist Award, 2000; Medal of Honor (sculpture), Nat Arts Club, 01; Catherine Lorrilard Wolfe Art Club Annual, 01; Medallic Art Award, Pen & Brush Club, 01; Nat Asn Women Artists Award (sculpture), 01. *Bibliog:* Articles in The NY Art Rev, 88, Sculpture Fundamentals, 88 & Women Artists in America, Appolo Bks, 88; Biographical Ency of Am; Painters Sculptors and Engravers of US; New York Art Review, Am Reference Publ Corp, 88; The Architect's Source of Artists & Artisans, Kraus Sikes, Inc, 93; International Artist Magazine, 2-3/2002, 14; Gallery & Studio 4-5/2002. *Mem:* Nat Asn Women Artists (vpres, 94-96, pres, 97-99); Sculptors League NY; New York Soc Women Artists; Artists Equity NY; Catherine Lorrilard Wolfe Art Club; NY Soc Women Artists (Sculptor Chair 96-99); Nat Asn Women Artists (bd dirs 2006). *Media:* Metal, Welded. *Specialty:* Kerygma Gallery, American Contemp Artists. *Interests:* Mucic and theatre. *Publ:* Dictionary of American Painters and Sculptors, Appolo Bks, 88; Women Artists in America, Appolo Books, 98; Contemporary Women Artists, St James Press, 99. *Dealer:* Kerygma Gallery 38 Oak St Ridgewood NJ; Sculpture Showcase 156 S Main St New Hope PA. *Mailing Add:* 428 Sagamore Ave Teaneck NJ 07666

INDIVIGLIA, SALVATORE JOSEPH
PAINTER, INSTRUCTOR
b New York, NY, Nov 16, 19. *Study:* Leonardo da Vinci Art Sch; Sch Indust Arts; Pratt Inst, BA; fresco & mural painting with Alfred D Crimi; also with Buck Ulrick, Nicholas Volpe, Earl Winslow & George Harrington, Jr. *Work:* USN Combat Art Collection, Washington, DC; Grumbacher & Sons Collection, NY; Mutual Benefit Life Insurance Co, NJ; Annin Flag Co & Morris Davis Collection, Emily Lowe Found, NY. *Comn:* Assisted Alfred D Crimi with hist mural for Northampton, Mass, 40, Gen Anthony Wayne Mural for Wayne, Pa, 41 & Bowery Mission Mural for Bowery Mission, NY, 42. *Exhib:* Allied Artists Am, 48-98 & 1999-2000; Am Watercolor Soc Ann, NY, 53-83 & 1999-2004; Audubon Artists Ann, NY, 53-2004; Joe & Emily Lowe Found Show, 55 & 60; Operations Palette, USN Combat Art, Smithsonian Inst, Wash, DC, 65; Nat Acad Design, NY, 65-75. *Pos:* Art dir, acct exec & vpres, formerly; off comdr, USN combat artist, 61-79. *Teaching:* Asst & instr, City Col New York, 46-69; private classes, 46-72; instr watercolor, East Williston Libr, New York, 60-72; instr fine & appl arts, Mechanics Inst, New York, 62-66. *Awards:* Pauline Law Award in Oil, Knickerbocker Artists, 74; Gold Medal Watercolor, 75; Liquitex Watercolor Award, Allied Artists Am, 97. *Mem:* Artists Fel (pres, 60-63); Am Watercolor Soc (dir, chmn, 53-72), Allied Artists Am (secy, 59-62); Knickerbocker Artists (vpres, 57-59); US Naval Acad Allemni Asn (assoc mem, 65-05). *Media:* Watercolor, Oil. *Collection:* McLean Library Hofstra Univ, NY; two WWII posters; paintings Viet Nam operations 1964-67, contributed 2004-05. *Publ:* auth, 8 Watercolors of Franklin Sq, Franklin Sq Hist Soc, circa, 51-53; Watch, USNR, 67; Naval Aviation News, 68; All Hands, Bur Naval Personnel, 69; auth, Watercolor page, Am Artist Mag, 71. *Mailing Add:* 974 Lorraine Dr Franklin Square NY 11010

INGALLS, EVE
SCULPTOR, PAINTER
b Cleveland, Ohio, Sept 29, 36. *Study:* Skowhegan Sch Art; Smith Col, BA, 58; Yale Univ Sch Art, BFA, 60, MFA, 62. *Work:* G D Searle Com Collection; Zimmerli Mus, New Brunswick, NJ; NJ State Mus, Trenton, NJ; Jersey City Mus, Jersey City, NJ; New Jersey State Coun on the Arts, Trenton, NJ; Schokland Mus, The Neth. *Exhib:* Butler Inst Am Art, 66; Art & Archit Gallery, Yale Univ, 77; Contemp Reflections, Aldrich Mus, 77 & 87; Cleveland Mus, 77, 80 & 86; Conn Painting, Sculpture and Drawing Traveling Exhib, 78; SoHo 20 Gallery, NY, 80, 81, 84, 86, 90, 92, 97, 99, 2004 & 2006; Conn Comm on the Arts, Hartford, 85; Columbus Mus Art, Columbus, Ga, 85; Paula Allen Gallery, NY, 87 & 88; New Brit Mus Am Art, 89 & 96; Kulturforum Monchengladbach, WGer; Conn Biennial, Bruce Mus, Greenwich, 91; Lyman Allyn Mus, New London, 92; Virginia Miller Gallery, Coral Gables, 93; Transmission, de Zaaijer, Amsterdam, The Neth, 98; Chesterwood Mus, Stockbridge, Mass, 2000; Sculpture Now, Berkshire Botanical Gardens, Stockbridge, Mass, 2002, Unmoored, Phillips Mus Art, Franklin & Marshall Col, Lancaster, Pa, 2002, 100 NJ Artists Make Prints, traveling show, 2002, Schokland Mus, The Neth, 2003; Art Forum Jarfo-Kyoto, Kyoto, Japan, 2005; Holland Paper Biennial, Coda Mus & Rijswijk Mus, 2006. *Teaching:* Instr painting & drawing, Silvermine Guild Sch Arts, 72-; vis lectr, Yale Univ, 79; lectr, State Univ NY, Col at Purchase, 85; vis asst prof, Trinity Col, Hartford, 91. *Awards:* Artist of the Year, Art/Place Gallery, Southport, Conn, 98; NJ Printmaking Fel, Rutgers Ctr for Innovative Print & Paper, Mason Gross Sch Arts, New Brunswick, NJ. *Bibliog:* William Zimmer (auth), rev, New York Times, 89, 91, 92 & 98; Pado Van De Velde (auth), Warm Onthal Voor, De Courant, Amsterdam, 98; Michael Rush (auth), Review, Art New England, 97; Jill Conner (auth), rev, Sculpture, 3/2005; Edward S. Casey, Earth Mapping, Chap 5, 2005. *Mem:* Sculptors' Guild, Int Sculpture Ctr. *Media:* Mixed. *Dealer:* SoHo 20/ Chelsea Gallery 511 West 25st New York NY 10001. *Mailing Add:* 9 Veblen Cir Princeton NJ 08540

INGBER, BARBARA
DEALER, COLLECTOR
b New York, NY, Apr 18, 32. *Study:* NY Univ. *Pos:* Dir, Barbara Ingber Assocs, 72-89; dir & cur, The Artists Mus, 89-. *Mem:* Mus Mod Art; Whitney Mus Am Art; Guggenheim Mus; Metrop Mus. *Specialty:* 20th century American art. *Collection:* Paintings, drawings, sculpture and photographs by contemporary American artists. *Mailing Add:* 16 North Chatsworth Ave Larchmont NY 10538

INGHAM, TOM (EDGAR)
SCULPTOR
b Puyallup, Wash, Feb 23, 42. *Study:* Self Taught. *Work:* Ball State Univ, Muncie, Ind; Univ Puget Sound, Tacoma, Wash. *Comn:* 14 Illus, Playboy Mag, Chicago, Ill, 74-88; poster, British Railways, London, Eng, 85; poster, Seattle Chamber Music Festival. *Exhib:* 8th Ann Exhib, Calif Mag, Palo Alto, 83; Physicians for Social Responsibility: Peace Forum & Art Exhib, Calif Polytech, San Luis Obispo, Calif, 86; 14th Ann Int Competition, Watcom Art Mus, Bellingham, Wash, 94; Biennial Competition, Tacoma Art Mus, Wash, 95; The Art of Paper, W Coast Paper Co, Kent, Wash, 96. *Awards:* Gold Medal, 23rd Ann, Soc Illusr, 80; Award of Excellence, 8th Calif Mag Exhib, 83; Third Prize, Puget Sound Area Exhib, Frye Art Mus, 90. *Media:* Handmade Asian Paper, Recycled Styrofoam. *Publ:* Contribr, Illusr 23 & 25, Soc Illusr, 82 & 84; Graphics Annual, Graphic Press Corp, Switz, 83; California Art Annual, Calif Mag, 83; Outstanding American Illustrators Today, Graphic-sha, Tokyo, 85

INGLE, JOHN S
PAINTER, EDUCATOR
b Evansville, Ind, Sept 18, 33. *Study:* Univ Ariz, BFA, 64, MFA, 66; Royal Acad Beaux Arts, Brussels, Belgium. *Work:* Metrop Mus Art, NY; Springfield Art Mus, Mo; Evansville Mus Arts & Sci, Ind; Phillip Morris Inc, NY; Chemical Bank, NY; Met Life Insurance Co, NY; Evansville Mus Art & Sci, Ind; and others. *Exhib:* Contemp Am Realism Since 1960, 81 & Works on Paper From the Collection of Jalene and Richard Davidson, 82, Pa Acad Fine Art; Every Object Rightly Seen, Univ Va Art Mus, Charlottesville, 82; 20th Century Am Watercolors Traveling Exhib, Gallery Asn NY State, 83; Contemp Images Watercolor, Univ Wis, Oshkosh, 83; Realist Watercolor, Univ Conn, Hartford, 83 & Fla Int Univ, 83; solo exhibs, Capricorn Gallery, Bethseda, Md, 79 Tatistcheff & Co, NY, 81, 83, 85 & 88 & Transco Energy Exhib Gallery, Houston, 85; Am Realism: Twentieth-Century Drawings and Watercolors, Art, San Francisco, 85; The Recognizable Image, Bruce Mus, Greenwich, Conn, 85; The Eye and the Heart: Watercolors of John Stuart Ingle, 88 & 89; Wadsworth Atheneum, Evansville Mus Arts & Sci, Hunter Mus; Realist Watercolors, Palmer Mus Art, Pa State Univ, University Park, 90. *Teaching:* Prof painting, drawing & design, Univ Minn, Morris, 66-. *Bibliog:* Hilton Kramer (auth), Critics choice, New York Times, 1/18/81; James Cooper (auth), article, News World, 1/18/81; John Driscoll (auth), Paradigms of reality, Am Artist, 3/82; Patricia C Johnson (auth), Ingle's watercolors an exhibit not to miss, Houston Chronicle, 2/16/85; Thomas Bolt (auth), John Stuart Ingle, Arts Mag, 11/85. *Media:* Watercolor. *Publ:* Auth, John Camp, the Eye and the Heart, Watercolors of John Stuart Ingle, Rizzoli Publ, 88

INGRAM, MICHAEL STEVEN
PAINTER
b Ft Campbell, Ky, Feb 13, 73. *Exhib:* represented in collections of World Grotto Gallery, Knoxville, Tenn, Knoxville Mus Art. *Collection Arranged:* Sir Real, The Art of Steve Ingram, World Grotto Gallery, 2006. *Bibliog:* Pluto Sports, Southern Comfort Skate Video, Thrasher magazine, 95. *Media:* Oil, Mixed Media. *Publ:* New Millennium Literary Magazine cover art, vol 1, ed 1 & 2, 97. *Dealer:* Brian C Irwin, 512 Post Oak Lane, Knoxville, Tenn, 37920

INJEYAN, SETA L
PAINTER
b Aleppo, Syria, May 3, 46; US citizen. *Study:* Beirut Univ Col, Lebanon, 69; Art Ctr Col Design, Pasadena, Calif, with Richard Diebenkorn, Lorser Feitelson, Llyn Foulkes, Ann McKoy & Peter Alexander, BFA, 76. *Work:* Kaloust Gulbenkian Found, Lisbon, Portugal; Wells Fargo Bank, Los Angeles; Eastern State Hosp, Medical Lake, Wash. *Exhib:* Art Rental Gallery, Los Angeles Co Mus Art, 80 & 92-93; one & two-person exhibs, Merging One Gallery, Santa Monica, Calif, 87, Parker-Blake Gallery, Denver, Colo, 89, Photo Art Gallery, Burbank, Calif, 91, El Camino Col, Torrance, Calif, 92, Brand Libr Art Galleries, Burbank, Calif, 92, Burbank Municipal Art Gallery, Calif, 93 & Brendan Walter Gallery, Santa Monica, Calif, 94 & 95; Art Coun Auction/Exhib, Butterfield & Butterfield, Los Angeles, 91; Unnatural Landscapes, Century Gallery, Sylmar, Calif, 94; Brendan Walter Gallery, Santa Monica, Calif, 94; Artists and Architecture, Artspace Gallery, Woodland Hills, Calif, 94; and others. *Awards:* First Place, Armenian Allied Arts Coun, 75; Best Show, Soc Art Ctr Alumni, Art Ctr Col Design, 76; Three Purchases Prizes, Wash State Arts Comn, 83. *Bibliog:* Nancy Kapitanoff (auth), Marks on the Earth, Los Angeles Times, 4/29/94; Nancy Kapitanoff (auth), Building an impression, Los Angeles Times, 5/13/94; Joe Futtner (auth), City of Dreams, NOHO Mag, 6/94. *Mem:* Artists Equity Asn; Los Angeles Inst Contemp Art; LALMA. *Media:* Miscellaneous Media. *Mailing Add:* 5610 Pinecone Rd La Crescenta CA 91214-1418

INNERST, MARK
PAINTER
b York, Pa. *Study:* Kutztown Univ, BFA. *Work:* Mus Modern Art, NY; Met Mus Art, NY; Mus Contemp Art, Los Angeles; Solomon R Guggenheim Mus, NY; Brooklyn Mus, NY. *Exhib:* The Long View, Mus Modern Art, NY, 94; Realism After Seven AM, Hopper House, Nyack, NY, 96; Art at Work: Forty Yrs of Chase Manhattan Col, Contemp Arts Houston, 99. *Media:* Arylic, Oil. *Dealer:* Paul Kasmin Gallery 293 Tenth Ave New York NY 10001. *Mailing Add:* 136 Emerald Ave West Cape May NJ 08204-1230

INOUE, KAZUKO
PAINTER
b Fukuoka City, Japan, Jan 14, 46; US citizen. *Study:* Mich State Univ, BFA & MFA. *Work:* Wichita State Univ Mus Fine Arts, Kans; Mich State Univ; Newark Mus, NJ. *Exhib:* Flint Inst Art, Mich, 73; one-woman shows, Razor Gallery, NY, 74 & O K Harris Gallery, 77; Soho Ctr Visual Artists, 78; Aldrich Mus Contemp Art, Conn, 79; Intersections, Allan Stone Gallery, 2006. *Teaching:* Vis artist painting & drawing, Mich State Univ, 73; lectr drawing, Eastern Mich Univ, fall 74. *Awards:* Awards, Chautauqua Art Ctr, 70 & Detroit Inst Arts, 72. *Bibliog:* Joseph Dreiss (auth), article, Arts Mag, 74; Michael Brenson (auth), article, 84, New York Times; Michael Brenson (auth), article, New York Times, 5/27/87. *Mem:* Col Art Asn Am. *Media:* Mixed. *Dealer:* Allan Stone Gallery 113 E 90th St New York NY

INOUE, KOZO See Kozo

INSLEY, WILL
PAINTER, DRAFTSMAN
b Indianapolis, Ind, Oct 15, 29. *Study:* Amherst Col, BA; Harvard Univ Grad Sch Design, MA(archit). *Work:* Kroller-Muller-Rijksmuseum, Otterloo; Kunsthalle Tubingen Mus, Ger; Australian Nat Gallery, Canberra; Mus Mod Art, NY; Indianapolis Mus Art, Ind; Addtl Group Shows; Joan Miro Found, Barcelona, Spain, 2004; Serralves Mus Contemp Art, Porto, Portugal, 2004; Kunsthalle Fridericianum, Kassel, Ger, 2005. *Comn:* Great Southwest Indust Park, Atlanta, Ga, 68. *Exhib:* One-man shows, Walker Art Ctr, Minneapolis, 68, Albright-Knox Art Gallery, Buffalo, NY, 68, Mus Mod Art, NY, 71, Hause Lange Mus, Krefeld, Ger, 73, Fischbach Gallery, NY, 73, Wurttembergischer Kunstverein, Stuttgart, Ger, 74, Mus Contemp Art, Chicago, 76 & Max Protetch Gallery, NY, 82 & 92, Will Insley: The Opaque Civilization, Solomon R Guggenheim Mus, NY, 84; Documenta 5, Kassel, 72; The Opague Civilization, Solomon R Guggenheim Mus, NY, 84; Hirschhorn Mus & Sculpture Garden, Washington, DC, 84; New Wall Fragments, Max Protetch Gallery, NY, 88; group-show, Mus Mod Art, NY, 2006. *Pos:* Artist in residence, Oberlin Col, 66 & Univ NC, Chapel Hill, 95; art critic, Univ NC, Greensboro, 67-68 & Cornell Univ, 69. *Teaching:* Instr art, Sch Visual Art, 69-. *Awards:* Nat Found Arts & Humanities Award, 66; Guggenheim Fel, 69; Gottlieb Found Grant, 94. *Bibliog:* Carter Ratcliff (auth), Fragments for a civilization, Art in Am, Vol 73, 4/75; Maurice Poirier (auth), A realm of logical insanity, Art News, Vol 83, 11/84; Donald Wall (auth), Will Insley: Buildings/ Fragments, Arts Mag, Vol 50, 11/75. *Media:* All. *Dealer:* Annemarie Verna Rontgenstrasse 44 8005 Zurich Switzerland. *Mailing Add:* 231 Bowery New York NY 10002

IPCAR, DAHLOV
PAINTER, ILLUSTRATOR
b Windsor, Vt, Nov 12, 17. *Study:* Oberlin Col, 33-34. *Hon Degrees:* Univ Maine, LHD, 78; Colby Col, DFA, 80; Bates Col, DFA, 91. *Work:* Brooklyn Mus, Metrop Mus Art & Whitney Mus Am Art, NY; Portland Mus Art, Maine; Colby Col Mus Art, Waterville, Maine; Bates Col, Lewistown, Maine. *Comn:* mural, Shriner's Children's Hosp for Crippled Children, Springfield, Mass, 79; mural, Kingfield Elementary Sch, Maine, 80; mural, Narragansett Elementary Sch, Gorham, 81; mural, Crescent Park Elementary Sch, Bethel Maine, 94; mural, Mid Coast Hosp Brunswick, Maine, 2000. *Exhib:* one-woman shows, Children's Mus, Oakland, Calif, 56, Portland Mus Art, Maine, 59, 63 & 70, 2000, Del Art Mus Libr, 76, Frost Gully Gallery, Portland, 77, 85 & 96, Hobe Sound Galleries, Fla, 79, Colby Col Mus Art, 80 & Mus Art, Olin Arts Ctr, Bates Col, Lewiston, Maine, 90; group exhibs incl, PA & Detroit Ann, 40; Colby Col Mus Art, 74; Maine State Mus, 76; Joan Whitney Payson Art Mus, Westbrook Col, 82-85; Frost Golly Gallery, Freeport, Maine, 2001 & 03, 2005. *Awards:* Deborah Morton Award, Westbrook Col, 78; Kerlan Award, Univ Minn, 98; Maryann Hartman Award, Univ Maine, 2003. *Bibliog:* Anne Commire (ed), Something About the Author Vol 49, Gale Research; Joyce Nakamura (ed), Something About the Author, Vol 8, Gale Research, 89; Maine Masters Proj, Dahlov Ipcar, Pcov, Video, 2001. *Media:* Oil, Watercolor. *Publ:* Auth & illusr, Calico Jungle, Knopf, 65; The Land of Flowers, Viking, 74; Lobsterman, Downeast, 80; My Wonderful Christmas Tree, Down East Books, 86; and others. *Dealer:* Thomas R Crotty Frost Gully Gallery 1159 US Rt 1, Freeport Maine, 04032

IPOUSTÉGUY, JEAN ROBERT
SCULPTOR, GRAPHIC ARTIST
b Dun-Sur-Meuse, France, Jan 6, 1920. *Study:* Ecole Primaire Super, BEPC, 37, Prix Nat Des Arts 7 es Prix hon, 77, Legion D' Honneur, 84. *Work:* Mus Mod Art, Solomon R Guggenheim Mus, NY; Nat Gallery, Londres, Angletree; Nat Gallery of Victoria, Melbourne, Australia; Mus Mod Art, Mus Beaubourg, Paris; Baltimore Mus Art; Mus St Pierre, Lyon; and others. *Comn:* Val de Grace, Etat Francais, Paris, 83; A La Lumiere de Chacun, Ambassade de France, Washington, 83; Ministre des Finances, France, Paris, 87; Rimbaud, Paris, 89; Celle, Osnabruck, Allemagne, 92; and others. *Exhib:* Solo exhibs, Sculptures & Dessins, Carlbserg Glyptotek, Denmark, 83, Heitland Found, Ger, 89, Dialog, 90 Prague, Czech, 90, Bobigny, Nevers, France, 91 & Oberhausen, Berlin, Allemagne, 92, Bourges, France, 93, Bremen, 94, Vitry, France, 94; Dun sur Meuse, (Mort De L'Eveque Neumann), France 95; Chateau De Montreal En Perigord, France, 96. *Awards:* Prix Bright, XXXII Biennale Venise, M Bright, 64; Dessins, 1er Prix Rijeka, Yogoslavia, 68. *Bibliog:* Gaudibert Pierre (auth), Ipousteguy, Cercle D'Art, Paris, 89; Ipousteguy, Parlons Evelyne Artaud, 93. *Mem:* Academie Royal de Belgique. *Media:* All Media. *Publ:* Auth, Leaders et Enfants Nus, Soleil Noir, 70; Ronds Dans L'O et Le Pessimisme, Eds Sigart, 76; Sauve Qui Peut Robin, Crasset, 78; Arcs et Traits, Gercle d'Art-Sarver, 89; Le Balmoral des Anxieux, Soleil Natal, 94. *Dealer:* 35 rue Chevreul Choisy le Roi France

IPPOLITO, ANGELO
PAINTER, EDUCATOR
b St Arsenio, Italy, Nov 9, 22; US citizen. *Study:* Ozenfant Sch Fine Arts, New York; Brooklyn Mus Art Sch, with Ferren; Meschini Inst, Rome, Italy; also with Afro, Rome. *Work:* Whitney Mus Am Art, Metrop Mus Art; Munson-Williams-Proctor Inst, Utica, NY; Phillips Gallery, Washington, DC; Norfolk Mus Arts & Sci, Va; Milwaukee Mus, Wis; and many others. *Comn:* Mural (oil painting), comn by Singer & Sons, now in collection of Montreal Trust Co, Que, 67. *Exhib:* Young Am, Whitney Mus Am Art, 57; Abstract Impressionism, Arts Coun, London, 58; Sao Paulo Bienal, Brazil, 61; Am Collages, Mus Mod Art, NY & Beuningen Mus, Rotterdam, 66; Retrospective, State Univ NY, Binghamton, 75; one-man shows, Borgenicht Gallery, NY, 75 & 86; plus others. *Teaching:* Instr painting, Cooper Union, 56-66; artist in residence, Mich State Univ, 66-71; assoc prof art, State Univ NY Binghamton, 71-76, prof art, 76-. *Awards:* Fulbright Fel to Florence, Italy, 58; Ford Found Artist in Residence to Arnot Gallery, 65; Tiffany grant, 79; and others. *Bibliog:* Dore Ashton (auth), Arte Americana contemporanea, Commentari, Lionello Venturi Rome, 55; Irving Sandler (auth), Angelo Ippolito Landscapes, Provincetown Advocate, 7/4/57; Alfred Frankenstein (auth), Professors tell a story at Bolles, San Francisco Chronicle, 10/1/61; and others. *Media:* Oil. *Publ:* Contribr, Italy Rediscovered (catalog), Munson-Williams-Proctor Inst, 55; contribr, It Is, spring 58; contribr, Nature in Abstraction, Whitney Mus Am Art, 58; and others. *Mailing Add:* State Univ NY Dept Art Binghamton NY 13902

IPSEN, KENT FORREST
GLASSWORKER, CRAFTSMAN
b Milwaukee, Wis, Jan 4, 33. *Study:* Univ Wis-Milwaukee, BS; Univ Wis-Madison, MS & MFA; also with Harvey K Littleton. *Work:* Milwaukee Art Ctr, Wis; Toledo Mus Art, Ohio; Corning Glass Mus, NY; Chrysler Mus, Norfolk, Va; Chicago Art Inst; and others. *Comn:* First Gov Awards for the Arts, State of Va, 79. *Exhib:* Vidrios, Estudio Actual, Caracas, Venezuela, 74; Wis Directions, Milwaukee Art Ctr, 75; Looking Forward, Fairtree Gallery, NY, 75; Relig & Art, Vatican Mus, 78; New Glass, Int Competition Corning Mus, 79; and others. *Teaching:* Asst prof glassworking, Mankato State Col, Minn, 65-68; assoc prof glassworking, Chicago Art Inst, 68-72; assoc prof glassworking & chmn dept crafts, Va Commonwealth Univ, 73-76, prof, 76-. *Awards:* Nat Endowment Arts, US Govt, 72 & 75. *Bibliog:* Lee Nordness (auth), Objects USA, Viking, 71; Ray Grover (auth), Contemporary Art Glass, Crown, 75. *Mem:* Am Craft Coun; Ill Craft Coun (pres, 70-72); Nat Coun Educ in Ceramic Arts; Nat Coun Art Adminr. *Media:* Glass. *Dealer:* Habatat Galleries 28235 Southfield Rd Lathrup Village MI 48076; Heller Gallery 965 Madison Ave New York NY 10021. *Mailing Add:* 715 Bowe St Richmond VA 23220-3011

IRELAND, DAVID
PRINTMAKER
b Bellingham, Wash, 30. *Study:* Western Wash State Univ, 48-50; Calif Col Arts & Crafts, BAA(indust design), 53; Laney Col, Oakland, studied plastics technol & printmaking, 72-74; San Francisco Art Inst, MFA, 74. *Work:* Mus Mod Art, NY; San Francisco Mus Mod Art; Whatcom Mus Art & Hist, Bellingham, Wash; Mass Inst Technol Gallery; Oakland Mus, Calif. *Comn:* Jade Garden, Washington Proj for Arts, Washington, DC, 84-85; Newgate (entryway sculpture), Landfill Preservation Area, Candelstick Point State Park, San Francisco, 85-87; Light-up Philadelphia (light schemes), Fairmont Park Art Asn, 87; outdoor sculpture, Three Rivers Art Festival, Pittsburgh, 87-88; vis artists apartment (functioning art work in collaboration with architect Henry Moss & Master craftsman John Sirois), Addison Gallery, Andover, Mass, 96. *Exhib:* Solo exhibs, Mus Mod Art, NY, 88, Hirshhorn Mus & Sculpture Garden, 90, Walter Art Ctr, Minneapolis, 92, Ruth Bloom Gallery, Santa Monica, Calif, 92, Laura Carpenter Fine Art, Santa Fe, NMex, 93, Mattress Factory, Pittsburgh, Pa, 93 & Gallery Am Acad Rome, Italy, 97, Everyday Art, Freddman Gallery, Pa, 2000, Reflections, Jack Shainman Gallery, NY, 2000, Christopher Grimes Gallery, Calif, 2001, Gallery Paule Anglim, San Francisco, Calif, 2001; Awards in the Visual Arts (traveling), Los Angeles Co Mus Art, 88; Colby Col Mus Art, Maine, 93; Self Portraits in Black and White by Eighty-Six West Coast Artists, Edith Caldwell Gallery, San Francisco, 93; Artist's Space, NY, 94; Issues of Image, Cheryl Haines Gallery, San Francisco, 94; Double Trouble: The Patchett Collection, Mus Contemp Art, San Diego, Calif, 98; Off the Wall, Ashville Art Mus, NC, 98; On the Ball: The Sphere in Contemp Sculpture, DeCordova Mus & Sculpture Park, Lincoln, Mass, 99; group exhibs, Seascape, Rapture, Mass Coll of Art, 2000, Eccentric Forms and Structures, Microsoft Art Collection, Wash, 2000, Christopher Grimes Gallery, Calif, 2000, Making the Making, Apex Art Curatorial Prog, NY, 2001. *Pos:* Artist-in-residence, Headlands Ctr Arts, Ft Barry, Calif, 86-87. *Awards:* Louis Comfort Tiffany Found Grant, 87; Am Acad Art, Rome, Italy, 97; Vis Award, Flintridge Found, 98. *Dealer:* IXL Art Servs San Francisco CA. *Mailing Add:* c/o Gallery Paule Anglim 14 Geary St San Francisco CA 94108

IRELAND, PATRICK
CONCEPTUAL ARTIST
b Ireland, 34. *Study:* Univ Col, Dublin, Ireland; Cambridge Univ; Harvard Sch Pub Health, Cambridge, Mass, MA. *Work:* Chase Manhattan Bank Collection, Metrop Mus Art, Mus Mod Art, NY; Butler Inst Am Art, Youngstown, Ohio; Nat Mus Am Art, Washington, DC; Kilkenny Gallery Mod Art, Hugh Lane Gallery Mod Art, Ireland;

Nat Gallery Australia; Hirshhorn Mus & Sculpture Garden, Smithsonian Inst, Washington; Metrop Mus Art, NY; Mus Modern Art, NY. *Exhib:* Cranbrook Acad, Bloomfield Hills, Mich, 81; Neuberger Mus, Purchase, NY, 82; Brooklyn Mus, NY, 83; Poetry and the Visual Arts, Univ NC, Charlottesville, 84; Univ Va, Charlottesville, 84; The Minimal Line, Bard Col, Annandale-on-Hudson, NY, 85; Galerie Hoffman, Friedberg, W Ger, 86; Summer Exhib, Charles Cowles Gallery, NY, 87; Detroit Inst Arts, Mich, 87; Art on Paper, Weatherspoon Art Gallery, Univ NC, Greensboro, 88; Pvt Works for Pub Spaces, RC Erpf Gallery, 88; Fuller-Gross Gallery, San Francisco, Calif, 89; solo shows, Elvehjem Mus Art, Univ Wis, Madison, 92, Butler Inst Am Art, 94, Brigham Young Univ Mus Art, 95, Crawford Munic Art Gallery, Cork, Ireland, 95, Old Yacht Club, Cobh, Ireland, 96, Orchard Gallery, Derry, N Ireland, 98 & Charles Cowles Gallery, NY, 98 & 99; New Talent - New Ideas, Charles Cowles Gallery, NY, 96; Art and the Am Experience, Kalamazoo Art Inst, Mich, 98; Works on Paper, A to Z, Charles Cowles Gallery, NY, 98; Gotham Group, Charles Cowles Gallery, NY, 98; Primarily Structural, PS I Contemp Art Ctr, Long Island City, NY, 99; Toward a Society for All Ages: World Artists at the Millenium, UN Visitors' Lobby, NY, 99. *Teaching:* Vis prof, Univ Calif, Berkeley, 67; adj prof, Barnard Col, Columbia Univ, 70; prof fine arts & media, Southampton Col & Long Island Univ, 97-. *Awards:* Mather Award Art Criticism, Col Art Asn, 65; Franklin Murphy Lectr, Spencer Mus, Univ Kans, 80. *Bibliog:* Ken Johnson (auth), article, NY Times, 10/23/98; Caoimhin Mac Giolla Leith, article, Artforum, 11/98; Thomas McEvilley (auth), An artist & his aliases, Art in Am, 05/99. *Mailing Add:* c/o Charles Cowles Gallery 537 W 24th St New York NY 10011

IRMAS, AUDREY MENEIN
COLLECTOR
Pos: Co-founding trustee, Audrey & Sydney Irmas Charitable Found, 83-, projects incl Audrey & Sydney Irmas Campus of the Wilshire Blvd Temple, Audrey & Sydney Irmas Los Angeles Youth Ctr; bd trustees, Mus Contemp Art, Los Angeles, 92-, pres, chmn, formerly, Hirshhorn Mus. *Awards:* Named one of Top 200 Collectors, ARTnews Mag, 2004. *Interests:* Photography. *Collection:* Contemporary art. *Mailing Add:* Audrey & Sydney Irmas Charitable Found 16830 Ventura Blvd Ste 364 Van Nuys CA 91436-2797

IRVIN, MARIANNE FANELLI
PAINTER, COLLAGE ARTIST
b Philadelphia, Pa, Sept 9, 47. *Study:* Philadelphia Col Art, with Karl Sherman, BFA (painting), 69; Md Inst Col Art, with Al Hurwitz, 85; Rudolph Steiner Col, Calif State Univ, Sacramento, with David Elkind, 89. *Comn:* Infant portrait studies, comn by Dr Norman J Santora, Upper Darby, Pa, 70; Portrait of Marie, comn by Clarence Carroll, Upper Darby, Pa, 81; vestments to honor the Holy Spirit, comn by Rev Patrick C Stephenson, American Canyon, Calif, 94; floral photog, cover art cd, Bouquet, Francesca & Leonardo, 2000; floral photog, Commemorative Poster, Purple Passion, Benefit Concert, Am Canyon, Calif, 2003; floral photg, cover art cd, A Christmas Rose, Francesca & Leonardo, 2003. *Exhib:* California Small Works, Calif Mus Art, Santa Rosa, 89 & 90; Napa Co Spring Fair, Calif, 89; Fairfield Regional Juried Art Show, Calif, 92; State of the Art 93 Int Invitational, New Eng Fine Arts Inst, Boston, Mass, 93; Festa Artisanos Juried, Am Canyon, Calif, 93. *Pos:* Art dept head fine arts, Rosemont Sch Holy Child, Pa, 82-84; founding artist bd mem, American Canyon Arts Found, Calif, 92-; art educ consult creative & mental growth, Butterfly Hope Nature Ctr, Denver, Colo, 93; artist-in-residence, Bransford Elem Sch, Fairfield, Calif, 94. *Teaching:* Adj art instr, Delaware Co Community Col, Media, Pa, 87 & 88, Napa Valley Col, Calif, 89-92; vis art instr Making Arts Grow in the Community, Fairfield Calif Civic Arts, 94-97. *Awards:* Anna Jones Mem Award, Main Line Ctr Arts Mem Group Exhib, 82; Best of Show, Festa Artisanos, City of American Canyon, 93; 1st Place Award abstract painting Festival of Artists Am Canyon, Calif, 95. *Bibliog:* Mary Wallis (auth), Napa Valley artists to open studios, Napa Valley Register, 9/92; Felix A Bedolla (auth), Local artist wins award, Artscan, Napa Valley Arts Coun, 5-6/94; Dan German (auth), Canyon artist puts her mark on festival, Napa Valley Register, 7/94. *Mem:* Nat Mus Women Arts; Int Imagery Asn. *Media:* Oil Paint on Silk, Pantone Letrafilm Matt Colors. *Publ:* Contribr, Contemporary Women Artist Desk Calendar, Bo Tree Publ, 89; Todays Great Poems, Famous Poets Soc, 94; Reflections of Light, Nat Libr Poetry, 95. *Dealer:* Muzzys Secret Garden Gallery Suisun City CA. *Mailing Add:* 915 Limewood St Suisun City CA 94585

IRVINE, BETTY JO
LIBRARIAN, INSTRUCTOR
b Indianapolis, Ind, July 13, 43. *Study:* Ind Univ, AB, 66, MLS, 69, PhD, 82. *Pos:* Fine arts slide librn, Sch of Fine Arts, Ind Univ, Bloomington, 66-68, asst fine arts libr, 68-69, fine arts librn, 69-. *Teaching:* Instr art bibliog, Sch of Fine Arts, Ind Univ, Bloomington, 69- & instr art librarianship, & Info Sci, 86-. *Awards:* Officer's Grant, Coun of Libr Resources, Washington, DC, 71; Teaching Excellence Recognition Award, Ind Univ, 2000. *Mem:* Am Libr Asn (vchmn-chmn-elect art sect, 78-79); Midwest Art Hist Soc (session chmn, 76); Art Libr Soc NAm (chmn, Standards Comt, 83 , vpres, 91 & pres, 91). *Res:* Organization and management of slide libraries; art library planning and design; women in libraries. *Publ:* Organization and management of art slide collections, Libr Trends, 1/75; coauth (with L Korenic), Survey of periodical use in an academic art library, In: Art Documentation, Bulletin Art Libr Soc NAm, 10/82; auth, Sex Segregation in Librarianship, Greenwood Press, 86; ed, Facilities Standards for Art Libraries and Visual Resources Collections, Art Libr Soc NA & Colo Libr Unltd, 91; auth, Chinese art libraries: developments and trends, Parts I-II, Art Libr J, 2000, 01. *Mailing Add:* c/o Fine Arts Libr Ind Univ Bloomington IN 47401

IRVING, DONALD J
ADMINISTRATOR, WRITER
b Arlington, Mass, May 3, 33. *Study:* Mass Col Art, BA, 55; Columbia Univ Teachers Col, MA, 56, EdD, 63. *Pos:* Chmn dept art & dir, Peabody Mus Art, George Peabody Col Teachers, Nashville, Tenn, 67-69; dir sch, Sch of the Art Inst Chicago, 69-83; dean, fac fine arts, Univ Ariz, Tucson, 83-90, prof art, 90-91, adj prof, 91-. *Teaching:* Teacher art, White Plains High Sch, NY, 58-60; instr art, State Univ NY Col Oneonta, 58-60; prof art & dean, Moore Col Art, Philadelphia, 63-67. *Mem:* Nat Asn Schs Art (treas & mem bd dir, 72-75); Union Independent Cols Art (bd dir, 72-, chmn bd, 79-); Nat Coun Art Adminr (bd dir, 73-); Fedn Independent Ill Cols & Univs (bd dir, 74-). *Res:* Application of industrial materials and techniques to contemporary sculpture. *Publ:* Auth Sculpture: Material and Process, Van Nostrand Reinhold, 70. *Mailing Add:* PO Box 974 Sonoita AZ 85637-0974

IRWIN, GEORGE M
PATRON, COLLECTOR
b Quincy, Ill, May 2, 21. *Study:* Univ Mich, BA, 43. *Hon Degrees:* Culver-Stockton Col, DFA, 73; Western Ill Univ, DHL, 90; Quincy Univ, Ill, DHL, 2000. *Pos:* Chmn bd, Am for Arts, Washington, DC, 62-72 & Ill Arts Coun, 63-71; mem bd, Mus Contemp Art, Chicago, formerly; mem bd, Ill State Mus & Mus Contemp Art, Chicago; pres, Quincy Soc Fine Arts, 47-77. *Awards:* Lifetime Award, Ill Arts Alliance Found, 90; Studs Terkel Lifetime Arts Award, Ill Humanities Coun, 99; R Driehaus Fedn Award, Landmarks Preservation Coun Ill, 99. *Mem:* Life mem Art Inst Chicago; Nat Trust Hist Preserv; and others. *Collection:* Twentieth century American artists. *Publ:* producer, Historic Quincy Architecture, 96. *Mailing Add:* 1636 Hampshire St Quincy IL 62301

IRWIN, LANI HELENA
PAINTER
b Annapolis, Md, Oct 27, 47. *Study:* Am Univ, Washington, BFA, 69, MFA, 74. *Work:* Nat Mus Am Art, Washington; Bayly Mus, Charlottesville, Va; Hirschorn Mus, Washington, DC; Huntington Mus, WVa; Corcoran Gallery Art, Washington, DC. *Exhib:* Md Biennial, Baltimore Mus, 74; 19th Area Exhib, Corcoran Gallery Art, Washington, 74; Graham Gallery, NY, 77; Huntington Mus, W Va, 2001; solo exhibs, Gallery K, 81, 83, 86, 94 & 98; Katharina Rich Perlow Gallery, NY, 96, 97, 2000 & 03; 179th Ann Art Invitational, Nat Acad Design, NY, 2004; The Figure in American Painting and Drawing 1985-2005, Ogunquit Mus Am Art, Ogunquit, Maine; What is Realism, Albemarle Gallery, London, 2005. *Awards:* Pollock-Krasner Found Grant, 95. *Bibliog:* Jill Wechsler (auth), Lani Irwin, Am Artist, 6/83; James Mann (auth), The metaphysical art of Lani Irwin, Am Arts Quart, spring 94; Jeff Wright (auth), Lani Irwin, Cover, summer 96; Gail Leggio (auth), The Interior Theater of Lani Irwin, Am Arts Quart, 2001. *Media:* Oil. *Dealer:* Katharina Rich Perlow Gallery 560 Broadway New York NY 10012. *Mailing Add:* Porziano 68 Assisi 06081 Italy

IRWIN, ROBERT
ENVIRONMENTAL ARTIST
b Long Beach, Calif, Sept 12, 28. *Study:* Otis Art Inst, 48-50; Jepson Art Inst, Los Angeles, 51; Chouinard's Art Inst, Los Angeles, 52-54; San Francisco Inst Art, Hon Dr, 79, Otis-Parson's Art Inst, Hon Dr, 92. *Hon Degrees:* Hon dr art, San Francisco Art Inst, 79, Otis-Parson's Art Inst, Los Angeles, 92. *Work:* Art Inst Chicago; Walker Art Ctr, Minneapolis, Minn; San Francisco Mus Mod Art, Calif; Mus Contemp Art, Lannen Found, Los Angeles; Mus Mod Art, Whitney Mus Am Art, NY; Mus Contemp Art, San Diego. *Comn:* 9 Spaces 9 Trees, Seattle, Wash, 83, 56 Shadow Planes, Old Post Off, Gen Servs Admin, Washington, DC, 83; Arts Enrichment Master Plan, Miami Int Airport, 86-88; Central Garden, J Paul Getty Mus, Los Angeles, 92-97; 1-2-3-4, Mus Contemp Art, San Diego. *Exhib:* Solo exhibs, Pace Gallery, NY, 92, Pace Wildenstein Gallery, Los Angeles, 98, Musee d'Art Contemporain de Lyon, France, 98, Dia Ctr Arts, NY, 98-99; retrospective, Whitney Mus Am Art, NY, 77, Mus Contemp Art, Los Angeles, Kunstverein, Cologne, Ger, Mus d'Art Moderne de la Ville, Paris & Reina Sofia, Madrid, Spain, 93-95, Mus of Contemp Art, Los Angeles (traveling), 93-95; Pace Wildenstein Gallery, 94, 98 & 99; Contemp Art in Transition-from the Collection of the Ho-Am Art Mus, Ho-Am Art Gallery, Seoul, Korea, 97; California Scheming Mus Contemp Art, Chicago, 98; Material Perfection: Minimal Art & its Aftermath Selectred from the Kerry Stokes Collection, Lawrence Wilson Art Gallery, Univ Western Australia, Perth, 98; and others. *Teaching:* John J Hill lect prof, Univ Minn, 81; Cullinan lect prof, Rice Univ, 87-88. *Awards:* MacArthur Found Award, 84; Guggenheim fel, 76; MacArthur fel, 84-89. *Bibliog:* Calvin Tompkins (auth), Knowing in Action, The New Yorker, 85; Rosalind Krauss (auth), Overcoming the Limits of Matter, Studies in Mod Art, Mus Mod Art, 91; Roberta Smith (auth), Matter Turned into Light & Space, New York Times, 92; and others. *Media:* All. *Publ:* Auth, Notes Toward A Model (catalog), Whitney Mus, 77; Set of Questions, American Artists on Art from 1940-1980, 80; Being and Circumstance: Notes Towards A Conditional Art, 85; The Hidden Structures of Art (Robert Irwin catalog), Mus Contemp Art, Los Angeles, 93; Robert Irwin: Getty Garden, Los Angeles: The J Paul Getty Mus, 2002. *Dealer:* PaceWildenstein 32 E 57th St New York NY 10022. *Mailing Add:* PaceWildenstein Gallery 32 E 57th St 2nd Fl New York NY 10022

ISAACS, AVROM
ART DEALER, PUBLISHER
b Winnipeg, Man, 26. *Study:* Univ Toronto, BA(polit sci & econ). *Pos:* Dir & owner, Isaacs/Innuit Gallery Eskimo Art, 70-; assoc fel, Calumet Col, York Univ, 70-; bd dir, Mus Textile, Toronto. *Awards:* LLD York Univ; Order of Can. *Specialty:* Early North American Indian art and artifacts; art of the Eskimo of all periods

ISAACS, CLAIRE NAOMI
ADMINISTRATOR
b San Francisco, Calif, Feb 12, 33. *Study:* Pomona Col, BA, 54; Ohio State Univ, 54-55; Univ Calif, Berkeley, 62-64; Univ Southern Calif, 71; Claremont Grad Sch, MA(20th century art hist), 75; Harvard Univ, cert art mgt, 77, Coro fel pub affairs for arts mgr, 79. *Collection Arranged:* Children's Book Illustrators (artmobile exhib), 67; Art of the African (traveling exhib), 69; Children's Art From Three Countries: Japan, Iran, USSR, 76; Int Child Art Collection, 1978-83 (auth, catalog), 83. *Pos:* Asst, Art Gallery, Univ Calif, Berkeley, 61-63; educ supvr, San Francisco Mus Mod Art, 63-66; asst dir & coordr, Visual Art Proj, PACE (Proj to Advance Creativity in Educ), San Bernardino, Inyo & Mono Co Sch, 66-69; dir, Jr Arts Ctr, Munic Arts Dept, Los Angeles, 70-80, Burnsdall Art Ctr, Los Angeles Affairs Dept, 80-83; dir cult affairs, City & Co, San Francisco Arts Comm, 83-. *Teaching:* Lectr art for deaf, Univ Calif Exten, Los Angeles, 72. *Awards:* Golden Grate Award, Western Asn Art Mus, 78. *Mem:* Am Asn Mus; Am Asn Youth Mus; Nat Art Educ Asn. *Publ:* Auth, Paul Klee and Galka Scheyer, Artforum, 62; The Art of Borrowing and Distributing Art for the Small Community, Visual Arts Proj, 70; ed, Proceedings of the Conference on Art for the Deaf, Jr League Los Angeles, 75; contribr, The Museum and the Visitor Experience, Western Regional Conf Am Asn Mus, 77. *Mailing Add:* 56 Roble Rd Berkeley CA 94705

ISAACS, RON
PAINTER, SCULPTOR
b Cincinnati, Ohio, Oct 14, 41. *Study:* Berea Col, BA, 63; Ind Univ, MFA, 65. *Work:* Huntsville Mus Art; McDonalds Corp, Oakbrook, Ill; Am Express, AT&T & Chase Manhattan Bank, NY. *Comn:* Three painted sculptures, Univ Hosp, Cleveland, Ohio, 94; painted sculpture, Menorah Park Foundation, Beachwood, Ohio, 02. *Exhib:* One-person exhib, Monique Knowlton Gallery, NY, 80, 82 & 85, Robert L Kidd Galleries, Birmingham, Mich, 85, Pittsburgh Ctr for the Arts, 86 & Sazama Gallery, Chicago, 92; More Than Land or Sky: Art from Appalachia, Nat Mus Am Art, Animal Image, Renwick Gallery, Smithsonian Inst, Washington, DC, 81; Realism Invitational, Southeastern Ctr for Contemp Art, Winston-Salem, NC, 82-83; Illusions, Greenville Co Mus Art, SC, 84; More Than Meets The Eye: The Art of Trompe L'Oeil, Columbus Mus Art, 85-86; The Medium as Illusion, Calif State Univ, Fullerton, 86; and others. *Teaching:* Instr fine arts, Sue Bennett Col, London, KY, 65-69; prof painting & drawing, Eastern Ky Univ, Richmond, 69-01; professor emeritus, 01-. *Awards:* First Purchase Awards, Preview 73, Col of Mount St Joseph, Cincinnati, Ohio, 72, Fifth Berea Drawing Biennial, Berea Col, Ky, 83. *Bibliog:* Madeleine Burnside (auth), Ron Isaacs (rev), Art News, 11/78; Dona Z Meilach (auth), Woodworking: The New Wave, Crown Publ, New York, 81; Phyllis George (auth), Kentucky Crafts, Handmade & Heartfelt, Crown Pubol, NY, 89. *Mem:* Am Crafts Coun; Nat Art Educ Asn. *Media:* Acrylic, Birch Plywood. *Publ:* True Lies (art/essay), Nouvei Object VI, Design House Publ, Seoul, Korea, 01. *Dealer:* Schneider Gallery 230 W Superior St Chicago IL 60610; Toni Birckhead Gallery 342 W 4th St Cincinnati OH 45202; Snyderman Gallery 303 Cherry St Philadelphia PA 19106. *Mailing Add:* 420 Adams Ln Richmond KY 40475-8764

ISAACSON, GENE LESTER
COLLECTOR, HISTORIAN
b Rugby, NDak, June 14, 36. *Study:* Concordia Col, Moorhead, Minn, BA, 58; Univ Northern Colo, MFA, 62; Univ Salzburg Orff Inst, Austria, 63-64. *Pos:* Bd trustees, Orange Co Ctr Contemp Art, currently; gallery dir, Rancho Santiago Col, Calif, 85-86, chmn dept art, 92-94. *Teaching:* Chmn dept art, Willamette Univ, 62-63, Santa Ana Col, 64-84; vis assoc prof art hist, Chapman Col, World Campus Afloat, 69-71; ed, Art Forum Newsletter, Calif, 81-91; art hist, Rancho Santiago Col, Santa Ana & Orange Coast Col, Costa Mesa, 85-. *Awards:* Profiles in Excellence, Staff Award, RS Col, 92. *Bibliog:* Richard E Ellinger (auth), Design and Color Structure, Int Press, 65. *Res:* Prehistoric and primitive art; African art; oceanic art; art collecting. *Collection:* Extensive survey of West African tribal sculpture; oceanic art, American Indian; United States and European modern painting and graphics. *Publ:* Coauth, Col Exhib Catalogs, Willamette Univ & Santa Ana Col, 62, 68, 72 & 77; auth, Monuments of African Sculpture, Santa Ana Col, 72; articles in Primitive Arts Newsletter, New York, African Arts, Univ Calif, Los Angeles & Western Humanities Rev; African Legacy, Orange Coast Col, 94; and many others

ISAACSON, LYNN JUDITH
PAINTER, SCULPTOR
b New York, NY, Nov 8, 1948. *Study:* Queens Col, with Herb Aach & Louis Finkelstein, MS(art educ), 74; Lehman Col, MFA(painting), 81. *Comn:* Relief construction, Oppenheimer & Co Inc, NY, 81; styrofoam & wood construction, Saratoga Construction Inc, Montreal, Que, 84. *Exhib:* Liberty and the Pursuit of Liberty, Nat Women's Caucus Arts, 86; Lehman Col Alumni Show, Lehman Col Art Gallery, Bronx, NY, 86; solo show, Soho Gallery, NY, 86 & 89; Vangarde Gallery, New London, Conn, 68, Soho Gallery, 90; Educ Alliance, NY, 92. *Pos:* Membership secy, Bd Dir, Women's Caucus Arts, 80-86. *Teaching:* Teacher fine arts & ceramist, Jr High Sch 117, Bronx, NY, 71-. *Awards:* Queens Youth Ctr Arts Award, Queens Col, 74. *Bibliog:* Ellen Lee Klein (auth), article, Arts Mag, 9/83. *Media:* Mixed Media on paper based on quilt design. *Publ:* Illusr, Working Big: A Teacher's Guide to Environmental Sculpture (coauths, John Lidstone & Clarence Bunch), Van Nostrand Reinhold Co, 75. *Dealer:* Soho Gallery 168 Mercer St New York NY 10012; Vangarde Gallery 331 Captains Walk New London CT 06320. *Mailing Add:* 229 E 21st St No 4 New York NY 10010-6433

ISAACSON, MARCIA JEAN
ARTIST, EDUCATOR
b Atlanta, Ga, Sept 25, 45. *Study:* Univ Ga, Athens, BFA & MFA. *Work:* Minn Mus Art, St Paul; High Mus Art, Atlanta, Ga; Greenville Coun Mus of Art, Greenville, SC; Fla House Rep, Tallahassee; Ala Powers Co; Duke Univ Mus Art, Durham, NC; Eastman Pharmaceuticals, Melvern Pa; Ark Art Ctr. *Exhib:* Drawings USA, Minn Mus Art, St Paul, 71 & 73; 35 Artists in the SE Traveling Exhib, High Mus Art; Southeastern Graphics Invitational: Drawing, Mint Mus Art, Charlotte, 79; West 79 & 84: Art and the Law, Minn Mus Art, St Paul; Drawing Show, Southeastern Ctr Contemp Arts, Winston-Salem, NC, 82; Kipnis Gallery, Atlanta, 81 & 82; Nat Drawing Invitational, Ark Art Ctr, Little Rock, 86; Ten Yrs Southeastern Seven, Southeastern Crt Contemp Arts, Winston-Salem, NC, 87; Duke Univ Mus of Art, Durham, NC, Nat Drawing Invitational Emporia State Univ, Emporia, KS. *Pos:* Selection panels, SECCA Grants, Southeastern Ctr Contemp Art, 77, Nat Endowment Arts Fel Grants, 80-81, Ill Art Coun Grants, 85 & Fla Art Coun Grants, 85. *Teaching:* Instr printmaking & drawing, Wesleyan Col, Macon, Ga, 70-73; asst prof drawing, Univ Fla, Gainesville, 73-80, assoc prof, 80-. *Awards:* Teacher of the Year, Col Fine Arts, Univ Fla, 77-78; Nat Endowment Arts-Southeastern Ctr Contemp Art Fels, 77; Fla Fine Arts Coun Fel, 79 & 89; Purchase Award, Davidson Col, NC, 73 & State Univ Col, NY, 75. *Media:* Pencil, Charcoal. *Mailing Add:* 1803 NW Tenth Ave Gainesville FL 32605-5311

ISAACSON, PHILIP MARSHAL
CRITIC, WRITER
b Lewiston, Maine, June 16, 24. *Study:* Bates Col, BA, 47; Harvard Law Sch, LLB, 50. *Hon Degrees:* Bowdoin Col, DFA, 83 & 84; Bates Col, DHL, 97. *Work:* Portland Mus Art, Maine. *Exhib:* Maine 2000, Maine Coast Artists, Rockport, Maine, 2000. *Pos:* Adv mem, Maine Lawyers & Accountants for the Arts, 94-; mem, Exec Adv Comt, Bates Col Mus Art, 96-; mem, Maine Hist Pres Comn, 98-. *Awards:* Boston Globe-Horn Book Awards, Honor Bk, 89; Cult Recognition Award, Maine Community Cult Alliance, 92. *Mem:* Maine State Comn Arts & Humanities (chmn, 75-). *Res:* The American eagle as a decorative device; architecture of Maine since 1920; esthetics of architecture. *Publ:* Auth, The American Eagle, NY Graphic Soc, 75; contrib, Marine Forms of American Architecture, Colby Col, 76; auth, Round Buildings, Square Buildings & Buildings that Wiggle Like a Fish, Knopf, 89; A Short Walk Around the Pyramids & Through the World of Art, Knopf, 93. *Dealer:* June Fitzpatrick Gallery 112 High St Portland Maine 04101. *Mailing Add:* 75 Park St Lewiston ME 04240

ISAACSON, RONALD G
GALLERY DIRECTOR, COLLECTOR
b Chicago, Ill, June 19, 48. *Study:* Northeastern Ill State Univ, BFA, 70. *Exhib:* Am Craft Expo, Am Craft Enterprises, St Louis, Mo, 78; Lakefront Festival of Arts, Milwaukee Art Inst, Wis, 79; Monument Sq Art Festival & Wisconsin Designer-Craftsman, Wustum Mus Fine Arts, Racine, 80; Beloit Festival of Art, Wis, 81; Great Lakes Regional Art Expo, Cleveland, Ohio, 82; Marretta Crafts Nat, Ohio, 82; Fountain Sq Arts Festival, Evanston, Ill, 86. *Collection Arranged:* Clay Concepts: Clay as a Vessel, 84, Adornments: Sculptural Jewelry, Gather of Glass: Contemporary Studio Glass & Teapots, 85, Kemenyffy Raku: New Works, 86, Mindscape Galley, Evanston, Ill. *Pos:* Regional mem, Evanston Arts Coun, 74-, adv, grant rev comt, 85-; ed adv, Crafts Report, 79-92; adv, Nat Glass Art Dealers Asn, 83-, arts & bus comt, Evanston Chamber Com, Ill, 84-; co-dir, Mindscape Gallery, Evanston, Ill, currently. *Bibliog:* Sheila Flanagan (auth), A professional approach to fine crafts, 79 & Sharon Shinn (auth), Mindscape collection shows it's stuff to Chicago corporations, 85, Decor Mag; The Gallery as an Art Form, Craft Marketing Yearbk, 84. *Mem:* Nat Crafts Planning Conf (regional mem, 74-); Am Crafts Coun (regional mem, 74-); Ill Arts Coun (regional mem, 74-). *Specialty:* Mixed. *Collection:* Contemporary American crafts 1960-, glass, fiber & ceramics. *Publ:* Coauth, Craft shop design and display marketing techniques, Craft Market News, 78; Publicity: A gallery's point of view, Ceramics Monthly, 80; Reaching new markets tary public relations & stalking the collector, Crafts Report, 85; Glass: The Seductive Media, Am Ceramics Soc, 86

ISAAK, NICHOLAS, JR
PAINTER, CONSERVATOR
b Manchester, NH, July 5, 44. *Study:* Boston Univ, BFA, 67, MFA, 69; spec study with Walter Murch, Robert Gwathmey & Karl Fortess. *Work:* Va Mus Fine Arts, Richmond; Western Ill Univ, Macomb; Fitchburg Mus Art, Mass; Northern Ill Univ, DeKalb; Bradley Univ, Peoria, Ill; and others. *Exhib:* Pa Acad Fine Arts 164th Ann, 69; one-man shows, Robinson Gallery, Va Mus Fine Arts, 71 & Maxwell Davidson Gallery, NY, 81; Chrysler Mus Art, Norfolk, Va, 72; Print Invitational, Pratt Grahics Ctr, NY, 73; Mod Printmakers, Rochester Inst Technol, NY, 74; 2nd Graphics Biennial, Metrop Mus, Miami, Fla, 75; Fitchburg Mus Art, Mass, 76; Regional Selections, Dartmouth Col Mus, Hanover, NH, 79. *Pos:* Conservator, 79-. *Teaching:* Instr printmaking, Norfolk State Col, Va, 69-72; asst prof painting, Boston Univ, Mass, 72-77; assoc prof printmaking & chmn dept, Keene State Col, NH, 77-81. *Awards:* Nat Teaching fel, Dept Health, Educ & Welfare, 69; Cert of Distinction, Va Artists Biennial, Va Mus Art, 71; Rosenthal Found Award, Am Acad & Inst of Arts & Letters, 79. *Media:* Oil; Etching. *Dealer:* Maxwell Davidson Gallery 43 E 78th St New York NY 10021

ISABEL, MCILVAIN
SCULPTOR, EDUCATOR
Study: Smith Col, BA; Pratt Inst, MFA. *Comn:* JFK Commission, 89. *Exhib:* Robert Schoelkopf Gallery, New York City, 82-87, Moore Gallery, Philadelphia, 93, Arnot Art Mus, Elmira NY; Numerous group exhibs in NY, Pa and Va. *Teaching:* Ast prof, & artist-in-residence Wash & Lee Univ, 1975-82; Vis assoc prof, Sweet Briar Col, 1977; assoc prof, Sch Visual Arts, Boston Univ, 1982-. *Awards:* Grantee Sculpture Fel award, Artists Found, Boston, 84. *Mem:* Nat Acad of Design (acad). *Mailing Add:* Sch of Visual Arts Rm 552 855 Commonwealth Ave Boston MA 02215

ISCHAR, DOUG
PHOTOGRAPHER
b Honolulu, Hawaii, Nov 20, 48. *Work:* Houston Mus Fine Arts. *Exhib:* Dark O'Clock, Sao Paulo Mus Mod Art, Brazil, 94; Photogrs Gallery, London, 94; Blum Helman Gallery, NY, 94; Mercer Union, Toronto, Ont, 95; solo exhib, Site Santa Fe, NMex, 96; Insight, San Diego, Calif, 97; Wooster Gardens, NY, 98. *Teaching:* Assoc prof, Univ Ill, Chicago, 89-. *Awards:* Nat Endowment Arts, 92; Ill Arts Coun, 98. *Mailing Add:* 5801 N Sheridan Rd Chicago IL 60660

ISERMANN, JIM
SCULPTOR
b Kenosha, Wis, Aug 25, 55. *Study:* Univ Wis, Milwaukee, BFA, 77; Calif Inst Art, MFA, 80. *Work:* Mus Contemp Art Los Angeles. *Comn:* Calendar, Fuji Oil, Osaka, Japan, 90, 91 & 92. *Exhib:* Solo exhib, Shag Paintings, Feature, NY, 89, 91, 92, 94 & 96 & Richard Kuhlenschmidt Gallery, Los Angeles, 89, Sue Spaid Fine Art, Los Angeles, Calif, 94, Richard Telles Fine Art, Los Angeles, 94, 96 & 98, Ynglingagatan 2, Stockholm, Swed, 95, Studio Guenzani, Milan, Italy, 97, Robert Prime, London, Eng, 97 & Fifteen: Jim Isermann Survey, Inst Vis Arts, Univ Wisc traveling exhib, Univ N Tex Art Gallery, Denton, Santa Monica Mus Art, Calif, Univ NC, Greensboro & Inst Contemp Art, Philadelphia, 98; Avant-garde in the '80's, Los Angeles Co Mus Art, 87; Material Conceits, Mint Mus, Charlotte, NC, 90; LAX 94 (catalog), Los Angeles Munic Art Gallery, 94; Surface de Reparation, FRAC Bourgogue, Dijon, France, 94; Guys Who Sew, Art Mus, Univ Calif, Santa Barbara, 94; Division of Labor: Woman's Work in Contemp Art (catalog), Bronx Mus Arts, NY, 95; Roommates, Mus Van Loon, Amsterdam, The Neth, 98; Los Angeles Times, Palazzo Re Rebaudengo per l'Arte Contemporanea, Italy, 98; Pop Abstraction, Penn Acad Fine Art, Philadelphia, 98; lovecraft, S London Gallery, UK, 98; and others. *Awards:* Fel, Nat Endowment Arts, 84 & 87; Fel, Art Matters, Inc, NY, 86. *Bibliog:* Holland Cotter (auth), Art in review, NY Times, 1/14/94; Hunter Drohojowska-Philp (auth), He will keep you in stitches, Los Angeles Times, 3/20/94; Michael Duncan (auth), rev, Art in Am, 10/94; and others. *Publ:* Coauth, The Best of Both Worlds, Art & Text, No 57, 5-7/97. *Mailing Add:* c/o Telles Fine Art 7380 Beverly Blvd Los Angeles CA 90036

ISHAQ, ASHFAQ
ADMINISTRATOR
Study: Govt Col, Lahore, Pakistan, BA; Univ, MPA, Punjab; Econ, George Washington Univ, PhD. *Awards:* Grantee Hesselbein Community Fel, Peter Drucker Found, 2001. *Bibliog:* (auth) Success in Small & Medium Scale Enterprises, 87; founder, editor ChildArt magazine, 98—. *Mem:* Int Acad Digital Arts and Scis (adv bd mem), World Psychiatry Asn. *Mailing Add:* Internat Child Art Found Ste 1225 1350 Connecticut Ave Northwest Washington DC 20036

ITALIANO, JOAN
SCULPTOR, LITURGICAL ARTIST
b Worcester, Mass. *Study:* Siena Heights Univ, PhB, Studio Angelico, MFA; Barry Univ Miami, Fla; Nino Caruso, Rome, Italy, Beani & Cacia Foundry; Pietrasanta, Italy. *Comn:* Tree of Life Fountain, Mary Manning Walsh Carmelite Home, NY, 71; Shrine to the American Saints (ceramic on wood), Our Lady of Good Counsel Church, W Boylston, Mass, 86; memorial panel (ceramic on wood), Mercy Ctr, Worcester, Mass, 90; Little Flower, Shrine to St Theresa (stoneware & granite), Boylston, Mass, 96; Processional Cross (enamel on copper & wood), Wellsley Col, Mass, 98. *Exhib:* Norton Gallery, West Palm Beach, Fla; Cantor Gallery, Holy Cross Col, Worcester, Mass; Pindar Gallery, NY; Women Exhibiting in Boston, Prudential Ctr; Wolfe Gallery, W Palm Beach, 96; and others. *Collection Arranged:* Mount Holyoke Col Mus; Norstar Security Trust, Rochester, NY; Bingham, Dana & Gould, Boston; Int Ctr for Ceramics, Rome, Italy; Brown, Rudnick, Freed & Gesmer, Boston. *Pos:* Dir, Art Gallery, Barry Col, 56-58; consult liturgical art, Dick Bros Archit Interiors, 62-72; dir, Studio Beato Angelico N, West Boylston, Mass, 59- & Studio Beato Angelico S, West Palm Beach, Fla, 91-; consult, Reader's Digest Art Trade Books, 93-96. *Teaching:* Instr sculpture, Barry Col, Miami, Fla, 56-58; assoc prof sculpture & ceramics, Col of the Holy Cross, 69-89, chmn fine arts dept, 77-80. *Awards:* First Prize in Sculpture, Palm Beach Art League 37th & 38th Ann; Bachelor Ford Fel, 76; Prize, Northeast Sculptors Assoc, Boston, 83 & 86; Fac Fel, Col Holly Cross, 88. *Bibliog:* Vivian Raynor (auth), review, Pindar Show, New York Times, 7/6/84; James Reil (auth), article, Worcester Mag, 5/20/81; George French (auth), Sculptor Joan Italiano's New Direction Is Right On Course, Evening Gazette, Worcester, Mass, 10/22/82; and many others. *Mem:* New Eng Sculptors, Asn; Int Sculpture Ctr; Lay Dominican. *Media:* All Media. *Res:* fired clay sculpture. *Dealer:* Art South 4401 Cresson St Philadelphia PA; Pindar Gallery 127 Greene St New York NY. *Mailing Add:* PO Box 175 West Boylston MA 01583

ITATANI, MICHIKO
PAINTER
b Osaka, Japan, May 8, 48. *Study:* Art Inst Chicago, MFA, 76. *Work:* Art Inst Chicago, Mus Contemp Art, Chicago. *Comn:* Jane Addams Found. *Exhib:* Shinjuku Park Tower, Tokyo; Solo exhibs, Alternative Mus, NY, 85, Rockford Mus, Ill, 87; Univ Wis, Milwaukee Art Mus, 92; Wright Mus, Beloit Col, Wis, 94; Nexas Contemp Art Ctr, Atlanta, 95; and others. *Teaching:* Prof painting & drawing, Art Inst Chicago, 79-. *Awards:* Fel, Nat Endowment Art, 80-81; Ill Arts Coun Artist's Grant, 84 & 85; John Simon Guggenheim Fel, 90-91. *Bibliog:* Betty Ann Brown & Arlene Raven (coauths), Exposures: Women & Their Art, Newspace Press; Lucy R Lippard (auth), Mixed Blessings, Pantheon Press; James Yood (auth), Michiko Itatani, Artforum, 3/94; and others. *Media:* Oil, Mixed Media Drawing. *Publ:* NAME Artbook II. *Dealer:* Fassbenter Gallery 309 W Superior Chicago IL 60610; Printworks Inc 311 W Superior Chicago IL 60610

ITCHKAWICH, DAVID MICHAEL
PRINTMAKER, ILLUSTRATOR
b Westerly, RI, Aug 18, 37. *Study:* RI Sch Design, BFA. *Work:* John Sloane Study Collection, Univ Del; Charles Dana Mus, Colgate Univ; NY Pub Libr; Munson-Williams-Proctor Inst, Utica, NY; Metrop Mus Art, NY. *Exhib:* Nat Print Exhib, Brooklyn Mus, NY, 70 & 72; Davidson Nat Print Show, Davidson Univ, 73-75; one-man shows, Munson-Proctor-Williams Inst, Utica, NY, 76, Newport Art Asn, RI, 78; Martin Sumers Graphics, 76; Nat Exhib, NY Soc Illusr, 78; and others. *Bibliog:* The visions of David Itchkawich, Intellectual Dig, 2/72; John Mattingly (auth), When Men Were Animals and Animals Were Men: A Study of the Graphic Work of David Itchkawich, Angelica Press, NY, 76; Suzanne Boorsch (auth), The pleasure of creation: The work of David Itchkawich, Print Collector's Newslett, 9-10/78. *Dealer:* Horizon Gallery 45 Christopher St New York NY 10014. *Mailing Add:* c/o FDR Gallery 670 Broadway New York NY 10012

ITURBIDE, GRACIELA
PHOTOGRAPHER
b Mexico City, Mex, May 16, 42. *Study:* Ctr Univ de Estudios Cinematograficos, Univ Nac Autonomade Mex, 69-72; studied with Manuel Alvarez, Bravo, 70. *Exhib:* Tres fotografas mexicanas, Galeria Jose Clemente Orosco, Mexico City, 75 & Midtown Y Gallery, NY, 76; one-woman shows, Casa de Cultura, Juchitan, Oaxaca, 80, Mus Modern Art, 82, Casa de la Cultura de Juchitán, Mex, 85, Cantonal Mus Fine Arts, Lausanne, 87, Side Gallery, Newcastle, Eng, 89, Mus Photog, Hokkaido, Japan, 90, Mus Photogr Arts, San Diego, Calif, 90, Mus Modern Art, San Francisco, Calif, 90, Mus Photog, Seattle, Wash, 91, Galería Visor, Valencia, 92, Mus Arte Moderno, Rio de Janeiro, Brazil, 93, Mus de la Photgraphie, 93, Univ Salamance, 94, Adair Margo Gallery, El Paso, Tex, 95, Gallery Contemp Photog, Los Angeles, Calif, 95 & Mus Fine Arts, Sante Fe, NMex, 2001; Ctr Georges Pompidou, Paris, France, 82; Retrospective, Mus Arte Contemporáneo Monterrey, Mex, 96 & Philadelphia Mus Art, Pa, 97-98. *Awards:* Production Grant, Centre Georges Pompidou, 83; Prize, UN, 86; W Eugene Smith Award, W Eugene Smith Meml Found, 87-88; Guggenheim Fel, 88; Grand Prize, Mois de la Photo, 88; Hugo Erfurth Award, 89; Int Grand Prize, 90; Award, Rencontres Photographiques, 91. *Mailing Add:* Apdo Postal 21-479 Ortega # 20 Coyaocan 91105 04000 Mexico

ITURRALDE, TERESA
ART DEALER, COLLECTOR
b Mexico City, Mex, Oct 7, 63. *Study:* Univ San Diego, BA, 85. *Pos:* Art dir, Iturralde Gallery, 87-; art consult, Calvin J Goodman, 88-, Levis Strauss & Co, San Francisco, Calif, 93-94. *Teaching:* Teaching asst photog, Univ San Diego, 85 & 86. *Bibliog:* Jeanne Beach (auth), Gallery to feature Latin American art, La Jolla Light, 3/26/87; Daniel Munoz (auth), New Mexico art gallery, La Prensa, San Diego, 4/3/87; Latin Am Art Mag, First Word p 6, & the Latin Am Market p 31, Inaugural Issue, 89; San Diego County, City Mag Local Gallery Owners, Vol 2, p 72, 90; Nancy Kapitanoff (auth), A shared obsession: two sisters passion for Latin American art, Los Angeles Times, 5/10/92. *Mem:* Los Angeles Art Galleries. *Specialty:* Contemporary Mexican and Latin American art. *Collection:* Contemporary art with emphasis on Mexican and Latin American art

IVERS, LOUISE H
HISTORIAN, ADMINISTRATOR
b May 30, 43. *Study:* Boston Univ, BFA, 64; Univ NMex, MA, 67, PhD, 75. *Teaching:* Prof art, Calif State Univ, Dominguez Hills, 71-. *Awards:* Sunbird Grant, Getty Ctr Educ Arts, 89; Women's Archit League Award, 94; Calif Coun for Humanities Grant, 2000; Evalyn M Bauer Found grant, 2002 & 2004. *Mem:* Soc Achit Historians. *Res:* 1920s and 1930s Architecture in California. *Publ:* Auth, Montezuma Hotel at Las Vegas Hot Springs New Mexico, J Soc Archit Historians, 74; Cecil Schilling, Jazz Age Architect, Carson: Calif State Univ, Dominguez Hills, 94; Cecil Schilling, Long Beach Architect, Southern Calif Quart, summer 97; Evolution of modernistic architecture in Long Beach, Southern Calif Quarterly, 86; Hugh Davies, Architect & Innovator, CSU Dominguez Hills, 2002; An Architectural Stylist, W. Horace Austin & Eclecticism in California, Calif St Univ, Dominguez Hills, 2005. *Mailing Add:* Calif State Univ Dominguez Hills 1000 E Victoria St Carson CA 90747

IVERSEN, EARL HARVEY
PHOTOGRAPHER, EDUCATOR
b Chicago, Ill, Jan 26, 43. *Study:* Univ Ill, Chicago Circle, BA, 70; RI Sch Design, MFA, 73. *Work:* Mus Mod Art, NY; Univ Colo Art Mus, Boulder; Sheldon Gallery, Univ Nebr, Lincoln; Spencer Art Mus, Univ Kans, Lawrence; Sioux City Art Ctr, Iowa. *Exhib:* The Great West, Denver Art Mus, 77; solo exhib, Mass Col Art, 78, Metropolitan Col, Denver, 78, Kresge Gallery, Mich State Univ, Ann Arbor, 80 & Sioux City Art Ctr, 82; An Open Land, Chicago Art Inst, 83; two-person exhib, Spencer Art Mus, Lawrence, Kans, 83. *Teaching:* Instr photog, Mass Col Art, 73-74; assoc prof design & photog, Univ Kans, Lawrence, 74-, photogr, Univ Theater, 81-. *Awards:* Excellence Award Photog, Univ & Col Designers Asn, 76; grant, 76 & fel, 83, Nat Endowment Arts. *Publ:* Illusr, Photo Art Mag, #12 & #14, 81; illusr, Erotic Photography, Demarais Press, 81; illusr, Kansas in Color, Regents Press Kans, 82. *Mailing Add:* Univ Kans Dept Design Lawrence KS 66045

IVES, COLTA FELLER
CURATOR, EDUCATOR
b San Diego, Calif, Apr 5, 43. *Study:* Mills Col, BA, 64; Columbia Univ, MA, 66. *Collection Arranged:* The Great Wave (auth, catalog), Metrop Mus Art, New York, 75; Felix Nadar Photog, Metrop Mus Art, New York, 77; The Painterly Print (coauth, catalog), Metrop Mus Art, New York, 80; Albrecht Durer & Holy Family, Metrop Mus Art, New York, 82; Eugene Delacroix: Drawings & Prints, Metrop Mus Art, New York, 84; Pierre Bonnard: The Graphic Art (coauth, catalog), Metrop Mus Art, New York, 89; Daumier Drawings (coauth, catalog), Metrop Mus Art, New York, 93; Goya in the Metrop Mus Art, New York, 95; Toulouse-Lautrec in the Metrop Mus Art (auth, catalog), New York, 96. *Pos:* Mem staff, Metrop Mus Art, New York, 66-, cur-in-charge, dept prints & illus bks, 75-93, cur, Dept Drawings & Prints, 93-. *Teaching:* Adj prof art hist, Columbia Univ, 70-87. *Awards:* First Place Award Exhib Catalog, Art Libr Asn New York, 75. *Mem:* Assoc Hist Nineteenth Cent Art, Print Coun Am (exec bd, 76-78, 84-86, vpres, 89-91). *Res:* Nineteenth century French drawings, prints and illustrated books. *Publ:* French Prints in the Era of Impressionism & Symbolism, Metrop Mus Art, New York, 89; coauth, Pierre Bonnard: The Graphic Art, Metrop Mus Arts, NY, 89; Daumier Drawings, Metrop Mus Arts, NY, 92; Toulouse-Lautrec, Metrop Mus Arts, NY, 96. *Mailing Add:* Dept of Prints & Photographs Metrop Mus Art New York NY 10028

IVEY, WILLIAM J
ADMINISTRATOR
b Detroit, Mich, Sept 6, 44. *Pos:* Dir, Country Music Found, 71-; chmn, Nat Endowment Arts, 98-. *Awards:* Billboard Country Liner Notes of Year Award, 74; Grammy Award Nominations, 75 & 83; Sr Res Fel, Inst Studies Am Music, 79-80. *Mem:* Pres, Comn Arts & Humanities; Acad TV Arts & Sci; Nat Acad TV Arts & Sci (bd govs Nashville Chap, 84-88); Writer's Guild Am; Nat Acad Rec Arts & Sci (trustee, 76-80, 88-89 & 91-95, vpres, 80-81 & 93-94, nat pres, 81-83, nat chmn, 89-91); plus many others

IWAMASA, KEN
EDUCATOR, PRINTMAKER
b Manzanar, Calif, Apr 28, 43. *Study:* Calif State Univ, Long Beach, BA, 66, MA, 72. *Work:* El Camino Col; City of Los Angeles; Rio Hondo Col. *Exhib:* One-man shows, Rio Hondo Col, 76 & Old Dominion Univ, 77; World Print Competition, San Francisco Mus Mod Art, Calif, 77; Detroit Nat Print Symposium, Cranbrook Acad Art, 80; Fantastic Art, Castle San Giorgo, Italy, 81; Works on Paper, Cheney-Cowles Mem Mus, Spokane, 81; Artist as Social Critic, Mich State Univ, Ann Arbor, 81; and others. *Teaching:* Asst prof drawing & printmaking, Univ Colo, Boulder, 72-. *Awards:* Grants & Purchase Awards from Scott Found, Japan Found & Univ Colo. *Media:* Screen, Lithography. *Dealer:* Miriam Perlman Gallery 505 N Lake Shore Dr Chicago IL 60611; Sebastian Moore Gallery 1411 Market St Denver CO. *Mailing Add:* 64 Huron Court Boulder CO 80303-4414

IWAMOTO, RALPH SHIGETO
PAINTER
b Honolulu, Hawaii, Sept 13, 27. *Study:* Art Students League, with John Von Wicht, Vaclav Vytlacil & Byron Browne, 48-49 & 51-53. *Work:* Butler Inst Am Art, Youngstown, Ohio; Herbert F Johnson Art Mus, Cornell Univ; State Found on Cult & Arts, Honolulu; Wadsworth Atheneum, Hartford, Conn; Zimmerli Mus Art Rutgers Univ, New Brunswick, NJ. *Exhib:* solo shows, Columbia Mus Art, SC, 59, Elmira Col, NY, 68 & St Mary's Col, Md, 89, Gallery Onetwentyeight, NY, 2001, David Findlay Jr, Gallery, NY, 2004; Bergen Co Mus, NJ, 83; Contemp Mus, Honolulu, 90; New Britain Mus, Conn, 2003; Wellesley Col, Davis Mus, Mass 2004; Real Art Ways Ctr, Hartford, Conn, 2004; First Hawaiian Ctr, Contemp Mus, Hawaii, 2005; Nat Acad Mus, NY, 2005. *Awards:* Purchase Prize, Butler Inst Am Art, 57; Fel, John Hay Whitney Found, 58; Grant, Adolph & Esther Gottlieb Found, 87; Pollock-Krasner Found Grant, 2002. *Bibliog:* K Ichida (auth), article, Ichimai Art Mag, Tokyo, 12/80; Helen A Harrison (auth), article, NY Times, 12/29/85; Fred Camper (auth), Review, Chicago Reader, 10/17/97; Jeffrey Wechsler (auth), Preface to catalog, Findlay Gallery Show, 04; Elisa Decker (auth), Review, Art in Am, 1/05. *Mem:* New York Artists Equity. *Media:* Acrylic, Oil. *Publ:* Auth, Octagon Concepts. *Mailing Add:* 463 West St A-1110 New York NY 10014

IZUKA, KUNIO
SCULPTOR, PAINTER
b Tokyo, Japan, Mar 2, 39. *Study:* Otis Art Inst, Los Angeles Co; Art Students League. *Work:* Mus Mod Art Tokyo, Japan. *Comn:* Monumental sculpture, Warner Commun, Los Angeles, 72. *Exhib:* First Int Exhib Mod Sculpture, Hakone Open-Air Mus, Japan, 69; Exhib Contemp Japanese Art, Mus Mod Art, Rio de Janeiro, 71 & Milan, Italy, 72. *Teaching:* Asst instr sculpture, Art Students League, 68-69. *Awards:* Purchase Prize, 50th Anniversary Show, Otis Art Inst Los Angeles Co, 68; Second Prize, Exhib Contemp Japanese Art, New York, 72. *Mem:* Sculptors Guild; Japanese Artist Asn New York. *Media:* Metal; Oil

J

JAAR, ALFREDO
SCULPTOR
b Santiago, Chile, Feb 5, 56. *Study:* Instituto Chileno Norteamericano de Cultura, Chile, 79, Universidad de Chile, Santiago, Chile, 81. *Work:* Found L'Arche de la Fraternite, La Defense, Paris; High Mus Art, Atlanta, GA; La Jolla Mus Contemp Art, CA; Lannan Found, Los Angeles, CA. *Exhib:* Mus Nat d'Art Mod, Paris, 89; Brooklyn Mus, NY, 89; San Francisco Mus Modern Art, Calif, 90; The Sch Art Institute Chicago, IL, 90; solo exhibs, NY, 87, Institute Contemp Art, 88, Galerie Gabrielle, Maubrie, Paris, France, 88, Brooklyn Mus, NY, 89, Galerie Barbara Farber, Amsterdam, The Neth, 89, New Mus Contemp Art, NY, 90, Carnegie Mellon Art Gallery, Pittsburgh, PA, 90; Mus Contemp Photog, Chicago, 95; Islands, Nat Gallery Australia, 96; Thinking Print, Mus Mod Art, NY, 96; Mach/Onmacht, MUAKA, Antwerp, 96; Happy End, Kunsthalle Dusseldorf, 96; and others. *Awards:* John Simon Guggenheim Foun Grant, 85; NY State Coun Arts Grant, 85. *Bibliog:* Tzvetan Todorov (auth), Documenta 8; Vicenc Altaió, Plus Ultra; David Levi Strauss, Camera work. *Mailing Add:* 252 Lafayette St Apt 3 E New York NY 10012

JABBOUR, MONA AMAL
EDUCATOR, PAINTER
b Lebanon, Oct 22, 60. *Study:* Chelsea Sch Art, 79; Beirut Univ Col, Lebanon, BS, 86; Pratt Inst, MFA, 90. *Exhib:* One-woman show, Pratt Inst, NY, 90 & Agial Gallery, Beirut, Lebanon, 92; Salon d'Aviomne, Sursock Mus, Beirut, 93; Ann Alumni Artists Exhib, Lebanese Am Univ, Beirut, 97 & Graphic Art in Lebanon, 98. *Teaching:* Instr fine arts, Lebanese Am Univ, 92-97 & asst prof, 97-. *Awards:* Sheikh Fayed Student Award, Beirut Univ Col, 86. *Mem:* Nat Asn Schs Art & Design. *Media:* Mixed Media

JACHNA, JOSEPH DAVID
PHOTOGRAPHER, EDUCATOR
b Chicago, Ill, Sept 12, 35. *Study:* Univ Mo Photo-Jour Workshop, 57; Ill Inst Technol Inst Design, with Aaron Siskind, Harry Callahan & Frederick Sommer, BS(art educ), 58, MS(photog), 61. *Work:* George Eastman House, Int Mus Photog, Rochester, NY; Art Inst Chicago; Photog Collection, Exchange Nat Bank of Chicago; Mass Inst Technol; Mus Mod Art, NY. *Exhib:* Solo exhibs, Art Inst Chicago, 61, Nikon Salon, Tokyo, 74, Visual Studies Workshop Gallery, Rochester, NY, 79, Chicago Ctr Contemp Photog, 80, Focus Gallery, San Francisco, 81 & Tweed Mus, Duluth, Minn, 86; Photog: Midwest Invitational, Walker Art Ctr, Minneapolis, 73; Photographers and the City, Mus Contemp Art, Chicago, 77; Second Sight, Carpenter Ctr Visual Arts, Harvard Univ, 81; Josephson, Jachna & Siegel: Chicago Experimentalists, San Francisco Mus Mod Art, 88; Vanishing Presence, Walker Art Ctr, Minneapolis, 89. *Collection Arranged:* Co-cur with Gary Minnix: Richard Nickel, Photographs, fall 1972, Harold Allen, Photographs, spring 1975, Ward Gallery, Univ Ill, Chicago; Robert Stiegler, Photographs, Gallery 400, Univ Ill, Chicago, fall 1986. *Teaching:* From instr to asst prof photog, Inst Design, Ill Inst Technol, 61-69; from asst prof to prof photog, Univ Ill, Chicago Campus, 69-; workshops, Peninsula Sch Art, Door Co, Wis, summers 69-71. *Awards:* Fac Grant Color Photog, Univ Ill, Chicago Circle Campus, 72; Ferguson Grant, Friends of Photog, Carmel, Calif, 73; Nat Endowment Arts, 76; John Simon Guggenheim Mem Found Fel, 80. *Bibliog:* Landscape illusions, In: Photography Year 1974, Time-Life Bks, 74; John B Turner (auth), Joseph D Jachna, Photo-Forum, Auckland, NZ, 75; Light Touching Silver (monogr), Chicago Mus Photog, 80. *Publ:* Art in America, New Talent Issue, 62; Camera Mainichi '74-9, 74; Photog & Art-Interactions since 1946, 87; Landscape As Photograph, Yale Univ Press, 85; Vanishing Presence, Walker Art Ctr & Rizzoli, 89. *Dealer:* Stephen Daiter Gallery 311 W Superior Chicago IL. *Mailing Add:* 5707 W 89th Pl Oak Lawn IL 60453

JACIR, EMILY
PHOTOGRAPHER
b Palestine, 70. *Study:* Univ Dallas, BA(art), 92; Memphis Col Art, MFA, 94; Whitney Ind Study Program, NY City, 98-99. *Work:* Mus Modern Art, Arnhem, The Neth, 2003, Herbert F Johnson Mus, Cornell Univ, NY, 2001, Queens Inter, Queens Mus Art, 2002, Made in Palestine, Art Car Mus, Houston, 2003, Whitney Biennial, Whitney Mus Am Art, 2004, Cheekwood Mus Art, Nashville, 2004. *Exhib:* One-woman shows, Anderson Ranch Arts Ctr, Snowmass Village, Colo, 97, Eastfield Col Gallery, Mesquite, Tex, 97, Everywhere/Nowhere, SPACES, Cleveland, 99, From Paris to Riyadh (Drawings For My Mother), Univ Gallery, US, Sewanee, Tenn, 2000, New Photog: Bethlehem to Ramallah, Debs & Co Project Room, NY, 2002, Where We Come From, 2003, Belongings, O K Ctr Contemp Art, Linz, Austria, 2003, The Neth, 2003, Los Angeles Inter Art Biennial, Frumkin Duval Gallery, Santa Monica, Calif, 2003, Artspace Annex II, New Haven, Conn, 2003, Woher wir kommen, Künstlerhaus, Bremen, 2004, Den I: a på Moderna: Emily Jacir: Where We Come From, Moderna Museet, Stockholm, 2004, The Khalil Sakakini Cult Ctr, Ramallah, 2004, Nuova Icona, Venice, 2004, Kunstraum Innsbruck, Innsbruck, 2004, Accumulations, Alexander & Bonin, NY, 2005; group shows, 7th Ann McNeese Nat Works on Paper, McNeese State, Lake Charles, La, 94, Women in Art: 12 Texas Women, Contemp Art Ctr, Houston, 97, Xmas, Kent Gallery, NY, 99, Free for All, Temporary Art Services, Chicago, 2000, Carnival in the Eye of the Storm; War/Art/New Technol, Pacific Northwest Col Art, Portland, Ore, 2000, Greater NY, PS I Contemp Art Ctr, Long Island City, 2000, Strangers/Estrangers, PS I Clocktower Gallery, NY, 2001, 2001, Made in Transit, Vacancy Gallery, NY, 2001, Unjustified, Apex Art, NY, 2002, Submerged, Nuremberg, 2002, Right2Fight, Sarah Lawrence Col, Bronxville, NY, 2002, Settlement, Gallery 400, Chicago, 2002, Global Priority, Hester Art Gallery, Univ Mass, 2003, Shatat, Colo Univ Art Galleries, Boulder, 2003, VEIL, Inst Int Arts, London, 2003, 8th Istanbul Biennial, 2003, 100 Cuts, Gallery 312, Chicago, 2004, Empire: Videos for a New World, Md Inst Col Art, Baltimore, 2004; Cover Girl: The Female Body & Islam in Contemp Art, Ise Cult Found, NY, 2004, Neither Here Nor There: Video Artists Navigate Cult Displacement, Election, Am Fine Arts, NY, 2004, Sometime: Six Works for Film & Video, Anthony Reynolds Gallery, London, 2004, Desenhos: A-Z, Porta 33, Funchal, Ilha da Madeira, 2005. *Mailing Add:* c/o Debs & Co 525 W 26th St New York NY 10001

JACKLIN, BILL (WILLIAM)
PAINTER, PRINTMAKER
b Hampstead, London, Eng, Jan 1, 43. *Study:* Walthamstow Sch Art, Essex, BA(painting), 64; Royal Col Art, London, MA(painting), 67. *Work:* Victoria & Albert Mus & Brit Mus, London; Metrop Mus, NY; Mus Mod Art, NY; Yale Ctr British Art, New Haven, Conn; Tampa Mus Mod Art. *Comn:* Mural, Cesar Pelli & Assoc, Washington Nat Airport, DC; painting futures market, Bank of England, London, 88; tapestry, DeBeers, London, 94. *Exhib:* Mus Mod Art, NY, 72; British Painting Today, Mus Mod Art, Paris, 73; British Painting 1952-77, Royal Acad Art, London, 77; Directors Choice, Tampa Mus Art, Fla, 87; Metrop Mus, NY, 90; Britain & Sao Paulo Biennale 1951-91, Brit Coun, London, 92; Urban Portraits NY 1986-92 (with catalog), Mus Mod Art, Oxford, Eng, 92-93; Urban Portraits Hong Kong, Brit Coun Hong Kong, 93-95; New Acquisitions, 20th Century Wing, Metrop Mus Art, NY, 96-97; L'ecole Londres, de bacon a Bevan, Found Vierny, musee Maillol, Paris, 98. *Pos:* Artist-in-residence, Hong Kong. *Teaching:* Instr painting, Numerous Art Cols Gt Brit, 67-75. *Awards:* Bursary Award, Arts Coun London, 75. *Bibliog:* John Russell Taylor (auth), Bill Jacklin Recent Work, Marlborough Gallery, 87 & Bill Jacklin (monograph), Phaidon Press; Robert Rosenblum (auth), Urban Portraits, Marlborough Fine Art Catalogue, 88; Tina Eden Productions (dir), Bill Jacklin in New York (film), 92; Phoebe Hoban (auth) The Connected Image, Marlborough Catalogue, New York, 99; Jill Llyod (auth) Sihouettes & Shadows New York City, Marlborough Catalogue, London, 2000. *Mem:* Assoc mem Royal Acad; Royal Acad London. *Media:* Oil; All Media. *Dealer:* Marlborough Gallery Inc 40 W 57th St New York NY 10019

JACKOBOICE, SANDRA KAY
ARTIST
b Detroit, Mich, Jul 22, 36. *Study:* Mich State Univ, East Lansing, 1956; Aquinas Col, Grand Rapids, Mich, BA, 1989; post graduate study with prominent Am artists. *Work:* City Hall, Bielsko Beals, Poland; Downtown Mgt bd, Grand Rapids, Mich; Corp Off, Monarch Hydraulics, Grand Rapid, Mich. *Comn:* West Mich Iris Soc, New Hybird Iris, Grand Rapids, Mich; St. Roberts Church, Ada, Mich; plus mant pvt comn. *Exhib:* Great Lakes Pastel Soc, Juried Exhib, Midland, Mich, 1999, 2003; Girl Scouts of Am Invitational Exhib, Grand Rapids, Mich, 2002; Int Assoc of Pastel Soc, Demonstrator's Exhib, Albuquerque, NMex, 2003; Artist in Residence, Franciscan Life Process Ctr, Lowell, Mich, 2003; Pastel Soc of Am, Invitational Exhib, Dunedin, Fla, 2004; plus many other solo & group exhibs. *Pos:* Co-found, pres, Great Lakes Pastel Soc, 1997-2001, bd adv & satellite coord, 2001-; exhib coordnr, Peninsular Club, Grand Rapids, Mich, 1997-2001; found, adv to bd of dir, Southwest Fla Pastel Soc, 2001-02; found, Pastel Group of Southwest Fla, 2001; vpres & mem ch, Int Asn Pastel Soc, 2005-. *Teaching:* Coordnr, instr, pastel classes, Grand Rapids Art Mus, 2000-01; pastel instr, Von Liebig Art Ctr, Naples, Fla, 2001-; workshop instr, Marco Island Art Ctr, Marco Island, Fla, 2002-; pastel Instr, Aquinas Col Emer Prog, Grand Rapids, Mich, 2004. *Awards:* West Mich Iris Soc, 1994; Botanical Images award, 1995, 96; Great Lakes Pastel Soc, 2003. *Mem:* United Arts Coun, Collier Co, Fla (bd mem); Pastel Soc Am (signature mem); Artist Alliance; Great Lakes Pastel Soc; Southwest Fla Pastel Soc (life mem). *Media:* Pastel, Acrylic. *Interests:* painting, photography, golf, travel. *Publ:* Artists Photo Reference Flowers, North Light Books, 2002; Pastel Artists Int Mag, 3rd edition; Getting to Know Pastel, brochure IAPS Convention, 2003; Original Pastel Under Sail, The Artist Mag, 2003; Pastel on Canvas, Pastel Jour, 2004; The Ultimate Guide to Painting from Photographs, North Light Books, 2005. *Mailing Add:* 8111 Bay Colony Dr Unit 704 Naples FL 34108

JACKSON, CHARLOTTE
PAINTER, INSTRUCTOR
b New York, NY, Nov 21, 1926. *Study:* Traphagen Art Inst, 1943-45. *Work:* White House, Washington, DC; NYC Courthouse, Mayor's Mansion, NY; Royall Cornwall Gallery & Mus, Minneapolis, Minn; Joe Franklin TV Show (exhib), NY; and many mus & corp collections throughout the world. *Comn:* Hester St, comn by Phil Coffaro (of Art Expo) NY, 1975; Cesars Palace, comn by decorator, Las Vegas, Nev, 1979; Cover of Plate Collector Magazine (self portrait), Kermit, TX, 1980; Lynn's Rose, Dover Financial Corp & NBSR, NY, 1981; Sands Hotel, comn by decorator, Las Vegas, Nev, 1982. *Exhib:* Brooklyn Mus, Brooklyn, NY, 1975; Whitney Mus, NYC, 1977. *Collection Arranged:* Pictures on Exhibition, 1978, 1979, 1981; Somerset Mus, 1990-91. *Pos:* Art dir, Southwest Art, NYC, 1994-96. *Teaching:* instr oil painting, Pearl Paint, Fla, 2004-. *Media:* Oil. *Publ:* Henry Youngman (auth), Art That I Like, Dalton Publishing, 1984; Ray Johnson (auth), Realism Art, Dalton Publishing, 1985; Ray Johnson (auth), The Art of Flowers, Ray Johnson, 1985. *Mailing Add:* 7537 Fairfax Dr #H Tamarac FL 33321

JACKSON, HARRY ANDREW
PAINTER, SCULPTOR
b Chicago, Ill, Apr 18, 24. *Study:* Art Inst Chicago, 31-38; with Ed Grigware, Cody, Wyo, 38-42; Brooklyn Mus Art Sch, with Hans Hofmann, 46-48; Univ Wyo, Hon Dr, 86. *Work:* Whitney Mus Western Art, Cody; Vatican Mus, Rome; Minn Inst Arts; Woolarac Mus, Bartlesville, Okla; Am Mus Gt Brit, Bath, Eng; Met Mus of Art, NY. *Comn:* Stampede, 60 & Range Burial, 66 (oil murals), Whitney Gallery Western Art; Sor Capanna (monument), Piazza dei Mercanti, Rome, 62; painted sculpture of John Wayne (for cover), Time Mag, 8/8/69; Sacagawea, Buffalo Bill Historical Ctr, Cody, Wyo; Official Monument to John Wayne (heroic bronze), Beverly Hills, Calif, 84; Sacagewa (patinaed), Santa Barbara, Calif, 85. *Exhib:* Nat Acad Design, NY, 64, 65, 67, 68 & 70; Gilcrease Mus, Tulsa, Okla, 80; retrospective, Buffalo Bill Hist Ctr, Cody, Wyo, 81 & Univ Wyo Art Mus, 87; Palm Springs Desert Mus, Calif, 81; J Poole Gallery, London, 82; Trailside Gallery, Scottsdale, Ariz, 83; one-man show, Brooklyn Mus, NY, 48, retrospective NY Metro Mus of Art, 87. *Pos:* Off combat artist, USMC, 44-45; founder fine art foundry, Camaiore, Italy, 64-, Harry Jackson Studios, Italy, 65-; Chief Exec Officer, Harry Jackson Studios (formerly Wyo Foundry Studios, Inc), Cody, Wyo, 71-; founder, Western Arts Found, 74-; foundry, partner, Jackson-Mariani Fine Art Foundry, Camaiore, Italy, 85-98; founder, Harry Jackson Art Mus, Cody, Wyo, 94. *Awards:* Fulbright Grant, 54; Samuel Finley Breese Morse Gold Medal, Nat Acad Design, 68; Silver Medal, Nat Cowboy Hall of Fame, 71. *Bibliog:* M Amaya (auth), article, Connoisseur, 79; L Pointer & D Goddard (auth), Harry Jackson, Abrams Publ, 81; Harry Jackson, Forty Years of His Work 1941-81, Wyo Foundry Studios, 81; Harry Jackson, Thirty Years in Versillia, City Camaiore, Italy, 85; and others. *Mem:* USMC Combat Corresp Asn; Nat Sculpture Soc; Fel Am Artists Prof League; assoc mem Nat Acad Design (academician). *Media:* Oil; Bronze. *Publ:* Contribr monograph catalog, Kennedy Galleries, 69; auth, Lost Wax Bronze Casting, Northland Press, 72 & Van Nostrand Reinhold, 79; Harry Jackson. *Mailing Add:* PO Box 2836 602 Blackburn Cody WY 82414

JACKSON, HERB
PAINTER, PRINTMAKER
b Raleigh, NC, Aug 16, 45. *Study:* Davidson Col, BA, 67; Philips Univ, Marburg, WGer; Univ NC, MFA, 70. *Work:* Brit Mus, London; Libr Cong, Washington; Victoria & Albert Mus, London; Brooklyn Mus Art, NY; Baltimore Mus Art, Md; Whitney Mus Am Art, NY; Minneapolis Inst Arts; Mint Mus, Charlotte, NC. *Comn:* Mural, Vail Commons, Davidson Col, 84; First Union Nat Bank, 88. *Exhib:* One-person exhibs, Mint Mus Art, Charlotte, NC, Springfield Art Mus, Mo, & Fundacao Calouste Gulbenkian, Lisbon, Portugal, Ashville Mus Art, NC, Greenville Mus Art, Greenville NC, 2000, Fayetteville Mus Art, Fayetteville, NC, 2003; Mint Mus Art, Charlotte, NC, 68, 70 71, 79 & 81; Am Acad & Inst Arts & Letts, NY, 81 & 87; Brooklyn Mus Art, 81; Knoxville World's Fair, Tenn, 82; Contemp Arts Ctr, New Orleans, La, 88; Kunstsammlungen der Veste Coburg, Ger, 88; Lorenzelli Fine Art, Milan, Italy, 89; Exhib Hall of Union Moscow Artists, Moscow, USSR, 89; Samuel P Harn Mus, Gainesville, Fla, 90; Stetson Univ, Deland, Fla, 2006; Group Exhibs: Utah Mus Art, Salt Lake City, 1998, Thomas McCormick Gallery, Chicago, 2002, Peace Tower, Whitney Mus Art, NYC, 2006. *Teaching:* Prof fine art, (Douglas C Houchens Professorship) Davidson Col, 69-. *Awards:* Southeastern Ctr Contemp Art Grant, 81; Artist Fel, 84; NC Award, 1999. *Bibliog:* Dr Roger Lipsey (auth), Herb Jackson Drawings at the Mint Museum, Arts, 6/83; Dr Donald Kuspit (auth), Herb Jackson: The Archeological Surface, 11/88; Frank Getlein (auth), Herb Jackson: Vitreographs, 8/90. *Mem:* Col Art Asn Am; Southeastern Col Art Conf. *Media:* Acrylic, Graphics. *Dealer:* Stremmel Gallery 1400 S Virginia St Reno NV 89502; Christa Faut Gallery 19818 North Cove Rd Ste E3 Cornelius NC 28031; Somerhill Gallery 3 Eastgate E Franklin St Chapel Hill NC 27514; Parchman Stremmel Gallery 110 W Olmos San Antonio TX; Art Gallery LTD 502 Pollock St New Bern NC 28562; Thomas Paul Fine Art 5622 Le Sage Ave Woodland Hills CA 91367; Julian Contemp Art 534 Brennan's Ct Avon Lake OH 44012. *Mailing Add:* PO Box 10 Davidson NC 28036

JACKSON, MARION ELIZABETH
HISTORIAN, EDUCATOR
b Saginaw, Mich, July 7, 41. *Study:* Univ Mich, PhD(art hist), 85, with Rudolf Arnheim, Evan Maurer, Marvin Eisenberg & Roy Rappaport. *Collection Arranged:* Inuit Sculpture (auth, catalog), Univ Mich Mus Art, 79; The Vital Vision: Drawings by Ruth Tulurialik (auth, catalog), Art Gallery Windsor, Ont, 86; Contemporary Inuit Drawings, Macdonald Stewart Art Ctr, Univ Guelph, 87; Ruth Weisberg - Paintings, Drawings, Prints 1986-1988, Univ Mich Sch Art, 87; Parr: Drawings, Mt St Vincent Univ, 88. *Pos:* Assoc dean, Univ Mich Sch Art, 86-91. *Teaching:* Lectr, art hist, Eastern Mich Univ, Ypsilanti, 83-84; assoc prof, Univ Mich Sch Art, 86-91, Carleton Univ, Ottawa, Can, 91-95; prof & chair, Art & Art His, Wayne State Univ, Detroit, Mich. *Mem:* Col Art Asn; Native Am Art Studies Asn; Nat Asn Humanities Educ; African Studies Asn; Brazilian Studies Asn. *Res:* Native arts, particularly North American Inuit art; folk arts; outsider arts; & art criticism; African American art. *Publ:* Contemp Print Drawings, Macdonald Stewart Art Ctr, 87; Ruth Weisberg: Paintings, Drawings, Prints, 1968-1988, Univ Mich Sch Art, 88; Tyree Guyton: Listen to His Art, Detroit Inst Arts, 90; auth, Pudlo: Thirty Years of Drawing, Nat Gallery of Can, 90; Inuit Women Artists: Voices from Cape Dorset, 94. *Mailing Add:* 1336 Nicolet Pl Detroit MI 48207

JACKSON, MATTHEW DAY
ASSEMBLAGE ARTIST
b Panorama City, Calif. *Study:* Univ Wash, Seattle, BFA, 1997; Rutgers Univ, Mason-Gross Sch Arts, New Brunswick, NJ, MFA, 2001. *Exhib:* San Titre, Boulder Mus Contemp Art, Colo, 1999; Rabbett Gallery, New Brunswich, NJ, 2001; Drift, Manasquan, NJ, 2002; Portland Mus Art Biennial, Maine, 2003; White, Black, Yellow, Red, Storefront 1838, NYC, 2003; Spiritual Hunger, Daniel Silverstein Gallery, NYC, 2003; Relentless Proselytizers, Feigen Contemp, NYC, 2004; Mommy! I! Am! Not! An! Animal!, Capsule Gallery, NYC, 2004; The Greater New York Show, PS1 Contemp Art Ctr, 2005; Bridge Freezes Before Road, Barbara Galdstone Gallery, Sticks & Stones, Perry Rubenstein Gallery, NYC, 2005; Whitney Biennial, Whitney Mus Art, NYC, 2006; one-man shows: By No Means Necessary, Chinati Gound, Marfa, Tex, 2004; Perry Rubenstein Gallery, 2005; Paradise Now, Port Inst Contemp Art, 2006. *Awards:* Scholar Skowhegan Sch Painting & Sculpture, Skowhegan, Maine, 2002; vis scholar Chinati Found, Marfa, Tex, 2004

JACKSON, OLIVER LEE
PAINTER, SCULPTOR
b St Louis, Mo, 35. *Study:* Ill Wesleyan Univ, BFA, 58; Univ Iowa, MFA, 63. *Work:* San Francisco Mus Mod Art & Fine Arts Mus San Francisco; Oakland Mus; Seattle Art Mus; New Orleans Mus Art; Mus Mod Art & Metrop Mus, NY; Portland Art Mus, Ore; High Mus, Atlanta; Mus Contemp Art, Chicago & San Diego; many others. *Comn:* Painting for state off bldg, San Francisco, Calif Arts Coun, 87; marble sculpture for Gen Servs Admin Bldg, Oakland, Calif, 88, 96. *Exhib:* Solo exhib,

Seattle Art Mus, 82, St Louis Art Mus, 90 & Crocker Art Mus, Sacramento, Calif, 93, Newport Harbor Art Mus, Newport Beach, Calif, 93 & Fresno Art Mus, 2000, Sert Gallery, Harvard Univ, 2002-2003; Biennial Exhib, Whitney Mus, 83; An Int Survey of Recent Painting and Sculpture, Mus Mod Art, NY, 84; States of War, Seattle Art Mus, Wash, 85; California Figurative Sculpture, Palm Springs Desert Mus, 87; The Appropriate Object, Albright-Knox Gallery, Buffalo, NY, 89. *Pos:* Vis artist, Art Inst Chicago, 69; artist in res, Wake Forest Univ, SE Ctr Contemp Art, 80 & NC Sch Arts, Winston-Salem, 80; vis artist, Univ Calif, Santa Barbara, 85, Univ Wash, Seattle, 85, Univ Ill, Champaign, 88, Univ Calif, Berkeley, 89, Univ Hawaii, Hilo, 93 & 2001, San Francisco Art Inst, 93, Calif Col Arts & Crafts Summer Invitational, Paris, 2000 & Harvard Univ, 2000. *Teaching:* Instr, Southern Ill Univ, East St Louis, 67-69, Oberlin Col, 69-70; prof art, Calif State Univ, Sacramento, 71-2002. *Awards:* Award in Painting, Nat Endowment Arts, 80; Eureka Fel, Fleishhacker Found, 93; Awards for the Visual Arts, Flintridge Foundation, 2004. *Bibliog:* Regina Hackett (auth), Oliver Lee Jackson (catalog), SE Ctr Contemp Art, 80; Thomas Albright & Jan Butterfield (co-auth), Oliver Jackson, Seattle Art Mus, 82; Robert Pincus (auth), Oliver Jackson, Iannetti-Lanzone Gallery, San Francisco, 88; Oliver Jackson, Fresno Art Mus, 2000. *Media:* Oil; Marble; Intaglio prints. *Dealer:* Artist Forum. *Mailing Add:* c/o Anne Kohs & Assoc 115 Stonegate Rd Portola Valley CA 94028

JACKSON, PAUL C
PAINTER

b Lawrence, KS, Mar 25, 68. *Study:* Mississippi State Univ, BFA, 1989; Univ of MO, MFA, 1992. *Work:* MO State Capitol, (gov's portrait), Jefferson City, MO; Mo Gov's Mansion, Jefferson City, MO; MO Supreme Court, Jefferson City, MO; Margaret Harwell Mus, Poplar Bluff, MO; Univ of MO, Columbia, MO. *Comn:* Tiber Spot Mosaic, Univ of MO, Columbia, MO, 2001; Mo Commem State Quarter, US Mint, Washington, DC, 2003. *Exhib:* Rocky Mtn Watermedia, Foot Hills Art Ctr, Golden, Colo, 1996; Kans Watercolor So, Wichita Art Mus, Wichita, Kans, 1996; Am Watercolor Soc, Salmagundi Club, New York City, 2006; MO Watercolor Nat, Christian Memorial, Fulton, MO, 2006; La Watercolor, St. Charles Place, New Orleans, La, 2006. *Collection Arranged:* First Glimpse Back, Pensacola Mus, 2000. *Pos:* judge, Alaska Watercolor Soc, 2003; judge, La Watercolor Soc, 2005. *Awards:* Hardie Gramatky Award, 1992; Distinguished Alumni, Univ of MO, 2001; Dong Kingman Award, Am Watercolor Soc, 2006. *Mem:* signature mem, Am Watercolor Soc, 1998. *Media:* Watercolor. *Publ:* Auth, Painting Spectacular Light Effects, North Light, 2000; illus, The Physicians Guide to Investing, 2005. *Mailing Add:* 2918 Bluegrass Columbia MO 65201

JACKSON, SARAH
SCULPTOR, GRAPHIC ARTIST

b Detroit, Mich, Nov 13, 24. *Study:* Wayne State Univ, BA, 46, MA, 48. *Work:* Joseph H Hirshhorn Collection, Washington, DC; Nat Gallery Can, Ottawa; Montreal Mus Fine Arts; Montreal Mus Contemp Arts; Fine Arts Collection, Smithsonian Inst, Washington, DC; Mus Mod Art, NY; Tate Gallery & Victoria & Albert Mus, London; Nat Postal Mus & Mus of Civilization Can. *Comn:* Dancer (bronze), Cloverdale Shopping Ctr, Toronto, 66; Metamorphosis (bronzes) & Mindscape (bronze hanging), Student Union Bldg, Dalhousie Univ; plastic & bronze sculpture, Mt Sinai Hosp, Toronto. *Exhib:* Artist in Residence Ser, Stony Brook Univ, NY, 89; Dreams Come True Exhib, Eye Level Gallery, Halifax, Nova Scotia, 89; Traveling, A Space Exhib, Artware: Artists Books, Toronto, 89; Artitudes, Int Art Competition, Green St Gallery, NY, 89; Copier Art Exhib, London, Olympic, Eng, Copier Art Festival, Tech Univ Nova Scotia, Copier Art Murals and Collectable Prints, Manuge Gallery, Halifax, Copier Art Mural Exhib, Hilton Hotel, Halifax, Nova Scotia, 89; one-woman shows, Micro Hall Art Center, WGer, 89, Westchester Comn Col, Valhalla, NY, 90, Copier Art Bookwords, WCBA, Minneapolis, 90; The Works Art Festival, 90; Int Soc Copier Artist, NY, 84; Nat Mus Women Arts, Wash, DC, 87; and many others. *Pos:* Artist-in-residence & dir, Arts & Technol Festival, 79- & dir, Summer Arts Celebration, 81-, Tech Univ NS; co-cur, Int Mail/Copier Art Exhib, 85; dir, Int Mail Copier Art Exhib and Art's & Technology Festival, Tech Univ, Nova Scotia, 85, Summer Arts Festival Tech Univ & Copier Arts Festival, Nova Scotia, 86, 87; initiator & co-cur, Int Mail Copier Art Exhib (with Bookworks), London, Eng, 87; guest artist, Mail/Copier Art Festival, Can Postal Mus, Can Mus Civilization, 92. *Teaching:* Lectr, Mexico City Col, 48, London Univ, 54-55, Tate Gallery, London, 54-55, Thomas More Inst, Montreal, 56, Nat Gallery, Ottawa, 57, Toronto Univ, 60-61, YMCA Adult Educ, Toronto, 62, St Mary's Univ, 63, Nova Scotia Col Art, 70, Dartmouth Adult Educ Div, 72-73 & Univ BC, 79; lectr, Tech Univ, Nova Scotia, 78-89. *Awards:* Award of Excellence, Art Mus Asn Am, 85; Ontario Arts Coun Grant, 74; Grant, Nova Scotia Govt, 90. *Bibliog:* Ramuna Macdonald (dir), Sarah Jackson Halifax (film), Nat Film Bd Can, 80; Elissa Bernard (auth), Women of Vision: Artists' shared experiences led to show in Tatamagouche, The Sunday Herald, 98. *Media:* Bronze; Graphics. *Publ:* Auth, Copier Art Bookworks (several titles), poetry & images. *Mailing Add:* 1411 Edward St Halifax NS B3H 3H5 Canada

JACKSON, SUZANNE FITZALLEN
PAINTER

b St Louis, Mo, Jan 30, 44. *Study:* San Francisco State Col, BA, 66; Sch of Drama, Design, Yale Univ, MFA, 90; Otis Art Inst, Los Angeles, with Charles Whi. *Work:* Adam Clayton Powell Jr, State Office Bldg, Harlem; Palm Springs Desert Mus; California African-Am Mus; Daniel, Mann, Johnson & Mendenhall, Co, Los Angeles; Indianapolis Mus Art; Jen Libr, Savannah Col of Art & Design, Ga. *Comn:* Peace Bird, Secy State Edmund G Brown, Jr, Sacramento, 72; Stephen Chase, Arthur Elrod & Assoc, Palm Springs, 74; Artful Living, William Chidester Co, Pac Design Ctr, Los Angeles, 75; mural, New Health Ctr, Los Angeles, 79; and many others. *Exhib:* solo exhibs, Calif State Off Bldg, Los Angeles, 81-82; Multi-Cult Art Inst, San Diego, 83; Fashion Moda, NY, 84; Ingber Gallery, NY, 84; Ankrum Gallery, Los Angeles, 84; Sargent Johnson Gallery, San Francisco, 85; Black Like Me Gallery, San Francisco, 86; African Am Artist in Los Angeles, A survey exhib: Pathways, 66-89; Calif African Am Mus & Los Angeles Munic Art gallery; Forever Free, Works by African-Am Women Artists Traveling Exhib, Ctr Visual Arts, Univ Ill, Normal, 80-82; 19-Sixties, Calif Mus African-Am Hist & Cult, Los Angeles, 81-89; Mus African-Am Art, Los Angeles, 85; Libr for the Performing Arts at Lincoln Ctr, New York City, 95; Savannah Int Airport, 96; John Slade Fly House, New Haven, Conn; York W Bailey, Penn Ctr, St Helena Island; World Festival of Art on Paper, Ljubjliana, Slovenia, 02; Int Biennale fur Bildende Kunst-Austria, 02; Thurgood Marshall Postal Stamp exhib, RED Gallery, Savannah, Ga, 03; Nine, Painting Faculty, Pinnacle gallery, 2003; Suzanne Jackson: Paintings & Monoprints, Pinnacle Gallery, Savanna, GA, 2005 & Marshall House Galleries, 2005-2006; Ars Femina, Stockholm, Sweden, 2002-2006. *Pos:* Vchairperson, Calif Arts Coun, 75-78; artist-coordr, Brockman Gallery Productions CETA Pub Art Prog, 77-78; Century City Cult Comn, 78-79; dir, Int Women's Writing Guild, 79-; proj dir, Cult Exchange Prog, Lagos, Nigeria/Wajumbe Cult Inst, San Francisco, 85-86. *Teaching:* Lectr, Calif Inst Women, 74; Idyllwild Sch Music & Arts, 81-82; chairperson, Fine Arts, painting, drawing & dance, Elliott Pope Prep Sch, 82-85; vis lectr, San Francisco State Univ, 87; asst prof/scenographer, St Mary's Col, Md, 94; prof painting, Savannah Col Art & Design, Ga, 96. *Awards:* Cave Canem Poetry Fel, 96-99; Scad Painting fac artist-in-residence, artlink at elizabeth found studios, New York City, 2002; Presidential fel fac develop in printing, Sauannah Col of Art & Design, 2003. *Bibliog:* Four Plus One (catalog), Nat Urban League Conf, San Francisco, 86; Gumbo Ya Ya, 95; St James Guide to Black Artists, St James Press/Schomberg Ctr for Res in Black Cult, 97. *Mem:* Int Women's Writing Guild; United Scenic Artists, Local 829; Costume Soc Am; Ctr Study Beadwork; St Mary's Women's Writing Group; Telfair Mus, Art fair comt Mem, 2002-2005; Col Art Asn Southeastern col Art. *Media:* Acrylic, Mixed Media. *Publ:* Auth, What I Love (paintings & poetry), Contemp Crafts, 72; Animal (paintings & poetry), continuity transcripts and features, 78. *Dealer:* Katharine T. Carter & Associates. *Mailing Add:* 15 W 41st St Savannah GA 31401-8984

JACOB, MARY JANE
CURATOR, HISTORIAN

b Queens, NY, Jan 5, 52. *Study:* Fla State Univ Study Ctr, Florence, Italy, 72; Univ Fla, Gainesville, BFA, 73; Univ Mich, Ann Arbor, 76. *Collection Arranged:* Magdalena Abakanowicz, 82; Dada and Surrealism in Chicago Collections, 84; Gordon Matta-Clark: A Retrospective, 85; Jannis Kounellis: A Retrospective, 85; British Sculpture since 1965: Tony Cragg, Richard Deacon, Barry Flanagan, Richard Long, David Nash & Bill Woodrow (co-curated with San Francisco Mus Mod Art), 87; all Mus Contemp Art, Chicago & traveling. *Pos:* Curatorial asst, Det Inst Arts, 76-77, from asst cur to assoc cur mod art, 77-80; chief cur, Mus Contemp Art, Chicago, 80-87. *Awards:* Nat Endowment Humanities Fel, 73-74 & 80-81. *Mem:* Nat Women's Caucus Art (adv bd, 79-80); Mich Coun Arts; Art Table Inc, 83-. *Res:* 20th century art with emphasis on American art of the 1920's and 1930's and contemporary American and European art. *Publ:* Contribr, The Amazing Decade: Women and Performance Art 1970-1980, Astro Arts Bks, Los Angeles, 83; auth, Anni Albers: A modern weaver as artist, In: The Woven and Graphic Art of Anni Albers, Smithsonian Inst Press, Washington, 85. *Mailing Add:* 707 W Junior Terr No 10 Chicago IL 60613-1524

JACOB, NED
PAINTER, LECTURER

b Elizabethton, Tenn, Nov 15, 38. *Study:* Pvt studies with Robert Gilbert, Robert Lougheed & Bettina Steinke. *Work:* Denver Art Mus; Indianapolis Mus Art; Whitney Gallery Western Art, Cody, Wyo; Albrecht Art Mus, St Joseph, Mo; Washburn Univ, Topeka, Kans. *Exhib:* One-man shows, Univ Sask, Saskatoon, Can, 59, Nat Cowboy Hall Fame & Western Heritage Ctr, Oklahoma City, 72, Birger Sandzen Mem Gallery, Lindsborg, Kans, 76, Whitney Gallery Western Art, 76, Frye Gallery, Seattle, 79, Coe Kerr Gallery, NY, 82, Wichita Art Mus, 83 & El Paso Mus Art, 83; Twenty-fifth Anniversary Exhib, James Fisher Gallery, Denver, 84; Mus of SW, Midland, Tex, 97. *Teaching:* Guest lectr, painting & figure drawing, Fechin Inst, Taos, NMex, 88-92, Art Students League, Denver, 89-94, Scottsdale Artists Sch, Ariz, 90-94 & Sun Valley Ctr Arts & Humanities, Idaho, 92. *Awards:* John F & Anna Lee Stacy Fel, 74. *Bibliog:* Sandra Dallas (auth), Ned Jacob, Fenn Galleries Publ Inc, 79; W Bradley (auth), Twenty-five Years--Ned Jacob, Artists of Rockies, 85; DW LaCour (auth), Artists in Quotation, McFarland & Co Inc, Jefferson, NC, 89. *Mem:* Salmagundi Club, NY; Chelsea Arts Club, London; Nat Arts Club, NY. *Media:* Oil, Charcoal; All. *Interests:* history and craft of traditional painting

JACOB, WENDY
EDUCATOR

Study: Williams Col, BA, 80; Sch of Art Inst Chicago, MFA, 89. *Work:* Whitney Mus Art, NY City, Krannert Art Mus, Univ Ill, Champaign, Cranbrook Art Mus, Cranbrook Acad Art, Kemper Mus Contemp Art, Kans City, Mass Mus Contemp Art, Kunsthaus Graz, Austria. *Exhib:* Galerie Walcheturm, Zurich, The Sch of the Art Inst of Chicago, Emmanuel Perrotin, Paris, Galerie Karin Schorm, Vienna, Milwaukee Inst Art & Design, Schipper and Krome, Cologne, Ger, Centre Nat d'Art Contemporain, Grenoble, France, Temple Gallery, Tyler Sch Art, Philadelphia, Cranbrook Acad Art, Bloomfield Hills, Mich, Mass Inst of Technol List Visual Arts Ctr, Cambridge, Chicago Project Room, Madison Art Ctr, Wis, Centre Georges-Pompidou, Paris, Forum for Contemp Art, St Louis, Kunsthaus Graz, Austria. *Pos:* Mem, HaHa artists collaborative, 89—. *Teaching:* Instr, performance dept The Sch of the Art Inst of Chicago, 93; asst prof, visual arts Mass Inst of Technol, Cambridge, 99; asst prof, dept sculpture Col Fine Arts Ill State Univ. *Awards:* Creative Capital Found Grant, 1999; Ill Arts Coun Artist's Fel Award, 1999; Bunting Inst Fel, Radcliffe Inst Advanced Study, Harvard Univ, 2004—05. *Mailing Add:* Mass Inst of Technol Visual Arts Prog 265 Mass Ave N51-317 Cambridge MA 02139

JACOBOWITZ, ELLEN SUE
CURATOR, DIRECTOR
b Detroit, Mich, Feb 21, 48. *Study:* Univ Mich, BA, 69, MA, 70; Courtauld Inst Art, 70-71; Bryn Mawr Col, PhD. *Collection Arranged:* American Graphics: 1860-1940 (auth, catalog), Rijkmuseum & Philadelphia Mus Art, 82; The Prints of Lucas van Leyden and His Contemporaries (auth, catalog), Nat Gallery Art & Boston Mus Fine Arts, 83; From Mantegna to Goya: Old Master prints from the Berman collection, Philadelphia Mus Art, 85; New Art on Paper, Philadelphia Mus Art, 88. *Pos:* Cur, Philadelphia Mus Art, 72-90; asst dir, Cranbrook Inst Sci, 91-. *Awards:* Smithsonian Grants, 77-78; Gold Medal, Netherlands Soc Philadelphia, 83; Fel, Nat Endowment Arts, 87. *Mem:* Print Coun Am (bd mem, 80-83); Print Club Philadelphia (bd mem, 78-84); Illustrated Bartsch (ed & bd mem); Neth-Am Amity Trust (bd mem, 81-). *Res:* Early 16th century Netherlandish printmaking; Am printmaking since the late 19th century; contemporary printmaking. *Publ:* Auth, Three Centuries of Chiaroscuro Woodcuts, Pa Acad Fine Arts, 73; contribr, Philadelphia: Three Centuries of American Art, Philadelphia Mus Art, 76; coauth, The Illustrated Bartsch--Lucas van Leyden, Abaris, 81. *Mailing Add:* Cranbrook Inst Sci 1221 N Woodward PO Box 801 Bloomfield Hills MI 48303-2824

JACOBS, DAVID (THEODORE)
SCULPTOR, KINETIC ARTIST
b Niagara Falls, NY, Mar 1, 32. *Study:* Orange Coast Col, AA; Los Angeles State Col, AB & MA. *Work:* Guggenheim Mus, NY; Mus Art, Richmond, Va; Otterbein Col, Ohio; Valley Mall, Hagerstown, Md; Hofstra Mus, Hempstead, NY; Otterbein Col, Ohio; Ohio State U. *Comn:* Cloud Fountain (sculptured fountain), Valley Mall Assoc, Hagerstown, Md, 74; bronze relief, Paul Radin Mem, Hofstra Univ Libr, 74; Ventura High, Deer Park High Sch, NY, 76; Rainframe (sculptured screen), Dawn-Joy Corp, NY, 76. *Exhib:* The Art of Assemblage, Mus Mod Art, NY, 61; numerous one-man shows, 61-95; 68th Am Exhib, Art Inst Chicago, 66; Sound, Light, Silence, Art That Performs, W R Nelson Gallery, Atkins Mus, Kansas City, 66; Inflatable Sculpture, Jewish Mus, NY, 69; Sound Sculpture, Vancouver Art Gallery, 73. *Pos:* Sculpture cur consult, Hofstra Mus, formerly. *Teaching:* Prof sculpture, Hofstra Univ, 62-95, chmn dept fine arts, 82-89; vis critic sculpture, Cornell Univ, New York Prog, 69 & 70, Baruch Col, City Col New York, 77-79. *Awards:* Res grant, Hofstra Univ, 68; Creative Artists Pub Serv Grant, 73 & 76; Artist-in-Sch Grant, Nat Endowment Arts & NYFA, Central HS, Valley Stream, 79. *Bibliog:* D J Irving (auth), Sculpture: Materials & Processes, Van Nostrand Reinhold, 68; Wayne Craven (auth), Sculpture in America, Crowell, 68; Chichura & Stevens (auths), Super Sculpture: Using Science, Technology and Natural Phenomena in Sculpture, Van Nostrand Reinhold, 74. *Media:* Aluminum, Rubber. *Mailing Add:* 51 Eighth Ave Sea Cliff NY 11579

JACOBS, FERNE K
WEAVER
b Chicago, Ill, 42. *Study:* Claremont Grad Sch, Calif, MFA, 76. *Work:* Royal Scottish Mus, Edinburgh; Am Craft Mus, NY; Wadsworth Atheneum, Hartford, Conn; Detroit Inst Arts, Mich; Oakland Mus, Calif. *Exhib:* Fiber Re/Evolution Traveling Exhib, Milwaukee Art Mus, Wis, 87; The Eloquent Object Traveling Exhib, Philbrook Mus Art, Tulsa, Okla, 89; Craft Today USA Traveling Exhib, Am Craft Mus, NY, 89-91; Four Artist Reflect 1971-1991 (with catalog), Soc Art in Crafts, Pittsburgh, Pa, 91; one-person exhib, Sybaris Gallery, Royal Oak, Mich, 92 & 99; Hand and the Spirit, Scottsdale, Ariz, 96; and others. *Pos:* Fel, Am Cross Coun, 95. *Teaching:* Int Col, Los Angeles, 78-; Haystack Mountain Sch Crafts, Deer Isle, Maine, 90. *Awards:* Nat Endowment Arts, 73-74, 77-78 & 90-91; Am Craft Coun. *Bibliog:* Rob Puller (ed), The Basket Makers Art, Contemporary Baskets & Their Makers, Clark Books, 86; Marcia & Tom Manhart (eds), The Eloquent Object, Philbrook Mus Art, Univ Washington Press, 87; A basket is, Am Craft Mag, 2-3/90. *Media:* Waxed Linen, Textiles

JACOBS, HAROLD
PAINTER, SCULPTOR
b New York, NY, Oct 29, 32. *Study:* Cooper Union, 53; NY Univ; New Sch Social Res; Sorbonne, Fulbright scholar, 61. *Work:* Whitney Mus Am Art, NY; Portland Art Mus, Ore; Kalamazoo Art Ctr; Philadelphia Mus Art; Pa Acad Fine Arts. *Comn:* Performance sculpture, Group Motion Dance Co; ltd ed, Akiba Acad, Merion, Pa; outdoor mural, Meridian Books, Philadelphia; sculpture, ARA lobby, Philadelphia; entrance mural, Le Bon Marche Dept Store, Paris, 98, 2000. *Exhib:* Solo exhibs, Pa Acad Fine Arts, 78 & Portland Ctr Visual Arts, Ore, 81; retrospective, Selected Works 1966-1985, Moore Col Art, 85; VIA Paris, 91; Asphalte, Paris, 92; Snyderman Gallery, Philadelphia, 96, 99; 3 Part Retrospective, France, 2001. *Teaching:* Prof painting, Moore Col Art, 66-89 & emer prof, 89-; prof emeritus, Moore College of Art. *Awards:* Nat Endowment Arts Collaboration Grant Visual & Performing Arts, 75; Distinguished Artist Award, Moore Col Art, 83. *Media:* Mixed. *Publ:* Harold Jacobs Selected Works 1966-1985 (exhib catalog & video tape), Moore Col Art, 85; Harold Jacobs Createur, L'espace Asphate, Paris, 92; Catalog of 3 part Retrospective, 2001. *Dealer:* Snyderman Gallery Philadelphia PA. *Mailing Add:* Le Grand Logis Ligre Par Chinon 37500 France

JACOBS, HELEN NICHOLS
PAINTER
b Kent, Conn, Feb 16, 24. *Study:* With Arthur Maynard & Spencer B Nichols. *Exhib:* Kent Art Asn, Conn, 75, 88, 93-06; Hudson Valley Art Asn, 78-06; Catharine Lorillard Wolfe Art Club, 80-88; Am Artists Prof League, NY & NJ, 81-06; Open Jury Show, Ridgewood Art Inst, 94-06. *Teaching:* Instr oil painting, Ridgewood Adult Sch, NJ, 68-72 & Ridgewood Art Inst, 71-96. *Awards:* Am Artists Prof League Award, 2000; Ridgewood Art Inst, 2000, 02-03; Norman Rockwell Mus Award, 04. *Mem:* Am Artists Prof League; Catharine Lorillard Wolfe Art Club; Kent Art Asn; Hudson Valley Art Asn; Ridgewood Art Inst. *Media:* Oil. *Publ:* auth, Housatonic River Summer, 2004. *Mailing Add:* 684 Terrace Dr Paramus NJ 07652

JACOBS, JIM
PAINTER, PRINTMAKER
b New York, NY, May 26, 45. *Study:* Boston Univ, BA; Bryn Mawr Col, study with Richmond Lattimore; Harvard Univ; Boston Mus of Fine Arts. *Work:* Rose Art Mus, Brandeis Univ, Waltham, Mass; Chase Manhattan Bank; Arman; Smith Mus. *Exhib:* Expressions of the Seventies, NY, 77; Elizabeth Weiner Gallery, NY, 79 & 80; Danforth Mus, Framingham, Mass, 81; Smith Mus, Springfield, Mass, 81; Gallery Yves Arman, 81 & 82; Oscarsson Siegeltuch & Co, NY, 86; and others. *Pos:* Archivist, Leo Castelli Gallery, 67-68. *Teaching:* Instr vase painting, Boston Univ, 65, Harvard Univ, 66, Bryn Mawr Col, 67; lectr, Boston Mus Fine Arts, Mus Sch, Boston, Harvard Univ; instr vase painting, Bryn Mawr Col, 67. *Awards:* Creative Artists Pub Serv Prog Grant, 81-82. *Bibliog:* Article, Art News, 6/80; article, Arts Mag, 5/81; article, Art Am, 2/83; Michael Komanecky & Virginia Fabbri Butera (coauth), The Folding Image: Screens by Western Artists of the ninteenth & twentieth centuries, (exhib catalog), Yale Univ Art Gallery & Nat Gallery Art, 84. *Media:* Lacquer, Board. *Dealer:* Oscarson Siegeltuch & Co 568 Broadway New York NY 10012. *Mailing Add:* 26 W 20th St New York NY 10011

JACOBS, PETER ALAN
SCULPTOR, EDUCATOR
b New York, NY, Jan 31, 39. *Study:* State Univ NY Col New Paltz, with Ilya Bolotowsky, BS(art educ), 60, MA(art), 62; Vanderbilt Univ-George Peabody Col, EdD(fine arts), 65. *Work:* Bloomsburg State Col, Pa; Col Mainland, Texas City, Tex; Muskingum Col, New Concord, Ohio; George Peabody Mus, Nashville, Tenn; Mus Satire & Humor, Bulgaria. *Exhib:* New Directions in Art, Beloit Mus, Wis; Wis Designer-Craftsman, Milwaukee Art Ctr & Wis Painters & Sculptors, 68 & 69; Southwest Invitational, Yuma, Ariz, 73 & 74; 65 one-man shows incl, Work on Tour by Ariz Arts & Humanities Comn, Ariz, Tex, Ohio & Wis, 74-75 & Univ Ohio, Univ Colo, Grand Canyon Art Ctr & Univ Wyo Art Mus; Banares Hindu Univ, Varanasa, India, 80; Mostra di Grafica, Soc Delle Belle Arti, Firenze, Italy, 83; 6th Int Biennial, Gabrova, Bulgaria, 83; Int Salon of Jazz Posters, Bydgoszcz, Poland, 85; 28th Ann Art Zone, Denver, 88; Mondak Art Ctr, Foothills Art Ctr, 2000-01. *Collection Arranged:* Ilya Bolotowsky Retrospective, Crossman Gallery, Univ Wis-Whitewater, 68 & Northern Ariz Univ Mus, 73; Andy Warhol, 81, Robert Rauschenberg, 81, Roy Lichtenstein, 82, James Rosenquist, 82, Sam Francis, 83 & Willem de Kooning, 84, Colo State Univ. *Teaching:* Chmn art dept, Univ Wis-Whitewater, 65-70; head dept art, Northern Ariz Univ, 70-74; dept chair & prof, Cent Mich Univ, 74-76 & Colo State Univ, 76-86, prof, 88; fac, Semester at Sea, Univ Pittsburgh, fall semester, 98; Univ Mediation Officer. *Mem:* Hon life mem Nat Coun Art Adminr (founder & chmn bd dir, 72-77); Col Art Asn Am; Mich Soc Arts, Lett & Sci (chmn fine arts div, 75); Nat Art Educ Asn; Native Am Art Study Asn. *Media:* Wood. *Res:* American Indian arts. *Interests:* Canoing, Camping, Fishing, Northwest Coast Native Arts. *Publ:* Auth, Visual Arts in the Ninth Decade, Nat Coun Art Adminr, 80. *Dealer:* Philip Bareiss Contemporary Exhibitions PO Box 2739 150 Ski Valley Road Taos NM 87571. *Mailing Add:* 1727 Rangeview Fort Collins CO 80524

JACOBS, RALPH, JR
PAINTER
b El Centro, Calif, May 22, 40. *Study:* With Evelyn Nadeau, Frederic Taubes & Abel G Warshawsky. *Work:* Beirut Art Mus, Lebanon; Continental Telephone Co, Ga. *Comn:* Many pvt collections in Can, Japan, Australia & SAm. *Exhib:* Rosicrucian Mus, San Jose, Calif, 63, 67 & 71; Coun Am Artists Soc Nat Exhib, NY, 64; Nat Exhib, Springville Mus Art, Utah, 65; Soc Western Artists Ann Exhibs, de Young Mus, San Francisco, 65 & 69; Armenian Allied Arts Ann, Los Angeles, 66; Monterey Co Exhib, Monterey Mus Art, 96. *Awards:* Soc Western Artists Ann Second Award for Silhouette in Morning Light, 64; Klumpkey Mem Award for Classic Nude, de Young Mus, San Francisco, 65; Second Place Award & Spec Peoples Choice Award, Monterey Co Fair, 95. *Mem:* Calif Art Club. *Media:* Oil. *Publ:* Award Winning Paintings, 1964, Prize Winning Paintings, 1965, 1966, Allied Publs, Inc; Exhibit 26, Mag Art, spring summer 1968. *Mailing Add:* PO Box 5906 Carmel CA 93921

JACOBS, SCOTT E
PAINTER, ILLUSTRATOR
b Westfield, NJ, Oct 24, 58. *Study:* Ducret Sch Design, NJ, 92; Parsons Sch Design, NY, 92; Airbrush Illus Getaway, 94-95. *Work:* Engineered Fasteners, St Louis; San Diego Chargers, Calif. *Comn:* 85 paintings, Harley Davidson, Milwaukee, 93-2000; painting, Sorrento Cheese, Hamburg, NY, 96; 8 paintings, Chevrolet Corp, Detroit, 96-98; painting, Mattel Corp, El Segundo, Calif, 97; painting, Porsche USA, Phoenix, 98. *Exhib:* Motorcycles as Art, Peterson Mus, Los Angeles, 96; Harleys 95th Anniversary, Milwaukee Pub, 98; Behes & Black Leather, St Louis Guild, 99. *Awards:* Varga Lifetime Achievement Award, Airbrush Action, 98; Rookie of Yr Award, Chevrolet Corp, 98. *Bibliog:* Neil Evans (auth), Biker Dreams, Epicenter Films, 97. *Mem:* Rancho Santa Fe Art Guild. *Media:* Acrylic. *Publ:* auth, Big Twin, Filapashy, 96, VQ Mag, Paisano Publ, 96, US Art Mag, MSP Commun, 96, American Iron, Tam Commun, 96, Art of Scott Jacobs, Airbrush Action, 2000, Easyriders, The Motorcycle Art of Scott Jacobs. *Dealer:* Segal Fine Art 594 S Arthur Ave Louisville CO 80027. *Mailing Add:* PO Box 2677 Rancho Santa Fe CA 92067

JACOBSEN, HUGH NEWELL
ARCHITECT
b Grand Rapids, Mich, Mar 11, 29. *Study:* Univ Md, BA, 51; Archit Asso Sch Archit, London, Eng, 54; BArch, MArch, Yale, 55. *Hon Degrees:* Gettysburg Col, LHD (hon), 74; Bradford Col, LHD (hon), 90; Univ Md, DFA (hon), 93. *Comn:* principal works incl; US Embassy, Paris, addition to US Capitol, two Smithsonian Mus (renovations), Southern Vt Art Ctr. *Exhib:* Fundação Armando Alvares Penteado in São Paolo, Brazil, 98; Nat Bldg Mus Retrospective in Washington DC, 99; Va Ctr for

Archit, 2005. *Pos:* Archit, with Philip Johnson, New Canaan, Conn, 55; archit, Keyes, Lethbridge & Condon, Wash, 57-58; principal, Hugh Newell Jacobsen, FAIA, 58. *Teaching:* Lectr, univs; vis prof, Univ Cairo, Egypt, 70. *Awards:* Nat Am Inst of Archit honor awards 69, 74, 78, 80, 85, & 88; AIA Centennial Award; AD Deans Design, 2005. *Mem:* Fel Am Inst of Archit; Nat Acad of Design (elected); Century Asn; Yale Club (New York City). *Publ:* Ed: A Guide to the Archit of Wash DC, 65; Hugh Newell Jacobsen Architect, (monogr), 88; Hugh Jacobsen Architect, Recent Work, (monogr), 94. *Mailing Add:* 2529 P St NW Washington DC 20007-3024

JACOBSEN, MICHAEL A
HISTORIAN, EDUCATOR, PAINTER
b Pasadena, Calif, June 4, 42. *Study:* Univ Calif, Santa Barbara, BA, 65, MA, 70; Columbia Univ, PhD, 76. *Work:* Calif Polytechnic Univ, Pomona. *Comn:* watercolors of N Am birds, various pvt collectors. *Exhib:* Craig Ellwood Archit Drawings, Cal Poly Gallery, 94; Jupiter & His Children, Ga Mus Art, 97. *Teaching:* Asst prof Renaissance art, Cleveland State Univ, Ohio, 73-77, Univ Ore, 77-79; assoc prof art, Univ Ga, 79-87; vis assoc prof art, Stanford Univ, 87, Univ Calif, Riverside, 88-89; lectr, Calif Polytechnic Univ, Ponoma, 89-99, assoc prof, 99-. *Awards:* Kress Fel, 72-73. *Mem:* Col Art Asn; Southern Calif Art Hist Soc. *Res:* Renaissance art history, Italian 15th century. *Publ:* Mantegna's battle of sea monsters, Art Bull, 12/82; Perspective in Mantegna's early panels, Arte Venenta, 83; Dolphins in Renaissance art, Studies in Iconography, fall 83; Durer's Johannes Kleberger Source, 91; Agostino diDuccio's Virtues, pages 13-18, Antichita Viva, 95; Back and Forth: The Renaissance and Mythology, pages 51-66, Archeologia Transatlantica, XVI, 98. *Mailing Add:* c/o Calif State Polytechnic Univ Art Dept 3801 W Temple Ave Pomona CA 91768-4071

JACOBSHAGEN, N KEITH, II
PAINTER, PHOTOGRAPHER
b Wichita, Kans, Sept 8, 41. *Study:* Kansas City Art Inst, Mo, BFA; Art Ctr Col Design, Los Angeles; Univ Kans, MFA. *Work:* Sheldon Mem Gallery, Lincoln, Nebr; Univ Kans Mus Art, Lawrence; Mus Art Okla Univ; Oakland Mus, Calif; Pasadena Art Mus, Calif. *Exhib:* A Sense of Place: The Artist & the Am Land, Sheldon Mem Art Gallery, Lincoln, Nebr, 74; Southern Ark Univ, Magnolia & Westark Community Col, Ft Smith, Ark, 78; In Respect of Space, Swan River Mus, Paola, Kans, 79; Group, Volga-Consalvo Gallery, Boston, Mass, 79; Corp Exhib, auspices of Minneapolis Art Inst, 79 & NAm Casualty Exhib, 79; and others. *Teaching:* Assoc prof art, Univ Nebr-Lincoln, 68-80. *Awards:* Owen H Kenan Award, 34th Ann Contemp Am Painting, 72; Frank Woods Fel, Univ Nebr, 75. *Bibliog:* Alan Gussow (auth), A Sense of Place: the Artist and the American Land (film), Nebr Educ TV, 74. *Media:* Oil. *Publ:* Contribr, Twelve Photographers: A Contemporary Mid-America Document, Mid-Am Arts Alliance, 78; Special report: Midwest art, Art in Am, 7-8/79; Artists work range through human emotions, Kansas City Star, 8/12/79; Cottonwood Rev, fall 79; In respect of space, Forum/Kansas City Artists Coalition, 12/79; and others. *Dealer:* Dorry Gates PO Box 7264 Kansas City MO 64113; Charles Campbell Gallery 647 Chestnut St San Francisco CA 94133. *Mailing Add:* c/o Kiechel Fine Art 5733 S 34th St Lincoln NE 68516

JACOBSON, ARTHUR
PAINTER, PRINTMAKER
b Chicago, Ill, Jan 10, 24. *Study:* Univ Wis, BS, 48, MS, 50. *Work:* Pa Acad Fine Art, Philadelphia; Mus NMex, Santa Fe; Ariz State Univ, Tempe; Phoenix Art Mus, Ariz; Dallas Mus, Tex. *Comn:* Exterior mural in marblecrete, Phoenix Jewish Community Ctr, Ariz, 62. *Exhib:* Solo Exhib, Watercolors, Kerr Ctr, Scottsdale, Ariz; Corcoran Biennial, Corcoran Mus, Washington, 57; The Print Club-Etching, Philadelphia Mus, 59; Dallas Print-Southwestern, Dallas Mus, 60; Northwestern Printmakers, Seattle Mus, 66; Drawing Exhib, Palace Legion Hon, San Francisco, 66; Denver Invitational, Denver Mus, 71; Watercolor USA, Springfield Art Mus, 80; Invitational, Elvehjem Mus Art, Madison, Wis, 80; Rise Found, Albuquerque, NMex. *Teaching:* Prof emer painting & drawing, Ariz State Univ, 56-88; guest prof painting, Univ Wis, 67-68. *Awards:* Purchase Award, Pa Acad Fine Arts, 59; Purchase Award, Dallas Mus, 60; First Prize, Scottsdale Fine Arts Mus, 75; Best of Show Award, Honolulu Watercolor Soc, 95. *Bibliog:* Univ Chattanoogs, 75; 100 American and European Drawings, Prentice-Hall, 81. *Media:* Oil, Watercolor. *Mailing Add:* PO Box 226 Bridgehampton NY 11932

JACOBSON, FRANK
ADMINISTRATOR
b Philadelphia, Pa, Sept 14, 48. *Study:* Univ Wis, BA, 70; Boston Univ Sch Fine Arts, MFA, 73. *Pos:* Exec dir, Arvada Ctr Arts & Humanities, 79-85; mgr, Theaters & arenas, Denver, 85-87; pres & chief exec off, Scottsdale Cult Coun, 87-. *Teaching:* Asst prof theater, Univ Mont, 73-75. *Mem:* Metrop Denver Arts Alliance (pres, 81-83); Asn Performing Arts Presenters (bd, 84-87). *Publ:* Auth, Performing Art Centers - Market the Arts, FEDAPT, 83; Municipal Connections, ACUCAA Bulletin, Vol 29, No 7, 86. *Mailing Add:* Scottdale Cultural Council 7380 E Second St Scottsdale AZ 85251

JACOBSON, LOUIS
CRITIC
Pos: Staff reporter, Wash City Paper, Wash, photog art critic. *Publ:* Contribr articles to ARTNews and Art on Paper mags. *Mailing Add:* Wash City Paper 2390 Champlain St NW Washington DC 20009

JACOBUS, JOHN M
EDUCATOR, HISTORIAN
b Poughkeepsie, NY, Sept 15, 27. *Study:* Hamilton Col, AB, 52; Yale Univ, MA, 54, PhD, 56. *Teaching:* From instr to asst prof, Princeton Univ, 56-60; from asst prof to assoc prof, Univ Calif, Berkeley, 60-63; assoc prof to prof, Ind Univ, Bloomington, 63-69; prof, Dartmouth Col, 69-. *Res:* Nineteenth & twentieth century art, both architecture & painting. *Collection:* Prints & graphic arts from 18th century to present. *Publ:* Auth, Philip Johnson, Braziller, 62; auth, Twentieth Century Architecture: The Middle Years, Praeger, 66; auth, Matisse, Abrams, 73. *Mailing Add:* 5 Hilltop Dr Hanover NH 03755-2317

JACQUARD, JERALD (WAYNE)
SCULPTOR
b Lansing, Mich, Feb 1, 37. *Study:* Mich State Univ, BA, 60 & MA, 62. *Work:* Kresge Mus, Mich State Univ, East Lansing; Kalamazoo Inst Art, Mich; Laumeier Sculpture Park, St Louis; Chicago Inst Art; Ind Univ Art Mus, Bloomington; Hamilton Corp I; Ind Mus of Art. *Comn:* Sculpture, Chicago Transit Authority, 74; Sculpture, Mich Manufacturing, Lansing, Mich, 94. *Exhib:* One-man shows, Detroit Inst Art, 65, Ill Inst Technol, 69, Univ Chicago, 70, Indianapolis Mus, 75, Kalamazoo, 89, South Bend Regional Mus Art, 93 & Grand Rapids Mus Art, 93; Bicentennial Sculpture for a New Era, Chicago, 75; restrospective, Kalamazoo Inst Art, 92, Ind Mus Art, 94 & 2002. *Teaching:* Assoc prof sculpture, Univ Ill, Chicago Circle Campus, 66-75; prof sculpture, Ind Univ, Bloomington, 75-2000, prof emeritus, 2000-. *Awards:* Fulbright Award, 63; Guggenheim Fel, 73; Nat Endowment Arts, 80; Eli Lilly Fel, 84. *Mem:* Int Sculpture Asn. *Media:* Steel, Bronze. *Publ:* Major Color Catalogue of Jacquard & His Art (from 75-94) to Accompany Traveling Mus Exhibitions, 92, 94, INd Hist Mus, & Ind Mus Art. *Mailing Add:* Ind Univ Dept Art Bloomington IN 47405

JACQUEMON, PIERRE
PAINTER
b Lyon, France, Aug 6, 35; US citizen. *Study:* Self-taught. *Work:* Goteborg Mus, Sweden; Magdalene Col, Cambridge, Eng; Mus d'Art Mod, Paris, France; St Paul Sch, NH; Ika-Shika Nat Univ, Tokyo, Japan. *Exhib:* One-man shows, Temple Gallery, London, 62, Bianchini Gallery, NY, 63, Weeden Gallery, Boston, 68, Berkshire Mus, Mass, 69 & Atrium Gallery, Geneva, Switz, 74, Weeden Gallery, Boston, Mass, 71, Temple Gallery, London, Eng, 72, Bernard Letu, Geneva, Switz, 80 Galerie Philadelphia, Paris, France, 81, Suzanne de Coninck, Paris, France, 82, Phoenix Gallery, NY, 85 & Gallery Juno, NY, 93 & 95; Inst Contemp Art, Boston, 70; Bertha Schaeffer Gallery, NY, 78; Abreu Gallery, NY, 83; Summer Show, Gallery Juno, NY, 95 & 97 & Small, 95. *Bibliog:* Pierre Jacquemon, Gallerie de Bellecour, Lyon, France. *Media:* Oil. *Dealer:* Gallery Jund 568 Broadway Suite 604B New York NY 10012. *Mailing Add:* 62 E Seventh St New York NY 10003

JACQUES, MICHAEL LOUIS
PAINTER, PRINTMAKER
b Barre, Vt, Apr 12, 45. *Study:* Boston Univ, BFA, 67; Univ Hartford Art Sch, MFA, 71; and with David Aronson, Conger Metcalf, Walter Murch & Paul Zimmerman. *Work:* Nat Collection Fine Arts, Smithsonian Mus, Washington; Mus Am Art, Washington; Philadelphia Mus Art; Chrysler Mus, Va; Mus Fine Arts, Boston; and many others. *Exhib:* Silvermine Nat, 80; All on Paper, 80; Acad Artists Asn Exhib, 80 & 81; Audubon Artists Exhib, 80 & 82; Am Artists Prof League Exhib, 82; Boston Printmakers Exhib, 84-85; represented in over 125 Nat Exhibs & over 40 one-man exhibs. *Pos:* Artist-in-residence, ABT Assoc, Cambridge, Mass, 80-81 & Va Mus, 81-82. *Teaching:* Instr art, Emmanuel Col, Boston, 71-73, assoc prof art, 73-88; fine artist, 88-; instr, Art Inst, Southern Calif, 93-. *Awards:* First Prize, Cooperstown Art Asn, 79; Charlotte Printmakers Purchase Award, 79; Am Artist Prof League Prize, 82; Hunterdon Art Ctr Award, 85. *Bibliog:* Paul T Nagano (auth), Michael Jacques-A Double Career in Art, Am Artist Mag, New York, 77; Jeanne B Kissane (auth), Beyond the Stereotype, Small Business, Vol IV, No 1, Worcester, Mass, 1/79; Sandra Angelo (auth), Painting in a Looser style, Am Artist Mag, New York, 2/94. *Mem:* Los Angeles Printmakers; Boston Printmakers; Copley Soc. *Publ:* Auth & illusr, Images of Age, ABT Bks, 81

JACQUES, RUSSELL KENNETH
SCULPTOR, PAINTER
b Springfield, Mass, Feb 19, 1943. *Study:* Boston Univ, BFA, 66. *Work:* DeCordova Mus, Lincoln, Mass; Abilene Fine Arts Mus, Tex; Mead Mus, Amherst, Mass; Nat Gallery Nova Scotia, Halifax; Boston Univ; and others. *Comn:* Kinetic wood sculpture, Nat Ballet Can, Toronto, 81; stainless steel sculpture, Boston Univ, 82; bronze & stainless steel sculpture, Tex Commerce Bank, Dallas, 82; bronze & stainless steel floor sculpture, First Bank Boston, 83; stainless steel sculpture, Hammerson Can Inc, Toronto, 83; Boston Ballet Co, 79-83. *Exhib:* Counterpoint at the Quadrangle, Springfield Fine Arts, Mass, 82; Boston Mus Fine Arts, 83; Interim I,II & III Chesterwood Outdoor Invitational, Stockbridge, Mass, 83; Abilene Christian Univ, Tex, 83; Brea Mus, Brea, Calif, 93; Whitney Mus Am Art, NY, 94; Bowers Mus, Santa Ana, Calif, 94; and many others. *Collection Arranged:* GTE Boston; Muskegon Art Mus; La Quinta Arts Found. *Teaching:* Instr basic drawing, Holyoke Community Col, 75, instr advan design & compos, 76. *Awards:* Second Place, Best in Show, 71 & Award of Excellence, 78, Springfield Art League, George Walter Vincent Smith Mus. *Bibliog:* Nancy Norcross (dir), The Emerging Artist (film), Mass Arts & Humanities Coun, 80; Outdoor Sculpture in the Berkshires II, Nat Trust Hist Preservation, Libr Congress, 7-9/80; Nancy Goebel (auth), article, Art Voices, 8/81; Claudia Elferdink (dir), Art in Common: Russell Jacques--Sculptor (film), Continental Cablevision Channel 57, Springfield, 83. *Media:* All. *Specialty:* stainless & bronze sculpture. *Mailing Add:* Russell Jacques Studio 48701 Shady View Dr Palm Desert CA 92260-6730

JACQUETTE, JULIA L
PAINTER
b New York, NY, Dec 17, 64. *Study:* Skowhegan Sch, 85; Skidmore Col, BS, 86; Hunter Col, MFA, 92. *Work:* Sheldon Mem Gallery & Sculpture Garden, Lincoln, Nebr; Mus Modern Art, New York City; Univ Ariz Mus Art, Tucson. *Exhib:* The Next Word, Neuberger Mus, Purchase, NY, 98; Mus Contemp Art, Sydney, Australia, 98; Mus Modern Art, New York City; Virtues and Vices, Judy Ann Goldman Fine Art, Boston, 2001; White Paintings, Michael Steinberg Fine Art, NY, 2004; I Dreamt, Tang Mus, Saratoga Springs, NY, 2004; My Houses, Michael Steinberg Fine Art, NY, 2006; Complicit!, Univ Va Art Mus, Charlottesville, Va, 2006. *Teaching:* RI Sch Design, 2005, 06; Princeton Univ, 2005, 06. *Awards:* Pollocl/Krasner Award, 94. *Bibliog:* Bon Bon of the Vanities, (style and entertaining supplement), NY Times Mag,. *Publ:* Julia Jacquette (auth), I Dreamt, publ by Tang Mus, 2004. *Dealer:* Michael Steinberg Fine Art NY. *Mailing Add:* 110 E 1st St New York NY 10009

JACQUETTE, YVONNE HELENE
PAINTER, PRINTMAKER
b Pittsburgh, Pa, Dec 15, 34. *Study:* RI Sch Design, 52-56, with John Frazier & Robert Hamilton; also with Herman Cherry & Robert Roche. *Work:* Staatliche Mus, Berlin; Colby Col Mus, Waterville, Maine; Stanford Mus, Stanford, Calif; Utah Mus, Salt Lake City; Hudson River Mus, Yonkers, NY. *Comn:* Five panel painting in oil, NCent Bronx Hosp, NY, 73; five color lithograph, Horace Mann Sch, Riverdale, NY, 74; mural installation for Fed Bldg & Post Off, Gen Serv Admin, Bangor, Maine, 79-82; Night View Wash DC, Jefferson Mem, 84; Triptych of Minneapolis (mural), First Bank, 85; prints, Provincetown Fine Arts Work Ctr, 1992, Zimmerli Mus Rutgers Univ, 1993, Bus Com for the Arts, 1994, Cleveland Print Club, 1999, Sch. Hardknocks Dance Theatre Workshop, New York City. *Exhib:* New Image in Painting, Int Biennial, Tokyo, Japan, 74; Brook Alexander Inc, NY, 82, 85, 88, 89, 92 & 95; solo shows, Currents 22, St Louis Art Mus, 83-84, Recent Paintings and Works on Paper, Berggruen Gallery, San Francisco, 84 & 91, Yurakucho Seibu-Takanawa Art, Tokyo, Japan, 85 & Tokyo Nightviews, Brooke Alexnder Inc, NY & Bowdoin Col Mus Art, Maine, 86, DC Moore Gallery, 97, 2000, 03 & 06, Mary Ryan Gallery, 97, Huntington Mus, 97; Survival of the Fittest II, Ingber Gallery, NY, 85-86; 19th Ann Acad-Inst Purchase Exhib, Am Acad & Inst Arts & Letters, NY, 87; Univ S Maine, Gorham, 98; Cantor Arts Ctr, Stanford Univ, 2002. *Teaching:* Instr, Moore Col Art, Philadelphia, 72; Vis artist & instr painting, Univ Pa, 72-76 & 79-82; vis artist, Nova Scotia Col Art, 74; instr, Parsons Sch of Design, 75-78; instr, Grad Sch Fine Arts, Univ Pa, Philadelphia, 79-84, Pa Acad Fine Arts Grad Sch Philadelphia, vis critic, 91-. *Awards:* Am Acad Arts & Letts, 90; John Simon Guggenheim Mem Found, 97-98; Nat Acad Painters Award, 1998; Nat Acad Print Award, 1999; and others. *Bibliog:* Carolyn Eyler (auth), Yvonne Jacquette, Maine Aerials, Univ S Maine, 98; Paul Mattick (auth), Art in America, Yuonne Jacquette at DC Moore, 12/2000; Robert Berlind (auth), Eye in the Sky, Art in America, March 2002. *Mem:* Artists Equity Asn; Nat Acad, Mem. *Media:* Oil, Pastel; Miscellaneous. *Specialty:* Contemporary Painting and Sculpture. *Interests:* Tibetan Buddhism. *Publ:* Illusr, Country Rush, Adventures in Poetry, 72; illusr, Aerial, Eyelight Press, 81; Jeff Wright and drawings, Toothpaste Press, 82; Jayne Anne Philips, 84; collabr, (with Rudy Burckhardt, film), Night Fantasies; coauth (with Maureen Owen), Erosion's Pull, 2004. *Dealer:* DC Moore 724 Fifth Ave New York NY 10019; Mary Ryan Gallery 24 W 57 St New York NY 10019. *Mailing Add:* 50 W 29th St New York NY 10001

JAE
SCULPTOR, JEWELRY DESIGNER
b Brooklyn, NY, Jan 9, 47. *Study:* Pace Univ, BA; pvt sculpture study with Bruno Lucchesi, New York & Italy, Jacques Lipschitz, Italy, Evangelous Moustakis, Greece & Manolo, Spain. *Comn:* Garden sculpture, comn by M Gumpel, US; garden sculpture, comn by Valerio Todisco, Italy; garden sculpture, comn by George Farah, US; garden sculpture, comn by L Toppall, US; garden sculpture, comn by JM Haft, US; and others. *Exhib:* Am Hellenic Soc, Athens, Greece; Brooklyn Visits the Met, Metrop Mus Art, NY; Nat Arts Club, NY; Black Hist Month, US Naval Acad, Annapolis, Md; Brooklyn Mus Art; Salmagundi Club, NY; Int Art Show, Pietrasanta, Italy; and many others. *Pos:* Founder, Jae's Arc (Art Rehab Ctr), theatrical prod, sculptress, currently. *Teaching:* Instr sculpture, pvtly; lectr art appreciation; lectr art therapy. *Awards:* Drama Desk Award, Say Good night Gracie. *Bibliog:* Article, Chicago Sun Times; article, Que Hacemos, Buenos Aires; Guerneri (film), The World of Jae, NY. *Mem:* Broadway League of Theater Producers; Newport Mus Art Asoc; Preserv Soc Newport, RI; Nat Mus Women in Arts; Metrop Opera Club. *Media:* Cast Bronze; Gold Silver, Gemstones. *Interests:* Opera, theatre, concerts & lectures; Dancing, tennis, exploring & traveling. *Publ:* Auth, article, Informacion, Alicanti, Spain; article, Costa Blanca News, Benedorm, Spain; Chicago Sun Times; Novidades, Mex. *Mailing Add:* 200 E 64th St New York NY 10021

JAEGER, BRENDA KAY
PAINTER, CRAFTSMAN
b Fairbanks, Alaska, July 20, 50. *Study:* Eastern Wash Univ, Spokane, Wash, BA, 72; Whitworth Col, Spokane, Wash, MAT, 76; research with Kohei Fukuda, Japan, 83, 84 & 89; Lower Columbia Col, Longview, Wash, cert Pulp & Paper Technol, 85; Wash State Univ, Vancouver, Master in Teaching, 96, K-8 cert, endorsements K-12 art, English, Japanese. *Work:* Alaskan State Coun Contemp Art Bank, Alyeska Pipeline Serv Co & Anchorage Mus Hist & Arts; Dean Witter Reynolds; Ketchikan Pioneers Home, Alaska; Standard Production Co. *Exhib:* The Cheney Cowles Mem Mus, Spokane, Wash; Handmade Paper Works, Anchorage Mus History & Art, Alaska, 79; Int Hand Papermakers Conf, Boston Sch Artisanry, Mass, 80, 8th Nevada Ann: Contemp Works of Paper, Sierra Nevada Mus Art, Reno, 81; 30th & 32nd Ann Southwest Washington Exhib, 83 & 85, State Capitol Mus, Olympia, Wash; Second Ann Patrons Watercolor Gala, Gallery of the Kresge Fine Art Ctr, Oklahoma City, 84; 45th Ann Exhib Northwest Watercolors, Bellevue Art Mus, Wash, 85; Ann Alaska Juried Watercolor Exhib, 90 & Winter Landscapes, 86, Anchorage Mus Hist & Art; Stonington Gallery, 86-92. *Pos:* Artist with studio, Brenda K Jaeger Art Studio, 78-. *Teaching:* Instr art, Whitworth Col, 74-75, Spokane Art Sch, 74-75, Art Arouse Prog, ESD 101, 74-75, Columbia Basin Col, 76-77 & Walla Walla Community Col, 76-77; vis artist, Wash State Cult Enrichment Prog, 75-76, 77-78; instr art, Univ Alaska, Anchorage, 78; pvt instr, 78-; artist-in-educ programs, Alaska, 85-, Utah, 88-92, Iowa, 88-90, Ore, 90-96, Auburn, Wash, 90-92; Lower Columbia Col, spring 87 & 88; Lower Kuskokwim Community Col, 88; Univ Alaska Southeast Islands Col, Petersburg, 90; head Art Dept, Pac Northern Acad, 96-. *Awards:* Best of Show, All Alaska Juried Watercolor exhib, 79, 81, 84 & 85; Best of Show, 32nd Ann Southwest Washington Exhib, 85; Allied Arts Juried Painting Show, 87; Eastern Wash Watercolor Soc Juried Competition, 83. *Bibliog:* Schiller (auth), The revolution in paper, Am Artist, 77; Beverly Plummer (auth), How does your garden grow, Fiberarts, 79. *Mem:* assoc Midwest Watercolor Soc; assoc Am Watercolor Soc; Northwest Watercolor Soc; assoc Nat Watercolor Soc. *Media:* Watercolor, Japanese Handmade Paper. *Publ:* Contribr, Flying Blind: Sunstruck at Merrill Field, & Breakfast, Vol VII, No 3, Calyx, summer 83; Shishaldinskaya, Northward J, Can, 83; illusr, Lake County Diamond, Tim Hunt (auth), Pope in Space, Barbara Blatner (auth) & 17 Toutle River Haiku, James Hanlen (auth), Intertext, 89; auth, Karasuyama Poems, Intertext, Anchorage, Alaska, 95; illusr, Lynx, 89 & 90. *Dealer:* White Bird Gallery Cannon Beach OR; Artique Ltd Anchorage AK. *Mailing Add:* Box 142252 Anchorage AK 99514

JAFFE, IRA S
EDUCATOR, CRITIC
b New York, NY, Aug 19, 43. *Study:* Columbia Univ, New York, AB, 64, MFA (cinema), 67; Univ SC, PhD (cinema), 75. *Pos:* Presidential lectr, Univ NMex, 84-86; dir, Int Cinema Lect Series & vpres Southwest Film Str, 88, head, Media Arts Prog, Univ NMex, 89. *Teaching:* Lectr cinema, Univ Southern Calif, Los Angeles, 70-72; assoc prof, Univ NMex, Albuquerque, 72-88, prof, 88-, chair dept media arts, 2001-03, assoc dean Col Fine Arts, 2001-02. *Mem:* Soc Cinema Studies; Univ Film and Video Asn. *Res:* Study of Charles Chaplin and Orson Welles; research centering on film theory and US Independent Cinema; women filmmakers in Third World cinemas. *Publ:* Auth, Film as the narration of space: Citizen Kane in Perspectives on Citizen Kane, GK Hall, NY, 96; Fighting Words: City Lights, Modern Times, The Great Dictator, Hollywood as Historian: Am Film in a Cultural Context, Univ Press, Ky, 83; Fool for love: the shifting frontier, Artspace, 86-87; co-ed, Women filmmakers and the politics of gender in third cinema, Univ Colo Press (for Frontiers: J Women Studies), 94; Redirecting the Gaze: Gender, Theory and Cinema in the Third World, State Univ NY Press, 99. *Mailing Add:* Col Fine Arts Univ NMex Albuquerque NM 87131

JAFFE, IRMA B
HISTORIAN, EDUCATOR
b New Orleans, La. *Study:* Columbia Univ, BS, MA, PhD. *Exhib:* Whitney Ann, Whitney Mus Am Art, 1964-1965; Conditional Commitment, Long Island Univ, 1966. *Pos:* Res cur, Whitney Mus Am Art, New York, 64-65; ed bd, Am Art J, currently; contrib ed, Art News. *Teaching:* Chmn dept art hist, Fordham Univ, 66-77, prof, 66-; prof art hist Fordham Univ, 66-87. *Awards:* Nat Endowment Humanities Fel, 73-74; Am Coun Learned Soc, 73 & 82; Award of Merit, Am Asn Mus, 84; Distinguished Serv Award, Fordham Univ, 86; Virgiliana Medal, Italian Encyclopedia Inst, 86; Knight in the Order of Merit of the Italian Republic; Ausonian Soc Cornaro Award. *Mem:* Col Art Asn Am; Am Studies Asn; Am-Italian Soc of Legions of Merit. *Res:* American art; Italian art and literature. *Interests:* Poetry, Italian Lit. *Publ:* Baroque Art: The Jesuit Contribution, 1970, John Trumbull. Patriot Artist of the Am Revolution, 1975; Coauth with Yvonne Korshak, Selections from the Permanent Collection of the Ark Art Center, 1983; ed, Paul Korshin, Ethics & Aesthetics in Eighteenth Century Am Art, 1986; Art of the Western World (chaps 6-9), 1989. *Mailing Add:* 880 Fifth Ave New York NY 10021

JAFREE See Geoffrey, Iqbal

JAGGER, GILLIAN
PAINTER, SCULPTOR
b London, Eng, Oct 27, 30. *Study:* Carnegie Inst Technol, BFA; Colorado Springs Fine Arts Ctr, with Vytlacil, scholar, 52; Univ Buffalo; Columbia Univ; NY Univ, MA. *Work:* Finch Col Mus, NY; Brompton's, Montreal, Que; Carnegie Inst, Pittsburgh. *Comn:* Portrait comns, 47-51. *Exhib:* Two-man & group shows, Loft Gallery, 55-57; one-man shows, Ruth White Gallery, NY, 61, 63 & 64; Finch Col Mus, 64; Lerner-Heller Gallery, 71, 73, 75 & 77; The Horse: Light & Motion, Lerner-Heller Gallery, NY, 75. *Pos:* Textile designer, Wamsutta Mills, Fruit of the Loom, 55-57. *Teaching:* Lectr art, Radio Free Europe, cols & prof art schs; instr painting, NY Univ, Post Col & New Rochelle Acad, formerly. *Awards:* Guggenheim Fel, 83. *Mailing Add:* Boice Mill Rd Kerhonkson NY 12446

JAIDINGER, JUDITH C CLARANN SZESKO
PRINTMAKER, PAINTER
b Chicago, Ill, Apr 10, 41. *Study:* Art Inst Chicago, BFA. *Work:* State Found Culture & Arts, Honolulu, Hawaii; Portland Art Mus, Ore; Ill State Mus, Springfield; Ashmolean Mus, Oxford, Eng; Kemper Group, Long Grove, Ill; Ukrainian Independent Contemp Art, USSR. *Comn:* Wood engraving, Face to Face, Ltd Ed, Penmaen/Busyhaus Publ, 85; wood engaving illustrations, comn by David R Godine, 2006. *Exhib:* West '79 The Law Exhib, Minn Mus Art; 3rd Int Biennial Print Exhib, Taipei Fine Arts Mus, Taiwan ROC, 87; Interprint '90, Int Print Exhib, LUIV Mus Hist of Religion & Atheism, Ukraine, USSR, 90; 23rd Bradley Univ Print & Drawing Exhib, Ill, 91; Wood Engraving Here & Now, Ashmolean Mus, Oxford, Eng, 95; San

Diego Art Inst, Calif, 92; Beyond Boundaries N Am Printmaking Exhib, Calif Soc Printmakers, Richmond, 97; Prints USA 2001, Springfield Art Mus, Mo, 01; Nat Printmaking 2001, Col of NJ, Ewing, 03; Solo exhib, How Well I Knew Her Not, Woodengravings Muskegon Mus Art, 2005-06. *Teaching:* Instr wood engraving, Office Field & Continuing Educ, Northeastern Ill Univ, 80-. *Awards:* Smithsonian Traveling Exhib Award, Contemp Am Drawings V, Norfolk Mus Arts & Sci, 71-74; Purchase Awards, Minot State Col, NDak, 70 & 77; Graphic Award, Int Competition Printmakers, Clary-Miner Gallery, Buffalo, NY. *Mem:* Soc Am Graphic Artists, NY; Soc Wood Engravers, Gt Brit; fel, Royal Soc Painter Printmakers Eng; Boston Printmakers Mass. *Media:* Wood Engraving; Opaque Watercolor, Mixed Media. *Publ:* Engravers Two, Silent Bks, Cambridge, Eng, 92; Endgrain: Contemporary Wood Engraving in North Am, 94; An Engraver's Globe, 02; Lancelot and the Lord of the Distant Isles, 2006; The Tale of Galehaut Retold, 2006. *Mailing Add:* 6110 N Newburg Ave Chicago IL 60631

JAKUB, JEFFREY ANDREW
PAINTER, ILLUSTRATOR
b Rahway, NJ, Mar 29, 43. *Study:* Newark Sch Fine & Indust Art, AA, 1963. *Work:* Newark Mus of Art, Newark, NJ; Greenville Mus of Art, Greenville, NC; Mary Kay Cosmetics Corp Hq, Dallas, Tex; The Palm Beach Co, NY; First South Bank Collection, 9 cities, NC. *Comn:* Peach Floral Painting, Rosalynn Carter, Whitehouse, Washington, DC, 1980; Grant: Sculpture/painting, NC State Beaufort Col, Washington, NC, 1996; Rural Churches Eastern NC, NC Coun for the Arts, Raleigh, NC, 1997; Paintings for Capitol Bldg, state Sen Marc Basnight, Raleigh, NC, 2003; Hackney Corp, Hodges Hackney, Washington, NC, 2006. *Exhib:* Dimensions Nat Exhib, Sawtooth Galleries, Winston Salem, NC, 2001-2004; Watercolor Soc NC, Artsspace Bank of Arts, Salem Col Raleigh, Winston Salem, NC, 2001-2005; Adirondack Int Exhib, Old Forge Arts Center, Old Forge, NY, 2004; Raleigh Soc Arts - Int, Meredith Col, Raleigh, NC, 2004; Am Watercolor Soc 139th Int, Salmagundi Club, NY, 2006. *Pos:* Pres & CEO, Jeff Jakub Design Hillsborough, NJ, 1973-; Exec Art & Advert Dir, Roots of Summit, NJ, 1963-1973; Creative Dir, WT Quinn Advert Agency, Somerset, NJ, 1983-1986. *Teaching:* Instr, advert, illus, life drawing, Spectrum Inst of Advert Arts, NJ, 1982-1984; instr, workshops, Boca Raton, Fla, Elizabeth City, NC, Balto, Md, 1984-2006; instr, oil, watercolor, Beaufort /Pittsburg Community Cols, 1986-1999. *Awards:* 57th Juried Edhib, Watercolor Soc NC, 2003; Second place, 59th Juried Exhibition, Watercolor Soc, NC, 2005; Nell Storer, 139th Int Awards, Am Watercolor Soc, 2006. *Bibliog:* Jakub Wins Triple Crown, Raleigh News & Observer, 1997; John Underwood (auth), He Paints Like a Native, Washington Daily News, 1997; Al Critcher (auth), Immortalized Artist Capture, Williamston Enterprise, 1999. *Mem:* Beaufort Co Arts Coun (pres), Washington, NC, 1994-1996; Watercolor Soc NC (signature mem, E Regional Chair), 2005-; Greenville Brushstrokes (nom pres), Greenville, NC, 2006-; Am Watercolor Soc; Assoc Artists Winston Salem, NC; Nat Watercolor Soc; Allied Artists Am; Southern Watercolor Soc. *Media:* Watercolor, Oil, Pen/Ink, Pastel, Charcoal. *Interests:* Interior Design, Fashion Design, Opera. *Dealer:* Riverwalk Gallery 139 W Main St Washington NC 27889; River Street Gallery 207 E River St Savannah GA 31401. *Mailing Add:* 104 Forecastle Ct Washington NC 27889

JALAPEENO, JIMMY (ALBERT) J BONAR
PAINTER, PHOTOGRAPHER
b Bryan, Tex, Jan 5, 47. *Study:* Univ Houston, 64-66; Univ Tex Austin, BFA(painting & photog), 66-69, Russell Lee's asst, 67-68; Univ Calif Davis, MFA(painting & photog), 71-73. *Work:* Towne Club, Dallas; MBank Austin; 3M Corp; Watson & Casey Co; Tex Com Bancshares; and others. *Comn:* Pub art piece, Robert Mueller Airport, Austin, 87-91. *Exhib:* Solo shows, Bois d'Arc Gallery, Austin, 80, Hadler-Rodriguez Gallery, Houston, 83 & 86 & Air Gallery, Austin, 85 & 88, Laguna Gloria Mus, Austin, 87 & Lyons Matrix Gallery, Austin, 94; My Blue Heaven, Tex Fine Arts Asn, 92; Young Tex Artists Series Reunion Exhib, Amarillo Art Ctr, 93; Austin Visual Arts Asn, 93; Small Works, Trax, Austin, 94. *Pos:* Photogr, Tex Hist Comn, Austin, 74-. *Teaching:* Lectr basic drawing, Univ Houston Art Dept, 73-74. *Awards:* Nat Endowment Arts Fel, 80 & 89. *Bibliog:* Photo portfolio, Riata Mag, 69; drawing portfolio, Calif Quart Mag, spring & fall 72; article, Tex Homes, 1/83. *Mailing Add:* PO Box 12304 Austin TX 78711

JAMES, A EVERETTE, JR
PATRON, WRITER
b Oxford, NC, Aug 22, 38. *Study:* Univ NC, AB, 59; Duke Univ Sch Medicine, MD, 63; Harvard Medical Sch; 66-69; Johns Hopkins, ScD, 71; Harvard Business Sch, 79; Royal Soc Med, London, 74. *Work:* Asheville Art Mus; US Embassies; Greenville Art Mus; Kenan Inst; John Hope Franklin Ctr, Duke Univ; Ctr for Honors, UNC; Boston Anthaneum; Cosmos Club; Mint Mus; Duke Univ; John Hopkins, Hickory Mus; Chickwood, Ctr for Study of the Am South, Greensboro Col; Martin Co Courthouse; Morris Mus; and others. *Exhib:* Southern Folk Art, 94-95; Antique Decoys, 94-95; NC Pottery, 94-95; NC Quilts, 97-98; Southern Women Artists (1840-1940), 98; NC Painters (1850-1950), 98; Southern Painters (1840-1940), 98-99; Southern Art, Huntsville Art, Mobile, Ala, 2003; African American Images, Nat Civil Rights Inst. *Collection Arranged:* The Ahls: An American Art Family (auth, catalog), 80-83; Spectrum of Portraiture, 82; James Collection, 83 & The American Scene, 83, University Club, Nashville; Eugene Healon Thomason Retrospective (catalog), 85; Royster Collection (catalog), 86; Pattie Royster James Collection, 87; Indiana Impressionism (catalog), 89; Collection Antique Waterfowl Decoys (with catalog), Tenn State Mus, 90; Tonalism and Nocturnes (catalog), 91; James Collection, 92 & Works on Paper, Cosmos Club, 93; The South (1840-1940), Knoxville Mus Art, Tenn, 92; Radiography & Art, New York, Washington, DC, London, Paris, Atlanta & Boston, 88-96; Southern Folk Art, Sawtooth Ctr, Winston-Salem, NC; Folk Art, Fine Arts Mus South, Mobile, Ala; Folk Art, Fisk Univ, Fayetteville State Univ, Elizabeth City State Univ & Nat Civil Rights Mus, Memphis, 94-98; Quilts, Ward Mus & Chapel Hill Mus, 98-99; Women Art of South, SC; Wesleyan, Merith, Asheville Art Mus; The South (1840-1940) Huntsville Art Mus, 2004; Hickory Art Mus, 2005; African Am Quilts, NC Farm Mus, Lucy Craft Ctr, 2005; and others. *Pos:* Ed, J Art Med; treas, bd mem, Int Soc Art Med; art comt, Cosmos Club; bd Am Visionary Art Mus; guest cur, Chapel Hill Mus Art,1999-2000, NC Pottery Mus, 2005-06. *Teaching:* Lectr Am Impressionism, Woman's Club, Centennial Club & Dixon Gallery, Memphis, Tenn, 81; instr, Philadelphia Antiques Show & Ark Art Coun, 86; African-Am Folk Tradition, Fisk Univ, 92; Elizabeth City State Univ, Women Artists (1840-1940), Chapel Hill, 98; Women's Studies UHC, 2003; John Hope Franklin Ctr, 2004; Morris Mus Art, 2005; AM Soc Ceramics, New York City, 2005; Miss Univ, 2005. *Awards:* Distinguished Med Alumnus, Duke Univ, 92; Carraway Award, Preservation NC, 94; Humanitarian Award, Duke Univ, 2003; Gold Medal, Am Roentgen Ray Soc, 03. *Bibliog:* Collections of Paintings in Hospitals, Int J Art in Med, 94; James Collection of Southern Folk Art, Ala Arts Coun, 94; Paintings in Hospitals, Royal Soc Medicine; Monograph African Am Quilts, 2004. *Mem:* Nat Trust Historic Preserv; Soc Preservation Tenn Antiquities; Explorer's Club; Cosmos Club; Alpha Omega Alpha. *Res:* Use of imaging techniques to evaluate paintings; visual physiology and art. *Interests:* Am Art, 1865-1940. *Collection:* American impressionism; American landscape; Antique Decoys, NC Pottery, Southern Folk Art; The South 1840-1940; NC Quilts; African-Am Quilts. *Publ:* Coauth, Digital Radiography; A Focus on Clinical Unity, 82; Certain radiographic techniques to evaluate paintings, Am J Roentgenology, 83; Digital radiography in the analysis of paintings, a new and promising technique, J Am Inst Consev, 83; auth, An introduction to Eugene Healan Thomason: The 'Ashcan Artist' who came to the mountains, Appalachian J, 83; Investing in American Impressionism, MD Mag, 83; Not every canvas is down for the count, Med Econ, 84; A physician's opportunity to contribute to the arts, The Pharos of Alpha Omega Alpha, summer 85; American Art: Thoughts of a Collector, 94; Essays in Folk Art, 01; North Carolina Art Pottery (1900-1960), 2003; Collecting Am Paintings, 2005. *Dealer:* Vose Gallery Newbury St Boston MA; Knoke Galleries Atlanta Ga; Foothills Gallery, Tryon NC. *Mailing Add:* 205 New Castle Pl Chapel Hill NC 27514

JAMES, ALFRED EVERETT
PAINTER, PHOTOGRAPHER
Study: RI Sch Design, BFA, 30; studied at Thurn Sch Mod Art & Hoffman Sch Mod Art. *Exhib:* Younger RI Artist Exhib, Vose Galleries, Providence, 29; Ann Exhib, Providence Art Club, RI, 29; Ann Ala Art League, Montgomery Mus Fine Arts, 40-80; Ann Army Exhib, W Palm Beach Mus, 43; 4th Ann Art Exhib, High Mus Art, Atlanta, 50; Ann Columbus Art Guild, Columbus Col, Ga, 82-98; Ann Columbus Mus Art Guild, Ga, 97. *Teaching:* Instr oil painting, Auburn Univ, Ga, 37-46 & Gallops Sr Ctr, Ga, 84-98. *Awards:* Ala Art League Purchase Award, Loveman, Joseph & Loeb, 50 & 53; Mary Houghton Mem Award, Ala Art League, 56. *Mem:* Columbus Artists Guild; Columbus Mus Guild. *Media:* Oil on Canvas. *Mailing Add:* 2406 Camille Dr Columbus GA 31906

JAMES, BILL (WILLIAM) FREDERICK
PAINTER, ILLUSTRATOR
b Manchester, Conn, Oct 7, 43. *Study:* Syracuse Univ, BFA, 65. *Work:* Dept Commerce, Montgomery, Ala; Panasonic, Japan; Business Weekly, NY; McGraw-Hill Pubs, NY. *Comn:* Mag illus, Tennis Mag, 91; mag & poster illus, Alfa Romeo, 91; mag illus, Golf Illus, 92; video illus, Rabbit Ears Productions, 92; card illus, NBA, 92; calendar, Panasonic, 95; 2 paintings, Fox News, 2005. *Exhib:* Knock'n on Heaven's Door, Am Watercolor Soc, 2003; Under Duress, Pastel Soc Am, 2003; Cornucopia Ballerinas, Natl Watercolor Soc, 2004; Cornucopia Ballerinas, Am Watercolor Soc, 2006; Been There-Done That, Pastel Soc Am, 2006. *Awards:* Silver Metal Award, Pastel Soc, Am, 93; Silver Metal Award, Am Watercolor Soc, 2001; Borse Miller Mem Award, Am Watercolor Soc, 2006; Maureen Bloomfield, Watercolor Masters, 11/2002. *Bibliog:* Jennifer King, Int Artist Mag, 1-12/2001; Maureen Bloomfield, The Pastel Journal, Oct 2004. *Mem:* Pastel Soc Am; Am Watercolor Soc; Nat Watercolor Soc; Knickerbocker Artists. *Media:* Pastel, Watercolor; Oil. *Publ:* Int Artist Mag, 12-01/01; Watercolor Magic Mag, 11/2003; Pastel Jour, 10/2004. *Dealer:* Telluride Gallery of Fine Art 130 E Colorado Box 1900 Telluride CO; Broden Gallery Ltd 218 N Henry St Madison WI; Art 4 Business, 161 Leverington Ave, Philadelphia, PA; Coconut Grove Gallery 2790 Bird Ave Coconut Grove FL. *Mailing Add:* 509 NW 35th St Ocala FL 34475

JAMES, CATTI
SCULPTOR, CONSULTANT
b Mount Vernon, NY, Oct 8, 40. *Study:* Boston Univ, BFA; Columbia Univ, MA. *Work:* Harlem Art Collection; Indianapolis Mus Art; NY State Art Collection; Govt Ctr, Plattsburgh, NY; Primary Indust, NY. *Comn:* Mural, Sepia Enterprises, Toledo, 72; costume design, Harry Belafonte Tour, 74 & Walter Nicks Dance Theater & Repertory Co, 74; cover design & book layout, Nat Bd, YWCA, 77; cover design, Girls Clubs Am, 78; cover design & book layout, Nat Bd, YWCA, 79; Environmental Design BAY STREET, Sag Harbor, NY; Installation, Collaboration with Betsy Damon, UN Decade of Women, Univ of Nairobi; Still Photography, GENERATIONS, (film) Girls Clubs of AM. *Exhib:* Contemp Black Artists in Am, 71 & Whitney Ann, Whitney Mus Am Art, 72; Wild Art Show, PS1, NY, 82; Ritual & Rhythm, Kenkeleba House Gallery, NY, 82; Collage & Assemblage, Gallery Hastings, Hastings-on-Hudson, NY, 83; Exchange of Sources: Expanding Powers, Calif State Stanislaus, Turlock, 83; Artists of the 80s, Los Angeles Co Fair, Pomona, 83; Solo Vertibrae, Wilma Jenanings Gallery, New York City; Mixed Media Constructions, Retrospective, Franklin Marshall Col, PA. *Teaching:* Art consult, Wiltwyck Sch Boys, 68-70 & Graham Sch, currently; instr anat, Col New Rochelle, 72; lectr African art & workshops on African design; Assoc Prof & Dir of Grad Art Ed Prog CCNY, New

York City; Teaching Artist, MOMA, New York City; Adj Prof, Hofsra Univ, New York City. *Awards:* Creative Artists Coun Grant in Painting, NY State Coun Arts, 71; PSC/CUNY Research Award; NEA-Visiting Artist Award; UN Decade of Women Womens Caucus for Arts, Naibroi Kenya; NYS Council on the Arts. *Bibliog:* Black artists in America (slides), Univ SAla & H Kress Found; Robert Doty (auth), Contemporary Black Artists in America. *Mem:* Am Crafts Coun; Univ Council on Art Education; Entitled; Black Women Artists; Inter Sculpture Ctr; Prof Staff Congress/CUNY. *Media:* Wood, sheet acrylic, hardware, fiber, and found materials. *Publ:* Auth, three articles in Arts & Activities Mag, 67-70; auth, A Black perspective on art, Black Enterprise Mag, 75. *Dealer:* Allan Stone Gallery 48 E 86th St New York NY 10028; Merton D Simpson Gallery 1063 Madison Ave New York NY 10028; Merton D. Simpson Gallery, 38 W 28th St NYC, 10001. *Mailing Add:* 6 Fulton St Hastings-on-Hudson NY 10706

JAMES, CHRISTOPHER P
PHOTOGRAPHER, PAINTER
b Boston, Mass, May 8, 47. *Study:* Cummington Community Arts, 68; Mass Col Art, BFA, 69; RI Sch of Design, MAT, 71. *Work:* Mus Mod Art, NY; Int Mus Photog, George Eastman House, Rochester, NY; Metrop Mus Art, NY; Boston Mus Fine Arts, Mass; Minneapolis Inst Arts Mus; and others. *Comn:* Subway steel enamel panels, Cambridge Arts Coun, 80. *Exhib:* One-man shows, Minneapolis Inst Arts, 77, Int Mus Photog, George Eastman House, 77, Centre d'Art Contemporain, Geneva, 79, Univ Ore Mus Art, 80, Witkin Gallery, NY, 81, 83, 85, 87 & 90; Weston Gallery, Carmel, Calif, 84, 86, 89 & 91, & Lizardi Harp Gallery, Pasadena, Calif, 87, 88 & 90; Mirrors and Windows, Mus Mod Art, NY, 78; Counterparts, Metrop Mus Art, NY, 82; and other one-man shows. *Teaching:* Asst prof photog & design, Greenfield Community Col, 71-78; artist-in-residence, Keene State Col, 77-78; lectr, Mass Inst Technol, Philadelphia Col Art, Univ Ore, Parsons Sch Design & RI Sch Design; instr, Chulalongkorn Univ, Bangkok, Thailand & Rencontres Internationales De La Photographie, Arles; prof, Harvard Univ, 78-91, Art Inst Boston, 91-. *Awards:* Daguerre, Niepce Medal, Phot-Univers USA/USSR, Minister of Foreign Affairs, Paris, 76; Mass Arts Found Fel, 78. *Bibliog:* Hilton Kramer (auth), New York Review, Esman, New York Times, 9/23/77; David Bourdon (auth), New York Review, Esman, Village Voice, 10/10/77; John Russell (auth), New York Review, Witkin, New York Times, 10/21/83. *Mem:* Soc Photog Educ. *Media:* Photo; Watercolor. *Publ:* Contribr, Alternative Photographic Process, Morgan & Morgan, 78; portfolio, Popular Photography, NY, 79; portfolio, American Photographer, NY, 79; cover & portfolio, Camera, Suisse, 4/79. *Dealer:* Witkin Gallery New York NY; Lizardi/Harp Los Angeles CA. *Mailing Add:* c/o Art Inst of Boston 700 Beacon St Boston MA 02215-2598

JAMISON, PHILIP
PAINTER
b Philadelphia, Pa, July 3, 25. *Study:* Philadelphia Mus Sch Art, 50. *Work:* Pa Acad Fine Arts, Philadelphia; Wilmington Soc Fine Arts, Del; Nat Acad Design, NY; Flint Inst Art, Mich; Frye Art Mus, Seattle, Wash; Nat Air & Space Mus, Washington, DC; Brandywine River Mus, Pa. *Comn:* NASA Artist for Apollo-Soyuz Space Launch, 75, Space Shuttle Mission 51-G, 85. *Exhib:* solo exhibs, Hirschl & Adler Galleries, NY, 59-80, Delaware Art Mus, 73, Janet Fleisher Gallery, Philadelphia, 77, Newman Galleries, Philadelphia, 82, 84, 86, 90 & 93, Ruthven Gallery, Lancaster, Ohio, 86 & Patricia Carega Gallery, Washington, DC, 85 & 87, Hahn Gallery, Philadelphia, 93, 98 & 2002; 200 Yrs of Watercolor Painting in Am, Metrop Mus Art, NY, 67; Chester Co Hist Soc, 1999; and others. *Pos:* Artist, Apollo Soyuz Space Launch, Kennedy Space Ctr, Fla, Nat Aeronautics & Space Admin, 75. *Teaching:* Instr watercolor, Philadelphia Col Art, 61-63. *Awards:* Dana Medal, Pa Acad Fine Arts, 61; Gold Medal of Honor, Allied Artists Am, 64; Nat Acad Design Prize, 67; Recipient Dawson medal Pa Acad Fine Arts, 1959, 77, Dana medal, 1961, first award Nat Arts Club, New York City, 1961; Dana medal, 1961, first award National Arts Club, New York City, 1961; Lena A Mason prize Nat Acad of Design, 1962; Samuel Finley Breese Morse medal Nat Acad of Design, 1969; Walter Biggs Mem award Nat Acad of Design, 1982; William Church Osborn prize Am Watercolor Soc, 1961, 79; medal of Honor Knickerbocker Artists, New York City, 1961; Bainbridge award Allied Artists Am, 1958, 60; first prize Wilmington Society Fine Arts, 1957, 59, 61; MW Zimmerman Mem prize Philadelphia Watercolor Club, 1963; Gold medal honor Allied Artists Am, 1964; Childe Hassam Fund purchase prize Am Acad of Arts and Letters, 1965; CFS award, 1966; Edgar A Whitney award, 1971; High Winds award, 1972; Whitney award, 1973; Ted Kautzky Memorial award, 1974; Ranger Fund purchase prize Nat Acad of Design, 1962, prize, 1967; Alfred Easton Poor award, 1999; Zella W Pine award, 2003; Pike prize, 2003; Adolph and Clara Obrig award, 1974; Thornton Oakley Memorial prize Philadelphia Watercolor Club, 1967; Gold medal Franklin Mint Gallery Am Art, 1974, Merit award Nat Watercolor Exhib, Springfield (Ill) Art Asn, 1979. *Mem:* Am Watercolor Soc; Philadelphia Watercolor Club; Nat Acad Design. *Media:* Watercolor, Oil. *Specialty:* Fine Arts. *Collection:* Pa Acad of Fine Arts, Boston Mus of Art, Brandywine River Ms, The Fine Arts Mus of San Francisco, Nat Acad of Design, NYC. *Publ:* Contribr, Am Artist Mag, 62; auth, Capturing Nature in Watercolor, 80; Making Your Paintings Work, Watson-Guptill, 84; A Painting Without Spirit is Like Flat Beer, pvt publ, 88; publ, I Hate People Who Refer to Works of Art As Pieces, 95. *Dealer:* Newman and Saunders Galleries 120 Bloomingdale Ave Wayne Pa 19087

JANIS, CONRAD
DEALER, COLLECTOR
b New York, NY, Feb 11, 28. *Collection Arranged:* Participated in arranging all exhibitions at Sidney Janis Gallery from New Realism, 62 through Sharp Focus Realism, 72; and others. *Pos:* Co-owner, Sidney Janis Gallery. *Specialty:* All historic movements in 20th century art to the present. *Collection:* Contemporary American art

JANJIGIAN, LUCY ELIZABETH
PAINTER, MURALIST
b Jerusalem, Palestine, Dec 14, 32; US citizen. *Study:* Heidelberg Col, Tiffin, Ohio, BA, 55; Emory Univ, Atlanta, Ga, MS, 56; Art Students League, with Robert Hale, 70, Fogerty, 71 & Glasier, 72; study with Victor D'Amico, 72-74; Stacy Wkshp Studio, New York, NY, 74-. *Work:* Am Cyanamid Hq, Wayne, NJ; Berliner Handels & Frankfurter Bank, NY; Mekhitarist Mus, Vienna, Austria; Gallery Phillip, Toronto; Arab Bank, NY. *Comn:* Two acrylic murals, St Leon's Church, Fairlawn, NJ, 81; acrylic mural, Armenian Evangelical Union of NAm, Los Angeles, Calif, 85; acrylic mural, Armenian Missionary Asn, Paramus, NJ, 87; Christmas cards & Christmas stamps-American Evangelical Church, NY, 87 & 89. *Exhib:* Passaic Co Community Col, NJ, 88; Convention Hall Philadelphia PA, 89; Capital Place Gallery, Trenton NJ; Heidelberg Col, Tiffin, Ohio, 90; Am Libr Mus Am Inc, Watertown, Mass, 92; one-person show, Presby Publ Corp, Louisville, Ky, 94; and others. *Pos:* Mem art comt, Armenian Gen Benevolet Union, Saddle Brook, NJ, 79-; bd trustees, Bergen Mus Arts & Sci, Paramus NJ, 84-90 & Artists for Mental Health, Paterson, NJ, currently. *Awards:* Hon Mention, Bergen Co Artists, 70; Hon Mention, Franklin Lakes Art Show, 72; First Place Acrylic Abstract, Gregg Galleries-Nat Arts Club, 81. *Bibliog:* Hope Noah (auth), article, Weekend Times, NJ, 8/88; Sean Siman (auth), The painterly conscience of Lucy Janjigian, Artspeak, 12/1/88; Nancy Kleinhenz (ed), Portraits of Inhumanity - The Advertizer Tribune, Tiffin OH, 10/2/90. *Mem:* Cath Artists of the 80's; Composers, Authors & Artists of Am; Burr Artists; Nat League Pen Women; Westside Arts Coalition & NY Artists Equity Asn Inc, NY. *Media:* Acrylic. *Mailing Add:* 268 Edgewood Rd Franklin Lakes NJ 97417-2007

JANKOWSKI, THEODORE ANDREW
PAINTER, MURALIST
b New Brunswick, NJ, Dec 14, 46. *Study:* Rhode Island Sch Design, 71; Cape Sch Art, 71-73, 80-86. *Work:* State Mus Reserve of Palace of Peter the Great, Leningrad, USSR; Hiroshima Peace Mem Mus, Hiroshima, Japan; Cigna Mus Art Collection, Philadelphia, Pa; Johns Hopkins Evergreen House Perm Collection, Baltimore, Md; Provincetown Art Asn Mus, Mass; Yad Vashem Holocaust Mus, Jerusalem. *Exhib:* Hensche & Friends, Michael Ingbar Gallery, NY, 88; Provincetown Mus, Mass, 93; State of the Art, Boston, Mass, 93. *Media:* Oil. *Dealer:* Green Flash Gallery Kawaehae Hawaii. *Mailing Add:* PO Box 791 Kapaau HI 96755

JANNETTI, TONY
PRINTMAKER, DESIGNER
b Yonkers, NY, May 27, 1947. *Study:* Pratt Inst, BFA, 69. *Work:* Mus Mod Art, NY; Yale Univ Art Gallery, New Haven; Philip Morris Collection, NY; IBM Collection, New York, Dallas, Hartford; Chase Manhattan Bank, NY; Zimmerli Mus, New Brunswick, NJ; and others. *Comn:* Rahini II, Edward Durrell Stone Asn, NY, 80. *Exhib:* Resurrection Show, 55 Mercer St Gallery, NY; Nimbus Gallery, Dallas, Tex, 83-85; Relief Painting in the 80s, Zimmerli Mus, 88; Marcus-Gordon Gallery, 89; invitational, Artists Space, 94. *Pos:* Creative consult, Fiji Co, 72-81; founder, Media Wall Design, 88. *Teaching:* Instr, Fordham Univ, 83-84. *Publ:* Auth, articles in Artforum, 9/81 & 9/86, New York Art Review, 88 & J of the Printworld, 92. *Mailing Add:* Bowery Studios 261 Bowery New York NY 10002-1201

JANNEY, CHRISTOPHER DRAPER
ENVIRONMENTAL ARTIST, DESIGNER
b Washington, DC, Mar 14, 50. *Study:* Princeton Univ, with Michael Graves & James Seawright, BA(archit, visual arts), 73; Mass Inst Technol, with O Piene, MS(environ art), 78. *Work:* Smithsonian Inst; Miami Art in Pub Places Trust; NationsBank Collection, Sacramento Metrop Art Comn; San Antonio Arts Comn, NY Metrop Transit Auth. *Comn:* REACH-NY, 96; Rainbow Pass, Coral Gables, Fla; Harmonic Runway, Miami Airport, 95; and others. *Exhib:* Soundstair, Boston Mus Fine Arts, 79, Walker Art Ctr, 80, Nat Gallery Art, 80, Corcoran Gallery Art, 80, Second Int Electronic Music Conf, Brussels, Belg, 81 & Santa Barbara Mus Art, Calif, 82; Sonic Pass, Miss Mus Art, Jackson, 81; Wall-to-Wall John Cage, Symphony Space, NY, 82; Inside Rhythms, Inst Contemp Art, Boston, 83; Steamshuffle (with catalog), Pub Art in Am, Philadelphia, Pa, 87; Heartbeat:mb, with M Baryshnikov, City Ctr, NY, 98. *Pos:* Res fel, Ctr Advan Visual Studies, Mass Inst Technol, 1978-92; chmn, Inst for Performance Sculpture Inc, 1987; coun mem, CEIS, Fulbright Found, 1995-. *Teaching:* Instr, Mass Col Art, 1984-85 & State Univ NY, Purchase, 1987; vis prof, Cooper Union Sch Archit, New York, RI Sch Design, 1995. *Awards:* Nat Endowment Arts Grant, 91; Mass Coun Grant, 91; New England Found Grant, 92. *Bibliog:* Daria Sommers (auth), The Elephant on the Hill (film), Smithsonian World, PBS, 6/86; Andy Scheleucan (auth), Studio 7 (film), WNEV-TV; Martha Teishner (auth), An Ear for Art, CBS This Morning, WCBS-TV, 95. *Media:* Sound, Electronics. *Publ:* Articles in The New York Times, 10/84 & 9/86 and People Mag, 10/79; Sand and communication, 4/94; Light Waves, Cover/Feature, Archit Record, 11/95. *Mailing Add:* 75 Kendall Rd Lexington MA 02173

JANNICELLI, MATTEO
PAINTER, PHOTOGRAPHER
b Newark, NJ, Aug 26, 35. *Study:* Montclair Art Mus, 61; study with Michael Lenson, 61-62; Kean Univ, BA(fine art), 76; Private Lessons with Vincent Nardone. *Work:* Hoffman LaRoche Pharmaceutical Corp, Nutley-Clifton, NJ; Munic of Bloomfield, NJ; Newark Pub Libr, NJ; Atlantic City Art Ctr, NJ; Micro Industrial Corp, Bayville, NJ; Kean Univ Mus Permanent Collection. *Comn:* Roman Antiquities (mural), Three Brothers Italian Restaurant, Old Bridge, NJ, 83-84. *Exhib:* NJ 28th Water Color Show, Morris Mus Arts & Sci, Morristown, NJ, 70; Am Art at Mid Century, Northfield YMHA, West Orange, NJ, 74; Jersey Five, Ocean Co Col, Toms River, NJ, 98; Jersey Five, Bay Head, NJ, 99; Brick 2000 Cult Arts Ctr, 2000; One man show, Anchor & Palette Gallery, Bay Head, NJ, 2004; Display Yarn Paintings, Georgian Court Univ,

Lakewood, NJ, 2001; Juried shows, Audubon Artist Art Soc, 2000-2006, TV Art Auction, Rosehill Auction Gallery, Englewood, NJ, 2006; Fabrick Show, Beyond the Stitch II, Artist Guild, Ocean Co, NJ, 2006. *Pos:* Pres, Bloomfield Art League, 70-73; vpres, Federated Art Asn NJ, 71-72; pres, Manasquan River Art Group, 1988-1991. *Teaching:* Instr watercolor, Newark Sch Fine & Indust Art, 70-75; instr painting, Artist & Craftsman Guild, Cranford, NJ, 72-73; instr graphics/printmaking, Annex Sch Art, Montclair, NJ, 72-73. *Awards:* Mixed Media Award, 24th Annual Sr Citizens State Show, 2000; Award, Ocean Co Senior's Art Show, 02; Diane B Bernhard Award for Merit, Audubon Artists 62nd Annual Nat Art Spirit Found, 2004. *Bibliog:* Ruth Ann Williams (auth), Graven images-featured artist, NJ Music & Arts Mag, 74; Esther Forman Singer (auth), The art part, Worrel Publ Surban News, 76; The Ocean Star Newspaper, 10/1/99; Encyclopedia Am Painters, Sculptors & Engravers of the US Colonial, 2002. *Mem:* Ocean Co Camera Club; Ocean Co Artist Guild; Manasquan River Group Artists (pres, 88-91); Audobon Artists; Allied Artists; Atlantic City Art Center. *Media:* Mixed Media, Sculptor, Graphic Arts, Fabric Collage. *Collection:* Ocean Co Col, NJ, 02; Carl Burger, sculpture, Nightmare; Dick LaBonte, drawing, Nude Study; Rhoda Yanow, drawing, Nude Study; Bill Nagengast Family, drawing, Landscape. *Publ:* illusr, Jersey Five, 99. *Dealer:* Ann LaBonte Neff 45 Mount St Bayhead NJ 08742; Anchor & Palette Gallery; Tycoon Art Gallery Manasquan NJ. *Mailing Add:* 257 McGuire Blvd Brick NJ 08724

JANOWICH, RONALD
PAINTER
b Baltimore, Md, 48. *Study:* Col Art Md Inst, BFA, 70, MFA, 72. *Work:* Metrop Mus Art, NY; Aldrich Mus Contemp Art, Ridgefield, Conn; Bank of Boston; Cleveland Mus Art, Ohio; Tate Gallery, London, Eng; and others. *Exhib:* The 1980's: A New Generation, Metrop Mus Art, NY, 88; solo exhibs, Galerie Malmgran, Goteburg, Sweden, 90, Galleri JMS, Oslo, Norway, 90, Monotypes 1989-90 (with catalog), Gallery Kuranuki, Osaka, Japan, 90, Compasse Rose Gallery, Chicago, Ill, 91, Galerie Lelong (with catalog), Paris, France, 91 & Pamela Auchincloss Gallery, NY, 92 & 94; Painting, 91 & Transcendence & Immanence, 92, Galerie Lelong, NY; Collaborations in Monotype from the Garner Tullis Workshop, Sert Gallery, Carpenter Ctr Visual Arts, 92; Inaugural Exhib, Tennisport Arts, Long Island City, NY, 92; Lillian Heidenberg Gallery, NY, 93; Shape, Pamela Auchincloss Gallery, NY, 94; After the Fall, Aspects of Abstract Painting 1970-Present, Newhouse Ctr Contemp Art & Snug Harbor Cult Ctr, NY, 97; and many others. *Collection Arranged:* Metrop Mus Art; Tate Gallery, London; Cleveland Mus Art; numerous pvt collections. *Teaching:* Assoc prof painting, drawing, 2 & 3-D design, printmaking & independent study, Lafayette Col, Pa, 80-85; drawing, Parsons Sch Design, NY, 84; vis artist, Prog Painting, Kent State Univ, Ohio, 92 & 96, Cleveland Inst, Ohio, 93 & 96, undergrad, grad painting & advanced drawing, Grad Seminar, Ohio State Univ, 96, undergrad & grad painting, Photo Seminar, Univ Fla, 96-98; vis asst prof, painting and drawing, Fla State Univ, 98-. *Awards:* Nat Endowment Arts Fel, 76, 89. *Bibliog:* Margaret Moorman (auth), Painting, ARTnews, 134, 11/91; David Carrier (auth), rev, Tema Celeste, 87-89, spring, 93; Vivian Raynor, Geometry now, NY Times, 10/24/97; and others. *Media:* Oil. *Publ:* Auth, On Horizontality: A Structural Approach, 82; Brice Marden at Pace, Art Gallery Rev, Fall 82; Contemp Abstract Painting (exhib catalog), Muhlenberg Col, Allentown, Pa, 83; Small Works: New Abstract Painting (exhib catalog), Lafayette & Muhlenberg Cols, 84; Black Oil: Aspects of Dimensionality, J Artists, No 6, spring 86; and others. *Dealer:* Pamela Auchincloss Gallery 601 W 26th St 12th Floor New York NY 10001. *Mailing Add:* 302 FAC PO Box 115801 Gainesville FL 32611-5801

JANOWITZ, JOEL
PAINTER
b Newark, NJ, Nov 29, 45. *Study:* Brandeis Univ, BA, 67; Univ Calif, Santa Barbara, MFA, 69. *Work:* Mus Fine Arts, Boston; Fogg Mus; Harvard Univ; Rose Art Mus; Brandets U, Waltham, Mass; Whitney Mus, Metrop Mus, Brooklyn Mus, Minneapolis Inst of Arts. *Comn:* Mural, Alewife Subway Sta, Mass Bay Transportation Authority, Cambridge, 85. *Exhib:* Whitney Biennial, Whitney Mus Am Art, NY, 73; Boston Watercolor Today, 76, A Private Vision: Contemp Art from the Graham Gund Collection, 83 & Recent Paintings and Sculpture 1944-1984, 85, Mus Fine Arts, Boston, Mass; Hassam Fund Purchase Exhib, Am Acad & Inst Arts & Lett, NY, 80 & 87; solo shows, Munroe, NY, 83, 86, 88 & 92, Bernard Toale Gallery, Boston, 87 & 98, Clark Gallery, Lincon, Mass, 2002; Herbert W Plimpton Collection of Realist Art, Rose Art Mus, Brandeis Univ, Waltham, MA, 95; Painting Ctr, NY, 96; Contemp Works on Paper: 1990-2000, Minneapolis Inst Arts, 1; Visions & Revisions, Mus of Fine Arts, Boston, 2003; solo: High Point Ctr for Printmaking, Minneapolis, MN, 2005. *Teaching:* Asst prof, painting & drawing, Brown Univ, Providence, RI, 73-75 & 77; instr painting, Harvard Univ Summer Sch, 80, 81, 94-98 Mus Fine Arts Sch, 85, 94-2000, Princeton Univ, 1997, Fine Art Work Ctr, Provincetown, Mass, 99-2005, Wellesley Col, 2003 to present. *Awards:* Artists Fel, Mass State Grants Artists, 75 & 79 & Nat Endowment Arts, 76 & 82; Hassam & Speicher Fund Purchase Award, Am Acad & Inst Arts & Lett, 80 & 87; Artists Fel, New York Found for Arts, 88. *Bibliog:* Greg Masters (auth), Joel Janowitz, Arts Mag, 12/84; Robert C Morgan (auth), New York in Review, Arts Mag, 9/88; Robert C Morgan (auth), Tactility & contrast: The Italian sojourn of Joel Janowitz, In: Between Modernism & Conceptual Art, McFarland Press, 97; Gerry Bergstein (auth), Art Feautre Joel Janowitz, Agni 53, Boston Univ, 2001; Francine Koslow Miller (auth), Joel Janowitz's Greenhouses, Art New England, 6-7/2002. *Media:* Oil, Watercolor. *Mailing Add:* 49 Grenville Rd Watertown MA 02472

JANS, CANDACE
PAINTER, PRINTMAKER
b Rockville Centre, NY, Oct 22, 52. *Study:* Wheaton Col, Norton, studied with Vaino Kola, BA, 74; Villa Schifanoia Grad Sch Fine Arts, Florence, Italy, MA, 75; RI Sch Design, studied with Wolf Kahn & Irving Petlin, MFA, 79. *Work:* Hunter Mus, Chattanooga, Tenn; Am Express Co, NY; Wheaton Col, Norton, Mass; Cabot Corp, Wellington Mgt Corp, Mass Financial Servs, Boston, Mass; TRW, Inc, Cleveland; Commerce Bancshares, Kansas City, Mo. *Exhib:* The Mood of New Eng, Boston Jubilee 350, Copley Soc, Mass, 80; Boston Now, Brockton Mus Triennial, Mass, 80; Contemp Boston Portraits, Boston Univ Gallery, Mass, 80; Collector's Gallery XVIII, Marion Koogler McNay Art Inst, San Antonio, Tex, 84; Group Show, Bayly Art Mus, Univ Va, Charlottesville, 87; one-woman shows, Fischbach Gallery, NY, 84, 86, 89 & 95 & Wheaton Col, Mass, 92, 2000; and others; Fischbach Gallery, One Woman Show, 2005. *Collection Arranged:* Springfield Art Mus, Springfield, MO. *Mem:* Boston Visual Artists Union; Women's Caucus Arts (Boston chap); Boston Athenaeum. *Media:* Oil, Lithography. *Dealer:* Larry DiCarlo Fischbach Gallery 210 Eleventh Ave 8th Fl New York New York 10001. *Mailing Add:* 291 Adams St Milton MA 02186

JANSCHKA, FRITZ
PAINTER, GRAPHIC ARTIST
b Vienna, Austria, Apr 21, 19. *Study:* Acad Fine Arts, Vienna, with A Paris Guetersloh. *Work:* Albertina, Vienna; Mus XXth Century, Vienna; Philadelphia Mus Art, Pa; Grafische Sammlung, Zurich, Switz; Hist Mus, Vienna. *Comn:* One Hundred Etchings to World Literature Edition, Harenberg, Dortmund, Ger; 36 Watercolors to 36 Poems by J Joyce, comn by Clyde Joyce, Vienna, 89. *Exhib:* Pa Acad Fine Arts, Philadelphia, 51-54; Graphische Sammlungen, Zurich, 72; Fantastic Realists, Wiener Schule, Near East & Far East Countries, 72-74; Die Wiener Schule de Phantastischen Realismus, Mus Am Ostwall, Dortmund, Ger, 79; XXth Century, Art Club, Oesterreich Mus, Vienna, 81; one-man shows, Orangerie Palais Auersperg, Vienna, 82, Rupertinum Salzburg, Austria, 87 & Illustration's To Sonne & Mond, Gallery at Oper, 89, My Choice: Joyce!, Cantor Fitzgerald, Gallery, Haverford Col, Haverford, PA, 2000; Graphic 24, Albertina, Wien, Austria, 96; Wake Tarot, Weatherspoon Art Mus, Art on Paper, Bianuel, NC, 2004. *Pos:* Vis artist, UNCG, 92. *Teaching:* Prof emer fine arts, Bryn Mawr Col, Pa, Fairbanks prof in Humanities emer. *Awards:* M Slaughter Teaching Award, 85; Gold Medal of Merit, City of Vienna, Austria, 89; Title Prof, Pres Austria, 75. *Bibliog:* J Norton-Smith (auth), A Tribute to James Joyce's Ulysses, Reading Univ, Eng, 73; Johann Muschik (auth), Janschka Monograph & Vienna school of fantastic realism, Jugend & Volk, Vienna/Munich, 74; Otto Breicha (auth), Der Art Club, Oesterreichs, J & V, Vienna, 81; The Larger Austria, Edition Tusch, Sotrifer, Vienna, 82. *Media:* Oil, Watercolor. *Publ:* Auth, 26 etchings to James Joyce's Ulysses, Rizet, 72; Vom Denken der Dichter, Bibliophile Taschenbuecher, Dortmund, WGer; contribr, After Surrealism, 72, auth, Ulysses Alphabet, 73 & contribr, After Classicism, 73, PropyLaen, Berlin, Germany. *Dealer:* Newman Galleries 1625 Walnut St Philadelphia PA 19103; Galerie Habarta A2824 Seebenstein Austria. *Mailing Add:* 1004 Sunset Dr Greensboro NC 27408

JANSEN, ANGELA BING
PAINTER, PRINTMAKER
b New York, NY, Aug 17, 29. *Study:* Brooklyn Col, BA; NY Univ, MA; Atelier 17, New York, with S W Hayter; Brooklyn Mus Art Sch. *Work:* Metrop Mus Art, Mus Mod Art & NY Pub Libr, NY; Philadelphia Mus Art; Art Inst Chicago; Tate Gallery, Victoria & Albert Mus, London, Eng; Brooklyn Mus; and others. *Exhib:* Brooklyn Mus Nat Print Exhib, 50, 70 & 76; Nat Exhib of Prints, Libr of Cong, Washington, DC, 69 & 71; Biennial de Venise, Italy, 72; Biennial of Graphic Art, Wein, 72 & 77; Lang of Print, Pratt Ctr, NY, 73; Solo Exhib, Gimpel & Weitzenhoffer Gallery, NY, 74, 78 & 80; Five Printmakers, Martha Jackson Gallery, NY, 75; Nat Print Exhib, NY, 76; Madison Art Ctr, Wis, 77; Now Drawing Is, Int Exhib, Imbashi Gallery, Kyoto, 78; Int Exhib original drawings, Rijeka, 80; Images, Printing, 81, Int Exhib, Bruxelles, 81. *Awards:* First Prize, Asn Am Artists, Int Miniature Print Exhib, 71; George Roth Prize, Philadelphia Print Club, 71 & 74; Grant for Printmaking, Nat Endowment Arts, 74-75; and others. *Bibliog:* Article, The Print Collector's Newsletter, 7-8/73; Judith Goldman (auth), The language of print, Review #I, Art Forum, summer 79; Francine Tyler (auth), Angela Jansen, Printmaker, ARTFORUM, Summer 79. *Media:* Etching, Painting. *Mailing Add:* 1646 First Ave New York NY 10028

JANSEN, CATHERINE SANDRA
PHOTOGRAPHER, ENVIRONMENTAL ARTIST
b New York, NY, Dec 14, 50. *Study:* Cranbrook Acad Art, Bloomfield Hills, Mich, BFA, 71; Acad di Belle Arti, cert, 72; Temple Univ, MFA, 76. *Work:* Philadelphia Mus Art; Ctr Creative Photogr; Fine Arts Mus Honolulu; Frans, Kline & French; Bell of Pa; ARA Co. *Exhib:* Unique Photographs: Multiple Sculpture, Mus Mod Art, NY, 73; Three Centuries of Am Art, Philadelphia Mus Art, Pa, 76; Am Family Portraits, Philadelphia Mus Art, 76; solo exhibs, Ctr Creative Photog, Tucson, Ariz, 83, Hicks Gallery, Bucks Co Community Col, Newtown, Pa, 84, Univ Va, Charlottesville, 85, Photog Resource Ctr, Boston, 87, Spaces Gallery, Cleveland, 88, Owen Patrick Gallery, Philadelphia, 89 & Moore Col Art, Philadelphia, 91; The Camera Rediscovered, Woodmere Art Mus, Philadelphia, 95; Complexity & Contradiction, Paley Design Ctr, Philadelphia, 96; and others. *Teaching:* Instr photog, Bucks Co Community Col, Newtown, Pa, 73-. *Awards:* Individual Artist Grant, Pa Coun Arts, 81, 88 & Nat Endowment Arts, 83; Cult Insertive Grant, 82 & 95. *Mem:* Pa State Coun Arts. *Publ:* Introduction to Visual Literacy, Curtis, Prentice Hall Publ, 88; Nancy Howell-Koehler, The Creative Camera, Davis Publ, 88; Photo Art Process, Davis Publ Inc, 91; Philadelphia Mag, Manayonic Art Festival, 95; Mildred Constantine & Laurel Reuter, Whole Cloth, Monticello Press, 98. *Mailing Add:* c/o Dept Art/Bucks Co Community Col Swamp Rd Newtown PA 18940

JANSEN, MARCUS ANTONIUS
PAINTER
b Manhattan, NYC June 28, 68. *Study:* Berufsfachschule for Design, Moenchengladbach, Ger, 1985-1986; Berufschule for Painters, Moenchengladbach, Ger, 3 yr Journeymanship, 1986-1989; US Army PLDC Leadership Course, Cert, 1995. *Work:* Nat Taiwan Mus Fine Art, Taiwan; Ford Motor Co Hq, Dearborn, Mich;

Tuskeegee Univ, Tuskeegee, Ala; Oasis Towers Jorge Perez (The Related Group of Florida), Ft Myers, Fla; Southwest Fla Mus Hist, Ft Myers, Fla. *Comn:* Mural (school), Berufsfachschule, Moenchengladbach, Ger, 1987; 4 Hist works of Art, Ford Motor Co, Dearborn, 2003; 11 Hist works of Art, Southwest Fla Mus Hist, 2006; Oasis Towers Permanent Collection, Jorge Perez (The Related Group of Florida), Miami Fla, 2006; and others. *Exhib:* Ford Motor Co Paintings, Charles H Wright Mus, Dearborn, Mich, 2003; Groupshow, Stricoff Fine Art Ltd, Chelsea, NY, 2003; Ft Myers an Urban Perspective, Southwest Fla Mus Hist, Ft Myers, Fla, 2006; Voice of a Generation, Am Art Gallery, Paris, France, 2006; Summer Survey, Lawrence Asher Gallery, Los Angeles, 2006; Urban Expressions, Alliance for the Arts, Ft Myers, Fla, 2006. *Awards:* New Artist of the Year Winner, Angel of the Arts Award, Alliance for the Arts, Ft Myers, 2005; Best Practice in Art & Cult Winner, Famous 100 artists book, World of Art, London, UK, 2005. *Bibliog:* Petru Russu (auth), Famous 100 Contemporary Artists, World Art Books, 2006; Mark L Tomkins (auth), Illuminations, Tenspeed Publ, 2006. *Mem:* Alliance for the Arts; Art League; Fla Art Cult Center; Am Acad Arts; Midtown West Assocs. *Media:* Mixed Media-Painting. *Publ:* Auth, Modern Urban Expressionism, Am Art Gallery, Paris, France, 2006

JAQUE, LOUIS
PAINTER
b Montreal, PQ, May 1, 1919. *Study:* Inst Appl Arts, Montreal. *Work:* Nat Gallery Can, Ottawa; Montreal Mus Fine Arts; Mus Quebec; Mus d'Art Contemporain, Montreal; Societe Publicite Editoriale Collection, Milan, Italy; Mus Sherbrooke; Mus Joliette. *Comn:* Mural, Quebec Pavilion, Expo 70, Osaka, Japan, 70; mural, Maison de Radio-Canada, Montreal, 72; mural, Place de la Bourse, Montreal, 74. *Exhib:* Europa 72, 3rd Int Exhib Painting, Milan, 72; Salon Int d'Art Contemp, Paris, 74 & 75; retrospective, Montreal Mus Fine Arts, 77; solo exhib, Can Cult Ctr, Paris, France, 78; Arte Universal a Traves de los Tempos, Mus Palacio Bellas Artes, Mex. *Collection Arranged:* Retrospective, 25 Years of Painting, Montreal Mus Fin Arts. *Teaching:* Instr design & design hist, Inst Applied Arts, Montreal, 59- 83. *Awards:* Jessie Dow Award, Montreal Mus Fine Arts, 60; Can Art Coun Grant to Artist, 64 & 72; Europa 72 Bronze Medal, City of Milan, 72. *Mem:* Founder Soc Prof Artists Que (pres, 64-65); Royal Can Acad. *Media:* Oil, Tempera. *Publ:* Art in New York, Time Mag, 10/31/69; Considerations over a concept, D'ars Mag, Italy, Nos 53 & 54; 16 Quebec painters in their milieu, La Vie Des Arts, 78; Monique Brunet-Weinmann (auth), Louis Jaque: le point de vue d'icare, La Vie Des Arts, spring 85; Monique Brunet-Weinmann (auth), Louis Jaque, 89. *Dealer:* Han Art Gallery 4209 Ste Catherine W Westmount PQ Can H3Z 1P6. *Mailing Add:* 6150 Ave du Boise Apt 3G Montreal PQ H3S 2V2 Canada

JAQUET, LOUIS
CONCEPTUAL ARTIST, PAINTER - ALL MEDIA
b Paris, France, Mar 27, 44. *Study:* Acad De La Grande Chaumiere, Paris, 65; Acad Julian, Paris, 66; Ecole Nat Superieure, Des Beaux Arts, Paris, 72. *Work:* Palais Des Expositions, Zurich, Switz; Mus Modern Art, Tel Aviv, Isreal; Mus Modern Art, Bologna, Italy; Palazzo Pitti Mus, Florence, Italy; Vatican Mus, Vatican City, Italy. *Comn:* Fresco 11x 13 painting, Swiss Govt, zurich, 85; painting, City Scape, Am Embassy, Paris, 96; painting, Vatican City, Pope John Paul II, Vatican City, 2004. *Exhib:* Int Biennal Exhib Contemp Art, Salsomaggiore, Terne, Italy, 82; Int Biennal Exhib, Graphic Arts, Tokyo, Japan, 83; Int Biennal Exhib, Contemp Art, Los Angeles, Calif, 84; Royal Acad, London, 84; Biennal Contemp Art, Palazzo Corsini, Rome, Italy, 84; Int Biennal Exhib, Zurich, Switz, 85; Int Biennal Exhib, Tsukuba, Japan, 86. *Awards:* First Prize, Tokyo Japan, Int Graphic Art Exhib, 85; Special Distinction Award, Tsubuka, Japan Int Biennal Exhib, 86; First prize, painting, Nat Exhib, Italy, 87. *Mem:* Maison Des Artistes, France; Routhschild Found, Paris, France. *Media:* Oil on canvas. *Publ:* Auth, The Israel J, J Aoilion, 83; auth, Gazzetta de Reggio, Annusca Campani, 84; auth, Il Popolo, Ivanna Arnaldi, Rome, Italy, 85; auth, E Benezit Dictionnaire, Librairie Grund, 98; auth, Giorgio Ruggeri, Louis Jaquet, Edision d'Arte Ghelfi, 2001. *Dealer:* Gallerie 454 15105 Kercheval Ave Grosse Pointe MI 48230. *Mailing Add:* c/o Gallerie 454 15105 Kercheval Detroit MI 48230

JARAMILLO, VIRGINIA
PAINTER
b El Paso, Tex, Mar 21, 39. *Study:* Otis Art Inst, 58-61. *Work:* Long Beach Mus Art, Calif; Pasadena Art Mus, Calif; Aldrich Mus Contemp Art, Ridgefield, Conn; Schenectady Mus, NY. *Exhib:* Whitney Mus Am Art Ann, NY, 72; Contemp Reflections 1971-72, Aldrich Mus Contemp Art, Ridgefield, 72; group exhib, Douglas Drake Gallery, Kansas City, Kans, 75 & one-man show, 76; plus others. *Pos:* Assoc dir & aesthet adv, Hybrid Inc, 72-74. *Awards:* Ford Found Grant, 62; Nat Endowment Arts, 72-73; Creative Artists Pub Serv Prog Grant, 75. *Bibliog:* F Bowling (auth), Outside the galleries: Four artists, Arts Mag, 11/70; Deluxe show, Houston Chronicle, 8/71; C Ratcliff (auth), The Whitney Annual, Part I, Artforum, 4/72. *Mem:* Nat Soc Lit & Arts. *Media:* Acrylic, Oil. *Res:* Religious architecture throughout Europe. *Publ:* Auth, Post-minimal artists, Arts Mag, 9/75. *Mailing Add:* PO Box 199 Prince St Sta New York NY 10012

JARDINE, DONALD LEROY
ADMINISTRATOR, GRAPHIC ARTIST, EDITOR
b Idaho Falls, Idaho, July 7, 26. *Study:* Weber Col, Ogden, Utah, CA, 48, Assoc Sci, 49; Univ Utah, BS, 50 & MS, 62; Univ Minn, Minneapolis, PhD, 75; studied with Farrell R Collett, Alvin Gittens, Arnold Friberg, Walter Wilwerding, Peter Busa & Reid Hastie. *Comn:* General Mills; 3-M; Gambles; and many others. *Pos:* Pres, Utah Art Educ Asn, 58-60; ed, The Illustrator Mag, 63-96; bd dir, Asn Prof Artists, 68-70. *Teaching:* Art teacher, Bountiful Sr High Sch, Utah, 51-62; assoc dir art educ, Westminster Col, Salt Lake City, 58-60; educ dir, Art Instr Sch, Minneapolis, 62-93; prof career art, Univ Minn, 68-83; dir educ, Palmer Writers Sch, 85-93. *Awards:* Distinguished Art Award, Weber State Univ; Teacher Year, Davis Co Sch Dist, 58. *Mem:* Asn Prof Artists (dir, 65-67); Art Instr Schs (vpres, 77); Art Dir Club; Nat Art Educ Asn (lectr, 74-75). *Media:* Ink, Oil. *Interests:* travel & photography. *Publ:* Auth, How to Sell Your Artwork, 63; Richard Lack's Atelier, Am Artist, 71; Creating Cartoon Characters, 89, Creating Cartoon Animals, 90, & The Art of Cartooning, 98, Walter Foster Publ Co; many articles in Wildlife Art Mag; Creating Cartoon Animals #2, Translated & Publ in Russia, 2004. *Dealer:* Kramer Gallery, MPLS. *Mailing Add:* 5554-1 Nathan Ln Plymouth MN 55442-3264

JARVIS, DONALD
PAINTER, INSTRUCTOR
b Vancouver, BC, 23. *Study:* Vancouver Sch Art, with hon, 48; also with Hans Hofmann, New York, 48 & 49. *Work:* Nat Gallery Can, Ottawa, Ont; Art Gallery Greater Victoria, BC; Vancouver Art Gallery; London Pub Libr & Art Mus; Can Coun Art Bank, Ottawa; and others. *Exhib:* Nat Gallery of Can, 55-65 & 69; Some Painters of the BC Mainland, Art Gallery of Greater Victoria, 65; Int Exhib of Drawings & Prints, Lugano, Switz, 66; one-man show, Vancouver Art Gallery, 49, 55 & 77; Coasts, The Sea and Canadian Art, Stratford, Ont, 79; and others. *Teaching:* Instr painting & drawing, Emily Carr Col of Art, 51-86. *Awards:* Emily Carr Scholar, Vancouver Sch Art, 48; Sr Arts Fel, Can Coun, 61. *Mem:* Royal Can Acad Arts. *Media:* Mixed Media

JARVIS, JOHN BRENT
PAINTER
b American Fork, Utah, Nov 28, 46. *Study:* Snow Col, AS, 65; Utah State Univ, BS, 71; Brigham Young Univ. *Work:* Brigham City Mus, Utah; Latter Day Saints Church Mus; Springville Mus Art, Springville, Utah. *Comn:* Painting, Latter Day Saints Church, 84. *Exhib:* Salt Lake Art Ctr Regional Show, 76; Am Watercolor Soc, NY, 76; one-man shows, Brigham Young Univ, Provo, Brigham City Mus, Bertha Eacles Gallery, Ogden, & Trivoli Gallery, Salt Lake City, Utah; Northwest Rendezvous Show, Helena, Mont, 89-90. *Awards:* Merit Award, Utah Painting & Sculpture, Utah Inst Fine Arts, 74; Ann Noye Watercolor, Salt Lake Art Ctr Intermountain, 76; Merit Award, Mormon Art Show, Brigham Young Univ, 77. *Media:* Multimedia, Watercolor. *Dealer:* Lido Gallery Park City Utah. *Mailing Add:* 1355 E 250 North St Pleasant Grove UT 84062-3054

JASHINSKY, JUDY
PAINTER, CURATOR
b Oconto Falls, Wis, Dec 27, 47. *Study:* Univ Wis, Stevens Point, BS, 70; Mich State Univ, MFA, 73. *Work:* Nat Gallery Art, Washington, DC; Springfield Art Mus, Mo; Univ Mich Sch Med, Ann Arbor; Smith-Barney, NY; Muskegon Mus Art, Mich. *Comn:* Portrait, comn by Mrs Gilbert Hart Kinney, Washington, DC, 91; 6 portraits, comn by Mary Hynes Berry, Chicago, 91-93; 50th Anniversary Screen, Meyer Found, Washington, DC, 94. *Exhib:* Contemp Am Indian Art, Smithsonian Mus Nat Hist, 84; Deutsch-Amerikanisches, Stadtische Galerie, Regensburg, Ger, 89; one-man shows, Washington Proj for the Arts, Washington, DC, 89, Susquehanna Art Mus, Harrisburg, Pa, 92-93 & Rosenberg Gallery, Goucher Col, Baltimore Md, 94; The Return of the Cadavre Exquis, The Drawing Ctr, NY, 93 & Corcoran Gallery Art, Washington, DC, 94; Artists Select, Artists Space, NY, 94; solo exhib, Roman Fever, Artemifia Gallery, Chicago, Ill, 98, Artists Mus, Washington, DC, 98, Academy Celebration 1616, Gibson Creatives, 98; Past, Present, Future, Clare Spitler, Ann Arbor, Mich, 98; Jolt, Baum Garther Gallery, Washington, DC, 99. *Collection Arranged:* Primal Painting, Marlboro Gallery PGCC, Largo, Md, 85; Memento Mori, Fondo del Sol Visual Arts Ctr, 90; Boudoir and Lupanar (catalog), Washington Proj for the Arts, Washington, DC, 95. *Pos:* Chair, Community Outreach Comt, Washington Proj Arts, 91-93. *Teaching:* Instr painting & drawing, Prince Georges Community Col, Largo, Md, 80-86, Trinity Col, Washington, DC, 84-87 & Westshore Community Col, Scottville, Mich, 90-93. *Awards:* American-Russian Cult Found, Sponsorship, Roman Fever Exhib, Artist Mus, Washington, DC, 89; New Forms Regional Grant, Painted Bride, Philadelphia, Pa, 93; Mayors Award Excellence, Service to the Arts, 92. *Bibliog:* Robert Bersson (auth), Beyond Painting & Sculpture, Worlds of Art, Mayfield Publ, 91; Mary McCoy (auth), Reviews, New Art Examiner, 1/93; Shenandoah, Wash & Lee Univ Review, 10/98. *Mem:* Washington Proj for the Arts; Coalition of Washington Arts. *Media:* Acrylic, Oil. *Publ:* Lost Work of Judy Jashinsky (catalog), 96. *Dealer:* Clare Spitler 2007 Pauline Court Ann Arbor MI 48103. *Mailing Add:* 115 10th St NE Washington DC 20002

JASUD, LAWRENCE EDWARD
PHOTOGRAPHER, EDUCATOR
b Chicago, Ill, Oct 26, 42. *Study:* Southern Ill Univ, BS(photog), 69; Ohio State Univ, MA(photog), 80. *Work:* J Paul Getty Mus; Univ Tenn, Knoxville; Schearing Plow Corp Coll, Memphis; Malone & Hyde Corp Coll, Memphis; Tokyo Col Photog. *Exhib:* Naked, Univ Colo, Boulder, 85; Magic Silver, Univ Northern Iowa, Cedar Falls, 91; Photog Book Arts in US, Univ Tex, San Antonio, 91; Brooks Biennial Invitational, Memphis Brooks Mus Art, 92; Windows on Tennessee, Cheekwood, Nashville, 94. *Teaching:* Assoc prof photog, Univ Memphis, 81-. *Awards:* Media Fel, Tenn Eastman Co, 87; Individual Artist's Fel, Tenn Arts Comn, 87; Dean's Creative Achievement Award, 96. *Bibliog:* Robert McGowen (auth), Memphis Brooks Biennial Catalog (essay), Memphis Brooks Mus, 92. *Mem:* Col Art Asn; Soc Photog Educ (reg secy, 83-86). *Publ:* Auth, Words, Sounds & Power, Logan Elm Press, 91; auth & illusr, A Portfolio of My "Myths & Rituals" Photographs, History of Photography, 92; auth, Memphis Brooks biennial catalog (essay), Memphis Brooks Mus, 94; Through a pinhole brightly, View Camera Mag, 95; Wisdom of the forest, Number: 30, 96. *Dealer:* Jay Etkin Gallery Memphis Tenn. *Mailing Add:* 244 S Greer St Memphis TN 38111-3434

JAUDON, VALERIE
PAINTER
b Greenville, Miss, Aug 6, 45. *Study:* Miss State Col Women, Columbus, 63-65; Memphis Acad Art, Tenn, 65; Univ Am, Mexico City, 66-67; St Martin's Sch Art, London, Eng, 68-69. *Work:* Hirshhorn Mus & Sculpture Garden, Nat Mus Women Arts, Washington, DC; Mus Mod Art, NY; Aldrich Mus Art, Ridgefield, Conn; Fogg Mus, Cambridge, Mass; Albright-Knox Art Gallery, Buffalo, NY; Birmingham Mus Art, Ala. *Comn:* Pilot (oil on canvas), Atlanta City Hall, Ga, 89; Freestyle (ceramic tile wall mural), Equitable Bldg, NY, 89; Reunion (3 acre paving plan, brick and granite), Municipal Bldg, NY, 89; Refraction (ceramic mural), Lab Sci Bldg, Staten Island, NY, 94; and others; Filippine Garden (grass & gravel garden) Thomas F Eagleton Courthouse, St Louis, MO, 2004. *Exhib:* Mus Mod Art, NY, 75; Hirshhorn Mus & Sculpture Garden, Washington, DC, 77; solo exhibs, Pa Acad Fine Arts, 77, Corcoran Gallery, Los Angeles, 81, Dart Gallery, Chicago, 83, Amerika Haus, Berlin, Ger, 83, Sidney Janis Gallery, NY, 83, 85, 86, 88, 90, 93 & 96, McIntosh/Drysdale Gallery, Washington, 85 & Miss Mus Art (with catalog), Jackson, 96, Stadel Mus, Frankfurt, Ger, 99; Von Lintel Gallery, NY, 2003, 2005; Nat Gallery, Washington, DC, 80; Mus Fine Arts, Boston, Mass, 82; Generations of Geometry, Whitney Mus Am Art at Equitable Ctr, NY, 87; Making Their Mark, Cincinnati Art Mus & traveling, 89. *Teaching:* Instr, Sch Visual Arts, New York, 83-84; assoc prof, Hunter Col, New York, 85, prof, 92. *Awards:* Vis Arts Fel Grant, Nat Endowment for the Arts, 88; Art Award, Excellence in Design, Art Comn, New York, 88; NY State Fel Painting, 92; Merit Award, Am Soc Landscape Archits, Ala Chap, 94. *Bibliog:* John Perreault (auth), Allusive depths: Valerie Jaudon, Art in Am, 10/83; Barry Schwabsky (auth), Degrees of symmetry, Art in Am, 10/96; Anna Chave (auth), Disorderly Order: The Art of Valerie Jaudon (with catalog), Valerie Jaudon, Mississippi Mus Art, Jackson. *Dealer:* Sidney Janis Gallery 100 W 57th St New York NY 10019; Von Lintel Gallery. *Mailing Add:* 44 King St New York NY 10014

JAWORSKA, TAMARA
FIBER ARTIST, TAPESTRY ARTIST
b Archangelsk, Russia, 28: Can Citizen. *Study:* State Acad Fine Arts, Poland, BFA, Fac Design Art Weaving, MFA; Royal Can Acad Arts, fel academician, Acad Italia Delle Arti e del Lavoro Fel Acad, Fel, York Univ, Toronto. *Work:* Nat Mus, Warsaw, Poland; Molson Can, Toronto; York-Hanover Corp, Toronto; JDS Investment Corp, Toronto; Nat Mus A Puschkin, Moscow, USSR; Can Embassy, Ryiadh, Saudi Arabia; Dept External Affairs, Can; Nat Mus Textile Art, Warsaw, Nat Mus Home Army, Krakóv, Poland; and many pvt collections. *Comn:* Tapestries-Gobelin, Olympia & York Co, Place Bell Can, Ottawa, 71 & Bank Montreal, Toronto, 75, Metrop Life Ins Co, Ottawa, 77, JDS Finch 1000, Toronto, 76 & var pvt collections in US, Can, Switz, Eng, Sweden & France. *Exhib:* Solo exhib, 7 Mus, Art Galleries, Spain, 80-91; retrospectives, Ctr Nat de la Tapisserie D'Aubusson, Galerie Inard, Paris, traveling abroad, 81-82, 84, 86, 89 & 91 & Royal Acad Arts, John B Aird Gallery, Toronto, 92; Centennial Exhib RCA, Toronto; Mus Appl Arts, Budapest, Hungary, 95; Mus Fine Arts/Drescen Design Zentrum, Ger, 96; Manifesto 96, Int Festival of Archit & Design, 96; Mayor Retrospective, Peak Gallery, Toronto, Can, 97, Gallery Solo, King City, Toronto, 2003. *Pos:* Dir pvt design-weaving art studio, Toronto, currently. *Teaching:* Instr post grad workshop design & weaving, Ont Col Arts, Can. *Awards:* Master Painter Honoris Causa, Acad Ital delle Arti; Gold Medal & First Prize, Int Art Competition, New York, 85; Gov Gen, 125th Anniversary Medal, 93; Order of Canada (CM), by HRH Queen Elizabeth II, Outstanding Achievements in Creative Arts, 94; Golden Jubilee Medal - by HRH Queen Elizabeth II. *Bibliog:* Tapestries by Tamara Jaworska (film), CBS Toronto, 70 & Tamara's Tapestry World, CBS Arts & Sci Prog in Film, Toronto, 75; film, Tapestries by Tamara, New Collection, CBC Arts Film, Toronto, 80; film (mini-series), A Modern Country, Tamara's Tapestry World, Textures & Canadian Reflections, Can Broadcasting Co; film, Portrait of the Artist, CHCH TV & CHEX TV; and articles in American & European variety mag, art mag, art books & daily newspapers. *Mem:* Royal Can Acad Arts; Acad Italia del Arti a del Lavoro. *Media:* Wool, Artificial Yarns. *Dealer:* Centre Nationale de la Tapisserie D'Aubusson Galerie Inard 39 Rue De Verneuil Paris France; Gallery Solo King City Toronto. *Mailing Add:* 49 Don River Blvd Toronto ON M2N 2M8 Canada

JAY, BILL
PHOTOGRAPHIC HISTORIAN, CRITIC
b Maidenhead, Berkshire, Eng, Aug 12, 40. *Study:* Berkshire Col Art, dipl; Univ NMex, MA & MFA; spec study with prof Van Deren Coke & prof Beaumont Newhall. *Work:* Int Mus Photog, Rochester, NY; Bibliotheque Nat, Paris, France; Art Mus, Univ NMex, Albuquerque; plus many pvt collections. *Exhib:* Mod Art, var locations in Brit & Europe, 67; Art Mus, Univ NMex, 76; one-man shows, Micro-Gallery, Phoenix, Ariz & Northlight Gallery, Tempe, Ariz, 77. *Collection Arranged:* Brit Documentary Photog 1850-1970, Brit Coun, 71; The English Scene, Tony Ray-Jones & Sir Benjamin Stone 1864-1914, 71, Inst Contemp Arts, London; plus others. *Pos:* Ed/dir, Album Mag, London, Eng, 69-71; dir photog, Inst Contemp Arts, London, Eng, 69-71. *Teaching:* from asst prof to assoc prof art hist, 19th century & 20th century photog, Ariz State Univ, Tempe, Ariz, 74-. *Mem:* Soc for Photog Educ (mem bd dir, 74-78); Royal Photog Soc Gt Brit (mem Royal comn, 72). *Res:* Photography of the 19th and 20th centuries, especially British topographical work of the wet-plate era. *Publ:* Auth, Robert Demachy: Photographs and Essays, 74, Acad Ed; auth, Victorian Cameraman: Francis Frith 1822-1898, 73 & Victorian Candid Camera: Paul Martin 1864-1944, 73, David & Charles; Negative/Positive: A Philosophy of Photography, Kendall-Hunt, 79; Addison House and Photography: Current Perspectives, Light Impressions, 79. *Mailing Add:* c/o Sch of Art Ariz State Univ Tempe AZ 85287

JAY, NORMA JOYCE
PAINTER
b Wichita, Kans. *Study:* Wichita State Univ; Art Inst Chicago; Calif State Univ, Long Beach. *Work:* Irvine Found; Edwin Morris Collection; Deloitte, Haskins & Sells. *Exhib:* Mystic Maritime Gallery, Mystic Seaport Mus, Mystic, Conn, 82, 83, 85, 90, 92 & 95; Coos Bay Art Mus, Ore, 94, 96 & 98; Frye Mus, Seattle, Wash, 97; Cummer Mus Art, Jacksonville, Fla, 97-98; Newport Harbor Nautical Mus, Newport Beach, Calif, 98-99. *Awards:* Best Show, Ford Nat Competition, 61; Artists Award, Chriswood Galleries, 73; First Place, Traditional Artists 10th Ann, 76; Best of Show Award, Newport Harbor Nautical Mus, Newport Beach, Calif, 99. *Bibliog:* Peter Rogers (auth), review, Sea Hist, winter 80-81; Contemporary Marine Art, Nimrod Press, 81; Rebecca Smith (auth), Norma Jay, West Coast Impressions, Nautical Quart, autumn 84; article, Antiques & Arts Weekly, 12/82; Yacht Portraits, Sheridan House. *Mem:* Fel Am Soc Marine Artists. *Media:* Oil

JEAN, BEVERLY (BEVERLY) JEAN STRONG
PAINTER, ART DEALER
b Eugene, Ore, Oct 1, 27. *Work:* Atlanta Bowe Co, Ga. *Pos:* Owner, Tiqua Gallery, Santa Fe, NMex, currently. *Media:* Oil Painting, Monoprints. *Specialty:* Contemporary paintings; antique folk art; American Indian art; colonial Mexican art. *Mailing Add:* 901 Paseo De la Cuma Santa Fe NM 87501-1254

JECK, DOUGLAS A
SCULPTOR
b Jersey City, NJ, 63. *Study:* Tenn Technol Univ, Cookeville, Tenn, 81-83; Appalachian Ctr Arts & Crafts, Smithville, Tenn, BA, 84-86; Sch Art Inst Chicago, Ill, MFA, 87-89. *Work:* Lamar Dodd Art Ctr, La Grange, Ga. *Exhib:* One-person exhibs, Appalachian Ctr Arts & Crafts, Smithville, Tenn, 85, Connell Gallery/Great Am Gallery, Atlanta, Ga, 91, Connell Gallery, Atlanta, 92, William Traver Gallery, Seattle, 95, 98 & 2000, Dorothy Weiss Gallery, San Francisco, 97, 98, Garth Clark Gallery, New York City, 2000; Death of Innocence, Sarratt Gallery, Vanderbilt Univ, Nashville, Tenn, 87; Doug Jeck & Jacqueline Saccoccio, Sch Art Inst Chicago, Gallery 2, 88, Chicago Fire II, Northwest Arts Coun, 88, New Talent I, 89, Doug Jeck & Lisa Pines, Contemp Art Workshop, 90, Tattoo, Randolph St Gallery, Chicago, Ill, 90; LaGrange National XVI, Lamar Dodd Art Ctr, Ga, 91; group exhibs Randolph St Gallery, Chicago, 89, David Adler Cult Ctr, Libertyville, Ill, 90, William Traver Gallery, Seattle, 93, 96, Getty Rymer Gallery, Sch Art Inst Chicago, 94, Garth Clark Gallery, 96, Dorothy Weiss Gallery, 97, Perimeter Gallery, Chicago, 98, Kennedy Mus Art, Athens, Ohio, 99, Scripps Coll, Claremont Calif, 99, Dolphin Gallery, Kansas City, Mo, 2000, Los Angeles Co Mus Art, 2000. *Collection Arranged:* Internat Mus Ceramic Art, Alfred, NY; Los Angeles Co Mus, Los Angeles; Johnson Was Collection, Chicago; Virginia A Groot Found, Chicago. *Pos:* asst program dir mus edn, The Artifact Ctr, Chgo, 89-91; grad critique panelist Sch Art Inst Chicago, 92; juror/panelist So Arts Fedn Regional NEA Fellowship Oanel, 95; outside reviewer Sch Art Inst Chgo, 97; juror Bellevue Art Mus, Wash, 98; mem community adv comt, Tacoma Art Mus, Wash, 98. *Teaching:* Asst prof art, NY State Col Ceramics, Alfred Univ; adj prof Sch Art Inst Chgo, 93; asst prof, NY State Coll Ceramics, Alfred Univ, 94; asst prof, Sch Art, Univ Wash, Seattle, 96-. *Awards:* Ill Arts Coun Artist Fel, 89; Nat Endowment Arts, Visual Artist Fel Grant, 90; Fel Award, Sch Art Inst Chicago, Ill, 89; Lamar Dodd Art Ctr Purchase Award, LaGrange Nat Exhibit, LaGrange, Ga, 91; Nat Endowment for Arts Travel Grant, 92; LaNapoule Found Award, France, 92; Visual Artists Fel Grant, Nat Endowment for Arts, 92; Virginia A Groot Found Grant, 97 & 98. *Bibliog:* Klaus Ottmann (auth), Tattoo, Flash Art, Jan/Feb, 90; Catherine Fox (auth), Clay figures come to life at Connell, Atlanta J & Constitution, Ga, 1/25/91; Jerry Cullum (auth), Douglas Jeck, Art Papers, Vol 15, No 3, 41, May/June, 91; Lisa Englander (auth), The Nude in Clay II: A Contemporary Reading of Sculptural Traditions, Perimeter Gallery, 98; Jo Lauria (auth), Color and Fire - Defining Moments in Studio Ceramics, 1950-2000, Rizzoli Internat Pubs, NY, 2000; Tatto-Review, New Art Examiner, 90; Doug Keck at Dorothy Weiss, Art in Am, 97; Doug Jeck/Deli Seigenthaler: Sculpture and Paintings, Art Papers, 92; Doug Jeck, Ceramic Art #17, 97; Reviews - Doug Jeck, American Ceramics, 91; others

JEFF
PAINTER, PHOTOGRAPHER
b Oakland, Calif, 1942. *Study:* Univ NMex, BFA, 71; Univ Wis-Madison, MFA & MA, 73. *Work:* Mus Mod Art, NY; Metrop Mus Art, NY; Moderna Museet, Stockholm, Sweden; Art Inst Chicago, Ill; Seattle Art Mus, Wash. *Exhib:* Recent Acquisitions, Metrop Mus Art, NY, 79; one-person exhibs, OK Harris Works Art, 79, The Destroyed Print (with catalog), Pratt Manhattan Ctr, 82, Univ Colo, 84, Bronx Mus Arts, 84, City Univ Grad Ctr Mall, 84, Orange Co Ctr Contemp Art, 89 & Univ Nev, Reno, 95; Recent Acquisitions, Art Inst Chicago, 84; Aldrich Mus Contemp Art, 88; 100th Birthday Celebration, Denver Art Mus, 93; 20th Century Art: Recent Accessions, Snite Mus Art, Univ Notre Dame, 93; Across Borders/Sin Fronteras (with catalog), Art Mus Americas, Washington, 94; What is a Print, Montclair Art Mus, NJ, 95; Temporarily Possessed: The Semi Permanent Collection (with catalog), New Mus Contemp Art, NY, 95. *Teaching:* Asst prof, Fashion Inst Technol, 76-. *Awards:* Res Found Grant, State Univ NY, 83-85; Fel, Nat Endowment Arts, 86-87. *Bibliog:* Grace Glueck (auth), Art: Beauties & Beasts at the Pratt Gallery, NY Times vol CXXXIII, 4/6/84; Michael Arkush (auth), Valley Calendar: Fall Brings a Diversity of Arts, Its New Its Local, Los Angeles Times, 9/21/90; Cathy Curtis (auth), Art Review: The focus of Death Has Clearly Departed, Los Angeles Times, 9/13/91. *Media:* Acrylic, Oil. *Mailing Add:* 114 Fulton St New York NY 10014

JEFFERS, WENDY JANE
CURATOR, ARTIST
b Providence, RI, Sept 5, 48. *Study:* Univ Mass, BFA, 71; Pratt Inst, MFA(painting), 74; also attended NY Inst Fine Arts, Art Students League, Tyler Sch Art, Am Univ, New Sch Social Research, Mass Col Art, Columbia Univ, Corcoran Mus Sch, NY Acad Art & Nat Acad Design. *Work:* Port Authority NY & NJ; Chase Manhattan Bank, NY; Continental Group, Stamford, Conn; Miller, Tabak & Hirsch, NY; pvt collections, Dr & Mrs Jack Aslanian, Mr & Mrs George Demeter, Mr & Mrs William Hayden; and many others. *Exhib:* The Icarus Odyssey, Guadalajara & Mexico City, 79; Wash Square East Galleries, NY Univ, 80; Paperworks 80, Hudson River Mus, Yonkers, NY, 80; AIR Gallery Invitational, NY, 82-85; one-person exhib, Bristol Art Mus, RI, 84; Fairleigh Dickinson Univ, NJ, 84; Sculptures-Drawings, Berkshire Artisans Art Ctr, Pittsfield, Mass, 84. *Collection Arranged:* First Nat City Bank Art Collection, New York, 73-74; Seven Decades at the Colony (auth, catalog), New York, 76; A Curators Choice: A Tribute to Dorothy C Miller, Rosa Esman Gallery, New York, 82; Niles Spencer A Portrait in Words and Images, Archives Am Art, New York, 90; Niles Spencer Exhib, Whitney Mus Am Art, Equitable Ctr, spring 90; Holger Cahill and Dorothy C Miller: An Exhibitiion of Paintings, Sculpture and Documents from the Decade 1929-1939, Archives of Am Art, 93. *Pos:* Independent cur. *Awards:* Max Beckmann Fel, Brooklyn Mus, 71-72; Graduate Fel, Pratt Inst, 73-74; MacDowell Colony Fel, 77. *Bibliog:* Kay Larson (auth), article, NY Mag, 3/1/82; Michael Kimmelman (auth), Review of Niles Spencer exhib, NY Times, 6/15/90; Michael Kimmelman (auth), Review of Archives Exhib, NY Times, 5/14/93. *Media:* Oil, Graphite. *Res:* Working on Catalogue Raisonne of Niles Spencer's painting and sculpture; Working on biography of Dorothy C Miller retired senior curator of the Museum of Modern Art. *Specialty:* Early 20th Century Am Modernism. *Publ:* Niles Spencer, Whitney Mus Am Art, 90; Dorothy C Miller: A Profile, New Eng Antiques J, 5/90; Holger Cahill & Am Art J Arch Am Art, fall 92 & Holger Cahill & Am Folk Art, Antiques Mag, 9/95; auth, Abby Alderich Rockefeller: patron of the modern antiques magazine, 11/2004. *Mailing Add:* 61-63 Crosby St New York NY 10012

JELLICO, NANCY R
PAINTER, SCULPTOR
b LaGrange, Ga, Sept 22, 39. *Study:* Colo Inst Art, Denver, with John Jellico & Charlie Dye, diploma, 60; Univ Denver, with John Witaschek, 81; CA-10 Wkshp, Kerrville, Tex, 86. *Comn:* The Good Things Don't Change (four paintings), 82, sculptures: Bunch Quitter, 83, He Ain't Heavy, 84, Head to Head, 88 & Lendin' a Hand, 90, The Upjohn Co, TUCO Div, Kalmazooo, Mich; Flag design, ProRodeo Hall of Champions & Mus of the Am Cowboy, Colo Springs, 83; archit sculpture (to scale), St Thomas Sem, Denver, Colo, 85, 88 &90. *Exhib:* Mountain Oyster Club's Ann Contemp Western Art Show, Tucson, Ariz, 1984-2000; Classic-Am Ann Western Art Show & Sale, Beverly Hills, Calif, 87-90 & 94; solo exhib, Nat Cowgirl Hall Fame, Hereford, Tex, 90; Women Artists & the West, Tucson Mus Art, Ariz, 91-94; Happy Canyon Western Art Invitational, Pendleton, Ore, 91-97; Wyoming Western Images, Murisaki Gallery, Tokyo, Japan, 92; Spirit of the Great Plains, Mus Nebr Art, Kearney, 98, 2000. *Pos:* Registrar, Colo Inst Art, Denver, 61-65. *Teaching:* Instr figure drawing & anatomy, Colo Inst Art, 64-65. *Awards:* Warren Richardson Award (first place), 83, C M Charlie Russell Award, 85, Hon Mention, 86, Western Regional Ann Art Show & Sale, Cheyenne, Wyo; Artist of the Year & Best Show/Oil-base Medium, Rushmore Prof Fine Artists Show, Rapid City, SD, 85; Inducted into Colo Inst Art Hall of Fame, Denver, Colo, 91. *Bibliog:* Deborah S Borg (auth), article, Equine Images, fall 89; Shirley Behrens (auth), article, Art of the West, 3-4/90; Ann Thompson (auth), article, Wild West, 2/95. *Mem:* Will James Soc. *Media:* All Media. *Publ:* Illusr of five art textbooks, Int Correspondence Schs, 60-65; Portrait of Franklin Booth for feature article, Am Artist Mag, 66; Portrait of Pawel Kontny for feature article, Artists Rockies & Golden West Mag, 81; auth & illusr, feature article in: Int Cowboy Mag, Surrey, Eng, 12/87-1/88. *Mailing Add:* 85558 479th Ave Amelia NE 68711-3233

JENCKS, PENELOPE
SCULPTOR
b Baltimore, MD, Mar 23, 36. *Study:* Hans Hoffmann Sch, 55; Swarthmore Col, student, 56; Skowhegan Art Sch, 57; Boston Univ, BFA, 58; Stuttgart (Ger) Kunstakademie, 59. *Exhib:* One-woman shows, Fitchburg (Mass) Art Mus, 76, Landmark Gallery, New York City, 77 & 81, Art Inst Boston, 78, Helen Shlein Gallery, Boston, 81 & 85; group shows, at USIS, Amerika Haus, Freiburg, Ger, 60, Nat Inst Arts & Letters, New York City, 66, Mass Coun Arts & Humanities, Boston, 66, Thayer Acad, Braintree, 71, Boston Visual Artists Union, 74, Pa State Univ Mus Art, 74, Kennedy Galleries, New York City, 77, GVW Smith Art Mus, Springfield, Mass, 77, Clark Univ Mus Worcester, Mass, 78, Mass Artists Found Fed Reserve Bank, Boston, 80, Danforth Mus, Framingham, Mass, 80 & 84, Rose Art Mus Brandeis Univ, 82, MacDowell Colony Benefit, Cambridge, Mass, 83, Brockton Mass Art Mus, 83, Currier Gallery Art, Manchester, NH, 84, Fitchburg Art Mus, 84, Newton Arts Ctr, 85, Boston Univ, 86, Alchemy Gallery, Boston, 87, Helen Bumpus Gallery, Duxbury, Mass, 89, Rising Tide Gallery, Provincetown, Mass, 89, Contemp Sculpture, Chesterwood, Stockbridge, Mass, 89. *Pos:* Instr, Braintree (Mass) Art Asn, 71-72, Art Inst Boston, 75-79, Boston Col, Newton, Mass, 78. *Teaching:* Resident, MacDowell Colony, 75, 76, 78, & 87; prof, Saltzman vis artist Brandeis Univ, Waltham, 81-83; guest lectr, in field, currently. *Awards:* Commendation for Design Excellence, Nat Educ Asn, 81; grantee Brandeis Univ, 83; Henry Hering Mem Medal, Nat Sculpture Soc, 88. *Mem:* Nat Acad. *Mailing Add:* c/o Nat Acad Design 1083 Fifth Ave New York NY 10128

JENDRZEJEWSKI, ANDREW JOHN
SCULPTOR, ADMINISTRATOR
b Fremont, Mich, July 1, 46. *Study:* Tyler Sch Art, Rome & Philadelphia, BFA, 68; Wash Univ, St Louis, MFA, 73. *Exhib:* Show Case Show, Water Tower, Louisville, Ky, 85; Omnibus '88 Invitational, Herron Gallery, Indianapolis, Ind, 88; 40th Ann Four State Ilmoian, Quincy Art Ctr, Ill, 90; Midwest Sculpture, South Bend Regional Mus Art, Ind, 90; Indian Sculpture Invitational, Munster Art Ctr, Ind, 94. *Pos:* Mus technician, Univ Mich Mus Art, 73-75. *Teaching:* Prof art & sculpture & art dept chmn, Vincennes Univ Jr Col, 77-. *Bibliog:* Steve Mannheimer (auth), The Vincennes group, Indianapolis Star, 10/31/82; Marion Garmel (auth), Strong entries in Omnibus Exhib, Indianapolis News, 7/14/84; Hollis Sigler (auth), Jurer's Statement, 20th Ind Artists Catalog, 85. *Mem:* Nat Asn Sch Art & Design; Mid Am Col Art Asn. *Media:* Miscellaneous. *Mailing Add:* 404 N Fifth St Vincennes IN 47591-2106

JENKENS, GARLAN F
CURATOR, PAINTER
b Stamford, Tex, Aug 26, 49. *Study:* N Tex State Univ, Denton, BFA, 74, MFA, 76; Univ Ore, Eugene, PhD, 82. *Work:* N Tex State Univ Collection, Denton; Koger Corp, Exec Ctr, Little Rock, Ark; Corvallis Art Ctr Collection, Ore; Mountain View Community Col, Dallas, Tex; Worthen Banking Corp, Pine Bluff, Ark. *Exhib:* Amarillo Competition, Amarillo Art Ctr, Tex, 75; Watermark, Issac Hathaway Fine Art Ctr, Pine Bluff, Ark, 88; Stockton Nat IV, Haggin Mus Art, Calif, 88; Ark Art 91, Henderson State Univ, Arkadelphia, 91; The Arkansas Collection, Univ Ark, Little Rock, 91; The Inaugural Exhib: Selected Ark Artists, Collector Gallery, Washington, DC, 92; Dramas Recent Works by David Bailin, Arts & Sci Ctr, SE Ark, Pine Bluff, 93 & Artists of the Am West, 93; David Bailin, Works on Paper, Hathaway Howard Arts Ctr, Univ Ark, Pine Bluff, 94, Signs, Sentences and Symbols, 95, Environmental Surfaces; Speaking Through Textures, 95 & Surreal Journeys, 95; New Works, Baum Gallery Fine Art, Univ Cent Ark, Conway, 96, Impressions of Arkansas, 96, An Anthology, 96; and others. *Collection Arranged:* Mark Chagall: Illustrations for the Old Testament (auth, catalog), 88; Frederick Remmington: Illustrator of the Old West (auth, catalog), 89; Drawing: A Survey of the 20th Century (auth, catalog), 90; A Treasury of American Prints (auth, catalog), 91; Dali: The Divine Comedy (50 woodcuts; auth, catalog), 92; Recent Paintings: Frits van Eeden, Artist-in-Residence (auth, catalog), Brevard Mus Art, Melbourne, Fla, 93; John M Howard Retrospective: 1947-1977, 94. *Pos:* Dir & chief cur, Baum Gallery, Univ Cent Ark, currently. *Teaching:* Instr, Art Dept, Univ Cent Ark, Comway, currently; instr, Univ N Tex, Denton. *Awards:* Purchase Award, Tex A&I Invitational, 76; Purchase Award, 2nd Ann Juried Exhib, 81; Purchase Award, 5th Nat Biennial, 87. *Mem:* Am Asn Mus; Southeastern Mus Asn; Col Art Asn; Nat Art Educ Asn. *Media:* All. *Mailing Add:* c/o Baum Gallery Univ Cent Ark 201 Donaghey Ave Conway AR 71601

JENKINS, DONALD JOHN
CURATOR, HISTORIAN
b Longview, Wash, May 3, 31. *Study:* Univ Chicago, BA & MA. *Collection Arranged:* The Woodcut in Japan, 1700-1969, 69 & Japanese Folk Art and Ukiyo-e Prints, 83, Portland Art Mus, Ore; Ukiyo-e Prints & Paintings, The Primitive Period 1680-1745 (auth, catalog), Art Inst Chicago, 71; Louis V Ledoux, Collecting Ukiyo-e Master Prints (auth, catalog), Japan House Gallery, New York, 73; Masterworks in Wood: China and Japan (auth, catalog), Portland Art Mus & Asia House Gallery, New York, 76; Images of a Changing World: Japanese Prints of the Twentieth Century (auth, catalog), St Louis Art Mus, Los Angeles Co Mus Art, Carnegie Inst Mus Art & Portland Art Mus, 83; Perspectives 11, Contemp Japanese Graphics, 88; Portland Art Mus, Ore; Perspectives 13, Shoichi Ida, 89; The Floating World Revisited (auth, catalog), Portland Art Mus & Cleveland Mus Art, 93-94; Imperial Tombs of China, 95; Design & Installation of 5000 sq ft of new Asian galleries at PAM, 94-97. *Pos:* Asst cur, Portland Art Mus, 66-68, cur, 74-75 & dir, 75-87, cur Asian Art, 87-2004, chief curator, 97-2001; assoc cur Oriental art, Art Inst Chicago, 69-74. *Teaching:* Instr art hist, Mus Art Sch, Portland, Ore, 63-65; lectr hist art, Univ Mich, Ann Arbor, 74; vis instr, Dept Art, Univ Chicago, 74; vis prof hist Japanese art, Reed Col, Portland, 86-87. *Awards:* Uchiyama Susumu Award, Japan Ukiyoe Soc, 93; Order Rising Sun, with Gold Rays & Rosette, Govt Japan, 94. *Mem:* Japan Am Soc; Portland Classical Chinese Garden Bd. *Res:* Japanese prints and paintings of the Ukiyo-e School. *Publ:* Auth, Handbook of the Asian Collection of the Portland Art Mus, 81; article, Ukiyoe, Encyclopedia of Japan, Kodansha, 83; Painting of the Floating World, The Bulletin of the Cleveland Mus Art, 9/88; Facing the Future, Revisiting the Past, The New Wave, Twentieth Century Japanese Prints from the Robert O Miller Collection, Bamboo Publ, Hotei Japanese Press, 93; Shunsho & the Katsukawa School, essay Vol 3 of the catalog of the Buckingham Print Collection, Art Inst Chicago, Princeton Univ Press, 94. *Mailing Add:* Portland Art Museum 1219 SW Park Portland OR 97205

JENKINS, MARY ANNE KEEL
PAINTER, INSTRUCTOR
b Pitt Co, NC, Nov 20, 29. *Study:* Ferree Sch Art, Raleigh, NC; E Carolina Univ, Greenville; NC State Univ Sch Design, Raleigh; San Carlos Art Sch, Mexico City. *Work:* Weatherspoon Art Mus; NC State Univ Gallery Design; Greenville Art Mus; Wilson Collection, Univ NC, Chapel Hill; NC Mus Hist, Raleigh; HC Taylor Art Gallery, A&T State Univ, Greensboro, NC; NC Mus Art, Raleigh; Minn Mus Art, Minneapolis. *Comn:* Interior mural, Radio Station WPTF, Raleigh, 71; Philip Morris, 82; mural, First Union Nat Bank, Raleigh, 91, Chamber Commerce, Raleigh, 91. *Exhib:* NC Mus Art, Raleigh; Danville Art Mus, Va, 82; Raleigh Munic Bldg Exhib, 88 & 93; Duke Univ Law Sch, 98; 50-yr retrospective, Greenville Art Mus, 99-2000; Women Artsist, Greenville Mus Art, 04; Four Decades, Gallery C, Raleigh, NC, 05; The Best in NC, Gallery C, Raleigh, 2006. *Teaching:* Instr advanced painting, Pullen Art Ctr, Raleigh. *Awards:* Drawings USA Purchase Award, Minn Mus Art, St Paul, 71; Purchase Award & Hon Mention, Piedmont Exhib, Mint Mus, Charlotte, NC, 77; Raleigh Art Achievement Award, 87; Raleigh Medal of Art, 94; 12th Nat Jury Show, Paul Lindsay Sample Mem Award, Chautauqua Exhib of Am Art, 1969. *Bibliog:* Rubel Romero (auth), Ten Best (All That Was Great in 88) Our Critic's Choices - Deep Perspective, Spectator Mag, 1/89; Blue Greenberg (auth), Jenkins Exhibit: A

Whole & It's Parts, The Durham Morning Herald, 4/29/90; Dick Bell (auth), A lifetime devoted to art, Spectator, 5/26/94; Mary Anne Keel Jenkins, A retrospective, Greenville Mus Art, 2000. *Mem:* NC Mus Art (life). *Media:* All Media. *Dealer:* Gallery C 3532 Wade Ave Raleigh NC 27607. *Mailing Add:* 2600 Oxford Rd Raleigh NC 27608

JENKINS, PAUL
PAINTER
b Kansas City, Mo, July 12, 23. *Study:* Kansas City Art Inst & Sch Design, 38-41; Art Students League, 48-52, DH, 73. *Work:* Mus Mod Art, Whitney Mus Am Art & Solomon R Guggenheim Mus, NY; Tate Gallery, London, Eng; Mus Art Mod & Ctr Georges Pompidou, Paris; Stedelijk Mus, Amsterdam, Holland; Corcoran Gallery Am Art, Washington; and others. *Comn:* Medal, Inst French Civilization & Cult, NY Univ, 85; performance of Shaman to the Prism Seen, Paris Opera, 87; painted 2 kilometers of silk for performance at the Great Hall of the People, Peking Prism, 87. *Exhib:* Butler Inst Am Art, Youngstown, Ohio, 86; L'Opera de Paris, 87; Corcoran Gallery Art, Washington, DC & watercolor traveling show: Gimpel Fils Gallery, London; Gallery Art Point, Tokyo; Galarie Patrice Trigano, Paris; Musee de Nice, Galeries de Ponchettes et d'Art; Gimpel Weitzenhoffer Galerie, NY; Houston Mus Fine Arts, Tex; Painted silks, Int Comt for Safeguard of Venice & the Great Wall of China, 88; solo exhibs, Yoshii Gallery, Paris, 93, Assoc Am Artists, NY, 93, Paquale Iannetti Gallery, San Francisco, 94, Gallery Art Point, Tokyo, 94, L'Eau et la Couleur, France, traveling, 94, La Maison Francaise, NY Univ, 94 & Manchester Craftsmen's Guild, Pittsburgh, Pa, 94; one-man retrospective, Mus Fine Arts, Houston, San Francisco Mus Art & Palm Springs Desert Mus; Mus Mod Art, NY; Whitney Mus Art, NY; Solomon R Guggenheim Mus, NY; Tate Gallery, London, Eng; Mus Art Mod, Centre G Pompidou, Paris. *Awards:* Commandeur Arts & Lettres, France, 83; Cambridge Acad (Hon), Wales, 98; Benjamin West Clinedinst Medal Artists, Fel, NY, 2000. *Bibliog:* Pascal Bonafoux (auth), Paul Jenkins: Conjunctions and Annexes, Editions Galilee, Paris, 91; Frank Anderson (auth), L'Eau et la Couleur, Presence d'Art Contemporain, 94; and others. *Mem:* Century Asn; La Maison Francaise, NY Univ; Nat Acad, NY. *Publ:* Coauth, Anatomy of a Cloud, Abrams, 83; auth, dance-drama, Shaman to the Prism Seen, Paris, Opera, 5/87; coauth, Conjunctions and Annexes, Eds Galilee, Paris, Eng & Fr eds, 91; Seven Aspects of Amadeus and the Others, Eds Galilee, Paris, 92; Shaman to the Prism Moon, 94. *Dealer:* Assoc Am Artists 20 W 57th St New York NY 10019; Joseph Richards Gallery 1045 Madison Ave New York NY 10021

JENKINS, TWINNY
PAINTER, SCULPTOR
b Salem, Mass, May 6, 22. *Study:* New England Sch Art & Design; studied with color expert Harry Bartnick, 82; Montserrat Col Art; studied with Roger Martin, 84. *Hon Degrees:* Copley Soc Boston, dipl for Artistic Distinction, 87. *Work:* Pres Wm Clinton Collection Archives; Sakura Color Products Corp, Osaka, Japan; Salem City Hall. *Comn:* State House, comm by Gov Edward J King, Boston, 82; Salem City Hall, comm by Mayor Jean Leveque, Salem, 82; New England Power Plant, Salem, Mass, 85. *Exhib:* One-woman shows, Copley Soc, Boston, 87, Montserrat Col Gallery, Beverly, 85, Hooper Mansion Gallery, Marblehead, 82 Winfiskey Gallery, Salem State Col, Salem, Mass, 77; one-woman retrospective, Twinny Jenkins House Mus, Salem, Mass, 88-. *Awards:* Honor Award, Copley Soc Boston, 87. *Bibliog:* Henry Ferrini (producer), My Little Hands (video), 89; Liliya Guttsenok (producer), Twinny's Art Life (video), CNN, 93; also articles in Yankee Mag, 88 & Greater Boston Community Develop, 84. *Media:* All Media; Clay

JENKINS, ULYSSES SAMUEL, JR
VIDEO ARTIST, MURALIST
b Los Angeles, Calif, Sept 19, 46. *Study:* Southern Univ, BA, 69; Otis Art Inst, MFA, 79. *Work:* Calif Inst Arts, Santa Clarita; Long Beach Mus Art; Am Mus Moving Image, Astoria, NY; Electronic Arts Intermix, NY. *Comn:* Mural hist of motor vehicles, Calif Dept Motor Vehicles, Los Angeles, 76; Cake Walk (vid doc), Houston Conwill, NY, 83; Being Witness: The Haids Proj (doc), Headlands Ctr Arts, Sausalito, Calif, 91. *Exhib:* James D Phelan Awards, San Francisco Mus Art, 93; Int Festival Electronic Arts, San Paulo & Rio de Janerio, Brazil, 94; When Worlds Collide, Mus Mod Art, NY, 94; New Media Research/The Art & Virtual Environments Proj, Baniff Ctr for Art, Alta, Can, 94; Governor's Conf on Art & Technology VI, Calif Arts Coun, Santa Claria, 95; and others internationally. *Pos:* Artistic dir, Othervisions Studio, 83-. *Teaching:* Vis lectr video art, Univ Calif, San Diego, 79-81, Otis Parsons Art Inst, Los Angeles, 85; asst prof, Univ Calif Irvine, 93-. *Awards:* NEA Grant, 80, 82 & 95; Calif Arts Coun Fel, 86-97; Black Filmmakers Hall of Fame, 90 & 92. *Bibliog:* Judith Wilson (auth), Black Artist 87-88, Garland Press, 89; Lorraine O'Gady (auth), Interview of Maren Hassinger, Hatch Billops Collections Inc, 93. *Mem:* Bay Area Video Coalition, San Francisco (bd mem, 90-96). *Media:* Video & Performance Art, Telecommunications Art. *Publ:* Auth, Video visions, electronic dreams, Oakland Mus & Mus Calif, 90; Doggerel Period: California Arts Council Multi-cultural Grant, pvt publ, 91; What are you going to do after you drink up the ocean?, Video Networks, 92; Scratching the belly of the beast, Film Forum Catalog, 94; Headlands virtual ritual, Headlands J, 94. *Dealer:* The Electronic Arts Intermix 536 Broadway 9th floor New York NY 10012. *Mailing Add:* 6527 West Blvd Inglewood CA 90302-1845

JENNERJAHN, W P
EDUCATOR, PAINTER
b Milwaukee, Wis, June 15, 22. *Study:* Univ Wis, Milwaukee, BS, 46; Univ Wis, Madison, MS, 47; Black Mountain Col, with Josef Albers, 48-50; Acad Grande Chaumiere, Paris, 50; Acad Julian, Paris, 50-51; also with Gerard Wagner, Dornach, Switz, 78 & 81. *Work:* Josef Albers Found; Black Mt Col Art Mus; AT&T; AVIS. *Comn:* Stained glass panel, Long Island Jewish Hosp, NY; stained glass mural, comn by Dr Fredrick Lane, Great Neck, NY; stained glass mural(with John Urbain), JFK Airport Int Hotel; murals for eight ships(with Elizabeth Jennerjahn), Mil Sea Transport Serv; painting, Avis World Hq, Garden City, NY. *Exhib:* Exhib Momentum, Chicago; Milwaukee Ann, Univ Wis; Birmingham Ann, Ala; Dulin Ann, Tenn; Black Mountain Col Invitational, Johnson City, Tenn. *Teaching:* Art teacher, Black Mountain Col, NC, 49-50, Cooper Union, 52-54, Hunter Col, 53 & Elderhostel Prog, N Ariz Univ, Sedona; prof art, Adelphi Univ, 54-87; retired. *Awards:* Tiffany Found Grant, 52; Adelphi Univ Humanities Grants, 62, 68 & 84. *Media:* Oil, Watercolor. *Publ:* Illusr, Respect for Life, 74; contribr (with Geo K Russell), Laboratory Investigations in Human Physiology, MacMillan, 78. *Dealer:* Art in Living Spaces Cornville Ariz. *Mailing Add:* 707 Rainbow Tr Sedona AZ 86351

JENNEY, NEIL
PAINTER, SCULPTOR
b Torrington, Conn, Nov 6, 45. *Study:* Self taught. *Exhib:* One-man exhibs, Galerie Rudolf Zwirner, Cologne, WGer, 68, Noah Goldowsky Gallery, NY, 70, Blum Helman Gallery, NY, 75 & Matrix Gallery, Wadsworth Atheneum, Hartford, Conn, 75-76, The Bad Yrs 1969-70, Seven Paintings from 1969, 98 Greene St Loft, NY, 73, Blum/Helman, NY, 75, Univ Calif Art Mus, Berkeley, 82, Contemp Arts Mus, Houston, Stedelijk Mus, Amsterdam, The Neth, La Mus, Humlebaek, Denmark, Kunsthalle, Basel, Switz, 82, Oil & Steel Gallery, NY, 84, Neil Jenney Paintings & Sculpture 1967-1980, Carpenter & Hochman Gallery, NY, 85, Barbara Mathes Gallery, NY, 87, Vivian Horan Fine Art, NY, 88, Collection in Context Neil Jenney: Natural Rationalism, Whitney Mus Am Art, NY, 94, Gagosian Gallery, NY, 2001; New Image, Whitney Mus Am Art, NY, 78-79; 60-80 Attitudes-Concepts-Images, Stedelijk Mus, Amsterdam, 82; Annina Nosei Gallery, NY, 83; Whitney Mus, NY, 94; group exhibs Hal Bromm Ballery, NY, 77, Inst Art & Urban Resources, NY, 77, Holly Solomon Gallery, NY, 77, Whitney Mus Am Art, NY, 77, 78, Met Mus Art, NY, 77, Fine Arts Mus San Francisco, 77, Pushkin Mus, Moscow, 77, The Hermatage, Leningrad, 77, Palace of Art, Minsk, 77, New Mus Contemp Art, NY, 78, Albright-Knox Art Gallery, Buffalo, 78, Newport Harbor Mus, Newport Beach, 78, Oakland Mus, 78, Cincinnati Art Mus, 78, Art Mus South Tex, Corpus Christi, 78, Krannert Art Mus, Univ Ill, Champaign, 78, Blum/Helman Gallery, NY, 78, 80, Audrey Strohl Gallery, Memphis, 79, Marian Goodman Gallery, NY, 80, Neue Galerie-Sammlung Ludwig, Aachen, Ger, 80, Nordjyllands Kunstmuseum, Aalborg, Denmark, 80, Mus Contemp Art, Los Angeles, 83 & 87. *Bibliog:* Mark Stevens (auth), Neil Jenney: Art is a social science, Portfolio, Vol 4, No 3, 5-6/82; Julia Brown & Bridget Johnson (coauth), Charles and Doris Saatchi: Notes, In: The First Show: Painting and Sculpture from Eight Collections, 1940-1980, Mus Contemp Art, Los Angeles, 83. *Publ:* Auth, Anti-Illusion: Procedures-Materials, Whitney Mus Am Art, 69; When Attitude Becomes Form, Kunsthalle, Bern, 69; article, Allen Mem Art Mus Bull, Vol 27, No 3, spring 70. *Mailing Add:* 151 Chapel Rd Winchester CT 06098

JENNIFER, TODD
FILMMAKER
b Colombo, Sri Lanka. *Study:* Calif Univ, San Diego, MFA. *Exhib:* The Girls Nervy, 1995; Chronic, 1996; Darling Internat (with MM Serra), 1999; Fear of Blushing, 2001; The Time We Killed, 2004; group shows: Toronto Film Festival, Kill Your Timid Notion: Dundee Contemp Arts Festival, Whitney Biennial: Day for Night, Whitney Mus Am Art, 2006; Shadows Choose Their Horrors. *Pos:* Found, Sparky Pictures, Inc, 2000. *Teaching:* Vis asst prof & electronic arts, Yale Univ, New Haven; instr (part-time), Bard Col, Milton Avery Sch Arts, Cooper Union, Millennium film workshop. *Awards:* grantee Jacob K Fel, 1997-2001; Andrea Frank Found grant, 1999; We Are Going Home, Film Co-op award, Ann Arbor Film Festival, 1999; Juror's Citation, Black Maria Film Festival, 1999; Cinematography award, Cinetexas Film Festival, 2000; Recipient Princes Grace award, 2000; Critics prize, Berlin Film Festival, Outstanding Artistic Achievement; Outfest, Best NY, NY Narrative Feature, Tribeca Film Festival. *Mailing Add:* Sparky Pictures Inc PO Box 136 Planetarium Sta New York NY 10024

JENNINGS, JAN
WRITER
b Chicago, Ill, Apr 4, 43. *Study:* Northwestern Univ, Evanston, BSJ; Univ Mo-Columbia, grad studies journalism & art. *Pos:* Art writer, San Diego Tribune, Calif, 71-88; asst dir mus, Mingei Int Mus World Folk Art, San Diego, 90-91; writer, publicist art & humanities, Univ Calif, currently; art dir, writer, The Frederic Whitaker and Eileen Monaghan Whitaker Found, San Diego, Calif, 01-. *Mem:* San Diego Mus Art; San Diego Mus Contemp Art; Mingei Int Mus World Folk Art. *Res:* artists Frederic Whitaker and Eileen Monaghan Whitaker. *Collection:* Various collections from representational works to abstract, op, pop & animation. *Publ:* Free-lance writer with contributing features to Southwest Art Mag, Am Artist, Western Art Digest, Art of California, Ranch & Coast; Contrasts That Complement: Eileen Monaghan Whitaker - Frederic Whitaker (auth), Marguand Books Inc, Seattle, 04. *Mailing Add:* 1750 Galveston St San Diego CA 92110

JENRETTE, PAMELA ANNE
PAINTER, COSTUME DESIGNER
b Ft Bragg, NC, Aug 24, 47. *Study:* Univ Tex, BFA, 69. *Exhib:* Clean, Well-lighted Place (two-artist show), Austin, Tex, 71; Whitney Biennial, NY, 75; Cologne Art Festival, Ger, 75; one-artist show, Artists Space, New York, NY, 75. *Pos:* Studio asst, Lawrence Poons, New York, 71-75. *Awards:* Competition Award, Conde Nast, 69. *Bibliog:* Martha Utterback (auth), Texas, Artforum, 1/71. *Media:* Acrylic, Watercolor

JENSEN, BILL
PAINTER
b Minneapolis, Minn, Nov 26, 45. *Study:* Univ Minn, BFA, 68, MFA, 70. *Work:* Whitney Mus Am Art, Metrop Mus Art & Mus Mod Art, NY; Worcester Mus Art, Mass; Fogg Art Mus, Cambridge, Mass; Los Angeles Co Mus Art, Calif; Chase Manhattan Bank, NY; and others. *Exhib:* solo exhibs, Mus Mod Art, 86, Grob Gallery,

London, 91, Margo Leavin Gallery, Los Angeles, Calif, 91, Mary Boone Gallery, NY, 93, 95, 96, 98, 01, 03, Nielson Gallery, Boston, 94, Patricia Faure Gallery, Santa Monica, Calif, 95, Joan T Washburn Gallery, NY, 96, Joseloff Gallery, Hartford, Conn, 99, Danese Gallery, NY, 00, Galerie Felix Ringel, Düsseldorf, Ger, 2001; Mary Boone Gallery New York City, 93, 95, 98, 2001 & 2003; Celebrating Modern Art: The Anderson Collection, San Francisco Mus Mod Art, 2000; Danese Gallery, New York City, 2000, 2002 & 2004; Painting Abstraction II, NY Studio Sch, 2001; Art Downtown: NY Painting & Sculpture, Wall St, New York City, 2002; Tex Gallery, Houston, 2003; A Bend in the Road: Paintings and Works on Paper, Maier Museum of Art, Randolph-Macon Woman's Col, Va, 2003; Clear Intentions, Rotunda Gallery, Brooklyn, 2003; Contemporary Voices: Works from The UBS Art Collection, Mus Modern Art, NY, 2005; Paint It With Black, Betty Cunningham Gallery, NY, 2005. *Teaching:* Instr, Univ Minn, 65-70, Brooklyn Mus Art Sch, 71-75 & York Col, Queens, NY, 72-73. *Awards:* Artist's Fel, Nat Endowment Arts, 85-86; Am Acad Arts & Letters Award, 97; Guggenheim Fel, 98. *Bibliog:* Eric Gibson (auth), Bill Jensen, Art News, 1/96; John Yau (auth), Epiphany & Surrender: The recent paintings of Bill Jensen, LINGO, 3/96; Pepe Karmel (auth), Bill Jensen recent drawings, NY Times, 4/5/96; Jed Perl (auth), The Unvarnished Truth, Modern Painters, 4/98; Robert Smith (auth), Bill Jensen and Leonardo Drew, The NY Times, 9/98; Tom Breidenbach (auth), Bill Jensen, Artforum, 12/98; Lance Esplund (auth), Truth or Dare, Modern Painters, 4/99; Ken Johnson (auth), Bill Jensen, The NY Times, 4/21/2000; Rachel Youens (auth), The Manhattan Scene, The Brooklyn Rail, Feb 2001; Ken Johnson (auth), Bill Jensen, The NY Times, 3/16/2001; Mario Naves (auth), Art Submits to Mary Boone in Dealer's Chelsea Atrium, The New York Observer, 3/19/2001. *Mem:* Creative Artists Pub Serv Prog; Fel, Nat Endowment for Arts; Nat Acad. *Media:* Oil, Gouache. *Mailing Add:* c/o Mary Boone Gallery 745 Fifth Ave New York NY 10151

JENSEN, CLAY EASTON
SCULPTOR, EDUCATOR
b Salt Lake City, Utah, Mar 14, 52. *Study:* Univ Utah, Salt Lake City, BFA, 75; Univ Calif, Berkeley, MA, 78, MFA, 79. *Work:* Oakland Mus, Calif; Crocker Art Mus, Sacramento, Calif. *Comn:* Sculpture, Fed Reserve Bank, San Francisco, Calif, 83; sculpture, Syntex Corp, Palo Alto, Calif, 84; sculpture, AT&T, Pleasanton, Calif, 84; sculpture, William Wilson & Assocs, San Mateo, Calif, 86; sculpture, Dealy, Renton & Assocs, Oakland, Calif, 86. *Exhib:* Solo exhibs, San Francisco Mus Mod Art (with catalog), Calif, 83, Fuller Cross Gallery, San Francisco, 85 & 88, Christopher Grimes Gallery, Santa Monica, Calif, 90, Erickson & Elins Gallery, San Francisco, 92; Utah Mus Fine Arts, Salt Lake City, 75; New Affirmations, Oakland Mus, Calif, 80; MFA Exhib, Univ Art Mus, Univ Calif, Berkeley. *Teaching:* Assoc instr, Univ Utah, Salt Lake City, 75-76; vis fac, Calif Col Arts & Craft, 80-82, asst prof, 87-; guest lectr sculpture, Univ Calif, Berkeley, 84-85; asst prof, San Jose State Univ, 84-85 & 89-90. *Awards:* Fel, Nat Endowment Asn, 78; Soc Encouragement Contemp Art Award, San Francisco Mus Mod Art, 83. *Bibliog:* Alfred Jan (auth), article, in: Images and Issues, 1/84; Suzaan Boettger (auth), rev, in: Art Forum, 4/84; Robert McDonald (auth), Rural Urban Dichotomies, Vol XIIII, No 39, Art Week, 11/19/83; James Scarborough (auth), Galactic Perspective Clay Jensen at Christopher Grimes Gallery, Vol 21, No 35, Artweek, 10/90. *Media:* Painted Steel, Cast Bronze. *Dealer:* Erickson & Elins Gallery San Francisco CA; Morgan Gallery Kansas City MO. *Mailing Add:* 951 62nd St Emeryville CA 94608

JENSEN, DEAN N
DEALER, CRITIC
Study: Univ Wis, BA; Roosevelt Univ, Chicago; Univ Chicago. *Collection Arranged:* Center Ring: The Artist (auth, catalog), Milwaukee Art Mus, Columbus Mus Art, NY State Mus, Albany & Corcoran Gallery Art, 81; Material Obsessions: Folk and Outside, Art from Wisconsin Collections (auth, catalog), Milwaukee Inst Art & Design, 89. *Pos:* Art ed & critic, Milwaukee Sentinel, Wis, 67-87; owner, Dean Jensen Gallery, Milwaukee, 87-. *Teaching:* Milwaukee Inst Art & Design, 91-. *Awards:* Res & Study Fel, Univ Mich, 85-86. *Res:* Contemporary art; Circus as a theme in art. *Publ:* Auth, The Biggest, The Smallest, The Longest, The Shortest, Wis House, 75; Reunion in Hell: The Drawings of Paul Caster, Perimeter Press, 82; contribr, Art News, Arts, Midwest-Art & others. *Mailing Add:* c/o Dan Jenson Gallery 759 N Water St Milwaukee WI 53202

JENSEN, LEO
SCULPTOR, PAINTER
b Montevideo, Minn, July 10, 26. *Study:* Walker Art Ctr, scholar, 46-48. *Work:* US Info Agency, Washington, DC; Brown Univ; Walker Art Ctr, Minneapolis, Minn; Mattatuck Mus, Waterbury, Conn; Achenbach Col, San Francisco; bronze & concrete Spool-Frog sculpture, Windham, Conn, 2000; Mark Twain Libr, Redding, Conn; Acad for Educ Develop, Washington, DC; bronze fountain, Vinnies Restaurant, Old Saybrooke, Conn, 2000. *Comn:* construction, Macmillan Publ Co, NY, 68; polychrome relief, Med World News, NY, 70; Wood Model for Spool-Frog Bridge sculpture, Windham, Conn, 95; four 3000 lb bronze frogs for bridge, Willimantic, Conn, 2001. *Exhib:* Solo exhibs, Amel Gallery, NY, 64-65, Sakovitz Gallery, Houston, 64, New Britain Mus Am Art, Far Gallery, NY 73, Arras Gallery, NY, 76, A Book Gallery, San Francisco, 78, Frank Fedele Gallery, NY, 81, Vorpal Gallery, NY, 87, Mattatuck Mus, Waterbury, Conn, 90, Childers Gallery, Ft Lauderdale, Fla, 91; group shows, Butler Inst Am Art, Ohio, 53, Mattatuck Mus, Conn, 90; Mus Mod Art, 64 65, Am Mus Nat Hist, 82, NY; Milwaukee Art Ctr, 65; Chicago Hist Soc, 81; Baseball Hall Fame, 83; Castle Gallery Col, New Rochelle, NY, 87; Hollycroft Int, 96; and other mus in 64 countries. *Pos:* Founder, Wildcat Fine Art Trust, New Haven, Conn, 88. *Bibliog:* M B Scott (auth), The Artist & the Sportsman, Renaissance, 68; D Z Meiloch (auth), Contemporary Art With Wood, Crown, 68; H N Abrams Publ, Champions of Am Sport, Smithsonian Inst, 81. *Mem:* Artists Equity Asn. *Media:* Bronze, Wood; Acrylic, Watercolor. *Mailing Add:* PO Box 264 Ivoryton CT 06442

JERDON, WILLIAM HARLAN
PAINTER, INSTRUCTOR
b Hamilton, Ohio, May 30, 44. *Study:* Bowling Green State Univ, 66, MA, 72, MFA, 73. *Work:* Western Reserve Hist Soc, Cleveland, Ohio. *Comn:* mural, Standard Oil Ohio, Cleveland, Ohio, 84; mural, Good Year Aerospace, Akron, Ohio, 84; mural, Chase Brass & Copper Co, Inc, Cleveland, Ohio, 85; mural, Deloitte, Haskins, Sells Accounting, Cleveland, Ohio, 85. *Exhib:* 55th Ann Exhib, Toledo Mus Art, Toledo, Ohio, 73; 36th Ohio Artist and Craftsmen show, The Massillon Mus, Massillon, Ohio, 74; invitational painting exhib, Southern Alleghenies Mus Art, Loretto, Pa, 78; Butler Inst Am Art, Youngstown, Ohio. *Pos:* educ testing adv, Educ Testing Serv, Princeton, NJ, 86-87; continuing researcher, Nat Arts Educ Research Ctr, NY Univ, NY, 87-88; test writer, Educ Testing Serv, Princeton, NJ, 88-89. *Teaching:* teacher, Art & Photog, Cleveland Heights High Sch, Cleveland Heights, Ohio, 66-97; instr, Drawing, Cleveland Inst Art, Cleveland, Ohio, 78-80; instr, Drawing & Painting, Ringling Sch Art and Design, Sarasota, Fla, 2001-2003. *Awards:* US Presidential Distinguished Teacher Award, White House Comn on Presidential Scholars, 85; Fel for Teachers of the Arts, John F Kennedy Ctr for the Performing Arts, Washington DC, 86; Honors Fel, RI Sch Design, Providence, RI, 87. *Bibliog:* Timothy Dvin (auth), Heights teacher sees honors, The Plain Dealer, 6/10/86; Helen Cullinan (auth), Fitting tribute to gallery head, Cleveland Plain Dealer, 7/31/91; Susan Chapman (auth), Englewood's Bill Jerdon, Sarasota Herald Tribune, 6/3/2004. *Mem:* Sarasota Portrait Artists Asn. *Media:* Oil, Charcoal, Graphite. *Publ:* auth, A Course of Study for Art History, Cleveland Heights, Univ Heights BOE, 74; auth, A Course of Study for Photography, Cleveland Heights, Univ Heights BOE, 75; auth, A Course of Study for Advanced Photography, Cleveland Heights, Univ Heights BOE, 75; auth, A Course of Study for Studio Problems, Cleveland Heights, Univ Heights BOE, 76; auth, A Course of Study for Advanced Studio Problems, Cleveland Heights, Univ Heights BOE, 76. *Dealer:* Dabbert Gallery 76 S Palm Ave Sarasota Fla 84236. *Mailing Add:* 600 Artist Ave Englewood FL 34223

JERGENS, ROBERT JOSEPH
PAINTER, EDUCATOR
b Cleveland, Ohio, Mar 18, 38. *Study:* Cleveland Inst Art; Skowhegan Sch Painting & Sculpture; Yale Univ, BFA & MFA; Am Acad in Rome. *Work:* Cleveland Mus Art; NAm Col, Rome, Italy; Skowhegan Sch Painting & Sculpture; Brooklyn Art Mus; and others. *Comn:* Cleveland Pub Libr, 60 & 89. *Exhib:* Cleveland Mus Art, 57-64; Exhib by US Info Agency; Mus Mod Art, NY; Corcoran Gallery Art, Washington, DC; Mostra Univ, Rome; and others. *Teaching:* Instr design, Cooper Union, formerly; instr drawing, Sch Art & Archit, Yale Univ, formerly; instr design, Cleveland Inst Art, currently. *Awards:* Prix de Rome, 60 & 61; Mary C Page Grant, 61; Prize, Cleveland Mus Art, 61; and others. *Mailing Add:* 5356 Regency Dr Cleveland OH 44129-5961

JERINS, EDGAR
PAINTER
b Lincoln, Neb, June 12, 58. *Study:* Pa Acad Fine Arts, 80. *Work:* Ark Art Ctr, Little Rock; Mus of Nebr Art, Kearney, Nebr. *Exhib:* My Friend, My Brothers, Payne Gallery, Moravian Col, PA, 2004; one man exhib, Tatistchett Gallery, NY; Traditions and Departures, Mentors and Protoges, Vose Gallery, Boston, MA; collectors exhib, Ark Art Ctr, Ark, 2004; Re-Presenting Representation VI, Arnot Art Mus, Elmira, NY. *Awards:* Elizabeth Greenshilds Found Grant, 80; Caroline Gibbons Granger Mem Award, Pa Acad, 87; The Pollock-Krasner Found Grant, 2004; The Elizabeth Found for the Arts Grant, 2003; George Sugarman Found Grant, 2002; ED Found Grant, 2001. *Bibliog:* Helen A Harrison (auth), 76 Artworks review 86 & 87, Islip Mus Show, 89, NY Times. *Mem:* Fel, Pa Acad Fine Arts; Copley Soc, Boston. *Media:* Oil, Pastel. *Dealer:* Portraits Inc 985 Park Ave New York NY 10028; Tatischeff Gallery 529 W 20th 9th Flr New York NY 10011. *Mailing Add:* 326 E 84th St No 4C New York NY 10028

JERRY, MICHAEL JOHN
EDUCATOR, CRAFTSMAN
b Grand Rapids, Mich, Aug 18, 37. *Study:* Sch Am Craftsman, Rochester Inst Technol, AAS & BFA, 60, MFA, 63; Cranbrook Acad Art, 60-62. *Work:* Wustum Mus Fine Art, Racine, Wis; Mus Contemp Crafts, NY; Metrop Mus of Art, NY; Brooklyn Mus Art, NY. *Exhib:* Int Trade Fair Jewelry Exhib, Munich, Ger, 71; The 6th Goldsmiths Expos, Kersnikova, Yugoslavia, 72; Goldsmiths, Renwick Gallery, Washington, DC, 74; Contemp Metals US, Downey Mus Art, Calif, 85; Am Pewter Guild Design Competition, James Michener Mus, Pa, 94. *Teaching:* Assoc prof metalsmithing, Wis State Univ, Menomonie, 63-70; prof metalsmithing, Syracuse Univ, 70-. *Mem:* Am Crafts Coun; Soc NAm Goldsmiths. *Media:* Metal. *Publ:* Contribr, American jewelry, Design Quart, 59; Philip Morton, Contemporary Jewelry, Holt, 69; Objects: USA, Viking, 70; The Craftsman in America, Nat Geog Soc, 75; Metalsmith, Vol 8, fall 88 & Vol 1, Winter 92. *Mailing Add:* Syracuse Univ Dept Art Syracuse NY 13244-1010

JERVISS, JOY
PRINTMAKER
b Palmerton, Pa, Feb 14, 41. *Study:* C W Post Col, & Empire State Col; apprentice to Andre Girard. *Work:* Colgate Univ Libr & Syracuse Univ Art Collection, NY; Bibliot Nat, Paris; Miami Mus Mod Art, Fla; Ariz State Univ, Tempe; Princeton Univ Art Mus, NJ; Lehigh Univ Art Galleries, Pa; Art Inst of Zanesville, Ohio. *Pos:* Art exhib dir, N K Winston Corp, New York, 66-73; pres, United Press & Pallet, Northport, NY, 68-; founder, Northport Art League, 71-. *Teaching:* Asst instr printmaking, North Shore Community Arts Ctr, Great Neck, NY, 66-68; instr printmaking, Union Free Sch Dist 4, Northport, NY, 70-72; instr, BOCES III, 82-86. *Media:* Etching. *Mailing Add:* 84 Ocean Ave Northport NY 11768

JESSEN, SHIRLEY AGNES
PAINTER
b Brooklyn, NY, Jan 23, 21. *Study:* New York Sch Applied Design Women, scholar, cert, 39; Fashion Art Inst, Rockefeller Ctr, 40; also with Lou Eisele, Frederick Lehman, Paul Wood & Norman Nodell, 60-99; Huntington Town Art League, 1992-2003; Long Island Coun Arts, 91-99. *Work:* Sotheby Art Auctions; Channels 13: Art & Auctions, 79-87; Channel 21 Art Auctions, 79-87. *Exhib:* One-woman exhibs, Shelter Rock Libr, Roslyn, NY, 96, Garden City Libr, 96, Art League Long Island, 98, 99 & 04, Huntington Art Coun, 99, Unitarian Universalist Church, Garden City, 2000, Farmingdale Libr, 2000, Township Oyster Bay, 2000-03, Adelphi Univ, 2005 & others; Winthrop Univ Hosp, 50-2003; St Pauls Cult Arts Exhib, Garden City, 96; Directors Invitational, Chelsea Art Ctr Cult Arts, Muttontown, 96-2003; Gold Coast Art Show, AHRC, Brookville, 96; Planting Fields Art Show, Coe Estates Hist Park, 96; Island Landmark Exhib, Mill Mus, 97; and others. *Pos:* Illusr, Wantagh Parent Teachers Asn, 50-65; illusr, United Cerebral Palsy, 59-75; illusr, Nassau Co Med Soc Auxilary, 59-95; illusr, Georgia O'Keeffe, Community Club, 88 & 93-. *Teaching:* Expo Films 70-71; On the Casino, Community Club of Hempstead and Garden City, 2003. *Awards:* Cash Award, Suburban Art League, 81; Finalist, Lincoln Ctr, 81 & 82; Am Artists Mag; Award of Excellence in Oil, Town of Oyster Bay, 2004. *Bibliog:* David L Shirey (auth), Critical Rev, NY Times, 3/9/80; Book review, NY Art, 87-91; Robert Clarke (auth), Critical Rev, Garden City Life, 4/25/96. *Mem:* Freeport Arts Coun; Long Island Arts Coun Freeport; Knickerbocker Artists, NY; Art League Long Island; Allied Artists Am; hon life mem, bd dir, pres Nassau Co Med Soc Alliance. *Media:* Oils, Acrylics; Watercolor, pen and ink. *Publ:* Newsday, New York Times, Garden City Life, Garden City News, 96-2005. *Mailing Add:* 15 St Pauls Crescent Garden City NY 11530-1409

JESSUP, ROBERT
PAINTER
b Moscow, Idaho, July 18, 52. *Study:* Univ Wash, Seattle, BA(art hist), BFA(painting), 75; Univ Iowa, Iowa City, MA(painting), 77, MFA(painting), 78. *Work:* Metrop Mus Art, NY; High Mus Art, Atlanta, Ga; Huntington Art Gallery, Univ Tex, Austin; Roswell Mus & Art Ctr, NMex. *Comn:* Relief painting, comn by Doanld B Anderson, Roswell, NMex, 81; painting, comn by Robert Dornbush, Atlanta, Ga, 85. *Exhib:* Solo exhibs, Roswell Mus, NMex, 81, Nicola Jacobs Gallery, London, Eng, 84, Jan Turner Gallery, Los Angeles, 86, Zola-Lieberman Gallery, Chicago, 86 & Ruth Siegel, Ltd, NY, 86; New Figurative Painting, Asheville Art Mus, NC, 85; Painting & Sculpture Today, Indianapolis Mus Art, Ind, 86; Landscape, Seascape, Cityscape, Contemp Arts Ctr, New Orleans, La, 86. *Teaching:* Lectr & vis artist painting, Ohio State Univ, Columbus, Ohio, 81-82; asst prof painting, Ga State Univ, Atlanta, 82-83 & Cornell Univ, Ithaca, NY, 83-86. *Bibliog:* John Russell (auth), Aspects of the figure, New York Times, 7/2/82; Theodore F Wolff (auth), How artists improve, Christian Sci Monitor, 7/2/86. *Media:* Oil on Canvas & Linen; Charcoal on Paper. *Dealer:* Ruth Siegel Ltd 24 W 57th St New York NY 10019. *Mailing Add:* 2329 Salado St Denton TX 76201-7953

JESWALD, JOSEPH
PAINTER
b Leetonia, Ohio, May 17, 27. *Study:* Acad Julian, Paris; with Fernand Leger, Paris; Columbia Univ. *Work:* Hirshhorn Mus; Neuberger Mus; Addison Gallery Am Art; Rockefeller Found. *Pos:* Founder, Montserrat Col Art, Beverly, Mass. *Mailing Add:* 4417 Mink Rd Sarasota FL 34235-5119

JEWELL, JOYCE
PAINTER, PRINTMAKER
b Washington, DC, Oct 11, 45. *Study:* Montgomery Col, Md, AA, 65; Am Univ, Washington, DC, BA, 67; George Washington Univ, MFA, 72; Tamarind Inst Lithography, NMex, 74. *Work:* Montgomery Co Contemp Print Collection, Md; Owensboro Federal Savings & Loan Asn, Ky. *Exhib:* 19th Area Exhib, Corcoran Gallery Art, Washington, DC, 74; Irene Leache Mem Art Exhib, Chrysler Mus, Va, 78, 80; Va Printmakers, 1979, Va Mus Fine Arts, 79; 17th Bradley Nat Print & Drawing Exhib, Lakeview Mus, 79; Mid-Am Nat Art Exhib, Owensboro Mus Fine Art, Ky, 80; 22nd Area Exhib: Works on Paper, Corcoran Gallery Art, 80; Collage & Assemblage: A Nat Invitational Traveling Exhib, Miss Mus Art, Jackson, Miss, 81-83; Maryland Biennial: Works on Paper, Baltimore Mus Art, 83-84. *Pos:* Graphic designer, John Hoskins & Assocs, Arlington, Va, 67-71. *Teaching:* Prof design, drawing, etching & lithography, Montgomery Col, Md, 71-. *Awards:* Printmaking Award, Montgomery Co Juried Art Show, 78; Mid-Am Volunteers Purchase Award, Owensboro Mus Fine Art, 80; Owensboro Federal Savings & Loan Purchase Award, Mid-Am Nat Art Exhib, 80. *Bibliog:* Article, Gargoyle Mag, No 17/18, 81; Collage & Assemblage, Miss Mus Art, 81. *Media:* Collage. *Mailing Add:* c/o Montgomery Col 7600 Takoma Ave Takoma Park MD 20912-4197

JEYNES, PAUL
SCULPTOR, PAINTER
b Millburn, NJ, 27. *Study:* Yale Univ, BA, 49; with Frank Eliscu, 74. *Comn:* Tiger, US Filter Corp, NY, 76; Cougar & 2 Cubs, Rye Country Day Sch, NY, 90; Dog & Cat, Bide-A-Wee, NY, 99. *Exhib:* Allied Artists, NY, 84-93; St Hubert's Giralda, 88-90; Nat Acad Design, 90; Central Park Zoo, NY, 90; Olympia and York, NY, 91. *Pos:* Dir, Art Founders Guild Am Inc, 79-88; Ed, The Artist's Foundry 79-99. *Awards:* First Prize for Wondrous Wildlife, Cincinnati Zoo, 83; Gold Medal, Allied Artists, 85; St Hubert's Giralda Award of Distinction, 89; and others. *Mem:* Soc Animal Artists Inc; Allied Artists Am Inc. *Media:* Acrylic, Cast Bronze. *Mailing Add:* 305 E 70th St New York NY 10021

JEZIK, ENRIQUE
SCULPTOR, ENVIRONMENTAL ARTIST
b Codoba, Arg, Aug 1, 61. *Study:* Nat Sch Fine Arts, Buenos Aires, Arg, 87. *Work:* Mus Nac Bellas Artes, Buenos Aires, Arg; Mus Arte Contemporaneo Carrillo Gil Mexico. *Exhib:* Algunos Especimenes, Mus Universitario Chopo, Mexico City, 93; one-man shows, Mus Universitavio Chopo (with catalog), Mexico City, 91, Esculturas, Mus Arte Mod, Toluca, Mexico, 92 & Observaciones, Mus Arte Contemp Carrillo Gil, Mexico City, 95; In-site 94, Traveling Exhib, 94; Libro-objecto, Centro Wilfredo Lam, Havanna Cuba, 95; 70-80-90, Mus Nac Bellas Artes, Buenos Aires, Arg, 95. *Awards:* Sculpture Mention, Ministry Cult, Arg 87 & 88; Mention, State of Mexico Govt, 90. *Bibliog:* Cuauhtemos Medina (auth), Enrique Jezik, escultor en Braille, La Jornada, 93; Luis Felipe Ortega (auth), Trayectos exteriores, Exhib Catalog, 96. *Dealer:* Galeria Nina Menocal Zacatecas No 93 Col Roma Mexico DF Mexico 06700

JILG, MICHAEL FLORIAN
PAINTER, PRINTMAKER
b Albert, Kans, June 28, 47. *Study:* Fort Hays State Univ, BA, 69 & MA, 70; Kent State Blossom Festival, with Jack Tworkov, Alex Katz & James Melchert, 70; Wichita State Univ, with John Fincher, MFA, 72. *Work:* Joslyn Art Mus, Omaha, Nebr; Wichita Art Mus, Kans Arts Commission; Purdue Univ Galleries; Alice and Hamilton Fish Libr, Garrison, NY. *Comn:* George Washington Mural Project, Ellis Bicentenial Comt, Kans, 76; St Ann (painting), St Ann Parish, Olmitz, Kans, 81; mural proj, Sherridan Coliseum. *Exhib:* Mid-Am V, Nelson Gallery Art, Kansas City, Mo, 74; Mainstreams 74, Herman Fine Art Ctr, Marietta, Ohio, 74; Selected Kansas Artists, Kans State Capital, Topeka, 77; Allied Artists Am, Nat Acad Galleries, NY, 77-78; 1st Kans Artists Competition, Judicial Bldg, Topeka, 81; Kans Watercolor Soc Five State Exhib, Wichita Art Mus; 11th Ann Paper in Particular Nat Exhib, Columbia Col, Md; The Intaglio Process: Print Consortium Traveling Exhib; Images Women Prints, Embassy of US, Bonn, Ger, 88; Artists: A Kansas Collection, 89. *Teaching:* Prof painting, Ft Hays State Univ, 81-. *Awards:* Junior League Omaha Purchase, 70; Purchase Award, Kans Arts Commission, 80; Cash Award, Kans Arts Commission, 81; Kans Govs Artist, 91; FHSU Disting Scholar, 2001. *Bibliog:* The Best Kansas Arts & Crafts, 88; Erotic Art by Living Artists, 89; A Kansas Collection, 89. *Mem:* Kansas City Artists' Coalition; High Plains Printmakers; Hays Arts Coun (mem bd dir, currently); Boston Printmakers; Kans Watercolor Soc; Gabinetto Disegni E Stampe Degli Uffizi, Florence, Italy (scholar mem). *Media:* Drawing, Acrylic; Intaglio. *Specialty:* Contemporary art. *Dealer:* Strecker-Nelson Gallery Manhattan KS. *Mailing Add:* Dept Art Ft Hays State Univ 600 Park St Hays KS 67601

JOANNOU, DAKIS
COLLECTOR
Study: Cornell Univ, BCE; Columbia Univ, MCE; Doctor in Archit, Univ Rome. *Collection Arranged:* Dakis Joannou coll, Athens. *Pos:* Chmn J&P-Avax SA, Athens, 2000-; pres, exec bd dir, J&P Group, Cyprus; chmn Athenaeum Hotel & Touristic Enterprises SA, Athens, J&P Avax, SA, YES Hotels & Restaurants, Athens; chmn bd, dir, DESTE Found Contemp Art, Athens; bd trustees, New Mus contemp Art, NY; Int dirs, Council Solomon R Guggenheim, NY, MOCA, LA, TATE, London. *Mem:* Tate Modern Council. *Collection:* Contemporary art. *Mailing Add:* 9 Fragoklissias St Athens 15125 Greece

JOELSON, SUZANNE
PAINTER
b Paterson, NJ, Jan 12, 52. *Study:* Bennington Col, BA, 69. *Work:* Eli Broad Collection, Los Angeles; New Sch, Chase Manhattan Bank & CW Post Col, NY. *Exhib:* Solo exhibs, Wolff Gallery, NY, 88, Fernando Alcolea Gallery, Bacelonea, 90, White Columns, NY, 90 & Lipton/Owens Co, NY, 94; McNeil Gallery, Philadelphia; Lipton/Owens Co, NY, 95; Debs & Co, NY, 98; and others. *Teaching:* Instr painting & color, Sch Visual Arts, 89-; instr painting, Columbia Univ, 91-97, Chautagua Inst, 94-95; instr masters painting prog, Bard Col, NY, 99; instr masters fine arts, NY Univ. *Awards:* Nat Endowment Arts Fel, 87. *Bibliog:* Robert Mahoney (auth), Suzanne Joelson at Debs & Co, Time Out/NY, 12/10/98; Ken Johnson (auth), Suzanne Joelson at Debs & Co, NY Times, 12/11/98; Alexi Worth (auth), Suzanne Joelson at Debs & Co, New Yorker, 12/21/98. *Media:* Painting. *Specialty:* Contemporary art. *Publ:* Auth, In Her Own Voice, Bomb, fall 87. *Dealer:* Debs & Co New York City. *Mailing Add:* 530 Canal St New York NY 10013

JOFFE, BERTHA
DESIGNER
b St Petersburg, Russia; US citizen. *Study:* New York-Phoenix Sch Design, Sch Art League Indust Scholarship, 30-31; City Col New York, BS; Teachers Col, Columbia Univ, MA; NY Univ Inst Fine Arts, Carnegie Tuition Scholarship, 40-42, Art Students League, studied with William Zorach, Winold Reiss & Oronzio Maldarelli. *Comn:* Drapery designs for leading hotels; design on drapery fabric, UN Staff Dining Rm. *Exhib:* Artists for Victory, Metrop Mus Art, NY, 42; Art in Business Exhib, NY, 42; Int Textile Exhib, Weatherspoon Art Gallery, Univ NC, 44; Renaissance Fair, Summit, NJ, 78; Watercolors & Lithographs, On Air Exhib, WNET-TV, NY, 80, 82 & 83; Maplewood Cult Comn Art Exhib, Mem Libr, NJ, 87. *Pos:* Freelance textile designer, 42-; designer women's wear, French Fabrics Co, New York, 62-66; designer home furnishing fabrics, M Lowenstein & Sons, New York, 67-77. *Teaching:* Instr textile & costume design, City Col New York, 40-43; docent art hist, Metrop Mus Art, 41. *Awards:* World Who's Who Commerce & Industry; Int Who's Who Art & Antiques; The World Who's Who Women. *Mem:* Soc Arts, Religion & Contemp Cult, NY. *Media:* Watercolor, Tempera. *Mailing Add:* 333 Elmwood Ave No P5005 Maplewood NJ 07040-2491

JOHANNINGMEIER, ROBERT ALAN
PAINTER, WRITER
b St Louis, Mo, Aug 29, 46. *Study:* Kansas City Art Inst, BFA, 68. *Exhib:* Sun Carnival, Mus Fine Art, El Paso, Tex, 67; Allied Artists Am, NY, 80; Audubon Artists Ann Exhib, NY, 80; Grand Nat Exhib, NY, 80 & 81. *Teaching:* Instr, Old Masters Painting Techniques Workshop. *Awards:* First Place, Tri-State Art Exhib, Carlsbad Area Art Asn, NMex, 68. *Bibliog:* Flo Wilks (auth), Radiating harmony, SW Art, 82; Arejas Vitkauskas (auth), American scene, Worldwide News Bur, 83; Trish Garrigus (auth), Art of investing/collecting, Ctr Econ Revitalization, 83. *Media:* Oil. *Res:* Artistic styles and painting techniques from 1400 to the present; topics of special interest to collectors. *Publ:* Auth, The protection of works of art, Art & Commun, 79, Art as investment, 79; auth & illusr, The Art of Investing While Collecting, Art & Commun, 83, Our Culture Crisis, 87 & How to Inspire Our Family and Appreciate Our Heritage, 92. *Dealer:* Galerie Kornye 2530 Fairmount St Dallas TX 75201. *Mailing Add:* 812 N Edwards Carlsbad NM 88220

JOHANSEN, JOHN MACLANE
ARCHITECT
b NY City, June 29, 1916. *Study:* Harvard Univ, BS, 39; Harvard Grad Sch Design, MArch, 42. *Pos:* Principal, Johansen-Bhavnani, New York City, 73-89; pvt practice, 89—. *Mem:* Fel Am Inst of Archit (honor award 72, medal of honor NY, 76); Am Acad in Rome, Nat Acad of Design, Am Acad Arts and Letters (Brunner award 68), Architectural League (NY pres, 68-70); Nat Acad. *Publ:* auth, A life in the Continuing Modern Archit

JOHANSON, GEORGE E
PAINTER, PRINTMAKER
b Seattle, Wash, Nov 1, 28. *Study:* Portland Mus Sch, Ore; Atelier 17, NY. *Work:* Nat Collection, Washington, DC; Chicago Art Inst; NY Pub Libr; Victoria & Albert Mus, London, Eng; Oldham Co Coun, Eng; and many others. *Comn:* Civic Auditorium, Portland, 69; Portland Bldg, 88; Bremerton High Sch, Wa, 89; Ore State Univ, Corvallis, 92; Peninsula Park, Portland, 98. *Exhib:* Calif Palace Legion Hon, San Francisco; Am Embassy, London, Eng; Seattle Art Mus; Portland Art Mus, Ore; Univ Ariz, Tucson; Univ Ill; Western NMex Univ; Palm Springs Desert Mus, Calif; Univ Houston, Tex. *Pos:* Pres, Northwest Print Coun, 81-83. *Teaching:* Instr painting & printmaking, Portland Mus Art Sch, 55-80; lectr, Reed Col, Portland, Ore, 77; instr printmaking, La State Univ, Baton Rouge, 92. *Awards:* First Ed Award, Ore Arts Comn, 76; Award, Ore State Fair, Salem, 77; Governors Award for the Arts, 92; and others. *Bibliog:* Bruce Guenther (auth), 50 Northwest Artists, Chronicle Bks, 83; Lois Allen (auth), Contemporary Art in the Northwest, Craftsman House, 95 & Northwest Printmakers, 97; Equivalents, Portland Art Mus, 2001. *Mem:* Portland Art Asn; Northwest Print Coun (pres, 83). *Media:* Oil, Etching. *Publ:* Creator, Etching and Color Intaglio (film), 73 & Printmaker (film), 76; Drawings Retrospective, Univ of Oreg, 89. *Dealer:* Pulliam-Deffenbaugh Gallery 522 NW 12th St Portland Ore 97210. *Mailing Add:* 2237 SW Market St Dr Portland OR 97201

JOHANSON, PATRICIA
SCULPTOR, ENVIRONMENTAL ARTIST
b New York, NY, Sept 8, 40. *Study:* Brooklyn Mus Art Sch; Art Students League; Bennington Col, BA, 62; Hunter Col, MA, 64; City Col Sch Archit, BS & BArch, 77. *Hon Degrees:* Mass Col Art, Hon DFA, 95. *Work:* Mus Mod Art, NY; Storm King Art Ctr, Mountainville, NY; Dallas Art Mus, Tex; Metrop Mus Art, NY; Nat Mus Women Arts, Washington. *Comn:* Fair Park Lagoon, Dallas, Texas, 81-86; Endangered Garden, Candlestick Cove, San Francisco Arts Commission, 87-97; Park for a Rainforest, Amazonas, Brazil, 92-; Nairobi River Park, Kenya, 95-; Ulsan Dragon Park, Yukong Ltd, South Korea, 96-. *Exhib:* Art of the Real, Mus Mod Art, NY, Grand Palais, Paris, Kunsthaus, Zurich & Tate Gallery, London, 68-69; Women in Am Archit, Brooklyn Mus, NY, 77; Recent Acquisitions, Mus Mod Art, NY, 79; Am Drawings in Black & White, Brooklyn Mus, 80; Recent Acquisitions, Metrop Mus Art, 82; Fragile Ecologies, Queens Mus, NY, 92; Creative Solutions to Ecological Issues, Dallas Mus Natural Hist, 93; Differentes Natures, La Defense, Paris & La Virreina, Barcelona, 93-94; Tres Cantos Da Terra, Nat Mus Fine Arts, Rio de Janeiro, 93; Cosmic-Maternal, Gallery Nikko, Tokyo, 94; Chalk Circle, Michael Fuchs Galerie, Berlin, 97; Jardin 2000, Villa Medici, Rome, 2000; Ecovention, Contemp Arts Ctr, Cincinnati, 02; A Minimal Future, Mus Contemp Art, Los Angeles, 04. *Pos:* Design consult, Consolidated Edison Corp, NY, 72, Yale Univ, 72, Bartholomew Consolidated Sch Corp, Columbus, Ind, 73, Int Year Child Comm, 79, Corning Park, Albany, 82, Fair Park, Dallas, 82, Pelham Bay Park, NY, 84 & Cathedral Sq, Sacramento, 84; San Francisco Clean Water Prog, 88; Pub Art Master Plan, Rockland Co, New York, 90; mem, Omame Proj, Earth Summit, Brazil, 92 & Global Forum, Kyoto, Japan, 93; Sanart, Ankara, Turkey, 97; City Plan, Brockton, Mass, 97 & Petaluma, Calif, 98; cons, Oikos, Yukong Ltd & Seoul Develop Inst, South Korea, 96-99; grants selection com, Nat Endowment Arts, Washington, DC, 00; Designer, French Embassy Cultural Srvs, New York, 2000, Salt Lake City Planning & Design, 2003, Duluth, Minn Planning & Design, 2004-06 & Zhang Jia Jie, National Forest Park, China, 2004; cons, City of Salina, Kans, Carollo Engrs, 01-05. *Teaching:* Vis prof art, State Univ NY, Albany, 69; vis artist, Mass Inst Technol, 74, Oberlin Col, 74 & Alfred Univ, 74; lectr, Colby Col, Maine, 81; West Texas State Univ, Canyon, 88, & Mass Col Art, 94; seminar, Yale Univ, 89; Olesen Fel, Bennington Col, 91-92, Calif State Univ, Monterey Bay, 97, 99, 2006. *Awards:* Guggenheim Fel, 70 & 80; Gold Medal, Accademia Italia Delle Arti, 79; Governor's Grand Achievement Award, Envision Utah, 2004. *Bibliog:* Balken, Debra & Lucy R Lippard, Patricia Johanson: Drawings & Models for Environmental Projects, 69-86, Berkshire Mus, Pittsfield, Mass, 87; Barbara Matilsky (auth), Fragile Ecologies, Rizzoli, 92; Kelley Caffyn (auth), Art and Survival: Patricia Johanson's Environmental Projects, Islands Institute, 2006. *Mem:* Global Forum Arts Group, NY. *Publ:* Architecture as Landscape, Princeton J, Vol 2, 85; Art and Survival: Creative Solutions to Environmental Problems, Gallerie Monogr, Vancouver, BC, 92; La Ville Comme Forme D'Art Ecologique: La Trace de Rocky Marciano, Les Annales Recherche Urbane, Paris, No 85, 99; Beyond Choreography: Shifting Experiences in Unicivilized Gardens, Landscape Design and the Experience of Motion, Dumbarton Oaks, 2003; Fecund Landscapes: Art and Process in Public Parks, Landscape and Art, London, Number 29, 2003. *Mailing Add:* 179 Nickmush Rd Buskirk NY 12028

JOHNS, CHRISTOPHER K(ALMAN)
PAINTER, EDUCATOR
b Racine, Wis, Dec 2, 1952. *Study:* Univ Wis, Milwaukee, 71-73; San Francisco Art Inst, BFA, 75; Stanford Univ, MFA, 77. *Work:* Continental Bank, Chicago, Ill; Best Products Co, Richmond, Va; Univ Wis, Platteville; Stanford Univ, Calif; Charles Wustum Mus Fine Art, Racine, Wis. *Exhib:* West-the Law, Minn Mus Art, St Paul, 79 & 80; Hassam Fund Purchase Exhib, Am Acad & Inst Arts, NY, 80; Abstraction in Louisiana, 80 & Festival of New Work, 84, Contemp Art Ctr, New Orleans, La; View from Southeast Wis, Charles Wustum Mus, Racine, Wis, 81; Southern Abstraction, City Gallery, Raleigh, NC, 87; solo exhibs, Union Gallery, La State Univ, Baton Rouge, 83, Univ Ala, Huntsville, 91 & Art at Koll, New Orleans, 97, Sylvia Schmidt, 2001, Albert Blue Gallery, Baton Rouge, La, 2000; Perimeter Gallery, Chicago, 98, 02; Abstraction, Sylvia Schmidt Gallery, New Orleans, 99, Images of Water, 02; Return of the Men, Peltz Gallery, Milwaukee, 02; New Artists Show, Baton Rouge Gallery, La. *Pos:* vis artist, David & Julia White Artists Colony, Costa Rica. *Teaching:* Instr painting, Charles Wustum Mus, 77-78; prof painting & drawing, La State Univ, Baton Rouge, 79-. *Awards:* Southern Arts Fedn Artists Fel, 88; Visual Arts Grant, State of Louisiana Arts Div, 86. *Bibliog:* Juliana Harris-Livingston (auth), Abstraction still not convinced, Figaro, New Orleans, La, 8/80; Christopher Fischer (auth), Three Abstractionsits. New Orleans Art Rev, La, 99. *Media:* Oil. *Dealer:* Sylvia Schmidt Gallery New Orleans, LA; Perimeter Gallery, Chicago, Ill. *Mailing Add:* 864 Albert Hart Baton Rouge LA 70808

JOHNS, JASPER
PAINTER
b Augusta, Ga, May 15, 1930. *Study:* Univ SC. *Work:* Victoria & Albert Mus, London; Mus Mod Art & Whitney Mus Am Art, NY; Albright-Knox Art Gallery, Buffalo, NY; Wadsworth Atheneum, Hartford, Conn; Mus Mod Art, Paris; San Francisco Mus Mod Art, Calif; Stedelijk Mus, Amsterdam, Neth; Hirshhorn Mus & Sculpture Garden, Washington, DC; Tate Gallery, London; Moderna Museet, Stockholm; Kunst Mus, Basel; White Flag, 1955; Flag, 1955; False State, 1959; Study for Skin, 1962; Seasons, 1986. *Exhib:* One-man shows, Mud Mod Art, 68, 70 & 92, Cana Art Gallery, Seoul, Korea, 91, Gagosian Gallery, NY, 92, Prints & Drawings from the Castelli Collection, Palaus de Luppe, La Fondation Vincent Van Gogh, Arles, France, 92, Milwaukee Art Mus, Wis, 92, Galeria Weber Alexander Cobo, Madrid, Spain, 92; Mus Contemp Art, Chicago, 71-72; Art Inst Chicago, 74; Walker Art Ctr, Minneapolis, 74; Saidye Bronfman Ctr, Montreal, 80; Pace Gallery, NY, 80; Whitney Mus Am Art, NY, 80; Hirshhorn Mus, Washington, DC, 80; Stedelijk Mus, The Neth, 80; Margo Leavin Gallery, Los Angeles, 81; Leo Castelli Gallery, NY, 81; Hotel des Arts, Paris, France, 92; Mus Mod & Contemp Art, 92. *Pos:* Dir, Found Contemp Performance Artists, 63-. *Awards:* Recipient 1st prize Print Biennale Ljubljana, Yugoslavia, prize IX Sao Paulo (Brazil) Biennale; Skowhegan medal for painting Skowhegan Sch of Painting and Sculpture; Skowhegan medal for graphics; Mayors award of Hon for Arts and Culture City of NY; Wolf prize for painting, Wolf Found; Int prize Venice Biennale, 1988; Nat Medal of Arts; The White House; named to SC Hall of Fame, 1989. *Bibliog:* C Kelder (auth), Prints: Jasper Johns at Hofstra, Art in Am, 3/73; D Ward (auth), Jasper Johns drawings, Arts Rev, 9/74; J Reichardt (auth), The rendering is the content, Archit Design, 12/74. *Mem:* Am Acad Arts and Letters (Gold medal for graphic art); Royal Acad Arts; Nat Inst Arts and Letters; Am Acad Arts and Scis. *Mailing Add:* PO Box 642 Sharon CT 06069-0642

JOHNSEN, MAY ANNE
PAINTER
b Port Chester, NY. *Study:* With John Carroll. *Work:* St Mary's Church, Hudson, NY; also in pvt collection of Philip Schyler, Albany, NY. *Comn:* Fire Equipment 1890's (painting), Tsaawassa Fire Dept, Brainard, NY, 53. *Exhib:* Women Artist in Am from 20th Century to Present; Int Exhib, Smithsonian Inst; Drawing Int, Barcelonia, Spain; Knickerbocker Nat Exhib, NY; Catherine Lollilard-Wolfe Nat Show, NY; Int Miniature Art Show, NC, WVa, NMex & Ark; and others. *Awards:* Silvermine Guild Marine Award, 59; First Prize, Columbia Co Fair, 59; Ohio Marine Award, Ohio Miniature Soc, 69; and others. *Bibliog:* Article, La Rev Mod, 68. *Mem:* Assoc mem Miniature Painters, Sculptors & Gravers Soc Washington; Miniature Art Soc NJ; Am Soc Marine Painters; charter mem World Fedn Miniaturists. *Media:* Mixed. *Specialty:* Watercolor. *Interests:* Marine, landscape sculpting, etchings, watercolor miniatures. *Dealer:* Squillaci Gallery 524 Summit Ave Schenectady NY 12307. *Mailing Add:* Rte 20 PO Box 5 Brainard NY 12024

JOHNSON, ANITA LOUISE
PAINTER, GRAPHIC ARTIST
b Silver Creek, NY, Oct 22, 31. *Study:* Albright Art Sch, Buffalo, NY, BFA, 1952; Grad Courses (art), Univ Buffalo, 1963-1968. *Work:* City Hall, Buffalo, NY; Buffalo Gen Hosp; Inland Div Ford Motor Co, Dayton, Ohio; Women & Childrens Hosp, Buffalo, NY; Blue Cross Western NY, Buffalo, NY. *Exhib:* Director's Choice, Albright Art Gallery, Buffalo, NY, 1990; Invitational Studio Exhib, Burchfield-Penny Center, Buffalo, NY, 1994; Solo Exhibs, Garrett Club, Buffalo, NY, 1994, Studio Arena Theatre, Buffalo, NY, 1995, Upstairs at Sutherlands Gallery, Buffalo, NY, 1996, 1995, Arts Coun Buffalo Erie Co, Buffalo, NY, 2001, and numerous others; Nat League Pen Women, Center for Tomorrow, State Univ Buffalo, NY, 1995; Carnegie Cult Center,

Nat League Pen Women, Tonawanda, NY, 1997; Somarts Gallery Invitational, San Francisco, Calif, 1999; Buffalo Soc Artists, Castellani Mus Art, Niagara Falls, NY, 2005; Niagara Frontier Exhib, Kenan Center, Lockport, NY, 2006. *Pos:* Asst art Dir, Buffalo Courier Express, Buffalo, NY, 1952-1981; art dir, Buffalo News, Buffalo, NY, 1981-1991. *Awards:* Merit Award, Theodore Roosevelt Hist Mansion, Buffalo Soc Artists, 1987; 2nd Prize Oil, Kenan Center, Lockport Savings Bank, 1993; Award, Nat League Am Pen Women, Kenan Center, 2000; and numerous others. *Mem:* Buffalo Soc Artists (bd dirs, 1980-1985 & 1987-1992, pres, 1989-1990); Nat League Am Pen Women of W NY; Hallwalls Contemp Art Center. *Media:* Acrylic, Oil, All Media. *Mailing Add:* S 5677 Sterling Rd Hamburg NY 14075

JOHNSON, AUDEAN See Audean

JOHNSON, BARBARA LOUISE
PAINTER, PRINTMAKER
b Worcester, Mass, Nov 10, 27. *Study:* Univ Miami, Fla, 46-48; Smith Col, Mass, AB, 50; Univ Calif-Berkeley, 51; Univ Mich, BS, 57, MFA, 59. *Work:* Zimmerli Mus, Rutgers Univ; Contemp Art Mus, Chamalieres, France; Monterey Peninsula Mus Art; Am Express Int, Tokyo; Banco Int, Lima, Peru; others. *Comn:* 17 mixed media pieces, Lodge at Pebble Beach, Calif, 94; 180 mixed media works on paper, Inn at Spanish Bay, Pebble Beach, Calif, 96. *Exhib:* Los Angeles Printmakers Ann, 88-94; Contemp Am Prints, Barbican Ctr, London, 89; Norske Grafikere, Oslo, Norway, 93; Spencer Mus Art, Univ Kans, 95; Univ Wis, 95; Hunterdon Mus, Clinton, NJ; Los Angeles Print Making Soc, Exchange Exhib, Belfast, Ireland, 2006. *Collection Arranged:* A. Expres Int; Tolman Collection- Tokyo, Japan; Baer & Assoc, Att, Palo Alto, CA; Bank of Boston, MA; Life Scan Corp, Pebble Beach Corp, Seagete Corp, Scotts Valley, Ca; PES Environmental Inc, Novato; Read-Rite Corp, Milpitas, CA; Mus of Contemporary Art, ChamaLieres, France; Sp.-Bay resort, Pebble Beach, CA; Pan-Pacific Corp, Guatemala; Tolber Int Design, J. Knutsen Int Design-San Francisco, Ca; The Spa at Pabble Beach, CA. *Teaching:* Jr H S High School, Mclean, Va; Senior Citizens, Carmel, CA. *Awards:* Leila Sawyer Mem Award, 87, Shelley Sterling Mem Award, 89 & Medal Honor & Jack Key Cotton Mem Award, 91 Nat Asn Women Artists, NY; Dorothy Tabak Mem Award; Nat Asn Women Artists, Collage, 2006. *Bibliog:* Jeanne Davidson (auth), Barbara Johnson/artist & printmaker, Print World, spring 87. *Mem:* Calif Soc Printmakers; Los Angeles Printmaking Soc; Nat Asn Women Artist, NY; Carmel Art Asn, Calif. *Media:* All. *Interests:* Travel & Reading. *Publ:* Journal of the Print World. *Dealer:* Winfield Gallery PO Box 7393 Carmel CA 93921; Carmel Art Asn PO Box 227 Carmel CA 93921; The Gallery 329 Primrose Rd Burlingame Calif 94010; RFA 200 Kansas St San Francisco 94103; Jeanne Davidson: Fine Prints, N.Y.C. *Mailing Add:* 3548 Greenfield Pl Carmel CA 93923-9441

JOHNSON, BARBARA PIASECKA
COLLECTOR, PATRON
b Staniewicze, Poland, Feb 25, 37. *Study:* Univ Wroclaw, Poland, MA(art hist), 65. *Collection Arranged:* Opus Sacrum, (auth, catalog), Royal Castle, Warsaw, Poland, 90 & Liechtensteinische Staatliche Kunstsammlung, Vaduz, Liechtenstein, 91, Musee de la Chapelle de la Visitation, Monaco, 95-; Cultural Heritage in Europe, Jan Vermeer, St Praxedis, Wawel Royal Castle, Krakow, Poland, 91-92; The Flight into Egypt, Musee de la Chapelle de la Visitation, Monaco, 97; Saint Praxedis, Musee de la Chapelle de la Visitation, Monaco, 98. *Pos:* Trustee, dir, chairperson, The Barbara Piasecka Johnson Found, currently; trustee, chairperson, The Paderewski Ctr, currently; pres, Centrum Ignacego Paderewskiego, currently; mem, Chmns Counc Metrop Mus Art, New York, 86; mem, Collectors Comt Nat Gallery Art, Washington, DC, 80-91; mem, US Dept State Fine Arts Coun, 78-85; mem, Coun Found Univ Wroclaw, 91-92; trustee & dir, Atlantic Found & Harbor Branch Found, 72-85; bd mgrs, Wistar Inst Philadelphia, 89-91. *Awards:* Polish Am Congress Heritage Award, 89; Living Legacy Award, 94; Order of St Charles Officer decoration (for serv to Principality of Monaco), conferred by HSH, Prince Rainer III, 95. *Bibliog:* Antoni Dzieduszycki (auth), Love is Greater Barbara Piasecka Johnson & Eleven Arts Inc (prods, film), 90; Roger M Williams (auth), Wealth in the Service of Poland, Found News, 1-2/91. *Collection:* Paintings 13th-19th Century (emphasis on old masters); Furniture & Decorative Arts 16th-19th Century (emphasis on French Furniture); Sculpture 15th-19th Century. *Mailing Add:* 4519 Province Line Rd Princeton NJ 08540

JOHNSON, BRENT
PAINTER
b Tyler, Tex, Aug 25, 41. *Study:* Cent State Univ, BFA, 67; Univ Okla; Univ Md. *Comn:* Okla Dept Wildlife Conservation, 2006. *Exhib:* Watercolor USA, Springfield Art Mus, Mo, 75; Am Watercolor Soc, Nat Acad Design, NY, 75-81; La Ann, La Mus Art, Shreveport, 76; Delta Art Asn, Ark Art Ctr, Little Rock, 76; San Diego Nat Watercolor Exhib, Cent Fed Tower, 77; Rocky Mountain Nat Watermedia Exhib, Foothills Art Ctr, Golden, Colo, 77; Arts for the Parks, 2002; and others. *Pos:* Bd dir, Oklahoma City Arts Coun, 79-80. *Teaching:* variour workshops. *Awards:* Mercantile Bank Award, Watercolor USA, 75; Bus Community Award, Rocky Mountain Nat Watermedia Exhib, 77; John Young Hunter Mem Award, Am Watercolor Soc, 81. *Bibliog:* Lynn Martin (auth), Today's art, Syndicate Mag Inc, 74; Dean G Graham (auth), Outdoor Oklahoma, Okla Dept Wildlife, 1/76; Marcia Lionberger (auth), Oklahoma Art Gallery, Wall & Wall Publ Co Inc, fall 81. *Mem:* Prof Artist Asn Okla (pres, 77-78); Whiskey Painters Am. *Media:* Watercolor, Acrylic. *Dealer:* Windward Gallery 2111 Strand Galveston TX; Windberg Gallery 229 N Main St Salado TX. *Mailing Add:* 513 Sweetgum Oklahoma City OK 73127

JOHNSON, BRUCE (JAMES)
PAINTER
b Riverside, Calif, May 6, 44. *Study:* Univ Hawaii, Honolulu, BFA, 66; El Camino Col, Gardena, Calif; Calif Col Arts & Crafts, Oakland, MFA, 70. *Exhib:* James D Phelen Awards Exhib, Calif Palace of Legion of Honor, San Francisco, 69; Western Wash State Nat Drawing & Small Sculpture Exhib, Western Wash State Univ, Bellingham, 70; San Francisco Art Inst Centennial Exhib, 71 & Work on Paper, 73, San Francisco Mus Mod Art; Grids, Inst Contemp Art, Univ Pa, Philadelphia, 72; Eighteen Bay Area Artists, Los Angeles Inst Contemp Art, 76 & Univ Calif, Berkeley Art Mus, 77; Art Hawaii Ann, Honolulu Acad Arts, 78, 79 & 83; Artists Hawaii Cult Exchange Exhib, Ohio & Manila, 80-81. *Teaching:* Instr art, Santa Rosa Jr Col, Calif, 72-76; lectr drawing, Univ Hawaii, Honolulu, 78-79; instr, Honolulu Acad Arts, 81. *Awards:* MacDowell Colony Fel, 71; Young Artist Award, Contemp Art Comt of Oakland Mus Art Guild, 73. *Bibliog:* Judith L Dunham (auth), Johnson and Linhares, Artweek, 3/73; Alfred Frankenstein (auth), She's somebody to watch, San Francisco Chronicle, 4/3/73. *Media:* All Media. *Mailing Add:* 3318 Woodlawn Dr Honolulu HI 96822

JOHNSON, CAROL M
CURATOR
b Quincy, Mass. *Study:* Mass Col Art, BFA, 80; Univ Md, College Park, MLS, 88. *Collection Arranged:* Carl Van Vechten & Miguel Covarrubias, About Face, 94; Am Daguerreotypes, 1842-1862, online exhibit (http://locweb2 loc gov/pp/daghtml/dagabt.html); Ansel Adam's Photogs of Japanese-Am Internment at Manzanar, 2002; Civil War Photogs, Stereograph Cards, 2005. *Pos:* cur photog, Libr Cong, Prints & Photog Div, Washington, 99-. *Mem:* Am Asn Mus. *Publ:* Auth, Panoramas of Duluth, Minn, History of Photography, 92; Faces of Freedom: Portraits from the American Colonization Society Collection, Daguerreian Ann, 96; coaruth, Eyes of the Nahon: A Visual Hist of the US, 1997; Gathering History: The Marion S Carson Collection of Americana, 99. *Mailing Add:* 405 Windover Ct NW Vienna VA 22180

JOHNSON, CECILE RYDEN
PAINTER, PUBLISHER
b Jamestown, NY. *Study:* Augustana Col, AB; Pa Acad Fine Arts; Art Inst Chicago; Am Acad Fine Arts; Univ Colo; Univ Wis. *Work:* Chicago Mus Sci & Indust; Davenport Munic Mus; Macalester Col; General Mills; Minn Mining. *Comn:* Trans World Airlines; Rockefeller Resorts; Jamaican Govt; CBS/World Tennis; Official artist (lithographs), 1980 US Lake Placid Olympics & 1990 Winter Olympics, Albertville, France; and many others. *Exhib:* Am Watercolor Soc; Washington Watercolor Soc; US Info Agency & State Dept Traveling Exhib to Europe, Asia, Africa & South Am; one-man shows, Davenport Munic Mus & Hudson River Mus; US Tennis Open, Nat Stadium, 83; Grand Central Gallery; and others. *Teaching:* Instr workshops, Ghost Ranch, Abiquiu, 82, Bermuda, 83. *Awards:* Catharine Lorillard Wolfe Art Club Gold Medal; Prizes, Am Watercolor Soc, Knickerbocker Artists & others. *Bibliog:* Feature article, Am Artist, 1/83; Kent (auth), 100 Watercolorists, Watson Guptill; Creating in Watercolor (film), Crystal Productions; Feature Article, Am Artist, 5/86. *Mem:* Am Watercolor Soc; Hon mem Nat Arts Club; Soc Illusr; hon mem Nat League Pen Women; Allied Artists, Audubon Soc. *Media:* Watercolor, Acrylic. *Res:* World travel. *Specialty:* Am Swedish Inst-Scandinavian Artists in USA. *Interests:* Winter Sports, Landscapes/Water. *Publ:* Contribr, illus, 42 issues Skiing Mag & Ski Impact Mag. *Mailing Add:* Des Artistes One W 67th St New York NY 10023-6200

JOHNSON, CHARLES W, JR
EDUCATOR, HISTORIAN
b New York, NY, Apr 7, 38. *Study:* Westminster Col, BMEd, 60; Union Theol Seminary, MSM, 62; Ohio Univ, PhD, 70. *Teaching:* Asst prof, State Univ NY Col New Paltz, summer 66; From asst prof art hist to assoc prof, 67-81, Univ Richmond, prof, 82-, chmn dept fine arts, 67-; Pro Art Hist, Chmn, Dept of Art & Art History, 67-2003; Sr Fel & Scholar, Jepson Sch Leadership Studies, Univ Richmond, 2005. *Awards:* Pres Citation, Westminster Col, 95; SCHEV Outstanding Faculty Award, 96; Golden Key Intl Hon Soc, (hon mem), 2002. *Mem:* Col Art Asn Am; Popular Culture Asn of South; Prog Enhancing Teaching Effectiveness, (ch); Univ Richmond Trustee Committee. *Interests:* Italian & Northern Renaissance art, Mannerism & the Baroque; Survey of art: Early Renaissance through Modernism; 18th Century Studies. *Publ:* The Renaissance Print in Social Context, Exhibi Catalogue, Univ of Richmond, 99; The World of Stefano della Bella(1610-1664), Italian Printmaker, Univ of Richmond & The Virginia Mus of Fine Arts, 2001; Eighteenth Century Prints Catalogue, UR, 2005. *Mailing Add:* Jepson School of Leadership Studies Univ of Richmond Richmond VA 23173

JOHNSON, D'ELAINE A HERARD See D'Elaine

JOHNSON, DEAN P
SCULPTOR
Study: SDak State Univ, Brookings, 74-77; Minneapolis Col Art & Design, Minn, 78-79; Univ Wyo, BFA, 80, MA, 81, MFA, 90. *Exhib:* Solo shows, Ctr Contemp Arts, Santa Fe, NMex, 88, Laramie Co Community Col, Cheyenne, Wyo, 89, Casper Col, Wyo, 90 & Nicolaysen Art Mus, Casper, Wyo, 91; Ctr Contemp Arts, Santa Fe, NMex, 90; Wash State Arts Comn, Olympia, 91; Rock Springs Fine Arts Ctr, Wyo, 92; and others. *Awards:* Wash State Arts Coun Comn, 90; Individual Artist Grant, 90 & Fel, 91, Wyo Arts Coun; New Forms: Regional Initiative Grant, Nat Endowment Arts, Rockefeller & Warhol Founds, 92. *Bibliog:* Nancy Melich (auth), Art: range-riding curator hunts best of the west, Wall St J, 28, 8/27/85; Ted Pinkowitz (auth), Installation, constructions, environments, New Art Examiner, 55, 6/88; Thomas Patin (auth), Dean Johnson at the Center for Contemporary Arts, Santa Fe, Artspace, 53, fall 88; and others. *Mailing Add:* 3717 Pioneer Ave Cheyenne WY 82001

JOHNSON, DIANA L
GALLERY DIRECTOR, CURATOR
b New York, NY, July 13, 40. *Study:* Radcliffe Col, Harvard Univ, BA, 62; Brown Univ, MA, 71. *Pos:* Assoc cur prints & drawings, Mus Art, RI Sch Design, 69-76, actg chief cur, 74-76, cur prints, drawings & photogs & chief cur, 76-79, actg dir, 78-79; dir, Brown Univ, David Winton Bell Gallery, 90-. *Mem:* Print Coun Am (treas, 82-89);

Asn Col & Univ Mus & Galleries (RI rep, 90-); Am Fed Arts (exhib comt). *Publ:* Auth, Spaces (exhib catalog), 78 & Fantastic Illustration and Design in Britain 1860-1930, 79, Mus Art RI Sch Design; Reprise: The Vera G List Collection, 91 & coauth, The Collections of Brown Univeristy, 92, Brown Univ. *Mailing Add:* David Winton Bell Gallery List Art Center Brown Univ 64 College St Providence RI 02912-9021

JOHNSON, DIANE CHALMERS
HISTORIAN, EDUCATOR
b Dubuque, Iowa, Jan 3, 43. *Study:* Harvard Univ, Radcliffe Col, BA(fine arts), 65; Univ Kans, MA(art hist), 67, PhD(art hist), 70. *Teaching:* prof modern European Am art history, Col Charleston, dept chair, 70-78 & 91-2001. *Awards:* Nat Endowment Humanities Res Fel, 81-82; Addlestone Chair Am Art, Col Charleston, 89-94. *Mem:* Col Art Asn Am; Historians Am Art Asn; SECAC. *Res:* Nineteenth and twentieth-century European and American art; Art Nouveau and Symbolist art; Picasso's late work. *Publ:* Auth, Odilon Redon's apocalypse de Saint-Jean, Arts Va, 72; American Art Nouveau, Harry N Abrams Publ, 79; Picasso's Papiers Colles, In: XXVI Int Congress for the History of Art, Univ Pa Press, 89; Albert P Ryderts Siegfried and the rhine maidens, Am Art, 94; contribr, American Symbolist Art: Nineteenth Century, 2004. *Mailing Add:* 59 Smith St Charleston SC 29401

JOHNSON, DONALD RAY
HISTORIAN, PRINTMAKER
b Poteau, Okla, Jan 14, 42. *Study:* Northeast Okla State Col, BA, 63; Univ Okla, MFA, 70 & MA, 71. *Work:* Topeka Publ Lib, Topeka Kans; Baker Art Found; Dickinson State Col, NDak. *Comn:* Lithograph, Kans Cult Arts, 73. *Exhib:* Lithography 1969, Fla State Univ, 69; Images on Paper, Jackson, Miss, 71; Graphics 71, Western NMex Univ, 71; Santa Fe Trail Ctr, Larned, Kans, 81; Ft Hays State Univ, 71; Mulvane Art Ctr, Washburn Univ Topeka, Kans, 88; Baker Art Found, Liberal Kans, 88; and others. *Teaching:* Assoc prof art hist, Emporia Kans State Univ, 70-; chmn, div art, Emporia Kans State Univ, 84. *Awards:* Emporia Kans State Univ Grants, 73, 75, 76, 78, 80-82; Wenner-Gren Found Grant, 83; Kans Comt Humanities Grant, 85. *Mem:* Col Art Asn. *Res:* American West during the 19th century; Santa Fe Trail through Kansas; mound builders in eastern Oklahoma

JOHNSON, DOUGLAS WALTER
PAINTER, CERAMIST, PUBLISHER
b Portland, Ore, July 8, 46. *Study:* Self-taught. *Work:* Permanent Collection, Mus NMex, Santa Fe; Am Nat Collection, Am Nat Ins Co, Galveston, Tex; NMex State Capitol Bldg, Santa Fe; De Vries Insurance Agency, St Joseph, Mich; Hotel Eldorado, Santa Fe, NMex. *Comn:* Rio Grande (mural), El Dorado Hotel, Santa Fe, NMex. *Exhib:* Inner Sanctums, Gerald Peters Gallery, Santa Fe, NMex, 88; Contemp miniatures, J N Bartfield Gallery, NY, 89; Birds of Magic, Gerald Peters Gallery, Santa Fe, NMex, 90; 35 Yr Retrospective Exhib, NMex State Capitol, Governors Gallery, Santa Fe, 93; Flowers, Pots & Trains, Parks Gallery, Taos, NMex, 96; Hist Windows, Nedra Mattrucci Gallery, Santa Fe, NMex, 01. *Teaching:* Prime-Time sch proj drawing & painting, Espanola Sch District, 93-94. *Awards:* Jurors Award, NMex Biennial, Mus NMex, 73; Second Prize Award, Watercolor NMex, NMex Watercolor Soc, 74; Santa Fe Opera Poster, NMex, 81; Cert of Achievement, US Dept Agr Nat Forest. *Bibliog:* Douglas Johnson (auth), Cliff-Dweller, NMex Mag, 4/94; Robert Ewing (auth), Birds of Magic, Douglas Johnson, 90; Robert Ewing (auth), Painters Odessey, Clear Light Publ, Santa Fe, NMex, 97. *Media:* Casein on Paper, Clay. *Specialty:* Contemporary and work of Dead American Masters; Spanish Colonial period, New Mexico; Archeology of above. *Interests:* History, Southwestern Pre-history (1050-1450 AD Pueblo Indians). *Collection:* Soutwest Indian. *Publ:* NMex Mag Calendar, 06; Spanish Colonial Churches of NMex, Obsidian Mountain, 03; and numerous others. *Dealer:* JN Bartfield NY NY; Fenn Galleries Santa Fe NM; Parks Gallery Taos NMex; Nedra Matteucci Gallery Santa Fe NMex. *Mailing Add:* PO Box 9 Coyote NM 87012

JOHNSON, ERIN (STUKEY)
PAINTER, SCULPTOR
b New York, NY. *Study:* Studied with Jacque Lipchitz, Italy, 73 & Wattana Wattanapan, 91-94; Rhodes Col, BA, 73. *Work:* Highland Terrace Med Ctr, Murfreesboro City Hall, Murfreesboro, Tenn; Childrens Discovery House Mus, Murfreesboro, Tenn; Jane Voohrees, Zimmerli Mus, Rutgers, NJ. *Exhib:* Cheekwood, Nashville Artist Guild, Tenn, 95; Ann Nat Asn Women Artists, NY, 95, 96, 97 & 98; Tenn All State, Parthenon Mus, Nashville, 95-97; Tenn Watercolor Soc, Hunter Mus, Chattanooga, 96; One Woman Show, Ctr Arts, Tenn; Nat Asn Women Artists Ann; ASCA Ann, City Hall, Murfreesboro, 2004; 2 women show, Murfreesboro Center for Arts, 2005. *Pos:* Docent, Masterworks & Jacksonian Exhib, Tenn State Mus, Nashville, 91-92; gallery supv, Murfreesboro Art League, 91-96. *Teaching:* Instr art, elem & high sch. *Awards:* 1st & 2nd Place & Best Show, Murfreesboro Art League, 93 & 94; Juror Award, Tenn Watercolor Soc, 96; Featured Artist, Ann Parade Artists, 96; ASCA 2nd Place, 2003. *Bibliog:* Clinton Confehr (auth), Acquisition of art, Daily News J, 92; Arlyn Ende (auth), Visual impressions, Daily News J, 93; Susan Knowles (auth), Art in recovery, Nashville Scene, 93. *Mem:* Nashville Artist Guild (pres, 94-95); Nat Asn Women Artists; Am Soc Contemp Artists; Tenn Asn Craft Artists. *Media:* Mixed Media, Sculpture. *Dealer:* James Ben Gallery & Studio Franklin TN; Midtown Gallery Nashville TN. *Mailing Add:* 2211 Shannon Dr Murfreesboro TN 37129

JOHNSON, EUGENE JOSEPH
HISTORIAN
b Memphis, Tenn, May 22, 37. *Study:* Williams Col, BA, 59; NY Univ, MA, 63, PhD, 70. *Teaching:* Prof art, Williams Col, Williamstown, Mass, 65-, chmn art dept, 78-80, 90-91. *Mem:* Soc Archit Hist; Renaisance Soc Am. *Publ:* Auth, S Andrea in Mantua, the Building History, 75; Charles Moore, Building & Prog, 86; coauth, Memphis: Archit Guide, 90; coauth, Drawn from the Source, The Travel Sketches of Louis I Kahn, 96. *Mailing Add:* Williams Col Dept Art 15 Lawrence Hall Dr Williamstown MA 01267-2607

JOHNSON, GUY
PAINTER
b Fort Wayne, Ind, 27. *Study:* Fla State Univ, MA, 52. *Exhib:* Solo exhibs, Hundred Acres Gallery, NY, 71 & 72, Gallerie Fabian Carlsson, Gothenberg, Sweden, 74, Stefanatti Gallery, NY, 74, Basel Int Art Exhib, Switz, 78, Galerie d'endt, Amsterdam, The Neth, 78 & Galerie Arenthon, Paris, 89; Tomasulo Gallery, Union Col, Cranford, NJ, 85; Art in the Armory, NY, 88; Trains and Planes: The Influence of Locomotion in Am Painting, traveling exhib, 89-90; 79th Ann Exhib, Maier Mus Art, Randolph-Macon Women's Col, Lynchburg, Va, 90; other one-man exhibs, Louis K Meisel Gallery, 79, 83, 85, 87, 88, 89 & 90. *Teaching:* Murray State Univ, Ky, 53-56, Lee Col, Tex, 56-63, Univ Bridgeport, Conn, 64-68. *Bibliog:* Jose Pierre (auth), Guy Johnson, Editions Pilipacchi, 88; John L Ward (auth), American Realist Paintings 1945-1980, UMI Res Press, 89; Chiong Yiao Chen (auth), A small bite of the Big Apple - Small-scale works of art from New York galleries, Maier Mus Art, Randolph-Macon Women's Col, 90. *Publ:* Les Hyperrealistes Am, Eds Filipacchi, Paris, France, 73; Superrealism, E P Dutton, Co, New York, 75; Superrealist Painting and Sculpture, William Morrow Co, New York, 80; Cover illus, Harper's 5/87; American Realist Painting 1945-1980, UMI Res, Inc, Chicago, 88. *Mailing Add:* c/o Louis K Meisel 141 Prince St New York NY 10012

JOHNSON, HOMER
EDUCATOR, PAINTER
b Buffalo, NY, Dec 24, 25. *Study:* Pa Acad Fine Arts with Julius Bloch & Hobson Pittman, 46-52; Studies at Balkan Bridges to Peace, Kragujevac, Serbia, 2002. *Work:* Butler Inst Am Art, Youngstown, Ohio; Smith, Kline & French Labs, Philadelphia; Pa Acad Fine Arts. *Exhib:* Pa Acad Fine Arts Regional; W Village Meeting House, Brattleboro, VT, 88; Artists House, Philadelphia, 93 & 95; Atlantic Community Col, 96; Southern Vt Art Ctr, 96; Main Line Unitarian Church, Devon, Pa, 99; The Hill Sch, Pottstown, Pa, 2000; Exhibs, S Vt Art Gallery, Windham Art Gallery, Brattleboro, Vt & Philadelphia Sketch Club, 2000-2005. *Teaching:* Instr, Pa Acad Fine Arts & Fleisher Art Mem. *Awards:* Purchase Prize, Am Watercolor Soc, 72; First Prize Aqueous Media, Philadelphia Watercolor Club, 79; Percy Owens Award, Distinguished Pa Artist, 93; Dene M Louchheim Fac Fel, Fleisher Art Mem, 95; Crest Award, Philadelphia Watercolor Club, 97. *Mem:* Am Watercolor Soc. *Media:* Watercolor, Acrylic. *Dealer:* Artists House Gallery Philadelphia Pa 19106

JOHNSON, J STEWART
CURATOR, CONSULTANT
b Baltimore, Md, Aug 31, 25. *Study:* Swarthmore Col, BA; Univ Del, Winterthur Prog in Early Am Cult, MA; Harvard Univ, Loeb Fel. *Pos:* Cur decorative arts, Newark Mus, 64-68; cur decorative arts, Brooklyn Mus, 68-73, vice dir collections, 70-72; consult contemp glass, Corning Mus Glass, 73-74; cur decorative arts, Cooper-Hewitt Mus Design, 75-76; cur design, Mus Mod Art, New York, 76-86; Consult design & archit, Dept 20th Century Art, Metrop Mus Art, 90-. *Teaching:* Boston Univ, 86-87; FIT, 88-90. *Mem:* Victorian Soc Am (pres, 66-69); Am Friends of Attingham Park (pres, 80-83). *Publ:* Auth, Eileen Gray: Designer, 79; The Modern American Poster, 83. *Mailing Add:* Dept Twentieth Century Art Metrop Mus Art 1000 5th Ave New York NY 10028-0198

JOHNSON, JAMES ALAN
PAINTER, EDUCATOR
b Malden, Mass, Apr 2, 45. *Study:* Mass Col Art, Boston, BFA, 67; Wash State Univ, Pullman, MFA, 70. *Work:* Denver Art Mus, Colo; Minneapolis Mus Fine Arts; Mus Mod Art, NY; Chicago Art Inst; San Francisco Art Inst. *Exhib:* Artist Book Works, Chicago, 90; Multiples, Nexus Gallery, Atlanta, 90; CAGE Gallery, Cincinnati, 91; Walker's Point Ctr Arts, Milwaukee, 93; First Sightings Recent Modern & Contemp Acquisitions, Denver Art Mus, 93; 34d Ann NY Digital Salon (with catalog), Sch Vis Arts, 95; Options 1, Denver Art Mus, 96; The View from Denver (with catalog), Mus Moderner Kunststiftung, Ludwig Wien, Vienna, Austria, 97; Strong Words: Art, Text and Lang, Arvada Ctr Arts & Humanities, Arvada, Colo, 98. *Teaching:* Instr graphics, dept archit, Wash State Univ, Pullman, 70; asst prof painting & drawing, Univ Colo, Boulder, 70-78, assoc prof, 78-95, asst chmn, 88-91, prof, 95-, chmn, dept fine arts, 2002-. *Bibliog:* John Fisher (auth), James Johnson at University of Colorado Art Galleries, Artspace, summer 81; Print Collectors Newsletter, 89; Umbrella, 93. *Media:* All Media. *Publ:* Auth, A Thousand Words, Boulder, 91; Words on Works, Leonardo, Vol 25, No 1, 92; Index, 94; and others. *Dealer:* Robischon Gallery 1740 Wazee Denver CO 80202; Amos Eno Gallery 59 Franklin St B2 New York NY 10013. *Mailing Add:* Fine Arts Dept Univ Colo Campus Box 318 Boulder CO 80309

JOHNSON, JAMES EDWIN
GRAPHIC DESIGNER
b Minneapolis, Minn, Feb 18, 42. *Study:* Col St Thomas, Minneapolis; Minn Col Art & Design, with Robroy Kelly & Joe Luca, BFA. *Work:* Minneapolis Col Art & Design; Nat Gallery Fine Arts. *Comn:* Bicentennial pinwheel (outdoor graphic wind piece), Ft Worth Art Mus, Tex, 76; commemorable collage, Dayton-Hudson Found. *Exhib:* Making the City Observable, Int Design Conf, Aspen, Colo, 72; World Crafts

Coun, Oaxtepec, Mex, 76; Images of an Era: The Am Poster 1945-1975 Int Traveling Exhib, 76; Exhib of Design Process, Clara M Eagle Gallery, Murray State Univ, 77. *Pos:* Graphic designer, Gen Mills & IBM Corp, 66-70; head graphic design dept, Walker Art Ctr, Minn, 70-78; partner, Johnson plus Johnson Graphic Design, 78-. *Teaching:* Instr graphic design, Minneapolis Col Art & Design, 71-79; instr, Hamlin Univ, 74; vis lectr, St Cloud Univ, Univ Minn, Duluth, Bemidje Univ & Moorhead Univ. *Awards:* Cert Distinction, Creativity Eighty, 81; Oliver Award Merit, 81; Champion Papers Award, 82. *Bibliog:* Article, Design Quart 94/95, 75; The show awards exhib, Format Mag, 76; Publication design awards 1977, Soc Publ Designers, 77. *Mem:* Minn Graphic Designers Asn (mem coun, 77); Am Inst Graphic Arts; Soc Publ Designers; Fed Design Registry. *Publ:* Designer, American Indian Art: Form and Tradition, Walker Art Ctr, 72; designers, The Great American Rodeo, Ft Worth Art Mus, 75

JOHNSON, JOYCE
WRITER, SCULPTOR

b Newton, Mass, July 12, 29. *Study:* Escuela de Artes Oficios y Tecnicos, Madrid, Spain, with Don Ramon Mateu, cert; Sch of Mus Fine Arts, Boston, with Harold Tovish & Oscar Jespers, cert, grad fel. *Work:* Cushing Acad, Ashburnham, Mass; Cape Cod Conserv, Barnstable, Mass; Provincetown Art Asn & Mus; Habitat, Belmont, Mass; de Cordova Mus, Lincoln, MA; Cape Mus of Fine Arts, Dennis, MA. *Comn:* Sculpture, Botanical Gardens, Cornwall, Eng, 85; High Head, Commemorative Plaque, 89. *Exhib:* One-woman exhib, Annhurst Col, South Woodstock, Conn, 74 & Cape Cod Conserv, 83, 85 & 86; 20-Year Retrospective, Wellfleet Art Gallery, Mass, 77; Art in Transition--A Century of the Mus Sch, Mus Fine Arts, Boston, 77; Cape Mus, 88, 91 & 92; Chandler Gallery, 88-91; Addison-Holmes Gallery, 96-; Central Conn State Univ, 97; Forest Hills Cemetery 150th ann, sculpture show, 98-; Forest Lawn Cemetary, 100th ann, Buffalo, NY, 99-; Retrospective, Cape Coo Mus of Art Dennis MA, 2005. *Pos:* Asst dir, Beaupre Arts Ctr, Stockbridge, Mass, 59-62; dir-founder, Nauset Sch Sculpture, North Eastham, Mass, 68-71; dir & founder, Truro Ctr for the Arts, Mass, 72-94; trustee, Lower Cape Arts Coun, 84-88; writer, Cape Codder Newspaper, currently; founder-Mem, Peaked Hill Trust to Save Dune Shacks, 85; founder, Outer Cape Artists Residency Consortium, 95; Exhib Comt, Provincetown Art Asn & Mus, 95-00; Steering Comt, Campus Proviencetown and Highland Ctr, Cape Cod Nat Seashore, 99-. *Teaching:* Instr sculpture from life, Cape Cod Conserv, Barnstable, Mass, 73-87, Truro Ctr for the Arts, Truro, Mass, 74- & Provincetown Mus Sch, 83-89. *Awards:* First Prize Pictorial Photograph, New Eng Press Assoc, 85; First Prize Sculpture, New Eng Ann, Cape Cod Art Asn, 91. *Bibliog:* Articles in Cape Arts, Cape Codder, Cape Cod Times & Boston Globe, 72-94. *Mem:* Provincetown Art Asn (trustee, 76-78); Castle Hill. *Media:* Wood Carving, Clay. *Specialty:* Fine Arts. *Interests:* History, Photography. *Publ:* Joyce Johnson Cape Cod Arts, 2001; Truro Center for the Arts-30th Anniversary The Cape Codders, July 11, 2001; Listed in Who's Who in American Art and Who's Who in Women since 1978. *Dealer:* Addison Gallery 45 S Orleans Rd Orleans MA 02653. *Mailing Add:* PO Box 201 Truro MA 02666

JOHNSON, KAYTIE
CURATOR

b San Francisco, July 26, 64. *Study:* Ariz State Univ, BA, 87; Ariz State Univ, MA, 01. *Exhib:* Leaving Aztlaír, Ctr for Vis Art, Denver, Limn Gallery, San Francisco, 2005; DePauw Biennial: Contemp Art in the Midwest, Richard E Deeler Art Ctr, DePauw Univ, 2005; Skirting the Line: Conceptual Drawing, 2006; Chuck Ramirez: Deeply Superficial, 2006; Sally Heller: Material Minutiae; Anena One, Santa Monica Ctr Contemporary Art, Louisville, Ky. *Pos:* dir, cur Univ Galleries, Mus, Collections, Richard E Peeler Art Ctr, DePauw Univ, 03-. *Mem:* Asn Latin Am Art. *Res:* Contemporary Latina/o, Mexican, Chicana/o and border art. *Publ:* Contemporary Chicana and Chicano Art: Artists, Works, Culture and Education, Bilingual Rev/Press, 02; St. James Guide to Hispanic Artists: Profiles of Latino and Latin American Artists, Bilingual Rev/Press, 02. *Mailing Add:* DePauw Univ Richard E Peeler Art Center 10 W Hanna St Greencastle IN 46135

JOHNSON, LEE
PAINTER, EDUCATOR

b Albion, Nebr, Nov 9, 35. *Study:* Minneapolis Col Art & Design, BFA; Skowhegan Sch Painting & Sculpture, with Alex Katz; Univ NMex, MA. *Work:* Denver Art Mus, Colo; Roswell Mus & Art Ctr, Roswell, NMex; Mus of NMex, Fine Arts, Santa Fe; Jonson Gallery, Univ NMex, Albuquerque, NMex; and others. *Exhib:* 1st Ann Painting Invitational, Mus NMex, 68; Masterpieces from the Mus of NMex, McNay Art Inst, San Antonio, Tex, 70; Five Artists from Colo Traveling Exhib, Rocky Mountain Coun Arts, 71-72; Rocky Mountain Coun Arts Traveling Exhib, Eight Western States, 72; 8 West Biennial, Grand Junction, Colo, 72-74; one-man show, Western Ctr Arts, Grand Junction, Colo, 96; ARSC Traveling Exhib, Sic Univs & Colls, 1999-2001. *Pos:* Asst dir-cur, Roswell Mus & Art Ctr, NMex, 62-68; dir, Gunnison Coun on Arts & Humanities, Colo, 73-75. *Teaching:* Instr drawing & painting, Eastern NMex Univ, Roswell, 62-67; asst prof drawing & painting, Western State Col, Gunnison, Colo, 68-81, prof art, 84. *Awards:* First Prize Painting, 8 West Biennial, W Co Art Ctr, 74; Artist-in-Residence Grant, Roswell Mus & Art Ctr, 75. *Mem:* Mid-Am Col Art Asn; Col Art Asn. *Media:* Acrylic, Watercolor. *Mailing Add:* c/o Dept Art Western State Col Colo Gunnison CO 81230

JOHNSON, LESTER F
PAINTER, EDUCATOR

b Minneapolis, Minn, Jan 27, 19. *Study:* Minneapolis Sch Art; St Paul Art Sch; Chicago Art Inst. *Exhib:* 10 Independents, Guggenheim Mus, NY, 72; 70th Am Exhib, Art Inst Chicago, 72; Minn Mus Art, 73; Whitney Mus Am Art, 73; From the Imagination, Green Mountain Gallery, NY, 78; Homo Sapiens, Aldrich Mus Contemp Art, Ridgefield, Conn, 82; Martha Jackson Mem Collection, Nat Mus Am Art, Washington, 85; Chicago Art Fair, Ill, 87, 88 & 89; NJ Ctr Visual Arts, Summit, 87; Aldrich Mus Contemp Art, 87; Int Art Fair, Los Angeles, Calif, 88 & 89; Parrish Art Mus, Southampton, NY, 88; solo exhibs, David Barnett Gallery, Milwaukee, Wis, 89 & 94, Gimpel Weitzenhoffer Gallery, NY, 90, Donald Morris Gallery, Detroit, Mich, 91, Eva Cohon Gallery, Chicago, Ill, 92, Margaret Lipworth Gallery, Boca Raton, Fla, 92 & 94, Los Angeles Int Jack Rutberg Gallery, Calif, 93 & Ed Thorp Gallery, NY, 94; Paris-NY-Kent Fine Art, Kent, Conn, 90; Eva Cohon Gallery, Chicago, 92; Peter Findlay Gallery, NY, 96. *Teaching:* Artist-in-residence, Univ Wis, Milwaukee, 64; adj prof painting, Yale Univ, New Haven, Conn, 64-89, dir, studies grad painting, Sch Art & Archit, 69-74; retired. *Awards:* Guggenheim Fel, 72; Guggenheim Fel Painting, 73; Creative Arts Award Painting, Brandeis Univ, 78. *Bibliog:* Paul Schimmel & Judith Stein, The Figurative Fifties, Rizzoli, NY, 88; George Zabriskie (dir), Lester (film), New York: Brandon Films; Harry Rand (auth), Lester Johnson, Art Mag, 10/90. *Mem:* Am Acad Design; Coun Am Acad Design; assoc Nat Acad Design. *Mailing Add:* PO Box 7582 Greenwich CT 06836

JOHNSON, LESTER L
PAINTER, EDUCATOR

b Detroit, Mich, Sept 28, 37. *Study:* Univ Mich, BFA, 73, MFA, 74. *Work:* Detroit Inst Arts; Osaka Univ Arts, Japan; St Paul Co, Minn; The Tougaloo Col Art Collections, Miss; Univ Mich Mus Art; Fed Res Bank Chicago-Detroit Br. *Comn:* Martin Luther King Community Ctr, Holtzman and Silverman Companies, Farmington Hills, 82; Bishop Int Airport, Flint, 94. *Exhib:* Art for Technology: A Reunion of Mural Artists, Martin Luther King Neighborhood Network, Detroit, 2000; Appreciation and Insight, Nicolet Area Technical Col, Rhinelander, Wis, 2001; A Cult Heritage: Selected Works of African Am Art From the DIA's Collection, Detroit Inst of Arts, 2001; Intercambio 2001, Centro de Memoria e Cult dos Correios, Salvador, Brazil; Jordan Road Gallery, Sedona, Ariz, 2003; Reverberations, Contemp Art by African-Amerian Artists of Southeastern Mich, Klemm Gallery, Siena Heights Univ, Adrian, 2004; Pluperfect Plural, Buckham Gallery, Flint, 2005. *Pos:* Participant dept, art and art hist 3d Annual African Am Lecture Series, Wayne State Univ, 2000, int conference on African Influences in the Visual Arts of the Ams, 2001. *Teaching:* Prof drawing & painting, Col for Creative Studies, Col Art & Design, 75-. *Awards:* Andrew W Mellon Found Proj Res/Travel Grant, 82 & 84; Mus African-Am Hist, 83; Recognition Award, African-Am Music Festival,90. *Mailing Add:* Collection for Creative Studies 201 E Kirby St Detroit MI 48202-4034

JOHNSON, LOIS MARLENE
PRINTMAKER, EDUCATOR

b Grand Forks, NDak, Nov 17, 42. *Study:* Univ NDak, BS, 64; Univ Wis-Madison, MFA, 66. *Work:* Philadelphia Mus Art; Elvehjem Art Ctr, Madison; McCray Gallery, Univ NMex, Albuquerque; Univ NDak, Grand Forks; Adolph Behn Mem Collection, NY. *Comn:* Poster, Philadelphia Mus Art, 72. *Exhib:* Soc Am Graphic Artists, NY, 65-67, 70 & 71; Northwest Printmakers Int, Seattle, 68; Am Color Print Soc, 68-72; Silk Screen, Philadelphia Mus Art, 72; 18th Biennial Exhib, Brooklyn Mus, NY, 72; and others. *Teaching:* From asst prof to assoc prof printmaking & chmn dept, Philadelphia Col Art, 67-. *Awards:* Abraham Hankins Award, Am Color Print Soc, 68; Award, Prints in Pa, 69; Eyre Medal, Philadelphia Watercolor Club, 71. *Mem:* Print Club; Am Color Print Soc (coun, 68-72); Philadelphia Watercolor Club (bd dir, 72); Soc Am Graphic Artists; Philadelphia Art Alliance. *Media:* Intaglio, Silkscreen. *Publ:* Contribr, Artist proof, Pratt Graphic Ctr, 67. *Dealer:* The Print Club 1614 Latimer St Philadelphia PA 19102

JOHNSON, MARK M
MUSEUM DIRECTOR

b Rochester, Minn, Dec 10, 50. *Study:* Univ Wis, Whitewater, BA(art hist), 74; Univ Ill, Urbana-Champaign, MA(art hist) & cert arts mus studies, 76. *Collection Arranged:* Idea to Image: Preparatory Studies from the Renaissance to Impressionism (auth, catalog), Cleveland Mus Art, 80; Japanese Woodblock Prints: Themes & Techniques, Cleveland Mus Art, 80; Photographs by Yousuf Karsh, traveling, 87-98; Am Drawing Biennial, Muscarelle Mus Art, Va, 88, 90, 92 & 94; King William's Praise: Romeyn de Hooghe's Etchings of William III (auth, catalog), Muscarelle Mus Art, Va, 89; Literacy through Art (auth, catalog), Muscarelle Mus Art, 90; Contemp Abstract Painting: Resnick, Reed, Laufer & Moore, Muscarelle Mus Art, 91; Contemp Inuit Drawings, Muscarelle Mus Art, Va, 93; Nissan Engel: Nouvelles Dimensions (auth, catalog), Muscarelle Mus Art, Va, 94; Hans Grohs: An Estatic Vision (auth, catalog), Montgomery Mus Fine Arts, 96; After History: The Paintings of David Bierk (auth, catalog), Montgomery Mus Fine Arts, 2000; Ginny Ruffner (auth, catalog), Montgomery Mus Fine Arts (traveling), 2003-05. *Pos:* Lectr mus ed, Art Inst Chicago, 76-77; cur art hist, Cleveland Mus Art, 77-81; asst dir & cur Europ painting, Krannert Art Mus, Ill, 81-85; dir, Muscarelle Mus Art, Va, 85-94, Montgomery Mus Fine Arts, Ala, 94-. *Teaching:* Instr art hist, Cuyahoga Col, Cleveland, 77-81; instr mus studies, Univ Ill, Urbana-Champaign, 81-85 & Auburn Univ, Montgomery, 95-2005; instr art hist & mus studies, Col William & Mary, 85-94. *Awards:* Numerous grants for mus opers, conserv, exhibs, res, educ & mus studies. *Mem:* Am Asn Mus; Col Art Asn; Nat Art Educ Asn; Asn Art Mus Dirs; Int Coun of Mus. *Mailing Add:* Montgomery Mus Fine Arts PO Box 230819 Montgomery AL 36123-0819

JOHNSON, MARTIN BRIAN
ILLUMINATOR, ASSEMBLAGE ARTIST

b Elmer, NJ, 51. *Study:* Va Polytechnic Inst; Va State Univ, BArchit, 74; Univ NC, Chapel Hill, MFA, 77. *Work:* Ball State Univ, Muncie, Ind; The Vogel Collection, Nat Gallery Art, Washington, DC; Chrysler Mus, Norfolk, Va; Works in public collections, Dallas, Mus. *Exhib:* Pleady Entreaty, Va Mus Fine Arts, Richmond, 90; Hesheunisallforone (44 4 x 4S 30 part), Southeastern Ctr Contemp Art, Winston

Salem, NC, 92; Forty-Four Four by Fours, Art Mus Western Va, Roanoke, Va, 94; New Works Fellowships (with catalog), City Gallery Contemp Art, Raleigh, NC & Arlington Mus Art, Tex, 94; Cheekwood Mus Art, Nashville, Tenn, 95; Nexus Contemp Art Ctr, Atlanta, Ga; Forinstance Gallery, Richmond, Va, 2005. *Pos:* pres, Va Marketing Assocs; owner, operator, Forinstance Gallery, Richmond, Va, currently. *Awards:* Northern Telecom Fel, City Gallery Contemp Art, Raleigh, NC, 93. *Bibliog:* Allan Schwartzman (auth), article, Arts Mag, 1/80; Donald B Kuspit (auth), articles, Art Am, 9/83, Artforum, 5/85; Linda McGreevy (auth), article, Arts Mag, 5/88. *Media:* Gesture, Oeuvre. *Specialty:* The Lifetime Oeuvre Evolution of Martin Johnson's works. *Interests:* Jazz, food, eternity. *Dealer:* Forinstance Gallery 107 E Cary St Richmond VA 23219. *Mailing Add:* PO Box 29 Virginia Beach VA 23458

JOHNSON, MIANI (MARIANNE) GUTHRIE
DEALER, CONSULTANT
b New York, NY, July 14, 1948. *Study:* Barnard Col, BA. *Pos:* Dir, Willard Gallery, currently. *Media:* All. *Specialty:* Contemporary painting and sculpture. *Mailing Add:* c/o Willard Gallery 12 E 12 St New York NY 10003

JOHNSON, RICHARD A
PAINTER, EDUCATOR
b Minneapolis, Minn, Feb 26, 42. *Study:* Minneapolis Col Art & Design, BFA, 65; Washington Univ, St Louis, Mo, MFA, 67; Am Acad in Rome, fel, painting, Prix de Rome, Italy, 68. *Work:* Longview Mus Art, Tex; R J Reynolds Indus, Winston-Salem, NC; Phillip Morris, NY; Pan Am Life, New Orleans; Katz & Bestoff Inc, New Orleans. *Exhib:* Walker Biennial, Walker Art Ctr, Minneapolis, 66; Tex Painting & Sculpture, Dallas Mus Fine Arts, 71; Photo Realism & Abstract Illusionism, Pittsburgh Arts & Crafts Ctr, 78; Operation Update 1979, Longview Mus, Tex, 79; Reality of Illusion, Denver Mus Art, 79; Illusion, Southeastern Ctr Contemp Art, Winston-Salem, NC, 83. *Teaching:* Chmn, Dept Fine Arts, Univ New Orleans, 79-, instr painting, 80, assoc prof painting, drawing & design, currently. *Awards:* Rockefeller Artist-in-Residence Grant, Southeastern Ctr Contemp Art, Winston-Salem, NC, 80. *Bibliog:* Mary King (auth), Two artists on display, St Louis Post-Dispatch, Mo, 5/74; Ted Calas (auth), Art scene, Figaro Newspaper, New Orleans, 10/79; Harry Schwalb (auth), Trick and treat, Pittsburgher Mag, Vol II, No 8, 79. *Mem:* Artists' Equity Asn La (vpres, 76-78). *Media:* Mixed. *Dealer:* Galerie Simonne Stern 2727 Prytania St New Orleans LA 70130; Watson-DeNagy 1106 Berthea Houston Tex

JOHNSON, RICHARD WALTER
SCULPTOR, INSTRUCTOR
b Glen Cove, NY, Aug 11, 46. *Study:* State Univ NY, Oneonta, BA, 72; State Univ NY, Albany, MA, 76. *Work:* Fla Atlantic Univ; State Univ NY, Albany. *Comn:* Ground Zero Sculpture Park, Howe Cave, NY, 93. *Exhib:* Sculpture Now, Gallery 151, Palm Beach, Fla, 86; Steel & Iron, John Lavine Gallery, Palm Beach, 87; New Sculpture, Eugenia Palacios Gallery, Palm Beach, 94; Steel Forms, Florence Gallery, Palm Beach, 95; Steel in Focus, Woodbull Art Ctr, Milford, NY. *Pos:* Founder, Bear Trap School, Fla, 80-; sculptor in residence, Ground Zero Sculptture Park, 93-. *Teaching:* vis prof, sculpture, Vero Beach Ctr Arts, Fla, 2000; vis instr, Glimmer Glass Creative Learning Ctr, Cooperstown, NY, 2006. *Awards:* Key Bank Award, 84; Sculpture Award, NY State Fair, 93; Sculptor in Residence, Blackwood Sculpture Space, Maryland, NY, 2005. *Bibliog:* Les Krantz (auth), American artists, Am References, 90, NY Art review, 91. *Mem:* Cooperstown Art Asn; Upper Catskill Art Asn; Int Sculpture Ctr. *Mailing Add:* 217 LEONARD RD Maryland NY 12116-2307

JOHNSON, ROBERT FLYNN
CURATOR, HISTORIAN
b Jersey City, NJ, Mar 20, 48. *Pos:* Cur asst, Worcester Art Mus, Mass, summer 72; asst cur prints & drawings, Baltimore Mus Art, 73-75; cur in chg, Achenbach Found Graphic Arts, Fine Arts Mus San Francisco, 75-. *Teaching:* San Francisco Art Inst, 81. *Awards:* Nat Endowment Arts Fel, 75. *Mem:* Print Coun Am; Print & Drawing Soc of Baltimore Mus Art (vpres, 74-75); Bay Area Graphic Arts Coun (adv). *Res:* American prints of the 19th and 20th century; 19th century French drawings. *Publ:* Auth, American Prints, 1870-1950, Univ Chicago Press, 76; Lucian Freud Works on Paper, Thames & Hudson, 89. *Mailing Add:* 126 20th Ave San Francisco CA 94121-1308

JOHNSON, RONALD W
HISTORIAN, EDUCATOR
b Rockford, Ill, July, 29, 37. *Study:* Calif State Univ, San Diego, BA, 59 & MA, 63; Univ Calif, Berkeley, MA(hist art), 65 & PhD(hist art), 71. *Teaching:* Asst prof hist art, Univ Iowa, Iowa City, 70-73; prof hist art, Humboldt State Univ, Arcata, Calif, 73; vis instr hist art, Univ Calif, San Diego, 76; vis instr hist art, Univ Calif, Berkeley, 81. *Mem:* Col Art Asn Am. *Res:* Picasso's and late 19th century art; emphasizing conceptual relationships between art and poetry. *Publ:* Auth, Picaasso's old guitarist and the symbolist sensibility, Artforum, 12/74; Dante Rossetti's Beata Beatrix and the new life, Art Bulletin, 12/75; Poetic pathways to Dada: Marcel Duchamp & Jules Laforgue, 5/76, Vincent van Gogh and the vernacular: His southern accent, 6/78 & Picasso's Demoiselles d'Avignon and the theatre of the absurd, 10/80, Arts. *Mailing Add:* Humboldt State Univ Dept Art Arcata CA 95521

JOHNSON-ROSS, ROBYN
PAINTER, WRITER
b San Francisco, Calif, Jan 1, 46. *Study:* George Washington Univ, Washington, DC, BA, 68. *Comn:* Corcoran Gallery Art, Washington, DC. *Exhib:* 10+10+10: Washington Artists 1982, Corcoran Gallery, 82; Woman as Protagonist, Rosenberg Gallery, Goucher Col, Baltimore, Md, 92; solo exhib, Attitudes of the Flesh, Gallery 10, Washington, DC, 94; Black Art, Rockville Arts Pl, Md, 95; MOCA Biennial: The Figure, Mus Contemp Art, Washington, 96; Arts Sites 96: Presenting the Nude, DC Arts Ctr, 96. *Pos:* Writer, KOAN Mag, Washington, DC, currently. *Awards:* Fel, Nat Endowment Arts, 87-88. *Media:* Oil. *Mailing Add:* 1706 Lamont St NW Washington DC 20010

JOHNSTON, BARRY WOODS
SCULPTOR
b Florence, Ala. *Study:* Ga Inst Technol, B(arch), 69; Art Students League, with Joseph De Creeft; Pa Acad Fine Arts, with Walker Hancock, Harry Rosen & Tony Greenwood; Nat Acad Fine Arts, with Michael Lantz; also studied in Italy, with Enzo Cardini & Madame Simi. *Work:* The Vatican Mus, Rome; Martin Luther King Libr, Georgetown Univ & Lutheran Church Reformation, Washington, DC; CBN Univ, Va. *Comn:* Medal, Ann Letelier Moffitt Award, Inst Policy Studies, Washington, DC; Journey to Jerusalem, US Citizens Cong, Washington, DC; lobby centerpiece, Fentress Cancer Ctr, Hillside Methodist Hosp, Waco, Tex; Sen Sparkman bust, C of C, Hartsell, Ala; Wedlock (sculpture), Lafayette Ctr, Washington, DC; Mariner, Hampton, Va; Mother & Child, Evanston, Ill. *Exhib:* One-man shows, St John's Church, 75, George Washington Univ Libr, 76, Folger Shakespeare Libr, 79, Washington, DC & City Hall, Hampton, Va, 86, Columbia Art Ctr, 93, Md Fedn of Art Gallery on the Circle, Annapolis, 95, Mulligan Gallery, Virginia Beach, Va, 95, Worldwide Gallery, Atlanta, 95, James A Michener Art Mus, Doylestown, Pa, 99; Four Realists, Foundry, Georgetown, 76; Nat Sculpture Soc Ann Group Show, NY, 80-86; Martin Luther King Libr, 83; Allied Artists Am Exhib, NY, 86; Centre Int D'Arte Contemporian, Paris, France, 86; Arts Festival, Castello di Besozzo, Italy, 86; Bucca di Magra, Massa, Italy, 87. *Awards:* Second Prize for Figurative Sculpture, Ga Marble Fest, 83; Pres Award Nat Arts Club Ann, 94; Cassidy Meml Award, Salmagundi Club, 98. *Mem:* Nat Sculpture Soc; Founder, Art For Humanity Found (pres, 78-81); Am Medallic Sculpture Asn. *Media:* Clay, Bronze. *Publ:* Auth, articles in Sculpture Rev, winter 85-86 & spring 86, Sculptor's Int, vol 3, 84 & spring 86. *Mailing Add:* 2423 Pickwick Rd Gwynn Oak MD 21207-6635

JOHNSTON, PHILLIP M
CURATOR, MUSEUM DIRECTOR
b Texarkana, Tex, July 24, 44. *Study:* Baylor Univ, BA(cum laude), 66; Southern Methodist Univ, MA, 68; Univ Del, MA, 74. *Collection Arranged:* Victorian Furnishings from Armsmear and the James Goodwin House, 75, American Indian Baskets in the Wadsworth Atheneum, 76, Ancient Art of Peru: the Etherington Collection, 76, Glass from Six Centuries, 76, Art in Seventeenth Century New England (auth, catalog), 77 & Gerrit Thomas Rietveld, Designer (auth, catalog), 80, Wadsworth Atheneum, 80; Courts & Colonies: The William & Mary Style in Holland Eng & Am (co-auth, catalog), Cooper-Hewitt Mus & Carnegie Mus Art, 87- 88; Kansas City Collects Contemp Ceramics (auth, catalog), Nelson-Atkins Gallery, 89. *Pos:* Assoc cur dept decorative arts, Wadsworth Atheneum, Hartford, Conn, 73-75, cur decorative arts, 75-78, chief cur & cur decorative arts, 78-82; cur decorative arts & head antiquities, Oriental & decorative art, Carnegie Mus Art, Pittsburgh, Pa, 82-, dir, 88-96; vpres, Soc Preserv New Eng Antiq, 96-98; dir, Mus Art, RI Sch Design, 98-. *Teaching:* Instr dept English, Hannibal-LaGrange Col, Mo, 67-68 & Southern Methodist Univ, 68-71. *Res:* American silver and furniture, contemporary American ceramics. *Publ:* Ed, English Silver: The Elizabeth B Miles Collection, Wadsworth Atheneum, 76; auth, Eighteenth and nineteenth century American furniture in the Wadsworth Atheneum, Antiques, 79; Dialogues between designer and client: furnishings proposed by Leon Maricotte to Samuel Colt in the 1850s, Winterthur Portfolio, Winter 84; The William and Mary style in New York, Antiques, 88; American Silver in the Cleveland Mus Art, 94. *Mailing Add:* RI Sch Design Mus Art 224 Benefit St Providence RI 02903-2723

JOHNSTON, RANDY JAMES
CERAMIST, SCULPTOR
b Austin, Tex, 50. *Study:* Univ Minn, Minneapolis, BFA(studio art), 72; studied with Tatsuzo Shimaoka Mashiko, Japan, 75; Southern Ill Univ, Edwardsville, MFA, 90. *Work:* Dustin & Lisa Hoffman, Los Angeles; Univ Art Mus, Ariz State Univ, Tempe; Univ Art Mus, Univ Minn, Minneapolis; Burke Found, NY; Banff Sch Art, Alberta, Can; Minneapolis Inst Arts, Minn; Los Angeles Co Mus, Calif. *Exhib:* Solo shows, Viterbo Col, LaCrosse, Wis, 83, Wis Acad Sci, Arts & Lett, Madison, 87, Pro Art, St Louis, Mo, 87 & 90; Manchester Inst Arts & Sci, NH, 92; Babcock Gallery, NY, 95; Seibu, Tokyo, Japan, 98; DAI Icki Arts, NY, 99; Lacoste Gallery, Concord, Mass, 2000. *Pos:* Studio, River Falls, Wis, 72-; guest cur, Col St Catherine Gallery, St Paul, Minn, 77; consult, Minneapolis Sch Art & Design, Minn, 77, St Cloud State Col, Minn, 78 & adv bd, Northern Clay Ctr, St Paul, Minn, 91. *Teaching:* Guest lectr, var univ & col, 74-2000; teacher, Rochester Art Ctr, 73-74 & 76, Univ Minn, Quadna Summer Art Ctr, 76, 78 & 79, Univ Minn Studio Arts, 78-79 & Bergen Sch Art, Norway, 81; assoc prof art, Univ Wis, River Falls, 92-98; workshop, Univ Wis-Stout, 87; Emily Carr Sch Art, Vancouver, BC, 88; Southern Ill Univ, Edwardsville, 89; spec asst prof, Kansas City Art Inst, Mo, 92; Huara Huara Studio, Santiago, Chile. *Awards:* Craftsmen's Apprenticeship, 78-79, Craftsmen's Fel, 78-79 & Visual Arts Fel, 90-91, Nat Endowment Arts; Individual Artist Fel, Proj Grant, Wis Art Bd, 83; Bush Artists Fel, 98. *Bibliog:* Am Craft, 12/90-1/91; Fragile Blossoms Enduring Earth, 89; Warren MacKenzie, An Am Potter, 91; Coil Minoque/Sanderson (auth), Wood Fired Ceramics. *Publ:* Wood firing, Vol II, No 1, 83 & article, winter 89, Studio Potter; Between two fires, essay, Am Wood Fired Catalog, Univ Iowa, 91; Portfolio, Ceramics Monthly, 10/91; Ceramic Art & Perception, No 16, 94; Color and Fire, Rizolli Publ Lauria. *Dealer:* Trax Gallery Berkeley CA; Babcock Gallery New York NY. *Mailing Add:* N 8336 690th St River Falls WI 54022

JOHNSTON, RICHARD M
SCULPTOR, EDUCATOR
b Kankakee, Ill, Sept 22, 42. *Study:* El Camino Jr Col; Calif State Col, Long Beach, BA; Cranbrook Acad Art, MFA. *Work:* Weber State Col; Salt Lake Co Bar Asn; Cranbrook Acad of Art. *Comn:* Steel wall sculpture, Western Airlines, Los Angeles, 69; bronze wall sculpture, Telemation Inc, Salt Lake City, Utah, 71; gold leaf/steel sculpture, Sun Valley Ski Corp, Idaho, 71; Temple Kol Ami, Salt Lake Int Ctr. *Exhib:*

Craftsman USA, Los Angeles Co Mus Art, 66; Nat Crafts Exhib, Univ NMex, 68; Inter-Mountain Biennial, Salt Lake Art Ctr, 70; 73rd Western Ann, Denver Art Mus, 71; Nat Small Sculpture & Drawing Show, San Diego State Col, 72; one-man show, Salt Lake Art Ctr, 80. *Teaching:* Prof, Univ Utah, 68-90, Calif State Univ, San Bernadino, 90. *Awards:* First Prize, Sterling Silversmiths, 68; Purchase Award, Utah Mus Fine Art, 69; Purchase Award, Salt Lake Art Ctr, 70. *Media:* Metal. *Mailing Add:* 528 Amigos Dr Ste A Redlands CA 92373-6258

JOHNSTON, ROY
PAINTER, HISTORIAN
b Tyrone, N Ireland, June 12, 36. *Study:* Belfast Col Art, BA & NDD, 66; Cardiff Col Art & Univ S Wales, DAE, 69; Trinity Col, Univ Dublin, PhD, 89. *Work:* Ulster Mus, Belfast, N Ireland; Hugh Lane Munic Gallery Mod Art, Dublin, Ireland; Arts Coun Great Britian, London, Eng; Munson-Williams Proctor Inst, Utica, NY; Univ Ulster, Coleraine, N Ireland. *Comn:* Posters for the environment, 70, wall relief, 76 & suite of six drawings, 82, Arts Coun N Ireland, Belfast; tapestry mural, Univ Col Galway, 73. *Exhib:* Irish Imagination, Corcoran Gallery, Washington, 72; Aos Og, Mus d'Art Moderne, Paris, France, 73; retrospective, Hugh Lane Munic Gallery Mod Art, Dublin, 85; Artists of Central NY, Munson-Williams Proctor Inst, Utica, NY, 89; The Abstract Irish, Right Bank Gallery, Brooklyn, NY, 92; Ateliers D'Artistes De Pont-Aven, Mus De Pont-Aven, France, 93; Albany Ctr Gallery, NY, 94; and others. *Collection Arranged:* Roderic O'Conor Vision & Expression (exhib catalog), Hugh Lane Munic Gallery Mod Art, Dublin; Roderic O'Conor (1860-1940), Retrospective (exhib catalog), Mus de Pont-Aven, France, 84 & Ulster Mus, Belfast & Barbican Art Gallery, London, 85. *Teaching:* Lectr, fine art, Univ Ulster, Belfast, 69-87; prof, drawing & painting, Skidmore Col, Saratoga Springs, NY, 87-94; Eastern Mich Univ, 94. *Awards:* Carroll Prize Painting, Irish Exhib Living Art, Carroll & Co, 73; Walker Painting Award, An Oireachtas, Dublin Scott, Tallon, Walker, 78; Key Bank Prize, Cooperstown Nat, Key Bank, 88 & 89. *Bibliog:* Dorothy Walker (auth), The Intelligent Eye, Hibernia Review, 72; Dr Brian Kennedy (auth), Roy Johnston 1965-1985, Arts Coun N Ireland, 85; Cyril Barrett (auth), Roy Johnston, Art Monthly, 85. *Mem:* Col Art Asn Am; Nat Asn Sch Art & Design. *Media:* Acrylic, Oil. *Res:* School of Pont-Aven and the life and work of Roderic O'Conor 1860-1940. *Publ:* Auth, Systems and Art, Introspect, 75; Sean Scully, Circa Mag, 82; Roderic O'Conor in Brittany, 84 & Roderic O'Conor: The Elusive Personality, 85, Irish Arts Review; O'Conor Gravures, Arts de L'Ouest, Rennes, 86. *Dealer:* Oliver Dowling Gallery 19 Kildare St Dublin Ireland 2; Bell Gallery 162 N Woodward Birmingham MI. *Mailing Add:* 4 Bull Run Drive Oxford OH 45056

JOHNSTON, THOMAS ALIX
PAINTER, PRINTMAKER
b Oklahoma City, Okla, June 4, 41. *Study:* San Diego State Col, BA, 65; Univ Calif, Santa Barbara, MFA, 67; Atelier 17, Paris & Atelier Lacouriere et Frelaut, Paris, 80. *Work:* Henry Art Gallery, Univ Wash & Seattle Art Mus, Seattle; Portland Art Mus; Mod Art Mus, Kobe, Japan; Royal Collection, Riyadh, Saudi Arabia; and others. *Exhib:* 52nd Biennial, Libr Cong, Washington, DC & Blackfish Gallery, Portland, 84; NW Ann, Seattle Art Mus, 72 & 92, Evergreen State Col, 80, Wash; Black and White Drawings by 150 Americans 1970-1980, Brooklyn Mus, 80; Davidson Gallery, Seattle, 82 & 91; Francine Seders Gallery, Seattle, 84, 86 & 87; Galerie Jean Claude Riedel, Paris, 89; McIntosh Gallery, Atlanta, Ga, 93; IXL Gallery, San Francisco, 94; Second Int Graphic Art, Prague, Czech Rep, 99; Evergreen State Col, Olympia, Wash, 2001; Northlight Gallery, Everett, Wash, 2002; Anthropomorphic Consciousness, Joe's Garage, Olympia, Wash, 2005. *Collection Arranged:* 25 American Print Artists, La Jeune Gravure Contemporaine, Paris, 95. *Pos:* Dir, Western Gallery, Western Washington Univ, 83-87; auth & ed, Western Gallery News, Western Wash Univ, 83-88. *Teaching:* Prof art, Western Wash Univ, prof emeritus. *Awards:* First Place/Graphics, 14th Northern Calif Ann, Calif State Univ, Chico, 70; Purchase Award, 57th NW Ann, Seattle Art Mus, Wash, 72; Artist in Residence, Chateau Suduiraut, Sauternes, France, 93. *Bibliog:* Nicholson, Baker (auth), Discards, The New Yorker, 94; Fred Moody (auth), It's in the Cards, Seattle Weekly, 98; Simeona Hoskova (ed), Labyrinth, The Ministry of Culture of the Czech Republic, 98. *Media:* Intaglio, Acrylic, Oil. *Publ:* Illusr Concerning Poetry, Western Wash Univ, 73-80; The Ventriloquist, R Huff, Univ Press Va, 77; Beyond the veil: The etching of Helen Loggie, Whatcom Mus, 79; Du Regard a la Vision, Lacouriere Frelaut, Paris, 94. *Mailing Add:* PO Box 12593 Olympia WA 98508-2593

JOHNSTON, WILLIAM RALPH
ADMINISTRATOR, CURATOR
b Toronto, Ont, Feb 15, 36. *Study:* Univ Toronto Trinity Col, Hon BA, 59; NY Univ Inst Fine Arts, MA, 66. *Collection Arranged:* Anatomy of a Chair: Regional Variations in 18th Century Furniture Styles, Metrop Mus, New York, 62; J W Morrice (with catalog), Montreal Mus Fine Arts, Nat Gallery Can, 68. *Pos:* Cur, Robert Lehman Collection, New York, 62-63; gen cur, Montreal Mus Fine Arts, 64-66; asst dir, Walters Art Gallery, 66-83, assoc dir, 83-. *Awards:* Fel, Am Wing, Metrop Mus Art, 63-64. *Mem:* Am Ceramic Circle; Victorian Soc Am. *Res:* 18th & 19th century painting & decorative arts. *Publ:* Coauth, Japonisme, Cleveland Mus; auth, The Nineteenth Century Paintings in The Walters Art Gallery, Baltimore, 82; coauth, Alfred Jacob Miller, Artist on the Oregon Trail, Ft Worth, 82; Masterpieces of Ivory from the Walters Art Gallery, 85; Alfred Sisley, London, 92; William and Henry Walters, The Reticient Collectors, J.H.U. Press, Baltimore, MD, 99; The Triumph of French Painting (coauth), London, 2000; The Faberge Menagerie, (coauth), Baltimore, 2003. *Mailing Add:* Walters Art Mus 600 N Charles St Baltimore MD 21201

JOHNSTON, YNEZ
PAINTER, PRINTMAKER
b Berkeley, Calif, May 12, 20. *Study:* Univ Calif, Berkeley, MFA, 46. *Work:* Mus Mod Art, Whitney Mus Am Art & Metrop Mus Art, NY; Hirshhorn Mus & Sculpture Garden, Washington, DC; Milwaukee Art Ctr, Wis; plus others. *Comn:* Etchings, Int Graphic Arts Soc, NY; drawings, Washington Gallery Mod Art, Washington, DC, 65; etchings, Roten Galleries, Baltimore, Md, 66-67; etching, Los Angeles Co Mus, 81. *Exhib:* One-man retrospective, San Francisco Mus Art, 67, Kennedy Mus Am Art, Athens, Ohio, 97; Mekler Gallery, Los Angeles, 72, 74, 77, 82, 84 & 88; Mitsukoshi Galleries, Tokyo, Japan, 77; Worthington Gallery, Chicago, 83, 86 & 88; Retrospective Exhib Paintings, Sculptures, Prints 1950-1992, Fresno Art Mus, Calif, 92; Schmidt-Bingham Gallery, NY, 98; The Norton Simon Mus of Art, Exhib of 30 Works owned by the Mus, 2004. *Teaching:* Instr etching, Colorado Springs Fine Arts Ctr, 54-56 & Univ Judaism, 67; instr painting, Calif State Univ, Los Angeles, 66-67, 69 & 72-73; instr, Otis Art Inst of Parsons Sch of Design, Los Angeles, 78-81; artist-in-residence, Fullerton Col, 82. *Awards:* Guggenheim, 52; Tamarind Fel, 66; Nat Endowment Arts, 82 & 86. *Bibliog:* Theodore F Wolff (auth), Christian Sci Monitor, 86; John Berry (auth), View from the wind palace, Mankind Mag, 75; Gerald Nordland (auth), Ynez Johnston, Grassfield Press (in coop with Univ Ohio), 96. *Media:* Mixed Media, Acrylic. *Interests:* literature, fiction, poetry. *Dealer:* Tom d'Alessandro Tomlyn Gallery Tequesta Fla; Tobey Moss Gallery Los Angeles Calif. *Mailing Add:* 579 Crane Blvd Los Angeles CA 90065

JOHNSTONE, MARK
CONCEPTUAL ARTIST, CURATOR
b St Louis, Mo, 53. *Study:* Colo Col, BA, 75; Univ Southern Calif, MFA, 82. *Work:* Calif Mus Photog, Univ Calif, Riverside; Nestle, Nat Acad, Glendale, Calif; Centro Documentazioni Arti Visive E Archivo/Rosamilia, San Giorgio, Italy; Biblioteque Nat, Paris, France. *Comn:* many multi-media productions comn in Colo, Calif & Idaho, 97-. *Exhib:* One-man show, Vista: Some Landscape Observations, Calif Mus Photog, Riverside, 81; Ten Yr Selection, Martin Schweig Gallery, St Louis, Mo, 87; Recent Work, Min Gallery, Tokyo, Japan, 88; and others. *Collection Arranged:* Joe Deal: Southern California Photographs, 1976-86, Los Angeles Munic Art Gallery, 77-89, 92; Eileen Cowin and John Divola, Recent Work, No Fancy Titles, La Jolla Mus Contemp Art, Calif traveling, 85; Robert Mapplethorpe & Edward Weston, The Garden of Earthly Delights (traveling), Calif Mus Photog, Riverside, 95. *Pos:* Contrib ed, Artweek, 77-89; series content adv, The Photographic Vision, KOCE-TV PBS, Huntington Beach, Calif, 83-84; vpres, cur exhibs, Security Pac Corp, Los Angeles, 88-92; adminr, Pub Arts Div, Cult Affairs Dept, City of Los Angeles, 95-01; phot ed, Int Doc mag, 2004-; consultant public art, City of Ketchum, ID, 2006-; arts comnr, City of Hailey, ID, 2006-. *Teaching:* Vis prof photog, Colo Col, Colorado Springs, summers 79-83; lectr hist photog, Calif State Univ, Fullerton, 81-88. *Bibliog:* Colin Gardner (auth), Calendar-Galleries, Los Angeles Times, 9/6/85; Suzanne Muchnic (auth), A focus on creativity, Los Angeles Times, 3/1/87; Chuck Nicholson (auth), Exploring Culture & Photography, Artweek, 4/29/89; plus others. *Media:* Miscellaneous Media. *Res:* Contemporary photography & art. *Publ:* Auth, The photographs of Larry Burrows, In: Observations: Essays on Documentary Photography, 84, Friends of Photog; Melting the Material World, Fotokritik, 6/86; Contemporary Art in Southern California, Craftsman House, 99; Epicenter-San Francisco Bay Area Art Now, Chronicle Books, 02. *Mailing Add:* PO Box 4350 Hailey ID 83333

JOLLEY, DONAL CLARK
PAINTER
b Zion Nat Park, Utah, Oct 20, 33. *Study:* Brigham Young Univ, BS, 59; with Glen Turner, J Roman Andrus. *Work:* First Nat Bank Nev, Reno; San Bernardino Co Mus, Redlands, Calif; Aerospace Corp, El Segundo, Calif; Church of Jesus Christ of Latter-Day Saints, Salt Lake City; Brigham Young Univ; Smithsonian Inst; Mayo Clinic. *Comn:* McDonald's, Lake Arrowhead, Blue Jay, Calif. *Exhib:* One-man shows, Brigham Young Univ, 75 & 81 & Univ Nev, Reno, 78; Traditional Artists, San Bernardino Co Mus, Redlands, 76-79 & Fine Arts Inst, 78-79 & 91; Kimball Art Ctr, Park City, Utah, 86; Peppertree Ranch, 88-2006; Mid Am Indian Ctr, Wichita, Kans, 90; Autry Mus, Los Angeles, 96; Segil Gallery, Monrovia, Calif, 2006; Art for Heaven's Sake, Redlands, Calif, 2006. *Pos:* Jr illusr, Space Technol Lab, Redondo, Calif, 60-61; sr illusr, Aerospace Corp, El Segundo, Calif, 61-71. *Teaching:* Instr painting, San Bernardino Valley Col, 73-81. *Awards:* Brand XII Award, 83; Riverside Centennial Award, 83; Gold Medal, Am Indian & Cowboy Artists, 90 & 94, Bronze, 92; Best of Show, San Dimas, Calif, 2004; and others. *Bibliog:* Fred Kiemel (auth), Making a presentation brochure self-promotion, Camera Life Mag, 5/80; Peggy & Harold Samuels (coauths), Contemporary Western Artists, 82; Patricia Dunsmore (auth), Elan Mag, 11/88; Gerald F Brommer (auth), Understanding Watercolor, 93; The Best of Watercolor, Schlemm & Nicholas, 95. *Mem:* Nat Watercolor Soc (vpres, 91); Watercolor West (vpres, 78, 79 & 97-98). *Media:* Watercolor, Acrylic. *Dealer:* Studio Gallery 26375 Apache Tr Rimforest CA 92378. *Mailing Add:* 26375 Apache Trail Rimforest CA 92378

JONAITIS, ALDONA
HISTORIAN, ADMINISTRATOR
b New York, NY, Nov 27, 48. *Study:* State Univ NY, Stony Brook, BA, 69; Columbia Univ, with Douglas Fraser, MA, 72, PhD, 77. *Exhib:* Chiefly Feasts: The Enduring Kwakiutl Potlatch, Am Mus Nat Hist, 91. *Pos:* Vpres pub progrs, Am Mus Nat Hist, 90-93; dir, Univ Alaska Mus, 93-. *Teaching:* Prof art, State Univ NY, Stony Brook, 88-90; prof anthrop, Univ Alaska, Fairbanks, 93. *Awards:* Chiefly Feasts, Winner, Am Asn Mus Curs Comt Award for Excellence in Exhib, 91. *Mem:* Native Am Art Studies Asn; Am Asn Mus; AAM/ICOM. *Res:* Northwest Coast Indian art. *Publ:* Auth, Art of the Northern Tlingit, Univ Wash Press, 86; From the Land of Totem Poles: The

Northwest Coast Indian Art Collection at the American Museum of Natural History, Univ Wash Press, 88; A Wealth of Thought: Franz Boas on Native American Art, Univ Wash Press, 93; Chiefly Feasts: The Enduring Kwakiutl Potlatch, Univ Wash Press, 91; A Wealth of Thought: Franz Boas on Native American Art, 95; Looking North: Art From the Univ of Alaska Mus, 98; The Yuguot Whalers' Shrine, 99. *Mailing Add:* Univ Alaska Mus PO Box 756960 Fairbanks AK 99775

JONAS, JOAN
VIDEO ARTIST, CONCEPTUAL ARTIST
b New York, NY, July 13, 36. *Study:* Mount Holyoke Col, BA(art hist), Mass; Boston Mus Sch, Mass; Columbia Univ, NY, MFA, 65; Sch Mus Fine Arts, Boston. *Work:* Mus Mod Art, NY. *Exhib:* The Video Show, Serpentine Gallery, London, 75; one-woman shows, Anthology Film Archives, NY, 75, Inst Contemp Arts, Los Angeles, 75, Stedelijk Mus, Amsterdam, Kunstmuseum, Bern, Van Abbemuseum, Eindhoven, Holland, San Francisco Mus Art & Univ Art Mus, Berkeley; Artists Mus, Lodz, Poland, 91-92; Solo exhib incl, Infinito Botanica, ArtPace, San Antonio, 1996, Tableau Vivant, The Alamo, San Antonio, 1998, New Painting y Mas, Galeria Ortiz, San Antonio, 1999, Infinito Botanica: NY, Ctr Curatorial Studies, Bard Col, 1999, Mexique, El Museo del Barrio, New York City, 2000, Untitled Grid No. 7, Infinito Botanico: St Louis, Des Lee Gallery, Wash Univ 2001, SHOP, Jessica Murray Projects, Brooklyn, 2001, Dust in the Wind, NY Pub. Art Fund, 2002, Market Squared, Galeria Ortiz, San Antonio, 2002, Nacho de Paz (and Other TexMex Miracles), Frederieke Taylor Gallery, New York City, 2002, Pan in the Park, Laumeier Sculpture Park, St Louis, 2003; group exhibs incl, San Antonio Sculpture Symposium, 1989, Planta de Arte Nuclear, San Antonio, 1990, Tex Dialogues, Shrines, Milagros Contemp Art Gallery, San Antonio, 1992, El Impacto de Dos Mundos, Art Space Gallery, New Haven, Conn, 1992, Closets: Queer Experience, Esperanza Peace and Justice Ctr, San Antonio, 1993, Hispanic Artists of 1993, Guadalupe Cult Arts Ctr, San Antonio, 1993, The Illusive Object, Diverse Works, Houston, 1993, Blue Star VIII, Blue Star Art Space, San Antonio, 1994; Synthesis and Subversion: A Latino Direction in San Antonio Art, Art Gallery Univ Tex San Antonio, 1995, Double Trouble: Mirrors/Pairs/Twins/Lovers, Blue Star Art Space, San Antonio, 1995, Tres Proyectos Latinos, The Business of Art, Instituto Cult de Mexico, San Antonio, 1998, Trade, Salon 300, Brooklyn, 1998, The Ecstatic, Trans-Hudson Gallery, New York City, 1999, Yard Sale, Downtown Arts Project, New York City, 2000, Texans in the Whitney, Arthur Roger Gallery, New Orleans, 2000, Infinito Botanico, Downtown Arts Project, New York City, 2000, City Lights: Art Walk, Comite Colbert, New York City, 2000, Ultrabaroque: Aspects of Post-Latin Am; Art (traveling exhib), 2000-03, Hopscotch, Gallery Art, Kean Univ, NJ, 2001, Lost in Space, Gary Tatinsian Gallery, New York City, 2001, Caribbean Biennial, Santo Domingo, Dominican Republic, 2001 ARS01-KIASMA, Infinito Botanica: Spain, ARCO, Madrid, 2002, Parklife, MetroTech Center, Brooklyn, 2002-03, Dreamspaces/Entresuenos, Deutsche Bank, New York City, 2003, Ballroom Marfa, Tex, 2004. *Pos:* Guest lectr, Yale Univ, New Haven, Conn, 74, Princeton Univ, 74 & Minneapolis Col Art, Minn; vis artist, Otis Art Inst, Los Angeles, Calif, 75, Minneapolis Col Art & Design, 79, Wright State Univ, Dayton, Ohio, 80 & Long Beach State Col, Calif, 80. *Teaching:* Assoc prof, Hunter Col, 85-88; tutor, Rijksakademie, Amsterdam; prof dept archit, prof, acting dir visual arts prog; Joined fac, Mass Inst of Technol, Cambridge, Mass, 2000. *Awards:* Creative Artists Pub Serv Prog, 72, 73 & 75; Nat Endowment Arts Grant, 73 & 75; Maya Dern Award in Video, Am Film Int, 88; Rockefeller Award, 90; and others; Recipient Hiroshima Art Prize, 1998, Kepes Art Prize, Council for Arts, Mass Inst of Technol, 2004, Artist Award for Distinguished Body of Work, Col Art Asn, 2004. *Bibliog:* Wulf Herzgenrath (auth), Video Ein Neue Medium in der Bildenden Kunst, Mag Kunst, Mainz, 7/74; Marcus Guterich (auth), Art Presented According to the Evolution Principle, Kunst Kunst Kunst, Cologne, Ger, 74; Howard Junker (auth), Joan Jonas: The mirror staged, Art Am, 2/81. *Media:* Mirrors; Videotape. *Publ:* Auth, Organic Honey's visual telepathy, Drama Rev, New York, 72; coauth, Show Me Your Dance, Art & Artists, London, 10/73. *Dealer:* Electronic Arts Intermix 536 Broadway New York NY. *Mailing Add:* Mass inst of Tech Visual arts Program 265 Mass Ave Cambridge MA 02139

JONES, ALLEN CHRISTOPHER
PAINTER, PRINTMAKER, SCULPTOR
b Southampton, Eng, Sept 1, 37. *Study:* Royal Col Art, London, 59-60; Hornsey Col Art, London, NDD & ATD, 59-61. *Work:* Mus Mod Art, NY; Tate Gallery, London; Chicago Mus Art; Mus 20th Century Art, Vienna, Austria; Stedelijk Mus, Amsterdam, Neth; and others. *Comn:* Sculpture, Liverpool Garden Festival, 84; sculpture, Frederick R Weisman Found, Los Angeles, 84-85; sculpture, British Airport Authority, Heathrow Airport, 90; Darcey Bussell (portrait), National Portrait Gallery, London, 94; sculpture, Swire Properties, Hong Kong, 97; Sculpture at Goodwood, 98; Chatsworth, Derbyshire, 2000; GlaxoSmithKline World HQ, London, 2001; Taikoo Place, Hong Kong, 2002/3; The Red Mansion Foundation, London & Beijing. *Exhib:* One-man show, Fruit Market Gallery, Edinburgh, 75 & Barbican Art Gallery, London, 95; retrospective, Inst Contemp Art, London, 78 & Walker Art Gallery, Liverpool, 79; The Folding Image, Nat Gallery Art, Washington, DC, 84; Pop Art, Royal Acad, London, 91-92 & Musee Des Beaux-Arts, Montreal, 92-93; The Portrait Now, Nat Portrait Gallery, London, 94; Allen Jones Prints Retrospective, Barbican Art Gallery, London, 95; Kunsthalle Darmstadt, 96; Trussardi, Milan, 98; SmithKline Beecham, London, 2000; Galleria d'Arte Maggiore, Bologna, 2002; Palezzo dei Seite, Orrielo, 2002; Gallery Levy, Hamburg, 2001, 2003; Regal Acad Arts, London, 2002. *Pos:* Trustee, British Mus, 90-99. *Teaching:* Guest prof painting, Univ S Fla, 68-69, Univ Calif, Los Angeles, 77 & Hochschule de Kunste, Berlin, 82-83. *Awards:* Prix Des Jeunes Artists, Paris Biennale, 63; Art & Work Award (sculpture, London Bridge City), Wapping Arts Trust, London, 89; Heitland Found Award, Ger, 95. *Bibliog:* Marco Livingstone (auth), Allen Jones: Sheer Magic, Thames & Hudson, 79; Charles Jencks (auth), Allen Jones, Acad Ed, 93; Marco Livingstone (auth), Allen Jones Prints, Prestel, 95; and others. *Mem:* Royal Acad Arts. *Media:* Paint; Prints; Sculpture. *Specialty:* Contemporary Art (in all cases). *Publ:* Illusr, Allen Jones Figures, Galerie Mikro, Berlin, 69; Allen Jones Projects, 71 & Waitress, 72, Mathews Miller Dunbar, London. *Dealer:* Thomas Levy Galerie Osterfeld Strasse 6, 22529, Hamburg; Galleria d'Arte Maggiore, Via D'Azeglio 15, 40123, Bologna, Italy; Galeriw HDorotheer Strasse, 511, A-1010 Vieena, Austria. *Mailing Add:* 41 Charterhouse Sq London EC1M 6EA United Kingdom

JONES, BEN
PAINTER, SCULPTOR
b Paterson, NJ, May 26, 42. *Study:* Sch Visual Arts; NY Univ, MA; Pratt Inst, MFA; Univ Sci & Technol, Kumasi, Ghana, New Sch Social Research. *Work:* Newark Mus, NJ; Howard Univ; Studio Mus, NY; Johnson Publ, Chicago. *Exhib:* Mus Mod Art; Studio Mus in Harlem; Black World Arts Festival, Lagos, Nigeria; Newark Mus, 77; Fisk Univ, 77; Bishop Col, Dallas, Tex, 78; solo shows, Newark Mus, 84, NJ State Mus, 84 & 96, Jersey City Mus, NJ, 94 & Jadite Gallery, 96, 97 & 98; Gallery 62, NY, 83 & Dallas Conv Ctr, 85; Mus Am Life & Cult, Dallas, Tex, 86; Pa Acad Art, Philadelphia, 86; Montclair Mus, NJ, 87 & 92; Dallas Mus Art, Tex, 89; High Mus Art, Atlanta, Ga, 90; Milwaukee Art Mus, 90; Newark Mus, NJ, 91; Md Inst, Col Art, Baltimore, 97; Southshore Art Ctr, Chicago, Ill, 98; and others. *Pos:* Art dir, Urban League Essex Co Exhib, 72. *Teaching:* Prof art, Jersey City State Univ, NJ, currently; adminr, Alumni Faculty, currently; coordr Fine Art, BFA Comt & adv bd, Afro Studies Ctr. *Awards:* Nat Endowment Arts, 74-75; NJ Arts Coun Grant, 77-78 & 83-84; Delta Sigma Theta-Excellence in the Arts, 85; and others. *Bibliog:* Articles, Art Am, 71; articles, New York Times, 72 & 82-85. *Mem:* World Print Coun; Nat Conf Artists. *Res:* African art and culture in WAfrica and Paris, France. *Mailing Add:* 117 Kennsington Ave Apt 206 Jersey City NJ 07304

JONES, CARTER R(UTHVEN), JR
SCULPTOR
b Mount Kisco, NY, Mar 6, 45. *Study:* Sch Visual Arts, with Edward Giobbi, 64-65; Boston Mus Sch, dipl, 69; pvt study in Paris, 69-71. *Work:* Brookgreen Gardens, Pawleys Island, SC; Numismatic Mus, NY; pvt collections of William Maxwell, NY, Beauford Delaney, Paris, Vera Newman, Croton on Hudson, NY, Herman Schneider, Martha's Vineyard Mass, Humfer Noyse, Portland, OR; British Mus, London, Eng; Smithsonian Inst, Washington, DC. *Comn:* 25 portraits (sculpted), comn in Boston, NY & Paris; Walt Disney Prodns, 81-; Henson Assocs, 86-; Warner Bros, 94-; Nickelodeon, 95-; over thirty-five medallions and coins executed for various mints incl Medallic Art Corp, The Lincoln Mint, Judaic Heritage Soc and Art Medals Inc. *Exhib:* Am Towers, NY, 96-97, 2000; Lever House, NY, 81, 83, 90; Numismatic Mus, NY, 83, 84; Boston Mus Sch, 69; Nat Sculpture Soc, NY, 91, 2000; Atelier 14, NY, 98; 515 Greenwich Studio Complex, NY, 99. *Collection Arranged:* Brookgreen Gardens, Pawleys Island, SC; Numismatic Mus, NY; Nat Sculpture Soc, Slide Libr; pvt collections of William Maxwell, NY; Beauford Delaney, Paris; Vera Newman, Croton on Hudson, NY; Herman Schneider, Martha's Vineyard, Mass; Humfer Noyse, Portland, Ore. *Teaching:* Instr human & animal anatomy, Sch Visual Arts, New York, 80-82; The Compleat Sculptor; instr The Compleat Sculptor, 2000-. *Awards:* Art Dirs Award, Art Dirs Am, 79; Youth Award, Nat Sculpture Soc, 80; Nat Sculpture Soc Award, 81; Art Dir's Award, New York, 84; Nat Sculpture Soc Fel, 85-. *Bibliog:* Arthur Williams (auth), The Sculpture Reference. *Mem:* Fel Nat Sculpture Soc; Soc Artists Anatomists; Am Medallic Sculpture Asn (pres 83 85); Am Anatomy Asn. *Media:* Clay, Bronze. *Interests:* The human and animal figure. *Mailing Add:* 39 Bond St Apt 2 New York NY 10012-2427

JONES, CHARLOTT ANN
EDUCATOR, MUSEUM DIRECTOR
b Jonesboro, Ark, May 27, 27. *Study:* Col St Scholastica, BA, 62; NTex State Univ, MS, 70; Pa State Univ, PhD, 78. *Collection Arranged:* Anuskiewicz Silkscreen Prints, 83, Rauschenberg Purina Chow Prints, 83 & Anuskiewicz, Judd, Marisol Prints, 83, Stephens Collection; The Figure and Other Paintings, 83; Paintings and Ceramics, 83; Arkansas Treasures: Twenty Outstanding Black Arkansans (auth, catalog), 87; Delta Genius: Clementine Hunter; A Personal Statement: Arkansas Women Artists (auth, catalog), Arkansas Arts Ctr, Little Rock & Nat Mus Women Arts, Washington, 92. *Pos:* Dir emer, Mus Ark State Univ 83-98; cur Nat Mus Women Arts, Ark. *Teaching:* Dir children's art, Charlott Jones Sch Art, Jonesboro, Ark, 72-; asn prof art, Ark State Univ, Jonesboro, 75-90. *Bibliog:* Alumni Profiles, Col St Scholastica Times, spring 89. *Mem:* Nat Art Educ Asn; Ark Art Educ; Am Asn Mus; Ark Women in Higher Education; Ark Mus Asn. *Media:* Mag articles. *Res:* Free will in art making. *Publ:* Auth, The wellspring of Dylan, English J, 66; Women and art, Delta Kappa Gamma Bulletin, 82; contribr, Gifted and Talented in Art Education (monogr), Nat Art Educ Asn, 83; Eugene B Wittlake, Ark Biographies, 99

JONES, CYNTHIA CLARKE
COLLAGE ARTIST, GRAPHIC ARTIST
b Brooklyn, NY, Aug 12, 38. *Study:* Brooklyn Mus, 53-57; Art Students League Art Career Sch, 57-58; Hunter Col, with L Kimmel, 63-65. *Work:* Nat Mus Women Artists, Washington, DC. *Exhib:* One-woman show, Queens Pub Libr, Jamaica, NY, 86 & Int Art Gallery, Jamaica, NY, 93; Works on Paper, Gallery Ten, Rockford, Ill, 94; Works On/Off Paper, Queens Community Col Art Gallery, Bayside, NY, 94; Concept to Depiction, Cork Gallery Lincoln Ctr, NY, 94; Violence in the Media, St Johns Univ Gallery, Jamaica, NY, 94; Colorado Coalition for Abstinence traveling art show, Boulder, 94-95; Collection 94 traveling show, Towson State Univ, Baltimore, Md, 94-95; Juried Show, Upsteam People Gallery, 2005; Liturgical Arts & Sacred juried show, Riverside Interchurch juried show, 2006; Invitational Summer, Upsteam People Gallery, 2006. *Awards:* Fine Arts & Painting Award, Queensboro Soc, 73; France Lieber Mem Award, Nat Asn Women Artists Ann, Nat Asn Women Artists, 92 & Kreindler Mem Award, Nat Asn Women Artists, 95; Lill Award, Int Art Gallery, 93.

Bibliog: Lisa A Rue (auth), Art for Awareness, Friends First, 94. *Mem:* Nat Asn Women Artists; Artists Equity New York; Col Art Asn; Womens Caucus for Art; Guild Am Papercutters. *Media:* Kiri-e. *Publ:* Illusr, Scholastic Mag, 57; Statistics Department Baruch Col, 73; Employers Local 384 Newsletter; logo designer, International Art Gallery, 92; Kiri-e method featured, North Light Mag, 95; Christians In, In the Visual Arts Directory, 2000; Cutpaper, featured in Daniel Smith (catalog) summer 2005-2006. *Mailing Add:* 113-32 Mayville St Saint Albans NY 11412

JONES, DAVID LEE
SCULPTOR, ASSEMBLAGE ARTIST
b Columbus, Ohio, Feb 26, 48. *Study:* Kansas City Art Inst, BFA, 70; Univ Calif, Berkeley, Marion Davies Fel, 72, MFA, 73; studio asst to Peter Voulkos, 70-72. *Work:* San Francisco Mus Art; Univ Art Mus, Berkeley; DeSaisset Mus & Art Gallery, Univ Santa Clara, Calif; Oakland Mus, Calif; G B Cafe Wednesday (Division MOCA). *Exhib:* Solo exhibs, San Jose State Univ, 71, Daniel Weinberg Gallery, San Francisco, 73, Michael Walls Gallery, NY, 75 & Braunstein/Quay Gallery, San Francisco, Calif, 84, 87, 91 (with catalog, essay by Paul Karlstrom) & 92; San Francisco Mus Art, 74; Whitney Biennial Am Painting & Sculpture, Whitney Mus Art, NY, 75; Calif Painting & Sculpture--The Mod Era, San Francisco Mus Art & Nat Collection Fine Arts, Washington, 76-77 (catalog); The California Artists, Huntsville Mus Art, 77; New Bay Area Printing & Sculpture (cataloged), Calif State Univ, Northridge, 82; Almost Functional, Richard/Bennet Gallery, La, 89; Here and Now-Rene DiRosa Col (catalog), Oakland Mus, 94; Breaking Traditions: Artists Who Use Glass, Univ Calif Mus, Blackhawk, 94 (catalog); Glass: Linking Art & Science, MIT Mus, Cambridge, Mass, 96; Doors, Walls, ows, Univ Calif-Berkeley, 98; Fallout, Meridian Gallery, San Francisco, Calif, 2000. *Awards:* Soc Encouragement Contemp Art Grant, 74; Individual Artists Grant, Nat Endowment Arts, 74. *Bibliog:* Ellen Lubell (auth), David Jones, Art Mag, 6/74; Al Frankenstein (auth), numerous reviews in San Francisco Chronicle & Examiner. *Media:* All Media. *Mailing Add:* PO Box 8872 Emeryville CA 94608

JONES, DONALD GLYNN
PAINTER, ILLUSTRATOR
b Lyons, Kans, Jan 20, 35. *Study:* Univ Okla, BFA, 58; Bongart Sch Art, with Sergei Bongart, Rexburg, Idaho, 83. *Exhib:* 29th Ann, Soc Illusrs, NY, 87; Nat Soc Painters in Casein & Acrylic, Nat Arts Club, NY, 87, 90, 92-2006, Lotus Club, NY, Award Exhib, 92; Allied Artists of Am, Nat Arts Club, NY, 87, 96; 55th Midyear Exhibition, Butler Inst, Youngstown, Ohio, 91, 66th Midyear Exhib, 2002; Audubon Artists, Nat Arts Club, NY, 92, 93, 94, 98-2001, 2005; Rocky Mountain National, Foothills Art Ctr, Golden, Colo, 95, 98, 99, 2002; Watercolor USA, Springfield Art Mus Mo, 2001, 2004, 2005. *Awards:* Juror's Award, 42nd Ann Nat, Colo Springs Art Guild, 86, Merit Award, 86; Dr David Soloway Mem Award, 39th Ann, Nat Soc Painters in Casein & Acrylic, 92; Madonna Aldredge Mem Award, 25th Ann, Rocky Mountain Nat, 98; Jane Gottleib-Brown Award, Assoc Artists of Southport, NC, 86; Nat Soc Painters in Casein & Acrylic, 2003; Juror's Award, Watercolor USA, 2004; Winsor Newton Award, 52nd Ann, Nat Soc Printers in Casein & Acrylic, 2005. *Mem:* Nat Soc Painters in Casein & Acrylic, NY; Audubon Artists, NY; Rocky Mountain Nat Watermedia Soc; Watercolor USA Honor Soc. *Media:* Acrylic. *Publ:* contribr, Illustrators 29, Soc Illusrs, 88; contribr, The best of acrylic painting, Rockport Publs, 96. *Mailing Add:* 6812 Sandlewood Dr Oklahoma City OK 73132-3911

JONES, DOUG DOUGLAS MCKEE
PAINTER, SCULPTOR
b Sewell, Chile, Oct 16, 29; US citizen. *Study:* San Diego Fine Arts & Crafts; San Diego State Col; Los Angeles Art Ctr Col Design, grad; also with Lorser Feitelson, Audubon Tyler, Leon Franks, Sergei Bongart, Dan Greene & Harley Brown. *Work:* Hall of Champions, Univ San Diego, Calif Western Sch Law, Aerospace Mus, San Diego, Calif. *Comn:* Portraits, Mayor Charles Dail, San Diego & Mayor Kiyoshi Nakarai, Yokahama, San Diego Chap, Am Inst Architects, 63; 43 portraits, Int Aerospace Hall Fame, San Diego, 64-72; portrait, Gen Claire Chenault, Flying Tigers Asn, 71; portrait, Marie Winzer, Scripps Hosp; and others. *Pos:* Owner & dir, The Jones Gallery, 64-; art appraiser, currently. *Awards:* Merit Award, New York Portrait Club, 79. *Mem:* Sr mem Am Soc Appraisers; Am Portrait Soc. *Media:* Oil, Pastel. *Specialty:* Paintings and sculpture by distinguished 19th and 20th century American artists. *Publ:* Auth, article, Southland Artist Mag & illusr cover. *Mailing Add:* c/o The Jones Gallery 2710 Summit Dr Escondido CA 92025

JONES, ELIZABETH A B (MRS LUDWIG GLAESER)
SCULPTOR, PHOTOGRAPHER
b Montclair, NJ, May 31, 35. *Study:* Vassar Col, BA, 57; Art Students League, 58-60; Scuola Arte Medaglia, Rome, Italy, 62-64; Acad Brasiliero de Belas Artes, Hon dipl, 69. *Work:* Royal Mint Mus, Eng; Montclair Art Mus, NJ; Smithsonian Inst, Washington, DC; Italian Mint Mus, rome. *Comn:* Gold medallion, Pope John Paul II, gift of Ital State to Pope, 79; bronze sculpture (multiple), Female Head, Res Lab Inauguration, Revlon Corp, NY, 83; portrait gold medal, Nelson A Rockefeller Ann Pub Serv Award, 88; gold medal, Sloan-Presbyterian Hosp Women, NY, 90; Am Asn Mus Ann Award for Philanthropy, 93; and many others. *Exhib:* Fedn Int Medaille FIDEM, 63-92; solo shows, Tiffany & Co, 66-68; Smithsonian Inst, Washington & Nat Sculpture Soc, NY, 71, 78 & 88; Photog, Univ Md, 81; retrospectives, Vassar Col, 82 & Ital Mint, Rome, 89; Tyler Sch Art, Rome, 82; Sights Unseen, Philadelphia, 97; Arts Forum Gallery, NY, 2000. *Pos:* Chief sculptor-engraver, US Mint, 81-90; General Partner, L'Atelier LP, Chiago, 93-. *Awards:* Outstanding Sculptor of the Year, Am Numismatic Asn, 72; Int Coin of the Year Award, Numismatic News, 83, 84 & 87. *Bibliog:* Velia Johnson (auth), Dieci Anni di Studi Medaglistica, Milan, 79; Giulio Andreotti (preface), Jones-Dalla Zecca di Roma alla United States Mint (retrospective exhib catalog), Rome, 89; David Bowers (auth), Commemorative Coins of the United States-A Complete Encyclopaedia, Wolfeboro, NH, 91; and many articles in numismatic mags & newspapers in the US & Italy. *Media:* Metal, Cast, Miscellaneous Media. *Publ:* Reflections on the Gold Coinage of the Twentieth Century, Am Numismatic Soc, COAC Proceedings, No 6, New York, 90

JONES, FRANKLIN REED
PAINTER, WRITER
b Needham, Mass, May 18, 21. *Work:* Mus Art, Sci & Indust, Bridgeport, Conn; Conn Audubon Soc, Fairfield; Monarch Capitol Insurance co, Springfield, Mass; Blue Cross Blue Shield Hq, Pittsburgh, Pa. *Exhib:* Am Watercolor Soc, NY, 77; De Cordova Mus, Lincoln, Mass, 77; Berkshire Mus, Pittsfield, Mass, 77; Ellsworth Nat Exhib, Simsbury, Conn, 77; Old Forge Art Ctr, NY, 94. *Pos:* Asst to dir, Famous Artists Sch, 58-74. *Teaching:* Instr painting, Famous Artists Sch, Westport, Conn, 53-58. *Awards:* Award of Excellence, Ellsworth Gallery, Simsbury Cult Comt, 77; Privet Prize, Adirondack Nat Exhib, 83 & 84; Cert of Merit, 27th Ann Nat Exhib, Soc Illus, 85; and others. *Bibliog:* Fred Whitaker (auth), The Paintings of Franklin Jones, Am Artist Mag, 66. *Mem:* Am Watercolor Soc, Dolphin Fel. *Media:* Acrylic, Watercolor. *Interests:* Photog, Writing. *Publ:* Contribr, Acrylic Watercolor Painting, 70 & Complete Guide to Acrylic Painting, 71, Watson-Guptill; auth, The Pleasure of Painting, 75 & Painting Nature: Solving Landscape Problems, 78, North Light; illusr, Gray's Sporting J, 77. *Mailing Add:* 1037A Heritage Village Southbury CT 06488

JONES, FREDERICK
PRINTMAKER
b Llanymymech, Wales, Mar 6, 40. *Study:* Cardiff Col Art, Wales; Univ Pittsburgh; Univ Wis-Madison; print workshop, London & Atelier 17, Paris. *Work:* Lakeview Ctr for Arts, Peoria, Ill; Brit Mus, London; Victoria & Albert Mus, London; Krannert Mus, Univ Ill; Southern Ill Univ, Carbondale; Ill State Mus, Springfield, Ill; plus others. *Comn:* Large three part drawing, Ill State Libr, 92. *Exhib:* Int Print Biennial, Seoul, Korea, 71; Mid-Am Exhib, Montreal, Can, 71; Nat Image on Paper Show, Springfield, Ill, 72; Nat Print & Drawing Show, Macomb, 75; Heartland Painters Exhib, Bloomington Art Ctr, Ill, 92. *Teaching:* Lectr design drawing, Chester Col Art, Eng, 66-68; prof printmaking, Western Ill Univ, 68-, gallery dir, 69-71. *Awards:* First Prize for Drawing, Ill State Fair, 94; Grants,The Ill Landscape Portfolio, 97; Stipend Award, Western Ill Univ, Art in Pub Places, 97, Ill Humanities Coun Award, 2000; Landscape Workshop Award, Arrowmont Sch Arts and Crafts, Tenn, 2000; plus others. *Bibliog:* Mack Stegmaier (auth), Fred Jones, Am Artist, 2/88. *Media:* Pastel, Charcoal, Watercolor. *Dealer:* J Rosenthal Fine Arts 230 W Superior Chicago IL 60610; Peoria Art Guild 1831 N Knoxville Peoria IL 61603. *Mailing Add:* c/o Dept Art Western Ill Univ Macomb IL 61455

JONES, JAMES EDWARD
PAINTER, PRINTMAKER
b Paducah, Ky, Jan 27, 37. *Study:* Philadelphia Col Art, with Henry Pitz, Benton Spruance & Jerome Kaplan, dipl (illus), 60, fel, 56-61, BFA, 61; Univ Pa, with Barnett Newman, Angelo Seville, David Smith, Richard Stankiewicz & James Van Dyke, MFA, 62. *Work:* McDonogh Sch, Md; Dennison Univ; Smith Mason Gallery; The Studio Mus in Halem, NY; Soc Art & Culture, Columbia, Md; Columbia, MD Print Consortim Col; Morgan State Univ Coll, MD Princess, Anne MD; Newark Pub Libr, Newark NJ, 2001 (45 prints); and others. *Comn:* Prints, Heritage Mus, Baltimore, Md, 93; paintings, Great Blacks in Wax Mus. *Exhib:* juried shows, Baltimore Mus 63-67; Corcoran, Wash, DC, 68; Del Fine Arts Mus, 68; Baltimore Co Campus, Univ Md, 79; Smith Mason Gallery, Washington, DC, 79, 80 & 82; Morgan State Univ, 83; Burkett Gallery, Md, 88; Senoje Gallery, Baltimore, 90; Morgan State Univ Ann Fac Show, 90, 91, 92 & 94; Eulipion Gallery, Baltimore MD, 2000; Newark Pub Lib, 2002; Morgan St Univ, Convergence, 2003. *Collection Arranged:* The Senoje Collection, Balt, 89-2002. *Pos:* Dir, The Senoje Collection, Balt, 90-91, exec dir, 91-92, 96 & 98-2005. *Teaching:* From assoc prof to prof art educ, painting & printmaking, drawing & visual arts, Morgan State Univ, 62-93; instr, Dundalk Community Col, 77-78, Baltimore City Community Col, 94-98 & Sojourner Douglass Col, 94-98. *Awards:* Stewart Art Award, NJ State, 56; Univ Pa Fel & Thorton Oakley Creative Achievement Award, 62; Morgan State Univ Grant, 63-68; Huntsville Mus Art, Huntsville Ala Invitational, 80. *Mem:* Print Consortium (Kansas City); The Senoje consortum, Founder in 1989: Dir. *Media:* All Media. *Res:* Transformations, catalouge of photographs from 1957-2005. *Specialty:* The Senoje Collection, Representing 8 artists, New York, Baltomore, MD. *Collection:* 45 prints in permenent collection, Newark public Lib. *Publ:* Dr. Weaver Cur Convergence Catalouge, 2003; Morgan State Univ. *Dealer:* The Senoje Collection; Eulipion Gallery Baltimore Md. *Mailing Add:* 2930 Silver Hill Ave Baltimore MD 21207

JONES, JANE
PAINTER
b Denver, Colo, Apr 3, 53. *Study:* Metrop State Col, BS, 76; Regis Univ, MLS, 2005. *Work:* St Louis Univ Mus, Mo; Marriott Corp, Bethesda, Md. *Exhib:* Oil Painters Am Exhib, Chicago, 92; Realism, Packersburg Art Ctr, WVa, 94, 95; Lekae Gallery, Scottsdale, Ariz, 96, 98, 99, 2003 & 05; Turner Art Gallery, Denver, Colo, 98; Am Art in Miniature, Gilcrease Mus, Tulsa, Okla, 2000, 01, 02, 04 & 06; Horizon Fine Art, Jackson, Wyo, 2001; Horizon Fine Art, 2001; Nat Mus Wildlife Art, 2001-2006; Realism Invitational, Santa Fe, NMex, 2001 & 02; West Valley Art Mus,Phoenix, Ariz, 2003; Colo Hist Mus, 2004. *Collection Arranged:* Marriott Corp, Bethesda, Md; St. Louis Univ Mus, St. Louis, Mo. *Teaching:* inst art hist, art apreciation, painting & drawing, Red Rocks Community Coll, 90-2006; Metrop State Col 2005-2006. *Awards:* Juror's Choice Award, Conty Lines, Arvada Ctr Arts, 91; Floral Award, Am Artists Prof League, NY, 92, 94, 99; Juror's Choice Award, Colo Artist Asn, 97; Florence and Ernst Thorne Thompson Mem Award, Allied Artists Am, 2002; Vera C

Rosenhaft Award; Am Artists Prof League, 2004. *Mem:* Am Artists Prof League (assoc); Allied Artists Am; Int Guild Realism. *Media:* Oil. *Specialty:* Contemp Realism. *Collection:* St Louis Univ Mus; Marriott Corp. *Dealer:* Lekae Gallery 7106 E Main Scottsdale AZ 85251. *Mailing Add:* 9141 W 75th Pl Arvada CO 80005

JONES, JUDY VOSS
PRINTMAKER, PAINTER
b Winston-Salem, NC, Dec 26, 49. *Study:* Univ Ga, BFA, 72, MFA, 76. *Exhib:* Birmingham Biennial, Birmingham Mus Art, Ala, 83; Drawing Invitational, Va Mus Art, Richmond, 85; Works on Paper, Nexus Gallery, Atlanta, Ga, 87; Selections From Winstone Press, NC Mus Art, Raleigh, 88; Still-Life/Variations of a Theme, Sarat Gallery, Vanderbilt, Univ, Nashville, Tenn, 89; Visual Arts Fels Retrospective, SC State Mus, Columbia, 90; SC Contemp Artists, Owensboro Mus Fine Art, Ky, 91; and others. *Teaching:* Assoc prof drawing & printmaking, Converse Col, Spartansburg, SC, 76-92. *Awards:* SC Individual Artist Fel, SC Arts Comn, 81 & 87. *Dealer:* Mary Praytor Gallery 26 S Main St Greenville SC 29601. *Mailing Add:* 230 Milledge Cir Athens GA 30605

JONES, KRISTIN See Jones & Ginzel

JONES, LIAL A
MUSEUM DIRECTOR
Study: Univ Del, BA, 79; Mus Mgt Inst, Univ Calif, Berkeley, 96. *Pos:* Assist dir, Del Art Mus, Wilmington, 79, deputy dir, Chief Exec Officer; dir, Crocker Art Mus, Sacramento, 99-. *Awards:* Recipient Art Educator of Year, Art Educators of Del, 93, Paul Getty Trust Scholarship, 96. *Mailing Add:* Crocker Art Mus 216 O St Sacramento Sacramento CA 95814

JONES, LOIS SWAN
WRITER, HISTORIAN
b Dallas, Tex, July 3, 27. *Study:* Univ Chicago, PhB, 47, BS, 48, MS, 54; NTex State Univ, PhD, 72; Ctr Univ d'Ete des Pyrenees, Univ Toulouse, summer 75. *Pos:* Conductor, Le Petite Cercle d'Art, Dallas, 60-79; auth, narrator & photogr, Five Nights in Europe, Dallas Country Club, 63-75; co-owner, Swan Jones Prodns, 92-. *Teaching:* Lectr art hist, Univ Tex, Arlington, 69-70; from asst prof to prof art hist, Univ NTex, Denton, 72-92, emer prof, 92-. *Awards:* Commendation, Catholic Audio Visual Educ, 93 & 95; Distinguished Serv Award, Art Libr Soc NAm, 97; Worldwide Books Publ Award, 2000. *Mem:* Art Libr Soc NAm; Col Art Asn; Visual Resources Asn. *Res:* Art bibliography and research methodology; Christian iconography; art & the Internet. *Publ:* Auth, Art Libraries & Information Services, Acad Press, 86; Art Information: Research Methods & Resources, Kendall/Hunt, 78, 84 & 90; The Development of Christian Symbolism Video Series: Madonna & Child, 92, Crucifixion & Resurrection, 94, Heaven or Hell: The Last Judgment, 94, Virgin Mary in Art, Swan/Jones prod, 96; Art Information and the Internet: How to Find It, How to Use It, Oryx Press, 98. *Mailing Add:* 3801 Normandy Dallas TX 75205

JONES, LOU MARY LOUISE HUMPTON
PAINTER, SCULPTOR
b West Chester, Pa. *Study:* Pa State Univ, BA(Eng lit), 49; with Gene Davis, 68-72; George Mason Univ, Fairfax, Va, BA(art hist), 77; Corcoran Sch Abroad, Leeds Univ, Eng. *Work:* Phillips Collection, Washington, DC; Northern Va Community Col, Alexandria; Am Embassies, Damascus, Syria, Bern, Switz & Bamako, Mali; Univ DC, Washington. *Comn:* Nat Mus Women Arts, Washington. *Exhib:* 19th Area Show, Corcoran Mus, Washington, DC, 74; Va Artists, Va Mus, Richmond, 77 & 79; Coastal Exchange Show, Richmond, 88; New Ways to Collage, George Mason Univ, Fairfax, Va; New Work on Paper, Susan Conway Gallery, 90; Arlington Showcase III, 94; Global Focus, NMWA, Washington; UN Conf on Women, Bejing, China; Gallery K, Washington DC, 94 & 96; Marymount Univ, Arlington, Va, 1999-2000; Gallery 10, Washington, DC, 2000. *Pos:* Panelist, Women Visual Arts, Women's Ctr, Washington, DC, 75, Artists Survival, Univ Md, 78, Am Univ, 79 & Corcoran Sch Art, Washington, DC, Md Inst Art, Baltimore; art consult, Am Corrections, DC, 77-80; dir educ, Athenaeum Mus, Alexandria, Va, 85-; docent, Phillips Collection, Washington, DC, 90. *Teaching:* Instr drawing-mixed media children, Corcoran Gallery, Washington, DC, 75-80; vis prof, Univ Md, 81; adj prof, Marymount Univ, Arlington, Va, 85-94 & Geo Mason Univ, Fairfax, Va, 89-. *Awards:* Purchase Award, Northern Va Community Col, 75; Fel, Va Ctr Creative Arts, Sweet Briar, 81; Artist Equity Award, Form & Substance. *Bibliog:* Jan Allen (auth), article, Washington Times, 10/83; Pam Kesseler (auth), Yellow and gold, Washington Post, 7/88; Michael Welzenbach (auth), Lou Jones at Conway Carroll, Washington Post, 7/89; Mary McCoy (auth), Ellipse in Arlington, Washington Post, 8/94. *Media:* Paper, Collage. *Mailing Add:* 329 Maple Ave Falls Church VA 22046

JONES, MICHAEL BUTLER
SCULPTOR, FREELANCE CURATOR
b Chicago, Ill, Oct 7, 46. *Study:* Ohio State Univ, BFA, 68, MFA, 78. *Comn:* Ten outdoor murals, Nat Endowment Arts, Dayton, Ohio, 73; 18 outdoor murals in Ohio & Chicago; ten ceramic landscapes, State of Ohio, Columbus, 74; sixteen commemorative bas relief terra cotta panels, Univ Minn, Minneapolis, 85. *Exhib:* Dayton Art Inst, Ohio, 85; Massillon Mus, Ohio, 87; Cleveland Ctr for Contemp Art, Ohio, 88; Cleveland Inst Art, 89; Ohio Univ, 89; Ohio Craft Mus, 95. *Collection Arranged:* Film Installations: Works by Paul Sharits, Bill Lundberg, Anthony McCall & Al Wong, 87; Craft As Content: Nat Metals Invitational, 87; Takaaki Matsumoto: Installation Proj & Design Works, 88; Dan Friedman: Installation Proj & Design Works, 91; Printed Matter, 92. *Pos:* Dir, Univ Gallery, Wright State Univ, Dayton, Ohio, 78-82 & Univ Akron, 85-91. *Awards:* Ohio Arts Coun Fel, 80. *Bibliog:* Pam Houk (auth), Gary Bower & Michael Jones, Am Ceramics, 86. *Mem:* Artists' Orgn Cols Ohio; Col Art Asn; Am Craft Asn. *Media:* Clay, Steel. *Publ:* Ed, Athena Tacha: Tape Sculptures, 78 & Regional Fel Recipients Traveling Exhib Cat, Wright State Univ, 79; Ed, Pyramidal Influence in Art, 79, Triad, Sculpture Projects, 81 & Ten Solo Exhibitions, 82, Wright State Univ, Dayton, Ohio; Aspects of Perception, Bard Col & Va Commonwealth Univ, Richmond, 82; coauth, Film Installation Works, Univ Akron, Ohio, 86; Harold Kitner, Univ Akron, 88. *Mailing Add:* 790 Wright St Yellow Springs OH 45387

JONES, NORMA L
PAINTER
b Morrisonville, Ill. *Study:* Univ Houston, Clear Lake City, 75-76; Univ NMex; Univ Mo; Tex Univ; Washington Univ, St Louis; also studied with Rex Brandt, George Post & Edward Betts. *Work:* Banco de Brazilia, Pondereille Oil Co; Tex Instruments Co, Tenneco; AMACO, Houston; Bank Am, NMex. *Comn:* D Regan, Manhatten, NY; Susan Davis, Las Cruces, NMex; Mr & Mrs Ron Biagi, Balboa Island, Calif; Mr & Mrs Randy Luck, Rochester Hills, Mich. *Exhib:* Am Watercolor Soc, Nat Acad, NY; Watercolor USA, Springfield Mus, Mo; Western Fedn, Albuquerque Mus, San Diego & Houston; Magnifico 94; Western Fedn, San Antonio & traveling, 96; Rocky Mountain Nat, 97; Nat Collage Soc, 97; Watercolor USA, 98; Arts Crawl, Albuquerque, NMex, 2000. *Teaching:* Instr, Pickwickian Schools, Houston, Texas & various workshops in Houston & Albuquerque. *Awards:* Merit Award, Western Fedn, San Antonio (traveling), 96; Rocky Mountain Nat Award, 97; Purchase Award, Watercolor USA, 98; Masterworks of NMex Award, 2000. *Bibliog:* Article in NMex Mag, 5/92; Gerald Brommer, Collage Techniques (bk), 97; article in Albuquerque Arts Mag, 3/98. *Mem:* NMex Watercolor Soc Signature Group; Soc Layerists Multi-Media; Southwestern Fedn Watercolorists; North Coast Collage Soc; Am Univ Asn. *Media:* Acrylic, Mixed Media. *Publ:* Contribr, Twelve New Mexico Landscape Painters. *Dealer:* Dartmouth St Gallery Albuquerque NM; Weyrich Gallery Albuquerque NM; Patrician Design Albuquerque NM; THe Johnsons Madrid NM; Vladimir Fine Arts Kalamazoo Mich. *Mailing Add:* 9312 Las Calabazillas NE Albuquerque NM 87111

JONES, PATTY SUE
PAINTER, CURATOR
b New Orleans, La, Aug 18, 49. *Study:* Auburn Univ, 67-69 & 74; Univ Calif, Los Angeles, photog with Robert Heinecken, BA, 72, MA, 74; Univ Wash, with Jack Lenor Larsen, summer 75. *Work:* Yuma Fine Arts Ctr, Ariz. *Comn:* Paintings, Regent Hotels Int, Beverly Hills, Calif, 74; tapestry, Fluor Corp, Irvine, Calif, 78; tapestry, Security Pac Bank, Topanga Canyon, Calif, 79. *Exhib:* Tucson Mus Art, Ariz, 75; Ariz State Univ, Tempe, 79; Security Pac Hq, Los Angeles, 81; Occidental Col, Los Angeles, 81; Los Angeles Inst Contemp Art, 81; and many others. *Collection Arranged:* Robert Delgado, Mural Making: The Process, 80, The Mask: Object and Image, 80, Paper: Cast/Torn/Formed, 80 & California Dada, 80, Old Venice Jail Gallery, Venice, Calif. *Pos:* Dir's coun mem, Yuma Fine Art Ctr, Ariz, 76-77; cur exhibs, Old Venice Jail Gallery, Venice, Calif, 79-81. *Teaching:* Teaching asst, Univ Calif, Los Angeles, 73-74; instr, Ariz Western Col, Yuma, 74-77, Ariz State Univ, Tempe, 75-76 & St Mary's Col, Los Angeles, 82. *Awards:* Purchase Award, 10th Ann Southwestern, 75. *Bibliog:* Laurel Meinig (auth), Artists-in-residence (catalog), Yuma Art Ctr, Ariz, 76; William Wilson (auth), Lint drawings (review), Los Angeles Times, 80. *Media:* Oil. *Publ:* Contribr, Spectrum: New directions in color photography, Univ Hawaii, 79. *Mailing Add:* 311 North Ave 66 Los Angeles CA 90042

JONES, PIRKLE
PHOTOGRAPHER
b Shreveport, La, Jan 2, 1914. *Study:* Calif Sch Fine Arts, cert, 49. *Hon Degrees:* Grant in photography, NEA, 77; Cert of Recognition, Nat Urban League, 61; Doct Fine Arts, San Francisco Art Inst, 04. *Work:* San Francisco Mus Mod Art; Art Inst Chicago; Ctr Creative Photog, Univ Ariz; Yokohama Mus, Japan; Mus Mod Art, NY; Metropolitan Mus Art, NY; Nat Mus Modern Art, Koyoto, Japan. *Comn:* Commemorative UN Portfolio, Bank Am, San Francisco, 55; The Story of a Winery, Paul Masson, John Bolles, San Francisco, 59; Courthouses, Bicentennial Proj, Joseph E Seagram Inc, NY, 75. *Exhib:* Photog in the Twentieth Century, Nat Gallery Can, 67; A Photog Essay on the Black Panthers, De Young Mus Art, 68, Studio Mus Harlem, 70, Hopkins Ctr, Dartsmouth Col, 70 & Univ Calif, Santa Cruz, 70; Courthouse, Photographs from the Segrams' Collection, Mus Mod Art, NY, 78; Messages From West Coast, Photo Gallery Int, Tokyo, 79; Curator's Choice: By John Humphery, San Francisco Mus Mod Art, 80; Awards of Honor, A Documentary Exhibition, San Francisco Arts Commission, Gallery, Bank Am, World Hq, San Francisco, 83; Photog in California: Pushing the Boundaries 1945-1980, San Francisco Mus Mod Art, 84; Made in Calif: Arrt, Image & Identity, 1900-2000, Los Angeles (Calif) Co Mus Art, 2000-01; Pirkle Jones, 60 yrs in Photog, Santa Barbara Mus Art, 2001-2002; Berkeley Art Mus, Berkeley, Calif, 2003; Pirkle Jones & the Changing California Landscape, San Francisco Mus Modern Art, 2003-2004. *Teaching:* Instr photog, Calif Sch Fine Arts, 52-58, Ansel Adams Workshops, Yosemite Nat Park, 66-74 & San Francisco Art Inst, 70-97; master class, Univ Calif, Santa Cruz, 84, 88. *Awards:* Award Hon Photog, A Documentary Exhib, San Francisco Arts Comn, 83. *Bibliog:* Ansel Adams (auth), article, US Camera Mag, 10/52; Nancy Newhall (auth), article, Aperture Mag, 56; Robert Holmes (auth), article, Brit J Photog, 10/80. *Publ:* Auth, Portfolio One, Commemoration Signing United Nations Charter, private publ, 55; coauth, Death of a valley, Aperture Mag, 60; The Vanguard, A Photographic Essay on the Black Panthers, Beacon Press, 70; auth, Berryessa Valley The Last Year, Vacaville Mus, 94; auth, Pirkle Jones California Photogrpahs, Aperture, 2001; co-auth, Black Panthers 1968, Greyball Press, 2002. *Dealer:* Shapiro Gallery, 49 Geary Ste 208, San Francisco, CA, 94108. *Mailing Add:* 663 Lovell Ave Mill Valley CA 94941-1086

JONES, RONALD LEE, JR
EDUCATOR, WRITER
b Beckley, WVa, Dec 4, 42. *Study:* Concord Col, BS, 64; Ariz State Univ, MA, 68; Univ Md, PhD, 75. *Pos:* Contrib ed, Art Voices, S Palm Beach, Fla, 78-; chmn, WVa Arts & Humanities Comn, Capitol Complex, Charleston, 78-; secy, Int Coun Fine Arts Deans; pres, Fla Arts Deans Network. *Teaching:* Prof art & chmn dept, Shepherd Col, Shepherdstown, WVa, 69-, chmn, Div Creative Arts, formerly & dean, Sch Arts, formerly; Col Fine Art, dean Univ S Fla, currently. *Mem:* Nat Art Educ Asn; Nat Coun Policy Study Art Educ; Col Art Asn, WVa (pres, 71, 72 & 75); Nat Asn Arts Adminr; Nat Asn State Art Agencies; Tampa Mus Art (bd trustees). *Res:* Aesthetic response; writing art criticism for art journals. *Publ:* Auth, A re-examination of Mittler's efforts toward modern art attitude, Studies in Art Educ, 75; contribr, Artists in Schools: Analysis and Criticism, Univ Ill Bur Educ Res, 78; auth, Phenomenological analysis effects on aspective perception: a review, Rev Res in Visual Arts, 78; Critical reviews of artists, Art Voices/S 78-80; Phenomenological balance and the aesthetic response, J Aesthetic Educ, 79. *Mailing Add:* c/o Col Fine Art Univ S Fla 4202 E Fowler Ave FAH 110 Tampa FL 33620

JONES, RONALD WARREN
ARTIST, CRITIC
b Ft Belvoir, Va, July 8, 52. *Study:* Huntington Col, BA, 74; Univ SC, MFA, 76; Ohio Univ, PhD(art hist), 81. *Work:* Baltimore Mus Art; Moderna Museet, Stockholm, Sweden; Whitney Mus Am Art, Moca, La; Mus Mod Art, NY. *Comn:* Pritzker Park, City of Chicago; and others. *Exhib:* High Mus Art, Atlanta, 86; Metro Pictures, NY, 87-90; Metro Pictures, NY, 87 & 88; Sebui Mus, Tokyo, 90; Mind Over Matter Whitney Mus Am Art, NY, 90; Galerie Lehman, Switz, 92 & 94; Sonnabend Gallery, NY, 93; Metro Pictures, 97. *Teaching:* RI Sch Design, 88-90; Yale Univ, 89-98; Sch Visual Arts, 89-90; chmn, Visual Arts Div & dir, Digital Media Ctr, Sch Arts, Columbia Univ, 98; provost, Art Ctr Col of Design, 2000-. *Awards:* Mellon Found Stipend, 83; Fel, Nat Endowment Visual Artist, 84. *Bibliog:* Peter Halley (auth), Ronald Jones, Marcel Duchamp, and the New South (catalog essay), San Jose Mus Art; Richard Flood (auth), Ronald Jones (catalog essay), Isabella Kacprzak, Koln; Roberta Smith (auth), The New York Times, 88-90; Eleanor Heartney (auth), Ronald Jones at Metro Pictures, Art in Am, 1/88. *Mem:* Col Art Asn. *Publ:* Auth, various articles, essays & reviews, in: Artforum, Parkett Arts Mag, C Mag, Art in Am, Artscribe & Flash Art. *Dealer:* Metro Pictures 150 Greene St New York NY; Sonnabend Gallery New York NY. *Mailing Add:* Art Center 1700 Lida St Pasadena CA 91103

JONES, RUTHE BLALOCK
PAINTER, EDUCATOR
b Claremore, Okla, June 8, 39. *Study:* Bacone Col, with Dick West, AA; Univ Tulsa, with Carl Coker, BFA; Northeastern State Univ, Tablequah, Okla, MS. *Work:* Mus Am Indian, Heye Found, NY; Indian Arts & Crafts Bd, US Dept Interior, Washington, DC; Heard Mus, Phoenix; Philbrook Art Ctr, Tulsa; Williams Performing Arts Ctr, Tulsa, Okla. *Comn:* Minnetrista Cult Ctr, Muncie, Ind, 93. *Exhib:* Contemp North Am Indian Painting, Mus Natural Hist, Smithsonian Inst, Washington, DC, 82; Am Indian Community House, NY, 82; Southeastern Indian Artists, Fine Arts Ctr, Atlanta, Ga, 88; 9th Symposium, Int Soc Polyaesthetic Educ, Schloss Mittersill, Austria, 90; Moving the Fire, Official Okla State Event 1993 Pres Inaguration, Washington, DC, 93; Watchfall Eyes Invitational, Heard Mus, Phoenix, Ariz, 94; From the Earth X, Am Indian Contemp Arts, San Francisco, Calif; Symbols of Faith and Belief Gil Crease Mus, Tulsa, Okla 2000-; Visions and Veeces Milbrook Mus, Tulsa, 1998-. *Teaching:* Instr art, Bacone Col, Muskogee, Okla, 79-85, 87-. *Awards:* First Painting Award, Red Earth Art Competition, Oklahoma City, 90; Gov Award, State Capitol, Oklahoma City, 93; Crumbo Mem Award, SWAIA Indian Market, Santa Fe, NMex, 94. *Bibliog:* J Snodgrass (auth), Handbook American Indian Artists, Mus Am Indian, 67; H Meredith (auth), The Bacone School of Art, Chronicles Okla, LVIII, No 1, spring 80; article, Okla Today, Vol 35, No 4, 7-8/85. *Mem:* Southwestern Indian Art Asn, Santa Fe, NMex; Indian Arts & Crafts Asn, Albuquerque, NMex; Jacobson Found, Norman, Okla. *Media:* Watercolor, Acrylic, Graphics. *Res:* Ceremony of Delaware and Shawnee tribes of Indians; traditional American Indian painting. *Specialty:* Native Am Art. *Publ:* Mini Myths and Legends of Oklahoma Indians, Wise, Lu Celia, 78; State of Oklahoma Indian Education Curriculum Guides, 78; Bacone Indian University: A History, Williams & Meredith, 80; Auth, Keepers of Culture, (exhib catalog), Anniston Mus of Natural Hist, Ala, 88; Legends of Tree Delaware Indians (cover art), 99. *Dealer:* Native American Art 323 S Main Mall Tulsa OK 74172 74145; Indian Images Box 3621 Evansville IN 47735. *Mailing Add:* 517 S Woodlawn Ave Okmulgee OK 74447-5347

JONES, THEODORE JOSEPH
SCULPTOR, PRINTMAKER
b New Orleans, La, Sept 14, 38. *Study:* Xavier Univ, BA; Mich State Univ, MA; Univ Mont, MFA; Fla A&M Univ, cert; Fisk Univ, cert. *Work:* Johnson Publ Co, Chicago; Mus African Art, Washington, DC; First Am Nat Bank, Nashville. *Exhib:* One-man exhibs, Ala A&M Univ, Normal, 75, Tenn State Mus, 75 & Creatadrama Art Gallery, Bloomington, Ind, 75; 17th Tenn All-State Artists Exhib, Centennial Park Galleries, Nashville, 77; From These Roots Exhib, Tenn State Mus, Nashville, 77; Smith-Mason Galleries, Washington, DC, 77; and many others. *Pos:* Touring artist, Tenn Arts Comn, 70-; art consult, Claiborne Ave Design Team Symp, New Orleans, La, 74-. *Teaching:* Instr art, Fla A&M Univ, 65-68; from assoc prof to prof art, Tenn State Univ, 68-. *Awards:* Tenn State Univ Grant, 70; Third Place Sculpture, Tenn Art League, 74; Lyzon Galleries Award Graphics, Cent South Exhib, 75. *Bibliog:* Clara Hieronymus (auth), Ted Jones Exhibition, Tennessean Newspaper, 75; Kenneth Weedman (auth), article, Sculpture Quart, 75. *Mem:* Tenn Lit Arts Asn; Southern Independent Artists Asn; Southern Asn Sculptors; Southeastern Graphics Coun; Tennessee Art League. *Publ:* Contribr, Galaxy III Communication Arts Seminar Basic Holography, 74; ed, Faculty exhibition catalogs & brochures, Tenn State Univ, 74-75; auth, Thoughts and Verses (poetry and prints), 75 & Masonite-Printing: A New Approach in Relief Printing, 77, New Dimension Studio, Nashville. *Mailing Add:* 1003 Cross Bow Dr Hendersonville TN 37075-9403

JONES, THOMAS WILLIAM
PAINTER
b Lakewood, Ohio, Aug 13, 42. *Study:* Cleveland Inst Art, dipl, 64. *Work:* City of Seattle Selects II (For Pub Collection of Seattle City Light, Wash); Rainier Bank Collection, Pac Northwest Bell Collection, Seattle; Pac Car & Foundry & Eddie Bauer, Inc, Seattle. *Comn:* 25 landscape paintings, Gen Tel Co of the Northwest, Everett, Wash, 68; paintings of Old Holland, Western Int Design Serv, St Francis Hotel, San Francisco, 72; paintings for bd dirs, Seattle First Nat Bank, 74; four seasonal landscapes & 60th anniversary catalog cover, Eddie Bauer Inc, Seattle, 75, 80 & 82; Presidential Christmas Card, comn by White House, 85, 86, 87, 88; Vice Presidential Christmas Card, 2002-2003. *Exhib:* One-man show, Frye Art Mus, Seattle, 73 & 99; 154th Nat Acad Design, NY, 79; Northwest Art Today, 75, Works on Paper, 75 & Wash Open, 79, Seattle Art Mus; Artists of Am, Denver, 81-98; Nat Acad of Western Art & Prix de West, Oklahoma City, 81-2006; Celebration of Northwest Art, Gov's Mansion, Olympia, Wash, 84. *Awards:* Ted Kautzky Mem Award, Am Watercolor Soc, 75 & Bronze Medal of Honor, 79; First Place, Water Media, Rocky Mountain Nat, 76; Silver Medal, Nat Acad Western Art, 84 & Gold Medal, 87. *Bibliog:* Auth, Watercolor page, Am Artist, 9/79; Southwest Art feature article, Southwest Art Inc, (9/85 & 12/96); Patricia Black Bailey (auth), article, US Art, 1/90; Art in the White House-A Nations Pride-White House Hist Asn, 92; Myrna Zanetell (auth), Art of the West, Duerr & Tierney, 2004; Mary Evans Seeley, Season's Greetings from the White House, Presidential Christmas Corp, 2005. *Mem:* Hon mem Fed Can Artists. *Media:* Watercolor. *Dealer:* Howard Portnoy Gallery 6th & Dolores Carmel CA 93921; Galleries Sternberg 875 N Michigan Ave Ste 2850 Chicago Il 60611. *Mailing Add:* 18226 Dubuque Rd Snohomish WA 98290-8534

JONES, TONY
EDUCATOR
Pos: Dir, Glasgow Sch Arts, 80-86; pres, Sch Art Inst Chicago, 86-92; dir, Royal Col Art, London, 92-96; pres & co-Chief Exec Officer, Sch Art Inst Chicago, 96-. *Awards:* Named Hon Dir Bd, Osaka Univ Arts (Japan), 2000; Hon Prof, Univ Wales, 95; recipient Scotland's Newbery Medal, 86. *Mem:* Fel: Royal Col Art; Am Inst Architects. *Mailing Add:* Sch Art Inst of Chicago Office of the Pres 37 S Wabash Chicago IL 60603

JONES, W LOUIS
PAINTER, SCULPTOR
b Durham, NC, Feb 22, 43. *Study:* Pa Acad Fine Arts; E Carolina Univ, BS; Cranbrook Acad Art, MFA. *Work:* Metrop Life Ins, Boston; RJR/Nabisco Winston-Salem; Exxon; Nations Bank; Citicorp. *Exhib:* Solo exhibs, Arwin Gallery, 66-79, Kornblee Gallery, NY, 77, 78, Greenhill Ctr, Greensboro, NC, 86, Davidson Co Art Guild, 90; Am Realism: Realist Invitational, SECCA, Winston-Salem, 83; San Francisco Mus Mod Art, 86; DeCordova & Dana Mus, Lincoln, 86; Univ Tex, Austin, 86; Northwestern Univ, Evanston, 86; Williams Col Mus, Williamstown, Mass, 87; Abron Art Mus, 87; Madison Art Ctr, Wis, 87. *Teaching:* Skidmore Col, 69-74, La State Univ, Baton Rouge, 79, Univ SC, Columbia, 80. *Awards:* Purchase Awards, Arnkot Mus, Elmira, 73, Jacksonville Art Mus, 77, Russell Sage Col, Troy, 78, Berkshire Art Mus, Pittsfield, 76, Univ Nebr, Omaha, 78; Grant NY State Coun on the Arts, 73. *Mem:* Nat Soc Painters in Casein; Am Asn Univ Prof. *Media:* Acrylic; Wood. *Publ:* Watercolor 88 by American Artist, Polymer Painting by Russell O Woody, 88; American Realism from the James Collections, 86. *Mailing Add:* c/o Marita Gilliam Inc Art Gallery 912 Williamson Dr Raleigh NC 27608

JONES & GINZEL
SCULPTORS
Jones: b Washington, Aug 1, 56; Ginzel: b Chicago, Ill, July 14, 54. *Study:* Jones: St Martin's, London, 78-79, RI Sch Design, BFA, 79, Yale Univ, MFA, 83; Ginzel: self-taught. *Work:* Mus d'Arte Contemporanea, Prato, Italy; Wadsworth Atheneum, Hartford, Conn; Brooklyn Mus, NY; Kunsthalle, Basel, Switz; Targetti Art Light Collection, Florence, Italy. *Comn:* Mnemonics, Battery Park City Authority, 92, Occulus, Metrop Transit Authority, NY, 99; Principia, Ore Convention Ctr, Portland, 90; Plethora, Arts Am Prog, New Delhi, India, 91; Diaxiom, Com Sq One, IM Pei & Partners, Philadelphia, Pa, 91; Apostasy, 1996 Olympic Arts Festival, Woodruff Park, Atlanta, 96; Metronome, One Union Sq, NY, 99; Tevereterino, Rome, Italy, Polarities, Kans City Airport. *Exhib:* Ad Infinitum, Whitney Mus Am Art at Philip Morris, NY, 85 & 88; solo exhibs, Va Mus Fine Arts, (catalog), 86, New Mus Contemp Art, NY, 86, Wadsworth Atheneum, 88, List Visual Arts Ctr, Mass Inst Technol, Cambridge, 88; Interaction, 88 & Metathesis, Aldrich Mus Contemp Art, Ridgefield, Conn; Antithesis (with catalog), Kunsthalle, Basel, Switz, 89; Axis, Mechanika, Contemp Arts Ctr, Cincinnati, Ohio, 90-92; Synchysis, Chicago Cult Ctr, Ill, 93; Apotheosis (with catalog), Pub Art Fund Inc, NY, 94; Ellipsis, Aquario Romano, Rome, 95; Enigmas, Frederieke Taylor, NY, 96. *Teaching:* Ginzel: Instr Sculpture, Sch Visual Arts, NY, 85-; Jones: instr sculpture, Philadelphis Col Art, 86; Both: lectr, Tyler Sch Art, Philadelphia, 87 & 94; vis artists, Yale Univ, New Haven, Conn, 88 & 96, Cornish Sch Art, Seattle, Wash, 88, RI Sch Design, Providence, 89 & 96 & Harvard Univ, Cambridge, Mass, 89. *Awards:* Fel, Nat Endowment Arts, sculpture, 86 & 94; Pollock-Krasner Found, 94; Rome Prize, Am Acad Rome, Italy, 94-95; Louis Comfort Tiffay Found, 91. *Bibliog:* Edith Newhall (auth), Happening Time and Again, NY Mag, 10/25/99; David Masello (auth), New York's 50 Best Works of Art in Public Places, City & Co, 99; Tom Finkelpearl (auth), Dialogues in Public Art, MIT Press, 2000. *Mem:* Int Sculpture Ctr. *Media:* Mixed Media. *Dealer:* Frederieke Taylor, 535 W 22nd St New York NY 10001. *Mailing Add:* 289 Bleecker St New York NY 10014

JONSSON, TED (WILBUR)
SCULPTOR
b Berkeley, Calif, Oct 2, 33. *Study:* Univ Calif Davis, BFA(philos fine art), 52-57; Univ Wash, MFA(sculpture), 62-64. *Work:* City of Seattle, Permanent Works Collection, Wash; Seattle Art Mus, Wash; Manoogian Collection, Detroit, Mich; Fed Reserve Bank San Francisco, Seattle, Wash; Wash State Art Collection; Alaska Coun on the Arts; Seattle Pub Art Collection. *Comn:* Seattle Water Dept (fountain), City of Seattle, Wash, 75; Seattle Int Airport (sculpture), Port of Seattle, Wash, 72; Univ Alaska (sculpture), Alaska Coun Arts, Anchorage, 76; Olympia Tech Col (sculpture), Wash State Art Comn, 79; Fed Reserve, New Plaza (sculpture), Fed Reserve Bank San Francisco, Seattle, Wash, 91; Fountain, SAP Labs Inc, Palo Alto, Calif, 98; Kennelly Commons (sculpture fountain), Green River Col, auburn, Wash, 2005. *Exhib:* West Coast Now, Current Art from Western Seaboard, Traveling West Coast Mus Show, 68; Govenor's Invitational Int, Olympia, Wash, 69, 72, 73, 75 & 76; Art in Pub Places, Henry Gallery, Univ Wash, 72; Northwest 77, Seattle Art Mus Pavillion, Wash, 77; Northwest Invitational, Artists Today: Part II, Seattle Mod Art Pavillion, 77; Seattle Sculpture 27-87, Bumberbiennial, 87; Northwest Ann, Seattle, 90; Barcelona/Seattle exhib, Seattle, 90, Barcelona, Spain, 91; Holland Meets the USA, Galerie Daneel, Amsterdam, 92; Hungary/USA Exchange, Galeria Vizual Art, Galeria Ava Gera, Budapest, Hungary, 93. *Pos:* Cur, Wash State Capitol Mus, 62-63; art curator, Washington State Capitol Mus, Olympia, 62. *Teaching:* Art instr sculpture, Highline Community Col, Midway, Wash, 68-79; sculpture instr, Calif State Univ, Humbolt, 88-89; sculpture tech instr Humbolt State Univ, 89-90. *Awards:* First Prize, Pacific Northwest Ann, Spokane Mus Art, 67; Sculpture Award, Ann Exhib Northwest Painting & Sculpture, Seattle Art Mus, 73; Visual Arts Honors Award Outstanding Visual Artist, Wash State Art Comn, 87; and others. *Bibliog:* Louis G Redstone (auth), Art and Architecture & Public Art New Directions, McGraw-Hill, 79; John Beardsley (auth), Art in Public Places (pg 135), 1981; Charlie B Tomlins (auth), Water Sculpture USA, Univ Tex Press, 86; CB Tomlins (auth), Water Sculpture USA, Univ Tex Press, 1986. *Mem:* Artist Equity Wash State Chap Nat Affil (vpres 86-92); Int Sculpture Ctr; Artist Trust; The Artist Group (charter mem, bd dir 71, bd dir 72, 73, vice chair bd dir 74, 75, pres 77). *Media:* Stainless Steel, Granite, Water. *Interests:* Sailing, flying, skiing. *Dealer:* OK Harris Gallery 383 W Broadway New York NY 10012; Davidson Galleries 313 Occidental S Seattle WA 98104. *Mailing Add:* 805 NE Northlake Way Seattle WA 98105

JOOST-GAUGIER, CHRISTIANE L
ADMINISTRATOR, HISTORIAN
b Ste Maxime, France; US citizen. *Study:* Radcliffe Col, BA(hon); Harvard Univ, MA, PhD; Univ Munich, postgrad; Endowed Postdoc Fel AAUW. *Hon Degrees:* Harvard Univ, Phi Beta Kappa (hon), 2005. *Pos:* Independent Scholar. *Teaching:* Asst prof Renaissance art, Tufts Univ, 69-75; prof Renaissance art, NMex State Univ, 75-85, head art dept, 75-81; prof Renaissance art, Univ NMex, 85-2000, chair art dept, 85-87; Smithsonian Inst, lectr; Univ Maryland, lectr. *Mem:* Col Art Asn (bd dir, 80-86); Nat Coun Arts Administrators; Renaissance Soc Am (coun); Women's Caucus Art (adv bd); 16th Century Soc; and others. *Res:* Venetian drawings, series of famous men and women; Quattrocento art in Florence and Venice; Lombard architecture; Raphael and Rome; Michelangelo; intellectual history; Greek and Roman lit history, The Pantheon; Pythagoreanism in the renaissance. *Interests:* Art history as intellectual history. *Publ:* Auth of var articles in Gazette des Beaux-Arts, Art Bull, Zeitschrift fuer Kunstgeschichte, Commentari, Antichita Viva, Acta Historiae Artium, Artibus et Historiae, Arte Lombarda, Arte Veneta, Storia dell'Arte, Studi Veneziani; auth, The Selected Drawings of Jacopo Bellini, Raphael's Stanza della Segnatura: Meaning and Invention; auth, Measuring Heaven: Pythagoras and His Influence on Thought and Art in Antiquity and the Middle Ages; auth, Finding Heaven: Pythagoras & His Influence on Thought & Art in the Renaissance. *Mailing Add:* 2475 Virginia Ave NW #801 Washington DC 20037

JORDAN, BETH MCANINCH
PAINTER
b Corn, Okla, Nov 23, 18. *Study:* Southwestern State Univ, grad; Taber Col, Hillsboro, Kans; also with Jack Vallee, Millard Sheets & others. *Work:* Okla Art Ctr, Southwest Christian Col, State of Okla Collection of Okla Art & Humanities Coun; Oklahoma City Arts Coun; Kerr Conv Ctr; and over 50 corp collections. *Exhib:* Okla Nat Printmakers & Watercolor Show, 61; Southwestern Watercolor Soc Regional & Open, Dallas, Tex, 67, 69 & 71; 8 State Exhib Painting & Sculpture Ann, Okla Art Ctr, 71; Watercolor USA, Springfield, Mo, 73 & 79; Okla Artists Ann, Philbrook, Tulsa, 61-72; Butler Inst Am Art, Youngstown, Ohio, 78; one-person show ann for the past 32 yrs; Audubon artists, NY; Nat Womens Show, NY. *Pos:* Art bd, Omiplex, Kirkpatrick Gallery, formerly. *Teaching:* Instr painting & drawing, pvt classes, 60-70; instr painting & drawing, Okla Sci & Art Found, 62-66. *Bibliog:* Oklahoma City Key & Oklahoma City Down Towner, 85. *Mem:* Southwestern Watercolor Soc. *Media:* Watercolor, Pencil, Collage. *Dealer:* Linda Howell & Assocs Inc 6432 N Western Ave Oklahoma City OK 73116. *Mailing Add:* 1606 Drakestone Ave Oklahoma City OK 73120-1207

JORDAN, GEORGE EDWIN
HISTORIAN, CONSULTANT
b Ky, Oct 29, 40. *Study:* Univ Ky; Ringling Sch Art, Sarasota, Fla, BFA; ETenn State Univ. *Pos:* Cur, Reece Mus, Johnson City, Tenn, 66-69; cur Am art & registrar, New Orleans Mus Art, La, 69-72; art critic, New Orleans Times-Picayune, La, 74-77, ed, World of Art column, 77-79; freelance art writer, lectr, appraiser & consult, 79-; contrib ed, Art & Auction, 81-84; co-ed, New Orleans Art Rev, 82-; auth, Critics Choice monthly column, Go Mag, 83-88; guest cur, Seldom Seen Figures, Arts Coun New Orleans, 86. *Teaching:* Guest instr hist contemp painting, Adult Educ, Tulane Univ, 76-79; instr painting & art hist, New Orleans Acad Fine Arts, 84-85; vis scholar, Hist New Orleans Collection, 2001-02. *Res:* Artists who worked in New Orleans and the Southeast, late 18th, 19th and early 20th centuries. *Publ:* auth, Louisiana Artists 19th Century, WYES-Educ Television, New Orleans, 72-73; contribr, Encyclopedia of New Orleans Artists, 1718-1918, Historic New Orleans Collection, 87; auth, Josephine Crawford, In: Eight Southern Women Artists (catalog), Greenville County Mus of Art; coauth, Complementary Visions of Louisiana Art, Hist New Orleans Collection, 96; contribr (film), Brothers in Art, Ellsworth & William Woodward & their Art in the South, Hist New Orleans Collection, 97; auth, Geoge L Viavant, Artist of the Hunt, Hist New Orleans Collection, 2003. *Mailing Add:* 745 Lakeside Dr Bridgeport CT 06606

JORDAN, JACK
ADMINISTRATOR, SCULPTOR
b July 29, 27; US citizen. *Study:* Langston Univ, BA; Univ Iowa, MA; Ind Univ, MS; State Univ Iowa, MFA; Okla Univ; Ind Univ, DEd. *Work:* State Univ Iowa Mus, Iowa City; Atlanta Univ Art Mus, Ga; Okla Art Ctr, Oklahoma City; Golden State Ins Co, Calif; Afro-Am Cult Heritage Ctr, Dallas, Tex Anatomy of A Fowl (sculpture), Sutton Estate, Ardmore, Okla. *Comn:* Come Ye Children (sculpture), Bethany United Methodist Church, New Orleans, 71; Mural, Bell Baptist Church, 80; mural, Second Hwy Baptist Church, 81; mural, Guiding Light Baptist Church, 81; mobile mural, 100 yrs struggle for freedom, Nat Afro-Am Mus, Wilberforce, Ohio & wood sculpture, Forgive Them For They Know Not, 92. *Exhib:* NY Archit League & Nat Sculpture Soc; Nat Competitive Art Show, Walker Art Ctr, Minneapolis & El Mira Art Gallery, Pismo Beach, Calif; Nat Art Show, Carnegie Inst Int, Pittsburgh, Pa; Atlanta Art Gallery; Sculpture 81, Counterpoint Guild Nat Exhib of 16 Selected Black Sculptors, NY, 81; New Orleans Mus Art, 89; Downtown Gallery, New Orleans, 90; and others. *Collection Arranged:* Emancipation Centennial Nat Art Exhib, 63; New Orleans Bicentennial Art Exhib, Bicentennial Comn New Orleans, 74; Black Family Bicentennial Art Show, 75. *Teaching:* Head art dept, Claflin Univ, Orangeburg, SC, 49-50, Allen Univ, Columbia, SC, 52-55 & Langston Univ, Okla, 57-61; prof & head art dept, Southern Univ New Orleans, 61-90. *Awards:* Sculpture Awards, Joslyn Art Mus, Omaha, Nebr & Walker Art Ctr, Minneapolis; nine Nat Sculpture Awards, Atlanta Art Gallery, 50-73; and others. *Bibliog:* Cedric Dover (auth), American Negro Art, New York Graphic Soc, 60; Kaye Teall (auth), Black History of Oklahoma, Okla Pub Sch Title III, Elem & Sec Educ Act, 71; Judith W Chase (auth), Afro-American Arts & Crafts, Van Nostrand Reinhold, 71. *Mem:* Okla Art Asn; Nat Conf Artists (vpres, 65, pres, 66-67); Creatadrama Soc; Nat Conf Artists (chmn bd trustees, 83-); New Orleans Ctr Creative Arts (treas, 83-87). *Media:* All

JORDAN, JOHN L
SCULPTOR, VIDEO ARTIST
b Houston, Tex, Dec 21, 44. *Study:* Art League of Houston, 66; studied with John Howley, St Kilda, Australia, 83. *Work:* Catskill Alliance for Peace, Woodstock, NY; Woodstock Mus, NY; Collection of Tammy DeMichael, Woodstock, NY. *Comn:* Billboard mural, US Air Force, Ellington AFB, Tex, 66. *Exhib:* Homage to Dali with Fried Eggs, Manhattan Pub TV, NY, 91; Clouds Gallery, Woodstock, 92-98; Intimate Views, Woodstock Artists Asn, 94; Hiroshima on the Hudson, Town Hall, Woodstock, NY, 2000; Woodstack Guild 5x7 Show, 2001; WATV-Ceramics Dept, Mugathon, Woodstock, Guild of Artists & Craftsmen, 2005. *Pos:* Artist & designer, Jerusalem Jewels, Hawaii, 77-85; art dir, Gaudeamus Jordan, Woodstock, NY, 88-; art rep, Whitney Morse Art Group, New York, 88-91; producer & host, Ramble On, WATV, Woodstock, NY, 90-2006; exec producer, Woodstock Winter Video Festival, 94; producer, Woodstock Music Asn, 2002-05. *Teaching:* Art teacher, Onteora Sch Dist, Phoenicia, NY, 88-91. *Awards:* Spec Award, Am Fedn Gem & Mineralogical Soc Nat Show, Astrohall, 82; Exhib Award, Montgomery Co Fair, Conroe, Tex, 85; Exhib Award, Allentown Art Mus, Pa, 88. *Bibliog:* Ron Ronck (auth), Arts scene, Honolulu Advertiser, 84; Kevin O'Brian (auth), Woodstock Times, NY, 12/29/88; Sharon Cherven (auth), Woodstocks' Jordan Romances the Stones, Daily Freeman, Kingston, NY, 11/27/89; Artist Creates Dali tribute triptych, Art Bus News, 3/90; Julie Knipe (auth), Judge throws out claim, Globe-Times, Bethlehem, Pa, 5/17/90. *Mem:* Woodstock Artists Asn, NY; Woodstock Guild Artists, NY, 89-; Woodstock UFO Network. *Media:* All Media. *Publ:* Homage to Dali with Fried Eggs (video), 92; Peter Max in Woodstock (video), 94; Pete Seeger on Solar (video), 97; The Dharma Bums in Woodstock (video), 2002-05; The Sand Painters of Tashi Lhunpo Monastery (video), 2002. *Mailing Add:* c/o/ John Jordan PO Box 932 Woodstock NY 12498

JORDAN, WILLIAM B
HISTORIAN, CONSULTANT
b Nashville, Tenn, May 8, 40. *Study:* Washington & Lee Univ, BA, 62; NY Univ, MA, 64, PhD, 67. *Hon Degrees:* So Methodist Univ, LHD, 95. *Pos:* Chmn div fine arts, Meadows Sch of the Arts, Southern Methodist Univ, 67-73, dir, Meadows Mus, 67-81; deputy dir, Kimbell Art Mus, 81-90; bd trustees, Chinati Found, Marfa, Tex, 2001- & Nasher Found, Dallas, 2001-. *Teaching:* Assoc prof Span art hist, Southern Methodist Univ, 68-75, prof Span art hist, 75-81. *Awards:* Spanish Knight Awards, Order of Isabel la Catolica, 86; Vassari Award, Dallas Mus, 86; Order of Civil Merit, 88. *Mem:* Am Soc of Hispanic Art Hist Studies (gen secy, 76-78); Hispanic Soc of Am. *Publ:* Auth, Juan van der Hamen y Leon, Univ Microfilms, 67; The Meadows Museum: A Visitor's Guide to the Collection, Meadows Mus, 74; El Greco of Toledo (catalog), Toledo Mus Art, 82; Spanish Still Life in the Golden Age: 1600-1650 (catalog), Kimbell Art Mus, 85; Still Lifes of Juan Sanchez Cotan, Museo del Prado, 92; Spanish Still Life from Velazquez to Goya (catalog), Nat Gallery, London, 1995; Juan van der Hamer y Leon & the Court of Madrid, Yale Univ Press, 2005. *Mailing Add:* 3601 Turtle Creek Blvd Dallas TX 75219

JORGENSEN, AURORA DIAS See Dias-Jorgensen, Aurora Abdias

JORGENSEN, BOB (ROBERT) A
PAINTER, INSTRUCTOR
b Long Island, NY Dec 1, 28. *Study:* Pratt Inst, Brooklyn, NY, 45-46; SUNY, Farmingdale, Assoc (art), 48; Fitchburg State Col, teaching cert, 77. *Exhib:* Am Watercolor Soc, Salmagundi Club, NY, 96; Birds in Art, Leigh Yawkey Woodson Art Mus, Wausau, Wis, 96, 98; Nat Arts Club, NY, 96-2000; Am Artists Prof League, Salmagundi Club, 96-2000; Nat Acad Design, NY, 2000; Butler Inst Am Art, 2001. *Awards:* Air Float Systems Award, Hudson Valley Art Asn, 99; Past Pres's Award, RI Watercolor Soc Nat, 2000; Silver Medal of Honor, Allied Artists of America, 2001. *Bibliog:* Final Touch, WIldlife Arts Mag, 11/99. *Mem:* Allied Artists Am; New Eng Watercolor Soc (bd dir); Hudson Valley Art Asn; RI Watercolor Soc (bd dir, 1st vp, 96-99, pres, 99-2001, instr watercolor, 96-99); American Artists Prof League, (fel). *Media:* Watercolor. *Dealer:* Premier Image Gallery, Ashland, MA; Artica Gallery, Duxevry, MA. *Mailing Add:* 20 Woodland Rd Ashland MA 01721

JORGENSEN, FLEMMING
PAINTER
b Aalborg, Denmark, May 29, 34; Can citizen. *Study:* Art Sch Denmark. *Work:* Can Coun & Nat Gallery Can, Ottawa, Ont; McGill Univ; Univ Victoria; Winnipeg Art Gallery, Man. *Exhib:* 2nd Biennial Int Prints, Paris, France, 70; one-man shows, Marlborough-Godard, Montreal, Que, 72, Gallery Allen, Vancouver, 74, Bau-Xi Gallery, Victoria, 75 & Gallery Mira Godard, Toronto, 76; Kyle's Gallery, 79-83; North Park Studio, Victoria, 85. *Pos:* Vpres, Metholin Int Summer Sch Arts, currently. *Teaching:* Instr, Univ Victoria, BC, Lester B Pearson Col, currently. *Awards:* Can Coun Arts Bursary, 69 & 71. *Dealer:* Gallery Mira Godard 22 Hazelton Ave Toronto ON Can. *Mailing Add:* MISSA 650 Pearson College Dr Victoria BC V9C 4 V9C 4H7 Canada

JORGENSON, DALE ALFRED
EDUCATOR, ADMINISTRATOR
b Litchfield, Nebr, Mar 20, 26. *Study:* Harding Col, Ark, philos with J D Bales, BMus, 48; George Peabody Col, Tenn, MA, 50; Ind Univ, aesthetics with John Mueller, PhD, 57; Harvard Univ, cert arts admin, 72. *Pos:* Retired. *Teaching:* Prof aesthetics, Bethany Col WVa, 59-62; dir fine arts, Milligan Col, Tenn, 62-63; head fine arts div & teacher aesthetics, Northeast Mo State Univ, 63-87; retired. *Mem:* Am Soc Aesthetics; Midwest Col Art Asn. *Res:* Aesthetics and elementary aesthetics for contemporary students. *Publ:* Auth, The campus and the arts, Proceedings of the Nat Asn Sch Music, 70; Preparing the educator for related arts, Music Educr J, 5/70; The French lieutenant's woman, or to forego manipulation, Christianity Today, 5/11/73; Theological-Aesthetic Roots in the Stone-Campbell Movement, Thomas Jefferson Univ Press, 1/89; The Life & Legacy of Franz Hauser, Southern Ill Univ Press, 95. *Mailing Add:* 1512 S Cottage Grove Kirksville MO 63501

JOSEPH, STEFANI A
PAINTER, EDUCATOR
b Newport, Gwent, Eng. *Study:* Ruskin Sch Drawing & Fine Art, Oxford Univ, BA, 75; Royal Acad Sch, London; Savannah Col Art & Design, Ga, MFA, 2001. *Work:* St Hilda's Col, Oxford Univ, Eng; Templeton Col, Oxford, Eng; Sr Common Room, Westminster Col, Oxford, Eng; Isle of Wight Area Health Authority, Newport, Eng; St Bartholomew's Hosp, London. *Comn:* Portraits of profs, St Hilda's Col Oxford Univ, England. *Exhib:* Ibizagrafic, Mus Contemp Art, Ibiza, Spain, 86; Seoul Print Biennial, Mus Contemp Art, Korea, 88; group exhib, Mus Mod Art, Oxford, 88 & The Gallery Cork St, London, 97; Perpignan Biennial, Mus Contemp Art, France, 90; Selections, Broome St Gallery, NY, 98; 98 China Art Expo, China Int Exhib Ctr, Beijing, 98; Warren-Britt Galleries, Ala State Univ, 2000; juried exhib, The Hite Art Inst, Univ Louisville; State Capitol Gallery, Atlanta, Ga, 2001; Franklin Sq Gallery, Southport, NC, 2001 & 2002; Faces of Woman, Las Vegas Arts Coun, 2003; Red Gallery, Savannah, 2003; Art with a Southern Drawl, Univ Mobile, Ala, 2003; Trinidad Natl Fine Art Exhib, AR Mitchell Mus, CO, 2003 & Galerie Gora, Montreal, 2003; Art Now Galeria Zero, Barcelona, 2004; Miami Art Fair, The Chattahoochee Valley Art Mus, 2004; The Babcock Sch Bus Mgt and Sch of Law, Wake Forest Univ, NC, 2004; Fine Art Exhib, Mountain Valley Arts Council, 2005; Franklin Square Gallery, 2006; Jan & Gary Dario Gallery, 2006; Palm Beach Community Col, Lake Worth, Fla, 2006; solo exhibs, Mountain Valley Arts Coun, Guntersville, Ala, Annette Howell Center for the Arts, Valdosta, Ga, 2006. *Teaching:* Prof found studies, Savannah Col Art & Design, 93-. *Awards:* Prize winner, Ann July Nat Exhib, Franklin Sq Gallery, 2002; Prize Winner, Winterfest Fine Art Exhibit, 2005; Presidential Fel, Savannah Col Art & Design, 2005. *Bibliog:* Zoe Randall (auth), Duplicity and Intrigue, Connect Savannah, 99; Daniel Smith (auth), Meeting With Mystery, The Ga Guardian, 99. *Mem:* Southeastern Col Art Asn. *Media:* Oil on Canvas. *Dealer:* Off The Wall Gallery Savannah GA; Bender Fine Art Marietta GA; Galerie Gora, Montreal. *Mailing Add:* 24 E Liberty St Apt 22 Savannah GA 31401

JOSEPHSON, KENNETH BRADLEY
PHOTOGRAPHER, ASSEMBLAGE ARTIST
b Detroit, Mich, July 1, 32. *Study:* Rochester Inst Technol, BFA, 57; Inst Design, Ill Inst Technol, MS, 60. *Work:* Mus Mod Art, NY; Art Inst Chicago; Ctr Creative Photog, Univ Ariz; Mus Contemp Art, Chicago; Bibliot Nat, Paris. *Comn:* Great Ideas Series (assemblage), Container Corp Am, Chicago, 81; photog mural, SBI, Fla A&M Univ, 86. *Exhib:* The Photographer's Eye, Mus Mod Art, NY, 64; solo exhib, Art Inst Chicago, 71, Mus Art, Univ Iowa, Iowa City, 74, Fotoforum, Kassel, Ger, 78 & Mus Contemp Art, Chicago, 83; Painting in the Age of Photog, Kunsthaus, Zurich, 77; Mirrors and Windows, Mus Mod Art, NY, 78. *Teaching:* Prof photog, Art Inst Chicago, 60-; exchange teacher, Konstfackskolan, Stockholm, Sweden, 66-67; assoc prof, Univ Hawaii, Honolulu, 67-68; vis prof, Univ Calif, Los Angeles, 81-82. *Awards:* Fels, Guggenheim Mem Found, 72 & Nat Endowment Arts, 75 & 79; Ruttenberg Arts Found Grant, 83. *Bibliog:* Alex Sweetman (auth), Reading the bread book--a ten page note, Afterimage, 3/74; Floris M Neussüs (auth), Kenneth Josephson: The illusion of the picture, Fotoforum, Kassel, Ger, 78; Lynne Warren & Carl Chiarenza (auths), Kenneth Josephson, Mus Contemp Art, Chicago, 83. *Publ:* Auth, The Bread Book, pvt publ, 73; contribr, New American imagery, Camera, Switz, Vol 53, No 5, 74; The Photographer's Choice, Addison House, 75; Nude: Theory, Lustrum Press, 79; Kenneth Josephson, Mus Contemp Art, Chicago, 83. *Dealer:* Rhona Hoffman Gallery 312 N May St Suite 104 Chicago IL 60607

JOSTEN, KATHERINE ANN
CONCEPTUAL ARTIST, DIRECTOR
b Dayton, Ohio, Feb 27, 49. *Study:* Ohio Univ, BS, 71; Atlanta Col Art, BFA, 81; Univ Wis, Madison, MFA, 86. *Work:* Tucson Mus Art; Ariz State Univ Mus Art, Tempe. *Exhib:* Origins, Univ Ariz Mus Art, 87; 23rd Southwestern Traveling Exhib, Northern Ariz Univ, Flagstaff, 90; Ariz Artist Mus Collection, Ariz State Univ Art Mus, 93; Ariz Biennial, Tucson Mus Art, 93 & 99, Wide Open Spaces, 94; Earth, Man & Spirit, Sun Cities Art Mus, Ariz, 95; Global Art Proj Exhib, Nat Inst Arts, Taipei, Taiwan, 98, Tucson Mus Art, Ariz, 99; Women Artists in the Mus Collection, Tucson Mus Art, 99; Dirs Choice, Tucson Mus Art, Ariz, 2000. *Pos:* Founder & dir, Global Art Proj, Tucson, Ariz, 93-. *Teaching:* Instr color & design, Univ Ariz, 90-91; adj fac basic design, color & design, painting, Pima Col, Tucson, 87-2000. *Awards:* Pollack-Krasner Found Grant, 94; Rockefeller Found Flow Fund Grant, 98; 2002, UNESCO Peace Prize Nominee; and many others. *Bibliog:* Carrie Rothburd (auth), Serendipidy in Action: A Conversation with Katherine Josten on the Global Art Project, The Cath Found, Vol XIV, No 2, Seeds Unfolding, 97; Timothy Gassen (auth), Art connects the world: Tucson woman rides herd on Global Art Project, Ariz Daily Star, 2/19/98; Kristen Coughlin (auth), Artist organizes third biennial worldwide art exchange, Crafts Report, 4/98; and others. *Mem:* Tucson Mus Art; Ariz State Univ Art Mus. *Publ:* Auth, Visions of Global Unity: Inspired Images from the Global Art Project, Artifact Press, 96. *Mailing Add:* 840 E Elm St #2 Tucson AZ 85719-3914

JOW, PAT See Kagemoto, Patricia Jow

JOYAUX, ALAIN GEORGES
MUSEUM DIRECTOR
b Lansing, Mich, Oct 28, 50. *Study:* Mich State Univ, BFA(studio), 75, MFA, 77, MA(art hist), 78. *Collection Arranged:* European Tools From the 17th Century to the 19th Century (auth, catalog), 81; American Naive Painting: The Edgar William and Bernice Chrysler Garbish Collection (auth, catalog), Flint Inst Arts, 82; The Elisabeth Ball Collection of Paintings, Drawings and Watercolors: The George and Frances Ball Foundation (auth, catalog), 83; Childe Hassam in Indian (auth, catalog), 85; Europ & Am Paintings & Sculpture: Selected Works (auth, catalog), 94. *Pos:* Asst dir, Flint Inst Arts, Mich, 78-83; dir, Ball State Univ Mus of Art, 83-2003 Retired. *Mem:* Am Asn Mus; Intermuseum Conserv Asn. *Res:* Late 19th century European art; Degas. *Mailing Add:* Antiques & Plunder 22 North Sycamore St Petersburg VA 23803

JOYCE, J DAVID
PHOTOGRAPHER, SCULPTOR
b Kindersley, Sask, Jan 7, 46. *Study:* Carleton Univ, Ottawa, BA, 69; Univ Ore, Eugene, MA, 72, MFA, 75. *Work:* Seattle Arts Comn Portable Works Collection; City of Seattle; State of Ore; City of Eugene, Ore. *Comn:* Univ Ore Mus Art, Eugene, 82, Hult Ctr Performing Arts, Eugene, 83 & Mid-Valley Arts Coun, Salem, Ore, 83; photosculpture theatre sets, Eugene Ballet Co, 82; photosculptures, Univ Ore Mus Art, Eugene, 82, Hult Ctr Performing Arts, Eugene, 83 & Mid-Valley Arts Coun, Salem, Ore, 83; City of Eugene, 86 & 88; State of Ore, 86; Seattle Arts Comm, 86; Mahlon Sweet Airport, Eugene, Ore. *Exhib:* Solo exhib, Triton Mus Art, Santa Clara, Calif, 83, Univ Ore Mus Art, Eugene, 85, Northwest Artists Workshop, Portland, Ore, 85, Maryhill Mus, Goldendale, Washington, 86, Ore State Univ, Corvallis, 86, Murcuse Pfeifer Gallery, NY, 87, 89 & Fine Arts Mus, Long Island, NY, 91; Alternative Image II, Kohler Art Ctr, Sheboygan, Wis, 83; Segmentations, Friends Photog, Carmel, Calif, 83; Theatre of Gesture, Los Angeles Ctr Photog Studies, 83; Electrostatics Int, Cleveland State Univ, 84. *Teaching:* Asst prof film, Loyola Univ, Montreal, 75-76; instr mass communication & design, Lane Community Col, Ore, 78-. *Awards:* First Place, Washington-Oregon Juried Art Competition, Maryhill Mus, 85; Oregon Artists Fel, 86. *Bibliog:* The Photographic Sculpture of David Joyce, Nat Pub Radio, 7/10/87; articles in Darkroom Photography Mag, 10/85, 1/86 & 2/88. *Media:* Life Size Photographic and Photocopy Sculpture. *Dealer:* Marcuse Pfeifer Gallery 568 Broadway Suite 102 New York NY 10012; Susan Spiritus Gallery 3333 Bear St Suite 330 Costa Mesa CA 92626. *Mailing Add:* 990 Madison St Eugene OR 97402

JOYNER, JOHN BROOKS
HISTORIAN, MUSEUM DIRECTOR
b Baltimore, Md, Nov 24, 44. *Study:* Univ Md, BA, 66, MA, 69. *Collection Arranged:* Asian & African Art, Towson State Univ, 72-73; Permanent Collections, Univ Calgary, 75-76; George Rickey Sculpture, South Bend Art Ctr, 82; Patronage in Southern Art Mus, The Grand Tour, 88; Art of the Eighties: Selections from the Whitney Mus, 90. *Pos:* Dir, Nickle Arts Mus, Univ Calgary, 75-81, South Bend Art Ctr, Ind, 83-87 & Montgomery Mus Fine Arts, formerly, Gilcrease Mus, currently. *Teaching:* Lectr art hist, Towson State Univ, Baltimore, 72-74, Univ Calgary, Can, 72-80 & Univ Alta, Edmonton, Can, 80-83. *Mem:* Asn Art Mus Dirs; Am Asn Mus; Int Coun Mus. *Res:* 19th-20th century Europe & American painting & sculpture; Arshile Gorky's drawings & Canadian art. *Publ:* Auth, The Drawings of Arshile Gorky (monogr), Univ Md, 69; auth, Stephen Andrews-Banff, Art Mag, 10/77; auth, Printmaking in Alberta, Art Mag, 2/77; ed, the Sculpture of George Rickey (exhib catalog), South Bend Art Ctr, 85; auth, Marion Nicoll RCA, Masters Gallery Ltd, 80. *Mailing Add:* Gilcrease Mus 1400 Gilcrease Museum Rd Tulsa OK 74127

JU, I-HSIUNG
EDUCATOR, PAINTER
b Kiangyin, China, Sept 15, 23. *Study:* Nat Univ Amoy, China, AB(Chinese art), 47; Univ Santo Tomas, Manila, BFA, 55, MA(hist), 68. *Work:* Philippine Cult Ctr, Manila; Nat Mus Hist, Taipei, Taiwan; Int Ctr, Univ Conn; DuPont Art Gallery, Washington & Lee Univ; F&M Ctr, Richmond, Va; and others. *Comn:* 14 murals, Gulf States Paper Corp Nat Hq, Tuscaloosa, Ala, 70-71; and others. *Exhib:* South-East Asian Art Contest, Manila, 57; Asian Arts Festival, Univ Philippines, Manila, 65; Philippine & Japan Joint Art Exhib, Nat Mus Hist, Taipei, 66; 10th Japan Nan-ga-in Exhib, Tokyo, Kyoto & Osaka Mus, 70; Nat Painting & Calligraph Exhib, Nat Gallery, Taipei, 70 & 74; five one-man shows, Xiamen, Fuzhou, Shanghai, Beijing, Shenyang, 91 & 94; Taipei, Sun Yet-sen Mem Mus, Manila, Philippines, 97; Asia Gallery, Princeton, NJ; CG Gallery, 98; Caren Ctr, College Park, Md; Jiang-yin Cult Ctr, China, 98. *Teaching:* Lectr Chinese arts, Univ Maine, Univ NH, Univ Vt, Univ Conn, 68-69 & Va Mus Fine Arts, Richmond, 69-89; prof art, Univ Va & Washington & Lee Univ, 69-89, prof emer, 89-; vis prof, Fudan Univ, Shanghai, China & Xiamen Univ, China. *Awards:* Art Educator of the Year, Taiwan, 74; Spec Award for Contrib to the Arts, Nat Mus of Hist, Taipai, 78; Outstanding Achievement in field of Art, Philippine Chinese Asn Am, 96. *Mem:* Col Art Asn Am; Am Asn Univ Prof; Princeton Art Coun. *Media:* Ink, Acrylic. *Publ:* Auth, About Art, 59; Book of Bamboo, Book of Orchids (3rd & 4th eds), A Collection of Recent Landscape Paintings by Ju Nat Mus of Hist, Taipai, 76; Book of Chrysanthemum, 84, Book of Plum, 88, Art Farm Gallery, 1st ed; illusr, Beyond the Good Earth, Art Farm Gallery, 91; I-Hsiung Jus Landscape Painting Book II, Golden Production Inc, Hong Kong, 96. *Dealer:* E & J Frankel 1040 Madison Ave New York NY 10021; CG Gallery 10 Chambers St Princeton NJ 08542

JUAREZ, ROBERTO
PAINTER
b Chicago, Ill, 52. *Study:* San Francisco Art Inst, BFA; Univ Calif, Los Angeles, 78-79. *Work:* Newark Mus, NJ; Atlantic Richfield Co, Los Angeles; Gulf & Western, NY; Goldman & Sachs, NY; Rutgers Univ, New Brunswick, NJ; Metrop Mus Art, NY; General Mills Corp, Minneapolis, Minn. *Comn:* 25' X 9 1/2' mural painting, Tri Am, Coral Gables, Fla, 90; Miami Beach Police Station, 93; NY Pub Sch, 94. *Exhib:* New Wave, NY, Inst Art & Urban Resources, PS1, NY, 81; New Visions, Aldrich Mus, 81; Back to the USA, Kunstmuseum, Luzern, Theinisches Landesmuseum, Bonn & Wurttembergischer Kunstverein, Stuttgart, 83 & 84; Am Artist as Printmaker, Brooklyn Mus, 83-84; An Int Survey of Recent Painting and Sculpture (with catalog), Mus Mod Art, NY, 84; New Am Painting: A Tribute to James & Mari Michener, Archer M Huntington Art Gallery, Univ Tex, Austin, 84; Blast, 84 & Double Vision, 85, B-Side Gallery, NY; Innovative Still Life, Holly Solomon Gallery, NY, 85; This Way-This Way, Thorpe Intermedia Gallery, Sparkhill, NY, 85; solo exhib, San Francisco Art Inst, Calif, 77, Robert Miller Gallery, NY, 77, 81, 84, 86 & 87, Staller Ctr Arts, State Univ NY, 91; Midtown Payson Galleries, NY, 92; Betsy Rosenfield Gallery, Chicago, Ill, 92; Neuberger Mus, State Univ NY, 92-93. *Pos:* Artist-in-residence, Gulf & Western Co, Altos de Chavon, Dominican Republic, 84; painting workshops, Anderson Ranch, Aspen, 88, 89 & 90. *Teaching:* Vis artist, Pilchuck Glass Ctr, Stanwood, Wash, 91; vis artist, Yale Univ, Norfolk, Conn, 91; vis artist, Anderson Ranch, Snow Mass, Colo, 92. *Bibliog:* Roberta Smith (auth), article, Village Voice, 12/81; Grace Glueck (auth), article, New York Times, 1/28/83; Susan Hapgood (auth), article, Flash Art, 3/83. *Media:* Oil, Acrylic. *Dealer:* Robert Miller Gallery 41 E 5th St New York NY 10022. *Mailing Add:* 303 E 8th St New York NY 10009

JUDD, DE FORREST HALE
PAINTER, EDUCATOR
b Hartsgrove, Ohio, Apr 4, 16. *Study:* Cleveland Inst Art, grad, 38, post grad scholar, 39; Colorado Springs Fine Arts Ctr, with Boardman Robinson, 39-42. *Work:* Cleveland Mus Art, Ohio; Dallas Mus Fine Arts, Tex; Beaumont Mus Art, Tex; Univ Tex, Austin; Southern Methodist Univ. *Exhib:* Am Painting Today, Metrop Mus Art, 50; Tex Contemp Artists, Knoedler Gallery, NY, 52; New Accessions, USA, Colorado Springs Fine Arts Ctr, 52; Ten Texas Painters, Frank Perls Gallery, Beverly Hills, Calif, 53; Texas Painting & Sculpture, 20th Century, Southern Methodist Univ, 71. *Teaching:* Prof painting, Southern Methodist Univ, 46-82, prof emer, 82. *Awards:* First Prize, Cleveland Mus Art, 41; E M Dealey Purchase Award, Tex Painters & Sculptors Exhib, 50; First Prize, 2nd Ann Exhib, Beaumont Mus Art, 53. *Media:* Oil, Acrylic. *Mailing Add:* 1604 Concord Pl Carrollton TX 75007-2925

JUDGE, MARY FRANCES
PAINTER
b Minneapolis, Minn, July 31, 35. *Study:* Col New Rochelle, NY, BA (art), 61; Univ Notre Dame, Ind, MFA (painting), 71. *Work:* Carnegie Mus, Pittsburgh, Pa; Springfield Col Gallery, Ill; Nobles Co Art Ctr, Worthington, Minn; Lee Co Cult Ctr, Ft Myers, Fla; Oak Ridge Mus, Tenn; and other pvt and pub collections; New Britain Mus of Art, New Britain, Conn. *Comn:* Interpretive Family Portraits, New York City, Stockholm; Pvt Residence Frescoes, Ceyras, France, 1992. *Exhib:* Midwest Biennial, Joslyn Mus, Omaha, Nebr, 72; Ann Mid-States Exhib, Evansville Mus, Ind, 71; Brooks Mus Art, Memphis, Tenn, 70 & 71; one-woman show, Moody Gallery, Austin, Tex, 72, Contemp Gallery, Dallas, 73, Reflections Gallery, St Louis, Mo, 73, Hansen Galleries, NY, 77-78, Dolly Fiterman Gallery, Minneapolis, Minn, 80, Ross Gallery, Scottsdale, Ariz, 81, Rosenberg Libr, Harris Gallery, Galveston, Tex, 83, Max Gallery, NY, 85, Leonarda Di Mauro Gallery, NY, 88, Univ Tex, Dallas, 84-90, Lee Co Alliance Arts Cult Ctr, Ft Myers, Fla, 92 & Oak Ridge Art Mus, Tenn, 94, Monogramma Galleria, Rome, Italy, 2001; Beverly Gordon Gallery, Dallas, Tex, 87; Leonarda Di Mauro Gallery, NY, 88; All Out, Long Island Univ, Brooklyn, NY, 94; Recycling with Imagination, Portland, Ore, Phoenix, Ariz, NY & Pittsburgh, Pa, 94-2000; Minneapolis Inst Arts, 2000-01; solo exhib, Digital Sandbox Gallery, New York City, 2003. *Pos:* Mem bd, Dallas Mus Fine Arts, Tex, 76-77. *Teaching:* instr, Col of New Rochelle, New York City. *Awards:* Strathmore Nat Art Award, Scholastic Art Awards, Strathmore Papers, 50; Bixby Portrait Award, St Louis Artists Guild, 71. *Bibliog:* Articles in Arts Mag, 3/77 & 10/78; Terry Trucco (auth), Artnews, 5/79; Marian Courtney (auth), article, New York Times, 6/26/83; Dennis Wepman (auth, article), Manhattan Arts, 90; Knoxville News Sentinel, 5/15/94; David Howard (dir), Mary Frances Judge (film); Il Giornale D'Italia, 6/22/2001. *Mem:* St Louis Women Artists (bd mem, 72-74); Artist Equity (NY & bd mem Dallas, 74-78); Nat Asn Female Execs; Nat Soc Graphologists. *Media:* Mixed media painting. *Specialty:* Contemporary abstracts. *Interests:* graphology, ann painting trip to Italy. *Collection:* Giovanni Morabito, Rome. *Publ:* Bovarchè, II editizone, Italy. *Dealer:* Dolly Fiterman Fine Arts 100 University SE Minneapolis MN 55414; Galleria Monogramma Rome Italy. *Mailing Add:* c/o Dolly Fiterman Fine Arts 100 University Ave SE Minneapolis MN 55414

JUDSON, JEANNETTE ALEXANDER
PAINTER, COLLAGE ARTIST
b New York, NY, Feb 23, 12. *Study:* Nat Acad Design, with Robert Phillip & Leon Kroll; Art Students League, with Vaclav Vytlacil, Charles Alston, Carl Holty & Sidney Gross. *Work:* US State Dept & Hirshhorn Mus, Washington, DC; Brandeis Univ; Mus NMex; Columbia Univ, Brooklyn Mus, Fordham Univ & NY Univ, NY; and many other pub and pvt collections. *Exhib:* One-man shows, Pa State Univ, 69, NY Univ, 69, Syracuse Univ House, NY, 75 & Am Standard Gallery, 80; Key Gallery, NY, 80-83; Bodley Gallery, 67, 69, 71 & 73; and others. *Awards:* Am Soc Contemp Artists Award, 76, 78, 85 & 94, D Feigen Mem Award, 77, Am Soc Contemp Artists; Nat Asn Women Artists Award, 79; Lillian Hellman Award, Nat Asn Women Artists. *Bibliog:* Articles in Arts Mag & Art Moderne, 69-80. *Mem:* Nat Asn Women Artists; Am Soc Contemp Artists; Artists Equity New York. *Media:* Acrylic, Mixed Media. *Mailing Add:* 1130 Park Ave New York NY 10128

JUDSON, WILLIAM D
CURATOR, HISTORIAN
b New London, Conn, Dec 10, 39. *Study:* Williams Col, BA, 60; Oberlin Col, MA, 68; Yale Univ. *Collection Arranged:* 73 var vis artist presentations, 75-. *Pos:* Cur film & video, Mus Art, Carnegie Inst, Pittsburgh, 75-; panelist media arts, Nat Endowment Arts, 78-; bd mem, Pittsburgh Filmmakers Inc, 74-. *Teaching:* Adj inst film hist, Univ Pittsburgh, 73-. *Mem:* Col Art Asn; Ohio Valley Regional Media Arts Coalition (pres, 80-); Am Film Inst; Am Fedn Arts (film adv bd, 78-). *Res:* Early film history; documentary film; experimental film; 20th century art

JUGO DE VEGETALES See Thompson, Jack

JUHAROS, STEPHEN
PAINTER
b Budapest, Hungary. *Study:* Royal Hungarian State Univ Fine & Indust Arts, MA (arts). *Work:* Royal Hungarian Mus Fine Art, Budapest, Hungary; City Art Mus, Budapest, Hungary; Nat Mus of Fine Art, Budapest, Hungary; Mus Midland, Tex; Mus Hall Pres, Gettysburg, Pa; Largest church mural on continent, Pittsburgh, Pa; mural, History of Northern Arizona Univ, Flagstaff, Ariz. *Comn:* Over 400 collections, Ireland, Eng, Finland, France & Ger; Joseph Cardinal Mindszenty, for Cardinal Spellman; Archbishop of US; Ambassador to Brazil; Pres Dwight D Eisenhower. *Exhib:* Various Art Exhib, NY, NJ, New Eng, Ala, Mich & Fla; Int Art Exhib, Mex, Hungary, Ger, French Riviera, Madrid & Spain. *Collection Arranged:* Mrs. Viola Babbitt, Flagstaff, Ariz; James Kemper, Former Ambassador to Brazil; Dr T Hicks, Ariz; Barry Goldwater, US Senator; Al Zink, Esquire. *Pos:* Art instr prog, Flagstaff Television, formerly; owner, Treasure Art Gallery & Studio, currently. *Teaching:* instr, art classes, Ger, formerly; instr, arts, Acad Arts, NJ, formerly; instr, art classes, Flagstaff, Prescott & Sedona, Ariz, formerly. *Awards:* Many first place awards; Gold Medal of Inst, Rome, Italy; Three First Prizes & Honorable Mention, Montclair Mus Art Exhib, NJ, 53. *Mem:* Nat Soc Am Impressionists (found mem); Individualists of Sedona, Fraternal Asn Artists, Sedona, Ariz; Masters Art, Royal Hungarian State Univ Fine & Indust Art, Budapest Hungary. *Media:* Oil, Watercolor. *Res:* History books. *Specialty:* Traditional fine art. *Interests:* History, travel, hiking. *Dealer:* Casey Gallery Scottsdale AZ; Lindsey Gallery Caramel by the Sea CA; Newman Gallery Philadelphia PA; Treasure Art Gallery Sedona AZ; Hudgens Gallery of Fine Art Flagstaff AZ; Gallery Andrea Scottsdale AZ. *Mailing Add:* Treasure Art Gallery 2855 Highway 179 Sedona AZ 86336

JULIO, PAT T
EDUCATOR, CRAFTSMAN
b Youngstown, Ohio, Mar 1, 23. *Study:* Wittenberg Col, BFA, with Ralston Thompson; Univ NMex, MA, with Raymond Jonson & Lex Haas; Univ Colo, with Robert Lister; Ohio State Univ, with Edgar Littlefield; Tex Western Col, with Wiltz Harrison. *Comn:* Stained glass windows, Episcopal Good Samaritan Church, Community Church & pvt collections. *Exhib:* Denver Art Mus, 50 & 63; Pueblo Art Mus, 60; Pueblo Col, 60 & 69; one-man shows, Pueblo Art Mus, 64 & Western State Art Gallery, 69. *Teaching:* Prof art, Western State Col, 71-. *Mem:* Col Art Asn Am; Western Art Asn; Am Ceramic Soc; Am Crafts Coun; Inst Indian Studies; and others. *Mailing Add:* 145 Silver Sage Dr Gunnison CO 81230

JUNG, KWAN YEE
PAINTER
b Toysun, China, Nov 25, 32; US citizen. *Study:* Chinese Univ Hong Kong New Asia Col, BA(painting), 61; San Diego State Univ, postgrad studies, 68. *Work:* Springville Mus Art, Utah; San Diego Chinese Hist Mus, Calif; Nat Acad Mus, NY; Hickory Mus Fine Art, NC; San Bernadino Art Asn, Calif. *Exhib:* Calif Nat Watercolor Soc Ann,

72-79; Watercolor USA, 72 & 75; Am Watercolor Soc Ann Exhib, 73-78; Nat Acad Design Ann, 74, 82, 86 & 92; one-man shows, Univ Hong Kong, 75, Edward Dean Mus, Calif, 77 & US Int Univ, San Diego, 83; group exhib, Water to Women Margaret Cross Gallery, Old Pasadena, Calif, 95, May Snow Kim's Art Gallery, Rowland Heights, Calif, 95, Co-art Int Gallery, Vancouver, British Columbia, Can, 96, Kruglak Gallery, Mira Costa Col, Oceanside, Calif, 97, San Diego Chinese Hist Mus, 97, The Earl & Birdie Taylor Libr, San Diego, 98, 174th Ann Exhib Nat Acad of Design, 99. *Collection Arranged:* Springville Mus, Utah; San Diego Chinese History Mus; Nat Acad Mus, NY; Hickory Mus Art, NC. *Pos:* Commercial artist advertising dept Hong Kong Soy Bean Products Co, 61-63; owner Jung's Gallery, La Jolla, California, 76-78; freelance artist, instructor, demonstrator San Diego, 78—. *Awards:* Am Watercolor Soc Award, 76, 78, 87 & 98; Best of Show, Sumi-E Soc Am, 79; Merit Award, Nat Acad Design, 92. *Bibliog:* interview, Artist-TV 51, San Diego, 83; article in SW Art Mag, 1/83; article in Western Arts Digest, 5-6/86; article in Watercolor Mag, 98. *Mem:* Nat Watercolor Soc; Am Watercolor Soc; Nat Acad Design. *Media:* Watercolor, Oil. *Publ:* Special Focus on California, Art Voices, 2/83; Splash 1 & 2, America's Best Contemporary Watercolor, North Light, 91 & 92; Kwan Y Jung & Yeewah Jung, Art of Calif, 11/92; Chinese Brush Painting Step by Step, NorthLight Books, 2003. *Dealer:* Kim Art 1015 Nogales St No 118 Rowland Heights CA 97148

JUNG, YEE WAH
PAINTER
b Canton, China, Sept 4, 36; US citizen. *Study:* Chung Man Art Sch, WuHun, China, 54-58; Chinese Univ Hong Kong New Asia Col, 58-62. *Comn:* The Tours of Confucius (mosaic painting), Facade of Ambassador Hotel (with Chiu Fung Poon), 59. *Exhib:* Watercolor USA, 73-75 & 88; Nat Acad Design, 74; Butler Inst Am Art, 74; Mira Costa Col, Kruglak Gallery, Calif, 97; San Diego Hist Chinese Mus, Calif, 98; Taiwanese Am Ctr, Calif, 2000. *Awards:* First Place, Southern Calif Expo Art, Del Mar, 71; Calif Nat Watercolor Soc Award, Watercolor USA, 73-78; Watercolor USA Award, Calif Nat Watercolor Soc, 77; First Prize, 25th Art Festival Exhib, 88; Seventh Ann King's Award, Advent Fine Arts Exhib, 89. *Bibliog:* Interview, Spectrum-TV 10, San Diego, 82; article, SW Art Mag, 1/83; Betty Lou Schlemn & Tom Nicholas (auths), The Best of Watercolor, Rockport Publ Inc, 96. *Mem:* Nat Watercolor Soc; Watercolor USA Hon Soc. *Media:* Oil, Watercolor. *Publ:* Auth, Environmental Escape, Southwest Art, 1/83; Splash 1, America's Best Contemporary Watercolor, North Light, 91; Kwan Jung & Yeewah Jung, Art of Calif, 11/92; Abstract in Watercolor, 96. *Dealer:* Kim Art 1015 Nogales St 118 Rowland Heights. *Mailing Add:* 5468 Bloch St San Diego CA 92122

JURINKO, ANDY (ANDREW) FLOYD
PAINTER
b Phillipsburg, NJ, June 17, 39. *Study:* Kutztown State Col, Pa, 57-58; Philadelphia Mus Col Art, 61-63. *Work:* Sports Mus NEng, Boston, Mass; Nat Baseball Mus & Hall Fame, Cooperstown, NY. *Exhib:* Diamonds Are Forever, traveling exhib, 87-90; Diamond Gold, Nat Baseball Mus, 89; Gallery Henoch, NY, 89; Sports Mus New Eng, Cambridge, Mass, 93; Mickey Mantle's, NY, 94. *Teaching:* Instr illus, Philadelphia Col Art, 87-88. *Bibliog:* Subject of Sportslook, ESPN, 6/89; Baseball Mag, ESPN, 8/89; New York Mag, 8/92. *Media:* Acrylic, Oil. *Publ:* The Art of Baseball, Harmony Books, 90; Shibe Park, Princeton, 91; Fenway, Putnam, 92; Baseball: A Treasury of Art & Literature, Hugh Levin Assoc, 93; Treasury of Baseball, Publ Int, 94. *Dealer:* Gallery Henoch 80 Wooster St New York NY 10012. *Mailing Add:* 125 Cedar St New York NY 10006-1017

JURNEY, DONALD (BENSON)
PAINTER
b Rye, NY, Jan 7, 45. *Study:* Pratt Inst, NY, 71-72; Art Students League, 79. *Work:* Mus City of New York; Hudson River Mus, Yonkers, NY; Bank Am, San Francisco, Calif; Oakland Mus, CA. *Comn:* Lobby Paintings, Clorox Co, Oakland, Calif. *Exhib:* Berkshire Art Asn, Berkshire Mus, Pittsfield, Mass, 80; Silvermine Guild, New Canaan, Conn, 80; 45th Ann Mid-Year Exhib, Butler Inst, Youngstown, Ohio, 81; Parrish Art Mus, Southampton, NY, 81; 159th Ann Exhib, Nat Acad, NY, 84; 163rd Ann Exhib, Nat Acad, 88. *Awards:* C R Gibson Award, 31st New Eng Exhib, 80; Award of Merit, 62nd Nat Exhib, Springfield Art League, 81; Special Award, 19th Ann Exhib, Putnam Arts Coun, 81. *Bibliog:* Eric Widing (auth), Donald Jurney, 11/82 & M Stephen Doherty (auth), Motifs for landscape painting, 2/84, Am Artist; film, Reflections on the Hudson, CBS-TV, 9/84. *Mem:* Century Asn. *Media:* Oil, Watercolor. *Dealer:* Hoorn-Ashby Gallery 766 Madison Ave New York NY 10021. *Mailing Add:* 110 Hitch Pond Cir Seaford DE 19973-6221

JUROVICS, TOBY
CURATOR
Study: Univ NC, BA (art hist and english), 1988; Univ Del, MA (art hist), 1992. *Collection Arranged:* Emmet Gowin: Aerial Photographs, 1998; Photographs by Barbara Bosworth, 2000; Robert Adams: From the Missouri West, 2004. *Pos:* With Princeton Univ Art Mus, NJ, 1991-2006, assoc cur photog, cur photogr; cur photogr, Smithsonian Am Art Mus, Washington, DC, 2006-. *Mailing Add:* Smithsonian American Art Museum Victor Bldg 750 Nineth St NW Washington DC 20001

JUSTIS, GARY
SCULPTOR, KINETIC ARTIST
b Wichita, Kans, Apr 4, 53. *Study:* Wichita State Univ, BFA, 77; Sch Art Inst Chicago, MFA, 79. *Work:* Mus Contemp Art, Borg-Warner Corp, Chicago; Ill State Mus, Springfield; Krannert Mus Art, Champaign, Ill; Alexandria Mus Art, La; US Equities Corp, Chicago, Ill; Durindol Inc, Chicago, Ill. *Comn:* Wall sculpture, Carson's Int, O'Hare Int Airport, Chicago, 87; sculpture, Carson's Int, O'Hare Int Airport, 90; Garden Park Comn, Gary Justis & LJ Douglas, Evanston, Ill, 92. *Exhib:* solo exhibs, Compass Rose Gallery, Chicago, Mus SE Tex, Klein Art Works, Chicago, Tough Gallery, Chicago, Mus Sci & Indust, Chicago, 82, Chicago Cult Ctr, 85 & Alexandria Mus Art, La, 86, The Causal Garden, Compassrose Gallery, Chicago, 88, Quiet Works 1989-91, Compassrose Gallery, 91, Functionality, Kinetic Sculpture, Midland Ctr Arts, Mich, 98-99, This is the thing, Klein Art Works, Chicago, 2000, Head on Horizon, Tarble Art Ctr, Eastern Ill Univ, 2001; Painting & Sculpture Today, Indianapolis Mus, 84; Art Inst Chicago, 84; Ten Yrs of Collecting, Mus Contemp Art, Chicago, 84; PULSE Nat Exhib, Edwin A Ulrich Mus Art, Wichita, Kans, 92; Nature of the Machine, Chicago Cult Ctr, 93; Art in Chicago, 1945-1995, Mus Contemp Art, 96; Incrementum: Selected Works 1979-1996, Klein Artworks & Tough Gallery, Chicago, Ill, 96; Sound & Vision, Rockford Art Mus, Rockford, Ill, 98; Chicago Abstraction, Klein Art Works, Chicago, 99; Contemporary Figurative Scupture, Tweed Mus ARt, Duluth, Minn, 2000. *Teaching:* Instr sculpture, Sch Art Inst Chicago, 86-; adj asst prof, Univ Ill, Chicago, 88-89; guest lectr, Northwestern Univ, Chicago, 91-98; asst prof, Ill State Univ, 98-. *Awards:* Edward L Ryerson Fel Award, 79; Nat Endowment Arts Grant, 84 & 90; Ill Arts Coun Fel, 84. *Bibliog:* Judith Russi Kirshner (auth), Gary Justis--MSI, Art Forum, 12/82; Dan Cameron (auth), New generation of Chicago artists, Art News, 10/84; Michael Bonesteel (auth), article, Art in Am, 6/85; James Yood (auth), article, Artforum, 12/88; Lauri Dahlberg (auth), article, Dialogue Mag, 90. *Media:* Miscellaneous Media. *Publ:* Auth, Speakeasy, New Art Examiner, Summer 90. *Mailing Add:* Ill State Univ School of Art Campus Box 5620 Normal IL 61790

JUSZCZYK, JAMES JOSEPH
PAINTER, PRINTMAKER
b Chicago, Ill, Jan 30, 43. *Study:* Univ Ill, Urbana, 60-62; Cleveland Inst Art, BFA(Ford Found Grant), 66; Univ Pa, MFA(fel), 69. *Work:* Chase Manhattan Bank; Merill Lynch Int Zurich; Swiss Bank Corp; Krannert Art Mus, Univ Ill; NJ State Mus. *Comn:* Chromos Electronic AG Zurich, 6/88. *Exhib:* One-man shows, Gimpel Hanover Galerie, Zurich, Switz, 75, 77 & 82, Jan Cicero Gallery, Chicago, 80, 83, 87 & 92, Galerie Knostruktiv Tendens, Stockholm, Sweden, 82 & 85, ACP-Viviane Ehrli Gallery, Zurich, Switz, 88, 93 & 94, Found Construct & Concrete Art, Zurich, Switz, 91, Long Island Univ, 97 & Stadtishes Kunstmuseum, Singen, Ger, 97; Eight Abstract Painters, Inst Contemp Art, Univ Pa, 78; Geometric Abstraction: A New Generation, Inst Contemp Art, Boston, 81; Am Abstract Artists 50th Anniversary Exhib, Bronx Mus Fine Art, NY, 86. *Pos:* Guest artist-in-residence, Ill State Univ, 79 & 96, Atelierhaus, Zurich, Switz, 86; artist consult, Lascaux Colours & Restauro, Zurich, 95-. *Teaching:* Vis artist, Ohio State Univ, 89, Lacoste Sch Arts, France, 94; adj prof, City Col New York, 96. *Awards:* Pollock-Krasner Found Grant, 95. *Bibliog:* Katrina Vatsella, Pius Sidler & Corey Postiglione (auths), Haiku Geometry II (exhib catalog), 90; Willy Rotzler (auth), Bilder 1990, Rational und Meditativ Zur Malerei von James Juszczyk (exhib catalog), 91; Peter Killer & Corey Postiglione (auths), James Juszczyk (monograph), 92. *Mem:* Am Abstract Artists; Found Art Theory & Educ; Col Art Asn. *Media:* Acrylic on Canvas; Lithography, Silkscreen. *Dealer:* Ohm Design 225 LaFayette St No 809 New York NY 10012; ACP Viviane Ehrli Galerie Austrasse 38 CH-8045 Zurich Switz

K

KABAKOV, ILYA
CONCEPTUAL ARTIST, PAINTER
b Soviet Union, 33. *Study:* Moscow Surikov Inst Art, 51-57. *Work:* Mus Mod Art, NY; Mus Nat d'Art Mod, Ctr Georges Pompidou, Paris, France; Stedelijk Mus, Amsterdam, Holland; Ludwig Mus, Cologne, Ger; Mus Contemp Art, Ghent, Belg; Brooklyn Acad of Music; Espace Lyonnais pour l'Art Contemporain, Lyon, France, 96; Kunsthalle Hamburg, Ger, 96; Mus of Ludwig, Köln, Ger; Hochhaus zür Palme, Zurich, Switzerland, 97; Moenchehaus Mus fuer Moderne Kunst, 98; Nagoya City Mus, Japan; Mus of Contemp Art, The Netherlands, 99; The Dialogue, Kunstwegen, Stadische Galerie Northern, 99; The Fountain, Middlebourg, Holland, 2000; Singen 2000, Hier da und Dort, 2000. *Comn:* Whose Wings are These? (outdoor permanent installation), Cent Mus, Utrecht, Holland, 91; The Blue Dish (outdoor permanent installation), Expo '92, Scville, Spain, 92; costumcs & sets for "Life with an Idiot", Neth Opera, Amsterdam, Holland, 92; School No 6, Chinati Found, Marfa, Tex, 93; The Last Step (monument) to immigrants from Europe to America, Bremerhaven, Ger. *Exhib:* Dislocations, Mus Mod Art, NY, 91; solo exhibs, Hessisches Landesmuseum, Darmstadt, Ger, 94, Ctr Nat d'Art Contemporain, Grenoble, France, 94, Mus Contemp Art, Helsinki, Finland, 94, Nat Mus Contemp Art, Oslo, Norway, 94 & Mus d'Art Mod, Ctr Georges Pompidou, Paris, 95Deweer Art Gallery, Otegem, Belgium, 98, Mus van Hedendaagse Kunst, Antwerp, Belg, 98, Thaddaeus Ropac Gallery, Salzburg, 98, Moenchehaus Mus fuer Moderne Kunst, Goeslar, Ger, 98, Irish Mus Mod Art, Dublin, 98, Stadtgallery, Heerlen, The Neth, 98, Sprengel Mus, Hannover, Ger, 98, 99, Mito Tower, Japan, 99, Amsterdam Fonda Noor de Kunst, The Neth, 99, Duke Univ Mus, NC, 99, Tate Gallery, London, 2000, Junstmuseum, Bern, 2000, Lia Rumma Gallery, Naples, Italy, 2000, Aspen Art Mus, Colo, 2000, Galerie Clara Maria Sels, Duesseldorf, others; Barbara Gladstone Gallery, NY, 96; Mus d'Art Contemporain, Lyon, France, 96; and others. *Teaching:* Prof installation art, Staedelschule, Frankfurt, Ger, 92. *Awards:* Arthur Koptcke Award, Kopcke Found, Copenhagen, Denmark; Max Beckman Prize, Frankfurt, Ger, 93; Joseph Beuys Prize, Beuys Found, Basel, Switz, 93; The Ludwig Prize, Friends of the Mus of Ludwig, Aachen, 89; The Chevalier of Fine Arts Medal, Ministry of Culture, Paris, France; Art Critics Asn Award, 97; The Kaiserring Trager, Stadt Goslar, 98. *Bibliog:* Jean-Hubert Martin & Claudia Jolles (auths), The Window, Benteli, 85; 68 Installations, Ctr Georges Pompidou, Paris, 95; Amei Wallach (auth), Ilya Kabakov, Abrams (in prep). *Media:* Installation. *Publ:* Contribr, (with Yuri Kuper), 52 Dialogues on the Communal Kitchen, Ateliers

Municipaux d'Artists, Marseille, France; auth, Life of Flies, Cologne, Ger: Kolnischer Kunstverein, Ed Cantz, 92; Five Albums, Mus Contemp Art, Helsinki, Finland, 94; Die Kunst der Installation, Munchen, Akzente Hanser Verlag, 96; Music on the Water, Koln, Walter Konig Verlag, 96; and others. *Mailing Add:* c/o Barbara Gladstone Gallery 515 W 24th St New York NY 10011

KADLEC, KRISTINE
COLLAGE ARTIST, WRITER
b Green Bay, Wis, 53. *Study:* Pasadena City Col, AS, 98. *Exhib:* Weave Collage, Borders Bookstore, Glendale, Calif, 2002; Reuse/Recycle w/Paper Weave Collage, Los Angeles Fine Arts Bldg, Los Angeles, Calif, 2003; Czech into Paper Weave Collage, Consulate of Czech Republic, Westwood, Calif, 2004. *Awards:* Project Grant, Artistic Recycling, Yellow Fox Found, 2002; Project Grant, Reuse/Recycle w/Paper Weave Collage, Puffin Found, 2003; 3rd Place, Casa Verdugo Libr Juried Exhib, Glendale Art Asn, 2003. *Bibliog:* Shannon Wilkinson (auth), Take Charge of your Marketing, Art Calendar Magazine, 2003; Michelle Taute (auth), Collage your way to Creativity, Artist's Sketchbook, 2003; Dian Page (auth), That's Life, Green Bay Press Gazetter, 2004; Scrap & Stamp Arts Magazine, Scott Publications, 2005; Artist's Sketchbook Magazine, F & W Publications, 2005. *Media:* Paper-Weave Collage, Representational. *Publ:* Notions (art), American Sewing Guild, 2000; Artists' Magazine (Art) F & W Publ, 2002; Fiberarts Magazine (Art), Interweave Press, 2005. *Mailing Add:* 1949 N Vermont Ave # 9 Los Angeles CA 90027-1873

KAERICHER, JOHN CONRAD
PRINTMAKER, EDUCATOR
b Springfield, Ill, June 30, 36. *Study:* Millikin Univ with David Driesbach, BFA, 59; Univ Iowa, with Mauricio Lasansky, Stuart Edie, James Lechay & Robert Knipschild, MFA, 63. *Work:* Univ Iowa; Millikin Univ; Dordt Col; Northwestern Col Iowa; plus pvt collections. *Comn:* Medal, Northwestern Col, 66. *Exhib:* Kottler Galleries, NY; Va Polytech Inst Ann; Benjamin Galleries, Chicago; Iowa Printmakers Invitational, Iowa Arts Coun, Des Moines; Maastricht Int Printmaking Bienale, The Neth; selected prints Private Collection of Msters 20th Printmaking, Arkansas State Univ; 32 one-man shows; 115 group shows. *Pos:* Found & gallery dir, Northwestern Col, 63-79 & 81-97, found, bldg dir & coordr permanent collection, Bushmer Art Ctr, 66-. *Teaching:* Prof printmaking & drawing, 63-, chmn art dept, 63-84, rotation chmn art dept, 89-2005 & emeritus prof (art) 6/2005-, Northwestern Col, Iowa. *Awards:* Creative Prod Grants Northwestern Col Iowa, 66, 68, 75, 77, 81, 84 & 94 for sabbatical leaves. *Bibliog:* Rev of NY exhib in Park East Periodical; Kaericher and His Art (video), Television, newspaper articles. *Mem:* Mid-Am Col Art Asn; Iowa Print Group; Northwestern Printmakers. *Media:* Drawing, Printmaking, Intaglio printmaking, drawing. *Publ:* Survey of Iowa Printmakers. *Mailing Add:* 202 Arizona NW Orange City IA 51041

KAGAN, ANDREW AARON
HISTORIAN, CONSULTANT
b St Louis, Mo, Sept 22, 47. *Study:* Wash Univ, AB, 69; Harvard Univ, MA, 71, PhD, 77. *Collection Arranged:* Samuels Collection. *Pos:* Contributing ed, Arts Mag, NY; critic art & architecture, St Louis Globe-Democrat, Mo; consultant, principal, Andrew Kagan, PhD & Assocs. *Teaching:* Critic-in-residence, Bennington Col, Vt, 72-73; vis prof art hist, Wash Univ, St Louis, Mo, 80-81. *Awards:* Ford Found Res Grant. *Bibliog:* Musikforschung, 39, 86; Publ Weekly, 9/20/93; Chronicle of Higher Education, 8/95. *Mem:* Wed Night Soc. *Res:* Paul Klee studies; theory of absolute art; 18th & 20th century art hist, theory, criticism; 19th & 20th century architectural history & criticism. *Interests:* restoring historic bldgs; golf. *Publ:* Marc Chagall, Abbeville, 89; Paul Klee at the Guggenheim Mus, 93; contribr, Dictionary of Art, Grove's/McMillan; Absolute Art, Gottingen, 93, Grenart/Green, 95; and others; Improvisations: Notes on Pollock and Jazz, Avalon, 2000; Paul Klee - Art & Music, 83, 87. *Mailing Add:* 15021 Claymoor Ct Suite 8 Chesterfield MO 63017

KAGEMOTO, HARO
FILMMAKER, PHOTOGRAPHER
b Tokyo, Japan, Jan 9, 1952; US citizen. *Study:* Sch Modern Photog, NJ, cert, 72; Univ Hawaii, Manoa, BFA, 77; State Univ NY, New Paltz, MFA, 79. *Work:* Everson Mus Fine Art, Syracuse, NY; Erie Art Mus, Mich; Libr of Cong, Washington, DC; Calif Mus Photog, Santa Barbara; Guggenheim Mus, NY. *Exhib:* 53rd Ann Nat Acad Design, NY, 78; Selected Works, Woodstock Artists Asn, NY, 79; Prints & Drawing Invitational, Mariam Graves-Mugar Gallery, New London, NH, 81; Leisure Am, Tampa Mus Art, Fla, 83; Classical Photographs, Boston Mus Art, 83; Dada Duchamp Exhib, Colby-Sawyer Col, New London, NH, 83; Alaskan Mail Art Exhib, Ketchikan Arts Coun, 83 & 84; Games 92, St Cloud, Minn, 92; Contained Art, Central Mich Univ, Mt Pleasant, 97; Small Works, Finley Community Ctr, Santa Rosa, Calif, 97; and others. *Pos:* Production mgr & asst dir, Wonderland Productions, San Francisco, 83-88, dir, 89-; contract off, San Francisco State Univ, 2000. *Teaching:* Instr etching-intaglio, Communications Village Ltd, Kingston, NY, 77-79; vis artist photo-silkscreen, Univ Calif, Berkeley, 80-83; vis lectr printmaking, San Francisco State Univ, 83. *Awards:* Charles Eugene Banks Award, Honolulu, Hawaii, 77. *Mem:* Am Film Inst; Am MENSA, San Francisco Mus Modern Art. *Media:* Video Art, Documentary. *Collection:* Everson Museum of Art, Library of Congress, University of Hawaii. *Mailing Add:* 2806 Truman Ave Oakland CA 94605-4847

KAGEMOTO, PATRICIA JOW
PRINTMAKER, PAINTER
b New York, NY, Feb 20, 52. *Study:* Syracuse Univ Sch Art, NY, 70-71; Hunter Col, City of New York, 71-72; State Univ NY, New Paltz, BFA, 75; Printmaking Workshop, New York, studied with Robert Blackburn, 84. *Work:* Collection of Bellevue Hosp, NY; Printmaking Workshop, NY; Calif Mus Photog, Riverside; The Robert Blackburn Printmaking Workshop Collection at the Library of Congress, Washington, DC; and other public, corporate and private collections. *Comn:* Intaglio print eds, Communications Village Ltd, Kingston, NY, 75. *Exhib:* Mohawk-Hudson Regional, Univ Art Gallery, State Univ NY, Albany, 76, Schenectady Mus, 77, Albany Inst Hist & Art, NY, 78; Invitational Art Exhib, Ctr Galleries, Albany, NY, 83; Affirmations of Life, Kenkeleba House, NY, 84; In a Stream of Ink, Col Art Gallery, State Univ NY, & Alumni Printmakers' Invitational, New Paltz, NY, 84; All Media I, Woodstock Artists' Asn, NY, 85 & 91; Games '92, St Cloud, Minn; Contained Art, Cent Mich Univ Art Gallery, Mt Pleasant, 97; Small Works, Finley Comm Ctr, Santa Rosa, Calif, 97; and others. *Pos:* Consult printer, Printmaking Workshop, NY, 84; exhib auditor, NY State Coun Arts, NY, 84-87; gallery asst, Watermark/Cargo Gallery, Kingston, NY, 88-91. *Teaching:* Instr etching & color viscosity, Commun Village Ltd, Kingston, NY, 75-80; vis artist color viscosity printing, State Univ Col, Fredonia, NY 78; dir children's print workshop linocuts, Woodstock Libr, NY, 89. *Awards:* Am the Beautiful Award, Printmaking, Am the Beautiful Fund, 76; First & Second Place Graphics, Sullivan Cult Ctr, Catskill Art Soc, 83; Ulster Co Decentralization Grant, Intaglio Prints, NY State Coun Arts, 89. *Bibliog:* Graphic Arts, Educ Audio Visual Inc, 77; Liam Nelson (auth), Harris and Jow merit High Watermarks, The Daily Freeman, 89; Steven Kolpan (auth), Intaglio dragons, Woodstock Times, 89. *Mem:* Ansel Adams Ctr for Photog; Nat Mus of Women in Arts; San Francisco Mus of Modern Art. *Media:* Color Viscosity Intaglio Prints; Acrylic, Watercolor. *Mailing Add:* 2806 Truman Ave Oakland CA 94605-4847

KAGLE, JOSEPH L, JR
PAINTER, MUSEUM DIRECTOR, ART HISTORIAN
b Pittsburgh, Pa, May 2, 32. *Study:* Carnegie Mus Sch Art, 38-51; Dartmouth Col, AB, 55; Univ Colo, MFA, 58, UALR, MEd, 84. *Hon Degrees:* Tbilisi Fine Arts Acad, Tbilisi, GA, Hon Prof Art, 2002; Mongolia Univ Art & Culture, Hon Prof Art, 2004. *Work:* Southeast Ark Arts & Sci Ctr, Pine Bluff; Alcoa Collection, Pittsburgh; Nat Mus Taiwan, Taipei; Kimon Friar Collection, Athens, Greece; Sanford Besser Collection, Little Rock, Ark; Am Embassy, Tbilisi, Ga. *Comn:* Concrete mural, Hafa Adai Theatre, Agana, Guam, 72-73; mosaic mural, State Arts Coun, Univ Guam, 74; concrete mural, Nat Endowment for Arts, Agana, Guam, 75; acrylic painting, Bank of Guam, Agana, 75; sculptures, comn by lawyer in Guam, 75. *Exhib:* One-man show, US Info Serv Lincoln Ctr, Taipei, Taiwan, 75, Tyler Mus & Art Ctr, Waco, 98; Image of the South Pacific, Nat Mus Taiwan, Taipei, 76; NY State Ann, Arnot Mus, 77; Lakeview Series, Southeast Ark Arts & Sci Ctr, Pine Bluff, 79; retrospective, Hopkins Ctr, Dartmouth Col, Hanover, NH, 80; Prague Tex Exhib, Czech Repub, 94; Arts Ctr of Waco, Tex, 99-2000; Chicago Int Art Exhib, Lincoln Park, 2001; Nat Gal, Tbilisi, GA, 2002 & 03; Red Car Gal, Ulaan-Baatar, Mongolia, 2004. *Collection Arranged:* Buddhist Hell Scrolls (auth, catalog), travel exhib throughout South, 80; John Howard and Friends, group show of minority art, 80; Southeast Ark Arts & Sci Ctr Permanent Collection, 80; Wildlife Collection Ann Exhib, 80; Arkansas Annual, 80; Texas Artists Exhib, 94. *Pos:* Exec dir, Southeast Ark Arts & Sci Ctr, 78-84, Brockton Art Mus, 84-87, Art Ctr Waco, 87-; Freelance, Waco Herald-Tribune, 88-. *Teaching:* Assoc prof art & chmn dept, Keuka Col, Keuka Park, NY, 64-68; assoc prof & artist-in-residence, Wash State Univ, 65-66; assoc prof art, World Campus Afloat, 68-69; prof art & chmn dept, Univ Guam, 70-76, McLennan Community Col, Waco, Tex, 90-2005, Tbilisi State Acad Art, 2001-2002; staff, inst of Art and Culture, Ulaan Baatar, Mongolia, 2004, Kingwood Col, TX, 2006. *Awards:* First Award in Painting, Cheney Cowles Mus, 66; Pac Artist of Yr, Am Inst Architects, Pac Chap, 77; Grant, Found Proj Scholar, 83 & 84; Fulbright Scholar, 2001, Fulbright Specialist, 2003-; Hon Rubait, Georgian Artist Union, Tbilisi; Hon Faculty, State Acad Art, Tbilisi. *Bibliog:* State Council on the Arts Artists of Guam, Nat Endowment for Arts, 74; Getting better all the time, PB Com (Paul Greenberg), 78; Work by J Kagle, Dartmouth Col, 80. *Mem:* Col Art Asn; Am Mus Asn; Southeast Mus Asn; Mid Southern Watercolorists; Tex Asn Mus; Rotary Club Southwest, 2006-; Rotary Global History Fellowship, Peace Historian, 2006-. *Media:* Acrylic, Watercolor, Collage, Pen, Ink, Art Consultant. *Res:* Oceanic Art, Georgian Artists and American Architecture and Painting. *Specialty:* Contemporary Art. *Interests:* Painting, Writing, Museum Consulting, Architecture. *Collection:* Oriental and Modern American Art. *Publ:* Auth, The Twenty-Four Hour Day, China Press, 75; Osiik is Dead, Glimpses, Guam, 76; contribr, The Future is Now, Com Press, 80; auth, Long walks at twilight and dawn, Islands Mag, 80; The good old boy of art, Art Consortium, 80; An American Supra, 2003. *Mailing Add:* 3758 Glade Forest Dr Kingwood TX 77339

KAHAN, ALEXANDER
DEALER, CONSULTANT
Study: State Univ NY. *Pos:* Owner, Alexander Kahan Fine Arts Ltd, New York, currently. *Mem:* Appraisers Asn Am. *Specialty:* Paintings and graphics of 19th and 20th century. *Collection:* Appel, Matta, Dubuffet, De Chirico, Riopelle, Calder, Dufy, Miro, Francis, Chagall, Picasso, Renoir, Marini & Utrillo, Vlaminck, Metzinger & Valtat. *Mailing Add:* 565 West End Ave New York NY 10024

KAHAN, LEONARD
DEALER, PAINTER, ART APPRAISER, CONSULTANT
b Bronx, NY, Jan 21, 35. *Study:* Pratt Inst, BFA, 57; Brooklyn Col, MFA, 64; studied Brooklyn Mus Art Sch, 48, Art Students League, NY, 51-52. *Exhib:* Grand Central Art Gallery, New York City, 55, CCC Gallery, Brooklyn, 55, 58, Pratt Inst, 57, Walt Whitman Gallery, NY, 62, Copland Gallery, Woodstock, NY, 66, 67, Satori Gallery, NYC, 67, Ashby Gallery, New York City, 70, 81, 82, Varsovie Gallery, NYC, 82, 83, Lee Witkin Gallery, New York City, 83, Ledel Gallery, New York City, 83; NJ Ann Photog Contest, 85; Mus Mod Arts, Buenos Aires, Argentina, 90, 91; Otterbein Col Art Gallery, Cleveland, 92; Frederick Clement Gallery, Montclair, NY, 97; Univ Colo Art Gallery, 99; Watermark/Cargo Gallery, Kingston, NY, 2000, 02; Woodlands Gallery, West Orange, NJ, 2002; Angel Orensanz Found Ctr for Arts, New York City, 2002, Printmaking Coun NJ, 2003, Washington Square East Galleries, 2003. *Pos:*

retired owner, L Kahan Gallery, Inc; curator, Queensborough Community Col Art Gallery, Queens, NY, 2003-05. *Teaching:* art lectr, Queens Col, 68-70; art lectr, Brooklyn Col, 63-68; art instr, Brooklyn YMCA, 61-63; asst dir, art instr, Community Cult Ctr, Brooklyn, 56-58. *Mem:* Appraisers Asn Am. *Media:* Acrylic, Collage. *Specialty:* African art. *Mailing Add:* 16 Moran Rd West Orange NJ 07052-2252

KAHAN, MITCHELL DOUGLAS
MUSEUM DIRECTOR, HISTORIAN
b Richmond, Va. *Study:* Univ Va, BA, 73; Columbia Univ, univ fel, 73, MA, 75; City Univ NY Grad Sch, univ fel, 75-76, MPhil, 79, PhD, 83. *Collection Arranged:* Art Inc: American Paintings from Corporate Collections (coauth & ed, catalog), Montgomery Mus & Brandywine Press, 79; American Paintings of the Sixties and Seventies: Selections from the Whitney Museum of American Art (auth, catalog), Montgomery Mus, 80 & Roger Brown (coauth, catalog), 80; Nicholas Africano (auth, catalog), 83 & Heavenly Visions: Art of Minnie Evans (auth, catalog), 86, NC Mus. *Pos:* Cur painting & sculpture, Montgomery Mus Fine Arts, Ala, 78-82; cur Am & contemp art, NC Mus Art, 82-86; dir, Akron Art Mus, 86-; vpres, Intermus Conserv Asn, 88-90, pres 90-92 & 94-95. *Awards:* Helena Rubinstein fel, Whitney Mus Art, 76; Smithsonian fel, Nat Collection Fine Arts & Hirshhorn Mus, 76-78; Nat Endowment fel, 87; Distinguished Mus Prof Award, Ohio Mus Asn, 2003. *Mem:* Col Art Assoc, Intermus Conserv Assoc (trustee 1986-95, pres 1990-92, 95), Asn Art Mus Dirs, Akron Area Arts Alliance (pres 2003-04), Akron Roundtable (pres, 2001). *Res:* American art, contemporary art. *Publ:* Contribr, Robert Colescott: Pride & Prejudice in a Retrospective, San Jose Mus, 87; coauth, Akron Art Museum: Art Since 1850, An Introduction to the Collection, 2001. *Mailing Add:* Akron Art Mus 70 E Market St Akron OH 44308

KAHN, CECILY
PAINTER
Study: Int Sch Graphics, Venice, Italy, 80-81; Calcografia Nazionale, Rome, Italy, 80-81; RI Sch Design, BFA, 81. *Exhib:* Eighteen Graphic Artists in Venice, Segno Grafica Gallery, Italy, 81; Brooklyn in Profile, Pan Arts Gallery, NY, 83; Prints from teh Workshop of Cone Editions, Gallery North, Setauket, NY, 87, Family Lines, 90; NY City Works by 21 Artists, 1 Penn Plaza, NY, 88; Group Show, Blondies Contemp Art, NY City, 91; Beneath teh Surface, Tribeca 148 Gallery, NY, 92; Signs of Life, The Policy Bldg, NY City, 93; Painters Painting II, The Painting Ctr, NY City, 94; Emerging Artists, 1995; All in a Family, the New Britain Mus Am Art, Conn, 97; Maine Debuts Since 79, Maine Coast Artists, Rockport, 97; Small Works, Kendall Art and Design, Hudson, 97; Relatively Speaking: Mothers and Daughters in Art, NewHouse Ctr Contemp Art, Staten Island, 94-97; A Welcome Exchange, Temple Bar Gallery, Dublin Ireland, 99; Dialogue and Discourse, Dolan Ctr Gallery, Long Island, 2001; Rhythmic Renderings, Elsa Mott Eves Gallery, NY, 2002; Inspired by the Land, Attleboro Mus, Mass, 2002; Abstract Dilemmas, Martin Art Gallery, Allentown, Pa, 2002; A Family Affair, Katherina Rich Perlow Gallery, NY City, 2002; Variations: Abstractions X4, 2003; The Gift of Art, 2003; Lohin Geduld Gallery, NY, 2004; A Kaleidoscope of Color: Recent Paintings, Thomas Dean Fine Art, Atlanta, 2005

KAHN, DEBORAH
PAINTER, EDUCATOR
Study: Kans City Art Inst, BFA. *Work:* Hood Mus, Dartmouth Col; Albright-Knox Mus. *Exhib:* Exhibs incl, Bowery Gallery, Les Yeux du Monde, Swarthmore Col, Pierogi 2000, Ruth Siegal Gallery, George Hemphill & David Adamson Galleries. *Teaching:* Asst prof, Am Univ, Wash, DC, 89—; Guest artist, Dartmouth Col, Swathmore Col, RI Sch Design, Chautauqua Sch Art, Nat Women's Mus, Univ IA Sch Art, Vt Studio Ctr. *Awards:* Fel Guggenheim Mem Found, 2004. *Mailing Add:* Am Univ Dept Art Watkins Bldg 116 4400 Massachusetts Ave NW Washington DC 20016

KAHN, KATIE (KATHRYN) ANNA
PAINTER
b Chicago, Ill, Oct 21, 49. *Study:* Univ Chicago, 67-68, Calif Col Arts & Crafts, BFA, 74; Yale Univ Sch Art, MFA, 76. *Exhib:* solo exhibs, Field Gallery, Martha's Vineyard, Mass, 72, 79, 83, Studio I, Oakland, Calif, 73, Leedy-Voulkos Gallery, Kansas City, Mo, 89, Transco Gallery, Houston, 93, Merwin Gallery, Ill Wesleyan Univ, Bloomington, 99, Univ Tex of the Permian Basin, Odessa, 99, Roswell Mus & Art Ctr, NMex, 00, Concordia Gallery, Bronxville, NY, 01, Artemisia Gallery, Chicago, Ill, 03, Gallery 1756, Chicago, 97, 99, 02, Atlantic Gallery, NY, 03; selected group exhibs, Swarthmore Col Art Gallery, 76, Fairweather Hardin Gallery, Chicago, 80, 85, 86, Katherine Lincoln Press, San Francisco, 82, Berkeley Art Ctr, Calif, 83, 84, World Print Coun, San Francisco, 83, Euphrat Gallery, De Anza Col, Cupertino, Calif, 83, 84, 59th & 60th Ann Crocker-Kingsley Exhibs, 84, 85, San Francisco Arts Comn Gallery, 84, Arts Coun of San Mateo, Belmont, Calif, 85, Walnut Creek Civic Art Gallery, Calif, 85, 87, Chabot Col Gallery, Hayward, Calif, 85, Pro Arts, Oakland, Calif, 85, 86, Atlantic Gallery, NY, 86, Col of Lake Co, Grayslake, Ill, Kohler Art Ctr, Sheboygan, Wis, Sonnenshein Gallery, Lake Forest Col, Ill, Adler Cult Ctr, Libertyville, Ill, 86, Alternative Space, Kansas City, Mo, 88, The Watson-Ess Gallery, Kansas City, Mo, 88, Clara Hatton Gallery, Colo State Univ, Ft Collins, 88, Leedy-Voulkos Gallery, Kansas City, Mo, 88, Mark Four Gallery, Lincoln, Nebr, 88, New Gallery Bemis Found, Omaha, 88; Esther Saks Gallery, Chicago, 89, 90, Evanston Art Ctr, Ill, 90, Lawndale Art and Performance Ctr, Houston, 90, 93, Sewall Art Gallery, Rice Univ, Houston, 91, 93, Transco Gallery, Houston, 91, Dolphin Gallery, Kansas City, Mo, 92, Barnes-Blackman Galleries, Houston, 93, Col of Santa Fe Arts Gallery, NMex, 96, Jack Olson Gallery, Northern Ill Univ, DeKalb, 96, West End Gallery, Houston, 96, 97, 98, New Bedford Art Mus, Mass, 97, Northern Ill Univ Art Gallery, Chicago, 98, Beverly Art Ctr, Chicago, 98, Carlson Tower Gallery, N Park Univ, Chicago, 00, Artemisia Gallery, Chicago, 01, Kingsbury St/Stable Studios, Chicago, 02, Atlantic Gallery, NY, 02, 03. *Pos:* juror Ragdale Found, Lake Forest, Ill, 88-91, Kansas City, Art Coalition, Mo, 89, Roswell Mus & Art Ctr, NMex, 00, Artist-in-Residency Program, 96; lectr, workshops, studio visits, panels, critiques, Calif Col Arts & Crafts, Oakland, 85, 86, Univ Calif, Berkeley, 86, Vassar Col, Poughkeepsie, NY, 86, Kansas City Art Inst, Mo, 87, Univ Houston, 91, Rice Univ, Houston, 93, 94, Randolph Macon Women's Col, Lynchburg, Va, 94, Jack Olson Gallery, Northern Ill Univ, DeKalb, 96, 03, Gallery 1756, Chicago, 97, 99, SAIC, Chicago, 97, Ill Wesleyan Univ, Bloomington, 99, Albuquerque Arts Soc, NMex, N Park Univ, Chicago, 00, Concordia Col, Bronxville, NY, 01. *Teaching:* teaching asst, printmaking dept, Calif Col Arts & Crafts, Oakland, 73; instr, Educ Ctr Arts, New Haven, Conn, 75, Blackhawk Mountain Sch Art, Colo, 81, ASUC Studios, Univ Calif, Berkeley, 84-85, San Francisco State Univ, 84 & 85, and Walnut Creek Civic Arts, Calif, 85-87; vis lectr, Rice Univ, 91, 94-95; asst prof, Kansas City Art Inst, Mo, 87-89, spec asst prof, 91-92; assoc prof, Northern Ill Univ, DeKalb, currently. *Awards:* res fel, Ragdale Found, Lake Forest, Ill, 84, Roswell Mus & Art Ctr, NMex, 99-00, Ucross Found, Clearmont, Wyo, 02; fel Yale Summer Sch Music & Art, Norfolk, Conn, 73; nat visual artist grant, Nat Endowment Arts, 93-94. *Bibliog:* WFMT Fine Arts Radio, Chicago, 80; New Art Examiner, 80, 89; Oakland Tribune, 86; Omaha World Tribune, 88; KKFI Radio, Kansas City, Mo, 89; Kansas City Star, 89; Where two realities meet, Southern Accents, 91; Creative partners, Houston Post, 91; The Standard Times, New Bedford, Mass, 97; Gulf Coast, 97; Faces are startling revelations, Chicago Sun Times, 99; Vision Mag, Roswell Daily Record, 99; Abstract paintings that cross barriers of time and place, NY Times, Westchester ed, 01. *Dealer:* Gallery 1756 1756 Sedgewick Chicago IL; Atlantic Gallery, New York. *Mailing Add:* 1759 N Cleveland Ave Chicago IL 60614

KAHN, NED M
ENVIRONMENTAL ARTIST, SCULPTOR
b New York, NY, Feb 16, 60. *Study:* Univ Conn, Storrs, BA, 82. *Work:* NC Mus Life & Sci, Durham; Exploratorium Mus, San Francisco; Parc De La Villette, Paris, France; Saibu Mus Art, Fukouka, Japan; NY Hall Sci, Queens. *Comn:* Regenerating landscape, Wash State Arts Coun, Puyallup, 90; greenhouse proj, San Francisco Arts Comn, 91; Vortex Tower, Liberty Sci Ctr, Liberty Park, NJ, 92; wavespout (breathing sea), City of Ventura, Calif, 93; primordial garden, Chevron Corp, San Francisco, 94. *Exhib:* Multimediale 2, Ctr Art, Karlsruhe, Ger, 91; Rotunda Gallery, Canary Wharf, London, Eng, 92; NC Mus, Durham, 92; Momentum Gallery, Ventura, Calif, 92; Mole Antonelliana, Torino, Italy, 92; and others. *Pos:* Artist-in-residence, Exploratorium Mus, San Francisco, 82-, Headlands Ctr Arts, Calif, 87-88, NY Hall Sci, Queens, 88-89. *Awards:* Sculpture Fel, Nat Endowment Arts, 91; Bernard Osher Cult Award, Jewish Community Endowment, 92; Nat Endowment Arts Award, 94. *Bibliog:* Adam Gopnick (auth), Talk of the town: twister, New Yorker Mag, 11/88; Bruce Weber (auth), Works in progress, New York Times Mag, 3/89; Jeff Greenwald (auth), Local color, SF Mag, 3/90. *Media:* Environmental. *Mailing Add:* 11650 Graton Rd Sebastopol CA 95472

KAHN, ROBIN
CONCEPTUAL ARTIST, COLLAGE ARTIST
b New York, NY, Jan 17, 61. *Study:* Barnard Col, Columbia Univ, BA (art hist), 82; Pratt Inst, MFA, 85. *Work:* Nat Mus Women Arts, Washington. *Comn:* Capsula de Tiempo Cordoba, Seville, Spain, 92; Another Useful Household Product, SOS Int, 94 Capiacabana, Extremadura Spain & NY, 96-97; Capiacabana, Extremadura Spain & NY, 96-97. *Exhib:* Effected Desire, Carnegie Mus Art, Pa, 92; solo exhibs, Aim High & Do Your Best, Jersey City Mus, 93, Kim Light Gallery, Los Angeles, Calif, 94, Susan Inglett Gallery, NY, 95 & 97, Proj Room, Esso Gallery, NY, 98; Bad Girls, New Mus Contempo Art, NY, 94; The Feminine Image, Nassau Co Mus Art, 97; Raise the Roof, White Columns, NY, 98; The Jewel Box, Gaga Gallery, NY, 98; Seeing Money, Rotunda Gallery, Brooklyn, 98; Ha Selections from the Mirth Collection, Terrain Gallery, San Francisco, 98; and others. *Pos:* Organizer & cur prom copy events & performances, SOS Int, 93-94. *Awards:* Fel Grant, Nat Endowment Arts, 87 & 89; Support Grant, Art Matters Inc, 88 & 96; City Grant, Creative Time, NY, 95. *Bibliog:* Elizabeth Hess (auth) She wove a brand New Jersey, Village Voice, 6/93; Ingrid Schaffrer (auth), Reviews: Robin Kahn, Artforum, 2/96; Andrea Codrington (auth), Milking Dada: Robin Kahn, World Art No 2, 96. *Mem:* Founding mem SOS Int; founding mem Agencia de Viaje; 4 Works Found, NY. *Media:* Miscellanous Media. *Publ:* Ed, Spec Issue, 92, Prom Copy, 93, Time Capsule: A Concise Encyclopedia by Women Artists, 95, SOS Int; Reveres of a Spinster, MIS Dias Press, 97. *Dealer:* Susan Inglett 100 Wooster St New York NY 10012. *Mailing Add:* 114 Mercer St New York NY 10012

KAHN, SUSAN B
PAINTER
b New York, NY, Aug 26, 24. *Study:* Parsons Sch Design; also with Moses Soyer. *Work:* Albrecht Gallery Mus, St Joseph, Mo; Montclair Mus, NJ; Butler Inst Am Art, Youngstown, Ohio; Reading Mus, Pa; Joslyn Art Mus, Omaha, Nebr. *Comn:* Two Paintings, M Riklis, chmn Rapid Am Corp, 86-87. *Exhib:* One-person shows, ACA Galleries, NY, 64, 68, 71, 76 & 80, Albrecht Art Mus, St Joseph, Mo, 74 & NY Cult Ctr, 74; Nat Acad Design, 70; Butler Inst Am Art, 73; St Peter's Col Art Gallery, Jersey City, NJ, 78; Heidi Neuhoff Gallery, 89; Sindin Galleries, 956 Madison Ave, 96; ACA Galleries Group Show, 2000; plus others; Tyler Mus, Tex; St Laurence Mus, Univ Mus, Canton, NY; Farleigh Dickinson Mus, Rutherford, NJ; Syracuse Univ Mus, Syracuse, NY; Sheldon Swope Gallery, Terre Haute, IN; Cedar Rapids Art Ctr, IA; Edwin Ulrich Mus, Wichita, KS; Johns Hopkins School of Int Studies, Johns Hopkins Univ, Washington, DC. *Awards:* Nat Arts Club Award, 67; Famous Artists Sch Award, 67 & Anne Barnett Mem Prize, 81, Nat Asn Women Artists; Solveig S Palmer Award, 87; Dorothy Schweitzer Award, 90; Audrey Hope Shirk Mem Award, 117th Ann Nat Assoc Women Artists Show, 2006. *Bibliog:* Marshall Matusow (auth), Art Collectors Almanac, Jerome E Treisman, 65; Lincoln Rothschild (auth), Susan Kahn, Asn Univ

Presses Inc, 80. *Mem:* Artists Equity Asn; Nat Asn Women Artists. *Media:* Oil. *Collection:* Geller Lobel; L Davis Collection; Fabrikant; Strasser; Pack Gilrod; Lipman; Moses Sayer; Chaim Gross; Samuel Gross; many others. *Publ:* Contribr, How to Paint a Prize Winner, 65. *Mailing Add:* 870 United Nations Plaza New York NY 10017

KAHN, TOBI AARON
PAINTER, SCULPTOR
b New York, NY, May 8, 1952. *Study:* Hunter Col, New York, BA(summa cum laude), 76; Pratt Inst, New York, MFA, 78. *Work:* Solomon R Guggenheim Mus, Jewish Mus & Swiss Bank Corp, NY; Ft Wayne Mus, Ind; Nat Gallery Art, Washington, DC; Houston Mus Art. *Comn:* Paintings, Mitchell & Co, Boston, 85; painting, First City Corp, NY, 86; sculptures for set designs, Solomons Dance Co, 88, Muna Iseng Dance Proj, Elizabeth Swados, 90; sculpture, Robert Lee Blaffer Trust For New Harmony, Ind, 93. *Exhib:* A View of Nature, Aldrich Mus, Ridgefield, Conn, 86; The New Romantic Landscape, Whitney Mus Am Art, Stamford, Conn, 87; Art on Paper, Weatherspoon Art Gallery, Greensboro, NC, 88; Golem Danger, Deliverance & Art, Jewish Mus, NY, 88; Contemp Landscapes: Five views, Waterworks Visual Arts Ctr, Salisbury, Va; Eco-92, Mus Mod Art, Rio de Janeiro, Brazil, 92; solo shows, Thomson Gallery, Minneapolis, Minn, 93, Mary Ryan Gallery, NY, 93 & Allene Lapides Gallery, Santa Fe, NMex, 94; Metamorphoses, Houston Mus Fine Art, Tex, 97-99; Landscape at the Millennium, Albright-Knox Art, Buffalo, NY, 2000; plus others. *Teaching:* Lectr, Sch Visual Arts, NY, 86-. *Bibliog:* Douglas Dreishpoon (auth), Tobi Kahn, the essence of vision, Arts Mag, 1/85; Michael Brenson (auth), article, New York Times, 11/6/87; Susan Kandel & Elizabeth Hayt-Adkins (coauths), article, Art News, 1/88; Holland Cotter (auth), Tiobi Kahn, New York Times, 11/26/93; Susan Kleinman (auth), Blending modern art with objects of the spirit, New York Times, 4/26/2000; Jeff Daniel (auth), Kahn's works reflect the sea and the sky, but they're not landscapes, Saint Louis Dispatch, 3/29/98; Tobi Kahn: Correspondence, Edwin A Ulrich Mus of Art, 2000. *Mem:* Col Art Asn. *Media:* Acrylic; Wood, Bronze. *Dealer:* Harmon-Meek Gallery 601 5th Ave South Naples, FL 34102; Hoops - Epstein Galleries 2631 Colquitty Houston Texas 77098. *Mailing Add:* 1223 Jackson Ave Long Island City NY 11101-5501

KAHN, WOLF
PAINTER
b Stuttgart, Ger, Oct 4, 27. *Study:* New Sch Social Res, with Stuart Davis; Hans Hofmann Sch; Univ Chicago, BA, 51. *Work:* Whitney Mus Am Art, Mus Mod Art & Metrop Mus Art, NY; Houston Mus Fine Arts; Los Angeles Co Mus Art, Calif; Brooklyn Mus, NY; Asheville Art Mus, Asheville, NC; Nat Bank Tulsa, Tulsa, Okla; Port Authority NY & NJ; Summit Art Ctr, Summit, NJ; Transamerica Corp, Charlotte, NC. *Comn:* Portraits, Jewish Theological Sem, NY, 67 & 68; landscape, comn by Young Smith, Litchfield Plantation, SC, 70; The Four Seasons, AT&T Hq, NY, 85; 2000 K Street, Washington, 87; Designed First Day of Issue for UN Philatelic Collection, 92; The Atlantic Golf Club, Bridgehampton, NY, 95; Color etching comn by the Am Acad & Inst Arts & Letters for their 100th Anniversary. *Exhib:* Whitney Mus Am Art, 57, 58, 60, 61 & 77; Albright-Knox Art Gallery, 58; Pa Acad Fine Arts, 61 & 65; Dallas Mus Art, 62; Students of Hans Hoffmann, Mus Mod Art, NY, 63; Am Places, Corcoran Gallery Art, 79; Recent Acquisitions, Metrop Mus Art, NY, 79-80; The Janss Collection, San Francisco Mus Mod Art, 85; solo shows, Stremmel Gallery, Reno, Nev, 95, Grace Borgenicht Gallery, NY, 95, Boca Raton Mus Art, Fla (traveling to Butler Inst Am Art), 96, Vered Gallery, East Hampton, NY, 96 & D C Moore Gallery, NY, 96; Color, Brattleboro Mus, Vt, 95; Inaugural Exhib, DC Moore Gallery, 95; Pastels by Ten Contemp Artists, DC Moore Gallery, NY, 96; Contemp Directions, Abstraction & Realism, Jacqueline Holmes & Assoc Inc, Jacksonville, Fla, 96; solo, Ameringer / Yohe Fine Art, Boca Raton, Fla, 2002-2003, New York, NY, 2003-2004; Mus fur Kunst und Gewerbe, Hamburg, Ger, 2001; Ogden Mus Southern Art, New Orleans, 2006; Westport Arts Ctr, Westport, Conn, 2004; Provincetown Art Asn & Mus, 2006; group, Invited! Works on Paper, First St Gallery, New York, NY, 2001; Holiday Group Exhib, Lisa Kurts Gallery, Memphis, Tenn, 2002; Jerald Melburg Gallery, Inc, Charlotte, NC, 84-96 & 2005; Hans Hofmann: The Legacy, The Painting Ctr, New York, NY, 2005; AmericanMasters, Recent Acquisitions, Marianne Friedland Gallery, Naples, Fla, 2006. *Teaching:* Vis assoc prof painting, Univ Calif, Berkeley, 60-61; adj assoc prof painting, Cooper Union, NY, 60-77; artist-in-residence, Dartmouth Col, 84. *Awards:* Guggenheim Fel, 67-68; Hassam Fund Purchase Award, Am Acad & Inst Arts & Lett, 79; Ranger Fund Purchase, Nat Acad Design, 79; Prize, Nat Acad Design, 87; Am Artist Achievement Award, 93; Lifetime Achievement Award, Vt Coun on the Arts, 98; Hon Degree Dr Fine Arts, Wheaton College, 2000. *Bibliog:* David Pagel (auth), Wolf Kahn at Babeor, Art & Auction, 9/94; Justin Spring (auth), Wolf Kahn, Abrams Publ, New York, 96; Autumn's artist, CBS Sunday Morning, 10/20/96. *Mem:* Nat Acad Design; Am Acad & Inst Arts & Lett (trustee). *Media:* Oil, Pastel. *Publ:* Connecting incongruities, Art Am, 11/92; gently down the stream, Art New Eng, 10-11/93; Wolf Kahn Paints the South, Morris Mus, Augusta, Ga, 99; Mus Fuer Kunst und Gewerbe, Hamburg, Ger, 00; Wolf Kahn Pastels, Abrams Publ, New York, 2000; Wolf Kahn's America, Abrams Publ, New York City, 2003; auth, Stout Shines at BMAC Show, Brattleboro Reformer, 9/21/2000; auth, Artist's Notebook: Belgium, Travel & Leisure, 9/2000; auth, A Reader's Response to Life at the Vermont Studio School, The Brooklyn Rail, 12/2003-1/2004; auth, Allan Kaprow (1927-2006), The Brooklyn Rail, 5/2006. *Dealer:* Reynolds Gallery Richmond Va; Thomas Segal Gallery Baltimore MD; Ameringer Yohe Fine Art New York NY; Jerald Melberg Gallery Charlotte NC; Marianne Friedland Gallery Naples Fla; Addison Ripley Fine Art Washington DC; Stremmel Gallery Reno Nev

KAIDA, TAMARRA
PHOTOGRAPHER
b Lienz, Austria, 46. *Study:* Goddard Col, Plainfield, Vt, BA, 74; State Univ NY, Buffalo, MFA, 79. *Work:* Ctr Creative Photog, Tucson, Ariz; Int Mus Photog, George Eastman House, Rochester, NY; Santa Fe Mus Fine Arts, NMex; Mus Mod Art, NY; Polaroid Corp, Cambridge, Mass; and others. *Exhib:* Curator's Choice, Lieberman and Saul Gallery, NY, 89; Current Works, Gallery Kansas City Artists Coalition, Mo, 89; group show, Anderson Ranch Arts Ctr, Aspen, Colo, 89; solo exhib, Fine Arts Gallery, Rhode Island Sch Design, 89 & OPSIS Found Gallery, NY, 90; Arizona Photographs: The Snell and Wilmer Collection, Ctr Creative Photog, 90; Photog Book US, 91. *Collection Arranged:* Contemporary European Portraiture, Northlight Gallery, Ariz State Univ, Tempe, 83; Mixed Signals: Photographs with Text (co-cur Rod Slemmons), Northlight Gallery, Ariz State Univ, Tempe, 88. *Pos:* Asst dir educ dept, Int Mus Photog at George Eastman House, Rochester, NY, 76-79. *Teaching:* Vis lectr, Ariz State Univ, 79-80, asst prof, 80-85, assoc prof, 85-; prof, Sch Art, Katherine K Herberge Col Fine Arts, Tempe, Ariz. *Awards:* Fel, Nat Endowment Arts, 86; Photography Fel, Ariz Comn Arts. *Publ:* Coauth (with Rita Dove), The Other Side of the House, Pyracantha Press, Ariz State Univ Sch Art, 88; auth, Tremors from the Faultline, Visual Studies Workshop Press, 89. *Dealer:* Califia Books San Francisco CA. *Mailing Add:* PO Box 139 UBUD Gianyar Bali Indonesia 80571

KAIMAN, CHARLES
PAINTER
b New York, NY, July 12, 47. *Study:* Art Students League New York, with Edwin Dickinson, Jean Liberte & Sol Wilson, 60-66; New York Univ, BS, 69; study with Joseph De Martini & Gerritt Hondius. *Work:* Exodus, Arden Heights Blvd Jewish Ctr, Staten Island, NY. *Exhib:* Solo exhibs, AAA Gallery, Detroit, Mich, 72 & Roko Gallery, NY, 75; Allied Artists Ann, NY, 75 & 77; Jersey City Mus, NJ, 78; Audubon Artists Ann, NY, 81; Recent Paintings, Prince Street Gallery, NY, 82, Blue Mountain Gallery, 84, 87, 88, 90, 92, 94, 97 & 98 & Wesleyan Col, 97. *Pos:* Treas, Prince St Gallery, 81-83 & Blue Mountain Gallery, 88-. *Bibliog:* Staten Island Advance, 98. *Media:* Oil, Watercolor

KAINEN, JACOB
PAINTER, PRINTMAKER
b Waterbury, Conn, Dec 7, 09. *Study:* Art Students League, with Nicolaides, 26; NY Univ Eve Sch Archit, 36-38; Pratt Inst, grad, 30; Corcoran Sch Art, hon DFA, 92. *Work:* Whitney Mus Am Art, Metrop Mus Art & Mus Mod Art, NY; Art Inst Chicago; Phillips Collection, Nat Gallery Art, Nat Mus Am Art, Washington; Hirshhorn Mus & Sculpture Garden; Addison Gallery Am Art; and many others. *Comn:* Mixed media color print, Smithsonian Assocs, Cleveland Print Club, 77; Floor medallion, Nat Airport, Washington, 94. *Exhib:* Corcoran Gallery Art Painting Biennial, 57; one-man shows, Roko Gallery, NY, 64-66, Pratt Manhattan Ctr, NY, 72, Lunn Gallery, Washington, 76-79 & 81-82; Print Retrospective, Nat Collection Fine Arts, Baltimore Mus Art, 76-77; Jacob Kainen, Five Decades as Painter, Nat Collection Fine Arts, 79; Nancy Drysdale Gallery, Washington, 91; Painting Retrospective, Nat Mus Am Art, Addison Gallery Am Art, Andover, Mass, Equitable Gallery, NY 93-94; Print Retrospective, Portland Mus Art, Ore, 93-94. *Bibliog:* Jacob Kainen (film), Nat Mus Art, Smithsonian Inst, 82; Harry Rand (auth), Jacob Kainen, Arts Mag, 83; William C Agee & Avis Berman (coauth), Jacob Kainen, retrospective catalog with 100 color reproductions. *Media:* Oil. *Mailing Add:* 27 W Irving St Chevy Chase MD 20815

KAINO, GLENN
SCULPTOR
Exhib: Group shows include Whitney Biennial, Whitney Mus Am Art, 2004; The Bronx Mus Art; Studio Mus, Harlem; Walker Arts Ctr; Int Film Festival Rotterdam. *Pos:* Co-founder, Deep River Gallery, LA; head programming and creative dir, Universal Music Group and Sony Music Entertainment joint venture; chief creative officer, Napster, formerly; exec vpres creative and online, IMF: The International Music Feed, 2006-. *Teaching:* Prof, UCLA and Univ Southern Calif, formerly. *Mailing Add:* IMF: The International Music Feed 2220 Colorado Ave Santa Monica CA 90404

KAISER, BENJAMIN
SCULPTOR, DESIGNER
b Tel Aviv, Israel, July 2, 43; US citizen. *Study:* San Jose State Univ, BA, 77, MFA, 79. *Work:* Mus Contemp Art in Glass, Valencia, Spain; City Palo Alto, City San Jose, Calif. *Comn:* Fountain, Villa Monterey Country Club, Phoenix, 82; glass panels, Rolm Corp, San Jose, Calif, 83. *Exhib:* New Glass Int Exhib, Corning Mus Art, 79; Contemp Glass: Australia, Canada, USA and Japan, Nat Mus Mod Art, Kyoto & Tokyo, Japan, 81; Int Directions in Glass Art, Art Gallery Western Austalia, Perth, 82; Sculptural Glass, Tucson Mus Art, 83; Vicointer 83, Mus Contemp Art in Glass, Valencia, Spain, 83. *Teaching:* Instr glass-blowing, Bezalel Acad Art & Design, Jerusalem, 72-74. *Media:* Glass, Stainless Steel. *Mailing Add:* 9209 Wollaston Way Elk Grove CA 95624

KAISER, CHARLES JAMES
PAINTER, GRAPHIC ARTIST
b Milwaukee, Wis, Mar 10, 39. *Study:* Layton Sch Art, Milwaukee; Univ Wis, Milwaukee, BFA, MS & MFA; painting with John Colt, Robert Burkert & Laurence Rathsack. *Work:* Wustum Mus, Racine, Wis; Union Art Gallery, Univ Wis, Milwaukee; Civic Art Collection, Munic Bldg, Springfield, Ill; Marquette Univ & Miller Brewing Co Corp, Milwaukee. *Comn:* Portrait, Pres of Mount Mary Col, Milwaukee, Wis, 82. *Exhib:* Five shows, Watercolor USA, Springfield, Mo, 62-72; Northwest Miss Valley Artists Invitational, Ill State Mus, Springfield, 66; Calif Nat Watercolor Soc, Laguna Beach, 70 & 72-73; Exhib Contemp Am Painting, Palm

Beach, Fla, 70; Chicago & Vicinity, Chicago Art Inst, 71; Wis Directions, 75 & 78, Wis Artists Make Toys, 79 & Drawing: The Fundamental Art, 81, Milwaukee Art Mus. *Teaching:* Prof art, Mount Mary Col, 73-. *Awards:* Calif Nat Watercolor Soc Purchase Award, Butrijamp Found, 70; Madison Salon Graphic Art Drawings & Prints Award, Wis State J; Wis Watercolor Soc Award for Excellence, 71. *Media:* Oil, Watercolor; Prismacolor Pencil. *Publ:* Phyllis Carey (ed), Wagering on Transcendence, Cover Illus, Sheed and Ward, 97; cover illus, Gaylord Nelson (intro), Celebrating Door County's Wild Places, Prairie Oak Press, 2001. *Mailing Add:* 5028 N Diversey Blvd Milwaukee WI 53217

KAISER, DIANE
SCULPTOR, EDUCATOR
b Brooklyn, NY, May 27, 46. *Study:* Brandeis Univ, BA(Hon Scholar); Columbia Univ, MFA; additional study with Peter Grippe & Sahl Swarz. *Work:* Columbia Univ; Inst for Advanced Study. *Comn:* Amherst Arts Lottery, 90 & 92; Westwood Arts Lottery, 95; Westwood Educ Found, 96 & 98. *Exhib:* Contemp Reflections, Aldrich Mus Contemp Art, Ridgefield, Conn, 75; Mus Fine Arts, Springfield, Mass, 81; 14 Sculptors Gallery, NY, 85; Outdoor Sculpture of Chesterwood, Mass, 86-87; Outdoor Sculpture of Stamford Mus & Nature Ctr, Conn, 88; solo exhib, Mus Fine Arts, Springfield, Mass, 89; Outdoor Sculpture at Bradley Palmer State Park, Mass, 92; and others; Outdoor Sculpture installation, Duxbury Art Complex, 97. *Collection Arranged:* Drawings & prints, independent exhib prog, Comt Visual Arts Inc, New York, 77; The Living Room: sculpture and furniture, 14 Sculptors Gallery, New York, 86. *Teaching:* Chmn & instr art dept, Chapin Sch, New York, 70-79, St Hilda's & St Hugh's Sch, New York, 90-; vis artist, Dwight-Englewood Sch, NJ, 76; instr, Northfield-Mount Hermon Sch, Northfield, Mass, 79-80; lectr art dept, Smith Col, Northampton, Mass, 80-83; asst prof art, Elms Col, Chicopee, Mass, 90-94; dir art, Westwood Pub Schs, Mass, 94-; instr advanced placement art, Fitchburg State Col Prof Develop Ctr, 1999-. *Awards:* MacDowell Colony Fel, 73; Teachers Fel, Skidmore Col, 97. *Mem:* Col Art Asn; Mass Dirs Art Educ; Nat Art Educ Asn. *Media:* Clay, Wood. *Publ:* Contribr, Children, Clay & Sculpture. *Mailing Add:* 15 Fairview Rd Canton MA 02021

KAISER, S(HARON) BURKETT
PAINTER
b 46. *Study:* Calif State Univ, Northridge, 64-65, San Diego, BA, 69; Brandes Art Inst, 82-83; Calif Art Inst, 84-88, study with Russ Sergei Bongart, 82-85; studies with Charles Movalli, 93-98. *Work:* Princess Cruise Lines. *Exhib:* Art Expo, Los Angeles, Calif, 91; Tokyo Inst Art Show, Japan, 92; California Art Club-85 Yrs of Art, Carnegie Art Mus, Oxnard, Calif, 94; Calif Heritage Gallery, San Francisco, 96; one woman show, Premier Gallery, Fredricksberg, Va, 96; and many other one-person & group shows. *Bibliog:* Molly Siple (auth), article, Calif Art Club Newslett, 1/95; M Stephen Doherty (auth), Creative Oil Painting, Rockport Publ; Oil highlights, Am Artist, 96. *Mem:* Signature mem Calif Art Club. *Media:* Oil. *Dealer:* Colville Publishing 2909 Oregon Court Torrance CA 90503

KAISER, VITUS J
PAINTER
b Erie, Pa, May 3, 29. *Study:* NC State Col; Veterans Sch, Erie, with Joseph Plavcan; Univ Pittsburgh. *Work:* Erie Pub Libr. *Exhib:* Am Drawing Biennial, Norfolk Mus, Va, 71; Albright-Knox Art Gallery, Mem Gallery, Buffalo, 72; Butler Inst Am Art, 73; Am Drawings III, Portsmouth, Va, 80; Am Drawings, Smithsonian Inst traveling exhib, 81; and others. *Mem:* Erie Art Mus; Soc Watercolor Painters Pa; NPAA; and others. *Media:* Multimedia. *Interests:* Painting & Drawing. *Mailing Add:* 551 W 26th St Erie PA 16508

KAISH, LUISE
SCULPTOR, PAINTER
b Atlanta, Ga. *Study:* Syracuse Univ, with Ivan Mestrovic, BFA & MFA; Escuela de Pintura y Escultura, Mexico City, Mex; Taller Grafico. *Work:* Whitney Mus Am Art, NY; Jewish Mus, NY; Rochester Mem Art Gallery, NY; Smithsonian Inst; Metrop Mus Art, NY; Nat Mus Am Art, Washington. *Comn:* Ark of Revelations (bronze), Temple B'rith Kodesh, Rochester; Great Ideas of Western Man & Walter Paepke Award Sculpture, Container Corp Am; Christ in Glory (bronze), Holy Trinity Mission Sem, Silver Spring, Md; ark doors, menorahs, eternal light (bronze), Temple Beth Shalom, Wilmington, Del; Continental Grain Co, NY. *Exhib:* Sculpture USA, Metrop Mus Art, NY; Recent Sculpture USA, Mus Mod Art, NY; Albright-Knox Mus, Buffalo; Hopkins Ctr, Dartmouth Col, Hanover, NH; Whitney Biennials, Whitney Mus Am Art, NY; one-man shows, Minn Mus Art, Staempfli Gallery, NY, Rochester Mem Art Gallery & Jewish Mus, NY; plus others. *Pos:* Artist-in-residence, Hopkins Ctr, Dartmouth Col; vis artist, Univ Wash, Seattle & Univ Haifa, Israel. *Teaching:* Prof sculpture, Columbia Univ, NY, 80-93, chmn div painting & sculpture, 80-86, emer prof, 93-. *Awards:* Guggenheim Fel Creative Sculpture; Louis Comfort Tiffany Grant Creative Sculpture; Rome Prize Fel in Sculpture, Am Acad, Rome; Arents Pioneer Medel, Syracuse Univ. *Bibliog:* Roger Lipsey (auth), An Art of Our Own, the Spiritual in Twentieth Century Art, Shambhala, 88; Gerrit Henry (auth), Luise Kaish: A Lyrical Essay Vol 62 No 7, Arts Mag, 3/88; Charlotte Streifer Rubinstein (auth), American Women Sculptors: a history of women working in three dimensions, GK Hall, 90. *Mem:* Century Asn; Am Acad in Rome (emer trustee, currently); Nat Acad Design. *Media:* All. *Dealer:* Kaish Studios 610 W End Ave Apt 9A New York NY 10024. *Mailing Add:* 610 W End Ave Apt 9A New York NY 10024

KAISH, MORTON
PAINTER, EDUCATOR
b Newark, NJ, Jan 8, 27. *Study:* Syracuse Univ, BFA; Acad de la Grande Chaumiere, Paris; Ist d'Arte, Florence; Acad delle Belle Arti, Rome. *Work:* Brooklyn Mus, NY; British Mus, London; Whitney Mus Am Art; Metrop Mus, NY; Nat Mus Arts, Smithsonian Inst, Washington, DC. *Exhib:* Young Am Printmakers, Mus Mod Art, NY, 53; one-man shows, Staempfli Gallery, NY, 64-89, New Sch Social Res, 74 & Hollis Taggart Galleries, NY, 93-96; Art Inst Chicago, 64; Whitney Mus Ann Am Painting, 66; Am Inst Arts & Lett, 66, 73 & 74; US Info Serv, Italy, 72; Minn Mus Art, 75; Springfield Mus Art, 75; Taft Mus, 82; USIA Jerusalem, Israel, 85. *Teaching:* Prof painting & drawing, Fashion Inst Technol, State Univ NY, 73-; instr, New Sch, 74-77 & Art Students League, 74-82; artist-in-residence, Dartmouth Col, 74 & Univ Haifa, Israel, 85; vis prof, Queens Col, 79, Univ Wash, Seattle, 79 & Boston Univ, 87; vis artist, Columbia Univ, 86; FIT, Univ Florence, 90-. *Awards:* Appointed: New York State Univ Fac Exchange Scholar, 87; Benjamin Altman Landscape Prize, Nat Acad Design, 89; Andrew Carnegie Prize, Nat Acad Design, 92. *Bibliog:* R Bass (auth), article, Art News 11/83; R Martin (auth), article, Arts Mag, 11/86; S Doherty (auth), article, Am Artist, 12/93. *Mem:* Academican Nat Acad Design; Artists Fel; Century Asn. *Media:* Oil, Acrylic. *Dealer:* Hollis Taggart Gallery 48 E 73 St New York NY 10021; Irving Gallery Palm Beach FL. *Mailing Add:* 610 West End Ave New York NY 10024

KAKAS, CHRISTOPHER A
PRINTMAKER, PAINTER
b Dayton, Ohio, Dec 11, 41. *Study:* Miami Univ, Ohio, BFA, 66; Univ Iowa, MA, 68, MFA, 69. *Work:* Minneapolis Inst Art; Sheldon Mem Art Gallery, Univ Nebr, Lincoln; Mus Art & Archit, Univ Mo, Columbia; Cleveland Mus Art, Ohio; Rockford Col, Ill; and others. *Exhib:* Metrop Mus, Coral Gables, Fla, 80; Univ SDak, Vermillion, 80; one-man shows, Hiestand Art Gallery, Miami Univ, Oxford, Ohio, 80, Montgomery Mus Fine Arts, Ala, 82 & Sarratt Gallery, Vanderbilt Univ, Nashville, Tenn, 86; Rockford Int, Rockford Col, 83; 40th NAm Print Exhib, Brockton, Mass, 88; Biennial Exhib Contemp Southern Art, Huntsville, Ala, 88; Artists Proof, 89; Greenville Mus Art, NC, 89. *Teaching:* Asst prof, Syracuse Univ, NY, 75-76; asst prof art, Western Ky Univ, Bowling Green, 76-78; assoc prof, printmaking, Univ Ala, Tuscaloosa, 78-. *Awards:* Purchase Awards, 1st Ann Nat Print Exhib, San Diego State Univ, 68, 2nd Ann Nat Print Exhib, Ga Comn Arts, 71 & 4th Annual Nat Print Exhib, Moravian Col, 85; Award, Rockford Int, 83; Award, 6th Alabama Works on Paper, 85. *Mem:* Col Art Asn; Los Angeles Printmaking Soc; Southern Graphics Coun. *Media:* Intaglio, Lithograph; Gouache, Acrylic. *Dealer:* Miriam Perlman Inc Lake Point Tower Suite 1902 505 N Lake Shore Dr Chicago IL 60611; Maralyn Wilson Gallery 2010 Cahaba Rd Birmingham AL 35223. *Mailing Add:* Univ Ala Dept of Art PO Box 870270 Tuscaloosa AL 35487-0270

KALB, MARTY JOEL
PAINTER, EDUCATOR
b Brooklyn, NY, Apr 13, 41. *Study:* Mich State Univ, BA, 63; Yale Univ, BFA, 64; Univ Calif, Berkeley, MA, 66. *Work:* Klutnick Nat Jewish Mus, Washington; Metrop Mus Art, NY; Cleveland Mus Art, Ohio; Libr Cong, Washington; JB Speed Art Mus, Louisville; and many others. *Exhib:* Nat Drawing Competition Gallery, 84, NY, 95; Witness & Legacy, Contemp Art about the Holocaust, Columbus Mus Art, Ohio, 95; Invitational Survey Painting, Columbus, Ohio, 95; 171st Ann Exhib, Nat Acad Design, NY, 96; Nat Mid Yr Exhib, Butler Inst Am Art, 97 & 2002; Ind Univ, 98; Mus Art South Bend, Ind, 99; Fla Holocaust Mus, St Petersburg, 2000; Sinclair Col, Dayton, Ohio, 2003. *Teaching:* Instr, Univ Ky, 66-67; assoc prof painting, Ohio Wesleyan Univ, 67-81, prof, 81-. *Awards:* Chess Award for Drawing, Columbus Art League, 91; Steidel Award for Visual Arts, Columbus Art League, 96; Fabri Prize for Graphic Work, Nat Acad Design, 96. *Bibliog:* Numerous articles in NY Times, Dialogue & Columbus Dispatch; M Baigell (auth), Jewish American Artists and the Holocaust; The Holocaust's Ghost: Writings on Art Politics, Law and Education. *Mem:* Col Art Asn Am; Ohio Art League. *Media:* Acrylic, Pastel. *Publ:* feature story, Art of Our Time, Dayton Art Inst, 87; review, The Photographs of Joseph Albers, Allen Mem Art Mus, 1/3/88; rev, Art in Europe and America, Wefner Ctr, Ohio State Univ, 5/90; auth, New Currents, Recent Art in Spain, Riffe Gallery Col, Ohio; Labyrinth of the Spirit, Smithson, Fox, Viola, Serrano, Lancaster, Ohio. *Dealer:* Art Access 540 S Drexel Ave Columbus OH 43209. *Mailing Add:* 165 Griswold St Delaware OH 43015

KALINA, RICHARD
PAINTER, PRINTMAKER
b New York, NY, May 21, 46. *Study:* Univ Pa, BA, 66. *Work:* Indianapolis Mus Art; Norton Gallery Art, Palm Beach, Fla; Lehman Brothers Kuhn Loeb, Inc & NY Univ, NY; Amstar Corp; Pa Acad Fine Arts; and others. *Exhib:* Solo exhibs, O K Harris Gallery, NY & Jack Glenn Gallery, Los Angeles, 70, Tibor de Nagy Gallery, NY, 79, 80, 82 & 84, Piezo Electric (with catalog), NY, 86 & 87, Elizabeth McDonald Gallery, NY, 88-89, Diane Brown Gallery & Ledis Flam Gallery, 92 & Lennon, Weinberg Gallery, NY, 93, 95, 98, 2001, 2003 & 2006; Sidney Janis Gallery, NY, 90; Lennon Weinberg Gallery, NY, 92; Pamela Auchincloss Gallery, NY, 92; Diane Brown Gallery, NY, 92; and others. *Pos:* sr critic, Yale Univ; vpres & bd dir, Int Asn Art Critics, USA sect; contrib ed, Art in Am. *Teaching:* Lectr, Art New York City Prog, State Univ NY, 77, Montclair State Col, 91 & Yale Univ, Norfolk, Conn, 91; painting panel discussion, NY, 79 & Morton G Neumann Family Found, NY, 80; panel discussion, Sch Visual Arts, NY, 81, New Sch, 88, Hunter Col, 89 & Inst Contemp Art, PS1, 90; sem, Aspen Inst Humanistic Studies, Baca, Colo, 82; studio lectr, Bates Col, 89 & Drew Univ, 90; art hist fac, Bennington Col, Vt, 89-90, panel discussion, 91; artist-in-residence, Fordham Univ, Col Lincoln Ctr, NY, 90, chmn dept theatre and visual arts, prof studio art & art hist, 90-; vis artist, Glassel Sch Art, Houston Mus Art, Tex, 91 & New York Univ, Grad Sch Art, 91. *Awards:* Visual Arts Fel, Nat Endowment Arts, 92. *Bibliog:* Robert C Morgan (auth), The new end game, 1-3/92 & Alain Kirili (auth), Interview with Richard Kalina, 4-5/92; Steven Henry Madoff (auth), A new lost generation, Art News, 4/92; Richard Kalina, Bomb, winter 92. *Media:* Oil on Canvas. *Publ:* Imagining the Present: Context, Content & the Role of the Critic, Routledge Press, London & NY, 2006; contribr ed, Art in America. *Mailing Add:* 44 King St New York NY 10014-4960

KALISH, HOWARD
SCULPTOR
Study: Cooper Union Art Sch; NY Studio Sch. *Exhib:* Solo shows at Bowery Gallery, NY, 73, 75, Armstrong Gallery, NY, 87, Denise Bibro Fine Art, NY, 2001; group shows at Bowery Gallery, NY, 70, 94; State Univ NY, Albany, 70; First Street Gallery, NY, 73; Green Mountain Gallery, NY, 77; Prince Street Gallery, NY, 77; Pratt Manhattan Ctr, NY, 80; Kent State Univ Art Gallery, 81; Gallery 120, NY, 81; 55 Mercer Street Gallery, NY, 81; Nat Acad Design, NY, 82; Sculpture Ctr, NY, 82; Queens Mus, NY, 83; Sutton Gallery, NY, 83; Artists Choice Mus, NY, 84; Henry Street Settlement House, NY, 88; Sculptors Guild, NY, 90; 110 Green Street, NY, 91; Cast Iron Gallery, NY, 91, 93, 95; Kyoto Art Gallery, Japan, 93; Chesterwood Mus, Stockbridge, Mass, 94, 98, 99, 2000; Lever House, NY, 94; Union League Gallery, NY, 95; Lycoming Col, Williamsport, Pa, 95; FFS Gallery, NY, 95; Stamford Mus, Conn, 96; Williamsburg Art and Historical Ctr, Brooklyn, 97; Fordham Univ, Lincoln Ctr, NY, 97; Calif State Univ, Art Gallery, Fullerton, 97; Vedanta Gallery, Chicago, 99, 2000; Long Beach Island Found for Arts, Loveladies, NJ, 99; Waterside Gallery, W Stockbridge, Mass, 2000; Art Ctr of the Capitol Region, Troy, NY, 200; Wyndy Morehead Fine Arts, New Orleans, La, 2001. *Pos:* Exec bd mem Sculptors Guild, NY; bd dirs Artists Choice Mus, NY. *Teaching:* Prof, Nat Acad, NY, NYU, Nassau County Mus Art Sch, Roslyn, NY, Brooklyn Mus Art Sch; vis artist Kent State Univ, Ohio. *Awards:* Nat Endowment for Arts Sculpture Grant. *Mem:* Nat Acad (acad, 2004). *Media:* pigmented cement, steel, bronze. *Mailing Add:* PO Box 220088 Brooklyn NY 11222

KALISHER, SIMPSON
PHOTOGRAPHER
b New York, NY, July 27, 26. *Study:* Ind Univ, BA, 48. *Comn:* photo essay, refugee camp in Lavrion, Greece, Intergovernmental Commission for Europ Migration (ICEM), 56; one yr grant for photog essay Syracuse, NY, NY Coun on the Arts, 68-72; various corp including PepsiCo, Phillip Morris, IBM, AT&T, and others. *Exhib:* Four Directions in Photog, Albright-Knox Art Gallery, 64; Hist of the Picture Story, Mus Mod Art, NY, 67; Harlem on My Mind, Metrop Mus Art, NY, 68; Photog in Am, Whitney Mus, 75; Mirrors and Windows, Mus Mod Art, NY, 78 & traveling, 78-80; Discovering Am, Art Inst Chicago, 78; solo exhibs, Voltaire Gallery, New Milford, Conn, 80, Art Inst Chicago, George Eastman House, Rochester, NY, Akron Mus Art, Ohio & Image Gallery, NY; Summer Stock, Witkin Gallery, 81; Am Children, Mus Mod Art, 81; Conn Craftsmen, Pump House Gallery, Hartford, Conn, 90; Poses & Gestures, Mus Mod Art, 94; Am Photog 1890-1965, Musee Nat d'Art Mod, Paris, 96; Railroad Men, Keith de Lellis Gallery, NY, 98; Making Choices, Walker Evans & Co, Mus Modern Art, NY, 2000; The City Seen, Everson Mus Art, Syracuse; and others. *Collection Arranged:* Mus Mod Art, NY; Corcoran Gallery, Washington DC; Mus Fine Art, Houston; Everson Mus Art, Syracuse, NY; Milwaukee Mus; and others. *Teaching:* Instr photog, Sch Visual Arts, NY, 80-83. *Bibliog:* Thomas H Garver (auth), 12 Photographers of the American Social Landscape, 67; Robert Doty (ed), article, Photogr in America, 74; Ian Jeffrey (auth), Time Frames. *Publ:* Auth, Railroad Men: Photographs and Collected Stories, Clarke & Way, 61; Propaganda and Other Photographs, Addison House, 76; illusr, Clinical Sociology, 79. *Dealer:* Keith de Lellis Gallery 47 East 68 St New York NY 10128. *Mailing Add:* 395 South End Ave #33J New York NY 10280

KALLENBERGER, KREG
SCULPTOR
b Austin, Tex, 50. *Study:* Univ Tulsa, Okla, BFA, 72, MA, 74. *Work:* Mus Fine Arts, Boston; Detroit Inst Arts; Los Angeles Co Contemp Art; Hokkaido Mus Art, Sapporo, Japan; High Mus Art, Atlanta. *Comn:* Glass & marble 5 x 5 x 5, SW Res Inst, San Antonio, 96; glass & marble, City of Tulsa Water Treatment, Okla, 98. *Exhib:* Collecting Am Decorative Arts & Sculpture, Mus Fine Art, Boston, 91; Glass from Ancient Craft to Contemp Art, Morris Mus, Morristown, NY, 92; Form & Light, Am Craft Mus, NY, 94; Glass Today by Am Studio Artist (with catalog), Mus Fine Art, Boston, 97; Glass, Owensboro Mus Fine Art, Ky, 97; Glass Today, Cleveland Mus Art, 97; Masters of Contemp Glass (with catalog), Indianapolis Mus Art, 97; Glass, Los Angeles Co Mus Art, 98. *Pos:* Technician, Pilchuck Glass Ctr, Stanwood, Wash, 83; juror, Mid-Am Arts Alliance Fel Awards, Kansas City, Mo, 87, artist in residence, Rocky Mountain Nat Park, 95; juror & speaker, Okla Scholastic Art Awards, Tulsa, 95. *Teaching:* adj prof art, Univ Tulsa, 1979-1984. *Awards:* Bronze Medal, Int Art Competition, Olympics, Los Angeles, 84; Nat Endowment Arts Fel Grant, 84; Silver Prize, Int Exhib Glass Kanazawa, Japan, 95. *Bibliog:* Many articles in various books and magazines, 81-97; Dan Klein (auth), Glass a Contemporary Art, Rizzoli Int, 89; Tsuneo Yoshimizu (auth), Survey of Glass in the World, Kyoryudo Publ Ltd, Tokyo, 92; Patrick Frank (auth), Artforms, Rev 7th Ed, pages 218-19, Prentice Hall, 2004. *Media:* Glass. *Dealer:* Leo Kaplan Modern 965-A Madison Ave New York NY 10021; Habatat Galleries Mich & Fla; Holsten Gallery Stockbridge Mass. *Mailing Add:* 221 W Woodrow Pl Tulsa OK 74106

KALLIR, JANE KATHERINE
ART DEALER, WRITER
b New York, NY, July 30, 54. *Study:* Brown Univ, Providence, RI, AB, 76. *Exhib:* NY State Mus, Albany, 83; Austrian Nat Gallery, 90; San Diego Mus Art, 94 & 2001; Orlando Mus Art, 2001; Museo del Vittoriano, Rome, 2001; and others. *Pos:* Dir, Galerie St Etienne, New York, 79-. *Teaching:* Guest lectr, Mus Am Folk Art, New York, 82-85, NYU, 82-85, Nat Gallery Art, 94, Ft Lauderdale Mus Art, 96, Mus Mod Art, 97, Int Found for Art Rsch, 98, Wexner Ctr, Columbus, Ohio, 99, San Diego Mus Art, 2001, Columbus Mus Art, 2002 & Clark Art Inst, 2002. *Awards:* Silver Medal for Service to the Austrian Nation; Elic foure Literary Award, France. *Mem:* Art Dealers Asn Am (bd dir, 93-96); Art Table. *Res:* Austrian & German expressionism; international naive art, especially in its relationship to modernism. *Specialty:* Klimt, Schiele, Kokoschka, Kubin, Kollwitz, Grandma Moses, Modersohn-Becker, Corinth, Sue Coe. *Publ:* Auth, Austria's Expressionism, 81; Viennese Design and the Wiener Werkstaette, Braziller, 86; Gustav Klimt: 25 Masterworks, 89; Egon Schiele: The Complete Works, 90 & 98; Richard Gerstl/Oskar Kokoschka, 92; Egon Schiele, 94; Egon Schiele: 27 Masterworks, 96; Grandma Moses in the 21st Century, 2001; Egon Schiele: Watercolors and Drawings, 2003; and others. *Mailing Add:* c/o Galerie St Etienne 24 W 57th St New York NY 10019

KAM, MEI K
PAINTER, INSTRUCTOR
b Chungshan, Guangdong, China, Aug 7, 38; US citizen. *Study:* New York Univ, Cert Interior Decor, 67; Art Students League, New York, 77-78; Edgar Whitney Workshop, New York, 79-82. *Work:* Pastel Soc Am, Nat Art Club, NY. *Comn:* Watercolor paintings, US Coast Guard, Washington, DC, 84-85. *Exhib:* Three Contemp Artists, NY Univ Prog Bd, 86; 121st Exhib, Am Watercolor Soc, NY, 88; Hudson Vally Art Asn Ann, Westchester Co Ctr, 82-88; Audubon Artists Ann, Nat Art Club, NY, 80 & 88; Nat Acad Design, 92. *Teaching:* Instr watercolor, Salmagundi Club, NY, 82-85 & Jackson Heights Art Club, Queens, NY, 85-86; instr pastel, Pastel Soc Am, NY, 87. *Awards:* Award of Excellence, Charles Davis Mem Fund, 85; Artist Fel Award, Elizabeth K Ellis, 86 & 87; Morilla Canson Talens Award, Pastel Soc Am, 87. *Bibliog:* Dorothy Hall (auth), Art and Artists, Park East, 1/82; Palmer Poroner (auth), The Problem of Conservative Art, ArtSpeak, 4/16/84. *Mem:* Salmagundi Club; Pastel Soc Am; Hudson Valley Art Asn; Knickerbocker Artists; US Coast Guard Artists; Audubon Artists Inc. *Media:* Watercolor, Pastel. *Publ:* Contribr, Readers' pictures exhibited, The Artist (Eng), 8/81; Drawing with Pastels by Ron Lister, Prentice-Hall, 82. *Mailing Add:* 45-23 Union St Flushing NY 11355

KAMEN, REBECCA
SCULPTOR, EDUCATOR
b Philadelphia, Pa, July 8, 50. *Study:* Pa State Univ, BS, 72; Univ Ill, MA, 73; RI Sch Design, MFA, 78. *Work:* Uniweave Co Showroom, Chicago; IBM, Baltimore, Md & Raleigh, NC; Tower Construction, Bethesda, Md; Gannett Corp, Roselyn, Va; Advisors Financial, Vienna, Va; Capital One; KPMG Peat Martwick Corp; Inst Def Analysis. *Comn:* Welded steel sculpture, Lynhaven Career & Vocational Ctr, Columbia, SC, 75; welded steel sculpture, Lancaster High Sch, Lancaster, SC, 75; laminated wood wall relief, Pa State Univ, 76. *Exhib:* Works on Paper, 80, Collage on Paper, 81, Corcoran Gallery Art; Collage and Assemblage, Miss Mus Art, Jackson, 81; Joe Guy/Rebecca Kamen, Leslie Cecil Gallery, NY, 87; Primitivism, Artscape 1987, Baltimore, MD, 87; Rebecca Kamen: Recent Painting & Sculpture, Winston Gallery, Washington, 88; Jones Troyer Fitzpatrick Gallery, Washington, 90 & 92; Abstract Icons, Roanoke Mus Arts, Va, 92; Cortland Jessup Gallery, Provincetown, Mass, 93 & 94; Across Borders/Sin Fronteras, Art Mus Americas, Washington, 94; Traces: Connecting Drawing & Sculpture, Md Art Place, Baltimore, 95; Portsmouth Mus, Va, 96; Am Ctr Physics, 2005; McLean Project Arts, 2005; plus many others. *Pos:* Artist-in-residence, SC Arts Comn, 74. *Teaching:* Prof sculpture, Northern Va Community Col, Alexandria, 78-. *Awards:* Award, Alexandria Sculpture Fest, Alexandria, Va, 83; Sculpture Award '84, Washington, 84; Pub Art Trust, 84; Va Mus Art Fel, 2000; Pollack Krasner Grant, 2006; and others. *Bibliog:* Eric Gibson (auth), Garden blends indoors, outside, Washington Times, 92; Mary McCoy (auth), Sowing the seeds of two cultures, Washington Post, 94; Mary McCoy (auth), On common ground, art takes root, Washington Post, 95; and others; Sarah Tanguy (auth), Sculpture Mag, 2006. *Mem:* Int Sculpture Ctr; Washington Sculptors Group. *Media:* Wood, Mylar, Wire. *Dealer:* Carla Massoni Gallery, 203 High St, Chestertown, Md, 21620. *Mailing Add:* 1554 Great Falls St McLean VA 22101

KAMINSKY, JACK ALLAN
PHOTOGRAPHER, PRINTMAKER
b New Brunswick, NJ, Sept 8, 49. *Study:* Brooklyn Col, BS, 72, MFA(fel), 75. *Work:* LaGrange Col, Ga; Arch Am Art, Smithsonian Inst, Washington, DC. *Comn:* Graphic designs, Off of Neighborhood Govt & New York Mass Transit Authority for Eastern Pkway Subway Sta, 74. *Exhib:* Brooklyn Scenes by Brooklyn Artists, Brooklyn Mus Community Gallery, 79; Summer Exhib, Salmagundi Club, NY, 79; Doors & Chairs & Windows, Snug Harbor Cult Ctr, Staten Island, NY, 79, Never Fail Imagery Show, Sch Mus Fine Arts, Boston, 80; Invitational, Henry Hicks Gallery Ltd, Brooklyn, NY, 81; Rotunda Gallery, Brooklyn Borough Hall, Brooklyn, 82; Queens Mus Commercial Gallery, Queens, NY, 83; Brooklyn Mus, Brooklyn, NY, 84; Gallery 72, Omaha, Nebr, 85; Wiesner Gallery, Brooklyn, NY, 87; Soho Photo Gallery, NY, 88; Lever House, NY, 88; Stuhr Mus, Grand Island, Nebr, 90; Gov's Mansion, Lincoln, Nebr, 90. *Pos:* Photogr, Aunt Len's Doll & Toy Mus, 74-; gallery asst, Ann Kendall Richards Inc, NY, 81-88; photogr, PEN, NY, 84-; asst dir photo dept, Baby Togs, NY, 88-. *Teaching:* Head graphics & photog dept, Brooklyn Mus Art Sch, 73-85; instr photog, Pratt Inst Continuing Educ, Brooklyn Botanic Gardens, 85; Long Island Univ, Continuing Educ, Brooklyn, NY & The Educ Alliance, NY, 85-. *Mem:* US Coast Guard Artists; Salmagundi Club. *Publ:* NY Woman Mag, 88. *Mailing Add:* 1760 Marine Pkwy Brooklyn NY 11234

KAMM, DAVID ROBERT
PRINTMAKER, EDUCATOR
b West Union, Iowa, Jan 22, 52. *Study:* Wartburg Col, BA, 74; Univ Iowa, with Mauricio Lasansky, MA, 86, MFA, 88. *Work:* Vatican Collection Mod Art, Rome, Italy; Fine Art Asn, Ho Chi Minh City, Vietnam; Elon Col Fine Arts Collection, Elon Col, NC; Univ Iowa; Int Mus Collage, Assemblage & Construction, Cuernavaca, Mex; Art Colle, Sergines, France. *Comn:* Two ed original prints, Red Fox Inn, Waverly, Iowa, 73; original print, for The Prairie Suite: A Study of Place, Grinnell Col, Iowa, 2001. *Exhib:* Bradley Nat Print & Drawing Exhib, Peoria, Ill, 89; Pac States Nat Biennial Print Exhib, Hilo, Hawaii, 90; Points of Reference, CSPS Arts Ctr,

Cedar Rapids, Iowa, 92; Harper Nat Print & Drawing Exhib, Palatine, Ill, 94; Pages from a Small World, Charles H MacNider, Mason City, Iowa, 96; Schoharie Co Nat Small Works Exhib, Cobleskill, NY, 97; The Print & the Process, Albrecht-Kemper Mus Art, St Joseph, Mo, 2000; Sanctuary, Concordia Col, Moorhead, Minn, 2003; Nat Drawing & Small Sculpture Show, Corpus Christi, Tex, 2005. *Pos:* Residency artist, Iowa Arts Coun, 78-88; gallery coordr & preparator, Luther Col, 89-. *Teaching:* Asst prof art printmaking & drawing, Luther Col, Decorah, Iowa, 90-; Instr art appreciation & drawing, NE Iowa Community Col, Calmar, 92-2001. *Awards:* Fulbright Study in Russia, Iowa State Univ, 92; Purchase Award, Davidson Col, 93; Proj Grant, Iowa Arts Coun, 1997, NEH Summer Inst, Ferrum Col, Va, 2002. *Mem:* Found Art Theory & Educ; Print Consortium, Kansas City, Mo; Col Art Asn. *Media:* Collage, Printmaking. *Publ:* Auth, Art within the Liberal Arts, National Conference Proceedings, Sch Visual Arts, NY, 93; Etchings of Roi Patridge, Print World, 94; I Know What I Like, Fate in Review, Univ Hawaii, 94-95; Coauth, From Aasland to Zorn, Agora, Luther Col, 95; auth, Resurrecting Content, Fate in Review, Univ Hawaii, 97-98; auth, Touching the Aesthetic Elephant, Fate in Review, NE Tex Community Col, 02-03; illus, Marguerite Wildenhain: A Diary to Franz, South Bear Press, Decorah, IA, 2005. *Mailing Add:* 607 John St Decorah IA 52101

KAMM, DOROTHY LILA
PAINTER, WRITER
b Chicago, Ill, Apr 6, 57. *Study:* Northern Ill Univ, BFA, 79; Sch Art Inst Chicago, MFA, 84. *Comn:* 9-piece dresser set, comn by Dr & Mrs Michael Dennis, Ft Pierce, Fla, 89; set of 33 name stands, comn by Mr & Mrs Tommy Bruhn, Ft Pierce, Fla, 90; Urn, 92 & Framed painting on porcelain canvas, comn by Richard Rendall, Cincinnati, 93; Framed painting on porcelain canvas, comn by Dr Shirley Dunbar, Naples, Maine, 96; Nativity set, comn by Linda Geary, Stuart Fla, 11/97. *Exhib:* Art-i-ture: Furniture by Artists, Ctr Arts, Stuart, Fla, 90 & 91; Lighthouse Gallery, 90; Porcelain Fine Art Gallery, Denver, 94; A E Bean, Backus Gallery, Ft Pierce, Fla, 97; Hand Painted Porcelain, Hist Soc Martin Co, Elliot Mus, Stuart, Fla, 97. *Teaching:* Instr basic design & advance interior design, MacCormac Jr Col, Chicago, Ill, 81-84; instr color light & sound, Dayton Art Inst, Ohio, 85; instr china painting, Art Gallery, Smithfield Col, Stuart, Fla, 88-94, Martin Co Coun Arts, Stuart, Fla, 94-2000 & St Lucie West, 2000-. *Awards:* Purchase Award, 26th Ann Lighthouse Gallery Art & Craft Festival, 89; Merit Award, Art Assoc's Martin Co, 93. *Bibliog:* For Mother with Love, Traditional Home Mag, 4/91; Dorothy Kamm, China Decorator, 94 Porcelain Sets from Interior Finishes, 5-6/91; Ingrid Nordemar (auth), Artists Medium Is China Syndrome, Tribune, 10/17/97; Ike Crumpler (auth), Opening up to china an expert guides others on painting porcelain, The News, 10/15/2000; Sharon Wernlund (auth), Painted porcelain a passion for Port St Lucie Woman, The palm Beach Post, 7/17/2000; Susan S Frackelton (auth) Woman of Fire, Sinsinawa Dominicans, 2004. *Mem:* Int Porcelain Artists & Teachers Inc; Nat League Am Pen Women, (vpres, 90-96); Am Asn Univ Women; Fla State Asn Porcelain Artists (corr sec 99-). *Media:* Porcelain. *Publ:* Ed, Dorothy Kamm's Porcelain Collector's Companion, 92; Painting Dresden Flowers, Brit Porcelain Artist & China Decorator, 94; Creating depth & shadow using warm & cool tones, China Decorator, 1/95; Garnering Design Inspiration from old Porcelains, British Porcelain Artists, 1-2/97; auth, Victorian Inspiration, 2/97, Garden Triptych, 6/97 & Winter Landscape in Lavender Light, 11/97, China Decorator; Judy Knight (auth), Decorating with Hand Painted Porcelain, Country Collectibles, summer 2000; American Painted Porcelain: collectro's Identification & Value Guide, Collector Books, 97, reprinted, 99; Comprehensive Guide ot American Painted Porcelain Antique Trader Books, 99; Painted Porcelain Jewelry & Buttons, Collector Books. *Mailing Add:* 10786 Grey Huron Ct Saint Lucie West FL 34986

KAMPF, AVRAM S
EDUCATOR, CURATOR
b Jan 1, 20. *Study:* New York Univ, BA, 51; New Sch Social Res, MA, 53; PhD, 62; Columbia Univ, with Meyer Schapiro, Rudolph Wittkover & Julius Held. *Collection Arranged:* Avraham Ofek, Paintings (auth, catalog), Catherine Noren, The Camera of My Family (auth, catalog), Luise Kaish, Sculpture (auth, catalog), 73 & Jewish Experience in the Art of the 20th Century, 75-76 (auth, catalog), Jewish Mus, NY. *Pos:* Chief cur, Jewish Mus, New York, 71-76; dir & founder, Haifa Univ Art Gallery, Israel, 78-85. *Teaching:* Prof art hist, Montclair State Col, 57-; assoc mem art hist, Columbia Univ, 61-65; vis prof art hist, Hebrew Univ, Haifa Univ, Jerusalem, 76-. *Awards:* Fulbright lectr, Hebrew Univ, 66; Kenneth B Smilen Literary Award, Jewish Mus, 84; Mus Award Original Res, Israel Mus, 85. *Mem:* Col Art Asn; Interfaith Forum on Religion & Archit; Hebrew Union Congregation-Comn Art & Archit. *Res:* Jewish motifs in Twentieth Century art. *Publ:* Auth, Contemporary Synagogue Art, Jewish Publ Soc, 65; The Jewish Mus, An institution adrift, Judaism, 68; Aspects of the relationship to architecture, painting and sculpture, Scripta Hierosolymitana, 72; Jewish Experience in the Art of the Twentieth Century, Bergin & Garvey, 84; Ardon, the Bauhaus and the search for transcendence, Tel Aviv Mus, 85. *Mailing Add:* 372 Central Park W New York NY 10025

KAMYS, WALTER
PAINTER, EDUCATOR
b Chicago, Ill, June 8, 17. *Study:* Art Inst Chicago, 43, with Hubert Ropp, Louis Ritman & Boris Anisfeld; also with Gordon Onslow-Ford, Mex, 44. *Work:* Regional Contemp Art Collection, Fargo, ND; Boston Pub Libr; Albion Col, Ohio; Thorne-Sagendorph Art Gallery, Keene, NH; and others. *Exhib:* One-man shows, Bertha Schaefer Gallery, NY, 55, 57 & 60, New Vision Ctr Gallery, London, Eng, 60 & East Hampton Gallery, NY, 70; Recent Drawings, USA, Mus Mod Art, 56; 22nd Int Watercolor Biennial, Brooklyn Mus, 63; Inst Contemp Art, Boston, 66; Smithsonian Inst, 68; retrospective, Herter Art Gallery, Univ Mass, 86; Works on Paper, Nada-Mason Gallery, Mount Herman Sch, Northfield, Mass, 90; Overview - Thorne - Sagendorph Art Gallery, Keene, NH. *Collection Arranged:* Wright State Univ Art Gallery; Westfield State Col; Univ Mass Fine Arts Ctr; NY Univ; Univ Vt, Burlington Art Mus; Smith Col; Mt Holyoke Col; Soc Anonyme Col, Yale Univ; Harvard Univ. *Teaching:* Instr art, Putney Sch, Vt, 45; G W V Smith Art Mus, Springfield, Mass, 47-60; prof painting & drawing, Univ Mass, 60-87, dir, Art Acquisition Prog, 62-74, emer prof, 87-. *Awards:* Prix de Rome, 42; Boston Art Festival Award, 55; Award, Drawing & Small Sculpture Shows, Ball State Teachers' Col, Art Gallery, Muncie, Ind, 61-62; Westfield State Col Purchase Prize, 68. *Bibliog:* Harriet Janis & Rudi Blesh (auth), Collage: Personalities, Concepts, Techniques, Chilton, 62; Morris Risenhoover & Robert T Blackburn (auths), Artists as Professors, Conversations with Musicians, Painters, Sculptors, Univ Ill Press, 76; The Societe Anonyme & The Dreier Bequest, Yale Univ. *Mailing Add:* N Main St Sunderland MA 01375

KAN, DIANA
PAINTER, LECTURER
b Hong Kong, Mar 3, 26; US citizen. *Study:* With Chang Dai Chien, China, 46; Art Students League, with Robert Johnson & Robert B Hale, 49-51; Ecole Beaux Arts, Paris, with Paul Lavelle, 52-54. *Work:* Nat Acad Design, Metrop Mus Art, NY; Philadelphia Mus Art; Nelson Gallery, Atkins Mus, Kansas City, Mo; Nat Hist Mus, Taiwan. *Comn:* Lotus painting, Nat Hist Mus, Taiwan, 71. *Exhib:* Royal Acad Arts, London, Eng, 64; Royal Soc Painters, London, 64; Nat Acad Design, NY, 67-86; one-man shows, Elliott Mus, 67, 74 & 86, Nat Hist Mus, Taiwan, 71 & NY Cult Ctr, 72; Hobe Sound Galleries, Fla, 76 & 86; Nat Arts Club, 79; and others. *Teaching:* Instr watercolor, Art Students League, New York, 85. *Awards:* John Pike Mem Award, Nat Acad Design, 87; Silver Medal of Honor, 88, Gold Medal of Honor, Distinguished Achievement, 90, Knickerbocker, NY; Gold Metal Honor, Salmaqundi Club, 97. *Bibliog:* Sheila Elliot (auth), The art of Chinese painting--Diana Kan, Artists Mag, 8/86; Shu-I (auth), Profile of Diana Kan, Cosmopolitan Mag, 2/87; Daria Sommers (dir), Eastern Spirit, Western World: A Profile of Diana Kan (film), Elliot Mus Production, Stuart, Fla, World Premiere, Mus Fine Art, Boston, 88. *Mem:* Nat Acad Design; Fel Royal Soc Arts, London, Eng. *Media:* Watercolor. *Publ:* Auth, How and Why of Chinese Painting, 74; auth, articles, Am Artists Mag, 74 & 86. *Dealer:* China 2000 Fine Art 5 East 57th St New York NY 10022; Midtown Payson Gallery 11870 SE Dixie Hwy Hobe Sound FL 33455. *Mailing Add:* The Nat Arts Club 15 Grammercy Park S New York NY 10003

KAN, KIT-KEUNG
PAINTER
b Quangdong Province, China, Dec 7, 43. *Study:* Studied Chinese painting with Leung Pak-Yu, Chou Yat-Fung and Kan Maytin, 58-62; Univ Md, PhD, 75. *Work:* Hong Kong Mus Art; Am Asn for Advancement of Sci, Washington, DC; Chinese Univ Hong Kong; Am Embassy, Moscow; Art Bank, US Dept of States, Washington, DC. *Exhib:* one-man shows, Robert Brown Contemp Art, Wash, DC, 86, 87, 89, 91, 92 & 94, Hsiung Shih Gallery, Taipei, 88 & 91, Roberts Gallery, Tawson State Univ, Baltimore, 89 & 92, Alisan Fine Art, Hong Kong, 90 & 96 & Taipai Fine Arts Mus, 95; Lung Men Gallery, Taipei, 97; Del Ctr for Contemp Art, Wilmington, 2002; Kwang Hwa Information & Cult Ctr, Hong Kong, 2002; Hood Col, Frederick, Md, 2003; Harmony Hall Reg Ctr, Ft Wash, MD, 2004; Grotto's Fine Art, Hong Kong, 2005. *Awards:* First Prize, Watercolor, Open Art Competition, Chatham Gallery, Hong Kong, 64; First Prize, Ann Fine Art Exhib, Greater Reston Art Ctr, Va, 82. *Bibliog:* Washington Post, 12/26/87, 9/17/93, 9/25/93 & 10/7/2004; Asian Art News, 3/95 & 7/95; Kit-Keung Kan's Paintings: 1965-1995, Hsiung Shih Art Books Co Ltd, Taipei, 95. *Mem:* Artist Equity; Coalition Washington Artists. *Media:* Chinese Ink, Watercolor on Rice Paper, Chinese Calligraphy. *Dealer:* Grotto's Fine Art 2F 31C-D Wyndham St Hong Kong; Lung Men Art Gallery 218-1 Chunghsiao East Rd Sec 4 Taipei Taiwan; Robert Brown Gallery 2030 R St NW Washington DC 20009; B Damer Gallery 2650 Frankfort Ave Louisville KY 40206. *Mailing Add:* 6809 Tammy Ct Bethesda MD 20817

KAN, MICHAEL
HISTORIAN, ADMINISTRATOR
b Shanghai, China, July 17, 33; US citizen. *Study:* Columbia Col, BA(art hist & archeol), 53; State Univ NY Agr & Tech Col Alfred, MFA(ceramics & sculpture), 57; Columbia Univ, MA(art hist), 69, MPhil, 74. *Collection Arranged:* African Art & Simpson Collection, Brooklyn Mus, 70; guest cur, Ancient Art of West Mexico, Los Angeles Co Mus Art, 70; curatorial consult, African Art Tribal Art from West Africa, Portland Mus, 71; curatorial consult, Pre-Columbian Art in the Collection of Jay C Leff, Allentown Mus, 72; Detroit Collects African Art, 77; Treasures of Ancient Nigeria: Legacy of 2000 Years, 79. *Pos:* Assoc cur primitive art, Brooklyn Mus, 68-70, cur, 70-73, chief cur, 73-76; cur African, Oceanic & New World cult, Detroit Inst of the Arts, 77-. *Teaching:* Lectr art hist, Univ Calif, Berkeley, 64-66; lectr art Eastern Asia, Finch Col, 66-67; lectr African art, NY Univ, 70-. *Mem:* Mus Collaborative Inc (trustee, 75); Am Asn Mus. *Res:* The art of early cultures of pre-Columbian Peru and pre-Columbian Mexico; African art education. *Publ:* Contribr, Early Chinese Art and the Pacific Basin, 68; auth, African Sculpture, 70; coauth, Ancient Art of West Mexico, 70. *Mailing Add:* 10 Shore Rd Danbury CT 06811

KANE, BILL
PHOTOGRAPHER, ASSEMBLAGE ARTIST
b Holden, Mass, Feb 18, 51. *Study:* Univ Mass, BA, 73; San Francisco State Univ, MA, 78. *Work:* Mus fur Moderne Kunst, Frankfort, Ger; San Francisco Mus Mod Art; Carnegie Mellon Inst, Pittsburgh, Pa; The Oakland Mus, Calif; Stanford Univ, Calif. *Comn:* Neon installation, Washington Project Arts, Washington, 81; photo/neon mixed media, Southland Corp, Dallas, Tex, 82; mixed media, sculpture, Heathman Hotel, Portland, Ore, 84; photo/neon mixed media, Cognata & Assocs, San Francisco, 84;

photo/neon mixed media, NW Ayer Advert, NY, 89. *Exhib:* Contemp Glass, Nat Mus Tokyo & Kyoto, 81; Int Directions in Glass Art, Nat Gallery Victoria, Melbourne, Australia, 83; Examining the Perimeters of 20th Century Photog, San Francisco Mus Mod Art, 85; dalla Pop Art Americana, alla Nuoua Figurazuove, Padiglione d'Art Cont, Milano, Italy, 87; Explorations, extending the boundaries of cont photog, Mus Contemp Photog, Chicago, 87; Am Art Today, Fla Int Univ Art Mus, Miami, 92; Modernosm, San Francisco, Calif, 04. *Awards:* Photog Award, Eyes & Ears Found, 79 & 84; Nat Endowment Arts, Photog, Fel, 80; Nat Endowment Arts, Painting, Fel, 91. *Bibliog:* Bill Kane-Photo/Neon Works, Boca Raton Ctr Arts, 82 & Foster Goldstrom Inc, 83; Carl Little (auth), Bill Kane at Foster Goldstrom, Art Am, 12/89; Rudy Stern (auth), Contemporary Neon, Retail Reporting Corp, 90. *Media:* Neon, Paint, Wood. *Publ:* Auth, Bill Kane, Selected Photography and Neon Works, Foster Goldstrom, Inc, 83; Extending the Perimeters of Twentieth Century Photography, San Francisco Mus Mod Art, 85; Dalla Pop Art Americana, alla Nuova Figurazione, opere del Museod' Arte, Moderna di Francorforte, Padiglione d'Arte Contemporanea, Milano, 87. *Dealer:* Modernism 685 Market St San Francisco Calif 94105

KANE, BOB PAUL
PAINTER
b Cleveland, Ohio, July 11, 37. *Study:* Cornell Univ; Art Students League, with Will Barnet; Pratt Inst. *Work:* Joseph H Hirshhorn Collection; Palm Springs Desert Mus; Pa Acad Fine Arts; Joseph H Hirshhorn Mus & Sculptor Garden, Washington, DC; Butler Inst Am Art, Youngstown, Ohio. *Exhib:* Solo shows include Journey into Color, Hollis Taggart Galleries, NY, 2006; group shows include Collector's Choice, Okla Art Ctr, 68; Biennial of the Painters of the Mediterranean, Nice, France, 73; Biennial of Menton, France, 73; Bertha Schaefer Gallery, NY, 68, 70, 72 & 74; Galerie Marcel Bernheim, Paris, 70, Albright-Knox Mus, 73; Ankrum Gallery, Los Angeles, 69, 74, 79 & 81; Harmon-Meek Gallery, Naples, Fla, 89-99; Butler Inst Am Art, Youngstown, Ohio, 95; Am Embassy, Tokyo, Japan & Am Embassy, Bern Switz, 88-94. *Teaching:* Instr painting & art hist, Mt Clair Col, 69-70; instr painting & art hist, NY Univ, 69-70. *Bibliog:* Richard Boyle (auth), Bob Kane, Mus Munic St Paul de Vence, 72. *Media:* Oil. *Dealer:* Bertha Schaefer Gallery 41 E 57th St New York NY 10022; Ankrum Gallery 657 N La Cienega Blvd Los Angeles CA 90069. *Mailing Add:* 125 Riverside Dr No 2F New York NY 10024

KANE, MARGARET BRASSLER
SCULPTOR
b East Orange, NJ, May 25, 1909. *Study:* Syracuse Univ; Art Students League; also with John Hovannes; Colo State Christian Col, Hon PhD, 73. *Work:* US Maritime Comn; Nat Mus Am Art; Smithsonian Inst, Washington; Nat Asn Women Artists; Zimmerli Art Mus, Rutgers Univ; Bruce Mus, Greenwich, Conn; numerous pvt collections; plus others; Packer Collegiate Inst, Brooklyn, NY. *Comn:* Plaque for Burro Monument, Fairplay, Colo. *Exhib:* NY Metrop Mus; Whitney Mus Am Art, NY; Philadelphia Mus Int Sculpture Exhibs; Pa Acad Fine Arts; Nat Mus Tour of Treasures from the Smithsonian Am Art Mus, 2000-01; Hist Exhib 18902-1970s, Zimmerli Art Mus, 1999-2000; Scenes Am Life, Watson Guptill Publ, NY, 2003. *Pos:* Juror, Am Mach & Foundry Co, 57. *Teaching:* Lectr, Creative Approach to Sculpture. *Awards:* First Anna Hyatt Huntington Prize, 42 & Medal of Hon for Sculpture, 51, Nat Asn Women Artists; Henry O Avery Prize, NY Archit League, 44; Owl Award Arts, Nat League Am Pen Women Inc, 91; plus others. *Bibliog:* Greenwich Mag, Dec, 91; The Enourina Figure 18902-19702 (catalog), Zimmerli Mus, 12/12/99; The Enduring Figure Collection. *Mem:* Nat Asn Women Artists; fel Int Inst Arts & Lett; emer mem Pen & Brush, Inc, Mem Emer, 92; founding & lifetime mem Sculptors Guild, Inc. *Media:* Wood, Marble, Bronze. *Specialty:* Six-foot square limewood panel pedestal sculpture. *Interests:* Woodcarvings tracing the evolution of mankind, 1938-2000. *Collection:* Donald Trump; Rene Anselmo; Betty Rigg; Archie Andrews. *Publ:* Reproductions, In: Contemporary American Sculpture, 48, Contemporary Stone Sculpture, 71, crown; contribr ann reproductions, 50-77, feature articles, 90 & 93, Greenwich Time Publ, 50-77; article, Am Artists, 1/70; Auth, reproductions of wood carvings used by McGraw-Hill, 73; Am References (artists), 89. *Mailing Add:* 30 Strickland Rd Cos Cob CT 06807-2729

KANEGIS, SIDNEY S
DEALER
b Winthrop, Mass, Sept 6, 22. *Study:* Boston Mus Fine Art Sch. *Pos:* Owner & dir, Kanegis Gallery, Boston, 50-. *Specialty:* Modern master graphics. *Mailing Add:* 244 Newbury St Boston MA 02116-2403

KANG, IK-JOONG
PAINTER, SCULPTOR
b Cheong Ju, Korea, July 21, 60; US citizen. *Study:* Pratt Art Inst, New York, MFA, 84; Hong IK Univ, Seoul, Korea, BFA, 86. *Work:* Whitney Mus Am Art; Mus Contemp Art, Los Angeles; Bronx Mus Art, NY; Sam Sung Cult Found, Seoul, Korea. *Comn:* Queens Main St Subway Sta, Metrop Transit Authority, NY, 91; Occupational Training Ctr, Dept Cult Affairs, NY, 92; San Francisco Int Airport, San Francisco Art Comn, Calif, 94. *Exhib:* One-man show, Queens Mus Art, NY, 92; Multiple Dialogue, Whitney Mus Am Art, 94, & Eight Thousand Four Hundred Ninety Days of Memory, 96; Throw Everything Together and Add, Capp St Proj, San Francisco, 94 & Korean Pavillion, Venice, Italy, 97; Habana Int Biennial, Centro Wifredo Lam, Cuba, 96; Three Hundred Sixty Five Days Eng, Contemp Arts Forum, Santa Barbara, Calif, 96; The Year of the Tiger, Ludwig Mus, Aachen, Ger, 98. *Awards:* Joan Mitchell Found Fel, 96; Special Merit Award, 47th Venice Biennale, 97; Louis Comfort Tiffany Found Fel, 98. *Bibliog:* Arlene Raven (auth), Throw Everything Together and Add (rev), Village Voice, 12/9/90; Grace Glueck (auth), 8,490 Days of Memory (rev), NY Times, 8/2/96; Carol Lutfy (auth), Artish profile: Ik-Joong Kang, Art News, 3/97. *Media:* All Media. *Mailing Add:* 628 E 20th St No 1A New York NY 10009

KANGAS, GENE
SCULPTOR, AUTHOR
b Concord, Ohio, May 22, 44. *Study:* Miami Univ, BFA; Bowling Green Univ, MFA; Univ Ky. *Work:* Butler Inst Am Art, Ohio; City Miami, Fla; City Upper Arlington, Ohio; Case Western Reserve Univ & Cleveland Pub Libr, Cleveland. *Comn:* Sculptures, Cuyahoga Co Justice Ctr, Cleveland, Ohio, 77, Frank J Lausche State Off Bldg, Cleveland, 80, Case Western Reserve Univ, Cleveland, 81, Dade Co, Miami, Fla, 83, Coral Springs, Fla, 84, Boynton Beach, Fla, 85. *Exhib:* Sculpture Invitational, Art Acad Cincinnati, 80; City of Upper Arlington Sculpture Invitational, Columbus, Ohio, 82; Art Assemblage, Columbus, Ohio, 82; Invitational Sculptor Exhibs; and numerous group and one-man exhibs. *Teaching:* Instr sculpture, Univ NC, 68-71; asst prof sculpture, Cleveland State Univ, 71-75, assoc prof, 75-84, prof, 84-. *Awards:* Univ Res Grant, Univ NC, 68-70; First Prize in Sculpture, Cleveland Mus Art, 75; RCAC Res Grant, Cleveland State Univ, 91-93; and others. *Bibliog:* Hollander (auth), Plastics for Artists and Craftsmen; Campen (auth), Outdoor sculpture in Ohio; McCelland (dir), Public Sculpture of Cleveland (film), 82. *Media:* Metal, Wood. *Publ:* Coauth, Decoys; A North American Survey, Hillcrest Publ, 83; Decoys, Collector Bks, 91; Collectors Guide to Decoys, Wallace-Homestead Publ, 92; New World Folk Art, Cleveland State Univ Publ, 92. *Mailing Add:* Cleveland State Univ Euclid Ave at E 24th Cleveland OH 44115

KANIDINC, SALAHATTIN
CALLIGRAPHER, DESIGNER
b Istanbul, Turkey, Aug 12, 27. *Study:* Defenbaugh Sch Lettering, under Roger I Defenbaugh; Zanerian Col Penmanship, text lettering under John P Turner; State Univ Iowa, cert lettering, under Prof Meyer; Univ Minn, cert lettering; Univ Calif, cert advert. *Work:* The White House, Washington, DC; Independence Hall, Philadelphia; Franklin Mint Mus Medallic Art, Franklin Ctr, Pa; Peabody Inst Libr, Baltimore, Md. *Comn:* Presidential designs, Tiffany & Co, NY, 70; Genius of Michelangelo Medals, Franklin Mint, 71; medal design, Fedr Turkish-Am Socs, NY, 73; Christmas Card Design, UNICEF, NY, 73 & 91; postage stamp designs, United Nations, 78, 82 & 86; and others. *Exhib:* 1000 Yrs of Calligraphy & Illumination, Baltimore, 59; Bertrand Russell Centenary Int Art Exhib, London, 72-73. *Pos:* Chief calligrapher, Deniz Basimevi MD, Istanbul, Turkey, 50-61; lettering artist, Buzza-Cardozo, Anaheim, Calif, 62-64; asst art dir, Rust Craft Publ, Dedham, Mass, 64; lettering specialist-designer, Tiffany & Co, New York, 64-72; owner-creative dir, Kanidinc Int, New York, 72-82; graphic design eng, NBC-TV, 82-91; corp design cons, 92-. *Awards:* First Prize, Ann McKay Christmas Card Contest, 74. *Mem:* Int Asn Master Penmen & Teachers Handwriting; Int Ctr Typographic Arts; Queens Coun Arts; Soc Scribes & Illuminators; Int Graphological Soc; Handwriting Analysts Int. *Media:* Ink, Gouache. *Publ:* Contribr, Alphabet Thesaurus, Vol II, III, 65-71; contribr, Turkish-Am Encycl Dig. *Mailing Add:* 33-44 93th St Jackson Heights NY 11372

KANOVITZ, HOWARD
PAINTER
b Fall River, Mass, Feb 9, 29. *Study:* Providence Col, BS, 49; RI Sch Design, 49-51; with Franz Kline, 51-52; Inst Fine Arts, NY Univ, 59-61. *Work:* Whitney Mus Am Art, NY; Ludwig Mus, Cologne, Ger; Hirshhorn Mus & Sculpture Garden; Mus Boymans-Van Beuningen, Rotterdam, Holland; Metrop Mus Art, NY; and others. *Comn:* The Opening, 180 Beacon Corp, Boston, 67; A Death in Treme, Florists Transworld Delivery Collection, Detroit, 71; Collector's Wall, FK Johnssen, Essen, Ger, 71. *Exhib:* Whitney Mus Am Art Ann, NY, 72; Dokumenta 6, Kassel, Ger, 77; Guild Hall, Easthampton, 78; Hamburg Kunstverein, Hamburg, Ger, 79; Akad der Kunste, Berlin, Ger, 79; Kestner-Gesellschaft, Hannover, 79; Parrish Art Mus, Southampton, 88; Art Mus, Fla Int Univ, Miami, 89. *Teaching:* Instr painting & design, Brooklyn Col, 61-64; instr 2-D design, Pratt Inst, 64-66; prof painting, Southampton Col, 77-78; Sch Visual Arts, New York, 80-85. *Awards:* Berlin Deutscher Akademischer Austauschdienst, 79-80. *Bibliog:* Peter Sager (auth), Neue Formen des Realismus, Mag Kunst, 71; Sam Hunter (auth), Howard Kanovitz's new paintings, 4/75 & Michael Florescu (auth), Kanovitz, the new work, 2/79, Arts Mag. *Media:* Acrylic. *Dealer:* Howard Kanovitz 361 N Sea Mecox Rd Southampton NY 11968. *Mailing Add:* 361 N Sea Mecox Rd Southampton NY 11968

KANTER, LORNA J
PAINTER, PRINTMAKER
b Passaic, NJ, Apr 10, 31. *Study:* Am Art Sch, AAS (4 yr merit cert completion), 62; Pratt Graphics Art Ctr (scholar), 63; Art Students League (scholar), 77-80. *Work:* White House, Washington; Ronald W Reagan Libr, Simi Valley, Calif; Intrepid Sea/Air/Space Mus, NY; Douglas MacArthur USO, NY; Colonial Williamsburg Found, Va,. *Comn:* Portrait of Gen Douglas MacArthur & George Washington, comn by Military Order of Purple Heart, Intrepid Mus, NY, 85; Two Portraits of Pres Ronald Reagan, comn by Military Order of Purple Heart, White House Washington & Intrepid Mus, NY, 86. *Exhib:* Traveling Exhib, Fairleigh Dickinson Univ, Teaneck, NJ, 64; 30th Ann Painters & Sculptors Soc NJ, Jersey City Mus, 71; Libby Girl Among the Flowers, Cartier Inc, NY, 86; Realism Today, Am Artist Mag Nat Competition, Carol Siple Gallery, Denver, Colo, 88-89; Sundance Gallery, Bridgehampton, NY, 96. *Teaching:* Portraiture & Drawing, Am Art Sch, New York, 65-66. *Awards:* Green Ribbon, Nat Arts Club, Knickerbocker Artists, 64, Artist Yr Award, Salmagundi Club, Beaux Arts, Inc, 84; Nat Competition, Award, Am Artist Mag, 88-89. *Bibliog:* Mermelstein (auth), Dreams of gold & ancient queens, Herald-News, 85; A portrait of courage, NY Post, 85; Daryln Brewer (auth), Er-satz masterpieces for your home, NY Times, 90. *Mem:* New York Artists Equity; Beaux Arts Inc; life mem, Art Students League. *Media:* Oil, Drawing Mediums. *Publ:* Auth, Pain & TMJ: The Experience & Survival of a Patient, Mod Nutrition News, 87; Col Craig House Garden, (lithographs world-wide), ART Inc, 89. *Mailing Add:* 24 Janice Terr Clifton NJ 07013-4214

KAPHEIM, THOM
PRINTMAKER, PAINTER
Study: Northern Ill Univ, BFA(sculpture), 67, MFA(prints & drawing), 71. *Work:* Ill State Mus, Springfield. *Pos:* Chmn art dept, Wauconda High Sch. *Mailing Add:* c/o Gerhard Wurzer Gallery 1217 S Shepherd Houston TX 77019

KAPLAN, FLORA EDOUWAYE S
EDUCATOR, CURATOR
Study: Hunter Col, BA (cum laude); Columbia Univ, MA; Grad Ctr, City Univ New York, PhD, 76. *Hon Degrees:* Chieftancy Equiv, Honorary Edo, Benin, Nigeria. *Collection Arranged:* Time Landscape, Greenwich Village, NY, 74; Images of Power: Art of the Royal Court of Benin, Grey Gallery & Study Ctr, NY Univ, 81; Women in Museums, Citibank, New York, 82; In Splendor & Seclusion: Royal Women & Art of the Court of Benin, Nigeria (photographs), 82, 84-85 & 86-90; Art of the Royal Court of Benin, Benin Nat Mus, Benin City, Nigeria, 85; Fragile Legacy: The Photographs of S O Alonge, As Cultural & Political History, Nigeria, Benin Cult Ctr, Nigeria, 97. *Pos:* Cur, Dept Primitive Art & New World Cult, Brooklyn Mus, NY, formerly; consult, Dahesh Mus, NY, 88-; ed adv bd, Encycl Cult Anthrop, 93-95; ed bd, NY Univ Electronic J Sci & Arts, NY Univ Ctr Digital Media, 95-; co-ed, Mus Meanings (bk series), Routledge Ltd, London, 97-; Exhib Comt, Nat Parks Serv: Statue of Liberty, Ellis island, 98-; Ed Bd, Mus and Soc, Leicester Univ Press, United Kingdom, 2003-; Ed Bds: Adv Bd, Mem Revista de Museos de Mexico y del Mundo, 2003-; Reviewer, Fullbright Awards, 2003-2004. *Teaching:* Adj lectr, Herbert H Lehman Col, City Univ NY, 70-73, lectr, 73-74, grad fel, 74-76; adj asst prof, Dept Anthrop, NY Univ, 76-77, asst prof, 77-84, assoc prof & dir, 84-90, prof & dir, Cert Prog Mus Studies, Grad Sch Art & Sci, 90-99, prof anthropology & mus studies, 90-. *Awards:* Fulbright fel, Univ Benin, Nigeria, 83-85; NY Univ Humanities Coun Challenge Fund Grant, 88; Ford Found Grant & Samuel H Kress Found Grant, Intl Conference, Guardians of Monuments and Memory: Case Studies in Urban Conservation and Mus in the Middle East, 97-99. *Mem:* African Studies Asn; fel Am Anthrop Asn; fel NY Acad Sci; Am Asn Mus; Soc Visual Anthrop; Inter Coun Mus. *Res:* Art and Culture of Benin (Nigeria), Mus Theory. *Publ:* Auth, Iyoba, The Queen Mother of Benin: Images and Abiguity in Gender and Sex Roles in Court Art, Vol 16, No 3, 386-407, Art Hist, 9/93; ed & contribr, Museums and the Making of "Ourselves:" The Role of Objects in National Identity, Univ Leicester Press, Pinter Publ, London, 3d edit, 98; auth, Exhibitions as communicative media, In: Museum, Media, Message, Routledge Press, London, 95; ed & contribr, Queens, Queen Mothers, Priestesses and Power: Case Studies in African Gender and Power, Annals of the New York Academy of Sciences, Vol 810, 97; Benin Art and Culture, 03; Introducing Mus Studies, 03; author, A Mexican Folk Pottery Tradition: Cognition and Style in Material Culture in the Valley of Puebla, Carbondale, Southern Illinois Univ Press, 94. *Mailing Add:* 140 Nassau St New York NY 10038-1501

KAPLAN, ILEE
PRINTMAKER, ADMINISTRATOR
b Los Angeles, Calif. *Study:* Univ Calif, Berkeley, BA; Calif State Univ, Long Beach, MA. *Exhib:* Solo exhibs, Folk dance, 81, New Woodcuts, 87, Night Life Series, 89, Studio 1617, Los Angeles & Angels Gate Cult Ctr, San Pedro, Calif; Recent Works, Chamberlain Gallery, San Juan Capistrano, Calif, 91; Four Directions, Platt Gallery, Univ Judaism, Los Angeles, 92; Downey Mus, Calif, 94; Woodprints, Pearl Cunnard Gallery, Ohio State Univ, Mansfield, 95. *Pos:* Adminr, Brockman Gallery Productions, Los Angeles, 82-84; mem adv bd, Mus Studies prog, Rancho Santiago Community Col, Santa Ana, Calif, 88; assoc dir, Univ Art Mus, Calif State Univ, Long Beach, 84-; steering comt, Pub Corp Art, Long Beach, Calif, 86, 87 & 88; grant rev panelist, Inst Mus Serv, 92; selection panel, Long Beach Adv Comt Pub Art, 92. *Teaching:* Instr art, Calif State Univ, Dominguez Hills, Carson, 83; lectr, Calif State Univ, Long Beach, 85 & 88. *Awards:* Fel, Nat Endowment Arts, 87; Fel, Calif Arts Coun, 90; Distinguished Artist Award, Pub Corp Artists, 92. *Bibliog:* A brand-new arts council celebrates Jewish artists with its first show, Los Angeles Times, 11/18/88; Kaplan's work is strong, Kalamazoo Gazette, 11/89; People fire Kaplan's palette, Press Telegram, 9/91. *Mem:* Pub Corp Arts (bd dir, allocations comt); Angel's Gate Cult Ctr; Am Asn Mus; Pub Art, Long Beach, Calif (adv comt); Arts of (APSORA, Cambodian Ctr, Lon Geach, Calif (adv bd). *Publ:* Auth, The arts in Long Beach, Long Beach Citizen News. *Dealer:* Studio 1617 1617 Silverlake Blvd Los Angeles CA 90026. *Mailing Add:* 1865 Ashbrook Ave Long Beach CA 90815

KAPLAN, JACQUES
COLLECTOR, DEALER
b Paris, France, Oct 22, 24. *Study:* Sorbonne Univ, France, PhD. *Awards:* Croix de Guerre. *Bibliog:* Articles in New York Times, 66, Life Mag, 68, Time & Newsweek. *Collection:* Contemporary American art, 19th century European art and the Old Masters. *Mailing Add:* 15 Jennings Rd South Kent CT 06785

KAPLAN, JULIUS DAVID
HISTORIAN
b Nashville, Tenn, July 22, 41. *Study:* Wesleyan Univ, Middletown, Conn, BA; Columbia Univ, MA & PhD. *Collection Arranged:* Symbolism, Europe and America at the End of the 19th Century, 80, Gaston Lachaise, Sculpture and Drawings, 80, Kate Steinitz, Art and Collection, Avant-Garde Art in Germany in the 1920's and 1930's, 82 & Selections from The Edward-Dean Museum of Decorative Arts, 84, Art Gallery, Calif State Univ, San Bernardino; The Evans Collection of Oriental Ceramics, 88; The Dechter Collection of Greek Vases, 89. *Teaching:* Lectr, Colby Col, Waterville, Maine, 66; asst prof, Univ Calif, Los Angeles, 69-77; assoc prof art hist, Calif State Col, San Bernardino, 77-, chmn dept, 78-82, prof, 82-, assoc dean grad prog, 86-, dean grad studies, 89-, res & fac develop, 91-99. *Awards:* Grant-in-aid, Am Coun Learned Socs, 77; Nat Endowment Arts Grant, 81; Calif Art Coun Grant, 81, 82 & 83; Fine Arts Comt, City of San Bernardino, Calif, 88. *Mem:* Col Art Asn. *Res:* Academic and official art in France, 1850-1900. *Publ:* Auth, The religious subjects of James Ensor 1877-1900, Revue Belge d'Archaeol d'Hist l'Art, 66; Gustave Moreau, Los Angeles Co Mus Art, 74; Gustave Moreau, UMI Res Press, 82. *Mailing Add:* Dept Art Calif State Univ 5500 University Pkwy San Bernardino CA 92407

KAPLAN, LEO
ASSEMBLAGE ARTIST, COLLAGE ARTIST
b Binghamton, NY, Jan 21, 12. *Study:* Rochester Inst Technol, 32. *Work:* Chase Manhattan Bank, NY; Everson Gallery, Syracuse; Memorial Art Gallery & Bausch & Lomg, Rochester, NY; Skidmore Col, Saratoga Springs, NY; Eastman Kodak Co; Welch's, Westfield, NY; Xerox Corp, Stamford, Conn; B'nai B'rith Mus, Washington; Coral Springs Mus, 01; Elaine Baker Gallery, Boca Raton, Fla. *Comn:* The Humanities, Monroe Community Col, Rochester, NY, 66; AMF Inc, White Plains, NY, 78; Kodak Centennial, Lincoln First, Rochester, 79; Regents Publ, NY, 83; Rochester Tel Co, 85. *Exhib:* One-man shows, Two Rivers Gallery, Binghamton, NY, 68 & Univ Miami Calder Gallery, 90; Miss Mus Art, Jackson, 81; Hunter Mus, Chattanooga, 82; Mus Art, Ft Lauderdale, 82, 83 & 88-90; Tampa Mus, 83; Schmidt Ctr Gallery, Fla Atlantic Univ, Boca Raton, 98; Coral Springs Mus, Fla, 2001 & 04. *Awards:* Best of Show, Brockport State Univ, 66; Ida Abrams Award, Mem Art Gallery, Finger Lakes, 71; Merit Award, 82, Hortt Jurors Award, 90, Ft Lauderdale Mus, Fla, 90. *Publ:* Article in Southwest Ariz, 91. *Dealer:* Elaine Baker Gallery Boca Raton FL 33431; Loring Gallery Sheffield MA. *Mailing Add:* 5310 Buttonwood Ct Tamarac FL 33319

KAPLAN, MURIEL
SCULPTOR, COLLECTOR
b Philadelphia, Pa, Aug 15, 24. *Study:* Cornell Univ, BA, 46; Sarah Lawrence Col, Grad Work, 58-60; Oxford Univ, Eng, cert, 71; Art Student's League, NY, 75-88. *Work:* Columbia Univ Law Libr, New York, NY; Brandeis Univ, Waltham, Mass; Lyndon Johnson Libr, Univ Tex, Austin; John F Kennedy Sch, Jerusalem, Israel; Johnson Mus, Cornell Univ, 98. *Comn:* portrait bust, Vera List, 75; portrait bust, Charles E Smith, 90; portrait bust, Bel Kaufman, 93; portrait bust, Morris Levinson, 97; portrait bust, Frank Rhodes, Cornell Univ pres, 98. *Exhib:* Allied Artists Am Ann, Nat Acad Art, NY, 58-73; Nat Asn Women Artists Ann, Fed Bldg, NY, 66-85; Artists and Engineers in Technology, Brooklyn Mus, NY, 68; Artist's Guild, Norton Mus Art, Palm Beach, Fla, 81-90; Folk Art Exhib, Barrington Mus, Delray Beach, Fla, 84; Art in Pub Places, Govt Ctr, West Palm Beach, Fla, 85-86 & 88, Northwood Inst, West Palm Beach, Fla, 93; Armory Art Ctr, 2000; Nat Sculpture Soc, NY, 2000; Nat Asn Women Artists, 2006. *Collection Arranged:* Works of Wayne Thlebaud, Ernest Trova, Janet Fish & Larry Rivers; Viola Frey, Patti Warahina. *Pos:* Secy, Comt to Estab Art Mus, Westchester, NY, 56-58; co-chair, First Televised Art Auction, WNET, NY, 64; mem, Comt Art in Pub Places, Palm Beach, Fla, 83-84; art adv bd, Boca Raton Mus Art, Fla, 88-90; bd dir, Palm Beach Co, Coun Arts, 92-94, Armory Art Ctr, West Palm Beach, Fla, 93-. *Teaching:* Instr portrait sculpture, pvt studio, 66-70; instr, Armory Sch, 87-92. *Awards:* Sculpture Prize, Nat Asn Women Artists Ann, 66; Robert Kennedy Humanitarian Award, Settlement House, New York, 68; Portrait Award, Allied Artists Am Ann, 69; First Prize Sculpture, Barrington Mus Art, 84; Sculpture Prize, Norton Art Mus, 88; Best in Show, Nat Asn Women Artists, 2006. *Bibliog:* Dorothy Ann Flor (auth), Casted characters, Ft Lauderdale Sun Sentinel, 5/17/84; Muriel Kaplan Keeps Ahead in the Sculpture Business, Arts Mag, 7/92; Jan Sjostrom (auth), Kaplan: Through A sculptors eyes, Palm Beach Daily News, 1/23/94. *Mem:* Art Students League; Nat Asn Women Artists; Nat Sculpture Soc; Norton Gallery & Sch Arts, Lect Sponsor; Soc of 4 Arts, Palm Beach, Fla; Int Sculpture Ctr. *Media:* Clay, Bronze. *Specialty:* portraits. *Collection:* works of Wayne Thlebaud, Ernest Trova, Janet Fish & Larry Rivers. *Dealer:* Portraits Inc 7 W 51st St New York NY 10019. *Mailing Add:* 115 Lakeshore Drive North Palm Beach FL 33408

KAPLAN, PHYLLIS
PAINTER, COMPUTER ARTIST
b Brooklyn, NY, 50. *Study:* Cooper Union, BFA, 72; Domus Acad, post grad studies, 85. *Work:* Nat Mus Women Arts, Washington, DC; Mitsubishi pvt collection, Japan; Sharjah Arts Mus, United Arab Emirates; Col Univ S Fla, Col Marine Sci; Col City of Balatonfured, Hungary. *Exhib:* Bershire Art Asn, Berkshire Mus, Pittsfield, Mass, 70; Three Rivers Arts Festival, Carnegie Mus Art, Pittsburgh, Pa, 95-96 (catalogs); Global Focus, Nat Mus Women Arts, Beijing, China, 95; Heat Exhaustion, Fine Arts Mus Long Island, Hempstead, NY, 96; 14th & 15th Juried Exhib, Fine Arts Mus Long Island, NY, 96 & 97; Halpert Biennial, Appalachian State Univ, Boone, NC, 97 (catalog); World Artists for Tibet, Blue Mountain Gallery, NY, 98; 1st Int Biennial, Trevi-Flash Art Mus, Trevi-Perugia, Italy, 98 (catalog); one-person shows Kings Gallery, Brooklyn, NY, 74, Long Island Univ, Brooklyn, 75, Tribeca Gallery, NY, 97, Verge, Manhattan Mini Storage, NY, 99; Mayfair, Open Space Gallery (catalog), Allentown, Pa, 2000; Sharjah Arts Mus, United Arab Emirates, 2000; 4th Ann Juried Exhib, Canajoharie Libr & Art Gallery, Canajoharie, NY, 2000 & 2002; Snapshot, Contemp Mus, Baltimore, 2000; New Symbols, Montgomery Col, Rockville, Md, 2002; Virtue, Visual Art Gallery, St Paul, MN, 2000; 35th Int Exhib, San Bernardono Co Mus, Calif, 2000-01; Sharjah Int Arts Biennial, Sharjah, United Arab Emerites, 2001; Univ S Fla, Col of Marine Sci, St Petersburg, 2001; Cambridge Art Asn, Nat Prize Show, MA, 2001; Viziraros Gallery, Budapest, Hungary, 2004; Central EU Gallery, selections from HMC Residency Collection, Budapest, Hungary, 2006. *Collection Arranged:* LandShapes, Orgn Independent Artists, 96; Flights of Fantasy, Broadway Mall, 97. *Pos:* artist in residence, F J Music Sch, Balatonfured, Hungary, 2002. *Teaching:* instr oil painting, Monroe Co Arts Coun, 2001. *Awards:* Hon Mention, Orgn Ind Artists Salon Show, 94; Hon Mention, 1st Int Biennial Female Artists, Art Addiction Gallery, 94; Artists Space/Independent Project Grant, 99; Hon Mention, Mayfair, 2000; Univ S Fla, Award Best in Show, 2001, Hon Mention, Canajoharie Libr & Art Gallery, 2003. *Bibliog:* Carey Lovelace (auth), Dreamlike

visions, Newsday, 8/2/96; Jane Shapiro (auth), Heats on over at FAMLI, The Herald, 8/22/96; Chris Geiger (auth), Fantasy flies in West Side Arts Coalition Group Show, Artspeak, 1/98. *Media:* Acrylic, Oil, Computer Artist. *Publ:* Contribr, Artist Exhibits, Kings Courier, 74; 1st Annual Organization of Independent Artists Calendar, Orgn Ind Artists, 94; Reality, Villager, 94; Pierrepont Place Brooklyn Heights, Brooklyn J Arts, 94; Looking out on artistic landscapes, Courier Lifestyles, 96. *Mailing Add:* 213 W Sarah St Milford PA 18337

KAPLAN, SANDRA
PAINTER, PRINTMAKER
b Cincinnati, Ohio, May 23, 43. *Study:* Art Acad Cincinnati, with Julian Stanczak, 60-61; Pratt Inst, with Richard Lindner & Lennart Anderson, BFA(with hons), 65; City Univ New York, 68-70. *Work:* ALCOA Pittsburgh, Pa; Am Express Co, Inverness Park, Colo; Hyatt Regency Hotel, Dubai, United Arab Emirates; Blue Cross, Blue Shield, Denver; Neiman Marcus Corp Hqs, Los Angeles. *Comn:* Vail Athletic Club, 79; Saudi Arabia, 5-panel watercolor; Standard Textile Corp, Cincinnati; monotypes, Fairmont Hotels, San Jose & Chicago, 87; watercolors, Marriot Hotel, Hong Kong; Art in Public Places, watercolor, Colo Coun Arts, 89; mural, Univ Colo Sch Pharmacy, 94. *Exhib:* Dubins Gallery, Los Angeles, 88 & 90; Eva Cohon Galleries Ltd, Chicago & Highland Park, 89; Olson Larsen Gallery, Des Moines, Iowa, 90; Arvada Ctr Arts, 91; Nicolaysen Art Mus, Casper, Wyo, 92; Wave Hill Gallery, Riverdale, NY, 95; Boulder Mus Contemp Art, Boulder, Colo, 97; Laura Paul Gallery, Cincinnati, 98; Cline Fine Art, Santa Fe, 99 & 2000; Mizel Ctr for the Arts, Denver, 03; and others. *Teaching:* Instr painting & design, Arapahoe Community Col, 74-75; art instr, Metrop State Col, 77-78; guest art instr, Denver Univ, 78-79; instr painting, Art Students League Denver, 01-. *Awards:* First Place, Rocky Mountain Regional Print Show, 82; Ludwig Vogelstein Found Grant, Phillip Morris Fel, Yaddo Artists Colony, 86; Best of Show, Colo Art Expo; Covisions Grant, Colo Coun on the Arts, 86. *Bibliog:* Roberta McIntyre (auth), summer's garden, Focus, Santa Fe, 10/87; Carole Katchen (auth), Watercolor, the very large picture, Artists Mag, 9/88; Lynn Kari Petrich (auth), Painting floral objects, Am Artist/Watercolor, 89; Christian Science Monitor, 12/2/91; The New York Times, 8/13/95; The Rocky Mountain News, 5/30/03; The Denver Post, 5/2/03; interview with Suzanne McCarroll, KCNC TV News 4, 6/17/03. *Mem:* Trustee, Mus of Contemporary Art/ Den; Friday Club (discussion). *Media:* Watercolor; Oil. *Publ:* Illusr, Rationale, 65; contrib, Art Work, No Commercial Value, Grossman, 71; Landscapes (catalog), Arvada Ctr Show, 91; Human and/or Nature (brochure), Nicolaysen Mus, 92. *Dealer:* Sharks Inc 2020 9th St Boulder Colo 80302; Wm HAVU Fine Art 1040 Cherokee St Denver Colo 80204; Olson Larsen Gallery 203 5th St W Des Moines Iowa 50265. *Mailing Add:* 2939 S Lafayette Dr Englewood CO 80113

KAPLAN, STANLEY
PRINTMAKER, MURALIST
b Brooklyn, NY, Sept 4, 25. *Study:* Cooper Union Sch Art, cert fine arts, 49; NY Univ, BS, 52; Pratt Inst, New York, MS, 68. *Work:* Metrop Mus Art, NY; Brooklyn Mus, NY Pub Libr; Columbia Univ; Philadelphia Mus Art; Newark Mus Art; Challahoochee Valley Art Mus; Portland Art Mus; Hunterdon Mus Art, NJ. *Comn:* Murals, AT & T Community Develop Corp, NY & Fla, 73, 74 & 75; mural, Manuche's Restaurant, NY, 62; Illustrations of Poetry, 94. *Exhib:* 45 one person shows: ACA Gallery, New York City, 1954 to Stone Metal Press Gallery, 2004; 170 group shows: Libr of Cong, Wash, DC, 1951 to Allied Artist of Am, 2004; Old Print Shop Gallery, NYC. *Pos:* Mgr, Tortoise Press, 78-. *Teaching:* Art teacher, Levittown Pub Schs, NY, 54-59; prof art, Nassau Community Col, Garden City, 65-95. *Awards:* Sixth Ann Competition Award, Port Washington Pub Libr, 71; Purchase Award, Soc Am Graphic Artists 55th Nat Print Exhib, 77; Philladelphia Watercolor Soc, 04; Academic Artis Asso, 2004; Puffin Foundation, 2004; Allied Artists of Am, 2004; 30 awards all together. *Mem:* Soc Am Graphic Artists (vpres, 72-74, pres, 76-78); Southern Graphic Council; Mid Am Print Council; Albany Print Club. *Media:* Woodcut, Etching, Book Art. *Specialty:* Prints, maps, books. *Interests:* Music, Films, Travel. *Publ:* Nassau Review, Jewish Currents, Wordsmith, KAVR Pub, Tortoise Press; and many others. *Dealer:* The Old Print Shop NYC. *Mailing Add:* 47 Trapper Ln Levittown NY 11756

KAPLINSKI, BUFFALO
PAINTER, WATERCOLORIST
b Chicago, Ill, May 25, 43. *Study:* Art Inst Chicago; Am Acad Art. *Work:* Denver Pub Libr-Western Art Collection; Johns-Manville, Denver, Colo; Denver Art Mus; Dallas Power and Light, Tex; United Bank, Denver, Colo; Petro-Lewis, Denver, Colo; Eastman-Kodak, Windsor, Colo; and others. *Comn:* Fredrick Ross Co, Denver; Prudential Bache Securities, Denver; painting, Red Rocks vistor ctr, 03. *Exhib:* Grand Junction Group Art Show, Western Colo Ctr for the Arts, 03; Taos Art Fest, Total Art Gallery, 03; one man show, The Art Center, Grand junction, Colo, 04; Rist Canyon Art Exhib, Belvue, Colo, 04; one man show, Pinon Gallery, Littleton, Colo, 2006; and many others. *Teaching:* Instr, Colo Inst Art, Univ Denver; instr watercolor, Art Students' League, Denver, 88-94. *Awards:* Southwestern Biennial Hon Mention, NMex Arts Mus, Santa Fe; Nat Cowboy Hall of Fame, Oklahoma City, Okla, 93; Artist of the West, Pioneer Mus, Colorado Springs, 93; Best of Category Award, Mitchell Mus, Trinidad, Colo; Plum Creek Wine Label, Los Angeles Co Fair Wine Competition, 01; plus others. *Bibliog:* Article in Am Artist Mag, 8/72; article, Artists Rock; Harold & Peggy Samuels, Contemp Western Artists, 11/82; articles in Am Artist, 6/84 & Art West Mag, 9-10/84; Harmon S Graves (auth), Passionate Landscape/Painting Journeys of Buffalo Kaplinski, Sunstone Press, Santa Fe, NMex, 2006. *Media:* Acrylic, Watercolor. *Specialty:* Fine Art Landscape. *Interests:* Christian evangelism & tool collecting. *Dealer:* Total Arts Gallery 122A Kit Carson Rd Taos New Mexico 87571; Columbine Galleries 211 Old Santa Fe Trail Santa Fe New Mexico 87501; Pinon Fine Art 2510 W Main St Littleton Colo 80120. *Mailing Add:* PO Box 44 Elizabeth CO 80107

KAPP, DAVID
PAINTER
b New York, NY, Jan 3, 53. *Study:* Windham Col, BFA, 74; Queens Col, MFA, 77. *Work:* Metrop Mus Art; Mus of the City NY; Mus Art, RI Sch Design, Providence; NC Mus Art, Raleigh; Microsoft Corp, Redmond, WA. *Exhib:* Brooklyn Paperworks, Brooklyn Mus Art, NY, 82; The Art of this Century, Mus Art, RI Sch Design, Providence, 91; The Technol Muse, Katonah Mus Art, NY, 91; NY, NY Recent Cityscapes, NC Mus Art, Raleigh, 95; Graphics from Solo Impressions, Albright Knox Gallery, Buffalo, NY, 96; All in a Family, New Britian Mus Am Art, CT, 87; New New York Views, Mus City NY, 99; Beyond the Mountains (Contemp Urban Land), Muskegon Mus Art, Mich, 2000. *Teaching:* vis critic, Brances Univ, Waltham, MH, Nov 99. *Awards:* Hassam Purchase Prize, 79; CAPS Fel Painting, 82; Am Acad Nat Inst Arts & Letters, 94. *Bibliog:* Robert Pinars (auth), Style Shucks, Art Mag, 82; Michael Brenson (auth), David Kapp, NY Times, 12/87; Robert Edelman (auth), Painted Streets - Urban Grids, Working the Grid, Hard Press Inc, 2000. *Mem:* Nat Acad Design. *Mailing Add:* 305 Canal Ave New York NY 10013

KAPP, E JEANNE
PAINTER, PHOTOGRAPHER
b Hagerstown, Md, Oct 16, 33. *Study:* Studies in Los Angeles Valley Col, 66-69, Univ Utah, 85-90; cert interior design, Los Angeles Interior Design Sch, 69-82; Joseph Raphael Workshop, 76; Univ Utah, 76-82; Earl Pierce Civic Arts, 85-90. *Work:* Univ Calif Presidential Residence, Kensington. *Comn:* McLaren Lodge (painting), comn by Mrs James Cooney, San Francisco, Calif, 95. *Exhib:* Festival 83, Mus Natural Hist, Salt Lake City, 83; Utah 84, Mus Fine Art, Salt Lake City, 84; Five Star Art, Salt Lake Art Ctr, 84; Salon Des Nations, Centre Int D'Art, Paris, France, 84; Painting Eden, Calif Heritage Gallery, San Francisco, 96; Valley Landscape, Danville Fine Arts Gallery, Calif, 97; Inspirations from the Earth, Gallery Concord, Calif, 98; Fall Exhib, Valley Art Gallery, Walnut Creek, Calif, 98; Invitational Exhibs: Mt Diablo, Robert Butler Gallery, Vineyards, Jessel Gallery, Napa, Calif, 2005-2006. *Pos:* Cur fine arts, Contra Costa Co Libr, Pleasant Hill, Calif, 95-98. *Awards:* Alamo Danvill Artists Award, 90-95; Lamorinda Arts Alliance Award, 95-97; 2nd Place Oil, Las Juntas Artists, 97, 1st Pl, 98; 1st Place, Contra Costa Co Fair, 98; 2nd Place, Discover Art League, 2000. *Bibliog:* Utah 81, Utah Travel Coun, 1981; Various articles in Contra Costa Times, 89-97. *Mem:* Alamo-Danville Artists Soc (circuit leader, 90); Las Juntas Artists (juror's asst, 92); Oil Painters Am; Benicia Fine Arts; Lamorinda Arts Alliance. *Media:* Oil. *Publ:* auth, The Am Connection, Pub Creative Art Enterprises, 1985; Guide Book of Western Aritist, Art of the West Mag, 2001. *Dealer:* Valley Fine Art Gallery 1661 Botelho Dr Walnut Creek CA 94549; Danville Fine Art Gallery 233 Front St Danville CA 94526. *Mailing Add:* 411 Donegal Way Lafayette CA 94549

KAPROV, SUSAN
PAINTER, MURALIST
b New York, NY, Aug 11, 46. *Study:* City Col New York, BA, 67; Dartmouth Col, Hanover, NH, MA, 68. *Work:* Mus Mod Art & Metrop Mus Art, NY; Corcoran Gallery Art, Washington, DC, Nat Mus Am Art, Washington, DC; Brooklyn Mus; Rose Art Mus; Gernsheim Col, Waltham, Mass. *Comn:* Austin Co, Atlanta, Ga; Reeves Communication Corp, NY, 81; NASA, Washington, DC, 81 & 92; Prudential Insurance Co, 82; Hexcel Corp, 83; City of NY; Port Authority, NJ, 90; Liberty Sci Ctr, 92. *Exhib:* Prints: Acquisitions 1973-76, Mus Mod Art, NY, 77; one-man show, Hayden Planetarium, NY, 78 & Brooklyn Mus, 81; Recent Acquisitions, Nat Mus Am Art, Washington, DC, 78; Art-Technol, Philadelphia Print Club, 79 & 92; Alternative Imaging Systems, Everson Mus, Syracuse, NY, 79; installation, Granite Gallery, Nat Mus Am Art, 83-84; Fay Gold Gallery, Atlanta, 90; Neikrug Gallery, NY, 92; Midtown Y Gallery, 92; Women Artist of the NASA Art Program, National Mus of Women in the Arts, Washington DC, 2001; NY Visions, Merrick Gallery, St Petersburg, Fla, 2002; Digtial 2004, NY Hall of Science; Convergence, Fort Collins CO Mus of contemp Art, 2005; Project Diversity; Rotunda Gallery, 2005. *Teaching:* Sch Visual Arts, NY, 92. *Awards:* MacDowell Colony Fel, 71 & 73; Ossabaw Island Proj Fel, 73; Creative Artists Pub Serv fel, NY State Coun on Arts, 79-80; Palenville Interarts Ctr, Palenville, NY, 96; Brandywine Workshop, Philadelphia, PA, 96. *Bibliog:* Donald Saff (auth), History of American Printmaking, Holt, Rinehart, Winston, 77; Ellen Lubell (auth), article, Art in Am, 81; V Butera (auth), article, Arts Mag, 81. *Mem:* Am Inst Architects, NY Chap. *Media:* Fired Enamel on Glass, Glass Mosaic, Mixed Media Prints, Photography, Drawing. *Interests:* Architecture, archaeology, science. *Publ:* New York Arts/Berliner Kunst: Susan Kaprov; Capturing the Public Sphere, feature article by John Perreault; The Public Review, 5/2003; NY Times 3/2003. *Mailing Add:* 149 Willow St No 5C Brooklyn NY 11201-2259

KAPSALIS, THOMAS HARRY
PAINTER, SCULPTOR
b Chicago, Ill, May 31, 25. *Study:* Sch Art Inst Chicago, BAE, 49, MAE, 57; Fulbright Grant, Ger, 53-54. *Work:* Main Bank, Chicago, Ill; Elmhurst Col, Ill; Art Inst Chicago, Ill; Ill State Mus, Springfield. *Exhib:* Chicago & Vicinity Exhib, 12 times, 50-81 & Contemp Drawings from 12 Countries, 52, Art Inst Chicago; 27th Biennial Exhib Contemp Painting, Corcoran Gallery Art, Washington, DC, 61; Visions-Painting & Sculpture: Distinguished Alumni 1945 to Present, Art Inst Chicago, 76; two-person exhib, Art Inst Chicago, 79; Chicago: Some Other Traditions, Madison Art Ctr, Wis, 83; Artists Choose Artists, 83, Hyde Park Art Ctr, Chicago; one-man shows, NAME Gallery, 85 & Roy Boyd Gallery, Chicago, 86 & 88; faculty sabbatical exhib, Art Inst Chicago, 87; int art expn, Navy Pier, Chicago, 86; Am Prints 1900-1960, Art Inst Chicago, 92; Quad City Arts Exhib, Art Works S/R Gallery, Rock Island Ill, 91 & 92; Am Prints 1900-1960, Exhib, Art Inst Chicago, Print & Drawing Dept; The New Eng Fine Art Inst Nat Exhib Am Contemp Art, Boston, Mass, 93; Union League Civic & Arts Found Auction, Chicago, Ill, 93; 55th Ann Exhib featuring work by 55 artists who have shown at the ctr from 1939 to the present, Hyde Park Art Ctr, Chicago, Ill,

94; Just Good Art, Hyde Park Art Ctr Benefit Auction, Chicago, Ill, 94, 95, 96, & 98; Ox-Box Benefit Auction, Sch Art Inst Chicago, Ill, 94, 95, 96 & 97; Lake Forest Art Expo, W Lake Forest Train Station, Ill, 96; Don Baum Says: Chicago Has Famous Artists Exhib, Hyde Park Art Ctr, Chicago, Ill, 96; Wellness House Gala Art Auction 96, Hinsdale, Ill, 96; Altered Object, Hyde Park Art Ctr Benefit Auction, 99; Just Good Art, Hyde Park Art Ctr Benefit Auction, 2000 & 02; The Big Picture Show: Size Does Matter, Betty Rymer Gallery, Sch Art Inst, Chicago, 2003. *Teaching:* Prof drawing & painting, Art Inst Chicago, 52-2006; lectr painting, Northwestern Univ, Chicago & Evanston, 58-71. *Awards:* Huntington Hartford Found Grant, 56 & 59; Pauline Palmer Prize, 60 & Jule F Brower Prize, 69, Art Inst Chicago. *Bibliog:* Meilach & Seiden (auth), Direct Metal Sculpture, Crown, 66; Meilach & Hinz (auth), How to Create Your Own Designs, Doubleday, 75; Ivy Sundell (auth), Art Scene, 2000; and others. *Media:* Acrylic, Oil, Metal Welded, Wood. *Dealer:* Robert Henry Adams Gine Art 715 North Franklin Chicago Il 60610; Corbett vs Dempsey Modern Art & Uncommon Objects 1120 N Ashland Ave 3d Floor Chicago IL 60622. *Mailing Add:* 5204 N Virginia Ave Chicago IL 60625

KARAFEL, LORRAINE
WRITER, CRITIC
b Orange, NJ, Nov 29, 56. *Study:* Univ of Paris IV, Sorbonne, France 76; Ecole du Louvre, Paris, France, 76 & 77; Univ Florence, Italy, 77; Rutgers Col, New Brunswick, NJ, BA, 78; New York Univ Inst Fine Arts, MA, 84; Columbia Univ, Sch of Arts, MFA, 87. *Pos:* Assoc cur spec exhib progs, Nat Gallery of Art, Washington, DC, 90-94. *Teaching:* Instr, Parsons Sch Design, New York, 86-90 & 94-; vis lectr, Rutgers Col, New Brunswick, NJ, 89- 90; lectr, George Mason Univ, Fairfax, Va, 92-. *Mem:* Int Art Critics Asn, Am Branch. *Publ:* Auth, Master of the Moulin Rouge, Art News, 86; contribr, paintings in the Louvre, Stewart, Tabori & Chang, 87; contribr, American Art 1913-1993, Royal Acad Arts, London, 93; auth, Decorative Objects in the Paintings of Veneer, Antiques, 96. *Mailing Add:* 12 E 95th St New York NY 10128

KARAWINA, ERICA (MRS SIDNEY C HSIAO)
PAINTER, STAINED GLASS ARTIST
b Ger; US citizen. *Study:* Studied in Europe; also with Frederick W Allen & Charles J Connick, Boston. *Work:* Contemp Mus, Honolulu; Mus Mod Art, NY; Boston Mus Fine Arts; Libr Cong, Washington, DC; Honolulu Acad Arts; State Found Cult Arts. *Comn:* Crux Gemmata (faceted glass in concrete), Manoa Valley Church, Honolulu, 67; six windows of faceted glass, St Anthony's Church, Kailua, Oahu, Hawaii, 68; This Earth is Ours (faceted glass), News Bldg Foyer, Honolulu Advertiser, 72; four faceted glass mosaic murals, Hawaii State Off Bldg, Honolulu, 75; ceiling (faceted glass), Circuit Ct, Honolulu, 84; Hawaii, Hawaii (faceted glass mural), Campus Ctr, Diamond Head, Kapiolani Col, Honolulu, 88. *Exhib:* Dance Int, Rockefeller Ctr, NY, 37; Competition of State of Mass, NY's Fair, 39; Protestant Orthodox Ctr, NY World's Fair, 64; one-man shows, China Int Inst, Taipei, Taiwan, 56 & Contemp Arts Ctr, Honolulu, 77; Ryan Gallery, Kailua, 81; plus others. *Pos:* Draftsman stained glass, Connick Studios, Boston, 30-33; designer stained glass, Burnham Studios, Boston, 35-38. *Teaching:* Butera Sch of Art, Boston, 47-48. *Awards:* John Poole Mem Prize, Honolulu Acad Arts, 52; James C Castle Award, Narcissus Art Festival, Honolulu, 61. *Bibliog:* Jean Charlot (auth), Exhibition of stained glass, 5/53; Joanne Shaw (auth), Echoes of universality, Vol 72, No 9, Paradise of Pac; Francis Haar & Murray Turnbull (ed), Artists of Hawaii, Vol II, 77; Hawaii Doe (vcr cassette), Karawina, 85. *Mem:* Honolulu Print Makers; Honolulu Acad of Arts; Hawaii Artists League; fel Int Inst Arts. *Media:* Stained Glass. *Publ:* Contribr, From Maui to Mainz, 56-57 & From Hawaii to Holland, 63, Stained Glass

KARDON, CAROL
PAINTER, INSTRUCTOR
b Mt Vernon, NY. *Study:* Art Students League, New York, 55-56; Bennington Col, Vt, BA, 56; Univ Pa, Grad Sch Fine Arts, spec student, 70; also studied with Wolf Kahn, Dan Greene & Albert Handell, Barnes Found, Merion, Pa. *Work:* Shell Oil; Bon Secours Mem Reg Med Ctr, Mechanicsville, Va; RJ Reynolds Industs; Shearson Lehman Brothers; Smith, Barney, Harris & Upham Co; and others. *Comn:* William Penn House, Philadelphia; Chester Valley Country Club, Malvem, Pa. *Exhib:* Cheltenham Award Show, Mus Philadelphia Civic Ctr, Pa, 80 & Cheltenham Art Ctr, Pa; one-woman shows, Gross McCleaf Gallery, Philadelphia, Pa, 80-82 & 84 & Gallery Ave Kobe, Nishinomiya Hyogo, Japan, 87; Great Swamp XXV Exhib, Nabisco Brands Corp, East Hanover, NJ, 85; Ann Exhib, Pastel Soc Am, NY, 86, 87, 89 & 92; group show, Neville-Sargent Gallery, Chicago, Ill, 89-92; Cooper Gallery, Lewisburg, WVa; Carspecken-Scott Gallery, Wilmington, Pa. *Teaching:* Pastel & color, Main Line Ctr Arts; landscape workshop in Santa Fe, NMex, Pa Acad Fine Arts, Philadelphia, 91. *Awards:* Pastel Soc Am Plaque Award, Salmagundi Club, New York, 96; Marion Strueken-Bachmann Award for Landscape, Pastel Soc Am, New York, 96; Pastel Soc W Coast Award, 96. *Mem:* Pastel Soc Am; W Coast Pastel Soc; Salmagundi Club, NY. *Media:* Pastel, Oil. *Publ:* Contribr, Best of Pastel, Rockport Publ, 96. *Dealer:* Carspecken-Scott Gallery Wilmington DE; Summa Gallery New York NY. *Mailing Add:* 248 Beech Hill Rd Wynnewood PA 19096

KARDON, DENNIS
PRINTMAKER
Study: Yale Univ, BA(cum laude), 73; study prog, Whitney Mus Am Art, 73. *Work:* Jewish Mus; JV Speed Mus; Boston Mus Fine Art; Nat Mus Am Art; Fogg Art Mus. *Exhib:* One-person shows, Barbara Toll Fine Arts, NY, 81, 84, 86 & 89, Studio Space, Simon Watson, NY, 90, A/D, NY, 90 & Richard Anderson Fine Arts, NY, 96; Painting & Sculpture Exhib, Am Acad Arts & Letts, NY, 93 & 46th Ann Am Acad Purchase Exhib, 94; Building a Collection: The Dept of Contemp Art, Mus Fine Art, Boston, 93; Design Biennial: Mirrors, Parrish Art Mus, Southampton, 94; Inside Out, Psychological Self-Portrait & In the Flesh, Aldrich Mus Contemp Art, Conn, 95; Being Human, Mus Fine Arts, Boston, 96; Too Jewish? Challenging Traditional Identities, Jewish Mus, NY, San Francisco, Los Angeles & Baltimore, 96. *Awards:* NY Found Arts Grants, 87; Louis Comfort Tiffany Found Grant, 91; John Simon Guggenheim Mem Fel, 98. *Bibliog:* Robert Mahoney (auth), Dennis Kardon, Richard Anderson Fine Arts, Time Out NY, 3/13-20/96; Pepe Karmel (auth), Art in review, NY Times, 3/22/96; P C Smith (auth), Dennis Kardon at Richard Anderson (illus), Art Am, 7/96. *Mailing Add:* 2 Charlton St No 2 New York NY 10014

KARDON, JANET
MUSEUM DIRECTOR, CURATOR
b Philadelphia, Pa. *Study:* Temple Univ, BS(educ), 55; Univ Pa, MA(art hist), 66; Am Mgt Asn, 86. *Hon Degrees:* Moore Col Art, Hon Dr Humanities, 84. *Collection Arranged:* Seventies Painting (auth, catalog), Univ Arts, 78, Siah Armajani (auth, catalog), 78, Alice Avcock (auth, catalog), 78 & Point (auth, catalog), 78; David Salle (auth, catalog), Inst Contemp Art, 86, traveling, 86-87; Robert Kushner (auth, catalog), Inst Contemp Art, 87, traveling 87-89; Robert Mapplethorpe: The Perfect Moment, Inst Contemp Art, 87, traveling, 87-89; Building a Permanent Collection: A Perspective on the 1980's Explorations: The Aesthetic of Excess (auth, catalog) & Costumes by Pat Oleszko, Am Craft Mus, 90; History of Twentieth Century Craft Three Volumes - The Ideal Home, Craft in the Machine Age, Revivals, Diverse Traditions, 93-96. *Pos:* Dir exhibs, Univ Arts, 75-78; consult & panelist, Nat Endowment Arts, 75-, mem overview panel mus prog, 84, 85 & 89; dir, Inst Contemp Art, Univ Pa, 79-89 & Am Craft Mus, 89-96; visual arts panel mem, Pa Coun Arts, 78-83, vchmn, 82-83 & 88; US Comnr, Venice Biennale, 80; spec proj panel mem, Pa Coun Arts, 78-83, panel mem, Art in Pub Spaces, Vet Admin, 80, Nat Endowment Arts Mus Seminar, Baltimore Mus Art, 81, Inter-Arts Prog, Nat Endowment Arts, 84, oversight panel, Visual Arts Prog, 89 & 90; consult, Artists Spaces Site Visitations, Visual Arts Prog, Nat Endowment Arts, 80, Inter-Arts Site Visitations, 83-84; session leader, Am Kunsthalle, Col Art Asn, 83; chair, Frank Jewitt Mather Award in criticism, Col Art Asn, 84; bd advs, Awards in Visual Arts, Southeastern Ctr Contemp Art, 84-; chair selection panel Int exhibs, US Info Agency, 87. *Teaching:* Lectr, Gwynedd Mercy Col, 67, Univ Arts, 68-75; vis assoc prof, Fashion Inst Technol & Pratt Inst, 97-99. *Awards:* Helena Rubenstein Fel, Whitney Mus Am Art, 75; Nat Endowment Arts Res Grant, 78. *Bibliog:* Ron Javers (auth), Art breaking, Philadelphia Mag, 2/91; Patricia Malarcher (auth), American Craft Museum launches centenary project, Crafts Report, 2/91; Leslie Ferrin (auth), Controversy breeds confrontation at American Ceramics Annual Art of Collecting Symposium, Crafts Report, 5/91; and others. *Mem:* Col Art Asn; Pa Coun Arts; Am Asn Mus; Asn Art Mus Dirs. *Res:* Twentieth century; post-World War II; earthworks performance sculpture. *Publ:* Auth, Lenore Tawney: A Retrospective (exhib catalog), Am Craft Mus, 90; The History of Twentieth-Century American Craft: a centenary project - 3 Vol 1900-1945 Am Craft Mus. *Mailing Add:* 150 E 69th St Apt 12J New York NY 10021-5704

KAREKEN, MICHAEL RAYMOND
PRINTMAKER, PAINTER
b Washington, DC, July 16, 61. *Study:* Yale Univ Summer Sch Music & Art, 82; Bowdoin Col, BA, 83; Brooklyn Col, MFA, 86; Skowhegan Sch Painting & Sculpture, 88. *Work:* Walker Art Ctr, Minneapolis Inst Arts, Minn; Minn Mus Am Art & Minn Hist Soc, St Paul. *Exhib:* Selections 42, Drawing Ctr, NY, 88; Art and the Law, Nev Mus Art, Reno, 95 & Springfield Mus Art, Ohio, 95; Drawings Midwest, Minn Mus Am Art, Minneapolis, 96; Earth Air Fire Water, Minneapolis Inst Arts, Minn, 96; Invitational Exhibition of Painting & Sculpture, Am Acad Arts & Letters, NY, 97; 173rd Ann Exhib, Nat Acad Mus, NY, 98; 175th Ann Exhib, Nat Acad Mus, 2000; Solo show Groveland Gallery, Minneapolis, Minn, 99. *Teaching:* Lectr painting, drawing & printmaking, Minneapolis Col Art & Design, Minn, 96-. *Awards:* Artist Fel, New York Found Arts, 88; Artist Fel, Minn State Arts Bd, 96; Louise Nevelson Award, Invitational Exhib Painting & Sculpture, Am Acad Arts & Letters, 97; Bush Found Fellowship, 2000; Artist Fellowship, Minn State Arts Bd, 2000; Printmaking Award, Nat Acad of Design, 2000. *Mem:* Col Art Asn. *Mailing Add:* 3215 S Humboldt Ave Minneapolis MN 55408

KARIMI, REZA
PAINTER
b Isfahan, Iran, Aug 23, 46, US citizen. *Study:* Sch Fine Arts, Isfahan, 66; Queens Col, Univ NY, BA, 76 & Brooklyn Col, MFA, 78. *Exhib:* Memories of Iran, Borghi & Co, NY, 90, Mina Renton Gallery, London, 92 & Hammer Galleries, NY, 93; Harrison Celebrates Art (A Tricentennial Tribute), Neuberger Mus Art, Purchase, NY, 96; New York City in 1997, Hammer Galleries, NY, 97; World of Drawing and Watercolor, The Dorchester, London, 98. *Awards:* Grant, Ancient Persepolis, Fine Arts Ministry, Iran, 66; 1st Prize, Prof Show, Putnam Arts Coun, 87. *Bibliog:* Portrait of an Artist (film), 92 & Exhibition Review at Hammer (film), 93, Aftab Productions, WNYC TV Network. *Mem:* Am Inst for Conservation; Putnam Arts Coun. *Media:* Watercolor, Oil on Canvas. *Publ:* Contribr, Technology in the service of art, Armon Mag, 9/91; Interview with Reza Karimi (painter), Ispand Mag, Summer 93; Exceptional images, Golchin Publ, 7/94; He views simplicity & creates the sublime, Persian Heritage, Fall 96; Hunter of light & memories, Golchin Publ, 5/98. *Dealer:* Art Restoration Inc PO Box 29 School St Mahopac Falls NY 10542. *Mailing Add:* School St PO Box 29 Mahopac Falls NY 10542

KARIYA, HIROSHI
CONCEPTUAL ARTIST
b Kamaishi, Iwate Pref, Japan, Apr 14, 48. *Work:* New Mus Lib, NY; Inst Contemp Art, Univ Pa, Philadelphia; McCarthy Arts Ctr, St Michaels Col, Winooski, Vt; Kubo Mus, Mooka, Japan. *Exhib:* Sign of the Times 1993, Art Tower Mito, Ibaraki, Japan, 94; Sutra; One thing in everything; Everything in one thing, Inst Contemp Art, Univ Pa, Philadelphia, 90; Sutra, Exit Art, NY, 89; Sound Show, PS 1 Mus, NY, 79; Int

Drawing Biennale, Camden Arts Ctr, London, 79; World Print Competition, San Francisco Mus Art, 77. *Bibliog:* Kay Larson (auth), Sound Show, Village Voice, 10/29/79; Edward J Sozanski (auth), Contemplating creation, rebirth, Philadelphia Inquirer, 3/18/90; Miki Miyatake (auth), Signs of hope, Japan Times, 4/17/94. *Media:* Multi Media. *Mailing Add:* 143 S Eighth St No 3B Brooklyn NY 11211-6167

KARLEN, MARK
EDUCATOR
b Philadelphia, Pa. *Study:* Inst Design, Ill Inst Technol, BS, 52; New Sch Soc Res, New York, grad studies, 54-55; Union Inst, PhD, 83. *Pos:* Interior designer & architect, Karlen & Assoc, Philadelphia, 85-94; dean art & design, Fashion Inst Technol, New York, 94-. *Teaching:* Assoc prof & chmn, Dept Interior Design, Univ Cincinnati, 74-79; assoc prof, Mt Vernon Col, Washington, 82-85; prof & chmn, Interior Design Dept, Moore Col Art, Philadelphia, 88-94. *Mem:* Am Inst Architects; Interior Design Educators Coun; Found Interior Design Educ; Am Soc Interior Designers. *Publ:* Auth, Space Planning for the NCIDQ Exam, MGI Mgt Inst, 89; Space Planning Basics, Van Nostrand Reinhold, 92; Lighting Design for the NCIDQ Exam, MGI Mgt Inst, 93. *Mailing Add:* Fashion Inst Technol Seventh Ave at 27th St Rm D350 New York NY 10001

KARLEN, PETER H
EDUCATOR, WRITER
Study: Univ Calif, Berkeley, BA(hist), 71; Univ Calif, Hastings Col Law, JD, 74; Univ Denver Col Law, MS(law & society), 76. *Pos:* Art attorney, self-employed, 78-86, owner, Peter H Karlen, A Prof Law Corp, 86-; writer, Artlaw column, 79-; contrib ed & columnist, Artweek, 79-95, Art Calendar, 89-96; Art Cellar Exchange, 89-92; Equine Images, 92-95. *Teaching:* Lectr law & the arts, Univ Warwick Sch Law, 76-78; adj prof, Univ San Diego Sch Law, 79-84; adj prof, Western State Univ Col Law, 76, 79, 80, 88 & 92. *Mem:* Am Soc Aesthetics; Brit Soc Aesthetics. *Res:* Property rights in aesthetic creations; expert opinions, fakes & forgeries; artist's moral rights. *Publ:* Auth, What is art? A sketch for a legal definition, Law Quart Rev, 78; Legal aesthetics, Brit J Aesthetics, 79; Moral rights in California, Univ San Diego Law Rev, 82; Aesthetic quality & art preservation, J Aesthetics & Art Criticism, 83; Fakes, forgeries, & expert opinions, J Arts Mngmt & Law, 86; Appraiser's Responsibility for Determining Fair Market Value, Cloumbia - VLA, J Law & Acts, 89. *Mailing Add:* 1205 Prospect Ste 400 La Jolla CA 92037

KARLSTROM, PAUL JOHNSON
HISTORIAN, ADMINISTRATOR
b Seattle, Wash, Jan 22, 41. *Study:* Stanford Univ, BA(Eng lit), 64; Univ Calif, Los Angeles, MA(art), PhD, 73. *Collection Arranged:* Venice Panorama (auth, catalog), Grunwald Ctr for Graphic Arts, Univ Calif, Los Angeles, 69; Louis M Eilshemius in the Hirshhorn Museum Traveling Exhib (auth, catalog), 78; Claude Buck (auth, catalog), Glastonbury Gallery, San Francisco, 83. *Pos:* Asst cur, Grunwald Ctr for the Graphic Arts, Univ Calif, Los Angeles, 67-70; guest cur, Smithsonian Inst Traveling Exhib Serv, Washington, 77; dir, West Coast Regional Ctr, Arch Am Art, Smithsonian Inst, San Francisco, 73-91, San Marino, 91-03; mem adv bd, Humanities West; bd dir, Integrated Arts, Bay Area Video Coalition & Southwest Art Hist Coun, formerly; secr, Va Steele Scott Found; vp Noah Purifoy Found. *Teaching:* Instr Renaissance to mod art, Calif State Univ, Northridge, 72-73; vis instr mus practices, Calif Col Arts & Crafts, Oakland, 76. *Awards:* Samuel H Kress Fel, Nat Gallery Art, Washington, 70-71; Acad Distinction, Col Fine Arts, Univ Calif, Los Angeles, 74. *Mem:* Calif Hist Soc (edit bd); Oral Hist Asn; Am Studies Asn. *Res:* American art and culture, 19th and 20th century. *Publ:* The Spirit in the Stone: Visionary Art of James W Washington, Jr, Univ Washington Press, 89; Turning the Tide: Early Los Angeles Modernists 1920-1956, Santa Barbara Mus Art, 90; Fletcher Benton, Harry N Abrams, 90; ed, On the Edge of America: California Modernist Art, 1900-1950, Univ Calif Press, 97; contrib, Diego Rivera: Art and Revolution, INBA, 99, The Complete Jacob Lawrence, Univ Wash Press, 2000, Reading California, Univ Calif Press, 2000. *Mailing Add:* 73 Carmelita St San Francisco CA 94117

KARN, GLORIA STOLL
PAINTER, PRINTMAKER
b New York, NY, Nov 13, 23. *Study:* Art Students League; also with Eliot O'Hara & Samuel Rosenberg. *Work:* Yale Univ; Brooklyn Mus; Pittsburgh Pub Schs; Carnegie Inst Mus Art; Westinghouse Collection. *Exhib:* Assoc Artists Pittsburgh Ann, 49-; Butler Inst Am Art Ann, 61; one-man shows, Pittsburgh Plan for Art, 65, Carnegie Inst Mus, 66 & North Hills Art Ctr, 78, 83 & 91; Sacred Arts Show, St Stephens, Pittsburgh, 66; Acqueons Open, 98 & 2000; work exhib several Pittsburgh Art Shows, currently. *Pos:* illusr, cover artist, Pulp Mags, 41-49. *Teaching:* Instr painting & collage, North Hills Art Ctr, 65-; instr, Community Col Allegheny Co, 73-79. *Awards:* Carnegie Inst Purchase Prize, 60; Westinghouse Purchase Prize, 66; Third Prize, Pittsburgh Watercolor Soc, Aqueous Open, 98, Hon Mention, Waterworks, 2002; Second Prize, North Hills Art Ctr, 2000, 2001, 2002, 2003, First Prize, 2002. *Bibliog:* Rusty Hevelin (auth), Pulpcon 30 Guest of Honor, the Pulpster #11, 2001; John Wooley (auth), Pulp Adventures (interview by auth), 2001. *Mem:* Assoc Artists Pittsburgh; Group A, Pittsburgh (pres, 66-70); Pittsburgh Ctr Arts (bd mem, 69-72); North Hills Art Ctr (bd mem, 70-72 & 78-80, pres, 80-81); Pittsburgh Watercolor Soc (bd mem 2000-2006). *Media:* Oil, Watercolor; Etching, Lithography. *Mailing Add:* 151 Louise Rd Pittsburgh PA 15237

KARNES, KAREN
CERAMIST, CRAFTSMAN
b New York, NY, Nov 17, 25. *Study:* Brooklyn Col, BA, 46; NY State Col Ceramics, Alfred Univ, 51; Sesto Fiorentino, Italy, 50-51. *Work:* Am Crafts Mus, NY; Everson Mus, Syracuse, NY; Metrop Mus Art, NY; Del Mus Art, Wilmington; Philadelphia Mus Art, Pa; Mus of World Folk Art, Calif; and many others. *Comn:* Fireplace, sink & garden seats, comn by Jack Lenor Larsen, Easthampton, NY, 62. *Exhib:* High Styles: Am Design Since 1900, Whitney Mus Am Art, NY (traveling), 85; Kamper Gallery, Kansas City Art Inst, Mo, 86; N Eng Ceramic Vessels, Westminster Gallery, Boston, Mass, 86; Art in Craft Today: Poetry of the Physical, Am Craft Mus, NY, 86; The Arts at Black Mt Col, Grey Art Gallery, NY (traveling), 87; Fired with Enthusiam, Campbell Mus, Camden, NJ (traveling), 87; one-person exhib, Hadler/Rodriguez Gallery, La, 81, NY, 81, 82 & 85, The Hand and the Spirit, Scottsdale, Ariz, 86, 88, 90 & 93, Stratton Arts Festival, Stratton, Vt, 86 & Garth Clark Gallery, NY, 87, 90, 92, 94, 97, 99, 2000; JoAnn Rapp Gallery, Ariz, 98; group exhibs, Garth Clark Gallery, NY, 2001; Los Angeles Co Mus of Art, Calif, 2000. *Collection Arranged:* Salt Glazed Ceramics, Hadler Rodriguez Gallery, 77. *Teaching:* Instr, clay seminar/workshop, Bloomsburg State Univ, Pa, Penland Sch Crafts, 71; art craft workshop, Soc Ed, Eng, 70 & 73, kiln workshop, Bowling Green State Univ, Ohio, 73; craftsman-in-residence, Hunter Col, CUNY, 75-76, Del Art Mus, 76; instr, Royal Col Art, London, 77, Southampton Col LI Univ, summer prog 78-80; Frog Hollow Craft Ctr, Middlebury, Vt, 80-82, 85 & 89; Camberwell Sch Art, London, 86. *Awards:* Artists Fel, Vermont Coun Arts, 88; Vt Gov Award Excellence Art, 97; Gold Medal, Am Craft Coun, 98; and others. *Bibliog:* Reggie Hynes (auth), Karen Karnes Workshop, Ceramic Review, 82; Mary E Harris (auth), The Arts at Black Mountain Col, MIT Press, Cambridge, Mass, 87; Zelanski & Fisher (coauths), Appreciating the Visual Arts, John Calmann & King, 88. *Dealer:* Garth Clark Gallery. *Mailing Add:* 188 Whitehill Loop Morgan VT 05853

KARP, AARON S
PAINTER
b Altoona, Pa, Dec 7, 47. *Study:* State Univ NY Col Buffalo, BA, 69; Ind Univ, MFA, 73. *Work:* Guggenheim Mus, NY; Albuquerque Mus, Albuquereue Airport & Univ NMex Art Mus, Albuquerque; Ackland Art Ctr, Chapel Hill, NC; Roswell Mus, NMex; American Airlines Corp & ITT Corp, Dallas, Tex; and many others. *Exhib:* One-man exhibs, Janus Gallery, Santa Fe, NMex, 88 & 90, Watson Gallery, Houston, Tex, 89, Katherina Rich Perlow Gallery, NY, 89 & 91, State Univ NY, Albany, NY, 90, Barclay Simpson Gallery, Lafayette, Calif, 90, Robischon Gallery, Denver, Colo, 91, Amarillo Art Ctr, Tex, 92, Helander Gallery, Palm Beach, Fla, 92, Barclay Simpson Fine Art, Lafayette, Calif, 92, Eva Cohon Gallery, Chicago, 93 & 95, Erikson & Elins Fine Art, 94, Sandy Carson Gallery, Denver, 97, Craighead-Green Gallery, Dallas, 97, 2000 & 02, Elliot Smith Contemp Art, St Louis, 98, Lee Hansley Gallery, Raleigh, NC, 99, Duke Univ Fine Art Gallery, Durham, NC, 2000, R Duane Reed Gallery, St Louis, 2001 & 05, Tercera Gallery, San Francisco, 2002, Carson-Masuoka Gallery, Denver, 2002, William Havu Gallery, Denver, 2004; School of the U, Fine Art Mus, Univ NMex, Albuquerque, 2000; Man and Nature, Adair Margo Gallery, El Paso, Tex, 2001, Finca Las Culebras, 2003; Colored By Process, Contemp Art Gallery, Colo State Univ, Colorado Springs, 2002; Systems, Duke Univ, Durham, NC, 2006; For Lack of Focal Point, Albuquerque Mus, NM, 2006; and others. *Pos:* Oper supervisor, Guggenheim Mus, 74-75; dir, E Carolina Univ Gallery, Greenville, NC, 77-79. *Teaching:* Asst prof, Univ NMex, Albuquerque, 79-84. *Awards:* Artist-in-Residence Grant, Roswell Mus & Art Ctr, NMex, 81 & 85, Anderson Ranch Art Ctr, Snowmass, Colo, 98, Djerassi, Woodside, Calif, 2000, MacNamara Found, Westport Island, Maine, 2004 & Fundacion Valparaiso Mojacar, Spain, 2006; Research Allocation Grants, Univ NMex, Albuquerque, 82; Exxon Corp Purchase Award, Guggenheim Mus, New York, 84; Grants MacDowell Colony, Peterborough, NH, 2000, Pollock-Krasner Found, 2001, John Anson Kittredge Found, 2002 & Julia and David White Artists' Colony, Ciudad Colon, Costa Rica, 2003. *Bibliog:* Diane Waldman (auth), Emerging Artists 1978 to 1986: Selections from the Exxon Series (catalog), Solomon R Guggenheim Mus, 87; Louise Krasniewicz (auth), review, The Times Union, Albany, NY, 3/17/90; Sandy Ballatore (auth), Aaron Karp, Artspace, 9-10/90. *Media:* Acrylic. *Dealer:* Erickson & Elins Gallery 345 Sutters St San Francisco CA. *Mailing Add:* 7811 Guadalupe Trail NW Albuquerque NM 87107-6507

KARP, DIANE R
EDUCATOR
Study: Univ Pa, PhD in art hist. *Work:* Mus Nat Hist, NY; Philadelphia Mus Art, 1985. *Exhib:* Exhib incl with Dan Fox In Time of Plague, Am; exhib incl Art, Medical & the Human Condition, Philadelphia Mus Art, 1985. *Pos:* Cur-Ars Medica Phil Mus Art; dir New Observations Mag, Santa Fe Art Inst, 2001-. *Teaching:* Prof, 20th century art hist. Temple Univ. *Publ:* auth: (exhib catalogue) Ars Medica, 1985. *Mailing Add:* Santa Fe Art Inst 1600 St Michaels Dr Santa Fe NM 87505

KARP, RICHARD GORDON
PAINTER, LECTURER
b Brooklyn, NY, May 17, 33. *Study:* City Col New York, BBA(advert) & MA(fine art); Brooklyn Mus Art Sch, with John Bageris. *Work:* Aankoop Gemete, Stedlijk Mus, Amsterdam, Neth; Northern Ill Univ, DeKalb. *Exhib:* Stedlijk Mus, Amsterdam, 70; RAI Exhib, Amsterdam, 70; Heckscher Mus, Huntington, NY, 74; Viridian Gallery, NY, 77; Parrish Mus, South Hampton, NY, 78. *Bibliog:* Julie Attkiss (auth), Karp, riding his intuition, Holland Herald, 3/69. *Mem:* Visual Artist & Gallery Asn; Artists Equity. *Media:* Oil & Mixed Media. *Dealer:* Ronald Hunnings Inc 139 Spring St New York NY 10012; Kunsthandel K 276 Keizersgracht 276 Amsterdam Netherlands. *Mailing Add:* 1201 Queen Anne Rd Teaneck NJ 07666

KARSH, YOUSUF
PHOTOGRAPHER
b Armenia, Dec 23, 08; Can citizen. *Study:* With John H Garo, Boston; hon degrees from 27 univs among others. *Work:* Metrop Mus Art & Mus Mod Art, NY; Nat Portrait Gallery, London, Eng; Nat Gallery Can, Ottawa, Ont; Biblioreque Nat, Paris; Chicago Art Inst; and many others. *Exhib:* One-man shows, Boston Mus Fine Arts, 68, Corcoran Gallery Art, 69, Seattle Art Mus, 70, Mus Mod Art, Tokyo, 71-81, Mus Sci

& Industry, Chicago, 77-79, Mus Photogr & Film, Bradford, Eng, Int Ctr Photogr NY, 83 & Nat Portrait Gallery, London, 83; Major Retrospective, Mus Fine Art, Boston, 97; Detroit Inst Art, 98; Nat Portrait Gallery, Australia, 99; plus many others, incl Nat Gallery Australia & Alberta, Can. *Pos:* Trustee, Photog Arts & Sci Found, 65-72; photog adv, Expo 70, Osaka, Japan, 96-70. *Teaching:* Vis prof photog & fine arts, Ohio Univ, 68-70 & Emerson Col, 72-73. *Awards:* Can Coun Medal, 65; Silver Shinola Award, Boston Univ, 83; Companion of Can, Can Govt, 90; and many others; Silver Shinola Award, Boston Univ, 83; Companion of Can, Can Govt, 90. *Bibliog:* Forsee (auth), Yousuf Karsh, In: Five Famous Photographers, 70; featured article, Reader's Digest, 2/77; featured on Sixty Minutes, Columbia Broadcasting System, 5/77; Harry Rasky (dir), Karsh: The Searching Eye (film), 85. *Mem:* Hon fel Royal Photog Soc; Dutch Treat Club, NY; Rideau Club, Ottawa; Royal Can Acad Arts; Prof Photog Asn Can; Century Club; hon fel Prof Photog Am. *Media:* Film. *Publ:* Auth, Karsh Portraits, 76; Karsh Canadians, 78; Karsh: a Fifty Year Retrospective, 83; American Legends, 92; Karsh: A Sixty Year Retrsopective, 96. *Mailing Add:* 2 Commonwealth Ave Boston MA 02116

KARWOSKI, RICHARD CHARLES
PAINTER, EDUCATOR
b Brooklyn, NY, Oct 3, 38. *Study:* Pratt Inst, with Richard Lindner & Jacob Landau, BFA, 61; Columbia Univ, MA, 63. *Work:* Okla Art Ctr, Oklahoma City; Everson Mus, Syracuse, NY; Wichita Mus, Kans; Detroit Art Inst, Mich; Butler Inst Am Art, Youngstown, Ohio. *Exhib:* Watercolor USA, Springfield, Mo, 80; Winterscape, Guild Hall Mus, East Hampton, NY, 81-82; Pittsburgh Watercolor Soc Ann, 81-83; Pelham Arts Ctr, NY, 83; Guild Hall Mus, 50 Artists View the South Fork, East Hampton, 85-86; Retrospective: 1970-86, Saatchi & Saatchi Compton Advert Inc, NY, 86; Mich Watercolor Soc, Drasl Art Ctr, 86; Wagner Col, Kade Gallery, Staten Island, NY, 87; Retrospective: 1963-1988, Aritawagh Hall, Springs, East Hampton, 88; Watercolor Bright & Beautiful, Guild Hall Mus, 88; and others. *Pos:* Dir, Grace Gallery, New York City Tech Col, Brooklyn, 70-80, assoc dir, 81; adv comn mem, Art & Design High Sch, NY, 77-, pres, Alumni Asn, 80-. *Teaching:* Prof painting & design, New York City Tech Col, 69-. *Awards:* Okla Watercolor Soc President's Award, 84; Nat Arts Club Salzman Award, 85; Northlight Book Award, Wamaroneck Artist Gold, 85; and others. *Bibliog:* Chauncey Howell (reporter), NBC News, 74; John Perrault (ed, critic), article, SoHo Weekly News, 11/27/75; Helen A Harrison (auth), article, New York Times, 2/3/80. *Mem:* Salmagundi Club; Pa Soc Watercolor Painters; Audubon Soc of Artists; Nat Arts Club; NY Artists Equity (bd dir, 82-84). *Media:* Watercolor, Oil. *Publ:* Auth, The contour color method, The Artists Mag, 4/86; contribr, Art in Society, The Arts Academe, Univ Wis, 76; auth, Am Artist Mag Watercolor page, Bill Publs, 3/79; contribr, Footwear, Van Nostrand, 79; illusr, The Intimate Hour (bk jacket), Avery, 79; auth, The Watercolor Page, Am Artist Mag, Mar 79; contribr, Pratt Reports, Pratt Inst, spring, 81; auth, Watercolor Bright and Beautiful, Watson Guptill, 10/88. *Dealer:* Nancy Stein Art Consult New York NY; Gallery East East Hampton NY

KASH, MARIE (MARIE KASH WELTZHEMER)
PAINTER, GRAPHIC ARTIST
b Akron, Ohio, May 5, 60. *Study:* Univ Cent Okla, Edmond, Okla, BA(com art), 82; studies with Alan Flattman, Sally Strand & Lorenzo Chavez. *Work:* Goddard Art Ctr, Ardmore, Okla; Corp: Laureate Psychiatric Clinic & Hosp, Tulsa, Okla; Coca Cola, Moscow; Am Bank & Trust, Edmond, Okla; Lawyers Title Oklahoma City Inc. *Comn:* Pvt portrait, comn by Mr & Mrs Sherwood Taylor, Norman, Okla, 89, 90, 93 & 97; pvt portrait, comn by Mr & Mrs Bill Hodges, Edmond, Okla, 91, 96 & 2000; Pvt Portrait, Mr & Mrs Daivd Rainbolt, 89, 97, 2003; pvt Portrait, Mr & Mrs John Baumert, 99, 2000, 2001, 2005; Accounting Firm Off of Tullius Taylor Sartain & Sartain. *Exhib:* 19th, 21st & 25th Ann Open Exhib, Pastel Soc Am, NY, 91, 93 & 97; solo exhibs, Goddard Art Ctr, Ardmore, Okla, 93, 2005 & Kirkpatrick Gallery Okla Artists, Oklahoma City, 95; Telluride Pastel Invitational, Telluride Gallery, Colo, 95; Person to Person, W Valley Art Mus, Ariz, 97; and others. *Pos:* Graphic media artist, Okla Water Resources Bd, Oklahoma City, 84-88. *Awards:* Stephen Leitner, Esq Award, 19th Ann Open Exhib, Pastel Soc Am, 91; First Award Excellence, 11th Ann Exhib, Pastel Soc Southwest, 91; Best Show, Okla Art Workshop 11th Ann Juried Exhib, Tulsa, 94. *Bibliog:* John Brandenburg (auth), Paintings Capture Music for the Eyes, The Daily Oklahoman, 9/8/95; The Best of Pastels, Rockport Publ, 96; The Pastel Journal, Taking the Temperature of Color for Strong Complementary Contrasts, by, Ruth Summer, May/June, 2000. *Mem:* Pastel Soc Am (sig mem); Pastel Soc Southwest (sig mem); Okla Pastel Soc. *Media:* Pastel, Watercolor. *Dealer:* MA Doran Gallery 3509 S Peoria Tulsa OK 74105; Telluride Gallery of Fine Art, 130 E Colorado Ave Telluride CO 81435. *Mailing Add:* 2513 Woodruff Rd Edmond OK 73013

KASHDIN, GLADYS SHAFRAN
PAINTER, EDUCATOR
b Pittsburgh, Pa, Dec 15, 21. *Study:* Art Students League, with Stefan Hirsch; Univ Miami, BA(magna cum laude), 60; Fla State Univ, with Karl Zerbe, MA, 62, PhD(humanities), 65. *Work:* Tex Tech Mus, Lubbock; Futan Univ, Shanghai, China; Columbus Mus Arts, Ga; Mus Sci and Industry, Tampa; Jan Phatt Libr,Tampa. *Comn:* Silkscreen eds, LeMoyne Art Found, Tallahassee, Fla, 70, 71 & 73; City of Tampa Publ Art Prog, Oil, Acrylic Large Paintings, 2004-05. *Exhib:* 28th Ann Brooklyn Mus, 44; one-woman shows, Palm Beach Art, LeMoyne Art Found, Tallahassee, 66-74, Columbus Mus Arts, Ga, 73, 76 & 83, Univ SFla, 75, 81 & 2002, Tex Tech Mus, 78, Fla Dept of State, Tallahassee 85 & 86, Kresge Mus Art, E Lansing, Mich, 87, Ferris State Univ, Mich, 89, Fla A&M, Tallahassee, 91 & Tampa Mus Art, 96-97; Fla State Univ, Appleton Mus Art, 99, 2001-2002; Mus Sci and Industry, Tampa, 2003. *Collection Arranged:* Dr & Ms Cecil Mackey, pvt collection, Mich; Univ So Fla, Colleges of Bus, Social Studies, Special Collections Libr; Mus Sci and Indust; Wheeler, Herman, Hopkins & Lagor, Pa; Dr & Ms William Dalton, pvt collection. *Pos:* Photogr, Shafran Co, NY & Fla, 38-60. *Teaching:* Instr & dir oil painting, Adult Educ, Palm Beach Co, Fla, 56-60; instr watercolor, Thomasville Art Guild, Ga, 61-62; prof humanities, Univ SFla, Tampa, 65-87, Humanities Visual Arts Workshops, 66-71, prof emer humanities, 87-. *Awards:* Gold Medal, Univ Miami, 60; Citizens Award, Mus Adv Bd, Hillsborough Co, 84; Phi Kappa Phi Artist-Scholar Award, 87; Award of Merit, Norton Mus Art, 1957, 60, 63. *Bibliog:* Dr Hans Juergensen (auth), Kashdin's Everglades series, 73 & Herb Allen (auth), Local rivers series theme, 75, Tampa Tribune; Pam Renner (auth), Gladys Kashdin: An artist in her sun-lit years, Bay Life, 79; Gladys Shafran Kashdin: The Creative Spirit, 1999; Gladys Shafran Kashdin: Gaia's Daughter, 2001, rev ed, 2003; Gladys Shafran Kashdin: In Retrospect, 95-96. *Mem:* Tampa Mus Art; Metrop Mus Art; Nat Mus Women in Art. *Media:* Watercolor, Acrylic. *Publ:* Auth, A new approach to a humanities-visual arts workshop, Humanities J, fall 70; Life long education for women--general & liberal studies from their point of view, Perspectives, winter 74; Women artists and the institution of feminism in America, SEASA, 79; auth, In Retrospect, Tampa Mus Art, 96. *Mailing Add:* 441 Biltmore Ave Temple Terrace FL 33617

KASKEY, RAYMOND JOHN
SCULPTOR, ARCHITECT
b Pittsburgh, Pa, Feb 22, 43. *Study:* Carnegie Mellon Univ, BA(archit), 67; Yale Univ, Sch Art & Archit, also sculpture with Erwin Haver, 69. *Work:* Mus Mod Art, NY; First Interstate Bank, Ore; Kaiser Permanente, Portland, Ore. *Comn:* sculpture, Portland Bldg, Ore, 85; sculpture, Harold Washington Library Ctr, Chicago, 90; sculpture, Nat Law Enforcement Officers Memorial, Washington, DC. *Exhib:* Nat Sculpture Soc Ann, Equitable Gallery, NY, 80 & 81; Barbara Fendrick Gallery, Washington, DC; John Nichols Gallery, NY, 86; Barbara Fendrick Space, NY, 88. *Teaching:* Asst prof arch & design, Univ Md, College Park, 69-76; vis critic, Yale Univ, New Haven, Conn, spring 77 & Kans State Univ, Manhattan, spring 78. *Awards:* Mrs Louis Bennett Prize, 82 & Henry Hering Mem Medal, 86, Nat Sculpture Soc; Creative & Performing Arts Award, Univ Md, 70 & 72. *Bibliog:* video, Portlandia, Rogers Cable Network, Ore; Hail, Portlandia, Art News, 12/85; article, Archit Mag, 12/85; article, Newsweek, 7/86; article, Mus & Arts, 10/88. *Mem:* Nat Sculpture Soc; Am Inst Archit. *Media:* Bronze, Stone. *Dealer:* Barbara Fendrick Gallery 3059 M St NW Washington DC 20007. *Mailing Add:* 2221 Hall Pl NW Washington DC 20007-1837

KASNOWSKI, CHESTER N
COLLAGE ARTIST, CONCEPTUAL ARTIST, PAINTING
b Perth Amboy, NJ, Jan 23, 44. *Study:* Dayton Art Inst, Ohio, BFA, 71; Tulane Univ, New Orleans, La, MFA, 73. *Work:* Brooklyn Mus, NY; Guggenheim Mus & Whitney Mus Am Art, NY; Stedelijk Mus, Amsterdam. *Exhib:* One-person exhibs, Ball State Univ, Muncie, Ind, 74 & McKissick Mus, Columbia, SC, 78; Contemp Arts Ctr, New Orleans, La, 78; Dartmouth Col Galleries, Hanover, NH, 79; Class Portrait, Robert Hull Fleming Mus, Burlington, Vt, 81; Invitational, Franklin Furnace, NY, 82. *Teaching:* instr, watercolor, acrylic painting, currently. *Awards:* Nat Endowment Arts Grant, 74; Drawing Grant, 78 & Spec Mention, Illuminated Thoughts Exhib, 79, Vt Coun Arts. *Media:* Acrylic. *Dealer:* Bertha Urdang Gallery 23 E 74th St New York NY 10021; Northstar Gallery Manchaster Vt 05255. *Mailing Add:* PO Box 1 Weston VT 05161

KASS, DEBORAH
PAINTER
b San Antonio, Tex, 52. *Study:* Art Student's League, 68-70; Whitney Mus Independent Study Prog, 72; Carnegie-Mellon Univ, BFA(painting). *Work:* Guggenheim Mus; Cincinnati Mus; Mus Mod Art, NY; Whitney Mus Am Art; Mus Fine Arts, Boston; Jewish Mus. *Exhib:* Jose Freire Gallery, 94 & 95; Nohear: Incandies cent, La Mus Art, Homlebeac, Denmark, 96; The Prophecy of Pop, Contemp Art Ctr, New Orleans, La, 97; In Your Face, Andy Warhol Mus, Pittsburgh, Pa, 98; Art on Paper, Weatherspoon Gallery Art, Greensboro, NC, 98; The Warhol Project: The Neucombe Art Gallery, Tulane Univ, New Orleans, 99; one person shows, Chmn Ma, Jose Freire Fine Arts, New York City, 1993, Barbara Krakow Gallery, Boston, 1994, Arthur Roger Gallery, New Orleans, 1998; My Andy: A Retrospective, Jose Freire Fine Art, New York City, 1995, Kemper Mus Contemp Art and Design, Kansas City, Mo, 1996. *Teaching:* Distinguished vis artist, RI Sch Design, 90, 91; vis artist, Art Inst, Chicago, 93, Boston Mus Sch Fine Arts, 93, State Univ NY, Purchase, 94 & Skowkegan Sch Painting & Sculpture, 97. *Awards:* Fel, NY State Found Arts, 91; Art Matters, 92; Fel, Art Matters Inc, 92 & 96. *Bibliog:* Roberta Smith (auth), Women artists engage the enemy, NY Times, 8/16/92; Holland Cotter (auth), NY Times, 1/15/93; Holland Cotter (auth), Art in Am, 6/94. *Mem:* Col Art Asn. *Dealer:* Arthur Roger Gallery New Orleans LA

KASS, RAY
PAINTER
b Rockville Centre, NY, Jan 25, 44. *Study:* Univ NC, BA, 67, MFA(painting), 69; also painting with Keith Crown, 67 & John Cage, 83-90. *Work:* Addison Gallery Am Art, Andover, Mass; Boston Pub Libr; Art Mus Western Va, Roanoke; Univ Mass, Amherst; Montgomery Mus Art, Ala; Norton Mus Art, W Palm Beach, 02. *Comn:* Ethyl Corp, Richmond, Va; Grayco Corp, Richmond, Va. *Exhib:* Allan Stone Gallery, NY, 72, 75, 77, 81 & 86, Addison Gallery Am Art, 74, Osuna Gallery, Washington, DC, 79, 84 & 88 & Southeastern Ctr Contemp Art, NC, 80; Reynolds Gallery, Richmond, Va, 91 & 95; Franz Bader Gallery, Washington, DC, 93 & 95; Art Mus Western Va, Roanoke, 93; AVC Contemp Arts, NY, 2000-2002. *Collection Arranged:* John Cage: New River Watercolors (auth, catalog), Va Mus, Richmond, 88; Morris Graves: Vision of the Inner Eye, Braziller, NY, 83. *Pos:* Guest cur, Phillips Collection, Washington, DC, 80-83; Dir, Mountian Lake Workshop, Va Tech Found, 85-. *Teaching:* Asst prof painting, Va Polytechnic Inst, Blacksburg, Va, 76-81, assoc prof, 81-84, prof, 84-. *Awards:* Individual Artists Grant, Nat Endowment Arts, 81; Va Mus

Artists Fel, 84; and others. *Bibliog:* Donald B Kuspit (auth), Painting in the South: 1564-1980, Va Mus, Richmond, 80; Theodore F Wolff (auth), How Nature Engages Artists, Christian Sci Monitor, 6/29/90; Donald B Kuspit (auth), Images of the Winged Earth: The Painting of Ray Kass, Art Mus Western Va, Roanoke, 93. *Mem:* Col Art Asn Am; Folk Art Soc Am; Jargon Soc. *Media:* Watercolor, Oil. *Res:* On-going collaborative art projects of the Mountain Lake Workshop of the Virginia Tech Found. *Publ:* Auth, Morris Graves: Vision of the Inner-Eye (book), Braziller, NY, 83; auth, Sounds of the Inner-Eye: Mark Tobey, John Cage, Morris Grave, Univ of Wash Press, Seattle, 2002. *Dealer:* Reynolds Gallery 1514 W Main St Richmond VA 23220; A.V.C. Contemporary Art 41 E 57th St New York 10022. *Mailing Add:* 1360 N Fork Rd Christiansburg VA 24073

KASSNER, LILY
HISTORIAN, CRITIC
b Mexico City, Mex, Nov 16, 40. *Study:* Universidad Nacional Autonoma de Mexico, Mexico City, Mex, BA (hist), 65, MA (art hist), 76 & PhD (art hist), 97. *Collection Arranged:* Transicion y Ruptura, Europalia 93, Noortman Gallery, Maastricht, Holland, 93; La Escultura Mexicana al fin del Milenio, Europalia 93, Park Leopold Vindictive Laan, Oostende, Belgium, 93; Actualidad Plastica en Mexico, Europalia, 93, Provincaal Mus Voor Moderne Kunst, Oostende, Belgium, 93; Francisco Zuñiga: Homenaje, 94 & Ricardo Martinez Homenaje, 94, Museo del Palacio de Bellas Artes, Instituto Nacional de Bellas Artes, Mexio City, Mexico; Cur on EDS Collection, 96-97; Collab, Catalogue, Mexico Eterno Exhibition, Palacio de Bellas Artes, Mexico Petit Palais, France, Musco Marco, Monterrey, Mexico, 99; Catalog, Helen Escobedo Exhibition, Estar y No Estar, Moca V Nam, Mexico; Catalogue Expression del Nuevo Milenio Presencia de Mexico, Museo de Arte Contemporaneo, Puerto Rico, 2001; Catalogue Santiago Calatrava, V Nam, Mexico; Collab, Aztecs Catalogue Royal Acad Arts Exhibition, UK, 2002; Collab, Catalogue, La Estetica de Jesus Reyes, Ferreira Exhib, Mexico, 2002; Research Cur, Article, Tiempo, Piedra Y Barro, Exhibition, UNam Mexico, Centro Cultural Santo Domingo, Oaxaca, Macay, Youcatan, 2002-2003; Collab, Acqua-Wasser, Catalogue, V Nam, Goethe Inst, Mexico, 20033. *Pos:* Coordr (second state of El Espacio Escultorico), Universidad Nacional Autonoma de Mexico, Mexico City, 80-83, dir, Urban Art Laboratory of Experimentation, Coordinacion de Humanidades, 80-83, dir genl artes plasticas Universidad Nacional Autonoma de Mexico, 2000-2004; adv plastic arts, Instituto Nacional de Bellas Artes, Mexico City, Mex, 92-95; researcher, Coordinacion de Difusión Cultural, UNAM. *Teaching:* Instr mod & contemp sculpture, Universidad Iberoamericana, Mexico City, Mex, 78-80, instr hist Mex sculpture, 78-80; Studies Ctr for Culture & Arts, Casa Lamm, Mexico, 2004-2006. *Awards:* From Nat Research Syst Nat Researcher, 2001-04; Cult Inst for Mex-Israel, 99; Recognition from the State Secy, PR, 2001; Diploma Colegio de San Ildefenso, AC, V Nam, Mex, 2003. *Mem:* Vocalia de Arte Urbano, Instituto Mexicano de Administracion Urbana, Mexico, City; Departamento de Artes Plasticas de la Universidad Metropolitana, Mex (mem-adv, 97-98); Directors Council Music Acad, Palacio de Mineria, AC V Nam, Mex; plus others. *Media:* Contemporary sculpture and comparative analysis of sculptoric tendencies. *Res:* Influence of pre-Hispanic on modern and contemporary Mexican sculpture. *Interests:* new tendencies on Mexican Contemporary Art, 60-present. *Publ:* Auth, Jesus Reyes Ferreira: Su Universo Pictorico, Coleccion de Arte NC 34, Universidad Nacional Autonoma de Mexico, 78; La Figura en la escultura Mexicana, Bancreser, Mex, 86; Armando Morales, Americo Arte Editores, 95; Diccionario de Escultores Mexicanos del Siglo XX, 97 & Mathias Goeritz: Vida y Obra, Consejo Nacional para la Cultura y Artes, 97; La Geometria Sensual de Sebastian, Circulo de Arte, Dir, GRAL de Publicaciones CNCA, Mexico, 2000-2002; Chucho Reyes, Editorial RM First & Second Edition, Mexico, 2000-2002; Augusto Escobedo Circulo de Arte, Dir GRAL de publicaciones, CNCA, Mexico, 2004; Vicente Ganduia, Crupozurich, Mexico, 2004; Diccionario de Escultores Mexicanos del Siglo XX, Third Ed, Digital Library, CNCA, 2005; Yolanda Gutierrez, Circulo de Arte, CNCA, Mex, 2006. *Mailing Add:* Sierra Guadarrama 33-4 Mexico DF 11000 Mexico

KASSOY, BERNARD
PAINTER, PRINTMAKER
b New York, NY, Oct 23, 14. *Study:* City Col New York, BSS(cum laude), MSE(fine arts); Cooper Union Art Sch, grad, 37; also with John Ferren, Isaac Soyer, Arthur Osver & Arun Bose. *Work:* Public and Corporate Collections: Butler Inst Am Art, Slater Mem Mus, Univ Georgia Mus, WPA Fed Art Project, Bocour Artist Colors, The Kheel Collection, Cornell Univ, NY State Hist Assoc, NY Pub Libr Photo and Print Collection, The Reba and David Williams Print Collection, The Bronx Inst, Lehman Col, Arch Am Art, Smithsonian Inst; and others. *Comn:* Birdiness (film photog & editing), Bd Educ, High Sch Music & Art, NY, 57; Stage set design for Fiddler on the Roof, Apricot Theatre, NY, 88; Slides of an Aquamanile Bronze, Metrop Mus Art, NY. *Exhib:* Showcase, Bronx Coun Arts, NY, 68-69; Nat Acad Design, NY, 68 & 75; 28 Contemporaries, Bronx Mus Arts, NY, 71; Int Sculpture Exhib, Pietrasanta, Italy, 76 & Forte dei Marmi, Italy, 76; one-man shows, Ward-Nasse Gallery, NY, 79, Mid-Hudson Art & Sci Ctr, Poughkeepsie, NY, 79, Vladeck Hall Gal, Bronx, NY Retrospective, 89 & Woodcuts, Pioneer-Smithy Gallery, Cooperstown, NY, 91 & Etchings, 96; Ward Nasse Gallery, NY, 86; Bronx Mus Arts, NY, 85-86; Pioneer Gallery, Cooperstown, NY, 88, 91 & 97; ACA Gallery, NY, 54. *Pos:* Painter, Fed Art Proj, NY, 36; World War II, US Army Photog, 42-46; World War II S.E.A.C., draftman, US Army, 45. *Teaching:* Instr fine arts, High Sch Music & Art and other NY High Schs, 39-72; instr lithography, City Col NY, 66-67 & Nat Acad Design, 68; instr painting & mem fac, Harriet FeBland Advan Painters Workshop, New Rochelle, NY, 74-. *Awards:* Merit Award, 58th Ann, Art Dirs Club, 79; Award Merit, Pastel Soc Am, 81; Award in Painting, Am Soc Contemp Artists Ann, 84, 93, 98; Florian Kramer Mem Award in Painting, City Col Art Alumni Exhib, 85; Artist Fel, Va Ctr Creative Arts, 86, 88, 91 & 95. *Bibliog:* Contemporary Graphic Artists, 87. *Mem:* Artists Equity Asn NY (bd dir, 62-, secy, 75-78); Contemp Artists Guild; Am Soc Contemp Artists (vpres, 83-85); Pastel Soc Am; Int Asn Artists, UNESCO (delegate, US comt), 83. *Media:* Oil, Watercolor; Woodcut, Etching. *Publ:* Illusr, ed drawings, NY Teacher News, 50-60; Therapeutic Dance/Movement, Human Sci Press, 79; illusr, WWII US Army Serv Publ; illusr, WWII US Army Photography, 42-46. *Dealer:* Pioneer Gallery Cooperstown NY. *Mailing Add:* 130 Gale Pl Bronx NY 10463

KASSOY, HORTENSE
SCULPTOR, PAINTER
b Brooklyn, NY, Feb 14, 17. *Study:* Pratt Inst, grad; Columbia Univ Teachers Col, with Oronzo Maldarelli & Charles J Martin, BS & MA; Am Artists Sch, with Chaim Gross; Studied sculpture with Sabl Swarz & Oronzio Maldarelli; Studied advanced printmaking at Lehman Col with Arun Bose. *Work:* Slater Mem Mus, Norwich, Conn; Bocour Artists Colors, Inc; Amalgamated Houses. *Comn:* Maternal Force (marble sculpture), Amalgamated Housing Coop Towers, Bronx, NY, 71. *Exhib:* Sculpture Today, Toledo Mus & Toronto Mus, 47; Nat Acad Design, NY, 71; 28 Contemporaries, Bronx Mus Art, 71, Ann, 72, Yr of the Woman, 75; Brooklyn Mus, Contemp Artists Guild, 74; 150th Ann, Nat Acad Design, 75; solo exhibs, Caravan House Gallery, NY, 75, Women in the Arts Gallery, 78, Vladeck Gallery, 81, 85 & 97, Ward-Nasse Gallery, 86 & Pioneer Gallery, Cooperstown, NY, 87, 91, 97 & 2002; Int Sculpture Exhib, Forte dei Marmi, 76, Pietrasanta, 76, Italy; Am Soc Contemp Artists Ann, 79-2006; Palisades Gallery Inaugural Exhib, Hudson River Mus, 82; Between the Wars, Bronx Mus, NY, 85-86; Retrospective, Vladeck Gallery, 2002; Mini-Retrospective, Smithy Pioneer Gallery, 2002. *Pos:* Chmn visual arts, Bronx Coun Arts, 73-76; corresp secy, US Comt, Int Asn Art (UNESCO), 79-89. *Teaching:* Instr sculpture, painting & 3D design, Evander Childs High Sch, Bronx, 61-72; instr sculpture, Harriet FeBland Advan Workshop, 75-80. *Awards:* Grumbachers First Prize in Watercolor, Painters Day at World's Fair, 40; Erlanger Award in Sculpture, 80 & Rizzoli Award in Sculpture, 83, Am Soc Contemp Artists, 90, 92, 94, 96 & 2000, 2002; Fel, Va Ctr Creative Arts, 86, 88, 89, 92, 94 & 96; Jeane Pierce Walker Prize for Sculpture, 2002. *Bibliog:* David Howard (dir), Hortense Kassoy (film). *Mem:* Artists Equity Asn, NY (bd dir, 71-75 & 79-83, vpres, 75-79 & adv bd, 89-91); Contemp Artists Guild; Am Soc Contemp Artists (assoc pres, 87-89 & vpres, 90-94, 99-2000 & 2003); Fedn Modern Painters & Sculptors. *Media:* All Media, Watercolor. *Dealer:* Smity-Pioneer Gallery Cooperstown NY. *Mailing Add:* 130 Gale Pl Apt 6B Bronx NY 10463

KASTEN, KARL ALBERT
PAINTER, PRINTMAKER
b San Francisco, Calif, 1916. *Study:* Marin Col; Univ Calif, AB, MA; Univ Iowa, with Lasansky; Hans Hofmann Sch Art. *Work:* Victoria & Albert Mus, London, Eng; Mus Mod Art, NY; Auckland City Mus, New Zealand; Mus Beaux-Arts, Rennes, France; Los Angeles Co Art Mus; and others. *Comn:* Painting, Reno, comn by Carter R King, 90. *Exhib:* Art Inst Chicago Am Painting Ann, 60; Contemp Am Painting & Sculpture, Univ Ill, 69; Achenbach Found Graphic Arts, San Francisco, 75; World Print III Traveling Exhib, 80-81; National Printmaking Invitational, Fla State Univ; Inst Franco Am, Rennes, 95; and others. *Collection Arranged:* Muser des Beaux Arts, Rennes, France; Victoria & Albert Mus, London; Auckland City Mus, Aukland, New Zealand; Crocker At Mus, Sacramento, Calif; Oakland Mus Art, Oakland, Calif; Portland Art Mus, Portland, Ore; Achenbach Collection, San Francisco, Calif. *Teaching:* prof emeritus. *Awards:* Creative Arts Inst Fel, 64 & 71; Tamarind Lithography Fel, 68; Distinguished Artist Award, Calif Soc Printmakers, 97; plus others. *Bibliog:* McClelland and Last (auths), The California Style, Hilcrest, 85; Susan Landauer (auth), Breaking Type: The Art of Karl Kasten, Ctr for the Book, 99; D Acton (auth), The stamp of impulse: abstract impressionist prints, Worcester Art Mus, 2001. *Mem:* Calif Soc Printmakers (coun mem, 72-76); Berkeley Art Ctr (bd mem); Print Consortium. *Media:* Etching, All Media. *Res:* Paul Gauquin's printmaking techniques. *Interests:* Collecting ethnic art. *Collection:* Egon Schiele, Luca Cambiaso, Paul Gauguin & Emile Bernard. *Dealer:* Annex Gallery Santa Rosa CA; Robert Green Fine Arts Mill Valley CA. *Mailing Add:* 1884 San Lorenzo Ave Berkeley CA 94707

KASTNER, BARBARA H
PAINTER
b Perryton, Tex, Dec 2, 36. *Study:* San Antonio Art Inst, 75-78; Tex Tech Univ, BS, 59, MS 64. *Work:* Nebr Wesleyan Univ, Lincoln; Omaha Airport Authority, Nebr; Pillsbury Int Hq, Minneapolis; AT&T, Northwestern Bell Tel Co, Omaha, Nebr; CONAGRA, Omaha, Nebr; Northwestern Bell Tel Co, Omaha, Nebr; Norwest Corp, Omaha, Nebr. *Exhib:* Rocky Mountain Nat Watermedia Exhib, Foothills Art Ctr, Golden, Colo, 79, 82, 83, 92; Nat Watercolor Soc Exhib, Brea Civic & Cult Ctr, Los Angeles, 81, 82, 89; Watercolor USA, Springfield Art Mus, Mo, 83 & 94; Ann Exhibs, Nat Acad Design, NY, 84, 90 & 92; two-person exhibs, Joslyn Mus Art, Omaha, Nebr, 85 & 87; Allied Artists Am Exhib, Nat Arts Club, NY, 86; Am Watercolor Soc Exhib, NY, 77, 82, 83, 85, 90, 91 & 94. *Collection Arranged:* Impact, The art of Nebraska Women, Ed by Dora Hagge, pub by Impact, Inc w support of Nebraska Arts Council, 88. *Pos:* Bd dir, Tex Watercolor Soc, 78-79, San Antonio Watercolor Soc, 77-79; chairperson, Rocky Mountain Nat Watermedia Exhib, Golden, Colo, 95; juror of awards, Am Watercolor Soc, 91; appointed mem, Evergreen Area Coun for the Arts, Evergreen, Colo, 92-95. *Awards:* Ogden M Pleissner Mem Award, Nat Acad Design, 90; Walter Greathouse Medal, Am Watercolor Soc, 90, Elsie & David Wu Sect-Key Mem Award, 94; Mary A Desser Award, Nat Soc Painters in Casein & Acrylic, New York, 93. *Bibliog:* Roger Catlin (auth), Flatness of summer landscape transformed into art, Omaha World Herald, 7/25/82; Stephen Doherty (auth), Five ways to strengthen your landscapes, Watercolor '91, Am Artist's Mag, spring; Maureen Bloom (auth), Night visions, Watercolor Magic, 11/2000; Katherine Mesch (auth), Against the Night, The Artists' Mag, 8/2005; Kathleen H Sutton (auth), Barbara Kastner: Capturing the Mystery Just Outside Your Door, Elevated Living Mag, 11/2005-12/2005. *Mem:* Am Watercolor Soc (juror awards, 91); Nat Watercolor Soc; Alliance for Contemp Art,

Denver, Colo. *Media:* Casein, Acrylic. *Publ:* auth, Making night scenes sparkle, Artists Mag, 4/91; Contributed to Dramatize Your Paintings with Tonal Value, by Carole Katchen Northlight Publ, 93; Color & Light for the Watercolor Painter by Christopher Schink, Watson Guptill, 95; Have Watercolor Crayons, WIll Travel, Watercolor Magic Mag, Summer, 2001; Landscape Lessons, Watercolor Magic Handbook, 7/2002; Watercolor Yearbook, publ Watercolor & Magic, 2003. *Mailing Add:* 30012 Troutdale Ridge Rd Evergreen CO 80439

KATANO, MARC
PAINTER
b Tokyo, Japan, July 17, 52. *Study:* Calif Col Arts & Crafts, Oakland, BFA(with distinction), 75. *Work:* RT Metro Col Greens Sta Comn, Sacramento, 87; San Francisco Arts Comn at San Francisco Int Airport, 88. *Exhib:* One-man shows, Stephen Wirtz Gallery, San Francisco, 80, 83, 86, 87, 91, 94 & 95, Sharon Traux Fine Art, Venice, Calif, 93, Gallery Fresca, Tokyo, Japan, 94, Thomas Babeor & Co, La Jolla, 95, Bently Gallery, Scottsdale, Ariz, 95, La Art Core Ctr, Calif, 97 & Stremmel Gallery, Nev, 97; Traditions Transformed, Oakland Mus, 84; GH2 Gallery, 92; Contemp Japanese-Am Artists in Calif, PacTel Corp, Walnut Creek, Calif, 92; "Drawings from LA", Galleria Finarte, Na Goya, Japan, 92; Gallery IV, Los Angeles, 93; Galleria Finarte, Nagoya, Japan, 93; Organized Nature, Korean Cult Ctr, Los Angeles, 94; Inaugural Exhib, LA Artcore, Los Angeles, 94; SF to BC, Elizabeth Leach Gallery, Portland, 94; Equinox: An Autumn Group Exhib, Thomas Babeor & Co, La Jolla, 95; All Things Great but Small V, Stremmel Gallery, Reno, 95; Newance, Stephen Wirtz Gallery, San Francisco, 96; California Painting Sampler, Bank Am Art Collection, San Francisco, 97; Works on Paper, Stephen Wirtz Gallery, San Francisco, 98. *Awards:* KQED Award, Crown Zellerbach Inc, 80; award, Soc Encouragement Contemp Art, 81. *Bibliog:* Dorothy Burkhart (auth), Generations of abstractions, San Jose Mercury News, 1/20/89; Dare Michos (auth), A legacy of abstraction, Artweek, 2/25/89; Betsy Oberthier (auth), Visions Art Quart, fall 93. *Media:* Oil, Acrylic. *Mailing Add:* c/o Stephen Wirtz Gallery 49 Geary St San Francisco CA 94108

KATAYAMA, TOSHIHIRO
PAINTER, DESIGNER
b Osaka, Japan, July 17, 28. *Study:* Self-taught. *Work:* Fogg Art Mus, Harvard Univ, Cambridge, Mass; De Cordova Mus, Lincoln, Mass; Ohara Mus Art, Kurashiki, Japan; Toyama Mus Mod Art, Japan; Setagaya Art Mus, Tokyo; and others. *Comn:* Granite wall sculpture (26' x 100'), Ohara Mus Art, Kurashiki, 91; grand floor landscape design, incl steel sculpture & water fall (33' x 15' x 35'), Pasonic Hdq Off, Tokyo, 92; stone sculpture (granite 150 tons) & wall relief (wood & plaster 12' x 120'), Mitsui Fire & Marine Insurance, Hq, Chiba, 94; theater foyer-wall mural (copper 10' x 40') & corridor-wall mural (9' x 115'), JT Hq Bldg, Kobe, 98; monumental sculpture (titanium & stainless steel), World Health Orgn Hq, Kobe, 98; and others. *Exhib:* Graphic Image, Cent Mus Mod Art, Tokyo & Kyoto Nat Mus, Japan, 73 & 74; one-man shows, Am Inst of Graphic Arts, NY, 68, Rose Art Mus, Brandeis Univ, 71, Kunstler Haus, Wine, Austria, 77 & Nantenshi Gallery, Tokyo, 78, 80, 83, 86, 89 & 96; and others. *Pos:* Art dir, Nippon Design Ctr, Tokyo, 60-63; graphic designer, Geigy, Basel, Switz, 63-66; dir, Carpenter Ctr Visual Arts, Harvard Univ, 90-93. *Teaching:* Prof graphic design, visual & environ studies, Harvard Univ, Cambridge, Mass, 66-95; prof emeritas, Harvard Univ. *Awards:* Artist (in Architectural space work) of the Year, 98. *Bibliog:* The Work of Toshi Katayama, Kajima Inst Publ Co, 81. *Mem:* Alliance Graphique Int (head official, Zurich, 75). *Media:* Mixed. *Publ:* Coauth, Three Notations, Rotations with Mr Octavio Paz, Harvard Univ, 74; Toshi Katayama's class work at Harvard Univ, Musashino Art Univ, Tokyo, 93. *Dealer:* Nantenshi Gallery 3-6-5 Kyobashi Chuo-Ku Tokyo Japan. *Mailing Add:* c/o Carpenter Ctr Harvard Univ 24 Quincy St Cambridge MA 02138

KATCHEN, CAROLE LEE
PAINTER, WRITER
b Denver, Colo. *Study:* Ripon Col, Wis; Univ Colo, Boulder, BA(cum laude), 65. *Work:* Northwest Community Hosp, Arlington Heights, Ill; AGIP, Houston, Tex; Cherry Creek Nat Bank, Denver Symphony Orchestra, Denver, Colo; Mus Outdoor Art, Englewood, Colo; Penrose Community Hosp, Colorado Springs; Baptist Methodist Ctr, Little Rock, Ark; Gene Codes Corp, Ann Arbor, Mich; and others; Children's Hosp, Little Rock, Ark; St Joseph's Hosp, Hot Springs, Ark. *Exhib:* Solo exhibs, Centro Colombo-Americano, Bogota, Colombia, 74, Mus Southwest, Midland, Tex 82, River Market Artspace, Little Rock, Ark, 99 & Legacy Fine arts Gallery, Hot Springs, Ariz, 2000; 8 State Exhib Painting & Sculpture, Okla Art Ctr, Oklahoma City, 78; Midwestern Printmaking & Drawing, Tulsa Libr, Okla, 78; Rocky Mountain Nat Watermedia, Foothills Art Ctr, Golden, Colo, 80; Alliance Contemp Art, Denver Art Mus, 82; Pastel Soc Am Ann, Nat Arts Club, NY, 90; Pastels USA, Sacramento Fine Arts Ctr, 94; Pastel Society of the Southwest, Longview Art Mus & Irving Art Ctr, Tex, 95; Reynolds Gallery, Univ Pac, Stockton, Calif, 96; Am Inaugural Art Exhib, Washington, DC, 97; Ark Governor's Off, Little Rock, 97; IAPS Pastel Comp, Colo State Hist Mus, Denver, 98; Office of Senator Blanch Lincoln, Washington, DC, 2000, Ark Capitol Bldg, Little Rock, 2003; Solo exhibs, Telluride Gallery of Fine Art, Gelluride, Colo, 2002, Bryant Gallery, New Orleans, 2002, Alpha Gallery, Little Rock, 2002, Gallery Central, Hot Springs, 2003, Gore Creek Gallery, Vail, Colo, 2004, Legacy Gallery, Hot Springs, 2005. *Pos:* Contrib ed, Today's Art & Graphics, NY, 80-81 & The Artist's Mag, Cincinnati, 86-. *Teaching:* lectr, Rocky Mountain Col Art & Design, Denver, 83-85; lectr, Univ Calif Artsreach, Los Angeles, 88-89. *Awards:* Outstanding Achievement in Art, West Valley Col, 70; Outstanding Working Woman, US Dept Labor, 82; Kans Pastel Soc Award, Pastel Soc Am, 90; and others. *Bibliog:* John Jellico (auth), Drawing from life, Am Artist Mag, 9/75; Betty Harvey (auth), Carole Katchen, Artists of the Rockies, 76; Barbara Moss (auth), Profile, Design Notes, 92; Ellis Widner (auth), Artist in Residence, AR Democrat-Gazette, Little Rock; Susan Pierce (auth), Hot Springs Artist has a Story to Tell, Active Years, 99; Chuck Dodson(auth), Bon Voyeur, Number Mag, 2000. *Mem:* Pastel Soc Am; Int Asn Pastel Soc (bd dir, Golden Mentor award); Hot Springs Music Festival. *Media:* Pastel, Oil, Bronze sculpture. *Publ:* Auth, Dramatize Your Paintings with Tonal Value, 93; Painting With Passion, North Light Books, 94; Make Your Watercolors Look Professional, 95, How to Get Started Selling Your Art, 96, 200 Great Painting Ideas for Artists, 98, North Light Bks, Ohio; illusr, That Sweet Diamond, Atheneom, 98; Express Yourself with Pastels, Int Artists Books, 2000. *Dealer:* Gore Creek Gallery 158 Gore Creek Dr Ste 132 Vail CO 81857; Telluride Gallery of Fine Art 130 E Colo Ave Tellluride CO 81435; Legacy Gallery 804 Central Ave Hot Springs AR 71901; American Legacy Gallery 5911 Main St Kansas City MO 64113; Alpha Gallery 11809 Hinson Rd Ste 100 Little Rock AR 72212. *Mailing Add:* 624 Prospect Ave Hot Springs AR 71901

KATO, KAY
CARTOONIST, ILLUSTRATOR
Study: Pa Acad Fine Arts; Am Acad Dramatic Arts. *Work:* NJ Gov Brendan Byrne; Newark Pub Libr Spec Collections, 57 cartoon originals from weekly column, depicting libr programs & events, 92; NJ Gov Thomas Kean; Bob Hope. *Comn:* Cover, Am Tel & Tel Mag, 54; book jacket for The Television-Radio Audience and Religion, Harper & Bros, 55; cover, Today's Living, NY Herald-Tribune, 57; also covers for Christian Sci Monitor, Sat Eve Post & others. *Exhib:* One-woman shows, RC Vose Galleries, Boston, 45, Boston Pub Libr, 45, Newark Pub Libr, 92, Newark Mus, 80 & 93, Montclair State Col, 87 & Belleville Pub Libr, 89; Montclair Art Mus, 53, 56 & 57; At Man and His World, Int Salon of Cartoons, Montreal, Que, 75-88; traveling shows, West Caldwell Pub Libr, Livingston Pub Libr & Passaic Pub Libr, 92; and others. *Pos:* Columnist, "On location in Jersey", weekly cartoon column, Sunday Star Ledger, 64-95. *Teaching:* Instr, Cambridge Ctr Adult Educ, Mass, 44-47; instr, South Orange & Maplewood Adult Sch, 63. *Awards:* First Prize Award for Cartoons, NJ State Fedn Women's Clubs, 77 & 78; Plaque Award, Newark Mus Paleontology Prog, 79 & Livingston Hist Soc, 90; Special Reception, Gov Kean & Secy of State Jane Burgio, State House, 89. *Bibliog:* Foremost Women in Communication, Foremost Am Publ Corp, 70; Essex Co Libr Prog, Channel 3, Cablevision TV, 79. *Publ:* Contribr, This Week, Nation's Bus, NY Times Mag, Parade, Am Weekly & others; Staten Island Advance, 77; Marriage and Family Reality, Harper & Row, 89; auth, Park Art, Sunday Star Ledger Collection Columns, Donning Co Publ, 4/99; and others. *Mailing Add:* 60 Chapman Pl Glen Ridge NJ 07028

KATSELAS, MILTON GEORGE
PAINTER, ART DEALER
b Pittsburgh, Feb 22, 33. *Study:* Carneige-Mellon Inst, BFA, 54. *Work:* Beverly Hills Playhouse & Klein, Gardner & Assoc, Calif; also pvt collection of Tasso Katselas, Pittsburgh. *Exhib:* Emily Lowe Painting Competition, NY, 65; solo exhibs, Gallery PS 962, Los Angeles, 86, 275 La Cienega, Los Angeles, 89 & Green Gallery, Santa Monica, Calif, 93; Four, Gallery 258, Beverly Hills, Calif, 95. *Media:* Acrylic, Mixed Media. *Specialty:* Contempory American Art. *Publ:* Auth, Dreams into Action, Dove Press, 96. *Dealer:* Gallery 258 258 S Robertson Blvd Beverly Hills CA 90211. *Mailing Add:* 254 S Robertson Blvd Beverly Hills CA 90211

KATSIFF, BRUCE
PHOTOGRAPHER, MUSEUM DIRECTOR
b Philadelphia, Pa, Dec 10, 45. *Study:* Philadelphia Col Art, 64-65; Rochester Inst Technol, BFA, 68; Pratt Inst, MFA, 73; Oxford Univ, 85-87. *Work:* George Eastman House, Rochester, NY; Am Arts Doc Ctr, Exeter, England; Allentown Art Mus, Pa; Erie Art Mus, Pa. *Exhib:* Photog as Printmaking, Mus Mod Art, NY, 68; Vision & Expression, Int Mus Photog, 69; Philadelphia Mus Art, 70; Underground Gallery, NY, 70; Pa Acad of Fine Arts, 73; Pa Photogrs, Allentown Art Mus, 87; Am Photogrs; Taingin, China, 87; Pa Acad Fine Arts, 90; Santa Fe Photo Ctr, 88; Woodmore Art Mus, 02; Legacy Gallery, 97; Krasdale Gallery, 99; River Run Gallery, 2005. *Pos:* Eastman Kodak, 67-69; dir, James A Michener Art Mus, 90-. *Teaching:* Prof art, Bucks Co Community Col, 69-, chmn art & music, 75-89 & Thomas Edison Col, 76-78. *Awards:* PA Art Fel, 89. *Bibliog:* Gene Thorton (auth), Photography Review, NY Times, 70; A D Coleman (auth), article, Village Voice, 71. *Mem:* Am Asn Mus; Soc Photographic Educators. *Mailing Add:* Box 28 Lumberville PA 18933

KATZ, ALEX
PAINTER
b New York, NY, July 24, 27. *Study:* Cooper Union; Skowhegan Sch; Colby Col, Maine, Hon Phd, 85. *Work:* Mus Mod Art, Metrop Mus Art, Whitney Mus Art, NY; Art Inst Chicago; Los Angeles Co Mus Art, Calif; Brooklyn Mus, NY; Philadelphia Mus Art, Pa; and others. *Comn:* Mural, Harlem Sta, Chicago. *Exhib:* Retrospective exhibs, Wadsworth Atheneum, 71, Whitney Mus & Va Mus, 74-75 & 86; 32nd Biennial Exhib Contemp Am Painting, Corcoran Gallery Art, Washington, DC, 71; Queens Mus, Flushing, NY, 80; Recent Drawings, Mus Mod Art, NY, 81; print retrospective, Brooklyn Mus, NY, 88; Seibu Mus Art, traveling, Tokyo, Japan, 88; NC Mus Art, traveling, Raleigh, 90; drawing retrospective, Mus Art, Munson-Williams-Proctor Inst, travelling, Utica, NY, 91; Robert Millery Gallery, 96-97; solo exhibs, Jablonka Galerie, London, Eng, 97, Saatchi Gallery, London, Eng, 98, Cult Found, Ger, 98, Galerie Thaddaeus Ropac, Paris, France, 98, Galerie Barbara Thumm, Berlin, Ger, 98, PS1 Contemp Art Ctr, Long Island City, NY, 98 & Centro Cult Recoleta, Buenos Aires, Argentina, 98; Views from Abroad: European Perspectives on Am Art, Mus fur Moderne Kunst, Ger, 1/31/97-5/4/97; Cartoon and Paintings, Albertina Mus, Vienna, Austria, 2004-2005; The Univ S Fla, Tampa, 2005; CAC Malaga, Malaga, Spain, 2005; Colby College Art Mus, Waterville Maine, 2005; Neue Editionen, Sabine Maximilian Verlag, Munich, Ger, 2005; The Sixties, Pacewildenstein Gallery, New York, NY, 2006; Alex Katz In Maine, Pa Acad Fine Arts, Philadelphia, 2006; and others. *Teaching:* Adj prof, Yale Univ, 62-63, NY Univ,

83-84. *Awards:* John Simon Guggenheim fel, 72; Nat Endowment Arts grant, 76; Mary Buckley Award Achievement, Pratt Inst, 97; and others. *Bibliog:* Simon Shama & Dave Hickey (auths), Alex Katz Under the Stars: American Landscapes 1951-1995 (exhib catalog), The Inst for Contemp Art/PS 1 Mus, NY, 96; David Sylvester & Merlin James (auths), Alex Katz - Twenty Five Years of Painting (exhib catalog), The Saatchi Gallery, London, Eng, 98; Zdenek Felix & Carter Radcliff (auths), Alex katz Cutouts (exhib catalog), Hamburg: Deichtorhallen Hamburg, 2003. *Mem:* Am Acad and Inst Arts & Letters, 88. *Media:* Oil on canvas. *Res:* Colby College Mus Art, Waterville Maine, Katz archives. *Dealer:* Pace Wildenstein New York City. *Mailing Add:* c/o Pace Wildenstein 32 E 57th St New York NY 10022

KATZ, DON
SCULPTOR, STAINED GLASS ARTIST
b Chicago, Ill, Feb 14, 25. *Study:* Art Inst Chicago, 46-47; Art Students League, NY, 48-49; Ctr D'Art Sacre, Paris, 50-51. *Comn:* door carvings, Temp Beth Esmeth, Brooklyn, NY, 55; door carvings, Temp Anch Chesed, Youngstown, Ohio, 57; Ark (carving), comn by Vassar J Cerrill, Poughkeepsie, NY, 58; stained glass, Richmond J Ctr, Va, 59; stained glass, Bayside JC, Queens, NY, 68. *Mem:* NY Artist Equity; Audubon Artists. *Media:* Wood, Glass. *Mailing Add:* 59-15 47th Ave Woodside NY 11377

KATZ, LEANDRO
ASSEMBLAGE ARTIST, FILMMAKER
b Buenos Aires, Arg, June 6, 38; US citizen. *Study:* Univ Nac Buenos Aires, BA, 61; Pratt Graphic Arts Ctr, 65-67. *Work:* Rare Book Collection, Houghton Libr, Harvard Univ; Ruth & Marvin Sackner Arch, Fla; Mus Mod Art Rare Book Libr, NY; Brooklyn Mus Collection; Julia & Horacio Herzberg Collection; Museo de Barrio, NY; Museo de Arte Moderno, Argentina; Sterling Meml Libr, Yale Univ. *Exhib:* Cineprobe, Mus Mod Art, NY, 79; The Lunar Alphabet, Clocktower, NY, 80; Metropotamia, PS1, Long Island City, 81; The Judas Window, Whitney Mus Am Art, 82; Orpheus Beheaded, RI Sch Design Mus, 83; 1987 Whitney Biennial Exhib, Whitney Mus Am Art; The Decade Show, New Mus Cont Art, 90; El Museo Del Barrio, 96; Art Inst Chicago, 98; and others; Museo Nacional de Beaux Artes Bienal, 2002. *Teaching:* Fac mem pre-Columbian art, Sch Visual Arts, NY, 71-; fac mem semiotics & cinema, Brown Univ, 81-; fac mem, Film Dept, New Sch Social Res, NY, 86-; fac mem, Dept Commun, Film Prog, William Paterson Univ, retired. *Awards:* Fel, Nat Endowment Arts, 79 & 94; Fel, Guggenheim Mem Found, 80; Fel, Rockefeller Found, 93; New York State Coun on the Arts Grant, 98. *Bibliog:* Lucy Lippard (auth), Overlay, Pantheon Books, 83; Dore Ashton (auth), American Art Since 1945, Oxford Univ Press; Susana Torruella Leval (auth), Recapturing History, Col Art Asn, 92; Jacqueline Barnitz (auth), Twentieth Century Latin American Art, Univ of Tex Press. *Media:* Photography, Language Assemblages, Film, Ditigal Imaging. *Res:* Latin Am subjects; Photographic installations and prints. *Publ:* Self Hypnosis, TVRT Press, 75; Auth, The Milk of Amnesia, CEPA & The Visual Studies Workshop Press, 85; 27 Windmills, Viper's Tongue Books; Burnt Book/Libro Qvemado, Nexus Press, 95; Che/Loro, Viper's Tongue Press, 98, Chegueuara in Bolivia: A Chronology, Viper's Tongue Books, 2001. *Mailing Add:* 341 Lafayette St #10 New York NY 10012

KATZ, MORRIS
PAINTER
b Poland. *Study:* Ulm, Ger & Gunsburg; with Hans Facler; Art Students League, NY, 50-56. *Work:* Evansville Mus Arts & Sci, Ind; Jr Col Albany, NY; Butler Inst Am Art, Youngstown, Ohio; St Lawrence Univ Giffiths Art Ctr, Canton, NY; Univ Art Gallery, State Univ NY Binghamton. *Comn:* Pope Paul VI painting, comn by Thomas A Dexter, 65; pictures, Smithsonian Inst; mural, City of NY, comn by Detective Endowment Assn, NY; mural, Synagogue, Brooklyn, NY. *Exhib:* Instant live art shows, more than 10,000 throughout the world; 6000 oil paintings, JA Olson Co, Winona, Miss, 60-63; Morris Katz Int Art Studio, NY. *Pos:* art cons, Bd Edn, New York City, 88-68. *Teaching:* Instr, Learning Annex, NY. *Awards:* World's Most Prolific and Speedy Artist, The Guiness Book of World Records, 1980-. *Bibliog:* Howard Jacobson (auth), Root Schmoots, Penguin; Bob Garfield (auth), Waking up Screaming, Scribner; Sondra Farrel (auth), One Minute Super Stars; Jane & Michael Stern (auth), The Encyclopedia of Bad Taste, Harper Collins; William E. Geist (auth), City Slickers, New York Times. *Mem:* Am Guild of Variety Artists; Int Platform Asn; Artists Equity Asn; Int Arts Guild Monaco; Am Fedn Television & Radio Artists; Am TV Arts & Sci. *Media:* Oil, Pencil. *Publ:* Auth, Paint Good and Fast, Sterling Publ, NY, 1985; The Presidents of America, Jerusalem-Simonim; auth, Up Late with Joe Franklin, Scribbner. *Mailing Add:* 247 W 29th St New York NY 10001-5275

KATZ, TED
PAINTER, EDUCATOR
b Philadelphia, Pa, July 29, 37. *Study:* Franklin & Marshall Col, AB, 59; Art Students League, 61-65; Acad Grande Chaumiere, Paris, 64-65; Harvard Univ, Grad Sch Educ, 68-72, EdM, 69, EdD, 72. *Exhib:* John F Kennedy Ctr; Demuth Found; Philadelphia Col Art; Moore Col Art; Millersville Univ. *Pos:* Fel, Grad Sch Educ, Harvard Univ, 68-72; dir Aesthetic Education Proj, Northwest Regional Educ Lab, Portland, Ore, 71-72; dir, Ford Found Proj, Inst Am Indian Arts, Santa Fe, NMex, 72-75; dir, Appalachia Regional Arts Prog, NC Arts Coun, Raleigh, NC; chief educ div, Philadelphia Mus Art, Pa, 77-84; dep dir, Ore Art Inst, Portland, 84-86. *Teaching:* lectr, Philadelphia Col Art, 78-84. *Awards:* Grant, Carnegie Corp; Grant, Ford Fund; Grant, Nat Endowment Arts. *Bibliog:* Howard Taubman (auth), Awakening the defeated, New York Times, 11/12/66; Museums as Schools, Newsweek, 10/15/79; Museums for a New Century, a Report of the Commission on Museums for a New Century, Am Asn Mus, Washington, 84. *Media:* Aquamedia. *Publ:* Auth, Art as a Reflection of Human Concerns and Other Common Denominators, In: Museums, Adults & the Humanities: A Guide for Educational Programming, Am Asn Mus, Washington, 81; Museums & Schools: Partners in Teaching, Pa Dept Educ, Harrisburg, 84; The Philadelphia Museum of Art Institute as research and development, Arts & Learning Spec Interest Group Proceedings J, Am Educ Res Asn, 84; coauth, Understanding & Creating Art (with Golstein, Kowalchuk & Saunders), West Pub Co, St Paul, Minn, 2nd ed, 91. *Dealer:* Butters Gallery Ltd 223 NW 9th Ave Portland OR 97209. *Mailing Add:* c/o Butters Gallery Ltd 520 NW Davis St Portland OR 97209

KATZEN, HAL ZACHERY
DEALER
b Baltimore, Md, July 16, 54. *Study:* San Francisco Col Art; Johns Hopkins Univ; Md Inst Col Art, BFA, 76. *Pos:* Asst dir, B R Kornblatt Gallery, Baltimore, Md, 76-78; assoc dir, Transworld Art, Alex Rosenberg Gallery, formerly; owner & dir, Katzen/Brown, Hal Katzen Gallery. *Mem:* Appraisers Asn Am. *Specialty:* Contemporary art, American painting and sculpture. *Mailing Add:* 305 E 40th St New York NY 10016-2189

KATZENBERG, DENA S
CONSULTANT, CURATOR
b Baltimore, Md. *Study:* McCoy Col of Johns Hopkins Univ; New York Sch of Interior Design. *Collection Arranged:* Great Am Cover-Up: Counterpanes of the 18th & 19th Century (auth, catalog), 71, Contemp Egyptian Folk Tapestries, 73, Blue Traditions: Indigo Dyed Textiles & Related Cobalt Glazed Ceramics from the 17th Century through the 19th Century (auth, catalog), 73-74, And Eagles Sweep Across the Sky: Indian Textiles of the North American West (auth, catalog), 77, Baltimore Album Quilts (auth catalog), 81-82, Imperial Costume from the Manchu Dynasty, 82, Baltimore Mus of Art. *Pos:* Consult Cur, Baltimore Mus Art, currently. *Mem:* Centre Int d'Etude des Textiles Anciens, Lyon, France; Needle & Bobbin Club, NY. *Res:* History of Indigo dye, Irish textile printing and manufacturing; North American Indian weaving; Baltimore album quilting. *Collection:* Textiles. *Publ:* Auth, Copper plate-printed Irish textile, Antiques, 4/77. *Mailing Add:* 22 Blythewood Rd Baltimore MD 21210-2402

KATZIVE, DAVID H
ADMINISTRATOR
b San Francisco, Calif, Mar 23, 42. *Study:* Brown Univ, BA; Univ Chicago, MA. *Pos:* Chief educ div, Philadelphia Mus of Art, 70-76; consult, Art Park, Lewiston, NY, 74-; asst dir, Brooklyn Mus, 76-81; dir, DeCordova Mus, 81-. *Teaching:* Instr art hist, Univ Chicago Exten, 66-68 & Ill Inst Technol, Chicago, 68-70. *Mem:* Am Asn Mus; Col Art Asn; Art Mus Asn; Asn Art Mus Dirs. *Mailing Add:* 57 Hicks St No 2 Brooklyn NY 11201-1356

KATZMAN, LAWRENCE (KAZ)
DESIGNER, CARTOONIST
b Ogdensburg, NY, June 14, 22. *Study:* Univ Pa, BS; Art Students League, with Reginald Marsh. *Pos:* Vprcs & chmn bd, Kaz Inc, 47-56, chmn & Chief Exec Officer, 56-98; pres & chmn bd, Kaz Int, 98-2000; dir, World Bus Coun, World Pres Orgn, Metrop Pres Orgn & Princeton Rev, currently; chmn emer, Kaz Inc, 2000-; treas, Nat Cartoonists Soc, Milt Gross Fund, 90-2006. *Awards:* Silver Cup of City of Bordighera, Italy, 59; Palma d'Oro, 66; Silver T-Square, Nat Cartoonists Soc; Salon of Humor, Bordighera, Italy; Gold Key Award, Nat Cartoonists Soc, 2005. *Mem:* Art Students League; Nat Cartoonists Soc (dir); Cartoonists Guild; Authors Guild. *Publ:* Auth & illusr, For Doctors Only, Eng, 60; Prima y Dopo i Pasti, Italy, 60; and other bks & cartoons in mags & newspapers throughout the world; illusr, greeting cards & bks, Gibson-Buzza; Headlines(TM) Acrostic Type Puzzles (2 vols), Random House, 93; many other books & cartoon collections in many languages. *Mailing Add:* 101 Central Park W New York NY 10023

KAUFMAN, GEORGE S
PATRON
Study: Ohio State Univ, BS; NYU, MS. *Pos:* Chmn, Kaufman Astoria Studios, currently; pres, Kaufman Realty Corp. *Mem:* Real Estate Bd, NY; Midtown Real Estate Owners Asn (pres, currently); Whitney Mus Am Art, New York City (trustee, currently). *Mailing Add:* Kaufman Astoria Studios 34-12 36th St Long Island City NY 11106

KAUFMAN, GLEN
PRINTMAKER, EDUCATOR
b Ft Atkinson, Wis, 32. *Study:* Univ Wis, BS, 54; Cranbrook Acad Art, MFA, 59; State Sch Arts & Crafts, Copenhagen, Denmark, 60. *Work:* Am Craft Mus, NY; Art Inst Chicago; Nat Mus Mod Art, Kyoto, Japan; Cleveland Mus Art; Renwick Gallery, Smithsonian Inst. *Exhib:* Solo exhibs, Gallery Maronie, Kyoto, Japan, 84, 85 & 86, Wacoal Ginza ArtSpace, Tokyo, Japan, 84, 87, 89, 90, 94 & 96, Allrich Gallery, San Francisco, Calif, 90, Itami City Crafts Ctr, Osaka, Japan, 91, Azabu Mus Tokyo, Japan, 91, Ba Tang Gol Arts Ctr, Seoul, Korea, 94, Gallery Gallery, Kyoto, Japan, 96, Wacoal Ginza Art Space, Tokyo, Japan, 96, Brown/Grotta Gallery, Wilton, Conn, 98, Joanne Rapp Gallery, Scottsdale, Ariz, 98 & One an dTwo Am Ctr, Nashville, Tenn, 2000; Am Craft Mus, NY, 86, 87 & 95; Tour of Asia, Arts Am Prog, 88-89; Tour of Europe, Arts Am Prog, 89-93; Renwick Gallery, Smithsonian Inst, Washington, DC, 92-93; Art Inst Chicago, Ill, 93; Group exhibs, The Cleveland Mus Art, Ohio, 98, The Ctr Contemp Crt, St Louis, Mo, 99 & Singapore Art Mus, 99. *Collection Arranged:* Am Craft Mus, NY; The Art Inst Chicago, Ill; Ba Tang Gol Art Ctr, Seoul, Korea; The Cleveland Mus Art, Ohio; Itami City Craft Ctr, Hyogo, Japan; H M de Young Meml Mus, San Francisco, Calif; Nat Mus Modern Art, Kyoto, Japan; Renwick Gallery, Smithsonian Inst, Washington, DC; Wichita Art Assn, Kans. *Pos:* area chair, Fabric Design; dir, Study Abroad Program, Japan. *Teaching:* Assoc prof art, Univ Ga,

Athens, 67-72, prof art, 72-; vis lectr, Sch Textiles, Royal Col Art, London, Eng, 76; prof art, Univ Ga. *Awards:* Fel, Nat Endowment Arts Visual Artists, 76 & 90 & Am Craft Coun, 88; Univ Ga Creative Res Medal, 88; Silver Prize, Itami Craft Ctr, Osaka, Japan, 89. *Bibliog:* Jeon Myung-Ok (auth), Visual experiences with grids, Monthly Crafts, 12/89; Marypaul Yates (auth), Pacific inspiration: the textiles of Glen Kaufman, Am Craft, 8/91; Katherine Westphall (auth), The Surface Designers Art, Lark Bks Publ, 93. *Mem:* Am Craft Coun; hon life mem, Surface Design Asn. *Media:* Silkscreen. *Publ:* Co-auth, Design on Fabrics, Van Nostrand Reinhold Publ, 67, 76 & 81; Fields of Indigo and White: The Shibori Kimono of Japan, Ga Mus Art Publ, 89; 4th International textile competition 94 Kyoto, spring 95, The gleam of gold, fall 95 & surface design in Japan, winter 97, Surface Design J. *Dealer:* Brown/Grotta Arts, Wilton, Conn. *Mailing Add:* 190 Harben Pl Athens GA 30606

KAUFMAN, HENRY
PATRON
b Wenings, Ger, Oct 20, 27. *Study:* NYU, BA, 48; Columbia Univ, MS 49; NYU, PhD, 58. *Hon Degrees:* NYU, LLD, 92; Yeshiva Univ, LHD, 86. *Pos:* Asst chief, econ res dept Fed Reserve Bank NY, 57-61; with Salomon Brothers, Inc, New York City, 62-88, gen partner, 67-88, mem exec comt, 72-88, managing dir, 81-88, chief econ, charge bond market res, industry & stock res & bond portfolio analysis res & corp bond res depts, also vchmn; Pres, Money Marketeers, NY Univ, 64-65; founder, Henry Kaufman & Co, 88-; bd dir, Lehman Brothers Holdings Inc, 95-. *Mem:* Am Econ Asn; UN Asn (bd dir, co-chmn econ policy coun, currently); Coun Foreign Relations; Econ Club New York City (dir, currently); Whitney Mus Art (trustee, currently). *Mailing Add:* c/o Whitney Mus Am Art 945 Madison Ave New York NY 10021

KAUFMAN, IRVING
PAINTER, EDUCATOR
b New York, NY, Oct 4, 20. *Study:* Art Students League; NY Univ, BA & MA. *Work:* Univ Mich Mus Art; Saginaw Mus Art; Ohio State Univ; Parke-Davis Co; Columbia Univ Law Libr. *Exhib:* Various group shows and one-man exhibs. *Teaching:* Assoc prof art, Univ Mich, Ann Arbor, 56-64; prof art, City Col New York, 64-86, emer prof, 86-; vis prof art educ, Teachers Col, Columbia Univ, New York, 86-90. *Awards:* Manual Barkan Award, Nat Art Educ Asn, 81; Lowenfeld Mem Lectr, Nat Art Educ Asn, 88. *Mem:* Inst Study Art in Educ (pres, 72); Col Art Asn Am; Univ Coun Art Educ. *Media:* Oil. *Publ:* Auth, Art & Education in Contemporary Culture, 66; contribr, Concepts in Art Education, 70; New Ideas in Art Education, 72; ed, Arts Issue, Curriculum Theory, Network, 74; contribr, Arts in Society, 75; auth, Studies In Art Educ, 88; and others. *Dealer:* Rehn Gallery 655 Madison Ave New York NY 10021. *Mailing Add:* 525 E 86th St #4G New York NY 10028

KAUFMAN, JANE
PAINTER, SCULPTOR
b New York, NY, May 26, 38. *Study:* Cornell Univ, 56-58; NY Univ, BA, 60; Hunter Col, MFA, 65. *Work:* Whitney Mus Am Art, NY; Wooster Mus Fine Arts, Mass; Mus Mod Art S Australia, Canberra; Brooklyn Mus, NY; Aldrich Mus Contemp Art, Ridgefield, Conn; and others. *Exhib:* One Man's Choice, Dallas Mus Fine Arts, Tex, 69; Highlights of 1970 Season, Aldrich Mus Contemp Art, Ridgefield, Conn, 70; solo exhibs, Whitney Mus Am Art, 71 & 73, Droll/Kulbert Gallery, NY, 78 7 80, PM & Stein Gallery, NY, 82, Bernice Steinbaum Gallery, NY, 85 & 88, Art in General, NY, 98; Corcoran Gallery Art, 72 & 73; Critic's Choice, Lowe Art Gallery, Syracuse Univ, NY & Munson-Williams-Proctor Inst Mus Art, Utica, 77; Decorative Art: Recent Works, Douglas Col Gallery, New Brunswick, NJ, 78; Intricate Struct-Repeated Images, Tyler Sch Art, Philadelphia; Contemp Screens, Mus through United States, 86; Absolute Henri, Henri Gallery, Washington, DC, 91; Bellas Artes Gallery, NY, 92; Labor of Love, New Mus Am Art, NY, 96; and many others. *Teaching:* Instr fine arts, New York Pub High Schs, 60-69; Lehman Col, Bronx, NY, 69-70, Bard Col, Annandale-on-Hudson, NY, 71-73 & Brooklyn Mus Art Sch, 72-73; lectr, Queens Col, 73-74; vis artist, workshops & lect, var cols & univs, US & Can, 74-; instr fine arts, Cooper Union Sch Art, New York, 81-92; instr, State Univ NY Westchester Community Col, Valhalla, 96-97. *Awards:* Guggenheim Fel, 74; Nat Endowment for Arts Fels, 79 & 89; Creative Artists Pub Serv Prog Grant for sculpture, 81. *Mailing Add:* 151 W 18th St New York NY 10011

KAUFMAN, JASON EDWARD
CRITIC, EDITOR
Study: Univ Urbino, Italy, Studies in Italian Art and Language, 83; Univ Rochester, NY, BA(art hist), 84; Rutgers Univ, New Brunswick, NJ, MA(art hist), 87. *Pos:* Sr ed, Jour Art, New York City, 90-91; NY corr Art Newspaper, NY, 91-; film evaluator panelist, Prog for Art on Film (joint prog of the Metrop Mus Art & J Paul Getty Trust), NY, 93; panelist ARCO, Feria Int de ARte COntemporaneo, Madrid, 95; ARTnewsletter, publ of ARTnews, 94-98. *Mem:* Asn Int des Critiques D'Art; Am Asn Mus. *Publ:* Contrib articles to prof jour.; art critic (reviews for exhib), contract writer The Am Friends of the British Mus, British Mus, London, England, 1994-95, (videodisc) Nat Gallery Art, Wash, DC, 1994, contrib (freelance articles) AICA Newsletter, Am Arts Quarterly, Appraiser, Art & Antiques, Art & Auction, Artnet mag, ARTnews, Artpapers Assoc Press, Atelier, Baltimore Sun, Bergen Record, Ctr for Experimental Perceptual Art Journal, Diario 16, Drawing, Everything Art, Insight Mag, Kalías: revista de arte, Latin Am Art, Los Angeles Cty Mus of Art Graphic Arts Coun Newsletter, Los Angeles Times, New Art Examiner, The NY Sun, Review: Latin Am Lit and Arts, Saab Mag, Sculpture, Sculpture Review, Smithsonian Mag, Spotlight, The Springfield Republican, The Standard-Times, Times Literary Supplement, Ultimas Noticias The Wall Street Jour, The Wash Post, The Wash Times, The World & I., writer, observer for session on "The arts and social capital in Am," Harvard Univ, John F. Kennedy Sch of Govt; The Saguaro Seminar: Civic Engagement in Am, Cambridge, Mass, 1999. *Mailing Add:* Art Newspaper 594 Broadway Ste 406 New York NY 10012

KAUFMAN, LORETTA ANA
SCULPTOR, PAINTER, INSTRUCTOR
b New York, NY, 46. *Study:* Palm Beach Jr Col; Univ Tampa. *Work:* Westpoint Stevens, NY; Arcadia Ctr, Pretoria, SAfrica; Bank Am, London, Eng; Environ Res Found, Wash; Oconee County Sch Dist, SC; and others. *Exhib:* Solo exhibs, Exhibit A Gallery, Savannah Col Art & Design, Ga, 87, New Work, Piedmont Craftsmen Ctr, Winston-Salem, NC, 90; NCECA Clay Nat, Ariz State Univ Art Mus, Tempe, Touring, 91-92; SC State Mus, Columbia, 94; From the Ground Up, Austin Mus Art, Tex, 98; Appalachian Ctr for Crafts, Tenn, 2002; Power of Excellence, Southeastern Ctr, Contemp Art, Winston, Salem, NC, 2004; TACA Biennial Tenn State Mus, Nashville, Tenn, 2004. *Pos:* Cur, Tri State Sculptors Exhib, Spartanburg Co Arts Ctr, SC, 91. *Teaching:* Instr, sculpture, Greenville Co Mus Art, SC, 88-90, SC Arts Comn, 88-94; vis artists ceramics, Greenville Co Sch Dist, 89-90, Univ SC, Columbia, 93; artists-in-residence sculpture, Shriner's Hosp Crippled Children, Greenville, SC, 90-91; artist-in-residence ceramics, Spartanburg Co Sch Dist, SC, 96. *Awards:* First Place, 3rd Ann Monarch Tile Nat Ceramics Competition, 88; Purchase Award, 2nd Ann NCNB Exhib, 89. *Bibliog:* Ann Spencer (auth), Exhibit to feature noted sculpture, Charlotte Observer, NC, 12/29/89; Olivia Fowler (auth), Interview with a Sculptor, Montgomery, Ala Lakeside Living Mag, 90; Dr Kathryn Bennett (auth), Tri State Sculptors, Atlanta Art Papers, 5-6/91; and others. *Mem:* Artists Equity Asn; Piedmont Craftsmen; TACA. *Media:* Clay; Oil. *Publ:* Contribr, Monarch tile national, Ceramics Monthly, 11/1/88. *Dealer:* Carlisle Consulting PO Box 140781 Nashville TN 37214. *Mailing Add:* 5221 Whispering Valley Dr Nashville TN 37211

KAUFMAN, MICO
SCULPTOR
b Romania, Jan 3, 24; US citizen. *Study:* Acad Fine Arts, Rome & Florence, Italy, 47-51. *Work:* Bronze sculpture, Rouses Mem, Lowell, Mass, 80; Homage to Women (bronze sculpture), Hist Nat Park, Lowell, Mass, 84; Claude Debussy (bronze sculpture), Univ Mass, Lowell Campus, Mass, 87 & St Germain en Laye, France; Italia (bronze sculpture), Town Hall, Lowell, Mass, 87; Ann Sullivan & Helen Keller "Water", Agawam, Mass, 92 & Tewkesbury, England, 85; bronze sculpture, Muster Park Fountain, Tewksbury, Mass, 92; Touching Souls, United Methodist Church, tewkesbury, MA, 93, Tewkesbury Abbey, Tewkesbury, England, 99; The Spirit of the Marathon, Bronze, Marathon, Greece, 2004. *Comn:* Official Ford VPres Commemorative Medal, 73; Official Ford Pres Commemorative Medal, 74; 200 Bicentennial Medals, Danbury Mint; Official Pres Reagan/VPres Bush Medal, 85; Official Pres Bush Commemorative Medal, 89. *Exhib:* Int Fedn Medal Producers, Lisbon & Port, 79, Florence, Italy, 83, Stockholm, Swed, 85, Commemorative Medal, Colo, 87, Freedom British Mus, London, Eng, 92; Prudential Art Festival, New Eng Sculpture Soc, 69; Helsinki, Finland, 90; retrospective, Am Numismatic Soc, 92; Budapest, Hungary, 94. *Teaching:* Instr sculpture, Boston Ctr Adult Educ, 59-62, New Eng Sch Art, Boston, 69-70 & Nashua Arts & Sci, 70-71; instr sculpture, New Eng Sch Art, Boston, 69-70 & Nashua Arts & Sci, 70-71. *Awards:* Alma & Ulysses Ricci Award for Best Conservative Painting or Sculpture, Rockport Art Asn, 67; Sculptor of Year, Houston, Tex, 78 & J Sanford Saltus Award for Signal Achievement in Art of the Medal, Am Numismatic Soc, 92. *Bibliog:* Ann Schecter (auth), Vivid sculptural works, 11/19/67 & Perlinax (auth), Maggie Walker Medal, 11/11/71, Lowell Sun, Mass; Brenda Badolato (auth), The sculpture of Mico Kaufman, Lawrence Eagle Tribune, Mass, 6/18/68. *Mem:* life fel Nat Sculpture Soc; New Eng Sculpture Asn; Cambridge Art Asn; Rockport Artists Asn; Nat Soc Lit and Arts; Fel Am Numismatic Soc; Am Medallic Sculpture Asn; Federation Internationale de la Medaille. *Media:* Bronze, Stainless Steel. *Publ:* Auth, The Making of Mold Block and Case, 60; Your most penetrating portrait ever, Nat Sculpture Rev, 72. *Mailing Add:* 23 Marion Dr Tewksbury MA 01876-1224

KAUFMAN, NANCY
ART ADVISOR, WRITER
b Woonsocket, RI. *Study:* Boston Univ, AB(art hist), 60; Univ Calif, Berkeley, art & archit hist. *Comn:* Matt Mullican (wall relief), Zeckendorf Co, 89; Harry Roseman, bronze (wall relief), J P Morgan & Co, 90; Andrew Leicester Maya Linn, LIRR, 94. *Exhib:* Studio to Site: Pub Art NY, 93. *Collection Arranged:* New York City Transit Authority, Livingston Plaza Facility, 92; Haight Gardner Poor & Havens, 87; St Luke's/Roosevelt Hosp, 93-. *Pos:* Dir visual arts referral serv, Creative Artists Pub Serv prog, 74-79; bd dir, Ctr for Arts Info, 78-83; partner, Kaufman Randolph Tate, Fine Art Services, 79-83; pres, Nancy Kaufman Fine Art Servs, 83-; search cons, Opportunity Resources, Inc, 96-. *Teaching:* Mem fac, New Sch Social Res, 84-86. *Bibliog:* At home with art (column), House Beautiful, 83-86. *Mem:* Arttable (bd dir, 90-93); Asn Prof Art Adv (bd dir 83-88). *Mailing Add:* 305 W 86th St New York NY 10024

KAUFMAN, STUART MARTIN
PAINTER, ILLUSTRATOR
b Brooklyn, NY, Dec 1, 1926. *Study:* Pratt Inst, New York, 45-46; Art Students League, New York, 46-48; study with Howard Trafton, Frank V DuMond & Frank Reilly. *Work:* Newark Mus Art, NJ; Minneapolis Inst Fine Art, Minn; Metrop Mus Art, Lehman Collection. *Comn:* commn by Jeanne Vanderbilt, Charles Engelhard Jr, B Rionda Bragh, Stephen Smith, Katherine Beach, Mrs. John Heminway, David Daniels, Bernard Rabin. *Exhib:* Annual Invitational, Montclair Mus, NJ, 57-64; Selected NJ Artists, Newark Mus, 58, 59, 64 & 65; Invitational Exhib, Chicago Art Inst, 61; Realistic Am Art, Butler Inst Am Art, Youngstown, Ohio, 62; Fine Arts Festival, San Diego Mus, Calif, 64; 20th Century Realists, Hirschl & Adler Gallery, NY, 65; Annual Exhib, Nat Acad Design, NY, 66; Invitational Ann Exhib, Soc Illusrs, NY, 66; Davis Gallery, NY. *Pos:* Illusr book cover paintings, Simon & Schuster, 61-83, CBS Publ-Fawcett, 70-82, Dell Publ, 83-95, Warner Publ, 84-86 & St Martins Press, 86. *Teaching:* Heritage Art Sch, S Orange, NJ; Armory Art Sch, W Palm Beach, Fla; JCC

Art Sch, Boca Raton, Fla. *Awards:* George R Beach Prize, 58 & Traditional Oils, 64, Montclair Mus Art; Guri Seaver Mem Award, Art Inst Chicago, 61. *Bibliog:* Esther Forman Singer (auth), Figure paintings of Stuart Kaufman, Am Artist, 72. *Media:* Oils. *Dealer:* Stace Allison Segal 2401 NW 64th St Broken Sound Boca Raton, FL 33496. *Mailing Add:* 6050 S Verde Trail Apt 403 Boca Raton FL 33433-4466

KAUFMANN, ROBERT CARL
ART LIBRARIAN
b Birmingham, Ala, Apr 27, 37. *Study:* Birmingham Southern Col, Ala, BS(Fr & hist), 61; Sch Libr Serv, Columbia Univ, New York, MSLS, 65, MA candidate in art hist, 65-69. *Pos:* Asst librn, Fine Arts Libr, Columbia Univ, New York, 64-68, fine arts librn, 68-69; librn, Cooper-Hewitt Mus, Smithsonian Inst, New York, 65-; art libr, Div Art, Donnell Br, New York Pub Libr, 69; art & archit librn, Yale Univ, New Haven, Conn, 71-74. *Awards:* Joe Delmore Langston Award, Ala Libr Asn, 63; Comt to Rescue Italian Art Res Fel, Bibliot Naz Centrale, Florence, Italy, 69-71. *Mem:* Victorian Soc Am; Art Libr Soc NAm. *Res:* Nineteenth century furniture and decorative arts; subject headings for twentieth century decorative arts. *Mailing Add:* 220 W 93rd St No 11A New York NY 10025

KAULITZ, GARRY CHARLES
PRINTMAKER, PAINTER
b Rapid City, SDak, Oct 6, 42. *Study:* Rochester Inst Technol, BFA & MFA. *Work:* Anchorage Mus Hist & Art; Art Inst Chicago; Humana Inc; Am Life Insurance; Art Acad China. *Comn:* Steeltect Industs, Louisville; Norton Hosp, Louisville. *Exhib:* One-man shows, JB Speed Art Mus, Louisville, 71, Bellarmine Col, Ky, 76 & 90, Brookhaven Col, Tex, 79, 2001, Bear Gallery, Fairbanks, Alaska, 2000, Ind Univ Southeast, New Albany, 2000 & Alaska Pacific Univ, 2000; Int Miniature Print Exhib, NY, 78; Print Club of Philadelphia, 79-80; Freichen Int Print Exhib, 80; Crackow Biannual, 80; Decker Morris, AK, 95 & 98; Univ Alaska, 97; Colorprint USA, 98; Prints Across the Pacific, 98; and others. *Teaching:* Prof printmaking, Louisville Sch Art, 68-82; vis artist, Brookhaven Col, Tex, 79, 83 & 88 & Southern Ill Univ, 79; guest speaker, Detroit Print Symposium, 80; instr, Univ Louisville, 87-93; prof printmaking, Univ Alaska, 93-. *Awards:* Evansville Mus Ann Exhib Award, 68; Arthur D Allen Mem Award, Regional Fine Arts Biennial, 71; Alsmith Fel, 92; and others. *Bibliog:* Sarah Lansdell (auth), Review of work, 2/71 & Linda Bousch (auth), A printmaker's excursion into fact & fantasy, 2/75, Courier-J & Times; Mike Dunham (auth), Anchorage Daily News, 11/97; Julie Decker (auth), Kebreakers, Alaska's Most Innovative Artists, 99. *Mem:* Southern Print Coun; NW Print Coun; Mid-Am Print Coun. *Media:* Oil; Mixed Media. *Publ:* Auth, A Portfolio of Prints & Poems, pvt publ, 73. *Dealer:* Decker Morris Gallery Anchorage AK. *Mailing Add:* c/o Univ Alaska 3211 Providence Dr Anchorage AK 99508-4614

KAUPELIS, ROBERT JOHN
PAINTER, EDUCATOR
b Amsterdam, NY, Feb 23, 28. *Study:* State Univ NY Col Buffalo, BS; Albright Art Sch, cert; Teachers Col, Columbia Univ, MA & EdD. *Work:* Univ Mass; Atlanta Art Inst; NY Univ Art Collection; Mich State Univ; Burchfield Art Ctr, Buffalo, NY; and others. *Exhib:* Over 60 one-man shows incl Image South Gallery, Atlanta, Ga, 77-79 & 82, Schenectady Mus, 80, Andre Zarre Gallery & Hudson River Mus, NY, 83; Univ Alaska, Fairbanks, 86; Kingsboro Community Col, Brooklyn, 87; Jack Gallery, NY, 87, 88, 90; Gallery Camino Real, Boca Raton, Fla, 90; Alan Brown Gallery, Hartsdale, NY, 90; Circle Gallery, Chicago & Denver, 90, 91; Reece Gallery, NY, 93; Hurlbutt Gallery, Greenwich, 96; Flywheel Gallery, Piermont, NY, 97; Quick Art Ctr, St Bonaventure, NY, 98; The Studio, Armonk, NY, 2002; Gallery in the Park, Cross River, NY, 2005; Gallery 25N, Peekskill, NY, 2005. *Teaching:* Pub sch of NY State, 51-56; New Paltz State, instr, 53-55; TC Columbia Univ, instr, 58-85; Prof of Art & Art Education, NY Univ, retired. *Awards:* Prize for Sculpture, New Eng Ann, 69; Painting Prize, Silvermine New Eng Ann, 73, 2000, First Prize, 79 & 80; Outstanding Alumni Award, 2005. *Bibliog:* Herbert Livesey (auth), The Professors, Charterhouse, 75; Gerald M Monroe (auth), Teaching drawing: The personal approaches of Robert Kaupelis, Drawing, 5-6/79 & Am Artist, 8/81; Ruth Bass (auth), article, Arts, 9/83. *Mem:* Am Soc Contemp Artists; Artists Equity; Silvermine Guild Artists; Univ Coun on the Arts; Katonah Mus Artists Asn (coun). *Media:* Acrylic, Oil. *Publ:* Auth, Learning to Draw, 66 & Experimental Drawing, 80, Watson-Guptill; John Canaday (auth), NY Times, 10/72; William Zimmer (auth), NY Times, 4/91. *Dealer:* Gallery M 290 Fillmore St Denver CO 80206; The Studio 2 Maryland Ave Armonk NY 10504; Gallery 25N Peekskill NY. *Mailing Add:* 988 Barberry Rd Yorktown Heights NY 10598

KAVANAGH, CORNELIA KUBLER
SCULPTOR, DESIGNER
b April 8, 40. *Study:* Barnard Col, BA (art hist), 62; Teacher's Col, Columbia Univ, MA, 72. *Comn:* stone sculptures, comn by Merinoff Family, Lake Success, NY, 96; bronze sculpture, Kirshenbaum & Bond, Partners, NY, 97; Bronze Lion (sculpture), Lancaster Vineyards, Napa, Calif, 2000; bronze sculpture, comn by Leventhal Family, Tenafly, NJ, 2000; Long Wharf Theater, New Haven, Conn; Marnier-Lapostolle, Paris, France, 2005. *Exhib:* Art Asia, Hong Kong Convention Ctr, 91; 22nd Annual Competition, Stamford Mus & Nature Ctr Conn, 92; Five from Connecticut, Norwalk Community Col Conn, 95; Five Winners, Discovery Mus, Bridgeport, Conn, 97; Qualita Fine Art Gallery, Las Vegas, 2000; Connecticut Women Artist Inc, Univ Hartford, 2000; Art of Northeast, Silvermine Guild Arts Ctr, New Canaan, Conn, 2000; Bronze, Plaster, Stone, Tucker Robbins Gallery, NY, 2001; The Shape of Time, Kirshenbaum Bond & Ptnrs, NYC, 2002; Art Place, Yale Physicians Building, New Haven, 2002; Garden Art Pequot Library, Southport, Conn, 2002; Tucker Robbins, NY, 2004; Sculpture Invitational Mill Brook Gallery, Concord, NH, 2004; Improvisation on a Square, Blue Mountain Gallery, NY, 2004; Openasia, Venice, Italy, 2004; Art Place, Yale Univ Med Sch, New Haven, Conn, 2005; Hargate Art Gallery, St Pauls Sch, Concord, NH, 2005; La Biennale de Venice, Venice, Italy, 2005; The Tsunami Project, Blue Hour, Blue Mountain Gallery; NY, Zane Bennett Contemp Art, Santa Fe, NMex; Sofa Chicago, Chicago, Ill; The Elements - Water, Gallery Contemp Art, Sacred Heart Univ, Fairfield, Conn, 2006. *Awards:* Discovery Mus Best Sculpture, Bridgeport, Conn, 97; Amidor Mem Award for Stone Sculptue, New Canaan, Conn, 2000; CT Women Artists, Inc, Jurors Choice, 2003. *Bibliog:* Vivien Raynor (auth), Local Show of the Northeast, Wider Themes, NY Times, 95; Betty Tyler (auth), Art 2000, The Norwalk Hour, 2000; Martha S Scott (auth), Cornelia Kubler Kavanagh, 2001; Robert Mahoney, Cornelia Kubler Kavanagh Sculpture; Mark Treatise, The Shape of Time, NY, 2001; Victor M Cassidy, NY, Cornelia Kubler Kavanagh Sculpture Mag, May, 2003; De grandes Paolo, A Bridge Between E & W at Openasia, 2004. NY Arts Nov/Dec, 2004; Paolo DeGrandis, Victor Cassidy (coauths), Venice Biennale show catalog, 2005; William Zimmer (auth), Tsunami Project Rev, 1/2006. *Mem:* NSS; Conn Women Artists Inc. *Media:* Stone, Bronze. *Dealer:* Blue Mountain Gallery 530 W 25 St NY; Zane Bennett Contemporary Art 826 Canyon Rd Santa Fe NM 87501. *Mailing Add:* 24 Point Rd South Norwalk CT 06854

KAVLESKI, CHARLEEN VERENA
CONCEPTUAL ARTIST, SCULPTOR
b Ellenville, NY, Nov 19, 42. *Study:* Orange Co Community Col, AA, 63, AAS, 64; John Herron Sch Art, 64; State Univ NY, New Paltz, BS, graduate studies fine arts, 65-72. *Work:* Crosscurrents; Franklin Sq Gallery, Southport, NC; Shimizu Am Corp, Durham, NC; pvt individual collections; Nat Asn Women Artists, New York City; and others. *Comn:* Installation of painted constructions, comn by Dr Gustav Gavis, Monticello, NY, 94 & comn by Dr Goddard Lainjo, Middletown, NY, 95. *Exhib:* One-man shows, Westbroadway Gallery, NY, 82 & 83, Amos Eno Gallery, NY, 86, 87, 90, 91, 94, 97, 98, 99, 2001, 03 & 05; Stockton National, Haggin Mus, Calif, 85; Three Rivers Arts Festival, Pittsburgh, Pa, 86, 87 & 89; 51st Ann National, Butler Inst Am Art, Youngstown, Ohio, 87; Mohawk-Hudson Regional, Schenectady Mus, NY, 89; Measure for Measure, NY Acad Sci, 92; Nat Asn Women Artists Millenium Collection (touring), NY, 1992-2005; Shimizu Am Corp, Durham, NC; Nat Asn Women Artists ann exhibs, 1992-2005; Beck Gallery, Hurleyville, NY, 2003; Sullivan Co Mus & Cult Ctr, Hurleyville, NY, 2003; Plotkin Gallery, Dobbs Ferry, NY, 2006. *Collection Arranged:* Franklin Square Gallery, Southport, NC; Shimizu Am Corp, Durham, NC. *Pos:* Treas & bd mem, Amos Enos Gallery, 91-94. *Teaching:* Art teacher, Monticello Central, NY, 1968-99; art adv ed, lit & art mag, Monticello Middle Sch, NY, 1989-99. *Awards:* First Place-Installation, Nepenth Mundi Emerald City Classic, 87; Miriam E Halpern Mem Award, 105th Ann Exhib, Nat Asn Women Artists, 94 & Clara Shainess Mem Award, 107th Ann Exhib, 96. *Bibliog:* Les Krantz (auth), The New York Art Review, Am References, 88, Times Herald Record, 97, Temple Emanuel of Great Neek and Great Neck Record, 97, Sullivan County Dem, 97, 2001, 03 & 05. *Mem:* Nat Asn Women Artists; NY State Art Teachers Asn; Ret Teachers Asn NY; Catskill Art Soc. *Media:* Miscellaneous Media. *Interests:* Art history; contemporary art; antiques; collectibles. *Dealer:* Amos Eno Gallery 594 Broadway New York NY 10012. *Mailing Add:* 530 W 25th St New York NY 10001

KAWA, FLORENCE KATHRYN
PAINTER
b Weyerhaeuser, Wis, Feb 24, 12. *Study:* Minneapolis Sch Art, 30-34; Univ Wis, Milwaukee, BS, 40; La State Univ, Baton Rouge, MA, 44; summers, Black Mountain Col, 44, Columbia Univ, 46-48, Cranbrook Acad Art, 51, Mass Inst Technol, 56 & Leeds Col Art, Eng, 70. *Work:* Univ Wis, Madison; La Art Comn, Baton Rouge; US Info Agency for Am Embassies; Pub Bldgs Admin for Marine Hosps; Hoover State Office Bldg, Des Moines, Iowa. *Exhib:* Int Watercolor Biennial, Brooklyn Mus, 51, 55, 57, 59 & 61; Ann Exhib Contemp Am Sculpture, Watercolor & Drawings, Whitney Mus Art, NY, 53; Nat Competition Watercolors, Drawings & Prints, Metrop Mus Art, NY, 53; Contemp Watercolor in the US, sponsored by US Embassy Cult Div, France, 53; 20th Century Am Graphic Arts, US Info Agency Touring Foreign Mus, 56-57; one-man show, Des Moines Art Ctr, 76. *Teaching:* Asst prof painting & design, Fla State Univ, 46-62; prof painting & design, Drake Univ, 64-78, emer prof, 78-. *Awards:* Edmundson Award for Best Work in Any Medium, Des Moines Art Ctr, 70, Esther & Edith Younker Award, 77; 13th Midwest Biennial Purchase Award & Best in Show, Joslyn Mus, Omaha, 74; plus others. *Media:* Oil, Watercolor. *Dealer:* Olson-Larsen Gallery 203 Fifth St West Des Moines IA 50265

KAWASHIMA, TAKESHI
PAINTER, SCULPTOR
b Takamatsu City, Japan, Jan 13, 1930. *Study:* Musashino Univ Art, 51-56; Art Students League New York, 66. *Work:* Mus Mod Art, NY; Ohara Mus Art, Kurashiki; Tokyo Metrop Mus Art; Tokushima Prefectural Mus Mod Art, Tokushima City, 88; Hiroshima City Mus Contemp Art, 99; Okazaki City Mus, 2000; State Univ, Pottsdam, NY; Frederick R Weisman Art Found; and others. *Comn:* Tokyo Life Insurance Co, Ltd, Tokyo, 89; Takamatsu City Libr, Takamatsu City, 92; Mita Copy, NJ, 92; Kawachi-Nagano City Ctr, Osaka, 92; Hachioji City Art & Cult Hall, Tokyo, 94; and others. *Exhib:* Mus Modern Art, New York, NY 1965-66 & 67; Wadell Gallery, New York, NY, 67, 69 & 72; Aldrich Mus Contemp Art, Ridgefield, Conn, 67; Nat Mus Art, Osaka, Japan, 77; Tradition & Today, Bargen Mus Art Sci, NJ, 83; Japan: Dynasty '83, Sante Webster Gallery, Philadelphia, 83; Japanese Contemp Painting, 1960-80, Mus Mod Art, Gunma, 84; retrospective show (solo), Takamatsu City Mus Art, Takamatsu City, 89; solo exhib, Haenah-Kent Gallery, NY, 95, Walter Wickiser Gallery, 98, State Univ, Potsdam, 2004 & Mitchell Algus Gallery, NY, 2006; and others. *Collection Arranged:* Hosetsu Ohtsuka Calligraphy (auth, catalog), 82. *Awards:* Silvermine Prize, 18th Ann New Eng Exhib, New Canaan, Conn, 67. *Bibliog:* Udo Kulterman (auth), The new painting, Frederick A Praeger, 69; Joseph Love (auth), Art Int, 71; Holland Cotter (auth), NY Times, 04/21/2006. *Media:* Acrylic, Oil, Watercolor; Stone, Metal.

Publ: Contribr, Decoration art, 72 & The base of sculpture, 78, Shincho-Sha; New York for twelve years, Shikoku Shinbun, 76; auth, I Love New York, essay, US Japan Publ New York, Inc, 104, 92; contribr, Exclusive, Soho, Seikatsu-no-tome-sha, 54, 89; Chronicle of Art, Vol 6 1976-1989, Mainichi News Paper, 74-75, 91. *Dealer:* Nantenshi Gallery 3-6-5 Kyobashi Chuo-ku Tokyo Japan. *Mailing Add:* 11 Mercer St 2F New York NY 10013-2079

KAWECKI, JEAN MARY
SCULPTOR, GALLERY DIRECTOR
b Liverpool, Eng; US citizen, June 24, 1926. *Study:* Liverpool Col Art, Eng; Art Career Sch, New York; also with Douglas Prizer. *Work:* Hoffman LaRoche Pharmaceutical Co; First Montclair Housing, NJ; The Carrier Found, Belle Mead, NJ; Noyes Mus Art. *Comn:* Wall sculpture, First Montclair Housing Corp, 83; Site-Specific Works for Temple Anshe Emeth, New Brunswick, 87; Eight Sculptures, Ctr Women Policy Studies, Washington, DC. *Exhib:* Nat Miniature Soc, Nutley, NJ, 75; Audubon Artists, Nat Acad Design, NY, 78; Newark Mus, 78; Nabisco World Hq, 79; solo show, NJ Inst Technol, 80-; Bergen Mus, 81; Montclair State Col, 90; NJ Arts Ann, 1998 & 2001. *Pos:* Free lance illusr mag, London, Eng, 46-51, Sol Vogel & Am-Mitchell Publ, New York, 51-53, Tobias Meyer & Nebenzahl, New York, 58-66; co-founder & dir, Doubletree Coop Art Gallery, Upper Montclair, 74-88; vpres, co-founder, exhib chair, Studio Montclair Inc, An Asn of Prof Visual Artists, 1997-. *Awards:* Patrons Award, Hudson Artists at the Bergen Mus, 76; Sculpture Award, Audubon Artists at Nat Acad Galleries, New York, 78; First Prize, St John's Ann Juried Show, Newark, 79, 86. *Bibliog:* Anne Betty Weinshenker (auth), M & A on Art, NJ Music & Arts, 12/76; Eileen Watkins (auth), article in Star Ledger, 87; Betty Freudenheim (auth), article in Sunday NY Times, 89. *Mem:* Artists Equity Asn NY; Doubletree Coop Gallery (dir & chmn hanging comt & spec shows, 74-88); Women Artists Montclair. *Media:* Found Stone, Metal & Epoxy. *Publ:* Work on Cover of Geraldine R Dodge Found Ann Report. *Dealer:* Scott Broadfoot Broadfoot & Broadfoot Gallery Boonton NJ. *Mailing Add:* c/o Studio Montclair Inc 108 Orange Rd Montclair NJ 07042

KAY, REED
PAINTER, WRITER
b Boston, Mass, Mar 29, 25. *Study:* Sch Mus Fine Arts, Boston, dipl, 49, with Karl Zerbe. *Work:* Cape Ann Hist Mus, Gloucester, Mass; De Cordoa Mus, Lincoin, Mass; Rose Art Mus, Brandeis Univ, Waltham, Mass; Wellingyon Mauagement, Boston, Mass; Wiggin Collection, Boston Pub Libr. *Exhib:* Kanegis Gallery, Boston, 56; Boris Mirski Gallery, Boston, 64, 65; A Selection of Am Art, Inst Contemp Art, Boston, 76; Art in Transition, Mus Fine Arts, Boston, 77; one-man exhib, Alpha Gallery, Boston, 78, 83, 90, 96, 2000, 2002 & 2005; Circle Gallery, Washington, 86; Amherst Col, 73, 94; Boston Athenaeum, 96; Danforth Mus Art, Framingham, Mass, 95; Nat Acad, NY, 98, 2004, 2005; Univ NH, 2000; Cape Ann Hist Mus, Gloucester, Ma, 2002; Boston Univ Art Gallery, 2002; and others. *Teaching:* Instr painting, Sch Mus Fine Arts, Boston, 49-50, 51-56; instr painting techniques, Skowhegan Sch Painting, Maine, 52-60; instr painting, Boston Univ, 56, prof painting, 68-. *Awards:* James William Paige Traveling Fel, 50-51; Artist Fel Grant for Painting, Nat Endowment Arts, 81-82. *Bibliog:* articles, Christian Sci Monitor, 6/21/65, Boston Globe, 2/14/65 & 12/27/81, Boston Herald, 2/23/90, Middlesex News, 10/8/95. *Mem:* Nat Acad (acad, 2003). *Media:* Oil, Gouache. *Res:* Effects of painter's materials and media on aesthetic qualities of pictures and the way they change with age. *Publ:* Auth, The Painter's Companion, Webb Bks, 61; contribr, World Bk Encycl, 72-88; The Painter's Guide to Studio Methods & Materials, Doubleday, 72 & rev ed, Prentice-Hall, 83. *Dealer:* Alpha Gallery 38 Newbury St Boston MA 02116. *Mailing Add:* 109 Rawson Rd Brookline MA 02445-4509

KAYE, DAVID HAIGH
TEXTILE ARTIST, DESIGNER
b Kingston, Ont, 47. *Study:* Ont Col Art, Toronto, AOCA; Univ Guelph, BA; Cranbrook Acad Art, Bloomfield Hills, Mich, MFA. *Work:* Jean A Chalmers Collection of Contemp Can Crafts, Ont Crafts Coun, Toronto; Can Coun Art Bank, Ottawa; Nat Mus Mod Art, Kyoto, Japan; Massey Found Collection, Ottawa; Prudential Insurance Co Am, Toronto. *Comn:* Linen & Jute (tapestry), comn by P Farlinger, Glouchester News, Toronto, 74; Relief Illusion (tapestry), comn by L Gladstone, Videogenic Corp, Toronto, 81; Relief Illusion Number Two (tapestry), comn by Helena Hernmarck & Niels Diffrient, Ridgefield, Conn, 82. *Exhib:* 100 Yrs: Evolution of the Ontario College of Art, Art Gallery Ont, Toronto, 76; Fiberworks, Cleveland Mus Art, Ohio, 77; Fiber Works: Americas & Japan, Nat Mus Mod Art, Kyoto & Tokyo, Japan, 77 & 78; Engaged Reliefs, Macdonald Stewart Art Ctr, Guelph and traveling, 82-83; Canada Mikrokosma, Barbican Ctr, London, Eng, 82 & Textilmuseum, Krefeld, WGer, 83; Tapices Canadienses Contemporaneos, Palacio de Cristal, Madrid, Spain, 83; Here and Now-Canadian Fibre Art, Cambridge Arts Ctr, Cambridge, Ont, 86; and others. *Awards:* Lt-Gov's Medal, Grad Medal, Ont Col of Art, 72; Can Coun Short-Term Grant, Ottawa, 75 & 78; F Javier Sauza Arts Award, 80; Craftsmen Grant, Ont Arts Coun, Toronto. *Bibliog:* M E Bevlin (auth), Design Through Discovery, Holt, Rinehart & Winston, 77; S W Keene (auth), Toronto artist seeks integrity of idea, materials, technique, Weaving & Fiber News, Homer, NY, 80; J Parkin (auth), Art in Architecture, Visual Arts, Ont, 82. *Media:* Natural Fibers, Mixed Media. *Mailing Add:* 128 Dovercourt Rd Toronto ON M6J 3C4 Canada

KAYE, MILDRED ELAINE
INSTRUCTOR, PRINTMAKER
b New York, NY, Sept 24, 29. *Study:* Ind Univ, Ind, 51; Montclair State Col, MA, 77. *Work:* Works to 95: Serigraph: After 95, Primarily Digital Art, also various traditional media. *Comn:* Logos and corporate images; illustration of filmstrips for Troll Assoc; Portraits, Graphic Designer. *Exhib:* Solo Shows; Kurth Cottage Gallery; Hamilton House Mus, Montclair, NJ; Norman Alexander Art Gallery, Scarsdale, NY; Talli's Gallery, NY; Gallery North, Paramus, NJ; Gallery One, Montclair State Univ; Vineyard Gallery, NY; Group shows; Art Inst of Calif, San Francisco; Missouri Western State Col; Williamsburg Art and Historic Ctr; Cleveland Mus of Art; Silicone Valley Mus of Art; Salmagundi Club NY; Audubon Artists; Salmagundi Club; Mus of the City of NY; United Nations Bldg (Millennium Collection); Times Sq Lobby Gallery. *Collection Arranged:* Nabisco Brands; John Herron Institute, Indianapolis; Am Cultural Center, Taipei; NJ Board of Education, Trenton; Cisco Systems; Leonard Boucour Co; Passaic Community Coll; Indiana Univ, Bloomington IN; Montclair State Univ, NJ;. *Pos:* Art ed, Am Book Co, 52-56; Illus, Film Strips, 60-65; graphic designer, Guy-Mar Printing, 65-72; cur, Summerfun Theater, 93- & NJ State Bd of Educ Bldg, 98-. *Teaching:* Graphic design, Bergen Co Vocational Schs, 72-99; art, Art Ctr Northern NJ, 90-95. *Awards:* Director's Choice; Mo Western State Col; Showcase Award; Manhattan Arts Int; Int Mac World Digital Gallery, Int Small Works Show; Bergen Mus, Best in Show; Fair Lawn Art Asn First Prize; Image used for poster, MacWorld Expo, San Francisco; Atrium Gallery, First Prize Experimental; First Prize, Cork Gallery (Lincoln Ctr); Pen and Brush Invitational, HM. *Bibliog:* Segment on exhibit (film), NJ Nightly News, 11/81; Henry Doren (auth), The face of the coin, NJ Artform, 12/81; Art in Orange County, 83; The New York Art Review. *Mem:* Charter Member of Salute to Women in the Arts; Nat Asn Women Artists (vpres); Nat Print Consortium, Pen & Brush; Studio Montclair; Steering Committee Art Educators of NJ. *Media:* Serigraph, Computer. *Specialty:* Fine Arts. *Interests:* Art History, especially Surrealism; the web. *Publ:* Auth, The Want Ad, 10/80, The Other Side of the Coin, 12/80, The Layout and Paste-Up, Self Taught, 8/81, Introduction to Typography, 10/81 & Introduction to Copyfitting, 2/82, NJ Artforms; dir, The Carousel, an Idyl (animated film), 86; Life Cycles: 2 Flatworms (scientific animated film), 86; Gallery Guide, 2000. *Dealer:* Nathans Gallery 1205 McBride Ave West Paterson NJ 07026; Talli's Fine Arts 132 E 82nd St New York NY 10028; Ward-Nasse Gallery, New York City. *Mailing Add:* 87 Kern Pl Saddle Brook NJ 07663

KAYSER, THOMAS ARTHUR
CONSULTANT, DESIGNER
b Milwaukee, Wis, Oct 4, 35. *Study:* Layton Sch Art, 58; Cranbrook Acad Art, 59; Mus Mgt Inst, Berkeley, 80. *Collection Arranged:* The American Indian/The American Flag, 76; The Art of Haute Couture, 78; German Expressionism from Western Michigan, 79; Kalamazoo Collects Photography, 80; Super Realism from the Morton G Neumann Collection, 81; New Image/Pattern & Decoration from the Morton G Neumann Collection, 83; A Century of Caring, 86; Light Dreams, Kalamazoo Inst Arts, Mich, 87; The Cutting Edge, 88; John Himmelfarb: Meetings in the Garden, 89. *Pos:* Asst dir, Flint Inst Arts, Mich, 65-78; exec dir, Kalamazoo Inst Arts, Mich 78-89; pres, Tom Kayser & Assoc, 89-; dir, Gilmore Car Mus, Hickory Corners, Mich, 94-. *Mem:* Am Asn Mus; Art Mus Asn; Mich Mus Asn; Mich Coun Arts (chmn adv bd); hon mem & founder Dirs Art Mus Mich; Midwest Mus Asn. *Mailing Add:* 2132 Rambling Rd Kalamazoo MI 49008

KAZ, NATHANIEL
SCULPTOR, INSTRUCTOR
b NY, NY, Mar 9, 17. *Study:* Art Students League, with George Bridgman, Samuel Cashwan & William Zorach. *Work:* Metrop Mus, Whitney Mus & Brooklyn Mus, NY; NY Univ, NY; Larry Aldrich Mus, Conn. *Comn:* Wood relief, US Treas Dept, US Post Off, Hamburg, PA; cast aluminum relief, Binghamton Col, NY; limestone relief carving, Vine St Temple, Nashville, Tenn; Gordian Knot (bronze relief), Northern Valley Englewood Savings Bank, Leona, NJ; four cast bronzes & large wood carving, Temple Beth Emeth, Albany, NY; and others. *Exhib:* Whitney Mus Am Art, NY; Metrop Mus Art, NY; Mus Mod Art, NY; Art Inst Chicago; Philadelphia Mus Fine Arts, Pa; World's Fairs, Chicago, NY & San Francisco, 39; Nat Acad Design, NY, 74, 76, 79, 81, 86, 88. *Teaching:* Instr sculpture, Art Students League of NY, currently. *Awards:* Grant, Nat Inst Arts & Lett; First Prize, Nat Monument Competition, UN Gen Assembly; Sculpture Prize, Brooklyn Mus, NY, 48 & 52; Alfred G B Steel Mem Prize, 148th Ann Exhib, Pa Acad Fine Arts, 53; Medals of Honor, Audubon Artists, 60, 81, 83, 84 & 87; Agop Agopoff Award, Nat Acad Design, 88. *Bibliog:* Ray Wisniewski (dir), A Small Bronze Mask: A Portrait of the Sculptor Nathaniel Kazas Revealed in His Work (film), George C Arcaro, 56. *Mem:* Sculptor's Guild; life mem, Art Students League; Audubon Artists; Nat Sculpture Soc Fel; Assoc Nat Acad Design. *Media:* Bronze, Marble. *Mailing Add:* Art Students League 215 W 57th St New York NY 10019-2193

KAZOR, VIRGINIA ERNST
CURATOR
b Detroit, Mich, Sept 28, 40. *Study:* Univ Southern Calif, BA, MA. *Collection Arranged:* Separate Realities (catalog), 73; 24 From Los Angeles (with catalog), 74; Dreams for Sale: The Great Work of Hollywood Still Photographers 1927-1949, 76; Greene and Greene: Architecture and Related Design of Charles Sumner Greene and Henry Mather Greene, 1894-1934 (with catalog), 77; The Barnsdall Projects: Drawings by Frank Lloyd Wright, 80; Frank Lloyd Wright: Designs for Hollyhock House, 86; Frank Lloyd Wright in Los Angeles 1919-1926: An Architecture for the Southwest (with catalog), 88. *Pos:* Curatorial asst mod art, Los Angeles Co Mus Art, 65-68; cur, Los Angeles Munic Art Gallery, 70-78 & Frank Lloyd Wright's Hollyhock House, 78-. *Mem:* Los Angeles Bicentennial Orgn (chmn mus comt, 74-); Soc Archit Hist, Southern Calif Chap (pres, 81-83, exec bd, 83-86). *Mailing Add:* Hollyhock House Barnsdall Park 4800 Hollywood Blvd Los Angeles CA 90027

KEANE, BILL
CARTOONIST
b Philadelphia, Pa, 22. *Hon Degrees:* Penn Col, IA, LHD, 81. *Work:* Bil Keane Original Cartoon Collection, Syracuse Univ; Int Mus Cartoon Art, Cartoon Art Mus, San Francisco; Ohio State Univ. *Pos:* Staff artist, Philadelphia Eve Bull, 45-59; creator & nat syndicated cartoonist, The Family Circus, 60, Channel Chuckles, 54-77.

Awards: Best Syndicated Panel Cartoonist, Nat Cartoonists Soc, 69, 71 & 74; Reuben Award, 82; Siver T Sq, 2001. *Mem:* Nat Cartoonists Soc. *Media:* Pen and Ink. *Interests:* Traditional jazz music; tennis. *Publ:* Auth, 57 paperback collections, Fawcett; 8 cartoon books, Andrews & McMeel, Guideposts Books. *Mailing Add:* 5815 E Joshua Tree Ln Paradise Valley AZ 85253

KEARNEY, JOHN (W)
SCULPTOR
b Omaha, Nebr, Aug 31, 24. *Study:* Cranbrook Acad Art, Bloomfield Hills, Mich, 45-48; Univ Stranieri, Perugia, Fulbright Grant Italy & Ital Govt Grant Sculpture, 63-64. *Work:* Mus Contemp Art, Standard Oil Bldg & Mus Sci & Indust, Chicago; Detroit Children's Mus; Mitchell Mus, Mt Vernon, Ill; Edwin A Ulrich Mus of Art, Wichita, Kans; New Sch Social Res, NY; and others. *Comn:* Large outdoor sculptures, Wichita State Univ, Chicago, Chicago Park Dist, Wichita Coliseum & Lincoln Park Zoo, Chicago, 82; King Ranch, Tex; Interfirst Plaza, Dallas; large outdoor bronze, Oz Park, Chicago, Ill; Mitchell Mus, Mt Vernon, Ill; 4 large outdoor works, Staley Transportation, Munster, Ind, 2000; bronze, Goudy Sch, Chicago, Ill, 03; Tin Man, Cowardly Lion, and ScareCrow. *Exhib:* Am Fulbright Artists, Palazzo Venezia, Rome, 64; one-man shows, ACA Galleries, NY, 65, 69, 72, 74, 76 & 79, 2003-2004: Ill Inst of Technol, 76 & 98, Ulrich Mus of Art, Wichita, 76 & Contemp Art Workshop, Chicago, 81 & 84; two-man show, Art Inst Chicago, 77; Cherrystone Gallery, Wellfleet, Mass, 80 & 92; Goldman-Kraft Gallery, Chicago, 85; Group Gallery, 87, Berta Walker Gallery, Provincetown, Mass, 92-95, 97 & 2005; Retrospective, Mitchell Mus, Mt Vernon, Ill, 94. *Pos:* Dir, Contemp Art Workshop, Chicago, 49-90, pres, 92-; mem adv bd, Art Inst Art Rental & Sales Gallery, Art Inst of Chicago; juror, Sch Art Inst Chicago, 96. *Teaching:* Instr sculpture, Contemp Art Workshop, Chicago, 50-70 & Mundelein Col, 70-71; instr, Fine Arts Work Ctr, Provinceton, Mass, 96. *Awards:* Man of Year, Adult Educ Coun Chicago, 62; Fulbright Award, Italy, 63 & 64; Ital Govt Grant, 63 & 64; vis artist, Am Acad in Rome, 85, 92, 98, 03; and others. *Bibliog:* Articles, People Mag, 10/16/89, Chicago Mag, 6/89, Chicago Sunday Tribune, 5/10/92; Nickalodeon - TV, With Linda Ellerbee, 10/5/97, KDFN-TV, Fox News Time for Kids, Dallas, 10/2/98 & 10/12/98, KERA TV, On the Record, 10/4/98. *Mem:* Provincetown Art Asn & Mus (vpres, 62-70); Fine Arts Work Ctr, Provincetown (adv bd). *Media:* Bronze, Welded Steel Bumpers. *Interests:* Italian Renaissance Art, Egypt, Southeast Asia. *Collection:* Mus of Contemporary Art, Chicago Field Mus, Chicago; Mitchell Mus, Mt Vernon, IL: Ulrich Mus, Wichita, Provincetown Art Assoc. & Mus City of Chicago; State of IL Mus, Springfield; Detroit Childrens Mus; Cranbrook Mus; New School for Social Research, NYC; Standard Oil Building, Chicago; Oakton Comm College, Desplaines, IL; Mundelein College, of Loyola Univ, Chicago; Northwestern Univ, Evanston; Peace Mus, Chicago; Francis Parker School-Chicago; Plus Dozen of other Public and private Collection, Fayetteville Arkansas Youth Ctr. *Publ:* Provinceton Arts Mag, 2005. *Dealer:* ACA Gallery 529 W 20th St New York NY 10011; Contemporary Art Workshop 542 W Grant Pl Chicago IL 60614; Berta Walker Gallery Provincetown MA 02657. *Mailing Add:* 830 Castlewood Terr Chicago IL 60640

KEARNEY, LYNN HAIGH
ADMINISTRATOR, CURATOR
b Chicago, Ill. *Study:* Northwestern Univ, BA, 49; Harvard Univ/Harvard Bus Sch, cert arts admin,78. *Exhib:* Weaving Art Inst of Chicago, 54. *Collection Arranged:* exhibs, Contemp Art Workshops. *Pos:* dir, Contemp Art Workshop, Chicago, 1951-80, co-dir, 1980-91, dir, 1992-; Mid-North Assoc, Board, 81-84; Oriana Singers, Advisory Board, 85-present; trustee, Francis Parker Sch, Chicago, 1981-84, Provincetown Art Asn & Mus, 1980-84, Dedalus Found (Robert Motherwell Found), 1991-; panelist, Chicago Off Fine Arts, Sch Art Inst Chicago, 1994. *Teaching:* Visiting Artist Am Acad in Rome, 92-98, 2003. *Bibliog:* Beverly Price (auth), Off the Record with Rob Weller, ABC/TV documentary, 5/81; Barbara Varro (auth), Man who turns bumpers into beasts, Chicago Sun Times, 3/22/81. *Mem:* Provincetown Arts Asn & Mus (trustee 80-84); Chicago Artists Coalition; Nat Asn Artists Org; Field Mus. *Media:* Exhib Curated of Emerging Art, All Media. *Specialty:* Young emerging artists, contemp art, all media. *Interests:* Italian renaissance; early cults; egyptology; Tibetan, Budhism, Southeast Asian Art. *Publ:* Auth, Bumper Art, Body Engineering J, 10/76. *Mailing Add:* 830 Castlewood Terr Chicago IL 60640

KEARNS, JAMES JOSEPH
SCULPTOR, PAINTER
b Scranton, Pa, Aug 7, 24. *Study:* Art Inst Chicago, BFA, 51. *Work:* Mus Mod Art & Whitney Mus Am Art, NY; Newark Mus Art; NJ State Mus, Trenton; Nat Collection Fine Arts, Smithsonian Inst & Hirshhorn Mus, Washington, DC; Hirshhorn Mus, Washington, DC. *Exhib:* Nat Inst Arts & Lett, 59; Whitney Mus Am Art Ann, 59-61; Johnson Wax Collection, World Tour, 62-67; Pa Acad Fine Arts, Philadelphia, 64-65; The Figurative Tradition, Whitney Mus Am Art, 80; one-man shows, Rider Col, NJ, 87, Dir Choice, Hunterdon Art Ctr, 87 & Trenton State Mus, 88; Continuities, Rider Univ, 2006. *Pos:* Mem bd gov, Skowhegan Sch Painting & Sculpture, 64-70. *Teaching:* Instr drawing, painting & sculpture, Sch Visual Arts, 60-90; instr sculpture, Fairleigh-Dickinson Univ, 62-63; instr painting & sculpture, Skowhegan Sch Painting & Sculpture, summers 62-65. *Awards:* Nat Inst Arts & Lett Grant, 59. *Bibliog:* Selden Rodman (auth), Conversations With Artists, Devin Adair, 57 & The Insiders, La State Univ, 60; Lee Nordness (auth), Art USA Now, Viking, 63. *Media:* Bronze, Fiberglass. *Publ:* Illusr, Can these bones live, New Directions, 60; illusr, The Heart of Beethoven, Shorewood Press, 62. *Dealer:* Grippi Gallery 315 E 62nd St New York NY 10021. *Mailing Add:* 452 Rockaway Rd Dover NJ 07801

KEARY, GERALDINE
PAINTER
b Salt Lake City, UT, Feb 22, 35. *Study:* Diablo Valley Jr Col, 1977-88; Workshops with Charles Movalli. *Comn:* Kaiser Permante; City of Clayton; Alameda Fair Bd; San Mateo Fair Bd. *Exhib:* Am Watercolor Int Exhib, Salmugundi Club, NY, 1993, 94 & 95; Sixth Ann Oil Painters of Am, Quast Galleries, Taos, NMex, 1997; Calif State Capital, Off of Gray Davis, San Francisco, Calif, 1999; Seventh Int Exhib, Cornel Mus, Delray Beach, Fla, 2003; Nat Watercolor Exhib, Muckenthaler Cult Ctr, Fullerton, Calif, 2004; Trition Mus Art; Coos Bay Mus Art; Oxnard Maritime Mus. *Teaching:* instr, Martinez Adult Sch, 1975-76. *Awards:* Donor's Award, Nat Watercolor Soc, 1993; Best Landscape, Calif State Fair, 1995; Third place, Calif Watercolor Asn Nat, 1997; Painters of Am Award, 2006. *Bibliog:* Greenville Killeen, Acrylic Technics, Northlight Books, 1994; Al Barnes, Paint the Wonders of Water, Artist's Mag, 1999; Loraine Crouch, Acrylic Essentials, Artist's Mag, 2002. *Mem:* Am Watercolor Soc, Signature; Nat Watercolor Soc, Signature; Calif Watercolor Asn, Signarture; Int Soc of Marine Painters, Signature; Northwest Watercolor Soc, Signature; Calif Art Club; Acrylic & Cassein Painters; Nat Acrylic Painters Asn. *Media:* Acrylic, Cassein & Oils. *Dealer:* Marin Soc of Artists PO Box 203 Ross Calif 94957; Art Concepts N Calif Blvd Walnut Creek Calif 94596. *Mailing Add:* 3870 Canyon Way Martinez CA 94553-3716

KEATING, DAVID NELSON
PHOTOGRAPHER, ASSEMBLAGE ARTIST
b Rye, NY, Sept 5, 62. *Study:* Yale Univ, New Haven, Conn, BA, 85; Univ NMex, Albuquerque, MA(studio art-photog), with distinction, 91, MFA(studio art-photog), with distinction, 94; Calif Inst Arts, Santa Clarita, 92. *Work:* Univ Art Mus, Albuquerque, NMex. *Exhib:* Solo exhibs, John Sommers Gallery, Univ NMex, Albuquerque, 90 & 91, Calif Inst Arts, 92, Graham Gallery, Albuquerque, NMex, 94, Univ Art Mus Downtown, Albuquerque, 95 & George Eastman House, Int Mus Photog & Film, 96; Disclosing the Myth of Family, Betty Rymer Gallery, Art Inst Chicago, 91; Pvt & Pub, Betty Rymer Gallery, Art Inst Chicago, 92; Dwellings of Introspection, San Jose Inst Contemp Art, Calif, 92; Photobiographers, Atlanta Gallery Photog, 92; The Mediated Image: Am Photog in the Age of Info, Univ Art Mus, Albuquerque, 93; Current Fictions, Mus Photog Arts, San Diego, 96; group show, Ctr Contemp Arts, 99. *Awards:* Van Deren Coke Fel, Univ NMex, Albuquerque, 91; Photogrs & Friends United Against AIDS, Art Matters Inc, 92; Visual Arts Fel Photog, Nat Endowment Arts, 94. *Bibliog:* Casey Fitzsimmons (auth), Turning the tables, Artweek, 9/19/91; Deborah Willis (auth), Imagining Families: Images and Voices (exhib catalog), Smithsonian Inst, 94; James Crump (auth), (Dis)regarding plaque art, New Art Examiner, 4/95. *Media:* Mixed Media

KEAVENEY, SYDNEY STARR See Starr, Sydney

KECK, JEANNE GENTRY
PAINTER
b Goochland Co, Va, Nov 29, 38. *Study:* William & Mary Col, 58-59; Dayton Art Inst, 74-75; Berkshire Sch Contemp Art, 91; Vt Studio Ctr, 92; special study with Don Dennis, Fred Leach, Nita Engle, Glen Bradshaw, Al Brouillette, Robert Lassig, Ed Betts, Frank Webb, Maxine Masterfield & Marilyn Phillis; independent studio prog, Assisi, Italy, 93. *Work:* Green Brokers, Englewood, Colo; Ford Aerospace & Communication Corp, Hanover, Md; Fed Reserve Bank, Baltimore, Md; Anne Arundel Hosp, Annapolis, Md; Nation's Bank, Charlotte, NC; and others. *Exhib:* One-person show, Springfield Art Mus, Ohio, 78-79, Twentieth Century Gallery, Williamsburg, Va, 86, Md Fed Arts, Annapolis, 84 & 87, C Grimaldis Gallery, Baltimore, Md, 89 & Md Hall Creative Arts, Annapolis, 89 & 94; Southern Watercolor Soc, Oklahoma City, 86; Ruby Blakeney Gallery, Savage Md, 91; Virginia Lynch Gallery, Tiverton, RI, 92; Brenda Taylor Gallery, Boston, Mass, 94; Taylor Gallery, Lynchburg, Va, 94; and others. *Teaching:* Instr painting, Fairborn Art Asn, Ohio, 77-81; instr watercolor, brush & palette, Wright-Patterson AFB, Ohio, 80. *Awards:* Bronze Medal, Ohio Watercolor Soc, 84; Silver Award, Mid Atlantic Regional, 84; Second Award, Southern Watercolor Soc, 86. *Bibliog:* Jeanne Dobie (auth), Making Color Sing, Watson-Guptill, 86; Mark St John Erickson (auth), Economy & expression, Williamsburg Gazette, Va, 86; Jeanne Dobie & Marilyn Phillis (auth), Watercolor Techniques for Releasing the Creative Spirit, 92. *Mem:* Md Fedn Art (mem bd dir, 82-86); Ohio Watercolor Soc; Baltimore Watercolor Soc (juror, 84); Ga Watercolor Soc; Pa Soc Watercolor Painters; Annapolis Watercolor Club (pres, 83-84, vpres, 84-86). *Media:* Acrylic, Oil. *Publ:* Auth, Making Color Sing, Watson-Guptill, 86. *Dealer:* Brenda Taylor Gallery New York NY; Virginia Lynch Gallery Tiverton RI. *Mailing Add:* 1117 Kalmia Ct Crownsville MD 21032-2126

KEECH, JOHN H
PAINTER
b Winston-Salem, NC, May 28, 1943. *Study:* Washington Univ, BFA, 65; Univ Iowa, MFA, 68. *Work:* Masur Mus Art, Monroe, La; The Stephens Collection & Ark Art Ctr, Little Rock; Muhlenberg Col, Allentown, Pa; United Parcel Serv, Greenwich, Conn. *Exhib:* Third Ann Fla Nat, Fla State Univ, Tallahassee, 88; In Search of Am Experience, Fed Plaza, NY, 89; New Am Talent, Laguna Gloria Art Mus, Austin, Tex, 89; St Mary's Col, Notre Dame, Ind, 93; Sam Houston State Univ, Huntsville, Tex; Acme Art Co, Columbus, Ohio, 98; Kansas City Artist Coalition, Kansas City, Mo, 98. *Teaching:* Asst prof painting & drawing, Ark State Univ, 68-78, assoc prof, 78-89, prof, 89-. *Awards:* Best of Show, 10th Monroe Nat Ann Exhib, Masur Mus Art, La, 73; Merit Awards, Multiple Media Exhib, Erie Art Ctr, 74 & Spar Nat Art Exhib, 83; Third Ann Fla Nat, Fla State Univ, Tallahassee; New Am Talent, Austin, Tex, 89; 22nd Bradley Nat Print & Drawing Exhib, Peoria, Ill; Nat Endowment for Arts Fel Award, Mid-Am Art Alliance, 92. *Media:* Oil, Plexiglass. *Publ:* Auth, Jazz-Eye, private publ; contrib, Two Untitled Works, River City Review, 85. *Mailing Add:* PO Box 43 State University AR 72467

KEEGAN, DANIEL T
DIRECTOR
Study: Univ Wis, BA; Southern Ill Univ, MFA. *Pos:* Dir, Kemper Mus Contemp Art, Kans City, Mo, San Jose Mus Art, 2000-. *Teaching:* Teacher WVa Wesleyan Col, Avila Col, Kansas City. *Mailing Add:* San Jose Mus Art 110 S Market St San Jose CA 95113-2383

KEEGAN, KIM E
ADMINISTRATOR, SCULPTOR
b Mt Kisco, NY, Apr 18, 55. *Study:* Univ NH, BA(studio art), 84; Plymouth State Col, MEd, 98. *Pos:* Dir admis, Columbus Col Art & Design, 86-87; vpres prog, NH Inst Art, 87-96; dean fac, Monserrat Col Art, Beverly, Mass, 97-. *Mem:* NH Art Educators Asn (pres, 94-95); Nat Art Educators Asn; Am Asn High Educ; Asn Supv & Curric Develop. *Publ:* Auth, Customer Satisfaction, Course Trends, 12/92. *Mailing Add:* 190 Brook St Manchester NH 03104

KEELER, DAVID BOUGHTON
PAINTER
b Cleveland, Ohio, Feb 11, 31. *Study:* Cleveland Inst Art, dipl; Case Western Reserve Univ, Cleveland. *Work:* Cleveland Inst Art, Ohio; Cleveland Art Asn; Nat Mus Am Art, Washington, DC. *Exhib:* Cleveland Mus Art Regional, 60-63, 65, 67, 74 & 76; Butler Inst Am Art Nat, Youngstown, Ohio, 60 & 62; Corcoran Gallery of Art, Washington, DC, 65 & 69; one-man shows, 323 Gallery, Alexandria, Va, 65; Studio Gallery, Alexandria, Va, 66; Barbara Fielder Gallery, Washington, DC, 76; Wolfe St Gallery, Alexandria, 77; Studio Gallery, Washington, DC, 83; Curzon Gallery, Boca Raton, Fla, 89 & 91; Soc Four Arts Nat, Palm Beach, Fla, 91; Boca Raton Mus All Fla Show, 99. *Pos:* Preparor & exhib designer, Cleveland Mus Art, 61-64; tech asst to cur, Nat Collection Fine Arts, Washington, DC, 66-71 & chief exhib & design, 72-85. *Bibliog:* Andrew Hudson (auth), article, Washington Post, 10/65 & 10/66; Ben Forgey (auth), article, Washington Evening Star, 4/76. *Mem:* Boca Raton Mus Artist Guild. *Media:* All Media. *Dealer:* Lazzaro Signature Gallery Fine Art 184 W Main Gtonghton Wis 53589. *Mailing Add:* 399 NE 20th St Boca Raton FL 33431-8136

KEELEY, SHELAGH
HISTORIAN, PAINTER
b Oakville, Ont. *Study:* York Univ, Toronto, BA (art hist), 77. *Work:* Mus Mod Art, NY; Art Metropole, Toronto; Art Gallery Ontario, Toronto; Walker Art Ctr, Minneapolis; Nat Gallery Can, Ottawa. *Exhib:* Works from the Permanent Collection, Nat Gallery, Can, 91; Drawn in the Nineties, Independent Inc, NY Traveling Exhib, 92-94; X Mostra da Gravura, Musea da Gavura Cidada de Curitiba, Brazil, 92; Natural Sci, John Gibson Gallery, NY, 92; La Fabbrica di Seta Arezzo, Italy, 92; From the Intimacy of the Page, The Power Plant, Toronto, 92; solo-exhibs, Art Metropole, Toronto, 90, Defabriek, Eindhoven, 91, Granary Books, NY, 91 Nexus Contemp Art Ctr, Atlanta, 91, Axe Né-7, Hull Quebec, 92, Contemp Mus, Honolulu, 92, Exit Art, NY, 93; and many others. *Pos:* Asst cur, Art Gallery York Univ, 79-81; artist in residence, Imadate Paper Workshop, Japan, 89; De Fabriek, Eindhoven, Holland, 91; Banff Centre, Alberta, 91; PS 1 Studio, NY, 91-92. *Teaching:* Painting instr, Emily Carr Col Art, Vancouver, 86. *Awards:* Lower East Side Printshop, NY, 90; Pyramid Atlantic, Washington, 91; Nexus Press Book Residency, Atlanta, 93. *Mailing Add:* c/o Pelavin Editions 13 Jay St New York NY 10013-2848

KEENA, JANET LAYBOURN
PAINTER, DESIGNER
b St Joseph, Mo, Sept 11, 28. *Study:* Univ Kans; Univ Calif, Los Angeles; Am Acad Art, Chicago. *Work:* Albrecht Mus, St Joseph, Mo; Arthur Andersen & Co, Washington; NY Marriot Hotel; AARP Hq, Washington DC. *Comn:* AARP Hq, Washington; Oliver Carr Co. *Exhib:* Albrecht Art Mus, 72; Ark Art Ctr, Little Rock, 72; Richmond Mus, Va, 72; Henoch Gallery, NY; Nat Arts Club Ann, NY; South Bend Regional Mus Art, 94; Nelson Atkins Mus Art, Kansas City, Mo. *Teaching:* Artist-in-residence, William Jewell Col, 73. *Awards:* First Publ Award, Fine Arts Discovery Mag, 70; First Prize, Renwick Mus Award, Nat Arts Club Ann, Mo State Fair, 71 & 72 & Northern Va Community Col. *Bibliog:* Donald Hoffmann (auth), Art in Mid-America, Kansas City Star, 5/69 & 5/74; Jean Trusty (auth), Art, Kansas City Squire Mag, 4/71; R C Seine (ed), Contemporary American Artists, La Rev Mod, Paris, 11/71. *Mem:* Nat Arts Club, NY; Washington Women's Art Asn. *Media:* Oil, Watercolor. *Dealer:* Foxhall Gallery 3301 New Mexico Ave NW Washington DC 20016; Marin Price Gallery 7022 Wisconsin Ave Chevy Chase MD 20815. *Mailing Add:* 19412 Pompano Ln # 107 Huntington Beach CA 92648

KEENE, PAUL
PAINTER
b Philadelphia, Pa, Aug 24, 1920. *Study:* Philadelphia Mus Sch & Univ Pa, 39-41; Tyler Sch Art, Temple Univ, 45-48; Acad Julien, Paris, 49-51; Whitney Fel, 52-54. *Work:* Pa Acad Fine Arts, Philadelphia Mus & Afro Am Mus, Philadelphia; Brandywine Workshop; James Michner Mus, Doylestwon, Pa. *Comn:* History of University (mural), Johnson C Smith Univ; mural, Philadelphia Redevelop Authority. *Exhib:* Pa Acad Fine Arts, 52-53 & 68-69, Lagos Mus, Nigeria, 61; Master Series, Carnegie Libr, Pittsburgh, 70; one-man show, Festac-Lagos, Nigeria, 79; Afro Am Mus, Philadelphia, Pa, 90, Michner Mus, Doylestown, Pa, 91; Painting Show, Morgan State Univ, Baltimore, Md, 80; Alfred Deshong Mus, Widener Univ, 81; group shows, Philadelphia Mus, 92 & Brandywine Workshop, Philadelphia, Pa, 93; Print Image Gallery, Brandywine Workshop, Philadelphia, Pa; group show, Hampton Univ Mus, Va. *Teaching:* Prof painting, Centre D'Art, Port-au-Prince, Haiti, 52-53; assoc prof drawing & painting, Philadelphia Col Art, 54-68, chmn basic art prog, 63-66; prof drawing & design, Bucks Co Community Col, Newton, 68-85. *Awards:* Alumni Award, Temple Univ, 67; Alumni Award, Philadelphia Col Art, 72; Van der Zee Award, Brandywine Workshop, Philadelphia, Pa, 90. *Bibliog:* Lewis-Waddy (auth), Black artists on art, Contemp Crafts, 71; Archives in America, Art J, 89; Color in Contemporary Painting, LeClair, 91. *Media:* Mixed. *Mailing Add:* 2843 Bristol Rd Warrington PA 18976

KEENER, POLLY LEONARD
ILLUSTRATOR, WRITER
b Akron, Ohio, July 14, 46. *Study:* Conn Col, New London, BA, 68; Kent State Univ, 67; Princeton Univ, NJ with Kurt Weitzman, 68. *Work:* Stan Hywet Hall Found & West Point Market, Akron, Ohio. *Comn:* Numerous pvt & corp illus comns, 78-. *Exhib:* 13th Ann Baycrafters Show, Baycrafters Gallery, Bay Village, Ohio, 75; Group Christmas Show, Mus Nat Hist, Cleveland, Ohio, 79; Our Own Show, Soc Illus Mus Am Illus, NY, 91; Univ Akron Fac Traveling China Exhib, 92-93; Traveling Cartoon Show, Ohio/Mich Chap Nat Cartoonists Soc, 96-98. *Pos:* Pres, Keener Corp, Akron, Ohio, 77-; mem, bd trustees, Stan Hywet Hall Found, Akron, 79-; part-time graphic designer, freelance, 79-; mem bd trustees, Womens Hist Proj, Akron, 93-96; mem bd dir, Nat Cartoonists Soc, 97-2001. *Teaching:* Instr soft sculpture, Univ Akron, 79-84, cartooning, 79-; cartooning, Northeastern Ohio Univs Col Med, 92-95. *Awards:* Unsung Hero Award, Jr League of Akron, 88; Woman of the Year in Creative Arts, Women's Hist Proj, 89; Artist of the Year, Heidleberg Col, 98. *Bibliog:* Suzanne Severin (auth), Tooned in, Northern Ohio Living Mag, 7/93; Erica Barkemeyer (auth), Cashmakers: artful entrepreneur, Cash Saver Mag, 2/94; Becky Snyder (auth), Polly Keeners labor of love: Cartooning, Focus Newspaper, 11/94; Cartoon Art Puts Message on Wall at 'Berg', Tribune Newspaper, Tiffin, Ohio. *Mem:* Soc Illusrs, NY; Nat Cartoonists Soc, Great Lakes Chap. *Media:* Pen & Ink, Watercolor. *Res:* History, techniques and psychology of cartooning. *Publ:* Illusr, Eat Dessert First, Fairlawn Press, 87; auth, Interview with Mischa Richter, Cartoonists Profiles Mag, 88; illusr, It's Our Serve, Jr League, Long Island, 89; auth, Cartooning, Prentice Hall, 92; illusr, 80 + Great Ideas for Making Money At Home, Walker & Co, New York, 92; Writers Little Instruction Book, Writers World Press, Aurora, Ohio, 97; illusr, Hamster Alley (cartoon strip), DBR Media, 3/2000-; and others. *Mailing Add:* 400 W Fairlawn Blvd Akron OH 44313

KEERL, BEAT
PAINTER, PHOTOGRAPHER
b Basel, Switz, Mar 21, 48, US citizen. *Study:* Layton Sch Art, Milwaukee, Wis, BFA, 70; Rutgers Univ, MFA, 72. *Work:* Am Express Co, World Hq, NY; Union Bank of Switz, NY; Zimmerli Art Mus, New Brunswick, NJ; Los Angeles Co Mus Art. *Exhib:* Alexander Milliken Gallery, 78, 80 & 81; Peter Nojer Gallerie, Zurich, Switz, 82 & 84; Graham Mod Gallery Nuc, 89 & 91; The Camera's Eye (auth, catalog), Los Angeles Co Mus Art, (traveling), 94 & 95; The Painted Photograph, Wyo Univ Art Mus, 97. *Awards:* Nat Endowment Arts, 81 & 87. *Bibliog:* Ann Wooster (auth), Photo/Alchemy (exhib catalog), Frredius Gallery, 92; Jill Kyle (auth), Painted Photography, Spot Mag, 86; Jo Ann Lewis (auth), Galleries, Washington Post, 88. *Media:* Oil on Photograph. *Mailing Add:* 71 Mercer St New York NY 10012

KEEVER, KIM
PHOTOGRAPHER, PAINTER
b New York, NY, May 13, 55. *Study:* Old Dominion Univ, Norfolk, Va, BS, 76. *Work:* Mus Mod Art & Metrop Mus, NY; Chrysler Mus, Norfolk, Va; Brooklyn Mus, NY; Hirshhorn Mus, Washington. *Exhib:* Irene Leach Exhib, Chrysler Mus, Norfolk, Va, 86; Recent Acquisitions, Mus Mod Art, NY, 86; M-13 Gallery, NY, 86; Brody's Gallery, Washington, 88; Queens Mus, NY, 92; Art Space, Raleigh, NC, 96; De Chiara/Stewart Gallery, NY, 98, 2000; Fotogalerie Wein, Vienna, Austria; Fassbender Stevens, Chicago, Ill; Cornell Dewitt, NY; David Floria Gallery, Aspen, Colo, 2004; Feigen Contemporary Gallery, NY, 2005; Carrie Secrist Gallery, Chicago, 2006. *Bibliog:* Everett Potter (auth), Kim Keever & Promises, Promises, Arts Mag, 86; Klaus Ottman (auth), Supermannerism, Flash Art, 86; Garett Holg (auth), rev, Art News, 2002; Ed Leffingwell (auth), rev, Art in Am, 2005. *Media:* Cibachrome, Video; Oil. *Publ:* Auth-illusr, Yes & No, Prints & Poetry, Kaldewey Press, 82; illusr, Twenty Love Poems and a Song of Desperation (Pablo Naruda, auth), Kaldewey Press, 89. *Dealer:* Cornell Dewitt 525 W 26th St New York NY 10012. *Mailing Add:* 204 E Seventh St New York NY 10009

KEHLMANN, ROBERT
CRITIC, ARTIST, CURATOR
b Brooklyn, NY, 42. *Study:* Antioch Col, Ohio, BA, 63; Univ Calif, Berkeley, MA, 66. *Work:* Corning Mus Glass, NY; Leigh Yawkey Woodson Art Mus, Wausau, Wis; Hessisches Landes Mus, Ger; Mus Art Decoratifs, Lausanne, Switz; Hokkaido Mus Mod Art, Japan; Mus Für Zeitgewoössische Glasmalerei, Langen, Ger; Toledo Mus Art, Ohio; Oakland Mus, Calif; Mus Arts & Design, NY. *Comn:* Lincoln Sq Res Lobby, NY; Four Seasons Hotel, San Francisco. *Exhib:* New Stained Glass, Mus Contemp Crafts, NY, 78; New Glass, Corning Mus Glass, NY, 79; World Glass Now, Hokkaido Mus Art, Sapporo, Japan, 91; Int Directions in Glass Art, Art Gallery Western Australia, Perth, 82; Glass Now 93, Yamaha Corp, Japan, 93; Oakland Mus, Calif, 86; Craft Today USA, Am Craft Mus, NY, 89-90; Hist Am Glass, Corning Mus Glass, NY, 89; 25 yr retrospective, Hearst Art Gallery, St Mary's Col, Moraga, Calif, 96. *Collection Arranged:* Current Trends in Glass (auth, catalog), Walnut Creek Civic Art Gallery, Calif, 80; Emerging Artists in Glass (auth, catalog), Calif Crafts Mus, Palo Alto, 81; Glass Art Nat, Downie Mus Art, Calif, 86; Inaugural exhib, Mus Glass, Tacoma, Wash. *Pos:* Contributing ed, Glass Art Mag, Oakland, Calif, 75-76; ed, Glass Art Soc J, Seattle, Wash, 81-84; contrib ed, New Glass Work Mag, 87-88. *Teaching:* Instr Glass Design, Calif Col Arts & Crafts, Oakland, Calif, 78-80, 90 & Pilchuck Glass Ctr, Stanwood, Wash, 78-80; instr design, Miasa Bunka Ctr, Miasa, Japan, 85. *Awards:* Craftsman's Fel Grant, Nat Endowment Arts, 77; Art Critic's Fel Grant, Nat

Endowment Arts, 78. *Bibliog:* Grace Glueck (auth), Art People, The New York Times, 2/10/78; Johannes Schreiter (auth), Die Glasbilder von Robert Kehlmann, Neues Glas, 3/81; Interview: Robert Kehlmann, Stained Glass Art, Japan, fall 85; Paul Smith (auth), Poetry of the Physical, Craft Today, 86; Susanne K Frantz (auth), Contemp Glass, H N Abrams, 89; Janet Koplos (auth), Robert Kehlmann at the Hearst Art Gallery, Art in Am, 9/96. *Mem:* hon life mem Glass Art Soc (bd dir, 80-84 & 89-92). *Media:* Glass; Drawing. *Specialty:* www.robertkehlmann.com. *Publ:* Auth, Schaffrath: Stained glass and mosaic, Craft Horizons, 2/78; Stained glass in the USA today, Canada Crafts, 10-11/78; Glasfenster der siebziger jahre, Kunst Und Kirche, Linz, Austria, 4/79; The legacy of Johan Thorn Prikker, 4/15/85 & Glass of the 80s, 8/87, Am Craft; 20th Century Stained Glass: A New Definition, Kyoto Shoin Co Ltd, Kyoto, Japan, 92; The Inner Light: Sculpture of Stanislau Libensky and Jaroslava Brychtova, Univ Wash Press, 2002. *Dealer:* Heller Gallery New York NY. *Mailing Add:* 2207 Rose St Berkeley CA 94709

KEHOE, PATRICE
PAINTER
b Atlanta, Ga, Feb 13, 52. *Study:* Duke Univ, 70-72; Univ NC, Chapel Hill, BFA, 73; Washington Univ, St Louis, Mo, MFA, 77. *Exhib:* 22nd Area Exhib: Works on Paper, Corcoran Gallery Art, Washington, DC, 80 & The Washington Show, 85; Maryland Biennial, Baltimore Mus Art, 80; one-person shows, Osuna Gallery, Washington, DC, 83, 86 & 88, Jones, Troyer, Fitzpatrick Gallery, Washington, DC, 91, Anton Gallery, Washington, DC, 93 & Univ Md, Col Park, 98; two-person show with W C Richardson, Va Mus Fine Arts, Richmond, 86; Recollections: Washington Artists at WPA, 1975-88, Washington, 88; Works of Distinction: Selected Donations and Lends, Nat Mus Women Arts, Washington, DC, 91; Artsides Eleven, Washington Area Show, 96; Strictly Painting, McLean Ctr Arts, Va, 96. *Teaching:* Assoc prof painting & drawing, Univ of Md, College Park, 77-. *Awards:* Louis Comfort Tiffany Award, 82; Visual Arts Fel Grant, Nat Endowment Arts, 88; Individual Grant, Univ Md, 98. *Bibliog:* Howard Risati (auth), Patrice Kehoe, Artforum, 91; Mary McCoy (auth), A shift of energy, an earthly glow, Washington Post, 90; Lee Fleming (auth), Patrice Kehoe at Anton, Washington Post, 93. *Mem:* Washington Project for the Arts, DC. *Media:* Oil. *Dealer:* Anton Gallery Washington DC 20009. *Mailing Add:* 4309 Sheridan St University Park MD 20782

KEISTER, STEVE (STEPHEN) LEE
SCULPTOR
b Lancaster, Pa, Aug 22, 49. *Study:* Tyler Sch Art, Philadelphia & Rome, BFA, 70, MFA, 72. *Work:* Whitney Mus Am Art; Mus Contemp Art, Chicago; Dallas Mus Fine Arts; Lannan Found, West Palm Beach, Fla; Mus Contemp Art, Los Angeles; High Mus Art, Atlanta; Milwaukee Art Mus. *Exhib:* New Work-NY, New Mus, 78; Eight Sculptors, Albright-Knox Gallery, Buffalo, 79; solo exhib, Options, Mus Contemp Art, Chicago, 80; Biennial, 81, Selected Painting & Sculpture Acquired Since 1978, 82 & Minimalism to Expressionism, 83, Whitney Mus Am Art; Beelden-Sculpture 1983, Rotterdam Arts Coun, The Neth, 83; Language, Drama, Source & Vision, New Mus, NY, 83. *Teaching:* Instr, Sch Visual Arts & New York Univ. *Awards:* Pollock Krasner Found Scholar, 87; Nat Endowment Arts Fel, 88. *Bibliog:* Peggy Kutzen (auth), article in Arts Mag, 5/81; Prudence Carlson (auth), Otherworldly geometrics, Art in Am, 10/81; Jeanne Silverthorne (auth), article in Artforum, 1/83. *Media:* Plywood, Miscellaneous Media. *Publ:* Steve Keister: Recent Work (exhib catalog), 88; Steve Keister: Sculpture (exhib catalog), Nina Freudenheim Gallery, Buffalo, 90

KEKY-MAGYAR, EVA
PAINTER, GRAPHIC ARTIST
b Sopron, Hungary; Australian citizen. *Study:* Studied with Erne Agoston, Sopron, Hungary, 55 & Johnny Friedlander, Paris, France, 60; State Acad Visual Arts, Karlsruhe, WGer, 56-59. *Work:* Art Gallery NSW, Sydney, Australia; Commonwealth Collection, Canberra, Australia; Smithsonian Inst; Deryne Mus, Debrecen, Hungary; Nat Gallery, Graphics Collection, Prague, Czech Repub. *Awards:* Trienale of Graphic Arts, Prague, 94. *Bibliog:* Printmaking, Sydney, 65; Renate Gross (auth), Kuntstmarkt, Art Factum, 93; Encyclopedia of Living Artists, Art Network, 92, 93 & 95. *Mem:* hon mem Masaryk Acad Fine Arts, Prague. *Media:* Encoustic, Glasstextile; Computer. *Dealer:* O'Delle Abney 591 Broadway 3rd Floor New York NY 10002

KELBAUGH, ROSS J
COLLECTOR, HISTORIAN
b Baltimore, Md, June 13, 49. *Study:* Univ Md, BA, 71; Johns Hopkins Univ, MLA, 77. *Exhib:* Baltimore Collects, Baltimore Mus Art, 82; Solomon Nunes Carvalho, Jewish Hist Soc, Baltimore, Md, 89; Threads of Life, Jewish Hist Soc, 91; A House Divided, Md Hist Soc, 91; Southern Shadows, Atlanta Hist Ctr, 96. *Mem:* Daguerreian Soc; Am Photog Hist Soc; Regional Photog Group. *Res:* Photographic history of 19th and early 20th century Maryland and other Mid-Atlantic states. *Collection:* Nineteenth century photographic portraiture of the Victorian era. *Publ:* Auth, Directory of Maryland Photographers, 1839-1900, 89, Directory of Civil War Photographers, Vol 1-3, 90-93, Hist Graphics; Introduction to Civil War Photography, Thomas Publ, 91; Monumental Daguerreotypes of Baltimore, Daguerreian Soc, 94. *Mailing Add:* 7023 Deerfield Rd Baltimore MD 21208-6008

KELLAR, JEFF
SCULPTOR
b Washington, DC, Sept 25, 49. *Study:* Univ Pa, BA, 71, film with Rudy Burkhardt. *Work:* Univ S Maine, Gorham, Maine; Portland Mus Art, Maine; Mus Am Art, Philadelphia, Pa; Portalnd Mus Art, Maine; Farnsworth Mus, Rockland, Maine. *Comn:* Arc Temple Bet Ha-Am, Portland, Maine, 87; exterior sculpture for the Percent for Art Prog, Kennebunk Sch System, Kennebunk, Maine, 90; interior sculpture, Sanford Sch System, Sanford, Maine, 90; interior sculpture, Freeport Sch System, Maine, 92; interior sculpture, Belfast Sch System, Maine, 92. *Exhib:* Artist Designed Furniture, Norton Gallery Art, W Palm Beach, Fla, 86; Ten, Portland Mus Art, Portland, Maine, 88; Interstices, Farnsworth Mus, Rockland, Maine, invitational, 89; Art That Works, traveling exhib, 14 mus across the country, 90-93; one-man shows, Gallery Camino Real, Boca Raton, Fla, 91, Portland Mus Art, Maine, 95, Univ Southern Maine, Gorham, 95, Dean Velentgas Gallery, Portland, Maine, 96 & Gallery Joe, Philadelphia, 97; Retrospective, Univ Maine, Farmington, 94; The Unbroken Line, Mus Am Art, Philadelphia, 97. *Pos:* Adv panel, Maine Arts Comn, 88-91; Gov's Adv Bd, Maine Aspirations Compact, 88. *Teaching:* Artist-in-residence, Sculpture, Univ S Maine, Gorham, 87; instr, Haystack Mountain Sch Crafts, 87. *Awards:* Design Award, Maine Times Design, Maine Times, 87; Individual Artist fel, State of Maine, 96; Penna Acad Fine Art Fel Purchase Award, 97. *Bibliog:* Sherry Miller (auth), Ten, Portland Mus Art, Art New Eng, 6/88; Shirley Jacks (auth), rev, Art New Eng, 7-8/90; Martha Severins (auth) essay, Portland Mus Art Bull, 11/90; and others. *Mem:* Int Sculpture Ctr. *Media:* Miscellaneous Media. *Publ:* Contrib, Designing Furniture, Taunton Press, 89; Maine Art Now, Dog Ear Press, 90. *Mailing Add:* 7 Wolcott Ave Falmouth ME 04105

KELLAR, MARTHA ROBBINS
PAINTER, INSTRUCTOR
b Alamogordo, NMex, 49. *Study:* Murray State Univ, Ky, 67-69; NMex State Univ, Alamogordo, 79-81, spec study with Ramon Froman, Albert Handell, David Leffel, Sherrie McGraw. *Comn:* Oil portraits, Col Bus Admin & Econ, NMex State Univ, Las Cruces, 92. *Exhib:* Pastel Soc Am Nat Open, Nat Arts Club, NY, 85-86 & 87; Salmagundi Club Non-Member Exhib, NY, 86, 87 & 93; Catherine Lorillard Wolfe Art Club Ann Exhib, Nat Arts Club, NY, 87; Carlsbad NMex Reg Art Mus, 98; Audubon Artist Ann Nat Exhib, Salmagundi Club, NY, 2000; Am Women Artists Ann Nat Exhib, Contemp Southwest Galleries, Santa Fe, N Mex; Nita Stewart Haley Mem Libr, 27th Ann Art Show, Midland, Tex, 2005. *Teaching:* Instr pastel, oil painting, Kellar Art Studio, La Luz, NMex, 86-; instr figure drawing, Eastern NMex Univ/Ruidoso, NMex, 91-. *Awards:* Andrews/Nelson/Whitehead, Pastel Soc Am Nat Open, 85; J B McReynolds Mem, Salmagundi Club Non-Members Exhib, 87; Degas Award, Pastel Soc West Coast Nat Open, 89. *Bibliog:* Steve Wall (auth), Unity, harmony & clarity: the life and work of Martha Kellar, Mountain Passages Mag, winter/spring 92; T Nicholas & JC Terelak (eds), The Best of Oil Painting, Rockport Publ. *Mem:* Pastel Soc Am; Pastel Soc West Coast. *Media:* Oils, Pastels. *Interests:* Asian antiquities. *Dealer:* Henington Fine Art 1703 Llano St Suite 343 Santa Fe NMex; Ann Buell Fine Art Sudderth Plaza Ruidoso NM. *Mailing Add:* Three Robin Ln La Luz NM 88337

KELLER, FRANK S
PAINTER
b Minneapolis, Minn, Aug 31, 1951. *Study:* Creighton Univ, Nebr, 69-70; Univ Minn, Minneapolis, BA, BFA, 74; Pratt Inst, MFA, 77. *Work:* Phillips Collection; Mus Art, Carnegie Inst, Pittsburgh; Mus Fine Arts, Houston; Edwin A Ulrich Mus Art, Wichita, Kans; Philips Collection, Washington, DC; and others. *Exhib:* Minnesota Artists, Rochester Art Ctr, 72 & 74; Baltimore Mus Art, 75; solo exhibs, 57th St Galleries, NY; Ariz Nat Painting Exhib, Scottsdale Ctr Arts, 78; Art in Embassies, Dept State, Am Embassy, Bonn, WGer, 79-; Am Works on Paper: 100 Yrs of Am Art History Traveling Exhib, 83-85. *Awards:* Purchase Award, Baltimore Mus Art, 75. *Bibliog:* Ann Sargent Wooster (auth), article, Art News, 5/77; Peter Frank (auth), article, Village Voice, 1/2/78; Christa Lancaster (auth), Frank Keller: Tending the formal tradition, Arts Mag, 11/81. *Mem:* Visual Artists & Galleries Asn. *Media:* Drawing, All Media. *Publ:* Auth, Frank Keller-Paintings 1975-1981 (exhib catalog), 81. *Mailing Add:* 57 Thompson St 6A New York NY 10012

KELLER, MARTHE
PAINTER
Study: Boston Univ, 66-69; Temple Univ, Tyler Sch Art, Rome, Italy, 68; Maryland Inst Col Art, BFA(painting), 70; George Washington Univ, MA(art therapy), 73. *Work:* Metrop Mus Art, Mus Mod Art & Whitney Mus Am Art, NY; Fogg Art Mus, Harvard Univ; Am Mission, Ambassador's Residence, Vienna, Austria; Barbara Guggenheim, Inc; plus many others. *Exhib:* Biennial, Baltimore Mus Art, 77; one-man shows, Albuquerque Arts Ctr, Univ NMex, 78, Whitaker Found Mus, Palermo, Italy, 82, Stephen Rosenberg Gallery, NY, 86, 87, 89 & 93, Conlon Gallery, Santa Fe, 90, Galleria Plurima, Udine, Italy, 91, Galleria Turchetto, Milan, Italy, 94 & Halsey Gallery, Col Charleston, SC, 94, Kaufman Fine Art, NY, 97 & 98, Atrium Gallery, Univ of Conn, 99 & Art Resources Transfer, NY, 2000; The Persistence of Abstraction (with catalog), Edwin A Ulrich Mus Art, Wichita, Kans, 92; The Persistance of Abstraction, Noyes Mus, Oceanville, NJ, 94; Galerie Guth-Maas & Maas, Reutlingen, Ger, 96; Ohio State Univ, Columbus, 96; Recent Acquisitions, Metrop Mus Art, NY, 99; San Jose Mus Art, Calif, 99; Woman and Geometric Abstraction, Rubelle & Norman Schaffler Gallery, Pratt Inst, Brooklyn, 2000; Irresolution, Painting and Photog, Rosenberg & Kaufman, NY, 2000; Toward the New: Am Abstract Artists, Hillwood Art Mus, Brookville, NY, 2000; and others. *Pos:* Draftsperson, Sol Lewitt wall drawing retrospective, Wadsworth Atheneum, Hartford, Conn, 81, John Weber Gallery, 82 & 85 & Paula Cooper Gallery, 82; vis artist, Whitaker Found, Palermo, Italy, 82, Univ Calif, Santa Barbara, 87, NY Studio Sch, NY, 89, Sch Art Inst Chicago, 90 & RI Sch Design, 93; co-founder, Directions of Broadway Exhib Space, NY, 83-84; judge, Ann Student Awards, Kingsborough Community Col, NY, 91. *Teaching:* Guest lectr, Quarto Liceo Artistico, Rome, Italy, 80, Primo Liceo Artistico, Brera, Milan, Italy, 81 & Sarah Lawrence Col, 91; instr, Sch Art Inst Chicago, Oxbow, Mich, 91, drawing marathon, NY Studio Sch, NY, 92; lectr, Princeton Univ, NJ, 91-92; guest artist, Ringling Sch, 97 & Hunter Col, 98. *Awards:* NY Found Arts Fel, 89; Nat Endowment Arts Fel, 89; MacDowell Colony Fel, 90. *Bibliog:* Tiffany Bell (auth), Martha Keller, Art In Am, 9/97; Ken Johnson (auth), Art guide, NY Times, 10/30/98; Mario Naves (auth), Reveiw, New Art Examiner, 3/99. *Mem:* Abstr Am Artists Asn. *Mailing Add:* c/o Stephen Rosenberg Gallery 115 Wooster St New York NY 10012

KELLEY, DONALD CASTELL
GALLERY DIRECTOR
b Boston, Mass. *Study:* Sch of Mus Fine Arts, Boston, dipl; Yale Univ, BFA & MFA. *Work:* numerous pvt collections. *Pos:* Gallery dir, Boston Atheneum, 68-90; retired. *Specialty:* Contemporary New England Artists. *Interests:* Work of 20th century American contemporary artists and photographers. *Dealer:* D.C. Kelley. *Mailing Add:* 22 Oak St Charlestown MA 02129-1811

KELLEY, DONALD WILLIAM
PRINTMAKER, SCULPTOR
b Tulsa, Okla, July 20, 39. *Study:* Univ Tulsa, with Alexandre Hogue & Duayne Hatchett, BA, 62; Claremont Grad Sch, MFA, 66; Univ NMex with Garo Antreasian, 66; Tamarind Lithography Workshop, Los Angeles, 66-69. *Work:* Los Angeles Co Mus Art, Los Angeles; Mus Mod Art, NY; Norton Simon Mus Art, Pasadena, Calif; Nat Gallery Art, Washington, DC; Univ NMex Art Mus, Albuquerque, NMex; Pub Libr Cincinnati; and others. *Exhib:* One-man shows, Not in NY Gallery, Cincinnati, 75, Antioch Col, 75 & Cincinnati Invitational Awards Exhib, Cincinnati Art Mus, 75, Clay Street Press Gallery, Cinciccati, 2005; Alternative Landscape, Contemp Art Ctr, Cincinnati, 72; Environ Sculpture--Proposals for Sawyer Point Park, Contemp Arts Ctr, Cincinnati, Ohio, 77; Persistent Vision, Claremont Grad Sch, 85; Six Contemp Printmakers, Suzanna Terrill Gallery, Cincinnati; 18th Korean Int Contemp Prints, Seoul, Korea, 2003; Earth: Adoration/Rarishment, Flat File Galleries, Chicago, 2004. *Collection Arranged:* Pushing Boundaries: Lithographs from Nine American Fine Art Presses, Exhibtion Curator. *Teaching:* Prof art, Univ Cincinnati, 69-75, currently; vis artist lithography, Antioch Col, 75. *Awards:* Ohio Arts Coun Artists Project Grant, 97. *Bibliog:* Jules Engel & Ivan Dryer (auth), Look of a lithographer (film), Tamarind Lithography Workshop, 69; Kristin L Spangenberg (auth), Cincinnati Invitational Awards Exhibition: Drawings and Prints, Midwest Art, 3/75. *Media:* Lithography. *Publ:* auth Pushing Boundaries: Lithographs from Nine American Fine Art Presses (exhib catalog), DAAP Galleries, Univ Cincinnati, 98. *Mailing Add:* c/o Fine Arts Dept Univ Cincinnati 6335 Dept Art & Archit Cincinnati OH 45221

KELLEY, HEATHER RYAN
PAINTER, DRAFTSMAN
b New Haven, Conn, Jan 19, 54. *Study:* Southern Methodist Univ, BFA, 75; Northwestern State Univ, MA, 84. *Work:* Univ NDak; Austin Peay State Univ, Clarksville, Tenn; Southern Methodist Univ, Dallas; Univ Maine, Presque Isle; James Joyce Ctr, Dublin, Ireland; Univ Kans, Fort Hayes; Harry Ransom Humanities Rsch Ctr, Austin, Tex; Appalachian State Univ, Boone, NC. *Comn:* Mural-scaled painting, St Patrick Hosp, Lake Charles, La, 92; devotional paintings (series), Our Lady of Lourdes Hosp, Lafayette, La. *Exhib:* solo exhib, Sum of the Parts, Hooks-Epstein Galleries, Houston, Tex, 98, James Joyce Ctr, Dublin, Ireland, 97; Mixed Media, Slidell Cult Ctr, La, 98; What is Drawing Now?, Weber State Univ, Ogden, Utah, 2000; In Celebration of James Joyce, Am Irish Historical Soc, NY, 2001; Round One, Hooks Epstein Galleries, Houston, 2002; TABOO X Portfolio - Print Gumbo, Southern Graphics Conference, 2002, Ulane Univ, 2002, Fine Arts Academy, Poznan, Poland, 2002; Nat Small Painting Exhib, Wichita Ctr for Arts, 2002; Recent Drawings, Prints and Photographs, La State Univ, Baton Rouge, 2002; 36th Nat Drawing and Small Sculpture Show, Delmar Col, Corpus Christi, Tex, 2002. *Teaching:* vis lectr art, McNeese State Univ, 82-84, asst prof, 84-90, assoc prof, 90-96, prof, 96-; Endowed prof, Col Lib Arts, 93-94, 95, 96; Jack V Noland Endowed Professorship Chair, Col Lib Arts, 2001-04. *Awards:* Distinguished Fac Award, McNeese State Univ, 87; Best of Show, 21st Ann Juried Exhib, Masur Mus, 94; Artist of the Year, Arts & Humanities Coun SW La, 97; Ind Artist Grant, La Divsn of Arts, 95; Shearman Rsch Fel, 88, 89, 91, 2000. *Mem:* Col Art Asn; Phi Kappa Phi (South Central Artist award 2001-04). *Media:* Oil, Collage. *Res:* James Joyce's Finnegans Wake. *Specialty:* paintings, prints, mixed media works. *Dealer:* Hooks-Epstein Galleries Houston. *Mailing Add:* 821 S Division St Lake Charles LA 70601

KELLEY, MIKE
PAINTER
b Detroit, Mich, 54. *Study:* Univ Mich, Ann Arbor, BFA, 76; Calif Inst Art, Valencia, MFA, 78. *Work:* Mus Contemp Art, Los Angeles & Los Angeles Co Mus Art; Whitney Mus Am Art, Mus Mod Art & Guggenheim Mus, NY; Boston Mus Art; Mus Contemp Art, Chicago. *Exhib:* Solo shows include Museu d'Art Contemporani de Barcelona, Rooseum, Malmo, Sweden & Stedelijk Van Abbemuseum, Eindhoven, The Neth, 97, Destroy All Monsters: Postmodern Multimedia and Musical Mutations, Ctr Contemp Art, Seattle, 2000, Memory Ware, Jablonka Galerie, Cologne, Ger, 2001, Selected Works 1982-1990, Skarstedt Fine Art, NY, 2002, The Poetry of Form: Part of an Ongoing Attempt to Develop an Auteur Theory of Naming, Galerie Daniel Templon, Paris, 2002, Reversals, Recyclings, Completions, and Late Additions, Metro Pictures, NY, 2002, Memory Ware, Wood Grain, Carpet, Galleria Emi Fontana, Milan, Italy, 2003, The Uncanny, Tate Liverpool, 2004, Day Is Done, Gagosian Gallery, NY, 2005; group shows include Currents 7: Work in Action, Milwaukee Art Mus, Concord Gallery, NY, 85; Spectrum: Natural Settings, Corcoran Gallery Art, Washington, DC, 86; Contemp Diptychs: Divided Visions, Whitney Mus Am Art, Conn, 87; Avant-Garde in the Eighties, Los Angeles Co Mus Art, 87; Awards in the Visual Arts 7, Los Angeles Co Mus Art & traveling, 88; Aldrich Mus Contemp Art, Ridgefield, Conn, 91; Songs of Innocence/Songs of Experience, Whitney Mus Am Art, Equitable Ctr, NY, 92; Recent Narrative Sculpture, Milwaukee Art Mus, Wis, 92; Post Human, Musee d'Art Contemporain, Pully/Lausanne, Switz, 92; Ars Pro Domo, Mus Ludwig, Cologne, 92; Schurmann Sammlung, Ludwig Forum fur Int Kunst, Aachen, Ger, 92; Re: Framing Cartoons, Wexner Art Ctr, Ohio State Univ, Columbus; Wounds: Between Democracy and Redemption in Contemp Art (with catalog), Moderna Musett, Stockholm, Sweden, 98; Los Angeles Times, Palazzo Re Rebaudengo per l'Arte Contemporanea, Guarene, Italy, 98; Plaisir Deplaisir, Musee d'art contemporain, Bordeaux, France, 98; Crossings, Kunsthalle, Vienna, 98; Out of Actions: Between Performance and the Object, 1949-1979 (with catalog), Mus Contemp Art, Los Angeles, MAK-Austrian Mus Applied Arts, Vienna, Museu d'art Contemporani de Barcelona, Spain & Mus Contemp Art, Tokyo, 98; Artists Take on Detroit, Detroit Inst Arts, 2001; Music in Me, Geselleschaft für Aktuelle Kunst, Bremen, Ger, 2002; Last Spring in Paris, Patrick Seguin Gallery, Paris, France, 2002; Whitney Biennial, Whitney Mus Am Art, 2002; Do It, Soo Visual Arts Ctr, Minneapolis, 2003; Outlook: Int Art Exhib Athens, Factory, Athens Sch Fine Arts, Athens, Greece, 2003; The Not-So-Still-Life. A Century of Calif Painting and Sculpture, San Jos Mus Fine Art, 2003; Monument To Now: The Dakis Joannou Collection, DESTE Found Contemp Art, Athens, Greece, 2004; WOW (The Work of the Work), Henry Art Gallery, Univ Washington, 2004. *Awards:* Louis Comfort Tiffany Found Grant, 84; Nat Endowment for Arts Visual Artists Fellowship Grant, 85; Artists Space Interarts Grant, 86; Awards in the Visual Arts Grant, 87; Nat Endowment for Arts Mus Program Exhib Grant, 90; Skowhegan Medal in Mixed Media, 97; Univ Mich Sch Art and Design Distinguished Alumnus Award, 98; Calif Inst Arts Distinguished Alumnus Award, 2000; John Simon Guggenheim Memorial Found Fellowship. 2003. *Bibliog:* Diane Shamash (auth), A History Lesson, Art in Am, 10/98; Carlo McCormick (auth), Mike Kelley, Juxtapoz, fall 98; Martha Schwendener (auth), Mike Kelley, Time Out, New York, 6/25/98-7/2/98; and others. *Media:* Mixed Media. *Publ:* Auth, Mike Kelley: From Timeless/Authorless No 9, 18, 30, 34, 44, 66, Whitewalls: A Journal of Language and Art, No 38, 96; coauth, Fresh Acconci, Snowflake 3, No 26, 96; auth, Mike Kelley: Repressed archit memory replaced by psychic reality, Archit NY, No 15, 96; Mike Kelley on the aliens among us, World Art, 11/14/97; coauth, Sod and Sodie Sock, Wirtschaft, Austria, 9/23/98. *Mailing Add:* c/o Metro Pictures 519 W 24th St New York NY 10011

KELLEY, RAMON
PAINTER
b Cheyenne, Wyo, Feb 12, 39. *Study:* Colo Inst Art. *Work:* Santa Fe Art Mus, NMex; Marietta Col, Ohio; Mus Native Am Cult, Spokane, Wash; Tex Tech Univ Mus, Lubbock; Charles & Emma Frye Mus Fine Art. *Exhib:* Ann Exhib, Am Watercolor Soc, 71-77; Mainstreams, Marietta, Ohio, 72, 75 & 76; Allied Artists Am, 72, 73 & 74; Nat Arts Club Pastel Exhib, 74; Pastel Soc Am, 75-79; and others. *Awards:* Artists & Dealers Award, Mus Native Am Cult, 79; Mem Award Portrait, Pastel Soc Am, 79; Best of Show Medal, Kalispell Art Show & Auction, 79; and others. *Mem:* Pastel Soc Am (juror, 78), Nat Arts Club; Am Watercolor Soc (nat juror); Allied Artists Am; Pastel Soc Am. *Media:* Oil, Watercolor. *Publ:* Contribr, Am Artist Mag, 3/69 & 12/72 & Southwest Art Mag, 11/73; contribr, Joe Singer's How to Paint Figures in Pastel, Watson-Guptill, 76; coauth, Ramon Kelley Paints Portraits & Figures, Watson-Guptill, 77. *Dealer:* Canyon Rd Art Gallery 710 Canyon Rd Santa Fe NM 87501. *Mailing Add:* c/o Ventana Fine Art 400 Canyon Rd Santa Fe NM 87501-2718

KELLNER, TATANA
PHOTOGRAPHER, PRINTMAKER
b Prague, Czech, Nov 21, 50; US Citizen. *Study:* Univ Toledo, BA, 72; Rochester Inst Technol, MFA, 74. *Work:* US Holocaust Mus, Washington; Nat Mus Women Art, Washington; Toledo Mus Art, Ohio; Metrop Mus Mod Art, NY; Pepsico Co, Purchase, NY. *Exhib:* Retrospective, Queens Mus Bulova Ctr, NY, 91, Hartwick Col, Oneonta, NY, 94, Bloomsburg Univ, Pa, 95, Soc Contemp Photog, Kansas City, Mo, 95 & Univ Toledo, Ohio, 97; Photo Nominal 95, Forman Gallery, Jamestown, NY, 95; Between Spectacle & Silence, Photog Resource Ctr, Boston, 95; solo exhibs, Floating Gallery, Winnipeg, Man, Can, 96, Univ Arts, Philadelphia, 97, Marist Col, Poughkeepsie, 97 & Ft Lewis Col, Durango, Colo, 97; A Woman's Place (with catalog), Monmouth Mus, NJ, 96; Goldstrom Gallery, NY, 98; Eye Witness, Ctr for Photog, Woodstock, NY, 2000; CEPA Gallery, Buffalo, NY, 2002. *Pos:* Artistic dir, Women's Studio Workshop, Rosendale, NY, 74-; vis artist, Univ Southern Maine, 97. *Awards:* Individual Artist Fel, NY Found Arts, 92 & 96; Banff Ctr Arts, 95. *Media:* Miscellaneous Media. *Specialty:* Monique Goldstrom. *Publ:* contrib, Century of Artists' Books, Granary Books, 95, Our Grandmothers, Welcome Enterprises, 98 & Shaping Losses: Cultural Memory & the Holocaust, Univ Ill Press, 98. *Dealer:* Goldstrom Gallery New York NY. *Mailing Add:* 552 Binnewater Rd Kingston NY 12401

KELLY, ARLEEN P See Schloss, Arleen P

KELLY, ELLSWORTH
PAINTER, SCULPTOR
b Newburgh, NY, May 31, 1923. *Study:* Pratt Inst, 41-42, Hon DFA, 93; Boston Mus Sch, 46-48; Ecole Des Beaux-Arts, Paris, 48-49; Bard Col, DFA(hon); Royal Col Art, London, Hon Dr, 97. *Work:* Metrop Mus Art, Whitney Mus Am Art, Guggenheim Mus & Mus Mod Art, NY; Art Inst of Chicago, Ill; Mus Contemp Art, Los Angeles; Stedelijk Mus, Amsterdam, Holland; Nat Gallery of Art, Washington, DC; Tate Gallery, London; Philadelphia Mus Art; St Louis Art Mus, Mo; and others. *Comn:* sculpture, Ryda & Robert H Levi Sculpture Garden, 88; painting, IM Pei, Morton H Meyerson Symphony Ctr, Dallas, Tex, 89; sculpture, Carre d'Art, Musee d'Art Contemporain, Nimes, France, 93; Tokyo Int Forum, Japan, 96; Boston Fed Courthouse, Boston, 98; and others. *Exhib:* solo exhibs, Inst Contemp Art, Boston, 63-64, Albright-Knox Gallery, 72 & 80, Mus Mod Art, NY, 78, 90, 99, Whitney Mus Am Art, 82, 2003, Art Inst Chicago, 89, Margo Geavin Gallery, LA, 91, John Berggruen Gallery, San Francisco, 91, Paula Cooper Gallery, NY, 91, Galerie Nationale du Jeu De Paume, Paris, 92, Westfalisches Landesmuseum, Munster, Ger, 92, Matthew Marks Gallery, NY, 92, 94, 96, 98, 99 & 2001, Tate Gallery, London, 93, Metrop Mus of Art, NY, 98, Boston Univ Art Gallery, 98, New Britain Mus of Am Art, Conn, 98, Newcomb Gallery of Art, Tulane Univ, La, 98, Bemis Ctr for Contemp Art, Omaha, Nebr, 98, Fogg Art Mus, Cambridge, Mass, 99, High Mus of Art, Atlanta, 99, Art Inst Chicago, 99, Kunstmuseum Winterthur, Switz, 99 Stadtische Galerie im

Lenbachhaus, Munich, Ger, 99, Mittchell-Innes & Nash Gallery, NY, 99, Dela Art Mus, Wilmington, 99, The Drawing Ctr, 2002, Mus of Contemp Art, San Diego, Calif, 2003; Geometric Abstraction & Minimalism in Am, Solomon R Guggenheim Mus, 89; Biennial Exhib, Whitney Mus Am Art, 91; The Art of this Century, Guggenheim Mus, 92; Haus der Kunst, Munich, 96; Metrop Mus Art, NY, 98; William Hayes Fogg Art Mus, Harvard Univ, Cambridge, Mass, 98. *Awards:* Smithsonian Inst Award, Smithsonian Inst, 99; Edward MacDowell Medal, MacDowell Colony, 99; Praemium Imperiale, Japan Art Asn, 2000. *Bibliog:* Francesco Bonami (auth), Spotlight: Ellsworth Kelly, Flash Art, 3-4/93; Louis Inturrisi (auth), Tales of the Palazzo Cenci, Archit Digest, 4/93; Daniel Shapiro (auth), African Art Life, ArtNews, 5/94. *Mem:* Nat Inst Arts & Lett; Fel Acad Arts and Scis; Nat Acad of Design (acad, 1994-). *Publ:* Auth, Fragmentation and the single form, Artists Choice, Mus Mod Art, NY, 90. *Mailing Add:* c/o Matthew Marks Gallery 523 W 24th St New York NY 10011

KELLY, FRANKLIN WOOD
CURATOR, HISTORIAN
b Richmond, Va, June 1, 53. *Study:* Univ NC, Chapel Hill, BA(art hist), 74; Williams Col, Mass, Kress Fel, MA(art hist), 79, Univ Del, Newark, PhD(art hist-outstanding dissertation), 85. *Collection Arranged:* Problems in Connoisseurship and Conservation, Minneapolis Inst Arts, 85; The Early Landscapes of Frederic Edwin Church (with catalog), Amon Carter Mus, 84; Frederic Edwin Church (with catalog), Nat Gallery Art, 89-90; Winslow Homer (with catalog), Nat Gallery Art, 95-96. *Pos:* Cur asst, Va Mus, Richmond, 75-77; assoc cur paintings, Minneapolis Inst Arts, 83-85; asst cur Am art, Nat Gallery Art, Washington, DC, 85-87, cur Am art, 87-88; cur collections, Corcoran Gallery of Art, Washington, DC, 88-90; cur Am & Brit painting, Nat Gallery Art, Washington, DC, 90. *Teaching:* Univ Md, 90, Princeton Univ, 91 & Univ Del, 95; adj assoc prof, Univ Md, 91. *Awards:* Kress Fel, Ctr Advan Study, Nat Gallery Art, Washington, 81-83. *Mem:* Col Art Asn. *Res:* American art, specializing on 19th century landscape painting, especially that of Frederic Edwin Church and Thomas Cole; Winslow Homer, George Bellows. *Publ:* auth, Portraits of John Durand, Antiques Mag, 82; Thomas Cole's paintings of Mount Etna, Arts in Va, 83; The Early Landscapes of Frederic Edwin Church, 87; Frederic Edwin Church & The National Landscape, 88; Frederic Edwin Church, 89. *Mailing Add:* Nat Gallery Art 2000 B S Club Dr Landover MD 20785

KELLY, KEVIN T
PAINTER
b Covington, Ky, Sept 6, 60. *Study:* Art Acad Cincinnati, BFA (magna cum laude), 87. *Exhib:* Solo exhibs, Bruce R Lewin Gallery, New York City, NY, 95, 96, Marta Hewett Gallery, Cincinnati, Ohio, 96 & Suzanna Terrill Gallery, Cincinnati, Ohio, 99, Sex, Flames and Tracers, C-Pop Gallery, Detroit, 2001, End Games, Linda Schwartz Gallery, 2002, Mr Bad Example, Kidder-Smith Gallery, Boston, 2003, Beyond the Pale, Carnegie Arts Center, Covington, Ky, 2004, Drawings, Manifest Creative Res Gallery and Drawing Center, 2005, Stasis Quo, Dayton Art Inst, 2005; group shows include C Stands For., C-Pop Gallery, Detroit, Mich, 99; Pop and Circumstance, Media Bridges, 2004; The Director Selects, Trinity Gallery, Atlanta, Ga, 2004; Skin Deep, 708 Walnut St, 2004; Carnivale d'Expose, Carnegie Visual and Performing Arts Center, 2005; Welcome Back: Alumni Invitational, Ruthe G Pearlman Gallery, Art Acad Cincinnati, 2006; Cincinnati Timeline, Phyllis Weston-Annie Bolling Galleries, 2006. *Pos:* Studio asst to Tom Wesselmann, 89-94. *Teaching:* Guest lectr, Artists Reaching Classrooms, Artworks Inc, Cincinnati, 99-2000; instr, Baker Hunt Found, Ky, 2002-; adj instr, Art Acad Cincinnati, 1998-. *Awards:* Al Smith Fel, Ky Arts Council, 2000. *Bibliog:* Lee Horvitz (auth), Kelly at Marta Hewett Gallery, Antenna Arts Mag, 8/96; William Livingstone (auth), The Current Revival of Pop Art, www.Texaco.com, 11/99; Diane Heilenman (auth), View Points: Cover Art, Louisville Courier Jour, 7/2000; Vick Prichard (auth), Postmodern Provocative: Kevin Kelly's Pop Art More Than Skin Deep, The Sunday Challenger, 2004; Sara Pearce (auth), Pop in to these must-see shows, Cincinnati Enquirer, 2005, Artist takes off on American pop culture, 2005; Ron Rollins (auth), Let's talk about sex (or not), Dayton Daily News, 2005; Jud Yalkut (auth), Sexplosion: The provocation super-graphics of Kevin T Kelly, Dayton City Paper, 2005. *Media:* Acrylic. *Publ:* contribr, Business as Usual (exhib catalog), Marta Hewitt Gallery, 92, The Big Pig Gig (exhib catalog), Cincinnati Art Mus, 2000 & New American Paintings, Vol 28, 2000; New American Paintings Vol 28, Open Studios Press, Wellesley, Ma, 2000; New American Paintings Vol 46, Open Studios Press, 2003; Stasis Quo, Dayton Art Inst, Ohio, 2005. *Dealer:* Bruce R Lewin Fine Art 136 Prince St New York NY 10012; Kidder-Smith Gallery, Boston, Mass; Trinity Gallery, Atlanta, Ga; Phyllis Weston/Annie Bolling Gallery, Cincinnati, Ohio

KELLY, MARY
CONCEPTUAL ARTIST, SCULPTOR
b Ft Dodge, Iowa, June 7, 41. *Study:* Col St Teresa, Minn, BA, 63; Pius XII Inst, Florence, Italy, MA, 65; St Martins Sch Art, London, 68-70. *Work:* Zurich Mus, Switz; Australian Nat Gallery, Canberra; Arts Coun Gr Brit; Tate Gallery, London, Eng; Art Gallery of Ont, Can, Vancouver Art Gallery, New Mus, NY. *Comn:* New Hall, Cambridge Univ, New Mus, NY. *Exhib:* Solo exhibs, Postmasters Gallery, NY, 89 & 93, New Mus Contemp Art, NY, 90, Vancouver Art Gallery, Can, 90, Knoll Gallery, Vienna & Budapest, 91, Mackenzie Art Gallery, Can, 92, Herbert Johnson Mus Art, Cornell Univ, 92, C Zilkha Gallery, Wesleyan Univ, 92; Barbara Toll Fine Art, NY, 90, The Decade Show, New Mus, 90; Whitney Mus Am Art, 91; Carnegie Mus Art, 92; PostMasters Gallery, NY, 93; Galleri F15, Norway; Uppsala Konst Mus, Sweden, 94; Helsingfors Stads Konst Mus, Finland, 94; and others. *Pos:* Dir studio, independent study program, Whitney Mus Am Art; dir, studios Ind Study Prog Whitney Mus Am Art, New York City, 1989-1996. *Teaching:* Vis artist & fel, New Hall Col, Cambridge Univ, England, 1985-1986; Regents lectr, Univ Calif, Los Angeles, 94-95; prof-interdisciplinary study UCLA. *Awards:* Visual Arts Fel, Nat Endowment Arts, 1987. *Bibliog:* Parveen Adams (auth), The Art of Analysis, Fall, No 58, 10/91; Emily Apter (auth), Fetishism and Visual Seduction in Mary Kelly's Interim, Fall, No 58, 10/91; Laura Mulvey (auth), Impending Time: Mary Kelly's Corpus, Lapis, 92. *Mem:* New Mus Contemp Art (adv bd); X Art Found. *Media:* Miscellaneous Media. *Publ:* Auth, Interim, New Mus Contemp Art, New York, 90; Pecunia Olet, Top Top Stories, City Lights Books, San Francisco, 91; Magiciens de la Mer(d), Art Forum, New York, 91; Gloria Patri, Wesleyan Univ, Pvt Pub, 92; Mary Kelly, Selected Writings, The MIT Press, 95. *Mailing Add:* c/o Postmasters 459 19th St New York NY 10011-3803

KELLY, ROBERT JAMES
PAINTER, GRAPHIC ARTIST
b Billings, Mont. *Study:* Moorhead State Univ, BA, 80; Sch Commun Arts, 91. *Work:* Southern Plains Indian Art Mus, Anadarko, Okla; Northern Wolf Mus, Sci Mus Minn & Smithsonian Inst, Ely. *Comn:* Wolf dance costume (with Wolf Feather Artist Cooperative), Sci Mus Minn, Ely, 83; mixed media sculpture, (with Wolf Feather Artist Cooperative), First Bank, Duluth, 84; GBW O/C painting, pvt collector, Minneapolis, 89; mapping servies O/C, pvt collector, Minneapolis, 90; three paintings, Arusa Inc, Minneapolis, 91. *Exhib:* 7th Ann Art From the Earth, Galleria, Norman, Okla, 83; Heart of the North, Raven Gallery, Edina, Minn, 84; Invitational Exhibit, Southern Plains Indian Art Mus, Anadarko, Okla, 85; Artist Soc Int Exhib, Juried, San Francisco, 87; Transmutations, Red Gallery, Minneapolis, 90. *Pos:* art dir, VideoAge, Minneapolis, Minn; artist-in-residence, White Earth Indian Reservation Sch, summer 1987. *Mem:* Minn Artists Asn; HTML Writers Guild; Graphic Artists Guild. *Media:* Oil on Canvas, Pastel on Paper. *Mailing Add:* 18097 Liv Ln Eden Prairie MN 55346-4108

KELLY, WILLIAM JOSEPH
DRAFTSMAN, PAINTER
b Buffalo, NY, May 4, 43. *Study:* Philadelphia Col Art, BFA; Prahran Col Adv Educ; Nat Gallery Sch, Australia, MA. *Work:* Mus Mod Art, Melbourne, Australia; Guernica Mus, Spain; Acad Belle Art, Perugia, Italy; Durban Art Gallery, South Africa; United Nations, Geneva, Switz; Australian Nat Gallery, Canberra. *Exhib:* one-man shows, Prince St Gallery, NY, 74, Acad Belle Arti, Perugia, Italy, 75 & William Kelly: Realism in Transition, Butler Inst Am Art, 82; Tapestry & the Australian Painter, Nat Gallery, Melbourne, 79; Australian Printmaking, Brown Univ, 80; Gerstman-Abdallah Fine Arts, Cologne, Ger, 86; William Kelly: The Peace Project, Mus Mod Art, Australia, 93; The Peace Project Exhib, Chautauqua Inst, NY, 94; United Nations Human Rights Folio, Durban S Africa, 99; Guernica Document, Guernica Mus, Spain, 2000-2001; Humanist Art/Symbolic Sites, Int Exhib, 2005-; Heart & Mind, Tarra Warra Mus Art, Melbourne, 2006; William Kelly: Prints, Shepparton Art Gallery, Australia, 2006. *Pos:* Dean sch art, Victorian Col Arts, Melbourne, 75-81. *Teaching:* Instr, Victorian Col Arts & Nat Gallery Sch, Melbourne, Australia, Philadelphia Col Art & others; vis artist, Chautauqua Inst, NY, 94. *Awards:* Australian Film Comn Grant, 83; Australian Violence Prevention Award, 94; Guernica Award for Collaboration Art, 2001; Courage of Conscience Award, USA, 2006. *Bibliog:* Wayne Tindall (dir), William Kelly/Painter & Projects, Video Documentary 30 min, 87; Anna Clabburn (ed), William Kelly: A Contemporary Tragedy, Moma, Australia, 93; Karen Lotter (ed), Universal Declaration of Human Rights Exhib Catalog, Durban, S Africa, 99; Iratxe Momoitio (ed), Art Towards Reconciliation, Guvernica Mus, Spain, 2000; William Kelly (ed), Art & Humanist Ideals: Contemporary Perspectives, MacMillan Publ, 2000 & 2003; Phillip Ashton (dir), William Kelly/Guernica/Gernika: Plaza of Fire & Light (film), 2006. *Mem:* Hon life mem Australian Ctr Contemp Art; Founding mem Urban Design Forum. *Media:* Acrylic; Charcoal. *Res:* Substancial research in humanist art over four centuries leading to the publication of Art and Humanist ideals. Contemporary perspectives. *Publ:* Auth, Drawing Now, Artist's Choice Mus Newslett, NY, 4/80; Imaged art: The subjectified aspect in the age of new figuration, Artists Choice Mus J, New York, fall 82; Intro to Contemporary Australian Drawing, Macmillan Co, 86; ed, Violence to Non-Violence: Prints from the Peace Project, Craftsman House / Sydney Publ, 94; A Contemporary Tragedy (catalogue), Mus Modern Art, Melbourne, 93; Markers Along the Way: William Kelly, Shepparton Art Gallery, Australia, 2006. *Mailing Add:* c/o Archive of Humanist Art PO Box 368 Prahran 3181 Australia

KELM, BONNIE G
MUSEUM DIRECTOR, ADMINISTRATOR, CONSULTANT
b Brooklyn, NY, Mar 29, 47. *Study:* Buffalo State Univ Col, BS(art educ), 68; Bowling Green State Univ, MA(art hist), 75; Ohio State Univ, PhD(arts admin), 87. *Collection Arranged:* Art in Columbus-50 Years, Columbus Mus Art, 80; Three Views from Columbus (with catalog), Arts Consortium, Cincinnati, 81; Artworks: A Tribute to Women Artists (with catalog), Columbus Cult Arts Ctr, 83; Connections: An International Exhibition of Visual Arts & Cultural Artifacts), (with catalog), Ohio State Univ Galleries, 85; Into the Mainstream: Contemporary American Folk, Naive and Outsider Art), (with catalog), Miami Univ Art Mus, 90; Traditions, Transitions & Transformations, Yearlong Exhib Prog, 92; Collecting by Design: The Allen Collection, 94; Barbara Hershey: A Retrospective, 96; Facing the Past: Portraits from the Permanent Collection, 99; Georgia O'Keefe in Williamsburg, 2001; (with catalog), out of site: Selections fron the Glazer Collection, 2005. *Pos:* Pres bd trustees, Columbus Inst Contemp Arts, Ohio, 77-81; founding dir, Bunte Gallery, Franklin Univ, Columbus, Ohio, 78-88; Miami Univ Art Mus, Oxford, Ohio, 88-96; chair, Art in Pub Places Grant Panel, Ohio Arts Coun, 91-94; bd trustees, Ohio Mus Asn, 93-96; bd trustees, US Nat Comt, Int Coun Mus, 97-2004; bd dir, Asn Univ & Col Mus & Galleries, 98-2006; bd dir Int Com Univ Mus, AAM Accreditation Visiting Com, 99-; dir, Miami Univ Art Mus, Oxford, Ohio, 1988-96, Muscarelle Mus Art, Col Wm & Mary, Williamsburg, Va, 96-02 & Univ Art Mus, Santa Barbara, 2002-06. *Teaching:* Prof art hist, Franklin Univ, Columbus, Ohio, 76-88; vis prof art ed/admin, Ohio State

Univ, Columbus, 80-83; assoc prof arts admin, Miami Univ, Oxford, Ohio, 88-96; assoc prof art & art hist, Col William & Mary, Williamsburg, Va, 96-02, adj prof art hist, Univ Calif, Santa Barbara. *Awards:* Fulbright Award, USIA & Neth Am Comn for Educ Exch, 88; NEH Summer Sem Fel, 92; Marantz distinguished Art Educ Award, Ohio State Univ, 95; Cur's Award, Southeastern Mus Assn, 2001. *Bibliog:* Mark St. John Crickson (auth), The Daily Press, Va, 5/2002; Charles Donlan (auth), ArtScene, Santa Barbara News Press, 2/2004; Lorraine Wilson (auth), Glazer Exhibit is Out of Site, Santa Barbara News Press, 1/2005. *Mem:* Am Asn Mus; Int Coun Mus; Col Arts Asn; Intarnat Coun of Mus; Internat Com of Modern Art; Western Mus Conf. *Res:* Modernist women artists; feminist art history; art & ritual. *Publ:* Contribr, Into the Mainstream: Contemporary American Folk, Naive & Outsider, Miami Univ Art Mus, 90; Aminah Robinson, Kunstforum Int, 91; Traditions, Transitions & Transitions, Visual Arts Res, 92; Museums as interpreters of culture, Arts Management, Law & Society, 93; Madge Tennent: Contested Images from Paradise (bk chap), Modernism, Gender & Culture, Garland Publ Inc, 97; Hottest Ticket in Town, Va Gazette, 01; Author, editor Georgeia O'Keeffe in Williamsburg, 2001; Contributor, Lot:EK-MOU, 2001; others. *Mailing Add:* 7098 Sunland Ave La Conchita CA 93001

KELMAN, MAUREEN S
SCULPTOR, EDUCATOR

b Cleveland, Ohio, July 14, 52. *Study:* Monmouth Col, BA (art, cum laude), 74; Univ Mass, Dartmouth, MFA (visual design), 81; Nantucket Island Sch Art & Design, with Kathy Kelm, 80; Carriage House Handmade Paperworks, Boston, with Donna Koretsky, 81, 86, Elaine Koretsky, 81, others; Penland Sch Crafts, with Jo Ann Giordano, 91, Ana Lisa Hedstrom, 2000; Haystack Mountain Sch Crafts, with Walter Nottingham, 83, Margaret Prentice, 84 & Kai Chan & Betty Oliver, 88, Anne Wilson, 93; research & study in Japan, with Shioko Fukumoto, Sieki Kikuchi & Sadako Sakurai, 87. *Work:* Cannabis Press Collection, Kasama, Japan. *Comn:* 30 fabric banners, Community Col RI, Warwick, 86; 7 woven sculptures, comn by Elizabeth Webbing, Pawtucket, RI, 86; Water Lines (site specific sculpture), Providence Parks Dept; fabric banner installation, RI Hosp, 95; fabric banners, RI Hosp, Providence. *Exhib:* Int Textile Fair Exhib, Kyoto, Japan, 87; Influences-Innovations, Torpedo Factory Art Ctr, Alexandria, Va, 92; Contemp Shibori, Int Shibori Symp, Nagoya, Japan, 92; RI Women Artists, Bell Gallery, Brown Univ, 95; Across Rhode Island: Ten Sculptors, South Co Art Asn, RI, 95 & 96; Worcester Ctr for Crafts, Mass, 97; White House Blue Room Christmas Tree, 98; many others. *Pos:* juror, RI State Coun Arts, 82, 88, 2000; artist-in-residence, Bristol Community Col, Mass, 80-81; selection comt mem, Gallery One, Providence, 84-85, bd dir, publicity dir, 93-95; co-juror Warren Mem Art Exhib, Warwick Art Mus, RI, 89. *Teaching:* instr art dept, Community Col RI, Warwick, 81-85, asst prof, 85-91, acting co-chair, 93, assoc prof, 91-97, prof, 97-; instr surface design, RI Sch Design, Providence, 90, 95-97; instr weaving & basketry, Frissell Mus, Oaxaca, Mex, 91-92; instr fiber structures, Haystack Mountain Sch Crafts, 94, 98, 2000-02; adj fac fibers dept, Mass Col Art, 96-97; vis artist, guest lectr, Int Textile Conf, Kyoto, 87, Brown Univ, 91, RI Sch Design Mus Art, 92, Providence Art Club, 93, RI Weaver's Guild, 94, Mass Coll Art, 96, 98, 99, New Eng Weaver's Sem, 99; adj instr, Univ Mass, Dartmouth, 78-80, 85, Fuller Mus Art, Mass, 80, 89, Haystack Mountain Sch Crafts, 83, 88, 93, Mass Coll Art, 84, 86, Horizons Craft Sch, 88-2000, Frissell Mus, Oaxaca, Mex, 91, 92, Concord-Assbet Sch, Mass, 92 & Vt Col, 96, 98. *Awards:* Spec Mention Award, May Show, Cleveland Mus Art, 80; Visual Artist's Fel, Nat Endowment Arts, 90. *Mem:* Col Art Asn; Am Craft Coun; Surface Design Asn. *Media:* Fiber, Mixed Media. *Publ:* Fiberarts Mag, 11-12/95; contribr, Rhode Island Women Speak, An Anthology of Authors and Artists, Nat Mus Women in Arts, 97; numerous catalogs. *Mailing Add:* 15 Eames St Providence RI 02906

KELMENSON, LITA
SCULPTOR, EDUCATOR

b Buffalo, NY, June 30, 32. *Study:* Albright Art Sch, Cert, 53; State Univ NY, Buffalo, BS, 54; Queens Col, NY, MS, 64. *Work:* Mari Galleries of Westchester Ltd, Mamaroneck, NY; Nat Asn Women Artists Collection, Jane Voorhees Zimmerli Art Mus, Rutgers, State Univ NJ. *Exhib:* Nat Asn Women Artists Exhib, Bergen Community Mus, NJ, 83 & Monmouth Mus Fine Arts, NJ, 87; Nassau Co Mus Fine Arts, Roslyn, NY, 88; Invitational, In the Best Tradition, Heckscher Mus; Fine Arts Mus Long Island, Hempstead, NY, 91; Social Stigmas, Tribeca 148 Gallery, NY, 92; A View of One's Own, Zimmerli Art Mus, Rutgers Univ, 94; Derived from Wood, Ormond Mem Art Mus, Ormond Beach, Fla, 2003; 3Deluxe, Mason Murer Fine Art, Atlanta, 2005; Parrish Art Mus, Southampton, NY, 2005. *Pos:* Adv bd, Islip Art Mus, 76-79. *Teaching:* Vis lectr plastic sculpture, Adelphi Univ, Garden City, NY, 74; assoc prof, Hofstra Univ, Hempstead, NY, 75-76; adj prof, Nassau Community Col, Garden City, NY, assoc prof. *Awards:* Spec Award, Nassau Co Mus Fine Art, 88; Chase Manhattan Award for Works on Paper, 89; Medal Honor & Amelia Peabody Mem, Nat Asn Women Art, Amelia Peabody Estate, 90. *Bibliog:* Malcolm Preston (auth), Social commentaries, Newsday, 1/12/82; Phyllis Braff (auth), Inner concepts, outer forms, NY Times, 1/15/89; Helen Harrison (auth), Grace and intrigue highlight sculpture, NY Times, 7/9/95, Interactive Elements, 4/14/02. *Mem:* Nat Asn Women Artists; Artist-Craftsmen New York; Orgn Independent Artists. *Media:* Wood, Polyester Resin. *Publ:* Auth, A wholesome commitment, The Graphic, 82; A sense of Mexico, Spanish Today, 85, Nat Art Educ Asn J, 85; An historical perspective, NY State Art Teachers Asn J, 88; The Sculpture Ref by Arthur Williams. *Mailing Add:* 199 N Marginal Rd Jericho NY 11753

KELSEY, JOHN
DIRECTOR, WRITER

Study: Comparative Lit, student, Columbia, Univ; Film Production student, NYU. *Exhib:* Group shows at Whitney Biennial: Day for Night, Whitney Mus Am Art, NYC, 2006. *Pos:* Writing consult (films), Synthetic Pleasures, 1996; writer Artforum Mag, 2004; Co-dir, Reena Spaulings Fine Art Gallery, NYC; Permanent mem, Bernadette Corp, NYC. *Mailing Add:* Reena Spaulings Fine Art 165 E Broadway 2nd Fl New York NY 10002

KELSEY, ROBIN E
EDUCATOR

Study: Harvard Univ, PhD, 2000. *Teaching:* Asst prof, hist of art and archit Harvard Univ. *Awards:* Recipient Arthur Kingsley Porter Prize, Col Art Assoc for essay "Viewing the Archive; Timothy Sullivan's Photogs for the Wheeler Survey, 1871-74", 2004; fel, Sterling & Francine Clark Art Inst, Williamstown, Mass, 2004. *Mailing Add:* Harvard Univ Dept Hist Art Archit Sackler Mus 485 Broadway Cambridge MA 02138

KELSO, DAVID WILLIAM
PRINTMAKER, ART DEALER

b Van Nuys, Calif, Jan 29, 48. *Study:* Univ Calif, Riverside, BA, 69; Univ Calif, Berkeley Extension with Kathan Brown, 71. *Work:* Rutgers Archives, Zimmerli Mus, New Brunswick, NJ; US Dept of State, Washington; Fine Arts Mus San Francisco; Gilkey Ctr Graphic Arts, Portland Art Mus, Ore; McNay Art Mus, San Antonio, Tex. *Exhib:* Folio 73, San Francisco Mus Mod Art, Calif, 73; Prints Calif, Oakland Mus, Calif, 75; Third and Sixth Hawaii Nat Print Exhib, Honolulu Acad Arts, 75 & 83; Art in Pub Places, Cheney Cowles Mem Mus, Spokane, Wash, 77; Bay Area Fine Art Presses, Walnut Creek Civic Arts Gallery, Walnut Creek, Calif, 78; Six Printmakers, San Francisco Mus Mod Art, Calif, 78; Selections from the Rutgers Archives, Grolier Club, NY, 85; Process Prints, Richmond Art Ctr, Calif, 86; Intaglio Printing in the 1980's (catalog), Zimmerli Mus, Rutgers Univ; Directions in Bay Area Printmaking: Three Decades (catalog), Palo Alto Cult Ctr, 92; Bay Area Fine Art Presses, Off of Mayor Frank Jordan, San Francisco, 93; Bay Area Prints, Amerika Haus, Stuttgart, Ger, 93; A Fifteen Yr Survey, Mulligan - Shanoski Gallery, San Francisco, 95. *Collection Arranged:* Achenbach Found, San Francisco, Calif; Citibank, New York, NY; Fairmont Hotel, Chicago, Ill; Portland Art Mus, Oreg; Hewlett Packard, Calif; McNay Mus, Tex; US Dept State, Washington, DC. *Pos:* Founder, dir, Made in California Intaglio Press, Oakland, 80-. *Awards:* Int Print Exhib, Purchase award, Portland Art Mus, Ore, 96; Janet Turner Nat Print Competition, Hon mem, Nat Print Competition, Calif State Univ, Chico, 97; 14th Nat Exhib, Purchase Award, Los Angeles Printmaking Soc, 97. *Bibliog:* Abrams (auth), Printmaking in America: Collaborative Prints and Presses 1960-90, Northwestern Univ Press,1995. *Mem:* Graphic Arts Coun; Los Angeles Printmaking Soc. *Media:* Intaglio Printmaking. *Specialty:* Contemporary intaglio prints (primarily Calif Artists). *Interests:* bicycling; social dancing. *Collection:* Achenbach Found, San Francisco; Citibank, NYC; Fairmont Hotel, Chicago; Portland Art Mus, Oreg; Hewlett Packard, Calif; McNay Mus, Tex; US Dept State, Washington, DC. *Publ:* Auth, Frank Lobdell: Proofing for Prints, Print Collector's Newsletter, 88; Printing Gertrude (catalog), San Francisco Mus Mod Art Rental Gallery, 96; Auth, August Francois Gay (catalog), Monterey Mus Art, 97; S Solscheck Walters (auth), The California Printmaker, 1996; auth, Consuming Art, ZYZZYVA, 1999; My montercy in the etching of anguot francios Gay, Naticiau de montercy, Montercy history and art asn, Vol. VIV, No.3, 20-50, summer 2005. *Dealer:* SFMOMA Rental Gallery Bldg A Ft Mason San Francisco CA 94123; Printworks Ltd. *Mailing Add:* 3246 Ettie St No 16 Oakland CA 94608

KELTNER, STEPHEN (LEE)
SCULPTOR, EDUCATOR

b Eugene, Ore, Apr 1, 49. *Study:* Roanoke Col, Va, BFA, 72; Pratt Inst, New York, MFA, 76. *Comn:* Wall Work, Belevue Hosp, NY, 83. *Exhib:* One-man shows, Piedmont Gallery, Martinsville, Va, 72, Va Mus, Roanoke, 73, Dorsey Gallery, Roanoke, 74, Col New Rochelle, NY, 94; AIR Gallery, NY, 86-87; Mus Discovery & Sci, NY, 93; Downey Mus Art, Calif, 93; Trenton City Mus, NJ, 94; Silicon Gallery, 95; Convergence IX, Providence, RI, 96; Greene Gallery, Ridgefield, Conn, 97; Anita Shapolsky Gallery, NY, 96; Fordham Univ, Ridgefield, Conn, 97; Montclair Art Mus, NJ, 97. *Teaching:* Adj prof sculpture, State Univ NY, Purchase, 86, Brooklyn Col, City Univ NY, 93- & Col New Rochelle, 94-96. *Awards:* Biennial Cert of Distinction, Va Mus, Richmond, 73; Grants, Nat Endowment Arts, Va Arts & Humanities and others, 73-80; Artist in Residence, NY State Coun Arts, 78-79. *Mem:* Sculptors Guild (vpres, 93-95, pres, 93-95); Int Sculptors Ctr. *Media:* Steel. *Mailing Add:* 109 Sterling Pl Brooklyn NY 11217

KEMBLE, RICHARD
PRINTMAKER, SCULPTOR

b Erie, Pa, Nov 7, 32. *Study:* Trenton State Col, NJ, BA; Pratt Graphics Art Ctr, study with Carol Summers. *Work:* IBM; Newark Mus, NJ; NJ State Mus, Trenton; US Info Agency; Mitchner Mus, Doylestown, Pa. *Comn:* Sculpture, Mercer Hosp, Trenton, NJ; altarpiece & vestments, St Andrews Church, Yardley, Pa, 72; cake, Mus Contemp Crafts, NY, 73; Circle F Industry, Trenton, 73; sculpture, Gloucester Co Col, NJ, 75. *Exhib:* Albright Knox Art Gallery, Buffalo; Mus Mod Art, Sao Paulo, Brazil; Philadelphia Mus Art, Pa; Forager House Collection, Nantucket, Mass, 86, 88, 90, 93, 96, 98, 2000 & 2001; Nantucket Mem Airport, Mass, 94, 96, 98 & 99. *Collection Arranged:* Mue Modern Art, NYC; Phila Mus; Mus Modern ARt, Sao Paulo, Brazil; NJ State Mus, Trenton; Newark Mus, NJ; Nantucket Hist Assn, Mass; Boston Public Libr, Mass; Art in Embassies; Nat Gallery Art, Washington. *Teaching:* Instr printmaking, Pratt Inst, 67-78, Long Beach Island Found Arts & Sci, Loveladies, NJ,

73; artist-in-residence, North Country Sch, 73-80 & NJ State Coun Arts, 74-75. *Awards:* Purchase Award, NJ State Mus, 70; Printmaker's Fel, Nat Endowment Arts, 74-75; NJ State Coun Arts Grant, 78. *Bibliog:* Richard Kemble Woodcuts (catalog), Int Print Soc, New Hope, Pa, 84; Franz Geierhaus (auth), The Creative Act, Int Print Soc, New Hope, Pa, 85; film doc, Richard Kemble, Media Ctr Trenton State Col, NJ, 85. *Mem:* Pratt Graphic Arts Ctr; Soc Am Graphic Artists; Am Color Print Soc. *Publ:* Auth, The Quiet Forest (portfolio), Forager House Studio, Washington Crossing, Pa, 77. *Dealer:* Forager House Collection Po Box 1076 Nantucket MA 02554; Lucky St Gallery 1120 White St Key West FL 33040. *Mailing Add:* c/o Forager House Collection PO Box 1076 Nantucket MA 02554

KEMENYFFY, STEVEN
CERAMIST, EDUCATOR
b Budapest, Hungary, Aug 18, 43; US citizen. *Study:* Augustana Col, Rock Island, Ill, BA, 65; Univ Iowa, Iowa City, MA, 66, MFA, 67. *Work:* Everson Mus, Syracuse, NY; State Univ NY, Geneseo; Butler Inst Am Art, Youngstown, Ohio; Smithsonian Inst, Washington, DC; Cincinnati Art Mus, Ohio; Erie Art Mus, Pa. *Comn:* Ceramic wall murals (with Susan Kemenyffy), Rohm & Haas Pharmaceutical, Philadelphia, Pa; Kaiser Permanente Med Ctr, Irvine, Calif; Int Fur Co, Montgomery, Ala; Scott Enterprises, Erie, Pa; Penn Bank, McBrier Properties Group, Erie, Pa; and numerous pvt commissions. *Exhib:* Ceramics '70 Plus Wovenforms, Everson Mus, Syracuse; Ceramic Sculpture Invitational, Univ of NC, Chapel Hill, 77; Soup Soup, Beautiful Soup, Campbell Mus, Camden, NJ, 83; 75 Yrs of Pittsburgh Art, Its Influences, Carnegie-Mellon Univ, Pa, 85; Pattern & Decoration Contemp Approaches, Craftsman Potters Asn, London, Eng, 88; A Festival of Ceramics, Rufford Craft Ctr, Nottinghamshire, Eng, 88; Nat Ceramics 88, New Zealand Soc Potters Inc, Wellington, NZ, 88; Raku-Arts, Kansas City Contemp Art Ctr, Kansas City, Mo, 89; Exhib 280: Works OffWalls, Huntington Mus Art, WVa, 89; J M Kohler Art Ctr, Sheboygan, Wis, 90; Celebrating Clay, Miller Gallery, Cincinnati, Ohio, 90; Cent Pa Festival of the Arts Crafts Nat 24, Zoller Gallery, State Col, Pa, 90; Traveling Craft Exhib, Pittsburgh, Pa, 90; Miller Gallery, Cincinnati, Ohio, 92; Ceramics Invitational Exhib, Kipp Gallery, Ind Univ Pa, 92; Am Crafts, Cleveland, Ohio, 92; Figurative Clay, Claytrade, Portland, Ore, 92. *Teaching:* Prof Ceramics, Edinboro State Col, Pa, 69-, Edinburgh Art Col, Edinburgh, Scotland, 85, Miami Univ, Oxford Ohio, 86, San Diego Potters Guild, Calif, 87, Nat Ceramics 88, Wellington, NZ, 88, Ringling Sch Art & Design, Sarasota, Fla, 88; Int Experimental Ceramic Studio, Kecskemet, Hungary, 87, Congresso Nacional De Technicas Para Arte Ceramica, San Paulo, Brazil, 89, Phoenix Col, Ariz, 90, Bussum, Holland, 90, Fla Community Col Jacksonville S Campus, Fla, 90; Kingston, RI, 91, Walnut Creek, Calif, 91, Toronto, Ont, Can, 91, Renwick Gallery Nat Mus Am Art, Smithsonian Inst, Washington, DC, 91, Eastern Ky Univ, Lexington, 92. *Awards:* Cash Ceramic Award, Cleveland May Show, Cleveland Mus Art, 72; Nat Endowment Arts Grant, 77; Assoc Artists of Pittsburgh Ann Award, Carnegie Mus, 83. *Bibliog:* John Gibson (auth), Contemporary Pottery Decoration, Chilton Bk Co, Radnor, Pa, 87; Steve Branfman (auth), Raku, A Practical Approach, Chilton Bk, Randnor, Pa, 91; Susan Peterson (auth), The Craft & Art of Clay, Prentice Hall, Englewood Cliffs, NJ, 92. *Mem:* Nat Coun Educ Ceramic Arts; Pittsburgh Craftsman Guild; Pa Guild Craftsmen; Assoc Artists Pittsburgh. *Media:* Clay. *Dealer:* Sybil Robins Craftsman Gallery Scarsdale NY; Fenton Moore Buffalo NY. *Mailing Add:* c/o Edinboro Univ Dept Art Edinboro PA 16444

KEMENYFFY, SUSAN B HALE
ARTIST
b Springfield, Mass, Oct 4, 41. *Study:* Syracuse Univ, New York, BFA, 63, study with Robert Marks; Univ Iowa, Iowa City, IA, 66, study with Mauricio Lasansky, MFA(with hons), 67. *Work:* Philadelphia Mus of Art, PA; The Internat'l Cermic Mus, Kecskemet, Hungary; Everson Mus, Syracuse, NY; Smithsonian Inst, Renwick Gallery, Washington, DC; Cincinnati Art Mus; Canton Art Inst, Ohio; Carnegie Inst Mus Art, Pittsburgh, Penn. *Comn:* Kaiser Permanente Med Ctr, Irvine, Calif; The Tom Ridge Ctr at Presque Isle, Erie, PA; The School Dist of the City of Erie, PA; Rohm & Haas, Philadelphia, Pa; Ubukata Indust Co, Inc, Nagoya, Japan; St Vincents Hosp, Erie, Pa. *Exhib:* Ann Exhib, Assoc Artists Pittsburgh, Carnegie Mus Art, Pittsburgh, Pa, 78-82, 83-87, 88 & 90-92; Keramia Fesztival, Vigado Galeria, 97 & Nemzetkozi Szimpozium, 97, Tolgyfa Galeria, Budapest, Hungary; The Scottish Gallery Edinburgh, Scotland; Rufford Craft Center, Eng; Lerchenborg Slot Kalundborg, Denmark; Hungarian Cult Inst Stuttgart, Ger. *Pos:* Chairwoman Emer, Pa Council on the Arts. *Teaching:* Escuela Madrilena de Ceramica de la Moncloa; Edinburgh Col Arts Edinburgh, Scotland, 85; Miami Univ, Oxford, Ohio, 86; Ringling Sch Art & Des, Sarasota, Fla, 88; lectr at numerous univs and art asns, 78-98. *Awards:* Nat Endowment Arts Grant, 73 & 77; Assoc Artist's Pittsburgh Award, Carnegie-Mellon Mus, 81, 83 & 87; and others; Pa Honor Roll of Women, 96; Distinguished Pennsylvanian, Gannon Univ, Erie, 01; Women Making History, Erie, PA, 2005. *Bibliog:* Susan Peterson (auth), The Craft & Art of Clay, Prentice Hall, 92, 96 & 99; Shawn Irwin Sims (auth), American Ceramics: The Female Body in Clay Form, 94; Robert Piepenburg (auth), The Spirit of Clay, A Classic Guide to Ceramics, Pebble Press, 96; Marriage of true minds, Donald Miller Premier, Pittsburgh Post-Gazette, 97. *Mem:* Assoc Artists Pittsburgh; Pittsburgh Craftsman Asn. *Media:* Printmaking, Graphics. *Interests:* Landscape Design. *Publ:* Illusr, Write tough, Poems by Peggy Godfrey, Behrend Quart, Pa State Univ, 95; The Making of a Garden, Logan House, Pa, 97; Surface design, J Surface Design Mag, Vol 22, No 4, 98; contribr & illusr, Designing the world (photo & essay), Erie-Chautaugua Mag, 97; The Heritage Mag; The Making of the East High Tile Mural, 2001. *Mailing Add:* Raku Place 4570 Old State Rd McKean PA 16426

KEMP, FLO
PRINTMAKING
b Oct 21, 41. *Study:* Montclair State Col, NJ, BA, 63; Hofstra Univ, NY, MA, 73. *Work:* Securities Exchange Comn, Manhattan Savings Bank, NY; United Jersey Bank, NJ; Mikasa, Tokyo; Art in Embassy Program, US State Dept, Taipei. *Comn:* Seiskeya Ballet Prog Cover, Seiskeya Ballet Studios, St James, NY; Gurneys Resorts Etching, Gurney's Inc, Montauk, NY; holiday cover, Herald, 95. *Exhib:* Marbella Art Gallery Exhib, NY, 91; Local Color, Northport Galleries, Northport, NY, 95; The Environment, Elaine Benson Gallery, Bridgehampton, NY, 95, 96; print travel show, Nat Asn Women Artists, 98; Catherine Lorillard Wolfe Ann Exhib, 2000 & 06; CW Post Traveling Exhib, Gallery North, Setauket, NY, 2000-06. *Pos:* Vpres, Northport Galleries, NY, 88-90; chmn, Nat Travel Print Exhib, Nat Asn Women Artists, 90-92, asst chmn, 95-96. *Awards:* Landscape Award, Wash Sq, New York, 98; Nat Asn Women Artists Graphics Award, Los Olas Mus, Fla, 97; Best of Show Award, 2D, Ann Arbor State St Art Festival, 00; 1st in Graphics Award, Mystic Art Festival, 00; First in Graphics, Peltenhouse Square Art Festival, Philadelphia, 2003; Best of Category, Duneiden Festival Art, Fla, 2003, 04. *Mem:* Nat Asn Women Artists; Huntington Art League; East End Arts Coun; Nat Asn Independent Artists; Catherine Lorillard Wolfe Asn. *Media:* Etching. *Publ:* Jour of Forestry, 2/01 cover. *Mailing Add:* Box 2202 Setauket NY 11733

KEMP, JANE
LIBRARIAN, EDUCATOR
b Davenport, Iowa, Apr 10, 44. *Study:* Univ Iowa, BA, 66; Univ Pittsburgh, MLS, 71. *Collection Arranged:* Col Fine Arts Collection Ann Exhib; Gerhard Marcks Centenary (auth, catalog), 89; Marguerite Wildenhain: Her Life & Works (auth, catalog), 96; Pond Farm Collection (auth, catalog), 2003. *Pos:* Supervisor, Fine Arts Collection, Luther Col, 81-, spec collections librn, 97-. *Teaching:* Prof bibliog instr, Luther Col, 81-, prof art collections care, 90-; prof, Paideia Prog (intendisciplinary Eng/Hist), 2004. *Mem:* Am Libr Asn, Arts Section; Asn Col & Res Libr; Asn Col & Univ Mus & Galleries; Iowa Mus Asn. *Res:* Academic art collection management; research on artists represented in college fine arts collections. *Interests:* Art collection registration methods; art conservation techniques; art collection promotion ideas. *Publ:* Auth, Bibliography in Kath, Ruth, The Letters of Gerhard Marcks & Marquerite Wildenhain, Iowa State Univ Press, 91; Art in the Library, J Acad Librarianship, 94; coauth, Displays & Exhibits in College Libraries, Am Libr Asn, 97; principal auth, Fine Arts Collection website, http://finearts.luther.edu. *Mailing Add:* Luther Col Fine Arts Collection Decorah IA 52101

KEMP, PAUL ZANE
EDUCATOR, SCULPTOR
b Apache Creek, NMex, Nov 6, 28. *Study:* NMex Highlands Univ, BA, 50, MA, 54; Cranbrook Acad Art, MFA, 60. *Exhib:* Tex Fine Arts Asn Ann Citation Show, Austin, 69 & 70; 8th Baytown Ann, Tex, 74; Metals Invitational Show, 81 & Blue Bonnets and Other Flora, 86, Cult Activities Ctr, Temple, Tex; The Art Ctr Cent Tex Biennial, Waco, Tex, 89, retrospective, Baylor Univ, Waco, Tex, 93; and others. *Teaching:* Asst prof art, Baylor Univ, 61-64, assoc prof, 64-69, prof, 69-. *Awards:* Jurors Choice, Tex Fine Arts Asn Citation Show, 69 & 70; Purchase Entry, Ark Art Ctr, 69; Cash Award, 8th Baytown Ann, 74. *Media:* Sheet Metal, Miscellaneous Media. *Publ:* Contribr & illusr, Tex Trends Art Educ, spring 69. *Mailing Add:* 14200 Wagner Dr Waco TX 76712-9645

KEMPE, RICHARD JOSEPH
COLLECTOR, CURATOR
b New York, NY, Oct 28, 22. *Study:* New York Univ, BS, 47; PhD, 53; Univ Oslo, cert, 48. *Collection Arranged:* Metrop Young Artists Show, Nat Arts Club, 58 & 59; Sch Paris Exhib, Nat Arts Club, 63; Books and Graphics of the Cobra Artists, City Gallery, New York City Dept Cult Affairs, 86. *Pos:* UN Delegate to World Conf on Intellectual Property (WIPO), Stockholm, 67. *Mem:* Centro De Artes Creativas, De Cuernava, Calif. *Interests:* Modern and contemporary art, collection also contains extensive group of artists' books, currently emphasizing artwork of young Mexican artists. *Publ:* Ed, Cobra Prints Cobra Books, Franklin Furnace Arch Inc, 86; contribr, Hendrik Glintenkamp: un debujante norteamericano en Mexico, 1917-1920, Inst Nac de Bellas Artes, Mexico, 87. *Mailing Add:* Rio Lerma 156-502 Mexico 06500 Mexico

KEMPER, RUFUS CROSBY & MARY BARTON STRIPP
COLLECTOR
b Rufus: Kansas City, Mo, Feb 22, 27. *Study:* Phillips Accad, Andover, Mass, 42; Univ Mo; Beta Theta Pi. *Hon Degrees:* LLD (hon), William Jewel Col, 1976; DFA (hon), Westminster Col, 1983. *Pos:* Joined, City Nat Bank & Trust Co (now UMB Financial Corp), Kansas City, 50; exec vpres, UMB Financial Corp, 57-59, pres, 59-71, chmn & Chief Exec Officer, 71-2000; sr chmn, UMB Financial Corp & UMB Bank, 2000-2004; retired, 2004; hon trustee, Thomas Jefferson Found; mem nat comt Whitney Mus Am Art, New York City; comnr Nat Mus Am Art, Wash; founder, chmn bd trustees, The Kemper Mus Contemp Art, Kansas City, 94-; trustee, Kemper family found; founder, mem bd dir, The Agriculture Future of Am, 96-. *Awards:* Recipient Key Man Kansas City Jr CofC, 52; Distinguished Serv, 64; Man of Yr Award, Kansas City Press Club, 74; Outstanding Kans Citian Award Native Sons Kansas City, 75, 82; 1st Advocacy Award Mid-Continent Small Bus Asn, 80; Banker Adv of Yr Award, Small Bus Admin, 81; Lester Milgram Humanitarian Award, 82, Man of Yr Award Downtown, Inc, 82, Pirouette Award Kansas City Ballet Guild and Kansas City Tomorrow Alumni Asn, 83; fac Alumni Award Univ Mo Columbia Alumni Asn, 82; Mo Arts Coun Award, 84; Kansas City Chancellor's Medal Univ Mo, 84; Distinguished Serv Award St Paul Sch Theology, 87; Advocacy Award Mo Citizens for the Arts, 87; Outstanding Patron of Excellence in the Arts & Archit Am Inst Archit - Kansas City, 94; VIP Leadership Award Centurions Leadership Prog Greater Kansas

City CofC, 95; Kans Citian of Yr, 97; named one of Top 200 Collectors ARTnews Mag, 2004. *Mem:* Am Royal Asn (vpres, bd dir, currently); Clubs: River, Carriage, Kansas City Country, Kansas City, 1021, Mo, Chathan, Mass, Garden of the Gods, Cheyenne Mountain Country (Colorado Springs, Colo). *Interests:* Sailing, tennis, horseback riding & raising cattle. *Collection:* Old Masters, Modern & Contemporary Art. *Mailing Add:* Kemper Mus Contemp Art 4220 Warwick Blvd Kansas City MO 64111

KEMPNER, HELEN HILL
COLLECTOR, PATRON
b Houston, Tex, Jan 30, 38. *Pos:* Bd trustees, Contemp Arts Mus, Houston, 77-, vpres, 77-78, secy, 78-79, pres, 79-. *Collection:* Contemporary paintings and sculpture; primitive, mostly African art. *Mailing Add:* Contemp Art Mus 5216 Montrose Blvd Houston TX 77006-6598

KENDALL, THOMAS LYLE
CERAMIST, ADMINISTRATOR
b St Louis, Mo. *Study:* Ill State Univ, BS, 71, MS, 73. *Work:* Ill State Univ, Normal; Kalamazoo Inst Arts, Mich; Mich Arts Coun, Lansing; Cooper Hewitt, NY. *Comn:* Large scale out door sculptures, Battle Creek, Mich, 89; Large sclare sundial sculpture, Kalamazoo, Mich, 2000. *Exhib:* Columbus Mus Art, Ohio, 75 & 79; Marietta Col, Ohio, 78; Raku V-Nat, Peters Valley, NJ, 79; solo exhib, Craft Alliance Gallery, St Louis, Mo, 81; Mich Ceramics, 83; Functional Ceramics Invitational, St Louis, 85; Wooster Col, 86; Karen Kendall Gallery, 89; Kalamazoo Inst Arts, 94; Carnagy Ctr Art, 94; Diversity in Clay, Muskegon, Mich, 2000. *Collection Arranged:* Contemporary Ceramics: The Artist's Viewpoint (auth, catalog), 77. *Pos:* Dir, Sch Kalamazoo Inst Arts, 83-96, fac, 73-96; exec dir, Hand Workshop Art Ctr, 96. *Teaching:* Chmn, Dept Ceramics, Kalamazoo Inst Arts, Mich, 73-96; vis fac ceramics, Kalamazoo Col, 84-86, 94-96 & 98-99; vis artist, Penland Sch Crafts, 81 & 84 & ceramics, Truro Art Ctr, 83 & 84; instr ceramics, SIAS Western Mich Univ, 87-96. *Awards:* First Place, Battle Creek Craft Biennial, 79; Purchase Award, Kalamazoo Art Competition, 83; Cash Award, Mich Ceramics, 83, Kalamazoo Arts Festival, 99; Functional Ceramics Nat Exhib award. *Mem:* Nat Conf Educ Ceramic Arts; Am Crafts Coun. *Media:* Clay. *Publ:* Auth, Computerized glass calculation, Ceramics Monthly, 12/83. *Dealer:* Synchronicity Glen Arbor MI. *Mailing Add:* 10936 Three Mile Rd Plainwell MI 49080

KENDRICK, MEL
SCULPTOR
b Boston, Mass, 1949. *Study:* Trinity Col, Hartford, BA, 71; Hunter Col, New York, MA, 73. *Work:* Metrop Mus Art, Whitney Mus Am Art, Brooklyn Mus, NY; Addison Gallery Am Art, Andover, Mass; Storm King Ctr, Mountainville, NY; Centro Cult Art Contemporaneo, Mexico City, Mex; Walker Art Center, Minneapolis, Minn; High Mus Art, Atlanta, Ga; Baltimore Mus Art, Md. *Exhib:* Solo exhibs, John Weber Gallery, NY, 83, 85, 87, 89 & 92, Margo Leavin Gallery, Los Angeles 84, 88 & 90, Barbara Krakow Gallery, Boston, Mass, Univ Mass Gallery, 86, Contemp Arts Mus, Houston, 86, St Louis Art Mus, Mo, 87, Galeria 57, Madrid, Spain, 87, C Grimaldii Gallery, Baltimore, MD, 90 and others; Biennial Exhib, Whitney Mus Am Art, 85; Art of the 80s, Metrop Mus Art, NY, 88; Four Am: Aspects of Current Sculpture, Brooklyn Mus, NY, 89; Baltimore Mus Art and Grimaldis Gallery, MD, 90; John Weber Gallery, NY, 92; Guild Hall Mus, NY, 92; and others. *Awards:* Grants, Creative Artists Pub Serv Prog, 74 & 78; Nat Endowment Arts, 78 & 81. *Bibliog:* Michael Boodro (auth), Mel Kendrick's Calculated Risks, Art News, p 104-109, 5/91; Michael Kimmelman (auth), In Westchester, Sculpture Meets Nature, NY Times, 7/19/91; Kay Larson (auth), Summer Stock, New York, p 60, 9/2/91; Miles Beller (auth), Interlocking Parts, Art News, No 13, p 24, 4/9/92; Jed Perl, Through a Blighted Landscape, New Criterion, 9/92. *Dealer:* Margo Leavin Gallery 810 N Robertson Blvd Los Angeles CA 90069

KENNA, MICHAEL
PHOTOGRAPHER
b Widnes, Cheshire, Eng, Nov, 20, 53. *Study:* Upholland Col, Lancashire, Eng, 65-72; Banbury Sch Art, Oxfordshire, 72-73; Col Printing, London, HND Distinction, 73-76. *Work:* Australian Nat Gallery, Canberra; Bibliotheque Nationale, Paris, France; San Francisco Mus Mod Art; Fox Talbot Mus, Lacock, Eng; Milwaukee Art Mus; Victoria & Albert Mus, London. *Exhib:* Arbres, Georges Pompidou Ctr, Paris, France, 82; solo exhibs, Fox Talbot Mus, Lacock, Wiltshire, Eng, 83 & Bampton Arts Ctr, Oxfordshire, 84; 20th Century Photographs, Hololulu Acad Arts, Hawaii, 84; Madison Art Ctr, Wis, 85; Chateau d'Eau Mus, Toulouse, France, 86; Nicephore Niepce Mus, Chalon-Sur-Saone, France, 86; Gallery Min, Tokyo, Japan; Photographers Gallery, London, 87; Mus Ludwig, Cologne & Kunstverein Gottingen, Fed Repub Ger, 87. *Teaching:* Friends of Photography, San Francisco, Calif. *Awards:* Friends of Imogene Cunningham Award, San Francisco, Calif, 81; KQED/Zellerbach Award, San Francisco, Calif, 81. *Bibliog:* Jean Francois Chevrier (auth), Michael Kenna: Photographs, Stephen Wirtz Gallery & Weston Gallery, 84. *Publ:* Michael Kenna 1975-1987 (exhib catalog), Gallery Min, Tokyo, Japan; Michael Kenna - Night Walk, San Francisco Friends of Photography. *Mailing Add:* c/o Weston Gallery PO Box 655 Carmel CA 93921

KENNEDY, GENE (EUGENE) MURRAY
PHOTOGRAPHER, EDUCATOR
b San Diego, Calif, Mar 13, 46. *Study:* San Diego State Univ, BA, 69, MA, 76. *Work:* Mus Mod Art, NY; Cent Wash Univ; San Diego Natural Hist Mus & San Diego State Univ, San Diego; Hallmark Contemp Collection, Kansas City; Calif State Libr. *Exhib:* One-man shows, Moore Col Art, 83 & 89, San Diego Nat Hist Mus, 83, Lightwork Gallery, Sacramento, 86, 87 & 89, Northern Ill Univ, 87, Univ Calif Exten, 88, Univ the Paciic, 88; group exhibs, San Francisco Camerawork, 83, Purdue Univ, W Lafayette, 85, Mus Contemp Photog, 85; View Point Gallery, Sacramento, 94; Univ Pacific, Stockton, 94; and others. *Collection Arranged:* Robert Bechtle: Reference and Realism in Four Modes, 78, Fletcher Benton Sculpture, 79 & Helen Levitt: Color Photographs, 80, Tom Holland: Works from 1969-1979, 80, Manuel Neri: Twenty Years, 81 & Helen Shirk: Metalwork, 81, Grossmont Col Gallery, El Cajon, Calif. *Pos:* Dir, Art Gallery Grossmont Col, 73-81; The Darkroom, Sacramento, 86-. *Teaching:* Instr photog, San Diego State Univ, 70-73, Grossmont Col, El Cajon, Calif, 72-81, Univ Calif, San Diego, 82-83, Maine Photographic Workshops, 82; Univ The Pacific, 87-88; Univ Calif, Davis, 89; Sierra Col, Rocklin, Calif, 89-91; Cosumnes River Col, Scramento, 90-91. *Awards:* Spec Award of Excellence, Moore Col Art, 83; Nat Endowment Arts Grant, 84. *Bibliog:* Portfolio: Photographs by Gene Kennedy, J Am Photog, 3/85; Jan Haag (auth), Gene Kennedy: Ravaged Landscapes, View Camera Mag, 3/89; Gary F Kurutz (auth), Violations of the Landscape: The California Photography of Gene Kennedy, Calif State Libr Found Bull, 7/90. *Mem:* Soc Photographic Educ; Friends of Photog. *Media:* Photography. *Publ:* Ed, Garry Winogrand, 76, ed & illusr, Carol Shaw-Sutton: Crossing Over, 78, Viewpoint: Ceramics 78 & 79, 78 & 79 & ed, Helen Levitt: Color Photographs, 80, Grossmont Col Publ. *Dealer:* The Darkroom 708 57th St Sacramento CA 95819

KENNEDY, JAMES EDWARD
PAINTER, SCULPTOR
b Jackson, Miss, Sept 30, 33. *Study:* Ala State Univ, BS; Ind Univ, MAT(painting); Spring Hill Col. *Work:* Johnson Publ Co Collection, Chicago. *Exhib:* Atlanta Univ Nat Exhib, 60-64; Eastern Shore Art Gallery, 67; Birmingham, Ala Festival Arts Centennial Exhib, 72; Ala State Univ, 72; Univ WFla, 73. *Teaching:* Prof art hist & painting, Univ S Ala, Mobile, 68-, chmn dept art, currently; guest instr Afro-Am art, Morehead State Univ, Minn, summer 72. *Awards:* Afro-Am Art Slide Grant, 69 & Ethnic-Am Minority Art Slide Libr Grant, 71, Samuel H Kress Found. *Bibliog:* Afro-American Artists, Boston Pub Libr, 73. *Mem:* Nat Conf Artists; Col Art Asn Am. *Publ:* Coauth, An Afro-American Slide Project, Art J, 70-71 & An Afro-American Art and Artist's Finders Index, Am Revolution Bicentennial Comn, Washington, DC, 73. *Mailing Add:* 5408 Gaillard Dr Mobile AL 36608-2532

KENNEDY, MARLA HAMBURG
ART DEALER, CURATOR
b Newark, NJ, Jan 3, 61. *Study:* Art Students League, 78; Barnard Col, Columbia Univ, BA(summa cum laude), 83. *Collection Arranged:* Terrae Motus, Naples, Italy, 86; A Decade of Contemporary Painting, Tokyo, 93; A History of Landscape Photography, Los Angeles, 94; Kissing, 95; Wedding Days, 96. *Pos:* Dir's assoc, PSI Inst Art & Urban Resources, New York, 85-86; assoc dir, Galerie Lucio Amelio, Naples, Italy, 85-89; dir, Richard Green Gallery, Los Angeles, 89-92, Angles Gallery, Los Angeles, 92-94, G Ray Hawkins Gallery, Los Angeles, 93-96, Howard Greenberg Gallery, New York, 96-. *Specialty:* Photography, vintage and contemporary. *Publ:* Coauth, Terrae Motus, Motta, 85; The Nude and Nobuyoshi Araki, H2O Ltd, 94; Kissing, H2O Ltd/Graystone, 95; Wedding Days, H2O Ltd, 96

KENNEY, DOUGLAS
CERAMIST, CLAY SCULPTOR
b San Diego, Calif, 1962. *Study:* San Diego Mesa Col, AA, 83; San Diego State Univ, BFA, 85; Rochester Inst Technol, Scholar, 87, MFA(ceramics), 89. *Comn:* Three custom relief tile disks on plywood, comn by Carole Kraus, 92. *Exhib:* solo exhibs, Creative Arts Gallery, San Antonio, 92, Gallery Authentique, Roslyn, 93, Santa Fe Connection, Tex, 95, Artables Gallery, Houston, 95, Cube Gallery, Shigaraki, Japan, 96, Funaoka Gallery, Otsu, Japan, 96 & Gallery Tao, Tokyo, Japan, 96; US Artists 93, Native to Neon, Philadelphia, 93; Galveston Arts Ctr, Tex, 94; Clay for the Wall, Salt Lake City Art Ctr, 95; RIT Alumni Exhib, NCECA, Rochester, 96; Exhib of Works Born at the Park, Shigaraki Ceramic Cult Park Mus, 96; Six Shigaraki Artists, Shiga Ikeda Cult Ctr Hall, Otsu City, Japan, 96; Five Int Ceramic Artists, La Galerie ART PRESENT, Paris, France, 96; To Art Space, Seoul, Korea, 97; Gallery 500, Elkons Park, Pa, 97; Mind's Eye Gallery, Scottsdale, Ariz, 99; Art Inc Gallery, San Antonio, Tex, 99. *Teaching:* Instr ceramics, San Antonio Col, 89-95; guest lectr, Univ Calif-Davis, 90; guest lectr/workshop, Univ Tex, San Antonio, 91, Jingdezhen Porcelain Sculpture Factory, China, 93, Jewish Community Ctr, San Antonio, 93, SW Tex State Univ & Galveston Col, 94; Artist-in-residence, Shigaraki Ceramic Cult Park, Japan, 95-96. *Awards:* Patron Purchase Award, Wichita Nat, 88; Wallace Mem Libr Purchase Award, 89. *Bibliog:* Karen Robin (auth), Douglas Kenney-Geometric Perspectives, Ceramics & Art Perception No 18, 94; Joy Onozuka (auth), Just spinning his wheels, Tokyo Daily Yomuri English Newspaper, 2/16/96; review, Asahi Daily Newspaper, 2/16/96; Karen Robin (auth), Geometric Perspectives, feature art, Ceramics: Art & Perception, No 18, pgs 51-53, 12/94. *Mem:* Col Art Asn; Am Craft Coun; Nat Coun Educ Ceramic Arts. *Media:* Clay; Enamel on Metal. *Publ:* Am Craft, Gallery Sect, B/W photo, 12/89, 1/90 & 8-9/92; Art Calender Mag, B/W cover photo & statement, 12/90; Raku: A Practical Approach, B/W photo & statement, Chilton Bk Co, 91; Raku Integrations, Ceramics Mo, 6-8/91; color photog, Deco Deco, Japanese Interior Design Mag, 2/92; Airbrush Action, article (6 pages w/color photos), 98. *Mailing Add:* 700 Bond Ave Santa Barbara CA 93103

KENNEY, ESTELLE KOVAL
ART THERAPIST, PAINTER
b Chicago, Ill, Feb 15, 28. *Study:* Sch Art Inst Chicago, with Joshua Kind, BFA, 76, MFA, 78; registered art therapist, ATR; Chicago Inst Psychoanalysis, TEP grad, 78; Loyola Univ Chicago, 82-. *Work:* Ill State Mus, Springfield; Union League Club Chicago. *Exhib:* The Chicago Connection, traveling, 76-77; Contemp Issues--Works on Paper by Women, Woman's Bldg, Los Angeles, plus others, 77-78; solo show, Renaissance Soc, Bergman Gallery, Univ Chicago, 80; Navy Pier, Chicago, 80; Artists Urban Gateways, 81; and others. *Pos:* Art therapist, Grove Sch Handicapped, Lake

Forest, Ill, 72-77, New Triar E & C, Spec Educ, Winnetka, Ill, 77-78, Cove Sch Learning Disabled, Evanston, Ill, 79-81 & North Shore Inst Therapy through Arts, Winnetka, Ill, 79-81; contrib ed, Format Mag, 78-. *Teaching:* Art therapy lectr, Univ Ill Circle Campus, Chicago, 77 & Nat Col Educ, Evanston, Ill, 77; dir art therapy prog, Loyola Univ Chicago, 81-. *Awards:* First Purchase Prize, Union League Club of Chicago, 74 & Ill State Mus, Springfield, 75. *Mem:* Ill Art Educ Asn; Nat Art Educ Asn; Am Art Therapy Asn; Ill Art Therapy Asn (pres). *Media:* Enamel, Watercolor. *Publ:* Auth, Joshua Kind: Naive painting in Illinois, Format Mag. *Dealer:* Sonia Zaks Gallery 620 North Michigan Ave Chicago IL 60611. *Mailing Add:* 3830 N Clark St Chicago IL 60613

KENNINGTON, DALE
PAINTER
b Savannah, Ga, Jan 25, 35. *Study:* Huntington Col, Montgomery, Ala, BA; Univ Ala, BA(art), 57; Auburn Univ, MFA. *Work:* Butler Inst Am Art, Youngstown, Ohio; Columbus Mus Art, Ga; Cheekwood Mus Art, Nashville, Tenn; Mobile Mus Art, Ala; Maitland Art Ctr, Fla. *Exhib:* Cheekwood Nat Contemp Paintings, Cheekwood Mus Art, Nashville, 94; Nat Mid-Yr Show, Butler Inst Am Art, Youngstown, Ohio, 94-96; Getting Real, Fitchburg Mus Art, Maine, 95; Alabama Impact, Huntsville Mus Art, 95; Time & Place Traveling Exhib, Mobile Mus Art, 96; Encounters (with catalog), Huntsville Mus Art, Ala, 97; one-man show, Wiregrass Mus, Dothan, Ala, 97; Body & Soul, Contemp Southern Figures, Cummer Mus Art, Jacksonville, Fla, 98. *Awards:* First Place Award, Nat Contemp Painting Competition, 91; First Place Award, Ala Contemp Women Artists, Ala State Coun Art, 93; Jurors Merit Award, La Grange Nat XX Biennial, Chattahoochee Art Mus, 98. *Bibliog:* Daniel MacAlpine (auth), Like Clockwork, Am Style, 96; Karlin Mcarthy (auth), Developing an eye, SW Art, 97. *Media:* Oil on Canvas

KENNON, ARTHUR BRUCE
EDUCATOR, EDITOR
b Mine la Motte, Mo, Feb 18, 33. *Study:* Southeast Mo State Univ, BS, 58, Southern Ill Univ, MFA, 67, Univ Mo, Specialist Art Educ, 74. *Hon Degrees:* PhD Art Ed-Kappa Pi. *Pos:* Coord first ABC Art Program, St Louis Art Mus, Ferguson-Florissant Sch Dist, 91-92; Evaluator Fine Arts Survey, State La Dept Educ, Arts/Humanities Div, 91. *Teaching:* Dir Art Educ, Desloge Mo Pub Schs, 59-64; coordr art, Ferguson & Florissant Mo Schs, 64-; adj fac art & educ, Webster Univ, Webster Groves, Mo, 70. *Awards:* Art Educator of the Year, Mo Art Educ Asn, 78; Outstanding Contributions to Art Educ, Nat Arts Educ Asn, 79; Host Comt, NAEA Conv, Kansas City, 90. *Bibliog:* Jean Dean (auth), Art Leaders, Northwest Journal, 10-10-88; Clarissa Start (auth), Creative Way, St Louis Post Dispatch, 7-15-88; Garnet Leader (auth), Our New President, The Sketch Book, Spring 88; John Archibald (auth), Art Kennon, St Louis Post-Dispatch, 11/89. *Mem:* Royal Soc Encouragement Arts (Fel); life mem Kappa Pi Int Hon Art Fraternity (pres); Mo Art Educ Asn (pres, 76-78); St Louis Art Supervisors Asn (pres, 65-67); Berkeley Community Teachers Asn (pres 66-67 & 72-73); St Louis Suburban Retired Teachers Asn, 2006-. *Publ:* Auth, Art is Basic, Kappa Pi, 87; Andy Warhol, Kappa Pi Sketch Book, Spring 87; ed, The Sketch Book of Kappa Pi (mag) Kappa Pi, 76-; auth, Arts Integration in the Elementary Curriculum, La Dept Educ, 92. *Mailing Add:* 9321 Paul Adrian Dr St Louis MO 63126-2607

KENNON, ROBERT BRIAN
PRINTMAKER, HISTORIAN
b St Louis, Mo, Oct 5, 65. *Study:* Webster Univ, St Louis, Mo, BFA(printmaking), 87; Univ Iowa, MA(art), 89, MFA, 90, MA(art hist), 93. *Work:* Slovenija Int Art Club, Slovenia, Europe; The Print Club, Albany, NY; The Md Printmakers Inc, Baltimore; The Print Consortium, Kansas City, Mo; The Print Club, Philadelphia. *Exhib:* Spiritual Visions, Webster Univ Regent's Col, London, Eng, 91; Md Print Exhib, Univ Brasilia, Brazil, 93; Calif Print Soc Exhib, Mission Cult Museo, San Francisco, 93; 17th Nat Open Competition, Schenectady Mus, 93; Diversity & Vision, Triton Mus Art, Santa Clara, Calif, 94; Spiritual Visions, ND State Univ, Fargo, ND, 98; Soc of Am Graphic Artists, 68th Nat Members Exhib, NY, 2000; Triton Mus Art, Santa Clara, Calif, 2001; Spiritual Visions, Med Coast Fine Arts Gallery, Quad-City Airport, Moline, Ill, 2002. *Pos:* Co-owner & dir, Albion Print Studio, Marion, Iowa, 90-. *Teaching:* Asst prof, Mt St Clare Col, Clinton, Ia, 96- & Franciscan Univ, Clinton, Ia, 96-. *Awards:* Gabor Peterdi Award for Printmaking, Soc Am Graphic Artists. *Bibliog:* Hope Greer (auth), Earth rock & sky, Levenworth Times, 93; Ralph Slatton (auth), Landscapes, Greenville Sun, 93; Liz Greenbaum (auth), Metamorphic Insights, Bloomington Arts Ctr, 93; Ralph Slatton (auth), Featured Artist Robert Kennon, In Print, 98. *Mem:* Calif Soc Printmakers; Print Club Albany Inc; Md Printmakers Inc; Fla Printmakers Soc; Soc Am Graphic Artists; LA Printmakers Soc. *Media:* Printmaking

KENT, H LATHAM
PAINTER
b Mass, June 20, 30. *Study:* Vesper George Sch Art, 51, Boston, Mass; apprentice with Artie McKenzie, Fla. *Exhib:* Coral Gables Art Gallery, Coral Gables, Fla; Int Boat Show Art Exhibs, Miami Beach, Fla; Gingerbread Sq Gallery, Key West, Fla; The Wilson Gallery, Dennis, Mass; Aries East Gallery, Brewster, Mass; Dodge House Gallery, Chatham, Mass; Lyman Eyer Gallery, Provincetown, Mass. *Pos:* Artist, Steve Hannagan, NY 51-54 & Bronzini of NY, 54-57; Com artist, Coco-Cola, Union Pacific Railroad, Libbey Glassware & Admiral, currently; pres & off, Southern Chapter, Am Arist Prof League, formerly. *Mem:* Copley Soc, Boston, Mass; Int Soc Marine Painters, Fla; Am Artists Prof League, SFla (pres, 78-83); Provincetown Art Asn & Mus. *Media:* Oil. *Specialty:* Traditional Am Art. *Mailing Add:* 501 Commercial St Apt 3A Provincetown MA 02657-2443

KENTON, MARY JEAN
PAINTER, ENVIRONMENTAL ARTIST
b Fayette Co, Pa, 1946. *Study:* Pomona Col, Claremont, Calif, BA, 68; San Francisco Art Inst, MFA, 74. *Work:* Mattress Factory, Pittsburgh, Pa; Seton Hill Univ, Greensburg, Pa; Laughlin House Property, Grindstone, Pa. *Comn:* Painting, The Floating Rectangles, comn by John Cage, 90; design & lighting for Merce Cunningham's Breakers, comn jointly by Merce Cunningham Dance Co & Boston Ballet, 94. *Exhib:* Geometry of Color, Laughlin House Property, Grindstone, Pa, 89; Mary Jean Kenton: A Survey, 1973-1990, Allegheny Col Art Galleries, Meadville, Pa, 90; Carnegie Int 1991, John Cage Proj, Carnegie Mus Art & Mattress Factory, 91-92; Roly Wholyover A Circus, Los Angeles Mus Contemp Art, 93, Menil Collection, Houston, Guggenheim Mus, Soho, Mito Art Towers, Japan, Philadelphia Mus Art, Pa, 94-95; Paintings, Mattress Factory, Pittsburgh, Pa, 98; Botanica, Tweed Mus Art, Duluth, Minn, 99; New Paintings & Garden Commision, Seton Hill Univ, Greensburg, Pa, 99; Waynesburg Col, Pa, 2005; Westmoreland Co Community Col, Youngwood, Pa, 2005; Westmoreland Mus Am Art Biennial, Greensburg, Pa, 2006. *Pos:* Ed (for Pittsburgh), New Art Examiner, 86-94; contribr, Sculpture, 96-2001. *Teaching:* adj fac, Westmoreland Co Community Col, Youngwood, Pa, 2002-; adj prof, Waynesburg Col, Pa, 2003-. *Awards:* Fel in Art Criticism, Pa Coun Arts, 88, 91 & 94. *Bibliog:* Sheena Wagstaff (auth), Earth Colors, Pittsburgh Mag, Pa, 22-23, 8/92; Kathleen M Dlugos (auth), Mary Jean Kenton: Mattress Factory, exhib rev, New Art Examiner, 12/98-1/99; Robert Raczka (auth), Mary Jean Kenton's Freedom (with limits), Pa State Jour Contemp Criticism, #3, pp34-38; Anna Kisselgoff (auth), Painterly Contemplation in Cunningham's "Breakers", NY Times, 3/11/94, pC3. *Mem:* Heritage Coun, Nat Road Heritage Corridor of Pa, 2006. *Media:* Oil, Watercolor; Horticultural Material. *Interests:* interaction between artmaking and the natural world, and the way in which theory colors perception. *Publ:* Auth, Mary Jean Kenton: The Geometry of Color, pvt publ, 89; Points of View IV: Artist's Choice (catalog, essay), Westminster Col Art Gallery, New Wilmington, Pa, 92; Legacy 2, New Art Examiner, 3/95; Recent Additions to the Geometry of Color, pvt publ, 96, updated 2003. *Mailing Add:* Box 42 Merrittstown PA 15463

KENYON, COLLEEN FRANCES
PHOTOGRAPHER, ADMINISTRATOR
b Dunkirk, NY, Aug 6, 51. *Study:* Skidmore Col, Saratoga Springs, NY, BS, 73; Ind Univ, Bloomington, with Henry Holmes Smith in photog, MFA, 76. *Work:* Mus Mod Art, NY; Int Mus Photog, George Eastman House, Rochester, NY; Akin, Gump, Strauss, Hauer & Feld Corp Collection, NY; Metrop Mus Art, NY; Avon Collection, NY. *Exhib:* Mirrors & Windows: Am Photog Since 1960, Mus Mod Art, NY, 78; one-person show, Foto Gallery, NY, 80, Camerawork Gallery, San Francisco, 80, Sacred Childern, ARCO Ctr Visual Art, Los Angeles, Calif, 80, Color & Hand-Colored Photographs, Silver Image Gallery, 81, Catskill Ctr Photog, Spring 82, Shadai Gallery, Tokyo, 93 & Gallery 292, NY, 97; 15 yrs retrospective, Kleinert Gallery, Woodstock, NY, 86; Pleasures & Terrors of Domestic Comfort, Mus Mod Art, NY; Pleasures and Terrors of Domestic Comfort, Mus Mod Art, NY (traveling, Baltimore Mus Art, Los Angeles Co Mus Art), 91-93; Artists Who Work, Kleinert-James Arts Ctr, Woodstock, NY, 95; Double Feature, Syracuse Stage, NY, 95; fac exhib, Woodstock Sch Art, NY, 96; Eye of the Beholder, ICP, NY, 97; The Passion, Kingston, NY, 98. *Pos:* exec dir, Ctr for Photog, Woodstock, NY. *Teaching:* Instr photog, Slippery Rock State Col, Pa, Jan-May, 77; instr photog, Bard Col, Annandale, NY, winter 79; residency Va Ctr for Arts, 98, Nantucket Sch Art & Design, 96, 99. *Awards:* Photog Fel, NY Found Arts, 89; Agfa Corp Award, 94; Mats Grant, Yaddo Artists Colony, Saratoga Springs, NY, 95. *Bibliog:* Catherine Marx (ed), Right Brain Left Brain Photography, Amphoto, Watson-Guptill, New York, 94; Grace & George Schaub (auths & eds), Marshall's Hand Coloring Guide & Gallery, G&G Schaub, 95; Fine Art Photography, Graphis Press, Switz, 96. *Mem:* Soc for Photog Educ; Women's Caucus for Art; Nat Asn Artists Orgn; Am Fedn Arts. *Media:* Photography; Painting. *Dealer:* Sarah Morthland Gallery New York NY

KEOUGH, JEFFREY
DIRECTOR
b Concord, Mass, Oct 30, 53. *Study:* Sch of the Mus Fine Arts, Boston, Mass. *Pos:* Dir of Exhibs, Mass Col Art, currently. *Mailing Add:* Mass Col Art Baklar & Huntington Gallery 621 Huntington Ave Boston MA 02115

KEPALAS
SCULPTOR, PAINTER
b Vilnius, Lithuania; US citizen. *Study:* Ont Col Art, Toronto; Brooklyn Mus Sch Art. *Work:* Pa Acad Fine Arts, Philadelphia; Univ Mass Art Gallery, Amherst; Libr & Mus Performing Arts, Lincoln Ctr, NY; Lithuanian Mus, Adelaide, Australia; Mus Mod Art Lending Serv, NY. *Comn:* Bronze bust, Mr Louis Horst, NY, 62; bronze bust, Mrs Gunilla Kessler, NY, 71; bronze bust, Mr Robert Spring, 87; bronze reliefs of 4 American Saints: Frances Cabrini, John Neumann, Elizabeth Ann Seton & Isaac Jogues, 92. *Exhib:* Pa Acad Fine Arts, Philadelphia, 68; Silvermine Guild Artists Ann, New Canaan, Conn, 69; Jersey City Mus, NJ, 69-71; Phoenix Gallery, NY, 70, 72, 74, 76, 78-81 & 84. *Awards:* First Prize, Coun Advan Lithuanian Cult, Chicago, Ill, 78; Accademico d'Italia con Medaglia d'Oro, Salsomaggiore, Italia, 80; Doris Kreindler Mem Award, Am Soc Contemp Artists, 83. *Bibliog:* Edgar Buonagurio (auth), Elena Kepalas, Art Mag, 6/79; Elena Kepalas Bronze Sculptor, New York Arts J, 79; Palmer Poroner (auth), Discoveries in Arts, Art Speak, 11/81. *Mem:* Am Soc Contemp Artists; Metrop Painters & Sculptors. *Media:* Bronze; Acrylic, Oil. *Mailing Add:* 1047 2nd St Apt 10 Santa Monica CA 90403-3612

KEPETS, HUGH MICHAEL
PAINTER, PRINTMAKER
b Cleveland, Ohio, Feb 6, 46. *Study:* Carnegie-Mellon Univ, BFA, 68; Ohio Univ, MFA, 72. *Work:* Metrop Mus Art, NY; Philadelphia Mus Fine Arts; Cleveland Mus Art; Libr Cong, Washington, DC; Yale Univ Art Gallery; and others. *Comn:* Cover, Paris Rev 65, spring 76; City Walls Inc, NY, 76; Outdoor three dimensional wall painting, Three Rivers Arts Festival, Pittsburgh, 82. *Exhib:* Cleveland Mus Art, 68-93; Brooklyn Mus, NY, 72 & 76; 35th Midyear Show, Butler Inst Am Art, 72; Works on Paper, Va Mus Fine Arts, Richmond, 74; one-man shows, Fischbach Gallery, NY, 74, 76 & 78, Marcus/Gordon Assoc, Pittsburgh, 81, Roger Ramsay Gallery, Chicago, 84 & 88, David Adamson Gallery, Washington, 86 & 92, Randall Beck Gallery, Boston, 76, 79, 86 & 89 & Brenda Kroos Gallery, Cleveland, 93 & 96; Boston Printmakers 27th Ann, Boston Mus Fine Arts, 75; West '79/The Law, Minn Mus Art, St Paul, 79; Am Acad Arts & Lett, NY, 78 & 80; plus many others group and solo exhibs. *Awards:* Nat Endowment Arts Grant, 76; Cleveland Arts Prize, 79; Creative Artists Pub Serv Grant, 80. *Dealer:* Brenda Kroos 1300 W 9th St Cleveland OH 44113. *Mailing Add:* 13 Chinmoy Ln New Milford CT 06776

KEPNER, RITA
SCULPTOR
b Binghamton, NY, Nov 15, 44. *Study:* Elmira Col, NY, 62-63, Harpur Col, State Univ NY, BA, 66, Okla Univ, 88; Seattle Pac Univ, 90; Western Wash Univ, 91-92; City Univ, MA, 98. *Hon Degrees:* Acad Bedriacehse Calvatore, Italy, hon MFA, 84. *Work:* Warsaw Mus, Poland; Seattle City Collection, Wash; Kenmore Libr; Wash Mutual, Seattle; Children's Hosp, Seattle; Cowlitz Indian Tribe, Wash. *Comn:* wood Sculpture, City of Znin, Poland, 76; wood sculpture, City of Zalaegerszeg, Hungary, 77; bronze sculpture, Develop Authority, Seattle, 78; granite sculpture, Seattle Publ Libr, 78; cast stone sculpture, US Army Corps of Engineers, Savannah, Ga, 94 & 96. *Exhib:* Artist in the City, 75, Seattle Art Mus, Wash, 77; Int Sculptors, Znin, Poland, 76 & Zalaegerszeg, Hungary, 77; Am Artist in Poland, Zoliborg Mus, Warsaw, 81; Am Artist in Wiesbaden, Die Roemer, Ger, 88; Quimper Arts, Port Townsend, Wash, 93 & 94; Univ Art Mus, State Univ NY, Binghampton, 96; Ichikawa, Japan, 97; Bruskin Gallery, Port Townsend, Wash, 98; Arts Alliance Gallery, Port Townsend, Wash, 2002, 03 & 04; Gallery 9, Port Townsend, 2004. *Pos:* artist-in-residence, Seattle, 75, 77-78. *Teaching:* Instr Sculpture Experimental Col, Univ Wash, 72-74; master sculptor, Evergreen Col Internship Prog, Olympia, Wash, 74-78. *Awards:* Appointed Visual Arts Ambassador-informal-between USA & Poland, 76-81; Kosciuszko Found Travel Grant Award Winner, 75, 76, 79, 81. *Bibliog:* Something Happened in Seattle, NEA Newslett, 76; David Miller (dir, video), Rita Kepner Sculptor, 81; Stephanie Irving (auth), In support of the arts, Peninsula Mag, fall 91; Symon Bojko, Polish American Artists, Warsaw, Poland, Women Artists of Am, Vol 2. *Mem:* Bainbridge Island Arts & Humanities Coun (founder, 86); Int Artists Asn UNESCO, Paris; Artists Equity Asn; Int Artists Coop, Edelvecht, Ger; Quimper Arts, Port Townsend, Wash; Gallery 9. *Media:* Sculpture, stone, wood, ceramic, bronze and drawing. *Specialty:* local artists. *Interests:* Art, educ, reading, gardening, writing, editing, sailing. *Publ:* Contribr, Northwest Art, The Arts, Leonardo Mag, Poland Mag, Polska Panorama, Seattle Post Intelligencer. *Dealer:* Gallery 9 North Olympic Artists Cooperative. *Mailing Add:* 1012 Water St Port Townsend WA 98368

KERMES, CONSTANTINE JOHN
PAINTER, PRINTMAKER
b Pittsburgh, Pa, Dec 6, 23. *Study:* Carnegie-Mellon Univ, BFA; also with Victor Candell, Leo Manso, Glenn Bradshaw, Catherine Liu & Frank Lloyd Wright. *Work:* Lancaster Mus Art, Pa; Notre Dame Art Mus, South Bend, Ind; Stockmanshove Mus, Damme, Belgium; Pa State Univ, University Park; Lebanon Valley Col, Pa; Pennsylvania State Univ, PA; Elizabethtown Col, PA; Kutztown Univ, Kutztown, PA; Lancaster Mus of Art, Lancaster, PA. *Comn:* Murals, Pa Hist & Mus Comn, Cornwall Mus, 68; Fontrier Found, Paris; assemblage murals, Ford New Holland, Pa & Brussels, Belg; Farm & Indust Equip Inst, Wrigley Bldg, Chicago. *Exhib:* Design Rev, Smithsonian Inst, Washington, DC, 69; solo exhibs, Grimaldis Gallery, Baltimore, 79, Reading Mus, 80, ten solo shows at Seligmann Gallery, NY & Demuth Found Gallery, Lancaster Mus Art, 93; Pa Watercolor Soc, 79, 80, 84 & 85; Hancock Shaker Mus, Pittsfield, Mass, 89; Art of the State, William Penn Mus, 2000; Dumuth Mus, Lancaster, Pa, 2000-2003; Westmooreland Mus of Am Art, Greensburg, Pa, 2003-2004; and many others. *Awards:* Traveling Exhib Painting Prize, Petrol Industs, 71; Award Oxford, Md Ann Exhib, 91 & 92; Best Show, Lancaster Mus Art Summer Show, 96; Top Award, Berks Art Alliance, Hazelton, Pa, 2000; Philadelphia Watercolor Soc Award, 2003-05; Mid-Atlantic States Exhibit, 2001. *Bibliog:* Morse (auth), Shakers & Worlds People, Dodd Mead, 80; Horgan (auth), Shaker Holy Land, Harvard Press, 82; S Stein (auth), Shaker Experience in America, Yale Univ Press, 92. *Mem:* signature mem Penna Watercolor Soc & AWS; signature mem, Baltimore Watercolor Soc. *Media:* Oil, Acrylic, Watercolor; Woodcut, Lithography. *Publ:* Auth, Shaker Architecture, 70; auth & illusr, American Icons, 75; Folk images of rural Pennsylvania, Pa Folklife, 6/75 & 6/81; Symbols of Love in Folk Art, 87. *Dealer:* Jacques Seligmann Gallery 5 E 57th St New York NY 10022. *Mailing Add:* 981 Landis Valley Rd Lancaster PA 17601

KERN, ARTHUR (EDWARD)
EDUCATOR, SCULPTOR
b New Orleans, La, Oct 27, 31. *Study:* Tulane Univ La, BA, 53, MFA, 55. *Exhib:* One-man shows, Ariz State Univ, 74 & Int Sculpture Conf, Tulane Univ, 76; South Houston Gallery, NY, 75. *Teaching:* Asst prof drawing, Univ Southwestern La, 67-69; assoc prof painting & sculpture, Tulane Univ La, 69-, assoc chmn dept art, 72-. *Media:* Apoxy. *Mailing Add:* 500 State St New Orleans LA 70118

KERN, KAREN R
PAINTING
b March 1952. *Exhib:* Artisan Gallery, Northport, NY; Isis Gallery, Port Wash, NY; Environ Sculpture Exhib, Schure Plaza, Old Westbury, NY; Nassau Co Celebration of Arts, Nassau Co Mus, Roslyn, NY; Women in Visual Arts Exhib, Univ Okla; Long Island Artists, Heckscher Mus, Huntington, NY; Amsterdam, Whitney Int Fine Art, Chelsea, New York City. *Collection Arranged:* Sessions Data Placement, Glen Cove, NY; Morton Commun, Great Neck, NY; Apollo Co, NY; Admiral Commun Co, NY; Deloitte, Haskins & Sells, Inc, One World Trade Ctr, NY. *Pos:* asst, photo realism, Audrey Flack, formerly

KERNE, BARBARA DAVIS
ART DEALER, PAINTER
b New York, NY, Jan 1, 39. *Study:* Brooklyn Col, BA, 58; Univ Md, College Park, MA, 69. *Work:* Corcoran Gallery Art & Libr Cong, Washington; Norton Gallery Art, Palm Beach, Fla; Franz Masereel Ctr Graphic Arts, Kasterlee, Belg; Univ Tenn, Knoxville. *Comn:* Dreaming of Spring (painting), Grand Hyatt Hotel, Washington, 86; Tow Path (oil/linen painting), Potomac Community Ctr, Md, 88; Ellipse Garden (oil on linen), Signet Bank Corp Collection, Washington, 89. *Exhib:* Solo exhibs, Franz Bader Gallery, Washington, 90, Addison-Ripley Fine Art, Washington, 93 & 95, Anne Arundel Community Col, Arnold, Md, 95 & Montgomery Col, Rockville, Md, 96; Three Visions, Wash Proj Arts, Washington, 95; State of the Art, Md Art Place, Baltimore, 95; Graphic Legacy, Nat Mus Women Arts, Washington, 95; Global Focus, Nat Mus Women Arts, Washington, 96; Metamorphosis, Corcoran Gallery Art, Washington, 96. *Teaching:* Prof art, Montgomery Col, Rockville, Md, 72-. *Awards:* Va Ctr Creative Arts Fel, Mt St Angelo, Sweet Briar, Va, 92 & 94; Individual Artist Award for Visual Arts/Paintings & Works on Paper, Md State Arts Coun, 96. *Bibliog:* William Dunlop (interviewer), Around Town, WETA, PBS, 1/19/95; Percy North (auth), Barbara Kerne: Recent works on canvas and paper, Wash Rev, Vol XX, No 6, 4-5/95; J W Mahoney (auth), Barbara Kerne at Addison-Ripley, Art Am, 12/95; A A Every (dir), Barbara Kerne, Educator/Artist (video), public television, 92. *Mem:* Soc Am Graphic Artists; Calif Printmakers Soc; Col Art Asn; S Graphics Coun Bd 90-91 (secy, 89-90); Coalition Washington Artists (secy, 88, 89, 90 & 91). *Media:* Oil; Intaglio. *Dealer:* Addison-Ripley Gallery Ltd 9 Hillyer Ct NW Washington DC 20008

KERNS, ED (JOHNSON), JR
PAINTER
b Richmond, Va, Feb 22, 45. *Study:* Va Commonwealth Univ, BFA; Md Inst Col Art, Baltimore, with Grace Hartigan, MFA. *Work:* Aldrich Mus Art, Ridgefield, Conn; Chase Manhattan Bank, NY; Edward Albee Found, NY; Citicorp, NY; Corcoran Gallery, Washington, DC. *Exhib:* Albright-Knox Art Gallery, Buffalo, NY, 71 & 72; San Francisco Mus Mod Art, 78; Pa Acad Fine Arts, 82; Ben Shahn Gallery, NJ, 89; Muhlenberg Col Ctr Arts, Allentown, Pa, 91; Williams Ctr Arts Gallery, Easton, Pa, 92 & 93; Open Space Gallery, Allentown, Pa, 92; one-man show, M-13 Gallery, NY, 95 & 97; State Theatre Gallery, Easton, Pa, 98; Ruffino de Tamayo Print Mus, Mex, 98. *Pos:* Head art dept, Lafayette Col, Easton, Pa. *Teaching:* Eugene H Clapp, Prof humanities & art, Lafayette Col, Easton, Pa, 80-. *Awards:* Art Achievement Key, Va Commonwealth Univ, 67; Artist of the Year, Larry Aldrich Assoc, New York, 71. *Bibliog:* Articles, Arts Mag, 1/79 & Artforum, 1/80, Art News, 12/84, Morning Call, 1/90, The Express, 2/90 & Philadelphia Inquirer, 6/91. *Mem:* Col Art Asn. *Media:* Acrylic, Collage. *Publ:* Coauth (with Loder), Tracks in the Straw, 85, Eavesdropping on the Echoes, 87 & Wrestling the Light, Luriamedia Press, 91. *Dealer:* Howard Scott 520 W 20th St New York NY 10012. *Mailing Add:* Lafayette Col Dep Art Easton PA 18042

KERRIGAN, MAURIE
SCULPTOR, PAINTER
b Jersey City, NJ, Apr 28, 1951. *Study:* Moore Col Art, Philadelphia, Pa, BFA, 73; Art Inst Chicago, MFA, 77; Whitney Mus Am Art, 77. *Work:* Philadelphia Mus Art & Please Touch Mus, Philadelphia, Pa; Lanon Found, Palm Beach, Fla; Phillips Collection, Smithsonian Inst, Washington, DC; Nat Women's Mus, Washington, DC; Best Corp Collection, NC. *Comn:* Mural, Candy Corns Visit Chicago, Pippers Alley, Chicago, Ill, 76; exterior sculpture, Three Boats, Reading Mus, Reading, Pa; sculpture, The Muse 34th Vessel, Am Express Col, NY. *Exhib:* Chicago & Vicinity, Art Inst Chicago, Ill, 77; Contemp Drawings, Philadelphia Mus Art, Pa, 79; Projects IV, Inst Contemp Art, Philadelphia, Pa, 80; Awards in the Visual Arts I, Nat Mus Am Art, Washington, DC, 82-83; De Moines Art Ctr, 82-83; Denver Art Mus, 82-83; one women show, Rockin, Philadelphia Mus Art, 87, Walkin, Pennsylvania Acad Fine Art, 89. *Pos:* Pres, Kerrigan Painting Co. *Awards:* Artist Fel, Pa Coun Art, 82; MacDowell Colony Fel, 86 & 87; Penny McCall Found Award, 87. *Bibliog:* Jean Silverthorne (auth), Maurie Kerrigan, Arts, 12/79; Ann-Sargent Wooster (auth), Maurie Kerrigan at Touchstone, Art in Am, 12/81; Wendy Slatkin (auth), Maurie Kerrigan, Arts, 5/83. *Mem:* Women's Caucus Art; Int Sculpture Ctr. *Media:* Handmade Paper, Wood; Oil Pastels. *Dealer:* Max Hutchinson Gallery 131 Green St New York NY 10012. *Mailing Add:* 1714 North St Philadelphia PA 19130-3307

KERSELS, MARTIN
CONCEPTUAL ARTIST, ILLUSTRATOR
Study: Univ Calif, Los Angeles, BA(art), 84, MFA(art), 95. *Exhib:* Stephen Wirtz Gallery, San Francisco, 97; Biennial (with catalog), Whitney Mus Am Art, NY, 97; W-139, Amsterdam, 97; Cahors Festival, France, 99; Melbourne Biennial, Australia, 99; and others. *Publ:* David Schafer (auth), rev, Art Papers, 5-6/98; William Wilson (auth), Commotion pulls viewer into artist's wacky life, LA Times, 10/21/98; Michael Darling (auth), The fat man sings, LA Weekly, 10/30/98-11/4/98. *Mailing Add:* c/o Deitch Projects 76 Grand St New York NY 10013-2220

KERSLAKE, KENNETH ALVIN
PRINTMAKER, EDUCATOR
b Mt Vernon, NY, Mar 8, 30. *Study:* Pratt Inst, 50-53, with Calvin Alberts & Philip Guston; Univ Ill, Urbana, with Lee Chesney, BFA, 55 & MFA, 57; Tamarind Lithography Workshop with Garo Antreasian, 64. *Work:* Libr Cong, Washington; Brooklyn Mus, NY; Nat Gallery Art, Washington; Samuel P Harn Mus Art, Gainesville, Fla; Boston Mus Fine Arts; Portland Mus Art; Krann Art Mus Art, Univ Ill, Champaign; and others. *Exhib:* 30 Yrs of Am Printmaking, 20th Ann Exhib of Prints, Brooklyn Mus, NY; one-man shows, Oxford Gallery, Eng & Univ SC, Spartenburg; Am Prints & Printmaking, Pratt Graphic Ctr, NY; Graphics Invitational, Mint Mus, Charlotte, NC, 81; 30 Am Printmakers, Ohio State Univ, Columbus; retrospective, Samuel P Harn Mus Art, Gainesville, Fla, 96; and others. *Teaching:* Distinguished serv prof, Univ Fla, Gainesville, 58-, emer prof, currently; artist-in-residence, Univ Mo, Columbia, summer, 81; prof art, Univ Ga Studies Abroad Prog, Cortona, Italy, summer, 82; artist-in-residence, Univ Tex, Austin & Univ Ala, 10/96. *Awards:* Distinguished Fac Award, Univ Fla, 79; Grant, Frans Masereel Graphic Centrum, Kasterlee, Belgium; Teacher of Yr, Col Fine Art, Univ Fla, 87. *Bibliog:* H Williams (auth), Notes for a Young Painter, Prentice-Hall, 63; R Fichter (auth), Three Florida artists using photography, Fla Arts, 5/78; portfolio, Art Visions, Winter Park, Fla. *Mem:* Boston Printmakers; Print Club, Philadelphia; Soc Am Graphic Artists; Southern Graphic Coun, Pres, 90-92; Fla Printmaking Soc. *Media:* Intaglio, Painting; Digital Arts. *Dealer:* Arts On Douglas New Symrna Beach FL; Blue Spiral 1 Gallery 38 Biltmore Ave Asheville NC 28820. *Mailing Add:* 1114 NW 36th Dr Gainesville FL 32605

KERSWILL, J W ROY
PAINTER
b Bigbury, Eng, Jan 17, 25; US citizen. *Study:* Plymouth Col Art, Eng; Bristol Col Art, scholar. *Work:* Wyo State Art Gallery; Mus Mountain Man; Grand Teton Natural Hist Asn Nat Park, Wyo; Jefferson Nat Expansion Mem, St Louis, Mo; Dept Interior Nat Collection, Washington, DC. *Comn:* Hist murals, Alpenhof Teton Village, Wyo, First Nat Bank, Englewood, Colo & Key Bank, Cheyenne, Wyo. *Exhib:* Am Artists Prof League Ann, NY, 50-. *Mem:* Am Artists Prof League; Artist Equity Asn. *Media:* Watercolor, Oil. *Dealer:* Hi Country Art. *Mailing Add:* Box 2440 Box 1089 Polson MT 59860

KERTZER, ANITA ELIZABETH
PAINTER, SCULPTOR
b Ottawa, Ont, Can. *Study:* Ottawa Sch Art; Banff Sch Fine Arts; Ringling Sch Art, Fla. *Work:* Parliamentary Portrait Gallery, Ottawa, Can. *Comn:* Prime Minister Pearson, Can. *Exhib:* Salon de Paris, Louvre (Grand Palais), Paris, France, 86; Fed Brit Artists, Pall Mall, London, Eng, 86-98; Pastel Int, Casa Loma, Toronto, Ont, 87; Nouveaux Maitres de L'image, Vieux-Ports, Montreal, Que, 89; North America's Most Innovative Pastel Painters; Ill Mus Art, Quincy, 90; retrospective, Univ SFla, Sarasota, 92 & 98. *Pos:* Pres, Pastel Soc Can, 84-; Premier Pastelist of Can. *Teaching:* Instr portrait, Manatee Art League, Fla, 86-98, Longboat Key Art Ctr, Fla, 96-. *Awards:* Mention Honorable, Salon de Paris, Institut de France, 86; Giffuni Plaque, Nat Arts Club, Pastel Soc Am, 87; First Prix Pastel, Nouveaux Maitres Image, APAQ, Que, 89. *Mem:* Pastel Soc Can (pres, 84-); Pastel Soc Am; Can Conf Arts; Soc Pastellistes France; Sarasota Art Asn, Fla; Can Inst Portrait Artists. *Media:* Oil, Pastel. *Publ:* Auth, Best of USA Pastels II, 99; Best of Canadian Pastels, 2000

KERZIE, TED L
PAINTER, EDUCATOR
b Tacoma, Wash, May 10, 43. *Study:* Wash State Univ, Pullman, BA, 65; Claremont Grad Sch, Calif, MFA, 72; Calif State Univ, Bakersfield, MAH. *Work:* Power Mus, Sydney, Australia; Wayne Anderson Collection, Boston; Luigiani Rossi Collection, Milan, Italy; Arco Collection Visual Arts, Los Angeles; Reader's Digest Collection, NY; Stouffers, Capital Group, Los Angeles; Merv Griffin, Palm Desert. *Comn:* Stouffers, Dion-Ross. *Exhib:* Solo show, Cirrus Gallery, Los Angeles, 80, Sherry Frumkin Gallery, Santa Monica, Calif, 91; Tengin Salon Gallery, Fukuoka, Japan, 81; Ten Calif Colorist Traveling Exhib; Valerie Miller Gallery, Palm Desert, Directors Guild, Hollywood, Calif, 92; Adamar Fine Arts, Miami, Fla, 94; West Coast Process Art, Bakersfield Mus Art, Calif, 97; and others. *Collection Arranged:* Los Angeles Abstract Painting (catalog), Univ Calif, Riverside, 80. *Pos:* Vpres, TRT Enterprises Casting Agency, Bakersfield, Calif; captain, photograph eng, USAF, 66-71, Motion Picture Off, 70-75. *Teaching:* Asst prof fine arts, Scripps Col & Claremont Grad Sch, Calif, 73-76; prof fine arts, Calif State Col, Bakersfield, 76-, summer arts, 86-. *Awards:* Bautzer Award for Univ Advance Planning, 98-99. *Bibliog:* William Wilson (auth), article, 80 & Suzanne Munchnic (auth), article, 8/81, Los Angeles Times; Melinda Wortz (auth), article, Art News, 80 & 83; Pick of the week, LA Weekly, 11/91. *Mem:* Aircraft Owners & Pilot Asn; Angel Flight Pilots. *Media:* Acrylic, Mixed Media. *Dealer:* Adamar Fine Arts 177 NE 39th St Miami FL 33137. *Mailing Add:* Dept Art California State Col 9001 Stockdale Hwy Bakersfield CA 93309

KESSLER, ALAN
PAINTER, SCULPTOR
b Philadelphia, Pa, Oct 15, 45. *Study:* Philadelphia Col Art, BFA; Yale Univ Summer Sch, Norfolk, Conn, Yale fel, 66; Md Inst Col Art, Baltimore, Hoffberger fel painting, MFA, 69. *Work:* Am Fedn Arts, NY; NY Univ Collection; Brockton Art Mus, Mass; Rose Art Mus, Brandeis Univ; State Univ NY Col Cortland. *Exhib:* One-man shows, Brown Univ, 77, O K Harris Gallery, NY, 77, 79, 80, 83, 85 & 89, Everson Mus Arts, Syracuse, NY, 78 & Morgan Gallery, Kansas City, Mo, 78; Directions, Hirshhorn Mus, Washington, DC, 79; Real, Really Real, Super Real, Directions in Contemp Am Realism, 81 & 82; and others. *Teaching:* Instr painting & drawing, Md Inst Col Art, 68-69; instr, Hudson River Mus, 74; asst prof art, Brown Univ, 77-82. *Awards:* First Prize in Painting, Acad Arts, Easton, Md, 68; Elizabeth T Greenshields Mem Found Grant in Painting, Montreal, 74; Artist in Residence Grant, Nat Endowment Arts, Del State Arts Coun, 75-76. *Bibliog:* Gregory Battcock (auth), Super Realism a Critical Anthology, Dutton, 75; Vivian Radnor (auth), Art: While waiting for tomorrow, New York Times, 10/23/77; Kim Levin (auth), Preview exhibition wood sculpture, O K Harris Gallery, Arts Mag, 10/77. *Media:* Polychrome, Wood. *Mailing Add:* 305 Camino Cerrito Santa Fe NM 87501

KESSLER, HERBERT LEON
EDUCATOR
b Chicago, Ill, July 20, 41. *Study:* Univ Chicago, BA, 61; Princeton Univ, MFA, 63, PhD, 65. *Teaching:* From asst prof to prof hist art, Univ Chicago, 65-76; prof, Johns Hopkins Univ, 76-, chmn dept, 76-90 & 95-98, Dean, Sch Arts & Sci, 98-99; Richard Krautheimer guest prof, Bibl Hertziana, 96-97. *Mem:* Fel Medieval Acad Am; Col Art Asn; Fel Am Acad Arts & Sci. *Res:* Medieval art. *Publ:* Frescoes of the Dura Synagogue & Christian Art, Dumbarton Oaks, 90; Studies in Pictorial Narrative, Pindar, 94; The Poetry and Paintings of the First Bible of Charles the Bald, Mich, 97; Rome 1300: On the Path of the Pilgrim, 2000; Spiritual Seeing: Picturing God's Invisibility in Medieval Art, 2000; Old St. Peter's and Church Decoration in Medieval Italy, 2002. *Mailing Add:* Dept Hist Art Johns Hopkins Univ Baltimore MD 21218

KESSLER, JANE Q
CURATOR, WRITER
b Charlotte, NC, June 14, 46. *Study:* ECarolina Univ, BS, 69; Yale Univ Printroom, 82; Boston Pub Libr Printroom, 83. *Collection Arranged:* Harvey Littleton: Glass, 78; Southeastern Graphics Invitational (auth, catalog), 79-82; Southeastern Contemporary Metalsmiths (auth, catalog), 80 & 81; Contemporary American Prints from the Permanent Collection of the Mint Museum (auth, catalog), 83; Ida Kohlmeyer: Thirty Years (auth, catalog), 83; Southern Comfort/Discomfort, 87, Made in America, 88, Va Beach Arts Ctr; Counterbalance: LeWitt, Tinguely, Peart, Bechtler Gallery, 91; RSV: 6 Artists Respond, Bechtler Gallery, 92; Chiaroscuro, Montgomery Mus Biennial, Ala, 94; I Found Context, installations, 96; North Carolina Pottery Mus, permanent installation, 96-97. *Pos:* Cur exhibs, 78-84, cur contemp art, Mint Mus, 84-88; principal partner, Curs' Forum, 88-94, Artcentral Inc, 94; bd dir, Penland Schs; Chmn & founder, CONTEXT Visual Art Ctr; consult & cur, Carillon Gallery, Shorenstein Co, 95-. *Awards:* Prof Fel Grant, Nat Endowment Art Mus. *Bibliog:* Interview, New Arts Examiner, 86 & Fiber Arts, 94. *Mem:* NC Print & Drawing Soc (pres bd, 83); Southeastern Col Arts Conf (bd dirs, 82-85); Southern Graphics Coun; World Print Coun; Am Crafts Coun Southeastern Assembly; Southeastern Mus Coun. *Res:* Regional exhibitions of prints, drawings and crafts; history of American prints; southern art; American crafts; crafts of the Southern Appalachians. *Publ:* auth, Un-making it, Art Papers, 85; Rude Osonik, Am Craft, 90; Randy Schull, NC State Univ; auth, From Mission to Market, Appalachian Crafts (catalogue essay), Am Craft Mus, New York, 94; Southern Arts & Crafts (catalogue essay), Mint Mus, 96. *Mailing Add:* 10300 Mt Olive Rd Mount Pleasant NC 28124-9647

KESSLER, JON A
SCULPTOR
b Yonkers, NY, Jan, 57. *Study:* State Univ NY, Purchase, BFA, 80; Whitney Mus Independent Study, Studio Prog, NY, 81. *Exhib:* Solo exhibs, Kestner-Gesellschaft, Hannover, 94, Luhring Augustine, NY, 94, Salzburger Kunstverein, Salzburg, 94, Neue Galerie am Landesmuseum Joanneum, Graz, 94, Puerto de Santander, 94, The Augustus Saint Gardens Mem, Cornish, NH, 96 & Univ Arts, Philadelphia, 97; The Lyon Biennial, Lyon, 95; Everything That's Interesting Is New, Athens Sch Fine Arts, Greece, 96; New York Hist Soc, 96; Exposure, Luhring Augustine, NY, 96; Sites of Chinatown, Mus Chinese Am, NY, 96; Family Values, Hamburger Kunsthalle, Hamburg, 97; Kunst, Arbeit, Sudwestdeutsche Landesbank, Stuttgart, 98; Crossings, Kunsthalle, Vienna, 98; and many others. *Bibliog:* Joshua Decter (auth), Don't Look Now (catalog), Thread Waxing Space, New York, 1-2/94; Peter Winter (auth), Hoflich Grusst der Goldfisch, Frankfurter Allgemeine Zeitung, 4/22/94; Neville Wakefield (auth), Jon Kessler: Luhring Augustine Gallery, Artforum, 10/94; and many others. *Mailing Add:* 40 White St New York NY 10013

KESSLER, LEONARD H
ILLUSTRATOR
b Akron, Ohio, Oct 28, 21. *Study:* Carnegie Inst of Tech, BFA(painting & design), 49. *Work:* De Grummond Collection, Univ Southern Miss; Kerlan Collection, Univ Minn. *Awards:* New York Times 10 Best Illus Children's Books, 54, 55 & 57. *Mem:* Soc Illusr; Graphic Artists Guild; Author's League; Author's Guild; Soc Children's Books Writers. *Media:* Pen & Ink, Pencil, Watercolor, Markers, Acrylic. *Publ:* Auth & illusr, Old Turtles, 90 Knock-Knock, 91 Greenwillow; Here Comes Strikeout rev ed, Harper Collins, 92; illusr, Is There a Penguin at your Party?, Simon & Schuster, 94; Is There a Gorilla in the Band?, Simon & Schuster, 94; Kick Pass & Run, New illus ed, 96; Last One is a Rotten Egg, rev ed, Harper Collins, 99; auth, Mr Pine's Purple House, 2002, Mr Pine's Mixed-up Signs, 2003, Mrs. Pine Takes a Trip, 2005, Republished by Purple House Press. *Mailing Add:* 1624 Treehouse Cir Sarasota FL 34231

KESSLER, LINDA
PAINTER, PHOTOGRAPHER
b Brooklyn, NY, Aug 20, 54. *Study:* Brooklyn Col, with Lee Bontecou, BA, 75; Atelier apprentice to Anton P Russev, New York, 81-85; Art Students League, with David Leffel, Frank Mason & Thomas Fogarty, New York, 81-88. *Work:* Hosp for Joint Diseases/Orthopaedic Inst, NY; La Posada de Las Monjas, San Miguel de Allende, Mex; Mt Sinai Hosp, NY; and others. *Comn:* Portrait, Colin Gallery, NY, 90; portrait, Paulo De Castro, Sao Paulo, Brazil, 92; portrait, Esther & Dennis Rodriguez, Sao Paulo, Brazil, 92; landscape, Julia Newton, Venice, Calif, 94. *Exhib:* Westbeth

Gallery, NY, 93; Womens Show, Pratt Inst, Brooklyn, NY, 94; Nat Asn Women Artists, 395 W Broadway Gallery, NY, 94; Recycling with Imagination, AIA Gallery, Pittsburgh, Pa, 96; Brazilian Contemp Art, Boston City Hall Gallery, Mass, 97; Offspring, Brooklyn, NY, Feminist Expo, Baltimore, Md, 2000; 112th Ann Exhib Nat Asn Women Artists, NY, 2001; Cork Gallery, Lincoln Square, NY, 2002; Images Against War, Gallery Lichtblick, Cologne, Germany, 2003; Real Brooklyn - A Day in Our Life, Borough Hall, Brooklyn, NY, 2003; Peaceworks, Times Square Lobby Gallery, NY, 2003; Benefit Show, Muskegon Pregnancy Services, Mich, 2004. *Pos:* Coordr, Art & Play Therapy, Hosp for Joint Diseases/Orthopaedic Inst, New York, 82-86; photogr, owner, Focus Pocus, A Fine Art Photography Studio, New York, 97-. *Teaching:* Pvt painting lessons in Sao Paulo, Brazil, 91-92; fine art tchr, Alternative Jr/Sr HS, Brooklyn, NY, 2000-. *Awards:* First Prize, John Howard Sanden Portrait Competition, Art Students League, New York, 88; Best Show Award, Micro/Macro Exhib, Helio Gallery, New York, 89; Ada Cecere Mem Award, Nat Asn Women Artists, 395 W Broadway Gallery, New York, 94. *Bibliog:* Will Grant (auth), Varied generations, varied dimensions, Artspeak, New York, 12/90; Audrey Bernard (auth), For art's sake, Daily Challenge, New York, 11/90; Liam Nelson (auth), Drawn to sculpture, Kingston Daily Freeman, NY 9/90; Best of Acrylic Painting, Rockport Pubs, 96; Landscape Inspirations, Rockport Pubs, 97; plus others. *Mem:* New York Artists Equity; Nat Asn Women Artists; Nat Arts Educ Asn; Am Soc Media Photographers; Professional Women Photographers. *Media:* Acrylic, Mixed Media. *Interests:* Fgn travel, cross-country skiing. *Publ:* Auth The Rainbows End, The Int Libr Photography, 2000. *Dealer:* JJ Brookings Gallery San Francisco, CA. *Mailing Add:* Focus Pocus 85 Livingston St Brooklyn NY 11201

KESSLER, MARGARET JENNINGS
PAINTER
b Auburn, Ind, Aug 15, 44. *Exhib:* Top 100, Nat Arts for the Parks Show, traveling, 89. *Teaching:* Instr painting workshops internationally. *Awards:* Silver, 82, Bronze, 83, Gold Medal, 89 & 94, Grumbacher Art Awards; Hon Mention, Am Artist's Prof League, Salmagundi Club, NY, 84; Gold Medal, Oil Painters Am Regional, San Antonio, 94; and others. *Bibliog:* Article, Southwest Art Mag, 12/84; article, Watercolor Mag, fall 93. *Mem:* Signature mem Artists & Craftsmen Asn (pres, 85-86). *Media:* Oil. *Publ:* North Light Mag, 4/85 & The Artists' Mag, 1/85, 2/85 & 1/88; contribr, cover, The Artist's Mag, 2/85; Painting Better Landscapes, Watson-Guptill Publ, New York, 87; Everything You Ever Wanted to Know About Oil Painting, Watson-Guptill Publ, New York, 93. *Mailing Add:* 330 Ridgehaven Pl Richardson TX 75080-2569

KETCHAM, RAY WINFRED, JR
DEALER, DESIGNER
b Hartford, Ala, Dec 4, 22. *Study:* Ringling Sch Art, Fla, 46-48. *Comn:* Home Calendar, Coca-Cola Company, 55-67; mural, Delta Airlines, 66. *Pos:* Owner, Ray Ketcham Gallery, 66-. *Awards:* Freelance Artist of the Year, Professional Artists Asn Atlanta Inc, 65. *Specialty:* Nineteenth & early twentieth century American & European paintings. *Mailing Add:* 540 Forestdale Drive NE Atlanta GA 30342

KETCHUM, ROBERT GLENN
PHOTOGRAPHER, CURATOR
b Los Angeles, Calif, Dec 1, 47. *Study:* Univ Calif, Los Angeles, with Heinecken & Teske in photog, BA(design, cum laude), 70; Brooks Inst, 71; Calif Inst Arts, MFA(photog), 74. *Work:* Mus Mod Art & Metrop Mus Art, NY; Los Angeles Co Mus Art, Los Angeles; Nat Mus Am Art & Corcoran Gallery, Washington, DC. *Comn:* Seafarm (book), comn by Harry N Abrams, Int Ocean Inst, NY, 77; portfolio, traveling exhibit, Lila Acheson Wallace Fund, NY, 82-84; color portfolio of Alaska, The Wallace Ford Fund, NY, 82-84; Chattahoochee Suite, Cousins Properties, Atlanta, Ga, 85-87; color portfolio, Cleveland Found, Gund Found, Akron Art Mus, Ohio, 86-. *Exhib:* White House, Washington, DC, 79; Smithsonian Traveling Exhib Service, 80-84; Am Photogr and Nat Parks Traveling Exhib, 81-83; one-man exhib, Sheldon Mem Art Gallery, Lincoln, Nebr, 84; Lyndon Johnson Libr, Austin, Tex, 84; Nat Mus Am Art, 85; and others. *Pos:* Cur, Nat Park Found, DC, 78-; bd trustees, Los Angeles Ctr Photog Studies, 75-81, pres & exec dir, 79. *Teaching:* Founder & teacher photog workshop, Sun Valley Ctr Arts & Humanities, 71-73; instr photog, Calif Inst Arts, 75; instr & adv bd, Appalachian Arts Ctr, Highlands, NC, 82-. *Awards:* Nat Park Found Award, 78 & 79; Mat Res Award, Ciba-Geigy, 79; NY State Coun on the Arts Grant, 85. *Bibliog:* Suzanne Muchnic (auth), Ketchum, Evert at Municipal, Los Angeles Times, 6/14/83; Gene Thorton (auth), Critics choice/photography, New York Times, 12/29/85; Margaret Moorman (auth), New York Reviews/Robert Glenn Ketchum, Art News, 3/86. *Mem:* Friends Photog. *Media:* Cibachrome Color Prints, Books. *Publ:* Coauth, Outerbridge, Los Angeles Ctr Photog Studies, 76; auth, Photographic Directions: Los Angeles 1979, Security Pac Bank, 79; Landscape Photographers and America's National Parks, Nat Park Found, 79; The Hudson River and the Highlands, Aperture, 85. *Mailing Add:* 696 Stone Canyon Rd Los Angeles CA 90077

KETNER, JOSEPH DALE
MUSEUM DIRECTOR, CURATOR
b Anderson, Ind, Oct 30, 55. *Study:* Ind Univ, BA, 77, MA, 80. *Collection Arranged:* Grace Hartigan, 81 (with catalog), 81; Beautiful, Sublime & Picturesque (with catalog), 84; Carl F Wimar (with catalog), 91; Robert S Duncanson (with catalog), 93; A Gallery of Modern Art (with catalog), 94; Art & Science: Investigating Matter, Catherine Wagner (with catalog), 97. *Pos:* Cur-registr, Ft Wayne Mus Art, Ind, 79-82; cur, 82 & dir, 89-98, Washington Univ Gallery Art; cur, Ros Art Mus at Brandeis Univ, Waltham, Mass, 98-. *Mem:* Midwest Art Hist Soc, Univ Mus Comt (co-chair, 92); incorporating mem, St Louis Area Mus Collaborative. *Publ:* Auth, Continuing Search of Grace Hartigan, Artnews, 81; Robert S Duncanson: Late Literary Landscapes, Am Art J, 83; coauth, Beautiful, Sublime, & Picturesque, Washington Univ, 84; Carl F Wimar: Chronicler of the Missouri, R Amon Carter/Abrams, 91; auth, Emergence of the African-American Artist, Univ Mo, 93. *Mailing Add:* Rose Art Mus Brandeis Univ Mailstop 069 PO Box 9110 Waltham MA 02454

KETTLEWOOD, BEA CARD
PAINTER, STAINED GLASS ARTIST
b Pompton Plains, NJ, Jun 7, 29. *Study:* Kean Univ, BS, 1951; New York Univ, MA, 1955, EDD (creative art), 1972. *Work:* Arnot Mus, Elmira, NY; Rutgers Univ, New Brunswick, NJ; Jersey City City Hall, Jersey City, NJ; Nairn Old Parish, Nairn, Scotland; Paterson Library, Paterson, NJ. *Comn:* stained glass window designs, Chilton Mem Hospital, Pompton Plains, NJ, 1990, Morristown Mem Hospital, Morristown, NJ, 1994, Rehabilitation Inst, Morristown, NJ, 1995, Hackettstown Community Hospital, Hackettstown, NJ, 2000; 3 stained glass windows, 1st Reformed Church, Pompton Plains, NJ, 86; oil painting Nairn Church comn by Choir of 1st Reformed, Nairn Scotland, 97. *Exhib:* State Show, Montclair Mus, Montclair, NJ, 1962; Burr Artists Show, Jersey City Mus, Jersey City, NJ, 1968; Juried Open Show, Farnsworth Art Mus, Rockland, ME, 1969-77; Juried Open Show, New Eng Fine Arts Inst, Boston, MA, 1993; Ellasue Open, Trenton City Mus, Trenton, NJ, 1996; Juried Open Show, Monmouth Mus, Lincroft, NJ, 1998; Art From The Start, Suny-Orange, Middletown, NY, 2004; Juried Open Show, Butler Inst of Am Art, Youngstown, OH, 2005. *Pos:* retired art educator 33 yrs. *Teaching:* Educator & dept chmn, New Milford High, New Milford, NJ, 1951-1984; lectr art & art hist, free lance, 1984-. *Mem:* Ringwood Manor Asn Arts, 91-; Maine Art Gallery 62-2004; Arts Coun Orange Co, NY Gallery Comt 85-95; Women's Caucus for Art NJ, NY chap, 80-95. *Media:* Oil, Watercolor. *Res:* Visual Space in Painting: 49-69; Hist Am Archit. *Specialty:* Maine Artists. *Interests:* Am Archit; Writing. *Dealer:* Brush and Easel Gallery Nobleboro Vt. *Mailing Add:* 45 Wilrue Pkwy Pompton Plains NJ 07444-1717

KETTNER, DAVID ALLEN
ARTIST, EDUCATOR
b Sunman, Ind, Oct 19, 43. *Study:* Skowhegan Sch Painting and Sculpture, 64; Cleveland Inst Art, BFA, 66; Ind Univ, MFA, 68. *Work:* Pa Acad Fine Arts; Philadelphia Mus Art, Pa; Rutgers Univ, Col Arts & Sci, Camden, NJ. *Exhib:* Six Self-Portraits 1975 Series, Whitney Mus Am Art, NY, 76; 41st Int Eucharistic Congress Liturgical Arts Exhib, Civic Ctr, Philadelphia, 76; Philadelphia Houston Exchange, Inst Contemp Art, Philadelphia, 76; Recent Acquisitions, Philadelphia Mus Art, 77; Am Drawing Show, Fine Arts Gallery, San Diego, Calif, 77; Contemp Drawing, 78 & A Bach Transcription, 81, Pa Acad Fine Arts. *Teaching:* Assoc prof painting & drawing, Philadelphia Col Art, 68-. *Bibliog:* Victoria Donohue (auth), article, Philadelphia Inquirer, 10/9/81. *Mailing Add:* Dept Painting Broad & Pine Sts Univ of the Arts 320 S Broad St Philadelphia PA 19102-4994

KEVESON, FLORENCE
PAINTER, ILLUSTRATOR
b New York, NY. *Study:* Cooper Union Art Sch, art degree; Art Students League, Ford Found Scholar; also with Sidney Gross & Leo Manso. *Comn:* Woodstock Hist Soc. *Exhib:* Albany Inst Hist Art Ann, 68-72; solo exhib, Silvermine Guild Artists, 69 & Marist Col, 72; Wadsworth Atheneum Mus Ann, 69-77; Berkshire Mus Ann, Pittsfield, Mass, 70-80; Painters & Sculptors, Bergen Mus, Paramus, NJ, 70-83; Butler Inst Ann, 72; Nat Arts Club, 82-89; Academy of Art and Letters. *Pos:* Illusr, Conde Nast Publ, 49-52; free-lance illusr, 53-. *Awards:* Shandoff Award, Berkshire Ann, 70; G Paley Award, Nat Asn Women Artists Ann; Michael M Engel Award, Am Soc Contemp Artists; Audubon Artists, 85; Pen & Brush Inc, 95-2005. *Mem:* Audobon Artists; Am Soc Contemp Artists; Nat Asn Women Artists; Silvermine Guild; Pen & Brush Inc. *Media:* Oil. *Collection:* CD Morris; Rudolf Collectors. *Publ:* Illus in Vogue, McCalls, Good Housekeeping, Glamour, Harpers Bazaar, Seventeen; and others. *Dealer:* La Boette Gallery New York NY. *Mailing Add:* 314 E 201 St Bronx NY 10458

KEVORKIAN, RICHARD
PAINTER
b Dearborn, Mich, Aug 24, 37. *Study:* Pa Acad of Fine Arts, Philadelphia, 58; Richmond Prof Inst, BFA(painting), 61; Calif Col of Arts & Crafts, Oakland, MFA(painting), 62. *Work:* Mus Genocide, Yerevan, Armenia; Fed Reserve, Richmond, Va; Southeastern Ctr for Contemp Art, Winston-Salem, NC; IBM, Washington; PBS KAMU, Col Sta, Tex; Va Commonwealth Univ, Richmond, Va; Banco Nat, Lima, Peru. *Exhib:* Painting in the South, 1564-1980, traveling exhib, Va Mus Fine Arts, Birmingham Mus Art, Nat Acad Design, NY JB Speed Art Mus, & New Orleans Mus Art; Southern Abstraction: Five Painters, Traveling Exhib, Univ Tenn, Clemson Univ, NC State Univ & Cheekwood Fine Arts Ctr, Nashville, Tenn; Contemp Art Acquisitions, Equitable Gallery, NY; 35 Southeastern Artists, High Mus, 76; Southeast 7, Southeastern Ctr Contemp Art, Winston-Salem, 77; Leicester Polytech, Eng; Marita Gilliam Gallery, Raleigh, NC; Eric Schindler Gallery, Richmond, Va; Univ Guam; Muggleton Gallery, Auburn, NY; plus others. *Pos:* vis artist, Nat Col Art & Design, Dublin Ireland; Central School Art and Design, London, Eng; Loughborough Col Art, Leicester, Eng; Winchester, Col Art, Eng; Ulster Col, Belfast, Northern Ireland. *Teaching:* Instr painting, Richard Bland Col, Petersburg, Va, 61-64; prof & chmn dept of painting & printmaking, Va Commonwealth Univ, Richmond, 64-, prof emer, 92. *Awards:* Individual Sr Artists Grant (painting), Nat Endowment Arts, 72; Southeastern Ctr Contemp Arts Grant (painting), 76; Guggenheim Fel Painting, 78; Traveling Fel Va Mus Fine Arts, 61-62. *Mem:* Nat Coun of Art Adminr. *Media:* Oil, acrylic. *Specialty:* Visual Arts. *Interests:* Fishing, Hunting, Cooking. *Dealer:* Aaron Gallery 1717 Connecticut Ave NW Washington DC 20009. *Mailing Add:* 7909 Rock Creek Rd Richmond VA 23229

KEY, TED
CARTOONIST, ILLUSTRATOR-CHILDRENS BOOKS
b Fresno, Calif, Aug 25, 1912. *Study:* Univ Calif, Berkeley, BA, 33. *Work:* Brandywine Mus; George Arents Research Libr; Syracuse Univ; Int Mus Cartoon Art; Ohio State Cartoon Libr. *Pos:* Creator, Hazel, daily panel syndicated by King Features, 1943 & Hazel TV series (NBC & CBS); creator (cartoon features), Hazel, Peabody & Sherman, Bullwinkle & Rocky Show, 59, Diz & Liz, Jack & Jill Mag, 61-71, Positive Attitude Posters, 65-; Writer for several TV series, NBC & CBS, formerly; ideas for many Saturday Evening Post covers; creator, Hazel, 43, The Saturday Evening Post; assoc editor, Judge Mag, 37-39; playwright, NBC Radio Production, The Clinic, in anthology, Best Broadcasts of 1939-40; creator & writer 3 Walt Disney Studios feature movies: Million Dollar Duck, Gus, The Cat From Outer Space. *Awards:* Best Syndicated Panel Award, Nat Cartoonists Soc, 77. *Mem:* Nat Cartoonists Soc; Writers Guild Am W. *Publ:* Published 21 books; Illus, How to Develop Your Thinking Ability. *Mailing Add:* 1694 Glenhardie Rd Wayne PA 19087

KEYSER, WILLIAM ALPHONSE, JR
CRAFTSMAN, PAINTER, SCULPTOR
b Pittsburgh, Pa, July 30, 36. *Study:* Carnegie-Mellon Univ, Pittsburgh, BS, 58; Sch Am Crafts, Rochester Inst of Tech, MFA (furniture design), 61; Sch Art, Rochester Inst Tech, MFA (painting), 2006. *Work:* Am Crafts Mus, NY; Artpark, Lewiston, NY; Eastman Kodak Co, Rochester, NY; Mem Art Gallery, Rochester, NY; Sheldon Mus of Fine art, Univ Neb, Lincoln. *Comn:* Subway Benches, Sculptures, Mass Bay Transportation Auth, 84; complete sanctuary furnishings, St Mary's Church, Rochester, NY, 87; Rochester Top 100, annual award sculpture, Peat Marwick & Rochester Chamber of Commerce, 1987-2006; bench, sculpture, Art Park, Lewiston, NY, 1986; baptistry, St Joseph's of Penfield, NY, 87; chapel furnishings, Diocesan Ctr, Roman Catholic Diocese, Rochester, NY, 2003. *Exhib:* Nat Invitational Furniture Show, Mendeocino Calif, 90; Craft Art Western NY, Burchfield-Penny Art Ctr, Buffalo, NY, 1990, 1994 & 2006; Kanazawa Arts & Crafts Competition, Kanazawa, Japan, 91; Contemp Crafts NY, NY Mus, Albany, NY, 97; NY State Biennial, NY State Mus, Albany; Studio Furniture: Fine Art Invitational, Memphis Col of Art, 2000; The Maker's Hand: Am Studio Furniture, 1940-1990, Mus Fine Arts, Boston, Mass, 2003; Graduate Thesis Exhib, Bevier Gallery, Rochester Inst Tech, Rochester, NY, 2005. *Teaching:* Prof Emeritus furniture design, Sch Am Crafts, Rochester Inst of Technol, 62-97-, chmn crafts, 81-89. *Awards:* Young Americans Award, Am Crafts Coun, 62; Craftsmen's Fel, Nat Endowment for the Arts, 75; Distinguished Alumnus, Rochester Inst Tech, 1987; Fel Am Craft Coun, 97; Merit Award, Carnegie Mellon Univ, 1998; Award of Distinciton, The Furniture Soc, 03. *Bibliog:* Jonathan Fairbanks (auth), American Furniture 1620 to the Present, 81; Dona Z Meilach (auth), Woodworking: The New Wave, Crown Publ, 81, William Keyser and the MBTA Bench Project (video), Rochester Inst Technol, producer, 84; and others; Edward S. Cooke Jr, Gerald W R Ward & Kelly H L'ecuyer (auths), The Maker's Hand-Am Studio Furniture 194 to 1990, 2003. *Mem:* Am Crafts Coun; Furniture Soc. *Media:* All Media. *Publ:* Auth, Steam Bending--Heat and Moisture Plasticize Wood, 77 & Portfolio: W A Keyser, The Challenge of Churches, 79, Fine Woodworking, Taunton Press; Where Designs Are Born, Home Furniture, Taunton Press, 95. *Dealer:* Pritam & Eames East Hampton NY; Snyderman Gallery Philadelphia Pa. *Mailing Add:* 8008 Taylor Rd Victor NY 14564

KHACHIAN, ELISA A
PAINTER
b Worcester, Mass, May 6, 35. *Study:* RI Sch Design, BS, 57; Fairfield Univ, graphic art, 82; Silvermine Col Art. *Work:* Pvt collection, Town of Fairfield, Conn. *Exhib:* Southern Vt Art Ctr; Juried Exhib, Javitts Ctr, Nat Asn Women Artists, NY, 88; Conn Watercolor Soc, New Brit Mus Am Art, 90; First Show Mus, Katonah Mus, NY, 92; Conn Women Artists, New Brit Mus Am Art, 92; Art of the Northeast, 97; Discovery Mus, 98; and others. *Pos:* Art asst, RI Sch Design, Spec Talents, 56-57; art educ, W Concord Sch System, 57-58. *Teaching:* Problem solving, Darien Art Soc, 87-91. *Awards:* Conn Women Artists Award, Merchants Bank & Trust, 89; Seven Awards, 50th Ann Conn Watercolor Soc, 90; Best Drawing/Painting, Discovery Mus, 98; Women's Caucus for Art; Silvermine Art Guild; Art Place Coop Gallery. *Mem:* Nat Asn Women Artists; Silvermine Guild Ctr for the Arts; Conn Women Artists; Conn Watercolor Soc; New Haven Paint & Clay. *Media:* Watercolor, Collage, Printmaking. *Publ:* Auth, Watercolor, 96; auth, Splash, National Asn Women Artists, Zimmerli Mus, Rutgers Univ, 8/2005 & 9/2006. *Mailing Add:* 213 Hollydale Rd Fairfield CT 06430

KHALIL, CLAIRE ANNE
PAINTER
b Boston, Mass, Feb 20, 44. *Study:* Emmanuel Col, BA, 65; Acad di Belle Arte, Florence, Italy, 65-66. *Work:* Am Stock Exch, NY; Janss Found, Sun Valley, Idaho; Venus--the Bittkers-New Haven, Conn, 75. *Comn:* Red Brick House, comn by Gloria Garfinkel, NY, 81; Sweet Briar, comn by Stephanie Axinn, NY, 82; The House of the Three Gables, comn by Carol Butz, NY, 82; Sun Valley and the Janss Collection with Dove, comn by Glenn Janss, Idaho, 84. *Exhib:* Focus on Realism: Selections from the Collection of Glenn C Janss, traveling exhib throughout US, 85; Fireworks: Am Artists Celebrate the Eighth Art, Butler Inst Am Art, Youngstown, Ohio, 85. *Bibliog:* Alvin Martin (auth), American Realism--Twentieth Century Drawings and Watercolors, San Francisco Mus Mod Art & Harry N Abrams, 86. *Dealer:* Nancy Hoffman 429 W Broadway New York NY 10012. *Mailing Add:* c/o Nancy Hoffman Gallery 429 W Broadway New York NY 10012-3766

KHALIL, MOHAMMAD O
GRAPHIC ARTIST, PRINTMAKER
b Burri, Khartoum, Sudan, Jan 8, 36; US citizen. *Study:* Khartoum Tech Sch, dipl, 60; Acad di Belle Arte di Firenze, dipl, 66. *Work:* Metrop Mus Art, NY; Smithsonian Inst; Libr Congress; Mus Mod Art, Osaka, Japan; Mus Grenoble, France. *Exhib:* 17th Print Biennial, Brooklyn Mus, 70; solo exhibs, Bronx Mus, 87, Inst du Mon de Arab, 87, Nat Mus Am Art, Washington, 95; group exhib, Herbert F Johnson, Ithaca, NY, 93. *Teaching:* Instr printmaking, New Sch Social Res, 70-, Pratt Inst, Brooklyn, 71-83, Parson Sch Desgin, 88-, NY Univ, 91-. *Awards:* Grant, Bronx Coun on Arts, 87; Bronze Prize, Osaka Triennial, 91; First Prize, Int Biennial Cairo, 93. *Mem:* Nat Acad. *Mailing Add:* c/o Mary Ryan Gallery 24 W 57th St New York NY 10019

KHALILI, NASSER DAVID
COLLECTOR
b Isfahan, Iran, 45. *Study:* Studied computer sci, Queens Col, New York City; Univ London, PhD, 88; Boston Univ, 2003, LHD(hon). *Pos:* Owner The Khalili Collections, 70-, which incl The Nour Found - The Nasser D Khalili Collection of Islamic Art, The Khalili Collection of Spanish Damascene Metalwork, The Kibo Found - The Khalili Collection of Japanese Art, The Khalili Collection of Swedish Textile Art; also owner Favermead property co; Assoc research prof & mem governing body Sch Oriental and African Studies, Univ London; Int bd overseers Tufts Univ, Mass, 97-; bd trustees Boston Univ, 2003-; co-founder, chmn Maimonides Found, London; co-founder, mem bd dir, Iran Heritage Found, 95-; endowed Nasser D Khalili Chmn of Islamic Art, Univ London, The Khalili Research Ctr for the Art and Material Cult of Middle E, Univ Oxford. *Awards:* Decorated Knight Commander of the Royal Order of Francis I (KCFO), Medaglia Pontifica Pope John Paul II, Knight of the Equestrian Order of Pope St Sylvester (KSS); named Trustee of the City of Jerusalem, 96; named one of 200 Top Collectors, ARTnews mag, 2004; hon fel, Univ London. *Mailing Add:* The Nour Found Nasser D Khalili Collection Islamic Art London England W1X5NL United Kingdom

KHEEL, CONSTANCE
PAINTER
b New York, NY, 45. *Study:* Bennington Col, Bennington, Vt, BA(painting & sculpture), 67. *Work:* Nat Gallery Mod Art, Santo Domingo, Dominican Repub; The Newark Mus, NJ; Herbert F Johnson Mus Art, Ithaca, NY; Aldrich Mus Contemp Art, Ridgefield, Conn; Mint Mus Art, Charlotte, NC. *Exhib:* Harcus-Krakow Gallery, Boston, Mass, 80; solo exhib, Andre Zarre Gallery, NY, 82, 84 & 86, Reece Galleries, NY, 88, RVS Fine Art, Southampton, NY, 88, Boinayel Galleria de Arte, Santo Domingo, 89, Leonora Vega, NY, 94; Williams Col Mus Art; Inst Cultura Puertorriquena, San Juan, PR; Univ Art Gallery, State Univ NY; and others. *Awards:* Fel, Nat Endowment Arts, 87. *Mem:* Nat Asn Women Artists. *Mailing Add:* Joslin Ln Buskirk NY 12028

KIDD, REBECCA MONTGOMERY
PAINTER
b Muncie, Ind, Nov 29, 42. *Comn:* Double portrait, comn by Delegate & Mrs Robert Bloxom, Mapsville, Va, 73; film illus, Effective Educ Systems, Essexville, Mich, 75; children's portrait, comn by Mr & Mrs Stephen B Tankard, Exmore, Va, 84; Civil War era portrait, comn by Mr & Mrs Louis Floyd, Exmore, Va, 86; double portrait, comn by Mrs Joanne Vankesteren Smith, Onancock, Va, 88. *Exhib:* The Pentagon, Arlington, Va, 74; Int Cong on Arts & Commun Exhib, Queen's Col, Univ Cambridge, Eng, 82; Int Platform Asn Conv Art Exhib, Hyatt Regency, Washington, DC, 84; solo exhib, Eastern Shore Chap Va Mus, Eastern Shore Community Col, Melfa, Va, 87. *Awards:* Popular Choice Award, & Merit Award, IPA Conv Exhib, 84. *Bibliog:* Art by Rebecca Kidd shown, Daily Times, Salisbury, Md, 1/17/82; Artist Rebecca Kidd recieves IPA Awards, Eastern Shore News, Va, 8/23/84. *Mem:* Visual Artists & Galleries Asn. *Media:* Oils, Pastels. *Dealer:* Roadside Gallery Main St Melfa VA. *Mailing Add:* 9 Lake St Onancock VA 23417

KIDWELL, MICHELE FALIK
HISTORIAN, WRITER
b New York, NY, June 1, 44. *Study:* Hunter Col, New York, BA(cum laude), MA. *Pos:* Art tour guide, various mus & galleries, 78-99; sales & appraisals for courts, attorneys, charities & pvt clients, 85-; judge, Cong Arts Caucus, 91; cur, Fedn Protestant Welfare Agencies, 93; exec comt, Hunter Col Art Gallery; bd, Bacchanalia. *Teaching:* Fac, New Sch Univ, 78-2002, NY Univ, 84-90 & Col New Rochelle, 91; lectr in field 78-. *Mem:* Nat Arts Club; Jewish Community Relations Coun; Landmarks and parks Committee, Community Bd 7; Women Working At Home. *Res:* Italian illuminated manuscripts. *Mailing Add:* 495 West End Ave Apt 1K New York NY 10024

KIEFERNDORF, FREDERICK GEORGE
PAINTER, EDUCATOR
b Milwaukee, Wis, May 12, 21. *Study:* Univ Wis, BA & MS. *Work:* Springfield Art Mus, Mo; Mo State Hist Soc Permanent Collection (painting requested 75); Wis Salon Art, Madison; Sch Ozarks, Point Lookout, Mo; Pittsburgh State Col, Kans. *Exhib:* Ann Delta Show, Little Rock, 67 & 74; Ten Painters of Missouri, Traveling Exhib, Mo State Coun Arts, 68; Springfield Art Mus Midwest Exhib, 72; retrospective exhib, Park Central Gallery, 81; two-man show, Jordan Creek Gallery, 85; show of drawings & paintings, Springfield Art Mus, 88; Emer Fac Exhib, Southwest Mo State Univ Design Gallery, 96. *Teaching:* Prof art, Southwest Mo State Univ, 53-81. *Awards:* Purchase Award, Springfield Art Mus, 56 & 65 & Award of Merit, 67; Purchase Award, Sch Ozarks, 70 & Award of Merit, 81. *Bibliog:* Edgar A Albin (auth), article in Art Voices/South, 7-8/78; Edgar A Albin (auth), article in Springfield Mag, 1/87; Gregory Thielen (auth), Journeys Near & Far, Springfield Art Mus, 88. *Media:* Polymer, Vinyl Cement. *Mailing Add:* 1748 Madaline Springfield MO 65804

KIEFFER, MARY JANE
PAINTER
b Chicago, Ill. *Study:* Am Acad Art, 37-38; Maholy-Nagi Sch Design; Art Inst Chicago. *Comn:* Numerous pvt comns. *Exhib:* Pasadena Soc Artists Ann, Riverside Art Mus, 68; Invitational, Nat Acad Design, NY, 68; Utah State Univ, Logan, 74-80; Brand XII, Brand Libr, Glendale, Calif; Nat Watercolor Soc Ann, Palm Springs Mus, Calif; Rocky Mountain Nat, Colo Art Mus; Downey Mus, 90; Los Angeles Co Century Gallery. *Awards:* First Award & Purchase Award, Laguna Art Mus, 74, Bruggen Ann Award, 76 & Del Mar Col Ann Award, 79, Nat Watercolor Soc, 55-85; Purchase Award, Utah State Univ Gallery, Logan. *Mem:* Nat Watercolor Soc (pres, 77-78); Pasadena Soc Artists (pres, 81-82). *Media:* Watercolor. *Publ:* Contribr, Expressive Watercolor Techniques, Davis, 82. *Mailing Add:* 1252 Inverness Dr Pasadena CA 91103

KIELKOPF, JAMES ROBERT
PAINTER
b St Paul, Minn, July 13, 39. *Study:* Minneapolis Sch Art, BFA, 65; Grand Marias Art Colony, summer 63; Skowhegan Sch Painting, summer 64. *Work:* Walker Art Ctr, Minneapolis Inst Art. *Comn:* First Bank Minneapolis, Minn, 82; Republic Bank, Houston, Tex, 83; 3M Corp, St Paul, Minn, 90. *Exhib:* Walker Art Ctr Biennial, 64 & 66; Minneapolis Inst Art Biennial, 67; Interchange, Dallas Mus Fine Arts, Tex, 72; Landmark Ctr, St Paul, 79; Minneapolis Inst of Art, Minn, 86; SDak Art Mus, Brookings, 90. *Media:* Acrylic, Oil. *Dealer:* Thomas Barry Fine Arts 400 First Ave N Suite 304 Minneapolis MN 55401. *Mailing Add:* 1963 Ashland Ave Saint Paul MN 55104-5831

KIENHOLZ, LYN
PATRON, ADMINISTRATOR
b Chicago, Ill. *Study:* Sullins Col; Md Col Women. *Exhib:* Cowin-Divola (catalog), La Jolla Mus Contemp Art & nat & Europ tour, 85-87; Off the Beaten Track (brochure), Wight Gallery, Univ Calif, Los Angeles, 88; Chinese Influence on West Coast Artists (catalog), Taiwan Mus Art, 88; Lee Miller Photographer (book), Corcoran Gallery Art, nat & int mus tour, 89-93; Individual Realities (catalog), Sezon Mus Art, Tokyo & Japan tour, 91; 12 Artists for Havana, Cuba Biennale, 94; Architecture for the New Millenium (catalog), MOCA Taipei, Taiwan, Macau, and China, 2002-04; LA 1955-1985 (catalog), Centre Pompidou, Paris, 2006. *Pos:* Asst to artist Edward Kienholz, 66-74; exec dir, Beaubourg Found, Ctr Pompidou, Paris, 77-81; founder & chmn, Calif-Int Arts Found, Los Angeles, 81-. *Bibliog:* Hunter Drohojowska (auth), Carrying a torch for Olympic artists, Los Angeles Herald Examiner, 7/31/83; Suzanne Muchnic (auth), Lyn Kienholz puts sculpture on a pedestal, Los Angeles Times, 6/2/84; Carolyn Mitchell (auth), It Takes ability and connections to establish an arts Foundation, Chattanooga Times, 12/24/85; Jody Leader (auth), C/IAF on a roll, Los Angeles Reader, 7/11/86; Suzanne Muchnic (auth), Museum leaders to get eyeful of Los Angeles, Los Angeles Times, 9/18/90; Charles Koppelman (auth), The Matchmaker, LA Times, 2/26/06, Life, Times, KCET-TV, 4/18/2006. *Mem:* Artists Equity; Comite Int Musees d'Art Moderne. *Interests:* All forms of contemporary art. *Publ:* Memoria: Cuban Art of the 20th Century, 2003. *Mailing Add:* 2737 Outpost Dr Los Angeles CA 90068

KIHLSTEDT, MAJA
PAINTER, PRINTMAKER
b Stockholm, Sweden. *Study:* The Royal Danish Art Academy, MA, 73-77; Yale School of Art, Norfolk Summer Scholarship Program, 79. *Work:* Nokia, Stokholm, Sweden; Se Banken, Stockholm, Sweden; Nordbanken, Stockholm, Sweden; Virginia Ctr for the Arts, Sweet Briar, VA; Ohrling, Reveco, Lybrant, Stockholm, Sweden. *Exhib:* Stockholm Int Art Fair, Jan Eric Lowenadler Gallery, Stockholm, Sweden, 97; Painting Object, Gallery Bergman, Stockholm, Sweden, 2000; Anima-Numina-Ogo-Mammo, Cortland Jessup Gallery, NY, 2001; Biennale Int Dell'Arte; Transformations, The Sakai City Mus, Sakai Japan, 2001; Beatles, Beasts, and Mystical Beings, SUNY Westchester, Valhalla, NY, 2002; Encaustic Works Biennale, Marist Col Art Gallery, Poughkeepsie, NY, 2003; AAF Contemp Art Fair, Gallery Galou, NY, 2004. *Awards:* Fel, Yaddo Corp, 82; Fel, The McDowell Colony, 82. *Bibliog:* Joel Silverstein (auth), Trace, Essay in Exhibition Catalog, 97; Ricki Neuman (auth), Maja Kihlstedt Far Pris, Sveivska Dag Bladet, 4/3/2002; Susan Hamburger (auth), Painting and the Self After Postmodernism, Waterfront Weekly, 97. *Media:* Painting, Drawing. *Dealer:* Mats Bergman, Gallery Bergman Storgatan 28, Stokholm, Sweden; Patricia Cazoha, Gallery Galou, 237 Kent Ave, Williamsburg, Brooklyn, NY, 11211. *Mailing Add:* 6W 28th St New York NY 10001-6409

KIJEK, MANON CATHERINE (MANON CATHERINE CLEARY)
PAINTER, DRAFTSMAN
b St Louis, Mo, Nov 14, 42. *Study:* Wash Univ, BFA, 64; Temple Univ, MFA, 68. *Work:* Corcoran Gallery Art & Nat Mus Women in Arts, Washington, DC; Mem Art Gallery, Univ Rochester, NY; Brooklyn Mus, NY; Phoenix Art Mus, Ariz; Utah Mus Fine Arts, Salt Lake City; Chicago Art Inst, IL; Colgate Univ, The Picker Art Gallery, Hamilton, NY; Kasteev State Mus, Almaty, Kazakhstan. *Comn:* Portait, Dr Luther Terry, 89; Painting, Am Embassy, Lima, Peru, 95. *Exhib:* Images of the 70's: 9 Washington Realists, Corcoran Gallery Art, Washington, DC, 80; Taft Menagerie, Taft Mus, Cincinnati, Ohio, 81; An Am Bestiary, Inst Contemp Art, Richmond, Va, 81; Am Drawings in Black & White, Brooklyn Mus, NY, 81; Perspectives on Contemp Am Realism: Works of Art on Paper from the Collection of Jalane and Richard Davidson, Pa Acad Fine Art & Chicago Art Inst, 82-83; Twentieth Century Am Drawings: The Figure in Context, traveling exhib, Int Exhib Found, Terra Mus Am Art, Okla Mus Art, Nat Acad Design, 84-85; Pintura e Desenho De Manon Cleary, Centro de Arte de Arte Moderna, Gulbekian Found, Lisbon, Portugal, 85; Art Exchange, Tretyakov Gallery, Moscow, 90; 16th Ann Nat Drawing Exhib, Norman Eppink Art Gallery, Emporia State Univ, 92; Drawing on the figure, Edna Carlsten Gallery, Univ Wis, 93; Nat Showcase Exhib, Alternative Mus, NY, 96; Artsites 96, Corcoran Gallery Art, Washington, 96; Most 96, Kasteev State Mus, Almaty, Kazakhstan, 96; The Female Gaze: 4 Washington Women Draw Men, Montgomery Col, Rockville, Md, 96; Gardner's Delight, Nat Mus Women in the Arts, Washington, 00; Contemp Am: Relaist Drawings: The Jalone & Rich Collection, Art Inst Chicago, 99-00; Manon Cleary, Body iun Question, Md Art Pl, 97; Manon Cleary, The Body in Question, Md Art Place, 97; Realist Drawings, The Jalane and Richard Davidson Collection, Art Inst Chicago, 99-00. *Pos:* Guest artist, Herning Hoiskoke, Denmark, 80; artist-in-residence, Ucross Found, Wyo, 84-96, Bridge Asn, Almaty, Kazakhstan; artist-in-residence, Coca Cola, Mobil Oil, Cosmic Observatory Project, Almaty Kazakhstan, 97. *Teaching:* Instr fine arts, State Univ NY, Oswego, 68-70; prof fine arts, Univ DC, Washington, DC, 70-93, actg chairperson art dept, 85-86 & 90-91 & assoc dean, Col Lib & Fine Arts, 92-94, acting coord, Art Prog, 94-00; Acting Dir Univ Gallery, 98-2000, Retired, 2005. *Awards:* Fac Res Award, Univ DC, 83, 89, 00; Mayor's award for Outstanding Contrib to an Artistic Discipline, 99; Pres' award for teaching, Univ DC, 01; Individual Artist Grant, DC Com for the Arts, 02. *Bibliog:* Jose Sommer Ribeiro & Lee Fleming (auths), Pintura E Desenho de Manon Cleary, Gulbeukian Found, 85; Clint Brown & Cheryl Mclean (coauths), Drawing from Life, Holt Reinhart & Winston, 94; Paul Cummings (auth), Dictionary of Contemporary Artists, 6th ed; Ruth Fine, Ramond Hernandez, and Mark Pascale (auths), Contemporary Am Realist Drawing, Art Inst Chicago Press, 99-00. *Mem:* Col Art Asn; Washington Review (bd mem). *Media:* Oil, Graphite. *Dealer:* Addison/Ripley Gallery 9 Hillyer Ct Washington DC 20008. *Mailing Add:* 1736 Columbia Rd NW Washington DC 20009-2815

KIKUCHI-YNGOJO, ALAN
PHOTOGRAPHER, COLLAGE ARTIST
b San Francisco, Calif, Feb 6, 49. *Study:* Diablo Valley Col, 67-69; Univ Calif, Davis, BA, 71, MFA, 75. *Work:* Metrop Mus Art, Alternative Mus, NY; Clarence Kennedy Gallery, Polaroid Corp, Cambridge, Mass; Cleveland Mus Art; Erie Art Ctr, Pa. *Exhib:* Contemp Icons, San Francisco Mus Mod Art, 75; Beyond Photog, Alternative Mus, NY, 80; US Art Now, Gotesborgs Konstforening, Sweden, 81; Painting and Sculpture Today, Indianapolis Mus Art, 82; Counterparts, Metrop Mus Art, NY, 82; solo exhib, Triton Mus Art, Santa Clara, Calif, 82; Recent Acquisitions, Clarence Kennedy Gallery, Polaroid Corp, Cambridge, Mass, 83; Seven Am Artists, Cleveland Mus Art, 83. *Awards:* Nat Endowment Arts Fel, 81. *Bibliog:* Grace Glueck (auth), article in New York Times, 1/15/82; Lynn Zelevansky (auth), article in Art News, 4/82; Christopher French (auth), Redefining figures, Art Week, 7/3/82. *Dealer:* Hal Bromm Gallery 90 W Broadway New York NY 10013. *Mailing Add:* 1615 18th St Apt 24L San Francisco CA 94107-2378

KILAND, LANCE EDWARD
PAINTER, PRINTMAKER
b Fargo, NDak, Nov 27, 1947. *Study:* Moorhead State Univ, BA, 69; Southern Ill Univ, MFA, 71. *Work:* Walker Art Ctr, Minneapolis; Art Inst Chicago; Milwaukee Art Mus; Minneapolis Inst Arts. *Exhib:* Mid-States Art Exhib, Evansville Mus Art, Ind, 70; Biennial Exhib, Whitney Mus Am Art, NY, 83; Rooted in NDak, NDak Mus Art, Grand Forks, 84; 39th Biennial Am Painting, Corcoran Gallery Art, Washington, 85; Viewpoints, Walker Art Ctr, Minneapolis, 85; Recent Acquisitions: Emerging Artists, Walker Art Ctr, Minneapolis, 86; Print & Drawing Exhib, Minneapolis Inst Arts, 88; Landmark Editions, NDak Mus Art, Grand Forks, 91; New Acquisitions, Art Inst Chicago, 91 & Contemp Prints and Portfolios, 92; Bewildered Image 2, Minneapolis Inst Arts, 95. *Teaching:* North Hennepin Community Col, Minneapolis. *Bibliog:* Eleanor Heartney (auth), Lance Kiland, 1/84 & Mason Riddle (auth), Lance Kiland, 10/85, Arts Mag; Chris Waddington (auth), Lance Kiland at Thomson, Art in Am, 6/89. *Media:* Oil; Lithograph & Woodcut. *Publ:* Landfall Press, Chicago; Landmark Edits, Minneapolis. *Mailing Add:* 800 Ithaca Ln N Plymouth MN 55447

KILB, JENNY
PAINTER, MURALIST
b Cincinnati, Ohio, Mar 3, 52. *Study:* Cincinnati Art Mus, 60-70; Dept Painting & Sculpture, Carnegie-Mellon Univ, 70-72. *Work:* NASA Art Collection, Washington, DC; Casa Grande Art Mus, Casa Grande, Ariz; Deming (New Mex) Airport Collection. *Comn:* Award Objects, Excell in Environment (sculptures), City of Tucson, Ariz, 92; exterior mural (16 X 60 Ft), Tucson Arts Dist Partnership, Ariz, 93; exterior mural, Southwestern Paints, Tucson, Ariz, 94; exterior mural, Oracle Pub Libr, Ariz, 94. *Exhib:* Ten Yrs of Feminist Art Invitational, Murray State Univ, Ky, 95; 26th Ann Exhib, Palm Springs Desert Mus, 95; Showcasing the Woman's Voice Invitational, Louisville Visual Art Asn, Ky, 95; Paper Trail West 1996, Snowgrass Inst Art, Cashmere, Wash, 96; solo exhib, Barn Gallery, Rancho Linda Vista, Oracle, Ariz, Edge of the Cedars Mus, Utah, 97, Ready, Set, D'Art, Benefit for Tucson Mus Art, 1998/2000. *Pos:* Artist in residence, Cincinnati Planetarium, Ohio, 78-79; founder & chair, Oracle Festival Fine Art, Oracle, Ariz, 92-96. *Awards:* 1st & 3rd Place, Landscapes of My Mind, Casa Grande Art Mus, 94; Prof Develop Grant, Ariz Comn Arts, 96; Grant, Four Corners Sch Outdoor Educ, 96; Writing Award, Southwest Writers' Workshop, 1998. *Bibliog:* M Wilson (auth), Ribbons of Color, Ariz Arts & Travel, 1 & 2/84; M Wilson (auth), Jenny Kilb, Kalei Colorscapes, Southwest Art, 12/84. *Mem:* Women's Caucus Art; Earth Angels Artists. *Media:* Color Pencil, Acrylic. *Publ:* Auth, Border Beat Arts J, 97; auth, Dispatch: Oracle (arts commentary), 97; auth, Pilgrim, A Sarah Farling Mystery (novel), Painted Lady Publ, 2002. *Mailing Add:* 474 N Broad St Globe AZ 85501

KILEY, KATIE
PRINTMAKER, PAINTER
b Decatur, Ill, 1951. *Study:* Attended Clarke Col, Dubuque, Iowa; St Ambrose Univ, BA (art), 74; Univ Iowa, MA, 87; Iowa State Univ, MFA, 89. *Exhib:* Drawings, Prints and Paintings, Muchnic Gallery, Atchison, Kansas, 98; Whiskey Gods and Cold Black Beads: Drawings, Paintings and Prints, Alfons Gallery, Milwaukee, 95; Girls! Girls! Girls! Jacqueline Ross Gallery, Chicago, 98; Paintings, Drawings and Prints, Dartmouth Col, 98; Gossamer Veils, Figge-Moss, Stoney Brook Sch, NY, 2000; Conversations, Quigley Gallery, Clark Col, Dubuque, Iowa, 2003; Constructing the Figure, Augustana Col, Rock Island, Ill, 2003; Printmaker's Traveling Show: The Prairie, Grinell, Iowa, 2003; Kiley and Koiso, Midcoast Gallery, LeClaire, Iowa, 2004; Venus Envy, Midcoast Bucktown Gallery, Davenport, Iowa, 2005; Nat Acad Mus, NY, 2006. *Pos:* Mem advertising dept Deere & Co, 72-73. *Teaching:* Prof art St Ambrose Univ. *Mailing Add:* c/o del Mano Gallery 11981 San Vicente Blvd Los Angeles CA 90049

KILGUSS, ELSIE SCHAICH
PAINTER, INSTRUCTOR
b Manhattan, NY, Aug 4. *Study:* RI Sch Design, cert botanical and sci illustration, MAT course, BS (advertising); Cape Cod Sch Art; studies with Henry Hensche, Lois Griffel, Charles Sovek and others. *Work:* Alfred Butler & Co, numerous locations worldwide. *Comn:* landscapes, Caribbean Villas, St John, Virgin Island, 92; portraits, comn by N Barker, Newport, RI, 99; portrait, comn by Laurell C Tripp, RI. *Exhib:* Warwick Art Mus, RI, 87, 89, 90, 91, 95, 97, 99; NewPort Art Mus, RI, 90, 95, 98; Sheldon Fine Art, 2000-2005; one-woman shows Warwick Mus Art, 2000, 2001, Newport Mus Art, 90-95, The Gallery at Chatham, Mass, 90-99, Dodge House Gallery, Providence, 99, Cafe Gallery, 98-99; exhibs Providence Art Club Gallery, 91, 93, 95, 97, Artists Gallery, Wickford, 90, Helme House, Kingston, RI, 90, 91, 95, 97, 98, 99, Art Ocean State, Wickford, 90, 91, 94, 95, 96, 97, 98, Spring Bull Gallery, Newport, RI, 93, 99. *Pos:* instr, painter, art, Studio ZWEI, currently. *Teaching:* instr various art asn, mus, and privately, 80-. *Mem:* Providence Art Club; Wickford Art Asn (pres, 90, 91); RI Watercolor Soc; Newport Artists Guild; South Co Art; Oil Painters Am (asst mem, currently); Am Watercolor Soc. *Media:* Oil, Watercolor. *Specialty:* Fine Art Gallery & Studio. *Publ:* illustr, RI Sch Design Catalog, 92; contribr, Providence Mag, 94. *Mailing Add:* Studio Zwei 14 Pojac Point Rd North Kingstown RI 02852

KILIAN, AUSTIN FARLAND
PAINTER, EDUCATOR
b Lyons, SDak, Sept 19, 20. *Study:* Augustana Col, SDak, BA, 42; Univ Iowa, MFA, 49; Acad Montmartre, Paris, with Fernand Leger, 51; Mexico City Col, 52; Ohio State Univ, 55; Univ Calif, Los Angeles, 66. *Work:* D D Feldman Collection, Dallas; Univ Iowa Galleries, Iowa City. *Exhib:* Laguna Gloria Mus Citation Regional, Austin, Tex, 58; Art Asn New Orleans, Delgado Mus, 59; Made in Tex by Texans, Dallas Mus Contemp Arts, 59; San Diego Art Instr Show, Art Ctr La Jolla, Calif, 61; Inland Empire Country Club Fac Exhib, San Bernardino, 81; Living Desert, Palm Desert, Calif, 85; and others. *Collection Arranged:* Waco Art Forum Mus Regional Shows, 59; San Diego Art Guild Shows, Fine Arts Gallery, 61; Art In All Media, Southern Calif Expos, Del Mar, 63-70; Col of the Desert Shows, 70-. *Pos:* Chief Exec Officer, Kilian Studios, 88-; PDN Photog. *Teaching:* Instr photog, Univ Idaho, 49-50; head dept art, Dillard Univ, 50-53; asst prof, Baylor Univ, 53-59; chmn dept art, Calif Western Univ, 59-64; assoc prof, Col Desert, Calif, 70-86, head dept art, 86-87 & prof emer, 87-. *Awards:* Art Asn New Orleans Third Award, Delgado Mus, 52; Sons of Herman Award, San Antonio, Tex, 55; Purchase Award, D D Feldman Exhib, 68. *Bibliog:* Henry Burnett & Orville Voigt, Today Painting (Video Series), Col Desert, 80-85; William Hemmerdinger (auth), Collectors, Palm Springs Life Mag, 12/81. *Mem:* Art Hist Southern Calif; Palm Springs Desert Mus; Col Art Asn Am; Am Fedn of Arts. *Media:* Collage, Oil. *Specialty:* wide format color prints. *Publ:* Auth, Catalog loan exhibition of notable works from the Metropolitan, 52, Culture makes a face, KABC-TV, Hollywood, 62, The Two Californias (catalog), 63, Southern California Exposition, Art in All Media (catalogs), 63-70 & article, San Diego Eve Tribune, 6/14/64. *Mailing Add:* 73286 Juniper St Palm Desert CA 92260-4702

KILLEEN, MELISSA HELEN
DEALER, GALLERY DIRECTOR
b Binghamton, NY, Oct 28, 55. *Study:* Syracuse Univ, NY, BFA(cum laude), 76; Johnson Atelier Tech Sch Sculpture, NJ, cert, 78. *Collection Arranged:* Wood Biennial (twelve wood designer-craftsmen; auth, catalog), 78, 80 & 82; Monumental Sculpture Traveling Exhib, 79 & 82; Monumental Weaving, 83; Com Bank, Hq & Br, NJ; Traveler's Mortgage Serv Hq, Cherry Hill, NJ; Jefferson Bank, Philadelphia, Pa. *Pos:* Craft coordr, By Hand Crafts Gallery, NJ, 76-77; mgr, Richard Kagan Gallery, Pa, 78-79; dir & owner, The Gallery at 401, Magnolia, NJ, 79-; owner & dir, Landsman Gallery, 82-; vpres, ArtMarkit Inc, 82-; appraiser, Am Soc Appraisals, 88; art fair/fund raising event planner, 82-. *Teaching:* Asst dept chairperson ceramic shell & plastics, Johnson Atelier, NJ, 76-79. *Mem:* Sr mem Am Soc Appraisers; Am Craft Coun. *Specialty:* Contemp fine art, monumental sculpture and graphic art, corporate art consultation, appraisals. *Mailing Add:* c/o Landsman Gallery 401 S White Horse Pike Magnolia NJ 08049-1069

KILLMASTER, JOHN H
ENAMELIST, PAINTER
b Allegan, Mich, Dec 2, 34. *Study:* Soc Arts & Crafts, Detroit, Mich; Hope Col, BA; Univ Guanajuato, Mex, Cranbrook Acad Art, MFA. *Work:* Boise Gallery Art & Boise Cascade World Hq Collection, Boise, Idaho; FMC Corp, Chicago, Ill; Albertsons Inc, Boise, Idaho; Enamel Mus, Coldsprings, KY; Idaho First Nat Bank; Sunshine Mining; and others; The Herret Ctr for Arts at the Col of Southern Idaho, Twin Falls, ID. *Comn:* Sculpture, Portland Arts Comn, 78-79; murals, Wash State Art Comn, 79, Ore Arts Comn, 80. *Exhib:* San Francisco Mus Mod Art, Calif, 79-80; Nat Mus Am Art, Smithsonian Inst, 79-80; Denver Art Mus, 80; Int Enamel Exhib, Sumida Gallery, Tokyo, Japan, 93; The Cutting Edge, Exhibtions, Frey Art Mus, Seattle, WA, 94; St Petersburg & Moscow Int Enamel Exhib, Russia, 94; Contemp Int Enamelist Exhib, Canadian Clay & Glass Mus, Can, 94; Crossing Boundaries-Enamel Int, Waterloo, Ont, Can, 99; Am Enamels, Tacoma, Wash, 2000; 9th Int Juried Enamel Exhib, Evergreen State Col Gallery, Olympia, Wash, 2003; Looking Forward-Glancing Back, Northwest Designer Craftsmen at 50 Exhibition, Whatcom Mus Art, Bellingham, WA, 2005; Drawing Power, Nat Automotive Hist Collection, Detroit Pub Libr, Mich, 2005-2006. *Pos:* illusr, designer, Allied Artists, 55-56; Blythe, Ambrose & Noyes, 56-58; Illusr & designer, Ladriere Art Studio, Detroit, 58-61. *Teaching:* Asst prof painting, Ferris State Col, 69-70; prof art, Boise State Univ, 70-; instr art, Grand Marais Art Colony, Minn, 85. *Awards:* Governor's Award for Excellence in the Arts, Idaho, 78; Scholar Boise State Univ Found, 95; Woodrow W Carpenter Award, Int Enamelist Soc, 2001. *Bibliog:* The Calif Art Review, Krantz, 89; Art Masters (video), BSU, 89; The Dictionary of Enameling-History Technique, 97; Enameling with Professionals, L Bachrack Pub, 2000; Contemp Enameling Art & Techniques, Schiffer Publishing Ltd, Atglen, Pa, 2006. *Mem:* NW Designer Craftsman Asn; Nat Enamelist Guild, Washington, DC; Enamelists Guild West, San Diego; Enamalist Soc; Intl Enamelist Soc. *Media:* Acrylic, Enamel. *Res:* Innovative approaches/techniques and styles in contemporary architectural large scale enameling. *Publ:* Glass on metal, Int J, 83, 89, 90, 91, 95, 2000 & 2002. *Dealer:* Random Modern Gallery, Tacoma, Wash; Image Maker Artist Consortium Boise ID; Basement Gallery, Boise, ID. *Mailing Add:* 9180 JR Way Middleton ID 83644

KIM, CHEONAE
PAINTER, PRINTMAKER
b Inchon, Korea, Sept 17, 52. *Study:* Southern Ill Univ, BA, 83, MFA, 86. *Work:* Printworks, Chicago; Bock Gallery, Northwestern Univ, Evanston, Ill; Glasgow Sch of Art and Design, Scotland; Milwaukee Art Mus, Wisc. *Exhib:* Speak, Randolph Street Gallery, Chicago, 92; On Condition, Gallery 400, Univ Ill, Chicago, 92; Is Poetry Visual Art?, Turman Gallery, Ind State Univ, Terre Haute, 93; Abstract-Chicago, Klein Gallery, Chicago, 93; one-person show, Forum for Contemp Art, St Louis, 94. *Teaching:* Vis asst prof drawing & print, Southern Ill Univ, Carbondale, 91-93, vis instr silkscreen, 93-. *Awards:* Nat Endowment Arts Visual Artists Fel, 93; Distaff Side, Women's Artists, 1st Award, Mitchell Mus, Mt. Vernon, Ill; Rickert-Ziebold Trust Award, Southern Ill Univ, Carbondale, Ill. *Bibliog:* David McCracken (auth), Randolph Street show speaks volumes, Chicago Tribune, 1/92; Deborah Wilk (auth), On condition, New Art Examiner, 4/93; Robert Duffy (auth), Power lives, St Louis Post-Dispatch, 4/94. *Media:* Acrylic, Oil. *Dealer:* Elliot Smith Gallery 4727 McPherson Ave St Louis MO. *Mailing Add:* 1925 Brown Pl Murphysboro IL 62966

KIM, PO (HYUN)
PAINTER
b Korea; US citizen. *Study:* Univ Ill, MFA (fel), 57. *Hon Degrees:* LHD. *Work:* Chicago Art Inst, Ill; Solomon R Guggenheim Mus, NY; Seoul Art Ctr, Korea; Kwangju City Art Mus, Korea; NJ Power & Lighting Co; Seoul Nat Mus Contemp Arts, Korea. *Exhib:* one-man shows, Kornblee Gallery, NY, 61, Squibb Gallery, Princeton, NJ, 79, Gallery Mod Art, Munich, West Ger, 80, Art Alliance, Philadelphia, Pa, 80; Kwangjn City Mus Art, Korea, 96; Painting & Sculpture Today, Indianapolis Mus Art, Ind, 78; Korean Drawing Now, Brooklyn Mus, NY, 81; one-man retrospective, Seoul Arts Ctr, Korea, 95; Park TYU Sook Gallery, Seoul, Korea, 1996; Nahi Gallery, Long Island, NY, 98; Gallery Korea, NY, 2000; Nat Mus Contempory Art, Seoul, Korea, 2000; Gary Snyder Gallery, NY, 2002; many others; Po Kim and Sylvia Wald Gallery, Kwangsi, Korea, 2002-. *Collection Arranged:* Int Gallery, Smith Sonian Inst, Washington, 2003; Tenri Cultu Ins, NY, 2004. *Teaching:* Instr, New York Univ, 61-62; prof, Chosum Univ Korea, 46-55. *Media:* Oil, Acrylic. *Mailing Add:* 417 Lafayette St New York NY 10003

KIMBALL, WILFORD WAYNE, JR
LITHOGRAPHER, DRAFTSMAN
b Salt Lake City, Utah, July 15, 43. *Study:* Southern Utah State Col, BA, 68; Univ Ariz, MFA, 70; Tamarind Inst, Albuquerque, NMex, fel printing, 70-71, Master Printer, 71. *Work:* Tamarind Collection, Albuquerque, NMex; Brooklyn Mus; Libr Cong, Washington, DC; Lessing J Rosenwald Collection, The Philadelphia Mus of Art & Nat Gallery Fine Arts, Washington, DC. *Exhib:* Brooklyn Mus Biennial Print Exhib, NY, 78; 56th Ann Philadelphia Competition, The Print Club, 80; Colorprint USA, Texas Tech Univ, Lubbock, Tex, 80; Tenth Anniversary Exhib, Tyler Mus Art, Tex, 81; one-man shows, Phoenix Art Mus, Ariz, 81, Art Mus STex, 81 & Thirty Am Printmakers Invitational, Univ Gallery Fine Art, Ohio State Univ, 82; Seventh British Int Print Biennale, Cartwright Hall, Bradford, W Yorkshire, Eng, 82; and others. *Pos:* Artist-in-residence, Roswell Mus & Art Ctr, NMex, 72. *Teaching:* Lectr lithography, Univ NMex, 71; vis lectr lithography, Univ Wis, Madison, 72-73 & summers 73 & 74; asst prof lithography & drawing, San Diego State Univ, 73-74; asst prof lithography, Calif State Univ, Long Beach, 74-75; asst prof lithography & drawing, Univ Tex San Antonio, 75-77; lectr lithography, San Diego State Univ, 77-78; prof lithography, Ariz State Univ, Tempe, 78-84 & Brigham Young Univ, Provo, Utah, 84-; prof lithography, Brigham Young Univ, 84-. *Awards:* William H Walker Purchase Award, 55th Philadelphia Ann, 79; Purchase Awards, 17th Bradley Nat Print & Drawing Exhib, 79 & Vermillion '79 Nat Print & Drawing Competition, 79. *Media:* Lithography. *Mailing Add:* 185 S 1300 E Pleasant Grove UT 84062-3025

KIMBRELL, LEONARD BUELL
HISTORIAN
b Archibald, La, Aug 3, 22. *Study:* Northwestern State Univ, La, BA, 42; Univ Ore, MS, 50, MFA, 54; Univ Iowa, PhD, 65. *Work:* Univ Ore, Eugene; Portland Art Mus, Ore. *Pos:* Contrib ed, Artweek, 71-81; art critic, NW Mag, 81-; Art appraiser. *Teaching:* Prof art, Eastern Ore Col, 54-61; prof art, Portland State Univ, 61-, head dept art & archit, 76-84; Prof Emer, 93. *Awards:* Purchase Award, Portland Art Mus, 53. *Mem:* Col Art Asn; Soc Archit Historians. *Res:* Cranach's nudes in the light of Luther's ethics; Alexander Pope as failed painter; guide to art in the Pacific Northwest; Rodins at Maryhill; Betty Feves: Ceramist. *Publ:* Auth, Some new light on Astoria Column, Festshrift: Marion Ross, Soc Archit Historians, 76. *Mailing Add:* 1785 SW Montgomery Dr Portland OR 97201-2482

KIMES, DON
PAINTER, EDUCATOR
b Oil City, Pa, Nov 18, 50. *Study:* Westminster Col, BA, 75; Univ Pittsburgh, grad studies, 75-77; Brooklyn Col, City Univ NY, MFA, 80; NY Studio Sch, cert, 78; studied with Agostini, Bell, Campbell, McNeil, Vicente, Heliker, Matter & Carone. *Work:* Chautauqua Inst, NY; Mass Inst Technol, Cambridge, Mass; Mus dell'Acad Belle Arti Pietro Vannucci, Italy; Univ Chicago; Conn State Univ; Watkins Collection, Am Univ, Washington. *Exhib:* Paperworks, Brooklyn Mus, NY, 82; Nat Acad Design, NY, 86; Baltimore Mus, Md, 86; solo exhibs, Madison Mus, Wyo, 93, Cy Katzen Gallery, Washington, 93, Nat Acad Sci, Washington, 93, Casa de Cult, Villahermosa, Mex, 93, Galleria Isa, Italy, 95, Amerika Haus, Munich, 96 & Rocca Paolina, Perugia, Italy, 96; Corcoran Gallery Art, 94 & 96; Galleria di Arti Vivre, Milan, 95; Piazza Broletto, Perugia, Italy, 95; Anton Gallery, Washington, 96. *Pos:* Co-founder & sr critic, Inst Int dell'Arte é Architettura. *Teaching:* Instr painting, State Univ NY, Stonybrook, 79; instr painting, NY Studio Sch, NY, 80- & chmn bd govs, 83-85; artistic dir, Chautauqua Inst Sch Arts, 85-; artist-in-residence, Conn State Univ, 87-88; assoc prof art, dept chmn, Am Univ, Washington, 88-. *Awards:* Yellowstone Nat Park, US Dept Interior Award for Artist Residency, 93; Artist Residency, Camerata di Todi, Italy, 94-95; Mellon Award, Munich, Ger, 96. *Bibliog:* Rossella Vasta (auth), Il Corriere dell'Umbria, Italy; Cynthia Kraman (auth), Don Kimes, The artist as philosopher, Sunstorm Mag, 88; Barbara Rose (auth), Heavy Metal, Don Kimes' New Work (exhib catalog), Acad Belle Arti Pietro Vannucci, Italy, 96. *Media:* Miscellaneous Media, Prints. *Publ:* Auth, In Praise of Space: 19th Century American Landscape, Westminster Press, 76; From Landscape to Collage, Ecker Press, 86; coauth, Chadakoin Review, An Interview with Agostini & Portfolio Reproduction. *Dealer:* Marie Tapparo 15 S Montague Arlington VA 22204. *Mailing Add:* Chautauqua Sch Art PO Box 1098 Chautauqua NY 14722-1098

KIMMEL-COHN, ROBERTA
DEALER, WRITER
b Milwaukee, Wis, Feb 1, 37. *Study:* Sophie Newcomb Col, with George Rickey; Univ Wis; Boston Univ Sch Fine & Appl Arts, BFA. *Pos:* Art dir, McGraw-Hill Publ Co, New York, 61-62, Macmillan & Co, 64-65 & Walker & Co, 65-67; pres, Roberta Kimmel Advert, New York, 67-; partner, Kimmel/Cohn Photog Arts, New York, 74-. *Bibliog:* Surrealism in advertising, Art Dir Mag, 70; article in Art Dir Ann, 72; People in the news, New York Times, 74. *Specialty:* Photography; Man Ray; nineteenth and twentieth century art. *Publ:* Auth, Erste Landung, portfolio of photographs by George Grosz, 77; Man Ray: Vintage Photographs, Rayographs and Solarizations, 77; In Artist's Homes, Clarkson Potter Inc. *Mailing Add:* 41 Central Park W New York NY 10023

KIMMELMAN, HAROLD
SCULPTOR
b Philadelphia, Pa, Feb 20, 23. *Study:* Cape Sch Art, Provincetown, Mass; Pa Acad Fine Art, Philadelphia. *Comn:* Burst of Joy, The Gallery, Philadelphia, 77; Marino Monument, Casa Enrico Fermi Corp, Philadelphia, Pa, 77; Man Helping Man, Am Col Cardiology, Bethesda, Md, 79; Hol; Hand in Hand, Merck Sharp & Doehme, West Point, Pa, 88; Volume III, Drexel Univ, 89. *Exhib:* Pa Acad Fine Arts, 68; Philadelphia Civic Ctr Show, 71; Woodmere Art Mus, 98. *Awards:* Braverman Karp Prize for sculpting, 68; May Audubon Prize for sculpting, 69. *Bibliog:* Sculpture of a City, Walker Publ Co, 74. *Mem:* Artists Equity Asn (pres, Philadelphia Chap, 72); fel Pa Acad Fine Arts. *Media:* Stainless Steel, Bronze. *Mailing Add:* 538 W Carpenter Ln Philadelphia PA 19119

KIMMELMAN, MICHAEL
CRITIC
b New York, NY, May 8, 58. *Study:* Yale Univ, BA(summa cum laude), 80; Harvard Univ, MA(art hist), 82. *Pos:* Music critic, Atlanta J Constitution, 84, Philadelphia Inquirer, 85-87; culture ed, US News & World Report, Wash, DC, 87; art critic, New York Times, 88-90, chief art critic, 90-. *Teaching:* Lectr in field; sr fel, Nat Arts Journalism Program Columbia Univ, 2000. *Awards:* Named a finalist in criticism for the Pulitzer Prize, 2000. *Publ:* Auth: Portraits: Talking With Artists at the Met, the Modern, the Louvre and Elsewhere, 1999 (named Notable Book of Yr, Wash Post and The Times, named Best Book of Yr, Publs Weekly); contribr to the NY Review of Books, articles to other mags. *Mailing Add:* c/o NY Times 229 W 43rd St New York NY 10036-3959

KIMPTON, JEFFREY S
ADMINISTRATOR
Study: Augustana Col, Rock Island, Ill, Attended political sci & pre-law, 68-70; Univ Ill, BS in music educ, cum laude, 73; Univ Ill, MS in music educ & sch admin, 75; Am Mgt Assoc, Cert in corp financial mgt & accounting, 95. *Pos:* Dir inst, educ Yamaha Corp Am, 88-96; dir, pub engagement Annenberg Inst Brown Univ, 96-99; dir, sch music Univ Minn, 99-2003, prof music educ, 99-2003; pres, Interlochen Arts Acad, 2003-. *Teaching:* Var teaching & adminr positions, Pub Sch Syst, Wichita, Kans, Apple Valley, Minn, Corinth, NY, 73-88. *Mailing Add:* Interlochen Arts Acad Off of the Pres PO Box 199 Interlochen MI 49643

KIMURA, RIISABURO
PAINTER, PRINTMAKER
b Yokosuka, Japan, Oct 13, 24. *Study:* Yokohama Univ, 47; Hosei Univ, Tokyo, 54. *Work:* Mus Mod Art & Brooklyn Mus, NY; Nat Mus Mod Art, Kyoto, Japan; US Info Agency; City of Hamburg, WGer; and many others. *Comn:* Print ed, Brooklyn Mus, 75. *Exhib:* one-man shows, JICC, Washington, DC, 91, Gallery Aunkan, Osaka, Japan, 91, Artra Gallery, NY, 92 & Tokyo Kyota Osaka Yokohama Sendai, Art Mus Ginza, Tokyo, 95, Sendai City Mus, 99, Williamsburg Art & Hist Ctr, NY, 2000 & Ono City Off, Fukul, Japan, 2001, trav exhib, Tokyo, Yokohama, Osaka & Kyoto, Japan, 2005-2006; USA Pavillion Expo 70, Osaka, Japan, 74; Japanese Artists in the Americas, Nat Mus Mod Art, Kyoto, Japan, 74; Boston Printmakers Exhib, Brockton Art Ctr, Mass, 74; Nora Gallery, NY, 85; Jewish Community Ctr, Minneapolis, Minn, 85; Col Women's Asn Print Show, Am Club, Tokyo, 86-2001; Pratt Inst, NY, 88; Machida City Mus Graphic Arts, Japan, 92; Brooklyn Mus, NY, 95; New Am Art Show, Mayor's Off, NY, 98; 48th CWAJ Print Show, Am Club, Tokyo, Japan, 2003; Resounding Print Show The Gibson Gallery Col, Univ MD, 2004; Los Angeles Co Mus Art, 2005; Art Mus of SUNY, 2005; Libr Congress, Washington, DC, 2006. *Awards:* Int Biennal Print Award, Tokyo, 70. *Bibliog:* Art News, 10/79; Interior Design, 1/79; Art Am, 3/80. *Mailing Add:* 463 West St No G-361 New York NY 10014

KIND, JOSHUA B
EDUCATOR, CRITIC
b Philadelphia, Pa, Nov 5, 33. *Study:* Univ Pa, Philadelphia, BA, 55; Columbia Univ, PhD, 67. *Pos:* Chicago ed, Art News, New York, 64-70; dir, Oxbow Summer Sch Art, Saugatuck, Mich, 67-68; contrib ed, New Art Examiner, Chicago, 75-85. *Teaching:* Instr art hist, Northwestern Univ, Evanston, Ill, 59-62; instr humanities, Univ Chicago, 62-65; vis prof art hist, Sch of Art Inst Chicago, 64-76; asst prof art hist & humanities, Ill Inst Technol, Chicago, 65-69; prof art hist, Northern Ill Univ, DeKalb, 69-. *Awards:* Nat Endowment for the Arts Critics Fel, 77. *Mem:* Col Art Asn; Soc Architectural Historians. *Res:* Modernism; creativity and the avant-garde; Renaissance iconography; modern architecture. *Publ:* Auth, Rouault, 69; Art and the corps of women, 3/78 & The corruption of Norman Rockwell, 1/79, New Art Examiner; contribr, World Bk Year Book & Encyclopedia Britannica Yr Bk, 70-; contrib, Contemp Artists, 1st, 2nd & 3rd ed; contrib, Int Dict of Art and Artists, vol 2, 90. *Mailing Add:* 5619 Dunham Rd Downers Grove IL 60516-1247

KIND, PHYLLIS
ART DEALER
b New York, NY. *Study:* Univ Pa, BS, 54: Univ Chicago, MA, 65. *Pos:* Dir, Phyllis Kind Galleries, Chicago, 67-98, New York, 75-. *Mem:* Am Art Dealers Asn. *Specialty:* Representing major Chicago artists introducing exhibitions and selected works by other major contemporary American & Russian artists, also specializing in Outsider, Art Brut and Haitian art. *Collection:* Direct from Moscow, Phyllis Kind Gallery, 1987. *Mailing Add:* c/o Phyllis Kind Gallery 136 Greene St New York NY 10012

KINDAHL, CONNIE
WEAVER, CRAFTSMAN
b Decatur, Ill. *Study:* Univ Ill. *Comn:* Prudential Insurance Co, Washington, DC, 84; Med W Community Health Plan, Chicopee, Mass, 84; Alpha Chi Omega Sorority, Amherst, Mass, 84; Harvard Community Health Fac, W Roxbury, Mass, 86; Dow Chemical Co, Chicago, Ill, 86. *Exhib:* 2-man show, Western New Engl Col, Springfield, Mass, 83; Wichita Nat Decorative Arts Exhib, Wichita, Kans, 85; 8th Ann Vahki Exhib, Mesa, Ariz, 86; Fiber/Fiber, Convergence 86, Toronto, 86; Rugs: Contemp Handwoven Floorcoverings, Mus Am Textile Hist, North Andover, Mass, 86. *Teaching:* Instr rug weaving, Weavers Guild Boston, 84-86 & Augusta Heritage Ctr, Davis & Elkins Col, 88. *Awards:* Chairmans Choice in Fiber, Wesleyan Potters, 82, Special Recognition Award, Nassau Co NY Fiber Arts Forum & Exhib, 85 & First Prize in Rugs, New Eng Weavers Seminar, 85. *Bibliog:* Elizabeth French (auth), Connie Kindahl, Shuttle Spindle & Dyepot Handweavers Guild Am, 86. *Mem:* Am Craft Coun; Handweavers Guild Am; Worcester Craft Ctr; Leverett Craftsmen & Artists. *Media:* Fiber. *Publ:* All White Overshot Rug, spring, 82, Rugs on a Three-End Block Draft, Weavers J, spring 84; Boundweave Rug on an Overshot Threading, Shuttle Spindle & Dyepot, 86. *Mailing Add:* RR 2 364 Daniel Shays Hwy Pelham MA 01002

KINDERMANN, HELMMO
PHOTOGRAPHER, PAINTER
b Lancaster, Pa, Oct 11, 47. *Study:* Tyler Sch Fine Art, Temple Univ, BFA, 69; study of photog, Visual Studies Workshop, Rochester, NY, 71-73; State Univ NY Buffalo, MFA, 73. *Work:* Miss Art Asn, Jackson; Visual Studies Workshop, Rochester, NY; St Lawrence Univ, Canton, NY; Alternative Mus, NY. *Exhib:* Images, Dimensional, Movable, Transferable, Akron Art Inst, Ohio, 73; New Approaches, Ctr for Exploratory and Perceptual Arts, Buffalo, NY, 75; New Photog/76, Cent Wash State Col, Ellensburgh, 76; Photo/Synthesis, Herbert F Johnson Mus of Art, Ithaca, NY, 76; Auto as Icon, Int Mus Photog, George Eastman House, Rochester, NY, 79; and others. *Pos:* Cur, US Eye Photo Exhib, Nat Fine Arts Comt, XIII Olympic Winter Games, Lake Placid, NY, 78-. *Teaching:* Asst prof photog, Lake Placid Sch Art, Ctr for Music, Drama & Art, NY, 73-81. *Awards:* Purchase Prize, Images on Paper, Miss Art Asn, 71. *Mem:* Soc for Photog Educ; Col Art Asn Am; Photog Instr Asn; Friends of Photog. *Publ:* New Photographics/76, Cent Wash Col, 76; contribr, Works and Process,

CMDA Publ Co, 76; contribr, Photo/Synthesis, Herbert F Johnson Mus Art, 76; contribr, The Photograph Collectors Guide, Lee Witkin & Barbara London, NY Graphic Soc; contribr, Uniquely Photographic, Quiver No 5, Honolulu Acad Arts; and others. *Mailing Add:* 1830 Rose Tree Ln Havertown PA 19083-2728

KING, BRIAN JEFFREY
ENVIRONMENTAL ARTIST, PUBLISHER
b Des Moines, Iowa, Oct 22, 52. *Study:* studied with Ronald Mallory, 1990-93; studied with Gustav Likan, 1994-96; studied with Armand G Winfield 2002-05. *Hon Degrees:* D Emeritus, NLP Inst Austin. *Work:* Zilker Botanical Gardens, Austin; Austin History Ctr. *Comn:* 2 paintings, comn by Joseph & Joan Kullman, NYC; World's largest single canvas painting, comn by Robert Cox, Tex. *Exhib:* Ball in the jack Gallery, 2003-05; Death of the Unknown Artist, 99; 11-11 Art Show, 95. *Collection Arranged:* Shining Golden Suns LLC. *Pos:* artist; art dir, Picture Paper Mag, 94; cofounder, 11-11 Art Show, 95. *Teaching:* freelance teacher, digital art techniques. *Awards:* first art mag on the net, The Picture Paper-Priceless, 94. *Bibliog:* Michael Barnes (auth), World art party, Austin Am Statesman, 11/95; The Picture Paper, Excel Mag, Austin Am Statesman, 8/95. *Mem:* World Art Party; NMex Film Commission; NMex Culture Net. *Res:* Y2K Studies. *Specialty:* social, political and environmental art. *Interests:* culture, politics, education. *Publ:* coauth, Mankind's Millennium Manual, 99; coauth, Secrets of the Cavemen, 2000; ed, The Picture Paper Art Mag, Victoria Vranich, 94-97, publ, 95-97; various Prentice Hall Tech Manuals. *Dealer:* Ball in the Jack Gallery. *Mailing Add:* 1202 Morningside Dr NE Albuquerque NM 87110

KING, CLIVE
PAINTER, DRAFTSMAN
b Feb 11, 44; Brit citizen. *Study:* Exeter Col Art, dipl AD, 66; Goldsmiths Col Art, Univ London, dipl, 67. *Work:* Found Today's Art, Nexus Gallery, Philadelphia; Oxford Brookes Univ, Eng; Cyfarthfa Castle Mus, Wales, Eng; Dartmouth Col, Conn; Carol Damian Col, Fla Internat Univ, Mus Mod Art, Wales. *Exhib:* One-man shows, Glynn Vivian Art Gallery, Swansea, Eng, 90, Barbican Ctr, London, 91, Art Mus, Fla Int Univ, Miami, 96, 1708 Gallery, Richmond, Va, 97, Raymond Lawrence Gallery, Atlanta, 98 & Mus Mod Art, Wales, Eng, 99; Southern Arts Fedn Fel Exhib, Southeastern Ctr Contemp Art, Winston-Salem, NC, 96; Mus Mod Art, Wales, 99; Whitworth Art Gallery, Manchester, UK, 99; Nat Mus of Wales, 2000; Raymond Lawrence Gallery, Atlanta, 2000; Lowe Art Mus, Miami, 2000. *Pos:* Chair, Art Dept, Fla Int Univ, Miami, 92-98. *Teaching:* Sr lectr visual art, Salisbury Col Art, Eng, 74-79, Oxford Brookes Univ, Eng, 79-92; grad dir MFA program, Fla Internat Univ, Wales, 2000-. *Awards:* Southern Arts Fedn Fel, Southeastern Ctr Contemp Art, Nat Endowment Art, 96; Ann Artists Award, 1708 Gallery, Southeastern Col Art Conf, 97; Individual Artist Fla Fel, Traveling Exhib Prog, Fla Div Cult Arts, 98. *Bibliog:* Bernadine Heller-Greenman (auth), Clive King, Art Papers, 95; Carol Damian (auth), Clive King, Southern Arts Fedn Rev, 97; Nona Hieman (auth), Interview with Clive King, Southeastern Col Art Conf Rev, 97. *Mem:* Col Art Asn, Southeastern Col Art Asn. *Media:* Acrylic. *Res:* SW Native Am ancient sites. *Specialty:* drawing. *Publ:* auth, Painting the Drawing. *Dealer:* Raymond Lawrence Gallery, Atlanta; Barbara Gullman Gallery, Miami. *Mailing Add:* 27021 SW 119th Ct Homestead FL 33032

KING, ELAINE A
CURATOR, HISTORIAN
b Oak Park, Ill, Apr 12, 47. *Study:* Northern Ill Univ, BS, 68, MA, 74; Columbia Col, Chicago, photog hist with Arthur Siegel; intern, George Eastman House, summer 77; Northwestern Univ, PhD, 86, with Howard Becker, Leland Roloff, Charles Kleinhaus & Donald Kuspit & Jim Brekenridge; Cert Art Appraisal, New York Univ, NY, 2002. *Pos:* Cur, Dittmar Mem Gallery, Northwestern Univ, 77-81; dir, Hewlett Art Gallery, Carnegie-Mellon Univ, 81-89; corresp ed, Dialogue Mag, 84-89; dir, Carnegie-Mellon Univ Art Gallery, 85-91; independent cur, freelance, 91-; art critic in residence, Del Ctr Contemp Art, Wilmington, 92; exec dir & chief cur, Contemp Arts Ctr, Cincinnati, 93-95; guest cur, III Master Graphics Biennial, Gyor, Hungary, 95 & 97, 99, 2001, 03, 05. *Teaching:* Lectr art dept, Northwestern Univ, 77-81; prof art hist & critical theory, Carnegie-Mellon Univ, 81-; sr research fellow, Smithsonian Am Art Mus, 2002; short-term research fellow, Nat Portrait Gallery, 2001; disting art historian in residence, Am U, Internat Program, Italy, 2006. *Awards:* The Trust for Mutual Understanding Grant, 94; Art Critic Fel, Pa Arts Coun Grant, 89, 95, 99, 2000; Fac Develop Grant, Carnegie Mellon Univ, 89, 96, 99, 2002; Irex Grant, 2001; Research Fel, Ctrl European Cult Inst, 2002. *Mem:* Col Art Asn (midwestern bd dir, 97-2003); Art Table & Am Asn Mus, Mountain Lake Criticism Symp (bd dir, 81-91); Asn Int Art Critics; Am Asn Historians Am Art; Am Asn Mus; Am & Popular Culture Asn; Col Art Asn. *Interests:* sailing, gardening, reading, cooking, travel, cats. *Publ:* Art in a Kaleidoscope Era, In: After the Fall Aspects of Abstract Painting since 1970 (exhib catalog), Newhouse Ctr Contemp Art, 97; Fictional Theatricality in Cyber Space (exhib catalog), Jersey City Mus, 98; Mel Bochner, CMU Press, 85; Global Tranaesthetics within a Post-Modern Enlightenment Project, Grapheion, 1/2000; Enigmatic Sculpture, Magdalena Jetelova, Sculpture, 5/2000; many others; Barry LeVa, 68-88; Elizabeth Murray, 89; New Generations: Chicago, 90; New Generations: New York, 91; auth, Ethics in Vis Arts, Allworth Press, 2006; Ethics and the Visual Arts, 2006. *Mailing Add:* 5013 W Cedar Ln Bethesda MD 20814

KING, GEORGE G
DIRECTOR
Study: Attended, Bennington Col; Md Inst Col Art, BFA. *Pos:* Prog dir, Cooper-Hewitt Nat Design Mus, Smithsonian Inst, New York City; exec dir, Katonah Mus Art; dir, Georgia O'Keeffe Mus, Santa Fe, 1998-. *Mailing Add:* Georgia O'Keeffe Mus 217 Johnson St Santa Fe NM 87501

KING, LYNDEL IRENE SAUNDERS
MUSEUM DIRECTOR
b Enid, Okla, June 10, 43. *Study:* Univ Kans, BA, 65; Univ Minn, MA, 71, PhD, 82. *Pos:* Asst dir, Art Mus, Univ Minn, 76-78, dir, 78-; dir, Exhibs & Mus Relations, Control Data Corp, 79, 80-81; exhib coordr, Nat Gallery Art, 80; dir, Art Mus, Univ Minn, 81-, Weisman Art Mus, 93-. *Teaching:* Art hist, Mus Studies, Univ Minn, 79-. *Awards:* Recipient Cult Contrib of Yr award, Minneapolis CofC, 78; Honor award, Minn Soc Archit, 79. *Mem:* Am An Mus, Int Coun Mus, Upper Midwest Conservation Asn (pres bd dir, 1980-); Minn Asn Mus (steering comt, 1982); Art Mus Asn Am (vpres bd dir, 1984-89); Asn Col and Univ Mus and Galleries (vpres, 1989-92); Asn Art Mus Dir (bd trustees, 1998-, chmn art issues comt, 1998-2000, chmn tech commun comt, 2000); Am Fedn Arts Bd, currently. *Res:* Nineteenth century England, especially interaction of arts and society. *Publ:* Auth, Exhibition diplomacy, Mus News, 79; Museums and special exhibitions, Art J, 80; The industrialization of taste: The Artunian of London, UMI Research Press, 85. *Mailing Add:* Weisman Art Mus 333 E River Rd Minneapolis MN 55455

KING, MYRON LYZON
DEALER
b Hampton Bays, NY, Oct 22, 21. *Study:* David Lipscomb Col, Peabody Col, BA. *Pos:* Lyzon Pictures & Frames, Inc, Nashville. *Bibliog:* George Minzel (auth), Portrait of a Flying Lady, Turner Publ. *Specialty:* Contemporary American art; Sterling Strauser, Paul Lancaster, Malva and David Burlink. *Mailing Add:* 932 Evans Rd Nashville TN 32704-4034

KING, RAY
SCULPTOR, LIGHT ARTIST
b Philadelphia, Pa, July 4, 50. *Study:* Burleighfield House, Loudwater, Bucks, Eng, 75-76. *Work:* Nat Mus Am Art, Washington; Victoria & Albert Mus, London, Eng; Corning Mus Glass, Corning, NY; Best Products, Richmond, Va; Chasco Co, Jericho, NY; E I Dupont de Nemours & Co, Wilmington, Del. *Comn:* Philadelphia Beacons, (four illuminated 42 feet high glass, stainless steel, granite base, light column torches), Avenue of the Arts, Philadelphia, Pa, 94; Light Wave, Rowan Col, Glassboro, NJ, 94; Bristol Beacon, Market Street Wharf, Pa, 95; Sky Garden, Davee Libr, Univ Wisc-River Falls, 96; Double Helical Projections, Iowa State Univ, Ames, 96. *Exhib:* Pa Acad Fine Arts, Philadelphia, 79; Denver Art Mus, Colo, 87; J B Speed Art Mus, Louisville, Ky, 88; Va Mus Fine Art, Richmond, 88; Huntsville Mus Art, Ala, 89; Oklahoma City Art Mus, 89; Contemp Philadelphia Artists, Philadelphia Mus Art, 90; Lane Gallery, San Diego, 93; Galleria, St Petersburg, Fla, 93; Nat Mus Jewish Hist, Philadelphia, 94; Gallery Am Craft, Wheaton Village, Millville, NJ, 95; Urban Glass, Brooklyn, NY, 96. *Pos:* Panelist, fel grants, Nat Endowment Arts, 81; mem bd dir, NY Experimental Glass Workshop, 81-88. *Awards:* Nat Endowment Arts Fel, 84; Pa Coun Arts Fel, 86; Edwin Guth Mem Award, Illuminating Eng Soc, 88. *Bibliog:* Vilma Barr (auth), The Best of Neon, 92; Robert Kehlman and Kyoto Shoin, (coauths), 20th Century Stained Glass: A New Definition, 92; Penny Balkin Back (auth), Public Art in Philadelphia, 92. *Mem:* Int Sculpture Soc; Am Craft Coun. *Media:* Glass, Metal; Light. *Publ:* Contribr, Public Art in Philadelphia, 92; 20th Century Stained Glass: A New Definition, 92; The Best of Neon, 92; The Best of Stained Glass, 91; numerous articles & photograph periodicals. *Mailing Add:* 835 N 3rd St Philadelphia PA 19123

KING, VICTORIA VRANICH KILLOUGH
PUBLISHER, PAINTER
b Lubbock, Tex, Feb 15, 56. *Study:* studied with Gustav Likan, 1994-96; studied with Armand Winfield, 2003-05. *Work:* State of Oreg Gov's Collection, Salem; Zilker Botanical Gardens, Austin, Tex; Austin History Ctr. *Exhib:* Global Art Show, Austin, 94; 11.11 Art Show, Austin, 95; Mojo Art Show, Austin, 99; Death of the Unknown Artist, Austin, 99; Ball in the Jack Gallery, 2003-05. *Pos:* Publ, The Picture Paper Mag, 94-97; cofounder, World Art Party-Austin Tea Party, 95. *Awards:* first art mag on the internet, The Picture Paper-Priceless, 94. *Bibliog:* Michael Barnes (auth), World art party, Austin Am Statesman, 11/95; The Picture Paper, XL Mag, Austin Am Statesman, 8/95. *Mem:* World Art Party; NMex Film Commission; NMex Culture Net. *Media:* Acyrlic. *Specialty:* social, political and environmental art. *Publ:* coauth, Mankind's Millennium Manual, 1999; coauth, Secrets of the Cavemen, 2000. *Dealer:* Ball in the Jack Gallery. *Mailing Add:* 1202 Morningside Dr NE Albuquerque NM 87110

KING, WILLIAM
SCULPTOR
b Jacksonville, Fla, Feb 25, 25. *Study:* Univ Fla, 42-44; Cooper Union Art Sch, 45-48; Brooklyn Mus Art Sch, 49; Academia de Belle Arti, Rome, 49-50; Cent Sch, London, 52. *Work:* Univ Calif; Cornell Univ, Ithaca, NY; Hunter Mus, TN; Syracuse Univ, NY; Los Angeles Co Mus, Calif; Brandeis Univ, Waltham, Mass; Metrop Mus Art, Whitney Mus & Solomon R Guggenheim Mus, NY; and many pvt collections; Mus Modern Art. *Comn:* Mural, SS United States, 52; mural, Bankers' Trust, NY, 60; sculpture, Miami-Dade Jr Col, Fla, 72; sculpture, State Univ NY, Potsdam, 73-74; sculpture, Detroit Med Ctr, 79; sculpture, Madison Art & Civic Ctr, Wis, 79; sculpture, Lincoln Libr, Ft Wayne, Ind, 80; sculpture, Palo Alto, Calif, 86; sculpture, Fla State Coun Arts, Lakeland, 87; sculpture, Broward Co Fla, 90; sculpture, City of Philadelphia, 95. *Exhib:* Whitney Mus Am Art, Mus Mod Art & Guggenheim Mus, NY; Philadelphia Mus Art; Los Angeles Co Mus Art; retrospective, San Francisco Mus Art, Calif, 70 & 74; solo exhibs, San Francisco Mus Art, 70, Wadsworth Atheneum, Hartford, 72, Hunter Mus, Chatanooga, Tenn, 87, Peconic Gallery, NY, Brunnier Gallery & Mus, Iowa, 90, Extension Gallery Inc, NJ & Hokin Gallery Inc, Fla, 91; Nat Acad Design, NY, 89; Brenau Univ, Gainesville, Ga, 91; Coming of Age of Am Sculpture, Lehigh, Pa, 91-92; Mus Art, Ft Lauderdale, Fla, 92; 40 Yrs of Works in Wood, Sheridan Past Gallery, 94; Lizan-Tops Gallery, E Hampton, NY, 98; and

others. *Teaching:* Instr sculpture, Brooklyn Mus Sch Art, 52-55; lectr sculpture, Univ Calif, Berkeley, 65-66; instr sculpture, Art Students League, 68-69, Univ Pa, 72-73 & State Univ NY, 74-75. *Awards:* Fulbright Fel, 49-50; St Gaudens Medal, Cooper Union, 64; Creative Artists Pub Serv Proj Grant, 74; Gold Medal, Nat Acad Design, New York, 86. *Bibliog:* S Schwartz (auth), New York letter: William King, Art Int, 11/72; John Sanders (auth), Photography Year Book 1973, London, 72; Hilton Kramer (auth), The Age of the Avant-Garde, London, 74. *Mem:* Nat Arts Club NY; Nat Acad Design (pres, 93-); Am Acad Arts & Letts. *Dealer:* Alexandre Gallery 41 E 57th St New York NY 10022. *Mailing Add:* 21 Saddle Lane East Hampton NY 11937

KINGSLEY, APRIL
CURATOR, CRITIC, LECTURER
b New York, NY. *Study:* Inst Fine Arts, NY Univ, BA(art hist) & MA; City Univ NY Grad Ctr, 86, MPhil, PhD, 2000. *Collection Arranged:* Paintings That Paint Themselves Or So It Seems, 2005; Blast From the Past: Art of the 1960's (catalogue), 2006. *Pos:* Cur, Kresge Art Mus, MSU. *Teaching:* Sch of Visual Arts, 1973-1990. *Bibliog:* Judy K Collischan van Wagner (auth), Women Shaping Art, 84-. *Mem:* Int Art Critics Asn; CAA; MAHA. *Res:* Conceptual art; Abstract Expressionism; Ashcan realism; Realism; Figurative Expressionism; Art in the Toon Age. *Publ:* Auth, Mary Shaffer (exhib catalog), Habatat Galleries, Aspen, Colo, 94; Fiber: Five Decades from the Permanent Collection of the American Craft Museum (exhib catalog), 95; Arturo Alonzo Sandoral: A Retrospective, Univ Ky Art Mus, 98; Alvin Loring: On a Spiralling Trajectory, Neuberger Mus Art, 98; John Clem Clarke, The Am Way, Allentown Art Mus, 98; Abstract Expressions in Context in 300 Years American Paintings: The Montclair Art Mus Collection, 99; The Paintings of Alice Dalton Brown, 2002; Art in the Toon Age, 2004. *Mailing Add:* 2449 Wild Blossom Ct East Lansing MI 48823-7203

KINGTON, LOUIS BRENT
SCULPTOR, CRAFTSMAN
b Topeka, Kans, July 26, 34. *Study:* Univ Kans, BFA, 57; Cranbrook Acad Art, MFA, 61. *Work:* Mus Contemp Crafts, NY; Mint Mus of Craft and Design; Univ Wis-Milwaukee; Renwick Gallery, Smithsonian Inst, Washington, DC; Ill State Mus, Springfield; and others. *Comn:* Memphis Botanical Garden, Tenn; Friendship Hall, Nakajo, Japan; Rend Lake Col, Ina, Ill. *Exhib:* North Am Goldsmiths, Renwick Gallery, Smithsonian, Washington, DC, 74; Am Crafts for the Vatican Mus, Rome, 78; Towards a New Iron Age, Victoria & Albert Mus, London, 82; Craft Today, Poetry of the Physical, Am Craft Mus, NY, 86; The Eloquent Object, Philbrook Art Ctr, Tulsa, Okla, 87; City on a Hill: 20 Yrs of Artists at Cortona, Italy, 89; Artists from Ill, Kunstlerhas Palas, Bregenz, Austria, 91; and others. *Teaching:* Prof metal smithing, Southern Ill Univ, Carbondale, 61-96; retired. *Awards:* Craftsman Fel, Nat Endowment Arts, 75 & 82; Am Craft Coun, Gold Medal for Excellence; Artist Fel, Ill Arts Coun, 85; L Brent Kington chair at Southern Ill Univ Carbondale created in his honor, 2006. *Mem:* Soc NAm Goldsmiths (pres, 70-74); Am Crafts Coun (trustee, 76-80); Artists-Blacksmiths Asn NAm (dir, 75-79). *Media:* Metals. *Res:* Symbolic objects denoting authority, social distinction and ritual. *Specialty:* Fine Crafts, Painting, Sculpture. *Interests:* 20th Century Painting, Sculpture, Ethnic Arts. *Dealer:* Duane Reed Gallery St Louis MO and Chicago IL. *Mailing Add:* c/o Sch Art & Design Southern Ill Univ 1100 S Normal Ave Carbondale IL 62901

KINIGSTEIN, JONAH
PAINTER, DESIGNER
Study: Cooper Union Art Sch, 41-43; Grande Chaumiere, Paris, 47-51; Belle Arte, Rome, Fulbright Fel, 53-54. *Work:* Mus Mod Art, NY; Albright-Knox Art Gallery, Buffalo, NY; Nelson Gallery Art; Washington Mus; Ain Herod Mus, Tel-Aviv, Israel; also in pvt collections. *Exhib:* Butler Inst Am Art, Youngstown, Ohio, 56; Young Americans, Whitney Mus Am Art, NY, 57; Nat Acad Arts & Lett, 68; one-man shows, ACA Gallery, 68 & Rittenhouse Gallery, Philadelphia, 75; Washington Irving Gallery, NY, 82; Art & the Law, Landmark Ctr, St Paul, Minn, 82; Rittenhouse Gallery, Philadelphia, 82; Pindar Gallery, NY, 88 & 92; Student Univ Art Gallery, Univ Mass, 90; and others. *Teaching:* Brooklyn Mus Art Sch, 70. *Awards:* Fulbright to Italy, 53; Louis Comfort Tiffany Found Award, 62; Perkins-Elmer Prize, 62; and others. *Mem:* Nat Acad NY. *Publ:* Lee Nordness (auth), Art USA Now, Viking Press, 62; Laurence Shmeckabier (auth), Syracuse Univ Collection, 64; Barry Schwartz, The New Humanism, 74; Catalogue of the Collection of American Art at Randolph-Macon Womens College, Univ Va, 77. *Mailing Add:* 738 Westminster Rd Brooklyn NY 11230

KINKADE, CATHERINE
PAINTER, PRAINTMAKER
b Westfield, MA, Apr 3, 40. *Study:* Boston Univ, BA, 1962; Montclair Mus Sch Art. *Work:* Pastel Soc Am Permanent Collection, NY; Nat Asn of Women Artists UN Millenium Collection, NY; Nature Conservancy Collection, Shelter Island, NY; Grand Cen Galleries Permanent Collection, NY; Exxon-Mobil Hq Permanent Collection, NY. *Comn:* Morristown Wetlands (10' 4 panel oil), Tiffany & Co, 1990; Change Water (20' oil Triptych), AT&T, 1991; Near Chatsworth (oil), BASF, 1994; Third River (6 panel monotype), Am Savings Bank, 1997; Wisteria (8' oil), Dai Kitchi Japanese Restaurant (Tatami Rm), 1999; Champagne (oil & wine bottle label), Angelbecks & Gruet Vineyards, Bethon, France, 2000. *Exhib:* Solo exhibs, Reflections, Pen & Brush, NY, 1990; La Champagne, Frederick Clement Gallery, Montclair, NJ & NY, 1999; Centennial Nat CLWAC Traveling Exhib, US, 1990-1991; Montclair Colony Past & Present, Montclair Art Mus, Montclair, NJ, 1997; Connections, Kunstlerbund, Graz, Austria, 2003; Master Pastelists, Butler Inst, Butler, Ohio, 2003; Expos Int: Salons des Artists Contemporains, 2003, 2004, 2005. *Pos:* Instr (pastel painting/color plein air landscape), Montclair Art Mus Sch of Art, 1981; Artist in Residence (landscape en plein air), Van Vleck House & Gardens, 1996. *Awards:* Nat Arts Club (top award), Pastel Soc Am Nat Ann, 1982; Gold Medal of Honor, Catherine Lorillard Wolfe Art Club Nat Ann, 1989 (pastel), 1993 (oil); Best in Show, Pen & Brush Ann, 1989. *Bibliog:* Kristina Feliciano, ed (auth), Best of Pastels, Rockport, 1996; Kristen Park (auth), In the Taoist Tradition: An Interview with Landscape Painter, Catherine Kinkade, TCM World Newspaper, 2002; The Art of Pastel (Art de Pastel en France), 2006. *Mem:* Pastel Soc Am (signature mem 1981, master pastelist 1985); Catharine Lorillard Wolfe Art Club (vpres exhibs & painting 1984-1987); Viridian Print Studio (exec dir 1996-); Art du Pastel en France (2003); Nat Asn Women Artists (1999). *Media:* Oil, Pastel, Watercolor. *Publ:* Contribr, Meditative Approach to Plein Air Painting, Pastelogram, publ of the Pastel Asn Am, 2003. *Dealer:* Walker-Kornbluth Art Gallery 7-21 Fair Lawn Ave Fairlawn NJ 07410; Avila Fine Arts (art consult) 1850C Burnt Mills Rd Bedminster NJ. *Mailing Add:* 257 Midland Ave Montclair NJ 07042

KINNAIRD, RICHARD WILLIAM
PAINTER, EDUCATOR
b Buenos Aires, Arg, Nov 19, 31; US citizen. *Study:* Univ Mich, Ann Arbor, 49-51; Carleton Col, Northfield, Minn, BA, 53; Art Inst Chicago, 52; Univ Ill, with Lee Chesney, MFA, 58. *Work:* Seattle Mus of Art; NC Mus of Art, Raleigh; Hanes Knitting Corp & R J Reynolds Corp, Winston-Salem, NC. *Comn:* Thomas Wolfe Mem Sculpture, class gift to Univ NC-Chapel Hill, 66; pediment sculpture, Mint Mus of Art, Charlotte, NC, 72. *Exhib:* Award Winners Exhib of Chicago No-Jury Show, Art Inst of Chicago, 57; Southeastern Ann Painting & Sculpture, High Mus, Atlanta, Ga, 66; Experimental Media, Corcoran Gallery of Contemp Art, Washington, DC, 70; Painting & Sculpture Exhib, Mint Mus of Art, 71; Third Ann Contemp Reflections, Aldrich Mus of Contemp Art, 73; solo exhibs, Sandhurst Art Coun, Aberdeen, NC, 78 & Rowan Art Ctr, Salisbury, NC, 79; Selections from the Collection, Aldrich Mus Contemp Art, Ridgefield, Conn, 78; Patron Art Patron, Southeastern Ctr Contemp Art, 79; Exhib of Works by Tenn Valley States Artists, Tenn Valley Auth Washington Visitors Ctr, DC, 79. *Collection Arranged:* Univ Evansville Fine Arts Exhib, Ind, 73. *Teaching:* Instr printmaking & etching, Auburn Univ, Ala, 60-64; from instr to assoc prof painting, Univ NC, 64-76, prof painting, 76-. *Awards:* Purchase Award, Third Ann Contemp Reflections, Aldrich Mus of Contemp Art, 74; First Painting Award, Spring Mill Ann Art Exhib, Spring Mills Corp, Lancaster, SC, 76; First Award, 40th Ann NC Artists, NC Mus of Fine Art, Raleigh, 77. *Media:* Acrylic, Oil. *Mailing Add:* c/o Dept Art Univ NC Hanes Art Ctr CB 3405 Chapel Hill NC 27599

KINNEE, SANDY
PAINTER, PRINTMAKER
b Port Huron, Mich, Mar 30, 47. *Study:* Univ Mich, Ann Arbor, BFA(printmaking), 69, grad study, 70; Wayne State Univ, Detroit, MFA(printmaking), 76; Atelier 17, Paris, France, 79. *Work:* Metrop Mus Art, NY; Mus NMex, Santa Fe; Evergreen State Col; Portland Art Mus; Allen Art Mus, Oberlin, Ohio; Madison Art Ctr, Wis; and others. *Exhib:* Works on Handmade Paper, Mus Mod Art, NY, 76; Paper as Medium, Smithsonian, traveling, 78-80; Fans, Philadelphia Mus Art, Pa, 79; one-man shows, Coburn Gallery, Colo Col, 92, 1/1 Gallery, Denver, Colo, 92, Art Selection, Zurich, Switz, 94 & TAK Gallery, Schann, Liechtenstein; Art Multiple, Dusseldorf, Ger, 95; SAGA/FICA Edition, Paris, France, 95; 1/1 Gallery, Denver, Colo, 95; Art Selection, Zurich, Switz, 97. *Awards:* Purchase Award, Southwest Biennial, Mus NMex, Santa Fe, 78; Printmakers Fel, Western States Art Found, 79; Pollack Krasner Found Grant, 87. *Bibliog:* Jules Heller (auth), Papermaking, Watson-Guptill, 78; Virginia Butera (auth), Sandy Kinnee, Arts Mag, 6/81; Suzanne M Singletary (auth), Sandy Kinnee, fans and kimonos, Artspace, 1/82. *Media:* Handcolored Intaglio on Handmade Paper; Watercolor. *Publ:* Papermaking (film), Crystal Productions, Aspen, Colo, 80; An Introduction to Printmaking (slide ser) & Printmaking with Basic Equipment (slide ser) Crystal Production, Aspen, Colo, 83; & auth, Fans, bridges, kimonos and the role paper plays in my work, Print Club, Philadelphia, 81; Printmaking (film), Crystal Prod, Aspen, Colo, 83. *Dealer:* Art Selection Zurich Switz. *Mailing Add:* 1202 N Institute Colorado Springs CO 80903

KINNEY, GILBERT HART
COLLECTOR, ADMINISTRATOR
b New York, NY, May 11, 31. *Study:* Yale Univ, BA, 53 & MA, 54; John F Kennedy Sch, MPA, 73. *Pos:* Trustee, 74-77, 78- & chief exec officer, 77-78, Corcoran Gallery of Art, Washington, DC; trustee, Archs Am Art, 74-88, 89-91, pres, 78-82; trustee, Am Fed Arts, 78-, pres 2000; dir, Am Arts Alliance, 85-91; trustee, Yale Art Gallery, 91-. *Collection:* Major emphasis post-war American painting and sculpture, also European 20th century painting and sculpture, South and Southeast Asian sculpture especially bronzes. *Mailing Add:* 19 E 72nd St Apt 9A New York NY 10021

KINOSHITA, GENE
ARCHITECT
b Vancouver, BC, Jan 18, 35. *Study:* Univ BC, BArch (honors), 59; Yale Univ, MArch, 62. *Comn:* McMaster Univ Art Gallery & Libr, Hamilton, Ont, 89-93; Scis Complex, Univ Western Ont, London, 89-91; Whitby Mental Health Ctr, Ont, 91-97; Fenbrook Inst, Gravenhurst, Ont, 94-98, YMCA, Sarnia-Lambton, 95-98; Art Gallery Windsor, Ont, 2000; Univ Toronto Pharmacy Bldg, 2002. *Exhib:* Traveling Exhib Can Art Mus, Royal Can Acad Arts, 67; Can Unit Masonry Awards Prog Traveling Exhib Can, 72; Ont Masons Rels Coun, Traveling Prov Exhib, 73; Am Inst Arch & Am Correctional Asn Traveling Show, 80; Royal Can Acad Gallery, 87; 3rd Int Conf on Justice Archit, 98. *Pos:* Principal, Moffat Kinoshita Architects Inc, 65-2005; Principal, Cannon Design, 2005-. *Teaching:* Univ Toronto Sch Archit, 69-71 & 80-84. *Awards:* Ont Asn Archit Award of Excellence for Royal Ont Mus & NY Aquatic Ctr, 87 & 89; Gov Gens Award in Archit, for Queen Elizabeth Terraced Galleries of the Royal Ontario Mus, Toranto, 1986; Merit Award for Alumni Ctr, Univ Guelph, Ont, 89; Award of Excellence, Ont Asn Archit, 89; Order of da Vinci Medal, Ont Asn Archit, 2004; and

45 others. *Mem:* Ont Asn Archit; academician Royal Can Acad Arts (pres, 84-88); Ont Col Art (hon trustee); Art Found Greater Toronto (pres, 93-95); fel Royal Archit Inst Can; and others. *Collection:* Can Art of Royal Can Acad Art Academicians of abstr minimalist paintings & abstr landscape paintings & prints & of Japanese prints of 18th & 19th century artists. *Publ:* Auth, The ROM: A new lease on life, Canadian Collector, 7-8/82; Museums are for people, the evolution of a design concept, Rotunda Mag, Vol 15, No 2, 82. *Mailing Add:* 278 Sheldrake Blvd Toronto ON M4P 2B6 Canada

KINSTLER, EVERETT RAYMOND
PAINTER, INSTRUCTOR
b New York, NY. *Study:* Nat Acad Design, New York; Art Students League, with DuMond; also, John Johansen & Jas Montgomery Flagg; Rollins Col, Hon DFA, 83. *Hon Degrees:* Hon DFA, Rollins Col, 1983; Hon DFA, Lyme Acad Col Art, 2002. *Work:* Metrop Mus Art, NY; Carnegie Inst, Pittsburgh; Brooklyn Mus; Smithsonian Inst, Washington; Mus City NY; Butler Inst Am Art; and others; Nat Portrait Gallery, Washington, DC (71 works). *Comn:* Portraits of Pres George Bush; Secy State James Baker; off White House Portrait of Pres Gerald R Ford, Pres Ronald Reagan, Pres Bill Clinton, 5 US Secs of State; portraits of John Wayne, Katharine Hepburn, Tom Wolfe, Gene Hackman, Peter O'Toole, Paul Newman, Donald Trump, official NYC mayoral portrait of Rudolph Giuliani; portraits of presidents of following universities: Yale, Harvard, Princeton, Chicago, Oklahoma, Brown, Pa & Boston; and others. *Exhib:* One-man shows, Grand Cent Art Galleries, 83, Lotos Club, NY, 72, Lluisa Gallery, Mich, 81, Artists of Am, Denver, 81-90, Rollins Col, Fla, 83 & Hollis Taggart Gallery, 94, New York Creative, Mus City of NY, 2006; ann exhibs Am Watercolor Soc; ann exhibs Nat Acad Arts; ann exhibs Nat Acad Design; and others. *Teaching:* Instr painting & drawing, Art Students League, 70-; instr Nat Acad Design Sch. *Awards:* Nat Arts Club, 1959-1967; Silver Medal, Audubon Artists, 1988; Gold Medal, Allied Artists, 1996; Copley Medal, Nat Portrait Gallery, 2000; Medal, Nat Acad Design, 2003; Gold Medal, Salmigundi Club, NYC, 2005; Copley Soc, 2006. *Bibliog:* Articles, Am Artist, 1/72 & 7/84, People, 7/14/76, Saturday Evening Post, 82, Southwest Art, 3/82, Artists of Rockies, summer 83 & Art Times, 4/88, NY Times, 12/89. *Mem:* Nat Arts Club; Nat Acad Design; Am Watercolor Soc; Life mem, Players Club; Life mem Lotos Club; Yale Club; Audubon Artists; Allied Artist of Am; Copley Soc (Boston); Pastel Soc of Am (Hall of Fame); Lambs Club (life); Players Club (life). *Publ:* Painting Faces, Figures & Landscapes, Watson-Guptill, 81, rev, 95; Everett Raymond Kinstler.An Artist's Journey, PBS Documentary, 2002; auth, My Brush With History, 2005; auth, The Artists Journey Through the Popular Culture, 2005; auth, Paints Ahead, TV documentary, 2006. *Dealer:* Vose Galler, Boston; Matteucci Gallery, Santa Fe; Richland Fine Art, Tennessee. *Mailing Add:* 15 Gramercy Park New York NY 10003

KIOUSIS, LINDA WEBER
PAINTER, ILLUSTRATOR
b Cleveland, Ohio. *Study:* Cleveland Inst Art, dipl, Case Western Reserve Univ, BS, MA. *Work:* Univ Mo Hosp & Clinic, Columbia; Ohio Watercolor Soc; Salem Pub Libr, Ohio; Arches Paper Co; Binney & Smith Inc, Pa; and others. *Comn:* Soc Corp, Cleveland, Ohio, 93; Paintings, Children's Oncology Serv Northeastern Ohio, Inc, 94. *Exhib:* Mainstream America: Collection of Phil Desind, Butler Inst Am Art, Youngstown, Ohio, 87; Am Realism, Parkersburg, WVa, 89; Choices and Decisions, Chelsea Galleries, Beachwood, Ohio, 90; Watercolor Now, Springfield Art Mus, Mo, 91; Watercolor USA, Mo, 91; 34th Ann Chautauqua Nat Exhib Am Art; Woman's Touch, Glass Growers Gallery, Erie, Pa, 91; Art Inspired by Architecture, Great Northern Corp Ctr, Ohio, 92; Graphic Watercolors, Sandusky Cult Ctr, Ohio, 92; Northwest Watercolor Soc, Wash; Cleveland Clinic SW, Ohio; Daniel Smith Artists' Materials, Wash; Farmington Mus, NM. *Teaching:* Instr, Ohio Watercolor Soc, 97. *Awards:* Best of Show, Santa Fe Trail Days, Colo, 99; Best of Show, Baycrafters, Ohio, 2000; 1st Prize, Western Colo Watercolor Soc, 2000; Best of Show, Ohio Watercolor Soc, Nat Canton Art Mus, Ohio; Best of Show, Winterfest 2002, Guntersville, AL. *Bibliog:* Marilyn Phillis (auth), Watermedia Techniques for Releasing the Creative Spirit; Who's Who of Am Women, Marquis, 96; Watercolor Magic, F&W Publ, spring 2001. *Mem:* Ohio Watercolor Soc; Pa Watercolor Soc; Watercolor USA Hon Soc; Nat Asn Women Artists; Midwest Watercolor Soc; Sylvan Grouse Guild; Tex Watercolor Soc; Ala Watercolor Soc; Western Colo Watercolor Soc. *Media:* Transparent Watercolor. *Dealer:* Glass Growers Gallery Erie PA; The Bonfoey Co 1710 Euclid Ave Cleveland OH 44115. *Mailing Add:* 8968 Snow Rd Parma OH 44130-2117

KIPNESS, ROBERT
PAINTER
b Brooklyn, NY, 31. *Study:* Univ Iowa, BA, 52, MFA, 54. *Work:* British Mus, Brooklyn Mus Art, Carnegie Mus Art Pittsburgh, Fitzwilliam Mus Cambridge, Libr. Congress, Metrop Mus Art NY City, Mus Fine Arts Boston, Nat Acad of Design NY City, Nat Mus Am Art Washington, DC, NY Pub. Libr, Philadelphia Mus Art, Ashmolean Mus Oxford, Victoria & Albert Mus London, Whitney Mus Am Art New York City. *Exhib:* Exhib incl The Contemporaries, New York City, 59-67, FAR Gallery, New York City, 68-75, AAA, New York City, 77, Hirschl & Adler, New York City, 77-80, Jane Haslem Gallery, Wash, 76-98, Redfern Gallery, London, 95-98, Butler Inst Am Art, 99, Weinstein Gallery, San Francisco, 2000-04, Beadleston Gallery, New York City, 2003; rep in collections of Art Inst Chicago, Bibliotheque National de France. *Awards:* Recipient Speicher-Hassam Purchase award, Am Acad & Inst Arts & Letters, 88; Daniel Serra-Baduc Mem award, Audubon Artists, 98; Rembrandt Graphics award, Boston Printmakers, 99. *Mem:* Royal Soc Painter Printmakers, UK; Nat Acad of Design (acad, Cannon prize 99). *Mailing Add:* Davidson Galleries 313 Occidental Ave S Seattle WA 98104

KIPNISS, ROBERT
PAINTER, PRINTMAKER
b New York, NY, Feb 1, 31. *Study:* Art Students League; Wittenberg Col; Univ Iowa, BA & MFA. *Hon Degrees:* Wittenberg Univ, hon PhD, 79; Ill Col, hon Dr Letters, 89. *Work:* Whitney Mus Am Art, NY; The British Mus, UK; and others; Metrop Mus, NY; Biblioteque Nationale de France, Paris; Pinakothek Moderne, Munich, Ger. *Comn:* Presentation Print, The Albany Print Club, 95; Porteolio Print, Art Students League, 01. *Exhib:* Recent Acquisitions, Whitney Mus Am Art, 72; one-man shows, Mus de Arte Moderno, Cali, Colombia, 75 & 80 & Enatsu Gallery, Tokyo, 88 & 90, Beadleston Gallery, NY, 01, 03, New Orleans Mus Art, 06; III Bienal Americana de Artes Graficas, Museo La Tertulia, Cali, Colombia, 76; one-man retrospective, Asn Am Artists, NY, 77 & Wichita Falls Mus, Tex, 97; Redfern Gallery, London; Butler Inst Am Art, Ohio, 99; Brit Mus, 2000; Am Acad Arts and Letters invitation, 88; Ashmolean Mus, Oxford, Eng, No Day Without a Line, Diploma Prints of the Royal Society of Painter-Printmakers, 99; Fitzwilliam Mus, Cambridge, Eng, Recent Acquisitions, 99; The Nat Acad Design, NY, Papertrail: Works on Paper From the Collection, 2000; The British Mus, London, Recent Acquisitions, 2000; Royal Acad Summer Show, London, 01; one-man shows, New Orleans Mus Art, New Orleans, La, Harnett Mus, The Univ Richmond, Richmond Vt, Orlando Mus Art, Orlando, Fla, Paintings & Drawings of the 1960's, SKH Gallery, Great Barrington, Mass, Millenia Gallery, Orlando, Fla, 2006; many others. *Awards:* Prize, Nat Acad Design, 76, 80 & 81; Medal Honor, Audubon Artists, 82, 97-98; Award, Soc Am Graphic Artist, 2000; Am Acad Arts and Letters Purchase Prize, 88. *Bibliog:* Robert Kipniss: The Graphic Works, Abaris Books, 80; Robert Kipniss, Intaglios, 1982-2004, Hudson Hills Press, New York & Manchester, 2004; Seen in Solitude: The Prints of Robert Kipniss from the James F White Collection, The New Orleans Mus Art, Publ, 2006. *Mem:* Nat Acad Design; Boston Printmakers; Soc Am Graphic Artists; Century Asn, NY; Royal Soc Painter-Printmakers, London, 98. *Media:* Oil; Mezzotint. *Publ:* Illusr, Poems of Emily Dickinson, Thomas Y Crowell, 64; Collected Poems of Robert Graves, Anchor Doubleday, 66; Poems of Rilke, Limited Ed Club, 81; Printmaking Today, London, 96. *Dealer:* Redfern Gallery, London; Weinstein Gallery, San Francisco, CA; Beadleston Gallery, New York, NY. *Mailing Add:* Hudson House PO Box 112 Ardsley On Hudson NY 10503

KIPP, LYMAN
SCULPTOR
b Dobbs Ferry, NY, Dec 24, 29. *Study:* Pratt Inst, 50-52; Cranbrook Acad Art, 52-54. *Work:* Whitney Mus Am Art, NY; Albright-Knox Art Gallery, Buffalo; High Mus of Art, Atlanta, Ga; Univ Ala, Huntsville; State NY Albany Mall. *Comn:* Sculpture for Post Off & Fed Off Bldg, Van Nuys, Calif; sculpture, Village Lake Placid, NY; Grosse Pointe Libr, Mich. *Exhib:* Four Whitney Mus Am Art Sculpture Ann, 64-70; Sculpture in Environ, NY, 67; Cool Art, 68 & Highlights of the Season, 68, Larry Aldrich Mus, Conn; Art of the Real, Mus Mod Art, NY & London, 68, & Paris & Berlin, 69; Change of View, Larry Aldrich Mus, 75; Sculpture in the Constructivist Tradition, Hamilton Gallery, NY, 77; Urban Structures-Monumental Sculpture, Nat Endowment Arts Traveling Exhib originated in Akron, Ohio, 77-79; Art in Pub Places, Ferris State Col, Mich, 79. *Teaching:* Instr sculpture, Bennington Col, 60-63; asst prof sculpture, Hunter Col, 63-66, prof & chmn dept, 75-; prof sculpture & chmn dept, Lehman Col, 66-75. *Awards:* Guggenheim Fel, 66; Fulbright Grant, 66; City Univ Fac Res Awards, 70 & 75. *Mailing Add:* c/o Ianuzzi Gallery 7070 N 59th Pl Paradise Valley AZ 85253

KIRK, JEROME
SCULPTOR, KINETIC ARTIST
b Detroit, Mich, 23. *Study:* Mass Inst Technol, BS. *Work:* San Francisco Mus Mod Art, Sheldon Art Gallery, Univ Nebr; Phoenix Art Mus, Ariz; Storm King Art Ctr, Mountainville, NY; and others. *Comn:* Thirty maj sculpture comn in pub places; Standing Waves, Univ Calif, Berkeley, 80; Torsive Undulations in Space, TRW Hq, 85; Avion, Koll Ctr, Irvine, Calif, 86; Lunaire, Bayside Bus Park, Fremont, Calif, 91; Optimus, Matrix Essentials Inc, Cleveland, 94; and others. *Exhib:* Sculpture Potsdam, NY, 77; 28 solo and 57 group exhibs; Louis K Meisel Gallery, NY, 76, 87 & 88; Artluminium La Gallery d'Art Lavalin, Montreal, 89; Erickson/Elins Gallery, San Francisco, 92, 95, & 98; Erickson Gallery, Healdsburg, Calif, 2002 & 05; and others, 2002, 05, 06. *Teaching:* Invited lectr, Univ Mont, 96. *Bibliog:* Exploring Visual Design, Selleck, Worcester, Mass, 87; Environmental Art, Shoichiro, Tokyo, 91; La Sculpture En Acier, Clerin, Paris, 93; and others. *Media:* Aluminum, Stainless Steel. *Res:* Designs for vertical axis wind energy turbines. *Specialty:* Fine art, painting and sculture. *Dealer:* Louis K Meisel Gallery 141 Prince St NY NY 10012; Erickson Gallery 324 Healdsburg Ave Headsburg Calif 95448. *Mailing Add:* 5648 Bacon Rd Oakland CA 94619

KIRKHAM, GRAHAM
COLLECTOR
b Edlington, Doncaster, Eng, Dec 14, 44. *Study:* Bradford Univ, PhD (hon). *Pos:* Founder, DFS Furniture Co, 69- exec chmn, currently. *Awards:* Decorated Commander of the Royal Victorian Order (CVO); Created Baron Kirkham, of Old Cantley in the Co of South Yorkshire, 99; named one of Top 200 Collectors, ARTnews Mag, 2004. *Collection:* 19th & 20th Century British & French painting. *Mailing Add:* DFS Furniture Co Bentley Moore Ln Adwick-le-St Doncaster South Yorkshire United Kingdom DN6 7BD

KIRKPATRICK, DIANE
HISTORIAN
b Grand Rapids, Mich, June 28, 33. *Study:* Vassar Col, BA, 55; Cranbrook Acad Art, MFA, 57; Univ Mich, Ann Arbor, MA, 65, PhD, 69. *Collection Arranged:* Chicago: The City and Its Artists, Univ Mich Art Mus, Ann Arbor, 78; The Fair View: Representations of the World's Columbian, Exposition of 1893, Terra Mus Am Art,

Chicago & Univ Mich Art Mus, 93. *Pos:* Manuscript & layout ed, Fideler Publ Co, Grand Rapids, Mich, 57-58; dir children's educ, Grand Rapids Art Mus, Mich, 60-62; dir film & video studies, Univ Mich, 77-78. *Teaching:* asst prof to assoc prof, Univ Mich, 72-82, prof, 82-. *Mem:* Col Art Asn Am; ACM SIGGRAPH; Soc Photog Ed. *Res:* Contemporary art, including photography, film, video and computers. *Publ:* Religous photography in the Victorian age, 83 & Science, Art, and the human image, 85, Mich Quart Rev; Holography and the art-technology scene, Holography Redefined, 84; The Artists of the 16: Backgrounds and Continuities, 90; La Fotografia ala Nuova Techologia, 92. *Mailing Add:* Hist of Art Dept Univ Mich 110 Tappan Hall Ann Arbor MI 48109-1357

KIRSCHENBAUM, BERNARD EDWIN
SCULPTOR
b New York, NY, Sept 3, 24. *Study:* Cornell Univ; Inst Design, Chicago, BA. *Work:* Storm King Art Ctr, Mountainville, NY. *Comn:* Sculptures, Spectrum II, Mass Inst Technol, Cambridge, 68 & Walkthrough, J Patrick Lannan Found, Palm Beach, Fla, 69. *Exhib:* Sculpture in Environment, Cent Park, NY, 67; Cool Art: Abstraction Today, Newark Mus, NJ, 68; Painting & Sculpture Today, Indianapolis Mus Art, 70; Three NY Artists, Corcoran Gallery Art, Washington, DC, 73; Sculpture in the Fields, Storm King Art Ctr, 74. *Awards:* Guggenheim Fel Sculpture, 72. *Dealer:* Sculpture Now Inc Max Hutchinson 142 Greene St New York NY 10012. *Mailing Add:* 180 Park Row New York NY 10038

KIRSHNER, JUDITH RUSSI
CURATOR, CRITIC
b St Louis, Mo, Nov 24, 42. *Study:* Barnard Col, BA, 64; Bryn Mawr, MA, 69. *Collection Arranged:* Claes Oldenburg, The Mouse Mus, 77; June Leaf-Retrospective, 78; Gordon Matta-Clark, Circus-Caribbean Orange, 78; Vito Acconci-Retrospective: 1969-80, 80; Contemporary Chicago Painters-Two Decades, 86. *Pos:* Chief cur, Mus Contemp Art, Chicago, 76-81; cur, Terra Mus Am Art, 85-86. *Teaching:* Asst prof art criticism & contemp art, Sch of the Art Inst Chicago, 81; dir Sch Art and Design, Univ Ill, Chicago, prof art history, dean Col Architecture and teh Arts, currently. *Mem:* Col Art Asn; Int Art Critics. *Publ:* Auth, Tom Otterness' frieze, 83 & Non-u-ment: Gordon Matta-Clark, 85, Artforum; The possibility of an avant-garde, Formations, 85; numerous reviews in Artforum and numerous mus catalog essays. *Mailing Add:* Univ Ill Dept Art 303 Jefferson Hall 935 W Harrison Chicago IL 60607-7039

KIRSTEIN, JANIS ADRIAN
PAINTER, INSTRUCTOR
b Louisville, Ky, Jul 7, 55. *Study:* Ind Univ, Bloomington, 73-75; Univ Louisville, BA, 77; Univ Mass, MFA, 81. *Comn:* painting, Don Rigazzio, 2000. *Exhib:* Int Juried Art Competition, Mussavi Art Ctr, NY, 89; Mid Am Biennial Nat Art Exhib, Solomon Guggenheim Mus, NY, 89; La Asociacion Cult Peruano Británica, Lima, Peru, 2002; One woman exhib, Zephyr Gallery, Louisville, Ky, 2002 & 04; Alternate Views: Approaches to Abstraction, Univ Louisville Hite Art Gallery, 2004; Int Photog Competative Exhib, Greeley Sq Gallery, NY, 2004; Hasselblad Int Photo Competition, Linz, Austria, 2004. *Pos:* art critic, Courier-Journal Newspaper, 77-78. *Teaching:* instr fine arts, Western Hills High Sch, Ky, 89-; instr fine arts, Governor's Scholars Program, Ky, 95; instr 2D design, Univ Louisville, Ky, 2000-. *Awards:* Al Smith Fel Ky Nat Found for the Arts, 83, 2000; Ky Found for Women Fel, 87. *Mem:* Nat Art Educ Asn; Louisville Visual Art Ctr Asn. *Media:* Acrylic, Pastel & Digital Art. *Publ:* illustr, Am Voice Literary J, Ky Found for Women, 87. *Dealer:* Zephyr Gallery 610E Market Louisville KY 40205. *Mailing Add:* 2001 Spring Dr Louisville KY 40205

KIRSTEN-DAIENSAI, RICHARD CHARLES
PAINTER, PRINTMAKER
b Chicago, Ill, Apr 16, 20. *Study:* Art Inst Chicago; Univ Wash; also study in Japan, 58-89. *Work:* Seattle Art Mus; Bell Tel Co; Libr of Cong, Washington, DC; Metrop Mus Art, NY; Tokyo Mus Mod Art, Japan. *Exhib:* Seattle Art Mus, numerous shows, 45-69; Frye Mus, Seattle, 60-65 & 69; Gov Invitational, 67; Collector's Gallery, Bellevue, Wash, 67; Richard White Gallery, Seattle, 68; Kirsten Gallery, Seattle, 75-89; plus many others. *Awards:* Purchase Prize, Univ Ore, 68; Purchase Prize, Seattle First Nat Bank, 69; plus others. *Bibliog:* Article, Arts Asia Mag, 1-2/79. *Mem:* Northwest Watercolor Soc (pres, 68 & 69); Artists Equity (pres, Seattle Chap, 52-56), Seattle Chap mem, 89. *Media:* Watercolor, Acrylic; Mixed Media. *Mailing Add:* c/o Kirsten Gallery 5320 Roosevelt Way NE Seattle WA 98105-3629

KIRSTEN-HONSHIN, NICHOLAS
PAINTER
b Seattle, Wash, 1947. *Study:* Univ Wash, 65-66. *Work:* King Co; Pac Northwest Bell; Peoples Nat Bank; Rainier Bank; Safeco Ins Co. *Exhib:* Stillwater Gallery, Seattle, 83; Return Gallery, Taos, NMex, 84; Mysterium Gallery, Boulder, Colo, 88; solo shows, Kirsten Gallery, Seattle, 79-81, 83, 85 & 88. *Pos:* Dir, Kirsten Gallery, Invisible Frame Shop & Kirsten Gallery Publ, 77-. *Publ:* Life Goes On, Wildflower Productions, 95

KISCH, GLORIA
SCULPTOR
b New York, NY, Nov 14, 41. *Study:* Sarah Lawrence Col, BA, 63; Boston Mus Sch, 64-65; Otis Art Inst, Los Angeles, BFA & MFA, 69. *Work:* Milwaukee Art Mus; Los Angeles Co Art Mus; Palm Springs Art Mus, Calif; Neuberger Mus, Purchase, NY; Va Mus Fine Arts, Richmond; and others. *Publ:* The Rocker, Bernice Steinbaum (auth), Rizzoli Publs; International Furniture Design for the 90's, Libr Applied Design; Product Design 4, Libr Applied Design

KISSIK, KATHY LYNNE
PAINTER; PHOTOGRAPHER
b Nov 14, 68. *Study:* Tufts Univ, BFA, 1992; Sch Mus Fine Arts, cert (Traveling Scholar), 1993; Univ NSW, cert (etching), 2000. *Work:* Attleboro Mus; Mus Fine Arts, Boston, Mass; Diamond Hill Vineyards, Cumberland, RI; Masterman, Culbert & Tully, Boston, Mass; The Bradley Galleries, Milwaukee, Wis. *Comn:* mural, RSPCA, Booklyn, NY, 94; painting, Sch Mus Fine Arts, Boston, Mass, 95; Alpha Gallery, Boston, Mass. *Exhib:* 5th Yr Show, Mus Fine Arts, Boston, 93; One-woman show, Alpha Gallery, Boston, 96; New Eng Triennial, Fuller Mus, Brockton, Mass, 97; Emerging Artists, Southeast Mus Photog, Dayton, Fla, 98; 16th Ann Juried Exhib, Pleiades Gallery, New York City, NY, 98; The Least Possible Words, Philharmonic Ctr Arts, Naples, Fla, 99; Windows, Dana M McCutcheon, Berkeley, Calif, 2000; Group show, Ray Hughes Gallery, Sydney, Australia, 2001-02. *Teaching:* instr Montessori, Sydney, Australia, 94, instr woodoworking, Tauntor, Mass, 95; instr Attleboro Mus, Mass, 96-2000. *Awards:* Artist Project Grant, RISCA, 98, Photography Fel, 99. *Bibliog:* Bill Van Siclern (auth), Art Spotlight, Providence Jour, 96; Cate McQuaid (auth), Grid Grief & House of Gifts, Boston Globe, 96; Janette Sears (auth), Attleboro Mus Auction, Sun Chronicle, 2000. *Media:* All Media. *Dealer:* Alpha Gallery 14 Newbury St Boston MA 02116. *Mailing Add:* 189 Pound Rd Cumberland RI 02864

KITAJ, R B
PAINTER, PRINTMAKER
b Cleveland, Ohio, 1932. *Study:* Cooper Union Advan Sci & Art, New York, 50-51; Acad Fine Art, Vienna, 51-52; Ruskin Sch, Univ Oxford, dipl, 60; Royal Col Art, grad, 61; Univ London, Hon Dr, 82; Royal Col Art, Hon Dr, 92; Cal Col Art & Craft, Hon Dr, 95; Univ Durham, Hon Dr, 96. *Work:* Mus in the US & Europe; Metropolitan Mus of Art, NY; Cleveland Mus of Art, Ohio; Royal Coll of Art, London, Eng; Israel Mus, Jerusalem; High Mus, Atlanta, Ga; Whitney Mus of Am Art, Ny. *Exhib:* One-man shows, Marlborough Fine Art, London, 63, 70, 74, 80, 85-86 & 94, Marlborough Gallery, NY, 65, 79, 85-86 & 95, Kunsthalle, Dusseldorf, 82, Hamburg Kunsthalle, 91, V & A Mus, London, 94 & RB Kitaj: A Retrospective, Tate Gallery, London, Los Angeles Co Mus, Calif & Metrop Mus Art, NY, 94, Nat Gallery, London, 2001-02, Abbot Hall Art Gallery, 2002, La Louver Gallery, Venice, Calif, 2003; Retrospective (with catalog), Hirshhorn Mus, Washington, 81; Kunsthalle, Dusseldorf, 82; traveling retrospective, Tate Gallery, London, Los Angeles Co Mus Art, Calif & Metrop Mus Art, NY, 94-95; and others. *Teaching:* Vis lectr, Slade Sch, Univ London; vis prof, Univ Calif, Berkeley & Univ Calif, Los Angeles. *Awards:* Skowhegan Medal for Drawing, New York, 85; Golden Lion for Painting, Venice Bienalle, 95; Order of Arts & Lett, Repub France, 96; Chavalier des Arts et des Lettres, Repub of France, 96; Wollaston Award to the best painting in the Summer Exhib, Royal Acad, London, 97; Hon Doctorate, Spertus Coll, Chicago, Ill, 99; Hon Doctorate, Durham Univ, 96, Hon Doctorate, Calif Coll of Arts, 95. *Bibliog:* Ken Johnson (auth), RB Kitaj: Views of a fractured century, Art in Am, 3/95; Jason Kaufman (auth), Who will stand up for Kitaj, Art Newspaper, 4/95; John Ash (auth), RB Kitaj, Metrop Mus Art, Artforum, XXXIII, No 9, 5/95. *Mem:* Inst Arts & Letts, NY; Royal Acad London; Nat Acad Design. *Publ:* Auth, A Painter's Tale, Sight & Sound, 7/91; Automat 1929 by Edward Hopper, Telegraph Mag, 9/11/93; Boxing, Art Rev, 9/93; Little Imitations of My Life, Independant on Sunday, 6/12/93; Matisse's Violinist at the Window, A brush with genius, Guardian, 10/24/95. *Dealer:* Marlborough Gallery 40 W 57th St New York NY 10019. *Mailing Add:* c/o Marlborough Fine Arts Ltd 6 Albermarle St London W1X 4BY England United Kingdom

KITAO, T KAORI
HISTORIAN, EDUCATOR
b Jan 30, 33; US citizen. *Study:* Univ Calif, Berkeley, AB(archit), 58, MA(art hist), 61; Harvard Univ, PhD(art hist), 66. *Pos:* Chmn, Swarthmore Col, 75-81; vpres, Int Soc Comparative Study Civilizations, 80-83. *Teaching:* Asst prof hist archit, RI Sch Design, 63-66; asst prof art hist, Swarthmore Col, 66-68, assoc prof, 68-75, prof, 75-, William R Kenan prof, 93-. *Awards:* Lindbeck Distinguished Teaching Award, 98. *Mem:* Col Art Asn; Soc Archit Historians. *Res:* Philadelphia architecture; comparative semiotics, east and west; Bernini and Baroque Rome; streets. *Publ:* Auth, Circle and Oval in the Square of St Peter's, NY Univ Press, 74; contribr, La prospettiva rinascimentale, Centro Di, Florence, 80. *Mailing Add:* 540 Westminster Ave Swarthmore PA 19081

KITTREDGE, NANCY (ELIZABETH)
PAINTER
b Ellsworth, Maine, 38. *Study:* Vesper George Sch Art, Boston, 56-57; Univ NH, Durham, 57-59; Univ Maine, Orono, BA, 61; Univ Miami, Coral Gables, Fla, MA, 63. *Comn:* Portrait, Univ Maine Theatre Dept, Orono, 76; 24' x 36' Backdrop, World Premier, Broad Waters, Malashock Dance & Company, Old Globe Theatre, San Diego, 95. *Exhib:* solo exhibs, San Diego Mus Art, 81 & 90 & David Zapf Gallery, San Diego, 90, 93, 96, 98, 2001 & 05; Contemp Artists' Artists, Sylvia White Contemp Art, Los Angeles, 91; Local Productions: Painters of San Diego Co, Calif Ctr for the Arts, Escondido, Calif, 92; Elements, Los Angeles Munic Art Gallery, Los Angeles, 98; Lindenberg Gallery, NY, 2000; Oceanside Mus of Art, Oceanside, Calif, 2000; San Diego Mus Art, 2002. *Collection Arranged:* Household Corp, Chicago; Women's Clinic & Family Health Care Ctr, Los Angeles; Indust Metals South Inc, New Orleans; Dow Theory Lett Inc, La Jolla, Calif; Luce, Forward, Hamilton & Scripps, San Diego; Univ Maine, Orono; San Diego Mus Art; Laguna Mus Art, Calif. *Teaching:* Instr Tulane Univ, New Orleans, 68-69. *Mem:* Nat Mus Women in Arts. *Media:* Oil, Mixed Media. *Specialty:* Fine Art; Oils. *Interests:* poetry; philosophy. *Publ:* American Artists: An Illustrated Survey of Leading Contemporary Americans, Krantz Publ Co, Chicago, 85; San Diego Artists, Artra Pub Inc, Encinitas, Calif, 88; The California Art Review, 2nd ed, Am References Publ Corp, Chicago, 89. *Dealer:* David Zapf Gallery 2400 Kettner Blvd Ste 104 San Diego CA 92101. *Mailing Add:* 13646 Mira Montana Dr Del Mar CA 92014

KJOK, SOL
PAINTER
b Lillehammer, Norway, Mar 16, 68. *Study:* Univ Vienna, Austria, BA, 1991; Univ Paris, Master in French Lit, 1992; Univ Cincinnati, MA, 1993-96; Parsons Sch Design, New York City, MFA, 1998. *Work:* Cincinnati Art Mus, Ohio; Teckningsmuseet Nat Mus of Drawing, Laholm, Sweden; works in pub and pvt collections, USA, Austria, Belgium, Colombia, Eng, France, Ger, Norway, Sweden. *Exhib:* One-woman shows incl: Allegro Non Troppo, Brodie Gallery; Cincinnati, Ohio, 1996, Swirling-Sviv Tegnerforbundets Gallery, Oslo, Norway, 2001; Skeins and Veins, Samuel ST Chen Fine Arts Ctr, Conn, 2005; Strings of Beads, Perlestrenger, Galleri 27, Oslo, Norway, 2005; Swift & Slow, Nordic Heritage Mus, Seattle, Strings of Beads, Manifest Gallery, Cincinnati, 2006; Group exhib incl: Current Trends, Galleri Steen, Oslo, Norway, 2001; Night of 1000 Drawings, Artists Space, NY, 2002; 69th Juried Show, Arnot Art Mus, NY, 2003; Festival Mira! Lubolo, Casa de Am, Madrid, Spain, 2004; Working Artists in Brooklyn, Romo Gallery, Atlanta, Ga, 2005. *Pos:* Graphic designer, Agence Karen, Paris, formerly; dir, ind studies of Norwegian lang/cult, 1993-96; co-producer, Documentary Odd Nerdrum: Savor of Painting, 2002-; lectr (recent work), Center Conn State Univ, 2/2005; lectr (string series), Manifest Gallery, Cincinnati, 1/2006. *Teaching:* Teaching asst, art hist Univ Cincinnati, 1995-96; resident, Larroque Artists' Colony, Urt, France, 1997-98; teaching asst, painting Parsons Sch Design, New York City, 1997-98. *Awards:* Robert Rauschenberg's Found, 2001; Honorable mention in Exhib Am Art, RIC Inst, Chicago, 2004; Pub Project Grant Am-Scandinavian Found, New York City, 2005. *Bibliog:* Ellen M Rosenholtz (auth), Hopscotch: Associative Leaps in the Construction of Narrative, Painted Bride Art Center, Philadelphia, Pa, 2002; Balansekunstnaren Sol Kjok, Valdres, June 18, Pgs 12-13, 2005; Scandinavian in New York, Nordic Reach, No 15, Vol 18, 28-34, 2006. *Mem:* Col Art Asn; NBK, Norwegian Visual Artists; Tegnerforbundet (Nor Drawing Art Asn). *Dealer:* Romo Gallery Atlanta; Manifest Gallery Cincinnati; Galleri 27 Oslo. *Mailing Add:* 252 Green St Brooklyn NY 11222

KLAMEN, DAVID
PAINTER
b Dixon, Ill, Jan 20, 61. *Study:* Univ Ill, Urbana-Champaign, BFA, 83; Sch Art Inst, Chicago, MFA(painting), 85. *Work:* Mus Contemp Art, Chicago; Krannert Mus Art, Champaign, Ill; Ill State Mus, Springfield; Metrop Mus Art, NY; Nat Mus Contemp Art, Seoul, Korea. *Comn:* Large painting, Bartlit Beck, Chicago, Ill, 94. *Exhib:* Chicago & Vicintity Show, Art Inst Chicago, 85; Art and the Law, Rose Art Mus, Waltham, Mass, 88-89; Aids Found Exhib, Mus Contemp Art, Chicago, 89; solo show, Cedar Rapids Art Mus, Iowa, 91; Spirited Visions, Ill State Mus, Springfield, 92; Drawing New Conclusions, Art Inst Chicago, Ill, 92; Mind & Beast, Leigh Yawkey Woodson Art Mus, Wasau, Wis, 92-93; New Acquisitions, Metrop Mus Art, NY, 95; Art in Chicago, Mus Contemp Art, Chicago, 96; Embracing Beauty, Huntsville Mus Art, Ala, 97. *Teaching:* Instr art, Valpraiso Univ, Ind, 85; asst prof, Ind Univ, Gary, 85-91, assoc prof, 91-97, prof, 97-. *Awards:* Top Forty, Forty Under 40, Crains Chicago Bus, 94. *Bibliog:* Garrett Holg (auth), David Klamen, ArtNews, 10/93; Jeff Borden (auth), Forty under 40, Crains Chicago Bus, 9/26/94; Garrett Hold (auth), David Klamen, Art News, 4/97; and others. *Media:* Oil Paint. *Mailing Add:* c/o Richard Gray Gallery 875 N Michigan Ave Chicago IL 60611

KLARIN, KARLA S
PAINTER
b Los Angeles, Calif, Mar, 17, 53. *Study:* San Francisco Art Inst, BFA, 74; Otis Art Inst, Los Angeles, MFA, 78. *Work:* Los Angeles Co Mus Art; US Consulate, Berlin, Ger; Frederick R Weisman Collection; Loyola Law Sch; Atlantic Richfield Corp, Los Angeles. *Exhib:* Solo shows, Univ Redlands, 83, Claremont Grad Sch, Calif, 83, Karl Bornstein Gallery, Santa Monica, Calif, 84 & 86, Koplin Gallery, Los Angeles, 89, Tortue Gallery, Santa Monica, Calif, 92 & 95; Young Talent Awards: 1963-1983 (with catalog), Los Angeles Co Mus Art, 83; Landscape/Common Ground, Jan Turner Gallery, Los Angeles, 88; California Landscape Art Motif: Plein Air to Present, Downey Mus Art, 88; Natural Selection: The Terrain of Southern California, Riverside Art Mus, 88; California Artists from the Frederick Weisman Collections, Frederick R Weisman Mus Art, Pepperdine Univ, 96. *Awards:* Young Talent Award, Los Angeles Co Mus Art, 82. *Bibliog:* Suzanne Muchnic (auth), Karla Klarin, Los Angeles Times, 86; Suvan Geer (auth), Karla Klarin, Los Angeles Times, 10/20/89; Suzanne Muchnic (auth), Karla Klarin, Artnews, 12/92. *Dealer:* Tortue Gallery 2917 Santa Monica Blvd Santa Monica CA 90404. *Mailing Add:* 500 Ashland Ave Santa Monica CA 90405

KLAUBER, RICK
PAINTER
b July 7, 50. *Study:* Bard Col, with Murray Reich, BA, 72; apprentice to Helen Frankenthaler, residence apprenticeship with Robert Motherwell, 70-73. *Exhib:* One man shows, Artists Space, NY, 75, Long Point Gallery, Provinctown, Mass, 77, 79 & 81, Oscarsson-Hood Gallery, NY, 80 & Universal Fine Objects, Provincetown, Mass, 91 & 92, Brenda Taylor Gallery, NY, 98; Group Shows, Albright-Knox, Buffalo, NY, 81; The Drawing Room, AFR Fine Arts, Washington, DC, 88; Crosscurrents, Fine Arts Work Ctr, Provincetown, Mass, 90; In Full Effect, White Columns, NY, 90; Behind Bars, Threadwaxing Space, NY, 92; Drop Dead Painting, 103 Reade Street, NY, 94; Int Biennial, Janos Xantus Mus, Gyor, Hungary, 95; Galerie Ardrea & Wolfram Cornelissen, Georgenbon, Ger, 96; X-section, MMC Gallery, NY, 97; Brenda Taylor Gallery, NY, 1998-2000; KCC Gallery, CUNY, NY, 1996-2000. *Teaching:* Guest teacher drawing & painting, Bard Col, 84-90; School Visual Arts, 85-96; teacher drawing, watercolor painting, Parsons Sch Design, 1989-2000; teacher drawing & painting, Pratt Inst, 1996-2003; teacher art hist & drawing, Kingsborough Comm Col, 1996-2003. *Bibliog:* Tom Breidenbach (auth), Review in Art Forum, 11/98; John Yau (auth), article, Art in Am, 81; B H Friedman & Chris Busa (auth), Crosscurrents: the New Generation, East Hampton Ctr Contemp Art, 90. *Media:* Oil. *Publ:* Contribr, A bird is more (catalog on Robert Motherwell), Im Irker Gallery, St Gal, Switz, 71; auth, article on Fritz Bultman, Provincetown Arts, 86; contribr, Rosebud, Mudfish, 88. *Mailing Add:* 57 Prince St New York NY 10012

KLAUSEN, RAY
SCULPTOR
b Jamaica, NY. *Study:* Hofstra Univ, BA, 61; NY Univ, MA, 63; Yale Univ, MFA, 67. *Work:* Fla State Univ Mus; Columbus Cares Found, Columbus, Ohio; TDK Corp, Tokyo, Japan; Yamaguchi Mus, Osaka, Japan. *Comn:* Sculpture, Tallarico Inc, Beverly Hills, Calif, 91; sculpture, Telicos Corp, Newport, Calif, 91; sculpture, Merrill Lynch Magowan, Carmel, Calif, 91; sculpture, Sanyo Securities Co Ltd, Tokyo, Japan, 92; sculptures, Yokohama Royal Park Hotel Nikko, Yokohama, Japan, 93. *Exhib:* Solo exhibs, Fla State Univ Mus, 93, Long Beach Mus Art, Calif, 93, San Diego Art Inst, Calif, 93, Palm Springs Desert Mus, Palm Beach, Calif, 94 & La Quinta Sculpture Park, Calif, 94. *Teaching:* Guest lectr sculpting & theatre design, Yale Univ, 87, Fla State Univ, 93 & NY Univ, 94. *Awards:* TDK Art Grants, TDK Corp, 91 & 92. *Bibliog:* John Culhane (auth), Is it sculpture?, NY Times, 91; Peter Clothier (auth), Ray Klausen new sculpture, Catalog Essay, 91; Kawahara Keiko (auth), The art of Ray Klausen, Japan Art News, 92. *Media:* Welded Metal, Miscellaneous Media. *Dealer:* Eva Cohon 301 W Superior St Chicago IL 60610

KLAUSNER, BETTY
WRITER, CURATOR
b New York, NY, Aug 18, 28. *Study:* Wells Col, BA, 50. *Collection Arranged:* Masami Teraoka Erotica, 1968-1984, 84; Llyn Foulkes: Portraits, 86; Terry Allen, Big Witness (Living in Wishes), 87; Michael Singer, 87; Joan Snyder Collects Joan Snyder, 88; Home Show, 88. *Pos:* Dir, Contemp Graphics Ctr, Santa Barbara Mus Art, 78-81, Santa Barbara Contemp Arts Forum, 84-92. *Mailing Add:* 2100 Pacific Ave San Francisco CA 94115

KLAVEN, MARVIN L
PAINTER, EDUCATOR
b Alton, Ill, Apr 8, 31. *Study:* State Univ Iowa, BA & MFA. *Work:* Univ Iowa; Millikin Univ; Mayer Collection, Gilman Collection & Ill Bell, Chicago. *Exhib:* 24 Illinois Artists, 67; Chicago Sun Times Exhib, 68; 21st NMiss Valley Art Exhib, 68; Artists Who Teach, 69; Contemp Am Painting & Sculpture, 69. *Pos:* Dir, Decatur Art Ctr, Ill, 61-69 & Kirkland Art Gallery, 69-. *Teaching:* Asst prof drawing, Northern Ill Univ, 59-61; prof art dept, Millikin Univ, 61-. *Awards:* Tiffany Found Grant, 64. *Media:* Acrylic, Silk Screen. *Mailing Add:* Art Dept Millikin Univ 1184 W Main St Decatur IL 62522-2084

KLECKNER, SUSAN
PHOTOGRAPHER, FILMMAKER
b New York, NY, July 5, 41. *Study:* Art Students League, with Landes Lewitin; City Univ New York, Pratt Inst. *Comn:* Birth Film, Women's Interart Ctr & NY State Coun Arts, NY, 72; Another Look, Teleprompter & Women's Video Service, NY, 72; Desert Piece, Women Artist Filmakers, 82; media, Feast or Famine, Interart Theatre, 83. *Exhib:* Brooklyn Mus, NY, 72; film Festival, Whitney Mus Am Art, NY, 73 & Mod Mus, Paris, France, 74; Wild Art Show, Project Studio One, NY, 82; AIR Gallery, 82; Moonmade Space, 83; West 22nd St Show, 83. *Pos:* Dir photog workshop, Community Resource Ctr, NY, 68-70; co-dir, Women's Liberation Cinema, 70-71; founding coordr, Women's Interart Ctr, NY, 70-71; video ed, Women's Video News Service, 72-73; artist-in-residence, Cummington Sch Arts, 74 & Women's Interart Ctr, 82; co-dir, Workshops for Women, 80-83. *Teaching:* Asst chmn photog, Pratt Inst, NY, 70-74; consult writing, City Univ NY, 72-73; dir, Fresh Film Ctr Photog, NY Univ Undergrad Film Sch, NY, 73-74; instr, NY Inst Photog, 78-80, Int Ctr Photog, 82-, NY Univ/Int Ctr Photog grad prog, 83 & NY Univ performance studies, 83. *Awards:* Grant, Whitney Mus, NY State Coun Arts, 72. *Bibliog:* Gazzette, Ms Mag, 73; Rochelle Ratner (auth), Beyond the limits, Soho Weekly News, 80; Carrie Rickey (auth), Third wave, Village Voice, 81. *Mem:* Women Artists in Revolution; Feminists in the Arts; Womens Caucus Art; Peacock Brigade; Professional Women Photogr. *Media:* Video, Xerography; Pastel, Watercolor. *Publ:* Auth, A personal decade, Heresies, No 16, 83. *Dealer:* New Yorker Films 43 West 61st St New York NY 10011. *Mailing Add:* 335 94th St New York NY 10128-5618

KLEEBLATT, NORMAN L
CURATOR, CRITIC
b Bridgeton, NJ, 48. *Study:* Rutgers Univ, New Brunswick, NJ, AB(art hist), 71; Conserv Ctr, Inst Fine Arts, NY Univ, dipl(conserv) & MA, 75. *Exhib:* John Singer Sargent: Portraits of the Wentheimer Family, 1999-2000; Mirroring Evil: Nazi Representations/Contemp Art and Popular Cult, 2001. *Collection Arranged:* Painting a Place in America: Jewish Artists in New York 1900-1945, Jewish Mus, New York, 91 & Collecting for the Twenty-First Century: Recent Acquisitions and Promised Gifts, 93; Too Jewish? Challenging Traditional Identities Traveling Exhib, Jewish Mus, San Francisco, Univ Calif, Los Angeles, Armand Hammer Mus Art & Cult Ctr, The Contemp, Baltimore & Nat Mus Am Jewish Hist, Philadelphia, 96; An Expressionist in Paris: The Paintings of Chaim Soutine, Los Angeles Co Mus Art & Cincinnati Art Mus, 98; The Dreyfus Affair, 87; and many others. *Pos:* Susan & Elihu Rose Cur Fine Arts, Jewish Mus, NY, 95-05, curator, 2005-; planning cons Nat Found for Jewish Cult, 95, 96, 97, 98, 2000. *Awards:* Post-Grad Fel, Nat Mus Fel Act, 75-76; Presidence d'Honneur, Comite Scientifique, Societe Internationale d'histoire de l'Affaire Dreyfus, 94-; Mus Prof Fel, Nat Endowment Arts, 96. *Mem:* Col Art Asn; Am Asn Mus; Int Asn Art Critics; Coun Am Jewish Mus. *Publ:* Auth, Merdel The caricatural attack against Emile Zola, No 52, 54-58, Art J, fall 93; Identity politics: multivalent voices, No 83, 29-31 & 35, Art Am, 12/95; The other edge: Representing

ethnicity, gender and sexuality in New York, No 5, 22-36, Issues Archit Art & Design, 97; Autour du Corps d'Alfred Dreyfus, No 2, 37-42, Lee Cahiers du Judaisme, summer 98; Master Narritives/Minority Artists, No 57/3, 29-35, Art J, fall 98; Persistence of memory, Art in Am, 6/2000; Faith: The Impact of Judeo-Christian Religion on Art at the Millennium (catalog), The Aldrich Mus of Contemporary Art, 2000; plus many others. *Mailing Add:* 330 E 63rd St New York NY 10021

KLEEMANN, RON
PAINTER
b Bay City, Mich, July 1937. *Study:* Univ Mich, BS(design), 61. *Work:* Guggenheim Mus, Mus Mod Art, NY; Hirshhorn Mus, Washington; Indianapolis Mus Art; Univ Va Art Mus; Air & Space Mus, Washington; and others. *Comn:* Painting for reproduction, Corvette catalog, 86. *Exhib:* Mus Contemp Art, Chicago, 71; Wichita Mus, Wichita State Univ, Kans, 75; New Acquisitions, Mus Mod Art, NY, 77; Flint Inst Fine Arts, 78; Louis K Meisel Gallery, NY, 79, 83, 92 & 94; Rich Perlow Gallery, NY, 87; RH Love Galleries, Chicago, 87; Cheekwood Fine Arts Ctr, Nashville, Tenn, 92. *Pos:* Off artist, Indianapolis 500, 77-79 & Super Bowl XVII, Pasadena, Calif, 83. *Bibliog:* Andrea Mikotajok (auth), American Realists at Louis K Meisel, Arts Mag, 1/75; articles, Indianapolis News, 4/77 & Chicago Tribune, 10/77. *Dealer:* Louis K Meisel Gallery 141 Prince St New York NY 10012. *Mailing Add:* c/o Louis K Meisel Gallery 141 Prince St New York NY 10012

KLEIDON, DENNIS ARTHUR
EDUCATOR, DESIGNER
b Chicago, Ill, Sept 20, 42. *Study:* Bradley Univ, Peoria, Ill, 60-61; Univ Ill, Champaign, 61-64; Ill Wesleyan Univ, Bloomington, BFA(com art), 66; Ill State Univ, Normal, MS(sculpture), 67. *Work:* Massillon Mus, Ohio, Northern Ill Univ, DeKalb; Ill State Univ; Numa Ltd, Akron. *Comn:* Commemorative sculpture wall piece (wood, assemblage), Akron Nat Bank & Trust, Tuchman, Canute, Ryan & Wyatt, Architects, Rolling Acres Shopping Ctr, 76; promotional design, Scheeser & Buckley, Inc, Akron, 76; illustration, Hesselbart & Mitten Advert, Akron, 75 & Alsides, Inc, Akron, 75. *Exhib:* All-Ohio Exhib, Canton Art Inst, 71 & 72; Images, Nat Drawing Competition, Baldwin Wallace Col, Berea, Ohio, 72; Cleveland Invitational Exhib, Cooper Sch of Art, 72 & Lake Erie Col, 73; one-man show, Akron Art Inst, 76; and others. *Pos:* Designer/deliniator, Wight & Assoc, Downers Grove, Ill, 65-66 & Richard R Cramer, Architects, Hinsdale, Ill, 67; pres, Kleidon & Assoc, 75-. *Teaching:* Instr drawing, Univ Ill, Champaign, 67-69; From assoc prof to prof graphic design, Univ Akron, 69-. *Awards:* Res grants, Univ Akron, 70 & 77; First Place/Painting, All-Ohio Exhib, Canton Art Inst, 71; Merit Award/Design, Nat Univ & Col Designers Asn Design Competition, 75. *Bibliog:* Tex Tech Univ, Color Print USA (filmstrip), 71; Packaging education: The case for cooperation, Boxboard Container Mag, 11/79. *Media:* Acrylic, Vinyl. *Dealer:* Gallery 200 200 W Mound Columbus OH 43223. *Mailing Add:* 4670 Granger Rd Akron OH 44333-1312

KLEIMAN, ALAN
PAINTER, SCULPTOR
b Brooklyn, NY, Feb 20, 38. *Study:* Richmond Prof Inst, BFA; Cranbrook Acad Art, MFA; study with Oscar Kokoschka, Salzburg, Austria. *Work:* Mus Mod Art, Whitney Mus Am Art, Metrop Mus Art, NY; Carnegie Mus, Pittsburgh, Pa; Boston Mus Fine Art, Mass. *Comn:* Abstract fresco, Richmond City Fathers, Va, 57; rubber paint pool mural, comn by Mr & Mrs Pechenik, York, Pa, 60; abstract painted wall, Detroit Archit League, Mich, 65; abstract painted wall, City Walls, NY, 72. *Exhib:* Biennale, Sao Paulo, Brazil, 68; Silvermine, Conn, 70; Carnegie Inst Int, Pittsburgh, 71; In The Realm of the Monocramatic, Chicago & NY, 79; Painting About Painting, Paterson Col, NJ, 81; Beging, NY, 90; Elisabeth Harris Gallery, New York, NY, 94; O'Hara Gallery, New York, NY, 96; Robert Steel Gallery, New York, NY, 97; and others. *Pos:* Asst publicity dir, Artist Tenents Asn, 60-67; vpres, Grand St Artist Group, 70-75; chmn, Soho Artifacts, 71-75. *Awards:* Creative Artists Pub Serv fel & CETA grant, 78; Creative Artists Pub Serv Grant, 83; Nat Found Arts Grant, 90. *Bibliog:* Hans Van Deljen (auth), Alan Kleiman paints Europe, Frie Folkes, Amsterdam, 56; Arts Mag, 97; Review Mag, 97. *Media:* Watercolor, Oil. *Publ:* Auth, Painting Provincetown water, The Beacon, 61; Investigations into the light of red color, Arts, 76; Light dazzle and glow, The Soho Artist. *Dealer:* Area Code Gallery 31 Wooster St New York NY 10013. *Mailing Add:* 70 Grand St No 2 New York NY 10013

KLEIN, BEATRICE (T)
PAINTER, PRINTMAKER
b Lynchburg, Va, Feb 7, 20. *Study:* Md Inst Col Art, cert, 42; Art Students League, with Yasvo Kuniyoshi, 42-43; Va Commonwealth Univ, 71-74; study with Hans Hofmann, Provincetown, Mass, 44; Md Inst Col Art, Hon BFA, 95; MD Inst Col Art, BFA, 95. *Work:* Va Mus Fine Arts, Fed Reserve Bank, Nations Bank, Phillip Morris Co, Richmond, Va; Rocky Mount Art Ctr, NC. *Comn:* Dr Porter Vinson Prof of Medicine (portrait), 70, Dr George Oliver Pres (portrait), 75, Va Commonwealth Univ, Richmond; Mr Harry Schwarzchild Pres (portrait), Cent Nat Bank, Richmond, Va, 78; Rabbi Ariel Goldburg (portrait), Beth Ahabah Synagogue, Richmond, Va, 78. *Exhib:* Six-State Painting Exhib, Anderson Gallery, Va Commonwealth Univ, Richmond, 73; Nat Drawing & Photog Show, 2nd St Gallery, Charlottesville, Va, 75-76; Va Printmakers, Va Mus Fine Arts, Richmond, 76; Va Craftsmen, Va Mus Fine Arts, Richmond, Va, 80; Va Prints & Drawing, Va Mus Fine Arts, Richmond, 81; one-man retrospective, Artspace Gallery, Richmond, Va, 94; group exhib, The Figure Pastel Drawings, Artspace Gallery, Richmond, Va, 2003. *Awards:* Cert of Distinction, Va Mus Biennial, Va Mus Fine Arts, 55-59; Irene Leach Mem Prize, Chrysler Mus, Norfolk, Va, 58; 3rd Prize for Painting, State Painting Show, Anderson Gallery, Va Commonwealth Univ, 73. *Mem:* Richmond Artists Asn (pres, 60-64). *Media:* Oil, Watercolor; Silkscreen, Pastel. *Dealer:* Artspace Gallery 6 E Broad St Richmond VA 23226; Artifacts 1608 Harborough Rd Richmond VA 23233. *Mailing Add:* 10003 Cedarfield Ct Richmond VA 23233-1935

KLEIN, CECELIA F
HISTORIAN, EDUCATOR
b Pittsburgh, Pa, June 5, 38. *Study:* Oberlin Col, BA, 60, MA, 67; Columbia Univ, PhD with Douglas Fraser, 72. *Collection Arranged:* Art of Pre-Columbian Am, Meadow Brook Art Gallery, Oakland Univ, Rochester, Mich, 76; Mother, Worker, Ruler, Witch: Cross-Cultural Images of Women, Mus Cult Hist, Univ Calif, Los Angeles, 80. *Teaching:* Asst prof art hist, Oakland Univ, Rochester, 72-76; assoc prof art hist, Univ Calif, Los Angeles, 76-88, prof, 88-. *Awards:* Distinguished Teaching of Art History Award, Col Art Asn, 2000. *Mem:* Col Art Asn; Asn Latin Am Art. *Res:* Pre-Columbian art history, with emphasis on Aztec art/iconography. *Interests:* Relation Aztec art to social, historical & political context. *Publ:* Auth, The Devil and the Skirt: an Iconographic Inquiry into Prehispanic Nature of the Tzitzimime, In: Ancient Mesoamerica, 2000, In: Estudios de Cultural Nahuatl, 2000; None or All of the Above: Gender Ambiguity in Hahua Ideology, In: Gender in Prehispanic America: A Symposium at Dumbarton Oaks 12 and 13 October 1996, 2001; coauth (with Eulogio Guzman, Elisa C. Mandell, Maya Stanfield-Mazzi, and Josephine Volpe), Shamanitis: A Pre-Columbian Art Historical Disease, In: The Concept of Shamanism: Uses and Abuses, 2001. *Mailing Add:* c/o Dept Art Hist Dodd 100 Univ Calif 405 Hilgard Ave Los Angeles CA 90095

KLEIN, CYNTHIA
APPRAISER
Study: Univ Mass, Amherst, BA(art hist), BS (bus admin); Rutgers Univ, grad studies in Art Hist; Phi Beta Kappa. *Pos:* Specialist, paintings dept to dir, prints dept CG Sloan & Co Auctioneers, N Bethesda, Md, 91-2000; vpres, dir, prints dept Doyle NY, 2000-; Prints appraiser, Antiques Roadshow, WGBH-PBS, currently. *Mem:* Am Hist Prints Collectors Soc; Soc for Japanese Arts. *Mailing Add:* Doyle NY 175 E 87th St New York NY 10128

KLEIN, DORIS
PRINTMAKER, SCULPTOR
b New York, NY, Nov 10, 18. *Study:* Art Students League, with Sidney Gross; Works Progress Admin Sch, with James Leschay & Anton Refregier; also sculpture with Maurice Glickman. *Work:* Univ Maine Permanent Collection; New Sch Permanent Collection, NY. *Exhib:* Mus Belles Artes, Arg, 63; Maxwell Gallery, San Francisco, 67; Audubon Artists, 68; Roko Gallery, NY, 68-72; and many others. *Awards:* Best of Show, Jersey City Mus, 63-66; Marion K Haldenstein Mem Prize, Nat Asn Women Artists, 68; Grumbacher Award, Mamaroneck Artists Guild, 69; Fame and Fortune Contest winner, for writing sone "When You're With Me" arranged by Tommy Dorsey, sung by Frank Sinatra, 41. *Bibliog:* Hilton Kramer (auth), Rev of Roko show, New York Times, 68; Betty Chamberlain (auth), Philharmonic Hall program, 72. *Mem:* Nat Asn Women Artists. *Media:* All. *Publ:* Auth, Paintings & Poems by the Radio Poet, Longmeadow Press, 95; contribr, The Best of Metropolitan Diary, Mallioni Morris. *Mailing Add:* 1510 York Ave Apt 6B New York NY 10021-0751

KLEIN, ELLEN LEE
PAINTER, EDUCATOR
b New York, NY. *Study:* City Col New York, BA; Pratt Inst, MFA. *Work:* Thirteen Collection, NY; Hofstra Mus, Long Island, NY. *Exhib:* Solo exhibs, Green Mountain Gallery, NY, & Maples Gallery, Fairleigh Dickinson Univ, Sotheby's, NY; 15th Ann Art Show, Fairleigh Dickinson Univ; Cornell Med Ctr, NY; Eubie Blake Mus, Baltimore, Md; City Col, NY. *Pos:* Dir, Art Alumni Asn, City Col, NY & Settlement Arts Consortium, United Neighborhood Housing, NY; adminr, Sch Fine Arts, Nat Acad Design, NY, 80-94; critic & writer, ARTS Mag, NY, 82-88; dir humanities, Educ Alliance, NY, 95-98. *Teaching:* Adv, Robeson Ctr Gallery, Rutgers Univ, Newark, NJ; instr drawing & art hist, High Sch Music & Art, NY; adj prof contemp art, Jersey City State Col; instr painting, Usdan Ctr Creative & Performing Arts, Wyandanch, NY; adj prof, City Col NY. *Bibliog:* Lawrence Campbell (auth), article, Art News, 9/73; Klein at Phoenix, Park East, 3/76; Nina Ffrench-Frazier (auth), Gallery guide, Westsider, 4/27/78. *Mem:* Col Art Asn Am; Artists Equity; Am Asn Mus; City Col Art Alumni Asn; Int Council Mus; Nat Asn Female Execs. *Media:* Oil, Paper Collage. *Publ:* Auth, Toby Buonagario: More optical bounce to the ounce, 86, Beneath the surface of Terence La Noue, 86, All kinds of rational questions: An interview with Michael Goldberg, 86 & Debra Weier - in all Dimensions, 88, ARTs Mag; Manhattan Spotlight on Furman J Finck, Manhattan Spotlight, 4/88; auth, Bill Traylor: Observing Life, American Art Review, 99. *Mailing Add:* 139-12 84th Dr No 1F Briarwood NY 11435

KLEIN, LYNN (ELLEN)
PAINTER, PHOTOGRAPHER
b San Francisco, Calif, Apr 14, 50. *Study:* Univ Minn, BA, 74, MFA, 76; Cite Internationale des Arts, Paris, 84-86 & 98. *Work:* Philadelphia Mus Art; Oakland Mus, Calif; Walker Art Ctr, Minneapolis; Nat Libr Prints & Photographs, Paris, France; San Jose Mus Art, Calif; Crocker Art Mus, Calif; Mpls Inst Arts; NY Pub Libr. *Comn:* Mitsukoshi Manno Golf Club, Tokyo, 96; Renaissance Hotel, Hong Kong, 97; Miami Int Ariport, Fla, 2000; Fairmont Mayakoba, Cancun, Mex, 2004; Ritz Carlton, Palm Beach, Fla, 2005; and others. *Exhib:* West 81, Art & Law, 81, Lighter Shade of Pale, 90, Minn Mus Am Art, St Paul; one-woman show, Coffman Gallery, Univ, Minn, Minneapolis, 82, Print Club, Philadelphia, Pa, 85, Foster White Gallery, Seattle, 89 & Carolyn Ruff Gallery, 94, Robert Green Fine Arts, Mill Valley, Calif, 2000; Photog Invitational, Tweed Mus Art, 83; Textile Arts Int: Rauschenberg, Samaras & Klein, 90; San Francisco Bay Area Women Artists Mentors, San Francisco Art Comn Gallery, 96; US Art, San Francisco Int Art Expo, 96; The Painterly Print, Mill Valley, Calif, 96; Craftsman Guild & Calif Heritage Gallery, 98; California Artists at Achenbach, Palace Legion Honor, San Francisco, Calif, 2001; Visible Rhythm, San Jose Mus Art, 2003; NeoMod, Recent CA Abstraction, Crocker Art Mus, Sacramento, Calif, 2005; Editions LTD: Prints, Mpls Inst Art, 2006. *Pos:* vis artist, Textile Ctr Minn, 2003. *Teaching:*

Instr design, Univ Minn, 74-84; asst, Design Dept, Col Educ, 74-76, lectr, 76-84 & instr art educ, 78-80; asst, Midwest Conserv, Minneapolis, 79-83; vis fac, Quadna Mountain Lodge, Hill City, Minn, 78; vis artist, Iowa State Univ, 84 & Textile Ctr Mpls, 2003. *Awards:* Rockefeller Found Fel, 84-86; Jerome Found Printmaking Fel, Kala Inst, 89; Cite Int des Arts Residency, Paris, France, 98; others. *Bibliog:* Textilforum, Zeitgeossische, 3/93; Peter Selz (monograph) for solo exhib, 2000; Yoshiko Wada (auth), Memory on Cloth, 2002. *Mem:* Achenbach Graphic Arts Coun. *Media:* Oil; Miscellaneous Media. *Publ:* Double/Absent, Ed 15, Vermillion Editions, Diptych, 83; Wild Women, Ed 20, Blue Sky Press, 2002; Brave New World, Edition 20, Blue Sky Press, 2004. *Dealer:* Ira Wolk St Helena CA; Robert Green Fine Art Mill Valley CA

KLEIN, MICHAEL EUGENE
HISTORIAN, WRITER
b Philadelphia, Pa, July 30, 40. *Study:* Rutgers Col, New Brunswick, NJ, BA, 62; Columbia Univ, New York, MA, 65, PhD, 71. *Collection Arranged:* John Covert, 1882-1960 (auth, bk), Smithsonian Inst Press, 76. *Pos:* Vis cur, Hirshhorn Mus, 76. *Teaching:* Asst prof art hist, State Univ NY, Brockport, 71-73; asst prof, Univ SC, 73-77; asst prof, Western Ky Univ, 77-80, assoc prof, 81-. *Mem:* Col Art Asn Am. *Res:* American art of early 20th century, especially John Covert; Arnold Friedman; Meyer Schapiro. *Publ:* Auth, John Covert's time: Cubism, Duchamp, Einstein, a quasi scientific fantasy, summer 74 & John Covert's studios in 1916 and 1923, fall 79, Art J; Scotese collection at the Columbia Museum of Art, Southeastern Col Art Conf J, fall 74; auth, John Covert and the Arensberg circle, Arts Mag, 5/77. *Mailing Add:* Dept Art Western Ky Univ Bowling Green KY 42101

KLEINBAUER, W EUGENE
HISTORIAN
b Los Angeles, Calif, June 15, 37. *Study:* Univ Calif, Berkeley, with Walter Horn, BA & MA, 62; Princeton Univ, with Richard Krautheimer & Kurt Weitzmann, PhD, 67. *Pos:* Pres, Internat Ctr Medieval Art, 87-90. *Teaching:* Asst prof hist art, Univ Calif, Los Angeles, 65-72; chmn, Dept Fine Arts, Ind Univ, 73-76, chmn arts admin prog, 73-75 & fall 78, prof hist art, 77-, prof Near Eastern languages & cultures, 85- & chmn dept hist art, 92-95; Sam & Ayala Zacks vis prof hist art, Hebrew Univ, Jerusalem, 78; assoc dir, Henry Hope Sch Fine Arts, Ind Univ, 88-92; F L Morgan vis prof, Univ Louisville, 96-2006. *Awards:* Nat Endowment Humanities Fel, 76-77; Pres Award Distinguished Teaching, Ind Univ, 99. *Mem:* Col Art Asn Am; Int Ctr Medieval Art (mem bd dir, 70-73, 74-77 & 81-83, ed, GESTA, 80-83, pres, 87-90); Medieval Acad Am; US Nat Comt Byzantine Studies; Speculum (ed bd, 90-93). *Res:* Specialist in medieval art and architecture; historiography of Western art. *Publ:* E Kitzinger, Art of Byzantium & Medieval West, Ind Univ, 76; auth, Research Guide to the History of Western Art, Am Libr Asn, 82; Early Christian and Byzantine Architecture, GK Hall, 92; numerous scholarly articles & reviews; Saint Sophia in Constantinople, 99; Hagia Sophia, 04. *Mailing Add:* Dept Art History Indiana Univ Bloomington IN 47405

KLEINBERG, SUSAN
ARTIST
b Phoenix, Ariz. *Study:* Hunter Col with Bob Morris & Tony Smith, MA, 72; Pomona Col, BA; Univ Guadalajara, Univ Madrid, grad work. *Work:* Los Angeles Co Mus, Calif; Cincinnati Mus, Ohio; La Jolla Mus, Calif; Am Ctr Paris, France; IBM, NY & Paris, France; Venice Biennale Archive, Italy; White House Collection, Washington, DC; and others. *Comn:* Park-slides, Pomona, Calif, 75; Triptich paintings, Liebman, Adolph, Cherne, NY, 87, Rainen Corp, San Francisco, 88 & Media Ctr for Human Rights, NY, 90; 2 paintings, comn by Mrs L Levin, Los Angeles, Calif, 87; painting, Colo Open Lands, Land Trust, 89; painting, Univ Calif, San Diego, 91. *Exhib:* Los Angeles Co Mus, Calif, 79; Mass Inst Technol, Boston, 82; Mus Mod Art, NY, 82; Light/Walls, Am Ctr Paris/Beauborg, France, 87; Orton Collection, Cincinnati Mus, Ohio, 88; Sarabhai Collection, Ahmedabad, India; Arte Laguna, Milan, Italy, 95; Venice Biennale, Italy, 95; Studio D'Arte Barnabo, Venice, Italy, 96; Wilshire Blvd Temple, Los Angeles, 97; PSI, NY, 99; Venice Biennale, 01; Neuhof Gallery, NY, 02; Spec Projects, Chicago Inst Art Fair, 02; Tasende Gallery, La Jolla, Calif, 02; PSI/Mus Modern Art, 02; Mus Fine Arts, Buenos Aires, 02; Furture Democracy, Istanbul Biennale 2003, Akbank Headquarter, Istanbul, Turkey; Total Mus, Seul Korea, 2004; Istituto Veneto, 2005, Venice Italy; Anditoruium S Marganta Unirojvenice, Opening day of Venice Biennale, June, 2005. *Awards:* Nat Endowment Arts, 77; Max Beckman Award, Brooklyn Mus, 80; Am Acad Rome, 95 & 96; City of Venice Grant, 95; Ziegler Found grant, 95, award, 01, 02; Samsung Corp grant, 01-03. *Mem:* Soc Fels; Am Acad Rome; Nat Arts Club. *Media:* Paint, Drawing, Video. *Mailing Add:* 250 W 85th St 14-H New York NY 10024

KLEINMAN, SUE
PAINTER, LECTURER
b New York, NY. *Study:* Pratt Inst, Brooklyn, BFA; Caton-Rose Inst Fine Arts; New Sch Social Res, New York; Mus Mod Art, New York, with Zoltan Hecht & Donald Stacey; also with Raphael Soyer & Anthony Toney. *Work:* Brown Univ, RI; Fairleigh Dickinson Univ, Rutherford, NJ; Maimonides Hosp, Brooklyn; Mus Art, Ft Lauderdale, Fla. *Exhib:* Knickerbocker Art, 59 & Audubon Art, 60, Weiner Gallery, NY; one-woman shows, Lord & Taylor Gallery, NY, 76, Pompano Recreation Ctr, Pompano Beach, Fla, 80 & Pompano Beach Pub Libr, 83, 85, 86, 89, 91, 94, 96 & 98. *Pos:* Lectr & docent, Ft Lauderdale Mus Art, 73-96; instr art appreciation, Century Village, 84-85; vpres, Mus Art; vpres & prog chmn, Bnai Bnith; bd dir & founder, Ort-Pompano Chap. *Awards:* Bronze Medal, Village Art Ctr, 58; Silver Medal, Trade Bank New York. *Bibliog:* Jane Jaffe (auth), article, Manhattan E, 65; Dorothy Hall (auth), article, Park E, 69; Saint-Evermond (auth), article, France-Amerique, 69; Pompano Monday Paper, 87. *Mem:* Artists Equity Asn; Nat Women's Art Asn; Broward Art Guild; Boca Raton Art Ctr; ORT. *Media:* Oil and Palette Knife. *Dealer:* Contextual Gallery 813 E Los Olas Blvd Ft Lauderdale FL 33301

KLEINSMITH, BRUCE JOHN See Nutzle, Futzie (Bruce) John Kleinsmith

KLEMENT, VERA
PAINTER
b Danzig, Ger, Dec 14, 29; US citizen. *Study:* Cooper Union Sch Art & Archit, grad, 50. *Work:* Mus Mod Art, Jewish Mus, NY; Philadelphia Mus Art; Northern Trust Bank, First Nat Bank, Chicago; Smart Mus, Chicago; Mus Contemp Art, Chicago; Ariz Mus Art, Tucson; Art Inst of Chicago; Block Mus, Evanston Ill; Ill Art Mus, Springfield; Miami Univ Art Mus, Oxford; Davis Mus of Contemp Art, Sedalia, Mo; Davis Mus, Wellesley, Mass. *Comn:* Ed of etchings, NY Hilton/Rockefeller Ctr, 61; 27 1/2 ft & 2 ft painting, Kemper Ins Co, Long Grove, Ill, 75; painting, McCormick Place, Chicago. *Exhib:* Walker Art Ctr Invitational, Minneapolis, Minn, 77; Jewish Mus, NY, 82; one-woman show, Spertus Mus, 87; group show, Ill State Mus, Springfield, 90; Corcoran Gallery Art, Washington, DC, 94; Retrospective, Cult Ctr, Chicago, 99; one-person show, Ft Wayne Mus of Art, In, 02, Mary & Leigh Block Mus Art, 02, Univ Ariz Mus Art, Tucson, 01, Tarble Art Ctr, Ea Ill Univ, Charleston, 02. *Teaching:* Instr painting, Univ Ill, 68-69; asst prof art, Univ Chicago, 69-78, assoc prof, 78-86, prof, 87-95, prof art emeritus, 95-. *Awards:* Louis Comfort Tiffany Found Grant, 54; Guggenheim fel, 81-82; Nat Endowment Arts, 87; Pollock/Krasner Found Grant, 98-99; Ill Arts Coun Grant; Camargo Found Residence, Cassis, France, 2006; and others. *Bibliog:* William S Lieberman (auth), Printmaking & the American woodcut today, Perspectives USA, 53; Amy Goldin (auth), Vitality vs greasy kid stuff, Art Gallery Mag 4/72; article in Artists' Writings, publ by NAME, 77; Dore Ashton (auth), Two Part Connection: Vera Klement's Painting, Arts Mag, 3/84, retrospective catalog, A Question of Drawing, 89; James Yood (auth), Vera Klement, Artforum, 89; Donald Kuspit (auth), Vera Klenent's Poem-Paintings; Sue Taylor (auth) Vera Klement: Things Made Mythic. *Media:* Oil. *Specialty:* Maya Polsky Gallery, Chicago. *Dealer:* Maya Polsky Gallery Chicago IL. *Mailing Add:* 727 S Dearborn Chicago IL 60605

KLESH-BUTKOVSKY, JANE
GRAPHIC ARTIST, PAINTER
b Hazelton, PA, Feb 14, 57. *Study:* Madison Art Sch, under Robert Brackman & Bill Schultz; Cape Sch, under Henry Hensche; Annapolis Art Inst, under Cedric & Jonette Egli; Pocono Pines, Pa, under William Herring, Charles Sovek, Charles Ried, Charles Movaui at Pocono Pine, Pa,; Nat Acad Design, under Everette Raymond Kinstler & Sam Adouqui. *Work:* Hazelton Art League, Hazelton, Pa. *Exhib:* Nat Acad of Design 171st Ann Exhib, NY, 1995; Am Artists Prof League 75th Ann Exhib, NY, 2003; Am Impressionist Soc 5th Ann Exhib, Vero Beach, Fla, 2003; Allied Artist of Am 90th Ann Exhib, NY, 2003; Audubon Artists 63rd Ann Exhib, NY, 2005. *Teaching:* Instr, drawing, Luzerne Co Community League, 1995-. *Awards:* Am Artists Fund Award, Am Artists Prof League 75th, Am Artists Fund, 2003; Butler Inst of Am Allied Artists 90th, Butler Inst, 2003; Best of Show, Hazelton Art League 48th, Evelyn Graham, 2006. *Mem:* Audubon Artists; Pa Plein Air Soc (signature mem); Portrait Soc of Am; Am Impressionist Soc; Hazelton Art League. *Media:* Charcoal, Oil, Watercolor. *Mailing Add:* 216 W Chapel St Hazleton PA 18201

KLETT, MARK
PHOTOGRAPHER
b Albany, NY, Sept 9, 52. *Study:* St Lawrence Univ, BS, 74; State Univ NY, MFA, 77. *Hon Degrees:* Hon Dr, St Lawrence Univ, 2004. *Work:* Mus Mod Art & Whitney Mus, NY; Los Angeles Co Mus Mod Art & Los Angeles Co Mus Art, Calif; Art Inst Chicago, Ill; High Mus Art, Atlanta; J B Speed Art Mus, Louisville. *Exhib:* Solo exhibs, Los Angeles Co Mus Art, 84, Art Inst Chicago, 84, Kathleen Ewing Gallery, Washington, 94, Addison Gallery Am Art, Andover, Mass, 94, Scottsdale Ctr Arts, Ariz, 94, Nat Mus Am Art Smithsonian Inst, Washington, 94 & Pace Wildenstein McGill, NY, 95, Huntington Art Galleries, 99, Cleveland Art Mus, 98, The Huntington, San Marino, 99, Ariz State Univ, 2004, Nev Mus Art, Reno, 04, Neuberger Mus Art, Purchase, NY, 04, Frost Art Mus, Miami, 05; Photographs from the Last Decade, San Francisco Mus Mod Art, 88; Recent/Ancient Artifacts of the Southwest, Anderson Ranch Arts Ctr, Aspen, Colo, 88; Min Gallery, Tokyo, 88; Three Photographers, Harnett Gallery, Univ Rochester, NY, 88; L'Oeil de la Lettre Evidence of Man, Amon Carter Mus, Ft Worth, 89; On the Art of Fixing a Shadow, One Hundred and Fifty Yrs of Photog, Nat Gallery Art, Washington, 89; Panorama of California, Oakland Mus, Calif, 92; Hidden Faces, Paul Kopeikin Gallery, Los Angeles, 94. *Teaching:* Acad prof, Ariz State Univ, 82-; Regents prof art, Ariz State Univ, Tempe. *Awards:* Art Fel, Nat Endowment Arts, 79, 82, 84 & 93; Visual Arts Fel, AVA, 85; Creative Arts Award, Brandeis Univ, 90; Japan US Friendship Comn 95, Buhl Found, 99; fel, Guggenheim Found, 04. *Bibliog:* William L Fox (auth), View Finder: Mark Klett, Photography and the Reinvention of Landscape, Univ NMex Press, 2001. *Mem:* Soc Photog Educ. *Publ:* Coauth, Second View: The Rephotographic Survey Project, Univ NMex Press, 84; Headlands: The Marin Coast at the Golden Gate, Univ NMex Press, 89; One City/Two Visions, Chronicle Books, 90; Revealing Territory, Univ NMex Press, 92; Desert Legends, Henry Holt, 94; Third Views, Second Sights, Mus NMex Press, 2004; The Black Rock Desert, Univ Ariz Press, 2002. *Dealer:* Pace/MacGill New York. *Mailing Add:* 1136 S Ash Ave Tempe AZ 85281

KLINDT, STEVEN
ADMINISTRATOR
b Davenport, Iowa, Dec 18, 47. *Study:* Sch of Art, Univ Iowa, BA(studio art), 70, MA(photog), 74. *Collection Arranged:* Photograph Invitational, Galesburg Civic Art Ctr, Ill, 76; Proposals for Lake Sculpture, Evanston Art Ctr, Ill, 77; New American Photography (auth, catalog), Columbia Col, 82. *Pos:* Dir, Galesburg Civic Art Ctr, 74-76, Evanston Art Ctr, 76-79, Chicago Ctr Contemp Photog, Columbia Col Galleries, 79-83, Mus Contemp Photog, Columbia Col, 83-84, Tweed Mus Art,

Duluth, Minn, 84-89; exec dir, Queens Mus Art, New York, 89-93, Morris Mus, Morristown, NJ, 93-. *Teaching:* Mus studies MA program, Columbia Col, Chicago, 79-84; Visual Arts Admin, New York Univ, 92-. *Mem:* Col Art Asn; Am Asn Mus; Asn Art Mus Dirs; Park Ave Club. *Publ:* Ed, Jerry N Uelsmann, Photographs from 1975-1979, Columbia Col, Chicago, 80; Light Touching Silver-Photographs, Columbia Col, Chicago, 80; and others. *Mailing Add:* Morris Mus 6 Normandy Heights Rd Morristown NJ 07960

KLINE, HARRIET
PAINTER, PRINTMAKER, PAPERMAKER, SCULPTOR

b New York, NY, Sept 26 1916. *Study:* Hunter Col, BA; also with Isaac Soyer; Art Students League, with Robert Philipp & Morris Kantor; China Inst, NY, with Prof YC Wang, 45-59. *Work:* Grey Art Ctr, NY Univ; State Art Collection, Dresden, Ger; State Univ NY Col Oswego; Western New Eng Col, Springfield, Mass; Jane Voorhees Zimmerli Mus, New Brunswick, NJ; numerous pvt collections including Estate of Bill Blass, IBM, Estate of Malcolm Forbes. *Exhib:* Silvermine Nat Exhib, Silvermine Guild, New Canaan, Conn, 59, 74, 86 & 89; Solo exhibs, Selected Artists Gallery, NY, 60-75, Paper Work, 38th Ann, Butler Inst Am Art, 74 & Katonah Gallery, NY, 80; First Exhib Am Graphics, Albertinum Mus, Dresden, 80; First Nat Asn Women Artists, traveling show, Israel & Egypt, 82; Solo Moneyworks, Automation House, NY, 84, Schiller-Wapner galleries, NY, 88, Katonah Gallery, NY, 89 & Lobby Gallery, NY, 92; Five Moneyworks Canvases, Tiffany & Co, 89; Five Moneyworks Sculptures, Tiffany & Co, 92; retrospective, From Watercolors to Moneyworks, Katonah Village Libr Gallery, NY, 1998; Sterling Glen, Rye Brook, NY, 2006. *Teaching:* Instr, pvt classes, 59-68. *Awards:* Nat Asn Women Artists Works on Paper, 70, 72, 78, 80, 84, 90 & 95; Am Soc Contemp Artists Watercolors & Graphics Award, 79, 83 & 84, Works on Paper, 89. *Mem:* Nat Asn Women Artists; Am Soc Contemp Artists; life mem Art Students League; Katonah Mus Artists Asn (awards 2001, 2002). *Media:* Watercolor; Moneyworks. *Publ:* articles, NY Times, 5/22/88, 2/12/89, 8/15/92 & Westchester, 9/27/98; article, The Numismatist, 5/88; article, Coinage Mag, 6/88; article, Intercorp, 10/13/89; Spotlight, 10/98; and others. *Dealer:* Note: Moneyworks is a trademark; all rights reserved by artist. *Mailing Add:* 1200 King St c/o Sterling Glen Apt 341 Rye Brook NY 10573

KLINE, KATY
DIRECTOR

Pos: Cur, coord spec projects List Visual Arts Ctr, Mass Inst of Technol, Cambridge, dir, 1986-98; Bowdoin Col Mus Art, Brunswick, Maine, 1998-; Review panelist, Nat Endowment for Arts, Inst Mus Servs, Adolph and Esther Gottlieb Found; juror Del, Art Mus Biennial, Mid Atlantic Arts Found, RI Sch Design Mus Art, McKnight Found; vis comt, Williams Col Mus Art. *Awards:* Recipient Gyorgy Kepes Fel Prize, 1995. *Mailing Add:* Bowdoin Col Mus Art 9400 Col Station Brunswick ME 04011

KLING, VINCENT GEORGE
ARCHITECT

b East Orange, NJ, May 9, 16. *Study:* Columbia Univ, BA, 40; Mass Inst of Technol, MA, 42. *Pos:* Found, sr partner Kling Partnership, Philadelphia, 46-64; prin, Vincent G Kling & Assoc, 64-73; Kling-Lindquist Inc, 73-86; consult, archit, MARTA, Atlanta, 75 -; consult archit, Community Col, Philadelphia, 79 -; consult, archit, Seattle Transit, 83 -; Kling-Lindquist Partnership Inc, 86-87. *Awards:* Gold medal and diploma of honor City Coun of Quito, Ecuador, 1961; award of excellence Artists Guild of Delaware Valley, 1976; Recipient Am Inst of Archits Lifetime Achievement award, 2003. *Mem:* Fel Am Inst of Archit; Nat Acad (assoc, 87-91, acad, 91-); Am Inst of Archit (Philadelphia chap) (pres, 65-66); Fountainebleau Fine Arts and Music Sch Asn; Soc Am Regist Archit Clubs: Mass Inst of Technol of Philadelphia, Columbia of Philadelphia Lodges: Lions. *Mailing Add:* 1259 Birchrun Rd Chester Springs PA 19425

KLIPPER, STUART DAVID
PHOTOGRAPHER

b Bronx, NY, Aug 27, 41. *Study:* Univ Mich, Col Lit, Sci & Arts, BA, 62, Col Archit & Design, 62-63. *Work:* Walker Art Ctr, Minneapolis; Art Inst Chicago; Mus Fine Arts, Boston; Mus Mod Art, NY; San Francisco Mus Mod Art; and many others. *Comn:* Anasazi Plates, Univ Mich; Cray I Computer, Cray Res Inc; The World in a Few States, First Bank Systems, Minneapolis. *Exhib:* 20th Century Am Photogr, Atkins Mus Fine Art, Kansas City, 74; Multiple Strip Images, Walker Art Ctr, Minneapolis, 78; Am Photog in the 70's, Art Inst Chicago, 79; Recent Work, Minn Mus Art, St Paul, 80; Art Inst Chicago, 80; Duluth Photogrs, Tweed Mus Art, Minn, 82; Minn Mus Art, 82; Portents in the North: Radiation in Lapland, Minn Mus Art, St Paul, 88; one-man shows, Jewish Mus, NY, 88, Czechoslovakia Photog Festival, 91, Minneapolis Inst Art, 92, Thompson Gallery, Minneapolis, 92, Twentieth Century Photog Gallery, NY, 93, Fernbank Mus Natural Hist, Atlanta, 93 & McDougall Gallery Art, Christchurch, NZ, 94; Arctic and Antarctic Photogs, San Francisco Mus Mod Art, 89; On Antarctica 1989 (selections from), Mus Mod Art, NY, 91; Between Heaven and Home, Nat Mus Am Art, 92; Images from a Frozen Land, Arlington Ohio Art Ctr, Byrd Polar Inst, 92; Art from the Rain Forest, Fernbank Mus, Atlanta, 92; Our Town, Burdin Gallery, Aperture Found, NY, 93; Automotive Minn, pArts Gallery, Minneapolis, 93; plus many others. *Collection Arranged:* Seven Photogr (guest-cur), Art Gallery, Macalester Col, St Paul, Minn, 78. *Teaching:* Instr photog, Minneapolis Col Art & Design, 70-71, vis prof, 74-75 & 78; vis prof photog, Colo Col, Colorado Springs, 78, 79, 80, 89. *Awards:* J S Guggenheim Mem Found Photogr Fel, 79-80, 89-90; Antarctic Serv Medal, US Navy, 89; Selectee, Artist in Antarctica Prog, Nat Sci Found, 89, 91 & 93; and others. *Mem:* Minn Artists' Exhib Prog. *Publ:* Auth, The Art of the Twin Cities, Portfolio Mag, summer 80; Bearing South, The Press, Colo Col, 91; numerous photograph in Between Heaven and Home exhib catalog, Aperture Mag, Harper's Newsweek, ArtForum & Art News, 91 & 92; American in a Few States, In: The Creating of the North American Landscape, John Hopkins Univ Press, 93; High Latitudes, Aperture Press, 93. *Mailing Add:* 5044 Xerxes Ave S Minneapolis MN 55410-2226

KLITZKE, THEODORE ELMER
EDUCATOR, HISTORIAN

b Chicago, Ill, Nov 4, 1915. *Study:* Art Inst Chicago, BFA, 40; Univ Chicago, BA, 41, PhD, 53; Kansas City Art Inst, Hon DFA, 80. *Teaching:* Instr art hist, Univ Chicago, 46-47; asst prof art hist, State Univ NY Col Ceramics, Alfred Univ, 53-59; prof art hist & chmn dept art, Univ Ala, Tuscaloosa, 59-68. *Mem:* Am Studies Asn; Col Art Asn Am; Soc Archit Historians; fel Nat Asn Sch Art. *Res:* Social history of American art; 19th century French art; German expressionism; history of prints and drawings. *Publ:* Contribr, reviews in Col Art J & Art Bull, 59-; contribr, Alexis de Tocqueville and the Arts in America, Festschrift Ulrich Middeldorf, 68; auth, Melville Price Retrospective: 1920-1970, Frame House Gallery, 70; contribr, Hermann Wilhelm (catalog), 72. *Mailing Add:* 7918 Sherwood Ave Baltimore MD 21204-3600

KLOBE, TOM
GALLERY DIRECTOR EMER, EDUCATOR

b Minneapolis, Minn, Nov 26, 40. *Study:* Univ Hawaii, BFA, 64, MFA, 68; Univ Calif, Los Angeles, 72-73. *Work:* State Found Cult & Arts, Contemp Mus & Honolulu Acad Arts, Honolulu, Hawaii; City of La Mirada, Calif; Nat Orange Show Collection, San Bernadino, Calif; Downey Mus Art, Calif. *Comn:* Onizuka Ctr Int Astronomy, Hawaii; and others. *Exhib:* Artists of Hawaii, Honolulu Acad Art, 67 & 68; 9th Ann Southern California Exhib, Long Beach Mus Art, 71; Calif-Hawaii Regional, Fine Arts Gallery, San Diego, 71, 72 & 76; Ann Purchase Prize Competition, Riverside Art Mus, Calif, 72-74 & 76; solo exhib, Downey Mus Art, Calif, 74. *Collection Arranged:* Hawaii State Art Mus, 02; Honolulu Acad Art, 02-03; Philippine Gallery, 03; Crossings 03: Korea/Hawaii; Labor & Leisure, 05; Western Galleries, Honolulu Acad Arts, 05; Treasures Hamilton Libr, 05. *Pos:* Actg dir, Downey Mus Art, Calif, 76; dir, Univ Hawaii Art Gallery, Honolulu, 77-2006. *Teaching:* Prof design & Islamic & Medieval art hist, Univ Hawaii, Honolulu, 77-2006. *Awards:* Print Casebooks, Best in Exhib Design, Koa Furniture of Hawaii, 81, Greek and Russian Icons, 84, 2nd Int Shoebox Sculpture Exhib, 85, The Art of Micronesia, 86 & The Art of Polish Posters, 87; Chevalier de l'Ordre des Artes et des Letters, Rep of France, 2000; Clopton Award, Distinguished Community Serv, Univ Hawaii, 03; Living Treasure of Hawaii Award, 05. *Mem:* Hawaii Mus Asn. *Res:* Exhib design & interpretation. *Publ:* Ed, Int Shoebox Sculpture Exhib, Univ Hawaii Art Gallery, 82, 85, 88, 91, 94, 97, 2000, & 03. *Mailing Add:* Univ Hawaii Art Gallery Honolulu HI 96822

KLONARIDES, CAROLE ANN
VIDEO ARTIST, CURATOR

b Washington, DC, Apr 2, 1951. *Study:* Va Commonwealth Univ, Richmond, BFA(painting & printmaking), 73; Whitney Mus Independent Study Prog, New York, 72-73; New Sch Social Res, New York, MA(media studies), 83. *Work:* Mus Mod Art, NY; Ctr Georges Pompidou, Paris, France; Donnell Media Ctr, NY Pub Libr, NY; Mus Art, RI Sch Design, Providence; Contemp Arts Mus, Houston, Tex. *Comn:* 60 second video psa, Nat Asn Artists' Orgn, New York, Art Against AIDS, AmFAR; 6 1/2 minute video art tape, Channel Four, NYSCA, NYFA, United Kingdom, 88; 11 two-three minute videos, Olympia & York, NY, 88; 11 41 minute video, Wexner Ctr Visual Arts & BBC2 (United Kingdom). *Exhib:* Video: Heroes/Anti-Heroes, Contemp Arts Mus, Houston, Tex, 84; San Sabastion Film/Video Festival, San Sebastion, Spain, 84; Video Recent Acquisitions, Mus Mod Art, NY, 86; Films on Art, A Festival at the Mus Boymans-Van-Beuningen, Rotterdam, 86; Documenta 8, Kassel, Ger, 87; Digital Visions: Computers & Art, Everson Mus Art & IBM, Syracuse, NY, 87; Ghosts in the Machine, Channel Four, London, Eng, 88; Meet the Makers, Donnell Media Ctr, NY, 88; Reflections, Films by Artis, 7 Festival Int Du Film Sur l'Art, Montreal Can, 89; Electronic Landscapes, Nat Gallery Can Ottawa Ontario, 89; Reconstructed Realms, Long Beach Mus Art, Calif, 89; Video and the Computer, MOMA, New York City, 89; Into The Nineties: New Works/New Spaces, Wexner Ctr Visual Arts, Columbus, Ohio, 90; ImageWorld, Art and Media, Whitney Mus Am Art, 90. *Pos:* Programming dir, MCTV, 80-82; dir, Baskerville & Watson Gallery, NY, 83-87. *Awards:* Nat Endowment Arts Fel, New Genres, 87; NY Found Arts Fel, Collaboration (MICA-TV), 87. *Bibliog:* Marvin Heiferman & Lisa Phillips (auth), Imageworld, Whitney Mus Am Art 89-90; Regina Cornwell (auth), TV or Not TV, Contemporanea, 10/89 p 58-63; Robert H Pelfrey (auth), Art & Mass Media, Harper & Row, 85. *Mem:* Pub Art Fund (panelist, 88); Nat Endowment Arts (panelist, 88, site visitor, 89); Community Access Advisory Commt Brooklyn Community Access Television; NY Found Arts (bd gov). *Publ:* "Television for Real", Center Quarterly No 38, Volume 10, Number 2, Center for Photography at Woodstock, 89, 23-25; "It's Evening in America", Luso-Americanos de Arte Contemporanea, 7/4/89. *Dealer:* Electronic Arts Intermix 536 Broadway 9th Fl New York NY 10012. *Mailing Add:* c/o Long Beach Mus Art Media Art Ctr 2300 E Ocean Blvd Long Beach CA 90803

KLOPFENSTEIN, PHILIP ARTHUR
ADMINISTRATOR, HISTORIAN

b Lake Odessa, Mich, Apr 28, 37. *Study:* Mich State Univ, with Abraham Ratner & Linsey Decker, BFA; Western Mich Univ, with Harry Hefner, MFA; Harvard Univ, arts admin cert. *Exhib:* State Ark Educ Dept Traveling Exhib, 76-; Mid Southern Watercolor Soc Ann, 72-74. *Collection Arranged:* John Henry Byrd (1840-1880), Southeast Ark Arts & Sci Ctr, Pine Bluff, 70; Ernest Trova One-Man Exhib, 71; Art Inc II (Am paintings from Am corp collections), 80. *Pos:* TV writer & teacher, Ark Educ TV, Conway, 68-69; dir, Southeast Ark Arts & Sci Ctr, 70-76; exec dir, Augusta Richmond Co Mus, Ga, 77-79; dir, Montgomery Mus Fine Arts, Ala, 79-82; vpres,

Res and Reclamation, 83-88. *Teaching:* Instr, Paw Paw Pub Sch, Mich, 63-65; instr painting, watercolor & art educ, Little Rock Univ, 65-68; instr art hist, Auburn Univ, Montgomery, 84-85, Glenwood Pub Sch, 89-97; fed prog coord, Ctr Point Sch Dist, 97-. *Mem:* Am Asn Mus; Southeastern Mus Conf (regional rep, 74-75); Three Rivers Art Guild Inc. *Media:* Watercolor, Acrylic. *Res:* John Henry Byrd. *Publ:* Auth, John Henry Byrd (1840-1880), 71. *Mailing Add:* PO Box 890 Glenwood AR 71943

KLOSS, WILLIAM
HISTORIAN, WRITER
b Cleveland, Ohio, Dec 23, 1937. *Study:* Oberlin Col, BA, 62, MA, 68; Univ Mich, 72. *Collection Arranged:* More than Meets the Eye: the Art of Trompe l'Oeil (with catalog), Columbus Mus Art, Ohio, 85. *Pos:* Exhib coordr, Smithsonian Inst Traveling Exhib Ser, 74-78; founder & dir of tours, Washington Art Asn Inc, 78-; bd dir, Pyramid Atlantic Art Ctr, 95-97. *Teaching:* Asst prof art hist, Univ Va, Charlottesville, 69-72; lectr art hist, Smithsonian Study Tours, 78- & Sotheby's Inst, 88-; prof great artist Italian Renaissance, Teaching Co, 2004, prof history European art, 2005 & prof Dutch masters, 2006. *Awards:* Fulbright Scholar Study Art Hist in Rome, US Govt, 67-69; Presidential Appt, Comt for Preservation of White House, 90, 93, 97, 2002-. *Mem:* Col Art Asn of Am; Am Asn Mus. *Res:* Preparation of Senate Collection. *Publ:* Auth, Treasures from the National Museum of American Art, 85, Smithsonian; Samuel F B Morse, Harry N Abrams, 88; coauth, Treasures of State, 1991, Deceptions and Illusions, Nat Gallery Art, 2002 & US Senate Catalogue of Fine Art, 2003; auth, Art in the White House: A Nation's Pride, Harry N Abrams, 92. *Mailing Add:* 1824 Wyoming Ave NW Washington DC 20009

KLOTZ, SUZANNE
ASSEMBLAGE ARTIST, EDUCATOR
b Shawano, Wis, Oct 15, 44. *Study:* Washington Univ, St Louis, 62-64; Kansas City Art Inst, 64-66, BFA, 66; Univ Mo, Kansas City, 66-67; Tex Tech Univ, 70-72, MFA, 72. *Work:* Nat Mus, Smithsonian Inst; Spencer Art Mus, Lawrence, Kans; Scripps Col, Claremont, Calif; Munic Jerusalem, Israel; Phoenix Art Mus, Ariz; Mesa Centennial Conf Ctr, Ariz; San Antonio Mus Art, Tex; Minn Mus Art, St Paul. *Comn:* Sculpture, Roosevelt Park, Phoenix, Ariz. *Exhib:* one-person exhibs, Scottsdale Ctr Arts, 78, Phoenix Art Mus, 81 Spencer Art Mus, Lawrence, Kans, 82 & Mus STex, Corpus Christi, 83; Boise Gallery Art, Boise, Idaho; Cheney Cowles Mem Mus, Spokane, Wash; Ohio State Univ, Columbus; Purdue Univ, Lafayette, Ind; Aborigine & Klotz, N Ariz Univ Flagstaff, 91; Visions of Unity, Salt lake Art Center, Utah, 93; Ben Gurion Univ Negev Beer Sheva, Israel, 94; Childrens Art Exhib, West Bank, Israel, 91-94; Munic Gallery, Jerusalem, Israel, 94; Warriors & Dreamers, Joseph Gross Gallery, Univ Ariz, Tucson, 96; Threshold Gallery, Santa Monica, Calif, 98. *Pos:* art consult, Australian Aborigines, Berri, 91-92; intern, Collaborative Exhib, Salt Lake Art Ctr, Utah, 95. *Teaching:* Instr painting, drawing & design, Angelo State Univ, San Angelo, Tex, 72-75, assoc prof, 85-86; asst prof drawing & design, Scripps Col, Claremont, Calif, 76-78; vis prof, Univ Tex, San Antonio, spring 85; vis sculptor, Ariz State Univ, Tempe, 85-86 & Univ Utah, Salt Lake City, 91-92 & 95; Childrens Unity Art Workshops, Mineral Wells, Tex, Winter Haven, Fla, 96 & Taipei, Taiwan, 97; assoc prof studio arts. *Awards:* Craftsman Fels, 76 & 78 & Performance Grant, 83, Nat Endowment Arts; Gov Award, Ariz, 87; Outstanding Grad Student, Tex Tech Univ, Lubbock, 92; Ariz Visual Arts Fel, 99. *Bibliog:* Hubert Crehan (auth), Dream houses & fanciful creatures of Suzanne Klotz, St Louis Post Dispatch, Mo, 74; Berman & Pinto (auths), Creative Exploration Series, Merrick, 75; Dorian Hyland (auth), American Baha'i, Art Transcends, 98; and many articles in various magazines. *Mem:* Col Art Asn; Nat Asn Women Artists. *Media:* Mixed. *Publ:* Coauth, Everything's the Same, Country Western Press, 77; Everything's Different, 78; auth, Ties of the Heart, 2000. *Dealer:* Rizwan Gallery 1869 E Shawnigan Lake Rd Shawnigan Lake BC

KNECHT, JOHN
FILMMAKER, VIDEO ARTIST
b Iron Ridge, Wis, Mar 5, 47. *Study:* Univ Wis, Oshkosh, BS, 72; Idaho State Univ, MFA, 74. *Work:* Queens Mus, NY. *Exhib:* Solo shows, Collective for Living Cinema, 80, Mus Mod Art, NY, 85, Alternative Mus, NY, 92 & 94, Millennium, 95, Calif Inst Arts, Valencia, Arsenal Kino, Berlin, Ger, London Film Coop, London, Eng, Davidson Col, 95; Edinburgh Film Fest, Edinburgh, Scotland, 81 & 84; 2nd Video Biennial, Mus Mod Art, Columbia, 88; Am Film Inst Videofest, 94; Black Mariafest, 94; and others. *Pos:* Chair, art & art hist, Colgate Univ, 91-99; mem bd govs, Nat Conf Undergrad Res, 93-. *Teaching:* Asst prof, Univ Okla Sch Art, 74-78; assoc prof, Colgate Univ Dept Art & Art Hist, 81-93, prof, 93-; vis lectr, Brown Univ, spring 81. *Awards:* Lightworks Grant, 83; New York Found for the Arts Video Fel, 89; New Forms Fel Rockefeller & Nat Endowment Arts, 90. *Bibliog:* Mick Eaton (auth), Continuing the adventures of Adrian Block, Film Bulletin, London, 2/83; Lucy R Lippard (auth), A Different War, Real Comet Press; Robert Doyle (auth), Artists of Conscience, John Knecht: Iron. *Mem:* Sculpture Space, Utica, NY (bd dir, 92-95); NY Found Arts (artists adv bd, 97). *Media:* Film, Video. *Publ:* Friction/non-friction cinematograph, winter 91; Muses & fuses: Trama in the Technosphere, artists space catalogue on the work of Les LeVeque. *Mailing Add:* PO Box 83 Hamilton NY 13346

KNEPPER-DOYLE, VIRGINIA
PAINTER, ENVIRONMENTAL ARTIST
b San Francisco, Calif, Apr 6, 32. *Study:* Univ Calif, Berkeley, BA, 55; studied oil painting & drawing with Mex, Dominican & Uruguayan artists, 58-71; De Cordova Mus Art Sch, 71-72; Univ Geneva, Switz, printmaking, 75-78. *Work:* Marin Civic Ctr Frank Lloyd Wright Gallery, San Rafael, Calif; WACE USA, San Francisco, Calif; Strathmore Paper Corp. *Comn:* Painting of Washington, DC pres, Bendix Corp, Detroit, Mich, 80; painting of Washington, DC, Rause & Assoc, Philadelphia, Pa, 80; paintings of San Francisco, US Ambassador, Luxembourg, 90; painting of White House, Milk Lobby, Washington, DC. *Exhib:* Bay Arts, Cult Arts Gallery, Belmont, Calif, 89 & 91; Allied Artists Am Ann Exhib, Nat Arts Club, NY, 90; Biennale des Femmes, Le Grand Palais, Paris, France, 90; 4th Int Exhib, Mus Mougins, Mougins, France, 92; Fourth World's Conference on Women, Beijing, China, Sydney, Australia & Washington, DC, 95; and others. *Pos:* Art consult, Hanson Galleries, San Francisco, 83-85; mem, Arts & Open Space Comn, Belvedere, Calif. *Awards:* First Place for Watercolors, Dept State, Washington, 77, Second Place for Drawing, 78. *Mem:* Nat Mus Women Arts; Alliance Women Artists; Allied Artists Am; San Francisco Women Artists; Womens Caucus for Art. *Media:* Oil, Acrylic. *Dealer:* John Doyle 333 Fremont St San Francisco CA 94105. *Mailing Add:* 10 Tamalpais Cir Belvedere CA 94920

KNERR, ERIKA TILDE
PAINTER, MURALIST
b Lancaster, Pa, Oct 2, 62. *Study:* Tyler Sch Art, Philadelphia, BFA, 85; Sch Visual Art, New York, MFA, 88. *Comn:* Mural, Cent Park Zoo, Larson Co Environ & Exhibs, NY, 87; mural, Childrens Mus Manhattan, Sam Kornhauser Archit, NY, 90; mural, NY Hall Sci, Sam Kornhauser Archit, NY, 90. *Pos:* Art dir, New Observations Mag, 90-96. *Media:* Painting

KNIFFIN, RALPH GUS
GRAPHIC ARTIST
b San Carlos Reservation, Ariz, Nov 21, 46. *Study:* Inst Am Indian Art, Santa Fe, NMex, dipl; study with Allan Houser, Charles Loloma, Otellie Loloma & Fritz Scholder. *Work:* Gila Co Court House, Globe, Ariz; Sentry Ctr, Scottsdale, Ariz; San Carlos Indian Hosp, Ariz; Gallo Winery, Modesto, Calif; United Bank, Tempe & Phoenix, Ariz. *Exhib:* All Indian Art Show, Gallery La Luz, Alamagordo, NMex, 74; Scottsdale Nat Indian Art Exhib, Scottsdale, Ariz, 75 & 76; Nat Indian Art Show, Heard Mus, Phoenix, Ariz, 76; Invitational in Drawing, Heard Mus, Phoenix, Ariz, 77. *Awards:* Best of Show, Gallery La Luz, Alamagordo, NMex, 74; First Place, Scottsdale Nat Art Exhib, Ariz, 76; First Place Spec in Graphics, Heard Mus, Phoenix, Ariz, 76. *Bibliog:* Articles in Carefree Enterprise, 74 & Phoenix Cent News, 75; Maggie Wilson (auth), New Artist Stunned by Limelight Status, Ariz Repub, 76. *Media:* Pen & Ink. *Mailing Add:* c/o Gallery 3 3119 E Thomas Rd Ste B Phoenix AZ 85016-8024

KNIGHT, DAVID J
GALLERY DIRECTOR, EDUCATOR
b Tulsa, Okla, Mar 12, 66. *Study:* Ohio Wesleyan Univ, BFA, 88. *Pos:* Cur, Maritain Gallery, Loveland, Ohio, 89-93; gallery dir collections, Northern Ky Univ, 89-; internship, Advanced Studio Sem. *Teaching:* Instr, Northern Ky Univ, 90-. *Mailing Add:* Northern Ky Univ Dept Art Nunn Dr Highland Heights KY 41099

KNIGHT, WILLIAM
PAINTER, PRINTMAKER
b Miami, July 28, 42. *Study:* NY Studio Sch Painting, 1989-92; Pa Acad Fine Arts, 1990-91; Fleisher Art Meml, Philadelphia, 1992-95; Studies with Mel Leipzig, NJ, Joy Turner & Sylvia Hamers, Washington, DC. *Work:* pvt collections of J Seward Johnson, Dr Steven Gecha, Dr June Laval, Elizabeth Snow and many others. *Exhib:* one-man shows incl Princeton Univ, 1993, Johnson Arts Ctr, Litchfield, Conn, 1994, 1997, 2001, Widener Univ, West Chester, Pa, 1999, The Gallery at Schering-Plough, Madison, NJ, 2001, Ctr Experimental Psychotherapy, NY, 2002, 03, R & F Encaustics Gallery, Kingston, NY, 2005, Educational Testing Serv, Princeton, NJ, 2006; group shows incl TAWA in NY, Blue Mountain Gallery, NY, 1993, NY Inst Technol, 1994, Johnson Atelier, Hamilton, NJ, 1994, Ann Metro Show, City Without Walls, 1994, 96, 2001, & 2002, Johnson & Johnson Int Hq, 1995, Breaking the Rules, Katonah Mus, Katonah, NY, 2001, Charles Cowles Gallery, NY, 2002, Nat 2002, Cooperstown Art Asn, Cooperstown, NY, 2002, DCCA Open, Del Ctr Contemp Arts, Wilmington, Del, 2002; oil paintings, Delaware Art Mus, 2002-2004; Am Accad Arts & Letters Ann Exhib, 2003; Perkins Ctr for Arts, Moorestown, NJ, 2003; Ellarslie Mus, Trenton, NJ, 2004; Ceres Gallery, NY, 2004; Brodsky Gallery, Princeton, NJ, 2004. *Pos:* Painting Full time. *Awards:* Nat Acad Design Fel, 95; Exceptional Merit (top award), City Without Walls, 2000; Dodge Found Fel, Vt Studio Ctr Dodge Fund, 2002 & 2005; Byrdcliffe Arts Colony, 2006. *Mem:* City Without Walls; TAWA. *Media:* Oil, Encaustic, Pastel, Watercolor, Charcoal, Black Rubber. *Mailing Add:* Grant House 309 Wood St Burlington NJ 08016

KNIGIN, MICHAEL JAY
PAINTER, PRINTMAKER
b Brooklyn, NY, Dec 9, 42. *Study:* Tyler Sch Art, BFA. *Work:* Whitney Mus Art, Cooper Hewitt Mus, Japan Soc, NY; Nat Collection Fine Arts, US Dept State, Washington; Portland Mus Fine Arts, Ore; Mus Modern Art, Mexico City; Taiwan Mus. *Exhib:* Smithsonian Inst, Washington, 69; Albright-Knox Art Gallery, 70; Mus Mod Art Lending Serv, NY, 71; Recent Acquisitions, Whitney Mus Am Art, NY, 71; Sch Worcester Art Mus, Mass, 72; Israel Mus, Jerusalem, 76; Taiwan Mus, 77; Mus Mod Art, NY, 78; Nat Soc Illusr Show, 78-79; US Dept of State, Washington, 79; Foreign Corresp Club, Tokyo, 79; Brooklyn Mus, 83; Guild Hall Mus, EHampton, NY, 90; NASA Gallery, Cape Kennedy, Fla; and many exhibs both US & abroad. *Teaching:* Prof, Pratt Inst, currently. *Awards:* Ford Found Grant, Tamarind Lithography Workshop, 64; Clio Award, Art Direction, 79; NASA Art Team, 89-92. *Bibliog:* Suzanne Boorsch (auth), article, 78, Ann Jarmusch (auth), article, 79, Art News; Judy Goldman (auth), Art in America, 79; Irene Klotz (auth), article, Fla Today, 89. *Mem:* Soc Am Graphic Artists; Jimmy Ernst Artists Alliance. *Media:* All; Painting, Printmaking. *Publ:* Coauth, The Technique of Fine Art Lithography, 70; auth, Local Choice, Pratt Graphics Ctr, 72; The Contemporary Lithographic Workshop Around the World, Van Nostrand, Mexico City News, 85. *Mailing Add:* PO Box 95 Wainscott NY 11975-0095

KNIPPERS, EDWARD
PAINTER, PRINTMAKER
b Oklahoma City, Okla, Sept 7, 46. *Study:* Pa Acad Fine Arts, 67; Sorbonne, Paris, 68; Asbury Col, Wilmore, Ky, BA, 69; Int Summer Acad Fine Arts, Salzburg, Austria, with Zao Wou-ki, 70, with Otto Elgau & Wolfgang Zeiszner, 76; Univ Tenn, Knoxville, MFA, 73; S W Hayter's Atelier 17, Paris, fel, 80. *Work:* Int Summer Acad Fine Arts, Salzburg, Austria; Tenn Fine Arts Ctr, Cheekwood, Nashville; Vanderbilt Univ, Nashville; Billy Graham Mus, Wheaton, Ill; Univ Okla Mus Art, Norman; The Vatican, Rome, Italy; Cincinnati Art Mus, Cincinnati, Ohio; The Grunewald Print Col at the Armand Hammer Art Mus, LA. *Exhib:* Solo exhibs, Tenn Fine Arts Ctr, Cheekwood, Nashville, 74, Foxhall Gallery, Washington, DC, 82, 86 & 94, Wheaton Col, Ill, 83 & 86, Va Mus Fine Arts, 86-87, Univ Okla, Norman, Okla, 90, Roanoke Mus Fine Arts, Va, 90 & Touchstone Gallery, Washington, 95, The Cath Univ of Am, Wash, DC, 2002; one man shows, Brehm Center, Fuller Seminary, Pasadena, Calif, 2004; group shows, Los Angeles Co Mus, 85-86, New Expressionism, SE Ctr Contemp Art, Winston-Salem, NC, 87, Greenbelt Invitational, Castle Ashby, Northhampton, Eng, 92, Gallery Sotos, Thessaloniki, Greece, 94, Hope in the City, Union Station, DC, 1999; Urban Art Inst, Chattanooga, Tenn, 2000; Like a Prayer: A Jewish and Christian Presence in Contemp Art, (a group invitational), Tyron Ctr for Visual Art, Charlotte, NC, 2001; Foxhall Gallery, Washington, DC, 2005. *Pos:* Bd dir, Christians in Visual Arts, 80-05. *Awards:* Salzburg Prize, Int Summer Acad Fine Arts, Austria, 76; Va Prize for painting, Va Comn Arts, hon mention, 89 & 90; Arts Am Prog Award, Int Symp, Nea Fokea, Greece, 93. *Bibliog:* Howard N Fox (auth), Setting the stage, Los Angeles Co Mus Art catalog; Timothy Verdon (auth), Violence & Faith in Art of Edward Knippers, Univ Okla Mus Art; Theodore Prescott (auth), Edward Knippers: A Profile, Image, J Arts & Relig, 93; James Romaine, Objects of Grace, Conversations on Creativity and Faith, Square Halo Books, 2002. *Mem:* Christians in Visual Arts. *Media:* Oil; Intaglio, Block Prints. *Publ:* Reproduction, Life Mag, 12/94; Reproduction, In: Who Do You Say That I Am, MacMillian, NY, 96; auth, New American Paintings, The Open Studio Press, Mass, 96; contribr, The Old, Old Story, Sq Halo Books, Md, 2000; Rich Copley (auth) The Body of Christ, Lexington HeraldLeader, 3/14/04 (illusr); A Broken Beauty: Figuration, Narrative & Transcendent in North American Art, Ecrdmans, 2005. *Mailing Add:* 2408 Washington Blvd Arlington VA 22201-1116

KNOBLER, LOIS JEAN
SCULPTOR, PAINTER
b New York, NY, Feb 2, 29. *Study:* Syracuse Univ Col Fine Arts, BFA; Fla State Univ, MA. *Work:* Worcester Mus, Mass; Fla State Univ Mus; St Lawrence Univ, NY. *Exhib:* two-person show, Hillyer Gallery, Smith Col, Northampton, Mass, 76; solo exhib, Atrium Gallery, Univ Conn, Storrs, 83; Am Traditions in Watercolor, Worcester Art Mus, 87; Installation Vigil, Sesnon Art Gallery, Univ Calif, Santa Cruz, 94; Philadelphia Artists Artwork, City Hall, Philadelphia, Pa, 2000; Philadelphia Artists, Moore Col of Art, Philadelphia, Pa, 01; Philadelphia Int Airport, 2004-05. *Awards:* Greater Hartford Civic Arts Festival Award, 72. *Bibliog:* American Traditions in Watercolor: The Worcester Art Mus Collection, Abbeville Press, 87; Nouvel Object, Design House Publ, Korea, 98; International Survery of Fine Arts and Crafts, 98. *Media:* Miscellaneous Media. *Collection:* Worcester Art Museum, Mass. *Mailing Add:* 2041 Wallace St Philadelphia PA 19130

KNODE, MARILU
CURATOR, ADMINISTRATOR
b Calgary, Alta, Can, Aug 4, 59; US citizen. *Study:* Univ Grenoble, France, 81-82; Univ Kans, Lawrence, BA(art hist), 81; City Col New York, MA(mus studies), 84. *Collection Arranged:* Tony Cragg Sculpture (mid-career retrospective; with Paul Schimmel), 90; Different Stories (selections from permanent collection), 91; Mapping Histories (group show with Anne Ayres, auth, catalog), 91-92; Personal Inventory, Ellen Birrell & Nick Vaughn (auth, catalog); In Excess (group show), 94; Llyn Foulkes: Between a Rock and a Hard Place, 95. *Pos:* Sr cataloger, Mus Mod Art, New York, 84-88; Assoc cur, Newport Harbor Art Mus, Calif, 89-91, assoc cur, 91-92; independent cur, 91-94; cur, Huntington Beach Art Ctr, 94-96. *Mem:* Am Asn Mus; Col Art Asn. *Publ:* Contrib, Tony Cragg Sculpture: 1975-1990, 90, auth, Third Newport Biennial: Mapping Histories, 91, Sarah Seager, 93, Newport; auth, Interview with Nayland Blake, Connie Hatch & Kim Dingle, J Contemp Art, Newport, 92; and others

KNOEBEL, DAVID J
VIDEO ARTIST, WRITER
b Elysburg, Pa, July 19, 1949. *Study:* Yale Univ, with William Bailey, BA, 72; Skowhegan Sch, with William Stankiewicz, 72; also with George Sugarman, 79-82. *Work:* Indianapolis Mus Art. *Exhib:* Pool Proj, Artist's Space, NY, 80; Painting & Sculpture Today, Indianapolis Mus Art, 80; one-man show, Baruch Col, State Univ NY, 82; Gold Show, Mus Mod Art, NY, 82; Smart Art, Harvard Univ, 85; Primo Piano, Rome, Italy, 86; Pa Acad Fine Arts, Philadelphia, 96; Infos 2000, Ljubljana, Slovenia, 2000; Festival Int de Linguagem Electronica, Sao Paulo, Brazil, 2000; Web3D/VRML 2000 Conf, Monterey, Calif, 2000; Carmen Conde Anthology, Cartagena, Spain, 2006. *Teaching:* Vis artist, Marymount Int Sch, Rome, Italy, 85. *Bibliog:* Lisa Russ Spaar (auth), Lines Online: Poetry Journals on the Web, Chronicles of Higher Education, 11/6/2003; Roberto Simanowski (auth), Concrete Poetry in Digital Media, Dichtung-Digital, 3/2004; Rita Raley (auth), Reading Spaces, Iowa Web Rev, 9/2006. *Media:* Misc Media. *Publ:* auth catalog statement, Light, Islip Art Mus, 82; Words in Space, Ylem, 5-6/99; Euclid: Composing with Words in Space, Web Art & Poesie, 7/2000. *Mailing Add:* PO Box 312 Elysburg PA 17824

KNOLL, ISABEL A GIAMPIETRO See Giampietro, Isabel Antonia

KNOTT, DEE D
PAINTER, ILLUSTRATOR
b Flint, Mich, May 6, 43. *Study:* Mich State Univ, 61-62; Kendall Sch Design, 62-63. *Work:* Marriott Corp, Mich, 90; General Motors Corp, Detroit, Mich, 93; Governor Ji Lin, Changlin, People Republ of China, 94; Isuzu Corp Hq, Mich, 90; Prime Minister Takeshita, Japan, 93; and others. *Comn:* Paintings, Gen Motors, Detroit, 80, Nat 4-H Bldg, Washington, DC, 86, Mich Spec Olympics, Detroit, 86 & Cleo Laine Album Cover, Milton Keynes, Eng, 88; 5 paintings for the Premier of China, comn by Lee Iacocca, Detroit, 88. *Exhib:* 37th Nat Exhib, Butler Inst Am Art, Youngstown, Ohio, 78; Ga Watercolor Soc, Mus Arts Sci, Macon, Ga, 83; Retrospective/Knott, Detroit Inst Arts, 84; RI-Japan Exhib, Kawakami, Tokyo, Japan, 85; Watercolor USA, Springfield Art Mus, Mich, 85; Adirondacks Nat Exhib Am Watercolors, Old Forge, NY, 90; NC Maritime Mus, 94; Turner Street Gallery, Beaufort, NC. *Collection Arranged:* Nat Watercolor Soc First-Half Century Collection. *Awards:* Art League of Chicago Award, Midwest Watercolor Soc, 85; Huntington Bronze Medal, Catherine Lorillard Wolfe Nat Exhib, 86; Todah Moshe Award, Adirondack Nat Exhib Am Watercolors, 88. *Bibliog:* Sylvia Krissoff (auth), The Knott touch, Grand Rapids Press, 88; Corinne Abatt (auth), Dee Knott sees a beautiful gentle world, Birmingham Essentric, 88; Sherry White (auth), Beaufort Winds, an Intimate View by Dee Knott, News Times, Morehead City, NC, 94. *Mem:* Am Watercolor Soc; Nat Watercolor Soc; Rocky Mountain Nat Watermedia Soc; Catherine Wolfe Art Club Soc; Am Soc Marine Artists. *Media:* Transparent Watercolor. *Publ:* Auth, Capturing the moment, Artist Mag, 85; illus, Christmas Journey, Am Libr Soc Asn, Mich, 90; Cleo Laines Word Tour Publ, 90; Splash I, 92, Splash II, 94, Splash IV, Painting Ships, Shores & the Sea, 97, North Light Publ

KNOWLES, ALISON
PERFORMANCE ARTIST, PRINTMAKER
b New York, NY, Apr 29, 33. *Study:* Middlebury Col, Vt, 52-54; Pratt Inst, BFA, 56, Manhattan Sch Printing, 62; studied with Josef Albers, Rihard Lindner & Adolph Gottlieb. *Hon Degrees:* Hon Doctorate Fine Arts, 2003. *Work:* Mus of Mod Art Bk Collection, NY; Oakland Mus, Calif; Jean Brown Archives, Tyringham, Mass. *Comn:* The Identical Lunch (two self-portraits), comn by Alberto Zopellari, 77; Leone D'oro (silkscreen ed), comn by Francesco Conz, 78. *Exhib:* Coeurs Volants, with Marcel Duchamp, 67; The Big Book, Mus Contemp Art, Chicago, 67; Crazy Publishers, Gugggenheim Mus, 69; A House of Dust, Cal Arts Campus; SumTime, Everson Mus, Syracuse, NY, 74; 03 23 03, Montreal Mus Fine Arts, Can, 77; Walker Art Ctr, Minneapolis, Minn, 80; solo shows, Ruth & Marvin Sackner Archive, Miami Beach, Fla, 86, Unique Cloth & Paper Works, Nordyllands Kunstmuseum, Aalborg, Denmark, Finger Book 2 & Palimpsest Prints, 87-88, Seven Indian Moons, 90, Emily Harvey Gallery, NY, Indigo Island, Stadt Galerie, Saarbrucken, Ger, 94 & Basta Fagioli, Unimedia Galerie, Genova, Italy, 94, Sea Change and Footnotes, Emily Harvey Gallery, NY, 2000, Gallery 400, Chicago, Sound and Vision, Odense Performance Festival, Denmark, 2001, Time Samples, Emily Harvey Found, Venice, Italy, 2006, plus others; Women on the Verge, Wimmer Gallery, NY, 95; Retrospective, Indigo Island (with catalog), Stadtgalerie Saarbrucken, Ger, Ctr Contemp Art, Warsaw, Poland & Museet for Samtidskunst, Roskilde, Denmark, 95; Full of Beans, Bremen, Ger, 96; Queensland Art Gallery, Brisbane, Australia, 97; Out of Actions, Mus Contemp Art, Los Angeles, Calif, 98; Fraven Mus, Bonn, Ger, 98; Caterina Gualco Gallery, Genova, Italy, 98; and others. *Teaching:* Dir graphics lab, Calif Inst of the Arts, Valencia, 70-72; Fachhochschule, Hamburg, Ger, 94-. *Awards:* Guggenheim Fel, 68; Nat Endowment Arts, 81 & 85; Travel Grant, Deutscher Acad, Ger, 83; Teaching Residency, Sommerakademie für Bildende Kunst, Salzburg; Distinguished Artist Award for Lifetime Achievement, Col Art Asn, 2003. *Bibliog:* Tom Johnson (auth), Shoes, shoestrings & Gertrude Stein, Village Voice, 78; Kristen Stiles (auth), Something Fishy, 93; Robert C Morgan (auth), Ather the Deluge, 93. *Mem:* Printed Ed; The Performance Workshop. *Media:* Serigraphy, Silkscreen. *Publ:* Auth, spoken Text, Left Hand Bks; Natural Assemblages and the True Crow, Visual Studies Workshop Press, Rochester, NY, 80; A Bean Concordance, Printed Eds, 83; coauth (with George Brecht), The Red, The Green, The Yellow, The Black and The White, Brussels Ed, Lebeer-Hossman, 83; Bread & Water, Left Hand Books, 94; Book Footnotes, Gramary Books, NY, 2000; Auth, Time Samples, Granary Books, 2006. *Mailing Add:* 122 Spring St New York NY 10012

KNOWLES, RICHARD H
PAINTER, EDUCATOR
b Evanston, Ill, June 29, 34. *Study:* Grinnell Col; Northwestern Univ, Evanston, BA, 56; Ind Univ, MA, 61, studied with James McGarrell, Leon Golub & Albert Elson. *Work:* Ind Univ, Bloomington; Ark State Univ; State of Tenn Collection, Reece Mus, Nashville; Brooks Mem Mus Art, Memphis, Tenn. *Comn:* Tuquois Inn, Turcs & Cacos, 80; Harrah's Inn & Casino, E Chicago, IN, 2001. *Exhib:* Ten in Tennessee, Cheekwood Mus, Nashville, 86-87; Solo shows, Loyola Univ, New Orleans, 87 & Forest Project, W Tenn Regional Art Ctr, Humbolt, 98; Six Americans, Ark Art Ctr, Little Rock, 64; 50 States Exhib & Tour, Rockford Art Asn & Am Fedn Arts, 65-67; Am Painters & Sculptors, Colgate Univ, 75; Edinburgh Arts Festival, Scotland, 80; Two-person show, Memphis Ctr Contemp Art, 88; Arts in the Park, Memphis Brooks Mus Art, Fla, 98. *Pos:* Pres, Mid-Am Col Art Assoc, 86, 88; Publ, Untitled (art jour), currently. *Teaching:* Asst prof art, Univ Ark, 61-65; prof art, Memphis State Univ, 66-99, emer, 99-. *Awards:* Best Entry for Ark Artist, Delta Ann, 61 & 62; Painting Prize, Mid-South Exhib, 72. *Mem:* Sierra Club; Mid Am Col Art Asn. *Media:* Acrylic, Oil. *Specialty:* Jay Etkin Gallery: painting, drawing, seul, photog. *Interests:* Geology, Paleontology; Hiking; Writing. *Collection:* State Collections often & AR, Harrah's, Memphis Brooks Mus. *Dealer:* Jay Etkins Gallery Memphis. *Mailing Add:* 3814 N Berlinwood Cove Memphis TN 38133

KNOWLES, SUSAN WILLIAMS
CURATOR, CRITIC
b Washington, DC, Sept 1, 52. *Study:* Vanderbilt Univ, BA, 74, MA, 86; Peabody Col, MLS, 75. *Exhib:* An Enduring Legacy; ET Wickham: A Dream unguarded; Two paths to progress: WEB DuBois, Charles S Johnson and the New Negro Arts movement, 2001; Red Grooms: Selctions from the Graphic Work, traveling show, 2001-2005. *Collection Arranged:* The American Scene: 1900-1950 Traveling Print Show (auth, catalog), 83; A Decade of British & American Screenprints Traveling Show (auth, catalog), 85; A C Webb: The Skyscraper Drawings Architectural Perspectives (auth, catalog), 86; Spirit & Form: William Edmondson & Puryear Mims, 88. *Pos:* Registrar & art librn, Fine Arts Ctr, Cheekwood, Tenn, 81-85, cur collections, 85-87; visual arts coordr, Metrop Nashville Arts Comn, Tenn, 87-92; cur, Tenn Exhib, Nat Mus Women Arts, 92-94; acting gallery dir, Mid Tenn State Univ, Murfreesboro; Art Feature Producer, Nashville Publ Radio, 2003-. *Teaching:* 20th century art hist, O'More Col Design, 92; gallery practices, Mid Tenn State Univ; Cur Arts at the Airport, Nashville Int Airport 94-2005, independent cur. *Awards:* Fel: US Capital Historical Soc & Ctr for Historic preserv; Middle Tenn State Univ; grant: Tenn Arts Comn. *Mem:* Col Art Asn; Am Asn Mus. *Res:* Tenn Art & Archit; Contemp Artists. *Publ:* Tenn Ed, Art papers, 84-; Revs, New Art Examiner, 85-92; auth, Signatures Section: Center Stage Mag, 87-88; Living Artists: Four Installations, Knoxville Mus Art, 90; Pinkney Herbert (exhib catalog), Univ Little Rock, Ark; monthly art column, Nashville Scene, 91-94; An Enduring Legacy, Frist Center for the visual Arts, 2001; Art of Tenn, Frist Center for the visual Arts, 2003. *Mailing Add:* S W Knowles & Assocs 4225 Harding Pike Suite 507 Nashville TN 37205

KNOWLTON, DANIEL GIBSON
RESTORER, CONSERVATOR
b Washington, DC. *Study:* With Marian U M Lane, Washington; Boston Arts & Crafts, grad. *Work:* Univ Chicago Libr; Brown Univ Libr, Providence, RI; Dumbarton Oaks Libr, Washington; Harvard Univ Libr; Cornell Univ Libr; John Carter Brown Libr, Providence, RI. *Comn:* Epistle (gold & leather binding), Grace Church, Providence, 56; The Anguish of the Jews (gold & leather binding), comn by Ciro Scotti, Vatican Libr, 68; Comn to rebind 7 leather book shelves, Fall River Soc, 2000. *Exhib:* Hand bookbinding exhibs, Corcoran Gallery Art, 58; one-man shows, Bristol Hist Soc RI, 69, RI Sch Design, 71 & 75 & Ctr Bk Arts, NY, 75; Rockefeller Libr, Brown Univ, 81 & 91; Providence Hist Soc, 81 & 91; and others. *Pos:* Bookbinder, Brown Univ, 56-92; owner & bookbinder, Daniel G Knowlton Co, Longfield Studio, Bristol, RI, 74-98, 2001-2006. *Teaching:* Instr bookbinding, Daniel G Knowlton Co Longfield Studio Home Bindery, 74-96 & 98-2006. *Bibliog:* Yankee Damon (auth), article in Yankee Mag, 62; Ann Banks (auth), article in Brown Alumni Monthly, 71; Interview, Educ TV 36, Providence, RI, 74 & TV News WJAR-TV, 90. *Mem:* Miniature Painters, Sculptors & Gravers Soc, Washington; Guild Book Workers, NY; Ctr Book Arts, NY. *Media:* Bookbinding. *Mailing Add:* 1202 Hope St Bristol RI 02809

KNOWLTON, GRACE FARRAR
SCULPTOR, PHOTOGRAPHER
b Buffalo, NY, Mar 15, 32. *Study:* Smith Col, BA(art), 54; Columbia Univ Teachers Col, MA(art educ), 81. *Work:* Metrop Mus Art, NY; Newark Mus, NJ; Corcoran Gallery Art; Houston Mus Fine Arts; Victoria & Albert Mus, London, Eng; Brooklyn Mus, NY. *Exhib:* One-man shows, Henri Gallery, Washington, DC, 73, Razor Gallery, NY, 74, Parsons-Dreyfuss Gallery, NY, 79, Aaron Berman Gallery, 81, Susan Harder Gallery, 83, Twining Gallery, 85-86 & 87, Witkin Gallery, 86 & 87, Bill Bace Gallery, 89, Smith Col Mus Art, Mass, 92; Aldrich Art Mus, Ridgefield, Conn, 86; M 13, NY, 92 & 94; Katonah Mus, 93; Hirschl & Adler Mod, 95 & 97; Bates Coll Mus, 02; Neuberger Mus, 02; Collaborative Concepts Gallery, NY, 2003; John Davis Gallery, 2004; Van Brunt Gallery, Beacon, NY, 2006; Whirlwind Gallery, NY, 2006. *Pos:* Asst to cur graphic arts dept, Nat Gallery Art, Washington, 54-57. *Teaching:* Instr art, Arlington Co Pub Schs, 57-60; Pratt, 2000; Art Students League, 98-2005; William Patterson univ, 2003; Natl Acad Art, 2001; instr, Mixed Media, Art Students League, NY, 2006. *Awards:* Pub Art Fund Inc, 87; Outdoor Installation Proj Grant, EHampton Ctr Contemp Art, 89; Grant: Nadine Russel Endowed Chr, Louisiana State Univ, 2003. *Bibliog:* Three Spheres by Grace Knowlton (video), Mus Outdoor Arts, Denver, Colo, 89; Christine Liotta (auth), Sculpture: A Natural Order, Hudson River Mus, Yonkers, 9-10/91; Roberta Smith (auth), NY Times, 4/24/92. *Mem:* Century Asn. *Media:* Steel, Copper, Concrete. *Publ:* Auth, Grace Knowlton, Layers and Traces (exhib catalog), Smith Col Mus Art, 4-8/92. *Dealer:* John Davis, New York, NY; Lesley Heller, New York, NY. *Mailing Add:* 67 Ludlow Ln Palisades NY 10964

KNOWLTON, JONATHAN
PAINTER, EDUCATOR
b New York, NY, Feb 22, 37. *Study:* Yale Univ, BA; Univ Calif, Berkeley, MA. *Work:* Mus Mod Art, NY; Victoria & Albert Mus, London; Univ Calif Art Mus, Berkeley; La Jolla Mus Fine Art, Calif; Oakland Mus, Calif; Montreal Mus Fine Arts, Ont. *Exhib:* Survey '68, Montreal Mus Fine Arts, 68; 17th Nat Print Exhib, Brooklyn Mus, 70; Edmonton Art Gallery, 72; John Bolles Gallery, San Francisco, 73; Latitude 53, Edmonton, 75; Front Gallery, Edmonton, Alta; Vik Gallery, Edmonton, 89; Edmonton Art Gallery, 93; Fran Willis Gallery, Victoria, BC, 93. *Teaching:* Assoc prof drawing & painting, Univ Alta, 66-90. *Awards:* Purchase Award, Los Angeles Co Mus Art, 61; Fulbright Grant, 64-65; Can Coun Grant, 68-69. *Bibliog:* Phylis Matousek (auth), Knowlton travels many roads, Edmonton J, 11/14/84; The Nuclear Glare Has Its Own Beauty in A-Bomb, Soc, 89; Elizabeth Beauchamp (auth), Knowlton retrospective sheds light on local talent, Edmonton J, 6/l/90. *Media:* Acrylic, Oil, Watercolor. *Publ:* Auth, Riding the mainstream of modern imperatives, Interface, Vol 2, No 9, 11/79. *Dealer:* Fran Willis Gallery Victoria BC

KNOX, ELIZABETH
PAINTER
b June 13, 44. *Study:* Parsons Sch Design; New Sch Social Res; Art Students League scholar, with Robert Beverly Hale, 74. *Comn:* Athletic mural, Unity Col, Maine, 94. *Exhib:* Biennial Contmp Am Painting & Sculpture, Whitney Mus Am Art, NY, 75; Maine Maritime Flatworks Exhib, Reed Gallery, Univ Maine, Presque Isle, 95; Summer in Maine, Francesca Anderson Fine Art, Lexington, Mass, 95; December Show, O'Farrell Gallery, Brunswick, Maine, 95; Five Artists, Five Points of View, Round Top Ctr Arts, Damariscotta, Maine, 96; Contemp Master Drawings, Atrium Gallery, Campus Lewiston-Auburn Col, Maine, 96; Solo exhib, More than Meets the Eye, O'Farrell Gallery, Brunswick, Maine, 97; Tenth Anniversary Exhib, Round Top Ctr Arts, 98. *Teaching:* Instr painting & drawing, Round Top Ctr Arts, Damariscotta Maine, 91-. *Bibliog:* Philip Isaacson (auth), In Lewiston, a search for technique in the service of meaning, Maine Sunday Telegram 10/96; Jane Falla (auth), Elizabeth Knox, Digging for deeper meaning, Times Record, 11/96; Words and images, Lit Publ, Univ Southern Maine, 98. *Mem:* Golden Key Nat Hon Soc. *Media:* Oil, Graphite. *Mailing Add:* c/o Round Top Ctr for the Arts-Round Top Gallery Business Rte 1 Box 1316 Damariscotta ME 04543

KNOX, GEORGE
HISTORIAN, WRITER
b London, Eng. *Study:* Courtauld Inst Art, Univ London, BA, MA & PhD. *Hon Degrees:* Univ Victoria, DLitt, 96. *Collection Arranged:* Tiepolo Bicentenary Exhib, Fogg Art Mus, Cambridge, Mass, 70; Tiepolo Drawings, Staatsgalerie, Stuttgart, 70; Tiepolo: Tecnica e Immaginazione, Palazzo Ducale, Venice, 79; Piazzetta: Disegni, Incisioni, Libri, Manoscritti, Fondazione Giorgio Cini, Venice, 83; Piazzetta, A Tercentenary Exhibition, Nat Gallery Art, Washington, DC, 83; 18th Century Venetian Art in Canadian Collections, Vancouver Art Gallery, 89; Giandomenico Tiepolo: Disegni Del Mondo, Udine, Castello & Bloomington, Ind Univ Art Mus, 96-97. *Teaching:* Instr, Slade Sch Art, Univ London, 50-52; instr, King's Col, Newcastle, Univ Durham, 52-58; instr, Queen's Univ, Ont, 69-70; prof fine arts & head dept, Univ BC, 70-87, prof emer. *Awards:* Guggenheim Fel, 2000. *Mem:* Can Comn Hist Art; Comite Int d'Histoire de l'Art; Ateneo Veneto. *Interests:* Venetian 18th century art, particularly the drawings of the Tiepolo family, Piazzetta & Pellegrini. *Publ:* Domenico Tiepolo: Raccolta di Teste, Udine, 70; Giambattista & Domenico Tiepolo, The Chalk Drawings, Oxford, 80; Robert Lehman Collection VI: Italian 18th Century Drawings, New York, 87; Piazzetta, Oxford, 92; Pellegrini, Oxford, 95. *Mailing Add:* 3495 W 11th Ave Vancouver BC V6R 2K1 Canada

KNOX, SIMMIE
PAINTER
b 1936. *Study:* Temple Univ, BFA, MFA. *Comn:* Portrait, Martin Luther King, Jr, Bowie State Col, 1974; portrait, Frederick Douglass, Mus African Art, Washington, DC, 1975; portrait, Judge H. Carl Moultrie, The H. Carl Moultrie Courthouse, 1985; portrait, Supreme Court Justice Thurgood Marshall, 1989; portrait, Dorothy Height, Nat Council Negro Women, 1989; portrait, David and Joyce Dinkins, The Schomburg Collection, 1993; portrait, Col Rosemary McCarthy, US Army Nurse Corp, 1994; portrait, John V. Atanasoff, Cosmos Club, 1995; portrait, Muhammand Ali, 1995; portrait, Hank and Billye Aaron, 1996; portrait, Melvin Sabshin, Am Psychiatric Asn, 1997; Official Whitehouse portrait, President William Clinton and First Lady Hillary Clinton, 2004. *Exhib:* Biennial of Contemporary Am Painting, Corcoran Gallery Art, Washington, DC, 1971. *Pos:* Staff mem, Mus African Art, Washington, DC; portrait artist, 1981-. *Media:* acrylic, oil

KNUDSEN, CHRISTIAN
PAINTER, PHOTOGRAPHER
b June 3, 45; Danish citizen. *Study:* Sir George Williams Univ, BFA, 69. *Work:* Mus Fine Arts & Musee D'Art Contemporain, Montreal; Art Gallery Ont, Toronto; Vancouver Art Gallery, BC; Can Coun Art Bank, Ottawa. *Comn:* Painting, Govt Can Post Off, Que, 78. *Exhib:* Concordia Univ, Montreal, 74; Vancouver Art Gallery, 78; Montreal Mus, Que, 79; Glenbow Mus, Calgary, 80; Agnes Etherington Art Ctr, Kingston, Ont, 81. *Bibliog:* David Burnett (auth), Knudsen at Godard, Art Am, 1/78; David Burnett (auth), Christian Knudsen, Parachute No 11, summer 78; Robert Swain (auth), Christian Knudsen, Agnes Etherington Art Ctr, Kingston, Ont, 81. *Media:* Mixed Media; Silkscreen. *Dealer:* Paul Kuhn Fine Arts 722 11th Ave SW Caligary Aberta T2R 0E4 Canada. *Mailing Add:* 3827 Drolet St Montreal PQ H2W 2L3 Canada

KNUTSSON, ANDERS
PAINTER, CURATOR
b Malmo, Sweden, May 8, 37; US citizen. *Study:* Malmo Tech Col, Sweden, BSME, 67; Cincinnati Art Acad, 69. *Work:* Albright-Knox Art Gallery; Arkivmuseet, Lund, Sweden; Fleming Mus, Univ Vt, Burlington; Moderna Museet, Stockholm, Sweden; Univ Maine Mus Art, Orono; Williams Col Mus Art, Williamstown, Mass; and many other pub & pvt collections. *Exhib:* One-man shows, Helen Day Art Ctr, Stowe, Vt, 87, Keith Green Gallery, NY, 87, Gates of Light, Williams Col Mus Art, Williamstown, (catalog) Mass, 88, Bennett Siegel Gallery, NY, 90, edition Hylteberga, Skurup, Sweden, 90, Lightscapes, Univ Maine Mus Art, Orono, (catalog) 90, Stephen Solovy Gallery, Chicago, & Ami Gallery, Seoul, Korea, (catalog), 93; retrospective (catalog), Gray Art Gallery East Carolina Univ, Greenville, NC, 95; Roger Smith Gallery, NY, 95; Samuel Zacks Gallery, York Univ, Toronto, Can, 96; Manif (catalog), Art Fair, Seoul, Korea, 96; Hishult Konsthalle, Sweden, 98; Ystad Art Mus, Sweden, 99; Karlshamn Konshall, Sweden, 2000; Gallery AMI, Seoul, 2001; Merce Cunningham Studio, NY, 2002; Gallery 718, Brooklyn, NY, 2003; St. Thomas Aquinas Col, NY, 2004; Art Downtown, Deutsche Bank, NY, 2004; Gallery U, Cleveland, OH, 2005; Rosewood Gallery, Kettering, OH, 2005; Cool New York

Dance Festival, NY, 2005; Keutler Int Drawing Center, Brooklyn, NY, 2006. *Collection Arranged:* res cur, Yolélé Art Gallery, Brooklyn, NY, 2004; Clinton Hill Art Festival, Brooklyn, NY, 2004-2005; chief cur, Magnolia Tree Earth Center, Brooklyn, NY, 2005-2006. *Awards:* Liquitex Artist of the Month, 2003. *Bibliog:* Carlo McCormick (auth), Anders Knutsson and the Promise of Light, Anders Knutsson Lightscapes/Ljusskap, Univ Maine Mus Art, 90; Barnaby Ruhe (auth), Another Conceptual Category, Anders Knutsson: Lightscapes/Ljusskap, Univ Maine Mus Art, 90; Michael Duffy (auth), Anders Knutsson: The Experience of Light, E Carolina Univ, 95; and many others. *Media:* Oil, Wax, Acrylic, Pencil. *Mailing Add:* 93 Lexington Ave Brooklyn NY 11238

KOBAYASHI, HISAKO
PAINTER
b Tokyo, Japan, Jan 23, 46. *Study:* Univ Hawaii, BFA, 78; Pratt Inst, MFA, 80. *Exhib:* Brooklyn Artists, Brooklyn Mus, NY, 79, Walsh Gallery, Chicago, Ill, 97, Alex Gallery, Washington, DC, 97 & 98, Ise Art Found, NY, 98; one-person exhibs, DTW Gallery, NY, 94, Walter Wickiser Gallery, NY, 94 & 95, Cercles Des Collectioneurs D'Art Contemporain, Paris, France, 94, Galerie Ovadia, Nancy, France, 95, Walsh Gallery, Chicago, 96 & Masur Mus Art Monroe, La, 96; Southeby's Auction, Minn, 94; Ise Art Found, NY, 95; Roger Smith Gallery, NY, 95; James Michener Mus, Pa, 97; Hammond Mus, Salem, NY, 98; State Mus Munhen, Ger, 99. *Teaching:* Asst, Pratt Inst, 80. *Awards:* Semi finalist, CAPS Grants Awards, New York State, 81, 82. *Bibliog:* Robert Hicks (auth), Shape provides first idea, Villager, 3/94; Yoshiki Yamamoto (auth), Abstraction and the Contemporary World, Chugai Nippo, 10/94; New York art scene, Asahi Art News, 12/95. *Media:* Oil, All Media. *Mailing Add:* 55 Great Jones St New York NY 10012

KOBER, ALFRED JOHN
EDUCATOR, SCULPTOR
b Great Bend, Kans, June 3, 37. *Study:* Dodge City Col, AA, 58; Ft Hays State Col, BS(art), 60 & MS(art), 66. *Work:* Boise Gallery Art, Idaho; Ft Hays State Col. *Comn:* Two outdoor sculptures, Boise State Univ, 71 & 72; stainless steel sculpture, Bank of Idaho, Boise, 72; welded steel sculpture, Boise Cascade World Hq, Boise, 74; sculpture for Veterans Park, Boise, comn by Idaho Veterans, 76; stainless steel sculpture, Atlantic Richfield, Denver, 78; altar pieces, Central Lutheran Church, Yakima, Wash; restored two historic sculptures, City Payette, Idaho. *Exhib:* Ann Exhib Northwest Artists, Seattle, Wash, 69-74; Mainstreams, 72 & 77; LaGrange Nat Competition II, Ga, 75; 21st Ann Drawing & Small Sculpture Show, Ball State Univ, 75. *Teaching:* Instr art, Hutchinson Community Jr Col, Kans, 66-68; assoc prof sculpture, Boise State Univ, 68-78, assoc prof, 78, prof, 79, prof, 99, retired. *Awards:* Purchase Award, Grover M Hermann Fine Arts Ctr, Marietta, 72; Award of Excellence, Marietta Col, 72; Award, Ball State Univ, 75. *Mem:* Boise Art Asn. *Media:* Mixed. *Res:* Experimental sculpture techniques & materials; Emphasis metal casting. *Interests:* Metal engraving; custom jewelry. *Publ:* Art in Public Places. *Mailing Add:* 2024 Crystal Way Boise ID 83706-4346

KOCAR, GEORGE FREDERICK
PAINTER, ILLUSTRATOR
b Cleveland, Ohio, Sept 28, 1948. *Study:* Cuyahoga Community Col, Cleveland, Ohio, AA, 75; Cleveland State Univ, Cleveland, Ohio; BA, 77; Syracuse Univ, NY, MFA, 83. *Work:* Cleveland State Univ; Cent Mo State Univ, Warrensburg; Metro Gen Hosp, Cleveland, Ohio; Butler Inst Am Art, Youngstown, Ohio. *Comn:* Am Greetings Corp. *Exhib:* Butler Mid-Year Exhib, Butler Inst Art, Youngstown, Ohio, 81-85, 87, 94, 96, 98, 99, 01 & 02; one-person show, Central Mo State Univ, Warrensburg, 87, Lake Erie Col, Painesville, Ohio, 92, Studio Gallery, Cleveland, Ohio, 95, Lakeland Community Col, Kirtland, Ohio, 98 & Case Western Reserve Univ, Cleveland, Ohio, 99, Ohio State Univ, Newark, 2004, Mount Vernon Nazarene Univ, Ohio, 2004; Double Take, Firelands Asn Visual Arts, Oberlin, Ohio, 92; Creative Perception, Agora Gallery, NY, 94; Nat Juried Exhib, Phoenix Gallery, NY, 96; Illustrators Only, Visual Club, NY, 96; Art Space, Lima, Ohio, 2000; Montserrat, NY, 2000; Ashtabula Arts Ctr, Ohio, 01; Kocar/Benvenuto, Roy G BV, Columbus, Ohio, 03; Ohio State Univ, Newark, 2004; Mt Vernon Nazerene Univ, Vernon, Ohio, 2004; Fitton Ctr for Arts, Hamilton, Ohio, 2005; Ashtamola Arts Ctr, Ohio, 2006; and others. *Pos:* Pres, Flying Banana Studio, Bay Village, Ohio; master designer, Am Greeting Corp, 84-. *Teaching:* Part-time fac, Akron Univ, Ohio & Cleveland Inst Art; part-time fac, Ashland Univ, Ohio; part-time fac, Cuyahoga Community Col, Cleveland. *Awards:* Jurors Award, Butler Mid-Year Exhib, Youngstown, Ohio, 85 & 99; Best of Show, Ohio State Expo Ctr, Columbus, 99; Award, Soc Graphic Artists, NY, 2002. *Bibliog:* Cecily Firestein (auth), George Kocar High Energy Paintings, Manhattan Arts Int, 9-10/93; Jorge Santiago (auth), Creative perception, Artspeak, 9/94; Cindy Barber (auth), article, Cleveland Plain Dealer, 12/14/98. *Mem:* Saving & Preserving Arts & Cult Environ, Cleveland, Ohio; Northeast Ohio Illustration Soc (pres). *Media:* Acrylic, Watercolor. *Publ:* Illusr, Us against them, NY Times, 83; Is That You Laughing Comrade?, Citadel Press, 86; auth-illusr, Vacationing with a bunch of Maine-iacs, Cleveland Plain Dealer, 86; auth, Painting the world at large & Fine Art & Illustration-Bridging the Gap, 86, Artist's Mag; illusr, Cooking with Humor, 90. *Dealer:* Gallery 324 Erieview Galleria Cleveland OH. *Mailing Add:* 24213 Lake Rd Bay Village OH 44140

KOCH, ARTHUR ROBERT
PAINTER, EDUCATOR
b Meriden, Conn, Feb 26, 34. *Study:* Wesleyan Univ; RI Sch Design, with John Frazier, BFA, 57; Univ Wash, MFA, 61. *Exhib:* Art: USA: 59, NY; US Info Agency Painting Show, Europe, 62-66; Tex Painting & Sculpture of the 20th Century, 70-71. *Teaching:* Instr studio, Univ NH, 57-59; instr studio, El Centro Col, Dallas, 66-70; head dept studio art, Meadows Sch Arts, Southern Methodist Univ, 70-, assoc prof design & painting, 78-. *Awards:* Ft Worth Art Ctr Award, 70. *Mem:* Dallas Area Artists Equity Asn (pres, 70-71); Artists Equity Asn (vpres, 71); Blue Bonnets Anonymous (chmn, 71-72); Tex Asn Schs Art. *Dealer:* Contemp Fine Arts Gallery 2425 Cedar Springs Dallas TX 75201. *Mailing Add:* 11149 Lanewood Cir Dallas TX 75218-1906

KOCH, DAVID HAMILTON
PATRON
b Wichita, Kans, May 3, 1940. *Study:* MIT, BS 1962, MS, 1963. *Pos:* Res engineer and process design engineer, Amicon Corp, Cambridge, 1963-64, Arthur D Little Inc, Cambridge, 1964-67, Halcon Int Inc, NYC, 1967-70, Scientific Design Co, NYC; with Koch Industries Inc, Wichita, Kans, 1970-, exec vpres 1981-, bd dir; chmn bd dir, Chief Exec Officer, Chemical Technology Group LLC. *Mem:* Trustee, Guggenheim Mus, NYC, Mem Sloan Kettering, House Ear Inst, LA, John Hopkins Univ, The Prostate Cancer Found, LA; mem chmn's coun, Metrop Mus Art, NYC; bd dir, Am Mus Nat History, NYC, Aspen Inst, Colo, Earthwatch, Watertown, Mass, Inst of Human Origins, Ariz, Rochefeller U, NYC, MIT (life mem of corp), Reason Found, Santa Monica, CATO Inst, Washington, Citizens for a Sound Economy, Washington. *Mailing Add:* Koch Industries Inc 667 Madison Ave Floor 22D New York NY 10021-8029

KOCH, EDWIN E
SCULPTOR, PAINTER
b New York, NY, Feb 21, 15. *Study:* Mus Mod Art Sch; also with E Kramer. *Work:* Butler Inst of Am Art, Youngstown, Ohio. *Exhib:* Am Watercolors, Drawings & Prints, Metrop Mus Art, 52; Int Exhib Watercolors, Prints, Drawing, Pa Acad Design, 52; Int Watercolor Exhib, Brooklyn Mus, 53; Nat Acad Design, 58-75; var one-man shows. *Awards:* Framemakers Award, Silvermine Guild Artists, 62; Medals of Honor for Watercolor, 70 & Oils, 72, Painters & Sculpture Soc NJ; Grumbacher Award, Audubon Artists, 79. *Bibliog:* Brian O'Doherty (auth), One-man show, 62 & John Canady (auth), One-man show, 66, New York Times. *Mem:* Audubon Artists; Nat Soc Painters in Casein & Acrylic (bd dir, 75-); Knickerbocker Artists (vpres, 77-78); Painters & Sculptors Soc NJ (vpres, 74-); Am Vet Soc Artists (treas, 70-75). *Media:* Oil, Casein. *Mailing Add:* 109 Old Hoagerburgh Rd Wallkill NY 12589

KOCH, GERD HERMAN
PAINTER, EDUCATOR
b Detroit, Mich, Jan 30, 1929. *Study:* Wayne State Univ, BFA, 1951; Univ Calif, Los Angeles; Univ Calif, Santa Barbara, MFA, 1967. *Work:* Santa Barbara Art Mus; Los Angeles Co Mus Art; Univ Mont; Va State Mus Fine Art; Calif State Univ Long Beach. *Comn:* Design of Ash Grove (folk music cabaret), 58; large painting, Los Angeles Dance Theater, 1959; large painting, Wilshire Theater, Los Angeles, 1959-62. *Exhib:* Los Angeles Co Mus Art Ann, 59; solo exhibs, Esther Robles Art Gallery, Los Angeles, 59, 61, 63 & 65, Esther Bear Art Gallery, 65 & 67, Carnegie Art Mus, 88, Momentum City Art Gallery, 91, La Jolla Art Mus, Santa Barbara Co Art Mus, Long Beach, Calif & others; Univ NC, 66; Butler Inst Am Art, Youngstown, Ohio, 66; Calif Palace of Legion of Honor, San Francisco, 67; Calif Arts Festival, 68; Ferus Gallery, Los Angeles Landmark Gallery, 98; Studio Channel Islands Art Ctr; and others. *Collection Arranged:* curated exhib, Ventura Col, 1970-96; Studio Channel Islands Art Ctr, John Nava tapestry Project, Cathedral of our Lady of the Angels, LA, 2003. *Pos:* Founding mem bd dir, Art Ctr & Gallery on Campus Calif State Univ Channel Islands, 98-; mem acquisition comt, Ventura City Art Collection, 2000, 2001, 2003-2005; comnr, Pub Art Comn, Ventura, 2002-; mem task force, Ventura Cult Ctr, 2003-; founder, Venture Beautiful; bd mem, Focus on the Masters, 98-. *Teaching:* Painting workshops, 54-; prof painting & drawing, Ventura Col, 60-61 & 67-98; instr, Univ Calif Exten, 66-72; teaching asst to Kurt Kranz, Univ Calif, Santa Barbara, 67. *Awards:* Calif State Fair First Award, 63; M Grumbacher Inc Purchaser Award, Nat Watercolor Soc, 56 & 1st Purchase Award, 76; Art Gallery named in his honor, Studio Channel Islands Art Ctr, 2005. *Bibliog:* Prize Winning Oil Paintings, Allied Publ, 61. *Mem:* Nat Watercolor Soc; Ventura Art Asn. *Media:* Oil, Acrylic. *Res:* art history lectures on Van Gogh 98-2000. *Dealer:* Studio Channel Islands Art Ctr. *Mailing Add:* 444 Aliso St Ventura CA 93001

KOCH, PHILIP
PAINTER, DRAFTSMAN
b Rochester, NY, Mar 30, 48. *Study:* Oberlin Col, BA, 70; Ind Univ, MFA, 72; residency in Edward Hopper's Studio, 83, 86, 92, 94, 96, 98, 2000, 2002, 2004 & 2006. *Work:* Butler Inst Am Art; Ind Univ Fine Arts Mus; Minn Mus Am Art; Sheldon Swope Art Mus, Terre Haute, Ind; Washington Co Mus Fine Art, Hagerstown, Md; Saginaw Art Mus, MI; Cod Cod Mus Art, Mass. *Exhib:* Sheldon Swope Art Mus, 95; Butler Inst Am Art, 95; Midwest Mus Am Art, 95; Washington Co Mus Fine Arts, 95; Saginaw Art Mus, 96; Blanden Mem Art Mus, 98; Rahr-West Art Mus, 99; Cape Mus Fine Arts, 2003; Univ of Maryland Coll, 2004; Alpers Fine Art, Andover, Mass, 2005. *Teaching:* Instr painting, Cent Wash State Col, 72-73; prof, Md Inst Col Art, 73-. *Awards:* Ford Found Grant, 79; Mellon Grant, 84. *Media:* Oil, Pastel. *Publ:* Auth, Direct painting outdoors, Am Artist, 4/82; Edward Hopper and the American Imagination, Whitney Mus Am Art, 95; On Visiting Edward Hopper's Studio, Oberlin Mag, spring 95; A Vision of Nature: The Landscape of Philip Kody, Univ of Maryland Col, 04. *Dealer:* Jane Haslem Gallery 2025 Hillyer Place NW Washington DC 20009; Sommerville Manning Gallery 101 Stone Block ROw Greenville, DE 19807; Alpers Fine Art 2 Main St Andover MA. *Mailing Add:* 71 Penny Ln Baltimore MD 21209

KOCH, VIRGINIA See Greenleaf, Virginia

KOCHER, ROBERT LEE
PAINTER, EDUCATOR
b Jefferson City, Mo, Dec 19, 29. *Study:* Univ Mo-Columbia, AB & MA; also with Fred Shane & Paul Brach, Post Grad; Univ Iowa, Iowa City with Jean DeMarko & Robert Knipschild. *Comn:* Religious Feasts, Culver-Stockton Col Dining Hall, 57; outdoor sculpture, Duane Arnold Residence, Cedar Rapids, Iowa; Inaugural comn,

Coe Col pres, 96. *Exhib:* Mid-Am Ann, Kansas City, Mo, 60; All Iowa Artists, Des Moines Art Ctr Ann, 63-75; Miss Corridor Competition, Renwick Gallery, Washington, DC, 80; 32 one-person exhibs, Nat Surface Design Competition; one man retrospective, Cedar Rapids Mus Art, 97; Retrospective, Paul Engle Center, 2006. *Pos:* Dir, New York Term Coe Col, 78-80; curator, Coe Col Art Collections, 96-; co-dir, Coe Col Sesquicentennial, 2001. *Teaching:* Prof art, Coe Col, 59-; Marvin D Cone prof, 87-95, emer, 95-. *Awards:* First Prize Painting, All Iowa Artists, Des Moines Art Ctr, 69; Younkers Award; co-recipient, Eliza Hickok Kesler Service Award, 2006. *Bibliog:* Andrew Dolkart (auth), The Old Executive Building: A Victorian Masterpiece, Govt Publ Review, 85. *Mem:* Cedar Rapids Art Ctr (bd dir, 61-81), Iowa; Cedar Rapids Marion Coun Arts, Iowa; Friends Adv Bd, Univ Iowa Mus Art, 86-90. *Media:* Acrylic, Watercolor. *Mailing Add:* 3002 Ridgemore Dr SE Cedar Rapids IA 52403-1935

KOCHKA, AL
MUSEUM DIRECTOR, ADMINISTRATOR
b Paterson, NJ, June 28, 28. *Study:* Newark State Teachers Col, NJ, BS, 49; William Paterson Col NJ, MA, 68. *Pos:* Dir, NJ Coun Arts, Trenton, 76-78, Sangre de Cristo Arts & Conf Ctr, Pueblo, Colo, 79-84, Amarillo, Tex, 84-87 & Muskegon Mus Art, Muskegon, Mich, 88-93; fine art appraiser, 93-; emeritus, Mukegon Mus of Art, 2004. *Teaching:* Art teacher, Kinnelon High Sch, NJ, 63-68; art educ consult, NJ State Dept Educ, Trenton, 68-74, dir arts & humanities, 74-76; adj, Hope Col, Holland, Mich, 96-97. *Awards:* Art Educator of Yr, Art Educators NJ, 73; Mitchell A Wilder Award, Tex Asn Mus, 87. *Bibliog:* Frances Traher (auth), Sangre de Cristo Art Center hits its stride, Art West, Vol 6, 83. *Mem:* Mich Asn Mus; Midwest Mus Conf; Tex Asn Mus (bd trustees, 83-84); Mich Mus Asn (bd trustees, 91-94); Appraisers Asn Am, certified Am Art. *Publ:* Contribr, Dan Coen: The Lamar Series, Colorado Springs Fine Arts Ctr, 84; ed & contribr, Georgia O'Keeffe and Her Contemporaries, 85, Eight Modern Masters, 85 & Holy Family through the Ages, 86, Amarillo Art Ctr; contribr, Georgia O'Keeffe: Raissone Res Catalog, 2001. *Mailing Add:* 223 Main St Dennisport MA 02639

KOCHMAN, ALEXANDRA D
SCULPTOR-CLAY, PAINTER
b Poltava, Ukraine, 36. *Study:* Fashion Inst Technol, New York, AAS, 62; Northeastern Ill State Univ, Chicago, BA, 72; Univ Ill, Chicago, MFA, 78. *Work:* Ill State Mus, Springfield, Ill; State Ill Ctr Governor's Off, Chicago, Ill; John G Shedd Aquarium, Chicago; Milwaukee Pub Mus, Wis; Amoco Corp, Chicago, Ill; Harris Bank, Geneva, Ill; Siemens, Schaumburg, Ill; Saks Fifth Ave, Oakbrook, Ill; Ill Benectine Col, Lisle, Ill; Am Nat Bank, Trust & Rockford, Ill; Cirque Group, Chicago. *Comn:* Sculptural vessels, Swiss Bank, Chicago, Ill, 84; mural, Lincoln Properties Corp, Oakbrook, Ill, 86; ceramic wall sculpture, Barack, Forrazzano & Kirschbaum, Chicago, Ill, 87; Siemens Medical Systems (mural), Schaumburg, Ill, 87; wall sculpture, St Volodymyr & Olha Ukrainian Cath Church, Chicago, Ill, 88. *Exhib:* Women in Visual Arts, 89, Outstanding Am Craftsmen, 90, Judith Racht Gallery, Harbert, Mich; New Horizons in Art, North Shore Art League, Skokie, Ill, 90; Chicago Street Gallery, Lincoln, Ill; Biennale, Ukranian Fine Arts, Lviv, Ukraine, 91; Fine Art of Craft, Scottsdale Ctr Arts, Scottsdale, Ariz, 93; Port Royal Post Off, Port Royal, SC, 2002; Ukrainian Inst Mod Art, Chicago, 97; Dominican Univ, River Forest, 2001; plus many others. *Pos:* consult, Milwaukee Pub Mus, Wis, 80; Cur, The Permanent Collection, Ukrainia Inst of Mod Art, Chicago; juror, Ill Dept Nat Resources, Artisan Prog, 2001. *Teaching:* adj asst prof art & sculpture, Dominican Univ, River Forest, Ill, 83-. *Awards:* First Award, Oakbrook Invitational, Oakbrook C of C, 82; Governor's Purchase Award, Ill State Prof Exhib, State Ill, 86; First Award, Ill State Exhib, Springfield, 89. *Bibliog:* Yuri Myskiv (auth), Alexandra D Kochman and the world in balance, Ukrainian Weekly Rev; Patricia Weismental (auth), feature, Univ Ill Chicagoan, 90; Svito-Vyd, Literary Rev Mag, KyiV, Ukraine, 93; Carol Bradley (auth), Ceramics Monthly, 9/97. *Mem:* Chicago Artists' Coalition (bd mem, 82-82); Ukrainian Inst Mod Art (art juror, 79-). *Media:* Clay, oil. *Mailing Add:* 5453 N Virginia Ave Chicago IL 60625

KOCHTA, RUTH MARTHA
ART DEALER, PAINTER
b Ridgewood, NY, Jan 5, 1924. *Study:* Queens Col, New York, 65-68; Art Students League with Julian Levi, Rudolph Baranik, Bruce Dorfman & Leo Manso, 69-75. *Work:* First & Merchants Bank, Richmond, Va; Nat Bank NAm, NY; Fairleigh Dickinson Univ, Teaneck, NJ; Philathea Mus, Can; General Electric, Pittsfield, Mass. *Exhib:* Nat Acad, NY, 69; Audubon Artists Ann Exhib, NY, 70; Philathea Mus, Can, 72; Elizabet Ney Mus, Austin, Tex, 72; Heckscher Mus, Huntington, NY, 74; Wadsworth Atheneum, Hartford, Conn, 75; New Britain Mus, Conn, 75. *Pos:* Dir, Imperial Gallery, NY, 80-82; owner/dir, Clark Whitney Gallery, Lenox, Mass, 83-. *Media:* Oil. *Specialty:* Contemp paintings and sculpture. *Mailing Add:* 14343 Poplar Ave Flushing NY 11355-2320

KOCOT & HATTON
PAINTER, VIDEO ARTISTS
b Kocot b Northampton, Mass; Hatton b Kingston, Pa. *Study:* Kocot: Pa Acad Fine Arts, CFA, 67; Univ Pa, BFA(magna cum laude), 87; Hatton: Pa Acad Fine Arts, CFA, 68. *Work:* Hunt Manufacturing Co Inc Collection & Julius Bloch Collection, Philadelphia Mus Art, Pa; New Arts Prog, Kutztown, Pa; Fukuya Gallery, Hiroshima, Japan. *Comn:* photographs, Andy Warhol Mus, Pittsburgh, Pa, 99; video, Del Mus Art, Wilmington, 00. *Exhib:* Inst Contemp Art, Philadelphia, 99; Delaware Art Mus, Wilmington, 2000; Hunterdon Mus Art, Clinton, NJ, 02; Del Ctr for Contemp Art, Wilmington, 03; Tufts univ Art Gallery, Medford, Mass, 04; Atwater Kent Mus, Philadelphia, Pa, 04; Shore Ins Contemp: Arts, Long Beach, NJ, 2005; Larry Becker Contemp Art, Philadelphia, 2006. *Pos:* Panel mem, Moore Col Art, Philadelphia, Pa, 89 & Artists in Collaboration, Inst Contemp Art, Philadelphia, Pa, 96; guest cur, Nexus Gallery Found, Today's Art, Philadelphia, Pa, 97; vis artist, Pa Acad Fine Arts, Philadelphia, Pa, 98. *Teaching:* tchr Univ of the Arts, Philadelphia, Pa, 00, 02; vis artist, Pa Acad Fine Arts, Philadelphia, Pa, 98. *Awards:* Nat Endowment Arts Grant, 79; Fel, Pa Coun, 86 & grant, 89. *Bibliog:* Eileen Neff (auth), Scale/Ratio-review, ARTFORUM, 4/89; Anne Percy (auth), New Work on Paper-Hunt Collection, Philadelphia Mus, 96; Miriam Seidel (auth) Biennial 2000, Delaware Art Mus, 2000; margo Nash (auth), Motion and Nature, NY Times, 1/5/03; Edith Newhall, Philadelphia Inquirere, 4/14/2006. *Mem:* Inst Contemp Art; New Arts Prog; Philadelphia Mus Art; Pa Acad Fine Arts. *Media:* Painting, Video, Photography. *Dealer:* Larry Becker Contemp Art 43 N Second St Philadelphia PA 19106. *Mailing Add:* PO Box 2148 Philadelphia PA 19103

KOCSIS, JAMES PAUL
PAINTER
b Buffalo, NY, Apr 27, 36. *Study:* Philadelphia Col of Art, Univ of the Arts, dipl, 58. *Work:* Lessing J Rosenwald Collection, Nat Gallery Art, Libr of Cong, Washington; Albright-Knox Art Gallery, Buffalo, NY; Victoria & Albert Mus, London; pvt collections of HM Elizabeth, Queen of Eng, His Royal Highness Charles, Prince of Wales, The Right Hon Lord Kenneth Clark, Nancy & Ronald Reagan, Presidential Collection, The White House; Kendal Mus, Eng; Bodleian Libr, Oxford Univ, Eng; and others. *Exhib:* One-man shows, Crucifixion Exhib, Memory of Philadelphia Scourge Period, 72, Columbia Mus Art, SC, 74, Harvard Univ, Mass, 76, Univ Arts, Philadelphia, 76, Sydney Opera House, Australia, 79, Dhahran Central Libr, Saudi Arabia, 82, Jilin U Changchun, China, 82, United World Col Adriatic, Trieste, Italy & Southern Africa, Mbabane, 84-85, Italsider Steel, Genoa & Alessandria, Ital, 85, US Int Univ-Europe, London, 85, Univ Glasgow, Scotland, 85, James Joyce Mus, Dublin, Ireland, 85, Int Mus & Art Festival, Glamorgan, Wales, 85, Kendal Mus, Eng, 86; Oxford Univ, Eng, 88; Imo State Libr, Owerri, Nigeria, 89, Nat Arts Theater, Lagos, Nigeria, 89, Progress Bank Nigeria Ltd, Lagos, 89; Freedom Hall, Martin Luther King Jr Ctr & Atlanta-Fulton Public Libr, Atlanta, Ga, 90; US Mission to the UN, NY, 91; United Nations, NY, 91; Sopot and Gdansk, Poland, 91; Zentral-Bibliothek, Cologne, Germ, 92; Ger Am Inst: Saarbrucken, 92; Goethe Inst Am House, Frankfurt, Ger, 92; Freie Univ, Berlin, Germ, 94; Igneous Man Exhib, Missionaries of Charity, Mother Teresa, Calcutta, India, 95; Gandhi Peace Found, New Delhi, 95; Int, India Ctr, New Delhi, 95; Benjamin Franklin Libr, Mexico City, 98; Nat Mus & Libr, Casa de la Cultura Ecuatoriana Benjamin Carrion, Quito, Ecuador, SA, 98; Inst de Investigaciones Esteticias, Univ Nacional de Mexico, Mexico City, 98; Galaria Guillermo Kahlo, la casa de cultura, Jesus Reyes Heroles, Coyoacan, Mexico, 99; Elefterios Venizelos, Int Airport, Athens, Greece, 2003; Vikelaia Libr, Crete, 2003; Acad Athens Univ, Athens, Greece, 2003; Nat Academy Athens Libr, Athens, Greece, 2003; The Hermitage Mus, St Petersburg, Russia, 2005; Dostoevsky Mus, St Petersburg, Russia, 2005; Russian Accad Arts, St Petersburg, Russia, 2005. *Pos:* Illusr, children's books, 61-68; illusr & designer for Random House Publ & 20th Century Fox, 67; publ of catalogues, books, color prints & posters for nat & int distribution. *Teaching:* Instr drawing & pictoral compos, Philadelphia Col of Art Univ of the Arts, 65-67; lectr, Philadelphia Col of Art Univ of the Arts, Kutztown State Teachers Col, civic & social groups. *Awards:* Am Inst Graphic Arts Biannual Award, 68. *Bibliog:* Portia A Scott (auth), World Renown Artist to Bring Works to Martin Luther King Center, Atlanta Daily World, 3/9/90; Paul Willistein (auth), Art Takes Flight, Morning Call, 5/7/95; Dr Albert Nekimken (auth), Kocsis Scourged, Surviving the Art World, Paragon Press, 99; and others. *Media:* Oil on Linen. *Mailing Add:* PO Box 20782 Lehigh Valley PA 18002-0782

KODNER, MARTIN
ART DEALER, CONSULTANT
b St Louis, Mo, Nov 25, 34. *Study:* St Louis Col Pharmacy, BS, RPH, 56. *Pos:* Dir, Kodner Gallery, St Louis, Mo, formerly; dir, Kodner Gallery, currently. *Mem:* Am Appraisers Asn, NY. *Specialty:* American and European art of the 19th and 20th centuries; masters of the old west; impressionists, American and French. *Publ:* Auth, Oscar E Berninghaus, Gateway Heritage Publ, winter 83-84; Carl (Charles) Wimar, Gateway Heritage Publ. *Mailing Add:* c/o Kodner Gallery 9918 Clayton Rd St Louis MO 63124

KOEHLER, HENRY
PAINTER
b Louisville, Ky, Feb 2, 27. *Study:* Yale Univ, BA, 50. *Work:* Calif Palace Legion Honor, San Francisco; Speed Mus Art, Louisville, Ky; Parrish Art Mus, Southampton, NY; Thomasville Cult Ctr, Ga. *Comn:* Baseball murals, NY Mets, Shea Stadium, 64. *Exhib:* One-man shows, Calif Palace Legion Honor, 66, Speed Art Mus, 67 & Parrish Mus, 70; Wildenstein, London, 71, 73, 76 & 78; Aiken Racing Hall Fame, 78; Galerie La Cymaise, Paris, 82, 84, 87, 91, 95, 97 & 2005; Spink & Son, London, 90, 92 & 94; Ky Derby Mus, 93; Newhouse Galleries, NY, 94 & 96; Rafael Valls Ltd, London, 98, 2000, 2002, 2004 & 2006; Nat Mus of Racing, Saratoga, NY, 2003; Century Asoc, NY, 2005. *Pos:* Hon Trustee, Parrish Mus of Art, Southampton, NY. *Mem:* The Brook, NY; Whites, The Beefsteak, London; Century Asn, NY; Saratoga Reading Rms, NY; Southampton Club, NY. *Media:* Oil, Drawing. *Dealer:* Rafael Valls Ltd London England; Galerie La Cymaise Paris France. *Mailing Add:* 80 N Main St Southampton NY 11968

KOEHLER, RONALD GENE
SCULPTOR
b Cape Girardeau, Mo, Sept 9, 30. *Study:* Southeast Mo State Univ, Cape Girardeau, BS (art educ), 72, MAT, 75; Memphis State Univ, Tenn, with Harris Sorrelle, MFA (sculpture), 80. *Work:* Ark Arts Ctr, Little Rock; Del Mar Col, Corpus Christi, Tex; Tenn All-State Artist Collection, Nashville; W Palm Beach Int Airport, Fla; Hawaii

State Found on Culture & the Arts, Honolulu; Hechinger Tools as Art Collection, Washington, DC; National Building Mus, Smithsonian. *Comn:* sculpture installation, Our Lady of Victories Catholic Church, Cleveland, Miss, 91; Marble outdoor sculpture, Arrowmont Sch Arts & Crafts, Gatlinburg, Tenn, 97. *Exhib:* one-man show, Univ Ark, Little Rock, Ark, 2000, Miss Mus Art, Jackson, 2001 & Univ Memphis, 2002; 7th Int Shoebox Scultpure Exhib, Univ Hawaii, Honolulu, 2000; Westmoreland Art Natl, PA, 2000; Defining Idea in Wood, Tex, 2004; Northwest New Mexico Nat, NMex, 2004; Suitcase Exchange Show, USA & New Zealand, 2004; After Duchamp-a Global Exhib, WI, 2004; 39th Nat Del Mar Col, Tex, 2005. *Pos:* Int pres, Kappa Pi int Hon Art Fraternity, 98-. *Teaching:* GA Instr design, Memphis State Univ, Tenn, 78-80; instr sculpture, Delta State Univ, Cleveland, Miss, 80-82, assoc prof sculpture & printmaking, 84-93; staff asst, Arrowmont Sch Arts & Crafts, Gatlinburg, Tenn, 82-84; prof art, Delta State Univ, 93-. *Awards:* Purchase Award, Bi state Exhib, MS, 2004; Cottonlandia Mus, Greenwood, Miss, 2000, Crosstie Arts Festival, Cleveland, Miss, 2000 & Meridian Mus Art, Miss, 2001; Visual Artist Fel-Miss Arts Comn, 91-92; Best of Show Award, Fred Wells Nat Exhib, Nebr, 2000; Westmoreland Award, Westmoreland Art Nat, Pa, 2004. *Bibliog:* featured artist, Fine Wood Working Mag, No 62, 1/87, Gallery section, Am Craft Mag, Vol 47, No 4, 8/87; Woodwork Mag, No 23, 10/93; Arthur Williams (auth), Sculpture: Technique-Form-Content, Davis Publ, rev ed 95; Country Roads Mag, 12/99; Donald Meilach (auth), Wood Art TOday, Schiffer Publ, 2004. *Mem:* Int Sculpture Asn; Am Crafts Coun; Craftsman Guild Miss; Kappa Pi (int pres 98-). *Media:* Wood, Metal. *Publ:* Auth, Natural Dyes on Handmade Paper, Delta State Univ, 82; Arthur Williams (auth), The Sculpture Reference, Sculpture Books Publ, 2004; (ed) The Sketch Book, A Journal of Kappa Pi Intl Hon Fraternity. *Dealer:* Galeria Ortiz San Antonio TX; Art Under a Hot Tin Roof Jackson TN. *Mailing Add:* 400 S Bolivar Cleveland MS 38732-3745

KOENIG, ELIZABETH
SCULPTOR
b New York, NY, Apr 20, 37. *Study:* Sorbonne, Paris, 57; Wellesley Col, BA, 58; Yale Univ, MD, 62; Art Students League, New York, with John Hovannes, 63-64; Corcoran Mus Sch Art, with Heinz Warnecke & John Rood, 64-67. *Work:* Curator's Collection, Eugene O'Neill Mem Theater Found, Waterford, Conn; Art Students League, NY. *Comn:* Tenn marble carving, Washington Hebrew Cong, Washington, DC, 78; monumental bronze sculpture for front of Admin Bldg, George Meany Ctr Labor Studies, Silver Spring, Md, 82. *Exhib:* Ten Sculptors, Washington Womens Arts Ctr, Washington, DC, 77; retrospective 1963-1978 (auth, catalog), Lyman Allyn Mus, New London, Conn, 78 & Rotunda, Pan-Am Health Orgn, Washington, DC, 78; Finalist Exhib, Outdoor Sculpture Competition, Rockville Munic Gallery, Md, 78; 11th Ann Sculpture Conf, Meridian House Int, Washington, DC, 80; Sculpture & Prints, Cath Univ Am, 80; 35 Yr Retrospective, Foundation Henri Harpignies, Paris, France, 99; one-woman show, Foxhall Gallery, 77, 85 & 99; one-woman show, La Galerie Myrian H., Paris, France, 2006. *Collection Arranged:* The Mystique of Metal, Art Barn, Nat Park Serv, Washington, DC, 85. *Awards:* First Prize for Sculpture, 70 & Second & Third Prizes for Sculpture, 71, Tri-State Regional Sculpture Exhib, Montgomery Co Art Asn. *Bibliog:* Patricia Raymer (auth), From iron to gold, Washington's metal artists, Washingtonian Mag, 75; Robert Spring (auth), New projects: Sculpture for the George Meany Center, In: The Artists Foundry for Practicing Sculptors, Vol 5, No 1, 82. *Mem:* Artists Equity Asn, Washington, DC (vpres, 77-83); life mem Art Students League, NY; Int Sculpture Ctr. *Media:* Stone, Bronze. *Interests:* Reading & Gardening. *Collection:* Marble Carving in Permanent Collection of Regional Center for Women in The Arts, West Chester, PA, 2003. *Publ:* Auth, Monumental torso, Washington Artists News, 81. *Dealer:* Foxhall Gallery 3301 New Mexico Ave NW Washington DC 20016; Miller Gallery 2715 Erie Ave Cincinnati OH 45208. *Mailing Add:* 9014 Charred Oak Dr Bethesda MD 20817

KOENIG, JOHN FRANKLIN
PAINTER, PHOTOGRAPHER
b Seattle, Wash, Oct 24, 24. *Study:* US Army Univ, France, 45; Univ Wash, 48, Sorbonne, Paris, 48-51. *Work:* Mus Art Mod, Paris, France; Ctr Nat Art Contemp, Paris; Mus Western Art, Tokyo; Seattle Art Mus; Mus Art Contemp, Montreal; Musee National d'Art Moderne, Ctr National d'Art et de Culture Georges Pompidou; Nat Mus Art, Osaka, Japan; Musee del'Etat, Luxembourg. *Comn:* Mural & glass windows (with Wogenscky), CHU Hosp, St Antoine, Paris, 65. *Exhib:* Galerie Arnaud, 52-74; Carnegie Inst Int, Pittsburgh, 64; retrospectives, Seattle Art Mus, Wash, 70, Works 1947-1992, Mus de Metz, Montbeliard, Albi, 93; one person exhibs, Fuji Television Gallery, Tokyo, 77, Tacoma Art Mus, 80, Paris Art Ctr, 82, Galerie Treize, Montreal, 83, Galerie Kutter, Luxembourg, Greg Kucera Gallery, Seattle, 83, Nat Gallery Iceland, Rekajavik, 85 & Carolyn Staley Gallery, Seattle, 86; Foster-White Gallery, 71-95; Seattle Style, 5 French Mus, 86-87; Traveling Exhib, 21 Mus & Cult Ctrs France, 90-92; and others; Galerie Sievi, Berlin, 2000. *Pos:* Cur, Seattle Parks Dept Centennial, 84 & John Pence Gallery, San Francisco, 84; commr Les Annees le Combat, Mus France, 99-2000. *Teaching:* Artist-in-residence, Sch Appl Arts, Istanbul, 76. *Awards:* Prix Critiques Art de Presse Parisienne, 1st Biennale Paris, 59; Named Officer de l'Ordre des Arts et es Lettres, France, 86, Commandant, 89; Medaille de Vermeil, City of Paris, 86. *Bibliog:* Pierre Restany (auth), John Franklin Koenig, Galerie Arnaud, Paris, 60; Michel Ryon (auth), John Franklin Koenig, Galerie Arnand, Paris, 69; Liliane Thorn-Petit (auth), John Franklin Koenig, Radio-Television Luxem, Bourgeoise, 75; film, Fuji Televison, Tokyo, Japan, 77. *Media:* Acrylic, Oil. *Publ:* Coauth, John Franklin Koenig, 65-70; ed, La Danse Contemporaine, Fayard, Paris, 80. *Mailing Add:* 400 18th Ave E Seattle WA 98112

KOENIG, PETER L
PAINTER, CURATOR
b Hungary, Sept 10, 33. *Study:* Mass Col Art, BFA, 59; Cranbrook Acad Art, MFA, 61; Harvard Univ, EdM, 71; further study-Warsaw Acad Fine Arts; Boston Univ; Mass Inst Technol. *Work:* RI Col, Providence; Univ NDak, Grand Forks; Weber State Col, Ogden, Utah; Prahran Col, Melbourne, Australia; Ctr Contemp Art, Great Falls, Mont. *Exhib:* Butler Inst Am Art, Youngstown, Ohio, 63; Boston Arts Festival, 64; Pa Acad Fine Arts, Philadelphia, 66; solo exhib, Harvard Univ, Cambridge, Mass, 71, Ctr Contemp Art, Great Falls, Mont, 85, Univ Hawaii, 91, Fitchburg Mus, Mass, 92, Heritage Plantation of Sandwich, Mass, 92, Mass Col Art, 93; Salt Lake Art Ctr, Utah, 75; Cataumet Art Ctr, Mass, 98. *Collection Arranged:* Utah Artist Today, Brigham Young Univ, Utah, 77; Rodger P Kingston: Photographs, Univ Ark, 80; Rituals of the Land, Art Complex Mus, Duxbury, Mass, 86; New Horizons: 19th Century American Marine Painting (auth, catalog), Art Complex Mus, Duxbury, 88; Falmouth: A Visual Legacy, Cape Mus Fine Arts, Mass, 88. *Pos:* Dean, Art Dept, Prahran Col, Melbourne, Australia, 76-79; cur, Art Complex Mus, Duxbury, Mass, 85-89; art critic, Enterprise Newspaper, Mass & Bradenton Herald, Fla; exib dir, Art Ctr Sarasota, Fla, 98-2003; Dir, Twin Palms Studio. *Teaching:* Prof painting & drawing, RI Col, Providence, 63-67; chmn art dept, Wheelock Col, Boston, 67-71 & Weber Col, Utah, 71-76; prof, Univ Ark, 79-82; lectr, Univ Hawaii, 90. *Awards:* Provincetown Workshop Fel, Mass, 61; McDowell Fel, 64; Fulbright Grant, 64-65; US Bicentennial Grant, 76. *Mem:* Am Asn Mus; New Eng Mus Asn; Col Art Asn Am; Falmouth Artists Guild; Honolulu Acad Fine Arts. *Media:* Acrylic, Photography, Conceptual Art. *Interests:* Sailing, Bicycling, Swimming, Film. *Publ:* Auth, Rituals of the Land: Native American Art of the Colorado Plateau, Art Complex Mus, 86; Falmouth: A Visual Legacy, Teaticket Press, 87. *Dealer:* Picchi Gallery Piazza di Brancoli Lucca Italy 55050; Cataumet Art Ctr Mass. *Mailing Add:* PO Box 1223 Osprey FL 34229

KOENIG, ROBERT J
MUSEUM DIRECTOR, EDUCATOR
b Jersey City, NJ, June 6, 35. *Study:* Pratt Inst, BS(art educ), 57; Yale Univ, BFA, 59, MFA, 61; New Sch Soc Res; Columbia Univ Sch Gen Studies; Gen Elec Mgt Prog Mus Adminrs. *Exhib:* Wood, Fiber, Clay and Metal in African Art, The African Art Mus of the SMA Fathers, NJ, 1999; Eloquent Threads: The Language of African Textiles and Costumes; Perspectives on African Art, The African Art Mus of the SMA Fathers, NJ, 2000; Asanti Brass Miniatures from the Collections of AfrikaCentrum, Cadier en Keer, The Neth, 2001; Five Cultures of Africa: African Art from the Collections ofthe SMA African Art Mus, 2002; Design for Living Traditional Arts of Sub-Saharan Africa from the Collections of the SMA African Art Mus, 2002; Textile Art of the Bakuba: Velvet Embroideries in Raffia from the Collection of Sam Hilu, 2003; Beauty and the Beasts: Kifwebe Masks of the Songye, Luba and Related Peoples of the Congo, 2003. *Pos:* Exhib designer, Newark Mus, NJ, 61-63; asst dir, Morris Mus Arts & Sci, 69-76; from asst dir to assoc dir, Montclair Art Mus, NJ, 76-80, dir, 80-93; juror/evaluator, AAM Accreditation Comm, NJ State Coun on Arts & Inst Awards, 85-88; bd dir, NJ Mus Coun, 85-87, Long-range Planning Comn, 87-88; Md State Coun Arts, 87; Vietnam Mem Comp, 88; dir, Noyes Mus, Oceanville, NJ, 91-93 & African Art Mus, SMA Soc, Tenafly, NJ, 95-; pres, Composers Guild, NJ, 96-2001. *Teaching:* Instr art, Pub Schs, Union City, NJ, 63-69, Bloomfield Col, NJ, 89-90, Montclair State Col, NJ, 88-89, Univ Pa, 90 & Berkshire Sch Contemp Art, North Adams, Mass, 92; adj prof, Stockton State Col, Pomona, NJ, 92-93; assoc prof museology, Seton Hall Univ, 94-97; lectr Montclair State Univ, 97-; lectr Jane Voorhees Zimmerle Art Mus, Rutgers Univ, 97-. *Awards:* First Prize, Grad Painting, Yale Univ, 60; Excellence Award, NJ Art Dir's Club, 90; Silver Medal, The Song of the Loom, Leipzig Int Bk Exhib, 90. *Mem:* MAAM, Gov NJ; Am Asn Mus; Nat Trust His Preservation; NJ Mus Coun; AAMD; Nat Arts Club; Yale Club, New York. *Res:* traditional arts of sub-Saharan Africa. *Specialty:* works assoc with the SMA workshop at Ekiti, Nigeria under Father Kevin Carroll, SMA; African pottery and textiles. *Interests:* African, Asian, ancient Greek and Roman art; 20th century and contemporary art. *Collection:* African Art Mus of SMA. *Mailing Add:* 23 Bliss Ave Tenafly NJ 07670

KOESTNER, DON
PAINTER
b St Paul, Minn, Nov 28, 23. *Study:* Minneapolis Sch Art, four yrs. *Work:* Brown Co Minn Courthouse; Dakota Co Minn Libr; Minn State Hist Soc Permanent Collection. *Comn:* Mural, St Olaf's Church, Minneapolis, 50; diorama-mural, Goodhue Co Hist Soc, Red Wing, Minn, 69. *Exhib:* Classical Realism Show, Springville Mus Art, Utah, 82; Amarillo Art Ctr, Tex, 83; Maryhill Mus Art, Goldendale, Wash, 83; The Painters of Light, Dallas, Tex, 83; Classical Realism Conf Show, Heritage Art Gallery, Alexandria, Va, 86; one-man show, Heritage Art Gallery, Alexandria, Va, 87, Minn River Sch Art, Burnsville, 96 & Johnson Heritage Post Gallery, Grand Marais, 96; Lancaster Art Festival, Lancaster, Ohio, 88; Beauty: A Rebirth of Relevance, Newington-Cropsey Found Gallery, Hastings-on-Hudson, NY, 96; East Coast Ideals-West Coast Concepts, Carnegie Art Mus, Oxnard, Calif, 97; Acad Art San Francisco, Calif, 97; Springville Mus Art, Utah, 97. *Teaching:* Instr oil painting & drawing, Minn Mus Art Sch, 70-75 & Atelier Lack, Minneapolis, 75-85. *Awards:* Grumbacher Award, Ogunquit Art Ctr Nat Exhib, 64; First Prize for oil painting, Minn State Fair, 66; Award, Am Artists Prof League, 68. *Bibliog:* video, Classical Realism, Heritage Art Gallery, 91; video, A Visit with Don Koestner, Minnestoa Public TV, WDSE, 95; New American Masters, The World and I Mag, 86. *Mem:* Am Soc Classical Realism (emeritus). *Media:* Oil. *Publ:* Essay, Landscape Painting, Realism in Revolution, Taylor Publ, Dallas, Tex, 85. *Dealer:* Master Framers 262 E Fourth St Paul MN 55101; Carver & Beard Galleries 800 La Salle Ave Minneapolis MN 55402-2006. *Mailing Add:* 5314 Williams Dr Silver Bay MN 55614

KOGAN, DEBORAH
PAINTER, ILLUSTRATOR
b Philadelphia, Pa, Aug 31, 40. *Study:* Philadelphia Col Art; Pa Acad Fine Arts, 58-62; Univ Pa, Albert C Barnes Found, 62-64. *Work:* Drexel Univ, Philadelphia, Pa; Libr Cong, Washington; Univ Minn, Minneapolis; Free Libr Philadelphia; Carnegie-Mellon Univ, Pittsburgh. *Comn:* Graphic murals, Chase Manhattan Bank, 69. *Exhib:* Pa Acad Fine Arts Bienniel, 67 & 69; Philadelphia Artists, Philadelphia

Mus Art, 73, 74 & 79; 110th Exhib Am Watercolor Soc, Nat Acad of Design, NY, 77; Am Women in Fine Arts, Moore Col Art, Philadelphia, 77; Mus Philadelphia, 79; US-Israeli Exchange Exhib, Tel Aviv, 78; Albright Col, 80; Soc Illustrators, 90, 91, 92, 94, 95 & 98; also many one-woman shows. *Teaching:* Univ of Arts, Philadelphia. *Awards:* Tiffany Grant, 68; Drexel Citation, 87; Carolyn W Field Award for Children's Lit, 88; Int Reading Asn Award, 90; Penn Book Award, 91. *Bibliog:* 21 Women Artists, Muse, 79; Sixth Book of Childrens Book Authors and Illustrators, HH Wilson Publ, 91; Something About the Author, Gale, 93; and others. *Mem:* Artists Equity Asn (mem bd dir, 77-79); Women's Caucus for Art; Muse: Woman's Collab (mem bd dir, 77-80); Authors Guild; Soc Childrens Bk Writers & Illustrators. *Media:* Acrylic; Watercolor. *Publ:* Star Gazing Sky, Crown, 91; illus, Apple Picking Time, Crown Publ, 94; Jackrabbit, Crown Pub, 96; illus, The Barn Owls, Charlesbridge, 2000; auth, illus, Hokusai: The Man Who Painted a Mountain, Farrar, Straus & Giroux, 2001; Sweet Dried Apples: A Vietnamese Wartime Childhood, Houghton Mifflin, 96. *Mailing Add:* 810 Southampton Ave Wyndmoor PA 19038

KOGOD, ROBERT & ARLENE
COLLECTOR
Study: Am Univ, BS 62. *Hon Degrees:* Am Univ, LLD(hon), 2000. *Pos:* Joined, Charles E Smith Companies, 59; co-chmn. & co-Chief Exec Officer, Charles E Smith Residential Realty Inc, 67-2001; bd trustees, merged with Archstone Communities Trust to become Archstone-Smith Trust, 2001-; bd regents, Smithsonian Inst., 2005; adv to pres, Am Univ, 2003-. *Awards:* Named one of Top 200 Collectors, ARTnews Mag, 2004. *Collection:* Modern & Contemporary Art, especially American Art. *Mailing Add:* Vornado Realty Trust 888 7th Ave New York NY 10019

KOHL-SPIRO, BARBARA
PRINTMAKER, PAINTER
b Milwaukee, Wis, Feb 10, 40. *Study:* Univ Wis Madison, BS(art hist); Univ Wis Milwaukee. *Work:* Milwaukee Art Ctr. *Comn:* Painting, comn by Golda Meier, 77. *Exhib:* Wis Painters & Sculptors, Milwaukee Art Ctr, 65; Washington Art, Washington Armory, DC, 77 & 78; NY Show, Allen Park Gallery, 77; Janus Gallery, Washington, DC, 78; Alex Rosenberg Gallery, 78-79; Voices of Past, Women in Jewish Art, Jewish Community Ctr, Washington, DC, 79. *Teaching:* Asst trainer of docents in art hist, Milwaukee Art Ctr, 78-. *Awards:* Pub Television Auction Award for Best in Show, 77. *Media:* Color and Fabric on Paper; Oil on Canvas. *Collection:* Milton Avery oils, Morris Lewis, Dubuffet, Hockney, Ralph Fasanella, Wayne Thiebold, Hepworth, Suttman, Saul Steinberg. *Dealer:* Michael Lord Gallery Milwaukee Wis. *Mailing Add:* 777 N Prospect Milwaukee WI 53202-4000

KOHLER, RUTH DEYOUNG
MUSEUM DIRECTOR, CURATOR
b Chicago, Ill, 41. *Study:* Smith Col, Northampton, Mass, BA; Univ Hamburg, Ger; Kunsthochschule, Hamburg, Ger; Banff Sch Fine Arts; Univ Wis, Madison; Lakeland Col, LHD, 84. *Pos:* Dir & mem, Kohler Found, Inc, Wis, 60-, pres 85-; asst dir, John Michael Kohler Arts Ctr, Sheboygan, Wis, 68-72, dir, 72-; mem, Wis Arts Bd, Madison, 73-81 & chmn, 74-77; mem, Wis Am Revolution Bicentennial Comn, Madison, 74-77; mem visual arts panel, Nat Endowment Arts, Washington, DC, 75-, mem visual arts mus panel, 76-78, mem, Selection Panel for Percent Art Prog Madison, Wis, 86. *Teaching:* Instr printmaking, Univ Alta, Calgary, Can, 64-66. *Awards:* Fel, Wis Acad Sci, Art & Letts, Madison. *Mem:* Nat Coun on Educ for Ceramic Arts, 90; hon bd James Renwick Alliance, Smithsonian Inst, 90; hon mem Col Fel Am Crafts Coun, 92. *Mailing Add:* 608 New York Ave Sheboygan WI 53081

KOHN, MICHAEL BUNDY
ART DEALER, CRITIC
b Los Angeles, Calif, Sept 20, 58. *Study:* Univ Calif, Los Angeles, BFA(art hist), 80; Inst Fine Arts, New York Univ, MA(art hist), 84. *Pos:* US ed, Flash Art Mag, 83-85; co-owner & dir, Garet/Kohn Gallery, New York, 83-84; co-owner, Turner-Kohn Gallery, Los Angeles, Calif, 85-. *Teaching:* Teaching asst, art hist, New York Univ, 83; vis teacher, Art Ctr, Pasadena, 86. *Awards:* Hill Rebay Fel, Guggenheim Mus, 83. *Res:* Recurring themes and motifs of historical styles in contemporary art and current social context. *Specialty:* Contemporary art from Europe, New York and Los Angeles. *Publ:* Auth, Carlo Maria Mariani and Neoclassicism, 1/82 & Mannerism and contemporary art, 3/84 Arts Mag; Styles and their social context in the East Village, Univ Calif, Santa Barbara Mus (exhib catalog), 10/84; Romantic visions, 1/85 & Hypermannerism, 6/86, Flash Art Mag

KOHUT, LORENE
PAINTER
b La Port, Tex, Nov 16, 29. *Study:* With Coulton Waugh & John Gould. *Work:* Court Gen Sessions, Washington, DC; Pa State Univ; Du Pont Co; Del State Col; Wesley Col; and others. *Exhib:* Ogunquit Arts Ctr 49th Nat, Maine, 69; Hudson Valley Art Asn, 42nd & 43rd Nat, White Plains, NY, 69-70; Nat Acad Design, NY, 70; Catharine Lorillard Wolfe Nat, NY, 80; Am Artist Prof League Grand Nat Exhib, 81. *Awards:* Gold Medal Oils, Hudson Valley Art Asn, 69; Gold Medal, Watercolor, Catharine Lorillard Wolfe Nat, 80; Gold Medal, Oil, Am Artist Prof League Grand Nat Exhib, 81. *Media:* Mixed Media, Alkyd. *Dealer:* Extra Touch of Class Alexandria VA 22312. *Mailing Add:* 706 Garwood St Smithville TX 78957

KOLBOWSKI, SILVIA
CONCEPTUAL ARTIST
b Buenos Aires, Arg, 53; US Citizen. *Study:* Franconia Col, New Hampshire, AA; Hunter Col, BS. *Work:* Mus Mod Art, NY; Roger Pailhas, Marseilles,; Whitney Mus Am Art, NY; Walker Art Ctr, Milwaukee. *Exhib:* Solo shows, Nature Morte Gallery, NY, 85 & 86, Interim Art, London, 88, Postmasters Gallery, NY, 88, 89, 92 & 97, Harry Winston Inc, NY, 90, Galerie Roger Pailhas, Paris, 92 & 95, American Fine Arts, 99 & 2002, NY, Western Front, Vancouver, BC, 2000, Seven, NY, 2001, American Fine Arts, NY, 2002, Y8, Hamburg, Ger, 2003 & Secession, Vienna, Austria, 2004; Group shows, Whitney Mus Am Art, 87, 88, 89 & 90; Material Ethics, Milford Gallery, NY, 88; New Directions, S Bitter-Larkin Gallery, NY, 90; Marginal Practices, Gracie Mansion Gallery, NY, 90; Summer exhib, Postmasters Gallery, NY, 91; DisContinuous Spaces, Storefront Art & Archit, NY & Sch Archit Gallery, Princeton Univ, 93; Commodity Image, Int Ctr Photog Midtown, NY, 93; House Rules, Wexner Ctr, Columbus, Ohio, 94; Architectures of Display, Archit League, NY, 95; Making Pictures: Photographs by Women, 1975-Present, Nicole Klagsbrun Gallery, NY, 96; Centre de Cultura Contemporania, Barcelona, 96 & Am Fine Arts, NY, 99; Whitney Biennial, Whitney Mus Am Art, 2000; PHAG Inc, NY, 2001; Walker Art Ctr, Minneapolis, Minn, 2002; Barbican Art Gallery, London, 2002; Arthur Ross Gallery, Columbia Univ, 2002; Piano Nobile, Geneva, Switz, 2004; Art Metropole, Toronto & Printed Matter, NY, 2004. *Pos:* fel, Inst Archit & Urban Studies, NY, 80-83; Ed bd, anymag, 93-94; ed, Oct Mag, 93-2000, adv bd, 2000-; adv bd, Michael Kalil Found, NY, 2003-. *Teaching:* Columbia Univ, 92-; lectr, Harvard Univ, Grad Sch Design, 97, Yale Univ, Sch Archit, 97 & Berlage Inst, Amsterdam, 98; Parsons Sch of Architecture, 99-; Whitney Mus Ind Study Program, 88-96; The Cooper Union, 2002 & 2005-2006. *Awards:* NY Found Arts Grant, 86 & 98; Nat Endowment Arts, 89. *Bibliog:* Martha Schwendeer (auth), Silvia Kolbowski, Closed circuit, Time Out, 6/26-7/13/97; Reinold Martin (auth), Closed circuit, Texte zur Kunst, No 28, 11/97; Simon Leung (auth), Best of 2004 Books, Artforum, 12/2004; David Joselif (auth), Navigating the New Territory, Artforum, summer 2005; Mignon Nixon (auth), On the Couch, 10/2005; Mignon Nixon (auth), She-Fox, Women Artists at the Millenium, 2006. *Media:* Multi-Media/Video, Text, Photography, Sculpture. *Dealer:* American Fine Arts Co 22 Wooster St New York 10013. *Mailing Add:* 222 Park Ave South # 11C New York NY 10003

KOLDORF, IRENE JANET
SCULPTOR
b Newark, NJ, Aug 8, 25. *Study:* Pratt Inst, Brooklyn, NY, 43-44; Kean Col, Union, NJ, BA(art educ), 70; Rutgers-Newark Mus Training Prog, cert, 80; workshop, Pietra Santa, Italy, 96. *Work:* Am Soc Parenteral & Enteral Nutrition, Washington; Breaux Mart, New Orleans, La; Pvt Collections, Dr & Mrs Murray Pine, Maplewood, NJ. *Comn:* Metal figures, Temple Sha'Arey Shalom, comn by the Lippy family, Springfield, NJ, 82; Artisians of Ancient Rome (2 marble heads), Newark Mus, NJ, 98. *Exhib:* Art by Design, Princeton, NJ, 88; Monmouth Mus, Lincroft, NJ, 85, 89, 94 & 96; Trenton City Mus, NJ, 89 & 94; Zimmerli Mus, East Brunswick, NJ, 89; Gaelan Gallery, Whippany, NJ, 2001, 2002, 2003; Grounds for Sculpture, Hamilton, NJ, 2001; Catherine Lorillard Wolfe Art Club, New York City, 2002; and others. *Pos:* Founder & corresp secy, Springfield Asn Creative Arts, Springfield, NJ, 63-68. *Teaching:* Teacher sculpture, Westfield Summer Wkshp, NJ, 75-84; docent humanities, Newark Mus, NJ, 80-94; artist-in-residence, Artists League Cent NJ, 85 & 86, 90 & 92; demonstr sculpture, East Brunswick-TV Channel 8, 85, 86 & 90. *Awards:* Best in Show, Springfield Asn Creative Arts, NJ, 65; Hon mention, Middlesex Co Mus, NJ, 85; Second Place, Wahington Sq Outdoor Art Exhib, New York, NY, 85; Awards, Catherine Lorillard Wolfe Art Club & Nat Arts Club, New York, 90 & 92. *Bibliog:* Ann Betty Weinshenker (auth), article, NJ Music & Arts, 78. *Mem:* Sculptors Asn NJ (docent, 81-82, secy, 83-, pres, 88-89); Artists League Cent NJ; Int Sculpture Ctr, Washington; Women's Caucus Arts; Summit Art Ctr, NJ; Sculptor Asn (pres, NJ, 88-); Catherine Lorillard Wolfe Art Club. *Media:* Wood, Stone, Metal. *Mailing Add:* 21 Garden Oval Springfield NJ 07081

KOLISNYK, PETER
PAINTER, SCULPTOR
b Toronto, Ont, Nov 30, 34. *Study:* Western Tech Sch Toronto, Ont, with Fred Fraser, Julius Griffith, Margaret Aitken & George Griffin, 51-54. *Work:* Art Gallery Ont, Toronto; Art Bank, Can Coun, Ottawa; Winnipeg Art Gallery, Man; Queen's Silver Jubilee Art Collection, Govt Ont, Toronto; Ukrainian Inst Mod Art, Chicago. *Comn:* Agnes Etherington Gallery, Queens Univ, Kingston, Ont; Peterboro Art Gallery. *Exhib:* One-man exhibs, Art Gallery Ont, 77-78, Mercer Union, Toronto, 83 & Art Gallery Lindsay, 83; Montreal Mus Fine Arts, 60, 62, 67 & 69; Fourth Biennial Exhib Can Art, Nat Gallery Can, Ottawa, 61; Art Gallery Ont, Toronto, 67, 69, 70, 72 & 77; Albright-Knox Art Gallery, 68; A Plastic Presence, San Francisco Mus Art, and others, 69-70; 49th Parallels--New Canadian Art, Mus Contemp Art, Chicago, and others, 71; Contemp Outdoor Sculpture, Guildwood Hall, Toronto, 82; Rational Alternatives, Harbourfront Art Gallery, Toronto, 83; Works on Paper, Ukrainian Inst Mod Art, Chicago, 83; and many others. *Pos:* Cur, Cobourg Art Gallery, 64-69; trustee, Art Gallery Ont, 82-. *Teaching:* Dir & lectr art, Glendon Col, York Univ, Toronto, 75-; instr, Prison Arts Found, Kingston, Ont, 78 & Emily Carr Col Art, Vancouver, 82-. *Awards:* Sculpture Award, Ont Soc Artists, 72; Can Coun Sr Arts Grant, 75-76; Ont Arts Coun Grants, 75, 77-79 & 81-83. *Bibliog:* Clara Hargittay (auth), article, Art Mag, 5-7/82; David Nasby & Fern Bayer (coauth), Art for Architecture, Govt Ont, 82. *Mem:* Can Artists Representation Ont; Can Soc Painters Watercolour; Ont Soc Artists; Royal Can Acad Arts. *Media:* Watercolor; Miscellaneous. *Mailing Add:* c/o Ukranian Inst Mod Art 2320 W Chicago Ave Chicago IL 60622-4722

KOLLER-DAVIES, EVA
ASSEMBLAGE ARTIST, PAINTER
b St Peternov, Rumania, Jan 29, 25; Can citizen. *Study:* Cent Tech Sch, 43; Ont Col Art, Toronto, 68-70; Univ Toronto, 72-73. *Work:* Permanent collection, Ctr Arts, Vero Beach, Fla, 92. *Exhib:* Five Abstract Artists, Gallery of Riverside Theatre, Vero Beach, Fla, 86; solo exhib, Indian River Community Col Gallery, Fla, 86, Gallery of Brevard Community Col, Melbourne, Fla, 88 & McAlpine Ctr Arts, Ft Pierce, Fla, 89; Fla Artists, Ctr for Arts, Vero Beach, 88; Ont Soc Artist, McDonald Gallery, Toronto, 88; Abstract Artists from the Permanent Collection, Ctr for Arts, Vero Beach, Fla, 96. *Media:* Acrylic, Mixed Media. *Mailing Add:* 788 Acacia Rd Vero Beach FL 32963

KOLODZEI, NATALIA
ADMINISTRATOR, CURATOR
b Moscow, Jan 8, 74. *Study:* State Univ NJ, BA in Art Hist with hons, 98; Phi Beta Kappa. *Exhib:* Body Politics: Selections from the Kolodzei Collection of Russian & Eastern European Art, Resnick Gallery, Long Island Univ, 3-4/99; 4+4: Two Generations of Russian Avant-Garde, Mimi Ferzt Gallery, NY, 2001; New Identities New Forms: Contemporary Russian Women Artists from the Kolodzei Collection, Georgetown Univ Art Galleries, Washington, DC, 3/2002; Women in Art: Three Generations of Women Artists, Long Island Univ, NY, 2003; A Retrospective of the Works by Petr Belenok, United Nations, NY, 2003; From Leningrad to St Petersburg: 25 Years of Art, Chelsea Art Mus, NY, 12/2003-5/2004; Finding Freedom: Forty of Soviet & Russian Art, Bergen Mus Art & Science, NJ, 2004 & Leepa-Rattner Mus Art, Fla, 2005; The Federal Assembly: A Project by Sergei Kalinin & Farid Bogdalov, Moscow Mus Modern Art, 2004 & Central Exhib Hall, St Petersburg, Russia, 2005; Oleg Vassiliev: Memory Speaks (Themes & Variations), State Tretyakov Gallery, Moscow, 2005 & State Russian Mus, St Petersburg, Russia, 2006; plus many others. *Collection Arranged:* Kolodzei Collection of Russian & Eastern European Art. *Pos:* Exec dir, Kolodzei Art Found, Inc, Highland Park, NJ, 91-; adv bd, Russian Am Forum, NY, 95-; cur, Bergen Mus Art & Sci, Chelsea Art Mus, New York City, 2005. *Awards:* Named Hon Citizen of State of Okla, Gov of Okla, 93. *Mem:* Am Asn for Advancement of Slavic Studies, Int Salon Soc (ambassador 1996-); Int Art Fund, Print Club NY; NY Russian Club; Golden Key Nat Hon Soc; AICA; Asn Art Historians, Russia. *Publ:* auth, Unknown Segal at the Hermitage, Iskusstvo, 10-11/2002, 16; auth, James Rosenquist. Retrospective, Iskusstvo, 11-12/2003, 23; auth, First Illustrated Constitution of Russia, in: Art Constitution, Moscow, 2003, 14-15; auth, Four Visions: Transcultural New Jersey, in: Transcultural New Jersey: Diverse Artists Shaping Culture & Communities, Rutgers Univ, NJ, 2004-2005; coauth (with Tatiana Kolodzei), Our Collection. Some Facts, Sobranie, 2006, 108-115; auth, The American National Exhibition of 1959, Pinakotheke, 22-23, 2006, 78-84; plus many others. *Mailing Add:* 123 S Adelaide Ave Apt 1N New Brunswick NJ 08904-1614

KOLOSVARY, PAUL PALKO See Palko Kolosvary, Paul

KOLTUN, FRANCES LANG
COLLECTOR, LECTURER
b New York, NY. *Study:* Brooklyn Col, BA; Columbia Univ, MA. *Pos:* Ed, writer & broadcaster, NBC & Syndicated Radio on Collecting, 70-. *Mem:* Drawing Soc. *Collection:* Nineteenth and twentieth century drawings and etchings. *Publ:* Numerous articles on art. *Mailing Add:* 45 E 66th St New York NY 10021

KOMAR, VITALY See Komar and Melamid

KOMAR AND MELAMID
PAINTER, PRINTMAKER
b Moscow, USSR, Komar Sept 11, 43, Melamid July 14, 45. *Study:* Stroganov Inst Art & Design, Moscow, USSR, 67. *Work:* Whitney Mus Am Art; Stedeliyk Mus Amsterdam; Guggenheim Mus, Mus Mod Art & Metrop Mus Art, NY. *Comn:* Murals, Liberty as Justice, NY Percent For Art Prog, 94; mural, Unity, First Interstate Bank Bldg, Los Angeles, Calif, 93. *Exhib:* Solo exhibs, Wadsworth Atheneum, Hartford, Conn, 78, Mus Mod Art, Oxford, Eng, Mus Decorative Art, Paris, France, 85, Neuen Gesellschaft für Gildende Kunst, Berlin, 88, Brooklyn Mus, 90; Counterparts and Affinitees, Metrop Mus Art, NY, 82; Reallegory, Chrysler Mus, Norfolk, Va, 83; An Int Survey, Mus Mod Art, NY, 84; The Biennale of Sydney, Australia, 86; Documenta 8, Kassel, 87; Fifty Yrs of Collecting: An Anniversary Selection, Sculpture of the Modern Era, Solomon R Guggenheim Found, 87; FIAC Paris, 89; Brooklyn Mus, 90. *Teaching:* Instr visual art, Moskov Regional Art Schole, 68-76. *Awards:* Grant, Nat Endowment Arts, 82. *Bibliog:* Umberto Eco (auth), Bevente Breznev Cola, L'Espresso, 76; Robert Hughes (auth), Through the ironic curtain, Time Mag, 10/25/85; Gary Indiana (auth) Komar and Melamid confidential (cover story), Art in Am, 6/85; Jan Frazier (auth), Profile, The New Yorker, 12/86; Jean-Hubert Martin (auth), L'art da da da de Komar et Melamid, Art Press, N103, 5/86; Carter Ratcliff (auth), Komar and Melamid, Abbeville Press, 89. *Publ:* Coauths, The barren flowers of evil, 3/80 & In search of religion, 5/80, Artforum; Death Poems, NGBK-Nichen, Ger, 88

KOMARIN, GARY
PAINTER
b New York, NY, Sept 14, 51. *Study:* Albany State Univ, studied with Richard Stankiewicz, BA, 73; New Sch Social Res, 74; New York Studio Sch, studied with Paul George, 74; Art Students League, studied with Gabriel Laderman, 75; Brooklyn Mus Sch, 75; Boston Univ Sch Fine Arts, studied with Philip Guston, MFA(painting), 77. *Work:* AT&T, NY; Boston Univ; Stevens Corp, Ark; United Bank Houston; Prudential Ins Co; and others. *Comn:* Painting for Clarendon House Project, Liebman & Liebman, NY, 80; painting on paper, comn by chmn bd trustees, Kimball Art Mus, Ft Worth, Tex, 85; Chris Thompson album (cover painting), Atlantic Records. *Exhib:* Solo exhibs, Mus Art, Univ Ore, Eugene, 81, Maxwell Davidson Gallery, NY, 85, Helander Gallery, Palm Beach, 88, Brian Reddy, Little Silver, NJ, Sandler/Hudson Gallery, Atlanta, Ga, 91, Klarfeld/Perry Gallery, NY, 92 & others; East Village and NY-New Work (with catalog), Moos Art, Fla, 85; Best of Season, Helander Gallery, Fla, 86; Dog Days of Summer, Littlejohn Smith Gallery, NY, 86; Morris Mus Biennial, NJ, 88; and others. *Teaching:* Asst prof painting & drawing, Hobart & William Smith Cols, Geneva, NY, 77-78, Univ Ore, 80-81 & Southern Methodist Univ, Dallas, 81-84. *Awards:* Finalist, Int Art Competition, Los Angeles, 83; 1st Prize, 19th Ann Painting Competition, Houston, 83; Philip Hulitan Award, Soc of Four Arts, Palm Beach, 86. *Bibliog:* Carol Everingham (auth), A comical view of American dream lost, Houston Post, 11/85; Pam Perry (auth), Stories in paint, Atlanta Constitution, 11/85; W Zimmer (auth), The mentor shines through at show in Little Silver, 87, Summer splendors outside the city, 87, New York Times; Eileen Watkins, Surrealist loads canvas with images so viewer can find something new, New York Times, 87; and others. *Mem:* Col Art Asn. *Media:* Oil on Canvas, Oil on Paper. *Dealer:* Klarfeld/Perry 472 Broone St New York NY 10012. *Mailing Add:* Six Kevin Dr Flanders NJ 07836-9731

KOMAROFF, LINDA
CURATOR
Work: Auth: The Golden Disk of Heaven: Metalwork of Timurid Iran, 1992; Co-cur (with Stefano Carboni) (exhibs) The Legacy of Genghis Kahn: Courtly Art and Culture in Western Asia, 1256-1353 (Alfred H Barr Junior Award for exhib catalogue, Col Art Assoc, 2004). *Pos:* Fac dept art, Hamilton Col, NY, 86; cur, Metrop Mus Art, New York City; cur Islamic art, head dept ancient and Islamic art, Los Angeles Co Mus Art, 95. *Awards:* Fulbright Scholar Grant, 80-81, 88-89; Recipient Media Award, Muslim Pub Affairs Coun, 2003. *Mailing Add:* LA Co Mus Art 5905 Wilshire Blvd Los Angeles CA 90036

KOMODORE, BILL
PAINTER, EDUCATOR
b Athens, Greece, Oct 23, 32; US citizen. *Study:* Tulane Univ La, BA, 55 & MFA, 57; Hans Hofmann Sch, Provincetown; also with Mark Rothko. *Work:* Whitney Mus Am Art; Des Moines Art Ctr, Iowa; Nat Gallery Art; Walker Art Ctr; Milwaukee Mus Art; Hamilton Gallery Art, Ont, Canada; Dallas Mus Art, Tex; Barrett Collection, Dallas, Tex. *Exhib:* One-man shows, Haydon Calhoun Gallery, Dallas, 61, Howard Wise Gallery, NY, 65 & 67, Automation House, NY, 73, DW Gallery, Dallas, 81, 83 & 84, Eugene Binder Gallery, Dallas, 87 & Studio Gallery, Brookhaven Col, 96; The Responsive Eye, Mus Mod Art, 64; Albright-Knox Art Gallery, Buffalo, NY, 65 & 68; Whitney Mus Am Art, NY, 65 & 68; 12 Artists from North Texas, Dallas Mus Fine Arts, 79; First Texas Triennial (with catalog), Contemp Arts Mus, Houston, 88; Texas II, San Francisco Mus Modern Art, 88; three-man show (McManaway, Komodore, Gummelt), Baylor Univ Gallery, Waco, Tex, 90; The Vessel, Dallas, Tex, 90; Bill Komodore/Jay Sullivan, Irving Arts Ctr Gallery, Tex, 91; Jansen-perez Gallery, San Antonio, Tex, 92; The Establishment Exposed, Dallas Visual Art Ctr, 96; Content Drives Form: Recent Works of Bill Komodore, Meadows Mus, Dallas, Tex; Komodore, Art Mus South Tex, Corpus Christi, 1/99; Bill Komodore: Poetry in Paint, Pillsbury Peters Fine Art, Dallas, 2000; The Gaze, Gerald Peters Gallery, Dallas, 2005; Not Dead Yet: Persistence of the Figure in Contemporary Art, Landmark Arts, Tex Tech U., 2006; Modalities of the Visible: A Survey of Contemporary Art in North Texas, Forum Gallery, Brookhaven Coll Ctr for Arts, Dallas, 2002; Bill Komodore & Laurence Scholder, Art League, Houston, 2002. *Teaching:* Vis artist, Mary Washington Col, 73-76, Richland Col, Arts Magnet High Sch, Dallas, 77-78, Brookhaven Col, Dallas, 81-90, Dallas Theatre Ctr, 81-84 & Univ Tex, Dallas, 82-88; painter, prof, Southern Methodist Univ, 89-. *Awards:* Assistance League Houston, 97; First Prize, Whitney Mus (dir) David Ross, 97; Legends Award, Dallas Visual Arts Ctr, 97. *Bibliog:* Melissa Morrison (auth), article Dallas Morning News, 8/90; Dee Mitchell (auth), Article Dallas Morning News, 9/97; Janet Kuther (auth), Article Dallas Mooney News. *Media:* Oil, Watercolor. *Publ:* Illusr, Fishes of Lake Pontchartrain, Tulane Univ Press, 54; contribr, Contemporary American Painting and Sculpture, Univ Ill Press, 65; Young America, 1965, Whitney Mus Am Art, 65; auth, Komodore (color catalog), Dallas Visual Art Ctr, Meadows Mus, Dallas, Tex & Mus South Tex, Corpus Christi, 97. *Dealer:* Gerald Peters Fine Art 2913 Fairmount Dallas TX. *Mailing Add:* c/o Southern Methodist Univ Div Art Rm 1640 0AC Dallas TX 75275

KONDOS, GREGORY
PAINTER, EDUCATOR
b Lynn, Mass, 23. *Study:* Calif State Univ, Sacramento, BA, MA. *Exhib:* Am Acad Arts & Letters, New York City, 93. *Pos:* Chmn, Art Dept, 62-82. *Teaching:* Fac, Sacramento City Col, 56-62; artist in res, Yosemite Nat Park; guest instr, Univ Calif, Berkeley, Univ Fla, Monterey Mus. *Awards:* Recipient Dillon Collection prize, Winter Invitational, Calif Palace, Legion of Hon. *Mem:* Nat Acad of Design (acad, 95). *Mailing Add:* Gregory Kondos Art Gallery 3835 Freeport Blvd Sacramento CA 95822

KONG, YOUNGHEE See Doe, Willo

KONOPKA, JOSEPH
PAINTER
b Philadelphia, Pa, Oct 6, 32. *Study:* Cooper Union, grad, 54; Columbia Univ, 55. *Work:* Butler Inst Am Art, Youngstown, Ohio; Nat Mus Am Art, Washington, DC; Mus Art, Brigham Young Univ, Utah; Tucson Mus Art, Ariz; Vatican Mus, Vatican City; Hickory Mus Art, Hickory, NC; NY Pub Libr; Archives of Am Art, Smithsonian Inst, Washington, DC; Biggs Mus Am Art, Dover, DE; Saginaw Art Mus, Mich; Springfield Art Mus, Springfield, Mo; Elmhurst Art Mus, Ill. *Exhib:* Butler Inst Am Art, 74, 77, 79, 82, 84 & 87; Brooklyn Mus, 76, 78 & 81; Recent Acquisitions, 81, Drawing from Permanent Collections, 82 & On the 20th Century, 83, Monclair Art Mus, NJ; Atlantic City Art Ctr, 89, 90 & 96; Bergen Mus, Paramus, NJ 91; South Bend Regional Mus Art, Ind, 98; Harn Mus Art, Gainesville, Fla, 98; Selections from Permanent Collection, Ogunquit Mus Am Art, Maine, 1999; The Human Factor, Sunrise Mus, Charleston, WVa, 2000; Molvane Art Mus, Collecting & Connecting, 2003; New Jersey Historical Soc, Changed Lives, 2nd Anniversary Sept 11, Sept-Nov, 2003; Univ Mus, Southern Ill Univ, Carbondale, Ill, 2004; Jersey City Mus, Constructing Am III: Industry & Modernity, 2005; Recent Acquisitions to the Swope Collection, Swope Art Mus, 2005; Recent Accessions on Exhibit, Springfield Art Mus, Ill, Dec-Jan, 2006; and many others. *Pos:* Scenic artist, NBC TV 52-2006, Late night with David Letterman, 82-93, Late Night with Conan O'Brian, 93-06. *Awards:*

Purchase Awards, Newark Mus, 68 & NJ State Mus, 70; Medal Honor, NJ Painters & Sculptors Soc, 71; Purchase Awards, Ocean City Art Ctr, NJ, 70 & Atlantic City, NJ, 71. *Bibliog:* Articles, Arts Mag, 2/73 & 12/75; Sunday New York Times, 76 & Newark Star-Ledger, 10/79 & 1/82; article, NJ Art Form Mag, 3-4/81; article, Szymon Bojko, Polish-American & Polish Artists in Contemporary American Art, 2002. *Mem:* Assoc Artists NJ (vpres, 77-85); Nat Soc Painters in Casein & Acrylic Inc; Clifton Asn Artists, NJ; United Scenic Artists; Atlantic City Art Asn. *Media:* Acrylic. *Res:* Smithsonian Institution, Archives of American Art. *Dealer:* Capricorn Gallery 10236 River Rd Potomac MD 20854; Nathans Art Gallery 1205 McBride Ave West Paterson NJ 07424. *Mailing Add:* 26 Snowden Pl Glen Ridge NJ 07028

KOOB, PAMELA NABSETH
CURATOR
b Boston, June 28, 48. *Study:* Stanford Univ, BA, 70; Harvard Grad Sch Edn, MAT, 71; Hunter Col, SCUNY, MA, 97. *Exhib:* A Permanent Record of What has been Accomplished: Highlights from the Permanent Collection, Art Students League of NY, Forbes Galleries, NY, 2004. *Collection Arranged:* Curator, A Century on Paper: Prints by Art Students League Artists, 2002; Curator, Edward Hopper's New York Movie, 98. *Pos:* Cur, Art Students League of NY, 98-. *Awards:* Richard M Kaye Scholarship, Hunter Coll, NY, 97. *Mem:* Coll Art Asn; AAM. *Publ:* Giorgio de Chirico and America, Hunter Coll, 96; Edward Hooper's NY Movie, Hunter Coll, 98; A Century on Paper, Art Students League of NY, 02. *Mailing Add:* 215 W 57th St New York NY 10019

KOONS, DARELL J
EDUCATOR, PAINTER
b Albion, Mich, Dec 18, 24. *Study:* Bob Jones Univ, BS, 51; Western Mich Univ, MA, 55; Eastern Mich Univ. *Work:* Butler Inst Am Art, Youngstown, Ohio; Mint Mus Art, Charlotte, Gov Mansion, Columbia, SC State Art Collection Mus Art, SC; Gibbes Gallery, Charleston, SC. *Comn:* Series of paintings hist scenes city of Greenville, comn by Tom Styron (dir Greenville Co Mus), 2004. *Exhib:* Acquavella Galleries, NY, 64 & 66; Springfield Mus Art Nat, Mass, 65; Soc Four Arts Nat, Palm Beach, Fla, 67; one-man shows, Mint Mus, Charlotte, NC, Wash Co Mus Art, Hagerstown, Md, Columbus Mus, Columbus, Ga, Jesse Besser Mus, Alpena, Mich; Art Embassies Prog, US State Dept, 90. *Pos:* Painter, currently. *Teaching:* Instr art, Homer Community Schs, 52-54; Bob Jones Univ, 55-98, drawing & painting instr, retired. *Awards:* Purchase Awards, Guild SC Artists, 63, Davis Assocs, Chattanooga, Tenn, 65 & Wake Forest Univ Gallery Contemp Art, 65. *Bibliog:* Steve Yates (auth), Greenville's noted barn painter, Sandlapper, 3/68. *Mem:* Upstate Visual Artists. *Media:* Watercolor, Acrylic. *Dealer:* Hampton III Gallery Wade Hampton Blvd Taylors SC 29687. *Mailing Add:* 6 Yancy Dr Greenville SC 29615

KOONS, JEFF
PAINTER, SCULPTOR
b York, Pa, 55. *Study:* Md Inst Col Art, Baltimore, 72-75 & BFA, 76; Art Inst Chicago, Ill, 75-76. *Exhib:* Retrospective (with catalog), Stedelijk Mus, Amsterdam, The Neth, 92, San Francisco Mus Mod Art, Calif, 92, Staatsgalerie Stuttgart, Ger, 93, Aarhus, Denmark, 93 & Walker Art Ctr, Minneapolis, Minn, 93; A Survey 1981-1994, Anthony d'Offay Gallery, London, Eng, 94; solo exhibs, Mus Contemp Art, Sydney, Australia, 95, Galerie jerome de Noirmont, Paris, France, 97, Guggenheim Mus Bilbao, Spain, 97,Anthony d'Offay Gallery, London, Eng, 98, Deste Found, Athens, Greece, 99, Deutsche Guggenheim, Gerlin, Ger, 2000 & Gagosian Gallery, Los Angeles, 2000; Playpen & Corpus Delierium (with catalog), Kunsthalle Zurich, Switz, 96; a/drift, Ctr Curatorial Studies Mus, Bard Col, Annandale-on-Hudson, NY, 96; Art at Home - Ideal Standard Life (with catalog), Spiral Garden, Tokyo, Japan, 96 & Gallery Seomi, Seoul, Korea, 96; It's Only Rock and Roll: Rock and Roll Currents in Contemp Art, Phoenix Art Mus, Ariz, 97; Belladonna, Inst Contemp Arts, London, Eng, 97; Family Values: Am Art in the Eighties and Nineties (with catalog), Scharpff Collection, Hamburger Kunsthalle, Hamburg, Ger, 97; Autoportraits, Galerie Municipale du Chateau d'Eau, Toulouse, France, 97; Multiple Identity: Amerikanische Kunst 1975-1995 Aus Dem Whitney Mus of Am Art (with catalog), Kunstmuseum Bonn, Ger, 97 & Castello di Rivoli, Mus d'Arte Contemporanea, Rivoli, Italy, 97; Objects of Desire: The Modern Still Life (with catalog), Mus Mod Art, NY, 97; Futuro Presente Passato: La Biennale di Venezia (with catalog), Venice, Italy, 97; Envisioning the Contemp: Selections from the Permanent Collection, Mus Contemp Art, Chicago, Ill, 97-98; On the Edge: Contemp Art from the Werner and Elaine Dannheisser Collection (with catalog), Mus Mod Art, NY, 97-98; A House Is Not A Home, Ctr Contemp Art, Amsterdam, The Neth, 97; Dramatically Different (with catalog), Ctr Nat D'Art Contemporain de Grenoble, France, 97-98; Kunst, Arbeit (with catalog), Sudwest LB Forum, Stuttgart, Ger, 97-98; Art in the 20th Century: Collection from the Stedelijk Mus Amsterdam (with catalog), Ho-Am Art Mus, Seoul, Korea, 98; Tuning Up #5, Kunstmuseum Wolfsburg, 98; Rene Margritte and the Contemp (with catalog), Mus voor Mod Kunst, Oostende, Belg, 98; Urban, Tate Gallery, Liverpool, Eng, 98-99; Interno - Esterno/Alterno (with catalog), FENDI, NY, 98; A Celebration of Art, Hirshhorn Mus & Sculpture Garden, Washington, 99; Am Century, Part II, Whitney Mus Am Art, NY, 99; Innocence and Experience, Mus Mod Art, NY, 2000, Pop and After, 2000, Matter, 2000, MoMA 2000, 2000, Actual Size, 2000 & Collaborations with Parkett: 1984 to Now, 2001; Reflections, Monika Sprüth Philomene Magers, Munich, 02, Penetration, Friedrich Petzel Gallery, New York City, 02, Penetration, Marianne Boesky Gallery, New York City, Shopping, Tate Liverpool, 02; Air, James Cohan Gallery, New York City, 03; Leckerbissen, Fischerplatz-Galerie, Ulm, 03. *Bibliog:* Roberta Smith (auth), Jeff Koons: Easyfun, NY Times, 99; Robert Hicks (auth), Jeff Koons brings art to the people, Villager Preview, 12/1/99; Robert Rigney (auth), Kitsch and Tell, Artnews, 3/2000. *Publ:* authThe Jeff Koons Handbook, 93; coauth (with Thomas Kellein) Jeff Koons Pictures 1980-2002, 03; coauth (with Robert Rosenblum and David Sylvester) Jeff Koons Easy Fun Ethereal, 03. *Dealer:* Sonnabend 420 W Broadway New York NY 10012

KOOPALETHES, OLIVIA KOOPALETHES ALBERTS
PAINTER, PRINTMAKER
b New York, NY. *Study:* Cooper Union for the advancement of Sci & Art, New York, 43, 44, 45; study with Wallace Harrison, New York, 46-49; Atelier Fernand Leger, Paris, 49; Atelier Andre Lhote, Paris, 50; Roberto DeLamonica, 76-79, Krishna Reddy, New York Blackburn Workshop, 80 & Shou Ping Liao, 81, Tenafly, NJ. *Work:* Jane Vorhees Zimmerli Art Mus, Rutgers Col, New Brunswick, NJ, 2003. *Exhib:* Solo shows, On Paper, New City Libr, NY, 89, L'Atelier Gallery, Piermont, NY, Greek Consulate Cult Ctr, Greek Embassy, NY, 92, Gallery Interchurch Ctr, NY, 94, Intermission Gallery, John Harms Ctr, Englewood, NJ, 95 & Bergen Mus Arts & Sci, Paramus, NJ, 96 & Gannon Univ, Schuster Gallery, Erie, Pa, 98-99, Arts Guild of Rahway, NJ, 01, Pleiades Gallery, New York City, 01, Studio 4 West, NY, 01, Audubon Artists, 02, Belskie Mus, NJ, 03, Maniotis Art Ctr, Boston, 03, Berlox Laboratories Corp, Wayne, NJ, 04; League of Transient Beauty, Aspects of Flowers, Invitational, Lever House, NY, 92; Critical Eye, Am Soc Contemp Artists, Broome St Gallery, 92; Ridgewood Art Inst, NJ, 92; Nat Asn Women Artists traveling print show, 92-93; Audubon Artists 52nd Ann, NY, 92; Audubon Artists Ann, NY, 95 & 96; Invitational Exhib (auth catalog), Pleiades Gallery, NY, 96; Nat Asn Women Artists Traveling Show, 96-99; Hunterdon Art Ctr, Clinton, NJ, 97; Painters Affiliate, Johnson & Johnson, New Brunswick, NJ, 97; City Without Walls, 18th Ann Metro Traveling Show, Newark, NJ, 99; Seton Hall, Newark, 99; Pleiades Gallery, New York City, 2000; Audubon Artists, 58th Ann Exhib, New York City, 2000; Am Soc Contemp Artists 82nd Ann Exhib, 2000; World Paper Challenger II, Dana Libr, Rutgers, Newark, NJ, 2003; Am Soc Contemp Artists, 85th & 86th Ann, New York City, 2003-2004; Int Soc Experemental Artist De Vos Mus, Marquette, Ill, 2006; 13th Ann Edward House Art Ctr, Nyack, NY, 2006; Nat Asn Women Arts, 2006; Karpeles Libr Mus, Newburg, NY; Port of Call Gallery, Warwick, NY. *Pos:* Historian, Nat Asn Women Artists, 89-97; violinist Bergen Philharmonic Orch, Teaneck, NJ; Bergen Co Teen Arts Festival, Art Critique, 99-2005. *Teaching:* Monitor printmaking, Robert DeLamonica Art Ctr, 79-81, Shou Ping Lian Art Ctr, Tenafly, NJ, 81-82. *Awards:* Honorable Mention, Montclair State Art Gallery; Grumbacher Silver Medal, Best in show, Salute to Women in the Arts, 93; Myra Biggerstaff Award, Nat Asn Women Artists 107th Ann, 96 & 108th Ann, 97; Am Soc Contemp Artists Award, 80th Ann Exhib, 98; Salute to Women in the Arts, Award of Excellence, Art Ctr Northern NJ, New Milford, NJ, 2002, 2nd Prize, 2005; Nat Asn Women Artists 117th Ann Dorothy Schweitzer Mem Adwards, Reading, Pa, 2006. *Bibliog:* EC Lipton (auth), Art Speak, NY, 10/92; Evonne E Courtros (auth), Hellenic Times, NY, 2/94; David Messer (auth), article, Bergan Mus Newsletter, 9-12/96; Ed McCormack (ed), Immediacy to an Ancient Medium, Gallery & Studio, Nov-Dec 2003/Jan 2004. *Mem:* Nat Asn Women Artists (hist, 6/87-5/91); Am Soc Contemp Artists; Printmaking Coun NJ; Audubon Artists Inc, NY; Art Ctr Painting Affil NJ; Salute to Women in the Arts NJ; Hellenic Am Womes Soc of NJ; Art from Detritus, NY; Int Soc Experimental Artist (ISEA), Fort Worth, Tex. *Media:* Wax Crayon, Colored Pencil; Encaustics. *Publ:* Contribr, Pages of Revelation, Artbuilders Inc, 86; 100 Years: A Centennial Celebration of National Association of Women Artists, Nassau Co Mus Fine Arts, Roslyn Harbor, NY, 88; Joanne Mattera (auth), Encaustic Painting: Contemporary Expression in the Ancient Medium of Pigment Wax, Watson Guptill. *Dealer:* Leader Associates, Wayne, NJ; Artvue, Mahawah, NJ. *Mailing Add:* 12 Cambridge Way Alpine NJ 07620

KOOYMAN, RICHARD E
CRAFTSMAN
b Grand Rapids, Mich, Oct 1, 56. *Study:* Grand Valley State Univ, BFA, 79; Ohio State Univ, MFA, 82. *Exhib:* Objects Gallery, Chicago, 87, 88, 90 & 93; Detroit Gallery Contemp Craft, Detroit, 89 & 93; The Works Gallery, Philadelphia, Pa, 93; Smithsonian Craft Show, Smithsonian Inst, Washington, DC, 93 & 94; Twist Gallery, Portland, Ore, 93; Bennett Galleries, Knoxville, Tenn, 94; Nancy Sach Galleries, St Louis, Mo, 94. *Awards:* Mich Coun Arts, 89; Nat Endowments Arts, 89; Mich Gov Award Arts, 90. *Mem:* Am Craft Coun; Col Art Asn; Nat Coun Educ Ceramic Arts. *Mailing Add:* c/o Tvedten Fine Art Gallery 284 E Third St Harbor Springs MI 49740

KOPF, SILAS
CRAFTSMAN
b Warren, Pa, 49. *Study:* Princeton Univ, AB(archit), 72; with Wendall Castle, 74-76; Ecole Boulle, France. *Work:* Gannett Corp; Scovill Corp; pvt Collections of Anne & Ronald Abramson, Washington, DC, Walda & Sydney Bestoff, New Orleans, La, Janice & Robert Diamond, NY, Sylvia & Donald Gerson, Ft Myers, Fla and many others. *Comn:* Craft work, Steinway & Sons, NY. *Exhib:* Wisteriahurst Mus, Holyoke, Mass, 86; Workbench Gallery, NY, 86; A C E Crafts at the Armory, NY, 87; Artful Objects: Recent Am Craft, Ft Wayne, Ind, 89; solo exhibs, Gallery Henoch, NY, 90, 92, 95 & 2001; Conservation by Design (nat touring exhib), 95-97. *Collection Arranged:* Mus of Art & Design, NY; Smith Col, Northamton, Mass; Yale Univ, New Haven, Conn. *Awards:* Craftsman's Fel, Nat Endowment of Arts, 88; New Eng Found Arts Fel, 97. *Bibliog:* Articles in fine woodworking, Am Craft, NY Times, Boston Globe, Art in New Eng, La, Marqueterie (France) & Art and Practices of Marquetry (Britian). *Mem:* Furniture Soc. *Dealer:* Gallery Henoch 555 W 25th St New York NY. *Mailing Add:* 20 Stearns Ct North Hampton MA 01060

KOPLOS, JANET
COLLECTOR, EDITOR
Study: Univ Minn, BA; Ill State Univ, MA. *Pos:* Ed, Minichi Daily News, Tokyo; ed, Art Material Trade News, Atlanta, GA; contrib ed, Fiberarts, Art Papers, New Art Examiner; sr ed, Art in America, NYC, 90 . *Awards:* Recipient, Nat Endowment Arts Award, Art Critic's Fel. *Publ:* coauth, Unexpected: Artists' Ceramics of the 20th Century, Laura De Santillana Works, 2002. *Mailing Add:* Art in America Brant Art Publications 575 Broadway New York NY 10012

KOPLOWITZ, ALICIA
COLLECTOR
b Sept 12, 52. *Pos:* Took control with sister Esther of family co Construcciones y Contratas SA, 90; Construcciones y Contratas SA (Cysca) merges with Fomento de Obras y Construcciones SA (Focsa) to become Fomento de Construcciones y Contratas SA (Fed Commun Comn), 92, vchmn, 92-97, sold shares to sister, 97; owner, investment co, Omega Capital, currently. *Awards:* Named one of Top 200 Collectors, ARTnews Mag, 2004. *Collection:* Old Masters & Modern Art. *Mailing Add:* Found Alicia Koplowitz Paseo de la Castellana 28-4 Madrid 28046 Spain

KOPPELMAN, CHAIM
PRINTMAKER, EDUCATOR
b New York, NY, Nov 17, 20. *Study:* Am Artists Sch; Art Col Western Eng, Bristol; Ozenfant Sch Fine Arts; Aesthetic Realism with Eli Siegel & Ellen Reiss. *Work:* Victoria & Albert Mus, London; Mus Fine Arts, Caracas, Venezuela; Mus Mod Art, Metrop Mus Art & Whitney Mus Am Art, NY; and many others. *Comn:* Eli Siegel Meml, Druid Hill Park, Baltimore, 02. *Exhib:* Merida Rapp Graphics, Louisville, Ky, 85; 161st Ann, Nat Acad, 86; 10th Int Small Works Ann, NY, 86; Print Club, Philadelphia, 88; Alternative Mus, NY, 88; Brooklyn Mus, 89; Beatrice Corde Gallery, NY, 99; and others. *Pos:* Consult, Aesthetic Realism Consultations, 71-. *Teaching:* NY Univ, 47-55, Brooklyn Col, 50-60, State Univ NY, New Paltz, 52-58 & Sch Visual Arts, 59-. *Awards:* Creative Artists Pub Serv Grant, 76; Cannon Prize, Nat Acad, 86 & 89; 10th Ann Int Small Works Exhib Award, 86; Philadelphia Mus Purchase Award, Print Club, 87; Prize, Nat Acad, 89 & 93; Silver Medal, Audubon Ann, 96; Lifetime Achievement Award, Soc Am Graphic Artists, 2005. *Bibliog:* Barry Schwartz (auth), The New Humanism, Praeger, 74; Una Johnson (auth), American Prints and Printmakers, Doubleday; Fritz Eichenberg (auth), The Art of the Print, Abrams, 76; Joan Lukach (auth), Hilla Rebay: In Search of the Spirit in Art, 83. *Mem:* Nat Acad Design; Soc Am Graphic Artists (former pres). *Media:* Etching, Miscellaneous Media. *Publ:* Co-auth, Aesthetic Realism: We Have Been There, 69; auth, This Is the Way I See Aesthetic Realism, 69; illusr, Damned Welcome, Definition, 72; contribr, Sunstorm Mag, 85; auth, J of the Print World, 87, 88, 89 & 92. *Dealer:* Susan Teller Gallery 568 Broadway New York NY 10012. *Mailing Add:* 498 Broome St New York NY 10013

KOPPELMAN, DOROTHY
PAINTER, CONSULTANT
b New York, NY, June 13 1920. *Study:* Brooklyn Col; Am Artists Sch; Art Students League; studied Philosophy of Aesthetic Realism with Eli Siegel, founder, now with Ellen Reiss. *Work:* Yale Univ, New Haven, Conn; Hampton Inst, Va; Mus of Jewish Family, Durham, NC; Nat Mus Women Arts, Washington, DC; Savannah Col Art Design, Ga. *Exhib:* Rian Gallery, 61; Museum Mod Art, New York City & Columbus Gallery Fine Art, 62; City Art Mus St Louis & Walker Art Ctr, 63; Baltimore Mus Art; 161st Ann Juried Exhib, 86, 165th Juried Exhib, 90, Nat Acad Design, NY; Hudson Guild, 88 & 90; Drawing Ctr, 93; Audubon Juried Ann, 96 & 98, Levitan Gallery, 96; Atlantic Gallery, 97-98, 2000-2003; 175th Juried Exhib Nat Acad Design, NY, 2000; Beatrice Conde Gallery, 2000; Terrain Gallery, 61, 2002, 2003. *Pos:* Dir, Terrain Gallery, 55-83 & Visual Arts Gallery, 62-64; pres, Aesthetic Realism Found Inc, 73-87. *Teaching:* Instr art, Adult Educ, Brooklyn Col, 52-75; consult Aesthetic Realism, 71-; instr, Nat Acad, Sch Fine Arts, 88, 89, 96 & 98; instr, critical inquiry, Aesthetic Realism Fedn, New York, 80-. *Awards:* Prize Painting, Brooklyn Soc Artists, 60; Tiffany Found Grant, 65-66; T Lindner Award for Painting, 96; Clara Shainess Award for Painting, 99. *Bibliog:* Emily Genauer (auth), article, NY Herald Tribune, 62; revs, Art News, 59, 61 & 62, NY Times, 62. *Mem:* NY Artist's Equity; Am Soc Contemp Artists. *Media:* Oil,Printmaking. *Specialty:* Contemp Art. *Collection:* Nat'l Mus Women in the Arts; Wash Co Mus Art; Libr Cong. *Publ:* Coauth, Aesthetic Realism: We Have Been There, 69; illusr, Children's Guide to Parents & Other Matters, 71, 2003; Van Gogh, Sunstorm, 84; Chardin, Tenn Tribune. *Dealer:* Terrain Gallery, 141 Greene St. NYC 10013; Atlantic Gallery 40 Wooster St New York NY. *Mailing Add:* 498 Broome St New York NY 10013

KOPRIVA, SHARON
PAINTER, SCULPTOR
b Houston, Tex, Feb 11, 48. *Study:* Univ Houston, with J Alexander & J Surls, BS, 70, MFA, 81. *Work:* Mus Fine Arts, Sante Fe, NMex; Mus Fine Arts & Menil Mus, Houston, Tex; Lowell Mus, Miami, Fla. *Comn:* Sculpture, ZZ Top, Billy Gibbons, Houston, 90; Grant, Mid America, 92; Cultural Arts Coun, Houston, 92 & 95. *Exhib:* Mus Fine Arts, Sante Fe, NMex, 86; Ctr Contemp Art, Mexico City, 87; Mus SE Tex, Beaumont, 91; Mus Fine Arts, Houston, Tex, 94; Nat Mus Am Art, Washington, 96; Menil Mus 2001; Mus Fine Arts, Shanghai, China; Nat Mus Lima, Peru, 2006; and others. *Collection Arranged:* Barrett, Menil, Houston MFA, Oshman Collection. *Pos:* Bd mem, Orange Show Found, Houston, 89-. *Teaching:* Teach fel, Univ Houston, 81; vis artist, Tex Tech & NDak State Univ, 90. *Awards:* First Place, Blaffer Gallery, Univ Houston, 88; Sculpture Grant, Diverse Works, Houston, 90; Texas State Artist Year 2005. *Bibliog:* S Bell (auth) & Gambrell (auth), articles in: Art Am, 87 & 89; Ed Hill (auth), article, Art Forum, 90; C Anspon (auth), Art News, 2000 & Sculpture, 2000; Houston Contemp Art, MFA Shanghai 2006. *Media:* Oil, Pencil; Bone, Paper-Mache. *Dealer:* Allan Stone Gallery New York NY 10016; Pillsbury-Peters Dallas TX; Lewelley Gallery, Santa Fe, NMex. *Mailing Add:* 1317 Arlington Houston TX 77008

KOPYSTIANSKY, IGOR
CONCEPTUAL ARTIST, PAINTER
b Lvov, Ukraine. *Work:* Art Inst Chicago; Mus Mod Art, Saint-Etienne, France; Mus Mod Art, Berlin; Ludwig Forum for Int Art, Aachen, Ger; Ludwig Mus, Palais Lichtenstein, Vienna; Art Gallery NSW Sydney; Mus Mod Art, Frankfurt, Ger; Folkwane Mus, Essen, Ger. *Exhib:* One-man shows, Berlinisehe Galerie-Mus Mod Art, Berlin 91, Kunsthalle Dusseldorf, 94 & Folkwang Mus, Essen, 99; 9th Biennial of Sydney, Art Gallery NSW, Sydney, 92; Cocido y Cruelo, Centro Arte Reina Sofia, Madrid, 94; 22nd Biennial of Sao Paolo, Brazil, 94; 4th Istanlul Biennial, Instanbul, Turkey, 95; 2nd Johannesburg Biennale, 97; Lyon Biennale, 97; First British Biennial, Liverpool, 99; Int exhibs, Change of Scene, 99; Venice Biennial Aperto, 1988; Documenta XI, Lisson Gallery, London; Sprengel Mus, Hannover, Ger. *Awards:* Fel, DAAD Artists Prog, Berlin, Ger, 90. *Bibliog:* Barry Schwabsky (auth), Igor & Svetlana Kopystiansky, Arts Mag, 2/89; Andy Grundberg (auth), Art, too, finds a summer home, NY Times, 8/24/90; Helena Kontova (auth), An interview with Igor & Svetlana Kopystiansky, Flash Art Intl, 93; B Schwabsicy (auth), Igor & Svetlana Kopystiansky, Artforum, 12/2002. *Media:* Installation, Painting; Video, Photography. *Interests:* videoing; sculpting; photography. *Publ:* Coauth, Igor & Svetlana Kopystiansky, DAAD, 91; auth, The Museum, Kunsthalle Dusseldorf, 94; coauth, In the Tradition, Creation No 2, Madrid, 94. *Dealer:* Lisson Gallery London 52-54 Bell St London NW1 5DA England. *Mailing Add:* 526 W 26th St No 608 New York NY 10001

KOPYSTIANSKY, SVETLANA
CONCEPTUAL ARTIST, PHOTOGRAPHER
b Voronez, Russia, Nov 11, 1950. *Work:* Metrop Mus Art, NY; Art Inst Chicago; Ludwig Forum for Intl Art, Aachen, Ger; Mus Mod Art, Berlin, Ger; Art Gallery NSW, Sidney; Mus Mod Art, Frankfurt, Ger. *Exhib:* One-woman show, Berlinische Galerie, Mus Mod Art, Berlin, 91, Kunsthalle Dusseldorf, Ger, 94, Kunsthalle Helsinki, Finland, 94; 22nd Biennial of Sao Paolo, Brazil, 94; Cocido y Crudo, Centro Arte Reina Sofia, Madrid, 94; solo exhibs, Kunsthalle Dusseldorf, 94, Kunsthalle Helsinki, Finland, 95, Mus Mod Art, Bode Mus Berlin & Some Assembly Required, Art Inst Chicago, 96; 4th Istanbul Biennial, Turkey, 95; Lyon Biennale, 97; Johannesburg Biennale (with catalog), 97; Change of Scene 1999, Mus Mod Art, Frankfurt Am Main, Sculpture Projects in Munster, 97; The First British Biennial, Liverpool, 99; Examining Painting, Whitechapel Art Gallery, London & Mus Contemp Art, Chicago, 99; One-woman show, Documenta XI, Ger, 2002, Lisson Gallery London, 2002, Sprengel Mus, Hannover, Ger, 2002. *Awards:* DAAD Artists Prog, Berlin, Ger, 1990. *Bibliog:* Barry Schwabsky (auth), Igor & Svetlana Kopystiansky, Arts Mag, 2/89; Andy Grundberg (auth), Art, too, finds a summer home, NY Times, 8/24/90; Helena Kontova (auth), An interview with Igor & Svetlana Kopystiansky, Flash Art Intl, 10/93; Barry Schwebsky (auth), Igor & Svetlana Kopystiansky, Artforum, 12/2002. *Media:* Installation Sculpture, Painting; Video, Photography. *Interests:* sculpting; painting; videoing. *Publ:* Coauth, Igor & Svetlana Kopystiansky, DAAD, 91; auth, Short Stories by Anton Cuckhov, Stop Over Press, Berlin, 93; coauth, In the Tradition, Creation No 2, Madrid, 94; auth, The Library, Kunsthalle Dusseldorf, 94; The Shadow of Gravitation, Art Inst Chicago, 96. *Dealer:* Lisson Gallery London 52-54 Bell St London NW1 5DA England. *Mailing Add:* 526 W 26th St No 608 New York NY 10001

KORD, VICTOR GEORGE
PAINTER, INSTRUCTOR
b Satu Mare, Romania, Sept 16, 1935; US citizen. *Study:* Cleveland Inst Art; Yale Univ, BFA, 58, MFA, 60. *Work:* Whitney Mus Am Art, NY; Cleveland Mus Art, Cleveland; Aldrich Mus, Ridgefield, Conn; Madison Art Ctr & Univ Wis, Madison, Wis; Elvehjem Art Ctr, Univ Wis. *Exhib:* Chicago Art Inst, 62; solo exhibs, Richard Gray Gallery, Chicago, 67, Univ SFla, Tampa, 68, Galerie Ricke, Cologne, Ger, 70 & Univ Ill, Champaign, 70; Cleveland Mus Art, Ohio, 68; Lyrical Abstraction, Whitney Mus Am Art, NY, 71; New Am Abstract Painting, Vassar Col, Poughkeepsie, NY, 72; Invitation 77 - Ten Painters, Walker Art Ctr, Minneapolis, 77; Made in Virginia, Reynolds-Minor Gallery, Richmond, 84; group exhib, Kathryn Sermas Gallery, NY, 90; two-man show, Kathryn Sermas Gallery, NY, 90; and others. *Pos:* Co-ed, New Arts Examiner, Richmond Off, 83-87. *Teaching:* Univ Ill, Champaign, 60-65; Univ Wis, Madison, 65-81, chair, 79-81; chair & prof, Va Commonwealth Univ, Richmond, 81-87; prof art, Cornell Univ, Ithaca, NY, 87-. *Awards:* Guggenheim Fel, 62. *Mem:* Fed Arts Coun Richmond, Va (bd dir, 83-87); Am Abstract Artists. *Mailing Add:* 245 Henry St Brooklyn NY 11201

KOREN, EDWARD B
CARTOONIST, ILLUSTRATOR
b New York, NY, Dec 13, 35. *Study:* Columbia Univ, BA, 57; Atelier 17, Paris, with SW Hayter; Pratt Inst, MFA, 64. *Hon Degrees:* Union Col, LHD, 84. *Work:* Fogg Mus, Cambridge, Mass; Princeton Univ Mus; RI Sch Design Mus; US Info Agency; Libr Cong; and others. *Exhib:* Exposition Dessins d'Humeur, Soc Protectrice d'Humeur, Avignon, France, 73; Art from the NY Times, Soc Illusr, NY, 73; Art from the New Yorker, Grolier Club, 75; Terry Dintinfass Gallery, NY, 75-77, 79 & 91; Koren: Prints and Drawings 1954-1981 Traveling Exhib, State Univ Albany, NY, 82-83; Virginia Lynch Gallery, Tiverton, RI, 99, 2000, 2001, 2002; Middlebury College Mus Art, 2006; and others. *Pos:* staff artist, The New Yorker Magazine. *Teaching:* Adj prof art, Brown Univ, 64-2006. *Awards:* Third Prize, Biennale Illusr, Bratislava, Czech, 73; Ten Best Childrens Bks of Yr, New York Times, 73; Prix d'Humour, Soc Protectrice d'Humour, Avignon, France, 76; John Simon Guggenheim Fel, 70-71. *Mem:* Authors Guild; Soc Am Graphic Artists. *Media:* Pen & Ink. *Publ:* Auth, The Hard Work of Simple Living, Chelsea Green, 98; Pet Peeves, 2000; Travelling While Married, Algonquin Books, 2003; auth, illusr, very Hairy Harry, Harper Collins, 2003; illusr, The New Legal Seafoods Cookbook, Broadway Books, 2003; The Lunious Monster's Sky-High Fly Pie, 2006. *Mailing Add:* Box 464 Brookfield VT 05036

KORENIC, LYNETTE MARIE
LIBRARIAN
b Berwyn, Ill, Mar 29, 50. *Study:* Univ Wis, Madison, MFA, 79 MA, Libr Sci, 81, MA, Art History, 84. *Pos:* Asst art librn, Fine Arts Libr, Ind Univ, 82-84 & Arts Libr, Univ Calif, 84-88; head arts libr, Univ Calif, Santa Barbara, 88-. *Mem:* Art Libr Soc NAm (secy 83-84, vpres 89, pres 90, past pres, 91; Col Art Asn; Am Libr Asn. *Res:* 18th, 19th and 20th century American art; history of photography. *Publ:* Coauth, Survey of Periodical Use in an Academic Art Library, 82, Grant Development Strategies for Large and Small Libraries, 90, ARLIS/NA Publ. *Mailing Add:* Univ Calif Arts Libr Santa Barbara CA 93106

KORMAN, BARBARA
SCULPTOR, ASSEMBLAGE ARTIST
b New York, NY, Apr 8, 38. *Study:* Art Students League; NY State Col Ceramics, Alfred Univ, BFA(cum laude), 59, MFA(Grad Fel), 60; State Univ NY Col, Purchase. *Work:* In many pvt and pub collections throughout the world. *Exhib:* Albright-Knox Art Gallery, Buffalo, NY, 60; Metrop Mus Art, NY, 76; Queens Mus, NY, 81; Overseas Press Club, NY, 88; Tiffany & Co Windows, NY, 92; Heckscher Mus, Huntington, NY, 95 & 96; Eisenhower Hall Gallery, West Point Acad, NY, 96; Exhibs Grounds for Sculpture, 2001; and others. *Pos:* Photogr - producer, audio-visual educ packages, 78-85; designer, producer Sculpture Studio 62-. *Teaching:* instr sculpture & stage design, NY Bd Educ, 61-91. *Awards:* Outstanding Art Educator Award, 77; Jeffrey Childs Willis Mem Prize Sculpture, 84; and many others; Brio-Bronx award for sculpture, 98; Yosemite Renaissance XVII award for sculpture, 2002; Coun Am Artist Soc award, 2002. *Mem:* Nat Asn Women Artists; Int Sculpture Ctr; Bronx Coun Arts; Katonah Mus Artist Asn. *Media:* Metal Cast, Painted Wood

KORMAN, HARRIET R
PAINTER
b Bridgeport, Conn, Dec 10, 47. *Study:* Skowhegan Sch Painting & Sculpture, summer 68; Queens Col (NY), BA, 69. *Work:* Weatherspoon Art Gallery, Univ NC, Greensboro; Solomon R Guggenheim Mus, NY; Maier Mus Art, Lynchburg, Va; Solomon R Guggenheim Mus, NY; Maier Mus of Art, Lynchburg, VA; Weatherspoon Art Gallery, Greensboro, NC. *Exhib:* Solomon R Guggenheim Mus, 71; Whitney Mus Am Art, 72, 73, 74 & 95; solo exhibs, Willard Gallery, NY, 80, 83 & 87, Sorkin Gallery, NY, 90 & Lennon, Weinberg Inc, NY, 92, 94 & 96, Lennon Weinberg, Inc, NY, 2001 & Daniel Weinberg Gallery, Los Angeles, Calif, 2002; Abstract Expressionism: An Ongoing Legacy, Gallery Kohn Pederson Fox & Gallery Hastings-on-Hudson, NY, 94; Directions in Am Abstraction: A New Decade, Southern Alleghenies Mus Art, Loretto, Pa, 94; Directions in Am Abstraction: A New Decade, Southern Alleghenies Mus Art, Loretto, Penn, 94; Lennon, Weinberg Inc, NY, 95 & 96; After the Fall: Aspects of Abstract Painting Since 1970, Snug Harbor Cult Ctr, Staten Island, NY, 97; Turning the Corner, Abstraction at the End of the Twentieth Century, Hunter Col, NY, 97; group exhibs, Texas Gallery, Houston, TEX, 2001 & Lennon Weinberg Inc, NY, 2002, Nat Acad Mus, NY, 2006; Retrospective (with catalog) After the Fall: Aspects of Abstract Paintings Since 1970, Snug Harbor Cult Ctr, 97 & Turning the Corner-Abstraction at the End of the 20th Century, Bertha and Karl Leubsdorf Gallery, Hunter Col, CUNY, 97. *Teaching:* vis faculty, Bennington Col, Vermont, 83; vis artist MFA program, Va Commonwealth Univ, 84; Richmond Printmakers Workshop, VA, 86 & 87; adj fac, Queens Col, CUNY, 90-93 & Fashion Inst of Technol, NY, 89-. *Awards:* Theodoron Found Award, 71; Nat Endowment Arts Fel Grant, 74, 78 & 93; NY Found Arts, Grant, 91; Yaddo Residency Grant, Sararoga Springs, NY, 96; Edward Albee Found Residency Grant, Montauk Point, NY, 97. *Bibliog:* Ken Johnson (auth), Harriet Korman at Lennon, Weinberg, Art Am, 11/94, Saul Ostrow (auth), Strategies for a New Abstraction, Tema Celest, autumn 91; Alfred Corn (auth), Harriet Korman at Lennon, Weinberg, Art in America, 4/7; Alfred Corn (auth), Artforum, 97; Harriet Korman at Lennon, Weinberg, New York Times, 3/9/2001. *Media:* Oil. *Dealer:* Lennon Weinberg Inc 560 Broadway Suite 308 New York NY 10012-3945

KORN, HENRY
MUSEUM DIRECTOR, WRITER
b Sept 19, 45. *Study:* Johns Hopkins Univ, AB, 68. *Pos:* Arts comn & found dir, City of Santa Monica, Calif, 86-90; cult affairs mgr, City of Irvine, Calif, 90-93; pres & mus dir, Guild Hall of East Hampton, NY, 93-99. *Teaching:* Adj instr, Johnson State Col, Vt, 84; practicum seminars on pub arts and cult diversity for local government agencies, 86-93; Dir Art & Cult, City of Beverly Hills, Calif, 99-; Dir, City of Beverly Hills Munic Gallery, 99-. *Awards:* Nat Endowment Arts Fel Fiction, 78; City Livability Award, US Conf Mayors, 89; Award of Excellence, Calif Parks & Recreation Soc, 91. *Bibliog:* Carissa Katz (auth), Guild Hall: a hot summer, East Hampton Star, 5/97; Robert Lipsyte (auth), Long on celebrity, short on charity, NY Times, 8/98. *Mem:* Mus Asn NY State. *Publ:* Contribr, Connoisseur, Art & Auction, LA Weekly; auth, Muhammad Ali Retrospective, 77, A Difficult Act to Follow, 82 & Marc Chagall, 85, Staten Island Advance & Congress Monthly

KORNBLATT, BARBARA RODBELL
DEALER
b Baltimore, Md, Jan 25, 31. *Study:* Community Col Baltimore, AA; Goucher Col, with Hilton Brown, BA. *Pos:* Dir, B R Kornblatt Gallery, Washington, DC; founder, dir, Fine Art, Baltimore; bd director, Shriver Hall, Baltimore, currently. *Teaching:* Lectr, Smithsonian Inst & Baltimore Hebrew Univ; leads art educ trips. *Awards:* served on art advisory panel for Internal Revenue Serv, 86-89. *Bibliog:* Articles in Sun, 5/26/76, News Am, 9/23/79 & Baltimore News Am, 11/2/80. *Mem:* Art Table. *Specialty:* Contemporary American sculpture, prints and painting. *Mailing Add:* c/o Shriver Hall Ste 105 3400 N Charles St Baltimore MD 21218-2698

KORNBLUM, MYRTLE
PAINTER, PRINTMAKER
b Chicago, Ill, Aug 18, 1909. *Study:* Washington Univ, St Louis; Univ Miami, Coral Gables, studied with Hans Hoffman. *Exhib:* City Art Mus, St Louis, Mo, 60-62; Print Club NY, 60; Art USA, Madison Sq Garden, NY, 60; Libr Cong, Washington, DC, 63; Silvermine Printmakers, New Canaan, Conn, 65; Atkins Mus Fine Art, Kansas City, Mo; Joslyn Mus, Omaha, Nebr; one-woman shows, St Louis Artists Guild, 70-81 & Norton Gallery, St Louis, Chicago, Kansas City, Madrid & Haifa; and others. *Awards:* First Prize, New Testament Show, Temple Israel, St Louis Co, Mo, 70; Second Prize, 70 & First Energy Prize, 75, St Louis Artists Guild. *Mem:* St Louis Artists Guild; Acad Prof Artists; Community Women Artists. *Media:* Collagraph, Woodcut. *Mailing Add:* St Louis Artist Guild 2 Oak Knoll Park St Louis MO 63105-3008

KORNBLUTH, FRANCES
PAINTER, ASSEMBLAGE ARTIST
b New York, NY, July 26, 20. *Study:* Brooklyn Col, BA, 40; Brooklyn Mus Art Sch, 55-59; Pratt Inst, MAE, 62. *Work:* Aetna & Cigna Collections, Hartford, Conn; Quinebaug Valley Community Col, Danielson, Conn; Doctor's Coun, NY; Gestalt Inst, Cleveland, Ohio; Hudson River Mus, NY; Chrysler Mus, Norfolk, Va; Altos de Chavon Found, Dominican Republic; pvt collections of Jamie Wyeth, Southern Island, Maine and other pvt collections in US, Can, Dominican Republic, Eng, Italy & Israel. *Exhib:* 158th Ann Exhib Pa Acad Fine Arts, Philadelphia, 63; 32nd & 42nd Conn Artists Ann, Slater Memorial Mus, Norwich, Conn, 75 & 85; Joan Whitney Payson Gallery Art, Portland, Maine, 83; 78th & 83rd Ann Exhib, Conn Acad Fine Arts, William Benton Mus, Storrs, 88 & 94; Conn Vision, Mattatuck Mus, Waterbury, 89; Prudence Crandall Mus, Canterbury, 93 & 94; Homer Babbidge Libr, Univ Conn, 96; solo exhib incl Artworks Gallery, Hartford, Conn, 69, 81, 91, Pradis Gallery, East Douglas, Mass, 97, Slater Mem Mus, Norwich, Conn, 2001; and numerous others. *Pos:* Estab & taught program for gifted elem in Thompson, Conn, 80-84. *Teaching:* Lectr art, Univ Conn, 70 & 71 & Annhurst Col, Woodstock, Conn, 79-80, Adelphi Univ, Garden City, NJ, Hofstra Univ, Hempstead, NY, Dowling Col, Oakdale, NY, Mills Col, New York City; instr & dir gifted educ, Thompson Pub Sch, Conn, 72-76. *Awards:* Knox Found Finalist for Commission, Hartford, 90; Miriam E Halpern Mem Award, 92; Shortell Award, 95; 1st Prize in Painting, 57th Ann Artists Exhbn, Slater Meml Mus, Norwich, Conn, 2000; Award for Solo Exhib, Collages and Constructions, Slater Meml Mus, Norwich, 2001; Lifetime Achievement Award, Brooklyn Col, NY, 2000; Work on Paper Award, Conn Acad Fine Arts, Conn, 2004; and numerous others. *Bibliog:* Jude Schwendenwein (auth), Color & Light Permeate Kornbluth Show, Hartford Courant, Conn, 6/15/91; Susan Wadsworth (auth), Frances Kornbluth: Paintings & Constructions, Art New England, Boston, Mass, 8-9/91; Alicia Craig Faxon (auth), Frances Kornbluth: Points of Departure, Art New Eng, Boston, Mass, 10-11/95. *Mem:* Nat Asn Women Artists; Conn Acad Fine Arts; Women Artists Monhegan Island; Northeast Conn Art Guild; Showcase for Collage; Arts/Worcester. *Media:* Acrylic; Mixed Media; Constructions; Collage. *Interests:* Film, music. *Publ:* Monhegan: the Artists Island. *Dealer:* Lupine Gallery Monhegau Island Maine 04852; Celebrations Pomtret CT. *Mailing Add:* 134 Buckley Hill Rd North Grosvenordale CT 06255

KORNETCHUK, ELENA
DEALER, HISTORIAN
b Ger, June 10, 48; US citizen. *Study:* Univ Md, College Park, BA, 70; Univ Iowa, MA, 72; Georgetown Univ, PhD, 82. *Collection Arranged:* The Graphics of Estonia, Latvia and Lithuania, Russian Images Ltd, 78, Contemporary Russian Painting, 78 & Kaplan's Lithographs, 79; Retrospective of Anatolii Kaplan, Russian Images Ltd, Pittsburgh, 79. *Pos:* Partner, Masterworks Int, Chicago, 76-78; pres, International Images, Ltd (aka Russian Images, Ltd), Sewickley, Pa, 78-; lectr, contemp art in the USSR, Univ Pittsburgh, 85-; mem, bd dir, Carnegie-Mellon Univ Art Gallery, Pittsburgh, 85-; cur Eastern Europ Art, New Eng Ctr Contemp Art, Brooklyn, Conn, 86-. *Teaching:* Instr Russian lang, lit & cult, Univ Iowa, 70-72 & Univ Md, College Park, 73-75. *Mem:* Asn Advan Slavic Studies, Stanford, Calif, 71-; World Affairs Coun, Pittsburgh, 78-; Sweetwater Art Ctr, Sewickley, Pa (bd dir, 80-84); Asn Advan Baltic Studies, Mahwah, NJ, 82-; Am Coun Study Islamic Soc, Villanova, Pa, 85-; Am Latvian Artists Asn, NY, 85-. *Specialty:* Contemporary art from Russia, Latvia, Estonia, Bulgaria and other countries of Eastern Europe. *Collection:* Contemporary art from the USSR, Japanese wood engravings. *Publ:* Auth, Contemporary Russian printmaking: An overview, Graphics Mag, 10-11/79; Contemporary Soviet prints: A national diversity, Print News, 10/80; Inars Helmust and the Latvian graphic tradition, spring 82, Nature printing: Robert Little and Renata Sawyer, spring 83, Prints today: Holland summer, 83 & The watercolors of Dzemma Skulme, spring 86, J Print World. *Mailing Add:* International Images Ltd 514 Beaver St Sewickley PA 15143-1779

KORNHAUSER, ELIZABETH MANKIN
MUSEUM DIRECTOR, CURATOR
b Tenafly, NJ, June 24, 50. *Study:* Boston Univ, BA, 72, PhD, 88; State Univ NY, Cooperstown, MA, 76. *Work:* Wadsworth Atheneum Mus Art, Hartford, Conn; Brooklyn Mus, Long Island Hist Soc, Brooklyn, NY; Smith Col Art Mus, Northampton, Mass; Yale Art Gallery, New Haven, Conn. *Collection Arranged:* Brooklyn Before the Bridge, 82-83; Ralph Earl, 91-92; American Paintings at the Wadsworth Atheneum, 2 vols, 96; New Worlds from Old: Australia and American 19th Century Land, 98-99; Alfred Stieglitz, Georgia O'Keeffe and American Modernism, 99; Caldar in Connecticut, 2000. *Pos:* cur Am art, Wadsworth Atheneum, 83-95, deputy dir, chief cur, 95-99; acting dir, Wadsworth Atheneum Mus Art, 2000. *Teaching:* lectr Am art hist, Trinity Col, Hartford, Conn, 89-2000. *Bibliog:* John Updyke (auth), Alfred Stieglitz, Georgia O'Keeffe and American Modernism, NY Rev Books, Spring 99; James Fenton (auth), New Worlds from Old, NY Rev Books, Fall 99; Robert Hughes (auth), article, Time Mag. *Mem:* Arch Am Art; Am Studies Asn; Col Art Asn; Am Asn Mus Dirs. *Mailing Add:* Wadsworth Atheneum Mus Art 600 Main St Hartford CT 06103

KORNMAYER, J GARY
PAINTER, PHOTOGRAPHER
b Omaha, Nebr. *Study:* San Diego State Univ, 59-61; Nat Univ, San Diego, BA, 70, MA(audio-visual commun), 74. *Work:* Riverside Art Mus, Calif. *Comn:* Tex Hist, Nat Univ, San Diego, 73 & Am Hist of Slavery, 74; stations of cross, St Charles Borromeo Church, Morganton, NC, 98. *Exhib:* One-man shows, Soho Gallery, NY, 75-78, Inst Mex NAm Relaciones Cult, Mexico City, Inst Allende, San Miguel Allende, Mex, 80, San Diego Art Inst, 89, 92 & 93 & Tryon Art Ctr, NC, 96; Calif-Hawaii Biennial, Fine Arts Gallery, San Diego, 76; San Diego Art Inst, Calif; Upstairs Gallery, Tryon, NC, 96, 97, 98, 99 & 2000; Village Gallery, Flat Rock, NC, 98; Tryon Arts Gallery, Tryon, NC, 2002; Conn Gallery, Lambrum, SC, 2002; Spartanburg Co Art Mus, Spartnaburg, SC, 2005. *Pos:* Photogr, Gen Dynamics Corp, San Diego, 58-60, sr audio-visual commun, 60-69, mgr graphics commun, 80-92; mem adv bd, Carolina Foothills Artisan Ctr, 99-. *Awards:* Distinctive Merit, San Diego Art Director's Soc, 65; Second Place, Fine Arts Gallery San Diego, 68; First Place Purchase Award, Riverside Art Mus, 70. *Bibliog:* Hedy O'Beil (auth), J Gary Kornmayer, artist, Arts Mag, 10/77; Hal Gray (auth), Horizons, Channel 39, 12/77; In the Public Interest, City of San Diego, Channel 2, 1/78. *Mem:* San Diego Fine Arts Soc-Art Guild (mem bd dir, 68-70); Span Village Art Asn (mem bd dir, 72-74, pres, 74-78); San Diego Art Inst (mem bd dir, 90-93, pres, 93-94). *Media:* Mixed Media. *Dealer:* Upstairs Gallery PO Box 553 Tryon NC 28782; Carolina Foothills Artisan Ctr, PO Box 517, Chester, SC, 29323. *Mailing Add:* 3350 River Rd Columbus NC 28722

KOROT, BERYL
VIDEO ARTIST, PAINTER
b New York, NY, Sept 17, 45. *Study:* Univ Wis, 63-65; Queens Col, BA, 67. *Work:* Chase Manhattan. *Comn:* Video opera, The Cave, with Steve Reich, 93; Video opera, Three Tales, with Steve Reich, 2002. *Exhib:* Solo exhibs, Everson Mus, Syracuse, 75 & 79, Castelli Gallery, NY, 77 & Whitney Mus, 80; group shows include Yesterday and After, Mus des Beaux Arts, Montreal, 80; Burden, Kos, Korot, San Francisco Art Inst, 81; Paintings, John Weber Gallery, 86; Videoskulptor, Kolnischer Kunstuerein, Zurichkunsthaus, Berliner Kunstverein, 89; Carnegie Inst Art, Points of Departure: Origins in Video, Pittsburgh, 90; 1993-94 Exhib Video Installation Tour: Whitney Mus, 93, Düsseldorf Kunsthalle, 94 Reina Sofia, Madrid, 94, Mus Moderne d'Ascq, Lille, 94; performance work, Hindenbrg Spoleto Festival, 98; 2 installations, Mass Col Art, 99; video projection, Am Century Post 2, Whitney Mus, 2000; video installation, Frankfort, History Mus, 2000; Travelling video opera, Three Tales, Vienna, Berlin, Amsterdam, Torino, Lisbon, London, Paris, NY, Charleston, Perth & Hong Kong; American Century at Whitney Mus, 2001; video installation, Jewish Mus Paris, 2002; video installation, PBS, 2005; DMZ, S Korea, 2005. *Teaching:* Sch Visual Arts, 76-78; Montgomery Fel Dartmouth Col, 2000. *Awards:* Nat Endowment Arts Grant, 75, 77 & 79; NYSCA Grant, 78; John Simon Guggenheim Fel, 94. *Bibliog:* and others; Andrew Clements (auth), rev, The Guardian, 5/18/2002; Keith Potter (auth), rev, The Independent, 5/18/2002; Justin Davidson (auth), rev, NY Newsday, 10/13/2002. *Media:* Video, Computer. *Publ:* Ed, Radical software, Vol I & Vol II, Gordon & Breach Sci Publ, 72-74; Video Art, Harcourt, Brace, Jovanovich (in press). *Mailing Add:* 114 Horseshoe Hill Rd Pound Ridge NY 10576

KOROW, ELINORE M See Korow-Bieber, Elinore Maria Vigh

KOROW-BIEBER, ELINORE MARIA VIGH
PAINTER, EDUCATOR
b Akron, Ohio, July 31, 1934. *Study:* Cleveland Inst Art, with Rolf Stoll, Paul Riba & John Teyral; Sienna Heights Womens Col; Sawyer Col Bus. *Work:* Hebrew Acad, Cleveland Heights, Ohio; Berkowitz Kumin Mem Chapel; Cleveland Play House Gallery; Bd Rm, Blue Cross/Blue Shield, Cleveland, Ohio; Cleveland Clinic Found; Kent State Univ, School Fashion & Kent Mus; Temple EmanuEl, Cleveland Heights, Ohio; First Congregational Church, Akron; Univ of Akron, Stitzlein Alumni Center, OH. *Comn:* Rabbi Boruch Sorotzkin, Pres of Rabbinical Col Telshe, Wickliffe, Ohio; George Hilden, Pres of Osco Drugs, Chicago; Jerome Weinberger, Pres Gray Drugs, Cleveland; Charles Walgreen, Pres Walgreen Drugs, Chicago; double oil portrait, Stitzlein Alumni Ctr, Univ Akron, Ohio, 98; and others; Mrs Burton D Morgan, Kent State Univ; Cantor Irvin Bushman, Temple EmanuEl, Cleveland Heights, Ohio; Pres William Luntz, Luntz Corp, Canton, Ohio; Pres Stewart Turley, Eckert Drug, Clearwater, Fla; Producer Syd Friedman, Channel 35, Fairview Park, Ohio. *Exhib:* Butler Inst Am Art, Youngstown, Ohio, 68-70; Nat Acad Design, NY, 73; World Trade Ctr, Am Artists Prof League, NY, 80; one-woman show, Chagrin Valley Little Theatre, Ohio, 80, Nat Acad Design, NY, 73; Miniature Painting Show, Bath, Ohio, 81; All Ohio-Canton Art Inst, 88; Boston Mills Nat Show, Peninsula, Ohio, 88; Mansfield Art Mus, 88; Invitational, Fairmont Fine Arts Ctr, Novelty, Ohio, 2002; Massillon Mus, 2002; Lynn Kottler Galleries, New York City, 1974; Stan Hywet Hall & Gardens, Akron, OH; Spring Exhib, Women's Art League of Akron, OH, 2006; and many others. *Pos:* Staff artist & designer, Am Greeting Corp, Cleveland, 57-58 & 71-73; owner, Elinore Korow: Portraits, Shaker Heights, Ohio, 1973-94, Akron, Ohio, 1994-. *Teaching:* Instr painting, drawing & portraiture, Eastern Campus Elders Prog, Cuyahoga Community Col, 79-, Univ Akron, 95-; lectr, Ancient Egypt, Cleveland Clinic Found: Oasis, 96. *Awards:* 2nd Prize Geo Mayer Galleries, Akron, Ohio, 2000; Best in Show Award, First Annual Juried Show, Women's Art League, Akron, 2000; Honorable Mention Award, Akron Soc Artists and Womens Art League of Akron, Almond Tea Gallery, Chyahoga Falls, Ohio, 2000; Best of Show, Stan Hywet Hall & Gardens, Akron, OH. *Bibliog:* Review, Northern Ohio Live Mag. *Mem:* Charter mem Ohio Watercolor Soc; Women's Art League Akron (pres 99-2000); Am Portrait Soc; Am Artists Prof League; signature mem Akron Soc Artists; Am Pastel Soc; Akron Soc Artists; and others. *Media:* All. *Dealer:* Copper Moon Gallery 3807 Brecksville Rd Richfield OH 44286. *Mailing Add:* 923 Mayfair Rd Akron OH 44303

KORSHAK, YVONNE
HISTORIAN, EDUCATOR
b Chicago, Ill. *Study:* Radcliffe Col, BA, 58; Univ Calif, Berkeley, with D A Amyx, H Chipp, J K Anderson & J Bony, MA(classical archeol), 66, PhD(art hist), 73. *Collection Arranged:* Selections from the Adelphi Univ Art Collection (co-ed, catalog), 79. *Teaching:* Prof, Adelphi Univ, 75-, chairperson dept art & art hist, 79-82, dir mus studies prog, 79-. *Awards:* Award Merit, 88, President's Award, 90, Adelphi Univ; Award Merit, Am Ash Mus. *Mem:* Charter mem Long Island Art Historians Asn; Col Art Asn Am; Archeol Inst Am; Asn Ancient Historians; Am Soc 18th Cent Studies. *Res:* Eighteenth-nineteenth century French painting; classical Greek art; iconography and hidden imagery. *Publ:* coauth, Selections from the Permanent Collections of the Arkansas Arts Center, 83; auth, Realism and Transcendent Imagery: Van Gogh's Crows over the Wheatfield, Pantheon 43, 85; Frontal Faces in Attic Vase Painting of the Archaic Period, Chica, 87; The Liberty Cap as a revolutionary symbol in America and France, Smithsonian Studies in Am Art, 10/87; "Paris and Helen" by Jacques Louis David: Choice and judgement on the eve of the French Revolution, Art Bull, 3/87. *Mailing Add:* 1025 Fifth Ave New York NY 10028

KORTENHAUS, LYNNE M
CONSULTANT, CURATOR
b Long Branch, NJ, Jan 11, 51. *Study:* RI Sch Design, Providence, BFA, 73, MFA, 75; Florence, Italy, independent study, 74-75, hons. *Pos:* Asst dir, Arvest Galleries, Boston, Mass, 75-78; art consult, pvt-corp insts in Boston, 78-79; New Eng rep, Phillips Fine Art Auctioneers & Appraisers, 79-82; dir marketing & corp sales, Haley & Steele Gallery, 83-84, fine arts consult & cur, 84-. *Teaching:* Instr lithography, RI Sch Design Printmaking Workshop, 73-75. *Bibliog:* Article in Corporate Artnews, 6/85; article in Designers West, 8/85. *Mem:* Appraisers Asn Am; Appraisers Registry; Newbury St League (vpres & auction chairperson). *Media:* Appraisal

KORTLANDER, WILLIAM
PAINTER, HISTORIAN
b Grand Rapids, Mich, Feb 9, 25. *Study:* Mich State Univ, BA; Univ Iowa, MA & PhD. *Work:* Columbus Mus Art, Ohio; Schumacher Gallery, Capital Univ, Columbus, Ohio; Chubu Inst, Nagoya, Japan; Huntington Mus, WVa; Chemical Bank & AT&T, NY. *Exhib:* Pa Acad Fine Arts, Philadelphia, 65; Wadsworth Atheneum, Hartford, Conn, 65; AM Sachs Gallery, NY, 66, 68 & 79; Corcoran Gallery, Washington, 68; Baltimore Mus, Md, 68; one-man show, Haber/Theodore Gallery, NY, 80, 82 & 84, Foster Harmon Gallery, Sarasota, Fla, 86 & 87 & Gallery V, Columbus, Ohio, 96; Nat Mus Am Art, Smithsonian Inst, Washington, 81; The Shanghai Exchange, Shanghai Teachers Univ, Peoples Repub China, 88; Collectors Gallery, Invitational Albright-Knox Art Gallery, Buffalo, NY, 94; Out of this World, Mansfield Art Ctr, Ohio, 98; Gallery V, Columbus, Ohio, 98, 2000; One Person Show; Fitton Ctr for Creative Arts, Hamilton, Ohio, 2004; Invitational Shows: Gallery V, Columbus, OH, 2005-2006. *Pos:* Prof Emer of Art, Ohio Univ, 1994. *Teaching:* Instr art hist, Lawrence Univ, 54-56; asst prof art hist, Univ Tex, Austin, 56-61; vis asst prof art hist, Mich State Univ, summer 60; prof painting, Ohio Univ, 61-94. *Awards:* Painting of Year, Mead Corp, 65; Baker Award, Ohio Univ, 67. *Bibliog:* Doc, Kortlander & Kortlander, WOUB TV, Athens, Ohio, 84; Nicholas Roukes (auth), Acrylics Bold & New, Watson Guptil, 86; Kay Koeninger (auth), Sharing a familial sense of place, The Columbus Dispatch, Ohio, 2/8/98. *Media:* Multimedia. *Res:* Iconography of 15th Century Flemish Painting. *Publ:* Auth, Painting with Acrylics, Van Nostrand Reinhold, 73. *Mailing Add:* 7414 Angel Ridge Rd Athens OH 45701

KORZENIK, DIANA
WRITER, PAINTER
b New York, NY, Mar 15, 41. *Study:* Vassar Col, Oberlin Col, BA, 61; Columbia Univ, Art Hist Masters; Havard Grad Sch of Edu, D of Ed, 72. *Work:* Diana Korzenik Collection of Am Art Edn, Huntington Libr & Mus, San Marino, Calif. *Comn:* J P Getty Trust; Art-Making & Education. *Exhib:* 4 Decades of Painting (retrospective), Boston. *Collection Arranged:* Exhibitions on Nineteenth Century America, 86 & Drawn to Art: Fruitlands, 88, Univ NH; Korzenik Collection of American Art Education, Huntington Mus Libr, San Marino, Calif; Drawn to Art res, Am Antiquarian Soc. *Pos:* Prof emeritus, Mass Col Art. *Awards:* Fel, Woodrow Wilson-Ford Found, 62; L L Winship Lit Award, Boston Globe, 86; City of Boston Pro Arts Serv in the Arts Award, 92; Am Libr Asn LEAB Award, 05. *Bibliog:* David Perkins (auth), Project Zero, J Aesthetic Educ; Howard Gardner (auth), Art, Mind & Brain & Artful Scribbles, Basic Books Inc; Clair Golomb (ed), The Development of Artistically Gifted Children; Drawn to Art 19th Century American Dream, Univ Press New England, 1986; Objects of American Art Education, Huntington Library Press, 2006. *Mem:* Nat Art Educ; Caucus Social Theory & Art Educ; Mus Fine Arts; Ephemera Soc Am; Col Art Asn; Women's Caucus Art; Am Antuquerian Soc; Mass Hist Soc. *Media:* Painter and writer on art. *Res:* History of Am Art edn. *Publ:* Framing the Past, Nat Art Educ Asn, 92; Art Making & Education, Ill Univ Press, 93; Gifted Child Artists, Ehrlbaum, 94; co-ed, The Cultivation of American Artist, Oak Knoll Press; auth, Drawn to Art, 1986; Objects of American Art Education, Huntington Lib Press, 04. *Mailing Add:* 7 Norman Rd Newton MA 02161

KOS, PAUL JOSEPH
SCULPTOR, EDUCATOR
b Rock Springs, Wyo, Dec 23, 42. *Study:* Georgetown Univ, 61-62; San Francisco Art Inst, BFA, 65, MFA, 67. *Work:* Ft Worth Art Mus, Tex; Mus Mod Art & Mus Conceptual Art, San Francisco; Mus Mod Art, NY; Inst Contemp Art, Univ Pa; Everson Mus Art, Syracuse, NY. *Comn:* Floating (sculpture), Winery Lake, Napa, Calif, 68, Wind (sculpture), 69 & Performance (sculpture), 70; Secy of State, State Arch Bldg, Calif State Arts Comn, Sacramento, 90; Art in Transit, San Francisco Arts Comn, 90; Poetry Garden, Bechtel Corp, San Francisco, 91; Poetry Sculpture Garden

with poet Robert Hass, Fremont Properties, San Francisco, 99-00; Tunnel/Chapel di Rosa Art Preserve, Napa, Calif, 97. *Exhib:* solo exhibs, Laguna Art Mus, 90, Univ Art Gallery, San Diego State Univ, 91, JB Speed Mus, 92, Gallery Paule Anglim, San Francisco, 92 & 95, Col Notre Dame, Belmont, Calif, 94, Sculpture Furnished, 95 & Sculptural Allegories, Gallery Paule Anglim, San Francisco, 98; 1:1, Refusalon, San Francisco, 2000; Open House, Art on Site 1, San Francisco, 2000; Univ Art Mus, Berkeley, 2003; Grey Gallery, New York City, 2003; Mus Contemp Art, San Diego, 2004; Inst Contemp Art, Cincinnati, 2004. *Teaching:* San Francisco Art Inst, 78-. *Awards:* John Simon Guggenheim Mem Fel, 90; Nat Endowment for Arts & FONCA, 97; Flintridge Found, 1999-2000; Fleiskacker Found Fel, 2005. *Dealer:* Gallery Paul Anglim 15 Geary St San Francisco, Ca 94108. *Mailing Add:* Gallery Paul Anglim 15 Geary St San Francisco CA 94108

KOSCIANSKI, LEONARD J
CONCEPTUAL ARTIST
b Cleveland, Ohio, Apr 20, 52. *Study:* Cleveland Inst Art, BFA, 77; Univ Calif, Davis, MFA, 79. *Work:* Metrop Mus Art & Arnot Mus, NY; Philadelphia Mus Art; Cleveland Mus Art; Chase Manhattan Bank; Newport Harbor Mus, Calif; Milwaukee Mus Art; Chicago Art Inst. *Exhib:* Beast: Animal Imagery in Recent Painting, PS 1, NY, 82; one-man shows, Phyllis Kind Gallery, 83, 84, 86, 87, 88, 89, 90 & 91, Arthur Roger Gallery, New Orleans, 90 & 92, Fendrick Gallery, Washington, DC, 91, Robert Berman Gallery, Santa Monica, 92, OK Harris, NY, 95, Right Gallery, 96 & Cumberland Gallery, Nashville, Tenn, 96; New Narrative Paintings, Metrop Mus Art, NY, 83; Narrative Paintings, Mex City, 84; Innocence & Experience, Greenville Co Mus Art, SC, 85; The 1980's: A New Generation, Metrop Mus Art, NY, 88; Am Art Today: Contemp Landscape, Art Mus, Fla Int Univ, Miami, 89; Since 1980: New Narrative Painting, Phoenix Mus Art, Ariz; Harmony and Discord: Am Landscape Today, Va Mus Fine Arts, Richmond, Va; Twenty Yrs of Landfall Press, Landfall Gallery, NY; The Landscape in Twentieth-Century American Art, traveling, Tampa Mus Art, Fla, Greenville Co Mus Art, SC, Madison Art Ctr, Wis, Grand Rapids Art Mus, Mich, 92; and others throughout US. *Teaching:* Asst prof art, Univ Tenn, Knoxville, 80-84 & Univ Md, College Park, 84-87; instr, Arrowroot Sch, Gatlinburt, Tenn, 80-; lects & workshops at numerous institutions. *Awards:* Fels, Awards Visual Arts, 83 & Nat Endowment Arts--Southeastern Ctr Contemp Arts, 83; Individual Artist Fel, Nat Endowment Arts, 85 & 89; Rockefeller Found Scholar, Bellagio, Italy. *Bibliog:* Helen L Kohen (auth), Landscape Show Rich in Tradition, The Miami Herald, 1/15/89; Alan G Artner (auth), Cinematic Canvas: Koscianski's predator art employs many idioms of film, Chicago Tribune, 2/16/89; Pat Van Gelder (auth), Animals as subjects in Contemporary Art, Am Artist, 5/89. *Media:* Oil on Canvas, Pastel on Paper. *Dealer:* Wright Gallery 41 E 57th St 11A New York NY; Robert Berman, 2525 Michigan Ave C2 & D5 Santa Monica CA 90404

KOSCIELNY, MARGARET
SCULPTOR, DRAFTSMAN
b Tallahassee, Fla, Aug 13, 40. *Study:* Tex Woman's Univ, with Toni Lasalle; Univ Ga, BA(art hist) & MFA, with Irving Marantz, Joseph Schwarz, Charles Morgan, Gabor Peterdi, Arthur Deshaise, Kenneth Kerslake. *Work:* Jacksonville Art Mus; Ga Art Mus. *Comn:* Omni, Norfolk, Va, 75; Hyatt Hotel, Nashville, 76; Fla Senate, 78; Atlanta Airport, 80; AT&T, Jacksonville, 83; Stage Set Designs, The Magic Flute, Univ NMex, 87; and others. *Exhib:* Two-man exhib, Contemp Gallery, St Petersburg, 75; Four Jacksonville Artists, Cummer Gallery, Fla, 76; one-person shows, Vanderbuilt Univ, Nashville, Tenn, 77, Univ Conn, 81 & Univ NMex, 87; Flight Patterns, Third Floor Gallery, Atlanta, Ga, 80; and many others. *Pos:* Asst to dir, Cummer Gallery Art, 69-74; cur, Kamal Col, Jacksonville, Fla, 78-98. *Teaching:* Instr printmaking, Jacksonville Univ, 67 & Jacksonville Art Mus, 68. *Awards:* Nat Endowment Arts Grant Fla Arts Coun, 76; Nat Competition, Atlanta Airport Comn, 79. *Bibliog:* Photos & Essays, Kalliope, 79. *Mem:* Arts Assembly (1976). *Media:* Three-Dimensional Drawing, Assemblage; All Media. *Dealer:* www.margaretkoscielny.com. *Mailing Add:* 1254 Belvedere Ave Jacksonville FL 32205-7941

KOSHALEK, RICHARD
MUSEUM DIRECTOR
b Wausau, Wis, Sept 20, 41. *Study:* Univ Wis, Madison; Univ Minn, Minneapolis, BA(archit), MA(art hist). *Collection Arranged:* 9 Artists-9 Spaces (auth, catalog), 70; Stephen Antonakos: Outdoor Neons, 75; Dan Flavin: Drawings, Diagrams & Spaces, 75; Larry Bell: The Iceberg & It's Shadow, 75; Robert Irwin: Continuing Responses, 75-76; The Great American Rodeo (auth, catalog), 76 & 77; Ronald Bladen: Outdoor Sculpture Proposals, 78; Warburton Ave: The Architecture of a Neighborhood, 78; John Mason: Installations From the Hudson River Series, 78; Richard Serra: Elevator 80; and many others. *Pos:* Cur, Walker Art Ctr, Minneapolis, 67-72; asst dir, Nat Endowment Arts, 72-73; dir, Ft Worth Art Mus, 74-76; dir, The Hudson River Mus, 76-80; deputy dir, Mus Contemp Art, Los Angeles, formerly, dir, currently. *Teaching:* Pres, Art Ctr Col of Design, 1999-. *Awards:* IBM Int Fel; Nat Endowment Arts Fel. *Mem:* Art Prog, Chase Manhattan Bank; Yale Univ Coun Comt on Art Gallery & Brit Art Ctr. *Publ:* Auth, Midwest Photographers, Walker Art Ctr, 72. *Mailing Add:* President Art Center College of Design 1700 Lida Street Pasadena CA 91103-1999

KOSS, GENE H
SCULPTOR, EDUCATOR
b La Crosse, Wis, Nov 17, 47. *Study:* Univ Wis, River Falls, BS, 74; Tyler Sch Art, Temple Univ, Philadelphia, MFA, 76. *Work:* The Lannan Found, Palm Beach, Fla; Univ Wis, La Crosse; Tyler Sch Art, Temple Univ, Philadelphia; One Canal Place, New Orleans; New Orleans Mus Art. *Comn:* Ceramic sculpture, Schie Eye Inst, Philadelphia, 76; steel & glass sculpture, Contemp Art Ctr, New Orleans, La; sculptural rondels for stained glass windows, Toura Synagogue, New Orleans, La. *Exhib:* One-man shows, Univ Southwestern La, Lafayette, 76, Newcomb Art Sch, Tulane Univ, New Orleans, La, 77, Perception Gallery, Houston, 86, Arthur Roger Gallery, New Orleans, La, 82, 84, 90, 92, 94 & 96, 98, 2001, 2002, Newcomb Col/Tulane Univ, Dept Art, New Orleans, La, 86, Public Sculpture, Baton Rouge Gallery, La, 2002; Third Biennial Lake Superior Int Craft Exhibit, Tweed Mus Art, Minn, 75-77; Marietta Col Crafts Nat, Ohio, 76; 55th Ann Exhib, Meadows Mus Art, Shreveport, La, 77; Glass Art Soc Invitational, Contemp Art Ctr, New Orleans, La, 85, Southern Abstraction, 88, Artists/Architects Collaboration Drawing and Models, 91 & Glass and Iron, 93; 3500 Yrs of Glassmakers, New Orleans Mus Art, La, 86, Contemp Crafts in the Urban Environment, 93 & 100 Yrs of Ceramic Art, 1894 - 1994: A Newcomb Faculty Retrospective, 94; Innovations I-Glass Sculpture, Masur Mus Art, Monroe, La, 91; The Vessel Transformed, Pensacola Mus Art, Fla, 92; Nat Glass Show, Judy Youens Gallery, Houston, Tex, 94; Outdoor Sculpture, Penland, NC, 95; Sculpture Object Functional Exposition, Chicago, 97; 20th Anniversary Exhib, Arthur Roger Gallery, New Orleans, 98; Int Cast Glass, Belvetro Gallery, Miami, Fla, 98; Between Grains of Sand and Microchips, Silverstein Gallery, NY, 2000. *Collection Arranged:* Louisiana Craftsmen Show, 77-78 & Glass & Ceramics Student Show, 77-78, Newcomb Art Sch, Tulane Univ, New Orleans. *Pos:* Cur, Nat Glace Sculpture Exhib, Perception Gallery, 84; exhib coordr, Glass Invitational Contemp Art Ctr, 84; reg coordr, Glass Art Soc Conf, New Orleans, La, 85; consult steel molds, Blenko Glass, Wheeling, WVa, 90. *Teaching:* Instr glass, Tyler Sch Art, Temple Univ, Philadelphia, summer 76; assoc prof ceramics & glass, Newcomb Art Sch, Tulane Univ, New Orleans, 76-81 & 81-; instr, mixed media sculpture, Pilchuck Glass Sch, Seattle, Wash, 93; adv, New Orleans Sch Glass Works, La, 90. *Awards:* Face-Wilson Art Found Travel Grant, Newcomb/Tulane Univ, New Orleans, La, 91-92; Research Grant, Tulane Grant Univ, New Orleans, La, 90; Necomb Found Fel Grant, Newcomb Col/Tulane Univ, New Orleans, La, 91 & 92. *Bibliog:* Gene Koss (auth), Sculptural Glass, Glass Art Soc J, Process used in fabrication my sculpture, 85-86; Marcia Vetrocq (auth), Report from New Orleans: Marching On, Art Am, 97; Doug McCash (auth), Big Glass in the Big Easy, Glass, 97. *Mem:* Glass Art Soc; Am Crafts Coun; Nat Coun on Educ in Ceramic Arts; Contemp Art Ctr; La Crafts Coun (mem standards comt bd, 77-78). *Media:* Glass, Ceramics. *Publ:* Auth, The techniques of manufacture, In: Vasilike Ware: An Early Bronze Age Pottery Style in Crete, Paul Astroms Forlag, Sweden, 77; Gene Koss (auth), Sculptural Glass, Glass Art Soc J, Process used in fabrication my sculpture, 85-86; Marcia Vetrocq (auth), Report from New Orleans: Marching On, Art in America, 97; Doug Mc Cash (auth), Big Glass in the Big Easy, Glass, 97. *Dealer:* Perception Galleries Glass Art Houston TX; Arthur Roger Galleries New Orleans LA

KOSSOFF, LEON
PAINTER
b London, Eng, 1926. *Study:* Royal Col Art, London; St Martin's Sch Art; Bordugh Polytechnic. *Work:* Tate Gallery, London; Chicago Art Inst; Brit Coun, London; Art Gallery NSW, Australia; Cleveland Mus Art. *Exhib:* Venice Biennale (traveling), 95-96; one-man retrospective, Tate Gallery, London, 96; Drawn To Painting, LACMA, 99, Poussin Landscapes by Kossoff, J Paul Gotty Mus, 99. *Publ:* Drawn To Painting, Richard Kendall, Merrell Publishers, 99. *Dealer:* La Louver 45 N Venice Blvd Venice CA 90291. *Mailing Add:* c/o LA Louver Gallery 45 N Venice Blvd Venice CA 90291

KOSTA, ANGELA
ASSEMBLAGE ARTIST, WRITER
Study: Louis Ritman, 1964; Art Inst Chicago, 76-78. *Exhib:* solo exhibs, Main St Art Gallery, Chicago, 65, Spectrum Gallery, 83 & San Diego Mus Art, 85-88, 94, 96 & 99, San Diego; Yokohama Citizens' Gallery, Japan, 92; William Grant Still Art Ctr, Los Angeles, 93; Art Inst Nat, San Diego, 96, 2001; Studio 21, San Diego, Calif, 2005-2006; Whitney Mus Am Art, Biannual, NY, 2006. *Awards:* Purchase Award, New Horizons Art, North Shore Art League, 77; Best of Show Awards, Artists Guild Ann, San Diego Mus Art, 87 & 88; San Diego Art Inst, 89, 2001. *Bibliog:* Miller (auth), article, Los Angeles Times, 6/2/82; Lewinson (auth), article, San Diego Union, 4/7/83; Ollman (auth), article, Los Angeles Times, 11/20/87. *Mem:* San Diego Artists Guild; San Diego Mus Contemp Art. *Media:* Mixed Media; Collage, Painting. *Publ:* Paper art, Fiberarts Mag, 84; Abakanowicz retropective, 11/6/84 & Judy Chicago's project, 7/7/85, San Diego Union; Banham by design, Reader, 4/24/86; Teacher/student interface: two views of education, Fiberarts Mag, 87. *Mailing Add:* 5268 Mt Alifan Dr San Diego CA 92111

KOSTABI, MARK
PAINTER, SCULPTOR
b Los Angeles, Calif, Nov 27, 60. *Study:* Fullerton Community Col, 78; Calif State Univ, Fullerton, 79-81. *Work:* Mus Mod Art & Guggenheim Mus, NY; Memphis Brooks Mus Art, Tenn; Metrop Mus, NY; Groninger Mus, Holland; Brooklyn Mus; Corcoran Gallery Ary; Nat Gallery Mod Art, Rome. *Comn:* Shopping bag design, Bloomingdales, NY, 86; mural, Palazzo dei Priori in Arezzo, Italy, 88; To See Through is Not to See Into (public sculpture), San Benedetto del Tronto, Italy, 88; album covers, Guns 'N' Roses -Use Your Illusion & Ramones -Adios Amigos. *Exhib:* solo exhibs, Azabu Mus, Tokyo, 93, Seibu, Osaka, Japan, 93, Nicolae Gallery, Columbus, Ohio, 94, Hanson Gallery, New Orleans, 94, Studio Gastaldelli, Milan, 94, Sony Tower, Osaka, Japan, 94, Martin Lawrence Galleries, Newport Beach, Los Angeles, NY & San Francisco, 94, Parco, Tokorozawa & Kichijoji, Japan, 94, Giovanni Di Summa Gallery, Rome, Italy, 94, Meitetsu, Nagoya, Japan, 94, Arlene Bujuse Gallery, East Hampton, NY, 94 & Studio Spaggiari, Milan, 94; L'Immagine Galleria d'Arte Contemporanea, Arezzo, Italy, 98; Blu Art Arte Moderna, Alba Adriatica, Italy, 98; Martin Lawrence Galleries, Sherman Oaks & San Francisco, Calif, NY, 98, 99; Galerie Le Jardin des Arts, Jingumae & Aoyama, Toyko, 98; Galleria Pio Monti, Rome, 99; Palazzine Azzurra, San Benedetto de Tronto, Italy, 99; Studio G, Milan, 99; ArteCapital, Brescia, Italy, 2000; Trevi Flash Art Mus Int Contemp Art, Trevi, Italy,

2000; Guastalla Arte Moderna e Contemporanea, Forte dei Marmi, Italy, 2000; Temple Gallery, Temple Univ, Rome, 2000; one man retrospective, Mitsukoshi Mus, Toyko, 92, Art Mus of Estonia, Tallinn, 98. *Pos:* Designer consumer prods, swatch watches, album covers, T-shirts, ties, glasses, lighters, book covers, puzzles, posters & ltd ed vases; producer, Inside Kostabi, NY; writer of monthly advice column, Ask Mark Kostabi, Artnet.com & Artists Pick, Shout Mag. *Teaching:* lectr, worlwide. *Awards:* Proliferation Prize, East Village Eye, 84. *Bibliog:* Walter Robinson (auth), Mark Kostabi at Hal Bromm, Art in Am, 84; features in many articles in the New York Times, People, Vogue, Vanity Fair, Playboy, Forbes, New York Mag, Artforum, Art in Am, ARTnews, Arts, Flash Art & Tema Celeste. *Media:* Oil on Canvas. *Publ:* Auth, Kostabi: The Early Years, Office Suite, Sadness Because the Video Rental Store was Closed & numerous others, self publ, 81; illusr, East Village 85, 85 & auth, Upheaval, 85, Pelham Press; Soho New York, Egret Press, 86; profiled on 60 Minutes, Eye to Eye with Connie Chung, A Current Affair, Nightwatch, The Oprah Winfrey Show, Lifestyles of the Rich & Famous, West 57th, CNN, MTV & numerous TV programs throughout Europe & Japan; I Did it Steinway (CD), 98; auth, Sadness Because the Video Rental Store Was Closed, Kostabi: The Early Years & Conversations with Kostabi. *Dealer:* Ronald Feldman 31 Mercer St New York NY 10013

KOSTECKA, GLORIA
PAINTER
b Bloomfield, NJ. *Study:* Am Art Sch, NY; Traphagen Sch Fashion, NY; Prosopon Shc Iconology, NY. *Comn:* St John The Baptist Orthodox Ch, Alpha, NJ. *Exhib:* Federated Art Asn Exhib, NJ State Mus Cult Ctr, Trenton, 77; Nat Soc Painters Casein & Acrylic 24th Exhib & Nat Audubon Soc Exhib, Nat Acad Galleries, NY, 77 & 78; Am Artists Professional League, Bergen Co Mus, NJ, 80; Nat Soc Painters Casein & Acrylic 28th Ann Exhib, Nat Arts Club, NY, 81 & 85. *Awards:* Travel Awards, Nat Soc Painters Casein & Acrylic, 81-85 & Wash Square Outdoor Art Exhib, 81-83. *Mem:* Nat Soc Painters Casein & Acrylic; Am Portrait Soc. *Media:* Acrylic, Pencil. *Mailing Add:* 23 Elmwood Dr Clifton NJ 07013

KOSTELANETZ, RICHARD
MEDIA ARTIST, WRITER
b New York, NY, May 14, 40. *Study:* Brown Univ, AB(with honors), 62; Kings Col, London, Fulbright Scholar, 64-65; Columbia Univ, MA, 66. *Work:* Book-Art Books: Mus Mod Art; Humanities Res Ctr, Univ Tex, Austin; Videotapes: Anthology Film Archives, NY; Franklin Furnace, NY; Visual Poetry, The Sackner Archive of Concrete and Visual Poetry. *Comn:* Videotapes Synapse, Syracuse Univ, 75; holograms, Cabin Creek Ctr, Work & Environ Studies, 78; audiotapes, Westdeutscher Rundfunk, 82, 83 & 89; audiotapes, Am Pub Radio, St Paul, Minn, 84; holograms, Dennis Gabor Lab, Mus Holography, 85. *Exhib:* Imaged Words & Worded Images, NY Univ, 70; one-man shows, Video Writing, Anthology Film Archives, NY, 75 & 76, Visual poems, Nonsyntactic Prose, Minimal Fiction, Numerical Art, Chistopher Stephens, NY, Univ Toledo, 75-77; Audio Art, The Kitchen, NY, 78; Book Art, PS 1, Long Island City, NY & Tulsa Pub Libr, 78; Wordsand (retrospective work in several media), Simon Fraser Univ, Univ Alta, Cornell Col, Iowa, Calif State Univ, Bakersfield, Miami Dade Community Col, Vassar Col, 78-81; Rik Gadella, Int Artists Books, 96. *Collection Arranged:* Language & Structure in North Am, traveling exhib throughout Can & US, 75-77. *Pos:* Co-founder & publ, Assembling & Assembling Press, 70-82; stipendiat, DAAD Berliner Kunstperprogramm, Ger, 81-83. *Teaching:* Vis prof, Am studies & eng, Univ Tex, Austin, 77; Master Artist, Atlantic Ctr for the Arts, 2001; vis prof theater, grad fac, Hunter Col, CUNY, 2002. *Awards:* Guggenheim Fel, 67; Visual Arts Grant, 76, 78, 79 & 85 & Media Arts Grant, 81, 82, 85, 86, 89 & 90, Nat Endowment Arts; Pollock-Krasner Fel, 2001; and others. *Bibliog:* Tom Johnson (auth), Intermedia Lives, Village Voice, 10/4/76; George Myers Jr (auth), Scavenger Art & Richard Kostelanetz, An Introduction to Modern Times, Lunchroom, 82; SoHo: The Rise and Fall of an Artist's Colony, Routledge, 2003. *Mem:* Nat Artworkers; Found Independent Video & Film; Int Asn Art Critics; PEN. *Media:* Books, Print, Audio, Video, CD-Rom, Holography, Film. *Res:* Polyartistry; literary intermedia (sound & visual poetry). *Collection:* visual literature, paintings, drawings, black and white, cultural magazines' self-retrospectives. *Publ:* Wordworks: Poems New & Selected, 93; A Dictionary of the Avant-Gardes, 93; An ABC of Contemporary Reading, 95; Crimes of Culture, 95; John Cage: (ex)plain(ed), 96; John Cage: A Documentary Monograph, 70, 91; Language and Structure in North America, 74; Thirty-Five Yrs of Visible Writing, Koja, 2004. *Mailing Add:* Prince St Sta PO Box 444 New York NY 10012-0008

KOSTER, MARJORY JEAN
PRINTMAKER
b Grand Rapids, Mich, Feb 9, 26. *Study:* Univ Mich Exten Night Sch, 47-64; Pratt Graphic Workshop, New York, summer 64. *Work:* Metrop Mus Art, NY; Brooklyn Mus Art, NY; also pvt collection of Harold Joachim; Detroit Art Inst, Mich; Grand Rapids Art Mus, Mich; and others. *Exhib:* Ann Exhib Prints & Drawings, Oklahoma Art Ctr, 67; 7th Ann Mercyhurst Col Nat Graphics Exhib, Erie, Pa, 67; 3rd Nat Print & Drawing Exhib, Western Mich Univ, Kalamazoo, 68; 16th Nat Print Exhib, Brooklyn Mus, 68; 1st Nat Print Exhib, Honolulu, 71. *Mem:* Nat Inst Arts & Lett. *Media:* Woodcut. *Mailing Add:* 940 Maynard Ave NW Grand Rapids MI 49504-3659

KOSTYNIUK, RONALD P
SCULPTOR, EDUCATOR
b Sask, July 8, 41. *Study:* Univ Sask, BSc & BEd; Univ Alta, BFA; Univ Wis, MS & MFA. *Work:* Edmonton Art Gallery, Alta; Saskatoon Art Gallery, Sask; Kresge Art Found, Detroit, Mich; Can Coun Art Bank, Ottawa, Ont; Ft Lauderdale Mus, Fla; Glenbow Art Mus, Calgary, Univ of Calgary, Calgary: Univ of Saskatchewan, Saskatoon:; Univ of Manitoba, Winnipeg; Mackenzie Art Mus, Regina; Winnipeg Art Gallery, Winnipeg; Univ of Lethbridge, Lethbridge; Alta Foundation for the Arts, Edmonton; Saskatchewan Allied Arts Board, Regina, Sask;. *Comn:* Relief mural, exec off Paul Albertsen Ltd, Winnipeg; sculpture, Asn Bldg, Calgary; sculpture, City of Edmonton Recreational Complex, Edmonton; Silvermans, Winnipeg, Manitoba; Amoco Petroleum Ltd, Calgary, Alta. *Exhib:* One-man shows, Mem Univ, St John's, Nfld, 73, Sarnia Art Gallery, Ont, 74, Univ Moncton, NB, 74, Mt St Vincent Univ, Halifax, NS, 75 & Univ Calgary, Alta, 78; Kunst Int, Hippe Halle, Gmunden, Austria, 89; Art Concrete, Mus Archit, Wroclaw, Poland, 90; L'Idee-Systematisole Koncrete en Konstruktieve Kunst, Zoetermeer, The Neth, 90; Concept/Form, Cult Art Centrl Munic Athens, Greece, 91; City as a Memory, Chicago Athenaeum, Chicago; Sci in the Arts-Arts in the Sci, Hungraian Acad of Fine Arts, Budapest; Concrete Art, Mondriaanhaus Mus, Amersfoort, The Neth; Innovation, Kongresshous Mus, Gmunden, Austria; Int Constructive Art, Millenarium Ctr, Budpest; Int Overview of Constructive Art, Galerie Konkrete, Sulzberg, Ger. *Teaching:* Prof design & sculpture, Univ Calgary, Alta, 71-, head grad studies, dept art. *Awards:* Can Council Arts Bursary, 69; Foreign Exchange Scholar, External Affairs Govt Can, 78; Killam Resident Fel, Univ Calgary, 79. *Bibliog:* Jan Van der Marck (auth), Relief sculpture, 69; John Stocking (auth), Relief sculptures, Arts Mag, 75; John Graham (auth), Kostyniuk's reliefs, Vie des Arts, 75; Marion Andres (auth), Kostyniuk's constructed reliefs, Art Post, 86; Virgil Hammock (auth) Prairie Visions: The art of Ron Kostyniuk, Art Focus, 92; Kay Burns (auth) Ron Kostyniuk: The Saskatchewan Road Map Series, Artichoke, 2000; Joan Kendrick (auth), Kostyniuk's Road Map Series, Art Focus #73, 2002. *Mem:* Royal Can Acad Art; Univ Art Asn; Can Conf of the Arts. *Media:* Plastics, Metals. *Publ:* Auth, The Evolution of the Constructed Relief 1913-1979 & Art and Sources, Univ Calgary; Neo-Constructions, Univ Calgary; An Antropomorphic Architecture, Univ Calgary; Saskatchewan Road Map Series, Univ of Calgary, 2001. *Mailing Add:* 4907 Viceroy Dr Calgary AB T3A 0V2 Canada

KOTASEK, P MICHAEL
PAINTER, LECTURER
b Endicott, NY, Sept 2, 62. *Study:* Syracuse Univ (studied under Jerome Witkin & Murray Tinkleman), BA, 1985; Private study from Burt Silverman, 1988-1990. *Exhib:* Philadelphia Watercolor Soc Ann Exhib, 1999, 2001-2003; Cooperstown Art Asn Ann Nat Exhib, Cooperstown, NY, 99, 2001-2002 & 2004; Am Artists Professional League, Salmagundi Club, NY, 1999, 2002, 2005; Art Asn Harrisburg, Harrisburg, Pa, 2003; Allied Artists of Am, Nat Arts Club, NY, 2003, 2005; Local Landscapes, Grenning Gallery, Sag Habor, NY, 2005; 4 Artists Invitational, Harrisburg Art Asn, Harrisburg, Pa, 2006; Man and Nature, Grenning Gallery, Sag Harbor, NY, 2006. *Pos:* Freelance Illusr, 1985-1993. *Awards:* Allied Artists of Am Gold Medal of Honor, Allied Artist of Am, NY, 2003; Henry Gasser Mem Award, Allied Artists of Am, NY, 2004; Frank C Wright Mem Award, Am Artists Professional League, NY, 2005; AAPL Medal of Hon, Am Artists Prof League, NY, 2002; Heitland Mem Award, Philadelphia Watercolor Soc, Bryn Mawr, Pa, 2003; Thomas Moran Mem Award for Watercolor, Salmagundi Club, NY, 2003. *Bibliog:* Int Showcase of Award Winners, Allied Artists of Am, Int Artist Mag (issue 36), 2004; Annette Hinkle (auth), Grenning Gallery: New Views of Old Haunts, Sag Harbor Express, 2004; Joshua Rose (auth), Man and Nature in the Hamptons, Am Art Collector (issue 9), 2006. *Mem:* Philadelphia Watercolor Soc (signature mem). *Media:* Egg Tempera, Watercolor, Graphite Pencil. *Publ:* Every Picture Tells a Story, Watercolor Magic Mag, winter 2001. *Dealer:* Grenning Gallery 90 Main St PO Box 3049 Sag Harbor NY 11963. *Mailing Add:* 2600 Yale St Endicott NY 13760

KOTIK, CHARLOTTA
CURATOR, HISTORIAN
b Prague, Czech, Dec 13, 40; US citizen. *Study:* Kunsthistorisches Inst, Univ Wien, 65; Charles Univ, Prague, BA(art hist), 66, MA(art hist), 68. *Collection Arranged:* Jiri Kolar: Transformations (auth, catalog), 78; On Paper, About Paper (auth, catalog), 80; Jennifer Bartlett (auth, catalog), 80; Figures: Forms and Expressions (auth, catalog), 81; Fernand Leger: Retrospective (auth, catalog), 82; John Cage: Scores and Prints (coauth, catalog), 82; Charles Clough, Recent Work (auth, catalog), 83; Second Western States Exhib (auth, catalog), 84; Expendable Ikon: Works by John McHale (auth, catalog), 84; Francois Morellet: Systems (auth, catalog), 84; Working in Brooklyn: Sculpture (auth, catalog), 85; Monumental Drawing: Works by 22 Contemporary Americans (auth, catalog), 86; Third Western States Biennal (auth, catalog), 86; Working in Brooklyn: Painting (auth, catalog), 87; 4 Americans: Aspects of Current Sculpture (auth, catalog), 89; Working in Brooklyn: Installations (auth, catalog), 90; Grand Lobby Installation Series (auth, brochures), 84-93; Louise Bargeois: Recent work, 45th Venice Biennale (brochure), 93; Louise Bargeois: Locus & Memory, Works 1982-1993, (coauth, catalogue) 1994. *Pos:* Cur asst, Jewish Mus, 58-61 & Nat Gallery, 61-64, Prague, Czech; assoc & asst cur, Nat Trust, Prague, Czech, 67-70; cur, Albright-Knox Art Gallery, Buffalo, 70-83; cur, Brooklyn Mus, NY, 83-, chair dept painting & sculpture, 92-. *Teaching:* Tutor fine arts, Empire State Col, Buffalo, NY, 77-79; adj asst prof, State Univ NY Buffalo, 79-83; instr art hist, Sch Visual Arts, NY, 90-. *Awards:* Frederick R Weisman Art Found Award for outstanding achievement in contemp art, 91; Munic Art Soc Cert of Merit for the Grand Lobby Ser, 91; Nat Endowment Arts & US Info Agency, selected to curate Louise Bourgeois, the exhib to represent US in the 1993 Venice Biennale. *Mem:* Adolph & Esther Gottlieb Found Inc, NY (bd dir); Art Table Inc; Nat Endowment Arts (panelist & field rep); Arts Action Coalition, NY (bd dir); City Arts Workshop Inc, NY (bd dir); Experimental Intermedia Found Inc, NY (bd dir). *Res:* Contemporary American art and architectural history. *Publ:* Co-auth, Contemporary Art 1942-72, Collection Albright-Knox, 72; Albright-Knox Art Gallery, Paintings and Sculpture from Antiquity to 1942, 78; Fernand Leger, Abbeville Press, 81; contrib auth, The Play of the Unmentionable: An Installation by Joseph Kosuth at The Brooklyn Museum, New Press, with Brooklyn Mus, 91. *Mailing Add:* Dept Painting & Sculpture Brooklyn Mus Brooklyn NY 11238

KOTOSKE, ROGER ALLEN
PAINTER, SCULPTOR
b South Bend, Ind, Jan 4, 33. *Study:* Univ Notre Dame, Ind, 50-52; Univ Denver, Colo, BFA, 54, MA, 56. *Work:* Rockhill Nelson Gallery, Kansas City, Mo; State Univ NY Col Oswego; Denver Art Mus; Franklin Mint, Philadelphia. *Comn:* Large outdoor sculpture, City of Denver, 68. *Exhib:* Artist Teacher Today USA, State Univ Oswego, NY; one-man shows, Pollock Gallery, Southern Methodist Univ, Dallas, 69 & James Yu Gallery, NY, 76; Report from Soho, Grey Gallery, NY, 76; Contemp Am Painting & Sculpture, Indianapolis Mus Art, 78; Ill Painters Traveling Exhib, 81-; 22nd Biennial Works on Paper Exhib, Univ Del, Newark, Del, 86; Int Exhib, Chinese Nat FA, Beijing, 87; Greater Midwest Int III, Mo, 88. *Teaching:* Prof art, Univ Denver, 58-68 & Univ Ill, Urbana, 68-. *Awards:* Purchase Awards, Nelson-Atkins Mus, 59 & State Univ Oswego, NY, 68. *Bibliog:* Meilach & Kowal (co-auth), Sculpture Casting, Crown Publ, 72; Meilach (auth), The Artist Eye, Regnery Press, 72; Verhelst (auth), Sculpture: Tools, Materials and Techniques, Prentice-Hall, 73 & 88. *Mem:* FATE. *Media:* Acrylic; Wood. *Mailing Add:* 1611 W White St Champaign IL 61820

KOTTEMANN, GEORGE & NORMA
COLLECTORS
Dr Kottemann, b St Louis, Mo, Aug 17, 31; Mrs Kottemann, b Springfield, Ill, Jan 1, 32. *Collection:* Contemporary paintings, prints, sculpture, glass and ceramics. *Mailing Add:* 3300 N Bigelow Peoria IL 61604

KOTTING, JOEY
ARTIST
Exhib: Exhibs incl White Columns, White Room Gallery, 98, Atrocity Exhibition, Yvon Lambert, 2004, Print Publishers Spotlight: Universal Limited Art Editions, Barbara Krakow Gallery, 2004. *Awards:* Fel Guggenheim Mem Found, 2004. *Mailing Add:* c/o Barbara Krakow Gallery 10 Newbury St Boston MA 02116

KOUNS, MARJORIE K
PAINTER, PHOTOGRAPHER
b Elmhurst, Ill, Aug 4, 57. *Study:* Studied sculpture with Mary Rose Carroll, 78; Ill Wesleyan Univ, Bloomington, 79. *Work:* Franklin Furnace Archive Inc, NY; Ben Franklin Univ Hosp, Berlin, Ger. *Comn:* Satellite Mural Proj, Mothers Ctrs, Hamburg, Stuttgart, Munich, Ger, 97; Docu murals, Nat Cong Neighborhood Women, Washington, DC, 97; Well Lit Chess Pieces, project for Washington Sq Park, New York City; Body as Canvas, New York City, Miami, Los Angeles, Calif. *Exhib:* Made by Hand, 4th UN Conf on Women, Beijing, China, 95; Trans Hands, UN Habitat, Taskisla Univ, Istanbul, Turkey, 96; Beijing-One Yr Later, UN Int Hq, NY, 96; solo show, USIS Am Haus, Berlin, Ger, 97; Art of Change, Times Sq Gallery, NY, 98; Sarkahc Neves (Seven Chakras) Pub Art Installation, Times Sq Gallery, NY, 99. *Pos:* Professional Voice-Over. *Awards:* Materials for the Arts, H 2 Timeline, New York Dept Cult Affairs, 83. *Bibliog:* Annabel Walker (auth), Hands off to writer handsome work, Hong Kong Standard, 1/7/96. *Mem:* Artists' Circle, New York, NY. *Media:* Paint. *Mailing Add:* 15 Minetta St New York NY 10012

KOVATCH, JAK
PAINTER, PRINTMAKER
b Los Angeles, Calif, Jan 17, 29. *Study:* Univ Calif, Los Angeles, 46; Chouinard Art Inst, Los Angeles, 47-49; Calif Sch of Art, Los Angeles, 49-50; Univ Southern Calif, Los Angeles, 51; Los Angeles City Col, 55-56; Art Students League, spec study with Michael Ponce de Leon, 72 & 75. *Work:* Fogg Mus Art, Harvard Univ; Libr Congress; Joseph Hirshhorn Collection; Fairfield Art Collection, Town Hall, Conn; John Slade Ely House Collection, New Haven; Art Mus, Joinville, Brazil; Univ Miss. *Exhib:* Los Angeles Co Mus Art, 49, 54 & 55; Boston Mus Fine Arts, 54; Libr Congress, 54; Butler Inst Am Art, 54; M H de Young Mem Mus, San Francisco, Calif, 54; Mus Mod Art, NY, 56; Wadsworth Antheneum, Hartford, Conn, 58 & 72-76 & 79; Audubon Artists Inc, Nat Acad Galleries, NY, 73 & 78 & Nat Arts Club, NY, 79-95; Boston Ctr Arts, 76; Nat Acad Design Exhib, 77 & 80; Honolulu Acad Arts, Hawaii, 77 & 85; Print Club, Philadelphia, Pa, 78; Metrop Mus Art, Tokyo, Japan, 87 & 88; Taiwan, Rep of China, 88 & 91; Barbican Art Ctr, London, Eng, 89; Hammond Mus, North Salem, NY, 92; Lever House, NY, 95; Fed Hall, NY, 96; Salmagundi Club, NY, 97; Rensselaerville Inst, NY, 97; and 600 others. *Pos:* Student asst, Lynton Kistler Lithography Studio, Los Angeles, 52-53; animation dept, Walt Disney Prod Inc, Burbank, Calif, 53-54; Commercial Illustration, 57; mem selection comt, Conn Comn on the Arts, Percent for Art Prog, Hartford, 87-88. *Teaching:* Instr, Famous Artists Schs Inc, Westport, Conn, 57-59, New York City Col Exten Div, 59-60; prof design, Univ Bridgeport, Conn, 62-94; ethyl prof, Indust Design, 88-94; fac, Silvermine Sch Art, New Canaan, Conn, 94-. *Awards:* Merit Award, The Print Club of Albany, Inc, Schenectady Mus, NY, 92; Award, Stamford Mus, Conn, 94, 95 & 2000; Painting Award, New Britain Mus Am Art, Conn, 97; Mellon Fel, Vis Fac Prog, Yale Univ, 79-81, 83; Printmaking Grant, Conn Com Arts, 83, 84; More than 180 Awards & Honors. *Mem:* Audubon Artists (dir graphics, 95); Artists Equity; Westport Arts Ctr Conn; Los Angeles Printmaking Soc; Silvermine Ctr Arts; and others. *Media:* Miscellaneous Media; use of Etching inks for impasto passages in paintings, combined with oil washes on 300 LB hot press water color paper. *Specialty:* contemporary & old masters. *Interests:* Many years x-ray experience with the human figure-combined with experimental real or imaginary forms has had significant influence on images used in painting and graphics. *Dealer:* Silvermine Ctr for Arts Inc 1037 Silvermine Rd New Canaan CT 06840-0411; Left of the Bank Gallery 185 Sound Beach Ave Old Greenwich CT. *Mailing Add:* 34 Sasco Creek Rd Westport CT 06880

KOVATCH, RONALD R
CERAMIST
b S Bend, Ind, June 12, 53. *Study:* Kansas City Art Inst, BFA, 76; Southern Ill Univ-Edwardsville, MFA, 87. *Work:* Kansas City Art Inst, Mo; St Mary's Col, South Bend, Ind; Evansville Mus Art & Sci, Ind; Marian Col, Indianapolis; Valparaiso Univ, Ind; Univ Wis, Whitewater. *Exhib:* Solo exhibs, Lill St Gallery, Chicago, 90, Univ Notre Dame, ISIS Gallery, Ind, 91, Gallery Nine, Univ Ill, Urbana-Champaign, 91, and others; Fresh Ideas from Familiar Faces, Ill Ceramic Invitational, Parkland Col Art Gallery, Champaign, 92; Containers Revisited, Nat Coun Educ for the Ceramic Arts, Tyler Art Gallery, Tyler Sch Art, Temple Univ, Philadelphia, 92; Evanston Art Ctr, Ill, 97; Outguild Mus, Northern Ill State Univ, Dekalb, 97; and many others. *Pos:* Owner/operator, pottery studio, Vernon, Ind, 78-85; many workshops & lectrs, 88-91. *Teaching:* Vis artist/instr ceramics, Sch Art Inst, Chicago, 88; vis asst prof ceramics, Sch Fine Arts, Ind Univ, Bloomington, 88-89; asst prof ceramics, Univ Ill, Urbana-Champaign, Sch Art Design, 89-. *Awards:* Visual Artist Fel Grant, Nat Endowment Arts, 90; Visual Artist Fel, Ill Arts Coun, 91 & 96. *Mailing Add:* 303 N Orchard St Urbana IL 61801

KOVINICK, PHILIP PETER
WRITER, HISTORIAN
b Detroit, Mich, July 4, 24. *Study:* Calif State Univ, Chico, BA & MA. *Collection Arranged:* Co-curator, Canyons, Arroyos & Oases: Desert Landscape in Southern California, 1900-1985, 85; Reaching the Summit: Mountain Landscapes in Calif, 1900-1986, 86; The Woman Artist in the Am West, 1860-1960, 76. *Awards:* Western Heritage Award, Outstanding Art Book of Yr, 98. *Mem:* Collegium Western Art (pres); Laguna Art Mus Hist Collections Coun (charter mem); Archives Am Art; Huntington Libr Reader, San Marino, Calif. *Res:* Book on John Frost, Planned for Publication in late 2007. *Publ:* coauth, Women artists: The American frontier, Art News, 12/76; coauth, An Ency of Women Artists of the American West, Univ Tex Press, Austin, 98; coauth Publications in So Calif Art, Vol VI, Dustin Publs, Los Angeles, 99; coauth, Western Women Artists, 98; contribr, Grove's Encyclopedia of Am Art Before 1914, 2000; An encyl (auth) The Woman Artist in The American West, 1860-1960. *Mailing Add:* 4735 Don Ricardo Dr Los Angeles CA 90008

KOWAL, CAL (LEE)
CURATOR, PHOTOGRAPHER
b Chicago, Ill, Sept 4, 44. *Study:* Univ Ill, Chicago (art & art hist), 67; Ill Inst Technol, Inst Design, MS (photog), 71. *Work:* Art Inst Chicago, Ill; Cincinnati Art Mus, Ohio; De Cordova Art Mus, Lincoln, Mass; Miami Art Mus, Oxford, Ohio; Chase Manhattan-Ohio Banks, Cincinnati. *Comn:* Silkscreen, SHV NAm, Cincinnati, Ohio, 81; Collaborative Effort (with Peter Bodnar III), Louisville Water Tower Art Asn, 85. *Exhib:* National Photog Invitational, Anderson Gallery, Richmond, Va, 75; OK Art, Contemp Art Ctr, Cincinnati, Ohio, 76; solo exhibs, True-False, Carl Solway Gallery, Cincinnati, 83 & Univ Dayton, Ohio, 85; Representation Strategies in Contemp Photog, Southern Ill Univ, Carbondale, 85; 5 in Color: The Constructed Photograph, Warren Lee Ctr, Vermillion, SDak, 86. *Collection Arranged:* Daniel Brown Collection, Middlebury Col, Vt, 81; All Ohio Photography File, Art Acad Cincinnati, 83; Extended Vision (auth, catalog), Ponderosa, Inc, Dayton, Ohio, 84; Mus Contemp Photog, Columbia Col, Chicago, 94. *Pos:* Cur photog, Carl Solway Gallery, 82-86. *Teaching:* Sr fac photog & drawing, Art Acad Cincinnati, Ohio, 71-; guest prof, Miami Univ, Oxford, Ohio, 76-78; vis artist, Sch Art Inst, Chicago, 84-85. *Awards:* Artist-in-Residence, Syracuse Univ, 77; Ohio Arts Coun Fel, 82; Soc Contemp Photog Award, Current Works, Kans, 85. *Mem:* Contemp Art Ctr (bd trustees); Soc Photog Educ (Midwest bd). *Media:* Mixed Media & Drawing; Photographic Assemblages. *Publ:* Auth, Book Full of Spoons, Rose-Pose Publ, 75; T-Shirts Are Tacky, 76, This Space Reserved, 79; Soft Color, portfolio, Self-Publ, Cincinnati, Ohio, 84; Unfamiliar House Series, 86. *Dealer:* Toni Birckhead Gallery 342 W 4th St Cincinnati OH 45202. *Mailing Add:* 2543 Cleinview Ave Cincinnati OH 45206-2101

KOWAL, DENNIS J
SCULPTOR, WRITER
b Chicago, Ill, Sept 9, 37. *Study:* Art Inst Chicago; Univ Ill, Navy Pier; Southern Ill Univ, BS, 61, MFA, 62. *Work:* Gillette Corp, Boston; Lakeforest Col, Ill; Inst Contemp Art, Boston; Babson Col, Wellesley, Mass; Bank New Eng Corp hq, Boston; Fed Reserve Bank, Boston; Newsweb Corp, Chicago. *Comn:* Photon II, Sarasota Season of Sculpture, 00-01; Enigma, Sarasota Season of Sculpture, 02-03; Remembrance, Temple Beth Israel, Longboat, Fla, 04; Menorah, Fla Holocaust Mus, St Petersburg, Fla, 04; Remnant Series 25, Sculpture, Key West, Fla, 05; Iris, Sarasota Season of Sculpture, 05-06. *Exhib:* One-man exhib, Mead Art Mus, Amherst Col, Mass, 78, NC Mus Art, Raleigh, 78, Gilbert Gallery Ltd, Chicago, Ill, 79, Boston Fine Arts Gallery, Mass, 84, Beaulieu Art Gallery, Cambridge, Mass, 88 & Mount Holyoke Col Mus, Mass, 88; Mead Art Mus, Amherst Col, Mass, 78; NC Mus Art, 78; Gilbert Gallery Ltd, Chicago, 79; Kristopher Lindsay Gallery, Sarasota, Fla, 94; John & Mable Ringling Mus Art, Sarasota, Fla, 94; pub sculpture, Navy Pier, Chicago; Sarasota Season of Pub Sculpture, 00-01, 02-03, 05-06. *Pos:* Artist-in-Resident, Dartmouth Col, 70-71, Univ Ga, 73, Amherst Col, 77-78, Milton Acad, 77, Maudslay State Park, Newburyport, Mass, 88-90; vis artist, Pinellas Co Arts, St Petersburg, Fla; panelist Fla Arts Coun, 99. *Teaching:* Prof sculpture, Columbus Col Art, Ohio, 63-64, Frostburg Col, Frostburg, Md, 64-65, Univ Ill, Champaign, 66-70 & Mass Col Art, Boston, 71-72; vis lectr, Univ Ga, 73. *Awards:* Numerous awards, 70-; Artist-in-Resident & Fel, Yaddo, Saratoga Springs, NY, 70, Macdowell Colony, Peterborough, NH, 65, 72, Vietnam Veterans Mem Commonwealth, Mass, 86-; Nat Endowment Arts Matching Grant, Babson Col, Wellesley, Mass, 76; Vietnam Vets Mem Award Commonwealth of Mass, 86-90; Cultural Recognition Award Fla Dept of State Millennium, Photon 11, 2000. *Bibliog:* Rituals of celebrations, Dennis Kowal, Decade Mag, 79; 100 year philosophy, Sarasota Art Rev, 91; Dateline (Channel 4 with

K Kirshner): public art, voodoo dolls and politics, Sarasota, Fla, 94; Symbols: Signs of Our Times, CG Jung Soc, 2000; plus others. *Mem:* Inst Contemp Art, Boston, Chicago; Boston Visual Artists Union; Pub Art Comt, City Sarasota, Fla (vchmn, formerly, chmn, currently); Sarasota Anglers Club; Int Game Fish Asn; Int Sculpture Ctr; Mangrove Fly Fishing Club; Coastal Conservation Asn. *Media:* Mixed Media. *Collection:* artifacts. *Publ:* Contribr, Contemporary Wood Sculpture, 68, contribr, Contemporary Stone Sculpture, 69 & auth, Casting Sculpture, 72, Crown; auth, Artists speak, NY Graphic Soc, 76; The Link, An Artist of Modern Time, Boston Univ Press, 88; Public Art in Greater Boston, Harvard Common Press, 88; Art, money & politics-public art, Sarasota Art Rev, 91; Cultural Wars - Critique and Affirmation Series #29, Artarget News, 1997; Liberal Arts?, Forbes Pub, 1999; Direct Metal Sculpture, Schiffer Pub, 2001. *Dealer:* DJ Kowal Studios 508 Osprey Ave South Sarasota FL 34236. *Mailing Add:* 508 Osprey Ave S Sarasota FL 34236

KOWALKE, RONALD LEROY
PAINTER, PRINTMAKER
b Chicago, Ill, Nov 8, 36. *Study:* Univ Chicago, 54-56; Art Inst Chicago, BFA, 54-56; Rockford Col, BA, 59; Cranbrook Acad Art, MFA, 60. *Work:* Mus Mod Art & Metrop Mus Art, NY; Libr Cong & Nat Gallery, Washington, DC; Rockford Col, Ill; Boston Pub Libr; The Contemp Mus, Honolulu; The Samuel P Hard Mus Art, Gainesville, Fla, 93. *Comn:* interior wall, The Europa Ctr Econ Study, Mannheim, Ger, 97; Windows of Fire, The Hawaii Convention Ctr, 98. *Exhib:* Nat Print Exhib, Calif Soc Etchers, San Francisco Mus Art, 65; 15th Ann Print Exhib, Brooklyn Mus, 66; New Directions 1982, Hawaii Artist League, Amfac Plaza Gallery, 82; Hawaii '82-Works on Paper, Univ Hawaii, Hilo, 82; Hawaii Craftsman '82, Amfac Plaza Gallery, 82; two-man exhib, Structures, Art Loft Gallery, Hawaii, 83; Easter Arts Festival, Ala Moana Art Ctr, Hawaii, 83. *Teaching:* Instr design, Northern Ill Univ, 60-61; instr drawing, design & printmaking, Swain Sch Design, New Bedford, Mass, 61-64; assoc prof art, Univ Hawaii, 69-72, prof, 72-. *Awards:* Purchase Awards, Honolulu Acad Arts, 69 & 71; Faculty Res Grant, Univ Hawaii, 69 & 70; Faculty Travel Grants, Univ Hawaii, 79 & 82; Spec Projects grant, Univ Hawaii, 90, Travel grant, 91; Distinguished Citizen award, Chopin Soc Hawaii, 93; fellowship Ctr Arts and Humanities, 94. *Bibliog:* Dantes Inferno: A Portfolio of Ten Etchings, Impressions Workshop, Boston, 70; Gentle Words and Gentle People: A Portfolio of Ten Etchings, Univ Hawaii, Honolulu, 71; Artists of Hawaii, Vol 11, Univ Hawaii Press, 77. *Mem:* Honolulu Printmakers. *Dealer:* Associated American Artists Inc 663 Fifth Ave New York NY 10022; Ferdinand Roten Inc 123 W Mulberry Baltimore MD 21201. *Mailing Add:* 1590 Ulupii St Kailua HI 96734-4443

KOWALSKI, DENNIS ALLEN
CONCEPTUAL ARTIST
b Chicago, Ill, May 14, 38. *Study:* Univ Ill, Chicago(archit), 55-57; Sch Art Inst Chicago, BFA(sculpture), 62; Sch Art Inst Chicago, MFA(sculpture), 66. *Work:* Gov State Univ; Ill State Univ; Art Inst Chicago; Mus Contemp Art, Sidley & Austin, Chicago; Prudential, Newark, NJ; Indianapolis Mus Art. *Comn:* Outdoor sculpture, Univ of Chicago, 75. *Exhib:* Art Inst Chicago, 65-66, 75 & 80; one-man shows, NAME Gallery, 76, 80 & 95, Marianne Deson Gallery, Chicago, 78, 81, 83, 86 & 89, Deson/Saunders Gallery, Chicago, Art Acad Cincinnati, 91, Robert Morrison Gallery, NY, 92, Beret Int Chicago, 93 & 97 & Bonafide Gallery, Chicago, 2000; Redefining the Object, Cleveland Ctr Contemp Art & Wright State Univ, Dayton, Ohio; Generations I Chicago, Carnegie Mellon Univ Gallery, Pittsburgh, Pa; West Art and the Law, traveling, 91; Mindy Oh Gallery, Chicago, 94; group shows, Total Mus Contemp Art, Seoul, Korea, Nat Mus Art, Seoul, Korea & Mus Contemp Art, Chicago, 96; and many others. *Teaching:* Assoc prof sculpture, Univ Ill, Chicago, 70-. *Awards:* Nat Endowment Arts Fel Grant, 75; Grant, Ill Arts Coun, 80, Fel, 80 & 84; Spec Assistance Grant, Ill Arts Coun, 95. *Bibliog:* Alan Artner (auth), articles in Chicago Tribune, 10/7/83 & 4/25/86 & 6/2/89 & 93; Garret Holg (auth), rev, Art News, 9/89; Tim Porges (auth), Contemporanea, Chicago Reviews, 5/90; James Yood (auth), rev, New Art Examiner, 12/91; Kathryn Hixson (auth), Review Flash Art, 11-12/91; and others. *Mailing Add:* 4134 N Damen Ave Chicago IL 60618

KOWALSKI, LIBBY R
FIBER ARTIST, EDUCATOR
b Chicago, Ill, Jun 29, 40. *Study:* Millikin Univ, BA, 62; Colorado State Univ, BFA, 79; Cranbrook Acad Art, MFA, 81. *Work:* Kresge Art Mus, ELansing, Mich; Dowd Fine Arts Gallery, Cortland, NY; IBM, Southfield, Mich; Unisys, Washington; General Motors, Detroit, Mich. *Exhib:* Fiber Structure Nat, Downey Art Mus, Downey, Calif, 88; Black & White, Gayle Willson Gallery, Southhampton, NY, 89; Small Works Invitational, Ctr Tapestry Arts, NY, 89; Fiber Explorations, State Univ NY, Stony Brook, 89; solo exhib: Space/Place/Fragment, Ctr Tapestry Arts, NY, 91; and others. *Teaching:* Prof weaving & surface design, State Univ NY, Cortland, 82-; fibers, Chautauqua Sch Art, summers 87-91; designer/owner, CTD Studio, Hand Weaving & Design Studio, New York, 89-; adj fibers, Grad Prog, Syracuse Univ, 91. *Awards:* Visual Artists Prog Grant, NY State Coun on Arts, 85; Computer Graphics, Stipend, Research Found State Univ New York, 86. *Bibliog:* Else Regensteiner (auth), Geometric Design in Weaving, Schiffer Publ, 86; Tom Milligan (auth), Libby Kowalski: her work (film), WSKG, 4/90. *Mem:* Am Craft Coun; Col Art Asn. *Media:* Fibers. *Publ:* Contribr, Fiberarts Design Book, 80; contribr, Ithaca Women's Anthology, 89. *Dealer:* Yaw Gallery Birmingham Mich. *Mailing Add:* 32 Union Sq E Ste 216 New York NY 10003

KOWALSKI, RAYMOND ALOIS
PAINTER
b Erie, Pa, June 21, 33. *Study:* Pa State Teachers Col, Edinboro; Cleveland Inst Art, BFA, 77. *Work:* State of Pa Educ Syst. *Exhib:* May Show, Cleveland Mus Art, 69-71 & 83; Preview 71, Mt St Joseph's Col, Cincinnati, 71; Butler Mus Show, Youngstown, Ohio; one-man show, Green Mansion Gallery, Cleveland, 79, Bluffton Col, Ohio, 79, Ohio Mus Beachwood, 87, Lmeek Gallery, Cleveland, Ohio, 2005; Ohio State Fair, 79; Willoughby Fine Arts Ctr, Ohio, 79; Shaker Hist Mus, 90. *Pos:* Designer, Am Greetings Corp, Cleveland, 59-65, art dir, 65-, managing art dir, 73-, dir, Creative Planning, 81, dir design, 83; Exec dir design, 85; consult, Carlton Cards Ltd, United Kingdom, 93-95. *Teaching:* Instr design, Cooper Sch Art, Cleveland, 69-70; instr painting for local art groups, 70-; guest critic, RI Sch Design, Sr Proj, 90; guest instr, Columbus Col Art & Design, Parsons Sch Design, 92. *Awards:* Award, Jewish Community Ctr Ann, Cleveland Heights, 79; Award, Erie Art Ctr Ann, Penn, 79; Ohio State Fair, 81; and others; Fine Arts Show Awards, B P Am Gallery, Cleveland Ohio, 87 & 88; Am Greetings Corp Fine Arts Show, Cleveland Playhouse Gallery. *Bibliog:* Helen Borsick (auth), article in Cleveland Plain Dealer Suppl, 68; Ray Kowalski--painter of houses, Wonderful World Ohio, 10/69; Ray Kowalski-House Painter, WKYC-TV, Cleveland. *Mem:* Soc Illusrs; Int Arts Comt-UNICEF, 96-97. *Media:* Acrylic, Collage, Watercolor, Digital imagery. *Interests:* Digital photography, landscape design. *Mailing Add:* 2429 Derbyshire Rd Cleveland OH 44106

KOZLOFF, JOYCE
PAINTER, MOSAIC ARTIST
b Somerville, NJ, Dec 14, 42. *Study:* Carnegie Inst Technol, BFA, 64; Columbia Univ, MFA, 67. *Work:* Metrop Mus Art, Mus Mod Art, NY; Nat Gallery Art, Wash; Albright-Knox Art Gallery, Buffalo, NY; Brooklyn Mus, NY; Mass Inst Tech, Cambridge; Nat. Mus. of Am Art, Wash; Nat Gallery of Art, Wash; Mus of Modern Art, NY. *Comn:* Pasadena, The City of Roses, Maguire Thomas Partners, Plaza las Fuentas, Pasadena; I S 218, NY Percent for Art Program, Art Comn City of NY, 91; History of Visual Style in Hollywood Movies, 7th and Flower Station, Southern Calif Rapid Transit District's Metro Rail Proj, 91-93; Around the World on the 44 Degree Parallel, Minn Percent for Art in Pub Places, 94; Wash Nat Airport, Metrop Wash Airports Authority, 94; and others. *Exhib:* one-woman exhibs, Mint Mus, Charlotte, NC, 80, Renwick Gallery, Smithsonian Inst, Wash, 80-81, Joslyn Art Mus, Omaha, Nebr, 82, Hunter Mus Art, Chattanooga, Tenn, 87, Nancy Drysdale Gallery, Wash, 92, Galerie Feurle, Cologne, Ger, 92, State Univ NY, Old Westbury, 92 & Allrich Gallery, San Francisco, 93, Baruch Coll, NY, 2000, Albuquerque (NMex) Mus, 2000, DC Moore Gallery, NY, 2001; Utopian Visions, Mus Mod Art, NY, 87; Architectural Clay, Clay Studio, Philadelphia, 93; The Lure of the Local, Colo Univ Art Galleries, Boulder, 94; Exhibs incl Payson Galleries, New York City, 95, DC Moore Gallery, New York City, 96-2001, Boston Univ Art Gallery, 2000, Whitney Mus Contemp Art, New York City, 99-2000, Nat Mus Women in the Arts, Washington, 2001; represented in permanent collections of Metrop Mus Art, New York City, Mus Modern Art, New York City, Nat Gallery of Art, Wash DC; auth of Patterns of Desire, 2000; coauth, W Robert Kushner, of Boy's Art, 2003; Ann Exhib Am Acad, Rome, 2000; Nat Mus Fine Arts, Buenos Aires, 2000. *Teaching:* Instr ACE prog, Queens Col, Flushing, NY, 71-72; instr, Sch Visual Arts, 73-74, Art Inst Chicago, 75, Syracuse Univ, 77, Univ NMex, 78, Brooklyn Mus Art Sch, 78-79, Washington Univ, St Louis, Mo, 86, Cooper Union, New York, 90 & Rutgers Univ, New Brunswick, NJ, 92; adv bd, Pub Art Fund, 84-86 & Dept Art, Carnegie Mellon Univ, 92-96; bd dir, Col Art Asn, 85-89; Chicago Art Institute, Sch Visual Arts, New York City, Cooper Union, New York City. *Awards:* Yaddo Fel, Saratoga Springs, NY, 84; Rockefeller Found Grant, Bellagio, Italy, 92; Djerassi Resident Artists Prog, Woodside, Calif, 94; Jules Guerin Fel, Rome Prize, Am Acad, Rome, 1999-2000; Grantee Yaddo Fel, Sarasota Springs NY, Diane Wood Middlebrook Fel, Rockefeller Found, Bellagio, Italy, Jules Guerin Fellowship, Am Acad, Rome, Italy, Nat Endowment for the Arts. *Bibliog:* Eleanor Heartneg (auth), A necessary transgression, The New Art Examiner, 11/88; Allan Schwartzman (auth), Monumental trouble, Elle, 9/89; Peggy Phelan (auth), Grimes of passion, Artforum, 5/90; and many others; Kaplan, Janet (auth.) Revisiting the Age of Discovery Art in Am, 99; Frankel, David, Art Forum, 99. *Mem:* Nat Acad. *Media:* Ceramic Tiles, Glass Mosaic. *Publ:* Auth, From the other side: Public artists on public art, Art J, winter 87; Patterns of Desire, Hudson Hills Press, NY, 90; The Question of gender in art, Tema Celeste, autumn 92; Forum: On motherhood, art and apple pie, Meaning, 11/92; Joyce Kozloff, Generation of Fel, Nat Endowment Arts, Wash, 93; auth: of Patterns of Desire, 2000; co-auth:, w. Robert Kushner, of Boy's Art, 2003. *Dealer:* DC Moore Gallery 724 Fifth Ave New York NY 10012. *Mailing Add:* 152 Wooster St New York NY 10012

KOZLOFF, MAX
PHOTOGRAPHER, WRITER
b Chicago, Ill, June 21, 33. *Study:* Univ Chicago, BA, 53, MA, 58; Inst Fine Arts, NY Univ; Fulbright scholar, France, 62-63. *Exhib:* One-man shows, Holly Solomon Gallery, NY, 77, 79 & 80, Marlborough Gallery, NY, 82, PPOW Gallery, NY, 93; Nat Ctr Performing Arts, Bombay, India, 96; and others. *Pos:* Art critic, The Nation, 61-69; NY corresp, Art Int, 62-64; contrib ed, Artforum, 63-74, exec ed, 74-76. *Teaching:* Instr, Calif Inst Arts, 70-71 & Yale Univ, 74; prof photog, Sch Visual Arts, NY, 89-00; and many others. *Awards:* Pulitzer Fel Critical Writing, 62-63; Frank Jewett Mather Award Art Criticism, 66; Guggenheim Fel, 68-69; Nat Endowment Arts Criticism Fel, 84; Int Ctr Photog Writing Award, 90. *Publ:* Auth, Cubism Futurism, 74; Photography and Fascination, 79; The Privileged Eye, 87; Duane Michals Now Becoming Then, Twelve Trees Press, 90; Lone Visions, Crowded Frames, Univ NMex Press, 94; NY Capital Photography, Yale Univ Press and Jewish Mus, 02. *Mailing Add:* 152 Wooster St New York NY 10012

KOZLOW, RICHARD
PAINTER, SCULPTOR
b Detroit, Mich, May 5, 26. *Study:* Cass Tech, Detroit; Detroit Soc Arts & Crafts. *Work:* Smithsonian Nat Mus Am Art, Washington; State Mich Libr, Archives Mus, Lansing, 88; Detroit Inst Arts; Iris & Gerald Cantor Collection, Stanford Univ, Calif; Wayne State Univ, Detroit; and others. *Comn:* Sky Series (three paintings), Ford Motor Co, NAAO Bldg, Dearborn, Mich, 80; The Opera's Not Over (painting), Yaffe

Assocs, Southfield, Mich, 81; Great Ideas of Western Man Series, Container Corp Am; Wine labels (five paintings), Muer Corp Restaurants, 89-90; painting, Mona Lizautuers-Les Auteur Restaurant, Royal Oak, Mich, 90. *Exhib:* Victims Series, Birmingham Temple, Farmington Hills, Mich & Meadowbrook Mus Art, Rochester, Mich; Regional Ann, Butler Inst Am Art, Ohio, 52; retrospectives, Detroit Inst Arts, 64 & Art Gallery Windsor, Ont, 77; Lithographs from Mourlot Graphics, Hudson River Mus, NY, 70; solo exhibs, Ohio Univ, Athens, 82 & Am Embassy, Madrid, Spain, 84, Black, White and Bronze, Janice Cherach Gallery of Detroit Jewish Community Ctr, West Bloomfield, Mich, 97, Victims Series, Swords into Plowshares Gallery & Peace Ctr, Detroit, Mich, 98, Holocaust Univ Mich, 99; traveling exhib, Nat Inst (Mex) Bellas Artes - San Miguel Allende, Aguas Calientes & Guanajuato, 91; Distinguished Artist Award and Exhib, Birmingham Temple Ann Arts Show, Farmington, Mich, 97; Lost Drawings, Early Yrs Exhib, Gallery on Main, Royal Oak, Mich, 98. *Teaching:* Instr & dept head, Detroit Soc Arts & Crafts, 50-60; instr spec workshops, Birmingham-Bloomfield Art Asn, Mich, 70-79, & 90; artist-in-residence, Inst Allende, San Miguel Allende, Gto, Mexico, formerly; instr special travel workshops, Costa Rica, 81, Smokey Mountains, 81 & Mexico, 82. *Awards:* Founders Soc Award, Mich Artist Exhib, Detroit Inst Arts, 63; Mich Found Arts Award, 82; Outstanding Achievement Award, Birmingham Temple, 89; Lois and Alvin Spector Found Arts Award. *Bibliog:* Wendon Blake (auth), Complete Guide to Acrylic Painting, Watson-Guptill; LJ Feinberg (auth), cover painting & biog, J Am Med Asn, 1-26/90; Aimee Exgas (auth), To Life: The Art of Richard Kozlow, Jour Jewish Hist Soc Mich, 2004. *Media:* All. *Publ:* Auth & illusr, Of Man's Inhumanity to Man, Lark Press, 65. *Dealer:* Kozlow Studio MI. *Mailing Add:* 176 Suffield Ave Birmingham MI 48009-1239

KOZLOWSKI, EDWARD C
PAINTER, DESIGNER
b Bridgeport, Conn, Mar 11, 27. *Study:* Butera Sch Fine Art, 47; Whitney Sch Art, portrait with Simka Simkovitch, dipl, 51; Yale Sch Design, color with Josef Albers, BFA, 54. *Work:* Yale Univ, New Haven, Conn; Brittex; Citytrust; IBM; General Electric; Xerox; pvt collection of Al Pacino. *Exhib:* Conn Yale Artists, Yale AA Gallery, New Haven, 76; 2nd Ann Int Soc Arts, Foothills Art Ctr, Golden, Colo, 79; 27th Ann Nat Soc Painters Casein & Acrylic, Nat Arts Club, NY, 80; 3rd Ann, Salmagundi Club, NY, 80; 156th Ann, Nat Acad Design, NY, 81. *Pos:* Staff artist, Bridgeport Post, Conn, 47-54; advert designer, Int Silver Co, Meriden, Conn, 54-56; dir packaging develop, Warner Packaging, Bridgeport, Conn, 56-64; owner, Edward C Kozlowski Design Inc, New York, 64-83. *Teaching:* Instr design, Pratt Inst, Brooklyn, 65-69 & Parson Sch Design, 83-86. *Awards:* Best Show, 20th Ann, Barnum Festival Soc, 80; Best Acrylics, 20th Ann, Barnum Festival Soc, 80; Frederick Lowey Award, Salmagundi Club, 81. *Mem:* Salmagundi Club; Conn Classical Arts; Am Inst Graphic Arts; Advertising Club Fairfield Co (pres, 64-65). *Media:* Acrylic, Watercolor; Conte, Pencil, Lithograph, ink. *Publ:* Coauth, The Package Designer Looks At Packaging Materials, Packaging Design, 64; Contribr, Changing Times, Indust Design, 75; Auth, Job Sheet: A Better Link Between Packager and Marketer, Product Mgt, 76. *Dealer:* Art/Place 400 Center St Southport CT; Moviehouse Gallery Main St Millerton NY. *Mailing Add:* 74 Columbine Dr Trumbull CT 06611-4603

KOZMON, GEORGE
PAINTER
b Cleveland, Ohio, Apr 22, 60. *Study:* Cleveland Inst Art, Ohio, BFA, 82. *Work:* Cleveland Mus Art, Ohio; Erie Art Mus, Pa; DuPont, Detroit, Mich; IBM, Armonk, NY; Butler Inst Am Art, Youngstown, Ohio; and others. *Comn:* canvas (4ft x 6ft), Goodyear Tech Ctr, Akron, 85; Canvas, Gateway Arena, Cleveland Indians; painting on masonite (3ft x 5ft), Turner Construction, Columbus, 86; 5 (5ft x 8ft) canvases, Univ Hosp, Cleveland, 89, 9 paintings on aluminum, Key Corp, Cleveland, 99. *Exhib:* Gov Residence Invitational, Columbus, Ohio, 85; The Artist Obsessed: Architecture Perceived, Fendrick Gallery, Washington, DC, 866; Sande Webster Gallery, Philadelphia, 89 & 91; one-man show, Quan/Schieder Gallery, Toronto, Robert Kidd Gallery, Thrive an artspace 2005; two-man show, Deson/Saunders Gallery, Chicago, 94 & Eleuation art 2006, Groupshow on the wall, cleveland state Univ, 2006; Directors Choice Show, Virginia Miller Gallery, Miami. *Collection Arranged:* Thrive an artspace, 2005. *Pos:* dir, Cain Park Art Festival, Cleveland Heights, Ohio, 97-; founder/owner, Thrive an artspace; indipendant cur, High art gallery. *Teaching:* Vis lectr, Mid Am Col, Art Asn, 84; instr, drawing & archit, Cleveland Inst Art, 85-86, life drawing, 2000-. *Awards:* Ohio Coun Individual Fel, 84-85; Ohio Arts Coun Visual Artists Fel, 84, 87, 91 & 95; Nat Endowment Arts Individual Artists Fel, 87-88; and others. *Bibliog:* Gerorge Kozmon (video), Goodyear, 84; A brush with buildings, Washington Post, 4/12/86; Am artist watercolor, Evolving subject mater, 2003. *Mem:* World Fedn Hungarian Artists; Cleveland Hungarian Am mus. *Media:* Acrylic on Paper & Canvas. *Publ:* Auth, Art in the Midwest, Am Artist, 84; City whites, Cleveland Mag, 84; Drawing a line of departure, Cleveland Mus Art, 84; On the wall, Cleveland State Univ, 2006; and numerous catalogues. *Mailing Add:* 360 Timberidge Tr Gates Mills OH 44040

KOZO
PRINTMAKER
b Osaka, Japan, June 18, 37. *Study:* Keio Univ, Dipl Art, 60. *Work:* Mus Mod Art, Paris, France; Royal Libr Belg, Brussels; Mus Mod Art, Calcutta, India; Osaka City Mus, Japan; Keio Univ, Tokyo, Japan. *Comn:* Mural, Siege Social Fougerolle, Paris, France, 74; mural, Dresdner Bank, Frankfort, Ger, 79; mural, Siege Social Itocyu, Tokyo, Japan, 80; mural, Villas Presidentielles, Bagdad, Iraq, 82; mural, Dresdner Bank, Singapore, 85. *Exhib:* Salon de Mai, Mus Mod Art, Paris, France, 63-68; solo exhibs, Mus Chartres, France, 73, Cent Mus, Tokyo, Japan, 85 & Hakone Open-Air Mus (with catalog), Kanagawa, Japan, 92. *Awards:* Grand Prix de Serigraphie, Paris, France, 69; Grand Prix du Contemp Art, Tokyo, Japan, 71. *Bibliog:* Bernard Gheerbrandt (auth), Kozo Lavis, FRT Races, 83; Jacques Busse (auth), Dictionary of Art, E Benezit, 93. *Media:* Oil, Silkscreen. *Publ:* Sculptures of Crystal, Daum, 80; Post Cards, Posters, Nouvelles Images, 80; Ed, Tapestries, Robert Four, 82; Portfolio of Silkscreen, Multiple Impressions, 85; Kimono, Juraku, 86

KRAAL, LIES
PAINTER
b Rotterdam, Holland, July 23, 37. *Hon Degrees:* 2005 Cola Award City of Los Angeles. *Work:* Laguna Mus Art, Calif; Panza Collection, Milano, Italy; La Coleccion Jumex, Mexico City. *Comn:* LA Coleccion Juniex Mus, Mexico City, 2002. *Exhib:* 2 Dimensions, Univ Tex, El Paso, 84; Exemplary Contemp, Univ Calif, Santa Cruz, 87, 88; Lies Kraal, Claremont Univ, Calif, 2000; Jumex Mus, Mexico City. *Teaching:* guest artist, Painting's Edge, Idyllwild Arts, Calif; resident, Chinati Found, Marfa, Tex, 2003; Vis Artist Residency Chinati Fond, Marfa, Tex, 2003. *Awards:* COLA Fel, City of LA Cultural Affairs Dept, 2005. *Bibliog:* Rosanna Albertini (auth), Lies Kraal, Claremont Grad Univ, 2000. *Media:* Acrylic. *Specialty:* Contemporary Art. *Dealer:* Susanne Vielmetter 5795 West Washington Blvd. Culver City, CA, 90232; Charlotte Jackson Fine Art 200 W Marcy St Ste 101 Santa Fe NM 87501. *Mailing Add:* 724 Milwood Ave Venice CA 90291

KRAFT, CRAIG ALLAN
SCULPTOR, CURATOR
b Ames, Iowa, Dec 7, 49. *Study:* Univ Wis-Madison, BA & MA; Atlantic Ctr Arts (Stephen Antonokos-Artist Residence Prog), New Smyrna Fla, 88. *Work:* French Consulate, New Orleans, La; Dorsey Law Firm, Minneapolis, Minn; Zimmering & Zinn Inc, NY; Epco, Bensalem, Pa; Int Machinist Asoc, Washington. *Comn:* Maitland Surgical Ctr, Fla, 88; 30' acrylic & neon with cross faders, Rouse Co, Washington, 91; Five Famous Washingtonians in neon, Pennsylvania Ave Dev Corp, Washington, 93; auditorium marquee, 96, Falling Rising Man, Admin Bldg, 98, RI Sch Design. *Exhib:* DC Sculpture Now, Sumner Sch Mus, Washington, 89; Transformations, Washington Sq, Washington, 90; one-man show, Zenith Gallery, Washington, 90 & 94, Reston Art Ctr, Va, 92, Perry House Galleries, Arlington, Va, 97 & Traveling Light, Seto, Japan, 98; Electric Eclectic, Ctr Contemp Art, North Miami, Fla, 93; Outdoor Sculpture Competition Exhib, Western Carolina Univ, NC, 95; Pop Ups, Socrates Sculpture Park, Long Island City, 95-96; Convergence Art Festival & Intern Sculpture Conf, Providence, RI, 96. *Collection Arranged:* Light as a Helping Hand traveling exhib, 94. *Pos:* Artistic dir, Glen Echo Neon Restoration, Washington, DC, 90. *Teaching:* Instr neon/light sculpture, Int Sculpture Ctr Conf, 90, Smithsonian Inst, 90-. *Awards:* Neon Lit Art Nat Winner, St Publ, Cincinnati, Ohio, 88, 89, 90 & 96; Visual Arts Grant, Nat Endowment Arts & DC Arts & Humanities, 93 & Small Proj Grant, 97; Masterworks, Convergence XI, Providence, RI, 98. *Bibliog:* Personal interview, Channel 9 WUSA, 91; Christian Schiess (auth), Interviews with light artists, St Publ, 93; Fox News Network, Neon Exhibition-Craig Kraft, 94. *Mem:* Washington Sculpture Group. *Media:* Light Sculpture. *Publ:* Auth, Neon (instrnl video), 97. *Mailing Add:* 931 R St NW Washington DC 20001

KRAFT, STEVE
DESIGNER
b Los Angeles, Calif, Dec 5, 46. *Study:* Univ Calif at Berkeley, B(Arch). *Work:* De Young Mus, San Francisco; Oakland Mus, Calif. *Comn:* Reception area work in cherrywood & glass, Osborne McGraw-Hill, Emeryville, Calif, 87; construction in steel & nylon, Saatchi & Saatchi, San Francisco, 88; collection case, Richard Diebenkorn, Healdsburg, Calif, 90; assemblage in red oak & steel, Bechtel Corp, Richmond, Calif, 91; furniture for private residence/studio, Wolf von dem Bussche, Berkeley, 96. *Pos:* Owner/design dir, Kraft Furniture, 78-. *Media:* Wood, Metal. *Mailing Add:* 2300 Foothill Blvd Oakland CA 94601

KRAKOW, BARBARA L
DEALER
b Boston, Mass, June 9, 36. *Study:* Boston Univ, BA, 58. *Collection Arranged:* Internat Contemporary Art, 45-. *Pos:* Pres, Harcus-Krakow Gallery, Boston, 64-83, Barbara Krakow Gallery, 83-; art adv panel, Internal Revenue Service, 80-84; membership comt, Art Dealers Asn Am, 85-; bd mem, Art Auction AIDS Action Comt, 85, co-chairperson, 86; cur, Ninth Ann Drawing Show, Boston Ctr Arts, 88. *Teaching:* Lectr, Harvard Arts Mus, 11/86. *Awards:* Honored by Boston YWCA, Tribute to Women Entrepreneurs, 86. *Mem:* Art Table Inc; Art Dealer Asn Am; Int Fine Print Dealer Asn. *Specialty:* Internat art 1945 to present, paintings, sculpture, drawings and prints. *Mailing Add:* Barbara Krakow Gallery 10 Newbury St Boston MA 02116

KRAMARSKY, WERNER & SARAH-ANN
COLLECTOR
Pos: Bd trustees, Mus Modern Art, New York City, 98-, life trustee, 2003-, mem drawing comt, 94-, vchmn, 98-, mem comt on archives, libr & res, 97-; chmn bd, Andy Warhol Found; bd dir, UCLA Hammer Mus, currently. *Awards:* Named one of Top 200 Collectors, ARTnews Mag, 2004. *Collection:* Modern & Contemporary drawings, especially American Art. *Mailing Add:* 560 Broadway New York NY 10012-3938

KRAMER, BURTON
DESIGNER, EDUCATOR
b New York, NY, 32. *Study:* Inst Design, Ill Inst Technol, BSc (visual design), 54; Royal Col Art, London, Eng, 55-56; Yale Univ Sch Fine Arts, MFA (design), 57; with Josef Albers, Paul Rand, Alexey Brodovitch & Bradbury Thompson. *Hon Degrees:* Ont Col Art and Design, Can, Hon D, 2003. *Work:* Smithsonian Inst, North Am Life Assurance. *Comn:* Identity program design, Can Imperial Bank Com, Can

Broadcasting Corp, Copps Coliseum, Reed Paper, Can Craft Coun, Teknion Furniture, Science North, Nat Res Coun Can, Onex Packaging, Gemini Group & St Lawrence Centre Arts. *Exhib:* Can Graphic Design, Tokyo, Japan, 75; Spectrum Can, Montreal, 76; VI Poster Biennale, Warsaw, Poland, 76; RCA Designers 78, Toronto, 78; Graphic Designer Can Best of '80's, Art Dirs Show, Toronto, 85; Logo Biennale, Ostend, Belgium, 94; Pekao Gallery, Toronto, 99; Peak Gallery, Toronto, 2001-2002; Kabat-Wrobel Gallery, Toronto, 2003; Arta Gallery, Toronto, 2005; Fran Hill Gallery, Toronto, 2005; Siano Gallery, Philadelphia, 2006; CorBraun Gallery, Westport, Ont, Can, 2006. *Pos:* Chief designer, Halpern Advert, Zurich, Switz, 62-65; dir corp graphics, Clairtone Sound Corp, 66-67; pres, Kramer Design Assocs Ltd, Marketing Commun & Design, 67-2001. *Teaching:* Mem design fac, Ont Col Art, 78-98. *Awards:* Graphic Designers Can, 85; Lifetime Achievement Award, Arts Toronto, 99; Order Ont, 2003. *Bibliog:* Article, Studio Mag, Toronto, 85; First Choice, Tokyo, 89; Idea Mag, Tokyo, 92. *Mem:* Royal Can Acad Art; fel Graphic Designers Can (pres, 75-77); Alliance Graphique Int. *Media:* Acrylic. *Interests:* Art, antiquities, architecture, music, books and travel. *Collection:* Foundation for Constructive Art, Calgary, Alberta & pvt collections. *Publ:* Auth & contribr, Top trademarks and symbols of the world, Milan, 74; auth & ed, Idea Mag, Tokyo, 75 & 85; auth, Canadian Interiors, Toronto, 75; Appl Arts Quart, 90; Essays on Design, 9/97. *Dealer:* Oeno Gallery Ont; CorBraun Gallery Westport Ont. *Mailing Add:* Kramer Design Assoc Ltd 103 Dupont St Toronto ON M5R 1O4 Canada

KRAMER, HARRY
PAINTER
b Philadelphia, Pa, Mar 20, 39. *Study:* Philadelphia Col Art, BFA in painting, 1962; Yale Univ, MFA in painting, 1965. *Work:* group exhib Hudson River Mus, Yonkers, NY, 1983, NY Studio Sch, 1985, Nat Acad of Design, 1994, 95, 96, 2001, US Embassy, Vienna, 2002, Ameringer and Yohe Fine Art, Boca Raton, 2002, 2003; pvt collections, Brooklyn Mus Art, Corcoran Gallery, Metrop Mus Art, Nat Acad of Design, Ketcham and McDougal Found, NJ, Detroit Inst of Art, Chase Manhattan Bank. *Exhib:* One-man shows: Brata Gallery, New York City, 1972, 55 Mercer Gallery, New York City, 1973, 74, 76, 81, Forum Gallery, Maryland, 1977, Ted Greenwald Gallery, New York City, 1983, Gruenebaum Gallery, New York City, 1985, 87, Charles Cowles Gallery, New York City, 1991, 94, 98, 2003, Bill Bace Gallery, 1993, Ameringer and Yohe, 2003 & 05, Ober Gallery, Kent, Conn, 2006. *Teaching:* Prof, Queens Coll, Flushing, NY, 1970; Instr, NY Studio Sch, 1968-73; NYU, 1968-69. *Awards:* Fel NY State Coun on Arts, 1973, 77; Fel Nat Endowment for Arts, 82; Faculty Res Grant Queens Col, 83, 94, 95, 96. *Mem:* Nat Acad (acad, 94). *Media:* Oil. *Mailing Add:* Ameringer and Yohe 20 W 57th St New York NY 10019

KRAMER, HILTON
CRITIC, EDITOR
b Gloucester, Mass, Mar 25, 28. *Study:* Syracuse Univ, BA; Columbia Univ; New Sch Social Res; Harvard Univ; Ind Univ. *Pos:* Assoc ed & feature ed, Arts Digest, 54-55; managing ed, Arts Mag, 55-58, ed, 58-61; chief art critic & art news ed, New York Times, formerly; ed in chief, New Criterion, 82-; columnist, Arts & Antiques Mag; art critic, New York Observer, 87-. *Teaching:* Lectr art today. *Publ:* Auth, The Age of the Avant-Garde, Farrar, Straus & Giroux, 74; contribr, Arts Mag, Partisan Rev, Commentary, New Repub, New York Rev Bks, Encounter, Art in Am, Artforum, The Hudson Rev, Artscanada & others

KRAMER, JAMES J
PAINTER
b Columbus, Ohio, Oct 24, 27. *Study:* Cleveland Sch Art; Western Reserve Univ; Ohio State Univ. *Work:* Monterey Peninsula Mus Art, Calif; Georgetown Hist Soc, Colo; United Bank Denver; Univ Nevada, Reno; Colo Heritage Ctr Mus, Denver; and others. *Comn:* Illustration, Trail Guide, Ventana Chapter, Sierra Club, 69; program cover, Orchestra Santa Fe, 84-85; Sixth Street (watercolor), Georgetown Soc, 85; NMex Community Found, 94; NMex Symphony Orchestra, 98. *Exhib:* Mus Western Art, Denver, Colo, 84; Southwestern Realism, NMex Mus Fine Art, Santa Fe, 90 & Taiwan Mus, 91; Am Art in Miniature, Gilcrease Mus, Tulsa, Okla, 1990-2000; Millicent Rogers Mus, Taos, NMex, 92; Royal Watercolour Soc, London, Eng, 92; Artists of Am, Colo Hist Mus, Denver; Prix de West, Nat Cowboy Hall Fame, Okla City; and others. *Teaching:* Watercolor workshop, Mont Art Educ Asn, Great Falls, 74; watercolor workshop, Soc Western Artists, Fresno, Calif, 75 & Ghost Ranch, Abiquiu, NMex, 80; instr, Valdes Art Workshp, Santa Fe, NMex, 85-95 & Scottsdale Artists' Sch, Ariz, 86-88. *Awards:* Gold Medal, Calif Art Club, 73; Silver Medal, Nat Acad Western Art, 89; Frederic Remington Award, Nat Acad Western Art, 91; and others. *Bibliog:* Stephen M Parks (auth), James Kramer, Skill can destroy soul, Art Lines, 9/84; Suzanne Deats (auth), James Kramer, Focus/Santa Fe, 6-7/87; John Villani (auth), Watercolorist displays stroke of genius, NMex Mag, 5/92. *Media:* Watercolor. *Publ:* Contribr, The Watercolor Page, Am Artist Mag, 73; contribr, 40 Watercolorists & How They Work, 76 & Executive Diary, 76, Watson-Guptill; Painting Small & Watercolor and Gouache (films), Okla Co Libr, 77; Distinguished Artist of Yr Calendar, NMex Mag, 93. *Dealer:* Claggett/Rey Gallery Vail CO; Altermann Galleries Dallas TX and Santa Fe NM

KRAMER, LINDA LEWIS
PAINTER, COLLECTOR
b New York, NY, Mar 25, 37. *Study:* Scripps Col, Claremont Calif, with Paul Soldner, BA, 59; Sch Art Inst, Chicago, MFA, 81. *Work:* Mus Contemp Art, Chicago; Purdue Univ, W Lafayette; Univ Ill, Carbondale; Allan Chasonoff Ceramic Collection, Mint Mus Art, Charlotte, NC; Mary & Leigh Block Mus Art, Evanston, Ill. *Exhib:* One-woman shows, "Three Cultures, Red, Yellow & Blue", Univ Ariz, Tucson, 84, Chicago Cult Ctr, 86, Still Light, Evanston Art Ctr, Luminous Light, Tough Gallery, Chicago, 93 & Pool, Franklin Sq Gallery, Chicago, 94; Alternative Spaces, Mus Contemp Art, Chicago, 84; 80th Exhib, Art Inst, Chicago, 84; Material & Metaphor, Chicago Cult Ctr, 86; Retrospective, Hyde Park Art Ctr, Chicago, 99; Evanston Arts Coun, Noyes Cult Arts Ctr, 2003; Corbett vs Dempsey, 2005. *Pos:* Comt mem, Evanston Art Ctr Exhibs, 91-. *Teaching:* Instr, Columbia Col, 93; Sch Art Inst, 95; Urban Gateways, Chicago, 96. *Awards:* Ill Arts Coun Grant, 84, 96; Levy Found Prize, 80th Chicago & Vicinity Exhib, 84, 89; Karolyi Found Grant, Vence, France, 89. *Bibliog:* Diane Douglas (auth), Material & Metaphor, Chicago Pub Libr Cultural Ctr, 86; Patty Carroll (auth), Spirited Visions, Univ Ill Press, 91; Ivy Sundell (auth), Art Scene Chicago, Crow Woods Pub, 2000. *Mem:* Mid-west Clay Guild (vpres, 86, treas, 90); Evanston Art Ctr (exhib comt, 96); Artemisia Gallery (bd, 97-); Art after 5-Chair-Evan AM Art Ctr, 2005. *Media:* Miscellaneous Media, Installations. *Collection:* Chicago imagists first and second generation, Hairy Who Sch. *Publ:* Auth, Natural & Cultural Energy, Leonardo Mag, 87; Retrospective Catalog, Hyde Park Art Ctr, Chicago, 99. *Dealer:* Printworks 311 W Superior Chicago 60610; Corbett vs Dempsey, 1120 N. Ashland, Chicago, 60622. *Mailing Add:* 370 Glendale Ave Winnetka IL 60093

KRAMER, LOUISE
MURALIST, SCULPTOR
b New York, NY. *Study:* Cooper Union, cert, 44; Hofstra Univ, BA, 68; Hunter Col, MA, 70. *Work:* Nassau Community Col, Hempstead, NY; Mus Fine Art, Univ Iowa, Iowa City; Brentwood High Sch, NY. *Comn:* Mural, Int Ladies Garment Workers' Union, Local 23-25, NY, 85. *Exhib:* Two Women Sculptors, RI Univ Gallery, Kingston; Emerging Real, Storm King Art Ctr, Mountainville; one-woman show, Nassau Co Mus Fine Arts, Roslyn; Women Choose Women, NY Cult Ctr; Calif Col Arts & Crafts Print Show, San Francisco Mus Art; Printmaking, New Forms, Whitney Mus, NY; AIR Gallery, NY, 75, 78, 81, 83 & 85; Working Women, Am Fedn State Co & Munic Employees; 18th Nat Print Exhib, Brooklyn Mus, 86. *Teaching:* Artist-in-residence, sculpture, Univ Iowa, Iowa City, 78; lectr sculpture, Arrandale Sch, Great Neck, NY. *Awards:* North Shore Community Arts Award, Great Neck, 75; Fel Printmaking, NY State Coun Arts, 76; Nat Endowment Arts Fel Printmaking, 76. *Bibliog:* Lizzie Borden (auth), Louise Kramer, Artforum, 72; Kate Linker (auth), Louise Kramer, Arts Mag, 5/77. *Mem:* Women in the Arts; Women's Caucus Arts. *Media:* Steel, Brass. *Dealer:* AIR Gallery 63 Crosby St New York NY 10012. *Mailing Add:* 26 Beaver St New York NY 10004

KRAMER, MARGIA
CONCEPTUAL ARTIST, VIDEO ARTIST
b Brooklyn, NY. *Study:* Art Students League; Brooklyn Col, BA; Inst of Fine Arts, New York Univ, MA(art hist); performance/dance study with Yvonne Rainer & Simone Forti. *Work:* Mus Mod Art, NY; Allen Mem Art Mus, Oberlin, Ohio; New York Pub Libr; Univ Calif, San Diego; Temple Univ; Carnegie/Mellon. *Comn:* Secret (video), Ill Arts Coun, Chicago, 81; Progress (Memory) I (video), Visual Studies Workshop, Rochester, NY, 83; New Wozzeck (video) Jerome Found, 85; Obelisk for Raymond Williams (pub sculpture), Pub Art Fund Inc, NY, 88; I a Wo/Man (multi-media), San Francisco Artspace, 89. *Exhib:* Jean Seberg-The FBI-The Media, Mus Mod Art, NY, 81; Progress (Memory) II, Whitney Mus Art, 84; Surveillance, Los Angeles Contemp Exhibs (LACE), 87; Social Engagement: Women's Video in the 80's, Whitney Mus Art, 87; Democracy and Politics, Dia Art Found, 88; Committed to Print, Mus Mod Art, 88; A Different War: Vietnam in Art, Akron Art Mus, traveling exhib, 89-92; Making Their Mark: Women Artists move into the Mainstream 1970 to 1985, Cincinnati Art Mus, traveling exhib, 89-90. *Pos:* Television studio technician, Morgan Guaranty Trust Co & WNYC-TV Channel 31, 82-83; ed, Upfront Mag, 84-85; panelist, NY Found for the Arts, 86. *Teaching:* Vis asst prof, painting & drawing, Duke Univ, 79-80; asst prof painting & drawing, Univ of Ill, Chicago, 80-81; asst prof film & video, Univ of Hartford, 83-84; artist in residence, Mass Inst Technol, 89. *Awards:* Artists Fel, Nat Endowment Arts, 76, 82 & 90; Fel, NY Found Arts, 88; Fel Mass Coun Arts Humanities, 89. *Bibliog:* Lucy Lippard (auth), Get the Message? A Decade of Art for Social Change, 84 & A Different War: Vietnam in Art, 90; Branda Miller & Deborah Irmas et al (auths), Surveillance, 87; Deborah Wye (auth), Committed to Print, Social and Political Themes in Recent American Printed Art, 88. *Mem:* Asn of Ind Video & Filmmakers, Inc; Col Art Asn. *Media:* Multi-media, Video; Graphics, Books. *Publ:* Coauth (with Vanalyn Green), Against Inner Exile, Upfront Mag, No 2, winter 81/82; auth, Disinformation Warfare, A Breaking of Codes in Painting and Video, Red Bass Mag, No 10, Fla, winter/spring 86; Cracking the Concrete: Interventionist Posters, Upfront Mag, winter 86/87; Andy Warhol et al, The FBI File on Andy Warhol, 88; The Warhol File, Andy Warhol: Film Factory, London, 89. *Dealer:* Video Data Bank Art Inst Chicago Jackson Blvd & Columbus Dr Chicago Ill; Printed Matter Inc 7-9 Lispenard St New York NY

KRAMLICH, RICHARD & PAMELA
COLLECTOR
Study: Northwestern Univ, BA(hist), 57; Harvard Univ, MBA, 60. *Pos:* With, Kroger Co, Cincinnati, 60-64; joined, Gardner & Preston Moss, Boston, 64, exec vpres, 68—69; gen partner, Arthur Rock & Assoc's, 69—78; co-founder & gen partner, New Enterprise Assoc's, Menlo Park, Calif, 78—; founder, New Art Trust, 97—; bd dir, Celetronix, Decru, Fabric7Systems, Financial Engines, Force10 Networks, Foveon, Graphic Enterprises, Informative, Zhone Technol, Visual Edge Tech, Silicon Valley Bancshares, 2005—, adv mem bd, 2003—2005; bd dir, UCSF Found, Bay Area Video Coalition, currently; vchmn bd, dir, San Francisco Exploratorium, currently. *Awards:* Lifetime Achievement Award 2001; Named one of Top 200 Collectors, ARTnews Mag, 2004; recipient Lifetime Achievement Award in Entrepreneurship & Innovation, Lester Ctr for Entrepreneurship & Innovation, Haas Sch Bus, Univ Calif, Berkeley, 2005. *Mem:* Nat Venture Capital Asn (pres, 92—93, chmn, 93—94). *Collection:* Video & new media art. *Mailing Add:* 3699 Washington St San Francisco CA 94118

KRANE, SUSAN
CURATOR, MUSEUM DIRECTOR
b Gary, Ind, June 8, 54. *Study:* Carleton Col, BA(magna cum laude), 76; Columbia Univ, MA, 78, Univ Colo, MBA, 2000. *Collection Arranged:* Art at the Edge: Barbara Ess (auth, catalog), 92; Art at the Edge: Alison Saar (auth, catalog), 93; Tampering: Artists & Abstraction Today, (auth, brochure) 94; Tangle of Complexes: Photography in Mexico, 96; Enrique Chagoya, 97; Nene Humphrey: A Wild Patience, 98; Out of Order: Mapping Social Space (co-auth, catalog), 2000; Let's Walk West: Brad Kahlhamer, 04. *Pos:* Rockefeller Found Intern, Walker Art Ctr, Minneapolis, 78-79; asst cur, Albright-Knox Art Gallery, Buffalo, NY, 79-82, assoc cur 83, cur 83-87; cur, 20th Century Art, High Mus Art, 87-95; dir, Univ Colo Art Galleries, 1996-2001; dir, Scottsdale Mus Contemp Art, Arizona, 2001-. *Teaching:* Adj prof art hist, State Univ NY, Buffalo, 80-86; adj prof, Emory Univ, Atlanta, 88-95; asst prof, Univ Colo, Boulder, 96-. *Awards:* Norton's Curators' Fel, 94. *Mem:* Art Table; Col Art Asn. *Publ:* Lynda Bengolis: Dual Natures, Univ Wash Press, 90; Max Weker: The Culnist Decade, Univ of Wash Press, 91; Graven Images in Barbara Rowe, Castellani Art Mus, Niagara Falls, NY, 91; Matrix: Nene Humphrey, Winthrop Univ, Rock Hill, SC, 92; Equal Rights & Justice, 94; and others. *Mailing Add:* Scottsdale Mus Contemp Art 7374 E Second St Scottsdale AZ 85251

KRANKING, MARGARET GRAHAM
PAINTER, LECTURER
b Florence, SC, Dec 21, 30. *Study:* Am Univ, Washington, DC, BA(summa cum laude), Clendenin Fellow in Art Hist), 52. *Work:* Fed Nat Mortgage Asn, AT&T & Wall St J, Washington, DC; US Gen Accounting Off; Marsh & McClennan Cos; Nat Coun Educ, Washington, DC; Hospice Montgomery Co, Md; Art in Embassies: Mission Off UN, Official Residence Ambassador to UN, Hon John Bolton; US Coast Guard Hall of Heroes; and others. *Comn:* Portrait, Rear Admiral Harold C Train & Admiral Harry D Train II, comn by Mrs Harold C Train, Washington, DC, 71; portrait, Dr Cecile Bolton Finley, Univ Va, Mrs Joseph V Marcoux, Alexandria, Va, 79; Charles H Jones, 83 & Harry A Tow, 85, Water Pollution Control Fed, Washington, DC; Children's Nat Med Ctr, Washington, DC; Navy Fed Credit Union Hq, Vienna, Va, 97. *Exhib:* 7th Ann Area Show, Corcoran Gallery Art, Washington, DC, 52; Maryland Biennial, Baltimore Mus Art, 74 & 76; Rocky Mountain Nat Watermedia Exhib, Foothills Art Ctr, Golden, Colo, 85, 86, 88 & 92; Retrospective, Florence Mus, 91; Shada Gallery Invitational, Riyadh, Saudi Arabia, 91; Bicentennial Exhib, Belle Grove Plantation, Middletown, Va, 94; Washington Co Mus Invitational, Hagerstown, Md, 96; Government House Invitational, Annapolis, Md, 97 & 98; Black Rock Ctr, Germantown, Md, 2002. *Pos:* Asst to head of publications, The Nat Gallery of Art, 52-53; official US Coast Guard artist, 86-. *Teaching:* Guest instr, Amherst Col, Mass, 85; Woman's Club, Chevy Chase, Md, 97-2006. *Awards:* First Place, Area 87 Exhib Paintings & Graphics, Fairfax Co Coun Arts, Va, 87; Ross Family Award, Adirondacks Nat Exhib Am Watercolor, Old Forge, NY, 88; George Gray Award, US Coast Guard Art Prog, 91 & 98; and others. *Bibliog:* Charles Sullivan (auth), Numbers at Play, Rizzoli, New York, 92; Christine Unwin (auth), The Artistic Touch I, II & III, Creative Art Press, 94, 96 & 98; Phil Metzger (auth), The North Light Guide to Materials and Techniques, North Light Books, 96; Phil Metzger (auth), The Artist's Illustrated Encyclopedia, North Light Books, 2001. *Mem:* Transparent Watercolor Soc; Potomac Valley Watercolorists (pres, 81-83); Southwestern Watercolor Soc; Southern Watercolor Soc; Nat Watercolor Soc; Am Watercolor Soc; Houston Watercolor Soc; Balt Watercolor Soc; Western Fedn of Watercolor Socs. *Media:* Watercolor, Pastel. *Specialty:* Paintings, sculpture. *Publ:* Auth, The watercolor page, Am Artist Mag, 5/88; auth, Add Watercolor Page, Am Artist Mag, 10/2002. *Dealer:* McBride Gallery 215 Main St Annapolis MD 21401. *Mailing Add:* 3504 Taylor St Chevy Chase MD 20815

KRANTZ, CLAIRE WOLF
CRITIC, CURATOR
b Chicago, Ill, Jun 22, 38. *Study:* Therapy, Univ Ill, BS in Occpl, 61; Stanford Univ, Post grad, 78; Sch Inst of Chicago, BFA, 79; Sch Inst of Chicago, Postgrad, 83; Phi Kappa Phi. *Work:* Solo and two-person exhib incl Bade Mus, Berkeley, Calif, 1997; var others; group exhib incl Spertus Mus, Chicago, 1994, Clarke House Mus, Chicago, 2004; var others; organized exhib for inst incl: The Spertus Mus, The State of Ill Mus. *Exhib:* Solo and two-person exhib incl Gallerie S&H De Buck, Belg, 1989, Galerie Paula Kouwenhoven, Delft, The Neth, 1990, Galerie Blankenese, Ger, 1991, Sazama Gallery, Chicago, 1992, Chicago Cult Ctr, 1993, Perimeter Gallery, Chicago, 1997, 2002, Wash State Univ, Pullman, 1997, Kedia Kabun Gallery, Yogyakarta, Indonesia, 1998, Contemp Art Ctr of Peoria, Ill, 2000, I Space Gallery, 2002, Toomey-Tourell Gallery, San Francisco, 2002, Flatfile Photog Gallery, Chicago, 2004, various others; group exhib incl Walker Gallery Art, 1981, Art Inst Chicago, 1981, AIR Gallery, New York City, 1991-2003, NY Arts Gallery, New York City, 2003, various others; organized exhib for inst incl: U-Turn E-Mag, Wood St Gallery, Ukrainian Inst Modern Art; freelance art critic for nat art publ, incl Art in Am. *Pos:* occupational therapist, 61-76. *Teaching:* lectr, at var univs in the US, Europe, and Indonesia. *Mem:* Chicago Art Critics Assoc. *Mailing Add:* 711 S Dearborn #401 Chicago IL 60605-2308

KRASHES, BARBARA
PAINTER
b New York, NY. *Study:* Art Students League, with Reginald Marsh, Julian Levi & Vaclav Vytlacil; NY Univ, BS; Hunter Col, NY; Educ Alliance, with Chaim Gross; New Sch Social Res, NY. *Work:* Ulrich Mus Art, Wichita, Kans; St Lawrence Univ Mus, Canton, NY; Valley Bank, Springfield, Mass; Walter Kidde Constructors, Inc, Cincinnati, Ohio; Hood Mus Art, Dartmouth Col, Hanover, NH. *Exhib:* Art: 1965, Am Express Pavilion, NY World's Fair; Am Abstract Artists, Riverside Mus, NY; Fordham Univ at Lincoln Ctr, NY; NY Univ; Hyde Collection, Glens Falls, NY; Tyler Art Gallery, SUNY, Oswego, NY; Myers Fine Arts Gallery, SUNY, Plattsburgh, NY; Brooklyn Mus, NY; Newark Mus, Newark, NJ. *Pos:* Art dir, Adult Educ Ctr, New York, 61-93. *Awards:* George B Bridgman Mem Scholar, Art Students League, NY. *Bibliog:* Art World Problems (tape), Today's World, Fordham Univ, 73. *Mem:* Fedn Mod Painters & Sculptors, Inc (past pres), NY; life mem Art Students League, NY; NY Artists Equity Asn, Inc. *Media:* Mixed-Media, Acrylic. *Interests:* Painting and Art History. *Collection:* Hood Museum of Art, Dartmouth College; St Lawrence University Museum, Ulrich Museum of Art; Collections in Austria, England, Germany, Israel, Italy & United States. *Publ:* The New York Arts Calendar (spec issue) for NY World's Fair Am Express Show, 65; Feigin Memorial Collection (catalog), St Lawrence Univ; Female Artists in the United States: A Research and Resource Guide to Women Painters 1900-1985, Nat Endowment Humanities; Experimental Works, Fedn Mod Painters & Sculptors, NY. *Mailing Add:* 77 W 85th St New York NY 10024-4161

KRASNYANSKY, ANATOLE LVOVICH
PAINTER, ARCHITECT
b Kiev, Ukraine, USSR, Feb 26, 30; US citizen. *Study:* Kiev State Inst Fine Art & Archit, MA, 53. *Work:* Kiev State Artist's Union Collection, Ukraine, USSR; Dalzell Hatfield Gallery Collection (Int Watercolor Masters), Los Angeles; Stanford Univ, Palo Alto, Calif; Los Gatos Mus, Calif; Dyansen Galleries; and others. *Comn:* Restovration of Potemkin and Marble Palases, State, St Peterburg, Russia, 52-53; Central Art Pavilion, Exhibs Artists Union, State, Kiev, Ukraine, 55-58; Restoration of Historical Alexandria Park, State, Uman, Ukraine, 61-68; Metro Station Politechnical Inst, State, Kiev, Ukraine, 69; Ampitheatre & Corp Bldg, Renaissanse Guild Inc, Long Beach, Calif, 84-85. *Exhib:* Russian Artist's in USA, Stanford Univ, Palo Alto, 81 & contemp Russian Artists, UCLA; solo exhibs, Stanford Univ, Palo Alto, 82 & Dyansen Galleries, Beverly Hills & Coho, NY, 88-90; Contemp Russian Artists in Exile, Univ Calif, Los Angeles, 82; Russian Art in USA, Los Gatos Mus, Calif, 82; group & solo exhibs, Dyansen Galleries, Boston, San Diego, Washington & Tokyo, 88-91; and others. *Pos:* Principal archit designer, Inst Tech Aesthetics, Dept Interior Design, Kiev, Ukraine, 68-74; principal designer & art dir, Central Ukraine Pavilion Republican Exhibs, Kiev, 74; set designer, Universal Studios, Hollywood, 78-84; independent consult archit design & presentation, Univ Calif, Los Angeles, 83; dir design & art, Renaissance Guild Inc, Long Beach, Calif, 84. *Teaching:* Lectr aesthetic design & art, Kiev Inst Tech Aesthetic, Ukraine, 69-73. *Awards:* First Prize, Interiors and Art for Metro, Politechnical Inst, State, 60; Second Prize, Monument of Potemkin Uprising in Odessa, State, Ukraine, 65; ABC Certif Appreciation Prof Contrib Acad Award Shows, Hollywood, 76-77. *Media:* Watercolor, Acrylic. *Dealer:* Dyansen Galleries of USA 131 Varick St New York NY 10012; Park West Gallery 29469 Northwestern Southfield MI 48034. *Mailing Add:* 871 S Bundy Dr Los Angeles CA 90049

KRATE, NAT
PAINTER
b New York, NY, Aug 26, 18. *Study:* WPA Art Sch, New York, 34-35; Pratt Inst, New York, 35-36; Art Students League, 36-38 & 46-47. *Work:* Berkshire Mus, Pittsfield, Mass; Mus Arts & Sci, Daytona Beach, Fla; Van Wezel Performing Arts Hall, Sarasota, Fla; Fla WCoast Symphony Hall, Sarasota. *Comn:* Thirteen wall murals, 1st Army Hq, Govs Island, NY, 42-43; 11 portraits, comn by different individuals, 80-93; ann report cover art, Fla Progress Corp, St Petersburg, Fla, 90. *Exhib:* Solo-shows, Becket Art Gallery, Mass, 78, Welles Gallery, Lenox, Mass, 81, Ana Sklar Gallery, Bal Harbor, Fla, 85, Foster Harmon Galleries Am Art, Sarasota, Fla, 86, 89, 92 & 94, Arvida Gallery, Longboat Key, Fla, 86, Longboat Key Art Ctr, Fla, 89 & Donn Roll Galleries, Sarasota, Fla, 94; Fla Figure Show, Brevard Mus, Melbourne, Fla, 93; 43rd Ann All Fla, Boca Raton Mus, Fla, 94; Fla Artist Group, Mus Arts & Sci, Daytona Beach, Fla 94; 4th Biennial Exhib, Huntsville Mus, Ala, 94. *Teaching:* Instr figures, Longboat Key Art Ctr, Fla, 84-86, Sarasota Art Asn, Fla, 86-87 & Ringling Sch Art & Design, Sarasota, Fla, 89-90. *Awards:* Silver Medal of Hon, Knickerbocker Artists USA, 93; Elizabeth Morse Genius Award, 94; Houser Award, Soc 4 Arts, Palm Beach, 95; Best in Show, Charlotte City, Art Guild, National Exchange, Punta Fla, 04. *Bibliog:* Carol Parker Rife (auth), Artful ways, Gulfshore Life Mag, 90; Profile & portfolio, Arts & Sci Quart, 92; Laura Stewart (auth), State artists show-cased, Daytona Beach News J, 94. *Mem:* Knickerbocker Artists USA; Fla Artist Group; Am Artists Prof League; Sarasota Co Arts Coun. *Media:* Oil. *Publ:* Mag illus, Fawcett Publ, New York, 48. *Dealer:* Donn Roll Galleries 1415 Main St Sarasota FL 34236; Mickelson Gallery 707 G St NW Washington DC 20001; Zenith Gallery 413 7th St NW Washington DC 20004. *Mailing Add:* 4737 Sweet Meadow Cir Sarasota FL 34238

KRATZ, MILDRED SANDS
PAINTER
b Pottstown, Pa. *Study:* With Whitney & Burns, Portugal & Greece. *Work:* Franklin Mint Mus; General Mills; Goodyear Inc; Fitchburg Mus; Motorola; and others. *Comn:* Franklin Mint. *Exhib:* Nat Acad Design, NY, 73-93; 105 one-woman shows incl, Fitchburg Art Mus, Mass, 75; Wistariahurst Mus, Holyoke, Mass, 79; Dyer-York Mus, Saco, Maine, 80; Canton Art Inst, Ohio, 80; William Penn Mus, Pa; Retrospective, The Hill Sch, Pottstown, Pa, 93. *Pos:* Judge & juror, Pa, Fla, Ohio, Ind, etc, 85-96. *Teaching:* Artist-instr, Queen Elizabeth II, New York to Eng, 75; res artist, Cunard Line, 75-96. *Awards:* Six gold medals, misc exhibs, 75-88; Pa Senatorial Citation, 77; Grumbacher Award, Watercolor USA, 82; Awards, Water Soc Ohio, 83-90. *Bibliog:* Mildred Sands Kratz - Contemporary Artist, PBS Show. *Mem:* Hon Soc Watercolor USA; Am Watercolor Soc; Am Artist Prof League; Pottstown Area Artists Guild (co-founder & pres, 66); Ohio Watercolor Soc; Allied Artists Am; hon mem Philadelphia Watercolor Club. *Media:* Watercolor. *Publ:* Illusr, Nat Antiques Rev, 71; Stories of French Creek, 73; auth, Watercolor page, Am Artist Mag, 73; illusr, Prints, 83; Palette Mag, 83; Stitchery, 86-96. *Dealer:* WM Ris Galleries Stone Harbor NJ; Upwyth Art Skippack Pa. *Mailing Add:* 17406 Heather Oak Pl Tampa FL 33647

KRAUS, JILL GANSMAN
COLLECTOR
b Philadelphia, Pa, Oct 25, 52. *Study:* Carnegie Mellon Univ, BFA, 74; RI Sch Design, MFA, 77. *Pos:* Designer Accesocraft, New York City, 77-78, Cadoro, New York City, 78-79; asst to dir, design Monet Jewelry, 79-81; sr designer, Swank Inc, 81-85; product marketing mgr, Marvella, 85; vpres design & training, Swarovski Jewelry US Ltd, New York City, 92; Avon Products, New York City, 97. *Awards:* Named one of Top 200 Collectors, ARTnews Mag, 2004. *Mem:* Friends of the Carnegie Int (co-chmn, currently); Carnegie Mellon Univ (bd trustees, currently); World Studio Found, New York City (bd dir, currently); New Mus Contemp Art (bd trustees, currently); Pub Art Fund (bd trustees, currently). *Collection:* Contemporary Art

KRAUS, PETER STEVEN
COLLECTOR
b Aug 12, 52. *Study:* Trinity Col, Hartford, Conn, BA (econ), 74. *Pos:* partner, Goldman, Sachs & Co, New York City, 94, co-head fin, inst group, investment banking div, 98-2001, co-head pvt wealth mgt, 2001, co-head investment mgt div, 2001-, also managing dir & mem mgt comt. *Awards:* Named one of Top 200 Collectors, ARTnews Mag, 2004. *Mem:* Trinity Col, (Charter trustee, 98-); Calif Inst Arts (bd overseers, currently); Friends of the Carnegie Int (co-chair, currently). *Collection:* Contemporary Art. *Mailing Add:* Goldman Sachs & Co 85 Broad St New York NY 10004

KRAUS, (ERSILIA) ZILI
SCULPTOR, JEWELER
b Satchinez, Timisoara, Romania; US citizen. *Study:* Graphic Sketch Club, Philadelphia, Pa, 28-30; Nat Acad Design with Leon Kroll, 30-32; Barnes Found, Pa, 33-35; Samuel S Fleisher Art Mem with Frank Gasparro, 62-74; Inst Allende, San Miguel de Allende with Enrique Lopez, 72-81. *Work:* Cinnaminson Town Hall, NJ; Burlington Co Libr, Westhampton, NJ. *Comn:* Resurrection (mural), Calvin Presbyterian Church, Pa, 35; Yearbook (cover illustration), Columbia Univ Sch Pub Health & Admin, NY, 67. *Exhib:* Earth Edge, Painting, Montreal Mus Fine Art, Quebec, 56; Sculpture, Fleisher Art Mem, Philadelphia, Pa, 67-72; Sculpture, Woodmere Art Mus, Philadelphia, Pa, 68-86, jewelry, 80-85; Sculpture, Cheltenham Art Ctr, Pa, 70-84; Sculpture, Da Vinci Art Alliance, Philadelphia, Pa, 72-84; Sculpture, Burlington City Cult & Heritage Comn, Mt Holly, NY, 84-87. *Collection Arranged:* Membership Show, Cinnaminson Art Centre, 66-67; Triboro Artists, Burlington Co Libr, 69; jewelry, Cheltenham Art Ctr, Pa, 85; jewelry, Woodmere Art Mus, Philadelphia, 83-92. *Pos:* Textile designer, Shapiro & Co, New York, 45-48. *Teaching:* Instr painting, Art League Long Island, Queens, NY, 50-51 & Northern Burlington City Region High Sch, Columbus, NJ, 64-65; instr beginning & advanced painting, Cinnaminson High Sch, NJ, 65-76. *Awards:* First Prize, jewelry (man's neckpiece), Woodmere Art Mus, Philadelphia, 83 & 91; Oscar d'Italia, sculpture, Accademia Italia, Italy, 85; Purchase, ring, Cheltenham Twp Art Ctr, Pa, 85. *Mem:* Woodmere Art Mus, Germantown, Pa; Leonardo Da Vinci Art Alliance, Philadelphia; Cheltenham Township Art Ctr, Cheltamham, Pa; Nat Mus Women Arts, Washington, DC. *Media:* Wood, Pastel; Metal, Gem Stones. *Interests:* Designing creative jewelry (men's and women's). *Publ:* Burlington Co Times, 91. *Mailing Add:* 255 Sloboda Ave Mansfield OH 44906

KRAUSE, BONNIE JEAN
MUSEUM CONSULTANT
b La Crosse, Wis, Sept 20, 42. *Study:* Viterbo Col, BA, 64; Southern Ill Univ, MS, 68. *Collection Arranged:* US Grant: Man of Peace, Man of War, traveling exhib, 83; Bits and Pieces: Southern Illinois Tradition in Rag Rugs, traveling exhib, 90; Olynthus 348 B C: The Destruction and Resurrection of a Greek City, traveling exhib, 92; New Deal Art: Images of Mississippi, 94-95, exhib & traveling exhib; Waves of the Future, 98. *Pos:* Dir, Ill Ozarks Graft Guild, Southern Ill Univ, 80-81, cur hist, Univ Mus, 81-85, sr develop specialist, 85-90; dir univ mus, Univ Miss, 90-2000. *Teaching:* Instr art marketing, Southern Ill Univ, 74-76. *Bibliog:* Palmer Hudson (auth) Mississippi Folklorist: Mississippi Folklife, Vol. 32, No 1. *Mem:* Ozark States Folklore Soc; Miss Hist Soc; Miss Folklore Soc. *Publ:* Family of the Hills: The Bridgemans of the Pine Hills, US Forest Serv, 85; coauth, German Americans in the St Louis Region 1840-60, Mo Hist Soc, 89; Auth, Bits and Pieces: The Southern Illinois Tradition in Rag Rugs, Mid-American Folklore, Vol XXI, No 1, Spring 93; The Mary Bure Mus, Oxford Mississippi, as a WPA Community Art Center, 39-42. *Mailing Add:* 141 Haw Creek Mews Dr Asheville NC 28805

KRAUSE, DOROTHY SIMPSON
PAINTER, COLLAGE ARTIST
b Mobile, Ala, Sept 22, 40. *Study:* Montevallo Univ, BA, 60; Univ Ala, MA, 62; Pa State Univ, DEd, 68. *Work:* Smithsonian Am Art Mus, Washington, DC; Zimmerli Mus Rutgers Univ; DeCordova Mus; Boston Mus Fine Arts; Danforth Mus Art, Framingham, Mass. *Comn:* Mural, Trinity Place, Boston, 98; Herman Miller (mural), Holland, Mich, 98; murals, prints, Fed Reserve Bank, Boston, 2002-03. *Exhib:* Solo exhib, Ctr Creative Imaging, Camden, Maine, 94, NE Sch Photog, Boston, Mass, 94, Wellesley Col, 95 & Dana Hall, 99; Univ Mass, Lowell, 99; Simmons Col, 2000; Creiger-Dane Gallery, 2000; Art Complex Mus, Duxbury, Mass, 2001; Evos Arts Institute, Lowell, 2002; Fla Gulf Coast Univ, 2002; New Eng Sch Photog, 2003; Judi Rotenberg Gallery, Boston, 2003, 04, 05; Danforth Mus Art, Framingham, Mass, 2003; Havard Med Sch, Boston, 2006. *Pos:* Artist-in-residence, Ctr Creative Imaging, 91-94; corp cur, Iris Graphics, Bedford, Mass, 93-98; cons, Hewlett-Packard, 2006-. *Teaching:* Assoc prof art educ, Va Commonwealth Univ, Richmond, 69-74; prof computer graphics, Mass Col Art, Boston, Mass, 74-2000, prof emeritus, 2000-. *Awards:* Frank Procter Whiting, Cooperstown 1993 Nat; IDAA award, 2003. *Bibliog:* Colin Wood (auth), Dorothy Krause & the Trinity Place Project, Design Graphics, 9/98; Harald Johnson (auth) Mastering Digital Printmaking, 2002 &05; Jeremy Sutton & Daryl Wise (auths), Secrets of Award Winning Digital Artists; Richard Noyce (auth), Printmaking at the Edge, 2006; Bruce Wands (auth), Art of Digital Age, 2006. *Mem:* Womens Caucus Art; Col Art Asn; Boston Printmakers; Photog Resource Ctr; others. *Media:* Digital Collage, Mixed Media. *Publ:* Fractal Design Painter Creative Techniques, Hayden, 96; Painting with Computers, Rockport, 96; The Painter 5 WOW! Book, Peachpit Press, 2002; Photoshop 5 Bible, 98, Painter 5 Studio Secrets, 98, IDG Bks. *Dealer:* Judi Rotenberg Boston Mass; Nan Mulford Gallery Rockport Maine. *Mailing Add:* 32 Nathaniel Way PO Box 421 Marshfield Hills MA 02051

KRAUSE, GEORGE
PHOTOGRAPHER
b Philadelphia, Pa, Jan 24, 37. *Study:* Philadelphia Col Art. *Work:* Mus Mod Art, NY; Bibliot Nat, Paris; Libr Cong, Washington, DC; Philadelphia Mus Art; Houston Mus Fine Art. *Exhib:* Five Unrelated Photographers, Mus Mod Art, NY, 63; one-man shows, George Eastman House, Rochester, NY, 75, Mus Bellas Artes, Caracas, Venezuela, 76, Witkin Gallery, NY, 78, Houston Mus Fine Art, 78, Am Acad Rome, 79 & Pa Acad Fine Art, Philadelphia, 82; one-man Retrospective, Houston Mus Fine Art, 92. *Teaching:* Assoc prof photog, Bucks Co Community Col, Newtown, Pa, 73-75; prof photog, Univ Houston, 75-99, ret; dir photog workshops, Venice Photog Biennale, Italy, summer 79; artist in residence, Am Acad Rome, 79-80; hon prof photog, E Tex State Univ, 88. *Awards:* Guggenheim Found Grants, 67 & 76; Prix de Rome, 76; Nat Endowment Arts, 73 & 79; and others. *Bibliog:* Mark Power (auth), George Krause I, Monog Toll & Armstrong, 72; Nancy Hellebrand (auth), I Nudi-George Krause, Photo Rev, 80; Arno Minkkinen (auth), article, Contemp Photogr, 81; Anne Tucker (auth), George Krause: A Retrospective, Rice Univ Press. *Mem:* Am Acad Rome. *Media:* Silver Gelatin, Mixed Media. *Publ:* Illusr, The photographer's eye, 66 & Looking at pictures, 73, Mus Mod Art; auth, I Nudi (catalog), Mancini, 80. *Dealer:* Photographs Do Not Bend Gallery 3115 Routh St Dallas TX 75201; George Krause 291 E Summit Dr Wimberley TX 78676. *Mailing Add:* c/o Photographs Do Not Bend Gallery 3115 Routh St Dallas TX 75201

KRAUSS, ROSALIND E
HISTORIAN, CRITIC
b Washington, DC, Nov 30, 40. *Study:* Wellesley Col, BA, 62; Harvard Univ, PhD, 69. *Collection Arranged:* Joan Miro: Magnetic Fields, Guggenheim Mus, 71; 200 Years of American Sculpture, Whitney Mus Am Art, 76; Richard Serra, Mus Mod Art, New York, 85. *Pos:* Assoc ed, Artforum, 71-76; ed, October Mag, 76-. *Teaching:* Assoc prof art hist, Mass Inst Technol, 65-71; lectr, Princeton Univ, 72-74; prof, Hunter Col, 75-90, Columbia Univ, 92-. *Awards:* Guggenheim Found Fel, 71; Mather Award Criticism, Col Art Asn, 72. *Res:* Theory and criticism of modernist art; history of photography. *Publ:* Auth, Terminal Iron Works: Sculpture of David Smith, Mass Inst Technol Press, 71; Passages in Modern Sculpture, Viking Press, 77; Sculpture of David Smith: Catalog Raisonne, Garland Press, 78; The Originality of the Avant-Garde and Other Modernist Myths, Mass Inst Technol Press, 84. *Mailing Add:* Columbia Univ 116th & Broadway New York NY 10027-6902

KRAVIS, HENRY R
COLLECTOR
Study: Claremont-McKenna Col, BA in Econ, 67; Columbia Univ, MBA, 69. *Pos:* partner, Bear Stearns; founding partner, Kohlberg Kravis Roberts, 76-, sr partner 87-; bd dir, PRIMEDIA Inc, 91-; leadership council, bd trustees, Claremont-McKenna Col, Metropolitan Mus Art, Mount Sinai Hosp, currently; co-chair Partnership for NYC, chair Columbia Bus Sch Council. *Awards:* Named on of Top 200 Collectors, ARTnews Mag, 2004. *Collection:* Old Master drawings and paintings, Impressionist art, 20th-century art, French furniture. *Mailing Add:* Kohlberg Kravis Roberts & Co Ste 4200 9 W 57th St New York NY 10021

KRAVIS, JANIS
DESIGNER, ARCHITECT
b Riga, Latvia, Oct 20, 35; Can citizen. *Study:* Sch Archit, Univ Toronto. *Exhib:* Royal Can Acad Arts, Nat Gallery Can, Ottawa, 70. *Awards:* Ont Tourist Accommodation Award, 67; Ont Eedee Design Award, 67; 25 Year Merit Award in Archit Excellence, Ont Asn Archit, 91. *Mem:* Ont Asn Architects; Asn Can Indust Designers; Royal Can Acad Art; Royal Archit Inst Can. *Mailing Add:* 38 Cedarbank Crescent Toronto ON M3B 3A4 Canada

KRAVIS, MARIE-JOSEE
COLLECTOR
b Ottawa, Ont, Can, Sept 11, 49. *Study:* Univ Que, BA, 70; Univ Ottawa, MA, 73. *Hon Degrees:* Univ Windsor, Laurentian Univ, LLD. *Pos:* Financial analyst, Power Corp Can Ltd, 69-70; spl asst to solicitor gen, Govt Can, 71-73; sr economist, Hudson Inst, 73-76, exec dir, 76-94, sr fellow, 94-; bd mem, exec comt mem, Mem Can Coun for Rsch on Social Sci & Humanities, 82-86, Can Govt Comn Adv Bd, 82-89, Consultative Comt on Financial Inst, Govt Que, 84-90; vchmn, Royal Can Comn on Nat Passenger Transp, 90-92; bd dir, Ford Moter Co, 95-, Vivendi Universal, 2001-, Interactive Corp, 2001-; vchmn, bd trustees, Mus Modern Art. *Awards:* Named one of Top 200 Collectors, ARTnews mag, 2004. *Collection:* Old Masters, Impressionism, 20th century art & French furniture

KRAVITZ, WALTER
SCULPTOR, PAINTER
b Chicago, Ill, Oct 25, 38. *Study:* Art Inst Chicago, BFA(fel), 64; Syracuse Univ, MFA, 67. *Work:* Hirshorn Mus, Washington. *Comn:* Suspended sculptures, Washington Conv Ctr, 86 & Niagara Falls, NY wintergarden; stairwell installation, Wash Proj Arts, 83; Muddy Branch Sch, Montgomery Co, Md; cabin, John Md Ice

Rink, 90; Montgomery Col Fine Arts Ctr, 92. *Exhib:* PS1, NY, 82; Franz Bader Gallery, Washington, 86-88; SE Ctr Contemp Art, 87; Corcoran Gallery Art, 92 & 94; Gallery K, Washington, 93 & 94; Sullivan Co Mus, NY, 93-96; and others. *Teaching:* Prof design & painting, Philadelphia Col Art, 69-74; prof painting & drawing, George Mason Univ, 76-. *Awards:* DC Comn Individual Artist Grant, 83, 87 & 89; Va Mus Fel, 88. *Mailing Add:* 614 A St SE Rear Washington DC 20003

KRAVJANSKY, MIKULAS
PAINTER, PRINTMAKER, DESIGNER
b Rudnay, Slovakia, May 3, 28; Can citizen. *Study:* Acad Muzas Art, Bratislava, Slovakia, PSV, 57. *Hon Degrees:* Magister of Arts. *Work:* Simon Fraser Univ; White Mountain Acad Arts; Wilfred Laurier Univ; Can Union Col; many others. *Comn:* Stucco mural, Nitra City Hall, Czech, 55; mobile sculpture, Dept Rec & Parks, Bratislava, 59; mural, Toronto City Hall, 69; mural, City of Napa, Calif, 96; mural, Humboldt Bay, Southport Landing, Calif, 97. *Exhib:* Binale of Fine Arts, Sao Paolo, Brazil, 57 & 61; Scenography, Int Cult Ctr, Cairo, Egypt, 66; ETC Opera Designs, Nat Opera, Budapest, Hungary, 67; Nat Canadian Exhib, Toronto, 72; Group of Contemporarists, tour of SAm cities, 72; Art Expo, Javitz Comr Ctr, NY, 80-88; one man shows, Dyansen Galleries, NY, Los Angeles, San Francisco, San Diego, New Orleans & Boston. *Pos:* Head scenographer, State Theatre, Presov, Czech, 59-64; head art & design dept, Czechoslovak TV, Bratislava, 64-68; artistic dir, Black Box Theatre of Can, 69-78; owner, MK Publ Co. *Teaching:* Lectr scenography, Acad Arts, Bratislava, 57-58; asst prof design, Acad Muzas Art, Bratislava, 65; asst master art design, Humber Col, Toronto, 69-75. *Awards:* Gold Medal, Bienale of Sao Paulo, 65, 67. *Bibliog:* Stage Design Throughout the World Since 1950; Harap, London, 60; Genesis (film), Gregor Film, Toronto; Paintings the Towns (film), RJD Enterprises, Los Angeles, 97; Artists of California (film), Mountain Production, 93. *Media:* All Painting Media; Intaglio Printing. *Mailing Add:* 7 Penny Lane Wasaga Beach ON L9Z 1N4 Canada

KREBS, PATSY
PAINTER
b Oakland, Calif. *Study:* Claremont Grad Sch, MFA, 76. *Work:* Santa Barbara Mus Art, Calif; Berkeley Art Mus; Mills Col Mus. *Exhib:* Solo exhibs, Bluxome Gallery, San Francisco, Calif, 87, Mincher Wilcox Gallery, San Francisco, Calif, 89, Dorothy Goldeen Gallery, Santa Monica, Calif, 90, 92 & 93, Stephen Rosenberg Gallery, NY, 90 & 92, Sun Valley Ctr Arts & Humanities, Idaho, 91 & 94, Haines Gallery, San Francisco, Calif, 92, 94, 96 & 99, M-13 Gallery, NY, 93, San Marco Gallery, San Rafael, Calif, 96, Ginsler, San Francisco, 97, Greg Kucera Gallery, San Francisco, 2001; The Uncommon Book: I Thought Hope was Home, Artists Sun Valley Ctr for Arts & Humanities, 97; Drawing, Haines Gallery, San Francisco, 98; Illuminated Under White Light, RB Stevenson Gallery, Calif, 98; Core, Stark Gallery, New York City, 99; Greg Kucera Gallery, Seattle, 99; Minimalism Then & Now, Berkeley Art Mus, Calif, 2001; and many others. *Teaching:* Instr, Mt San Antonio Col, Walnut, Calif, 77-78, Los Angeles City Col, 78-79, Calif State Univ, 80, San Francisco State Univ, 86-88, Calif Col Arts & Crafts, Oakland, 90-91, Dominican Col, San Rafael, Calif, 92-93 & San Francisco Art Inst, 88-. *Awards:* Support Grant, Nat Endowment Arts, 91; Support Grant, Marin Arts Coun, 92; Pollack-Krasner Found Grant, 95. *Bibliog:* Pamela Hammond (auth), Patsy Krebs: the fullness of abstraction, Art Space Mag, 92. *Media:* Acrylic and Watercolor on Paper and Canvas. *Dealer:* The Haines Gallery 49 Geary St San Francisco CA 94108. *Mailing Add:* PO Box 446 Inverness CA 94937

KREBS, ROCKNE
SCULPTOR
b Kansas City, Mo, Dec 24, 38. *Study:* Kans Univ, Lawrence, BFA, 61. *Work:* Phillips Collection, Smithsonian Inst, Corcoran Gallery Art, Hirshhorn Mus & Sculpture Garden, Washington; Philadelphia Mus Art, Pa; Ft Worth Art Mus, Tex; Contemp Art Ctr, Cincinnati, Ohio. *Comn:* Crystal Willow (24 ft x 19 ft glass, steel & searchlight sculpture), 88; The Red River Bridge (neon, laser, search lights & fiber optics), comn by City Shreveport, 93; permanent laser beam structure, CNN Ctr, Atlanta, 96; Good Luck World (laser animation), 96; Inclined Planes, Urban Scale Lasers, comn by Ruder & Finn, Johnstown, Pa, 89; Good Luck World comn by Indianapolis Mus Art, 96. *Exhib:* Sculpture Am Directions, Nat Mus Am Art, Washington, 75; The Source: An Urban Scale Laser Enviroment, Nat Mall, Washington, 80; Urban Scale Lasers: Columbus, Ohio, 82, Mt Wilson to CALTECH, Pasadena, 83, Fountain Sq, Cincinnati, Ohio, 84, Memorial Art Gallery & Univ Rochester, NY & others through 96; Laser exhibs: Cleveland Ctr Contemp Art, Ohio, 87; Mapplethorpe Projection, Corcoran Gallery Art Facade, Washington, 89. *Pos:* Bd dir, Wash Project Arts, 80-84 & Coalition of Wash Artists, Washington, 82-89, Artist Equity, Nat VP, 94-. *Awards:* Individual Artist Fel Grant, Nat Endowment Arts, 70; JS Guggenheim Fel, 72; Night Beautiful Award, Fla Power & Light Co, 87; Illumination Engineering Soc Award, 87; Distinguished Merit Award, Md Col Art & Design, outstanding leadership Behalf Artists Rights, Md, 89. *Bibliog:* Paul Richard (auth), The city at night is light, Wash Post & News Serv, 73; Nina Felshin (auth), article, Art Int, 5/74. *Media:* Light. *Publ:* Coauth, Rockne Krebs, Artist on Their Art, 68 & Walter Hopps, and Nina Felshin, Three Washington Artists, 70, Art Int; Jane Livingston, Art & Technol Catalog, Los Angeles Co Mus, 71; Nina Felshin, Projected Images (catalog), Walker Art Ctr, 74; Sam Hunter, American Art, Abrams, 79; Rockne Krebs, a retrospective of drawings 1965-1982 (catalog). *Dealer:* Jay Belloli, Baxter Art Gallery, Caltech, Pasadena. *Mailing Add:* 1428 U St NW Washington DC 20009

KREGER, PHILIP
DIRECTOR
b Detroit, Mich, Aug 9, 52. *Study:* Columbus Col of Art, BFA, 74. *Collection Arranged:* Russian Realism: Paintings from Behind the Iron Curtain, 00; Scenes of Am Life: Treasures from the Smithsonian Am Art Mus, 00; Buffalo Bill's Wild West, 00; To Conserve A Legacy: Am Art from Historically Black Col and Univ, 01; A Brush With History: Painting From the National Portrait Gallery, 01; Herb Alpert: Music for Your Eyes, 01; The Best of Tennessee, 01; Royalty & Elegance: Selections From the Pat Kerr Collection, 02. *Pos:* Mus exhib dir, Tenn State Mus, 83-. *Teaching:* Prof introduction to design, Oakridge Assoc Univs, 1975. *Mem:* Am Asn Mus; Industrial Design Soc Am. *Interests:* Magic Lanterns of Laser Light. *Collection:* Holography. *Publ:* Herb Alpert, exhib design & film appearance, Music for Your Eyes, 01. *Mailing Add:* Tenn State Mus 505 Deaderick St Nashville TN 37243

KREILICK, MARJORIE E
MOSAIC ARTIST, EDUCATOR
b Oak Harbor, Ohio, Nov 8, 25. *Study:* Ohio State Univ, BA, 46, MA, 47; Cranbrook Acad Art, MFA, 52; apprentice to Gulio Giovanette, Rome, 56; Am Acad in Rome, FAAR, 63. *Work:* Joslyn Mus, Omaha, Nebr; Columbia Mus Art, SC. *Comn:* Marble pebble mural, Wonderland Shopping Ctr, Livonia, Mich, 59; ten marble murals, State Off Bldg, Milwaukee, 63; mosaic foucault pendulum, Augustana Univ, Sioux Falls, SDak, 67; marble mosaic mural, Mayo Clinic, Rochester, Minn, 69; marble mosaic pool, Telfair Acad Arts & Sci, Savannah, Ga, 73. *Exhib:* Palace of Expos, Rome; Minn Mus Art, St Paul; solo show, Archit League, NY; Fairweather Hardin Gallery, Chicago. *Pos:* Univ of Wisconsin, Madison, WI, 53-92. *Teaching:* Instr-docent design, Toledo Mus Art, 48-51; from instr to prof design-sculpture, Univ Wis-Madison, 53-92, prof emer, 92-. *Awards:* Univ Wis Grant, 60; Prix de Rome, Am Acad in Rome, 61; Edwin Austin Abbey Fel, Am Acad in Rome, Italy, 61-63; Research Grant, Univ of Wis-Madison, 65,70,76,79,80, (mosaic studio asistant); Univ of Wis-Madison Grant from Chancellor's Office for Design, 68. *Mem:* Nat Soc Mural Painters; Int Asn Contemp Mosaicists, Ravenna, Italy. *Media:* Marble Mosaic. *Publ:* Contribr, Art in Architecture, 69; Art in Architecture, Louis Redstone, 68, McGraw Hill Source Book of Architectural Ornament, Brent Brolin, 82, Van Nostrand Reinhold; Inquiring About Comunities, Robert Tabachnick, Holt, Rinhart, Winston; Friends Around the Corner, G.F. Kenney, Lyons, and Carnahan. *Mailing Add:* 2713 Chamberlain Ave Madison WI 53705-3719

KREITZER, DAVID MARTIN
PAINTER
b Ord, Nebr, Oct 23, 42. *Study:* Concordia Col, BS, 65; San Jose State Univ, MA, 67. *Work:* Santa Barbara Mus, Calif; San Diego Mus, Calif; Joseph Hirshhorn Found, Washington, DC; Sheldon Gallery, Univ Nebr; Bakersfield Mus, Calif. *Comn:* Woman's Place & US Army Corps of Engrs, covers for Atlantic Mag, 70; California & the War, cover for Motorland Mag, 70; Tristan und Isolde (opera posters), Seattle, 81. *Exhib:* One-man shows, Am Art Since 1850, 68, Maxwell Gallery, San Francisco, Ankrum Gallery, Los Angeles, 71, 75, 77 & 79-81, Gumps Gallery, San Francisco, 81; Benedictine Art Awards, NY, 69; 6th Mobile Ann, Ala, 71; Adelle Mus Fine Arts, Dallas, 83; Stary-Sheets Gallery, Los Angeles, 92. *Teaching:* Instr painting, San Jose State Col, 68; instr life drawing, Poly State Univ, San Luis Obispo, Calif, 83. *Awards:* Ciba-Geigy Award, 71. *Bibliog:* Currant Mag, 6/75; Am Artist, 4/82. *Media:* Watercolor, Oil. *Dealer:* Summa Gallery 527 Amsterdam Ave NY 10024. *Mailing Add:* 1442 12th St Los Osos CA 93402

KREMERS, DAVID
CONCEPTUAL ARTIST
b Denver, Colo, 60. *Study:* Self-taught, Paris, 76-82. *Work:* San Francisco Mus Mod Art; Denver Art Mus; Panza Coll, Milano, Italy; Eli Broad Family Found, Santa Monica, Calif; Norton Coll, Santa Monica, Calif. *Exhib:* Facing the Finish (traveling), San Francisco Mus Mod Art, 91; The 8th Day, Landesmuseum, Linz, Austria, 93; Centennial Greetings, Denver Art Mus, Colo, 93; Veered Science, Huntington Beach Art Ctr, 95; solo show, ACME, Santa Monica, Calif, 95; Art Meets, Royal Acad, Copenhagen, 96; Boretum, Mondridan Found, The Neth, 98; In the Polka Dot Kitchen, Otis Col, 98. *Pos:* Distinguished Conceptual Artist, Caltech, 97. *Awards:* Colo Fedn for Art New Talent, Univ Colo, 94. *Bibliog:* Kenneth Baker (auth), David Kremers, Art News, 5/92; David Pagel (auth), Virtual reality, Los Angeles Times, 9/17/93; Louwrien Wijers (auth), Art meets science & spirituality in a changing economy, Acad Editions, 96. *Publ:* Contribr, Genetische Kunst-Kunstelisches Leben, PVS Verlager, 93; auth, Science Fair (exhib catalog), Thomas Solomon, 93; Growing reality, Zing Mag, 96; Delbruck paradox version 2, Art J, 96. *Dealer:* ACME 6750 Wilshire Blvd Los Angeles CA 90034. *Mailing Add:* 3031 S Ash St Denver CO 80222-6704

KREMPEL, RALF
PAINTER, ASSEMBLAGE ARTIST
b Groitzsch, Saxony, Ger, June 5, 35. *Work:* Libr Congress, Washington; European Patent Office Den Haag; World Intellectural Property Organ, Geneva; Mus Borna; Mus Groitzsch; Contemp Art Mus: di Rosa Preserve, Napa, Calif. *Exhib:* Le Salon des Nations, Ctr Int d'Art Contemp, Paris, 85; Art Contemporain Cabinet des Dessins, Espace Delpha, Paris, 86; Galerie Salammbo-Atlante, Paris, 87-93; Stadtgalerie, Groitzsch, 91-93; Museumsgalerie, Borna, 93; Museumsgalerie, Groitzsch, 94. *Pos:* Inventor & designer of Visual Commun Syst, world-wide message relay & depicting method employing colors rather than letters in transmission & presentation. *Teaching:* guest lectr Wiprecht Gymnasium, Groitzsch. *Awards:* Invite d'Honneur, Le Salon des Nations, SOCAP, Geneva, Switz, 85. *Mem:* Mus Soc; Forderverein Mus, Borna. *Media:* Acrylic; Colored Ceramic-Porcelain-Glass Tiles. *Res:* Evolution as the origin of the multiple species. *Publ:* Auth, numerous patent bulletins & statements; auth, 2 USA & European Patents and 3 Registered Trademarks: Visual Communication System, Krempel Code & Art with a Message; auth, Trilogy: Order of the Universe, Codex for the Cosmos. *Dealer:* San Francisco Painter Magnate Rincon Ctr San Francisco CA 94119-3368; Stadtgalerie Bruehl 2 04539 Groitzsch Germany. *Mailing Add:* 2400 Pacific Ave San Francisco CA 94115-1275

KREN, MARGO
PAINTER, EDUCATOR
b Houston, Tex, Dec 1, 39. *Study:* Univ Wis, Madison, BS, 66; Univ Iowa, MFA, 79. *Work:* Acad Arts and Design, Tsinghue Univ, Beijing; Deakin Univ, Melbourne, Australia; Emprise Fin Corp, Wichita, Tex; Mariana Beach Mus Art, Kansas State Univ, Manhattan; McAllen Int Mus, Tex; and others. *Exhib:* New Harmony Gallery Contemp Art, Ind, 98; Iowa State Univ, Ames, 2001; Spencer Mus Art, Univ Kans, 2001; Olson-Larson Gallery, Des Moines, 2001; River Gallery, Chelsea, Mich, 2001; Vanderbilt Univ, Nashville, 2002; The Waiting Room, New Orleans, 2002; and others. *Pos:* Panelist, Arts Midwest/NEA Regional Visual Arts Fel Selection, 88; Mid-Am Art Alliance panelist, Nat Endowment Arts Regional Fels, 92, New Eng Found Arts panelist, 96. *Teaching:* Prof painting, drawing, Kans State Univ, Manhattan, 71-2003; artists residencies, Ragdale Found, Lake Forest, Ill, 86, Va Ctr Creative Arts, Sweet Briar, 87 & Yaddo, Saratoga Springs, NY, 89; vis artist prof, Tilin Col Art, Changchua, China, 2005. *Awards:* Nat Endowment Arts Grant, 82; Kans Gov Art Award, 89; Kans State Univ Distinquished Grad Fac Mem Award, 89-90; Kans Arts Comn Fel, 2000. *Bibliog:* Novelene Ross (auth), Margo Kren/dreams and memories, Women Artist News, winter 86-87; Andrew Svedlow (auth), Within the mask: contemplation of works by Georgia O'Keeffe and Margo Kren, Kans Quart, Vol 19, No 4, 87; Leland Warren (auth), Margo Kren: Intimate experience and spaces of paintings, Kans Quart, Vol 24, No 1, spring 93. *Mem:* Kansas City Artist Coalition (pres, 82-83); Nat Women's Caucus for Art; Col Art Asn. *Media:* Oil, Acrylic. *Publ:* Auth, Philomene Bennett, a Kansas City artist, 82 & Michael Meyers, a Chicago performance artist, 85, Kans Quart. *Dealer:* Strecker-Nelson Gallery Manhattan, KS; Olson-Nelson Gallery Des Moines IA. *Mailing Add:* 2912 Tatarrax Dr Manhattan KS 66502-1978

KRENECK, LYNWOOD
PRINTMAKER, EDUCATOR
b Kenedy, Tex, June 11, 36. *Study:* Univ Tex, BFA, 58, MFA, 65. *Hon Degrees:* Collection of Art Inst of Chicago, Ill. *Work:* Fine Arts Gallery San Diego, Calif; McNey Art Inst, San Antonio, Tex; Print Collection, Philadelphia Mus Art; Mus Contemp Art Knoxville, Tenn; Art in Embassies Prog, US State Dept; Okla Art Ctr, Oklahoma City; High Mus, Atlanta; Royal Mus Art, Antwerp, Belgium. *Exhib:* Libr Cong Nat Print Show, 75; Nat Invitational Print Exhib, Visual Arts Ctr, Anchorage, Alaska, 89; The Passionate Eye Group Show, Laguna Gloria Arts Mus, Austin, Tex, 92; three-person show, Kalamazoo Inst Arts, Mich, 92; Tex Select Invitational, Wichita Falls Fine Art Mus, 93; Nat Touring Screen Print Show, Boston Mus Fine Arts Sch, 93; Nat Printmaking Invitational, Univ Miami, Fla, 95; 177th Ann Exhib, Nat Acad Art & Design, New York City, 02. *Teaching:* Prof printmaking, Tex Tech Univ, 65-; vis artist, Univ Ulster, Belfast, Northern Ireland, 95, Diocesan Sch, Auckland, NZ, 96, Seacourt Collab Press, United Kingdom & Royal Acad Art, Gent, Belgium, 2000. *Awards:* Purchase Prize, Boston Printmaker's Ann Exhib, 78 & 79; Purchase Prize, Works on Paper Int Exhib, Auburn Univ, 86; Gerson Lieber Prize, 64th Nat Soc Am Graphic Artists Ann Competition, New York, 91. *Bibliog:* EC Cunningham (auth), Printmaking, A Primary Form of Expression, Univ Colo Press, 92; Julia Ayres (auth), Printmaking Techniques, Watson-Guptill Publ, NY, 93; Glen R Brown (auth), J Print World, spring 95; Malone Yingxue (auth), Contemporary American Printmaking, Wampler, Jilin Fine Arts, China, 99; Isabel Howe (auth), Lynwood Kreneck-Printmaker, Texas Tech Univ Press, 2003. *Mem:* Southern Graphics Coun; Boston Printmakers; Philadelphia Print Club; Los Angeles Print Soc; Soc Am Graphic Artists. *Media:* Screenprinting, Drawing. *Res:* Research and development of techniques for new water base screen print inks; Visiting Artist in Residence, Ohio State University, 1986 to enhance R&D; Various articles and manual published in 1988. *Publ:* The complete printmaker, McMillan & Co, NY, 89; article, Sch Arts Mag, 88. *Dealer:* Charles Adams Gallery Kingsgate Shopping Ctr Lubbock TX. *Mailing Add:* 3209 45th St Lubbock TX 79413-3513

KRENS, THOMAS
MUSEUM DIRECTOR, EDUCATOR
b New York, NY. *Study:* Williams Col, BA, 69; State Univ NY, Albany, MA, 71; Yale Univ, MPPM, 84. *Hon Degrees:* State Univ NY, DHL, 89. *Collection Arranged:* The Restoration of Thomas Hart Benton, 85; The Peggy Guggenheim Collection, Venice, Italy, 88-. *Pos:* trustee, Williamstown Regional Art Conserv Lab, 83-85; stategic planning consult, Brooklyn Mus, 84-86; consult Solomon R Guggenheim Mus, NYC, 86-88, dir, 88-; adv comt mus proj Nat Educ Asn, Am Fedn Arts, Washington; trustee Solomon R Guggenheim Found, 88-. *Teaching:* asst prof art history Williams Col, Williamstown Mass, 72-80, dir artist in residence prog, 76-80, dir mus art, 81-88. *Mem:* Asn Art Mus Dirs; Aspen Inst Italia; Soc Kandinsky Ctr/Georges Pompidou; Gesellschaft fur Moderne Kunst am Mus Ludwig; Coun For Relations; AFA; Yale Univ Coun (art gallery comt, Brit Art Ctr com). *Publ:* auth Jim Dine Prints, 1970-77, 77; The Prints of Helen Frankenthaler, 80; The Drawing of Robert Morris 1956-82, 82; Robert Morris The Mind/Body Problem, 94; The Great Utopia The Russian and Soviet Avant-Garde, 1915-32. *Mailing Add:* c/o Guggenheim Mus Soho 1071 5th Ave New York NY 10128-0112

KRENTZIN, EARL
SCULPTOR, SILVERSMITH
b Detroit, Mich, Dec 28, 29. *Study:* Wayne State Univ, BFA, 52; Cranbrook Acad Art, MFA, 54; Royal Col Art, London, Fulbright Fel, 57-58. *Work:* Detroit Inst Art, Mich; Cranbrook Galleries, Bloomfield Hills, Mich; St Paul Art Ctr, Minn; Jewish Mus & Mus Contemp Crafts, NY; Hirshorn Mus, Washington, DC. *Comn:* Enamel plaque, Gloria Dei Lutheran Church, Detroit, 54; Menorah, Temple Israel, Detroit, 63; metal sculpture, Westland Shopping Ctr, Detroit, 65; plus many pvt comn of silver sculptures. *Exhib:* One-man shows, Kennedy Galleries, NY, 68-75, Detroit Inst Art, 78 & Oshkosh Mus, 82; NJ State Mus, Trenton, 70; Jewelry USA Traveling Exhib, Am Crafts Mus, 84-; Masters Am Metalsmithing Mus Ornamental Metalwork, Memphis, 88; Toys Designed by Artists, Ark Arts Ctr, Little Rock, 89-2005; and others. *Teaching:* Instr art, Univ Wis-Madison, 56-60; vis prof silversmithing, Univ Kans, 65-66; vis prof metalwork, Fla State Univ, 69. *Awards:* Fulbright Fel, 57-58; Nat Decorative Arts Exhib, Wichita Art Ctr, Kans, 66; Tiffany Grant, 66. *Bibliog:* Article, Am Mag, 11-12/82. *Media:* Miscellaneous Media. *Interests:* Collecting art, antiques & old toys. *Publ:* Auth, Centrifugal casting, Craft Horizons Mag, 11/54. *Mailing Add:* 412 Hillcrest Grosse Pointe Farms MI 48236

KRESCH, ALBERT
PAINTER
b Scranton, Pa, 1922. *Study:* Brooklyn Col, BA; NY Univ, MA; studied with Hans Hoffman at Hans Hoffman Art Sch. *Exhib:* Solo show at Salander O'Reilly Galleries, NY, 2002; group shows at Gallery Neuf; Thorne Art Gallery, Kean State Col, NH; Prince Street Gallery, NY; Jane Street Gallery, NY, 48; Cornell Univ, NY, 76; Hobart & William Smith Gallery, 77; Landscape Anthology, Green Mountain Gallery, NY, 88; Contemp Realist Gallery, 89, 90; Bowery Gallery, NY, 89; Art and Friendship, Selections from the Nell Blaine Collection, Tibor de Nagy Gallery, NY, 98, 2003; Ctr Figurative Painting, 2000; Mus Modern Art, NY, 2006. *Teaching:* Prof Brooklyn Col, Queens Col, Pratt Inst. *Awards:* Fulbright fel. *Mem:* Nat Acad (acad, 2005). *Media:* Acrylic, Oil

KRESTENSEN, ANN M
CERAMIST, SCULPTOR
b Baltimore, Md, Apr 4, 39. *Study:* Md Inst Art, 60 & Hon BFA, 96. *Comn:* Ceramic vesseles & triptych (silk painting), ALB Fed Bank, Las Cruses & Corrales, NMex, 85. *Exhib:* Baltimore Regional Show, Baltimore Mus Art, Md, 60; Everson Mus Gift Gallery Show, Everson Mus, Syracuse, NY, 82. *Pos:* Craft rep, MNex Arts & Crafts Fair, 79-81; Southwest Arts & Crafts Festival, 88-90. *Teaching:* Instr pottery, Acad Arts, Easton, Md. *Awards:* Merit Award, NMex Clay, 83; Jurors Choice, Acad Arts, Easton, 95; Best of Show, Acad Art Mus, Mem Show, 2003. *Mem:* Am Crafts Coun; Acad Arts, Easton, Md. *Media:* Clay, Painting. *Mailing Add:* PO Box 96 Bozman MD 21612

KRETSCHMER, MELISSA
SCULPTOR
b Santa Monica, Calif, 62. *Study:* Art Ctr Col Design, Pasadena, Calif, BFA, 86, MFA, 88. *Work:* Allianz, Berlin, Ger; Wadsworth Atheneum, Hartford, Conn. *Exhib:* Julian Pretto, NY; Gallerie Tschudi, Glarus, Switz; Art Miami '98, Fla; Long Beach Mus Art, Calif; Vereniging voor Culturele Informatie en Actueel Prentenkabinet, Hasselt, Belg; Wadsworth Atheneum, Hartford, Conn; PS1 Mus, Long Island City, NY; Caledonian Hall, Royal Botanic Garden, Edinburgh; Ace Gallery, Los Angeles, Calif; Geukens & De Vil, Knokke, Belgium; Galerie Frank, Paris; Eric Stark, NY. *Bibliog:* Saul Ostrow & David Pagel (auths), Assemblage, Bricollage and the I: Meg Cranston, Melissa Kretschmer and Maya Lin, Bomb Mag, No 35, spring 91; Juan Cruz (auth), Carl Andre/Melissa Kretschmer, Art Monthly, No 220, 10/98; Duncan MacMillan (auth), Reflected glory, Scotsman, 8/27/98; Collette Chattonpadhyay (auth), Exhibition Review, Sculpture Mag, 6/02; Kyle MacMillan (auth), Exhibit Clearly Compels, Denver Post, 2001; Lilly Wei (auth), Transparent Facade: From New York to Los Angeles, Catalogue Essay, Otis Art Inst Gallery, 99. *Media:* Glass, Tar, Beeswax, Printing Ink, parafin. *Publ:* Claude Briand-Picard (auth), Ready-Made Color: La Couleur Importee, Positions & MCA, 2002. *Dealer:* Arnaud Lefebvre 30 Rue Mazarine 75006 Paris France; Rule Modern & Contemp 111 Broadway Denver CO 80203; Geukens & De Vil Zeedijk 735 8300 Knokke Belgium; Ace Gallery 5514 Wilshire Blvd Los Angele CA

KREZNAR, RICHARD J
PAINTER, SCULPTOR
b Milwaukee, Wis, May 1, 40. *Study:* Univ Wis, BFA; Brooklyn Col, MFA; Inst Allende, Mex. *Work:* Walker Art Ctr, Minneapolis; Milwaukee Art Mus, Wis; Univ Wis, Madison; Colgate Univ, Hamilton, NY; Sidney Lewis Best Co; and others. *Exhib:* Pa Acad Fine Arts, 63; Butler Inst Am Art, 65; Milwaukee Art Mus, 66; Wis Directions, Milwaukee Art Mus, 75; one-man shows, Paley & Lowe Inc, 72 & OK Harris Gallery, NY, 74, 76 & 83, Jefferson Pub Libr, NY, 94, Atelier Gallery, NY, 94 & Stewart Int Airport, NY, 98, Del Art Ctr Gallery, Narrowsburg, NY, 99; Thorpe Intmedia Gallery, Sparkill, NY, 83; Mattingly-Baker Gallery, Dallas, Tex; Century of Alumni Art, Univ Wis, Milwaukee, 85; Del Arts Ctr Gallery, Narrowsburg, NY, 95; Nutshell Arts Ctr, NY, 96 & 98; Liberty Mus & Arts Ctr, NY, 97 & 98; Beck Gallery, Sullivan Co Mus, NY, 98; and others. *Teaching:* Instr studio art courses, Brooklyn Col, 64-73, asst prof, 74-79; instr, Parsons Sch of Design, 78; instr sculpture, Skowhegan Sch Painting & Sculpture, 78; instr sculpture, Philadelphia Col Art, 80-82 & Cooper Union, NY; vis artist, Univ Wis-Milwaukee, 84. *Awards:* Ford Found Purchase Award, 62 & 64; Prizes, Milwaukee Art Ctr, 62, Wis Salon of Art, 63 & Walker Art Ctr, 64. *Media:* Oil. *Publ:* auth At Home with Art, 99. *Mailing Add:* Mauer Rd Callicoon Center NY 12724-0218

KRIEG, CAROLYN RUTH
PHOTOGRAPHER, PAINTER
b Vancouver, Wash, Dec 14, 53. *Study:* Westmont Col, 72-73, American Col in Paris, 73-74, Portland State Univ, 74-75, Univ Calif, Santa Barbara, BA, 76; Marylhurst Col, 84-86; Univ Wash, 87-88. *Work:* Seattle Art Mus; Biblioteque National, Paris, France; Mus Comtemp Photography, Chicago; Portland Art Mus, Oreg; Hofter Mus Art, Helena, Mont; and others. *Comn:* photo mural, Seattle Arts Comn, 90; Wash State Arts Comn, 90, 91, 93, 94, 96. *Exhib:* Women in Photog Int, Acad Fine Arts, Catania, Italy, 90-92; Mementos, William Reagh Los Angeles Photog Ctr, Calif, 93; Predatory Visions, St Lawrence Univ, Canton, NY, 94; one-women shows, Seattle Art Mus, 94, Goddard Ctr Visual & Performing Arts, Ardmore, Okla, 96, Holter Mus, Helena,

Mont, 96, Dahl Cent Gallery & Fine Arts, Rapid City, SDak, 97, Art Mus Missoula, Mont, 2001, Sun Valley Art Ctr, Idaho, 99; NW Int Art Competition, Whatcom Mus Art, Bellingham, Wash, 96; Beyond Novelty, Mus Contemp Photog, Columbia Col, Chicago, 2003; Celebrating Women in the Arts, Frye Art Mus, Seattle, 2003; United States Embassy, Rangoon, 2002-2006. *Pos:* Vpres photo coun, Seattle Art Mus, Wash, 89-92; vis scholar/artist, Univ Mont, Missoula, 93. *Teaching:* Everett Community Col, Wash, 2001; Pacific Luth Univ, Tacoma, Wash, 2001, 2003 & 2006. *Awards:* First Place Purchase Award, Positive/Negative, Slocumb Gallery, 91; Juror's Award Best of Show, Artquake, 93; Juror's Award, Current Works, Soc Contemp Photog, 95. *Bibliog:* Matthew Kangas (auth), Carolyn Krieg at Cliff Michel, Art in Am, 93; Rod Slemmons (auth), Documents NW: Interior Vision, Seattle Art Mus, 94, Predatory Visions, St Louis Univ, Richard F Brush Gallery, 94,; Rod Slemmons (auth), Carolyn Krieg: A Photographic Survey, Traces and Memories, Holter Mus, of Art, Helena MT, 96; Rod Stemmons (auth), Carolyn Krieg: Predator, Prey & Prayer, Augen Gallery (catalog); International Invitational, Benham Gallery, Seattle, 90, Art Works for Aids, NW Aids Found, Seattle, 90; Paint Me a Poem: A Canvas of Words, King Co Pub Art Prog, King County Poetry and Art on Buses, Seattle, 99; Silver Anniversary Art Auction, Missoula Art Mus, 93, 96; Eye of the Camera: Photographs from the 3M Corporate Art Program, Heather Otis, 96, Ten Years 1986-1996, Laura Russo Gallery, 96,; New American Talent, Laura Trippi, Laguna Gloria Art Mus, Austin, TX, 90; Positive/Negative National Exhibition, M K Wegmann, Slocumb Gallery, Johnson City, TN, 91. *Mem:* Ctr Contemp Arts, Seattle. *Media:* Altered Photography; Prints. *Specialty:* Contemporary Art and Prints. *Publ:* Twelfth Annual Works From the Heart, Cheney Cowles Mus, Spokane WA, 97 Human References, Marks of the Artist, Beth Sellars, Seattle Art Commn, 97; Society for Contemporary Photography, Current Works 1995, Leedy Voulkos Art Ctr, Kansas City, MO, 95; Seattle Poets and Photographers: A Millenium Reflection, Rod Slemmons, J T Stewart, Univ of Wash Press, Seattle Arts Commn, 99. *Dealer:* Augen Gallery 817 SW 2d St Portland OR 97204; Lorinda Knight Gallery, 1220 3rd Ave, Seattle, WA, 98101; Robischon Gallery 1740 Wazee St Denver CO 80202; Dana Gallery 246 N Higgins Ave, Missoula, MT 59802; Hanson Howard Gallery 82 N. Main St, Ashland, OR, 97520. *Mailing Add:* 23511 53rd Ave SE Bothell WA 98021-8040

KRIEGER, FLORENCE
SCULPTOR, PAINTER
b New York, NY. *Study:* Cooper Union Art Sch, BA, 35; Nat Acad Fine Arts, 40; Art Students League, 45; study with Jose DeCreeft & Robert Brackman. *Comn:* Medals, Bd Educ, NY, 35; Art Students League, 63; steel & bronze scorpion & lion, Crewe Group of Companies, NY, 70; bronze wall hangings, Elisofon Gallery, NY, 75; bronze menorah & eternal light, Westminster Chapels, NY, 80. *Exhib:* The Dream, Riverside Mus, NY, 52; Peace, Allied Artists, NY, 55; solo exhib, Long Island Univ Gallery, Brooklyn, NY, 63; The Am, Nat Acad Design, NY, 75; Wind Song, Pacem in Terris Gallery, UN, NY, 79; Mother Love, Salmagundi Club, NY, 83; Pray for Peace, Knickerbocker Artists, NY, 84; Women, Audubon Artists, NY. *Pos:* Dir, Fine Arts Sculpture Co, NY; pvt lessons in painting, 86-90. *Teaching:* Instr sculpture, NY Sch Indust Art, 38-42 & Gallery 7, Brooklyn, 80-86. *Awards:* Merit Award, Riverside Mus, Civil Serv Comn, 52; Salmagundi Club Award, Second Ann Exhib, 79; Knickerbocker Mem Award, 34th Ann Exhib, 84; Merit Award, Brooklyn Mus. *Bibliog:* Close Up article, New York Post, 80; John Korez (auth), profile, Villager, 81. *Mem:* Catherine Lorillard Wolfe Art Club Inc; Knickerbocker Artists; Nat Asn Women Painters & Sculptors; Audubon Artists; Am Artists Prof League. *Media:* All. *Publ:* Auth, article, 90th Anniversary Catherine Lorillard Art Club, NY Times. *Dealer:* Ed Elisofon Galleries 115 E 9th St New York NY. *Mailing Add:* Gallery 7 & Art Studios 8759 19th Ave Brooklyn NY 11214

KRIEGER, RUTH M
PAINTER, PRINTMAKER
b Newark, NJ, May 17, 22. *Study:* With Stuart Davis, 41; Moses Soyer, 42; Newark State Col, BA, 43. *Work:* State Mus, Trenton, NJ; Miss Art Asn, Jackson; Rosenberg Libr, Galveston, Tex; Burndy Engineering Co, Norwalk, Conn; Montclair State Col, NJ. *Exhib:* Conn Acad, Hartford Atheneum, Conn, 71; Audubon Artists, Nat Acad Gallery, NY, 71; Boston Printmakers, Boston Mus Fine Arts, Mass, 72; Ann Small Sculpture & Prints, Butler Inst, Youngstown, Ohio, 72; Assoc Artists of NJ, Montclair Art Mus, NJ, 74; Drawing Invitational, Hunterdon Co Art Ctr, Clinton, NJ, 81; Assoc Artists of NJ, Nabisco Galleries, Parsippany, NJ, 81. *Awards:* Clyde L Carnahan Award, 70 & 72; Second in Oils, Nat Acad New York, 70 & Conn Acad Ann, 71. *Mem:* Assoc Artists of NJ (pres 78-80, bd mem 74-); Artists Equity Asn of NJ. *Media:* Oils, Acrylic; Seriagraph, Cliche Verre. *Dealer:* Little Gallery Raleigh NC. *Mailing Add:* 454 Prospect Ave No 142 West Orange NJ 07052

KRIEGER, SUZANNE BARUC
PAINTER, LECTURER
b Jan 31, 1924. *Study:* Studied oil painting with Esphere Slobotkina; self-taught batik. *Work:* Nassau Community Col, NY; Schoenfeld Med Art Asn, New York, NY. *Comn:* Mural, Radium Treatment Room, Franklin Gen Hosp, Valley Stream, NY, 66; murals & decorations, Saddle Rock School Disco, Great Neck, NY 75; vignette for brochure, Designers Showcase, 84 & 85. *Exhib:* Parrish Art Mus, Southhampton, NY, 68; Arts Festival, Nat Arts Pavilion, NY, 70; Festival of Arts, Brooklyn Mus; Art Exhib, Heckscher Mus, Huntington, NY; Versions of Our World Today, Donnell Libr, NY, 80; Salmagundi Club, NY; NY State Pre-Biennial Art Exhib, Lever House, NY, 83; Art Exhib of the 80's, Union Carbide Bldg, NY; Nassau Co Fine Arts Mus. *Pos:* Co own, 1st Co-op Gallery, Long Island, currently. *Teaching:* Instr arts & crafts, Creative Develop Prog, 7-11 Club, Great Neck, NY, 66-71 & Summer Wkshp, Saddle Rock Elem Sch, 66-72; instr seniors art, Continuing Educ Res Ctr, Queens, NY; art progs, Osborne Sch, Rye, NY, currently. *Awards:* First Prize Batik, Salmagundi Club, 75; Second Prize Watercolor, 44th Nat Art League Spring Exhib, 80. *Bibliog:* Jeanne Paris (auth), review, Long Island Press, 70; A Smith (auth), Wall with a view, New York Daily News; Malcom Preston (auth), Unusual work, Newsday, Long Island. *Mem:* Nat Asn Am Pen Women; Long Island Craftsman Guild; Nat Art League; Artists Net-Work Long Island. *Media:* Batik; Pen and Ink. *Publ:* Contribr, Little Neck Then and Now, Banner Publ, 84. *Dealer:* Glass Gallery 315 Central Park W New York NY 10025. *Mailing Add:* 40 Schenck Ave Great Neck NY 11021-3641

KRIEMELMAN, SHEILA M
PAINTER, EDUCATOR
b Honolulu, Hawaii, Sept 15, 41. *Study:* Univ Mo, BS(art educ), 63; Col New Rochelle, MS(studio art), 83; Studies with Roy Lichtenstein, Larry Rivers & Eric Fischl, Long Island Univ, 87. *Work:* Bell Atlantic Corp, Paramus, NJ; Honolulu Acad Art, Hawaii; Iona Col, New Rochelle, NY; Quigley Publ, Larchmont, NY; and other corp collections. *Comn:* Wall mural (collab with Leroy Cox), Arthur Murray Studios, Wilmette, Ill, 77; wall mural, Willard Sch, Evanston, Ill, 78; canvas mural (17' x 12'), Mussavi Gallery, Soho, NY, 87. *Exhib:* Nat Asn Women Artists, 93-96; Art of the Northeast USA, Silvermine Galleries, Conn, 94; Dachau 1933-1945, Wildcliff Ctr Arts, New Rochelle, NY, 94; KOA Gallery, Honolulu, Hawaii, 95; Klutznik Mus, Washington, 97. *Teaching:* Assoc prof fine art, Iona Col, New Rochelle, NY. *Awards:* Best in Show, Mamaroneck Artists Guild Juried Show, 83; Molly Canady Award, Nat Asn Women Artists 104th Juried Show, 93; Grace Huntley Pugh Award (First Place), Mamaroneck Artists Guild 36th Ann Exhib, 94. *Bibliog:* Ed McCormack (auth), Sheila Kriemelman & the art of social witness, Artspeak, 4/94; Catherine Drillis (auth), Triumph of the human spirit, Manhattan Arts, 4/94; Deborah Scates (dir), Dachau, An Artists Response, Va Cable TV, 4/94. *Mem:* Nat Asn Women Artists; NY Soc Women Artists; NY Artists Equity; Col Art Asn; Mamaroneck Artist Guild Inc (bd mem, 81-91). *Media:* Acrylic, Watercolor. *Publ:* Auth, Craighead, the litany of the great river, cross currents, Am Asn Relig & Intellectual Life, 92. *Mailing Add:* 148 Greene St New York NY 10010-3288

KRIENKE, KENDRA CLIVER See Daniel, Kendra Cliver Krienke

KRIESBERG, IRVING
PAINTER
b Chicago, Ill, Mar 13, 19. *Study:* Art Inst Chicago, BFA, 41; Escuela de Artes Plasticas, Esmeralda, Mexico City; NY Univ, MA, 72. *Work:* Mus Mod Art, Whitney Mus Am Art, Jewish Mus, NY; Detroit Inst Art; Chase Manhattan Bank & Ciba-Geigy, NY; Cincinnati Mus Art; Rose Mus Boston; Nat Mus Am Art, & Corcoran Mus, Washington, DC; Kresge Art Mus, Lansing MI; National mus of Am Art, DC; Butler Inst, Ohio. *Comn:* Mural, Beth Emet, Evanston, Ill, 72; Peace Dove Banner, NY Cult Ctr, 82. *Exhib:* One-man shows, St Louis Mus Art, Mo, 53, Everson Mus, 80, Rose Mus, Boston, 81 & Washington Univ Art Gallery, St Louis, 82; 16 Americans, Mus Mod Art, NY, 54; 10 Independents, Guggenheim Mus, NY, 71; Emotional Impact, Am Mus Asn, 86-87. *Teaching:* Prof painting, Yale Grad Sch, 62-70 & State Univ NY, 71-76, Columbua Univ, 77-79. *Awards:* Fulbright Grant, 65-66; Guggenheim Mem, 76; Nat Endowment Arts, 81; NY Found, 91; Pollock-Krasner Award, 2002. *Bibliog:* Allan Kaprow (auth), Kriesberg & Nature, Art Int, 6/64; Dore Ashton (auth), Kriesberg Dintenfass Gallery, 78; Geo Preston (auth), Kriesberg, Arts Mag, 12/87; Art in America, Elisa Decker. *Mem:* Nat Acad. *Media:* Oil, Sculpture, Clay. *Publ:* Auth, Looking at Pictures, Ford Found, 56; Art, The Visual Experience, Pitman, 65; Working with Color, Van Nostrand Reinhold, 86. *Dealer:* Peter Finday Gallery 41 E Madison New York NY 10022; Lori Bookstein Gallery, 37 West 57St, NY 10019. *Mailing Add:* 32 Washington Sq W #7W New York NY 10011-9156

KRIMS, LES
PHOTOGRAPHER, CONCEPTUAL ARTIST
b Brooklyn, NY, Aug 16, 42. *Study:* Cooper Union, New York, BFA; Pratt Inst, Brooklyn, MFA. *Work:* Mus Mod Art, NY; Nat Gallery Can, Ottawa; Musee Nat d'Art Moderne, Centre Georges Pompidou, Paris; George Eastman House, Rochester, NY; Bibliot Nat, Paris. *Exhib:* Le nu photographié (catalog), Galerie d'Art du Consul Gen Bouche-du-Rhone, Aix-en-Provence, France; Making Light: Wit and Humor in Phtoography, The Francis Lehman Loeb Art Ctr, Vassar Col, Poughkeepsie, NY, 2000; Photographs for Sick Kids, The Royal Hosp for Sick Children, Edinburgh, Scotland, 2001; The Peter C Bunnell Collection, Princeton Univ Art Mus, 2002; One man shows, Les Krims, Forum de l'Image, Toulouse, France, 2002; Revelation: Representations of Christ in Photog, Hotel de Sully, Paris & The Israel Mus, Jerusalem, 2002; The Photographers Edge, Carl Solway Gallery, Cincinatti, 2002; Hexenwahn: Ängste der Neuzeit, (catalog), Deutsches Historisches Mus, Berlin, 2002; two person, Form and Femininity, The MacLaren Art Ctr, Barrie, Ont, 2003; Venus in Furs, Neue Galerie am Landsmus Joanneum, Graz, Austria, 2003. *Teaching:* prof art, Buffalo State Col, 69-81, prof, 81-. *Awards:* State Univ NY Res Found Grant & Grant-in-Aid, 70 & 71; Nat Endowment Arts Fel, 71, 72 & 76; NY State Coun Arts Grant, 71, 73 & 75. *Bibliog:* Jacques Bloesch (auth), Jacques Désires de photographies, Le Scorpion Bleu, Geneva, 2001; Alain Roger (auth), Nus et paysages, Edits Aubier, 2001; Les Krims, Actes Sud, Arles, France, 11/2005. *Media:* Dye Coupler, Silver Prints; Inkjet Print. *Publ:* Illusr, Grafisk Form Mag, 90; The Sun, Tokyo, Japan, 91; contribr & illusr, Det Iscenesatte Fotografi (by Mette Sandbye), Forlaget Politisk Revy, Copenhagen, Denmark, 92; illusr, Foto Taschenkalender, Atium Verlag/Michale Klant Publ, Heidelberg, Ger, 92; contribr & illusr, Images, Centre de la Photographie Geneve, Geneva, Switz, 93; Le Chat Essentiellement, Paris, Nathan/Delpire, 2000. *Mailing Add:* 187 Linwood Ave Buffalo NY 14209

KRINSKY, CAROL HERSELLE
EDUCATOR, HISTORIAN
b Brooklyn, NY, June 2, 37. *Study:* Smith Col, BA, 57; NY Univ, MA, 60, PhD, 65. *Teaching:* Prof fine arts, NY Univ, 65-. *Awards:* Millard Meiss Publ Award, 88; Design Arts Grant, Nat Endowment Arts, 94; Distinguished Teaching of Art Hist Award, Col of Art Asn, 2004. *Mem:* Soc Archit Historians (NY chap pres, 79-81, nat

pres, 84-86); Col Art Asn; Int Ctr Medieval Art; Columbia Sem on the City (co-chmn, 93-95); Byzantine Studies Conference, Soc Am City Regional Planning Hist. *Res:* Recent native American architecture; architecture in New York and Chicago; European synagogue architecture; Representing group identity in modern architecture; 15th C Flemish Painting. *Publ:* Vitruvius De Architectura, Wilhelm Fink Verlag, 69; Rockefeller Center, Oxford Univ Press, 78; Synagogues of Europe: Architecture, History & Meaning, Archit Hist Found, MIT Press, 84; Gordon Bunshaft of Skidmore, Owings & Merrill, Archit Hist Found, MIT Press, 88; Contemporary Native American Architecture: Cultural Regeneration & Creativity, Oxford Univ Pr, 96

KROLL, DAVID
PAINTER
b Phoenix, Ariz, Feb 27, 56. *Study:* San Francisco Art Inst, BFA, 80; Art Inst Chicago, MFA, 86. *Work:* First Nat Bank Chicago; Gund Collection, Cambridge, Mass; Microsoft Corp, Redmond, Wash; Philip Morris Mgt Corp, NY; Prudential Ins Co, Newark, NJ. *Exhib:* One-man exhibs, Sch Art Inst Chicago, 85, NAME Gallery, Chicago, 88, Betsy Rosenfield Gallery, Chicago, 89, 91 & 93, Betsy Rosenfield Gallery, Chicago Int Art Expo, 90 & Jamison/Thomas Gallery, NY, 92; Revelations: Artists Look at Religion, Gallery 2, Sch Art Inst Chicago, 91; Still Alive: Contemp Still Life, Rockford Col Art Gallery, Ill, 91; Light, Milwaukee Inst Art & Design, 92; Artfair/Seattle, Betsy Rosenfield Gallery, Seattle, 92; From America's Studio: Drawing New Conclusions, Betty Rymer Gallery, Sch Art Inst Chicago, 92; May 1992, Betsy Rosenfield Gallery, Chicago Int Art Expo, 92; Nature Fabrilis, Steibel Modern, NY, 92; and others. *Teaching:* Vis artist painting, Art Inst Chicago, 86-91. *Bibliog:* Wade Wilson (auth), David Kroll, New Art Examiner, 12/91; Susan Snodgrass (auth), David Kroll at Betsy Rosenfield Gallery, Art Am, 1/92; Holland Cotter (auth), Nature Fabrilis, NY Times, 7/3/92. *Media:* Oil on Linen. *Mailing Add:* c/o Lisa Sette Gallery 4142 N Marshall Wy Scottsdale AZ 85251

KROLL, LYNNE FRANCINE
PAINTER, COLLAGE ARTIST
b San Mateo, Calif, Dec 18, 43. *Study:* Brooklyn Community Col, AAS, 63; Rockland Found Arts, 68; workshops with numerous masters, 79-2006; Ed Betts Master Class Watermedia Juried, 93Wolf Kahn, 98, Anna Tomchyk, 99, Maggie Taylor's Digital Collage, 2002. *Work:* Broward Co Main Libr, Ft Lauderdale, Fla; Coral Springs Med Ctr, Fla; Anne Kolb Nature Ctr, Hollywood, Fla; Jane Vorrhees Zimmerli Art Mus; and others; Intl Mus Collage, Assemblage & Construction, Mexico; Artecolle, the Mus& Gallery of Collage Sergines, France. *Comn:* Brass welded copper doors depicting external flame, Mania Nudell Holocaust Learning Ctr, Davie, Fla; brass welded copper doors, Belle Terre Bldgs, Coral Springs, Sunrise, Davie & Boca Raton, Fla, 77. *Exhib:* New Art, S Fla, Fel Recipients, Mus Contemp Art, Miami, 98; Nat Soc Painters in Casein & Acrylic, Salmagundi Club, NY, 98, 2001-06; Under the Influence, Ft Lauderdale Mus Art, 2000; Birth of Widsom, Soc Layerists in Multimedia, Santa Fe, NMex, 2000; Millennium Collection, UN, 2002; Wish You Were Here, Cork Gallery, Lincolm Ctr for Performing Arts, New York City, 2002; Catharine Lorillard Wolfe Art Club, 107th Natl Exhibit, Natl Arts Club, NY, 2003; In the Spotlight, and Award Winners Invitational, Nat Asn Women Artists, Fifth Ave Gallery, NY, 2003; Allied Artists of Am, 89th, 90th, 91st St, Ann, 2002-2004; Am Watercolor Soc 138th, 139th Ann Internat Exhib, Salmagundi, Club, NY, 2005, 06; Watercolor USA, 2006; Springfield Art Mus, Mo. *Awards:* South Fla Cult Consortium Fel Award, Nat Endowment Arts, 98; 1st Pl Watermedia Award, Catharine Lorillard Wolfe Art Club Mem Exhib, 2006; Art Students League NY Award, Audubon Artists 63d Ann Exhib, 2006; Dr Irving Silver Meml Award, Nat Assoc Women Artists 115th Ann Exhib. *Bibliog:* Artists Profile, Broward Cult Quart, Spring 98; Artists Profile, Art Trends Mag, Glycee Ed, Aug/Sep 98; How Rutgers Women's Collection Grows, NY Times, 9/15/2002. *Mem:* Nat Asn Women Artists; Soc Layerists Multi-Media; signature mem Tex Watercolor Soc; Nat Asn Painters Casein & Acrylic; Catharine Lorillard Wolf Art Club; Nat Collage Soc; Fla Watercolor Soc; Audobon Artists; Allied Artists Am. *Media:* Mixed Media, Computer, Photography, Watercolor. *Publ:* Auth, Abstracts in Watercolor, 96, Painting: The Best of Watercolor Composition, 97 & Best of Watercolor I, II, III, 95, 96, 98, Rockport Publ; auth, Bridging Time & Space, Artwork & Essays on Layered Art, Soc Layerists Multimedia, 99; Best of Photography, Pub Photographers Forum, 98, 99, 2000, 2001, 2002; Collage in All Dimensions, Nat Collage Soc, 2006. *Dealer:* Orlando Mus Art, Gallery Gift Shop, Orlando, FL; Aquarian Age Boca Raton FL. *Mailing Add:* 3971 NW 101st Dr Coral Springs FL 33065

KRONSNOBLE, JEFFREY MICHAEL
PAINTER, EDUCATOR
b Milwaukee, Wis, Feb 9, 39. *Study:* Univ Wis-Milwaukee, BS, 61; Univ Mich, Ann Arbor, MFA, 63. *Work:* Mus Fine Arts, St Petersburg, Fla; Addison Gallery Am Art, Andover, Mass; Nat Gallery Art, Washington, DC; Fla Capitol Bldg; New Orleans Mus Art; and others. *Comn:* Portrait, Univ S Fla Med Sch. *Exhib:* Chicago & Vicinity Exhib, Art Inst Chicago, 61-63; one-man shows, New Orleans Mus Art, 67, Univ Fla, Gainesville, 75 & ACA Galleries, NY, 79, 81, 84 & 86; 25 Yr Retrospective Exhib, Polk Mus Art, Lakeland, Fla, 90. *Teaching:* Prof art, Univ SFla, 63-. *Awards:* Thomas B Clarke Prize, Nat Acad Design, New York, 80; William A Paton Prize, Nat Acad Design, New York, 81. *Bibliog:* Barbara Gallati (auth), Jefferey Kronsnoble, Arts, 12/81; Katherine Duncan (auth), Jeffrey Kronsnoble, A Retrospective, Catalogue Essay, Polk Mus Art. *Media:* Mixed, Oil. *Dealer:* Clayton Galleries Tampa FL. *Mailing Add:* PO Box 302 Mountain City GA 30562

KRONZON, ZIVA
PRINTMAKER, SCULPTOR
b Haifa, Israel. *Study:* Bezalel Acad Art, Jerusalem, student. *Work:* Nat Mus Women in Arts, Washington, DC; Israel Nat Mus, Jerusalem, Israel; Sprengel Mus, Hanover, Ger; Herbert Johnson Mus, Ithaca, NY; Art Student League, NY. *Exhib:* Terra Interdicta II, Blanis Mus, Mongevideo, Uruguay, 96; Parer Sculr Jures, Gerhard Harcks House, Bremen, Ger, 97; Terra Interdicta I, Yad Levanim, Petach Tikva, Israel, 98; New Works, Ashdod Mus, Israel, 98. *Awards:* Herman Struck Prize, oil painting, Bezalel Acad Art, 88; HRCA Sculpture Award, Hudson River Mus, 89; Inernat Art Critic Award, Montecideo, Uruguay, 90. *Media:* Paper. *Publ:* Michael Brenson (auth), Ziva Kronzon, NY Times, 88; Martha Viale (auth), Infrequent Expressions, El Pais, Montevideo, 96; Karin Stelwag (auth), Lehm Und Blut, Stutgart Zeitung, 98. *Mailing Add:* 315 E 86th St Apt 20M New York NY 10028

KROPF, JOAN R
CURATOR, LECTURER
b Cleveland, Ohio, Aug 4, 49. *Study:* Cleveland Art Inst; Cooper Sch Art; Cuyahoga Community Col; St Petersburg Jr Col; Eckerd Col, BA; Calif State Univ, MA;. *Collection Arranged:* Cancelled Graphic Plates, 75; Hiram College Graphics Show, 76; Erotic Art by Dali, 76; Dali's Anamorphoses, 77; Dali/Hasman Photog Exhib, 78; Important Dali Statements & Surrealist Documents, 79; Women: Dali's View, 79; Homage to Gala, 82; Secret Life Drawings, 82; Flor Dali, 83; Lucas Collection, 85; Dali's Divine Comedy, 85; Dali Sculpture, 86; Surrealist Drawings, 88; Many Faces of Dali-Lacroix Photographs, 89; The Alchemy of the Philosophers, 90; Dali's Graphic Art, 92; Homage to the Masters: Vision Nouvelle, 93; Dali The Early Years, 94; Dali by the Book, 96; Dali by Design, 97; Surrelism in Am, 1998; The Mouse Adventure, 2000; Dali Objects/Dali Fetishes, 2002; Dali in Am Collection, 2004; Dali Revealed, 2005; Dali Under the Influence, 2005. *Pos:* Asst deputy dir, Salvador Dali Mus, Cleveland, 71-75, dir, 76-82, cur, 83-89, co-exec dir, 90 & cur, collection, 92-, deputy dir, 2000-. *Mem:* Am Asn Mus. *Publ:* Auth, Secret Life Drawings, 82 & Flor Dali (photographs), 83, Salvador Dali Mus; auth, Dali's Divine Comedy, Surrealist Drawings, Docent Training Manual; Dali's Animal Crackers; collabr The Official Catalog of Graphic Works of Salvador Dali, Dali Japan, 99; Dali Objects, 2002; Dali, Jadan, 2006. *Mailing Add:* c/o Salvador Dali Mus 1000 Third St S St Petersburg FL 23701

KRUEGER, LOTHAR DAVID
PAINTER, EDUCATOR
b Two Rivers, Wis, Sept 19, 19. *Study:* Milwaukee State Teachers Col, Wis, BS, 42; Univ Wis-Madison, MS, 47; Univ Iowa, with Mauricio Lassansky in printmaking, grad, 50; Ohio State Univ, Columbus, grad art hist, 53. *Work:* Wis Mem Union, Madison; Am Inst Architects, Ark Arts Ctr, First Nat Bank Little Rock & Pulaski Savings & Loan, Little Rock, Ark. *Exhib:* 6 Ann Exhibs Art, Springfield Art Mus, Mo, 48-67; 9 Midwestern Delta Exhibs, Ark Art Ctr, Little Rock, 60-75; St Paul Art Ctr, 63 & 64-65; 10th Midsouth Exhib, Brooks Mem Gallery, Memphis, Tenn, 65; Ann, Ark Arts Ctr, Little Rock, 80; 22nd Ann, Oklahoma Arts Ctr, 80; and others. *Collection Arranged:* Am Inst Architects Art Collection, Ark Artist Exhib, traveling since 66; Arts, Crafts & Design Fair, Ark Distinguished Artists Collectors Exhib, 74. *Pos:* Vpres, Ark Educ Asn, 65-66, pres, 66-68. *Teaching:* Instr painting & drawing & ed, Northern Iowa Univ, Cedar Falls, 47-51; prof painting & drawing, Univ Ark, Fayetteville, 53-81, prof emer, 81-. *Awards:* First Place, Ark Artist Exhib, Am Inst Architects, 60-61 & 77; Honorable Mention, 12th Ann Delta Regional, Ark Arts Ctr, 69; Purchase Prize, Ark Arts Ctr, 80. *Bibliog:* Edgar A Albin (auth), An expert in abstract expressionism, Ark Democrat, 61 & The Arts, Sunday News & Leader, Springfield, Mo, 72. *Media:* Acrylic, Watercolor. *Mailing Add:* c/o North Dak Mus Art PO Box 7305 Grand Forks ND 58202

KRUG, HARRY ELNO
PRINTMAKER, EDUCATOR
b Oshkosh, Wis, Aug 20, 30. *Study:* Univ Wis-Milwaukee, BFA; Univ Wis-Madison, MS. *Work:* Libr of Cong, Washington, DC; Nelson-Atkins Art Gallery, Kansas City, Mo; US Info Agency; Springfield Art Mus, Mo; Ohio Univ Galleries. *Exhib:* 22nd Am Color Print Exhib, Am Color Print Soc, 63; 6th Nat Print Exhib, Silvermine Guild Artists, New Canaan, Conn, 67; 19th Ann Exhib, Boston Mus Fine Arts, Mass, 68; Teacher-Artist Today, State Univ NY Col Oswego, 69; Hopman, Krug, Ecker, Galerie Feursee, Stuttgart, 70. *Pos:* Crafts dir, Spec Serv, Ger. *Teaching:* Prof & chmn printmaking, Pittsburg State Univ, currently. *Awards:* Mid-Am Ann Purchase Award, Nelson-Atkins Art Mus, Kansas City, 60; Sonia Watter Award, Am Color Print Soc, Pa, 62; Prize for Graphics, Jersey City Mus, NJ, 68. *Bibliog:* Kenneth W Anvil (auth), Serigraphy, Prentice Hall, 65; John Ross & Clare Romano (auth), The Complete Screenprint & Lithograph. 72; John Ross & Clare Romano (auth), The Complete Printmaker, Free Press, 72; Screen Printing, Watson-Suptill Publications, 73. *Mem:* Boston Printmakers; Philadelphia Print Club. *Media:* Serigraphy, Lithography. *Mailing Add:* 1113 S 220th St Pittsburg KS 66762-6851

KRUGER, BARBARA
CONCEPTUAL ARTIST, FILM CRITIC
b Newark, NJ, Jan 26, 45. *Study:* Syracuse Univ, 65; Parsons Sch Design; Sch Visual Arts, 66. *Work:* Floor mosaics in five locations, Fisher Col of Bus, Ohio State Univ, Columbus, 98; Op Ed page, The NY Times, 7/26/98; display windows, Saks Fifth Avenue, NY, 2000; Untitled, banner billboards at 8th Ave/42nd St and Washington St/West Side Hwy, Pub Art Fund & Whitney Mus Am Art, 2000. *Exhib:* solo exhibs, Monika Spruth Gallery, Koln, WGer, 87, 90, Nat Art Gallery, Wellington, New Zealand, 88, Mary Boone Gallery, NY, 89, 91, 94, 97, Galerie Bebert, Rotterdam, The Neth, 89, Fred Hoffman Gallery, Santa Monica, Calif, 89, Duke Univ Mus Art, Durham, NC, 90, Parrish Art Mus, Southampton, NY, Mus Contemp Art, Los Angeles, 99, Galerie Yvon Lambert, Paris, 99, Whitney Mus Am Art, NY, 2000, South London Gallery, 01, Ctr Arte Contemp, Siena, Italy, 02; Castello di Rivoli, Turin, Italy, 89; Ctr Georges Pompidou, Paris, France, 89; Kalamazoo Inst Arts, Mich, 98; Ga Mus Art, Athens, 99; Galerie Yvon Lambert, Paris, 2000; Mus des Beaux-Arts, Lille, France, 2002, Schirn Kunsthalle, Frankfurt, Ger, 2002. *Collection Arranged:* Pictures and Promises, The Kitchen, New York, 81; Artists' Use of Language, Franklin Furnace,

New York, 83; Creative Perspectives in American Photography, Hallwall's Gallery, Buffalo, NY, 83. *Teaching:* Vis artist, Calif Inst Art, Art Inst Chicago & Univ Calif, Berkeley; prof art Univ Calif Los Angeles, currently. *Awards:* Creative Artists Serv Progr Grant, 76-77; Nat Endowments Arts Grant, 83-84; Golden Lion Award for Liftetime Achievement, Venice Biennial, 2005. *Bibliog:* Robert C Morgan (auth), Barbara Kruger, Arts Mag, 4/89; Carol Squires (auth), Diversionary (Syn) tactics/Barbara Kruger has a way with words, Bijutsu Techo, 4/89; Therese Lichtenstein (auth), Barbara Kruger's After-Effects: The Politics of Mourning, Art and Text, 7/89; Frederick Garber (auth), Re Positioning: The Syntaxes of Barbara Kruger, Univ Hartford Studies in Lit, 9/89; Maia Damianovic (auth), Scandali a New York, Tema Celeste, Jan 98; David Frankel (auth), Barbara Kruger, Artforum, Feb 98; Carissa Katz (auth), Barbara Kruger: The Place of Art, The East Hampton Star, 7/23/98; Erica-Lynn Gambino (auth), Barbara Kruger, The Parrish Art Mus, Sculpture, 1/99; David L Jacobs (auth), Gendered Engendered, Camerawork, Oct 99; Suzanne Muchnic (auth), Barbara Kruger, Art News, Jan 2000; Lane Relyea (auth), Barbara Kruger, Artforum, Feb 2000; Diane Armitage (auth), Barbara Kruger Q & A, The Magazine (Santa Fe), May 2000; Anne Wehr (auth), Ism she lovely?, Time Out New York, 7/6/2000; Kim Levin (auth), Shortlist: Barbara Kruger, The Village Voice, 2000; Hilton Kramer (auth), Greed Is Really Bad, Says Designer Kruger, The New York Observer, 8/21/2000; Marie-Pierre Nakamura (auth), Barbara Kruger, Art Actuel, Sept 2000; Eric Miles (auth), Barbara Kruger, Tema Celeste, Oct 2000; Claire Bishop (auth), Interview with Barbara Kruger, Make, Dec 2000; Raphael Rubinstein (auth), Barbara Kruger at the Whitney Museum, Art in America, Mar 2001; and many others. *Media:* Mixed. *Publ:* Auth, Picture/Readings, 79; No Progress in Pleasure, 82; contribr, film criticism, Artforum. *Mailing Add:* 24 Lancaster Ln Monsey NY 10952

KRUKOWSKI, LUCIAN
PAINTER, EDUCATOR
b Brooklyn, NY, Nov 22, 29. *Study:* Brooklyn Col, BA, 52; Yale Univ, BFA, 55; Pratt Inst, MS, 58, Washington Univ, St Louis, PhD, 77. *Work:* St Louis Art Mus, Mo; Fogg Mus, Mass; San Francisco Art Mus, Calif. *Comn:* Outdoor wall painting, Nat Endowment Arts, St Louis, 72; outdoor wall painting, HBE Corp Bldg, St Louis, 83. *Exhib:* Staempfli Gallery, 58 & 62 & Cee-je Gallery, NY, 67, Loretto Hilton Gallery, 70, Moore Gallery, St Louis, 75 & 78 & Burns Gallery, St Louis, 81; Long Island Univ, NY, 85; Messing Gallery, St Louis, Mo, 92. *Teaching:* Prof art, Pratt Inst, 55-69, chmn dept fine arts, 67-69; prof art & dean, Sch Fine Arts, Washington Univ, 69-77, prof philos, 77-. *Mem:* Am Soc Aesthetics; Am Philos Asn. *Publ:* A basis for attributions of art, J Aesthetics Art Criticism, fall 80 & Artworks that end and objects that endure, winter 81; commentary on Beardsley's fiction as representation, Synthese 46, 81; Adorno & atonal music (rev), Bucknell, 84; Art and Concept, Univ Mass Press, 87; Aesthetic Legacies, Temple Univ Press, 92. *Mailing Add:* 665 S Skinner Blvd Apt 10 D St Louis MO 63105-2350

KRULIK, BARBARA S
DIRECTOR, MUSEOLOGIST
b June 13, 55. *Study:* Pa State Univ, Univ Park, BA (art hist), 76; Reinwardt Acad, Amsterdam Sch Arts, The Neth. *Collection Arranged:* Oil Sketches from the Ecole des Beaux Arts, 87; Painters by Painters, Portraits from the Uffizi Gallery, 88; 19th Century Polish Painting, 88; Women in Mex, 90; Helene Schjerfbeck: Finland's Modernist Rediscovered, 92; Hallowed Haunts: The Drawings & Watercolors of Charles Addams, 91-92; Darkness & Light: Swedish Drypoint Etchings, 93; Artists By Artists, Forum Gallery, 93; Sidney Simon: A Retrospective, Provincetown Art Asn, Mass, 95; Derriere Guard: An Exhibition, Kitchen Ctr Video, Music & Dance, NY, 97; Radical Views: George Grosz and Philip Evergood, Forum Gallery, NY, 98. *Pos:* Asst dir, 83-89, Nat Acad Design, interim dir, 89-90, deputy dir, 90-92; guest cur, New York City AIA Archit Design Awards exhib, 86, 87 & 90; assoc dir, Forum Gallery, 92-94; dir, Grad Sch Figurative Art, NY Acad Art, 94-97; mgr, Magpie Music Dance Co, 2001-; mgr, Warren & Consorten, 2006-. *Teaching:* Guest lectr, Fashion Inst Technol & Mus Studies Prog, 87 & 88; Univ Pa, continuing educ, 92, Kalamazoo Art Inst, 93; guest lectr, mus managment, Reinwardt Acad, Amsterdam, Neth, 99 & 2005. *Mem:* Am Asn Mus; Int Coun Mus; Initiative Group, Exhib Platform. *Publ:* Auth, Raphael Soyer, Forum Gallery, New York, 95; writer, Art Dealers Asn Am Report, summer 96 & spring 97; Marjukka Kaminen, Galleria Bronda, Helinski, Finland, 98; Radical Views, Forum Gallery, NY, 98; Jules Pascin, Forum Gallery, NY, 2001; Sean Henry, exhib catalog, Berkely Square Gallery, London & Forum Gallery, NY, 2001; contribr, Patrick Huse & the object as data carrier, Stenersen Mus, Oslo, Norway, 2001; Charles Matton, Forum Gallery, 2002; From Monumentality to Intimacy, Diana Moore exhib catalog, Forum Gallery, NY, 2004; Questioning Beauty: attraction & repulsion in the art of Silvia B., Sculpture Magazine, 7/2005. *Mailing Add:* 2e Jacob van Campenstraat 112 II Amsterdam 1073XX Netherlands

KRUPP, BARBARA D
PAINTER
b Elyria, Ohio, July 1, 42. *Study:* NY Sch Art, with Graham Nixon, Lowell Ellsworth AWS & Fred Leach AWS, 97. *Work:* Massillon Mus Art, Massillon, Ohio; Mansfield Art Ctr, Mansfield, Ohio; Osceola Bd City Commissioners, Osceola, Fla; Five Points Plaza Bldg & Mike Bieber, Sarasota, Fla. *Comn:* 6 pieces Art Collection, John Calys, Leesbury, Va, 2006. *Exhib:* Not Just Another Perfect Face, Mansfield Art Ctr, Mansfield, Ohio, 97; Salon D'Out, Isabelle Duncan Mus, Paris, France; Poems of Reality, Ariel Gallery, New York, NY; Gasparilla Arts, Tampa Mus, Tampa, Fla, 2004; Colors, Orange Ctr for Contemp Arts, Orange, Calif, 2005; Blooms of Summer & Abstract Nature, Dabbert Gallery, Sarasota, Fla, 2006. *Awards:* Best Show, Piegon Key Art Festival, 2004; Best Show, Marquette, Mich, 2006. *Mem:* Rockport Art Asn; NAIA; Ohio Arts & Crafts Counc. *Media:* Acrylic. *Mailing Add:* 2125 Seagrape Dr Vero Beach FL 32963

KRUSKAMP, JANET
PAINTER
b Grants Pass, Ore, Dec 10, 34. *Study:* Chouinard Art Inst, Los Angeles and pvt study. *Work:* Rosicrucian Egyptian Mus, San Jose & Triton Mus Art, Santa Clara, Calif; Springville Mus Art, Utah; Alexandria Mus Art, La; La Grange Col, Ga; and others. *Comn:* Seven paintings, Cowden Ranch, 74; painting, Burger King, 75; Challenge-Cook Brothers, 76; two paintings, Jet Air, Inc, 76; painting, Anning-Johnson & Co, 89; Bicentennial Event, comn by San Jose Bicentennial, 76; Bentley House Publ, 99. *Exhib:* Soc Western Artists Ann, M H De Young Mus, San Francisco, 71; Soc Western Artists, Rosicrucian Egyptian Mus, 72; Mainstreams, Marietta Col, Ohio, 75; solo exhibs, Rosicrucian Egyptian Mus Gallery, 70, 73, 76 & 86, Springville Mus Art, Utah, 78, San Jose Mus Art, 80 & Charles & Emma Frye Mus Art, Washington, 74; San Jose Mus Art, Calif, 80; Redding Mus Art, Calif, 80; and others. *Pos:* artist, juror. *Teaching:* pvt instr, 40 yrs. *Awards:* Soc Western Artists Ann First Place Oils, 70; Trustees' Award & Andy Trophy, Grand Galleria Nat Art Competition, Seattle, 72, First Prize & Purchase Prize, 73; and others. *Bibliog:* Janice Loveos (auth), Janet Kruskamps America, Southwest Art, 6/75; Ted Bredt (auth), Beauty From the Commonpalce, Calif Today; Robert Sher (auth), Portraits to Products, Abbink Comm Group, 2/2003. *Mem:* Nat Mus Women Arts, Washington, DC; Los Gatos Art Asn (pres, 69). *Media:* Oil, Egg Tempera, Watercolor. *Publ:* Painting From Your Own Photos. Another View, Northlight Mag, 2/79. *Dealer:* Bentley Publishing Group Walnut Creek CA

KUANG, TING SHAO
PAINTER
b Beijing, Oct 7, 39, US citizen. *Study:* Cent Acad Arts & Crafts, Beijing, BA, 62. *Work:* Ginza Art Mus, Tokyo, Japan; Yunnan Fine Art Mus, China; Nat Mus China, Beijing; Shanghai Fine Art Mus, China; Great Hall of the People, Beijing, China. *Comn:* The Beautiful & Mysterious XiShuang Ban Na, Great Hall of the People, Beijing, 79; Light of Human Rights, UN, 93; Motherhood, UN, 94; cover & stamps, 4th Conf Women UN 50th Anniversary, 95. *Exhib:* Solo exhibs, Ginza Art Mus, Tokyo, Japan, 88, Tainan Fine Art Mus, China, 91, Historic Mus Art, Beijing, China, 92 & Shanghai Mus Art, China, 92. *Teaching:* Oil painting, Traditional Chinese painting, Etch-Yunnan Inst Arts, Kunming, 62-80; lectr, Dept Visual Arts, Univ Calif Los Angeles Exten, 83. *Awards:* Best of Show, Univ SC Martin Luther King Fine Arts Competition, 84; Gold Key of Milbrea, Mayor Mountain View, 94. *Bibliog:* Anna Macdonnell (auth), Segal Fine Art, 89; Tetsuro Murobushi (auth), Kodansha Ltd, 89; Ann Wicks (auth), People's Publ House, 91. *Mem:* Chinese Artists Asn (chmn, 91-). *Media:* Chinese Stone Painting. *Publ:* Contribr, The Art of Ting Shao Kuang, Kodansha, 89; Ting Shao Kuang Serigraphs, Segal Fine Art, 91; Painting Paradise-The Art of Ting Shao Kuang, People's Fine Art Publ House, 92; Ting Shao Kuang Serigraphs, Dainppon Printing Co, 94

KUCHAR, KATHLEEN ANN
PAINTER, EDUCATOR
b Meadow Grove, Nebr, Feb 4, 42. *Study:* Kearney State Col, BA, 63; Ft Hays Kans State Col, MS, 66; Brooklyn Mus Art Sch, Max Beckmann Mem scholar, 66-67, with Reuben Tam, 67; Wichita State Univ, MFA, 74; Santa Reparata Graphic Art Ctr, Florence, Italy, 91. *Work:* Wichita State Univ Art Gallery; Ft Hays State Univ Art Gallery; Nebr Arts Collection; Crescent Cardboard Co Collection; Biblical Arts Ctr, Dallas, Tex. *Exhib:* Watercolor USA, Springfield Art Mus, Mo, 68, 79, 80, 84, 85, 91 & 94; one-person shows, Nat Design Ctr, NY, 68 & Biblical Arts Ctr, Dallas, Tex, 88; Am Watercolor Soc Exhib, NY, 79; group show, Ariel Gallery, NY, 88. *Teaching:* Instr art, Minden Pub Schs, Nebr, 63-65; assoc prof painting-design, Ft Hays State Univ, 67-78, prof, 78-2001. *Awards:* Pilot Award Outstanding Prof at Ft Hays State Univ, Hays, Kans, 80; Nat Endowment/Mid-Am Arts Fel, 86; Governor's Visual Artist, State of Kans, 93. *Bibliog:* Rev in Art News, 68 & Art Rev, 69; Female Artists, Past & Present, Women's Hist Res Ctr, Inc, 74; Rev in Manhattan Arts, 88; New York Art Rev, 88. *Mem:* Rocky Mountain Nat Watermedia Soc; Kans Watercolor Soc; Nat Watercolor Soc; Watercolor-USA-Honor Soc. *Media:* Acrylic; Watercolor Monotype. *Dealer:* Hand Artes Gallery Truchas NMex; Gallery A Taod NMex

KUCHTA, RONALD ANDREW
MUSEUM DIRECTOR, EDITOR
b Lackawanna, NY. *Study:* Cape Cod Sch Art, Provincetown, Mass, 53-57; Kenyon Col, Gambier, Ohio, BA, 57; Case Western Reserve Univ, Cleveland, Ohio, MA(art hist), 62; Mgt Inst, Cornell Univ, 79. *Comn:* US Commisioner for the 3rd World Ceramic Biennial, 2005. *Collection Arranged:* Modern Mexican Painting, 70; Tantra (with catalog), 70; Interior Vision, European Abstract Expressionism, 1945-1960 (with catalog), 70; Animals in African Art (with catalog), 73; 15 Abstract Artists--Los Angeles, 73; New Works in Clay, 76; Provincetown Painters, 77; Diversions of Keramos: American Clay Sculpture 1925-1950, 83; Robert Beauchamp: American Expressionist, 84; Syracuse China Ctr Study Am Ceramics, 87; Continuity and Transformation, Contemporary Japanese Ceramics, 92; Sublime Forms, Enigmatic Visions, CJCS, 98. *Pos:* Cur, Chrysler Art Mus, 61-68, Santa Barbara Mus Art, 68-74; dir, Everson Mus Art, 74-95; assoc, Loveed Fine Arts, NY, 95-; ed, Am Ceramics, NY, 95-; chmn, Longhouse Res Art Comt, E Hampton, NY, 97-; trustee Moca, NY, Watershed Ctr for Ceramic Arts, Edgecomb, Maine; trustee, Kulaev Cult Heritage Fund, Los Angeles, CA, 2004. *Teaching:* Adj prof museology, Syracuse Univ, 74-94. *Awards:* Service to the Arts Award, Cult Resources Coun, Syracuse, 92; Award for Contributions to Am Art, Fonda del Sol Arts Ctr, 93; Commending dir, NY State Senate Resolution 317, Everson Mus Art, 95. *Mem:* Am Asn Mus Dir; Int Coun Mus; Nat Arts Club, NY; Nat Conf Educ Ceramic Art; Int Acad Ceramics, 92; Friends of Contemp Ceramics. *Media:* Ceramics. *Res:* Int contemp ceramics. *Specialty:* Ceramic sculpture. *Collection:* Contemporary Ceramics. *Publ:* Acquired Identities: And Other Observations on Contemporary Ceramics by an Acquisitive Museum Director,

Ceramics, Art & Perception, Sydney, 93; In the beginning was the word: Takako Araki's ceramic bibles, Am Ceramics, Vol II, No 1, 93; The past is present-ceramics at the end of the twentieth century, Ceramics Art & Perception, Sydney, Australia, 12/96; From the Earth: Clay, Water & Fire, 96; The Emergence of 6 Taiwan Artists, 96; plus many others; From the Earth: Clay, Water & Fire, 96; The Persistence of Craft, Major Themes in Contemp Ceramics, London, 2002. *Dealer:* Loveed Fine Arts 575 Madison Ave New York NY 10022. *Mailing Add:* 60 Sutton Place S New York NY 10022

KUCKEI, PETER
PAINTER, STAINED GLASS ARTIST
b Husum, Schleswig-Holstein, Ger, May 25, 38. *Study:* Staatliche Kunstschule Bremen, 61; Staatliche Akademie de bildenden Kuenste, Stuttgart, 63. *Work:* Landesmuseum Schleswig-Holstein, Ger; Kunsthalle Emden, Ger; Staatsgallerie Stuttgart, Ger; Mus Karlsruhe, Ger; Assoc Art Amsterdam, Holland. *Comn:* Stained glass windows, Maritim ProArte Hotel, Berlin, Ger, 95; Glaswork, Dorint Hotel, Berlin, Ger, 97. *Exhib:* Modus Vivendi 11 Ger Painters, Mus Wiesbaden, Ger, 85; Image of Shakespeare, Kunstforum Berlin, Ger, 86; solo exhibs, Landesmuseum Oldenburg, Ger, 88, Kunsthalle Wilhelmshaven, Ger, 89 & Staedtischer Kunstverein Paderborn, Ger, 92; Masterpieces from the Collection of Henri Nannen, Kunsthalle Emden, Ger, 90 & 96; The Large Format, Emsdettener Kunstverein, Ger, 93; Painting, Galerie Ricker, Heilbronn, Ger, 97; Galerie Kuckei & Kuckei, Berlin, Ger, 98; Galerie Schutte, Essen, Ger, 98; Between Inst & Construction, Galerie MB Art, Stuttgart, Ger, 98. *Teaching:* Drawing, Staatliche Akademie, Stuttgart, 86-87. *Awards:* DEUBAU Award, Ger, 79; BDA Award, Niedersachsen, Ger, 80 & 82; Walter Hesselbach Award, Ger, 80. *Bibliog:* W Hennig (auth), Monumente Documente, AM-Gruppe, 85; Dr J Schilling (auth), Drawings and Gouaches, Galerie Schueppenhaur, 86; Dr Peter Reindl (auth), Peter Kuekei Landesmuseum Oldenburg, 88. *Media:* Oil on canvas. *Publ:* Auth, Peter Kuckei San Francisco (portfolio), Nau-Verlag, Berlin, 95; Yan Geling, Peter Kuckei, San Francisco, 95. *Dealer:* Galerie Rieker Friedrich-Ebert-Brucke 74019 Heilbronn Germany; Galerie Kuckei & Kuckei Linienstr 158 (HOF) 10115 Berlin-Mitte Germany. *Mailing Add:* Studio Kuckei 240 N Dixie Hwy Bay 20 Hollywood FL 33020

KUCZUN, ANN-MARIE
PAINTER, ILLUSTRATOR
b Springfield, Mass. *Study:* Bay Path Jr Col, ABS; Univ Colo, Boulder. *Work:* Pratt Community Col, Kans; EF Hutton & Co, Colo; US West, Colo & Wyo; Ellsworth Hist Soc, Kans; US Embassy, Nicosia, Cyprus, Greece; Microsoft Corp, Wash. *Comn:* Bookcover, Roberts-Rinehart Inc, Boulder, Colo; bookcover, Natural Resources Ctr, Boulder, Colo; illus & bookcover, Island Press, Covelo, Calif. *Exhib:* Nat Arts Club, NY; solo-shows, Sangre De Cristo Arts Ctr, Pueblo, Colo, 88-89 & Andrew J Macky Gallery, Univ Colo, Boulder, 92; CU Art Galleries, Univ Colo, Boulder, 93; Colo Hist Mus, Denver, 94 & 98; Womens Studio Workshop Gallery, Rosendale, NY, 94; Colo Springs Art Ctr, 98; Denver Art Mus, Colo; Int Asn Pastel Socs, 98; Int Watermedia, Colo Springs, 2000; Dos Chappel Outdoor, Colo, 2003. *Pos:* Freelance illusr, Univ Colo, John H Breck, Inc, Buxton Corp, WWLP/TV, Roberts Rinehart Inc Publ; pub, Roberts-Rhinehart Inc; Auth, designer, of Illustr book, cd, book, transfiguration of Christ Orthdox Cathedral; A guide to its Art & Architectue, 2004. *Awards:* 1st Prize, Sangre De Cristo Arts Ctr, Pueblo, Colo; Purchase Award, Pratt Community Col, Kans, 80; Art in Pub Places award, Colo Arts Coun, 97; Merit award, Int Asn Pastel Socs, 98; Gold award, Pikes Peak Art Asn, 2000; Best of Show, Pixelated Palette & Paintbrush, 2002. *Bibliog:* features with color photos in Boulder Daily Camera, 77-2004; Southwest Art, 5/88; NY Art Rev, 3rd Ed; 2000 Outstanding Artists & Designers of the 20th Century, Internat'l Biographical Center, Cambridge, England, 2001; Fine Art News, 2003, Color, Illustrated. *Mem:* Colo Pastel Soc; Int Asn Pastel. *Media:* Watermedia, Pastel; Digital Collage. *Interests:* Genealogy and travel. *Publ:* Collage Techniques, Gerald Brommer, Watson-Guptill, 94; Open Studios (dir/catalog), 95 & 97; article, Women's Mag, 8/97; Bravo, 2000; illusr, Wilbraham-Hampden Times, 2002; illusr, Bus News, NYC, 2/2003. *Mailing Add:* 930 Miami Way Boulder CO 80305

KUEHN, EDMUND KARL
PAINTER, LECTURER
b Columbus, Ohio, Aug 18, 1916. *Study:* Columbus Art Sch, cert, 38; Art Students League, cert, 39. *Work:* Columbus Gallery Fine Arts; Capital Univ, Battelle Mem Inst; Springfield Art Mus. *Exhib:* Keny Gallery, 82-96. *Collection Arranged:* Paintings from Columbus Homes, 63; Jean Crotti in Retrospect, 65; The Gordian Knot, 67; Works by David Blythe, 68. *Pos:* Cur, Columbus Gallery Fine Arts, 39-43, asst dir, 62-67, cur collections, 67-76. *Teaching:* Asst prof drawing & painting, Ohio State Univ, 46-47; assoc prof drawing & painting, Columbus Col Art & Design, 52-62. *Mem:* Columbus Art League; Am Asn Mus. *Media:* Miscellaneous Media. *Mailing Add:* 828 City Park Ave Columbus OH 43206

KUEHN, FRANCES
PAINTER
b New York, NY, Feb 16, 43. *Study:* Douglass Col, Rutgers Univ, BA, Rutgers Univ, New Brunswick, MFA. *Work:* J B Speed Art Mus, Louisville, Ky; Weatherspoon Art Gallery, Univ NC; Power Inst, Univ Sydney, Australia; Allen Mem Art Mus, Oberlin, Ohio; New Jersey State Mus, Trenton; and others. *Comn:* Portrait for private collection, 72. *Exhib:* Whitney Mus Ann, 72 & Biennial, 73; one-woman shows, Douglass Col Libr, 73, Max Hutchinson Gallery, 73 & 74 & A M Sachs Gallery, NY, 78, Phoenix Gallery, NY, 01, William Paterson Univ, Wayne, NJ, 02; Contemp Portraits by Well-Known Am Artists, Lowe Art Mus, Coral Gables, Fla, 74; Selections in Contemp Realism, Akron Art Inst, Ohio, 74; Mitchell Algus Galley, NY, 02; Artists on the Edge, Douglass Col Libr, 05. *Teaching:* Artist-in-residence, Rice Univ, 80. *Awards:* NJ State Coun Arts Artist's Fel, 78-79; Nat Endowment Arts Artist's Fel, 82-83. *Bibliog:* Phyllis Derfner (auth), Frances Kuehn, Art Spectrum, 2/75; Lynn Miller & Sally Swenson (auths), Lives and Work, Talks with Women Artists, Scarecrow Press, 81. *Media:* Acrylic. *Mailing Add:* 789 West End Ave Apt 4D New York NY 10025-5417

KUEHN, GARY
SCULPTOR, GRAPHIC ARTIST
b Plainfield, NJ, 1939. *Study:* Drew Univ, NJ, BA(art hist), 62; Rutgers Univ, NJ, MFA, 64. *Work:* NJ State Mus, Trenton; also in pvt collections of Richard P Kaplan, NY, Roy Lichtenstein, NY & Robert Scull, NY; Albertina Mus, Vienna, Austria; Whitney Mus Am Art, NY. *Exhib:* One person exhibs, Douglas Drake Gallery, Kansas City, 74, 76, 80, 82, 87, 89, 91 & 93, Art Galaxy, NY, 85, Margarete Roeder Gallery, NY, 86, 90, 91, 93, 95 & 98, Galerie Julie Kewenig, Frechen, Ger, 86 & 88, Rudolf Zwirner Gallery, NY & Koln, Ger, 86 & Galerie Sylvia Menzel, Berlin, Ger, 87; Elements of Style, NY, Deson-Saunders Gallery, Chicago, Ill, 89; Aus Meiner Sicht, Galerie Rolfe Ricke, Kolnisher, Kunstuerien, Ger, 89; Made in NY, Williams Ctr Arts, Easton, Pa, 89; New Aquisitions, Lehmbruch Mus, Duisberg, Ger, 91; Galerie Rudolf Zwirner, Koln, Ger, 91; Gallery Artists, Douglas Drake Gallery, NY, 92; Kuehn Marioni Smith, Margarete Roeder Gallery, NY, 92; Adding It Up, Print Acquisitions 1970-1995, Mus Mod Art, NY, 95; Sculptures, Boxes, Paintings, Cucalon Gallery, NY, 96; White, Mitchell Algus Gallery, NY, 98; and many others. *Teaching:* Instr, Fairleigh Dickinson Univ, NJ, 65, Drew Univ, NJ, 65-68, Sch of Visual Arts, New York, 68, Hochshule fur Bildende Kunst, Braunschweig, Ger, 70, & Douglass Col, 73; prof, Rutgers Univ, 73-. *Awards:* Nat Endowment Arts Grant, 77; DAAD Fel, Berlin, 79; Greenburger Award, 90. *Dealer:* Margaret Roeder Gallery 545 Broadway New York NY 10012. *Mailing Add:* 133 W 24th St New York NY 10011

KUEHNL, CLAUDIA ANN
GOLDSMITH
b Kenosha, Wis, Aug 11, 48. *Study:* Philadelphia Col Art, Pa, BFA, 70; State Univ NY Col, New Paltz, MFA, 74. *Exhib:* Contemp Am Gold-Silversmiths, Corcoran Gallery Art, Washington, DC, 72; Southern Tier Arts & Crafts Exhib, Corning Mus, NY, 74; Jewelry & Metal Objects from the Society of North Am Goldsmiths (Europ traveling show); Holstein Gallery, Palm Beach, Fla, 83; Gene Barth Gallery, Oklahoma City, 85; Cross Creek Gallery, Malibu, Calif, 86; Fergus-Jean Gallery, Columbus, Ohio, 89; Gayle Willson Gallery, Southampton, NY, 94; plus many others. *Teaching:* Asst prof, art appreciation, two dimensional design & drawing, Suffolk Co Community Col, Selden, NY, 75- & metalsmithing & jewelery, Southampton Col, NY, 76-79 & art dept drawing; tech mgr, Gesswein, Thailand, 89-90. *Awards:* Nat Endowment Arts Fel, Crafts, 75-76. *Mem:* Soc NAm Goldsmiths; Am Crafts Coun; NY State Craftsmen Inc. *Media:* Gold, Stone. *Publ:* Jewelry concepts, Technology, Oppi Untrach; auth, Murray Bouid, Jewelry Making; Metal Smith, spring 87. *Dealer:* Works Gallery Jobs Lane Southampton NY 11968; Works Gallery 1250 Madison Ave New York NY 10128. *Mailing Add:* Box 622 Quogue NY 11959

KUEMMERLEIN, JANET
FIBER ARTIST
b Dearborn, Mich, Jan 10, 32. *Study:* Detroit Soc Arts & Crafts, 50-51; Cranbrook Acad Art, with Harry Osaki, 51-52. *Work:* Chicago Art Inst; Rochester Inst Technol; Ga Inst Technol; Smithsonian Nat Gallery Art; 3M Corp. *Comn:* Fiber relief sculpture, Gen Serv Admin, Richmond, Calif, 76; fiber mural, Williams Ctr, Tulsa, 80 & State Bar Calif, Sacramento, 80; fiber & sculpture, State Fed Savings, Tulsa, 82; fiber relief sculpture, Richardson-Vicks, Shelton, Calif, 83; fiber relief, Z J Loussac Libr, Anchorage, Alaska; fiber mural, DuPont, Wilmington, Del. *Exhib:* Five Fiber Artists, Sheldon Mem Gallery, Lincoln, Nebr, 63; Objects USA Traveling Exhib, US & Europe, 69; Forms in Fibre, Chicago Art Inst, 71; Am Craft Exhib, Dallas Mus, 72; Craft Invitational, San Diego Mus Fine Art, 74; Art in Worship, Mus Contemp Crafts, NY, 74; Women, Fiber, Clay & Metal, Bronx Mus, 77; Fiberworks, Cleveland Mus, 78. *Collection Arranged:* Contemporary Crafts (auth, catalog), Rockhurst Col, 64. *Awards:* Awards, Univ Kans, 65-69 & Am Inst Archit, 69-71, 75-79 & 88. *Bibliog:* Louise Schulteis (auth), Artist in fiber, Kansas City Star, 71; Irene Reynolds (auth), Fiber artist, Kansan Mag, 76. *Mem:* Mo Coun Arts; Am Craft Coun. *Media:* Fiber. *Publ:* Contribr, Textile Art in the Church, Abingdon Press, 71; contribr, Quilting, Patchwork, Applique, Trapunto, 74 & Soft Sculpture, 74, Crown; contribr, The Place of Art in the World of Architecture, Chelsea House, 80; contribr, Sewing Machine Craft Book, Van Nostrand Reinhold, 80. *Mailing Add:* 7701 Canterbury St Shawnee Mission KS 66208-3946

KUHLMAN, WALTER EGEL
PAINTER, EDUCATOR
b St Paul, Minn, Nov 16, 18. *Study:* St Paul Sch Art, with Cameron Booth, 36-40; Univ Minn, BA, 41; Tulane Univ, 45-46; Calif Sch Fine Arts, 47-50; Acad Grand Chaumiere, Paris, 50-51. *Work:* San Francisco Mus Mod Art; Oakland Mus, Calif; NY Metrop Mus Art; Nat Mus Art, Washington, DC; Mus Mod Art, Rio de Janiero; De Saisset Mus, Santa Clara, Calif; Minn Mus Art; Laguna Mus Art, Calif; and many others. *Exhib:* One-man shows, The Carlson Gallery, Historic Survey of Bay Area Abstr Expressionist Art in San Francisco, 1945-1960, Calif Palace of the Legion of Hon, 56-64, Walker Art Ctr, Minneapolis, Stanford Univ Gallery, Santa Barbara Mus Art, Charles Campbell Gallery, San Francisco, 81, 83, 85 & Bolles Gallery, San Francisco; 20-yr Retrospective, De Saisset Mus, 69, 40-yr Retrospective, Sonoma State Univ Gallery; Petit Palais Mus, Paris; Painting & Sculpture in California: of the Moden Era, Smithsonian Inst; NY World's Fair; San Francisco Mus Mod Art; group show, Period of Exploration 1945-1950, Oakland Mus, Calif, 73; UC Davis, Directions in Bay Area Painting, A Survey of Three Decades; traveling exhib, San Francisco Mus Mod Art, Laguna Arts Mus, Calif & Nat Acad Design, 95; Dark Ave

Armory Ann Int Fine Print Exhib, NY, Virginia Mus Modern Art Am Paintings, Petit Palais Mus, Paris, Mus of Modern Art, Sao Paulo British Mus, London, Nat Mus Am Art, Phillip Memorial Gallery, Washington, DC, Oakland Mus Art, Calif, Laguna Mus of Art, Calif, 98, The Menil Collection, Houston, Cleveland Mus Art, Mus Modern Art, San Francisco Mus Modern Art, Salander O'Reilly Gallery, NY; and others. *Teaching:* Stanford Univ; Calif Sch Fine Arts; Univ NMex, 60-65; Univ Santa Clara, 66-69; prof painting & chmn dept art, Sonoma State Univ, Calif, 69-, emer prof. *Awards:* Fel, Cummington Found, Mass, 42, Graham Found, Chicago, 57, Calif Arts Coun, 83, Maestro Award; Calif Arts Coun Award, Outstanding Calif Working Artist & Teacher; Tiffany Found, NY; Graham Found, Chicago. *Mem:* Nat Acad Design. *Media:* Oil, Monoprints. *Mailing Add:* 27 Glen Ct Sausalito CA 94965

KUHN, AUDREY GRENDAHL
PRINTMAKER, FIBER ARTIST
b Chicago, Ill, May 3, 29. *Study:* Univ Mich, Ann Arbor, BA(design), 52; Skidmore Col, 72; Russel Sage Col, Troy, NY, grad study art educ & printmaking, 73-75. *Work:* Mus Mod Art, Haifa, Israel; Mayo Clinic, Rochester, Minn; Norton Simon Co, NY; Corp Sci & Technol, Indianapolis; Hudson Valley Community Col, Troy, NY. *Exhib:* Artexpo NY, Jacob Javits Ctr, NY, 79-89; solo exhib, Ctr Gallery, Albany, 85; group exhib, Ctr Gallery, Albany, 92; Print Club Albany Ann, Schenectady Mus, 92; Am Craft Coun, Columbus, Ohio, 94; Mindscape Gallery, Evanston, Ill, 94-95. *Awards:* Second Prize, Stockade Art Show, Stockade Asn, 91; Second Prize, Art in the Park, Saratoga Co Arts Coun, 92; First Prize, Saratoga Arts Coun, 95; Finalist, Hawks And Heroes Contest, Internat Quilt Festival, Yokohama, Japan, 2000; Juror's Award of Excellence, Rehoboth Art League, Del, 93, 2000. *Bibliog:* Sharon Shinn (auth), Mixed media prints, 3/89 & Monotypes: The unique prints, 3/91, Decor Mag. *Mem:* Print Club Albany (treas & chmn presentation print comt, 89-91); Designer Crafts Coun Schenectady Mus; Graphic Artists New York (treas, 76); Rehoboth Art League; Ctr Galleries, Albany. *Media:* Serigraph with Intaglio; Fiber Design. *Interests:* Physical Fitness, Sewing, Knitting, Travel. *Dealer:* Dan Greenblat Gallery D&D Bldg Third Ave New York NY

KUHN, BOB
DRAFTSMAN, PAINTER
b Buffalo, NY, Jan 28, 20. *Study:* Pratt Inst, 3 yrs; Art Students League. *Work:* Nat Cowboy Hall Fame, Oklahoma City; Genesee Country Mus, Rochester, NY; Thomas Gilcrease Mus, Tulsa, Okla; Nat Mus Wildlife Art, Jackson, Wyo; Autry Nat Ctr, Glendale, Calif. *Comn:* many pvt & public commisions. *Exhib:* One-man show, Abercrombie & Fitch, NY, 65 & two-man show, 67, Tryon Gallery, Nairobi, Kenya, 73; Animals in Art, Royal Ont Mus, Toronto, 75; Wildlife, Images in Painting and Sculpture, Royal Ont Mus, 90; Gilcrease Rendesvous, 94; Retrospective Show, Nat Mus Wildlife Art, 2002; Nat Cowboy & Western Heritage Mus. *Teaching:* several workshops. *Awards:* Two Gold Medals, Nat Cowboy Hall Fame; Five Medals of Honor, Soc Animal Artists; Prix de West, Nat Cowboy Hall of Fame, 91; Rungius Medal, Nat Mus Wildlife Art, 92. *Mem:* Soc Animal Artists. *Media:* Acrylic on Masonite. *Publ:* Auth, Animal Art of Bob Kuhn, Watson-Guptill, 73; contribr, Classic African Animals, Winchester, 73; illusr, The Art of Bob Kuhn, Masters of the Wild Series, Briar Patch Press, 89; Wild Harvest, Sporting Classic Press, 97. *Mailing Add:* 4100 Avenida del Cazador Tucson AZ 85718

KULICKE, ROBERT M
CRAFTSMAN, PAINTER
b Philadelphia, Pa, Mar 9, 24. *Study:* Philadelphia Col Art; Tyler Sch Arts, Temple Univ; Academie Leger, Paris, 49-51. *Work:* Philadelphia Mus Art; Hirshhorn Mus & Sculpture Garden; Mus Art, Pa State Univ. *Comn:* Frames designed: Welded Metal (for Mus Modern Art, New York City, 60, Knoll Welded Metal, 61, Plexibox, 64, Metal Section, 67-68. *Exhib:* Silvermine Guild, 64; Art Inst Chicago; Dayton Art Inst, Ohio; 100 Yrs of Am Realism, Am Fedn Arts, 65; Whitney Mus Am Art, NY, 69; one-man exhibs, Kornblee Gallery, NY, 70-73, Davis & Long Co, NY, 74-80, Mus Art, Penn State Univ, 78, Davis & Langdale Co, NY, 81-, Columbia Mus Art & Sci, SC, 83, John C Stoller & Co, Minneapolis, Minn, 85, John F Warren, Philadelphia, 88, Campbell-Thiebaud Gallery, San Francisco, 91 & 94, Locks Gallery, Philadelphia, Pa, 92 & Courtyard Gallery, Wash Studio Sch, 93, Campbell-Thiebaud Gallery, San Francisco, Davis & Langdale Co, New York City, 1981-2000. *Pos:* Co-dir, Kulicke Stark Acad, NY, formerly. *Teaching:* Instr, Univ Calif, 64 & 70; instr, Jewelry Arts Inst, NY, 64-, dir, 74- & assoc, 87-. *Awards:* Int Design Award, Am Inst Interior Designers, 68; assoc mem Nat Acad Design, 88. *Mem:* Assoc mem Nat Acad; Jewelry Arts Inst. *Media:* Oil, Pastel. *Mailing Add:* 320 W 90th St New York NY 10024

KULTERMANN, UDO
ART HISTORIAN, ARCHITECTURAL HISTORIAN
b Stettin, Ger. *Study:* Univ Greifswald, Ger, 47-50; Univ Munster, 50-53. *Hon Degrees:* Hon doct degree Estonian Academy of Art, Tallinn, Estonia, 2004. *Comn:* Consultant to Public Sculpture, Duisburg, Ger, 1965-67; advisor to Melen Gallery Contemp Art, Essen, Ger, 1965-67. *Exhib:* Monochrome Painting, 60, Kasimir Malevic, 60, Ad Reinhardt, Francesco Lo Savio & Jef Verheyen, 61, Glass Chain, 62, Eisenstein, 64, Fangor, 64, City Art Mus, Leverkusen, Ger, Lygia Clark, Galerie Thelen, Essen, Ger, 68, Lucio Fontana, 62; Andy Warhol, 65; Piero Manzoni, 67; Robert Graham, 67. *Pos:* Dir, City Art Mus, Leverkusen, Ger, 59-64; consult to art collectors, galleries and govt agencies. *Teaching:* Prof hist & theory archit, Washington Univ, 67-, Ruth & Norman Moore Prof Archit, 86-94, emer prof, 94-. *Awards:* Distinguished Fac Award, Wash Univ, 85; Corresponding Mem Croatian Acad Sci Arts, Croatia, 97. *Bibliog:* S Giedion (auth), Neues Bauen in der Welt Zu dem Buch von Udo Kultermann, Neue Zuercher Zeitung, 1/10/66; Rudolf Bisanz (auth), Art History, Which Way, Art J, 93; Karina Tyerr (auth), Kunst und Winklichkeit, Zeitsdinft fue Aesthetik und Allgeuseire Kunztwissenscheft 41, 1991; Daniel Baumann (auth), Coffee Table and Avantgarde, Art Press, 2000. *Mem:* Nat fac humanities, arts & sciences, Atlanta, GA. *Res:* History of art history; African culture; Third World architecture; Eastern European architecture; contemporary art; Theory of art. *Publ:* History of Art Theories From Prehistory to Present, Wissenschaftliche Buchgesellschaft (rev ed 98); Ed St James Modern Masterpieces, The Best of Art, Architecture, Photography and Design Since 1945, Detroit Visible Ink Press, 97; Basilica of Maxentius, Verlag und Datenbank fuer GeistesWissenschaften, Weimar, 97; Contemporary Architecture in the Arab States-Renaissance of a Region, McGraw-Hill, NY, 99; Ed, Architecture in South and Central Africa, Vol VI, World Architecture: A Critical Mosaic 1900-2000, Thirty Years After The Future of the Past, Kiado Publ, Budapest, 2002; Architektur and Revolution: the Visions of Boullée and Ledoux, Kiado Publ, Budapest, 2003; Gesdrichte der Kunstgeschichte-Der Weg einer Wisenschaft, Munich (rev ed 1990), Prentel Publ; Art and Life, The Function of Intermedia, New York, Universe Books, 1970. *Mailing Add:* 300 Mercer St No 17B New York NY 10003

KUMAO, HEIDI ELIZABETH
PHOTOGRAPHER, KINETIC ARTIST
b California, 1964. *Study:* Univ Calif, Davis, BA&BS, 88; Sch Art Inst Chicago, MFA, 91. *Work:* Philadelphia Mus Art. *Comn:* Installation of cinema machines, Washington Project for the Arts, Washington, DC, 93. *Exhib:* solo shows, Washington Proj Arts, Washington, DC, 93, Art in General, NY, 93, Hallwalls Contemp Art Ctr, Buffalo, NY, 94, Contemp Arts Center, Cincinnati, 96, Alternative Mus, NY, 97, Introductions, Braunstein-Quay Gallery, San Francisco, 98, Center for Arts Yerba Buena Gardens, San Francisco, 99, Lisa Sette Galery, Scottsdale, Ariz, 99 Three Rivers Art Gallery, Pittsburg, Pa, 2001, Creative Capital Found, Emerging Fields, NY, 2004, Wired Wear, Mott Community Col Art Gallery, Flint, Mich, 2005.; Houston Ctr Photog, Houston, 96; Ariz State Univ Art Mus, 96; The Alternative Mus, NY, 97; Joan Miro Found, Barcelona, 98; Yerba Buena Ctr Arts, San Francisco, 98; Zoetropia, Zeum, San Francisco, 99; Womentek, Peninsula Fine Arts Ctr, Va, 2000; Arrested Development, Castle Gallery, Col New Rochelle, NY, 2002; Still, Ann Arbor Film Festival, 2003; Listen to Me, Detriot, 2003; Tart, Klein Gallery, Chicago, 2004; Only Skin Deep: Changing Visions of the American Self, Int Ctr Photog, NY, 2004; Thought Crimes: The Art of Subversion, Diverseworks, Houston, 2005; Brides of Frankenstein, San Jose Mus Art, 2005; Nat Acad Mus, NY, 2006. *Teaching:* Vis asst prof photog, Univ Maryland Baltimore County, 1991-92; res fellow arts, Univ Mich, Ann Arbor, 1995-96, Roman J Witt vis asst prof, 2001-03; vis asst prof photog, Syracuse Univ, 1992-95, 1997-98; instr, sculpture dept, RI Sch Design, 1997; adj faculty, dept art and art history, City Col NY, 1997. *Awards:* Philadelphia Mus Art Purchase Prize, Print Club, 91. *Bibliog:* Ann Barclay Morgan (auth), Heidi Kumao: tied, Artpapers, 5/94; Martha McWilliams (auth), Transformers, Washington City Paper, 10/22/93; Elizabeth Licata (auth), Heidi Kumao, Artforum, 94; and others. *Mem:* Col Art Asn. *Media:* Photography. *Mailing Add:* Univ Mich Sch Art and Design 200 Bonisteel Blvd Ann Arbor MI 48109

KUMLER, KIPTON (CORNELIUS)
PHOTOGRAPHER, LECTURER
b Cleveland, Ohio, June 20, 40. *Study:* Cornell Univ, BEE, 63, MEE, 67; Mass Inst Technol, with Minor White, 68-69; Harvard Univ, MBA, 69; spec study with Paul Caponigro, 70. *Work:* Mus Mod Art, Metrop Mus Art, NY; Mus Fine Arts, Boston; Victoria & Albert Mus, London; Int Mus Photog, George Eastman House, Rochester, NY. *Comn:* Essay on Danish Archit in Frederiksted, St Croix, Landmark Soc, 75-76; Photog Surv, Del Water Gap, Nat Endowment Arts, 76-77. *Exhib:* Recent Acquisitions, Boston Mus Fine Arts, 74; Addison Gallery Am Art, 74; solo exhibs, NJ Mus, Trenton, 78, Photog Place, Philadelphia, 79, Cronin Gallery, Houston, 80, Harcus Krakow Gallery, Boston, 80 & Worcester Art Mus, Mass, 80; and others. *Collection Arranged:* Traveling Exhib, Nat Endowment Arts Survey Work, NJ, 77-78. *Teaching:* Instr photog, Project Inc, Cambridge, Mass, 69-72; instr advan photog, Maine Photog Workshops, Rockport, 77-80. *Awards:* Nat Endowment Arts Photog Survey Grants, Peters Valley, NJ, 76-77 & Boston Hist Survey, 80-81; Mass Coun Arts Photog Fel, 77. *Publ:* Contribr, Camera, Lausanne, Switz, 70; contribr, Popular Photography, 75; auth, Kipton Kumler: Photographs, 75 & Plant Leaves, 78, David Godine; contribr, Print Letter, Zurich, 77. *Dealer:* Marcuse Pfeifer Gallery 825 Madison Ave New York NY 10016; Harcus Gallery 7 Newbury Boston MA 02116. *Mailing Add:* 28 Beaver Pond Rd Lincoln MA 01773

KUN, NEILA
PHOTOGRAPHER
b Philadelphia, Pa, Feb 8, 51. *Study:* Tyler Sch Art, Temple Univ, BFA, 72, MFA, 94. *Work:* Bibliotheque Nat, Paris, France; NY Pub Libr; Ctr Photog, Woodstock, NY; Lehigh Univ; Villanova Univ, Pa. *Comn:* Sculpted obverse coin of the realm, Guyana one penny piece, Franklin Mint, Pa, 77; sculpted coin for Queen Elizabeth's silver anniversary for Brit Virgin Island, Franklin Mint, Pa, 79. *Exhib:* Works on Paper (catalog), Beaver Col, 89 & 94; Mems Show, Philadelphis Art Alliance, Pa, 90; solo show, Muse Gallery, Philadelphia, Pa, 93; group show, Fachhochschule Bielefeld Fachbereich Design, Ger, 93 & Berman Mus, Ursinus Col, Collegeville, Pa, 94. *Teaching:* instr, De Ctr for the Arts Wilmington, 2001; instr, Phoenixville Art Ctr, 2003-; instr, Montgomery Co Community Col West, 2003-. *Awards:* Abbington Photo Show, 87; Award of Merit, Artists Equity Show, 88 & 94; Griffiths Award, MainLine Ctr Arts, 94; Friends Award, Widner Univ, Chester, Pa, 2002; Leeway Found, Window of Opportunity Award, 2004; Philadelphia Mus Art, Purchash Award, Perkins Art Ctr, 2005. *Bibliog:* Daphne Landis (auth), Speaking for Themselves, The Artist of South Eastern Pennsylvania, 2003; One of a Kind, Artist's Book Traveling Show (exhib catalog), spanish/english ed, 1996. *Mem:* Soc Photog Educ; Friends Photog; Artists Equity; Print Club, Philadelphia. *Media:* Non-Silver Processes Cyanotype, Gum Bicromate Prints. *Collection:* Philadelphia Mus Art; Brooks Art Mus, Memphis, Tenn;

Mus Modern Art/Franklin Furnace/Artist Book Collection, NY; St Louis Mus Art; Montclair Art Mus, NJ. *Publ:* Article, Popular Photog, 2/90; coauth (with Ava Blitz & Jennifer Schmidt), Delaware Center for Contemporary Art, Art & Community 4, Visual Art Residencey Prog, 2001-2002; Art Matters, Celebrating Philadelphia's Artist Legacy, Woodmere Art Mus, 2000. *Mailing Add:* 1007 E Cedarville Rd Pottstown PA 19465

KUNC, KAREN
PRINTMAKER, EDUCATOR
b Omaha, Nebr, Dec 15, 52. *Study:* Univ Nebr-Lincoln, BFA, 75; Ohio State Univ, MFA, 77. *Work:* Nat Mus Am Art, Smithsonian Inst, Washington, DC; Libr Cong, Washington, DC; Worcester Art Mus, Mass; Mus Mod Art, NY; Nat Art Libr, Victoria & Albert Mus, London; and others. *Comn:* Woodcut print, Madison Print Club, 94; Suite of Prints, Zimmerli Art Mus, Rutgers Univ, 95; Artist Book, Nat Mus Women Arts, Washington, 96; Label Image, Benziger Winery Imagery Series, Glen Ellen, 96; Artist's book, Women's Studio Workshop, NY, 98. *Exhib:* World Print III, San Francisco Mus Mod Art, 80; one-woman shows, Columbus, Ohio Mus Art, 83, Sheldon Mem Art Gallery, Lincoln, Nebr, 84, Joslyn Art Mus, 95, Gallery APA, Nagoya, Japan, 95, Davidson Galleries, Seattle, 95, Felix Jenewein Gallery, Kutna Hora, Czech Repub, 96, Hafnarborg Inst Cult & Fine Art, Iceland, 96 & Galleria Harmonia, Jyvaskyla, Finland, 96, Galerie Dumont 18, Geneva, Switz, 2000; Tradition & Innovation 1500-1989, Calif Palace Legion of Honor, San Francisco, 89; National Mus Women in Arts, Washington, 1991, Elvehjem Mus Art, Univ Wisconsin, Madison, 93, 9th Seoul Int Print Biennale, 94; Recent Acquisitions, Nat Mus Am Art, 95; Dressing the Text: The Fine Press Artists Book, Art Mus Santa Cruz Co, 95; Ibizgraphic 96, Int Biennial, Mus Art Contemp, Spain, 96; Carved Block Prints in the Americas, Graphic Studio Gallery, Tampa, 96; Sightlines, Int Invitational, Edmonton, Can, 97; Int Print Exhib, Portland Mus Art, 97; 8th Int Biennial, Taipei Fine Art Mus, Taiwan, 97; The Sense of Touch, Women Printmakers, Ceres Gallery, NY, 97; 4th Sapporo Print Biennale, Hokkaido Mus Mod Art, Japan, 98; 2nd Int Triennial Graphic Art, Prague, 98; Between Nature and Culture: American Prints, Felix Jenewein Gallery, Kutna Hora, Czech Republic, 99; Relativities, Bankside Gallery, London, 2000; Int Artists Print Exhib, Hyndai Arts Centre Gallery, Ulsan, Korea, 2001; 5th Am Print Biennial, Marsh Art Gallery, Univ Richmond Mus, Va, 2002; 4th Egyptian Int Print Triennale, Cairo and Alexandria, Egypt, 2003; VII Int Art Triennale Majdanek, State Mus, Lublin, Poland, 2004; Biennale Int d'Estampes Contemporaine de Trois-Rivieres, Quebec, Can, 2005; Book as Art: Twenty years of Artists' Books, Nat Mus Women in Arts, Washington, DC, 2006; and others. *Collection Arranged:* Represented in permanent collections Mus of Modern Art, New York, National Mus Am. Art, Smithsonian Insti, Washington, Libr. Congress, Washington, Worcester (Mass) Art Mus, Sheldon Memorial Art Gallery, Univ Nebraska, National Art Libr., Victoria and Albert Mus, London, Mus Modern Art, New York City, Brooklyn Mus Art, Fogg Art Mus Harvard Univ. *Pos:* Gallery dir, Univ Nebr, 88-91; research fellow Kyoto Seika Univy, Japan, 93; visiting artist Icelandic Coll Arts & Crafts, Rekyavik, 95; dir Mid-Am print coun conf, Printmaking Relevance/Resonance, 2004. *Teaching:* Prof printmaking, Univ Nebr, Lincoln, 83-97; vis asst prof, Univ Calif, Berkeley, 87; vis artist/teacher, Carleton Col, Northfield, Minn, 89; vis prof, Univ Mich, Ann Arbor, 99; artist in residence, Nagasawa Art Park, Tsuna, Japan, 2001; Willa Cather prof, Univ Nebr, 2003-. *Awards:* Sponsors Prize, 5th Sapporo Int Print Exhib, Japan, 2000; Artist of Yr Award, Nebr Gov Arts Award, 2000; Boston Printmakers NAm Print Exhib, 2000; Purchase award, Bradley Nat Print & Drawing Exhib, 2001; Lincoln Arts Coun Award, 2003; Sally R Bishop Master Faculty Fel, Ctr for Book Arts, 2005; Milw Art Mus Award, 2006; and others. *Bibliog:* Mendelowitz, Faber, Wakeham (co-auth), A Guide to Drawing, Wadsworth/Thomson Learning, 2005; Bob Nugent (auth), Imagery: Art for Wine, Imagery Estate Winery Art Collection, 2005; Hilda Raz (auth), Visionary Evidence, Davidson Galleries, 2005. *Mem:* Nat Acad NY; Soc Printmakers; Col Art Asn; Nebr Art Asn; Calif Soc Printmakers. *Media:* Woodcut, Artist Books. *Collection:* Mirror of the Wood: A Century of the Woodcut Print in Finland, 2005. *Dealer:* Atrium Gallery 4729 McPherson Ave St Louis MO 63108; Davidson Galleries 313 Occidental Ave S Seattle 98104; Robischon Gallery 1740 Wazee St Denver 80202. *Mailing Add:* 1557 N 32nd Rd Avoca NE 68307

KUNCE, SAMM
CONCEPTUAL ARTIST, SCULPTOR
b Los Angeles, Calif, Oct 16, 56. *Study:* San Francisco Art Inst, 86; Mason Gross Sch of the Arts; Bard Col, MFA, 89. *Work:* Mus Mod Art, NY; Mus Contemp Art, Chicago; Bauhaus Kunstlerbarten, Weimar, Ger; Mus Mod Art, Tusla, Slovenia. *Comn:* outdoor earthwork, Polish Cen Contemp Art, Oronsko, Poland, 98; outdoor earthwork, Bauhaus Univ, Weimer, Ger, 99; outdoor earthwork, Sacred Heart Univ, Fairfield, Conn, 2000; outdoor earthwork, S Eastern Cen Contemp Art, Winston-Salem, NC, 2000. *Exhib:* Living with Contemp Art, Aldrich Mus Contemp Art, Ridgefield, Conn, 95; Configura 2, Fishmarket Gallery, Ehrfurt, Ger, 95; Botanica, Tweed Mus (traveling), Duluth, Minn, 99; Samm Kunce, Thomas Ruben Gallery, Ger, 99; Samm Kunce: Dune, John Gibson Gallery, NY, 99; LIfe Cycles, S Eastern Cen Contemp Art, Winston-Salem, NC, 2000; Garden & Memory, Medici Palace, Rome, Italy, 2000; Samm Kunce: Rough, Gallery Contemp Art, Fairfield, Conn, 2000. *Awards:* Louis Comfort Tiffany Award, 97. *Bibliog:* Susan Harris (auth), Samm Kunce, Art in Am, 9/95; Susanne Altmann (auth), Samm Kunce, Kunstforum, 7/99; Tom McDonough (auth), Samm Kunce@John Gibson, Art in Am, 11/99. *Dealer:* John Gibson Gallery 568 Broadway New York NY 10012. *Mailing Add:* 55 Flatbush Ave Ext Brooklyn NY 11201

KUNIN, MYRON
COLLECTOR
Pos: CEO, vchm bd dirs, Regis Corp, Edina, Minn; pres, Curtis Squire Venture Capital Inc. *Mem:* Minn Inst Arts (lifelong trustee). *Collection:* Collector of old masters & contemporary art. *Mailing Add:* Regis Corporation 7201 Metro Blvd Edina MN 55439-2103

KUNSCH, LOUIS
PAINTER, COLLAGE ARTIST
b Bronx, NY, Dec, 37. *Study:* Art Students League New York, 61-65, Sch Visual Arts, NY, 70-72. *Work:* Queens Borough Community Col, NY; Printmaking Workshop, NY; Libr of Congress, Capital Heights, Md. *Exhib:* Ball State Univ, Ind; Jamaica Arts Ctr; Berkshire Mus, Mass; Purdue Univ, Ind; solo shows, Main Street Gallery, Brewster, NY, 75, Long Beach Libr, 77, The Exhibitionists, Jamaica, 77, PS 1, Long Island City, 79, Queens Borough Libr, NY, 91 & 94 & LaGuardia Community Col, NY, 92; Works on Paper, Gallery BAI, 95; Queens Mus Art, NY, 2000. *Pos:* bd dirs, Artists Talk On Art, NY. *Awards:* Ford Found Scholar, 64-65. *Mem:* Art Students League. *Media:* ink & watercolor on paper. *Dealer:* Franklin 54 Gallery 181 Christopher St New York NY. *Mailing Add:* 31-65 138th St Flushing NY 11354

KUNSTLER, MORTON
PAINTER, ILLUSTRATOR
b New York, NY, Aug 28, 31. *Study:* Brooklyn Col; Univ Calif, Los Angeles; Pratt Inst, cert, 50. *Hon Degrees:* Dr Fine Arts, Shanandoah Univ, Winchester, VA. *Work:* USAF Mus, Boulder, Colo; San Mateo Co Historical Mus, Calif; US House Reps, US Senate & The White House, Washington, DC; Lowie Mus Anthrop, Berkeley, Calif; Nassau Co Mus Fine Arts, Roslyn, NY; Mus Am Hist, Smithsonian Inst, Washington, DC. *Comn:* Paintings, National Geographic, Washington, DC, 66-69; six paintings, American Cyanamid, NJ, 71-76; four paintings, NY Bank for Savings, NY, 76; seven paintings, Rockwell Int, Pa, 80; Cram & Foster, 80. *Exhib:* One-man shows, Hammer Galleries, NY, 77, 79, 81-82, 85-86 & 89, USN Mem Mus, Washington, DC, 79 & 82 & Pittsburgh Ctr Arts, Pa, 81; Mus Westward Expansion, St Louis, 89; Dunnegan Gallery, Bolivar, Mo, 91; Hammer Galleries, 92, 93, 95, 98, 2000, 2003, 2004; Nat Military Park, Gettysburg, 92; Hall Valor Mus, New Market Battlefield, Va, 92; NC Mus Hist, Raleigh, 95; and others; Mus of the Confederacy, Richmond, VA, 2000; Nat Civil War Mus, Harrisburg, PA, 2002; Booth Western Art Mus, Cartersville, GA, 2005. *Awards:* Henry Timrod, Southern Culture Award from the Order of the Stars & Bars; Jefferson Davis, Southern Heritage Award; Pratt Inst Alumni Achievement Award. *Media:* Oil, Watercolor. *Publ:* Gettysburg, Turner Publ, 93; The Am Spirit, Rutledge Hill Press, 94; The Confederate Spirit, Rutledge Hill Press, 2000; Gods & Generals, Greenwich Workshop Press, 2002; The Civil War Art of Mort Kunstler, Greenwich Workshop Press, 2004. *Dealer:* Hammer Galleries 33 W 57th St New York NY 10019. *Mailing Add:* Cove Neck Rd Oyster Bay NY 11771

KUNZ, SANDRA THURBER
PAINTER
b London, Conn. *Study:* Principia col; Art Students League. *Work:* Monmouth Mus; Morris Mus of Arts & Sci; Bergen Mus of Art & Sci; AT&T; Nabisco World Hq. *Exhib:* Nat Acad of Design, 90; Monmouth Co Arts Coun Juried Show, 95; New London Art Soc and Gallery, 96. *Awards:* The Tucker, Anthony & RL Day Award, Garden State Watercolor Soc; Shrewsbury State Bank Award, NJ Watercolor Soc; Watercolor Award, Long Beach Island, 99. *Mem:* NJ Watercolor Soc; Garden State Watercolor Soc; Princeton Art Asn; Ocean Co Artists' Guild; Monmouth Co Arts Coun. *Media:* Miscellaneous Media. *Publ:* article, The Best of Watercolor, 97. *Mailing Add:* 249 Daffodil Dr Freehold NJ 07728

KUOPUS, CLINTON
PAINTER, EDUCATOR
b Detroit, Mich, Dec 8, 42. *Study:* US Navy Photog Intelligence Sch, 63; Eastern Mich Univ, Mich State Univ, Wayne State Univ. *Work:* Mich Educ Asn; Hiram Col, Ohio; J Walter Thompson Advert Agency; Lake Erie Col Permanent Collection; Pub Collection, Cedar City, Utah. *Exhib:* Source Detroit Exhib, Cranbrook Mus Art, Bloomfield Hills, Mich, 76; May Show Exhibs, Cleveland Mus Art, Ohio; Butler Inst Am Art, Youngstown, Ohio, 79; 38th Cedar City Nat, Utah, 79; Print Collaboration-Stewart and Stewart, Detroit Inst Art 91 & Kansas City Art Mus, 91-92. *Pos:* Photog interpreter, US Navy, 62-66; fac dir exhibs, Parsons Sch Design, 83-. *Teaching:* Photog intelligence training petty off, US Navy, 64-66; instr visual art, Bloomfield Hills Schs, Mich, 70-75; asst prof art, Lake Erie Col, Painesville, Ohio, 75-80, 82-83; adj fac, Youngstown State Univ, 80-82 & Univ Akron, 81-82; foundations fac, Parsons Sch Design, 83-, dir of exhib, 88-. *Media:* Multimedia. *Mailing Add:* 1790 Poppleton Dr W Bloomfield MI 48324-1149

KUPER, YURI KUPERMAN
PAINTER
b Moscow, USSR, July 5, 40; British citizen. *Study:* Academy of Art, Moscow. *Work:* Pushkin Mus, Tretiakov Gallery, Moscow; Nat Found Contemp Art, Ministry of Cult, Paris; Nat Gallery, Oslo; Bank of Am; Univ Chicago; Nat Libr of Congress, Washington, DC; Thew Sainsburg Collection, Univ Norwich; Veno Royal Mus, Kiyoharu Shirakaba Mus, Tokyo. *Exhib:* Centre Culturel, Jerusalem, 72, Haaken Galerie, Oslo, 81, Claude Bernard Galerie Paris, 83-88, NY, 86-89, Krugier Galerie, Geneve, Switz, 83, Galerie Rambert, Paris, 89; solo-show, Yoshii Gallery, Tokyo, 91 & 92, Yoshii Found-Kiyoharu Mus, 91, Valois Gallery, Paris, 91, Hesdin Gallery, Paris, 92, Yoshii Gallery, NY, 92, Sala Alternativa Gallery, Caracas, 92. *Bibliog:* David Newman (auth), Arts, 3/81; John Russel (auth), Maugunal exhib, NY Times, 10/83; John Berger (auth), Vuri Kuper Paintings, Claude Bernard, 10/83. *Publ:* Illusr, L'Angoisse du Roi Solomon, Emile Ajar (auth), 79; Notre Dame de Paris performed at the Nat Theatre, L'Opera de Paris, 88; Tristane and Isolde, Imprimerie Nationale, Paris in the series Le Livre de Art, 89; My Sister, Life, Boris Paternak (auth), Ltd-Eds Club, New York, 90; Nouvelles de la Russie Rouge, Imprimerie National, Paris, 91-92

KURAHARA, TED N
PAINTER, EDUCATOR
b Seattle, Wash, July 16, 25. *Study:* St Louis Sch Fine Arts, Washington Univ, with Paul Burlin, BFA, 51; Bradley Univ, Peoria, Ill, with Leon Engers, MA, 52. *Work:* Museo Civico, Taverna, Italy; Univ Sidney, Australia; Brooklyn Mus; Huntington Gallery, WVa; Malmo Konsthal, Malmo, Sweden; Columbia Univ, New York City,

NY; Pratt Inst, Brooklyn, NY; Des Moines Art Ctr. *Comn:* Comune Di Torgiano, Italy. *Exhib:* Woodside-Braseth Gallery, Seattle, 80; Anders Tornberg, Lund, Sweden, 81, 84, 91 & 98; Leif Stahle Gallery, Paris, France, 87; Anita Shapolsky Gallery, NY, 87-94; Kiyo Higashi Gallery, Los Angeles, Calif, 95, 97, 99 & 2002; Pardo-Lattuada Gallery, New York City, 2002-05; Robert Pardo, Artefact Gallery, Milan, Italy & Zurich, Switz. *Pos:* Dir, Springfield Art Asn, Ill, 53-55 & Emily Lowe Gallery Hofstra Univ, Long Island, NY. *Teaching:* Prof art, Grad Fine Art, Pratt Inst, Brooklyn, NY; prof art, Pratt Inst, Brooklyn, 70-06, chairperson painting & drawing dept, 80-83. *Awards:* Yaddo Fel, 78; Guggenheim Found Grant, 85; Nat Endowment Arts Grant, 86. *Bibliog:* Donald B Kuspit (auth), Kuraharas Paintings, 84; J Sans (auth), A propos du travail de Kurahara, L'oeilk, Paris; Corinne Robins, Panel Paper, Asia Soc, N.Y.C., 2000; cagalog essay Robert Lee, Asian Am Arts Center, N.Y.C., 2000. *Mem:* Abstract Am Artists. *Media:* Acrylic, All Media. *Dealer:* Kiyo Higashi Gallery Los Angeles CA; Anders Tornberg Gallery Lund Sweden; Pardo-Lattuada Gallery New York NY; Artefact Gallery, Milan, Italy & Zurich, Switz. *Mailing Add:* 78 Greene St New York NY 10012

KURHAJEC, JOSEPH A
SCULPTOR
b Racine, Wis, Oct 13, 38. *Study:* Univ Wis, BS, 60, MFA, 62. *Work:* New Sch Social Res, NY; Espanol Mus Contemp Art, Madrid, Spain; Mus Mod Art, NY; Chicago Art Inst; Walker Art Ctr, Minneapolis, Minn. *Comn:* Bronze cone, Allan Stone, Purchase, NY, 71; bronze sculpture, Norman Shaifer, Brooklyn Heights, NY, 71. *Exhib:* Am Fedn Art Traveling Exhib, 64; Sculpture Ann, Whitney Mus Am Art, NY, 64, Young Am, 65; Espanol Mus Contemp Art, 69; Ten Independents, Guggenheim Mus, NY, 72; Basel Art, 76. *Pos:* owner, dir, Treadwell Mus Fine Art, NY. *Teaching:* Asst prof, Cornell Univ, 65-66; asst prof, Newark Sch Indust & Fine Art, 67-69; asst prof, Univ Wis-Stout, 71-73, State Univ NY, New Paltz, 73-74, Lo Studiolo, Rome, 74-83. *Awards:* Int Fur Designers Award, 83. *Mem:* Sculptors Guild, NY. *Dealer:* Treadwell Museum Fine Art Treadwell NY 13846. *Mailing Add:* 178 Rue Raymond Losserand Apt 3104 Paris 75014 France

KURKA, DONALD FRANK
PAINTER,
b Chicago, Ill, July 29, 30. *Study:* Syracuse Univ, BFA, 52; Art Inst Chicago, MFA, 56; NY Univ, PhD, 68. *Comn:* IBM; Hosp Corp Am; Hilton Hotels; Stouffers, Tenn Valley Authority; and others. *Exhib:* Contemp Prints, Libr Cong, 55; solo exhib, McClung Mus, Univ Tenn, Knoxville, 78; Hunter Mus, Chattanooga, Tenn, 81 & 91 & Here & Now, Greenville Cty Mus Art, SC, 89; Mus Art, Evansville, Ind, 88; Palazzo Caselli, Cortona, Italy, 90; Centro de Bellas Artes, Maracaibo, Venezuela, 90; Acad Fine Arts, Helsinki, Finland, 92; Vermont Studio Ctr, 93; Arrowmont, Gatlinburg, Tenn, 94-2001; Ewing Gallery, Univ Tenn, 2000. *Pos:* Vis artist, Fine Arts Acad, Helsinki, Finland, 92, Vt Studio Ctr, 93, Fine Arts Acad, Bratislava, Slovakia, 94, Arrowmont Sch Arts & Crafts, Gatlinburg, Tenn, 94-2001, Mt Artists Refuge, 95, Univ Tex, San Antonio, 96, Clemson Univ, 96, & Ringling Sch Art, Sarasota, Fla, 98-99. *Teaching:* Prof painting, Southampton Ctr, Long Island Univ, 69-77, dir, Div Fine Arts, 73-77; prof & head dept art, Univ Tenn, Knoxville, 77-93. *Awards:* Vandergrift Award, Art Inst Chicago, 55; Best in Show, Long Island Painters, Hecksher Mus, 73; Art-in-residence, Univ Ga, Study abroad prog, Cortona, Italy, fall, 90; 1st Prize Photog, 18th Ann Selby Gardens, Sarasota, Fla, 99. *Mem:* Nat Coun Art Adminr; Nat Asn Schs Art & Design; Col Art Asn. *Media:* Acrylic, Oil. *Publ:* Auth, Fact, Fiction, Fantasy-Exhib Catalog essay, Ewing Gallery, Univ Tenn, 87; catalog, The Art of Carl Sublett, Ewing Gallery, Univ Tenn, 2000. *Dealer:* Art 4 Bus Philadelphia PA; Soho Myriad Inc Atlanta GA

KURLANDER, HONEY W
PAINTER, INSTRUCTOR
b Brooklyn, NY. *Study:* Parsons Sch Design; NY Univ; Pratt Inst, Brooklyn, BA. *Work:* De Seversky Conf Ctr, Greenvale, NY; Dietz Mus, Wasserberg, Ger; C W Post Col Art Ctr, Brookville, NY; Gregory Mus Traveling Collection, Hicksville, NY; Reddon Collection, Paris, France. *Comn:* Western scenes of horses & oil drilling, Rotan-Mosle, Tulsa, Okla, 81; Waldorf Astoria, NY & Stanford Ct, Calif, Hospitality Valuation Serv Inc, Mineola, NY, 83-87; Roslyn, Turn of the Century (2 murals), Jolly Fisherman, Roslyn, NY, 84; Fulton Street Ferry Landing (mural), Thomas M Quinn & Sons Inc, Astoria, NY, 85; Mural, Comn by Friends Oyster Bay, E Norwich Libr. *Exhib:* Long Island Artists, The Heckscher Mus, Huntington, NY, 66-68; Exposition Intercontinental, The Palace, Monaco, 65; Traveling Art Exhib, Gregory Mus, Hicksville, NY, 70-; solo exhib, Adelphi Univ, Alumni House Gallery, Garden City, NY, 77; First Int Art Competition, Am Artist Mag, Marion, Ohio, 78; NLAPW Nat Exhib, Goethe Hall, Sacramento, Calif, 78; Exhib of Oil Paintings, Salmagundi Club, NY, 78; Celebration of the Arts, Nassau Mus Fine Art, Roslyn, NY, 83; NLAPW Nat Biennial, Arlington, Va, 2000. *Collection Arranged:* Dietz Mus, Wasserberg, Germany; Grumbacher Collection, NYC. *Pos:* Freelance textile designer, 49-58; Freelance children's bk illustr, 50-60. *Teaching:* Instr, painting, E Meadow High Sch, New York, 58-60 & Kurlander Studio, Old Westbury, NY, 59-2000. *Awards:* Best of Show, Malverne Artists 28th Ann, Greenwich Savings Bank, 72; Best of show, excellence & first prize, NLAPW, 78-2000; Best of show, NY State Juried Art Exhib, Lever House, 87; Best of show, C W Post, 90. *Bibliog:* Tom Cullen (auth), Looking back-the art of success, Long Island Com Rev, 9/72; Jeanne Paris (auth), Many faces of nature, Newsday, 9/79; Malcolm Preston (auth), Two definitely modern realists, Newsday, 4/84. *Mem:* Nat League Am Penwomen; Salmagundi Club; Art League Nassau Co. *Media:* Acrylic, Oil. *Publ:* auth, Best of Flower Painting, North Light Books, 98. *Dealer:* Robley Gallery Old Northern Blvd Roslyn NY 11576; Garden City Galleries Ltd 923 Franklin Ave Garden City NY 11530. *Mailing Add:* 6185 Wooded Run Dr Columbia MD 21044

KURTZ, ELAINE
PAINTER
b Philadelphia, Pa. *Study:* Philadelphia Col Art, BA; Barnes Found, Merion, Pa, 64-65. *Work:* Philadelphia Mus Art, Pa; Nat Mus of Am Art, Libr of Cong, Corcoran Mus Art & Nat Gallery Art, Washington, DC; and others. *Exhib:* solo shows The Corcoran Mus Art, Washington, DC, 2000, Kouros Gallery, NY, 01, 03, Troyer Gallery, Washington, DC, 95, 01; Nat Mus Am Art, Selections From the Martha Jackson Meml Collection, Washington, DC; XXIV Prix Int D'Art Contemporain de Monte Carlo, 90; Herbert F Johnson Mus, Woman Artists, Cornell Univ, NY, 83; Int Festival of Painting at Cagnes-sur-Mer, US Entry, 81; New Acquisitions "Here and There", The Israel Mus Jerusalem, 99; Pertaining to Philadelphia, Philadelphia Mus Art, 84. *Awards:* Silver Star Alumni Award for Painting, Philadelphia Col Art, 77. *Bibliog:* Jo Ann Lewis (auth), Abstracts by Elaine Kurtz, Wash Post, 82; Maximum Impact Minimalism, Wash Post, 88; Nicole Lewis (auth), Arts Beat, Washington Post, 00; Olivia W Douglas, "Nanno Degroot-Elaine Kurtz, Art News, 95; Elaine Kurtz, "Alluvial Paintings", Corcoran Mus Art, 2000. *Media:* Acrylic on Canvas, Mixed Media on Canvas. *Publ:* Contribr, The Clouds-Prose Poems by Harry Rand (10 original lithographs), Dove Press, Washington, DC, 97; Poems, Lynne Honickman, Intro by Anais N18 8 original prints by 8 artists, 83; Original Seriagraph, White Spectrum, Inst of Contemp Art, Univ of Pa, 80. *Dealer:* Troyer Gallery Washington DC; Kouros Gallery 23 E 73 St New York NY 10021. *Mailing Add:* 17 E 16th St 8th Flr New York NY 10003

KURYLUK, EWA
PAINTER, SCULPTOR
b Cracow, Poland, May 5, 46. *Study:* Acad Fine Arts, Warsaw, MFA & MA, 70. *Work:* Biblio Nat, Paris; Graphische Sammlung Albertina, Vienna, Austria; Nat Mus, Warsaw, Poland; Kettle's Yard Mus, Cambridge, Eng; Bass Mus Art, Miami Beach, Fla. *Comn:* Wall piece, Nat Humanities Ctr, Res Triangle Park, NC, 89. *Exhib:* Textile Sculpture, Mus des Beaux Arts, Lausanne, Switz, 85; 40th Int Festival, Richard Demarco Gallery Edinburgh, 86; Membranes of Memory, Centro de Arte y Comunicacion, Buenos Aires, 86; Fourth Int Triennale Drawing, Mus Archit, Wroclaw, Poland, 88; Polish Women Artists and the Avant-garde, Nat Mus Women in Arts, Washington, 91; and others. *Pos:* Ed, Cahiers Litteraires, Paris, 82- & Formations, 83-, Private Arts, 92-. *Teaching:* Prof acad film, Lodz, 79-80, Inst Applied Theater Sci, Giesseh, WGer, 86, New Sch, New York, 88-, Univ Calif, San Diego, 92 & New York Univ, 94-. *Awards:* Rockefeller Fel, Nat Humanities Ctr, 88; Bronze Medal, 4th Int Triennale Drawing, 88; Asian Cult Coun Fel Japan, 91. *Bibliog:* Jan Kott, E White & E Grabska (coauths), The fabric of memory, Ewa Kuryluk: Cloth works 1978-1987, Formations, 87; Ewa Kuryluk, Drawings and Installations, ZPAP, Warsaw, 94; Janet Koplos (auth), Art and Textiles, Art in Am, 2/96. *Mem:* Int Art Critics Asn; PEN. *Media:* All Media, Cloth. *Mailing Add:* 504 W 110 St Apt 3A New York NY 10025

KURZ, DIANA
PAINTER, EDUCATOR
b Vienna, Austria; US citizen. *Study:* Brandeis Univ, BA(fine arts, cum laude); Columbia Univ, MFA(painting). *Work:* Corcoran Gallery Art, Washington, DC; Rose Art Mus, Brandeis Univ, Mass; Brooklyn Botanic Garden, Brooklyn, NY; Jewish Mus, Vienna, Austria; Historisches Mus der Stadt Wien, Vienna, Austria. *Comn:* Mural, comn by Howard Finkelstin, NY, 85. *Exhib:* Brooklyn Mus, 75; solo exhibs, Snug Harbor Cult Ctr, 82, Rider Col, 84, Alex Rosenberg Gallery, NY, 84, Palais de Justice, Aix-En-Provence, France, 86, Brooklyn Botanic Garden, 89, Mercer Co Community Col, 90, Thomas Ctr Gallery, Gainesville, Fla, 91, Austrian Consulate Gen, NY, 95, Santa Fe Gallery, Gainesville, Fla, 98 & Bezirks-Mus Josefstadt Vienna, Austria, 98, Trenton City Mus, NJ, 2002, Holocaust Mus & Study Ctr, Spring Valley, NY, 2003, St Joseph's Col, Patchogue, NY, 2003; Bergen Mus Art, NJ, 93; Trenton City Mus, NJ, 94; Clymer Mus, Univ Tex, 95; Nat Mus Women Arts, 97; Blue Mountain Gallery, NY, 98. *Teaching:* Lectr drawing, Philadelphia Col Art, 68-73; adj lectr art, Queens Col, NY, 71-76; vis prof art, Pratt Inst, 73; vis asst prof, Univ Colo, 78; vis asst prof art, State Univ NY Stony Brook, 79; vis artist painting, Va Commonwealth Univ, 80; vis artist painting, Cleveland Inst Art, 80-81, Sch Art Inst Chicago, 87, Oxbow Sch Art, Mich, 88 & Vermont Studio Ctr, 90. *Awards:* Fulbrignt Grant, 65-66; Am Ctr Residency, Paris, 85-86; Artist in Residence, Vienna, Austria, 97. *Bibliog:* Lawrence Alloway (auth), catalog, Queens Col, 72; Lawrence Campbell, Art in Am, 5/84; Arlene Raven (auth), catalog, Steon Hall Univ, 2002. *Mem:* NY Artists Equity Asn (bd dir); Fine Arts Fedn of NY. *Media:* Oil, Watercolor. *Publ:* Mother Massage, Dell Publ, 92; East meets west (article), Am Artist Mag, 12/92; cover illusr Attitudes Mag, Jewish Fed Pub, NJ, spring 2000. *Mailing Add:* 152 Wooster St New York NY 10012

KURZEN, AARON
PAINTER, SCULPTOR, ASSEMBLAGE ARTIST
b St Paul, Minn, 20. *Study:* Art Students League, NY, 38-39; Hans Hofmann Sch, NY; Acad de Brera, Milan, Italy; Univ Guadalajara, Mex; studied with Yasuo Kuniyoshi, Cameron Booth, Giorgio de Chirico, Rome & Hans Hofmann. *Work:* Mass Inst Technol Mus, Cambrige; Mus Holography, NY. *Exhib:* Brooklyn Mus, NY; Silvermine Guild Artists, New Canaan, Conn; Audubon Artists Ann Exhib, Nat Acad Design Galleries, NY, 67-90; Prince St Gallery, NY, 91; Solo exhib, Willoughby Wallace Libr Gallery, Stony Creek, Conn, Mus Holography, NY, 82, Minn State Fair, St Paul, Ashby Gallery NY. *Teaching:* instr, painting, Quinnipiac Col, formerly; instr, painting, Mt Carmel, Conn, formerly; insr, life drawing, NY Univ, formerly; instr, art, Dalton Sch, NY, 91-. *Awards:* Silver Medal of Honor, sculpture, Audubon Artists, Nat Arts Club, NY, 2001. *Mem:* Audubon Artists, NY. *Media:* Oil, Metal, Clay & Wax. *Specialty:* Figurative, Envisionary & Assemblages. *Mailing Add:* PO Box 3233 Branford CT 06405

KUSAMA, YAYOI
SCULPTOR, PAINTER
b Matsumoto City, Japan, 29; US citizen. *Study:* Art Students League, NY, 57; Kyoto Arts & Crafts Sch, Japan, 59. *Work:* Chrysler Mus, Provincetown, Mass; Stedelijk Mus, Amsterdam. *Exhib:* Solo exhibs, Fuji Television Gallery, Tokyo, 84, Missoni Boutique, Yura Kucho-Marion Seibu, Tokyo, 85, Tamagawa-Takashimaya, Tokyo, 86, Musee Municipal Dole, 87, Soul Burning Flashes, Fuju Gallery, 88, Ctr Int Contemp Art, NY, 90 & Oxford Mus, Eng, 90; Le Japon des Avantgarde, Centre Georges Pompidou, Paris, 86; Japanese Art Today, San Diego Mus, 86; Opening Show, Meguro Mus Art, Tokyo, 87; Objet, Tsukashin Hall, Osaka, 87; Second Int Contemp Art Fair, Los Angeles, 88; Chicago Int Art Expos, 88; Art-Kites Traveling Show, 88-92; and many others. *Pos:* Pres & found, Japan Ed Co, 77-. *Publ:* auth: Manhattan Suicide Addict, 78, Christopher Homosexual Brothel, 83, Lost in Swapland, 92; Woodstock Phallus Cutter, 88; Publ, Between Heaven and Earth, 88; contribr articles to mag and newspapers. *Mailing Add:* c/o Frank Born Arts 866 Capp St San Francisco CA 94110

KUSNERZ, PEGGY ANN F
EDITOR, HISTORIAN
b Detroit, Mich, Jan 12, 47. *Study:* Univ Mich, BA(art hist), 71, MLS, 71, MA(Am cult), 82, PhD(Am cult), 92. *Collection Arranged:* Images of Old Age 1790 to Present (coauth, catalog), SITES Exhib, 79. *Pos:* Head librn exten serv & mus librn, Univ of Mich, head art, archit libr, 80-94, asst to dean, 94-97, lectr, 94-99, assoc editor, History of Photography, 01. *Teaching:* Art: Hist of Photog, Am Culture: Res Methods, Univ of Mich. *Mem:* Col Art Asn; Am Studies Asn; Soc Photog Educators. *Media:* Photography. *Res:* History of photography. *Interests:* History of photography & panoramic photography. *Publ:* Ed, Architecture Library of the Future, Ann Arbor Univ of Mich Press, 89. *Mailing Add:* 804 Sycamore Ann Arbor MI 48104

KUSPIT, DONALD BURTON
HISTORIAN, CRITIC
b New York, NY, Mar 26, 35. *Study:* Columbia Univ, BA; Yale Univ, MA(philos); Univ Frankfurt, PhD(philos); Pa State Univ, MA(art); Univ Mich, PhD(art hist). *Hon Degrees:* Davidson Col, 93; San Francisco Art Inst, 96; Univ Ill, 98. *Pos:* Contrib ed, Artforum, Sculpture; ed, Art Criticism, currently; adv bd, Centennial Review. *Teaching:* Prof art hist & philos, State Univ NY Stony Brook, 78-; A D White prof at large, Cornell Univ, 91-96. *Awards:* Fel, Nat Endowment Humanities, Nat Endowment Arts, Fulbright Comn, Guggenheim Found & Ford Found, 73-74; Frank Jewett Mather Award Distinction in Art Criticism, Col Art Asn, 83; Citation Distinguished Serv to Visual Arts, Nat Asn Sch Art & Design, 97; and others. *Bibliog:* The Rebirth of Painting in the Late 20th Century, 2000, Psychostrategies of Auant-Grade, 2002, The End of Art, 2004, Cambridge Univ Press; Dialectic of Decadence, Allworth New York, 2003. *Mem:* Col Art Asn Am; Am Soc Aesthet; Am Inst Art Critics; Am Psychoanalytic Asn. *Publ:* Chihuly, Abrams, 97; Hans Hartung, Antibes, 98; The Rebirth of Painting in the Late 20th Century, Cambridge Univ Press, 2000; Redeeming Art: Critical Reveries, Allworth, 2000; Psychostrategies of Avant-Garde Art, Cambridge Univ Press, 2000. *Mailing Add:* Dept Art SUNY Stony Brook NY 11794-5400

KUSTERA, CARTER
CONCEPTUAL ARTIST, SCULPTOR
b Sault Ste Marie, Ontario, Sept 1, 62. *Study:* Algonquin Col, 82; Ont Col Art, 85. *Work:* Israel Mus, Jerusalem; Wake Forrest Univ, Winston-Salem, NC; Allem Mem Art Mus, Oberlin, Ohio; Bard Coll, Annadale-on-Hudson, NY. *Exhib:* Open 93: Emergency, Aperto, Biennale Venezia, 93; Fall from Fashion, Aldrich Mus Contemp Art, 93; Prospect 93, Frankfurter Kunstverein, Ger, 93; Am Art Today, Art Mus Fla Univ, Miami, 94; Home Video Redefined, Ctr Contemp Art, N Miami, Fla, 94; Take a Gook Look at Yourself, Hudson River Mus, Westchester, NY, 95; Caravanserri Contemp Art, Pascara, Italy, 95. *Awards:* Arts Grant B, Can Counc, 91; Pollack/Krasner Found, 93; NY Found Arts Grant, 96. *Bibliog:* An art bazaar abuzz, NY Times, 93; Grace Glueck (auth), Who's editing Kustera?, NY Observer, 93; Kate Taylor (auth), A spoof of talk TV, Toronto Globe & Mail, 94. *Media:* Conceptual Art

KUTNER, JANET
CRITIC, WRITER
b Sept 20, 37; US citizen. *Study:* Stanford Univ, 55-57; Southern Meth Univ, BA, 59. *Pos:* art critic, Dallas Morning News, 70-. *Awards:* Art Critics Award, Nat Endowment Arts, 76-77; Art Critics Fel, Nat Gallery Art, 91; Legand Award, Dallas Ctr for Contemp Art, 2005. *Mem:* Am Asn Mus; Int Coun Mus; Art Table. *Publ:* Coauth, David McManaway, Contemp Art Mus, Houston, 73; auth, James Surls, Tyler Mus Art, 74; various reviews of Texas exhibits for Artnews Mag, 75-. *Mailing Add:* Dallas Morning News Communs Ctr Dallas TX 75265

KUWAYAMA, GEORGE
CURATOR, HISTORIAN
b New York, NY, 25. *Study:* Williams Col, BA; Inst Fine Arts, NY Univ; Univ Mich, MA, PhD. *Collection Arranged:* Arts Treasures from Japan (ed & auth, catalog), 65; Contemporary Japanese Prints (auth, catalog), 72; Ceramics of Southeast Asia (auth, brochure), 72; Ancient Ritual Bronzes of China (auth, catalog), 76; Chinese Jade from Southern California Collections (auth, catalog), 77; Chinese Ceramics: The Heeramaneck Collection (auth, catalog), 73; The Joy of Collecting: Far Eastern Art from the Lidow Collection (auth, catalog), 80; The Bizarre Imagery of Yoshitoshi (co-auth, catalog), 80; Far Eastern Lacquer (auth, catalog), 82; Japanese Ink Painting (ed & auth, catalog), 85; Shippo: The Art of Enameling in Japan (auth, catalog), 87; The Quest for Eternity: The Sculptural Development of Ceramic Funerary Figures in China (ed & contribr), 87; Imperial Taste: Chinese Ceramics from the Percival David Foundation, The significance of Chinese Ceramics in the East and West (ed & contribr), 89; Ancient Mortuary Traditions of China (ed), 91; New Perspectives on the Art of Ceramics in China (ed), 92; Chinese Ceramics in Colonial Mexico (auth, catalog), 97. *Pos:* Cur Oriental art, Los Angeles Co Mus Art, 59-69, sr cur Far Eastern art, 69-96, sr cur emer, 96-. *Teaching:* Instr Chinese painting, Univ Calif, Los Angeles, 62; instr Far Eastern painting, Univ Southern Calif, 63; Univ Hawaii, 2000. *Awards:* Freer Fel, Univ Mich, 55; Hackney Fel, Am Oriental Soc, 56; Inter-Univ Fel, Ford Found, 57. *Bibliog:* Craig Clunas, rev Art in China, China Review Int, vol 6, no 1, 1999. *Mem:* Asn Asian Studies; Chinese Art Soc; Japan Soc; Int House Japan; Col Art Asn. *Res:* Far Eastern art and archaeology. *Publ:* Ed & contribr, The Great Bronze Age of China: A Symposium, Los Angeles Co Mus Art, 83; Archaeological Objects, Ceramics and Lacquer Works, Arts of Asia, 3-4/89; Beauty and Utility: the Lacquered Baskets of China, Orientations, 11-12/89; Watt and Ford, East Asian Lacquer: The Florence and Herbert Irving Collection, J Asian Studies, Vol 52, No 1, rev ed, 2/93; Qiangjin Lacquer, in Bulletin of the Oriental Ceramic Soc, Hong Kong, No 10, 92-94; Japan, Enamels, The Dictionary of Art, vol 17, pp 377-379, London, 1996; Chinese Ceramics in Colonial Peru, Oriental Art, vol XLVI, no 1, 2000; co-auth (with Anthony Pasinski) Chinese Ceramics in the Audiencia of Guatemala, Oriental Art, vol XLVIII, no 4, 2002; catalog entries in The Grandeur of Vicereal Mexico, Mus Fine Arts, Houston, 2002. *Mailing Add:* Los Angeles Co Mus Art 5905 Wilshire Blvd Los Angeles CA 90036

KUWAYAMA, TADAAKI
PAINTER, SCULPTOR
b Nagoya, Japan, Mar 4, 32. *Study:* Tokyo Univ Art, BFA, 56. *Work:* Albright-Knox Art Gallery, Buffalo, NY; Worcester Art Mus, Mass; Wadsworth Atheneum, Hartford, Conn; Larry Aldrich Mus, Ridgefield, Conn; Herron Art Mus, Indianapolis; and others. *Exhib:* Systemic Show, Guggenheim Mus, NY, 66; Plus by Minus, Today's Half-Century, Albright-Knox Art Gallery, 68; Kunst Wird Material, Nationalgalerie, Berlin, 82; Gegenwart Ewigkeit, Martin Gropius Bau, Berlin, 90; Scream Against the Sky, Guggenheim Mus & San Francisco Mus Mod Art, 94-95; Stiftung fur Konkrete Kunst, Reutlingen, Ger, 95; Kawamura Mem Mus, Japan, 96; and others. *Awards:* Nat Coun Arts Grant, 69; Adolph & Esther Gottlieb Found Grant, 86. *Bibliog:* Robert C Morgan (auth), Sculpture Mag, July/August, 2000. *Media:* Acrylic, Oil; Mixed Media. *Dealer:* Gallery Yamaguchi Osaka Japan; Renate Bender Munich Germany; Tamada Project Tokyo; Galeriekonig Germany. *Mailing Add:* 136 W 24th St New York NY 10011

KWAK, HOON
PAINTER
b Seoul, Korea, July 9, 41; US citizen. *Study:* Fine Art Col, Seoul Nat Univ, BFA, 63; Calif State Univ, Los Angeles, MA, 80, Long Beach, MFA, 82. *Work:* Security Pac Nat Bank, Los Angeles; Exec Life Insurance, Los Angeles; Mod Art Mus, Seoul, Korea; Manatt, Phelps, Rothenberg & Tunney Co, Los Angeles; Bear Stearns & Co, Los Angeles. *Comn:* Paintings, Conrad Hilton, Chicago, 85 & Compri Hotel, Aurora, Colo, 85. *Exhib:* Spokane Nat exhib, Cheney Cowles Mem Mus, Spokane, 81; 6 Artists, Nagasaki Prefecture Mus, Nagasaki, Japan, 81; 61st Nat Watercolor Soc exhib, Palm Springs, Calif, 81; New Comers, 81 & Only Los Angeles, 86, Los Angeles Municipal Art Gallery; Show-1 Winter, 81, Additional Space Expose V, 82 & 1 To 1, 85, Rental Gallery, Los Angeles Co Mus Art. *Awards:* Purchase Award, Minot State Col, NDak, 81; Past Pres Award, Nat Watercolor Soc, 81; Invitational Exhib Award, Pensacola Col, 82. *Media:* Acrylic, Oil. *Mailing Add:* 23602 Clearpool Pl Harbor City CA 90710-1113

KWIECINSKI, CHESTER MARTIN
EDUCATOR, PAINTER
b Youngstown, Ohio, July 7, 24. *Study:* Kansas City Art Inst, BFA & MFA; Kansas City Univ; Youngstown Univ. *Work:* Butler Inst Am Art, Youngstown, Ohio; El Paso Mus of Art, Tex. *Comn:* Historical murals, McSorley Colonial, Pittsburgh, Pa, 54; murals (with Bill Rakocy), Colonial House and Congo Rm, Youngstown, Ohio, 60 & Alberini Restaurant, Niles, Ohio, 65. *Exhib:* Mo State Fair, 49 & 50; Albright-Knox Gallery Art, Buffalo, NY, 52; El Paso Regional show, 76; one-man show, Butler Inst Art, Youngstown Ohio, 62. *Pos:* Mus dir, Abilene Fine Arts Mus, Tex, 73-80. *Teaching:* Instr, Warren City Schs, Ohio, 54-66; assoc prof painting, Col of Artesia, NMex, 67-71. *Awards:* Best Local Art, New Year Show, Butler Inst Am Art, 42; Purchase Award, Carlsbad Art Asn, NMex, 68; Purchase Award, Hobbs-LLano Estacado, Hobbs Art Asn, NMex, 69. *Mem:* Am Asn Mus; Tex Asn Mus; Permian Basin Mus Asn, 78. *Media:* Watercolor, Oil. *Publ:* Guest art ed, Abilene Reporter News, 74; auth, articles, Pigment & Form, 64

KWONG, EVA
SCULPTOR, CERAMIST
b Hong Kong, 54. *Study:* Oxbow Summer Sch Painting, Saugatuck, Mich, 74; RI Sch Design, Providence, BFA, 75; Tyler Sch Art, Temple Univ, MFA, 77. *Work:* Cranbrook Art Mus, Bloomfield Hills, Mich; Finnish Craft Mus, Helsinki, Finland; Butler Inst Am Art, Youngstown, Ohio; Slippery Rock State Univ, Pa; Shigaraki Ceramic Cult Park Mus, Japan; Racine Art Mus, Racine, Wis; Minneapolis Inst Art, Minn; Wright State Univ, Dayton Ohio. *Comn:* Bacteria, Diatoms and Cells, 2004 Nat'l Inst of Infections Disease Ctr for Disease Control of Preventions, Atlanta, GA. *Exhib:* Lill St Gallery, Navy Pier, Chicago, Ill, 91 & 92; solo shows, South Bend Mus Art, Ind, 93 & The Clay Place, Pittsburgh, Pa, 94; group shows, Everson Mus Art, Syracuse, NY, 93, Newark Mus, NJ, 93, Akron Art Mus, Ohio, 93, Cleveland State Univ, 93, Bellevue Art Mus, Wash, 93, Cleveland Mus Art, 94 & Craft Mus, Columbus, Ohio, 94; McDonough Mus Art, Youngstown, Ohio, 96; Carleton Col, Northfield, Minn, 96; plus many others; Minneapolis Inst Art, Minn; others. *Teaching:* Instr for numerous drawing & ceramic workshops throughout US & abroad; part-time fac, Kent State Univ, 89-. *Awards:* Ohio Arts Coun Fel, 88, 94, 99 & 2004; Nat

Endowment Arts, 88; Pa Coun Arts Fel, 85 & 87. *Bibliog:* Article, Monthly Craft Mag, Seoul, Korea, Vol 1, No 9, 54-55, 11/88; Barbara Tannenbaum (auth), Ohio Perspectives: 5 Sculptors, Akron Art Mus, 93; Tom E Hinson (auth), The Invitational: Artists of Northeast Ohio, Cleveland Mus Art, 94. *Media:* Clay, Paper. *Dealer:* William Busta Gallery 2021 Murray Hill Rd Cleveland OH 44106; Sybaris Gallery 301 W Fourth St Royal Oak MI 48067; Sherrie Galleries

L

LABAT, TONY
CONCEPTUAL ARTIST, SCULPTOR
b Nov 14, 51. *Study:* San Francisco Art Inst, BFA, 78, MFA, 80. *Work:* Mus Mod Art, NY; George Pompidou, Paris, France; Long Beach Mus Art, Calif; Newport Harbor Art Mus, Newport Beach, Calif; Open Heim Collection, Bonn, Ger. *Comn:* Installations, Works Progress Admin, Washington, 85, Capp St Proj, San Francisco, 87 & Mus Contemp Art, Los Angeles, 88. *Exhib:* Am Art of the late 80's traveling exhib, Boston & Europe, 88; Fuller-Gross Gallery, San Francisco, Calif, 88; Bay Area Media, San Francisco Mus Mod Art, 90; Idealist, Ingrid Raab Gallery, Berlin, 90. *Teaching:* Prof performance/video, San Francisco Art Inst, 85-; prof media, Univ Calif, San Diego, 86-87. *Awards:* Grant, Nat Endowment Arts, 87; Fleishhacker Found Grant, 87; Engelhard Award, Boston, 88; Asn Visual Artists. *Bibliog:* Jan Butterfield (auth), Object Poem, Henry Art Gallery, 86; Alfred Jan (auth), A Critique of Culture, High Performance, 87; Carlo McCormick (auth), Tony Labat, Artspace, 87. *Media:* Performance, Video. *Mailing Add:* c/o San Francisco Art Inst 800 Chestnut St San Francisco CA 94133

LABLE, ELIOT
SCULPTOR
b Apr 24, 37. *Study:* Ohio Univ, BA, 59; New Sch, 70-73; Brooklyn Mus Art Sch, 72-73. *Work:* City Art Mus Helsinki, Finland; Bd Educ; Pub Art for Pub Schs; Museo de Arte, Costarricense, Costa Rica; Mus Modern Art, Helsinki, Finland. *Comn:* Coop Tech HS Comn; Root Mem Outdoor sculpture; Creative Path, Flushing Town Hall, Flushing, NYC, 2005; Queen Council Exhib, 2005; Bd of Dir Nurture, Art, Guggenheim Mus. *Exhib:* Reflections Ann, Aldrich Mus Contemp Art, 76; 55 Mercer St Gallery, 84 & 86-96; Gallerie Pelen, Helsinki, Finland, 87, 88 & 94; Gallerie Ostermahl, Stockholm, Sweden, 88; Contemp Mus Costa Rica (auth, catalog), 92; Impremo Atelier Print Show (auth, catalog), Helsinki, Finland, 92 & 94; Bothnia Ice Sculpture Competition (with catalog), Oulu Art Mus, Finland, 96; and others; Cooptech Pub Comn, New York City, 99; Long Island City Art Frenzy, New York City, 2001; Chelsea Studio Gallery, New York City, 2002; Dam Struhltraber Gallery, NY, 2002; Queens Coun on the Arts Exhib, NY, 2003. *Teaching:* Adj lectr, LaGuardia Col; mem fac, Brooklyn Mus Art Sch, 78-85, LaGuardia Col, 85-. *Awards:* Nat Endowment Arts Artist in Residence Grant, 83; Fulbright Grant, 94; Kellogg Found Grant, 96-97. *Bibliog:* Kivirinta (auth), Helsinki Sanomat, review, 1/92; Pessi Rautio (auth), Review Helsinki Sonomas, 94; Diane Nahas (auth), review, Woodside Queens Gazette, 5/95; Marja Salmela (auth), review, Helsingen Sonomat, 2/96; James Della Fiora (auth), review, The Villager, 5/96; Natasha Sweeten (auth), review, 11211, 2002. *Mem:* Fulbright Asn. *Media:* Welded Steel. *Collection:* PorkKana Col, Helsinki, Finland; Contemp Mus, Helsinki, Finland; City Mus, Helsinki, Finland; Contemp Mus, Costa Rica. *Publ:* Auth, Galerie (catalog), Pelin, 88 & 94; Contemporary Museum, Costa Rica (catalog), 92. *Mailing Add:* 43-01 21st St Long Island City NY 11101

LA BOBGAH, ROBERT GORDON
SCULPTOR, VIDEO ARTIST
b Montreal, Que, Nov 22, 36. *Study:* Concordia Univ, Montreal, BA, 62; Western Mich Univ, Kalamazoo, MA, 67. *Work:* Nat Gallery Alvethorpe, Libr Congress, Washington, DC; Nat Gallery Can, Ottawa; Philadelphia Mus Art; Andy Warhol Mus; Hijikata Tatsumi Mem Archive, Tokyo; Kazuo Ohno, Tokyo. *Comn:* Ceramic murals, Hamburg Bros, Pittsburgh, Pa, 77; stages of the cross in ceramic, Immaculate Conception Church, Clarion, Pa, 78. *Exhib:* Carnegie Inst Art, Pittsburgh, Pa, 87 & 92; Pittsburgh Biennial, Pittsburgh Ctr, 94; Brew House, Space 101, NEA, Pittsburgh, Pa, 98; Soc of Sculptors, Pittsburgh, Pa, 2002; Pittsburgh Filmakers, Pa, 2005; Artists Upstairs, Pittsburgh, Pa, 2006. *Teaching:* Instr, Pittsburgh Ctr Arts, Pa, 88-91. *Awards:* Purchase Award, Erie Art Mus, 87; Jurors Award, Auburn Works on Paper, Ala, 86 & Westmoreland Mus Art, 86; Gloria Fitzgibbons Award, Pittsburgh, 92; Print Group Award, PGI, 2000. *Bibliog:* Murry Horn, Monogr, Pittsburgh Biennial, 9/94; article, PGH City Paper, 2/2000; NEA Forecast Regional, Space 101, Catalogue, Pittsburgh, Pa, 98. *Mem:* Soc Sculptors, Pittsburgh; Pittsburgh Soc Artists; Philadelphia Print Club. *Media:* Mixed Media. *Publ:* Coauth, The Paper Bird Handmade Book, Pvt publ, 72; Book I: The Book of Unnabeable Rites of Mystery, Unique Press, 2000; Book II: The House Song of the Theatrical Bamboo Cutter, Unique Press, 2003; Pittsburgh Post-Gazette, 6/2005; Pittsburgh City Paper, 6/2006. *Dealer:* DeVechis Gallery Philadelphia PA; Gallerie Chiz, Pittsburgh, Pa; Space Gallery, Pittsburgh, PA. *Mailing Add:* 319 S Atlantic Ave Pittsburgh PA 15224-2310

LABONTE, DICK
PAINTER
b Battle Creek, Mich, 21. *Study:* Colgate Univ, NMex; Chicago Acad Fine Arts, Ill; studied with Alfred Krakusin & John Hennigan. *Work:* Cocktails at White House, Pres & Mrs Bill Clinton; White House, Washington, DC; Cocktails at White House, Pres & Mrs George Bush; Schering-Plough Corp, NJ; Manasquan Libr, NJ; Borough Hall, Bay Head, NJ. *Comn:* Holiday on Wall St, McGraw Hill Publ, 79; Spring Lake 1892, Spring Lake Hist Soc, 92. *Exhib:* Anchor & Palette Gallery, Bay Head, NJ; William Ris Galleries, Stone Harbor, NJ; Foligraph Galleries, Falls Church, Va; Solo exhib, Anchor & Palette Gallery, Bay Head, NJ, Peck Sch, Morristown, NJ, Artists Guild Ocean Co, NJ, Main St Gallery, Manasquan, NJ; Lovelandtown Mus, Bay Head, NJ,; Schering-Plough Corp, NJ. *Teaching:* instr, NJ artists groups & sch's, currently. *Mem:* Manasquan River Group Artists, NJ; Artists Guild Ocean Co, NJ. *Media:* Acrylic, Oil. *Specialty:* Americana and nostalgia themes, NJ beach scenes. *Publ:* auth, Paintings of the Jersey Shore and More, Jersey Shore Publications. *Dealer:* LaBonte Prints Inc PO Box 96 Bay Head NJ 08742. *Mailing Add:* Anchor & Palette Gallery PO Box 96 45 Mount St Bay Head NJ 08742

LABRIE, CHRISTY
STAINED GLASS ARTIST, PAINTER
b Portsmouth, NH, June 24, 43. *Study:* Boston Ctr Adult Ed, Sacred Heart Hosp Sch Nursing, Manchester. *Work:* Healing & Restoration Office, Mission Ch, Boston; Carmelite Monastery, Concord, NH; LaSalette Shrine, Attleboro, Mass (lost in fire 99); St Anselm Col, Manchester, NH (one of earliest works). *Comn:* Numerous pvt comns. *Exhib:* Southhampton Glassworks & Galerie, Palm Beach, Fla; Sheafs Warehouse Mus, Portsmouth, NH. *Pos:* emergency rm nurse; quality reviewer and coding analyst; clin research nurse, Peter Bent Brigham Hosp, Joslin Diabetes Found, USDA Human Aging at Tufts U, Boston. *Teaching:* Classes, lectures & assembly, Archdiocesan Choir Boy Sch, Cambridge, Mass. *Awards:* Award Medal, Outstanding People of the 20th Century, Intl Biographical Centre, Cambridge, Eng, 98. *Mem:* Our Lady's Rosary Makers. *Media:* Stained Glass; Acrylic Paints. *Publ:* Illusr, cover artist, Yankee Mag, 1/76 & Our Lady's Missionary, 10/76, Soul Mag, 9-10/86; Christmas card, Healing & Restoration Ministry, 90 & 91; contribr, Randy the Rooster (children's book); coauth of several abstracts & papers publ in sci/med j. *Mailing Add:* PO Box 580 Rye Beach NH 03871

LACHAPELLE, DAVID
PHOTOGRAPHER
Study: Art Student's League & Sch Visual Arts, NY. *Exhib:* LaChapelle Land, Staley-Wise Gallery, NY, 96. *Awards:* VH1 Fashion Award, Photographer of the Year; Infinity Award Applied Photog, Int Ctr Photog, 97. *Publ:* Auth, LaChapelle Land, Callaway Ed/Simon & Schuster. *Mailing Add:* c/o Staley Wise Gallery 560 Broadway New York NY 10012

LACHMAN, AL
PAINTER
b Bronx, NY, Oct 17, 36. *Study:* Syracuse Univ, 1953-54; Art Students League, 1955-60; studied with Robert Phillip & Americo DiFranza. *Work:* Walt Disney Corp Collection, Orlando, Fla; Hershey Corp Collection, Pa; Ford Motor Co, Detroit, Mich; Domino Pizza Collection, Detroit, Mich; Central Libr Denver, Colo. *Exhib:* Pastels Only, Salmagundi Club, NY, 83; Cherry Creek Nat Art Show, Cherry Creek Found, Denver, Colo, 90; Las Olas Nat First Show, Las Olas Mus, Fla, 91; Gasparilla Nat Arts Show, Tampa Mus, Fla, 92; Boca Raton Art Show, Crocker Mus, Fla, 93; Nat Art Show, Bruce Mus, Greenwich, Conn, 94; Contemp Eye, Michener Mus, New Hope, Pa, 2005. *Collection Arranged:* Northwest Airlines; Walt Disney Corp Collection; Univ Ga Law Sch; Baptist Hosp, Fla; Sun Bank. *Pos:* Founder, PSA for Pastels only, Nat Arts Club, NY. *Teaching:* instr, workshops int, currently. *Awards:* Best of Show, Las Olas Nat Art Show, Las Olas Mus Art, 91; Best of Show, Giffuni Mem Award, Pastel Soc Am Nat, 92; Best of Show, Naples Nat, Eden Found, 2000. *Bibliog:* P Sessler (auth), Artists Mag, F&W Publ, 94; Krachen (auth), Best of Pastel, North Lights Books, 96; P Metzger (auth), Artists Encyl, North Light Books, 2000. *Mem:* Pastel Soc Am (dir bd control, formerly); Pastel Soc Can; Salmagundi Club; Pastel Soc Kans; Nat Drawing Asn. *Media:* Acrylic, Oil. *Publ:* contribr, Pastel Interpretations, North Light Books, 95; contribr, Best of Pastel, North Light Books, 96; contribr, Artists Encyl, North Light Books, 2000; Contribr, Artists of the River Town, River Arts Press, 2002. *Mailing Add:* Lachman Gallery 39 North Main St New Hope PA 18938

LACK, RICHARD FREDERICK
PAINTER, INSTRUCTOR
b Minneapolis, Minn, Mar 26, 28. *Study:* Minneapolis Sch Art; R H Ives Gammell Studios, Boston. *Work:* Maryhill Mus Fine Arts, Washington; Elizabeth T Greenshields Mem Found Collection, Montreal, Que; Springville Mus Art, Utah; Newark Mus Art, NJ. *Comn:* Six portraits of Joseph P Kennedy, Jr, comn by Ambassador Kennedy & Kennedy Found, NY; portraits of Gov Wendell Anderson and Gov Albert Quie. *Exhib:* Allied Artists Am, 53; Boston Arts Festival, 53 & 54; Nat Acad Design Ann, 55; Twin City Biennial, Minneapolis Inst Arts, 62; Am Artists Prof League Nat, 67-73; solo exhibs, Brigham Young Univ, Provo, Utah, 72 & St Thomas Acad, St Paul, Minn, 77; Classical Realism - The Other Twentieth Century (traveling show), Tex, Wash, Utah, 83; Minneapolis Inst Arts, 88; The Relevance on Beauty, NY, 94. *Teaching:* Found dir & instr painting & drawing, Atelier Lack, Minneapolis, 69-. *Awards:* First Prize, Copley Soc, Boston, 62; Gold Medal, Am Artists Prof League, 67 & 73 & Margaret Fernald Dole Prize for Best Portrait, 72; and others. *Bibliog:* D Jardine (auth), Richard Lack's atelier system of training painters, Am Artist Mag, 6/71; Stephen Giertson (auth), Richard Lack, An American Master, ASCR, 2001. *Media:* Oil, Pastel. *Publ:* Auth, On the Training of Painters and Notes on the Atelier Program, 79 & Classical Realism, The Other Twentieth Century, 82, Atelier Lack Inc; Realism in Revolution, Taylor, 85; Contribr & ed, Classical Realism Quart & The Classical Realism J. *Mailing Add:* 5827 Louis Ave Minnetonka MN 55343

LACK, STEPHEN
PAINTER, FILMMAKER
b Montreal, Que, Aug 27, 46. *Study:* Columbia Univ, New York, with Tony Padovano, 66; McGill Univ, BA, 67; Inst Allende, San Miguel, Mex, MFA, 69; Ecole des Beaux, Montreal; Otis Art Inst, Los Angeles. *Work:* Australian Art Gallery, Canberra; MTV & NY Pub Libr, NY; Print Div, New York Pub Libr; Quadracci Col, Imperial Oil,

Pewaukee, Wis; Jerusalem Mus, Israel; Elmhurst Mus, Chicago, Ill. *Comn:* Mural, Societe Int Transporte Aeronautique, Switz, 88; Artes Magnus, Ancienne Manufacture Royale, De Limoges, France; Rutgers Archives Print-making, Voorhees Zimmerleig Mus, New Brunswick, NJ; Grey Art Gallery, NY. *Exhib:* Weatherspoon Art Gallery, Univ NC, 89; solo exhibs, Galerie Daniel, Montreal, 90, Galerie Nadeau, Philadelphia, 91, Galerie Dresdnere, Toronto, 91, 93 & 95, Joyce Goldstein Gallery, NY, 95 & 97, Simon Dresdnere Gallery, Toronto, Can, 93, Gallery Dijkstra, Belg, 96 & Leo Kamen, Toronto, Can, 97; Motion as Metaphor, Birginia Beach Ctr Arts, 91; Rutgers Mus, NJ, 92; Hopper Mus, Nyack, NY, 96; The Edge of Innocence (with catalog), Lyman Allyn Mus, New London Ctr, 98-99; Gallery One, Toronto, 99, 01; Gallery Dyjhstra, Antwerp, Belgium, 00; Dorfman Projects Bronze Edit, 01; NY Acad Art Benefit, 01. *Teaching:* Artist-in-residence, Fla State Univ, Ancienne Manufacture, Royale, Limoges, France, Banff Inst, Alta, Can, 87; studio workshop, Long Island Univ, 88; artist-in-residence, Ford Motor Co, Dearborn, Mich; lectr, New York Artists Studio Workshop & Ford Moter Co, Detroit. *Awards:* Nat Endowment for the Arts, 87 & 93; Canada Council Award, 91. *Bibliog:* Timothy Cohrs (auth), Stephen Lack print portfolio, Arts Mag, 4/88; Eileen Myles (auth), Steven Lack: one man show, Art Am, 12/89; Katie Clifford (auth), Art News, 3/99. *Media:* Paint on Canvas. *Publ:* Auth, Just Get Me Out of Here, Eldindean Press, 87. *Dealer:* Joyce Goldstein Gallery 39 Wooster St New York NY 10013; Leo Kamen Gallery 80 Spadina Ave Suite 406 Toronto ON M5V 2J3

LACKEY, JANE W
FIBER ARTIST
b 48. *Study:* Calif Col Arts & Crafts, BFA, 74; Cranbrook Acad Art, MFA, 79. *Work:* Nelson-Atkins Mus Art, Kansas City, Mo; Johnson Co Community Col, Overland Park, Kans; Art Options, NY; Am Craft Mus; James A Michener Collection Kent State Univ, Ohio. *Exhib:* Solo exhibs, Charlotte Crosby Kemper Gallery, Kansas City Art Inst, Mo, 82, Hokin/Kaufman Gallery, Chicago, 88, Textile Art Ctr, Chicago, 93, Gallery Art, Johnson Co Community Col, Overland Park, Kans, 94, I Space, Chicago, 94, Sybaris Gallery, Royal Oak, Mich, 95, 98, Grand Arts, Kansas City, Mo, 96, Roy Boyd Gallery, Chicago, 97, 00, 02, Cranbrook Art Mus, Bloomfield Hills, Mich, 99, Dolphin Gallery, Kansas City, Mo, 00; 14th Int Biennial of Tapestry, Mus Cantonal Beaux-Arts, Lausanne, Switz, 89; St Louis Art Mus, 95; Cloth Reveries, Macalester Col Art Galleries, St Paul, Minn, 96; Regional Expressions, NDak Mus Art, Grand Forks, 97; Off the Map, Paint Creek Ctr Arts, Rochester, Mich, 97; Cranbrook: POSTOPIA, Craft & Folk Art Mus, Los Angeles, 99; Remnants of Memory, Asheville Art Mus, NC, 2000; Ctr Galleries, Detroit, 01, 02; Dolphin Gallery, Kansas City, Mo, 02. *Collection Arranged:* Detroit Inst Arts; Am Craft Mus; Arthur Andersen and Co, Chicago; Xerox Corp, Washington, DC; Sigal Corp, Washington, DC. *Pos:* Guest cur, Muskegon Mus Art, 79; juror, Wichita Art Mus, 81; juror, Lawrence Arts Ctr, 82; co-cur, Charlotte Crosby Kemper Gallery, Kansas City Art Inst, 92; juror, Art Ctr, 91; juror, Adams Mem Gallery, 88; artist in residence, Cranbrook Acad of Art, Mich. *Teaching:* Prof & dept chair, Fiber Dept, Kansas City Art Inst, 80-; numerous vis artist lect, Art Inst Chicago, Calif Col Arts & Crafts, Cranbrook Acad Art, Kent State Univ, Vis Artists Consortium, Univ Kans, Haystack Sch Arts & Crafts. *Awards:* Nat Endowment Arts, 84 & 88; US/France Exchange, Nat Endowment Arts, 89; Grand Arts Exhib Grant, Margaret Hall Silva Found, 95-97; Ill Arts Coun Artists Fel Award, 97. *Bibliog:* Garrett Holg (auth), Art News, 11/95; Marsha Miro (auth), Detroit Free Press, 3/95; Alice Thorson (auth), Kansas City Star, 11/95. *Media:* Mixed Media, Drawing. *Dealer:* Roy Boyd Gallery 739 N Wells Chicago IL 60610

LACKTMAN, MICHAEL
CRAFTSMAN, JEWELER
b Philadelphia, Pa, Mar 1, 38. *Study:* Pa State Col, 57-61; Cranbrook Acad of Art, Bloomfield Hills, Mich, 61-63; Kunsthaandverskolen, Copenhagen, Denmark, 65-66. *Work:* Pa State Col, Millersville, Pa; Cranbrook Acad Art, Bloomfield Hills, Mich; Metrop Art Mus, NY; Chicago Art Inst; Philadelphia Art Mus; and others. *Comn:* Liturgical metalry, Redeemer Lutheran Church, Livermore, Calif, 71; Kiddusch cup, Brandeis Univ, Waltham, Mass, 63. *Exhib:* California Design VI, Crocker Art Mus, Sacramento, 69; California Design XI, Pasadena Art Mus, 71; Metal Experience, Oakland Art Mus, Calif, 71; 4th Int Jewelry Exhib, Schmuckmuseum, Pzorheim, Ger, 72; Diamond Today: Int Jewelry Exhib, NY, 75. *Collection Arranged:* The Brooklyn Mus; Art Inst Chicago; Philadelphia Art Mus; Met Mus Art; Oakland Art Mus; Dallas Art Mus; Milwaukee Art Mus. *Pos:* Prof emeritus. *Teaching:* Asst prof design, Univ Calif, Berkeley, 66-73, Univ Chile, Santiago, 72-73; prof jewelry & metalsmithing, Univ Wis-Milwaukee, 73, art prof, 1973-95. *Awards:* Louis Comfort Tiffany Grant, 63; Ford Found Grant, 72-73; Nat Endowment Humanities Grant, 75. *Bibliog:* Articles & photographs of work, Art & Archit, 71 & Playboy Mag, 75. *Mem:* Am Craftsman Coun; San Francisco Bay Asn; Sterling-Silversmiths Guild Am; Scand-Am Found; Col Art Asn. *Media:* Jewelry, Metals. *Mailing Add:* 573 Park Estates Sq Venice Park FL 34293

LACOM, WAYNE CARL
PAINTER, GRAPHIC ARTIST
b Glendale, Calif, Oct 11, 22. *Study:* Art Ctr Sch, 42; Chuoinard Art Inst, 43-44; Jepson Art Inst, 45-46; Univ Calif Exten, 50. *Work:* Brand Libr Gallery, Glendale, Calif, Los Angeles Unified Sch Dist; Hawaiian Airlines; Brand Libr, Glendale, Calif; Lahaina Restoration Found. *Comn:* Bronze sculpture, Flamingo Hotel, Las Vegas, 70; painting, Hawaiian Airlines, Honolulu, 71; stained glass window, comn by Mr & Mrs Taub, Encino, Calif, 72; painting, Security Pacific Bank, Glendale, Calif, 75. *Exhib:* Artists of Los Angeles & Vicinity, Los Angeles Co Mus Art, Calif, 50; Watercolor Exhib, Santa Barbara Art Mus, Calif, 52; Pasadena Mus Art, Pasadena, Calif, 53; Denver Mus Art, Colo, 54; Cuernavaca Art Mus, Mex, 55; Lahaina Restoration Found Mus, Lahaina, Hawaii, 88; Heritage Mus, Calif Watercolorist, Santa Monica, Calif, 2004; Bakersfield Mus Art; Sullivan Goss Gallery, Santa Barbara, Calif. *Pos:* Pres, Int Art Serv, 78-. *Teaching:* Instr watercolor, Los Angeles Unified Sch Dist, Adult Educ, 47-78; Instr, School of the Arts, E Los Angeles City College, 80-90. *Awards:* First Place, Glendale Art Asn, 48; Best of show, Catalina Art Fest, 89; Best of Show, Lahaina Town Exhib, Lahaina, Hawaii, 93 & 98. *Bibliog:* The Creative Hand (video), Los Angeles Unified Sch Dist, 73; California Watercolors, 1850-1970, Hillcrest Press. *Mem:* Nat Watercolor Soc (pres, 65-66); Artists for Educ Action (treas, 67-73). *Media:* Watercolor, Acrylic. *Publ:* Transparent Watercolor, 73 & Landscapes, 77, Davis Publ; Palette Talk, Grumbacher, 75; The California Style, Hillcrest Press, 85; The California Romantics, Artra, 86; McClelland & Last (auths), California Watercolors 1850-1970, Hillcrest Press, 2003. *Dealer:* Village Gallery 120 Dickenson St Lahaina HI 96761; Gordon McClelland PO Box 3564 San Clemente CA 92672. *Mailing Add:* 16703 Alginet Pl Encino CA 91436

LACY, SUZANNE
CONCEPTUAL ARTIST, WRITER
b Wasco, Calif, Oct 21, 45. *Study:* Bakersfield Col, Calif, AA, 65; Univ Calif, Santa Barbara, BA (zoological scis, with honors), 68; Calif Inst Arts, MFA (social design), 73; Studied with Judy Chicago, Sheila de Bretteville & Allan Kaprow. *Comn:* Martk Taper Forum, Los Angeles, Calif, 73; Studio Watts Workshop, Los Angeles, Calif, 75-77; Nev Humanities Com, Las Vegas, 78; Law Enforcement Assistance Asn, Los Angeles, Calif, 79; Center Music Experiment, San Diego, Calif, 83. *Exhib:* One-woman shows, Montgomery Gallery, Pomona Col, 83; Video Art: A History, Mus Mod Art, NY, 83; Committed to Print, Mus Mod Art, NY, 88; Full Circle (installation), Chicago, 93; Underground (installation), Three Rivers Art Festival, Pittsburgh, 93; The Roof is on Fire, Oakland, 94; Auto on Edge of Time, Snug Harbor Cult Ctr, NY, 94; Auto on the Edge of Time: A Retrospective of Works on Violence, Snug Harbor Cutl Ctr, Staten Island, NY, 94; In a Different Light, Univ Art Mus, Berkeley, Calif, 95; Out of Action, Mus Contemp Art, Los Angeles, 98; and others. *Pos:* Mem nat adv bd, Art Dept, Carnegie Mellon Univ, 92-; artist in residence, Oakland Sharing Vision, 96-2000; city arts comnr, City of Oakland, Calif, 99-2001, mayor's task force edn, 99; mem adv bd, Attidunal Healing Connection, Oakland, Calif, 2000-. *Teaching:* Minneapolis Col Art & Design, 85-86; Sch Art Inst Chicago, 86; vis artist, Carleton Col, 87; dean, Sch Fine Arts, Calif Col Arts & Crafts, 87-97; spec asst to pres serv learning, Ctr Art and Pub Life, Calif Col Arts and Crafts, 97-98, dir, 98-; mem edn and arts task force, Oakland Unified Sch Dist, Calif, 2001; mem supt's task force schs, Alameda Co Office Educ, 2001. *Awards:* Individual Artists Fel, Nat Endowment Arts, 79, 81, 85 & 92 & Media Arts Grant, 92; Guggenheim Fel, 92; Award Pub Serv, NY Benevolence Coun, 95; Grant, Surdna Found 96, 97 & 98, Inst Noetic Scis and Fetzer Inst, 98, Nathan Cummings Found, 98, 99 & 2000, Fleishhacker Found, 99, Tides Found, Potrero Neuvo Fund, 99, Levi Strauss Found, 99, Morris Stulsaft Found, 99, Richard and Rhonda Goldman Fund, 99 & Oakland Found Children and Youth, 99; Fel, Creative Works Fund, 98 & Flintridge Found, 2000; many others. *Bibliog:* Jennifer Fisher (auth), Interperformance: the live tableaux of Suzanne Lacy, Janine Antoni, and Marina Abramovic, Art Jour, 97; Meiling Cheng (auth), Sacred naked nature girls, TDR: Jour Performance Studies, Summer/98; Katy Deepwell (auth), Suzanne Lucy on new genre public art, n.paradoxa 4, 99; Charles R Garoian (auth), Performing Pedagogy: Toward an Art of Politics, SUNY Press, 99; Nic Paget-Clarke (auth), An Interview with Suzanne Lacy: Art and Advocacy, In Motion Mag, 11/2000. *Mem:* Los Angeles Inst Contemp Art; The Woman's Bldg (mem bd, 74-79); Women's Caucus Arts (nat bd, 79-82). *Media:* Theatrical and Non-Theatrical Performance; Installation, Books and Video. *Publ:* ed, Mapping The Terrain: New Genre Public Art, Bay Press, 94; Affinities: Thoughts on An Incomplete History in The Power of Feminist Art, Abrams, 94; co-auth, Jo Hanson, Susan Steinman, WCA, 97; ed, Mapping the Terrain: New Genre Public art, Bay Press, Seattle, 95; auth, Prostitution notes, Veiled Histories: The Body, Place and Public Art, Critical Press, 97. *Mailing Add:* 28 Privateer St Apt 5 Marina Del Rey CA 90292-6761

LADD, BETH
PAINTER
b Bennington, Vt, Aug 15, 44. *Study:* Sch Mus Fine Arts, Tufts Univ, BFA, 70; Harvard Grad Sch Design, MLA, 75. *Comn:* Hologram, Warner Lambert Co, Morris Plains, NJ, 70. *Exhib:* Lasers & Holograms traveling exhib, Mus Contemp Art, Chicago, 70, Ft Lauderdale Mus Art, Fla, 71 & Akron Art Mus, 71; Oil Paintings, Pindar Gallery Soho, 90; Time Out of Time, Bromfield Gallery, 91; Time Out of Time, Umbrella Ctr Arts, Concord, Mass, 91; Seventh Triennial Exhib, Fuller Mus Art, Brocton, Mass, 93; Weeping Beech Series, Digital Equip Corp, Marlboro, Mass, 94. *Awards:* Norman T Newton Award, Harvard Grad Sch Design, 72 & Ford Found Grant, 75. *Bibliog:* Christine Temin (auth), Critic's tip, Boston Globe, 11/1/90; Nancy Stapen (auth), Artists who create personal images of the divine, Boston Globe, 9/12/91; Christine Temin (auth), Fuller Triennial, Boston Globe, 6/4/93. *Media:* All Media. *Publ:* Coauth & illusr, Wetlands and the WaterCycle (monogr), MA Audubon, 75; A Method for Resource Analysis, Ulster Co EMC, 75; illusr, An Introduction to Groundwater and Aquifers (monogr), 83 & Mapping Aquifers and Recharge Areas (monogr), 84, MA Audubon; contribr, New American Paintings, Open Studios Press, 92

LADER, MELVIN PAUL
HISTORIAN, EDUCATOR
b Auburn, NY, Jan 30, 47. *Study:* State Univ NY, Albany, BA, 69, MA, 72; Univ Del, PhD, 81. *Collection Arranged:* Peggy Guggenheim Collection, Solomon R Guggenheim Mus, Venice, 87; Arshile Gorky Drawings Retrospective, Whitney Mus of Am Art, 2003. *Pos:* exhib consult, Stephen Mazoh & Co, New York, 94 & Gagosian Gallery, New York, 98. *Teaching:* Prof art hist, George Washington Univ, 78-. *Awards:* Mus Fel, Smithsonian Inst, 77-78; Fel, Rockefeller Found, 78. *Mem:* Col Art Asn; Arch Am Art; Catalogue Raisonne Scholars' Asn. *Res:* Abstract expressionism; twentieth century American art; modern art patronage. *Publ:* Auth,

Graham, Gorky, DeKooning and the Ingres revival in America, 78, Howard Putzel: Proponent of surrealism and abstract expressionism in America, 82 & Arshile Gorky's The artist and his mother, 1/84, Arts Mag; Arshile Gorky, Abbeville, NY, 85; Peggy Guggenheim's Art of This century in Peggy Guggenheim's Other Legacy (exhib catalog), Solomon R Guggenheim Mus, 87; David Porter's Personal Statement: A Painting Propjecy, 1950, Archives of Am Art Jour, 88; Arshile Gorky: A Modern Artist in the Academic Tradition in Arshile Gorky: Works on Paper (exhib catalog), Peggy Guggenheim Collection, Venice, 92; The Paintings of Charles Seliger: Nature and Vision (intro), Charles Seliger: Redefining Abstract Expressionism, 2003. *Mailing Add:* Dept Art George Washington Univ 801 22nd St NW Washington DC 20052

LADERMAN, GABRIEL
PAINTER, EDUCATOR
b Brooklyn, NY, Dec 26, 29. *Study:* Atelier 17, with S W Hayter 49 & 52; Hans Hofmann Sch Fine Arts, 49; with DeKooning at studio, 49-50; Brooklyn Col, BA, 52; Cornell Univ, MFA, 57. *Work:* Meade Mus, Amherst, Mass; Glen C Janss Collection, Boise Art Mus; Nat Gallery Art, Washington, DC; FMC Corp, Chicago; Cleveland Mus Art; Mus Fine Arts, Boston; and pvt collections of Edward Pillsbury, Robert Natkin, Malcolm Holtzman, William Bailey & Davidson Collection; plus others. *Exhib:* Brooklyn Mus, 58 & 59; Am Sense of Reality, Milwaukee Art Ctr, 69; Trends in Contemp Realist Painting, Boston Mus Fine Art, 74; one-person exhibs, Inst of Int Educ, UN, NY, 78, Nat Mus Malaysia, Kuala Lumpur, 82, Cornell Univ, 82, Meade Mus, Amhurst Col, Mass, 83, Joel Berger Gallery, Provincetown, Mass, Contemp Realist Gallery, San Francisco, 87 & 90 & Jessica Darraby Gallery, Los Angeles, 87; Contemp Am Realism Since 1960, Pa Acad Fine Arts, traveling to Va Mus Fine Arts, Oakland Mus, Gulbenkian, Lisbon & Germanische Nationalmuseum, Nuremberg, 81; Narrative Painting, Fla Int Univ Mus, Miami, 88; Joel Berger Gallery, Provincetown, Mass, 88; 100th Anniversary Exhib, Pratt Inst, New York City Gallery, traveling to Brooklyn Campus, 88; The Nude, One Penn Plaza, NY, 88; Storytelling: Narrative Painting, NJ Ctr for Visual Arts, 88; Objects Observed: Contemp Still-life, Gallery Henoch, NY, 90. *Pos:* Provost's tenure comt, Yale Univ, 82; juror, Nat Endowment Arts, 83, NY State Coun on Arts, 85-86; invited commentator, MacArthur Found, 86, 87 & 88; invited judge, Univ Va, 88. *Teaching:* Asst prof, State Univ NY, 57-59, Pratt Inst, 59 68; artist in residence, La State Univ, 66-67; prof, Queens Col, 66-, chmn, 79-82; vis prof, grad sch, Yale Univ, 68-69, 81, 83 & 89; fac, Skowhegan Sch Painting & Sculpture, 70 & 71; instr painting, Tanglewood Inst, 73 & Yale-Norfolk Sch, 74; founding dir summer landscape prog, Queens Col, 80-81; visiting critic & guest lectr at many cols, univs and institutions throughout US, Australia & Asia. *Awards:* Fulbright Fel to Italy, 62-63; Nat Endowment Arts Sr Fel, 81-82, 82-83 & 86-87; Ingram Merrill Found, 75-77 & 84; JS Guggenheim Fel, 88; Altman prize for Figure Painting 170th Annual Exhib of Nat Acad, 1995, vis Artist Univ Pa, 1997, juror Bowery Gallery Exhib, 96, vis distinguished prof Am Univ, 94-95, Washington. *Bibliog:* Don Gray (auth), Laderman at Schoelkopf, Artworld, 86; Jed Perl (auth), review article, New Criterion, 87; John L Ward (auth), American Realist Painting 1945-1980 (2 reproductions), UMI Res Press, Ann Arbor, 89. *Mem:* Nat Acad. *Media:* Oil, Pastel. *Collection:* represented in permanent collections Witherspoon Mus, Cleveland Mus, Mus Fine Arts, Boston, Brandeis Univ Art Mus, Chase-Manhattan Bank, A.D. White Mus Cornell Univ, Nat Gallery Art, Muzium Negara, Kuala Lumpur, Mead Mus Amherst Coll, Glen S. Janss Collection Boise Art Mus, Federal Maritime Commission Corp. Chicago, Archdiocese of Baton Rouge, Fidelity Bank Collection, Philadelphia, Sierra Club; curator of juried exhibition Bowery Gallery, 96, "Poetic Dimensions in the Modern Still Life," Emily Lowe Gallery, Hofstra Mus, 2005. *Publ:* Auth, Outer Light, Ann XXXV, Artnews, 11/69; Unconventional Realists, Part II, Sculpture, Artforum, 70; Notes from the Underground, Artforum, 70; Use and Misuse of the Past and Too Recent Past, Artforum, 71; Morandi, Col Art J, summer 82. *Dealer:* Schoelkopf Gallery 825 Madison Ave New York NY 10021. *Mailing Add:* 760 West End Ave No 3E New York NY 10025

LADOUCEUR, PHILIP ALAN
ADMINISTRATOR, DIRECTOR
b Syracuse, NY, Nov 6, 50. *Study:* State Univ NY, MA, 80; studied with Kenneth Lindsay & Albert Boime. *Collection Arranged:* Teacher and Student, 95; Ohio and the Civil War, 96; Diverse Visions Invitational, 96; Waters, Classic Forms, 97; Jim Wallace & Laura; Leslie Cope Retrospective, 97; Ceramic Int Exhib, 98. *Pos:* Dir, Blanden Art Mus, 91-94 & Zanesville Art Ctr, 95-. *Mem:* Am Asn Mus; Col Art Asn. *Mailing Add:* Zanesville Arts Ctr 620 Military Rd Zanesville OH 43701

LA DUKE, BETTY
ARTIST
b Bronx, NY, Jan 13, 33. *Study:* Denver Univ, 1950; Cleveland Inst Art, 1951-1952; Inst Allenoe, San Miguel, Mexico, 53; Calif State Univ, Los angeles, BA; Calif State Univ, Los Angeles, MA. *Comn:* Three Monkeys, Lion King Parade, Disney Land, Calif, 1997. *Exhib:* The Field Mus, Chicago; Hampton Univ Art Mus, Hampton, Va, 2000; Africa from Eritrea with Love, Dallas Mus of Art, Dallas, Tex, 2001; Africa: Myth, Magic and Reality, Hudgens Art Ctr, Duluth, Ga, 2001; Chattanooga African Am Mus Art, Chattanooga, Tenn, 2001; Dallas Mus Art, Tex, 2001; From Africa with love, William King Art Ctr, Abingdon, Va, 2002; Capitol Children's Mus, Washington, DC, 2003; Smith Robinson Mus, Jackson, Miss, 2003; and several others; one person circulating exhibs: Dreaming Cows, Heifer Int, Africa: Myth, Magic & Reality, Children of the World, Latin American Transitions, Surviving War, Dreaming Home, Chiapas Mexico: Land & Liberty, Celebrating Women's Creative Hands & Spirits; and many others. *Collection Arranged:* Hallie Ford Mus of Art, Willamette Univ, Salem, Oreg; Portland Art Mus, Oreg; Schneider Art Mus, So Oreg Univ, Ashland, Oreg. *Teaching:* prof of art, So Oreg Univ, Ashland, 64-96; art teacher, Stevenson Jr High, Los Angeles, Calif, 60-64; prof of art emeritus, Southern Ore Univ, 1964-1996. *Awards:* Oreg Gov's Award for the Arts, 93; Ziegfield Award, Nat Art edn Asn, 96. *Bibliog:* (auth) Gloria Orenstein, Multi Cultural Celebrations, The Paintings of Betty La Duke, Pomegranate, 90; (auth) Susan Ressler, Women Artists of American West, 2003; (auth) Mc Farland Video, Brian Varady, Africa Between Myth and Reality and An Artists Journey from the Bronx to Timbuctu, So Oreg Univ, 96; Ore Art Heritage Film, 2006. *Mem:* Art Coun/Africa Studies Asn; Internat Soc Educ Through the Arts/Nat Art Edu Asn. *Media:* Acrylic. *Res:* Work with Heifer Int, 2003-2006. *Interests:* Women and Art in Non-Western Socs. *Collection:* Documenting Heifer Int projects to alleviate world hunger. *Publ:* Companras: Women, Art & Social Change in Latin America, City Lights, San Francisco, 1985; auth, Africa Through the Eyes of Women Artists, 90; auth,Women Against Hunger, a Sketchbook Journey, Africa World Press, 97; Auth, Africa: Women's Art, Women's Lives, Africa World Press, 97; Women Artists: Multi Cultured Visions, Africa World Press, 1997. *Mailing Add:* 610 Long Way Ashland OR 97520

LAEMMLE, CHERYL
PAINTER
b Minneapolis, Minn, Aug 11, 47. *Study:* Humboldt State Univ, BA, 74; Washington State Univ, MFA, 78. *Work:* Eli Broad Family Found; Metrop Mus Art & Chase Manhattan Bank, NY; Frederick R Weismann Found; Corcoran Mus Art, Washington, DC; Walker Art Ctr, Minneapolis; Gen Mills, Minneapolis, Minn; High Art Mus; and others; Nat Mus Women in the Arts, Washington. *Exhib:* An Int Survey of Recent Painting & Sculpture, Mus Mod Art, NY, 84; From NY, Ace Contemp Exhib, Los Angeles, Calif, 88; Making Their Mark; Women a Move in the Mainstream 70-85, Cincinnati Art Mus, 89; Real Illusion, Whitney Mus Art at Equitable Ctr NY, 90; In the Looking Glass, Mint Mus Art, Charlotte, NC, 91; La Femme Surreal & the Frozen Narrative, Visual Arts Ctr, Calif State Univ, Fullerton, 91; I, Myself & Me, Twentieth Century & Contemp Self Portraits, Midtown Payson Galleries, NY, 92; Midtown Payson Gallery, NY 94; Duane Reed Gallery, St Louis, Mo, 98; one-woman shows, Sharpe Gallery, NY, 84, 86, Holin Kaufman Gallery, Chicago, 86, Mus of Art, Wash State Univ, Pullman, 90, Faye Gold Gallery, Atlanta, 92. *Awards:* Fel, Creative Artists Pub Serv Prog, 80; Vera G List Award, 84; Painting Fel, Nat Endowment Arts, 85-86 & 86-87. *Bibliog:* Lisa Peters (auth), article, Arts Mag, 5/83; Richard Armstrong (auth), article, Art Forum, summer 83; Ronny Cohen (auth), article, Art News, summer 83; William Zimmer (auth), Art walk, Village Voice, 4/1/86. *Mailing Add:* 536 N Broadway Nyack NY 10960

LAESSIG, ROBERT
PAINTER, ILLUSTRATOR
b West New York, NJ, Nov 15, 13. *Study:* Art Students League; also study in Ger. *Exhib:* Philadelphia Watercolor Soc, 64-70; Allied Artists, NY, 70-72; Pittsburgh Watercolor Show, 78; Ohio Watercolor Show, 78-79; Am Watercolor Show, 79. *Pos:* Pres, Robert Laessig Fine Arts Co, West Richfield, Ohio, 69-71 & Quail Ravine Studios, Inc, Peninsula, Ohio, 85-89; Senior art consultant Am. Greetings, Inc; painting represented in collections Norfolk Mus Art, Cleveland Mus Art, Springfield Inst Fine Art, Denver Mus Art; designer personal Christmas cards President Lyndon B Johnson, 1964-66, Gov Celeste, Ohio, 83 90; Pub of prints Art Beats, Salt Lake City; assoc with Gallery One, Mentor, Ohio. *Awards:* Prizes, Am Watercolor Soc, 70 & 71, Wichita Centennial, 70 & Pittsburgh Watercolor, 80; Pitts Watercolor Society, 81, award Mainstreams Marietta, Ohio, 83; Adirondack Nat Show, Old Forge, NY, 82-83; Gold medal, Ohio Watercolor Soc, 87 & 88; Lifetime Achievement award, Fairmount Ctr, Ohio, 2003; and numerous others. *Mem:* Nat Acad (assoc 64-94, academician, 94-); Dolphin Club; Am Watercolor Soc; Ohio Watercolor Soc; Am Watercolor Soc. *Mailing Add:* 26376 John Rd Olmsted Township OH 44138-1277

LAFAYE, BRYAN F
MUSEUM DIRECTOR, EDUCATOR
Study: La Col, Ba, 91; Clemson Univ, MFA, 93. *Collection Arranged:* Will Henry Stevens (paintings; auth, catalog), Am Modernist, 95; Salvation on San Mountain (photos; auth, catalog), Neel & Springer, 96; Abstract Perceptions: Gary Chapman (paintings), 97; Leroy Archuleta: A to Z (NMex folk art), 97; On the Road: T H Benton(paintings), 98. *Pos:* Cur, Alexandria Mus Art, La, 94-96; dir, Univ Art Mus, Univ Southern La, Lafayette, 96-. *Teaching:* Instr drawing, La Col, Pineville, 94-96; inst art hist, La State Univ, Alexandria, 96; asst prof art hist, Univ SW La, Lafayette, 96. *Awards:* Exhib Award, Lannan Found, 95 & Los Angeles Div Arts, 98; Int Partnership Award, Am Asn Mus, 97-99. *Mem:* Am Asn Mus; La Asn Mus (first vpres); Southeastern Mus Conf. *Res:* American Modernism; Contemporary Art from the American South. *Publ:* contribr, Emery Clark, Univ Art Mus, 98. *Mailing Add:* Univ Southwestern La Univ Art Mus USL Drawer 42571 Lafayette LA 70504

LAFFOLEY, PAUL (GEORGE), JR
PAINTER, ARCHITECT
b Cambridge, Mass, Aug 14, 35. *Study:* Brown Univ, Providence, RI, BA, 58; Harvard Grad Sch Design, apprenticeship with Mirko Basaldella, 59-62; apprenticeship with Frederick J Kiesler, 62-63; Dept Archit, Mass Inst Technol, 64-65; Boston Archit Ctr, 67-69. *Work:* Addison Gallery Am Art, Andover, Mass; Brockton Mus Art, Mass; Mus Fine Arts, Boston; First Nat Bank Chicago; Grand Rapids Art Mus, Mich. *Comn:* The Elvis Project (8 paintings), Country Music Mag, NY, 88-94. *Exhib:* 18th Bienal Int de São Paulo, Brasil, 85; The Triennial, Brockton Art Mus, Mass, 87; Boston Now: Projects, Inst Contemp Art, Boston, Mass, 87; Images of Death in Contemp Art, Haggerty Mus Art, Milwaukee, Wis, 90; Re: Framing Cartoons, Wexner Ctr for Arts, Columbus, Ohio, 92; Du Fantastique Au Visionnaire, Zitelle Cult Exhib & Commun Ctr, Venice, Italy, 94; Kent Gallery, NY, 98, 99, 2001; Austin Mus Art, Tex, 99. *Pos:* Pres & dir projs, Boston Visionary Cell Inc, Boston, Mass, 71-. *Awards:* Fel in Painting, Mass Artists Found, Boston, 89; Studio Fel, Marie Walsh Sharpe Art Found Space Prog, New York, 91-92; Gottlieb Award Individual Support, 97, 98. *Bibliog:* Ken Johnson (auth), Paul Laffoley at Kent, Art in Am, 12/89; Roger G Denson (auth),

The new metaphysical art & its legacy, Tema Celeste, No 26, 7-10/90; Donna Kossy (auth), Kooks: A Guide to the Outer Limits of Human Belief, Feral House, 94. *Mem:* Founding mem Boston Visual Artists Union. *Media:* Acrylic, Oil. *Publ:* Contribr, Unbuilt America: Forgotten Architecture in the United States from Thomas Jefferson to the Space Age; Sulfur 17: A literary tri-quarterly of the whole art, Eastern Mich Univ, Ypsilanti, Vol VII, No 2, 11/86; auth, The Phenomenology of Revelation, Kent Fine Art Inc, 89; contribr, Blast: Number 3: Remaking Civilization, X-Art Found Inc, 94. *Dealer:* Kent Gallery 67 Prince St New York NY 10012. *Mailing Add:* c/o Boston Visionary Cell Inc 36 Bromfield St Suite 200 Boston MA 02108

LAFLEUR, LAURETTE CARIGNAN
PAINTER
b Manchester, NH, Nov 14, 1939. *Study:* Notre Dame Col, 80; NH Inst Art, 81. *Comn:* individual paintings for collectors. *Exhib:* group shows, at Saco Merchants Asn, 1993-2006, Kennebunk River Club, 2001, Carlyle Place, 2002-04, Keene Ashuelot Park, 1993-2006, Milford, NH, Park Show, 2003, South Portland (Maine) Park Show, 1994-2005, Andover, Mass, Show, 1994-2006, Lawrence Heritage Park Show, 2003, Plymouth NH, Park Show, 1993-2006, Art Affair in the Country, 2005-2006, Animal Rescue League Show, 2006, Greeley Park Show, Nashua, NH, 2005-06; One-woman shows, Hooksett Pub libr, 99, Barnes & Noble Bookstore, 96, Peterborough NH Libr, 2005; two-person shows, Keene, City Hall, 2003, Chesterfield, Pub Libr, 2003, Chesterfield Granite Bank, NH, 2003. *Pos:* artist, 76-; Cashier, Pru-Bache Securities, Manchester, 86; off mgr, Shockley & Assoc Advertising, Amherst, NH, 87-88; accounting clerk, State of NH Admin Serv, Concord, 93-96. *Awards:* Recipient Awards; Manchester Park Shows, 85-86, Greeley Park shows, 88, Deerfield Fair, 93-95, Saco, Maine, 94, Am Mothers Inc, Augusta, Maine, 95, Andovers Art in the Park, 2005, Art Affair in the Country, 2005. *Mem:* Keyes Art Group; Andover Artists Guild (past pres); Keene Art Asn; Manchester Artists Asn (secy, pres); Nashua Artists Asn. *Media:* Acrylic, Oil, Watercolor. *Mailing Add:* 11 Heather Dr Hooksett NH 03106-1538

LAFON, DEE J
PAINTER, SCULPTOR
b Ogden, Utah, Apr 23, 29. *Study:* Weber State Col; Univ Utah, BFA, 60, MFA, 62; also with Francis de Erdley, Phil Paradise & Marquerite Wildenhain. *Work:* Utah State Fine Art Collection, Salt Lake City; Okla Art Ctr, Oklahoma City; Philbrook Art Mus, Tulsa, Okla; Univ Okla, Norman; Dillard Collection, Univ NC, Greensboro. *Comn:* Wood sculpture, Univ Okla, 72. *Exhib:* Am Drawing Bienniale, Norfolk, Va, 69; Int Miniature Prints Show, Pratt Graphic Ctr, NY, 70; Midwest Bienniale, Omaha, Nebr, 72; one-man shows, Springfield Art Mus, Mo, 78 & Goddard Art Ctr, Ardmore, Ore, 78. *Teaching:* Instr ceramics & drawing, Weber State Col, 62-64; assoc prof painting & drawing, ECent State Col, 64-, chmn dept art, 79-. *Awards:* Eight State Exhib Purchase Award, 70; Hon Mention, Midwest Bienniale, 72; Tulsa Regional Painting & Drawing Award, 72. *Mem:* Okla Designer Craftsman. *Media:* Oil, Multi-media. *Dealer:* Oklahoma Art Ctr 3113 General Pershing Blvd Oklahoma City OK 73118; Ben Pickard Gallery 541 NW 39th St Oklahoma City OK 73118. *Mailing Add:* 904 Tarkington Dr Norman OK 73071-0868

LAGORIA, GEORGIANNA MARIE M
MUSEUM DIRECTOR, CURATOR
b Oakland, Calif, Nov 3, 53. *Study:* Gonzaga Univ, Florence, Italy, 74; Santa Clara Univ, Calif, BA, 75; Univ San Francisco, MA, 78. *Collection Arranged:* The Candy Store Gallery (with catalog), 80, Contemp Hand Colored Photographs (with catalog), 81, Northern California Art of the Sixties (with catalog), 82 & Artist and the Machine 1910-1940 (with catalog), 86, de Saisset Mus, Santa Clara, Calif; Judy Dater: Twenty Years, traveled through US & Spain, 86; The Laila and Thurston Twigg-Smith Collection, 93. *Pos:* Asst dir, de Saisset Mus, Santa Clara Univ, Calif, 78-83, dir, 83-86; dir, Palo Alto Cult Ctr, Calif, 86-91, Contemp Mus, Honolulu, 95-; adv bd, Wiegand Gallery, Col of Notre Dame, Belmont, Calif; consult, 91-95. *Awards:* Publ Support Grant, Ahmanson Found, 81; Nat Endowment Arts, 85-86; NAS fel, Stanford Grad Sch Bus, 02. *Mem:* ArtTable; Calif Asn Mus (bd, 87-89); Western Mus Conf of Am Asn Mus; Hawaii Mus Asn (pres, 2000-02). *Res:* Modern and contemporary art, craft, and design with an emphasis on the West Coast. *Publ:* Contribr, Judy Dater: Twenty Years, Univ Arizona, 86; contribr, Persis Collection of Contemp Art, Honolulu Advertiser. *Mailing Add:* 47-665 Mapele Rd Kaneohe HI 96744

LAGUNA, MARIELLA
PAINTER, PRINTMAKER
b New York, NY. *Study:* NY Univ (archit); New Sch; Brooklyn Mus Art Sch; Adelphi Univ; Pratt Graphic Ctr. *Work:* Rockefeller Family; Brooklyn Col; also in many pvt & indust collections. *Comn:* Portraits & wall paintings, pvt & indust. *Exhib:* Pa Acad Fine Arts, Philadelphia, 64; Allied Artists Am Ann, 64; Nat Acad Design Ann, 64; Salvatora Rosa, Naples, Italy, 72; Pallazzo Vechio, Florence, Italy, 72; and many others. *Pos:* Colorist, Lawrence Laguna Architect, 60-; interior designer (free lance). *Teaching:* Instr art, Baldwin, Oceanside, Rockville Centre Pub Schs continuing educ workshops, 57-; St Margret Sch, Va & Lincoln Ctr, NY. *Awards:* Gold Medal (First Prize), Hofstra Univ, 61; Medal of Honor, Nat Asn Women Artists, 67; Ann Award, Am Soc Contemp Artists, 83 & 89; and many others; 13 Resident Fels. *Bibliog:* Newspaper interviews, Taos, Long Island Press, News Day, San Jose Mercury News, Calif & others. *Mem:* Artist Equity of New York, Inc; Nat Asn Women Artists, Inc; New York Soc Women Artists; Contemp Artists; Nat Asn Women Artists. *Media:* Oil, Acrylic; Watercolor, Pastel. *Dealer:* Karol Kamin New York NY. *Mailing Add:* 1521 Wiley St Hollywood FL 33020-6522

LAHR, J(OHN) STEPHEN
PAINTER, EDUCATOR
b Lincoln, Nebr, Aug 5, 43. *Study:* Univ Nebr, Lincoln, BFA, 68, with James Eisentrager, MEd, 72, EdD, 79. *Work:* Univ Nebr, Omaha; Joslyn Art Mus, Omaha; Pensacola Jr Col, Fla, 86. *Exhib:* Paper in Particular, Columbia Col Gallery, Mo, 81, 82 & 83; Mid-Four Regional Competition, Nelson Gallery Art, Atkins Mus, Kansas City, Mo, 81 & 82; Watercolor Missouri, William Woods Col, Fulton, 83 & 84; two-person exhib, Joslyn Art Mus, Omaha, 83; Kans Watercolor Soc Ann Competition, Wichita Art Mus, 85; Pensacola Nat Landscape Exhib, 86; Ga Watercolor Soc Ann Nat Exhib, Macon Mus Arts & Sci, 89 & 92. *Collection Arranged:* Missouri Folk: Their Creative Images, Folk Arts Exhib, 82; Sichaun Fine Arts Acad Exhib, Fine Arts Gallery, Valdosta State Col, Ga, 86 & 89; Valdosta Work on Paper I and II, Fine Arts Gallery, 88-89; Artoberfest (juried exhib), Cult Arts Ctr, 91-94. *Pos:* State art dir, Nebr Dept Educ, Lincoln, 74-79. *Teaching:* Instr art, Lincoln Pub Sch, Nebr, 69-72 & Univ Nebr, Lincoln, 72-73; asst prof art educ & studio, Univ Nebr, Omaha, 78-80; asst prof art educ & painting, Univ Mo, Columbia, 80-85; assoc prof, head dept art & gallery dir, Valdosta State Col, Ga, 85-89, prof art dept, 91. *Awards:* Purchase Awards, Joslyn Art Mus, 80 & Univ Nebr, Omaha, 82; Pensacola Nat Pruchase Award, 86. *Mem:* Nat Art Educ Asn; signature mem Am Watercolor Soc; Ga Art Educ Asn (bd mem); Ga Watercolor Soc; ASCD; Phi Delta Kappa. *Media:* Watercolor, Intermedia. *Res:* Methods of art instruction; Mixed Media Constructions; art educator profiles. *Publ:* Auth, Handbook for Art Education, Nebr Dept Educ, 78; Who teaches art: Report of recent surveys, In: Studies in Art Educ, Nat Art Educ Asn, 83-84; Health Hazards in the Artroom, EAEA J, 91; Missouri Folk: Their Creative Images (videographer) Libr of Congress, 84; Postmodernism: An Overview of Theory, Resources in Edn, 2000. *Mailing Add:* Valdosta State Univ Art Dept Valdosta GA 31698

LAHTINEN, SILJA (LIISA) TALIKKA
PAINTER, PRINTMAKER
b Lumivaara, Finland, 54. *Study:* Helsinki Univ, BA & MA, 69; Atlanta Col Art, BFA, 83; Col Art, Md Inst, MFA, 86; Acad Int Greci Marino. *Hon Degrees:* Associated Academician, Accademia Internacionale, Vinzaglio, Ital, 2002. *Work:* In the Spirit of Fluxes, Santa Barbara Mus Art, Calif; Peanut Gallery, Albany Mus Art, Ga; Excellent Ctr Art & Cult, Grover Beach, Calif; Saint-Marg-in-the-Woods Col Gallery, Ind; Womens Studio Workshop, Rosendale, NY. *Exhib:* Color: The Divine Madness, Ward-Nasse Gallery, NY, 96; Myths, Milagros and Magic, Ward-Nasse Gallery, 96; Printmakers Renaissance, Rolling Stone Press Gallery, 96; Coca Cola Co: New Americans, Spruill Arts Ctr, 96; Fullgrown Art, Woodruff Arts Ctr, 96; Nuutti Galleria, Finland, Virrat, 2003, 04 & 05; and others. *Pos:* Artist, Silja's Fine Art Studio, Marietta, Ga, 78-. *Awards:* Int Art Competition Cert of Excellence in Printmaking, 88; State of Ga award, Women in Visual Arts, 97; Honorable mention, Women in Arts, Latin Mus Art, Miami, Fla, 2004; Premio Alba, Meriti Artistici, Ferrara, Ital, 2003. *Bibliog:* Susan Randall (auth), A guardian of the earth, Manhattan Arts Int, 1-2/94; Claude le Suer (auth), Nature and Mysticism in the Art of Silja T Lahtinen, Artspeak, 12/94; Joseph Merkel (auth), Silja Talikka Lahtinen, Karelian Girl, Artspeak, 1/95. *Mem:* Orgn Independent Artists; Ga Artists Registry; Am Craft Coun; Roswell Fine Arts Alliance; WCA of Ga (found mem); Am Art Therapy Asn. *Media:* Oil, Acrylic on Canvas; Mixed Media. *Interests:* Shamanism. *Collection:* Chatachoochee Mus of Art, Ga. *Publ:* Contribr, Encyclopedia of Living Artists, Vols 2-10, Art Network Press, 87-96; Erotic Art by Living Artists, Directors Guild Publ, 88; The Art of Lovemaking, An Illustrated Guide, Prometheus Bks, 92; cover, Downtown, 5/26/93; contribr, The Guild, Gallery and Designers Editions, Kraus Sikes Inc, 94-96, 2003-05; Printworld Dir, 2005. *Dealer:* Ward-Nasse Gallery 178 Prince St New York NY 10012; Rolling Stone Press Gallery 432 Calhoun St Atlanta GA. *Mailing Add:* 5220 Sunset Trail Marietta GA 30068

LAHTINEN-TALIKKA, SILJA See Lahtinen, Silja (Liisa) Talikka

LAI, WAIHANG
PAINTER, EDUCATOR
b Hong Kong. *Study:* Chinese Univ Hong Kong, BA, 64; Claremont Grad Sch & Univ Ctr, MA, 67. *Comn:* Painting of McBryde Mill, A&B Inc, 75 & 77. *Exhib:* Watercolor USA, Springfield Art Mus, Mo, 69; The Best in the West, Edward-Dean Mus, Calif, 70; Philadelphia Watercolor Club Exhib, Philadelphia Civic Ctr Mus, 72; one-man shows, Phoenix Art Mus, Ariz, 67, Kauai Mus, Hawaii, 71, 72, 92, 93, 2003 & 2004, Kahana Kii Fine Art Gallery, 82, & Princeville Galleries, Hawaii, 85, Kilohana Galleries, Hawaii, 89, & Kauai Mus, Hawaii, 92 & 93; Am Watercolor Soc Ann Exhib, 85; solo exhib, Art & Soul Gallery, Hawaii, 2001; Kauai Com Coll Performing Arts Ctr Gallery, 98. *Teaching:* Vis prof art, Ariz State Univ, Tempe, summer 67; asst prof art, Maunaolu Col, Maui, Hawaii, 68-70; prof, Kauai Community Col, 70-04. *Awards:* First Place for Watercolor, Maui Co Creative Arts Exhib, Hawaii, 68; Bronze Medal Honor, Univ Hawaii Bd Regents, 92; Hon Excellence in Teaching Award, 93. *Mem:* Am Watercolor Soc; Philadelphia Watercolor Soc; Kauai Watercolor Soc (pres); Kauai Oriental Art Soc (pres, currently). *Media:* Watercolor, Acrylic. *Publ:* Auth, The Chinese Landscape paintings of Waihang Lai, 66; The Watercolors of Waihang Lai, 67 & Waihang Lai, Watercolor Calendar, 78; illusr, The Tao of Practice Success, 91; Advertisements for acupuncturists, 92. *Mailing Add:* PO Box 363 Lihue HI 96766

LAICO, COLETTE
COLLAGE ARTIST, PAINTER
b New York, NY. *Study:* Art Students League; Marymount Col, Haystack Mtn Sch Art & Crafts. *Comn:* Paintings, Am Int Life Assurance Co, NY, 89. *Exhib:* Monmouth Mus Fine Arts, Monmouth, NJ, 87; ann exhib Silvermine Guild Gallery, 86-96; ann Nat Asn Women Artists, NY, 87-96; Conn Gallery, Marlborough, 88, 89 & 90; Greenwich Art Soc, 88-96; Hudson River Mus, Yonker, NY, 89; solo show, Hammond

Mus, North Salem, NY; ann Bedford Asn Art Show, 2003-2005. *Teaching:* Instr art/craft, Westchester Art Workshop, 71-86; instr colonial art/crafts, Westchester Comm Col, 76-80; instr quilting, Scarsdale Adult Sch, 79-92. *Awards:* Gerald Kandler Mem Award, Womans Club Whiteplains, 89 & Mamaroneck Artists Guild, 86; Elizabeth Morse Genius Award, 88 & Sara Winston Mem Award, 92, Nat Asn Women Artists; Randolf Ghitwood Award, Greenwich Art Soc, 92; First Prize Mixed Media, Ann Art Exhib, Bedford Art Asn, 2005. *Bibliog:* Dorothy Friedman (auth), Artist Explores "Arts", Greenwich Time, 1/19/90; Janet Koplos (auth), article, Advocate & Greenwich Time, 2/18/90; The Designers Sourcebook, Guild Publs, eds, 92-96. *Mem:* Silvermine Guild Ctr Arts; Katonah Mus Artists Asn; Artists Equity Asn; Nat Asn Women Artists; Katonah Mus (bd mem 2004-2006). *Media:* Mixed Media. *Mailing Add:* 510 Forsyth Lane #401 Edmonds WA 98020

LAING, RICHARD HARLOW
ADMINISTRATOR, ARTIST
b Ypsilanti, Mich, Apr 19, 32. *Study:* Eastern Mich Univ, BS(art), 54; Wayne State Univ, MA(printmaking, sculpture), 60; Pa State Univ, DEd(art educ, art), 76. *Comn:* Fountain (bronze & stainless), comn by Paul Vortman, Denton, Tex, 62; wall sculpture, comn by Blazier Comn for Civic Ctr, Denton, Tex, 66; three stainless steel sculptures, Pa State Univ, University Park, 67-68; bronze sculpture fountain, Ewing-Miller Assoc, Terre Haute, Ind, 68; 10 piece stained glass design & construction, Elizabeth's Restaurant, Meadville, Pa, 77. *Exhib:* Wabash Valley Regional Exhib, Terre Haute, Ind, 71; Allegheny Col Galleries, Pa, 78; Theil Col Galleries, Grove City, Pa, 78; Butler Mus Art, Youngstown, Ohio, 79, Goldsboro Arts Coun Exhib, NC, 80; Witherspoon Gallery, Greensboro, NC, 88; and others. *Pos:* Develop specialist cult affairs, ECarolina Univ, Greenville, 83-. *Teaching:* Instr design shop, Col Art & Design, Univ Mich, 54-55; instr studio art & humanities, Edsel Ford High Sch, 55-60; asst prof studio art & art educ, NTex State Univ, 60-68; art head dept & assoc prof, Ball State Univ, Muncie, Ind, 68-71; prof & chair, Edinboro State Col, Pa, 71-79; dean, Sch Art, ECarolina Univ, Greenville, NC, 79-83, prof art, 83-. *Awards:* First Cash Prize/Painting, Eastern Ind Artist Exhib, Muncie Art Asn, 69 & 71; Community Arts Award, Greenville, NC, 80. *Mem:* Col Art Asn; Am Asn Univ Prof; Nat Asn Sch Art & Design; Nat Coun Art Adminr; Nat Art Educ Asn. *Media:* Mixed. *Mailing Add:* 204 Pineview Dr Greenville NC 27834-6434

LAING-MALCOLMSON, BONNIE
MUSEUM DIRECTOR, PAINTER
b Seattle, Wash, Dec 16, 52. *Study:* Pac Northwest Col Art, BFA, 77; Mont State Univ, MFA, 91. *Pos:* Dir acad affairs & admis, Pac Northwest Col Art, 81-87; exec dir, Beall Park Art Ctr, Bozeman, Mont, 91-94, Paris Gibson Sq Mus Art, Great Falls, Mont, 94-. *Teaching:* Adj prof art appreciation & art hist, Mont State Univ, 93. *Mem:* Am Asn Mus; Mont Art Gallery Dir Asn; Mont Asn Mus. *Mailing Add:* c/o Paris Gibson Sq Mus Art 1400 First Ave N Great Falls MT 59401

LAIOU, ANGELIKI E
EDUCATOR
b Athens, Greece, Apr 6, 41. *Study:* Univ Athens, 58-59; Brandeis Univ, BA(summa cum laude), 59-61; Harvard Univ, MA, 62, travel grants, 64-65, PhD, 66. *Pos:* Dir, Dumbarton Oaks, Washington, DC, 89-. *Teaching:* Instr, Univ La, New Orleans, 62; instr, Harvard, 66-69, asst prof, 69-72, prof Byzantine hist, 81-; assoc prof, Brandeis, 72-75; prof, Rutgers, 75-81; vis prof, Princeton, 81. *Awards:* Guggenheim Fel, 71-72 & 78-79; Rutgers Univ Res Coun grants; Am Coun Learned Soc Fel, 88-89. *Mem:* Phi Beta Kappa; Medieval Acad Am; Am Comt Byzantine Studies; Greek Comt Study South-Eastern Europe; Am Sch Classical Studies Athens. *Mailing Add:* 1735 32nd St NW Washington DC 20007

LAKE, JERRY LEE
PHOTOGRAPHER, EDUCATOR
b Manhattan, Kans, Apr 1, 41. *Study:* Va Commonwealth Univ, Richmond Professional Inst, BFA, 66; Ohio Univ, Athens, MFA, 68. *Work:* Corcoran Gallery Art, 69; Kodak Corp, 85; Bibliotheque Nat, Paris, 84-85; Nat Inst Health, 86. *Exhib:* One-man shows, Sign of Jonah Gallery, Washington, DC, 69 & Northern Va Community Col, 69; Fac Exhib, Corcoran Gallery Art, 68-70; Corcoran Gallery Art, 69; Unpeopled Spaces Traveling Exhib; Biennial Exhib, Va Mus, 81; In Celebration: Art at George Washington University, The Art Barn, Washington, DC, 82; Fac Show, Dimock Gallery, Washington, DC, 83-90; The Ritz, Washington DC Proj Arts, 83; 1734 Gallery, 83; Best of Kathleen Ewings Gallery, 83 & 86; Nat Juried Exhib, NY, 84. *Teaching:* Dir photog prog, Corcoran Sch Art, 68-71; head photog section, George Washington Univ, 71-; prof photo, George Washington Univ. *Bibliog:* Benjamin Forgey (auth), Designed for design, Washington Post, 83; Jo Ann Lewis (auth), Professorial pictures, Washington Post, 83. *Mem:* Soc Photog Educ; Int Photog Soc; Am Asn Col Prof. *Publ:* Contribr photog, Horizon Mag, 75-76 & America Mag, 76; contribr cover photog, Environmental Action, 12/77. *Dealer:* Kathleen Ewing Gallery 1609 Connecticut Ave Washington DC 20009. *Mailing Add:* PO Box 82 Rte 3 Lovettsville VA 20180-9803

LAKE, RANDALL
PAINTER, PRINTMAKER
b Long Beach, Calif, Aug 2, 47. *Study:* Acad Julian, Paris, 67; Univ Colo, BA, 69; Ecole Superieure Beaux Arts, Paris, 72; Atelier 17, Paris, 72-73; Univ Utah, MFA, 77. *Work:* Springville Mus Art, Utah; Am Embassy, Am Libr, Paris; Utah State Arts Collection. *Comn:* Oil paintings of Jerusalem, Mormon Church, Salt Lake City, 79; portrait Willard Eccles, Weber State Col, 81; portrait Nellie Tayloe Ross, Wyo State Capitol, Cheyenne, 82; portrait Dr Leonard W Jarcho, Univ Utah Med Sch, 83; Val A Browning, St Benedict's Hosp, Ogden, Utah, 85; Mayor Ted Wilson, City & Co Bldg, Salt Lake City, 86. *Exhib:* Salon D'Automne, Grand Palais, Paris, 70 & 72; Salon De Mai, Musee D'Art Mod, Paris, 72; Utah Painting & Sculpture, Mus Fine Arts, Univ Utah, Salt Lake City, 75-76; Intermountain Biennial, Salt Lake Art Ctr, 76; Assoc Utah Artists Bicentennial Exhib, Salt Palace, Salt Lake City, 76. *Pos:* Assoc dir, Guthrie Inst Fine Arts, 73-78, painter in residence, 80-. *Teaching:* Assoc instr, Univ Utah, 76-78; Scottsdale Artists' Sch, 92-93. *Awards:* First Place, Asn Utah Artists Bicentennial Exhib, 76; Purchase Award, Deseret News Show, 78, Utah Arts Co, 84; Gold Medal, April Salon, Springville Mus Art, 81; Purchase Award, Utah Arts Coun, 84. *Bibliog:* Genevieve Breerette (auth), A travers les galeries, Le Monde, 71; Lois Collins (auth), Painters of the Guthrie, Expression Mag, 81; Diane Casella Hines (auth), Randall Lake-traditional realist, Am Artist Mag, 2/3/84; article, Randall Lake-Revivalist, Southwest Art Mag, 9/85. *Media:* Oil, Pastel; Gouache. *Dealer:* John Pence Gallery 750 Post St San Francisco CA 94109. *Mailing Add:* 158 E 200 S Salt Lake City UT 84111-1556

LAKE, SHELLEY
PHOTOGRAPHER, ARTIST
Study: RI Sch Design, BFA, 76, MIT, MS, 79; Cleveland Chiropractic Col, D of Chiropractic. *Pos:* Tech dir (films), The Last Starfighter. *Teaching:* Teacher, aesthetics, Northhampton, Mass; and prof photog. *Awards:* Three CLIO awards; Nicograph award, Japan, first place; AT&T Image Competition; grantee

LAKES, DIANA MARY
PAINTER
b Sussex, NJ, Aug, 12, 1948. *Study:* Russell Sage Col, BA, 1970; State Univ of NY, Albany, MSW, 1971. *Work:* Musee D'Art Naif Max Fourny, Paris, France; Le Musee Int D'Art Naif, Quebec, Can; Theatre on the Lake, Chicago, Ill; Gallerie Je Reviens, Westport, Conn. *Exhib:* Pittori Naifs a Guiglia, 5th Salone Int, Modena, It, 1999; The Naive Painters in Castelvetro, Castelvetro, It, 2001; US Embassy, Montevideo, Uruguay, So Am, 2001; Gallerie Je Riviens, Wesport, Conn, 2001; solo exhibs: The Cedar Rapids Mus of Art, Cedar Rapids, IA, 2003, Leigh Yawkey Woodson Art Mus, Wausay, Wis, 2005. *Bibliog:* Se De Lee, Magic of Naive:1992, Sonje Mus of Contemp Art, 1992; Jean Florman, Paintings, Io City Press Citizen, 1995; Auth: Amanda Pierre, Artist in Wonderland, desmoines Register, 2002. *Mem:* Wis Watercolor Soc. *Media:* Acrylic, Watercolor. *Mailing Add:* 1225 Edgehill Dr Madison WI 53705-1414

LALIN, NINA
PAINTER
b Mar 9, 35. *Study:* Hofstra Univ, BA(art & english), 56; Art Students League, 70 & 80-82; studies with Barbara Nechis, Daniel Greene & Dong Kingman, 84, 86 & 87. *Work:* Am Labor Mus, Paterson, NJ. *Exhib:* Natural Forms, Soc Experimental Artists, Bradenton, Fla, 92; Forest Floor, Salmagundi Club, NY, 93; Rythems II, Ramapo Col Gallery, NJ, 94; Two Women, Fairleigh Dickenson Gallery, Hackensack, NJ, 94; Natural Forms, Cork Gallery, NY, 94. *Teaching:* Art teacher, pvt studio work, 76-94, YMHA, Wayne, NJ, 91-92. *Awards:* Buckett Award, Greenwich Village Arts Show, 85; Merit Award, Soc Experimental Artists Soc, 92; Excellence Award, Salute, Cork Gallery, 94. *Bibliog:* Alexandra Shaw (auth), Salute to women in arts, Manhattan Arts Mag, 9/94. *Mem:* Salute Women Arts; Nat Asn Women Artists; Int Soc Experimental Artists. *Media:* Oil, Watercolor. *Dealer:* Shannon Art Gallery Wayne NJ 07470. *Mailing Add:* 10 Bonita Terr Wayne NJ 07470

LALLY, JAMES JOSEPH
DEALER, CONSULTANT
b Mt Vernon, NY, Apr 18, 45. *Study:* Harvard Univ, BA, 67; Columbia Univ, MBA, 68, MIA, 70. *Pos:* Dir, Chinese Works of Art Dept, Sotheby Parke Bernet NY, Inc, formerly, dir, Sotheby Parke Bernet Hong Kong, Ltd, formerly; pres, Sotheby's NAm, formerly, J J Lally Co, currently. *Specialty:* Chinese works of art (ceramics, archaic bronzes, jades, sculpture, paintings and the minor arts). *Mailing Add:* JJ Lally & Co 41 E 57th St 14th Fl New York NY 10022

LA LUMIA, FRANK
PAINTER
b Chicago, Ill, Aug 9, 48. *Study:* Am Acad Art, 72-73. *Work:* Mus NMex, Santa Fe; Americana Mus, El Paso, Tex; Southern Utah State Coll, Cedar City; Albuquerque Mus, NMex. *Exhib:* Nat Watercolor Soc Ann, Laguna Beach Mus Art, Calif, 78; one-man show, Charles & Emma Frye Mus, Seattle, 79; two-man show, Americana Mus, El Paso, Tex, 87. *Awards:* Wildlife Award, Arts for Parks Ann Exhib, Jackson, Wyom, 2001; Best of Show, Tex Watercolor Soc 50th Ann Exhib. *Bibliog:* Joy Murphy (auth), feature article, SW Art, 89; feature article, SW Art, 10/94; Pleinar Painting in Watercolor & Oil (auth), North Light Pubs. *Mem:* Nat Watercolor Soc (signature mem); Plein Air Painters Am (signature mem); Oil Painters Am (signature mem). *Media:* Oil, Watercolor. *Publ:* Auth, Plein Air Painting in Watercolor and Oil, North Light Pub. *Dealer:* Cogswell Gallery 223 Gore Creek Dr Vail CO 81657; Columbine Gallery 211 Old Santa Fe Tr Santa Fe NM 87501

LAMAGNA, CARLO
EDUCATOR
Study: Col Holy Cross, BA in English; Univ Mass, MA in art hist. *Teaching:* Prof & Chmn, art dept NYU. *Mailing Add:* NY Univ 82 Wash Sq East New York NY 10003

LA MALFA, JAMES THOMAS
SCULPTOR, EDUCATOR
b Milwaukee, Wis, Nov 30, 37. *Study:* Univ Wis, Madison, BS, 60, MS, 61 & MFA, 62; studied sculpture with Leo Steppat & printmaking with Alfred Sessler. *Work:* Memphis Acad Art; Univ Wis, La Crosse; Neville Art Mus, Green Bay, Wis. *Comn:* Relief sculpture, Phillips Hall, Univ Wis, Eau Claire, 66, Theater Bldg, Univ Wis Ctr, Marinette, 95; sacred sculpture, Wittenberg Univ, Ohio, 68. *Exhib:* Springfield Art Ctr,

Ohio, 67; Print & Drawing Nat, Minot State Teachers Col, NDak, 70; 29th Northeastern Wis Art Ann, Green Bay, 70; 23rd Ohio Ceramic & Sculpture Ann, Butler Inst Art, 71; One man show, West Bend Gallery of Art, 2000-2001; UW Marinette sculpture garden, 2000, 2003; Northeastern Wis Tech Inst, 2003. *Teaching:* Instr visual arts, Univ Wis-Eau Claire, 63-66 & Wittenberg Univ, 66-69; asst prof, Univ Wis, Green Bay, 69-72; assoc prof, Univ Wis Ctr, Marinette, 72-. *Awards:* A System of Sculpture Invitational, Univ Wis, Milwaukee Art Dept, fall 91; Best of Show, 52nd Annual Exhib, Neville Mus Art. *Bibliog:* JJ (auth), article, Art News, 4/64; Pierre Mornand (auth), Expositions diverses review, Rev Mod, 11/71. *Mem:* Coalition of Active Sculpture Teachers (pres, currently). *Media:* Multi. *Mailing Add:* U Wis Ctr Marinette 750 W Bay Shore St Marinette WI 54143

LAMANTIA, JAMES
ARCHITECT, PAINTER
b New Orleans, La, Sept 22, 23. *Study:* Tulane Univ La, BSArch, 43; Harvard Univ Grad Sch Design, BArch, 47; Skowhegan Sch, 47. *Work:* NO Mus Art; High Mus Atlanta; Colby Col Mus, Maine. *Comn:* Dairy & Belvedere, Central Park, NY. *Exhib:* Simonne Stern Gallery, New Orleans, 87. *Pos:* Emer prof archit, Tulane Univ. *Teaching:* Held var teaching positions at several major univs. *Awards:* Prix de Rome, 48-49; Fulbright fel, Italy, 49-50; Fulbright prof archit, Univ Jordan, Amman, 78-79. *Bibliog:* Equal arts of James Lamantia, Archit Forum, 52. *Media:* Oil, Acrylic. *Collection:* Architectural drawings; Piranesi prints; Rare Architectrual Books. *Mailing Add:* 539 Bienville St New Orleans LA 70130

LAMANTIA, PAUL W ZOMBEK
PAINTER
b Chicago, Ill, Jan 20, 1938. *Study:* Art Inst Chicago, BFA, 66, MFA, 68. *Work:* Koffler Found Collection, Nat Collection Fine Arts, Smithsonian Inst; Dennis Adrian Collection, Chicago; Art Inst of Chicago, Ill; David & Alfred Smart Mus, Chicago; Cincinnati Mus Art, Ohio; and others; Mus Contemp Art, Chicago. *Exhib:* What They're Up To In Chicago Traveling Exhib, Nat Gallery Can, Ottawa, 72-73; North, East, South & Middle: An Exhib on Contemp Am Drawing, Corcoran Gallery Art & Ft Worth Art Mus, 75-76; Works on Paper, Art Inst Chicago, 77; one-man retrospective, Hyde Park Art Ctr, Chicago, 82; Chicago Imagism, A 25 Yr Survey, Davenport Mus Art, Iowa, 94; Post-War Chicago Works on Paper & Sculpture, David & Alfred Smart Mus, Univ Chicago, Ill, 95; Art in Chicago, 1945-1995 (with catalog), Mus Contemp Art, Chicago, 96; Don Baum says' Chicago Has Famous Artists, Hyde Park Art Ctr, Chicago, 96. *Collection Arranged:* Art Inst Chicago, Chicago, Ill; Mus Contemp Art, Chicago, Ill; Nat Mus Am Art, Smithsonian Inst, Wash DC; Madison Art Center, Madison, Wis; The Collection of Jean Dubuffet, Paris, France; Cincinnati Art Mus, Cincinnati, Ohio; The Figge Art Mus, Davenport, Iowa; The Wright Mus Art, Beloit, Wis; The Ukrainian Inst Mod Art, Chicago, Ill. *Teaching:* Creative Seminar Proj, Columbia Col, Chicago, Ill, 94 & 98, Cincinnati Acad Art, Art Inst Chicago, Loyola Univ Chicago. *Awards:* Logan Prize, Art Inst Vicinity Show, Chicago, 84. *Bibliog:* David Elliott (auth), Cunning painter of the smart set, Chicago Sun-Times 3/29/81; Dennis Adrian (auth), Sight Out of Mind, Essays & Criticism on Art, UMI Research Press, 10/85; Lynn Gamell, Ernest Hartmann & Donald Kuspit (auths), Dreamworks: Artistic and Psychological Perspectives, State Univ, NY & Cornell Univ Press, 99; James Yood (auth), Paul Lamantia, New Art Examiner, Mar, 1996. *Media:* Oil, Mixed Media. *Mailing Add:* 315 W Concord Pl Chicago IL 60614

LAMARCA, HOWARD J
DESIGNER, EDUCATOR
b Teaneck, NJ, July 11, 34. *Study:* Cooper Union Art Sch, scholar, 52-56, cert graphic arts, 56; Columbia Univ, BFA, 60; Syracuse Univ, grad asst, 60-62, MFA, 62. *Collection Arranged:* James Gordon Irving-Painter, 71; Grant Reynard-Painter, 71; Charles Shedden, Sculptor-Ralph Didriksen, Painter, 71; George Fish, Painting-Shirley Yudkin, Paintings, 72; Marion Lane, Painting Retrospective, 72; Arnoldo Miccoli-Painter, 73; Sam Weinik-Painter, 74; Erna Will-Sculptor; Eleanor Smoler-Painter, 74; Batiks--Giovanna Bellia La Marca, Co Col Morris, 76; Batik & Calligraphy Exhibit, Dwight-Englewood Sch, 85; Korean Graphic Design Exhib, Hillwood Mus, Brookville, NY, 98; NY Art Dir Club, 98. *Pos:* Advert art dir, Givaudan Advert, New York, 57-; dir, Bergen Community Mus, 71-74; sem dir Europ advert, Paris, France, Dusseldorf & Frankfurt, Ger, Zurich, Switz & Milan, Italy, 78-84; European Art Tour, Milano, Venice, Florence, Rome, 90. *Teaching:* Asst prof art, Trenton State Col, 74-80; assoc prof art, Co Col of Morris, 74; adj asst prof, Parsons Sch Design, 79-81; chmn art dept & prof art, C W Post Ctr, Long Island Univ, 80-; lectr, Musashino Art Univ Tokyo, Meiji Gakuin Univ, Yokohama & Tokyo, Hoseo Univ, Hanyang Univ & Kyung-yi Univ, Korea, 97. *Awards:* Graphics Design Award, New York, 79 & 81. *Mem:* Soc Scribes; Art Dir Club NY; Col Art Asn Am; Am Inst Graphic Arts; Univ & Col Design Asn. *Media:* Graphics, Calligraphy. *Publ:* Auth, An analysis of Gauguin's-What are We? Where Do We Come From? Where Are We Going?, Artist Mag, London, 3/62; An analysis of the facade of San Marco, Eleven Mag, spring 72; Some Thoughts on Design, City Univ New York, 74; Ethics & aesthetics, Focus, 76; Another Hillwood, Ventures in Res, 2/86. *Mailing Add:* Three Crescent Ave Cliffside Park NJ 07010

LAMARRE, PAUL
CONCEPTUAL ARTIST, SCULPTOR
b Detroit, Mich. *Study:* Univ Mich, BFA, 78. *Work:* ICA, London, Eng; New Mus Contemp Art, NY; Montecarotto Mail Art Mus, Italy. *Comn:* Bldg installation, comn by Andrew Klink, Los Angeles, 89-90; bldg installation, comn by Helen Jacobs, NY, 90. *Exhib:* one-person shows, Hallwalls, Buffalo, NY, 83 & Dooley Le, Cappellaine Gallery, NY, 92; Starving Artists Cook Book, Anthology Film Archives, NY, 89; EIDIA Show, Barbara Braathen, NY, 89; New Fabricants, Richard Green Gallery, Los Angeles, 90; Store Show, Richard/Bennett Gallery, Los Angeles, 91; Value, NY, 91; and others. *Awards:* CAPS Fel, New York, 82; Video Fel, New York Found, 87. *Bibliog:* Luca Neri (auth), Il Ricettario Dell Artista, Lei Mag, 89; Robert Mahoney (auth), Quiet desperation, Arts Mag, 89; Judd Tulley (auth), Art speak, Taxi Mag, 89; Hal Rubenstein (auth), Mirabella Mag, 91. *Mem:* Asn Independent Video & Filmakers; NY Artists Equity Asn; Media Alliance. *Media:* Installations, Video. *Publ:* Coauth, Starving Artists' Cook Book, EIDIA Publ, 91; Starving Artists' Banquet, NY Times, 92. *Mailing Add:* 426 E Ninth St No 1C New York NY 10009

LAMB, DARLIS CAROL
SCULPTOR, PAINTER
b Wausa, Nebr. *Study:* Univ Nebr, Omaha; Creighton Univ, Omaha; Red Rocks Community Col; studied sculpture with Stanley Bleifield, Lloyd Glasson & Francisco Zuniga; Columbia Pacific Univ, BA, MA. *Work:* Gannett Found, Denver; Nebr Hist Soc, Lincoln; First Fed Savings & Loan Asn of Lincoln, Omaha; Benson Park Sculpture Garden, Loveland, Colo; Am Lung Asn; Space Found, Colorado Springs, Colo; Colorado Springs Osteopathic Foundation, Colo. *Comn:* Spirit of Health (sculpture, bas reliefs & medallions), Am Lung Asn, Colorado Springs & Denver, Colo, 84-89; sculpture, Loveland High Plains Arts Coun, Colo, 88, 2001, 03; Hall of Fame Medal, Space Found, Colo, 97; Col Osteopathic Found, 99. *Exhib:* Northern Am Sculpture Exhib, Foothills Art Ctr, Golden, Colo, 83, 84, 86, 87, 90 & 91; Catherine Lorillard Wolfe, NY, 83, 85, 89, 91, 93, 2004-2005; Nat Sculpture Soc, NY, 85, 91, 95, 97, 2003-06; 161st Exhib, Nat Acad Design Gallery, NY, 86; Allied Artists, NY, 92 & 95; Pen & Brush, NY, 93, 95, 96, 98 & 2000. *Teaching:* instr, terra cotta sculpture Ruidoso Art Sch, Ruidoso, NMex, 94, 95, Loveland Acad Fine Arts, Loveland, Colo, 1995, Curtis Ctr for Arts & Humanities, Greenwood Village, Colo, 2000, St Mary's Acad, Denver, 1998. *Awards:* C Percival Dietsch Award, Nat Sculpture Soc, 91; Horse's Head Award Best Sculpture, Catharine Lorillard Wolfe Art Club, 94 & Hon Mention, 96 & Medal of Honor, 98 & 2005; Roman Bronze Award, Pen & Brush, 95; Bronze medal for Sculpture, 99; Harriet W Frishmuth Memorial Sculpture award, 2002; Paul Manship Memorial Sculpture award, 2001. *Bibliog:* Gary Michael (auth), article, Southwest Art Mag, 1/89 & 7/99; Betty Lane (auth), Footprints in the sand, Elan Mag, 5/90; Christina Reid (auth), Artists medal is out of this world, Villager, 7/17/97; Darlis Lamb, SWA Mag, 7/99; Focus Santa Fe, 8-9/2005. *Mem:* Catharine Lorillard Wolfe Art Club; North Am Sculpture Soc. *Media:* Clay, Cast Metal; Watercolor, Oil. *Dealer:* Howard Mandville Kirkland, Wash; Peterson-Cody Gallery Santa Fe NMex. *Mailing Add:* 5515 S Kenton Way Englewood CO 80111

LAMB, MATT
PAINTER, SCULPTOR
b Chicago, Ill. *Work:* Nat Treasury, Washington; Spertus Mus Judaica, St Xavier Col & State of Ill Collection, Chicago; Vatican Mus, Italy; Mus Contemp Art, Ferrara, Italy. *Comn:* Life of Christ (9 tarps), Mannheim Cathedral, Ger. *Exhib:* Carl Hammer Gallery, Chicago, 90; Galerie Berlin, Ger, 92; Galeria Praxis Arte Int, Mexico City, 93; Galerie Kasten, Mannheim, Ger, 95; Madness & Matt Lamb, Fasshender Gallery, Chicago, 96; State of Ill Gallery, Lockport, Ill, 96; Rockford Art Mus, Ill, 97; Galeria Punto, Valencia, Spain, 97; Mus Contemp Art, Ferrara, Italy, 97; Fassbender Gallery, Chicago, 98. *Bibliog:* Michael Bonesteel (auth), Lamb of God, Carl Hammer Gallery, 90; James Yood et al (auths), Matt Lamb, Fassbender Gallery, 94; Donald Kuspit (auth), Madness and Matt Lamb, Fassbender Gallery, 96; and others. *Media:* Oil on canvas. *Mailing Add:* c/o Judy Saslow Gallery 300 W Superior Chicago IL 60610

LAMBERT, ED
PRINTMAKER, PAINTER
b Atlanta, Tex, Jan 27, 49. *Study:* Tex Tech Univ, BFA & MFA. *Exhib:* Pratt Graphic Ctr Int Miniature Print Exhib, 75; Mach I Int Print Exhib, Metrop Mus Art, Miami, Fla, 75; one-man shows, M E's Gallery, Houston, 83 & Charlton Art Gallery, San Antonio, 86; Animal Magnetism, Nueva Street Gallery, San Antonio, 90. *Teaching:* Prof printmaking, Del Mar Col, Corpus Christi, Tex, 74-, chmn art dept, 80-. *Bibliog:* Joseph A Cain (auth), Profile, Art Voices South, 7-8/80; Dan Goddard (auth, rev), San Antonio Express News, 7/19/90. *Media:* Etching, Airbrush. *Dealer:* Nueva Street Gallery 507 E Nueva St San Antonio TX 78205. *Mailing Add:* 607 Del Mar Corpus Christi TX 78404

LAMBERT, PHYLLIS
ARCHITECT, DIRECTOR
b Montreal, Que, Jan 24, 27. *Study:* Vassar Col, BA, 48; Ill Inst Technol, with Myron Goldsmith & Fazlur Khan, MS(archit), 63. *Hon Degrees:* McGill Univ, DLitt, 86; Concordia Univ, LLD, 86; Univ of Windsor, LLD, 89; Pratt Inst, DFA, 90; Queen's Univ, DCL, 90; Univ of British Columbia, Dlitt, 92; Univ of Victoria, LLD, 93; Univ of New Brunswick, Dlitt, 95; Emily Carr Inst of Art and Design, Dlitt, 98; Univ of Waterloo, LLD, 00; Dartmouth Univ, Hon Dr, 01; Spertus Inst of Jewish Studies, Hon Dr, 01; Univ du Québec à Montréal, Hon Dr, 02; Ryerson Univ, Hon Dr, 04. *Work:* Saidye Bronfman Ctr, with Webb, Zerafa & Menkes, YWHA, Montreal, 63-68; Jane Tate House Renovation, with Arcop Assoc, Phyllis Lambert off & residence, Montreal, 74-76; Small Cinema, with Arcop Assoc, pvt house, Montreal, 75-76; Biltmore Hotel Renovation, with Gene Summers, Los Angeles, Calif, 76-77; Can Ctr Archit, Consult Archit, with Peter Rose, Montreal, 84-89. *Comn:* Court House: A Photographic Document, (exhib catalog), with Richard Pare, 77-80. *Exhib:* Retrospective (auth, catalog), 4th Fl Gallery, Seagram Bldg, NY 77; Cooper-Hewitt Mus, NY, 83; Art Inst Chicago, 83; Nat Gallery Can, Ottawa, 84; Musee Nat d'art moderne, Ctr Georges Pompidou, Paris, 84; Montreal Mus Contemp Art, Chicago, 2001-02. *Collection Arranged:* Joseph E Seagram & Sons Inc Collection, 54-; Can Indian Exhib, 69 & Aaron Siskind Exhib, 70, Saidye Bronfman Centre, Montreal; Seagram Plaza: Its Design & Use, Seagram Bldg, New York, 77. *Pos:* Dir planning, Seagram Bldg, NY, 54-58; dir, Seagram Bicentennial Proj, Co Courthouse in the US, 74-; founder/dir, Can Ctr for Archit, 79; Commissioner, Int Confederation Archit Mus, 79; project dir,

renovation of Ben Ezra Synagogue, Cairo, Egypt, 81. *Teaching:* Lectr, Urban Studies Prog and Dept of Hist, Concordia Univ, Montreal, 82-83; Final Yr Reviews, École d'Archit, Faculté de l'aménagement, Université de Montréal, 85; Adj Prof, Sch of Archit, McGill Univ, Montreal, 86-; Final Yr Reviews, Sch of Arch, McGill Univ, 89-92; Assoc Prof, Faculté de l'aménagement, École d'Archit, Univ de Montréal, 89-; Guest Prof, Atelier Triptyque, Faculté d'aménagement, École d'Archit et paysage, Univ de Montréal, 92; Final Yr Reviews, Sch of Archit, Univ of Waterloo, Ontario, 93. *Awards:* 25-year Award Excellence, Am Inst Archit, 84; Gold Medallist, Royal Archit Inst of Can, 91; Hon Mem: Am Inst of Archit, NY Chap, 96; Life mem, Coun of the Ontario Asn of Archit, 03; Fel of the Am Inst of Archit, Hon, 03. *Bibliog:* Paul Goldberger (auth), "A Treasurehouse for Architecture," NY Times, 5/7/89; Various auth, "Profiles darchitectes d'aujourd'hui"; auth, ARQ: La Revue d architecture, issue devoted to Phyllis Lambert, 12/95; Blair Kamin (auth), "Talking frankly with 'Joan of Architecture,'" Chicago Tribune, 2/19/02. *Mem:* Royal Can Acad Arts; Soc du Patrimoine Urbain de Montreal (pres, 79); Soc Archit Historians (dir, currently); Int Confederation of Archit Mus (ICAM); Fonds d'investissement de Montréal (FIM), (pres, bd dir, 96-). *Res:* United States County Courthouse Photographic mission, Institute for Advanced Study, Princeton, New Jersey. *Specialty:* promoting public understanding, and widening thought and debate on the art of architecture, its History, theory, practice, and role in society today. *Collection:* Architectural drawings from the 16th century to the 20th century; photographs of the 19th and 20th century; manuscripts and books on architecture. *Publ:* contribr, Court House, Horizon Press, spring 78; auth, The archit mus: "a founders perspective," J of the Soc of Archit Hist, 9/99; auth, Mies Immersion, Mies in America, 01; auth, Love in the Time of the WTC, Log, 2004. *Mailing Add:* Can Centre for Architecture 1920 Baile St Montreal PQ H3H 2S6 Canada

LAMBRECHTS, MARC
PAINTER, PRINTMAKER
b Lier, Antwerp, Belg, Sept 14, 55. *Study:* Higher St Lucas Inst, Brussels, Belg; Art Sch, Bratislava, Czech (govt scholarships); Pratt Inst, New York. *Work:* Aldrich Mus Contemp Art, Conn; Flemish Community, Belgium; Gemeentekrediet, Belg; Kidder & Peabody, NY; Terra's Interno, Tokyo, Japan; PROTEK Pharmaceutical, Bern, Switzerland; David & Lucile Packard Found, Los Altos, Calif; Saks Fifth Ave; Terra's Interno, Tokyo Japan; Kidder & Peabody, NY; Stichting Paulus Dommelhof, Eindhoven, Holland; Davidsfonds Nat'l, Belgium. *Comn:* Portfolio of Etchings, Rotary Club, Antwerp, Belg, 81 & Univ Brussels, 89; Portfolio-Works on Paper, Flemish Investment Co. *Exhib:* Solo exhibs, Gallery Fontainas, Brussels, Belg, 88, Arts Club Washington, DC, 89, Tibor de Nagy Gallery, NY, 91, Hugieia Art Gallery, Belg, 92, Jeffrey Coploff Fine Art, Ltd New York City, 2002; Salon des invites, Brussels, Belgium Moba Art, Brussels Belgium, 2003; A Walk Through Mini-mini Space, Joie Lassiter Gallery, Charlotte, North Caroline Recent Works, Van den Brande-Wauters in Assoc with The Peak, Singapore, 2004. Sediments, Joie Lassiter Gallery, Charlotte, NC, 2005; Recent Acquisitions, Aldrich Mus Contemp Art, Conn, 88; Hudson River Open '89, Hudson River Mus, NY, 89; Art of Northeast USA, Silvermine Galleries, Conn, 91; A Taste of Belgium, Bryant Galleries, Atlanta, Ga, 91; 100 Yrs Belgian Art, L'Arc de Defence, Paris, France, 90; VUB, Free Univ Brussels, Belg, 91; Am Abstraction: A New Decade, Southern Alleghenies Mus Art, Loetto, Pa, 94; Galerie Ute Brummel, Dortmund, Ger, 97; Galeri Faider, Brussels, Belgium, 97; Kunst Forum, Schelderode, Belgium, 98; Joie Lassiter Gallery, Charlotte, NC, 99; Jeffrey Coploff Fine Art, Ltd, NY, 2002; One Land, Eight Belgian Artists, Frieda and Roy Furman Gallery at the Lincoln Ctr, New York City, 2002; The Big Picture, Arthaus, San Francisco, 2002; Arthaus of Paper, Arthaus, San Francisco, 2002; Interior Motives, Arthaus, San Francisco; Le Bateau Fou, West Hampton, NY; Musee de le Gravure, La Louviere, Belgium (Collection Emile Lanc), 2003; Olympic Truce: Pieces of Peace, Olympic Arts Fest 2004, Organized by the Greek Embassy; Inside Stories, Arthaus, San Francisco; Greatest Hits, Arthaus, San Francisco, 2004; In The Mix; Getting Real; No Contest, Arthaus, San Francisco, 2005; Within Our Walls, Trizec Properties, Charlotte, NC, 2005; AAF Contemp Art Fair, NY, 2005 & 2006; and many others. *Pos:* cur, 26 Am Artists, Campo & Campo, Antwerp, Belgium, 99. *Teaching:* Guest prof, Higher Inst Fine Arts, Antwerp, Belgium, 1997-2004. *Awards:* First Prize, Young Belgian Graphic Artists, Rotary Club, 81; Cert Excellence, printmaking, Int Art Competition, New York, 87; Medal in Printmaking & Cert Excellence in Small Works, USA Major Art Competition, Los Angeles, 87; Olympic Truce: Pieces of Peace competition, Olympic Arts Festival 2004, Organized by the Greek Embassy. *Bibliog:* Alice Gray (auth), Art News, 1/92; Bourbon, NY Arts Mag, 11/98; Brooklyn Bridge, 3/97. *Media:* Mixed Media; Etching. *Specialty:* Contemporary Art. *Dealer:* Jeffrey Coploff Fine Art Ltd 526 W 26th St New York NY 10001; Joie Lassiter Gallery 318 E 9th St Charlotte NC 28202; Arthaus 1053 Bush St Suite #2 San Francisco CA 94109. *Mailing Add:* 158 S Oxford St Brooklyn NY 11217

LAMBRIX, TODD
SCULPTOR
b Livingston, NJ, 69. *Study:* Rutgers Univ, New Brunswick, NJ, BFA, 98; RI Sch Design, MFA, 2001; studied with Kuehn, Tom Butter, Dean Snyder. *Work:* Pvt collections. *Exhib:* Solo exhib, Bristol-Myers Squibb Gallery, Princeton, NJ, Slater Mem Mus, Norwich, Conn, Phoenix Gallery, New York City, Utopia of One Sol Koffler Gallery, Providence, RI, 2001; RI Sch of Design, 2001. *Teaching:* instr, Raritan Valley Community Col, currently; instr, RI Sch of Design, currently. *Awards:* VT Studio Residency Award, 96; Sculpture Award, Ct Acad Fine Arts, 2000. *Mem:* Col Art Asn. *Media:* Mixed; Wood and Metal. *Specialty:* Non-objective experimental. *Mailing Add:* 18 Lauriston St Providence RI 02906

LAMIS, LEROY
SCULPTOR, EDUCATOR
b Eddyville, Iowa, Sept 27, 25. *Study:* NMex Highlands Univ, BA, 53; Columbia Univ Teachers Col, MA, 56. *Work:* Albright-Knox Mus; Des Moines Art Ctr; Whitney Mus Am Art; Joseph H Hirshhorn Collection, Washington; Larry Aldrich Mus. *Comn:* NY State Coun Arts Award, 70. *Exhib:* Whitney Mus Am Art Sculpture Ann, NY, 64, 66 & 68; Responsive Eye, Mus Mod Art, NY, 65; Art Today, Albright-Knox Art Gallery, Buffalo, 65; one-man shows, Staempfli Gallery, NY, 66, 69 & 73 & Traveling Show, 69, JB Speed Mus, Louisville, John Herron Mus, Indianapolis, La Jolla Mus Art, Calif; Neuberger Collection, Smithsonian Inst & RI Sch of Design, 68; Am Sculpture, Univ Nebr, Lincoln, 70; Artists at Dartmouth, New City Hall, Boston, Mass, 71. *Pos:* Found & pres, PC Art Inc. *Teaching:* Asst prof, Cornell Col, 56-60; prof sculpture, Ind State Univ, Terre Haute, 61-89; artist in residence, Dartmouth Col, 70. *Media:* Plastics; computer art

LAMM, LEONID IZRAIL
CONCEPTUAL ARTIST, PAINTER
b Moscow, Russia, Mar 6, 28; US citizen. *Study:* Archit Acad, Moscow, 1947; Graphic Acad, Moscow, MFA, 1954. *Work:* Metrop Mus Art, NY; Solomon R Guggenheim Mus, NY; Stedelijk Mus, Amsterdam, Holland; Jewish Mus, NY; Tretiakovsky Gallery, Moscow. *Exhib:* Transit, State Russ Mus, 89; From Gulag to Glasnost: Nonconformist Art from Soviet Union, 1956-1986, Jane Voorhees Zimmerly Art Mus, New Brunswick, NJ, 95; Russian Jewish Artists in a Century of Change 1870-1988, Jewish Mus, NY, 95; Temporarily Possessed, New Mus Contemp Art, NY, 95; Re-inventing the Emblem: Contemp Artist Recreated a Renaissance Idea, Yale Univ Art Gallery, 95; Russian Conceptual Art of the 1980's, Duke Univ Mus Art, Durham, NC, 96; SOTs-ART, The New Mus of Contemp Art, NY, 86; The Colors of Money, Musee de la Poste, Paris, 91; New Acquisitions, Stedelijk Mus Amsterdam, 91; Non-Conformist Art from Soviet Union 1956-1986, Stedelijk Mus, Amsterdam, 97-98; Leonid Lamm: The Hall in the Hall, Herbert F Johnson Mus of Art, Cornell Univ, Ithaca, NY, 97; Leonid Lamm: Birth of an Image, Duke Univ Mus of Art, Durgham, NC, 98; Leonid Lamm: Birth of an Image, Jane Voorhes Art Mus, New Brunswick, NJ, 00; The State Russian Mus, St Petersburg, 2002; Abstraction in Russia, XX Century; Soviet Artists, Jewish Themes, Jane Vorhees Zimmerli Art Mus, New Brunswick, NJ, 2003; Global Village: the 1960's, Montreal Mus Fine Art, 2003-2004; Iakov Chernikhov & Leonid: Codes of Geometry, Nat Center Contemp Arts, Moscow, 2005. *Teaching:* Prof painting & drawing, Graphic Acad, Moscow, 62-73 & 76-82. *Awards:* Silver Medal, Int Book Fair, Leipzig, Ger, 59; 2000 Outstanding People of the 20th Century Medal & Diploma, Int Biographical Ctr Cambridge, CB2 3QP, Eng, 98. *Bibliog:* John Bowlt (auth), A Catafalque of the Senses, Eduard Nakhamkin Fine Art, New York, 90; Donald Kuspit (auth), Leonid Lamm's Homage to Yakov Chernikhov, Howard Schickler Fine Art, New York, 94; Eleanor Heartney (auth), Leonid Lamm: Birth of an Image (exhib catalog), Duke Univ Mus Art, 98. *Mem:* Iakov Chernikhov Int Found, Moscow, Sofia, NY (codir). *Media:* Multi Media; Installation. *Dealer:* Westwood Gallery 758 Broadway 1st fl New York NY 10012; Sloan Gallery Oxford Office Bldg 1612 17th St Denver CO 80202; Guelman Gallery 7/7 Malaya Polyanka 109180 Moscow Russia; IZO Gallery, 4 Davies St, London, W1K 3DL. *Mailing Add:* 310 E 23rd St Apt 3A New York NY 10010

LAMONTAGNE, ARMAND M
SCULPTOR, PAINTER
b Pawtucket, RI, Feb 3, 38. *Study:* Studied in Florence, Italy. *Comn:* 7-foot wood sculptures of Babe Ruth, 84 & Ted Williams, 85, Baseball Hall of Fame, Cooperstown, NY,; portrait of gov, Providence, RI, 87; life size wood sculptures of Larry Bird, Bobby Orr, Carl Yastrzemski, New Eng Sports Mus; life size bronze sculpture of Ted Williams, Ted Williams Mus, Hernando, Fla; life size wood sculpture of Gen George Patton, Patton Mus, Ft Knox, Ky. *Awards:* Russell Grinell Found Grant, 64. *Media:* Wood. *Mailing Add:* 405 Bungy Rd N North Scituate RI 02857

LAMONTE, ANGELA MAE
PAINTER
b New Britain, Conn, 1944. *Study:* Catan-Rose Inst Fine Arts,Cert, 67; Nat Acad Fine Arts, Study with Hugh Gumpel, 69; City Col, New York, MFA, 77; Bank St Col, MS, 82. *Exhib:* Malcolm King Faculty Exhib, Harlem State Off Bldg Gallery, 81; Art '84 Tobago, Int Art Convention, Trinidad-Tobago, Wis, 84; Boniface Gallery, Cathedral of St John the Divine, NY, 86; Gallery M, NY, 87; Gallery Art 54, NY, 88; Atlantic Gallery, NY, 1990, 92, 93, 96, 97, 98, 99, 2000, 2001, 2002; Multi-Media Arts Gallery, NY, 91-94; Atlantic Gallery, NY, 2003, 2004. *Pos:* Adv coun mem, New Century Artists Inc, New York, currently. *Teaching:* Prof art, painting & drawing, Malcolm King Col, New York, 79-89, chairperson art dept, 84-89. *Awards:* Louis Comfort Tiffany Found Scholar Award, 69; Louis La Beaume Award, Nat Acad Fine Arts, 70; Art Alumni Pres Award, City Col New York, 83. *Media:* Oil; Multi-Media. *Publ:* Art exhibit to benefit Malcolm-King, New York Voice, 9/81; article, New Britain Herald, 9/86; article, Hartford Courant, 9/87; article, Amsterdam News, 1/88; article, New Britian Herald, 8/93. *Mailing Add:* 149 W Fourth St New York NY 10012

LAMOUREUX, MARIE FRANCE
ART DEALER, GALLERY DIRECTOR
b Montreal, Can, 61. *Study:* Univ Montreal, Quebec, Can, 83; Univ Quebec, Rivieres, Quebec, Can, 91; Banff Sch Fine Arts, Banff, AB, 83. *Collection Arranged:* Exposition Speciale Du Canada, Mass, 2002; Nomadic Current: Louis Hughes, Lamoureux, 2004; Body & Soul, Gisele L'Epicier, Lamoureux, Ritzenhoff Gallery, Quebec, 2004; Today, The Light with Bertrand Tremblay, Ritzenhoff Gallery, Quebec, 2005; Modern Layers, Miklos Rogan, Lamoureux Ritzenhoff Gallery, Quebec, 2005. *Pos:* Art dir, Galerie Lamoureux Ritzenhoff, Montreal, Quebec, Can, 2000-. *Bibliog:*

Cynthia Ashton (auth), Libamah Review, Vandance Publ, 84; Max Wyman (auth), Review, Anna Wyman Dance Theatre, Vandance, 86; Robert Bernier (auth), Etablir Maîtres Demain, Parcours Informateur, 2004. *Specialty:* Canadian emerging contemporary & Canadian masters. *Collection:* Canadian Masters & Canadian contemporary works. *Publ:* auth, Le Ballon Rouge (book), Ed Pierre Tisseyre, 89; auth, Du Pur Expressionism & Contemporain, L'Action Gam, 93 & 2004; auth, Le Nubisme (prog), Centaur Theatre, 97; auth, Le Nubisme (prog), Theatre Rideau Vert, 97; auth, Québec Art, Canadian Art, Its Vitality, Our Pride, 2006. *Mailing Add:* Galerie Lamoureux Ritzenhoff 1428 Sherbrooke West Montreal PQ H3G 1K4 Canada

LAMPASONA, EYDI
ARTIST
b Jan 9, 55. *Study:* Fla Atlantic Univ, BFA, 1999; Vt Col, Union Inst Univ, MFA, 2007. *Work:* Coral Springs Mus, Fla; art Collection Mus, Sergines, France; Int Mus of Collage, Mex City, Mex; Mus of Art, Ft Lauderdale, Fla. *Exhib:* 8th Ann Exhib, Huntsville Mus Art, Ala, 1999; Under the Influence, Mus of Art, Ft Lauderdale, Fla, 2000; One woman exhibs; Selections, Coral Springs Mus, Fla, 2001, 2002; Wish you were here, Lincoln Ctr, NY, 2002; Eleventh Ann Int Exhib, Rosen Mus, Boca Raton, Fla, 2002; Eighty-second Ann Nat Watercolor Soc, Mont Serrat Col, San Pedro, Calif, 2002; All Mixed, Alliance for the Arts Ctr, Ft Myers, Fla, 2004; All Fla 55th Ann Exhib. *Teaching:* Art Instr, Coral Springs Mus of Art, 1997-2002; art instr, summer art dir, Boca Raton Mus Art Sch, 2001-; educ, Golden Acrylic Paint Co, 2001-. *Awards:* Best in Show, Ninth Annual Int Exhib, 2001; best in show, Indoctrination, Fla Atlantic Univ, 2001; second place, Image, Boca Mus, 2003. *Bibliog:* Playbill, Palm Beach, Cover and Featured Artist, 1998; State Port Pilot, NC, Art Review, Newspaper, 1999, Sun Sentinel City Link, Art Review, Newspaper, 2000. *Mem:* Int Soc of Experimental Artists, (pres, 2004); Nat Watercolor Soc (signature mem); Nat collage Soc (signature mem); Soc of Layerists in Multi-media (signature mem); The Artists Assoc. *Publ:* Int Mag, Nat Publications, 2001; Contribr, Composition and Design, North Light Books, 2003; The Art of Layering, Nelson/Dunaway, 2004; Collage in all Dimensions, Gardner, 2005. *Mailing Add:* 11035 Baybreeze Way Boca Raton FL 33428

LAMPITOC, ROL PONCE
PAINTER, PRINTMAKER
b Laoag City, Philippines; Can citizen. *Study:* Univ Philippines Sch Fine Arts, 52; Univ Windsor, 74; Nat Art Seminars, with John Howard Sanden, cert, 80. *Work:* Malacanang Palace & US Embassy, Manila, Philippines; St Claire Col Art Collections, Windsor, Ont; Univ Toronto, Chemical Eng, Ont; Centenary Hosp, Scarborough, Ont; Univ Toronto's Emmanuel Theological Col, Ont; and others. *Comn:* Pres Carlos Garcia & vpres Diosdado Macapagal, comn by Pablo Bustamante, Quezon City, Philippines; Mayor Richard Daley (portrait), comn by Philippine Consul Gen Sulit, Ill; Pres Harry Truman (portrait), US Embassy, Manila, Philippines; Bishop Georgiji (life-size portrait), Serbian Orthodox Diocese, Can; Prof Silcox Woodsworth, Woodsworth Col, Toronto, Ont; and others. *Exhib:* SEast Asian Art Conference, Art Asn Philippines, Manila, 57; Art Gallery, Windsor, Ont, 74; Pastel Soc Am, Nat Arts Club, NY, 74, 76, 77 & 79; 6th Int Art Friendship, Int Friendship Asn Japan, Tokyo, 81; Filipino Artist North Am, Nat Archives, Ottawa, Ont, 81; Pastel Soc Can Nat Arch, Ottawa, Ont, 88. *Pos:* Serigraphist, Quezon City, Philippines; asst art dir, Piercell Merchandising, Windsor, Ont, 73-80; painter & master printer, Atelier Lampitoc, Agincourt, Ont, 80-. *Teaching:* Instr painting, St Clair Col Continuing Educ, 73-74; instr painting, Windsor Art Gallery, 74. *Awards:* First Prize, Art Asn Philippines, 72; First Prize & most popular piece, Blue Mountain Found Arts, Collingwood, Ont, 87; First Prize, Nat Award Maison de la Culture, Pastel Soc Can, 89. *Bibliog:* Dorothy Hall (auth), Art & artists, Park East, New York, 1/10/77; Liane Faulder (auth), Famed in the Philippines, Toronto Star, Ont, 7/31/84; Carlota Rubio (auth), Art to Live with, Vision Hispano Americana, 1/15/88; Kalayaan (Lala) Garcia (auth), Lampitoc's Studio Fills with Artistic Energy, Philippine Reporter, 4/93; and others. *Mem:* Visual Arts Ontario; Pastel Soc Canada; Portrait Club New York; Philippine Artists Group. *Media:* All; Serigraphy, Silkscreen. *Dealer:* Harbour Gallery 1697 Lakeshore Rd W Mississauga ON Can L5J 1J4; Five Signatures Toronto ON. *Mailing Add:* 25 Tunmead Sq Scarborough ON M1B 1X1 Canada

LAMUNIERE, CAROLYN PARKER
PAINTER - ACRYLIC, OIL
b Cleveland, Ohio, Nov 22, 42. *Study:* Skidmore Col, BA(art hist), 65. *Work:* Berkshire Mus, Pittsfield, Mass; Needham, Harper, Steers Advert, Chicago; Am J Psychiatry, Washington; Sybil & Stephen Stone Collection, Brocton Mus, Mass; Art in Embassies, Washington. *Exhib:* Through the Looking Glass, Reflected Images in Am Art, Hecksher Mus, Huntington, NY, 84; 100 Yrs, 100 Artists, Nat Asn Women Artists, NY & Franz Bader, Wash, 89; Earth, Sea, Sky, Adelphi Univ, Long Island, NY, 91; Elaine Beckwith Gallery, Jamaica, Vt, 98; Hand Artes Gallery, Truchas, NMex; Women Made Gallery, Chicago, Ill, 98; Joyce Robbins, Group Show, Santa Fe, NMex, 2000; Munson Gallery, 9/11 Group Show, Santa Fe, NMex, 2001. *Awards:* Michael Engel Award, Nat Soc Painters in Acrylic & Casein; Runner Up Govesnors Award, Md; 1st & 2nd Mural Awards, Sign of the times, Int Competition. *Mem:* Nat Soc Painters Acrylic & Casein, NY; Nat Soc Women Artists, NY. *Media:* Acrylic and Oil. *Interests:* French Preservation. *Publ:* Contemporary Women Artists Calendar, Wash, Recreation Register; Better Homes & Gardens, 79 & 85; NY Times Gallery Guide, 81, 82 & 86; William & Mary Review, 92 & 93; The Best of Acrylic Painting, 97; Collectors' Guides, Santa Fe, Taos, NMex, 1998-2002; 100 Southwest Artists. *Dealer:* Hand Artes Gallery Truchas NM; Elaine Beckwith Gallery Jamaica VT; Johnson Gallery Madrid NMex. *Mailing Add:* 2953 Plaza Blanca Santa Fe NM 87500

LANCASTER, MARK
PAINTER
b Yorkshire, Eng, May 14, 38. *Study:* Dept Fine Art, Univ Newcastle-upon-Tyne, Eng, 61-65; Bootham Sch, York. *Work:* Victoria & Albert Mus & Tate Gallery, London; Arts Coun of Northern Ireland, Belfast; Allen Art Mus, Oberlin, Ohio; Art Gallery of S Australia, Adelaide; Mus Mod Art, NY. *Exhib:* One-man shows, Rowan Gallery, London, Eng, 65-90, Walker Art Gallery, Liverpool, Eng, 73 & Multiples, NY, 75; British Drawings: The New Generation, Mus Mod Art, NY, 67; Six Artists (toured Britian), Victoria & Albert Mus, London, 67; Young British Artist (traveling), Mus Mod Art, NY, 68; British Painting, Hayward Gallery, London, 75; Tate 79, Tate Gallery, London; Am Painting: the 80's, Grey Art Gallery, NY, 79; 2 X Immortal Int Tour, 94-98. *Pos:* Artist-in-Residence, King's Col, Cambridge, Eng, 68-70; designer, Merce Cunningham Dance Co, NY, 74-80, artistic adv, 80-84, artist & designer, 85-; asst to Jasper Johns, 74-85. *Teaching:* Instr, Dept Fine Art, Newcastle Univ, Eng, 65-66; Bath Acad Art, Corsham, Wiltshire, Eng, 66. *Awards:* Purchase Prize, Brit Int Print Biennale, Bradford, 70; NY Dance & Performance Award, 89. *Bibliog:* Mark Lancaster, Betty Parsons Gallery, article in New York Times, 10/74; John Russell (auth), Lancaster sets the stage for Cunningham, Art Am, 7-8/79; Richard Shone (auth), Mark Lancaster, Burlington Mag, 7/80; and others. *Publ:* Andy Warhol Remembered, Burlington Mag, 3/89

LANCASTER, VIRGINIA (GINNY) JANE
EDUCATOR, PAINTER
b Mulberry, Kans, Feb 7, 30. *Study:* Santa Rosa Jr Col; Univ Calif, Berkeley; Sonoma State Univ. *Hon Degrees:* Teaching Degree, Fine & Applied Arts & Related Technologies. *Work:* Mendocino Co Mus, Willits, Calif. *Exhib:* Birds of a Feather, Marin Co Libr, San Rafael, Calif, 71, Some Things I Love, 72 & Kid Stuff, 73; View from the Air, Sonoma State Univ, Cotati, Calif, 72, 150 Yrs of Work by Sonomo Co Women Artists, 80 & Generations, 86; Japanese Arts, George & Elsie Wood Libr, St Helena, Calif, 80; Caprice, Santa Rosa Community Col, Calif, 83; Homage to Japanese Art, Finley Community Ctr, Santa Rosa, Calif, 98. *Teaching:* Art, Sonoma State Col, 73-74, Napa Valley Col, 74-81 & Santa Rosa Jr Col, 75-79. *Mem:* Watercolor Artists Sonoma Co. *Media:* Miscellaneous Media. *Interests:* Avid gardener, Flying Private Pilot (retired list); Interior Design: making curtains, slipcovers, and Historical Houses. *Publ:* Contribr of several articles in Directions Mag, 73-74. *Mailing Add:* 638 Wright St Santa Rosa CA 95404

LANCEL MCELHINNEY, JAMES
PAINTER, EDUCATOR
b Abington, Pa, Feb 3, 52. *Study:* Skowhegan Sch of Painting & Sculpture, 73; Tyler Sch of Art of Temple Univ, BFA, 74; Yale Sch of Art, MFA, 76. *Work:* Yale Art Gallery; Danville Mus Fine Art & Hist; Camden Co Hist & Cult Comn; Asheville Art Mus; Greenville Art Mus; and many others. *Comn:* Reading Co, Philadelphia, 90; Carillon Space, Charlotte, NC, 97; Chrysler Mus, Norfolk, Va, 98; Hampton Roads Palimpsest, Chrysler Mus, Norfolk, Va, 98. *Exhib:* Challenge Exhib, Fleisher Art Mem, Philadelphia Mus Art, 83; Contemp Philadelphia Artists, Philadelphia Mus Art, 90; Philadelphia Int Art Expo, FAN Gallery, 94; Second Street Gallery, Charlottesville, Va 95; Linda Hayman Gallery, Boca Raton, Fla, 91; Lee Hansley Gallery, Raleigh, NC, 96 & 2000; Greenville Art Mus, NC, 96; Hickory Mus, NC, 97; Asheville Art Mus, 96; Chysler Mus Art, 98; Fan Gallery, 98; Crowded Prairie, Ucross, Sheridan, Wyo; Nicolaysen Mus, Casper, Wyo, 2000. *Pos:* artist-in-residence, Harper's Ferry Nat Hist Park. *Teaching:* Milwaukee Inst Art & Design, 91-93; vis artist, Carolina Univ Sch Art, 94; residency, Town of Ayden, NC, vis artist; asst prof, head drawing & painting, Univ Colo, Denver, 98, dir Univ Colo Denver/Comune di Feltre (Italy) Exchange Program, 2000-. *Awards:* Visual Arts Fel, Nat Endowment Arts, 87; Partners in Arts Grant, Richmond Va Arts Coun, 95; Jr Fac Res Grant, Univ Colo, Denver, 2000. *Bibliog:* Kate Dobbs Airial (auth), Beauty in battlefields, Independent Weekly, Raleigh, NC, 10/2/96; Jim Walter (auth), New American Painting, June 1998 Capturing the Battlefield, Art & Antiques Mag, summer 98; John Warner (producer), Virginia Currents (TV doc), WCVE-TV 23 & WHRO-TV (PBS), Richmond & Norfolk, Va, 98. *Mem:* Col Art Asn; Save Hist Am; Asn Preserv Civil War Sites; Foote Family Asn; Spotsylvania Preserv Soc (bd). *Media:* Oil, Watercolor. *Interests:* representational painting; figure portraits; landscape & landscape theory; preservation. *Publ:* New Art Examiner, 86; rev, Art & Antiques, 98; newspaper revs, Philadelphia, Los Angeles, Chicago, Conn, NC, Va, Washington DC, Colo, 80-2000. *Dealer:* Fraidoon Al-Nakib FAN Gallery 311 Cherry St Philadelphia PA 10106; Lee Hansley Gallery 6 W Martin St Suite 201 Raleigh NC 27601

LAND-WEBER, ELLEN E
PHOTOGRAPHER, EDUCATOR
b Rochester, NY, Mar 16, 43. *Study:* Pembroke Col, 1961-1963; Univ Mich, 1964; Univ Iowa, BA (Art Hist), 1965; Univ Iowa, MFA, 1968. *Work:* Int Mus of Photog, George Eastman House, Rochester, NY; San Francisco Mus Mod Art, Calif; New Orleans Mus Art; Libr Cong, Washington, DC. *Comn:* Bicentennial Doc Proj on Archit of Courthouses in US (in collab with 23 other photogrs with assigned geog areas), Seagram's Inc, NY, 75-76. *Exhib:* One-person shows, San Francisco Mus Mod Art, 78, Bard Col, Annandale on Hudson, NY, 79, Focus Gallery, San Francisco, 80 & Shadai Gallery, Tokyo, 83, Views and Portraits of Turkey, Daley Civic Ctr, Chicago, 98, Portrait of Turkey, Southeastern Okla State Univ, Durant, Okla, 99, To Save a Life: Stories of Holocaust Rescue, Humbolt State Univ First Street Gallery, Eureka, Calif, 2000, plus others; Portrait of Turkey: Ellen-Land Weber, Visual & Performing Arts Ctr Gallery, Southeastern Okla State Univ, Durant, Okla, 2000; Water in the West, First Street Gallery, Eureka, Calif, 2000; Fish On/No Fish: Hupa Tribal People & Trinity River Water, Morris Graves Mus, Eureka, Calif, 2001; Water in the West, FotoFest 2004, Williams Tower Gallery, Houston, Tex, 2004; Threads of Vision: Weaving a Life in Photog, Humboldt State Univ, Eureka, Calif, 2005; plus numerous others.

Teaching: Instr photog, Univ Calif Extension, Los Angeles, 70-74; asst prof photog, Humboldt State Univ, Arcata, Calif, 74-79, assoc prof, 79-83, prof, 83-; prof emer art, Humboldt State Univ, 2006. *Awards:* Fel, Nat Endowment for Arts, 75, 79, 82; Fel, Felbright, 93-94; Grant, Polaroid Artist's Support, 90, 92, 93; Humboldt State University Scholar of the Year, 2005. *Mem:* Soc for Photog Educ, mem since 73 to present (nat treas, 79-81, nat secy, 81-83). *Res:* Photographic digital imaging. *Interests:* Photography, Travel. *Publ:* Women of photography: an historical survey, San Francisco Mus of Mod Art, 75; Translations, Herbert F Johnson Mus, Ithaca, NY, 79; Courthouse, a Photographic Document, Horizon Press, 79; The Passionate Collector, photographs by Ellen Land-Weber, Simon & Schuster, 80; Photography and Art, Interactions Since 1946, Grundberg & Gauss, Abrams, 87; auth, To Save a Life: Stories of Holocaust Rescue, Univ Ill Press, 2000. *Dealer:* Craig Krull Gallery Santa Monica CA. *Mailing Add:* 790 Park Pl Arcata CA 95521

LANDAU, ELLEN GROSS
HISTORIAN, CRITIC
b Philadelphia, Pa, Feb 27, 47. *Study:* Cornell Univ, BA, 69; George Washington Univ, MA, 74; Univ Del, PhD, 81. *Collection Arranged:* America in the War: An Exhibit by Artists for Victory Inc (auth, catalog), Libr Cong, Washington, DC, 83; Jackson Pollock-Lee Krasner: Kunsterpaare, Kunstierfreunde (auth, catalog), Kunstmuseum, Bern & Switz, 89; Lee Krasner's collages 1953-55 (auth, catalog), Jason McCoy, Inc, 95-96. *Pos:* Res asst to chief cur, Corcoran Gallery Art, 69-71; asst cur hist properties, Nat Trust for Hist Preserv, 73-76. *Teaching:* prof art hist & chair, Case Western Reserve Univ, 82-. *Awards:* Rockefeller Found Fel, 78-79; Am Coun Learned Soc Fel, 85-86; Cleveland Arts Prize for Literature, Women's City Club, 91; John S Diekhuff Award Distinguished Grad Teaching, Case Western Reserve Univ, 93. *Mem:* Col Art Asn; Mid-West Art His Soc; Am Culture Asn; Catalogue Raisonne' Scholars Asn; Asn Hist Am Art. *Res:* Post 1945 American art; abstract expressionism; women's studies (gender issues); critical theory. *Publ:* Auth, Jackson Pollock, 89 & Lee Krasner: A Catalogue Raisonne, 95, Abrams. *Mailing Add:* Dept Art Hist & Art Case Western Reserve Univ Mather House 11201 Euclid Ave Cleveland OH 44106-7110

LANDAU, EMILY FISHER
COLLECTOR, ADMINISTRATOR
b Glen Falls, NY. *Pos:* Founding mem, Nat Mus Women Arts, 87; trustee, Whitney Mus Am Art, NY, 87-, vpres, 90-, co-chmn contemp comt, 94-; charter mem, US Holocaust Mem Mus, 92; mem chmn's coun, Mus Mod Art, NY, 92-, mem comt prints & illus bks, 85-, mem comt painting & sculpture, 97-; bd dir, Site Santa Fe, 94; bd dir, Georgia O'Keefe Mus, Santa Fe, 96; founder, Fisher Landau Ctr for Treatment of Learning Disabilities; partner, Fisher Bros, New York City, pres 84-91; mem chmns coun, Mus Modern Art. *Awards:* Decorated Chevalier, Order Arts & Letts, France; Hon Dr, Yeshiva Univ, NY, 98; named one of Top 200 Collectors, ARTnews Mag, 2004, 2006. *Mem:* Metrop Club, Doubles, & Palm Beach Co Club. *Collection:* Contemporary American art. *Publ:* Contribr, Jasper Johns: The Screenprints (exhib catalog), 96; Mishoo Cosmopolitan Cat (children's storybook), 2000

LANDAU, JON & BARBARA
COLLECTOR
Study: Brandeis Univ, 68. *Pos:* mgr, for Shania Twain, Natalie Merchant, formerly; producer, albums for MC5, Livingston Taylor, Jackson Brown, Bruce Springsteen, formerly; mgr, for Bruce Springsteen, Train, Patti Scialfa, currenty; founder, co-owner Jon Landau Mgt, currently; Rock critic, Crawdaddy!, Boston Phoenix, Rolling Stone, The Real Paper, currently. *Awards:* Named one of Top 200 Collectors, ARTnews Mag, 2004. *Collection:* Old Master painting & sculpture, 19th century French painting; American modernist art. *Publ:* Auth, It's Too Late to Stop Now: A Rock and Roll Jour, 72. *Mailing Add:* Jon Landau Mgt 80 Mason St Greenwich CT 06830

LANDAU, MYRA
PAINTER, MURALIST
b Bucarest, Rumania; Mex citizen. *Study:* Studied with Oswaldo Goeldi, Authodactic engraving on metal in painting. *Work:* Mus Mod Art, Mexico; Pinqcoteca del Estado, Sao Paulo, Brazil; Casa de Las Americas, Habana, Cuba; Univ Veracruzana, Xalapa, Mexico; Casas de Cultura, Mexico; and others. *Exhib:* Mus Mod Art, Mexico City, 75 & 87; Centro de Estudios del er Mundo, Mexico City, 77; Casa de La Cultura, Recife-Pe, Brazil, 78; Gallery Arte Global, Sao Paulo, Brazil, 78; Mus Mod Art, Salvador, Brazil, 78; Mus Carrillogil, Mexico City, 79; Univ Metrop Mexico City, 80; Ctr Cult Mexique, Paris, 83; Instituto Italo, Latino Americano, Roma, Ital. *Pos:* Docente-Facultad de Artes Plasticas, 74-75; investigadora, Inst de Investigaciones; esteticas, Univ Veracruzana, 75-. *Bibliog:* Teresa del Conde (auth), 12 Expresiones plasticas de hoy, Bancreser, 11/88; Raul Renan & Berta Taracena (auth), Diez años de la Galeria Metropolitana, Univ Autonoma Metropolitana, 89. *Mem:* Foro de Arte Contemporaneo, Mexico City. *Media:* Linen, Pastels. *Publ:* Si Sabes Ver, Univ Veracruzana, 76; Textos Legirles Ritmos Ile Gibles, Univ Veracruzana, 85; Ritmos, Univ Autonoma Nacional de Mexico, 86. *Mailing Add:* Alfaro 6 Xalapa Veracruz Mexico

LANDFIELD, RONNIE (RONALD) T
PAINTER
b Bronx, NY, Jan 9, 47. *Study:* Art Students League, 62-63, 94; Kansas City Art Inst, Mo, 63; San Francisco Art Inst, 64-65. *Work:* Mus Mod Art, Whitney Mus Art, Metrop Mus Art, NY; Hirshhorn Mus of Art, Washington; RI Sch of Design Mus, Providence; Walker Art Ctr, Minneapolis, Minn. *Comn:* Mural (painting 11 ft x 20 ft), Westinghouse Corp & I Chermayoff, Pittsburgh, Pa, 70. *Exhib:* Whitney Ann & Biennial Exhib of Am Painting, NY, 67, 69 & 73; Lyrical Abstraction, Whitney Mus of Am Art, 71 & Aldrich Mus of Contemp Art, Ridgefield, Conn, 71; Art for Your Collection, RI Sch of Design, Providence, 71; Recent Acquisitions, Mus of Mod Art, NY, 72; one-man shows, Andre Emmerich Gallery, NY, 73-75 & 75, Linda Farris, Seattle, Wash, 78, 79, 81, 84, 87 & 89, Sarah Rentschler Gallery, NY, 78 & 79, Medici-Berensen, Miami, Fla, 79, Stephen Rosenberg Gallery, NY, 94 & Nicholas/Alexander Gallery, NY, 94; Charles Cowles Gallery, NY, 80, 82-84; Hokin Gallery, Miami, Fla, 85 & 87; Hokin-Kaufman Gallery, Chicago, 85 & 87; Stephen Haller Fine Arts, NY, 87, 88, 89 & 90; Claudia Carr Gallery, 99; Salander - O Reilly Galleries, NY, 2000; Heidi Cho Gallery, NYC, 2005. *Teaching:* Instr fine arts, Sch of Visual Arts, New York, 75-89; instr, Art Students League NY, 1994-. *Awards:* Gold Medal, San Francisco Art Inst, Calif, 65; Cassandra; Nat Endowment Arts, 83; Pollock/Krasner Foundation, Grants 1995, 2001. *Bibliog:* Noel Frackman (auth), article, Arts, Vol 50, No 1, 9/75; Phyllis Tuchman (auth), article, Art News, Vol 77, No 3, 3/78; Lisa Messinger (auth), The landscape in Twentieth-Century American art: selections from the Metropolitan Museum of Art, Rizzoli, NY, 91; Cohen Mark Daniel (auth) Ronnie Landfield: New Works on Paper, Claudia Carr Gallery, Exhibition Rev Mag, 4/99. *Media:* Acrylic, Watercolor. *Dealer:* Salander-OReilly Galleries 20 E 79th St New York NY 10021. *Mailing Add:* 31 Desbrosses St New York NY 10013

LANDIS, ELLEN JAMIE
CURATOR, HISTORIAN
b Chicago, Ill, May 6, 41. *Study:* Univ Calif, Berkeley, BA; Univ Vienna, 60-61; NY Univ, Inst Fine Arts, MA. *Exhib:* Mus Menagerie, 91; El Couse, 91; Unbroken Threads, 92; Human Factor: Figurative Sculpture Reconsidered, 93; Man on Fire (auth, catalog), Luis Jimenez, 94; Zones of Experience: The Art of Larry Bell, 97; Tibet: Tradition & Change, 98; Silent Thigs, Secret Things: Still Life from Rembrandt to the Millennium, 99; Cast of Characters Figurative Sculpture, 2000. *Collection Arranged:* Homage to Rodin (coauth, catalog), Los Angeles Co Mus Art, Los Angeles, 67; Rodin Bronzes from the Collection of B Gerald Cantor (auth, catalog), Am Fedn Art, 70; Vincent Van Gogh, Baltimore Mus Art, 70; Four Americans in Paris: The Collections of Gertrude Stein and Her Family, Baltimore Mus Art, 71; Early 20th Century European Masterpainters, 77, Indian Art Today (auth, catalog), 77, Metro Youth Art (auth, catalog), 77 & Albuquerque Artists I (auth, catalog), 77, Mus Albuquerque; Reflections of Realism (auth, catalog), 79 & Katachi: Form and Spirit in Japanese Art, 80, Albuquerque Mus; Here and Now, 35 Artist in New Mexico (auth, catalog), 81, West-Southwest (auth, catalog), 82, In Place, 82, Eve Laramee, 83 & Hiroshige, 83 Albuquerque Mus, Wilson Hurley, 85; Adventures West, 89; Printers Impressions, 90. *Pos:* Cur, painting & sculpture, Baltimore Mus Art, 70 & 71, Albuquerque Mus, 77-2004; actg cur, Robert Gore Rifkind Collection, Beverly Hills, Calif, 72; bd dir, Actors Theater, Albuquerque, NMex, 79-81; bd adv, Artspace Mag, 78-93; art cur, Albuenque Mus, 77-; bd trustees, Comprehensive Art Publ, Ohio, 80-; mem, Writers Comt, Am Asn Mus; independent cur, 2004-. *Teaching:* Lectr introd to art, Yuba Col, Marysville, Calif, 76-77. *Awards:* The Chris Award, Homage to Rodin, Film Coun Greater Columbus, 69; Building Bridges Award, Univ NMex, 98; The Albuquerque Mus Dir's Award, 2000; Albuquerque Arts Alliance Bravos Award, 2000. *Bibliog:* Contemporary Personalities, Accademia' Italia' Delle Arti e Del Lavoro, 82; International Who's Who of Professional & Business Women, 1st ed, autumn 88. *Mem:* Col Art Asn; Am Asn Mus; SW Art Hist Coun (pres, 92-98). *Res:* Centralized research in areas of 19th Century and 20th Century art. *Publ:* Coauth, The David E Bright Collection, Los Angeles Co Mus Art, Los Angeles, 67; Matisse in Baltimore, Television Spec, 71; Carl Redin (exhib catalog), 84 & Wilson Hurley: A Retrospective Exhibition (exhib catalog), Albuquerque Mus, 85. *Mailing Add:* 7112 Osuna NE Albuquerque NM 87109

LANDREAU, ANTHONY NORMAN
EDUCATOR
b Washington, DC, Apr 2, 30. *Study:* Cath Univ Am, with Kenneth Noland; Black Mountain Col, NC, with Kline, Fiore & Rice, BA, 54; Temple Univ, MA, 93, Temple Univ, PhD, 96. *Collection Arranged:* Smithsonian Travelling Exhib Serv, 69-71; Carnegie Inst, 78-79; Textile Mus, 83-85. *Pos:* Exec dir, Textile Mus, Washington, DC, 67-75; cur educ, Carnegie Inst Mus Art, Pittsburgh, 75-81; pres, Int Collection Inc, 81-88; grad studies prog Anthrop, Temple Univ, Philadelphia, 88, research assoc, currently. *Teaching:* Instr weaving-design, Black Mountain Col, 54-56; lectr hist textiles, Univ Md, 75; asst prof, Manor Jr Col, 93-. *Awards:* Near E Res Ctr Grant, rug studies in Turkey, 73; Nat Endowment Arts prof Fels, study in Turkey, 73 & study in USSR, 75; Turkish res proj, Nat Endowment Humanities, 80. *Mem:* Am Anthrop Asn; Asn Feminist Anthrop; Am Ethnological Soc; Am-Turkish Asn (bd mem, 74-); Iran-Am Soc (bd mem, 74-). *Res:* Folk weaving, particularly in the Middle East. *Publ:* Auth, Yoruk, The Nomadic Weaving Tradition in the Middle East, Carnegie Inst, 78; Carpets and rugs, Encycl Americana, 80; Flowers of the Yayla, Textile Mus, 83; Anatolian Rug Weaving, Mirror of Change, Temple Univ, 96

LANE, ALVIN S
COLLECTOR
b Englewood, NJ, June 17, 18. *Study:* Univ Wis, PhB; Harvard Univ Law Sch, LLB; New Sch Social Res, with Seymour Lipton. *Pos:* Chmn comt on art, NY Bar Asn, 63-65; mem bd overseers fine arts, Brandeis Univ, 66-70; mem adv bd to NY Atty Gen on Art Legis, 66-71; secy & trustee, Aldrich Mus Contemp Art, 69-76, dir & vpres, 79; Soho Ctr for Visual Artists Inc, 74-83; bd dir, Artists Equity Asn, NY, Creative Artists Pub Serv Prog, Inc, 82-84; 20th Century Art Soc, High Mus Art, 86-95; Drawing Committee, Whitney Mus Am Art, 91; The Elverjem Mus Art Coun, 92. *Collection:* Modern and contemporary sculpture and sculptors' drawings. *Publ:* Auth, How the bar can assist the art community, New York Bar Asn, 65; The case of the careless collector, Art in Am, 65; Disclosure on disclosure, Print Collector Newslett, 74. *Mailing Add:* 35 E 38th St New York NY 10016

LANE, JOHN RODGER
MUSEUM DIRECTOR, HISTORIAN
b Chicago, Ill, Feb 28, 44. *Study:* Williams Col, BA, 66; Univ Chicago, MBA, 71; Harvard Univ, AM, 73, PhD, 76. *Hon Degrees:* San Francisco Art Inst, Hon Doc Fine Arts, 95. *Collection Arranged:* Stuart Davis: Art and Art Theory, Brooklyn Mus & Fogg Art Mus, 78; Modernist Art from the Edith and Milton Lowenthal Collection, Brooklyn Mus, 81; Robert Bourdon: Auto Rex, Carnegie Inst, 82; The Groups: Paintings by Archie Rand, Carnegie Inst, 83; Abstract Painting and Sculpture in America, Carnegie Inst, San Francisco Mus Mod Art, Minneapolis Inst Art & Whitney Mus, 83-84; Carnegie International, Carnegie Inst, 85; Ross Bleckner, 88 & Don Van Vliet, San Francisco Mus Mod Art, 88; Frida Kahlo, Diego Rivera, & Mexican Modernism from the Jacques & Natasha Gelman Collection, San Francisco Mus Mod Art, 96; Maria Botta: The SFMOMA Project, San Francisco Mus Mod Art, 95; Sigmar Polke: Recent Paintings and Drawings, Dallas Mus of Art & Tate Modern, 2002-03; Lothar Bumgarten: Carbon, Dallas Mus Art, 2004. *Pos:* Asst dir, Fogg Art Mus, 74; exec asst to dir, Brooklyn Mus, 75-78, adminr curatorial affairs, 79, asst dir curatorial affairs, 80; dir, Carnegie Mus Art, 80-86, San Francisco Mus Mod Art, 87-97; Eugene McDermott dir, Dallas Mus Art, Tex, 99-. *Teaching:* Teaching fel art hist, Harvard Univ, 73-75. *Mem:* Am Asn Mus; Int Coun Mus; Asn Art Mus Dirs; Williams Col Mus Art (vis comt); Asn Art Mus Dir (trustee 00-02). *Res:* 20th century American Art. *Publ:* Auth, New York: The Brooklyn Mus, Stuart Davis: Art and Art Theory, 78; co-ed (with Susan C Larsen), Abstract Painting and Sculpture in America 1927-1944, Carnegie Inst & Harry N Abrams, Inc, 83; co-ed (with Saskia Bos & John Caldwell), 85, Dalls Mus Art 100 Years, 03, Gerhard Richerter, 65-04, Lothar Baugmarten: Carbon, 04; contribr, The Barney A Ebsworth Collection Catalog, St Louis Art Museum, 87; Stuart Davis, American Painter, The Metrop Mus Art, 91; exec ed, The Making of a New Museum, San Francisco Mus Mod Art, 95. *Mailing Add:* c/o Dallas Mus Art 1717 N Hardwood Dallas TX 75201-2398

LANE, LOIS
PAINTER, PRINTMAKER
b Philadelphia, Pa, Jan 6, 48. *Study:* Yale Summer Sch Music & Art, 68; Philadelphia Col Art, BFA, 69; Yale Univ Sch Art & Archit, MFA, 71. *Work:* Whitney Mus Am Art, Mus Mod Art, NY; Albright-Knox Gallery, Buffalo, NY; Des Moines Art Ctr, Iowa; Mus Fine Art, Houston; Nat Gallery of Art, Washington, DC. *Exhib:* New Image Painting (with catalog), Whitney Mus Am Art, 78; Whitney Biennial (with catalog), Whitney Mus Am Art, 79; Selections from Art Lending, Mus Mod Art, NY, 80; Inst Contemp Art, Va Mus Fine Arts, Richmond, 81; post MINIMALism (with catalog), Aldrich Mus Contemp Art, Ridgefield, Conn, 82; one-person exhibs, Pa Acad Fine Arts, Philadelphia, 82, Willard Gallery, NY, 83, 85 & 87, John Berggruen Gallery, San Francisco, 87, Barbara Mathes Gallery, NY, 88 & 89, Barbara Krakow Gallery, Boston, 89, Hood Mus Art, Dartmouth Col, Hanover, NH, 90 & Barbara Toll Fine Arts, NY, 91 & 93; Some Recent Acquisitions, Mus Mod Art, NY, 83; 47th Nat Midyear Exhib, Butler Inst Am Art, Ohio, 83; Visions of Childhood: A Contemp Iconography, Whitney Mus Am Art, NY, 84; Recent Acquisitions, Albright-Knox Art Gallery, Buffalo, NY, 84; The Hunt Collection, Philadelphia Mus Art, Pa, 88; Permanent Collection, Mus Mod Art, NY, 91; The Print Club Residences, Print Club Philadelphia, Pa, 91; 5 Artists Living and Working in Warwick, NY, 91; Crossing Over, Changing Places, Print Club Philadelphia, Pa, 91; Selected Prints from Spring Street Workshop, Tomasulo Gallery, Cranford, NJ, 91; Apocalypse and Resurrection, Gallery Three Zero, NY, 92; Herbert F Johnson Mus Art, Cornell Univ, Ithica, NY, 92; and others. *Awards:* NY State Coun Arts Creative Artists Pub Serv Prog Grant, 77; Nat Endowment Arts Fel Painting, 78. *Bibliog:* Lisa Liebman (auth), Lois Lane: Barbara Toll Gallery, Artforum, Vol XXX, No 7, 107, 3/92; Nancy Malloy (auth), Lois Lane: Barbara Toll, Art News, Vol 91, No 3, 124-5, 3/92; Jerry Saltz (auth), Let us now praise artist's artists, Art & Auction, 74-115, 4/93. *Media:* Oil; Etching; Monotypes. *Publ:* Contribr, New Image Painting, Whitney Mus, 78; American Painting: the Eighties, Barbara Rose/Vista Press, 79. *Mailing Add:* 35 Drew Rd Warwick NY 10990

LANE, MARION ARRONS
PAINTER, SCULPTOR
b Brooklyn, NY. *Study:* Brooklyn Mus Art Sch, with Manifred Schwartz & Reuben Tam; Pratt Inst, NY; Art Students League, with Morris Kantor; Wm Paterson Col, NJ, BA; Rutgers Univ, with Leon Golub, MFA. *Work:* Bergen Mus Paramus, NJ; R Sunshine, B Feigen, N. Levine. *Exhib:* Pleiades Gallery, NY, 76, 77 & 2005; Williams Ctr, Rutherford, NJ, 90; Nabisco Corp Hq, 95; Broome St Gallery, 96; Edward Williams Col, NJ, 99; Retrospective Exhib, Westbeth Gallery, 2000; Pleiades Gallery, NY, 2005. *Teaching:* Instr, art appreciation & drawing, Bergen Community Col, 80-86; art therapist, 86-99. *Awards:* Edward Albee Found, NY, 1983; NJ State Council on Thearts Fellowships, 1983 & 1988; Richard Florsheim Art Fund Grant, 1999; Valparaiso Found Grant, Mojaca, Spain, 2002; Julia and David White Found Grant, Costa Rica, 2003; Residency Grant, Va Ctr for the Cult Arts, 2004. *Bibliog:* Hedy Obeil (auth), article, Arts Mag, 10/77; Deborah Jerome (auth), article, Record, 82; Eileen Watkins (auth), article, in: Newark Star Ledger, 4/86 & 9/90. *Mem:* Life mem Art Students League. *Media:* Acrylic, Oil Paint; Sheetmetal. *Collection:* Bloomfield College Museum; Bergen County Museum. *Publ:* Changing Perspectives, The Art of Marion Lane; Auth, Retrospective Catalog, 2000. *Dealer:* Kerygma Gallery Ridgewood NJ; Boston Art Boston MA; Pleiades Gallery NY. *Mailing Add:* 55 Bethune St G 119 New York NY 10014

LANE, ROSEMARY LOUISE
PRINTMAKER, SCULPTOR
b San Francisco, Calif, Dec 6, 44. *Study:* Calif Col Arts & Crafts, Oakland, with Ralph Borge, Robert Bechtle & Roy DeForrest, BFA, 66; Calif State Univ, Hayward, 70; Univ Ore, with Laverne Krause & Ken Paul, MFA, 73. *Work:* Univ Ore Art Gallery, Eugene; Brussels Art Mus, Belg; Fran Masereel Ctr Graphics, Kasterlee, Belg. *Comn:* Artwork, comn by Martha Dupont, The Sanctuary, Wilmington, Del, 89-90. *Exhib:* One-person exhib, Pa State Univ Invitational, 83, Prints & Cast Paper, Wilmington, 83 & Relics of Hope, 86, Art Loop, Wilmington, Del, 89, Inner Visions, Del State Arts Coun, Wilmington, 95; Int Print Biennial, Silvermine Guild Artists, New Caanan, Conn, 94; Art for Peace, Prints, Youth & Creative Arts Ctr, Troitsk, Russia, 94; Lane/Schwab (2 person exhib), John M Clayton Hall, Univ Del, Newark, 94; Okla State Univ, 97; Southern Graphics Coun Conf, Univ SFla, Tampa, 97. *Teaching:* Vis instr printmaking, Univ Ore, Eugene, 73-74; from instr printmaking, drawing & papermaking to assoc prof, Univ Del, Newark, 74-867, prof, 88-. *Awards:* Merit Award, Int Juried Art Exhib, Mussavi Gallery, New York, 85; Purchase Awards, 5th, 15th & 17th Nat Print & Drawing Exhib, Minot State Col, NDak; Art for Peace Grant, People to People Int, 94. *Bibliog:* Lisa Lyons (auth), Rosemary Lane, Artvoices, 1-2/80; Patricia Wright (auth), Rosemary Lane/Muse Gallery, Art Express, 12/81; Penelope Bass Cope (auth), Artist goes with her feminine instincts, Wilmington J, 11/83. *Mem:* Soc Am Graphic Artists; Los Angeles Printmaking Soc; Philadelphia Print Club; Int Graphic Arts Found. *Media:* Bichromate Prints; Handmade Paper Casts. *Mailing Add:* 50 Cummings Ct Bear DE 19701

LANE, WILLIAM
PAINTER
b Kalamazoo, Mich, Jan 12, 36. *Study:* Univ Calif Los Angeles, BA, 58, MA, 61. *Work:* Home Savings & Loan Collection, Los Angeles, Calif; Security Pac Bank, Los Angeles, Calif; Toronto Dominion Bank, Los Angeles, Calif; Price, Waterhouse & Co, Los Angeles, Calif; 1st Independent Gallery, Santa Monica, Calif, 93. *Exhib:* One-man shows, Palos Verdes Art Mus, 69, La Jolla Mus Art, 67, Studio Cafe, Corona Del Mar, 88, St Luke's Episcopal Church, Long Beach, Calif, 89; 20th Century European & Am Watercolors, Long Beach Mus Art, Calif, 88; 6 + 35, FHP Hippodrome Gallery, Long Beach, Calif, 91; Seductive Geometry, Los Angeles Abstr Art, Olga Dollar Gallery, San Francisco, Calif, 91; Aspects of Figural Painting in Southern California, Tatistcheff Gallery, Santa Monica, Calif, 91; Schick Art Gallery, Skidmore Col, Saratoga Springs, NY, 95; Fig Gallery, Santa Monica, Calif, 96 & 99; Defined Edge, Century Gallery, Sylmari, Calif, 98. *Pos:* Art gallery dir, Rio Hondo Col, Whittier, Calif, 98-99. *Teaching:* Prof art, Rio Hondo Col, Whittier, Calif, 69-; vis asst prof painting, Univ Calif Los Angeles, 76-77. *Awards:* Purchase Awards, City Art Festival, Los Angeles, 60, 66; Nat Endowment Arts Fel, 87. *Media:* Acrylic, Watercolor. *Specialty:* Paintings. *Dealer:* Fig Gallery Santa Monica Calif. *Mailing Add:* 2203 E 10th St Long Beach CA 90804

LANG, CAY
PHOTOGRAPHER
b Long Beach, Calif, Feb 5, 48. *Study:* Calif State Univ, Fresno, BA, 76; San Francisco Art Inst, MFA, 79. *Work:* Mediateque, Henin Veaumont, France; De Saisset Mus, Santa Clara, Calif; Los Angeles Co Mus Art; Bibliotheque Nat, Paris, France. *Exhib:* Laguna Beach Mus Art, Calif, 85; Camden Art Ctr, London, Eng, 85; Mus Mod Art, Ft Mason, San Francisco, 86; De Saisset Mus, Santa Clara, Calif, 88; Palais de Tokyo, Paris, 88. *Teaching:* Univ Calif Berkeley Exten, 90; Calif State Univ, San Francisco Exten, 90; Univ Calif, Davis, spring 91 & 92. *Awards:* Fel, MacDowell Colony, 87; Proj Grant, Polaroid Corp, 87; Visual Arts Fel, Am Pen Women, 88-89. *Bibliog:* Hans Eberhard Hess (auth), Blumenwunder aus Kalifornien, Phototecnik Mag, 4/86; Portfolio, Photo Design, 7/88; Evelyn Roth (auth), Body language, Am Photogr, 7/88. *Dealer:* Galerie Michele Chomette 24 Rue Beauborg 75003 Paris France; Benteler-Morgan Gallery, Houston, Tex. *Mailing Add:* 1506 62nd St Emeryville CA 94608

LANG, DANIEL S
PAINTER
b Tulsa, Okla, Mar 17, 35. *Study:* Northwestern Univ, Evanston; Univ Tulsa, BFA, with Alexandre Hogue; Univ Iowa, MFA, 59, with Mauricio Lasansky. *Work:* Mus Mod Art, NY; Art Inst Chicago; Libr Cong, Washington; Nelson-Atkins Mus Fine Art, Kansas City; Victoria & Albert Mus, London; and others. *Comn:* Beneficial Management Group, NJ, 82. *Exhib:* Boston Mus Fine Arts, 61; Sherry French Gallery, NY, 84; Hokin Gallery, Palm Beach, Fla, 91; William Hardie Gallery, Glasgow, Scotland, 92; Elliot Smith Gallery, St Louis, Mo, 94; Cline Gallery, Santa Fe, NMex, 94; plus many others. *Teaching:* Asst prof painting, Art Inst Chicago, 62-64, Wash Univ, 64-65; vis artist, Ohio State Univ, 68-69, Univ SFla, fall 72; adj prof, Univ Utah, 84-; dir summer art prog, Univ Tulsa, Montone, Italy, 95-. *Mem:* NY Artists Asn; Chelsea Arts Club, London, Eng. *Media:* Multimedia. *Publ:* Auth, Daniel Lang: Trees/Water/Silence, A selection of paintings from 1975 through 1986, 86

LANG, GARY
PAINTER, LECTURER
b Los Angeles, Calif, 1950. *Study:* Chouinard Art Inst, BFA, 70; Calif Inst Arts, BFA, 73; Yale Univ, MFA, 75. *Work:* Wadsworth Atheneum; Detroit Inst Art; Madison Art Ctr, Wis; Brooklyn Mus; Contemp Art Mus, Univ S Fla, Tampa; Portland (Maeine) Mus Art; pvt collections. *Comn:* Outdoor sculpture, NEA, New Haven, Conn, 73; wall painting mural, Mark Quint Gallery, La Jolla, Calif, 90; wall painting mural, Margaret Lipworth Fine Arts, Boca Raton, Fla, 92; site tape construct, Haags Gemeentemuseum, The Hague, Neth, 96; tape construct, Crosby St Projects, NY, 96. *Exhib:* Whitney Mus Art, 72; Brooklyn Painters, Brooklyn Mus, 87; New Work, Albright-Knox Mus, 88; Sailing to Byzantium-with Disenchantment, Sergio Tossi Arte Contemp, Prato, Italy, 93; Collection of Julian Pretto, Wadsworth Atheneum, 96; Hague Proj, Haggs Gemeentemuseum, The Neth, 96; solo shows, Quint Gallery, La Jolla, Calif, 97, Galerie Zurcher, Paris, France, 97 & 99, Brian Gross Fine Art, San Francisco, Calif, 98, 99, 2001, Claremont Grad Univ, Calif, 98, Stark Gallery, 2001, Crocker Plaza, Dan Fransisco, Calif, 2001, Yoshi Hirai, Japan, 2001, Gallerie Trabant, Vienna, 2001, Mus of Contemp Art, San Diego, Calif, 2001, Pub Garden Comn,

Carlsbad, Calif, 2001, Ouint Contmp Art, San Diego, Calif, 2001; Drawing From Life, Stark Gallery, NY, 97; Anniversary Shows 1973-1997, Galeria Cadaques, Spain, 97; Projects, Galerie Zurcher, Paris, France, 98; Cool Painting, Brian Gross Fine Art, San Francisco, Calif, 98; Davis St Inaugural, Butters Gallery Ltd, Portland, Ore, 99; I Love NY, Mus Ludwigh, Koln, Ger, 98; Haulin' Ass, Pierogi 2000 Flat Files (Armed and Dangerous), Yerba Buena Ctr, San Francisco, 2000; Lobby Installation: Mus Contemp Art, San Diego, 2001; Eckert Fine Art, Naples, Fla, 2000. *Teaching:* Lectr, Univ Calif Los Angeles, Clairmont Col, Calif, State Univ Am, NY,Yale Univ, 96, Ariz State Univ, Phoenix, 97, Empire State Col, NY, 99; prof grad archit, Univ Pa, 98. *Awards:* Fulbright/Hayes Travel Grant, USA/Spain, 75-77; Elizabeth Found Arts Grant, 95, Int Studio Program Award, 2000; Adolph and Esther Gottlieb Found Grant, 98. *Bibliog:* Kenneth Baker (auth), Cool Paintings Radiate Heat, San Francisco Chronicle, 12/12/1998; Donald Kuspit, Lynn Garwell & Hartmann (coauths), Dreamworks: Artistic and Pscychological Perspectives, SUNY & Cornell Univ Press, 99; Dan Bennett (auth), Beginning this season, living art will bloom in Carlsbad's flower fields, Los Angeles Times, 3/16,2000; and others. *Media:* Acrylic

LANG, J T
PRINTMAKER, EDUCATOR
b Maple Shade, NJ, Dec 24, 31. *Study:* Philadelphia Col Art, cert; Tyler Sch Art, BFA, BS(educ) & MFA; Barnes Found, with Violette De Mazia; also with Toshi Yoshida, Hirooyuki Tajima & Yuji Abe, Tokyo. *Work:* Philadelphia Mus Art; Cincinnati Mus Art; Birmingham Mus Art; State Dept, Washington, DC; Philadelphia Libr Collection. *Comn:* Large ed/woodcut, Print Club Philadelphia, 65, Exodus (litho ser), Pearl Fox Gallery of Elkins Park, 71; color litho ed, La Salle Col, Philadelphia, 74; John Baptist de La Salle, La Salle Col, Philadelphia, 81. *Exhib:* Japan Print Soc Ann, Tokyo, 62, 63, 65 & 66; one-man print shows, Yoseido Gallery, Tokyo, 65 & Birmingham Mus, Ala, 74; USA Print Workshop Exhib, Cincinnati, 67; Am Color Print Soc Ann, Philadelphia, 68-81. *Teaching:* Asst prof Western cult, Aoyama G Univ, Tokyo, 63-67; vis lectr printmaking, Tyler Sch Art, Philadelphia, 68-70; asst prof printmaking & Asian art hist, LaSalle Col, Philadelphia. *Awards:* Purchase Award, Pa Acad Fine Arts, 69; Outstanding Printmaker Award, Philadelphia Bd Educ, 73; Tyler Art Sch Award of Honor, 84. *Bibliog:* Dorothy Grafly (auth), Summer print show, Sun Bull, Philadelphia, 7/30/67; Richard L Bell (auth), Prints of J T Lang (video tape), Springfield High Sch, 4/71; Sally Ann Harper (auth), Lang/printmakers, La Salle Collegian, 3/27/73. *Mem:* Am Color Print Soc (coun mem, 72-); Philadelphia Print Club; Col Art Teacher's Asn; Philadelphia Watercolor Club, 87-. *Media:* All. *Dealer:* Pearl Fox Gallery 104 Windsor Ave Melrose Park Philadelphia PA 19126. *Mailing Add:* LaSalle Univ Philadelphia PA 19141

LANG, RODGER ALAN
SCULPTOR, EDUCATOR
b Chicago, Ill, Feb 9, 42. *Study:* Cornell Col, BA(art); Univ Wis-Madison, with Don Reitz & Harvey Littleton, MA(art) & MFA. *Work:* Brooks Mem Art Gallery, Memphis, Tenn; Mesa Col, Grand Junction, Colo; American Craft Mus, New York City. *Comn:* Ceramic tile wall mural, US West Corp, 78; ceramic tile wall mural, State of Colo, 80. *Exhib:* 49th Ann May Show, Cleveland Mus Art, Ohio, 67; Clayworks: 20 Americans, Mus Contemp Crafts, NY, 71; Wichita Nat, Wichita Ctr Arts, Kans, 90; NAm Sculpture Exhib, Foothills Art Ctr, Golden, Colo, 95; 52nd Wis Painters & Sculptors Ann, Milwaukee Art Ctr, 96. *Teaching:* Instr, Cleveland Inst Art, 66-70; assoc prof, Metrop State Col, 70-77, prof, 77-. *Bibliog:* Rose Slivka (auth), Laugh-in in clay, Craft Horizons, 10/71; Civilizations in clay, Craft Horizons, 12/77; Old Pecos Mus, Ceramics Mo, 4/90. *Mem:* Nat Coun Educ Ceramic Arts. *Media:* Ceramics, Wood, Mixed Media. *Dealer:* Inkfish Gallery Paul Hughes 949 Broadway Denver CO 80203. *Mailing Add:* 1655 Hoyt St Lakewood CO 80215-2913

LANG, WENDY F
ADMINISTRATOR, PHOTOGRAPHER
b Cleveland, Ohio, Feb 15, 38. *Study:* Skowhegan Sch Painting Sculpture, Maine, 54-56; Antioch Col, BA(design), 61; Stanford Univ Grad Sch, MA(Hispanic-Am Studies), 63; Col Mex, 63; Inst Hautes Etudes Am Latine, Paris, 64-65; Los Angeles City Col, 73-77; Abram Freeman Occupation Ctr, 81; Calif State Univ, Northridge, 81-82. *Work:* Nara Mus, Japan. *Exhib:* Butler Inst Am Art, Youngstown, Ohio, 78; Canton Inst Art, Ohio, 78; Friends Photog, 78; Downey Mus Art, Los Angeles Ctr Photog Studies, 78; Tenth Ann Int Photog Meet, Arles, France, 79; San Francisco Camera Work, Herbert Asherman Gallery, Cleveland, Ohio; Clarence Kennedy Gallery, Cambridge, Mass; one-woman show, Cleveland Playhouse Gallery; and many others. *Pos:* Coordr, Photog Mus, Los Angeles, 80-81; photogr, var freelance, 84-; interpreter, Pasadena City Col Hearing Impaired prog, 81-83, var freelance, 84-; bd dir, Damien Proj, Los Angeles, treas, 90. *Teaching:* Instr, Los Angeles City Col Community Serv, 79-82; instr, Parsons Workshops, 1990-93. *Awards:* Outstanding Student Award, Los Angeles City Col, 76. *Bibliog:* Photographic Artists & Innovators, 83. *Mem:* Soc Photog Educ; Friends Photog, San Francisco; Ctr Creative Photog, Tucson, Ariz; Int Ctr Photog, NY; Mus Photog. *Media:* Film & Digital. *Publ:* co-illusr, Ballet Box, RCA Records, 79; contribr & coauth, Sequences: Baptism of Eros II, Peterson's Photog, 6/79; cover photog, Wolf Mag Lett, spring 91 & fall 91; article, Manuscripts Mag, 99. *Dealer:* Picture Arts Stock Photo Agency. *Mailing Add:* 1231 Kipling Ave Los Angeles CA 90041-1616

LANGAGER, CRAIG T
PAINTER, SCULPTOR
b Seattle, Wash, July 5, 46. *Study:* Minn State Univ, Bemidji, BS(art), 71; Univ Ore, Eugene, MFA(art), 74. *Work:* Brooklyn Mus Art, NY; Denver Art Mus, Colo; Metrop Mus Art, NY; Winnipeg Art Gallery, Manitoba, Can; Seattle Art Mus; Whatcom Mus History & Art, Bellingham, Wash; Tacoma Art Mus. *Comn:* One Percent for Art Purchase, Seattle Arts Comn, Wash, 78; wall relief, comn by Ann Gerber, Seattle, Wash, 79; sculpture, comn by Gordon Hanes, Winston-Salem, NC, 82; sculpture, Niagara Frontier Transporation Authority, Buffalo, NY, 82-83. *Exhib:* Solo exhibs, Susan Caldwell Gallery, NY, 83 & 84, Inst Contemp Art, Boston, 82, Ruth Siegal Ltd, NY, 86, Bemidi State Univ, Minn, 86, William Traver Gallery, 91 & Security Pac Gallery, Seattle, 91-92; Painting & Sculpture Today, Indianapolis Mus Art, Ind, 82 & 86; Dialogues (with catalog), Winnipeg Art Gallery, 84; Body and Soul: Aspects of Recent Figurative Sculpture (with catalog), Contemp Art Ctr, Cincinnati, 85 & traveled 85- 87, Art Mus Asn Am, San Francisco; Totems, Edith Baker Gallery, Dallas, 88; Small and Stellar, Ruth Siegel Ltd, New York City, 89; 20th Anniversary of the Visiting Artist Prog, CU Art Galleries, Univ of CO at Boulder, 92; 5th Int Shoebox Sculpture Exhib, Univ of Hawaii Art Gallery, Honolulu, 94. *Collection Arranged:* Bank of CA Collection; Brooklyn Mus of Art, Brooklyn, NY. *Pos:* Coord, Earthworks: Land Reclamation as Sculpture Symp, King Co Arts Comn, Seattle, Wash, 78-79. *Teaching:* Chmn, fine arts dept, Cornish Inst, Seattle, Wash, 76-78; vis artist, sculpture, Syracuse Univ, NY, winter 82; Univ Colo, Boulder, spring 85; vis prof, sculpture & painting, Western Wash Univ, Bellingham, 89-90. *Awards:* Minn State Arts Grant, Minn Coun Arts, Minneapolis, 75; Whitney Found Grant, New York for Dartington Col Arts, Eng, 77. *Bibliog:* Kim Levin (auth), Craig Langager, Critical Distance-Cloning for a New Society, (catalog essay) Issues, New Allegory II, Inst Contemp Art, Boston, 82; Hackett, Regina Review, Twenty Years, 1970-1990 Prints, and Installation by Craig Langager, Seattle Post-Intelligencer, November 20, 91, C15; 5th Int Shoebox Sculpture Exhib (catalog), Univ Hawaii, Manoa, 94. *Mailing Add:* 2970 N Shore Rd Bellingham WA 98226

LANGDO, BRYAN RICHARD
ILLUSTRATOR, WRITER
b Denville, NJ, Jan 7, 73. *Study:* Art Student's League of NY, Studied with Harvey Dinnerstein, Michael Burban, Jack Henderson, Michael Pellitieri, 1990-1991, 1992-1995; Rutgers Col, BA, 1998. *Exhib:* The Original Art, Mus of Am Illus at the Soc of Illusr, 2002. *Teaching:* Instr, Somerset Art Asn, Bedminster, NJ, 2005-. *Media:* Watercolor, Pencil. *Publ:* Auth & illusr, The Dog Who Loved the Good Life, Henry Holt, 2001; illusr, Joe Cinders, Henry Holt, 2002; illusr, Cat and Dog, Harper Collins, 2005; illusr, Mummy Math: An Adventure in Geometry, Henry Holt, 2005; illusr, The Best Time of Day, Gulliver Books, 2005; illusr, The Stuffed Animals Get Ready for Bed, Harcourt, 2006; illusr, Patterns in Peru: An Adventure in Patterning, Henry Holt, 2007. *Mailing Add:* 189 Delacy Dr Plainfield NJ 07060

LANGER, SANDRA LOIS (CASSANDRA)
ART APPRAISER, HISTORIAN
b Woodridge, NY, Dec 18, 41. *Study:* Univ Miami, BA, 67, MA, 69; NY Univ, PhD, 74. *Collection Arranged:* Beyond Survival: Old Frontiers, New Horizons; Robert R Presto Collection, Mus City of NY. *Pos:* Contrib critic, Art Papers, 74-79; independent art hist & critic, New York, 86; co-dir, Psych-Arts Soc, currently; exec appraiser, free-lance writer, critic, grants & publ adv, currently; contrib ed, Women Artists Book Review; critic at large, Women's Art J; dir, Private Eye: Noir Arts Ltd; Cassandra Langer & Assocs Fine Art Appraisal Servs, currently; contrib, Women's Art J. *Teaching:* Asst prof mod-contemp art, Fla Int Univ, 73-78; asst prof to assoc prof, Univ SC, Columbia, 78-86; vis assoc prof, Hunter & Queens. *Awards:* Smithsonian Post-Doctorial Fel, Nat Mus Art, 84. *Bibliog:* Harper Collins (auth), A Feminist Critique, 96; auth, Whats Right with Feminism, 2000. *Mem:* Col Art Asn; Int Asn Art Critics; Am Soc Journalists & Authors; Pen & Appraiser Asn Am; PEN. *Res:* Deconstructing Romaine Brooks; critical overview; contemporary art and criticism, feminism and post modernism; deco-noir connections between film & photography. *Publ:* Co-ed & contribr, Turning points & sticking places: Feminist art criticism, Col Art J, 91; Mother and Child in Art, Cresent/Random House Bks, 91; New Feminist Criticism Art, Identify, Action, 94; auth, Romaine Brooks Beyond the Mask; Joan Synder, Eva Hesse: The wisdom of Nothing, 2006; and others. *Mailing Add:* 32-22 89th St Apt 605 Flushing NY 11369-2179

LANGFORD-STANSBERY, SHERRY K
ENVIRONMENTAL ARTIST, PAINTER
b North Platte, Nebr, Oct 29, 44. *Study:* Pvt study with G Leslie Smith, 67-70, Kansas City Art Inst, 69-72. *Work:* Searcy Co Bank, Marshall, Ark; Tenneco, Houston, Tex. *Comn:* Great Blue Heron, NW Ark Audubon Soc, Fayetteville, Ark, 84; Red Wolf, Wolf Sanctuary, Eureka, Mo, 87; River Otters, Little Rock Zoo, 87; Mountain Lion, Little Rock Zoo, 92; Mexican Wolf, Wolf Sanctuary, Eureka, Mo, 92; and others. *Exhib:* Okla Wildlife Art Festival, Camelot Hotel, Tulsa, Okla, 82-91; Arts Crafts & Design Fair, Robinson Conv Ctr, Little Rock, Ark, 82-92; Art Happening, St Louis, Mo, 84-96; Cheyenne Audubon Wildlife Exhib, Conv Ctr, Cheyenne, Wyo, 85; Wildlife Art Walk, St Louis Zoo, Mo, 85-88; Nat Wildlife Art Fest, Doubletree Inn, Overland Park, Kans, 88-2000; and others. *Collection Arranged:* One-woman Exhibition, Fort Smith Art Ctr, 86 & 89. *Pos:* Litho-artist, Hallmark Cards, 62-64. *Awards:* Best of Show, Okla Wildlife Art Fest, 88 & 91; Best of Show, Nat Wildlife Art Exhib, 88, 94, 95, 96, 97, 98, 99, 2000; Artist of Year, Ark Wildlife Fed, 88, 91, 92, 94 & 95, 96, 97, 98, 2000; Best of Show, Red River Revel, Shreveport, La, 89; Best of Show, Best Bald Eagle, Best Pencil, Okla Wildlife Art Festival, 90. *Bibliog:* Doris Freyder (auth), Wildlife Artist, Ozarks Mountaineer, 10/82; Terry Horton (auth), article, Arkansas Out of Doors, 10/88. *Mem:* Eureka Springs Guild of Artists & Craftspeople. *Media:* Pencil, Watercolor. *Publ:* Illusr, Trees, Shrubs & Vines of Arkansas, Ozark Soc; A Shadow in the Forest, JB George, Vantage Press. *Dealer:* White Oak Studio PO Box 937Harrison AR 72602; Quicksilver The Nature Gallery 99 Spring St Eureka Springs AR 72632. *Mailing Add:* PO Box 937 Harrison AR 72602

LANGLAND, TUCK
SCULPTOR, EDUCATOR
b Minneapolis, Minn, Oct 6, 39. *Study:* Univ Minn, BA(art), 61, MFA(sculpture), 64. *Work:* Ind Univ, Univ Notre Dame, South Bend; Midwest Mus Am Art, Elkhart, Ind; St Paul Acad & Summit Sch, Minn; Minn Mus, St Paul. *Comn:* Violin Woman (bronze), South Bend, Ind, 82; Polymnia (bronze), Ft Wayne, Ind, 84; Madeline Bertrand (bronze), Niles, Mich, 87; Flak Bait (bronze), Air & Space Mus, Smithsonian Inst, 94; Legacy (bronze), Goshen Ind Pub Libr, 97. *Exhib:* One-man shows, Small Bronzes, traveling, Eng, 77-78, Tweed Mus, Duluth, Minn, 78, Reflections, South Bend Art Ctr, Ind, 80, Mid-West Mus Am Art, Elkhart, Ind, 84; Concurrent Themes, South Bend Art Ctr, 87, SW Mich Col, 94, Hillsdale Col, Mich, 96 & Filli Gallery, Chi, 96; Cantigny, Ill, 94, 95, 96, 97 & 98; Serravezza, Italy, 96; Chesterwood, Mass, 97; and others in US & Eng. *Teaching:* Asst lectr sculpture, Carlisle & Sheffield Cols o -Art; Eng: 64-67; asst prof sculpture; Murray State Univ, 67-71; assoc prof & Chmn dept fine arts, Ind-Univ; South-Bend, 71-82, prof, 82; vis lectr; Stoke-on-Trent, Eng, 77-78; Hoosier Salon Show, Indianapolis, 1980, 82, 84, 85, 86 (Outstanding Work in Sculpture awards), collections incl: Midwest Mus Am Art, Elkhart, Ind, Calhoun St Pedestrian Mall, Ft Wayne, Ind, Beatrice Foods, Chicago, Morris Civic Auditorium, S Bend, Univ Minn, Minneapolis, Ind Univ at South Bend, Notre Dame Univ, S Bend, Minnesota Mus Art, St Paul; nat exhib incl: Nat Acad of Design, New York City, 1982, 83, 99, Salmagundi Club, New York City, 1982, 83, 99, Terrace Gallery Show (Honorable Mention award), Palenville, NY, 1982, Audobon Artists, New York City, 1984, Nat Sculpture Society (Liskin Prize 1986), New York City, 1985; invitational exhib include: Royal Festival Hall, London, 1980, Promega, Madison, Wis, 1996, Lyme Acad, Conn, 1997, Chesterwood, Mass, 1997. *Awards:* Best of Show, Northern Ind Arts Asn, 83; Liskin Prize, Nat Sculpture Soc, 85; Outstanding Work in Sculpture, Hoosier Salon, 88, 90, 93, 94, 95, 98 & Best of Show, 97. *Mem:* Artists Equity; Fel, Nat Sculpture Soc; Nat Acad; Nat Sculptor's Guild. *Media:* Bronze. *Interests:* Choral singing, swimming. *Publ:* Auth, Practical Sculpture, Prentice Hall, Englewood Cliffs, NJ, 88. *Dealer:* Columbine Loveland CO; Sculpture Showcase New Hope PA. *Mailing Add:* 12632 Anderson Rd Granger IN 46530

LANGMAN, RICHARD THEODORE
GALLERY DIRECTOR
b Philadelphia, Pa, June 9, 37. *Study:* Cornell Univ, 54-55; Univ Calif, Berkeley, BA(urban design), 60. *Collection Arranged:* Alice Neel, Paintings, 74; Clayton Pond, Paintings & Graphics, 74; Graphics of the 70's (Int Graphics Show), 75 & Craft Art (Nat), 77, Langman Gallery; Bruce Evans, Paintings, SICA, 78 & 80, Constructions, 80; Andy Warhol, Paintings & Graphics, 83. *Pos:* Dir, Langman Gallery, Jenkintown, Pa. *Specialty:* Contemporary painting and sculpture. *Mailing Add:* 218 Old York Rd Jenkintown PA 19046-3244

LANGSTON, MARY VIRGINIA
SCULPTOR, PAINTER
b Winterville, NC, Oct, 19, 45. *Study:* Univ NC, BA(political sci & hist), 68; Corcoran Sch Art, 1984-1988, 1990. *Work:* Greenville Mus Art, NC; Contemp Art Mus of Monte Catini, Italy; Nat Mus Women in Arts, Washington, DC. *Comn:* painting, Kathy Moore, Alexandria, Va; painting, Maggi Castelloe, Marshall, Va; painting, Paul Castelloe, Raliegh, NC. *Exhib:* Light in Tabacco Barn, Greenville Mus of Art, NC, 98; Light in Tabacco Barn, Danville Mus of Fine Arts & Hist, Va, 2003. *Pos:* Res asst, Nat Portrait Gallery, Wash, DC, 68-70. *Awards:* Merit Award, The Athenaeum, Alexandria, 84; First Place, fine arts, Corcoran Sch Art, 87; resident fel, Va Ctr for Creative Arts, Sweet Briar, Va, 94, 98 & 2006. *Bibliog:* Women Artists: Works from the Greenville Mus Art Collection, (exhib catalog), Greenville Mus Art, NC, 3/2001; Acceleration 30 years at high speed at Gallery 10, LTD, (exhib catalog), 2004; US Embassy, Banjul, The Gambia, Art in Embassies Prog, Dept State, 2005. *Mem:* Wash Sculptors Group; Gallery 10 LTD (exec bd, 2001-). *Media:* Misc Media. *Interests:* Travel; Gardening. *Publ:* Co-auth, The Light in the Tobacco Barn (catalog), Greenville Mus Art, 98. *Dealer:* Gallery 10 Washington DC. *Mailing Add:* 3718 Veazey St NW Washington DC 20016-2229

LANIGAN-SCHMIDT, THOMAS
ASSEMBLAGE ARTIST, INSTRUCTOR
b Elizabeth, NJ, Jan 16, 48. *Study:* Pratt Inst, Brooklyn, NY, 65-66; Sch Visual Arts, New York, 67; studied pvt with Jack Smith & Charles Ludlam, 70-74. *Work:* Metrop Mus Art, NY; Albright Knox Mus, Buffalo, NY; Mus d'Art Contemporain, Lausanne, Switz; Ludwig Mus, Aachen, Ger; Nelson Atkins Gallery, Kansas City. *Exhib:* Venice Biennale, The Pluralist Decade, USA Pavillion, Venice, Italy, 80; 20th Century Art from the Metrop Mus NY, Queens Mus, Flushing, NY, 83; Arte, Ambiente, Scena, Venice Bienale Italy, 84; Content: A Contemp Focus, Hirshorn Mus & Sculpture Garden, Washington, DC, 84; Sacred Images in Secular Art, Whitney Mus, NY, 86; Contemp Diptychs, Whitney Mus (Equitable), NY, 87; Americana Installation, Groninger Mus, The Neth, 87; 1991 Biennial Exhib, Whitney Mus Am Art, NY, 91. *Pos:* Bd govs, Skowhegan Sch Painting & Sculpture, 91-. *Teaching:* Instr MFA prog, Sch Visual Arts, 89-; resident artists studio, Skowhegan Sch Painting & Sculpture, 91-. *Bibliog:* Robert Atkins (auth), The center show, Village Voice, 5/26/89; Roberta Smith (auth), The return of Tzarina Tatlina, NY Times, 4/24/92; Tzarina Tatlina, New Yorker, 4/92. *Media:* Scotch Tape, Plastic Wrap. *Publ:* Contribr, Ornamentalism, Robert Jensen & Patricia Conway (auths), Oitter/Crown, 82; Once a Catholic, Peter Occhigrasso (auth), Houghton/Mifflin, 88. *Mailing Add:* c/o Holly Solomon Gallery 222 W 23rd St Ste #425 New York NY 10011

LA NOUE, TERENCE
PAINTER, EDUCATOR
b Hammond, Ind, Dec 4, 41. *Study:* Ohio Wesleyan Univ, BFA, 64; Hochschule für Bildende Künste, West Berlin, Fulbright Scholar, 65; Cornell Univ, MFA; Ohio Wesleyan Univ, DFA. *Work:* Roy Neuberger Mus, Purchase, NY; Corcoran Gallery Art, Washington; Indianapolis Mus Art; Carnegie Inst; Whitney Mus Am Art, Guggenheim Mus, Brooklyn Mus & Mus Mod Art, NY; Albright-Knox Gallery. *Exhib:* Philadelphia Mus Art; Carnegie Int, Pittsburgh; Albright-Knox Gallery, 71; Indianapolis Mus Art, 72; one-man shows, Nancy Hoffman Gallery, 74-78 & 80, Galerie Farideh Cadot, Paris, 77, 78 & 80, Arts Club Chicago, 83, Siegel Contemp Art, NY, 83, 85-88 & 90, Andre Emmerich, 88-89 & 92, Heland-Wetterling Gallery, Stockholm, Sweden; 9th Paris Biennial Am Art, 75; Philadelphia Mus Art, 77; 34th Corcoran Biennial of Am Painting; Iran-Am Soc, 78; and others. *Teaching:* Asst prof art, Trinity Col, 67-72; prof art & head dept, La Guardia Col, 72-84. *Awards:* Nat Endowment Art Grant, 72 & 83; Guggenheim Fel, 82. *Bibliog:* Numerous articles in Art in Am, Arts Mag, NY Times & Art News, 76-; Dore Ashton (auth), Terence La Noue (monograph), Hudson Hills Press, 92. *Media:* Acrylic on Canvas

LANSDON, GAY BRANDT
PRINTMAKER, JEWELER
b San Antonio, Tex, Dec 6, 31. *Study:* Univ Houston, Tex, BFA, 65; Mus of Fine Arts Sch, Houston, 66-68; Sam Houston State Univ, MFA, 75. *Work:* Univ Houston, Univ Ctr; Sam Houston State Univ; Shell Oil Co; Xerox Corp; Price Waterhouse; and others. *Comn:* 16 paintings, comn by Dr Robert Stewart, Houston, 67; serigraph, comn by Jean Geeslin, Huntsville, Tex, 69; three printed fiber panels, Bellville State Bank, Tex, 72. *Exhib:* 15th Ann Tex Craftsman, Dallas Mus Fine Arts, 71; Colorprint USA, Lubbock, Tex, 75; Third Nat Print Exhib, Univ Southern Calif, Los Angeles, 75; 14th Midwest Biennial, Joslyn Art Mus, Omaha, Nebr, 75; Purdue Univ Small Print Exhib, 76; Five Texas Jewelers, Austin, 92; The Art of Jewelry, 94. *Teaching:* Instr art, Houston Mus Fine Arts, Tex, 69-71; art dept fac, Univ Houston, Cent Campus, 71-82, coordr printmaking, 76-82; mem fac continuing educ, Univ Tex, Austin, currently. *Awards:* Jurors' Merit Awards, SW Graphics Invitational, 72 & Dimension X, 76, Houston Art League; First Prize, Baytown Ann, 78. *Bibliog:* Kit Van Cleave (auth), Gay Lansdon: Mixed-media printmaking, Today's Art, 2/77. *Mem:* Soc N Am Goldsmiths. *Media:* Mixed. *Dealer:* Artisans Gallery at the Arboretum 10000 Research Blvd Suite 258 Austin TX 78759. *Mailing Add:* 11631 River Oaks Tr Austin TX 78753

LANSDOWNE, JAMES FENWICK
PAINTER
b Hong Kong, Aug 8, 37. *Study:* LLD, Univ Victoria. *Hon Degrees:* Univ Victoria, LLD, 1980. *Work:* Ulster Mus, Belfast; Montreal Mus Fine Arts; Art Gallery of Greater Victoria; Beaverbrook Found; Audubon House, NY. *Comn:* Rare Birds of China, 32 watercolor paintings, LE (300) collotype portfolio. *Exhib:* Lab Ornithol, Cornell Univ, 68; Nat Mus Natural Hist, Smithsonian Inst, Washington, DC, 69; Animals in Art, Royal Ont Mus, Toronto, 75; retrospective, Vancouver Art Gallery, 81; Scripps Inst Oceanography, La Jolla, Calif, 81; and others. *Awards:* Order of Canada; Order of BC. *Mem:* Royal Can Acad Arts. *Media:* Gouache, Watercolour. *Interests:* Antiques, book collecting, ornithology. *Publ:* Coauth, Birds of Northern Forest, 66; Birds of Eastern Forest, Part I, 68 & Part II, 70; auth, Birds of the West Coast, Part I, 76 & Part II, 80; illusr, Rails of the World, 76; A Guide to the Behaviour of Common Birds, Donald Stokes, 71. *Dealer:* Winchester Gallery Victoria BC; Feheley Fine Arts Toronto Ont. *Mailing Add:* 941 Victoria Ave Victoria BC V8S 4N6 Canada

LANSNER, FAY
PAINTER
b Philadelphia, Pa. *Study:* Tyler Sch Fine Art, 45-47; Art Students League, 47-48; Hans Hofmann Sch, 48-50; also with Leger & L'Hote, Paris, 50-51. *Work:* Weatherspoon Art Mus, Greensboro, NC; NY Univ Art Collection; Corcoran Gallery Art, Washington; Newsweek Mag, Metrop Mus Art, NY; Neuberger Mus, State Univ NY Col, Purchase; and others. *Exhib:* Corcoran Gallery Art, Washington, 67 & 77; Albright-Knox Art Gallery, Buffalo, NY, 67; Mus Mod Art, NY, 69; 17th Brooklyn Mus Print Ann, NY, 70; Hans Hofmann as Teacher, Metrop Mus Art, NY, 79; Denver Art Mus, traveling, 89-90; Twentieth Century Women Artists, Knoxville Mus Art, 89-90; Poets & Painters, Brooke Alexander Gallery; Drawings: A Contemp View, Arlene Bujese Gallery, 94. *Teaching:* Lectr, New Sch, 74, Mabel Douglass Col, 75. *Bibliog:* Elsa Honig Fine (auth), American Women Artists: The 20th Century, (catalog); Rose Slivka (auth), East Hampton Star, 84, 86, 87, 91, 92, 93 & 94; Robert Long (auth), Perspectives, Southampton Press, 89, 91, 92, 93 & 94. *Publ:* Auth, Barbara Riboud, Craft Horizons Mag, 4/72. *Dealer:* Arlene Bujese 66 Newtown Lane East Hampton NY. *Mailing Add:* 317 W 80th St New York NY 10024

LANTZY, DONALD MICHAEL
ADMINISTRATOR, PRINTMAKER
b Wilmington, Del, May 8, 42. *Study:* Philadelphia Col Art, Pa, BFA, 65; Temple Univ, Tyler Sch Art, MFA, 69. *Work:* Temple Univ, Philadelphia, Pa; West Chester State Col, Pa. *Exhib:* Solo exhib, Pa Acad Fine Arts, 77 & Gross/McCleaf Gallery, 79, Philadelphia, Pa; US Int Studies, Naples, Italy, 81; Temple Abroad, Rome, Italy, 81; Lowe Art Gallery, Syracuse, NY, 83. *Pos:* Assoc dean, Tyler Sch Art, Philadelphia, Pa, 74-75 & dir, Temple Abroad, 79-82; dean, Col Visual & Performing Arts, Syracuse Univ, NY, 82-. *Media:* Drawing, Painting. *Mailing Add:* Syracuse Univ 200 Crouse Col Syracuse NY 13244-1010

LANYON, ELLEN
PAINTER, PRINTMAKER
b Chicago, Ill. *Study:* Art Inst Chicago, with Joseph Hirsch, BFA, 48; State Univ Iowa, with M Lasansky, MFA, 50; Courtauld Inst, Univ London, with Helmut Reuhman. *Hon Degrees:* DHL, Lincoln Col. *Work:* Art Inst of Chicago & Mus Contemp Art, Chicago; Walker Art Ctr, Minneapolis; Nat Mus Am Art, Smithsonian Inst; Metrop Mus Art & Brooklyn Mus, NY. *Comn:* Mural, Workingmans Coop Bank, Boston, 81; Mural, State Ill Bldg, Chicago, 83; Art in Public Places (mural), Police & Court Facil, Miami Beach, Fla; Miami Beach, TMA, 97; Mural, Rise of Chicago, Ill

State Capitol, Srpingfield, 89; Mural, Riverwalk Gateway, City of Chicago, 2000; Hiawatha Lrt Murals, Minneapolis, 03. *Exhib:* Art Inst Chicago, 46-81; Corcoran Gallery Art Ann, 61; The Figure, Mus Mod Art, NY, 62; solo exhibs, Printworks Gallery, Chicago, 89 & 93, Struve Gallery, Chicago, 90 & 93, Berland Hall Gallery, NY, 92 & Andre Zarre Gallery, NY, 94 & 97, Chicago Cult Ctr, 2000; Landscape, Whitney Mus; Am Realism, San Francisco Mus Art, 85; 25 yr retospective (traveling), Krannery Mus, Univ Ill, 87-88; Realism & Realities, Voorhees, Mus, Rutgers Univ, 89; Pretto-Berland Hall, NY Struve Gallery, Chicago, 90; Face to Face, Chicago Cult Ctr, 92; Artists Sketchbook, Nat Mus Women Arts, 94-95; Art in Chicago 1945-1995, Mus Contemp Art, Chicago, 96; Contemp Classicism, Neuberger Mus of Art, 99; Transformations, 30 yr retrospective, Nat Mus for Women in the Arts, 99, 2000; Chicago Loop, Whitney Mus of Am Art, Stamford, Conn, 2000; Nat Acad Mus Bi-Annuals, 99, 2001,2003,2005; Am Acad Arts & Letters-Invitational, 2004. *Pos:* Mem, Col Art Asn Bd Dirs, 78-82; CAA Art Journal Ed Bd, 79-92; Nat Acad of Design-Council Mem-2001-; Chair Ex Comm, 2004-2006. *Teaching:* Instr painting & dir, Ox Bow Summer Sch of Painting, Saugatuck, Mich, 60-2005; vis artist-lectr, Stanford Univ, 73 & Univ Calif, Davis, 73 & 80; vis artist & fel, Inst Arts & Humanistic Studies, Pa State Univ, 74; vis artist, State Univ Iowa; instr painting, State Univ NY Purchase, 78-, Parsons Sch Design, 79-80 & Sch Visual Arts, 80-83; instr painting, Cooper Union, 79-82, assoc prof, 83-92; instr painting, Anderson Ranch, 94-96 & Vt Studio Sch, 95, 97, 2001. *Awards:* Nat Endowment Arts Grant, 74 & 87; Yaddo Fel, 74-75, 76 & 98; Hereward Lester Cooke Found, 81; Florsheim Found Grant, 99; Puchase Am Acad Arts & Letters, 2004. *Bibliog:* Donald Kuspit (auth), Strange Games (catalog essay), 87; Christopher Lyon (auth), Recent Drawings, 90; Eleanor Heartney (auth), Monograph Essay, 92; and others; Lucy Lippard (auth), Under the Wing of Survival (catalog essay), 83; Debra Bricker Balkin (auth), Transformations (catalog essay), 99; Paintings of the 60's (auth) Franz Schultz Catalog Essay, 2005. *Mem:* Col Art Asn (bd dir, 77-81); Nat Acad 1997; Elected to the Century Asn NY 2005. *Media:* Acrylic, Prismacolor; Lithography. *Res:* 19th Century engravings & restoration. *Specialty:* Contemp paintings, drawings, prints. *Publ:* The Weasel by Annie Dillard, 82; White Walls, autumn 82; Mirabai Versions by Robert Bly, 84; Wonder Production, Vol 2, Landfall Press, 71; The Wandering Tattler, Perishible Press, 75; Index Print Studio, Cambridge, UK, 2003. *Dealer:* Printworks Ltd 311 W Superior Chicago 60610; Valerie Carberry Gallery, 875 N. Michigan, Chicago, 60611. *Mailing Add:* 138 Prince St New York NY 10012

LAPALOMBARA, CONSTANCE
PAINTER
b Brooklyn, NY, Dec 13, 35. *Study:* Manhattanville Col, BA, 57; Yale Univ, with William Bailey, 76-77; Tyler Sch Art, Temple Univ, MFA, 82. *Work:* Banca Commerciale Italiana, NY; First Union Bank, New Haven, Conn; Enichem USA, NY; Italiana Gas Industriale, Milan; Southern New Eng Tel, New Haven, Conn; New Haven Pub Libr; Univ Conn Health Ctr, Farmington. *Exhib:* Guido io vorrei., Palazzo Ducale, Mantua, Italy, 93; Ezra Stiles Col, Yale Univ, New Haven, 2000; A Moveable Feast, Zeuxis, Westbeth Gallery, NY, 2003; Industrial Beauty, George Billis Gallery, NY, 2004; Bachelier Cardonsky Gallery, Kent, Conn, 2004; Italia, Brickwalk Gallery, West Hartford, Conn, 2005; Points of View, Kehler Liddell Gallery, New Haven, Conn, 2005; Between Perception & Invention, Sharon Arts Ctr, Peterborough, NH, 2005; Around the Corner, Fenn Gallery, Woodbury, Conn, 2005; New Haven, Gallery 195, Conn, 2006. *Teaching:* instr painting & drawing, Southern Conn State Univ, 84-85. *Awards:* Painting, Ingram Merrill Found, 84; Grant, Schohair Co Arts Council, 98; Artists Fel, Conn Comn on the Arts, 2000. *Bibliog:* Andrew Forge (auth), The Clarity of American Light (catalog), Gabbiano Gallery, 93; T O'Shaughnessy (auth), The Cleansing Breeze of Everyday Objects, Waterbury Republican, 99; John Hollander (auth) Landscape Painting, 1960-90: The Italian Tradition in Am Painting Catalog, Gibbes Mus, Charleston, SC; J Harris (auth), A Different Landscape, Italy-Italy Mag, 2003; M Mullarkey (auth), Industrial Beauty Review, New York Sun, 2004; J Birke (auth), Elm City, New Haven Register, 3/2005; C Tyler (ed), Artists Next Door, Partnership for Conn Cities (publ), New Haven, 2006. *Mem:* Col Art Asn; Conn Acad Fine Arts; Conn Watercolor Soc; Conn Women Artists; New Haven Paint & Clay. *Media:* Oil. *Dealer:* Sandro Manzo-Gabbiano New York-Rome; Wingspread Gallery Northeast Harbor ME; P Siemon Fenn Gallery Woodbury CT. *Mailing Add:* 50 Huntington St New Haven CT 06511

LA PELLE, RODGER
PAINTER, DEALER
b Philadelphia, Pa, July 31, 36. *Study:* Univ Pa; Pa Acad Fine Arts. *Work:* Free Libr Philadelphia, Pa; Munson-Williams-Proctor Mus, Utica, NY; Mus Mod Art, NY. *Exhib:* Nat Exhib, Pa Acad Fine Art, Philadelphia, 58, Calif Palace of Legion Honor, San Francisco, 62 & San Francisco Art Mus, Calif, 63; La Pelle Galleries, 85-88, 92 & 94. *Pos:* Owner, Rodger La Pelle Galleries. *Awards:* Silver Medal, Cologne, Ger, 56; Cresson Traveling Scholar, Pa Acad Fine Art, 61; Moss-Graff Prize, Cheltenham Ann Exhib, 88; Lucy Glick Prize, 01. *Mem:* Fel Pa Acad Fine Arts (past pres). *Media:* Oil, Pencil. *Specialty:* Contemporary painting, sculpture and graphics. *Publ:* Art Matters. *Mailing Add:* c/o La Pelle Galleries 122 N Third St Philadelphia PA 19106-1802

LA PIERRE, THOMAS
PAINTER, PRINTMAKER
b Toronto, Ont, Dec 28, 30. *Study:* Ont Col Art, AA; Ecole Beaux Arts; Atelier 17. *Hon Degrees:* AOCA; RCA. *Work:* Montreal Mus Fine Art, PQ; Art Gallery Mississauga, MacLaren Art Ctr; Art Gallery Hamilton, St Catherines & Art Gallery Ont, Ont; Art Gallery Ont; Art Gallery Peel. *Exhib:* Sao Paulo Biennial, 63; Atlantic Provinces, 74; WCoast traveling exhib, Burnaby Art Gallery; Dimensions of Realism, Milan, Italy, 78; Sichuan Fine Art Inst, Chong Quing, China, 88; Rodman Hall, St Catherines, Ont, 88; Martin Sumers Art Gallery, NY, 89; The Arena of Heart and Mind, Works from 1972 to 1992 (with catalog), Art Gallery of Peel. *Teaching:* Instr drawing & painting, Ont Col Art, 58-95. *Awards:* Woolfitt Award for Painting Watercolor, 89; Trillium Workshop Award for Painting in Watercolor, 93; Arts & Lett Club Award for Painting in Oil, 98. *Bibliog:* William McElcheran (auth), Dialogue with demons, Arts Can, 70; Robert Percival (auth), 20th Century mystic, Art Mag, 75; Paul Duval (auth), article in Art Mag, 76 & 77. *Mem:* Can Soc Painters in Watercolour; Royal Can Acad Arts. *Media:* Oil, Watercolor; Lithography. *Publ:* Limited edition bk, lithographs, drawings & paintings, 1975-1980. *Dealer:* Kinsman Robinson Galleries Toronto ON. *Mailing Add:* 2067 Proverbs Dr Mississauga ON L4X 1G3 Canada

LAPINSKI, TADEUSZ (A)
PRINTMAKER, EDUCATOR
b Rawa Mazowiecka, Poland, June 20, 28; US citizen. *Study:* Acad Fine Arts, Warsaw, Poland, BA, 54, MFA, 55. *Work:* Academia Abertina Collection, Turin, Italy; Albertina Mus, Vienna, Austria; Bibliotheque Nationale, Paris; Calif Palace of Legion of Honor, San Francisco; Ctrl Inst Art, Beijing; Frick Collection, NYC; Hirshhorn Mus, Washington, DC; Libr of Congress, Washington, DC; and others. *Exhib:* Am Print in Venice, 77; one-man exhibs, Baak Gallery, Cambridge, Mass, 79, Bacardi Art Gallery, 79, Forum Gallery, Zagreb, Yugoslavia & Klevit Gallery, Washington, DC; Central Inst Art, Beijing, Peoples Repub China, 88; Mus City Torun, Poland, 92; solo exhibs, District Mus Art, Torun, Poland, 92, Sci Soc Plock Art Gallery, Poland, 93 & Dist Mus Zuhafdow, Poland, 94, Nat Mus of Art, Tien Jin, People's Rep China, Cork Gallery, Lincoln Ctr NY, Tadeusz Lapinski: Recent Lithographs, Kennedy Galleries, New York City, Gallery Lambert, Paris, Graphics by Lapinski, Mus Contemp Art, Sao Paolo, Brazil, Mus Modern Art, New York City, Tadeusz Lapinski Color Lithographs, Miami Mus Modern Art, Fla, House of Prints Gallery with Miro and Hass, Toronto, Can, Gallerie ULUS, Belgrade, Yugoslavia; 36th Biennale of Art, Venice, Italy. *Teaching:* Assoc prof lithography, Univ Md, 72-82, prof, 83-; instr, Grodzisk Mazowiecki, Poland, 56-63, 65-67; vis artist/lectr, Pratt Graphics Ctr, New York City, 63-64 & 68-69, Univ Brazil, Porto Alegre, 67-68. *Awards:* First Prize, Int Print Festival Vienna, 78; Second Prize, World Print, Paris, 80; Outstanding Achievement Award, 81 & Honor Awards, 86, Univ Md; Statue of Victory, World Prize Calvatone, Italy, 85. *Bibliog:* Fritz Eichenberg (auth), The Art of the Prints, Abrams, 77; Jane Haslem (ed), American Paintings and Graphics, Washington, DC; Lillian Dobbs (auth), Lapinski prints are unique, hard to find, Miami News, 11/16/79. *Mem:* Soc Am Graphic Artists; Painters Sculptors Soc of NJ (vpres, 72-76); Washington Printmakers Soc; Soc Graphic Arts, NY. *Media:* Lithography. *Dealer:* Jack Walsh Gallery Woodbine MD. *Mailing Add:* 10413 Eastwood Ave Silver Spring MD 20901

LAPKUS, DANAS
CURATOR, CRITIC
b Siauliai, Lithuania, Apr 4, 64; US citizen. *Study:* Vilnius Art Acad, MA(art hist), 89; Univ Ill, Chicago, MA, 95. *Collection Arranged:* Death: Born in the USA, Lemont Lithuanian Art Mus, 93; The Form of My Life, Comtemp Art Ctr, Vilnius, 96; Smuggled Art, Balzekas Mus, Chicago, 96 & Perfection in Exile, 97; Visions of Love, Chicago Cult Ctr, 98. *Pos:* Pub relations dir, Contemp Art Ctr, Vilnius, Lithuania, 89-90; chief cur, Balzekas Mus Lithanian Cult, Chicago, 91-. *Mem:* Midwest Mus Coun; Chicago Registrars Comt; Lithuanian Am Fine Arts Asn (bd mem, 95-); Ethnic Cult Preserv Coun, Chicago (bd mem, 97-). *Publ:* Numerous contemp art articles in Draugas Daily Paper, 91- & Metmenys Mag, 93-. *Mailing Add:* Balzekas Mus Lithuanian Culture 6500 S Pulaski Rd Chicago IL 60629

LA PLANT, MIMI
PAINTER, EDUCATOR
b San Francisco, Calif, Jan 7, 43. *Study:* Col of Marin, 68; Santa Rosa Jr Col, AA, 72; Univ Calif, Berkeley, BA, 74; Humboldt State Univ, MA, 82; Univ Calif Santa Barbara, MFA, 91. *Work:* Humbolt Cult Ctr, Eureka, Calif; Humboldt State, Santa Barbara Mus Art. *Comn:* Monotypes, Bank of Del Mar, Calif, 83 & Prudential Life Insurance Co, & Bank of Colo, 84; six monoprints, Dow Chemical, San Diego, Calif; large monotype, ANA Hotel, Japan 85. *Exhib:* Crocker-Kingsley Ann, Crocker Mus, Sacramento, Calif, 86; West Coast Works On/Of Paper, 87 & 88; Locus, San Luis Obispo Art Ctr, 92; 3 Abstract Painters, Foxhall Gallery, Washington, DC, 92; Introductions 92, Weintraub, Sacto, Calif; and others. *Collection Arranged:* Martin Wong, The Eureka Years, Humboldt State, First St Gallery, 1999. *Teaching:* Lectr painting, drawing, color theory, Humboldt State Univ, Ancata, Calif. *Awards:* Regents fel, Univ Calif, Santa Barbara; Assoc Faculty of Yr Award, Col of the Redwoods, 2000; Best of Show, RAA Juried Show, 2002. *Bibliog:* Belle McDonnell (auth), Mimi La Plant: An artist for all seasons, Times Standard Newspaper, 9/88. *Mem:* Humboldt Arts Coun; The Ink People; Ancata Artisans Coop. *Media:* Oil, Acrylic; Monotype, Pencil, Mixed Media. *Publ:* Auth, Monoprint: Painting or printing, Mendocino Art Ctr Mag, 7/87. *Dealer:* San Francisco Mus Mod Art Artist's Gallery San Francisco CA. *Mailing Add:* PO Box 832 Arcata CA 95518

LAPLANTZ, DAVID
JEWELER, SCULPTOR
b Toledo, Ohio, June 12, 44. *Study:* Bowling Green State Univ, with Hal Hasselschwert, BS(art), 66; Cranbrook Acad Art, with Richard Thomas, MFA, 69; Southern Ill Univ, with Alex Bealer, 70. *Work:* St Paul Art Ctr, Minn; Nat Mus Mod Art, Kyoto, Japan; Nat Mus Am Art, Smithsonian Inst, Washington, DC; Am Craft Mus; Schmuck Mus, Pforzheim, Ger; and others. *Comn:* Commemorative (scale model of house), Civil Rights Group, Detroit, 67; Smithsonian Mus, Wash; Nat Mus Modern Art, Kyon, Japan; Oakland Mus Art, Calif; Schmuck Mus, Pfarzheim, Ger. *Exhib:* For the Table Top, 80-83 & Contemp Am Jewelry: US Info Agency Arts Am, 85-87, traveling shows, Am Craft Mus; Gold as Gold-Alternative Materials in Am Jewelry, Renwick Gallery, Smithsonian Inst, Washington, DC, 81-84; Contemp

Jewelry-the Americas, Australia, Europe, Japan, Nat Mus Mod Art, Tokyo & Kyoto, Japan, 84; Jewelry USA, Nat Competitive Exhib, Am Crafts Mus & NAm Goldsmiths Soc, 84-86; Sixth Int Jewelry Ornament for the Head and Hair Competition, Pforzheim, Ger, 85-86; Gems & Jewels, New Acquisitions, Oakland Mus Art, 94-95; and others. *Teaching:* Instr, Inst Am Indian Arts, Santa Fe, NMex, 67-68, Flint Community Jr Col, Flint, Mich, 68-69, Kent State Univ, 77-78, Colo State Univ, 69-70, San Diego State Col, 70-71 & Humboldt State Univ, 71-2002, ret. *Awards:* Fulbright Scholar, New Zealand, 85; Merit Award, North Am Goldsmith Biennial Exhib, Phoenix Art Mus, Ariz; Scholar of the Year, Humboldt State Univ, 94. *Bibliog:* Articles in Crafts Horizons, 69-70 & 75, Goldsmith J, 80 & Art Craft Mag, 80; article, Ornament Mag, Vol V, No 4, 82; Chuck Evans (auth), Jewelry: Contemporary Design & Techniques, Davis Publ, 83; Peter Dormer & Ralph Turner (coauth), The New Jewelry-Trends and Traditions, Thames & Hudson, London, 85. *Mem:* Am Craftsman's Coun; Soc NAm Goldsmiths. *Media:* All. *Publ:* Contribr, Contemporary Jewelry, rev ed, 76; Jewelry Concepts & Technology, 83; auth, Artists Anodizing Aluminum, Press de LaPlantz, 88; ed, Jewelry Metalwork Survey, 1991, Press de LaPlantz, 91; contribr, Workshop Notes: Metals, Brynmorgan Press, 93

LAPLANTZ, SHEREEN
BOOK ARTIST, WRITER
b Glendale, Calif, Feb 9, 1947. *Study:* Los Angeles State Univ, BA, 68; Cranbrook Acad Art, 69; private instruction, Maori, 1985, Akwasasne Mohawk Tribe, 1982. *Work:* Mendocino Art Ctr, Calif; Murray St Univ; Nat Mus Women in the Arts; Mariott Libr, Univ Utah; Rare Book Room, Detroit Free Libr; Judicia Archives, Chicago. *Exhib:* Virginia Beach Arts Ctr, Va, 82; Eve Mannes Gallery, Atlanta, 82; Seattle Ctr, 83; Gallery 8, La Jolla, 83; Manyfold II, Donnell Libr Ctr, NY, 2000; Changing Pages, Univ Strathclyde, Glasgow, Scotland (traveling exhib; hard cover catalog), 1998-1999; one-person shows, Los Angeles State Univ, Murray State Univ, Ky, Jumboldt State Univ, New York City Libr, Humboldt Co Libr. *Pos:* Publ, Press de LaPlantz, Bayside, Calif, 81-. *Teaching:* Instr fiberarts, Col Redwoods, Eureka, Calif, 74-77; tchr various workshops, including Univ Minn Split Rocks Summer Arts Program, Duluth, 1995-2002; tchr bookbinding. *Awards:* Textiles Awards, Spring Show, Redwood Art Asn, 73 & 75; Cash Award, Calif Crafts IX, Crocker Art Gallery, 75. *Bibliog:* Dona Meilach (auth), Basketry Today, Crown, 79; Fiberarts Design Book, Hastings House, 80; Fiberarts Design Book II, Hastings House, 1983. *Mem:* Handweavers Guild Am; Am Crafts Coun. *Media:* Paper. *Publ:* Auth, Baskets and curls, Shuttle, Spindle & Dyepot, 1981; auth & ed, Plaited Basketry-The Woven Form, Press de LaPlantz, 1982; contrib ed, ARC, 1982; auth, Handwoven, Basketry Materials Guide, 1983; The artist in business, Humboldt Bay Sheep & Wool Newslett, 1983; The Art and Craft of Handmade Books, Lark Books, 2001; Innovative Bookbinding: Secret Compartments & Hidden Messages, Press de La Plantz, 1997; Cover to Cover: Creative Techniques for Making Beautiful Books, Journals & Albums, Lark Books, 1995; Twill Basketry: A Handbook of Techniques & Styles, Lark Books, 1993; The Mad Weave Book, Press de LaPlantz, 1984; Plaited Basketry: The Woven Form, Press de LaPlantz, 1982

LAPOINTE, FRANK
PAINTER, PRINTMAKER
b Port Rexton, Nfld, May 11, 42. *Study:* Ont Col of Art, AOCA, 66. *Work:* Can Coun Art Bank, Pub Works, Canada; Univ Ore, Corvallis; Nat Gallery Can, Ottawa; Art Gallery Ont, Toronto. *Comn:* Nfld postcard ser: What do you think of Jack?, Mem Univ Art Gallery Jubilee Portfolio, St John's, Nfld, 75; stainless steel & aluminum mirror sculpture, Fed Bldg, Grand Falls, Nfld, 79; lithograph portfolio, Can Saltfish Corp, 81; lithograph ed, For Sale, Mem Univ, St Johns, Nfld, 85; lithograph ed, Contrasts, Nfld Teachers' Asn, 90; mural, Trinity Arts Ctr, NF, 2000; lithograph, The Stone Age, Nat Gallery of Can. *Exhib:* 5 Salon Des Vendanges De Cognac, Cognac, France, 85; 25 Yrs of Art, Nat Touring Show, Mem Univ Art Gallery, 86; Door as a Circular Passage, Mem Univ Gallery, St John's, Nfld, 86; Out of the Studio, Mem Univ Gallery, St John's, Nfld, 90; Nfld Art, Salle de la Renaissance, Bordeaux, France, 92; Hidden Values, Art Gallery Nova Scotia, Halifax, 94; Land And Sea, Queen's Univ, Belfast, Ireland, 95; Land And Sea Tour of Ireland, Cork, Waterford, Sligo & Dublin, 96. *Pos:* Asst cur & art specialist, Art Gallery, Mem Univ, St John's, Nfld, 70-72, cur, 72-73; resident printmaker, St Michael's Printshop, Nfld, 81-82; guest cur, Art Gallery, NS Halifax, 83; visual arts coordr, Sound Symp, St John's, Nfld, 83, 88 & 90; colour/design consult, Enterprise Nfld, 91-92; visual art cons, Rising Tide Asn, 97-2003. *Teaching:* Instr painting & printmaking, Dundas Valley Sch of Art, Dundas, Ont, 69-70, design & color, Cobot Col, St Johns, 93 & 94; lectr, aesthet design, Mem Univ, St John's, Nfld, 88, 90 & 91. *Awards:* Silver Medal, 67 & Bronze Medal, 68, Nfld Arts & Lett, Govt Nfld; Can Coun Grant, 77; Can Coun Grant, 86. *Bibliog:* Joe Bodolai (auth), Visit to Newfoundland, 75-76 & Peter Bell (auth), Frank Lapointe/Gerald Squires, 76-77, Artscanada; Peter Bell (auth), Oberheide, Wright, Lapointe, Vie des Arts, Montreal, winter 76; Visions Artists and the Creative Process, TV Ont, 82. *Mem:* Can Soc of Painters in Watercolor; St Michael's Printshop; CARFAC Nat Toronto; Nfld Sound Symp. *Media:* Watercolor, Acrylic; Lithography, Etching. *Dealer:* Red Ochre Gallery, 96 Duckworth St, St Johns, NL, A1C 1E&. *Mailing Add:* Box 11 Port Rexton NL AOC 2H0 Canada

LA PORTA, ELAYNE B
PAINTER, PRINTMAKER
b Wilton, Conn. *Study:* Lesnick Sch Art with Steve Lesnick, 68-79; pvt study with Arnold Hitchcock, 68 & Cliff Segerclum, 68; Acad Fine Arts, Florence, Italy, 69. *Work:* Biblical Arts Ctr, Dallas, Tex; Villonova Univ, Pa, 91; St Bernadette Inst Sacred Art, Albuqurque, NMex. *Exhib:* Univ New Orleans, La, 91; Paul VI Inst Arts, Washington, DC, 91; Marion Libr, Dayton, Ohio, 91; West Bend Gallery Fine Arts, Wis, 92; Billy Graham Sacred Arts Ctr, 93. *Bibliog:* Beije Howell (auth), Historical biblical art by Elayne La Porta, Santa Monica Outlook, 10/80; Judee Quillum (auth), Elayne La Porta Artist, Art Voices South, 1/80; A D Hopkins (auth), Elayne La Porta Biblical Artist Las Vegas Review J, 11/83. *Mem:* Catholic Fine Arts Soc, NY; Catholic Artists of the 90's, NY; Midwest Asn Relig Talent Inc, Milwaukee, Wis; Int Registry Relig Women Artists, Fresno, Calif. *Media:* Oil. *Dealer:* Billy Graham Ctr Mus Wheaton IL 60187. *Mailing Add:* 443 Blackridge Dr Henderson NV 89015

LARAMEE, EVE ANDREE
SCULPTOR, CONCEPTUAL ARTIST
b Los Angeles, Calif, Jan 6, 56. *Study:* San Diego State Univ, BA, 78; San Francisco Art Inst, MFA, 80. *Work:* Albuquerque Mus Art, NMex; Mus Mod Art, NY; Fogg Mus, Harvard Univ, Cambridge, Mass; MacArthur Found, Chicago, Ill; Mus Contemp Art, Chicago. *Comn:* Site-specific installation, Zilkha Gallery, Wesleyan Univ, Middletown, Conn, 90; site-specific installation, Mus Contemp Art, Chicago, Ill, 92; pub art comn, San Diego State Univ, 97; Mass Inst Technol, List Visual Art Ctr, Cambridge, Mass, 99. *Exhib:* Galerie des Archives, Paris, France, 95; Venice Biennalle, 97; Mass Inst Technol List Ctr Visual Art, 99; Mass Mus Contemp Art, 2000; Getty Mus, Los Angeles, 2001; Koln Art Fair, Ger, 2002; Georgia Mus of Art, Athens, 2003; Kuntehalle Palazzo Liesfal, Basel, Switz, 2004. *Pos:* Artists Exhib Bd, Rotunda Gallery, Brooklyn; founding ed coun, Blast/Xart Found; bd dir, Int Artists Mus, Lodz, Poland. *Teaching:* Adj prof sculpture, NY Univ, 89-94; part-time prof art grad studies, RI Sch Design, 92-93; vis prof sculpture, Mass Inst Technol, Cambridge, 92; fac, Col Art, Md Inst, 94-96 & Cooper Union, 95; sculpture fac, Sarah Lawrence Col, 97-98, prof, 97-2001; Fairfield Univ, Dir of Visual Arts Prog 2001-2004; Md Inst Col of Art, Chair of Interdisciplinary Sculpture, 2004-. *Awards:* Fel, NY Found Arts, 89; sculptor-in-residence, Guggenheim Mus, 92; Nat Endowment Arts Regional Fel, 95, Educ & Access Grant, 98; NY Found for the Arts Grant, 2003; Pollock Krasner Found Grant, 2004; Mac Dowell Colony Fel, 2001, 2003, 2004. *Bibliog:* Nicolas de Oliveria, Nicola Oxley & Michael Petry (auths), Installation Art, Smithsonian Inst Press, 94; Making Sense: Five Installations on Sensation, The Katonah Mus, Katonah, NY, 96; A Permutational Unfolding: Eve Andree Laramee, Mass Inst Technol, 99; Linda Weintraub; In the Making, DAP Press, 2003; Jochen Gerz; Anthology of Art, Dumont Pub, 2003; Anna Hanigman; Questioning Authority; A Connersation with Eva Andrea Larance, Sculpture Mag July/Aug 2002; Jennifer MacGoregor Sugar Mud; Hudson River Projects, Wave Hill 2003; Steve Wilson, Infomation Art; Intersection of Art, Science, & Techology, MIT Press, 2001. *Mem:* Blast/The X Art Found, NY; Col Arts Asn; Nat Speleological Soc. *Media:* All; Installation. *Res:* Environmental issuses, place/space/site. *Specialty:* Art and Science. *Publ:* Auth, Notes on Sculpture, Albuquerque Mus, 83; The Eroded Terrain of Memory, Wesleyan Univ, 90; Inventing Wilderness: The National Parks, New Observations Mag, 91; Artists Project, J Contemp Art, 92; Wandering, Innerscapes; Anthology, of Artists Writing, Trieste, 98; A Permutational Unfolding: Art and the Culture of Science, Brazilian Nat Asn for Researchers in Visual Arts, 99; Only Questions- Interaction; Artistic Practice on the Network, Eyebeam/DAP Press, 2001; Netherzone; A Psychogeographical Force, Art Journal Mag, Fall 2004. *Mailing Add:* 126 Java St Brooklyn NY 11222

L'ARCHEVEQUE, ANDRE ROBERT
PAINTER, ILLUSTRATOR
b Montreal, Que, Apr 12, 23. *Study:* Ecole des Beaux Art, Montreal, MA, 42, Sir George Williams Sch Art, 43, Famous Artists Sch, New York, 49. *Work:* City of Montreal Pub Collection, Que; Chateau de Ramezay Mus, Montreal; Govt of Can Pub Collection, Ottawa; Texaco Can, Toronto; Bankers Asn Can, Montreal. *Comn:* Great Moments, large painting, Prudential Insurance Co, Toronto, Ont, 72; painting, Arab Repub Egypt, Cairo, 85; design for Quebec Pavillion, World Exhib, Govt of Que, 68. *Exhib:* Traveling exhib across US & Can, 75; solo exhibs, retrospective, Montreal, Toronto & Ottawa, 82 & Chateau de Ramezay Mus, Montreal, 85. *Pos:* Ed illusr, Pocket Books, 48-58; advert illusr, 52-72. *Awards:* First Prize, Watercolor & Drawing Exhib, Vancouver Air Command. *Bibliog:* Guy Boulizon (auth), Poetry of Nature, catalog, 82; videocassette, Prudential Insurance Co, 82; Nathalie Legris (auth), Andre L'Archeveque, Editions Marcel Broquet. *Media:* Oil, Acrylic; All Media. *Publ:* Illusr, World Book Encyl, 76; auth & illusr, Meditation, Bernard Desroches, 87. *Dealer:* Galerie Bernard Desroches 1144 Sherbrooke St Montreal PQ H7R 1K4 Canada

LARICO, BENJE
PAINTER
Study: Albuquerque, NMex, 73; Whitney Mus Independent Study Prog, 74; Wash Univ, St Louis, Mo, BFA, 72; Bennington Col, Vt, MA, 76. *Exhib:* Salon de Montrouge, France, 84; Daniel Weinberg Gallery, Los Angeles, Calif, 84; Am Acad Rome, Italy, 85; Abstractions in Process, Artists Space, NY, 87; Nordster Collection, Grey Gallery, NY, 88; Trisha Brown Benefit Auction, Paula Cooper Gallery, NY, 90; Molica Gallery, NY & Rome, Italy, 92. *Awards:* Prix de Rome, Am Acad Rome, 84-85; Grant, NY Found Arts, 88; Grant Painting, Nat Endowment Arts, 89. *Media:* Miscellaneous Media. *Mailing Add:* 358 Broadway New York NY 10013

LARKIN, EUGENE
DESIGNER, EDUCATOR
b Minneapolis, Minn, June 27, 21. *Study:* Univ Minn, BA & MA. *Work:* Mus Mod Art, NY; Nat Gallery Art & Libr Cong, Washington, DC; Art Inst Chicago; Addison Gallery Am Art, Andover, Mass; Nat Collection of Fine Arts, Smithsonian Inst, Washington, DC; and others. *Comn:* Int Graphic Arts Soc; Gen Mills Corp; Bus Wk; Minneapolis Soc Fine Arts; US Info Agency. *Exhib:* US Info Agency Traveling Exhib to Iran, Italy, France, Spain & Ger; one-man shows, Minneapolis Inst Art & Hamline Univ, 68; State Univ NY Albany, 69; Univ Calif, Long Beach, 69; Univ Minn, 74, 78, 81, 87, 91 & 92; Anderson & Anderson Gallery, 91, 92 & 94. *Teaching:* Instr, Kans State Col, Pittsburg, 48-54; head printmaking dept & chmn fine arts div, Minneapolis Sch Art, 54-69; prof, Design Dept, Univ Minn, Minneapolis, 69-91. *Awards:* Walker Art Ctr, 60 & Washington Watercolor & Print Exhib, 63; Rockford Biennial, 83; plus many others. *Mem:* Am Asn Univ Prof; Col Art Asn Am. *Media:* Woodcuts, Lithographs, Oil. *Publ:* Auth, Design: The Search for Unity, William C Brown, 88

LARKIN, (DR) JOHN E, JR MD
COLLECTOR, PATRON
b St Paul, Minn, Nov 8, 30. *Study:* Univ Minn, BS & MD; Harvard Univ. *Pos:* trustee, Minn Mus Art, Minn Soc Fine Arts & Minn Inst Art, formerly; benefactor, Minn Inst Art, Minn Mus Art & Weisman Mus; accessions comt, Minneapolis Inst Art. *Collection:* American art. *Mailing Add:* 7 Yellow Birch Rd Dellwood White Bear Lake MN 55110

LARMER, OSCAR VANCE
PAINTER, EDUCATOR
b Wichita, Kans, July 11, 24. *Study:* Minneapolis Sch Fine Arts, cert painting; Univ Kans, BFA; Wichita State Univ, MFA. *Work:* Nelson Gallery of Art, Kansas City, Mo; Kans State Univ, Manhattan; Wichita State Univ, Kans; Wichita Art Asn Gallery; Kans Univ, Lawrence; and others. *Comn:* Medallion, Kans State Col Centennial, Manhattan, 61; President's Medallion, Kans State Univ, 74; painting, Kans 4-H Found, Kans State Univ, 77; Gift Print Artist, Kans State Univ, Manhattan, Kans, 98. *Exhib:* Mid-Am Exhib, Nelson Gallery Art, Kansas City, Mo, 52-70; Watercolor USA, Springfield Art Mus, Mo, 57 & 68; Rocky Mountain Exhib, Denver Art Mus, Colo, 65; 45th Ann 17-State Exhib, Springfield, Mo, 75; Nat Watercolor Exhib, La Watercolor Soc, 76; Works of Art on Paper, Nat-Western Ann, Western Ill Univ, Galesburg, 76; Summer Invitational, Nelson Gallery of Art, Kansas City, Mo, 77, 79, 81, 84 & 86; Kansas Landscapes-Touring Invitational, 85-86; Burke Armstrong Gallery, Taos, NMex, 91-92; Kans Watercolor Soc Seven State Exhib, Wichita Art Mus, Kans, 98; One-man exhibs, Hutchinson Art Assoc, Shaeffer Art Mus, Barton Co Community Col, Great Bend, Beach Art Mus, Kans State Univ, Manhattan & Columbian Gallery, Wamego, Kans, 98. *Pos:* Asst dir, Wichita Art Mus, Kans, 53-55. *Teaching:* Prof drawing & painting, Kans State Univ, Manhattan, 56-89, head art dept, 67-71, emer prof, 90-. *Awards:* Purchase Awards, Smoky Hills Art, Hadley Med Ctr, 77, Kans Watercolor Soc, United Bank & Trust, 77, Prairie Exhib, 83 & Showcase Manhattan, 90; Winner, Kansas Postcard Series No 13, 90. *Bibliog:* V W Bell (auth), The Kansas Art Reader, Univ Kans Press, 76. *Mem:* Nat Col Art Asn; Mid-Am Col Art Asn; Kans Watercolor Soc; Kans Fedn Art. *Media:* Watercolor, Oil. *Publ:* Coauth, A Foundation for Expressive Drawing, Burgess Publ, 83. *Dealer:* Strecker-Nelson Gallery Manhattan, KS. *Mailing Add:* 2441 Hobbs Dr Manhattan KS 66502

LARNER, LIZ
SCULPTOR
Exhib: solo exhib include Margo Leavin Gallery, LA, 1988; Galerie Peter Pakesch, Vienna, Austria, 89; 303 Gallery, NYC, 89; Galleri Nordanstad-Skarstedt, Stockholm, Sweden, 90; Stuart Regen Gallery, Los Angeles, CA, 91; Peter Pakesch, Vienna, Austria, 92; Jennifer Flay Galerie, Paris, France, 93; Kunsthalle Basel, Basel, Switzerland, curated by Peter Pakesch, 97; Regen Projects, Los Angeles, CA, 98; Museum of Contemporary Art, Los Angeles, 2001; Museum of Contemporary Art, Chicago, 2002; Regen Projects, LA, 2005; group exhib include LACE Annual, 1987; Nothing Sacred, Margo Leavin Gallery, 87; Fed Reserve Plz, NYC, 89; Inst Contemporary Art, U Penn, 90; Renaissance Soc, Chicago, 91; Modern Mus Contemporary Art, LA, 92; James Corcoran Gallery, 93; Barbara Gladstone Gallery, 2000; Gallery at Green St, NYC, 2002; Inst Contemporary Art, London, 2004; Mus Modern Art, London, 2005; Whitney Biennial, Whitney Mus, NYC, 2006. *Mailing Add:* 5406 Monte Vista St Los Angeles CA 90042

LAROCHE, LYNDA L
CRAFTSMAN, DESIGNER
b Urbana, Ill, May 23, 47. *Study:* Montgomery Col, AA, 69; Univ NMex, BFA, 71; Indiana Univ, MFA, 76. *Work:* Indiana Univ Art Mus; Indianapolis Mus Art. *Exhib:* Fine Art Jewelry in Am, Cross Creek Gallery, Malibu, 86; Twice Gifted, Workbench Gallery, NY, 86; US Metal, San Francisco State Univ, 89; Art: Jewelry and Metalsmithing, Col Design, Iowa State Univ, Ames, 89; Fortunoff Silver Competition, NY, 90; Nat Metals Exhib, Mesa Arts Ctr, Ariz, 90; Expressions: Jewelry in the 1990's, Contemp Arts Ctr, Cincinnati, 91; The Collector's Eye, Am Craft Mus, NY, 91; Am Revelations, Nat Ornamental Metal Mus, Memphis, 96-98, Cleveland Ctr, Middlesborough, Eng, 98, Surrey Int Art, Eng, 98 & Soc Con Crafts, Pittsburgh, 98; Benchmarkers: Women in Metal, Nat Ornamental Metal Mus, Memphis, 98 & Skidmore Col, NY, 99; and others. *Pos:* Adv Panel for the Crafts, Indiana Arts Comn, 83-86; bd mem, Soc N Am Goldsmiths, 88-92; founder & chair, SNAG Educ Endowment, 91-94. *Teaching:* Vis asst prof, Indiana Univ, 78-79, 86 & 90, Montgomery Col, 79 & 88, Miami Univ, Oxford, Ohio, 88-89, SDak State Univ, 92; asst prof, Indiana Univ Penn, 97-. *Awards:* First Prize, Sterling Design Competition, Sterling Silversmiths Guild Am, New York, 76; Nat Endowment Arts, fel, 84, 87 & 93. *Mem:* Soc Am Silversmiths; Col Arts Asn; Soc NA Goldsmiths. *Media:* Sterling Silver, Gold. *Publ:* Auth, Master Metalsmith: Alma Eikerman, Metalsmith, winter 83; Randy Long: Recent Metalwork, Metalsmith Exhib Review, fall 84. *Mailing Add:* 360 North 8th St Indiana PA 15781

LARRAZ, JULIO F
PAINTER
b Havana, Cuba, Mar 12, 44. *Work:* Westmoreland Co Mus Art, Greensburg, Pa; Archer M Huntington Art Gallery, Univ Tex, Austin; Pa State Univ, Philadelphia; Mus Artc Mod, Bogota, Colombia; Mus Monterrey, Mexico, 87. *Exhib:* One-man exhibs, Nohra Haime Gallery, NY, 83, 84, 85, 86, 88, 89, 90, 91 & 92, Foire Int d'ArRt Contemp, Grand Palais, Paris, 83, Museo de Monterrey, Mex, 87, Ron Hall Gallery, Miami, 91, 92, & 93, Krannert Art Mus, Univ Ill, Urbana-Champaign, 92, Alonso Art, Artfi, Bogota, Colombia, 93, Alonso Art, Feria Iberoamericana de Arte, Caracas, Venezuela, 93; Work on Paper, Atrium Gallery, St Louis, 90; Prints, Collen Creco Gallery, Nyack, NY, 90. *Awards:* Cintas Found Fel, Inst Int Educ, 75; Am Acad Arts & Lett Award, 76. *Bibliog:* Barbara Duncan (auth), Lines of Vision, Washington, DC, 69; David Bourdon (auth), New York reviews Julio Larraz, Art Am, 3/87; Ruth Bass (auth), New York reviews Julio Larraz, Art News, 10/88; Edward Sullivan (auth), Julio Larraz, Hudson Hills Press, NY, 89. *Media:* Oil, Watercolor. *Publ:* Contrib, The Eye Witness to Space, Abrams, 70; illusr, The Perfect Wagnerite, Time-Life Bks, 72; The Whitehouse Enemies, New Am Libr, 73; contribr, Still the flypaper of politics, New York Times Mag, 74; New York Mag. *Dealer:* Nohra Haime Gallery 41 E 57th St New York NY 10022. *Mailing Add:* c/o Gary Naoler Fine Art 3306 Ponce de Leon Blvd Coral Gables FL 33134

LARSEN, D DANE
CERAMIST, SCULPTOR
b Oct 21, 50. *Study:* Harvard Univ, BA, study with William Reimann, Rudolf Arnheim & Buckminster Fuller; Univ Calif, Study with Ron Nagle; San Francisco State Univ, MA, study with Charles McKee, Hayward King, Dale Roush, Daniel Rhodes & Paul Soldner. *Work:* San Francisco State Univ Ceramics Collection; Carpenter Ctr for the Visual Arts, Harvard Univ, Cambridge, Mass; Oakland Mus, Calif; Prieto Gallery, Mills Col, Oakland. *Exhib:* Calif Ceramics & Glass, Oakland Mus; The Calif Craftsman, Monterey Peninsula Mus Art, Monterey, Calif; Marietta Col Crafts Nat, Grover M Hermann Fine Arts Ctr, Marietta, Ohio; Designer-Craftsman Nat, Richmond Art Ctr, Calif; Calif Crafts X, E B Crocker Gallery & Mus, Sacramento; Nat Cone Box Show, Kans Univ Union Gallery, Lawrence. *Pos:* Consult & dir of ceramics prog, San Rafael City Recreation Dept, 77-. *Teaching:* Instr ceramics, Col of Marin, Kentfield, Calif, 76- & Columbia Jr Col, Calif, summer 77; Art Acad, San Francisco, Calif, 80-84. *Awards:* Cash Awards, Calif Craftsman, 76, San Jose Mus Art, 76 & 76 & Civic Arts Gallery, 77. *Mem:* San Francisco Potters Asn; Am Crafts Coun; Col Art Asn. *Media:* Clay, Wood. *Dealer:* Meyer, Fort Mason Ctr San Francisco CA 94123. *Mailing Add:* PO Box 150973 San Rafael CA 94915-0973

LARSEN, ERIK
CONSULTANT, EDUCATOR
b Vienna, Austria, Oct 10, 11; US citizen. *Study:* Inst Superieur Hist Art & Archeol, Brussels, Belg, BA; Cath Univ Louvain, MA & PhD; restoration with Jef Lammens, Ghent & Jules Defort, Brussels. *Hon Degrees:* Janus Pannonius Univ, Dr, Pecs, Hungary. *Work:* Flowers, Fla Landscapes and Seascapes. *Exhib:* Copacabana Palace, Rio de Janeiro, Brazil, 46; Art League Gallery, Hernando Fla, 99; Appleton Mus, Ocala, Fla, 2004. *Collection Arranged:* Georgetown Univ Art Collections, Washington, DC. *Pos:* Dir & ed-in-chief, Pictura; Belg Govt Cult Mission in Brazil, 46-47. *Teaching:* Res prof art, Manhattanville Col Sacred Heart, 47-55; instr, Sch Gen Studies Exten Div, City Col New York, 48-55; from lectr to vis prof, Georgetown Univ, 55-58, assoc prof fine arts, 58-63, prof fine arts, 63-67, head dept fine arts, 60-67; prof hist art, Univ Kans, 67-80, dir, Ctr Flemish Art & Cult, 70-80, prof emer art hist, 80-; guest prof, Univ Salzburg, Austria, 88. *Awards:* Knight's Cross and Officer, Order of Leopold & Knight's Cross, Order of the Crown, Belg; Laureate, Inst France, Prix Thorlet, 62; mem, Jury Taras Shevshenko Mem, Washington. *Bibliog:* Die Post-Familie aus der Sicht von Frans Hals, Jahrgang, 8/2001; Die Vorstudie zum Stich, Zu Anton van Dycks Portat des Antwerpener Bildhauers Hubertus van den Eynden, Jahrgang, 2/15/2001; and numerous others. *Mem:* Appraisers Asn Am; Asn Dipl Hist Art & Archeol, Cath Univ Louvain. *Media:* Oil. *Res:* History of northern baroque and northern renaissance art. *Interests:* reading, music, swimming, Karate. *Publ:* Auth, Frans Post, Interprete du Bresil, Colibris Editora, Amsterdam-Rio de Janeiro, 62; coauth with Jane P Davidson, Calvinistic Economy and 17th Cent Dutch Art, Univ Kans Publ, 79; auth, Rembrandt, Peintre de Paysages: Une Vision Nouvelle, Publ d'Histoire l'Art & l'Archeologie Univ Louvain, 83; 17th Cent Flemish Painting, Luca Verlag, Freren, WGer, 85; The Paintings of Anthony Van Dyck, two vols, Luca Verlag, WGer, 88; and others. *Mailing Add:* 511 S Washington St Beverly Hills FL 34465

LARSEN, JACK LENOR
DESIGNER, WRITER
b Seattle, Wash, Aug 5, 27. *Study:* Univ Wash, BFA, 50; Cranbrook Acad Art, MFA, 51. *Hon Degrees:* RI Sch of Design DFA (hon), 82; Parsons Sch of Design PhD (hon). *Work:* Mus Mod Art, NY; Victoria & Albert Mus, London, Eng; Stedelijk Mus, Amsterdam, Holland; Cooper-Hewitt Mus Decorative Arts & Design, NY; Art Inst Chgo; Archives of Am Art, Washington; Royal Scottish Mus, Edinborough; Israel Mus, Jerusalem; Kunstindustrietmus, Copenhagen. *Comn:* Theatre curtain, comn by Charles Luchman Asn for Phoenix Civic Plaza, Concert Hall, Ariz, 72; Act curtain, St Charles Cultl Ctr, Commissioned by Powell/Kleischmidt, 78; Carpet, wall and window fabrics, leather upholstery for Trustees Dining Room, Met Mus Art, 92. *Exhib:* One-man show, Mus Decorative Art, Copenhagen, Denmark, 76; Retrospectives, Stedelijk Mus, Amsterdam, 68, Mus Fine Arts, Boston, Mass, 71, Renwick Gallery, Washington, DC, 72 & Fashion Inst Technol, NY, 78; 30 Yrs of Creative Textiles, Mus des Arts Decoratifs, Pavillon de Marsan, Louvre, Paris, 81. *Collection Arranged:* Co-dir, Wall Hangings, Mus Mod Art, NY, 70. *Pos:* Chmn, Haystack Sch, 76-81; pres, Am Crafts Coun, 81. *Teaching:* Dir fabric design dept, Philadelphia Col Art, 61-63; artist-in-residence, Royal Col Art, London, 75; affiliate prof, Univ Wash. *Awards:* Neiman-Marcus Award, Distinguished Serv in the Field of Fashion; Trailblazer Award, IFDA; Collab Award for Excellence in Design; Gold Medal, Am Crafts Coun, 96; Textile Design Inst medal, 96; Hall of Fame award, Interior Design Mag, 99. *Mem:* Am Crafts Coun (bd trustees, 54-, pres, 81-90, pres emer, 90-); Royal Soc Art, London; Am Inst Interior Designers (hon fel); Art Club Chicago, Brooklyn Botanical Garden, Ctr Internat. de la Tapisserie, Contemp Craft Asn Met, Mus Art, Omicron Nu; Life Mem Metrop Mus Art; Color Asn of US (adv bd). *Publ:* Auth, The Dyer's Art, 76; coauth, The Art Fabric: Mainstream, 81; Interlacing: The Elemental Fabric, Kodahsha; Material Wealth: Living with Luxurious Fabrics, 89; auth, Jack Lenor Larsen: A Weaver's Memoir, 98. *Mailing Add:* 55 Park Ave New York NY 10016

LARSEN, JOHN CHRISTIAN
EDUCATOR, LIBRARIAN
b Menominee, Mich. *Study:* Univ Mich, BDes, 50, MA(art hist), 51, MALS, 55, PhD, 67. *Pos:* Reference librn, Fine Arts Dept, Detroit Pub Libr, Mich, 54-57; head art div, Mich State Libr, Lansing, 57-61; art reference, Am Libr Asn. *Teaching:* Instr bibliog fine arts, Sch Libr Sci, Univ Mich, Ann Arbor, 65-68; asst prof bibliog visual arts, Col Libr Sci, Univ Ky, Lexington, 68-71; asst prof lit fine arts, Sch Libr Serv, Columbia Univ, New York, 71-77; assoc prof bibliog visual arts, Sch Libr Sci, Northern Ill Univ, De Kalb, 77-88. *Mem:* Art Libr Soc NAm; Am Libr Asn; Asn Col & Res Libr; Victorian Soc Am (bd mem, 75-76). *Res:* Use of information resources in visual arts. *Interests:* Evaluation of reference materials treating visual arts; education of art librarians. *Publ:* Auth, A seminar in fine arts bibliography, J Educ Librarianship, 70; The use of art reference sources in museum libraries, Spec Libr, 71; The education of fine arts/music librarians, Libr Trends, 75; Museum Librarianship, Shoe String Press, 85; Researcher's Guide to Archives, Shoe String Press, 88

LARSEN, MERNET RUTH
PAINTER, EDUCATOR
b Houghton, Mich, June 2, 40. *Study:* San Francisco Art Inst, with Nathan Olivera, 60; Univ Fla, with Hiram Williams, BFA, 62; Univ Ill, 62-63; Ind Univ, with James McGarrell & William Bailey, MFA, 65. *Work:* Univ Okla; Okla Art Ctr; Fla House of Rep; General Telephone Co; Ind Univ; Tampa Mus Art; Fla Gulf Coast Art Ctr; plus others. *Exhib:* Thirteen Young Artists You Should Collect, Okla Art Ctr, 65; Mid-Am Ann, Nelson Gallery, Kansas City, Mo, 66; Realism & Figuration, Fla State Univ Mus, Tallahassee, 71; All Fla Painters, St Petersburg Mus, 76; one-person show, Mont State Art Gallery, Bozeman, 77, Ea Ill Univ, 97; Realism & Metaphor, Jacksonville Mus and others, 80; Artists Choice, Swain Sch Design, 82; Southern Absraction, New Orleans & Raleigh, NC, 87; Sarasota Biennial, Ringling Mus Art, 2000; Univ S Florida Contemp Art Mus, Tampa, Fla, 2002, 2006. *Teaching:* Vis instr, Univ Okla, Norman, 65-67; prof painting & drawing, Univ SFla, 67-; instr, Cath Univ Milan, Rome, Italy, summer 70; vis artist painting, Ridgewood Sch Art, NJ, 73-74 & Mont State Univ, Bozeman, winter, 77; vis asst prof drawing, Yale Univ, fall 76; instr, Yale, Norfolk, 79. *Awards:* Fel Nat Endowment, 88, 89; USF Reasearch Grants to China, Japan & India, Fla Ind Artists, 89; Disting Teacher Award, USF. *Media:* Oils, Acrylic, Mixed Media. *Dealer:* Mira Mar Gallery Sarasota FL

LARSEN, PATRICK HEFFNER
PAINTER, SCULPTOR
b Port Arthur, Tex, July 11, 45. *Study:* Lamar Univ, BBA, 68; Sam Houston State Univ, teacher cert, 69; Stephen F Austin State Univ, MA, 70, MFA, 73. *Work:* Stephen F Austin State Univ, Nacogdoches, Tex; First Nat Bank of Ark, Little Rock; Univ Cent Ark, Conway. *Exhib:* Okla Art Ctr, Oklahoma City, 70 & 72; 16th & 17th Ann Delta Exhib, Ark Art Ctr, Little Rock, 73 & 74; one-man shows, Ft Smith Art Ctr, Ark, 75 & SArk Art Ctr, El Dorado, 76; 54th Ann Exhib, Meadows Mus of Art, Shreveport, La, 76; Rocky Mountain Ann Watercolor Exhib, Foothills Art Ctr, Golden, Colo, 77; Ariz Nat Painting Exhib, Scottsdale Art Ctr, Ariz, 77. *Teaching:* Asst prof painting, drawing, sculpture, watercolor & design, Univ Cent Ark, Conway, 70-80, assoc prof, 80-. *Awards:* First Place & Purchase Award, Fifth Ann Ark Artist Exhib, Southeastern Ark Art Ctr, 72; First Place in 19th Invitational Exhib of Ann Ark State Festival, 76; Top Award, 18th Ann Ark Oil Painting Exhib, 77. *Mem:* Nat Art Educ Asn; Ark Art Educ Asn. *Media:* Acrylic, Watercolor; Wood. *Mailing Add:* 6 Salem Rd Conway AR 72032-3388

LARSEN, SUSAN C
CURATOR, HISTORIAN
b Chicago, Ill, Oct 3, 46. *Study:* Knox Col, Galesburg, Ill, 64-66; Northwestern Univ, BA, 68, MA, 72, PhD, 75; Graves Found Fel, 80. *Collection Arranged:* Abstract Painting and Sculpture in America 1927-44 (auth, catalog), Mus Art, Carnegie Inst, Pittsburgh, Pa, 83; Edward Hopper, Whitney Mus, 89; Art in Place: 15 Years of Collecting, Whitney Mus, 89. *Pos:* guest lectr, series of lectures on Richard Diebenkorn, Los Angeles Co Mus Art, Los Angeles, 77; mem adv bd, Archives Am Art; chief cur, Farnsworth Art Mus, currently. *Teaching:* Asst prof hist of art, Carleton Col, Northfield, Minn, 74-75; from assoc prof to prof hist of art, Univ Southern Calif, Los Angeles, 75-; cur permanent collection, Whitney Mus Am Art, New York, 88-90; adjunct cur permanent collection, Whitney Mus Am Art, 90-91. *Mem:* Col Art Asn Am; Am Studies Asn; Southern Calif Art Historians Asn. *Res:* Abstract art of the 1930's; WPA in New York City; contemporary art in California; American folk art. *Publ:* Coauth, A Conversation with Richard Diebenkorn, J Los Angeles Inst Contemp Art, summer 77; auth, exhib catalogue, Vija Celmins, Newport Art Mus, 12/79; Richard Tuttle, Baxter Art Gallery, 79; CY Twombly, Newport Art Mus, 10/81; Selections from 8 Collections (catalog), Mus Contemp Art, Los Angeles, 83; coauth, Art in Place, Whitney Mus Am Art, 89; regular contribr, Art News Mag, Artweek & Artforum. *Mailing Add:* c/o Farnsworth Art Mus 352 Main St Box 466 Rockland ME 04841-0466

LARSON, JANE (WARREN)
CERAMIST, WRITER
b San Francisco, Calif, June 2, 22. *Study:* Swarthmore Col; Univ Rochester, BA(Eng, cum laude); Univ Calif, Los Angeles, sculpture with Anna Mahler; Antioch Univ, Visual Arts Ctr, MFA(ceramics). *Work:* Wash Co Mus of Art, Hagerstown, Md; Oak Ridge Community Art Ctr, Tenn; Collection of Works by Maryland Artists, Univ Md Col; Renwick Gallery, Washington, DC. *Comn:* Columnar mural (5' x 1' x 1'), Johns Hopkins Sch Int Studies, Washington; outdoor wall mural (3' x 30'), Energy & Life Art Ctr, Oak Ridge, Tenn, 92; Am Ctr Physics; Ten Molecules that Shaped the World (lobby mural), Univ Md Chemistry Dept, 97; Molecules that Matter to Medicine (mural), Nat Libr Med, List Hill Bldg. *Exhib:* One-person shows, Am Asn Advan Sci, Washington, 90 & Studio Gallery, Washington, 92 & 95; Sculpture on the Grounds, Rockville Civic Ctr Mansion, Rockville, Md, 92; Water Features, Franklin Sq Exhib Space, Washington, 92; Sculpture in the Garden, Univ Md, Univ Col, 94-95; Archival Clay Canvas, Creative Partners Gallery, Bethesda, Md, 96; three garden murals with water, Residence Inn, Wis Ave, Bethesda, Md. *Teaching:* Instr ceramics, Oak Ridge Community Art Ctr, Tenn, 63-66; workshops, slab construction, Kiln Club of Washington, 81; Potter's Guild, Annapolis, Md, 81; instr slab ceramics, Inst Learning Retirement, Am Univ, Washington, 83-84 & 86 & 94; part-time teacher. *Awards:* First Prize, Ceramic Guild Juried Show, 87; Kiln Club of Washington, 93; First Prize Ann Shows, Ceramic Guild, 94. *Bibliog:* Bethesda artist's flowers will bloom forever here, The Chronicle, Bethesda, Md, 5/8/85; C Stapleton (auth), Tomorrow's antiques, The Washingtonian, 5/79; L Ellicott (auth), Jane Larson, Clay Tales, EyeWash, 2/92. *Mem:* Artists Equity; Kiln Club Washington; Bethesda Ceramic Guild, Md; Int Sculpture Ctr. *Media:* Stoneware Clay, Ancient Glazes. *Res:* Art objects of the past that take the squared vessel form; clay's connection to scientific theories of Gaia and the Origin of Life. *Collection:* Origins of modern ceramics, particularly Japanese Iga, Hanada, Leach & Picasso. *Publ:* Bethesda: An artist's perspective, New Art Examiner, 4/87; Ceramics & the Homeless, Ceramics Mo, 4/89; Language in ceramics, Ceramics Mo, 10/95; Chemistry in Art, Chemical Intelligencer, 98; Stalking the Wild Tile, Tile Found, 97-98; We Need More Permanent Records, Cosmos Club J, 10/2000. *Dealer:* ARTSEEN Inc. *Mailing Add:* 6514 Bradley Blvd Bethesda MD 20034

LARSON, JUDY L
DIRECTOR
b Glendale, Calif, Mar 9, 52. *Study:* Univ Calif, Los Angeles, BA, 74, MA, 78; Inst Lib Arts, Emory Univ, Atlanta, PhD, 98. *Collection Arranged:* American Engravings before 1820 (with catalog), Am Antiquarian Soc, 79-84; Enchanted Images (auth, catalog), Santa Barbara Mus, 80; American Illustration (auth, catalog), Glenbow Mus, 85-86; Georgia Printmakers, (auth, catalog), High Mus, Atlanta, Ga, 86. *Pos:* actg asst cur Los Angeles Co Mus Art, 78; Sr cataloger, Am Antiquarian Soc, Worcester, Mass, 78-85; cur Am Art, High Mus, Atlanta, Ga, 85-98; exec dir, Art Mus W Va, Roanoke, 98-02; dir, Nat Mus Women in Arts, Washington, 02-. *Teaching:* Lectr hist prints, Assumption Col, fall 84 & Emory Univ, spring 86-88. *Res:* 18th and 19th century American Painting, federal period printmaking & illustration 1880-1925. *Publ:* auth American Illustration 1890-1925, 86; Contribr, William M Harnett Metrop Mus Art, New York, 265-275, 92; ed, Graphic Arts & the South: Proceedings of the 1990 North American Print Conference, Univ Ark Press, 93; coauth, American Paintings at the High Museum of Art (exhib catalog), Hudson Press, 94. *Mailing Add:* Nat Mus Women in Arts 1250 New York Ave Washington DC 20005

LARSON, KAY L
CRITIC, WRITER
b Cedar Rapids, Iowa. *Study:* Pomona Col, Claremont, Calif, with Mowry Baden, BA(philos, art practice), 69. *Pos:* Art critic/writer, Real Paper, Cambridge, Mass, 72-75; assoc ed, ARTnews, 75-78; art critic/writer, Village Voice, 79-80; art critic, NY Mag, 80-94; freelance writer, NY Times, 94-; managing ed, Cur: The M Jour, 2003-. *Teaching:* Instr & adj prof, NY Univ, 90-98; Writing Tutor, Ctr for Curatorial Studies, Bard Col, Annandale-on-Hudson, NY, 2003-. *Awards:* Nat Endowment Arts Critic Grants, 78 & 80; Japan Found Study Grant, 86. *Mem:* Int Art Critics Asn

LARSON, PHILIP SEELY
SCULPTOR, EDUCATOR
b Ventura, Calif, July 21, 44. *Study:* Univ Minn, Minneapolis, BA, 66; Columbia Univ, PhD, 71. *Work:* Walker Art Center, Minneapolis; Inst Art, Guggenheim Mus; NY General Mill Hq, Minneapolis; Chemical Bank Hq NY, Chicago Tribune; Hq Chicago, Lehman Bros, NY. *Comn:* Interior design & installation, Collection of Keyboard Instruments, Schubert Club, Landmark Ctr, St Paul, 79. *Exhib:* Hanson-Cowles Gallery, Minneapolis, 77; Glen Hanson Gallery, Minneapolis, 79 & 81; Emergent Americans, Guggenheim Mus, NY, 81; Mus Art, RI Sch Design, 83; Thomson Gallery, Minneapolis, 83,94; Walker Art Center, 1994, 2000. *Collection Arranged:* Burgoyne Diller, 71; DeKooning: Drawings & Sculptures (auth, catalog), 74; Naives/Visionaries (auth, catalog), 74; World Architecture in Minnesota, 78; Prairie School Architecture in Minnesota, Iowa and Wisconsin (auth, catalog), 82. *Pos:* Cur, Walker Art Ctr, Minneapolis, 70-75; frequent contribr, Print Collector's Newsletter. *Teaching:* Prof, Minneapolis Col Art & Design, 75-. *Awards:* Artist's Fel, Nat Endowment Arts, 79 & 81. *Mem:* Nat Trust for Hist Preserv. *Media:* Cast Iron, glass, screenprinting. *Publ:* 60 Scholarly articles on prints & drawings. *Dealer:* Bockley Gallery, Minneapolis. *Mailing Add:* 1527 W Franklin Ave Minneapolis MN 55405-3102

LARSON, SIDNEY
EDUCATOR, MURALIST
b Sterling, Colo, June 16, 23. *Study:* Univ Mo, AB & MA; Univ Okla; also with Thomas Hart Benton. *Work:* State Hist Soc, Mo; Munic Bldg, Jefferson City, Mo; Columbia Col; Columbia Pub Libr. *Comn:* Social History of Insurance, Shelter Ins Co, Columbia, Mo, 59; Social History of Ceramics & Metal, Riback Industs, Columbia, 67; mural, Munic Bldg, Jefferson City, Mo, 85; mural, Guitar Bldg, Columbia, Mo; mural, Boone Co Courthouse, Columbia, Mo. *Pos:* Mus cur, State Hist Soc, Mo, 61-. *Teaching:* Instr, Oklahoma City Univ, 50-51; Univ Mo-Columbia, summers; prof art, Columbia Col, 51-. *Awards:* Huntington Hartford Found, 62; Distinguished Serv Award, State Hist Soc, Mo, 89; Mo State Arts Coun Award, 91. *Mem:* Nat Soc Mural Painters; Am Inst Conserv Hist Artistic Works. *Res:* Private, federal, state and municipal painting restorations. *Publ:* Auth, Introduction to Fred Shane Drawings, 64; articles on Thomas Hart Benton, 69, 74 & 75 & auth, Conservation of a Bingham, 72, Mo Hist Rev; Chap in: Thomas Hart Benton Artist-Writer-Intellectual, 89. *Mailing Add:* 1408 Whitburn Dr Columbia MO 65203-5172

LARSON, WILLIAM G
PHOTOGRAPHER, EDUCATOR
b North Tonawanda, NY, Oct 14, 42. *Study:* State Univ NY, Buffalo, BS(art), 64; Inst Design, Ill Inst Technol, Chicago, MS(photog), with Aaron Siskind & Wynn Bullock, 67. *Work:* Mus Mod Art, NY; Philadelphia Mus Art; Los Angeles Co Mus Art; Baltimore Mus Art; Nat Gallery Can; J Paul Getty Mus. *Exhib:* Extending the Boundaries of Photog, Ctr Creative Photog, Tucson, 89; Artists Choose Artists, Inst Contemp Art, Philadelphia, 92; solo exhibs, Md Art Place, 94, RI Sch Design, 95 & Krannert Art Mus, 96, Cepa Gallery, Buffalo, 99, Visual Studies Workshop, Rochester, 2000, Arcadia U, 02, Renaissance Soc, 02, Art Inst Chicago, 03; Flora, Los Angeles Co Mus Art, 98; The Color Tradition, J paul Getty Mus, Los Angeles; Works from the Collection by Philadelphia Artists, Philadelphia Mus, 2000; group exhib, Univ Chicago, 03, San Francisco Mus Art, 2004, Howard Greenberg Gallery, NY, 2004. *Collection Arranged:* Philadelphia Mus of Art; Mus Modern Art, NY; Int Mus of Photography, George Eastman House; Los Angeles Co Mus of Art; San Francisco Mus Art. *Pos:* dir, grad Photography/Digital Imaging; dir, Md Inst Col Art. *Teaching:* Prof & dept chmn photog, Tyler Sch of Art, Temple Univ, Philadelphia, 67-; prof & dir grad studies photog, Col Art, Md Inst. *Awards:* Nat Endowment Arts, 71, 79, 86 & 92; Pa Coun Arts Fel, 83 & 88; Aaron Siskind Found Fel, 93; Guggenheim Fel, 82; Pew Fel, 02. *Bibliog:* S Perloff (ed), Lexigraphic portraits by William Larson, The Photo Review, 88; Bill Gaskins (auth), William Larson's Theatre du Monde, New Art Examiner, 10/94; Robert Hirsch (auth), Flexible Images, Exposure Vol 36: 1/2003; Eileen Neff (auth), Artforum, review, 9/2003; Taken by Design, NY Times Book Review, 12/2002. *Media:* Photography and Video. *Publ:* Photographing in the Studio, Hallmark, Inc, 94; Photomontage, Rockport Publ; A Century of Photography, 02; Taken by Design, 03; Seizing the Light, A History of Photography, 03. *Dealer:* Fern Shadd Photography 135 E 74th St New York NY; Charles Isaacs 19th & 20th Century Photography Malvern Pa. *Mailing Add:* 120 Hopwood Rd Collegeville PA 19426-2844

LARUE, JOAN MARRON
PAINTER
b Custer Co, Okla, Aug 19, 34. *Study:* Univ Okla, BA(fashion art), 56; workshop study with Sergei Bongart, William Reese, Ben Konis, Don Puttman, Jon Zahourek & Bettina Steinke, Hollis Williford, Richard Schmid, Harley Brown & Michael Lynch, 80-88. *Work:* Robert S Kerr Conf Ctr, Poteau, Okla; Mercy Health Ctr, Baptist Health Ctr, Presby Health Ctr & Okla State Senate Press Ctr, Oklahoma City; Frye Mus, Seattle, Wash; Okla State Art Collection. *Comn:* Mural size paintings, Senate Rooms, Okla State Senate, Oklahoma City, 83; mural, McCauley Plaza, comn by Sisters of Mercy, Oklahoma City, 86; Mural size paintings, Mercy Birthplace Ctr, 88. *Exhib:* Solo exhibs, Ft Smith Art Ctr, Ark, 70 & Okla Mus Art, Oklahoma City, 75; Midland Stewart Haley Memorial Show, 88, 89, 91 & 92; Plein Air Painters Am, 88, 89, 90 & 92; Philbrook Mus, Tulsa, Okla, 90 & 92; Okla Soc Impressionalists Traveling Show, 90; Gilcrease Mus Show, Petroglyphs in Okla, 93; and others. *Teaching:* Prof fashion arts, Univ Okla, 60-65; instr fine art, Okla Mus Art, Oklahoma City, 65-75; instr workshops, NMex, Okla, Tex & Hawaii, 75-80. *Awards:* First Place, Scottsdale Art Sch; Best of Show, Wrass, Cheyenne, Wyo. *Bibliog:* M J Van Deventer (auth), Painter and palette, Okla Home & Garden, 83; Lorene Marvin (producer), Oklahoma Original, Educ Television, OETA, 84; M J Van Deventer (auth), Joan Marron, excited student of life, Art Gallery Mag, 85; Susan Mcgarry (auth), Southwest Art Mag, 8/89; Walter Gray, Painting on Location (film), TV-KAUT, 89. *Mem:* Fashion Group Int (secy, 60); Oklahoma City Art Guild; Soc Am Impressionists; Plein Air Painters Am; Okla Soc of Impressionists. *Media:* Oil. *Dealer:* Dodson Gallery 7660 N Western Oklahoma City OK

LARZELERE, JUDITH ANN
TAPESTRY ARTIST
b Ann Arbor, Mich, Mar 17, 44. *Study:* Radcliff Col, 62-64; Univ Mich, BA, 67; Rutgers Univ, MFA, 74. *Work:* Iowa State Univ Libr, Ames; Am Craft Mus, NY; Radcliffe Col Harvard Univ, Cambridge, Mass. *Comn:* Silk wallhanging, Teradyne, Nashua, NH, 82; silk wallhanging, Biogen, Cambridge, Mass, 83; wallhanging, Putnam Investors, Boston, Mass, 88; wallhanging, Harper Indust, Inc, NY, 88; wallhanging, St Elizabeth's Hosp, Brighton, Mass, 94. *Exhib:* Quilt Nat, Athens, Ohio, 81, 83, 85, 87, 89 & 99; Quilt Art A Contemp View, Mus Max Berg, Heidelberg, Ger, 94; Visions, Mus San Diego Hist, Calif, 98; solo show, Bona Keane Gallery, Portland, Ore, 95; Sachen-Galerie, Switz, 95; and many others. *Pos:* Studio artist, 78-. *Teaching:* Penland Sch, NC, 90; Arrowmont Sch, Gatlinburg, Tenn, 90; Haystack Sch, Deer Isle, Maine, 98 & 2003; Banff Center, Calgary, Alberta, 91. *Awards:* Mass Cult Coun Grant, 93; Best Show, NY Quilt Festival, 95; Berkshire Taconic Trust-grant, 99, 2004. *Bibliog:* Visions Catalog, C&T Publ, 90, 94 & 98; New Wave Quilt Collections I & II by Setsuko Segawa, 91 & 93; Quilt Art A Contemporary View, Textilmuseum Max Berg Catalog, 94; 80 Leaders of the Quilt World, Nihon-Vogue, 94; Contemporary Quilts from the James Collection, AQS, 95; Quilts: A Living Tradition, Hugh Lauter Levin, 95; plus others; The Art Quilt, Hugh, Lauter, Levin, 97; The 30 Distinguished Quilt Artists of the World, Tokyo, Japan, 2003; Am Quiltmaking 1970-2003, Eleanor Levie (auth), 2004. *Mem:* Am Craft Coun; Friends Fiber Arts Int; Am Craft Council, S Co Art Assoc. *Media:* Contemporary Quilts, Strong Color. *Interests:* gardening, canoeing, bird-watching. *Publ:* Auth, Beyond log cabin, Threads, Tauton Press, 2/86; contribr, Fiber Expressions: The Contemporary Quilt, Schiffer Publ, 87; America's Glorious Quilts, Hugh Lauter Levin, 87; Fiberarts Design Book III, Lark Press, 88; auth, Quilting strip by strip, Threads, Tauton Press, 8/88. *Dealer:* Gross McClief Gallery 127 S 16th St Philadelphia PA 19102; Penny N Art Quilts 1017 Cathcart Way Stanford CA 94305; Alianza, Boston, MA; Gross McClief Gallery, Philadelphia, PA

LASANSKY, LEONARDO
DRAFTSMAN, PRINTMAKER
b Iowa City, Iowa, Mar 29, 46. *Study:* Univ Iowa, BGS, 71, MA, 72 & MFA, 72; also with Byron Burford & 15 Stuart Edie. *Work:* Brooklyn Mus, NY; Princeton Univ Mus; Philadelphia Mus Art; Achenback Collection, San Francisco; Nat Mus, Krakow, Poland; Libr of Cong, Washington, DC; Mus of Art, Grenchen, Switz; Minneapolis Inst Art; Nat Gallery of Art, Washington, DC; Hood Mus, Dartmouth Col. *Comn:* Portrait, Christopher Columbus, James Ford Bell Libr. *Exhib:* Int Print Biennale, Krakow, Poland, 80; one-man show, Dartmouth Col, Hood Mus, 82; Premio Int, eiella, Italy, 87; Bienal de San Juan, Grabado Lationamericano, Puerto Rico, 88-98; Am Embassy, Belgrade, Yugoslavia, 89-90; Prefectural Mus Art, Fukuoka, Japan, 90; Mus Art, Ball State Univ, 96. *Collection Arranged:* Espana: The Legacy of War: Works by Francisco Goya, 97; Africa: A Legacy in Memory, Material Differences, Mus for African Art, NY, 2004; Icons of Perfection: Figurative Sculpture from Africa, 2005-2006. *Pos:* Adv panel, Minn State Arts, 88-90; dir of exhib, Hamline Univ, 97. *Teaching:* Prof art, Hamline Univ, 72-, chmn fine arts div, 80-85, acting chmn art dept, 90-91; artist-in-residence, Dartmouth Col, 82; chair studio arts & art hist dept, 95-; chair fine arts div, 98-; artist-in-residentce, lifetime appointment, Hamline Univ, 2004-. *Awards:* Purchase Award, 5th Nat Hawaii Print Exhib, Honolulu, 80; Purchase Award, 4th Miami Int Print Exhib, Fla, 80; Distinguished Alumni Award, Univ Iowa, 81; Drawing Award, Berkshire Mus, Pittsfield, Mass, 82; and others. *Bibliog:* John Wilford Knopf (auth), The Mysterious History of Columbus, 91; New York Times, ed page, 1/2/91 & mag, Sect 6, 8/11/91; Columbus & The Age of Discovery, Morrow, 91. *Mem:* Nat Acad. *Media:* Intaglio. *Publ:* auth (introduction), Icons of Perfection: Figurative Sculpture from Africa, Hamline Univ Press, 2006. *Dealer:* Jane Haslem Washington DC. *Mailing Add:* Print Dept Hamline Univ 1536 Hewitt Saint Paul MN 55104

LASANSKY, MAURICIO L
PRINTMAKER, DRAFTSMAN
b Buenos Aires, Arg, 14; US citizen. *Study:* Superior Sch Fine Arts, Arg; Iowa Wesleyan Col, Hon DA, 59; Pac Lutheran Univ, Hon DFA, 69; Carleton Col, Northfield, Minn, Hon DA, 79; Coe Col, Iowa, Hon DFA, 85. *Work:* Art Inst Chicago; Mus Mod Art, NY; Libr Cong, Washington, DC; Uffizi Gallery, Florence, Italy; Mus Arte Contemp, Madrid, Spain; and over 100 univs & galleries, US & abroad. *Exhib:* One-man shows, Mauricio Lasansky: Selections from 30 Yrs of Printmaking, The Nazi Drawings, Palace Fine Arts, Mexico City, 69, Dickinson Col, Carlisle, Pa, 72 & 74, Third Int Biennial Mexico, 80, and over 160 others; Whitney Mus Am Art, NY, 71; and others. *Pos:* Virgil M Hancher chair (emer), Univ Iowa, 67. *Teaching:* Dir, Free Fine Arts Sch, Villa Maria, Cordoba, Arg, 36 & Taller Manualidades, Cordoba, 39; vis lectr, Univ Iowa, 45, asst prof art, 46, assoc prof, 47, prof, 48-, res prof, 65-67, Virgil M Hancher Distinguished Prof, 67-84, res prof, 71-72; Lucas lectr, Carleton Col, 65; Virgil M Hancher prof emer, 1984-. *Awards:* Guggenheim Fel, 43, 44, 45, 53 & 63; Distinguished Teaching of Art Award, Col Art Asn, 80; Nominated for Wolf Found Award in the Arts, Jerusalem, Israel,82; Hon Award Arts & Humanities Comn for the Aging, 83; Acad, Nat Acad Arts & Design, NY, 90. *Bibliog:* Kevin Kelly (producer & dir), Lasansky Printmaker, Univ Iowa Video Ctr. *Mem:* Col Art Asn Am (bd dir, 70-); life mem Nat Acad; Nat Acad Fine Arts, Buenos Aires, Argentina; Fel, Inst Advan Study, Ind Univ, Bloomington; LA, Soc Printmakers (hon artist 2001). *Media:* Etching. *Mailing Add:* Lasansky Corp 216 E Washington St Iowa City IA 52240-3926

LASCH, PAT
SCULPTOR
b New York, NY, Nov 20, 44. *Study:* Queen Col, NY, BA, 70; Ga State, MFA, 90. *Work:* Queens Col, City Univ NY; Mus Mod Art, Metrop Mus Art, NY, Oberlin Mus, Ohio; Prudential Insurance Co, NJ; Rutgers Univ, New Brunswick, NJ. *Comn:* Hommage: 1929-1979 (sculpture), Mus Mod Art, NY, 79, Kiresky Art Mus, Lansing, Mich, 2000; Womens Mus, Washington; Nat Acad Design, NY. *Exhib:* Solo exhibs, AIR Gallery, NY, 73, 77, 79 & 80, Kathryn Markel Gallery, NY, 81, 84 & 85, Lerner Heller Gallery, NY, 81, Albright-Knox Gallery, Members' Gallery, Buffalo, NY, 84, McIntosh Drepdale Gallery, Washington, 85, Marilyn Pearl Gallery, NY, 88 & 90 & Paridiso, Il Ponte Gallery, Rome, Italy, NH Acad Design, New York City, 01; Contemp Women: Consciousness & Content, Brooklyn Mus Art Sch, NY 77; Out of the House, Whitney Mus Am Art Downtown, NY, 78; The Cooked & the Raw, Thomas Segal Gallery, Boston, Mass; Controlling Woman, Sculpture Ctr, NY, 93; Bad Girl Show, New Mus, NY, 94; 20 yr retrospective, AIR Gallery, NY, 94; Controlling Woman: aka True Love, Hampshire Gallery, Mass, 94; and other solo exhibs. *Pos:* Guest panelist, Soho Ctr Visual Arts, NY, 77; lectr, Art Inst Chicago, currently. *Teaching:* Parson's Sch Design, 78-88, RI Sch Design, 89-90 & Univ Mass, Amherst, 91-. *Awards:* Special Proj, NY St Coun Arts, 84-85; Pollock-Krasner, 87; New Eng Found Arts, 95; and others. *Bibliog:* Ellen Lubell (auth), When a good gallery folds, Village Voice, 4/11/85; Vivien Raynor (auth) article, NY Times, 10/4/85; Jeff Weinstein (auth), It's heaven when you, Village Voice, 10/22/85. *Mem:* Soc Fels AAR; Nat Acad. *Media:* Mixed. *Publ:* Auth, AIR, Artforum, 11/80, 70; If You Make A Mistake Put A Rose On It, 85. *Dealer:* Judy Goldman Fine Arts 11 Newbury St Boston MA; Marilyn Pearl Gallery New York NY 10012

LASKE, LYLE F
SCULPTOR, EDUCATOR
b Green Bay, Wis, May 10, 37. *Study:* Univ Wis, Platteville, BS, 59; Univ Wis, Madison, MS, 61 & MFA, 65; Univ Minn, 68. *Work:* Plains Art Mus, Moorhead, Minn. *Exhib:* Solo exhib, Walker Art Ctr, Minneapolis, Minn, 66; Artists of Central NY, Everson Mus Art, Syracuse, 71; Draw and Small Sculpture Show, Ball State Univ, Ind, 74; Miss River Crafts Show, Memphis, Tenn, 77; Am Woodcarvers, Craft Ctr, Worchester, Mass, 78; New Handmade Furniture, Am Craft Mus, NY, 79; Beyond Folk, Minneapolis Inst Art, Minn, 84. *Teaching:* Instr, Wis State Univ, Platteville,

62-64; prof sculpture, Moorhead State Univ, Minn, 65-97, retired, 97; assoc prof, New York State Univ Col Oneonta, 70-71. *Media:* Wood. *Publ:* American woodcarvers, Craft Horizons, 4/78; Air-powered tools, Fine Woodworking, 1-2/79; Some abrasive facts, Fine Woodworking, 3-4/80; Woodworking: The New Wave, Crown Publ, 81; Fine Woodworking Techniques 3, The Taunton Press, 81. *Mailing Add:* 28433 Junco Dr Nevis MN 56467

LASKER, JOE (JOSEPH) L
PAINTER, ILLUSTRATOR-CHILDRENS BOOKS
b Brooklyn, NY, June 26, 18. *Study:* Cooper Union Art Sch, cert, 39; Escuela Universitaria de Bellas Artes, Mex, 48. *Work:* Whitney Mus Am Art, NY; Philadelphia Mus Art; Springfield Mus, Mass; Joseph H Hirshhorn Collection, Washington, DC; and others. *Comn:* Murals, US Pub Works Admin, Post Off, Calumet, Mich, 41, Milbury, Mass, 42 & Henry St Settlement Playhouse, NY, 48. *Exhib:* Pa Acad Fine Arts Ann, 47-53; Whitney Mus Am Art Ann, 47-58; Nat Acad Design Ann, NY, 47-82; Kraushaar Galleries, NY, 51-; and others. *Teaching:* Instr, College City, NY, 47; Assoc prof painting, Univ Ill, 53-54. *Awards:* Abbey Mem scholar, 46-47; Prix de Rome fel, 50-51; Guggenheim Fel, 54; Nat Inst Arts & Lett Grant, 68; Nat Acad Design, 80. *Bibliog:* 19 Young Americans, Life, 3/20/50; Goodrich & Bauer (auth), American art of our century, Praeger, NY, 61; Figurative Tradition, Whitney Mus Am Art, NY, 61; Mothers Can Do Anything, 1972(auth), He's My Brother, 1974(auth), Tales of a Seadog Family, (auth)1974, Merry Ever After (best illustrated children's book, NY Times, 1976, Notable Bk of Year Am Libr Asn 1977), (auth)1976, The Strange Voyage of Neptune's Car, (auth)1977, Lentil Soup, (auth)1977, Nick Joins In, (auth)1980, The Do-Something Day, (auth)1982, The Great Alexander the Great, (auth)1983, Tournament of Knights, (auth)1986. *Mem:* Nat Acad. *Media:* Oil, Watercolor. *Mailing Add:* c/o Kraushaar Gallery 724 Fifth Ave New York NY 10019-4106

LASKER, JONATHAN
PAINTER
b Jersey City, NJ, 48. *Study:* Sch Visual Arts, NY, 75-77; Calif Inst Arts, Valencia, Calif, 77. *Work:* Mus Ludwig, Cologne; The Corcoran Gallery of Art, Washington; The Hirshhorn Mus & Sculpture Garden, Smithsonian Inst, Washington; Wacoal Art Ctr, Tokyo; and others. *Exhib:* Fortieth Biennial Exhib of Painting, Corcoran Gallery Art, Washington, 87; Post-Abstract Abstraction, Aldrich Mus Contemp Art, 87; The Kaldewey Press, Thomas J Watson Libr, Metrop Mus Art, NY, 88; New Acquisitions, Hirshhorn Mus & Sculpture Garden, Washington, 91; one-person exhibs, Ctr Contemp Art (with catalog), Rotterdam, 93, Galleri Lars Bohman, Stockholm, 94, Bravin Post Lee (with catalog), NY, 94, Galeria Soledad Lorenzo, Madrid, Spain, 95, LA Louver, Venice, Calif, 95, Galleria Milleventi, Turin, Italy, 97 & Galerie Thaddaeus Ropac, Paris, 2000; Am Painting Now (with catalog), Eva Menzio, Turin, Italy, 94; ARS 95 Helsinki, Mus Contemp Art, Helsinki, Finland, 95; Reconditioned Abstraction, Forum for Contemp Art, St Louis, 96; Pop/Abstraction, Mus Am Art, Pa Acad Fine Arts, 98; Mixed Bag: Summer Group Show, Schmidt Contemp Art, St Louis, 99; Arte Americana: Ultimo Decennio, Mus d'Arte della Citta di Ravenna, 2000; Kevin Bruk Gallery, Miami, Fla, 2001; Thomas Schulte, Berlin, 2002; Nat Acad Mus, NY, 2006. *Awards:* Nat Endowment Arts Fel, 87 & 89; New York Found Arts Fel, 89. *Bibliog:* Gerhard Mack (auth), Jonathan Lasker im Kunstmuseum, Kunst-Bull, 6/98; Katy Siegal (auth), Jonathan Lasker: Selective Identity, ArtForum, 9/99; Kenneth Baker (auth), Odd Abstractions, San Francisco Chronicle, 10/28/2000. *Publ:* auth, Not a First, Kaldewey Press, 89; auth, Plastic Made Perfect: Measuring Mondrian: The New Math, Artforum, 9/95; auth, Jonathan Lasker: Complete Essays 1984-98, Edgewise Press, 98. *Mailing Add:* c/o Sperone Westwater 415 W 13th St #2 New York NY 10014-1104

LASKIN, MYRON, JR
CURATOR, HISTORIAN
b Milwaukee, Wis, Apr 7, 30. *Study:* Harvard Univ, AB, 52, AM, 54; Inst Fine Arts, NY Univ, PhD, 64. *Collection Arranged:* Fountainebleau, Nat Gallery Can, 73; J Paul Getty Mus. *Pos:* Cur Europ art, Nat Gallery Can, 68; cur paintings, J Paul Getty Mus, Malibu, Calif, 84-89. *Teaching:* Asst prof art hist, Washington Univ, 61-66. *Awards:* Italian Govt Grant, NY Univ, 59-60; Villa I Tatti Fel, 65-67, Kress Fel, 66-67, Harvard Univ. *Res:* Italian 16th and 17th century painting. *Publ:* Contribr, Burlington Mag, Art Bulletin, Arte Illustrata & others. *Mailing Add:* 17601 Tramonto Dr Pacific Palisades CA 90272

LASTER, PAUL
CONCEPTUAL ARTIST
b Flint, Mich, Oct 14, 51. *Study:* Univ Houston, Tex, 71-72; Fashion Inst Technol, New York, 76-80; New Sch for Social Res, New York, 81-84, with Lisette Model and Ian Wilson; Cooper Union, 84-85. *Work:* Art Inst Chicago; Whitney Mus Am Art, NY; Nat Mus Am Art, Smithsonian Inst, Washington; Los Angeles Co Mus Art, Calif; Brooklyn Mus Art, NY. *Exhib:* One-man shows, 91, The Greenberg Gallery, St Louis, 92, Hamiltons Gallery, London, 92, Galerie Baudoin Lebon, Paris, 92, Richard Levy Gallery, Albuquerque, 93, Mark Moore Gallery, Santa Monica, 93, Michael Klein Gallery, NY, 96 & photo solo (with catalog), 102 Prince St Space, NY, 97 & 98; The Photog of Invention, Nat Mus Am Art, Washington, DC, Mus Contemp Art, Chicago & Walker Art Ctr, Minneapolis, 89-90; Departures Photog 1923-90, Denver Art Mus, Joslyn Art Mus, Omaha & Pittsburgh Ctr Arts, 91-92; Dark Decor, San Jose Mus Art, Fla Gulf Coast Art Ctr, Belleair & The Alberta Col Art, Calgary, 92-93; The Return of the Cadavre Exquis, The Drawing Ctr, NY, Corcoran Gallery Art, Washington & Carnegie Mus Art, Pittsburgh, 93-94; True Stories, Betsy Senior Gallery, NY, 94; Interventions, UBU Gallery, NY, 95; Collection in Context (with catalog), Thread Waxing Space, NY, 96; Smallest Show on Earth, Richard Levy Gallery, Albuquerque, NMex, 97; Affirm Identity (with catalog), Kingsborough Community Col Art Gallery, Brooklyn, NY, 97; Empire State Pride Agenda Benefit, NY, 97; photo solo (with catalog), 102 Prince St Space, NY, 97 & 98; Emergency Art Fund, Pat Hearn Gallery, NY, 97; Obsession (with catalog), Rotunda Gallery, Brookly, NY, 97; Sex/Industry, Stefan Stux Gallery, NY, 97; 100, Holland Tunnel Proj Space, Brooklyn, NY, 98; Regarding Duchamp, Abraham Lubelski Gallery, NY, 98; A Brooklyn Salon, Rotunda Gallery, Brooklyn, NY, 98; The Winter Show, Charles Cowles Gallery, NY, 98; A Room with A View, Sixth at Prince Fine Arts, NY, 99. *Pos:* Adj cur photog, PS1 Mus, NY, 87-88; photog cur, Independent Curators, Inc, NY, 88-90. *Awards:* Nat Endowment Arts, 85 & 89; Art Matters, Inc, 88 & 89; Change, Inc, 89. *Bibliog:* Stuart Servetar (auth), article, New York Press, 2/7-13/96; Howard Halle (auth), article, Time Out/New York, 2/21-28/96; Paul D Miller (auth), WEBS, Axis Press, Brooklyn, NY, 99. *Media:* Miscellaneous Media. *Publ:* Auth, exhib catalog, Hirschl & Adler Modern, New York, 90; exhib catalog, Runkel-Hue-Williams, London, 91. *Mailing Add:* 313 Clinton St New York NY 11231

LASUCHIN, MICHAEL
PRINTMAKER, PAINTER
b Kramatorsk, Russia, July 24, 23; US citizen. *Study:* Rostow Col Art, USSR, 40-41; Philadelphia Col Art, BFA, 70; Tyler Sch Art, Temple Univ, MFA, 72. *Work:* Libr Cong, Washington; Philadelphia Mus Art; Nat Libr Print Collection, Paris; Mus Mod Art, Barcelona; Brooklyn Mus Art; and others. *Comn:* Print, Print Club Philadelphia, 74; print, Pratt Graphics Ctr, NY, 80. *Exhib:* 11th Int Exhib Graphic Arts, Mus Mod Art, Ljubljana, Yugoslavia, 75; 3rd Int Drawing Biennale, Cleveland, Eng, 77; Ninth Norwegian Int Print Triennale, Fredrikstad, Norway, 89; Interprint Lviv '90, Lviv, USSR, 90; Int Print Triennale, Crakow, Poland, 97. *Collection Arranged:* Permanent collections include Philadelphia Mus Art, Brooklyn Art Mus, Mus Modern Art, New York, Mus Modern Art, Barcelona, Spain, Libr. National, Paris, Berlin Mus of Art, Russian State Mus, Tretjakow Gallery, Moscow, Pushkin Mus, Moscow, Victoria Albert Mus, London; traveling group exhib, "A Legacy of Excellence: Artistic Achievements of Older Pennsylvanians," 2004. *Teaching:* Prof printmaking, Univ Arts, 72-92. *Awards:* Grumbacher Gold Medal Award, Nat Watercolor Soc, 81; Purchase Award, Honolulu Acad Fine Art, 85; Venture Fund Award, Melon Found, 87; and others. *Bibliog:* Cynthia B Frost (auth), Paintings suggest, Daily Pennsylvanian 11/20/74; Bill Southwell (auth), Exhibiting new talent, Drummer, 4/22/75; Dorothy Grafly (auth), Art contrasts, Art in Focus, 4/75. *Mem:* Boston Printmakers; Nat Watercolor Soc; Soc Am Graphic Artists; Nat Acad; and others. *Media:* Watercolor, Printmaking. *Publ:* Interpolated Voids, 71; Contribr, Folio '76. *Dealer:* art4business Philadelphia PA. *Mailing Add:* 120 E Cliveden St Philadelphia PA 19119

LATOUR, IRA HINSDALE, JR
PHOTOGRAPHER, HISTORIAN
b New York, NY, Nov 28, 1919. *Study:* San Francisco Art Inst, studied with Ansel Adams, Edward Weston & Minor White, 38-39, 45-46, 48 & 49; Univ Calif, Berkeley, BA, 67; Calif State Univ, Chico, MFA, 75. *Work:* Mus Mod Art, NY; Mus Mod Art, San Francisco; Oakland Mus, Calif; Smithsonian Nat Mus, Washington; Monterey Peninsula Mus Art, Calif. *Comn:* Mexico (mural) Mexican Pavillion, Golden Gale Int Expo: Nat Railways of Mexico, San Francisco, 39-40. *Exhib:* Monterey Photog Tradition: Monterey Peninsula Mus Art, Calif, 86, 87 & 88; Centennial Exhibi, Anthropology Mus, Calif State Univ, Chico, 87; The Weston Yrs: Edward Weston Centennial Exhib, Mus Mod Art, Mexico City, 88; Fifth Int Photog Art, Nat Mus, Beijing, China, 89; Faces & Figures of the 20th Century, House of Parliament, Prague, 2001; Josef Sudek Gallery, Prague, 2001; solo exhibs, Monterey Peninsula Mus Art, Calif 89, Fifty Yrs of Photog, Magale Gallery & Meadows Mus, Shreveport, La, 90. *Pos:* Dir photog, Hq US Army, Europe, 52-53; dir media film, Int Media Co GMBH, Frankfurt, Ger & NY, 59-66. *Teaching:* Asst prof photogr, San Francisco State Col, 55-59; prof art hist, Calif State Univ, Chico, 68-93. *Awards:* Motion Picture Excellence Award, San Francisco Int Film Festival, 65; Blue Ribbon Award, Am Film Festival, New York, 65; Bronze Medal, Int Film & TV Festival New York, 83; Artist of the Year, San Francisco Elder Arts, 2003. *Res:* History of 20th century California photography. *Publ:* Auth, Westcoast photography: Does it really exist?, Photography, London, 57; Considerations: Jean Despojols, Artist in Indochina, Univ J, 84; coauth, The Monterey Photographic Tradition: The Weston Years, Monterey Peninsula Mus, 86; Silver Shadows: A Directory & History (Early Photography), Chico Mus, 93. *Dealer:* Carl Mautz 15472 Shannon Way Nevada City CA 95926. *Mailing Add:* 487 Pasco Companeros Chico CA 95928

LATTANZIO, FRANCES
PHOTOGRAPHER, EDUCATOR
b Detroit, Mich, Oct 2, 49. *Study:* Univ Mich, BFA, 71, MFA, 73. *Work:* Bank of Ind & Vincennes Univ, Ind; Madison Plaza Corp & Hyatt Int Corp, Chicago; Ind State Univ, Terre Haute. *Exhib:* One-person exhib, Quincy Col, Ill, 86; Midwest Photograph Invitational VI, Univ Wis, Green Bay, 90; Creative Images, Indianapolis Art League, 88; The Known/The Unknown, Briscoe Gallery, Miss State Univ, 88; Hand-Manipulated Photog, Buckham Fine Arts Proj, Flint, Mich, 89. *Teaching:* Assoc prof photog, Ind State Univ, Terre Haute, 75-; adj asst prof photog, St Mary of the Woods Col, Ind, 80. *Awards:* Engraph Award, Engraph Inc, 81. *Bibliog:* Cheryl Bopp (auth), article, Arts Insight, 3/80. *Mem:* Col Art Asn; Soc Photog Educ; Friends of Photog; Arts Illiana. *Media:* Silver Prints; Hand-colored. *Publ:* Illusr, Figurative Contexts, Turman Gallery, 83. *Mailing Add:* 1500 S Sixth St Terre Haute IN 47802-1638

LAU, REX
PAINTER, PRINTMAKER
b Trenton, NJ, Feb 26, 47. *Study:* Sch Visual Arts. *Work:* Met Mus Art, NY; Solomon R Guggenheim Mus, NY; Albright-Knox Art Gallery, Buffalo, NY; Yale Univ Art Gallery, New Haven; Libr Congress, Washington. *Comn:* large panel painting, IBM Corp, Los Angeles, 85; large panel painting, Coca-Cola USA, Atlanta, 88. *Exhib:* Ten

Narrative Paintings, Met Mus Art, NY, 83; Nueva Pintura Narrative, Museo Rufino Tamayo, Mexico City, 84; New Horizons in Am Art, Solomon R Guggenheim Mus, NY, 85; The Barry Lowen Collection, Mus Contemp Art, Los Angeles, 86; Selections from the Exxon Series, Solomon R Guggenheim Mus, NY, 87; A New Generation, the 1980s, Met Mus Art, NY, 88. *Awards:* Pollock-Krasner fel, 95. *Bibliog:* Stephen Westfall (auth), Rex Lau, Ruth Siegel Gallery, 85; Gerrit Henry (auth), Rex Lau, Art in America, 87; Donald Kuspit (auth), Rex Lau, Galerie Objecta, Munich, 92. *Media:* Oil. *Dealer:* Kouros Gallery 23 East 73rd St New York NY 10021. *Mailing Add:* PO Box 697 Montauk NY 11954

LAUB, STEPHEN
SCULPTURE
b Oakland, Calif, July, 10, 45. *Study:* Univ Calif, Berkely, BA, 69, MA, 70. *Work:* Mus Mod Art & Donnelle Media Ctr, New York Pub Libr, NY; GOT A Gruppen AB (consortium), Stockholm, Sweden; Kunsthaus, Zurich, Switz; Fine Arts Mus, Houston, Tex. *Exhib:* Extended Photog, Fifth Biennale, Vienna Mus, Austria, 81; Venice Biennale 1984, Venice Exhib Hall, Italy, 84; Spatial Relationships, Mus Mod Art, NY, 85; Alles und noch viel mehr, Kunstmuseum, Bern, Switz, 85; Images of Am Pop Cult, Laforet Mus, Tokyo, 89; On the Edge: Photog & Sculpture, Cleveland Ctr Contemp Art, Ohio, 90; Ealan Wingate Gallery, NY, 91; Power: Its Icons, Myths, Indianapolis Mus Art, Ind, 91; Stephen Wirtz Gallery, 95; Invitational Exhib, Guild Hall, East Hampton, NY, 2005. *Teaching:* Assoc prof sculpture, Rutgers Univ, NJ, 87-. *Awards:* Fulbright Fel, Italy, 71-72; Artist's Fel, Nat Endowment Arts, 78-79; Artist's Fel, NY Found Arts, 89-90. *Bibliog:* Roberta Smith (auth), Stephen Laub, NY Times, 3/25/88; Charles Hagen (auth), Stephen Laub at Koury Wingate, Artforum, summer 88; Janet Koplos (auth), Stephen Laub, sculpture, 9/10/91. *Media:* Wood. *Mailing Add:* 735 E 9th St #4RW New York NY 10009

LAUB-NOVAK, KAREN
SCULPTOR, PAINTER, PRINTMAKER, WRITER
b Minneapolis, Minn, Aug 25, 37. *Study:* Carleton Col, Northfield, Minn, BA; State Univ Iowa, with Mauricio Lasansky, MFA; Sch Vision, Salzburg, Austria, with Oskar Kokoschka. *Work:* Carleton Col; Yale Univ; St Vincent's Archabbey; Continental Bank, Chicago; Pac Sch Relig; and others. *Comn:* 12-ft bronze statue of Norman Borlaug, 1971 Nobel Peace Prize Winner, Cresco, Iowa; bronze statuettes for Ann Sci Awards, Iowa Bio-Technol Asn, 89; bronze crucifix, Paulist Church, Grand Rapids, Mich, 89; bronze tributes for Empower Am, 95; bronze crucifix, The Vatican, 95; bronze, glass The Threshold Award, The Becket Fund, 98-2003; bronze sculpture, Manhattan Inst; bronze sculpture pres Import Export Bank of US. *Exhib:* One-woman shows, Rochester Art Ctr, Minn, 70, Rockefeller Found, 74, Univ Tenn, 74, Pac Sch Relig, 74 & Yale Univ, 75, Des Moines Art Ctr; William Sawyer Gallery, San Francisco; Los Robles Gallery, Palo Alto, Calif; Fuller Mus, Brockton, Mass, 96; Foxhall Gallery, Washington, 99-2000; and many others. *Pos:* Freelance illusr, Books, Mag & Newspapers, 80-2000; ed adv, Momentum Mag; freelance writer, various publ, 98. *Teaching:* Instr drawing, Carleton Col, 61-62; lectr, Georgetown Univ, Stanford Univ, Syracuse Univ, Mt Vernon Coll & Univ Calif, Riverside. *Awards:* Kokoschka Award, Salzburg, Austria. *Bibliog:* L P Ruotolo (auth), A new apocalypse, Motive Mag, 66. *Mem:* Int Sculpture Soc. *Media:* Oil, Lithography, Bronze & Glass Sculpture. *Collection:* Yale University, Carleton Collect, St Vincents Arch Abbey & Stonehill College. *Publ:* Illusr, Skunk named Zorrie (children's bk), 72; Art Creativity & The Sacred (bk) Essay; The Art of Deception (article); various other articles and reviews thru 2002. *Dealer:* Foxhall Gallery 3301 New Mexico Ave NW Washington DC 20016. *Mailing Add:* 3211 Northampton St NW Washington DC 20015

LAUCK, ANTHONY JOSEPH
SCULPTOR, EDUCATOR
b Indianapolis, Ind, Dec 30, 08. *Study:* John Herron Art Sch, Indianapolis, dipl prof grade in sculpture; Corcoran Sch Art, Washington, DC, cert advan study in sculpture & painting; Art Students' League, NY, also with Oronzio Maldarelli, Ivan Mestrovic, Carl Milles, Hugo Robus & Heinz Warneke. *Work:* Pa Acad Fine Arts, Philadelphia; Corcoran Gallery Art, Washington, DC; Butler Inst Am Arts, Youngstown, Ohio; Indianapolis Mus Art; Gary Art Ctr, Ind; Grand Rapids Mus, Mich. *Comn:* Set of facet windows, Congregation of Holy Cross, Ind Prov, Moreau Sem Chapel, Univ Notre Dame, 53; limestone image of Our Lady of the Univ, Univ Notre Dame, 63; 12 stained glass windows, Ursuline Motherhouse, Chatham, Ont, Can, 64; Basswood Sculpture Triptych, St Joseph Hosp, Mishawaka, Ind. *Exhib:* Fairmount Park Art Asn Int Exhib, Philadelphia, 48; Nat Exhib Art, Pa Acad Fine Arts, 49 & 53; Ind Artists' Exhib, Indianapolis Mus Art, 50, 51, 54 & 56; Audubon Artists, Nat Acad Arts, NY, 52-75; Mus Midwestern Am Art, Elkhart, Ind; Night Prayer, Terracotta, John Blank Ctr Arts, Mich City, Ind, 94. *Collection Arranged:* The Work of John B Flannagan, Art Gallery, Univ Notre Dame, 61, The German Expressionists, 70 & The Graphic Work of Georges Rouault (with introd), 72. *Pos:* Conf planning comt, Mid-Am Col Art Asn, 67-72; comt acquisitions, Snite Mus Art, Notre Dame Univ. *Teaching:* Chmn art dept, Univ Notre Dame, 50-73; dir, Art Gallery, Univ Notre Dame, 54-74. *Awards:* Monk at Prayer (limestone), Pa Acad Art, 53; The Wife of Lot (terra cotta), Indianapolis Mus Art, 54; Whirlpool Nat Sculpture Competition, Krasl Art Ctr, St Joseph, Mich, 86-. *Bibliog:* Dean A Porter (auth), Anthony Lauck: Sculptor, 70 & Edward Fischer (auth), The many facets of Anthony Lauck, 73, Univ Notre Dame Art Gallery Publ. *Media:* Wood, Stone

LAUDER, EVEYLN H
COLLECTOR
b Vienna, 40. *Study:* Hunter Col, BA. *Hon Degrees:* Muhlenberg Col, Hon degree, 96. *Pos:* educ dir, Estée Lauder Cos, New York City, 59, vpres, sr corp vpres, 89-. *Awards:* Spirit Achievement Award, Albert Einstein Col Med, 1991; named one of 75 Most Influential Bus Women, Crain's Newspaper, 96; Mary Waterman Award, Breast Cancer Alliance, 1998; Humanitarian Award, Coun Fashion Designers Am, 2001; Award for Excellence in Philanthropy, Sloan-Kettering, 2001; Top 200 Collectors, ARTnews Mag, 2004, 2006. *Mem:* founder of The Breast Cancer Res Found, the largest nat orgn dedicated solely to breast cancer res; implementing breast cancer awareness prog from Pink Ribbon campaigns to illuminating world landmarks in a pink glow for Breast Cancer Awareness Month. *Collection:* Modern Art, especially Cubism. *Publ:* Photographer: (book) The Seasons Observed, 94, An Eye For Beauty, 2002. *Mailing Add:* Estee Lauder Cos 767 5th Ave New York NY 10153-0023

LAUDER, JO CAROLE
COLLECTOR
Mem: The Ronald S Lauder Found (bd dir, currently); Int Coun Mus of Modern Art (pres, currently); Ind Cur Int, Mt Sinai MedCtr (bd trustees, currently); Friends of Art & Preservation in Embasies (chmn, bd dir, currently). *Collection:* Old Masters; 19th & 20th Century Art, especially German. *Mailing Add:* Mus Modern Art 11 W 53rd St New York NY 10019

LAUDER, LEONARD ALAN
ADMINISTRATOR, COLLECTOR
b New York, NY, Mar 19, 33. *Study:* Wharton Sch, Univ Pa, BS, 54. *Pos:* chmn, pres, Whitney Mus Am Art, formerly; With, Estée Lauder, Inc, 58-, exec vpres, 62-75, pres, 72-82, pres, chief exec off, 82-; vchmn bd, CFTA, 76-79; trustee, Aspen Inst for Humanistic Studies, 78; bd govs, Joseph H Lauder Inst Mgt and Int Studies, 83; bd dir, Adv Comn on Trade Negotiations, 83-87. *Awards:* Philanthropist of Yr, Greater NY Chap of Nat Soc of Fund Raising Execs, 93; Am Art award, Whitney Mus of Am Art, 96; Am Spirit award, Nat Retail Fedn, 98; Ellis Island Medal of Honor, 2000; Named one of Top 200 Collectors, ARTnews mag, 2004. *Collection:* Modern art including Picasso, Braque, Leger and Gris. *Mailing Add:* Estee Lauder Cosmetics Inc 767 5th Ave New York NY 10153

LAUDER, RONALD STEPHEN
COLLECTOR, PATRON
b New York, NY, Feb 26, 44. *Study:* Univ Paris, degree (in French Literature) 64, BS (in int business), 65; Univ Brussels, cert, 66. *Pos:* Chmn, Estee Lauder Int Inc, currently; chmn, Clinique Lab Inc, currently; chmn bd, Mus of Modern Art, currently; vis comt for Medieval Art, Metropolitan Mus Art, currently; trustee, Mt Sinai Med Ctr, 81-; trustee, Mus Modern Art, New York, 75-, chmn, 95-; pres, Neue Galerie, New York City, 2001-. *Awards:* Ronald S Lauder Drawing Galleries, Mus of Modern Art; Ronald S Lauder Drawing Gallery, Mus Modern Art, named in his hon, 84; Great Cross of Order of Aeronautical Merit, Spain, 85; decorated Great Cross of the Order of Aeronautical Merit with White Ribbon, Spain, 85; Ordre de Merit, France, 85; Recipient Ordre De Merit, France, 85, Distinguished Pub Serv medal award Dept Defense, 86; Medal for Distinguished Pub Serv, Dept Defense, 86; Named One of the World's Richest People, Forbes Mag, 99-2002; Named one of the Top 200 Collectors, ARTnews magazine, 2004, 2006. *Collection:* Old Masters, 19th and 20th Century art, especially German. *Publ:* Auth, Fighting Violent Crime in America, 85. *Mailing Add:* Lauder Investments Inc Ste 4200 767 Fifth Ave New York NY 10153-0023

LAUF, CORNELIA
CURATOR, ART HISTORIAN
b May 26, 61. *Study:* Oberlin Col, BA, 83; Columbia Univ, MA, 85; PhD, 92. *Collection Arranged:* Natura Naturata (An Argument for Still Life), Josh Baer Gallery, New York, 89; Flux Attitudes (auth, catalog), New Mus Contemp Art & Hallwalls, 92; The Wealth of Nations (auth, catalog), Warsaw, 92. *Pos:* Independent cur, 87-. *Teaching:* New Sch for Social Res, 95. *Awards:* Wolfgang Stechow Mem Prize, Oberlin Col, 81- 82, Oberlin Col Alumni Fel, 85-86; University Fel, 83-84, President's Fel, 84-86, Columbia Univ Travel Grant, 86, Samuel H Kress Fel, 89-90, Columbia Univ. *Publ:* Auth, Joseph Beuys, Seven Days (rev), 11/88; Franz Erhard Walther, Arts, 2/89; Talents and Gewgaws, Artscribe, 9-10/89; On reading some drawings of Reuys, Arts, 3/90; Collection Handbook, Guggenheim Mus, 92; Andre Cadere, Mus Mod Art, Paris & PSI, New York, 92. *Mailing Add:* 591 Broadway New York NY 10012

LAUFER, SUSAN
PAINTER
b Tuckahoe, NY, Dec 8, 50. *Study:* Art Students League, NY, 70; Boston Univ, Mass, BFA, 72; NY Univ, MA, 76. *Work:* Albright Knox Art Gallery; Brooklyn Mus; Denver Mus Art; Metrop Mus Art, New Mus, Am Express Bldg, Chemical Bank, E F Hutton, Shearson Leaman Bros, Swiss Bank Co, NY; Screen Actors Guild, Los Angeles; Harris Bank, IBM, Fed Reserve Bank, Chicago; and others. *Exhib:* Solo shows, Univ Conn, 90, Germans van Eck Gallery, NY, 90 & 91, Ctr Contemp Art, Chicago, 91 & 92, Betsy Sr Fine Arts, NY, 92, Camino Real Gallery, Boca Raton, Fla, 94; Chicago Mus Contemp Art, Ill, 91; Denver Art Mus, Colo, 92; Cleveland Ctr Contemp Art, Ohio, 92; Camino Real Gallery, Boca Raton, Fla, 94-96; Pace Eds, NY, 94; Michael Lord Gallery, Milwaukee, Wis, 1994-2000; Calif Mus of Art, Santa Rosa, 97; Greenville Co Mus Art, SC, 98; NY Studio Sch, 2000; and others. *Teaching:* Vis lectr, var univ, mus & col. *Awards:* Nat Endowment Arts, 84 & 92; Ariana Found, Endowment, NY, 85; Ferkauf Found, NY, 85. *Bibliog:* Gregory Galligan (auth), Susan Laufer (exhib catalog), Germans van Eck Gallery, NY, 90; Allan Artner (auth), Susan Laufer, The Chicago Tribune, 1/25/91; Phyllis Braff (auth), In The Abstract, Susan Laufer, The NY Times, 7/2/95; and others. *Publ:* Illustr, The Ruin Revived, Branden Press, Boston, Mass, 86; contribr, The Richard Maslow Collection (exhib catalog), 87; auth, Lines of Vision (exhib catalog), 89; illusr, Stone Heart (cover), No 26, fall 89 & auth, Literature and the Visual Arts, No 27, fall 89, Pequod, Nat Poetry Found, NY; Lifeline Series (cover), Storyline Press, 93. *Mailing Add:* 53 Crosby St New York NY 10012

LAUGHLIN, MORTIMER
PAINTER
b San Francisco, Calif, July 24, 18. *Study:* Hollywood Art Ctr, Calif, 41; Abbott Art Sch, Washington, DC, 45; Art Students League, New York, 46. *Exhib:* Mus Mod Art, NY; Stamford Mus, Conn; San Francisco Mus Art, Calif; Newport Art Asn, RI; Silvermine Art Asn, Conn; Albany Inst Hist Art, NY; Art USA, NY; one-man shows, Bartholet Gallery, 80-85, 88 & 90 & Gelabert Gallery, 91-2006. *Bibliog:* Les Krantz (ed & publ), Am Artists: An Illustrated Survey of Leading Contemp Am, 85; Les Krantz (auth), The NY Art Rev, 88. *Mem:* Metrop Mus Art. *Media:* Mixed Media. *Dealer:* Gelabert Gallery 255 West 86th St New York NY 10024. *Mailing Add:* Rd 1 Box 8 Susquehanna PA 18847

LAUHAKAIKUL, THANA
INSTRUCTOR, SCULPTOR
b Thailand, Jan 3, 41. *Study:* Silpakorn Univ, Bangkog, BFA (sculpture), 68; Mass Col Art, MS (art edn), 74. *Work:* Nat Mus, Bangkok. *Comn:* mixed media paintings, Sofitel Raja Orchid Hotel, Korn-Kaen, Thailand, 96; monument Great King Nareasuan, Thai Govt, Ayuthaya, Thailand, 2000. *Exhib:* one-man shows, Site Specific, Japan Island, Rayong, Thailand, 92, Texas Artist Series III, Univ Texas, Arlington, 93, 933 Window Works, Alexandria Mus Art, La, 93, Installation, Diverse Works Artspace, Houston, 94, Installation, Silom Artspace, Bangkok, 94; The Celebration of HM The King's 6th Birthday Ann, Nat Mus, Bangkok, 99-2000. *Teaching:* prof sculpture, Univ Tex, Austin, 79-

LAURENCE, GEOFFREY F
PAINTER
b Patterson, NJ, 49. *Study:* Byam Shaw, with Bridget Riley & Bill Jacklin, LCAD, 68; St Martins, with Frederic Gore & John Hoyland, BA, 71; NY Acad, with Eric Fischl & Vincent Desidirio, MFA(cum laude), 95. *Work:* London Borough of Camden, London, Eng; Mus Fine Art, Santa Fe, NMex. *Exhib:* Solo shows include Iswaswillbe, Meisel Arts Ctr, Denver, Colo, 2005, The Reality of Things: New Paintings and Drawings, LewAllen Contemp, N Mex, 2006; group shows include Tolly Cobbold Touring Show, Eng, 78; 5th Int Kunstaustellung, Freiburg, Ger, 92; Dialogues with Visual Tradition, NY Acad, 98; The Am Scene, Taos Mus, 99 & 2000; Artists on the Edge, Yeshiva Univ Mus, NY, 2002; Representing Representation VI, Arnot Mus, Elmira, NY, 2003; 15, Las Vegas Mus, Nev, 2005. *Teaching:* instr anat/painting, Acad Realist Art, Seattle, 1999; instr fine art, Santa Fe, 2000; instr anatomy, Seatte Acad Art, 2000-2005; instr fine art, Armory Arts Center, West Palm Beach, Fla, 2003; instr, anatomy drawing, Andreeva Portrait Acad, 2005. *Awards:* Walter Erlebacher Award, 95; J Epstein Travel Award, 95. *Bibliog:* Malin Wilson (auth), Albuquerque J, 97; Wesley Pulka (auth), Albuquerque J, 97; Lynn Cline (auth), New Mexican, 98; Ori Z Soltes (auth), Fixing the World, Univ Press New Eng. *Media:* Oil. *Dealer:* Lewallen Contemp 129 West Palace Ave Santa Fe NM 87501. *Mailing Add:* 1550 B Pacheco # 8 Santa Fe NM 87505

LAURIDSEN, HANNE
PAINTER, SCULPTOR
b Esbjerg, Denmark; US citizen. *Study:* Univ Calif, Berkeley, BA(art & art hist), 80; Univ Calif, San Diego, MFA, 82. *Work:* Mus Mod Art, NY; Paterson Mus, NJ; Buhl Collection, New York City. *Exhib:* Arrivals, Guild Hall Mus, E Hampton, NY, 83 & Mem Exhib, 98-2006; Who is the Monster, Galleri Jansen & Norgaard, Copenhagen, Denmark & Galerie Gerry Salant, Paris, France, 84; Parrish Art Mus Juried Exhib, Southampton, NY, 94; Mixed Media Installation, Gallery Bai, Barcelona, 96; Black & White with Picasso, Matisse, Dubuffet, Goldstrom Gallery, NY, 98; Good Against Evil Installation, Goldstrom Gallery, 99; Exhibs in Denmark, 2005-2006. *Bibliog:* Hannes Universe, Channel 2TV, Denmark, 90; Marion Wolberg Weiss (auth), Artist of the Hamptons, Dans Paper, Bridge Hampton, NY, 3/14/97; The Seven Stations of OJ, Fox TV, Channel 5 News, 97. *Mem:* Guild Hall Mus, East Hampton, NY; Parrish Art Mus, Southampton, NY. *Media:* Paintings, Sculpture, Photography. *Publ:* Auth, Shadows, High Performance, Los Angeles, spring-summer, 82. *Dealer:* H7L Studio 517 E 11 St New York NY 10000. *Mailing Add:* 517 E 11th St No 2 New York NY 10009

LAUTTENBACH, CAROL L
PAINTER
b New Haven, Conn, Nov 26, 34. *Study:* Washington Sch Art, (honors in oils & watercolors), 67. *Hon Degrees:* Washington Sch Art, Certificate Award, 1967. *Work:* Mus Des Duncan, Paris. *Comn:* Soundview Special Care Ctr, 76; Schiavone Corp, 80, Yale-New Haven Hosp, 82, New Haven Conn; Vet Mem Med Ctr, Meride, Conn, 84; Unholtz Corp, Wallingford, Conn, 84. *Exhib:* Conn Acad Fine Arts, Wadsworth Athenium, Hartford, Conn, 76; Int Art Competition, Palm Beach Art Galleries, New Orleans, La & Palm Beach Fla, 83; Grand Salon des Surindependants, Mus des Duncan, Paris; Nat Soc Painters in Casein & Acrylic, Am Acad & Inst of Arts & Letters, NY; Conn Acad Fine Arts, New Britain Mus Am Art, Conn, 93; New Haven Paint & Clay Club, John Slade Ely House, Conn, 94. *Collection Arranged:* Many. *Pos:* Artist. *Awards:* Beazley Realtors Award, Mt Carmel Art Asn, Hamden, 2000; Harvey Fuller Award, Arts & Crafts Asn Meriden, Inc, 2001; Mayor Carl Amento Award, Mt Carmel Art Asn, Hamden, 2002; Utrech Art Supplies Award - Hamden Art League, 2004; Dusa Chiropractic Center Award - Hamden Art League, 2005; Best Theme Award - Arts & Crafts Assn Meriden, 2005. *Bibliog:* Drawing Anthology International, Regina Publ, 74. *Mem:* Conn Acad Fine Arts, Hartford; Shoreline Alliance for Arts, Guilford, Conn; Provincetown Art Asn, Mass; Int Soc Artists, Marion, Ohio; life mem Wallingford Hist Soc. *Media:* Acrylic. *Specialty:* Specializes in Fine Arts. *Publ:* In need of sunshine?, Guilford Courier, 3/10/2005. *Dealer:* Carriage House Gallery Ltd 23 Bostn St Guilford CT 06437; Frame Shop Gallery 147 Post Rd E Westport CT 06880; Mary Lous Fischer Gallery, LTD, 23 Boston St, Guilford, CT. *Mailing Add:* 39 Ridgewood Rd Wallingford CT 06492

LAVADOUR, JAMES
PAINTER
b Adams, Ore, 49. *Work:* Seattle Art Mus, Wash; Portland Art Mus, Ore; The Heard Mus, Phoenix, Ariz; Wash State Arts Comn, Olympia; Seattle Arts Comn, Wash. *Comn:* Art in Public Places, Wash State Arts Comn, Olympia, 83, 85 & 87; NW Major Works Project, 89, Seattle Arts Comn, Wash. *Exhib:* Northwest Now, Tacoma Art Mus, Wash, 86; Crossed Cultures: 5 Contemp Native Northwest Artists, Seattle Art Mus, Wash, 89; Northwest Viewpoints: James Lavadour, Portland Art Mus, Ore, 90; Shared Visions: Native Am Sculptors and painters in the 20th Century, The Heard Mus, Phoenix, Ariz, 91; Land, Spirit, Power: First Nations at the National Gallery of Canada, Nat Gallery Can, Ottawa, Ont, 92. *Awards:* Ore Arts Fel, Ore Arts Comn, 86; Nat Printmaking Fel, Rutgers Univ, 90; Betty Bowen Mem Recognition Award, Seattle Art Mus, 91. *Bibliog:* Linda E Evans (auth), The Undiminished Landscape, Security Pacific Gallery, San Francisco, Calif, 90; Iona Chelette (auth), Northwest Southwest: Painted Fictions, Palm Springs Desert Mus, 90; Margaret Archuleta (auth), Shared Visions, The Heard Mus, 91. *Media:* Oil on Linen. *Mailing Add:* PO Box 1191 Pendleton OR 97801

LAVERDIERE, BRUNO E
SCULPTOR
b Waterville, Maine, May 13, 37. *Work:* Patrick Lannan Found; Everson Mus, Syracuse, NY; Columbus Mus, Ohio; Am Craft Mus, NY. *Exhib:* Mus Contemp Crafts, 77; Everson Mus, Syracuse, NY, 77; Fine Arts Gallery, State Univ NY-Cortland, 91; Franklin Parrasch Gallery, NY, 91. *Teaching:* Adj instr, Adirondack Community Col, 77-. *Awards:* Grants, Nat Endowment Arts, 76 & 90; NY Found Fel, 87. *Mailing Add:* 497 A Stony Creek Rd Hadley NY 12835

LAVIN, IRVING
HISTORIAN
b St Louis, Mo, Dec 14, 27. *Study:* Cambridge Univ, Eng, 48-49; Washington Univ, BA, 49; NY Univ, MA, 52; Harvard Univ, MA, 52, PhD(Sheldon Fel), 55. *Teaching:* Lectr hist art, Vassar Col, 59-62; from assoc prof to prof, NY Univ, 63-73; prof, Sch Hist Studies, Inst for Adv Study, 73-. *Awards:* Fulbright Fel, 61-63; Am Coun Learned Soc Fel, 65-66; Guggenheim Found Grant, 68-69. *Mem:* Fel Am Acad Arts & Sci; Corpus Ancient Mosaics Tunisia (mem steering comt, 69-); Nat Comt for the Hist of Art; Comite int d'histoire de l'art. *Res:* Art of late antiquity; Renaissance and Baroque sculpture. *Publ:* Auth, Bernini and the Crossing of Saint Peter's, Arts, Archaeol Inst Am & Col Art Asn Am, 68; Five new youthful sculptures by Gianlorenzo Bernini and a revised chronology of his early works, 68, Bernini's death, 72 & Divine inspiration in Caravaggio's two St Matthews, 74, Art Bull; Bernini and the Unity of the Visual Arts, Oxford Univ Press, 80; Drawings by Gianlorenzo Bernini from the Museum der Bildenden Kunste, Princeton Univ Press, 81. *Mailing Add:* 56 Maxwell Ln Princeton NJ 08540

LAVIN, MARILYN ARONBERG
EDUCATOR, HISTORIAN
b St Louis, Mo, Oct 27, 25. *Study:* Washington Univ, BA, 47, MA, 49; Univ Rome, cert, 52; Inst Fine Arts, NY Univ, PhD, 73. *Teaching:* Prof hist art, Princeton Univ, 75-; vis prof, Yale Univ, 78 & Univ Md, 79-80. *Awards:* Charles Rufus Morey Book Award, Col Art Asn, 77. *Mem:* Col Art Asn Am (mem bd dir, 79-83); Renaissance Soc. *Res:* Italian Renaissance painting with special interest in work of Piero della Francesco and history of fresco painting. *Publ:* Auth, The Corpus Domini Altarpiece of Urbino, Art Bull, 67; Piero Della Francesca: The Flagellation, Penguin, Viking, 72; 17th Century Barberini Documents & Inventories of Art, NY Univ Press, 75; Piero della Francesca's Baptism of Christ, Yale Univ Press, 81; The Eye of the Tiger: Department of Art & Architecture, Princeton Univ Press, 83. *Mailing Add:* 56 Maxwell Ln Princeton NJ 08540

LAVINE, STEVEN DAVID
EDUCATOR, WRITER, ADMINISTRATOR
b Sparta, Wis, June 7, 47. *Study:* Stanford Univ, BA, 69; Harvard Univ, MA, 70, PhD, 76. *Pos:* Asst dir arts & humanities, Rockefeller Found, 83-86, assoc dir, 86-88; selection panelist Input TV Screening Conf, Montreal, Can, and Granada, Spain, 1985-86; Consultant Wexner Found, Columbus, Ohio, 1986-87; bd dir, KCRW-FM Nat Pub Radio, 89-, Endowments Inc, 94- & KCET Pub Broadcasting, 98-2004; visi comt, J Paul Getty Mus, 1990-1997; consultant in field; co-dir. Arts and Govt Prog, The Am Assembly, 1991; co-chair, Arts Coalition for Acad Progress, Los Angeles Unified Sch Dist, 97; bd trustees, Cotsen Family Found, 2000-; mem archit, selection jury Los Angeles Cathedral, 1996, Architect LA, 1998-; adv. committee, The Asia Soc, Southern Calif Ctr, 1998-. *Teaching:* Asst prof Eng, Univ Mich, Ann Arbor, 74-81; fac chmn, Salzburg Seminar on Mus, 1989. *Awards:* Ford Grad Prize Fel, Harvard Univ, 69-74, Charles B Dexter Traveling Fel, 72; Horace H Rackham Resident Fel; Univ Michigan Faculty Recognition Award, 80; Children's Freedom Award, Children's Mus Los Angeles, 2001. *Mem:* Los Angeles Philharmonic (bd dir, 94-2004); J Paul Getty Mus (vis comt, 90-97). *Publ:* Co-ed, The Hopwood Anthology: Five Decades of Am Poetry, Ann Arbor Univ Press, 81; The Writer's Craft, Mich Quart Rev 21, 82; International Jewish Writing: From the Bellagio Conference, Prooftexts 4, 84; The Politics of Public Culture, 92, Smithsonian Inst Press. *Mailing Add:* Calif Inst Arts Off Pres 24700 McBean Pkwy Santa Clarita CA 91355-2397

LAW, JAN
PAINTER
b Newton, Mass, May 24, 46. *Study:* Mus Fine Arts, Boston, Mass, 59; Paris Am Acad, 79; Wellesley Col, 81; Pine Manor Col, BA, 82. *Work:* Paris Am Acad Art Gallery, Paris, France; Goddard Hosp, Brockton, Mass; Childrens Hosp, Boston, Mass; Bay State Med Ctr, Springfield, Mass. *Exhib:* Solo exhib, Jan Law Watercolors,

Decorators Showhouse at Plympton Ct, Boston Jr League, Sudbury, Mass, 90, Jan Law Painting & Prints, Swain Gallery, Dover, Mass, 2000; Art Expo, Jacob Javits Convention Ctr, NY, 93, 98, 99 & 2000; Art Expo Europe Int Convention Ctr, Eng, 94; group exhib, So this is Art, Wellesley, Mass, 95, Small Paintings, Medfield, Mass, 98, Art Show with Edna Hibel, Wellesley, Mass, 2002; Calif Art Expo, Int Convention Ctr, Calif, 98. *Teaching:* instr, drawing & painting, Children's Art Studio, Wellesley, Mass, 93-94. *Bibliog:* Margaret Fitzwilliam (auth), Happenings Artists Exhib, Wellesley Townsmen, 83; Victoria Fraza (auth), So they call this Art, The Tab, 95; Eric Shacker (auth), Artis Mag, Will Steigerwald Publ, 6-7/2005. *Media:* Acrylic, Oil, Watercolor, Art Dealer. *Dealer:* Brent Theriault 63 Fitts Rd Ashford CT 06278; Robert Belcher 804 Central Ave Hot Springs AR 71901. *Mailing Add:* 1 Lantern Ln Natick MA 01760-5640

LAWALL, DAVID BARNARD
HISTORIAN, MUSEUM DIRECTOR
b Detroit, Mich, Aug 27, 35. *Study:* Oberlin Col, BA, 56; Princeton Univ, MFA, 59 & PhD, 66. *Collection Arranged:* A B Durand 1796-1886 (auth, catalog), Montclair Art Mus, 71; Small Paintings Toward a Renewal of Classicism, 74-79, Anton Refregier (auth, catalog), 77, Image of Post-Modern Man, 79 & Ernest Fiene/Leon Kroll, New Still Life & Landscape Painting, 87, New York Gallery Show, 88, Univ Va Art Mus. *Pos:* Cur, Univ Va Art Mus, 71-85, dir, 85-90. *Teaching:* Instr, Univ Mo, Columbia, 60-61; instr, Ohio State Univ, Columbus, 61-64, asst prof, 64-68; assoc prof, Univ Va, Charlottesville, 69-. *Awards:* Fel, Nat Endowment Humanities, 69. *Mem:* NY Acad Art (exec bd, 81-90); Am Asn Univ Profs. *Publ:* Auth, Asher Durand: Art and Art Theory, 77 & Asher Durand: Catalog of Paintings, Garland, 78; ed, John Barber, 92. *Mailing Add:* 108 Bollingwood Rd Charlottesville VA 22903-1706

LAWRENCE, ANNETTE
CONCEPTUAL ARTIST, EDUCATOR
b Rockville Center, NY, Jan 28, 65. *Study:* Hartford Art Sch, Univ Hartford, BFA, 86; Md Inst Col Art, MFA, 90. *Work:* Dallas Mus Art; Mus Fine Arts, Houston; Art Pace Ctr Contemp Art, San Antonio; Goldman Sachs & Co, NYC; Jack S Blanton Mus Art, Austin. *Exhib:* Gender: Fact or Fiction, Laguna Gloria Mus Art, Austin, Tex, 92; Texas Collection, Modern Postmodern, Mus Fine Arts, Houston, 96; Finders/Keepers, Contemp Art Mus, Houston, 97; Art on Paper, Weatherspoon Art Gallery, Univ NC, Greensboro, 97; 1997 Whitney Biennial, Whitney Mus Am Art, NY, 97; Transparent/Opaque, Univ Mich Mus Art, Ann Arbor, 2000; Concentrations:36, Dallas Mus Art, Dallas, 2000; Theory Glassell Sch Art, Mus Fine Arts, Houston; audio visual: Recent Drawings by Annette Lawrence, Sweeney Art Gallery, Riverside, Calif, 2003. *Pos:* Artist in residence, Community Artists Collective, Houston, Tex, 90-91 & Proj Bridge, Houston, Tex, 92-93. *Teaching:* Asst prof painting, Univ NTex, Denton, 96-, assoc prof, painting and drawing, 2002-. *Awards:* Cult Art Coun Houston Artist Award, 94; Awards to Artists, Kimbrough Fund, Dallas Mus Art, 94; Skowhegan Camille Cosby Award for African Am Artists, 96. *Bibliog:* Janet Kutner (auth), Annette Lawrence at Gerald Peters Gallery, Art News, 4/98; Valerie Laupe Olsen (auth), Annette Lawrence: Theory (monograph), 03. *Media:* Mixed Media. *Dealer:* Dunn and Brown Contemporary 5020 Tracy St Dallas Texas 75205; Betty Cuningham Gallery 541 W 25th St New York NY 10001. *Mailing Add:* PO Box 3093 Denton TX 76202

LAWRENCE, HOWARD RAY
DESIGNER, EDUCATOR
b San Francisco, Calif, Mar 21, 36. *Study:* Univ Calif, Berkeley, BA(Arch), 62, MA(sculpture), 64. *Exhib:* Cad Cam Sculpture, Ecole Polytechnic, Paris, France, 93 & 95; Silicon Gallery, Philadelphia, 95. *Pos:* Archit apprenticeship, US, 65-69. *Teaching:* Asst prof archit, San Francisco City Col, 69-70, Hampton Inst, Va, 70-71, Univ Kans, 71-72, Pa State Univ, 72-, Birmingham Polytech, Eng, 78 & St Martin's Sch Art, London, 81. *Awards:* Harry Lord Ford Sculpture Prize, Univ Calif, 64. *Mem:* Asn Col Sch Archit; Environ Design Asn. *Media:* Freehand Drawing, Sculpture. *Publ:* Design Interconnections, pending

LAWRENCE, JAMES A
PAINTER, PHOTOGRAPHER
b San Mateo, Calif, May 23, 1910. *Study:* Univ Calif, Davis, grad, 33; Art Ctr, Los Angeles, art & photog, with Barse Miller, Will Connell & Charles Kerlee, 35-37; Chouinard Art Inst, Los Angeles, with Phil Paradise & Ricco Lebrun, 38; Art Students League, 40; New York Sch Mod Photog; also with illusr Louis J Rogers, San Francisco, 34. *Work:* Ford Collection, Dearborn, Mich; Calif Hist Soc. *Comn:* Ford Times Publications 1948-1960, Inc, 60. *Exhib:* One-man shows, Reed Galleries, NY, 41, Gump Galleries, San Francisco, 43 & Univ Nev, 53; Golden Gate Int Exhib, San Francisco; Art Inst Chicago; Metrop Mus Art, NY; Los Angeles Co Mus Art; and others. *Pos:* Tech photogr, Pagano Inc, New York, 40-41; mem, Nev State Coun Arts, 67-71. *Teaching:* Guest instr watercolor, Stanford Univ, spring 48; also pvt students in watercolor at var periods. *Awards:* Cert Merit & Gold & Silver Medals, Golden Gate Int Exhib, 40-41; Am Artists Prof League, 42; Terry Art Inst Award; and others. *Mem:* Nat Watercolor Soc. *Media:* Watercolor. *Publ:* Contribr, Ford Times, Sunset Mag, US Camera & Carson Valley-Historical Sketches; photogr, Sunset Mag, Calif, 40-49; Calif Art Rev, 1st ed, 90. *Mailing Add:* Rock Creek Ranch 1198 Centerville Lane Gardnerville NV 89410

LAWRENCE, JAYE A
SCULPTOR, CRAFTSMAN
b Chicago, Ill, Jan 8, 39. *Study:* Univ Ariz, BFA, 60; Ariz State Univ, MFA, 75. *Work:* Ariz State Univ Collection, Tempe; Pac Lutheran Univ Collection, Tacoma, Washington; Yuma Fine Arts Asn Collection, Ariz; Won Kwang Univ, Korea. *Exhib:* Teapot Image, Faith Nightingale Gallery, San Diego, Calif, 89; Return of the Magnificent 11, Cova Gallery, San Diego, 90; Hand Made for the Table, Folktree Collections, Pasadena, Calif, 91; Int Artist Exhib 92, Gallery 2000, Seoul, Korea, 92; Artisan Showcase, Newport Harbor Art Mus, Newport Beach, Calif, 93 & 94; Inaugural, Arveda Gallery, La Jolla, Calif, 96; Allied Craftsman, Hyde Gallery Grossmont Col, El Cajon, Calif, 96; Spectrum Revisited, Next Door Gallery, San Diego, Calif, 96; Brooch the Subject, Next Door Gallery, San Diego, Calif, 96; Artists chairs, Folk Tree Collections, Pasadena, Calif, 96. *Teaching:* Instr leather art, Grossmont Col, El Cajon, Calif, 81. *Awards:* Best of Show, 3rd Ann Phoenix Jewish Community Ctr Show, 69; Purchase Award, 4th Ann SWestern, 69; 12th Ariz Ann Award, 69; First Award Region XX, Tex Fine Arts Asn, Lubbock, Tex, 82. *Bibliog:* Marilyn Hagberg (auth), Jaye & Les Lawrence, 10/73 & Erik Gronborg (auth), Jaye Lawrence, 8/74, Craft Horizons; Carolyn Russell (auth), Rope forms sculpture, Daily Times Advocate, 4/28/74. *Mem:* Am Crafts Coun; Allied Craftsmen San Diego (corresp secy); COVA; NCECA. *Media:* Rawhide, Hog Casing; Wood. *Dealer:* Arveda Gallery 5624 La Jolla Blvd La Jolla CA 92037. *Mailing Add:* 2097 Valley View Blvd El Cajon CA 92019

LAWRENCE, LES
CERAMIST, SCULPTOR
b Corpus Christi, Tex, Dec 17, 40. *Study:* Southwestern State Col, Okla, BA, 62; Tex Tech Univ; Ariz State Univ, MFA(ceramics), 70. *Work:* Whitty Mus, San Antonio; Phoenix Art Mus, Ariz; E B Crocker Art Gallery, Sacramento, Calif; Pac Lutheran Univ, Tacoma, Wash; Ariz State Univ Collection, Tempe; Sheraton Hotel, Los Angeles, Calif; Southern Conn State Univ. *Exhib:* Les Lawrence, Southplains Col, Tex, 82; Am Crafts Traditions, San Francisco Airport, Calif, 84; Ceramic Festival II, Univ Art Collections, Ariz State Univ, 85; The Cup Exhib, Salem Art Asn, Ore, 86; 200 Tea Pots, Springfield Art Asn, Ill, 87; Birthday Party, Kohler Art Ctr, Sheboygan, Wis, 88; Ceramic Ivitational, Sikes Gallery, Millersville Univ, Pa, 89; Visiting Artist, Monarch Tile Nat Exhib, San Angelo Tex Mus Art, Tex, 90; Ceramic Conjunction, Long Beach Mus Art, Calif, 77; Great Am Foot, Mus Contemp Crafts, NY, 78; Solo exhibs, Gallery 2000, Seoul, Korea, 92, San Diego Mus Art, Calif, 93 & Schneider Gallery, Chicago, 94; and others. *Teaching:* Instr ceramics-sculpture, Hardin-Simmons Univ, Abilene, Tex, 66-68; prof ceramics, Grossmont Col, El Cajon, Calif, 70-; vis artist, Northern Iowa Univ, Cedar Falls, 88. *Awards:* Tex Watercolor Soc 16th Ann First Purchase Award, San Antonio Art League, 67; First Purchase Award, Region 20 Tex Fine Arts Asn, 68; Calif Crafts IX Purchase for E B Crocker Art Gallery, 75; Distinguished Alumni, South Plains Col, Tex, 87. *Bibliog:* Les Lawrence, Ceramics Monthly, 4/74 & 4/93; Studio potter, San Diego Ceramics, 93; Susan Delainey (auth), Les Lawrence New Vision Ceramics, Ceramic Art & Perception, 93. *Mem:* Am Crafts Coun; Allied Craftsmen San Diego (secy, 74); Nat Coun Educ for Ceramic Arts. *Media:* Clay. *Dealer:* Lawrence Arts 2097 Valley View Blvd El Cajon CA 92019; Martha Schneider Gallery 230 W Superior St Chicago IL 60610. *Mailing Add:* 2097 Valley View Blvd El Cajon CA 92021

LAWRENCE, MATTHEW R
PRINTMAKER, PAINTER
b York, Eng, Mar 15, 65; US citizen. *Study:* Brighton Polytech, Eng, BFA, 88; Tyler Sch Art, Philadelphia, MFA, 96. *Exhib:* Dual Voices, Cazenovia Col, NY, 95; Monolithic Impressions, Franklin & Marshall, Lancaster, Pa, 95; Recent Woodcuts, Kansas City Artist Coalition, Mo, 95; Journey to the Ctr of Blob, Millersville Univ, Lancaster, Pa, 95; The Revenge of the Blob, Penn State Univ, 96. *Teaching:* Sr lectr printmaking, Univ of the Arts, Pa, 91-. *Awards:* Art Matters Inc Fel, 95; Nat Endowment Arts, Works on Paper, 95; Pa State grant, 96. *Bibliog:* Wendy McDaris (auth), Elvis & Marilyn 2X, Rizzoli Bks, 94; Susan Tallman (auth), The Contemporary Print, Thames & Hudson, 96. *Mem:* Col Art Asn; Print Ctr Philadelphia. *Media:* Woodcut

LAWRENCE, RODNEY STEVEN
PAINTER
b Flint, Mich, Feb 20, 51. *Study:* Flint Community Jr Col; Univ Mich, BFA(magna cum laude), 73. *Comn:* Painting, First Nat Park Bank, Livingston, Mont, 74; illus, Dept Interior, Washington, 82; Hamilton Collector Plates, 88 & 92. *Exhib:* CM Russell Mus, Great Falls, Mont, 76-79; Nat Wildlife Art Show, Kansas City, 80; Birds in Art Nat Tour, Leigh Yawkey Woodson Mus, Wausau, Wis, 83; Wildlife: The Artist's View, 90 & 93. *Teaching:* Beartooth Wildlife Workshop, Big Timber, Mont, 92 & 95; Cedar Bend Farm Artist's Workshop, 94; Wa-Wa-Sum Workshops, Grayling, Mich, 95-96. *Awards:* Mich Wildlife Artist of Yr, Mich United Conserv Clubs Art Contest, 81; Trout Stamp Design Winner, Trout-Salmon Stamp Contest, 81, 87, 92 & 95 & Duck Stamp Winner, Waterfowl Stamp Contest, 83, 90 & 95, Mich Dept Nat Resources. *Bibliog:* Subject of many TV interviews on work and awards won, 81-86; Am interview with wildlife artist Rod Lawrence, Small-Towner, 83; Go mid-west young man, Midwest Art, 84; Who's Who mag, 11/88; Traverse Mag, 11/89. *Mem:* Outdoor Writers Asn Am; Mich Outdoor Writers Asn. *Media:* Acrylic on Panel, Oil. *Publ:* Illusr, Fred Bear's Field Notes, The Adventures of Fred Bear, Doubleday, 76; Complete Guide to Walleye Fishing, Willow Creek Press, 80; The Pigeon River Country, Asn Pigeon River Country, 85; Bear Paw Tackle (catalog cover), 91; Painting Wildlife Textures, Step by Step, Northlight Bks, 97. *Dealer:* Mill Pond Press Inc 310 Center Court Venice FL 34292. *Mailing Add:* 9320 M72 SE Kalkaska MI 49646-9780

LAWRENCE, SIDNEY S
PAINTER, WRITER
b San Francisco, Calif, 48. *Study:* Univ Calif, Berkeley, BA(art hist), 72; Univ Calif, Davis, 72-74, MA, 80. *Work:* Lerner Development Cos; Fed Reserve Bank, Richmond, Va; Lalo Mir, Buenos Aires, Arg. *Comn:* Robert E Lee IV portrait, comn by Cong Jim Leach, Wash, 1998. *Exhib:* Solo exhib, Gallery K, Washington, 83, 85, 88, 92, 96 & 2001, & Braunstein/Quay, 97 & Robert Lehman Art Ctr, Brooks Sch,

Mass, 2001; Contemp Self-Portraits from the James Goode Collection, Nat Portrait Gallery, Washington, 93; Beyond Likeness: Unconventional Portraits, Montgomery Col, Md, 94; Black Art, Rockville Arts Place, Md, 95; Rockwellian Times, 57 N Artspace, Washington, 2000; Distner Fine Arts, 2005. *Collection Arranged:* Roger Brown Retrospective 87-88, Hirshhorn Mus & Natl Tour, Washington, DC; Houston Conwill, Boyd Webb, Alison Saar, Tony Ourster, Ron Mueck, 1988-2003; Ghirardelli: 50 Yr Show, Mus Italo-Am, San Francisco, 1999. *Pos:* pub affairs officer, Hirshhorn Mus & Sculpture Garden, Smithsonian Inst, Washington, 75-2003; DC corresp, artnet.com, 2004; Arts consultant, Katzen Am Univ, 2005. *Awards:* Award of Merit Mus Italo-Am, Am Asn State & Local Hist, 2000. *Bibliog:* Florence Rubenfeld (auth), Sidney Lawrence, Mus & Arts Washington, 9-10/88; Pat Kolmer (auth), Sidney Lawrence: Wall Reliefs and Drawings, Wash Rev, 6-7/92; Joe Shannon (auth), Sidney Lawrence, Art Am, 7/96; Mark Jenkins (auth), Flat & 3-D, 2005. *Mem:* Int Asn Art Critics. *Publ:* Co-auth, Music in Stone: Great Sculpture Gardens of the World, Scala Bks, 84; auth, Art after modern art, 10/84, What a relief! New forms in art, 2/86, Artists collect, 9/87, Marching to a different drummer in art, 6/88, Photographs--the artist's secret weapon, 5/89, The 80's--world of paradox echoed in art, 3/90, & Latin Legacy--how four pioneers fueled modern art, 6/92, Smithsonian News Service; Houston Conwill--Markings on the Sand, Hirshhorn Works 1989, Washington, 90; Directions-Boyd Webb, 91; Directions - Alison Saar, 93; Directions-Tony Oursler: Video Dolls with Tracy Leipold, Hirshhorn Mus, 98; Ghirardelli: Portrait of a Family, 1849-1999, Mus Italo-Am, San Francisco, 2000; Directions - Ron Mueck, 2002; Review various shows for Art Am, Wash Post, Smithsonian & Wall Street J, 2004; Roger Brown's Gift, Fed Reserve Art Prog, 2005. *Mailing Add:* 1240 29th St NW Washington DC 20007

LAWRENCE, SUSAN
ART DEALER, CONSULTANT

b New York, NY, Dec 10, 39. *Study:* Univ Kans, BA, 61. *Pos:* Dir, Lawrence Gallery, Kansas City, Mo, 76-84; co-dir, Batz-Lawrence Gallery, Kansas City, Mo, 84-88; Lawrence Fine Art, Kansas City, Mo, 88-97; bd dir, UM-KC Gallery Art, Kansas City, Mo, 88-93, Film Soc Greater Kansas City, 91-, & Ko-Arts, supporting Tango in Kansas City, 2000-; founder & mem dir, Film Soc Greater Kansas City; Susan Lawrence Fine Art, Kansas City, Mo, 98-. *Mem:* Kansas City Art Gallery Asn (pres, 83-84, treas, 86); Westport Gallery Asn, Kansas City, Mo (founder & pres, 78-83); Contemp Art Soc, Kansas City (secy, 86). *Specialty:* Contemporary fine art, paintings and original prints by American and European artists, including regional artists. *Mailing Add:* 804 W 48th Ste 305 Kansas City MO 64112

LAWSON, KAROL ANN
MUSEUM DIRECTOR, CURATOR

b Davenport, Iowa, Nov 10, 58. *Study:* Sweet Briar Col, BA, 81; Univ Va, MA, 83, PhD, 88. *Collection Arranged:* Nobody Knows the Trouble I've Seen: The Paintings and Prints of Lamar Baker, Columbus Mus, Ga, 96; Maier Mus, Va, 2001; The View from Here: The Contemp Landscape, Maier Mus, Va, 2002; Women I Have Known: A Survey of work by Benny Andrews, Maier Mus, 2003; All of Me, Margrit Lewczuk, Maier Mus, 2004; Heart of the Matter: Recent Work by Elizabeth Murray, 2005; Some Kind of Wonderful: Sculpture by Jim Clark & Tara Donovan, 2006. *Pos:* rsch asst, Nat Mus Am Art, Smithsonian Inst, Wash DC, 87-91; dir collections, Columbus Mus, Ga, 91-99; dir, Maier Mus Art, Lynchburg, Va, 99-. *Teaching:* instr, Univ Va, 82-84, St Mary's Col, Maryland, 86 & Randolph-Macon Women's Col, 99-. *Awards:* pre-doctoral fel, Nat Mus Am Art, Wash, DC, 85-86; post doctoral fel, John Carter Brown Libr, Providence, RI, 87; Post Doctoral Fel, Huntington Libr & Art Collections, San Marino, Calif, 92. *Mem:* Am Asn Mus; Va Asn Mus; Southeastern Mus Conf; Col Art Asn; Asn Historians Am Art; Asn of Col and Univ Mus and Galleries. *Res:* 19th, 20th centuries and contemp Am Art; early landscape imagery in the work of Charles Willson Peale. *Publ:* auth, Charles Willson Peale's John Dickinson: An American Landscape As Political Allegory, Proceedings Am Philos Soc, 92; auth, An Inexhaustible Abundance: The National Landscape Depicted in American Magazines 1780-1820, J Early Repub, 92. *Mailing Add:* Randolph-Macon Woman's Col Maier Mus Art 2500 Rivermont Ave Lynchburg VA 24503

LAWSON, THOMAS
PAINTER, WRITER

b Glasgow, Scotland, 1951. *Study:* Univ St Andrews, MA, 73; Univ Edinburgh, MA, 75; Grad Sch City Univ NY, Phil, 81. *Work:* Chase Manhattan Bank, NY; Brooklyn Mus, NY; Scottish Arts Coun, Edinburgh; City New York; Arts Coun Gt Brit, London; and others. *Comn:* Temporary mural, Manhattan Munic Bldg, Dept Gen Serv, NY; temporary mural, Dunstan Soap Works, First Tyne Int, Gateshead, Eng, 90; sculpture, Circulo de Bellas Artes, Madrid, 91. *Exhib:* The Heroic Figure, Contemp Arts Mus, Houston, 84; Civic Virtues, City Univ Grad Ctr Hall, NY, 86; Sydney Biennale, Art Gallery NSW, 86; Painting, Brooklyn Mus, Brooklyn, 87; solo exhib, San Diego Mus Contemp Art, La Jolla, 87; A Forest of Signs, Mus Contemp Art, Los Angeles, 89; First Tyne Int, Gateshead, UK, 90; 10 Yr Survey Exhib, Third Eye Ctr, Glasgow, Scotland, 90; El Sueno Imperativo, Circulo Belles Artes, Madrid, 91; Monumental Propaganda, Independent Curs, NY & Moscow, 93; Painting in the British Arts Coun, UK galleries, 94-95; Sleeper, Edinburgh, 01. *Pos:* Cur consult, The Drawing Ctr, NY, 78-81; ed, Real Life Mag, NY, 79-91; coed, Afterall Journal, London & Los Angeles, 2002. *Teaching:* Instr, Sch Visual Arts, NY, 81-89; vis artist, Calif Inst Arts, spring 87 & 89, dean, 91-; grad instr, Rhode Island Sch Art Design, 87 & 88. *Awards:* Nat Endowment Arts Fel, 82-83, 85-86 & 88-89; Proj Grant, Art Matters Inc, 86-87; Bellagio Ctr Residency, Rockefeller Found, 97. *Bibliog:* Richard Martin (auth), article, 11/84 & Ronald Jones (auth), article, summer 85, Arts Mag; Jeanne Silverthorne (auth), Third Eye Centre (monogr & exhib catalog), Glasgow & Anthony Reynolds, London, 90; Scott Rothkopf (auth), Art Forum, April, 2002. *Mem:* Col Art Asn; Artists Equity; Nat Asn Artist Run Orgn. *Media:* All. *Publ:* Guilt by Association, IMMA, Dublin, 92; Jet Lag & Iron Hard Jets, The British Art Show (exhib catalog), 95; Attempting Community (exhib catalog), Drawing Ctr, New York, 96; Allan McCollum, Art Press, Los Angeles, 96; Looking For Something to Read, 02; The Unbearable Lightness of Painting: Laura Owens, 03; Mining for Gold, Slected Essays, 1979-1996, JRP/Ringier, Zurich, 2004. *Dealer:* Anthony Reynolds Gallery 60 Great Marlborough St, London, WIF 7B5. *Mailing Add:* 127 Wilton Dr Los Angeles CA 90004

LAWSON-JOHNSTON, PETER, II
PATRON

Study: Trinity Col, BA; Columbia Univ, MS(real estate develop). *Pos:* Managing partner, Jack Primus Partners LP, Harper Partners; trustee, Solomon R Guggenheim Found, chmn, investment comt, currently; dir & vpres, Elgerbar Corp; sr partner, Guggenheim Brothers, dir, Harry Frank Guggenheim Found, chmn, investment comt; dir emer, Charles A & Anne Morrow Lindberg Found. *Mailing Add:* c/o Solomon R Guggenheim Found 1071 Fifth Ave New York NY 10128-0173

LAWSON-JOHNSTON, PETER ORMAN
PATRON

b New York City, Feb 8, 27. *Study:* Univ Va, 1951. *Pos:* Reporter, yachting editor, Balt Sun Papers, 1951-53; exec dir, Md Classified Employees Asn, Balt, 1953-54; pub info dir, Md Civil Def Agency, Pikesville, 1954-56; dir, Zemex Corp, New York City, 1960-, vpres 1966-72, vchmn 1972-75, pres 1975-76, chmn 1975-2003; dir, Feldspar Corp 1959-2003, sales mgr 1956-60, vpres sales 1961-66, vpres 1966-72, chmn1972-81. *Mem:* Trustee, Solomon R Guggenheim Mus, 1964, vpres bus admin 1965-69, pres 1969-95, chmn 1995-98, hon chmn 1998-; pres adv bd, Peggy Guggenheim Collection; dir, Harry Frank Guggenheim Found, 1968-, chmn 1971-; partner, Guggenheim Bros, 1962-70, sr partner 1971-; Pilgrims of US, Carolina Plantation Soc, US Sr Golf Asn, Edgartown Yacht Club, Edgartown Reading Room Club, Jupiter Island Club, Brook Club, Yeamans Hall Club. *Publ:* Auth, Growing Up Guggenheim: A Personal History of a Family Enterprise, 2005. *Mailing Add:* 25 W 53rd St 16 New York NY 10019-5401

LAWTON, FLORIAN KENNETH
PAINTER, LECTURER

b Cleveland, Ohio, June 20, 21. *Study:* Cleveland Sch Art, 42 & 48-50; John Huntington Polytech Inst, 48-49; Cleveland Col, 48-49. *Work:* Cleveland Mus Art; Miami Univ, Oxford, Ohio; pvt collection of King Kahlid, Saudi Arabia; Duramax Inc, Middlefield, Ohio; Hiram Col, Ohio; Charles Miller Jr. & Paul Miller families, S Russell, Ohio; and others. *Comn:* Cleveland Citiscape, Ohio Bell Tel Co, 79; Rotek Co, Hamburg, Ger, 88; Nat Engineering Co, Cleveland, Ohio; TRW Inc, Cleveland; Carret & Co, NY; Cleveland-Clinic, Cleveland, Ohio; and others. *Exhib:* Cleveland Mus Art, 78-84; Butler Mus Am Art Nat, Youngstown, Ohio, 77-88; Nat Watercolor Soc, All-West Traveling Exhib, Los Angeles, 77-80; Salmagundi Club, NY, 78-80; Ky Watercolor Soc, Owensboro Mus, 79; Retrospective, Butler Mus Am Art, Youngstown, Ohio, 89; Am Watercolor Soc, NY; Watercolor USA, Springfield, Mo; and others. *Pos:* Art consult, Cleveland, Ohio, 72-; adv, Orange Arts Coun, Ohio, 77-; critic, 82-. *Teaching:* Instr painting & watercolor, Cleveland Inst Art, 81-; instr watercolor, Orange Arts Coun, Ohio, 77-; pvt classes. *Awards:* Grand Buckeye Leaf Award, Nat Watercolor Soc, 81; Peoples Choice Award, Great Lakes Regional, 82; First Prize & Larry Quackenbush Award, Hudson Ann, 82; Ohio Watercolor Soc, 80-84, 86, 88; Boston Mills Ann First, 86-87, 88, 89. *Bibliog:* Modern art review, Revue Mod Desarts, Paris, France, 6/70; Amish Romance (doc film), Scripps-Howard TV, Hiram Col, 75. *Mem:* Ohio Watercolor Soc; Am Watercolor Soc; Ky Watercolor Soc; Pa Watercolor Soc; Nat Watercolor Soc; Hilton Head, SC Watercolor Soc. *Media:* Mixed, Watercolor. *Res:* hist of dowtown Cleveland; Ohio canal system. *Publ:* Auth, Watercolor page, In: American Artist, Watson-Guptill, 70; featured artist, fine arts prints, Mill Pond Press, Venice, Fla; Artists Mag, 3/96; Artists Mag, 11/2000; Int Artists Mag, 1-2/2001. *Dealer:* Bonfoey Co Cleveland OH; Mill Pond Press Venice FL. *Mailing Add:* 410-29 Willow Cir Aurora OH 44202

LAWTON, JAMES L
SCULPTOR, EDUCATOR

b Louisville, Ky, July 28, 44. *Study:* Louisville Sch Art, Ky; Murray State Univ, Ky, BS; Kent State Univ, Ohio, MFA. *Work:* Western Mich Univ, Kalamazoo; City Hartland, Mich; City of Detroit, Mich; Williamston Publ Sch, Mich; Am Asian Soc, NY; Kresge Art Mus, East Lansing, Mich. *Comn:* Three Trusses Plus painted steel sculpture, Cass Park, City Detroit, 77-78; Past, Present, Future, 99, Williamston Publ Sch, Mich; Forest of Hands, Mason Pub Sch, Mason, Mich, 98. *Exhib:* A Road Show, juried, Contemp Art Inst Detroit, 85-86, Traveling; Saginaw Art Mus, Mich, 91; Invitational, Structure, Object Event, Art Ctr Battle Creek, Mich, 92; solo exhibs, Otherwise Gallery, Lansing, Mich, 94 & Fine Arts Gallery, DeWaters Art Ctr, Flint, Mich, 95; Group exhibs, New Regionalism, Detroit Artist Market, Detroit, 97, The Formal Issue: The State of Sculpture in Mich Univs, Midland Ctr for Arts, 03, Denison Univ Art Gallery, Granville, OH, 04; Summer Int Sculpture Ctr Exhib, Grounds for Sculpture, Hamilton, NJ, 2003; Invitational Outdoor Sculpture Exhib, Brighton, Mich, 06-. *Collection Arranged:* cur, 2005-2006 Fringe Festival, Mich State Univ, E Lansing, Mich; cur, Art on the Edge & Beyond: MSU's Fringe Events 06-07, Mich State Univ, E Lansing, Mich. *Pos:* Co-cur, The 12th Biennial & Beyond Boundries, Kresgo Art Mus, ELansing, Mich, 91 & 92; co juror, Wassenberg Art Ctr Ann, Van Wert, Ohio, 94. *Teaching:* prof sculpture, Mich State Univ & Kresge Art Ctr. *Awards:* Best of Show, 22nd Ann Paint & Sculpting Competition, Lansing, Mich; Mich State Univ Grants, 68, 79, 90 & 94; '89 Col Res Leave & Grant Awards; Best of Show, Mich Artist Exch; Battle Creek Art Ctr, Battle Creek, Mich; 1st Place Nat Sculpture Exch, Cen Mich Univ, Mt Pleasant, Mich, 84. *Bibliog:* Darlene B Damp (article), Saginaw News, Mich, 9/91; Leslie Cavell (auth), article, Lansing Capital

Times, 12/93; Grace Schott (auth), article, Flint J, 3/95; Arthuir Williams (auth), The Sculpture Reference, Sculpture Books Publ; Dennis Nowrocki (auth) Art in Detroit Public Places, Wayne State Univ Press; Christopher R. Young (auth), The Flint Journal, 9/04. *Mem:* Int Sculpture Ctr; Detroit Artist Market; Contemp Art Inst Detroit. *Media:* All Media. *Dealer:* Detroit Artist Market Detroit Mich. *Mailing Add:* 3485 Zimmer Rd Williamston MI 48895-9184

LAWTON, NANCY
PAINTER, GRAPHIC ARTIST
b Calif, Feb 28, 50. *Study:* Calif State Univ, San Jose, BA, 72; Mass Col Art, MFA, 80. *Work:* Ark Art Ctr Mus; The Brooklyn Mus; Chicago Art Inst; HJ Heinz Corp; Metrop Mus Art; Smithsonian Am Art Mus. *Comn:* Portrait of HJ Heinz, Heinz Corp, Pittsburgh, 84, Maurice & Richard Robinson, Scholastic, NY, 92. *Exhib:* Am Drawings in Black & White: 1970-1980, 80 & Gene Baro Collects, 83, Brooklyn Mus; San Francisco Mus Modern Art, Calif, 73; one-woman show, Brooklyn Mus, 83 & Victorian Munroe Gallery, 93; Drawing, Ark Art Ctr Mus, Little Rock, 84, 88, 92, 93 & 2003; The Art of Drawing III, Staempfli Gallery, NY, 84; gallery artists, Victoria Munroe Gallery, NY, 85, 87, 88 & 92; Realism Today, Nat Acad Design & Butler Inst Am Art, 88; Hunt Inst Botanical Documentation, Carnegie Melon Univ, Pittsburgh, Pa, 2001-2002; Arnot Art Mus, Elmira, NY, 2001-2003; Hirschl & Adler Galleries, NY, 2002-2006; John Pence Galleries, San Francisco, 2004; Vose Galleries, Boston, 2004; Telfair Mus Art, Savannah, 2006. *Teaching:* Instr printmaking & drawing, Mass Col Art, Boston, 79-80, instr drawing, 80-81; artist-in-residence, Noble & Greenough Sch, Boston, 90. *Awards:* Mellon Found Scholar, 82; NY State Creative Artist Pub Serv Award, 83; Grant, New York Arts Develop Fund, 85. *Bibliog:* Daniel Mendelowitz (auth), A Guide to Drawing, 93; Townsend Wolfe (auth), About Face, 2001; James White & Lugene Bruno (auth), 10th International Exhibition of Botanical Art, 2001. *Media:* Pencil & Silverpoint on Paper. *Dealer:* Hirschl and Adler Galleries New York NY. *Mailing Add:* 78 Willett St Albany NY 12210

LAWTON, THOMAS
HISTORIAN, EDITOR
b Somerset, Mass, Feb 5, 31. *Study:* RI Sch Design, 49-50; Durfree Tech Inst, BS(design), 53; State Univ Iowa, MFA, 59; Harvard Univ, 59-63, PhD, 70; Stanford Chinese Language Training Ctr, 63-64. *Pos:* Assoc cur Chinese art, Freer Gallery Art, 67, cur Chinese art, 70, asst dir, 71-77, dir, 77-87, dir Freer Gallery Art and Arthur M Sackler Gallery, 82-87, senior res scholar, 87-; ed-in-chief, Artibus Asiae, 93-. *Teaching:* Instr Chinese art, Smithsonian Assoc, 70 & George Washington Univ, 70-71 & 74-75, Franklin P Murphy Lecturer, 89; lectr, Harvard Univ, Cambridge, Mass, Princeton, NJ, Yale Univ, New Haven, Conn, Univ Va, Charlottesville, Oxford Univ, Eng, Shanghai Mus, Shanghai, Mus Rietberg, Zurich, Switzerland. *Awards:* Fel, Ford Found, 59-61, Fulbright, 63-66; John D Rockefeller 3rd Fund Grant, 66-67; Charlottesville/Albemarle Found for the Encouragement of the Arts Award for Meritorious Contrib to World of Arts, 87. *Bibliog:* Jessica Rawson (auth), Chinese jade from the Neolithic to the Qing, Artibus Asiae 56, No 1-2, spring 96; William Watson (auth), The Arts of China to AD 900, Artibus, Asiae 56, No 1-2, spring 96. *Publ:* Coauth, Freer: A legacy of Art, NY: Harry Abrams, 93; auth, Yamanaka Sadajiro: Advocate for Asian art, Orientations, 1/95; John C Ferguson: A fellow feeling of fallibility, Orientations, Vol 27, No 3, 3/96; Rubbings of Chinese bronzes, Bulletin of Mus of Far Eastern Antiquities, Vol 67, 97; A Time of Transition: Two Collectors of Chinese Art, Spencer Mus, Univ Kan, 97; New Perspectives on Chu Culture in the Eastern Zhou Period; ed, Arthur M Sackler Gallery, Washington, DC, 91; co-auth, Freer: A Legacy of Art, Freer Gallery Art, Washington, DC, 93. *Mailing Add:* Freer Art Gallery Jefferson Dr at 12th St SW Washington DC 20560

LAXSON, RUTH
CONCEPTUAL ARTIST
b Roanoke, Ala, 1924. *Study:* Auburn Univ; Atlanta Col Art. *Work:* Mus Mod Art, NY; New York Pub Libr; Yale Univ; Getty Ctr, Malibu, Calif; Sackner Collection, Miami; Victoria & Albert Mus, Tate Gallery, London; Univ Alta, Edmonton; Brown Univ; RI Sch Design; Emory Univ; Woodruff Lib; pvt collections. *Comn:* 2 lithographs, Rolling Stone Press. *Exhib:* Amerikanischer Buchkunst, Zeitgenssische Handpressendruke, Hamburg, 93; Int Survey Artists Bks, Atlanta Col Art, 94; Installation-Arts Festival Atlanta, 95; Artist Page, Art Papers, 96; Int Traveling Exhib Artists' Bks, Am Fedn Arts, 98; The Next Word, Newberger Mus, State Univ NY, 98; Connections/Contradictions, Carlos Mus, Emory Univ, 98; Drawings & Books, The Contemp, Atlanta, 99; Identity in the New Millennium, Eyedrum, 2000; Expert Narrative in Artists' Books, La State Univ, Baton Rouge, 2000; one-women exhib, paintings & drawings, Marcia Wood Gallery, 2002, Chairs Project, Emory Univ, 2003. *Pos:* dir, artist, Press 63 Plus, Atlanta. *Teaching:* Vis artist, Agnes Scott Col, Atlanta, 91; Atlanta Col, 91-92; Univ Iowa, 96. *Awards:* Acquistions Grants, Ga Coun Arts, 89 & 90; Resident Fel, Hambidge Ctr, 95; Arts Festival Atlanta Exhib, 95; Ga Women in the Visual Arts Grant, 97; CGR Scholarship, Hambridge Ctr, 98; Nexus Press Residency, 2000. *Bibliog:* Johanna Drucker (auth), The Century of Artists Books, 95; Pattie Belle Hastings (auth), interview, J Artists' Bks, 97; Jerry Cullum (auth), review, Re-Tell the Tale, 98; Rene Hubert (auth), The Cutting Edge of Reading: Artists' Books. *Mem:* Atlanta Col Art Alum; Atlanta Contemp Arts Ctr. *Media:* Printmaking, Multimedia. *Specialty:* Marcia Wood Gallery, encaustic and works on paper. *Publ:* Imaging, 91; Some Things are Sacred, 91; Wheeling, 92; Measure up, 95; Letters to the Ether/Other, 96; Retell the Tale, Art Papers, 98; Muse Measures, 99; Mythos Chronos Logos, 2000; A Hundred Years of: Lex Flex 2003. *Dealer:* Califia Books San Francisco; Marcia Wood Gallery Atlanta; PABA Gallery, New Haven, CT. *Mailing Add:* 2298 Drew Valley Rd Atlanta GA 30319

LAY, PATRICIA ANNE
SCULPTOR
b New Haven, Conn, Aug 14, 41. *Study:* Rochester Inst Technol, MFA; Pratt Inst, BS. *Work:* NJ State Mus, Trenton; Rochester Inst Technol; IBM; Rutger Univ; Henie-Onstad Mus, Oslo. *Comn:* Montclair State Col, 85 & 96. *Exhib:* Solo Shows, Douglass Col Women Artists Series, 73, NJ State Mus, 74, Jersey City Mus, 87 & Condeso/Lawler Gallery, NY, 92; Contemp Reflections, Aldrich Mus, Ridgefield, Conn, 75; Whitney Mus Am Art Biennial, 75; Structures: 13 NJ Artists, Montclair Art Mus, 84; Noyes Mus, NJ, 89; NY: Clay (traveling), Norway, 95-96; Six Artists: The 1990's, NJ State Mus, 96; Transcending Boundaries, Mi Qiu Modern Art Workshop, Coll Fine Arts, Shanghai Univ, China, 99; 1999 East and West, Soho 20 Gallery, 99; Lives and Works, The Exhibition, Ceres Gallery, NY, 2000; NJ Fine Arts Annual, Jersey City Mus, 2002; Wish You Were Here Too! AIR Gallery, NY, 2003; Altars, Icons and Symbols: Exploring Spirituality in Art, Noyes Mus, NJ, 2004. *Teaching:* Asst prof sculpture, State Univ NY Buffalo, 68-69; instr ceramics, Wagner Col, 69-71; lectr ceramics, Hunter Col, 71-72; prof sculpture & ceramics, Montclair State Univ, 72-. *Awards:* NJ State Coun Fel in Sculpture, 84 & 88; Am Scandinavian Found, 96. *Bibliog:* Leon Nigrosh (auth), Claywork, 75, 2nd ed, 86 & Low Fire: Other Ways to Work in Clay, 80, Davis Publ; Susan Peterson (auth), The Craft & Art of Clay, Prentice Hall, NJ, 92, 2nd ed, 95; J Arbeiter, B Smith & S Swenson (auths), Lives & Works: Talks with Women Artists, Vol II, Scarecrow Press, 96. *Media:* Clay, Metal. *Mailing Add:* 77 Grand St Jersey City NJ 07302

LAYNE, BARBARA J
INSTRUCTOR
b Seattle, Wash, Jan 12, 52. *Study:* Univ Colo, BFA, 79; Univ Kans, MFA, 82. *Work:* SC State Art Collection, Columbia; Cent d'Art Graphique, Romainmotier, Switz; Fed Reserve Bank Richmond, Charlotte, NC. *Exhib:* The HUB, Lincolnshire, Eng, 2005; Montreal Centre Contemp Textiles, 2006; Int Biennale Design, France, 2006; The Canadian Embassy, Washington, DC, 2007. *Teaching:* prof fibres, Concordia Univ, Montreal, 89-. *Awards:* Hexagram Research Grant, 2003-2006; Principal Investigator, CFI Infrastructure Grant, 2004-2007; Social Science & Humanities Research Grant, 2005-. *Bibliog:* Betty Ann Brown (auth), Expanding Circles, 96; Kim Sawchuk (auth), Barbara Layne & Ingrid Bachmann, Parachute Mag, 96; Mark Newport (auth), Fiberarts, 98; and others. *Mem:* Col Art Asn; Textile Soc Am. *Media:* Electronic Textiles. *Res:* Interactive textiles & wearable computing at the Hexagram Institute for Media Arts & Technology, Montreal. *Publ:* Auth, Paper Art in America, Leopold Hoesch Mus, Duren, WGer, 86; auth, Migrant Textiles, Telos Art Publ, 2001; auth, Barbara Layne (catalog), Portfolio Collection, Telos Art Publ, 2003. *Mailing Add:* Dept Studio Arts Concordia Univ EV2-823 1515 St Catherine W Montreal PQ H3G 2W1 Canada

LAZARUS, FRED, IV
ADMINISTRATOR
b New York, NY, Jan 1, 42. *Study:* Claremont McKenna Col, BA, 64; Harvard Univ, MBA, 66. *Hon Degrees:* Osaka Univ for the Arts, 2001. *Pos:* Staff Assoc Nat Coun for Equal Bus Opportunity, Wash, 69-71; pres Wash Coun for Equal Bus Opportunity, 71-74; exec Asst to chmn Nat Endow for Arts, Wash, 75-78; pres Md Inst Col Art, Baltimore, 78; Exec asst to chmn, Nat Endowment for Arts, 75-78; pres, Md Inst Col Art, 78-; trustee, Alliance for Ind Col's Art, 78-91, chmn, 84-86, 89-91; founding chmn, Nat Coalition for Educ Arts, 88-90; trustee, St Paul's Sch, 88-96, Am Coun for Arts, 80-97, secy, 91-94; trustee, Am for the Arts, 98-2001, Md Art Place, 88-96; trustee emer, Partners for Livable Places; bd dir, Afro-Am. Newspapers, Baltimore, 90-2003, Baltimore Artists Housing Corp; chmn, Baltimore Coun for Equal Bus Opportunity, 91-2000, trustee, Md Ind Col & Univ Asn, 78-, vchmn, 95-99, chmn, 99-2003; mem, Thurgood Marshall Mem Statue Comn, 96-98; chmn, Greater Baltimore Cult Alliance, 2001-; vchmn, Asn Ind Col's Art & Design, 92-96; bd dir, Midtown Develop Corp, currently. *Awards:* Mayor's Award, 88. *Mem:* Md Independent Cols & Univs Asn (chmn); Am Coun Arts (chmn, 96); Nat Coalition Educ Arts (chmn, 87-89); Partners Livable Places (trustee emer); Am Arts (chmn 96-99); Greater Balt Cult Alliance (chmn, 2002). *Mailing Add:* Md Inst Col Art 1300 W Mount Royal Ave Baltimore MD 21217-4134

LAZARUS, LOIS
PAINTER
b Brooklyn, NY, Aug 25, 1931. *Study:* Cooper Union, Art/Arch, 1952; Univ of Miami, BA, 1965; Hofstra Univ, MA, 1975. *Work:* San Francisco Mus of Mod Art, San Francisco, CA; Los Angeles Mus of Mod Art, Los Angeles, CA; El Paso Mus, El Paso, TX; De Young, San Francisco, CA. *Exhib:* New Painters, Archives of Venice Biernale Contemp Art, Venice, Italy, 1952; Los Angeles Co Painters, Los Angeles Mus of Mod Art, Los Angeles, CA, 1957-65; San Francisco col, San Francisco Mus, San Francisco, CA, 1957-73; Miami Painters, El Paso, El Paso, TX, 1968; Norton Gallery, Palm Beach, FL, 1970; De Young Mus, San Francisco, CA, 1979-84; Retrospect, Pratt Inst, New York, NY, 2005. *Teaching:* adj prof painting, Pratt Inst, New York, NY, 2003-06, adj prof architecture, 2003-06. *Media:* All Media. *Publ:* Auth, contribr, With These Hands They Built A Nation, 1979; auth, contribr, Country Is My Music, 1983. *Mailing Add:* 792 Columbus Ave Ste 2E New York NY 10025

LAZENBY, DEXTER
CONCEPTUAL ARTIST
b Overbrook, Pa, 55. *Study:* Conn Col, 73; Univ Md, College Park, 75; Tufts Univ & Sch Mus Fine Arts, BFA, 79; Sch Mus Fine Arts, Boston, Mass, dipl, 81, cert, 83. *Work:* Mus Fine Arts & First Church of Christ Scientist, Boston, Mass; Tufts Univ, Medford, Mass; Whitehead Inst Biomedical Res, Cambridge, Mass; Prudential Insurance Co Am. *Exhib:* Solo exhibs, Nielsen Gallery, 83, 86 & 90, Foster Gallery, Mus Fine Arts, 85, Boston, Mass; Traveling Scholars, Mus Fine Arts, Boston, Mass,

83 & 87; Currents, Inst Contemp Art, Boston, Mass, 89; Exploring the Figure through Sculptured Forms, Newport Art Mus, RI, 90; Common Ground II: Sculpture, Hurst Gallery & Nielsen Gallery, 90; Summertime Exhib, Nielsen Gallery, Boston, Mass, 92; Nielsen Gallery, Boston, Mass, 92; Frick Gallery, Belfast, Maine, 92; Nielsen Gallery, Boston, 99; O'Farrell Gallery, Brunswick, Maine, 2001. *Awards:* Visual Artists Fel for Sculpture, Nat Endowment Arts, 86; Pollack-Krasner Found Grant, 87; Engelhard Award, 88. *Bibliog:* Robert Taylor (auth), Sculpture at De Cordova Explores Edge of 90's, Sunday Boston Globe, 1/7/90; Nancy Stapen (auth), Ancient Art Meets Today in Exhibit, Boston Herald, 3/16/90; David Raymond (auth), De Cordova Museum and Sculpture Park, Lincoln Sculpture on the Edge, Art New England, 3/90; and many other reviews. *Mailing Add:* 1114 H Rd Acton ME 04001-6011

LAZUKA, ROBERT
ARTIST
Study: Art Inst Chicago, BFA (painting); Ariz State Univ, MFA. *Exhib:* Rep in permanent collections, Whitney Mus Art, NY, Smithsonian Nat Mus Am Art, Wash, DC, Nelson-Atkins Mus Art, Kansas City, MO, Clemson Univ, SC, Chattahoochee Valley Art Mus, Ga, Baseball Hall Fame Mus. *Pos:* Prof Sch Art, Ohio Univ, 84-, interim dir. *Mem:* Col Bd Advanced Placement Prog (mem, 88-, chief fac consultant, studio art 96-2000, devel comt). *Mailing Add:* c/o Ohio Univ School of Art 417 Seigfred Hall Athens OH 54701

LAZZARI, MARGARET R
PAINTER, EDUCATOR
b St Louis, Mo, 53. *Study:* Wash Univ, St Louis, Mo, MFA, 77. *Work:* Hartzell Corp, St Paul, Minn; VH Investment Group, Minneapolis, Minn; Transco Corp, Houston; Ralston Purina Co, St Louis, Mo; Piper, Jaffrey & Hopgood Inc, Minneapolis, Minn. *Exhib:* Solo exhibs, Rio Hondo Col, Whittier, Calif, 92, Fisher Gallery, Univ Southern Calif, Los Angeles, 92, John Thomas Gallery, Santa Monica, Calif, 94, Patricia Sweetow Gallery, Napa, Calif, 95, Art Works Gallery, Riverside, Calif, 95-96 & El Camino Col, Torrance, Calif, 96; Generations, Gwenda Jay Gallery, Chicago, 95; Encore, Art Works Gallery, Riverside, Calif, 96; Trans/Figure, Rio Hondo Col, Whittier, Calif, 96; Re-Masters: New Images from Old Sources, Rancho Santiago Col, Santa Ana, Calif, 96. *Pos:* Chair, SITE Gallery, Los Angeles, 89, Found Art, Theory & Educ Nat Conf, Sch Art Inst Chicago, 90 & S Calif Women's Caucus Art Ann Conf, Univ Calif, Los Angeles, 90; co-chair, Col Art Asn Studio Session Panel, San Francisco, 89; panelist, Found Art, Theory & Educ, Col Art Asn Ann Meeting, New York, 90, Finegood Gallery, West Hills, Calif, 90, Bakersfield Mus Art symp, Calif, 91 & Col Art Asn Ann Meeting, Boston, 96; co-cur, Vital Signs, Los Angeles Munic Art Gallery, 95. *Teaching:* Instr, Clarke Col, Dubuque, Iowa, 79-82; asst prof, Stephen F Austin State Univ, Tex, 82-86; lectr, St Francis Col, Ft Wayne, Ind, 89; assoc prof, Sch Fine Arts, Univ Southern Calif, Los Angeles, presently. *Awards:* Zumberge Res & Innovation Fund Fel, Univ Southern Calif, 92; Visual Artist Fel Works on Paper, Nat Endowment Arts, 95; Apple Computers Inc Proj Grant, Univ Southern Calif & Apple, 96. *Bibliog:* David DiMichele (auth); Vital Signs at LA Municipal Art Gallery, ArtWeek, 12/95; Nancy Kay Turner (auth), Margaret Lazzari, ArtScene, 9/96; Devorah Knaff (auth), For painter, practice makes profundity, Press Enterprise, Riverside, Calif, 10/20/96. *Mem:* Col Art Asn (comt electronic info, 90-93, artists lifetime acheivement award comt, 92-93, nominating comt, 92, chair nominating comt, 93); S Calif Women's Caucus Art (vpres, 88-90, pres, 90-91). *Publ:* Auth, Curriculum viva, art of the persona by Latinos in Los Angeles, Visions, spring 92; Material output, Framework, Vol 6, No 2, 93; Vital signs (essay, exhib catalog), Los Angeles Munic Art Gallery, 95; coauth (with C Lee), Art and Design Fundamentals, Van Nostrand Reinhold, 90; auth, Practical Handbook for the Emerging Artist, Harcourt Brace, 95. *Dealer:* Gwenda Jay Gallery 301 W Superior 2nd Floor Chicago IL 60610; Art Works Gallery 4649 Brockton Ave Riverside CA 92506. *Mailing Add:* 1717 23rd St Manhattan Beach CA 90266

LAZZARINI, ROBERT
SCULPTOR
b Parsippany, NJ, 65. *Study:* Parsons Sch Design, Grad, 85; Sch Visual Arts, NY City, BFA, 90. *Work:* Current/Undercurrent: Working in Brooklyn, Brooklyn Mus Art, 1997, The Whitney Biennial, Whitney Mus Art, 2002, first solo mus exhib, robert lazzarini, Va Mus Fine Arts, 2003-04 (Award for Best Exhib of Digital Art, Inter Asn Art Critics/USA, 2005). *Exhib:* Group exhibs, Intercourse, Mustar, Brooklyn, 94, Soup, 10, Brooklyn, 94, Second Independents Biennial, Galeria El Bohio, New York City, 94 & 96, Self Images, HBO Corp Gallery, New York City, 96, Gramercy Int, Gramercy Hotel, Gina Fiore Salon, New York City, 96, Genuine Fiction, W-139, Amsterdam, 97, Gramercy Int, Gramercy Hotel, Pierogi 2000, New York City, 97, Current/Undercurrent: Working in Brooklyn, NY Drawers, Gasworks Gallery, London, 97, The House, Manchester, 97, Invitational 98, Stefan Stux Gallery, New York City, 98, Multiple Sensations, Yerba Buena Ctr for the Arts, San Francisco, 2000, Haulin' Ass, Post, Los Angeles, 2000, Minutiae, Southeastern Ctr for Contemp Art, Winston-Salem, NC, 2000, Pierogi Flat Files, Block Artspace, Kansas City, Mo, 2001, Bitstreams, Brent Sikkema Gallery, New York City, 2001, Situated Realities: Works from Silicon Elsewhere, Md Inst Col Art, 2002, On Perspective, Gallery Faurschou, Copenhagen, 2002. *Awards:* Visual Arts Grant, NY Found for Arts, 85 & 86

LE, AN-MY
PHOTOGRAPHER
b Vietnam, 1960. *Study:* Stanford Univ, BA, 82, MS, 85; Yale Univ Sch Art, MFA(photog), 93. *Work:* Mus Mod Art & Metrop Mus, NY; Mus Fine Arts, Houston; Mus Mod Art, San Francisco; Bibliotheque Nationale, Paris. *Exhib:* MFA Thesis Exhib, Art & Archit Gallery, Yale Univ, 93; Wings of Change: Images of Contradiction and Consensus, Dir Guild Am, Los Angeles, 93; Building, Dwelling, Thinking, Lowinski Gallery, NY, 94; Picturing Asia Am: Communities, Cult, Difference (traveling exhib), Hunt Gallery, Webster Univ, St Louis & Silver Eye Ctr Photog, Pa, 94-96; Picturing Communities, Houston Ctr Photog, 97; New Photog 13, Mus Mod Art, NY, 97; Re-Imaging Vietnam, Fotofest, 98; Vietnam, Scott Nichols Gallery, San Francisco, 99. *Pos:* Staff photogr, Compagnons du Devoir, France, 86-91; freelance photogr, 93-. *Teaching:* Asst, Photog Dept, Yale Univ Sch Art, 92; lectr photog, Art Dept, Stanford Univ, 96, Continuing Studies Dept, 97, Fordham Univ & NY Univ, 98; vis asst prof, Bard Col, 99. *Awards:* Blair Dickenson Mem Award, Yale Univ Sch Art, 93; Photog Fel, NY Found Arts, 96; John Simon Guggenheim Mem Found Fel, 97. *Mailing Add:* 23 W Eighth St Apt 4C New York NY 10011

LE, DINH
PHOTOGRAPHER
Study: Univ Calif, Santa Barbara, BA(fine arts), 89; Sch Visual Arts full scholar, 90-92, New York, MFA(photog, digital imaging), 92. *Comn:* Accountability? (poster/postcard proj), Creative Time, NY & Los Angeles, 92; Race, Gender & Sexuality (poster proj), Painted Bride Gallery, Philadelphia, 93; Collaboration, Bronx Mus, Montefiore Family Health Ctr, NY, 96; Biography Memorial, Bronx Coun Arts, Woodlawn Cemetary, NY, 95. *Exhib:* Solo exhibs, Univ Ctr Art Gallery, Santa Barbara, Calif, 89, Art Studio Gallery, Santa Barbara, Calif, 89, Midtown Y Photog Gallery, NY, 90, Los Angeles Contemp Exhibs, 91, Visual Art Gallery, NY, 92 & Tyler Sch Art Gallery, Elkins, Pa, 92; Nat Mus Art, Kyoto, Japan, 92; Inst Contemp Art, Boston, 94; retrospective (traveling), Betteravia Gallery, Santa Maria, Calif, Elverhoy Mus, Solvang, Calif & Ro Snell Gallery, Santa Barbara, Calif, 94; San Francisco Mus Mod Art, 94; Points of Entry (traveling, with catalog), Friends Photog, Ansel Adams Ctr, San Francisco, Calif, 95; Portland Inst Contemp Art, Ore, 96; The Present (H)OUR, Oakland Mus, Calif, 96; A Labor of Love, New Mus, NY, 96; CEPA Gallery, Buffalo, NY, 97-98. *Awards:* Individual Fel, Art Matters Inc, NY, 92; Dupont Fel, Art Inst Boston, 94; Photog Fel, Nat Endowment Arts, 94-95. *Bibliog:* Karen Lipson (auth), An angry voice from Vietnam, NY Newsday, 12/8/92; Joanne Silver (auth), East and west woven into art, Boston Herald, 2/16/94; Cate McQuaid (auth), For Christ's sake, Boston Phoenix, 3/3/94. *Dealer:* CEPA Gallery 617 Main St Suite 201 Buffalo NY 14203. *Mailing Add:* 13055 Silver Creek St Moorpark CA 39021

LEA, LAURIE JANE
SCULPTOR, ASSEMBLAGE ARTIST
b Atlanta, Ga, May 7, 1948. *Study:* Newcomb Col, with Frank Boles, 66-67; Univ Colo, Boulder, with Gene Matthews & Frank Sampson, BFA, 70; Univ Ga, Athens, apprenticed with William Thompson, 78-79. *Work:* Ga Arts Coun, State Art Collection, Ga; Macon Mus Arts & Sci, Ga; Danville Mus Fine Art & Hist, Va. *Exhib:* Am Drawings, Smithsonian Inst Exhib, Portsmouth, Va, 76; USA: Portrait of the South, Palazzo Venezia, Rome, Italy, 84; Birmingham Biennial, Birmingham Mus Art, Ala, 85; National Women Artists Invitational, Clemson Univ, 86; Ut Och In, Malmo Kuntshall, Malmo, Sweden, 86; At the Edge, Laguna Gloria Art Mus, Austin, Tex, 88; one person shows, AIR Gallery, NY, 91, Vessels of the Spirit, Dolgenos Newman & Cronin Exhib Space, NY, 92, Artspace, Southern Arts, Portsmouth, Eng, 92 & touring exhib, Russell Cotes Mus, Bournemouth, Eng, 94; group shows, On Common Ground, Brooklyn Waterfront Artists Coalition, NY, 90, Urban Resurrection, The Gas Station, NY, 90, Elements of Drawing, AMMO Artists Exhib, NY, 91, Crossings II (catalog), Long Island Univ, NY, 92, 1-5 Show, NY, 92, The Machine in the Garden Revisited, Kingsborough Community Col, Brooklyn, NY, 93 & Aspex Gallery, Portsmouth, Eng, 94. *Pos:* Art dir, Common Cup Alternative Art Space, Atlanta, 72-77; bd dir, Ga Artists Int Exhib Fund, 84-87, Fulton Arts Coun, Atlanta, Ga, 84-87. *Teaching:* Vis artist, Atlanta Pub Schs & Trinity Schs, 74-81. *Awards:* Artists Grants, Artists Space, New York, 90; Exchange fel & Southern Arts Grant, Arts Coun Gt Brit, 92 & 94; Adolph & Esther Gottlieb Found Award. *Bibliog:* Creating an Artwork (videotape), WETV 30, PBS, 83. *Media:* Man-made Materials; Mixed. *Dealer:* Fay Gold Gallery 3221 Cains Hill Place NW Atlanta GA 30305. *Mailing Add:* 175 Columbia Hgts Apt 1A Brooklyn NY 11201-2156

LEA, STANLEY E
PAINTER, PRINTMAKER
b Joplin, Mo, Apr 5, 30. *Study:* Pittsburg State Univ, BFA; Univ Ark, MFA. *Work:* Smithsonian Inst & Libr Cong, Washington; Brit Mus, London; Inst Mex Norteamericano, Mex City; Mus Fine Arts, Houston. *Comn:* Collagraphs, Hyatt Regency Hotel, Houston, 72; paintings, Ft Worth Nat Bank, 73, Citizens Bank, Richards, Tex, 74, Am Nat Bank, Austin, 74 & USAA Bldg, San Antonio, 74; City of Hunstville (mural), Bradford Hotel, Dallas, Tex. *Exhib:* 48th Ann Soc Am Graphic Artists, NY, 67; Mainstreams Int, Marietta, Ohio, 68; Watercolor USA, Springfield, Mo, 69; 148th Ann Nat Acad Design, NY, 73; Nat Color Print USA, Lubbock, Tex, 74. *Teaching:* Prof printmaking & painting, Sam Houston State Univ, Huntsville, Tex, 61-93; vis prof, Mus Fine Arts, Houston, 68-71. *Awards:* Arts Nat, Tyler, Tex, 62; 4th Ann Print & Drawing, Ark Art Ctr, 70; Award, 68th Nat Tex Fine Arts, 79. *Bibliog:* Gerald F Brommer (auth), Art of Collage, Davis, Publ, Inc, 78. *Mem:* Col Art Asn; Southern Graphics Coun. *Media:* All Media. *Mailing Add:* 3324 Winter Way Huntsville TX 77340

LEACH, ELIZABETH ANNE
ART DEALER, WRITER
b Salinas, Calif, Mar 2, 57. *Study:* Scripps Col, Claremont, Calif, BA, 79; study with Arthur Stevens, Roland Reiss & Carl Hertel. *Collection Arranged:* Architecture of Monterey Peninsula (coauth, catalog), Monterey Mus, 76; Permanent Collection, Heathman Hotel, 84; co-cur, Curator's Choice, Ore Art Inst, 86; cur, Corporate Collections, Ore Business Committee Arts, Heathman Hotel, 86 & 89; cur, Photography Collection, Tonkin Torp Galen Marmaduke & Booth, 90. *Pos:* Asst dir, Galerie de Tours, Pebble Beach, Calif, 76; consult for archit survey, Hollywood

Revitalization Comt, 78; dir, Elizabeth Leach Gallery, Portland, Ore, 81-, chair, Visual Arts Comt, Artquake, 87-89; adv bd, Artfair Seattle, 90-. *Bibliog:* Megan McMorran (auth), Leach Will Agree, Bus J Mag, 8/13/84; Dorothy Smith (auth), article, in: Daily J Commerce, 11/8/84; Stephanie Martin (auth), article, in: Pac Northwest Mag, 4/85; Randy Gragg (auth), A Gallery for Our Time, Oregonian, 5/91. *Mem:* Portland Ctr Visual Arts (bd mem, 84-); Ore Art Inst; Chair of Visual Art Comt Artquake, 87. *Specialty:* Contemporary fine art. *Publ:* Auth, Art as an investment, Inst Managers & Prof Women, 81

LEACH, MADA (MADELINE) KLEIMAN
PAINTER
b Chicago, Ill, Dec 3, 39. *Study:* Duke Univ, 59; Meredith Col, BFA, 71; Art Inst Chicago, BFA & BAE, 64. *Work:* Cincinnati Bell Collection, Ohio; Louisville Arts Collection, Ky; Universal Bank, Orange, Calif; Strohmeier Collection, Frankfurt, Ky. *Comn:* Mural, Allergan Pharmaceutical, Irvine, Calif, 88. *Exhib:* Aqueous '81, Ky Watercolor Soc, Frankfurt Libr, Ky, 81; Cincinnati Bicentennial, Cincinnati Art Mus, Ohio, 81; Laguna Art Festival, Laguna Beach, Calif, 83-89; Traditionalist Show, Brea Ctr Arts, Brea, Calif, 84; Newport Festival of the Arts, Newport Beach, Calif, 86. *Pos:* Prog coordr, Festival Arts, Laguna Beach, Calif, currently. *Teaching:* Art instr, Art Inst Chicago, 64-65, Oakpark Schs, Ill, 65-68 & North York Bd Educ, Ont, Can, 75-80. *Awards:* Best of Show, Nature Interpreted, Josephine Rollman Mus, Cincinnati, 80; Strathmore Paper Award, Ohio Watercolor Soc, 81; Art Club Trust Award, Ky Bluegrass Competition, 82. *Mem:* Laguna Outreach Community Arts (vpres, currently). *Media:* Watercolor, Acrylic. *Dealer:* Art Angles 3411 E Chapman Ave Orange Ca 92669

LEAF, JUNE
PAINTER, SCULPTOR
b Chicago, Ill, 1929. *Study:* Roosevelt Univ, Chicago, BA(art educ), 54; Inst Design, Chicago, MA(art educ), 54; DePaul Univ, LHD, 84. *Work:* Mus Mod Art, NY; Art Inst Chicago & Mus Contemp Art; Smithsonian Inst, Washington, DC; Madison Art Ctr, Wis; Col Cape Breton, Sydney, NS, Can. *Exhib:* Torment, Whitney Mus Am Art, NY, 70; solo exhibs, Col Cape Breton Art Gallery, Sydney, NS, 82, Dalhousie Art Gallery, Halifax, NS, 82, NDak Mus Art, 83, Optica Gallery, Montreal, Can, 85, Edward Thorp Gallery, NY, 85, 88, 95 & 97, A Survey of Painting, Sculpture and Works on Paper, 1948-1991, traveling, Wash Proj Arts, DC, 91 & Works on Paper, 1969-1970, Va Lust Gallery, NY, 91; Edward Thorp Gallery, NY, 86-98; Phyllis Kind Gallery, Chicago, Ill, 89; Collector's Choice, Ctr Arts, Vero Beach, Fla, 92; Terra Firma-Five Immigrant Artists, Art Gallery, Mt St Vincent Univ, NS, Can, 93; Deplacements, La Chambre Blanche, Que, Can, 94; Prodigal Daughter, Rockford Col Art Gallery, Ill, 95; Sniper's Nest: Art that has Lived with Way R Lippard, Bard Col, NY, 95; Small as a Way of Working, Owen Art Gallery, Mount Allison Univ, New Brunswick, Can, 96; Women Chicago Imagists, Rockford Art Mus, Ill, 96; Making Music, Champion Int Corp, Stamford, Conn, 97; Body Double, Winston Wachter Fine Art, NY, 98. *Pos:* Instr painting & drawing, Art Inst Chicago, 54-58, Parson Sch Art & Design, NY, 66-68. *Awards:* Can Coun Arts Award, 78 & 84; Nat Endowment Arts, 89; Alumni, Award, Chicago Inst Technol, 96. *Bibliog:* John Yau (auth), Original desire, ARTS Mag, 11/91; Nancy Stapen (auth), June Leaf's emphatically female figure Imagery, Boston Globe, 12/91; Let us now praise artist's artists, Art & Auction, 4/93. *Media:* All Media. *Mailing Add:* 7 Bleecker St New York NY 10012

LEAF, RUTH
PRINTMAKER, INSTRUCTOR
b New York, NY. *Study:* New Sch Social Res, New York, with Anthony Toney; Atelier 17 with William Stanley Hayter. *Work:* NY Univ; US Info Agency; Bowdoin Col Mus Art; Colgate Univ; Portland Mus; Lib of Congress; Northeastern Univ; and others. *Exhib:* Sala Exposiciones, Escuela Nac Artes Plasticas, 67; Boston Mus, 70; De Cordova Mus, Mass, 71; Soc Am Graphic Artists, NY, 71; Galerie Art & Gravure, Paris, 72; Northeast Col, Maine; The Print Found, New York City. *Collection Arranged:* permanent collection at Northeastern Univ. *Pos:* Consult, Colby Col, Maine. *Teaching:* Instr intaglio, NShore Community Art Ctr, 69-. *Awards:* Purchase Awards, Libr Cong, 46, Hofstra Univ, 63 & Olivet Col, 67; Nassau Mus Prize, 94. *Bibliog:* Ron Perkins (auth), Artists at Work--Filmstrip 4, Jam Handy Sch Serv, 70; Interview with artist, Art in the World radio prog, Nassau Community Col. *Mem:* Soc Am Graphic Artists; Print Club, Philadelphia; Los Angeles Print Soc. *Media:* Graphics, Paper Works. *Publ:* Auth, Intaglio Printing Techniques, Watson-Guptill; Etching, Engraving & Other Intaglio Techniques, Dover. *Dealer:* Robin Ficara; Sondra Mayer; Carolin Silver. *Mailing Add:* 711 Boccaccio Ave Venice CA 90291

LEANDRE, JUAN (JOAN)
GRAPHIC ARTIST
Work: Whitney Biennial, Whitney Mus Am Art, 2004. *Comn:* Retroyou.org, 1999-. *Pos:* Organizer OVNI Scanner, Barcelona, 92—99; auth, MAP Series Maga Assemble Proj, 94—96; mem, Oigo Rom Proj Inst Universitari del Audiovisual, Barcelona, 96—98

LEARSY, RAYMOND
COLLECTOR, PATRON
b Luxembourg. *Pos:* mem, Nat Coun Arts, 1982-88; trustee, Whitney Mus Am Art. *Awards:* Named on of Top 200 Collectors, ARTnews Mag, 2004; Gertrude Vanderbilt Whitney Award, 2004. *Collection:* Contemporary art. *Mailing Add:* c/o Woodrow Wilson Int Ctr One Woodrow Wilson pl Wilson Council 1300 Pennsylvania Ave NW Washington DC 20004 3027

LEARY, DANIEL
DRAFTSMAN, PRINTMAKER
b Glens Falls, NY, July 20, 55. *Study:* Antioch Col, Yellow Springs, Ohio, BFA, 79; Syracuse Univ, MFA, 96. *Work:* Spencer Mus Art, Univ Kansas, Lawrence; Milw Art Mus; Munson-Williams-Proctor Inst Mus Art, Utica; NY Pub Libr; Toledo Mus Art, Ohio; and others. *Exhib:* One-man shows, Printworks Ltd, 88, Hyde Collection, Glens Falls, NY, 90, Printworks Gallery, Chicago, 91 & 95, Blanden Mem Art Mus, Ft Dodge, Iowa, 92, Bobbit Visual Arts Ctr, Albion Col, Mich, 93, Sharon Campbell Gallery, Greenville, SC, 94 & Western Mich Univ, 94; Group exhibs incl Voorhees Zimmerli Art Mus, Rutgers Univ, 90; Bradford Art Mus & Galleries, West Yorkshire, Eng, 90; Contemp Art Ctr, Cincinnati, Ohio, 91. *Awards:* New York Found Arts Fel, 88; Nat Endowment Arts, 89; Glens Falls Found Grant, 89. *Bibliog:* Alan G Artner (auth), Leary portraits etched with discernment, Chicago Tribune, 1/6/89; Gordon Ligocki (auth), Young artist drawing powerful figures, The (Hammond, Indiana) Times, 8/24/90; Alan G Artner (auth), Leary drawings reflect rare craft, insight, Chicago Tribune, 10/4/91. *Media:* Etching, Miscellaneous Media. *Dealer:* Printworks Gallery 311 W Superior St Suite 105 Chicago IL 60610. *Mailing Add:* 5670 NYS Rt 86 Apt 2 Wilmington NY 12997

LEATHERDALE, MARCUS ANDREW
PHOTOGRAPHER
b Montreal, Que, Sept 18, 52. *Study:* Ecole Des Beaux Arts, Montreal, 70-73; Art Ctr, Los Angeles, BFA, 74; San Francisco Art Inst, BFA(hon student), 75-77. *Work:* Madison Art Ctr, Wis; Australian Art Gallery, Canberra; New Orleans Mus Art, La; Vienna Mus Mod Art, Austria; Art Inst Chicago, Ill. *Exhib:* Solo exhibs, London Regional Art Gallery, Ont, 83, Rheinisches Landes Mus, Bonn, Ger, 84, Greathouse Gallery, NY, 84, 85, 86 & 87, Claus Runkel Fine Arts, London, Eng, 88, Wessel O'Connor Gallery, NY, 89, Fay Gold Gallery, Atlanta, Ga, 90 & Fahey Klein Gallery, La, 90; Brent Sikkema, NY, 90; Arthur Roger Gallery, New Orleans, 91, NY, 92; Galerie del Conte, Milwaukee, 92; Galerie Bardamu, NY, 93. *Awards:* Nat Endowment Arts Award for Photog, 84. *Bibliog:* Brook Adams (auth), Marcus Leatherdale 1984-1987, Greathouse Gallery, New York, 88; Peggy Cypher (auth), Marcus Leatherdale, Arts, 89; Ali Anderson Spivy (auth), Argonaut, 94. *Dealer:* Fahey-Klein Gallery Los Angeles CA; Brent Sikkemma Fine Arts 155 Spring St New York NY 10012. *Mailing Add:* c/o Fahey Klein Gallery 148 N La Brea Ave Los Angeles CA 90036

LEATHERS, WINSTON LYLE
PAINTER, PRINTMAKER
b Miami, Man, Dec 29, 32. *Study:* Univ Man, BFA, 56, Univ Mex, 57-58; Man Teachers Col, 60; Univ BC, 61. *Work:* Can Coun Collection; Winnipeg Art Gallery; Univ of Fife, Scotland; Edmonton Art Gallery. *Comn:* Environmental wall mural, Roghmans Ltd, Winnipeg, 73; low relief concrete wall mural, Porv of Man, Portage La Prarie, 77; mural, IKOY Archit Partnership, Winnipeg, Man, 77; low relief wall mural, BACM Co Ltd, Winnipeg, 78. *Exhib:* Paris Int Print Exhib, France, 72; Bermuda Biennial, 72; Brit Fedn Int, 73; Int Print Exhib, Zurich, Switz, 74; Manisphere Int, Moorehead, Minn, 75. *Collection Arranged:* Univ of Mex, Contemp Gallery of Art, Mexico City, 57; University of BC, 61; Western Canadian Art Circuit Traveling Exhib, Winnipeg Art Gallery, 66-67; British Fedn of Artist Gallery, London, Eng, 68; Winnipeg Art Gallery, 74. *Pos:* Man art curric revision comt, Prov of Man, 61-66; art adv, Libr Comn, City of Winnipeg, 76-. *Teaching:* Prof design & drawing, Univ of Man, 69-. *Awards:* Sr Can Coun Grant for Printmaking, 67-68 & Proj Grant for Printmaking, 73, Can Coun; Purchase Award, Man Soc Artists, Winnipeg, 76. *Bibliog:* Prof Vann (auth), Perspective--Winston Leathers, Univ Man, 69; Philip Fry (auth), Manitoba Artists, Winnipeg Art Gallery, 72; Ann Davis (auth), Cosmic Variations--Winston Leathers, Winnipeg Art Gallery, Bulletin Mag, 6/75. *Mem:* Can Artists Representation (pres, 72); Royal Can Acad Arts; Brit Fedn of Artists, Eng; Can Soc of Printmakers; Can Soc of Graphic Artists. *Dealer:* Thomas Gallery Osborne St Winnipeg MB Can. *Mailing Add:* 55 Roslyn Crescent Winnipeg MB R3L 0H6 Canada

LEAVEY, JOHN CHRISTOPHER
PAINTER
b Bronx, NY, Mar 21, 37. *Study:* studied under George Grosz, Robert Beverly Hale, Edwin Dickinson, Arts Students League, New York City, 55-61 (scholar, 60). *Hon Degrees:* Fel, Am Acad in Rome. *Work:* Museo Della Citta Roma; Hirschhorn Collection Nat Gallery, Washington, DC; Readers Digest Collction, Pleasantville, NY; Atelier-AJE, NY; Dickinson Col, Carisile, Pa; Pfizer Co, NYC. *Comn:* mural, Am Acad Rome, 70; mural, Pfizer Co, New York City. *Exhib:* Annual Exhib, Nat Acad Design, NY, 61, 63, 78, 88 & 90; Anniversary, Mus Della Citta Roma, 70; 4 Am Painters, Am Acad Rome, 72; Audubon Artists, Nat Arts Club, New York City, NY, 94 -2005; 5 Landscape Painters, Mus Art, Springfield, Mass, 97; Blue Mountain Gallery, New York City, 80, 84, 87 & 89, 90-2005; Southern Vt Art Ctr, 96 & 98, 2003-2005. *Pos:* Scenic Painter, Metropolitan Opera, 85-88, NYC; Paperhill Playhouse, NJ, 88-2001. *Teaching:* instr Reniassance Art & art history, St Stephens Sch, Rome, Italy, 72-73; instr painting landscapes, Southern Vt Art Cen, 2000-2002; instr, Reninassance Art, 2003. *Awards:* Prixde Rome 70-71; Louis Comfort Tiffany Grant, 65; B Altman Figure Prize Nat Acad of Design, 88; RB McNeely Award, Audubon Artists, 95; Art Students League Award, Audubon Artists, 00. *Mem:* United Scenic Artists US; Fel Am Acad Rome; Art Students League; Audubon Artists; Southern Vt Artists; Art Students League. *Media:* Oil, Acrylic. *Dealer:* Elaine Beckwith Gallery Jamacia Vt; Blue Mountain Gallery NYC. *Mailing Add:* 32 Union Square E New York NY 10003-3209

LEAVITT, THOMAS WHITTLESEY
MUSEUM DIRECTOR
b Boston, Mass, Jan 8, 30. *Study:* Middlebury Col, AB, 51; Boston Univ, MA, 52; Harvard Univ, PhD, 58. *Collection Arranged:* New Renaissance in Italy (auth, catalog), Pasadena Art Mus, Calif, 58; Piet Mondrian (auth,catalog), Santa Barbara Mus Art, Calif, 65; American Portraits in California Collections (auth, catalog), Santa

Barbara Mus Art, 66; Brucke (auth, catalog), Cornell Univ, 70, Georg Kolbe (auth, catalog), 72; Seymour Lipton (auth, catalog), Herbert F Johnson Mus Art, 73; Directions in Afro-American Art, 74; Painting Up Front (auth, catalog), Herbert F Johnson Mus Art, 81; Masters of Contemporary Art in Poland, 86; Agnes Denes, Cornell Univ, 92; Unto the Fifth Generation: The Vanderbilts as Artists (auth, catalog), Newport Art Mus, 95. *Pos:* Asst to dir, Fogg Art Mus, 54-56; exec dir, Fine Arts Comn, People to People Prog, 57; dir, Pasadena Art Mus, 57-63, Santa Barbara Mus Art, 63-68, Andrew Dickson White Mus Art, Cornell Univ, 68-72 & Herbert F Johnson Mus, Cornell Univ, 73-91; dir mus prog, Nat Endowment Arts, 71-72, mem mus adv panel, 72-75; trustee, Am Fed Arts, 72-91 & Newport Art Mus, 95-2001; interim dir, RI Sch Design Mus, Providence, 93-94, Newport Art Mus, RI, 94-95; interim dir, Menil Collection, Houston, Tex, 99-2000. *Teaching:* Lectr Am art, Univ Calif, Santa Barbara, 64-65; prof hist art, Cornell Univ, 68-92. *Awards:* Distinguished Serv to Mus Award, Am Asn Mus, 97. *Mem:* Col Art Asn Am; Am Asn Mus (coun mem, 76-79, vpres, 80-82, pres, 82-85); Asn Art Mus Dirs (pres, 77-78); Independent Sector (bd mem, 80-84); Am Fedn Arts; Williamstown Regional Art Conserv Lab (pres, 85-87, bd dir, 88-91). *Res:* American 19th & 20th century painting. *Publ:* auth, Artists & Museums: Tensions and Intentions, Q A J Art, Cornell Univ, 5/89; intro in: Agnes Denes, Herbert F Johnson Mus Art, 92; many others; Let the Dogs Bark: George Loring Brown and the Critics, Am Art Rev, 74. *Mailing Add:* 25 Water Way Saunderstown RI 02874

LEAVITT, WILLIAM
PAINTER, PHOTOGRAPHER
b Washington, DC, Nov 27, 41. *Study:* Univ Colo, BA, 63; Claremont Grad Sch, MFA, 67. *Work:* San Diego Mus Contemp Art, La Jolla, Calif; Boysmans Mus, Rotterdam, Holland; Mus of Contemp Art, Los Angeles, Calif. *Exhib:* Reconsidering the Object of Art: 1965-75, Mus Contemp Art, Los Angeles, 95; Made in Calif 1980-2000, Los Angeles Co Mus of Art, 2000. *Teaching:* Instr post studio art, Calif Inst Art, 75-76; instr Marymount Col, Rancho Palos Verdes, Calif. *Awards:* Art Fel New Genre, Nat Endowment Arts, 91; J Paul Getty Fel, 93; John Simon Guggenheim Mem Fel, 98. *Dealer:* Manjo Leavin Gallery 812 N Robertson Blvd Los Angeles, CA 90069. *Mailing Add:* c/o Margo Leavin Gallery 812 N Robertson Blvd Los Angeles CA 90069

LEBECK, CAROL E
CERAMIST, PAINTER, EDUCATOR
b Spokane, Wash, Sept 8, 31. *Study:* Univ Calif, Los Angeles, BA (cum Laude), 56, MA (ceramics); Swed State Sch Design, Stockholm, Sweden, HKS (ceramics). *Work:* Los Angeles Co Cult Art Asn, Brand Libr, Los Angeles; Marietta Col, Ohio; Univ Ariz; Triad Gallery, San Diego; Portnoy Ltd, Scarsdale, NY; The American Hand, Georgetown, DC; The Sculpture Gallery, San Diego; Spectrum Gallery, San Diego; Celebrations Gallery, San Diego. *Exhib:* California Women in Crafts, Craft & Folk Art Mus, Los Angeles, 77; California Crafts X, Crocker Art Gallery, Sacramento, 77; Viewpoint: Ceramics, 1978, Grossmont Col Gallery, El Cajon, Calif; Celebrations Gallery Invitational: Dinner for Eight, San Diego, 79; West Coast Clay Spectrum, Security Pac Bank, Los Angeles, 79; Spectrum Gallery, San Diego, 81, 83; and many others. *Teaching:* Instr ceramics, Grossmont Col, El Cajon, Calif, 62-85. *Awards:* Fel, Swed Am Inst Grant, 58-59; Purchase Award, Marietta Crafts Nat, 75; Award of Merit, California Crafts X, 77. *Bibliog:* Rolando Giovanni (auth), The Seragraph in Ceramics, Art School and Industry, Faenza Editrice, 83. *Mem:* Allied Craftsmen of San Diego (corresp secy, 75); Nature Conservancy; Sierra Club; Nat Wildlife Fedn. *Media:* Clay, Mixed. *Mailing Add:* 10436 Russell Rd La Mesa CA 91941

LEBEJOARA, OVIDIU
PAINTER, SCULPTOR
b Ciupa Arges, Romania, Dec 14, 52; US & Romanian citizen. *Study:* N Tonitza Sch Art, Bucharest, BFA, 73; Otis Parsons Inst Art, Los Angeles, BA, 88; Syracuse Univ, MA, 98. *Exhib:* Contemp Portraits, Barnsdall Art Ctr, Los Angeles Municipal Art Gallery, Calif, 96; Art Addiction, Int Art Gallery Stockholm, Sweden, 96; Ucci Gallery, NY, 96; Pasadena Art Space, Calif, 96; Retropective Expozition, Minister of Cult, Romania, 96; City Los Angeles Cult Affairs Dept, Munic Art Gallery, 97; Art Addiction Int Art Gallery Stockholm Sweden March Award of Merit, 97; Institut Int D'Arts Plastiques, Grand Prix Du Japon, Saporo, Japan, 97; Art World Gallery, SOHO NY, 97; Absolut Chalk, a street festival in Pasadena, Calif, 97; New World Art Ctr, NY, 98; First Int Biennial Trevi Flash Art Mus, Palazzo Lucarini Trevi, Perugia, Italy, 98; Forth Ann Int Minature Art Show, Seaside Art Gallery, NC, 98; Open Call Exhib SCalif Artists, City Los Angeles, Cult Affairs Dept, 98; Flecher Gallery, Woodstock, NY, 2000; The Millenium Art Collection, 2003; Limnar Gallery, NY, 2003; LA Mart Art, Los Angeles, 2004; Word Art Collection, Holland & Korea, 2004; Infusion Gallery, Los Angeles, 2005; Romanian Future, Viitorul Romanese Romanian-Am Soc Art & Science, Mariot Hotel, Los Angeles, 2006. *Pos:* Artist, Siderma, Bucharest, Romania, 79-96, Los Angeles Signs & Graphics, 87-94, Art & Signs, Burbank, Calif, currently. *Awards:* Award of Merit, Calif State Fair, 91. *Bibliog:* Interview, Romanian TV-CLUJ, Ovidiu Suciv, 8/93; Interview, Dreptatea Newspaper, Pan Iserna, 10/93; Interview, Cotidianul II, Sanda Aronescu, 10/93; Origini (Roots), 94 & 2000; George Nicolescu (auth), Mondo Mag, 96; Glendace News Press, 97; Cetatea Culturala, 2000; Interview, Origini, Gabriel Stanesu, 2003. *Mem:* Am Pastelist Asn; Knickerbockers Artist Asn; Graphic Artists Guild, NY; New World Art Ctr, NY; Am Acad Arts & Sci (Romanian); Literart, Asn Romanian. *Media:* Oil, Acrylic; Tempera, Clay. *Publ:* Visalia Star, 91; Magazin Int, Universul, Micromagazin-Romanian Mag, Artspeak, The Villager, Actualite Departmentale Sub Ovest-French Mag, 95; Luceafarul Romanesc, Can, 97; Origini, (Roots), Romanian Art Mag, 99. *Dealer:* Agora Gallery 560 Broadway Soho NY 10012. *Mailing Add:* 8306 Crenshaw Blvd Apt B Inglewood CA 90305-1721

LEBEY, BARBARA
PAINTER, PRINTMAKER, WRITER
b Newark, NJ, Feb 28, 39. *Study:* Sarah Lawrence Col, BA, 59, Emory Univ Sch Law, JD, 70. *Work:* Princeton Univ Art Mus, NJ; Carter Presidential Ctr, Atlanta; Robert B Coggins Collection of Woman Artists, Marietta, Ga; Vanderbilt Collection; Newark Mus Art; Hunter Mus; Albany Mus, Ga, 90. *Comn:* Floral Still Life, comn by President & Mrs Jimmy Carter, 86; Seacoast Garden (painting), comn by Pat Conroy, 87; Springtime in Buckhead (commemorative print), Greater Atlanta C of C, Buckhead Sesquicentennary, 88; Walter B Ford Collection, 90. *Exhib:* Rablen West, Vero Beach, Fla, 90; Little Acorn Gallery, Dunwoody, Ga, 90; Leon Loard Gallery Fine Arts, Montgomery, Ala, 90; Foster Harmon Galleries, Sarasota, Fla, 92; Omell Galleries, London, St James, Eng, 92; and others. *Pos:* Bd dir, Ga Vol Lawyers Arts. *Awards:* Gold Medal, Artists in New Eng, Vt Co Arts, 85; Award of Merit, Robert B Coggins Collection, Trammel Crow Co, 88; Governor's Award for Ga Women in the Visual Arts, 97. *Bibliog:* Diana Brown (auth), Gardens of painted delights, Southern Homes, 87; Robert Nesbitt (auth), Artist realizes her dream, Inside Buckhead, 87. *Mem:* Atlanta Artists Club; Collectors Club, High Mus Art, Atlanta; Internat Women's Forum. *Media:* Oil, Watercolor; All Media. *Publ:* auth, Family Engagements, Longstreet Press, 2001. *Mailing Add:* 3065 E Pine Valley Rd NW Atlanta GA 30305

LEBOFF, GAIL F
PHOTOGRAPHER
b Brooklyn, NY, June 6, 1950. *Study:* State Univ Ala, 71-73; New York Univ, BS, 80, MA(studio art-photo), 82. *Work:* Coca-Cola Collection, Atlanta, Ga. *Comn:* Work in Genre of Art Work, comn by Poumans, Queens, NY, 85-86. *Exhib:* New Works, Bergen Mus Art & Sci, NJ, 83; Print Collection Color, Brooklyn Mus, NY, 84; Seeing is Believing, Alternative Mus, NY, 85; Images of Icon (traveling exhib), Johnson & Johnson, NJ, 86-87; Taking Liberty, NY State Mus, Albany, 86; Chairs, Witkin Gallery, NY, 87. *Teaching:* Instr, Sch Visual Arts, NY, currently. *Mem:* Women's Caucus Art; Soc Photogr Educ. *Mailing Add:* 451 Broome St No 12W New York NY 10013

LEBRON, MICHAEL A
CONCEPTUAL ARTIST, GRAPHIC ARTIST
b St Louis, Mo, July 19, 54. *Study:* Cooper Union, BFA, 76. *Work:* Mus Mod Art, NY. *Exhib:* Havana Bienal, 94; El Mus Del Barrio, 94. *Awards:* NY Found Arts Fel, 86; David Dinkins Excellence in Arts Award, 87; Nat Endowment Arts Fel, 90. *Bibliog:* Richard Goldstein (auth), A spectre is haunting the MTA, Village Voice, 82; articles in NY Times, 92 & 93, Art Direction, 93, Village Voice, 93 & Archive (Lurzers Int), 94. *Mailing Add:* 36 Cooper Sq No 7F New York NY 10003

LE BRUN, CAROL
CRITIC, DEALER
b Rochester, NY, May 2, 42. *Study:* Marymount Manhattan Col, BA, 64. *Pos:* Art ed & critic, Boston Herald Traveler, Mass, 66-72 & Boston Herald Am, 72-73; art critic, Christian Sci Monitor, 73-; pub relations dir, Boston Arts Festival, 85; vpres, Aruest Galleries, Inc, Boston, 73-81. *Res:* Turn of the century American impressionists, New England artists & 19th & 20th century European artists. *Publ:* Contribr, Sunday Herald Traveler Mag, Boston Arts Mag, Europe Mag, Sunday Herald Am Mag, Christian Sci Monitor, Quincy Patriot Ledger & Boston Herald

LECHTZIN, STANLEY
GOLDSMITH, EDUCATOR
b Detroit, Mich, June 9, 36. *Study:* Wayne State Univ, BFA; Cranbrook Acad Art, Bloomfield Hills, Mich, MFA. *Work:* Mus Am Crafts, NY; Detroit Inst Arts; Schmuckmuseum Pforzheim, Ger; Philadelphia Mus Art; Goldsmiths Hall, London; Yale Univ. *Comn:* Silver mace, Temple Univ, 66; Longwood Col, 74; paten, 41st Int Eucharistic Cong, Philadelphia, 76. *Exhib:* One-man shows, Mus Contemp Crafts, NY, 65, Lee Nordness Galleries, NY, 69, Int Jewelry Exhib, Tokyo, Japan, 73 & Goldsmiths Hall, London, 75; Philadelphia: Three Centuries of Am Art, Philadelphia Mus Art, Pa, 76; 20th Century Jewelry, Electrum Gallery, London, Eng, 85; Hong-ik Ann Exhib, Walker Hill Art Ctr Mus, Seoul, Korea. *Teaching:* Prof metalsmithing, Tyler Sch Art, Temple Univ, 62-, chmn metals/jewelry 62-, chmn dept crafts, 65-79 & 85-88. *Awards:* Nat Endowment Arts Craftsmen's Grant, 76 & 85; Pa Governor's Award in Crafts, 84; Art Achievement Award, Wayne State Univ, 94. *Bibliog:* Karl Schollmayer (auth), Neuer Schmuck, Ernst Wasmuth-Verlag, Ger, 74; C E Licka (auth), Stanley Lechtzin: Technic and the organic paradigm, Metalsmith, summer 82; Michael Dunas (auth), Conversations on Technology, Philosophy of the Physical, Metalsmith, summer 88. *Mem:* Soc NAm Goldsmiths (mem bd dir, 70-75); Am Crafts Coun; Col Fels Am Crafts Coun. *Media:* Metal, Plastic. *Res:* Electroforming of gold jewelry; computer aided design & manufacture for crafts. *Publ:* Auth, Electrofabrication of metal, Craft Horizons, 64; contribr, Metal Techniques for Craftsmen, 68; auth, Museum of Contemporary Crafts (brochure), 69; contribr, Contemporary Jewelry, 70. *Dealer:* Helen Drutt Gallery Philadelphia PA. *Mailing Add:* PO Box 8816 Beech & Penrose Ave Elkins Park PA 19027

LECKY, SUSAN
PAINTER
b Los Angeles, Calif, July 19, 40. *Study:* Univ Southern Calif, BFA; also Europ travel. *Work:* Los Angeles Co Mus; Bloomington Fed Savings & Loan, Bloomington, Pontiac & Streator Br. *Exhib:* solo exhibs, Millikin Univ, Decatur, Ill, 83, Eastfield Col, Mesquite, Tex, 85, Conduit Gallery, Dallas, Tex, 86, ETex State Univ, Commerce, Tex, 86, Brazos Gallery, Richland Col, Callas, Tex, 91, Art Ctr, Waco, Tex, 92, LA Thompson Gallery, Dallas, Tex, 95, Irving Art Ctr, Tex, 98, Longview Mus Art, Tex, 2001, Art Centre Plano, Tex, 2001, Continental Gallery, Dallas, 2002, Brookhaven Col, Dallas, 2006 & others; Looking at the Earth, Nat Air & Space Mus, Smithsonian

Inst, Washington, 86-87; Masur Mus, La, 91, 93, 95, 96, 97, 2000, 2003; Abstraction II, Doshi Ctr Contemp Art, Harrisburg, Pa, 96; Horace Cardwell Competition, Meadows Gallery, Mus ETex, Lufkin, 96; 15th Ann Sept Competition, Alexandria Mus Art, La, 96; 3rd Ann Nat Exhib, State of Art Gallery, Ithaca, NY, 96; Decumano Secondo Verona, Italy, 97; Capino Veronese, Italy, 98; Warehouse Living Arts Ctr, Corsecann, TEx, 98, 99, 20000, 2001, 2002; Art with a Southern Draw, Mobile, Ala, 98, 99, 2001; Dishman Competition, Beaumont, Tex, 95, 96, 97, 2002; Art In the Metropolis, Ft Worth, Tex, 2001-2004; Arthouse on Routh, Dallas, Tex, 2003-2004; Asn League of Houston Celebrates Tex Art, 2005 & 06; Bath House Cultural Ctr, Dallas, 2006; and many others. *Pos:* Restorer, Univ Ill Libr, 73-; art critic, New Art Examiner, 76-78; pub lect, Millikin, Decatur, Ill, 83, Eastfield Col, Mesquite, Tex, 85, East Tex Univ, Commerce, 86, Univ Tulsa, 86, 99, Richland Col, Dallas, 89, Tex Woman's Univ, Denton, 89, Webster Univ, St Louis, 91, Art Ctr, Waco, Tex, 92, Circolo della Kosa, Verona, Italy, 97. *Teaching:* Vis artist, Univ Tulsa, Okla, 88 & 99. *Awards:* 60th Nat Windsor & Newton Award for acrylics, Cooperstown, NY, 95; People's Choice Award, Whitehorse Living Arts Ctr, Corsicana, Tex, 98; and others. *Bibliog:* Joe Kagle (dir), The Studios (video), Art Ctr, Waco, Tex, 92. *Media:* Acrylic, Colored Pencil. *Mailing Add:* 12116 Brookmeadow Ln Dallas TX 75218

LE CLAIR, CHARLES
PAINTER, EDUCATOR
b Columbia, Mo, May 23, 14. *Study:* Univ Wis, BS & MS, 35; Acad Ranson, Paris, 36; Columbia Univ, 40-41. *Work:* Butler Art Inst; Carnegie Inst Mus; Albright-Knox Art Gallery, Buffalo, NY; Provincetown Art Asn & Mus; McNay Art Inst, San Antonio. *Exhib:* Butler Inst Am Art, Youngstown, Ohio, 51, 56 & 71; Whitney Mus Am Art, NY, 51-56; Int Watercolor Exhib, Brooklyn Mus, 59; Nat Acad Design Ann, 60; Pa Acad Fine Arts, Philadelphia, 63 & 65; Am Acad & Inst Arts & Lett, 78; 60 Yr Retrospective, Villanova Univ, Philadelphia, 98; Susquehanna Art Mus, Harrisburg, Pa, 2003. *Teaching:* Assoc prof painting, Chatham Col, 46-52, chmn dept art, 46-60, prof painting, 52-60; dean, Tyler Sch Art, Temple Univ, 60-74, prof painting, 60-81, chmn dept painting & sculpture, 79-81, prof emer, 81-. *Awards:* Ten Awards, Assoc Artists Pittsburgh, 46-; Ford Found Fel Advan Educ, 52-53; Pennell Mem Award, Pa Acad Fine Arts, 65. *Media:* Oil, Watercolor. *Publ:* Auth, A Salute to William Pitt (catalog), Chatham Col, 58; Education of the Artist, Alumni Rev, Temple Univ, 1/62; The Art of Watercolor: Techniques and New Directions, Prentice-Hall, 85; Color in Contemp Painting, Watson-Guptill, 91; The Art of Watercolor, Watson-Guptill, rev ed 99. *Dealer:* Gross McCleaf Gallery 126 S 16th St Philadelphia PA 19102. *Mailing Add:* 2 Franklin Town Blvd Apt 1714 Philadelphia PA 19103-1231

LEDGERWOOD, JUDY C
PAINTER
Study: Art Acad Cincinnati, BFA, 82; Sch Art Inst Chicago, 84. *Work:* Metrop Mus Art, NY; Mus Contemp Art, Chicago, Ill; Milwaukee Mus Art, Milwaukee, Wis; Chicago Pub Libr. *Exhib:* Solo exhibs, Robbin Lockett Gallery, Chicago, 89, 90 & 92, Scott Hanson Gallery, NY, 89, Richard Green Gallery, Santa Monica, Calif, 91, Hanes Art Ctr Glass Gallery, Chapel Hill, NC, 92, Germans Van Eck Gallery, NY, 93, Feigen, Inc, Chicago, 93, 95 & 97 & Renaissance Soc, Chicago, 99, Feigen Contemp, NY, 2000, Concept Art, Pittsburgh, Pa, 2001, Sunny Days, 1301 PE, Los Angeles, Calif, 2002; Changing Views, Feigen, Inc, Chicago, 94; Nature, Revolution: A Gallery Proj, Ferndale, Mich, 94; Regional Biennial, Fort Wayne Mus Art, Ind, 94; Chicago Abstract Painters, Evanston Art Ctr, Evanston, Ill, 95; Inaugural Exhib, Mus Contemp Art, Chicago, 96; New Works, Feigen Inc, Chicago, 97; Exploiting the Abstract, Feigen Contemp, NY, 98; Weatherspoon Art Gallery, UNC, Greensboro, 2000; Search for Love, Gallery 312, Chicago, Ill, 2001; Chicago Artists in the New Millenium, Union League Club of Chicago, Ill, 2003. *Awards:* Wilder Travelling Fel, 82; Ill Arts Coun Chmn's Grant, 85; Nat Endowment Arts, 93; Biennial Competition, Louis Comfort Tiffany Found, 97; CIRA Grant, Northwestern Univ, 99; Univ Res Grant, Morocco, Archit, Decoration, Light, 2000. *Bibliog:* Alan Artner (auth), Art: Judy Ledgerwood, Chicago Tribune, 1/17/92; Joe Scanlan (auth), Why paint?, The Renaissance Soc Univ Chicago Newsletter, winter 92; Susan Snodgrass (auth), Review of exhibitions: Chicago, Art in Am, 4/92; Artner, Alen (auth.) Chicago Tribune, 93, 99. *Dealer:* Feigen Contemporary 535 W 20th St New York NY 10011. *Mailing Add:* 314 S Cuyler Oak Park IL 60302

LEE, BARBARA
COLLECTOR
b July, 45. *Study:* Simmons Col, BA. *Hon Degrees:* Boston Univ, MSW. *Pos:* chmn bd dir, Inst Contemp Art, Boston, MA; Pres, dir, treas, Barbara Lee Family Found, Cambridge, MA; founding chairwoman, contemp Arts prog, Isabella Stewart Gardner Mus, Boston, MA; co-founder, The White House Project, 97. *Awards:* recipient George Alden Leadership award; Opening Doors Award, Womens Inst for Housing Devel, 2002; Named one of top 200 collectors, ARTnews Mag, 2004, 2006; named to 100 Women who Run this Town, Boston Mag. *Collection:* Modern and contemp art by women. *Mailing Add:* 131 Mt Auburn St Ste 2 Cambridge MA 02138

LEE, BRIANT HAMOR
HISTORIAN, EDUCATOR
b New Haven, Conn, May 6, 38. *Study:* Carnegie-Mellon Univ; Adelphi Univ, BA; Acad de Belle Arti, Rome, Cert de Frequenza; Univ Italiana per Stranieri-Perugia; Ind Univ, MA; NY Univ; Mich State Univ, PhD. *Comn:* Over 100 theatrical productions, Scenographer, (in collaboration with staging dir); 25 theatrical productions, staging dir & scenographer, 64-. *Pos:* Design engineer, Kliegl Lighting, New York, 63-64; ed, J Empirical Research in Theatre, 80-85. *Teaching:* Instr scenography, US Int Univ, San Diego, Calif, 62-63; asst prof scenography, Bradley Univ, Peoria, Ill, 67-68; prof theatre, Bowling Green State Univ, Ohio, 96. *Awards:* Undergrad Alumni: Asn Master Teacher Award Finalist, Bowling Green State Univ, 96-97. *Mem:* Am Theatre Asn; Speech Commun Asn; Am Soc for Theatre Res; Ohio Theatre Alliance; Ohio Community Theatre Asn. *Media:* Watercolor, Ink. *Res:* Late 18th century European theatre architecture and theatrical staging. *Publ:* Auth, Pierre Patte, Late 18th century lighting innovator, Theater Survey, 76; The origins of the box set in the late 18th century, Theatre Survey, 78; Corrugated Scenery, Oracle Press, 82; Understanding Microcomputers & Microcomputer Wordprocessing, Bowling Green State Univ, 85; European Post-Baroque Neoclassical Theatre Architecture, Mellon Press, 96. *Mailing Add:* 336 S Church St Bowling Green OH 43402-3719

LEE, CATHERINE
SCULPTOR, PAINTER
b Pampa, Tex, Apr 11, 50. *Study:* San Jose State Univ, BA, 75. *Work:* Stadtische Galerie im Lenbachhaus, Munich; Mus Mod Art, NY; Tate Gallery, London; Mus Art, Carnegie Inst, Pittsburgh; US Dept State, Washington, DC. *Exhib:* Selected Works, Albright-Knox Mus, Buffalo, NY, 87; Artists in the Abstract, Weatherspoon Gallery, Univ NC, Greensboro, 90; Biennale de Sculpture, Monte Carlo, Monaco, 91; Geteilte Bilder, Das Diptychon in der neuen Kunst, Mus Folkwang, Essen, Ger, 92; Stadtische Galerie im Lenbachhaus, Munich, 92; Neue Galerie der Stadt Linz, Austria, 92; Contemp Prints, The Tate Gallery, London, 94; 29th Ann Exhib of Art on Paper, Weatherspoon Art Gallery, 94; US Print/Grafilkkaa USA Garner Tullis Workshop, Retretti Art Ctr, Finland, 95; Mizuma Gallery, Tokyo, Japan, 95; Galerie Karsten Greve, Köln, Ger, 95; Serienbilder-Bilderserien, Städtische Galerie im Lenbachhaus, Munich, 96; ArtPace, A Found for Contemp Art, San Antonio, Tex, 96; Sonoma State Univ Art Gallery, 97; Galleri Weinberger, København, 98; Bemis Art Found, Omaha, Nebr, 98; San Diego State Univ Art Gallery, 99; Lafayette Col Art Ctr, Easton, Pa, 99; Galerie Lelong, NY, 99; Die Kunst der Gegenwart Im Lenbachhaus München, Städtische Galerie im Lenbachhaus, Munich, 99; Galeria Carles Taché, Barcelona, Spain, 2000; Lyman-Allen Art Mus, New London, Conn, 2000. *Teaching:* Artist-in-residence, Minneapolis Col Art & Design, Minn Inst Art, 82; vis asst prof painting, Univ Tex, San Antonio, 83, vis asst prof sculpture; adj asst prof, Columbia Univ, NY, 86-87. *Awards:* Creative Artists Pub Serv Prog Fel Painting, 78; Nat Endowment Arts, Painting Grant, 89. *Bibliog:* John Russell (auth), Bright young artists, New York Times, 5/18/86; Demetrio Paparoni (auth), A Conversation with Catherine Lee, Tema Celeste, 2/92; David Carrier & Helmut Friedel (auths), Catherinne Lee, Outcasts, Stadtische Galerie im Lenbachhaus, Munich, 92; Carter Ratcliff & Faye Hirsch (auths), Catherine Lee, The Alphabet Works, Univ of Wash Press, 2d edit, 99. *Media:* Bronze; Oil. *Dealer:* Galerie Lelong 526 W 26th St New York NY 10001; Galerie Karsten Greve 5 Rue Debelleyme 75003 Paris France. *Mailing Add:* 106 Spring St New York NY 10012-3814

LEE, DAVID (TZEH-HSIAN)
PAINTER
b Hupei, China, Mar 24, 44. *Study:* NJ Inst Technol, MA, 69; Ridgewood Art Inst, 80 & 90. *Work:* Zhejiang Mus, Hangzhou, Zhejiang, China. *Exhib:* Allied Artists Am Ann Exhib, Nat Arts Club, NY, 87-89, 91, 93, 94, 97, 99 & 2000; Pa Watercolor Soc Ann Exhib, Port Hist Mus, Philadelphia, 87; NJ Watercolor Soc 50th Anniversary Exhib, Montclair Art Mus, 88; Am Watercolor Soc Ann Open Exhib, Salmagundi Club, NY, 90 & 2000; Art Competition Winners, Artist's Mag, Cincinnati, 91; Watermedia, Challenge of Champions, 2003; Int Exhib of the Watercolor Art Soc, Houston, Tex, 2003. *Awards:* Bergen Mus Art & Sci Juror's Award, Open Juried Art Exhib, 83, 86 & 87; NJ Watercolor Soc Award, 44th Ann Open Exhib, 86; Winsor & Newton Award, Am Artist Prof League 60th Grand Nat Exhib, 88. *Bibliog:* Estelle F Sinclaire (auth), Watercolor Soc Show, Arts Tues, Princeton Packet, 10/2/84; Eileen Watkins (auth), Art (critique), Star-Ledger, 9/11/87; Carole Katchen (auth), Winning strategies for landscape painting, Artists Mag, 12/91. *Mem:* Allied Artists Am Inc; Am Artists Prof League Inc; Hudson Valley Art Asn; NJ Watercolor Soc (historian, 93-2000). *Media:* Watercolor. *Publ:* Add Asian accents for tranquility in watercolor magic, Artists Mag, 93; A Boy in the Field, in: The Best of Portrait Painting, 98 & Needle Works, in: Splash 6, 2000, North Light Bks; Lotus Pond, in: The Best of Watercolor, Rockport Publ, 99; Butterflies, in: The Best in Watercolor, Splash 8, North Light Books, 2004. *Mailing Add:* 186 Hickory St Washington Twp NJ 07676

LEE, DORA FUGH
PAINTER, SCULPTOR
b Peking, China, Aug 16, 30; US citizen. *Study:* With Prince Pu Ju, Chao Meng-chu & Yen Shao-Hsiang, Peking, China; additional study with sculptor, Pietro Lazzari, Washington. *Work:* China Inst, NY; Pearl Buck Found, Philadelphia; Smithsonian Inst & Nat Cathedral, Washington; The Willard Hotel, Washington; Johns Hopkins Medical Ctr, Baltimore, Md; Nat Portrait Gallery, Smithsonian Inst; and others. *Comn:* Sears House, Washington. *Exhib:* Watercolor USA, Springfield, Mo, 75; sculpture Mainstreams, Marietta Col, Ohio, 76; Am Watercolor Soc Traveling Exhib, 76-92; Franz Bader Gallery, Washington, 76-96. *Teaching:* Pvt lessons in Chinese traditional painting & calligraphy, Smithsonian Inst, Washington, 83-84; Chinese calligraphy, George Washington Univ, 82. *Awards:* Best of Show, 68, First Prize/Watercolor, 71 & 72, Montgomery Co Art Asn Traveling Exhib, Am Watercolor Asn, 76; North Light Award, Nat Sumei Soc, 85. *Mem:* Washington Watercolor Asn; Nat League Am Pen Women; Am Watercolor Soc. *Media:* Oil, Watercolor; Clay. *Dealer:* Courtyard Gallery Beijing China. *Mailing Add:* 6305 Orchid Dr Bethesda MD 20817-5613

LEE, ELLEN WARDWELL
CURATOR
b Indianapolis, Ind, Feb 5, 49. *Study:* Smith Col, Northampton, Mass, BA, 71. *Collection Arranged:* William McGregor Paxton, 79; The Aura of Neo-Impressionism: WJ Holliday Collection, 83; More than Red, White and Blue: Am Paintings from the Permanent Collection of Indianapolis Mus Art, 89; Seurat at Gravelines: The Last Landscapes, 90. *Pos:* Assoc cur painting & sculpture,

Indianapolis Mus Art, 75-84, cur, 84-89 & sr cur, 89-91, chief cur, 91-. *Mem:* Am Asn Mus; Int Coun Mus. *Res:* Late 19th early 20th century American & European painting and sculpture. *Publ:* William McGregor Paxton, Nat Acad, Indianapolis Mus Art, 79; auth, The Aura of Neo-Impressionism: The WJ Holliday Collection, Indianapolis Mus Art & Ind Univ Press, 83; Seurat at Gravelines: The Last Landscapes, Indianapolis Mus Art, 90; Seurat Centenary (bk revs), Art J, Vol 51, No 2, 104-107, summer 92; Beyond the blackluster: Good exhibitions in small packages, Cur, Mus J, Vol 37, No 3, 172-184. *Mailing Add:* 3705 Spring Hollow Rd Indianapolis IN 46208-4169

LEE, ERIC MCCAULEY
MUSEUM DIRECTOR, HISTORIAN
b Clinton, NC, Feb 23, 66. *Study:* Yale Univ, New Haven, Conn, BA, 88, MA, 91, PhD, 97. *Collection Arranged:* Transls: JMW Turner and Printmakers, Yale Cent British Art, 93; Weitzenhoffer Collection French Impressionism: Fred Jones Jr Mus Art, Univ Okla, 2000; The Art of Taos: The Thams Collection. *Pos:* asst cur paintings, Yale Cent British Art, New Haven, Conn, 95-96; acting dir Fred Jones Jr Mus Art, Univ Okla, Norman, 97-98, dir, 98. *Teaching:* asst prof art hist, Sch Art, Univ Okla, Norman, 97-. *Mem:* AAM, Accreditation Visitining Committee; Col Art Asn; Midwest Art History Soc. *Res:* 18th-20th century European and American art. *Publ:* co-auth, Fred Jones Jr Mus of Art at the Univ of Oklahoma: Selecteo Works, Univ of Oklahoma Press, 2004

LEE, GERALDINE See Hooks, Geri

LEE, JANIE C
CURATOR
b Shreveport, La, Apr 22, 37. *Study:* Sarah Lawrence Col, BA, 59. *Mem:* Art Dealers Asn Am (vpres, 84-86, bd dir, 84-88 & 92). *Publ:* Auth, Master Drawings 1918-1985, spring 86; Ink Drawings 1890-1986, spring 87; Master Drawings, 1877-1987, spring 88; Abstract Expressionist Drawings 1941-1955, fall 88; Master Drawings 1859-1989, fall 89. *Mailing Add:* 3711 San Felipe Rd #4E Houston TX 77027

LEE, JOHN KEMP
ARTIST
b Hartford, Conn. *Study:* Dartmouth Col, BA; Maine Col Art, BFA; Univ Pa, MFA. *Exhib:* Solo shows include Blue Mountain Gallery, Soho, NY City, 95, South Vt Univ Arts, Manchester, Vt, 98, Univ Wis, La Crosse, 99, Norwich Univ, Northfield, Vt, 2001, Aughinbaugh Art Gallery, Messiah Col, Grantham, Pa, 2002, Kouros Art Gallery, NY City, 2003, 2005; group shows include Nat Acad Design, NY City, 2006. *Teaching:* Adj asst prof studio art Dartmouth Col, Hanover, NH, 84-. *Awards:* Individual Artist grant, Vt Council ARts, 2000-2001. *Mailing Add:* Kouros Gallery 23 E 73rd St New York NY 10021

LEE, KATHARINE C
DIRECTOR
b Detroit, Mich, Dec 12, 41. *Study:* Vassar Col, BA(art hist, magna cum laude), 63; Fulbright Scholar, 63-64; Harvard Univ, MA, 66; Knoxville Col, Il, Hon Dr Humane Letters, 96. *Collection Arranged:* Prairie School Furniture: Wright, Elmslie, Maher, 72, Art Deco: Trends in Design, 73, Collection of Contemporary Art of Mid-America Club, Chicago, 76-78, Artists View the Law of the 20th Century (auth, catalog), 77, Renaissance Soc & Smart Gallery, Univ Chicago; Some Recent Art from Chicago (auth, catalog), Ackland Art Mus, Univ NC, 80. *Pos:* Asst cur, Toledo Mus Art, Ohio, 68-70; dir exhib, Renaissance Soc, Univ Chicago, 71-73, cur collections, Smart Gallery, Univ Chicago, 73-79; cur, Ackland Art Mus, Univ NC, Chapel Hill, 79-82; asst dir, Art Inst Chicago, 81-85, dept dir, 85-91; dir, Va Mus Fine Arts, currently. *Teaching:* Mus course in hist mus & collection inst, Univ Chicago, 78; Getty Trust/Am Fed Art Mus Inst Fac, 91-93. *Awards:* Ford Found Grant in Mus Curatorial Training Internship, 66-68. *Mem:* Am Asm Mus (accreditation comn, 96-); AAMD (trustee, 96-, mem comt, 98-); CAA. *Mailing Add:* Va Mus Fine Arts 200 N Blvd Richmond VA 23220-4007

LEE, LARA
PRODUCER, FILMMAKER
b Brazil. *Study:* NY Univ. *Work:* Prufrock, B&W, 91, Neighbors, 92, Am Autumn Wind, 93, Synthetic Pleasures (full length documentary), 96, Architettura, Modulations-Cinema for the Ear (full length documentary), 98, Caipirinha Music Record Label, 97, Oblique (film) & Beneath the Borqa in Afghanistan, 2001, Caipirinha Music Record Label. *Exhib:* Munich Film Festival, Ger, 93; Breckenridge Festival of Films, Colo, 93; Univ Cincinnati Film Soc, 93; Humboldt Film Festival, Calif, 93; Women in Film, Hollywood, 94; Jerusalem Film Festival, Israel, 94; Bombay Int Film Festival, India, 94; S Beach Film Festival, Miami, 94; Int Outdoor Short Fest - Flickerfest, Australia, 95; Whitney Biennial, Whitney Mus Am Art, NY, 97; and many others. *Pos:* Producer & programmer, Sao Paulo Int Film Festival, 84-89; establisher film production company, Caipirinha Productions

LEE, LI LIN
PAINTER
b Jakarta, Indonesia, Oct 11, 55; US citizen. *Study:* Univ Pittsburgh, BS, 78. *Work:* Ameritech Servs, Chicago; Arthur Anderson & Co, Chicago; Art Inst Chicago; Philip Morris Co Inc, NY; Prudential Ins Co Am, Newark, NJ. *Exhib:* Solo Exhibs, LaSorda-Iri Gallery, Los Angeles, 88, Reicher Gallery, Barat Col, Lake Forest, Ill, 89, Tilden-Foley Gallery, New Orleans, 89, E M Donahue Gallery, NY, 89, 90, 91 & 92, Li-Lin Lee, New Works, Richard Iri Gallery, Los Angeles, 90, Betsy Rosenfield Gallery, Chicago, 90 & 92; Artfair/Seattle, Betsy Rosenfield Gallery, 92; Wall Project, Sculpture Center, Benefit Exhib, NY, 92; The Rectangled Bank, E M Donahue Gallery, NY, 92; May 1992, Betsy Rosenfield Gallery, Chicago Int Art Expo, Chicago, 92; and others. *Bibliog:* S G (auth), Li Lin Lee at Blum Helman Gallery, LA Times, 5/89; John Yau (auth), Li Lin Lee at E M Donahue Gallery, Artforum, summer 89; John Brunetti (auth), Li Lin Lee at Betsy Rosenfield Gallery, New Art Examiner, 5/92. *Media:* Oil on Burlap, Enamel on Wood. *Dealer:* E M Donahue Gallery 560 Broadway No 304 New York NY 10012. *Mailing Add:* 853 W Lawrence Ave Chicago IL 60640-4212

LEE, MACK
ART DEALER
Study: Hampshire Col, BA, 75. *Pos:* Own & dir, Lee Gallery, 81-. *Mem:* Asn Int Photog Art Dealers (bd mem, currently). *Media:* Photographs. *Res:* George Kendall Warren, James Wallace Black, Southworth & Hawes, Eugene Cuvelier, Adalbert Cuvelier, Gustave LeGray, Charles Negre, Henri LeSecq, Charles Marville, Edouard Baldus, Gertrude Kasebier, George Seeley, Karl Struss, Alfred Stieglitz. *Specialty:* 19th c Am, British & French photos; photo-secessionists & circle of Alfred Stieglitz; 20th c Am photos before 1980. *Publ:* Auth, Fifteenth Anniversary Show (exhib, catalog), Pvt Publ, 96; California in the 1930s, Photographs By Lange Levenson, and Noskowiak (exhib, catalog) pvt publ, 96; Camera Work, pvt publ, 12/97; Naturalist Photography 1880-1920, pvt publ, 9/98. *Mailing Add:* Lee Gallery 9 Mount Vernon St Winchester MA 01890

LEE, MARGARET F
PAINTER
b South St Paul, Minn, May 19, 22. *Study:* Rochester Art Ctr, with Adolph Dehn, Arnold Blanch & Robert Birmelin, 60-74; John Pike Watercolor Sch, Woodstock, NY, 72; watercolor with Zoltan Szabo, 74; Japanese woodblock with Toshi Yoshida, 74; Univ Minn, BA(art), 75. *Work:* YMCA-YWCA Permanent Collection, Rochester, Minn. *Exhib:* One-man show, Augsburg Col, Minneapolis, 73; 17th & 18th Int, Galerie Int, NY, 73-74; Mainstreams USA, Marietta Col, Ohio, 74; Am Painters in Paris, French Ministry & Paris City Coun, 75; Arts of Asia Gallery, Rochester, Minn, 75-77; and others. *Teaching:* Lectr Japanese Sumi-e, Winona Art Ctr, Minn, 74; instr Japanese painting, Rochester Art Ctr, 74. *Awards:* First Place, Northern Lights 75, St Paul, 75; Award of Excellence, Arts Omnibus, 76, St Paul; Award, Midwest Watercolor Soc Exhib, Minn Mus of Art, St Paul, 77. *Mem:* Minn Artists Asn; Sumi-e Soc Am, NY; Twin City Watercolor Soc, Minneapolis, Minn. *Media:* Acrylic, Sumi Ink; Watercolro. *Dealer:* Southeastern Minn Visual Artists Gallery 16 First St SW Rochester MN 55901. *Mailing Add:* 295 W 4th St Zumbrota MN 55992

LEE, MARY VIRGINIA
MURALIST, PAINTER
b Clinton, Okla, Nov 19, 24. *Study:* Am Univ, 43-45. *Work:* Phillips Mem Gallery, Washington; St Laurance Cathedral, Amarillo, Tex. *Comn:* Stations of the Cross, 81 & 12th Chapter Revelations (mural), 81, Parish Church, Montalto, Parma, Italy; Stations of the Cross, Epiphany Church, Oklahoma City, Okla, 84; two stained glass rose windows, St Peter's Church, Guymon, Okla, 85; sanctuary mural, St Joseph's Church, Hong-Kong, 93. *Exhib:* New Mexico Artists, Okla Art Ctr, Oklahoma City, 51; Alcove Exhib, NMex State Gallery, Santa Fe, 54; Traveling Group Show, NMex State Gallery, Santa Fe, 55; Alcove Exhib, NMex State Gallery, Santa Fe, 57; and others solo exhibs. *Bibliog:* Peter Seracino Inglott (auth), The Art of Mary Virginia Lee, Arte Cristiana, Scvola Beato Angelico, Milano, Italy, No LXIX, 8-9/81. *Mem:* Nat Asn Women Artists; hon mem Kappa Pi. *Media:* Oil, Acrylic. *Mailing Add:* PO Box 132 Clinton OK 73601

LEE, NELDA S
DEALER
b Gorman, Tex, July 3, 41. *Study:* Tarleton State Col, AA, 61; N Tex State Univ, BFA, 63; Tex Tech Univ, Lubbock, grad study, 65 & San Miguel de Allende Art Inst, Mex, 65. *Work:* Delgado Mus of Art, New Orleans, La; El Paso Mus of Art, Tex. *Comn:* Portrait of late Sam Jones, Supt Rising Star Pub Sch, comn by Student Coun, 66; designed terrazo marble floors, Sweetwater High Sch, comn by Balfour Co, Tex, 67; student ctr, Tarleton State Univ, comn by Student Coun, Stephenville, Tex, 68. *Exhib:* Artist of SE in Tex, Delgado Mus Art, New Orleans, La, 64; Tex Fine Arts Asn Traveling Exhib, 64-67; Int Designer-Craftsmen Exhib, El Paso Mus, Tex, 65; Tex Watercolor Soc Exhib, Elizabeth Ney Mus, San Antonio, Tex, 67. *Collection Arranged:* President Carter's Inaugural Reception Exhib, The Capitol, Washington, DC, 77. *Pos:* Owner-operator, Nelda Lee Inc, 67-; mem, Tex Comn Arts, 93-99. *Teaching:* Chairperson art dept, Ector High Sch, Odessa, Tex, 63-68. *Awards:* First Place Sculpture, Artist of the SE in Tex, Delgado Mus of Art, 64; First Place Design, Int Designer-Craftsmen Exhib, 65; First Place Mixed-Media, Tex Fine Arts Exhib, 65. *Bibliog:* Scheryl Vannoy (auth), Texas art dealer stages exhibition at Capitol, San Angelo Standard Times, 77; article, SW Art Mag, 80; Carrie Steenson (auth), A rare work of art, Business Mag, 81. *Mem:* Am Soc of Appraisers; Tex Asn Art Dealers (pres, 79-91). *Specialty:* Eighteenth--twentieth century English and American masters. *Interests:* Scholarships funded for art students. *Publ:* Auth, History of Art in Odessa, Texas, Permian Basin Hist Ann, 69; coauth, Painter of a vanishing America, SW Art, 74. *Mailing Add:* 2610 E 21 St Odessa TX 79761

LEE, THOMAS H
COLLECTOR
b 44. *Study:* Harvard Univ, B, 65. *Pos:* With, First Nat Bank Boston, 66-74, mgr high tech leading group, 68-74, vpres, 73-74; chmn, TH Lee Mezzanine; chmn, Chief Exec Officer, THLee Putnam Ventures; founder, chmn, Chief Exec Officer, Thomas H Lee Partners, Boston, 1974-2005; founder, chmn, Chief Exec Officer, Lee Equity Partners LLC, NY City, 2006-; nat adv bd, JP Morgan; dir, Metris Cos Inc, Miller Import Corp, Wyndham Int Inc, Snapple Beverage Corp, Gen. Nutrition Cos, Playtex Products Inc, Vail Resorts Inc, 1993, Safelite Glass Corp, Vertis Holdings Inc, First Security Servs

Corp; Established Henry Rosovsky Fund, Fac of Arts & Scis, Harvard Univ, 84; trustee Intrepid Mus, Lincoln Ctr for Rockefeller Univ, NY Univ Med Ctr, Mus Modern Art, NY City; vpres bd, Whitney Mus Am Art, currently. *Awards:* Named one of Top 200 Collectors, ARTnews mag, 2003-06. *Collection:* Modern and contemporary art, Egyptian art

LEE-SISSOM, E (EVELYN) JANELLE SISSOM
PAINTER
b Oakland, Calif, Feb 11, 34. *Study:* Art Instruction, Inc; Watkins Inst; Univ Tenn. *Work:* Parthenon Galleries & Mus, Tenn State Mus & Opryland Hotel's Collection Tenn Art, Nashville; Sunkist Corp Off, Atlanta, Ga; Tenn Valley Authority Corp Offices & Visitors Ctr, Knoxville, Tenn. *Comn:* Painting, Cookeville General Hospital, Tenn, 81. *Exhib:* 26th Nat Soc Painters Casein & Acrylic, Am Acad & Inst Arts & Letters, NY, 79; 22nd Traveling, Nat Soc Painters Casein & Acrylic, 79-80; 2nd Ann Open, Salmagundi Club, NY, 79; Grand Nat, Am Artists Prof League, NY, 79 & 80; one-woman show, Parthenon Galleries, Nashville, Tenn, 79 & 81. *Awards:* Third Award, 17th Tenn All-State, 77; Grand Award, 13th Central S, 78; Lyzon Art Gallery, 16th Central South, 81. *Mem:* Assoc mem Nat Soc Painters Casein & Acrylic; Am Artists Prof League; Tenn Art League; Cumberland Arts Soc Cookeville Tenn (bd dir, 75-80). *Media:* Acrylics. *Publ:* Contribr, Tennessee Conservationist, Tenn Dept Conserv, 78; Int Soc Artists Communicator, Billboard Publ, 79; illusr cover, Key: Nashville, Silversmith, 82; contribr, Nashville, Advantage Publ, 83. *Mailing Add:* 1151 Shipley Church Rd Cookeville TN 38501-7730

LEEBER, SHARON CORGAN
ART DEALER, CONSULTANT
b St Johns, Mich, Oct 1, 40. *Study:* Univ Wyo; Cent Mich Univ; Nat Open Univ, Washington, Trinity Univ. *Work:* Int Sculpture Park, Liberty Hill, Tex; Barnwell Art Ctr, Shreveport, La; Univ Tex, Arlington; Dallas Mus Fine Arts, Univ Tex, Dallas & Brookhaven Col, Dallas, Tex; Del Mar Col, Corpus Christi, Tex; Lone Star Park, Grand Prairie, Tex, 97; and others. *Comn:* Univ Tex, Arlington, 76; Arlington City Hall, Tex, 76; large welded male, Incarnate Word Col, San Antonio, Tex, 77; Veterans Meml Park, Irving, Tex, 2000; and others. *Exhib:* Tex Fine Arts Nat, Austin, 69; one-man retrospective show, Elizabet Ney Mus, Austin, 71; Tex Sculpture & Painting, Dallas, 71; Dallas Art, City Hall, Dallas, Tex, 78; Big Name Artists Show, Dallas, 78 & 79; Johannesburg Mus Art, The Fashion Designers Group of SA, Crafts Coun of S Africa, Pretoria Technikron, S Africa; plus others. *Collection Arranged:* Curatorials: Two From Texas, Two From London, Read Stremmel Gallery, 88; The Italian Show, Crescent Gallery, Dallas, Tex, 88; Beaux Arts Ball Fine Arts, Dallas Mus Art, 90; Plaza of the America's Glass Collection, 92; Similarities, Beverly Gordon Gallery, Dallas, Tex, 92; Dale Chihuly Glass & Drawing Exhib, Plaza Gallery, Dallas, Tex, 92; Dale Chihuly at Gerald Peters Gallery, Dallas, Tex, 94. *Pos:* Pres, Archit Arts Co, 80-; trustee, Florentine Found Art, 85-86. *Teaching:* Instr photog, El Centro Col, Tex, 71-81, Univ Tex, Dallas, 76-77. *Awards:* Purchase Awards, Shreveport Mus, 69 & Dallas Mus Fine Arts, 78. *Bibliog:* Thelma Neuman (auth), The Mirror Book, 78; L Haacke (auth), Art is more comfortable, Dallas Times Herald, 3/30/78; High Profile - Dallas Morning News, 92. *Mem:* Int Women's Forum; Artists Equity Asn (secy, Dallas Chap, 72-73); Dallas Women's Forum; and others. *Media:* Welded Steel, Glass. *Interests:* Travel. *Publ:* Nat Asn Indust & Off Parks Publ Series: How to Acquire for Your Development, #5, 87. *Mailing Add:* 6410 Dykes Way Dallas TX 75230-1816

LEEDS, VALERIE ANN
CURATOR, WRITER
b Summit, NJ, Jan 22, 58. *Study:* Univ Rochester, BA, 1979; Syracuse Univ, MA, 1981; City Univ New York, PhD (Douglass Fellowship in American Art, Dissertation Travel Fellowship), 2000. *Collection Arranged:* At the Water's Edge: 19th & 20th Century American Beach Scenes, Tampa Mus of Art, 1989; The Portraits of Robert Henri, Orlando Mus of Art, FL, 1994; An American Palette: Works from the Beck Collection, Mus of Fine Arts, St. Petersburg, FL, 2000; Robert Henri: The Painted Spirit, Gerald Peters Gallery, New York, 2005; Andrew Wyeth: American Master, Boca Raton Mus of Art, 2005. *Pos:* Cur assist, Whitney Mus of Am Art, New York, 1982-1984; Researcher & assoc, Spanierman Gallery, New York, 1984-1986; Cur exhibs, Tampa Mus of Art, 1987-1990; Cur Am Art, Orlando Mus of Art, 1990-1996; Independent cur, ed and writer, 1996-; Adjunct cur Am Art, Flint Inst of Arts, 2000-. *Teaching:* Adj prof, Eckerd Col, St. Petersburg, Fl, 2000. *Awards:* NEA Grant, NEA, 1995. *Mem:* Assoc of Art Editors. *Res:* 20th century Am art. *Interests:* art of Robert Henri, Ernest Lawson & the Ashcan Sch. *Mailing Add:* 728 Sergeantsville Rd Stockton NJ 08559

LEEDY, JIM (JAMES A LEEDY)
SCULPTOR, PAINTER
b McRoberts, Ky, Nov 6, 30. *Study:* Spec study with Shoji Hamada, 55 & Marguerite Wildenhain, 56; William & Mary Col (now Va Commonwealth), with Buckminster Fuller, BFA, 57; Columbia Univ, 57; Southern Ill Univ, MFA, MS, 58; Ohio State Univ, 58 & 59; Mich State Univ, MA(art hist), 59. *Work:* Am Craft Mus, NY; Nelson-Atkins Mus Art, Kansas City; Everson Mus Art, Syracuse; Los Angeles Co Mus, Calif; Ringling Mus, Ft Lauderdale. *Comn:* ceramic mural, Himeji Int Cult Ctr, Japan, 88; ceramic mural & column proj, Works Festival, Emonton, Alta, 92; steel sculpture, H&R Block Svc Ctr, Kansas City, Mo, 99; Large Scale Ceramic Sculpture, Taipei Co Yingko Ceramics Mus, Taiwan, 2001; Millennium Wall Sanbao, Jingdeshen, Jiangxi, China, 2004. *Exhib:* Solo shows, Am Craft Mus, 68, John Michael Kohler Art Ctr, Sheboygan, Wis, 71, Int Cult Ctr, Himeiji, Japan, 97, Contemp Art Ctr, Kansas City, Mo, 90 & Rochester Arts Ctr, Minn, 91 & 98, Richard A Beasley Art Mus & Gallery, Ariz, 97, Albrecht-Kemper Mus of Art, St Joseph, Mo, 2000, Taipei Co Yinko Ceramics Mus, Taiwan, 2001; traveling exhibs, Mus Mod Art, Paris, France, Spanish Mus Art, Madrid, Spain, Lilejevalche Mus, Warsaw, Poland, Palace of Fine Arts, Brussels, Belg, Arts Crafts Mus, Cologne, Ger, 70, Mus Mod Art, Stockholm, Sweden, 87, Denmark, The Neth & Finland, 92, Winter Olympics, Norway, 94, Fine Arts Mus, Lillehammer, Norway, 94 & Mus Applied Arts, Trondhiem, Norway, 94, Nat Coun Educ Ceramic Arts, 95, Color and Fire: Defining Moments in Contemp Ceramics, 1950-2000, Los Angeles Co Mus of Art and Other Venues; Surrealism, Retretti Arts Ctr, Suomi, Finland, 87; Raku-Transforming the Tradition, Kansas City Contemp Art Cttr, Mo, 89; Contemp Am Ceramics, Nelson-Atkins Mus, Kansas City, Mo, 90; Gallery 465, Sedona, Ariz, 2003; Weisspollack Gallery, NY, 2004. *Teaching:* Prof art hist, Univ Mont, Missoula, 59-64; prof art hist, Ohio Univ, Athens, 64-66; prof sculpture, Kansas City Art Inst, 66-. *Awards:* Distinguished Acheivement Award, Kansas City Art Inst, 95-; Project Grant, Margaret Silva Found, 1996-2000; Lifetime Achievement Award, Charlotte St Found, 2003. *Bibliog:* Matthew Kangas (auth), Prehistoric modern, Am Craft, 6-7/90; Laura Caruso (auth), Material, Process and Paradox: The Art of Jim Leedy, Leedy Voulkos Gallery, 91; Ole Lislerud (auth), Jim Leedy: An American Original, Ceramics: Art & Perception, 97; Matthew Kangao (auth), Jim Leedy: Artist Across Across Boundaries, 2000; Bruce Hellander (auth), Jim Leedy, Fire in a Brickyard, Weisspouack, 2003. *Mem:* Hon mem Nat Coun Educ Ceramic Arts; Am Inst Architects. *Media:* Clay, Paint. *Specialty:* Contemporary Art. *Dealer:* Leedy Voulkos Art Ctr Gallery 2012 Baltimore Kansas City MO 64108; Weisspollack Gallery NY NY. *Mailing Add:* C-12 Rte 4 Lake Lotawana MO 64086

LEEPA, ALLEN
PAINTER, EDUCATOR
b New York, NY, Jan 9, 19. *Study:* Am Art Sch New York, scholar; Art Students League; New Bauhaus, Chicago, scholar; Columbia Univ, BS, MA & EdD(scholar, dean's fel); Sorbonne & Grande Chaumiere, Paris. *Work:* South Bend Mus Art, Ind; Royal Acad, Scotland; Grand Rapids Mus, Mich. *Comn:* Mural, Ingham Co Arts Comn, State Wide Mich Competition, 84. *Exhib:* Mus Mod Art, NY, 53; Sao Paulo Biennale, Brazil, 63; one-man show, Galerie La Cour d'Ingres, Paris, 63; Mus Art Mod, Paris, 64 & 65; Retrospective, Hofstra Univ, 65; and many others. *Teaching:* Instr art, Hull Sch, Chicago, 37-38; Brooklyn Art Ctr, 39-41; Brooklyn Mus & Metrop Mus Art, 40-41; prof art, Mich State Univ, 45-. *Awards:* Painting, Fulbright Award, Paris; Childe Hassam Painting Award, Am Acad Arts & Lett, 69; Ford Found Grant, 70; Statewide Mural Competition, Mich, 80; Painting, Ford Found, SAm; and others. *Bibliog:* Michael Seuphor (auth), Abstract Painting, 62 & Dictionary of Abstract Art, 63, Abrams. *Mem:* Am Asn Univ Prof; Mich Acad Arts, Sci & Lett. *Media:* Acrylic on Canvas. *Publ:* Auth, The Challenge of Modern Art, Barnes, 49 & 61; contribr, articles in Humanities in Contemp Life, 60, New Art, 66, Minimal Art, 68 & New Ideas in Art Educ, 73; auth, Abraham Rattner, Abrams, 74; and others. *Dealer:* Leepa Gallery of Fine Arts 210 S Pinellas Ave Tarpon Springs Fla

LEEPER, DORIS MARIE
SCULPTOR, PAINTER
b Charlotte, NC, Apr 4, 29. *Study:* Duke Univ, BA, 51, hon PhD, 97; Stetson Univ, hon PhD, 97. *Work:* Nat Mus Am Art, Washington, DC; Miss Mus Art, Jackson, Miss; Columbus Mus Art, Ohio; 180 Beacon Collection, Boston, Mass; Wadsworth Atheneum, Hartford, Conn. *Comn:* Fiberglass sculpture, Alpert Investment for Forum 303, Arlington, Tex, 71; 160 modular unit wall sculpture, Hunter Mus Art, Chattanooga, Tenn, 73-75; enamel painting, Int Bus Machines, Atlanta, Ga, 76; concrete sculpture, Regional Serv Ctr, Jacksonville, Fla, 78; stainless steel wall sculpture, Orlando Int Airport, Fla, 83; Atlantic Ctr Arts, New Smyrna Beach, Fla, 96. *Exhib:* One-person shows, Hunter Mus Art, Chattanooga, 75 & 79, Ringling Mus Art, Sarasota, 76, Southeastern Ctr Contemp Art, Winston-Salem, NCar, 77, Norton Gallery Art, West Palm Beach, Fla, 79, Anniston Mus Natural Hist, Ala, 80, Pensacola Mus Art, Fla, 96-97; Six Fla Sculptors, Thomas Ctr, Gainesville, Fla, 89; Five Sculptors, Stetson Univ, Deland, Fla, 91; 2nd Int Ephemeral Sculpture Exhib, Fortaleza, Brazil, 91-92; one-person retrospective, Cornell Fine Arts Mus, Rollins Col, Winter Park, Fla, 95; and many others. *Awards:* Nat Endowment Arts Grant, 72; Artist-in-Residence Fel, Rockefeller Found, 77; Fine Arts Coun Fal Grant, 77. *Bibliog:* An interview with Doris Leeper, Enjoy, 73; Virginia Watson Jones (auth), Contemporary American Women Sculptors, Oryx Press, 86; Charlotte S Rubinstein (auth), Am Women Sculptors, 90. *Mem:* Atlantic Ctr Arts, New Smyrna Beach, Fla (mem adv coun & founder); LaNapoule Art Found, France (int adv coun); Volusia Co Cult Arts Adv Bd, Fla. *Media:* All; Miscellaneous. *Dealer:* Albertson-Peterson Gallery 329 Park Ave S Winter Park FL 32789; Arts on Douglas 123 Douglas St New Smyrna Beach FL 32168

LEESMAN, BEVERLY JEAN
PAINTER, WRITER
b Lincoln, Ill, Apr 22, 53. *Study:* Ill State Univ, Normal, Ill, BS, 1976; Springfield Col in Ill, Springfield, AA, 1973. *Comn:* Dinosaur Mural (3 walls), Gold Cup Gymnastics, Albuquerque, NMex, 2002-03; Southwest theme & faux walls, Andrew's, Albuquerque, NMex, 2001-02; Dragon Image in Watercolor for Kempo Karate Studio, Alburquerque, NM. *Exhib:* 18th Ann Exhibit, NE Watercolor Soc, Goshen, NY, 1994: 2003-2004; 2002 33rd River Road Show, La Art and Artists' Guild, Baton Rouge, La, 2002; Salmagundi Club 26th Ann Non-mem Juried Exhib, NY, 2003; 26th Int Exhib of WAS-H, Houston, Texas, 2003; Hilton Head Art Leaques Nat Juried Art Exhib, SC, 2003; Allied Artist of Am, NY, 2004; Catherine Lorillard Wolfe Art Club Juried Nat'l Show, NY, 2003-04; Watercolor West Brea, Calif, 2004; Taos Exhib of Am Watercolor VII, 2004, Taos, NMex. *Awards:* Dick Blick award,Aqueous Open, Dick Blick Supplies, 1995; Bd Dirs award, Fall 2002 Exhibit, NMex Watercolor Soc, 2002; 2nd place, 2002 33rd River Show, La Art & Artists' Guild, 2002; Am Artist Mag Award, Watercolor West, 2004; Richard Ochs Award, Northeast Watercolor Soc, 2004;. *Bibliog:* North Suburban Snapshot, Syracuse Herald Journal, 12/21, 94; Deidre Neilen (auth), An eye for detail: Beverly Leesman thrives on painting the complicated,

Syracuse New Times, 2/15/95; Jewish Link, 2002. *Mem:* Am Artist Prof League (signature mem); Nat Asoc Women Artists; Juried mem of Watercolor West; Signature mem of Northeast Water CO, Soc. *Media:* Watercolor. *Interests:* my family. *Collection:* private col. *Publ:* Art Critic,Syracuse New Times, 93-97; Watercolor Studio; Pleen Air Mag, 2004; Artist Mag, 2004-05

LEESON, TOM
PAINTER, SCULPTOR
b Chicago, Ill, Mar 16, 45. *Study:* Ball State Univ, BS, 68, Univ Calif, Los Angeles, MA, 71. *Work:* Los Angeles Co Mus Art, Calif; Santa Monica City Col Art Gallery, Calif. *Comn:* Painting comn by Lynda Resnick, Los Angeles, 86. *Exhib:* Current Concerns, Part 2, Los Angeles Inst Contemp Art, 75; The Object Observed, Los Angeles Munic Art Gallery, 78; Deja Vu: Masterpieces Updated, traveling exhib, Western Asn Art Mus, 83; Setting the Stage, Los Angeles Co Mus, 85-86; one person exhib, Ovsey Gallery, Los Angeles, Calif, 86, 89 & 95. *Teaching:* Vis lectr drawing, Univ Calif, Los Angeles, 77-79, lectr, 83-90, vis asst prof, 91-94; vis lectr drawing & sculpture, Univ Calif, Santa Barbara, 82. *Bibliog:* Howard Fox (auth), Setting the Stage, Los Angeles Co Art Mus Art, 85; David Helfrey (auth), Suspending disbelief, Visions Mag, Spring 88. *Media:* Oil, Acrylic; All Media. *Mailing Add:* 4748 W Washington Blvd Los Angeles CA 90016

LEET, RICHARD (EUGENE)
MUSEUM DIR (RETIRED), PAINTER
b Waterloo, Iowa, Sept 11, 36. *Study:* Univ Northern Iowa, BA, 58, MA, 65, with Ansei Uchima, Ted Egri, Paul R Smith & John Page; Univ Iowa, 61-64, with Stuart Edie & Robert Knipschild. *Work:* Mus Art, El Paso, Tex; Charles H MacNider Mus, Mason City, Iowa; Waterloo Munic Galleries, Iowa; Des Moines Art Ctr; Sioux City Art Ctr, Iowa. *Comn:* Art-in-State Bldg proj, Brenton Ctr, Iowa State Univ, Ames, Iowa, 95. *Exhib:* Ann Midyear Show, Butler Inst Am Art, Youngstown, Ohio, 69, 75 & 77; Midwest Biennial, Joslyn Art Mus, Omaha, 72, 74 & 76; Tweed Mus Art, Minn, 80; Mabee-Gerrer Mus Art, Shawnee, Okla, 87; Watercolor USA, Springfield Mus Art, Mo, 88, 94, 2002, 04 & 06; Land of the Fragile Giants (touring), Brunnier Art Mus, Iowa State Univ, 94-96; Art-in-Embassies, Cambodia & Leet: 30 Yrs of Painting (retro), touring, 95-97; 57th Juried Exhbn, Sioux City Art Ctr, Iowa, 2001; one-person shows, over 60. *Pos:* Mus dir & founding dir, CH MacNider Mus, 65-2001. *Teaching:* Instr art, Oelwein Community Schs, Iowa, 58-65; instr painting & drawing, CH MacNider Mus, Mason City, Iowa, 65-85. *Awards:* Esther & Edith C Younker Painting Award, Iowa Artist's Show, Des Moines Art Ctr, 78; Lifetime Distinguished Serv Award, Midwest Mus Conf, 95; Patron Purchase award, Watercolor USA, 2002, 2006. *Bibliog:* Mark Stegmaier (auth), An Artful Balance, Iowan Mag, spring, 88; Richard Leet: Artist/Administror (exhib catalog), Charles H MacNider Mus, 95; The Art of the Matter, The Rotarion, 6/96. *Mem:* Iowa Arts Coun (mem coun, 70-76); Iowa Mus Asn (pres, 78-80, life mem, Hall of Fame, 2001); Iowa Watercolor Soc (signature mem). *Media:* Watercolor. *Publ:* Portfolio, Selections from the Yucatan Sketch Books of Lawrence Mills, 81; He Pulled Lots of Strings, Monograph accomp Bil Baird Mem Exhib, 88; auth & designer, 25 Selections American Art, Charles H MacNider Mus (collection catalog), 91; auth, Charles Atherton Cumming-A Deep Root for Iowa Art, Am Art Rev, vol 2, 4/97; contribr, American Puppetry, PT Dirks, 2004. *Dealer:* Henry W. Myrtle Gallery, Cedar Falls. IA. *Mailing Add:* 1149 Manor Dr Mason City IA 50401

LEETARU, ILSE
PRINTMAKER
b Tallinn, Estonia, Oct 27, 15; US citizen. *Study:* Deutshe Meistershule, Munich, Ger, 48-49; Sch Visual Arts New York, 63-66; Grande Chaumiere, Paris, 67-70; Neo Sch, New York, 90. *Work:* Hosp Corp Am, Nashville; Tartu Art Mus, Estonia; Tallinn Art Mus, Estonia; Florean Mus, Romania; Zlmmerli Art Mus, NJ. *Exhib:* Artistes USA, Galeries R Duncan, Paris, 76, 78 & 81; Nat Asn Women Artists USA, Am Cult Ctr, Tel Aviv, Israel, 81 & Cairo, Egypt, 82; Nat Asn Women Artists, Dept Cult Affair, NY Gallery Exhib, 81; Estonian Art, Civic Ctr, Toronto, Can, 85; Galeria Cultura, Campinas, Brazil, 88; Hanga Ann, Metrop Mus, Tokyo, 85, 87; solo print exhibs, Art Mus, Tartu, Estonia, 90 & Art Mus, Tallinn, Estonia, 91; Art Mus, Talling, Estonia, 96; Toronto, Can, 2000; Raciborz, Poland, 2000. *Awards:* First Prize, Nat Asn Women Artists, 78; Medaille de Bronze, Akademia r Duncan, Paris, 81; Nat Women Asn Artists, NY, 98 & 2000. *Bibliog:* Endel Koks (auth), Estonian graphic artist, Stcokholm, Sweden, 79; P Reets (auth), Estonian art in exile, Stockholm, Sweden, 80; Vaba Eesti Sona, 2000. *Mem:* Nat Asn Women Artists. *Media:* All Media. *Dealer:* Artfull Eye M F Glintock 12 N Union St Lambertville NJ 08530. *Mailing Add:* 555 Kappock St Bronx NY 10463-6420

LEETE, WILLIAM WHITE
PAINTER
b Portsmouth, Ohio, June 12, 29. *Study:* Yale Univ, BA, 51, BFA, 55 & MFA, 57. *Work:* De Cordova Mus, Lincoln, Mass; Cleveland Mus, Ohio; Worcester Mus, Mass; Univ Mass; Bank of America, Providence, RI; Providence Mayflower Trust Bank; Mechanics Nat Bank, Worcester, Mass; 180 Beacon St Corp, Boston; various pvt collections. *Exhib:* New Eng Contemp Artists, Boston, 63 & 65; Silvermine Guild, Conn, 66; Art in Embassies, Inst Contemp Arts, Boston, 66; Structured Art, De Cordova Mus, 69; Young New Eng Painters, John & Mabel Ringling North Mus, Fla; Portland Mus & Currier Gallery, Manchester, 69; Newport Art Asn, RI, 70, 75; Decordova Mus, Decordova Collects, Lincoln, Mass, 78; Hypergraphics Int 7, Kansas City, Mo, 85; Conn Col Arts and Tech Symposium, 89, 91, 93; numerous shows at Univ of RI, Kingston incl Digital Prints, 00. *Teaching:* Assoc prof art, Univ RI, 57-74, prof, 74-95, prof emeritus, 95-. *Media:* Acrylic. *Mailing Add:* 202 Silver Lake Ave Wakefield RI 02879-4291

LEGGETT, ANN VAUGHAN
PAINTER, PRINTMAKER
b New York, NY, Oct 6, 41. *Study:* Sarah Lawrence Col, Bronxville, NY - 1958-60; Art Students League, New York City - 1960-63; apprenticeship with Frank Mason - 1960-63. *Work:* Mus of the City of New York; Princeton Univ Library, NJ; Town Hall, West Tisbury, Mass; Wabash Col, Crawfordsvile, Ind. *Comn:* Portrait of Arnold Fischer, West Tisbury, Mass, 1984; 7 Libyan Horseman (oil), Mission to U.N. of Libyan Arab Jamahiria, New York, 1992. *Exhib:* Painting New York, Mus of the City of New York, 1983; One-man show, Nat Arts Club, New York, 1961, 74 & 86, 500th Anv Bartolome de las Casas, Princeton Univ Libr, NJ, 1976, Wabash Col, Crawfordsville, Ind, 1978; Two-man show, Union League Club, New York, 1990; Hammond Mus, North Salem, NY, 2005. *Awards:* Best Vineyard Subject, Martha's Vineyard Agr Soc, Cattle Show & Fair, 1965; 3 Montague Award Pastel, Nat Arts Club, Pastel Soc of Am, 1974; Award for Portrait, Nat Arts Club, Bruce Stevenson, 1976. *Mem:* Japanese Artists Asn of New York. *Media:* Oil, Miscellaneous Printmaking, Small Sculpture, Pastel. *Publ:* Susan Meyer (auth), 20 Figure Painters, Am Artist/Watson-Guptill, 1979; Carol Donnell Kotrozo, Art That Addresses Life, Southwest Art, 1980; Kay Larson (auth) Italian Fantasies, New York Facts, New York Living Magazine, 1983. *Dealer:* Fielder & Fielder 440 North Rd Chilmark Mass 02535; GC Lucas Gallery 4930 N Pennsylvania St Indianapolis IN 46205. *Mailing Add:* 13-22 Jackson Ave Long Island City NY 11101

LEGRADY, GEORGE
PHOTOGRAPHER
b Budapest, Hungary. *Study:* Goddard Col, B; San Francisco Art Inst, M. *Exhib:* one-man shows, Rovaniemi Art Mus, Finland, 95, Ansel Adams Center, San Francisco, Calif, 96, Can Mus Contep Photography, Ottawa, 97-98, Nat Gallery Can, Ottawa, 97-98, Mus Contemp Art, Los Angeles, 98; Everybody's Talking, Gemeente Mus Helmond, The Neth, 96; Burning the Interface, Mus Contemp Art, Sydney, Australia, 96-98; Dawn of the Magicians, Nat Gallery, Prague, Czech Republic, 97; Tracing, Kunst und Austellungshalle der Bundesrepublik, Bonn, Ger, 97-98; Anticipation - Version 4.0, Centre d'art Contemporain, Geneva, Switz, 98; Contact Zones, Cornell Univ, Itahaca, NY, 99-2000; Transitional Spaces, Rotunde, Siemens Headquarters, Munich, Ger, 2000. *Teaching:* vis prof, N Tex State Univ, Denton, 77 & Calif Inst Arts, Valencia, 82-84; lectr, Univ Western Ont, Can, 78, asst prof, head visual arts dept, 78-81; asst prof photog and computer media, Univ Southern Calif, Los Angeles, 84-88; assoc prof, San Francisco State Univ, Calif, 89-97; prof electronic media, Merz Acad, Stuttgart, Germany, 96-2000; vis scholar, Hungarian Fine Arts Acad, Budapest, 94; vis assoc prof, Univ Calif, Los Angeles, 98; prof digital media, Univ Calif, Santa Barbara, 2000-. *Awards:* New Voices, New Visions Prize, Voyager Company, 94; Visual Fel, Nat Endowment Arts, 95; Computer Integrated Media Award, Can Coun, 96 & 97. *Res:* Integration of a theoretical framework with exploration of the potential of emerging technologies for new forms of cultural narrative. *Publ:* Artintact 3 (CD Rom), ZKM, Karlsruhe, Ger, 96; Actualizing the Virtual (CD Rom), revue virtuelle, Centre George Pompidou, Paris, France, 96. *Mailing Add:* Univ Calif Santa Barbara Art Dept Santa Barbara CA 93106

LEGRAND, YOLENE
PAINTER, MURALIST
b Port-Au-Prince, Haiti. *Study:* Art Students League, NY, with Kay Hazelip, Peter Homitzky, Leatrice Rose, 92-97 & Sam Adoquei, Landscape Workshop, 99; David Leffel Portrait Painting Workshop. *Comn:* cityscape mural, St Paul RE, NY, 96. *Exhib:* One-woman shows, La Maison Francaise Gallery, Columbia Univ, 95, Verve Art Gallery, Leuven, Belgium, 96, NY Pub Libr, 96, Hamilton Landmark Gallery, NY, 99, L'Alliance Francaise, Washington DC, 99, Shea Stadium, NY, 2000, 101 Hudson St Gallery, Jersey City, NJ, 2000, Alliance Francaise de Miami, 2002, Dennis Public Libr, Dennisport, Cape Cod, Mass, 2004, Wellfleet Public Libr Art Gallery, Cape Cod, Mass, 2006, Univ Col Art Gallery, Fairleigh Dickinson Univ, NJ, 2006, Hampton Bays Public Libr Art Gallery, Long Island, NY, 2006; group shows, Musee du Pantheon Nat Haitien, 99, Wet Paint, Newport Art Mus, RI, 2001, Salmagundi Club, Audubon Artists, 2002, Vanderbilt Gallery, Nantucket, Mass, 2002-03, Am Mus of Nat Hist, 2004, Pen & Brush Club Juried Exhib, 2004-2005, Nicole Gallery, Chicago, 2005, Dorsey's Art Gallery, NY, 2005, Makeready Press Gallery, Montclair, NJ, 2006, Taiwan Ctr, NY, 2006. *Teaching:* art teacher, Brooklyn Mus, 98-; artist-in-residence, Glen Ridge Elem Sch, 98-; instr, adult painting workshops. *Awards:* Lower Manhattan cult coun grant, 2000; Contribr to the World Art, Manhattan Borough Pres, 2004. *Bibliog:* Numerous newspaper articles, 95-98; News-Leader, NJ, 1/27/99; Haitian Times, 3/15/2000, 2/6/02; Miami Times, 9/12/02, 10/3/02; Miami Today, 9/12/02; The Miami Herald, 9/13/02, 10/4/02. *Mem:* Art Students League NY; Audubon Artists, Inc (treas, 2003-); Allied Artists of Am. *Media:* Oil and Pastel. *Interests:* Landscape. *Publ:* covers, Tribes Magazine, fall 2005. *Mailing Add:* Studio # 807 32 Union Square East New York NY 10003

LEHMAN, ARNOLD L
MUSEUM DIRECTOR, CURATOR
b New York, NY, July 18, 44. *Study:* Johns Hopkins Univ, BA, 65, MA, 66; Yale Univ, MPhil, 68, PhD, 74. *Collection Arranged:* Archit of World Fairs (auth, catalog), Dallas Mus Fine Arts, Tex, 72; Boom or Bust, Am Painting from World War I through 1939, 74; Art Deco, 74; Judaica from Am Collections, 75; The Vanderbilts: Collectors, 75; Am Magic Realists (auth, catalog), 76; World of Haitian Printing, (auth, catalog), 77; 50 Years of Cuban Painting, 77; Oskar Schlemmer (ed, catalog), 86, Benjamin West, 89; A Grand Design: The Art of Victoria & Albert Mus, 97. *Pos:* Chester Dale Fel, Metrop Mus Art, New York, 69-70; dir, Urban Improvements Prog, New York, 70-73; Parks Coun, New York, 73-74; dir, Metrop Mus & Art Ctr, Miami, Fla, 74-79; dir, Baltimore Mus Art, Md, 79-97; dir, Brooklyn Mus Art, NY, 97-. *Teaching:* Lectr art hist, Cooper Union Sch Art & Archit, New York, 69-71; Hunter Col, City Univ

New York, 71-72; adj prof art history Johns Hopkins, Balt, 86-97. *Mem:* Am Asn Mus Dirs (pres, 90-91, trustee, 86-92). *Res:* American architecture and urban planning; American painting, 20th century; late 19th century French painting. *Publ:* Arnold Lehman (editor), Oskar Schkmmer, Abrams, 86; contribr A Grand Design, Abrams, 97. *Mailing Add:* Brooklyn Mus Art 200 Eastern Parkway Brooklyn NY 11238-6052

LEHR, JANET
DEALER
b New York, NY, June 7, 37. *Study:* New York Univ, BA, 55; Brooklyn Law Sch, LLB/JD, 58. *Exhib:* 19th & 20th Century Landscape Photog, Munich State Mus, 78; Luminist Art, NGA, Washington, DC, 78; Robert Demachy, Yale Univ Art Mus, 81; History of Photog, Art Gallery New S Wales, Australia, 94; Horatio Ross, Scottish photographer 1850s, Yale Univ, Brit Ctr for the Arts, 93. *Pos:* Co-partner, Gallery 6M, 62-72; owner, Janet Lehr Inc, 72-; co-owner, Vered Gallery, East Hampton, NY, 88-. *Mem:* Founding mem Asn Int Photog Art Dealers; Antiquarian Booksellers Am. *Res:* Photographically illustrated books of the 19th century. *Specialty:* Fine vintage photographs of both the 19th and 20th century; exceptional contemporary; Milton Avery, Wolf Kahn, Leonard Baskin, Paul Georges and Rediscovery 1930-1950. *Publ:* Auth, Talbot's Role in the History of Photography, Antiquarian Bookman, J Chernofsky, 78; John Thomson, History of Photography, 1/80; and 32 catalogs. *Mailing Add:* 891 Park Ave New York NY 10021

LEHR, MIRA T(AGER)
PAINTER
b New York, NY, Sept 22, 38. *Study:* Vassar Col, BA, 56; Boston Mus Sch, 57; Robert Motherwell & James Brooks, 68 & 69; Nieves & Billmyer, 60-80. *Work:* Univ Tex Mus, Tyler; Bass Mus, Miami Beach, Fla; Suntrust Banks, FL; Frances Lehman Loeb Art Center, Poughkeepsie, NY; Bacardi Collection, Miami, Fla. *Comn:* Large scale wall piece, Art Enterprises Inc, Chicago, 86; monoprints, Interterra Corp, Miami, 88; Stephanie Odegard Collection: Rugs, 2005. *Exhib:* A Century of Women's Achievements, La Worlds Fair, New Orleans, 85; Ann Hortt Mem, Ft Lauderdale Mus, Fla, 86 & 89; Ann Exhib Contemp Am Paintings, Soc of 4 Arts, Palm Beach, Fla, 87-90; Cuban Mus, Miami, Fla, 89; 6 Artists-NY/Miami, Mus of Contemp Art, Miami, Fla, 94; Elaine Baker Gallery, Boca Raton, Fla, 2003; Bernie Steinbaum Gallery, Miami, Fla, 2004; Miami/Dade Community Col, 2004; Fay Gold Gallery, Atlanta, GA, 2004; Flomenhaft Gallery, NY, 2005. *Pos:* Chmn, Continuum Inc, 80-89 & Art in Public Places, Miami Beach, Fla, 85-91; trustee, Art in Pub Places, Dade Co, 86-90. *Awards:* Purchase Award, First Ann Works on Paper, Univ Tex, 86; Purchase Award, Belmont Towbin Found, 90; Grumbacher Award, Nat Orgn Women Artists, New York, 93. *Bibliog:* Linda Nochlin (auth), article, Best Mag, 10/5/90; Elisa Turner (auth), Luria group poses lively dialogue, Miami Herald, 6/6/90; Andrew Delaplaine (auth), The Myriad Colors of Mira Lehr, YES Mag, Vol I, No 4, 8/5/94; Mira Lehr: Visual Imprints by Courtney Curtis; Florida Design, Florida Design, Inc, Winter, 2003/2004. *Mem:* Womens Caucus Art (bd dir, 83-86); Nat Asn Women Artists; Nat Asoc of Mus, 2005. *Media:* Acrylic, Mixed Media. *Dealer:* Elaine Baker Gallery; Gallery 608 Banyan Trail Boca Raton FL 33431; Fay Gold Gallery, Atlanta, GA; Flomenhaft Gallery, NY, NY. *Mailing Add:* 5215 Pine Tree Dr Miami Beach FL 33140

LEHRER, LEONARD
PAINTER, PRINTMAKER
b Philadelphia, Pa, Mar 23, 35. *Study:* Philadelphia Col Art, BFA, 56; Univ Pa, MFA, 60. *Work:* Mus Mod Art & Metrop Mus Art, NY; Nat Gallery of Art, Corcoran Gallery & Libr Cong, Washington; Philadelphia Mus Art. *Comn:* Paintings, Kreissparkasse, Hildesheim, Ger, 90. *Exhib:* Brooklyn Mus Print Show, 72; one-man shows, Utah Mus Fine Arts, 73 & 82 & Marian Locks Gallery, Philadelphia, 74, 77 & 84; Galerie Kuhl, Hannover, Ger, 79, 82 & 91; 4th Miami Int Print Biennial, 80; Myung Sook Lee Gallery, NY, 97; Crecloo Art Gallery, NY 2004; Albright Col Freedman Gallery; Int Ctr Cultural Mgt (ICCM), Salzburg, Austria; and others. *Pos:* chair, Nat arts adv comt, Col Bd, 93-06; trustee, Int Print Ctr, New York, 94-. *Teaching:* Prof art & chmn dept, Univ NMex, 70-74; prof art & dir, Sch Art, Ariz State Univ, Tempe, 77-90; chair, Dept Art & Art Prof, New York Univ, 91; dean, Sch Fine & Performing Arts, Columbia Col, Chicago, 01-. *Awards:* First Prize, Fourth Miami Int Print Biennial, 80; Heitland Found Prize, Celle, Ger, 80; Gold Medal Award, Nat Soc Arts & Letters, 81; Fulbright Scholar Grant to Greece, 01; Fulbright Sr Scholar AIA Grant to Greece, 03-; and others. *Bibliog:* VD Coke (auth), The Painter and the Photograph, Univ NMex Press, 72; Fritz Eichenberg (auth), The Art of the Print, Abrams, 76; EA Quensen (publ), The Art of Leonard Lehrer, WGer, 86. *Media:* Collage, Lithography. *Publ:* Auth, articles, Art J, 74; Col Bd Review, 94; The Tamarind Papers. *Dealer:* Myungsook Lee Gallery New York NY. *Mailing Add:* Sch Fine & Performing Arts Columbia Col Chicago 600 S Michigan Ave Chicago IL 60605-1996

LEIBER, GERSON AUGUST
PRINTMAKER
b Brooklyn, NY, Nov 12, 21. *Study:* Art Students League; Brooklyn Mus Art Sch; DFA (hon), Bar Ilan Univ, Israel, 93. *Work:* Metrop Mus Art, NY; Whitney Mus Am Art, NY; Nat Gallery Art, Washington, DC; Libr Cong, Washington, DC; Boston Mus Fine Arts. *Comn:* Print eds, Asn Am Artists & Int Graphic Arts Soc. *Exhib:* One-man shows Oakland (California) Mus, 60, New York City, 61-64, 68-69, 72, 76, 85, 95-96, 98-99; Am Prints Today, USA, NY, 59; Cincinnati Int Biennial, 60; Fine Arts Mus Long Island (NY), 91, Steinbaum-Kraus Gallery, 98, Denise Bibro Gallery, East Hampton, 2001, 2003, Guild Hall Mus, 2003; exhib in numerous nat and int; Am Prints, in Russia, Rome, Italy, Mexico City, Mex & Salzburg, Ger; Libr Cong Exhibs; and many others. *Pos:* vpres, Judith Leiber, Inc, New York City, 63. *Teaching:* Instr graphics & illus, Newark Sch Fine & Indust Art, 61-68. *Awards:* Tiffany Fels, 57 & 60; Purchase awards Brooklyn Mus, 53-66 & Hunterdon Co Art Ctr 6th nat print exhib, 1962 Soc Washington Printmakers prize, 62; Audubon Medals of Honor for Graphics, 63-65; Sonia Watter award Am Color Print Soc, 68, 1000 Purchase award Asn Am Artists, 68, John Taylor Arms Mem prize Nat Acad of Design, 71; Am Nat Print Exhib Prize, Assoc Am Artists Gallery. *Bibliog:* Frank Getlein (auth), Bite of the Print, Potter, 63; Hooten & Kaiden (auth), Mother and Child in Modern Art, Meredith Corp. *Mem:* Asn Nat Acad; Soc Am Graphic Artists (pres, 78-80); Audubon Artists. *Media:* Intaglio. *Publ:* Illusr, Crisis (poem), Oxhead Press, 69. *Mailing Add:* 446 Old Stone Hwy East Hampton NY 11937-3191

LEIBERT, PETER R
CERAMIST, SCULPTOR
b New York, NY, Mar 13, 41. *Study:* Buffalo State Univ, BS(art educ), 63; Indiana Univ, MS(art educ), 67, MFA(ceramics, with distinction), 67. *Comn:* Wall relief, Conn Col, 93. *Exhib:* one-man shows, Portogallo Gallery, NY, 69, Cooper Union, NY, 71 & Kogei Gallery, Dobbs Ferry, NY, 74; Lyman Allyn Mus, New London, Conn, 80 & 96; New Port Art Mus, RI, 88; Pritman & Eams Gallery, East Hampton, Long Island, 88; NAC Gallery, Norwich, Conn, 88-96. *Teaching:* Artist in residence, Haystack Mountain Sch Crafts, Deer Isle, Maine, 78; prof ceramics, Conn Col, 67-, chmn dept art, 78-93; prof art. *Awards:* Purchase Prize, Rose Arts Festival, Norwich, Conn, 70-78 & 83; Best in Clay, 22nd Ann Exhib, 78 & First Prize for Sculpture, New Eng Regional Exhib, 83, Mystic Art Asn. *Mem:* Am Crafts Coun; Nat Coun Educ Ceramic Arts; Soc Conn Craftsmen. *Media:* Ceramics; Mixed. *Publ:* Illusr, Back to gum prints, Camera 35, 70 & A portfolio of photography, Pukka, 70; contribr, The artist as photographer, Conn Col Alumni News, 71. *Mailing Add:* 201 Cummings Art Ctr Conn Col Box 5473 270 Mohegan Ave New London CT 06320-4196

LEIBOWITZ, BERNICE
PAINTER, EDUCATOR
b Brooklyn, NY, Nov 2, 29. *Study:* Hunter Col, BA, 50, MA, 53; Art Students League, 55. *Work:* Schering-Plough Collection, Madison, NJ, 81 & 82. *Exhib:* Affiliate Group Show, Newark Mus, NJ, 78; Art of the North East, Silvermine Art Guild, New Canaan, Conn, 90; The New Romanticism, Pleiades Gallery, NY, 90; Art From New York City, Hispano 20 Gallery, Barcelona, Spain, 90; Art Educators as Artists, Glassboro State Col, NJ, 90. *Pos:* Bd dir, Arts Ctr, 80-, chmn, 89-. *Teaching:* Instr fine art, Bergen Community Col, 74-. *Bibliog:* Meredith Hall (auth), Bernice Leibowitz' Haunting Images, Art Speak, 3/90; Eileen Watkins (auth), Celebration of Spring, Sun, Star Ledger, 2/87; Carnival of Color, Manhattan Arts, 11/87. *Mem:* Nat Asn Women Artists; Artists Equity. *Media:* Acrylic. *Mailing Add:* 144 N Terrace Pl New Milford NJ 07646-1208

LEICESTER, ANDREW JOHN
ENVIRONMENTAL ARTIST
b Birmingham, Eng, Mar 5, 48. *Study:* Portsmouth Polytechnic, England, BA, 69; Manchester Polytechnic, England, MA, 70; Univ Minn, Minneapolis, MFA, 72. *Work:* Walker Art Ctr; Sheldon Mem Art Gallery. *Comn:* Riverwalk at Piers 3 & 5 (promenade and overlook), Philadelphia, Pa, 90; Genetic Eng Bldg (roof, facade and atrium), Iowa State Univ, Ames, 90; Zanja Madre (watergarden), Los Angeles, 92; Courtyard, Minn Hist Ctr, St Paul, 95; Ghost Series (5 ceramic murals) Pa Cent Sta, NY, 95. *Exhib:* Invitation, 75 & The River--Images of the Mississippi, 76, Walker Art Ctr; Proposals for Sawyer Point, Contemp Art Ctr, Cincinnati, 77; Artpark, Lewiston, NY, 78; Art on the Beach, Creative Time, Battery Park, NY, 80; Artists Gardens & Parks, Hayden Gallery, 81; Nature-Sculpture, Wurttembergischer, Kunstverein, Stuttgart, WGer, 81; The Artist As Social Designer, Los Angeles Co Mus Art, 85; The Texas Landscape 1900-1986, Mus Fine Arts, Houston, 86. *Pos:* Bd dir, Pub Art St Paul, Minn. *Teaching:* Instr sculpture & drawing, Carleton Col, Minn, 73-74; instr sculpture, Minneapolis Col Art & Design, 75-80; instr, Sch Landscape Archit, Univ Minn, St Paul, 85; vis fel, Royal Melbourne Inst Technol, Australia, 86. *Awards:* Fel, Minn Arts Bd, 80-81, Nat Endowment Arts, 81-82, Bush Found, 77, 83, 90, McKnight Found, 85 & Fed Transportation Authority, 95. *Bibliog:* John Beardsley (auth), The New Urban Landscape, Earthworks and Beyond, Abbeville Press, 89; Garth Rockcastle (auth), Ethics in Paradise, VIA Mag, Vol 10, 90; Donlyn Lyndon (auth), Conceiving a Courtyard, PLACES Mag, Vol 6, No 3, 90. *Media:* Mixed. *Publ:* Double Crossing, a George Washington Memorial for Dade County Courthouse, Flagler St, Miami, 87; Cincinnati Gateway, Main Entrance to Bicentennial Commons Part, Cincinnati, 88; Riverwalk at Piers 3 & 5, Delaware Avenue, Philadelphia, 90

LEIGH, HARRY E
SCULPTOR, PAINTER
b Buffalo, NY, Nov 7, 31. *Study:* Albright Art Sch, dipl, 52; State Univ NY, Buffalo, BA, 53; painting with Richard Pousette-Dart, 56-60; Columbia Univ, MA, 59; TC Columbia Univ, prof dipl, 62; studied sculpture with Peter Voulkos, 1959-60, NY. *Work:* Va Mus Fine Art, Richmond; Birchfield Penney Art Collection, Buffalo; Ulrich Mus Art, Wichita, Kans; John Dean, Tappan, NY; Pratt Inst, Bklyn. *Exhib:* Albright-Knox Art Gallery, Buffalo, NY, 52, 53 & 57; Everson Mus, Syracuse, 61; OK Harris, NY, 72, 74, 78, 05, Sighting & Collection Selection, Anderson Gallery, Buffalo, NY, 93; Community of Creativity: A Century of Mac Dowell Colony Artists, Currier Gallery Art, Manchester, NH, 96; Nat Acad Design, NY, 97; Wichita Art Mus, Kans, 97; Interpreting the River, Blue Hill Cult Ctr, Pearl River, NY, 98; 26 sculptures, Artist in Their Studios, Rockland Ctr for Arts, Nyack, NY, 99; Silvermine Guild Art Ctr, 51st Ann Exhib, Art of the Northeast, New Canaan, Conn, 2000. *Collection Arranged:* The Constructed Image, Rockland Center for Arts, West Nyack, NY. *Awards:* MacDowell Fel, artist-in-residence, 68, 69, 70, 72, 74, 75, 83, 85 & 86; Yaddo Fel, artist-in-residence, 72, 79, 80, 87, 90, 96, 2001, 02, 03, 04, 05; Creative Arts Prog Serv Fel, 78-79; Hand Hollow Found Fel, 80; Artist-in-residence, Thorpe Intermedia Gallery, 88. *Bibliog:* Martin Last (auth), rev, Art News, 1/69; Elizabeth Frank Perlmutter (auth), article, Art News, 9/74; Grace Glueck (auth), Harry Leigh & Keith Long, NY Times, 5/12/78; and others. *Mem:* MacDowell Fel Comt (treas, 80-93). *Media:* Wood, Bricks; House Paint, Oil. *Dealer:* OK Harris 383 W Broadway New York NY 10012. *Mailing Add:* 340 Haverstraw Rd Suffern NY 10901

LEIGHTON, DAVID S R
ADMINISTRATOR
b Regina, Sask, Feb 20, 28. *Study:* Queen's Univ, BA; Harvard Univ, MBA, DBA. *Hon Degrees:* Windsor Univ, LLD; Queen's Univ, LLD. *Pos:* Dir, Sch Fine Arts, Banff Ctr, 70-82; Dir, Nat Ctr for Mgt Res Develop, Univ Western Ont, 86-99; chmn, Nat Arts Ctr, Ottawa, 99-. *Teaching:* Prof, Univ Western Ontario, 56-70, 86-93. *Bibliog:* auth, co-auth, 9 books on Marketing; co-auth, ARtists Builders & Dreamers, 83; co-auth, Making Boards Work, 97. *Mailing Add:* 10948 Old River Rd RR 3 Komoka ON N0L 1R0 Canada

LEIGHTON, PATRICIA MACINNES
ENVIRONMENTAL ARTIST, SCULPTOR
b Greenock, Scotland, July 8, 50; Brit citizen. *Study:* Edinburgh Col Art, Scotland, BA(drawing & painting), 70-74; Sch Fine Art, Poznan, Poland, with Prof Magdalena Abakanowicz, MA, 74-76. *Work:* Univ Glasgow, Scotland; St Albans Abbey, Eng; Kyoto Mus, collab with Neagu, Japan; Djerassi Found, Woodside, Calif; Grizedale Gallery in the Forest, Hawkshead, Eng. *Comn:* Motorola-M8, Motorola, Easter Inch, Scotland, 92-93; Scottish Office, Dept of Transportation, England, 96; Stirling Coun, Scotland, 96; GSA Comn, Rooseville, Mont, 2000; Ilindentci, Bulgaria, 2000. *Exhib:* solo exhibs, AIR Gallery, London, Eng, 80, Third Eye Ctr, Glasgow, Scotland, 82, Newcastle Polytechnic Gallery, Eng, 83 & Kala Inst, Berkeley, Calif, 83; M8 Project Launch, Scottish Nat Gallery of Modern Art, 93; Drawing Ctr, New York City, 93; C Grimaldis Gallery, Baltimore, Md, 98; Susquehanna Art Mus, Harrisburg, Pa, 99; Whitaker Ctr for Sci & Arts, Harrisburg, Pa, 99. *Awards:* Res fellow, Dept of Fine Arts Univ Northumbria, Newcastle-Upon-Tyne, Eng; Grantee, Pollock-Krasner Found, 95. *Bibliog:* Art In America, Scotsman, 6/18/93; The Times, 2/93; The Herald, 93. *Media:* All

LEIPZIG, ARTHUR
PHOTOGRAPHER, EDUCATOR
b Brooklyn, NY, Oct 25, 18. *Study:* Photo League, 42; Paul Strand Workshop, 46. *Work:* Mus Mod Art, NY; Brooklyn Mus; Nat Gallery Art, Ottawa; Art Inst Chicago; Nat Mus Am Art, Washington, DC; Bank Am Art Prog, San Francisco; Bibliotheque Nationale, Paris; Consolidated Freightways Collection, San Francisco; The Jewish Mus, NY; Houston Mus Fine Arts; Mus Folkwang, Essen, Ger; and others; Intl Ctr Photogrpahy; Mus Contemp Art, Madison, Wis; The Columbus Mus Art, Columbus, Ohio. *Exhib:* New Faces, Mus Mod Art, NY, 46, Xmas Sale of Photographs, 53, Family of Man (with catalog), 55 & From the Mus Collection, 58 & Metrop Mus Art, Photog as a Fine Art, 61 & 62; Photo League, Int Ctr Photog, 78, Mus City New York City Play, 88, Frumkin Adams Gallery, NY, 90; Photographs of Jewish Life Around the World, Nassau & Queens Mus, NY, 82; Brooklyn Mus, Classic Photograph Mus Collection, 87; Hist Photog from Calif Collection, San Francisco, 89; one-man shows, Photofind Gallery, NY, 90, Frumkin/Adams Gallery, 92 & Port Washington Libr, 94, Growing up in NY, Milwaukee Inst Art & Design, Arthur Leipzig, A Tribute to Influence, Firehouse Gallery, 2001, On Assignment with Arthur Leipzig, Hillwood Mus Art, Columbus Mus Art, Stritch Univ, Milwaukee, Wis, 2005-2006,; Musee de la Civilisation, Quebec City, 90; The Sporting Life, High Mus, Atlanta; Stickball, Mus City NY, 94; Growing up in NY, Mus City NY, 95 & 96, Univ Md, 96; A World View, Howard Greenburg Gallery, 98; and others. *Pos:* Staff photogr, PM Newspaper, 42-46 & Int News Photo, 46-47. *Teaching:* Dir photog & prof art, Long Island Univ, 68-. *Awards:* Nat Urban League Award, 67; Excellence in teaching, David Newton, 89; Winner, Lucie Award for Outstanding Achievement in Fine Art, Photography, 2004. *Bibliog:* Jacob Deschin (auth), Six great teachers, 35 M Photog, 74; Documentary Photography, Time Life Books, 83. *Mem:* Am Soc Mag Photogr. *Publ:* Contribr, The Family of Man, Mus Mod Art, 55; Photography Yearbook, Fountain Press Ltd, 57, 59, 62 & 72; The Family of Children, Ridge Press, 77; auth, Photography & social change, Ventures in Res, 78; Sarah's Daughters, 88; Growing up in New York, 95; auth, On Assignment with Arthur Leipzig, 2005. *Dealer:* Howard Greenberg Gallery 41 E 57th St, New York, NY. *Mailing Add:* 378 Glen Ave Sea Cliff NY 11579

LEIPZIG, MELVIN DONALD
PAINTER
b Brooklyn, NY, May 23, 35. *Study:* Yale Univ, BFA, 58; Pratt Inst, MFA, 72. *Work:* NJ State Mus, Trenton; Montclair Art Mus, NJ; Noyes Mus, Oceanville, NJ; Whitehouse Collection, Washington; Cooper-Hewitt Mus, NY; Whitney Mus; Springville Mus, Utah; Univ Pa Archit Archives, Phila. *Comn:* Painting, Marriott Hotel, Princeton, NJ, 87; portraits, Mercer Co Community Col, Trenton, NJ, 75 & 93; painting, Mercer Med Ctr, Trenton, NJ, 93. *Exhib:* One-man shows, Telefair Acad, Savannah, Ga, 72, Montclair Art Mus, NJ, 84, NJ State Mus, Trenton, 85, Wash Co Mus, Hagerstown Md, 87, Brevard Art Ctr & Mus, Melbourne, Fla, 88, Trenton City Mus, NJ, 90, Hot Springs Art Ctr, Ark, 91; Retrospective, Trenton City Mus, NJ, 84, NJ State Mus, Trenton, 98 & Gallery Henoch, NY, 2000, 02, 03 & 05. *Teaching:* Instr woodcutting, Queens Col, 66-73; prof art hist & painting, Mercer Co Community Col, 68-. *Awards:* Fulbright Grant Paris, US Govt, 58; NJ State Coun Arts Fel, 92; Grant, Nat Endowment Art 95-96. *Bibliog:* William Zimmer (auth), The Making of a Gifted Realist, NY Times 12/84; Vivien Raynor (auth), Trenton: A Leipzig Semi Retrospective, NY Times 6/85; Mel Leipzig, The New Yorker, 10/2000, Gerard Haggerty (auth), 3/2006; Anne Fabbri (auth), defining The Subject with the Background, 8/2003; Edward Leffingwell (auth), Mel Leipzig at Gallery Henoch, 4/2006. *Mem:* Trenton Artists Workshop Asn (bd mem); Mercer Co Cult & Heritage Comn (comnr). *Media:* Acrylic. *Specialty:* Realist art. *Dealer:* Gallery Henoch 555 W 25th St New York NY 10001. *Mailing Add:* 38 Abernethy Dr Trenton NJ 08618

LEIS, MARIETTA PATRICIA
PAINTER
b Newark, NJ. *Study:* Univ Calif, Santa Monica Community Col, Parson, 78-82; Univ NMex, Albuquerque, MA, 85 & MFA, 88. *Work:* St Mary's Home, Manitowoc, Wis; Univ NMex, Health Servs & Div Continuing Educ Conf Ctr; Ross Labs, Columbus, Ohio; State Capitol, Santa Fe, NMex; Corrales Sr Ctr, Corrales, NMex; Albuquerque Art Mus, NMex; Resort at Summerlin, Las Vegas; Hudson Valley Hosp Ctr, Peekskill, NY; and others. *Comn:* NMex State Libr, Santa Fe. *Exhib:* Solo exhibs, In Between Architectonic Artworks, Pt I, Univ MNex, Albuquerque, 88, Pt II, Dartmouth St Gallery, Albuquerque, 88, Marietta Patricia Leis: The Pentimento Series, Pac Int Art Gallery, Palo Alto, Calif, 91, Textures of Italy, Univ NMex Continuing Educ Conf Ctr, Albuquerque, 93, Illuminations, The Casements, City Cult & Civic Ctr, Ormond Beach, Fla, 94, Excerpts from the Marietta Robusti Tintoretto Store, Jonson Gallery, Univ NMex, Albuquerque, 96, The Marietta Robusti Tintoretto Story, NDak, 97; Man & Nature, Stone House Gallery, Fredonia, Kans, 88; Pindar Nat Invitational, 5 Artists, Pindar Gallery, Soho, NY, 89; Graven Images, Chememekta Community Col, Salem, Ore, 93; Two Artists, Clatsop Community Col, Astoria, Ore, 94; MOSTRA 94, Mus Ital Americano, San Francisco, 94; Two Views, Montana State Univ, Billings, 95; Visible Whispers, Univ Gallery of Bridgeport, Conn, 99; Past Influence / Present Use, Sun Valley Ctr for Arts, Vt, 2000; one-women show, Patricia Carlisle Gallery, Sante Fe, NMex & W Valley Mus, Surprise, Ariz, 2001; and others. *Teaching:* Instr art & drawing, Univ NMex, Albuquerque, 85-88, art & contemp art, 88-. *Awards:* Artist Grant, Artist Space, New York, 89; Hon Distinction, Int Art Biennial-Mus, Hisico, Capranica, Italy; Artists Grant, ED Found, 94, 95 & 96; Artist Grant, Connemara Conservancy, Dallas, Tex, 98; Artist in Residence, Weir Farm Tevst, Wilton Conn & Schneider Mus, Ore. *Bibliog:* O Reed, Jr (auth), Multimedia artist likes viewers touch, to feel her work, Albuquerque Tribune, 3/2/93; S Randall (auth), She works in every medium you can imagine, Albuquerque J, Bosque Beat, Metro Plus, 4/27/93; L Stewart (auth), Secret garden blooms in illuminating exhibit, Daytona Beach Sunday News J, 7/17/94. *Mem:* Albuquerque United Artists; Col Art Asn. *Media:* Oil, All Media. *Publ:* auth, Three Artists in touch, Albuquerque Journal, W Pulkka, 10/31/99; Alegacy Framed (brochure), Jonson Gallery, 96. *Dealer:* Patricia Carlisle Fine Art 554 Canyon Rd Sante Fe NM 87501. *Mailing Add:* PO Box 1866 Corrales NM 87048

LEITES, ARA (BARBARA) L
PAINTER; EDUCATOR
b Hamilton, Ohio, June 3, 42. *Study:* Miami Univ, BFA, 64 & MFA, 67; studied with Judi Betts, Betty Lou Schlemm, Robert Wade, Milford Zornes, Louise Cadillac, Maxine Masterfield & Al Brouillette. *Work:* Springfield Art Mus, Mo; Dayton Art Inst, Ohio. *Exhib:* Cincinnati Art Mus Ann & Biennal, Ohio, 66 & 67; Audubon Artists Ann Exhib, Salmagundi Club, NY, 89, 94, 97, 99; Nat Watercolor Soc Ann, Muckenthaler Cult Ctr, Fullerton, Calif, 91, 2000; Foothills/Rocky Mountain Nat, Foothills Art Ctr, Colo, 91, 98, 2001-2003; Allied Artists Ann, Nat Arts Club, NY, 94, 96, 2004; Watercolor USA, Springfield Art Mus, Mo, 97, 2000; Watercolor Hon Soc Biennial, Springfield Art Mus, Mo, 97; Intern soc Acrylic Painters, 97-2000, 2002-2006; NAPA UK, Westminister Gallery, London, 99; Soc Watercolor Artists-Ft Worth, 2001, 2000, 1997, 1996, 1995, 1993; Okla Nat Watercolor Soc, 2002, 1998, 1997, 1993, 2003-2005; Eastern Wash Watercolor Soc, 2002, 1997; San Diego Watercolor Soc, 2001, 1995; Pittsburgh Watercolor Soc, 2001, 2000, 1999, 1997, 1994; Int Soc Experimental Artists, 2001, 2000, 1999, 1998, 1997, 2003-2004; Ariz Aqueous,1992, 1994, 1996-1999, 2005; Philadelphia Watercolor Asn Soc, 2000, 1998, 1996, 1992; Northwest Watercolor Soc, 2000, 1999; Ariz Watercolor Asn, 1998, 1999, 2003, 2005; Soc Watercolor Artists, 1999, 2002-2003, 2006; Am Watercolor Soc, 1999; Wyoming Watercolor Soc, 1999; Red River Watercolor Soc, 1997; Parkersburg Art Ctr, 1997, 1996; Western Colo Watercolor Soc, 1996, 1995; Northeast Watercolor Soc, 1996, 1993; Madison Avenue Art Gallery of Tenn, 1996; Calif Nat Watercolor Soc, 1996; Soc Experimental Artists, 1992-1994, 1996-2004; Nat Congress of Art and Design, 1995; Mid-Atlantic Regional Watercolor Exhib, 1995, 1994, 1993; Watercolor Today, Conn, 1992. *Pos:* Bd dir, Woodstock Guild Craftsmen, NY, 78-79; co-dir, Kleinert Gallery, Woodstock Guild, 78-79; reg rep, Calif Watercolor Soc, 98-. *Teaching:* instr drawing & painting Georgiana Bruce Kirby Preparatory High Sch, 98-2001 & 2005-, head visual arts dept, 99-2001. *Awards:* Winsor Newton Award, Ky Watercolor Soc, 96; Eastern Wash Watercolor Soc for Best of Show, 97, Merit award, 2002; Swede Johnson Memorial Award, Rocky Mountain Nat, 98; Chairman's award-Most Experimental Painting, Soc Watercolor Artists, 2002; Ga Peach award, Ga Watercolor Soc, 2002, Travel Show Selection, 1997; Best of Show award, Okla Nat Watercolor Soc, 2002, Tulsa Art Clubs award, 1997; Merit award, Eastern Wash Watercolor Soc, 2002; Watermedia, Int soc experimental Artist Houston, Tex, 2003; 23rd Adirondacks Nat Exhib Am Watercolors Award, Dr. Donald & Helen Budd Burness Memorial, 2004-2005; Texas Watercolor soc 56th Annual Nat Exhib Award, 2005-2006. *Bibliog:* Edited by Dona LeCrone Walston, Fifty Years of Excellence - Tex Watercolor Soc, 1999; Finalist/Experimental Category, The Artist's Mag, Dec, 2000; International Artist, Feb/Mar, 2001; The Artist's Magazine, 2004; The Palette Magazine, issue 17, 3/2006-4/2006. *Mem:* Signature mem Nat Watercolor Soc; signature mem Tex Watercolor Soc; signature mem Ky Watercolor Soc; signature mem Nat Soc Painters In Casein & Acrylic; signature mem Nat Acrylic Painters Asn; Audubon Artists, Inc; Miss Watercolor Soc; Ga Watercolor Soc; Watercolor Soc Ala; Federation Canadian Artists; Mont Watercolor Soc; Taos Nat Watercolor Soc; Pa Watercolor Soc; Rocky Mountain Nat Watercolor Soc; Soc Layerists in Mixed Media; Santa Cruz Watercolor Soc; Mo Watercolor Soc. *Media:* Acrylic, Watercolor. *Interests:* skiing; surfing; carpentry. *Collection:* KMS Corp; Seattle Washington, 98121, 92; Dos Puertos Restuarante; Mexico City, Mexico, 94; Kastrea Corp; Mexico City, Mexico,94; Tane Internat'l; Mexico City, Mexico, 95; Ascala SA, Mexico City, Mexico, 96; Springfield Art Mus, Springfield, MO, 97; NAPA Exhib-England; Alizadeh Toosi, BBC World Serv, Persian Section, Strand, London WC2B 4PH Timothy Clarke, Farthings/Seymour Place, Mile Path, Hook Heath, Gu 22 OJX, 99; Angaria SA, Mexico City, Mexico, 2004. *Publ:* Contrib, Creative Watercolor: A Step By Step

Process, 95, Best of Watercolor, 95, Best Abstracts, 95, Best of Watercolor-Composition, 97, Rockport Press; Splash 5, Northlight, Bks, 98; Fifty Years of Excellence-TX Watercolor Soc, 99; Finalist/Experimental Catalog-Dec issue, pp 49; Chosen for inclusion in 2004 Limited Ed Calendar THE ARTISTS MAGAZINE, 2003; The Art of Layering, Making Connections, 2004, The Soc of Layerists in Mult-Media, Finalist/Experimental Category-December issue The Artists Magazine, 2004; Watercolor Magic (feature article), 8/2006. *Mailing Add:* 168 Oxford Way Santa Cruz CA 95060

LEITHAUSER, MARK ALAN
PAINTER, DESIGNER
b Detroit, Mich, June 22, 50. *Study:* Wayne State Univ, BA, 72, MA, 73, MFA, 74. *Work:* Nat Gallery Art; Brooklyn Mus; Libr Cong. *Exhib:* Michigan Focus, Detroit Inst Arts, 74; Boston Printmakers Nat Show, DeCordova Mus, Lincoln, Mass, 76; 30 Yrs of Am Printmaking, Brooklyn Mus, 76; Nat Printmakers Show, Libr Cong, 77; In Celebration of Prints, Philadelphia Art Alliance, 80; Nat Print & Drawing Competition, Dulin Gallery Art, Knoxville, Tenn, 81; Am Perspective, 81 & Close Focus, 87, Nat Mus Am Art; Recent Acquisitions on Paper, Corcoran Gallery Art, 81; solo exhibs, Coe Kerr Gallery, 89 & 92, Chrysler Mus, 93 & Corcoran Gallery, 93; Refiguring Nature, Mus Contemp Art, Ft Worth, 91. *Pos:* sr cur, chief design, Nat Gallery Art, 74-. *Awards:* Purchase Award, Nat Print Show, Libr Cong, 75, Nat Printmakers Show, Nat Mus Am Art, 77 & Nat Print & Drawing Exhib, Dulin Gallery Art, 81; Leslie Cheek Design Award, 88; Presidential Design Award, 84, 88, 92 & 95. *Media:* Painting, Etching. *Dealer:* Hollis Taggart Gallery 48 E 73rd St New York NY 10021. *Mailing Add:* 3614 Idaho Ave NW Washington DC 20016

LEIVA, NICOLAS
PAINTER
b Tucuman, Arg, Nov 11, 58. *Study:* Facultad Bellas Artes, Univ Nat, Tucuman, Arg, BA, 84. *Comn:* Oil on canvas mural, Tiro Fed Argentoin & Fac Art, Tucuman, Arg, 83; Wine Spec Ed, Bodegas San Pedro, 1992 Cosecha, Chile, 94; pub collections at Mus of Art, Ft Lauderdale, Fla, Mus Jose Luis Cueva, Mexico City, Museo de Arte Moderno, Santo Domingo, Dominican Republic, Miami-Dade Community Col, Metro-Date Cult Resource, Miami, Mus Fine Arts Tucuman, Argentina, Fundacion Garcia Lorca, Madrid, Empresas Lineas Maritimas Argentinas, Buenos Aires, Fondo Nacional de las Artes, Buenos Aires, Municipalidad de la Ciudad de Aguilares Collection, Tucuman. *Exhib:* Southern Art Fedn, Southeastern Ctr Contemp Arts, Winston Salem, NC, 97; Latin Am Artist, E Tenn Univ, 97; Contemp Latino Voice, McDonough Mus, Youngstown, Ohio, 98; El Gran Viaje, Ayala Mus, Manila, Philippines, 99; McCabe Contemp Art, Cape Town, South Africa, 99; Ceramic-Italian Edition, Art Palm Beach, Gary Nader Fine Arts, Coral Gables, Fla, 99; Accounts SE: Transience, Southern Ctr Contemp Art, NC, 99; Del 49 al Fin del Milenio, Centro Cult Eugenio Virla, Tucuman, Argentina, 99; Art Miami, Inoccentti Gallery Miami, 2000; Fla Atlantic Univ, Schmidt Ctr Gallery, Boca Raton, 2000; Arti Sacro, Centro Ital per le Arti e la Cultura, Rome, 2000; Lowe Mus, Fla Individual Fel, Miami, 2001; ArteBa, Buenos Aires, 2001; Arco, Angel Romero Gallery Madrid, 2001; Dante Vecchiatto Gallery, Serie: Jugutes para Adultos, Forti di Marmi, Italy, 2001; Ceramica, Correr Mus, Venice, Italy, 2001. *Teaching:* Prof art, Nat Univ Tucuman, Arg, 86. *Awards:* Hon Distinction Biennial Int, Valparaiso, Chile, 89; Fel, SFla Cult Consortium, Miami, 91; Southern Art Fedn, Nat Endowment Arts, Atlanta, 96; Fla Individual Fel, 2000. *Bibliog:* Ricardo Pao Llousa (auth), Miami & the Art of Being in Exile, Apalache Quant, No 38, 92; Gean Moreno (auth), Mapping the Mind's Journey: The Painting of Nicolas Leiva, Metrop Dade Cult Resource, 93; Carol Damian (auth), Nicolas Leiva: Magical Voyage, Gary Nader Ed, 95. *Media:* All Media. *Publ:* Contribr, Vivid Perspectives in Six Strokes, Americas, Vol 43, No 2, 91; Nicolas Leivwa: Enigma Como Origen del la Imagen, Gary Nader Ed, 93; Work of Miami Artist, The Jetzer, 95; Materia y simbolism en Nicolas Leiva, siglo XXI, cult sect, page 3, 95; En Torno A Nicolas Leiva, Miami Herald, 97

LEKBERG, BARBARA HULT
SCULPTOR
b Portland, Ore, Mar 19, 25. *Study:* Univ Iowa, BFA & MA, with Humbert Albrizio. *Hon Degrees:* Simpson Col, hon DFA, 64. *Work:* Montclair Mus Art, NJ; Des Moines Art Ctr, Iowa; Knoxville Art Ctr, Tenn; Whitney Mus Am Art; General Electric Collection, Fairfield, Conn. *Comn:* Three interior sculptures, Beldon-Stratford Hotel, Chicago, 53; three interior sculptures, Socony-Mobil Co, NY, 55; lobby relief, Riedl & Freede Advert, Clifton, NJ, 64; life-size figures, Bayfield Clark, Bermuda, 71 & 74; Orpheus (10 ft work), Simpson Col, Iowa, 84; life size figure, Trafalgar House Realty, NY, 86; Loie Fuller Dancing figure, Brookgreen Gardens, SC, 2005; and others. *Exhib:* Five Pa Acad Fine Arts Ann, Philadelphia, 50-62; Whitney Mus Ann, 52, 56; New Talent, Am Fedn Arts Traveling Show, 59-60; Recent Sculpture USA, Mus Mod Art, NY, 59; One-man shows, Sculpture Ctr, NY, 59, 65, 71, 75, 77 & 83, Percival Galleries, Des Moines, Iowa, 90, 95 & 2000 & Harmon Meek Galleries, Naples, Fla, 97, Century Asn, New York City, 2001; Traveling solo show, Birmingham Mus Art, Ala & Columbia Mus Art, SC, 73; Retrospective, Mt Holyoke Col Mus, Mass, 78; Contemp Sculpture at Chesterwood, Stockbridge, Mass, 88, 89, 94, 97, 2001, 2004; British Mus, London, 94; Meguro Mus, Tokyo, Japan, 2001. *Teaching:* Fac, Col New Rochelle, 80-84; Univ Arts, Phila, 81-2001; Nat Acad Design, New York City, 09-95. *Awards:* Am Inst Arts & Lett Grant, 56; Guggenheim Found Fels, 57 & 59; Grant, Richard Florsheim Art Fund, 98; and others. *Bibliog:* Wayne V Anderson (auth), American Sculpture in Progress 1930-1970, NY Graphic Soc, 75; Donald M Reynolds (auth), Masters of American Sculpture: The Figurative Tradition, Abbeville Press, 93; Nathan Cabot Hale (auth), Creative Welding, Overpress, 94; and others. *Mem:* Sculptors Guild; Nat Acad (acad, Saltus Gold medal 1990); Nat Sculpture Soc (sec, Fel, Gold medal, 1991). *Media:* Bronze, Steel. *Dealer:* Harmon-Meek Gallery Naples FL

LELAND, WHITNEY EDWARD
PAINTER, EDUCATOR
b Washington, DC, Apr 12, 45. *Study:* Memphis Acad Arts, BFA; Univ Tenn, Knoxville, MFA. *Work:* Springfield Art Mus, Mo; Hunter Mus Art, Chattanooga, Tenn; Nat Mus Am Art, Smithsonian Inst, Washington, DC; Ark Art Ctr, Little Rock; Chase Manhattan Bank, NY. *Exhib:* solo exhib, Cumberland Gallery, Nashville, 90, Slemp Gallery, Mountain Empire Community Col, Big Stone Gap, Va, 93; 33rd Chautauqua Nat Exhib Am Art, Chautauqua, NY, 90; H20 Color Exhib, Crossman Gallery, Univ Wis, Whitewater, Wis, 93; Watercolor USA, Springfield Art Mus, Springfield, Mo, 94; The Tenn Twelve: Contemp Painting Today, Tenn State Mus, Nashville, Tenn, 94. *Teaching:* Asst prof, Univ Tenn, Knoxville, 70-78, assoc prof, 78-86, prof painting, 86-. *Awards:* Fel Grant, Nat Endowment Art, SE Ctr Contemp Art, 77; Nominee, Eighth Ann Awards Visual Arts, SE Conf Contemp Art, Winston-Salem, NC, 88; Arches & Rives Paper Award, Arjo Wiggins USA, Springfield Art Mus, 92. *Bibliog:* Bennett Schiff (auth), In a Tobacco City the Arts are Put in Place-Out Front, Smithsonian, Vol 9, No 10, 1/79; Don Kurka (auth), Southern Abstraction, Art Papers, Vol 8, No 2, 3-4/84; Faith Heller (auth), Ten Years of 'Southeast Seven': An Abundance of Individual Visions, Arts J, 1/88. *Media:* Acrylic, Watercolor. *Dealer:* Cumberland Gallery Nashville Tenn. *Mailing Add:* 2205 Maplewood Dr Knoxville TN 37920-2754

LEMAY, HARRY ADRIAN
PAINTER & INSTRUCTOR
b Lewistown, PA, Dec 19,1929. *Study:* US Merchant Marine Academy, BS (with hon), 1952; Cooper Union, grad cert, 1958. *Work:* Library of Congress, Washington, DC; Museum of Radio & Television Broadcasting, NY & Los Angeles, CA. *Comn:* Graphic Design, Illus, Reader's Digest, Dell Books, New York, NY, 1959-65; Illus & Design, Columbia Record Club, New York, NY, 1960-63; Graphic Design, Life Magazine, Prom, NY, 1964; Package Design, Pfizer, Merk Sharf & Dome, NY, 1964; Lighting Design, Carnegie Hall-Folklorico Filipino, NY, 1973. *Exhib:* First Paperback Book Show, AIGA, New York, NY, 1959; LeMay-25 Year Retrospective, Kenny Gallery, Art & Design, NYC, 1980; LeMay-Solo Exhib, LaGuardia Community College, NYC, 1991. *Pos:* Mgr art & production, RCA Victor Recor Club, NYC, 1965-67; vp creative, Capitol Record Club, Los Angeles, CA, 1967-69; Art dir, Mann Assoc, New York, NY, 1960-64. *Teaching:* instr theater arts, design, drawing, Art & Deisgn, NYC, 1972-1991; instr life drawing, graphic design, Sch for the Arts, Los Angeles, CA, 1993-97; instr life drawing, Rustic Canyon Park La Brea Art Center, Los Angeles, CA, 1993-1998. *Bibliog:* NBC TV Series (mongr), You're Part of Art, 1970. *Mem:* Los Angeles Art, 1993-97; life mem Art Students League of New York. *Media:* Designer, Director, Draftsman, Educator, Graphic Artist, Illustrator, Insructor, Lecturer, Acrylic, Oil, Watercolor, Printmaker, Publisher. *Interests:* art book collecting; computer graphics. *Publ:* Medley Mag, 1965-66; Keynotes Mag, 1967-69; Dr. Cristina Carney (auth), LeMay Lines Through Time (monogr), Who's Who in America, Who's Who in the World; Calif Quar, U Calif Davis, 1981. *Dealer:* Jean Marc Gallery 906 N LaCienega Los Angeles, CA 90069. *Mailing Add:* 357 S Curson Ave #6B Los Angeles CA 90036

LEMAY, NANCY
PAINTER
b New York, NY, Sept 7, 56. *Study:* Sch Visual Arts, BFA, 78; NY Univ, 84. *Comn:* designer: (logotype design) Art Direction Mag, 85. *Exhib:* Group show, Wings N Water Festival (poster winner), 90. *Pos:* graphic designer, JC Penney, 87-89; art dir, Catch A Rising Star, 89; graphic designer, WNBC TV News Graphics, 89-90; graphics engineer, NBC Network News Graphics, 90-91, KCOP TV News, Los Angeles, 91-94, superv graphic designer, 1994-2000; graphic designer, KNBC-TV, 2000-2001. *Teaching:* teacher, Rustic Canyon, Santa Monica, Calif, 2001-, Abram Friedman Occupational Ctr, Los Angeles, 2001-; instr, animation, Abram Friedman Occupational Ctr, currently. *Awards:* Recipient 5 Los Angeles Area Emmy Awards, 96-99; Art Times Award, CL Wolfe Annual, Art Times Mag, 2004; Catherine Lorillard Wolfe Art Club's, 108th Annual Nat Juried Show, 2004. *Media:* Oil, Acrylic, Collage & Watercolor. *Collection:* Painting, bird watching, sculpture & photography. *Publ:* auth, White Graphics, 2001; contribr, MacWeek Mag, 89. *Dealer:* Caorl Sauvion Freehand 8413 W Third St Los Angeles Calif 90048. *Mailing Add:* 357 S Curson Ave Los Angeles CA 90036-5201

LEMIEUX, BONNE A
PAINTER
b Elmwood Park, Ill, Aug 3, 21. *Study:* Los Angeles Art League, 82-83; Studied with Jake Lee, 82-83; Los Angeles Valley Col, 82-84. *Work:* City of Los Angeles Permanent Art Collection; Norwalk City Hall, Calif; Ernie Pyle Sch, Bellflower, Calif; Salvation Army Tabernacle, Hollywood; Univ Southern Calif. *Comn:* Portrait of Mayor, City of Norwalk, 90; Hist Bldg, walleck, Shave, Stanard & Blender, Woodland Hills Calif, 90. *Exhib:* Women Painters W, Univ Del, Newark, 87; Am Contemp Masters Invitational, Dr Sun Yat-Sen Mem Hall, Taipei, Taiwan, 87; Old Bergen, Ky Highlands Mus, Ashland, 87; Artists Soc Int, E Co Performing Arts Ctr, El Cajon, Calif, 89; Seattle Art Mus, 96; San Bernardeno Mus, Calif, 96. *Teaching:* Art instr watercolor, Creative Art Ctr, Burbank, 91-. *Awards:* Art Store & More Award, 86; Bronze Medal, Artists of the Southwest, 88; Best of Show, Ocean House Fine Arts Exhib, 96. *Bibliog:* David Kozinski (auth), Bonnie LeMieux, versatile artist, Artists Market, 76; Ernest Kay (ed), Bonnie LeMieux, The World Who's Who of Women, 86; Judy Shay (auth), Arts Glendale News Press, 89. *Mem:* Valley Watercolor Soc; Women Painters W; San Fernando Valley Art Club (vpres, 77 & pres, 78); Collage Soc; assoc mem Am Watercolor Soc. *Media:* Watercolor, Oil. *Mailing Add:* 22855 Belquest Dr Lake Forest CA 92630

LEMIEUX, IRENEE
PAINTER
b Quebec, Aug 3, 31. *Study:* Laval Univ; Conserv de Musique de Quebec, Montreal; Fontainebleau, France. *Work:* La Minerve, Quebec. *Exhib:* Third Salon Int de la Riviera, Grasse, France; 3rd Salon Int de la Cote d'Azur, Chateau des Requiers; 2nd Salon Int du Carnaval de Nice; 2nd Salon Int de Baden-Baden, Allemagne, 73; 7th Grand Prix Int Painting & Sculpture, Antibes, 74; among others. *Awards:* First Prize with Gold Medal, 3rd Salon Int de la Cote d'Azur, 73; Spec First Prize with Gold Medal, Acad de Lutece, Paris, 73; Second Prize with Silver Medal, 7th Grand Prix Int Painting & Sculpture, 74; and others. *Bibliog:* Roland Laznikas (auth), article, 3/73 & Raymond Clermont (auth), article, 6/74, La Rev Mod, Paris; and others. *Mem:* Asn Beaux-Arts Cannes. *Media:* Acrylic. *Mailing Add:* 5 Ave du Pont Scott Quebec PQ G1N 3S3 Canada

LEMON, ROBERT S, JR
EDUCATOR, HISTORIAN
b Pittsburg, Kans, Oct 1, 38. *Study:* Univ Mo, Kansas City, BA, 62; Ohio Univ, MA, 69 & PhD, 75. *Pos:* Mem, Orlando Airport Art Selection Comt, Orlando Aviation Authority, Fla, 83-89; mem, bd visitors, Cornell Fine Arts Mus, Rollins Col, 82-. *Teaching:* Prof art hist, Rollins Col, Winter Park, Fla, 73-, chmn, art dept, 80-99, chmn art dept Marshall Univ, 99-01. *Mem:* Southeastern Col Art Conf (pres, 97-00); Col Art Asn. *Res:* Twentieth century American painting and sculpture. *Publ:* Auth, An interview with Lowell Nesbitt, Art Voices South, 78; The Figurative Pretext: A Comparative Explication of the Fiction of Alain Robbe-Grillet and the Painting of the Photo Realists, University Microfilms, 80; American Printmakers of the 30's (exhib catalog), Cornell Fine Arts Mus, 81; Photo Realism: Logical evolution from post-painterly abstraction, Southeastern Col Art Conf Rev, 87; Reliefs and Menhirs: The Sculpture of J G Naylor (exhib catalog), Univ Gallery of Gainesville, Fla, 88; Doris Leeper: A Retrospective (exhib catalog), Cornell Fine Arts Mus, 95. *Mailing Add:* Rollins Col 2676 Winter Park FL 32789

LENAGHAN, ANDREW
PAINTER
b New Brunswick, NJ, 65. *Study:* Cornell Univ, BFA, 87; Brooklyn Col, MFA, 89. *Exhib:* It Figures, SFA Gallery, Stephen Austin State Univ, Nacogdoches, Tex, 96; Fac Exhib, NJ Asn Independent Schs, Gladston, 89; Watchung Art Ctr, NJ, 90; ADF/NY Sch Interior Design Exhib, Int Design Ctr, Long Island, 91; Roundabout Theater, NY, 93; solo exhibs, Gerorge Adams Gallery, 96, 96 & 98; Going Places, George Adams Gallery, NY, 96; Mixing Business with Pleasure: Selections from the George Adams Gallery NY, Sawhill Gallery, James Madison Univ, Harrisonburg, Va, 97; Reflections of Taste: Am Art from Greenwich Collections, Bruce Mus, Conn, 97; ntpelier Sandelson Gallery, London, 97; Illumination, George Adams Gallery, NY, 98. *Teaching:* Instr painting, Rutgers Prep Sch, Somerset, NJ, 88-92. *Bibliog:* Ruth Bass (auth), Realism: when a rose is a rose, Art News, 2/96 & Artist Mag (Tai Pei), 96. *Media:* Oil. *Mailing Add:* c/o George Adams Gallery 41 W 57th St 7th Fl New York NY 10019

LENGYEL, ALFONZ
HISTORIAN, WRITER, MUSEOLOGIST
b Godollo, Hungary, Oct 21, 21; US citizen. *Study:* Miskolc Law Acad, JD, 48, 48-50; San Jose State Col, BA(art hist), 58, MA(art hist), 59; Inst Art & Archeol, Univ Paris, PhD(summa cum laude),64; London Inst Applied Res, Hon LDD, 75; Univ Budapest, studies in art hist, archaeology & museology. *Hon Degrees:* LLD. *Pos:* Adj cur, Detroit Inst Arts, 68-72; mem adv bd, US Dept Interior, 87-91; bd dir, Mus of Asian Art, Sarasota, Fla, 2001-05. *Teaching:* Asst prof art hist, San Jose State Col, 1961-63; mem fac, Univ Md Europ Div, Paris & Heidelberg, 63-68; prof art hist & classical archeol, Wayne State Univ, 68-72; prof & dir archeol prog, Northern Ky Univ, 72-77; dean & prof, Inst Mediterranean Art & Archeol, 77-82; coordr art hist & museology prog, Rosemont Col, 82-; prof art hist & cur, Goebel's Print Collection, Eastern Col, 85-87; adv prof, Fudan Univ, Shanghai, China, 87-; consult prof, Xian Jiaotong Univ, Xian, China, 88; Pres, Fudan Mus Found, 89-; US dir, Sino-Am Field Sch Archeol, Xian, China; founder, dean Inst Mediterranean Art and Archaeology, Cincinnati, Ohio, 77-82, editor, Bull of Mediterranean Archaeology. *Awards:* Rockefeller Grant, Vienna, 57, S H Kress Grant, 67; Smithsonian Grant, 68; Gold Medal, Brazil Acad Humanities, 75; Smithsonian-NEH Grant, 76; Lilly Grant, 82; Connelly Grant, 83; and others. *Mem:* Int Asn Classical Archeol; Soc Prof Archeol; Regist Prof Archeol; Col Art Asn Am; Archeol Inst Am; Int Coun of Mus (Zcom/Unesco); and others. *Res:* Contemp Chinese Art; Market Socialism & its impact on Chinese Culture & Econ. *Interests:* Chinese Cartoon Art. *Publ:* Auth, Quattrocento, Kendall-Hunt, 72; coauth, L'Art et le Monde Moderne, Larousse, 72; Lexicon der Kristlichen Ikonographie, Herder Verlag, 73; ed & coauth, The Archaeology of Roman Pannonia, Ky Univ Press, 80; Selected prints from the Goebel's Collection, Eastern Col, 89; ed, Etruscans, 69-74; Acta Toscana, 74-75; Can-Am Rev of Hungarian Studies, 74; Archaeology for Museologists, 2002; Chinese Chronological History, 2002; and others. *Mailing Add:* 4206 73rd Terr E Sarasota FL 34243-5112

LENHARDT, SHIRLEY M
PAINTER
b St Louis, Mo, Oct, 6, 34. *Study:* Univ Mo, BS(art ed), 74, MA (painting), 79, MFA (painting), 81. *Work:* Univ Mo Women's Ctr, Columbia, Mo; Univ Mo Chancellors Collection, Columbia, Mo. *Exhib:* Am Art Ann Middletown Fine Arts Ctr, Middletown, Ohio, 81-85; Ann Juried Nat Exhib, Ga Tech, Atlanta, 81 & 86; Vineyard Theatre Gallery, NY, 84; New Orleans Art Asn Nat, 84 & 88; Nepenthe Mundi Soc, Wichita, Kans, 86, 87, 88; Important Mo Women Artists, traveling exhib, 86; Missouri Women Artists, St Louis Univ, 91. *Collection Arranged:* Water: Moods & Reflections, 84, Shiao-Cai-Li-Chinese Artist, 86 & Salubi Onakufe-Nigerian Artist (auth catalog), 86 Hawthorn Gallery. *Pos:* Columbia Comm on the Arts, Columbia, Mo, 82-86 & Dir, Hawthorn Gallery Art, 84-87. *Teaching:* Columbia Adult Educ Painting, 70-, Drawing 75-81, Univ Mo, Columbia. *Awards:* Best of Show-Gold Medal, Black Forest Sch Creative Art, Int Exhib, 81; First Prize, Sno-Bird Gallery Nat Exhib, 86; First Prize, Emerald City Classic VI-VII, Nepenthe Mundi Soc, 87, 88. *Bibliog:* Tim Stokesberry (auth), A matter of style, Travel Host Mag, 5/85; Shawna Stallcup (auth), Images of women, Columbia Missourian, 9/6/85. *Mem:* Columbia Art League Exec Bd, 91-92. *Media:* Acrylic, Oil; Watercolor. *Mailing Add:* 1118 St Christopher St Columbia MO 65203

LENKER, MARLENE N
PAINTER, COLLAGE ARTIST
b Clifton, NJ, Mar 07, 32. *Study:* Fairleigh/Dickenson Univ, AA, 51; Montclair State Univ, MA, 76. *Work:* Bergen Mus, Paramus, NJ; Montclair State Col, Upper Montclair, NJ; St Barnabas Medical Ctr, Livingston, NJ; Pepsico Hq, Purchase, NY; Am Airlines, NY; Hoffman Laroche, NJ; Kidder Peabody, NY; Johnson & Johnson, NJ; Hewlett Packard, Tex & Calif; and many others. *Comn:* Okla State Bank, Okla; ASEA, Brown Boveri Inc, NJ; NJ Cent Power & Light; Guioiden Hq, NJ. *Exhib:* One-woman shows, David Gary Ltd, NJ, 83, Snug Harbor Cult Ctr, NY, 85, Adelle Taylor Gallery, Dallas, Tex, 86, Reece Galleries, NY, Bloomfield Cult Ctr, NJ, 91, David-Gary Gallery, NJ, 92, Art in Focus, NJ, 92, Forrest-Scott Gallery, NJ, 97 & Fredrick Clement Gallery, NJ, 98; group shows, Colorworks Gallery, Hilton Head Island, NC, 90, Hammond Gallery, Ohio, 93, Alva Gallery, New London, Conn, 2001, Mus New Art, Detroit, Mich, 2001, Intercultural Art Ctr Gallery, NY & many others; Miniature Invitational, Old Church Cult Ctr, Demarast, NJ, 90; Hummerick Mus, Cincinnati, Ohio, 90; Northcoast Collage Soc, Cincinnati Mus, Ohio, 90; Walton Art Ctr, Ark, 94; Jain/Maranuchi Gallery, NY, 94; David-Gary Gallery, NJ, 94; Gregory Gallery, Conn, 94; Williams Gallery, NJ, 95; Broadfoot & Broadfoot, NJ, 96; Nat Small Works, NJ, 96; Layer: Mining the Unconscious, Western NMex Univ, 96; Celtic Connections, Bradford Col, Mass, 98; Artium Gallery, Norwalk, Conn, 2000; Lippman Gallery, Short Hills, NJ, 2001; GJ Cloninger Gallery, NJ; one-person shows, Chase-Freedman Gallerys, West Hartford, Conn, The Beth Shalom Rodfe Zedek, Synagague, Chester, Conn, The Charter Oak Cultural Ctr, Hartford, Conn, 2006. *Pos:* Pres, West Essex Art Asn, 70-73. *Teaching:* Instr fine arts Caldwell Col, Caldwell, NJ, 77-79; lectr, Nat Acad, NY. *Bibliog:* Skye Griffith (auth), Lyrical Landscapes, Staten Island Advance, 85; J Taylor Basker (auth), Art Review, NY Art Forms, 87; Eileen Watkins (auth), A Sense of Special, Star Ledger, 89. *Mem:* Nat Asn Women Artists (selection jury, 82-83); Artists Equity - NY Chap; Soc Layerists in Multimedia (E Coast coord); North Coast Collage Soc; NJ Watercolor Soc; Soc Layerists in Multimedia. *Media:* Acrylic, Collage. *Publ:* Illusr, New Jersey Goodlife, Rene B Timpone, 88; contribr, New York Art Review, Krantz, 89; Layering (video) - An Art of Time and Space, 91; The Guild, Anniversary Ed, 95, 97 & 98; Bridging Time & Space, 99; The Art of Layering, Making Connections, 2004. *Dealer:* GJ Cloninger Gallery 39 E Hanover Ave Morris Plains NJ 07950; Old Town Gallery, Park City, UT; Harris Gallery, Houston, TX. *Mailing Add:* 28 Northview Terr Cedar Grove NJ 07009

LENNON, TIMOTHY
PAINTING CONSERVATOR
b Chicago, Ill, Sept 18, 38. *Study:* Loras Col, BA; Univ Notre Dame, MA; Art Inst Chicago. *Pos:* Conservator, Art Inst Chicago, 80-. *Mem:* Fel Am Inst Conserv Artistic & Hist Works; Fel Int Inst Conserv Artistic & Hist Works. *Mailing Add:* Art Inst Chicago Michigan Ave at Adams St Chicago IL 60603

LENT, BLAIR
ILLUSTRATOR, WRITER
b Boston, Mass, Jan 22, 30. *Study:* Boston Mus Sch, Cummings Mem travel fel to Switz & Italy, 1955, Bartlett travel fel to USSR, grad(hons), 1968. *Work:* Boston Pub Libr; Kerlan Collection, Univ Minn; Mazza Collection, Findlay Col, Ohio; Keene State Col, Keene, NH; Wichita Falls Mus, Wichita Falls, Tex. *Comn:* Why the Sun and the Moon Live in the Sky (animated film), ACI Films, NY, 71; Christmas card design, UNICEF. *Exhib:* Solo Show, Wiggin Gallery, Boston, 70; Work by Five Major Am Illustrators, Univ Art Gallery, Albany, NY, 72; Contemp Am Illusr Children's Bks, Rutgers Univ, 74-75; Brattleboro Mus, Vt, 80; Univ Conn, Storrs, 82. *Awards:* Silver Medal, Bienal Int Arte Grafice, Sao Paulo, Brazil, 65; Bronze Medal, Bienale Illustrators, Bratislava, Czech, 69; Caldecott Medal, Am Libr Asn, 73. *Bibliog:* Lee Hopkins (auth), Books Are By People, Citation, 69; Anne Commire (auth), Something About the Author, Gale, 72; and others. *Publ:* Auth (pseud Ernest Small) & illusr, Baba Yaga, Houghton Mifflin, 66; From King Boggen's Hall to Nothing-at-all, Little, 67; illusr, The Funny Little Woman, Dutton, 72; auth & illusr, Bayberry Bluff, Houghton Mifflin, 84; Molasses Flood, Houghton Mifflin, 92; illustr Beastly Feast, Henry Holt, 99; Ruby and Fred, Henry Holt, 2000; plus others. *Mailing Add:* Ten Dana St No 208 Cambridge MA 02138-5425

LENTZ, THOMAS W
MUSEUM DIRECTOR, CURATOR
Study: Claremont Men's Col, BA; Univ Calif, Berkeley, MA in Near Eastern Studies; Harvard Univ, MA(Islamic art), PhD(fine arts), 1985. *Work:* Cur Timur and the Princely Vision: Persian Art and Culture in the 15th Century, Los Angeles Co Mus Art. *Pos:* Cur, Asian art RI Sch of Design; asst cur, to cur, head Dept Ancient & Islamic, Art Los Angeles Co Mus Art; asst dir, res & collections Freer and Sackler Galleries Smithsonian Inst, Washington, DC, 92, deputy dir, to dir inter, art mus div; dir, Elizabeth and John Moors Cabot, Harvard Univ Art Mus, Cambridge, Mass, 2003-. *Mailing Add:* Harvard Univ Art Mus 32 Quincy St Cambridge MA 02138

LEON, DENNIS
SCULPTOR, EDUCATOR
b London, Eng, July 27, 33; US citizen. *Study:* Temple Univ, BSc(educ), 56; Tyler Sch Art, MFA, 57. *Work:* Philadelphia Mus Art; Oakland Mus Art; San Francisco Mus Mod Art. *Comn:* Chevron Corp, 86. *Exhib:* Pa Acad Fine Arts, 56, 64 & 68; Philadelphia Mus Art; James Willis Gallery, 73; Univ Calif, Davis, 74; JPL Fine Arts, London, Eng, 75; Am 76, San Francisco Mus Mod Art, 77; Hanson-Fuller Golden Gallery, San Francisco, 77, 79, 81-82 & 84-85; San Jose Mus Art, 81; and others. *Teaching:* Prof sculpture, Philadelphia Col Art, 60-72 & Calif Col Arts & Crafts, 72-; vis artist, Sheffield Polytech, Eng, 75 & 76. *Awards:* Guggenheim Fel, 67; Nat Inst Arts & Lett Award, 67; MacDowell Fel, 81; Djerassi Found Fel, 83 & 84; and others. *Media:* Mixed Media. *Publ:* Auth, Paul Harris, 73. *Dealer:* Fuller Goldeen Gallery 228 Grant Ave San Francisco CA 94108. *Mailing Add:* 1254 E 12th St Oakland CA 94606-4325

LEONARD, JOANNE
PHOTOGRAPHER, EDUCATOR
b Los Angeles, Calif, 40. *Study:* Univ Calif, Berkeley, BA, 62; San Francisco State Col, 63-64. *Work:* US State Dept; Am Arts Doc Ctr, Exeter, Eng; San Francisco Mus Art; Int Mus Photog, Rochester, NY; Stanford Univ Mus, Palo Alto; Crocker Art Mus, Sacramento, Calif; Oakland Mus; and numerous pvt collections. *Exhib:* One-person shows, MH de Young Mem Mus, 68, San Francisco Art Inst, 74, Calif, Laguna Gloria Art Mus, Austin, Tex, 80 & Orange Coast Col Photo Gallery, Costa Mesa, 84; Photo Trans Form, San Francisco Mus Mod Art, 81; San Francisco Mus Art, 71, 75, 82 & 85; Summer Light, Light Gallery, NY, 72; Seattle Art Mus, Wash, 76; Whitney Mus Am Art, NY, 78; Franklin Inst, Philadelphia, 83; Santa Barbara Mus Art, Calif, 82, 83 & 86; Detroit Inst Arts, 92; Univ Mich Mus Art, 92; Schlessinger Libr Gallery, Radcliffe Col, Cambridge, Mass, 95; Int Ctr Photog, NY, 97. *Teaching:* Lectr, San Francisco Art Inst, 73-75 & Mills Col, Oakland, Calif, 82-83 & 86; prof art, Univ Mich Sch Art, Ann Arbor, 78-. *Awards:* Phelan Award, 71; Nat Endowment, Photog Surveys Grant, 77; Josephine Nevins Keal Award, Univ Mich, 81. *Bibliog:* HW Janson (auth), History of Art, Abrams, New York, 86; de la Croix, Tansey & Kirkpatrick (auth), Gardner's Art through the Ages, Harcourt, Brace & Javonovich, San Diego, 91; Lucy Lippard (auth), Lost & Found (catalog essay), 92; and others. *Mem:* Soc Photog Educators; Col Art Asn. *Publ:* Sexual Discourses: From Aristotle to AIDS 1989, Univ Mich Press, 92; Modern Fiction Studies, Vol 40, No 3, John Hopkins Univ Press, 94; Mich Feminist Studies, No 11, 96-97; M Hirsch (ed), The Familial Gaze, Univ Press, New Eng, 98. *Mailing Add:* Sch Art Univ Mich 2000 Banisteel Blvd Ann Arbor MI 48109

LEONARD, ZOE
PHOTOGRAPHER
b Liberty, NY, 61. *Work:* Mus Contemp Art, Los Angeles; Mus Mod Art & Whitney Mus Am Art, NY; Philadelphia Mus Art, Pa; San Francisco Mus Mod Art, Calif; Univ Art Mus, Univ Calif, Berkeley. *Exhib:* One-person exhibs, Univ Art Mus/Pac Film Archives, Univ Calif, Berkeley, 91, Renaissance Soc, Univ Chicago, 93, Le Casa d'Arte, Milan, Italy, 95, Mus Contemp Art, N Miami, 97, Philadelphia Mus, Pa, 98, Centre National de la Photographie, Paris, France, 98 & Paula Cooper Gallery, NY, 99; Benefit Auction, New Mus Contemp Art, NY, 91; The Return of Cadavre (traveling exhib), Drawing Ctr, NY, Corcoran Gallery Art, Washington, DC, Found Contemp Art, Mexico City, Santa Monica Mus, Los Angeles & Forum Contemp Art, St Louis, Mo, 93; Sum of the Parts, Art Gallery Univ Hawaii, Manoa, 94; Nature Studies II, Univ Gallery Fine Arts Ctr, Univ Mass, Amherst, 95; Compulsion to Repeat: Repetition and Difference in Works from the Permanent Collection, Mus Contemp Art, Los Angeles, 97; Points of View: Photog from the Collection, Gallery 2, Univ Mass, Pac Film Archive, Univ Calif, Berkeley, 96; Gothic, Inst Contemp Art, Boston, 97; Whitney Mus Am Art Biennial, NY, 97; The Precious Image: Contemp Platinum Photog, Univ Art Gallery, Montclair State Univ, NJ, 98; The Mus as Muse: Artists Reflect, Mus Mod Art, NY, 99; many others in the US and abroad. *Mailing Add:* c/o Paula Cooper Gallery 534 W 21st St New York NY 10011

LEONG, LAMPO
PAINTER, EDUCATOR
b Guangzhou, Guangdong, China, July 3, 61; US citizen. *Study:* Guangzhou Acad Fine Arts, China, BFA, 83; Calif Col Arts, Oakland, MFA, 88; Cen Acad Fine Arts, Beijing, PhD-ABD, 2005. *Work:* Stanford Mus Art, Palo Alto, Calif; Asian Art Mus, San Francisco; Minneapolis Inst Arts, Minn; Macao Mus Art; Guangdong Mus Art, China. *Comn:* paintings, Epcot Ctr, Disney World, Fla, 98, Tokyo Westin, Japan, 94; granite medallion, City of San Francisco, 99; mural and paintings, Westin Surabaya, Indonesia, 1996; murals, U Mo, Columbia, 2005. *Exhib:* Solo exhibs, Rosicrucian Egyptian Mus, San Jose, 86, Luis De Camoes Mus, Macao, 86, Guangzhou Fine Arts Mus, Guangzhou, China, 88, Chinese Cult Ctr, San Francisco, 91, Cult Inst Macao, 98 & Guangdong Art Mus, China, 99; Art of China, Shanghai Mus Fine Arts, China, 97; Shining Stars: Four Cult Visionaries of Contemp Painting, Pacific Heritage Mus, San Francisco, Calif, 98; Contemp Paintings from Collection of Macao Art Mus, Zhuhai Mus, Guangdong, China, 2000; George E Ohr Nat Art Challenge, The Ohr-O'Keefe Mus of Art, Biloxi, MS, USA, 02; Englewood Arts Nat Juried Art Show, Mus of Outdoor Arts, Englewood, CO, 03; Int Contemp Ink Painting, Changliu Art Mus, Taoyuan, Taiwan, 05; Question, Cantor Ctr for Visual Arts, Stanford, Calif, 2004; Media 1 Art Biennial, Medial Mus, London, 2005; Han Zi Reinvented: The Rhythm of Chinese Script, Calif State U, Fullerton, 2006; Taipei Internat Ink Painting Biennial, Nat Taipei U Tech, 2006. *Collection Arranged:* Asian-Am Contemp Art Exhibit, Chinese Cult Ctr, San Francisco, CA, 86; Chinese Artists in Academia, Columbia Art League, Columbia, MO, St. Louis Community College-Forest Park, St. Louis, MO, Chesterfield Arts Gallery, Chesterfield, MO, 04; American Eyes: Works from Art Prof at UM-Columbia, Guangdong Mus of Art, Guangzhou, China, 04. *Teaching:* Asst Prof, brush painting, San Francisco State Univ, San Francisco, Calif, 96-01; Assoc Prof, painting, drawing & brush painting, Univ Missouri-Columbia, 2001-. *Awards:* First Prize, Santa Cruz Art League, 90; Gold Medal, XV Exposicao Coltctiva dos Artistas de Macau, Leal Senado de Macau, Macao, 98; Third Prize, Girardot Nat Juried Exhib, Arts Coun of Southeast MO, Cape Girardeau, 03; Best of Show, 42d Ann Juried Exhib, Sumi-e Soc Am, J Harrison Smith Fine Art Gallery, Clearwater, Fla 2005. *Bibliog:* Eileen Blodgett (auth), Painting Tao-featuring Lampo Leong's painting (video), San Francisco State Univ, 89; Betsy Crabtree (auth), A conversation with Chinese painter Lampo Leong, San Francisco Arts Monthly, 2/92; Manni Liu & Jung Park (auths), Bridging the old and the new Worlds, Asian Art News, Hong Kong, 9/97; Pamela Marquis (auth) Artist Profile, Lampo Leong, Creating A New Visual Language, Columbia Home, Columbia, MO, 2/02, pp14-18; Margey Fischer (auth), From Oppression to Expression, Vox Mag, publ by Columbia Missourian, Columbia, MO, Vol 7, Issue No 52, 1/05, pp. 2 & 7; Jenna Kaegel (auth), Global Expressions, Columbia Daily Tribune, 2002; Edmund Moy (auth), Chinese Calligraphy Meets Modern Computer Technology, Asian Week, San Francisco, Calif, 2000; Kevin Allton (auth), The Wild Calligraphy of Lampo Leong, Sublimation: Calligraphy by Lampo Leung, Creative Macau, Inst European Studies Macau, Macau Cultural Ctr, 2006. *Mem:* Chinese Am Cult Exchange Asn (co-founder & dir, 92-); Nat Oil & Acrylic Painters Soc, Osage Beach, MO; World Asn Chinese Artists; Nat Mod Meticulous Painting Soc; Nat Sumi-e Soc Am, Va Beach. *Media:* Modern Brush Painting, Acrylic/Oil and Watercolor, and Calligraphy. *Res:* My current research is in comparative study of painting and calligraphy, especially the spiritual expression of the Sublime. *Publ:* Auth, Lam-Po Leong's Paintings, Mus Macao Luis De Camoes, 86; illusr, Brushstrokes-Styles and Techniques of Chinese Painting, Asian Art Mus San Francisco, 93; auth, The Common Ground of Light & Gravity, Chicago: Art Media Resources, Ltd, 98; auth, Lampo Leong: Contemplation Forces, Inst Cult De Macau, 98; auth, Learning the Art of Chinese Brush Painting: The Landscape, Nature in Art, Chinese Brush Painting, San Francisco, Calif, Asian Art Mus, 01, pp 11-17; auth, Recoding the Roots: Genetic Reformation & Culture Synthesis in the Era of Globalization, Yishu Jour Contemporary Chinese Art, 2004; auth, The Deconstruction & Reformation of Genes, The Artistic Trend of Modern Chinese Ink & Wash Works in the Late 20th Century, Modern Ink & Wash Painting Series IV, 2001

LEOPOLD, RUDOLF & ELIZABETH
COLLECTOR
b Vienna, Mar 1, 25. *Study:* Univ Vienna, MD, 1953. *Pos:* Dir, Leopold Mus, Wien, Austria. *Awards:* Named one of The Top 200 Collectors, ARTnews Mag, 2004. *Collection:* German & Austrian Expressionist Art. *Mailing Add:* Leopold Mus Museumplatz 1 Wien 1070 Austria

LEOPOLD, SUSAN
SCULPTOR, MURALIST
b Chicago, Ill, July 13, 60. *Study:* Sch Visual Arts, BFA, 82. *Work:* Brooklyn Mus, NY; Chase Manhattan Bank; First National Bank Chicago, Ill; Bibliot Ctr, Firenze. *Exhib:* one-woman shows, Carnegie Mellon Univ Art Gallery, Pittsburgh, 87, John Weber Gallery, NY, 95 & 96, Saw Hill Gallery, James Madison Univ, Harrisonburg, Va, Peep Show, NY Kunsthalle; Miniature Environments, Whitney Mus Am Art, NY, 89; Rotunda Gallery, Brooklyn, NY, 95; Voyeur's Delight, Franklin Furnace, NY; Bare Bones - TZ Art, NY; Hosfelt Gallery, San Francisco; Nat Acad Mus, NY, 2006. *Teaching:* Artist-in-residence, Henry Street Settlement, NY, 94-95; prof, mixed media, Cooper Union, 96; Vis artist, archit, Pratt Inst, 96. *Awards:* Indo-Am Fel, 89; MacDowell Colony, 94; Djerassi Found, 96. *Bibliog:* David Rimanelli (auth), Susan Leopold at John Weber, Art Forum, 12/88; John Russell (auth), Some masterly work of microscopic stature, NY Times, 8/11/89; Ken Johnson (auth), Art in Am, 7/93. *Media:* All Media. *Publ:* A Labyrinthine World of Correlations, Aurea Found, 95. *Dealer:* John Weber Gallery 142 Greene St New York NY 10012. *Mailing Add:* c/o Jean Albano Art Gallery 215 W Superior Chicago IL 60610

LEPORE, JOAN
ARTIST
Study: The Yard School, (life drawing, anatomy & design), Montclair, NJ; Arts Student League, New York; NJ Center for Visual Arts (portraiture), Summit, NJ. *Exhib:* Monmouth Mus; Rider Univ; Cork Gallery, Lincoln Center, New York; Segreto Gallery, NMex; Louisa Melrose Gallery, Frenchtown, NJ; ISEA-Minnetrista Cultural Ctr, Muncie, Ind; Renee Foosner Gallery, Millburn, NJ; Nat Arts Club, New York City; Salmagundi Club, New York City; Banana Factory, Bethlehem, Pa; Ridgewood Art Inst, Ridgewood, NJ; Johnson & Johnson Corp, N. Brunswick, NJ 2005; one-man shows, Mirza Gallery, Fairfield, NJ, Korby Gallery, Verona, NJ, Gallery 9, Chatham, NJ, Robin Hutchins Gallery, Maplewood, NJ. *Awards:* Kent Day Coes, Allied Artists, 2003; Finalist, Artist Mag Experimental Category, 2002 & 2003; M-Shac Award of Excellence, 2003 & 2005. *Mem:* signature mem Nat Acrylic Painters Asn; signature mem Allied Artists; Int Soc of Experimental Artists; Soc of Layerists in Multi-Media; Nat Collage Soc; Am Watercolor Soc; Nat Watercolor Soc; Millburn-Short Hills Art Ctr; Morris Co Art Asn; Essex Watercolor Club; signature mem NJ Watercolor Soc; signature mem Nat Asn of Women Artists; signature mem Audubon Artists; signature mem Garden State Watercolor Soc. *Mailing Add:* 840 Vail Rd Parsippany NJ 07054

LERNER, ABRAM
MUSEUM DIRECTOR, PAINTER
b New York, NY, Apr 11, 13. *Study:* NY Univ, BA; also var art schs, NY & Florence. *Exhib:* One man exhib, Davis Gallery, NY; Brooklyn Mus; Pa Acad Fine Arts; ACA Gallery, NY; Peridot Gallery, NY. *Pos:* Asst dir, ACA Gallery, 45-55; asst dir, Artists Gallery, 55-56; cur, Hirshhorn Collection, 56-67, dir, Hirshhorn Mus & Sculpture Garden, Smithsonian Inst, 67-84; retired, 84-. *Awards:* Founding Dir Emer, Hirshhorn

Mus; Commander, Order Orange-Nassau; Chevalier L'Ordre Arts & Lettres. *Mem:* Arch Am Art (adv bd). *Publ:* Contribr mag & mus catalogs; auth, Gregory Gillespie, 77; ed, The Hirshhorn Mus & Sculpture Garden (inaugural catalog), Abrams, 74. *Mailing Add:* 98 Lewis St Southampton NY 11968

LERNER, ALEXANDRIA SANDRA
PAINTER
b Philadelphia, Pa. *Study:* Pa Acad Fine Arts, cert, 75; Philadelphia Col Art, BFA, 76. *Work:* Philadelphia Mus Art, Pa; Rutgers Univ, NJ; Art Inst Chicago, Ill; Houghton Libr, Harvard Univ; Franklin Furnace Archive, NY; Southern Alleghenies Mus. *Comn:* painting, Duke Energy Corp, Charlotte, NC. *Exhib:* 25 Pa Women Artists, Southern Alleghenies Mus, 79; Artists Books, Tweed Mus, Minn, 80; Speaking Volumes, AIR Gallery, NY, 80; Small Works, Washington Square East Gallery, NY, 81; Three Am Artists, ABF Gallery, Ger, 81; A Contemp Survey Art Books, Southern Alleghenies Mus, Loretto, Pa, 81; solo exhibs, Beyond the Garden Wall, Marian Locks Gallery, Philadelphia, 82 & Philadelphia Art Alliance, 89; Rutger's Nat, 85 & 86, Philadelphia Art Now, Philadelphia Mus Art, 90, Port Hist Mus, Philadelphia, 90; Harwood Mus, Taos, NMex, 91; Mangel Gallery, Phildelphia, Pa, 91; Contemp Landscape, Taos Art Asn, 93; Fenix Gallery, Taos, NMex, 96; solo exhib, Reflection, Morning and Evening, Harwood Mus of Art, Taos, NMex. *Collection Arranged:* Erotic Art, Nexus Gallery, Philadelphia, 80; Bookworks (auth, catalog), Nexus Gallery, Philadelphia, 80; A Contemporary Survey Art Books (auth, catalog), Philadelphia Art Alliance, 81; Women in Art, William Penn Mus, Pa, 81. *Pos:* Co-dir, Artist Book Project, Nat Endowment Arts & Pa Council Grants, 80-; co-dir, SYNAPSE: A Visual Art Press, Pa, 80-; mem bd, New Art Examiner, 84-88; dir, McNeil Gallery, Philadelphia, 85-88; adv bd, Harwood Mus, Taos, NMex. *Awards:* Stedman Fund Purchase Prize, Rutgers Univ, 76; Philadelphia Mus Purchase Prize, Cheltenham Art Ctr, 80; Purchase Award, Art Inst Chicago, 81; Best of Show, Fall Arts, Taos, NMex, 99; Grant, Nat Endowment Art, 2001; Acclaimed Artist Award, Art in Pub Places, NMex State Univ, Las Cruces, 2002. *Bibliog:* Ann Jarmusch (auth), The real realisme/Philadelphia's new image, Art News, 3/81; Martha Giever (auth), Artists books, alternative space or precious object?, Afterimage, 5/82; Edward Sozanski (auth), Works of Intensity by Sandra Lerner, Philadelphia Inquirer, 5/89; Miriam Siedel (auth), Sandra Lerner, New Art Examiner, 9/82. *Mem:* Found for Today's Art/Nexus (trustee 76-); Philadelphia Art Alliance (chmn 80-85); Fel Pa Acad Fine Arts; Citizens Arts in Pa; Artists Equity. *Media:* Mixed Media. *Publ:* Auth, Ruffled Passions, Visual Art Press, 80. *Dealer:* Fenix Gallery Thos NM. *Mailing Add:* PO Box 3172 Ranchos De Taos NM 87557

LERNER, LESLIE ALLEN
PAINTER
b Chicago, Ill, Dec 19, 49. *Study:* Univ Wis, Milwaukee, BFA, 74; San Francisco Art Inst, MFA, 76. *Work:* Oakland Mus Art, Calif; Corcoran Gallery Art, Washington; Fine Arts Mus San Francisco; Norton Gallery Art, West Palm Beach, Fla; Hallmark Print Coll, Kansas City, MO; and others. *Exhib:* One-man shows, Monterey Peninsula Mus Art 88 & Tampa Mus Art, 95; Recent Acquisitions, Fine Arts Mus San Francisco, 91; California Cityscapes, San Diego Mus Art, 91; Featuring Fla, Ringling Mus, Fla, 93; Mythic Narrative, Palo Alto Cult Ctr, Calif, 96; Greenville Co Mus of Art, Greenville, SC; Littlejohn Contemp, New York City, 99, 2000; Byron Cohen Gallery, Kansas City, MO, 97, 99; Susan Cummins Gallery, Mill Valley, Calif, 99; Bay Area Drawing, Triton Mus of Art, Santa Clara, Calif, 99; Univ of South Fla Contemp Mus of Art, Tampa, Fla, 99; Palo Alto Art Ctr, Calif, 99. *Teaching:* Fac fine art, Ringling Sch Art & Design. *Awards:* Achievement Award, Pollock-Krasner Found, 90; WESTAF-Nat Endowment Arts Western States Fedn Grant, 90; Fla State Individual Artist Grant, 98; Fla Individual Artists Fel, 98. *Bibliog:* Kristina McKenna (auth), Leslie Lerner, Los Angeles Times, 5/89; Stephen Mumford (auth), Leslie Lerner, Review Art, 12/96; Elra Shale (auth), Leslie Lerner, Review Art, 6/98; Dominique Nahas (auth), Review Art, 12/99; Joel Silverstein (auth), Review of Art, 12/99; Frank Celbuski (auth), Artweek, 9/2000. *Media:* Acrylic on Corrugated Ragboard. *Dealer:* Littlejohn Contemporary 41 E 57th St New York NY 10022. *Mailing Add:* 1233 14th St Sarasota FL 34236

LERNER, LOREN RUTH
EDUCATOR
b Montreal, Que, Nov 4, 48. *Study:* McGill Univ, BA, 69, MLS, 75; Univ Mich, MA(art hist), 72, Univ de Montreal, PhD, 97. *Pos:* Fine arts librn, Concordia Univ, Montreal, Que, 75-80, head libr media ctr & visual arts bibliographer, 81-91, spec servs & visual arts libr, 92-96 & assoc dean, res & grad studies, Faculty Fine Arts, 97-. *Teaching:* Lectr, Dept Art Hist, Concordia Univ, 82-95 & assoc prof, 96-. *Awards:* Thirteenth George Wittenborn Mem Award, Univ Toronto Press, 91; Melva J Dwyer Award, 92 & 97. *Mem:* Art Libr Soc NAm (Can Regional Rep, 82-85). *Res:* Art and architecture in Canada; Can film and video lit. *Publ:* Coauth with Elizabeth Sacca, Visual Arts Reference and Research Guide, Perspecto Press, Montreal, 83; auth, Collection evaluation in fine arts libraries, in: Current Issues in Fine Arts Collection Development, Art Libr Soc NAm, Tucson, 84; Other disciplines and art: an overview based on oral evidence, Art Libr J, Vol XII, No 4, 87; Memoires et theses en histore de l'art canadien & Annales d'histoire de l'art canadien, J Can Art Hist, vol X, No 1, 87, Vol XII, No 2, 88, Vol XIII, No 1, 90 & Vol XV, No 2, 94; co-ed, Art and Architecture in Canada: A Bibliography (Univ Toronto Press, 91 & Bibliography and Guide to Literature (Canadian film & video), 97, Univ Toronto Press. *Mailing Add:* Concorida Univ Dept Fine Arts Rm VA-424 1455 de Maisonneuve Blvd W Montreal PQ H3G 1M8 Canada

LERNER, MARILYN
PAINTER
b Milwaukee, Wis, Sept 19, 42. *Study:* Univ Wis, Milwaukee, BA, 64; Pratt Inst, New York, MFA, 66. *Work:* Merrill Lynch; McCrory Corp; Chase Manhattan Bank; Prudential Life Insurance; Progressive Corp. *Exhib:* Solo exhibs, John Good Gallery, NY, 87 & 89 & Robert Morrison Gallery, 92; Object Bodies, Depaw Univ-William Weston Clark Emerson Art Ctr, 93; Summer Salon Show, Robert Morrison Gallery, NY, 93; A Painting for Every Ticket, Fabush Gallery, NY, 93; Reconstructivism-New Geometric Paintings in NY, 95; After the Fall, Snug Harbor Cult Ctr, Staten Island, NY, 97. *Teaching:* Assoc prof sculpture, Baruch Col, NY, 80-; instr painting, Sch Visual Arts, NY, 89-. *Awards:* NY Found for the Arts, 90; Fulbright, Indo-Am Fel, 90-91; Adolph & Esther Gottlieb Individual Support Grant, 94. *Bibliog:* Terry R Meyers (auth), Controlled substance, Marilyn Lerner's recent paintings, Arts Mag, 9/89; John Yau (auth), rev, Art Forum, 5/89; Mary Jones (auth), Arts Mag, rev & illus, 2/91. *Media:* Oil Paint, Oil Pastel. *Mailing Add:* 133 W 21st St New York NY 10011

LERNER, MARTIN
CURATOR, HISTORIAN
b Brooklyn, NY, Nov 14, 36. *Study:* Brooklyn Col, BA, 59; Inst Fine Arts, New York, 62-65. *Collection Arranged:* Materpieces of the Art of India (with Richard Ettinghausen), Metrop Mus Art, 72; Indian Miniatures from the Jeffrey Paley Collection (auth, catalog), 74; Bronze Sculptures from Asia (auth, catalog), 75; Blue and White: Early Japanese Export Ware (auth, catalog), 76-77; Along the Ancient Silk Routes, Central Asian Art from Berlin, 82; Notable Acquisitions of Indian & Southeast Asian Art, Metrop Mus Art, 82; The Flame and the Lotus (auth, catalog), Metrop Mus Art, New York, 84; The Lotus Transcendent (auth, catalog), Metrop Mus Art, 91; Permanent Galleries South & Southeast Asian Art, Metrop Mus Art, 94. *Pos:* Asst cur Oriental art, Cleveland Mus Art, 66-72; vchmn in charge of Far Eastern art, Metrop Mus Art, NY, 72-76 & cur, Indian & Southeast Asian art, 76-; consult, Santa Barbara Mus Art, Akron Art Inst, Honolulu Acad Arts, and others; co-researcher for the Munson-Williams-Proctor Institute's 50th Anniversary reconstruction of the 1913 Armory Show; adv, for chaps on Asian Art in Dorra, H, Art in Perspective, NY, 72 & Gardner's Art Through the Ages, Sixth ed; Curatorial Ad for South and Southeast Asian Art 2004-. *Teaching:* Asst prof Oriental art, Univ Calif, Santa Barbara, 65-66 & Case-Western Univ, Cleveland, 68-71; lectr, Oberlin Col, Princeton Univ, Phoenix Art Mus, Christie's NY, Utah Mus Art, Asia Soc in India and Nepal, 71 & 73, and others; Adj Prof Columbia Univ, 2004. *Res:* Indian and Southeast Asian art; American Modernist Art. *Publ:* The Flame and the Lotus, Abrams, 84; coauth (with W Felton), Thai and Cambodian Sculpture: From the 6th to 14th Centuries, Philip Wilson, 89; coauth (with W Felten), Entdeckungen: Skulpturen der Khmer und Thai (exhib catalog), Mus fur Ostasiatische Kunst, Koln, 89; coauth (with S Kossak), The Lotus Transcendent (exhib catalog), Metrop Mus Art, 91; Ancient Khmer Sculpture, New York, 94; and others. *Mailing Add:* Dept Asian Art Metrop Mus Art 1000 Fifth Ave New York NY 10028-0198

LERNER, SANDRA
PAINTER, COLLAGE ARTIST
b New York, NY. *Study:* Pratt Graphic Ctr, New York, 66-68; Hofstra Univ, BA, 78; studied painting with Leo Manso, Jerry Okomoto and Harry Sternberg, studied calligraphy & philos with Soshi Kampo Harada, Kampo Kaikan, Kyoto & Sumera, Japan, 81. *Work:* Aldrich Mus Contemp Art, Ridgefield, Conn; Jane Voorhees Zimmerli Art Mus, Rutgers Univ, NJ; World Study Mus, Fukuoka, Japan; Kampo Mus, Kyoto, Japan; Heckscher Mus, Huntington, NY; Radford Univ, Va. *Comn:* LAND (environ stage set for Eiko & Koma; with Eiko & Koma & Robert Mirabel), Rockefeller Found Multi-Arts Production Fund, 92; set design (Eiko & Koma), Japan Soc, 95; set design, Hiroshima Mus, Japan, 93; set design, Jacobs Pillow, Mass, 98; Redford Univ, Redford, Va. *Exhib:* Solo exhibs, Kauffman Gallery, Houston, Texas, 84, 86 & 91, Dubins Gallery, Los Angeles, Calif, 86, 87, & 89, Kampo Mus, Kyoto, Japan, 84 & 93, June Kelly Gallery, NY, 90, 92 & 96, Anderson Gallery, Buffalo, NY, 92, Perimeter Gallery, Chicago, 92, Washington Art Asn Gallery, Conn, 97 & 2005, Zimmerli Mus, Rutgers, NJ, 98, Betty Parsons Gallery, 82, Kimberly Greer Gallery, Northpoint, NY & June Kelly Gallery, 2000 & 2004; Invitational Exhibs, Mino in Am, Mus of Fine Arts, Houston, 82 & Tokyo Mus, Japan, 84; Guild Hall Mus, Hampton, NY, 75, 83 & 87; Fundraiser Exhib, New Mus Contemp Art, NY, 85 & 86; Works on Paper, Dubins Gallery, Los Angeles, 87; Small Works, June Kelly Gallery, NY, 88; Free Spirits, Elaine Benson Gallery, Bridgehampton, NY, 91; Dubins Gallery, Los Angeles, 91; Perimeter Gallery, Chicago, 92 & 93; June Kelly: A Particular Vision, Anderson Gallery, Buffalo, NY, 94; A Woman's Place: Central Hall Gallery Artists in the 90's, Gallery North, Setauket, NY, 96; A Woman's Place: The Central Hall Gallery in the 70's, Mus at Stony Brook, NY, 96; The Shore Inst Contemp Arts, Long Branch, NJ, 2006. *Pos:* Artist-in-residence, Nassau Co Bd Coop Educ, 75; art coordr, Friends Sch, Old Westbury, NY, 75-. *Teaching:* Lectr, Nassau Co Mus Fine Arts. *Awards:* Purchase Grant, Aldrich Mus Acquisition, Nat Endowment Arts, 78; Consult on Arts, NY State Senate Spec Comt Arts, 78-86; Stipend to lectr in Japan, Int Commun Agency Grant, 81; and others. *Bibliog:* Jennifer Dunning (auth), dance review, NY Times, 11/5/91; David McCracken (auth), rev, Chicago Tribune, 8/21/92; Margaret Moorman (auth), rev, ARTnews, 10/96; John Canady (auth), NY Times, 5/9/76; Lowery Sims (auth), catalog, 82; Donald Kuspit (auth), catalog, June Kelly Gallery, 90 & 92; Johnson (auth), NY Times, 12/24/99; Gladstone (auth), Art News, 3/2000; and many others. *Media:* Oil, Acrylic; Mixed Media. *Specialty:* June Kelly Fine Arts Paintings, prints. *Dealer:* June Kelly Gallery 591 Broadway New York NY 10012. *Mailing Add:* Ten E 18th St 6th Flr New York NY 10003

LERNER-LEVINE, MARION
PAINTER, PRINTMAKER
b London, Eng, Oct 31; US citizen. *Study:* Art Inst Chicago, study with Paul Wieghardt, Max Kahn, Vera Berdich, Adrian Troy & Laura Van Pappelandam, BFA, 54; Chicago Graphic Workshop, 53-55; Manhattan Graphic Ctr, NYC, study with Vijay Kumar, Fred Mershimer, 2000-06. *Work:* Citibank & Bank Am; Bates Col Mus Art; Brooklyn Mus; US State Dept; Bryn Maur Col; Sprint World HQ; Bellevue Hospital Ctr, NY; Four Seasons Hotel, Beverly Hills, Calif. *Comn:* Printed Editions (6 etchings) for Orion Editions, NY, 85, 86, 88, 90, 91, 92, 94 & 96. *Exhib:* One-woman shows, NY Univ, 78, Watercolors, Foundry Gallery, Washington, DC, 80 & Paul Klapper Libr, Queens Col, NY, 81; Perlow Gallery, NY, 86; Carey Arboretum, 90; Prince St Gallery, NY, 71, 73, 75, 77, 79, 81, 83, 92, 95, 98, 02, 05; Bill Coffel Gallery (Monster Gallery), Brooklyn, NY, 2006; Watercolors: Wash Depot Gallery, Conn, 2006. *Teaching:* Lectr watercolor, Sch Gen Studies, Brooklyn Col, 76-80; instr drawing, Univ Calif, Los Angeles, 77; vis artist, Art Inst Chicago, 81 & Southeast Mo State Univ, 81; instr painting, Col Staten Island, City Univ NY, 81-82; instr, watercolor, Educ Alliance Art Sch, NY, 98-2000. *Awards:* Adolf & Esther Gottlieb Grant in Painting, 81; Creative Artists Pub Serv Program Fel, 83; Nat Endowment Arts Fel, 86; Residencies, Yaddo Found, Saratoga Springs, NY, 79, 80, 82; Am Acad and Inst Arts & Letters, Award in Painting, 80. *Bibliog:* Carter Ratcliff (auth), art rev, Art News, 71; Lawrence Campbell (auth), art rev, Art News, 73; Ruth Bass (auth), Art rev, Art News, 79; Anselm Hollo (auth), The Shelves of Paradise, Marion Lerner Levine's Watercolors, 79; Laurence Alloway (auth), The Nation, 1977 & 88; June Cutler (auth), Marion Lerner Levine, Am Artist, 84; Dynthia Dantzic (auth), 100 New York Artists, 2006; and others. *Mem:* Print Consortium; NY Artists Equity; Soc Am Graphic Artists (mem coun); Fedn Am Painters and Sculptors; Artist's Fellowship; Graphic Arts Council of NY; Grace Choral Soc Brooklyn Heights. *Media:* Oil, Watercolor; Etching. *Interests:* Choral singing; piano, botanical illus. *Collection:* Taipei Normal Univ Print Collection, Taiwan, Rep China & others. *Publ:* Mystery in the Garden, 86. *Dealer:* Orion Editions Gallery 168 W 86th St New York NY 10024; Prince Street Gallery 530 W 25th St New York NY 10001. *Mailing Add:* 359 Sixth Ave Brooklyn NY 11215

LEROY, HUGH ALEXANDER
SCULPTOR
b Montreal, Quebec, Oct 9, 1939. *Study:* Montreal Mus Fine Arts, Sch Art & Design, studied with Arthur Lismer, 57-62; Sir George Williams Univ, Montreal, dipl, 60; McGill Univ, Montreal, studied with Louis Dudek, 76-77. *Work:* Nat Gallery & Can Coun Art Bank, Ottawa; Montreal Mus Fine Arts & Mus d'Art Contemporaine, Montreal; Ont Arts Coun, Toronto; Dept of Defense, Ottawa; Concordia Univ, Montreal. *Comn:* Sculpture, McGill Univ, Montreal, 73; sculpture, York Univ, Toronto, 74; sculpture, Fed Govt Can, Ottawa, 74; sculpture, Banff Ctr, Alta, 78; Ministry Govt Serv Public Works, New Justice Bldg, Ottawa. *Exhib:* Solo exhibs, Eye Level Gallery, Halifax, NS, 82, Self Seal, Wynick/Tuck Gallery, Toronto, 84, Wynick/Tuck Gallery, Toronto, 86, Toronto Sculpture Garden, 87, Jenny Rose-Le Bonheur, Olga Korper Gallery, Toronto, 89, Olga Corper Gallery, Toronto, Ont, 89, 90, 92 & 95 & Univ Waterloo Artspace Gallery, Ont, 95; Sculpture in a Garden, Art Gallery Ont, Toronto, 84; Installation Piece, Wynick/Tuck Gallery, Toronto, 86; Chinese Exchange Exhib, Zhejiang Acad, China, 86; 49th Parallel, NY, 89; Site/Memory, Cleveland Ctr Contemp Art, Cleveland & Macdonald Stewart Art Ctr, Guelph, 91. *Pos:* Dean, fine arts dept, Montreal Mus Sch Art & Design, 66-69; chmn, sculpture dept, Ont Col Art, Toronto, Can, 69-70; dir, MFA program, visual arts dept, York Univ, North York, Ont, 83-86. *Teaching:* Assoc prof, visual arts, York Univ, Toronto, 74-75, 77-78 & 81-89; sculpture instr, Banff Centre, Alta, 79; Nova Scotia Col Art Design, Halifax, 81; vis lectr, Importance of Intuition, Sheridan Col, Toronto, 85; A Search for Personal Imagery, Dundas Valley Sch Art, 85. *Awards:* First Purchase Prize, Can Pavilion, Expo '67, Can Coun, 67; UNESCO Fel, 68; Royal Can Acad Fel, 75. *Bibliog:* John Bentley Mays (auth), A Muscular Surge in Daring Hues, Globe & Mail, Toronto, 5/7/87; Christopher Hume (auth), Toronto Star (rev), 1/19/89; Donna Lypchuk (auth), Hugh LeRoy, Olga Korper Gallery, C Mag #21, spring 89. *Media:* Mixed. *Publ:* Contribr, What the Dickens--, Archit Canada, Toronto, 67. *Mailing Add:* c/o Olga Korper Gallery 17 Morrow Ave Toronto ON M6R 2H9 Canada

LEROY, LOUIS
PAINTER
b Yuma, Ariz, Aug 18, 41. *Study:* Univ Ariz, with Andrew Rush, BFA, 70. *Exhib:* Chicano Affirmation & Resistance, White Gallery, Unic Calif, Los Angeles, 90. *Pos:* Owner, Salsa Graphics Studio, San Antonio, 80-. *Awards:* Chrystal Stairs Award, Asn Am Cult, 88-98. *Mem:* Asn Am Cult (Found bd mem, 85-). *Dealer:* Cruzitas Art Gallery San Antonio TX

LESH, RICHARD D
PAINTER, INSTRUCTOR
b Grand Island, Nebr, May 3, 27. *Study:* Univ Nebr; Univ Denver, BA & MA; Mexico City Col. *Work:* Omaha Nat Bank. *Exhib:* Midwest Biennial, 58; Nebraska Centennial, Joslyn Mus, Omaha, 67 & Sheldon Gallery, Lincoln, 68; Nebr Wesleyan Univ Painting Ann, Lincoln, 78. *Pos:* Pres, Nebr Art Coun, 68-69. *Teaching:* Instr painting & head dept art, Wayne State Col, 51-79, Colo State Univ, 82-88. *Awards:* Second Prize Painting, Midwest Biennial, Joslyn Mus, 55; First Prize Painting, May Show, Sioux City Art Mus, 58; First Prize Painting, Heritage Mus, Omaha, 79. *Mem:* Col Art Asn Am; Nebr Art Teachers Asn. *Media:* Acrylic, Lacquer. *Publ:* Baker Street J, Baker St West 1. *Mailing Add:* 1205 Lory St Fort Collins CO 80524

LESHYK, TONIE
SCULPTOR, DRAFTSMAN
b Toronto, Ont, July 5, 50. *Study:* Sheridan Col Sch Design, Mississauga, Ont, dipl, high hons, 73; Ont Col Art, dipl, high hons, 75, study with Colette Whitten & Ann Whitlock. *Work:* Art Bank, Can Coun Arts, Ottawa; Art Gallery Brant, Brantford, Ont. *Exhib:* Vancouver Art Gallery, BC, 74; Toronto-Los Angeles Exchange, Los Angeles Inst Contemp Art, 79; Small Sculpture (with catalog), 82 & The Shelter Drawings: Out of the Studio, 85, Harbourfront Gallery, Toronto; A Portrait Southern Alberta Art Gallery (with catalog), Lethbridge, Alta, 83; Shelter, Burlington Cult Ctr, 86; Scale, Alta Col Art Gallery, Calgary, 86; Bollinger-Leshyk, Oakville Galleries, 87. *Collection Arranged:* Guest cur, ACT Powerhouse, Montreal-Toronto Exchange, 79; Artist's Choice, Glendon Gallery, Toronto, 80. *Teaching:* Artist-in-residence, Activity Ctr, Art Gallery Ont, Toronto, 79-82; instr, mixed media & visual arts, North York, Ont, summers, 83-88, head prog, 83 & 86; instr, Found Drawing I & III, Univ Guelph, 86-87. *Awards:* Design Can Award, 74; Ont Arts Coun Proj Award, 79 & 88; Can Coun Arts Grants, 83 & 86. *Bibliog:* Otto Rapp (auth), Tonie Leshyk at the Southern Alberta Art Gallery, Artmag, No 63/64, 83; Marshall Webb (auth), Ghost house: In memoriam to a worthy opponent, Vanguard, 4/84; Val Greenfield (auth), No peace, no shelter, C Mag, No 8, winter 86. *Media:* Plaster, Mixed Media. *Publ:* Auth, Your Skilled Weapon, self-publ, 85. *Mailing Add:* 338 Delaware Ave Toronto ON M6H 2T8 Canada

LESKO, DIANE
MUSEUM DIRECTOR, CURATOR
Study: State Univ NY, Binghamton, AB, 71, MA, 75, PhD, 81; Phi Beta Kappa. *Collection Arranged:* Jon Corbino: An Heroic Vision, 87; Gari Melchers: A Retrospective Exhib, 90; Frederick Carl Frieseke: The Evolution of an Am Impressionist, 2001. *Pos:* Cur collections, Mus Fine Arts, St Petersburg, Fla, 85-89, sr cur collections & exhibs, 89-94, asst dir, 93-94; dir, Telfair Mus Art, Savannah, Ga, 95-. *Teaching:* Asst prof art hist, Lycoming Col, Williamsport, Pa, 78-85. *Awards:* Harpur Col Found scholar, 1968-71; SUNY-Binghamton grad fel in art hist, 1971-73; doctoral fel in art hist, 1978-79; Lycoming Col Doctoral Dissertation grantee, 1981; fac prof devel grantee, summer 1982; recipient AAM Excellence in Peer Review Serv Award, 2004; Visionary Award, Savannah Area Tourism and Leadership Coun, 2004. *Mem:* Asn Art Mus Dirs; South East Mus Conf; Nat Organization of Women; Women's Caucus for Art; Col Art Assoc. *Res:* Nineteenth and twentieth century European and American art. *Publ:* Auth, Il Faut Etre de Son Temps: Charles Negre as painter-photographer in mid-19th century France, Arts, 81; James Ensor, the Creative Years, Princeton Univ Press, 85; James Ensor and Symbolist Literature, Art J, 85; Jon Corbino: An Heroic Vision, 87; Gari Melchers: A Retrospective Exhib, 90; and others. *Mailing Add:* Telfair Mus Art PO Box 10081 Savannah GA 31412

LESLIE, ALFRED
PAINTER, FILMMAKER
b Bronx, NY, Oct 29, 27. *Study:* NYU, 1947-1949. *Work:* Mus Fine Arts, Boston, Hirshhorn Mus, Wash, Mus Contemp Art, Chicago, 1984; Newport Harbor Art Mus, 1985; Boca Raton Mus Art, 1989; St Louis Art Mus, 1991; rep in collections of Metrop Mus Art, New York City, Stedelijk Mus, Amsterdam, Kunstmuseum, Basel, Moderna Museet, Stockholm. *Exhib:* Joseloff Gallery, Univ Hartford, 1991, Oil & Steel Gallery, NY, 1992, Manny Silverman Gallery, Los Angeles, 1995. *Teaching:* Vis artist, Amherst Col, Youngstown State Univ; vis prof, painting Boston Univ. *Awards:* Recipient lifetime achievement award, Chicago Underground Film Festival; grantee Guttman Found for Avant-Garde Film, 1962. *Mem:* Nat Acad, Amer Acad Arts and Letters. *Publ:* films incl Pull My Daisy, 1959, The Last Clean Shirt, 1963, The Cedar Bar, 2002; auth of 100 Views Along the Road, 1988; founding ed, The Hasty Papers, 1959. *Mailing Add:* 313 E 6th St New York NY 10003

LESLIE, JIMMY
PAINTER, INSTRUCTOR
b Long Branch, NJ, Aug 18, 67. *Study:* Monmouth Univ, BA, 1990; NY Acad Art, MFA, 1993; Monmouth Univ, Vermont Studio Ctr (scholarship), 1999. *Work:* Johnson & Johnson Health Care Systems, Skillman, NJ; First Baptist Church, Red Bank, NJ; Monmouth Medical Ctr, Long Branch, NJ. *Exhib:* Surroundings, Johnson & Johnson Hq, New Brunswick, NJ, 2002; Take Home a Nude Charity Art Auction, Sotheby's Auction House, NYC, 2003; Places & Spaces, Ocean City Arts Ctr, Ocean City, NJ, 2004; Interiors, Louisa Melrose Gallery, Frenchtown, NJ, 2004; Recent Exteriors, Pottier Libr Gallery, Ramapo College, Mahwah, NJ, 2005; Small Landscapes, Mitchell Sanborn Gallery, Keyport, NJ, 2006. *Teaching:* Instr fine arts (assoc prof), St Johns Univ, Queens, NY, 1994-1999; instr, Brookdale Community Col, Lincroft, NJ, 1995-; instr, Monmouth Univ, W Long Branch, NJ, 1995-; owner/teacher, The Leslie Art Studio in the Jersey Shore Arts Ctr, Ocean Grove, NJ. *Awards:* Special Recognition, Figurative Small Works, Armory Arts Ctr, W Palm Beach, Fla, 1998; Special Recognition, All Media '99, Period Gallery Omaha, Nebr, 1999; Artist in Residency Award, Vt Studio Ctr, Johnson, Vt, 99. *Bibliog:* David Boyer (auth), Illuminating Show, Sunday Standard Times, New Bedford, Mass, 2003; Barbara Tompkins (auth), Gallery Highlights, Nouveau Mag, 2004; Jennifer Cattaui (auth), Art Stars, MAR Mag, Summer 2006. *Mem:* Monmouth Co Arts Coun; Shors Inst of Contemp Art. *Media:* Oil, canvas. *Interests:* Running; Surfing; Motorcycling. *Mailing Add:* 15 Sickles Pl Shrewsbury NJ 07702

LESLIE, JOHN
PAINTER, FINE ART PHOTOGRAPHER, SCULPTOR, DESIGNER
b Philadelphia, Pa, July 11, 23. *Study:* Murrell Dobbins Tech, with Harry Brodsky, 38-41; Philadelphia Graphic Sketch Club, Fleisher Art Mem, 39-42, Philadelphia Mus Sch Indust Art, Philadelphia Col Art, 44; Phil Music Academy, 65-67; Penn State Univ, 82. *Work:* Philadelphia Mus Art, Woodmere Art Mus & Samuel S Fleisher Art

Mem, Philadelphia, Pa; John F Kennedy Mem Libr & Mus, Boston, Mass; US Embassy, Paris, France & 22 other US Mus. *Comn:* Collaborative Designer, Gimbel Brothers Thanksgiving Day Parade, Philadelphia, Pa, 45; window dioramas, Bonwit Teller, 45-50 & Philadelphia Eagles Football Team, Pa, 46; theatrical stage sets, Bessie V Hicks Sch Dramatic Arts, Philadelphia, 46; Interior Wall Murals, Philadelphia Savings Fund Soc, 48; ltd edititon lithographic prints: Les Bouquinistes, The Last Days of Summer & Soldier of Fortune, Galerie Marjolé, Sanatoga, Pa, 87. *Exhib:* Upper Merion, Pa Cultural Center, 66; Janet Fleisher Little Galleries, Philadelphia, Pa & Paris, France, 67; Woodmere Art Mus, Philadelphia, Pa, 67-68, 79-80, 85, 89-90; Ursinus Col, Collegeville, Pa, 83; Philadelphia Sketch Club, 87; Art Expo NY City, 88; 1st Ann Galeria Exhib, NY, 88; NY Oil Pastel Asn, Smoke Rise Village, Kinnelon, NJ, 88; Photo Arts Group, Charlotte Co, Fla, 94-95; Englewood Art Guild Fine Art Photos Expos, Fla, 96; United Pastelists of Am, Upper Nyack On-the-Hudson, NY, 97; Lemon Bay Buzz Gallery, Englewood, Fla, 2001; Arts & Humanities Coun of Charlotte Co, Fla, 2003. *Pos:* Art dir, Duplex Display & Manufacturing Co, Philadelphia, Pa, 47-54; designer, Leslie Creations, Lafayette Hill, Pa, 54-67; creative dir, Kopy Kat Inc, Ft Washington, Pa, 68-77; art dir, Jesse Jones Indust Inc, Philadelphia, Pa, 78-79; auth weekly column on fine art photography, Lasting Impressions, Englewood Herald, Fla, 2000-. *Teaching:* Lectr fine art ltd edition prints, Galerie Marjole', Sanatoga, Pa, 87. *Awards:* King Prussia Fine Arts Award, Cult Ctr Upper Merion, Pa, 66; Japanese Graphic Arts Industry Award, 75; First Walter Emerson Baum Award for an Am Impressionist Painting, Sellers Mus, 95; Sellers Mus Award for Impressionism in Fine Art Photog, Bucks Co, Pa, 01; Artistic Merit Award, Playboy Mag, 58. *Bibliog:* Alan Bennett (auth), Crystal Mall concept: Leslie's plan for sculptured, functional downtown malls, Charlotte Sun Herald, 2/19/90; Peter Bartolotta (auth), National Memorial to Honor World War II Veterans Proposed by Charlotte Artist, You Mag, 11/96; Barbara Boyle Valentine (auth), Former Philadelphia Artist Remembers Bygone Era, Art Matters, 3/96. *Mem:* Oil Pastel Asn, NY; Woodmere Art Mus, Philadelphia; Englewood Photographers Asn, Fla; Boca Grande Art Alliance, Fla; Arts & Humanities Coun, Charlotte Co, Fla. *Media:* Oil Pastel, Soft Pastel; Fine Art Photography; Welded, Chromed Steel Sculpture. *Res:* Collaborative research-designer of 11 Coarctare residential homes, noted for their consolidated compactability, attenuated to utilize every sq ft. of living space with no connecting hallways, built in Englewood, Fl, 97-99. *Interests:* Opera, Jazz, Greco-Roman & Modern Architecture, Military Mus design & history, Performing arts theater, documentary film making. *Publ:* Illusr, Artist Honored: shows at world's largest art exhibition, Venice Gondolier, 3/19/88; Englewood artist tapped for prestigious NY Oil Pastel Asn, Boca Beacon, 3/25/88; Artist enters Hall of Fame, Gulfshore Life Mag, 5/89; Artist had brush with little theater scenery, The Review, 5/94; Profiles in art: Renowned artist turns vision to fine art photography, Sarasota Herald Tribune, 12/24/93. *Dealer:* Blueberry Hill Studios 6318 Zeno Circle Port Charlotte FL 33981. *Mailing Add:* 6318 Zeno Cir Port Charlotte FL 33981-5399

LESLIE, SEAVER
PAINTER
b Boston, Mass, Aug 22, 46. *Study:* RI Sch Design, BFA, 69 & MA, 70; with Peter Blake, London, Eng, 73-74. *Work:* Fogg Art Mus, Cambridge, Mass; The Continental Corp, Simpson, Thatcher & Bartlett, NY; Chase Manhattan Bank, NY; Chemical Bank, NY. *Comn:* Art Park, Lewiston, NY, 75. *Exhib:* Manhattan, Whitney Mus, NY, 82; New Talent NY, Sioux City Art Mus, 85-; Glen Ganss Collection, Mus Mod Art, 86 & Am Realism, Watercolors & Drawings, 86, Mus Mod Art, San Francisco; De Cordova Mus, Lincoln, Mass; 40 Yrs of Maine, Portland Mus Art, Maine, 91. *Pos:* Self employed painter. *Teaching:* Instr painting, RI Sch Design, 71-81, Parsons Sch Design, 80-82, Wellesley Col, 83-84; artist-in-residence, Univ Calif, San Diego, 84-85, 87-88 & Univ Tenn, Knoxville. *Awards:* Second Prize Painting, Providence Art Club, Hilton Kramer, 70. *Bibliog:* Addison Parks, (auth), Seaver Leslie, Arts Mag, 80; Edward Sozanski (auth), Seaver Leslie, Providence J, 82; Daniel Schulman (auth), Seaver Lesie, Arts Mag, 83. *Media:* Oil, Watercolor. *Publ:* West by East, RI Sch Design, 70; 12 Points--Putting the Case for Customary Weight and Measure, Am Customary Weight & Measure, 79. *Mailing Add:* Old Stone Farm PO Box 248 Wiscasset ME 04578

LESNICK, STEPHEN WILLIAM
PAINTER, INSTRUCTOR
b Bridgeport, Conn, Mar 22, 31. *Study:* Silvermine Col Art, BA, Art Career Sch, BA; also with Revington Arthur, Jon McClelland, Jack Wheat & Gail Symon; studied watercolor with Herb Olsen. *Work:* Elk's Western Helldorado Art Collection, Nev; Burndy Libr Arts & Sci, Norwalk, Conn. *Comn:* Indust paintings, Burndy Libr Art & Sci, 59; portrait of Gov mansion, comn by Gov Paul Laxalt, Carson City, 68; commemorative coin (Boulder Dam), Elks Lodge, Las Vegas, 71-78; medallion series, Nev State Mus, 77-. *Exhib:* All New Eng Art Exhib, Conn, 55; Layout & Design Int Art Competition, Japan, 63; Ann Conn Relig Art Exhib, 63 & 64; Ann Am Watercolor Soc Show, 68; Helldorado Western Art Exhib, Nev, 68; and thirty-three one man shows. *Pos:* Layout designer, Vacart Art Studio, Stamford, Conn, 60-65; art dir, Kelley & Reber Advert, Las Vegas, 65-66; illusr, EG&G, Inc, Las Vegas, 66-73; art ed, Las Vegas Sun, 70-; syndicated newspaper columnist, Art for Everyone; illusr, Marine Corps Gazette; one of founders, Las Vegas Art Mus; owner, Lesnick Art Products. *Teaching:* Instr art, Desert Art League, Boulder City, 65-66; instr art, Las Vegas Art League & Artists & Craftsmans Guild, Nev, 65-68 & Clark Co Community Col; owner & instr, Lesnick Art Studio, Las Vegas, 65-. *Awards:* Conn Relig Show, Hallmark Greeting Cards, 63 & 64; First Prize, Nev Bicentennial Commemorative Medallion, Franklin Mint, 72; Purchase Prize, Barnum Fest; First Prize & Purchase Award, Helldorado Western Art Show; Region I Winner ($3000), Nat Arts in the Parks, 87; Purchase Award, Nat Arts Parks, 96. *Bibliog:* Articles in Desert Scope, 69-71. *Mem:* Nev State Watercolor Soc; Soc NAm Artists. *Media:* All Media. *Mailing Add:* 1127 Westminster Ave Las Vegas NV 89119

LETENDRE, RITA
PAINTER
b Drummondville, Que, Nov 1, 28. *Study:* Ecole Beaux Arts, Montreal; P E Borduas, Montreal. *Work:* Nat Gallery of Can; Mus Art Contemporain, Montreal; Art Gallery of Ontario; Mus Beaux-Arts, Montreal; Long Beach Mus Fine Arts, Calif; Rose Art Mus, Brandeis Univ, Waltham, Mass; Mus Que; San Diego Art Gallery; Algoma Art Gallery, Sault St Marie; Royal Bank of Can; Coopers Lybrand, NY; Blue Cross/Blue Shield, Mich; and others. *Comn:* Wall painting, Calif State Col, Long Beach, 65; mural, Greenwin of Toronto, 71; wall painting, Benson & Hedges, Neil-Wyick Col, Toronto, 71; mural, J D S Investment, Sheridan Mall, Pickering, Ont, 72; Via Rail, Toronto Transit Corp, 78. *Exhib:* Int des Arts, Mus Beaux-Arts, 60; 5 Festival di due Mondi, Spoleto, Italy, 62; IV Biennale Can Painting, Tate Gallery, London, Eng, 63; Can Pavilion Expo 67, Montreal, 67; Que Pavilion, World's Fair, Osaka, Japan, 70; one-woman shows, Waddington & Gorce, Montreal, 97, Centre Culturel de Drummondville, 98, Galerie Madeline, Lacerte, Quebec, 98, Art Gallery of Algoma, Sault Ste Marie, Moore Gallery, Toronto & Simon Blais Gallery, Montreal; Achieving the Modern, Winnipeg Art Gallery, 92; Pastels du Quebec, Gallerie de L'UQAM, Montreal; La Crise De L'Abstraction, Les Annes 1950, Nat Gallery Can, 92; Art 2000, Stratford Art Gallery, 2000. *Awards:* Le Prix de Peinture, Concours Artistique Que, 61; Cagnes sur Mer, France, 63; Que Bourse de Recherche, 67; Can Arts Coun Sr Grant Award, 71. *Bibliog:* Jules Heller (auth), Printmaking Today, Holt, Rinehart & Winston, 71; Rita Letendre (auth), The Montreal Years 1953-1963, Concordia Art Gallery, 89; Gaston Roberge (auth), Rita Letendre: Woman of Light, Belle Publ, 97. *Mem:* Royal Can Acad Art. *Media:* Acrylic, Oil, Pastels. *Dealer:* Moore Gallery Toronto; Simon Blais Montreal. *Mailing Add:* 5420 Boul Saint-Laurent Ste 100 Montreal PQ H2T 1S1 Canada

LETHBRIDGE, JULIAN
PAINTER
b Colombo, Sri Lanka, 47. *Study:* Winchester Col & Cambridge Univ, Eng, 60-69. *Work:* Metrop Mus Art, NY; Tate Gallery Contemp Art Soc, London. *Exhib:* Solo shows, Julian Pretto Gallery, NY, 88, Daniel Weinberg Gallery, Los Angeles, 89, Paula Cooper Gallery, NY, 89, 92 & 95, Stuart Regen Gallery, Los Angeles, 91, Karsten Schubert Ltd, London, 93; From Here, Karsten Schubert Ltd, London, 95; changing group exhib, Turner Runyon Gallery, Dallas, 96; Susan Sheehan Gallery, NY, 96; On Paper II, Schmidt Contemp Art, St Louis, Mo, 96. *Awards:* Francis J Greenberger Award, 88. *Mailing Add:* c/o Paula Cooper Gallery 534 W 21st St New York NY 10011

LETTENSTROM, DEAN ROGER
PAINTER, EDUCATOR
b Superior, Wis, Sept 12, 41. *Study:* Univ Wis, Superior, BFA, 67; Univ Dallas, Irving, Tex, MA, 68; Skowhegan Maine, 68; Ohio State Univ, Columbus, Ohio, MFA, 69; MacDowell Colony, 73. *Work:* Chicago Art Inst Libr, Ill; Huntington Mus & Galleries, WVa; Tweed Mus Art, Duluth, Minn; Lutheran Brotherhood Co, Minneapolis; Ohio State Univ Galleries, Columbus. *Exhib:* Texas Painting & Sculpture, Dallas Mus Fine Arts, Dallas, Tex, 68; Solo exhibs, Five Yr Retrospective, Duluth, 90, St John's Univ, 93, Wis, 94; Nat Ann, Mo, 92; 38th Ann Nat, Calif, 92; Cheekwood Nat, 92; group tour, Stix, Wis, 93, Anderson & Anderson, Minneapolis, 93. *Teaching:* Assoc prof painting, Drake Univ, Des Moines, Iowa, 70-73; instr painting, Minneapolis Col Art Design, 77-78; assoc prof painting, Univ Minn, Duluth, 79-93, prof art, 94-. *Awards:* Honorable Mention, Nat PTG Exhib, Washington, Pa, 90; Wis State Arts Bd Develop Grant, 93; Honorable Mention, 7 State Regional, Duluth Art Inst, 94. *Mem:* Col Art Asn Am. *Mailing Add:* Art Dept Univ Minn Duluth MN 55812

LE VA, BARRY
SCULPTOR
b Long Beach, Calif, 41. *Study:* Calif State Univ, Long Beach, 60-63; Los Angeles Col Art & Design, 63; Otis Art Inst, Los Angeles County, BFA, 64, MFA, 67. *Work:* Whitney Mus, Mus Mod Art, NY; Rijksmuseum Kröller-Müller, Otterloo, Neth; Philadelphia Mus Art; Chicago Art Inst. *Exhib:* Solo exhibs, Tex Gallery, Houston, 85 & 89, Daniel Weinberg Gallery, Los Angeles, 86 & 89, Galerie Fred Jahn, Munich, WGer, 88, David Nolan Gallery, NY, 89 & 90, Rijkmuseum Kröller-Müller, 88, Carnegie-Mellon Art Gallery, Pittsburgh, 88, High Mus, Atlanta, 88, Tex Gallery, Houston, 89, Stactishes Mus Abteiberg, Monchengladbad, Ger, 89, Daniel Weinberg Gallery, Los Angeles, 89, David Nolan Gallery, 89 & 90, Sonnabend Gallery, NY, 91, Galerie Fred Jahn, Munich, Ger, 92, Galerie, Georges-Philippe, Vallois, Paris, 93, Nolan/Eckman Gallery, NY, 93 & Staatlichen Graphischen Sammlung Munchen, 94; The New Sculpture 1965-1975: Between Geometry and Gesture, Whitney Mus Am Art, NY & Mus Contemp Art, Los Angeles, 90; Immaterial/Objects, Whitney Mus Am Art, 91; Galerie Faust, Geneva, Switz, 91; New Editions, Nigel Greenwood Inc, London, Eng, 91; Am Art: 1930-1970, Lingotto, Torino, Italy, 92; European and Am Drawings 1961-1969, Nolan/Eckman Gallery, NY, 93; and others. *Teaching:* Instr, Minneapolis Col Art & Design, 68-70; instr adv sculpture, Princeton Univ, 73-74; instr grad sculpture, Yale Univ, 76 520 Barry LeVa: 1966-1988, Carnegie Melon Univ Press, 88. *Awards:* Young Talent Grant, Los Angeles Co Mus, 68; Fel Sculpture, Guggenheim Found, 74; Nat Endowment Arts Fel, 76. *Bibliog:* Barry LeVa: 1966-1988, Carnegie Melon Univ Press, 88; Fred Jahn (auth), Barry LeVa: Dreaded Intrusions-Institutional Templates, Verlag Fred Jahn, Munchen, 92; Barry LeVa: Zeichnungen, Munich Diary-African Sketchbook, Staalichen Graphischen Sammlung Munchen, 93. *Publ:* Auth, Notes on a piece by Barry Le Va, Studio Int, 11/71. *Mailing Add:* c/o Nolan Eckman Gallery 6th Floor 560 Broadway New York NY 10012

LEVEE, JOHN H
PAINTER, SCULPTOR
b Los Angeles, Calif, Apr 10, 24. *Study:* Art Ctr Sch & Chenard Sch, Los Angeles; Univ Calif, Los Angeles, BA, 48; New Sch Social Res, with Stuart Davis, Abe Rattner & Kunyoshi, 48-49; Acad Julian, Paris, grand prix, 51. *Work:* Mus Mod Art, Whitney Mus Am Art & Guggenheim Mus, NY; Corcoran Gallery Art, Washington, DC; Mus Mod Art, Paris; plus many others in pub & pvt collections. *Comn:* Wall, Architects, Chateau Vaudreuil, Paris, 71-72; walls, Bank Credit Com, Paris, 72-73; floor design, Sch Marne-le-Vallee, Paris, 75; walls & banners, Prudential Life Insurance Co, Los Angeles, 77; wall, (1700 sq ft), Col Chateauchinon, France, 86. *Exhib:* Salon de May, Paris, 54-89; Corcoran Gallery Art, 56-58; New Acquisitions, 57 & Young Am Painters, 57-58, Mus Mod Art, NY; Whitney Mus Am Art, 57, 58 & 66; Salon de Realities, 58-98; Haifa Mus Art, Isreal, 63; Phoenix Art Mus, Ariz, 64; Krannert Art Mus, Univ Ill, 65; Walker Art Ctr, Minneapolis, 65; Tel Aviv Mus, Israel, 69; Palm Springs Mus, Calif, 77; Comparisons, Paris, 80-2004; Salon des Grands et Juenes d' Aujour' hui 92-2004; Mus Saint Leo, France, 2004; and others. *Teaching:* Vis prof art, Univ Ill, 64-65, Washington Univ, 67, NY Univ, 67-68 & Univ Southern Calif, 70. *Awards:* Purchase award, Commonwealth Va Biannual, 66; Ford Fel, Tamarind Workshop, 69; Four Prizes, Woolmark Found, 74-75; First Grand Prix, First Biannual de Paris, 69. *Bibliog:* Calender of the Mus of Modern Art, 57; cover, Art In America, 57; Arts, 6/57. *Media:* Acrylic, Mixed Media; Plexiglas. *Specialty:* Modern and contemporary painting. *Collection:* African, pre-Columbian and contemporary painting and sculpture. *Dealer:* Gallerie Callu-Merile 17 Rue des Beaux Arts Paris 6; Gallerie Le gall Peyroulet 18 Rue Keller Paris 11. *Mailing Add:* 119 rue Notre Dame des Champs Paris France

LEVEN, ANN R
ADMINISTRATOR
b Canton, Ohio, Nov 1, 40. *Study:* Brown Univ, AB, 62; studio work at RI Sch of Design; Harvard Bus Sch, MBA, 64; Fogg Mus. *Work:* Brown Univ. *Pos:* Financial asst, 67-69, asst treas, 70-72 & treas, 72-79, Metrop Mus Art, NY; Mus Aid Panel (mem), NY State Coun on the Arts, 77-79; adv comt, Art Dept, Brown Univ; trustee, Artist's Choice Mus, 79-87; vpres, Chase Manhattan Bank, 79-83; trustee, Artists Choice Mus, 79-87 & NY Sch Interior Design, currently; staff liaison, Presidential Task Force Arts & Humanities, Nat Endowment Arts, 81; dir, Twyla Tharp Dance Found, 82-87 & Am Art's Alliance, 90-92; treas, Smithsonian Inst, 84-90; overseer, Hood Mus-Hopkins Ctr, Dartmouth Col, 84-91, chmn bd, 88-91; deputy treas, Nat Gallery Art, 90-94, treas, 94-. *Teaching:* Fac, Columbia Business Sch, 75-94. *Awards:* Minnie Nelen Hicks Prize, Brown Univ; NY State Outstanding Young Woman, 76. *Mem:* Womens Forum; Art Table; Am Asn Mus. *Publ:* Contribr, Cultural Institutions Across America: Functions and Funding; The Buck Starts Here: Enterprise and the Arts; coauth, Case Series on Metrop Mus Art, Harvard Bus Sch. *Mailing Add:* Nat Gallery Art Washington DC 20565

LEVENSON, RUSTIN S
CONSERVATOR, RESTORER
b Toledo, Ohio, July 19, 47. *Study:* Wellesley Col, BA, 69; Fogg Art Mus, Harvard Univ, cert conserv, 72. *Pos:* Conservator, Can Conserv Inst, 73-74 & Nat Gallery Can, 74-77, Ottawa, Ont; asst conservator, Metrop Mus Art, New York, 77-80; pres & head conservator, New York Conserv Assoc, 80-; Fla Conserv Assoc, 86-. *Awards:* Am Libr Asn Excellence Prize, Distinction in Scholarship and Conservation Prize, Col Art Asn, Boston Bookbuilders prize for design, 01, Seeing Through Paintings. *Mem:* Fel Int Inst Conserv; fel Am Inst Conserv (chmn Paintings group, 83-84); Nat Inst Conserv. *Publ:* Materials and techniques of early Quebec painters, J Can Art Hist, 83; A New Method for Loose Lining Contemporary Paintings, 87 & Emergency Conservation, 94, Am Inst Conserv; Seeing Through Painitings, Yale Univ Press, 2000; contbrib chpt, Authenticity in the Marketplace of Buying Selling and Collecting Visual Art, Oxford Univ Press, 2003; The Expert vs The Object, Oxford Univ Press, 2004. *Mailing Add:* 13291 Old Cutler Rd Miami FL 33156

LEVERING, ROBERT K
PAINTER, COLLAGE ARTIST
b Ypsilanti, Mich, May 22, 19. *Study:* Univ Ariz, AB, 42; Art Inst Chicago, 43; Art Students League, 55-56; Brooklyn Mus Sch Art with Reuben Iam, 59-61. *Work:* USAF Collection, Pentagon, Washington, DC; also in pvt collections. *Comn:* Portraits of Kennedy, Eisenhower, U Thant, Martin Luther King & Dag Hamerskjold; portraits, pres Am Express; portraits, pres Wells & Fargo; and other public & pvt comns. *Exhib:* Seven exhibs, New York City Ctr Gallery; Soc Illustrators Gallery, NY; Brooklyn Mus, 61; Mikelson Gallery, Washington, DC, 68; NY Art Dirs Club Exhib, 69. *Teaching:* Guest critic & lectr, Parsons Sch Design, 65-70, instr painting & drawing, 76-93. *Awards:* Gold Medal, 69 & Merit Awards, Soc Illusr; Citation, NJ Art Dirs Club, 69; Soc Publ Designers Award, 69. *Media:* Oil; Graphics, Miscellaneous Media. *Publ:* Illusr, leading nat mag, bks, newspapers, advert & ed. *Mailing Add:* 330 E 79th St No 10-D New York NY 10021

LEVI, JOSEF
PAINTER
b New York, NY, Feb 17, 38. *Study:* Univ Conn, BA, 59; Columbia Univ, 60. *Work:* Mus Mod Art, NY; Albright-Knox Gallery, Buffalo, NY; Aldrich Mus Contemp Art, Ridgefield, Conn; Krannert Art Mus, Univ Ill, Urbana; Des Moines Art Ctr; Corcoran Gallery, Washington, DC; Brooklyn Mus, NY; Newark Mus, NJ; and many others. *Exhib:* One-man shows, Stable Gallery, NY, 66 & 68-70, Art Club, Chicago, Ill, 67, Gertrude Kasle Gallery, Detroit, Mich, 71, AM Sachs Gallery, 75, 76 & 78, O K Harris Gallery, NY, 83, 85, 87, 90, 92, 94, 96 & 99, Harmon Meek Gallery, Naples, 96, 2001; Art Fair, Basel, Switz, 73; Mus Art, RI Sch Design, Providence, 76; Deja Vu: Masterpieces Updated, Western Asn Art Mus, 81-82; Westheimer Collection, Okla Art Ctr, Oklahoma City, 88; The Humanist Icon, Bayly Art Mus, Univ Va, 90; The Purloined Image, Flint Inst Arts, 93; Art After Art, Nassau Co Mus Art, 94; and others. *Teaching:* Artist-in-residence, Appalachian State Univ, Boone, NC, 69 & Pa State Univ, University Park, 76. *Awards:* Purchase Award, Univ Ill, Urbana, 66; Selected for New Talent USA, Art Am, 66. *Bibliog:* William Wilson (auth), In the eye of the beholder, Art News, 2/70; J Patrice Marandel (auth), Preface for Silkscreen Portfolio, Domberger, 71; Allen Ellenzweig (auth), Still life with art history: The collage paintings of Josef Levi, Arts Mag, 12/76; Martha Scott (auth), Josef Levi, Arts Mag, 3/85. *Mem:* New York Artists Equity Asn. *Media:* Acrylics, Graphite on Paper. *Dealer:* O K Harris 383 W Broadway New York NY 10021; Harmon-Meek Gallery Naples FL. *Mailing Add:* 171 W 71st St New York NY 10023

LEVIN, CAROL GELLNER
SCULPTOR
b Cincinnati, Ohio, Jan, 10, 43. *Study:* Ind Univ, BA, 64; Univ Chicago, MA, 66; Corcoran Sch Art, 69-78. *Work:* Exec Off Bldg, Rockville, Md; Torpedo Factory Art Ctr, Alexandria, Va; Amnesty Int & Children's Defense Fund, Washington, DC; Strathmore Hall Arts Ctr, Rockville, Md. *Comn:* Ceramic sculpture, City Alexandria, Va, 83. *Exhib:* Art This Way, Strathmore Hall, Rockville, Md, 91; Art in Embassies prog, US State Dept, 96-98; Everyday Life, Nat Sculpture Soc Exhib, 99; Nat Sculpture Soc Ann Exhib, Brookgreen Gardens, SC, NY, NY, 2000; Catherine Lorillard Wolfe Ann Exhib, NY, NY, 2000-2001; Invitational Exhib, Univ of Chicago, 2002; Invitational Exhib, Jane Haslem Gallery, Wash, DC, 2002 & 2004. *Pos:* Artist-in-residence, Capitol Children's Mus, Washington, DC, 90. *Awards:* Art League Awards, 94-95; Montgomery Co Artists Asn Grant, 96; Montgomery Co Arts Coun Grant, 96-97. *Bibliog:* Don Miller (auth), With tongue in cheek, Sculpture Review Mag, spring 86; Lab Sch Washington (auth), Sculpture: Carol G Levin, DC Area Artists, 93-; Ruth Palombo (auth), Clay sculptures reveal commonality of spirit, Gazette Newspapers, 10/93; The low down on high tech, The Washington Post, 9/26/99; Caution, Controversy Ahead, The Washington Post, 4/7/2000. *Mem:* Nat Sculpture Soc; Artists Equity Asn; Sculptors Group Int Sculpture Ctr. *Media:* Ceramic, Bronze; Bonded Bronze, Concrete, Mache. *Publ:* Auth, Sculptor's dilemma, Wash Post, 8/83; Auth, Good morning America, ABC, 4/2002. *Dealer:* Jane Haslem Gallery. *Mailing Add:* 105 N Union St No 30 Alexandria VA 22314

LEVIN, GAIL
HISTORIAN, PHOTOGRAPHER
b Atlanta, Ga. *Study:* Sorbonne, Paris,; Simmons Col, BA(art hist), Hon Dr, 96; Tufts Univ, MA,; Rutgers Univ, PhD(art hist), 76. *Hon Degrees:* Simmons Col, 96. *Work:* High Mus Art, Atlanta; Ctr for Photog, Woodstock, NY; Pollock-Krasner House, East Hampton, NY. *Exhib:* Solo exhibs, Mem Art Gallery, Univ Rochester, NY, 85, Cedar Rapids Art Mus, Cedar Rapids, Iowa, 86, Univ Iowa Mus Art, Iowa City, 87, Peale House Gallery, Pa Acad Fine Arts, Philadelphia, 87-88 & Univ Art Collections, Ariz State Univ, Tempe, Ariz, 88; Cress Gallery, Univ Tenn, Chattanooga, 95; Trustman Gallery, Simmons Col, Boston, 95; Provincetown Monument Mus, Mass, 96. *Collection Arranged:* Morgan Russell: Synchromist Studies, 1910-1922, Mus Mod Art, New York, 76; Synchromism and Am Color Abstraction, 1910-1925, Whitney Mus Am Art, 78; Abstract Expressionism: The Formative Years, traveling exhib, 78; Edward Hopper: Prints and Illustrations, 79 & Edward Hopper: the Art and the Artist, traveling exhib, 80; Visions of Tomorrow: New York and American Industrialization in the 1920s-1930s, Isetan Mus Art, Tokyo & traveling, 88; Marsden Hartley in Bavaria (traveling exhib), Emerson Gallery, Hamilton Col, Clinton, NY, 89-90; Changing Cultures: Recent Artist Immigrants from China (traveling exhib), Baruch Col Gallery, 91-92; The Poetry of Solitude: Edward Hopper's Drawings, Hunter Mus Art, Chattanooga, 95; Aaron Copland's Am, Heckscher Mus Art, Huntington, New York, 2000. *Pos:* Cur, Edward Hopper Collection, Whitney Mus Am Art, 76-84. *Teaching:* Instr, New Sch for Social Res, 73-75; asst prof art hist, Conn Col, New London, 75-76; vis asst prof, Graduate Sch, City Univ New York, 79-80; assoc prof, Baruch Col, New York, 86-88; Will & Ariel Durant Prof Humanities, St Peter's Col, Jersey City, NJ, 87-88; prof, Baruch Col & grad ctr of City Univ, New York, 89-. *Awards:* Yale Univ Grant, 92-93; Nat Endowment Humanities Grant, 93-95 & 98-99; Am Nat Bank Chair of Excellence, Univ Tenn, 95-96; NY Times Notable Book of the Year, 1995; George Wittenborn Mem Award, Spec Mention, 96; Los Angeles Times Book Prize Finalist in Biography, 97; Hadassah-Brandeis Inst Res Grand, 2001; Schlesinger Libr Res Support Grant, 2005-2006; Senior Fulbright Scholar to Japan, 2006; Pollock Krasner Stonybrook Found Res Fel, 2006-. *Bibliog:* Auth, Marsden Hartley in Bavaria Univ Pres New England, 89. *Mem:* Int Asn Art Critics; PEN Freedom to Write; Col Art Asn Am; Catalogue Raisonne Scholars Asn; Am Studies Asn. *Res:* Marsden Hartley Catalogue Raisonne; Lee Krasner biog; Yasuo Kuniyoshi. *Interests:* Twentieth century art. *Publ:* Theme and Improvisation: Kandinsky and the American Avant-grade, 1912-1950, Blufinch Press, 92; Edward Hopper: An Intimate Biography, 95; Edward Hopper: A Catalogue Raisonne, WW Norton & Co Inc, 95; Hopper's Places, Univ Calif Press, 2nd ed, 98; Aaron Copland's American: A Cultural Perspective, Watson-Gupfill Pubs, 2000; co-ed & contribr, Ethics and The Visual Arts, 2006. *Mailing Add:* c/o Baruch Col 1 Bernard Baruch Way b7-235 New York NY 10010

LEVIN, GOLAN
ARTIST
Study: Mass Inst of Tech, BS(art & design), 94, MS(arts & scis), 2000. *Exhib:* Solo shows at Moving Image Gallery, NY City, 2001, Bitforms Gallery, NY City, 2002, NTT InterCommunicationsCenter, Tokyo, Japan, 2006; group exhib include Whitney Biennial, Whitney Mus Am Art, 2004; Digital Sublime, Mus Contemp Art, Taipei, Taiwan, 2004; Interactions/Art and Technology, Am Mus Moving Image, NY City, 2004; Prix Arts Electronica, OK Centrum Gegenwartskunst, Linz Austria, 2004; The Algorithmic Revolution: On the History of Interactive Art, ZKM, Karlsruhe, Ger

2004; You Are Here: The Design of Information, Design, Mus, London, 2005; New Media: What, Neuberger Mus Art, Purchase, NY, 2005; OneDotZero9, Inst Contemp Art, London, 2005; ElectroScape, Duolun Zendai Art Mus, Shanghai, 2005; Rhizome ArtBase 101, New Mus Contemp Art, NY, 2005; Generator.X.Exhibition, Nat Mus Art, Architecture and Design, Oslo, 2005; Tokyo Digital Arts Festival, Tokyo, Japan, 2005; Software Art, DeCordova Mus and Sculpture Pk, Boston, 2006; Whitney Mus Artport and Tate Online, Net Art Comn, 2006; Emacao Art.ficial 3.0 Biennial, Itau Cultural Inst, Sao Paolo, Brazil, 2006. *Pos:* Mem res staff, Interval Res Corp, 94-98; res asst, Mass Inst of Technol Media Lab, 98-2000; consult, Design Machine, NY, 2000-02; composer of numerous interactive and multimedia compositions, performances, recording and other works. *Teaching:* Adjunct prof, Columbia Univ, 2000; vis artist and lectr, Cooper Union Sch Art, 2001-02; adj fac Parsons Sch Design, 2001-03; asst prof electronic time-based art, Sch Art. Carnegie Mellon Univ, 2004-. *Awards:* Named New Artist Under 30, Print Mag, 2002; recipient Bronze Medal, ID Mag Interaction Design Award, 2002; named one of Top 100 Young Innovators, Mass Inst of Technol Tech Review, 2004; Award Distinction, Net Art, Prix Ars Electronica, 2004; Artist's Grant, Emerging Fields Category, Creative Capital Found, 2006. *Publ:* Composer numerous interactive and multimedia compositions, performances, recordings and other works

LEVIN, HUGH LAUTER
PUBLISHER
b Rye, NY, July 2, 51. *Study:* Univ Pa, BA, 73, Wharton Sch, MBA, 84. *Pos:* Pres, Hugh Lauter Levin Assoc Inc, 74-; dir, Abrams Original Editions, 76-83, vpres, Harry N Abrams Inc, 81-83. *Mem:* Fine Art Publs Asn (treas, 82-85); Orgn Ind Artists. *Specialty:* Publication of illustrated books. *Mailing Add:* 9 Burr Rd Westport CT 06880-4220

LEVIN, KIM
CRITIC, CURATOR
Study: Vassar Col, AB; Yale-Norfolk Summer Sch Art; Columbia Univ, MA. *Collection Arranged:* CCA Ujazdowski Castle Warsaw, 92; Nordic Biennial, Arken Mus Copenhagen, 96-97; Henie-Onstad Kunstsenter, Norway, 92. *Pos:* NY corresp, Flash Art, 80-84; contribr, Village Voice, 81-. *Teaching:* Claremont Grad Sch Art, 87; vis prof, HISK, Antwerp, 01. *Awards:* Art/World Award for Distinguished Newspaper Criticism, 86; SECA Fel, San Francisco Mus Mod Art, 93; Annenberg/Getty Fel, 2003. *Mem:* Int Asn Art Critics (Am vpres, 84-90, Am pres, 90-92, int vpres, 92-96, int pres, 96-02). *Publ:* auth, Lucas Samaras, Abrams, 75; contribr, Theories of Contemporary Art, Prentice-Hall, 85; auth, Beyond Modernism, Harper & Row, 88; contribr, Beyond Walls & Wars: Art, Politics & Multi-Culturalism, Midmarch Press, 92; Co-auth. Trans Plant; Living Vegetation in Contemporary Art (Hatje Cantz), 2000. *Mailing Add:* 52 W 71st St New York NY 10023

LEVIN, MORTON D
PRINTMAKER, PAINTER
b New York, NY, Oct 7, 23. *Study:* City Univ NY, BS(art educ); studies in Paris, France; painting with Andre Lhote, sculpture with Ossip Zadkine, etching & engraving with Stanley W Hayter & etching with Federico Castellon; studied lithography, Pratt Graphic Arts Ctr, NY. *Work:* NY Pub Libr; Libr of Cong, Washington, DC; Hist of Med Div, Nat Libr Med, Md. *Comn:* Mural, Stained Glass, L Natali Inc, 79. *Exhib:* 4th-7th Ann Nat Exhib of Prints, Libr of Cong, 46-49; Nat Acad Design & Soc Am Etchers, Gravers, Lithographers and Woodcutters, Inc, 46-48; 46th Ann Watercolor & Print Exhib, Pa Acad Fine Arts, 48; Salon de Mai, Musee D'Art Mod, Paris, France, 51; Biennale Int d'Arte Marinara, Pallazzo del Academia, Genoa, Italy, 51; one-man shows, Galerie Breteau, Paris, France, 52, Winston Gallery, San Francisco, 77, 79-85 & 86-90 & Winston Gallery, 91-98; Winston Gallery, 2003-06. *Teaching:* Founder, dir & instr printmaking & painting, Morton Levin Graphics Workshop, San Francisco, Calif, 72-91. *Awards:* Hon Mention, 21st Ann Northwest Printmakers, Seattle Art Mus, 49; Bryan Mem Prize, The Villager Travel Exhib, New York, 64; Third Prize, Washington Sq Art Exhib, Inc, 64. *Bibliog:* Yellow Silk, J Erotic Arts, summer 90. *Media:* Etching, Woodcut; Watercolor, Oil. *Specialty:* Paintings: oils, acrylics, woodcuts, etchings. *Interests:* visual art. *Publ:* Contribr, Yellow Silk, No 34, summer 90. *Dealer:* Winston Gallery 414 Mason St Ste 704 San Francisco, CA 94102. *Mailing Add:* 1416 Broadway Apt 6 San Francisco CA 94109

LEVIN, ROBERT ALAN
GLASS BLOWER, SCULPTOR
b Baltimore, Md, Sept 25, 48. *Study:* Denison Univ, Granville, Ohio, BFA, 71; Penland Sch Crafts, NC, 71; Southern Ill Univ, Carbondale, MFA, 74. *Work:* Corning Mus Glass, NY; Ebeltoft Glasmuseum, Denmark; Contemp Glass Mus, Madrid, Spain; High Mus Art, Atlanta, Ga; Mus Am Glass, Millville, NJ. *Comn:* Business Awards, comn by Gov Jim Hunt, Raleigh, NC, 80 & 98, Entrepreneurial Sch Award, 94-2000. *Exhib:* New Glass, Corning Mus Glass, NY, 79; Int Directions Glass Art, Art Gallery Western Australia, 83; Thirty Yrs New Glass, 1957-1987, Corning Mus Glass, 87 & Toledo Mus Art, 88; Am Glassmaking - The First Russian Tour, Steuben Glass, NY, Decorative Applied & Folk Art Mus, Moscow & Hermitage, Leningrad, 90; The First Ten Yrs, Glasmuseum, Ebeltoft, Denmark, 96; L'Chaim: A Kiddush Cup Invitational, Jewish Mus, San Francisco, Calif, 97; Celebrating Am Craft, Kunstindustrimuseum, Copenhagen, Denmark, 97; Hsinchu Int Glass Art Festival, Hsinchu Cult Ctr, Taiwan, 97; A World of Glass, Int Glass Exhib, Hadeland Glassverk, Jevnaker, Norway, 97; World Exhibition of Art Glass, Steninge Castle, Stockholm, Sweden, 99; Hot and Cool: Contemp Glass Work, touring via Exhibs USA, 2000; Extending the tradition: crafts from the Carolinas, Ogden Mus of Southern Art, New Orleans, La, 01; Glass Goblets, Kentucky Mus of Arts & Design, Lousville, 04; Power of Excellence, Southeastern Ctr for Contemp Art, Winston Salem, NC, 04; 4th Cheongju Int Craft Exhib, Cheongju Art Ctr, Korea, 2005; Humor & Whimsy, Racine Art Mus, Wis, 2006. *Pos:* Artist-in-residence, Penland Sch, NC, 76-80 & Art Park, Lewiston, NY, 87. *Teaching:* Asst prof glass, Rochester Inst Technol, NY, 88; instr glass, Wanganui Col, NZ, Penland Sch Crafts; many workshops around the US. *Awards:* NC Arts Coun Fel, 80 & 96; NC Arts Coun Proj Grant, 89-90; S Arts Fed & Nat Endowment Arts Regional Visual Arts Fel, 95. *Bibliog:* Barbara Mayer (auth), Contemporary American Craft Art, 88; Susanne Frantz (auth), Contemporary Glass, 89; Spillman & Frantz (auths), Masterpieces of American Glass, 90; Glass Art, Peter Layton, 96; Contemporary Glass, Color, Light and Form by Leier, Peters and Wallace, 2001; Object Lessons: Beauty & Meaning in Art, Guild Publ, 2001; Dona Z Meilach (auth), Wood Art Today, 2003; Ronni Lundy (auth), In Praise of Tomatoes, 2004; 500 Glass Objects, Lark Books, 2006. *Mem:* Am Crafts Coun; Piedmont Craftsmen Inc (bd trustees, 86-89); Glass Art Soc (bd dir, 91-94); Tri State Sculptors; Southern Highlands Craft Guild; mem, Yancey Cty Cult Resource Commission 2002-2005. *Media:* Glass; Mixed Media. *Publ:* New Zealand Crafts, winter 90; Journal of the Glass Art Soc, 91; American Craft, 12/95-1/96 & 6-7/98; Craft Arts International, Australia, No 59, 2003. *Dealer:* Blue Spiral Gallery 38 Biltmore Ave Asheville NC 28801. *Mailing Add:* 669 Upper Browns Creek Burnsville NC 28714

LEVINE, DAVID
CARTOONIST, PAINTER
b Brooklyn, NY, Dec 20, 26. *Study:* Tyler Sch Fine Arts; Hans Hoffman Sch. *Work:* Hirshhorn Mus & Sculpture Garden, Washington; Cleveland Mus, Ohio; Brooklyn Mus, NY; Fogg Art Mus, Cambridge, Mass; Nat Portrait Gallery, Washington; Metrop Mus Art, NY. *Exhib:* Whitney Mus Am Art Sculpture & Drawing Ann, 60 & 63; David Levine & Aaron Shikler, Brooklyn Mus, 71; Butler Inst Am Art, 58, 60, 72; Caricature Show, Am Cult Ctr, Paris, 79; Philips Gallery, Washington, 80; Caricatures Eng 19th century authors, Morgan Libr, 81; Caricatures & Watercolors, Ashmolean Mus, Oxford, Eng, 87; with Aaron Shikler, Claude Bernard Gallery, 88; and others. *Teaching:* Sch Visual Art, Brooklyn Mus. *Awards:* Thomas B Clarke Prize, Nat Acad Design, 62; Guggenheim Fel; Gold Medal for Graphics, Am Acad & Inst Arts & Lett, 92. *Bibliog:* PA Dreyfus (auth), The double image of David Levine, Am Artist, 71. *Mem:* Century Asn; Am Acad Arts & Lett. *Media:* All Media. *Publ:* Illusr, The Man from MALICE, 66; Pins and Needles, 69; No Known Survivors, David Levine's Political Plank, 70; New York Rev Books; NY Mag; The Arts of David Levine, Knopf, 78; Aesop, Gambit, 75. *Mailing Add:* 161 Henry St Brooklyn NY 11201

LEVINE, EDWARD
PAINTER
b Detroit, Mich, Jan 10, 28. *Study:* Wayne State Univ, Southlands Sch Design. *Work:* Ameritech, Detroit, Mich; Mich Bell Tel, An Ameritech Co, Detroit, Mich; Miller, Canfield, Paddock & Stone, Bloomfield Hills, Mich. *Exhib:* Solo exhibs, Xochipilli Gallery, Birmingham, Mich, 86, 88 & 90; Macomb Community Col, Mt Clemens, Mich, 87; Animal Life in Contemp Art, House of Reps, Washington, DC, 88; Urban Scenes of the 80's, De Waters, Flint, Mich, 88; Urbanology, Nat Exhib on Art & The City, Detroit, Mich, 89; and others. *Awards:* Silver Scarab, Scarab Club, 85. *Media:* Oil. *Mailing Add:* 700 Lockwood Rd Royal Oak MI 48067

LEVINE, ERIK
SCULPTOR
b Los Angeles, Calif, Oct 31, 60. *Study:* Univ Calif, Los Angeles, 82; Calif State Univ, Northridge, 80-81. *Work:* Walker Art Ctr, Minneapolis, Minn; Mus Contemp Art, Los Angeles; High Mus Art, Atlanta, Ga; Albright-Knox Art Gallery, Buffalo, NY; Whitney Mus Am Art, NY; and others. *Comn:* Round House (sculpture garden), Walker Art Ctr, Minneapolis, Minn, 90; Faulconer Gallery, Grinnell Coll, 2001. *Exhib:* Enclosing the Void: 8 Contemp Sculptors, Whitney at Equitable Ctr, NY, 88; one-man shows, Louisiana Mus Mod Art, Humlebaek, Denmark, 89 & Fundacio Joan Miro, Barcelona, Spain, 89; 1989 Biennial Exhib, Whitney Mus Am Art, NY, 89; Awards in the Visual Arts 8, traveling, High Mus Art, Atlanta, Ga & La Jolla Mus Contemp Art, Calif, 89; CAC, Vassiviere, France, 92; Lenbachhaus, Munich, 93; Galerie Bernd Klueser, Munich, 93 & 95; Pfalz Galerie, Kaiserslautern, Ger, 98. *Awards:* Nat Endowment Arts, 87, 89; NY Fdn Arts, 87, 99; Guggenheim Fel, 92; Pollock Krasner, 86, 90, 99; Awards in the Visual Arts, 88. *Bibliog:* Renate Cornu (auth), Erik Levine, Halle Sud, Barcelona, 89; Richard Armstrong, Richard Marshall, Lisa Phillips (auth), 1989 Whitney Biennial, Whitney Mus Am Art, 89; Michael Kimmelman (auth), Erik Levine at Diane Brown Gallery, NY Times, 89. *Dealer:* Galerie Bernd Klueser, Munich, Germany; Galerie Georges-Philippe & Nathalie, Vallois, Paris

LEVINE, JACK
PAINTER
b Boston, Mass, Jan, 3, 15. *Study:* Study with Dr Denman W Ross, 29-31; also with Harold Zimmerman; Colby Col, Hon DFA, 46. *Work:* Metrop Mus Art, NY; Mus Mod Art, NY; Walker Art Ctr, Minneapolis; Art Inst Chicago; Whitney Mus Am Art, NY; Vatican Mus, Rome, Italy; Thyssen-Bornemisza; and many others. *Exhib:* one-man show, DeCordova Mus, Lincoln, Mass, 68; Mid Town Gallery, NY, 90 & 92; St Botolph Club, Boston, 92; Midtown Payson Galleries, NY, 93, 95; George Krevsky Fine Art, San Francisco, 94, 97; Brooklyn Mus of Art, 99; The Century Club, NY, 99. *Teaching:* Lectr, Art Inst Chicago, Skowhegan Sch Painting & Sculpture, Univ Ill, Pa Acad Fine Arts, Am Art Sch, NY & Cleveland Mus Art Sch; Home Video & TV Show, Feast of Pure Reason, Ch 13, PBS, NY. *Awards:* Guggenheim Fel, 45 & 46; Corcoran Gallery Art Award, 59; Altman Prize, Nat Acad Design, 75; plus others. *Bibliog:* Kenneth Prescott and Emma Stine Prescott (auths.) The Comple Graphic Workss of Jack Levine, Dover Press.; Rizzoli (auth.) Jack Levine by Jack Levine, 89. *Mem:* Nat Inst Arts & Letts; Artists Equity Asn; Am Acad Arts & Sci; Nat Acad Arts & Letts; Am Acad Arts & Letts (chancellor, 91-92, pres, 93); and others. *Dealer:* DC Moore Gallery 724 5th Ave New York NY. *Mailing Add:* 68 Morton St New York NY 10014

LEVINE, LES
VIDEO ARTIST, MEDIA SCULPTOR
b Dublin, Ireland, Oct 6, 1935; US citizen. *Study:* study, Cent Sch Arts & Crafts, London, Eng, 53-56. *Work:* Nat Gallery Can, Ottawa, Ont; Metrop Mus Art, Whitney Mus Am Art, Mus Mod Art, NY; Philadelphia Mus Art; Indianapolis Mus Art; Nat Gallery Australia, Canberra. *Comn:* Contact (sculpture), Gulf & Western Indust, 69. *Exhib:* One-man exhibs, Slipcover, Walker Art Ctr, 67, Star Garden, Mus Mod Art, NY, 67, I Am Not Blind, Wadsworth Atheneum, 76, Prayer Rug, Philadelphia Mus Art, 79, We Are Not Afraid, Lower Manhattan Cult Coun, NY Subways, 81, Blame God Inst Contemp Art, London, Eng, 85, Media Proj & Pub Advert, Mai 36 Gallery, Luzern, Switz, 88; Documenta, Kassel, Ger, 77 & 87; San Francisco Int Video Festival, 83; Committed to Print, Mus Mod Art, NY, 88; Consume or Perish & Pray for More, NY Found Arts, NY Subways, 89; Pub Mind: Les Levine's Media Sculpture and Mass Ad Campaigns, Everson Mus, Syracuse, 90; Ease Pain, NY Found Arts, NY, 92; Send Receive, The Language of Art, Kunsthalle Wien, Vienna, 93; and others; Art Can See, Galerie der Stadt Stuttgart, Ger, 1997; Celebrate Yourself, Brigitte March Galerie, Stuttgart, Ger, 2005. *Collection Arranged:* Open To New Ideas (organizer), Jimmy Carter Collection, Ga Mus Art, Athens, 77. *Pos:* Pres, Mus Mott Art, Inc, 71-. *Teaching:* assoc prof, NY Univ, 71-72, Columbia Univ, NY, 78; video prof, William Paterson Col, Wayne, NJ, 74-76. *Awards:* First Prize for The Star Machine, Sculpture Biennale, Art Gallery Ont, 68; Nat Endowment Arts Fel, 74 & 80; Gustav Klimt Award for Best Billboard, City of Vienna, 94; and others. *Bibliog:* David Bourdon (auth), Plastic art's biggest bubble, Life Mag, 8/69; Barbara Cavaliere (auth), Les Levine's ads---and more ads, Arts Mag, 3/81; Vivien Raynor (auth), Not Afraid in the Subway, New York Times, 5/21/82; and others. *Mem:* Nat Arts Club (vp 84-); Architectural League of NY (vp 69-70). *Media:* Videotape; Gold, Multimedia. *Publ:* The poets' encyclopedia, Unmuzzled Ox, Vol 4, No 4, New York, 79; publ, Media: The Bio Tech Rehearsal for Leaving the Body, Alberta Col Art, 79; Biennale van de la Critique, Palais des Beaux Arts, Antwerpen Charleroi, 79; auth, Handmade Etchings by Les Levine, Artist Profusions, 81; Blame God, Inst Contemp Art, London, Eng, 85; and others. *Dealer:* Bridgette March Galerie Stuttgart Germany. *Mailing Add:* 20 E 20th St New York NY 10003

LEVINE, MARTIN
PRINTMAKER, EDUCATOR
b New York, NY, May 14, 45. *Study:* Calif Col Arts & Crafts, MFA(printmaking); State Univ NY, Buffalo, BS(art educ). *Work:* Libr Cong, Smithsonian Inst, Washington; Brooklyn Mus; Mus Fine Arts, Boston; Art Inst Chicago, Ill; Victoria & Albert Mus, London, Eng; and many others. *Comn:* Two etchings of hist landmark (with ADI Gallery, San Francisco), Clorox Co, Oakland, Calif, 76; etching for portfolio, Pratt Graphics Ctr, NY, 81 & 84; etching (facade), Union League Club, Chicago, 83; etching for portfolio, Brigham Young Univ, 93. *Exhib:* Nat Acad Design Ann Exhib, 74, 76-79, 86 & 96; 30 Yrs of Am Printmaking, Brooklyn Mus, NY, 76; Int Print Biennale, Cracow, Poland, 78, 86, 91 & 94; XV Int Bienal, Sao Paulo, Brazil, 79; Chicago & Vicinity, Art Inst Chicago, 81 & 85; Int Exhib, Kanagawa, Yokohama, Japan, 92 & 95; Int Biennale, Maastricht, The Neth, 93; Int Biennale, Belgrade, Yugoslavia, 94 & 96; Int Print Biennale, Varna, Bulgaria, 95. *Teaching:* Asst prof printmaking, Northwestern Univ, Evanston, 79-86 & State Univ NY, Stony Brook, 86-. *Awards:* Nat Endowment Arts Printmaking Fel, 77; NY Found Arts, 94 & 95; plus over 100 nat & int awards. *Mem:* Audubon Artists; Soc Am Graphic Artists (pres, 95-); Nat Acad. *Media:* Intaglio, Lithography. *Dealer:* Jonathan Greenberg Inc 1100 Madison Ave Suite 5K New York NY 10028. *Mailing Add:* Staller Ctr for Arts State Univ of NY Stony Brook Stony Brook NY 11794-5400

LEVINE, PHYLLIS JEAN
PAINTER
b Cleveland, Ohio, Jan 23, 47. *Study:* Cuyahoga Community Col, AA, 71; Special study with Shirley Aley Campbell, 89-91. *Work:* Rocky River Pub Libr, City Hall, Ohio; Cuyahoga Community Col, Parma, Ohio. *Exhib:* 75th Ann Spring Show, Erie Art Mus, Pa, 98. *Media:* Acrylic on Canvas. *Mailing Add:* 301 Cornwall Rd Rocky River OH 44116

LEVINE, SHEPARD
PAINTER, EDUCATOR
b New York, NY, Feb 28, 27. *Study:* Univ NMex, BA & MA; Univ Toulouse, France. *Work:* Parnassus Hall, Athens, Greece; Ore State Univ; Arkia Airlines, Israel; Salem Art Mus; Valley Libr OSO, Univ Ore. *Exhib:* Am Graphic Arts Asn; Brooklyn Mus; Henry Gallery, Univ Wash; San Francisco Mus Art; Portland Art Mus, Ore; Spokane Art Mus; and others. *Teaching:* Lectr to mus & pvt groups; prof art, Ore State Univ, formerly, emer prof, currently; retired. *Awards:* Purchase Award, Univ Ore. *Media:* Oil, Mixed media. *Mailing Add:* 3750 NW Hayes Ave Corvallis OR 97330

LEVINE, TOM
PAINTER, PRINTMAKER
b Cincinnati, Ohio, Nov 16, 45. *Study:* Miami Univ, Oxford, Ohio, BA, 67; Univ Denver, MBA, 68; Univ Cincinnati, MFA, 74. *Work:* Mus Mod Art, NY; Cincinnati Art Mus; New York Pub Libr; Andover Col, Mass; Mass Inst Technol, Cambridge. *Comn:* Stage set (three paintings), Chase Manhattan Bank, NY, 81; painting, Heidelberg Inc, Cincinnati, 92. *Exhib:* Recent Acquisitions, Cincinnati Art Mus, 83; solo exhibs, Galerie Weunsche, Bonn, 86, Galerie Ursus-Presse, Dûsseldorf, 88, 90, & 92, Segacho Exhib Space, Tokyo, 90 & Munic Gallery, Esch Luxembourg, 90; Galerie Leo Castelli, 95; Galerie Wild, Frankfurt, 96; Galerie I D Dusseldorf, 96; and others. *Media:* Oil

LEVINE, TOMAR
PAINTER
b New York, NY, Mar 24, 45. *Study:* City Col New York, BA, 66; Brooklyn Col NY, MFA, 74. *Work:* New York Acad Med; Chemical Bank, NY; AT&T, NY; Guy Carpenter & Co Inc, NY; INA Corp, NY. *Exhib:* New Am Still Life, Westmoreland Co Mus Art, Greensburg, Pa, 79; Painted Light, Reading Mus, Reading, Conn, 83; Artists' Choice: The First Eight Yrs, Artists' Choice Mus, NY, 84; Am Realism-20th Century Drawings & Watercolors, San Francisco Mus Mod Art, San Francisco, Calif, 85; 161st Ann Exhib, Nat Acad Design, NY, 86; Deutsch-Amerikanisches Inst, Munic Gallery, Regensburg, WGer, 88-89. *Teaching:* Instr, The New Sch for Social Research, NY. *Awards:* Yaddo Fel, 84; Fel, Va Ctr Creative Arts, 85; Cummington Community Arts, 91. *Bibliog:* Bill Sullivan (auth), Tomar Levine, Arts Mag, 83. *Mem:* NY Artists' Equity. *Media:* Egg Tempera, Acrylic Oil. *Mailing Add:* 191 Claremont Ave No 43 New York NY 10027-4033

LEVINSON, JOEL D
PHOTOGRAPHER, CONCEPTUAL ARTIST
b Conn, Apr 24, 53. *Study:* Univ Calif, Berkeley, BA(communications), 75, MA(visual arts), 78. *Work:* Yale Art Mus; Winnipeg Art Gallery; Mus fur Kunst und Gewerbe; Minneapolis Inst Arts; Boston Mus Fine Arts; Baltimore Mus Art. *Exhib:* Addison Gallery Am Art, 80; Minneapolis Inst Arts, 82; Denver Art Mus, 83; Palm Springs Art Mus, 84; solo exhibs, Amerika Haus, Berlin, 87, Crocker Art Mus, 88, Marsha Mateyka Gallery, 89, J B Speed Art Mus, Louisville, 82, OK Harris, NY, 82, Art Mus STex, Corpus Christi, 83, Sprengel Kunstmus, Hanover, WGer, 85 & Milwaukee Art Mus, Wis, 86. *Awards:* Eisner Award, Univ Calif, 78. *Bibliog:* Content/Context, Artforum, 12/88; Media Art/Constructive Photography, Art, 1/89; Robert C Morgan (auth), Joel Levinson and the loss of representation, New Art Int, 2-3/90. *Media:* Photography, Collage-Montage. *Publ:* Auth, Joel D Levinson (photogr), PM Publ, 82; The Making of a Collection, Minneapolis Inst Arts, Aperture, 84; Fleamarkets, Braus Ed, 87; People and Places, Milwaukee Art Mus, 87. *Dealer:* Eric Frank Gallerie London Berlin

LEVINSON, MIMI W
PAINTER, LECTURER
b Kenosha, Wis, June 6, 40. *Study:* Carnegie-Mellon Univ, with Roger Anliker, BFA, 62; San Jose State Col, Frick Scholarship, 64. *Work:* Ga Railroad Bank Collection, Augusta; Mesa Vista Hosp, San Diego, Calif; New Delhi Handi Crafts Mus, India; Stow Collection Co, 2002. *Comn:* Stained glass wall mosaic, Casselhoff's, Pittsburgh, Pa, 62; painted fabric mural, Kaiser-Permanente, San Diego, Calif, 78; batiks, Hillcrest Psychotherapy Ctr, San Diego, Calif, 80. *Exhib:* Craftman's Guild Shows, Arts & Crafts Ctr, Pittsburgh, Pa, 66-67; Art Guild All Media, San Diego Mus Art, Calif, 75 & 81; Calif Crafts XI, EB Crocker Art Mus, Sacramento, 79; Exchange Exhib, Yokohama Art Ctr, Japan, 79; Textile Kunst, Krefeld, Ger, 88; Fibers Exhib, Brand Mus, Glendale, Calif, 91; duo solo shows, Jewish Community Ctr, San Diego, Calif, 91-92; Fibre Meets Fiber, Mansfield Mus, Eng, 92; Southwestern Col Art Gallery, Allied Craftsmen, 2000; Spanish Village Art Ctr, 2000; San Diego Hospice, San Mus of Art Artists Guild, 2000; Allied Craftsmen Next Door Gallery, 2001; Beyond Borders, South Western Col, Calif, 2003; One Person Show Wesley Palms Gallery, San Diego, Calif, 2004; Small Images, San Diego Calif, 2005; Allied Craftesman, Palomar Col Boehm Gallery, 2005; Colorado Springs Univ Gallery, 2005; Small Images, San Diego, Calif, 2006. *Teaching:* Instr art, Sunnyside Sch, Pittsburgh, Pa, 62-67; workshop leader batik-weaving, Convergence 76, Pittsburgh, Pa, 76; instr cult arts, Jewish Community Ctr, San Diego, Calif, 79-91; San Diego State Univ extended studies, 89-93; mgr, San Diego Japanese Friendship Garden, 92-98; guest lectr, 2003. *Awards:* First Prize, Augusta Art Asn, 71; Purchase Prize, Ga Railroad Bank, 72; Third Prize, Weaver's Guild, 75; Purchase Prize, Small Images, 2003. *Bibliog:* Dan Coyro (auth), Batik: How to turn wax and dye into art, The Sentinel, 75; Jan Jennings (auth), Natural history museum, San Diego Evening Tribune, 78; Elise Miller (auth), Womanism to surrealism, San Diego Mag, 79. *Mem:* Allied Craftsmen; Am Crafts Coun; Surface Design Asn; Calif Fibers (chmn, 77); San Diego Mus Art Guild. *Media:* Batik, Mixed. *Res:* Prepetion for Mus Lectures, 2002, 2003, 2005, Research for articles published; 2/2001 Arts de Mexico at the Minge International Mus in OBJECT 2001, Austrlia. *Specialty:* MM Crafts. *Interests:* Travel Asia. *Collection:* Georiga Railroad Bank, Kzists-Remanente San Yeidro Medical Clinic, San Diego; Vista Hill Foundation, Stow Collection, CO. *Publ:* Contribr, Crafts 1976, Southern Calif Designer Inc, 76; Exotic Needlework, Crown, 78; Artes de Mexico:Mingei International Mus, Object, 2001. *Dealer:* Next Door Art Gallery 2963 Beech St San Diego CA 92102. *Mailing Add:* 2119 29th St San Diego CA 92104-5505

LEVINSON, MON
SCULPTOR, PAINTER
b New York, NY, Jan 6, 1926. *Study:* Univ PA, BS. *Work:* Whitney Mus Am Art, NY; Joseph H Hirshhorn Collection, Washington, DC; NY Univ Art Collection; Rose Art Gallery, Brandeis Univ; Brooklyn Mus, NY; Albright-Knox Art Gallery, Buffalo, NY. *Comn:* Objects & 69; sculpture, Pub Sch 166, NY, 67; mural-sculpture, Housing & Redevelop Bd, Demountable Vest Pocket Parks, NY, 69; and others. *Exhib:* Plus by Minus, 68 & Paper about Paper, 80, Albright-Knox Gallery, Buffalo, NY; The Responsive Eye, Mus Mod Art, NYC, 1965; A Plastic Presence, Milwaukee Art Ctr, Wis, NY & San Francisco, 69-70; Whitney Mus Am Art Sculpture Ann, 70 & 73; Storm King Arts Ctr, Mountainville, NY, 72 & 75; Hirshhorn Collection, 74; Rosa Esman Gallery, NY, 76 & 77; Getler Pall Gallery, NY, 81; Fine Arts Mus, Long Island, 81; Andre Zarre Gallery, NY, 89; OK Harris Gallery, NY, 97; Mitchell Algus Gallery, NY, 1999; Solitary Cantori Dell'utopia, Museo Civico di Taverna, Italy, 2004. *Teaching:* Vis artist, C W Post Col, 70-72 & 76-77. *Awards:* Cassandra Found Award, 72; Creative Artists Pub Serv Prog Award, NY State Coun Arts, 74; Nat Endowment Arts Fel, 76. *Mem:* Am Abstract Artists. *Mailing Add:* 309 W Broadway New York NY 10013

LEVINTHAL, DAVID LAWRENCE
PHOTOGRAPHER
b San Francisco, Calif, March 8, 49. *Study:* Stanford Univ, AB, 70; Yale Univ, MFA, 73; Mass Inst Tech, SM, 81. *Work:* Mus Mod Art, NY; Corcoran Gallery Art, Washington; Los Angeles Co Mus Art, Calif; Amon Carter Mus, Fort Worth, Tex; Nat Gallery New Zealand, Wellington. *Exhib:* Photog and Art, Los Angeles Co Mus Art, 87; Avant-Garde in the 80's, Los Angeles Co Mus Art, 87; Surrogate Selves, Corcoran Gallery, Washington, 89; Photog of Invention, Nat Mus, Washington, 89; Constructed Realities, Kunstverein, Munich, Ger, 89; Devil on the Stairs, Inst Contemp Art, Philadelphia, Pa, 91; More Than One Photog, Mus Mod Art, NY, 92; Instant Imaging Stories, Mus Mod Art, Vienna, Austria, 92; solo shows, Univ Art Mus, Univ NMex, Albuquerque, 95, Judah L Magnus Mus, Berkeley, Calif, 96, Philadelphia Mus Judaica, Pa, 97 & San Jose Mus, Calif, 99; Devoir de Memoire, Recontres Int de la Photographie, Arles, France, 97; Same Difference, Chapman Univ Guggenheim Gallery, Orange, Calif, 98. *Teaching:* Instr, photog, Univ Neada, Las Vegas, 75-76. *Awards:* Artists Grant, Nat Endowment Arts, 90-91; Guggenheim Fel, 95. *Bibliog:* Andy Gundberg & Kathy Gauss (coauths), Photo & Art & Anne Hoy (auth), Fabrications, Abbeville Press, 87; Terrie Sultan (auth), Surrogate Selves, Corcoran Gallery, 89. *Mem:* Col Art Asn. *Specialty:* Contemporary Art. *Publ:* Coauth (with Garry Trudeau), Hitler Moves East, Sheed Andrews & McMeel, 77; illustr, Modern Romance, Univ San Diego, 85; Centric 35: David Levinthal, Calif State Long Beach, 89; American Beauties, Laurence Miller, 90. *Dealer:* Paul Morris Gallery, 465 W 23rd St, NY, 10011. *Mailing Add:* 32 W 20th St New York NY 10011

LEVIT, GINGER
ART DEALER, WRITER
b Philadelphia, Apr 2, 37. *Study:* Univ Pa, BA in French, 1959; Univ Richmond, MA in French, 1975; Va Commonwealth Univ, MA in Art History, 1998; studies at Ecole du Louvre, Paris; La Sorbonne, Paris, Cert, 1994; Alliance Francaise, Paris, Cert. *Work:* Horace Day, Carlyle House Garden; The Lyceum, Alexandria. *Collection Arranged:* Horace Talmadge Day, Fine Arts Am, Inc, 83; William Fletcher Jones, Jefferson Hotel, 84; Raoul Middleman: Westwood Club, Arts on the Square, Richmond Symphony Designers House, 87; Paintings with Provenance, Richmond Symphony Designer House, 01. *Pos:* dir, Fine Arts Am, Richmond, 82-84; Arts on the Square, Richmond, 84-85; organizer, cons, Art-I-facts, 89-; dir, Ginger Levit Atelier, Richmond, 87-; art critic, correspondent, WRFK-FM; art critic, correspondent, Va News Network; dir fund-raising & cmty outreach activities, Richmond Philharmonic; juror, Tidewater Artists' Asn, Spring 2003 Mystery exhib. *Awards:* Award, Va Press Women, 2001 & 2002; Ben Franklin award for cmty svc, Univ Pa, 1989; 2d Place, Va Press Women Commun Contest, 03; Painting Raffled WAC, 2004. *Bibliog:* Roy Proctor (auth), Chicago painter, Richmond News Leader, 10/26/1991; Carla Davis (auth), A fan of all things French, Richmond Mag, 12/2001; Roy Proctor (auth), Pick Your Time, Sip You Wine, Welcome to Ginger Levit's Atelier, Richmond Times-Dispatch, 4/6/2003; Roy Proctor (auth), Sip Your Wine, Take Your Time, Welcome to Ginger Lecit's atelier, Richmond Times-Dispatch, 4/6/2003. *Mem:* Va Press Women; Richmond Symphony Orch League (PR chmn 1998-); La Table Francaise (dir 1998-); Accueil Francais de Richmond. *Res:* Pierre Bonnard and Eduard Vaillard and their Jewish Patrons; Edgar Degas' monotypes become etchings for the 1938 Blaizot "La Famille Cardinal". *Specialty:* French painting from 1850 to New York Armory Show in 1913; French Impressionists; French Post-Impressionists; Nabis painters Bonnard and Vuillard; Regional American artists, 1900-1950 & contemporary. *Interests:* French paintings of the past 200 years. *Collection:* expatriate Frank Myers Boggs, Herri - Joseph Harpignies & William Fletcherjones, Horace Talmadge Day, Raoul Middleman. *Publ:* Auth, Mainly Monet, Mid Atlantic Antiques Mag, 2000, East Coast Blockbuster Exhibition, 12/2001 & Less is more - MIchelangelo at Atlanta's High Mus, 2001; auth, John Singer Sargent's Jewish Wertheimers, Richmond Jewish News, 2001; auth, John Singer Sargent's Jewish Wertheimers, Washington Jewish Week, 2001; auth, Touring the Brandywine Valley, Mid Atlantic Antiques News, 12/2002; auth, A golden legacy, Style Weekly, 2002; auth, American Impressionism at the Chrysler, Tidewater Women, 12/2002; Rarefed Air at Wenter Antigues Show, 2004. *Mailing Add:* 419 Dellbrooks Pl Richmond VA 23233

LEVIT, HÉLOÏSE BERTMAN See Levit, Ginger

LEVITT, HELEN
PHOTOGRAPHER, FILMMAKER
b New York, NY, 1918. *Work:* Mus Mod Art, Metrop Mus Art, NY; Boston Mus Fine Arts; Corcoran Gallery Art; Mus Fine Arts, Houston; Metropolitan Mus of Art, NY; Art Inst of Chicago, Ill; Whitney Mus of Am Art, NY. *Exhib:* Solo exhibs, Mus Mod Art, 43 & 74, Sidney Janis Gallery, 80, Corcoran Gallery Art, 80, Boston Mus Fine Arts, 83, Laurence Miller Gallery, 96, 2000 & Paris Photographie Centre, 01; Nat Mus Am Art, Washington, DC, 84; Dept Photog Galleries, Mus Mod Art, NY, 84-; Twentieth Century Photog, Mus Fine Arts, Boston, 84; The NY Sch (Parts 1 & 2), Corcoran Gallery Art, Washington, DC, 85 & Part 3, 86; Portraits from the Permanent Collection, Metrop Mus Art, NY, 86; Conclusive Beauty (with catalog), Whitney Mus Am Art, NY, 88; On the Art of Fixing a Shadow: One Hundred and Fifty Yrs of Photog (with catalog), Nat Gallery Art, Washington, DC & Art Inst Chicago, 89; Photog Until Now (with catalog), Mus Mod Art, NY, 89; The New Vision (with catalog), Metrop Mus Art, NY, 89; The Cherished Image, Nat Gallery Can, Ottawa, 89; Mus Mod Art, NY, 91, 94 & 95; Recent Acquisitions, Metrop Mus Art, NY, 96; History of Women Photographers (traveling exhib), NY Pub Libr, Nat Mus Women Arts, Washington, DC, Santa Barbara Mus, Calif & Akron Mus, Ohio, 96; NY Sch of Photog, Jan Kesner Gallery, Los Angeles, 98; Matrix/Berkeley Twenty Yrs, Berkeley Art Mus, Calif, 98. *Awards:* Guggenheim Fel, 59, 60, 80 & 81; Ford Found Fel, 64; Nat Endowment Arts Fel, 76; Master of Photog Award, Internat Ctr of Photog, 97; Outstandng Achievement in Humanistic Photog, Photog Adminrs. *Bibliog:* Walker Evans (auth), Quality: Its image in the arts, Atheneum, 69; John Szarkowski (auth), Looking at Photographs, Mus Mod Art, New York, 73; Roberta Hellman & Marvin Hosking (auths), Color Photographs by Helen Levitt, Grossmont Col, 80. *Publ:* Coauth (with James Agee), A Way of Seeing, Horizon, 81; Slide Show: The Color Photographs of Helen Levitt, 2005. *Dealer:* Jeff Fraenkel Gallery 49 Geary St San Francisco CA 94108. *Mailing Add:* c/o Laurence Miller Gallery 20 W 57th St New York NY 10019

LEVITZ, ILONA S
PAINTER, EDUCATOR
b Brooklyn, NY. *Study:* Vesper George Sch Art, Boston, Mass, 1965; Trinity Col, Private Tutorial, Hartford CT1970-1972; Hartford Art Sch, Univ Hartford, Studio Classes, 1975-1977; Wesleyan Univ, Grad Prog, Middletown, CT, 1978-1979. *Work:* Fierston Financial, West Hartford, Conn; Underwriters Servs, Farmington, Conn; COW Parade 2000, NY. *Exhib:* Juried Exhib, New Britain Mus Am Art, New Britain, CT, 1982; 40th CT Artist Exhib, Silvermine Guild, Norwalk, CT, 1983; Conn Vision, Mattatuck Mus, Waterbury, CT, 1992; Three Women Artists, Jewish Community Center, W Hartford, CT, 1994; Women in the Arts, Wavery Gallery, New Haven, CT, 1995. *Collection Arranged:* John Vivolo, folk artist, Hartford Ct Jewish Center, 1982; Chesire Art Asn, Chesire Art League, 1991; Art for the Cure, New Britain Mus Am Art, 2001; Joy of Art, Hosp for Spec Care, 2004. *Teaching:* Cezanne & Beyond, W Hartford Art League, 1995-2003; Master Class, Great Color, W Hartford Art League, 2003; Compos, Rhythem & Color Vision Painting, W Hartford Art League, 2004-2006. *Awards:* Garfield Award, New Haven Paint & Clay, 1982; Best Drawing, New Britain Mus Am Art, 1985; Purchase Award, Wintonbury Art Asn, 1991. *Bibliog:* Stacy Stowe (auth), Is it Really Art?, NY Times, 1999; Patricia Rosoff (auth), A Wealth of Painterly Talent, Hartford Advocate, 2003; Will Steigerwald (auth), Northernlight, Artis, 10/2005; Jane Gordon (auth), A Painted Life, Home Living, 2006. *Mem:* Hartford Jewish Community Center (co-chmn cult Arts Committee), 1981-1983; CT Acad Fine Art (board mem), 1996-1999; W Hartford Art League (board mem), 1999-2002; Farmington Valley Ats Center (finance committee), 2003-2006. *Media:* Acrylic, Oil, Watercolor. *Specialty:* Abstract paintings, mixed & acrylic media by I S Levitz. *Interests:* Arts activist, jazz, dance, theater. *Dealer:* Ilona S Levitz 27 Arts Center Ln Avon CT 06001. *Mailing Add:* 869 Farmington Ave West Hartford CT 06119

LEVKOVA-LAMM, INNESSA
CRITIC, CURATOR
b Moscow, Russ; US citizen, 39. *Study:* Leningrad Inst Film Eng, MD, 65; Moscow Inst Lang, 66-68. *Work:* Duke Univ Art Mus, Durham, NC. *Comn:* Jane Voorhees Zimmerli Mus of Art, NB, NJ; Shifting from Center to Margins: Moscow Conceptualism, 1980's-90's. *Exhib:* Women in Art Atrium Gallery, Morristown, NJ, 2000; Hackensack Art Ctr, NJ, 2001; Three Generations of Russian Women Artists, Salena Gallery, LI Univ Brooklyn Campus, 2002; 40 yrs of Soviet & Russian Art, The Bergen Mus Art, Paramus, NJ, 2003. *Collection Arranged:* Russian and Soviet Political Art, 87; Transit: Russian Art Between East and West (auth, catalog), 89; Back to Square One (auth, catalog), 91; After Perestroika (auth, catalog), 91. *Pos:* Freelance art critic, Literature Rev, Moscow, Russ, 64-81, Contempornia, NY, 88-91 & Flash Art, Milan, Italy, 91-97; pres, Imago Fine Art & Design, Inc, NY, 98-. *Mem:* Int Asn Art Critics; Nat Writers Union. *Media:* Photography; Digital art. *Res:* Modern and contemporary art; Russian art of twentieth century. *Interests:* Revision of Kazimir Malevich's works. *Publ:* Auth, Rustislav Lebedev, Eduard Nakhamkin Fine Art, 90; coauth, Kultur in Stali Nismus, Edition Temmen, Ger, 94; Birth of an Image, Duke Univ Mus Art, NC, 98; Aufder Suche Nach Einer Neuen Indetiat, Ed Temmen, Ger, 98; auth, Face of Square: Mysteries of Kazimir Malevich, Pinkotheke, Moscow, 2004, The Art Magazine, Moscow, 2004 & The Collection, Moscow, 2005. *Mailing Add:* 310 E 23rd St Apt 3A New York NY 10010-4735

LEVY, BERNARD
DEALER
b New York, NY, Feb 10, 17. *Study:* NY Univ, BA, 37. *Pos:* Pres, Bernard & S Dean Levy Inc, 73-2001, chmn, 2001. *Bibliog:* On Madison Avenue, Fortune Mag, 12/47; Rita Reif (auth), Antiques, NY Times, 10/76; Douglas Villiers (auth), Next Year in Jerusalem, Viking Press, 76. *Mem:* Art & Antique Dealers League Am (pres, five yrs). *Specialty:* American paintings; American antique furniture; silver; English and American ceramics. *Publ:* An American Tea Party Colonial Tea & Breakfast Tables 1715-83; Opulence & Splendor - The New York Chair 1690-1830; Vanity & Elegance - The Dressing Table & Tall Chest in America 1685-1785. *Mailing Add:* Bernard & Dean Levy Inc 24 E 84th St New York NY 10028

LEVY, DAVID CORCOS
ART HISTORIAN, EDUCATOR
b New York, NY, Apr 10, 1938. *Study:* Columbia Col, BA, 60; New York Univ, MA, 67, PhD, 79. *Work:* Guggenheim Mus, NY. *Pos:* Exec dean, Parsons Sch Design, New York, 70-89; chancellor, New Sch Social Res, New York, 89-90; pres & dir, Corcoran Gallery Art, Washington, DC, 91-05

LEVY, HILDA
PAINTER, SCULPTOR
b Pinsk, Russia. *Study:* Univ Calif, Berkeley, AB; Pasadena City Col; Jepson Art Inst; Univ Calif, Los Angeles; also with Adolph Gottlieb. *Exhib:* Nat Gallery Can, Ottawa, Ont; Libr of Cong, Washington, DC; Butler Inst Am Art, Youngstown, Ohio; San Francisco Mus Art & M H de Young Mem Mus, San Francisco; one-woman show, Calif Palace Legion Hon, Pasadena Mus & McNay Inst, Calif; and others. *Awards:* 40 local & nat awards. *Bibliog:* Edward Reep (auth), Content of Watercolor, Reinhold; Lawrence C Goldsmith (auth), Watercolor Bold & Free, Watson Guptill; Les Krantz (ed), Calif Art Rev, Am References. *Mem:* Nat Watercolor Soc; Bay Printmakers. *Media:* Wood, Jewelry

LEVY, MARK
WRITER, HISTORIAN
b New York, NY, June 24, 47. *Study:* Clark Univ, BA, 68; Ind Univ, MA, 70, PhD, 77. *Pos:* Comnr, Alameda Co Art Comn, 85-86. *Teaching:* Asst prof, Kenyon Col, 74-79 & Univ Nev, 80-81; prof, Calif State Univ, Hayward, 81-; vis prof advan art theory, Grad Prog, San Francisco Art Inst, 84-89; vis prof grad prog consciousness dept, John F Kennedy Univ, 94-. *Awards:* Samuel Kress Dissertation Fel, 73; Nat Endowment Humanities Fel, 77; Fulbright-Hays Grant, summer 91. *Mem:* Int Asn Art Critics; Found Shamonic Studies. *Res:* World sacred art. *Publ:* Auth, The Shaman is a Gifted Artist, High Performance, fall 88; Rilke, Letters on Cezanne, San Francisco Rev of Books, fall 88; Squeak Carnwath, Artspace, 1/2/89; Wayang Kulit as a model for performance art, High Performance, summer 89; Technicians of Ecstasy: Shamanism & the Modern Artist, Bramble Books, 93; The Void of Art, summer 2005. *Mailing Add:* 5510 Golden Gate Ave Oakland CA 94618

LEVY, PHYLLIS
PAINTER
b Brooklyn, NY, June 20, 27. *Study:* Cooper Union Art Sch, cert; San Francisco State, AB(art), MA(art educ); Colo Springs Fine Arts Ctr (scholar); Calif Sch Fine Arts (scholar). *Work:* Israel Mus, Jerusalem. *Exhib:* 15th Ann Watercolor, San Francisco Mus Art, Calif, 51; 26th Ann Women, San Francisco Mus Art, Calif, 51; Am Watercolor Drawings & Prints, Metrop Mus, NY, 52; Strathmore Hall Members Exhibs, 92, 93 & 94; Invitational, Strathmore Hall Arts Ctr Gallery, 93 & 94; Techno-Art, Rockville Arts Place, 94; Montgomery Co Art Asn Exhib, 94; solo exhibs, George Meany Ctr Labor Studies, 94 & Gaithersburg Coun Arts, Kentlands I Gallery, 94; plus many others. *Teaching:* Teacher art, Montgomery Co Pub Sch, 69-78. *Awards:* San Francisco Art Asn Prize, 51; Washington Watercolor Asn Award, 92; Montgomery Co Art Asn Award, 92 & 93. *Mem:* Artists Equity Asn; Rockville Arts Place; Montgomery Co Arts Coun. *Media:* Acrylic, Mixed Media. *Mailing Add:* 9202 Friars Rd Bethesda MD 20817-2321

LEVY, S(TEPHEN) DEAN
DEALER, GALLERY DIRECTOR
b New York, NY, Nov 17, 42. *Study:* Yale Univ, BA, 64. *Pos:* Vpres, Bernard & S Dean Levy, Inc, 73-. *Bibliog:* On Madison Avenue, Fortune Mag, 12/47; Rita Reif (auth), Antiques, New York Times, 10/76; Douglas Villiers (auth), Next Year in Jerusalem, Viking Press, 76. *Mem:* Art & Antique Dealers League. *Specialty:* American paintings, antique furniture, silver; English and American ceramics. *Publ:* Auth, An American Tea Party, Colonial Tea and Breakfast Tables 1715-1783; Opulence & Splendor, The New York Chair 1690-1830; Vanity & Elegance, The Dressing Table & Tall Chest in America, 1685-1785. *Mailing Add:* Bernard & Dean Levy Inc 24 E 84th St New York NY 10028

LEVY, TIBBIE
PAINTER
b New York, NY, Oct 29, 08. *Study:* Cornell Univ, with Arshile Gorky, AB; Art Students League; Acad Grand Chaumiere & Acad Andre Lhote, Paris, France; NY Univ, JD. *Work:* Contemp Art Soc Gt Brit; Mus Mod Art, Madrid, Barcelona & Bilbao, Spain; Princeton Univ Mus; Cornell Univ Mus; plus 40 other mus. *Exhib:* Bodley Gallery, NY, 60-70; Galerie Ror Volmar, Paris, 61; Sala Nebli, Madrid, 62; Galeria Forum, Madrid, 63; Portal Gallery, London, Eng, 63 & 65; plus others. *Teaching:* Lectr art. *Media:* Oil. *Dealer:* Bodley Gallery 787 Madison Ave New York NY 10021. *Mailing Add:* 2 Sutton Pl S Apt 3D New York NY 10022

LEW, FRAN
PAINTER
b March 29 1946. *Study:* Brooklyn Col, with Philip Pearlstein, BA(art), 66; Boston Univ Sch Fine & Applied Art, MFA, 68; Int Ctr Paintings & Costume Design, Palazzo Grassi, with Gregory Battcock, Master (glassblower) Seguso, Venice, Italy, 78; Art Student's League, with Daniel Greene, Robert Beverly Hale & John Howard Sanden, 78-79; Reilly League Artists, NY, with Cesare Borgia, 79-84. *Work:* State of Israel, New York Consulate; Cornell Mus; Fenster Mus; Maitland Art Ctr Mus; Matilda Cuomo (portrait), Brooklyn Hist Soc. *Comn:* portrait, Interpub Group of Co, NY, 84; portrait, First Lady New York State, comn by Am Cancer Soc, NY, 86; portrait of Gov Mario M Coumo, comn by coalition of Italo-Am Asn, NY, 90; portraits, comn by Tambrands Inc, Westchester, NY, 90; official state portrait, Gov Mario M Cuomo, Hall of Gov, Albany, NY, 95. *Exhib:* Palazzo Grassi Int Ctr Painting & Design Exhib, Venice, Italy, 78; Salmagundi Club, 85, 86 & 87; Am Artists Mag Golden Anniversary Exhib, John Pence Gallery & Grand Cent Art Galleries, 87; solo exhibs, Columbus Club, NY, 82, Manhattan Borough President's Art Gallery, 89, Pen & Brush Club, NY, 89 & Grand Cent Art Galleries, 90. *Teaching:* Instr art, Am Int Sch, Israel, 71-72; instr portrait drawing, Adult Educ, Katonah, White Plains, NY, 80-82; art chmn, instr, Palisades Park Schs, NJ, 73-80. *Awards:* Gold Medal, Knickerbocker Artists, 84; Corporate Prize, Am Artist Mag Golden Anniversary Nat Competition, 87; Solo Award-Best Show, Pen & Brush Oil Exhib, 87. *Bibliog:* eds, Drawings in the Golden Anniversary National Art Competition, Am Artist Mag, 6/87; Edward Rubin (auth), article, Manhattan Arts, 10/89; quoted, portrait of Governor Mario M Cuomo, Am Artist Mag, 6/93. *Mem:* Knickerbocker Artists; Hudson Valley Art Asn; Catherine Lorillard Wolfe Art Club; Pen & Brush Club; life mem, Art Students League. *Media:* Oil, Pastel, All Media. *Publ:* Member of the Issue, Northlight, 82. *Dealer:* Fine Arts Int The Volney 23 E 74th St Suite 7E New York NY 10021. *Mailing Add:* 120 Fanshaw C Boca Raton FL 33434

LEW, WEYMAN
PAINTER, PRINTMAKER
b San Francisco, Calif, Feb 17, 35. *Study:* Univ Calif, Berkeley, BS, 57; San Francisco Art Inst, with Jay deFeo, 65-66. *Work:* MH de Young Mem Mus, San Francisco; Univ Calif Mus, Berkeley; Inst Arte Contemporaneo, Lima, Peru; Santa Barbara Mus Art, Calif; Oakland Art Mus, Calif; Brooklyn Mus; San Francisco Mus Modern Art, Calif. *Comn:* Univ Calif Mus, Berkeley, 74. *Exhib:* One-man shows, MH De Young Mem Mus, 70, Inst Contemp Art, Lima, Peru, 70, Santa Barbara Mus Art, 71, Art Gallery Greater Victoria, BC, Can, 72, Bonython Art Gallery, Sydney, Australia, 72-75, Sande Webster Gallery, Philadelphia, 72, 74, 77, 80 & 84 & Int Art Exhib Hall, Beijing, China, 91; and many others. *Pos:* Dir, Kelley Galleries, San Francisco, 68; guest cur, Nan Hai Arts Ctr, Calif, 90-92, Chinatown Community Art Prog, San Francisco, 91 & 93. *Teaching:* Guest instr painting, drawing & serigraphy, MH de Young Mem Mus Art Sch, 70-71. *Awards:* Merit Award, San Francisco Art Festival, 80; Distinguished Award for Cult, Chinese Cult Found San Francisco, 91. *Bibliog:* Oriental Art Mag, Eng, Summer 91; Li Beige (auth), on Weyman Lew, Art Mag, 12/91, China; Guo Rui (auth), Weyman Lew, Four Seas Mag, Beijing, China, 1/92; and others. *Mem:* Calif Soc Printmakers; Chinese Cult Ctr (art adv bd), San Francisco; Asian Am Arts Found (art adv bd), San Francisco; Acad Art Col (galleries & prom adv bd), San Francisco. *Media:* Ink, Watercolor; Etching. *Publ:* Auth, Weyman Lew Sketches Away, Triton Assocs, 81; ed, Contemporary Chinese Painting, Nan Hai Co USA & Chinese Artists Asn, China Publ, 90; Weyman Lew, of Peoples and Places, Chinese Cult Found San Francisco, 91; Echoes of Oxford, illustrations by W Lew, Phillip Carlson, 91. *Dealer:* Sande Webster Gallery 2006 Locust St Philadelphia Pa 19103; Robin Gibson Gallery 278 Liverpool St NSW 2010 Australia. *Mailing Add:* PO Box 29036 San Francisco CA 94129

LEWCZUK, MARGRIT
PAINTER
Study: Queens Col, New York, NY, 52. *Exhib:* Solo exhibs, Brooklyn Mus, NY, 75, John Davis Gallery, Akron, Ohio, 82, Thorden Wetterling Gallery, Stockholm, Sweden, 87, Pamela Auchincloss Gallery, NY, 87, 89, 92 & 94, Dolan Maxwell Gallery, Philadelphia, Pa, 88 & Bjorn Wetterling Gallery, Gottenburg, Sweden, 91; Munson-Williams Proctor Mus, NY, 81; Faculty Invitational, Bennington Col, Vt, 83; Works on Paper, Allport Gallery, San Francisco, Calif, 89. *Pos:* Univ Conn, 99-. *Awards:* Nat Endowment Arts, 89. *Media:* Oil on Linen, Charcoal Pastel on Paper. *Publ:* Exhib Catalogues for Pamela Auchincloss Gallery, 87 & Thorden Wetterling Gallery, 87. *Mailing Add:* 79 Metroplitan Ave Brooklyn NY 11211-3932

LEWENZ, LISA
VIDEO ARTIST, PHOTOGRAPHER
b Baltimore, Md, Apr 1, 55. *Study:* Philadelphia Col Art, 73-74; Kans City Art Inst, 76-77; Art Inst Chicago, BFA, 78; Calif Inst Arts, MFA, 82. *Work:* New Eng Holocaust Found Collection, Boston; Mus Contemp Arts, Baltimore, Md; Hallmark Collections, Kans City; Tisch Photo Collections, New York Univ; Deutsches Historisches Mus, Berlin. *Comn:* John A Logan Col, Ill Arts Coun, Carbondale, 85; A Letter Without Words, Independent Television Serv, 95-99. *Exhib:* Solo exhibs, A View from Three Mile Island, San Francisco Camerawork, Calif, 87, A Letter without Words, 92 St Gallery, NY, 89, Gormley Gallery, Baltimore, Md, 91, E J Bellocq Gallery, Ruston, La, 91, Towards a More Perfect Union, Baltimore Mus Art, Md, 92 & Huntington Gallery, Boston, Mass, 92; Other Rooms, The Kunstraum, Washington, DC, 90; Visual AIDS, Mus Contemp Arts, Baltimore, Md, 90; Rotterdam Int Film Fest/CineMart, 96; IFFM/No Borders, NY, 96; PBS Nat Broadcast, 99; various film festivals incl Sundance, Berlin, Amsterdam, Vancouver, Edinburgh, Jerusalem & Gothenberg. *Collection Arranged:* Site Works, St Mary's Gallery, 87; Constructions, 90, Contemp Puerto Rican Painting, 90, Fifth Ann Nat Print & Drawing Exhibit, Gormley Gallery, 91. *Pos:* Dir, Unit One photog prog, Univ Ill, Champaign, 85-87 & Gormley Gallery, Col Notre Dame Md, Baltimore, 90-91; dir/coordr, site specific sem, St Mary's Col, Md, 87-88; dir, NoNet Productions, 94-. *Teaching:* Vis lectr photog, Minneapolis Col Art & Design, 84; vis asst prof photog, Univ Ill, Champaign-Urbana, 85-87 & New York Univ, 92; asst prof, St Mary's Col, Md, 87-88 & Col Notre Dame, Md, 89-93; vis asst prof, Rochester Inst Technol, 92; vis lectr, Cornell Univ, Johns Hopkins Univ, NY Univ, Rowan Univ, currently. *Awards:* Fulbright Hays Scholar, Sr Res Award Ger, Ger & Coun Int Exchange Scholars, 93 & 94; Nat Endowment Humanities Fel Berlin, 94; Fel, Anonymous Was a Woman Found, 98. *Bibliog:* Philadephia Inquirer, 10/98; Los Angeles Times, 4/5/99; New York Times, 4/5/99. *Mem:* Soc Photog Educ; Md Art Place, Baltimore (exec bd dir, 88-92); Col Art Asn; Baltimore Artists Housing Coop (co-pres, bd dir, 90-); Friends Photog. *Media:* Interdisciplinary Arts, Photography; Film, Video. *Publ:* Auth, 1984 A View from Three Mile Island, No Net Productions, 83; contribr, Nuclear Power, A Weapon for the Enemy, UCLA Press, 84; Visions Issue: Environmental Action, 85; Friends of the Earth J, 86. *Mailing Add:* PO Box 133 Madison Square Stn New York NY 10010

LEWIN, BERNARD
DEALER, COLLECTOR
b Ger; US citizen. *Study:* With Kurt Wagner, Berlin. *Exhib:* Ann shows, Castaneda, Cora, Coronel, Tamayo and others. *Pos:* Art dir, B Lewin Galleries, Palm Springs, Calif, 60-. *Awards:* Thirty-eighth Anniversary of Mexican Masters, Lifetime Achievement Award, City of Los Angeles; Lifetime Achievement Award, First Int Gallery Invitational, Chicago; Significant Contribution Award, City of Palm Springs. *Mem:* Art Dealers Asn. *Specialty:* Mexican masters, Tamayo, Siqueiros, Merida, R Martinez, R Coronel, Diego Rivera, Felipe Castenada, Gustavo Montoya and others. *Collection:* Mexican masters, American and European. *Mailing Add:* 254 E Lake Dr Palm Springs CA 92264-5582

LEWIS, CAROLE
SCULPTOR
b London, Eng, Dec 28, 34, US citizen. *Study:* Hana Geber Workshop, apprentice to Hana Geber, 79-82, Art Students League, New York, with Gustave Rehberger; painting with George Jo Mess, Indianapolis, Ind; Aida Foster Sch, London, Eng; Greycotes Sch, Oxford, Eng. *Work:* Am Collection, Mus Int Art, Sophia, Bulgaria; Gen Electric Corp, Fairfield, Conn; Mus Hudson Highlands, Cornwall, NY; Starrett

City Assoc, Brooklyn, NY; Seicomart Corp, Sapporo, Japan; and many other pub & pvt collections. *Exhib:* Group shows, Cleveland Mus Nat Hist, Ohio, 84; Cast Iron Gallery, Soho, NY, 91-93; Kyoto Gallery, Japan, 93; Krystal Gallery, Warren, Vt, 93-94; Wildlife in Midtown, Am Towers, NY, 94. *Awards:* Pietro & Alfrieda Montana Award, Nat Sculpture Soc, 91; Charles H Levitt Prize, Nat Asn Women Artists, 91; Vincent Glinsky Mem Award, Audubon Artists, 94. *Bibliog:* Sculpture: Technique, Form, Content, Williams, 94. *Mem:* Sculptors Guild; Nat Asn Women Artists; Fel Nat Sculptors Soc; Audubon Artists; Hudson River Contemp Artists. *Media:* Terra Cotta, Clay; Metal, Bronze. *Dealer:* Sculpture Ctr 67 E 69th St New York NY; Arlene McDaniel Galleries Simsburg CT. *Mailing Add:* 368 W 246th St Bronx NY 10471

LEWIS, DAVID DODGE
PAINTER
b Houlton, Maine, Dec 21, 1951. *Study:* Univ Southern Main, BD (art educ), 70-74; Sch of Mus of Fine Arts, Boston, 74-75; Art Students League, NY City, 78; East Carolina Univ, MA (painting), 80-81, MFA (painting), 84-87. *Exhib:* Stockton Nat Exhib, Haggin Mus, Calif, 97; 27th Bradley Nat Print and Drawing Exhib, Bradley Univ, Ill, 98; Vitreographs from the Littleton Studios, Blue Spiral Gallery, Asheville, NC, 99; Scene/Unseen, Eastern N Mex Univ, 99; Millennial Biennial: Nat Works on Paper, Univ Richmond, Va, 2000; Stone Tool Drawings, Longwood Ctr Visual Arts, Farmville, Va, 2001; The Sentient Object, McLean Project for Arts, Va, 2001; Hodges Taylor Gallery, Charlotte, NC, 2002; Biennial 2002, Peninsula Fine Arts Ctr, Newport News, Va, Faces/Reality, 2005; Americas 2000, Minot State Univ, N Dakota, 2004; Hand to Hand, Green Hill Ctr NC Art, 2005. *Teaching:* Graphics instr Penland Sch Crafts, NC, 84 & 85, drawing instr, 93, 95 & 2000; intsr Mayland Technical Inst, Spruce Pine, NC, 84; asst prof fine arts Hampden-Sydney Col, 87-93, assoc prof fine arts, 93-95, William W Elliot assoc prof fine arts, 95, prof, 2000-. *Awards:* Va Prize Arts, Prints and Drawings, 89; John Peter Mettauer Award Excellence in Res, Hampden-Sydney Col, 92. *Mem:* Col Art Asn; South East Col Art Conference; Va Art Hist Colloquium; Central Va Arts; Longwood Ctr Visual Arts; Va Mus Fine Arts. *Mailing Add:* 1004 Edmonds St Farmville VA 23901

LEWIS, DONALD SYKES, JR
PAINTER
b Norfolk, Va, Dec 13, 47. *Study:* Randolph-Macon Col, Ashland, Va, BA(fine arts); Univ Va, MA(hist of art). *Work:* Central Fidelity Bank, Norfolk, Va; Randolph-Macon Col, Ashland, VA; Sears, Roebuck & Co, Chicago, Ill; First & Citizens Bank, Warm Springs, VA. *Exhib:* Second Ann Invitational Juried Show, Gallery II, Norfolk, 77; 57th Ann Nat Apr Salon, Springville Mus Art, Utah, 81; One-man shows, Auslew Gallery, 82, Art Works Gallery, 94, Hermitage Found Mus, Norfolk, Va, 96 & Warm Springs Gallery, Va, 2000; Randolph-Macon Col, Ashland, Va 85; Twentieth Century Gallery, Williamsburg, Va, 85; Pennisula Fine Arts Ctr, Newport News, Va, 97; 20th Ann Juried Exhib, Pleades Gallery, NY, 2002; 25th Ann Open Non-mem Exhib, Salmagundi Club, NY, 2002; Am Artist Professional League, Inc; 75th Grand Nat Exhib, Salmagundi Club, NY, 2003. *Pos:* Vpres, Auslew Gallery, Inc, Norfolk, 73-76, dir, 76-83, pres, 83-95; adv comt, Chrysler Mus, 88-90; sec treas, Granby & Main Corp, 2004-05, pres, 2005-. *Teaching:* Instr Am art, Hermitage Mus, Norfolk, 75, 78 & 79 & Old Dom Univ, 75-76. *Bibliog:* Hampton Roads Virginia Guide to Visual Artists, Grunwald & Radcliff, 84. *Mem:* Chrysler Mus Art. *Media:* Oil. *Res:* Cataloging works of Herman Ottomar Herzog and his son, Lewis E Herzog. *Publ:* Auth, Emily Nichols Hatch (catalog), 74 & foreword, In: Carolyn Wyeth (catalog), 12/74, Auslew Gallery, Inc; Herman Herzog, Southwest Art Rev, 75; contribr, Carolyn Wyeth Exhibition Catalogue, R W Norton Art Gallery, Shreveport, La, 1/76; auth, Herman Herzog (1831-1932), German landscapist in America, Am Art Rev, 7-8/76; American Paintings of Herman Herzog (exhib catalog), Brandywine River Mus, 9/12-11/22. *Dealer:* Warm Springs Gallery Warm Springs VA; Beach Gallery Virginia Beach VA; Green Leaf Gallery, Duck, Inc, Main St Fine Art and Antique Mall, Kilmarnock, VA. *Mailing Add:* 708 Cavalier Dr Virginia Beach VA 23451

LEWIS, DOUGLAS
HISTORIAN, CONSULTANT
b Centreville, Miss, Apr 30, 38. *Study:* Lawrenceville Sch, NJ, dipl, 56; Yale Col, BA, 59 & 60; Clare Col, Cambridge Univ, BA, 62, MA, 66; Yale Univ, MA, 63, PhD, 67; Am Acad Rome, Chester Dale fel, 64, dipl, 65. *Collection Arranged:* African Sculpture, 70, The Far North (Am Eskimo & Indian Art catalog), 73; The Drawings of Andrea Palladio Traveling Exhib (catalog), 81; Renaissance Small Bronze Sculpture and Associated Decorative Arts (catalog), 83; Renaissance Master Bronzes (with preface to catalog), 86; The Currency of Fame (catalog contributor), Nat Gallery Art, 94. *Pos:* David E Finley fel Venetian art, Nat Gallery Art, Washington, DC, 65-68; cur sculpture, Nat Gallery Art, 68-2004; vchmn, Citizens Stamp Adv Comt, US Postal Serv, 85-2004; chmn, 2004-05; bd advisors, Oakley & Rosedown, La State Historic Sites; bd advisors, Natchez Literary & Cinema Celebration, Miss. *Teaching:* Asst prof baroque & romantic art, Bryn Mawr Col, 67-68; asst prof renaissance & baroque art, Univ Calif, Berkeley, spring 70; sem leader renaissance archit, Folger Inst, Renaissance Sem, Washington, DC, spring 72; adj prof, Renaissance & baroque art, Johns Hopkins Univ, 73-77; prof Renaissance art & archit, Univ Calif, Berkeley, fall 79; lectr, Iowa State Univ, Ames, 80; lectr, Georgetown Univ, 80-93; vis prof, Univ Md, 89-2003. *Awards:* Copley Medal, Smithsonian Inst, 81. *Mem:* Fel Am Acad in Rome; Soc Archit Historians; Col Art Asn Am; Belg-Am Educ Found; Centro Palladiano, Vicenza; and others. *Res:* Art and architecture in Renaissance Venice; monographic studies on Michele Sanmicheli, Jacopo Sansovino, Andrea Palladio, Baldassare Longhena, Francesco Muttoni & Galeazzo Mondella (Moderno). *Interests:* John James Audubon; Architecture of American South. *Publ:* Auth, The Late Baroque Churches of Venice, 67 & Garland, 79; The Drawings of Andrea Palladio, Nat Gallery Art, 81 (rev ed., 2000); coauth, Renaissance Master Bronzes, SITES, 86; Nat Gallery Art Systematic Catalog, Renaissance Blaquettes (2 vols), 2005, 06. *Mailing Add:* PO Box 74762 Baton Rouge LA 70874-4762

LEWIS, GOLDA
ASSEMBLAGE ARTIST, PAPERMAKER
b New York, NY. *Study:* With Vaclav Vytacil, Hans Hofmann & Jack Tworkov; Papermaking with Douglas Howell. *Work:* Ciba-Geigy Chem Co, Pfizer Pharmaceuticals, Ardsley, NY; Madden Corp, NY; Hercules Powder Co, Wilmington, Del; Foundations of Paper Hist, Haarlem, Holland; Cheney Pulp & Paper Co, Franklin, Ohio; and others. *Exhib:* Handmade Paper, Points & Unique Works, Mus Mod Art, NY, 76; New Ways with Paper, Nat Collection Fine Arts, Smithsonian Inst, Washington, DC, 77-78; solo exhibs, Int Biennale of Paper, Duren, Ger, Galerie Faust, Geneva, Switz, 86, Discerning Images Gallery, Montclair, NJ, 87 & Gallery Inter-Am Develop Bank, Wash, DC, 88, Musei Banco Cen, Plaza Oe La Cultura, San Jose, Costa Rica, 93, Claudia Carr Gallery, New York City, 97, Gallery Diev Donne Papermill, New York City, 2000; Petit Format De Papier, Cul-Des-Sarts, Couvin, Belg, 89; Paper in Art, Nysted Kunstforening, Int Paper Art Biannual, Denmark, 89; The Book Art Gallery, 91; Summer Drawing, Philippe Staib Gallery, 92; Anita Shapolsky Gallery, NY, 93 & 94; Museo Banco, Central Plaza de la Cultura, San Jose, Costa Rica, 93; Dieu Donne Gallery, NY, 2000; Retrospective 1961-2001, Am Mus Papermaking, Atlanta, Ga, 2003; group exhibs, Gallery 256, Provincetown, Mass, 57, Mus Mad Art, Libr, NY, 63-64, 76, Am Cult Ctr, Jerusalem, 84, Aaron Gallery, Washington, DC, 89, Anita Shapolsky Gallery, 92, 93, Rutgers Univ, New Brunswick, NJ, 2000, Soho Creative, NY, 2001; and others. *Pos:* Built, equipped & consult, Papermaking Dept, Wildcliff Mus, New Rochelle, NY, 77. *Teaching:* Instr, Ballard Sch, NY, 61-71; lectr, Marymount Manhattan Col, 71; Am Fedn Arts rent an artist workshop on paper and artists working in paper, 74; lectr & workshops handpapermaking, Univ Mass, Amherst, 78; lectr, Univ Costa Rica, San Jose, 83, 84, & 93, Leopold Hoesch Mus, Duren, WGer, 86, NJ Ctr Visual Arts, Summit, 88 & Studio Sch NY, 89, Francisco Amigetti Biennial, San Jose, Costa Rica-juried show, 91; and others. *Awards:* NY State Coun Arts Grant, 71; Award, Clayworks, 80; Florsheim Fund Grant, 92. *Bibliog:* Jack Kroll (auth), Art News (feature review), 63; Thelma Newman (auth), Innovative Printmaking, Crown Publs, 77; Bernard Toale (auth), The Art of Papermaking, Davis Publs, 83; International Paper Art Biannual (catalog), Nysted, Denmark, 89; Heidi Mae Bratt (auth), New York Women, New York Post, 97; Akira Kurosaki (auth) with reproduction, Handpapermaking, Creation of Paper, 2000; and others. *Media:* Handmade Paper. *Publ:* Auth, Conference Review of 1977 Handpapermakers' Conference, Women's Artists News, 78; auth, Douglas Howell Sketch Books, Craft Horizons, 76; auth, Craft World, conf review, Boston Univ, 81; My Adventures in Paper, ESM Documentation, 84. *Mailing Add:* 31 Union Sq W Studio 9C New York NY 10003

LEWIS, JOSEPH S, III
ADMINISTRATOR, SCULPTOR
b New York, NY, Feb 22, 53. *Study:* Hamilton Col, NY, BA, 75; studied with John Ashbery, Allen Ginsberg & David Shapiro, grad writing sem, Brooklyn Col, NY; Md Inst Col Art, Baltimore, MFA, 89. *Work:* Studio Mus Harlem, NY; Mark Twain Bank, St Louis, Mo; Univ Colo, Boulder; State Univ NY, Potsdam; Experimental Print Workshop, NY; Anderson Ranch, Colo; Cite des Arts, Paris. *Comn:* Wind Chime, Riverside Arts Found, Calif, 95; The Twelve Principles, Long Beach Blue Line, Metrop Transit Authority, Los Angeles; The Wall of Dignity, Mayors Comt Arts & Culture, Baltimore. *Exhib:* Chant Acapella, Mus Mod Art, NY, 78; No Justice No Peace, Calif Afro-Am Mus, Los Angeles, 92; Primary Peoples Cols & Shapes, Univ Galleries, Ill State Univ, Normal, 93; Synesthesia: Sound & Vision, San Antonio Mus Art, Tex, 94; Equal Rights & Justice, High Mus, Atlanta, 94 & Smithsonian Inst, Washington, 95; Disciples of the Hood, Joe Lewis & The Neo-Ancestralist, Contemp Arts Ctr, Cincinnati, 96; Darkroom Projects, Milan, 99; Made in California, Los Angeles Co Mus Art; PhotoAlchemy, Sharadin Gallery, Univ Penn, Kutztown, 2000. *Collection Arranged:* The Times Square Show, New York, 80; Fashion Moda Store, Documenta VII, Kassel, Ger, 82; The Face of Jazz 1954-1984, Raymond Ross, Hamilton Col, Clinton, NY, 84; The Gathering Storm: What is the Enemy Now, Md Art Place, Baltimore, 92; LA Freewaves(installations), The Geffen, Temporary Contemp/Mus Contemp Art, Los Angeles, 96. *Pos:* Publ, Appearances Mag & Press, NY, 76-89; dir, Fashion Moda, NY, 78-82; proj mgr, Jackie Robinson Found, NY, 87-90; adminr, Pub Art Prog, Cult Affairs Dept, Los Angeles, 92-94; proj mgr, Art for Rail Prog, Metrop Transportation Authority, Los Angeles, 94-95; chair, Dept Art, Calif State Univ, Northridge, 95-2001; dean, FIT Sch Art & Design, NY, 2001-. *Teaching:* Vis asst prof art, studio, Carnegie Mellon Univ, Pittsburgh, 91-92; fac studio & theory, Calif Inst Arts, Valencia, Calif, 91-95; vis fac, New Genre Studio, Univ Calif, Los Angeles, 92. *Awards:* Fel, Thomas J Watson Found, 75; fel, New Genre, Nat Endowment Arts, 82; fel, New Genre, Md State Arts Coun, 92. *Bibliog:* Lowery Stokes Sims (auth), The Mirror The Other: The Politics of Esthetics, Artforum, 90; Lucy Lippard (auth), Mixed Blessings: New Art in a Multicultural America, Partheon Books, 90; Tobey Crockett (auth), Joe Lewis at Robert Berman, Art in Am, 94; Julie Art (ed), Cultural Economics, 96; Urban Mythologies, The Bronx Represented Since the 1960's, The Bronx Mus, 99. *Mem:* Col Art Asn, NY; Side St Projs, Santa Monica, Calif (bd pres, 92-95); Am Soc Composers, Authors & Publ; Int Asn Art Critics; Mus Contemp Art, Baltimore (bd vpres, 90-92); Calif Lawyer For the Arts (bd mem, 2000-); Nat Coun Art Admin (bd mem, 2000-); Mary Lind Found (bd mem, 98-2000 & treas, 99-); Jackie Robinson Found, Scolarship Comt, Los Angeles. *Media:* Multimedia. *Publ:* auth, How to commit suicide in South Africa: The work of Sue Coe, Artforum, 4/82; Jean Michel Basquiat, Contemporanea, 8/88; Soul shadows: Urban warrior myths: The work of Dawn Dedeaux, Artspace, 4/93; Radcliffe Bailey at Fay Gold, Art in Am, 3/95; Jim McHugh at the High Museum, Art in Am, 6/96; The Bronx Represented Since the 1960's, The Bronx Mus, 99. *Dealer:* Robert Berman Gallery 2525 Michigan Ave No C2 Santa Monica CA 90404

LEWIS, LOUISE MILLER
GALLERY DIRECTOR, EDUCATOR
b St Louis, Mo, Dec 4, 40. *Study:* Univ Calif, Berkeley, BA, 63; Univ NMex, Albuquerque, MA(french), 66, MA(art history), 72. *Collection Arranged:* Contemporary Figuration: The Kamm Collection, 97; Patssi Valdez: Private Landscapes, 98; Akiko Arita: Exploring Native Culture in Japan, 98; Jane Dickson: Almost Home, 99; Editorial Drawings of the 20th Century, 2000; Lili Lakick, Sirens and other Neon Seductions, 2001; Von Dutch: An American Original, 2002; Museum of Disappearance: Max Almy and Teri Yarbrow, 2003; Free Range: Seven Los Angeles Artists, 2003; Contemp Chinese Quilts, 2004; Suchen Hung: The Red Sea Series, 2004; African Art in the Life Cycle, 2005. *Pos:* Cur, Univ NMex Fine Arts Mus, 66-72, actg dir, 72; assoc dir, Calif State Univ Northridge Art Gallery, 72-80, dir, 80-. *Teaching:* Asst prof, Calif State Univ, Northridge, 72-79, assoc prof, 79-83, prof art hist, 83-, interdisciplinary humanities prog, 90-96. *Mem:* Art Table. *Res:* Art and the media. *Specialty:* International & Contemporary Art. *Publ:* Auth, California Video in Xle Biennale de Paris, Mus d'Art Mod, 80; Future Video: Max Almy, LAICA Journal, 83; Where Art the Daumiers of Video Art, Media Arts, 85; Generation of Mentors, Nat Mus Women, 94; Pattsi Valdez, Private Landscapes, 98; Lili Lapich: Sirens and other Neon Seductions, 2001; Free Range: Seven Los Angeles Artists, 2003. *Mailing Add:* California State Univ/Northridge Art Gallery 18111 Nordhoff St Northridge CA 91330-8299

LEWIS, MARCIA
JEWELER-METALSMITH, INSTRUCTOR
b Washington, DC, Oct 7, 46. *Study:* Corcoran Sch, Washington, DC; San Diego Univ, Calif; Calif State Univ, Long Beach. *Work:* Mus Contemp Crafts, NY; Oakland Mus Art; Renwick Gallery Mus Am Art, Smithsonian Inst. *Exhib:* Int Handwerks Messe, Munich, Ger 71; Am Metalsmiths, DeCordova Mus, Lincoln, Mass, 73; Kunstindustri Mus, Copenhagen, Denmark, 73; Goldsmiths 74, Smithsonian Inst, Washington, DC, 74; Crafts of the NAmericas, Colo State Univ & Smithsonian Inst, 75; Calif Design 12, Los Angeles, 76. *Pos:* Apprentice goldsmith, Ingrid Hansen, Zurich, Switz, 71-72; asst silversmith, Tony Laws Studio Ltd, Londin, Eng, 72-73. *Teaching:* Instr metalsmithing & gen crafts, Univ Wis, Whitewater, 73-75 & San Jose State Univ, Calif, 75-76; assoc prof art, Long Beach City Col, Calif, 78-. *Awards:* Sterling Silversmiths Award, Design Competition, Silversmiths Guild, 69; George C Marshall Mem Fel, Denmark-Amerika Fondet, 72; Nat Endowment Arts Award, Washington, DC, 76. *Bibliog:* Beverly Edna Johnson (auth), Biographical, Los Angeles Times Home Mag, 72; Thelma Newman (auth), Containers, Crown Publ, 77; Oppi Untracht (auth), Jewelry Techniques for Craftsmen, Doubleday, 78. *Mem:* Soc NAm Goldsmiths. *Media:* Metal. *Publ:* Auth, Wearable aluminum ornaments, Calif State Univ, Long Beach, 77. *Mailing Add:* Dept Art Long Beach City Col 4901 E Carson St Long Beach CA 90808

LEWIS, MARY
SCULPTOR
b Multnomah, Ore, Jun 18, 26. *Study:* Univ Oreg, with Mark Sponenburgh, 45-50, BS(sculpture), 49; Oreg Div Am Asn Univ Women Mabel Merwin fel, 50, Syracuse Univ, with Ivan Mestrovic, 50, tech asst to Mestrovic, 51-53, MFA, 53. *Work:* Obadiah (4' mahogany and copper bird), Skunk Cabbage (marble), Waterbury Club, Waterbury, Conn, 64; Mother and Son (lifesize, rosewood) & alder tabernacle door, St John Medical Ctr, Longview, Wash, 84; The Resurrection (bronze relief), St Stephen's Episcopal Church, Columbarium, Longview, Wash, 91; Descent of the Holy Spirit (bronze relief, aumbry door), Trinity Cathedral Church, Sacramento, Calif, 96. *Comn:* Madonna and Child (4' diamenter maple relief) St Joseph's Church Chapel, Roseburg, Ore, 78; The Holy Family (maple relief), St Frederic's Church, St Helens, Oreg, 85; Mysteries of the Rosary (15 bronze reliefs), Peace Garden, The Grotto, Portland, Oreg, 89; Five Symbolic Bronze Reliefs, garden, St John Med Ctr, Longview, Wash, 2000; The Luminous Mysteries of the Rosary (5 additional bronze reliefs) Peace Garden, The Grotto, Portland, Ore, 2005. *Exhib:* Artists of Oregon, Portland Art Mus, 51 & 69; 12th & 14th Ann New Eng Exhibs, Silvermine Guild Artists, New Canaan, Conn, 61 & 63; 62nd & 63rd Ann Exhib, New Haven Paint & Clay Club, John Slade Ely Ctr, New Haven, 63 & 64; Solo exhib, Liturgical Arts, Invitational Exhib, Marylhurst Col, Oreg, 84; Gallery Genesis, Chicago, Ill, 88; Works of Faith, First Presbyterian Church Gallery, Portland, Oreg, 97, 98 & 2005; Gifts of the Spirit invitational, First Presbyterian Church Gallery, Portland, Oreg, 97, 99; Retrospective: 1944-2000, Fine Arts Gallery, Lower Columbia Col, Longview, Wash; plus others. *Pos:* Staff artist, GAF Corp Photo Div, Portland, Ore, 70-76. *Teaching:* Asst prof art, Nat Col Arts, Lahore, Pakistan, 58-60. *Awards:* Tiffany Traveling Scholar, 53; Fulbright Lectr, 58 & 59; Fel, Nat Col Arts, Liahore, Pakistan, 98. *Bibliog:* Virginia Watson-Jones (auth), Contemporary American Women Sculptors, (illus), Oryx Press, 86,; Featuring The Little Yellow Dinosaur and artist, Stereo World, Nat Stereoscopic Asn Inc, vol 28, number 2, 2001; Arthur Williams (auth), The Sculpture Reference (illus), 2004; Cathy Zimmerman (auth), Mary's Legacy, The Daily News, 9/25/2005. *Media:* Wood, Stone. *Publ:* Coauth & illusr, The Little Yellow Dinosaur, 71, illusr, In the Beginning--the Bible Story of Creation, Adam & Eve, Cain & Abel, 72, Jesus Christ, His Youth, Disciples, Miracles, 75, GAF View-Master; illusr, Beginning Sculpture, 2004; illusr, The Sculpture Reference, 2005. *Mailing Add:* 74394 Wortman Rd Rainier OR 97048

LEWIS, MICHAEL H
PAINTER, EDUCATOR
b Brooklyn, NY, Aug 10, 41. *Study:* State Univ NY Col, New Paltz, painting with Ben Bishop, George Wexler & Ilya Bolotowsky, BS, 63, MFA, 75; Mich State Univ, MA, 64. *Work:* Fogg Mus Art, Harvard Univ; Albertina Mus, Vienna, Austria; Portland Mus Art, Maine; Art Bank Prog, U.S. Dept of State, Washington D.C.; Colby Col Mus Art, Waterville, Maine. *Comn:* Oil portrait, comn by Edmund S Muskie, 83; cover paintings for The Magus of Strovolos, Homage to the Sun, Fire in the Heart and the Mountain of Science (all by Kyriacos Markides), 86, 87, 90, 01; 6 Paintings, comn by Colby Col Miller Libr, Waterville, Maine, 97. *Exhib:* Solo shows, Uptown Gallery, NY, 80, 88, 91, 93, 95, 97, 00, 03, Steven Scott Gallery, Owings Mills, Md, 94, 98, Aucocisco Gallery, Portland, Maine, 2003, 2004;, Univ Mo, St Louis, 96, Colby Col Mus Art, Waterville, Maine, 00; Group shows, Fogg Art Mus, Harvard Univ, 87-89, 93, Vose Art Gallery, Boston, Mass, 2000, 2003, 2004; Aucocisco Gallery, Portland, Maine, 03, 04, 06; Steven Scott Gallery, Owings Mills, Md, 92-98, 99, 2000-2006; Portland Mus Art Biennal, Maine, 98-99; and others. *Pos:* Mem, Maine Arts Comn, 72-78, visual arts adv panel, 79-81, adv panel roster, 94-2004. *Teaching:* Instr art, Kingston City Pub Schs, NY, 64-66; prof painting & drawing, Univ Maine, Orono, 66-, chmn, Dept Art, 75-81, acting assoc dean col arts & sci, 81-83, chmn, Dept Art, 87-93. *Awards:* Video Work of Art Grant, Maine State Arts Comn & Maine Pub Broadcasting Network, 83; New Eng Found Arts/Nat Endowment Arts-Regional Fel, Visual Artists (drawing), 90-91. *Bibliog:* Alicia Anstead (auth), Artist Explores Winter in Orono in Colby Show, Bangor Daily News, 1/27/00; Phillip Isaacson (auth) Art Review, Maine Sunday Telegram, 5/9/2004; Kristen Andresen (auth), Michael Lewis' Landscapes Plumb Deeper Regions, Bangor Daily News, 2/7/06; Bob Keyes (auth), Michael Lewis Sees the Light, Maine Sunday Telegram, 6/11/06. *Mem:* Maine Arts Comn (contemp artist devel prog comt, 99-2004). *Media:* Turpentine Wash (with Oils), Video. *Dealer:* Steve Williams Uptown Gallery 1194 Madison Ave New York NY 10128; Steven Scott Gallery 9169 Reisterstown Rd Owings Mills MD 21117; Andy Verzosa Ancocisco Gallery, 157 High St, P.O. Box 4111, Portland, Maine. *Mailing Add:* 104 Bennoch Rd Orono ME 04473

LEWIS, NAT BRUSH
PAINTER, INSTRUCTOR
b Boston, Mass, Dec 17, 25. *Study:* Pembroke Col, Brown Univ & RI Sch Design, AB; Art Students League; watercolor with Mario Cooper; also with Henry Gasser Art. *Work:* Am Asn Univ Women, Somerset Hills, NJ; Bloomfield Art League, NJ; Bergen Mus Arts & Sci; Zhejiang Mus, China. *Exhib:* Am Watercolor Soc, NY; Am Artists Prof League Grand Nat; Salmagundi Club Exhib; Hudson Valley Art Asn; Philadelphia Watercolor Club; and others. *Pos:* artist in residence, Hillside High Sch, NJ. *Teaching:* Adj prof art, Seton Hall Univ, 84-. *Awards:* Int Exhib Award, Philadelphia Watercolor Soc, 95-2000, Crest Award, 99; Grambacher Hall of Fame, 97. *Mem:* NJ Watercolor Soc (pres, 73-75); Am Artists Prof League; Hudson Valley Art Asn; Philadelphia Water Color Soc. *Media:* Watercolor, Oil. *Publ:* Palette Talk Mag, 83 & 97; Watercolor, Am Artist Publ, spring 93; The Best of Watercolor II & Painting Light and Shadow, Rockport Publ, 97; The Collected Best of Watercolor, 2002. *Mailing Add:* PO Box 187 Port Clyde ME 04855

LEWIS, PETER BENJAMIN
COLLECTOR
b Cleveland, Ohio, Nov 11, 33. *Study:* Princeton Univ, AB, 55. *Pos:* pres, chief exec off, The Progressive Corp, Ohio, 65-2000, Mayfield Village, 65-94, chmn bd, 2000; trustee, Solomon R Guggenheim Mus, 93, chmn, 98. *Awards:* Named one of the Top 200 Collectors, ARTnews Mag, 2004. *Collection:* Contemporary art including American conceptual art. *Mailing Add:* Progressive Corp 6300 Wilson Mills Rd Cleveland OH 44143

LEWIS, RONALD WALTER
PAINTER, EDUCATOR
b Atlanta, Ga, Jan 27, 45. *Study:* Ala Col, BS(art & bus), 67. *Work:* Birmingham Mus Art, Ala; Fayette Art Mus, Ala; Jefferson State Col, Birmingham; Sylacauga Mus, Ala; Columbus Mus, Calif; Fine Art Mus of South, Mobile, Ala. *Exhib:* Ala Watercolor Soc, Birmingham Mus Art, 71-77; Dixieland Watercolor & Drawing Show, Montgomery Mus Art, Ala, 73; Watercolor USA, Springfield Art Mus, Mo, 73-74; Rocky Mountain Nat Watercolor, Golden, Colo, 76; Mainstreams, Marietta Col, Ohio, 76-77; Southern Watercolor Soc, Nashville, Tenn, 77; and others. *Teaching:* adj fac, Univ Montevallo. *Awards:* One hundred awards including Ala Watercolor Soc & Southern Watercolor Soc. *Bibliog:* Stevens (auth), Ronald Lewis Paintings, La Revue Mod, Paris, 9/73. *Mem:* Ala Watercolor Soc (vpres, 73-74); Birmingham Art Asn (mem bd, 76-); Southern Watercolor Soc; Am Watercolor Soc; signature mem, Am Watercolor Soc. *Media:* Miscellaneous Media. *Publ:* Illusr, My Country Roads & Pappa's Old Trunk, 11/81, Buck Publ Co; Birmingham Mag, 7/83; Southern Accents Mag, winter 83; Artist's Mag, 4/90; Am ARtist Mag, 3/97. *Dealer:* Dumonde Fine Art New York; Bryant Gallery New Orleans LA. *Mailing Add:* 2728 Ossa Wintha Dr Birmingham AL 35243

LEWIS, SAMELLA SANDERS
PAINTER, HISTORIAN
b New Orleans, La, Feb 27, 24. *Study:* Hampton Inst, BS; Ohio State Univ, MA & PhD; Tunghai Univ, Taiwan; Fulbright fel, 62; Univ Southern Calif, 64-66; NY Univ Inst Fine Arts, 65; Hampton Univ, Va, LHD, 90. *Work:* Oakland Mus, Calif; Baltimore Mus Fine Arts; Va Mus Fine Arts, Richmond; High Mus, Atlanta, Ga; Atlanta Univ Mus Contemp Art. *Exhib:* Joseph Hirshhorn Collection, Palm Springs Mus, 69; Dimensions of Black, La Jolla Mus Art, 70; Two Generations of Black Artists, Calif State Univ, Los Angeles, 70; Smithsonian Inst Traveling Print Exhibs, 80-83; Print Club Invitational, Philadelphia, Pa, 83. *Collection Arranged:* Media, Style & Tradition - The California Artists, 81 & Wildlife Sculpture, A Bayou Heritage, 82, Calif Mus Afro-Am Hist & Cult; Artist-teachers, Univ Southern Calif, Santa Monica Place, 83; African Images in the New World, Los Angeles Calif, 83; Richard Hunt: Sculptures & Drawings, 86 & Jacob Lawrence: Paintings & Drawings, 89-91, Arts Am. *Pos:* Coordr educ, Los Angeles Co Mus Art, 69-70; ed-in-chief, Int Rev African-Am Art, 85; pres, Oxum Int, 87; art ed, Black Art Mag, 78. *Teaching:* Prof fine arts & head dept, Fla A&M Univ, 53-58; prof humanitics & art hist, State Univ NY, 58-68; prof art hist,

Scripps Col, 69, emer prof, 84-. *Awards:* NY State-Ford Found Grant, 65; Ford Found Research Grant, 81-82; Prof of Yr Award, Scripps Col, 84; Honor Award, Women's Caucus Art, 89. *Bibliog:* The Black Artists (film), Afrographics, 68; Focus, KNBC-TV, 68; article, Los Angeles Times, 70. *Mem:* Col Art Asn Am; Nat Conf Artists (co-chairperson, 70-73). *Res:* African, Asian and Afro-American art. *Collection:* Rare African works, including Bakuba in the 1890's; Caribbean and African-American Works. *Publ:* Co-ed, Black Artists on Art, Vols I & II, 69 & 71; auth, Art: African American (textbk), Harcourt, 76; The Art of Elizabeth Catlett, Mus African Am Art, 84. *Dealer:* Alan S Lewis & Associates Fine Arts. *Mailing Add:* 1237 Masselin Ave Los Angeles CA 90019-2544

LEWIS, STANLEY
SCULPTOR, PRINTMAKER

b Montreal, Que, Mar 28, 30. *Study:* Montreal Mus Fine Arts, 48-51; Inst Allende, San Miguel, Mex, scholars, 52-55; Elizabeth T Greenshields Mem Found grant, Florence, Italy, 56-59. *Work:* Nat Gallery Can, Ottawa; Montreal Mus Fine Arts; Jerusalem Mus, Israel; Samuel Zacks Collection; Primal Portraits (5 stone cut prints), Los Angeles Mus Natural Hist; and others. *Comn:* Sleeping Spirit (lava boulder), 53, standing nude (white marble), 53 & The Corngrinder (gray marble), 54, Inst Allende; late Samuel Bronfman, Can Jewish Cong, 66. *Exhib:* One-man shows, Montreal Mus Fine Arts, 52 & 59, Israel Art Auction Gallery, Tel Aviv, 65 & Nat Gallery Can, 71; Atelier J Lukacs, Montreal, 75, 76 & 78. *Teaching:* Instr sculpture, McGill Univ Sch Archit, 52, Montreal Mus Fine Arts, 61-63 & Saidye Bronfman Art Ctr, Montreal, 61-; lectr, The Eskimo Artist, Nat Film Bd, Montreal, 75. *Awards:* Prize, Concours Artistiques, Que, 59. *Bibliog:* Peter Olwyer (auth), article, Can Art, fall 55; Earle Birney (auth), article, Sat Night, 55; Folch (auth), article, Vie Arts, summer 59. *Mem:* Founding mem Que Sculptors' Asn; hon rep Int Acad Leonardo da Vinci. *Media:* Stone. *Res:* Contributed original research on Michelangelo's childhood and marble carving techniques to writing of Irving Stone's The Agony and the Ecstasy. *Publ:* Auth, The Stone Speaks, 53; Hands to Create Wonders, 61; Space, Man and Stone, 69

LEWIS, WILLIAM ARTHUR
PAINTER, EDUCATOR

b Detroit, Mich, Mar 20, 18. *Study:* Col Archit & Design, Univ Mich, BDesign, 48. *Work:* Butler Inst Am Art, Youngstown; Grand Rapids Mus Art; Univ Mich St Paul Art Ctr & Mus Art; Grinnell Col; and others. *Comn:* Acrylic paintings, Soc Mfg Engrs, Dearborn, Mich, 71 & Grand Rapids Jr Col, 86; Watercolor series, McNary Sr Serv Ctr, Detroit, 87; three portraits, 1st Unitarian Church, Ann Arbor, Mich, 90; watercolor, Sundew, Coast Guard Tender, T Dickenson Collection, Ann Arbor, 94; watercolor, Zeppelin L24 over Landau, P Reusch Zeppelin Collection, Findlay, Ohio, 96; watercolor (steel indus), Pro Coil Col, Canton, Mich, 98. *Exhib:* Five Ann Exhibs, Butler Inst Am Art, 54-65, 99; Drawing USA, Mus Mod Art, 56; Corcoran Gallery Biennial, Washington, & Am Fedn Art Tour, 57; one-man show, The Last Yr of the Civil War, Detroit Hist Soc, Mint Mus, Madison Col, Va, Eastern Mich Univ, Dearborn Hist Mus & others, 62-65 & An Art Student in US Navy 1941-45, 43 watercolors & drawings, Clements Libr Am Hist Univ Mich, 95; Drawing USA, St Paul Art Ctr, 63 & 66; Romance of Transportation, 2 paintings, invited, Mich Art Train, 93-95; One Man's View: WWII through eyes of Bill Lewis (50 paintings, drawings), US Navy Hist Ctr, Washington, DC, 97. *Pos:* Assoc dean, Sch Art, Univ Mich, Ann Arbor, 66-75 & 84-85; dir, Comn Accreditation, Nat Asn Schs Art, 72-75; chief reader, Advanced Placement Studio Art, Col Bd-ETS, 78-81. *Teaching:* Prof art, Sch Art, Univ Mich, Ann Arbor, 57-86, prof emer, 85. *Awards:* Rackham Sch Grad Studies Fac Res Grants for Last Year of the Civil War, 60-62; JMW Turner, 64; Distinguished Alumnus, Univ Mich Sch Art, 93. *Bibliog:* Hazen Schumacher (auth), The Painting Professor, Univ Mich TV Studios, 62; Louise Bruner (auth), Feelings of an artist, Toledo Blade, 64; Joanne Nesbit (auth), War Painter, Univ Record, Univ Mich, 95. *Mem:* Fel Nat Asn Schs Art & Design; Mich Watercolor Soc. *Media:* Watercolor, Acrylics. *Publ:* Auth & illusr, The Civil War--A contemporary approach, Dimension, spring 62; illusr, cover & article, Limnos, summer 69. *Dealer:* Preston Burke Gallery Inc 30448 Woodward Ave Royal Oak Mich 48073; River Gallery 121 Main St Chelsea MI 48118. *Mailing Add:* 2550 Traver Blvd Ann Arbor MI 48105

LEWIS, WILLIAM R
INSTRUCTOR, PAINTER

b Osceola, Iowa, Sept 23, 20. *Study:* Drake Univ, BFA, 49; Univ Wash; Ariz State Univ, MA, 52. *Work:* Ariz Western Col, Yuma; Glendale Community Col, Ariz; Scottsdale Civic Ctr, Ariz; Valley Nat Bank, Phoenix, Ariz; Thunderbird Bank, Phoenix, Ariz; Southwest Savs, Phoenix, Ariz. *Exhib:* Ariz Ann, Phoenix Art Mus, 61-68; Butler Art Mus Ann Midyear Show, 62; Am Watercolor Soc Ann, 63-65; Southwestern Invitational, Yuma, 67-72; Watercolor USA Traveling Show, 68. *Teaching:* Chmn dept art, S Mountain High Sch, Phoenix, 54-81. *Awards:* Ariz Ann First in Watercolor, Phoenix Art Mus, 62. *Mem:* Ariz Watercolor Asn (pres, 63-64). *Media:* Watercolor. *Interests:* Collecting Jukeboxes and Radios. *Publ:* Prizewinning Watercolors, 64. *Mailing Add:* 313 E 15th St Tempe AZ 85281-6611

LE WITT, SOL
PAINTER

b Hartford, Conn, Sept 9, 28. *Study:* Syracuse Univ, BFA, 49. *Work:* Stedelijk Mus, Amsterdam, Holland; Albright-Knox Art Gallery, Buffalo, NY; Art Gallery Ont, Toronto; Los Angeles Co Mus Art, Los Angeles, Calif; Mus Mod Art, NY; also many international museums. *Comn:* Indoor structure, Port Authority Allegheny Co, Pittsburgh, Pa, 84; outdoor structure, Art in Public Places, Chicago, Ill, 85; lobby floor, Theatre Royal de la Monnaie, Brussels, Belgium, 86; wall drawings, Equitable Hq, NY, 85 & Bankers Trust, London, Eng, 88; Disney Develop Women Co, Orlando, 91. *Exhib:* Sculpture Ann, Whitney Mus Am Art, NY, 67; Guggenheim Mus & Mus Mod Art, 71, Walker Art Ctr, 72 & 88, NY; San Francisco Mus Art, 75; Retrospective traveling exhib, Mus Mod Art (exhib catalog), NY, Mus Contemp Art, Montreal, Krannert Mus, Champaign, Mus Contemp Art, Chicago & La Jolla Mus, Calif, 78-79; Wall Drawings 1968-1981, Wadsworth Atheneum, Hartford & Paula Cooper Gallery, NY, 81; Wall Drawings & Structures, Stedelijk Mus, (exhib catalog), Amsterdam, 84; Drawings 1958-1992, Haags Gemeentemuseum, 92; and many other one-man & group shows. *Teaching:* Instr, Mus Mod Art Sch, 64-67 & Cooper Union, 67. *Bibliog:* EC Goosen (auth), The Art of the Real USA 1948-1968, Mus Mod Art, 68; Lucy R Lippard (auth), Minimal Art, Haags Gemeentemuseum, 68; Susanna Singer (auth), Sol LeWitt Wall Drawing, Kunsthalle, Bern, 92; and others. *Publ:* Auth, I am still alive: On Kawara, Studio Int, 70; Sentences on conceptual art, 7/71 & Sol Le Witt, 6/73, Flash Art, Milan; All wall drawings, Arts Mag, 2/72; Sentences on conceptual art, Uber Kunst, Cologne, WGer, 74; Lines in Two Directions & in Five Colors with All Their Combinations, Walker Art Ctr, 88. *Mailing Add:* c/o Susanna Singer 50 Riverside Dr New York NY 10024

LEWTON, VAL EDWIN
PAINTER, DESIGNER

b Santa Monica, Calif, 37. *Study:* Claremont Univ, Calif, MFA, 62. *Work:* Smithsonian Am Art Mus; Corcoran Gallery, Washington, DC; and others. *Comn:* Air shaft mural, DC Art Works, 88. *Exhib:* Ten Plus Ten, Corcoran Gallery Art, 82; The Washington Show, Corcoran Gallery Art, 85; From the Anacostia to the Potomac, WPA, Wash, 89; one-man shows, Plum Gallery, Kensington, Md, 83-85, Addison Ripley, Washington, 90, 93 & 99. *Collection Arranged:* Exhibition Designer for Robert Rauschenburg Retrospective, Nat Mus Am Art, 76; Decorative Designs of Frank Lloyd Wright, Renwick Gallery, 77; The Masterpieces of Louis Comfort Tiffany, Renwick Gallery, 89; Americans in Paris, The Phillips Collection, 96; Calder-Miro the Phillips Col, 2004; and others. *Pos:* Chief design & production, Nat Mus Am Art-Smithsonian Inst, 73-95. *Teaching:* Lectr art, Univ Calif, Riverside, 62-63 & Georgetown Univ, Washington, DC, 81-. *Awards:* Best in Exhib Design, Print Casebooks, 91-92. *Bibliog:* Harry Rand (auth), The watercolors of Val Lewton, Arts Mag, 5/80; and others. *Mem:* Am Asn of Mus. *Media:* Acrylic, Watercolor. *Publ:* Auth, Washington Review (column), 75-. *Dealer:* Addison Ripley Gallery 1670 Wisconsin Ave NW Washington DC 20007. *Mailing Add:* 1425 Manchester Ln Washington DC 20001

LEXIER, MICAH
SCULPTOR

b Winnipeg, Man, Nov 13, 60. *Study:* Univ Man, Winnipeg, BFA, 82; Nova Scotia Col Art & Design, Halifax, MFA, 84. *Work:* Art Gallery Ont, Toronto; Jewish Mus, NY; Vancouver Art Gallery, BC; The British Mus, London, England; Mus Contemp Art, Sydney, Aus; Nat Gallery Canada, Ottawa. *Comn:* Metro Hall, Toronto, 1992; Nat Trade Centre, Toronto, 97; Air Canada Centre, Toronto, 98; Agnes Etherington Art Ctr, Queens Univ, Kingston, Ontario, 1999; Toronto Transit Comn, Shepard/Leslie Subway Station, 00. *Exhib:* Un-Natural Traces, Barbican Art Gallery, London 91; Perspective 93, Art Gallery Ont, Toronto, 93; The Body as Measure, Davis Mus & Cult Ctr, Wellesley, Mass, 94; The Riddle of the Sphinx, Islip Art Mus, NY, 94; Alliances: The Family, Can Mus Contemp Photog, Ottawa, Ont, 94; Das Americas 11, Museu du Arte, de Sao Paulo, Brazil, 95; solo exhib, Open Studio Gallery, Toronto, Ont, 98, Robert Birch Gallery, Toronto, Ont, 98, McDonald Stewart Art Centre, Guelph (with catalog), 98, Charles H Scott Gallery, Emily Carr Inst Art & Design (with catalog), Vancouver, BC, 98, Dunlop Art Gallery (with catalog), Regina, Saskatchewan, 98, Musee de Art Contemp de Montreal, Quebec, 98. Trepanier Baer Gallery, Calgary, Whyte Mus Can Rockies, Banff, Alberta, Gitte Weise Gallery, Sydney, 99, Jack Shainman Gallery, NY, 99, Robert Birtch Gallery, Toronto, 2000, Agnes, Etherington Art Ctr Queen's U, Kingston, Ont, 2000, I Space Gallery Univ Ill, Chicago, 2000, Hallwalls, Buffalo, NY, 2000, Gitte Weise Gallery, Sydney, 2001, Gallery 111, (CD ROM), Univ Manitoba, Winnipeg, 2002, Jack Shainman Gallery, NY, 2003 & 05, Dazibao, Montreal, Quebec, 2004, Contemp Art Gallery, Vancouver, 2005, Michael Gibson Gallery, London, Ontario, 2006, Gitte Weise Galerie, Berlin, Germ, 2005 & 06; The World According to the Newest and Most Exact Observations, Tang Tchg Mus and Art Gallery, 2001; Light X Eight, The Jewish Mus, New York City, 2000; The Time of Our Lives, New Mus of Contemp Art, 1999; Making the Making, Apex Art, NY (brochure); Size Immaterial, Castle Mus, Norwich, Eng; Instant Criticism of Illusionism, Agnes Etherington Art Ctr, Kingston, Ontario; Open, Arcadia Univ Art Gallery, Glenside, Pa, 2004; Free Sample, Mt St Vincent Univ Art Gallery, Halifax, NS (catalogue), 2005; Funny Papers, Winnipeg Art Gallery, 2006. *Pos:* Bd mem, Eye Level Gallery, Halifax, NS, 84-86; organizer, Audio By Artists Festival, 84-86; bd mem, Power Plant, Toronto, 91-95. *Bibliog:* Robin Metcalfe (auth), Cross Reference, Confederation Ctr Art Gallery, 94; Michele Theriault (auth), Perspective 93, Art Gallery Ont, 93; M Fleming & N Tousley (auths), Book Sculpture, Oakville Galleries, 93; Sarah Milroy (auth), The art of brick and mortar, The Globe and Mail, Toronto, 11/3/2001; Eric Fredericksen (auth), Brick by Brick, Architecture Mag, NY, 3/2002; Michael Petry, Nicola Oxley & Nicolas de Oliveria (auths) Installation Art in the New Millennium, Thames & Hudson, 2003; Jerome Delgado (auth), Espaces Manipules, La Press, Montreal, Quebec, 10/21/2004; Christian Bok (auth), Still Counting, Canadian Art, (vol 22 no 1) Toronto, Ontario, Spring 2005; Gil McElroy, A Moment of Our Time: The Sculpture of Micah Lexier, Espace Sculpture (Issue #76), Montreal, Summer 2006. *Mem:* The Art Gallery of York Univ, Toronto, 1997 & 98 (bd mem); The Power Plant, Toronto, 1991-95 (bd mem); Eye Level Gallery, Halifax, 1984-86 (bd mem). *Media:* Sculpture. *Publ:* Co-ed (with Don Lander) Sound by artists, Art Metropole & Walter Phillips Gallery, spring 90; Making, Impulse, Vol 16, No 1, 91; Love Letters, Public 10, 94; An Artist & Books, Descant 90, The Book: Twenty Five Anniv, Part One, Vol 23, No 3, 95; A Minute of My Time, Gallery Largeness, Issue No 2, 10/96; If Then, Atopia Journal (issue 0.66), 2/2000; 9,

10, 11 Defile Vol 1 issue 1, Spring 2003; Lives & Works (4 consec texts), YYZ Mag, 5/2006. *Dealer:* Jack Shainman Gallery 560 Broadway 2nd Floor New York NY 10012; Birch Libralato 129 Tecumseth St Toronto Ontario M6J2H2; Trepanier Baer Gallery Suite 105 999 8th St SW Calgary Alberta T2R1J5; Gitte Weise Galerie Linienstrasse 154 Berlin Ger 10115

LEYRER, SHIRLEY D See Dani

LEYS, DALE DANIEL
EDUCATOR, DRAFTSMAN
b Sheboygan, Wis, Dec 10, 52. *Study:* Yale Univ, 73; Layton Sch Art, Milwaukee, BFA, 74; Univ Wis, Madison, MA, 75, MFA, 77. *Work:* Evansville Mus Arts & Sci, Ind; Kentucky Fried Chicken, Louisville, Ky; A B Chandler Med Ctr, Lexington, Ky; Hyatt Regency Hotel, Frankfort, Ky; Hospital Corp Am, Nashville, Tenn; Budd Co, Shellbyville, Ky; Univ Ky, Mus Art; Nationsbank, Charlotte, NC. *Exhib:* Evansville Mus Arts & Sci, Ind, 77, 78 & 80; Ball State Univ Art Gallery, Muncie, Ind, 78 & 83; Rutgers Univ, NJ, 80; Greenville Mus, SC, 81; Davenport Mus, Iowa, 81; J B Speed Art Mus, Louisville, Ky, 82; Cheekwood Fine Arts Ctr, Nashville, Tenn, 84; Nat Drawing Invitational, Univ Tenn, Knoxville, 84 & Wake Forest Univ, Winston-Salem, NC, 88; Canton Art Inst, Ohio, 86; Univ SC, Columbia, 87; Univ Ark, Little Rock, 88; Marshall Univ, Huntington, WVa, 89; Dale Leys Recent Drawing, Heike Pickett Gallery, Lexington, Ky, 90; Univ Mo, Columbia, 92; Springfield Art Mus, Mo, 92. *Teaching:* Prof drawing, Murray State Univ, 77-. *Awards:* Drawing Award, State Univ NY, Potsdam, 77; Graphics Award, Mid States Exhib, Evansville Mus, 80; Purchase Award, Appalachian State Univ, Boone, NC, 83; 1986 Regional Competitive Exhib Award, Paducah, Ky, 86; Drawing Excellence Award, All Ky Art Exhibit, Lexington. *Bibliog:* Jerry Spieght (auth), Dale Leys: Ideas and his work, Sch Arts, 78 & Dale Leys, Art Voices S, 78; Dialogue Mag, 90; Art Papers, 91. *Media:* Mixed Media. *Mailing Add:* 1313 Lawson Ln Murray KY 42071-8203

LEYVA, ALICIA
PAINTER
b Mexico City, Mex, July 7, 22. *Study:* Univ Nac de Mex; studies with Agapito Rincon Piña, 56-57; Inst Art de Mex, with Alfredo Guati Rojo, Erasto Leon Zurita & Manuel Arrieta, 72-74; studies with Fernando Casas, 77-79. *Work:* Patio de los Siete Príncipes, Oaxaca, Mex; Mus de la Zaragoza Alancón, Spain; Embajada de Mex, Madrid, Spain; Consulado de Mex, NY; La Pinacoteca de la Escuela Nac Preparatoria, Mexico City, Mex. *Comn:* Poster, Mex Red Cross. *Exhib:* Group exhibs throughout Mexico, 57-94; 31 solo exhibs, 69-94. *Teaching:* Imitation drawing, Inst Lestonac & Inst Asunción de Mex, formerly; art hist, Escuela Normal de Maestros; conferences & classes for 20 years. *Awards:* Medalla Sor, Juana Inés de la Cruz; Medalla Miembro, Fundador de las Bellas Artes de Mex; Pincel de Plata, Soc Acuarelistas. *Mem:* Soc Mexicana de Acuarelistas; Agrupación de Cataluña; Ky Watercolor Soc; AIPE-UNESCO. *Media:* Printed Literature. *Publ:* Illusr, History of Mexico, 58; Fomento Cultural de México; Artes de México, Arts & Artists Mag. *Mailing Add:* 3ra Cerrada San Bernabé No 42 San Jeronimo 10100 Mexico

LHOTKA, BONNY PIERCE
PAINTER
b La Grange, Ill, July 14, 42. *Study:* Bradley Univ, BFA, 64. *Work:* United Banks, Rocky Mountain Energy, Midland Savings & Loan, Denver; First Nat Bank, Boise; Nat Conf State Legislations, Charles Swabb, IBM, US West United Air Lines, Johnson Space Ctr, Mariott Hotels. *Exhib:* Allied Artists Am, Nat Acad Design, NY, 74, 76 & 77; Nat Watercolor Soc, Palm Springs Desert Mus, Calif, 74-81; Am Watercolor Soc, Nat Acad Design, 77; Nat Acad Design Exhib, 77, 79 & 81; One-man show, Wyo State Art Gallery, Cheyenne, 79. *Teaching:* Instr abstract watermedia & acrylic, Colo Watercolor Soc, summer 77 & Colo Artist Workshops, summer 78. *Awards:* First Nat Top Ten, Am Artist Mag, 78; Strathmore Awards, Strathmore Paper Co, 79; Century Award of Merit, Rocky Mountain Watermedia Exhib, 81. *Mem:* Nat Watercolor Soc; Audubon Artists; Nat Soc Painters in Casein & Acrylics; Rocky Mountain Nat Watermedia Soc. *Media:* Watermedia; Acrylic. *Publ:* Contribr, Watercolor page, Am Artist Mag, 77; Watercolor, The Creative Experience by Nochis, North Light, 79; article, Southwest Art Mag,3/81; Creative Seascape Painting, Watson Guptill; The Guild 5, 6 & 7, Kraus Sikes Inc, Madison, Wis, 90-92. *Dealer:* Ruth Bachofnen Gallery 1926 Colorado Ave Santa Monica CA 90401. *Mailing Add:* c/o Jack Meier Gallery 2310 Bissonnet Houston TX 77005

LI, CHU-TSING
HISTORIAN
b Canton, China, May 26, 20; US citizen. *Study:* Univ Nanking, China, BA (Eng lit), 43; Univ Iowa, MA(Eng), 49, PhD(art hist), 55; post-doctoral res, Harvard Univ, 59 & Princeton Univ, 60. *Pos:* Res cur, Nelson-Atkins Mus Art, Kansas City, 68-; vis prof fine arts, Chinese Univ, Hong Kong, 71-73, Grad Inst Art Hist, Nat Taiwan Univ, Taipei, 90-91; Andrew W Mellon vis prof fine arts, Univ Pittsburgh, Pa, 95. *Teaching:* From instr to prof art hist, Univ Iowa, Iowa City, 54-66; prof Oriental art, Univ Kans, Lawrence, 66-90, chmn, Dept Hist Art, 72-78, Judith Harris Murphy Distinguished prof art hist, 78-90; Judith Harris Murphy Distinguished Prof Art His Emer, 90-. *Awards:* Phi Tau Phi (Chinese Scholastic Hon Soc), Phi Beta Kappa (hon), Phi Beta Delta (Hon Soc Int Scholars). *Mem:* Col Art Asn; Midwest Art Hist Soc; Asn Asian Studies. *Res:* Chinese painting of the Sung, Yuan, Ming, Ch'ing, and Modern Period. *Publ:* Auth, The Autumn Colors on the Ch'iao and Hua Mountains, 65 & A Thousand Peaks and Myriad Ravines: Drenwatz Collection, 74, Artibus Asiae; Liu Kuo-sung, Development of a Modern Chinese Artist, 69 & contribr, Five Chinese Painters: Fifth Moon Exhibition, 70, Nat Gallery Art, Taipei, Taiwan; auth, Trends in modern Chinese painting, Artibus Asiae, 79; ed, Chinese Scholar's Studio: Artistic Life in the Late Ming Period, London: Thames and Hudson, 87; ed, Artists and Patrons: Some Social and Economic Aspects of Chinese Painting, Seattle: Univ Wash Press, 89. *Mailing Add:* Univ Kans Lawrence KS 66045

LI-LAN
PAINTER
b New York, NY, Jan 28, 43. *Study:* HS Performing Arts, New York, NY. *Work:* Guild Hall Mus, E Hampton, NY; Ohara Mus Art, Kurashiki, Japan; Parrish Art Mus, Southampton, NY; William Benton Mus Art, Storrs, Conn; Heckscher Mus, Huntington, NY; The Sezou Mus Art, Japan; Va Mus Fine Arts, Richmond; Weatherspoon Art Gallery, Univ NC, Greensboro; Ark Arts Ctr, Little Rock; Werner Kramarsky Col, NY. *Exhib:* Solo shows, O K Harris Gallery, NY, 83, 85 & 87, Franz Bader Gallery, Washington, 89, William Benton Mus Art, Storrs, Conn, 90, Lung Men Art Gallery, Taipei, Taiwan, 93, Art Proj Int, NY, 94 & 96, Lin & Keng Gallery, Taipei, Taiwan, 95, 97, 2001 & 2006, Rutgers Univ, New Brunswick, NJ, 2002, Nabi Gallery, New York, NY, 2004, Jason McCoy Inc, New York, NY, 2006; Yun Gee and Li-lan: Paintings by a Father & Daughter, Southampton Campus Fine Arts Gallery, Long Island Univ, NY, 88; William Benton Mus Art, Storrs, Conn, 90; PS 1 Mus, NY, 92; New Mus Contemp Art, NY, 94; Lin & Keng Gallery, Taipeu, Taiwan, 95, 97 & 2001; Group shows, Ar Embassies Prog, US Dept State, Brussels, 2000, Taipei, Taiwan, 2000, The Parrish Art Mus, Southampton, NY, 2000, Guild Hall Mus, East Hampton, NY, 2000. *Awards:* Artists Grant, Artists Space, NY, 88 & 90. *Bibliog:* David Ebony (auth), review, Art Am, 2/95; Phyllis Braff (auth), NY Times, 10/29/95; Alice Yang (auth, catalog), Art Projects International, 10/96; Joyce Brodsky (auth, catalog), 2001; Robert Berlind (auth), review, Art in America, Jan 2005; Peter Frank auth), Two Exhibitions, Doublevision & Nabi, NY & Los Angeles, CA, 2003-2004; Carter Ratcliff (auth, catalog), 2006. *Mem:* Artists Equity. *Media:* Oil, pastel, watercolor. *Interests:* writing, photography. *Publ:* Auth, Canvas with an Unpainted Part, An Autobiography, Asahi Newspaper Publishing, Tokyo, 76. *Dealer:* Jason McCoy Inc 41 E 57th St 11th Fl New York NY 10022; Nabi Gallery, 137 W 25 St, New York, NY 10001. *Mailing Add:* PO Box 1194 East Hampton NY 11937

LIANG, LANBO See Leong, Lampo

LIAO, SHIOU-PING
PAINTER, PRINTMAKER
b Taipei, Taiwan, Sept 2, 36. *Study:* Nat Taiwan Normal Univ, Taipei, BA, 59; Tokyo Univ Educ, Japan, MA, 64; Ecole Nat Superienredes Beaux Arts, Paris, 65-68. *Work:* Nat Mus Mod Art, Tokyo, Japan; Victoria & Albert Mus, London, Eng; Musee Municipal d'Art Mod, Paris, France; Cincinnati Art Mus, Ohio; New York Pub Libr; Metrop Mus Art, NY. *Comn:* Mural, Cathy Hospital, Taipei, 76; mural, Howard Plaza Hotel, Taipei, 83. *Exhib:* Salon de Mai & Salon d'Antonne, Musee Municipal d'Art Mod, Paris, France, 68; Nat Print, Brooklyn Mus, NY, 70; one-man shows, Taft Mus, Cincinnati, 70, Calif Palace Legion Honor, San Francisco, 73, Mus Mod Art, Liege, Belg, 92 & Taiwan Mus Art, 92; Int Print Biennial, Nat Mus Mod Art, Tokyo, Japan, 70; Oversize Print, Whitney Mus Am Art, NY, 71; Int Print Exchange Exhib, Mus Art, Soeul, Korea, 79; Five from the Orient, Bergen Co Mus, Paramus, NJ, 81. *Collection Arranged:* Paintings by Leading Overseas Artist (auth, catalog), Hong Kong Mus Art, 82; Contemporary Printmaking Asn (auth, catalog), Singapore, 82; The Art of Shiou-ping Liao, Taiwan Mus Art, 92. *Teaching:* Vis prof printmaking, Tsukuba Univ, Japan, 77-79; Daemen Col, Amherst, NY, 78; adj prof painting & printmaking, Seton Hall Univ, NJ, 79-; vis prof, Nanjing Inst Art, Spring 91. *Awards:* Silver Medal, Salon des Artistes Francais, Paris, 65; De Cordova Mus Purchase Prize, Boston Printmaker Show, 71. *Bibliog:* The Art of Shiou-ping Liao, Taiwan Mus Art, 92. *Mem:* Soc Am Graphic Artists; Chinese Graphic Soc Taipei (bd dir, 74). *Media:* Mixed Media; Watercolor, Oil. *Publ:* Auth, The Art of Printmaking, 74 & Appreciation of Modern Prints, 76, Taipei Lion Art Book Co. *Mailing Add:* 284 Center St Englewood Cliffs NJ 07632-1601

LIBBY, GARY RUSSELL
MUSEUM DIRECTOR, EDUCATOR
b Boston, Mass, June 7, 44. *Study:* Univ Fla, studied with Jerry Uelsmann, AA, BA, studied with Philip Hultman, MA; Tulane Univ, studied with Leo Steinberg, MA; studied with Jesse Poesch. *Collection Arranged:* Audubon: Birds & Animals, 75, The Third Empire Porcelains and Silver, 77 & Artistic Taste in Pre-Castro Cuba, (auth, catalog), 77, Mus Arts & Sci, Daytona Beach, Fla; 400 Years of Prints, Eight Cuban Masters, Sampson Hall Gallery, Stetson Univ, Deland, Fla, 77; Salon & Picturesque Photography in Cuba, 89; Chihuly: Form from Fire, 93; Celebrating Florida (auth, catalog), 95; Adams Rib: Sexual Mythology and The Roles of Women in Art, 97; Coast to Coast: The Contemporary Landscape in Florida (auth, catalog), 98; Dali over Daytona Paintings, Sculpture, Works on Paper by Salvador Dali, 2000; Young America, 20901. *Pos:* Dir, Mus Arts & Sci, Daytona Beach, Fla, 1977-2001, dir emeritus, 2001-; Dir 2003-2005. *Teaching:* Instr, Tulane Univ, New Orleans, La, 1968-71; asst prof humanities-art hist, Stetson Univ, 1972-73, asst prof art hist surv, 1972-77, vis prof, 1977-85. *Awards:* Lifetime Achievement Award, Fla Asn Mus, 98; Lifetime Achievement Award, Fla Art Dirs Asn, 2000. *Mem:* Southeast Col Art Conf; Col Art Conf; Col Art Asn; Am Asn Mus; Fla Mus Asn; Fla Art Mus Dirs Asn (pres-elect, 95-97); Fla Arts Coun (mem, 2005-). *Res:* Latin American: Cuban and Caribbean, 19th century English and American painting; Pre-Columbian ceramics; Florida art. *Collection:* Pre-Columbian, etchings, engravings, 19th century painting; Florida Art 19th-20th C. *Publ:* ed, Alexander Archipenko: Themes and Variations, Mus Arts & Sci, Daytona Beach, Fla, 90; Treasury of Indian Miniature Painting, 93; Cuba: A History in Art, 98; ed, Celebrating Florida.Works of Art from the Vickers Collection, 95; auth, Coast to Coast: The Contemporary landscape in Florida, 1999 (Gold Medal, SEMC); auth, Treasury of American Art, 2003. *Mailing Add:* 723 N Oleander Ave Daytona Beach FL 32118

LIBESKIND, DANIEL
ARCHITECT
b Poland, 46; naturalized, US. *Study:* Cooper Union, 70; Sch Comparative Studies, Essex, Eng, 72. *Hon Degrees:* Humboldt Univ, Berlin, Hon Dr, 97; Essex Univ, Eng, Hon Dr, 99; Univ Edinburgh, Hon Dr, 2002; DePaul Univ, Hon Dr, 2002; Univ Toronto, Hon Dr, 2004. *Work:* Victoria & Albert Mus, London, 96-; Jewish Mus, San Francisco, 98-; Jewish Mus, Berlin, 99; Felix Nussbaum Mus, Osnabrueck, 99; Westside Shopping & Leisure Ctr, Brunnen, Switz, 2001-; Imperial War Mus North, Manchester, Eng, 2002; German Military Mus, Dresden, 2002-; World Trade Ctr site, 2003-; London Metrop Univ, Grad Student Ctr, 2004; Dali Mus, Prague, 2004; Danish Jewish Mus, 2004; Bar Ilan Univ, Wohl Conv Ctr, Tel Aviv, 2005; Denver Art Mus, 2006. *Pos:* Head dept archit, Cranbrook Accad, 78-85; head, Inst Archit & Planning, Milan, Ital, 86-89; architect, Berlin, 90-2003 & NY, 2003-; designer, sets & costumes, Tristan, Opera Saarbrueken, 2001 & St Francis Assisi, Berlin Opera, 2003; cultural ambassador archit, CultureConnect Prog, US Dept State; Sr scholar, John Paul Getty Ctr; scholar, Royal Danish Accad & Am Israel Cultural Found. *Teaching:* Louis Sullivan prof, Chicago; Bannister Fletcher prof, Univ London; Louis Kahn prof, Yale Univ; Frank O'Gehry Ch, Univ Toronto; Cret ch, Univ Pa; guest prof, Harvard Univ, UCLA & Hochschule Weisensee, Ger. *Awards:* Golden Lion, Venice Biennale, 85; Award for Architecture, Am Acad Arts & Letters, 96; Citizen of Berlin Culture Prize, 96; Goethe Medallion for Cultural Contribution, 2000; Hiroshima Art Prize, 2001. *Mem:* European Accad Arts & Letters; Accad Arts; Fedn German Architects. *Publ:* auth, The Space of Encounter, Universe, 2001; auth, Breaking Ground: Adventures in Life & Architecture, Riverhead Books, 2004. *Mailing Add:* Studio Daniel Libeskind 2 Rector St 19th Fl New York NY 10006

LICCIONE, ALEXANDER
PAINTER, GRAPHIC ARTIST
b Rochester, NY, Jan 28, 48. *Study:* Acad di Belle Art di Brera Milan, Italy Fine Art Int, 69-72; Fla Atlantic Univ, Boca Raton, BFA, 78. *Work:* Pvt Collection, Brescia & Melfi (Potenza), Italy; murals, CitiBank, NY; ceramic statues, Dime Bank, NY; New Sch for Soc Res, NY Pub Libr, Avalanche Pictures, Financial Guaranty Ins Co, Cathedral Preparatory Seminary, NY; Teatro Contadino, Naples, Italy; ABC TV; Casa Argentina en Jerusalem Embassy, Israel; The Am War Libr Mus, Gardena, Calif; Academia Di Belle Arti Di Brera, Milan, Italy; Church and Friary of St Francis of Assis Ch, New York, NY. *Comn:* TV announcer's box, Yankee Stadium; La Campagna Ristorante (Little Italy), NY, 93; Cent Properties Movie & Theatrical Co, NY, 93-94; Murals, Limoncello/The Grotto, NY, 96; Am War Libr Mus, Gardenia, Calif, 2002. *Exhib:* Comedy Central, Harvard Lampoon, NY, 90; ABC TV, NBC TV, CBS TV, Universal Pictures & Guiding Light Soap Opera 90-2006; Apollo Prod, Comedy Hour, 93; NBC TV, Saturday Night Live, David Letterman, Conan O'Brien, NY, 90-2006; Michael Ingbar Gallery, NY, 93-98; Universal Film TV, Law & Order, NY, 93-2006; Instituto De Artes Visuais, Lisbon, Portugal, 94; Sex & the City, HBO, 2001; Sopranos, HBO, 2003; Special Victims Unit, 2003-2006; Two Weeks Notice (movie), Castle Rock Pictures, 2003; The Jury, 20th Century Fox, 2004; Rescue Me, Canterbury Prods, 2004; The Webster Project, Warner Bros, 2005; MTV Networks, 2005; and others. *Teaching:* Painting workshop, Ctr for the Arts, Vero Beach, Fla, 96. *Awards:* Int Platform Asn Bd Gov Award, 92; 2000 Notable Am Men Award, Distinguished Leadership Award & Personalities of Am Award, Am Biog, 91-92; Daytime Emmy Award (Sesame Street) & (One Life to Live, Nat Acad Television Art & Scis, 92-93, 94-95, 2000-01; Daytime Emmy Award, As the World Turns, Nat Acad TV Arts and Sci, 2000-01; Daytime Emmy Award, Sesame Street, Nat Acad TV Arts and Sci, 2004-05. *Bibliog:* Am References Inc, Chicago, 87-90; Am Biog Inst, 91 & 92; Vincenzo Tanzj (auth), Antologia Dei Poettie D'Artisti Italiani, Rizzoli Publ, 95; Ricreatori Dell 'Abiente, 95. *Mem:* Nat Stereoscopic Asn; Orgn Independent Artists, NY; Art Initiatives at Tribeca, NY. *Media:* Oil, Watercolor. *Publ:* Auth, Stereo (3-D) realism in oil, Nat Stereo World Mag. *Dealer:* Michael Ingbar Gallery 568 Broadway New York NY 10012. *Mailing Add:* 4 Heritage Lane Lagrangeville NY 12540

LICHACZ, SHEILA ENIT
PAINTER
b Monagrillo, Panama, Oct 9, 42; US & Panamanian citizen. *Study:* Our Lady of the Lake Univ, San Antonio, Tex, BS, 65; Inter-Am Univ, PR, MA(educ), 68. *Work:* Palm Springs Desert Mus, Calif; Vatican Mus, Mus Contemp Religious Art, Vatican, 83; Vanidades Gallery, Miami, Fla, 92; Holyshrine of First Miracle, Cana in Galilee, Israel, 98; Domus Galilenea, Galilee, Isreal, 98 & 2005; St Saviour's Monastery, Old Jerusalem, Israel, 99; Franciscan Monastery/Meml Ch of Holy Land, Washington, DC, 2001; Our Lady of Mt Carmel Church, Panama City, Panama, 2005. *Comn:* Painting, presented to King Juan Carlos of Spain by Panamian Govt; painting, presented to Pope John Paul II by Panamian Govt, 83; painting, presented to president of Peru by Panamian Govt, 86. *Exhib:* Solo exhibs, Feingarten Galleries, Los Angeles, 89, Arnold & Mabel Beckman Ctr, Nat Acads Sci & Eng, Irvine, Calif, 89, Art Gallery, Miami Herald, Fla, 92, Art Gallery, Dudley House, Harvard Univ, Cambridge, Mass, 93, Ctr Fine Arts, Miami, Fla, 94, Art Mus Am, Washington, 96, Cath Univ Santa Maria La Antigua, Panama City, 2002 & Smithsonian Ctr Latino Initatives, Washington, DC, 2002-03; Expresion Plastica Latinoamerica, Habitante Gallery, Panama City, Panama, 90; Rediscovering the Americas, Bacardi Art Gallery, Miami, Fla, 91; The Spirit of Faith in Painting, Sculpture & Jewelry, Am Cath Mus, NY, 92; Exposicion Jerusalem: Taller Creativo de Artistas de America Latina y Miami Fla, Jerusalem Munic Art Gallery, 96; Rediscovering the Americas, Bacardi Art Gallery, Miami, Fla, 91; Segundo Salon de Artes Iberoamericano, Inst Mex dea Artes, La Asn de Agregados Culturales, Wash, DC, 93; Ctr Fine Arts, Miami Art Mus, Summit Americas, Fla, 94; Art Mus Am, Washington DC, 96; Art Gallery Brikel Ave, Miami, Fla, 97 & 98; The First Int Loan Exhib, Smithsonian Inst, Washington, DC, 97; Latin Artists visit Jerusalem, Fla Mus Hisp & Latin Am Art, Miami, Fla, 97; Ibero Am Traveling/Touring Art Show, Cult Inst Israel, 99; Espacio Venezuela Gallery, Miami Fla, 2001; Francisco De Paula Santander Gallery, Miami, Fla, 2002; Weisman Mus Art, Pepperdine Univ, Malibu, Calif, 2005. *Pos:* ambassador at large, Republic of Panama, 95-; vpres (special mission), Universidad Catolica, Santa Maria, La Antigua. *Awards:* Hispanic Achievement Award, Chicago, Ill, 96; Outstanding Alumna of Year (Awarded for Service to the Profession), Our Lady of the Lake Univ, San Antonio, Tex, 85. *Bibliog:* Ralph Luce (auth), Sheila Lichacz, Artist, Santa Fean Mag, 7/90; David Briggs (auth), Inspired works, Assoc Press, 20/3/92; Tara B Reddy (auth), Constructing religious faith through fragments of the past, Harvard Crimson, 2/18/93; Philip Eliasord (auth), Sheila E Lichacz, the spirit and soul of Latin America (catalog), 12/94; Fr James Heinsch (auth), God;s Paintbrush, Holyland, spring 99. *Media:* Pastel, Oil, Pre-Columbian Montage. *Mailing Add:* 555 NE 34th St #2705 Miami FL 33137

LICHAW, PESSIA
PRINTMAKER, ARCHITECT
Study: Technion Tel-Aviv, Israel, BA, 64; Betzalel Acad, Jerusalem, 69-70; Art Students League, 76-80. *Work:* Jerusalem Mus; Art Students League, NY. *Comn:* Images reproduced, Marriott Hotel, Tex, 84, Hyatt Hotel, NY, 86 & Sheraton Hotel, Philadelphia, Pa, 88; Originals, Gurneys Inn, Montauk, NY, 87 & City Bank, NY, 88-90. *Exhib:* Duke Univ, NC, 80; Queens Mus, NY, 82; Gallery Sho, Tokyo, 87; Artful Framer, Honolulu, 90; Nassau Mus, Long Island, NY, 92-93. *Pos:* Architect, currently. *Awards:* Purchase Prize & Merit Scholar, 77; Mem prize, Nat Asn Women Artists, 84; 1st Prize, Nassau Mus, 93. *Bibliog:* Malcolm Preston (auth), Five approaches to graphics, Newsday, 2/7/80; Jeanne Paris (auth), Glen Cove's a gallery, Newsday, 4/18/80; Helen A Harrison (auth), Many shades of white, New York Times, 1/11/81. *Mem:* Nat Asn Women Artists; Artist Network Great Neck; Printmaking Workshop, NY; Art Students League, NY. *Media:* Monoprints. *Mailing Add:* Nine Hampton Ct Lake Success NY 11020

LICHTENBERG, MANES
PAINTER
b New York, NY. *Study:* Art Students League; with Fernand Leger, Paris; Acad Grande Chaumiere, Paris. *Exhib:* Philadelphia Acad Fine Arts; Nat Acad Design, NY; Mus Mod Art, Paris; Allied Artists Am, NY; Mus I'lle de France, Paris. *Awards:* Prix Othon Friesz, Paris, 61; Gold Medal of Honor, Allied Artists Am, 64; Prix Maurice Utrillo, Utrillo Found Int, Paris, 64. *Mem:* Allied Artists Am; Am Watercolor Soc. *Media:* Watercolor, Oil. *Mailing Add:* 163 Pine St Homosassa FL 34446

LIDEN, HANNA
PHOTOGRAPHER
b Stockholm, Sweden, 76. *Study:* Parsons Sch Design, NYC, BFA, 2002. *Exhib:* Exhib, group shows, You're Just a Summer Love but I'll Remember You When Winter Comes, 2005; Be In, The Volta Show, 2006; Noctambule, NYC, The Whitney Biennial, Whitney Mus Art, NYC, 2006; One-man show, And in Her Shadow Death, Rivington Arms Gallery, NYC. *Mailing Add:* c/o Rivington Arms 102 Rivington St New York NY 10002

LIEBER, EDVARD
PAINTER, FILMMAKER
b Rockville Centre, NY, Apr 11, 48. *Study:* Manhattan Sch Mus, 1966-1968; Sch Visual Arts, New York, BFA, 76; studies with Robert Mangold & Richard Artschwager. *Work:* Mus Mod Art, NY; Ga Mus Art, Athens; Guild Hall Mus, East Hampton, NY; Chase Manhattan Bank, NY; Miele Corp, Guttersloh, Ger; Sarah Lee Corp, Chicago. *Exhib:* Edvard Lieber Recent Work, Jason McCoy Gallery, NY, 1989; New York Collection 91-92, Albright-Knox Gallery, 91; The Perfect Likeness, Albany Mus Art, Ga, 93; Young Blood, Guild Hall Mus, East Hampton, NY, 93; Children in Crisis, Munchausen Mus, Goslar, Ger, 94; What's New, Heckscher Mus, Huntington, NY, 2000; Frontiers, Galería d'Art Horizon, Girona, Spain, 2004. *Teaching:* Instr music & arts, Sch Visual Art NY, 78-06; asst prof art hist, Cooper Union, NY, 93; instr masters of light, Sch Visual Arts, NY, 2001-2003. *Awards:* NY State Coun on the Arts award, 83; NY Found for the Arts Award, 93, 94; Found for Contemp Performance Arts, NY, 99. *Bibliog:* Mary Rawson (producer), Lyceum: Edvard Lieber, WQED-TV, 1/2/80; Amei Wallach (auth), Older works in a new light: Cy Twombly, Al Held, Evard Lieber, Newsday, 1/26/90; Lawrence Campbell (auth), Edvard Lieber, Art in America, 7/90; Phyllis Braff (auth), Range of Interpretation of the Intuitive, NY Times, 11/1997; Dore Ashton (auth), Just Because I Don't Say Something, Mod Painters, winter 2000. *Media:* Mixed Media. *Publ:* Contribr, Elaine de Kooning: Her world and persona, Christie's Newslett, 89; contribr, one Man Two Visions, Pergamon Press, 93; The 1940's, Washburn Gallery, 93; Willem de Kooning: Reflections in the Studio, Harry N Abrams Inc, 2000; Dear Jackson Pollock, Pollock-Krasner House, 2003. *Dealer:* Ekstrom & Ekstrom 417 E 75 St New York NY 10021. *Mailing Add:* 24 Hay Rd Shirley NY 11967-3715

LIEBER, LOFA
PAINTER & GALLERY DIRECTOR
b Mukacevo, Czech, Mar 15, 23. *Study:* Special study with John Pike, 1974; Studies with Stefan Locos, 1978. *Work:* San Francisco Mus Art, CA; Lowdens Veterans Mus, Las Vegas; Kings Co Med Ctr, Brooklyn; Yad Vashem Holocaust Mus, Israel; SCC Library, Brooklyn. *Comn:* Portrait, Kings Co Med Ctr, Brooklyn, 1965; Portrait, OHR Somavach Educ Ctr, Monsey, NY, 1995; Ghetto Scenery (portrait), Baby Togs Inc., New York, 1999. *Media:* Acrylic, Oil, Watercolot, Woodcut, Restorer, Gallery Director & Art Dealer. *Dealer:* Lolas Art Gallery 4813 16th Ave Brookyln NY 11204. *Mailing Add:* 1530 54th St Brooklyn NY 11219

LIEBER, THOMAS ALAN
PAINTER
b St Louis, Mo, Nov 5, 49. *Study:* Univ Ill, BFA, 71, MFA, 74. *Work:* Guggenheim Mus, Mus Mod Art, NY; San Francisco Mus Mod Art; Los Angeles Mus Mod Art; Tate Gallery, London; Cleveland Art Mus. *Exhib:* New Perspectives in Am Painting, Guggenheim Mus, 78-88; The Aesthetics of Grafitti, San Francisco Mus Mod Art,

Calif, 78, Fresh Paint, 82; San Francisco Bay Area Paintings, Univ Nebr, Lincoln, 84; Contemp Am Monotypes, Chrysler Mus, Norfolk, Va, 85; Maine Collects, Farnsworth Mus, Rockland, Maine, 89; monotype, Tate Gallery, London, 94; Farnsworth Mus, Rockland, Maine, 2000; Hackett Freedman Gallery, San Francisco, 2004. *Teaching:* Vis prof, Stanford Univ, 89; Vt Studio Sch, Johnson, Vt. *Awards:* Nat Endowment Arts, 75; Invited Artist, Trillium Press, 2002. *Bibliog:* Robert McDonald (auth), Physically finds its place, 76 & Tom Liebers environmental paintings, 77, Art Week; John Russell (auth), Younger Americans, NY Times, 83. *Mem:* Nat Acad (acad 1994-). *Media:* Oil, Watercolor. *Dealer:* John Berggruen 228 Grant San Francisco CA; Friesen Gallery Seattle WA. *Mailing Add:* Hackett Freedman Gallery 250 Sutter St San Francisco CA 94108

LIEBERMAN, LAURA CROWELL
ADMINISTRATOR, CRITIC
b Oak Ridge, Tenn, Apr 7, 52. *Study:* Pomona Col, 72; Swarthmore Col, BA, 74. *Collection Arranged:* Atlanta Women Artists: A Personal Survey, Atlanta Art Workers' Gallery, 78; 36 Women Artists (co-ed, catalog), Peachtree Ctr Gallery, Atlanta, 78; Nine Diverse Directions: Atlanta, Ga Southern Col, 83; Speaking Volumes, American Mus of Papermaking, 2002; Artists of Heath Gallery, Mus Contemp Art of Ga, 2002. *Awards:* Outstanding Ga Women in the Visual Arts, 92. *Bibliog:* Karen Wantuck (auth), Subjective (catalog), 78; Sherry Baker (auth), 36 women artists, Atlanta Gazette, 4/78; Clyde Burnett (auth), A personal survey, Atlanta J-Constitution, 7/78. *Mem:* Georgia Assembly of Community Arts Agencies; Georgia Asn of Mus & Gall. *Res:* Contemporary art in Atlanta, Georgia and the Southeast. *Specialty:* Georgia and Regional Artists. *Publ:* Co-ed, Other Harmonies, Atlanta Women's Poetry Workshop, 77; auth, Five Atlanta women artists, Southern Quart, Univ Southern Miss, 79; ed, Contracts for Artists, 83; and others; auth, William Christenberry: A Retrospective (catalog essay), 90; London to Atlanta: International Exchange (catalog), 91; ed, City Arts update (newsletter), 92; Artists of Health Gallery Catalog, 2002. *Mailing Add:* Three Spring Circle NW Atlanta GA 30318

LIEBERMAN, LOUIS (KARL)
SCULPTOR, DRAFTSMAN
b Brooklyn, NY, May 7, 44. *Study:* Brooklyn Mus Art Sch, cert, 64; Brooklyn Col, BA, 62; RI Sch Design, BFA, 69. *Work:* Metrop Mus Art, NY; Staten Island Mus, Richmond, NY; Philadelphia Mus Art, Pa; Aldrich Mus, Ridgefield, Conn; Brooklyn Mus, NY; and others. *Comn:* Wall relief, Aldrich Mus Contemp Art, Ridgefield, Conn, 73; Wall relief, Kenan Ctr, NY State Coun on Arts, Lockport, NY, 73; and others. *Exhib:* Solo exhibs, Root Art Ctr, Hamilton Col, Clinton, NY, 80, Harm Bouckaert Gallery, NY, 81; List Art Ctr, Hamilton Col, Clinton, NY, 82; Ellen Price, NY, 82, John Davis Gallery, Akron, Ohio, 83 & 85, Columbus Mus Art Collectors Gallery, Ohio, 84, John Davis Gallery, NY, 86; One Cubic Foot, Thomas J Watson Libr, Metrop Art Mus, NY, 83; A Sigh of Relief, Wilson Art Ctr, Rochester, NY, 87; Stephen Rosenberg Gallery, NY, 87-88; New Art on Paper, Hunt Paper Collection, Philadelphia Mus Art, Pa, 88; Paper Thick, Erie Art Mus, Pa, Art Mus, Santa Cruz, Calif, Hunter Mus, Chattanooga, Tenn, 88-89; Black, Gray and White, Henry Feiwel Gallery, NY, 89. *Pos:* Contribr art critic, New York Arts J, 78-79. *Teaching:* Adj lectr drawing, Brooklyn Col, NY, 71-78; adj lectr sculpture/design, Lehman Col, Bronx, 72-75; vis artist sculpture, Ill State Univ, Normal, 79; vis artist, Hamilton Col, Clinton, New York, 82. *Awards:* New York Found Arts, 84-85; Pollock-Krasner Found, 87; Adolph and Esther Gottlieb Found, 89-90; and many others. *Bibliog:* Brian Riverman (auth), article, Dialogue, 7/84 & 8/84; Holland Cotter (auth) articles, Arts Mag, 11/85, Art Am, 1/87; Stephan Westfall (auth) article, Arts Mag, 2/87. *Media:* Multimedia. *Mailing Add:* 16 Greene St New York NY 10013

LIEBERMAN, MEYER FRANK
PAINTER, PRINTMAKER
b New York, NY, Aug 28, 23. *Study:* Art Students League, with Reginald Marsh; Pratt Graphics Ctr, with Andrew Stasik. *Work:* Jewish Mus, NY; Presidential Residence, Jerusalem; Columbia Univ, NY; Brooklyn Col, NY; Woodstock Hist Soc, Woodstock, NY. *Exhib:* Drawing USA, Mus Mod Art, NY, 56; One-man shows, Bodley Gallery, 78, Night Gallery, 81, Terrance Gallery, 81; Work Art Gallery, Saugerties, NY, 86; Unison Learning Ctr, New Paltz, 89 & 95; Woodstock Artists Asn, 94; Lieberman Gallery, 96 & 99; Art Soc Kingston, 2000; Woodstock Artist ASN, 2002; Coffey Cal Kington, 2003; Half Moon Studio, Saugeties, 2004; Coffey Cal Kington, 2005. *Teaching:* Instr drawing, painting & composition, Art Life Craft Studios, New York, 64-68; instr drawing, collage painting & composition, Temple Emanu-El, Yonkers, NY, 66-74; instr drawing, painting & composition, Flatbush Jewish Ctr, Brooklyn, 67-78; instr, Temple Emanuel, Kingston, NY, 78-80; Gifted & Talented Prog, Onteora School Dist, New York, 85-88, mentor, 2000; sr art prog, Woodstock, NY, 84-. *Mem:* Woodstock Artists Asn; Art Soc Kingston, NY. *Media:* Oil, Watercolor. *Mailing Add:* 648 Zena Rd Woodstock NY 12498

LIEBERMANN, PHILIP
PHOTOGRAPHER, EDUCATOR
b Brooklyn, NY, Oct 25, 34. *Study:* Mass Inst Technol, BS & MS, 58, PhD(linguistics), 66. *Work:* Brooklyn Mus, NY; Mus RI Sch Design, Providence; Albright Knox Gallery, Buffalo, NY; Silver Bullet Gallery, Providence; Providence Athenaeum, RI; Happenhoffer Mus of Anthropology, Mass. *Comn:* Photographs, Book-Walking in Switzerland, The Mountaineers, Seattle, 85-87; US of the Alpine Tourist Comn; Alpine Parks of France & NW Italy, Mountaineers, 89; Switzerland's Mountain Inns, Countryman Press, 98 & 2000; Buddhist wall paintings of Mustang, Nepal, Getty Found. *Exhib:* Carl Siembab Gallery, Boston, 66; B Urdang Invitational Traveling Exhib, 84; Animal in Photog 1845-1985, Invitational Photographers' Gallery, London, 86; B Urdang Gallery 82, 84, 86, 89 & 92; Mus Rhode Island Sch Design, 94; OP Steker, Amsterdam, 96; AHappenrepper Mus Anthropology, Mass, 2000; and others. *Pos:* Prof, Brown Univ. *Awards:* Young Photog Award, Time-Life, 65; Sullivan Award, J Banigan Sullivan, 84 & 86; Guggenheim Fel, 87. *Bibliog:* Contemp Art in Rhode Island, 2001. *Media:* Black & White Photography. *Specialty:* Contemporary Art. *Interests:* Mountain Climbing, Classical Music, Art. *Publ:* Co-Auth, Walking in Switzerland, Mountaineers, 87; photogr, Alpine parks, France & Italy, Mountaineers, 94. *Dealer:* Bertha Urdang 23 E 74th St New York NY 10021. *Mailing Add:* 141 Elton St Providence RI 02906

LIEBLING, JEROME
PHOTOGRAPHER, FILMMAKER
b New York, NY, April 16, 24. *Study:* Brooklyn Col, with Walter Rosenblum, Milton Brown & Ad Reinhardt; New Sch Social Res, with Lew Jacobs & Paul Falkenberg; LLD Portland Sch Art, Maine. *Work:* Mus Mod Art, NY; Corcoran Gallery Art; Boston Mus Fine Art; Libr Cong; Minneapolis Inst Art. *Exhib:* The Photo League, Int Ctr Photog, NY, 78; Mirrors and Windows, Mus Mod Art, NY, 78; 14 Northeast Photographers, Boston Mus Fine Arts, 78; solo exhibs, Corcoran Gallery Art, 80, Fogg Art Mus, 82 & Portland Art Mus, Maine, 83; Am Children, Mus Mod Art, NY, 81; Northeast Perambulations, Addison Gallery, 82; Retrospective: Jerome Liebling Photographs, Minneapolis Inst Art, Minn, 95; Jerome Liebling Photographs, The Photographers Gallery, London, Eng, 95. *Teaching:* Prof photog & film, Univ Minn, Minneapolis, 49-69 & Hampshire Col, 70-83; prof, SUNY, New Platz, NY, 56-57; prof photog, Yale Univ, 76-77. *Awards:* Fels, Guggenheim Found, 77 & 81 & Nat Endowment Arts, 79. *Bibliog:* Estelle Jussim (auth), No 15, Friends Photog, 77; Alan Trachtenberg (auth), Jerome Liebling--Photographs, Univ Mass Press, 82. *Mem:* Soc Photog Educ (trustee, 73-78); Univ Film Study Ctr (vpres, 75-77). *Specialty:* Photography. *Publ:* Coauth, Face of Minneapolis, Dillon Press, 66; illusr, Photography Current Perspectives, Mass Rev, 77; The People, Yes (Photographs of Jerome Liebling), Aperture, New York, 94. *Dealer:* Howard Greenberg Gallery 120 Wooster St New York NY 10012. *Mailing Add:* 39 Dana St Amherst MA 01002

LIEBMAN, DR SARAH
EDUCATOR, PAINTER
b Brooklyn, NY. *Study:* Brooklyn Col, BA, 76, with Sam Gelber & Jerome Viola, MFA, 78, with Philip Pearlstein & Lee Bonticou; Pratt Inst, Grad Fel Fine Art, 77, with Richard Bove & Dr Ralph Wickiser; Teachers Col, Columbia Univ, EdM, 86, EdD, 90, with Justin Schorr & Maxine Green. *Exhib:* Mid East Traveling Exhib, Cult Affairs Ctr, US Embassy, Israel & Egypt, 81; Nat Asn Women Artists, 81-82; Ann Exhib, Catherine Lorillard Wolfe Art Club, NY, 82; Nat Coun Art Jewish Life, Lever House, NY, 83; Nat Asn Women Artists, Bergen Mus Art & Sci, Paramus, NJ, 83 & NY, 83-84; solo exhib, Macy Gallery, Columbia Univ, NY, 85. *Teaching:* Instr drawing & painting, Sephardic Community Ctr, 81-84; instr art hist appreciation, Brooklyn Col, NY, 83-87; instr art hist, appreciation & drawing, Univ Conn, 91-92. *Awards:* Marilyn Freeman Award, Brooklyn Col, 75; Elizabeth Elanger Award, Nat Asn Women Artists, 81; Binney & Smith Award, Catherine Lorillard Wolfe Art Club, 82. *Mem:* Nat Asn Women Artists; Nat Art Educ Asn; Audubon Artists; Artists Equity; Col Art Asn. *Media:* Oil, Pastel. *Collection:* Mary Private Collection. *Publ:* Adult Learners, Two Col Art Prog. *Mailing Add:* 1270 North Ave #B1 New Rochelle NY 10804-2601

LIEBMAN, NORMAN
PAINTER
b Newark, NJ, Oct 9, 33. *Study:* Rutgers Univ, AB, 55; Chautauqua Art Inst, 81-86. *Work:* Mus Art, Ft Lauderdale, Fla; Boca Mus Art, Fla; Mayo Clinic Found, Rochester, Minn; Polk Mus Art, Lakeland, Fla; Musé des Beaux Arts, Orleans, France; and others. *Exhib:* Hortt, 31, 32 & 34, Mus Art, Ft Lauderdale, Fla, 89, 90 & 92; Boca Mus Art 39th Ann Show, Boca Mus, Fla, 90; Soc of Four Arts, Soc 4 Arts Mus, Palm Beach, Fla, 90; Ctr for the Arts, Vero Beach, Fla, 95. *Awards:* All Fla Prize, Boca Mus Art, 90. *Mem:* SFla Art Ctr. *Media:* Acrylic, Oil

LIEBOWITZ, JANET
PAINTER, SCULPTOR
b New York, NY. *Study:* Art Students League; Am Art Sch; studied with Robert Reed, New Haven. *Work:* Elmira Col, NY; Bocour Artist Color Collection, NY; Butler Art Inst, Youngstown, Ohio; Albrecht Gallery, St Joseph, Miss; Griffith Art Inst, St Lawrence Univ, Canton, NY. *Exhib:* Artists Choice, Women for the Arts Found, NY, 77; Silvermine Gold of Art Ctr, Phoenix Gallery, NY; Elmira Col, NY; Wadsworth Atheneum, Hartford, Conn. *Collection Arranged:* Papyrus Abstracts, Wesport Weston Arts Coun, 82; Selections in Contemp Art, Wesport Weston Arts Coun, 83. *Awards:* Painters prize, Painters & Sculptors Soc NJ, 68; Nat Asn Women Artists, NY; Reginald March Scholar Art Students League. *Bibliog:* Michael Benedict (auth), Art Int, 66; John Caldwell (auth), Art Forms of Paperwork, NY Times, 8/82. *Mem:* Nat Asn Women Artists; Penwomen, Boca Raton Chap; Lighthouse Gallery, Tequesta, Fla; Artists Equity; Prof Artist Guild of Boca Raton Mus, Fla. *Media:* All. *Dealer:* Silvermine Guild of Artists New Canaan Conn. *Mailing Add:* 7535 Fairfax Dr Fort Lauderdale FL 33321-4360

LIFSON, HUGH ANTHONY
PAINTER, EDUCATOR
b New York, NY, Nov 7, 1937. *Study:* Studio 10, with Irving Marantz, 53-59; Univ Wis, with Warrington Colescott & S Zingale, 55-56; Wesleyan Univ, with R Limbach, AB, 59; Ind Univ, 60; Pratt Inst, with Robert Richenberg, James McGarrell, 61 & Univ of Ind. *Work:* Cedar Rapids Mus Art, Iowa; State Univ NY, Postdam; Wesleyan Univ, Middletown, Conn; St Leo Col, Fla; Davenport Munic Art Gallery, Iowa. *Comn:* Environment, Cedar Rapids Art Ctr, Iowa, 69. *Exhib:* One-person shows, Ohio State Univ, Columbus, 72, Ward Nasse Gallery, NY, 78; Mid Am Ann, St Louis Munic Mus, Mo, 68 & Nelson Atkins Mus, Kansas City, 84; USA The Figure, Mus Mod Art, NY;

South Bend 20th Century Ctr, Ind, 81. *Collection Arranged:* Richard Kostelenhotz, Carl Shorske, Alan Shestack. *Teaching:* Prof, Cornell Col, Mt Vernon, Iowa, 84 & 86-2000, prof emer, 2000-. *Bibliog:* Richard Kostelanetz (auth), Metamorphosis, Assembling Press, 81. *Media:* Acrylics, Polyofinics; Computer Graphics. *Publ:* Trobor Mag. *Dealer:* Wiederspan Gallery 1314 Mt Vernon Rd SI Cedar Rapids IA 52403. *Mailing Add:* 219 Sixth Ave N Mount Vernon IA 52314

LIGHT, KEN
PHOTOGRAPHER, EDUCATOR
b Bronx, NY, Mar 16, 51. *Study:* Ohio Univ, Athens, Ohio, BGS, 73; San Jose State Univ, MFA (photography), 98. *Work:* San Francisco Mus Mod Art, Calif; Calif Hist Soc, San Francisco; Int Polaroid Collection, Boston; Fed Reserve Bank, San Francisco; Houston Mus Fine Arts; Int Ctr Photog; Center Creative Photog; NY Pub Libr; Nat Mus Am Art; Albin O Kuhn Libr; Bancroft Libr; Santa Barbara Mus Art. *Comn:* Libr Congress, Am Folklife Ctr, 89 & 90. *Exhib:* Work, Oakland Mus, Calif, 77; Faces Photographed, San Francisco Mus Mod Art, 84; New Documentary Photog, USA Images Gallery, Cincinnati, Ohio, 89; San Joaquin Co Hist Soc & Mus Arts Station, Tifton, Ga, 90; Mus Contemp Art, Morelia, Mex, 90; one-man exhibs, The Eye Gallery, San Francisco, 91, Chovnick Gallery, NY, 91 & Pac Tel Corp Plaza Gallery, Walnut Creek, Calif, 92; Nev Mus Art-Weigand Gallery, 93; Italian Americans in the West, Libr Cong, 94; Track 16 Gallery, Santa Monica, Calif, 2005; Int Ctr Photog, 2005; SE Mus Photog, 2006. *Teaching:* Fac photog, San Francisco Acad Art 76-96; aj prof, cur, Ctr Photography, Univ Calif, Berkeley, 1983-; adj prof photog, Univ Calif, Berkeley 82-, San Francisco Art Inst, 2000. *Awards:* Nat Endowment Arts Photogrs Fel, 82 & 86; Dorothea Lange Fel, 87; Thomas M Stoke Int Journalism Award, 90; Cannon Photo Esaysity Award, Univ Mo, 92; NPPA Res Grant, 96; Open Soc Inst Grant, 2005. *Bibliog:* Mark Lapin (auth), Light on the Border, Photo District News, 88; Delta Time; Mississippi Photographs, 95; Tex Death Row, Univ Press Miss, 96; Aperture Witness in Our Time, Smithsonian, 2000. *Mem:* Soc Photog Ed; Am Fed Teachers. *Publ:* Contribr, The Circle of Life, Harper Collins Publ, 91; Mexico Through Foreign Eyes, WW Norton, 92; Time for a Witness, East Bay Guardian, 1/92; Granta, No 40, fall 92; Image Mag, San Francisco Examiner, 7/12/92; Witness in Our Time, Smithsonian Inst Press, 2000; Coal Hollow, Univ Calif Press, 2/2006. *Dealer:* Barry Singer Gallery. *Mailing Add:* 55 VIA Farallon Orinda CA 94563

LIGHT, MICHAEL RUDOLPH
PHOTOGRAPHER
b Clearwater, Fla, Aug 5, 63. *Study:* Amherst Col, BA(summa cum laude) 86; San Francisco Art Inst, MFA(photog), 93. *Work:* San Francisco Mus Mod Art; Los Angeles Co Mus; Getty Research Inst, Los Angeles; Victoria & Albert Mus, London; Am Mus Natural Hist, NY. *Exhib:* Blue Fall, Chrysler Mus, Norfolk, Va, 95; Southeast Mus Photog, 98; San Francisco Mus Mod Art, 99; Hayward Gallery, London, 99; Mus Contemp Art, Sydney, 2000; Mito Art Tower, Japan, 2001; Auditorium Arte, Rome, 2004; Mus Mod, Salzburg, 2005; Colo Univ Art Mus, Boulder, 2005; Art Tower Mito, Mito, Japan, 2006; Worcester Art Mus, Mass, 2006; Calif State Univ, Long Beach, 2006; solo exhibs, Nat Hist Mus LA County, Calif, 2005, Hosfelt Gallery, San Francisco, 2005, Hasselblad Center, Goteborg, Sweden, 2006, Hosfelt Gallery, NY, 2006, and many others. *Teaching:* Instr, Deep Springs Col, Calif, 2001 & 2006. *Awards:* Award for Full Moon: Best Visual Anthology of 99, 7th Ann Photo-Eye Book Awards, Santa Fe, 2000; Award for Full Moon: Kodak Fotobook Preis 99, Stuttgart, 99, Full Moon: Best Natural Sciences Book of Yr/Aesthetics, bild der wissenschchaft mag, Stuttgart, 99; Marin Arts Coun Grant, 94. *Bibliog:* Michael Read & Andy Grundberg (auths), Blue Fall, See Mag/Friends of Photog, 95; D Schumacher (auth), Michael Light: Ranch & Oblivion, Art Papers 9-10/95; S Jenkins (auth), Wonder words, Bay Area Reporter, 10/97; Jody Zellen (auth) Michael Light, Artpapers, Nov/Dec 2000; Christopher Knight (auth), Puzzling Landscapes Happily Lost in Space, Los Angeles Times, 8/4/2000; Sharon DeLano (auth), On Photography: Darkness Visible, The New Yorker, NY, 10/6/2003; Phillip Morrison (auth), Metaphorical Suns, Scientific American, NY, 1/2004; RC Baker (auth), Best in Show: Apocalypse Porn, The Village Voice, NY, 5/1/2006; Colin Westerbeck (auth), SUGAR, West Magazine, Sunday Los Angeles Times, 8/27/2006. *Mem:* Soc Photog Educ. *Media:* Photography. *Publ:* Ranch, Twin Palms Publ, NMex, 93; Full Moon, Knopf, NY, 99; 100 Suns, Knopf, NY, 2003. *Dealer:* Hosfelt Gallery 430 Clementina St San Francisco CA 94103. *Mailing Add:* PO Box 460428 San Francisco CA 94146

LIGHTON, LINDA
SCULPTOR, INSTRUCTOR
b Kansas City, Mo, Mar 10, 48. *Study:* Monterrey Inst Technol, Mex, 65-66; Fontainbleau Sch Fine Arts, France, 67; Factory Visual Arts, Seattle, Wash, 71-74; Western Wash State Col, Bellingham, 75; Univ Idaho, Moscow, 75-77; Kansas City Art Inst, BFA, 87-89. *Work:* also pvt collection of the Crown Prince of Brunei; H&R Block World Hq, Kansas City, Mo; Spence Mus, Lawrence, Kansas; Sprint Corp, Kansas City, Mo; Daum Mus, Sedalia, Mo; Johnson Co Community Col, Overland Park, Kans; Int Ceramic Mus, Incheon, Korea. *Exhib:* 1st World Bienniale Ceramics, Incheon Korea, 2001; Devine Porcelain, Vallauris, France, 2004; Int Bienniale de Manises, Valencia, Spain, 2005; 20th Int Ceramic Festival, Incheon, Korea, 2006; Int Acad Ceramics, Riga, Latvia, 2006. *Pos:* adv bd, Nat Coun Edn Ceramic Arts; bd dir, Rev Arts Mag & Kansas City Ballet; dir, Lighton Int Artists Exchg Program at Kansas City Artists Coalition, Kansas City, Mo; nat comt, Kemper Mus Contemp Art, Kansas City. *Awards:* Honorarium-Amerika Haus, Berlin, Ger, 94; Int Workshop Ceramic Arts, Tokoname, Japan, 96; Grant, Int Geramic Symposium, Hungary, 2003. *Bibliog:* Diane Timmerman (auth), Flower power, Kansas City Home Design, Vol 1, 10/96; Roderick Townley (auth), The Winding Road to Her Creativity, Kansas City Home Design, 9/99; Joshua Rose (auth), Working to Build Bridges, Kansas City Jewish Life, 97. *Mem:* Nat Coun Educ Ceramic Arts; founding mem, Kansas City Contemp Art Ctr, Kans; Kansas City Artist Coalition; Arts Partners of Kansas City (dir, bd mem & secy); Int Acad Ceramics, Carouge, Switz. *Media:* Clay, Metal. *Publ:* Auth, numerous articles, Nat Coun for Educ of Ceramic Arts J. *Dealer:* Sherry Leedy Contemporary Art 2004 Baltimore Ave Kansas City MO 64108. *Mailing Add:* 4620 Charlotte Kansas City MO 64110-1535

LIGON, GLENN
PAINTER
b Bronx, NY, 60. *Study:* RI Sch Design, 80; Wesleyan Univ, BA, 82; Whitney Mus Independent Study Prog, 85. *Work:* Boston Mus Fine Art & List Art Gallery, MIT, Boston; Mus Mod Art & Whitney Mus Am Art, NY; Carnegie Mus Art, Pittsburgh; Hirshhorn Mus & Sculpture Garden, Washington, DC; Philadelphia Mus Art. *Exhib:* Solo exhibs, White Columns, NY, 91, Wadsworth Atheneum, 92, Max Protetch Gallery, NY, 92, 93 & 94, Whitney Mus Am Art at Philip Morris, NY, 92, Hirshhorn Mus & Sculpture Garden, 93 & Ruth Bloom Gallery, Santa Monica, 94, Brooklyn Mus of Art, 96, San Francisco Mus Mod Art, Calif, 96, Ezra and Cecile Zilkha Gallery, Middletown, Conn, 97, Inst Contemp Art/Univ of Pennsylvania, 1998, St Louis Art Mus, 2000, The Studio Mus in Harlem, NY, 2001, Kuntsverein Munich, Ger, 2001, D'Amelio Terras, NY, 2001, Anthony Meier Fine Arts, San Francisco, Calif, 2002; Galerie Gilles Peyroulet, Paris, 94; Dark O'Clock, Museu de Arte Moderna de Sao Paulo, Brazil & Plug In Inc, Winnipeg, Manitoba, Can, 96; Biennale of Sydney: Jurassic Technologies Revenant, Art Gallery of New South Wales, Sydney, Australia, 96; La Biennale di Venezia, XLVII Esposizione Int D'Arte, Venice, Italy, 97; XXIV Bienal de Sao Paulo: Nucleo Historico: Antropofagia e Historia de Canibalismos, Brazil, 98; 3rd Kwangju Biennale: Man + Space, Kwangju, South Korea, 2000; group exhib: Skin Deep, Numark Gallery, Washington, DC, 2003, An Am Legacy: Art from the Studio Mus, The Parrish Art Mus, Southhampton, NY, 2003, Influence, Anxiety, and Gratitude, MIT List Visual Art Ctr, 2003, On the Wall: Wallpaper and Tableau, The Fabric Workshop and Mus, Philadelphia, Pa, 2003, Family Ties, Peabody Essex Mus, Salem, Mass, 2003, The Disembodied Spirit, Bowdoin Col Mus of Art, Maine, 2003. *Awards:* Dewar's Young Artists Recog Award, 90; Fel, Art Matters Inc, 90; Grant, Joan Mitchell Found, 96. *Bibliog:* Laura Cottingham (auth), The pleasure principal, Frieze, 5/93; Ralph Rugoff (auth), Panic in the tower: Who's afraid of the Whitney, Los Angeles Weekly, 5/7/93-5/13/93; Roberta Smith (auth), A 24 hour-a-day show on gaudy, bawdy 42nd Street, New York Times, 7/30/93. *Dealer:* D'Amelio Terras 525 W 22nd St New York NY 10011. *Mailing Add:* c/o D'Amelio Terras 525 W 22nd St New York NY 10011

LIJN, LILIANE
SCULPTOR, WRITER
b New York, NY, Dec 22, 39. *Study:* Ecole de Louvre, Paris, Sorbonne, Paris. *Hon Degrees:* Univ Warwick, D Litt (Doctor of Letters), 2005. *Work:* The Brit Coun; Chicago Inst; Bibliot Nat, Paris; Mus Fine Arts, Bern; Victoria and Albert Mus, London; plus many others. *Comn:* Extrapolation, Norfolk & Norwich Triennial Festival, Norwich, 81; Zigzag Blues, Churchill Plaza, Basingsteke, 87; Carbon Black, Nat Chemical Labs, London Argo, NH Schroder, Poole Dorset, 88; Inner Light (24' x 7' Welsh slate, neon), comn by Kumagai Gumi (UK) Ltd & Ranelagh Developments for Prudential Insurance hq, Reading, 92; Dragon's Dance (12'x13'x8', cast bronze), comn by Marks & Spencers for Culverhouse Cross, Cardiff, 94; Earth Sea Light Koan, St Mary's Hosp, Isle of Wight, 97; Inner Light, St Thomas' Hospital, London, 98; Zero Gravity Koan, Commune di Umbertide, Italy, 2004; Starslide, Evelina Children's Hospital, London, 2005. *Exhib:* Exhib, Mus d'Art Mod, Paris, 67 & Electra, 83; 20th Century Drawings & Watercolors, Victoria & Albert Mus, London, 85; Livres d'Artistes, Centre George Pompidou, Paris, 85; Liliane Lijn: Poem Machines 1962-1968, Nat Arts Libr, Victoria & Albert Mus, London, 93; Art Unlimited, South Bank Ctr Exhib, touring, 94; Catalyst for Care, Wellcome Found, 94; British Abstract Art II, Angela Flowers Gallery, London, 95; Liliane Lijn: Her Mothers Voice (with catalog), Eagle Gallery, London, 96; Chimeriques Polymeres, Mus d'Art Mod de la Vill de Nice, 96; Rubies & Rebels, Concourse Gallery, Barbican & touring, 96; Liliane Lijn: Poem machines & other book works, Nat Libr Gallery, Wellington & Govett-Brewster Gallery, New Plymouth, NZ, 98; solo exhib, Lara Vincy, Koans Gallerie, Paris, 97, Koans Shirley Day Ltd, London, 2000, Force Fields, Mus of Contemp Art, Barcelona, Hayward Gallery, London, 2000, Dream Machines, South Bank Nat Touring Exhib, UK, 2000; Light and Memory, Centro per l'Art Contemporanea, Rocca di Umvertide; Claudio Nardi, Florence, 2002; Liliane Lijn Works 1959-1980, Mead Gallery, Univ of Warwick, Coventry, 2005; Austin Desmond Fine Art, Eng & Co Gallery, London, 2006. *Awards:* Publishing Award, Art Coun GB, 81; Award, Arts Coun Bursary Holography, 82; LFVPA Prod Award, 97; Art Council of England, International Artist Fellowship Residency, Space Sciences Lab, Berkeley Univ of CA, 2005. *Bibliog:* Phillipa Scott (auth), New Sculpture (catalog), Gillian Jason Gallery, London, 90; David Mellor (ed), The Sixties Art Scene in London (catalog), Phaidon Press, London, 93; Art in the Electric Age, Frank Popper, Thames & Hudson, London, New York, Editions Hazon, Paris, 93; Light Matters, Women's Art Mag, Jan/Feb 95; Oliver Bennett (auth) May the force be with you, The Guardian Weekend, 7/15/2000; plus others. *Media:* All Industrially Used Materials. *Publ:* Auth, What is art?, Ostrich No 9, Northumberland, 9/73; Six Throws of the Oracular Keys, Ed de la Nepe, Paris, 82; Crossing Map, Thames & Hudson, 83; Imagine the Goddess, A Rebirth of the Female Archetype in Sculpture, Leonardo, Vol XX, No 2; Body and Soul: Interactions between the Material and the Immaterial in Sculpture, Vol 31, No, 1, 5-12, Leonardo, 98; Light & Memory, Thames & Hudson Ltd, London, 2002; Liliane Lijn: Works 1959-1980, Mead Gallery Cornerhouse Publ, 2005. *Mailing Add:* 28 Camden Sq London NW1 9XA United Kingdom

LILES, CATHARINE (BURNS)
PAINTER, PATRON

b Macon, Ga, 44. *Study:* Wesleyan Col BFA(magna cum laude), 79; Mercer Univ, MLS, 89; with Constantine Chatov, Rhett English & Ann Adams. *Work:* Univ Tex Med Sch, Houston; Art by Am Women, Louise & Alan Sellars Collection, Marietta, Ga; King & Spalding Attys, Washington, DC; Arnall Golden Gregory Atty, Macon, Ga; City of Macon, France. *Comn:* Macon Symphony, Southern Bel Co; Macon Cherry Blossom Festival; Mercer Med Sch. *Exhib:* Solo & group exhibs, People & Places, Middle Ga Col, 81, Faces & Figures, Mercer Univ, 82 & Pittura dal Muro, JH Webb Gallery, Macon, Ga, 84; Who Am I?, Mus Arts & Scis, Macon, Ga, 83; Paintings by Am Women, Mus Arts & Scis, 83, Brenau Col, Gainesville, Ga, 91, Etowah Art Coun, Cartersville, Moultrie Art Ctr & Kennesaw Col, Marietta, Ga, 92; Art by Am Women, Brenau Col, Gainesville, Ga, 91, Knoxville Mus Art, Tenn, 92 & St Petersburg Mus Art, Fla, 93. *Pos:* Owner & pres, Markwell Inc, Healthcare Marketing Liles & Assoc, 82-2001, retired; past pres, Macon Arts Alliance; past pres, Macon Mus Arts & Scis. *Teaching:* Instr figure drawing & portrait painting, Mercer Univ, 1/83-9/83. *Awards:* Best in Show Print, Addy Award, Ad Club Central Ga, 87 & 88; Outstanding Alumni Award, Wesleyan Col, 91; Cultural Award, Macon Arts Alliance. *Bibliog:* Paul E Sternberg (auth), Paintings by American Women: Selections from the Collection of Louise & Alan Sellars, 89 & Art by American Women, 91. *Mem:* Macon Arts Alliance; assoc mem Am Watercolor Soc; Middle Ga Art Asn; assoc mem Nat Watercolor Soc; Ga Watercolor Soc. *Media:* Watercolor, Oil. *Dealer:* Art By American Women 2120 Cornerstone Lane Marietta GA 30064. *Mailing Add:* PO Box 6218 Macon GA 31208

LILES, RAEFORD BAILEY
PAINTER, SCULPTOR

b Birmingham, Ala, July 20, 23. *Study:* Birmingham-Southern Col, 41-43, 46-47; Auburn Univ, BSEE, 49; Atelier Fernand Leger, Paris, France, 49-51. *Work:* Musee d'Art Mod, Eliat, Israel; Andrew Dickson White Mus Art, Cornell Univ; Corcoran Gallery Art, Washington, DC; Amos Andersons Konstmuseum, Helsingor, Finland; Alfred Khouri Collection, Norfolk Mus, Va; Boston Col Mus Art, Mass; Birmingham Mus Art, Ala; Grey Art Gallery, New York Univ, NY; New Sch Social Research, NY. *Comn:* Silk screen series, East Hampton Gallery, NY, 67; also pvt collections. *Exhib:* Salon d'Art Independent & Art Libre, Paris, 51; Salon Nouvelle Reality, Mus Mod Art, Paris, 55; Mirco Salon d'Avril, Iris Clert, Paris, 56; Birmingham Mus, 72; Solo shows, Gallery 8, Paris, 51, East Hampton Gallery, NY, 67, Gibbes Art Gallery, Charleston, SC, 75, Univ Ark, Little Rock, 78, EM Donahue Gallery, NY, 93 & 95. *Awards:* Prize, Students of Leger, 51; First Prize, Alpine Gallery, 58. *Bibliog:* Turpin (auth), L'Orleanais Dans Les Art, 52; Orinese (auth), Tour D'Expositions Combat, 55; Brown (auth), Review of expositions, Art Mag, 68. *Mem:* Birmingham Art Asn; Ala Watercolor Soc. *Media:* All Media. *Mailing Add:* 310 Riverside Dr Apt 702 New York NY 10025-4143

LILJEGREN, FRANK
PAINTER, INSTRUCTOR

b New York, NY, Feb 23, 30. *Study:* Art Students League, with John Groth, Dean Cornwell, Frank J Reilly, Arthur Schwieder & Saul Tepper. *Work:* Manhattan Savings Bank, NY; Am Educ Publ Inst, NY; New Britain Mus Am Art, Conn; Art Students League, NY; Univ Mus, Southeast Mo State Univ, Cape Giradeau, Mo. *Comn:* Pastel Portrait, First Presby Church, Van Wert, Ohio; Pastel of the Brumback Libr, Van Wert, Ohio. *Exhib:* Nat Acad Designs, NY; Coun Am Artists Soc, Lever House, NY, 64 & 67; Salmagundi Club, NY, 64-68; Acad Artists Asn, Springfield Fine Arts Mus, Mass, 66-70; OS Ranch Exhib, Tex, 77-80; Ft Wayne Mus Art, Ind, 79. *Teaching:* Instr painting, Westchester Co Art Workshop, White Plains, 66-77, Art Students League, 73-74, Wassenberg Art Ctr, Van Wert, Ohio, 77-80, Wright State Univ, 81-. *Awards:* Allied Artists Am Awards; Frank V Dumond Award, Salmagundi Club, 65 & 67; Medal of Merit for Oil Painting, Today's Art Mag, 71. *Bibliog:* Jo Mary McCormick-De Guyton (auth), Frank Liljegren and his old friends, Am Artist Mag, 2/72; Ralph Fabri (auth), Medal of merit winner in 58th A A A annual, Today's Art Mag, 3/72; Linda Evans (dir), Frank Liljegren - How Much is an Artist Worth - My Mentor, Myself, 93. *Mem:* Allied Artists Am (corresp secy, 67, exhib chmn, 68-76, pres, 70-72, dir, 72-76); Artists Fel; Salmagundi Club; life mem Art Students League. *Media:* Oil, Pastels. *Specialty:* Still Lifes in Oils & Pastels. *Interests:* Visiting Mus, Reading Biographies about Artists. *Collection:* St. Francis Univ, Ft Wayne, IND, (Permanent Collection). *Dealer:* Liljegren Galleries 203 S Cherry St Van Wert OH 45891-2006. *Mailing Add:* 203 S Cherry St Van Wert OH 45891-2006

LILLIE, LLOYD
SCULPTURE

b Wash, May 20, 32. *Study:* Boston Mus Sch, Diploma with highest honors; student, Skowhegan Sch Painting and Sculpture; student, Corcoran Sch Art, Wash; student, Academia di Belle Arti, Florence, Italy. *Exhib:* One-man shows incl St Botolph Club, Boston, Falmouth, Mass Pub Libr Bumpus Gallery, Duxbury, Mass, Cambridge Art Asn, Mirsky Gallery, Boston, Mount Ida Col, Newton, Mass, Milton, Mass Acad; exhib in group shows at Corcoran Gallery Art, Wash, Nat Sculpture Soc, New York City, Art Inst of Boston, Boston Pub Libr, Palazzo Mediceo, Seravezza, Italy, Nat Acad of Design Invitational, 98, Forest Hills Cemetery Invitational, Boston, 98, Forest Lawn Cemetery Invitational, 99, Nat Sculpture Soc, 2000. *Collection Arranged:* permanent collections Boston Pub. Libr, Am Embassy, Riyadh, Saudi Arabia, Col William and Mary, Va, Univ Va, Charlottesville, Jefferson Univ, Philadelphia. *Pos:* Boston Mus Sch traveling fel, 59; Camargo Found fel, Cassis, France, 90. *Teaching:* fac, Boston Univ, 61—95, prof art, 74—95, prof emer, 95—. *Awards:* Bronze medal, Nat Sculpture Soc, 91; Gov's Design award, for Curley Park, Boston, 1st prize in sculpture, Boston Arts Festival, 91; Recipient 1st prize in sculpture, Nat Acad of Design, 94; Sydney Simon prize in sculpture, 99. *Mem:* Nat Acad

LILYQUIST, CHRISTINE
EGYPTOLOGIST, CURATOR

b Glendale, Calif, Aug 15, 40. *Study:* Pomona Col, BA, 62; NY Univ, MA, 65, PhD, 71. *Collection Arranged:* Dir, Dendur Temple Installation, Metrop Mus Art, New York, 72-78, dir, Egyptian Reinstallation, 72-83, consult, Renovation of the Cairo Mus, 75-77 & cur, Mus Consortium for the Exhib Treasures of Tutankhamun, 75-79. *Pos:* Asst cur Egyptian dept, Metrop Mus Art, New York, 70-72, assoc cur in charge, 72-74 & cur, 74-; consult, New York City Dept Park & Rec (Cleopatra's Needle), 78-80. *Mem:* Col Art Asn. *Res:* Egyptian gold, Middle Kingdom arts. *Publ:* Ed, Tutankhamun Exhib Publ, Metrop Mus Art, New York, 76; auth, Ancient Egyptian Mirrors: From the Earliest Times Through the Middle Kingdom, Munchner Aegyptologische Studien 27, 79. *Mailing Add:* c/o Wallace Res Curatorship Egyptology Metrop Mus Art Fifth Ave at 82nd St New York NY 10028

LIMA, JACQUELINE (DUTTON)
PAINTER, DRAFTSMAN

b Niagara Falls, NY, Oct 28, 49. *Study:* Swain Sch Design, New Bedford, MA, BFA, 78; Brooklyn Col, City Univ New York, MFA, 80. *Comn:* Hand painted wearable buttons, Rotunda Gallery, Brooklyn, NY, 85; 22' Circular ceiling mural, comn by New York Bd Educ & New York Sch Construction Authority, 96; A Family Portrait, Collection of John & Diane Herzog, 97; Infinite Collection of Flory Gardner, 98. *Exhib:* One-person Exhib, Fairleigh Dickinson Univ, Becton Hall Gallery, Teaneck, NJ, 3/98; Law Offices of Fredy H Kaplan, 26 Broadway, NY, 97; Art from the Ridge, L Gallery, Moscow, Russ & Berlin, Ger, 98; Time and Place, Kleinert/James Art Ctr, Woodstock, NY, 98; Object & Photo (Process the Image), Eklektikos Gallery, Georgetown, Washington, DC & East Ashland, Phoenix, Ariz, 98; Kentler Int Drawing Space, Red Hook, Brooklyn, 98. *Collection Arranged:* On the Waterfront, Kentler Int Drawing Space, 97; Members Exhib, Plymouth Church Pilgrims, Brooklyn, NY, 91, 92 & 93. *Pos:* Dir, Blue Mountain Gallery, NY, 91-98; cur, Brooklyn Water Front Artists Coalition, 88-93, exhib, Brookwood Child Care, Brooklyn, NY, 92 & 93; art therapist, Psychiatric Inpatient Prog, Coney Island Hosp, Brooklyn, NY, 92-95. *Teaching:* Instr, Hist & Theory Design Workshop, MFA Prog, Brooklyn Col, City Univ New York, 94-96; instr landscape drawing & painting, Western Carolina Univ, Cullowhee, 97; instr drawing, computer graphics/illus, New York Art World, Desktop Publ, Avant Garde Film, Fairleigh Dickinson Univ, Teaneck, NJ, 94-98. *Awards:* Charles W Shaw Award, Brooklyn Col, 79 & 80; Dr Maury Leibovitz Art Award, Lotos Club, Artists Welfare Fund, 86. *Bibliog:* Review of the World is Round, Contemporary Panoramas, Vivian Raynor, The New York Times, Jan 89; Review, Jed Perl (auth), The New Criterion, May 90; Jed Pearl (auth), Gallery Going Four Seasons in the Art World, The New Criterion, Harcourt Brace Jovanovich, 5/91. *Mem:* Brooklyn Waterfront Artists Coalition (bd dir, 85 & 86, rec secy, 87, vpres, 88, pres, 89, consult, 90-94). *Media:* Oil and graphite, acrylic. *Publ:* Crysalis J of the Reproduction of Who Would Have Ever Thought, spring 88; Crossings, An Artists Book ed by Nedd: Heller, 91 & 92. *Mailing Add:* 353 Van Brunt St Brooklyn NY 11231-1245

LIMONT, NAOMI CHARLES
PRINTMAKER, PAINTER

b Pottstown, Pa. *Study:* Pa Acad Fine Arts, BFA; Pratt Graphic Ctr, with Michael Ponce de Leon; Barnes Found; Univ Pa, BFA; Tyler Sch Art, with Romas Viesulas, MFA; also with Jerome Kaplan. *Work:* Philadelphia Mus Art & Pa Acad Fine Arts; Yale Univ; Eastern Mennonite Col, Va; Univ Southern Calif; Rutgers Univ, NJ. *Comn:* Mural, St Christopher's Children's Hosp, Philadelphia, 65; Creation (folio of prints), Philadelphia Print Club, 67; Folio '76 (bicentennial folio), Graphics Guild, Cheltenham, Pa, 75; Folio of Prints, The Centennial of Sun Printing Co, 80. *Exhib:* Int Biannual Print Show, Print Club, 77; Nat Print Exhib, Cedar City, Utah, 78; Eye on the Seventies, Philadelphia Mus Art, 79; Int Miniature Print Exhib, NY, 79; Structures, Rosenwald Gallery, Van Pelt-Dietrich Libr, Univ Pa, Philadelphia; and others. *Teaching:* Artist-in-residence, Lock Haven State Col, 81; instr graphics, Abington Art Ctr, 84-89. *Awards:* Sun Oil Award, Earth Art Exhib, 75; Stella Drabkin Award & Bronze Medal, Am Color Print Soc, 76; Grumbacher Award, 81, Guild Book Workers, Del Valley Guild Book Workers. *Bibliog:* Bagnell & Sosin (coordrs), The Tyler Show working women artists from Tyler School of Art, Samuel Paley Libr, Temple Univ, 73; review, Art News, 9/80; review, Art Voices, 3-4/81. *Mem:* Philadelphia Watercolor Club; Guild Bookworkers

LIN, MAYA Y
SCULPTOR

b Athens, Ohio, Oct 5, 59. *Study:* Yale, BA, 81, MA(archit), 86, Hon Dr Fine Arts, 87. *Work:* Los Angeles Co Mus Art; Vietnam Veterans Mem, Washington, DC. *Exhib:* Prin work incl Vietnam Veterans Mem, Washington, 81; Am Women Artists - Par II, The Younger Generation, Sidney Janis Gallery, NY, 84; Jane Voorhees Zimmerli Art Mus, Rutgers State Univ, NJ, 85; Civil Rights Memorial, Montgomery, Ala, 86; Avant-Garde in the Eighties, Los Angeles Co Mus Art, 87; 60's-80's Sculpture Parallels, Sidney Janis Gallery, 88; Group Exhib, Rosa Esman Gallery, NY, 90; solo exhibs, Industrial Ecology, Bronx Community Paper Co Munic Art Soc, NY, 97, Recent Work, Gagosian Gallery, Beverly Hills, Calif, 99, Maya Lin: Between Art and Archit, Cooper Union, Arthur A Houghton, Jr Gallery, NY, 2000; Urban Mythologies: The Bronx Represented Since the 1960s, The Bronx Mus of the Arts, NY, 99; Powder, The Aspen Art Mus, Colo, 99; The cultural Desert, Bentley Gallery, Mayo Clinic Scottsdale, Mus of Contemp Art, Ariz, 2002. *Pos:* Design consult, Cooper-Lecky Partnership, Washington, DC, 81-82; archit designer, Peter Forbes & Assocs, Boston, 83, Batey & Mack, San Francisco, 84; archit apprentice, Fumihiko Maki & Assocs, Tokyo, 85; design assoc, Peter Forbes & Assocs, NY, 86-87; Maya Lin Studio, NY, 87-. *Teaching:* Archit studio instr, Phillips Exeter Acad, summer 82; head teaching asst, Yale Art Hist Dept, 84-85; vis prof, Yale Col Seminar, 86; vis lectr, Harvard Univ,

Sch Landscape Design, Cambridge, Mass, 88; Resident in Fine Arts Am Acad, Rome, 98; vis lectr, Portland Arts and Lects, 97, TED Conf, 99. *Awards:* Henry Bacon Mem Award, AIA, 84; Nat Endowment Arts, 88; Design 100 - Elements of Style, Metrop Home, 90; Am Acad of Arts and Letters, award in Archit, 96; LVMH, Sci pour L'Art Award, 96; Finn Juhl Award, Wilhelm Hansen Found, Copenhagen, 2003. *Bibliog:* Alice Hall (ed), Vietnam Mem, Nat Geographic, 5/85; Jonathan Coleman (auth), Time Mag, 11/6/89; Boundaries (auth), 2000. *Mem:* Natural Resources Defense Counc (bd mem, NY, 98-); Nat Acad Design; Nat Acad Arts and Letters. *Mailing Add:* c/o Gagosian 980 Madison Ave New York NY 10021

LIN, SARA
PAINTER, CALLINGRAPHER
b Tiawan, Mar 25, 40. *Study:* Worldjournal Col, 1966-1970; Dr Ma Sing-Foon Calligraphy, 1982-1990; Jason Chang art studio, NY, 1996. *Work:* Nat Hist Mus, Taipei, Taiwan. *Comn:* Bearo's Italian Restaurant, Conn, 2000; Terence Cardinal Cooke Healthcare Ctr, 2003; Taiwan Cult Ctr, Taipe Econ & Cult Office, NY, 2006. *Exhib:* Sara Lin's Pastel Exhib, Lin's Studio, Brooklyn, NY, 1999; Pastel Soc Am Ann Exhib, Nat Art Club, Manhattan, NY, 1999, 2003, 2005; Am Artist Prof League Ann Exhib, Salmagundi Club, Manhattan, NY, 2002-2004; Audubon Artist Inc Ann Exhib, Salmagundi Club, Manhattan, NY, 2002-2005; Allide Artists Am Inc Exhib, Nat Art Club, Manhattan, NY, 2004. *Pos:* Pastels demonstr, N Am Pastel Artists 4th Ann Show, 2002-2004; exhib ch, N Am Pastel Artists Exib, 2003-2006; Juror selection, Taiwan Ctr Int Pastel Juried Exhib, 2005-2006; Exhib chmn, NTD TV Childrens Art Competition, 2006. *Awards:* Grumbacher Gold Medal, Conn Pastel Soc 10th Ann Exhib, 2003; President's Award, Am Artists Prof League, NY, 2004; Art Spirit Found Dianne B Bernhard Award of Merit, Life, Audubon Artists Art Soc, 2005. *Bibliog:* Jason Chang (auth), Pastel World of Jason Chang, G&P Col Marshall Wei, 1999. *Mem:* Pastel Soc Am (signature mem); AudubonArtists Inc (full mem); Am Artists Prof League; NY Chinese Calligraphy Arts Soc; N Am Pastel Artist Asn (exhib chair). *Media:* Pastels, Chinese Painting. *Dealer:* Taiwan Cult Ctr 137-44 Northern Blvd Flushing NY 11354. *Mailing Add:* 1215 8th Ave Brooklyn NY 11215

LINCOLN, DIANE THOMAS
PAINTER, CURATOR
b Albany, NY Jan 19, 48. *Study:* studied Avila Univ, Kansas City, Mo, 66-68, Kansas City Art Inst, 66, Minn Univ, 69; Kans Univ, Lawrence, BAE, 71; Wichita State Univ, MFA, 76; Post Grad Res Ctr, Yugoslavia, cert, 85. *Work:* St Francis Regional Med Ctr, Wichita State Univ Alumni Collection, Kans; Archdiocese of Miami, Fla; Cath Church Exten Soc, Chicago, Ill; Pilgrimage USA-Kansas Interfaith Economic Development, tour sacred spaces in Kansas 85-current Consultation and Development; Sacred Space; A Collaborative Exhibition, WSU Ulrich Mus of Art and Children's Peace Pavillion, Independence, Kans, Temple of Christ, 2002. *Comn:* Renovation, St John's Chapel, Salina, Kans; mural, St Bernard's Roman Catholic Church, Ellsworth, Kans, 98; Art Direction, Commission Big Brothers, Big Sister of Wichita, Kans, Tile mural, Interactive, collaboraitive art project between children and adults; St Elizabeth Ann Seaton, Salina, Kans; Bishop Miege High Sch, Kansas City; St Mary's, Salina. *Exhib:* Our Lives, Women Experiences, Kans Univ Hays Ctr Gallery, Lawrence, 85; Wichita Exhibs, Wichita Art Mus, Kans, 87; Fac Exhibs, E Ulrich Mus, Wichita, Kans, 91; solo exhib, Marylhurst Col, Portland, Ore, 93; Marian Exhib, Pontifical Marian Res Ctr, Univ Dayton, Ohio, 94; Two Person Exhib Compassion In conjunction with the Tex Tech Univ Vatican Exhib Tex Technol Int Cult Ctr, Lubbock, Tex, 2003 April - Aug. *Collection Arranged:* Women in Arts Inc, 85; Art Forms Holocaust, Wichita State Univ, 88; Clayton Staples Gallery, 92; De Mattias Gallery, 92; Cath Diocese Wichita, Newman Col, 92. *Pos:* Art gallery owner, Phoenix Art Inst, 82-86; art gallery dir, Wichita State Univ, 86-92 & prog dir, decorative & ornamental painting design cert prog, Sch Art & Design; dir, Demattias Gallery, Kans Newrian Univ. *Teaching:* Asst prof art & theology, Kans Newman Col, 90-92; asst prof, Wichita State Univ, Sch Art & Design. *Awards:* Alpha Delta Kappa Award, Ore, 89; Brotherhood-Sisterhood, Nat Conf/Christians & Jews Holocaust Educator, 89; Col of Fine Arts, Wichita State Univ Awarded Creative Research Activities Award, 2003, Wichita, Kans; Best Art Dir Award Wichita Art and Humanities for Sacred Space; a collaborative exhib, Wichita, Kans. *Bibliog:* James Reimer (auth), 9th Int Conf-Future of Religion, Conrad Grebel, 87; Joan Mitchell (auth), Cultural renaissance, Wichita State Univ Mag, 90; David Ramsey (auth), Arch Mod Christian Art, 91. *Mem:* Arch Mod Christian Art; Kans Multi Cult Arts Alliance (pres, 92-94); Women in Arts Inc; Nat Conf Christians & Jews Inc. *Media:* All Media. *Res:* Sacred & liturgical art. *Publ:* Todays Liturgy Mag, Kansas City, Mo, 92; Ore Cath Press Missal/Mag, 92-93; Second Opinion, Park Ridge Ctr, Chicago, 93; A Review of Literature, Art and Public Affaire, Cresset, Valpairso Univ, 97; The Decorative Painter, Nat Soc Decorative Painters, Issue 4, 98. *Dealer:* Gallery Genesis 4201 S Archer Ave Chicago IL 60632. *Mailing Add:* 1602 Woodrow Ct Wichita KS 67203

LINCOLN, JANE LOCKWOOD
PAINTER, PRINTMAKER
b Exeter, NH, Mar 17, 50. *Study:* St Lawrence Univ, BA (studio), 72; Cape Sch Art, 84-87; Art New England, with Wolf Kahn, 91; Armory Art Center with Bill Scott. *Work:* Cahoon Mus Am Art, Cotuit, Mass; Cape Cod Mus Art, Dennis, Mass; 4 panel mural, McCarthy House, Sandwich, Mass; Dartmouth Hitchcock Med Center (4 print installation), Lebanon, NH. *Comn:* Landscape, comn by H Zimmerman, New Seabury, Mass, 2000; Landscape, comn by J Budd, Dover, Mass, 2000; Landscape, comn by R Hallagan, Dover, Mass, 2002; Landscape, comn by C Goldberg, Tamarac, Fla, 2004; 6 print series, comn by J Borak, Guilford, Conn, 2005. *Exhib:* Three Sisters, Manchester Inst, NH, 96; Cape Mus Natural History, Brewster, Mass, 98; Visions, Cape Cod Community Coll, Bamstable, Mass, 98, Generations, 2000; Biennial Alumni, St Lawrence Univ, Canton, NY, 98; Fields of Color, Cahoon Mus Am Art, Cotuit, Mass, 99, Signature, 2000, Snow Birds, 2003; Pastel Show Ellison Ctr for Arts, Duxbury, Mass, 2000; Signature, Cape Mus Fine Arts, Dennis, Mass, 2003; Illuminations, Mass Gen Hospital, Boston, 2002-03; Solo Exhib (62 landscapes), Cranberry Bogs, Cape Cod Mus Art, Dennis, Mass, 2005-2006. *Collection Arranged:* Cape Cod Mus Natural History, Brewster, Mass, 2004; Cahoon Mus Am Art, Cotuit, Mass, 2005; Cape Cod Mus Art, Dennis, Mass, 2005, 06; Wynne-Falconer Gallery, Chatham, Mass, 2005. *Pos:* Chair, Signature Pastel Partners Soc, Cape Cod, 2001-2006. *Teaching:* color theory, Falmouth Artists Guild, 89-2000, abstract, 2003; lectr color mixing, Bamstable Pub Schs, 95-2000; lectr color mixing, Cahoon Mus Am Art, 99; lectr color theory, Cape Cod Art Asn, Barnstable, 2004; lectr color, Cape Cod Community Col, Barnstable, 2003. *Awards:* Color Award, 22nd Faber Birren Nat, Stamford, Conn, 2002; Canson Award, Pastel Painters Soc Cape Cod, Chatham, Mass, 2006; Best Pastel, Falmouth Artists Guild, Falmouth, Mass, 2006. *Bibliog:* Exploring color with Jane Lincoln, The Pastel J, 2003; Jane Lincoln: Applying Color Theory to Painting the Landscape, The Pastel J, 2003; On Defining Personal Style, Pastelagram, Pastel Soc Am, Winter 2003; Mistress of the Bogs, Cape Codder, 2006. *Mem:* Mus Fine Arts Boston; Pastel Soc Am; Pastel Painters Soc Cape Cod (signature); Falmouth Artists Guild; Pastel Painters Maine; Creative Arts Ctr; Arts Coun, Martin Co, Fla; Printmakers Cape Cod. *Media:* Pastel, Oil, White-Line Woodblock Prints. *Publ:* coauth, Two for the Road, Am Artist,92; contribr, Exhibits Add Some Color, Boston Globe, 96, Liestyle & Arts, Cape Cod Times, 99; illusr, Take in Some Local Color-Spyglass, Cahoon Mus, 99; contribr, Guide, Art in Am, 2000. *Dealer:* Cape Gallery Framer 245 Rt 28 Falmouth MA 02540; Wynne-Falconer Gallery 492 Main St Chatham MA 02633; Jacob-Fanning Gallery PO Box 3033 Wellfleet MA 02667. *Mailing Add:* 441 Central Ave East Falmouth MA 02536

LINCOLN, RICHARD MATHER
CERAMIST, EDUCATOR
b Ann Arbor, Mich, Mar 1, 29. *Study:* Potters Guild, Ann Arbor, with Rhoda Le Blanc Lopez & J T Abernathy. *Work:* Dallas Mus Fine Arts; Witte Mus, San Antonio, Tex; Detroit Inst Arts; Davenport Art Ctr, Iowa. *Comn:* Mural, Apparel Mart, Dallas; mural, Ft Worth Children's Hosp, Tex; light fixtures, The Quadrangle, Dallas. *Exhib:* Eight Ceramic Nat & Int Exhibs, Everson Mus, Syracuse, NY, 54-68; Young Americans, NY, 56; Fiber, Clay & Metal, St Paul, Minn, 60; Miami Ceramic Nat, 60; five S Cent Regional Exhibs, Santa Fe, NMex, 62-71. *Teaching:* Assoc prof ceramics, Tex Christian Univ, 63-. *Awards:* Third Pottery Prize, Young Americans, 56; Purchase Award, Univ Mich Mus, 56; First Pottery Award, SCent Regional Exhib, 62. *Bibliog:* Texas potter--Richard Lincoln, Designers W, 11/70. *Mem:* Am Craftsmen Coun. *Mailing Add:* 4759 Westcreek Dr Ft Worth TX 76133-1371

LINDAHL, TONI
PAINTER
b Paterson, NJ, Nov 8, 49. *Study:* NY Univ, MA. *Work:* Volvo-White Corp Hq; Duke Univ; Lowes Co; Centura; Glaxo, Inc. *Comn:* Pastel paintings, Sheraton Hotel, Greensboro, NC, 84; Pastel paintings, Hilton Hotel, Altamonte, Fla, 85; Pastel paintings, Wachovia Bank-Trust Co, Winston-Salem, NC, 90; Pastel paintings, Women's Hosp, Chapel Hill, NC, 2000. *Exhib:* Danville Art Mus, Danville, Va; Art on paper Exhib, Weatherspoon Gallery, UNCG; NC in NY, Nat Arts Club, New York, NY; invitational, Greenhill Ctr for NC Art, Greensboro, NC; Pastel Soc Am Exhib, Nat Arts Club, New York, NY. *Awards:* Nat Juried Exhib Award, numerous awards; Master Pastelist Award, Pastel Soc Am; Joseph U Giffuni Found Award; Award for Best Pastel, Salmagundi Arts Club, 85; Best in Show, Henley Southwestern Spectrum, 91. *Bibliog:* The Best of Pastels, Portrait Inspirations & Floral Inspirations, Rockport Publ. *Mem:* Greenhill Ctr for NC Art; NC Pastel Soc; Assoc Artists of Winston-Salem; Degas Pastel Soc; Pastel Soc Am. *Media:* Pastel Artist. *Interests:* Environmental issues. *Dealer:* Solo Art Gallery Miller St Winston-Salem NC; 2AC Art Gallery 609 S Elm St Greensboro NC. *Mailing Add:* 546 Birch Creek Rd Mc Leansville NC 27301

LINDEMANN, ADAM
COLLECTOR
b 62. *Study:* Amherst Col, BA; Yale Univ Law Sch, JD. *Pos:* founder, pres & CEO, Mega Communications Co, NY, 98-; appointee, Bush-Cheney FCC Adv Comt, 2001. *Awards:* Nominated Top 200 Art Collectors, ARTnews, 2006. *Mailing Add:* Mega Communications 701 Dahlia St NW Washington DC 20012

LINDEMANN, EDNA M
MUSEUM DIRECTOR, EDUCATOR
b Buffalo, NY. *Study:* Univ Buffalo, BS(art, dist); Albright Art Sch; Northwestern Univ, MA(magna cum laude), 40; Cranbrook Acad Art; Columbia Univ, EdD, 56. *Collection Arranged:* Burchfield Int Exhib, 68; 150 Years of Portraitive in Western NY, 81; Charles Clough: Selections 1972-81, 83; Charles Cary Rumsey, Sculptor: 1879-1922, 83; Niagara Falls, New Impressions, 85; Burchfield and His Colleagues, 89. *Pos:* Dir cult affairs, State Univ NY, Buffalo, 65-68; dir, Burchfield Art Ctr, 68-85, emer dir, 85-; Burchfield-Penney Art Ctr Coun, 68-; chmn, Gallery, Asn NY State, 70-72, mem bd dir, 72-77. *Teaching:* Instr art educ, NY Univ, 49-56; prof design, State Univ NY, Buffalo, 56-85, emer prof, 85-. *Awards:* Focus Award for Outstanding Contribution to Cult Affairs, Western New York-Buffalo Courier Express, 76; Achievement Award, Am Asn Univ Women, 83; Citizen of Yr Award, Buffalo News, 85. *Mem:* Gallery Asn NY State (found mem & chmn, 72-75); Burchfield Art Ctr, Buffalo, NY (found dir, dir emer current); Art Appraisers Asn; Am Asn Mus; Buffalo & Erie Co Botanical Gardens Soc (bd dir, 86-). *Res:* A comparative analysis of museums devoted to one artist or a small group of artists in the United States, Canada and worldwide; Charles E Burchfield and other Western NY artists. *Publ:* Auth, Our Legacy of Art in Western New York, 72; ed, Edwin Dickinson, 77; Roycroft: Spirit for Today, 77; The American Landscape: Paintings by Allen D'Arrangelo, 79; Auth, Burchfield and his Colleagues: Artist/Dealer/Collector, 89. *Mailing Add:* 52 Behm Rd West Falls NY 14170

LINDENBERG, MARY K
PAINTER, INSTRUCTOR
b New York, NY, Feb 2, 21. *Study:* Hunter Col, BA, 42; Phi Beta Kappa; Pi Mu Epsilon; Magna Cum Laude. *Work:* numerous pvt collections. *Comn:* Christmas Cards, 92 & 93, Courage Cards; Calendars for Am Press, 67, 79, 81, 83, 90, 95. *Exhib:* Brockton Art Mus, Mass, 80; Newport Art Mus, RI, 81; Three-person Show, Providence Art Club, RI, 85; RI Watercolor Soc, Pawtucket, 88; Bierstadt Art Soc, New Bedford, Mass, 88, 93 & 95. *Pos:* Co-founder, Mass Art Week, 57-, New Bedford, Mass, Art Week, 81. *Teaching:* Instr watercolor, New Bedford YWCA, 78-92, Southeastern Mass Univ, 85. *Awards:* First Prize, Brockton Art Mus, 80; Prize for watercolor, Greater Fall River Art Asn, 90; First Prize for drawing, Bierstadt Art Soc, 88; First Prize, Middleboro Art Soc, 87; First Prize, Magic Palette Gallery, 95; First Prize, Westport Art Group, 89. *Bibliog:* Eleanor Roth (auth), Do artists have special perceptions?, AIM Mag, 74; article, Surprising ingredient of creativity, Living Mag, Singapore, 79. *Mem:* Bierstadt Art Soc; Marion Art Ctr; Westport Art Group; Renaissance Art Gallery Fall River. *Media:* Watercolor, Acrylic, Drawing, Abstract Collage. *Publ:* Auth, mem issue, North Light Mag, 80, 83 & 91; Variations on a theme of nature, Palette Talk Mag, 84; Getting started in teaching, Draw Mag, 86. *Dealer:* Lopoukhine Gallery Inc 125 Newbury St Suite 4 Boston MA 02116. *Mailing Add:* 20 Emerald Dr North Dartmouth MA 02747

LINDENFELD, LORE
CRAFTSMAN
b Wuppertal, Ger, Apr 27, 21. *Study:* Black Mountain Col, Color with Josef Albers, Grad Certificate, 48; Textile Study with Anni Albers & Trude Guermonprez; Rutgers Univ, MEd, 82. *Work:* Renwick Gallery, Nat Mus Am Art, Washington, DC; Mus Art & Design, formerly Am Craft Mus, NY; The Newark Mus, Newark, NY; NJ State Mus, Trenton, NJ; Josef & Anni Albers Found, Bethany, Conn. *Exhib:* Lore Kadden Lindenfeld, A Life in Textiles, Black Mountain Mus & Arts Ctr, Asheville, NC, 97; Textiles in Am Fashion, Inst Technol, NY, 98; Bauhaus: Dessau-Chicago, NY, Mus Folkwang, Essen, Ger, 2000; High Fiber, Renwick Gallery, Smithsonian Am Art Mus, Washington, DC, 2005. *Pos:* Textile Designer, Various Companies, 48-58; Docent, Princeton Univ Art Mus, 94-. *Teaching:* fac mem, Middlesex Co Col, 68-86; Instr Weaving, Haystack Mountain Sch Crafts, Deer Isle, ME, 70. *Awards:* Craft fel, NJ State Council of the Arts, 85. *Bibliog:* Sigrid Wortmann Weltge (auth), Lore Kadden Lindenfeld, A Life in Textiles, Black Mountain Mus Arts Ctr; Betty Freudenheim (auth), Rocky Imagery in Fiber, NY Times, 93; Jeff Glenn (auth), Path of Illumination: the Journey of Lore Kadden Lindenfeld, Fiber Arts, 88. *Media:* Fiber. *Publ:* Auth, Boris Aronson: Setting the Stage for Theatrical Inventions, Surface Design Journal, 90; auth, Contemporary Tapestry in Japan, Fiber Arts, 83. *Mailing Add:* 121 Harris Rd Princeton NJ 08540-3375

LINDER, CHARLES KEATING
SCULPTOR
b Pittsburgh, Pa, 67. *Study:* San Francisco Art Inst, BFA, 90; Univ Calif, Berkeley, MFA, 97; studied with David Nash & Larry Jordan; self taught. *Exhib:* Solo exhib, Brian Gross, San Francisco, Calif, 2000, Paula Boettcher Galerie, Berlin, Ger, 2002, Post Gallery, Los Angeles, Calif. *Pos:* found, Alternative Gallery, Refusalon, San Francisco, Calif, currently. *Awards:* Murphy Cadogar Award; Marian Hahn Simpson Fel, Univ Calif, Berkeley; Sobel Award, San Francisco Art Inst. *Mem:* Soc of Independent Artists. *Media:* Metal. *Mailing Add:* 630 Natoma St San Francisco CA 94103

LINDERMAN, EARL WILLIAM
PAINTER
b Endicott, NY, Jan 1, 31. *Study:* Albright Art Sch & NY State Univ Col, BS, 53; Pa State Univ, MEd, 56, EdD, 60. *Work:* Valley Nat Bank Art Collection, Phoenix; William C Brown Publ Co, Dubuque, Iowa; Portland Art Mus, Ore; Lowe Art Gallery, Univ Miami; Eckerd Col, St Petersburg, Fla; and others. *Exhib:* One-man show, Tally Richard's Gallery Contemp Art, Taos, NMex, 78-83; Marilyn Butler Fine Art, Scottsdale, Ariz, 80-84; Aberbach Fine Art, NY, 82; Salon D'Automne, Grand Palais,Paris, France, 82; Elaine Horwitch Galleries, Scottsdale, Ariz, 84-86; CG Rein Galleries, Scottsdale, Ariz, 88-97, Houston, 90-92, St Paul, Minn, 90-94 & Santa Fe, NMex, 90-91; and others. *Teaching:* Prof painting & drawing, Ariz State Univ, Tempe, 66-. *Awards:* Bronze Vessel Second Award, Plains Art Mus, Moorhead, Minn, 79. *Bibliog:* Jim O'Rourke (auth), Earl Linderman, 72-82 Retrospective, Plains Art Mus, 82. *Media:* Oil, Pastel. *Publ:* Auth, Invitation to Vision, 67, coauth, Developing Artistic and Perceptual Awareness, 4th ed, 79 & auth, Teaching secondary School Art, 2nd ed, 80, William C Brown; coauth, Crafts in the Classroom, Macmillan Publ Co, 77, 84; auth, Linderman: The True and Incredible Adventures of Doctor Thrill, Paradise House, 84

LINDGREN, CARL EDWIN
PHOTOGRAPHER, HISTORIAN
b Coeburn, Va, Nov 20, 49. *Study:* Univ Miss, BAE, 72, MEd, 77, EdS, 93; Col of Preceptors, London, FCP, 93; UNISA, DEdu, 99. *Work:* Ctr for Study of Southern Cult, Univ Miss; Ctr for Faulkner Studies, SE Mo State Univ. *Exhib:* Passing Shadows, Faulkner & Yoknapatawpha Conf, Ctr for Study of Southern Cult, 91 & 92, Cossett Gallery, Memphis, Tenn, 92 & Manduri Univ Mus, India, 93; Southern Delight, Fairfax Gallery, London, 93; various showings throughout US, Russia, India and Europe, 2002-04. *Teaching:* Lectr photo, Univ Miss, 79-81, darkroom tech, 91-93; prof hist, Am Military Univ. *Awards:* Cert of Excellence, India Int Photog Coun, 91; Ed Bronze Star Award, Photog Soc Am, 91, 92, 93 & 96. *Bibliog:* Rowan Oak, Royal Soc Arts J, 92; Dr Burl Hunt (auth), Passing shadows, Art Papers, 93; Penni Bolton (auth), From Oxford Street to Oxford; Ole Miss Alumni Rev, 93. *Mem:* Fel Royal Soc Arts, Eng; assoc Indian Int Photog Coun, Madra, India; mem Photog Soc Am. *Media:* Black and White photography. *Publ:* Illusr, Rowan Oak and Yoknapatawpha, The Cape Rock, 91; illusr & auth, The regional photographer, Photog Soc Am J, 92; auth, Teaching photography in the Indian school, Photo Trade Dir, 92; Enigmatic presence, Royal Soc Arts J, 93; illustr, Monuments to the past, Ole Miss Alumni Rev, 93. *Mailing Add:* 10431 Hwy 51 Courtland MS 38620

LINDGREN, CHARLOTTE
SCULPTOR
b Toronto, Ont, Feb 1, 31. *Study:* Univ Mich, BS; Can Coun studies in Finland, Sweden & Eng. *Work:* Canada Mus Civilization, Ottawa; Can Dept External Affairs, Ottawa; York Univ, Toronto; Winnipeg Art Gallery; Confederation Ctr Art Gallery, Charlottetown, PEI; McLaughlin Gallery, Oshawa; Art Gallery of Nova Scotia, Halifax. *Comn:* Ten Light Nets, Queen's Col, Nfld, 68; IBM Headquarters Conference Room, Toronto, 68; Discovery, Expo '70, Can Pavilion, Osaka, Japan, 70; Receptor, CBC Bldg, Montreal, 74; Weir, Fed Fisheries Bldg, Yarmouth, 77. *Exhib:* Montreal Mus Fine Arts, 66; Am Fed Arts, Threads of Hist, 66-69; Nat Art Gallery, Ottawa, 67; Art Gallery of Ont, 74; Can Cult Centre, Paris, France, 76; Harbourfront, Toronto, 80; IV Triennale, Poland, 81; Barbican Centre, London, Eng, 82; Mikrocosmo, Spain, Denmark, Ger, 83-85; Cool Sixties, Canadian Mus Civilization, Ottawa 2005. *Pos:* Mem adv arts panel, Can Coun; consult, Nat Capitol Commission, 78, Pangnirtung Tapestries, 78-81; vpres, Royal Can Acad Arts, 78-81; cur, The Knot Exhib, Mary Black Gallery, Halifax. *Teaching:* Mem fac, NS Col Art & Design, 78-79 & 81-82 & Banff Ctr Fine Arts, 79; vis prof, Royal Col Art, London, 83, 85 & 91. *Awards:* Haystack Sch Scholar Award, 64; Can Coun Arts Award, 65; First Prize Award, Perspective Competition Centennial Comn, Govt Can, 67; Ont Arts Coun Award, 87; presentation grant, Nova Scotia Arts Council; Golden Jubilee Medal, Queen Elizabeth II, 2002. *Bibliog:* C Fraser (auth), article, 6/66 & J Graham (auth), article, 7/71, Arts Can; L Rombout (auth), article, Vie des Arts, winter 67; J Murray (auth), article, Arts Atlantic, winter 80. *Mem:* Royal Can Acad Artists; Can Artists' Representation (NS rep). *Media:* Miscellaneous. *Mailing Add:* 1557 Vernon St Halifax NS B3H 3M8 Canada

LINDMARK, ARNE
PAINTER, INSTRUCTOR
b Poughkeepsie, NY, Oct 26, 29. *Study:* Pratt Inst; also watercolor with Edgar Whitney. *Work:* Huntington Gallery, WVa. *Exhib:* Am Watercolor Soc Traveling Exhibs, 66-79, 93-97; Nat Arts Club Ann, 69-94; Allied Artists Am, 71-94; Mainstreams 72, Marietta, Ohio, 72; Am Watercolor Soc Exchange Show, Sydney, Australia, 79. *Teaching:* Instr painting & watercolor, Huntington Gallery, summer 71; instr, South West Watercolor Soc, Dallas, 78-79, Mid-West Watercolor Soc, Wis, 79, Houston Art Group, 80, Pocono Pines Workshops, Pa, 82 & 83 & Seven S St Workshops, Rockport, Mass, 83, Monterey, Calif, 90-91, Washington, DC & Fairhope, Ala, 93. *Awards:* Samuel J Bloomingdale Mem Award, 73 & Edgar A Whitney Award, 74, Am Watercolor Soc; Ranger Fund Purchase Award, Nat Acad Design, 79; Millard Sheets Award, Am Watercolor Soc, 93. *Bibliog:* Wendon Blake (auth), Acrylic Watercolor Painting, Watson-Guptill, 70; Margit Malstrom (auth), Arne Lindmark, master of the watercolor scene, Am Artist Mag, 1/71; Frank Webb (auth), Watercolor Energies, 83. *Mem:* Am Watercolor Soc; Allied Artists Am; Hudson River Art Asn; Duchess Co Art Asn; Nat Acad Design. *Media:* Watercolor. *Publ:* Splash I, 92; Painting With the White of Your Paper, North Light Pub, 95; Splash 5, 98

LINDQUIST, EVAN
PRINTMAKER, EDUCATOR
b Salina, Kans, May 23, 36. *Study:* Emporia Kans State Univ, BSE, 58; Univ Iowa, MFA, 63. *Work:* Whitney Mus Am Art, NY; Uffizzi, Florence, Italy; Albertina Mus, Vienna, Austria; Nelson-Atkins Art Mus, Kansas City; Art Inst Chicago. *Exhib:* Prints by Seven, Whitney Mus Am Art, NY, 71; Boston Printmakers Ann Exhib, 71-75; Opera Bevilacqua La Masa, Venice, Italy, 77; two-men circulating exhib, Ark Arts Coun, 79-81; Gallerie V Kunstverlag Wolfbrum, Vienna, Austria, 79; Ark Arts Ctr, Little Rock, 83, 86, 87 & 2002; and others. *Pos:* Staff artist, Emporia State Univ, 58-60. *Teaching:* Prof printmaking & drawing, Ark State Univ, Jonesboro, 63-2003; Emer prof Art, 2003-. *Awards:* More than 60 awards including Boston Printmakers, 71-74 & Potsdam Prints, NY State Univ Potsdam, 72; Lifetime Achievement Award, Ark Arts Coun, 04; Distinguished Alumni Award, Emporia State Univ, 04. *Bibliog:* Julia S. Ayres, Printmaking Techniques, Watson-Guptill Pubs, 93; Robert Malone, Yingxue & Scott Wampler, Contemporary American Printmaking, Jilin Fine Arts Pub House, 99; Benny Shaboy, Evan Lindquist, StudioNotes, Benicia, 99-2000. *Mem:* Boston Printmakers; The Print Club, Philadelphia; Soc Am Graphic Artists; Southern Graphics Coun. *Media:* Engraving, Woodcut. *Dealer:* The Old Print Shop, NYC; Sara Howell Gallery, Jonesboro, Ark. *Mailing Add:* 4300 Hickory Lane Jonesboro AR 72401

LINDQUIST, MARK
SCULPTOR
b Oakland, Calif, May 16, 49. *Study:* New England Col, BA, 71; Pratt Inst; Fla State Univ, MFA, 90. *Work:* Metrop Mus Art, NY; High Mus Art, Atlanta, Ga; Dallas Mus Art, Tex; Nat Mus Am Art, Washington, DC; Philadelphia Mus Art; and others. *Comn:* Sculpture, Brockton Art Mus, Mass, 85; 3 sculptures, Nations Bank Corp Hq, Charlotte, NC, 93. *Exhib:* The Art of the Turned Bowl, Renwick Gallery, Smithsonian Inst, 78; Solo shows, Brevard Art Mus, Melbourne, Fla, 86, Franklin Parrasch Gallery, NY, 89, Gail Severn Galley, Ketchum, Idaho, 92, Snyderman Gallery, Philadelphia, 92 & Dorothy Weiss Gallery, San Francisco, Ca, 93; The Poetry of the Physical, Am Craft Mus, NY & traveling, 86-88; Mus Fine Arts, Boston, 91, Am Crafts: The Nation's Collection, Renwick Gallery, Smithsonian Inst, 92; Del Art Mus, 93; The Art of the Woodturner, High Mus Art, Atlanta, Ga, 93; Beyond Nature: Wood into Art (with catalog), Lowe Art Mus, Miami, Fla, 94; The White House Collection Am Art,

Renwick Gallery, Smithsonian Inst, 95; Revolutions in Wood: Mark Lindquist 25 yr Retrospective Hand Workshop Art Ctr, 95; Nat Mus Am Art, 96; The Founders' Circle Collection Inaugural Exhib & The Jane and Arthur Mason Collection, Mint Mus Craft and Design, Charlotte, NC 2000; Wood Turning in N Am since 1930, Renwick Gallery, Smithsonian Inst, Yale Univ & Minneapolis Inst Arts, 2001-2002; Kanazawa World Craft Forum, Kanazawa, Japan, 2003; Devos Art Mus, Marquette, Mich, 2005. *Teaching:* Instr welding & three-dimensional design, New Eng Col, 70-71; head of woodworking, Craft Ctr, Worcester, Mass, 77-78; assoc prof, Sch Archit, Fla A&M Univ, 88-89. *Awards:* MacDowell Colony Fel, NH, 79; Fel, NEA/Southern Arts Fedn, 1989; Hon bd member, James Renwick Alliance, 96. *Bibliog:* Nancy Means Wright (auth), Mark Lindquist: The Bowl Is a Performance, Am Craft Mag, 10/11/80; Janet Koplos (auth), Mark Lindquist at Franklin Parrasch, Art in America, 4/90; Robert Hobbs (auth), Mark Lindquist: Revolutions in Wood, (exhib catolog) 25 yr retrospective at Hand Workshop Art Ctr, Richmond, Va & Renwick Gallery of the Smithsonian Inst, 95. *Mem:* Phi Kappa Phi. *Media:* Wood, Photography. *Publ:* Auth, Spalted Wood, 77, Turning the Spalted Bowl, 78 & Harvesting Burls, 84, Fine Woodworking Mag; Sculpting Wood, Davis Press, 86. *Mailing Add:* 311 Glory Rd Quincy FL 32351

LINDROTH, LINDA
PHOTOGRAPHIC ARTIST, CURATOR

b Miami, Fla, Sept 4, 46. *Study:* Douglass Col, BA(art), 68; Rutgers Univ with Leon Golub, MFA(art), 79; also with Gordon Matta Clark & Garry Winogrand. *Work:* Mus Mod Art, Metrop Mus Art & Mus City of New York, NY; Bibliot Nat, Paris; NJ State Mus, Trenton; Polaroid Corp; High Mus Art, Atlanta; Ctr Creative Photog, Tucson, Ariz; Yale Univ; First Bank of Boston. *Exhib:* Solo exhibs, Newark Mus, NJ, 85-86, City Spirit Artists/The New Haven Found, 86 & Photo Structures 1982-1986, Aetna Inst Gallery, Hartford, Conn, 87; Pub Space in the New Am City/Atlanta 1996 Design Competition, Nexus Contemp Art Ctr, 94; Strokes of Genius: Mini Golf by Artists, DeCordova Mus, Lincoln, Mass, 95; 1994-95 Weir Farm Vis Artists, Aldrich Mus Contemp Art, Ridgefield, Conn, 95; 25 Years of Feminism, 25 Years of Women's Art, Rutgers Univ, New Brunswick, NJ, 96; Beyond the Picture Plane, Conn Comn Arts, Hartford, 96; Natural Immersion, Boston Ctr Arts, 96; Fellowship Exhib, Conn Comn on the Arts, Hartford, 2001; The Bunker with Craig Newick When the Earth Meets the Sky, Creative Arts Workshop, 2002. *Pos:* Founder & dir, Gallery Jazz Inc Art Gallery, New Haven, Conn, 84-87; guest cur, Aetna Inst Gallery, Hartford, 87; co-curator, Pump House Gallery, Hartford, 90-93; Pub Art Comn for Conn Children's Medical Ctr, Hartford, 95-96; coordr fine arts lectr series, Quinnipiac Univ, Hamden, CT, & asst & adj prof fine art, 98-; consultant & interior designer, Artspace Hartford and Artspace Norwich, Live/Work space for Artists, 96-99. *Teaching:* Instr photog, Douglass Col, New Brunswick, NJ, 77-79. *Awards:* Gold Award, Wilmer Shields Rich Awards for Excellence in Commun, 95; Fel Painting, Conn Comn Arts, 95-96; Nat Endowment Arts Regional Fel in Photog, New Eng Found Arts; Finalist, Howard Found, Brown Univ Fel in Art, 2001; Grant, Te Found, Inc, 2002. *Bibliog:* Judy Birke (auth), Art Review, New Haven Register, 10/16/94; Jude Schwendenwien, Art Review, Art New Eng, 12/95; Patricia Rosoff, Seeking to Recapture Paradise Lost, Hartford Advocate, 5/9/96; Linda Lindroth,(auth), Books and Articles. *Publ:* Contribr, New Jersey Photography, 74 & Photographic Process as Medium, 76, Rutgers Univ; Artists Books USA, Independent Cur Inc, 78; Virtual Vintag,e The Insider's Guide to Buying and Selling Fashion Online, Random House, 2002. *Mailing Add:* 219 Livingston St New Haven CT 06511-2209

LINDSAY, ARTURO
SCULPTOR, PAINTER

b Colon, Panama, Sept 29, 46; US citizen. *Study:* Cent Conn State Univ, BA, 70; Univ Mass, MFA, 75; New York Univ, doctoral studies ongoing. *Work:* Nat Union Cuban Writers & Artists, Havana; Slater Mem Mus, Norwich, Conn; Barnett-Aden Collection, Washington, DC; Royal-Athena Galleries, NY; Univ Mass, Amherst. *Comn:* Homage to our Musicians (mural), Craftery Gallery, Hartford, 78; Cinque (mural), Amistad Cult Resource Ctr, Hartford, 78. *Exhib:* Through Young Black Eyes, Wadsworth Atheneum, Hartford, 72-73; Caribbean Festival Arts, Nat Union Cuban Writers & Artists Mus, Havana, Cuba, 79; Black & Hispanic Art in Conn, Slater Mem Mus, Norwich, 80; Art in the Southwest, African Am Mus, Dallas, 81; Artists of the 80's, Los Angeles Co Mus, 83; Houston Artists, Midtown Art Ctr, 84; African Am Art in Pub & Pvt Collections in Atlanta, The High Mus, 84; Caribbean Art: African Currents, Mus Contemp Hispanic Art, Soho, NY, 86; Encuentro de Escultura, Museo de Arte Contemporaneo, Panama City, Panama; Plexus, Santuary of Saitria, Sardinia, Italy. *Pos:* Dir & owner, Galeria Arturo, Hartford, Conn, 79-83; exec dir, Midtown Art Ctr, Houston, 83-84; asst dir, Royal-Athena Galleries, New York & Beverly Hills, 84-. *Teaching:* Instr, Univ Hartford, Univ Conn & NH Col. *Awards:* First Prize, Atlanta Life Ann Exhib & Competition, Atlanta Life Insurance Co, 81. *Bibliog:* Jay Whitsett (dir), Looking Better, Conn Pub Television Show, 78; James Miller (auth), Ancestry & the Art of Arturo Lindsay, Int Rev of African Am Art, 85. *Mem:* Int Sculpture Ctr; Col Art Asn Am; Nat Conf Artists; Art Against Apartheid; Plexus. *Media:* Cast Metal; Multi-Media. *Mailing Add:* 4026 Birchwood Cove Decatur GA 30034-5251

LINDSAY, KENNETH C
HISTORIAN, WRITER

b Milwaukee, Wis, Dec 23, 1919. *Study:* Univ Wis, PhB, 41, scholar, 47, MA, 48, PhD, 51; Ecole du Louvre, Fulbright fel, 49. *Collection Arranged:* Marshall Glasier, An Exhibition of Paintings & Drawings, 59; Jean Leppien, Paintings, Watercolors, Graphic Works, 64; Architectural Process, Works of James Mowry, 67; The Works of John Vandelyn, 70; Angello Ippolito, Retrospective, 75. *Pos:* Mem, NY State Comn Arts, 66-67; coun archit & urban design, Binghamton, 67-68. *Teaching:* Asst surv, Univ Wis, 47-49; instr, Williams Col, 50-51; prof, State Univ NY Binghamton, 51-. *Awards:* NY State Res Found Grants, 67, 69 & 72. *Res:* Modern American painting. *Publ:* Co-auth, Method in Breughel's paintings, J Aesthet & Art Criticism, 15: 376-386; auth, Kandinsky in 1914 New York, Art News, 55; Kandinsky in Russia (catalog), Guggenheim Mus, 63; Les themes l'inconscient, XXe Siecle, 27: 46-52; Millet's Winnower rediscovered, Burlington Mag, 74; plus others. *Mailing Add:* Art Dept Binghamton University PO Box 6000 Binghamton NY 13902

LINDSTROM, GAELL
PAINTER, EDUCATOR

b Salt Lake City, Utah, July 4, 1919. *Study:* Univ Utah, BS; Calif Col Arts & Crafts, MFA; also with Roy Wilhelm, Gloucester, Mass. *Work:* Utah State Univ; Southern Utah State Col. *Comn:* Murals, Southern Utah State Col & Cedar City Pub Libr; mosaic mural, Utah State Univ Forestry Bldg, 61. *Exhib:* Am Watercolor Soc, 53 & 57; Calif Watercolor Soc, 57. *Collection Arranged:* Maynard Dixon Exhib, Southern Utah State Col, 55; Nat Ceramic Exhib, 57 & 58 & Nat Painting Exhib, 58, Utah State Univ. *Teaching:* Prof art, Southern Utah State Col, 53-56, Utah State Inst Fine Arts, 57-61 & Utah State Univ, 57-85. *Awards:* Prizes & Purchase Awards, Utah State Fair, 52-54; Utah State Art Inst, 54; Am Watercolor Soc, 57. *Mem:* Am Watercolor Soc; Nat Watercolor Soc. *Media:* All. *Mailing Add:* 825 Lava Pt Dr Saint George UT 84770-8725

LINEKER, BRUCE
MUSEUM DIRECTOR, CURATOR

Study: Duke Univ, BA(art hist), 86; Univ Southern Calif, MA(art history & mus studies), 90. *Collection Arranged:* American Life in American Art(permanent collection), Whitney Mus Am Art, 91; In/Outsiders from American South (auth, catalog), 92; Tim Rollins and KOS, Southeastern Ctr Contemp Art, 94, Willie Birch, 95 & Civil Rights Now (auth, catalog), 96. *Pos:* Asst to cur, Whitney Mus Am Art, 89-91; cur exhib, Montgomery Mus Fine Arts, Ala, 91-93; cur, Southeastern Ctr Contemp Art, Winston-Salem, NC, 93-95; exec dir, Light Factory, Charlotte, NC, 93-99. *Mem:* Am Asn Mus; Asn Historians Am Art. *Res:* 20th century American art; contemporary self-taught art; new media. *Publ:* Auth, Annual and Biennial Exhibition Record of the Whitney Museum of American Art, Sound View Press, 91; coauth, Women of the Photo League, pvt publ, 98

LINES, MARIAN B
PAINTER

b Atlanta, Ga, Dec 7, 15. *Study:* Studied at High Art Mus, 34; Art Students League with Will Barnet & I Olinsky, 58; pvt studies with Ed Ross, Joe Perrin & Jack Ramsey. *Work:* Represented in pvt & business collections in US, Japan & Neth. *Exhib:* Group shows, Hunter Mus, Chattanooga, Tenn, 62, Ringling Mus, Sarasota, Fla, 63, Macon Mus, Ga, 66, Miril Mus, Charlotte, NC, 68, W Ga Col, Carrollton, 84 & Ga Tech, Atlanta, 85; solo shows, Ada Arts Gallery, NY, 62, DeKalb Col, Decatur, Ga, 72. *Teaching:* Pvt instr painting, 65-. *Awards:* Honorable Mention, Hunter Mus, 62; Purchase Award, WGa Regional, 86; Judges Choice, Ga Artists Show, 86. *Mem:* Nat Asn Women Artists. *Media:* Acrylic, Oil

LINHARES, JUDITH
PAINTER

b Pasadena, Calif, Nov 21, 40. *Study:* Calif Col Arts & Crafts, Oakland, BFA, 63, MFA, 70. *Work:* Calif Palace Legion of Honor; Butler Inst Am Art, Youngstown, Ohio; Frederick Wiseman Found, Los Angeles; Achenbach Found, San Francisco Mus Mod Art; Mills Col Art Gallery, Oakland; and others. *Comn:* Airport, City of San Francisco. *Exhib:* solo exhibs, Gallery Paule Anglim, San Francisco, 78, 80, 83, 84, 85, 89, 94 & 2003, La State Univ Art Gallery, Baton Rouge, 79, Nancy Lurie Gallery, Chicago, 81, 89 & 90, Concord Gallery, NY, 82 & 83, Ruth Seigel Gallery, NY, 85, L A Louver, Venice, Calif, 86 & 88, Julie Sylvester Editions, NY, 89, Sonoma State Univ, Calif, 94 & Edward Thorpe Gallery, New York City, 97, 2001 & 2006,; Market Street Project, Newport Harbor Art Mus, Newport Beach, Calif, 73; Calif: 3 by 8 Twice, Honolulu Acad Art, Hawaii, 78, Triton Mus, Santa Clara, Calif, 89; 500 Yrs Since Columbus, Triton Mus, Santa Clara, Calif, 92; Conversation, ART Inc, New York City, 2000; Distilled Life, Bard Col, Hudson, NY, 2000; Figures of Invention, Hartwick Col Art Gallery, Oneonta, NY, 2000; Exurbia, Gallery Luisotti, Santa Monica, Calif, 2001; Pulp Fiction, Sanoma State Univ, Calif, 2001; The Pilot Hill Collection, Croker Art Mus, Sacramento, Calif, 2002; Arrested Development, Castle Gallery, Col New Rochelle, NY, 2002; Figures of Inventions, The Work Space, NY, 2003; Charmed, The Lower Eastside Girls Club, NY, 2004; Multiflorous: A Spring Affair, Edward Thorpe Gallery, NY, 2005. *Teaching:* Sch Visual Arts. *Awards:* Adaline Kent Award, San Francisco Art Inst, 76; Nat Endowment Arts Grant, 79 & 87; Fel, Guggenheim, 97 & 98; Anonymous Was A Woman Grant, 99; Civitella Ranierei Residency Grant, 2006. *Media:* Oil on Canvas, Gouache on Paper. *Dealer:* Gallery Paule Anglim 14 Geary St San Francisco CA 94108. *Mailing Add:* Edward Thorp Gallery 210 Eleventh Avenue New York NY 10001

LINHARES, PHILIP E
CURATOR

b Visalia, Calif, Aug 8, 39. *Study:* Calif Col of Arts & Crafts, BFA, MFA, 66; post-grad study in Florence, Italy, 72. *Exhib:* San Francisco Mus of Art, Calif, 65; Nev Art Gallery, Reno, 77; La Mus, Copenhagen, Denmark, 77; one-man shows, Berkeley Gallery, San Francisco, 70, Lone Mountain Col, San Francisco, 77 & Oakland Mus, 79; and others. *Pos:* Curatorial asst, Oakland Mus of Art, Calif, 67; dir exhib, San Francisco Art Inst, Calif, 67-77; artist-in-residence, South of Market Cult Ctr, San Francisco, 77-; dir, Mills Col Art Gallery, 78-. *Publ:* Auth, articles in Currant Mag, 75-76; California Communication, Sydney Biennale Exhib catalogue, Australia, 76. *Mailing Add:* c/o The Oakland Mus Art Dept 1000 Oak St Oakland CA 94607-4892

LINK, LAWRENCE JOHN
PAINTER, WRITER
b Oklahoma City, Okla, Sept 2, 42. *Study:* Univ Okla, BA, 65, MFA, 68. *Work:* San Francisco Mus Art; Smithsonian Inst; Osaka Univ Arts, Japan; Chase Manhattan Bank, NY; Ore State Univ Mus. *Comn:* Lithographs, World Print Orgn, 74. *Exhib:* 2nd Ann Hawaii Nat Prints Exhib, Honolulu Acad Arts, 73; World Print Competition 73, San Francisco Mus Art, 73; Nev State Mus, 75; Corcoran Gallery, Washington, 75; one-man show, Fred Jones Mem Mus, Okla, 78; Bold Statements: Painting, Southeastern Ctr Contemp Art, NC, 80; Pontiac Art Ctr, Mich, 83; Robert L Kidd Gallery, Birmingham, Mich, 87; Art Communications Int Juried CD-ROM, 95; Pre PostModern II, Patricia Swope Meml Gallery, Ohio, 2000; Bobbit Visual Arts Ctr, Mich, 2000; Mich Masters, Delta College, Bay City, Mich, 2005; Edmonton Contemp Arts Soc, Edmonton, Alberta, Can, 2004 & 2005. *Pos:* Mich ed, New Art Examiner, 83-. *Teaching:* Prof, Western Mich Univ, 77-. *Awards:* Purchase Award, World Print Competition, 73. *Bibliog:* Article, Information Technology, The Chronicle of Higher Education, 7/8/92; Article, Higher Ed Still a NeXT Priority, NeXTWORLD, summer 92; article, Digital Gallery, Digital Video, 3/94. *Media:* Acrylic, Video. *Publ:* Auth, Comment, Am Craft, 8/86; Walter Darby Bannard, Arts Mag, 10/86; The problem of imitation, New Work, 10/87; Font styles, ClarisWorks J, 10/92; Start thinking about fonts, ClarisWorks J, 2/92; 3-D Text Tips, Digital Video, 12/94; auth, Apollo on the muck, Newcrit, 1/2000, Susan Roth's Toughness, 4/2001 & Ideas don't matter, 4/2002; auth, Slippery Slope of Hope, Newcrit, 6/2005. *Mailing Add:* 3382 Sandra Dr Kalamazoo MI 49004

LINK, PHYLLIDA K
PAINTER, EDUCATOR
b New York, NY. *Study:* Sorbonne, Paris, France, art cert, City Univ NY, BA, MA, 87. *Work:* Pen & Brush Club, Nat Arts Club, World Trade Center, Avanti Gallery, NY; Glyptothek Mus, Copenhagen, Denmark. *Exhib:* Staten Island Mus, NY, 83; Pastellists-Women, Pen & Brush Club, NY, 84-89; Lever House Gallery, Pastel Soc Am Mems, NY, 87; Nabisco Gallery, Pastel Soc of Am Mems, East Hanover, NJ, 88; Milburn Playhouse Gallery, Pastel Soc Am Mems, Milburn, NJ, 90; Riverdale Art Gallery, NY, 97 & 2005. *Teaching:* Adj prof, St Peter's Col, Jersey City, NJ, 86- & Hudson Co Community Col, Jersey City, NJ, 88-93. *Awards:* New York Pub Libr Award for Best Libr Exhib Ann, 79; Pastel Soc of Am Salmagundi Club, NY, 81; Cert, Lever House, NY, 82. *Media:* Watercolor, Acrylic. *Publ:* City Univ NY Newsletter, 83; Saint Peter's Col Newsletter, 93; Hudson Co Community Col Newsletter, 93; St Peter's Campus Newsletter, 96, 97, 98 & 2000. *Mailing Add:* 226 West 242 St Apt 2B Riverdale NY 10471-4011

LINK, VAL JAMES
JEWELER, EDUCATOR
b Shreveport, La, Apr 28, 40. *Study:* Cranbrook Acad Art, Bloomfield Hills, Mich, MFA; Univ Tex, Austin, BFA; Del Mar Jr Col, Corpus Christi, Tex, AA. *Work:* Ark Art Ctr Mus, Little Rock; Sarah Campbell Blaffer Gallery, Univ Houston; Mus Contemp Crafts Touring Exhib, NY; Denver Art Mus & Am Crafts Coun Touring Exhib. *Comn:* Sic Holloware & jewelry works, comn by Mr C A Harlan, Birmingham, Mich, 67-68; commemorative cup, comn by Univ Houston for Mrs Sarah Blaffer, 73; sculptural awards, Am Petrol Inst, Washington, DC, 73 & 74; seven major jewelry pieces, comn by Kenneth Helfand, Mill Run, Pa, 74-75; and others. *Exhib:* The Goldsmith 70 Exhibition, Minn Mus Art, St Paul; Inter-D III, Crafts 74 Int, McAllen Int Mus, Tex, 74; Reprise, Int Exhib Metalsmithing Work, Cranbrook Acad Art, 75; Contemp Metalcrafts, Clifford Gallery, Pittsburgh Arts & Crafts Ctr, Pa, 77; Soc NAm Goldsmiths Nat Metalsmith 77, Phoenix Art Mus, Ariz & Henry Gallery Fine Arts, Univ Wash, Seattle, 77; Am Goldsmiths--Now, Soc NAm Goldsmiths, Steinberg Gallery, Wash Univ, 78; and others. *Teaching:* Instr jewelry & metal, Interlochen Arts Acad, Mich, 67-70; assoc prof & head jewelry & metal area, Univ Houston, 70-. *Awards:* First Place, 15th Tex Crafts Exhib, Dallas Mus Fine Arts, 71; Ark Art Ctr Mus Purchase Award, 71-72. *Bibliog:* Lisa Hammel (auth), Thank technology, New York Times, 6/20/70; Murray Bovin (auth), Photographic representation of work, In: Silversmithing, Bovin Publ, 4th ed, 73. *Mem:* Soc NAm Goldsmiths; Sterling Silversmiths Guild Am; Am Contemp Arts & Crafts Slide Libr; Am Crafts Coun; Tex & Houston Designer Craftsmen. *Media:* Gold, Silver. *Mailing Add:* 5531 Darnell St Houston TX 77096-1101

LINKER, KATE PHILIPPA
CRITIC
b New York, NY, July 22, 52. *Study:* Radcliffe Col, BA(magna cum laude), 72; Columbia Univ, 73. *Exhib:* Cur, Difference: on Representation & Sexuality, The New Mus, NY, 85. *Pos:* Assoc ed, Tracks J, New York, 75-77. *Teaching:* Prof Postmodern Theory, Grad Prog, Photog & Related Media, Sch Visual Arts, New York, 97-. *Mem:* Int Asn Art Critics; Col Art Asn. *Publ:* Auth, Meditations on a goldfish bowl: Autonomy and Analogy in Matisse, Artforum, 10/80; Public sculpture, Parts I & II, Artforum, 3/81 & 6/81; On Representation and sexuality, Parachute, 9-11/83; contribr, Love for Sale: The words and pictures of Barbara Kruger, Abrams, 90; Vito Accons, Rizzoli, 94. *Mailing Add:* 227 W 17th St New York NY 10011

LINN, JOHN WILLIAM
ADMINISTRATOR, WRITER
b Shanghai, China, May 25, 36; US citizen. *Study:* Art Inst Chicago; San Diego State Univ, BA & MA; Univ Ga, PhD; worked with Edmund B Feldman and Albert Christ-Janer. *Work:* San Diego State Univ Gallery, Calif; Paul Sargent Gallery, Eastern Ill Univ, Charleston; First Nat Bank, Springfield, Ill. *Exhib:* Ill State Fair Exhib, Springfield, 77; Provincetown Nat Print & Drawing Exhib, Mass, 77; Hot Springs Art Ctr Exhib, 91; Delta Exhib, Ark Arts Ctr, 91; Texarkana Exhib, 92; & others. *Collection Arranged:* Seven State Bicentennial Exhibition, Paul Sargent Gallery, Eastern Ill Univ, 9/77. *Pos:* Dir & owner, Art Cellar Gallery, San Diego, Calif, 65-67. *Teaching:* Assoc prof art hist, Eastern Ill Univ, 67-77, chmn dept art, 75-77; prof art hist & dean fine arts, Henderson State Univ, 77-90; dir, Joint Educ Consortium, 90-. *Awards:* Best in Show, All San Diego Co Col Exhib, San Diego State Univ, 63 & Del Mar Southern Calif Exhib, Del Mar Co Fair, 67; First Place, San Diego Co Exhib, San Diego Art Guild, John Paul Jones, 66; and others. *Bibliog:* Naomi Baker (auth), John Linn, San Diego Union, 64; Charlotte Steen (auth), Art rev, Art Forum, 65; Donovan Mailey (auth), Art Cellar Gallery, San Diego Mag, 65. *Mem:* Nat Coun Art Adminrs; Am Coun Arts. *Res:* Using the phenomenological method of art criticism in the analysis of art, particularly Chinese landscape painting. *Publ:* Auth, In praise of brevity, Acad Forum, 83; Arts of Asia, Christian Sci Monitor (several publ); numerous articles in Acad Forum & Art Papers. *Mailing Add:* 831 N 26th St Arkadelphia AR 71923-3605

LINN, JUDY
PHOTOGRAPHER
b Detroit, Mich, June 28, 47. *Study:* Pratt Inst, NY, BFA, 69. *Work:* Getty Collection, Los Angeles, Calif; Detroit Art Inst; Dallas Mus Fine Art. *Exhib:* Dallas Mus Fine Arts, Tex, 76; 4 Photographers, Padigione d'Arte Contemporanea, Milan, Italy, 80; NY, New Wave, PS 1, Queens, 81; Recent Work, Susane Hilberry Gallery, Birmingham, 82; Flowers, Detroit Art Inst, Mich, 85; Chain Reaction, Gallery 55, NY, 85; India Observed, Sandra Berler Gallery, Chevy Chase, Md, 86. *Teaching:* Adj asst prof photogr, Pratt Inst, Brooklyn, NY, 74-85. *Awards:* Artist Grant, Bob & Stephanie Scull, 85; Line II Publ Grant, 86. *Bibliog:* Oriole Farb (auth), article, Mass Rev, summer 74; Patti Smith (auth), Babel, Putnam, NY, 78; Sam Wagstaff (auth), A Book of Photographs, Grey Press, 78. *Dealer:* Gallery Onetwentyeight 128 Rivington New York NY 10002. *Mailing Add:* 252 Elizabeth St New York NY 10012

LINN, STEVEN ALLEN
SCULPTOR
b Chicago, Ill, May 3, 43. *Study:* Univ Ill, BS(floricult & ornamental hort). *Work:* Indianapolis Mus Art; Milwaukee Art Mus; Bayley Art Mus; Albany Art Mus, Ga; Mus Arts Decorative Lausanne, Switz; Nat Baseball Hall Fame; Mus Craft & Folk Art, Los Angeles, Calif; Mus Art and Hist, Anchorage, Alaska; Long Beach Art Mus, Long Beach, Calif; Mint Mus, Charlotte, NC; Natl Liberty Mus, Philadelphia, PA. *Comn:* One Colorado Plaza, Pasadena, Calif, 91; Louis & Susan Meisel Outdoor Sculpture Collection, Sagaponic, NY, 92; Fair Dept Stores, Worcester, Mass; Verrerie Ouvrier D'Albi, France, 96. *Exhib:* Rochester Mem, 79; Newport Art Mus, 79 & 86; Milwaukee Art Mus, 81; Corcoran Gallery Art, 82; Nat Baseball Hall Fame, 85; Mus D'Art Et Histoire, Geneva, Switz, 96; Aperto Vetro, Fondazione Levi Palazzo Giustinian Lolin, Venice, Italy, 98; Sofa, Chicago, 2000; Agropolis Mus, Montpellier, France, 2000; Musee de Design et D'Arts Appliques Contemporain, Luasanne, Switz, 2003. *Teaching:* Lectr theatre design, Smith Col, Northampton, Mass, 68-69; tech instr sculpture, Univ Calif, Santa Cruz, 71-74; asst prof, Pratt Inst, Brooklyn, NY, 86-; Cerfav, Vannesque Chatel, France, 2000-. *Awards:* Ward Sculpture Prize, Berkshire Mus, 68; Rome Prize, Am Acad in Rome, 75; MacDowell Colony Fel, 80; Pollock-Krasner Found Award, 85. *Bibliog:* Arthur Williams (auth), Glass: State of the Art II, 88; Cover, Art Today Mag, Summer 89; Nancy Kapitanoff (auth), Works pay tribute to special leaders, Los Angeles Times, 5/24/92; Lise Ott (auth) Steve Linn, Ceramique et Verre, 9-10/94. *Media:* Bronze, Glass, Wood. *Dealer:* Gallerie H D Nick 30250 Aubais France; Habatat Gallery, 4400 Fernlee, Royal Oak, MI, Sandra Ainsley Gallery, 55 Mill St, Toronto, Canada. *Mailing Add:* Ave Des Embruscalles 34270 Claret France

LINTAULT, ROGER PAUL
ADMINISTRATOR, EDUCATOR
b New York, NY, June 13, 38. *Study:* State Univ NY New Paltz, BS(art) with distinction, 60; Southern Ill Univ, MFA(sculpture & ceramics), 62. *Work:* Honolulu Acad Arts, Hawaii; Mus Contemp Crafts, NY; Warner Brothers Records, Los Angeles, Calif; Calif State Univ, San Bernardino. *Exhib:* Craftsmen USA, Los Angeles Co Mus Art, Calif, 66; Looking West 1970, Joslyn Art Mus, Omaha, Nebr, 70; one man show, Esther-Robles Gallery, Los Angeles, 75, Architectural Dreams and Visions, Ctr Gallery, Calif State Univ, 81; Calif State Univ, San Bernardino, 79 & Fullerton, 81; Janus Gallery, Los Angeles, 79; Contemp Bronze, Calif State Univ, San Bernardino, 87; Phantoms of Function: Evolution of Art in the Utilitarian, Riverside Art Mus, Calif, 91; Table, Lamp and Chair, Am Inst Archit, Inst Bus Designers, Ore Sch Arts & Crafts, Portland, 91. *Teaching:* Asst prof art, Univ Hawaii, Honolulu, 65-68; lectr art, Calif State Univ, Long Beach, 68-69; prof art, Calif State Univ, San Bernardino, 69-, chmn dept, 72-77 & 97-. *Awards:* First & Purchase Prizes, All Calif Art Exhib, Nat Orange Show, 74. *Bibliog:* Don Woodford (auth), Truth, illusion and Roger Lintault, 4/26/75, Artweek; Louis William Fox (auth), article, Artweek, 1/13/79; Suzanne Muchnic (auth), article, Ten tales of architecture, Los Angeles Times, 2/9/79. *Media:* Metal, Cast, Miscellaneous Media. *Mailing Add:* c/o Dept Art Calif State Univ 5500 University Pkwy San Bernardino CA 92407-2397

LINTON, HAROLD
PAINTER, ADMINISTRATOR
b Pittsburgh, Pa, Oct 1, 47. *Study:* Lowe Sch Art, Syracuse Univ, BFA, 69; Univ Wash Sch Art, grad study with Spencer Moseley, 69-70; Sch Art & Archit, Yale Univ, grad study with Al Held, MFA, 72. *Work:* Muskegon Mus Art, Mich; Syracuse Univ, NY; Yale Univ, New Haven, Conn; Childrens Hosp, Detroit, Mich; Pittsburgh Rehab Inst, Pa. *Comn:* Shaped canvas, Handleman Corp, Clawson, Mich, 77; shaped canvas in main lobby, Beaumont Hosp, Royal Oak, Mich, 95; shaped canvas on ceiling, Temple Israel, West Bloomfield, Mich, 95; shaped canvas in lobby, Birmingham Temple, Farmington Hills, Mich, 95; shaped canvas, reception area, US Embassy, Helsinki, Finland, 96-97. *Exhib:* Solo exhib, I Irving Feldman Gallery, West Bloomfield, Mich,

85, 87 & 90; Harold Linton Paintings: 76-86, Muskegon Mus Art, Mich, 87; Handleman Collection, Oakland Univ-Meadowbrook Art Gallery, Rochester, Mich, 88; Form & Content, Janice Charach Mus Gallery, West Bloomfield, Mich, 92; Abstract Image Makers, Cincinnati Mus Art-Chidlaw Gallery, Ohio, 93; Self Portraits, Muskegon Mus Art, Mich, 95. *Pos:* Asst dean, Col Archit & Design, Lawrence Technol Univ, 91-; prof, color & design, Univ Art & Design, Helsinki, Finland, 96-97. *Teaching:* Prof art & archit, Lawrence Technol Univ, 74-, creator, BFA Degree Prog Archit Illus, 91-92. *Awards:* George Hess Mem Award, Syracuse Univ, 68; Ellen Battell Stoeckel Fel Grant Painting, Yale Univ, 68; Publishers Grant, Texts on Color, Design & Drawing, Van Nostrand Reinhold, 82, 85, 88, 90, 91, 94 & 96. *Bibliog:* Charles Wallenschlager (auth), Basic Visual Concepts & Principles, WC Brown, 91; M Portillo & JH Dohr (auth), A study of color planning criteria used by noted designers, J Interior Design Educ & Res, 93. *Mem:* Nat Asn Schs Art & Design; Col Art Asn; Am Soc Archit Perspectives; Inter-Soc Color Coun. *Publ:* Coauth, Architectural Sketching in Markers, Van Nostrand Reinhold, 90; auth, Color Consulting, Van Nostrand Reinhold, 92; Sketching the Concept, McGraw-Hill/Design Press, 93; Color Forecasting, Van Nostrand Reinhold, 94; Portfolio Design, WN Norton & Co, 96. *Dealer:* I Irving Feldman Gallery 6606 Pleasant Lake Ct West Bloomfield MI 48331. *Mailing Add:* Tilkantori 3B30 00300 Helsinki Finland

LIOTTA, JEANNE
FILM DIRECTOR
b NYC, 60. *Exhib:* Exhibited group shows at Whitney Biennial; Whitney Mus Art, 2006; Int Film Festival, Rotterdam; Pacific Film Archives, Berkeley, Calif; Anthology Film Archives, NYC; Mus Mod Art, NYC. *Pos:* Vis artist Bard, San Francisco Art Inst; dir (films), Blue Moon, 1988; Soma Sema, 1988; Open Sesame, 1989; Fungus Eroticus, 1990; Dervish Machine, 1992; CiCi N'est Pas, 1997; What Makes Day & Night, 1998; Mukitkara, 1999; Struck by the Hand, 2001; Window, 2001; L'air du Temps, 2003; One Day This May No Longer Exist, 2005. *Teaching:* Film instr Sch, Mus Fine Arts, Boston. *Awards:* Fel MacDowell Colony, 2002; grantee Jerome Found, NY State Coun Arts Experimental Television Center. *Mailing Add:* SMFA Boston 230 The Fenway Boston MA 02115

LIPOFSKY, MARVIN B
SCULPTOR, GLASS ARTIST
b Barrington, Ill, Sept 1, 38. *Study:* Univ Ill, Urbana, BFA; Univ Wis-Madison, MS & MFA. *Work:* Kunstgewerbe Mus, Berlin; Metrop Mus Art, NY; Nat Mus Mod Art, Kyoto, Japan; Corning Glass Ctr, NY; Oakland Art Mus, Calif; Los Angeles Co Mus; Boston Mus Fine Arts; Milwauke Art Mus, Wis; Mus Arts & Design, NY; Philadelphia Mus Art; San Francisco Mus Mod Art; St Louis Mus Art, Mo; and many others. *Comn:* Glass, plastic, metal twin panels, Metro Media Bldg, Los Angeles, 69; Frank Lloyd Wright, Calif Col Arts & Crafts Founders Award, 72; reception sculpture, Pac Enterprises, Los Angeles, 90. *Exhib:* One-man shows, Gallery Marionie, Kyoto, Japan, 78 & 87, Florence Duhl Gallery, NY, 79, SM Galerie, Frankfurt, 81, Galerie L, Hamburg, 81, Betsy Rosenfield Gallery, Chicago, 82, Holsten Galleries, Palm Beach, 85 & 87, Habatat Galleries, Chicago, Ill, Marvin Lipofsky: Concourse Gallery, Bank of Am Bldg, San Francisco, 2003, Marvin Lipofsky: A Glass Odyssey, The Journey of an Am Master, Fresno Art Mus, Calif, 2005-2006, Marvin Lipofsky: A Journey in Glass, Calif Polytechnic Univ, San Luis Obispo, 2006; Reiley/Hawk Gallery, Cleveland, Ohio, 88; Leo Kaplan Modern (auth, catalog), NY, 89, 91 & 94; Union of Bulgaria Artists, Sofia, 91; Judah Magnes Mus, Berkeley, Calif, 94; Marvin Lipofsky World of Glass, Kennedy Art Ctr Gallery, Holynames Col, Oakland, Calif, 96; Venizio Aperto Vetro, Palazzo Ducalle, Venice, Italy, 98; Lipofsky in China, R Duane Reed Gallery, St Louis, Mo, 98; retrospective, Marvin Lipofsky: A Glass Odyessy, Oakland Mus Calif, 2003; Musee d'Art Contemporarian, Skopje, Yugoslvia; The Toledo Mus Art, Toledo, Ohio; The Detroit Inst Art, Detroit, Mich; Indianapolis Mus Art, Indianapolis, Ind; Nat Mus in Wroclaw, Wroclaw, Poland; Renwick Gallery of Nat Mus of Am Art, Smithsonian Inst, Washington, DC. *Pos:* Ed, Glass Art Soc J, 76-80; adv bd, Friends Bezalel Nat Acad Arts and Design, Jerusalem, Israel. *Teaching:* Asst prof design, Univ Calif, Berkeley, 64-72; prof & head glass dept, Calif Col Arts & Crafts, Oakland, 67-87; vis prof, Rietveld Acad, Amsterdam, Holland, 70, Bazalel Acad Art, Jerusalem, Israel, 71, Univ Calif Los Angeles, 73, Pilchuck Sch Glass, Stanwood, Wash, 74, 77, 81 & 88, Colo Mountain Col, Summervail, 81 & 83 & Miasa Bunka Ctr, Miasa, Japan, 87; vis artist, Konstfack Skolen, Stockholm, Sweden, 89 & Univ Ceramic & Glass, Helsinki, Finland, 89, Fundación Centro Nac del Vidrio, La Granja, Spain. *Awards:* Nat Endowment Arts Fels, 74 & 76; Col Fels, Am Craft Coun, 91; Hon Award for inspiration and instigation of Bayarea Glass Community, Calif Glass Exchg, 2002; Master of the Medium Award, James Renwick Alliance, Washington, DC, 2003; Lifetime Achievment in Art, Art Alliance Contemp Glass, SOFA, Chicago, 2005. *Bibliog:* Matthew Kangas (auth), Marvin Lipofsky: Concealing the Void, Glass, 9/97; Alberto Toso Fei (auth), Marvin Lipofsky a "muranese" in California, Vetro Mag, 10-12/2000; Suzanne Baizerman (editor), Marvin Lipofsky: A Glass Odyssey, Univ Washington Press, 2003; Dan Klein (auth), Marvin Lipofsky, Craft Arts Int, Australia, No 62, 2004; Matthew Kangas (auth), Craft & Concept, Midmarch Arts Press, NY, 2006. *Mem:* Int Comt Artists in Glass; hon life mem Glass Art Soc (pres, 78-80); Bay Area Studio Art Glass (pres, 93-); Dominik Bimann Soc (hon); Higarium Glass Art Soc (hon). *Media:* Sculpture. *Dealer:* Holsten Galleries Stockbridge MA; R Duane Reed Gallery St Louis MO. *Mailing Add:* 1012 Pardee Berkeley CA 94710

LIPPARD, LUCY ROWLAND
WRITER
b New York, NY, Apr 14, 37. *Study:* Smith Col, BA, 58; NY Univ Inst Fine Arts, MA, 62. *Hon Degrees:* Moore Col Art, Hon DFA, 72; San Francisco Art Inst, Hon DFA, 85; Maine Col Art, Hon DFA, 94; Mass Col Art, Hon DFA, 98; Chicago Art Inst, Hon DFA, 03. *Pos:* Free-lance writer, cult critic, cur; mem adv bd Franklin Furnace, New York City, 79-; co-found, bd dir, Printed Matter, New York City; bd dir, Ctr Study Political Graphics, Los Angeles, Time & Space Ltd, Hudson, NY, Sustainable Settings, Woody Creek, Colo, Earthworks Inst, Santa Fe; co-found WEB, Ad Hoc Women Artist's Comt, Heresies Collective and J Artists Call Against US Intervention in Cent Am, Political Art Documentation/Distbn; Bd dirs, Center Am Places Earth works Inst. *Teaching:* vis prof, Sch Visual Arts, New York City, Williams Col, Univ Queensland, Australia & Univ Colo, Boulder; lectr in field. *Awards:* Mather Award col art assoc; Art Table Award, 99; Southwest Book Award, 2002; Athena Award from RISD, 2004. *Bibliog:* Florence Pierce: In Touch With Light, 98. *Res:* Urban & rulral lanscapes; Native American Art. *Publ:* Auth 20 bks, incl, Eva Hesse, 76, Partial Recall, 92 The Pink Glass Swan, 95, The Lure of the Local, 97 & On the Beaten Track (in prep), 99; Author: Pop Art, 66, The Graphic work of Philip Evergood, 66; Changing: Essays in Art Criticism, 71; ed,Surrealists on Art, 70, Dadas on Art, 71; Tony Smith, 72; Six Yrs: The Dematerialization of the Art Object, 73; From the Ctr: Feminist Essays on Women's Art, 76; Sol Le Witt, 78, (with Charles Simonds) Cracking (Br?Werden), 79; The Sch of Paris, 65, (novel) I See/You Mean, 79; Ad Reinhardt, 81; contribr, monthly columns Village Voice, 81-85; Overlay: Contemp Art and the Art of Prehistory, 83; Get the Message? A Decade of Art for Social Change, 84; Mixed Blessings: New Art in a Multicultural Am, 90; A Different War: Vietnam in Art, 90; contrib ed,: Art in Am; founding editor El Puente de Galisteo, 97; Village Voice In These Times, Z Mag, also numerous articles to mag, anthologies, and mus catalogs, 64-; curator 50 exhibs; performer in guerrilla and street theater. *Mailing Add:* 14 Avenida Vieja Galisteo NM 87540

LIPPINCOTT, JANET
PAINTER, PRINTMAKER
b New York, NY, May 16, 18. *Study:* Colorado Springs Fine Art Ctr; Art Students League; San Francisco Art Inst; also with Emil Bisttram, Taos, NMex, 49. *Work:* Utah Fine Arts Mus, Salt Lake City; Columbia Fine Arts Mus, SC; Denver Art Mus, Colo; Roswell Mus & Art Ctr, NMex; Albuquerque Mus, NMex; Fine Arts Mus, Santa Fe, NMex. *Exhib:* Enthios Gallery, Santa Fe, NMex, 86; Fagen-Peterson Gallery, Scottsdale, Ariz, 87, 88, & 89; Fletcher Gallery, Santa Fe, NMex, 90; New Directions Gallery, Taos, NMex, 94; Fine Arts Mus, Santa Fe, NMex, 94; and others. *Teaching:* Instr, Santa Fe Community Col, NMex, 85-. *Awards:* Atwater Kent Award, Palm Beach, Fla, 63; Southwestern Biennial Award, Santa Fe, 66; Arts in Residence, Durango, Colo, 68. *Bibliog:* Artist of the month, Southwest Art Gallery Mag, 5/72. *Mailing Add:* c/o Karen Ruhlen Gallery 225 Canyon Rd #18 Santa Fe NM 87501

LIPPMAN, JUDITH
GALLERY DIRECTOR, EDUCATOR
b New York, NY, June 11, 29. *Study:* Syracuse Univ, BA, 49. *Collection Arranged:* Maryland Art in Legislative Spaces (auth, catalog), 80 & Maryland Art & Artists (auth, catalog), 81, Gen Assembly Md. *Pos:* Guest lectr, Col Notre Dame, Md, 74-76; dir & cur, 20th Century Am Art, Meredith Gallery Contemp Art, Baltimore, 77-; mem, Artistic Properties Comn, State of Md, 77-80; Capitol arts coordr, Gen Assembly Md, 80-; lectr, New Sch Social Res, New York, 80-81, Johns Hopkins Univ, 83-, Md Inst Col Art, 85. *Mem:* Am Inst Architects; Artists Equity Asn. *Specialty:* Contemporary American art and fine crafts. *Publ:* Coauth, Gene Davis, Ed Baynard, Dorothy Gillespie, 80, Arts Gallery. *Mailing Add:* Meredith Gallery Contemp Art 809 N Charles St Baltimore MD 21201

LIPPMAN, SHARON ROCHELLE
CURATOR, ART HISTORIAN AND THERAPIST
b New York, NY, Apr 9, 50. *Study:* Art Students League, 66-68; HS Art & Design, 68; Mills Col, City Col New York, BA(art hist), 72; NY Univ, MA(cinema studies), 76, grad studies, 87; New Sch Social Res, 68-70; Columbia Univ, 70. *Work:* Suffolk Co Legislature, 90-97; Dept Interior, Fort Wadsworth, NY 2001. *Comn:* Homage to NY-LI Baymen (mural), 85, Sunday in the Park (mural), Art Without Walls Inc, NY, 92; Arttherapy Program, Various Hospitals; South St Seaport, By Land, By Sea, NY, 2005. *Exhib:* Holocaust Art, Polish Consulate, NY, 2002; Homage to the NY Skyscraper, Battery Park, 2002; Central Park: Peace-Quiet, Central Park, 2003; Nassau Co Detention Ctr, WIthin These Walls, 2003; W Islip/Bellport Libraries, Spiritual Energy, 2005; Caged Free, Nassau County, Detention Ctr, 2005; Museum Without Walls-Rhapsody in Art, South St Seaport, New York City, 2006. *Collection Arranged:* Museum Without Walls (auth, catalog), Pub Space-Heckscher State Park, 85-86; Color Me/Color Blind, Helen Keller Ctr for the Blind, 93; Blind Illusions, Pub Space-William Rodgers Bldg, NY, 94; Home Sweet Home, William Rodgers Bldg, 94; The Illustrative Eye, 94 & Quietplaces, William Rodgers Bldg; Holocaust-The Polish Experience, Polish Consulate, New York, 98. *Pos:* Exec dir, Art Without Walls Inc, Sayville & New York, 85-; art therapist, cur, historian, artist & filmmaker, currently. *Teaching:* Instr painting/drawing, sculpture & filmaking, Sara Sch Creative Art, 76-85; instr painting-drawing, Art Without Walls Inc, Sayville, NY, 85-. *Awards:* Suffolk Co News Inspiration Award, 90; Suffolk Co Proclamation, 93; Newsday Leadership Award, 94; Nat Poetry Press Award, 96; Nat Women's Hist Month Award, 96; Long Island Hall of Fame, 2004; Suffolk Co News, Inspiration Award, 2005. *Mem:* Col Art Asn; Mus Mod Art; Metrop Mus Art; Univ Film Asn; Whitney Mus Am Art; Guggenheim Mus; Jewish Mus; Americans for the Arts. *Media:* Paint, Film. *Res:* Combine the social, aesthetic and historical elements of art theories with cultural and creative development through the ages. *Specialty:* Public Space. *Interests:* Expanding non-traditional American art 1930-present and social/historical international art. *Publ:* Auth, University Poetry Press, Nat Poetry Press, 68; Patterns, Idlewild Press, 68; Still Waters, Island Light Press, 83; America at the Millennium, Poetry, 2000. *Mailing Add:* PO Box 2066 New York NY 10185-2066

LIPPMANN, JANET GURIAN
PAINTER, GALLERY DIRECTOR
b New York, NY, May 10, 36. *Study:* Brooklyn Col, with Ilya Bolotowsky, Ad Reinhardt, Kurt Seligman, John Russell, Mark Rothko & Burgoyne Diller, BA(art educ), 56, MA(art educ), 60; NY Univ, with Knox Martin. *Work:* Reader's Digest Asn, Inc; Nat Arts Club; Newington Cropsey Mus; numerous pvt collections. *Exhib:* Solo exhibs, River Gallery, Irvington-on-Hudson, NY, 91, Nat Arts Club, NY, 91, 94, 98, 2001 & 2002; Conoisseur Gallery, Rhinebeck, NY, 92, 93, 94; Goodman Gallery, Southampton, NY, 91-92; RVS, Southampton, NY, 91; Nature Nutures, State Univ NY, 94, The Sky Above, The Earth Below, 2001; Newington Cropsey Mus, 2003; Irvington-on-Hudson Publ Libr, 2005; Sunnyside Fed S&L, Irvington, 2006. *Collection Arranged:* Columbia Univ Med Ctr; Bank of NY. *Pos:* Founder, pres & dir, The River Gallery, Irvington-on-Hudson, NY, 74-89; founder, pres & dir, Janet Lippmann Fine Arts, 89-. *Teaching:* Instr art, New York City, Cincinnati & Westchester Publ Sch, 56-74; Instr, Children's Art Series, Mt Vernon, 64-71; pvt instr, Adult Art Classes, Tarrytown, NY, 71-73. *Awards:* Nat Arts Club Award, 89; Hudson Valley Art Asn, 99; Art Spirit Found Award for pastel 2003. *Mem:* Nat Arts Club, NY; Salmagundi Club; Artists Fel Pen & Brush Club, NY; Hudson Valley Art Asn; Pastel Soc Am. *Media:* Oils, Pastels. *Specialty:* Paintings by American and international artists; Contemporary Realism by Iiving Am artists. *Interests:* Gardening, travel. *Collection:* Newington Cropsey Museum; Natural Arts Club, NY. *Publ:* Auth, Painting in Giverny, Am Artist, 3/88; Giverny Revisited, Am Artist, 11/91. *Dealer:* Janet Lippmann Fine Art

LIPSCHUTZ, JEFF
PAINTER, CURATOR
b Atlantic City, NJ, Oct 6, 50. *Study:* Ponoma Col, Claremont, Calif, BA (philos), 71; San Francisco State Univ, BFA, 83, MA (painting), 85, 87. *Work:* Playboy Enterprises Corp Headquarters, Chicago, Ill; Bergstrom-Mahler Mus, Neenah, Wis; Aurora Pub Art Commn, Ill,; JVC Corp Video-Art Collectoin, Tokyo, Japan; Vt State Art Coun Grant Award Archives, Burlington. *Exhib:* The Eagle Mountain Project, Triton Mus Art, Santa Clara, Calif, 91; Eagle Mountain: The Making of an Environmental Tragedy, Riverside, Calif, 91; The Art of Politics, Playboy Enterprises Corp Headquarters, 92; Built on Sand, McDonough Mus Art, Youngstown, Ohio, 93; Lion Invicational, Nat Jewish Mus, Washington, DC, 97; Mojave Desert Paintings, The Art Gallery, Brooklyn Col, NY, 98. *Pos:* dir, Priebe Art Gallery, Uviv Wisc, 92-. *Teaching:* from lectr painting to assoc prof, Univ Tex, Austin, 88-. *Awards:* 12th Annual Tokyo Video Festival, Japan, Works of Special Distinction Award, 90; London Int Film & Video Festival, Blue Seal Winner, 90; Arts Midwestern/NEA Individual Artist Painting Fel, 93. *Media:* Oil, Canvas. *Publ:* Across A Great Distance: Paintings from the Majove Desert, Berstrom-Mahler, 2000. *Mailing Add:* Univ Wis Oshkosh Allen Priebe Gallery 800 Algoma Blvd Oshkosh WI 54901

LIPSCOMB, GUY FLEMING, JR
PAINTER, INSTRUCTOR
b Clemson, SC, Apr 11, 1917. *Study:* Univ SC, BS, 38; 50 watercolor workshops, 67-2004; Art Students League, 75. *Hon Degrees:* U SC, D Arts. *Work:* Univ SC; Mus Washington, Ga; LaGrange City Mus, Ga; Columbia Col, SC; Rice Mus, Georgetown, SC; Greenville (SC) Art Mus; Columbia Art Mus. *Exhib:* Am Watercolor Soc, NY, 79; 2000, 2004 mem; Watercolor USA Nat, Springfield, Mo, 79; Rocky Mountain Nat, Golden, Colo, 80, 83 & 89; Butler Inst Am Art, 80; Nat Arts Club, NY, 80; Allied Artists Nat, NY, 81, 86 & 90; 100 Nat open juried shows; 17 Nat Juried Shows, 96, 23 Nat Juried Shows, 97 & 17 Nat Juried Shows, 98. *Teaching:* Instr watercolor & painting, Columbia Mus Art workshops and throughout USA & Can. *Awards:* Best of Show, Ky Nat Watercolor Soc, 82; Am Artists Prof League Award, New York, 82; Second Award, Guild SC Artists, 83; Gold Medal Knickerbocker Artist, 86; and many others. *Mem:* Ga Watercolor Soc; SC Watercolor Soc; Ky Watercolor Soc; Pa Watercolor Soc; Miss Watercolor Soc; Philly Watercolor Soc; and others. *Media:* Watercolor, Oil; Acrylic, Ink. *Publ:* Contribr, Art Voices, 82; North Light Mag; auth, Watercolor Go with the Flow, Warson Guptill Publ, 92. *Dealer:* Hampton Gallery Taylor SC; Carol Saunder Gallery Columbia SC. *Mailing Add:* 25 Joseph Walker Dr West Columbia SC 29169-6961

LIPSKY, PAT
PAINTER
b New York, NY, Sept 21, 41. *Study:* Cornell Univ with Alan Solomon, BFA, 63; Art Students League, 63-64; Hunter Col, with Tony Smith, MA, 68. *Work:* Hirshhorn Mus & Sculpture Garden; Whitney Mus Am Art, NY; San Francisco Mus Fine Arts; Walker Art Ctr; Brooklyn Mus; Wadsworth Atheneum; and others. *Exhib:* solo exhibs, Fairleigh Dickinson Univ, Rutherford, NJ, 68, Andre Emmerich Gallery, NY, 70, 72, 74, 75, Everson Mus Art, Syracuse, 71, London Arts Gallery, Detroit, 71, Berenson Gallery, Bay Harbor Island, Fla, 74, 76, Deitcher O'Reilly Gallery, NY, 76, Andre Zarre Gallery, NY, 78, 91, Promenade Gallery, Hartford, Conn, 87, Virginia Miller Gallery, Coral Gables, Fla, 94, Lori Bookstein Fine Art, NY, 97, Elizabeth Harris Gallery, 99, 2001, 2003, 2004; Chase Manhattan Bank, NY, 67, Allan Stone Gallery, NY, 69; Larry Aldrich Mus, Ridgefield, Conn, 70, 72, 74; Phoenix Art Mus, 70; Kansas State Univ, Manhattan, 70; Whitney Mus Am Art, NY, 71; Tyler Mus Art, Tex, 71; Cranbrook Acad Art Mus, Bloomfield Hills, Mich, 73; Grand Rapids Art Mus, Mich, 74; San Francisco Art Inst, 74; Toldeo Mus Art, Ohio, 74; Moravian Col Art Gallery, Bethlehem, Pa, 77; Sarah Rentschler Gallery, NY, 79; Univ Mass, Amherst, 87; Ruth Siegel Gallery, NY, 88; CS Schulte Gallery, Millburn, NJ, 92, 93, 94; Tribe Gallery, NY, 98; Snyder Fine Arts, NY, 96; Duke Univ, Durham, NC, 2004; DC Moore Gallery, NY, 2004; and many others. *Pos:* Mem adv coun, Col Art & Archit, Cornell Univ, 88-93. *Teaching:* Instr, Fairleigh Dickinson Univ, 68 & Hunter Col, 72; vis artist, San Francisco Art Inst, 74; instr, State Univ NY, Purchase, 79-80; assoc prof, Hartford Art Sch, Univ Hartford, 83-2002. *Awards:* Va Ctr Creative Arts Fel, 86 & 93; NY Found Arts Fel, 92; Grant, Winsor & Newton Paint Co, 92; Grant Gottlieb Found, 99; Grant Pollock-Krasner, 2000; plus others. *Bibliog:* Carol Damian (auth), Coral Gables, Artnews, 5/94; Charles Bernstein (auth), Pat Lipsky Sutton, Art Papers, 7/94; Across generational bounds, New York Times, 96. *Media:* Oil on Linen, Acrylic on Canvas. *Interests:* Gothic Architecture, Stained Glass Windows. *Mailing Add:* 526 W 26th St Ste 1011 New York NY 10001

LIPTON, BARBARA B
EDUCATOR, CURATOR
b Newark, NJ. *Study:* Univ Iowa, BA(art hist); Univ Mich, studied Oriental art with James Plummer, MA; Rutgers Univ, MLS. *Exhib:* One-woman photog exhib, Newark Mus, NJ, 78; Images of the Alaskan Eskimo, New Eng Found Arts, 80-82; Anchorage Mus, 81; Am Mus Nat Hist, NY, 81. *Collection Arranged:* Whaling Days in New Jersey (auth, catalog), 75 & Survival: Life and Art of the Alaskan Eskimo (auth, catalog), 77-78, Newark Mus, NJ; Arctic Vision: Art of the Canadian Inuit (traveling exhib, auth, catalog), Govt Can, 84-86; Treasures of the Tibetan Mus, 88; Village Life in Rajasthan (photog exhib), 2006-07. *Pos:* Art libr dir, Newark Mus, NJ, 70-75, spec proj consult 76-82; asst dir, Castle Gallery, Col New Rochelle, 83-84; guest cur, Govt Can, 84-86; dir, Jacques Marchais Mus Tibetan Art, 85-97; cons curator, Jacques Marchars Mus Tibetan Art, 2002. *Teaching:* Instr, sch continuing ed, Pratt Univ, Brooklyn, NY, 79; instr eskimo art, New Sch, New York, & Univ Vt, 86; Drew Univ, 98, New Sch NY, 98 & State Univ NY, 98; instr Native Am art, Drew Univ, 97; instr Asian art, New Sch, New York, 98-, Tibetan art, 2003; instr Tibetan art, SUNY, Purchase, 2003. *Mem:* Explorers Club. *Res:* Whaling history; life and art of the Alaskan and Canadian Eskimo; New Jersey history; archival Eskimo films; Tibetan art and history. *Collection:* Eskimo art and artifacts. *Publ:* Coauth, Westerners in Tibet, Newark Mus, 73; auth, John Cotton Dana and the Newark Museum, 79; exec producer, Village of No River (film), 81; Tibetan Visual Art in White Lotus, 91; Treasures of Tibetan Art, Oxford Univ Press, 96; auth, Survival: Life and Art of the Alaskan Eskimo, Morgan & Morgan; Arctic Vision: The Art of the Canadian Inuit, Canadian Arctic Producers; Whaling Days in New Jersey, The Newark Mus. *Mailing Add:* 282 Scotland Rd South Orange NJ 07079

LIPTON, LEAH
HISTORIAN, CURATOR
b Kearny, NJ. *Study:* Douglass Col, Rutgers Univ, BA, 49; Harvard Univ, MA, 50. *Collection Arranged:* Around the Station: The Town and the Train (with catalog), 78 & Family Connections: Portraits by Chester Harding (auth, catalog), 81, Danforth Mus Art, Framingham, Mass; A Truthful Likeness: Chester Harding and his Portraits (auth, catalog), Nat Portrait Gallery, 85; Charles Hopkinson: Pictures from a New England Past (auth, catalog), Danforth Mus Art, 88-89; Three New England Painters: Hosmer, Pooke, Woodward (auth, catalog), Danforth Mus Art, 91. *Pos:* Bd dir & adj cur Am Art, Danforth Mus Art, 80-. *Teaching:* Prof art hist, Framingham State Col, Mass, formerly, emer prof, currently. *Awards:* Distinguished Serv Award, Framingham State Col. *Mem:* Col Art Asn; Soc Archit Historians; Am Studies Asn. *Res:* 19th and 20th century American art & architecture; portrait painting in America especially New England; life and career of Chester Harding (1792-1866); American women artists, 1900-1940. *Publ:* Auth, William Dunlap, Samuel F B Morse, John Wesley Jarvis & Chester Harding: Their careers as itinerant portrait painters, 81, The brief life of the Boston Artists' Association, 1841-1851, 83 & Chester Harding and The Life Portrait of Daniel Boone, 84, Am Art J; Chester Harding in Great Britain, Antiques, 84; Yankee Painters in the South, Southern Quart, 88; The Boston Five: Pioneers of Modernism in Massachusetts, Am Art Review, 94. *Mailing Add:* Dept Art Framingham State Col 100 State St Framingham MA 01701

LIPTON, SONDRA
PAINTER, SCULPTOR
b New York, NY, Apr 24, 29. *Study:* NY Univ, sculpture with Vincent Glinsky. *Work:* Pres Lyndon B Johnson Libr & in private collections of Mrs Pierre du Pont II, Paul Mellon, Mrs Seward Mellon, Jacqueline Kennedy Onassis, Mrs Sybil Harrington. *Comn:* Mr & Mrs Ralph Baruch; Mr William Rondina. *Media:* Oil on Wood, Oil on Paper. *Mailing Add:* 419 E 57th St New York NY 10022

LIPZIN, JANIS CRYSTAL
FILMMAKER, PHOTOGRAPHER
b Colorado Springs, Colo, Nov 19, 45. *Study:* Ohio Univ, BFA; NY Univ; Univ Pittsburgh, MLS; San Francisco Art Inst, MFA; Pittsburgh Filmmakers Workshop. *Work:* Carnegie Mus Art, Pittsburgh; Di Rosa Found Napa, Calif; C Richard & Pamela Kramlich, Coll Media Art. *Comn:* Berkeley Art Mus, Berkeley, CA, 2003; San Francisco Cinematheque Sink or Swim, Site Specific Projection: Naval Compression: Prelude, 2001. *Exhib:* Mus Mod Art, NY, 85, 91 & 97; PS 1, NY, 88; Art Gallery Ontario, Can, 90; Pacific Film Arch, Berkeley, Calif, 90, 95, 99; Stadtkino, Vienna, Austria, 92; Yerba Buena Gardens Ctr Arts, San Francisco, Calif, 94; De Young Mem Mus, San Francisco, 95; Chinese Taipei Film Archive, Taipei, Taiwan, 2003; Whitney Mus Am Art, 2000. *Pos:* Media cur, Anne Bremer Mem Libr, San Francisco Art Inst, 74-76, chair dept filmmaking, 85-91 & 2004-2005; bd dir, Canyon Cinema Coop, 81-83; contribr ed, Artweek, 81-84; bd dir, Found Art in Cinema, San Francisco, 83-90; consult, Univ Wis, Milwaukee, 91. *Teaching:* Asst prof art in film & photog, Antioch Col, 76-80; prof filmmaking, San Francisco Art Inst, 78-, dir undergrad studio prog, 94-96; vis artist, San Francisco State Univ, 81. *Awards:* Ohio Arts Coun Individual Artist Grant, 78; Nat Endowment Arts Individual Artist Grant, 83; NEA Inter/Arts, New Genres with Sonoma Co Found, 90-91. *Bibliog:* Manohla Dargis (auth), The eight & narrow, Village Voice, 89; Steve Anker (auth), Testament to an orphaned art, Blimp Film Mag, Vienna, 92; Brian Frye (auth), Seasonal Forces, 95; Kathy Geritz (auth), I Came into an 8 MM World, Big as Life, MoMA Catalog, 99; Chun-Hui-Wu, Totally Control, Film Appreciation Journal, Taipei Chinese Film

Archive, 2001. *Mem:* Canyon Cinema Coop; NY Filmmakers Coop; Col Art Asn; Lux London; Scratch Cinema Paris. *Media:* Photography & Film. *Publ:* Auth, Looking for gems, Artweek, 81; Tribute to James Broughton, San Francisco Int Film Festival catalog; Addressing urban issues, Artweek, 83; Some Thoughts on Super-8 at the Close of the 20th Century (catalog), Viva 8 Festival, London, 96; Vaca Valley Visions: A Sense of Time and Place (catalog), Vacaville Mus, 96; Why Didn't I Work in Granite, 50 Years of Bay Area Film & Video, Pacific Film Archive, Berkeley, CA, 2005; Made by human Hands, Small Windows: The 2d San Francisco Art Inst, 8MM Film Festival Catalog, 2001. *Dealer:* Canyon Cinema Coop 2325 Third St Suite 338 San Francisco CA 94107; NY Filmmakers Coop 175 Lexington Ave New York NY 10016. *Mailing Add:* 2434 Bloomfield Rd Sebastopol CA 95472

LIS, JANET
PAINTER
b Cleveland, Ohio, Jan 9, 43. *Study:* Cleveland Inst Art, scholar, 57-61; Ohio Univ Sch Fine Arts, BFA, 65. *Work:* Hollywood Mus Art, Fla; Southeastern Ctr Contemp Art; Lauren Rogers Mus, Miss; Brevard Co, Fla Art Pub Places Prog, Savanna's Clubhouse, Merritt Island; State of Fla Art Pub Bldg Prog, Fla Regional Off Bldg, Miami. *Comn:* First United Methodist Church & First Church of Nazarene, Pompano Beach, Fla; First Baptist Church, Pampano Beach, FL. *Exhib:* Watercolor USA, 80 & 81; Piedmont Biennial, Mint Mus, Charlotte, NC; Ga Watercolor Soc Exhib, Columbus Mus Art, 81; Aqueous, Ky Watercolor Soc, 81; Realist Invitational, Southeastern Ctr Contemp Art, 83; Mainstream Am, 87 & 88 & Ann Mid-year Show, Butler Inst Am Art; San Diego Watercolor Soc Ann, 89; Watercolor Soc Ann 93. *Collection Arranged:* Phil Desind Colls, Butler Inst Am Art. *Teaching:* Boca Mus, Boca Raton, Fla. *Awards:* Purchase Awards, Southeastern Ctr Contemp Art, 79, Eastman Mem Found, Lauren Rogers Mus, 79; Cash Awards, Watercolor USA, 80, Arts Assembly of Jacksonville, 81 & Ann Mid-year Show, Butler Inst Am Art, 88; Mitchell Graphics Award, Fla Watercolor Soc Ann, 93. *Bibliog:* Lorraine Huber (auth), The colorful world of Janet Lis, Fiesta Mag, 9/75; Mary Crowe Dorst (auth), article, Art Voices, 11-12/81. *Mem:* Southern Arts Fedn; Fla Watercolor Soc. *Media:* Acrylic on Paper. *Dealer:* www.janlis.com. *Mailing Add:* 12 Sunset Ln Pompano Beach FL 33062

LISK, PENELOPE E TSALTAS
PAINTER, PRINTMAKER
b New York, NY, June 16, 59. *Study:* Bryn Mawr Col, Pa, AB(fine art printmaking), 81, with Fritz Janschka; Cranbrook Acad Art, Bloomfield Hills, Mich, MFA(printmaking), 85, with Steve Murakishi. *Work:* Detroit Inst Art, Mich; Nelson Atkins Mus, Kansas City, Kans; Newport Harbour Art Mus, Calif; Cranbrook Acad Art Mus, Bloomfield Hills, Mich; Muskegon Mus Art, Mich. *Exhib:* One-person shows, Limited Impressions, Cabrini Col, 88 & Chilton Co, 90, Radnor, Pa; Drawing '89, Trenton State Col, NJ, 89; 4 artists show, Villanova Univ, Pa, 90; Pavillion Gallery, Mem Hosp, Pennsauken, NJ, 92; Women's Caucus for Art, Jun Gallery, Philadelphia, 94; several group shows, Philadelphia area, 94-2000; The Episcopal Acad, Merion, Pa, 2002. *Collection Arranged:* Centennial Exhib, Baldwin Sch, 89. *Pos:* Gallery asst, Noel Butcher Gallery, Philadelphia, Pa, 85-87; Assoc Development Dir- Chester Springs, Studio, Chester Springs, PA, 2004. *Teaching:* instr, The Baldwin Sch, Bryn Mawr, Pa, 85, camp mgr, 98-2005. *Awards:* Purchase Prize, Nat Drawing, Mercer Co Cult & Heritage Comn, 87; 2nd Prize-Painting, Impressions VIII, Main Line Chamber Com & Sun Oil Co, 88; Mary Custanza Award in Painting- Main-Line Art Center, 2005. *Mem:* Artists Uniting Religion & Art; Main Line Art Ctr; Community Art Ctr; Chester Springs Studio. *Media:* Painting, Printmaking. *Mailing Add:* 2421 N Feathering Rd Media PA 19063

LITTLE, JAMES
PAINTER, PRINTMAKER
b Memphis, Tenn, July 21, 52. *Study:* Memphis Acad Arts, BFA, 74; Syracuse Univ, MFA(fels), 76. *Work:* Ark Arts Ctr, Little Rock; Everson Mus Art; Brooks Mus Art; Twentieth Century Fund, NY; Mrs RaFaella de Ussia Collection, Mex; and others. *Comn:* Oil painting, Stephen Mallory Assoc, NY, 77. *Exhib:* Solo exhib, Everson Mus, 76; Works on Paper, Albright-Knox Art Gallery, 83; Liz Harris Gallery; Chrysler Mus; Alice Bingham Gallery, Memphis; RI Mus Art, Directions in the 1990's, 90; Nat Acad Mus, NY, 2006; and many others. *Teaching:* Asst drawing, Syracuse Univ, 74-76; instr drawing & painting, Memphis Acad Arts, 77-78. *Awards:* Creative Artists Pub Serv Grant, 81. *Media:* Oil on Linen or Canvas. *Dealer:* June Kelly Gallery 591 Broadway New York NY; Sid Deutsch Gallery 29 W 57th St New York NY. *Mailing Add:* 315 Seventh Ave New York NY 10001-6005

LITTLE, KEN DAWSON
SCULPTOR
b Canyon, Tex, April 8, 47. *Study:* Tex Tech Univ, BFA, 70; Univ Utah, MFA, 72. *Work:* Art Pace, San Antonio; Phoenix Art Mus; Contemp Arts Found, Honolulu; Lannan Found, Palm Beach; Mus Contemp Craft; Ariz State Univ; Utah Mus Fine Art; plus many others. *Comn:* Woodland Park Zoo (outdoor work), Seattle Art Comn, Wash, 91. *Exhib:* One-man shows, Cheney Cowles Art Mus, Spokane, Wash, Portland Ctr Visual Arts, Ore, 86, Fabric Workshop, Philadelphia, Pa, 89, Diverseworks, Houston, Tex, 91, 94, Forum for Contemp Art, St Louis, 97, Amarillo Art Mus, Tex, 97, Ctr for Contemp Art, Fort Worth, Tex, 98, Finesilver Gallery, San Antonio, 99, City Mus, St Louis, 00, Galveston Art Ctr, Tex, 01, Hotel Pupik 01, Schrattenberg, Austria, 01, Southwest Sch for Art and Craft, San Antonio, 03, Salt Lake Art Ctr, Utah, 03; Art Pace, San Antonio, 95; Forum Contemp Art, St Louis, 97; Finesilver Gallery, San Antonio, Tex, 99; Galveston Art Ctr, Tex, 00; Field Mus, Chicago, 02; Fabric Workshop, Philadelphia, 03; Art House, Tex Fine Arts Asn, Austin, 03; and many others. *Collection Arranged:* Daniel Jacobs, NYC; McDonald's Corp, Sacramento, Calif; Richard Nelson Gallery, Univ Calif at Davis; Microsoft Corp, Seattle. *Teaching:* Grad teaching asst, Univ Utah, 71-73; instr art, Univ South Fla, 72-74; asst prof, Univ Mont, 74-78, Univ Okla, Norman, 80-85; vis prof, Alfred Univ, NY, 78 & Univ Calif, Davis, 79; assoc prof, Univ Mont, Chmn, 78-80; prof, Univ Tex, San Antonio, 88-. *Awards:* Western States Arts Found Fel, 77; Nat Endowment Arts Fel, 82-83 & 88-89; Art Pace Found AIR Fel, 95; Artist/Ondustry Residency Grant, John M Kohler Art Ctr, Wis, 98; BorderArt/GrensKunst Artist Residency Exchange Grant, Ger, 01; Virginia Groot Found Award for Excellence in Sculpture, 01, 02. *Bibliog:* Elizabeth Skidmor Sasser (auth), Ken Little at the San Antonio Art Inst, Artspace Mag, Vol 8, No 3, 84; Dave Hickey (auth), Ken Dawson Little: A Beastiary of damaged goods, Art Space Mag, summer 85; Glen R Brown (auth), Focus: Ken Little, Meaning in Masquerade, Sculpture Mag, Vol 17, No 7, summer 98. *Media:* Mixed. *Dealer:* Finesilver Gallery San Antonio TX. *Mailing Add:* PO Box 830085 San Antonio TX 78283-0085

LITTLE CHIEF, BARTHELL
PAINTER, SCULPTOR
b Lawton, Okla, Oct 14, 41. *Study:* Cameron Univ, Lawton, Okla; Univ Okla, Norman. *Work:* Southwestern Mus Los Angeles, Calif; Southern Plains Mus, Anadarko, Okla; Cahokia Mounds Hist Site, Collinsville, Ill; Mus Art, Univ Okla, Norman; Okla Hist Soc, Oklahoma City. *Comn:* Terra-cotta sculpture, US Dept Interior, Washington, DC, 69; tempera painting, US Dept Interior, Washington, DC, 81; fiberglass sculpture, US Dept Interior, Washington, DC, 85. *Exhib:* Am Indian Artist, Philbrook Art Mus, Tulsa, Okla, 78; Vestiges and Resurgence, Morris Mus, Morristown, NJ, 79; Am Contemp Paintings Traveling Exhib, SAm, 79; one-man show, Mus Art, Univ Okla, Norman, 79; Am Indian Art 1980's, Native Am Ctr Living Arts, Niagara Falls, NY, 81. *Awards:* 1st Prize Sculpture, 95, Printmaking, 97, 3rd Prize, Sculpture, 96, Printmaking, 89, 94 & 95, Red Earth Indian Art Show, Olka City, Okla; Grand Award, 91, 1st Prize Painting, 93, 2nd Prize, 95, 1st Prize Sculpture, 95 & 97 & 2nd Prize Sculpture, 95 & 96, Cherokee Nat Hist Mus, Tahlequah, Okla; & others. *Media:* Tempera, Gouache; Alabaster, Bronze. *Publ:* Auth, Kiowa Voices, Tex Christian Univ Press, 83. *Dealer:* Barbara Gallery 135 Palace Ave Sante Fe NM 87501. *Mailing Add:* Rt 3 Box 109A Anadarko OK 73005

LITTLETON, HARVEY K
EDUCATOR, GLASS BLOWER
b Corning, NY, June 14, 22. *Study:* Univ Mich, BDesign; Brighton Sch Art, Eng; Cranbrook Acad Art, MFA; Philadelphia Col Arts, Hon DFA, Rhode Island Sch Design, Hon DFA. *Hon Degrees:* Philadelphia Univ of Arts, Hon Dr (fine arts), 82, RISD, 96 & Univ Wis, Madison, 2000. *Work:* Toledo Mus Art, Ohio; Victoria & Albert Mus, London; Mus Mod Art & Metrop Mus Art, NY; Kunstmuseum, Dusseldorf, WGer; Philadelphia Mus Art, Pa. *Exhib:* Objects USA, Johnson Wax Collection, 69-72; 15th Triennale Exhib Archit & Decorative Art, 74; New Glass, Corning Mus Glass, 79-81; retrospectives, Mint Mus Art, 79, 99-2001 & Renwick Gallery, Smithsonian Inst, 84; and others. *Pos:* Bd trustees, Pilchuck Sch, Wash, Penland Sch, NC, currently. *Teaching:* Instr ceramic art, Toledo Mus Art Sch Design, 49-51; prof art, Univ Wis-Madison, 51-77, emer prof, 77-, chmn dept art, 64-67 & 69-71, univ res grants, 54, 57, 62, 72 & 75. *Awards:* Nat Endowment Art Fel, 78-79; Gold Medal, Am Crafts Coun, 83; NC Governor's Award for Fine Arts, 87; Citation for Distinguished Serv in the Visual Arts, Nat Asn Schs Art & Design. *Bibliog:* Colescott (auth), Harvey Littleton, 59 & Dido Smith (auth), Off hand glassblowing, 64, Craft Horizons; Joan Falconer Byrd (auth), Pioneer in American studio glass, Am Craft, 2-3/80; Harvey K Littleton, A Retrospective Exhib, High Mus Art, 84. *Mem:* Fel Am Crafts Coun (trustee, 57 & 59-64); hon mem Nat Coun Educ in Ceramic Arts; hon mem Glass Art Soc; Corning Mus Glass; hon life mem Am Ceramic Soc. *Media:* Glass. *Publ:* Auth, Erwin Eisch, 63 & Glass in the Ozarks, 73, Craft Horizons; Glassblowing--a Search for Form, Van Nostrand Reinhold, 72. *Dealer:* The Littleton Collection: Art Gallery 3690 N USL Ft Pierce FL 34949; Maurine Littleton Gallery 1667 Wisconsin Ave Washington DC 20007. *Mailing Add:* 232 E Ridge Dr Spruce Pine NC 28777

LITTRELL, DORIS MARIE
DEALER
b Apache, Okla, Apr 30, 28. *Pos:* Owner, Okla Indian Art Gallery, currently. *Specialty:* Native American arts, with emphasis on Oklahoma Indian artists and craftsman. *Mailing Add:* 2335 SW 44th St Oklahoma City OK 73119

LITWIN, RUTH FORBES
PRINTMAKER, PAINTER
b Omaha, Nebr, Apr 14, 33. *Study:* San Antonio Col, Tex, 50; Richland Col, Dallas, 78; Southern Methodist Univ, Dallas, with Wilbert Verhelst, 79, Brookhaven Col, Dallas, Tex, with Don Taylor, 91-96; Western Ky Univ, Seminars with Ivan Schieferdecker & Laurin Northesen, 91; Washington Univ Workshop, Dallas, Tex, studied with Peter Marcus, 94 & 96 & Dawn Guernsey, 94. *Work:* Mem Ctr Holocaust Studies, Dallas; Nat Mus Women Arts, Washington, DC; AH Belo Corp, Texas Instruments, Brookhaven Col, Dallas; North Lake Col, Irving, Tex. *Comn:* Memorial (cast bronze) & Eternal Light (cast bronze), Mem Ctr Holocaust Studies, Dallas, 83; Sculpture, Jewish Home for the Aged, 88. *Exhib:* Nat Mus Women Arts, Washington, DC, 91; Masur Mus Art, Monroe, La, 92; Nat Competition, S Bend Art Ctr, Ind, 92; retrospective, Northlake Col, Irving, Tex, 92; Wichita Falls Mus & Art Ctr, Tex, 93; Tom Peyton Mem Arts Festival, Alexandria, La, 93; Wise Women Speak, Nat Open, Dallas, 94; Global Focus: Women in Art and Cult, UN Fourth World Conf Women, Beijing, China, 95; La State Univ Nat Exhib, Baton Rouge, 98; Univ Richmond Mus, Va, 2000; North Lake Col, 2001; Irving Arts Center, 2003; and many others. *Awards:* Purchase Award, Brookhaven Col, 96; Northlake Col, 2002; Rowena Elkin Award, 97; Soc Int des Beaux-Arts Prix, 98; Calender Award, Figurative Sculpture, Tex Sculpture Asn, 2006. *Bibliog:* Rachel Amado Bortnick (auth), Spreading the Message of

Tolerance, 94; Bridget Knight (auth), article, Wichita Falls Times Record News, 94; Wade Wilson (auth), Master strokes in printmaking, 95; Mike Jacobs (auth), Triumph over Tragedy, 148 & 149. *Mem:* Tex Fine Arts Asn (dir, 78-79, pres, 80-82, state bd, 82-86); Dallas Visual Art Ctr, (charter mem, 81); Int Sculpture Asn; Mid Am Print Coun; Women's Caucus Art (bd mem, 84-86, vpres prog, 86); Embassies Prog Washington, DC, Angola Embassy; Tex Sculpture Asn. *Media:* Printmaker; Sculpture. *Interests:* Live theater, movies, reading & yoga. *Publ:* Auth, Tough Issues in Women's Art, The Washington Post, Washington, DC, 2/22/91; Univers de Arts, Le Mag de L'Information Artistique, 9/88 & 10/99

LITZ, JAMES C
PAINTER
b Buffalo, NY, Sept 17, 48. *Study:* Self-taught. *Work:* Mus D'Art Naif, Paris, France; Fenmore House, NY State Hist Soc, Cooperstown, NY; Mengei Int World Folk Art Mus, La Jolla, Calif; Vietnam Vets Art Group; New York State Hist Soc, Buffalo; and others. *Exhib:* Nat Int exhibs, Clary Miner Gallery, Buffalo, NY, 87-90; Vietnam Vets Arts Group Nat Touring Exhib, 87-98; The Magic of Naive Art Touring Exhib, 87-88; Mid-west Mus Am Art Touring Exhib, 87-88; 42nd Western NY Albright Knox Exhib, Buffalo, NY, 88 & 90; Burchfield Art Ctr Folk Art Exhib, Buffalo, 88; La Cite Naifs Hotel de Ville salon Richelieu Exhib, Paris, 89; Nat Baseball Exhib, Gallery 53, Cooperstown, NY, 90. *Awards:* Partner's Press Award, Albright Knox Western NY Exhib, 88; First Prize, Cooperstown Art Asn 55th Nat Art Exhib, 90. *Mem:* Cooperstown Art Asn; Mus Am Folk Art, NY. *Media:* Acrylic, Watercolor. *Publ:* Auth, article in Sunstorm Fine Arts Mag, Summer 94; contribr, mag cover, Reader's Digest, 99. *Dealer:* Benjamans Art Gallery 419 Elmwood Ave Buffalo NY 14222; Vern Stein Fine Arts 5735 Main St Williamsville NY 14221. *Mailing Add:* 241 Peppermint Rd Lancaster NY 14086

LIU, HUNG
PAINTER
b Changchun, China, Feb 17, 48. *Study:* Beijing Teachers Col, China, BFA, 75; Cent Acad Fine Art, Beijing, MFA equivalent, 81; Univ Calif, San Diego, MFA(visual arts), 86. *Work:* Dallas Mus Art; San Jose Mus Art; City San Francisco Pub Art Prog; Muscarelle Mus Art, Col William & Mary, Williamsburg, Va; Santa Barbara Mus Art, Calif; Nat Mus Am Art, Smithsonian Inst, Wash; M H de Young Mem Mus/Fine Arts Mus of San Francisco; Oakland Mus of Art, Calif; Jane Voorhees Zimmerli Art Mus, New Brunswick, NJ; San Francisco Mus Modern Art; and many others. *Comn:* Art and the Tao (permanent mural & installation), Univ Calif, San Diego, 86; Reading Room (permanent pub off-site mural installation), Kuo Bldg, Chinatown, San Francisco, Calif, 88; Map No 33 (permanent mural on hist San Francisco) Moscone Conv Ctr, San Francisco, 92; Fortune Cookie, San Jose Mus Art & City San Jose Collection, 95; The Long Wharf, No 1 Embacadero Ctr, Skydeck, 41st Fl, San Francisco, 96. *Exhib:* solo exhibs, Chrysler Mus Art (brochure), Norfolk, Va, 95-96, Mills Col Art Gallery (brochure), Oakland, Calif, 95-96, The Last Dynasty, Steinbaum Krauss Gallery, NY, 95, You Can't Go Home Again, Univ Nev, Donna Beam Fine Art Gallery, Las Vegas, 96, Col Charleston, SC, 97, Crealdé Sch Art, Winter Park, Fla, 97, A Survey, 88-98 (traveling exhib), Wooster Col Art Mus, 98, Rena Bransten Gallery (catalogue), San Francisco, 98, Schneider Mus Art, Ashland, Oreg, 98, Steinbaum Krauss Gallery, NY, 99, Byron Cohen Gallery, Kansas City, Mo, 00, Gallery of Contemp Art, Sacred Heart Univ, Fairfield, Conn, 00, LewAllen Contemp, Santa Fe, NMex, 00, Boise Art Mus, 01, Polk Mus Art, Lakeland, Fla, 02, and others; Gender Beyond Memory (with catalogue), Tokyo Metrop Mus of Photogr, Japan, 96; Am Stories: Amidst Displacement & Transformation, Setagaya Art Mus, Tokyo, Japan, 97; Into the 21st Century, Selections from the Permanent Collection, San Jose Mus of Art, Calif, 99; The View From Here, Tretyakov Gallery, Moscow, 2000; San Jose Mus Art, Calif, 2001, 2002; Rena Bransten Gallery, San Francisco, 2001. *Collection Arranged:* AT&T Corp; City of San Jose; Fort Wayne Mus Art, Ind; Dallas Mus Art; LA Co Mus Art; Mills Col, Oakland, Calif; Oakland Mus Art, Calif; Santa Barbara Mus Art; SPencer Mus Art, Univ Kans, Lawrence; Nat Mus Am Art, Wash, DC; Univ Ariz Mus Art, Tucson. *Pos:* Lectr at many Mus, Symps & Univs, 85-94. *Teaching:* Prof art, Cent Acad Fine Art, Beijing, China, 81-84; adj prof, Chinese Art Hist, Univ Tex, Arlington, 87; asst prof art, Univ N Tex, Denton, 89-90; asst prof, Mills Col, Oakland, Calif, 90-95, assoc prof, 95-. *Awards:* Nat Endowment Arts, 89 & 91; Humanities Award, San Francisco Women's Ctr, Calif, 96; Joan Mitchell Found Grant Award Painting, 98. *Bibliog:* Robin Caudell (auth), A view of life through political pictures, Press-Republican, 9/24-10/1/98; David Bonetti (auth), From chaos comes art, San Francisco Examiner, 8/24/98; Marc Awodey (auth), Drawing Conclusions?, Seven Days, 9/23/98. *Mem:* Col Art Asn. *Publ:* Numerous articles in Art forum & Artweek between 88 & 92; auth, Artist's Statements, Visions, fall 89; Artist's statements (catalog for an artist generated exhib in Dallas), Vessel, 5/90; auth, Five Terms, Two Letters, Meaning-Contemp Art Issues, No 7, 90; Art to Art: Expressions by Asian American Women (video), Asian Women United of Calif, 93. *Dealer:* Rena Bransten 77 Geary St San Francisco CA 94108. *Mailing Add:* c/o Rena Bransten 77 Geary St San Francisco CA 94108

LIU, KATHERINE CHANG
PAINTER, CURATOR
b Kiang-si, China; US citizen. *Study:* Univ Calif, Berkeley, MS, 66. *Work:* Lew Allen Contemporary, Santa Fe, NMex, 98 & 99; Watercolor Biennial, Parkland Col Gallery, Ill, 98; Rosaline Koener Gallery, NY, 2000; Gail Harvey Gallery, Calif, 99; AMA Gallery, Finland, 6/01; Chrysler Mus, Va; Virginia Mus; Utah State Univ Art Mus; Palm Springs Desert Mus, Calif. *Exhib:* Chicago Navy Pier Int Art Fair, 94; Taiwan Art Educ Inst Invitational, 94; Rosenfeld Gallery, 94; JJ Brookings Gallery, 96; Hong Kong Univ Sci & Technol, 96; plus many others; solo shows, Egelund Gallerie, Copenhagen, Denmark, 2002, Galerie Parsi Parla, Lyon, France, 2004, Jenkins Johnson Gallery, 2005. *Pos:* Invited juror & lectr for over 75 nat & regional exhibs & orgns; cur, Lewallen Contemp, Santa Fe, 2003-04; cur, Jenkins Johnson Gallery, San Francisco, 2005; cur, Gail Havey Gallery, Santa Monica, Calif, 2006. *Teaching:* Instr watercolor, Western Va Mus Arts, 75-79, Conejo Valley Art Mus, 80-82 & watercolor groups, US & Abroad; instr intensive studies seminar, TAOS, NM, 98-2006. *Awards:* Second Award, Nat Watercolor Soc, 79; Best show, Nat Watercolor Soc mem Show, 84; Gold Medal, Allied Artists Am, New York, 86. *Bibliog:* Emilia Siltavuori (auth), Sweden, 7/21/01; Mia Tykkylainan (auth), The Possibility of a Slow Paced Life, The Art of Katherine Chang Liu, Gallerie Ama, 7/12/01; Ryon Harms (auth), Painting the Layers of Katherine Chang Liu, Los Angeles Daily News, 4/7/03. *Mem:* Watercolor USA Hon Soc; Nat Watercolor Soc. *Media:* Painting, Monotype; Mixed Media. *Collection:* Inst of Contemp Art, Lyon France; Chrysler Mus; Va Mus; Palm Springs Desert Mus. *Publ:* Auth, The California Romantics, Robert Perine, Artra Publ, 87; Exploring Painting, Davis Publ; Painting the Spirit of Nature, Watson-Guptill; Watercolor and Collage Workshop, Watson-Guptill. *Dealer:* Gail Harvey Gallery Santa Monica CA; Lew Allen Contemporary Santa Fe NM; Sandra Walters Internat Hong Kong; Jenkins Johnson Gallery San Francisco Calif & Chelsea New York; Christel Dahlen Gallery Copenhagen Denmark. *Mailing Add:* 1338 Heritage Pl Westlake Village CA 91362

LIVERANT, GIGI HORR
PAINTER
b Portsmouth, NH, Apr 10, 50. *Study:* Paier Col of Art, BA, 1972; Studied under Robert Brackman, 1971-1973. *Work:* Lyman Allyn Mus, New London, Conn; Conn Col, New London, Conn; Pfizer, Groton, Conn; Aetna Insurance Co, Hartford, Conn; Conn Savings Bank, New Haven, Conn; Three Rivers Community Col, Conn. *Comn:* Mural, Old Lyme Inn, Old Lyme, Conn, 1976; Mural, Conn Savings Bank, New Haven, Conn, 1978; CowParade, CowParade Inc, NY, 2000; CowParade, CowParade Inc, Boston, Mass, 2006. *Exhib:* Pastel Soc of Am, Hermitage Foundation Mus, Norfolk, Va, 1982; Illumination, Lyman Allyn Mus, New London, Conn, 1983; Gigi Horr Liverant, Slater Mem Mus, Norwich, Conn, 1992; Gigi Horr Liverant, Lyman Allyn Mus, New London, Conn, 1996. *Awards:* Hurlimann Armstrong Award, Pastel Soc of Am, M Hurlimann Armstrong, 1979; Bd Dirs Award, Kansas Pastel Soc, 1988; Art Spirit Found, Pastel Soc of Am, Dianne B Bernhard, 2000. *Bibliog:* Claudia Becker (auth), Vibrant Renditions of Everyday Objects, Women in the Arts, 1995. *Mem:* Conn Women Artists (coun mem), 1983-1985, 2002-2006; Conn Pastel Soc (juror), 2003, 2005; Pastel Soc of Am; Conn Acad of Fine Arts. *Media:* Pastel, Oil. *Dealer:* Alva Greenberg Alva Gallery 54 State St New London CT 06320. *Mailing Add:* 43 School Rd Colchester CT 06415

LIVESAY, THOMAS ANDREW
MUSEUM DIRECTOR, ADMINISTRATOR
b Dallas, Tex, Feb 1, 45. *Study:* San Francisco Art Inst, 63-65; Univ Tex, Austin, BFA, 68, MFA, 72; Harvard Univ, 78. *Collection Arranged:* Five Austin Artists (with catalog), 74; The Amarillo Competition, 75 & 77; Charles Burchfield Selected Works (with catalog), 75; Henri Matisse Etchings, 75; American Masters, 75; Warren Davis Retrospective (with catalog), 75; American Images, 76, with Nat Endowment for the Humanities; Young Texas Artists Series, 76-78. *Pos:* Tech staff, Univ Tex Art Mus, Austin, 66-70; cur, Elisabeth Ney Art Ctr, Austin, 70-73; dir, Longview Mus & Art Ctr, Tex, 73-75; cur, Amarillo Art Ctr, 75-77, dir, 77-80; asst dir admin, Dallas Mus Fine Arts, 80-85; dir, Mus NMex, 85-. *Teaching:* Univ Okla, MLS/me prog, 87-. *Awards:* Roy Crane Award Fine Arts, Univ Tex, Austin, 68. *Mem:* Am Asn Mus; Tex Asn Mus (pres, 83-85). *Res:* Twentieth century American art with particular emphasis on sculpture. *Publ:* Coauth, Larson-Walsh-Sculpture, 74; auth, Young Texas Artists Series, 78; American Images, 78; coauth, Made in Texas, 79; auth, Russell Lee, 79; Ruth Abrams, New York Univ, 86

LIVET, ANNE HODGE
ADMINISTRATOR, CRITIC
b Ft Worth, Tex. *Study:* Wellesley Col, Mass, 59-61; Univ Tex, Austin, 61-62; Tex Christian Univ, Ft Worth, BA, 72, MA, 74. *Collection Arranged:* Brazos River: a Television Exhibition with Robert Rauschenberg, Viola Farber and David Tudor, Ft Worth Art Mus, 77, The Record as Artwork: from Futurism to Conceptual Art (ed & contribr, catalog), 77 & Stella Since 1970 (ed, catalog), 78; David McManaway: Works-Twenty Years (auth, catalog), Univ Gallery, Meadows Sch Arts, Southern Methodist Univ, Dallas, 79; The Works of Edward Ruscha (auth, catalog), San Francisco Mus Mod Art, Calif, 81; Infotainment, 18 Artists from New York (auth, catalog); Art Against AIDS (ed, catalog); The New Urban Landscape (co-cur & auth, catalog), World Financial Ctr. *Pos:* Dir performing arts, Ft Worth Art Mus, 74-78 & cur, 75-78; co-founder with Stephen Reichard, Livet Reichard Co Inc, 79-. *Awards:* Nat Endowment Arts Fel Mus Prof, 76; Inst for Art & Urban Resources Fel, New York, 78-79. *Publ:* Ed & contribr, Contemporary Dance, Abbeville Press, 78; Contemporary Art Southeast, Vol II, No 2, 79; contribr, All Sweet Things, Bomb Mag, winter 98 & Looking Up, Pub Art Fund, 99. *Mailing Add:* c/o Livet Reichard Co Inc 306 W 38th St 7th Fl New York NY 10018

LIVICK, STEPHEN
PHOTOGRAPHER
b Castleford, Eng, Feb 11, 45; Can citizen. *Study:* Self-taught. *Work:* Can Mus Contemp Photog, Ottawa; Mus Mod Art, NY; George Eastman House, Rochester, NY; Carnegie Mus Art, Pittsburgh, Pa; Corcoran Gallery Art, Washington. *Exhib:* Solo exhibs, George Eastman House, Rochester, NY, 75 & 77, Nat Film Bd Can, Ottawa, 76, 77, 82 & 83, Baltimore Mus Art, 78, McIntosh Gallery, Univ Western Ont, London, 81, 93, MacDonald Stewart Art Ctr, 83, 94 & Can Mus Contemp Photog, Ottawa, 92; Persona (with catalog), Nickle Arts Mus, Calgary, 82; Seeing People, Photogrs Gallery, London, Eng, 84; Contemp Canadian Photog, Nat Gallery Can, Ottawa, 85; Corcoran Gallery Art, Washington, DC, 89; Portside Gallery, Yokohama,

Japan, 98. *Awards:* Several grants, Can Coun & Ont Arts Coun. *Bibliog:* David Scopic (auth), Gum Bichromate Book, 91; Calcutta, Can Mus Contemp Photog, 92; Livick Metaphorical Transformations, 97; and others. *Media:* Gum Bichromate Printing. *Dealer:* Deleon White Gallery 1096 Queen St W Toronto ON Canada M6J 1H9. *Mailing Add:* 22A Maitland St 3rd Fl London ON N6B 3L2 Canada

LIVINGSTON, CONSTANCE KELLNER
COLLAGE ARTIST, SCULPTOR
b Brooklyn, NY. *Study:* Tyler Sch Fine Art, Temple Univ, MFA, 44; studies with Philp Evergood, 50, Victor Candell, 70. *Work:* Ardsley Gallery Libr, NY. *Comn:* Sculpture-lucite & bronze, Patent Lawyers Asn, New Haven, Conn, 79. *Exhib:* Photog & Sculpture, Mus Gallery, White Plains, NY, 85; Nat Acad Galleries, NY, 85; Hudson River Mus, Westchester, NY, 85 & 90; Stamford Mus, Conn, 90; Katonah Mus, NY, 93; NY Soc Women Artists, NY, 93-94. *Teaching:* High sch educ art, Metrop Mus Art, 79-83. *Awards:* Famous Artist Award, Nat Asn Women Artists; Audubon Artists Medal, Audubon Artists; First Prize Sculpture, Mamaroneck Artists. *Mem:* Nat Asn Women Artists; Silvermine Guild Artists; Art Place Gallery; Art Initiatives; Artists Equity Asn. *Media:* Collage; Lucite, Welded Steel. *Mailing Add:* One Sheldrake Ln New Rochelle NY 10804

LIVINGSTON, MARGARET GRESHAM
ADMINISTRATOR, PATRON
b Birmingham, Ala, Aug 16, 24. *Study:* Vassar Col, AB, 45; Univ Ala, MA, 46. *Pos:* Chmn bd, Birmingham Mus Art, 78-86, exec comn, 78- & chmn comp on collections, 86-. *Awards:* Silver Bowl Award for Contrib Arts, Birmingham Festival Arts, 67; Woman of Year, Birmingham, Ala, 86. *Mem:* Am Asn Mus. *Interests:* Art history, education, board administration & organization and publication of museums. *Collection:* American graphics and drawings. *Mailing Add:* 12 Country Club Rd Birmingham AL 35213

LIVINGSTON, VALERIE A
EDUCATOR, MUSEUM DIRECTOR
b Pittsburgh, Pa. *Study:* Univ SFla, BA(art hist), 77; Fla State Univ, MA(art hist), 80; Univ Del, PhD(art hist), 89. *Collection Arranged:* W Elmer Schofield: Proud Painter of Modest Lands (auth, catalog), Moravian Col, 88; Encountering the Narrative in the Work of Florence Putterman (auth, catalog), Susquehanna Univ, 93; Intimate Perceptions: Aesthetic Considerations of Photography Through the Microscope, Susquehanna Univ, 93; Chronicles of Pa Plain People, 94; Joseph Priestly in America: 1794 to 1804 (coauth, catalog), Dickinson Col, 94; James Fitzgerald: Spiritual Transformation, 97; Masters of the French Poster, Susquehanna Univ, 97; Public & Private Eyes: FSA Photography in Pennsylvania, 98; Monhegan Modernists: 1940-1970 from the Collection of John M Day, Susquehanna Univ, 2002; Cognac, Cafe & Clluture: The Art of the French Poster, Susquehanna Univ, 2003. *Pos:* Prof art hist, chmn art dept, mus dir. *Teaching:* Adj prof art hist, Moravian Col, 86-90; assoc prof art hist & head art dept, Susquehanna Univ, 90-, dir Lore Degenstein Gallery, 92-. *Mem:* Col Art Asn; Am Asn Mus; Mid-Atlantic Asn Mus; Asn Col & Univ Mus & Galleries; Asn Historians of Am Art. *Res:* American art; early 20th century & federal portraiture; abstract expressionist sculpture (Herbert Ferber); contemporary feminist painters; Pennsylvania Impressionists (W Elmer Schofield). *Specialty:* American Art; Decorative Arts; French Posters. *Publ:* Auth, W.Elmer Schofield: Proud Painter of Modest Lands, Moravian Col, 88; Encountering The Narrative in The Work of Florence Putterman, 93; Joseph Priestley in America, Dickinson Col, 94; Hans Moller Purveyor of Color: 1905-2001, 2002; Beyond Description: Abstraction in the Oil Paintings of James Fitzgerald, Monhegan Mus, 2001. *Mailing Add:* 444 N New St Bethlehem PA 18018

LIVINGSTONE, BIGANESS
PAINTER
b Cambridge, Mass. *Study:* Mass Col Art, BFA(painting), 50, MA; Univ Wis, Madison, MFA(painting), 80. *Work:* Chase Manhattan Bank Collection, NY; Merrimack Co Courthouse, NH; Neville Mus, Wis; Radcliffe Col, Cambridge, Mass; and others; Engineering Bldg, Univ Wis, Madison; Mass Col of Art, Office of the Pres; Goldberg moser O'Neill Advt, Calif. *Comn:* Mural, Cranwell Chapel, Lenox, Mass, 67. *Exhib:* DeCordova Mus, Lincoln, Mass, 58 & 60; Fitchburg Art Mus, Mass, 77; Arts & Sci Mus, Nashua, NH, 77; Bergstrom-Mahler Mus Neenah, Wis, 78; Elvehjem Mus, Wis, 84; Minneapolis Art Mus, 86; Milwaukee Art Mus, 86; Del Ctr Contemp Art, 89; David Barnett Gallery, Milwaukee, Wis, 91-93; Claudia Chapline Gallery, Stinson Beach, Calif, 95; Crocker-Kingsley, Crocker Mus, Sacramento, Calif, 2000; Rahr-West Mus, Monitowoc, Wis, 2000; Allen/Thomas Gallery, Neenah, WI, 2001; SFMOMA Artists Gallery Point Mason, Calif, 2001 & 06; The Art Foundry Gallery, Sacramento, Calif, 2005. *Pos:* Regional dir, City Spirit Grant, NH Comn Arts, 75; mem, adv bd, Cudahy Gallery, Milwaukee Art Mus, 84-85; mem, panel & artists grant awards, Wis Arts Bd, 86; juror, Fairfield City Gallery, Fairfield, CA, 2005. *Teaching:* prof art, Univ Wis, Fox Valley, Drawing & painting, 76-93, emer prof, 93-. *Awards:* Grant, Bunting Inst Independent Study, Radcliffe Col, Mass, 65; Univ Wis Painting Grants, 89 & 90; Grant: The George Sugarman Fdtn, Inc, 2003; and others. *Bibliog:* Ted Farah (auth), Art collecting for fun and profit; Bartlett Hayes (auth), Tradition becomes innovation; Who's Who in American Education, Nat Reference Inst, 93; Benny Shaboy (auth), StudioNotes Tres & Art Opportunities, CA, 2004. *Mem:* Soc Inst Fels, Radcliffe Col, Mass; Mass Col Art N Calif Alumni. *Media:* Acrylic, Oil. *Dealer:* San Francisco Mus Modern Art Artists Gallery Bldg A Ft Mason Ctr San Francisco CA 94123. *Mailing Add:* 100 Little River Ct No 2 Vallejo CA 94591

LIVINGSTONE, JOAN
SCULPTOR, EDUCATOR
b Portland, Ore, May 29, 48. *Study:* Beloit Col, Wis, 66-67, Portland State Univ, BA, 72, Cranbrook, Acad Art, Bloomfield Hills, Mich, MFA, 74. *Work:* Cranbrook Acad Art Mus, Peat Marwick Exec Ed Ctr, Chicago, The Robert Efannebecker Collection, Lancaster, Pa, Burke Hoffman Law Offices, Kansas City, Mo; Metrop Mus Art, NY; Mus Contemp Art, Chicago; and others. *Comn:* Buchner's Woyzeck, 71 & Shakespeare's King Lear, 72, set designs, Portland Shakespeare Co, Ore; Ionesco's Exit the King, set design, Androgyna Theatre Co, Portland, 76. *Exhib:* Solo exhibs, Figures and Curtains: 1980-84, 341 W Superior St, Chicago, Ill, 84, Joan Livingstone: Sculpture from 1980-85, Contemp Craft Assoc, Portland, Ore, 85, Joan Livingstone: Recent Sculpture and Collage, Tyler Gallery, Tyler Sch Art Temple Univ, Elkins Pk, Pa, 86, Joan Livingston: Recent Sculpture, 88, and Joan Livingstone: New Sculpture, 90, Artemisia Gallery, Chicago & Dennos Mus Ctr, Traverse City, Mich, 98; Mesh: Five Chicago Sculptors, Foster Gallery, Fine Arts Center, Univ Wisconsin-Eau Claire, Wis, 89; Armor: Seven Chicago Sculptors, Randolph St Gallery, Chicago, 89; Crossroads: Contemp Fiber, The Gallery of Contemp Art, Univ Colo, Colo Springs (catalog), 90; USA/Columbia: Fibers, Fla State Univ Gallery and Mus, Tallahassssee, traveling to Bogota, Medellin, Calle, Columbia through 91 (catalog); Sculpture Textile, 12th Biennial, Mus Cantonal des Beaux Arts, Lausanne, Switz, 85; Imagining Form: Six Sculptors, State of Ill Art Gallery, Chicago, 88; Armor: Seven Chicago Sculptors, Randolph St Gallery, Chicago, 89; The Chicago Show (with catalog), Chicago Cult Ctr, 90; Faculty Sabbatical Show, Betty Rymer Gallery, Sch Art Inst Chicago, 91; New Acquisitions: The MCA Collects, Mus Contemp Art, Chicago, 91; Gallery Artists, Laura Russo Gallery, Portland, Ore, 94; Assemblage, Ctr Galleries, Ctr Creative Studies, Detroit, Mich, 98; Embodiment, Ark Art Ctr, Little Rock, 99; All-Shook-Up, James Fuentes Gallery, NY, 1/2000; New Breed of Art, Mus of Contemp Art, Pontiac, Mich, 2/00; Er-Uptions, Gallery X, Harlem, NY, 5/2000; numerous others. *Pos:* Artist-in-residence, Banff Ctr Art, Alta, Can, 82-87; panelist, Imagining Form: Six Sculptors, State of Ill Auditorium, Chicago, 88; lectr, Prog for Artisanry, New Bedford, Mass, 88. *Teaching:* Asst prof fiber, Kansas City Art Inst, Mo, 76-80; head fiber dept, Cranbrook Acad Art, Bloomfield Hills, Mich, 80-82; assoc prof fiber debt, Art Inst Chicago, 83-. *Awards:* Individual Artist Fel, Nat Endowment Arts, 79, 86 & 92; Fel, The Louis Comfort Tiffany Found, 89; Individual Artist Grant, Virginia A Groot Found, 98. *Bibliog:* Grady Turner (auth), Liz-N-Val-Feted-N-Validated, Flash Art, 1/2000; James Fuentes (auth), Open Space, Zing Mag, summer issue 2000; Michael MacInnis (auth), Liz-N-Val, Gallery X, The New York Art World, summer 2000. *Media:* Mixed Media. *Publ:* New synthesized images, Impulse: New Images in Fabric, Detroit Artists Market, 84; Katarina Weslien: Transformations & other everyday events, Payson Gallery, 87; Keynote at Convergence, Chicago Artists Coalition News, Vol XVI, No 10, Chicago, 88. *Dealer:* Gallery X 23 W 129 St New York NY 10027; Galerie Gesellscnaft Auguststrase 83 D-10117 Berlin Germany. *Mailing Add:* Sch Art Inst Chicago 37 S Wabash Chicago IL 60603

LIZ-N-VAL
SCULPTOR, PAINTER
b Liz, Poland; Val, USSR. *Work:* Kassel Documenta Arch, Ger; Ludwig Mus, Cologne, Ger; Staats Galerie Grafische Sam Mlung, Stuttgart, Ger; Whitney Mus Am Art, NY; Detroit Inst Arts, Mich. *Comn:* Mural, Urban Jungle, 8 BC Club, NY, 85; Liz-N-Val Head, Steven Spielberg, NY, 87. *Exhib:* El Mundo De Mickey Mouse (with catalog), Cuartel Conde Duque, Madrid & Barcelona, 94-95; Liz-N-Val Fractal Realities, World Wide Web, Paris, France, 96; Liz-N-Val, New Breed of Art, MoMa, Pontiac, Mich, 2/2000; Liz-N-Val, Er-Ruptions, Gallery X, Harlem, NY, 5/2000; Art of Mail(ing), Wexler Ctr for the Arts, Columbus, Ohio, 9/2000; solo show, All Shook-Up, James Fuentes Gallery, NY, 2000, Liz-N-Val Monk Room, Monk Gallery, Brooklyn, 2002, Liz-N-Val Selected Art Sites, Henrybuilt, NYC, 2006; New Breed of Art, Mus New Art, Detroit, MI, 2001; Gefasse, Galerie Gesellschaft, Berlin, Ger, 2001; Hybrid @ Brooklyn Art and Hist Ctr, 2002; Kaboom Mus of New Art, Detroit, Mich, 2002; Smallworks Show, NY Univ, 2003; Sharjan Int Biennial, UAE, 2003; Space Travelers, Tribes Gallery, NY, 2004; Merry/Peace, Sideshow Gallery, Brooklyn, NY, 2004; Beautiful Dreamer, Spaces Gal, Cleveland, Oh, David Gibson (cur), 2005; X-Tremist, Gal X Isteinbul, 2005; ABC No Rio Benefit, Deitch Project, 10-05; Democracy Project, Art Ctr Gal, Missouri State Univ, 2006. *Collection Arranged:* Art Quake Event, First Art-Genes Portable Mus, 92; Decay & Growth, First Portable Am Mus, 93; Art Quake/Art After Post-Mod, First Art-Genes Mus, 93; Sex Quake-Art After Apocalypse, Show in the Form of a Book, Dia Printed Matter, 93; Mus Collection Part I, Art Mag, Venice, 96. *Teaching:* Liz; Instr getting from A to B, Sch Mus Fine Arts, Boston, 69-74; What Is Art?, Mass Col Art, Boston, 74-77. *Bibliog:* Eleanor Hartney (auth), Trash or Treasure, Art News, 88; Tracy Gray (auth), Liz-N-Val Signatures, New Art Int, 88; Grady Turner (auth), Liz-N-Val-Feted-N-Validated, Flashart, 1/2000; Interview by Lily Faust, Art Police, 2003; David Gibson, Catalogue, New Work, 2002; Pool Art Addict, M MacInnis, Daily News, 3/13/04; Sarah Valdez (auth), 2004 Art in America, Space Travelers, 12/04; Stephan Maine (auth), Artnet-Brooklyn Beat; Barbara Rosenthal (auth), Art After Art Event, Art Circles, 10/04; Mary Hrbacek (auth), Tribes Gallery's Space Travellers, NYARTS Mag, 7-8/2004; Chris Twomey (auth), Liz-N-Val, NYARTS Mag, 10-11/2006; Steven Psyllos (auth), Selected Articles, NYARTS Mag, 10-11/2006. *Mem:* Mus Abstract Realism (dir 90-). *Media:* Interactive Media. *Publ:* Liz-N-Val New Work, catalog, 2002; Space Travelers@Tribes Gallery (catalogue), 2004; Museum of Truth & Beauty@Pool Addict (Catalogue), NY, 2004. *Mailing Add:* 7 Mercer St New York NY 10013

LLEARSY, RAYMOND & MELVA BUCKSBANM
COLLECTOR
b Luxembourg. *Awards:* Named one of top 200 collectors, ARTnews Magazine, 2004; recipient Gertrude Vanderbilt Whitney Award for outstanding arts patronage & philanthropy (with Melva Bucksbaum), 2004. *Mem:* Whitney Mus Am Art, Tate Gallery. *Collection:* contemporary art. *Mailing Add:* 646 Willoughby Way Aspen CO 81611

LLEWELLYN, ROBERT
PRINTMAKER, EDUCATOR
b Baltimore, Md, May 9, 45. *Study:* Baltimore City Community Col, AA, 66; Morgan State Univ, BA, 68; Md Inst Col Art, MFA, 72. *Work:* Baltimore Mus Art, Md; Smithsonian Inst, Nat Gallery Art, & Nat Inst Health Washington; NY Pub Libr, NY. *Exhib:* Contemp Am Prints, Albrecht Mus, Mo, 86; Intergrafia '91, Bur Art Exhib, Cracow, Poland, 91; Earth Views 31, Rockville Art Pl, Md, 93; one-man show, Gomez Gallery, Md, 94; State of the Art, Md Art Pl, Md, 95; 18th Int, Kanagawa Perfectural Gallery, Japan, 95. *Teaching:* Prof printmaking, Frostburg State Univ, Md, 72-. *Bibliog:* Nicomeotes Aravz (auth), Amnesis Art, Lascaux Publ, 88; Robert Llewellyn, New Art Examiner, 3/89; Art Diary International, Giancarlo Politi Ed, 92. *Mem:* Am Print Alliance; Md Printmakers; Col Art Asn. *Dealer:* Walter Gomez/Gomez Gallery 836 Leadenhall St Baltimore Md 21230. *Mailing Add:* 12213 Bedford Rd NE Cumberland MD 21502-6811

LLOVERAS, CONNIE
ARTIST
b Havana, Cuba, Oct 16, 58. *Study:* Fla Int Univ, BFA, 80. *Work:* Museo de Arte Contemporaneo, Panama; Lowe Art Mus, Miami; Washington State Art Comn, Seattle. *Comn:* Knowledge Path, Hillsborough Co Art, Tampa, 97; Ybor City Streetscape Project, Hillsborough Co Art, Tampa, 00; Threshold, Gen Services Admin, Washington, DC, 00. *Exhib:* Tampa Pub Art, The Tampa Mus of Art, 01; Intuition, The Robert and Mory Montgomery Art Center, Boca Raton, 02; Connie Lloveras: Interior Gardens, David Rockefeller Ctr for Latin Am Studies at Harvard, Cambridge, 00; Connie Lloveras: Unspoken Words, Museo de Arte Contemporanco, Panama, 02. *Awards:* Best Sculptor Award, Women Explore the Eighties, 87; Artist in Residency Grant, State of Fla, Cult Affairs Office, 02. *Publ:* Ricardo Pau Llosa, Outside Cuba, Rutgers Univ 88; ed, Andrea O Reilly Herrera, Re-Membering Cuba, Univ Tex, 01. *Dealer:* The Americas Collection, Coral Galbes, Fla, 33134. *Mailing Add:* 8800 Old Cutler Rd Coral Gables FL 33156-2236

LLOYD WEBBER, ANDREW
COLLECTOR
b London, Mar 22, 48. *Pos:* Composer: (Broadway plays) Joseph and the Amazing Technicolor Dreamcoat, 68, 73, 91 (Tony nom best original score, 82), 2003; producer: (Broadway plays) Joseph and the Amazing Technicolor Dreamcoat, 73, 74, 78, 80, 91; composer, orchestrator (Broadway plays) Jesus Christ Superstar, 70 (Tony nom best original score, 72), composer, producer, 96, 98; composer: (Broadway plays) Jeeves, 75; composer, producer (Broadway plays) By Jeeves (revision of Jeeves), 96; producer: Jeeves Takes Charge, 75; composer: The Beautiful Game, 2000, The Woman in White, 2004; producer, orchestrator (films) Jesus Christ Superstar, 73, Evita, 96 (Tony award best original score, 80). *Awards:* Named a Living Legend Grammy, 89, created knight in Queen's Honours Birthday List, 92, elevated to peerage in New Years Honours list, 97; named one of The Top 200 Collectors, ARTnews Mag, 2004; recipient Grammy awards, 80, 83, 85, Triple Play award, Am Soc of Composers, 88, City and Music Ctr of Los Angeles, 91, Praemium Imperiale award for music, 95, Richard Rodgers award for contrib to musical theatre, 96, Bernard Delfont award for contrib to show business, 97, Acad award, 97; Achievements awards incl Acad award (Oscar), Golden Globe, Tony, Drama Desk, and Grammy; Top 200 Collectors, ARTnews Mag, 2006; Recipient Kennedy Ctr Award for Achievement in the Arts, 2006. *Bibliog:* (auth): The Complete Phantom of the Opera, 87, The Complete Aspects of Love, 9, Sunset Boulevard: from movie to musical, 93. *Mem:* Royal Col Music. *Collection:* 18th to 20th century paintings, especially the Pre-Raphaelites. *Mailing Add:* 22 Tower St London England WC2H 9NS United Kingdom

LO, BETH (ELIZABETH)
CERAMIST, EDUCATOR
b Lafayette, Ind, Oct 11, 49. *Study:* Univ Mich, Alpha Lambda Delta Scholar, 68, James B Angell Scholar, 69-70, BGS, 71; Purdue Univ, 67; State Univ NY, Alfred, 71; Eastern Mich Univ, 72; Univ Mont, Teaching Asst, 72-74, MFA(ceramics), 74. *Work:* Univ Wash Med Ctr, Seattle; Yellowstone Art Ctr, Billings, Mont; Hallmark Card Corp Ceramics Collection; Univ Mont & Missoula Mus Arts; also several pvt collections. *Exhib:* Baltimore Mus Art, 86; solo exhibs, Clark Fork Gallery, Missoula, Mont, 90, Holter Mus Art, Helena, Mont, 92, MIA Gallery, Seattle, Wash, 93 & 96, J Maddux Parker Gallery, Sacramento, Calif, 93 & 96 & Missoula Mus Arts, Mont, 95; New Orleans Mus Art, 94; Cult Connections, Spaces Gallery, Cleveland, Ohio, 95; Beyond the Rock Garden (with catalog), Wing Luke Asian Mus, Seattle, 96; Magic Mud, NW Ceramics Invitational (touring Idaho), 96; Nat Coun Educ Ceramic Arts Cup Show, Chicago Art Expo, Navy Pier, 96. *Pos:* Commerical art work, including album covers, magazine illustration, promotional material, backdrops & archaeological drawings, currently. *Teaching:* Instr high-fire pottery, raku, dung firing & introductory art, Bitterroot Community Art Proj, 73-77, co-founder, 75-; fine arts camp instr, Univ Mont, Missoula, summer 74, vis asst prof ceramics, 85-86, asst prof art, 86-90, assoc prof art, 90-96, prof art, 96-; porcelain workshop, Creative Arts Workshop, New Haven, Conn, 85; vis artist, Bismarck Jr Col, NDak, 85-86; demonstrator, Nat Coun Educ Ceramic Arts Conf, Cincinnati, Ohio, 90; lectr, Univ Wash, Seattle, 93 & 96, Wing Luke Asian Mus, Seattle, 96; workshop & lectr, Calif State Univ, Chico, 93 & SW Crafts Ctr, San Antonio, Tex, 93; panelist, Nat Coun Educ Ceramic Arts, New Orleans, 94 & Mont Arts Coun Fel Awards, 96; organizer & coordr, Woodstack '95 (symp & summer prog), 95; co-chair & panelist, NGO Forum on Women, Beijing, China, 95. *Awards:* Indiv Artist Fel, Mont Arts Coun, 86; Visual Arts Fel, Nat Endowment Arts, 95; Sch Fine Arts Distinguished Fac Award & Merit Award, Univ Mont, 95. *Bibliog:* Susan Biskeborn (auth), Artists at Work: 25 Northwest Glassmakers, Ceramicists & Jewelers, Alaska Northwest Bks, 90; Ceramics Monthly, 5/95; Ron Glowen (auth), rev, Artweek, 12/96. *Media:* Clay, Mixed Media. *Dealer:* MIA Gallery Seattle WA; J Maddux Parker Gallery Sacramento CA. *Mailing Add:* 408 Village Pl Missoula MT 59802

LOBDELL, FRANK
PAINTER
b Kansas City, Mo. *Study:* St Paul Sch Fine Art, Minn, 38-39; Calif Sch Fine Art, 47-50; Acad Grande Chaumiere, Paris, 50-51. *Work:* Los Angeles Co Mus, Stanford Mus, San Francisco Mus Art & Oakland Mus Art, Calif; Nat Gallery, Washington, DC; Am Acad & Inst Arts & Letters, NY; Nat Mus Am Art, Smithsonian Inst, Washington, DC; Nat Acad Design, NY; numerous others. *Exhib:* One man shows, Lucien Labaudt Gallery, 49; 3rd Biennial of Sao Paulo, Brazil, 55; Int Art of a New Era, Osaka, Japan, 58; Martha Jackson Gallery, 58, 60, 63, 72, 74; Kompas 4, West Coast USA, Van Abbemuseum, Eindhoven, 70; 32nd Biennial Am Painting, Corcoran Gallery Art, Washington, DC, 71; San Francisco Mus Art, 83; IPA Gallery, Boston, 92; Office of Mayor, City Hall, San Francisco, 93; Escape from the Vault: The Contemp Mus Collection Breaks Out, Contemp Mus, Honolulu, 2002; Solo exhibs Galerie Anderson-Mayer, Paris, 65, San Francisco Mus Art, 69, Wiegand Gallery, Col Notre Dame, Belmont, Calif, 81, San Francisco Mus Modern Art, 81, Stanford Univ Mus Art, 92, Art Exchange, San Francisco, 2000, others; Group Shows, Salon du Mai, Paris, 50, III Sao Paulo Biennial, 55, Whitney Mus Am Art, 62-63, 72, Guggenheim Mus, New York City, 64, Univ Ill, 74, 15 Calif Modernists, Fresno Art Mus, 95; represented in permanent collections, San Francisco Mus Art, Oakland Mus Art, Los Angeles Co Mus, Nat Gallery Washington, DC. *Pos:* vis artist/artist-in-residence NY Studio Sch Drawing, Painting & Sculpture, 86, Yale Univ Sch Art, 92, Tyler Sch Art, Temple Univ, 93, numerous others. *Teaching:* Prof art, Stanford Univ, 66-; California Sch Fine Arts, 57-65. *Awards:* Nealie Sullivan Award, San Francisco Mus Art, 60; Gold Medal for Distinguished Achievement in Painting Medal, Am Acad & Inst Art & Letts, 88, Acad Purchase Award, 1992, 1994; elected to Nat Acad Design, 98. *Bibliog:* Michel Tapie (auth), Frank Lobdell, David Anderson, Paris, 66; Walter Hoppe (auth), Frank Lobdell 1948-1965, Pasadena Art Mus, 66; Gerald Nordland (auth), Frank Lobdell, San Francisco Mus Art, 69. *Mem:* Nat Acad. *Media:* All. *Publ:* Frank Lobdell: The Art of Making and Meaning, (catalog) Hudson Hills Press, 2003; Landauer, Susan (auth), The San Francisco School of Abstract Expressionism, Berkeley: Univ Calif Press, 1996; Natsoulas, John et al (auths), The Beat Generation Galleries and Beyond, Davis, Calif: John Natsoulas Press, 1996; Plagens, Peter (auth), Sunshine Muse, New York: Praeger, 1974; others; numerous catalogs & brochures. *Dealer:* Hackett Gallery Freedman, 250 Sutter St 4th fl San Francisco 94108. *Mailing Add:* 2754 Octavia St Apt 3 San Francisco CA 94123-4311

LOBELLO, PETER
SCULPTOR, GRAPHIC ARTIST
b New Orleans, La, Nov 18, 35. *Study:* Sch Archit, Tulane Univ, 53-55, Newcomb Sch Art, 54-55. *Work:* Aldrich Mus Contemp Art; Geneva Mus Art, Switz; Phoenix Art Mus; Plains Art Mus, Moorhead, Minn; New Orleans Mus Art. *Comn:* Sculptures, Chateau Bellereve, Geneva, 74, Villa Savoia, Geneva, 76 & Hyatt Hotels Corp, NY, 80, bronze sculpture for Privy Coun Chamber, New Istana Palace, Bandar Seri Begawan, 84; Atrium sculpture, Madison Equities and Gery Advertising, NY, 85; Anodized aluminum lobby sculpture, One Paydras Plaza, New Orleans, 86. *Exhib:* Contemp Reflections 73, Aldrich Mus Contemp Art, 73; Selections from the Art Lending Service, Mus Mod Art Penthouse Gallery, NY, 78; Prospectus: 1970s, Aldrich Mus Contemp Art, 79; Robert Kidd Gallery, Detroit, 80; 21st Midwestern Invitational, Plains Art Mus, Moorhead, Minn, 80; Alexander Rosenberg Gallery, NY, 80; Inaugral Show, Alexander Carlson Gallery, NY, 80; Rutgers Univ, 83; Sarah Y Rentschler Gallery, NY City, 84; Wood, Water and Stone, 909 Third Ave, NY, 85; Sculptures Comtemporaries, Galerie Les Hirondelles, Tennay/Coppet, Geneva, Switzerland, 87, Un Choix de Plus, 89. *Bibliog:* Paul Goldberger (auth), 42nd St: The Grand Hyatt, New York Times, 9/22/80; Isabel Forgang (auth), At home with sculptor Peter Lobello, New York Daily News Tonight, 10/15/80; Ada Louise Huxtable (auth), Architecture view: Two new triumphant hotels, New York Times, 10/19/80. *Mailing Add:* 47-15 36th St Long Island City NY 11101

LOCHNAN, KATHARINE A
CURATOR, WRITER
b Ottawa, Can, Aug 18, 46. *Study:* Univ Toronto, BA, 68, MA, 71; Courtauld Inst, Univ London, Eng, PhD, 82; Univ Calif, Berkeley, cert mus mgt, 87, Ryerson Polytechnical Inst, cert bus admin, 91. *Pos:* Cur asst, Royal Ont Mus, 68-69; asst cur, Art Gallery Ont, 69-75, cur prints & drawings, 76-95, sr cur, 95-; volunteer asst, Brit Mus, 75-76; assoc fel, Massey Col, 94-; rev bd, Can Cult Property Export, 97-. *Teaching:* Fine arts dept, Univ Toronto, spring 93-96. *Awards:* J Paul Getty Trust Scholar, 87; Award of Merit, Ryerson Polytechnical Inst, 91. *Mem:* Print Coun Am (bd mem, 80-82); London House Asn Can (chmn bd, 81-84); William Morris Soc Can (vpres, 84-85); Toronto Hist Bd (vpres, 93-); Opera Atelier (bd mem, 94-). *Res:* 19th century French and English art, William Morris and Arts and Crafts Movement, Symbolism. *Publ:* Auth, The Etchings of James McNeill Whistler, Yale Univ Press, 84; Whistler's Etchings and the Sources of His Etching Style, 1855-80, Garland Publ, 88; co-auth, The Lithographs of James McNeill Whistler, Vol 1, Art Inst Chicago, 98. *Mailing Add:* 21 Mackenzie Crescent Toronto ON M6J 1S9 Canada

LOCKE, MICHELLE WILSON
CURATOR
b Dallas, Tex, June 10, 47. *Study:* Trinity Univ, San Antonio, Tex; Univ Tex, Austin, BFA. *Pos:* Assoc cur/registrar, South Tex Inst for the Arts. *Teaching:* Art appreciation, Del Mar Col, Corpus Christi, Tex, 91-98. *Mem:* Am Asn Mus; Col Art Asn; Tex Asn Mus. *Res:* Fifteenth Century French illuminated manuscripts. *Specialty:* Modern and Contemporary Art of the Region. *Mailing Add:* 1902 N Shoreline Dr Corpus Christi TX 78401

LOCKHART, SHARON
PHOTOGRAPHER, FILMMAKER
b Norwood, Mass, 64. *Study:* San Francisco Art Inst, BA; Art Ctr Col Design, Pasadena, MFA. *Work:* Boijmans Van Beuningen Mus, Rotterdam, Holland; Eli Broad Family Found, Santa Monica, Calif; Whitney Mus Am Art, NY; Mus Contemp Art, Los Angeles, Calif; Mus Mod Art, San Francisco, Calif. *Comn:* Photograph, BMW. *Exhib:* Whitney Biennial, Whitney Mus Amer Art, NY, 97; Sharon Lockhart, Kemper Mus, Kansas City, 98; Cinema Cinema: Contemp Art and the Cinematic Experience, Van AbbeMuseum, Eindhoven, 99; 2000 Biennial Exhib, Whitney Mus of Am Art, NY, 2000; solo exhibs, Interview Locations/Family Photographs, Blum & Poe, Santa Monica, Calif, 2001, Mus of Contemp Art, Chicago, Ill, 2001, Mus of Contemp Art, San Diego, Calif, 2001, Barbara Gladstone Gallery, NY, 2003; Pub Offerings, Mus of Contemp Art, Los Angeles, 2001, 2004; Art Gallery Ontario, Toronto, 2000, Chac Mool Gallery, Los Angeles, 2001, MCA Chicago, 2001, 2003, Galerie Volker Diehl, Berlin, 2001, Mus für Neue Kunst, Karlsruhe, Ger, 2003; Vedanta Gallery, Chicago, 2003; Int Cooperation Admin Boston, 2004; New Dirs/New Films, Mus Mod Art, NY. *Awards:* Rockefeller Found Fel, 2000; John Simon Guggenheim Mem Found Fel, 2001; Creative Capitol Grant, 2002; Alpert Award in the Arts nominee, 2002. *Bibliog:* Howard Halle (auth), Next Wave: 4 Emerging on Paper, 3/98; Roberta Smith (auth), Renew, NY Times, 3/98; Bernice Reynard (auth), Sharon Lockhart Photographers "Goshogaoka" (catalog essay), Blum & Poe, 4/98. *Media:* Film. *Publ:* Filmmaker, Shaun Khalil, A Woman Under the Influence, 96; Truce: Echoes of Art in an Age of Endless Conclusions, 97

LOCKS, MARIAN
ART DEALER, COLLECTOR
b Philadelphia, Pa. *Study:* Univ Pa; New York Univ; New Sch Soc Research; Moore Col, hon DFA, 90. *Pos:* Coordr, Ann New Talent Exhibs, Marian Locks Gallery, Philadelphia, Pa, 69-88, founding dir & dir emer, 68; corp art adv & cur, Philadelphia, Pa, 69; cur, Older Women Artists, Rosemont Col Gallery Show, formerly. *Awards:* Dean's Award, Am Mus Acad Fine Arts; Art Matters Award & Excellence in the Arts, 88; Mayor's Award, Philadephia, 95. *Mem:* Pa Acad Fine Arts; Inst Contemp Art, Univ Pa; assoc Philadelphia Mus Art; Art Table; Philadelphia Art Dealers Asn. *Specialty:* Gallery is internationally recognized as a showcase for contemporary area artists and 20th century masters. *Collection:* 20th century contemporary. *Dealer:* Locks Gallery. *Mailing Add:* c/o Locks Gallery 600 Washington Square S Philadelphia PA 19106

LOEB, DANIEL S
COLLECTOR
b 1962. *Study:* Columbia Univ, AB (economics), 84. *Pos:* Assoc EM Pincus & Co, 84; sr vpres distressed debt dept Jefferies & Co, 91-93; vpres high-yield sales Citigroup Inc, 94; founder and CEO Third Group LLC, NY City, 95-. *Awards:* named one of Top 200 Collectors, ARTnews Mag, 2006. *Mailing Add:* Third Point LLC 390 Park Ave New York NY 10017

LOEHLE, BETTY BARNES
PAINTER
b Montgomery, Ala, Mar 21, 23. *Study:* Auburn Univ, Ala, 40-42; Harris Sch Art, Nashville, Tenn, 42-46; Evanston Art Ctr, Ill, 63-67. *Work:* Ga Council Arts & Humanities, Atlanta; DeKalb Community Col, Clarkston, Ga; R J Reynolds Tobacco Co, Winston-Salem, NC; Coca-Cola Int, Atlanta. *Exhib:* Hunter Ann, Hunter Mus Art, Chattanooga, Tenn, 77; Piedmont Show, Mint Mus, Charlotte, NC, 77; Artists in Ga, High Mus, Atlanta, 78; Southern Watercolor Soc, 76-79, 81-85 & 89; Ala Watercolor Soc, 79-81, 83, 85, 89, 93 & 94; Ga Watercolor Soc, 79 & 81-87, 93 & 94; Ky Watercolor Soc, 81, 83, 85 & 94; Art in Ga, Albany Mus, Ga, 81. *Awards:* Purchase Award, Olin Mills Corp, Hunter Mus, 77; Hans Hofman Award, Southern Watercolor Soc, 79; Award, Southern Watercolor Soc, 80, Ga Watercolor Soc, 80, 82, 83, 85, 87 & 88. *Bibliog:* Pat Hetzler (auth), Betty Barnes Loehle, Art Voices Mag, 5-6/81. *Mem:* Artists Assocs Inc (pres 78 & 79); Atlanta Artists Club; Southern Watercolor Soc; Ala & Ky Watercolor Socs; Ga Watercolor Soc (bd dir, 80-87). *Media:* Mixed. *Dealer:* Little House on Linden Gallery 2915 Linden Ave Homewood Al 35209. *Mailing Add:* 2608 River Oak Dr Decatur GA 30033

LOEHLE, RICHARD E
PAINTER, ILLUSTRATOR
b Atlanta, Ga, 23. *Study:* Atlanta Col Art, 40; Harris Sch Art, grad cert, 48; Evanston Art Ctr, Ill, 67. *Work:* High Mus Art; Montgomery Mus Art, Ala; Ala Watercolor Soc, Birmingham; Ga Coun Arts & Humanities; Chicago Artists Guild. *Comn:* Produce portraits of yr's four inducttes to Ga Aviation Hall of Fame. *Exhib:* Ga Artists Show, High Mus, 74 & 76; Southern Watercolor Soc, Columbus Mus, 78 & 82; Ga Watercolor Soc, Macon Mus, 82; Ky Watercolor Soc, Owensboro Mus, 83; Southern Watercolor Soc, Asheville Mus, NC, 83; and others. *Awards:* Purchase Prize, Dixie Ann, Montgomery Mus Art, 72; Best in Show, Atlanta Arts Festival, 73 & Southern Watercolor Soc, 80 & 83. *Bibliog:* Edith Coogler (auth), Prize-winning artist, Atlanta Constitution, 6/28/70; S Coleman & C Anderson (auths), article, Southern Watercolor Soc Newslett, 83; Richard and Betty Loehle, Parallel Careers, Nat Television, Mod Maturity, No 252. *Media:* Oil, Acrylic; Watercolor. *Publ:* Coauth, Great American Depression Book of Fun, Harper & Row, 81. *Dealer:* Portrait Brokers of Am Inc 36 Church St Birmingham AL 35213. *Mailing Add:* 2608 River Oak Dr Decatur GA 30033

LOESER, THOMAS
SCULPTOR
b Boston, Mass, May 27, 56. *Study:* Haverford Col, BA, 79; Boston Univ, BFA(magna cum laude), 82; Univ Mass, N Dartmouth, Mass, MFA, 92. *Work:* Mus Art, RI Sch Design, Providence; Cooper Hewitt Mus, Brooklyn Mus, NY; Mus Fine Arts, Boston; Yale Univ Art Gallery, New Haven; other pvt collections; Mus Fine Arts, Houston; Elvejhem Mus Art, Madison, Wis; Milwaukee Mus Art. *Exhib:* Furniture by British Am & French Designers, Victoria & Albert Mus, London, Eng, 84; Material Evidence, Smithsonian Inst, Washington, DC, 85; Furniture for Postmodern Age, Queens Mus, NY, 85; New Furniture in Am, Mus Fine Arts, Boston, Mass, 89 & 91; Art That Works, Mint Mus Art, Charlotte, NC, 90; one-person show, Peter Joseph Gallery, NY, 92 & 95, Art Mus RI Sch Design, 93, Milwaukee Art Mus, 93, Ark Art Ctr Decorative Arts Mus, 93 & Leigh Yawkey Woodson Mus, Warsaw, Wis, 93; Additions, Distractions, Multiple Complications and Divisions, Peter Joseph Gallery, NY, 95; A Passion for Wood, Gallery Functional Art, Santa Monica, Calif, 95; 5: Fifth Anniversary Exhib, Peter Joseph Gallery, NY, 96; Wisconsin Triennial, Madison Art Ctr, 96; Sculpture, Objects and Functional Art, Navy Pier, Chicago, Ill, 97 & 98; In Case, Pritam & Eames Gallery, East Hampton, NY, 97; Re-evolution, Soc Arts & Crafts, Boston, Mass, 97; Am Craft, Renwick Gallery, Washington, DC, 97; Contemp North Am Furniture - A Survey of the Furniture Makers Art, Neuberger Mus Art, NY, 97; Small Works, Pritam & Eames Gallery, East Hampton, NY, 98; Brooklyn Mus, NY, 98; Please Be Seated, Yale Univ Art Gallery, Conn, 99. *Pos:* Bd trustees, Haystack Mountain Sch, Maine, 88-97; juror, Festival at the Lake Crafts Show, Oakland, Calif, 90 & Ill Arts Coun, 91; panelist, Nat Endowment Arts, 92. *Teaching:* Instr fine arts, RI Sch Design, 87-88; instr, Swain Sch Design, New Bedford, Mass, 87 & Univ Wis, Madison, 91-92, asst prof, 92-96, assoc prof, 96-; numerous lectures & workshops at various univs & insts; adj prof, Calif Col Arts & Crafts, Oakland, 89-90. *Awards:* Visual Artists Fel Grant, Nat Endowment Arts, 84, 88, 90 & 94; Finalist, Biennale Award Competition, Louis Comfort Tiffany Found, 97; Grad Sch Res Award, Univ Wis, Madison, 98-99. *Bibliog:* Christine Temin (auth), The fine art of furniture, Boston Globe Mag, 2/18/96; Caitlin Kelly (auth), Art meets craft, Art & Antiques, summer 96; Dan Mack (auth), The Rustic Furniture Companion: Traditions, Techniques, and Inspirations, Lark Books, Asheville, NC, 96. *Media:* Wood, All Media. *Publ:* Auth, Speakeasy, New Art Examiner, 9/92. *Dealer:* Pritam & Eames Gallery Easthampton NY; Leo Kaplan Gallery, New York. *Mailing Add:* 2826 Lakeland Ave Madison WI 53704

LOEWER, HENRY PETER
WRITER, ILLUSTRATOR
b Buffalo, NY, Feb 13, 34. *Study:* Albright Art Sch, Univ Buffalo, with Lawrence Calcagno & Anne Coffin Hanson, BFA, 58. *Work:* Hunt Inst for Botanical Doc, Carnegie-Mellon Univ, Pittsburgh, Pa; Catskill Art Soc, Hurleyville, NY. *Exhib:* Int Exhib of Botanical Drawings, Hunterdon Art Ctr, Clinton, NJ, 77; 4th Int Exhib of Botanical Art, Carnegie-Mellon Univ, Pittsburgh, Pa, 77-78; One-man show, Horticultural Soc of NY, 77. *Awards:* First Place, Garden Writers Am, 81, 84 & 92. *Media:* Pen and Ink, Watercolor. *Publ:* Illusr, Wildflower Perennials for Your Garden, Hawthorn, 76; auth & illusr, Gardens by Design, Rodale, 86; A World of Plants, Abrams, 89; The Wild Gardener, 91; The Evening Garden, 93. *Mailing Add:* 185 Lakewood Dr Asheville NC 28803

LOEWY, RAYMOND
DESIGNER, GRAPHIC ARTIST
b Paris, France, 1893. *Study:* Chaptel Col; Ecole de Lanneau. *Comn:* Design for Air Force One; design interiors for Saks Fifth Ave, Gimbels & Lord & Taylor; design trademarks & logos for greyhound, Coca-Cola, US Post Off, Borden, Exxon, Lucky Strike, Nabisco, TWA, Shell, Int Harvester, US Coast Guard, Newsweek & Canada Dry; designs for Saturn & Apollo progr & habitability designs for Skylab, NASA. *Exhib:* One-man retrospective, Smithsonian Inst, Washington, DC, 75; one-man show, Jack Gallery, NY, 79; Forum Design, Linz, Ger, 80; Aesthetics of Progress, Hayden Gallery, Mass Inst Techol, 84. *Awards:* Award of Recognition for Personal Contrib to Indust Design Prof, Indust Designers Soc Am; Gold Medal, Paris Fair; Grand Officer in the Legion of Honor, Govt France, 79. *Mem:* Am Soc Indust Design (founder, fel & former pres); Am Acad Achievement; Hall of Fame, Boston; fel Brit Royal Soc Art. *Publ:* Auth, Never Leave Well Enough Alone, 49; contribr, Space Race, Circle Fine Art, 86. *Mailing Add:* c/o Vance Kirkland Found 1311 Pearl St Denver CO 80203

LOFTUS, PETER M
PAINTER
b Washington, DC, Oct 27, 48. *Study:* Md Inst Col Art, BFA, 71; Univ Pa, 74. *Work:* Glen C Janss Collection; San Jose Mus Art, Calif; Hunter Mus, Chatanooga, Tenn. *Exhib:* Am Realism: 20th Century Drawings & Watercolors, San Francisco Mus Mod Art, traveling exhib, 85; Contemp Am Realism, Columbus Mus Arts & Sci, Ga, 85; The Realist Landscape, Robeson Art Ctr Gallery, Rutgers Univ, 85; The Subject is Water, Newport Art Mus, 88; The Face of the Land, Southern Allegheny Mus Art, 88; New Horizons in Am Realism, Flint Inst Arts (traveling exhib with catalog), 91. *Teaching:* Vis lectr painting, Univ Calif, Santa Cruz, 76-88. *Bibliog:* Fredy Kaplan (auth), Portfolio of regional landscapes, Am Artist, 2/84; Alvin Martin (auth), American Realism: 20th Century Drawings & Watercolors, Abrams, 86; West Art & the Law, West Publ Co, 87. *Mem:* Col Art Asn Am. *Media:* Watercolor, Oil. *Dealer:* Fischbach Gallery 24 W 57 St New York NY; Contemporary Realist Gallery 23 Grant 6th Floor San Francisco CA 94108. *Mailing Add:* 729 Western Dr Santa Cruz CA 95060-3032

LOGAN, DAVID GEORGE
METALSMITH, EDUCATOR
b Milwaukee, Wis, June 14, 37. *Study:* Univ Wis-Madison, BS, 63, with Arthur Vierthaler, MFA, 68; Univ Ill-Urbana, with Robert von Neumann, Jr, MA, 67. *Comn:* Art in Worship (slide series), Am Crafts Coun; Chalice Univ, Lutheran Church, E Lansing Mich, 85. *Exhib:* Michiana Crafts Competition, Lafayette, Ind, 72; 37th Ann Nat Crafts Competition, Cedar City, Utah, 78; Nat Invitational Exhib, Northern Mich Univ, 79; Nat Print & Small Sculpture Exhib, Copus Christi, 81 & 83; Marietta Crafts Nat, Ohio, 82; Invited Retrospective, Appalacian Crafs Ctr, Tenn, 92. *Pos:* Visiting Artist: Haystack Sch, 81; Arrowmout Sch, 86 & 88; Penland Sch, 94. *Teaching:* Art, Oregon Pub Schs, Wis, 63-66; asst prof art, Mich State Univ, 68-79; vis artist metalsmithing, Northern Mich Univ, summer 71 & 74; assoc prof art, ETenn State Univ, 79-; prof & chmn, E Tenn State Univ, 93. *Awards:* Haas Found Award, Nat Print & Small Sculpture Exhib, 83; 1st prize, Metal Media Exhib, Winston, Salem, NC, 90. *Mem:* Mich Art Educ Asn (pres, 71-72, ed newslett, 73-74); Nat Art Educ Asn; Am Crafts Coun; Soc NAm Goldsmiths; Tenn Art Educ Asn (bd mem, 81-). *Media:* Non-Ferrous Metals, Glass. *Mailing Add:* Dept Art East Tenn Univ PO Box 70708 Johnson City TN 37614-0708

LOGAN, FERN H
PHOTOGRAPHER, GRAPHIC ARTIST
b July 6, 45. *Study:* Pratt Inst, 63-65; State Univ NY, BS, 91; Art Inst Chicago, MFA, 93. *Work:* AC Buehler Library, Elmhurst Col, Ill; Harlem State Office Bldg, Schomburg Ctr Res Black Cult, Belvue Hosp Ctr, NY. *Exhib:* One-man shows, Artist Portrait Series, Gallery 62, NY, 85 & Memories in Non-Silver, Delta Arts Ctr, Winston-Salem, NC, 88; Imagining Families, Smithsonian Inst, Washington, DC, 94; Spectra '97 Nat Photo Biennial, Silvermine Guild Galleries, New Canaan, Conn, 97; Myth Am, Urban Inst Contemp Artists, Grand Rapids, Mich, 97; Digital Sorcery, Ctr Photo, Woodstock, NY, 98. *Pos:* Sr graphic designer, Equitable Life, 78-83; owner, Logan Photog & Design Studios, 83-89. *Teaching:* Lectr, photogr & graphics, Mich Tech Univ, 89-92; asst prof, Elmhurst Col, 92-95 & Southern Ill Univ, 95-. *Awards:* Sponsored Project Grant, Artist Protrait Series, NY Coun Arts, 85; Parks, Chavez King Teaching Fel, Mich Tech Univ, 89-92; Arts Fel Grant, Digital Portraits, Ill, 98. *Bibliog:* Norman Schreiber (auth), Pop photo snapshots, Popular Photog, 2/85; Deborah Willis (auth), Black Photographs 1940-1988, Garland, 88; Lara Farb (auth), Gumbo Ya Ya, Midmarch Press, 95. *Mem:* Soc Photog Ed. *Publ:* Illustr, Six Decades at Yaddo, Yaddo Publ, 86; contribr, I Too Sing America, Workman Publ, 92; I Hear a Symphony, Anchor Bks, 94. *Mailing Add:* 1 Loblolly Lane Carbondale IL 62901

LOGAN, GENE ADAMS
SCULPTOR, PAINTER
b Kickapoo, Kans, June 14, 22. *Study:* Southwest Mo State Univ, BS, 49; Univ Southern Calif, PhD, 60; Univ Ore, 65; Univ Kans, MFA, 67; also with Elden Tefft & Jan Zach. *Work:* El Camino Col Sculpture Garden, Torrance, Calif; included in over 300 pvt collections. *Comn:* Sculpture, Chase Nat Ins Co, Springfield, Mo, 66; sculpture, Westmont Industs, Santa Fe Springs, Calif, 75; sculpture, City of La Mirana, Calif, 77; office bldg, Am Alliance for Health, Physical Educ, Recreation & Dance, Reston, Va, 85. *Exhib:* One-man shows, Ankrum Gallery, Los Angeles, 70-72, 75, 78 & 82; Pioneer Mus & Haggin Galleries, Stockton, Calif, 78; Zantman Art Galleries, Carmel, Calif, 79, Palm Desert, Calif, 89; Townhouse Gallery, New Orleans, 80, 88; Crowther of Syon Lodge, London, Eng, 80. *Teaching:* Prof art anat, Southwest Mo State Univ, Springfield, 67-69; prof life drawing, Pasadena Sch Fine Arts, Calif, 70. *Awards:* First Award Sculpture, All-Calif Exhib, Laguna Beach, 60 & 61; Sculpture Gold Medal Award, Calif State Fair & Expos, Sacramento, 62. *Bibliog:* Michael Leopold (auth), Beverly Hills Mag, 4-5/78, Irene Lagorio (auth), Art & artists, Monterey Peninsula Herald, 2/9/79; Sharon Apfelbaum (auth), Art, Palm Springs Life Mag, 2/80; and others. *Media:* Brazed Sheet Copper, Bronze; Acrylic. *Dealer:* Zantman Art Galleries Sixth & Mission Carmel CA 93921; 73-925 El Paseo Palm Desert CA 92260

LOGAN, KENT
COLLECTOR
b 1944. *Study:* Wharton Sch Bus, grad. *Pos:* Sr partner Montgomery Securities, San Francisco, Calif, 90-99; bd dirs Clyfford Stills Mus, Denver, Colo, Aspen Art Mus, Aspen, Colo. *Awards:* named one of Top 200 Collectors, ARTNews Mag, 2000-. *Mailing Add:* 815 Potato Patch Dr Vail CO 81657-4428

LOGAN, VICKI
COLLECTOR
b 1947. *Study:* Vassar Col, BA in Italian. *Pos:* With publ dept Denver Art Mus, Colo; trustee San Francisco Mus Art, Calif. *Awards:* named one of Top 200 Collectors, ARTNews Mag, 2000-. *Mailing Add:* 815 Potato Patch Dr Vail CO 81657-4428

LOGEMANN, JANE MARIE
PAINTER
b Milwaukee, Wis, Nov 12, 1942. *Study:* Layton Sch of Art, Milwaukee, Wis, 61; Univ Wis, Milwaukee, BA, 63. *Work:* Stanford Univ Art Mus, Calif; The Jewish Mus, NY; James Michener Collection, Univ Tex, Austin; Allen Mem Art Mus, Oberlin Col, Ohio; Guggenheim Mus, NY. *Exhib:* AAA, Ulrich Mus, Wichita, Kans, 92; Collecting for the 21st Century: Recent Acquisitions: The Jewish Mus, NY, 93; Aishet Hayil, Yeshiva Univ Mus, NY, 93; Drawings, Leo Castelli Gallery, NY, 94; The Persistence of Abstraction, Noyes Mus, NJ, 94; plus many others. *Collection Arranged:* Diversity NY Artists (auth, catalog), Univ RI, fall 85; American Abstract Artists: New Work: New Mem, 87. *Bibliog:* Peter Frank (auth), revs, Artnews, 11/79 (auth), revs, Print Collector's Newslett, 11/82; Helen A Harrison (auth), NY Times, 6/89; William Zimmer (auth), NY Times, 8/28/94; Lilly Wei (auth), Art in Am, 5/95. *Mem:* Am Abstract Artists (mem bd dir, 86-). *Media:* Oil, Watercolor. *Publ:* Auth & illusr, Abstracts-Book III, 78; ed, Ecology and feminism issue, Vol 4, Art Heresies, 81; Art in New York Today: Idea Mag, Toyko, Japan, 8/88; Letters/Words: Jane Logemann; Naomi Spector; Hebrew Union Col Publ, 8/94. *Mailing Add:* 35 Bond St New York NY 10012

LOGOTHETIS, ARISTIDES
ARTIST
b Athens, Greece, 67. *Study:* Tuffs Univ Sch & Mus Fine Arts, Boston, BFA, 96; Univ New Orleans, MFA, 2001. *Exhib:* Solo shows include Meta-Perceptions, Duke Univ, Univ New Orleans, Schoolhouse Ctr Art & Design, Mass, 2001; groups shows at The Last Wave, Southeastern La Univ, Hammond, La, 99; Bing Bang, Isaac Delgado Community Col, New Orleans, 2001; Nat Acad, NY City, 2006. *Teaching:* Resident artist Scholoss Buchsenhausen, Innsbruck, Austria, 2001, Ft George, Annotto Bay, Jamaica, 2002

LOHRE, THOMAS GEORGE, JR
PAINTER, SCULPTOR
b Covington, Ky, July 17, 53. *Study:* Univ Ky, 71-73; Northern Ky Univ, BA, 76. *Work:* Beringer Crawford Mus, Covington, Ky; portrait Jesus, Mary & Joseph, Covington Cath High Sch, Park Hills, Ky; portrait St Agnes, St Agnes Grade Sch, Ft Wright, Ky; portrait Henry Williams, Over-the-Rhine Sr Ctr, Cincinnati, Ohio; portrait, Thomas More Col, Crestview Hills, Ky. *Comn:* 29 Portraits, Newport Storefront Restoration Proj, Ky, 96. *Exhib:* The Art of Tom Lohre, Carnegie Art Ctr, Covington, Ky, 80, HEREArt ART@-D2 exhib, NY, 99, The Great Tomaso Show, Visual History Gallery, Cincinnati, 02; One man show, Artists Asn, Nantucket, Mass, 88. *Pos:* Asst to Ralph Wolf Cowan, Portrait Painter, 80-81. *Awards:* Second Place Painting, Summer Fair, Cincinnati, Ohio, 78; Second Place, Fitton Art Ctr, 94; Grant, City Newport, Main St Restoration Comt, 96. *Bibliog:* Owen Findsen (auth), Lohre Mixes Art, People and Fantasy, Cincinnati Enquirer, 6/28/81; Terri Schierberg (auth), Thos Lohre Fine Artist and Landscape Painter, Northern Ky Univ Mag, 95; Steven Ramos (auth), Master Painter of Newport, City Beat, Cincinnati, 96. *Mem:* Northern Ky Heritage League; Friends Baker-Hunt Found, Covington, Ky. *Media:* Oil on canvas; Robotics. *Publ:* Auth, Greenwich Village Guidebook, St Martins Press, 94. *Dealer:* Visual Hist Gallery 3437 Michigan Cincinnati Ohio 45208. *Mailing Add:* 619 Evanswood Pl Cincinnati OH 45220

LOK, JOAN M
PAINTER
b Hong Kong, Apr 2, 62. *Study:* Hong Kong Polytechnic Univ, 83; Baruch Col, BBA, 88; Strayer Univ, MBA, 2005. *Work:* Mus Chinese Australian Hist, Melbourne; Walt Disney World Co, Orlando, Fla; New Longon Arts Soc & Gallery, New London, Conn; Phillippines Chinese Cult Ctr, Manila; Lingnam Art Asn Am, NY. *Comn:* calligraphy, Harrah's, Las Vegas. *Exhib:* Masters of Oriental Brush Painting, Raya Gallery, Victoria, Australia, 90; 20th Anniversary Exhib, Chinese Cult Ctr, Manila, Philippines, 96; Sumi-e Across Border, John B Aird Gallery, Toronto, Can, 96; Lingham Art Asn Exhib, Chinese Cult Inst, Boston, Mass, 97; Female Chinese Am Artists, Confusius Plaza Gallery, NY, 2001; 40th Anniversary juried exhib, Strathmore Hall Arts Ctr, Bethesida, MD, 2003; Solo exhib, Focus on China, Frelinghuysen Arboretam, Morristown, NJ, 2004, Mind to Paper, Slayton House Gallery, Columbia, MD, 2005. *Pos:* Vpres, Lingram Art Asn Am, NY, 92-94; Nat Pres, Sumi-e Soc Am, Wash, DC, 2002-. *Teaching:* instr, Plaza Art Materials, Towson, Md. *Awards:* Grumbacher Gold Medallion Award, Sumi-e Soc Am, 35th Annual juried show, Grumbacher Watercolors, 98, Best in Watercolor Award, Art for Art's Sake Exhib, Conn Audubon Soc, 99; Grand Prize Winner, Nat Cherry Blossom Festival, Art Contest, 2005. *Bibliog:* Mao-fen Yu (auth), Joan Lok - Artist of Cherry Blossom World J, 11/5/04; Susan DeFond (auth), Memory Blossoms Into a Winning Entry, Washington Post, 4/3/2005; Oksana Dragan (auth), HK-Born Artist Paints National Cherry Blossom Festival Poster, Voice of Am News, 4/11/2005. *Mem:* Sumi-e Soc Am, (nat pres, 2002-); Lingham Art Asn Am, (vpres, 92-94); Glastenburg Art Guild; Edison Arts Soc; Asn Chinese Calligraphy Am. *Media:* Sumi-e, ink & watercolor on rice paper. *Collection:* Delicate watercolor and ink on rice paper of floral and landscape combining Eastern and Western Styles. *Publ:* contribr, Best of Flower Painting, North Light Books, 97; contribr, Always Bright, Vol II, Painting by Chinese Am Artists, Homa & Sekey Books, 2001; contribr, Sumi-e Quarterly, Sumi-e Soc Am, 2002-05; back cover artwork, Sakura Celebration, 2005. *Dealer:* Radiant Brush GAllery PO Box 6271 Columbia MD 21045. *Mailing Add:* PO Box 6271 Columbia MD 21045

LOMAHAFTEWA, LINDA JOYCE
PAINTER, INSTRUCTOR
b Phoenix, Ariz, July 3, 47. *Study:* Inst Am Indian Arts, Santa Fe, NMex; San Francisco Art Inst, BFA & MFA. *Work:* Ctr Arts Indian Am, Washington, DC. *Exhib:* Riverside Mus, NY, 65; Mus NMex, Santa Fe, 65-66; Ctr Arts Indian Am, 67-68; San Francisco Art Inst Spring Show, 70-71; Scottsdale Nat Indian Art Exhib, Ariz, 70-71. *Teaching:* Asst drawing, San Francisco Art Inst, 70; painting instr, Asn Am Indian Arts, San Francisco, summer 72; asst prof Native Am studies, Calif State Col, Sonoma, 72-; lectr, Native Am Studies, Univ Calif, Berkeley, 74-76; instr painting, Inst Am Indian Arts, Santa Fe, NMex, 76-. *Awards:* Hon Mention for Oil Painting, Mus NMex, 65; First Place in Graphic Arts Purchase Award, Ctr Arts Indian Am, 67; Third Place in Drawing, Scottsdale Nat Indian Art Exhib, 70. *Bibliog:* Lloyd E Oxendine (auth), 23 contemporary Indian artists, Art in Am, 7-8/72. *Media:* Acrylic, Oil. *Publ:* Illusr, Indian Mag, 71; Weewish Tree, Am Indian Historian Press, 71; contribr, Art in Am, 72. *Mailing Add:* c/o Joyce Robins Gallery 201 Galisteo St Santa Fe NM 87501

LOMBARDI, DON DOMINICK
ARTIST
b Bronx, NY, Dec 16, 54. *Study:* Empire State Col, BS, 95. *Work:* The Library of Congress, Washington, DC; Empire State Coll, SUNY, Saratoga Springs, NY. *Exhib:* 31st Ann Open Exhib, Sanbernardino Co Mus, Redlands, Calif, 96; New Art Ann, Stamford Mus, CT, 96 & 97; After the Rain, Del Arts Ctr Gallery, Narrowsburg, NY, 03; Six Approaches, Marist Art Gallery, Marist Coll, Poughkeepsie, NY, 02. *Collection Arranged:* The Waking Dream, Castle Gallery, 98; Obsession Fool, Pelham Art Ctr, 98. *Pos:* Art critic, feature writer, New York Times, New York City, 98- and Sculpture Mag, Washington, DC, 99-. *Teaching:* Adj art prof, Westchester Community Col, Vallhalla, NY. *Awards:* Dorothy Mayhail Mem Award, Stamford Mus, 97; spl opportunity stipend, NY Found for the Arts, 97; resident, Reykjavík Art Mus, Iceland, 01. *Bibliog:* William Zimmer (auth), Narratives in Charcoal and Ink, The NY Times, 12/1/2002; Katherine Gass (auth), Refigured South Shore Arts Center, Art New England, 9/2002; William Zimmer (auth), The 20th Century, Two View Points in Sculpture and Collage, The NY Times, 1/18/1998. *Mem:* AICA. *Mailing Add:* PO Box 108 Valhalla NY 10595

LOMONACO, STEPHEN
PAINTER, INSTRUCTOR
b New York City, NY Sept 15, 1931. *Study:* National Acad of Design, 1973; Queens Col, NY, BA (cum laude) 1986; NY Workshop Sch of Art Therapy, 1994. *Work:* Mt Saint Mary Col, Newburgh, NY; Columbia Col of Physicians & Surgeons, NY; Am Embassy, Brussels, Belg. *Comn:* Portrait, Columbia Col, New York, 1981; award medal, Columbia Col, New York, 1982; mural, Bergenfield HS, Bergenfield, NJ, 1980; bronze statue, Silas Monstsier, VP First Nat City Bank, Nutley, NJ, 1974. *Exhib:* Pastel Soc of Am, Hermitage Mus, Norfolk, Va, 1976; Pastel Soc of Am, Monmouth Mus, Monmouth, NJ, 1977; 20 Am Artists-Invitational, Hermitage Mus, Norfolk, Va, 1978; Pastels Only, Queens Mus, NY, 1979; Nat Drawing Asn, Water Mill Mus, Long Island, 1987. *Pos:* Demonstr, M Grumbacker Inc, New York City, 1980-82; master pastelist, Pastel Soc of Am, NY, 1984-; art therapist, Sloan Ketterin Mem Hosp, NY, 1993-97. *Teaching:* Art instr, painting & drawing, LoMonaco Art Studio, NY, 1973-; art, painting & drawing, Midland Park-Waldwick HS, Midland Park, NJ, 1976-79; art, painting & drawing, Fairlawn Artist Prof League, Fairlawn, NJ, 1980-84. *Awards:* Bainbridge Award, Nat Arts Club, Bainbridge Co Inc, 1976; Louis Le Baume Mem Prize, Pastel Soc Am, LeBaume Fam, 1978; G&G Giffuni Purchase Award, Pastel Soc Am, Joseph Giffuni, 1980. *Mem:* Degas Pastel Soc (hon mem); Artist's Fellowship; Pastel Soc Am (co-founder). *Media:* Oil, Pastel, Watercolor, Clay, Wood. *Publ:* illusr, New Hope for Your Hair, Dutton Press, 1962-63; illusr, New Hope for Your Skin, Dutton Press; Article, Harbor Gallery Group Show, Long Island Press, 1976; contribr, How to Paint Figures in Pastel, Watson Guptil, 1976; LoMonaco at Gallery Nine, Bergen Record, 1977; illusr, Animals, Animals, Animals, ABC Television, 1981; SKH Gallery-Great Barrington, MA, Berkshire Eagle, 2004. *Dealer:* Sam Kasten S.K.H. Gallery 46 Castle St Great Barrington, MA 01230. *Mailing Add:* 4 E 89 St Apt 6F New York NY 10128

LONDIN, BARBARA
PAINTER
b New York, NY. *Study:* Art Students League, with George Grosz & Reginal Marsch, 50; New Sch Soc Res, with Julian Levi, 64-67. *Work:* Bass Mus, Miami Beach, Fla; Chrysler Mus, Norfolk, Va; Mint Mus, Charlotte, NC; NY Cult Ctr; Rose Mus, Brandeis Univ, Waltham, Mass. *Comn:* Mural, comn by Robert Londin, NY, 70. *Exhib:* One-women show, Mint Mus, Charlotte, NC, 73 & Dreitzer Mus, Brandeis Univ, Waltham, Mass, 75; The 80's - A Post Pop Generation, Southern Alleghanies Mus Art, 90. *Pos:* Pres, Phoenix Gallery, 88-90; rep, bd asn, Artist Run Galleries, 92. *Awards:* Cert Excellence, I A C, 88. *Mem:* Artist Equity. *Media:* Acrylic. *Publ:* Wilson Libr Bull

LONDON, ALEXANDER
COLLECTOR, PUBLISHER
b Paris, France; US citizen. *Study:* Lycee Montaigne, Paris; Univ Pa, MSChE; Columbia Univ, PhD Program. *Pos:* Pres, Marstin Printing Corp, 69-; publ (with catalog), Trade Publ, 70-; exec dir, Imprimerie Centrale Commerciale, Paris, 70-. *Awards:* Forty five typographical & printing design awards, 56-98; spec awards for illus in Kalevala, 54 & design of Holocaust catalog, 79, Grolier Bk Club. *Mem:* Printing Industry Metrop, NY; Assoc Graphic Arts. *Collection:* French Impressionists; French Montparnasse; American contemporary, botanicals & wildlife animation. *Publ:* Illusr, Kalevala, 54; contribr & graphic designs var art catalogs, art mag, bks & printed materials. *Mailing Add:* 350 Central Park W No 10 New York NY 10025

LONDON, ANNA
GRAPHIC ARTIST, SCULPTOR
b Poland, July 2, 13; US citizen. *Study:* Brooklyn Col, BA, 33; Columbia Univ, MA, 35; Ruth Leaf Workshop, 70-75. *Work:* Firehouse Gallery, Nassau Community Col, Garden City, NY; Berkshire Mus, Pittsfield, Mass; Queens Borough Community Col, Queens, NY. *Exhib:* CW Post Col, Greenvale, NY, 73 & 78; Heckscher Mus, Huntington, NY, 75; Parrish Mus, Southampton, NY, 79; Cork Gallery, Lincoln Ctr, NY, 80-90; Hudson River Mus, NY, 85; and others. *Awards:* Purchase Awards, Firehouse Gallery & Berkshire Mus; Prize, Nat Asn Women Artists. *Bibliog:* Ruth Leaf (auth), Intaglio Printmaking Techniques, Watson-Guptill, 76. *Mem:* Nat Asn Women Artists; Nat Mus Women Arts, Washington. *Media:* Monprints; Clay, Computer prints. *Interests:* Exploring computer art. *Dealer:* Graphic Eye Gallery 402 Main St Port Washington NY 11050. *Mailing Add:* 33 Larch Dr New Hyde Park NY 11040

LONDON, BARBARA
CURATOR
b Glen Cove, NY, July 3, 46. *Study:* Hiram Col, Ohio, BA, 68; Inst of Fine Arts, New York Univ, MA, 72. *Collection Arranged:* Projects: Video I-XXXII, 74-81, Loren Madsen, 75, Peter Campus, 76, Nam June Paik, 77, Bookworks, 77 (Sachs Gallery), Projects: Shigeko Kubota, 78, Video Viewpoints, 78-90, Laurie Anderson, 78, Donald Lipski, 79, Video from Tokyo to Fukui and Kyoto (auth, catalog), 79 & Sound Art, 79, Mus Mod Art, New York, Music Video 85, Bill Viola, 87, Barbara Steinman, 89, Gary Hill, 90; Tony Cokes, 91, Thierry Kuntzel, 91, Jana Sterbak, Mus Mod Art, 92. *Pos:* Asst int prog, Mus Mod Art, NY, 71-73, curatorial asst dept of prints & illus bks, 73-77, cur video prog, 77-. *Teaching:* Film Dept, NY Univ, 79-82. *Awards:* Fel, Nat Endowment Arts, 88. *Publ:* Auth, Video Letter of Shuntaro Tanileawa and Shuji Terayama, Camera Obscura, Los Angeles, 90 & Fall, 91; A Few Reflections on High Definition Video and Art, HDTV, Union Square Press, New York, 90; Gary Hill, Image Forum, Tokyo, 91; Electronic Explorations, Art in America, 5/92; Techno-Visions: Tradition and the Avant-Garde, Art 20/21 & Earthly Paradise: The Paintings of Po Kim, Seoul, Korea, 92

LONDON, NAOMI
SCULPTOR
b Montreal, Que, Oct 3, 63. *Study:* Marianopolis Col, dipl, 83; Concordia Univ, BFA, 87; Univ Southern Calif, Los Angeles, MFA, 92. *Work:* Montreal Mus Fine Arts, Que; Stewart Hall Art Gallery, Pointe Claire, Que; Can Coun Art Bank, Ottawa, Ont; Musee d'art de Joliette; Musee d'art contemporain de Montreal. *Exhib:* One-woman shows, La Chambre Blanche, Que, 92, Brewery Arts Complex, Los Angeles, Calif, 92, Galerie Samuel Lollouz, Montreal, Que, 92, 95 & 97, Galleri Kilen, Lulea, Sweden, 94 & Agnes Etherington Art Ctr, Kingston, Ont, 95, Stichting Kunst & Complex, Rotterdam, The Neth, 98; Fall from Fashion (with catalog), Aldrich Mus Contemp Art, 93; Snow Sculpture Symp, Lulea Sweden, 94; Knit, Mus Textiles, Toronto, Ont; A-Dress: States of Being, Winnipeg Art Gallery, Man, 95; Young Contemporaries, London Regional Art & Hist Mus, London, Ontario, 96; Bereft, Hallwalls Contemp Art Ctr, Buffalo, NY, 96; L'oeil du collectionneur, Musee d'art contemporain de Montreal, 96; Sprawl, Mercer Union, Toronto, Ontario, 97; Nouvelles acquisitions Pret d'oeuvres d'art, Musee du Quebec, 97; Naomi London & Penelope Stewart, Open Studio, Toronto, Ontario, 99; The Poetics of Aging, Art Gallery of Hamilton, Ontario, 99; Weaving the World, Yokohama Mus Art, Japan, 99. *Teaching:* Instr contemp sculpture, Concordia Univ, 93-96; fine arts instr, Dawson Col, Montreal. *Awards:* Short Term Grant, Can Coun, 94; Proj Grant, Conseil des Arts et des Lettres du Que, 94; Prix Rene Payant, Musee d'art contemporian, Univ Montreal, 95. *Bibliog:* James Campbell (auth), Naomi London, Galerie Samuel Lallouz, 92; Pierre Landry (auth), The origin of things, Musee d'art Contemporain, 94. *Media:* Mixed Media, Drawing. *Publ:* L'origine des choses (exhib catalog); Discursive Dress (exhib catalog), John Micheal Kohler Art Ctr, Sheboygan, Wis, 94; Dispersions indentitiaires: videogranies recents du Que (exhib catalog), Art Gallery Ont, Toronto, 95; Necessary Grief; Naomi London - Grieving Equipment (exhib catalog), Agnes Etherington Art Ctr, Kingston, Ont, 95; London Life Young Contemporaries 1996 (exhib catalog), London Reg Art & Hist Mus, Ont, 96; Sweets, Hope and the Passage of Time: Three Projects, 2005; Wordsmiths, 2006. *Mailing Add:* 2712 rue Coleraine Montreal PQ H3K 1S7 Canada

LONDON, PETER
PAINTER, EDUCATOR
b New York, NY, June 27, 39. *Study:* Queens Col, BA, 61; Columbia Univ, MFA, 62, EdD, 68. *Work:* Columbia Univ; Concordia Univ; Queens Col. *Comn:* Stainless steel sculpture, John Bowne High Sch, NY, 69. *Exhib:* Collection of Final Portraits, Nat Holocaust Mus, Washington, DC, Concordia Univ, Univ Maui, Columbia Univ & Turo Synagogue. *Pos:* Pres, Pub Arts Coun, Mass, 75-79; post doctoral fel, Lesley Col, Cambridge, Mass; art critic, New Bedford Mag; ed bd, Sch Arts Eastern Regional Dir, NAEA. *Teaching:* Asst prof art & art educ, Concordia Univ, 67-71; prof art & art educ, Mass Univ, Dartmouth, 71-. *Awards:* Traveling Fel to Israel, 83-84. *Mem:* Nat Art Educ Asn; Int Soc for Educ through Art; Int Art Educ Asn; NEng Art Therapy Asn. *Media:* Charcoal, Pastel. *Publ:* Auth, Taming of the American Imagination, Nat Art Educ Asn J, 74; Towards a New Philosophy of Art Education, Art for the Primary Level, 74; Trust and Education, Southeastern Mass Union J, 75; Alternative Careers in Art, Careers in Art, 79; No More Secondhand Art, Showbhalia, 89; Art as Transformation, NAEA J, 5/92. *Dealer:* Galerie Don Steward Sherbrook St W Montreal PQ Can

LONG, CHARLES
SCULPTOR
b Long Branch, NJ, 58. *Study:* Philadelphia Col Art, BFA, 81; Whitney Independent Study Prog, 81; Yale Univ, New Haven, Conn, MFA, 88. *Exhib:* Aldrich Mus Contemp Art, 95; Defining the Nineties, Mus Contemp Art, Miami, 96; Transformal, Wiener Secession, Vienna, Austria, 96; Now Here, La Mus Mod Art, Humlebaek, Denmark, 96; solo exhibs, Shoshana Wayne Gallery, Santa Monica, Calif, 96, Tanya Bonakdar Gallery, NY, 96 & 97, Galerie Camargo Vilaca, Sao Paulo, Brazil, 97, Galerie Nathalie Obadia, Paris 97, London Projs, 97 & Sperone, Milan, 97; Whitney Mus Am Art Biennial, 97; Performance Anxiety, Mus Contemp Art, Chicago, 97. *Awards:* Nat Endowment Arts, 94; Guggenheim Fel, 97. *Bibliog:* Raphael Rubinstein (auth), Raphael Rubinstein on Charles Long, Gana Art, 5-6/96; Noel (auth), Stereolab, Bunnyhop, Issue 7, 96; Mark Van de Walle (auth), Back to the future: Charles Long & Stereolab, Parkett, No 48, 96. *Dealer:* Bonakdar Joancou Gallery 521 W 21st New York NY 10011. *Mailing Add:* 192 E Third St Apt 2-D New York NY 10009

LONG, MEREDITH J
DEALER
b Joplin, Mo, Sept 14, 28. *Study:* Univ Tex, BA, 50, Law Sch, 50-51, 53-54. *Pos:* Pres, Meredith Long & Co, Houston, 57-. *Teaching:* Art prof. *Mem:* Art Dealers Asn Am; Am Fedn Arts; Am Asn Mus; Cult Arts Coun Houston; Archives Am Art (bd mem). *Specialty:* 19th and 20th century American art. *Publ:* Ed, Americans at Home and Abroad Catalogue, 71; Tradition and Innovation--American Paintings 1860-1870, 74; Americans at work and play, 1845-1944 (catalog), 80. *Mailing Add:* 2323 San Felipe Houston TX 77019

LONG, PHILLIP C
MUSEUM DIRECTOR
b Tucson, Ariz, 42. *Study:* Tulane Univ, BA, 65. *Pos:* Dir, Taft Mus Art, Cincinnati, Ohio, 94-. *Mem:* Asn Art Mus Dirs

LONG, ROSE-CAROL WASHTON
HISTORIAN, ADMINISTRATOR
b New London, Conn, Mar 1, 38. *Study:* Wellesley Col, BA, 59; Yale Univ, MA(hist art), 62, PhD(hist art), 68. *Collection Arranged:* Twentieth Century Prints, Godwin-Ternbach Mus, 83. *Teaching:* Lectr, Queens Col, City Univ NY, 67-69, asst prof, 69-78, assoc prof, 79-83, prof art hist grad ctr 84-, exec officer PhD prog, 85-2000. *Awards:* Nat Endowment Humanities Fel, 72-73; Am Coun Learned Soc Grant, 72-73 & 82-83; Guggenheim Fel, 83-84; CUNY Rsch Award, 96-97, 97-98, 2004-05; J Clawson Mills Art History Fel, Met Mus Art, 2000. *Mem:* Col Art Asn; Am Fedn Arts; Historians Ger Cent Europ Art (pres, 97-2001, treas, 2001-); Soc Historian Eastern Europ & Russ Art. *Res:* Pioneers of 20th century abstract painting; Kandinsky; German Expressionism; art in the Weimer Rupublic. *Publ:* Auth, Scholarship: Past, Present & Future Directions, German Expressionist Prints and Drawings, The Robert Gore Rifkind Ctr for German Expressionist Studies, 2 Vols, Los Angeles Co Mus Art, 89; auth & ed annotation, German Expressionism: Documents from the End of the Wilhelmine Empire to the Rise of National Socialism, GK Hall, Macmillan, 93 & Univ Calif Press, 95; Nationalism of Internationalism? Berlin Critics & the Question of Expressionism, Acts of the XXVIII International Congress of the History of Art, Vol III, Berlin, 93; auth, Vom Marchen zur Abstraktion: Kandinsky 1910 - Avantgarde oder regressiver Modernismus?, In: Der Fruhe Kandinsky, 1900-1910, Brucke Mus, pp 99-109, 94; Kandinsky re-visited, Art J, fall 96; contribr, Experiment 9, 2003 & Bauhaus Culture: From Weimar to the Cold War, Univ Minn Press, 2006. *Mailing Add:* 161 W 15th St No 6J New York NY 10011

LONG, TERESA LOZANO
ADMINISTRATOR, EDUCATOR
Study: Univ Tex, Austin, BA; Univ Tex, Austin, MA (educ); Univ Tex, Austin, PhD, 65. *Pos:* Res assoc, Tex Educ Agency, consult Div Compensatory Educ; res assoc, Tex Govs Comt Pub. Sch Educ; consult, Migrant Educ & Head Start Progressive US Off Educ; founder, Long Found, Austin, 99-. *Mem:* Nat Coun Arts; Nat Endowment for Arts. *Mailing Add:* The Long Found Ste 7C2 40 N IH 35 Austin TX 78701

LONG-MURPHY, JENNY
ART DEALER, CONSULTANT
b Ft Worth, Tex, June 26, 55. *Study:* Finch Col, AA, 75; Sarah Lawrence Col, Bronxville, BA, 77. *Pos:* Asst dir, Meredith Long Contemp, New York, 77-79, dir, 79-80; mgr, Adam L Gimbel Gallery, New York, 81-83; adminr, Christie, Manson & Woods Int, Am Paintings Dept, 84-86; adminr, Meredith Long & Co, Houston, Tex, 86-91; bd, Blaffer Gallery, Univ Houston, 88-94; consult. *Specialty:* 19th and 20th century American Art. *Mailing Add:* c/o Meredith Long & Co 4517 Oleander St Bell Aire TX 77401-5118

LONGAKER, MARK
CRITIC, WRITER
Pos: Gallery views writer, Georgetowner. *Mailing Add:* Georgetowner 1054 Potomac St Washington DC 20007

LONGHURST, ROBERT E
SCULPTOR
b Latham, NY, Feb 23, 49. *Study:* Adirondack Community Col, AS, 69; Kent State Univ, BA(archit), 75. *Comn:* Sticks & Stones (environ construct, wood & granite) pvt residence, Lake Placid, NY, 89; Blast (14' high granite & stainless steel), Ensign-Bickford Ind, Simsbury, Conn, 92. *Exhib:* One-man shows, Randall Galleries, NY, 82 & Louis Newman Galleries, Beverly Hills, Calif, 86. *Awards:* Friends Am Art, Butler Inst Am Art, 79; Helen Eisler Mem Award, Audubon Ann, 80. *Bibliog:* Alice Gilborn (auth), Reaching for Perfection, Adirondack Life, 9/83; Dick Burrows (ed), A New Twist, Fine Woodworking, 8/91; Ken Fieldhouse (ed), Landmarks, Landscape Design, J Landscape Inst, 2/93. *Mem:* Int Sculpture Ctr, Washington, DC. *Media:* Wood, Stone. *Mailing Add:* Potterbrook Rd RFD Box 351 Chestertown NY 12817

LONGO, ROBERT
SCULPTOR, PAINTER
b Brooklyn, NY, Jan 7, 53. *Study:* State Univ Col NY, Buffalo, BFA, 75. *Work:* Mus Mod Art, Solomon R Guggenheim Mus & Whitney Mus Am Art, NY; Walker Art Ctr, Minneapolis, Minn; Tate Gallery, London; Art Inst Chicago; Guggenheim Mus, NY; Albright-Knox Art Gallery, Buffalo, NY; Wadsworth Atheneum, Hartford, Conn; and many others. *Exhib:* Convergence & Dispersal, SEM Festival, Albright-Knox Art Gallery, 76; In Western NY, Albright-Knox Art Gallery, 77; Figures: Forms & Expressions, Albright-Knox Art Gallery, 81; Empire: A Performance Trilogy, Corcoran Gallery Art, Washington, 81; Eight Artists: The Anxious Edge, Walker Art Ctr, Minneapolis, 82; Focus on the Figure: Twenty Yrs, Whitney Mus Am Art, NY, 82; New Figuration in Am, Milwaukee Art Ctr, 82; 1983 Biennial, Whitney Mus Am Art, NY, 83; An Int Survey of Recent Painting and Sculpture, Mus Mod Art, NY, 83; The Human Condition: Biennial III, San Francisco Mus Mod Art, 84; Currents, Inst Contemp Art, Boston, 84; The Heroic Figure Traveling Exhib, Contemp Arts Mus, Houston, 84; solo exhibs, Brooklyn Mus, NY 85, Los Angeles Co Mus Art (traveling), 89, Galeria Joan Prats, Barcelona, 93, Metro Pictures, NY, 94, Genereux Grunwald Gallery, Toronto, Can, 94, Galerie Gana-Beaubourg, Paris, 95 & Galerie Lupke Frankfurt, Ger, 95, Superheroes, Lipanjepuntin Artecontemporanea, Triests, Ital, 2000, Robert Longo:1980-2000, Emilio Mazzoli Moderna, Ital, 2000, Robert Longo-Sigmind Freud, Judisches Mus, Berlin, Germ, 2002, The Freud Drawings, Museen Haus Lange und Hais Esters, Krefelder Kunstmuseen, Krefeld, Germ, Albertina Mus, Vienna, 2002; The Am Exhib, Art Inst Chicago, 86; Monumental Drawing: Works by 22 Contemp Americans, Brooklyn Mus, NY, 86; Avante-Garde in the Eighties, Los Angeles Co Mus Art, 87; Image World: Art & Media Cult, Whitney Mus Am Art, 89; Affinities and Intuitions: The Gerald S Elliot Collection of Contemp Art, Art Inst Chicago, 90; Power, Indianapolis Mus Art, 91; Allegories of Modernism: Contemp Drawing, Mus Mod Art, NY, 92; NY Unplugged, Gallery Cothem, Zeedijk, 94; Essence & Persuasion: The Power of Black & White, Anderson Gallery, 95; It's Only Rock & Roll, Contemp Arts Ctr, Cincinnati, Ohio, 95; Passions Privee, Mus d'Art Mod, Paris, 95; NY Unplugged II, Gallery Cotthem, Belg, 96; Drawings, Metro Pictures, NY, 2003. *Bibliog:* Elizabeth Licata (auth), Living with art, Artnews, 12/95; Johnny Mnemonic gets pinned, Flash Art, 1/96; Dike Blair (auth), Artist's dream machines: the films of Longo, Salle & Clark, Flash Art, 3/96. *Publ:* Dir, Tales From the Crypt: This'll Kill Ya (film), HBO, 92; Lifes A Beat (film), Markenfilm, Hamburg, Ger, 92; Give It (film), Icon Pictures, 92; Series showcasing films & videos directed by Robert Longo, Espace Lyonnais D'Art Contemporian, Lyon, France, 93; dir, Johnny Mnemonic (film), Coroloco Films, Tristar Pictures, 94. *Mailing Add:* c/o Metro Pictures 519 W 24th St New York NY 10011

LONGO, VINCENT
PAINTER, PRINTMAKER
b New York, NY, Feb 15, 23. *Study:* Cooper Union, Cert 46; Brooklyn Mus Art Sch, 49-50. *Work:* Libr Congress, Washington, DC; Mus Mod Art, Brooklyn Mus Art, Whitney Mus Am Art, NY; Nat Gallery Art, Washington, DC; Met Mus, New York City, NY. *Comn:* Enameled steel ballustrade, Ronald Reagan; Cesar Pelli Terminal, Nat Airport, Washington, DC, 1996. *Exhib:* Two Decades of Am Prints, Brooklyn Mus, NY, 69; One-man retrospectives, 15 Yr Print Retrospective, Corcoran Gallery & Detroit Inst Art, 70; Whitney Mus Painting Ann, NY, 71; Am Drawings, Whitney Mus, NY, 73; Fogg Mus, Libr of Cong, Metrop Mus Art, NY Mus Fine Arts, Boston Mus Mod Art; one-person shows Alfred Univ, 1978, Andrew Crispo, New York City, 1980, Adam Gimbel Gallery, New York City; Color in the Graphic Arts, Libr Congress, Washington, DC, 74; Thirty Years of Am Prints, Brooklyn Mus, NY, 76; Am Prints Process & Proofs, Whitney Mus, NY, 81; Condeso/Lawler Gallery, New York City, 1984, 85, 87, 89, 90, 93, Hunter Col Art Galleries, Career Retrospective, 2003; The Perstistence of Painting, Ulrich Mus, Wichita, Kans, 92; Painting, Print Retrospective, Hunter Col Art Galleries, 2003. *Pos:* Prof emer, inaugural older Phyllis and Joseph Caroff chair fine arts; asst dir Yale Univ Summer Art School, Norfolk, Conn, 1955-59, dir, 1969. *Teaching:* Prof art, Bennington Col, Bennington, Vt, 57-67, Hunter Col, NY, 67-. *Awards:* Fullbright Fel, 51; Fel Guggenheim, 71; Grant Nat Endowment Arts, 73; Citation for Prof Achievement, Cooper Union, 1973. *Bibliog:* Gene Baro (auth), Print Retrospective (catalog essay), Corcoran Gallery, 70; Judith Goldman (auth), American Prints: Process & Proofs; Louis Lomonaco (auth), Artes et Metier Graphique, Flammarion, 92. *Mem:* Am Abstract Artists; Nat Acad. *Publ:* Auth, A Debate on Abstraction (exhib catalog), Hunter Col, 88; Abstraction and Immanence, Hunter Col. *Dealer:* Condeso-Lawler 76 Greene St New York NY 10012. *Mailing Add:* 50 Greene St New York NY 10013-2663

LONGO-MUTH, LINDA L
PAINTER, INSTRUCTOR
b Nyack, NY, 1948. *Study:* Independent Study, Rome, Italy, 69; Southern Conn Univ, New Haven, BS, 70; independent study, Paris, France, 71; Montclair State Univ, NJ, MA, 75. *Work:* Cathedral St John the Divine, NY; Assoc Neurologists, Plainfield, NJ; Global Petroleum Corp, Waltham, Mass; Nat Multiple Sclerosis Soc; Helen Hayes Hosp. *Exhib:* NY Acad Sci, 92; World Trade Ctr, NY, 92 & 93; Paine Webber Corp Gallery, 93; Ueno Royal Mus, Tokyo, 94; Hakone Open Air Mus, Mt Fiji, Japan, 94; Birmingham Mus, Ala; IBM Gallery Sci & Art, 92-2003; Piermont Flywheel Gallery, NY. *Pos:* Bd advs, Resources for Artists with Disabilities, NY, 90-92 & bd dir, 92-; art advocate for artists with physical disabilities, Art's Coun Rockland, 93-94. *Teaching:* Instr studio art, Ramapo Central Sch Dist, Suffern, NY, 70-87; lectr, Mus Mod Art, Edward John Noble Ctr Symp Women Artists Disabled, 91 & Ramapo Col, Ramsey, NY, 94; symposium, Mus Modern Art, NY. *Awards:* Zvita & Joseph Akston Found Award, 91 & Dorothy Seligson Mem Award, 92, Nat Asn Women Artists; Guy Forde Mony Penney Award, Helen Hayes Hosp, 92. *Bibliog:* Robert Samuels (auth), Showing the true colors, in a new career, Gannett Newspapers, 7/2/89; Susan Leavitt (producer), video, CBS Affiliate WJW Life choices television prog, 91; Leslie Boyd (auth), Rockland artist profile in courage, Gannett Newspapers, 12/26/91. *Mem:* New York Artists Equity; Artists Space, NY; Nat Asn Women Artists; Arts Coun Rockland, Spring Valley, NY; NY Soc Women Artists. *Media:* Acrylic-on-Canvas. *Publ:* Contribr, NJ Rehab mag cover, 12/89; Mental and Physical Disability Law Reporter, Am Bar Asn, Washington, DC, Vol 16, No 3, 5-6/92. *Mailing Add:* 4 Reina Ln Valley Cottage NY 10989

LONGOBARDI, PAM
PAINTER, PRINTMAKER
b NJ, 58. *Study:* Exch student, Univ Utah, 78; Univ Ga, BFA(studio art), 81; Mont State Univ, Bozeman, MFA, 85. *Work:* Tweed Art Mus, Duluth, Minn; Kennedy Art Mus, Athens, Ohio; Deloitte-Touche and Freeman-Hawkins Attorneys, Atlanta, Ga; Corcoran Gallery Art, Washington, DC; Saks Fifth Ave, Atlanta, Ga. *Comn:* Painting,

Imagery Series Wine Label, 95 & 05; Paintings, MBL Life Assurance Corp, 95; Painting, Atlanta Hartsfield Int Airport. *Exhib:* Solo exhibs, San Francisco Mus Mod Art Rental Gallery, Calif, 90, Artemisia Gallery, Chicago, 90, Inst de Estudios Norte Americanos, Barcelona, Spain, 91, Kathryn Sermas Gallery, NY, 91 & 92, Lowe Gallery, Atlanta, 91, 93, 94 & 98, Santa Monica, Calif, 92, Czech Cult Ctr, 93, Animal/Beautiful (catalog), Lowe Gallery, Atlanta, Ga, 98, World World, Lowe Gallery, Atlanta, Ga, 2000, Visible/Invisable, Hartsfield Int Airport Atrium, Atlanta, Ga, 2000, Beyond the Frame, Knoxville Mus Art, Tenn, 2000, Damp Edge, Pearl of the Third Mind, collaboration with C Dongoski, Gallery Art, Univ Northern Iowa, Cedar Falls, Iowa, Pearl of the Third Mind, collaboration with C Dongoski, Gusto House Gallery/Free Space, Kobe, Japan and Thin Line Drawn, collaboration with C Dongoski, Bergen Gallery, Savannah Coll Art & Design, Savannah, Ga, 2002, Worlds within Worlds, Jacksonville Mus Mod Art; USA: Within Limits, Documenta Galeria de Arte Ctr for Book Arts, Sao Paulo, Brazil, 94; 3 Americans, Crossing Space, Portoguard, Venice, Italy, 96; Art and Science Int Exhib, 90th Anniversary Tsinghua Univ Global Symposium, Nat Mus Fine Art, Beijing, China, 2001; Barrister's Gallery, New Orleans, Louisianna, 2002; Art Chicago 2002 at Navy Pier, Fay Gold Gallery, Navy Pier complex, Chicago, Ill, 2002; Skin; Contemp Views of the Body, Jacksonville Mus Mod Art, Jacksonville, Fla, 2003. *Teaching:* Vis artist, Chicago Art Inst, 86, Dartmouth Col, Hanover, NH, 88, Univ Chapel Hill, NC, 88, Univ Northern Iowa, Cedar Falls, 89, Mason Art Ctr, San Francisco, 89 & La State Univ, Baton Rouge, 90; assoc prof art, Univ Tenn, Knoxville, 87-97, Ga State Univ, currently; assoc prof painting, Ga State Univ, 97-, assoc dean fine arts, 2001-2003; assoc prof art, Ga State Univ, 97-. *Awards:* SAF/Nat Endowment Arts Visual Arts Fel, 94; Visual Artist Fel, Tenn State Arts Comn, 96; Juror's Choice Award, Red Clay Survey, Huntsville Mus Art, Huntsville, Ala; Ga State Univ Sch Art and Design Summer Rsch Grant, Atlanta; Finalist, Atlanta Hartsfield Airport T-Terminal Comn Competition; Chancellor's Award for Rsch and Creative Achievement, Univ Tenn, 98; Major Pub Art Comn, Atlanta's Med Examiner's Facility, Fulton Co Arts Coun; Ga State Sch Art & Design Summer Rsch Grant, Atlanta; All Star Ball Comn, Metro Atlanta CofC and Atlanta Cult Affairs, 2000; Research Initiation Grant, Col Arts & Scis, Ga State Univ, Atlanta; TABOO Project Grant, Requiem exhib, Nexus Contemp Art Center, Atlanta; Finalist, Atlanta Hartsfield Airport E-Concourse Expansion Comn Competition, 2001; Oustanding Faculty Res Award, Ga State Univ, Atlanta, 2005; and others. *Bibliog:* Peggy Cyphers (auth), Pam Longobard, NY in Review, ARTS, summer 91; Carny Ladislav (auth), Pam Longobardi, Profil, Bratislova, Slovakia, 93; Peter Frank & Jerry Cullum (auths), Appeals, Oaths & Queries: Objects & Installations by Pam Longobardi (catalog), 94. *Mem:* Col Art Asn; Southeastern Ctr Contemp Art. *Media:* Mixed Media; Copper. *Res:* Relationship between humans & animals eco-feminism. *Specialty:* Contemporary Art. *Interests:* Scuba, snorkeling, surfing and yoga. *Collection:* Atlanta Hartsfield International Airport; Tweed Art Mus, Minnesota; Corcoran Museum of Art, Washington, D.C. *Publ:* Contribr, Scientific American, Vol 250, No 4, 84; Infinity Mag, Vols 2, 3, 4 & 5, 84-86; auth & contribr, Images of nature and power: Named and nameless, Vol 2, Peabody Review, 90; contribr, Divided World, La State Univ Printmaking Dept, 90; The Persistence of Myth, Wycross Press, Auburn, Ala, 90. *Dealer:* Metaphor Contemp Art Brooklyn NY; Sandler Hudson Gallery Atlanta Ga; Rentz Gallery Richmond Va. *Mailing Add:* 1090 NE Standard Dr Atlanta GA 30319

LONGVAL, GLORIA
PAINTER
b Tampa, Fla, Feb 7, 31. *Study:* Am Art Sch, New York, NY, with Raphael Soyer, 51-52; Art Students League, with Robert Brackman, 52-53; Nat Acad Design, with Robert Philip, 55-58. *Work:* Los Angeles Co Mus; Museo Nacional, Palacio de Bellas Artes, Havana, Cuba; Riverside Art Mus, Calif; Latino Mus History, Art & Cult, Los Angeles; Wifredo Lam Cent, Havana, Cuba. *Comn:* Drawing for Int Decade of Women, Woman Tours, Los Angeles, Calif, 75; portrait (oil), Boris Pillin, Los Angeles, 76; portrait, Sharon Davis, Los Angeles, 77; portrait (oil), Dr Gerald Newmark, Los Angeles, 80; portrait (oil), Polia Pillin, Los Angeles, 76. *Exhib:* One-person show, Paideia Gallery, Los Angeles, 1962-65; San Bernadino Co Mus, Los Angeles, 1985; Del Bello Gallery, Toronto, Can, 1986; Downey Mus, Calif, 1987; April Sgro-Riddle Gallery, Los Angeles, 1988; Radford Univ, Va, 1990; Lancaster Mus, Calif, 1990; Museo Nacional, Palacio de Bellas Artes, Havana, Cuba, 1991; Latino Mus History, Art & Cult, Los Angeles, 1995; London Univ, Eng, 1996; Riverside Art Mus, Calif, 1997. *Pos:* Vpres, Los Angeles Artcore, 86-87 & contrib ed, 86; visual arts adv, Los Angeles Poetry Festival, 90-96; cur, Latin Diaspora, Art n Barbee Gallery, Los Angeles, 92; bd dir, Brewery Art Asn, 99-2001. *Teaching:* Instr painting, Sch Fine Arts, Univ Judaism, 68-71; guest instr, Los Angeles Children's Mus, 87-88; guest artist, Yosemite Park, 94-97; lectr, Galeria, Las Americas, Los Angeles, 93 & Brandeis Univ Women, Los Angeles, 2002. *Awards:* First Hon Mention, Nat Acad Allied Artists Am, 59; First Prize, Multi Media Mini, San Bernardino Co Mus, 83; Winner, Gannett Billboard Competition, Los Angeles, 95. *Bibliog:* Betty Ann Brown (auth), Yesterday and Tomorrow, Calif Women Artists,1989; Margaret Lazzari (auth), Curriculum Viva, Visions Art Quart, 1992; Shifra M Goldman (auth), Dimensions of the Ams, 1994. *Mem:* Brewery Art Asn Los Angeles; Womens Caucus for Art; Comn Feminile de Los Angeles. *Media:* Acrylic, Oil. *Dealer:* M M Smith PO Box 93832 Los Angeles CA 90093. *Mailing Add:* 638 Moulton Ave Los Angeles CA 90031

LONIDIER, FRED SPENCER
PHOTOGRAPHER, EDUCATOR
b Lakeview, Ore, Feb 19, 42. *Study:* Yuba Col, Marysville, Calif, AA, 62; San Francisco State Col, BA, 66; Univ Calif, San Diego, MFA (photog & mixed media), 72; also with David Antin. *Work:* Long Beach Mus Art, Calif; Faith Flam, Studio City, Calif; Oakland Mus, Calif; New Mus Contemp Art, NY; Southern Calif Libr Social Studies & Research; Los Angeles Video Libr, Calif; Univ Calif, San Diego, Specials Collections Libr, 98; Studio for S Calif Hist, Los Angeles, 2006. *Exhib:* One person shows, Rutgers Univ Labor Educ Ctr, New Brunswick, NJ, 78, 85-86, Ironworkers Union, Local 657, 86, Univ & Col Labor Educ Asn, 86, Calif Fedn Teachers, 89 & 91, Walter/McBean Gallery, San Francisco Art Inst, 92, Gallery of Art, Univ of N Iowa, 97, Mission Cult Ctr for Latino Arts, San Francisco, 2000, Side St Projects, Los Angeles, Calif, 2001, Blue Oyster Gallery, Dundin City, New Zealand, 2002 & Truck-trailer traveling exhib to the maquiladora zones, 2003, Harcourt House Arts Centre, Edmonton, Can, 2005, and many others; Pressing Engagements: Socially Oriental Photog (catalog), Tuttle Gallery, McDonough Sch, Md, 89; Visual Sociology, Mendenhall Gallery, Whittier Col, Calif, 90; Work Prints: The Eye of the Photojournalist, Rough Gallery, 90; Int Ctr Photog, Midtown, NY, 93; Inst Contemp Art, Boston, 93; Laguna Art Mus, Calif, 94; High Mus, Atlanta, Ga, 95; Exit Gallery, Univ of Nevada, 98; ACME Art Co, Main Gallery space, Columbus, Ohio, 2000; and many more; group show, NAFTA, ACME Art Gallery, Main Gallery Space, Columbus, Ohio, 2000; group show (catalog), At Work: The Art of California Labor, SFSU Art Gallery, 2003. *Pos:* Consult Eye Gallery, San Francisco, Calif, 85. *Teaching:* prof, visual arts dept, Univ Calif San Diego, 72-2006. *Awards:* San Diego Acad Senate Res Grant, Univ Calif, 75-76, 78-80, 81, 82, 83-84, 86-87, 88-89, 89-90; Nat Endowment Arts Fel, 80-83; Labor Coun Award, San Diego - Imperial Counties Labor Coun, 89; Best Entry Award, S Shenere Gallery, Los Angeles, Calif, 2002-2003. *Bibliog:* Fred Glass (auth), A-V reference shelf, Labor Studies J, Vol 20, No 1, spring 95; Jim McVicker (auth), Labor link TV gives unions a voice on cable channels, The Worker, UFCW Local 135, 2/96; Fred Lonidier (auth), Dateline: San Diego, Calif, labor link TV, Community Media Rev, Vol 19, No 2, 96; Kate Callen (auth), Photographs that make a point, UCSD Perspectives, San Diego, summer 2001; Grant Kester (auth), Conversation pieces: diabolical encounters in modern art, Chapter five: community and communicability, UC Press, 2002. *Mem:* Los Angeles Inst Contemp Art; Col Art Asn Am; Soc Photg Educ; Univ Coun. *Media:* Photo, Text, Video & Slide. *Interests:* installation art concerning class struggle. *Publ:* coauth, Union Made: Artists Working with Unions, Upfront, NYPADD, New York, winter 83-84; Working with unions, Culture in Contention, Real Comet Press, Wash, 85; Working with Unions II, Democratic Communications in the Info Age, Garmond Press, Can, 92; Letters to the ed, Labor Studies Forum, spring 96; Setting aside our differences, Rethinking Marxism, Vol 8, No 4, summer 96; auth, UC Hates Unions II: Labor Relations at the Univeristy of California, New Indicator, 2002; auth, Corporations in Societies, The Grenoble Res Center, CIESIMA, Grenoble, France, 2002. *Mailing Add:* Univ Calif San Diego Visual Arts Dept 9500 Gilman Dr La Jolla CA 92093-0084

LOONEY, NORM
SCULPTOR, CONCEPTUAL ARTIST
b Seattle, Wash, Oct 31, 42. *Study:* Calif State Univ, Long Beach, MFA(drawing & painting). *Work:* World Expo, 88; Childrens Hosp, Los Angeles; Town Ctr Rancho Cucamonga, Calif; SW Tex State Univ; Anchorage Mus Art. *Comn:* Security Pac Nat Bank, Calif; Calif State Univ, Long Beach; Environetics Int, Los Angeles; Innovax Methods Group, Los Angeles; Naples Prof Ctr, Long Beach. *Exhib:* Los Angeles Co Mus Art; NC Mus Art, Raleigh; Birmingham Mus Fine Art, Ala; Montgomery Mus Art, Ala; Hunter Mus Art, Tenn; Miti Gallery, Stockholm, Swed, 77; Soc Prom Contemp Art, Athens, Greece, 77; Okla Art Ctr, Oklahoma City, 77; The Texas Thirty, Nave Mus, Victoria, Tex, 77; Mus Art & Hist, Anchorage, Alaska; and others. *Pos:* Artist-in-residence, City of Long Beach, Calif, 79-80. *Awards:* Fel, Yaddo Inc, NY, 77 & 95; Fel, Gottlieb Found Inc; Calif Arts Coun Grant. *Media:* Mixed, Large Scale Sculpture

LOPEZ, EUGENIO ALONSO
COLLECTOR
b Mexico City, 68. *Pos:* Dir marketing Grupo Jumex, Ecatepec, Mex; owner and founder Chac Mool Gallery, Los Angeles, 94-, Jumex Collection, Escatepec, Mex, 2001-; trustee Los Angeles Mus Contemp Art, New Mus Contemp Art, NY. *Awards:* named one of Top 200 Collectors, ARTNews Mag, 2006. *Mailing Add:* Chac Mool Gallery 8920 Melrose Ave Los Angeles CA 90069

LOPINA, LOUISE CAROL
PAINTER, PRINTMAKER
b Chicago, Ill, Nov 24, 36. *Study:* Chicago Art Inst; Purdue Univ, BS; study with Lawrence Harris & Don Dennis. *Work:* Cincinnati Nat Hist Mus & Cincinnati Club, Cincinnati; Cincinnati Club; Hartwood Club; Nissequoque Golf Club, St James, Long Island, NY; G & R Tackle Co; Dana Pointe Yacht Club; Hartwood Club; Colo State Univ Vet Teaching Hosp; Bank of Smithtown. *Comn:* Dioram A Blackgroups: Asistencia Mission, San Bernardino Co Mus, 92; Vol III, IV & V (illus), comn by Russell Annebel. *Exhib:* Soc Animal Artists Exhibs, anns 72-90; one-person exhibs, Air Univ Libr, Montgomery, Ala, 77, Christ Church Little Gallery, Kettering, Ohio, 80, The Cincinnati Club, Ohio, 81, Nissequoque Golf Club, St James, Long Island, NY, 86, Nat Mgt Asn, Local Chapter, Newport Beach, Calif; Nature Interpreted, Cincinnati Mus Natural Hist, 80, 82 & 84; Wondrous Wildlife, Cincinnati Zoo, 83; Outdoor Expo, Albany, NY, 85; Nature of the Beast, Southern Alleghenies Mus Art, 86; Prestige Gallery: 1st & 2nd Ann Original Art Showcase, Can, 89 & 90; Whaletail, East African Wildlife Soc, 91; Artist's Registry Exhib, Dog Mus, 92 & 94; Wildlife West Art Festival, San Bernardino Co Mus Found, 92, 93 & 94; The Contemp Canine: Works from the Artists Registry, The Dog Mus, St Louis, Mo, 94, 96-98; Natural Selections IV, J MacArthur Beach State Park; 2000 Ky Nat Wildlife Exhib, Henderon Fine Art Ctr; Artists Focus on Calif Skies, Calif Art Club, 02; Impressions of New Eng, Bennington Ctr for the Arts, 02-03. *Collection Arranged:* oil paintings, Ken Stewarts Lodge, Bath, Ohio, 02, 03. *Teaching:* Instr drawing & painting, USAF Acad-Officer's Wives Club, 72-75. *Awards:* Best in Show, Nat Nature Art Exhib, 78, 79 & 82; Selection for commemorative print, Snow Leopard Symposium, India, 85; Best in Show, San Clemente Art Club, Winter Juried Exhib, 2002, Spring Juried Exhib, 2003; Best Mission Painting $1000 Purchase Award, Socalpapa Juried Show

San Juan Capistrano, 6/2005. *Bibliog:* Al Rosen & Faith Every (dirs), Louise Lopina's Art on the Wild Side, television feature program, 2/78; article, A sampling of assorted artists, Dayton Mag, 5-6/81. *Mem:* Nat Audubon Soc; Nature Conservancy; Soc Animal Artists (past exhib co-chmn); Old English Sheepdog Club Am; Laguna Plein Air Painters Asn; Calif Art Club. *Media:* Oil, Watercolor; Lithography. *Publ:* Reptiles and Amphibians of Aullwood & Wild Flowers of Aullwood, Nat Audubon, 78; View from the top: Snow leopards, Color Print, 82; Old English Sheepdogs, 85, 92 & 97; Shetland Sheepdogs, 88 & 99; Bulldog, 90; Rottweiler, 92; Yellow Labrador & New Foundland, 96; Golden Retriever, 95; Australian Shepherd, 2001; Illustrated Vol 6 & 7 Russell Annabel's Trouble is where you find it, Head for the Hills. *Dealer:* Wildbrook Studio. *Mailing Add:* c/o Wild Brook Studio 7 Calle Agua San Clemente CA 92673

LORBER, D MARTIN H B
CONSULTANT, HISTORIAN
b Macon, Ga, July 22, 43. *Study:* Univ NC, BA, 65; City Col New York, BS, 91. *Interests:* Japanese Swords & Fittings; Korean, Song ceramics. *Publ:* Auth, Japanese Sword Fittings, 5/77 & Japanese Buddhist Paintings, 7/78, Arts of Asia; coauth, 100 Masterpieces from the Collection of Dr Walter Ames Compton, Christie's, 2/92; Parts I, II & III, In: Japanese Swords & Swords Fittings, Christie's, 92; auth, Japanese arms and armour at the Metropolitan Museum of Art, Orientations, 10/92; Japanese Buddhist Paintings in the NY Museums, Int Asian Art Fair Catalogue, 3/2001. *Mailing Add:* 304 E 20th St New York NY 10003-1813

LORBER, RICHARD
CRITIC, EDUCATOR
b New York, NY, Dec 9, 46. *Study:* Columbia Col, with Meyer Schapiro & Lionel Trilling, BA(lit & art hist), 67; Columbia Univ, with Meyer Schapiro & Linda Nochlin, MA(art hist), 70, EdD(art), 77. *Pos:* Ed, Dance Scope Mag, 74-; contrib ed, Arts Mag, 75-; community liaison, Mus of Mod Art, 76-77; critic & contribr, Artforum, Arts Mag, 77-; adv panelist, NY State Coun on Arts, 78-; proj dir, Nat Video Clearinghouse, 79-; consult, Electronic Arts Intermix, 81; pres, Fox-Lorber Assoc Inc, 81-. *Teaching:* Instr art hist, Parsons Sch of Design, 74-77; asst prof art & art educ, Grad Sch of Educ, NY Univ, 77-79. *Publ:* Coauth, The Gap, McGraw-Hill, 68; auth, articles in Arts in Soc & Filmmakers Newsletter, 77; contribr, Video Art, Dutton, 78; article, Videodance, Millenium Film J, 12/81. *Mailing Add:* c/o Fox Lorber Assoc 419 Park Ave S New York NY 10016

LORBER, STEPHEN NEIL
PAINTER, PHOTOGRAPHER
b New York, NY, Aug 30, 43. *Study:* Pratt Inst, BFA; Brooklyn Col, MFA; Yale Univ, Stoekel fel, 64. *Work:* Chicago Art Inst; Okla Art Ctr, Oklahoma City; Western NMex Univ, Silver City; Roswell Mus & Art Ctr, NMex; Am Tel & Tel Co; Chase Manhattan Bank, NY; and others; Harvard Univ Library; Queen Sofia Found, Madrid; Univ of Ill; US Dept of state; Nat Inst of Health; Art Mus of S Tex. *Exhib:* One-man shows, Milliken Gallery, NY, 81, 83 & 85; Contemp Arts Ctr, NY, 82; John Szoke Gallery, NY, 87; Goddard Ctr Arts, Ardmore Okla, 89; Chicago Int Art Expos, 89 & 90; Group show, The Kitchen, NY, 94; Guild Hall, South Hampton, NY, 94; Mus de la Ciudad, Madrid, Spain; and others. *Awards:* Artist in Residence Grant, Roswell Mus & Art Ctr, NMex; Yaddo Fel, 71 & 75; Nat Endowment Arts Fel, 76-77. *Bibliog:* Allen Ellenweog (auth), Arts Mag, 9/77; Stephen Yoskowitz (auth), Arts Mag, Vol 55, No 9, 5/81; Kramer, Hilton, NY Times, Dec 21, 71, Photo; Kramer, Hilton, NY Times, June 9, 73, Photo; Kramer, Hilton, NY Times, Dec 15,73; Martin, Richard, Arts & Artists, Gt Brit, Nov, 73; Brown, Richard, Arts Mag, Feb, 74; Ratcliff, Carter, Art Int, Apr, 75, Vol XIX, No 5 Photo; Hoestry, Ingelborg, Art Int, May, 75, Vol XIX, No 5 Photo; Henry, Garrit, Art News, Summer, 76; Kramer, Hilton, NY Times, Apr, 22, 77; Brody, Jacqueline, Print Col Newsletter. *Media:* All. *Mailing Add:* 709 County Rte Greenwich NY 12834

LORCINI, GINO
SCULPTOR, MURALIST
b Plymouth, Eng, July 7, 23; Can citizen. *Study:* Montreal Mus Sch Art. *Work:* Nat Gallery Can, Ottawa; Mus Art Contemporain, Montreal; Chase Manhattan Bank, NY; Art Gallery Ont, Toronto; Matsushita Corp, Tokyo; and others. *Comn:* Mural, Nat Arts Ctr, Ottawa, 68; mural, Montreal Forum, Que, 69; fountain sculpture, Ste Anne's Hosp, PQ, 70; sculpture, Nat Defence Bldg, Ottawa, 72; Ont Prov Court House, London, 73; Bell Canada, Trinity Sq, Toronto, 84; Cong Ctr, Ottawa, 85; CFPL Broadcasting Sta, London, Ont, 87. *Exhib:* Op from Montreal, Fleming-Hull Mus, 66; Sculpture 67, Toronto, 67; Surv 68, Montreal, 68; one-man traveling exhib, Atlantic Provinces Mus, Can, 69; 3-D Into the 70's, Art Gallery Ont, Toronto, 70; Constructivist Heritage, Harbourfront Gallery, Toronto, 81; and other group & one-man shows. *Teaching:* Asst prof painting & sculpture, McGill Univ, 60-68; resident artist, Univ Western Ont, 69-72. *Awards:* Jessie Dow Award, Montreal Mus Fine Arts, 65; Arts Award, Can Coun, 68. *Bibliog:* M Gaulin (auth), Sculptor Lorcini, Time, 68; D Sanders (auth), Gino Lorcini, Bus Quart, 71. *Mem:* Royal Can Acad Arts Coun. *Media:* Aluminum, Bronze. *Publ:* Coauth, Creative response, McGill J Educ, 67. *Mailing Add:* 326 Old Brock Rd Dundas ON L9H 5H6 Canada

LORD, ANDREW
SCULPTOR
b Rochdale, Eng, 50. *Study:* Col Art, Rochdale, 66-68; Cent Sch Arts & Crafts, Studied with Gilbert Harding-Green & Bonnie van de Wetering, London, 68-71. *Work:* Mus Art, Dallas, Tex; City Art Gallery, Leeds, Eng; Mus Beymans van Beuningen, Rotterdam; Mus Contemp Art, Los Angeles; Mus & Art Gallery, Portsmouth, Eng; and others. *Exhib:* Int Ceramics 72, Victoria & Albert Mus, & traveling exhib, London, 72; Postmodern Prints, Victoria & Albert Mus, London, 90; Act Up Benefit Exhib, Matthew Marks Gallery, NY, 91; Group show, Gagaosian Gallery, 92; Drawings 30th Anniversary Exhib, Leo Castelli Gallery, NY, 93; Solo exhib, Galerie Bruno Bischofberger, Zurich, 92, Carnegie Mus Art, Pittsburgh, 93, Gagaosian Gallery, NY 94; and many others. *Pos:* De Porceleyne Fles, Netherlands, formerly. *Teaching:* Vis lectr, Bath Acad Art, Eng, 75-80. *Awards:* British Coun Scholar, 74. *Bibliog:* Jerry Saltz (auth), Andrew Lord at 65 Thompson St, Art in America, 2/93; Peter Schjeldahl (auth), Nostalgie de la Boue, The New Yorker, 12/92; Peter Schjeldahl (auth), Excellent pot, Voice, 12/92. *Mailing Add:* c/o Baldwin Gallery 209 S Galena St Aspen CO 81611

LORD, CAROLYN MARIE
PAINTER, INSTRUCTOR
b Los Angeles, Calif, Oct 6, 56. *Study:* Painting Workshops, with Millard Sheets, George Post, Rex Brandt, Robert E Wood, 76-83; Principia Col, Elsah, Ill, BA(fine arts), 78; San Francisco Tapestry Workshop, with Jean-Pierre Larochette, 81. *Work:* Principia Col, Elsah, Ill; Scripps Col, Claremont, Calif; Bank A Levy, Ventura, Calif; Los Angeles Athletic Club, Calif; The Buck Collection, Calif. *Comn:* Painting for label, and auction, Beringer Brothers Vineyards, St Helena, Calif, 85; 3 paintings, Los Angeles Athletic Club, Calif, 97, 99. *Exhib:* One-woman shows, Northeastern Nev Mus, Elko, 85 & 90; Watercolor USA Watercolor Now, Springfield Art Mus, Mo, 91 & 97; Watercolor Biennial, Triton Mus, Santa Clara, Calif, 92, 94, 96, 98, 2000, 02; Midwest Watercolor Soc, Neville Pub Mus, Green Bay, Wis, 92; Gardens Real and Imagined, Sun Gallery, Hayward, Calif, 92; Art in Embassies Program, Lesotho, Zambia, 98, 99, Kolonia, 2002. *Teaching:* La Romita Sch Art, Terni, Italy, 91; Mendocino Art Ctr, Calif, 96; Saddleback Community Coll, 97, 98, 99 & 2000. *Awards:* Adirondack Award Second Place, Adirondack Nat Exhib, Rouse Co, Baltimore, 87; Juror's Award Second Place, San Diego Watercolor Soc, 88; Springfield Mus Cash Award, Watercolor USA, 88 & 96. *Bibliog:* Robin Worthington (auth), The lightness of being artistic, San Jose Mercury News, 3/21/90; M Stephen Doherty (auth), The Importance of the Figure, Watercolor '96; contribr, Learning from Life's Changes, Watercolor Magic, 98. *Mem:* Nat Watercolor Soc; Calif Art Club; Thunderbird Found Arts. *Media:* Watercolor on Paper. *Publ:* Illusr, Musings of a fence painter, 2/3/86, View at the end of the walk, 9/1/87 South seas Romeo and Juliet, 9/27/88, The Home Forum, Christian Sci Monitor; contribr, Exploring Painting, Davis Publ, 88; Color & Light for the Watercolor Painter, Watson Guptill, 95. *Dealer:* Nancy Dodds Gallery PO 6016 Carmel Calif 93921. *Mailing Add:* 1993 DeVaca Way Livermore CA 94550

LORD, MICHAEL HARRY
DEALER, CURATOR
b Milwaukee, Wis, Nov 19, 54. *Study:* Univ Wis-Milwaukee. *Pos:* Asst to dir, Irving Galleries, 68-77; owner & dir, Michael H Lord Gallery, 78-. *Mem:* Milwaukee Art Dealers Asn (pres, 81-); Wis Coalition Arts & Human Needs (bd dir, 83-). *Specialty:* Contemporary American art; masters in photography and sculpture. *Mailing Add:* 772 N Milwaukee St Milwaukee WI 53202-3705

LORELLI, ELVIRA MAE
SCULPTOR, PAINTER
b Upland, Calif. *Study:* Pomona Col, BA, 50; Claremont Grad Sch, Scripps Col, MA(art educ), 61; Claremont Grad Sch & Univ Ctr, MA(art), 69; Otis Art Inst, with Charlie White, Don Kingman, Renzo Femci & Joseph Martinek, 71-75, Pietra Santa, Italy, with Martini Pasqualini, Gigi Guadanuchi, Bigi Rinaldo & Bernice Schachter, 93-95. *Hon Degrees:* MA (art educ), Claremont Grad School, 61; MA (art), Claremont Grad School and Univ Ctr, 69. *Work:* Trona High Sch, Calif; Barstow Centennial Park, Calif; Mojave Valley River Mus, Barstow, Calif; Southwest Trading Post, Lake Arrowhead, Calif; Shoppers Lane Gallery, Convina, Calif; Schiffman Gallery, Hesperia, Calif; Little Red Caboose Originals, Barstow, Calif. *Comn:* Murals, Methodist Church, 84, Barstow, Calif; stained glass window, St Joseph Church, Barstow, 86; bronze reliefs, Rotary Club, Barstow, 90; sculptures, St Philip Neri, 96; sculptures, bronze relief, Montara Sch, Barstow, Calif, 99. *Exhib:* Around the World, Nat Art Appreciation Soc, New Orleans, 84; Chaffee Community Art Show, Ont Mus & Gallery, Calif, 86; Fine Arts Inst Ann Art Show, Mus Art, San Bernardino Co, Calif, 87; Sixth Ann Fine Arts Show, SW Sculptors Asn, Victoriville, Calif, 88; Calico Fine Arts Show, Calico Ghost Town, Calif, 84-97; JD Pelan Exhib, Los Angeles; Neberrys Spring Fine Art Festival; Searles lake Art Show, Trona, Calif; Indios Pilot Club of the Golden Sands int Invitational; Lorains Coffee Shop, Barstow, 2004-2005; Art by the Lake, Big Bear, Calif, 2005-2006; Barstow Chamber of Commerce, Calif, 2006; Idle Spurs Restaurant, Barstow, Calif, 2006; and others. *Pos:* Judge, Ft Irwin Ann Art Show & Barstow Ann Mardi Gras Parade. *Teaching:* Dept head art, art instr & prof, Barstow Community Col, 62-82; pvt painting & sculpture instr, El Mae Studio, Barstow, Calif, 62-97; instr art, Univ Calif, Riverside, 78-87, Chapman Col, 79-84 & Am Vets Home, Barstow, Calif, 96-2006; gate instr, Barstow Middle Sch, 96. *Awards:* Nat Art Appreciation Soc, 84; Artist of the Month, Holiday Inn, 93; Calico Ann Fine Arts Exhib, 96. *Bibliog:* Bill Deselms (auth), Desert Dispatch Feature, 90; Desert Dispatch, 93 & 96. *Mem:* SW Sculptors; Gem Carvers Guild Int; Fine Arts Inst; Chaffee Community Art Asn; Barstow Artists Guild (pres). *Media:* Bronze, Stone, Oils, Watercolor. *Res:* Art with and without music. *Interests:* Photography, bowling, line-dancing, hiking & gardening. *Publ:* Artists USA Inc, 1977-78; Directory of Portrait Artists, Am Portrait Soc, 85; Art at Pomona Galleries of the Claremont Colleges 1887 to 1987. *Mailing Add:* 29205 Exeter St Barstow CA 92311

LORENTZ, PAULINE
PAINTER, INSTRUCTOR
b Newark, NJ, Dec 28, 14. *Study:* Newark Sch Fine & Indust Arts, NJ, grad; Art Students League; also with John R Grabach, NA. *Exhib:* Am Artists Prof League Grand Nat, NY, 65, 67-69 & 86-96; Expos Intercontinentale, Monaco & Dieppe, France, 67-68; 24th Am Drawing Biennial, Norfolk Mus Arts & Sci, Va, 71; Nat

Exhib, Mus Fine Arts, Springfield, Mass, 71-73; Smithsonian Traveling Exhib, US, 71-73. *Teaching:* Instr, Summit Art Ctr, NJ, 62-87, Art Ctr NJ, Orange, 73-80 & NJ Ctr Visual Arts, 87-. *Awards:* Best Show Oil, Am Artists Prof League; Arts Atlantic Award, Gloucester, Mass, 72; Gold Medal Graphics, Am Artists Prof League, 90; and many others. *Bibliog:* Philbrook Smith (auth), article, NJ Mus & Arts Mag, 2/64; article, Palette Talk, Vol 32, 77; article, Am Artist Mag, 4/84. *Mem:* Am Artists Prof League (pres, NJ chap, 85-88, dir, 86-); Catharine Lorillard Wolfe Art Club; Hudson Valley Art Asn, NY; Acad Artists Asn, Mass; Rockport Art Asn, Mass. *Media:* Oil, Charcoal. *Mailing Add:* 20 Southview Dr Berkeley Heights NJ 07922

LORENZ, NANCY J
PAINTER
b North Plainfield, NJ, Dec 10, 62. *Study:* Univ Mich, BFA, 85; Tyler Sch Art, Temple Univ, MFA, 88. *Work:* NY Pub Libr & Studio Sofield, NY; Champion Paper, Cleveland, Ohio; MIA Insurance, San Francisco, Calif; Shinwa Med, Nagoya, Japan. *Comn:* Paintings, Soho Grand Hotel, NY, 96; paintings, Studio Sofield, NY, 96; paintings, Senayan Hotel, Yokahama, Japan, 96; paintings, Muscat Hilton, Muscat, Oman, 97; mural, Mulia Hotel, Jakarta, Indonesia, 97. *Exhib:* Skulptour X 7 USA, Kultur Forum, Munchengladbach, Ger, 91; Notes on Science, Genovese Gallery, Boston, Mass, 94; Lacques, Galerie Verneuil Saints-Peres, Paris, France, 98; Orly and Elsewhere, PDX, Ore, 98; Galerie Xippas, Paris; "Mother of Pearl Paintings," 2001; Exhibit, Jay Grimm, New York City, 2002. *Teaching:* RI Sch Design, 96. *Awards:* John Simon Guggenheim Mem Found Fel, 98. *Bibliog:* Mary Sherman (auth), Molecular models gone wild, Boston Globe, 90; Joan Kron (auth), No big deal, its just gold, NY Times, 95; Willoughby Sharp (auth), Nancy Lorenz talks to Willoughby Sharp, 97. *Mem:* Pierpoint Morgan Libr, NY, young fel, 96-. *Media:* Mixed Media. *Dealer:* PDX Portland OR. *Mailing Add:* 10 E 29th St Apt 42E New York NY 10016-7445

LORFANO, PAULINE DAVIS
PAINTER
b Westbrook, Maine, June 15, 28. *Study:* Maine Col Art, teaching cert, 50; Univ Maine, Orono, BS, 52; workshops with Diana Kan, Edward Betts & Ted Goeschner, 80-94, Tony VanHasselt, numerous others. *Hon Degrees:* Maine Col Art, Hon Fine Art, 00. *Work:* TRW, Washington; George Mason Univ, Fairfax, Va; MITRE, First Va Bank. *Comn:* Painting, comn by T Evans Curtis, Ariz, 89; painting, Nat Symphony Women's Comt, Washington, 89; landscape, S Cleary Decocator, Fla & Va, 90; murals, Possibilities for Design, Denver, 92-94. *Exhib:* Solo shows, Am Horticult Soc, Alexandria, Va, 88, Nat Wildlife Fedn, Vienna, Va, 89 & Sumner Mus, Washington, DC, 89, Green Springs, Annandale, Va, 3/01; Mid-Atlantic Regional, Strathmore Hall, Bethesda, Md, 98; Biennial Art Exhib, Univ Tampa, Fla, 98; Va Watercolor Soc, Portsmouth Mus, Va, 98; Foundry Gallery, 99; Hilton Head Art League, Hilton Head Island, SC, 98; juried, Int Soc Marine Painters, 97, 98, 99 & 00, Strathmore Hall, 00, Va Watercolor Soc, 00; Fisher Gallery, Schlesinger Arts Ctr, No Va Community Col, Alexandria, 2002; Dyn Corp Gallery, Reston, VA, 2003. *Pos:* Art bd chmn, Nat League Am Pen Women, 82-84; bd dir, Vienna Arts Soc, 86-97; bd dir, Wash Watercolor Asn, 97; juror, various Art Shows; art consult, art bd, NLAPW, 2004-06. *Teaching:* Asst prof art, drawing & painting, continuing educ, George Mason Univ, 78-82; teacher painting, Studio, 82-01; instr drawing & painting, Art Clubs & Fairfax Adult Educ, 82-94. *Awards:* Historic Preservation Award, Historic Vienna Inc, 98; Am Artist Award, 98; 3d Place, Quiet Waters Exhib, Potomac Valley Watercolorists, 2002. *Bibliog:* J B Hamilton (auth), Artist shares talent, The Arrow Of Pi Beta Phi, 88; Jennifer Barcus (auth), Artist & authors, The Arrow of Pi Beta Phi, 93; Brian Trompeter (auth), A Painter for All Subjects, The Connection Newspaper, 6/10/98; Donna Southworth (auth), Sense of Place, Elan Mag, 3/2002. *Mem:* Vienna Arts Soc (pres, 79-81, 88-90 & 2004-05); Int Soc Marine Painters (signature mem); Va Watercolor Soc (cochair 25th exhib); Baltimore Watercolor Soc (signature mem); Wash Watercolor Asn (Exec bd, currently). *Media:* Watercolor, Oil. *Specialty:* Vienna Art Center; JP Brehony Model Home. *Interests:* Painting seascapes, landscapes and still lifes; travel. *Mailing Add:* 402 Old Courthouse Rd NE Vienna VA 22180-3603

LORING, JOHN
PAINTER, PRINTMAKER
b Chicago, Ill, Nov 23, 39. *Study:* Yale Univ, BA, 60; Ecole des Beaux Arts, Paris, 61-64; printmaking with Johnny Friedlaender, Paris, 62-64. *Hon Degrees:* Pratt Inst, Hon DFA. *Work:* Metrop Mus Art, Whitney Mus Am Art, Mus Mod Art, NY; Art Inst Chicago; Boston Mus Fine Arts; Yale Univ Art Gallery. *Comn:* Mural, US Customs Serv, Main Hall, US Customhouse, World Trade Ctr, NY, 74; three posters, NY Cult Ctr, 74; murals, Prudential Life Insurance Co, Eastern Home Off, Woodbridge, NJ, 76; outdoor mural proj, Nat Endowment Arts, Scranton, Pa, 77; murals, Nat Hq, Western Savings, Philadelphia, 79. *Exhib:* Silkscreen: History of a Medium, Philadelphia Mus Art, 71; Realism Now, NY Cult Ctr, 72; One-man shows, Baltimore Mus Art, 72 & Long Beach Mus Art, Calif, 75; Biennale of Graphic Art, Ljubljana, Yugoslavia, 73 & 77; Intergrafia 74 & 76, Krakow, Poland; Painting & Sculpture Today, Indianapolis Mus Art, 74; Silkscreen Prints, Chicago Art Inst, 75; Pace Editions, NY, 77. *Pos:* Art ed, Deleg World Bulletin, UN, 72; contribr, Print Collector's Newsletter, 73-75 & Art in Am, 77-; assoc ed & contribr, Arts Mag, 73-; contrib ed, Archit Digest, 76-; design dir & sr vpres, Tiffany & Co, 79-. *Teaching:* Distinguished vis prof art, Univ Calif, Davis, 77. *Awards:* Fourth Prize, Intergrafia 74, Krakow; Edith Wharton Award, Design & Art Soc, New York, 88. *Bibliog:* Ellen Lubell (auth), John Loring, 2/74 & Mario Amaya (auth), John Loring, 2/78, Arts Mag; Robert Hughes (auth), Murals without walls, 6/79. *Mem:* Chelsea Arts Club, London. *Media:* Oil; Photo Silkscreens. *Publ:* A Tiffany Christmas, Doubleday, 97; Tiffany's 20th Century, 98; Tiffany Jewels, 99; Paulding Farnham, 2000; Tiffany's Lost Genius, 2000; Magnificent Silver, 2001; Louis Comfort Tiffany at Tiffany & Co, 2002; Tiffany Flora & Tiffany Fauna, 2003; Tiffany in Fashion, 2003. *Mailing Add:* 403 W 46th St New York NY 10036

LOSAVIO, SAMUEL R
SCULPTOR, PAINTER
b Baton Rouge, La, Mar 15, 52. *Study:* La State Univ, BFA, 73, MFA, 79. *Work:* Valencia Community Col, Orlando, Fla. *Exhib:* Surrealism Continued & Southeast 7-11, Southeastern Ctr Contemp Art, Winston-Salem, NC, 88; Louisiana Abstractions, Contemp Art Ctr, New Orleans, 88; Birmingham Biennial V, Birmington Mus Art, 89; 22nd Bradley Nat Print & Drawing Exhib, Bradley Univ, 89; Working on Paper, Contemp Am Drawing, High Mus Art, Atlanta, 90; 20th Anniversary Exhib, Contemp Art Ctr, New Orleans, 97. *Pos:* Asst dir, La Arts & Sci Ctr, Baton Rouge, 95-. *Teaching:* Asst prof, found coordr, Univ Fla, 90-93; lectr, Loyola Univ City Col, New Orleans, 93-96. *Awards:* Nat Endowment Arts Fel, 87 & 89; Juror's Award, Orlando Mus Art, Ann Juried Exhib, 90; New Fac Award, Univ Fla, 91; Southeaster Ctr for Cont Art/RJ Reynolds Southeastern Artists Fel, 87

LOSIER, MARIE
FILM DIRECTOR
b Boulogne, France, 72. *Exhib:* Group shows: Tribecca Film Festival; Int Film Festival; Rotterdam; Seoul Film Festival, Lausagne Film Festival; York Underground Film Festival; Lake Placid Film Festival; Whitney Biennial, Whitney Mus Art, 2006; Chick-chick, 2000; The Touch Retouched, 2001; Loula Meets Charlie, 2002; Marie-Onette, 2002; Broken Blossoms, 2002; The Passion of Joan of Arc, 2002; Sanitarium Cinema, 2002; Mike Kuchar is on My Roof, 2003; Lunch Break on the Xerox Machine, 2003; Bird, Bath & Beyond, 2003; Electrocute Your Stars, 2004; Eat Your Makeup!, 2005; The Ontological Cowboy, 2005; Flying Saucey!, 2006. *Pos:* Film programmer, Fr Inst, Alliance Francaise, NYC, 2000; dir (films), 2000-2006. *Awards:* Grantee Nat Art Studio Club Grant, 1997; NY State Coun Arts, 2004. *Mailing Add:* French Inst 22 E 60th St New York NY 10022

LOTRINGER, SYLVERE
WRITER
b Paris, France, Oct 15, 38; US citizen. *Study:* Ecole Pratique des Hautes Etudes, Paris, BA & MA, 65, PhD 67. *Exhib:* Too Sensitive to Touch, No Wave Cinema, Whitney Mus Am Art, NY, 97. *Collection Arranged:* Artand, Galerie Optica, Montreal, 93. *Pos:* Sr mellon critic, CAL Arts, Calif, 90-91; vis critic, Art Ctr, Pasadena, 91-99; consult, Mus Mod Art, New York, 96 & Banff Ctr, Alta, Can, 97-98. *Teaching:* Prof French Lit & Philo, Columbia Univ, 72-. *Bibliog:* Under the Sign of Semiotexte, Critique, 94. *Media:* Text, Video. *Publ:* Auth, Photography & Death, Interrupted Life, New Mus Contemp Art, 91; Art & The Commodification of Theory, Flash Art, Milan, 91; auth, Nancy Spero, Phaedon Press, London, 96; Becoming Duchamp, Crossings, Kunsthalle, Wien, Austria, 98; Consumed by Myths, Premises, Guggenheim Mus Soho, N, 98. *Mailing Add:* Columbia University 522 Philosophy Hall New York NY 10027

LOTZ, STEVEN DARRYL
PAINTER, GALLERY DIRECTOR
b Los Angeles, Calif, Dec 28, 38. *Study:* Univ Calif, Los Angeles, BFA, 61; Univ Fla, Gainesville, with Hiram Williams, MFA, 63; Acad Fine Arts, Vienna, Austria, 65-66. *Work:* Jacksonville Art Mus, Fla; Orlando International Airport; His Royal Highness, Prince Phillip, London; Alachua Pub Libr, Gainesville, Fla; Universal Studios, Orlando. *Comn:* Fla Solar Energy Ctr; Walt Disney World, Fla. *Exhib:* Appalachian State Univ, NC, 90; Stetson Univ, Deland, Fla, 88; Univ of Tampa, Fla, 89; Atlantic Ctr Arts, New Smyrna Beach, Fla, 95; Univ NFla, Jacksonville, 97. *Teaching:* Asst prof drawing & painting, Jacksonville Univ, Fla, 66-68; chmn, Univ Cent Fla, Orlando, 68-78, prof drawing & painting 68-; vis exchange instr, Edinburgh Col Art, 78-79 & 80-81. *Awards:* First Prize, Jacksonville Arts Festival, 65; First Prize, Ocala Arts Festival, Ocala Nat Bank, 69; State Fla Grant. *Bibliog:* Roger Ortmayer (dir), Space Cathedral (film), CBS TV, New York, 72; Frank Martin (auth), article, Art Voices South, 11-12/79; Egberdien Van Rossum (auth), article, Bres 99 Mag, 4/83. *Media:* Oil, Acrylic. *Mailing Add:* 626 Lake Ave Orlando FL 32801-3914

LOVE, FRANCES TAYLOR
WRITER, PUBLISHER
b Salina, Kans, Apr 25, 26. *Study:* Univ Tex, BA(journalism & speech); studied television writing, Univ Houston; sem in Gt Brit & other Europ study, Smithsonian Inst. *Exhib:* Bronze sculpture of Elise Carmichael, 1975-1994. *Collection Arranged:* Steamboats Along the Louisiana Bayous (auth, catalog), 69, 19th Century Painters in Louisiana (auth, catalog), 72, Louisiana French Furnishings: 1750-1830 (ed, catalog), 74, Haitian Voodoo Art (auth, catalog), 76 & Victorian Decorative Arts in Louisiana (auth, catalog), 77, Art Ctr Southwestern La. *Pos:* Pub relations dir, Lafayette Art Asn, 60-63; dir, Art Ctr Southwestern La, Lafayette, 65-83; dir, Univ La at Lafayette, 65-83. *Res:* Louisiana colonial decorative arts; Texas and Louisiana decorative art and architecture; Victorian decorative art. *Publ:* Auth & ed, My Home is Austin, Texas, 58 & Here is South Louisiana, 65, Tribune Press; Oil People: A Gap in Understanding; Louisiana French Homes & Furnishings, 1750-1830, 99; ed, Travelhost of Acadiana Mag, 82-92; The Magazine, RE: Art & Culture in South Louisiana, pvt publ, 94; auth, Permanent Collection of the Art Museum and the People Who Made It Possible, 2003. *Mailing Add:* Frances Love & Assoc Pub Relations & Pub Consultants PO Box 51998 Lafayette LA 70505

LOVEJOY, MARGOT R
MULTI-MEDIA, EDUCATOR
b Campbellton, NB, Can, Oct 21, 30. *Study:* Mt Allison Univ, with Alex Colville & Lauren Harris, 47-49; Univ Academie Julian, Paris, 49; St Martins Sch Art, London, cert (design & illus), 50; Pratt Graphics Ctr, New York, with Ponce de Leon, Stasik & Zimilies, 66-71. *Work:* Getty Inst; Bibliotheque Nat, Paris; Dresden Mus, Ger; Hunterian Mus, Glasgow; Mus Mod Art New York. *Exhib:* Solo exhibs PS1 Mus, Inst

Contemp Art, 87, Labyrinth, East End Arts, Phildelphia, 88, Alternative Mus, 90, Islip Art Mus, NY, 92, 99, Arronson Gallery, Philadelphia, 93 & Queens Mus Art, 95; Committed to Print, Mus Mod Art, NY, 88; Philadelphia Print Club Invitational, Pa, 89; At the Intersection of Cinema & the Book, Granary Books Gallery, NY, 92; Mostra da Gravura Mostra Am, Curitiba, Brazil, 92; Contacts/Proofs, Jersey City Mus, 93; Academic Spirit, NY State Mus, Albany, 93; La Disparition de L'Alphabet (with catalog), Galerie Toner, Paris, 94; Site Readings, Granary Books Gallery, NY, 94; Gallery, NY, 94. *Teaching:* Instr, Pratt Graphics Ctr, New York, 72-79 & Parsons Sch Design, New York, 75-78; prof visual arts, State Univ NY, Purchase, 78-. *Awards:* NY State Coun Arts Individual Artist Support Grant, 86; John Simon Guggenheim Fel, 87; Arts Int Grant, Queens Mus, 94. *Bibliog:* Artists of conscience, Art News, 4/92; Nancy Princenthal (auth), Cinematic books, Artist's Book Beat, Print Collector's Newslett, Vol XXV, No 4, 9-10/94; Christine J Russo (auth), Afterimage, 10/94. *Mem:* Col Art Asn. *Media:* Projection Installation; Mixed Media. *Publ:* Auth, Postmodern Currents: Art & Artist in the Age of Electronic Media, UMI Press, 89 & Prentice Hall, 92 & 97; Labyrinth, 91, The Book of Plagues & Paradoxic Mutations; Manifestations, Galerie Toner, Paris; Multiple Worlds: An Int Survey of Artists' Books (exhib catalog), Atlanta Col Art Gallery, Ga, 1-3/94; Art and the Computer, Encyclopedia of Computer Science, 4th ed, Ralston Reilly, London, 2000. *Mailing Add:* 166-04 81st Ave Jamaica NY 11432-1204

LOVELESS, JIM
PAINTER
b Saginaw, Mich, Apr 24, 35. *Study:* DePauw Univ, AB, 57; Ind Univ, MFA, 60. *Work:* Munson-Williams-Proctor Inst, Utica, NY; Gettysburg Col, Pa; Hale & Dorr Law Firm, Boston; Chase Manhattan Bank, NY; Colgate Univ, Hamilton, NY. *Comn:* Portrait, McMaster Divinity Col, Hamilton, Ont. *Exhib:* Munson-Williams-Proctor Inst Ann, Utica; one-man shows, Kalamazoo Col, Mich & Everson Mus, Syracuse, NY, 77 & Gettysburg Col, Pa, 90; New Visions Gallery, Ithaca, NY, 89; Cooperstown Art Asn, NY, 93; and others. *Teaching:* Asst prof studio & art hist, Hope Col, Holland, Mich, 60-64 & Univ Ky, Lexington, 64-66; prof studio & art hist, Colgate Univ, Hamilton, 66-98, prof emer, 98-. *Awards:* Heffner Award, Grand Rapids Mus Art Ann, 62; Yaddo Fel; Millay Colony Fel, 86. *Media:* Watercolor, Acrylic

LOVELL, MARGARETTA MARKLE
HISTORIAN, CURATOR
b Pittsburgh, Pa, 1944. *Study:* Smith Col, BA, 66; Univ Del, MA, 75; Yale Univ, PhD, 80. *Collection Arranged:* American Painting, 1730-1960: A Selection from the Collection of Mr & Mrs John D Rockefeller, 3rd, Nat Mus Western Art, Tokyo, 82; William Morris: The Sanford and Helen Berger Collection, Univ Mus, Univ Calif, Berkeley, 84; Venice: The American View, 1860-1920, Fine Arts Mus San Francisco & Cleveland Mus, 84-85; Celebrating William Morris, Huntington Libr & Art Galleries, Pasadena, Calif, 96-97. *Pos:* cur asst, Yale Univ Art Gallery, 72-75; cur Am Art, Fine Arts Mus San Francisco, 81-85; guest cur, Berkeley Art Mus, 84; guest cur, Huntington Libr Art Galleries, 96-97. *Teaching:* acting instr, hist of art, Yale Univ, 77-81; asst prof, Univ Calif, San Francisco, 81-85; vis assoc prof, Univ Mich, fall 89; asst. prof hist art, Univ Calif, 85-90; Duane A & Virginia S Dittman Prof Am Studies, Coll William & Mary, 90-92; assoc prof hist of art, Univ Calif, Berkeley, 92-2003; vis assoc prof art & archit, Harvard Univ, fall 98; Disting vis prof art & art hist, Stanford Univ, fall 2001; prof hist of art, Univ Calif, Berkeley, 2003-. *Awards:* Ralph Henry Gabriel Prize, Am Studies Asn, 81; Nat Endowment Humanities Res Fel, 89-90; Huntington Libr, R Stanton Avery Disting Fel, 1994-95; Charles Eldredge Prize, Smithsonian Am Art Mus, 2006. *Publ:* A Visitable Past: Views of Venice by American Artists 1860-1915, Univ Chicago Press, 89; Food photography and inverted narratives of desire, Exposure v 34: 1/2 summer 2001; Art in a Season of Revolution: The Artist, the Artisan, and the Patron in Early America, Univ Pa Press, 05. *Mailing Add:* Dept Hist Art - 416 Doe Libr No 6020 Berkeley CA 94720-6020

LOVELL, WHITFIELD M
PAINTER
b New York, NY, 59. *Study:* Cooper Union Sch Art, New York, BFA, 81. *Work:* Metrop Mus Art, NY; Libr Congress, Div Prints & Photographs, Washington, DC; New Sch Soc Res, NY; Ark Arts Ctr Found, Little Rock; Bronx Mus, NY; Nat Mus Am Art, Washington; Seattle Art Mus; Montclair (NJ) Art Mus. *Exhib:* Solo exhibs, Harlem Sch Arts, NY, 87, Jersey City Mus, NJ, 88, Lehman Col Art Gallery, NY, 93, SE Ctr Contemp Art, Winston-Salem, NC, 97, DC Moore Gallery, NY, 97, Andy Warhol Mus, Pittsburgh, Pa, 98 & Univ N Tex Art Gallery, Denton, 99, Neuberger Mus, NY, 2000, DC Moore Gallery, NY, 2000, Studio Mus in Harlem, NY, Rutgers Univ, NJ, 2001, Tubman Mus, Ga, 2001; The Family, Goddard Riverside Ctr, NY, 92; Ctr Fine Arts, Miami, Fla, 92; Allen Mem Art Mus, Oberlin, Ohio, 92; Portraits/Retratos, Intar Gallery, NY, 93; Duke Univ Mus Art, Durham, NC, 93; Current Identities: Recent Painting in the US, traveling, Cuenca Bienal, Equador, 93-96; Page 9: Artists Books Show, 450 Broadway Gallery, NY, 94; Trees, Midtown Payson Galleries, NY, 94; Identity Crisis, Puffin Found, NY, 94; Empowerment: The Art of African Americans, Krasdale Gallery, White Plains, NY, 94; Consecrations; The Spiritual in the Time of AIDS, Mus Contemp Relig Art, St Louis, Mo, 94; The Animal Show, Goddard Riverside Gallery, NY, 94; Resisting Categories, City Without Walls, Newark, NJ, 95; Murder, Wolfson Gallery, Miami Dade Col, Fla, Thread Waxing Space, NY, & Bergamot Station Arts Ctr, Santa Monica, Calif, 95; It's How You Play the Game, Exit Art/First World, NY, 95; African-Am Works from the Permanent Collection, Ark Arts Ctr, Little Rock, 95; Inaugural Exhib, DC Moore Gallery, NY, 95; Starting with Flowers, DC Moore Gallery, NY, 96; Dia de los Muertos, Lawndale Art Ctr, Houston, Tex, 96; Round 3 Installations, Proj Row Houses, Houston, Tex, 96; Nat Drawing Show, Ark Arts Ctr, Little Rock, 96; This is Why We Sing, Atrium Gallery, Morristown, NJ, 97; Real: Figurative Narratives in Contemp African Am Art, Bass Mus Art, Miami Beach, Fla, 97; Havana Biennal, Cuba, 97; An Assessment of Contemp Figuration, David Klein Gallery, Birmingham, Mich, 97; Major African-Am Artwork Exhib, Craven Gallery, W Tisbury, Mass, 98; Food For Thought: A visual Banquet, DC Moore Gallery, NY, 98; Urban Mythologies: The Bronx Represented Since the 1960s, Bronx Mus Arts, NY, 99; Soho 20, NY; Yale Univ Art Gallery, 2000; Meguro Mus, Tokyo, 2001; DC Moore Gallery, 2006. *Awards:* Mid-Atlantic Nat Endowment Arts Regional Fel, 92; Andy Warhol Mus Residency, 98; Artist-in-Residence, Univ N Tex, Denton, 99. *Bibliog:* Sallie Gaines (auth), Rundown row houses as art, San Francisco Examiner, 4/28/96; Joel Weinstein (auth.) Sculpture, 2001; Eduardo Costa (auth), Report from Havanna: the installation biennial, Art Am, 3/98; Cynthia Nadelman (auth.) Art News, 2000; Princenthal, Nancy (auth.) A World in One Room, Art in America, 2001. *Mem:* Nat Acad. *Publ:* Auth, The Bronx Celebrates Whitfield Lovell (exhib catalog), Lehman Col Art Gallery, New York, 93. *Dealer:* DC Moore Gallery 724 5th Ave New York NY 10019. *Mailing Add:* 405 E 13th St Apt 3 New York NY 10009

LOVING, CHARLES R
MUSEUM DIRECTOR, CURATOR
b Waukesha, Wis, Jun 2, 57. *Study:* Univ Wis, BFA, 80; Univ Utah, MFA, 82; Univ Utah, MA, 85. *Pos:* Asst coordr, Utah Arts Coun, Salt Lake City, 82-84; asst dir, Utah Mus of Fine Arts, 84-; juror, Park City (Utah) Arts Festival, 85-90; grants reviewer, Inst Mus Serv's, Wash, 88-89; dir, cur, Snite Mus Art, Univ Notre Dame, modern sculpture, 99-. *Mem:* Am Asn Mus (state rep, currently); Utah Fundraising Soc. *Mailing Add:* U Notre Dame Snite Mus Art PO Box 368 Notre Dame IN 46556

LOVING, RICHARD MARIS
PAINTER, PRINTMAKER
b Vienna, Austria, 24. *Study:* Fieldston Sch, Riverdale, NY, 39-42; Bard Col, Annandale, NY, 43-44; New Sch Soc Res, 46. *Work:* Art Inst Chicago; Joslyn Art Mus, Omaha, Nebr; First Nat Bank Chicago; Kemper Art Collection, Chicago; Mus Contemp Art, Chicago; Block Mus, Evanston, Ill; Smart Mus, Univ Chicago, Ill. *Comn:* Enamel triptych, Concordia Col, River Forest, Ill, 67; enamel & stainless wire, Graver Water Conditioning, Union, NJ, 68; vitreous enamel mural, Union Tank Car Corp, Chicago, 70. *Exhib:* Collector's Choice Exhib, Joslyn Art Mus, Omaha, Nebr, 68; Contemp Art in Midwest, Univ Notre Dame, 69; Karlsruhe-Chicago, Karlsruhe, WGer, 79; Chicago; Some Other Traditions, 83-85; Traveling Exhib, Abstract-Symbol-Image, Ill Arts Coun; Lerner Heller Gallery, NY, 82; Printworks Gallery, Chicago, Ill, 2003; Nat Acad Mus, NY, 2006. *Pos:* Founding ed, Chicago-Art-Write. *Teaching:* Prof painting & drawing, Sch Art Inst Chicago, 63-; Prof emer, Sch Art Inst, Chicago. *Awards:* Nat Endowment Arts Fel. *Media:* Oil on Canvas or Wood Panel, Vitreous enamel paintings, Printkaing, Drawing. *Dealer:* Print Works Gallery Chicago. *Mailing Add:* 1857 W Armitage Ave Chicago IL 60622

LOWE, HARRY
ADMINISTRATOR, DESIGNER
b Opelika, Ala, Apr 9, 22. *Study:* Auburn Univ, BA, 43, MFA, 49; Cranbrook Acad Art, 51 & 53. *Collection Arranged:* Stuart Davis Memorial, Nat Collection Fine Arts, Washington, DC, Art Inst Chicago, Univ Calif Art Galleries, Los Angeles & Whitney Mus Am Art, New York, 65; Deputy Commissioner, US Exhib, Venice Biennale, 66; The Charles Sheeler Exhibition, Nat Mus Am Art, Philadelphia Mus Art & Whitney Mus Am Art, 69. *Pos:* Dir, Tenn Fine Arts Ctr, Nashville, 59-64; cur, Dept Exhib & Design, Nat Mus Am Art, 64-72, asst dir opers, 72-74, asst dir, 74-81, acting dir, 81-82, deputy dir, 82-84, deputy dir emer, 84. *Teaching:* Prof art, Auburn Univ, 49-59; fac, Sem for Hist Adminrs, Williamsburg, Va, 65, 67-71. *Mailing Add:* 802 A St SE Washington DC 20003

LOWE, J MICHAEL
SCULPTOR, EDUCATOR
b Cincinnati, Ohio, 42. *Study:* Ohio Univ, BFA; Cornell Univ, MFA. *Work:* Butler Inst Am Art, Ohio; State Univ NY Col Potsdam; Cornell Univ; St Lawrence Univ, NY; Tyler Mus, Tex. *Comn:* St Lawrence Univ, 85. *Exhib:* San Diego Art Inst, Calif, 87 & 90; San Bernardino Co Mus, Calif, 89; NE Mo State Univ, 96 & 98; Lafayette Art Asn, La, 98; NW Art Ctr, NDak, 98; Art Forms Gallery, Manyunk, Pa, 99; Annual Drawing & Small Sculpture Show, Del Mar Col, Corpus Christi, Tex, 2000, 04, 05 & 06; Schweinfurth Mem Art Ctr, Auburn, NY, 2001, 02, 04 & 05; Studio, Middleburg, Va, 2004; Meadows Gallery, Denton, TX, 2006; Foothills Art Ctr, Golden, CO, 2006. *Teaching:* Instr fine arts, St Lawrence Univ, 66-67, asst prof, 67-72, chmn dept, 71-87, assoc prof, 72-78, prof, 78-, GL Flint prof, 97-2004; prof Emer, GL Flint, 2004. *Awards:* Purchase Awards, Tyler Mus Art, 70, Butler Inst Am Art, 72, Clinton Co Govt Bldg, 76 & Sculpture, Delmare Col, 2005; Second Award Sculpture, Cooperstown Art Asn, 91; Heymann Assoc Award, Lafayette Art Asn, 98; MacFadden-Dier Award, No Country Regional Exhib, NY, 2001. *Bibliog:* Dictionary of American Sculptors: 18th Century to the Present, Apollo Press. *Mem:* Int Sculpture Ctr. *Media:* Welded Metal. *Mailing Add:* 315 Blackstone Ave Ithaca NY 14850

LOWE, JOE HING
PAINTER, PASTEL
b Guangdong, China, July 13, 33. *Study:* with Bill Lawrence - 1957; with Lajos Markos - 1960; with Daniel Greene - 1962. *Work:* Univ Texas at Dallas, Tex; Union Co College, Cranford, NJ; US Navy Combat Artist Gallery, Washington, DC; Guangdong Mus of Art, Guangzhou, China; The Institute Mus of Chicago, Ill. *Comn:* Charles Rosendahl (portrait), comn by Vice Adm Charles Rosendahl, Lakehurst, NJ; Arleigh Burke (portrait), comn by Adm Arleigh Burke, Washington, DC, 1969; Hon Mark A Constantino (portrait), comn by Hon Mark A Constantino, Brooklyn, NY, 1975; George Barrowclough, comn by Dr & Mrs. Keith Brodie, Durham, NC, 2004; Dr. Robert Goldman (portrait), comn by Dr. Robert Goldman, Chicago, Ill, 2006. *Exhib:* Joe Hing Lowe Nostalgic Sentiments, Guangdong Mus of Art Guangzhou,

China, 2002; Allied Artists of Am, Museum of Texas Tech Univ, Lubbock, Tex, 2003; Allied Artists of Am, Huntsville Mus of Art, Huntsville, Ala, 2004; Allied Artists of Am, Bergstrom-Mahler Mus, Neenah, Wis, 2004; Allied Artists of Am, Danville Mus of Fine Art, Danville, Va, 2004. *Teaching:* instr oil & pastels, portait/figure, Ridgewood Art Inst, Ridgewood, NJ, 1980-. *Awards:* Exceptional Merit, Pastel Soc of Am, Kalikow Award, 1989; Award for Excellence, Allied Artists of Am, Dianne B. Bernhard, 2001; Award for Excellence, Hudson Valley Art Asn, Dianne B. Barnhard, 2002; Portrait Award, Pastel Soc of Am, 2004. *Bibliog:* Kristina Feliciano (auth), The Best of Pastel 2, Quarry-Rockport Publishers Inc, 1998. *Media:* Charcoal, Oil, Pastel Painting, Watercolor. *Publ:* auth, How to Paint Portrait in Pastel, Watson Guptill, 1972 & 1976. *Mailing Add:* 36 Greaves Pl Cranford NJ 07016

LOWE, MARVIN
PAINTER, PRINTMAKER
b Brooklyn, NY, May 19, 27. *Study:* Juilliard Sch; Brooklyn Col, BA, 54; Univ Iowa, MFA, 60. *Work:* Philadelphia Mus Art; Brooklyn Mus; NY City Publ Libr; Nat Collection Fine Art, Smithsonian Inst; Columbia Univ; and 88 others in USA & foreign countries. *Comn:* Paintings, Purdue Univ, West Lafayette, Ind, 90. *Exhib:* Libr Cong, 60, 62 & 65; Mus Mod Art, NY, 65; Brooklyn Mus, 67; Philadelphia Mus Art, Nat Print Exhib, 68 & 72; Two-person show, Am Embassy, Ankara, Turkey, 74; Solo exhibs, Weyhe Gallery, NY, 76, Zriny Gallery, Chicago, 77-83, Jean Albano Gallery, Chicago, 92, Printworks Ltd, Chicago, 87 & Purdue Univ, 88; Indianapolis Mus Art, 82-83; Kunstzentrum, Glende/Reinbek, Fed Repub Ger, 88; Privatgalerie Plewisast, Hamburg, Fed Repub Ger, 88; and 53 other one-person shows. *Teaching:* Prof fine arts & printmaking, Hope Sch Fine Arts, Ind Univ, 68-91, emer prof, 91-. *Awards:* Paul Sach Mem Purchase Prize, 61; Lessing J Rosenwald Purchase Prize, Philadelphia Mus 66; Fel, Nat Endowment Arts Artists Award, 75; and others. *Bibliog:* Thelma Newman (auth), Innovative printmaking, Crown Publ, 75; article in Print Collector's Newsletter, 7-8/83; American Artists, New York Art Review & Chicago Art Review, Am References Publ, 89; Thelma Newman (auth), Experimental Printmaking. *Media:* Acrylic; All Media. *Dealer:* Printworks Ltd W Superior St Chicago IL 60610; Privat Galerie Hamburg Ger. *Mailing Add:* 535 E Deone Cir Tucson AZ 85704-6923

LOWE, SARAH
CURATOR, WRITER
b Buffalo, NY, 56. *Study:* Vassar Col, Poughkeepsie, NY, BA, 80; Grad Sch & Univ Ctr, City Univ New York, MPhil(dissertation fel), 89 & PhD, 96 & studied hist with Linda Nochlin, 96. *Collection Arranged:* Consuelo Kanaga: An American Photographer (catalog), Brooklyn Mus, 93; Social Studies/Public Monuments, Ctr Photog Woodstock, NY, 93; Tina Modotti: Photographs (catalog), Philadelphia Mus Art, 95; Tina Modotti and Edward Weston: The Mexico Experience, Barbican Galleries, London, England, 2003. *Pos:* Mem bd dir, Lower E Side Printshop, NY, 95-97; co-chmn, Coll Art Asn Panel, Exile, Expatriation, and Relocation: Artists and Writers in Mexico, 1910-1950, Los Angeles, 99. *Teaching:* Adj asst prof, Hunter Col, City Univ, NY; BA & MA adv, Gallatin Sch, NY Univ. *Awards:* Dept Fel (PhD prog art hist), Grad Sch & Univ Ctr, City Univ NY, 84 & 85; Eliza Buffington Fel Grad Res, Vassar Col, Poughkeepsie, NY, 87; Kristie A Jayne Fel (PhD prog art hist), Grad Sch, City Univ NY, 92. *Mem:* Art Table Inc; Col Art Asn; Latin Am Art Asn; Women Writing Women's Lives. *Res:* European, American and Latin American art of the 19th and 20th centuries; history of photography; printmaking and works on paper; feminist theory and criticism; contemporary art; Italian Renaissance art. *Publ:* Auth, The House that Jack Built: The Politics of Domesticity (exhib catalog), Foreman Gallery, Hartwick Col, Oneonta, NY, 87; Frida Kahlo, Universe Books, NY, 91; Fixing form: The still lifes of Tina Modotti, Hist Photog, Vol 10, No 3, fall 94; guest ed, Hist Photog, 9/94; contribr, The Diary of Frida Kahlo, Harry N Abrams, New York, 95; Itinera, IIR Gallery, New York, 12/2002; Edward Weston: Life Work, Lodima Press, 2003. *Mailing Add:* 497 Pacific St No 4A Brooklyn NY 11217

LOWE, TRUMAN T
EDUCATOR, SCULPTOR
Study: Univ Wis, La Crosse, BS(art educ), 69; Univ Wis, Madison, Ford Found Doctoral Fel, 71-73, MFA(sculpture), 73. *Work:* Minn Percent Art; Ohio Arts Coun, Columbus; Eiteljorg Mus, Indianapolis; Denver Art Mus; Tucson Mus Art, Ariz. *Comn:* Ohio Art Coun, Columbus, 92; Eiteljorg Mus, Indianapolis, 94; Denver Art Mus, Colorado, 95; Tucson Mus Art, Ariz, 96; Native Am Sculpture, White House Sculpture Lawn, Washington, DC, sponsored by the Heard Mus, Phoenix, Ariz, 97. *Exhib:* Milwaukee Art Mus, 85; solo exhibs, Cardinal Stritch Col, Milwaukee, Wis, 93, Eiteljorg Mus Am Indian & Western Art, Indianapolis, 94, McMurray Col, Franksville, Ill, 95, Jan Cicero Gallery Exhib, Chicago, 95, Eagle Gallery, Price Doyle Fine Arts Ctr, Murrary State Univ, Ky, 96, UWM Art Mus, Univ Wis-Milwaukee, 97 & Ma-Shu, Jan Cicero Gallery, Chicago, Ill, 97; Nat Gallery Can, Ottawa, 92; Minneapolis Mus Art, 96; Native Streams, Ind State Univ, Terre Haute, 96; Shared Visions, Auckland & Wellington, NZ; Mississippi River, 10 States, 10 Artists, Memphis Col Art, Tenn, 96; Gifts of the Spirit, Peabody Essex Mus, Salem, Mass, 96; Watershed, Minneapolis Mus Art, Minn, 96; Native Streams, traveling exhib organized by Jan Cicero Gallery, Chicago, Ill, 96-97. *Pos:* Consultant for many programs, schs & councils, 79-93; cur, contemp art, Nat Mus Am Indian, 00-. *Teaching:* Vis lectr art, Emporia State Univ, Kans, 73-74; asst dean & coordr multi-cult prog, Univ Wis, Madison, 74-75, coodr, Native Am Studies prog, 75-88, asst prof, 75-84, assoc prof, 84-89, prof, 89-; Var lectures, workshops & confs at schs & universities, 80-96; served on var comts, bds & couns at Univ Wis, Madison, 82-; prof Univ Wis, Madison, 89-. *Awards:* Chancellor's Develop Grant, 91; Individual fel, Nat Endowment Arts, 94-95; Grad Sch Res Grants, Univ Wis, Madison, 95-96 & 96-97. *Bibliog:* Mary Abbe (auth), Two exhibits confront the elements, Star Tribune, St Paul, Minn, 6/15/96; Anne Pizey (auth), Native American roundtable, Daily Planet, Tellvride, Colo, 7/31/96; Robertson & McDaniel (auths), Truman Lowe, emerging sculptor, Sculpture, 9/96. *Dealer:* Jan Cicero Gallery 221 W Erie Chicago IL 60610. *Mailing Add:* 6101 Hawser Rd Madison WI 53705

LOWENTHAL, CONSTANCE
HISTORIAN
b New York, NY, Aug 29, 45. *Study:* Brandeis Univ, BA, 67; Inst Fine Arts, NY Univ, AM, 69, PhD, 76. *Pos:* Asst mus educator, Metrop Mus Art, NY, 78-85; exec dir, Int Found Art Res, NY, 85-98; bd dir, Int Art & Antiques Loss Register, Ltd, Ctr Educ Studies, 91-95; writer, Art Crime Update, Wall Street J, 88-97; dir, Comn Art Recovery, World Jewish Cong, 98-01; pres, Constance Lowenthal, Inc, 2000-; consultant art ownership disputes, NY City, 2001. *Teaching:* Fac mem art hist, Sarah Lawrence Col, Bronxville, 75-78. *Publ:* Auth, Lorenzo Ghiberti, Encycl Britannica 3, 74; Conrat Meit's Judith and a Putto at Brou, Marsyas, 74; Conrat Meit's Busts of Philibert le Beau, Festschrift Yvonne Hackenbroch, 83; Rev of Limewood Sculptors of Renaissance Germany, M Baxandall (auth), Renaissance Quart, 83

LOWNEY, BRUCE STARK
PAINTER, PRINTMAKER
b Los Angeles, Calif, Oct 16, 37. *Study:* NTex State Univ, BA; San Francisco State Univ, MA; Univ NMex, asst to Garo Antreasian; Tamarind Lithography Workshop. *Work:* Minneapolis Inst Art; Art Inst Chicago; Art Mus Univ NMex, Albuquerque; Oklahoma City Art Ctr; Libr Cong Collection, Washington; Mus Fine Arts, Santa Fe, NMex. *Exhib:* Whitney Mus Am Art Print Exhib, NY, 70; One-man shows, Martha Jackson Gallery, NY, 71, Hills Gallery, Santa Fe, 73 & Univ NDak, Grand Forks, 74; 23rd Nat Exhib Prints, Libr Cong, 73; and others. *Teaching:* Instr, Minneapolis Col Art & Design, Fort Lewis Col, Univ NMex & Univ Tex, Austin, formerly. *Awards:* Louis Comfort Tiffany Found Graphics Art Award, 69; Nat Endowment Arts Grant, 74; Western States Arts Found fel, 79; and others. *Bibliog:* Artists of 20th century New Mexico, Mus Fine Arts, Santa Fe, 92; Mary Carroll Nelson (auth), Artists of the Spirit, Arcus Publ, Sonoma, Calif, 94. *Media:* Oil, Lithography. *Publ:* Tamarind: Forty Years, Devon, U NMex Press, 2000; Printmaking in New Mexico 1960-1990, Clinton Adams (auth), Univ NMex Press, 1992. *Dealer:* Hirsch Fine Arts 3940 Loquat Ave Miami 33133; Robischon Gallery 1740 Wazee St Denver CO 80202. *Mailing Add:* 800 Oso Ridge Rte Grants NM 87020

LOWRY, GLENN D
MUSEUM DIRECTOR
b New York, NY, Sept 28, 54. *Study:* Williams Col, BA (magna cum laude), 76; Havard Univ, MA, 78, PhD (For Lang Area Studies Fel, 78 & 79, travel grants, 80 & 81) 82. *Hon Degrees:* PhD Fine Arts, Pennsylvania Academy of Fine Arts, 2000. *Collection Arranged:* From Concept to Context: Approaches to Asian & Islamic Calligraphy (coauth, catalog), Freer Gallery Art, Smithsonian Inst, 86; A Jeweler's Eye: Islamic Arts of the Book from the Vever Collection (coauth, catalog), Arthur M Sackler Gallery, Smithsonian Inst, 88; Timur & Princely Vision: Persian Art & Culture in the Fifteenth Century (coauth, catalog), Arthur M Sackler Gallery, Smithsonian Inst & Los Angeles Co Mus Art, Calif, 89; Variations on a Script: Islamic Calligraphy from the Vever Collection, Arthur M Sackler Gallery, Smithsonian Inst, 90. *Pos:* Res asst, Clark Inst, 76, Archeol Survey, Amalfi, Italy, 80; researcher, Islamic Collection, McGill Univ, 76-77; asst cur, Islamic Art, Fogg Art Mus, Cambridge, Mass, 78-80; cur, Oriental Art, Mus Art, RI Sch Design, 81-82; dir, Joseph & Margaret Muscarelle Mus Art, 82-84; cur, Near Eastern Art & coordr, Curatorial Dept, Arthur M Sackler Gallery & Freer Gallery Art, Smithsonian Inst, 84-90; dir, Art Gallery of Ontario, Toronto, 90-95; dir, Mus Mod Art, New York, 95-. *Teaching:* Instr, Wellesley Col, 81; Andrew S Keck vis prof, Am Univ, 90. *Awards:* Naumburg Book Award, Williams Col, 75, Karl E Weston Prize for Distinction in the Arts, 76; Spec Exhib Fund Award for Timur & Princely Vision, Smithsonian Inst, 87, Scholarly Studies Award, 90; Chevalier de L'ordre de Merite Arts and Letters, Fr Govt, 94. *Mem:* Asn Art Mus Dirs; Can Asn Mus Dirs. *Publ:* Auth, The house of Timur, Asian Art, Vol 2, No 2, 89; Humayun's tomb: Form, function and meaning in early Mughdal architecture, Muqarnas, Vol 4, 87; Fatehpur-Sikri-urban structures and forms, In: Proceedings to the International Symposium on Fatehpur-Sikri, Marg Publ, 87; Art of the Ancient Near East In: Asian Art in the Arthur M Sackler Gallery, 87; Iskandar Mirza and Early Timurid metalware, Orientations, 9/86. *Mailing Add:* Mus Mod Art 11 W 53rd St New York NY 10019-5496

LOWRY, NICHOLAS D
APPRAISER
b NY, 68. *Study:* Cornell Univ, BA(art hist), 90. *Pos:* Journalist, dir, poster dept, Swann Galleries, New York City, 95-; pres, principal auctioneer, 2001—; appraiser, Antiques Roadshow, WGBH-PBS, currently. *Teaching:* Teacher Eng, Prague, formerly. *Awards:* Named one of 100 Most Eligible Bachelors, Gotham Mag, 2004. *Mailing Add:* Swann Galleries 104 E 25th St New York NY 10010

LOY, JOHN SHERIDAN
PAINTER
b St Louis, Mo, Nov 4, 30. *Study:* Colorado Springs Fine Art Ctr, Colo; Wash Univ Sch Fine Arts, BFA, 54; Cranbrook Acad Art, Bloomfield Hills, Mich, MFA, 58. *Work:* Munson-Williams-Proctor Inst, Utica, NY; Utica Col, NY; Lincoln-Rochester Bank Collection, Rochester, NY; Hayes Nat Bank, Clinton, NY; Savings Bank Utica. *Exhib:* solo exhib, Kirkland Art Ctr, Clinton, NY, 92, Bonsack Gallery, St Louis, 98 &Gallery 15, Rochester, NY, 02; Cooperstown Art Asn Ann, NY, 95; Albany Inst Hist & Art Regional, NY, 96; Cazenovia Col, Cazenovia, NY, 97; Retrospective exhib, Kirkland Art Ctr, Clinton, 2005. *Pos:* Prog dir, Peoples Art Ctr, St Louis, 59; gallery dir, Munson-Williams-Proctor Inst Sch Art, Utica, NY, 78-86. *Teaching:* Instr drawing, Wash Univ, 59; instr drawing & painting, Munson-Williams-Proctor Inst, 60-91; instr drawing, Hamilton Col, 92. *Awards:* First Painting Prize, Cooperstown Art Asn, 71, 74, 76 & 77; Grand Prize, Cooperstown Art Asn, 83; Residency, Cite Int des Arts, Paris, 91. *Media:* Oil. *Mailing Add:* 13 Fountain St Clinton NY 13323

LOZOYA, AGUSTIN PORTILLO
PAINTER
b Mexico City, Mex, Nov 29, 60. *Work:* Mus Raly, Montevideo, Uruguay; Mus de Arte Contemporaneo de Monterrey, Nuevo Leon; Mus de Chopo, Galeria Arvil & Oscar Roman, DF, Mex. *Exhib:* Clasisismo en Mexico, Centro Cult Arte Cont, Mexico City, 90; Recauderias e Inhumanidades, Mus del Chopo, Mexico City, 90; 100 Pintores Mexicanos (with catalog), Mus de Arte Contemporaneo de Monterrey, NL Monterrey, 93; Autorretrato Anos 90, Mus de Arte Moderno, Mexico City, 96; The Richness of Diversity, Susquehanna Art Mus, Pa, 97. *Awards:* Fund for Artist Colonies, Mid Am Arts Alliance, 88; Intercambio de Residencias, Fonca, Mex, Nat Endowment Arts & Can Coun, 94. *Bibliog:* Luis Carlos Eherich (auth), Figuraciones y Desfiguros, Ed Diana, 89; various auths, Nueva Plastica Mexicana, Attame Ed, 97. *Mailing Add:* 3a De Guayaquil No 40 Frac Las Americas Naucalpan 53040 Mexico

LUBECK, GERALD LOUIS
PAINTER, PRINTMAKER
b Long Branch, NY, 42. *Study:* Nat Acad Design, NY, 61; studied with Maxwell S Simpson, Lajos Markos, Jonathan Talbot & Gerald Fried. *Work:* Franklin Mint Corp, Pa; Am Stock Exchange, NY; Sloanne Kettering Inst, NY; New Mus, NJ. *Exhib:* Greenwich Workshop; Salmagundi Club, NY; Gallery One, Mentor, Ohio, 94-2000; Solo exhib, Tilting at Windmills Gallery, Manchester, Vt, 80-2001. *Awards:* First prize, oils, Miniature Art Soc Fla; first prize, animal painting, NJ Miniature Art Soc; Best in Show, Wash Sq Outdoor Art Soc, NY, 73. *Mem:* Salmagundi Club, NY; Allied Artists Am, NY; Hudson Valley Art Asn; Miniature Art Soc Fla. *Media:* Oil. *Specialty:* Landscapes, still lifes & animals. *Mailing Add:* RT 346 PO Box 51 North Pownal VT 05260

LUBELL, ELLEN
CRITIC, WRITER
b Brooklyn, NY, Apr 7, 50. *Study:* State Univ NY at Stony Brook, with Lawrence Alloway, BA, 71. *Pos:* Contrib ed, Arts Mag, 72-79; dir, Landmark Gallery, NY, 73-75; ed/publ, Womanart Mag, Brooklyn, 76-78; art critic, Soho Weekly News, NY, 77-79; free lance contribr, Art Am, 81-84; art critic, Village Voice, NY, 84-91; free lance contribr, Newsday, 88-91; dir community, Inform, NY, 91-95, Child Care Action Campaign, NY, 95-99; free lance contribr, Newark Star-Ledger, 96-97; dir of Pub relations, The Children's Aid Soc, 99. *Teaching:* Instr art criticism & art journalism, Sch Visual Arts, NY, 79-80. *Awards:* Art Critics Fel, Nat Endowment Arts, 78. *Bibliog:* Corinne Robins (auth), The women's art magazines, Art Criticism, Vol 1, No 2, 79; Cynthia Nadelman (auth), Women artists: Self-images, Art News, 82; Grace Glueck (auth), Private gone public, NY Times, 6/28/85; The Power of Feminist Art 94, Harry N. Abrams, NY; Ed by N Bronde and M D Gaward. *Mem:* Int Asn Art Critics. *Res:* To explore the relationship between fine arts and popular culture and the meaning of this differentiation in contemporary society. *Publ:* Auth, Whatever happened to the women's artist movement, Womanart Mag, 77; Can museums collect contemporary sculpture? Soho Weekly News, 79; Park Slope: An Overview (catalog), Brooklyn Mus, 80; The corporate collector, 84 & Dia Foundation shaken, 85, Village Voice; Politics before culture in the Bronx, 87, Painting by numbers, 88 & Sudden Impasto, 89, Village Voice; Corporations and art: they mean business, 90, Variety; A new gallery scene grows in Chelsea, 97, The Star Ledger

LUCAS, BONNIE LYNN
PAINTER, INSTRUCTOR
b Syracuse, NY, Sept 20, 50. *Study:* Wellesley Col, BA, 72; Rutgers Univ, MFA, 79. *Work:* Zimmerli Art Mus, Rutgers Univ; New York Pub Libr Print Collection. *Comn:* Temple Soc Concord (synagogue), Syracuse, NY, 88; Commissioned Assemblage (To Life). *Exhib:* Solo exhibs, Leverett House, Harvard Univ, 76, Kathryn Markel Gallery, NY, 79 & Avenue B Gallery, NY, 85, 86 & 87, Souyun Yi Gallery, NY, 91 & Edith Blum Gallery, Col of the Atlantic, Bar Harbor, Maine, 94; People 81, Hudson River Mus, Yonkers, NY, 81; Basic Needs, Islip Mus, East Islip, NY, 85; The Doll Show: Artist's Dolls & Figurines, Hillwood Art Gallery, CW Post, Long Island Univ, 85; Tangents: Art in Fiber, Md Inst, Col Art, Baltimore, MD, 87; Frontiers in Fiber: The Americans, NDak Mus Art, 88; Alice and Look who else, Through the looking Glass, Bernice Steinbaum Gallery, NY, 88; Love and Charity: The Tradition of Caritas in Contemp Painting, Sherry French Gallery, NY, 89; Assemblages from the Permanent Collection, Jane Voorhees Zimmerli Art Mus, Rutgers Univ, New Brunswick, NJ, 89; group exhibs, Good-bye to Apple Pie: Contemp Artists View the Family in Crisis, DeCordova Mus, Lincoln, Mass, 92, USA Today, Dutch Textile Mus, Tilburg, The Neth, traveling, 93 & Home is Where the Art is, or, Hybrid Affairs, Nat Arts Club, NY, 96; Bonnie Lucas & Steven Hardy, Gallery Rebolloso, Minneapolis, Minn, 95. *Teaching:* Lectr, Montclair State Col, NJ, 83 & Jane Voorhees Zimmerli Art Mus, Rutgers Univ, 84; vis artist, Appalachian Univ, Boone, NC, 87, Univ Ariz Tempe, 88; Workshop artist, Artpark, Summer, 88, Md Inst Col Art, Baltimore, 92; instr, Parsons Sch Design Continuing Educ, New York, 88-94, Md Inst Col Art, Baltimore, 92; vis artist, Am Acad Rome, 89, Col of the Atlantic, Bar Harbor, Maine, 94, Carleton Col, Northfield, Minn, 95; instr, Art Dept, City Col New York, 96-. *Awards:* Stevens Traveling Fel, Wellesley Col, 89; Grant, Art Matters Inc, 90. *Bibliog:* Joan Marter (auth), Review, Arts Mag, Summer, 87; Michael Brenson (auth), Cosmopolitan Artworks along suburban byways, NY Times, 8/4/89; articles & reviews in var publ. *Media:* Oil, Watercolor. *Mailing Add:* 37 Spring St New York NY 10012-5723

LUCAS, CHARLIE
PAINTER, SCULPTOR
b Pinklily, Ala, 51. *Study:* Self taught. *Work:* Birmingham Airport, Ala. *Exhib:* Outside: Artist from Alabama, Montgomery Mus Fine Art, Ala, 91; Orphans in the Storm, Chatahoochee Valley Art Mus, Lagrange, Ga, 92 & Tucson Mus Art, Ariz, 94; Passionate Visions, New Orleans Mus Art, La, 93. *Pos:* Vis artist, Montgomery Mus Fine Arts & other various institutions. *Bibliog:* Dan Rathers, 60 Minutes, CBS News, 93. *Media:* Metal, Sculpture. *Dealer:* Robert Haardt Gallery. *Mailing Add:* c/o Anton Haardt Gallery 2714 Coliseum St New Orleans LA 36104

LUCAS, CHRISTOPHER
CONCEPTUAL ARTIST
b Durham, NC, Nov 13, 58. *Study:* Yale Summer Sch Music & Art, 79; Kans Univ, BA, 80. *Work:* High Mus Art, Atlanta, Ga; Carnegie Mus Art, Pittsburgh, Pa; Bayer, Pittsburgh, Pa; Chase Manhattan, NY; Prudential Insurance Company of America. *Comn:* Ill-Saw Sculpture Park, Korea, 97. *Exhib:* Solo exhibs, John Good Gallery, NY, 86, 87, 89 & 92, Paolo Baldacci Gallery, NY, 95, Guy McIntyre Gallery, NY, 98 & Mario Diancono Gallery, Boston, 2003; Primal Abstractions, Mario Diancono Gallery, Boston, 92; Galleria Nazionale d'Arte Moderna, San Marino, 93; Spazio Atac, Rome, 96; and others. *Awards:* Fel, Nat Endowment Arts, 87-88; Pollock-Krasner Found, 88; Fulbright Fel, Repub of Korea, 90-91. *Bibliog:* Joshua Decter (auth), Christopher Lucas, Arts Mag, 4/92; Kunie Sugiura (auth), BT-Bijutsu Tecno, Japan, 4/92; Janet Koplos (auth), Christopher Lucas, Art in Am, 6/92. *Media:* Wood, Paint. *Mailing Add:* 315 E Eighth St New York NY 10009-5202

LUCAS, GEORGETTA SNELL
PAINTER
b Harmony, Ind, July 25, 20. *Study:* Ind State Univ, BS, 42; Butler Univ, MS, 64; Ind Univ & John Herron Sch Art, 60-65. *Work:* Ind Univ/Purdue Univ Med Ctr & Indianapolis Public Sch Collection; Ind State Univ Permanent Collection, Terre Haute, Ind; Nat Asn Women Artists; Jane Voorhees Zimmerli Art Mus, Rutgers Univ, NJ. *Comn:* Noah Loading Ark, mural, comn by William Plummer, Frankfurt, Ger, 74; Reflections, memorial oil painting, M S D Perry Admin, Indianapolis, 78; Masonic Lodge No 1-1809, comn by Bridgeport Lodge No 163, Ind, 90. *Exhib:* NY World's Fair, Bourbon St Gallery, La Pavilion, 64; Nat Asn Women Artist traveling show, Fine Arts Acad, Calcutta, India, 65; Nat Asn Women Artist show, Casino Municipale Gallery, Cannes, France, 66; Mid State Exhib, Evansville Mus, Ind, 70; 100th Yr Celebration Show, Nat Asn Women Artists, Jacob Javits Bldg, NY, 89; Nat Biennial 1994 Art Show for Nat League of Am Pen Women, Lincoln Ctr, NY, 94. *Pos:* Ind State Art chmn, Alpha Delta Kappa, 73-77; pres, Ind Artists/Craftsmen Inc, 79-84 & 87-89, Ind Fedn Art Clubs, 86-87; art chmn, Gov Int Platform Asn, 83-2000; Ind State pres, Nat League Am Pen Women, 98. *Teaching:* Inst art, Plainfield City Schs, Ind, 46-49 & 50-52; Metrop Sch Dist of Wayne, Indianapolis, 52-68; Metrop Sch Dist of Perry Twp, Indianapolis, 68-81; lectr, Int Platform Asn, Wash, 75, 77-78, 82 & 84, Art Educators Asn Ind, 76, Prof Educators Ind Conv, 78, Ind Fedn Art Clubs, 88 & Ind Sch Women's Asn, 88. *Awards:* Indiana Artist/Craftsmen, 74; Silver Award, Int Platform Art, 78; Best of Show, Nat League Am Pen Women, 83 & 97 & Ind Fedn, Art Club Exhib, 97. *Bibliog:* Leonidas Smith (auth), Hoosier artist, Indianapolis Star Mag, 8/65; Donald Frick (auth), Batik-Filmstrip-TV Cube, Indianapolis Mus Art, 74; Mary Slayton (auth), Shares love of art, music, The Plainfield Messenger, 5/17/90. *Mem:* Nat Asn Woman Artist; Nat League Am Pen Women (Ind art chmn, 84-96); honorary life mem, Ind Artist/Craftsmen Inc (pres, 79-84 & 87-89); Int Platform Asn (chmn art comt, 86-); honorary life mem Ind Fedn Art Clubs (pres, 85-87); life mem, Ind State Teachers Asn; World Craft Coun. *Media:* Watercolor, Oil. *Publ:* Illusr, Why So Sad, Little Rag Doll?, E C Seale, 63; contribr, Former Harmony resident receives VIP treatment, Brazil Daily Times, 8/3/67; Georgetta Snell Lucas art work presented to ISU, The Tribune, 73; Art teachers to see demonstration, Daily Herald, 3/22/76; cover art, Biennial Issue, Nat League Am Pen Women Mag, 6/94. *Mailing Add:* 6990 E CR 100 N Apt 223 Avon IN 46123-9714

LUCCHESI, BRUNO
SCULPTOR
b Lucca, Italy, July 31, 26; US citizen. *Study:* Inst Arte, Lucca, MFA, 53. *Work:* Pa Acad Fine Arts, Philadelphia; Dallas Mus Fine Arts; Ringling Mus, Sarasota, Fla; Hirshhorn Mus, Washington, DC; Whitney Mus Am Art, NY; and numerous others. *Comn:* Sculpture, Trade Bank, NY, sculpture, Cornell Univ. *Exhib:* Whitney Mus Am Art, NY; Pa Acad Fine Arts; Corcoran Gallery Art, Washington, DC; Nat Inst Arts & Lett; Brooklyn Mus, NY; plus others; Solo exhibs incl Prince Arthur Gallery, Toronto, On, Can, 77, Foster-Harmon Gallery, Sarasota, Fla, 80, 86, Shirlee Raushbach Gallery, Bay Harbor, Fla, 83, Blue Hill Cult Ctr, Pearl River, NY, 84, Casey Gallery, Scottsdale, Ariz, 86. *Teaching:* Instr, Acad Fine Arts, Univ Florence, Italy, 50-57; instr, New Sch Social Res, 60-70; Nat Acad of Design, New York City, 70-80. *Awards:* Watrous Gold Medal, Nat Acad Design, 61; Gold Medal, Nat Arts Club, 63; S F B Morse Medal, Nat Acad Design, 65; Lion of S Marco award Holion Cult Soc, New York City, 81; and others. *Bibliog:* Bruno Lucchesi, Arts Mag, 68, 71, 75; Bronzes Spotlight Exhibitions, New York Herald Tribune, 11/26/61; Bronze Realists, Time, 6/1/70; Michael Brenson (auth), Bruno Lucchesi, New York Times, 2/3/84; Art from Life, New York Times, 11/29/85; Dorothy Adlow (auth), Bruno Lucchesi, Christian Science Monitor, 1/26/62. *Mem:* Sculptors Guild; Artists Equity Asn; Nat Acad; Am Asn Univ Prof. *Publ:* Co-auth (with Margit Malmstrom), Terracotta, Watson-Guptill Pubs, 77; co-auth (with Margit Malmstrom), Modeling the Head in Clay, Watson-Guptill Pubs, 79; co-auth (with Margit Malmstrom), Modeling the Figure in Clay, Watson-Guptill Pubs, 80. *Dealer:* Forum Gallery 745 Fifth Ave New York NY 10151. *Mailing Add:* 30 5th Ave No 4J New York NY 10011-8859

LUCE, C(HARLES) BEARDSLEY
CONCEPTUAL ARTIST
b Phoenix, Ariz, June 15, 47. *Study:* Amherst Col, BA, 69, Univ Wash, MAT, 71. *Work:* The City of Seattle, Seattle Art Mus, Wash; Libr Cong, Washington, DC; Prudential Insurance Co, Newark, NJ; Bell Tel Co & Gen Elec Co, Chicago, Ill; NYNEX, NY; Sackner Archive of Concrete & Visual Poetry, Miami, Fla. *Exhib:* The Cyclonic Collapse of the Teahouse, 78 & Aether House, 79, Seattle Art Mus; Luise Ross, NY, 84; Fuji Art Salon, Tokyo, Japan, 85; Stokker-Stikker Gallery, NY, 86; Gracie Mansion, NY, 90-91; Dessont Saunders, Chicago, 91; Luise Ross, 92, 96, 99; plus others. *Pos:* Dean etymology, Inst Study of Etymological Lessons, NY, 79 & chmn, art dept. *Awards:* Art Matters, 89; John Simon Guggenheim Fel, 91. *Bibliog:* John Paoletti (auth), Charles Luce: Light truths, Arts Mag, 4/82. *Media:* Mixed. *Dealer:* Luise Ross 568 Broadway 4 Flr New York NY 10012. *Mailing Add:* 360 W 36th St 5NW New York NY 10018

LUCERO, MANUEL F
CERAMIST
b San Diego, Calif, May 26, 42. *Study:* San Jose Univ, BA (art), 65, MA(art), 67; San Francisco Art Inst, post-grad study, 92-93. *Work:* Beswick Collection, Los Angeles, Calif; Oakland Art Mus & Antonio Prieto Mem Collection, Mills Col, Oakland, Calif; Ceramic Monthly Collection, Columbus, Ohio. *Comn:* Brian Wash Laundromat, San Francisco. *Exhib:* Solo exhibs, Calif State Univ, Chico, 70 & 75, Univ Nev, Las Vegas, 76; Introductions, Gallery Paule Anglim, San Francisco, Calif, 93; White: 10 in 10, San Francisco Art Inst, Calif, 94; Forecast: Shifts in Direction (with catalog), Mus NMex, Santa Fe, 94; Next to Nothing (with catalog), Ctr Arts at Buena Gardens, San Francisco, 94; La Panaderia, Mex DF, 95; Oakland Mus of Calif, Inst Contemp Art, San Jose, 96; Diego Rivera Gallery, San Francisco, 99. *Teaching:* Prof art, Calif State Univ, Chico, 68-; vis artist & instr, Univ Nev, Las Vegas, 76. *Awards:* Ceramic Monthly Award, 71; Ceramic Int Award, Alberta Col, Calgary, 73; Nat Endowment Arts Fel, 93. *Bibliog:* David Bonetti (auth), Still life, new fife at introductions, San Francisco Examiner, 7/16/93; Kenneth Baker (auth), Next to nothing, San Francisco Chronicle, 9/17/94; Rebecca Solnit (auth), Next to nothing, Art Issues, 11/94. *Dealer:* Gallery Paule Anglim 14 Heary St San Francisco CA 94108. *Mailing Add:* 1417 15th St San Francisco CA 94103

LUCERO, MICHAEL (LEWIS)
SCULPTOR
b Tracy, Calif, Apr 1, 53. *Study:* Humboldt State Univ, Arcata, Calif, BA, 75; Univ Wash, Seattle, MFA, 78. *Work:* Metrop Mus Art, New Mus Contemp Art, NY; Seattle Art Mus; Mus Tamayo, Mexico City; San Francisco Mus Mod Art; Everson Mus, Syracuse, NY; Los Angeles Co Mus of Art. *Comn:* Plaza Las Fuentas, Pasadena, Calif. *Exhib:* solo exhibs, Dorothy Weiss Gallery, San Francisco, 95, Mint Mus, 96, Am Craft Mus, 96, David Beitzel Gallery, NY, 96, Kemper Mus Contemp Art & Design, Kansas City, Mo, 97, Renwick Gallery, Smithsonian Inst, 97 & Carnegie Mus Art, 98, R Duane Reed Gallery, St. Louis, 98, Allene Lapides Gallery, Santa Fe, NMex., 98, David Bietzel Gallery, New York City, 99, Dorothy Weiss Gallery, New York City, 99, Renwick Gallery, Wash, 2001; Ctr for Contemp Art, Seattle, 95; Fay Gold Gallery, Atlanta, 96; Cohen, Berkowitz Gallery, Kansas City, Mo, 97; David Bietzel Gallery, New York City, 99; Art Mus at Fla Int Gallery, 2000; Everson Mus of Art, Syracuse, NY, 2000. *Collection Arranged:* Am Craft Mus, NY; Ark Art Ctr, Little Rock; Carnegie Mus Art, Pittsburgh; Dannheiser Found, NY; First Bank, Minneapolis, Minn; Mint Mus Art, Charolette, NC; The New Mus Contemp, NY; Seattle Art Mus, Wash; Toledo Mus Art, Ohio. *Teaching:* Instr, New York Univ, 79-80 & Parsons Sch Design, 81-82; guest lectr, RI Sch Design, Providence, 79. *Awards:* Ford Found Scholar, Univ Wash, 77-78; Nat Endowment Arts, 79, 81 & 84; Creative Artists Pub Serv Prog Fel, 81; Nettie Marie Jones Fel, Ctr. for Music, Drama, and Art, Lake Placid, NY; NEA fel, 79; Young Am award, Mus Contemp Craft Coun, New York City, 78; Ford Found scholarship, 1977-78. *Bibliog:* William Zimmer (auth), A new figure on the horizon, Am Ceramics, winter issue; The figure; a celebration, Grand Forks Herald, 11/13/81; John Perreault (auth), Good for the figure, Soho News, 12/1/81; Elisa Turner (auth), A Return to Beauty, The Miami Herald, 09/13/2000; Domonique Nahas (auth), American Art Today: Fantasies & Curiosities, Miami Florida International Univ, 2000; Catherine Fox (auth), Celebrating 20 years of Artistic Evolution, The Atlanta Journal-Constitution, 12/31/99; Lizzie Zucker Salt (auth), Manufacturing Validity, Art Papers, 7/99, 8/99. *Dealer:* David Beitzel Gallery 102 Prince St, New York, NY 10012

LUCEY, JACK
PAINTER, EDUCATOR
b San Francisco, Calif, Feb 11, 29. *Study:* Acad Art Col, San Francisco, 55; San Francisco Art Inst, 59; San Francisco State Univ, BA, 76. *Work:* USAF Mus, Nellis, Nev; Naval Aviation Mus, Pensacola, Fla; Hall of Justice Bldg, San Francisco; Trans World Airlines, NY; USAF Artist Prog, Andrews AFB, Washington. *Comn:* Murals of Alaska, Pac Orient Lines, San Francisco, 72; London Illus, Trans World Airlines, NY, 74; Irish Countryside Paintings; Irish Tourist Bd, Dublin, 75; US Coast Guard Aircraft Scene, US Coast Guard Air Sta, San Francisco, 77. *Exhib:* 29th Ann Soc Western Artists, MH De Young Mus, San Francisco; San Francisco Art Festival, Civic Ctr, 76; Zellerbach Invitational, Zellerbach Plaza, San Francisco, 76; Industrial Graphics Int, San Jose, 77; Watercolor Technique, Marin Co Watercolor Soc, Mill Valley, Calif, 77; Third Falkirk Ann, Falkirk Cult Ctr, San Rafael, Calif, 78; one-man show, Agura Art, Collection of 36 paintings and Drawings Representing California Agriculture Today, Calif Mus Design & Industry, Los Angeles, 86. *Collection Arranged:* Veterans Mem Mus, 79; one-man shows, Sport's Art, Zellerbach Art Mus, 80 & Aviation Art, Bohemian Club, San Francisco, Calif, 81. *Pos:* Graphics artist, Shell Oil Co, San Francisco, 52-56; art dir, Independent J, San Rafael, Calif, 56-; courtroom artist, CNN, San Francisco Bureau, ABC-TV, NBC News-TV, KRON TV-4 & KGO TV-7, San Francisco. *Teaching:* Instr illus, Col Marin, 75-; instr art, Acad Art Col, San Francisco, 76-77; instr graphics, Indian Valley Col, Novato, Calif, 78-. *Awards:* First Place Illus, San Jose State Univ, Calif, 77. *Mem:* Col Art Asn; Soc Western Artists; San Francisco Soc Commun Arts; Artists in Print; North Bay Advert Commun. *Media:* Oil, Watercolor. *Publ:* Illusr, The Alamo, Reader's Dig, 73; San Francisco Giants, San Francisco Mag, 78; Chemical facts of life, Standard Oiler Mag, Standard Oil of Calif, 78. *Dealer:* Allport Assoc Gallery 1000 Magnolia Ave Larkspur CA 94939. *Mailing Add:* 84 Crestwood Dr San Rafael CA 94901

LUCHS, ALISON
CURATOR, HISTORIAN
b Washington, DC, Oct 5, 48. *Study:* Vassar Col, Poughkeepsie, NY, BA, 70; Johns Hopkins Univ, Baltimore, PhD, 76. *Collection Arranged:* Early European Sculpture, (permanent collection), 99-2002. *Pos:* Res asst, Ctr Advan Study Visual Arts, Washington, 80-83, asst cur sculpture, 82-89, assoc cur early European sculpture, 89-; cur, Early European Sculpture, 96-. *Teaching:* Asst prof, Swarthmore Col, Pa, 76-77; asst prof, Syracuse Univ, NY, 77-80. *Awards:* Robert H Smith Res Leave Grant, 88 & 98; Ailsa Mellon Bruce Nat Gallery Art Curatorial Sabbatical Fel, Ctr Advan Study History of Arts, 92-93, 2003; Samuel H Kress Found Grant & CAA Millard Meiss Grant, 94-95. *Mem:* Ital Art Soc; Col Art Asn; Renaissance Soc. *Publ:* The Convent of Sta Maria Maddalena de'Pazzi and its Works of Art, Florence, 90-91; Coauth, Western Decorative Arts, Part I, Nat Gallery Art & Cambridge Univ Press, 93; auth, Tullio Lombardo and Ideal Portrait Sculpture in Renaissance Venice, 1490-1530, Cambridge Univ Press, 95; auth, Lorenzo From Life? Renaissance Portrait Busts of Lorenzo de Medici, The Sculpture Jour, 2000; auth, Woman in Anguish, Artibus et, 2003; entries Encyclopedia of Sculpture, 2004. *Mailing Add:* c/o Sculpture Dept Nat Gallery Art 2000B S Club Dr Hyattsville MD 20785

LUCIER, MARY
VIDEO ARTIST, PHOTOGRAPHER
b Bucyrus, Ohio, Jan 25, 44. *Study:* Brandeis Univ, BA, 65. *Work:* Whitney Mus Am Art; Stedelijk Mus, Amsterdam; Nat Gallery, Can; Am Film Inst; San Francisco Mus Mod Art. *Comn:* Equinox (video installation), Grad Ctr, City Univ New York, 79; Planet (video installation), Hudson River Mus, 80; Winter Garden (video installation), Lower Manhattan Cult Coun, NY, 82; Noah's Raven (video installation), Toledo Mus Art, 93; House By the Water, Spoleto, USA, 97; Floodsongs, NDak, Mus Art, 98. *Exhib:* Solo exhibs, Whitney Mus Am Art, 81, 85 & 86, Carnegie Inst, Pittsburgh, 83, Wadsworth Atheneum, Hartford, 86, Dallas Mus Art, 87, Mus Contemp Art, Los Angeles, 88, Greenberg Wilson, NY, 89 & 91 & City Gallery Contemp Art, Raleigh, NC, 91; Biennial Exhib, Whitney Mus Am Art, 83; Mus Mod Art, NY, 83; Walker Art Ctr, Minneapolis, Minn, 87; San Francisco Mus Mod Art, Calif, 88; Kolnischer Kunstverein, Berlin, 89; Hudson River Mus, Yonkers, NY, 90, 2nd Biennale of Nagoya, Japan, 91; Univ Galleries, Ill State Univ, 90; Whitney Mus Am Art, Greenberg Wilson, NY, 91; 2nd Biennale Nagoya, Japan, 91; Ronald Feldman Fine Arts, NY, 92; Lennon Weinberg, Inc, NY, 95 & Mus Mod Art, March-June, 99; Rhona Hoffman, Chicago, 96; and others. *Pos:* Artist-in-residence, WNET Channel 13, NY, 82. *Teaching:* Instr video art, Sch Visual Arts, 79-83, NY Univ, 88-; vis artist, Minneapolis Col Art & Design, 80, Cleveland Inst Art, 82, San Francisco Art Inst, 84, NY Univ, 88-90 & State Univ NY, Purchase, 92. *Awards:* Jerome Found Grant, 82; Media Arts Grant, Nat Endowment Arts, 83; Media Grant, NY State Coun Arts, 83; Guggenheim Mem Found Grant, 90; Anonymous Was A Woman Found, 97; and others. *Bibliog:* John Miller (auth), Mary Lucier, 2/90 & Kirby Gookin (auth), Mary Lucier, 4/91, Artforum; Arlene Raven (auth), Refuse refuge, Village Voice, 1/15/91; Ann-Sargent Wooster (auth), The garden in the machine, Arts Mag, 4/92; Nancy Princeonthal, Mary Lucier At Lennon Leinberg, Art in Am, 97, John Beardsley, Art and Landscape, Spacemaker Press, 98. *Mem:* Media Alliance, NY (bd mem, 81-82); Parabola Arts Found Inc (bd mem & secy, currently). *Publ:* Contribr, Women's Work, Allison Knowles, 75; ed & contribr, Video Art, Harcourt Brace Jovanovich, 76; contribr, Scenarios, Assembling, 80; Illuminating Video, Aperture, 91; Art and Performance: Mary Lucier, Johns Hopkins, 99. *Mailing Add:* 223 W 20th St No 4A New York NY 10011

LUCKNER, KURT T
CURATOR
b Stafford Springs, Conn, Dec 29, 45. *Study:* Georgetown Univ, AB(art hist); Stanford Univ, MA(art hist). *Collection Arranged:* Silver for the Gods: 800 Years of Greek and Roman Silver (int loaned exhib), Toledo Mus Art, Ohio, Nelson Gallery, Kansas City, Mo & Kimball Mus Art, Ft Worth, Tex, 77-78. *Pos:* Asst cur ancient art, Stanford Univ Mus, summer 69; curatorial asst, Toledo Mus Art, Ohio, 69-70, asst cur, 70-73, cur ancient art, 73-. *Mem:* Col Art Asn; Archaeol Inst Am (pres, Toledo Chap, 71-75). *Publ:* Auth, Art of Egypt-part I, Vol 14, No 1 & part II, Vol 15, No 3, Greek vases: Shapes & uses, Vol 15, No 3, African art, Vol 16, No 2 & Greek gold jewlery, Vol 17, No 1, Toledo Mus News. *Mailing Add:* 3452 Kenwood Blvd Toledo OH 43606-2807

LUDMAN, JOAN HURWITZ
WRITER, RESEARCHER
b Brooklyn, NY, Feb 1, 32. *Study:* Barnard Col, BA, 53; C W Post Col, Long Island Univ, MA, 71. *Comn:* essay, Mem Art Gallery, Univ Rochester, NY. *Pos:* Assoc, Mason Fine Prints, Glen Head, NY, 72-86. *Res:* American and European original prints; compiling catalog, Raisonne Paintings of Fairfield Porter. *Publ:* Coauth (with Lauris Mason), Print Reference Sources: A Select Bibliography 18th-20th Centuries, 75, 2nd ed, 79 & The Lithographs of George Bellows: A Catalogue Raisonne, 77, Kraus-Thomson Orgn Ltd; contribr, Cecile Shapiro, auth, Fine Prints: Collecting, Buying and Selling, Harper & Row, 76; co-ed (with Lauris Mason), Print Collector's Quart: An Anthology of Essays on Eminent Printmakers of the World, 77, Kraus-Thomson Orgn Ltd; auth, Fairfield Porter: A Catalogue Raisonne of his Prints, Highland House Publ, Inc, 81; Fairfield Porter: A Catalogue Raisonne of his Paintings, Watercolors and Pastels, Hudson Hills Press, 99. *Mailing Add:* 11758 Grove Ridge Ln Boynton Beach FL 33437

LUDTKE, LAWRENCE MONROE
SCULPTOR
b Houston, Tex, Oct 18, 29. *Study:* Univ Houston, BS; Coppini Acad Fine Art, San Antonio, with Waldine Tauch. *Work:* USAF Acad; Central Intellegence Agency Hq; White House; Pentagon; Lifesize Bronzes, Lyndon B Johnson Libr. *Comn:* Charging Bronze Rams, Johnson & Johnson Inc, San Angelo, Tex, 66; Dr Denton Cooley (bronze bust), St Lukes Hosp, Houston, 69; Eddie Wokecki (bronze bas relief), Rice Univ, Houston, 69; Pieta (bronze group), St Marys Sem, Houston, 74; Fiona O'Donnell (bronze bust), comn by Dr Manus O'Donnell, Houston, 74; works comn by President Ronald Reagan, John Wayne, General Robinson Risner, Maury Maucrick, Robert Kennedy and Martha Mitchell. *Exhib:* Nat Cowboy Hall of Fame. *Teaching:* Scottsdale Artist Sch, 89. *Mem:* Fel Nat Sculpture Soc; Coppini Acad Fine Arts; Royal Acad Brit Sculptors (corresp mem). *Media:* Bronze, Marble. *Mailing Add:* 10127 Whiteside Ln Houston TX 77043-4302

LUDWIG, ALLAN I
PHOTOGRAPHER, ART HISTORIAN
b New York, NY, June 9, 33. *Study:* Yale Univ, with Josef Albers, Charles Seymour, Jr & Erwin R Goodenough, Edmund S Morgan, BFA, 56, MA, 60, Bollingen Found fel, 60-63, PhD, 64. *Work:* Mus Fine Arts, Houston, Tex; Los Angeles Co Mus Art, San Francisco Mus Mod Art; Espace Photographique de Paris; Tokyo Inst Technol; Mus Mod Art, Metrop Mus, NY; Mus Photog Arts, San Diego; Yale Univ Art Gallery; Chrysler Mus, Norfolk, Va; New Orleans Mus Art; Los Angeles County Mus Art, Calif; Center Creative Photog, Tucson, Ariz. *Comn:* Kiyosato Mus of Photographic Arts, Kiyosoto, Japan; The Archives of American Art, Washington, DC; The New Orleans Mus of Art New Orleans, La. *Exhib:* Solo exhibs, Twining Gallery, NY, 87, Shaidai Gallery, Tokyo, Japan, 87, Cepa Gallery, Buffalo, NY, 87, White Columns, NY, 87 & 88, O'Kane Gallery, Houston, Tex, 88, XYZ Gallery, Ghent, Belg, 89, Farideh Cadot Gallery, NY, 88 & 90, Northern Light Gallery, Ariz State Univ, Tempe, 90, Galerie Farideh Cadot, Paris, France, 91, Pamela Auchincloss Gallery, NY, 92 & 94, Gallery 954, Chicago, 94 & Gallery at 777, Los Angeles, 94, Cepa Gallery, Buffalo, 95, Chrysler Mus, Norfolk, 95, Hudson River Mus Westchester, Yonkers, 95, Houston Ctr Photog, 95, Ricco/Maresca Gallery, NY, 99; Group exhibs, Insect Politics, Hallwalls, Buffalo, NY, 90, Animals, Houston Ctr for Photog, Tex, 90, Photog: 1980's Discovery & Invention, Art, 21-90, Basel Switz, 90, Natural History & Formaldehyde Photog, Musee Zoologique de l'Universite Louis Pasteur, Strasbourg, France, 90 & Natur Mus Senchenberg Forschungs Institut, Frankfort, WGer, 91, Ricco-Maresca Gallery, New York, NY, 2000 & 2002, List Gallery, Swarthmore Col, Pa, 2004, Farideh Cadot Gallery, Paris, 2005, Albin D. Kuhn Libr Gallery, Univ Md, 2006; Women Series, New Mus, New York, NY, 93, Parko Gallery, Tokyo, Japan, 93; Narcissism: Artist's Reflect Themselves, Calif Ctr Arts Mus, Escondido, Calif, 95; Rtrospective, Kemper Mus Contemp Art, Kansas City, 96-97, Chrysler Mus, Norfolk, 98, The Mus of photog Helsinici, Fineland, in visible Light, 99; Ricco/Maresca Gallery, NY, 2001-02; Marion Ctr, Col of Santa Fe, Santa Fe NMex, 2001; List Gallery, Swarthmore Col, PA, Extraordinary Bodies; Photographs from the Moiter Mus, 2005. *Collection Arranged:* Repulsion: The Aesthetics of the Grotesque, Alternative Mus, 86. *Pos:* Chmn bd, Alternative Mus, New York, 78-83, mem exec bd, 83-88; dir, Ludwig Portfolios, 81-88. *Teaching:* instr RI Sch of Design, Yale Univ, Dickinson Col, Syracuse Univ. *Awards:* Photog Fel, NJ State Coun Arts, 89-90; Grant, Agfa Corp, 90; Nat Endowment Arts Fel, 91; Am Coun Learned Socs Fel. *Bibliog:* Photography 150 Years: Its Light and Shadow, Col of Art, Nihon Univ, Tokyo Inst Technol, 178, 89; Kunstforum, pp 142-145, 3-4/90; Kath McQuaid (auth), Photo Surrealism, South End News, 2/15/90; Brooks Johnson (auth), Tableau Mort, Bull Chrysler Mus, summer 95; Photography Speaks; 150 Photographers speaks on Their Art, Ed,; Brooks Johnson, Aperture Foundation, 2004, pp 304, 305. *Media:* Installations using Photographs. *Res:* I am currently writing a book on Mummies, mannequins, wax figures, dolls, puppets, automatons and robots. *Publ:* Auth, Graven Images, Wesleyan Univ Press, 66, 75, 99; Holy Land USA, The Clarion, summer 79; Beyond Photography I, II, 81 & 82 & Seeing Is Believing, 12/85-1/86, Alternative Mus; Sermons in Stone, Franco Maria Ricci, 11/84; Repulsion: The Aesthetics of the Grotesque, Alternative Mus, 86. *Mailing Add:* 55 Prince St New York NY 10012-3432

LUDWIG, EVA
SCULPTOR
b Berlin, Ger, May 25, 23; US citizen. *Study:* Greenwich House Pottery, with Lu Duble, 58-62; Sculptor's Workshop, with Harold Castor, 64; Craft Students League, wood sculpture with Domenico Facci, 68; Queens Col, sculpture with Richard Miller, 80-81. *Exhib:* Nonmem Exhib, Nat Sculpture Soc, NY, 72; Ann, 81 & Artist of the Month, 82, Woodstock Guild Craftsmen; Pen & Brush Sculpture Exhib, 86, 87 & 88; Catherine Lorillard Wolfe Art Club Exhib, 88-99; Alliance Queens Artists, 88-95; Solo exhib, Queens Col Art Ctr, 92; and others. *Awards:* Best in Wood, 69 & Bert Wangler Mem Award, 72, Woodstock Guild Craftsmen; First Prize in Sculpture, Cooperstown Art Asn, 71. *Bibliog:* Molding Ideas Into Art, Q C Quad, 5/18/92; B Gogel (auth), Ludwig's Sculptures on Exhibition at Q C Art Center. *Mem:* Catherine Lorillard Wolfe Art Club. *Media:* Wood, Clay. *Mailing Add:* 57-44 164th St Flushing NY 11365

LUEBBERS, LESLIE LAIRD
MUSEUM DIRECTOR, HISTORIAN
Study: Wellesley Col, AB, 67; Johns Hopkins Univ, MA, 69; New York Univ, Inst Fine Arts, MA, 87. *Collection Arranged:* World Print Three, 80 & World Print Four, 83, San Fancisco Mus Mod Art; Am Woodcuts, USIA European Tour, 84-87; Mind & Matter, USIA Asian Tour, 89-92; Carroll Cloar & Art History: Komar & Melamid, Memphis State Univ, 91. *Pos:* Dir, World Print Coun, San Francisco, Calif, 79-84; dir, Int Art Projects, San Francisco & New York, 85-90; dir, Art Mus, Univ Memphis Tenn, 90-. *Mem:* Am Asn Mus; SE Mus Conf; Asn Col & Univ Mus & Galleries (chmn bd). *Res:* Prints: 19th & 20th centuries, contemporary art & architecture. *Publ:* Auth, Mind and Matter: New American Abstraction, USIA/World Print Coun, 90; Jean Fautrier: Prints of the Forties, Print Collector's News Letter, 91; American Abstraction in the 90's & Into the Abstract World (article), Taipei Fine Arts Mus, 92; Jean-Paul Riopelle: Prints and the Legend, Print Collector's News Letter, 92; Documenting the Invisible: European Images of Ottoman Women 1567-1867, Print Collectors Newsletter, 93

LUECKING, STEPHEN JOSEPH
SCULPTOR, EDUCATOR
b Belleville, Ill, Aug 11, 48. *Study:* Quincy Col, Ill, BFA, 70; Bradley Univ, Peoria, Ill, grad study, 71; Miami Univ, Oxford, Ohio, MFA, 73. *Work:* Ill State Mus, Springfield. *Comn:* Miami Sun Reservoir (with Margaret Lanterman), Miami Univ & Nat Endowment Arts, Oxford, Ohio, 80; State Ill, 89, 90, 95 & 96; Upwells, Univ Ill, 90; Caparo Steel, Farrell, Pa, 95; Chem-Life Bldg, Univ Ill. *Exhib:* Ill State Mus, Springfield, 78; Art Inst Chicago, 79; Contemp Arts Ctr, Cincinnati, 80; Chicago Cult Ctr, 81; Rockford Art Mus, 89; Roy Boyd Gallery, Chicago, 90; Mus Contemp Relig Art, 94; Snite Mus, Notre Dame Univ, 96. *Collection Arranged:* Seven Sculptors, 78 & Stuart Court Installations (auth, catalog), 81-82, DePaul Univ; Paul Caponigro & Charles Ross, Archaeoastronomy Am Conf, St John's Col, 79. *Pos:* Reviewer & essayist, New Art Examiner, 86-; Visual Arts Panelist, Ill Arts Coun 87, & 88. *Teaching:* Asst prof, Purdue Univ, West Lafayette, Ind, 74-76; prof, chair, DePaul Univ, Chicago, 76-; vis artist, Sch Art Inst Chicago, 79 & 86. *Awards:* Clussman Prize, Art Inst Chicago, 78; project grants, Ill Arts Coun, 78, 80 & 81; Pougialis Award, Columbia Col, 81. *Bibliog:* Alan Artner (auth), The Nation: Chicago, Art News, summer, 77; Holliday T Day (auth), Chicago Invitational, Art Am, 11/78; Wendy Hoffman-Yuni, article, New Art Examiner, 3/79. *Media:* Steel, Iron. *Publ:* Contrib, Sculpture Mag, 89-90; Am Crafts, 90; Am Ceramics, 91-92. *Dealer:* Roy Boyd 215 West Superior Chicago IL 60610. *Mailing Add:* 1934 W Bradley Pl Chicago IL 60613-3614

LUFKIN, MARTHA BG
LAWYER, LEGAL WRITER, ART LAW CORRESPONDENT
b Boston, Mass, May 7, 54. *Study:* Phillips Exeter Acad, Grad, 72; Yale Univ, BA(political Sci, magna cum laude), 76; Oxford (Eng) Univ, MLitt in Politics, 79; Columbia Univ, JD, 82. *Pos:* Collaborateur juridique, Law Offs of SG Archibald, Paris, summer, 81, 82; assoc Shearman & Sterling, New York City, 82-87; Bingham, Dana & Gould, Boston, 87-92; pvt practice, probate, estate settlement, wills and trusts Lincoln, 92-; legal writer, 95-. *Awards:* Sr Scholar Hertford Col, Oxford Univ, 78-79; Harlan Fiske Stone Scholar Columbia Law Sch, 82. *Publ:* Auth, humor column Lincoln J 92— (Humor prize New Eng Press Assoc 96, 97); Alfred Hitchcock Mystery Mag, 95, 97; US legal corr, art law corr The Art Newspaper, 97-; contribr, Art Antiquity and Law, J Cultural Property; written about antitrust investigations of the auction houses Sotheby's and Christie's; claims by Italy and Egypt to recover antiquities looted from their soil; and lawsuits related to Nazi-looted art

LUINO, BERNARDINO
PAINTER
b Latina, Italy, Mar 27, 51. *Study:* Accademia di Belle Arti, Rome & Florence, Italy, MA. *Comn:* Mural, Presso II Centro Incontri Marentino Fiat, Torino, Italy. *Exhib:* Solo exhibs, Galleria Lo Zibetto, 80, Galleria II Fante di Spade, 82, Milan, Italy; Biennale di La Spezia, La Spezia, 80; VII Nat Biennal of Figurative Art, Piacenza; I Int Biennal of Graphic Art, Museo Civico Riva del Garda, Centro Int, della Grafica Venezia, Trento, 82; Grafica Ital Contemporanea, Quadriennale Nazionale d'Arte di Roma, traveled USA and Can, 82; XXIV Biennale Nazionale d'Art, Palazzo della Permanente, Milan, Italy, 89. *Media:* Oil on Panel. *Publ:* Illusr, Luino, Fotolito Savaresi, 85. *Mailing Add:* c/o Gallery Henoch 555 W 25th St New York NY 10001

LUISI, JERRY
SCULPTOR, INSTRUCTOR
b Minneapolis, Minn, Oct 7, 39. *Study:* Nat Acad Design, cert, 68-72; Art Students League. *Work:* NY State Gov Mansion, Albany; Agriculture Hall Fame, Kansas City, Mo; Nat Acad Design, NY. *Comn:* BASF Corp, Parsippany, NJ, 81-83; Armento Archit Arts, Buffalo, NY, 87; Franklin Mint, 88; Medallic Art, 89; Reseal, NY, 89. *Exhib:* Nat Acad Design 70, 74 & 81; Allied Artists Am, 71, 72 & 75; Nat Sculpture Soc, 74-; Mus Fine Arts, Springfield, Mass, 77; Salmagundi Club, 80 & 81; Artists Prof League, NY, 89; and others. *Pos:* Deleg, Fine Arts Fedn, New York, 78-80; ed sculpture, Aristos Mag, 83. *Teaching:* assoc prof, Fine Arts Prog, Fashion Inst Technol, 72- & Nat Acad Design, 79-82. *Awards:* Greenshields Found Grant, 72 & 75; Anna Hyatt Huntington Award, Hudson Valley Art Asn, 80; John Gregory Award, Nat Sculpture Soc, 80; and others. *Bibliog:* Articles, Nat Sculpture Rev, fall 80. *Mem:* Nat Sculpture Soc; Acad Artists Asn; life mem Art Students League; Artists Prof League, New York. *Media:* Clay, Bronze. *Mailing Add:* 36 E 36th St New York NY 10016

LUKAS, DENNIS BRIAN
PAINTER, EDUCATOR
b Hamilton, Ont, June 21, 47. *Study:* St Michael's Sch Cantorum, Toronto, Dipl(ancient music); Doon Sch Fine Art, Ont, with Henri Masson, Carl Schaefer & Tony Onley; McMaster Univ, with Tony Urquhart; Montreal Mus Sch Fine Art, with Arthur Lismer, grad dipl; Atelier 17, Paris, France, with Stanley Hayter. *Work:* Munson-Williams-Proctor Inst, Utica, NY; Art Gallery Hamilton, Ont; Bibliot Nat, Paris; Montreal Mus Fine Arts; Art Gallery Greater Victoria, BC; and many others. *Exhib:* One-man show, Stable Gallery, Montreal Mus Fine Arts, Can, 70; Retrospective Eleven Yrs, McKenzie Gallery, Trent Univ, Peterborough, Ont, 74; Peripheries, Mus d'Art Contemporain, Montreal, 74; Young Contemporaries, Art Gallery of London, Ont, 75; Forum 76, Montreal Mus Fine Arts, 76; On View Visual Arts Ont (touring 14 mus), 76-77; traveling exhib, Ctr Cult, Drummondville, Que, 80;

Gallery 76, Ont Col Art, Toronto, 80; and others. *Teaching:* Instr drawing & painting, Montreal Mus Sch, Que, 71-74; lectr drawing & painting, Univ Toronto, Ont, 75-76; vis asst prof drawing & painting, Hamilton Col, Clinton, NY, 76-78. *Awards:* Can Coun Awards, 67, 68 & 72; Ont Arts Coun Awards, 74-76, 78, 80, 82-84 & 95; AJ Casson Award, Seneca Col, Willowdale, Ont, 78. *Bibliog:* Catharine Bates (auth), article, Montreal Star, 73; David Lehman (auth), Dennis Lukas Recent Work to 1977, Hamilton Col Ed; Andre Dupont & Henri Barras (coauth), Lukas, Ctr Cult, Drummondville, Que, 80. *Mem:* Montreal Mus Fine Arts (gov & benefactor). *Media:* All. *Publ:* Auth, The Role of Education in the Art World (four essays), Niagara Artists Co, 91; The Art of Zaire (essay), Grimsby Pub Art Gallery, 93

LUKASIEWICZ, NANCY BECHTOLD
ADMINISTRATOR, TAPESTRY ARTIST
b Berkeley, Calif, Dec 17, 50. *Study:* Carnegie-Mellon Univ, BFA, 73; Univ Ga, MFA(with hons), with Glen Kaufman, 75. *Work:* Dow Chemical Co, Horgan, Switz. *Comn:* Tapestry, Dow Chemical Co, Midland Mich, 73; 4 panel tapestry, Jaworksi, Athens, Ga, 81. *Exhib:* Fiber Structures Int, Carnegie Mus, Pittsburgh, 75; Regional Invitational, Nexus Contemp Art Ctr, Atlanta, 79; solo exhib, Reece Mus, Johnson City, Tenn, 81; Athens Artists, Savannah Col Art, Ga, 83; Habitat Show I, State Botanical Garden, Athens, Ga, 90. *Pos:* Fiber artist, 69-81; dir, Lyndon House Art Ctr, Athens-Clarke Co, Ga, 77-. *Awards:* Ga Coun Arts Proj Grants, 78-96; Athens Cult Award, Clarke Co, Ga, 88. *Bibliog:* Catherine Fox (auth), Review, Atlanta J Constitution, 79; Focus women, Athens Banner-Herald, 94. *Mem:* Handweavers Guild Am; Ga Mountain Crafts; Ga Asn Mus & Galleries. *Publ:* Auth, Directory of Resources Georgia Handweavers, Ga Coun Arts, 78. *Mailing Add:* 350 Belmont Rd Athens GA 30605-4904

LUKASIEWICZ, RONALD JOSEPH
PRINTMAKER, ADMINISTRATOR
b Pittsburgh, Pa, Apr 20, 43. *Study:* Carnegie-Mellon Univ, BFA; Univ Ga, MFA. *Work:* Pittsburgh Pub Schs, Pa; Dow Chemical Co, Midland, Mich; City of Athens, Ga; Bankers Trust Co, NC; and others. *Comn:* Suite of serigraphs, 73 & bound book of serigraphs, 73, Dow Chemical Co, Midland, Mich; modular sculpture, Scorpio Rising Workshop, Farmington, Ga, 73; modular sculpture, City of Athens, Ga, 77; suite of serigraphs, Thornet Furniture, Dallas, 81. *Exhib:* 10th Ann Piedmont Graphics Exhib, Mint Mus of Art, Charlotte, NC, 73; Assoc Artists Ann Show, Carnegie Mus, Pittsburgh, Pa, 73; Medals, Banners, Ribbons, Pittsburgh Arts & Crafts Ctr, Pa, 74; Ga Nat, Lyndon House Galleries, Athens, 76; Moving Parts & Captured Light, The Third Floor, Atlanta; Spectrum I, Lyndon House Art Ctr, Athens, Ga, 80; Western Carolina Univ, Cullowhee, NC, 81; Corvoll Reese Mus, 86; Color as Theory, Goethe Inst, Atlanta, Ga, 88; and others. *Pos:* Dir cult activities, Athens, Ga, 74-76; preparator, Ga Mus of Art, Univ Ga, 76-87; dir, Climax Press, 83-. *Awards:* Purchase Award, Assoc Artists of Pittsburgh, Pittsburgh Pub Schs, 72; Award, Lyndon House Art Ctr, 81. *Bibliog:* D Miller (auth), Exhibit review, Pittsburgh Post Gazette, 74; J Chappell (producer), Scorpio Rising (16mm film doc), 74; Screen Printing Today, WGTV Television, 74. *Mem:* Col Arts Asn; Asn Artist of Pittsburgh; Athens Art Asn. *Mailing Add:* 350 Belmont Rd Athens GA 30605-4904

LUKE , GREGORIO
MUSEUM DIRECTOR
Pos: Cult Inst Mex, Los Anageles; dir, Mus Latin Am Art, Long Beach, 99-. *Awards:* Recipient Mayoral Citation, Wash, DC, 92; Irving Leonard Award, Hispanic Soc of Libr of Congress, 95; Educ Award, March of Dimes, 2001. *Mailing Add:* Mus Latin Am Art 628 Alamitos Ave Long Beach CA 90802

LUKIN, SVEN
PAINTER
b Riga, Latvia, Feb 14, 34. *Study:* Univ Pa. *Work:* Albright-Knox Art Gallery, Buffalo, NY; Los Angeles Co Mus Art; Larry Aldrich Mus, Ridgefield, Conn; Univ Tex, Austin; Whitney Mus Am Art, NY; and others. *Exhib:* Univ Ill, Urbana, 65; Torcuato di Tella, Buenos Aires, Arg, 65; New shapes of Color, Stedelijk Mus, Amsterdam, The Neth, 66; Univ Colo, Denver, 67; Painting: Out From the Wall, Des Moines Art Ctr, Iowa, 68; New Work, Los Angeles Co Mus Art, 78; Gallery Face, Tokyo, 87; Mus Foreign Art, Riga, Latvia, 87; and others. *Awards:* Guggenheim Fel, 66; Pollock-Krasner Found Grant, 90. *Bibliog:* Sam Hunter (ed), New Art Around the World, Abrams, 66; Allen S Weller (auth), The Joys & Sorrows of Recent American Art, Univ Ill, 68; Gregory Battcock (ed), Minimal Art: a Critical Anthology, Dutton, 68. *Mailing Add:* 807 Ave of the Americas New York NY 10001

LUKKAS, LYNN C
VIDEO ARTIST
b Minneapolis, Minn, May 6, 56. *Study:* U Minn, BFA, 82; RISD, MFA, 88. *Exhib:* When Night Cries, Intermedia Arts Gallery, Minneapolis, Minn, 92; Unter(halt)una, Franklin Furnace Arch, NY, 93; Yield the Body, Walker Art Ctr, 93; WE, Alice Rogers Gallery, St Johns Univ, Collegeville, Minn, 93; When Night Cries, St Johns Univ-Col St Benedict, 94; Through the Body, Weisman Mus Art, Minneapolis, 96; Cleveland Performing Art Festival, 98; McKnight Found Fel Exhibn, Minn, 2000; One City Festival, Capetown, South Africa, 2001. *Teaching:* Asst prof, St Johns Univ, Collegeville, Minn, 88-95; asst prof, media art, time and interactivity, dept art, Univ Minn, 2000-. *Awards:* Jerome Found Travel Study Grant, 93, 2000; Nat Endowment Arts, 93; Minn State Arts Award Fel, 95; Bush Found Fel, 96-97; Women Film Makers Grant Media Artistss Resource Ctr, 96; McKnight Found Fel, 99. *Media:* Video, Electronic Media. *Publ:* Auth, The Oculus Projects, Col Arts Asn Jour, 1/2000

LUM, KEN (KENNETH) ROBERT
CONCEPTUAL ARTIST, PHOTOGRAPHER
b Vancouver, BC, Sept 26, 56. *Study:* Simon Fraser Univ, with Jeff Wall & Ian Wallace, BGS, 80; Univ BC, MFA, 85. *Work:* Kunst Mus Luzern, Luzern, Switz; Mus Boymans-Van Beuningen, Rotterdam, Neth; Stadtische Galerie im Lenbachhaus, Munich, Ger; Frac Bretagne, Frac Loire, France; Nat Gallery Can, Ottawa. *Comn:* Functional sculpture, Art Gallery Ont, Toronto, 94. *Exhib:* Solo exhibs, Kunst Mus Luzerne, Luzern, 91, Badischer Kunstverein, Karlsruhe, 93, Stadtische Galerie im Lenbachhaus, Munich 93, Stills Gallery, Edinburgh, 95, Camden Arts Centre, London, 95 & Frac Haute Normandie, Rouen, 96, Agency Contemp Art, Philip Nelson Gallery, London, 98; Carnegie Int, Carnegie Mus Art, Pittsburgh, Pa, 91; Sydney Biennale, Art Gallery NSW, Sydney, Australia, 92; Johannesburg Biennale, 97; Sao Paulo Biennale, 98. *Teaching:* Asst prof, Univ BC, Vancouver, 90-; guest prof, Kunstakademie, Munich, Ger, 92, L'Ecole des Beaux-Arts, Paris, 94-97. *Awards:* Killam Res Prize, 98; Outstanding Alumni Award, Simon Fraser Univ, 97. *Publ:* Auth, Speculations, Imschoot Ltd, 93. *Dealer:* Andrea Rosen Gallery 130 Prince St New York NY 10012. *Mailing Add:* Dept Fine Arts Univ BC 6333 Memorial Rd Vancouver BC V5T 1Z2 Canada

LUM, MARY
EDUCATOR
Study: Univ Mich, BFA; Rochester Inst Tech, MFA. *Exhib:* Work exhib at, Hallwalls, Buffalo, NY, INTAR Gallery, New York City, Wash Project for the Arts, Washington, DC, Southern Exposure, San Francisco, Art in General, New York City, Buffalo, Kean Col, Union, NJ, Printed Matter, New York City, Ernest Rubenstein Gallery, Univ Wis, Bernard Toale Gallery, Boston, Paris Project Room, 2002, Aldrich Contemp Mus Art, Ridgefield, Conn, 2004. *Teaching:* Mem fac, Sch Art & Design, Albert Univ, NY, 84—2004, prof painting, co-chair MFA prog in electronic integrated arts; mem fac, painting and drawing Bennington Col, Vt, 2005—. *Awards:* Grantee, Nat Endowment for the Arts, NY Found for the Arts, Constance Saltonstall Found for the Arts, NY State Coun on the Arts; residency, Cite Internationale des Arts, Paris, International Studio/Curatorial Program, New York, MacDowell Colony, Petersborough, NH, 2003; Radcliffe Inst Fel, Harvard Univ, 2004—05. *Mailing Add:* Bennington Coll 1 Coll Dr Bennington VT 05201-6003

LUMBERS, JAMES RICHARD
PAINTER
b Toronto, Ont, Oct 8, 29. *Study:* Ont Col of Art, Toronto, OCA, 50. *Work:* Ont Govt; Tenn-Ness Antiques; Sun Oil Co; and numerous other corp & pvt collections in USA, Canada, Bermuda & Europe. *Comn:* Portraits, Former Prime Minister John Diefenbaker, 72, Chief Dan George, 73, 83 & 85, The Toronto Symphony Orchestra, 85, Hockey Greats: Gordie Howe, Sr & Wayne Gretzky, 91, Sir Edmund Hillary, 92, Joe Montana, 92; 4 Paintings, Royal Can Mounted Police; painting, Home of Lucy Maud Montgomery, Univ Prince Edward Island, 2005. *Exhib:* One-man show, Royal Ont Mus, Toronto, Can; Ont Sci Ctr, Toronto; Kennedy Galleries Inc, NY, 72; Nature Can, Nat Mus Can, 73, 76-78; Sportsman's Edge Gallery, NY, 78; McMichael Can Collection, Toronto Dominion Ctr; Le Moyne Art Found, Tallahassee, Fla, 78; Several tours & exhib, Can, 85-97, 2000; and many others. *Pos:* Graphic designer, James Lumbers Graphics Ltd, Toronto, 62-; pres, James Lumbers Publ Ltd. *Teaching:* lectr, many art groups. *Awards:* Statue, Juvenile Diabetes Found, 90; Winner of the Can Collectible of the Year, 91. *Bibliog:* Can Press, 89; Documentaries on PBS (Fla); Moments in Time-The Art of James Lumbers, 95; BBS Network Interviews, 96; The Art of James Lumbers, 95. *Mem:* ret mem, Soc Animal Artists, NY; Explorers Club, NY. *Media:* Acrylic. *Collection:* Tenness Antiques Ltd, Toronto. *Publ:* Over 250 works in ltd eds; Art Bus News, 87-95, 2000-02; Art Impressions (feature), autumn 93; Can Art Buyers Guide (feature), 93. *Dealer:* Gallery Andrea, 7019 E Main St, Scottsdale, AZ, 85251. *Mailing Add:* 16 Esna Park Dr Unit 3 Ontario ON L3R 5X1 Canada

LUMMUS, CAROL TRAVERS
PRINTMAKER
b Hyannis, Mass, Nov 2, 37. *Study:* Colby Sawyer Col, New London, NH, AA, 57; Mass Col Art, Boston; Univ of Geneva, Switz; study color with Hannes Beckmann, Dartmouth Col, Hanover, NH. *Work:* Univ Wis, Madison, Wis; Lund-Wassmer Springville Mus Collection, Salt Lake City, Utah; Arts Bank, Concord, NH; Theodore Milton Wassmer Collection, Fairview Mus, Utah Snow Col, Ephraim; Ogunquit Mus Art, Harold Shaw Collection. *Comn:* Southern Editions, 78. *Exhib:* solo exhib, Manchester Inst Arts, NH, 75-77; three-women show, Colby Sawyer Col, New London, NH, 76 & 94; Royal Soc Miniature Painters & Gravers, World Exhib, London, Eng, 95; Cove Gallery, Wellfleet, Mass, 2003; Gallery Z, Providence, RI, 2004; Three Graces Gallery, Portsmouth, NH, 2005; Barn Gallery, Ogunquit, Maine, 2006; and others. *Pos:* Illusr, Cincinnati Mag, Ohio, 64-67, Yankee Mag, 93-94. *Awards:* Oil award, Fitchburg Mus Art, Mass, 73; Rosmond DeKalb Award, Currier Mus Art, 75; Miniature Painters & Gravers, Washington, 93 & 96. *Mem:* League NH Craftsmen; Cape Cod Performing Arts Asn; NH Comn Arts (advisory panel); Silvermine Guild Arts, Conn; Nat Asn Women Artists, NY. *Media:* Intaglio print. *Interests:* Italian Language, Opera, Cross Country Skiing. *Publ:* Illusr, Editiones del Norte (cover/book), Hanover, NH, 68. *Dealer:* Southern Editions 521 St Ann St Jackson Square New Orleans LA 70116. *Mailing Add:* PO Box 525 Barnstable MA 02630

LUMSDEN, IAN GORDON
DIRECTOR
b Montreal, Que, June 8, 45. *Study:* McGill Univ, Montreal, BA, 68; Mus Mgt Inst Univ Calif, Berkeley, 91. *Collection Arranged:* The First Decade (with catalog), Confedn Ctr Art Gallery & Mus, Charlottetown, PEI, 75; Wallace S Bird Mem Collection (with catalog), Beaverbrook Art Gallery, Fredericton, NB, 75; Bloomsbury

Painters & Their Circle (US & Can traveling exhib), 76-78; The Queen Comes to New Brunswick: Paintings & Drawings by Molly Lamb Bobak (Can traveling exhib), 77-78; Drawings by Jack Weldon Humphrey (Can traveling exhib), 77-79; The Murray and Marguerite Vaughan Inuit Print Collection (Can traveling exhib), 81-82; 20th Century British Drawing, Beaverbrook Art Gallery, 86; Drawings by Carol Fraser 1948-1986 (Can traveling exhib), 87-88; Gainsborough in Canada (with catalog), 91; Early Views of British North America, Can traveling exhib (with catalogue), 94; Sargent to Freud: Modern British Paintings & Drawings in the Beaverbrook Collection (with catalog), 98. *Awards:* Above & Beyond Award, City of Fredericton, NB, 98; J Paul Getty Trust Scholar, Mus Management Inst, 91; The Brit Coun Visitors' Grant, 78, 91, 96. *Mem:* Atlantic Prov Art Gallery Asn (chmn, 70-72); Can Mus Asn (secy-treas, 73-75); Can Art Mus Dirs Orgn (treas 73-75, 2d vpres 75-77, 1st vpres 77-83, pres 83-85, treas 98-); Secondary Art Sub-Comt for NB Schs; Am Asn Mus; Can Soc for Decorative Arts (nat coun 99-). *Res:* 19th & 20th century Canadian art; 20th century British painting. *Publ:* Auth, Warkov, No 66 & Forrestall: de l'expressionnisme a l'hyperrealisme, No 67, Vie des Arts; Artist in New Brunswick: George Neilson Smith, Can Antiques Collector, 5-6/75; L'agrandissement du Beaverbrook, Vie des Arts, Vol XXIX, No 116, 84; Art and Music in New Brunswick, In: New Brunswick Ship Portraiture in the Nineteenth Century: an Examination of the Work of John O'Brien, William Gay Yorke & Edward John Russell, Ctr Can Studies Mt Allison Univ, New Brunswick, Vol 3, pp 35-51, 87

LUND, JANE
PAINTER
b New York City, NY. *Study:* Pratt Inst; Queens Col, New Sch Social Research. *Work:* Nelson Gallery Found, Kansas City, Mo; de Saisset Mus, Santa Clara, Calif; De Cordova Mus, Lincoln, Mass; Boston Mus Fine Art, Mass; Mus Fine Arts, Springfield, Mass. *Exhib:* Self-Amused: The Contemp Artist As Observer and Observed, Fitchburg Art Mus, Mass, 93; Seventh Triennial Exhib, Fuller Mus Art, Brockton, Mass, 93; Invitational Exhib Painting & Sculpture, Am Acad Arts & Letts, NY, 94; Nothing Overlooked: Women Painting Stillife, Contemp Realist Gallery, San Francisco, Calif, 95; Jane Lund: New Pastel Paintings, Forum Gallery, NY, 97; The Figurative Impulse, Kendall Art Gallery, Miami Dade Community Col, Fla, 98; Contemp Am Realist Drawings: The Jalane & Richard Davidson Collection, Art Inst Chicago, 99-00; Transforming the Commonplace-Master of Contemp Realism, Susquchanna Art Mus, Harrisburg, Pa, 03; Precision, Forum Gallery, Los Angeles, 2003; 179th Ann Invitational Exhib, Nat Acad Design, New York City, 2000; and others; Jane Lund: My Work, Forum Gallery, New York City, 2005. *Teaching:* Instr drawing, Berkshire Community Col, Pittsfield, Mass, 72-81, Smith Col, 99-. *Awards:* Fel, Mass Coun Arts & Humanities, 79 & Bunting Inst Radcliffe Col, 85-86; Artist's Fel, Nat Endowment Arts. *Bibliog:* A realist portfolio, New Eng Monthly, 10/85; New American Paintings, Open Studios Press, 96; cover and feature article, Am Artist, 3/99, Pastel J, 10/2006; others. *Mem:* Pastel Soc Am. *Media:* Highly Finished Pastels, Watercolor Constructions. *Dealer:* Forum Gallery Inc 745 Fifth Ave New York NY 10151. *Mailing Add:* 366 Norton Hill Rd Ashfield MA 01330

LUNDBERG, THOMAS ROY
FIBER ARTIST
b Belle Plaine, Iowa, June 3, 1953. *Study:* Univ Iowa, BFA, 75; Ind Univ, MFA, 79. *Work:* Am Craft Mus, NY; Indianapolis Mus Art; Chase Manhattan Bank, NY; Kaiser Found, Health Plan of Colo, Denver. *Exhib:* Craft Today USA, Mus des Arts Decoratif, Paris & European Tour, 89-92; Conversations: Textiles about Textiles, The Textile Mus, Washington, 94; Contemp Fiber from St Louis Collections, St Louis Mus, 95; 5th Int Triennial of Miniature Textiles, Mus d Angers, France, 96, 97, 6th Int Triennial, 99-2000; Art in Fiber, Indianapolis Mus Art, 97; The Cutting Edge: Contemp Quilts, Am Craft Mus, NY, 97, Nos Plus Belles Histoires Brodees, Mus Nat des Art et Traditiones Populaires, Paris, 99. *Teaching:* Prof fiber art, Colo State Univ, 79-. *Awards:* Western States Arts Fedn Regional Fel, NEA, 95; Covisions Award Colo Coun on the Arts, 96, 2000. *Bibliog:* Barbara Lee Smith (auth) Celebrating the Stitch, Taunton Press, Newton CT, 91; Anne Morrell (auth) Contemporary Embroidery, Studio Vista, London, 94; Lippard, Lucy et al (auths) Parallaxis: 55 Points of View, Western States Art Fedn, 96. *Mem:* Surface Design Asn. *Media:* Embroidery, Fiber. *Dealer:* Hibberd McGrath Gallery 101 N Main Breckenridge CO 80424; Mobilia 358 Huron Ave Cambridge MA 02138. *Mailing Add:* 806 Sandy Cove Lane Fort Collins CO 80525-3383

LUNDBERG, WILLIAM
ASSEMBLAGE ARTIST, FILMMAKER
b Albany, Calif, 42. *Study:* San Jose State Univ, Calif, BA(art), 64; Univ Calif, Berkeley, MA(art), 66. *Work:* Guggenheim Mus, NY; Mus Art, RI Sch Design; Mus Contemp Art, Univ Sao Paulo, Brazil; Mus Mod Art, Niterio, Brazil; numerous others, pub & pvt. *Exhib:* One-man shows, Whitney Mus Am Art, NY, 82, Carnegie Inst Mus Art, Pittsburgh, Pa, 84, Emily Davis Gallery, Univ Akron, Ohio, 87, Langford Archit Gallery, Tex A&M Univ, College Station, Tex, 89, Ctr Res Contemp Art, Arlington, Tex, 91, Solar Grandjean de Montigny, Centro Cult da PUC, Rio de Janeiro, Brazil, 92, Mus Contemp Art, Univ Sao Paulo, Brazil, 92 & Blanton Mus, Univ Tex Austin, 99; group shows, Bill Lundberg-Regina Vater, Bridge Ctr Contemp Art, El Paso, Tex, 90, World Disorder, Cult Space, NY, 91, Trance Medial, Austin, Tex, 91, Installation, Mexic-arte, Austin, Tex, 92, Funiarte, Cult Inst Rio de Janeiro, 93, 34th Ann Invitational, Longview Art Mus, Tex, 93, Old & New Masters of Super-8 & Anthology Film Archives, NY, 94; Mirrors Edge, BildMusseet, Umea, Sweden, Vancouver Art, 2000-; Alternative Currents, McKinney Ave Contemp, Dallas, 2001; and many others. *Teaching:* Instr, New Eng Col, Arundel, Eng, 71-74; Md Inst Col Art, Baltimore, 83; Parsons Sch Design, New York, 84-85; assoc prof, Univ Tex-Austin, 85-2000, prof, 2000-. *Awards:* Fel New Genre, Nat Endowment Arts, 91; Fulbright Fel, Mus Contemp Art, Sao Paulo, 92; Teaching Excellence Award, Col Fine Arts, 93; Fac Res Award, Univ Tex, 94; and many others. *Media:* Film, Video. *Mailing Add:* 4901 Caswell Ave Austin TX 78751

LUNDEEN, GEORGE WAYNE
SCULPTOR
b Holdrege, Nebr, 48. *Study:* Hastings Col, Nebr, LBA, 71; Univ Ill, MFA(sculpture), 73; Accademia de Belle Arte, Italy, 74; Artist-in-residence Texas Agr & Mechanical Univ, Col Station, 78-79. *Hon Degrees:* Univ Nebr, PhD, 1999. *Work:* Nebr State Collection, Kearney; People's Republic China, Nat Gallery, Peking; Holdrege, Nebr; Botanical Gardens, Wichita, Kans; City of Carmel, Calif. *Comn:* lifesize Robert Frost, Dartmouth Col, 96; Jack Swigert, Statuary Hall, Capitol Bldg, Washington, DC, 97; Lewis & Clark monument, Great Plains Art Mus, Lincoln, Nebr, 2004; monument, Coors Field, Denver, 2005; High Plains Heritage Ctr, Chadron, Nebr, 2002; and others. *Exhib:* One-man shows incl: O'Brien's, Scottsdale, Ariz, Driscol's, Denver, Vail, Trails West, Laguna Beach; works incl(bronze sculptures) Michelle (Nat Acad Art Watrous Gold medal 82), Promise of the Prairie (Holdrege Nebraska award 83). Fulbright-Hays grantee, Florence, Italy, 73-74. Mem Nat Sculpture Soc (Bronze medal 81, 84, Silver medal 82), Allied Artists Am (Montana award 82); recipient, Pioneer award, Neb legislature, 95, Distinguished Nebraskan, Gov Neb, 95; North Am Sculpture Exhib, Foot Hills Art Ctr, 79-86; Allied Artists Am Ann, NY, 80-87; Nat Sculpture Soc Ann, NY, 80-88; Nat Acad Design Ann, NY, 80-86; Am Western Art Exhib, Peking Arts Gallery, China, 81. *Pos:* Fulbright-Hays Scholar, Florence, Italy, 73-74; artist-in-residence, Tex A&M Univ, 78-79. *Awards:* Art Castings of Colorado Award, NAm Sculpture Exhib, 83; N Am Sculpture Exhib, John Cavenaugh Mem Award, 86; Allied Artists Members & Assocs Award, 87; Pioneer award, Legislature of Nebr, 92; Distinguished Nebraskan, State of Nebr, 95; and others. *Bibliog:* John Jellico (auth), G W Lundeen, Artist of the Rockies & Golden West, spring 81; M Lantz & T Morgan (auths), The western art of 12 western sculptors, Nat Sculpture Review, fall, 80; Libby James (auth), George Lundeen, Southwest Art, 5/83; Judy Hughs (auth), the Sculpting Lundeens, Southwest Art, 8/93. *Mem:* Nat Sculpture Soc; Allied Artists Am; Nat Acad. *Media:* Bronze. *Mailing Add:* c/o Loveland Sculpture Gallery 338 E Fourth St Loveland CO 80537

LUNDIN, NORMAN K
PAINTER, EDUCATOR
b Los Angeles, Calif, 38. *Study:* Sch Art Inst Chicago, BA, 61; Univ Chicago, 61; Univ Cincinnati, MFA, 63; Univ Oslo, Norway, 63. *Work:* Mus Mod Art, NY; Detroit Inst Arts; Brooklyn Mus Art; Seattle Art Mus; Achenbach Found; Fine Arts Mus, San Francisco; Yale Univ. *Exhib:* Solo exhibs, Allan Stone Gallery, NY, Space Gallery, Los Angeles, Stephen Haller Fine Art, NY, Long Beach Mus Art, Calif, (catalog), Schmidt Bingham Gallery, NY, Am Realism, San Francisco Art Mus, (catalog), Sources of Light, Henry Art Gallery, Seattle; Whitney Mus Am Art, NY; Barnsdale Gallery, Los Angeles Munic Mus; Seattle Art Mus; Koplin Gallery, Los Angeles; Francine Seders Gallery, Seattle. *Pos:* Vis artist, Hornsey Col Art, London, Eng, 69-70, Ohio State Univ, Columbus, 75, San Diego State Univ, 78, Brighton Col Art, Eng, 79 & Univ Tex, San Antonio, 82. *Teaching:* Prof art, Univ Wash, Seattle, 64-. *Awards:* Grants, Fulbright Found, 63-64, Ford Found, 78-79 & Nat Endowment Arts, 83; Wash State Visual Artists Fel, Tiffany Found. *Bibliog:* Bruce Guenther (auth), Fifty Northwestern Artists, San Francisco Chronicle Books, 83; Lynn Gamwell (auth), West Coast Realism, Laguna Beach Mus Art, 83; Robert Flynn Johnson (auth), Norman Lundin: A Decade of Drawing & Painting, Univ Wash Press, Long Beach Mus Art, 90. *Media:* Oil, Acrylic. *Dealer:* Schmidt-Bingham Gallery 41 E 57th St New York NY 10022; Francine Seders Gallery Seattle; Koplin Gallery 464 N Robertson Blvd Los Angeles CA 90048. *Mailing Add:* 3419 E Denny Way Seattle WA 98122

LUNEAU, CLAUDE
SCULPTOR
b Paris, France, 35; Can citizen. *Work:* Can Coun Art Bank; Laurentian Univ, Sudbury; Windsor Art Gallery; Holdbrooks Holdings, Toronto; Mus Civilization, Ottawa. *Exhib:* Solo exhibs, Mira Godard Gallery, Toronto, Ont, 82 & 84, Olga Korper Gallery, Toronto, Ont, 86, 88, 91, 93 & 96, Moosart Gallery, Miami, Fla, 86 & Koffler Gallery, Toronto, Ont, 93; Glenbow Mus, Calgary, Alta, 83; Olga Korper Gallery, Toronto, Ont, 86, 88 & 89; Equinox Gallery, Vancouver, BC, 88; Robertson Galleries, Ottawa, Ont, 88; 49th Parallel, NY, 89; Structure: Claude Luneau & Greg Murdock, Gallery/Stratford, Ont, 90. *Awards:* Can Coun Project Cost Grant, 83, 84 & 85; Ont Arts Coun Material Assts Grant, 83 & Traveling Cost Grant, 86. *Bibliog:* Christopher Hume (auth), Essays in whimsy, 8/14/82, Heavy Metal, 8/31/84, Toronto Star; From the Heart: Folk Art in Canada, McLelland & Stewart, Toronto, 83; Peter Day (auth), Claude Luneau, Can Art, spring 86. *Mailing Add:* c/o Olga Korper Gallery 17 Morrow Ave Toronto ON M6R 2H9 Canada

LUNSFORD, JOHN (CRAWFORD)
HISTORIAN, CURATOR
b Dallas, Tex, Apr 15, 33. *Study:* Harvard Univ, AB(Eng lit), 54; Columbia Univ, MA(pre-Columbian art hist & archaeol), 67. *Collection Arranged:* The Clark and Frances Stillman Collection of Congo Sculpture (with catalog), 69; Arts of Oceania (with catalog), 70; The Romantic Vision in America (with catalog), 71; African Art from Dallas Collections (with catalog), 72; The Gustave and Franyo Schindler Collection of African Sculpture (with catalog), 75; Nora and John Wise Collection of Pre-Columbian Art, 76. *Pos:* Cur, Dallas Mus Art, 68-80, sr cur, 80-86; dir, Meadow Mus, Southern Methodist Univ, 96. *Teaching:* Adj prof art hist, Southern Methodist Univ, Dallas, 67-96. *Res:* The arts of pre-Columbian Meso-America and West and Central Africa; pre-Columbian Central and South America; native American art. *Mailing Add:* c/o Meadows Mus Southern Methodist Univ Dallas TX 75275

LUNTZ, IRVING
DEALER
b Milwaukee, Wis, Jan 9, 29. *Study:* Northwestern Univ. *Pos:* Pres & dir, Irving Galleries, Inc, Palm Beach, Fla, 59-. *Mem:* Art Dealers Asn Am; Appraisers Asn Am. *Res:* Nineteenth and twentieth century American and European painting; sculpture and graphics; photography. *Specialty:* Modern and contemporary painting, sculpture and photography. *Mailing Add:* 332 Worth Ave Palm Beach FL 33480

LUPORI, PETER JOHN
SCULPTOR
b Pittsburgh, Pa, Dec 12, 1918. *Study:* Carnegie-Mellon Univ, BFA, 42; Univ of Minn, MS(educ), 47; studied with Joseph Bailey Ellis & John Rood. *Work:* The Walker Art Ctr, Minneapolis, Minn; Ball State Teachers Col Art Gallery, Muncie, Ind; North Hennepin Community Col Art Gallery, Fridley, Minn; Albert Lea Pub Libr, Minn; Minn Alumni Asn Art Gallery, IDS Ctr, Minneapolis; Normandale Jr Col, Minn; Col of St Catherine, St Paul, Minn. *Comn:* Creation (ceramic bas-relief), Westminster Presbyterian Church, Minneapolis, 82; St Joseph tryptich (ceramic bas-relief), St Joseph Hosp, Dickinson, NDak, 84; Bishop Whipple (bronze), St Cornelia Church, Morton, Minn; Pentecost & Christ Welcoming (bronze) & 3 bronze reliefs, Univ St Thomas, St Paul, Minn, 96; 7 ft Madonna (bronze), Col St Catherine, 98; St Joan of Arc, Bronze, Church of St Joan Arc, Minn, 2000. *Exhib:* Ann Assoc Artist of Pittsburgh, Carnegie Inst of Art, Pa, 40-62; Biennial Exhib of Paintings & Prints, Walker Art Ctr, Minneapolis, 47-49; 1st Biennial Exhib Prints & Drawing, Minneapolis Inst of Arts, 50, 52-54; Six-State Sculpture Exhib, Walker Art Ctr, 47, 51; Ann Local Artists Exhibs, Minneapolis Inst of Arts, 47-48, 50-52; 16th Ceramic Ann Nat Exhib, Syracuse, NY, 51; Fine Arts Exhib, Minn State Fair Art Gallery, St Paul, 46-; one-man show, St Paul Mus of Art, 52; Retrospective 1936-1993, Col St Catherine, St Paul, Minn, 93. *Teaching:* Instr sculpture, Univ of Minn, Minneapolis, 46-49; asst prof, sculpture, Col of St Thomas, St Paul, Minn, 49-51; prof sculpture, The Col of St Catherine, St Paul, 47-92; Ceramic Sculpture, Northern Clay Ctr, Minneapolis, Minn, 92-. *Awards:* 2nd award in sculpture, Prix de Rome, NY, 41; Carnegie Inst Prize for Sculpture, Asn Artists Pittsburgh, 49; Emily Arsenberg Award, Asn Artists Pittsburgh, 62; total of 40 sculpture awards, 37-. *Mem:* Soc Minn Sculptors; Minn Artists Asn. *Media:* Ceramic, Bronze, Wood. *Interests:* Fishing, Traveling, Coin Collecting. *Mailing Add:* 5118 12th Ave S Minneapolis MN 55417

LUPPER, EDWARD
PAINTER
b NJ, Jan 4, 36. *Study:* With Wesley Lea, Frenchtown, NJ; Trenton Jr Col; Parsons Sch Design, New York; Calif Col Arts & Crafts, Oakland; San Francisco Art Inst; San Francisco State Col; M H de Young Mem Mus Sch, 78. *Work:* Bear Paintings, Teddy Bear Mus, Naples, Fla; Los Angeles Maritime Mus; DiRosa Collection of Contemp Calif Artist. *Comn:* Two paintings, Scott Newhall Collection, 80 & 82; Annedeen Hosiery Mills, 88. *Exhib:* Baltimore Mus Art, 55; San Francisco Mus Art, 60; Am Embassy, Belg, 77-78; solo exhib Debruyne Fine Arts, Naples, Fla, 2001, 02, 03, 04; Rick Moore Fine Art, Santa Fe, NMex, 03, 04, 05; America's Best Paint, Naples, Fla, 2002 & 2003; DeBruyne Fine Arts, 2004-2005. *Pos:* Artist, card line, Posters, Sunrise Publ, 88-89 & 90-95; artist, Great Am Puzzle Co, 97-98; Maggie Needlepoint Co, 98-99. *Teaching:* Puzzle line, bits & pieces, 2002, 2003; artist, Giclé Fine Art Prints, 2004-2006. *Awards:* Huntington Hartford Found Fel, 64; Courage Cards Art Search Award, 2000 & 2001; Courage Exclusive Art Card Award for the internet, 2003. *Bibliog:* Article, San Francisco Chronicle, 60, San Francisco Examr, 62 & 65 & Seattle Times, 71; articles in Naples Daily News, 86 & Naples Times, Fla, 86, 87, 88, 89 & 90-92. *Media:* Casein, Oil. *Publ:* Auth, articles in Playgirl, 74, Apartment Life, 9/74, Popular Gardening Indoors, 77, Eaton Paper Corp, 77-78, Sunrise Publ, 79-80, Gulfshore Life & Naples Guide, 86 & 91-92, Am Artist, 88, Artist Mag, 89 & Focus Mag, Fla; brochure, Delta Shiva Corp, 87-88; auth (catalog), America's Best Paint, Naples, FL, 2001; auth (catalog), Naples Daily News, 3/2003; auth, The Bottom Line 2005, The Carousel Magazine, 7/2005. *Dealer:* Debruyne Fine Art 275 Broad Ave S Naples FL 34102. *Mailing Add:* 69-784 Wakefield Rd Cathedral City CA 92234

LUQUE, JOSE ANTONIO
CRITIC, CURATOR
b Mexico City, Mex, June 5, 54. *Study:* Facultad de Filosofia y Letras, UNAM, lic en hist, 84. *Collection Arranged:* Mexican Art Renaissance, Nagoya City Art Mus, Japan, 89; Le Fete de la Mort, Musee de la Botanique, Brussels, 93; Orozco, Rivera y Siqueiros Ctr, Cult de Delem, Lisbon, 95. *Pos:* Deputy dir & fine arts dus, Instituto Nacional de Bellas Arts, Mexico City, 82-86, Mus Mod Art, Instituto Nacional de Bellas Artes, 87-88 & Palace Fine Arts Mus, Mexico City, 93-94. *Publ:* Auth, La ilusion de lo real: realismos/hiperealism, Instituto Nacional de Bellas Artes, 88; Raices de Oaxaca: Tamayo, Nieto, Toledo, Casa de Tiempo, 92; Aguila y sol, pintura Mexico, siglo XX, 93 & Oaxaca, magia de Mexico, 93, Europalia; Os grandes mestres: Orozco, Rivera, Siqueiros, Fund das Descobertas, Lisbon, 95. *Mailing Add:* Calle Dos 17A-1 San Pedro de los Pinos 03800 Mexico

LURAY, J (SCHAFFNER)
COLLAGE ARTIST, PAINTER
b Columbus, Ohio, Apr 14, 39. *Study:* Ohio State Univ; Columbus Col Art & Design, BFA(advert), 62. *Work:* Nat Educ Asn, KPMG Peat Marwick, Cleveland, Ohio; Marketing Mix Inc, St Louis, Mo; Commun Satellite Corp, Washington, DC; Magna Group, Inc, Belleville, Ill; Healthlink Inc, St Louis, Mo. *Comn:* Stifel Nicolaus & Co, St Louis, Mo; Monsanto Co, St Louis, Mo; Anheuser-Busch Inc, St Louis, Mo; Barnes Hosp, St Louis, Mo; Gen Am Life Insurance, St Louis, Mo; and others. *Exhib:* 19th Area Exhib, Corcoran Gallery Art, Washington, DC, 74; Nat Watercolor Soc Ann, Fullerton, Calif; Adirondacks Nat Am Watercolors; Allied Artists of Am 79th Ann; MOAK-Four State Exhib, 94 & 95, Springfield Mus Art, Mo; and others. *Pos:* Advert designer, W P Simpson, Columbus, Ohio, 60-62, Paul L Devaney Studio, Columbus, Ohio, 62-69 & Designers Two, St Leonard, Md, 69-03. *Awards:* Soloway Award, Allied Artists Am; Mary Hill Mem Award, Catherine Lorillard Wolfe 98th Exhib, 94; Int Soc Experimental Artist, 93, 94, 95 & 96. *Bibliog:* Rachel Wolfe (auth), Splash 4, 96 & Northlights Publ; Betty L Schlemm & Tom Nicholas (auths), The Best of Watercolor, Rockport Publ, 96; Betty L Schlem (auth), The Best of Painting Composition and the Best of Painting Color, Rockport Publg, 98. *Mem:* Signature mem Texas Watercolor Soc; Am Watercolor Soc; Signature mem Nat Watercolor Soc; signature mem Kans Watercolor Soc; Int Soc Experimental Artist. *Media:* Acrylic, Watercolor. *Dealer:* Torpedo Factory Art Ctr Alexandria VA 22314

LURIE, BORIS
PAINTER, SCULPTOR
b Leningrad, Russia, July 18, 24; US citizen. *Exhib:* Drawings USA, Mus Mod Art, NY, 59; Tenth Street NY Cooperative Movement, Houston Art Mus, Tex, 60; NY Libr, Mus Mod Art, 62; Recycling Exhib, Israel Mus, Jerusalem, 78; Arts & Politics, Karlsruehe Mus, Ger, 78; Counterculture Art, Am Info Serv, Paris,78; Graffiti-art, Nassauischer Kunstverein, Weisbaden, Ger, 89; Janos Cat Gallery, NY, 98; Naomi Salmon, 2003 & 2004. *Bibliog:* Ray Wishniewski (dir) Doom Show (film), New York, 62; Ami Goldman, No! Art-man, Film, New York, NY, 2004. *Media:* All. *Publ:* Auth, Leonardo, London, 78; coauth, No!, Ed Hundertmark, Cologne/Berlin, Ger, 88 & Neue Gesellschaft for Bildende Kunst Berlin, Ger, 96. *Dealer:* Galerie & Ed Hundertmark Cologne WGer Bruesselerstrasse 29. *Mailing Add:* 48 E 66th St New York NY 10021

LUSKER, RON
PAINTER, DESIGNER
b Chicago, Ill, Jan 28, 37. *Study:* Sch Art Inst Chicago, 54-60; Univ Ill, Chicago Circle, Ill State Gen Assembly scholar, 57-62; Univ Chicago, 62-63; Southern Ill Univ, Carbondale, BA, 65, MFA, 66. *Work:* Univ NC; Price Waterhouse, Chicago; Chase Manhattan; Southern Ill Univ; Aldrich Mus Contemp Art. *Exhib:* 14th Ann Painting & Sculpture Exhib, Peoria Art Ctr, Ill, 66; 70th Ann Midwest Painting Exhib, Art Inst Chicago, 67; Convocation Arts, Sculpture, State Univ NY Albany, 68; 4th Ann Art Exhib Sculpture, Staten Island, 69; Eastern Seaboard Regional 3rd Ann Sculpture Exhib, 70; plus others. *Teaching:* Instr art, Southern Ill Univ, Carbondale, 65-67; asst prof art, State Univ NY Stony Brook, 68-72; assoc prof art, Kingsborough Community Col, 72-74. *Awards:* Grad Sch for Sculpture Fel & Grant in Aid, State Univ NY Stony Brook, 69 & 70. *Bibliog:* Malcolm Preston (auth), Assemblages display intellectual fantasy, Newsday, 5/21/69; Claire White (auth), Exhibition review, Craft Horizons, 6/70; Albert Boime (auth), Cosmic artifacts: The work in lucite of Ron Lusker, Art J, winter 72. *Mem:* Am Craftsmen Coun; Col Art Asn Am; Ctr Study Democratic Insts. *Media:* Acrylic, Oils. *Publ:* Auth, New York: The season in sculpture, 8/70, The green meadow school, 8/70, The jewelry of Marci Zelmanoff, 12/70 & Attitudes, Brooklyn Museum, 70, Craft Horizons Mag. *Mailing Add:* 85 Mercer St New York NY 10012

LUTES, JIM (JAMES)
PAINTER
b Ft Lewis, Wash, Dec 5, 55. *Study:* Wash State Univ, BA, 78; Art Inst Chicago, MFA 82. *Work:* Mus Contemp Art & Art Inst Chicago; Mus Contemp Art, Ghent, Belg; Domaine de Kerguehennec, Locmine, France; Ill State Mus, Springfield; Progressive Corp, Pepper Pike, Ohio. *Exhib:* Chicago & Vicinity Show, Art Inst Chicago, 84; 39th Corcoran Biennial (catalogue), Corcoran Gallery Art, 84-86; Viewpoints (catalogue), Walker Art Ctr, 85; Whitney Biennial (catalogue), Whitney Mus, 87, 2006; Why Paint, The Renaissance Soc, Univ Chicago, 92; solo exhibs, Dart Gallery, 86, 87, 88, 91 & 92, Guy LeDune Contemp Art, Brussels, Belg, 93, Vera Van Laer Gallery (catalogue), Knokke-Heist, Belg, 93, Zolla Lieberman Gallery, Chicago, 94, 96 & 99, Mus Contemp Art (catalogue), Chicago, 94, Mus van Hedendaagse Kunst (catalog), Ghent, Belg, 95 & Ctr Creative Studies, Detroit, 96; Abstract Chicago, Evanston Art Ctr, 95; Pulp Fiction, Gallery A, Chicago, 95; Faculty Biennial, Univ Galleries, Normal, Ill, 95; Art Chicago: 1945-1995, Mus Contemp Art (catalog), Chicago, 96; Zolla/Lieberman Gallery Inc, Chicago, 96, 97, 98 & 99; Art Chicago 1997, Navy Pier, Chicago, 97; Linda Hodges Gallery, Seattle, Wash, 97; Denaturalized, Mus Contemp Art, Chicago; Les Objets Contiennent l'Infiniti, Ecole Superiure des Beaux-arts de Tours, France, 98; Zolla Lieberman Gallery, Chicago, Ill, 99; and many others. *Teaching:* Vis artist, Art Inst Chicago, 83-95 & 98; adj assoc prof abstract painting, Univ Ill, Chicago, 95; assoc prof, Ill State Univ, Normal, 95-99; assoc prof, Sch Art Inst Chicago, 98-. *Awards:* Ill Arts Coun Grant, 85, 99; Seven Awards in Visual Arts, 88; Nat Endowment Arts, 93; Louis Comfort Tiffany Found Award, 93. *Bibliog:* Kathryn Hixson (auth), Arts Mag, p 107-108, 4/91; Alan Artner (auth), Is Painting Dead, Chicago Tribune, 4/92; Robert Frank (auth), Kuntsforum Int, Bd 119, pages 178, 336, 392, 92; Alan Artner (auth), MCA's Three for all, Chicago Tribune, 12/11/94; Alan Artner (auth), Lutes delivers own brand of Commentary, Chicago Tribune, 11/7/96; Susan Snodegrass (auth), Art in Am, 2000. *Media:* Oil, Acrylic. *Dealer:* Zolla Lieberman Gallery 325 W Huron St Chicago IL 60610

LUTNICK, HOWARD W
PATRON
b New York, NY. *Study:* Haverford Col, BA(econ), 83. *Pos:* With Cantor Fitzgerald, New York City, 83-, pres & Chief Exec Officer, 91-, chmn, 96-; founder, chmn, pres & Chief Exec Officer, eSpeed, 99-; speaker in field, currently; trustee, Solomon R Guggenheim Mus, currently; bd managers, Zachary & Elizabeth M Fisher Ctr Alzheimer's Disease Res, Rockefeller Univ; bd trustee, exec comt, Intrepid Mus Found; bd managers, Haverford Col; bd dir, Tate Gallery Projects Ltd, Tate Mus. *Awards:* Recipient Distinguished Pub Serv Award, Dept Navy. *Mailing Add:* eSpeed Inc 135 East 57th St New York NY 10022

LUTZ, MARJORIE BRUNHOFF
PAINTER - WATERCOLOR, SCULPTOR - WOOD, STONE
b Cincinnati, Ohio, Jan 25, 33. *Study:* Art Students League, with Sidney Simon; Duke Univ, Empire State Col, BA, Summit Univ La, MA, Sculpture Ctr, NY. *Work:* Tuttleman Collection, Merion, Pa; David Whitcomb Collection, Hudson, NY; Morgan Sculpture Gardens, Ctr Hall, Pa; Southern Vt Art Ctr, Manchester, Vt. *Comn:* Early Bird, Todd Hunter Develop Corp,; welded steel abstract, Taft Steel Corp, NY, 81; Helios, David Whitcomb, Hudson, NY; La Petite Francaise, Dixon Collection, Dorset, Vt; Gaia, Alexander White Collection, Old Chatham, NY, Carl Sweet Winery, Sacramento, Sting Ray, 2000. *Exhib:* solo show, Southern Vt Art Ctr, 84, Elm St Gallery, Manchester, Vt, 96; Ginofor Gallery, Cambridge, NY, 90-99; The Sculpture Works, Santa Fe, NMex, 2000; Four Winds Gallery, Santa Cruz, NMex, 2000; Munson Gallery, Santa Fe, NMex; Grace Fine Art Gallery, Morristown, NJ; Art is Okay, Alberquerque, NMex. *Teaching:* Instr sculpture, Southern Vt Art Ctr, Manchester, Vt, 85-95, pvt instrn 95-. *Awards:* Doris Kriendler Mem Award, Am Soc Contemp Artists, 83. *Bibliog:* American Artist Illustrated Survey of American Contemporaries; Am Dictionary of Sculptors. *Mem:* Am Soc Contemp Artists; Southern Vt Art Ctr, (bd dir, 88-93, vpres, 88, pres, 89-92); Screen Dir Guild. *Media:* Stone, Wood, Watercolor on paper. *Publ:* Archit Dig, 7/94. *Dealer:* Grace Fine Arts Morristown NJ. *Mailing Add:* 16 Brilliant Sky Dr Santa Fe NM 87508

LUTZ, WINIFRED ANN
SCULPTOR, INSTRUCTOR
b Brooklyn, NY, May 6, 42. *Study:* Cleveland Inst Art, BFA, 65; Atelier 17, with Stanley William Hayter, 65; Cranbrook Acad Art, MFA, 68. *Work:* Cleveland Mus Art; Albright-Knox Art Gallery; Chicago Art Inst; Desert Mus, Palm Springs, Calif; Crocker Gallery, Sacramento; Newark Mus, NJ; Int Paper Corp, NY; Jan van Eyck Akademie, Maastricht, Neth; Mount Holyoke Col Art Mus, Mass; Nat Bank of Chicago. *Comn:* sculpture, Harrisburg Mem, Commonwealth Pa, 93; sculpture garden, The Mattress Factory, 92-97; sculpture garden Ctrs for Disease Control, Atlanta, Ga, 98-2000; basin Schuylkill River Park, Phila, 97. *Exhib:* One-man show, Paper Reliefs, Am Craft Mus, NY, 75, Marilyn Pearl Gallery, 77-79, 84-85, 86, 88 & 90 New Am Paperworks, Int Traveling Invitational Exhib, 82-86, Paper as Image, Arts Coun of Gt Brit, 83 & Dolan-Maxwell Gallery, Philadelphia, 90; Int Biennale Paper Art, Leopold-Hoesch Mus, Duren, Ger, 86 & 88; Light Cycle, Visual Arts Ctr of Alaska, Anchorage, 86; A Point of View--A Vista, Hewlett Gallery, Carnegie-Mellon Univ, Pittsburgh, 86; Paper Art, Mus Provencial, Hasselt, Belg, 88; Paper Makes Space, Nordyllandi Kunst, Denmark, 89 +251 Grand Lobby Installation, Brooklyn Mus, 90; A Natural Order, Hudson River Mus, Yonkers, NY, 90; Flour to Ceiling/Surface to Edge, Cranbrook AcadArt Mus, 92; The Prison as Site, Historic Eastern State Penetentiary, Phila, 95; Correspondence/Congruence, The Contemp Arts Ctr Cincinnati, Ohio, 95; Nature Morte: Contemp Still Life, Am Mus Pa Acad Fine Arts, 96; Threshold, ICA Univ Pa, 97; The Best of the Season, Aldrich Mus Contemp Arts, Ridgefield, Conn, 99. *Teaching:* Asst prof sculpture, Yale Sch Art, 75-81, assoc prof, 81-82; assoc prof sculpture, Tyler Sch Art, 82-99, Laura Carnell prof, 99-. *Awards:* Nat Endowment Arts Fel, 84; Creative Time Inc Project Grant, 89; Pa Coun Arts, 89; Francis J Greenburger Found, 90. *Bibliog:* Jean Feinberg (auth), Findings of Winifred Lutz, Craft Horizons, 4/79; Jules Heller (auth), Papermaking, Watson-Guptill, 78; Maureen Bloomfield (auth), Nuances of number, Dialogue, an Art J, 11-12/85; Kotik (auth), The cutting edge, Kalamazoo Ctr for Arts, 88; Peter Gruen (auth), Viewpoint, Vol 9, No 6, Dialogue, 11-12/86; Bloemink (auth), A Natural Order, Hudson River Mus, 90. *Mem:* Col Art Asn (Dist Teaching Visual Arts, 99). *Media:* All. *Publ:* Auth, Felting, Am Crafts Mag, 8-9/80; Casting to Acknowledge the Nature of Paper, Int Conf Hand Papermakers, Carriage House Press, 81; appendix of Non-Japanese Fibers for Japanese Papermaking, Weatherhill, 83; Surface is A function Of distance, catalog essay, the Detroit Inst Arts Founders Soc, 88; Shrinking To Expand, Carriage House Press, 88. *Dealer:* Gallery Joe 302 Arch St Philadelphia PA 19106. *Mailing Add:* 2316 Terwood Rd Huntington PA 19006-5509

LUZ, VIRGINIA
PAINTER
b Toronto, Ont, Oct 15, 1911. *Study:* Cent Tech Sch. *Work:* Robert McLaughlin Gallery, Oshawa, Ont; Can Dept External Affairs; Can Embassies; J S McLean Collection; London Art Mus; also in many pvt collections. *Exhib:* Ont Soc Artists, 45-83; Can Women Artists Show (traveling exhib to NY & Can), 47-49; Can Soc Painters in Watercolour, 47-75; Can Tours; Can Group Painters; Tribute to Ten Women, Sisler Gallery, Toronto, Ont, 75; and others. *Teaching:* Instr illus, Cent Tech Sch, Toronto, 40-74, dir art, 69-74. *Mem:* Ont Soc Artists; Royal Can Acad; Can Soc Painters in Watercolour. *Media:* Watercolor. *Mailing Add:* 602 Melita Cresent No 319 Toronto ON M6G 3Z5 Canada

LYFORD , CABOT
SCULPTOR, PAINTER
b Sayre, Pa, May 22, 25. *Study:* Skowhegan Sch Art, summer 47; Cornell Univ, BFA, 50; Sculpture Ctr, New York, 50-51. *Work:* Lamont Gallery, Exeter, NH; Addison Gallery Am Art, Andover, Mass; Wichita Mus, Kans; Indianapolis Mus, Ind; New Eng Ctr Continuing Educ, Durham, NH; Ogunquit Art Mus; Portland Mus Art, Maine; Hunter Mus, Chattanooga, Tenn; over 150 pvt collections. *Comn:* Sculpture, Mt Sunapee Summit, NH, 64; Harbor Sculpture (black granite), Portsmouth, NH, 75; black granite whale, Prescott Park, Portsmouth, NH, 79; sculpture, Voc Tech, Stratham, NH, 83; Albacore Park Submariner Mem, Portsmouth, NH; Berwick Sch, ME; and others. *Exhib:* Addison Gallery, Andover, Mass; Fitchburg Art Mus; Univ NH; Midtown Gallery, NY; Ogunquit Mus, Maine; Theme Sculpture Bronze, New Bedford Whaling Mus; Mus of Art, Portland, ME. *Teaching:* Instr sculpture, Phillips Exeter Acad, NH, 63-86. *Awards:* Prizes, City Manchester, 70 & NH Architects Asn, 71 & 74-77; Sculpture Prize, Nat Acad Design, 90. *Media:* Stone, Wood, Bronze; Watercolor. *Publ:* Contribr, Contemporary Stone Sculpture, 71. *Dealer:* Greenhut Gallery Portland ME; Harbor Square Gallery, Rockland ME. *Mailing Add:* 4 Fish Pt Rd New Harbor ME 04554

LYLE, CHARLES THOMAS
ADMINISTRATOR
b Duluth, Minn, July 16, 46. *Study:* Univ Minn, James Wright Hunt scholar, 67-68, BA(cum laude), 68; Univ Del, Hagley fel, 68-70, MA(Am hist), 71. *Pos:* Dir, Monmouth Co Hist Asn, Freehold, NJ, 71-78 & Hist Soc Del, 80-90; dir mus, Nat Trust for Historic Preservation, 78-80; dir, Md Hist Soc, Baltimore, 90-93; exec dir, Boscobel Restoration, Inc, Garrison, NY, 95-2005. *Teaching:* Vis instr, Mus Studies Dept, Univ Del; instr Am decor arts prior to 1900, Lincroft, NJ, 75-76; preserv prog, Gouchen Col, Towson, Md, 93-94; pub progs, Bard Grad Ctr Studies Decorative Arts, NY, 97. *Awards:* Scholar Am Friends, Attingham Summer Sch, 77. *Mailing Add:* PO Box 100 Chelsea NY 12512

LYLE, JANICE S
MUSEUM DIRECTOR
b Hawthorne, Calif, Sept 14, 49. *Study:* Calif State Univ, BA, 74; Univ Calif, Santa Barbara, MA, 77, PhD, 84. *Pos:* Asst cur art, Palm Springs Desert Mus, 84-85, dir educ, 85-94, exec dir, 94-. *Teaching:* Lectr, Univ Calif, Riverside, 83-90; lectr contemp art, Scripps Col, 84; lectr Am art, Univ Redlands, 91. *Awards:* Athena Award, Corp Bus Women of the Yr, 95; Desert Woman of the Yr Award, 2005. *Mem:* Calif Asn Mus (bd mem, 94-, pres 02-); Mus Educators Southern Calif (treas, 90-94); Art Table; Am Asn Mus; AAMD; CAM (pres, 02-04). *Publ:* Ed & contribr, William Blake in the Art of His Time (exhib catalog), Univ Calif Santa Barbara Art Mus, 76; auth, Handlist of Essick Blake Collection, Blake - An Illus Quart, 78; ed & contribr, The Anglo-American Artist in Italy (exhib catalog), Univ Calif Santa Barbara Art Mus, 82; auth, The Landscapes of Anders G Aldrin (exhib catalog), Mus Hist & Art Ontario, 83; coauth, Desert Art Collections (exhib catalog), Palm Springs Desert Mus, 85. *Mailing Add:* Palm Springs Desert Mus PO Box 2310 Palm Springs CA 92263

LYNCH, BETTY
PAINTER, INSTRUCTOR
b McAlester, Okla. *Study:* Univ Tex, BA, 38; workshops with Robert E Wood, 72-88; also with Leonard Brooks, Rex Brandt & Charles Reid, Eliot O'Hara, Millard Sheets. *Work:* Mus Southwest, Midland, Tex; Art Asn Richmond, Ind. *Exhib:* Tex Watercolor Soc, Witte Mem Mus, San Antonio, 67, 68, 75, 82 & 83; Sun Carnival Art Exhib, El Paso, Tex, 67; Southwestern Print & Drawing Exhib, Dallas Mus Fine Arts, 69; Western Fedn Watercolor Soc, San Antonio, Tex, 79 & Phoenix, Ariz, 82 & Lubbock, Tex, 90; Am Watercolor Soc, 83, 85, 87 & 88. *Teaching:* Workshop instr watercolor, Okla, Calif, Kans, Fla, Ariz, Vt, Tex, SC, Mont, NMex, Wis, Mich, Colo, Nev, England & Spain, 77-83 & Artists Coop Workshops, France, 85; instr watercolor, La Romita Sch, Terni, Italy, Bermuda, Iowa, Kanuga & NC, 83, 84, 85, 87, 88, 89, 90, 92, 93, 94, 95 & 97. *Awards:* Purchase Prize, Tex Watercolor Soc, 83; Ed Whitney Award, Am Watercolor Soc, 87; Best-In-Show, Watercolor Art Soc, Houston, 90. *Bibliog:* Florence Hutchinson Lonsford (auth), Spotlight on Kappa artists, The Key, 82. *Mem:* Tex Watercolor Soc; Midland Arts Asn; San Antonio Watercolor Group; Am Watercolor Soc. *Media:* Watercolor, Graphic Artist. *Publ:* Auth, Watercolor page, Am Artist Mag, 80; Travel Tips From the Pros, Am Artist Mag, 85; Featured in Western Art Digest's Watercolor Edition, 5/86; Artist En Route, sketches by Betty Lynch, pvt publ, 98

LYNCH, FLORENCE
GALLERY DIRECTOR
Study: BS; MA in Art Admin. *Pos:* With Salvatore Ala Gallery; independent cur, Japan, Ger, France, The Neth, Italy; found, cur, Florence Lynch Gallery, New York City. *Awards:* Named one of Seven Emerging Young Dealers in Chelsea, NY Arts Mag, 1999. *Mailing Add:* 531-539 W 25th St New York NY 10001

LYNCH, MARY BRITTEN
PAINTER, COLLAGE ARTIST, INSTRUCTOR
b Pruden, Ky, 32. *Study:* Univ Tenn, Chattanooga, BA; Provincetown Workshop, Mass, studied with Leo Manso & Victor Candell; Univ Tenn, Knoxville, 65; Long Island Univ, Southampton, NY, grad study, 1989, with Eric Fischl, Larry Rivers, Robert Dash, Miriam Schapiro & April Gornik. *Work:* Coca Cola, South Central Bell, Atlanta; Mohawk Industries, Ga; TJX Corp, Mass; Forrest City Enterprises, Ohio; Campbell Co Hist Mus, Tenn; TVA, Knoxville, Tenn; and others. *Exhib:* Okla Arts Ctr, Oklahoma City, 74; Nat Watercolor Soc, Calif, Am Watercolor Soc, NY; Miss State Col for Women; State Univ NY; Purdue Univ; Northern Nat, Nicolet Col, Wis; Nat Women in Arts Mus Arch, Washington, DC; Smithsonian Inst Arch; Vanderbilt Univ, Nashville, Tenn; and others. *Pos:* Founder, Lenoir City Arts Festival, Tenn, 63 & Tenn Watercolor Soc, 70; Visual Arts Adv Panel Tenn Arts Comn; Juror, Idaho Watercolor Soc, 2000. *Teaching:* Instr watercolor & acrylics, Hunter Mus Art, Chattanooga, 69-77, Watercolor Workshop, Univ Tenn, Chattanooga, 75, 85 & 86 & Chattanooga Christian High Sch, 80-86, Girl's Preparatory Sch & Baylor Sch summer progs, Chattanooga; WVa workshop instr, 2002. *Awards:* Cash Award 91 & Purchase Award, 92, Tenn Watercolor Soc; Purchase, Cash Award & Medal, Ky Watercolor Soc, 96; Purchase Award, Nat Watercolor Soc, Calif, 1994, Rocky Mountain Nat, 2001, 2002 & 2006, Ga Watercolor Exhib, 2000-2002, Adirondacks Nat Award, etc. *Bibliog:* Southern Artisans (film for TV), 73. *Mem:* founder Tenn Watercolor Soc (founder, 69, treas, 70, vpres, 71, pres, 72-); Watercolor USA Honor Soc (corresp secy); Am Watercolor Soc, NY; Ga Watercolor Soc; Southern Watercolor Soc. *Media:* Watercolor, Acrylic, Collage. *Res:* contemp minimalism. *Interests:* Books & Tennis.

Publ: Contribr, Am Artist Mag Watercolor, 90; Artists Mag, 94, 96 & 2000; Collage Techniques, Brommer, 94; 100 Ways: Still Life & Florals, 2005; Best of Drawing, North Light Publishing, 2007. *Dealer:* Art4Business Inc Philadelphia PA; C Smith Consultants Phoenix AZ; 1401 Gallery Chattanooga. *Mailing Add:* 1505 Woodnymph Tr Lookout Mountain GA 30750-2633

LYNCH, MATTHEW
ARTIST
b Ind, 69. *Study:* Ball State Univ, BFA, 92; Syracuse Univ, MFA, 95. *Exhib:* Exhib incl, Highwayscape, Weber State Univ, Ogden, Utah, 97, An Investigation of Trans-Archit in Western Am, 97, Rise Overrun, Plan B Evolving Arts, Santa Fe, 97, L'Arche, Ecole Nationale d'Art, Cergy, France, 98, SPARCH, Bemis Ctr Contemp Arts, Omaha, 98, Ship from the Desert, Maschinenhalle, Potsdam, Ger, 98, Moorgs Project, 98, Free Basin, Hyde Park Arts Ctr, Chicago, 2000, Spec, Renaissance Soc, Univ Chicago, 2001, Mood River, Wexner Ctr Arts, Columbus, Ohio, 2002, Documenta XI, Kassel, Ger, 2002, Session the Bowl, Deitch Projects, NY, 2002, Whitney Biennial, Whitney Mus Am Art, NY, 2004, InSITE, San Diego, 2005. *Pos:* co-found & mem, SIMPARCH, 96-; Ctr Land Use Interpretation, LA, 99 & 2003; L'Ecole Nationale d'Art, France, Columbus Col Art & Design, Ohio, 2001; Documenta XI, Kassel, Ger, 2002. *Teaching:* Lectr, Concordia Univ, Montreal, Can, formerly; lectr, Weber State Univ, Ogden, Utah, 97; resident, Brandenburgischer Kunstverein, Potsdam, Ger, 98; lectr Univ Utah, Salt Lake City, 99; asst prof, fine arts Col Design, Archit, Art & Planning, Univ Cincinnati, 2002-. *Awards:* Pollock-Krasner Grant, 97; NMex Arts Cou Grant, 97; Creative Capital Grant, 2002. *Mailing Add:* 1328 Pullan Ave Cincinnati OH 45223

LYNCH, THOM
PAINTER, MURALIST
b Newark, NJ, Jan 17, 47. *Study:* Self taught. *Comn:* mural restoration, Sumitt Playhouse, 2002. *Exhib:* Palmer Mus, Springfield, NJ, 95, Berkeley Heights Pub Libr, NJ, 95, Am Cyanamid, Princeton, NJ, 95, Berks Arts Coun, Reading, Pa, 97, Brion Gallery, Lambertville, NJ, 99; A Blast of Color, Watchung Arts Ctr, NJ, 94, Faces of Change, 94, Between a Thought and a Thing, 96, End of the Millennium, 96 & Anthropomorphic, 99; Ariel Gallery, Soho, NY, 90, Basile-Spingarn Gallery, Matawan, NJ, 91, Calif Mus of Art / Burbank Ctr, Santa Rosa, Calif, 95, Resurgam Gallery, Baltimore, 96, Simon Gallery, Morristown, NJ, 97, Orange Bear Music Club & Gallery, NY, 98; Berkshire Artisans, Pittsfield, Mass, 99, Trenton City Mus, NJ, 99, 2001; The Toy Show, Artists for Art, Scranton, Pa, 2000, It's Alive, Brion Gallery, 2000; Int Forum Art Initiative, Moscow, Russia, 2002; The Peace Mus, Chicago, 2003. *Collection Arranged:* curator,The World With Perforations, International Stamp Art Exhibit, Watchung Art Ctr NJ, 97. *Awards:* Grant, Union City Heart, 2001. *Bibliog:* A Fringe Benefit for the Gallery's Faithful, NY Times, 95; Into the 90's, Suburban Cable/NJ Public TV, 95; Diverse Artists Rally Around Common Themes, Courier News, 99; New Art Group Comes Alive, The Times of Trenton, 2000; New Art Group Finds a Common Thread and Develops a Theme, Star Ledger, 2000; Robert Henkes (auth), The Crucifixion in American Art, McFarland & Co, 5/2003. *Mem:* New Art Group. *Media:* Acrylic. *Dealer:* Brion Galleries 1293 Rt 179 Lambertville NJ 08853. *Mailing Add:* PO Box 195 Pottersville NJ 07979

LYNCH, TOM (THOMAS) MICHAEL
PAINTER, INSTRUCTOR
b Chicago Ill, Feb 22, 50. *Study:* Am Acad Art, Univ Ill. *Work:* Neville Pub Mus, Wis; Burpee Art Mus, Rockford, Ill; Sagamon State Univ, Springfield, Ill; Standard Oil Corp, Chicago; and others. *Comn:* A Man and His City (paintings), Chicago Coun Fine Arts, 78; Portrait of a City (paintings), IBM Corp, Green Bay, Wis, 79 & Calumet City, Ill, 80; Chicago at Night, Chicago Harbors & Chicago Cafes (paintings), Chicago Coun Fine Arts, 80; Calendars, US Open (golf), 90 & 91; Five menu covers for Wag Restaurant; and others. *Exhib:* US Open Artist, 92; Sr US Open Artist, 93; NAMTA Shows, 1990-2000; solo show, Am Embassy, Paris, 96. *Pos:* Consulting dir, Am Int Art Ctr, Des Plaines, Ill, 81-; dir art, Ill Watercolor Soc, currently; consult, Raphael Brush, France & Holbein Paint, Williston, Vt, Strathmore Artists Papers, Crescent Cardboard Co; columnist, Am Artist, 95-96. *Teaching:* Instr watercolor, Dillman's Sand Lake Lodge, Wis, 79-2001, Northwestern Ohio Watercolor Soc & Southwest Watercolor Soc, Dallas, 81-86 & Southern Ariz Watercolor Soc, Tucson & Phoenix, 81-86, tools of the trade instr, currently. *Awards:* Graphic Art Award, Chicago Artist Guild, 79; First Place, Int Soc Artists, 80; Ochs Award Co Orange Co Watercolor Soc. *Bibliog:* Steve Fosdick (auth), Chicago at night, Herald, 5/81; Leona Toppel (auth), Profile, Downtown News, 12/81; Steve Doherty (auth), article, Am Artists, 5/81; Linda Rhodes (auth), profile, Ozark Mag, 2/85; Sue McGarry (auth), Group profile, Southwest Art, 5/85; Fred Klein (auth), Profile, Wall St J. *Mem:* Soc Am Impressionists (exec comt). *Media:* Watercolor. *Publ:* Auth & illusr, Watercolor lesson with Tom Lynch, Crafts & Things Mag, 81; auth, Watercolor page, Am Artist Mag, 81; illusr, Winter in Sleepy Hollow, Ford Times Mag, 81; contribr, Ford Times, 1/82, 4/82 & 12/82 & Readers Digest, 82; auth, The Magic of Watercolor, Fun with Watercolor, Fun with Watercolor II, Fun with Watercolor III, 82; Saluagh techniques, Am Artist, 4/86

LYNCH-NAKACHE, MARGARET
PAINTER, SCULPTOR
b Hartford, Conn, Dec 17, 32. *Study:* RI Sch Design, BFA, 54; Beaux-Arts, Paris, cert, 56; Atelier Chapelain-Midy. *Work:* L'Ambassade du Liban, Paris; Our Lady Victory Church, Centerville, Mass; Les Embrunts, Les Essembres, France; Georgetown Univ Hosp, Washington; Inst Keguruan Dan Ilum Pendidikan, Yogyakarta, Indonesia. *Comn:* Blown Tulips, Sargi, Dakar, Senegal, 78; Paris Cityscape, Cameron, Royal Oak, Mich, 78; Roses, Dagommer Cie, Paris, 78; Madonna, Ostronic, Potomac, Md, 79; Green Dunes, McDonald, Wellesley, Mass, 83. *Exhib:* One-person show, La Galerie du Meridien, Paris, 79, Hunter House, Vienna, Va, 82 & Georgetown Univ Hosp, Washington, 85 & 87; Long Branch Nature Ctr, 81; Cape Cod Art Asn, 83; Sandscape Gallery at Munson Meeting, Chatham, Mass, 88; Oliver Bldg, Boston, 92 & 93; Old Selectman's Building Gallery, West Barnstable, Mass, 95; Waterstone's Booksellers, Boston, Mass, 96; Boston Athenaeum, 98; Boston Athemaeum, 2003; A to Z, CoSo, Boston, 2006. *Pos:* Artist, Universal Films, New York, 56-57 & Girl Scouts USA, Hq New York, 59-61; artist-in-residence, Art Barn, Washington, DC, 79; pres, Network For Artists, Kindred Art Collection & Host Exhib Ltd, McLean, Va, 79-85. *Awards:* Second Place, Cape Cod Art Asn, 56; Second Place, McLean Art Club, 79; Second Place, Dennis Art Festival, 81; Purchase Prize, Herdon Fine Art Exhib, 89. *Bibliog:* L Chauvin (auth), Margaret Nakache, Galerie Jardin des Arts, 2/75; E Holgren (auth), Whisperings and sharings, Alexandrian Mag, spring 78; J de Recqueville (auth), Carnet des arts, Paris-Tel, 1/79. *Mem:* McLean Proj Arts (bd mem, 88-91); Copley Soc Boston. *Media:* Watercolor, Oil, Bronze. *Publ:* Contribr, Cadette Girl Scout Handbook, Girls Scouts USA, 63; auth, Art royalties, Int Herald Tribune, 5/16/77; Art game letters, Washington Post Mag, 11/5/78. *Dealer:* Copley Soc Boston 158 Newbury St Boston MA 02116. *Mailing Add:* PO Box 68 West Hyannisport MA 02672

LYNDE, STAN
CARTOONIST, ILLUSTRATOR
b Billings, Mont, Sept 23, 31. *Study:* Univ Mont; Sch Visual Arts, New York, 56-57. *Exhib:* The Evolution of Rick O'Shay, Yellowstone Co Fine Arts Ctr, Billings, Mont, 63; The Paintings of Stan Lynde, Midland Nat Bank, Billings, 75. *Pos:* Creator, auth & artist comic strip, Rick O'Shay, Chicago Tribune-New York News Syndicate Inc, 58-77 & Latigo, Field Newspaper Syndicate, 79-83. *Awards:* Inkpot Award Achievement in Comic Arts, 77; Mont Gov Award Arts, 83. *Bibliog:* A History of the Comic Strip, 68; articles in Cartoonist Profiles Mag, 69, 70, 79 & 81; Comics of the American West, 77. *Mem:* Nat Cartoonist's Soc; Comic Arts Prof Soc. *Media:* Pen & Ink; Oil. *Publ:* Auth, Rick O'Shay and Hipshot--The Great Sunday Pages, Tempo Bks, 76; Rick O'Shay, Hipshot and Me, 90, The Bodacious Kid (novel), 96, Careless Creek (novel), 98, Cottonwood Publ

LYNDS, CLYDE
SCULPTOR, PAINTER
b Jersey City, NJ, June 22, 39. *Work:* Nat Mus Am Art, Washington; Butler Inst Am Art, Youngstown, Ohio; Wadsworth Atheneum, Hartfield, Conn; NY Univ; Marion Koogler McNay Art Inst, San Antonio, Tex; and others. *Comn:* scultpure, Greater Hartford Arts Coun, Conn, 2000, US Courthouse, Montgomery, Ala, 99, NJ State Capitol Plaza, Trenton, 98, IRS Central Computing Facility, Martinsburg, WVa, 98, AT&T Network Opers Ctr, Bedminster, NJ, 99, Eastern Conn State Univ, Willimantic, 98, Foley Sq Fed Office Bldg, New York City, 97. *Exhib:* Solo exhibs, Babcock Galleries, NY, 69, 71, 73 & 75, Corcoran Gallery Art, Washington, DC, 73, OK Harris Works of Art, NY, 86, 88, 91, 94 & 01, NJ State Mus, Trenton, NJ, 93, Butler Inst Am Art, Youngstown, Ohio, 94; Aldrich Mus, Conn, 88; La Mus de la Civilization, Que, Can, 89; Stadtmuseum, Dusseldorf, Ger, 90; Univ Calif, 90; Nicaf, Yokohama, Japan, 92 & 93. *Awards:* First Prize, Monmouth Col, 68; First Prize & Medal of Hon, Painters & Sculptors Soc, NJ, 68; NJ State Coun Arts Fel, 84; Fels, NJ State Coun on Arts, 84 & 89; Nat Design award, GSA, Washington, DC, 97. *Bibliog:* Harry Rand & Eleanor Heartney (auths), Buddha Seat, Sculpture Catalog, 4/89 & 7/90. *Media:* Stone, Light, Glass. *Publ:* Frederick Morgan, auth, Drawings, Poems of the Two Worlds, Verona, Italy. *Dealer:* OK Harris Gallery 383 W Broadway New York NY 10012; Gallery Camino Real 608 Banyon Tr Boca Raton FL 33431. *Mailing Add:* 20 Franklin Ave Wallington NJ 07057

LYNN, JUDITH
PAINTER, ILLUSTRATOR, TAPESTRY ARTIST
b Chicago, Ill. *Study:* Los Angeles Conservatory of Music, 59-62; Univ Vinenna, Austria, third in class, 64; Fashion Inst Technology, 87-91. *Hon Degrees:* Hon teaching degree, Conservatory de Musica Marcay, Venezuela, 84-85. *Work:* Ateneo De Los Teques, Venezuela. *Exhib:* solo exhib Casa de la Cultura, Marcay, Venezuela, 84; Simbolos de la Menthe, Galeria EuroAmericano, Caracas, Venezuela, 84; Mus opening, Bayside Historical Soc, Bayside, NY, 97; Watercolor Exib, The Pen & Brush Club, NY, 2001; The Gallery at Lincoln Ctr, NY, 2002-2004. *Awards:* 3rd place oils & acrylics, IV Salon Imagen Annual, Salon Imagen Y Grumbacher, 84. *Bibliog:* Anne Louis Volkenborn (auth), Realism is the Theme of new Exhibits Opening in Caracas, The Daily Journal, Caracas, Venezuela, 1/18/84; Christina Assai (prod), Juventud Venezolano, TV-Concert with Paintings-Judith Lynn, 84; Dan Paolantonio (dir/prod), Documentary: The Italian Fascination, Flaming Cesar Film Co, England, 87. *Mem:* Am Watercolor Soc; Nat Mus Women in the Arts. *Media:* Watercolor, Acrylic. *Publ:* Recuento- Volumen II- Numero 7, Arte Plural Magazine, Caracas; Ademas de Soprano, Pintora, El Aragueno, Maracay, Venezuela, 2/1/85. *Mailing Add:* 2109 Broadway New York NY 10023-2106

LYNNE, MICHAEL
COLLECTOR
b 41. *Pos:* Atty, Barovick & Konecky; partner Blumenthal & Lynne, 60-80; counsel New Line Cinema, 80-90, Chief Operating Officer, pres, 90-2001, co-chmn, co-Chief Exec Officer, 2001-; bd dir, New Line Cinema, 83-; Exec prod: (films) Lord of the Rings: The Fel of the Ring, 2001, Lord of the Rings: The Two Towers, 2002, Lord of the Rings: The Return of the King, 2003. *Awards:* Named one of Top 200 Collectors, ARTnews Mag, 2004-. *Mem:* mem, NY Bar; Bd mem, Mus of Modern Art, Citymeals-on-Wheels, Am Mus of the Moving Image, Drawing Ctr; chmn, Mus Comt of Guild Hall East Hampton. *Collection:* contemporary art. *Mailing Add:* New Line Cinema Corp 888 7th Ave Fl 20 New York NY 10106-0001

LYON, GILES ANDREW
PAINTER
b New York, NY, June 30, 67. *Study:* Sch Visual Arts, New York, 84-85; Rochester Inst Technol, NY, 85-86; RI Sch Design, Europ hons prog, Rome, BFA, 89; Glassell Core Fel, Mus Fine Arts, Houston, 89-91. *Work:* Mus Fine Arts, Houston; also pvt collections of Edward Albee, Barret Collection, Christophe de Menil & Walter Hopps. *Comn:* Painting, Edward F Albee Found, Montauk, Long Island, 92; painting, Crowley, Mark & Douglas Attys at Law, Houston, 93; painting, Ambassador Hotel, Providence, RI, 94. *Exhib:* Core Fels Exhib, Alfred Glassell Sch Art, Mus Fine Arts, Houston, 90 & 91; Drawing from Tex, Mus Fine Arts, Houston, 91; The Big Show, Alfred Glassell Sch Art, Mus Fine Arts, Houston, 91; solo exhibs, Mus Art Guise, Houston, 92, Lynn Goode Gallery, Houston, 92, 94 & 96, Nine Freudenheim Gallery, Buffalo, NY, 94, Cuadrante 2, San Miguel de Allende, Mex, 96, Alexandre De Folin, NY, 97, Drawing Room, Area, Brooklyn, NY, 97, Angstrom Gallery, Dallas, Tex, 98, Feigen Contemp, NY, 99, 02, others; Conventional Forms/Insidious Visions, Alfred Glassell Sch Art, Mus Fine Arts, Houston, 93; Tex Contemp: Acquisitions of the 90's, Mus Fine Arts, Houston, 93; Dots & Lines, 8th Floor Gallery, NY, 96; Fascination, Lobby Gallery, Deutsche Bank, NY, 96; Buttered Side Up, Hallwalls Contemp Arts Ctr (catalog), Buffalo, NY, 96; The Exchange Show (with Arena & Pierogi 2000), NY, 96; Greater NY, Mus of Morder Art, 2000, New Plasma, Folin/Riva, NY, 01; featured artist, Mixed Greens, New York City, 03; and others. *Collection Arranged:* Mus Fine Arts, Houston; Edward Albee, NYC; The Barrett Collection, Dallas; Ross Bleckner, NYC; Christophe de Menil, NYC; Walter Hopps, Houston. *Pos:* Artist-in-residence, Edward F Albee Found, Montauk, NY, 91. *Teaching:* Vis artist/lectr, RI Sch Design, 90, San Jacinto Col, Houston, Tex, 93. *Awards:* Nat Endowment Arts Fel Grant, Mid-Am Art Alliance, 94; Artist in Res, Edward F Albee Found, Montauk, NY, 91; Core Fel, Glassell Sch Art, Mus Fine Arts, Houston, 89-91. *Bibliog:* Elizabeth McBride (auth), Giles Lyon: Beauty and the blob, 9/94 & Elizabeth Licata (auth), Giles Lyon, Nina Freudenheim, 1/95, ArtNews; Frances Colpitt (auth), Report from Texas: Going against the grain, Art Am, 4/95; Tom Moody (auth), Giles Lyon, Lynn Goode, ArtForum, 5/95; Carol Kino (auth) The Emergent Factor, Art in America, 7/00; Grady T. Turner (auth) Beautiful dreamers: emerging American painters, Circa 2000, Flash Art, Jan./Feb. 2000; New American Paintings, No 32, Open Studios Press, Wellesley, Mass, 3/01; plus others. *Media:* Acrylic, Water based Mediums. *Dealer:* Lynn Goode Gallery 2719 Colquitt Houston TX 77098. *Mailing Add:* 212 Northwood Houston TX 77009

LYON, ROBERT F
SCULPTOR, EDUCATOR
b Queens, NY, Sept 3, 52. *Study:* Mercer Co Community Col, AA, 72; Col NJ, BA 74; Tyler Sch Art, MFA, 77. *Work:* New Orleans Mus Art; La Arts & Sci Ctr, La State Univ, Baton Rouge; John Michael Kohler Arts Ctr, Sheboygan, Wis; Lamar Dodd Art Ctr, LaGrange, Ga. *Comn:* Bronze & terra cotta reliefs, Pioneer Place Plaza, Portland, 89; Earth Day Commemorative Sculpture, City of Baton Rouge, La, 95. *Exhib:* Two-person invitational, Sam Houston State Univ, Huntsville, Tex, 91, Troy Stae Univ, Ala, 2003; Clay Alabama Invitational, Univ Montevallo, 95; one-man show, Millsaps Col, Jackson, Miss, 96, Chattahoochee Valley Art Mus, LaGrange, Ga, 97, Bradley Univ, Peoria, Ill, 98, Univ SC, Spartanburg, 2001 & McKissick Mus, Columbia, SC, 2003, McKissick Mus, Columbia, SC, 2003, Univ Ga, Athens, 2004; Teaching Art: A Regional Faculty Invitational, Columbus Mus, Ga, 98; three-person exhib, Blue Spiral 1 Gallery, Asheville, NC, 2000; Univ Ark, Little Rock, 2000; Triennial, SC State Mus, Columbia, SC, 2004. *Pos:* Vpres & bd dir, Baton Rouge Gallery, 93-94; conf coordr, Sculpt-Fest 94, Baton Rouge, La, 94; nominations comt Nat Asn Schs Art & Design; bd dir, Southeaster Col Art Conf. *Teaching:* Prof art sculpture, La State Univ, 78-95; prof & chair dept art, Auburn Univ, 95-97, Univ SC, 97-2002, prof sculpture, 2002-. *Awards:* Visual Artists Fel, Nat Endowment Arts, 84; Artist Proj Grant, Cult Coun Rockland Co, 97; Grant, Univ SC, 2002. *Bibliog:* Dorothy Biner (auth), Robert Lyon, Melding, Clay & Wood, Ceramics Art & Perception, Issue #52, Sidney, Australia, 2003. *Mem:* Int Sculpture Ctr; Southeastern Col Art Conf (co-chair 2001 conf); Artist-Blacksmith's Asn N Am; Nat Coun Art Admins; Tri-Stae Sculputors Ednl Asn. *Media:* Clay, Wood. *Collection:* University of Texas; Louisiana Arts & Science Center; New Orleans Museum of Art. *Publ:* Coauth, Vasilikeware: An Early Bronze Age Pottery Style in Crete, Paul Astroms Forlag, 79. *Dealer:* Blue Spiral 1 Asheville NC; City Art Gallery Columbia SC. *Mailing Add:* Univ S Carolina Dept of Art McMaster Col Columbia SC 29208

LYONS, BEAUVAIS
PRINTMAKER, EDUCATOR
b Hanover, NH, Feb 24, 58. *Study:* Alfred Univ, 77; Univ Wis, Madison, BFA, 80; Ariz State Univ, MFA, 83. *Work:* Philadelphia Mus Art; Kohler Art Libr, Madison, Wis; Univ SDak-Vermillion; Smith Col Rare Book Collection, Northampton, Mass; Smithsonian Mus Am Art; Block Mus, Northwestern Univ, Evanston, Ill. *Exhib:* Selections from the Hokes Archives, Print Club, Philadelphia, Pa, 92; Carnegie Mellon Univ, Pittsburgh, Pa, 94 & 2001; St Lawrence Univ, Canton, NY, 94, 2001 & 06; State Univ NY, Buffalo, 95; Erie Mus Art, Pa,95; Vanderbilt Univ, 2002; others. *Pos:* Dir, Hokes Arch, 83-. *Teaching:* Vis asst prof art, Weber State Col, Ogden, Utah, 84-85; asst prof, Univ Tenn, Knoxville, 85-89, assoc prof, 89, Ellen McClung Berry prof, 96--2005; Fulbright lectr, Art Acad Poznan, Poland, 2002. *Awards:* Southern Arts Fedn/Nat Endowment Arts Regional Fel, 88; Southeastern Col Art Conf Award for Creative Achievement, 94; Fulbight Fel, Poznan Acad of Art, 2002. *Bibliog:* Lawrence Weschler (auth), Mr Wilson's Cabinet of Wonder, Pantheon Bks, 95; Linda Hutcheon (auth), Irony's Edge: The Theory and Politics of Irony, NY & London Routledge, 95; Roy R Behrens (auth), History in the Making, 70-77, Print mag, 5-6, 97; Beaurais Lyons: folk art fabricator, Folk Art Messenger, Vol 15, No 1, spring 2002. *Mem:* Southern Graphics Coun (ed Graphic Impressions); Col Art Asn; Am Asn Univ Profs; Soc Metavisual Studies. *Media:* All Media. *Publ:* Auth, The excavation of the apasht: Artifacts from an imaginary past, Leonardo J, Vol 18, No 2, 85; Speakeasy, New Art Examiner, Vol 17, No 5, 1/90; Artistic Freedom and the University, Art J, Vol 50, No 4, winter 91; The Art of the Trickster, Archaelogy, 3-4/94, Vol 47, No 2. *Mailing Add:* Sch Art-Univ Tenn 1715 Volunteer Blvd Knoxville TN 37996-2410

LYONS, CAROL
PAINTER, PRINTMAKER
b Brooklyn, NY. *Study:* Art Students League, 60's; studies in painting with Chaim Gross, in 3-D composition with David Smith & in watercolor with Zoltan Szabo & Edgar Whitney. *Work:* Victoria & Albert Mus, London; Jane Voorhees Zimmerli Mus, Rutgers Univ, NJ; Hermitage, Russia; IBM Colleciton, Westchester Co, NY; Omni Mag, Pvt collection; New York City, 5th Ave Pub Libr Print Collection; Spencer Mus, Kansas; His Royal Highness Duke of Gloucerter; Buren Town Hall, Netherlands. *Comn:* Watercolors painting, comn by Mrs M Huebner, Dobbs Ferry, NY, 93; watercolors painting, comn by Mr & Mrs Cloder, Pelham, NY, 93; watercolors painting, comn by Dr & Mrs B Klutchko, Hastings, NY, 93; watercolors painting, comn by Dr & Mrs Paul Hertz, Briarcliff Manor, NY, 94; watercolor, comn by Sothebys Real Estate, 96. *Exhib:* Audubon Art Club, Nat Arts Club, NY, 80; Ann Juried Show, Berkshire Mus, Pittsfield, Mass, 82; one-person show, Nicholas Roerich Mus, NY, 89; By the Riverside, Mus London, 90; Big Paintings, Nat Asn Women Artists, Javits Bldg, NY, 94; Nat Asn Women Artist, West Broadway Gallery, Soho, NY, 94; Artgroup of Yonkers, Studioalvianarte, Castel di Sangro, Italy, 94; Chautauqua Inst, NY, 96; Palatine Village Hall, Pallatine, Ill; Whittier City Hall, Whittier, Calif; 911 Woodblock Remembances:; Knickbocker Art Club, New York City; Lorillard Wolf Art Club, New York City; Catharine Laramie Wyo, 2004; Print Zero Seattle, Wash; Donnell Libr Ctr, New York City, 2005. *Teaching:* Daring Drawing, Art in the Elem Sch, New York City, Irvington, NY. *Awards:* Best in show, Womanart Gallery, NY, 80; Bronze Medal, Mus of the Duncans, Paris, 81. *Bibliog:* Robert Fisher (auth), The Zen of watercolor, Am Artist, 90; Fred Nold (dir), Interview-Carol Lyons, Cable Channel 19-WDMC, 90; Michael Ward (auth), Letter from the editor, Artists' Mag, 11/94. *Mem:* Nat Archives Mus Women Arts; Bklyn Mus Archives; Albany Print Club, NY; Artists Equity, New York City; Barenforum.org-(global); and others; Int Soc Experimental Artists. *Media:* Watercolor, Handprint,Woodblocks, Decalcomania. *Publ:* Cover artist & contribr, The New Spirit of Watercolor, 89 & Watercolor Magic-Risk It, 93, F & W Publ; Watercolor '90, Watson Guptil, 90. *Mailing Add:* Box 247 Ardsley On Hudson NY 10503

LYONS, FRANCIS E, JR
ART DEALER, LECTURER
b Detroit, Mich, Feb 14, 43. *Study:* Oakland Univ, BA, 68; City Col San Francisco, studied archit, 73; Montgomery Col, Md, 74; Towson State Univ, Md, 88; Am Craft Coun, New York, 93. *Pos:* Co-founder, Xochipilli Gallery, Rochester, Mich, 70-72; gallery rep & nat mgr, Marson Galleries, Baltimore, Md, 74-81; owner, Frank Lyons Collection, Glens Falls, NY, 81-; consult & interim dir, Venable-Neslage Gallerie, Washington, 92-93, 2002. *Teaching:* Lectr, prints & printmaking, numerous cols, univs & art ctrs, 76-. *Specialty:* 19th and 20th century prints and photographs; Japanese ukiyo-e and sosaka-hanga; Am Europenan early photography. *Mailing Add:* PO Box 2306 Glens Falls NY 12801

LYONS, JOAN
PHOTOGRAPHER
b New York, NY, Mar 6, 37. *Study:* Alfred Univ, BFA, 57; State Univ NY, Buffalo, MFA, 73. *Work:* Visual Studies Workshop, Rochester, NY; Ctr Creative Photog, Tucson, Ariz; Mus Mod Art, NY; San Francisco Mus Mod Art; Minneapolis Art Inst. *Exhib:* In Sequence, Mus Fine Arts, Houston, 82; Facets of the Collection, Mus Mod Art, San Francisco, 83; one-woman show, Ctr Creative Photog, Tucson, 84; Beyond Words, Art of the Book, Mem Art Gallery, Rochester, 86; Evocative Presence, Mus Fine Arts, Houston, 88; La Camera Ciega, Mus Art Contemp, Seville, Spain, 88; New Photomontage, Cranbook Acad Art, Bloomfield Hill, Minn, 88. *Pos:* Dir, Visual Studies Workshop Press, 72-. *Teaching:* Adj instr visual studies, Visual Studies Workshop, 75-, State Univ NY, Brockport, 86-. *Awards:* CAPS Fel, NY, 75 & 81. *Bibliog:* Tom Dugan (auth), Photography Between Covers, Light Impressions, 80; Ann Tucker (auth), Target Collection, Mus Fine Arts, Houston, 84; Joan Foncuberta (auth), Phot Visions No 15, Barcelona, Spain. *Mem:* Soc Photog Educ. *Publ:* Auth Ten self-pub artist's bks, 72-; ed, Artist's Books, a Critical Anthology & Source Book, Visual Studies Workshop Press, 86. *Dealer:* Visual Studies Workshop 31 Prince St Rochester NY 14607. *Mailing Add:* 176 Rutgers St Rochester NY 14607

LYONS, LISA
HISTORIAN, CONSULTANT
b Minneapolis, Minn, Dec 13, 50. *Study:* Northwestern Univ, Evanston, Ill, BA(art hist), 72; Columbia Univ, New York, MA(art hist), 73. *Collection Arranged:* Scale & Environment: 10 Sculptors (contribr, catalog), 77, Nicholas Africano, 78, Eight Artists: The Elusive Image (auth, catalog), 79, Close Portraits (auth, catalog), 80, The Anxious Edge (auth, catalog), 82, Wegman's World (auth, catalog), 82, Walker Art Ctr, Minneapolis; 39th Biennial Cont Painting (auth, catalog), 85, Corcoran Gallery Art, Washington, DC; Nicholas Africano: Innocence & Experience (auth, catalog), 91, Siah Armajani: The Poetry Garden & Recent Works, 92 & Chris Burden and Lynn Davis, 92, Lannan Found, Los Angeles, Calif; Percept, Image, Oject, 94; Facts and Figures, 94. *Pos:* Fel, Toledo Mus Art, Ohio, 73-74; Rockefeller Found Fel, Walker Art Ctr, Minneapolis, 75-77, asst cur, 77-78, cur, 79-82; dir acquisitions, Mus Fund, Minneapolis, 83-89; dir art progs, Lannan Found, Los Angeles, Calif, 89-. *Publ:* Auth, Henri Matisse: 1914-1917, Arts Mag, 5/75; An interview with James Byrne, Studio Int, 5-6/76; contribr, The river: Images of the Mississippi, Walker Art Ctr, 76; auth, Chuck Close, Rizzoli Int Publ, 87; Siah Armajami: the poetry garden, Design Quart, MIT Press, 94. *Mailing Add:* 2000 DeMille Dr Los Angeles CA 90027

LYSUN, GREGORY
PAINTER, RESTORER
b Yonkers, NY, Oct 24, 24. *Study:* Art Students League, with Louis Bouche, Edwin Dickinson, John Groth, Robert Beverly Hale & Reginald Marsh, 47-53. *Work:* Art Students League; New Britain Mus Am Art, Conn; De Cordova Mus, Lincoln, Mass; Butler Inst Am Art, Youngstown, Ohio. *Comn:* Portrait of Ruth Taylor, Westchester Community Serv Coun, Inc, White Plains, NY, 75; restoration work of 6 paintings by Edward Gay, comn by Mrs S Gay Linville, Scarsdale, NY, 81; restoration work of painting by John Steuart Curry, comn by Eugene Curry, Armonk, NY, 81; restoration of John Stewart Curry's Portrait of a Gypsy, Jefferson Co Hist Soc, Oskaloosa, Kans, 82; restoration work of the Pieta, statue, comn by St Joseph's Church, Bronxville, NY, 91. *Exhib:* 35 Yrs in Retrospect, 36-70, Butler Inst Am Art Midyear Show, 71; 67th Ann Exhib Conn Acad Fine Arts, Wadsworth Atheneum Mus, Hartford, Conn, 77; Art Teachers Juries Exhib, Neuberger Mus, State Univ NY, Col at Purchase, 77; From the 1920's to the Present, Works from the League's Permanent Collection, Art Students League, NY, 77; Directors Choice Exhib, selections from DeCordova Mus, Lincoln, Mass, 78; Ann Allied Arts Am, 85; 75th Nat Exhib, Conn Acad Fine Arts, William Benton Mus, Storrs, Conn, 88; Exhib Paintings & Sculpture, Berkshire Art Asn, Berkshire Mus, Pittsfield, Mass, 98; Allied Artists Am Mem Exhib, Butler Inst Am Art, Youngstown, Ohio, 2001; 73rd Grand Nat Exhib of Am Artists Profl League, Salmagundi Club, 2001. *Teaching:* Instr painting & drawing, Westchester Art Workshop, Co Ctr, White Plains, NY, 69-, Pelham Art Ctr, 78- & State Univ NY Col, Purchase, 82-; instr painting & drawing & chmn, Dept Art, Fairview-Greenburgh Community Ctr, Greenburgh, NY, 72-. *Awards:* Alice Collins Dunham Award, Best Portrait, 73rd Nat Exhib, Conn Acad Fine Arts, 83; Conn Acad Prize, 76th Ann Exhib, Conn Acad Fine Arts, 86; 64th Grand Nat Exhib Director's Award, Am Artists Prof League, New York, NY, 92; Continuing Education's Outstanding Fac Award, State Univ NY Purchase, 96; and others. *Bibliog:* Helen Ganz Spiro (auth), Art students follow teacher's example, 82 & Painter takes students to a different world, 83, Gannett Westchester Newspapers; M Stephen Doherty (auth), Different Strokes, Am Artist Mag, 12/99; Nelly Edmondson Gupta (auth), In Front of the Easel to Capture Not Just an Image, But Spirit, NY Times, 4/21/02. *Mem:* Life mem Art Students League; Allied Artists Am (hon); Life Fel Am Artists Prof League; Conn Acad Fine Arts; Hudson Valley Art Asn. *Media:* Oil. *Publ:* Auth, The construction of a painting, Palette Talk, 79; illusr, The Best of Oil Painting, 96 & Landscape Inspirations, 98, Rockport Publ. *Mailing Add:* 481 Winding Rd N Ardsley NY 10502-2701

LYTLE, RICHARD
PAINTER, EDUCATOR
b Albany, NY, Feb 14, 35. *Study:* Cooper Union; Yale Univ, BFA & MFA; also with Josef Albers. *Work:* Mus Mod Art, NY; Yale Art Gallery; Nat Collection Art, Washington; Minneapolis Mus Fine Arts; Rockefeller Mansion Mus. *Comn:* Concrete relief mural, Fairfield Univ, 65. *Exhib:* 16 Americans, Mus Mod Art, NY, 59; Seattle World's Fair, 62; Whitney Mus Am Art Ann, NY, 63; Art: USA: Now, SC Johnson Collection, World Tour, 63-; one-man show, De Cordova Mus, Lincoln, Mass, 74; Hopkins Ctr, Dartmouth Col, 86; plus others. *Teaching:* Instr art, Yale Univ, 60-63, assoc prof, 66-81, prof 81-, actg dean, Yale Sch Art, 80-81, 90 & 94, prof Emer, currently; dean, Silvermine Col Art, 63-66. *Awards:* Fulbright Grant to Italy, 58; Prof Achievement Citation & Augustus St Gaudens Award, 85, Cooper Union. *Bibliog:* Art: USA: NOW, Viking Press, 63; 16 Americans, Mus Mod Art, 59; Artist Next Door, The partnership for conn cities, Inc,. *Media:* Oil, Watercolor. *Dealer:* Herbert Palmer Gallery, Los Angeles, Calif. *Mailing Add:* 14 Sperry Rd Woodbridge CT 06525

LYTTON, CONSTANCE B
PRINTMAKER, PAINTER
b New York, NY. *Study:* Col William & Mary; Art Students League; Ruth Leaf Studio: Atelier 778. *Work:* Wesleyan Univ, Middletown, Conn; Univ Chicago; Tama Art Univ, Tokyo, Japan; City Univ, NY; Queensborough Comm Col Art Gallery. *Exhib:* Solo exhib, Davison Art Ctr, Wesleyan Univ, Middletown, Conn, 66, Interchurch Ctr, NY, 94 & Port Washington Libr, NY; The Larger Print, Midge Karr Gallery, NY Inst Technol, Westbury, 90; Mus Southwest, Midland, Tex, 90; Zhejian Acad Fine Arts, Hangzou, China, 93; Hecksher Mus, Huntington, NY; Kanagawa Kenmin Hall, Yokohama, Japan, 94; Shelter Rock Gallery, Manhasset, NJ. *Pos:* Co-dir, Prints Etc, Whitestone, NY. *Awards:* Juror's Award, Conn Women Artist Ann, 74. *Mem:* Artist Equity; Nat Asn Women Artist; Hempstead Harbor Art Asn. *Media:* Etching, Monotype; Mixed Media. *Dealer:* Skidmore Asn 645 Snowden Lane Princeton NJ; Prints Etc 15-17 163 St Whitestone NY 11357. *Mailing Add:* 21 Schenck Ave Great Neck NY 11021

M

MAAS, MARION ELIZABETH
PAINTER
b Brooklyn, NY, Feb 27, 30. *Study:* Pratt Inst, BS, 51; New York Univ; Frank Reully Sch Art. *Exhib:* The Garden, Mill Pond House, St James, LI, NY, 89; 100 Yrs 100 Works Nat Asn Women Artists traveling exhib, Islip Art Mus, East Islip, NY, 89, Fine Arts Mus, Mobile, Ala, 89, Chattanooga Regional Mus, Tenn, 89, Longview Mus Art, Tex, 89, Kirkpatrik Art Ctr, Oklahoma City, 90; Centennial Celebration, Jehangir Art Gallery, Bombay & Baroda, India, 89-90. *Awards:* Best in show, Nat Art League, 86; First Prize, Nat Asn Women Artists, 87. *Mem:* Nat Asn Women Artists; Catherine Lorillard Wolfe Art Club; Nat Art League. *Media:* Acrylic, Oil, Watercolor, Mixed Media. *Dealer:* LI Daniels Gallery Rosendal NY Main St Rte 213. *Mailing Add:* 85-57 67th Rd Rego Park NY 11374

MACADAM, BARBARA A
EDITOR
Pos: Freelance writer, 83-; assoc ed, Review: Latin Am Lit & Arts, currently; sr ed, ARTnews Mag, currently. *Mailing Add:* ARTnews Mag 48 W 38th St New York NY 10018-0042

MACARAY, LAWRENCE RICHARD
PAINTER, EDUCATOR
b Elsinore, Calif, May 8, 21. *Study:* Whittier Col, BA, 51; Calif State Univ, Long Beach, MA, 55. *Work:* Bowers Mus, Santa Ana, Calif; San Bernardino Co Mus Art; Bertrand Russell Peace Found, Nottingham, Eng; Spectrum Press, Orange, Calif; pvt collection of art critic, William Wilson, Los Angeles Times; De Saisset Mus, Santa Clara, Calif,. *Comn:* Location oil paintings of Eng & Ireland, 75; Art Shelter Pgm, Brea, Calif, 97. *Exhib:* New Talent, NY, Los Angeles Co Mus Art, 71-72; Bertrand Russell Centenary Art Exhib, Nottingham, 73; Southern Calif Regional Print & Drawing Exhib, 73, 74 & 76; Long Beach Mus Art, 80; Joslyn Ctr Arts, Torrance, Calif, 82; Grants Pass Mus Art, Ore, 83; Prize Winner, La Mirada Festival of the Arts, 84; one man show, Joslyn Fine Arts Gallery, Torrance, Calif, 85; El Camino Col Exhib, 87. *Pos:* Art & travel ed, Torrance Press-Herald, Calif, 63-70. *Teaching:* Prof drawing & painting, El Camino Col, 62-88. *Awards:* Prize for Art Unlimited, Downey Mus Art, Calif, 74; Southern Calif Exposition Prize, Del Mar, 74; All Calif Art Exhib Prize, 76. *Bibliog:* Dictionary of American Painters, Sculptors & Engravers by Fieldings, 86. *Media:* Oil. *Publ:* Auth & illusr, Sketches from an Irish detour, Yankee Doodlers, 76; illusr, Yarns & tales from the Great Smokies, The Cataloochee Press, 78; auth & illusr, The DeSombre House, Orange Blossoms Into Art, Wordwise, 94. *Dealer:* Ruskin Fine Arts 3936 Walgrove Ave Los Angeles CA 90066. *Mailing Add:* 780 N Malden Ave Fullerton CA 92832

MACAROL, VICTOR
MULTIMEDIA ARTIST, PHOTOGRAPHER
b US. *Study:* Peabody Inst, Johns Hopkins Univ, Baltimore, post-grad study, 68-69. *Work:* NJ State Mus, Trenton; Zimmerli Art Mus, New Brunswick, NJ; Kunsthaus, Zurich, Switz; Mus de l'Elysée, Lausanne, Switz; Biblio Nat, Paris; Noyes Art Mus, Oceanville. *Exhib:* One-man exhibs, Paterson Mus, NJ, 92, Galerie FOMA, Hradec Kralove, Czech Repub, 92, Hunterdon Mus of Art, Clinton, NJ, 93, St Joseph's Univ Gallery, Philadelphia, 94, Galerie Mesmer, Basel, Switz, 98, Galerie Michel Ray, Paris, 01, Goldsmiths Gallery, Lambertville, NJ, 03, Front Room Gallery, Singapore, 03; Acquisitions Recentes, Mus de e'Elysee, Lousanne, Switz, 91; Images of Flatiron Building, Berry-Hill Gallery, NY, 91; Five Yrs of Collecting Photographs, Mus Mod Art, Ljubljana, Slovenia, 96; Mensch-Focus-Ort, Galerie Arte, Basel, Switz, 96; Spuren, Galerie Mesmer, Basel, Switz, 98; Schwarz auf Weiss, Galerie Mesmer, Basel, Switz, 99; Life of the City, Mus Modern Art, NY, 02. *Awards:* Fel Award, NJ State Arts Coun, 82 & 86; Distinguished Artist Award, NJ State Arts Coun, 87. *Bibliog:* Victoria Donohoe (auth), Macarol exhibits at St Joseph's Univ, Philadelphia Inquirer, 11/94; Wendy Heisler (auth), A Witty Reflection of the World, Princeton Packet, NJ, 4/97; Martina Wohlthat (auth), Kunst in Basel Basler Zeitung, Switz, 4/98; Daniel Shearer (auth), Invisibility in the Moment, Princeton Packet, NJ, 7/99; William Gordon (auth), Picture Perfect, The Star-Ledger, NJ, 4/02; Cheach Ui-Hoon (auth), Unmistakable 'American Feel', The Business Times, Singapore, 5/03. *Mailing Add:* 15 1/2 Van Houten St Apt 304 Paterson NJ 07505

MACAULAY, DAVID ALEXANDER
DESIGNER, ILLUSTRATOR
b Burton on Trent, Eng, Dec 2, 46. *Study:* RI Sch Design, BArchit, 69. *Work:* Cooper Hewitt Mus, New York; Toledo Mus Art; Mus Art, RI Sch Design. *Exhib:* Ann Int Exhib Children's Bk Illus, Bologna, Italy, 76-77; 200 Years Am Illus, Mus of Hist, New York, 77; Buildingbooks, 77 & Drawing the Line, 78, Montclair Art Mus, NJ; Children's Book Art, Monterey Peninsula Mus Art, Calif & Triton Mus Art, Santa Clara, Calif, 78-79. *Pos:* Free lance graphic designer & illusr, 72-. *Teaching:* Instr 2-dimensional design, RI Sch Design, 74-76, adj prof illus, 76-85, chmn dept, 77-79; vis lectr, Yale Univ, 78-79; vis instr drawing, Brown Univ, 82; vis prof art, Wellesley Col, 85. *Awards:* Caldecott Hon Medal, Am Libr Asn, 74 & 78; Deutscher Jungenbuchpreis (Best non-fiction picture book), Ger, 75; Medal, Am Inst of Archit, 78; MacArthur Fellow, John D and Catherine T MacArthur Found, 2006. *Bibliog:* Paul Goldberger (auth), Schede/Libri, Abitare, Edtrice Segesta, Milan, 5/76 & How to build a castle, New York Times, 11/77; Stefan Kanfer (auth), Books, Time Mag, 11/77. *Mem:* Providence Preserv Soc (trustee). *Media:* Pen & Ink. *Publ:* Auth & illusr, Cathedral, The Story of Its Construction, 73, City, A Story of Roman Planning and Construction, 74, Underground, 76, Rome, Antics, Shortcut, Black and White (Caldecott Medal), Great Moments in Architecture, 78, Motel of the Mysteries, 79, Help Let Me Out, 82, Mill, 83, The Amazing Brain, 84 & Baaa, 85, Twh Way Things WorkThe New Way Things Work, 98, Building Big, 2000 Houghton Mifflin; and many publications internationally. *Mailing Add:* c/o Space Gallery of Archit 39 W 67th St New York NY 10023

MACAULAY, THOMAS S
ENVIRONMENTAL ARTIST, SCULPTOR
b Marshfield, Wis, Jul 2, 46. *Study:* St Olaf Col, BA, 68; Univ Iowa, MA, 70, MFA, 71. *Exhib:* Solo exhibs, Twining Gallery, NY, 87, Harvard Univ, Cambridge, Mass, 88, Ind Univ, Bloomington, 89, Contemp Mus, Honolulu, 90, Univ Colo, Boulder, 90, La Pietra, Honolulu, 91 & Case Western Reserve Univ, 92. *Teaching:* Prof sculpture, Wright State Univ, Dayton, Ohio, 73-. *Awards:* Fel, Guggenheim Mem Found, 84; Fel, Asian Cult Coun, 87; Fel, Fulbright Scholar Research, Japan-US Educ Comn, 91. *Bibliog:* Donald Kuspit & Betty Collings (coauth), Macaulay's Sculptural Views of Perceptual Ambiguity, Dayton Art Inst, 86; Donald Kuspit (auth), Thomas Macaulay: The Circle Squared, Univ Del, 90; Ann Bremner (auth), Thomas Macaulay A Year,

Southern Ohio Mus, 90. *Mem:* Artist's Organization (pres, 87-92). *Media:* Outdoor Environments, Indoor Environments. *Res:* outdoor concrete forms & plant materials; commercial cardboard box forms & indoor environmental installations. *Publ:* Auth, Hawall Architect: Art in Architecture, Hawaii Coun-Am Inst Architects, 3/90. *Mailing Add:* 5510 Scarff Rd New Carlisle OH 45344

MACBIRD, ROSEMARY (SIMPSON)
PAINTER
b St Joseph, Mo, Nov 19, 1921. *Study:* Art Inst Chicago, 41-43; also with Robert Wood, 82, Zoltan Szabo, 82 & Charles Reid, 83. *Comn:* Watercolors, Santa Barbara Bank, Calif, 81, Lawrence Stewart, Phoenix, Ariz, 82, Norman G Oliver, Hollywood, Calif, 83, Bonnie & Alan Kay, Los Angeles, 90 & Barbara Alter, Newport Beach, Calif, 92. *Exhib:* Knickerbocker Artists Ann Exhib, Salmagundi Club, NY, 83-84; Catherine Lorillard Wolfe Women Artists of Am, 84-85; Allied Artists Am Ann Exhib, Nat Arts Club NY, 84-85; US Dept Immigration & Naturalization Serv Centennial Art Exhib, Images of Am Immigration, a three yr traveling exhib, Georgetown Univ Art Gallery, Washington, DC, Ellis Island NY, Atlanta Fulton Co Libr, Ga, John F Kennedy Mus & Libr, Boston, Mass, Transamerica Tower, San Francisco, Calif, Natural Hist Mus, Los Angeles, Calif, 91-93; Audubon Artists 52nd Ann Exhib, Nat Arts Club, NY, 94; Salmagundi 1994 Non-Member Art Exhib, Salmagundi Club, NY; 1994 Alumni Traveling Art Show, Sch Art Inst Chicago, 94; and others. *Awards:* Santa Fe Fed Bank Purchase Award, Watercolor West Ann Exhib, 80; Grumbacher Gold Medal & Cash Award, Knickerbocker Artists Ann Exhib, 83; Best Watercolor Artist in Show Award, Art-a-Fair Festival, 89; Windsor Newton Watercolor Award, Audubon Artists 1994 Exhib, Nat Arts Club, New York & Salmagundi Exhib, Salmagundi Club, New York, 94; and others. *Mem:* Nat Watercolor Soc (bd mem). *Media:* Watercolor, Oil. *Dealer:* Lu Martin Galleries 372 N Coast Hwy Laguna Beach CA 92651; Tidelands Publications 28912 Canyon Rim Dr Trabuco Canyon CA 92619. *Mailing Add:* 913 Ronda Sevilla Unit Q Laguna Hills CA 92653-4756

MACCLINTOCK, DORCAS
SCULPTOR, WRITER
b New York, NY, July 16, 32. *Study:* Smith Col, AB; Univ Wyo, AM; Lyme Acad Col of Fine Arts. *Comn:* Trophy, Collie Club Am Found, 88. *Exhib:* Animal Imagery, St Hubert's Giralda, 87-89; Wildlife Images, Central Park Zoo Gallery, NY, 90; Art & the Animal (traveling), Cleveland Mus Natural Hist, 91; Algonquin Park, Can, 95; Witte Mus, San Antonio, Tex, 96; Shot Tower Gallery, Columbus, Ohio, 97; Disney's Animal Kingdom, Orlando, Fla, 98; Wildlife Art, Sharon Arts Ctr, Peterborough, NH, 98; Art of the Animal Kingdom, Bennington Ctr Arts, Vt, 98-02; Cleveland Mus of Nat History, 99; Wildlife Exp, Parker Co, 2002; Nat Sculpture Soc Ann, SC and NY, 2002; two-person exhib, Hiram Blauvelt Art Mus, Oradell, NJ, 2003; Hiram Blauvelt Art Mus, Oradell, NJ, 04; Art of the Animal Kingdom IX, Bennington Ctr Arts, Vt, 04-06; Catharine Lorillar Wolfe Art Club 108th Ann Exhib, NY 04-06. *Pos:* Res assoc, Calif Acad Sci, San Francisco; cur affil, Peabody Mus, Yale Univ, New Haven, Conn. *Awards:* Children's Book Award, NY Acad Sci, 74; Smith Col Medal, 87; Anna Hyatt Huntington Award, Catharine Lorillard Wolfe Art Club, 2004. *Mem:* Soc Animal Artists Inc (mem exec bd, 76-, jury, 76-95); Am Soc Mammalogists; Auths Guild. *Media:* Bronze. *Publ:* Auth 11 books incl, A Raccoon's First Year, Scribners, 82; African Images, Scribners, 85; Phoebe the Kinkajou, 85; Red Pandas, 88; Animals Observed, 93; A Natural History of Raccoons, 2003. *Mailing Add:* 33 Rogers Rd Hamden CT 06517

MACDONALD, BETTY ANN KIPNISS
PRINTMAKER
b Brooklyn, NY, Aug, 36. *Study:* Adelphi Univ, BA, 58; Columbia Univ, MA, 60; Chinese Inst, 66-68. *Work:* Libr Cong; Mus Mod Art, Buenos Aires, Arg; Am Cult Ctr, New Delhi, India; New Orleans Mus Art; Montgomery Mus Art, Ala; NY Pub Libr; White House, Washington, DC; Cheremeteff Collection, Book Chamber Internat, Moscow, Russia; Portland Art Mus, Oreg; Nat Mus of Women in the Arts; Univ Richmond Mus, VA; Washington Co Mus Fine Art, Hagerstown, MD. *Comn:* Murals, comn by Washington Women's Investment Club, Washington, DC, 89, Community of Creative Non-Violence. *Exhib:* Los Angeles Printmaking Soc Exhib, Univ HI, Hilo, HI, 85; Prizewinners Exhib, Judicial Ctr, Fairfax, Va, 85; one-person shows, Dept Interior, Geological Survey, Reston, Va, 89, Washington Printmakers Gallery, Washington, 89, Bird-In-Hand Gallery, Washington, 92, 94 & 98; Univ Brazil, 94; Nat Mus Women Arts, 94-95; Book Chamber Int, Moscow, Russia; House Humor and Satire, Gabrovo, Bulgaria, 10, 12 & 16; Mus Modern Art, Buenos Aires, Argentina. *Collection Arranged:* Cheremeteff Collection, Am Cult Ctr, New Delhi, India; Nat Acad Mus, New York, 98; New Orleans Mus Art. *Pos:* Bd mem, Washington Print Club. *Teaching:* Instr art, Montshire Mus, 76-83, Lebanon Col, 83-84, Smithsonian Inst, 85-95 & Corcoran Gallery Art, 96. *Awards:* First Prize Printmakers VII, Wash Women's Art Ctr, 85; State Prize Copley Soc Exhib, Nat League of Am Pen Women, 86; Purchase Prize, Print Club Albany, 98; Award of Merit, State of Va Copley Soc, Boston, 87; Past Pres Award, Mus Fine Arts, Springfield, Mass, 83; Book as Art VI and VII, Nat Mus Women in the Arts, Washington, 94, 95; Purchase Award Prize, Delta Nat Small Prints Exhib, Ark State Univ, 2001; Best in Show in Small Prints, Big Impressions, Md Fedn Arts Cir Gallery, Annapolis, Md, 2002. *Bibliog:* Pamela Kessler (auth), Plum Gallery, Washington Post, 3/18/88; Mary McCoy (auth), Washington Printmakers Gallery, Washington Post, 8/22/91; Saiden Pakraven (auth), Washington Printmakers Gallery, Washington Post, 1/17/02; Paul Cassady (auth), J Print World, 8/2/2004. *Mem:* Life mem Art Student League; Nat Asn Women Artists; Los Angeles Printmaking Soc; Washington Area Printmakers; Soc Am Graphic Artists. *Media:* Etchings, Monoprints. *Res:* Aedrypoint and mazzotint series that will take the viewer on a journey into twilight worlds of the imagination. *Publ:* Contribr, Tilt: An Anthology of New England Women's Writing and Art, New Victoria Publ, 75; Orig Print Calender, Wash Area Printmakers, 87, 88, 89, 90, 91, 92, 93, 95 & 96; William & Mary Rev, 92, 93, 94, 95, 96, 97, 98, 99, 2000, 01, 02, 03; book cover, Adagio for Trumpet and Strings, Precipice, Contrasts and Kaleidoscopic Changes, Arsis Press. *Dealer:* Washington Printmakers Gallery 2106 R St Washington DC 20008; Living Gallery 20 S First St Ashland OR 97520; River Gallery 400 E 2d St Chattanooga TN 37403; Somerhill Gallery 3 Beargate E Franklin St Chapel Hill NC 27514. *Mailing Add:* PO Box 1202 Mc Lean VA 22101

MACDONALD, BRUCE K
EDUCATOR, HISTORIAN, ARTIST
b New York, NY, June 6, 33. *Study:* Trinity Col, BA, 61; Harvard Univ, MA, 67 & PhD, 73. *Exhib:* Spirit Door, Soruba Samadhi Gallery, Asheville, NC, 6/2000; When.Now?, Artworks, Asheville, 7/2001; Closed.Open, The New Art Ctr, Newton, Mass, 9/2001; Original Nature, 16 Patton, Asheville, 6/2003. *Collection Arranged:* Photographs Before Surrealism, Mus Mod Art, New York, 68; Nineteenth Century Painting from the Mus de Arte de Ponce, Mass Inst Technol, 74. *Pos:* Dir, Exhibs, Mass Inst Technol, Cambridge, Mass, 74-75; dean, Sch Mus Fine Arts, Boston, Mass, 76-93, first pres, 93-94, pres emer, 94-. *Teaching:* Instr, Univ Mass, Boston,72; vis fac mem, Harvard Univ, 76. *Mem:* Photogr Resource Ctr, Inc (bd trustees, 76-86); Cambridge Multicultural Arts Ctr (bd dir, 83-85); Pro Arts Consortium (pres, 92-93); New Art Ctr (bd gov 94-96). *Media:* Oil on Panel. *Publ:* Contrib auth, Brassai, Mus Mod Art, 68; The Quarry by Gustave Courbet, Boston Mus Fine Arts Bull, 69; Nineteenth Century Painting from the Museo de Art de Ponce, Mass Inst Technol, 74; contribr, Visual Dharma: The Buddhist Art of Tibet, Shambala, 75. *Dealer:* Beth Kantrowitz Randi Hopkins The Skirt Gallery Boston MA; 16 Patton Ave Asheville NC 28801. *Mailing Add:* 87 Dalby St Newton MA 02458

MACDONALD, COLIN SOMERLED
WRITER, PUBLISHER
b Ottawa, Ont, Mar 5, 25. *Study:* Self taught artist; also study with Mabel May ARCA. *Exhib:* One-man show, Little Gallery, Photog Stores, Ottawa, Ont, 62; Ottawa Born Artists, Univ Ottawa, 67. *Collection Arranged:* A dict of Canadian Artists in 8 Vols. *Pos:* Ed & publ, Dictionary Can Artists, 67-; pres-dir, Can Paperbacks Publ Ltd, 74-. *Awards:* Exploration Program Research Award, Can Coun, 85; Wintario/Heritage Ont grant, 87; Melva J Dwyer Award, Art Lib Soc N Am, 97; plus others. *Bibliog:* W Q Ketchum (auth), Faces of Ottawa, Ottawa J, 3/70; Nancy Baele (auth), One-man dictionary of artists, The Ottawa Citizen, 6/90; D Fetherling (auth), Artistic References, Books in Can, 11/93, MacLean's July 28, 2003, Closing Notes People by Sharon Doyle Driedger. *Media:* Oil Painting. *Res:* Biographical information on living and dead Canadian visual artists with bibliography and critical comments. *Interests:* Collecting books on ocean going ships; collecting art reference & history books. Support for: large Canadian combined opers, Combat Force - Peace Making/Peace Keeping & N Am Missile Defence system. *Publ:* Auth, Dictionary of Canadian Artists (Sylvia Safdie to Jori Smith), Vols I-VII (rev), 67-97; Vol 8 Part One (July, 2006). *Mailing Add:* 17 Gwynne Ave Ottawa ON K1Y 1X1 Canada

MACDONALD, ROBERT R
DIRECTOR, HISTORIAN
b Pittsburgh, Pa, May 11, 42. *Study:* Univ Notre Dame, BA, 64, MA, 65; Univ Pa, MA, 70. *Exhib:* The Face of Genius: Images of Eugene O'Neill, 87; On Being Jomeless: Hist Perspectives, 87; Within Bohemia's Boarders: Greenwich Village (1830-1930), 90; Broadway, 125 Urs Musical Theater, 91; Gaelic Gotham; A History of the irish in NY, 96; Berenice Abbott: Changing NY, 97; NY Begins, 98. *Collection Arranged:* New Haven Colony Furniture (ed, catalog), New Haven Hist Soc, 72; La Portrait Gallery (ed, catalog), 81 & Sun King: Louis XIV and the New World (ed catalog), 84, La State Mus. *Pos:* Dir, New Haven Hist Soc, 71-74, La State Mus, 74-85 & Mus City NY, 85-. *Teaching:* Assoc fel Am civilization, Yale Univ, 73-74; instr mus studies, Tulane Univ, 81; lectr mus studies, NY Univ, 86-. *Awards:* Order of Arts & Lett, French Repub, 85; Order of Isabella Catolica, Govt Spain, 85. *Mem:* Am Asn Mus (pres, 85-87); Am Asn State & Local Hist (mem coun, 78-80). *Res:* American folk art, social and cultural history. *Mailing Add:* c/o Museum of the City of New York Fifth Ave at 103rd St New York NY 10029

MACDONALD, SCOTT
CRITIC, EDUCATOR
b Easton, Pa, Oct 10, 42. *Study:* DePauw Univ, BA, 64; Univ Fla, MA, 66, PhD, 70. *Teaching:* Asst prof humanities, Univ Fla, 69-70; from asst prof to prof film & Am lit, Utica Col, 71-, dir, Art Gallery, presently. *Res:* Research regarding avant-garde filmmakers. *Specialty:* Upstate New York artists whose work poses a challenge to the local Utica-Rome community. *Publ:* Auth, The expanding vision of Larry Gottheim's films, 78; Surprise, The films of Robert Huot, Quart Rev Film Studies, 80; Interview with Taka Iimura, Part 1, Art & Cinema, 80; Interview with Robert Huot, Afterimage, 80; and others. *Mailing Add:* 5 Sherman St New Hartford NY 13413-2611

MACDONALD, WILLIAM L
HISTORIAN, WRITER
b Putnam, Conn, 21. *Study:* Harvard Col, AB, Harvard Univ, AM & PhD(Emerton Fel, Shaw Fel, Morse Fel, Vet Nat Scholar). *Teaching:* Instr, assoc prof, Yale Univ, 56-65; AP Brown prof, Smith Col, 65-80. *Awards:* AD Hitcock Prize, Soc Archit Historian, 86 & 96; George Wittenborn Award, 96; Int Book Award, Am Inst Architects, 97; Getty scholar, Getty Ctr for Fine Arts & Humanities, 85-86; fel Am Acad Rone, 54-56. *Mem:* Fel Am Acad Arts & Sci; Soc Archit Historians (dir, 58-64); Am Asn Archit Bibliogr. *Res:* History of architecture and urbanism; ancient, early Christian, Baroque & American architecture. *Publ:* Auth, The Pantheon: Design, Meaning and Progeny, 76; assoc ed & contribr, Princeton Encyclopedia of Classical Sites, 76; auth, Piranesi's Carceri: Sources of Invention, 79; The Architecture of the Roman Empire, Vol 1, rev ed 82, Vol 2, 86; Hadrian's Villa (with John Pinto), 95 & La Villa Adriana (with John Pinto), 97; Northampton Massachusetts Architecture, 76; Early Christian & Byzantine Architecture, 62. *Mailing Add:* 3811 39th St NW Washington DC 20016-2835

MACDONELL, CAMERON
PAINTER, MURALIST
b Elmira, NY, 38. *Study:* Col Educ, State Univ NY, Buffalo, BS (art educ); studied with John Davidson, Mort Grossman, Larry Calcognio & Trevor Thomas; independent study, Santa Barbara, Calif. *Work:* IBM. *Comn:* pvt collections. *Exhib:* Regional, Albright Knox Art Gallery, NY, 60; Regional, Santa Barbara Mus Art, Calif; Our Town Gallery, Santa Barbara, 74; Goleta Galleria, Calif, 75; one-man show, 76, regional group show, 76-79, Arnot Art Mus, Elmira, NY; Artists Gallery, Elmira, NY, 79-81; Clemens Ctr, Elmira, NY, 83; Chemung Canal Gallery, 88; NUS Traveling Exhib, 90 Group show. *Pos:* Art dir marketing develop, Art Frame Publ, Santa Barbara, Calif, 70-76; mgr Econoline advert, Asn Retarded Children, Elmira, NY, 77-81; graph artist, 81-90; designer, Art made famous publ, Santa Barbara, Calif, currently. *Teaching:* Instr, Studio 605, 84-90 & 96; Basic drawing, Aduentist sch, 2006. *Awards:* Silver Medallions, Bicentennials, City of Santa Barbara & Co of Santa Barbara, 76; Artistic Serv Award, OMRDD, NY, 79; Citation, State of New York, Arts In the Park, 80. *Bibliog:* Larry Griffis, Jr (auth), World of art, Buffalo Courier Express, 61; Trevor Thomas, Buffalo Evening News, 62; Lee Batten (auth), California Artists, Art Fame Publ, 75; Tom Page (auth), Brush with Greatness, Elmira Star Gazette, 1/91. *Mem:* Southern Tier Arts Asn (co-chmn, 79-80); Founder of the Arts in the Park, An Ann Event, Elmira, NY. *Media:* Woodcuts, Oil, Collages Acrylic. *Res:* Christian Prophesy. *Interests:* Combining traditional religious art with contemp. *Collection:* IBM Collection, Binghamton, NY. *Publ:* contribr, Reflections, 72 & illusr, Salvang, 75, Art Fame Publ. *Dealer:* The Sturdivant Gallery 912 Southport St Elmira NY 14904; Art & Frame Gallery Water St Elmira NY 14901. *Mailing Add:* Studio 605 605 Yale St Elmira NY 14904

MACDOUGALL, ANNE
ART DEALER, PAINTER
b Winchester, Mass, Apr 27, 44. *Study:* Abbot Acad; Randolph-Macon Woman's Col, AB(art); Syracuse Univ, grad study in art. *Work:* Boston Univ, Mus Fine Arts, Boston; Va Mus Fine Arts; DeCordova Mus, Lincoln, Mass; Indianapolis Mus. *Exhib:* Boston Printmaker's Nat, 74, 76 & 77; Nat Print, Trenton State, 79; Drawings, DeCordova Mus, 80; Nat Print & Drawing, NDak State, 81; Addison Gallery Am Art, 81; Grand Cent Galleries, NY, 89; Luise Ross Gallery, NY, 94. *Pos:* Dir, GW Einstein Gallery, NY. *Awards:* Va Ctr Fel, 78; MacDowell Fel, 80; Purchase Award, Berkshire Mus, 81. *Bibliog:* Meryle Secrest (auth), article, Washington Post, 4/5/75; Paul Ciano (auth), article, Jewish Advocate, 2/8/78 & 6/81; Dr John Driscoll (auth), The American Landscape Book, 98. *Mem:* Art Table, NY; Boston Printmakers; Boston Visual Artists Union; Cambridge Art Asn (vpres, 72-73); Int Fine Print Dealers Asn. *Media:* Watercolor. *Mailing Add:* 98 Riverside Dr New York NY 10024

MACDOUGALL, PETER STEVEN
CERAMIC ARTIST, SCULPTOR
b Willimantic, Conn, Oct 23, 51. *Study:* Northwestern Conn Community Col, 70-72; Alfred Univ, New York, BFA, 75; Wichita State Univ, Kans, MFA, 77. *Work:* Downey Mus Art, Downey, Calif; Elrich Mus, Wichita State Univ; Nelson Gallery, Alfred Univ, NY; and others. *Exhib:* Copperstown Ann, Copperstown Art Asn, NY, 79-80; Fingerlakes Show, Mem Art Gallery, Rochester, 80; Everson Mus, Syracuse, NY, 80; Artworks Gallery, Hartford, Conn, 81; Univ Dallas, Irving, Tex, 81; and others. *Teaching:* Instr ceramics, Wichita Art Asn, 76-78; asst prof, State Univ NY, Oswego, 78-82; asst prof, Middle Tenn State Univ, 82-87. *Awards:* Craft Award, Northwestern Community Col, 72; Jury Award, Hartford Civic Art Show, 75; Third Place, Adironack Invitational, 81. *Mem:* Col Arts Asn; Nat Coun Educ Ceramic Arts; Am Craft Coun. *Media:* Clay. *Dealer:* Hanover Gallery New York NY. *Mailing Add:* PO Box 119 Round Pond ME 04564

MACEK, M D (MILA D)
PAINTER
b Prague, Czech Repub. *Exhib:* Gallery 53, Cooperstown, NY, 89; Salvatore Ala Gallery, 92-94; State Gallery, Most, Czech Repub, 93; Exile v NY, Galerie Vaclava Spala Prague, 93; solo exhib, Galerie Maria Chailloux, Amsterdam, The Neth, 94; Color, Matter, Energy, Oberhausen, Ger, 95; Galerie Maria Chailloux, Amsterdam, 97; Chimeat Gallery, NY, 98; participant in the space prog, The Mary Walsh Sharpe Art Found, 98-99; Pollock-Krasner Found, 99; Elizabeth Found for the Arts Studio Program, 2000; Adolph & Esther Gottlieb Found Grant, Gallery Maria Chailloux, Amsterdam, 2001. *Awards:* Pollock-Krasner Found Grant, 90; Nat Endowment Arts, Fel, 93-94. *Dealer:* Galerie Maria Chailloux Amsterdam Holland. *Mailing Add:* Box 10 A Treadwell NY 13846

MACGAW, WENDY
SCULPTOR
b Detroit, Mich, Nov 16, 55. *Study:* Univ Mich Sch Art, BFA, 77; Cranbrook Art Acad, MFA, 79. *Work:* Detroit Inst Arts, Albert Kahn & Asn, Architects. *Exhib:* Young Americans: Award Winner, Am Craft Mus, NY, 82; Steel-Glass Sculpture: Wendy MacGaw, Detroit Int Art, Mich, 85; Invitational Metal Show, 3 Rivers Art Fest, Pittsburgh, Pa, 85; Glass Am, Heller Gallery, NY, 85; Mich Nat Endowment Art Fest, 1965-85, Detroit Focus Gallery, 86; Detroit Artists: Update, Cranbrook Art Mus, Bloomfield Hills, 86; Detroit Artists Artemesia, 88; Glass, 88. *Pos:* Co-owner, Artpack Serv, Detroit, Mich, 84-; mem, Speech, Detroit, 84. *Teaching:* Asst prof design, Ctr Creative Studies, Detroit, 79-; instr fine arts, 3-D Design, Wayne State Univ, Detroit, 83-84; instr art & writing, Detroit Inst Art, Mich, 83-84. *Awards:* Award winner, Young Americans: Metal, 80; Nat Endowment Arts Fel, 82-83 & 86-87; Creative Artist Grant, Mich Coun Arts, 84-85; Mich Coun Arts, 88-. *Mem:* Detroit Focus; Founders Soc Detroit Inst Arts. *Media:* Metal, Glass. *Mailing Add:* 28201 Wellington St Farmington MI 48334-3266

MACGREGOR, GREGORY ALLEN
PHOTOGRAPHER
b La Crosse, Wis, Feb 13, 41. *Study:* Univ Calif, San Francisco, MA(photog), 71; with Jack Welpott & Don Worth. *Work:* San Francisco Mus Mod Art, Calif; Oakland Mus, Calif; Chicago Art Inst, Ill; Mus Mod Art & Whitney Mus, NY. *Exhib:* On the Go, Fine Arts Mus, San Francisco, Calif, 78; Recent Work, OK Harris Works of Art, NY, 79 & 82; San Francisco Mus Mod Art, 82, 83, 87 & 88; The Calif Trail, Arch Mus, St Louis, Mo, 90, Nev Hist Soc Mus, 91 & Dept Interior Mus, Washington, 97; The Oregon Trail, Wash State Hist Mus, Tacoma, 95 & Ore State Hist Mus, Portland, 96; Explosions, Nichols Gallery, San Francisco, 96; Overland, the California Emigrant Trail, Managed by the California Humanities Council, 91-; Lewis and CLark, Traveling Nat Exhib, 2003-2007. *Teaching:* Asst prof & chmn photog, Lone Mountain Col, San Francisco, Calif, 70-78; prof photog, Calif State Univ, Hayward, 80-84, prof art, 80-, art dept chmn, 90-93. *Awards:* Oakland Artist Fel Award, 90. *Bibliog:* Ted Hedypath (auth), The real as surreal, Artweek, 2/25/80; Jim Hughes (auth), Proofsheet, Popular Photog, 6/80; Mark Levy (auth), article, Images & Issues, 10/82. *Mem:* Soc Photog Educ. *Publ:* contribr, Darkroom Dynamics, Curtin-London, 79; auth, Explosions, Headlands Press, 80; article, Art Comn, 6/83; illusr, Darkroom Mag, Vol 4, No 8, 82; Overland, The California Emigrant Trail, Univ NMex Press, 96; auth, Lewis & Clark Revisited, Univ Washington Press. *Dealer:* O K Harris 383 W Broadway New York NY 10012; Equivalents Gallery 1822 Broadway Seattle WA. *Mailing Add:* 6481 Colby St Oakland CA 94618-1309

MACHIN, ROGER
SCULPTOR
b Leicester, Eng, Jan 29, 55. *Study:* Brighton Polytechnic, MA, 78, Sch Inst Arts Chicago, MFA, 80. *Work:* De Paul Univ, Chicago; Niagara Univ, Niagara Falls, NY; Long Island Univ, CW Post Campus, NY; Taylor Univ, Upland, NY. *Exhib:* One & two person exhibs, NAME Gallery, Chicago, Ill, 79, De Paul Univ, Chicago, Ill, 81, Foster Gallery, Univ Wis, Eau Claire, 82, Marianne Deson Gallery, Chicago, Ill, 85, Ill Wesleyan Univ, Bloomington, 89 & Turman Gallery, Ind State Univ, Terra Haute, 92; Aggregate, State Ill Gallery, Chicago, 86; Exterior/Interior, Rockford Art Mus, Ill, 86; Eccentric Machines, Kohler Art Ctr, Sheboygan, Wis, 87; Down to the Sea, New House Gallery, Staten Island, NY, 87; Sculpture Chicago Alumni Exhib, Ill, 87; Movers & Shakers, DePree Art Ctr, The Neth, Mich, 88; Summer Hydra, Compass Rose Gallery, Chicago, 89; Sculpture: Part II, Betsy Rosenfield Gallery, Chicago, Ill, 90; Sculpture Invitational, Greater Lafayette Mus Art, Ind, 91; Sculpture, Ricky Renier Gallery, Chicago, Ill, 91; Exploring Maps, Turman Gallery, Ind State Univ, Terra Haute, 92; and other group & solo exhibs. *Pos:* Asst to Loren Madsen, 78-84; Proj mgr contemp installations, Westin Maui & Westin Kauai, 87 & Hyatt Regency Waikoloa, Hawaii, 88; dir & owner, Method and Materials Fine Art Rigging and Installation Co. *Teaching:* Instr, Univ Wis, Eau Claire, 82, Chelsea Sch Art, London, Eng, 83, W Surrey Col Art, Eng, 87, Brighton Poly Tech, Sussex, 87, Reading Univ, Eng, 87 & Ill State Univ, Normal, 88; head sculptor, Evanston Art Ctr, Ill, 88. *Awards:* Individual Artist Grant, Ill Arts Coun, 84, 85 & 86; Visual Arts Fel, sculpture, Nat Educ Asn, 86 & 88; Uncross Found Fel, Wyo, 89. *Bibliog:* Steve Luecking (auth), Chicago sculpture: A nuts and bolts eloquence, New Art Examiner, 10/88; Corey Postigilione (auth), summer hydra at compass Rose Gallery (rev), Dialogue, 12/89; many other mag & newspaper articles & revs. *Mailing Add:* 2556 W Thomas Chicago IL 60607

MACHIORLETE, PATRICIA ANNE
PAINTER, CRAFTSMAN
b Jersey City, NJ. *Study:* Fairleigh Dickinson Univ, BS, 67; Art Ctr NJ, 81; also workshops with Barbara Nechis & Arthur Barbour. *Work:* Allied Signal Corp, Morris Township, NJ; Pub Serv Elect & Gas Co, Newark, NJ; NJ Am Water Co, Short Hills, NJ; Drakes Cakes, Wayne, NJ; The Lanid Corp, Parsippany, NJ. *Comn:* 3 Water Colors, comn by Mr Neil Vanderdusen, Pres, Sony Corp Am, Mendham, NJ, 86. *Exhib:* 15th Ann Salmagundi Club, 84 & 89 & Knickerbocker Artists, 84 & 89, NY; one woman show, Beneficial Mgt Corp Gallery, Peapack, NJ, 87; NJ Watercolor Soc, Monmouth Mus, Lincroft, NJ, 88-91; NAWA Travel Exhib, Mus Southwest, Sewanee, TN, 91-92; 71st Ann Nat Watercolor Soc, Brea Civic Ctr, Calif, 91; 49th Ann Audubon Artists, Nat Arts Club, NY, 91. *Pos:* Newsletter ed, NJ Watercolor Soc, 91-; bd dir, Nat Asn Women Artists, 91-93, catalog chairperson, currently. *Teaching:* Childrens Workshops for Pub librs. *Awards:* Monmouth Mus Award, 46th Annual NJ WC Soc Exhib, 88; Grumbacher Medallion, Leonardo Da Vinci, 83; First Prize, 60th Anniversary Exhib, Essex Watercolor Soc, 93. *Mem:* Nat Asn Women Artists (bd dir & chairperson, 91-93); Garden State Watercolor Soc; Miniature Soc, NJ; Essex Watercolor Soc; NJ Watercolor Soc (bd dir, 91-, rec secy, 98-). *Media:* Watercolor; Furniture Painting. *Publ:* The Artist's Mag, 6/93. *Mailing Add:* 133 Autumn Ridge Rd Bedminster NJ 07921

MACK, CHARLES RANDALL
EDUCATOR, HISTORIAN
b Baltimore, Md, May 23, 40. *Study:* Univ NC, Chapel Hill, AB, 1962, PhD (hist art), 1972. *Collection Arranged:* Classical Art from Carolina Collections (auth catalog), Columbia Mus Art, SC & NC Mus Art, Raleigh, 74; A Campus Collects (auth catalog), Univ SC Mus, Columbia, 80; H Robert Bonsack: Figure Studies, Goethe Inst, Atlanta traveling exhib, 81-82; Turned to Tradition: Southeastern Folk Pottery Today (auth catalog), Columbia Mus Art, SC, 88; Paper Pleasures: Five Centuries of Drawings and Watercolors (auth catalog), Univ SC Mus, Columbia, 92-94; Two Traditions in Transition: Folk Potters of E Germany and Am South, McKissick Mus, Univ SC, Columbia, 98; Bunzlauer Style (auth catalog), Georgia Mus of Art, Athers, 2002; Enamelware Art, McKissick Mus, Univ SC, Columbia, 2003; Bonsack: Centenary Celebration (auth cCatalog), McMaster Gallery, Univ SC, Columbia, 2003. *Pos:* VPres Southeastern Col Art Conf, 2000-03, pres, 2003-. *Teaching:* Prof ancient

& Renaissance art, Univ SC, Columbia, 70-2005, William J Todd, Dist Prof Emer Italian Renaissance, 92-. *Awards:* Am Coun Learned Soc Trav Grant, 82, 89; Nat Endowment Humanities Grant, 84, 89; Am Phil Soc Grant, 94; Southeastern Col Art Conf Research & Publ award, 98, Exhib & Catalog award 93. *Mem:* Am Col Art Asn; Southeastern Col Art Conf (pres 75-76, bd mem 84-87, pres 2003-2005); Southeastern Chap Soc Archit Historians (bd mem 84-87, pres 91-92). *Res:* Fifteenth century Italian art and architecture; Southeastern folk pottery; Bunzlauer style pottery from eastern Germany. *Publ:* Pienza: The Creation of a Renaissance City, Cornell Univ, 87; Roman Remains: John Izard Middleton's Visual Souvenirs of 1820-23, Univ SC Press, 97; Fictive Spaces for Monastic Places, Arris, 2001; Just What the Medici Ordered, Arris, 2002; co-auth, Like a Sponge Thrown into Water: Franics Lieber's European Travel Journal of 1844-45, Univ SC Press, 2002; Botticelli's Venus: Antique Allusions and Medicean Propaganda, Explorations in Renaissance Culture, 2003; Looking at the Renaissance: Essays Towards Contextual Appreciation, Univ Mich Press, 2005; auth, Talking with the Turners: Conversations with Southern Folk Potters, Univ SC Press, 2006. *Mailing Add:* 122 Woodrow St Columbia SC 29205-3134

MACK, DANIEL R
DESIGNER, CRAFTSMAN
b Rochester, NY, Dec 23, 47. *Study:* Univ Toronto, BA, 70; The New Sch, New York, MA, 75; self-taught woodworker. *Work:* Cooper Hewitt Mus; Am Craft Mus; Mus Fine Arts, Houston; Mus Fine Arts, Boston; Yale Art Gallery. *Exhib:* Am Craft Mus, 87, 91 & 92; Cooper Hewitt Mus, 92. *Teaching:* Teacher rustic woodworking, Anderson Ranch Arts Ctr, Snowmass, Colo, 87-93 & Omega Inst Holistic Studies, 97-. *Awards:* Fel, NY Found Arts, 86 & 90; Fel, Mid-Atlantic Arts Found, 88. *Bibliog:* Rustic revival, Washington Post, 5/85; William Bryant Logan (auth), Rococo rustic, House & Garden, 11/86; many other articles in national magazines. *Media:* Natural Form Wood. *Publ:* Auth, Making Rustic Furniture, Sterling/Lark, 92; The Rustic Furniture Companion, Lark, 96; Simple Rustic Furniture, Lark, 99; Log Cabin Living, Gibbs-Smith, 99. *Mailing Add:* 14 Welling Ave Warwick NY 10990

MACK, WILLIAM L
PATRON
Study: NYU, BS; Wharton Sch, Univ Pa, 61. *Pos:* Pres, sr managing partner, The Mack Orgn, formerly; founder, sr partner, Apollo Real Estate Advisors LP, 93-; bd dir, Mack-Cali Realty Corp, 97-, chmn, 2000-; bd dir, Bear Stearns Companies Inc, 97-2004; bd trustees, Solomon R Guggenheim Mus, New York City, currently; vchmn, N Shore Long Island Jewish Health Systems; trustee, Univ Pa, bd overseers, The Wharton Sch, endowed $10 million for the William & Phyllis Mack Ctr for Technol Innovation, 2001. *Mailing Add:* 76 N 9 St Newark NJ 07107

MACKENZIE, DAVID, IV
PAINTER
b Los Angeles, Calif, Nov 8, 42. *Study:* Orange Coast Col, Costa Mesa, Calif, AA; San Francisco Art Inst, BFA & MFA; also with Ron Nagle & Tom Holland. *Work:* Oakland Mus Art, Calif; Mills Collage Art Gallery, Oakland, Calif; Oakland Mus, Calif; San Francisco Mus Mod Art, Calif. *Exhib:* One-man shows, San Francisco Art Inst, 73, Grapestake Gallery, San Francisco, 75, 76 & 80, A Ten Yr Survey, Bluxome Gallery, San Francisco, 83 & Angeles Gallery, Santa Monica, Calif, 89; 18 Bay Area Artists, Art Mus, Univ Calif, Berkeley, 75; Whitney Biennial, Whitney Mus Am Art, 75; Tough Stuff, San Francisco Mus Mod Art, 83; Bay Area Painting, San Francisco, 84; Sheldon Mem Art Gallery, Univ Nebr, Lincoln; Natural Order, Art in General, NY, 91; Painting Show, Ridge St Gallery, 96; Transport, NY, 97; Process & Image, Eklektikos Gallery, Washington, DC, 98; The Art of Absolute Desire, NY, 99; Straight Painting, NY, 2000; Viewpoints of Recent Developments in Abstract Painting, NY, 2001; Dialog and Discourse, NY, 2001. *Pos:* Guest cur, Los Angeles Inst Contemp Art, Los Angeles, 76, San Francisco Art Inst, 78 & Dialog and Discourse, Friends Acad, 2001; guest organizer, San Francisco Art Inst, 83. *Awards:* Nat Endowment Arts Grant, 75. *Bibliog:* Peter Frank (auth), On the Trail of the Exxon National, Nat Arts Guide, Vol 3, No 1, 81; Thomas Albright (auth), Art in the San Francisco Bay Area 1945-1980, Univ Calif Press; & others. *Mem:* Ridge St Gallery. *Dealer:* Angles Gallery Santa Monica CA. *Mailing Add:* 315 Columbia St Brooklyn NY 11231

MACKENZIE, HUGH SEAFORTH
PAINTER
b Toronto, Ont, June 19, 28. *Study:* Ont Col Art; Mt Allison Univ, BFA. *Work:* Montreal Mus Fine Arts, PQ; Art Gallery Ont & Univ Toronto, Toronto; Univ Waterloo; London Art Gallery, Ont; House Commons, Otttawa; and others. *Comn:* Portrait of LB Pearson, Dept State, Ottawa, 68. *Exhib:* One-man shows, Morris Gallery, Toronto, 63-77, Univ Waterloo, 75, Carleton Univ Art Gallery, Ottawa, 95 & Galerie Dresdnere, Toronto, 95; Montreal Mus Fine Arts, Que, 64 & 70; Lithographs in collabr with NS Col Art, Nat Gallery Can, 71; Bau-Xi Gallery, Toronto, 81, 82, 83, 85, 86, 88, 90, 92, 93, 97, 99, 2000, 02, 04; Hart House, Univ Toronto, 87; Peterborough, Art Gallery, 88; Robert McGlaughlin Gallery, Oshawa, Ont; Gallery Lambton, Sarnia, 2002; Bau-Xi Gallery, Toronto, 2006; and others. *Teaching:* Instr art, Ont Col Art, 68-91; retired. *Awards:* JWG Forster Award, Ont Soc Artists, 61; Can Coun Award, 70; AJ Casson Award for Teaching Excellence, Ont Col Art Alumni Asn, 91. *Bibliog:* Hale (auth), article, Arts Mag, 2/70; Duval (auth), High Realism in Canada, Irwin Clarke & Co, Ltd, 74; Michael Bell (auth), Transitions - Hugh MacKenzie: Painter/Etcher, Carleton Univ Art Gallery. *Mem:* Royal Can Acad. *Media:* Oil, Etching. *Specialty:* painting, prints, sculpture. *Dealer:* Bau-Xi Toronto. *Mailing Add:* 84 MacPherson Ave Toronto ON M5R 1W8 Canada

MACKILLOP, ROD
PAINTER, EDUCATOR
b Northampton, Mass, June 15, 40. *Study:* Tufts Univ, BA, 61, MFA, 68; Sch Boston Mus Fine Arts, with Jan Cox & Jason Berger, dipl, 68. *Work:* Ashville Art Mus, NC; Duke Univ; Davidson Col, NC. *Exhib:* 47th Ann Painting & Sculpture Competition, Southeastern Ctr Contemp Art, Winston-Salem, 79; Large Painting Invitational, Southeastern Ctr Contemp Art, Winston-Salem, 81; NC Artists Exhib, NC Mus Art, Raleigh, 84; Southern Exposure, Alternative Mus, NY, 85; one-man exhib, Asheville Art Mus, NC, 89, St Johns Mus Art, Wilmington, NC, 89 & Hickory Mus Art, NC, 90. *Pos:* Head art dept, Roxbury Latin Sch, Mass, 65-73. *Teaching:* Prof painting & art criticism, Univ NC, Charlotte, 73-. *Awards:* Purchase Awards, Mint Mus, 79 & 81, Weatherspoon Art Gallery, 84. *Bibliog:* Jane Kessler (auth), Rod MacKillop (article), Art Papers, 7-8/82; Jon Meyers (auth), Rod MacKillop (exhib rev), New Art Examiner, 5/86; Jane Kessler (auth), Rod MacKillop/Paintings 1972-1989, Asheville Art Mus, 89. *Mem:* Col Art Asn; Friends of Art, Charlotte, NC. *Media:* Acrylic Paint. *Dealer:* Hodges Taylor Gallery 119 E 7th St Charlotte NC 28202. *Mailing Add:* 1918 Ewing Ave Charlotte NC 28203-5767

MACKINTOSH, SANDRA
SCULPTURE, COLLAGE ARTIST
b Detroit, Mich, July 2, 44. *Study:* Ctr Creative Studies, Detroit, Mich. *Work:* Guggenheim Mus; Brooklyn Mus, NY; Newark Mus, NJ; Union Bank Switz, Zurich; Shearson Lehman, NY; Hood Mus, Dartmouth Col, NH. *Exhib:* Collage: The State of the Art, Bergen Mus Art & Sci, Paramus, NJ, 85; McNay Art Mus, San Antonio, Tex, 85; Constructed Sculpture in Wood, Brooklyn Mus, 92. *Collection Arranged:* Collection of Fox and Cook Archiecture Firm Ny, 2004. *Pos:* Dir, E Market St Gallery, Red Hook, NY. *Bibliog:* Maureen Mullarkey (auth), The Nation, 12/19/88. *Media:* Wood, Stone, Iron. *Dealer:* Cordier & Ekstrom 417 E 75th St New York NY 10021. *Mailing Add:* 54 Joy Rd Woodstock NY 12498

MACKLOWE, HARRY
COLLECTOR
b 38. *Study:* attended Univ Ala, NY Univ, Sch Visual Arts, NY. *Pos:* Founder & CEO Macklowe Properties, Inc, NY City. *Awards:* named one of Top 200 Collectors, ARTNews Mag, 2005-. *Mailing Add:* Harry Macklowe R E 142 W 57th St New York NY 10019

MACNEILL, FREDERICK DOUGLAS
PAINTER
b Boston, Mass, Sept 28, 29. *Study:* Vesper George Sch Art, 52-54, with Alphonse J Shelton, 69 & Arthur Safford, 70. *Work:* First Nat Bank, John Hancock Life Insurance Co & First Church Christ Scientist, Boston; Otis Elevator Co, NY; Raytheon Corp, Lexington, Mass. *Exhib:* Southern Vt Art Ctr, Manchester, 82; solo exhib, Guild Boston Artists, Mass, 82-84; Hudson Valley Art Asn, Westchester Co Ctr, White Plains, NY, 85; Arts for the Parks, Jackson, Wyo, 91, 92 & 94; Mystic Int Exhib, Conn, 92; Grand Teton Natural Hist Asn, Jackson, Wyo, 93; and others; Top 100 Art for the Park, 2004. *Pos:* Instr, Needham Art Ctr, Mass, 83-83. *Awards:* Helen Van Wyk Gold Medal, Rockport Art Asn, 2002; Mareeret Pearson Gold Medal, Rockport Art Asn, 2002; Maurice E Goldberg Meml Award, Rockport Art Asn, 2002; Alden Bryan Award, Mort Shore AA Asn, 2006; Popular Vot Award, Rockport AA, 2006; Art Whole Supple Award, N Shore Art Asn, 2006; plus many others. *Bibliog:* Article in Yankee Mag, 78; Print Catalogue, NY Graphic Soc Ltd, 84; article in Boston Globe, 95. *Mem:* Guild Boston Artists; Allied Artists Am; Am Artists Prof League; Rockport Art Asn; Hudson Valley Art Asn. *Media:* Oil, Watercolor. *Publ:* Best of Oil Painting, Rockport Pub; Best of Watercolor, Rockport Pub; Art From the Park, North Light Pub; Landscape Inspirations, North Light Pub; Painting Textures, Rockport Pub; illusr book & cover, The Crucifiction in American Art, Macfarland Publs. *Dealer:* Guild of Boston Artists Boston MA; Powers Gallery Acton MA; Gallery on the Green Woodstock VT; Mastcove Gallery Kennebunkport ME. *Mailing Add:* 23 Dana Rd Concord MA 01742

MACPHERSON, KEVIN
PAINTER
b NJ, Apr 9, 56. *Study:* N Ariz Univ, BFA, 78; Scottsdale Artists Sch, 86-. *Exhib:* Plein Air Painters Am, 87, 88, 89, 90, 91 & 94-; solo exhibs, Taos Art Gallery, NMex, 89 & Redfern Gallery, Calif, 94 & 96-98; Taos, Impressionist Show, 89, 90, 91 & 92; Ctr Arts Southwest, Santa Fe, NMex, 90; Am Art in Miniature Invitational, Gilcrease Mus, 94; Alumni Invitational Show, Northern Ariz Univ, 94; Greenhouse Gallery, 96 & 98. *Teaching:* Taos Art Inst, 7/89; oil painting workshops, Scottsdale Artists' Sch, 90-98; Macpherson workshop, 91-98. *Awards:* Best of Show, Amarillo Nat Landscape Competition, 87; Stacey Scholar, 90; Best Landscape, Oil Painters Am, 92. *Bibliog:* Artists' worth watching (article), Art Talk, 2/88 & 11/94; Focus, Santa Fe, 8-9/93; SW Profile, 5/93; and others. *Mem:* signature mem, Plein Air Painters Am (pres); hon signature mem Oil Painters Am. *Media:* Oil. *Publ:* Artist Mag, 10/93 & 10/98; Fill Your Oil Paintings with Light and Color, Northlight Publ, 1/98. *Mailing Add:* 12 Clint Rd Taos NM 87571

MAC WHINNIE, JOHN VINCENT
PAINTER, SCULPTOR
b Rockville Centre, NY, Apr 22, 45. *Study:* Southampton Col, NY, BA(magna cum laude), 71; studied with Fairfield Porter, Larry Rivers & Ilya Bolotowsky. *Work:* Guggenheim Mus; Brooklyn Mus; Phillips Collection; Walker Art Ctr; Parrish Art Mus. *Exhib:* Summer Loan Exhib, Metrop Mus Art, NY, 79; Art in Am Since World War Two, Guggenheim Mus, 79; 24th Ann Contemp Am Painting Exhib, Lehigh Univ, 79; Am Drawing in Black and White, Brooklyn Mus, 81; Am Acad & Inst Arts & Lett, NY, 81; Human Figure in Contemp Art, New Orleans Mus Contemp Art, 82; Poets and Artists of the Region, Guild Hall, East Hampton, NY, 82. *Awards:* First Prize Painting, Parrish Mus, Southampton, NY, 71; Excellence in Painting, Heckscher Mus, Huntington, NY, 74. *Bibliog:* David Shapiro (auth), Transcending photography, Art Int, 76. *Media:* Oil, Encaustic. *Dealer:* Marlborough Gallery New York NY. *Mailing Add:* Deerfield Rd Water Mill NY 11976

MADAN-SHOTKIN, RHODA
PAINTER
b New York, NY. *Study:* Pratt Inst, BFA, 59; Carl Schmalz Workshops 78-79; Charles Reid Workshops, 80-85. *Work:* Discovery Mus, Bridgeport, Conn; Fairfield Art Collection, Conn; Ctr Financial Studies, Fairfield Univ, Conn; Zimmerli Art Mus, New Brunswick, NJ. *Exhib:* Nat Asn Women Artists Traveling Exhib, 83-86; Ann Open Exhib, Salmagundi Club, NY, 83; Womens Art Exhib, Purdue Univ, West Lafayette, Ind, 84; 100 Yrs/100 Works, Fine Arts Mus South Mobile, Ala & Longview Mus Art, Tex, 89-90; Flowers & Figures, Fairfield Univ Ctr Financial Studies, 90; solo shows, Greene Art Gallery, Guilford, Conn, 93 & 2001, Galerie Jamault, France, 2001, In the Light, Rockwell Art Gallery, Wilton, Conn, 2005. *Awards:* Mildred Reilly Mem, 83, Gene Alden Walker Award, 85 & Martha Reid Mem Award, 87, Nat Asn Women Artists; Gene Alden Walker Award for watercolor, NAWA, 99; Koenig Art Prize, Brush and Palette Club, New Haven, Conn; Jared Phillip Apple Mem Award, NWA, 03. *Bibliog:* Thomas F Potter (auth), Art topics, Meriden Record J, 88-89; Shirley Gonzales, Watercolor's maturity, New Haven Register, 89; Judy Birke (auth), Other Interesting Works, New Haven Register, 2002. *Mem:* Nat Asn Women Artists; Conn Watercolor Soc; New Haven Paint & Clay Club; Westport Art Ctr. *Media:* Watercolor. *Publ:* Contribr, Pulling Your Paintings Together, Watson-Guptill, 85. *Dealer:* Greene Art Gallery 29 Whitfield St Guilford CT 06437; Rockwell Art Gallery 379 Danbury Rd Wilton Conn 06897. *Mailing Add:* Five Brookside Dr Westport CT 06880

MADDEN-WORK, BETTY I
PAINTER, HISTORIAN
b Chicago, Ill, Nov 12, 15. *Study:* Am Acad Art, Chicago; Northwestern Univ; Univ Ill, BFA; Inst Design, Chicago; with Herb Olson, Spain & Italy; John Pellew, Ireland & Eng; Tom Hill, Mex; Zornes, Vt. *Work:* City of Springfield, Ill; Repub China; Ill Col; Lincoln Col; Caterpillar Tractor, Peoria; pvt collections. *Comn:* 7 paintings, Springfield Mayor's Awards Arts, 98. *Exhib:* Midwest Watercolor Soc, 81, 86 & 89; Ill Dept of Transportation, 81 & State Fair Professional, 81, 85 & 90; Fla Celebration of Women, 84; one-man shows, Western Ill Univ, Macomb, 78 & Caterpillar Tractor Co, Peoria, 79; S Ill Med Sch, 92; Sangamon State Univ, 91 & 94. *Collection Arranged:* Arts and Artifacts of Illinois. *Pos:* Com artist & illusr, Consolidated Bk Publ, Chicago, 44-46; com artist, Evans, Work & Costa Advert, Springfield, Ill, 55-59; fashion illusr, SA Barker Co, Springfield, 59-61; tech asst art dept, Ill State Mus, 61-63, cur art, 63-78; calligrapher, Ill Supreme Ct, 80-2003. *Teaching:* Instr art, Art Asn, Springfield, 78-94 & Ft Myers Beach, Fla, 85-90. *Awards:* Springfield Pacesetters Achievements in the Arts Award, 69; City Purchase Award, Springfield, 83; First Prize, Fla, SW Regional, 85 & 88; Midwest Water Color Soc Award, 86. *Bibliog:* Betty Madden Work: Building on a Wet-into-Wet Base, Am Artist, Watercolor, 92. *Mem:* Ill Artisans; Springfield Art Asn; signature mem Transparent Watercolor Soc Am; Prairie Art Alliance; Delta Kappa Gamma (hon). *Media:* Watercolor, Ink. *Res:* Arts, crafts and architecture of Ill. *Interests:* Art history, painting, calligraphy. *Publ:* Auth, Art, Crafts and Architecture in Early Illinois, Univ Ill Press, 74; Living Museum, articles, Ill State Mus, 63-78. *Mailing Add:* 3950 Sumac Dr Apt 219 Traverse City MI 49684-7014

MADDOX, JERALD CURTIS
CURATOR, HISTORIAN
b Decatur, Ind, June 9, 33. *Study:* Ind Univ, AB, 55 & MA, 60; Harvard Univ, 60-61. *Hon Degrees:* Corcoran Sch Art, Hon Dr Fine Art, Wash, DC, 97. *Work:* Int Mus Photog, George Eastman House, Rochester, NY. *Collection Arranged:* American Photography: The Sixties, Univ Nebr Art Galleries, 66; Creative Photography 1869-1969, Libr Cong, Washington, DC, 70. *Pos:* Asst to dir, Univ Nebr Art Galleries, 63-66; head curatorial section, Prints & Photog Div, Libr Cong, 66-78, cur photog, 66-, collections planner & coordr, 78-87; consult photog, Northern Va Community Col, 77. *Teaching:* Instr art hist, NY State Univ Col New Paltz, 62-63. *Awards:* Mus Prof Fel, Nat Endowment Arts, 74. *Mem:* Col Art Asn; Soc Photog Educ (treas, 68-73). *Res:* History and criticism of photography. *Publ:* Auth, Essay on a tintype, 1/69 & Creative photography, 1869-1969, 1/71, Quart J Libr Cong; Photography in the first decade, Art Am, 7/8/73; How much is a photograph worth, After Image, 2/75; The Pioneering Image: Celebrating 150 years of American Photography, 6/89. *Mailing Add:* 4514 Highland Ave Bethesda MD 20814

MADDOX, JERROLD WARREN
EDUCATOR, PAINTER
b Ft Wayne, Ind, Mar 6, 32. *Study:* Ind Univ, BS, 54 & MFA, 59. *Exhib:* Recent Painting USA: The Figure, Mus Mod Art, NY, 62-63; Moods of Light, Am Fedn Art, 63-64. *Teaching:* Asst prof humanities, Monteith Col, Wayne State Univ, Detroit, 60-63; lectr painting & drawing, Regional Col Art & Crafts, Hull, Eng, 64; asst prof painting & drawing, Univ Ky, Lexington, 64-66; asst prof drawing & painting, Amherst Col, Mass, 66-69; assoc prof drawing & painting, Reed Col, Portland, Ore, 69-70; assoc prof drawing & painting, Ind Univ, Bloomington, 70-74; head prof, Kans State Univ, Manhattan, 74-; dir, Pa State Univ, University Park, 80-84, prof, 84-. *Mem:* Col Art Asn Am; Nat Coun Art Adminr (chmn, 82); Nat Asn Sch Art & Design. *Media:* Oil. *Publ:* Coauth, Images and Imagination: an Introduction to Art, 65. *Mailing Add:* 1495 W Pine Grove Rd Pennsylvania Furnace PA 16865-9422

MADIGAN, MARTHA
PHOTOGRAPHER
b Milwaukee, Wis. *Study:* Univ Wis-Madison, BS(art educ), 72; Ariz State Univ, grad studies, 72-73; Visual Studies workshop, Rochester, NY, 76; Sch Art Inst Chicago, MFA, 78. *Work:* Metrop Mus Art, NY; Philadelphia Mus Art, Pa; Art Inst Chicago, Ill; Milwaukee Art Ctr, Wis; Detroit Inst Arts, Mich; Calif Mus Photog, Riverside; Madison Art Ctr, Wis; Ill State Mus, Madison; Goldman Sachs Collection, NY; Colo Mountain Col, Breckenridge; Woodmere Art Mus, Phildelphia. *Comn:* Elements, CoreStates Ctr (First Union Ctr), Phildelphia, 96; Seasons, Temple Univ Children's Med Ctr, Phildelphia, 2000. *Exhib:* Solo exhibs, Cranbrook Acad Art, Bloomfield Hills, Mich, 81, Colo Mountain Col, Breckenridge, Amarillo Col, Tex, 83, Notre Dame Col, Baltimore, Md, Univ Mont, Missoula, 85, Hartwick Col, Oneonta, NY, St Joseph's Univ, Philadelphia, Pa, 86, Univ Arts, Philadelphia, Pa, 90, Michael Rosenfeld Gallery, NY, 94, Human Nature: Solar Photograms, Haggerty Mus Art, Marquette Univ, 96, Exploring Human Spirit, Manchester Craftsmen's Guild, Pittsburgh, 97 & Human Nature, Hollins Univ, Va, 2001; Philadelphia Photog Faculty, Art Inst Philadelphia, 83; Faculty Exhibition, Tyler Sch Art, Temple Univ, Philadelphia, Pa, 87; Under Construction: New Photomontage, Cranbrook Acad Art Mus, Bloomfield Hills, Mich, 88; Artists Gardens, Noyes Mus, Oceanville, NJ, 90; Photog for Children, James Danziger Gallery, NY, 91; Practicum Sponsors, Univ Arts, Philadelpia, Pa, 92; Midtown Flower Show, Midtown Payson Gallery, NY, 92; The Camera Rediscovered, Woodmere Art Mus, Philadelphia, 94; Expectations & Innovations: Photog Beyond Tradition, Ansel Adams Ctr Photog Edu Gallery, San Francisco, 95; Digital Dialects, New Paradigms, Creiger-Dane Gallery, Boston, 96; The Spirit in Art, US Embassy, The Vatican, Rome, 98; Bodies Edge, Artforms Gallery, Manayumk, Pa, 99; Wild Life, City Hall, Philadelphia Off Arts & Cult, 2000; Biennial 2000, Del Art Mus, 2000; The First Decade, Michael Rosenfeld Gallery, NY, 2000; Photog Faculty Exhib, Tyler Sch Art, Temple Univ, Pa, 2000; West to Wyeth, Woodmere Art Mus, Philadelphia, 2000; and others. *Teaching:* Asst prof photog, Dept Art & Art Hist, Wayne State Univ, Detroit, Mich, 78-79; chairperson, Dept photog, Tyler Sch Art, Temple Univ, Dept Graphic Arts & Design, 83-84, 89-, asst prof, 79-85, prof, 85-. *Awards:* Individual Artists Grant Photography, Nat Endowment Arts, 80; Artist Residency Fel, Acadia, Maine, 94-96; Leeway Found 1996 Grant Photog, Philadelphia; Visual Arts Fel (Photog), Mid-Atlantic Arts Found, 96; Artists Residency Fel, ASAP, Acadia, Maine, 97, 98, 99 & 2000. *Bibliog:* Andy Grundberg (auth), Review, NY Times, 8/90; Robert Hirsch (auth), Exploring Color Photography, William C Brown Publ, 92; Robin Rice (auth), Hometown Pomo Photos, Phildelphia City Paper, 8/9/96; Chris Macleod (auth), Embodying the Spirit, New York, 6/4/97; Gottfried Jager & Gudrun Wessing (auths), uber moholy-nagy, Kerber Veriag Bielefeld, Ger, 97; Marcia Aldrich (auth), Girl Rearing: Memoir of a girlhood gone astray, Norton, 98; Edward J Sozanski (auth), Regional artists meets a high standard in biennial, The Philadelphia Inquirer, 4/16/2000. *Mem:* Soc Photog Educ; Women's Caucus for Art; Col Art Asn. *Publ:* Philadelphia Weekly, Meeting on the Square: Four Photographers take on Rittenhouse at the Art Allience, 6/7/95; Woodmere Art Mus, Annual Report, 98; Norhtern Lights, Fire, 99; Human Nature, Penn Humanities Forum, Univ Pa, 2000; Animal Life Ivades City Hall, Art Matters, 4/2000. *Mailing Add:* 730 Carpenter Lane Philadelphia PA 19119

MADONIA, ANN C
CURATOR, ADMINISTRATOR
b New York, NY. *Study:* Hunter Col, City Univ New York, AB, 72, MA, 77; Hofstra Univ, cert(appraisal), 79. *Collection Arranged:* American Profile: Drawings by Norman Rockwell (auth, catalog), 80; Selected Paintings from Charles August Ficke Collection (auth, catalog), 80; Mexican Colonial Paintings in the Davenport Art Gallery, 83; Lindley American Collection, 84; Paul Norton Retrospective (auth, catalog), 85; Harute--Out Here: Swed Immigrant Arts Midwest Am, 85; Quad City Art Showcase (competitive exhib; auth, catalog), 86; Intent Artist (auth, catalog), 87; American Drawing Biennial (competitive exhib), 90, 92, 94, 96 & 98; Spirit of the South, 92; Sculpture of Alexander Galt, 92; Gifford Beal: Picture-Maker (co-auth, catalog), 93; Drawings and Watercolors by Hans Grohs (with catalog), 95; The European Phoenix: Selections from the Lania Collection of Contemporary Prints (with catalog), 96; Facing the Past: Protraits from the Permanent Collections (with catalog), 99; O'Keeffe in Williamsburg: A Re-Creation of the Artist's First Public Exhibition in the South (essay, catalogue), 2001; O'Keefe's Photo Essay, 2001; William & Mary Collects II, a Celebration, 2003. *Pos:* Cur collections, Davenport Mus Art, Iowa, 79-88; cur collections, Muscarelle Mus, Col William & Mary, Williamsburg, Va, 89-; actg dir, 2002-. *Teaching:* Adj instr art hist, Col William & Mary, Williamsburg, Va, 94-95 & 2003-2005. *Awards:* Curator's Award for Exhib, Southeastern Mus Conf, for Facing the Past: Portraits from the Permanent Collections, 98-99. *Mem:* Am Inst Conservation Artistic & Hist Works; Am Asn Mus; Col Art Asn; Asn Art Mus Cur. *Res:* American art. *Publ:* Auth, Davenport: 1836-1936--The Centennial Mural, 80, Ralph Albert Blakelock--poet of the landscape, 80, Limners and likenesses, 81, & The Mexican Colonial Collection, 83, Bulletin, Davenport Mus Art; Early contributions by Swedish painters in America (essay), In: Harut-Out Here: Swedish Immigrant Artists in Midwest America (exhib catalog), 85; Rubens Peal still life, Thomas Hart Benton lithographs, Bulletin, Davenport Mus Art, 86; Intent of the Artist (exhib catalog), 87; auth, Facing the Past: Portraits from the Permanent Collection (exhib catalog), 99; co-auth, Gifford Beal: Picture-Maker (exhib catalog), 99, co-author, Faith, Spirit, and Tradition (exhib catalog), 2000; Georgia O'Keeffein Williamsburg, 2001. *Mailing Add:* Col William & Mary Muscarelle Mus Art PO Box 8795 Williamsburg VA 23197-8795

MADSEN, LOREN WAKEFIELD
SCULPTOR
b Oakland, Calif, Mar 29, 43. *Study:* Reed Col, Portland, Ore, 61-63; Univ Calif, Los Angeles, BA, 66, MA, 70. *Work:* Mus Mod Art, NY; Georges Pompidou Ctr, Paris; Hirshhorn Mus, Washington, DC; Israel Mus, Jerusalem; Los Angeles Co Mus Art, Calif; Mus Contemp Art, San Diego, Calif. *Comn:* Brookhollow Atrium, San Antonio, Tex, 84; Horton Plaza, San Diego, Calif, 85; Chevy Chase Metro Bldg, Chevy Chase, Md, 85; Untitled, La Guardia Community Col, NY, 91; JR Kinschicyo Sta, Tokyo, Japan, 97; and others. *Exhib:* One man show, Mus Mod Art, NY, 75; Sculpture Made in Place, Walker Art Ctr, Minneapolis, Minn, 76; David McKee Gallery, NY, 76, 77, 82, 86, 90, 92, 96 & 98; Art First, London, 98; Six Billion Monkey, SUNY, Stony Brook, 99; Apex Art CP, NY, 99; Mus Contemp Art, San Diego, 00. *Teaching:* Instr painting & sculpture, Sch Visual Arts, New York, 87-88. *Awards:* New Talent Award,

Mod & Contemp Art Coun, Los Angeles Co Mus Art, 75; Nat Endowment Arts Fel Grant, 76 & 80; Hon Mention, Vietnam, Veterans Mem Competition, 81. *Media:* Wood, Steel. *Dealer:* David McKee Gallery 41 E 57th St New York NY 10022. *Mailing Add:* c/o David McKee Gallery 41 E 57th St New York NY 10022

MADSEN, METTE B
PAINTER
b New York, NY, Apr 6, 1955. *Study:* Calif Col Art & Sci, BFA, 78. *Work:* Smithsonian Inst, Washington, DC. *Exhib:* Old Masters-New Master, Vox Populi Gallery, NY, 84; East Village, Ctr Contemp Art, Montreal, Can, 85; Best & Brightest from East Village & Soho, Barbara Gillman Gallery, Miami, Fla, 86; Focus NY, Moosart Gallery; Embellishment of the Statue of Liberty, Benefit for Cooper-Hewitt Mus & Smithsonian Inst, NY, 86. *Media:* Oil on Canvas. *Mailing Add:* 184 Bowery St 2nd Fl New York NY 10012

MADSEN, ROY
SCULPTOR, WRITER
b Chicago, Ill. *Study:* Univ Ill; Univ Wyo; Univ Southern Calif, PhD; Am Acad Art, Chicago. *Comn:* William Shakespeare Sculpture, Old Globe Theater, San Diego, Calif. *Exhib:* Nat Sculpture Soc; Allied Artists; Audubon Artists; Loveland Ann Sculpture Invitational; Temecula Wildlife Art Exhib; Redlands Mus Wildlife Exhib; Mountain Oyster Club Invitational. *Teaching:* Syracuse Univ; prof emer, San Diego State Univ. *Awards:* Pietro & Alfreda Montana Award, Katherine Thayer Hobson Award & Michael Gressel Award, Hudson Valley Art Mus; Pres Award, Am Artists Prof League; John Spring Art Found Award, Nat Sculpture Soc; Elliot Liskin Award, Audubon Artists; Best of Show Award, Temecula Wildlife Art Exhib; Alfred Mitchell Award, La Jolla Art Asn; Screen Director's Guild Fellow Award; Huntington Hartford Fellow in Sculpture. *Mem:* Allied Artists; Am Artists Prof League; San Diego Mus Art Artists' Guild; Audubon Artists; Hudson Valley Art Asn. *Media:* Wax and Bronze. *Publ:* auth, The Impact of Film, Animated Film & Working Cinema; auth, articles in Southwest Art & Wildlife Art. *Dealer:* Prentice Gallery 17701 N Hwy 1 Fort Bragg Calif 95437; Can Heritage Art Co 10516 Islington Ave Kleinburg Ontario L0J 1C0 Can. *Mailing Add:* 6431 Lake Adlon Ct San Diego CA 92119

MADURA, JACK JOSEPH
PAINTER, INSTRUCTOR
b Chicago, Ill, Feb 6, 41. *Study:* Murray State Univ, BS(art), 64 & MA(art educ), 66; Northern Ill Univ, with Robert Kabak, MFA(painting), 70. *Work:* Sun Yat-Sen Univ, Guang Zhou, Republic of China; Kemper Insurance, Chicago, Ill; Cincinnati Bell, Ohio; Northern Ill Univ, DeKalb; Ill State Mus, Springfield; and others. *Comn:* Portrait of Ill, New State Libr, 90 & Ill State Mus, 92. *Exhib:* Chicago State Univ Flat Show, 74; Am Printmakers, London, Eng; Watercolor USA, Springfield Art Mus, Mo, 75, 77, 78, 80 & 81; Art Polish Am, St Louis, Mo; one-man show, Ill State Mus, 78; and others. *Teaching:* Instr drawing & painting, Somerset Community Col, Ky, 66-68; prof art, Lincoln Land Community Col, 70-. *Awards:* Awards for Watercolor, Ill State Fair Prof Show, 75, 76, 77, 82, 84 & 91; First Place, Strawn Gallery, Ill Col; Mayors Award for Outstanding Visual Artist, Springfield, Ill, 91. *Bibliog:* Janet Taylor (dir), An interview with Jack Madura, Sangamon State Univ, Springfield, Ill; Jack Madura in his Studio, TV Interview, Springfield Area Arts Coun; Jerry Speight (auth), Jack Madura Watercolorist, School Arts. *Mem:* Ala & Ky Watercolor Socs. *Media:* Watercolor. *Mailing Add:* Dept Art Lincoln Land Comm Col Shepherd Rd Springfield IL 62708

MADY, BEATRICE M
PAINTER, DIGITAL ARTIST
b New York, NY. *Study:* Univ Dayton, Ohio, BFA; Pratt Inst, MFA, Brooklyn, NY. *Work:* Johnson & Johnson, New Brunswick, NJ; Sydney & Francis Lewis Found, Richmond, Va; Drew Univ, Madison, NJ; Arenol Chemical Corp, NY; Dayton Art Inst, Dayton, Ohio; Pfizer, Morris Plains, NJ; Bristol-Myers Squibb, Plainsboro & Lawrenceville, NJ; Janssen Pharmaceutica, Titusville, NJ; Ortho Dermatological, Skillman, NJ. *Exhib:* solo exhibs, Jersey City Visual Arts Gallery, NJ, 88, Caldwell Col Gallery, NJ, 91 & Johnson & Johnson Gallery, New Brunswick, NJ, 92, Johnson & Johnson Consumer Product Div, Skillman, NJ, 93, Rabbet Gallery, New Brunswick, NJ, 96 & Maurice M Pine Gallery, Fairlawn, NJ, 97; Ten Yr Anniversary Exhib, Rabbet Gallery, New Brunswick, NJ, 94; Alternate Visions, Seton Hall Univ Law Sch, Newark, NJ, 95; Three Abstract Artists, Watchung Art Ctr, Watchung, NJ, 96; Merck Corp Hq, Whitehouse Station, NJ, 97; Lines of Direction, Ben Shahn Gallery, Wayne, NJ, 98; For the Sake of Beauty, City Without Walls Gallery, Newark, NJ, 98; Silent Poetry, Seton Hall Law Sch, Newark, NJ, 2000. *Teaching:* Prof computer graphics-graphic design, St Peter's Col, Jersey City, NJ, 98-; prof computer graphics, Parsons Sch of Design, NYC, 2001-. *Awards:* Ford Found Grant, 78; Painting Fel, NJ State Coun Arts, 85; Kenny Fel, 2003 & 2006. *Bibliog:* Courtney Slevin (auth), Beatrice Mady, Contemp Art Univ Collection, 4/6/87; Vivien Raynor (auth), City without walls expands its reach, NY Times, 7/7/96; Ralph Bellantoni (auth), Artists revel in the abstract, Courier News NJ, 2/96; Debora Rosenthal (auth), The First Underground Show, Art in Am, NYC, 11/84. *Mem:* Col Art Asn. *Media:* Oil, Digital. *Dealer:* Rabbet Gallery 120 Georges Rd New Brunswick NJ 08901. *Mailing Add:* 106-108 Hopkins Ave Jersey City NJ 07306

MAGDANZ, ANDREW R
GLASS BLOWER
b River Falls, Wis, Aug 23, 51. *Study:* Univ Wis, River Falls, Univ Wis, Madison, BFA, 76, with Harvey Littleton; Calif Col Arts & Crafts, MFA, 78, with Marvin Lipofsky. *Work:* Mus Fine Arts, Boston, Mass; Oakland Mus, Calif; Corning Mus, NY. *Pos:* Studio Artist, independent. *Teaching:* Head, glass dept, Rochester Inst Technol, 79-81; instr, Alchuk Sch Glass; instr, Haystack Sch Crafts. *Awards:* Nat Endowment Arts Grants. *Mem:* Am Craft Coun (bd dir, 88); Glass Art Soc; Soc Arts & Crafts, Boston. *Mailing Add:* 71 Appleton St Cambridge MA 02138-3356

MAGDEN, NORMAN E
FILMMAKER, VIDEO ARTIST
b Cleveland, Ohio, Apr 21, 34. *Study:* Cleveland Inst Art, BS, 57; Case Western Reserve Univ, MA, 58, PhD, 74. *Work:* Cleveland Mus Art; Butler Inst Am Art, Youngstown, Ohio; Canton Mus Art, Ohio. *Exhib:* Int Film Competition, London Amateur Film Festival, Eng, 84; Canadian Film Festival, Montreal, 86; Multi-Image Performance Works Traveling Exhib, 73-96. *Pos:* Art Critic, Akron Beacon J, 66-67; film panel, Ill Arts Coun, 77-79; pres, Mimesis Inc, Ill, 78-93. *Teaching:* Prof media arts, Northern Ill Univ, 67-93; prof & dept head, Dept Art Univ Tenn, Knoxville, 93-. *Awards:* Short Film Showcase, Nat Endowment Arts, 79-80; Fel, Ill Arts Coun, 89-90. *Mem:* Col Art Asn. *Media:* Media Arts Performance. *Publ:* Auth, Peerless Motor Co Plant No 1, 1906-1909, Hist Am Bldg Survey, 73; illusr, Pennis Oppenheim Retrospective, Mus Mod Art, Paris, 80; Auth, Robert Morris Meets Post Modernism, New Art Examiner, 86; illusr, Carnival, American Style, Mardi Gras at New Orleans, Univ Chicago Press, 90. *Mailing Add:* Univ Tenn Dept Art 1715 Volunteer Blvd Knoxville TN 37996-2410

MAGEE, ALAN
PAINTER, SCULPTOR
b Newton, Pa, May 26, 47. *Study:* Tyler Sch Art, 65-66; Philadelphia Col Art, 67-69. *Work:* Columbus Mus Art, Ohio; Fine Arts Mus San Francisco; Newark Mus & Rutgers Mus Art, NJ; Portland Mus Art & Farnsworth Art Mus, Maine; Norton Gallery Art, Fla; Art Inst Chicago. *Comn:* Illus novels, Graham Greene & Bernard Malamod, Pocket Bks, NY, 74; cover paintings for Time Mag, 78, 79, 81, 82 & 85; portfolio of paintings for the Atlantic: The Walls Around Us, 87; Mural, Earth Sci Bldg, Univ Maine, 97; Mural, Maine State House, 2000. *Exhib:* Fresno Art Ctr, Calif, 85; Meckler Gallery, Los Angeles, 86; Am Acad & Inst Arts & Letters, NY 87; Art and the Law (with exhib catalog), ann traveling exhib, 89, 90; traveling retrospective, Farnsworth Art Mus, Ringling Sch Art & Design, Cheekwood Ctr for the Arts, James A Michener Mus Art, 91-92; solo exhibs, Edith Caldwell Gallery, San Francisco, 92, 93, 95, 96 & 97 Newport Art Mus, RI, 94, San Jose Mus Art, Calif, 93, Kodak Ctr Creative Imaging, 92 & Hollis Taggart Gallery, NY, 99, Berlin Philharmonic, Berlin, Ger, 2000, Hackett-Freedman Gallery, San Francisco, Calif, 2000; plus many others. *Teaching:* Ctr Creative Imaging, 93 & 94. *Awards:* R&H Rosenthal Award, Am Acad Arts & Letts, 81; Am Bk Award, 82; Leo Meissner Prize, Nat Acad Design, 90. *Bibliog:* John Canaday (auth), A dazzling new realist painter, Saturday Rev Mag, 12/80; Theodore F Wolff (auth), The emergence of a gifted artist, Christian Science Monitor, 10/26/82; John Russell (auth), article in the New York Times, 10/22/82; Edgar Allen Beem (auth), Alan Magee, Arts Mag, 10/86; plus many others; Maureen Mullarkey (auth) NY Rev mag, 4/15/00. *Media:* All Media. *Publ:* Stones and Other Works, Harry N Abrams; Alan Magee 1981-1991, Farnsworth Art Mus; Alan Magee, Inlets, Joan Whitney Payson Gallery Art. *Dealer:* Hollis Taggart Gallery New York NY; Hackett Freedman Gallery San Francisco CA. *Mailing Add:* Pleasant Point Rd Cushing ME 04563-9507

MAGEE, ALDERSON
GRAPHIC ARTIST, PRINTMAKER
b Hartford, Conn, Oct 5, 29. *Study:* Univ Conn, BS; West Hartford Art League; also with Estelle Coniff & Walter Korder. *Work:* Leigh Yawkey Woodson Art Mus. *Comn:* Bald Eagle, United Technol Corp, 83. *Exhib:* Conn Acad Fine Arts, Wadsworth Atheneum, Hartford, 74; Federal Duck Stamp Art, Peabody Mus, Salem, Mass, 77; Birds in Art, Leigh Yawkey Woodson Art Mus, Wausau, Wis, 84-88; Experience the West, Mus Rockies, Bozeman, Mont, 84 & 85; Northwest Rendezvous, Helena, Mont, 85; Miniature Show '86, GWS Galleries, Carmel, Calif; The Legacy Continues, Smithsonian Inst, Washington, 88; Coastal Impressions II, GWS Galleries, Southport, Conn, 92; Miniature Show '92, GWS Galleries, Carmel, Calif. *Awards:* First Prize, Conn Acad Fine Arts, 74; Gold Medal, Hudson Valley Art Asn, 75 & Grand Nat Exhib, Am Artists Prof League, New York, 78. *Bibliog:* George Reiger (auth), The Wings of Dawn, 236, 80; Starting From Scratch, Midwest Art Mag, 3/87; Russell A Fink (auth), Duck Stamp Prints, rev, 92. *Mem:* Salmagundi Club; Hudson Valley Art Asn; Soc Animal Artists; Am Artists Prof League. *Media:* Scratchboard; Etching, Engraving. *Publ:* Contribr, Federal Duck Stamp Design, US Govt, 76; Sporting Classics Mag, 11-12/86 & 9-10/92; Smithsonian Studies Am Art, spring 89. *Dealer:* New Masters Gallery Carmel CA; Douglas Gallery Trumbull CT

MAGEL, CATHARINE ANNE
SCULPTOR, PAINTER
b La Grange, Ill, Nov 13, 56. *Study:* Kansas City Art Inst, BFA, 79; NY State Col Ceramics, Alfred Univ, MFA, 82; Int Sch Art, Todi, Italy, 89. *Work:* Het Kruithuis Mus, Neth; Kansas City Art Inst, Mo; NY State Col Ceramics; Archie Bray Found, Helena, Mont; Southern New Eng Telephone, New Haven, Conn. *Comn:* ceramic walkways & benches, Arts in Transit, St Louis, Mo, 96; bus, Bi-State Develop Agency, St Louis, Mo, 96-97; Arts in Transit (fence proj), Wellston Metrolink Sta, St Louis, Mo, 97; tile mural, Floodwall, comn by Trailnet, St Louis, 2001; mosaics, Mo Dept Conserv; carved brick wall, Cloud Co Hist Soc Mus, Concordia, Kans, 2006; others. *Exhib:* Solo exhibs, Paul Mellon Art Ctr, Walingford, Conn, 86, Creative Arts Workshop, New Haven, 87, & Fontbonne Col, St Louis, 96 & City Mus, St Louis, Mo, 97 & Mitchell Mus at CedarHurst, Mt Vernon, Ill, 2000; Muscarelle Mus Art, Col William & Mary, Williamsburg, Va, 93; Ceramics Now, Downey Mus Art, 94; Ceramics, Fontbonne Col, St Louis, 95; Signs of the Cross, Forum Contemp Arts, St Louis, Mo, 95; Common Materials/Uncommon Ideas, Elliot Smith Contemp Art, St Louis, Mo, 97; The Figure in Clay and Fiber, New Bedford Art Mus, Mass, 97; Ceramic Work, Gallery Int, Baltimore, Md, 2005; Solo exhib, Ceramic Sculptures & Works on Paper, Univ St Louis Gallery, Visio, 2005, Uncommon Experience/Common Ground, Regional Arts Comn, St Louis, Mo, 2005. *Pos:* Artist-in-residence, Ciudad Colony, the David & Julia White Artist Colony, Costa Rica, 2003, Vt Studio Ctr, 2006;

Anderson Ranch, Showmass, Colo, 90; gallery assoc, Pro-art Gallery, St Louis, 92-93. *Teaching:* sculpture, Trumbull Col, Yale Univ, 83-84 & Lindenwood Univ, St Charles, Mo, 2005; instr drawing, NY State Col Ceramics, 89; beginning sculpture or 3/D design, Wichita State Univ, 90; instr ceramic sculpture, Maryville Univ, 94-95; instr scenic painting, Webster Univ, St Louis, Mo, 95-2002; the art of sculpture luminaria, St Louis Mus, St Louis, Mo. *Awards:* Fels, Nat Endowment Arts, 86 & Conn Comn Arts, 86. *Bibliog:* St Louis Design Magazine, St Louis, Mo, 2003 & 2004. *Media:* Paintings, Works on paper, Ceramic Sculpture. *Specialty:* Fine Art. *Mailing Add:* 148 Slocum Ave St Louis MO 63119

MAGENTA, MURIEL
SCULPTOR, VIDEO ARTIST
b New York, NY, Dec 4, 1932. *Study:* Queens Col, BA, 53; Johns Hopkins Univ, MA(art hist), 62; Ariz State Univ, MFA, 65, PhD, 70. *Work:* Univ Art Collections, Ariz State Univ, Tempe; Valley Nat Bank, Phoenix; Prudential Life Insurance, Scottsdale. *Exhib:* Coiffure Carnival, video/sculpture installation, Kansas City Art Inst, Mo, 91, Gallery 10, Wash, 91, Madrid Int Festival of Films by Women, Spain, 91, Europ Film Festival, Osnabruck, Ger, 91, Medien Operative Berlin, Ger, 92; United Nations Fourth World Conference on Women, Beijing, China, 95; 5th Electro-Video Clip of ACREQ, Montreal, Que, Can, 96; Token City Multimedia Installation (auth, catalog), Ariz State Univ Art Mus, Tempe, 97; Inter-Soc Electronic Arts 97, Sch Art Inst Chicago, Ill, 97; Minn Nat Print Biennial, Univ Minn, Minneapolis, 98; Token City, Electronic Rituals, Inermedia Art Gallery, Minneapolis, 99; Token City, Dream Centenary CG Grand Prix, Aizu, 99, Tokyo, 99; Progress of the World's Women, United Nations Building, NY, 2000; Token City, Cyberslag Electronic Festival, Groingen, The Neth, 2000; Coiffure Carnival Sculpture (permanent installation) Galvin Theater Lobby, Ariz State Univ, Tempe, 2002; Times Square Installation, Computing Common Gallery, Ariz State Univ, 2003; Times Square, Brooklyn Int Film Festival, Brooklyn Mus Art, NY. *Pos:* Exec ed & designer, Hue Points Women's Caucus for Art Newsmag, 82-84; Woman Image Now: Arizona Women in Art J, Ariz State Univ, 80-90; resident artist fel, multimedia/electronic imaging, Inst Studies Arts, Ariz State Univ, 91-; proj dir, The World's Women On-Line, Website, 95-. *Teaching:* Prof inter-media art, Ariz State Univ, 69-; vis artist-in-residence studio art, Univ Wis, Madison, summer 79, St Mary's Col, Notre Dame Univ, 84. *Awards:* Ariz Siggraph Asn Award, 86; Grants for sculpture, film, video, computer arts, 74, 76, 79, 82-83, 84, 86, 88, 91, 92, 94, 95,2000, 2002, 2003, 2004; Mid-Career Achievement Award, Woman's Caucus for Art, 91. *Bibliog:* N Broude (auth), The Power of Feminist Art, Harry N Abrams, 94; J Heller (auth), North American Women Artists of the 20th Century: A Biographical Dictionary, Garland, 95; M Lovejoy (auth), Postmodern Currents: Art and Artists in the Age of Electronic Media, Prentice Hall, 96. *Mem:* Coalition Women's Art Orgn (nat vpres, 78-80); Women's Caucus Art (nat pres, 82-84); Col Art Asn; Women in Animation; Inter-Soc Electronic. *Media:* Installation, Computer,Video, All. *Publ:* Auth, Photographic Essay, Women Artist News, Eyewitness Nairobi: United Nations World Conference of Women, Nairobi, Kenya, 86; Woman Image Now: Arizona State University, Women's Studies Quart, 87; Coiffure Carnival: Muriel Magenta, Exhib Catalog Ctr Arts, 90; Coiffure Carnival, Women Arts Mag, Women Artists Slide Libr, London No 39, 3-4/91; co-exec ed, Muriel Magenta & Dan Collins, The Simulated Presence: A Critical Response to Electronic Imaging, 93; Token City Multimedia Installation (exhib catalog) Ariz State Univ Art Mus, Tempe, 97. *Dealer:* V TAPE Toronto. *Mailing Add:* 8322 E Virginia Scottsdale AZ 85257

MAGGS, ARNAUD CYRIL BENVENUTI
PHOTOGRAPHER, GRAPHIC ARTIST
b Montreal, Que, May 5, 26. *Study:* With Carl Dair, 50; Scuola Belle Arti Brera, Milan, 59; Three Schs, Toronto, 74. *Work:* Nat Gallery Can; Vancouver Art Gallery; Art Gallery Hamilton; Winnipeg Art Gallery; Can Mus Contemp Photogr; Vancouver Art Gallery; Musee d'art Contemporain de Montreal. *Comn:* Restaurant mural (photographs), Windsor Arms Hotel, Toronto, 67. *Exhib:* Solo exhibs, Photographs 1975-84, Art Gallery Hamilton & Winnipeg Art Gallery, 86, Numberworks, Macdonald Stewart Art Ctr, Guelph, 89, Neuberger Mus, Purchase, NY, 90, Saidye Bronfman Ctr, Montreal, 90, Southern Alberta Art Gallery, Lethbridge, 90, Presentation House Gallery, N Vancouver, 92; Sweet Immortality, Edmonton Art Gallery, 78; The Winnipeg Perspective, Winnipeg Art Gallery, 79; Portraits, Nat Film Bd Can, Ottawa, 81; Persona, Nickle Arts Mus, Univ Calgary, 82; Seeing People, Seeing Space, Photogr Gallery, London, Eng, 84; Responding to Photog, Art Gallery Ont, 84; Allocations, 49th Parallel, NY, 84; Numbering, Art Gallery, Hamilton, 90; Int British Print Bienalle, Brantford, Eng, 90; Spec Collections, Int Ctr Photog, Midtown, NY, 92. *Teaching:* Vis artist, Banff Ctr, Banff, Alta, 88. *Awards:* Gold Medal, Can Graphica Exhib, Montreal, 65; Can Coun Sr Arts Grants, 69, 81 & 84; Gershon Iskowitz Award, 91. *Bibliog:* John Bentley Mays (auth), The many faces of Maggs, Globe & Mail, Toronto, 1/19/86; Gary Michael Dault, (auth), The narrative and its double, C Mag, summer 89; James D Campbell (auth), Arnaud Maggs: Identification, C Mag, Spring 91. *Publ:* Arnaud Maggs, catalog, Centre Culturel Canadien, Paris, 80; Arnaud Maggs Selected Works 1981-83, catalog, Charles H Scott Gallery, Vancouver, 84; Auth, Arnaud Maggs Photographs 1975-1984, catalog, Nickel Arts Mus, Univ Calgary, 84; Arnaud Maggs Numberworks Catalog, Macdonald Stewart Art Centre, Guelph, Ont, 89. *Mailing Add:* 245 Carlaw Ave Toronto ON M4M 2S1 Canada

MAGNAN, OSCAR GUSTAV
PAINTER, SCULPTOR
b Cienfuegos, Cuba, Dec 16, 37. *Study:* San Alejandro, Habana, Cuba, with Mateo Dela Torriente, MFA; Oxford Univ, Eng, Master in aribus; Sorbonne, with Dufrenne, PhD(aesthet). *Work:* Brit Mus; Libr Congress; Smithsonian Inst; RCA Corp; NY Univ; and others. *Comn:* Three panel mural, Univ Autonoma, Dom Repub, 68; bronze statue, Haina, Dom Repub, 68. *Exhib:* Salzburg Int Biennial, 64; one-man shows, Palazzo Strozzi, Florence, Italy, 66 & Galerie Motte, Paris, 70; Int Fair, Basle, Switz, 72; Inter-Kunst-Infomaturien, Dusseldorf, Ger, 72; New Jersey Selects, Squibb Corp, Princeton, NJ. *Pos:* Dir art gallery, St Peter's Col, 72-, cur mus, 73-. *Teaching:* Prof aesthet-sculpture, St Peter's Col, Jersey City, NJ, 77-. *Awards:* Can Coun Fel, 64; Cintas Found Inst Int Educ Fel, 66; Guggenheim Found Fel, 68; Hereward Lester Cooke Found. *Mem:* Am Abstract Artists; Artists Fel. *Media:* Acrylic, Oil; Aluminum, Bronze. *Publ:* The Art of Oscar Magnan, Ramparts, 64; Le Figaro, Litteraire, Paris, 7-20-26/70; Searching for Truth, Jersey J, 89. *Dealer:* Susan Teller Gallery 568 Broadway New York NY. *Mailing Add:* 50 Glenwood Ave Jersey City NJ 07306-4606

MAGNO, LIZ
SCULPTOR, CONCEPTUAL ARTIST
b Philadelphia, Pa, Feb 3, 38. *Study:* Univ Arts & Montclair State Univ, BA & grad study; Moore Col Art; New York Univ. *Comn:* Outdoor sculpture, Mayfair Sculpture in the Park, Allentown, Pa, 87, 89 & 94; outdoor sculpture, Pa State Univ, Reading, 88, 91 & 93; mural, Paolo Di Matheis Arts Fest, Piano Veterale, Italy, 89; outdoor sculpture, Burlington Co Col, Pemberton, NJ, 93-94; sculpture, Mayfair 10th Anniversary, 96. *Exhib:* Noyes Mus, Oceanville, NJ, 94; Reading Art, Freedman Gallery, Albright Col, Pa, 94; Contemp Women Artists, Freyberger Gallery, Pa State Univ, Berks Campus, Reading, 94; Decentered (traveling exhib), 96; Contemp Arts Corridor (traveling exhib), 97. *Pos:* Freelance maskmaker/theatre designer. *Teaching:* Artist in residence, var Pa schs, Pa Coun Arts, Arts Educ Prog. *Bibliog:* Stan Schaffer (auth), Low tech - high interest, Morning Call, 11/21/91; Marilyn J Fox (auth), Natural order, Reading Eagle, 7/25/93; Susan Chase (auth), Profile: Liz Magno - Lehigh Valley Woman Mag, 1-2/97. *Mem:* Int Sculpture Ctr. *Media:* All Media. *Dealer:* Maria Feliz Gallery and Sculpture Garden 60 W Broadway Jim Thorpe Pa 18229. *Mailing Add:* 4601 Aspen Dr Walnutport PA 18088-9472

MAGNUSON, ERIC A
CONCEPTUAL ARTIST
b June 2, 59. *Study:* Eastern Mich Univ, BFA, 82; Calif Inst Art, MFA, 85. *Work:* Mus Contemp Art, Los Angeles, Calif; Orange Co Mus Art, Newport Beach, Calif; Bard Col Ctr Curatorial Studies, NY; Bass Mus Art, Miami Beach, Fla. *Exhib:* Chocolate, Swiss Inst, NY, 95; Just Past, Mus Contemp Art, Los Angeles, 96; 1997, Thomas Nordpanstad Gallery, NY, 97; In Terms of Color, Silverstein Gallery, NY, 99; The Body in Photographs, Ctr for Cutatorial Studies, Baro Col, NY, 2000. *Bibliog:* Exploring new territories, LA Herald, 89; Looking back in anger, Art Press, 95; Eric Magnuson, NY Times, 97. *Publ:* Coauth, Figure of Speech, Thomas Solomon, 93; contribr Fourty Newport Biennial 93, Newport Harbour Art Mus, 93, Chocolate, Swiss Inst, NY, 95, Abstract Eroticism, Cyrup Ltd, 96, Death and the Will to Live, New Observations, Vol 117, 98

MAGUIRE, HENRY POWNALL
HISTORIAN, WRITER
b Bath, Eng, May 20, 43. *Study:* Kings Col, Cambridge, BA, 65; Harvard Univ, PhD, 73. *Teaching:* Asst prof medieval art, Harvard Univ, 73-76 & Dumbarton Oaks, 76-79; asst prof, Univ Ill, Urbana-Champaign, 79-82, assoc prof, 82-88, prof, 88-. *Mem:* Col Art Asn; Archaeol Inst Am; Int Ctr Medieval Art; Medieval Acad Am. *Res:* Late Roman, early Christian and Byzantine art. *Publ:* Auth, Truth and convention in Byzantine descriptions of works of art, 74 & The depiction of sorrow in middle Byzantine art, 77, Dumbarton Oaks Papers; auth, Art and Eloquence in Byzantium, Princeton, 81; auth, Earth & Ocean, The Terresterial World in Early Byzantine Art, Penn State, 87; coauth, Art & Holy Powers in Early Christian House, Univ Ill, 89

MAHAFFEY, MERRILL DEAN
PAINTER, INSTRUCTOR
b Albuquerque, NMex, Aug 12, 37. *Study:* Mesa Col, Colo; Calif Col Arts & Crafts; Sacramento State Col, BA; Ariz State Univ, MFA, 66. *Work:* Ariz State Univ; Phoenix Art Mus; Tucson Fine Arts Ctr; Mus Am Art; Colorado Springs Fine Arts Ctr. *Exhib:* Joslyn Mus Biennial, Omaha, Nebr; Newport Art Mus, 79; Mus Am Art, Washington, DC, 79; San Francisco Mus Mod Art, 79; Sierra Nev Mus Art, 81; Fresno Art Ctr, 81; Tucson Art Mus, 82; Colorado Springs Fine Arts Ctr, 83. *Teaching:* Instr painting & art hist, Phoenix Col, 67-83; lectr & writer art hist Am West. *Media:* Acrylic, Oil. *Publ:* Auth, Merrill Mahafley Monumental Landscapes, Northland Press, 79. *Dealer:* Suzanne Brown Galleries Scottsdale AZ. *Mailing Add:* 4 Puerto Ct Santa Fe NM 87505-2256

MAHER, JANET LYNN
PRINTMAKER, COLLAGE ARTIST
b Waterbury, Conn. *Study:* So Conn State Col, New Haven, BS in Art Educ, 76, studies with Anna Held Audette and Nicolas Orsini; Univ NMex, Albuquerque, MA, 81, MFA, 96, studies with Garo Antreasian and Betty Hahn. *Work:* Nat Mus Women in the Arts Lib & Rsch Ctr, Washington; Tate Gallery Artists Books Collection, London; Franklin Furnace Artists Book Archive, Mus Mod Art, NY; Albuquerque Mus, NMex; Sch Art Inst Chicago Artists' Books Collection. *Comn:* New Mexico Quilt (ceramic tile mural), Santa Fe Arts Commn & Santa Fe Capitol Improvements Program, Oliver LaFarge Lib, Santa Fe, NMex, 1989; Los Alamos (ceramic tile bldg treatment), NMex Arts Divsn, Univ NMex, Los Alamos, 1990. *Exhib:* Cover to Cover: Experimental Bookworks invitational, Mus Fine Arts, Santa Fe, 84; One-woman show, Other's Voices, Ctr Contemp Art, Santa Fe, 86; Get It On Paper: Gallery Artists, Invited Artists, and Gemini GEL Selections, Linda Durham Gallery, Santa Fe, 91; Pyramid Atlantic Book Arts Fair Invitational, Corcoran Gallery Art, Wash, 95 & 99; Ida y Vuelta, La Menuiserie, Rodez, France, 98; The Ray Graham Collection or a Sampling Thereof, Albuquerque Mus, 2000. *Pos:* educ coord, Tamarind Inst, Albuquerque, NMex, 90-93. *Teaching:* asst prof fine arts, studio, Loyola Col, Balt, 97-, assoc prof, 2003. *Awards:* First Prize, 49th Ann Conn Women Artists Exhib, John

Slade Ely House, New Haven, Conn, 78; Award of Merit, New Mexico, Mus Fine Arts, Mus of NMex, Sante Fe, 87; Raymond Jonsen Prize for Exceptional Acad and Creative Achievement, Univ NMex, Albuquerque, 94; Community Serv Award, ANA/Harwood Community Garden, Albuquerque, 96; Purchase Award, Halpert Biennial, Appalachian State Univ, Boone, NC, 99; Critic's Residency, Md Art Place, Baltimore, 2000-2001. *Mem:* CAA; Am Print Alliance; Md Printmakers; So Graphics Coun. *Media:* Mixed Media; Collage. *Dealer:* Gallery 10 Ltd 1519 Connecticut Ave NW Washington DC. *Mailing Add:* Loyola College Dept Fine Arts 4501 N Charles St Baltimore MD 21210-2601

MAHEY, JOHN A
MUSEUM DIRECTOR
b Du Bois, Pa, Mar 30, 32. *Study:* Columbia Col, 50-52; Pa State Univ, BA & MA(art hist). *Collection Arranged:* Sarah Miriam Peale (with catalog), Peale Mus, Baltimore, Md, 68; Master Drawings from Sacramento (auth, catalog), E B Crocker Art Gallery, Calif, 71; Native American Art at Philbrook (auth, catalog), 80 & Painter of the Humble Truth, 84, Philbrook, Tulsa, Okla; Asian Art, San Antonio Mus Art, 86; Mexican Folk Art, San Antonio Mus Art, 87; The Art of Drawing (with catalog), Flint Inst Arts, 92. *Pos:* Asst dir, Peale Mus, Baltimore, 64-69; dir, E B Crocker Art Gallery, Sacramento, 69-72, Cummer Gallery Art, Jacksonville, 72-75 & Mem Art Gallery, 75-79; chief cur, Philbrook Art Ctr, Tulsa, 79-84; dir, San Antonio Mus Art, 84-89; dir, Flint Inst Arts, 89-. *Teaching:* Instr art hist, Sacramento State Univ, 70; adj prof, Univ Rochester, 75-79. *Awards:* Fulbright Fel, 62. *Mem:* Am Asn Mus; Asn Art Mus Dirs. *Res.* 19th century American painting; Rembrandt Peale. *Publ:* Auth, Letters of James McNeill Whistler to George Lucas, 67, The Lithographs of Rembrandt Peale, 69 & The Studio of Rembrandt Peale, 69; contributions to numerous exhibitions catalogs, 69-92. *Mailing Add:* 4645 N Progress Ave Harrisburg PA 17110

MAHLKE, ERNEST D
SCULPTOR, EDUCATOR
b Madison, Wis, Sept 15, 30. *Study:* Univ Wis, BS & MS; Inst Allende, Univ Guanajuato, Mex, MFA. *Work:* State Univ NY Oneonta; and many pvt collections. *Exhib:* Smithsonian Inst Traveling Exhibs, 55, 57 & 58; Smithsonian Inst, 55, 61 & 62; Cooperstown Art Asn Nat Ann, NY, 61-82, 66-81 & 89; Artists of Cent NY Regional Ann, Munson-Williams-Proctor Inst, Utica, NY, 68-79; one-man shows, Two Rivers Gallery, Binghamton, NY, 72, The Art Ctr, Albany, NY, 76 & State Univ NY Oneonta, 80; Drawing & Small Sculpture Show, Ball State Univ Art Gallery, 75, 79, 81 & 82; Sculpture 75 Nat, 75; Major Albany Sculpture Sites, 82; Art Faculty Invitation, State Univ NY, Oneonta, 95. *Pos:* Pres, Wis Designer Craftsmen, Milwaukee, 62; mem bd, Oneonta Art Ctr, NY, 77. *Teaching:* Assoc prof sculpture, State Univ NY Oneonta, 62-78, prof, 78-93. *Mem:* Am Craftsmen's Coun. *Media:* Wood, Metal. *Dealer:* Gallery 53 Cooperstown NY 13326. *Mailing Add:* Mary Brown Hill Rd Laurens NY 13796

MAHLMANN, JOHN JAMES
PUBLISHER, ADMINISTRATOR
b Washington, DC, Jan 21, 42. *Study:* Boston Univ, BFA, 62, MFA, 63; Univ Notre Dame, summer 62; Pa State Univ, EdD, 70. *Pos:* Asst exec secy, Nat Art Educ Asn, Washington, DC, 69-71, exec dir, 71-82; ed, Art Educ, 70-81 & Art Teacher, 71-80; exec ed, Design for Arts Educ, formerly; exec dir, Music Educators Nat Conf, 82-. *Teaching:* Grad asst, Boston Univ, 62-63; grad asst & res asst, Pa State Univ, 63-64, instr, 66-67, dir gallery, Art Educ Dept, 66-67, asst prof, Tex Tech Col, 67-69. *Mem:* Music Educators Nat Conf; Rotary, Am Soc Asn Exec. *Mailing Add:* 10703 Cross Sch Rd Reston VA 22091-5105

MAHMOUD, BEN
PAINTER, EDUCATOR
b Charleston, WVa, Oct 6, 1935. *Study:* Columbus Art Sch, Ohio, cert, 57; Ohio Univ, Athens, BFA, 58, MFA, 60. *Work:* Art Inst Chicago, Ill; Brooklyn Mus, NY; Krannert Mus, Univ Ill, Urbana; Austin Mus Art, Tex; Mus Contemp Art, Chicago; pvt collections include The Columbus Gallery of Fine Art, Ohio, St Lawrence Col, NY, Ball State Univ, Ind, Ill State Mus, Sunrise Mus, WVa, The Borg-Warner Collection, Chicago, Ill, The Kemper Collection, The Ill Bell Collection, AT&T Collection, Art Inst of Chicago, State of Ill Collection, Millikin Univ Collection, many others; Columbus Gallery of Fine Art; Austin Art Mus. *Comn:* Hapworth Med Ctr, NY, 86. *Exhib:* One-man exhibs, Lakeview Ctr Arts, Peoria, 74, Ill State Mus, Springfield, 76, Zaks Gallery, Chicago, 80, 83, 85, 86, 90, 94 & 96, Ill, Nardin Gallery, NY, 80 & Madison Gallery, Toronto, Can, 80, Smelik & Stokking Gallery, The Hague, The Neth, Ballard & Fetherston Gallery, Seattle, WA, 99; Chicago Collects Mahmoud, Northern Ill Univ, De Kalb, 81; Art Today, Indianapolis Mus, Ind, 84 & 86; Traveling Exhib, Art and the Law, 86-; retrospective, Rockford Art Mus, Ill; Zaks Gallery, 2000. *Pos:* Bd mem & chmn visual arts, Ill Arts Coun, 73-77. *Teaching:* Dist res prof art, Northern Ill Univ, 65-2001, distinguished prof emer, 2001-. *Awards:* Creative Activity Grants, Northern Ill Univ, 65-; Painting Fel, Nat Endowment Arts, 75. *Bibliog:* David Tenuse (auth), rev, Wash Post, 4/30/77; Robert Kaupelis (auth), Experimental Drawing, Watson-Guptill, 80; Carrie Rebora (auth), Ben Mahmoud, New Art Examiner, Vol 8, 81. *Media:* Acrylic, Drawing. *Specialty:* Contemporary art. *Publ:* Auth (with William V Dunning), Advice to Young Artists in a Post Modern Era, Syracuse Univ Press, 98. *Dealer:* The Patricia Rolzar Gallery 118 Central Way Kirkland WA 98033. *Mailing Add:* 6502 Summerfield Loop New Port Richey FL 34655

MAHON, ROBERT
PHOTOGRAPHER
b Wilmington, Del, Dec 28, 49. *Study:* Univ Del, BA, 72. *Work:* Mus Mod Art, Metrop Mus Art & New York Pub Libr, NY; Humanities Res Ctr, Austin, Tex; Philadelphia Mus Art, Pa; Fogg Mus, Harvard Univ, Boston, Mass; and others. *Exhib:* Big Pictures by Contemp Photographers, 83, Permanent Collection Exhib, 84-86, Multiple Images, 93, Mus Mod Art, NY; Recent Acquisitions, NY Pub Libr, 85; Philadelphia Mus Art, 89 & 95; A Force of Repetition, NJ State Mus, 90; Guggenheim Mus, Soho, 94; Newark Mus, NJ, 2003; Philosophy Box, New York City, 2005. *Awards:* Guggenheim Grant, 85-86; Rutgers Ctr Innovative Printmaking Fel, 96. *Publ:* Illusr, These Trees Stand, 81, & Between the Lions, 86, Carol Joyce; Themes and Variations, Station Hill Press, 82; auth & illusr, Tribute to Minor White, Aperture, 84; illusr, I-VI, John Cage, 90. *Mailing Add:* PO Box Q Stockton NJ 08559

MAHONEY, JOELLA JEAN
EDUCATOR, PAINTER
b Chicago, Ill, June 11, 33. *Study:* Art Inst Chicago, 51; Inst Allende, San Miguel, Mex, 54 & 55, Northern Ariz Univ, Flagstaff, BS(art & english), 55; Claremont Grad Sch, Calif, Fel, MFA(painting), 65. *Work:* Sedona Mus Art, Ariz; Sohio Corp, Houston, Tex; Am Express Office, Phoenix, Ariz; Claremont McKenna Col, Calif; Northern Ariz Univ. *Comn:* Painting, Mutual Life Insurance, Newport Beach, Calif, 75; painting, comn Weldon Diggs-Atty, Upland, Calif, 87; painting, Univ LaVerne, Laverne, Calif, 84. *Exhib:* Art-in-Embassies Program, US State Dept, Bhutan, Lybia & Indonesia, 70-90; Jamison Gallery, Sante Fe, NMex, 74; Laguna Beach Invitational, Laguna Beach Mus Art, Calif, 75; solo exhibs, NAU Art Gallery, Flagstaff, Ariz, 80, Austin Gallery, Scottsdale, Ariz, 84; 5 Arizona Artists, Van Buren-Hazelton Cutting Gallery, Boston, Mass, 88; Red Stone Gallery, 89 & 96. *Pos:* Bd dir, Sedona Mus Art, Ariz, 89-; docent, Mus Northern Ariz, Flagstaff, 89-; art comn, City of Sedona, Ariz, 90-. *Teaching:* Prof art, Univ LaVerne, LaVerne, Calif, 64-98, prof emer, 98-; interim co-coordr, Northern Ariz Univ, Sch Fine Arts, 2000. *Bibliog:* Morneen K Bratt (auth), Oil on Canvas (catalog), Northland Press, 85; Cal Poly Univ, Women's Work, Univ Press, 86. *Mem:* Sedona Arts Ctr; Coconino Ctr Arts, Flagstaff, Ariz; Mus Northern Ariz; PETA; SPCA. *Media:* Oil, Watercolor. *Res:* Paintings that honor the earth and hold up the beauty and mystery of natural SW Canyon, landforms, figurative themes, classical. *Dealer:* Lawrence S Green 310 Apple Ave Sedona Ariz 86336. *Mailing Add:* 495 Smith Rd Sedona AZ 86336

MAHONEY, MICHAEL R T
HISTORIAN, EDUCATOR
b Worcester, Mass, Jan 24, 35. *Study:* Phillips Acad, 53; Yale Univ, BA, 59; Courtauld Inst, Univ London, PhD, 65. *Pos:* Mus cur, Nat Gallery Art, Washington, DC, 64-69, ed, 68-69. *Teaching:* Prof art hist, Trinity Col, Hartford, 69-. *Res:* Seventeenth century art. *Publ:* Auth, Drawings of Salvator Rosa, Garland, 77; coauth, Wadsworth Atheneum Paintings II: Italy and Spain, Hartford, 91. *Mailing Add:* Trinity Col Dept Fine Arts Hartford CT 06106

MAI, JAMES L
PAINTER, EDUCATOR
b Cheyenne, Wyo, Mar 8, 57. *Study:* Univ Wyo, BFA, 82, MFA, 85. *Work:* Univ Wyo Art Mus, Laramie; Wyo State Mus & Art Gallery, Cheyenne. *Exhib:* Faber Birren Color Exhibition, Stamford Mus, Conn, 97; ANA 27, Holter Mus Art, Helena, Mont, 98; Nat Exhib, Muse Gallery, Philadelphia, 99; 3rd National Exhibition, Galllery West, Alexandria, Va, 2000; Hunter Mus Art, Chattanooga, Tenn, 2001; 9th National, Art Ctr Northern NJ, New Milford, 2001; Myth, Imagination, Legends, Art Spaces Gallery, Calif, Md, 2001; Greeley Sq Art Gallery, NY, 2001; Exclusively Contemp, Eleven East Ashland Gallery, Phoenix, Ariz, 2001; others. *Pos:* Registr & curatorial asst, Univ Wyo Art Mus, Laramie, 1980-85; gallery dir, Univ Wyo Gallery 234, Laramie, 1985 86. *Teaching:* Vis lectr design, Univ Wyo, Laramie, 1986; asst prof painting, Wenatchee Valley Col, Wash; assoc prof, dept chair Graceland Univ, Lamoni, Iowa, 1996-2000; assoc prof art, coord found, Ill State Univ, Normal, 2000-. *Mem:* Col Art Asn; Am Soc Aesthetics; Found in Art, Theory & Edn. *Media:* Acrylic, Oil. *Mailing Add:* Ill State Univ Sch Art Campus Box 5620 Normal IL 61790

MAIDOFF, JULES
PAINTER, PRINTMAKER
b New York, NY, May 6, 33. *Study:* City Col New York, BS, 55, MA, 56; New York Univ, advan study with Estaban Vicente. *Work:* Des Moines Art Ctr, Iowa; Rose Mus, Waltham, Mass; Mus Spirito Santos, Lisbon, Portugal; Mus Masaccio, S Giovanni, Italy; City of Pisa, Italy. *Exhib:* One-man shows, Contemp Art Mus, Pisa, 77, 20 Yrs in Italy, Mus Masaccio, S Giovanni, Italy, 93, Mus Spirito Santos, Lisbon, 94; Americans Abroad, Covent Garden, London, 89; Self Portraits with Family, Galleria Ciovasso, Milan, 91; Palazzo Dei Sette, Orvieto, Italy, 96-97; Pinocateca, City of Fabriano, 6/97. *Pos:* Artist & designer, Asterisk Assoc, New York, 60-73; artist & founder dir, Studio Art Ctr Int, Florence, Italy, 75-; Avore Cult Ctr, Oporto, Portugal, 98; juror, Nat Prize Italy, City of Serra, di San Quirico, 98. *Teaching:* Head art dept, painting & drawing, Studio Art Ctr Int, Florence, Italy, 75-97. *Awards:* Fulbright Grant; Stearns Award, City Col New York. *Bibliog:* Mario De Michelli (auth), Jules Maidoff, 20 Years in Italy (monogr), City of S Giovanni, 93; Carol Becker (auth), Work on the 5 years 91-96, Palazzo Dei Sette, 12/96. *Mem:* Col Art Asn; Nat Asn Schs Art Design; Asn Am Col Univ Progs Italy; Asn Indep Sch Art. *Media:* All Media. *Mailing Add:* Via de Ginori 13 Firenze 50129 Italy

MAIER, MARYANNE E
PAINTER
b Rochester, NY. *Study:* With Dana Gibson Noble, 75-77; Paier Col Art, dipl(fine arts), 77; with Charles Gruppe, 81. *Hon Degrees:* Fine Arts Degree (hon), Paier Col Art. *Work:* Juried shows in New England, NY, Fla. *Comn:* various institutions, banks, restaurants, mus. *Exhib:* Am Painters in Paris Exhib, 77; Audubon Artists, Nat Acad Galleries, NY, 79; Mus Art & Sci, Bridgeport, Conn, 80; Hudson Valley Art Asn, White Plains, NY, 80; Seascapes of New Eng, Hartford State Capitol, Conn, 83. *Pos:* Artist, writer, demonstrator, lectr. *Teaching:* Art instr, Post Acad Art, Cheshire, Conn & Milford Acad, Milford, Conn. *Awards:* Judge's Spec Award, Bridgeport Art League,

79; Best Painting, Sarasota Visual Arts; First Prize, Rockport Art Asn; Best of Show, Salmagundi, NY. *Bibliog:* Edward Meaney (auth), Family life, Lynn Item News, Mass, 76; Lynn Doherty (auth), In her eyes all the world is a canvas, Milford Citizen, 80. *Mem:* Nat League Am Pen Women; Conn Classic Arts; Milford Fine Arts; life mem Kent Art Asn; Salmagundi Club; Visual Art Ctr, Sarasota, Fla. *Media:* Oil, Acrylic. *Interests:* seascapes. *Mailing Add:* 259 John Ringling Blvd Sarasota FL 34236

MAILMAN, CYNTHIA
PAINTER, EDUCATOR
b Bronx, NY, Dec 31, 42. *Study:* Pratt Inst, BS, 64; Art Students League; Brooklyn Mus Art Sch; Rutgers Univ, MFA, 78; Video Cert, Studio Prod & Portapak Prod courses, Community Television, Staten Island, NY, 94. *Work:* Everson Mus, Syracuse; Staten Island Mus; The Jane Voorhees, Zimmerli Art Mus, New Brunswick, NJ; Prudential Life Ins Co, Newark, NJ; NJ State Mus, Trenton; The Port Authority NY & NJ; The Queensborough Community Col Gallery, Queens, NY. *Comn:* Mural, Citywalls Pub Arts Coun, Staten Island, NY, 77; mural, World Trade Ctr, Port Authority, NY; Cow Parade, NY, 2000. *Exhib:* Solo exhibs, SOHO 20 Gallery, NY, 74, 76, 78, 80, 83, 86 & 99, Everson Mus Art, Syracuse, NY, 81, Maurice M Pine Free Pub Libr, Fairlawn, NJ, 81, Fairleigh Dickinson Univ, Edward Williams Col, NJ, 82, Manhattanville Col, NY, 85, New House Gallery, Staten Island, NY, 87, Staten Island Visions, 88, Staten Island Inst Arts & Scis, 2000; Works from the Permanent Collection, Staten Island Mus, NY, 87; Open Studio Tour & Show, 87; Staten Island Invitational, Newhouse Ctr, NY, 89; Summer on Broome, SOHO 20 Gallery, NY, 89; Women Printmakers, Queensborough Community Col Gallery, 91; Women for Choice, Womans Caucus Art Int, NY, 92; Resolutions, Affirmations, Acclamations, Art Lab, Snug Harbor, Staten Island, NY, 92; Hallelujah Invitational, Ceres Gallery, NY, 93; The Pushpin Show, SOHO 20 Gallery, NY, 94; Island Views, Newhouse Ctr, Staten Island, NY, 98. *Collection Arranged:* Mural, Dow Jones, NJ. *Pos:* Lectr, 77-; Ci Huval Coun Found/CETA Artists proj, 78-80; adj art instr, Livingston Col, NJ, 78-80. *Teaching:* Instr art, Queensborough Community Col, 80-85, adj asst prof, 85-2005, retired. *Awards:* Group Studio Arts Tours Grant, Staten Island Coun Arts, 87; Individual Artists Grant, NY State Coun Arts, 87; Encore Grant, Staten Island Coun Arts & Humanities & NY State Coun Arts, 2000. *Bibliog:* Eric Maisel (auth), Artists Speak-A Sketchbook, Harper San Francisco, 93; Henry Abrams (auth), The Power of Feminist Art, Broude & Garrard, 94; Seeing Ourselves, F Borzello, Thames & Hudson, 98. *Mem:* NY Womens Caucus Art; Coun on Arts Staten Island; SOHO 20 Artists; Mud Land Soc for Renaissance Stapleton; Community Bd #1; Bd Member SI, NY. *Media:* Acrylic, Mixed Media. *Interests:* Bird watching, traveling, reading, guitar playing, community activist. *Collection:* Queenborough Community College Gallery, Bayside, NY; The State Mus of New Jersey, Trenton, NJ; The Everson Mus of Art, Syracuse, NY; The Staten Island Mus, Staten Island, NY; The Jane Voorhees Zimmerli Art Mus, New Brunswick, NJ; The Port Authority of NY & NJ; The Prudential Insurance Co of America, Newark, NJ. *Dealer:* Soho 20 Chelsea, 511 W 25th St, New York, NY 10005. *Mailing Add:* 52 Broad St Staten Island NY 10304

MAIN, TIM
PAINTER
b Pa, 60. *Study:* Carnegie-Mellon Univ, Pittsburgh, Pa, BFA(sculpture & photog), 82. *Exhib:* Nautical Interiors and Seascapes, installation, Public Image Gallery, NY, 84; The Goetz Piece, installation, 151 Ridge Space, NY, 86; Singular Visions, Art in General, NY, 87; Men's Work, Union Seminary Chapel, NY, 88; two-person show, PS 122 Gallery, NY, 89; A Dislpay at Vigah, installation, Rotunda Gallery, Brooklyn, 90; Floating Tile Mosaic, proj installation, Artpark, Lewiston, NY, 90. *Awards:* Yaddo, Saratoga Springs, NY, residency, 89; Fine Arts Work Ctr Fel, Provincetown, Mass, 89; Nat Endowment Arts Visual Artist Fel, 89. *Bibliog:* Guerilla Artist, Newsday Mag, 9/20/87; Rotunda Installation--The Phoenix, Brooklyn, NY, 5/24/90; The Main Idea, Niagara Gazette, Niagara Falls, NY, 7/6/90. *Mailing Add:* 59 Grand St Brooklyn NY 11211

MAINARDI, PATRICIA M
HISTORIAN, CRITIC
b Paterson, NJ, Nov 10, 42. *Study:* Vassar Col, AB, 63; Columbia Univ, 63-65; New York Studio Sch, 65-66; Brooklyn Col, City Univ New York, MFA, 76; Hunter Col, MA, 80; City Univ New York, MPhilos, 81, PhD, 84. *Pos:* Ed, Women & Art, 71-72; ed, Feminist Art J, 72-73, contrib ed, 73-74, reviews ed, 87-89; dir, Goddard MFA Visual Arts Prog, 78-81; contrib ed, Arts Mag, 79-; bd dir, Col Art Asn, 91-95; pres, Asn Historians 19th Century Art, 93-96; ed bd, Art Bulletin 91-, chair, 94-; co-chair, Columbia Univ Seminar on Women & Soc, 94-96. *Teaching:* Vis lectr, Pratt Inst, Mass Col Art, 73 & 74, Brooklyn Col, 76-78, Sch Visual Arts, 77 & Goddard Col, 77-81; asst prof, Harvard Univ, 84-85; prof, Brooklyn Col & Grad Sch, City Univ New York, 85-; vis prof, Univ Queensland, Australia, 88, Princeton Univ, 92, Williams Col, 94. *Awards:* Chester Dale fel, Nat Gallery Art, 81-82; Tools of Res Grant, NEH, 89; Paul Mellon Vis Sr Fel, Ctr Advan Study, Nat Gallery Art, 90; Grant-in-Aid, Am Coun Learned Soc, 89. *Mem:* Col Art Asn; Int Asn Art Critics; Am Hist Asn. *Publ:* Quilts: The Great American Art, Miles & Weir, 78; Art & Politics of the Second Empire, Yale Univ Press, 87; The End of the Salon, Cambridge Univ Press, 94. *Mailing Add:* 602 Carlton Ave Brooklyn NY 11238-3407

MAIOR, PHILIP
SCULPTOR
Study: Mott Community Col, 67-69; Aquinas Col, Grand Rapids, Mich, 71-72. *Work:* Lincoln Ctr Sculpture Garden, Ft Collins, Colo. *Exhib:* NAm Sculpture Exhib, Foothills Art Ctr, Golden, Colo, 90; Colo Open, Foothills Art Ctr, Golden, 94; Poudre Valley Art League, Lincoln Ctr, Ft Collins, Colo, 94; Governor's Invitational, Loveland Mus, Colo, 94; Allied Artists Am, NY, 94. *Awards:* Best of Show, Poudre Valley Art League, 90; Foothills Art Ctr Award, NAm Sculpture Exhib, 90; Best of Show, Colo Open, 94. *Media:* Clay. *Dealer:* Carol Siple Gallery 1401 17th St Denver Colo 80202. *Mailing Add:* 1034 Blue Spruce Loveland CO 80538-2861

MAISEL, DAVID
PHOTOGRAPHER, ENVIRONMENTAL ARTIST
b New York, NY, Apr 22, 61. *Study:* Princeton Univ, BA(visual arts, art hist), 79-84; Harvard Univ, MA (architecture) 88-89. *Work:* Metrop Mus Art, NY; Int Mus Photog, George Eastman House, Rochester, NY; Rose Art Mus, Brandeis Univ, Waltham, Mass; Brooklyn Mus Art, NY; Baudoin Col Art Mus, Maine. *Exhib:* Collection Visions: Twelve Contemp Photogrs, Rose Art Mus, Waltham, Mass, 86; New Acquisitions, New Work, New Directions, Int Mus Photog, George Eastman House, Rochester, 89; Selected Photographs from the Permanent Collection, Brooklyn Mus Art, NY, 89; The New Am Pastoral: Landscape Photog in and Age of Questioning, Int Mus Photog, George Eastman House, Rochester, NY, 90 & Whitney Mus Am Art, Equitable Ctr, NY, 90; Landscapes of Consequence, Aldrich Mus Contemp Art, Ridgefield, Conn, 91; Managing Eden, Ctr Photography, Woodstock, NY, 2003; Treading Water, Soc Contemporary Photography, Kansas City, Mo, 2003; Diversions & Dislocations; California's Owens Valley, Ctr Land Use Interpretation, LA, 2004; reGenerations: Environmental Art in California, Armory Crt Arts, 2004; No Man's Land: Contemporary Photographers and Fragile Ecologies, Halsey Galllery, Inst Contemporary Art, Col Charleston, SC, 2004; New Turf, Robert Hull Fleming Mus, Univ Vt, 2005. *Pos:* vpres bd dirs, Photo Alliance, 2002-04. *Teaching:* Instr photog, Cambridge Sch Weston, Mass, 84-85, Santa Fe Photog Workshops, 91; Int Ctr Photog, New York, 92-. *Mem:* Advert Photog Am. *Media:* Photographic prints. *Mailing Add:* David Maisel Photography 100 Ebbtide Ste 320 Sausalito CA 94965

MAISNER, BERNARD LEWIS
PAINTER
b Paterson, NJ, June 21, 1954. *Study:* Cooper Union Col Art, New York, BFA, 77. *Work:* Philadelphia Mus Art; Pierpont Morgan Libr & Philip Morris, Inc, NY. *Exhib:* Solo exhibs, Kathryn Markel Gallery, NY, 82 & 85, Stux Gallery, NY, 88; New Drawing in Am, The Drawing Ctr, NY, 84; Words-Pictures, Bronx Mus Art, NY, 84; Written Imagery, Fine Arts Mus Long Island, Hempstead, NY, 84; Precious, Grey Art Gallery, NY Univ, 84; Gold Illuminators, Metrop Mus Art, NY, 85; The Shape of Abstraction, Stux Gallery, Boston, 86. *Teaching:* Guest lectr, medieval manuscript illumination technique, Cloisters Mus & Metrop Mus Art, NY, 77- & J Paul Getty Mus, Malibu, Calif, 83. *Awards:* Best in Show Award, 77 & Jurors' Award, 86, New York Univ Small Works Show. *Bibliog:* Calvin Thompkins (auth), Artists' books, New Yorker Mag, 1/25/82; Lorraine Karafel (auth), Maisner exhibition--Markel Gallery, Arts Mag, 3/83; Grace Glueck (auth), Religion makes an impact, NY Times, 4/7/85; Arlene Raven (auth), Spirited, Village Voice, 3/8/88; Judy Schwendenwein (auth), Bernard Maisner, Art News, summer 88. *Media:* Painting, All Media. *Publ:* Auth, My molding, flowing conception of image and how it affects the universe, Tracks, A Journal of Artists' Writings, spring 77. *Mailing Add:* 56 Mount St Bay Head NJ 08742-4632

MAJDRAKOFF, IVAN
PAINTER, ASSEMBLAGE ARTIST
b New York, NY, June 19, 27. *Study:* Cranbrook Acad Art, with Wallace Mitchell. *Work:* Univ Minn Gallery; Minneapolis Inst Art; Cranbrook Art Mus, Bloomfield Hills, Mich. *Comn:* Black & white photo collage, Bronx State Hosp, NY, 71; Masonite outdoor mural, San Francisco Art Comn. *Exhib:* Pa Acad Art, Philadelphia; Detroit Art Inst, Mich; Walker Art Ctr, Minneapolis; San Francisco Mus Art; Drawing Exhib, Mus Mod Art, NY; Mass Inst Technol, 83; One man show, Cranbrook Mus, Bloomfield Hills, Mich, 86; Oakland Mus, 97. *Pos:* Actg dir, Univ Art Gallery, Univ Minn, 52-55; dir, Stanford Univ Gallery, 62. *Teaching:* Instr drawing & painting, San Francisco Art Inst, 57-97, prof emer, 98-; instr drawing, Stanford Univ, 57-58 & 68-69. *Bibliog:* Al Wong (auth), Portrait of Ivan (film), 68. *Media:* Acrylic, Ink. *Mailing Add:* Dept Drawing-Painting San Francisco Art Inst 800 Chestnut St San Francisco CA 94133

MAJESKI, THOMAS H
PRINTMAKER, EDUCATOR
b Council Bluffs, Iowa, Sept 14, 33. *Study:* Univ Omaha, BFA, 60; Univ Iowa, with Mauricio Lasansky, MFA, 63. *Work:* Philadelphia Mus Art, Pa; Sheldon Mem Art Mus, Lincoln, Nebr; Joslyn Mus, Omaha, Nebr; Mus Voor Schone Kunsten, Antwerp Belg; Guangzhou Acad Fine Arts, People's Rep China; and others. *Comn:* Opera Omaha 25th Annv Print Edition. *Exhib:* Prints, Watercolors & Drawings, Pa Acad Fine Arts, Philadelphia, 65; 17 State Exhib, Springfield Art Mus, Mo, 74; Colorprint USA, Tex Tech Univ, Lubbock, 74; Int Miniature Print Competition, Pratt Graphics, NY, 83; solo exhib, Sioux City Art Ctr, Iowa, 95; Univ Tex, Pan Am 2002; Laredo Art Ctr, Tex, 2006. *Teaching:* Prof printmaking, Univ Nebr Omaha, 63-, Reagents prof, 89, prof art, prof emeritus, 99. *Awards:* Purchase Awards, Philadelphia Print Club, 67, Nebr Centennial, 67 & Springfield Art Mus, 74; Univ Nebr Teaching Excellence Award. *Bibliog:* The Print Collector's Newsletter (NY May 1982, p 60). *Media:* Monotypes, Wall constructions. *Mailing Add:* 1315 Silver St Ashland NE 68003-1843

MAJORE, FRANK
PHOTOGRAPHER
b Richmond Hill, NY, Feb 9, 48. *Study:* Philadelphia Col Art, BS, 69. *Work:* Albright Knox Art Gallery, Buffalo, NY; Boston Mus Fine Arts; Brooklyn Mus; Los Angeles Co Mus Art; Whitney Mus Am Art, NY. *Exhib:* 1985 Biennial Exhib, Whitney Mus Am Art, NY, 85; Avant Garde in the Eighties, Los Angeles Co Mus Art, 87; The Photog of Invention, Nat Mus Am Art, Washington, 89; Pleasures and Terrors of Domestic Comfort, Mus Mod Art, NY, 91; This Sporting Life, 1878-1991, High Mus

Art, Ga, 92; one-man shows, Butler Inst Am Art, 91, John & Mabel Ringling Mus Art, 91; Commodity Image, Int Ctr Photog, NY, 93. *Awards:* Tiffany Award, 93; Photog Fel, Aaron Siskind Found, 93, John Simon Guggenheim Found, 96. *Bibliog:* Andy Grundberg (auth), Images that represent deep bites of forbidden fruit, NY Times, 1/26/86; Richard Martin (auth), Frank Majore, Arts Mag, 2/88; Ileen Sheppard (auth), Frank Majore: Dreamsville, Ringling Mus Art, 91. *Media:* Photography. *Mailing Add:* 181 Duane St New York NY 10013

MAKANOWITZKY, BARBARA
PASTEL
Study: Art Students League, NY; San Francisco Art Inst, Calif. *Exhib:* 11 solo shows; 20 and more juried shows in New Eng, Calif, NY and Wash, DC. *Teaching:* instr workshops, Sharon Arts Center, NH. *Bibliog:* Master Painters World Pastel Showcase, International Artist, 12/05-1/06; Pastel Journal, 7-8/05. *Mem:* Signature mem, Pastel Soc Am (PSA). *Media:* Pastel. *Interests:* Favorite subject to paint is the sea. *Dealer:* Big Sur Gallery Carmel Calif; The Ventana Gallery Big Sur Calif; Home Scapes Carmel Calif. *Mailing Add:* PO box 177 South Freeport ME 04078

MAKAVEJEV, DUSAN
FILMMAKER
b Belgrade, Yugoslavia, Oct 13, 32. *Study:* Acad Theater, Radio, Film & TV, Belgrade. *Exhib:* Films, Man is Not a Bird, 65, Love Affair: Or, the Case of the Missing Switchboard Operator, 67, Innocence Unprotected, 68, WR: Mysteries of the Organism, 71, Sweet Movie, 75, Montenegro, 81, The Coca-Cola Kid, 85 & A Night of Love, 95; and numerous others. *Awards:* Guggenheim Fel, 98. *Bibliog:* John Taylor (auth), Directors and Directions, New York, 75; Stanley Cavell (auth), On Makavejev on Bergman, Critical Inquiry, Chicago, No 2, 79; Dusan Makavejev in Film Dope, London, 12/87. *Publ:* Auth, A Kiss for Komradess Slogan, 64; Nevinost bez zastite, (Innocence Unprotected), Zagreb, 68; WR: Mysteries of the Organism, New York, 72. *Mailing Add:* Bulevar Lenjina 193 Belgrade Serbia 11070

MAKI, COUNTESS HOPE MARIE
PAINTER, INSTRUCTOR
b St Joseph, Mo, Jan 14, 38. *Study:* Self-taught. *Comn:* Masters of Art (4 x 8 ft oil painting), comn by His Eminence Prince John, Ormiston Palace, Tasmania, Australia, 92; Horses (4 x 12 ft oil painting), comn by Jerry Grimes, Santa Rosa Beach, Fla, 94. *Exhib:* One-woman show, Arts-Inter Salon Int Des Sekneurs de L'Art, Chateauneuf du Pape, France, 94; Salon Int des Seigneurs de L'Art, Palais des Congres Marseille, 94; Montserrat Gallery, NY. *Teaching:* Art instr, Okaloosa Walton Jr Col, Fla, 66-68, television art show, Channel 6-Ft Walton Beach, Fla, 73-75 & Pensacola Jr Col, Fla, 78-88. *Awards:* Women's Inner Circle Achievement Award, Am Biog Inst; Most Admired Woman of the Decade, Bd Int Res Am Biog Inst; Int Art Award, Salon Int Des Seigneurs de L'Art, France, 94; and others. *Mem:* Int Biog Asns, Cambridge, Eng; Int Platform Asn; hon mem Res Bd Advisors for Am Biog Inst. *Media:* Oils, Mixed Media. *Dealer:* Overseas European Corp PO Box 7152 Freeport NY 11520. *Mailing Add:* 3985 Langley Ave Pensacola FL 32504

MAKI, ROBERT RICHARD
SCULPTOR, PAINTER
b Walla Walla, Wash, Sept 15, 38. *Study:* Western Wash State Col, BA, 62; Univ Washington, MFA, 66; San Francisco Art Inst Summer Workshop, 67. *Work:* Western Wash Univ, Outdoor Sculpture Collection, Bellingham; Henry Art Gallery, Univ Washington; Stanford Univ; Nat Collection Am Art, Washington, DC; Seattle Art Mus. *Comn:* Seattle-Tacoma Int Airport; Expo Ctr, Portland, Ore; Wash State Univ, Pullman, Wash; Fed Bldg/Courthouse, Eugene, Oreg; Evergreen State Col, Olympia, Wash; Trimet, City of Portland, Ok; Wake Forest Univ, Winston-Salem, NC. *Exhib:* West Coast Now, Portland Art Mus & De Young Mus, 68; one-man shows, Richamond Art Ctr, 67, Michael Walls Gallery, San Francisco, 69, Seattle Art Mus, Wash, 73 & 84, Montana State Univ, 73, Portland Ctr Visual Arts, Ore, 74, Southeastern Ctr Contemp Art, Winston-Salem, NC, 78, Richard Hines Gallery, Seattle, Wash, 79 & 81 & Maki/Maki, World Trade Ctr East, Seattle, 99; Reality of Illusions, Herbert F Johnson Mus Art, Cornell Univ, 79; Images & Latitude, Mona Bismark Estate, Paris, France, 88; Ishikowa Perfectual Mus Art, Japan, 88; Lannon-Cole Gallery, Chicago, Ill, 92; Maki/Maki, Butters Gallery, Portland, Ore, 94; Robert Maki = Wood & Steel, Bryan Ohno Gallery, Seattle. *Pos:* Guest lectr at many schs & mus nationwide, 66-. *Teaching:* Hon lectr, Univ Wash, Seattle, 66-68; guest artist, Humboldt State Univ, Calif, 74; Rockefeller Artist-in-Residence Fel, Wake Forest Univ, 79; St Cloud State Univ, Minn; NY Univ; Univ Idaho, Pocatello; NC Sch Arts, Winston-Salem; Montana State Univ, Bozeman; Ariz State Univ, Tempe; Univ Oreg, Eugene. *Awards:* Hon Alumni Fel, Western Wash Univ, Bellingham, 93; Purchase Award, Wright Found, 80; Nat Endowment Arts Senior Sculpture Fel, 68, Drawing, 79 & Sculpture, 85; $30,000 King Co Hon Award, 90; Grantee Nat Endowment Arts, 68, 79, 85. *Bibliog:* Peter Selz & Tom Robbins (auth), West Coast report: The Pacific Northwest today, Art Am, 11-12/68; Jan Van de Marck (auth), Robert Maki at Center for Visual Arts, Art Am, 9-10/74; Bruce Guenther (auth), 50 NW Artists, 83; Matthew Kangas (auth), Limitless Geometry: Robert Maki Sculpture, Vol 17, No 8, 10/98; Sculpture Mag; Felicia Gonazles (auth) Maki/Maki - double vision, Met Living, Vol 2 No 3, 10/2000. *Media:* All. *Mailing Add:* 9154 NE Eglon Rd Kingston WA 98346

MAKI, SHEILA ANNE
PRINTMAKER, PAINTER
b Sudbury, Ont, Aug 31, 32. *Study:* North Bay Normal Sch, teacher cert, 51; Univ BC, Can, 67; Camden Arts Ctr, London, Eng; George Brown Col, Toronto, Canada. *Work:* Hamilton Art Gallery, Kitchener-Waterloo Art Gallery & Ont Inst Studies Educ, Toronto, Can; Metrop Mus & Art Ctr, Miami, Fla; Ore State Univ; Cornell Univ, Ithaca, NY; Nat Mus Civilization, Ottawa; Robert McLaughlin Gallery, Oshawa; Burnaby Art Gallery. *Comn:* Circling Around, (portfolio), Merritt Publ, Toronto. *Exhib:* Printmakers '82, Art Gallery Ont, Toronto, 82; Gloucester Co Col, Sewell, NJ; Int Print Soc, New Hope, Mass; Woodstock Pub Art Gallery, Woodstock, Ont; Glenhyrst Art Gallery of Brant, Brantford, Ont, 88; WKP Kennedy Gallery, North Bay, Ont, 89; Robert McLaughlin Gallery (auth, catalog), Oshawa, Ont, 94; Wilfrid Laurier Univ, Waterloo, 2000; and others. *Pos:* Visual artist. *Awards:* Hon Mention, 8th Burnaby Print Exhib, Burnaby Art Gallery, 75; and others. *Bibliog:* Elaine Sills (article), Art in a Dream, Home Decor, Can, 81; Mary Mason (auth), Artist, Glendon Univ, 85; Franz Geierhaus (article) J of the Printworld, fall 90; Joan Murray (auth), McLaughlin Gallery,. *Mem:* Boston Printmakers; Heliconian Club, Toronto (exec mem, 75-80 & 83-86, treas, 93-95 & secy, 86-88. *Media:* Serigraphy, Miscellaneous; Acrylic, Oil. *Dealer:* Venturgraph Int. *Mailing Add:* c/o Venturgraph Int 19-400 Esna Park Dr Markham ON L3R 3K2 Canada

MAKLANSKY, STEVEN V
CURATOR
b New York, NY, Nov 13, 63. *Study:* Sir Jon Cass Sch Art, London; Tulane Univ, BA, 85; NY Univ, MA, 88. *Collection Arranged:* Masterpieces from the Permanent Collection, 93; Asserting Equality, A Photographic Legacy of African-Am Identity, 93; Double Exposure, 94; Cameraderie - The Latent Sociology of Photo-History, 95; E J Bellocq, New Orleans, 96. *Teaching:* Vis prof hist photog, Univ New Orleans, 96. *Mem:* Oracle-Photog Curators Group; La Asn Mus; Nat Endowment for Humanities. *Publ:* Auth, Asserting equality, 10/93, Double exposure-re-pairing photographs, 4/94, Modest witness, the unknown photographer, 7/94, Photography by the numbers, 10/95, Arts Quart Mag; Handbook to the collection, New Orleans Mus Art, 96. *Mailing Add:* c/o New Orleans Mus Art One Collins Diboll Cir PO Box 19123 New Orleans LA 70124

MAKLER, HOPE WELSH
ART DEALER
b Philadelphia, Pa, Mar 24, 24. *Study:* Drexel Univ, BS; Bryn Mawr Col & Univ Pa, MA; Barnes Found. *Pos:* Owner & pres, Makler Gallery, Philadelphia, currently. *Specialty:* Twentieth century painting and sculpture

MAKSYMOWICZ, VIRGINIA ANN
SCULPTOR, WRITER
b Brooklyn, NY, Feb 19, 52. *Study:* Brooklyn Col, City Univ, NY, with Lucas Samaras, BA, 73; Brooklyn Mus Art Sch, 73-74; Univ Calif, San Diego, with Allan Kaprow, Eleanor Antin & Newton & Helen Harrrison, MFA, 77. *Comn:* Mural, BACA Downtown Cult Ctr, 78 & sculpture, NY Botanical Gardens, 79, Cult Coun Found, NY; St Thomas Episcopal Church, Lancaster, Pa, 2005; NY Botanical Gardens; Col Wooster, Ohio; Mesa Col & Univ Calif, San Diego; Allen Art Mus, Oberlin, Ohio; many pvt collections. *Exhib:* Lightweight Works, Mitchell Mus, Mt Vernon, Ill, 95; Cameo Appearances, St Joseph's Univ, Philadelphia, Pa, 98; Garden of Earthly delights, Phoenix Project Room, NY, 03; The Physical boundaries of this world, Ceres Project Room, NY, 02; Accumulated Intention, De Pauw Univ, In, 03; Corners, Mus of Contemp Art, Ft Collins, Co, 03; Sheltered, Williams Art Ctr, Lafayette Col, Easton, Pa, 05. *Collection Arranged:* African Objects & Ethnobotany Collection (with catalog), NY Botanical Garden, 79; Time, Form, Nature, Mind, 10 on 8, New York, 86; 24 Canadians in New York, Amos Eno Gallery, New York, 86; Funny Girls: Women, Humor and the Visual Arts, Maria Feliz Gallery, Jim Thorpe, Pa, 93. *Pos:* Exec dir, Amos Eno Gallery, New York, 83-86; articles ed, Art & Artists, New York, 86-89. *Teaching:* Vis asst prof sculpture, Oberlin Col, Ohio, 80-81; vis sculptor, Wayne State Univ, Detroit, 81-82; vis artist, Minneapolis Col Art Design, 90; vis asst prof art, Franklin & Marshall Col, Lancaster, Pa, 91-96; adj prof art, Moore Col Art & Design, Philadelphia, 96-98; asst prof art, Franklin & Marshall Col, Lancaster, Pa, 00-06, assoc prof art, 06-. *Awards:* Artist Fel in Sculpture, Nat Endowment Arts, 84-85; Artist Fel, Art Matters Inc, 88. *Bibliog:* Human body as metaphor, NY Times, 88; Political art with style & decorum, review of women, Philadelphia Inquirer, 92 & 96; A Rich Exhib of Paper Possibilities, NY Newsday, 94; Modern Perspective into Italy's Art, LA Times, 98; Yes Virginia, Phillips Mus (catalog essay), 2002; The Physical Boundaries of this World, Sculpture Mag, 2003. *Mem:* Col Art Asn; Women's Caucus Art; Int Sculpture Ctr. *Media:* Sculptural installation. *Interests:* Political and social issues. *Publ:* contribr, Sculpture Mag, Encylopedia of Sculptor, Art & the Public Sphere, Women Artist News, Atlanta Art Papers & Art & Artists. *Dealer:* TandM Arts, Philadelphia, Pa. *Mailing Add:* 3719 Lancaster Ave Philadelphia PA 19104-2334

MALAMED, LYANNE
PAINTER
b Alton, IA, 31. *Study:* Briar Cliff Col, Sioux City, IA, BA, 53; Univ IA, Iowa City; studied with Eugene Ludins & Mauricio Lasanski. *Work:* Bristol-Myers Squibb Co; Johnson & Johnson Corp Hq, New Brunswick, NJ; Rider Col, Lawrenceville, NJ. *Exhib:* Solo Exhib, Mercer Co community Col, Trenton, NJ, Marymount Manhattan Col Gallery, 97, Hunterdon Mus Art, Clinton, NJ, 2000, Atrium Gallery, Chubb Group Ins Co, Warren, NJ, 2001, Somerset Art Asn, Bedminster, NJ, 2004, Arts Counc the Morris Area, 2005; Carnegie Ctr, Princeton, NJ; Morris Mus, NJ; Artists League of Central NJ; Gallery at Bristol-Myers Squibb, Lawrencebill, NJ. *Awards:* Fel, NJ State Coun on Arts, 85-86; First prize, NYC Ctr Gallery; First prize, Des Moines Art Ctr. *Media:* Oil, Acrylic. *Mailing Add:* 900 Timberlane Bridgewater NJ 08807

MALDRE, MATI
PHOTOGRAPHER, EDUCATOR
b Geestacht, Ger, Apr 3, 47; US citizen. *Study:* Univ Ill, with Joseph Jachna, BA(design), 69; Inst Design, Ill Inst Technol, with Aaron Siskind, Arthur Siegel & Charles Swedlund, Encycl Britannica grant, 70-72, MS(photog), 72; also with Paul Caponagro, Jerry Uelsmann, Nathan Lyons & Les Krims. *Work:* Kalamazoo Art Ctr,

Mich; Humboldt Arts Coun, Eureka, Calif; Pasadena Mus Art, Calif; Visual Studies Workshop, Rochester, NY. *Exhib:* Int Photo Show, Chicago, 74; First Light & Light II, Humboldt Arts Coun, 75; Ill Photogr Traveling Exhibs, Ill State Mus, Springfield, 78 & 82; Freshworks 79, Va Mus Fine Arts, Richmond; Friends of Photog, Carmel, Calif, 79 & 80; Univ Wis, Green Bay, 80; and others. *Pos:* Photogr & lab technician, Encycl Britannica, Chicago, 70-74; consult photog & graphics, Chicago Urban Corps, 72-. *Teaching:* Asst prof photog, Chicago State Univ, 72-78, assoc prof, 78-; instr photog, Beverly Art Ctr, Ill, 73-. *Awards:* Grand Award, Photo Images '76, Springfield; Merit Award, Radius '76, Burdee Mus, Rockford, Ill; Purchase Awards, Ill Photogr, Ill State Mus, 78 & 82. *Mem:* Soc Photo Educ; Int Mus Photo, George Eastman House; Friends of Photography. *Media:* Black and White, Cibachrome. *Publ:* Illusr, Encycl Britannica & Britannica Bk of Yr, 70-74; illusr, Comptons Encycl & Comptons Yr Bk, 70-74; illusr, Great Ideas Today, 70-74; illusr, Chicago: Metropolis of the Mid-Continent, Kendel/Hunt Co. *Mailing Add:* 1727 W 104th Pl Chicago IL 60643-2807

MALENDA, JAMES WILLIAM
ENAMELIST, EDUCATOR
b Kingston, Pa, Sept 14, 46. *Study:* Miami Dade Community Col, 69; Kent State Univ, BFA, 71; State Univ NY, MFA, 75. *Work:* Roberson Ctr Arts & Sci, Binghamton, NY; Univ Ga, Athens; Nordenfjeldske Kunstridustrimuseum, Trondheim, Norway; House of Humour and Satire, Gabrovo, Bulgaria. *Comn:* Advent Wreath, St Paul's Cathedral, Peoria, Ill, 80; Crucifix, Salem Lutheran, Peoria, Ill, 80; Medallions-Putnam, Rothberg, Bradley Univ, Peoria, 85; Wall Sculpture, Reading Tube Co, Reading, Pa, 90. *Exhib:* Enameling: Art and Industry, Nat Ornamental Mus, Memphis, Tenn; Int Exhib Enameling Art in Japan, Tokyo CentMus, & Ueno Royal Mus, 81, 83 & 85; Wine, Cooper-Hewitt Mus, NY, 85; Die Kugel-Glas & Metall, Deutsche Goldschmiedehaus, Hanau, Ger, 86; Masterworks Enamel 87, Taft Mus, Cincinnati; L'Art de L'Email, 10th Biennale Int, Limoges, France, 90. *Teaching:* Instr enamel & metal, Mohave Community Col, Kingman, Ariz, 75-76; assoc prof, Bradley Univ, Peoria, Ill, 76-78 & Kutztown Univ, Pa, 87-. *Awards:* Enameling Award, Thompson Enamel Co, 90; Artists Fel, Ill Arts Coun, 84 & 86; Pa State System Grant, 90. *Mem:* Distinguished mem Soc NAm Goldsmiths. *Media:* Enamel, Metal. *Publ:* Coauth, A Sculptural breakdown of static three dimensional form through multi-positioning, Leonardo, Vol 19, Issue 4, 86; auth, A breakdown of static 3-D form through multi-positioning, Glass on Metal, Vol 5, nos 2 & 3, 4-6/86. *Dealer:* Gallery 500 Church/Old York Rd Elkins Park PA 19117. *Mailing Add:* Dept Art Educ/Crafts Kutztown Univ Kutztown PA 19530

MALER, M LEOPOLDO MARIO
SCULPTOR
b Buenos Aires, Arg, Apr 2, 37. *Study:* Univ Buenos Aires, law, 60; Int Asn Comparative Law, France, 62. *Work:* Tamayo Mus, Mex; Hess Collection, Napa, Calif; Fundacion San Telmo, Buenos Aires, Arg. *Comn:* Monument, Seoul Olympic Comt, Korea, 88; monument, Mayor of Madrid, Spain, 92; monument for World Cup, Folk Village, S Korea, 2002. *Exhib:* 1st Biennale of Latinamerican Art, Sao Paulo, Brazil, 78; Echoes & Reflections, Ctr Interamerican Relations, NY, 82; Venice Biennale, Italy, 86; Otros Diluvios, Cult Ctr, Buenos Aires, Arg, 87; Latinamerican Art, Mus OAS, Washington, DC, 90; and others. *Pos:* Prog producer, BBC World Serv, London, 62-77; dir, Napa Contemp Arts Found, 88-94. *Teaching:* Vis prof art, Middlesex Polytechnic, London, 71-74; dean design, Parsons Sch Design, Santo Domingo, 83-85. *Awards:* First Prize, Sao Paulo Biennale Art, 77; Guggenheim Fel, 77; Medal Art Merits, Madrid, Spain, 91. *Bibliog:* BBC's Arena (dir), Maler's Requiem (film), BBC, 79; Edward Lucie-Smith (auth), Art Now, 85; Jorge Glusberg (auth), Maler, New York Univ, 87. *Media:* Recycled Metals, Wood. *Interests:* psychology, sailing, ecology. *Collection:* Laffont Collection, Hess Collection, Helft Collection. *Dealer:* Norah Haime Gallery. *Mailing Add:* EPS #R1366 PO Box 025330 Miami FL 33102

MALLIN, JOEL
COLLECTOR
Study: Cornell Univ, BS; Columbia Univ, LLB; NY Bar, 61. *Pos:* Atty, Joel Mallin LLP, NYC; Chmn, Aldrich Mus, Conn. *Awards:* Named one of top 200 collectors, ARTnews magazine, 2004-. *Mem:* Manhattan Theater Club. *Collection:* Mod & Contemp Art, particularly sculpture

MALLIN, JUDITH YOUNG
WRITER, COLLECTOR
Study: Syracuse Univ, NY, 56; NY Univ, 57 & 87. *Pos:* Lectr, Courtauld Inst, London, 91; Art Inst, Chicago, 92; Sch Visual Arts, 92; estab, The Young Mallin Archive, 92. *Awards:* Who's Who in East. *Res:* Surrealism; women artists of the forties, creativity and aging. *Collection:* Surrealist, women artists of the forties. *Publ:* Auth, Muriel Streeter, Anna Howard Gallery, 90; Virgil Thomson's Swan Song, Avenue Mag, 90; Juliet Man Ray, London Ind & Quest, NY, 92; Edward James, Quest, NY, 92; View: Parade of Avant Garde 1940-47, Thunders Mouth Press, NY, 92. *Mailing Add:* 719 Greenwich St New York NY 10012

MALLORY, NINA AYALA
EDUCATOR, HISTORIAN
b Madrid, Spain; US citizen. *Study:* Columbia Univ, BArchit, 56, MA, 62 & PhD, 65. *Teaching:* Instr art hist, Rutgers Univ, New Brunswick, NJ, 65-66; asst prof renaissance, The Cooper Union, New York, 66-68; assoc prof renaissance & baroque, State Univ NY, Stony Brook, 68-86, prof, 86-. *Awards:* Fulbright Fel, US Govt, 63; Nat Endowment Humanities Grant, 84-86; S H Kress Found Grant, 84-86. *Mem:* Col Art Asn; Am Soc for Hispanic Art Hist Studies. *Res:* Seventeenth century Spanish art. *Publ:* Auth, Roman Rococo architecture from Clement XI to Benedict XIV, 1700-1758, Garland, 77; coauth, Painting in Spain 1650-1700, Princeton, 82; auth, Bartolome Esteban Murillo, Alianza, 83; El Greco to Murillo, Spanish Painting in the Golden Age: 1556-1700

MALLORY, RONALD
PAINTER, SCULPTOR
b Philadelphia, Pa, June 17, 39. *Study:* Univ Colo, BA, 51; Univ Fla, BArch, 55; Sch Fine Arts, Rio de Janeiro, with Roberto Burle Marx, 56; Acad Julian, Paris, 57. *Work:* Mus Mod Art, Whitney Mus Am Art, NY; Albright-Knox Mus, Buffalo, NY; San Francisco Mus Mod Art; Inst Contemp Art, Philadelphia; Smithsonian Inst, Washington, DC; many others. *Comn:* Port Authority NY, World Trade Ctr, 83; Allied Lyons Corp, London, 88. *Exhib:* Mus Mod Art, 66 & 68; Larry Aldrich Mus, Ridgefield, Conn, 67 & 68; Torcuato di Tella, Buenos Aires, Arg, 69; Univ Calif, Los Angeles, 69; Solo exhibs, Stable Gallery, NY, 66, 67, Esther Robles Gallery, Los Angeles, Bonino Gallery, NY, 72, 73, Salon Annuciatta, Milan, Italy, 72, 73, Hansen Fuller Gallery, San Francisco, 73, Iris Clert, Paris, 901 Canyon Road Gallery, Santa Fe, NMex, 96 & Mitchell Algus Gallery, NY, 2001; Whitney Mus Am Art; World Trade Ctr, NY, 86; Mus Mod Art, NY & San Francisco; Whitney Mus Sculpture Ann; Milwaukee Art Ctr; Hayward Gallery, London; San Jose Mus Mod Art; Many others. *Pos:* Artist consultant, Bunker Hill Proj, Los Angeles; cur, C Project (holograms), NY & Miami, 95-98. *Teaching:* Instr, Univ Calif, Berkeley, 72; guest lectr, San Jose Univ, Calif; artist-in-residence, Univ Calif, Berkeley, 72. *Awards:* Pollock-Krasner Grant, 99; Artists Fel, 99. *Bibliog:* Larry Aldrich (auth), New Talent USA, Art in Am (rev), 7/8; John Gruen (auth), The galleries-a critical guide, New York Herald Tribune, 3/26; Peter Schjeldahl (auth), New York Letter, Art Int, Arts Mag & In the Galleries. *Mem:* Artists Equity. *Media:* Holograms. *Dealer:* Mitchel Algos Gallery 25 Thompson St New York NY 10013; Bonino Gallery 48 Great Jones St New York NY. *Mailing Add:* 441 East 57th St New York NY 10022

MALO, TERI (A)
PAINTER, PRINTMAKER
b Whitinsville, Mass, July 20, 54. *Study:* Emmanuel Col, with Michael Jacques, BA, 76; Univ Mass, Amherst, with John Townsend & Fred Becker, MFA, 78. *Work:* Philadelphia Mus Art; IBM Inc, Rose Art Mus Brandeis Univ, Waltham, Mass; DeCordova Mus, Lincoln, Mass; Newport Art Mus, RI. *Exhib:* Philadelphia Int Print Exhib, Philadelphia Mus Art, 79; one-woman show, Pucker Gallery, Boston, 79, 80, 82, 83-92 & 96, JRS Gallery, Providence, RI, 86, 88, 92 & 95, Art Collectors Gallery, NY, 81, Danforth Mus, 98 & Mus Work and Cult, 2001; Miami Int Print Exhib, Fla, 80; Silvermine 13th Nat Print Exhib, 80; Prints, Heritage Mus, Sandwich, Mass, 82; Jerusalem to Boston, Mitchell Mus, Mt Vernon, Ill, 83; Prints & Pots, Newport Art Mus, 85; Danforth Mus, 88 & 92. *Teaching:* Instr studio arts, Danforth Mus, 78-, fine arts, Buffalo State Col, NY, 90-91. *Awards:* Blanche E Colman Award, 98. *Mem:* Fenway Studios Inc. *Media:* Oil, Watercolor; Monotype. *Dealer:* Crane Collection Gallery 564 Washington St Wellesley MA 02181; Powers Gallery 342 Great Rd Acton MA 01720. *Mailing Add:* Malo Studio 103 30 Ipswich St Boston MA 02215

MALO-SPRAWKA, THERESA A See Malo, Teri (A)

MALONE, JAMES HIRAM
PAINTER, WRITER
b Winterville, Ga, Mar 24, 30. *Study:* Morehouse Col, AA, 50; Ctr Creative Studies Col Art and Design, with Sarkis Sarkesian, AA, 59. *Work:* Pavilion Int, Montreal, Can; Knokke-Heist Mus, Knokke-Heist, Belgium; New York Fales Library, 1996; Teaching Mus South, 1999; 480 S Evelyn Pl, Tree Grove, 2006. *Comn:* Malone's Atlanta Book, Atlanta newspapers, Ga, 86-88; Wall mural, Atlanta Centennial Olympic Park Corp, 96; Urban Renewal Hist Makers, NY RepoHist Asn, 97; Walt Disney scenery, 01; Mural, Washington Park Libr, Atlanta, 2004; Vine City Tree Trunk deco public art, Atlanta, 2006. *Exhib:* One-man shows, Neighborhood Art Ctr, Atlanta, 85, C W Hill Sch Gallery, 90 & Alma Simmons Mem Gallery, Atlanta, 94, 95 & 96; Encore Invitational Exhib, Giving Art Back To The Community, Atlanta Projs Hq Off, Atlanta, 94; A Peanut Extravaganza, Art and Imagery of the Peanut Exhib (A nutty show), Albany Mus Art, Ga, 94; Atlanta Res Auburn Ave African Am Hist Gallery, 96; City Hall East Gallery; RepoHistory Installation, 98; McPheeter's Art Gallery, 99; Gallery on the Greene, 2000; Teaching Mus South, 2003; Contemp Studious Biennial, 2003; Homecoming: 20th Century, City Gallery East, 2005; and others. *Pos:* Graphic designer, Northgate Advert Agency, 68-80; art dir, artist-in-residence, Contemp Studios, 59-62; graphic designer, Altanta Newspaper, 81; advertising designer, Atlanta J & Constitution, Ga, 84; fine arts chmn, Black Arts Network and Advocacy, 86; ad hoc comn, Nat Black Arts Fest, 88; publ, Literacy Cartoon Simply Apply Yourself, Southeastern Publ, Atlanta, GA, 90-; columnist, Atlanta News Leader, 91. *Teaching:* instr mgr Spec Serv Arts/Crafts Shop, SC, 52; instr Contemp Art Studios, Detroit, Mich, 63; Instr art basics, Your Heritage House, Detroit, 70; instr Fisher YMCA, Detroit, Mich, 71; instr, Nexus Art Ctr, Atlanta, 94; instr Highland Park Jr Col, Detroit, Mich, 73; instr Metrop College, Atlanta, Ga, 2000. *Awards:* 1986 Bronze Jubilee, WPBA 30 Pub TV, 86; Hon Art Award, Ctr for Creative Studies Col Art and Design Alumni Exhib, 86; Art Award, Art With a Southern Drawl Exhib, Mobile Col, 93; Art Award, Atlanta Centennial Olympic Park, 97; Annie L McPheeters Community Medallion, Atlanta, 98; Sr Art Award, Million Man March, 98. *Bibliog:* Richard Gincel (auth), Artist's work enlivens TAP offices, Atlanta J/Constitution Newspaper, 94; Bo Emmerson (auth), Uncovering Buttermilk Bottom, Atlanta J Constitution, 95; Estella Zavala (auth), Writer Pushes Multiethnic Art for Disadvantaged Youngsters, Wave Newspapers, Calif, 95; Malone's Colorful World, Donna Angle(auth), Millionaire Magazine, 8/2000; Express Yourself Felicia Feaster (auth), Creative Loafing, 2000; Bold Strokes of Affection H M Cauley (auth), Atlanta Journal/Constitution 2002; Who's Who in Black Atlanta, 2004-2005. *Mem:* Visual Vanguard Art Asn; Nat Conf Artists, Atlanta; Int Black Writers Group, Atlanta; Contemporary Artists Detroit, 2006; Keep Atlanta Beautiful Board, 2006; Grove Park Arts Alliance (pres), 2006. *Media:* Acrylics, Enamel. *Publ:* Auth, Anthology of Black

Writers Poetry: Word Up, Beans & Rice Publ, 90; illusr/writer, No-Job Dad, Victory Press, Monterey, Calif, 92; Street Beat Newspaper Column, Atlanta News Leader, College Park, Ga, 92; contribr, Something About the Author, Gale, 96; Jone's Family Cart, Ahkeelah's Press, 97; and others. *Mailing Add:* 1796 North Ave NW Atlanta GA 30318-6441

MALONE, PATRICIA LYNN
PAINTER
b Kansas City, Mo, Dec 3, 30. *Study:* Kansas City Jr Col, 48; Kansas City Art Inst, 49-51; Univ Tulsa, 78-80. *Work:* Oklahoma Art Ctr, Oklahoma City; Transco Energy Corp, Houston, Tex; Hallmark-Crown Ctr, Kansas City, Mo; Univ Tulsa, Okla; McGraw Hill Pub co, NY; Crowe Donlevy, Hall, Estill, Hardwick & Nelson, McGraw Hill. *Comn:* Painting, Cancer Care Ctr, 88; Logsdon Woody, 89; painting, Fed Judge Dana Rasure for Fed Ct House, Tulsa, Okla, 99; Day Break, Bartlesville. *Exhib:* Watercolor USA, Springfield Mus, Mo, 81, 83 & 89; Am Watercolor Soc, Salmagundi Club & Canton Mus, NY, Ohio, 82-88; Midwest Watercolor, Neville Pub Mus, Green Bay, Wis, 83-86; Miniature Art Soc Fla, 93; Miniature Painters Soc Washington, DC, 93-94; and others. *Awards:* Phyllis France Award, Midwest Watercolor Soc, 85; First Place Watercolor, 4th Ann, Phillips Petroleum, 88; Third Place Still Life, Minature Painters Soc, Washington; First place Painting, Women's Show. *Bibliog:* Watercolor '87, Am Artist Mag, 87; Ward (auth), New Spirit of Watercolor, North Light, 89; Albert-Wolf (auth), Splash 91, North Light; and others. *Mem:* Am Watercolor Soc; Nat Watercolor Soc; Watercolor Soc; Nat Watercolor Okla; Transparent Watercolor Soc; Okla Visual Artist Coalition. *Media:* Watercolor, Pastel. *Collection:* McGraw-Hill Publishing Co, The Williams Co, The Univ Tulsa. *Dealer:* M A Doran Gallery 3509 S Peoria Tulsa OK; Art South, Philadelphia PA; Art4Business.com The Gallery at Kingspoint Tulsa Okla. *Mailing Add:* 2807 E 48th St Tulsa OK 74105

MALONE, PETER
PAINTER
b New York, NY, 50. *Study:* Teachers Col, Sch Visual Arts, Columbia Univ, BFA, 77, MA, 83. *Work:* Elizabeth de C Wilson Mus, Manchester, Vt; Munson Williams Proctor Inst, Utica, NY. *Exhib:* Stilled Life, Islip Mus, East Islip, NY; Southern Vt Arts Ctr, Manchester, Vt; Kirkland Arts Ctr, Clinton, NY. *Pos:* gallery dir, Kingsborough Community Col, CUNY, 00-. *Teaching:* adj asst prof, Kingsborough Community Col, CUNY, 84-. *Awards:* rsch grant, Profl Staff Congress, CUNY, 98, 02. *Media:* Oil on Linen. *Mailing Add:* Kingsborough Community Coll Art Gallery 2001 Oriental Blvd Brooklyn NY 11235

MALONE, ROBERT R
PAINTER, PRINTMAKER
b McColl, SC, 33. *Study:* Furman Univ; Univ NC, BA; Univ Chicago, MFA; Univ Iowa. *Comn:* several editions of intaglio & relief prints, Ferdinand Roten Galleries, Baltimore, Md, 66-69; two editions intaglio & relief prints, De Cinque Gallery, Hollywood, Fla, 67; color etching, Ill Arts Coun, 1st Print Comn, 73; several editions of lithographs, Lakeside Studio, Lakeside, Mich, 71-80; Capital Develop Bd, State Ill, 94-95; Sculpture for Third Millennium, Ill, 1994-95. *Exhib:* Solo exhibs, Elliot Smith Gallery, St Louis & Merida Galleries, Louisville, KY, 85 & 87, Rapp Gallery, Louisville, 90, 92, 93 & 96; New Talent in Printmaking, AAA Gallery, NY, 68; Biennial Print Exhib, Calif State Col, Long Beach, 69; Bienniale Int L'Estampe 1970, Mus Mod Art, Paris, 70; 26th Ann Exhib Boston Printmakers, De Cordova Mus, 74; Currents 29: Drawing in St Louis (with catalog), St Louis Art Mus, 85. *Collection Arranged:* Central Academy Fine Arts, Beijing; Humana Inc, Ky; Seven-Up Co, Mo; Emerson Electric Co, Mo; Gen Am Ins Co, Mo; NY Pub Libr; Calif Palace Legion Hon, San Francisc; Philadelphia Mus Art; Smithsonian Inst & Libr Cong, Wash. *Teaching:* Assoc prof painting & printmaking, Wesleyan Col, Macon, Ga, 61-68; assoc prof printmaking, WVa Univ, Morgantown, 68-70; assoc prof printmaking, Southern Ill Univ, Edwardsville, 70-75, prof, 75-2000, prof emeritus, 2000-. *Awards:* Recent Am Graphics Purchase Award, Univ Wis-Madison, 75; Southern Ill Univ Sr Res Scholar Award, 75 & 84; Purchase Award, Sixty Sq Inches, Purdue Univ, 94. *Bibliog:* Prize-winning Graphics, book 7, 1967; Motive Mag, 1968, 1969; Sun Courier Journal & Louisville Times, 11/2/69; Charleston Daily Mail, 07/21/70; New Art Examiner, Apr, 1975; Basic Design, Systems, Elements, Applications, 1983; West End Word, 2/7/85; NY Art Review, 1988. *Mem:* Col Art Asn Am; Southern Graphics Coun. *Media:* Oil, Acrylic; Lithography, Montotype. *Res:* The Redevelopment and Advancement of the Photo-Gelatin Process, 1975-76; Ford Fel, 1977; New Problems with Surface and Illusion in Printmaking, 1977-80; A Re-examination of large scale group portraits for the 1980's, 1982-86; A Contemporary view of the human condition, 1984-85. *Specialty:* Paintings. *Interests:* running; weight lifting. *Publ:* Contemporary American Printmakers, 1999. *Dealer:* Yvonne Rapp Gallery 2117 Frankfort Ave Louisville KY 40206. *Mailing Add:* 600 Chapman St Edwardsville IL 62025-1260

MALOOF, SAM
SCULPTOR
b Chino, Calif, Jan 14, 1916. *Work:* Minn Art Mus; Fine Art Mus, Boston; The White House, Washington DC; Phila Mus Art; Renwick Gallery, among others. *Exhib:* Smithsonian Inst, Washington, DC, 1970; Renwick Gallery, Smithsonian Am Art Mus, 1971, 1992, 2004; Mus Contemp Art, Chgo, 1976; Vatican Mus, Rome, 1978; Vice President's House, Washington, DC, 1980; J.M. Kohler Arts Ctr, Sheboygan, Wis, 1983; Barnsdell Art Ctr, LA, 1984; Navy Pier Joanne Rapp Gallery, 1993; Connell Gallery, Atlanta, Ga, 1996; Craft and Folk Art Mus, LA, 2003. *Pos:* with Vortox, 1934-39; Harold Graham Indust Designer, 1940-41; graphic artist, Millard Sheets, 1946-48; design project in Iran and Lebanon, US State Dept, 1959, design project in El Salvador, 1963. *Media:* wood. *Mailing Add:* c/o Sam and Alfreda Maloof Found Arts and Crafts 5131 Carnelian St Alta Loma CA 91701

MALPEDE, JOHN
PERFORMANCE ARTIST, DIRECTOR
b Wichita Falls, Tex, June 29, 45. *Study:* Univ Wis, BA, 68. *Work:* Out of the Public Eye, 84; Too Many Questions, 84; South of The Clouds, 86; No Stone for Studs Schwartz, 87; LAPD Inspects San Francisco, 89-90; Jupiter 35, 89-90; LAPD Inspects the Twin Cities, 91; LAPD Inspects Amsterdam, 91; LAPD Inspects London, 91; Call Home, 91-93; Give Up All Your Possessions and Follow Me, 93; Dead Dog & Lonely Horse, 94-95; Standing Up and Falling Down, 95; Bronx Train, 95; I Was Sleeping with My Eyes Open, 95; Avec Motard, 96; Pre-Existing Conditions, 97; Temporary Quarters (Hit & Run), 97; co-dir Ping-Pong, 99; GET, 99; Agents & Assets, 2000. *Exhib:* Solo performance, Same or Different, 81, Olympic Update: homelessness in Los Angeles, 84-85. *Pos:* Artistic dir, Los Angeles Poverty Dept, Theater, 86-; self-employed artist, NY Univ, 84-85. *Teaching:* Vis distinguished prof performance, Miami-Dade Community Col, 91; vis asst prof performance, Dept World Arts & Cult, Univ Calif, Los Angeles, 94; teacher, MFA Dir's Prog & Calif Col Arts and Crafts; vis fac mem, Amsterdam Sch for Advanced Research in Theater and Dance Studies, 95-96; vis dir dept undergrad drama, Tisch Sch Arts, NY Univ, 95; vis artist, Movement Research, 93, 95; vis fac, Columbia Col, Chicago, 92, Sch Art Inst Chicago, 90. *Awards:* Adalide Kent Award, San Francisco Art Inst, 87; Visual Arts Grant, Nat Endowment Arts, 88; Bessie Creation Award, Dance Theater Workshop, Los Angeles, Calif, 89; NY State Coun on Arts grant; NEA grant; Calif Arts Coun grant; Dance Theater Workshop Bessie Creation Award; Adeline Kent Award, San Francisco Art Inst; Durfee Sabbatical Grant & Los Angeles Theater Alliance Ovation Award for work with Los Angeles Poverty Dept. *Bibliog:* Thomas Lebhardt (auth), John Malpede, Southern Calif Performance Issue, Mime J, 91. *Mem:* Col Art Asn; Nat Performance Network (mem, steering comt 90-92); Los Angeles Festival (mem, steering comt, 93); City of Los Angeles Cult Affairs Dept (mem arts adv comt, 90-91); Liberty Hill Community (funding bd, 94); Peter Sellars' Old Stories New Lives Found; Social and Pub Art Resource Ctr. *Publ:* Co-dir, producer video LAPD Inspects the Twin Cities, 92; prodr video The Hunger Artist on Sports Incredible, (The Kitchen grant), 84. *Mailing Add:* PO Box 26190 Los Angeles CA 90026

MALTA, VINCENT
INSTRUCTOR, PAINTER
b Brooklyn, NY, Apr 9, 22. *Study:* Art Students League. *Work:* Univ of Minn; Philadelphia Mus; Immaculate Heart Col; Birmingham Mus Art. *Exhib:* Brooklyn Mus Biennial Print Exhib, 52; Metrop Mus Nat Exhib of Watercolors, 52; Pa Acad Fine Arts, 53; Brooklyn Mus Int Watercolor Exhib, 53; Nat Acad of Design, 53; Three-man show, Art Students League, 94. *Teaching:* Instr fine arts, painting, Art Students League, 66-. *Awards:* Emily Lowe Award, 52; Louis Comfort Tiffany Found Award, 54; Betti Salzman Award, Nat Arts Club, 77. *Bibliog:* Marlene Schiller (auth), Return of the art spirit, Am Artist Mag, 3/78; Art Showcase, Manhattan Cable TV, 5/25/83 & 10/12/83. *Mem:* Artist Equity; Artists' Fel Inc, NY. *Media:* Mixed. *Mailing Add:* 1960 60th St Brooklyn NY 11204

MALTZMAN, STANLEY
PAINTER, PRINTMAKER
b New York, NY, 21. *Study:* New York Phoenix Sch Design, degree, 48. *Work:* Schenectady Mus, NY; Hudson River Mus, Yonkers, NY; Carnegie-Mellon Univ; Mus Fine Arts, Springfield, Mass; Greene Co Savings Bank, Greenville, NY; and others; Met Mus Art, NY. *Comn:* Steuben Glass, Corning, NY; Danbury Mint, Norwalk, Conn; Fed Land Bank & Smith & Wesson, Springfield, Mass. *Exhib:* Berkshire Mus, Pittsfield, Mass, 79; Am Watercolor Soc, NY, 80; Monotypes, The Painterly Print, NY, 86 & Pastel Soc Am, 94; Pretty Deadly Poisonous Plants of Forest, Field & Garden, Bruce Mus, Conn, 95; Allied Artists Am, Nat Arts Club, 97; Gifts of Winter exhib, Carnegie Mellon Univ, 2000; Butler Inst Art, Ohio, 2004. *Collection Arranged:* Color Fields from the Evening Sky, 83; Inspirations from Nature, Elliot Mus, Stuart, Fla, 96. *Pos:* Cur, Greenville Comm Libr Gallery, 97-98. *Teaching:* Instr drawing & pastel, Hudson Valley Workshops, 87-2006; Arts in Educ Serv, Questar III & Boccs, 96; instr, watercolor & drawing workshops, Greenville Libr, 2005. *Awards:* First Prize, Conn Acad Fine Arts, 76; Ball State Univ Award, 81; Drawing Prize, Berkshire Mus, Pittsfield, Mass. *Bibliog:* Article, Am Artist Mag, 4/86; Kaatskill Life Mag, spring 96; Artists Mag, 98. *Mem:* Greene Co Coun Arts, Catskill, NY (visual arts coun); Pastel Soc Am; Am Artists Prof League, Hudson Valley Art Asn. *Media:* Watercolor, Pastel; Graphics. *Specialty:* Contemporary Landscape. *Interests:* Landscapes of the Masers, the various kinds of papers work on, ornitholoty. *Collection:* Prints, drawings, watercolors of the 20th century. *Publ:* Sounds of Mystery-Sounds of a Distant Drum, Holt, Rinehart, Inc, 67; Botanical Arts & Illustration, Carnegie-Mellon Univ, 77-78; Printworld Directory, 82, 83, 84 & 85; The Crayon, Olana Newsletter; Drawing Nature, Northlight Books, 95; Drawing Trees, NLight Bks, 99. *Dealer:* Windham Fine Arts 5380 Main St Windham NY 12496. *Mailing Add:* PO Box 333 Freehold NY 12431

MANCINI, JOHN
PAINTER
b Comiso, Italy, Jan 9, 25; US citizen. *Study:* Scuola d'Arte, Comiso, Italy, dipl; Liceo & Acad di Belle Arti, Palermo, Italy, BA; Art Students League; Columbia Univ. *Work:* Galleria Della Acad, Palermo, Italy; Bank Am & Wells Fargo Bank, San Francisco; Mus Ital Art, Stone Park, Ill; Galeria de Colecionistas, Mexico City. *Comn:* Frank Carrubba, Palo Alto, CA. *Exhib:* Crocker Mus Art, Sacramento, Calif, 67; Palace of Fine Art, San Francisco, 68; Heritage Gallery, Los Angeles, Calif; Mus Ital-Am, San Francisco, Calif; Gallery Europa, Palo Alto, Calif. *Collection Arranged:* Hespe Gallery, San Francisco, Calif; Herbert Palmer Gallery, Los Angeles, Calif; Wellington Mgt Co, Boston, Mass; Robert Doran, Chestnut Hill, Mass; Harry & Gwen Schlough, Hillsborough, Calif; Chuck Silverman, Houston, Tex; David Himmelberger, Palo Alto, Calif. *Pos:* Art dir, R W Graphics, Palo Alto, Calif, 66-70 & Mancini Design,

Mountain View, Calif, 70-90; Mancini Fine Art, San Mateo, Calif. *Teaching:* Art teacher painting, Scuola d'Arte, Comiso, Italy, 49-51. *Awards:* Gold Medal, Ital-Am Artists in USA, 77; Environ Protection Agency, San Francisco, 80; US Embassy, Bucharest, Rumania, 90-. *Bibliog:* E M Polley (auth), John Mancini, Artforum, 65; Thomas Albright (auth), John Mancini, San Francisco Chronicle, 73; R L P (auth), Los Angeles Times, 84; and others. *Media:* Oil, Acrylic. *Interests:* Travel to Rome, Florence for Renaissance Art. *Collection:* R Doran, Willington Mandg Co, R&C Schlough, R McKenzie, C Silverman. *Publ:* NY Graphics Soc Pub Group. *Dealer:* Hespe Gallery San Francisco CA 94123; Gallery Europa, Palo Alto CA 94301. *Mailing Add:* 604 Connie Ave San Mateo CA 94402

MANCUSI-UNGARO, CAROL
CONSERVATOR, EDUCATOR
Study: Conn Col, BA; NYU Inst Fine Arts, MA in hist of art and conserv. *Pos:* Chief conservator, The Menil Collection, Houston, 83-2001; found dir, Ctr for Tech. Study of Modern Art Harvard Univ Mus, Cambridge, Mass, 2001-; dir conserv, Whitney Mus Am Art, New York City, 2001-. *Teaching:* sr lectr, in hist of art and archit Harvard Univ, Cambridge, Mass. *Awards:* Recipient Col Art Asn/Heritage Preserv Award for Distinction in Scholar and Conserv, 2004. *Mailing Add:* Harvard Univ Art Mus 32 Quincy Ave Cambridge MA 02138

MANCUSO, LENI MANCUSO BARRETT
PAINTER, INSTRUCTOR
b New York, NY. *Study:* Brooklyn Mus Art Sch; Art Students League; Pratt Inst, NY; New Sch Univ, NY. *Work:* Newberry Collection, Detroit, Mich; First Nat Bank Boston; Portland Mus Art, Maine; Kresge Gallery, Ann Arbor, Mich; Mich Bell Tel; NH State Art Bank; US State Dept, Washington, DC; John Day Collection of Monhegan Art, ME. *Exhib:* Wadsworth Atheneum, Hartford, Conn, 78; one-man shows Lamont Gallery, Exeter, NH, 72, Univ Maine Art Mus, Orono, Maine, 77, Currier Art Gallery, Manchester, NH, 81, St Anselm Col, Goffstown, NH, 87, Manchester Inst Arts, NH, 87, Maine Arts Commn, Augusta, Maine, 95, Jubilant Light, Maine Ctr for Contemp Art, Rockport, Maine, 96; Maine Coast Artists, 78, 79 & 96; Leighton Gallery, 91; Danforth Gallery, 94; Maine Arts Comn, 95; Castine Arts Asn, Maine, 1999-2000; Trinity Gallery, Castine, Maine; Galerie am Neuen Palais, Potsdam, Ger, 2003; Ctr for Maine Contemp Art, 2004-2005. *Teaching:* Instr painting & head art dept, Proctor Acad, Andover, NH, 55-60; instr painting & watercolor, Currier Gallery Art Sch, Manchester, NH, 62-70; instr painting & compos, St Paul's Sch, Concord, NH, 67-75. *Awards:* Watercolor Prize, Portland Mus Art, Maine, 61 & Currier Gallery Art, NH, 68 & 81; First Prize, Danforth Gallery, 94. *Bibliog:* T Rawson (auth), Leni Mancuso at Manchester Institute, Art/New Eng, 3/87; Beyond Tradition, Bar Harbor News, 93; Kenneth Greenleaf (auth) For Mancuso, It's not light, but reflection, Maine Sunday Telegram, 6/2/96; Carle Little & Arnold Skolnick (eds), The Art of Maine in Winter, Down East Bks, Rockport, Maine, 2002; Robert Post (auth), Understanding Maine Winter, Down East Bks, 2003; C. Little & A. Skolnick (eds.), The Art of Monhegan Island, Down East Books, Rockport, ME, 2004. *Mem:* NH Art Asn; Deer Isle Artists' Asn; Col Art Asn; Union Maine Visual Artists; Maine Coast Artists. *Media:* Watercolor, Casein. *Publ:* In Rothkos's Cave, 20 original drawings and poems, Puckerbrush Rev Porfolio # 6, Winter/Spring 98. *Mailing Add:* PO Box 303 Castine ME 04421

MANDEL, JOHN
PAINTER
b New York, NY, Dec 6, 41. *Study:* Pratt Inst, BFA, 64. *Work:* Nat Gallery Australia; Pa State Univ. *Exhib:* Whitney Mus Am Art Painting Ann, 69 & 72; The Contemp Figure, A New Realism, Suffolk Mus & Carriage House at Stony Brook, NY, 71; In Sharp Focus, Sidney Janis Gallery, NY, 72; Indianapolis Mus Ann, Ind, 72; One-man shows, Max Hutchinson Gallery, NY, 71-73, 75 & 79. *Pos:* Assoc dean, Sch Art & Design, Calif Inst Arts. *Teaching:* Instr painting, grad & undergrad sch, Pratt Inst, 71-76; instr painting, Calif Inst Arts, 72-. *Awards:* Paul Mellon Fel, 79. *Bibliog:* John Canaday (auth), Art: The figure as defined by Mandel, 11/21/71 & Art: In Mandel's Art, superb control, 4/28/73, New York Times. *Mailing Add:* c/o Calif Inst Arts Art Sch 24700 McBean Pkwy Valencia CA 91355

MANDEL, MIKE
PHOTOGRAPHER, MOSAIC ARTIST
b Los Angeles, Calif, Nov 24, 50. *Study:* Cal State, Northridge, BA, 72; San Francisco Art Inst, MFA, 74. *Work:* Mus Mod Art, NY; San Francisco Mus Mod Art; Bibliot Nat, Paris, France; Mus Fine Arts, Houston; Calif Inst Photog, Univ Calif, Riverside; and others. *Comn:* Hearth (wood tile mosaic mural), NY, 93; 5 skaters, City San Jose, Calif, 94-96; Waiting, San Francisco Int Airport, 96-99; Atlanta Fed Ctr, Gen Serv Admin, Ga, 99-. *Exhib:* Evidence, San Francisco Mus Mod Art, 77; New Photog 5, Mus Mod Art, NY, 89; Making Good Time, Calif Mus Photog, Riverside, 90; Phelan Award Winners, San Francisco Camerawork, 90; Add Noise, Contract Design Ctr, San Francisco, Calif, 92; Sprung in die Zeit, Berlinische Galerie, Mus Moderne Kunst, Photographie und Architektur, Berlin, Ger, 92-93; The Turk & the Jew, World Wide Web, 96-97; Scene of the Crime, Armand Hammer Mus, Univ Calif, Los Angeles, 97; The Artists Book II, Fine Art Ctr, Taos, 98; 25/25, Southern Exposure, San Francisco, 99. *Teaching:* Instr photog, Cabrillo Col, Aptos, Calif, 83-93, Calif Col Arts & Crafts, 92-93; vis assoc prof photog, Sch Art Inst Chicago, 93-94; prof electronic imaging, Wash State Univ, Pullman, 95-; lectr, Univ Mass, Boston, 98, Mass Col Art, Boston, 98- & Sch Mus Fine Arts, Boston, 98-. *Awards:* Nat Endowment Arts Grants, 73, 76 & 88; Calif Arts Coun Grants, 78 & 80; Fulbright Fel, 97. *Publ:* Auth, Baseball-Photographer Trading Cards, 75; coauth, Evidence, 77; auth, San Francsico Giants: An Oral History, 79; coauth, Headlands: The Marin Coast at the Golden Gate, Univ NMex Press, 89; auth, Making Good Time, Calif Mus Photog, Univ Calif, Riverside, 89. *Mailing Add:* 124 Maplewood St Watertown MA 02472

MANDEL, SAUL
ILLUSTRATOR, PAINTER
b New York, NY, Jan 21, 26. *Study:* Studied fine arts, figure study & painting at Pratt Inst. *Work:* Hebrew Arts Inst, Mus Am Illus, New York Zoological Soc, NY; Air Force Mus, Smithsonian Inst, Washington; Israel Mus, Jerusalem; and others. *Comn:* Love Postage Stamp, 86, US Postal Serv; Six Postage Stamps, United Nations, 92. *Exhib:* US Info Serv Am Designers Traveling Exhib, E Europe, 63-65; Children from Around the World, Allied Chemical Bldg, NY, 64; Sicherheit Lernen-Unfalle Vermeiden, Int Plakatwettbewerb, Essen, WGer, 81; Japan Design Found, Semba Ctr, Osaka, Japan, 82; one-man show, Mus Am Illus, NY, 83; Sabbath Art Gallery, Glen Cove, NY, 83. *Teaching:* Prof graphic design, Long Island Univ. *Awards:* Award of Excellence, Soc Illusrs, 63; Gold Medal, 35th Nat Outdoor Advert Competition, Inst Outdoor Advert, 71; Gold Medal for Best Illus, Conn Art Dir Club, 78. *Bibliog:* Articles in Graphis Mag, Idea Mag, Art Direction, Mod Publicity, CA Mag, Upper & Lower Case Int. *Mem:* Soc Illusrs; NY Art Dir Club; Am Inst Graphic Arts. *Media:* Mixed. *Publ:* Twenty Years of Award Winners, Hasting House, 81

MANDELBAUM, ELLEN
STAINED GLASS ARTIST, PAINTER
b New York, NY, June 16, 38. *Study:* Ind Univ, AB, 60, MFA, 63; study with James McGarrell, Ludwig Schaffrath, Jochem Poensgen & Albinus Elskus. *Work:* Shoreham-Wading River Libr, Long Island, NY; Living Art Found, NY; Ind Univ, Bloomington; Nishida Mus, Toyama, Japan. *Comn:* Greater Baltimore Med Ctr, Md, 93; chapel windows, Adath Jeshurun Synagogue, Minnetonka, Minn, 95; 30' window wall, SC Aquarium, Charleston, 2000; 28 windows, Marian Woods Convent, Hartsdale, NY, 2001; Har Shalom, Potomac, MD, 2003; Toni Sihes (residence) CEO of the Holy Guild, 2003; B'Nai Shalom of Olney, MD, 2004; Susan Simon, Dir, Queens Col Art Ctr, 2004. *Exhib:* Solo exhibs, Ellen Mandelbaum, Painting & Glass Art, Queens Col Art Ctr, NY, 98; Int Exhib, Centre Int Du Vitrail, Chartres, France, 89; Hudson River Mus, Yonkers, NY, 90; Personal Visions Invitational, New Glass Workshop, NY, 91; The Glass Canvas, Soc Arts & Crafts, Boston, 93; Layers of Experience, Women's 4th Int Stained Glass Workshop, Park Tower Gallery, Tokyo, 95; Crawford Munic Art Gallery, Cork, Ireland, 97; GlassWorks, Gallery on the Hudson, NY, 2000; Int Women's Contemp Stained Glass, Foothills Art Ctr, Golden Colo, 2000; Reflections on Glass, Am Bible Soc, 02-03; Sense of Place, Toronto, 2004. *Pos:* Owner, Ellen Mandelbaum Glass Art, 81-. *Teaching:* Docent exhibs, Whitney Mus Am Art, 64-66; lectr mod painting, Hunter Col, 64-67; glass painting & archit glass classes & workshops, Ellen Mandelbaum Glass Art Studio. *Awards:* Judges Choice, Stained Glass Asn Am, Toronto, 85; Visual Art Award of Excellence, Mod Liturgy Mag, 87 & 89; Relig Art Award of Excellence, Am Inst Architects, 97; Ministry and Liturgy, Best of Show, 01-02. *Bibliog:* Synagogue with a view, Stained Glass, winter 95; Christopher Peterson (auth), The Art of Stained Glass, Rockport Press, 98; Ellen Mandelbaum: Painting and Glass Art (catalog), Queens Col Art Ctr, NY, 98; Lynn Nesmith (auth), South Carolina Aquarium, Archit Record, NY, 2000. *Mem:* Prof affiliate Am Inst Archit, NY; Stained Glass Asn Am; Interfaith Forum on Religion Art & Archit. *Media:* Stained Glass. *Publ:* Dada & surrealism show at the Museum of Mod Art, Artforum, 68; contribr, Glass Art in Architecture, Thoughts & Ideas, Poensgen, Dusseldorf, 88; auth, The Vence Chapel: Matisse's Legacy in Stained Glass, New Work, 88; New Glass, The Painterly Alternative, Professional Stained Glass, 92; Masterclass, Glass Craftsman, 12/96; Working wiht a Stained Glass Artist, Faith and Form, 02. *Mailing Add:* 39-49 46th St Long Island City NY 11104-1407

MANDELBAUM, LYN
PAINTER, PRINTMAKER
b New York, NY, Sept 7, 50. *Study:* Tyler Sch Art, Rome, 70-71, Philadelphia, BFA, 72, MFA, 74. *Work:* Philadelphia Mus Art; Otis Libr, Los Angeles; New York Libr; Jean Brown Arch, Tyringham, Mass. *Comn:* Mural, Byblos Dicoteque, Marigot, St Martin, 81. *Exhib:* Mus Mod Art, NY, 73; Images - Dimensional - Movable - Transferable, Akron Art Inst, Ohio, 73; Fed Reserve Bd, Washington, DC, 74; Pa State Univ Mus Art, 74; Photo-Synthesis, Johnson Mus Art, 76; two-person exhib, 14 Sculptors Gallery, NY, 80; solo exhib, Foundations Gallery, NY, 82. *Pos:* Founder & dir, Eastern Shore Press, Philadelphia, 74-76 & Street Ed Inc, New York, 79-; pres, Island Magic Inc, New York, 82-. *Teaching:* Lectr printmaking, Philadelphia Col Art, 76-78; instr, Tyler Sch Art, 77-78. *Awards:* Purchase Award, Univ Del, Newark, 71. *Media:* All. *Publ:* Auth, Moderate Expectations, 78 & Anita's Revenge, 78, pvt publ; Consider Yourself Lucky, Street Ed Inc, 79; Notes: Keep a Candle Burning, pvt publ, 80; Say, Street Ed Inc, 82. *Mailing Add:* 20 Desbrosses St New York NY 10013-1704

MANDLE, EARL ROGER
ADMINISTRATOR
b Hackensack, NJ, May 13, 41. *Study:* Williams Col, BA, 63; Art Students League; Inst Fine Arts, NY Univ, mus training cert & MA, 67; Metrop Mus Art; Victoria & Albert Mus. *Hon Degrees:* Univ Toledo, DFA, 83; Kenyon Univ, DFA, 86. *Collection Arranged:* 30 Contemporary Black Artists, 68; Catalogue of European Paintings, Minneapolis Inst Arts, 70; Dutch Masterpieces from the 18th Century, 71-72; Dutch Silver, 80; El Greco of Toledo, 82; The paintings of Jan Vermeer, Washington & The Hauge, 95. *Pos:* Assoc dir, Minneapolis Inst Arts, 67-71 & 72-74; assoc dir, Toledo Mus Art, 74-77, dir, 77-88; deputy dir, Nat Gallery Art, Washington, DC, 88-93; pres, RI Sch Design, 93-; US Ambassador Arts at Large, 96-. *Teaching:* Instr art, Phillips Acad, Andover, Mass, 63-64 & McBurney Sch, New York, 64-65; vis lectr, Univ Wis, 73; adj prof, Univ Toledo, 93; Robert Sterling Clark vis prof art hist, Williams Col, spring 93; part time fac, RI Sch Design, 95-96. *Awards:* Andover Teaching Fel, 63; Ford Found Mus Training Fel, 66; Nat Endowment Arts Fel, 74; Ohio Gov Award, 83; Knight of the Order of Isabel the Catholic, His Majesty Juan Carlos, King of Spain, 85. *Bibliog:* J Woelm (auth), Dutch Masterpieces from the 18th century (film), Woelm-Polister Prod, 72; J Canaday (auth), Dutch masterpieces from the 18th century,

New York Times, 72. *Mem:* Am Asn Mus; Am Arts Alliance; Asn Art Mus Dirs; Art Mus Asn; Col Art Asn; Nat Coun Arts; and many others. *Res:* Eighteenth century Dutch art and nineteenth century English art. *Publ:* Auth, Adriaen Coorte, a unique late seventeenth century Dutch still-life painter, Burlington Mag Publ Ltd; The Fine Arts and Human Values in Higher Education, Univ Toledo, 79; Lifelong Learning in the Humanities, Philadelphia, Pa, 12/79; Museums in cultural and temporal context, J Mus Educ, Vol 16, No 3, fall, 91; introd, Inaugural Catalog, Mus Am Giverny, 92. *Mailing Add:* c/o RI Sch Design 2 College St Providence RI 02903

MANDZIUK, MICHAEL DENNIS
COMPUTER ARTIST
b Detroit, Mich, Jan 14, 42. *Study:* Self taught. *Work:* Minn Mus Art, St Paul; Borg Warner Corp, Chicago; Kemper Ins Collection, Long Grove, Ill; Art Ctr Collection, Park Forest, Ill; Springfield City Collection, Ill. *Exhib:* Tex Fine Arts Asn Travel Shows, 71, 72 & 74; Boston Printmakers Nat, 72-74; Minn Mus Art Drawing Biennial, St Paul, 73; Butler Inst Am Art, Youngstown, Ohio, 73-75; one-man shows, Welna Gallery, Chicago, 74 & Ukrainian Inst Mod Art, Chicago, 75; Hunterdon Nat Print Show, 74; Okla Art Ctr Nat Print Show, 74; 22nd Art Conf, Univ Mich, 74; Mitchell Art Mus, Mt Vernon, Ill, 75; Battle Creek Art Ctr, Mich, 76. *Pos:* Artist-craftsman juror, Ann Arbor St Art Fair, 71; Retired graphic specialist, Ford Motor Co, formerly, 97; Developing computer graphic images. *Awards:* Best of Show Award; Old Capt Art Fair Award, Springfield, Ill, 73-74; Detroit Artist Market, 71-72. *Media:* Computer Images. *Mailing Add:* 7191 Kolb St Allen Park MI 48101

MANERA, ENRICO ORLANDO
SCULPTOR, PAINTER
b Asmara, Italy, Apr 4, 47. *Study:* Liceo Artistico, Acad Fine Arts, Rome, 67. *Work:* Museo D'arte Moderna, Spoleto, Italy; Galleria D'arte Moderna Rondanini, Rome, Italy; Museo Nazionale Della Grafica, Rome, Italy; Palazzo Del Governo, Bari, Italy; Archivio Storico Della Biennale Di Venezia, Venezia, Italy. *Comn:* Sculpture, Mus Mod Art, Spoleto, Italy, 79; painting, Salzano Inst, Rome, Italy, 80 & Puglie Region, Bari, Italy, 82; sculptures (five), Valadier Inst, Rome, Italy 84; sculpture, Colaco Real Estate/Land Developer, Calif, 90. *Exhib:* Pop Art in Italy, Palazzo Collicola, 80 & Norma Jean, Mus Mod Art, 82, Spoleto, Italy; Tribute to Man Ray, Art Inst, Rome, Italy, 81; Visioni Imperiali, Cortina Inst, Rome Italy, 90; Arte Rome 90, Palazzo Del Congressi, Italy. *Collection Arranged:* Guido Io Vorrei, Palazzo Ducale Mantova, 93; Messuno Tocchi Caino, Gillo Dorfles, European Parliament, Bruxelles, 93; Palazzo Esposizioni, Rome, 94; Contact Duccio Trombadori (catalog), Galleria Cortina, Rome, 93. *Awards:* Eight Premio Pittura, Martina Franca, Salvatore Basile, 80. *Bibliog:* Carmine Benincasa (auth), La Tavola Di Paro, Selecta, 6/79; Ruggero Marino (auth), Pop Art Don't Surrender, Il Tempo, 5/80; Arturo Carlo Quintavalle (auth), L'Assassino ê IL Mercante, Corriere Della Sera, 2/88. *Publ:* Next-Contact, Gillo Dorfles, Joyce E Co, Rome, 93; Principali Mostre in Italia, City Hall, Rome-Palazzo Deue Esposizioni-Rome, Italy, 93; Quelli Che Contano Those Who Count, Marsilio Editori, Venice, 94. *Mailing Add:* 120 Morningside Dr San Francisco CA 94132

MANES, BELLE
PAINTER
b New York, NY. *Study:* Cooper Union, BFA, 78. *Hon Degrees:* Cooper Union, BA. *Work:* General Electric, Unimin Corp; Pfizer Chemical; Cochran Corp; Chubb Insurance; Sanford Bernstein & Sons. *Exhib:* Katonah Gallery, Conn, 88, 2001, Art Place Gallery, Conn, 92; Faber Birren Color Award Show, Conn, 93 & 94, 2002; Broome St Gallery, NY, 95, Lehman Col Gallery, NY, 96; Northern Westchester Ctr for Arts, 2002; Flinn Gallery, Conn, 2005. *Teaching:* Instr art, Plainfield Community Ctr, NJ, 56-59 & privately, White Plains, NY, 62-64; mentor, Pratt Inst, 78. *Awards:* Medal Honor, Nat Asn Women Artists, 79; Top Silvermine Award, New England Show, 81. *Bibliog:* Jonothan Goodman (auth), Belle Manes at Branchville SOHO, Art News, 3/94; Vivian Raynor (auth), Artists and curators with country roots, NY Times, 1/95; William Zimmer (auth), Community expressed in mixed media, NY Times, 12/95; Sally Aldrich (auth), Katonah Mus, Interviewing Belle Manes, 2001. *Mem:* Nat Asn Women Artists; Silvermine Guild; Contemporary Artists Guild. *Media:* Oil, Acrylic. *Dealer:* Branchville Soho Gallery RR Sta Rtes 7 & 102 Ridgefield CT 06829. *Mailing Add:* 1097 North St White Plains NY 10605

MANES, PAUL
PAINTER
b Austin, Tex, May 4, 48. *Study:* Lamar Univ, Beaumont, Tex, BBA, 72, BFA, 83; Sch Fine Arts Hunter Col, NY, 84. *Work:* Metrop Mus Art & Guggenheim Mus, NY; Herbert Johnson Mus Art, Cornell Univ, Ithaca, NY; Houston Mus Fine Arts, Tex; Mus SE Tex, Beaumont; Detroit Inst Art. *Exhib:* Jan Turner Gallery, Los Angeles, 87, 90 & 92; Pascal de Sarthe Gallery, San Francisco, 88; Betty Moody Gallery, Houston, 88 & 93; C Grimaldis Gallery, Baltimore, 88; Marisa del Re Gallery, NY, 93, 93 & 94. *Bibliog:* Phyllis Tuchman (auth), Paul Manes (exhib catalog), Kouros Gallery, 89; Allison De Lima Greene (auth), Paul Manes (exhib catalog), Marisa del Re Gallery, 93; Bill Maynes (auth), Paul Manes (exhib catalog), Mus SE Tex, 92. *Media:* Oil, Mixed Media

MANGEL, BENJAMIN
DEALER
b Philadelphia, Pa, Jan 12, 25. *Pos:* Owner, Benjamin Mangel Gallery, Philadelphia, Pa. *Specialty:* Contemporary paintings and sculpture. *Mailing Add:* 1108 Saint Andrews Rd 1714 Rittenhouse Sq Bryn Mawr PA 19010-1936

MANGEL, DEBORAH T
ART DEALER, CURATOR
b Philadelphia, Pa. *Study:* Temple Univ, BA(art hist, summa cum laude). *Collection Arranged:* Annual Holliday Crafts Exhib, Paley Mus PCT & S, Philadelphia, 92-; one screen 2 souls 4 Hands (with catalog), Art in City Hall, Philadelphia, 96. *Pos:* Pres, Mangel Gallery, Philadelphia, 70-, Pa Acad Fine Arts, 83; dir mus shop, Paley Design Ctr PCT & S, Philadelphia, 92-. *Bibliog:* Karen Heller (auth), The art of the sale, Philadelphia Inquirer, 9/17/89; Edward J Solanski (auth), Art, Philadelphia Inquirer, 10/18/96; Edward Higgins (auth), Leader of a New Movement, Art Matters, 10-96. *Mem:* Friends Philadephia Mus Art; Collector's Circle, Pa Acad Fine Arts, Philadelphia; Arts Adv Bd, Univ City Sci Ctr, Philadelphia. *Specialty:* Contemporary art. *Mailing Add:* 1108 St Andrews Rd Bryn Mawr PA 19010

MANGIONE, PATRICIA ANTHONY
PAINTER, MURALIST
b Seattle, Wash. *Study:* Fleisher Art Mem, Philadelphia; Barnes Found, Merion, Pa. *Work:* Inst Contemp Art, Dallas; Fleisher Art Mem, Philadelphia; Fidelity Bank, Philadelphia; Univ Pa; Noyes Mus, NJ. *Comn:* Acrylic on wood mural, Continental Bank & Trust Co, Philadelphia, 69. *Exhib:* Newman Galleries, Philadelphia, 78; More Gallery, Philadelphia, 82; Am Col, Bryn Mawr, Pa, 93; Berman Mus, Collegeville, Pa, 94; Bryn Maur Col, Pa, 94. *Pos:* Illusr, Sicilia, Ital Govt Quart, 66 & 68; bd mem, Va Ctr Creative Arts, 82-. *Awards:* Six Yaddo Resident Fels, 62-79; Artistic Contrib Philadelphia, Artists Equity Asn, 82; First Prize & Medal, Philadelphia Sketch Club, 87. *Bibliog:* Burton Wasserman (auth), The Art of Patricia Mangione, Sims Press, 71; James R Mellow (auth), Mangione at Rehn Gallery, New York Times, 74; Victoria Donohoe (auth), Paintings by Pat Mangione, Philadelphia Inquirer, 82. *Mem:* Artists Equity Asn; Philadelphia Art Alliance; Main Line Ctr Arts. *Media:* Oil, Acrylic. *Publ:* Auth, Some observations on the experience of painting, Parapsychology Found, 70; Exercise in magic, Sunday Bulletin, Philadelphia, 71. *Dealer:* Newman Gallery 1625 Walnut St Philadelphia PA 19103

MANGLANO-OVALLE, IÑIGO
SCULPTOR
b Madrid, Spain, 61. *Study:* Williams Col, Mass, BA(art hist), 83; Art Inst Chicago, MFA(sculpture), 89. *Work:* Mus Contemp Art, MacArthur Found, First Nat Bank & Linc Group, Chicago; Bohen Found, NY. *Exhib:* Solo exhibs, Assigned Identities, Centre Gallery, Miami-Dade Col, Fla, 91, Balsero, Mus Contemp Art, Chicago, 97, WooferWoofer, Contemp Arts Ctr, Cincinnati, Ohio, 97, The El Nino Effect, ArtPace Found Contemp Art, San Antonio, Tex, 97, Garden of Delights, Southeastern Ctr Arts, Winston-Salem, NC, 98, Inst Vis Arts, Univ Wis, Milwaukee, 99, Max Protetch Gallery, New York City, 00, 03, Cranbrook Art Mus, Bloomfield Hills, Mich, 01, Barcelona Pavilion, Mies van der Rohe Found, Barcelona, 02; From America's Studio: Drawing New Conclusions & Los Encuentros, Betty Reimer Gallery, Art Inst Chicago, Ill, 92; Bookmarks, Northern Ill Univ Art Gallery, 92; Latin Am Art in Miami Collections, Lowe Art Mus, Univ Miami, Fla, 94; Xicano Progeny: Redefining the Aesthetic - Towards a New Vision of Am Cult, Mex Mus, San Francisco, 95; Correspondences/Korrespondenzen, Chicago Cult Ctr, 95; Art in Chicago 1945-1995, Mus Contemp Art, Ill, 96; Contemp Art Collections, Nelson Fine Arts Ctr, Ariz State Univ Art Mus, Phoenix, 98; Mus Contemp Art, San Diego, 00; Whitney Mus Am Art, New York City, 01; Mus Modern Art QNS, Long Island City, NY, 02; and many others. *Collection Arranged:* The Bohen Found, NYC; Guggenheim Found, NYC; MacArthur Found, Chicago; Whitney Mus Am Art; Art Inst Chicago; Mus Contemporary Art, Chicago & San Diego; ArtPace, San Antonio; Metrop Bank and Trust Collection, Highland Hills, Ohio; The Refco Collection, Chicago; The Linc Collection, Chicago; Fundacion Cisneros, Caracas, Venezuela. *Awards:* Artist Fel Award, Ill Arts Coun, 92 & Spec Proj Award, 93; Visual Artist Fel, Nat Endowment Arts, 95; Int Artist Residency Fel, ArtPace Found, San Antonio, 97; Media Arts Residency, Henry Art Gallery, Univ Wash, Seattle, 98-00; Media Arts Award, Wexner Ctr for the Arts, Columbus, Ohio, 97-01; John D and Catherine T MacArthur Found Fel, 01. *Bibliog:* Bonnie Clearwater (auth), Studio Visit, Trans, Vol 1, No 3 & 4, 97; Victor Zamudio-Taylor (auth), Where is the bleeding heart?, Atlantica, No 15, 82-91, spring 97; Miwon Kwon (auth), For Hamburg: Public art and urban identities, Kunst auf Schritt und tritt, image pg 95, Kulutrbehorde Hamburg, 97. *Mailing Add:* c/o Max Protech Gallery 511 W 22nd St New York NY 10011-1109

MANGO, ROBERT J
PAINTER
b Chicago, Ill, Jan 20, 51. *Study:* Art Inst Chicago, 65-69; Univ Ill, BFA, 70-73, MFA, 75-76; Univ NMex, MFA, 73-74. *Work:* Pvt corp & pub collections throughout the US & Europe. *Exhib:* One-man exhibs, Loyola Univ Art Gallery, 79, Merchants Manufactures Club Am, Chicago, 81, Gallerie Chastain, NMex, 83, Dillon Gallery, NY, 95, Gallery Radost, Prague, Czech Repub, 97, Gallerie Orangerie, St Paul de Vence, France, 97 & Gallerie Miro, Prague, Czech, 98. *Pos:* Owner & dir, Neo Persona Gallery, NY, 83-90. *Teaching:* Instr, Thorthan Community Col, 75-77, Seton Hall Univ, East Orange, NJ, 82-84 & Caldwell Col, Montclair, NJ, 84; dept head sculpture, Loyola Univ, Chicago, 77; Seton Hall Univ, E Orange, NJ, 82-84. *Bibliog:* Scott MacMillan (auth), Is It Art? (interview), Prague Bus J, 6/97; Prague Post Rev, 6/97; Robert Forrester, Jr (auth), Theshold Prague Rev, 6/97. *Mailing Add:* 178 Duane St New York NY 10013

MANGOLD, ROBERT PETER
PAINTER
b North Tonawanda, NY, Oct 12, 37. *Study:* Cleveland Inst Art, 56-60; Yale Univ, Fel, 59, BFA, 61, MFA, 64. *Work:* Solomon R Guggenheim Mus, Mus Mod Art, Metrop Mus Art & Whitney Mus Am Art, NY; Mus Fine Arts, Houston; Mus Contemp Art, LA, Calif; Albright-Knox Art Gallery; Art Inst Chicago; and many others. *Exhib:* The Living Object, the Art Collection of Ellen H Johnson, Allen Mem Art Mus, Oberlin Col, Ohio, 92; 15th Anniversary Exhib, Rhona Hoffman Gallery, Chicago, 92; Acad-Inst Invitational Exhib of Painting and Sculpture, Am Acad & Inst Arts & Letts, NY, 92; Galerie Lelong, NY, 92; Shapes and Position, Ritter Klagenfurt, Austria, 92-93; one artist & 2-person exhibs; Mus fur Zeitgenossische Kunst, Ger, 95, Annemarie Verna Galerie, Zurich, 97, Bonnefantenmuseum, Ger, 97 & Robert

Mangold, Mus Wiesbaden traveling exhib, Kunstmuseum, Switz, 98-99, Addison Gallery of Am Art, Phillips Acad, Andover, Mass (traveling), 2000-01; Then and Now: Art Since 1945 at Yale, Yale Univ Art Gallery, New Haven, 98; Masters of the Masters: MFA Fac of the Sch of Visual Arts, NY, 1983-1998, Butler Inst Am Art, Ohio, 98; and others. *Collection Arranged:* Bonafanten Mus, Maastricht, Neth; Hallen Fur Neve Kunst, Shaffhausen, Switz; Hirshhorn Mus & Sculpture Garden, Smithsonian Inst; Israel Mus, Jerusalem, Israel; Metropolitian Mus of Art, NY; Mus of Art, Dallas, Tex; Mus of Art, Cleveland, Ohio. *Teaching:* Instr art, Sch Visual Arts, 63-, Hunter Col, 64-65, Skowhegan Summer Art Sch, Yale-Norfolk Summer Art Sch, 69 & Cornell Univ, 70. *Awards:* Nat Coun on Arts Award, 66; Guggenheim Mem Grant, 69; Alexej von Jawlensky Award, Mus Wiesbaden, Ger, 96; Trustee, Yale Univ Art Gallery, 99; Elected Mem, American Acad of Arts & letters, 01. *Bibliog:* Judith Russi Kirshner (introd), The Refco Collection, Essays by Eleanor Heartney, Anne Rorimer & James Yood, Refco Group Ltd, Chicago, 90; Minimal Art (exhib catalog), Nat Mus Art, Osaka, 90; Geoffrey Blodgett & Elizabeth A Brown (auths), Robert Mangold: The Oberlin Window (essays), Allen Mem Art Mus, Oberlin Col, Ohio (exhib catalog), 92; Klaus Kertess (auth), Robert Mangold: The Attic Series (exhib catalog), Pace Gallery, New York, 92; Elizabeth Brown (auth), The living object, the art collection of Ellen A Johnson (exhib catalog), Allen Mem Art Mus Bull, Oberlin Col, Ohio, 92; and many others. *Mem:* Am Acad Arts & Letters; Nat Acad. *Publ:* Auth, Six Arcs, NY: Lapp Princess Press, Ltd, 78. *Mailing Add:* c/o Whitney Mus Am Art 945 Madison Ave New York NY 10021

MANGOLD, SYLVIA PLIMACK
PAINTER
b New York, NY, Sept 18, 38. *Study:* Cooper Union, cert, 59; Yale Univ Art Sch, BFA, 61. *Work:* Albright-Knox Art Gallery, Buffalo, NY; Yale Univ Art Gallery; Mus Mod Art, Whitney Mus Am Art, NY; Weatherspoon Art Gallery, Greensboro, NC; Walker Art Ctr, Minneapolis, Minn; Utah Mus Fine Arts; Brooklyn Mus; Detroit Inst Art. *Exhib:* One-person shows, Young Hoffman Gallery, Chicago, 80, Nocturnal Paintings, Contemp Arts Mus, Houston, 81, Paintings, Brooke Alexander Inc, 82, 84, 86 & 89, Rhona Hoffman Gallery, 85, Tex Gallery, Houston, Brooke Alexander, NY & Fuller Goldeen Gallery, San Francisco, 87; A Contemp View of Nature, Aldrich Mus, Ridgefield, 86-87; 15th Anniversary, Flander's Contemp Art, Minneapolis, 87; Anne Marie Verna Galerie, Zurich, 88; Group Show, Annemarie Verna Galerie, Zurich, 88; Landscape Anthology, Grace Borgenicht Gallery, NY, 88; The Unnatural Landscape, Fay Gold Gallery, Atlanta, 88; The Transformative Vision; Contemp Am Landscape Painting, Three Rivers Arts Festival, Pittsburgh; Making Their Mark, Women Artists Move into the Mainstream, 1970-1985, Cincinnati Art Mus, New Orleans Mus Art, Denver Art Mus & Pa Acad Fine Art, 89; A Decade of Am Drawing 1980-1989, Daniel Weinberg Gallery, Los Angeles, 89. *Pos:* Sr painting critic, Yale Univ, 95-98 & 2000. *Teaching:* Instr drawing, Sch Visual Arts, New York, 70, instr painting, 70-71 & 74-82. *Bibliog:* Michael Florescu (auth), Sylvia Plimack Mangold, Arts Mag, 3/84; Michael Brenson (auth), Sylvia Plimack Mangold, New York Times, 11/22/85; Jeanne Silverthorne (auth), Sylvia Plimack Mangold, Brooke Alexander Gallery, Artforum, 3/86; Kenneth Baker (auth), Gestures that work or don't, San Francisco Chronicle, 5/12/87; John L Ward (auth), American realist painting, 1945-1980, UMI Research Press, Ann Arbor, Mich, 89. *Mem:* Nat Acad. *Media:* Oil, Drawings. *Publ:* Auth, Inches and Field, Lapp Princess Press Ltd, New York, 78; Project for Artforum, two moods, Sylvia Plimack Mangold, Artforum, 2/88. *Dealer:* Alexander & Bonin 132 Tenth Avenue New York NY 10011. *Mailing Add:* 155 Bull Rd Washingtonville NY 10992

MANGOLTE, BABETTE M
FILMMAKER, PHOTOGRAPHER
b Montmorot, France, Oct 11, 41. *Study:* La Sorbonne, Paris, BA, 64; Ecole Nat Photographic & Cinematographie, Paris, 64-66. *Work:* Mus Mod Art, NY; Mus G Pompidou, Paris; New York Pub Libr; Australian Nat Libr, Canberra. *Pos:* Assoc prof, Visual Arts Dept, Univ Calif, San Diego, 89-. *Awards:* Prix de la Lumiere, Toulon Film Festival, France, 75; CAPS Fel, NY, 76; Pre-production Grant, NY State Coun Arts, 86. *Mem:* Asn Independent Video & Filmmakers; Media Alliance. *Mailing Add:* 319 Greenwich St New York NY 10013-3339

MANHART, MARCIA Y
ADMINISTRATOR, CURATOR
b Wichita, Kans, Jan 14, 43. *Study:* Univ Ariz, Tucson, with Maurice Grossman, 62; Univ Tulsa, Okla, with Duayne Hatchett, Tom Manhart & Alexandre Hogue, BA, 65, MA, 71. *Work:* Okla State Art Collection, Okla Arts Ctr, Oklahoma City; Ark Arts Ctr, Little Rock; Fred Jones Mem Mus Art, Univ Okla, Norman; Philbrook Mus Art, Tulsa; Univ Tulsa. *Exhib:* Southwestern Craftsmen Biennial, Mus Int Folk Art, Santa Fe, NMex, 65, 67, 71 & 75; Craftsmen USA '66, Dallas Mus Fine Arts, Tex, 66; Ceramic Nat, Everson Mus, Syracuse, NY, 68; Manharts, Fred Jones Mem Mus Art, Norman, Okla, 73; Ceramics Invitational, Little Gallery, Mus Contemp Crafts, NY, 74; Ann Print, Drawing & Crafts Exhib, Ark Arts Ctr, Little Rock, 74 & 76. *Collection Arranged:* Our Oklahoma Indian Heritage: The Old Ways, 76; Traders Cargo from the China Sea: The Gillert Collection of Southeast Asian Ceramics, 78; Nature's Forms--Nature's Forces: The Art of Alexandre Hogue, 84; The Eloquent Object, 87; The Sanford and Diane Besser Collection, 92. *Pos:* Dir, Alexandre Hogue Gallery, Univ Tulsa, Okla, 67-69; dir educ, Philbrook Art Ctr, Tulsa, 72-77, asst dir, 77-83, actg dir, 83-84, exec dir, 84-. *Awards:* One-man Award, Southwestern Crafts Biennial, Mus Int Folk Art, 71; George Wittenborn Mem Award; Harwelden Award, Tulsa Arts & Humanities Coun, 89. *Bibliog:* Garth Bethel (auth), Manharts, Craft Horizons, 74; Research and education, In: Your Portable Museum, Am Crafts Coun, 75; John Conrad (auth), Contemporary Ceramic Technique, Prentice-Hall, 79. *Mem:* Art Mus Asn; Asn Art Mus Dirs. *Media:* Clay, Porcelain. *Res:* Contemporary art in craft media. *Publ:* Auth, Alexandre Hogue: Nature's Forms/Nature's Forces, 84; The Search is Over Enter Janet Kardon, Art Today, 89; A Neglected History: 20th Century American Craft, 90; Objects and Drawings, The Sanford and Diane Besser Collection, 92; Charting a new educational vision-craft in the machine age (essay), 94. *Mailing Add:* Philbrook Art Ctr PO Box 52510 Tulsa OK 74152

MANHART, THOMAS ARTHUR
EDUCATOR, CERAMIST
b Canon City, Colo, July 16, 37. *Study:* Univ Hawaii; Univ Tulsa, BA & MA. *Work:* Ark Arts Ctr, Little Rock; Fred Jones Mem Art Mus, Univ Okla, Norman; Philbrook Art Ctr, Tulsa; Okla State Art Collection, Okla Art Ctr, Oklahoma City; Tulsa Performing Arts Ctr, Okla. *Exhib:* Nat Decorative Arts Exhib, Wichita, Kans, 61, 64 & 66; Southwestern Crafts Biennial, Santa Fe, NMex, 65, 72 & 75; Craftsmen USA, Dallas & NY, 66; Regional Prints, Drawings & Crafts Exhib, Little Rock, 67 & 75; Nat Craftsmen's Exhib, Wichita, 68, 70 & 72. *Pos:* State rep, Am Craft Coun, 66. *Teaching:* Instr ceramics, Univ Tulsa, 61-68, asst prof, 69-73, assoc prof, 74-91, prof, 91-. *Awards:* Nat Decorative Arts Exhib Medal of Honor, Wichita Art Asn, 66; Nat Merit Award, Craftsmen USA, Am Crafts Coun, 66; Okla State Art Collection, Okla Arts & Humanities Coun, 73. *Bibliog:* Gar Bethel (auth), Manharts, Craft Horizons, 74; Okla designer craftsmen exhib, Ceramics Monthly, 75. *Mem:* Am Crafts Coun; Okla Designer Craftsmen; Tulsa Designer Craftsmen (pres, 68). *Media:* Clay and Fibers. *Publ:* Contribr, Profile, Am Crafts Coun, 60; Craft Horizons, 66, 68 & 74-75, Cimarron Rev, 69, Tulsa Univ Alumni Mag, 69 & Ceramics Monthly, 75. *Mailing Add:* 5318 E Fifth St Tulsa OK 74112-2812

MANHOLD, JOHN HENRY
SCULPTOR
b Rochester, NY, Aug 20, 19. *Study:* Univ Rochester, BA; Washington Univ, St Louis, MA; New Sch, with Chaim Gross & Manolo Pasqual; also with Ward Mount. *Work:* City of West Orange, NJ; Mem Sloan-Kettering Hosp, NY; Pyrofilm Corp, Whippany, NJ; A J Levera Assocs, Madison, NJ; Jacques Piccard Inst, Bern, Switz; and others. *Comn:* Bronze bust, Kallman Assocs, Jersey City, NJ; four bronze busts, Col Med & Dent NJ, Newark, 69, 70 & 78; bronze figure, Bernard Koven, 71; bronze bust, SASS Mus, Gatlinburg, Tenn, 2004. *Exhib:* Allied Artists Am, 66; Audubon Artists Am, 67-69; Mainstreams '68 & '71, Grover M Hermann Fine Arts Ctr, Ohio, 68 & 71; Nat Sculpture Soc, 69; Am Artists Prof League, 70-72; and others. *Pos:* Dir sculpture, Ringwood Manor Asn Arts, 68-70, 1st vpres, 70-71. *Teaching:* Pvt instr, currently. *Awards:* Medal Honor for sculpture, State of NJ, 68; First Prize, Paris Int, 70; Second Prize Patrons Award, Painters & Sculptors Soc NJ, 71; John Subkis Award, Nat Arts Club, 71; and others. *Bibliog:* David Leis (auth), pictures in Life Mag, 69; Pierre Morand (auth), La section Americaine de la Salon del'arte Francaise, La Rev Mod, 70; Ruth Ann Williams (auth), Art of the Oranges, NJ Music & Art, 72. *Mem:* Acad Artists Asn; Am Artists Prof League; Nat Arts Club; Knickerbocker Artists; West Valley Art Mus (2006). *Media:* Marble, Bronze. *Specialty:* bronze. *Interests:* Precious metals-jewelry. *Mailing Add:* 26027 N 44th Ave Glendale AZ 85310

MANILOW, LEWIS
COLLECTOR, PATRON
b Chicago, Ill, Aug 11, 27. *Pos:* Pres, Mus Contemp Art Chicago, 76-81; mem of bd, Beaubourg Found, 78-. *Collection:* Contemporary art, Mannerist prints and Turkish rugs

MANN, FRANK
PAINTER, GRAPHIC ARTIST
b Washington, DC, Apr 22, 50. *Study:* George Wash Univ, Washington, with painter Gene Davis, BS, 79; Pratt Inst, Brooklyn, NY, MFA, 82. *Work:* Mus Mod Art, NY; Guggenheim Mus, NY; Corcoran Gallery Art, Washington; Nationalgalerie, Berlin, Ger; Mus contemp Art, Nice, France. *Comn:* Window drawing, Artist's Space, NY, 89; mural, Dept Cult Affairs, NY, 90; mural, NY State Coun Arts, Binghamton, NY, 90; outdoor mural, Art Around Park, NY, 92; Project for St. Cyrits Church, NY, 97. *Exhib:* Contemp Sensibilities, Cie, Mod et Contemporain, Paris, France, 91; Painting Today, Mus Mod Art, Buenos Aires, Arg, 91; First Int Biennial, Trevi Flash Art Mus Int Contemp Art, Trevi, Italy, 98; Similar Shapes in Painting and Sculpture, Walter Wickiser Gallery, NY, 98; Venice Italy Palazzo Correra a Santa Fosca, Italy, 98; Printmaking Today, Corcoran Gallery Art, Washington; Driven to Abstnaction (invitational), Brother Chapman Gallery, I and Col, New Rochelle, NY, 2005. *Pos:* Exec dir, Collab Projs, NY, 87-88; proj dir, Basic Arts Network, NY, 91-92; bd dir, Artist Equity, NY, 2000-01; vpres, Artists Equity, NY, 2003-2005; vpres, The Am Soc of Contemp Artists, NY, 2003-2005. *Teaching:* Guest lectr, Corcoran Sch Art, Washington, 78-79, Pa State Univ, Reading, 86-87, Pratt Inst, Brooklyn, 87-88 & Parsons Sch Art & Design, NY, 96-97; Parsons Sch of Design The New Sch Univ, NY, 96-99; Pvt Studio Instr, Painting and Drawing, 98-present; guest lectr, Iona Col, New Rochelle, NY, 2005. *Awards:* NY State Coun Arts, 89; Nat Endowment Arts, New Arts Prog, 89; New York City Dept Cult Affairs, 90; The Lorenzo IC Maonifico Medal in Painting, Biennale Invt'l Dell'Ante Contemporanea, Florence, Italy, 2001. *Bibliog:* Marcello Llorens (auth), Frank Mann, Mind of a Visionary, Art Al Dia, NY, 90; Mitchell Corber (dir), Eye of the ainter (film, 28 minutes), Pub Broadcasting System, 91; Susan Scutti, Painting the Velocity of Intuition, Cover Mag, 43, Vol 12, No 2; Franklin Sirman's, Notes to an Exhib, ASCA Art Bulletin, 2004. *Mem:* Drawing Soc, NY; Artists Equity, NY; Collab Projs, NY (prog dir, 87-88); Am Soc Contemp Artists, NY; Contemp Artists Guild, NY; The Assoc D' Art Int'l, Mirabel, France. *Media:* Oil on Canvas. *Publ:* contribr, Works of Art on Paper with George Nelson Preston, Mus Mod Art, Buenos Aires, 90 Night Rider, illustrated, Redstone Press, 90; Midnight Review, Rio Arts Proj, 91; illusr, Nerves, Domestic Press, New York, 91; contribr, Contemporary sensibilities, Cie Modern et Contemporain, Paris, France, 91; The Optical Machine: Some Observations on Artistic Vision, nap text(s), Vol 3, No 1, p 1, 98; ASCA, The Am Soc of Contemporary Artists, (Essay), 2003. *Dealer:* Walter Wickiser 568 Broadway New York NY 10012; Kim Foster Gallery, 529 West 20th St, 1st FL, NY, NY, 10011. *Mailing Add:* 212 E 34th St No 3E New York NY 10016

MANN, JAMES ROBERT
CURATOR, CRITIC
b Columbia, SC, Oct 5, 56. *Study:* The Citadel, BA, 78; Univ SC, PhD, 85. *Collection Arranged:* Art After Post-Modernism, 97; George Sturman Collection of African Art (auth, catalog), 98; Domenic Cretara Retrospective Exhibition, 98; Wm Thomas Thompson Retrospective Exhibition, 98; Asian Art Now, 2000; Eli Leven Retrospective Exhibition (auth, catalog), 2000. *Teaching:* prof Am Poetry, Fed Univ Rio de Janeiro, Brazil, 87-88; prof Brit Poetry, Catholic Univ Arg, Buenos Aires, 88-89; lectr Am Culture, Univ Grenoble, France, 90-91. *Publ:* auth, Metaphysical Ptg of Lani Irwin, Am Arts Quart, 94, Bruno Civitico' s Paintings, 95; auth, catalog, Holocaust Exhibition, Las Vegas Art Mus, 98

MANN, JEAN (ADAH)
CERAMIST, SCULPTOR
b Schenectady, NY, June 27, 27. *Study:* Mannes Col Music; Hunter Col, sculpture with Irma Rothstein; Donald Mavros Studio, 4 yr apprenticeship, 64, Chinese Brush painting with Jongsoon Chung, Kiln Building and pottery with Gerry Williams; Glaze Chemistry with Yvonne LaFean & Dr Louis Navias. *Hon Degrees:* Master Craftsmen/Educator, Soc for Connecticut Crafts, CT; Andrew J Alexander Award, Candlewood League of Artists, 2006; Kent Art Assoc. *Work:* Metrop Mus Art, NY; Smithsonian Inst Hist & Technol Dept, Washington, DC; Mus Art & Archeol, Univ Mo, Columbia; Mus Haaretz, Ceramics Mus, Tel Aviv, Israel; Everson Mus Art, Syracuse, NY; Yale Univ Art Gallery, New Haven, Conn; Martin Luther King Jr Ctr Non-Violent Social Change, Atlanta, Ga; Hammond Mus, North Salem, NY; Southern Conn, New Haven; Schenectady Mus, NY; Housatonic Mus Art, Bridgeport, CT; Cyrenius Booth Library, Newton, CT. *Exhib:* One-woman shows, Silvermine Guild, New Caanan, Director's Choice Invitational, 2000, Conn, 76, The Galerie, Chester, Conn, 81 & 82, GWS Gallery, Southport, Conn, 87, Hammond Mus, North Salem, NY, 1975, 77, 82, 85, 88, 89, 93, 94, 95, 99, 2001, Atelier Gallery, New Milford, Conn, 89, Weslayan Potters, Middletown, Conn, 89 & Variations, Riverton, Conn, 92; Silvermine Guild, New Canaan, Conn, 76-; Mark Twain Libr Art Show, Redding, Conn, 84-91; Mendelson Gallery, Washington Depot, Conn, 87; Exhib Contemp Netsuke, Yamada Co, Tokyo, Japan, 88; Ceramics - The Oriental Influence, Farmington Valley Ctr, Fisher Gallery, 89; Cyreniws Booth Lib, Newtown, Conn, 2003; and others. *Teaching:* Wheel, hand methods & sculpture, carving porcelain, Rescue: Vis Artist Prog, Danbury & Southbury, Conn, 69; carving porcelain, Brookfield Craft Ctr, Conn, 81-82; demonstrator Netsuke carving, George Walter Vincent Smith Art Mus, Springfield, Mass, 84; Phoenix Workshop, Goffstown, NH; co-instr with Gerry Williams, The Kick Wheel Studio, New Fairfield, Conn. *Awards:* Artist Award, The Galerie, Conn Comn Arts, 81; Master Craftsman Educator, Soc Conn Crafts, 96; Society of Creative Arts of Newton Award, SCAN Annual Juried Show, 2004. *Bibliog:* Betty K Leavitt (auth), Netsuke She, J Int Netsuke Collectors Soc, 83; Betty K Leavitt & C Randall (coauths), Netsuke: Superlative Pieces, Netsuke Kenkyukai Conv, 83; Diane Dowling (dir), Artist Jean Mann (film), Com Cast, 89; and others. *Mem:* Silvermine Guild; Am Crafts Coun; Brookfield Craft Ctr; Soc Conn Crafts; New Haven Paint & Clay Club; Oriental Brush Artists Guild; Candlewood League of Artists; Kent Art Assoc. *Media:* Porcelain. *Interests:* Carving, reading, photography. *Publ:* Auth, Tools for Carving Porcelain, 75 & Highfire Copper Reds on Porcelain, 79, Studio Potter; Arts of Asia, Photo & Ltr, 9-10/92. *Mailing Add:* c/o The Kick Wheel 154 Rte 39 New Fairfield CT 06812-4203

MANN, KATINKA
SCULPTOR, PHOTOGRAPHER
b New York, NY, June 28, 25. *Study:* Univ Hartford Art Sch, Conn; Pratt Graphic Arts, NY. *Work:* Brooklyn Mus, Guggenheim Mus, Mus Mod Art Study Collection, NY; Polaroid Int Corp, Boston; Williamsburg Savings Bank & Russ Togs Inc, NY; San Francisco Mus Mod Art; Brooklyn Mus, Guggenheim Mus, Polaroid Corp; Russ Togs Inc, San Francisco Mus Mod Art; Islip Art Mus. *Exhib:* One-man shows, Cent Hall Gallery, 74-84, Hansen Gallery, NY, 76-79 & Heckscher Mus, Huntington, NY, 77 & 84, 504 Gallery, NY, AIR Gallery, NY Art Gallery Pt Washington Libr, NY Pa Ulrich Mus Art, Konica Gallery, Tokyo, Art Gallery Port Washington Libr, NY, 96, Space 504 Gallery, NY, 98, Heckscher Mus Art, Bryant Libr, Roslyn, NY, 2001; Aldrich Mus Contemp Art, 78; Ulrich Mus Art, Wichita, Kans; NJ State Mus, Trenton; Nikon, NY; Konica Gallery, Tokyo, Japan; Condeso/Lawler Gallery, NY; plus many others; Toward the New, Hillwoor Art Mus, Allentown, Pa, 2000; Tabletop 2002, Hofstra Mus, Hempstead, NY; El Instituto Nacional de Bellas Artes, San Miguel de Allende, Mex, 2003; Artist, Neighbors, Friends, Heckscher Mus Art, Huntington, NY, 2003. *Pos:* Co-chmn & bd mem, Prof Artists Guild, 72-73; Am Abrst Artists, Treasurer, 89-96, 2002-. *Awards:* Judith Leiber Co Purchase Award, Soc Am Graphic Artists, 69; Polaroid Corp Award, 83. *Bibliog:* Art in the World, Rinehart Press, 75; articles, NY Times, 77, 81, 85 & 96; Helen Harrison (auth), Photographs That Confound, Central Hall Gallery; Valerie Natsios (auth), Katinka Mann: An Alternative, New York Times; Phyllis Braff (auth), Originality Stands Out in Sculptural Variety; NY Times, Helen Harrison, 2000; NY Times, Phillis Braff, 2001; Am Abstr Artists Journal, #4, 2000; Hechscher Mus, of Art, Huntington, NY, 2001; Exhib Brochure, Janie Welker, Curator, 2001; Hofstra Art Mus, Hempstead, NY, 2002; Martin Art Gallery, Women Artists, Past and Present, Catalog, 2002; The Morning Call, Go Art, Abstr Demand Attention, Feoff Gehman, 2002. *Mem:* Am Abstract Artists (treas); Prof Artists Guild (vpres, 69-71); Artists Equity Asn; Prof Women Photogr. *Collection:* B'kyn Mus, Brooklyn, NY; Islip Art Mus, E Islip, NY; Polaroid Int'l Corp, Cambridge, MA; Heckscher Mus, Huntington, NY; Hillwood Art Mus, Greenvale, NY; Russ Togs, Corp, New York, NY; Muchlenberg College, Allentown, PA; Williams Burg, Savings Bank, Brookyn, NY; Am Abstr Artists Print Protfolio 50 Anniv; Am Abstr Artists Print Portfolio 60 Anniv. *Dealer:* Central Hall Gallery 386 West Broadway New York NY 10012. *Mailing Add:* 290 9th Ave Apt 13H New York NY 10001

MANN, MAYBELLE
HISTORIAN, WRITER
b Joliet, Ill, May 27, 1915. *Study:* Queens Col, City Univ New York, BA(hist), 65; NY Univ, MA, 67, PhD, 72. *Exhib:* Francis William Edmonds Traveling Exhib, Int Exhib Found, 76-77; Walter Launt Palmer, Albany Inst Hist & Art, 84-85; Art in Fla, Fla Hist Mus, Jupiter, 99. *Collection Arranged:* Francis William Edmonds (auth, catalog), Stony Brook, NY, 75-76; The Am Art Union (auth, catalog), Whitney Mus Am Art, 77-78; St Augustine Artists (auth, catalog), H M Flagler Mus, Palm Beach, 84-85; Walter Launt Palmer (auth, catalog), Albany Inst Hist & Art, 84-85. *Pos:* Art critic, Times Herald Record, 74-83 & Jewish World, 82-85; cur, Light House Gallery, Tequesta, Fla, 87-. *Teaching:* Lectr Am art, NY Univ, 74-76; instr, New Dimensions, Palm Beach Cmty Col. *Res:* Nineteenth and early twentieth century American art. *Publ:* Francis Walter Edmonds, Gardner Publ, 77; Articles, Antiques, Art & Antiques & Am Art J; Walter Launt Palmer: Poetic Reality, ALM Assoc, 86 & Am Art Union Revised, 88, ALM Asn; Am Art Union revised, ALM Assoc, 88; contribr, The Art of Florida-Painters, Patrons and Pillagers, Pineapple Press, 99; Art in Florida, Pineapple Press, 99. *Mailing Add:* 3264 Cove Rd Jupiter FL 33458

MANN, SALLY
PHOTOGRAPHER
b Lexington, Va, 1951. *Study:* Putney Sch, 66-69; Bennington Col, 69-71; Friends World Col; Praestegaard Film Sch, Denmark & Aegean Sch Fine Arts, Greece (Year abroad prog) 73; Hollins Col, BA(summa cum laude), 74, MA, 75. *Hon Degrees:* Corcoran Col Art, DFA (hon), 2006. *Work:* Addison Gallery Am Art, Andover, Mass; Baltimore Mus Art, Md; Birmingham Mus Art, Ala; Boston Mus Fine Art, Mass; Corcoran Gallery Art, Hirshhorn Mus & Sculpture Garden, Nat Mus Am Art, Smithsonian Inst, Washington, DC; Metrop Mus Art, Mus Mod Art & Whitney Mus Am Art, NY; San Francisco Mus Art, Calif; Va Mus Fine Arts, Richmond; and many others. *Exhib:* Solo shows at Cleveland Ctr Contemp Art, Houk Friedman, NY, 96, Jane Jackson Fine Art, Atlanta, 96, Joel Saroka Gallery, Aspen, 96, Greg Kucera Gallery, Seattle, 96, Christian Larson, Stockholm, Sweden, 96 & Catherine Edelman Gallery, Chicago, 96, Kunsthall, Rotterdam, Amsterdam, 97, Edwynn Houk Gallery, NY, 99, Galerie Karten Greve, Paris, Milan, St Moritz, Cologne, 2001, Byron Mapp Gallery, 2001.; Sally Mann: The Lewis Law Portfolio (catalog, monogr), Corcoran Gallery Art, Washington, DC, 77; group shows include Un/Common Ground, Va Mus Fine Arts, Richmond, 88; Awards in the Visual Arts 9 (with catalog), New Orleans Mus Art, La, traveling, 90; Pleasures & Terrors of Domestic Comfort, Mus Mod Art, NY, 91; Biennial Exhib, Whitney Mus Am Art, NY, 91; Contemp Color Photog, Selections from the Collection, Metrop Mus Art, NY, 91; Who's Looking at the Family, Barbican Art Gallery, London, 94; Imagined Children, Desired Images, Wellesley Col, Mass, 95; ME, Dru Arstark Gallery, NY, 95; Visions of Childhood (auth catalog), Bard Col, NY, 95; 100 Yrs/100 Images (auth catalog), Frankfurter Kunstverein, Ger, 95; Picturing the South, High Mus, Atlanta, 96; Homeland of the Imagination (auth catalog), Nations Bank Plaza, Atlanta, 96; Hospice: A Photog Inquiry (auth catalog), Corcoran Gallery, Washington, 96; Hayward Gallery, London, 98; Va, Hist Soc, Richmond, 2000; Catherine Edelman Gallery, Chicago, 2000; Gagosian Gallery, NY City, 2006; presented in permanent collections of Corcoran Gallery Art, Washington, DC, Whitney Mus Am Art, NY, Mus Modern Art, The Metropolitan Mus Art, NY and Mus Fine Arts, Boston. *Pos:* Guest lectr, Honolulu Acad Arts, 89, Women Photog Conf, 89, Md Inst Art, 89, Bard Col, 89, San Francisco Cameraworks, 90, Photog-Retrospect/Prospect Conf 90 & many others. *Teaching:* Instr, Maine Photog Workshops, 85-89; Palm Beach Photog Workshops, 87-89; Ctr Photog Woodstock, 88 & 90; Int Ctr Photog, New York, 89; Image Found, Honolulu, Hawaii, 89; Okla Arts Found, 89; Friends Photog Workshops, 90. *Awards:* Fels, Nat Endowment Arts, 82, 88 & 92; fel, Southeastern Ctr Contemp Art, 89; fel, Artists Visual Arts, 89; Photogr Yr Award, Friends Photog, 95. *Bibliog:* Rev, San Francisco Chronicle, 10/6 & 10/9/96; rev, New City (Chicago), 10/17/96; rev, Chicago Tribune, 10/20/96. *Publ:* Auth, Photo Gallery Int 15th Anniversary (catalog), 94; An American Century of Photography (exhib catalog), Hallmark Cards/Harry Abrams Inc, 95; Over there, San Francisco, 9/1/96; A celebration of one hundred years, New York Times Mag, 6/96; Fotografie, GEO Extra, spring 96. *Mailing Add:* c/o Edwynn Houk Gallery 745 5th Ave Suite 407 New York NY 10151

MANN, WARD PALMER
PAINTER
b Detroit, Mich. *Study:* Detroit Inst Art, 33; Univ Mich, BS, 49. *Work:* Smithsonian Inst, Wash; Mem Art Gallery, Rochester, NY; US Coast Guard, Wash; Sawyer Libr, Gloucester, Mass. *Comn:* Cityscape, the New Buffalo, Marsh & McLennon, Inc, Buffalo, NY, 75; Birthplace of Xerography, Xerox Corp, Webster, NY, 80; oil painting, Webster Optical Co, NY, 80; US Air, Charlotte, NC, 90. *Exhib:* Ann Shows, Salmagundi Club, NY, 75-90; Foothills Art Ctr, Golden, Colo, 80; 31st Ann Knickerbocker Art, Salmagundi Club, NY, 81; Mystic Int, Mystic Seaport Mus, Conn, 92; Arts for Parks Competition Top 100, 94, 2001. *Pos:* Artist, critic, currently. *Awards:* Helen G Oehler Award, AAPL Grand Nat, 91; Macwin Tuttle Award, Salmagundi Ann, 94 & 99; Gorton's of Gloucester Award, North Shore Arts Asn, 94; Alden Bryan Award, Grand Nat, NYC, 2004. *Bibliog:* Walt Reed (ed), Ward Mann, artist, North Light Mag, 11-12/77; Artists of Rockport, Rockport Art Asn 60th, 70th, 75th & 80th Anniversary Eds,; The Artists Mag, 8/97. *Mem:* Rockport Art Asn; North Shore Arts Asn; Knickerbocker Artists USA; Oil Painters Am; Am Artists Prof League Fel. *Media:* Oil, Watercolor. *Publ:* Contribr, Best of Oil Painting, Best of Watercolor, Light & Shadow & Landscape Inspirations, Rockport Publ, Inc; Art for the Parks, North Light Books. *Dealer:* Mann Gallery 77 Rocky Neck Ave Gloucester MA 01930; Oxford Gallery 267 Oxford St Rochester NY 14607. *Mailing Add:* 163 Stony Point Tr Webster NY 14580

MANNINO, JOSEPH SAMUEL
SCULPTOR
b Chicago, Ill, 50. *Study:* Knox Col, Galesburg, Ill, BFA, 1971; Southern Ill Univ, Carbondale, MFA, studied with Robert Arneson. *Work:* Crocker Art Mus, Sacramento, Calif; Renwick Gallery, Smithsonian Inst, Washington, DC; Southern Alleghenies Mus, Loretto, Pa; Univ Ala, Birmingham. *Exhib:* San Angelo Mus, Tex; Everson Mus Art, Syracuse, NY; Mus Modern Art, San Francisco, Calif; Bruce Gallery, Univ Pa, Edinboro, 2000; solo exhib, Arlington Arts Ctr, Va, Three Rivers Art Festival, Ptitsburgh, Pa, Montpelier Cult Arts Ctr, Laurel, Md, Crocker Art Mus, Sacramento, Calif. *Teaching:* Instr, sculpture, ceramics, Carnegie-Mellon Univ, 86-. *Awards:* Individual Fel Award, Pa Coun Arts; Wash State Art Comn Award, Medical Lake, Wash; Artist-in-Residence Award, Kohler Arts Ctr, Sheboygan, Wis. *Mem:* Nat Coun on Educ for Ceramic Arts; Col Art Asn; Soc of Sculptors, Pittsburgh, Pa. *Media:* Clay, Stoneware, Porcelain, Terra Cotta. *Specialty:* Large scale ceramic sculptures. *Mailing Add:* 5531 Beacon St Pittsburgh PA 15217

MANNOR, MARGALIT
PHOTOGRAPHER, CONCEPTUAL ARTIST
b Tel-Aviv, Israel, Nov 16, 40. *Study:* Hebrew Univ, Israel, 60-63, Avni Inst Fine Arts, Tel Aviv, cert, 64-69; studied photography with Rae Russel, cert, NY, 76-77. *Work:* Brooklyn Mus, Mus City New York, Jewish Mus, NY Pub Libr, NY; Mus Fine Arts, Houston; Israel Mus, Jerusalem; Tel Aviv Mus, Israel; and many other pub & pvt collections. *Exhib:* People 81, Hudson River Mus, Yonkers, NY, 81; Inaugural Exhib, Hudson River Mus, Yonkers, NY, 82 & Ann Exhib, 83 & 85; Member Choice, Albright-Knox Art Gallery, Buffalo, NY, 86-92; solo exhibs, Ein Harod Mus, Israel, 91 & Negev Mus, Beer Sheva Israel, 95; Modern Times Through the Concerned Eye, Katonah Mus Art, 92; All-of-a-Piece, Katonah Mus Art, NY, 95; Photog, Mus Fine Arts, Houston, 96; Women of the World, A Global Collection of Art, White Columns Gallery, NY, 2000; and many others. *Awards:* First Prize, Grand Prix Int, La Principalite de Monaco, 71; Solo Prize Photog, People 81, Hudson River Mus, 81; Photog Prize, All-of-a-Piece, Katonah Mus Art, 95. *Bibliog:* Donald Kuspit (auth), Margalit Mannor, Art Forum, NY, 9/90; Mordechai Omer (auth), The Presence of the Absent (exhib catalog), Tel Aviv Univ, 5/91; William Zimmer (auth), 51 selections out of 1000, NY Times, 6/11/95; Shlomit Shakked (auth), Beheaded Ready (exhib catalog), Bineth Gallery, Tel Aviv, 11/98. *Media:* Mixed Media, Installation. *Dealer:* Schneider Gallery 230 W Superior Chicago IL 60610; Bineth Gallery 15 Frishman St Tel-Aviv Israel. *Mailing Add:* 28 Sage Terr Scarsdale NY 10583

MANOLAKAS, STANTON PETER
PAINTER
b Detroit, Mich, Jul 25, 46. *Study:* Univ Southern Calif, BA, 69. *Work:* Marriott Corp, Newton, Mass; Bechtel Industries Corp Collection, San Francisco, Calif; Datum Inc, Anaheim, Calif; Callagher & Heffernan, San Francisco, Calif; Wolverine Bronze, Roseville, Mich. *Comn:* Historic Boston Suite, Marriott Corp, 87. *Exhib:* Los Angeles Co AFL-CIO Exhib, Calif, 82-90; Calif Traditional Artists, Mus Natural Hist, San Bernadino, 83; City Art Exhib, Millard Sheets Gallery, Pomona, Calif; Second Ann Southern Calif Hist Fair, Heritage Sq Mus, Los Angeles; Dossin Great Lakes Mus, Detroit, Mich; Featured Artist Grand Opening Ave Maris Gallery, Domino's Farms Ann Arbor Mich, 2000. *Awards:* First Place, Union Artist Exhibit, Los Angeles Co AFL-CIO, 89. *Bibliog:* Julia Ayres (auth), Paper the Critical Support, Watercolor 87 Am Artist, 1/87. *Media:* Watercolor. *Publ:* Auth, A Visual Odyssey Through America's Past, Watercolor 90 Am Artist, 9/90. *Dealer:* Gallery 131 Glendale Calif; Art Angles Orange Calif; Progressive Art & Frame Design, Clawson, MI. *Mailing Add:* 2500 Las Flores Dr Los Angeles CA 90041

MANOOGIAN, RICHARD ALEXANDER
COLLECTOR
b Long Branch, NJ, July 30, 36. *Study:* Yale Univ, BA (econ), 58. *Pos:* Asst to pres Masco Corp, Mich, 58-62, exec vpres, 62-68, pres, 68-85, chmn & CEO, 85-; chmn Alex and Marie Manoogian Found; pres & treas Richard and Jane Manoogian Found; co-founder Mackinac Island Community Found, 2003; trustee Univ Leggett Sch, State Dept Fine Arts Comn, Founder's Soc, Detroit Inst Arts, Center Creative Studies, Nat Gallery Art. *Mem:* named one of Top 200 Collectors, ARTNews Mag, 2003-. *Mailing Add:* Masco Corp 21001 Van Born Rd Taylor MI 48180-1300

MANSARAM, P
PHOTOGRAPHER, PAINTER
b Mount Abu, India. *Study:* Sir J J Sch Art, Bombay, India, 54-59; State Acad Fine Arts, Amsterdam, fel, 63; Ryerson Polytech, Toronto, Can, cert(motion picture prod), 70. *Work:* Gemeente Mus, The Hague; Nat Gallery Mod Art, New Delhi, India; Mem Univ Gallery, St Johns, Nfld; NY Pub Libr; Art Gallery Mississaugα; Air India, Electrografia Mus Int, Cuenca, Spain; Art Gallery of Hamilton, Royal Ontario Mus, Toronto. *Comn:* 8 posters on India destinations (lasergraphic images), comn by Air India; San Tache Art Gallery, Mumbai, India, 2000; Faculty Club, McMaster Univ, 2004. *Exhib:* Solo exhibs, Gallery de Drie Hendricksen, Amsterdam, The Neth, 64, Burlington Art Ctr, 89, 95 & Grimsby Pub Art Gallery, Ont, 90 & Art Gallery of Mississauga, Toronto, 93; Pundole Gallery, Bombay, India, 92; Saske Gallery, Kushiro, Japan, 92; Museu D'Art De Sabadell, Barcelona, Spain, 92; Mus Nier Bator, Hungary, 92; Dhoomimal Art Ctr, New Delhi, India, 96; St Naubert Arts & Cult Ctr, Winnipeg, 97. *Awards:* First Prize, Bombay State Art Exhib, 59; First Prize, Colour & Form Soc Award, Toronto, 75; Ont Arts Coun Grant, 90 & 91. *Bibliog:* Manmohan Saral (auth), Kala Khete. *Mem:* Colour & Form Soc (pres, 78-79, lifetime mem); Visual Arts Ont; Bombay Art Soc, life mem. *Media:* Mixed Media. *Res:* Created Mansaram's Art of the Rocks, Site Specific Project in Progress, Mt Abu, India, 1997-. *Publ:* Contribr, Art-Life Mag, 2/4/86; Colour Documentation of 40th Anniversary Art Exhib of Color & Form Soc, Mississauga, 92; Lalit Kala Contemporary Mag, Issue 48, India. *Mailing Add:* 298 Gardenview Burlington ON L7T 1K6 Canada

MANSFIELD, ROBERT ADAMS
SCULPTOR, EDUCATOR
b Chicago, Ill, May 4, 42. *Study:* Minneapolis Sch Art & Design, 61-62; St Cloud State Univ, BA, 68; Univ Mass, Amherst, MFA, 70. *Work:* Univ Mass, Amherst; Smith Col Mus Art, Mass; San Diego State Univ; St Cloud State Univ, Minn. *Exhib:* Abstract Painting of 70's, DeCordova Mus, Lincoln, Mass, 71; Nat Juried Exhib, Austin Mus Art, 79; 13th Ann, Marietta Col, Ohio, 80; North Am Sculpture Exhib, Golden Col Art Ctr, Colo, 80; Corpus Christi Col Mus, Tex, 81; and others. *Collection Arranged:* New Directions, Univ Mass, 69; Twombly & Diao, Hampshire Col, 71; Arthur Hoener, San Diego State Univ, 76; Jerome Liebling Photographs, San Diego State Univ, 78. *Teaching:* Instr art, Smith Col, 70-71; asst prof art, Hampshire Col, 71-79; assoc prof art & head sculpture dept, San Diego State Univ, 76-. *Awards:* Second Prize, Southern Calif Expos, Del Mar, 77; Best of Show, Marietta Col, 80. *Bibliog:* Mary Vercauteren (auth), Robert Mansfield, Holyoke Transcript, 4/12/73; Edward Silver (auth), Elliptical construction, Advocate, 12/4/75; Susan Muchnic (auth), Sculpture is alive and well, Los Angeles Times, 1/22/79. *Mailing Add:* Sch Art Design & Art Hist San Diego State Univ 5500 Campanile Dr San Diego CA 92182-4805

MANSHIP, JOHN PAUL
PAINTER, SCULPTOR
b New York, NY, Jan 16, 27. *Study:* Harvard Univ, AB, 48; with George Demetrios; Brera Acad, Milan. *Work:* Nat Collection Fine Arts, Washington, DC; Long Beach Art Mus, Calif; New Britain Mus, Conn; Hamilton Col, Clinton, NY. *Comn:* Baptism of Christ, Baptistry, St John Martyr, NY, 63; Pentecost (fresco), Chapel Sisters of St Joseph, Pawtucket, RI, 65; Stations of cross, St Clements Church, Warwick, RI, 66; Resurrection (with Margaret Cassidy), St Anthony's Church, Springfield, Mass, 71; portrait of Judge O'Connor, Worcester Co Courthouse, 72. *Exhib:* Newhouse Gallery, 82; Gallery on the Green, 88. *Pos:* Pres, Rockport Art Asn, 81-85. *Teaching:* Instr drawing & painting, Marymount Col, New York, 63; instr, Minnetonka Art Ctr, 78. *Awards:* Ranger Fund Purchase Award, Nat Acad Design, 65; Gold Medal, Burckhardt Acad, Rome, 78; Rockport Art Asn, 83 & 94; Nat Arts Club, 91; North Shore, 93. *Mem:* Am Watercolor Soc; Nat Soc Mural Painters (secy, 72-75); North Shore Art Asn (dir, 70-72); Artists Equity NY; Salmagundi Club; and others. *Media:* Oil, Watercolors; Bronze. *Publ:* Auth, Paul Claudel, Commonweal, 55; Raphael, Cath Encycl Youth, 64; Paul Manship, Abbeville, 90; Sculptors of Cape Ann, Nat Sculpture Mag, 97. *Dealer:* Leonarda di Mauro Gallery New York NY. *Mailing Add:* 10 Leverett St Gloucester MA 01930

MANSION, GRACIE
ART DEALER
b Braddock, Pa, Oct 22, 46. *Study:* Clarion State Col, 64-66; Montclair State Col, BA, 79. *Exhib:* Small Works Show, 80 Wash Sq E, NY, 80; Neo York (collab with Judy Rifka), Univ Art Mus, Santa Barbara, 84. *Collection Arranged:* Harvard Bus Sch. *Pos:* Dir, Gracie Mansion Gallery, 82-. *Bibliog:* Peter Bach (auth), Gracie Mansion's Art Alive, Taxi Mag, 9/87; John Carlin (auth), Gracie's new mansion, Paper, 5/89; John Jost (dir), All the Vermeers in New York (film), 90 & (play & TV), 92. *Mem:* Art Table. *Specialty:* Contemporary art. *Publ:* Articles, Gracie Mansion, New York Talk, 9/84, 10/84 & 11/84; New York Woman Mag, 7-8/87, 9/87 & 4/88; Hope Batey & Deborah Gimelson, Gracie Mansion Manhattan Catalog, Fall/Winter

MANSPEIZER, SUSAN R
SCULPTOR
b New York, NY. *Study:* Art Students League, Corcoran Sch Art, 66-68; City Col New York, BA, 62, MA, 66. *Work:* Greenburgh Pub Libr, Elmsford, NY; Off Bldg, Chappaqua, NY; Alumni & Friends of La Guardia High Sch. *Exhib:* New Members, Silvermine Guild Artists, New Canaan, Conn, 90; Hudson River Mus, Grace Glueck, Juror, Yonkers, NY, 90; Kirkland Art Ctr, Clinton, NY, 91; Southwest State Univ, Marshall, Minn, 91; Silvermine Guild of Artists, New Canaan, Conn, 92; Viridian Gallery, NY, 87, 90 & 93; two-person show, Berkshire Artisans, Pittsford, Mass, 94; Onward Gallery-Nihom Bashi (exhib catalog), Tokyo, Japan, 9/94. *Teaching:* Instr drawing, Col of New Rochelle, NY, 74-75; instr collage, painting & drawing, Art Ctr of Northern NJ, 90-. *Awards:* Sculpture Invitational, Pelham Art Ctr; Ivan Karp, Best in Show, Soho Gallery 54, 88; Second Prize Sculpture, Katonah Libr, 93. *Bibliog:* Vivian Raynor (auth) rev, NY Times, 3/90 & 9/90; Cornelia Seckel (auth), rev, Art Times, 11/98. *Mem:* The Gallery at Hastings-on-Hudson, 79; Mamaroneck Artist Guild, 79-90; Viridian Gallery, 85-90; Artist Equity, 90; Silvermine Guild Artists. *Media:* Wood, Metal. *Publ:* Auth, Onward Gallery-Nihom Bashi (exhib catalog), Tokyo, Japan, 9/94; NY Art & Antique Guide Book, International Art Reference Inc, 94. *Dealer:* Walter Wickiser Gallery Inc 568 Broadway New York NY 10012. *Mailing Add:* 67 Autumn Ridge Rd Pound Ridge NY 10576

MANTER, MARGARET C
PAINTER
b Providence, RI, Feb 20, 23. *Study:* RI Sch Design, 42; Syracuse Univ, NY, BFA, 46; Workshops with Barse Miller, Ed Betts & Chen Chi, 66-72, Edward Betts, Virginia Cobb & Maxine Masterfield, 82-89. *Work:* Col of Atlantic, Bar Harbor, Maine; Thomas Col, Waterville, Maine; Univ Maine, Machias; Eastern Maine Med Ctr, Bangor; Central Maine Power Co, Augusta. *Exhib:* Maine Coast Artists, Rockport, Maine, 88 & 89; Nat Asn Women Artists, NY, 89 & 90; Western Ill Univ, 90; Watercolor USA, Springfield, Mo, 91; Soc Experimental Artists, Bradenton, Fla, 92; Union of Maine Visual Artists, Gilley Mus, 2002; Experimental Artists, Travis City, Mich, 2001; Collage Exchg, New Zealand, 2002; and many others. *Teaching:* Instr watercolor, YMCA, Bangor, Maine, 70-80; Instr design, Univ Maine, Orono, 80-. *Awards:* Purchase Award, Central Maine Power Exhibit, Central Maine Power Co, 90;

Cer Award, Int Soc Experimental Artists, 2000. *Bibliog:* Hollerbach & Schlemm (auth), Best of Watercolor Vol I & II, 99. *Mem:* Nat Asn Women Artists; Union Maine Visual Artists; Int Asn Experimental Artists. *Media:* Watercolor, Miscellaneous Media. *Publ:* Best of Watercolor, Rockport Publ, Mass, 96. *Mailing Add:* 1328 State St Veazie ME 04401

MANUAL, ED HILL & SUZANNE BLOOM
PHOTOGRAPHER, VIDEO ARTIST
b Springfield, Mass, Aug 30, 35; uzanne Bloom: b Philadelphia, Pa, Nov 25, 43. *Study:* Ed Hill: RI Sch Design, BFA, 57; Yale Univ, MFA, 60; Suzanne Bloom: Pa Acad Fine Arts, BFA, 65; Univ Pa, MFA, 68. *Work:* Mus Contemp Photog, Chicago; Los Angeles Co Mus Art; San Francisco Mus Mod Art; Int Mus Photog, Rochester, NY; Int Ctr Photography, NY. *Comn:* Site specific installation, Fotofeis & Scottish Arts Coun, Inverness, Scotland, 93; Cult Arts Coun Houston & Harris Co, Houston, Tex, 96; The Protracted Image, FotoFest, 2002. *Exhib:* Signs, The New Mus Art, NY, 85; Photog & Art, Los Angeles Co Mus Art, 87; Solo-shows, Forest/Products, Contemp Arts Mus, Houston, Tex, 91, Mus Contemp Photog, Chicago, Ill, 92, NY Int Ctr Photog, 93 & Scottsdale Ctr for the Arts, Ariz, 94; Wasteland, Fotografie Biennale, Perspektief, Rotterdam, The Neth, 92; Renewing Our Earth, US Pavilion, Taejon, Korea, 93; Forest of Visions, Knoxville Mus Art, 93; Photography's Multimpe Roles, Mus Conemp Photog, Chicago, 88; 6th Bienal Int de Pintura, Cuenca, Ecuador, 88; Two Worlds; the Collaberation of Ed Hill and Suzanna Bloom, Int Ctr Photog, NY, 2002. *Teaching:* Prof art, Univ Houston. *Awards:* Rockefeller Interdisciplinary Arts Fel, Nat Endowment Arts, 87; Artists' Fel Photog, Nat Endowment Arts, 92; Visual Artists Pub Proj, Nat Endowment Arts, 93; Pub Art and Urban Design, Cult Arts Coun, Houston and Harris Co, 96. *Bibliog:* Mark Dery (auth), Art & technology, Artnews, 2/93; Stephen Hobson (auth), Manual et in Arcadia Ego, Perspektief 47/48, 94; Anne Barclay Morgan (auth), Art & technology, Art in Am, 4/94. *Mem:* Soc Photographic Educators; Col Art Asn. *Media:* Digital Photography, Video. *Dealer:* Moody Gallery 2815 Colquitt Houston TX 77098. *Mailing Add:* 2520 White Oak Dr Houston TX 77009

MANUEL, K(ATHRYN) LEE
CRAFTSMAN
b Loma Linda, Calif. *Study:* San Francisco Art Inst, BFA, 59. *Work:* Richmond Art Mus, Va; Am Craft Mus, NY; M H De Young Mem Mus, San Francisco; Oakland Mus, Calif. *Exhib:* San Francisco Mus Mod Art, San Francisco, Calif, 58, 75, 76, 78 & 83; solo exhibs, Swain Sch Design, New Bedford, Mass, 73 & Calif State Univ, Hayward, Calif, 78; Folk & Craft Mus, Los Angeles, 80 & 82; Artisians Gallery, NY, 84; Phoenix Art Mus, Ariz, 86; Cleveland Ctr Contemp Art, Ohio, 87; Craft Today, USIA (Europe), 89-92. *Awards:* Nat Endowment Arts, 88. *Dealer:* Mobilia Cambridge MA 02138. *Mailing Add:* 358 Huron Ave Cambridge MA 02138

MANUELLA, FRANK R
DESIGNER, CONCEPTUAL ARTIST
b New York, NY. *Study:* Cooper Union Advan Sci & Art, BFA; Pratt Inst, MS. *Work:* NY Univ; McAllen Int Mus; Univ Tex. *Comn:* Mural, McAllen Int Mus, 83; mural, Harligen, Tex, 91; mural, City of McAllen, Tex, 2000. *Exhib:* one person show, Int Mus Art & Science, McAllen, Tex, 2006. *Collection Arranged:* permanent collection, Int Mus Art & Sci, 03. *Pos:* Pres, F R Manuella Associates, currently. *Teaching:* Asst prof light & color, Pratt Inst, 75-82; prof art, Univ Tex, 82-00; master prof of art & design, Univ Tex, 00-. *Awards:* Outstanding Faculty Award, Univ Tex, Pan Am Univ, 87, 90 & 95; Merit Award, McAllen Int Mus, 88; Govs Award for Outstanding Serv, 89. *Bibliog:* Carompsun, New York Time Mag, 12/1/68; Karen Fisher (auth), Five careers, Cosmopolitan Mag, 3/69; Reviews & previews, Art News, 1/71; Dr N Moyer (auth), Fine Arts Review, Festiva/The Monitor, 6/9/2006. *Mem:* Univ Tex (fac senate, 88-94); Univ Press Univ Tex (bd mem grad faculty). *Media:* Site-Specific, Mixed Media Installation. *Mailing Add:* Dept Art Univ Tex 1802 Ivy Ln Edinburg TX 78539

MANUS, CONNIE SANDAGE See Hendrix, Connie Sandage Manus

MANVILLE, ELSIE
PAINTER
b Philadelphia, Pa, May 11, 22. *Study:* Tyler Sch Fine Arts, Temple Univ, BFA, BS. *Work:* Temple Univ, Philadelphia; Butler Inst Am Art; Guild Hall Permanent Collection, East Hampton, NY; Univ Iowa. *Exhib:* Butler Inst Am Art, 56; Walker Art Ctr, 58; Dallas Mus, 63; 30 Yr Retrospective Exhib, Snug Harbor Cult Ctr, Staten Island, 83; The Art of Flowers, Moravian Col, 84; Focus on Realism, Glenn C Janss Collection, 85; Hermitage Found, Norfolk, Va, 85; Tyler Sch Fine Arts, Pa, 88; Butler Inst Am Art, 98. *Teaching:* Adj instr, Fashion Inst Technol. *Awards:* Purchase Award, Butler Inst Am Art, 78; Nat Endowment Arts Visual Artists Fel, 81 & 85; NY Fedn Arts Grant, 90. *Bibliog:* Paintings reproduced, Arts Mag, 6/75, 4/78 & 2/82, Art News, 10/78 & New York Times Art & Leisure Guide, 2/28/82. *Media:* Oil, Oil Pastel. *Mailing Add:* 175 Lexington Ave New York NY 10016

MAPES, DORIS WILLIAMSON
PAINTER
b Russellville, Ark, June 25, 20. *Study:* Little Rock Jr Col; Hendrix Col, Ark; Ark Arts Ctr, Little Rock; Rex Brandt's Sch Painting, cert, Corona del Mar, Calif; also with George Post, Millard Sheets, John C Pellew, Louis Freund, Edgar A Whitney, Robert E Wood, John Pike & Robert Andrew Parker, 72. *Work:* Winthrop Rockefeller Gallery, Petit Jean, Ark; Ark Col Mus, Batesville; Am Found Life Ins Co, First Nat Bank & Ark Arts Ctr, Little Rock; Advan Indust, Blythville, Ark; Pres Clinton, White House, Washington. *Exhib:* Mid-Southern Ark Arts Ctr, 71-89; Watercolor USA, Springfield, Mo, 75; Southern Watercolor Soc, Cheekwood Mus, Jackson, Miss, 77; solo exhib, Univ Ark, Little Rock, 78; Celebrating Ark Women Artists, Russell Senate Bldg, Washington, 91, 93 & 96; Celebrating Ark artist of the Future 95, Fed Bldg, Little Rock, Ark, 95. *Teaching:* Oil & watercolor painting, Dansarts Sch, Little Rock, Ark, 68-86; oil painting, Bella Vista Fine Arts Ctr Ark, 71; watercolor, Miss Co Col, Blytheville, Ark, 72-73. *Awards:* Top Show, Ark State Festival Arts, 68 & 75; First Award, Southern Artists Asn, 72; First Award, Mid-Southern Watercolorists 74 & 85; Top Award, Mid-Southern Watercolorists, 74, 84 & 85. *Bibliog:* La Revue Mod des Arts, Paris, France, 3/75; Some Remarkable Women of Arkansas, 77; Arts & Voices South, 7/79. *Mem:* Mid-Southern Watercolorists (pres, 70-72); Southwestern Watercolor Soc; assoc mem Am Watercolor Soc. *Media:* Watercolor, Acrylic. *Collection:* Historic Mus Ark, Little Rock, Ark; Ark Art Ctr, Little Rock, Ark; Springfield Art Mus, Springfield, Mo; Clinton Presidintal Libr, Little Rock, Ark. *Publ:* Art News, 9/94. *Dealer:* Louie's Gallery 1509 Mart Little Rock Ark 72202. *Mailing Add:* 622 N Bryan Little Rock AR 72205

MARABLE, DARWIN WILLIAM
HISTORIAN, CRITIC
b Los Angeles, Calif, Jan 15, 37. *Study:* Univ Calif, Berkeley, BA, 60; San Francisco State Univ, MA(art), 72; Univ NMex, PhD(hist photog), 80; studied with Beaumont Newhall & Van Deren Coke. *Exhib:* John Spencer Weir: Surreal Spaces, 2006; Diablo Valley Col Art Gallery, Pleasant Hill, Calif. *Collection Arranged:* Visual Dialogue Found Revisited, 1968-2000; JJ Brookings Gallery, San Francisco, Calif; Vilem Kriz Meml Exhib, 1996; Irwin Art Ctr, Col of Arts and Crafts, Oakland, Calif; The Crucifixion in Modern Art, Hearst Art Gallery, St Mary's Col, Moraga, Calif, 92. *Teaching:* Lectr art hist, San Francisco State Univ, 76-77 & 82; lectr art hist, St Mary's Col, Moraga, Calif, 90-91 & 94; lectr hist photog & criticism photog, Univ Calif, Berkeley Exten, 95-; San Francisco Art Inst & Acad Art U, San Francisco, CA, 2001. *Bibliog:* Julian Cox, Edmund Teske Memory and Sunthesis, Hist of Photog, 95; Jose Antonio Rodriguez, La Persistencia de lo Sagrado, Textos y Ensayos. *Mem:* Soc Photog Educ; Hist Photog Group; Friends Photog San Francisco, CA; Photo Alliance, San Francisco, CA. *Res:* Surrealism & American photography; crucifixion in 20th century art; Visual Dialogue Found, San Francisco. *Interests:* Travel, Genealogy, Photography. *Publ:* Auth, Leland Rice's photographs of the Berlin Wall, Shadow & Substance, 90; interview with Oliver Gagliani, Photo Metro, 12/92; Capturing chaos, the photomontages of John Heartfield, Wash Times, 8/94; The crucifixion in photography, Hist Photog, autumn 94; Visual Dialogue Found, Black and White Mag, 2001. *Mailing Add:* 166 Valley Hill Dr Moraga CA 94556

MARAIS
PAINTER
b New York, NY. *Study:* Acad de la Grande Chaumiere, Paris & self-taught. *Work:* J Aberbach Collection, Long Island, NY; Hugo Perls, NY Collection; Dr Milton Reder, NY; UNICEF Collection, NY; Theodora Settele Collection, NY. *Exhib:* Galerie Chantepierre, Aubonne, Switz, 72; Galerie Int, NY, 75; Cafe de la Paix Exhib, Paris, 79; PubTV Channel 13, 79-80; Galerie St Placide, Paris; Salon des Nations, Paris, 84. *Mem:* Visual Artists & Galleries Asn; Nat Soc Lit & Arts. *Media:* Oil. *Publ:* Art Diary, 82 & 83. *Mailing Add:* c/o Mary Rachel Brown 33 W 67th St New York NY 10023

MARAK, LOUIS BERNARD
CERAMIC SCULPTOR, EDUCATOR
b Shawnee, Okla, Sept 9, 42. *Study:* Univ Ill, Champaign-Urbana, BFA, 65; Alfred Univ, MFA, 67. *Work:* Krannert Art Mus, Univ Ill, Urbana; Western Gallery, Western Wash State Col, Bellingham; Utah Mus Fine Arts, Univ Utah, Salt Lake City; Henry Art Gallery, Univ Washington, Seattle; Los Angeles Co Mus Art, Calif; Oakland Mus, Calif. *Exhib:* San Francisco Art Inst Centennial Exhib, MH De Young Mem Mus, 71; Calif Ceramics & Glass, Great Hall, Oakland Mus, 74; Northern Calif Clay Routes: Sculpture Now, San Francisco Mus Mod Art; Am Porcelain: New Expressions in an Ancient Art, Renwick Gallery, Nat Collection Fine Arts, Washington, 80; Int Tea Party, Contemp Crafts Gallery, Portland, Ore, 84; Inaugural Exhib, New Am Crafts Mus, NY, 86; Ceramics from the Smits Collection, Los Angeles Co Mus Art, Calif, 87; Fired with Enthusiasm, an exhib contemp soup tureens, Campbell Mus, Camden, NJ, 87; Beyond Words: The Book as Metaphor for Art, Vol 2, Calif Crafts Mus, San Francisco, 90; 500 Yrs Since Columbus, Triton Mus Art, Santa Clara, Calif, 92; and others. *Teaching:* Instr art, Keuka Col, New York, 67-69; prof art, Humboldt State Univ, Arcata, Calif, 69-. *Awards:* Purchase Award, Utah Mus Fine Arts, 71; Nat Endowment Arts Craftsmen's Fel Grant, 75; Artist Fel Grant, Calif Arts Coun, 94. *Bibliog:* Lloyd Herman (auth), American Porcelain: New Expressions in an Ancient Art, Timber Press, 81; Paul J Smith and Edward Lucie-Smith (coauth), Craft Today: Poetry of the Physical, Weidenfeld & Nicolson, 86; Martha Drexler Lynn (auth), Clay Today, Contemporary Ceramists & Their Work, Chronicle Books & Los Angeles Co Mus Art, 90. *Mem:* Am Craft Coun. *Media:* Ceramics. *Dealer:* Leslie Ferrin 163 Teatown Rd Croton on Hudson NY 10520. *Mailing Add:* 1110 Freshwater Rd Eureka CA 95503-9558

MARANDER, CAROL JEAN
PAINTER, GRAPHIC ARTIST
b Minneapolis, Minn, Dec 30, 50. *Study:* Colo State Univ, BFA(with honors), 73; Col Santa Fe, Albert Handell, pastel workshop, 82. *Work:* Comlinear Corp Gallery, Fort Collins, Colo. *Comn:* Pastel paintings, Marriott Hotels, Charlotte, NC, Trumball, Conn, 90, Omaha, Nebr, 92; pastel painting, Tucson Nat Resort & Spa, Ariz, 91; pastel paintings, US Post Off, Norman, Okla, 92. *Exhib:* 12th & 13th Ann Exhib, Pastel Soc Am, NY, 84 & 85; 75th Ann Exhib, Allied Artists Am, NY, 88; Exposition Int, Societe des Pastellistes de France, Compiegne, 88; Biennial Exhib, 88, Fine Art Calendar Artists Exhib, 89, Viva l'amour Artists Invitational, 91, Loveland Mus & Gallery, Colo; one-woman show, Colorscapes, Loveland Mus & Gallery, Colo, 90. *Pos:* Graphic designer, Colo State Univ, Fort Collins, 76-. *Awards:* Ann & Richard Sauter

Award, 12th Ann Exhib, Pastel Soc Am 84; First Place Other Media, Colo Artists Asn State Show, 86; Pastel Soc Am Award for Pastel, Allied Artists of Am 75th Exhib, 88. *Mem:* Pastel Soc Am; Allied Artists Am; Degas Pastel Soc; Colo Artists Asn. *Media:* Pastel. *Dealer:* Kyle Belding Gallery 1110 17th St Denver CO 80202. *Mailing Add:* 1400 Elm St Fort Collins CO 80521-1623

MARANO, LIZBETH
SCULPTOR, PHOTOGRAPHER
b Newark, NJ, Dec 2, 50. *Study:* Wash Univ, BFA, 72; Columbia Univ, MA(art hist), 98. *Work:* Boston Mus Fine Arts; New York Pub Libr. *Exhib:* Solo shows, Baruch Col Gallery, NY, 82, Daniel Weinberg Gallery, San Francisco, 82 & Galleria Molica, Rome, Italy, 92; Am Acad & Inst Arts Letts, NY, 89; Molica GuidArte Gallery, NY, 90 & 91; Pino Molica, Rome, Italy, 92 & 93; Staatsgalerie, Stuttgart, 97. *Teaching:* Sculpture, Brandeis, 89-90; Drawing, Cooper Union, 95. *Awards:* Grant, Change Inc, 75; Rome Prize Fel, Sculpture, Am Acad Rome, Italy; Nat Endowment Arts, Sculpture, 78, 85 & 88-89. *Bibliog:* Paolo Balmas (auth), Entropia; Lizbeth Marano (exhib catalog), Galleria Molica, Rome, 92; Gabriella Dalesio (auth), Lizbeth Marano: Entropia, Segno, 111-112, 2-3/92; Enzo Bilardello (auth), L'Entropia di Lizbeth Marano, Corriere della Sera, 3/5/92; and others. *Mailing Add:* 108 Franklin New York NY 10013

MARASCO, ROSE
PHOTOGRAPHER, EDUCATOR
b Utica, NY, Dec 25, 48. *Study:* Syracuse Univ, BFA, 71; Goddard Col, with Todd Webb, MA, 81; Visual Studies Workshop, MFA, 91, with Nathan Lyons & Frank Gohlke. *Work:* Polaroid Int Collection; Portland Mus Art; Davis Mus & Cult Ctr, Wellesley Col; NY Pub Libr Photog Collection; Fogg Art Mus, Harvard Univ; Univ New Eng; Smithsonian Nat Mus Am Hist. *Comn:* Percent for Art Grant, Harrington Elementary Sch, Maine; Aegean Univ S Maine Cult Exchange, 1997; Open House, Portrait Mus Art, 2002. *Exhib:* solo exhibs, Portland Sch Art, Maine, 86, Farnsworth Mus, Rockland, Maine, 92, Davis Mus & Cult Ctr, Wellesley Col, 95, Latvia Photog Mus, Riga & Sarah Mortland Gallery, NY, 98; Photokina '88, Polaroid Inst Exhib; Perspectives, Portland Mus Art, Maine, 88 & 2001; Exhib Photo, Berkshire Mus, Pittsfield, Mass, 92; Marlborough Gallery, 98; Leafing, Sarah Mouthland Gallery, 2000; Photographing Maine 1840-2000, Maine Coast Artists, 2000; Circles, Sarah Morthand Gallery, 2003; Domestics Objects: Past & Present, Univ Southern Maine, 2004-2005; The Long View, Norma Marin Collection, Univ Maine Mus Art, 2005. *Collection Arranged:* Todd Webb-Photographs, Univ Southern Maine Art Gallery, 81; Work from Five Decades-Todd Webb (auth, catalog), New Eng Found Arts, Cambridge, Mass. *Pos:* Prof art, Univ Southern Maine, 2000-. *Teaching:* Instr & dept head photog, Munson-Williams-Proctor Inst, 74-79; assoc prof art Univ Southern Maine, 79-; instr photog, Portland Sch Art, Maine, 81-87. *Awards:* MacDowell Colony Residency Fel, 85; Polaroid Materials Grant, 86; Maine Arts Comn Artists' Fel, 90; Maine Humanities Coun Major Grant, 90-91; Womens Studio Workshop Fel, 94; Good Idea Grant, Maine Arts Comn, Project Maine/France Grant, Univ Southern Maine, 2006. *Bibliog:* Vince Aletti (auth), The Village Voice, 2/4/98; The New Yorker, 2/23/98; Lucy R Lippard (auth), The Lure of the Local, The Mar Press, 97. *Mem:* Soc Photog Educ (NE region treas, 88). *Specialty:* Vintage and contemporary photography. *Publ:* Auth, A personal reflection based on the SPE Questionnaire: Teaching and Learning, Exposure 20:1, 3/82; How to make slides of your artwork, In: The Percent for Arts Handbook, Maine Arts Comn, 85; The silhouette craft of Kaye Housel, In: The World and I, 87; Looking at Photographs, In: 20th Century Photographs from Collection of the Bowdoin Col Mus Art (exhib catalog), 88. *Dealer:* Sarah Mortland Gallery 511 W 25th St #709 New York NY

MARCA-RELLI, CONRAD
PAINTER, COLLAGE ARTIST
b Boston, Mass, June 5, 13. *Work:* Mus Mod Art, Whitney Mus Am Art, Solomon R Guggenheim Mus, NY; High Mus Art, Atlanta, Ga; Wadsworth Atheneum; Metrop Mus Art; Chicago Art Mus; Walker Art Ctr, Minneapolis, Minn; and others. *Exhib:* One-man retrospectives, Whitney Mus Am Art, 67, Ft Lauderdale Mus Art, 79 & Ringling Mus, Sarasota, Fla, 80; Art Inst Chicago; Am Fedn Arts, 67-68; The New Am Painting & Sculpture, Mus Mod Art, 69; New Sch Social Res, 69; Am Painting 1970, Va Mus Fine Arts, Richmond, 70; One-man exhibs, Galera Joan Prats Barcelona, Spain, 78, Marlborough Gallery, NY, 79, Hokin Gallery, Chicago, 81, Phoenix Gallery, Washington, 82, GMB Gallery, Birmington, Mich, 82, Riva Yares Gallery, Scottsdale, Ariz, 90 & Vered Gallery, East Hampton, 95; plus many others. *Pos:* Vis critic, Yale Univ, 54 & 59; resident artist, New Col, Sarasota, Fla, 66. *Teaching:* Vis prof, Univ Calif, Berkeley, 58. *Awards:* Logan Medal & Purchase Prize, Art Inst Chicago, 54, Kohnstamm Prize, 63; Ford Found Award, 59; Purchase Prize, Detroit Inst Art, 60. *Bibliog:* Parker Tyler (auth), Marca-Relli (monogr), 60; H Harvard Arnason (auth), Marca-Relli (monogr), Abrams, 62; Gerard Miracle & Harold Rosenberg (auth), Marca-Relli, Barcelona, Spain, 75; and others. *Mem:* Inst Arts & Lett. *Mailing Add:* c/o Rira Yares Gallery 123 Grant Ave Santa Fe NM 87501

MARCHESCHI, (LOUIS) CORK
SCULPTOR, EDUCATOR
b San Mateo, Calif, Apr 5, 45. *Study:* Col San Mateo, 63-66; Calif State Col, Hayward, 66-68; Calif Col Arts & Crafts, Oakland, MFA, 70; also with Mel Ramos & Paul Harris. *Work:* Bochum Mus, WGer; Milwaukee Art Ctr; Mus Mod Art. *Comn:* Principle Group, Des Moines, Iowa, 91; Victoria Peak, Hong Kong, 93; Ft Lauderdale Airport, 94; Rowan Col, NJ, 94; Louisville Sci Ctr, 94; and others. *Exhib:* One-man shows, Kunsthalle Dusseldorf, Ger, 76, Milwaukee Art Ctr, Wis, 76, Hanson-Cowles Gallery, Minneapolis, Minn, 77, Tubingen Mus, Ger, 78, Van Abbe Mus, Endhoven, The Neth 78, Nat Gallery, Berlin, Ger, 78 & Braunstien Quay, 95; New Mus, NY, 80; Rutgers Mus, 83; Paris Mus Mod Art, 84; Nat Gallery, West Berlin, 84; Braunstien Quay, San Francisco, 92; Morgan Gallery, Kansas City, Mo, 92; and others. *Teaching:* Assoc prof art & intermedia, Minneapolis Col Art & Design, 70-85 & San Francisco Art Inst, 87-92. *Awards:* Minn State Arts Coun Grant, 75; Bush Found Grant, 78; DAAD Berlin Artist Prog Grant, 78; Nat Endowment Art, 82-83. *Bibliog:* Paul Owen (auth), Energy works (16mm film), 71; Merike Weiler (auth), Art Can article, 73; Heiner Hepper (auth), Cork Marcheschi (film), Ger Pub Broadcasting, 75; George Tapley (auth), article in Arts Mag, 83. *Media:* Electricity, Found Objects. *Collection:* Art deco objects and architectural period writings. *Publ:* Auth, Objects for producing visual phenomena with high-voltage electricity, 73; Heat, light and motion, 74; Neon, 75; Energy as Sculpture, Prof Kornelia V Berswordt (catalog), Mus Glaskasten, Marl, Ger, 91. *Dealer:* Modernism 236 8th St San Francisco CA 94103. *Mailing Add:* 192 Connecticut San Francisco CA 94107-2415

MARCHINI, CLAUDIA H
PAINTER, MURALIST
b Lima, Peru, Feb 3, 59; US Citizen. *Study:* Memphis Col Art, BFA, 87; Univ Tex, MFA, 89. *Comn:* Images of Ore, Ore Advocates Arts Found, Ore State Capital Bldg, Salem, 94. *Exhib:* Crosscut Biennial, Portland Mus Art, Ore, 93, Oregon Biennial, 95; Expo Sicion de Pinturasy Esculturas, Mus Nac, Lima, Peru, 98; The End, Tacoma Art Mus, Wash, 99; NMex Photogr, Eastern NMex Univ, 99; Millennium Madonna, Grants Pass Mus Art, Ore, 2000; 20th Ann NW Int Art Competition, Whatoom Mus, Bellingham, Wash, 2000. *Awards:* Second Place, Lucy Lippard, 97; First Place, Southern Ore Art Exhibit, Am Asn Univ Women, 2000; Individual Artist Fel Grant, Ore Arts Comn, 2000. *Bibliog:* Marcia Goren Weser (auth),Interesting Group Show Marks Gallery Closing, San Antonio Light, 8/2/89; Soledad Garcia (auth), Claudia Cilloniz Entre Piedray Pintura, Cosas Mag, 1/97; Jeremias Gamboa (auth), Hibridaciaires de Claudia Cilloniz, Visto Bueno Mag, 4/98. *Media:* Oil on Marble. *Dealer:* San Francisco Mus Modern Art Rental Gallery San Francisco CA. *Mailing Add:* 874 NE 7th St Grants Pass OR 97526

MARCK, JAN VAN DER
HISTORIAN, CRITIC
b Roermond, Neth, Aug 19, 29. *Study:* Univ Nijmegen, BA, MA & PhD(hist art), 56; Univ Utrecht; Columbia Univ, 56-59. *Exhib:* Charles Biederman, 65 & Lucio Fontana, 66, Walker Art Ctr, Minneapolis; Pictures to be Read/Poetry to be Seen, 67, Christo: Wrap in Wrap Out, 69, Moholy-Nagy, 69 & Art by Telephone, 69, Mus Contemp Art, Chicago; Am Art: Third Quarter Century, Seattle Art Mus, 73; Herbert Bayer, 77 & Acquisitions, 74-78, Dartmouth Col; In Quest of Excellence, Ctr Fine Arts, Miami, Fla, 84; Reconnecting, Detroit Inst Arts, 87, Art in Israel Today, 91, Among Friends, 91-92 & Interventions, 95; The Art of Contemp Bookbinding, Bibliotheca Wittockiana, Brussels, Koninklijke Bibliotheek, Den Haag Bibiotheque historique de la Ville de Paris, 97; Art and the Am Experience, Kalamazoo Inst Arts, 98; Lucio Pozzi, Mus of New Art, Detroit, 01. *Pos:* Cur, Gemeentemus, Arnhem, Neth, 59-61; deputy dir fine arts, Seattle World's Fair, 61-62; cur, Walker Art Ctr, Minneapolis, 63-67; dir, Mus Contemp Art, Chicago, 67-70, Dartmouth Col Mus & Galleries, 74-80 & Ctr Fine Arts, Miami, 80-85; twentieth century art & chief cur, Detroit Inst Arts, 86-95; cur consult, Detroit Inst Arts, 98-2003. *Teaching:* Assoc prof art hist, Univ Wash, Seattle, 72-74; adj prof art history, Dartmouth Col, 74-80. *Awards:* Fel, Rockefeller Found, 57-59 & Aspen Inst, 74 & 94; CASVA, 86; Decorated officer, Order Arts & Lett, 98; Order of Orange-Nassau Knight's Medal, 2000. *Mem:* Grolier Club; Int Asn Art Critics; Asn Int de Bibliophilie; Amis de la Reliure Originals. *Publ:* George Segal, Abrams, 75; Herbert Bayer: From Type to Landscape, Am Fedn Arts, 77; Arman, Abbeville, 84; In Quest of Excellence, Ctr for Fine Arts, Miami, 85; Bernar Venet, Difference, 88; The Art of Contemporary Bookbinding, De Buitenkant, Amsterdam, 97; Art and the American Experience, Kalamazoo Inst Arts, 98; Lucio Pozzi, Corraini, 2001. *Mailing Add:* 8941 Nadine Huntington Woods MI 48070

MARCOUX, JOHN W
DESIGNER
b Greenfield, Mass, June 18, 22. *Study:* Boston Mus Sch Fine Arts, 48-52, 55. *Work:* Boston Mus Fine Arts; Ronald Abramson, Washington, DC; Warren Ruben & Bernice Wollman, NY; Mr & Mrs Patrick Coady, Washington, DC; Fred Fiandaca, Boston, Mass. *Comn:* Garment display case, 85, Nesmin mummy case, 86 & Coptic chapel replica, 88, Mus Art, RI Sch Design. *Exhib:* NAGA Gallery, Boston, Mass, 91; Calif Crafts Mus, San Francisco, 92; Northwest Gallery Fine Woodworking, Seattle, Wash, 92; Newport Art Mus, RI, 92; Conservation by Design (traveling), Renwick Gallery, Washington, DC; and others. *Pos:* Furniture design, Boston, Mass, 56-76 & Providence, RI, 76-. *Teaching:* RI Sch Design, 88; Peter's Valley Craft Ctr, 89; Bennington Col, 90; Haystack Mountain Sch Craft, Deer Isle, Mass, 94. *Awards:* Crafts Award, 87 & 88 & Visual Arts Fel, 89, RI State Coun Arts; Visual Arts Fel, Nat Endowment Arts Fel, 90; RI State Coun Arts Grant, 93. *Media:* Furniture. *Publ:* Contribr, Mus Art Calendar, RI Sch Design, 88; Fine Woodworking Design Book IV, 88 & Book V, 89; The Guild 7, Kraus Sikes Inc, 91-92; AMBIENTE, Euro Design Guide, 91; Art New Eng, 4-5/92. *Mailing Add:* 283 George St Providence RI 02906

MARCUS, ANGELO P
DEALER, COLLECTOR
Study: Cairo Univ, MA. *Pos:* Pres, Eagle Art Gallery, Inc, currently. *Mem:* Nat Cowboy Hall Fame. *Specialty:* Western art. *Collection:* Olaf Wieghorst, Frank McCarthy, Robert Lougheed, William Whitaker, George Marks, John Clymer, Don Crowley, James Bama & Norman Rockwell. *Publ:* Wall Street Journal. *Mailing Add:* c/o Eagle Art Gallery 1250 Prospect La Jolla CA 92037

MARCUS, GERALD R
PAINTER, PRINTMAKER
b New York, NY. *Study:* Art Students League, New York, with Jean Liberte, Julian Levy, Sol Wilson & Jacob Lawrence, 1963-68; City Col NY, BA, 1968. *Work:* Standard & Poor Inc; Am Reinsurance Co Inc; Columbia Presby Hosp; Art in Embassies Prog, US State Dept; Albany Print Mus; Iowa Biennial Archives, Univ

Iowa. *Exhib:* one-man show, Paul Klapper Art Ctr, Queens Col, NY, 1983 & Griffith Menard Gallery, Baton Rouge, La, 1984; Adirondack Life, Lake Placid Art Ctr, 1989 & 90; Trenton City Mus, NJ, 1993; Stockton Nat, Haggin Mus, Calif, 1996; 40th Ann Nat Print Exhib, Hunterdon Art Ctr, Clinton, NJ, 1996; Soc Am Graphic Artists 68th Ann Exhib, 2000 & 2004; Humanity, Printmaking Coun NJ, 2001; A Movable Feast, Zeuxis Westbeth Gallery, NY 2003; September 11th Memorial Portfolio, Am Print Alliance; New Prints 2005/Winter, Int Print Ctr, NY, 2005; 15th Biennial Exhib, Purdue Univ, 2006. *Awards:* Claire Romano Prize for Etching. *Bibliog:* Cynthia Nadelman (auth), rev, Art News, summer 82; Stephanie Rauschenbusch (auth), Finding the Catskills, Prospect Press, 11/23/86; Artzine, Review of solo show, May 2003; John Goodrich (auth), review, New York Sun, 2/9/2006. *Mem:* Art Students League; Soc Am Graphic Artists. *Media:* Oil, Watercolor; Etching. *Dealer:* Concept Arts Gallery 1031 S Braddock Ave Pittsburgh PA 15218; Prince St Gallery 520 W 25th St New York NY 10001. *Mailing Add:* 463 West St New York NY 10014

MARCUS, GWEN E.
SCULPTOR
b New York. *Study:* NY Univ; RI Sch of Design; Art Students League; Nat Acad Design; studied with Clemente Spampinato, Bruno Lucchesi, Edgar Whitney & Isaac Soyer. *Hon Degrees:* Hon, BS. *Work:* Chi Mei Mus, Taiwan; Brookgreen Gardens, SC. *Exhib:* Kerygma Gallery, Ridgewood NJ, 99-05; Chi Mei Mus, Taiwan, 2001-05; Frank T Sabin Gallery, London, Eng, 2001 05; Champs Hill, W Sussex, Eng, Cavalier Gallery, Greenwich, Conn, Grenning Gallery, Sag Habor, Reflections Gallery, Santa Fe, NMex, Morris & Whiteside Galleries, Hilton Head, SC, 2001-2006. *Awards:* Gold Medal Am Prof League, NY, 1994, 1996, 2005; Gold Medal, Audubon Artist, NY, 1997; Josephine Beardsley Sander Mem Award, Allied Artist Am, Inc, NY, 1999; Gold Medal Hon, Hudson Valley Art Asn, NY, 2000; Am Artists Fund Award, Am Prof League, NY, 2001. *Mem:* Am Medallic Sculpture Asn (bd dir, 96-99); Hudson Valley Art Asn, 2002; Nat Sculpture Soc (bd mem, 2003-05); Audubon Artists, 2005. *Media:* Bronze. *Mailing Add:* 401 E 80th St Apt#19E New York NY 10021

MARCUS, IRVING E
PAINTER, EDUCATOR
b Minneapolis, Minn, May 17, 29. *Study:* Univ Minn, BA, 50; Univ Iowa, MFA, 52. *Work:* Oakland Mus Art, Calif; Butler Inst Am Art, Youngstown, Ohio; Yale Univ Art Gallery, New Haven, Conn; Nelson Gallery, Univ Calif, Davis; also many pvt collections; and others. *Comn:* various reviews in mags. *Exhib:* One-man shows, Zara Gallery, San Francisco, 78 & 80, Artspace, Crocker Art Mus, 78 & 88, Southeastern Ctr Contemp Art, Winston-Salem, NC, 79, Joseph Chowning Gallery, San Francisco, 85 & 91, Kathryn Sermas Gallery, 90, Sacramento State Univ Gallery, 2006; Welcome to the Candy Store, Crocker Art Mus, Sacramento, Calif, 81; Seven Artists in California, Gallery Takano, Tokyo, Japan, 85; Vertigo: The Poetics of Dislocation, San Francisco Art Inst, Calif, 87; John Natsoulas Gallery, Davis, Calif, 93; Joseph Chowning Gallery, San Francisco, Calif, 95; Solomon Dubnick Gallery, Sacramento, Calif, 2003; The Pilot Hill Col, Crocker Art Mus, Sacramento, Calif, 2003. *Collection Arranged:* Minneapolis Inst of Art, Minneapolis, MN; Allen Art Mus, Oberlin, OH; Oakland Art Mus, Oakland, CA; Crocker Art Gallery, Sacramento, CA; Reed Col, Portland, OR; Wake Forest Univ, Winston-Salem, NC; New Britain Mus Am Art, New Britain, Conn; S Tex Mus, Corpus Christi, Tex. *Teaching:* Instr art, Oberlin Col, 55-56, Univ Hawaii, 56-57 & Blackburn Col, 57-59; prof painting & printmaking, Sacramento State Col, retired, chmn dept art, 66-69; artist-in-residence, Wake Forest Univ, NC Sch Arts, Winston-Salem, 79. *Awards:* Prizes, Denver Mus Art, 52 & 58 & Crocker Art Mus, 63. *Bibliog:* Thomas Albright (auth), An extraordinary artist, San Francisco Chronicle, 2/11/73; Thomas Albright (auth), Bay area mythmakers, Art Gallery Mag, 11/74; various reviews in mags. *Media:* Painting, Drawing. *Dealer:* Solomon Dubnick Gallery 2131 Northrup Ave Sacramento CA 95825; Osceola Gallery 4053 Harlan St Ste 305 Emeryville CA 94608. *Mailing Add:* 601 Shangri Lane Sacramento CA 95825

MARCUS, MARCIA
PAINTER, EDUCATOR
b New York, NY, Jan 11, 28. *Study:* NY Univ, BA, 47; Art Students League, 54, with Edwin Dickinson. *Work:* Whitney Mus Art, NY; Philadelphia Mus Art; Univ Colo, Boulder; Hirshhorn Mus; Neuberger Mus; and others. *Comn:* Private & Public Portrait Comns. *Exhib:* Young Artists, Whitney Mus Art, 60; Woman Choose Women, NY Cult Ctr, 73; Everson Mus, Syracuse, 75; Canton Art Inst, 84; Benton Gallery, 86; 100 Yrs Creativity: The MacDowell Colony, Currier Gallery, NH, 96. *Pos:* Vis critic, 64-. *Teaching:* Adj instr painting, Cooper Union Sch Art, New York, 70-71; assoc prof painting & drawing, La State Univ, Baton Rouge, spring 72; instr, Vassar Col, 73-74; vis artist, Cornell Univ, spring 75, Syracuse Univ, 76 & Purdue Univ, 77-78; asst prof, RI Sch Design; assoc prof, Univ Iowa, 79-80; adj assoc prof, Queens Col, 81, Ohio State Univ, winter 83 & Univ Calif, spring 89; adj assoc prof, Chautauqua Inst, 90. *Awards:* Ingram Merrill Award, 64 & 77; artist-in-residence, RI Sch Design, Ford Found, 66; Nat Endowment Arts, 91; Pollock Foundation, 93. *Bibliog:* Paul Cummings (auth), Smithsonian Archives Interview, 75; Noel Frackman (auth), The Attic Mind of Marcia Marcus, Arts, 9/75; Alexander Russo (auth), Profiles of Women Artists, Univ Press, 84. *Media:* Oil, Pastel. *Publ:* Art and the Law Catalogues, West Publishing, 81; 25 Year Retrospective, Canton Art Inst, 84; Auth, Mutiny and the Mainstream: Talk that changed Art 1975-1990, MidMarch Arts Press, 92. *Mailing Add:* 80 N Moore St 165 New York NY 10013

MARCUS, ROBERT (MRS) P
COLLECTOR, PATRON
b New York, NY, July 10, 23. *Study:* Northwestern Univ; Parsons School of Design, NY. *Pos:* Bd Dir, Palm Beach Coun Arts; founder, Mus Am Folk Art, NY. *Mem:* Philarmonic Orchestra Fla; Fla Cult Action Alliance. *Collection:* American Folk Art (exhibited in 11 museums as: Two Centuries of American Folk Art: Masterworks From the Collection of Mr & Mrs Robert Marcus) North American, Latin American & European Art. *Mailing Add:* 208 Sandpiper Dr Palm Beach FL 33480-3327

MARDEN, BRICE
PAINTER, PRINTMAKER
b Bronxville, NY, Oct 15, 1938. *Study:* Boston Univ, BFA, 58-61, with Reed Kay, Arthur Hoener & Hugh Townley; Yale-Norfolk Summer Sch Music & Art, 61, with Bernard Chaet & Jon Schueler; Sch Art & Archit, Yale Univ, MFA, 61-63, with Esteban Vicente & Alex Katz. *Work:* Mus Mod Art, Whitney Mus Am Art, NY; Walker Art Ctr, Minneapolis, Minn; Ft Worth Art Ctr, Tex; Stedelijk Mus, Amsterdam; and others. *Exhib:* Whitney Mus Am Art Ann, NY, 69, 77 & 83; Modular Painting, Albright-Knox Art Gallery, Buffalo, 70; Painting--New Options, Walker Art Ctr, 72; Documenta 5, Kassel, Ger, 72; Guggenheim Mus, NY, 75; A New Spirit in Painting, Royal Acad Arts, London, 81; Solo shows, St Louis Art Mus, 93, Kunstmuseum, Basel, 92, Mus Fur Gegnwartskunst, 93, Mus Friedericianum, Kassel, 93, Kunsthalle, Bern, 93, Secession, Vienna, 93, Stedelijk Mus, Amsterdam, 93, Stattliche Graphische Sammlung, Munich, 97, Kunstmuseum of Winthelthur, Switz, 97, Wexner Ctr for Arts, Columbus, Ohio, 97, Fogg Art Mus, Mass, 97, Whitney Mus of Am Art, NY, 98, Carnegie Mus of Art, Pittsburgh, 99, Miami Art Mus, 99, Hirshorn Mus, 99, Dallas Mus of Art, Tex, 99 & Serpentine Gallery, London, 2000, Drawing the Line, The Maier Mus of Art, Randolph-Macon Woman's Coll, Va, 2001, Boston Univ Alumni Gallery, 2002; Affinities, Hayden Gallery, Mass Inst Technol, Cambridge, 83; Paintings, Galerie Maeght Lelong, NY, 83; Anthony d'Offay Gallery, London, 88; Matthew Marks Gallery, NY, 91, 93, 95, 2002; Dia Ctr for the Arts, 91; The Tate Gallery, London, 91; Kunstmuseum Basel, 93; Kunsthalle Bern, 93; Biennale Di Venezia, Venice, Italy, 97; Staatliche Giraphische Sammlung, Munich, 97; William Hayes Fogg Art Mus, Cambridge, 98; Miami Art Mus, Fla, 99; Mixing Memory and Desire, Neues Kunstmuseum, Lucerne, 2000; Age of Influence, Reflections in the Mirror of Am. Culture, Mus. Contemporary Art, Chgo, 2000; Etchings, Margo Leavin Gallery, LA, 2001; Serpentine Gallery, London, 2001; Repetition in Discourse, The Painting Center, NY, 2001; Auras and Epitaphs, First Public Sch of Hydra, 2002; Drawing the Line: A Retrospective, Maier Mus Art, 2002; Rocks and Art, Nature Found and Made, Chambers Fine Art, NY, 2002; Looking East, Boston Univ Art Gallery, 2002; Attendants, Bears, and Rocks, Matthew Marks Gallery, NY, 2003; Forty Years, Richard Gray Gallery, Boston Univ, 2003; The Stage of Drawing: Gesture and Act, The Drawing Center, NY, 2003; Singular Forms (Sometimes Repeated), Guggenheim Mus, NY, 2004; A Minimal Future? Art as Object, Mus Contemporary Art, LA, 2004; Not Exactly Photographs, Fraenkel Gallery, San Francisco, 2004; An Empty Space, Akira Ikeda Gallery, NY, 2005; Contemporary Voices, Mus Modern Art, NY, 2005; Imagineless Icons: Abstract Thoughts, Gagosian Gallery, London, 2005. *Pos:* security guard, Jewish Mus, 63-64; gen asst to Robert Rauschenberg, 66; painting instr, Sch Visual Arts, NY, 69-74. *Bibliog:* Jeremy Lewison (auth), Brice Marden: Prints 1961-1991, 91; Brenda Richardson (auth), Brice Marden Cold Mountain, 92; Klaus Kertess (auth), Brice Marden: Paintings & Drawings, 92. *Mem:* Am Acad Arts & Letts; Nat Acad. *Media:* Oil. *Dealer:* Matthew Marks Gallery New York NY 10021. *Mailing Add:* 6 St Lukes Pl New York NY 10012

MARDER, TOD
HISTORIAN
Study: Columbia Univ, PhD. *Teaching:* Prof, Rutgers Univ. *Awards:* Rome Prize Art Hist, Am Acad Rome, 97. *Res:* Bernini's architecture; urban planning in Rome; classical traditions in architecture from antiquity to the present. *Publ:* Auth, Bernini's Commission for the Equestian Statue of Constantine in St Peter's, in An Architectural Progress in the Renaissance and Baroque, Pa State Univ papers in Art Hist, VIII, 92; Sisto V e la fontana del Mose (Sixtus V and the Fountain of Moses), in Sisto V Roma e Lazio, 92; Manfredo Tafuri, Ricerca del rinascimento: Principi, citta, archtetti, Art Bulletin, rev, 3/95; Bernini's Scala Regia at the Vatican Palace, Architecture, Sculpture, and Ritual, Cambridge Univ Press, 97; Bernini and the Art of Architecture, Abbeville Press, 98. *Mailing Add:* Rutgers Univ Dept Art Hist Voorhees Hall Hamilton St New Brunswick NJ 08903

MAREE, WENDY P
PAINTER, SCULPTOR
b Windsor, Eng, Feb 10, 38. *Study:* Windsor & Maidenhead Col, Eng, 59; studied with Vasco Lazzlo, London, 59-62. *Work:* Bronze sculptures, (two) Amnesty Int, Washington, DC; prt collections of HRH Prince Faisal, Saudi Arabia, Gena Rowlands, John Cassavetes & Nicky Blairs, Los Angeles, Calif, Guilford Glazer, Beverly Hills, Calif & June Allyson, Ojai, Calif; one painting & two sculptures, Petropavlovsk Mus Kamchatka, Russia. *Comn:* Bronze Statue (5 ft tall), Ingleside Inn, Palm Springs, Calif, 95. *Exhib:* Windsor Arts Festival, Eng, 48; Summer Viewers Delight, San Bernadino Mus, Calif, 88; one woman show, Lake Arrowhead Libr, Calif, 89; group show, Petropavlovsk Mus, Kamchatka, Russia, 93; Avant Guarde Gallery, Palm Springs, 96; LGO Galerie Des Arts, Palm Springs, 98. *Awards:* Second Place, Nat BBC Television Show, 50; Award, San Bernardino Co Mus, Redlands, Calif, 88; Award Of Merit, Gov of Kamchatka, Russia. *Bibliog:* Les Krantz (auth), The California Art Review, 89. *Mem:* Artist Guild of Lake Arrowhead, 88, Rowac Lake Arrowhead, 92. *Media:* Acrylic; Bronze. *Mailing Add:* 246 N Saturmino Dr Palm Springs CA 92265

MARGOLIS, MARGO
PAINTER
b Lawrence, Mass, Dec 24, 47. *Study:* Skidmore Col, BS, 70; Ind Univ, MFA, 72. *Work:* Philadelphia Mus, Pa; Chemical Bank, Shearson Lehman, Chase Manhattan, IBM Corp Hq, Estee Lauder, Prudential, Amarota Hess Corp, NY; General Mills, Minneapolis, Minn; Brook Mus; Am Can Co, Greenwich, Conn. *Exhib:* One-person shows, Brooke Alexander Gallery, NY, 77, 78, 80, Conn Col, New London, 77, Miami-Dade Col, Fla, 79, Richard Greene Gallery, NY, 87, Beth Urdang Fine Art, Boston, 89, 93, Esso Gallery, New York City, 97; Contemp Drawings, Pa Acad Fine Arts, Philadelphia, 7; Monoprints, Univ Maine, 88; Beth Urdang Gallery, Chicago, 91; Penzesenze, Perugia, Italy, 91; Mentors, Vox Populi, Philadelphia, Pa, 93; Contemp Prints, Quartet Gallery, NY, 94; Wayne C Brown Collection, Colby Col, Waterville, Maine, 94; Abstract Painting, Carolyn Roy Gallery, NY, 94; Art Exchange, Esso Gallery, NY, 96, 97; plus many others. *Collection Arranged:* Philadelphia Mus Art; Brooklyn Mus; Estee Lauder Corp, NYC; Prudential, NYC; Chase Manhattan Bank, NYC. *Teaching:* Prof painting, Tyler Sch Art, Temple Univ, 88. *Awards:* CAPS Grant, NY State Coun Arts, 77-78; Nat Endowment Arts Grants, 80-81, 87-88; Nat Endowment Arts Int Fel, 87-88. *Bibliog:* John Russell (auth), New York Times, 78, 80; Carter Ratcliffe (auth), Thick Paint, Univ Chicago, 78; Lee Edwards (auth), Margo Margolis, Arts Mag, 80; Miles Unger (auth), Art New England, 10/1993. *Media:* Oil, Paint. *Dealer:* Beth Urdang Gallery Boston MA; Esso Gallery 191 Christie NY. *Mailing Add:* 16 Crosby St New York NY 10013

MARGOLIS, RICHARD M
PHOTOGRAPHER, ARTIST
b Lorain, Ohio, June 10, 43. *Study:* Univ Americas, Mexico City, 64, Kent State Univ, BS, 69; Viusal Studies Workshop, 72; Rochester Inst Technol, MFA, 78. *Work:* Mus Mod Art, NY; Victoria & Albert Mus, London, Eng; Bibliotheque Nat, Paris, France; Int Mus Photog, Rochester, NY; Yale Univ Art Gallery, New Haven, Conn; and others. *Comn:* Treasures of Imperial Austria, photographed medieval armor & armory, Landeszeughaus-Graz, Austria (exhib catalog), Mus Fine Arts, Houston, 91; photographs, Rochester Int Airport. *Exhib:* One-person shows, Foto,NY, 76, George Eastman House, Rochester, NY, 79, Bridges-Symbols of Progress, Rochester's Big Trees, Spectrum Gallery, Rochester, 90, Nat Acad Sci, Washington, DC, 90 & Rochester's Pub Art Dawson Gallery, 92; St Lawrence Univ, Canton, NY, 77; Carpenter Ctr, Harvard Univ, Cambridge, Mass, 78; Creative Artists Pub Serv Prog Photog Show, Whitney Mus Am Art, NY, 78; Mem Art Gallery, Rochester, NY, 79; Eng Landscapes, Camden Arts Ctr, London, Eng, 81; Foto, NY, 83; Queens Mus Art, 91; Paul Cava Gallery, 93; String Room, Weus Col, 96; Phot-Eye Gallery, Sante Fe, NMex, 98. *Collection Arranged:* Personal Landscapes, Rochester Landscape in Various Media, Artworks Gallery, 80; Francis Murray & H Jones, Gallery 696, Rochester, 81; Photography-Art of the State (auth, catalog), State Univ NY, Brockport, 83 & NY State Mus, 83; New York Bridges, 86; Computers and Photography, Pyramid Art Center, Rochester NY, 89. *Teaching:* Instr photog, Penland Sch Crafts, 79, 80, 86, 90 & 94; adj instr photog, Nazareth Col, Rochester, NY, 79-81; asst prof photog, State Univ NY, Brockport, 81-88; vis artist, Chautauqua Inst, 83. *Awards:* Agr Lift Grant, 89; Grant, NY State Coun Arts, 90; Artist Award for Contrib to Community, AGR, 94. *Bibliog:* Owen Edwards (auth), Raveling the knot, Saturday Rev, 4/28/79; Owen Edwards (auth), The complex complex, Am Photographer, 6/81; Contemporary Photographers, 82-86; A Photographer's Vision, Upstate, 90. *Mem:* Soc Photog Educ (chmn, Northeast region, 83 & 85); Photogr Heritage Asn, (founder & chair); Nat Trust Hist Preservation; Soc Indust Archeol. *Media:* Photography. *Publ:* Bridges-Symbols of Progress Exhib Catalog, 91. *Mailing Add:* 250 N Goodman St Rochester NY 14607

MARGULES, GABRIELE ELLA
ILLUSTRATOR, PAINTER
b Tachau, Czech, May 30, 27; US citizen. *Study:* Cambridge Sch Art, Eng, nat dipl fine arts; Royal Acad Schs, London; New York, studies with Hans Hofmann, Camilo Egas & Norman Carton. *Work:* Kerlan Collection, Univ Minn Res Ctr for Children's Books, Minneapolis; Forbes Collection; pvt collections, Garrison, Cold Spring, Woodstock & Hudson, NY, San Francisco, St Louis & Geneve, Switz. *Exhib:* NY Ctr, 54-72; Jr Coun, Mus Mod Art, 54-72; NY Artists Equity, 54-72; Solo exhibs, Panoras Gallery, 57, NY Pub Libr, 60, Lieberman Studio, 98, Baronet Theatre, 70 & Garrison Art Ctr, 85 & 96; Hastings on Hudson Art Coun, 74; Garrison Art Ctr, 78-2000; Barrett House, 87-2000; Putnam Arts Coun, 88-2000; Howland Art Ctr, 90; Art Soc Kingston, 96-2000; Woodstock Artists Asn, 96-2000. *Awards:* Silver Medal-First Prize for Life Drawing, Royal Acad, London, 49; Best 100 illus children's bks, Am Inst Graphic Arts, 68 & 70; Best Show, Putnam Arts Coun, 89, 90 & 94; James D'Arcy Award, 99. *Mem:* Artists Equity of New York (coun mem, 66-70); Art Soc Kingston; Dutchess Co Art Asn; Woodstock Artist Asn; Garrison Art Ctr. *Media:* Sumi-e Ink, Watercolor; Pastel. *Interests:* Poetry, Pub Speaking. *Publ:* Illusr, Harper's Mag, 63; Out of the Ark, Atheneum, New York & Longman Young, London, 68; Bird Songs, Atheneum, 69

MARGULIES, ISIDORE
SCULPTOR, KINETIC ARTIST
b Vienna, Austria, April 1, 21. *Study:* Cooper Union Art Sch, New York, 38-40; State Univ NY, Stony Brook, with Robert White and James Kleege, BA(liberal arts), 74; CW Post Col, MA(art), 75; with Alfred Van Loan. *Work:* Hall of Fame, State Univ NY, Stony Brook; Brookgreen Gardens, Myrtle Beach, SC; Doane Col, Fla. *Exhib:* One-man shows at State Univ of NY Stony Brook Gallery, 73, Suffolk Mus, Stony Brook, 74, Wiener Gallery, New York City, 74, Harbor Gallery, Cold Spring Harbor, NY, 76; group exhibs incl Hecksher Mus, Huntington, NY, 73, 74, 75, Nat Mus Sport, New York City, 72; Far Gallery, New York City, 1979, R K Parker Gallery, New York City, 1979; Nelson Rockefeller Collection, 80-81; Nat Sculpture Soc ann, 82; Ambassador Gallery, Soho, NY, 90-91; Cathedral of St John the Devine, NY, 91; Joel Meisner Gallery, 91-96; Chesterwood DC French Nat Trust, Mass, 94; Nat Sculpture Soc, 96. *Teaching:* Asst prof, CW Post Col, Brookville, NY, 76-77. *Awards:* Recipient award of excellence Hecksher Mus, 78-79; Coun Am Artists Award, Nat Sculpture Soc, 79; Gold Medal, Nat Sculpture Soc, 80; C Percival Dietsch Sculpture Prize, Nat Sculpture Soc, 83; Silver Medal, Knickerbocker Artists, 89. *Mem:* Huntington Twp Art League (chmn, 76-78); fel Nat Sculpture Soc; Knickerbocker Artists; Nat Acad (nat academician 1994). *Media:* Bronze, Mixed. *Mailing Add:* 650 Washington Ave Plainview NY 11803-1827

MARGULIES, MARTIN Z
COLLECTOR
b Feb, 38. *Pos:* Real estate developer; pres Martin Z Margulies Found, Inc; owner Martin Z Margulies Sculpture Park, 94-, Margulies Collection at the Warehouse, Miami, Fla, 99-; co-founder Overtown Youth Center, Miami, Fla, 2003-; board dirs Arts for Learning, Miami, Fla. *Awards:* Named one of Top 200 Collectors, ARTnews Mag, 2004-. *Collection:* Modern and contemporary art, photography. *Mailing Add:* 445 Grand Bay Dr Key Biscayne FL 33149

MARI, M
PAINTER, PRINTMAKER
Study: Atlanta Sch Art, BFA; Butler Univ; Ga State Univ; Principia Col. *Work:* Mus Contemp Crafts, Slide Libr, NY; Vogue Fabrics Libr, Conde Nast, NY; Hunter Mus, Chattanooga, Tenn; Lily Endowment, Indianapolis, Ind. *Comn:* Batik wallhanging, Emory Univ, Atlanta, Ga; sculptured fabric wall relief, Kennedy Ctr, Tampa, Fla, 86; triptych, diptych, monoprints, Hyatt Regency, Albuquerque, NMex, 90; triptych, Dewitt Embassy, 90. *Exhib:* Midstates Painting Exhib, Evansville Mus Art, 72-74; Am Fiber Art, Ball State Univ, 74; Fibers Invitational, Austin Peay State Univ, 74; Spoleto Festival, 77; The Dyers Art, Cincinnati, Ohio, 78; Southern Graphics Coun Invitational, 86. *Teaching:* Instr batik, silkscreen & fabric painting, Ind Univ, Indianapolis, 69-72, instr painting & drawing, 72-77; instr painting, Herron Sch Art, 72. *Awards:* Objects 71, Textile Award, IMA, 71; Purchase Award, Bardstown Invitational, Ky, 73; Southeastern Arts Festival Painting Award, Atlanta, Ga, 70; Purchase Awards, Dekalb Coun for Arts Invitational, 84 & 85. *Bibliog:* Dona Meilach (auth), Contemporary Batik & Tie Dying, Crown, 73; Joanifer Gibbs (auth), Batiks Unlimited, Watson-Guptill, 74. *Mem:* Surface Design Int; Am Crafts Coun. *Media:* Oil on Canvas. *Publ:* Peachtree Papers, 85. *Mailing Add:* 2080 NW Bolton Rd Atlanta GA 30318-1106

MARIANI, CARLO MARIA
PAINTER
b Rome, Italy. *Study:* Acad Fine Arts, Rome, BA(painting), 56. *Work:* Tate Gallery, London, Eng; Kemper-Kansas City Art Inst, Kansas City, Mo; Philadelphia Mus Art, Franklin Mint, Philadelphia, Pa; Steve Bellagio Collections, Las Vegas, Nev; Millenium Hotel, NY; Lincoln Ctr, List Col, NY; Guggenheim Mus, NY; Philadelphia Mus Fine Art, Pa; Mus Modern Art, Rome, Italy; Mus Pallazo Forti, Verona, Italy. *Comn:* Crescent Hunt, comn by Hunt, Dallas, Tex, 88; Hotel Macklowe, comn by Macklowe, NY, 89; Borghese Coll, Rome, Italy. *Exhib:* An Int Survey of Recent Painting & Sculpture, Mus Mod Art, NY, 84; solo exhib, Assoc Am Artist, NY, 97, Premio Marche, Ancona, Italy, 97, Hackett-Freedman Gallery, San Francisco, Calif, 97, 99, 2000, Mus Modern Art, Bologna, Italy, 01, Spiritual Erosion, Axel Raben Gallery, NY, 2002, Hackett-Freedman Art Gallery, San Francisco, Calif, 2002; Documenta, Mus Contemp Art, Pontiac, Mich, 2000; Deja Vu, Katonah Mus Art, NY, 2000; Contemp Art in Progress, Mus Modern and Contemp Art, Rome, Italy, 2000; Smetena Hall Municipal Hall, Prague, Poland, 2000; Lincoln Ctr List Collection at the Gallery Lincoln Ctr, NY, 2000; and others; group exhibs, Between Earth and Heaven, Ostend Mus of Modern Art, Belgium, 2001, Tesori NascostiHidden Treasures, Mus del Corsi, Ital, 2001, Shoes or No Shoes? Mus of Modern Art, Belgium, 2001, Desire Mus of Modern Art, Ital, 2002; Bulgari Coll, Rome, Italy; Bellagio, Las Vegas, NV; Thirty Three Women, Thomas Amman, Zurich, Switz, 2003; Italian Master Drawings, Philadelphia Mus Art, 2004; Poggiale, Forconi, Florence, Italy, 2004. *Awards:* Feltrinelli Award for lifetime achievement in painting, Acad deiLincei, Rome, 98. *Bibliog:* Calvesi/Wolbert/Fox (auths), Carlo Maria Mariani, Inst Darmstadt, 91; Donald Kuspit (auth), Idiosyncratic Identities, Cambridge Univ Press, 96; Laura Cheribini (auth), Mortal Sin - Respectful Heresies, Cannaviello, Milan, Italy; David Ebony (auth), Carlo Maria Mariani, 2001; Robert Rosenblum, 2003; Edward Lucie-Smith, 2001 & 2003. *Media:* Oil, All Media. *Publ:* Aimee Fitzpatrick (auth), This Artist Is Not Content To Rest On His Laurels, The Southampton Press, 1/99; Matthew Kangas (auth), Of Mind and Matter, Seattle Times, 5/99; Barry Schwabsky (auth), Not To Be Looked At (exhib catalog), Hackett-Freedman Gallery, San Francisco, Calif, 99; Gerard McCarthy (auth) rev, Art in Am, 9/99; Gerard McCarthy (auth), Displacement and Continuity (exhib catalog), Hackett-Freedman Gallery, San Francisco, Calif, 2000; Howard Fox, Maurizio Calvesi, Utopia, Pamstadt, Germany, 91; David Ebony (auth), Carlo Maria Mariani, 2001; Allesandro Riva (auth), On the Appian Way, Italy, 2004. *Dealer:* Hackett Freedman Gallery 250 Sutter St San Francisco CA; Assoc Am Artists 20 W 57th St New York NY; Independent (Private Cur) www.carlomariamariani.com. *Mailing Add:* 171 W 71st St Apt 12E New York NY 10023-3801

MARIN, JAVIER
SCULPTOR
b Uruapan, Michoacan, Mex, 62. *Study:* Nat Acad Art San Carlos, 80-83; Nat Univ Mex, Mexico City. *Work:* Santa Barbara Mus Art, Calif; Mus Arte Contemp, Marco, Monterrey, Mex; Mus Art Mod, Mexico City; Gumbiner Found, Long Beach, Calif; Mus Barro, Caracas, Venezuela. *Exhib:* Clasicismo en Mexico, Ctr Cult/Arte Contemp, Mexico City, 90; Terra Incognita, Mus Arte Mod, Mexico City, 92; El

Cuerpo Arrebatado, Mus Art Contemp, Marco, Monterrey, Mex, 94; Bienal Barro de Am, Mus Barro, Caracas, Venezuela, 95; Re-Imagining the Avant Garde: Modernism & the Art of Latin Am, Santa Barbara Mus Art, Calif, 95; one-man show, Palacio Bellas Artes, Mexico City, 96. *Bibliog:* Susan Kandel (auth), Non-traditional tradition, Los Angeles Times, 12/16/93; Teresa del Conde (auth), El Cuerpo Arrebatado (exhib catalog), Marco Mus, 94; Suzanne Muchnic (auth), Javier Marin, Art News, 10/95. *Media:* Clay, Bronze

MARINER, DONNA M
PAINTER, WRITER
b Youngsville, Pa. *Study:* Art Inst Sch, 45; Studied with W Peterson, Edinboro Col; Ben F Stahl & John Kuller; Dr Baptist, Clarion Col, 65-75; studied with A Sanders, 69; Famous Artist Sch, Westport, Conn, 74; Penn State, 83-84; Long-Ridge Writer Group Sch, 94-95. *Work:* Mariner's Art Gallery, Warren, Pa; Clinton Wilder Mus, Irvine, Pa. *Comn:* Portraits in pastel, pvt collections, 72-94; wood carvings, Warren Co Comnrs Off, Pa, 78 & 79; wood carving and oil paintings, Gulf Oil Co, Cleveland, 79-81; clipper ships, seascapes, still lifes, oils & pastels, comn by M Glotz, Warren, Pa, 88-91; Still lifes & hist railroad sta scenes, C Gerber, Wilcox, Pa, 93-96. *Exhib:* Warren Art League Shows, 68-94; Bradford Art Festival, 69, 70, 76, 82 & 85; Int Chautauqua Art Shows, NY, 76 & 78; 4th Can Int Corning Exhib, Toronto, 80; Am Artist Mag Nat Competition, NY, 86; and others. *Pos:* publicity chmn, Warren Art League & Warren Art League Summer Art Festival, 89-93, historian, 88-94; student consult, Long Ridge Writer Group Sch, 95-. *Teaching:* Instr painting, Warren Art League, 72-75, Warren Art League, 74-94 & Mariner's Art Studio, 76-; instr crafts, Warren Art League, 80-90; instr, home studio, 2006-. *Awards:* Outstanding Achievement, 90; Golden Poet Award, 87-94; Master Pastels, 84-96; Master of Oils, 86-99. *Bibliog:* Elaine Rhodes (auth), Artist returns to work, Warren Times Observer, 6/82; E Gallenstein (auth), Artist, carver and writer, Chip Chaps Mag, 86; Dianne Anderson (ed & auth), Mariner honored, Warren Times Observer, 6/15/94 & 8/17/93. *Mem:* Warren Art League; Nat Woodcarvers Asn; Int Soc Poetry; World of Poetry; Nat Libr Poetry; Poetry Guild; Famous Poets Soc; Int Artistic Asn (1980-). *Media:* Pastels, Oils. *Interests:* Poetry. *Publ:* Auth, Quick tips, perfect blenders, Am Artist Mag, 12/82; Last Farewell to Dixie, World of Poetry, 1/11/91 & In: Where Dreams Begin, 8/4/92; Summer arts festival, Dailey Press, Warren Times Observer, Corry Evening J, Jamestown Post J & Titusville Herald Paper, Pa, 7/92; Falling In Love, In: Outstanding Poets 1994, Nat Libr Poetry, 1/8/94; Warning, No Cats Allowed, Short Short Story Competition, 9/20/94; Paradise, Poetry Guild, 12/28/97; Paradise, publ American Art at the Millenium & Best Poems and Poets of 20th Century; plus numerous others. *Dealer:* Girtons 16 Hertzel St Warren PA 16365; Such'a Deal Gallery Rte 62 North Warren Pa. *Mailing Add:* PO Box 563 Warren PA 16365-0563

MARINSKY, HARRY
SCULPTOR, PAINTER
b London, Eng, May 8, 1909; US citizen. *Study:* RI Sch Design; Pratt Inst. *Work:* Metrop Mus Art, NY; Lincoln Ctr, Fordham Univ; Syracuse Univ Art Mus; York Univ Mus; Hunt Botanical Libr, Carnegie-Mellon Univ; Mus of the Hist of Resistance, Stazzema, Italy; and others. *Comn:* Five bronze figures representing spirit of nationalism, Vet Mem Park, Norwalk, Conn, 66; St Francis, St James Episcopal Church, Danbury, Conn, 60, St Francis Col, 85 & Assisi, Italy, 86, bronze figures, Harlequin Plaza, Denver, Colo, 81-88; Alice in Wonderland (bronze groups), Englewood, Colo; Enlarged St Francis, Pietrasanta, Italy, 2000. *Exhib:* Mus Mod Art, NY; Art Inst Chicago, 47; Kendall Art Gallery, Wellfleet, Mass; Hammer Galleries, NY; Shayne Galerie, Montreal; Montclair Mus, NJ, 88; Westmoreland Mus Art, Greensburg, Pa; Brookgreen Gardens, SC; and others. *Awards:* Silvermine Guild Sculpture Award, 56; C Percival Dietsch Prize, Nat Sculpture Soc, 85 & Henry Hering Award, 88. *Mem:* Nat Sculpture Soc, NY. *Media:* Bronze, Watercolor. *Publ:* The Sculpture of Harry Marinsky, Hammer Publ, 82; Mus of Outdoor Art, Englewood, Colo. *Dealer:* Hammer Galleries New York NY

MARION, ANNE WINDFOHR
PATRON, ADMINISTRATOR, COLLECTOR
b Fort Worth, Tex, Nov 10, 1938. *Study:* Univ Tex, attended, Univ Geneva. *Pos:* Chmn, Burnett Oil Co; pres, Burnett Ranches Ltd, 6666 Ranch, Guthrie, Tex, Burnett Found, Forth Worth, Tex; Chmn, Georgia O'Keeffe Mus, Santa Fe; trustee, Kimbell Art Mus; trustee, former chmn & pres, chmn acquisition com, Modern Art Mus, Forth Worth; past trustee, Mus Modern Art, NYC; mem bd regents, Texas Tech Univ; dir emeritus, Nat Cowboy Hall of Fame; mem exec com, Forth Worth Stock Show; hon bd mem, Nat Cowgirl Hall of Fame, West Heritage Ctr. *Awards:* Great Woman of Tex, Fort Worth Bus Press, 1993; Charles Goodnight award, 1993; Golden Deed honoree, Fort Worth Exchange Club, 1993; Fern Sawyer award, Nat Cowgirl Hall of Fame, 1994; Gov award for excellence in the arts, NMex, 1996; Boss of the Plains award, Ranching Heritage Ctr, 2003; named one of Top 200 Collectors, ARTNews Mag, 2003-. *Mem:* Tex & SW Cattle Raisers Asn; Am Quarter Horse Asn. *Mailing Add:* Burnett Ranchers Ltd PO Box 130 Guthrie TX 79236

MARION, JOHN LOUIS
COLLECTOR
b NY City, Nov 27, 33. *Study:* Fordham Univ, BS, 56; Columbia Univ, post grad, 60-61. *Pos:* Sotheby Parke Bernet Inc, New York City, 60-, dir, 65-, vpres, 66-70, exec vpres, 70-72, pres, 72-87; chmn bd, Sotheby's Inc, 75-, hon chmn, currently; bd dir, Sotheby Holdings Inc, London, Mus NMex Syst. *Awards:* Named one of Top 200 Collectors, ARTnews Mag, 2004-. *Mem:* Appraisers Asn Am; Vintage Club; Shady Oaks Club; Eldorado Club; Lotos Club. *Collection:* 17th & 18th Century European Art; Modern & Contemporary Art

MARIONI, PAUL
SCULPTOR, GLASS BLOWER
b Cincinnati, Ohio, July 19, 41. *Study:* Univ Cincinnati, BA, 67. *Work:* Corning Mus Glass; Hessisches Landesmuseum, Darmstadt, WGer; Oakland Mus; Yamaha Corp, Tokyo; Mus Am Craft, NY. *Comn:* Light columns, Port Authority, Pier 69 Hq, Seattle, 93; The Further I Look, the More I See, Eye Clinic, Univ Med Ctr, Seattle, 93; shelter, Veterinary Teaching Hosp, Pullman, Wash, 96; pillars, Burbank Police/Fire Dept, 97; Water Equals Light, Seattle City Light, 97. *Exhib:* New Glass: A Worldwide Survey, Corning Mus Glass, World Tour, 78-82; 200 Objects, Corning Mus Glass, Russ Tour, 90-91; Int Conf on Environ Glass, Corning Mus Glass, NY, 93; 100 Yrs - Calif Crafts, Oakland Art Mus, Calif, 93; V Internationales, Glasmuseum Frauenau, Ger, 95; Light Interpretations: Menorah Invitational, Jewish Mus, San Francisco, 95; Pilchuck Pioneers, William Traver Gallery, Seattle, 95; cast glass, Contemp Crafts Gallery, Portland, Ore 96; Trashformations, Watcom Mus, Bellingham, Wash, 97. *Pos:* Dir, Canyon Cinema, San Francisco, 72-74; coordr glass prog, Summervail, Vail, Colo, 79-84; dir, Glass Art Soc, 84-86. *Teaching:* Lectr art, San Francisco Art Inst, 73-75; asst prof, San Francisco State Univ, 74-78; fac, Pilchuck Sch, Stanwood, Wash, 74-96. *Awards:* Nat Endowment Arts Grants, 75-76, 82 & 88; First Prize Archit, Fragile Art, 83. *Bibliog:* Otto Rigan (auth), New Glass, Simon & Schuster, 76; Narcissus Quagliata (auth), From Mind to Light, Mattole Press, 76; Julie Hall (auth), Tradition and Change, Dutton Press, 78. *Mem:* Glass Arts Soc; Northwest Glass Artists. *Media:* Glass. *Dealer:* Walter-White Gallery 7th & San Carlos PO Box 4834 Carmel CA 93921; William Traver Gallery 110 Union St Seattle WA 98101. *Mailing Add:* 4136 Meridian Ave No 1 Seattle WA 98103

MARIONI, TOM
SCULPTOR
b Cincinnati, Ohio. *Study:* Cincinnati Art Acad, 55-59. *Hon Degrees:* Soc Ind Artists, PhD, 70. *Work:* Mus Mod Art, NY & San Francisco. *Comn:* Logo, Western Asn Art Mus, 69; pub sculpture, Marin Co Civic Ctr, 88. *Exhib:* Sound Sculpture As, Mus Conceptual Art, 70; De Marco Gallery, Edinburgh, Scotland, 72; White Chapel, London, Eng, 72; Student Cult Ctr, Belgrade, Yugoslavia, 74; one-man show, Foksol Gallery, Warsaw, Poland, 75, Mod Art Gallery, Vienna, Austria, 79, Pellegrino Gallery, Bologna, Italy, 79, Kunst Mus, Bern, Switz, 80 & Ctr G Pompidou Mus, Paris, 80. *Collection Arranged:* All Night Sculptures, Mus Conceptual Art, 73; Art Against War, San Francisco Art Inst, 84; Elegant Miniatures from San Francisco, Belca House, Kyoto, Japan. *Pos:* Cur art, Richmond Art Ctr, 68-71; dir, Mus Conceptual Art, 70-84; ed, Vision, Oakland, 75-82. *Teaching:* Instr, Univ Calif, Berkeley, 79, Los Angeles, 86. *Awards:* Nat Endowment Arts, 79, 80 & 84; J S Guggenheim Grant, 80; Travel Grant, Asian Cult Coun, 86. *Bibliog:* Bill Berkson (rev), Artforum, 5/86; David Winter (rev), Artnews, 4/86; Terri Cohn (auth), Tom Marioni Sacred Geometry, Sculpture Mag, 3/98; and others. *Mem:* San Francisco Art Inst (bd dir, 74-). *Media:* Wood. *Publ:* The Return of Abstract Expressionism, 69; The San Francisco Performance, 72; Notes & Scores for Sounds, 72; Vision (California), 75, Vision (Eastern Europe), Vision (New York City), Vision (Word of Mouth), 80 & Vision (Artist Photographs), 81; Writings on Art 1969-1999, Crown Point Press; Beer, Art & Philosophy, Crown Point Press, San Francisco, Calif, 2003. *Dealer:* Margarete Roeder 545 Broadway New York NY; Paule Anglim 14 Gear St San Francisco. *Mailing Add:* 657 Howard San Francisco CA 94105

MARISOL
SCULPTOR
b Paris, France, 1930. *Study:* Ecole Beaux Arts, 49; Art Students League, 50; New Sch, Hans Hofmann Sch, 51-54; Moore Col Art, Philadelphia, Hon DFA, 69, RI Sch Design, Providence, Hon Dr Arts, 86; State Univ NY, Buffalo, Hon DFA, 92. *Work:* Mus Mod Art, NY; Whitney Mus Am Art, NY; Albright-Knox Art Gallery, Buffalo; Mus De Arte Contemporaneo, Caracas, Venezuela; Nat Portrait Gallery, Washington, DC; Rose Art Mus, Brandeis Univ, Waltham, Mass; Hakone Open Air Mus, Japan; Art Inst Chicago; and others. *Exhib:* One-woman exhibs, Sidney Janis Gallery, NY, 66, 75, 84 & 89, Boca Raton Mus Art, Fla, 88, Galerie Tokoro, Tokyo, 89, Nat Portrait Gallery (with catalog), Washington, DC, 91, Tenri Gallery, Cult Inst New York, NY, 92, NJ Ctr Visual Arts (with catalog), NJ, 92 & Marlborough Gallery (with catalog), NY, 98; Forms in Wood, Am Sculpture of the 1950's, Philadelphia Art Mus, 85; The Artist's Mother: Portraits & Homages, Heckscher Mus, Huntington, NY & Nat Portrait Gallery, Washington, 87; Urban Figures, Whitney Mus Am Art at Philip Morris, 88; Body Language: The Figure in the Art of Our Time, Rose Art Mus, Waltham, Mass, 90; Figures of Contemp Sculpture (1978-1990): Images of Man, Isetan Mus Art, Tokyo, Dakimoru Mus Art, Osaka-Umeda & Hiroshima City Mus Contemp Art, 92; The League at the Cape, Provincetown Art Asn & Mus, Mass, 93; Lateinamerikanische Kunst im 20 Jahrhundert, Mus Ludwig & Josef-Haubrich Kunsthalle, Cologne, Ger, 93; Museo de Arte Contempo Ranio, Caracas, Venezuela, 96; Latin Viewpoints: into the Mainstream, Nassau Co Mus Art, NY, 97; The Feminine Image (with catalog), Nassau Co Mus Art, NY, 97; Coming Off the Wall, Susquehanna Art Mus, Pa, 98; Rep in permanent collections at Mus Modern Art, New York City, Whitney Mus Am Art, Albright-Knox Gallery, Buffalo, Hakone Open Air Mus, Tokyo, Nat Portrait Gallery, Washington, Harry N Abrams Collection, New York City, Yale Univ Art Gallery, Art Inst Chicago, Metrop Mus, New York City, numerous others; pub installation Am Merchant Mariner's Memorial, Promenade Battery Park Pier A, Port of NY, New York City; and others. *Awards:* 11th Annual Art Comn Awards, Excellence in Design for Am Merchant Mariner's Mem, Art Comn City New York, 92; Medal of Honor, Nat Arts Club, New York, 95; Gabriela Mistral Inter Am Prize for Cult, Org Am States, 97; and others. *Bibliog:* Margaret R Lunn (auth), Marisol, NJ Ctr Vis Arts, Harvard Printing Co, 93; Roberta Bernstein (auth), Marisol, Art Lift Ltd, NY, 95; Willo Doe (auth), Interview with Marisol, Space, 82-87, 7/97. *Mem:* Am Acad Arts & Letters, 78; Nat Acad. *Publ:* Contribr, Robert Bernstein & Yoshiaki Turo (auths), Marisol, Galerie Tokoro, Tokyo, 89; Carol Anne Munsun (ed), Pop Art: The Critical Dialogue, Univ Mich Res Press, Ann Arbor, 89; Contemporary

American Women Artists, Cedco Publg, San Rafael, 91; Nancy Grove (auth), Magical Mixtures: Marisol Portrait Sculpture, Smithsonian Inst Press for Nat Portrait Gallery, 91; Margaret Lunn (auth), Marisol, NJ Ctr Visual Arts, Harvard Printing Co, 92; and many others. *Dealer:* Marlborough Gallery 40 W 57th St New York NY 10019. *Mailing Add:* 427 Washington St 7th Fl New York NY 10013

MARK, ENID EPSTEIN
PRINTMAKER, PHOTOGRAPHER
b New York, NY, 32. *Study:* Art Students League; Smith Col, BA; West Chester Univ, lithography with Victor Lasuchin. *Work:* Smith Col Mus Art; Univ Pa; Univ Del; Philadelphia Mus Art; Free Libr Philadelphia; Houghton Libr, Harvard Univ; Princeton Univ; Jewish Mus, NY; Israel Mus, Jerusalem; Toledo Mus of Art; Libr Cong. *Comn:* Germantown Friends School, Philadelphia, Pa; Two print ed, Ronbic Editions, Philadelphia, Pa; Nat Libr Can, Ottawa. *Exhib:* Solo exhibs, Swarthmore Col, Pa, 80, Shipley Sch, Bryn Mawr, Pa, 82, Smith Col, Mass, 85 & Princeton Univ Libr; Artist's Bookworks, Albright-Knox Art Gallery, Buffalo, 82; Philadelphia Bookworks, Moore Col Art, 82; Books by Printmakers, Print Club, Philadelphia, 82; Women: Self-Image, Philadelphia Art Alliance, 83; Artists of the Book, Boston Atheneum & Am Craft Mus, NY; Franz Bader Gallery, 88; Princeton Univ, 88; Contemp Philadelphia Artists, Philadelphia Mus Art, 90; Imprints, Six Philadelphia Photogrs, Old Dominion Univ, Norfolk, Va. *Pos:* Artist in residence, Springfield Sch Dist, Pa, 68-69. *Teaching:* Community Arts Ctr, Wallingford, Pa, 81-33. *Awards:* Beaver Col Purchase Award, 80; Del Art Mus Purchase Award, 81; Graphics Award, Cheltenham Arts Ctr, Pa, 83; Third Prize, Am Color Print Soc, Juried exhib, 87 & second prize, 88. *Bibliog:* Susan Teller (auth), Prints by women: A survey of graphic work, Assoc Am Artists, 86; Deborah Curtiss (auth), Introduction to Visual Literacy, Prentice-Hall, 86; Karen Fitzgerald (auth), Making reader friendly books, Ms Mag, 6/87. *Mem:* Am Color Print Soc; Cheltenham Graphics Guild, Pa; Artists Equity Asn; Southern Graphics Coun; Women's Caucus Arts. *Media:* Lithography, Drawing, Non-Silver Photographic Processes. *Publ:* Auth, Promises, 84, The Bewildering Thread, 86 & An Afternoon at Les Collettes, 88, Elm Press; Springs, 90. *Dealer:* Franz Bader Gallery 1701 Pennsylvania Ave Washington DC. *Mailing Add:* 275 S 19th St 3rd Floor Philadelphia PA 19103

MARK, MARY ELLEN
PHOTOGRAPHER
b Philadelphia, Pa, Mar 20, 40. *Study:* Univ Pa, BFA(painting & art hist), 62; Annenberg Sch, Univ Pa, MFA(photojournalism), 64. *Work:* Bibliot Nat, Paris; Australian Nat Gallery. *Exhib:* Women of Photog, Sidney Janis Gallery, NY, 76; Am Images, Int Ctr Photog, NY, 79; Likely Stories, Castelli Graphics, NY, 80; Color as Form, Corcoran Gallery Art, Washington, DC & George Eastman House, NY, 82; Faces, United Nations 40th Anniversary Photog Exhib, Berkeley, Calif, 85; Miami Beach, Walker Art Ctr, Minneapolis, 86; Santa Barbara Contemp Arts Forum, Calif, 86; 50 Yr of Modern Color Photog, Photokina, Cologne, Fed Repub Ger, 86; Ansel Adams & Friends, Scotsdale Ctr Arts, Ariz, 87; Homeless in Am Corcoran Gallery Art, Washington, DC, 88 & traveling; The Instant Likeness, Polaroid Portraits, Nat Portrait Gallery, Washington, DC, 88; solo exhibs, Arthur Ross Gallery, Univ Pa, Philadelphia, 96, Cleveland Mus Art, Ohio, 96, Mus Art, Fort Lauderdale, Fla, 97, El Centro de la Imagen, Mex City, Mex, 98 & Centro Fotografico Alvarez Bravo, Oaxaca, Mex, 98; India: A Celebration of Independence, 1947-1997, Philadelphia Mus Art, Pa, 97, Royal Festival Hall, London, Eng, 98, Palazzo Reale - Arengario, Milan, Italy, 98, Montreal Mus Fine Arts, Que, Can, 99 & Chicago Cult Ctr, 99; Defining Eye: Women Photographers of the 20th Century, St Louis Art Mus, Mo, 98, Mus Fine Arts, Santa Fe, NMex, 98, Mead Mus Art, Amherst, Mass, 98 & Wichita Art Mus, Kans, 99. *Teaching:* Numerous lect series & workshops nationally & internationally. *Awards:* Nat Endowment Arts Grants, 77, 79-80 & 90; John Simon Guggenheim Fel, 94; Int Ctr Photog Journalism Award, 97. *Bibliog:* Mary Ellen Mark: shoots from the heart, New York Woman, 1-2/87; The unflinching eye, New York Times Mag, 7/12/87; article in Bomb Mag, summer 89. *Publ:* Coauth, Streetwise, Univ Pa Press, 85; Homeless in America, Acropolis Books, 88; auth, Portraits, Edition Stemmle, 89; Rolling Stone - The Photographs, Simon & Schuster, 89; 25 Years, A Retrospective Book, Bulfinch Press, 92

MARK, PHYLLIS
SCULPTOR, ENVIRONMENTAL ARTIST
b New York, NY. *Study:* Ohio State Univ; New Sch Social Res, sculpture study with Seymour Lipton. *Work:* Dickerson-White Mus, Cornell Univ; Allentown Mus Art, Pa; RCA Collection; Corcoran Gallery Art, Washington; Ft Wayne Mus Art, Ind; and others. *Comn:* Birmingham Ctr, Mich, 75; Land Sail installation, Hofstra Univ Mus, 90. *Exhib:* Sculpture as Jewelry, Inst Contemp Art, Boston, 73; Works on Paper by Women Artists, Brooklyn Mus, 75; Cast Iron Gallery, 92 & 93; Washington Square Atrium, 93; Soho 20 Gallery, NY, 93, 94 & 95; FFS Gallery, NY, 94, 95 & 96; Guild Hall, East Hampton, NY, 95; Solo exhibs, Ivoryton, Conn, 96, Roger Williams Park, Providence, RI, 96, Stamford Mus, Conn, 96 & Lever House, NY, 96. *Pos:* Bd dir, Soho 20 Gallery, 86- & Artists Representing Environ Arts; ed, The Guild Reporter, Sculptors Guild, 86. *Awards:* Ind Arts Comn & Nat Endowment Arts Grant, 79. *Bibliog:* Ed McCormack, Artspeak, 3/92; Rose Slivka, East Hampton Star, 92, 94 & 95; Williamsport Sun Gazette, 95; and others. *Mem:* Artist Rep Environ Art (mem bd dir & treas, currently); Women's Caucus for Art; Sculptors Guild (bd mem & vpres publs, currently). *Media:* Painted Aluminum, Stainless Steel. *Publ:* Auth, Zen Kustlers Aus New York (exhib catalog), Reinesche Post Rev, 89. *Dealer:* Soho 20 Gallery New York NY 10013. *Mailing Add:* 801 Greenwich St New York NY 10014-1842

MARKARIAN, ALEXIA (MITRUS)
PAINTER, SCULPTOR, DESIGNER
b Binghamton, NY. *Study:* Art Students League, drawing & anatomy studies with Robert Hale; Broome Community Col, State Univ NY, Binghamton, AB. *Work:* Chattahoochee Valley Art Asn, La Grange, Ga. *Comn:* Small Shade Pavilion (sculpture), Cal Trans/City Heights Community Develop Corp, Garden Art Proj Site Specific Pub Art, San Diego, 93. *Exhib:* Solo exhib, Free Fall, Univ St Louis, 88, Dietrich Jenny Gallery, San Diego, 89, Artists Union Gallery, Moscow, USSR, 90, Oneiros Gallery, San Diego, 91, Terra Obscura, Traveling USA & Can, 91-93 & Red Venus Gallery San Diego, 94, Heart in a Fist, Simay Space, San Diego, 2001; group exhibs, Riverside Mus Art, Calif, 86; National Midyear Show, Butler Inst Am Art, Youngstown, Ohio, 86-87; Five Women Artists: A Southern Californiia Perspective, traveling, USA & Can, 86-88; Fla Nat, Fla State Univ, Tallahassee, 88; On the Horizon: Emerging in California, Fresno Arts Ctr & Mus, 88; Bestiary, Women's Bldg, Los Angeles, Calif, 88; Artists Union Gallery, Moscow, USSR, 90; Calif Ctr Arts, Escondido, 93, Centro Cult, Tijuana, Mex, 94; Munic Art Gallery, Los Angeles, 95; Temporary Situations, Mira Costa Col, 96; Hello Again, Oakland Mus Art, Calif, 99; Three Plus Three, Oceanside Mus Art, Oceanside, Calif, 2000; Schneider Mus Art, Ashland, Ore, 2000; Pure Painting, San Diego Visual Arts Prog, Earl & Birdie Taylor Libr, San Diego, Calif, 2006; and others. *Pos:* lectr, San Diego Art Inst Artist Series, 89-90; Isomata Master Class Series, painting, Idyllwild, Calif, 92; lectr, Art Mus Greater Victoria, BC, Can, 93; set designer, Mac Wellmans play A Murder of Crows, San Diego, Calif, 93; originator & producer, Phototropolis: Contemp Photog, Int Photo Exhib, San Diego, Calif, 95; designer, Cinewest Productions film, Love Always, 96. *Awards:* Bellinger Award, Gebbie Found, Chatauqua Exhib, 85; First Award, Fine Arts, Int Soc Airbrush Arts, Pasadena, Calif, 85; Permanent Collection Purchase Award, La Grange Nat, Ga, 88; Artists Fel, Calif Arts Coun, 90. *Bibliog:* Tony di Gessu (prod), interview, Channel 51-TV, San Diego, Calif, 10/26/85; Bill Van Siclen (auth), Art in Rhode Island, Providence J-Bull, 2/86; Leah Ollman (auth), At the Galleries (article), Los Angeles Times, 2/12/88, 10/1/89, 11/20/91; Robert L Pincus (article), San Diego Union Tribune, 10/19/89, 6/15/90, 8/20/92, 6/24/93, 3/16/00, 8/31/00, 5/31/01, 6/29/06; Art in America, Rev of Exhibs, 4/90; Robert L Pincus (auth), Art Review (article), San Diego Union, 12/91; Elizabeth Kidd (auth), Outlook Mag, Vol III, issue 2, (article), Edmonton Art Gallery, 92; Gene Grey (auth), Living (article), Binghamton Press, 2/92; Mus Mod Art San Francisco, Mus Store Catalog, Winter, 96; Susan Subtle (auth), San Francisco Focus, Gift of Garbage (article), 97; Seattle Post Intelligencer, Fashion, 2002. *Mem:* San Diego Art Inst (bd dir, 81-82); Artists Equity (vpres, 84-86); Artists Guild San Diego Mus Art (corresp secy, 84). *Media:* Acrylic, Miscellaneous Media. *Publ:* Illusr, The Red Flower, Crossing Press, 88; contribr, Art Jewlery Today, Schiffer Publ, 2003. *Mailing Add:* 1702 Primrose Dr El Cajon CA 92020-5649

MARKEL, KATHRYN E
DEALER
b Richmond, Va, Oct 19, 46. *Pos:* Co-owner, Kathryn Markel Gallery, New York, currently. *Media:* Work on Paper. *Specialty:* Specialty work on paper by contemporary American artists. *Mailing Add:* 22 Hobart St Bronxville NY 10708

MARKER, MARISKA PUGSLEY
PAINTER, WRITER, LECTURER, COLLECTOR
b San Francisco, Calif. *Study:* With Leon Berkowitz, Robert Newmann, Hank Harmon, Horace Day, Daniel Greene, Albert Handell, Henry Hensche, and others. *Work:* Nat Mus Fine Arts, Valletta, Malta; The White House Artists Easter Collection, Smithsonian Inst, Washington, DC; Fed Reserve Bd Governors Collection, Washington, DC; Dulin Gallery Art, Knoxville, Tenn; and others. *Comn:* Container Corp Am. *Exhib:* Two-person show, Nat Mus Fine Arts, Valletta, Malta, 76; one-person shows, Fed Reserve Bd Governors, Washington, DC, 81 & 84, Va Beach Art Ctr, 83, Gilpin Gallery, The Atholl Series, 88, among others; Continuum V, Dulin Gallery Art, Knoxville, Tenn, 84; US State Dept Art in Embassies Prog, US Embassy, Muscat, Oman, 86-90; and others. *Pos:* Bd mem, Art League Alexandria, Va, 69-70; Artist-in-residence, Hollin Meadows Sch, Fairfax Co, Va, 86. *Teaching:* tchr puppet classas, William Rockhill Nelson Gallery Art, Kansas City, Mo, 40's; tchr painting, Vet Admin Hosp, Kansas City, Mo, 50's; lectr, contemp Am folk art, Alexandria Lyceum, Va, 78, Va Mus, 80. *Awards:* Judged, Maine Artists, The Next Generation, Washington, DC, 90, for Maine Arts Comm & Maine State Soc. *Bibliog:* The Markers at the Museum of Fine Arts, Times Malta, 10/20/76; Teresa Annas (auth), Energetic Marker creates art with depth, 9/4/83; John Levin (auth), Illuminating images, a unique technique, 9/8/83; Pam Frese & Ansley Valentine, Mariska Marker (film), College of Wooster, OH, 2005; and others. *Media:* Miscellaneous media. *Res:* Max Schallinger, a rediscovered artist. *Publ:* Auth, Korean arts have a great potential, Feel of Korea, Holl M Corp, 66; Pebbles in the Pond, 5/20/94; also feature articles in Kansas City Star and catalogs for Northern Va Fine Arts Asn; assorted mag articles, 2000-2003. *Mailing Add:* 9082 Belvoir Woods Pkwy Fort Belvoir VA 22060

MARKETOU, JENNY
VIDEO ARTIST
b Athens, Greece. *Study:* Univ Athens, Greece, BA, 80; Corcoran Sch Art, Washington, DC, BFA, 82; Pratt Inst, Brooklyn, MFA, 86. *Comn:* Astoria: Dreams of New York, Metrop Transit Auth, NY, 92. *Exhib:* 114 + 114, Univ SFla Contemp Art Mus, Tampa, 93; one-man shows, Western Front Gallery, Vancouver, BC, 95, Gallery Anadiel, Old City, Jerusalem, Israel, 96, Aria Kappatos Gallery, Argostoli, Kefalonia, Greece, 97 & In Situ, Snug Harbor, Staten Island, NY, 97; The Invisible Force: Nomadism as Art Practice, Polk Mus Art, Lakeland, Fla, 95; Ethereal Images, Southeast Mus Photog, Daytona Beach Community Col, 96; Artist's Messengers of Peace, Eretz Israel Mus, Tel Aviv, 96; En Route to MEX, ART & IDEA, Old Mexico City, Mex, 96; Int Showcase, Women and the Art of Multimedia, Nat Mus Women

Arts, Washington, DC, 97; I Can Not Take My Eyes Off You (video proj), The Sculpture Garden, NY, 97; Projected Sites, Sixth Biennial Arts & Technol, Cummings Art Ctr, Conn Col, New London, 97. *Awards:* Visual Arts Fel Photog, Nat Endowment Arts, Washington, DC, 91; Found Hellenic Cult Grant, 96; Resident Artist Fel, Ariz State Univ, 97 & Banff Ctr Arts, Alta, Can, 97. *Bibliog:* Sania Page (auth), Women Beyond Borders, Antikenmuseum & Sammlung, 96; Rosa Martinez (auth), Manifesta I, Witte de With Mus Contemp Art, 96; Roy Ascott & Robert Rindler (auths), Techno-Seduction, Cooper Union, 97. *Mailing Add:* c/o Jayne H Baum Gallery 26 Grove St Suite 4C New York NY 10014

MARKLE, GREER (WALTER GREER MARKLE)
MUSEUM DIRECTOR, HISTORIAN
b Port Arthur, Tex, Apr 12, 46. *Study:* Univ Wyoming, BFA, 68; Univ Utah, MA, 76; Univ Ore, PhD, 99. *Collection Arranged:* Contemp Am Prints and Drawings, UMFA Traveling, 78; Utah Wilderness Photography, traveling, 78; Potter and Prints, Sun Valley Ctr, 81; Will Martin Retrospective, Schneider Mus Art, 87; Art of the Orient: Schneider Mus Art, Zundel Col, 88. *Teaching:* Instr art hist, Univ Utah, Salt Lake City, 76-78; lectr art admin, Radcliffe Col, Cambridge, Mass, 78-82; asst prof art hist, S Ore State Col, Ashland, 86-; prof, S Ore Univ. *Mem:* Col Art Asn; Ore Advocates Arts; Am Asn Mus. *Res:* Contemporary Am art and Italian Renaissance art; Diego Rivera's portrait of America: Marxism and Montage. *Publ:* Auth, Marilyn Levine and photorealism, Ceramics Monthly, 76; Utah wilderness photography, Utah Arts Coun, 78; Potters & prints, Sun Valley Ctr, 81; Handbook for traveling exhibitions, Cambridge, Mass. *Mailing Add:* Southern Oregon State Col Art Dept Ashland OR 97520

MARKLE, SAM
DEALER, SCULPTOR
b Winnipeg, Man, 33. *Study:* Self-taught. *Work:* Nat Art Bank, Ottawa; McLaughlin Mus, Oshawa. *Comn:* Neon installations (with Jack Markle), Alcan Aluminum, Head Off, Toronto, 70; United Trust, Head Off, 72, Famous Players Theatre, Four Seasons Hotel, 73, Sunoco Bldg, 73 & Concourse & Plaza, Hudson Bay Co, 73, Toronto, 74. *Exhib:* One-man shows, Pop Sign Art, Gallery Pascal, 64, Alpha 64, Four Seasons Hotel, 64 & Flower & Garden Show & Electric Gallery, Toronto, 71; New Media, Art Gallery Ont, 71; Espace V Gallery, Montreal, 74. *Pos:* Dir, Electric Gallery, Toronto. *Mem:* Prof Art Dealers Can (vpres, 75-78); Can Conf Arts. *Media:* Neon tubing. *Specialty:* Electric art exclusively. *Mailing Add:* The Brothers Markle Inc 3530 Pharmacy Ave Toronto ON MIW 257 Canada

MARKLEY, DORIS YOCUM
PHOTOGRAPHER, WRITER
b Philadelphia, Pa, Feb 1, 1921. *Study:* Philadlephia Mus Sch Indust Art, 39-43; Philadelphia Mus Art, with Martha Zelt, 72-75; Montgomery Co Community Col, 85-90; study with Naomi Limont, Tony Rosati, Hobson Pitman & Douglas Skinner; Temple Univ, Tyler Sch Art, 87-88. *Work:* Friends Cent Sch, Overbrook, Pa; Sun Oil Co, Radnor, Pa; Acad Notre Dame, Villanova, Pa; Southwestern Life Insurance Co. *Exhib:* Outreach, Philadelphia Mus Art, Pa, 77; Univ Del Ann, Newark; Women in the Arts Ann, William Penn Mem Mus, Harrisburg, Pa, 79; Salmagundi Club Ann, NY, 79; Allentown Art Mus Ann, Pa, 79; Hunterdon Art Ctr Nat Print Exhib, Clinton, NJ; Miami Int Print Biennial, Fla, 80; Abington Art Ctr Nat Photog Ann, Pa, 84 & 85; Nat Photog Ann, Perkins, NJ, 87-88. *Pos:* Photog asst, Montgomery Co Community Col, 84-86; feature writer & photogr, Montgomery Life, East Norriton, West Norriton, King of Prussia, Pa, 90-98, Main Line Mag, Berwyn, Pa, 90-95 & Pinhole Photogr, Renner, 94. *Awards:* Purchase Awards, Univ Del, Newark & Rembrant Graphic Arts, Stockton, NJ; Forbes Mag Award Graphics, Salmagundi Club Ann, 79; Best of Show, Ursinus Col, 83; Louise Clearfield Award Photog, Main Line Arts, 86; Grand Prize Black & White Photog, Norristown Borough, Pa, 86, 87 & 88; Mildred Hoffman Humor Award, St David's Christian Writers Conf, 90. *Mem:* Am Color Print Soc; Eastern Pa Chap Soc Children's Bk Writers & Illusrs; Phi Theta Kappa. *Media:* Photography, Written Word, Illustration. *Publ:* Auth, Pinhole J, NMex, 4/88. *Mailing Add:* 2325 Chestnut Ave Norristown PA 19403

MARKMAN, RONALD
PAINTER
b Bronx, NY, May 29, 31. *Study:* Yale Univ, BFA, 57 & MFA, 59. *Work:* Brooklyn Mus, NY; Art Inst of Chicago, Ill; Hirshhorn Mus & Sculpture Garden, Smithsonian Inst, Washington, DC; Metrop Mus of Art, NY; Mus of Mod Art, NY. *Comn:* Christmas Card, Mus Mod Art, 68; Drawing, Rockland State Hosp, NY, 72; five murals, Riley Children's Hosp, 86; Ortho Childcare Ctr, Raritan, NJ, 91. *Exhib:* Recent Acquisitions Show, Mus Mod Art, 59 & 66, Young Am, Whitney Mus Am Art, 60, Am Inst Arts & Letts, 77 & 89, NY; Young Am, Whitney Mus Am Art, 60; Chicago Biennial Print & Drawing Show, Art Inst Chicago, 64; Pa Acad Fine Arts Ann, 67, Tyler Sch Art, 76, Philadelphia; Am Painting, Butler Inst, Youngstown, Ohio, 67; Print Biennial, Brooklyn Mus, 68; Humor, Satire and Irony, New Sch for Social Res, 72; Indianapolis Mus Art, 72 & 74; Work by Students of Josef Albers, Harvard Univ, 74; one-man show, Kanegis Gallery, Boston, 59, Terry Dintenfass Gallery, NY, 65, 66, 68, 71, 76, 79, 82 & 85, Dart Gallery, Chicago, 80, & King Gallery, Indianapolis, 83 & 86; Mitchell Gallery, St John's Col, Annapolis, MD, 2005. *Teaching:* Instr, Univ Fla, 59, Art Inst Chicago, 60-64 & Indiana Univ, 64-95, retired, 95-. *Awards:* Fulbright Fel, 62-63; Lilly open faculty fel, 89; Ind Arts Comn, 90, 93. *Publ:* Metrop Mus of Art, Mus of Modern Art, Brooklyn Mus, Herbert Johnson Mus, Cornell Univ, New York, NY; Art Inst of Chicago, IL; Cincinnati Art Mus, Cincinnati, OH; Joseph H. Hirshhorn Collection. *Mailing Add:* 1623 St Margaret's Rd Annapolis MD 21401

MARKMAN, SIDNEY DAVID
ADMINISTRATOR, HISTORIAN
b New York, NY, Oct 10, 1911. *Study:* Union Col, Schenectady, NY AB, 34; Columbia Univ, MA, 36, PhD, 41. *Teaching:* Prof art hist, Univ Nac de Panama, 41-45; prof art hist, Duke Univ, 47-, actg chmn dept art, 61-62 & 75-78, prof emer, 81-; Morgan Prof, Univ Louisville, 84; distinguished vis prof, Tulane Univ, 86. *Awards:* Asn for Latin Am Art. *Mem:* Soc Archit Historians. *Res:* Colonial art, architecture & urbanization of Central America & Chiapas, Mexico. *Publ:* Auth, San Cristobal de las Casas, Escuela de Estudios Hispano Am, Seville, Spain, 63; Colonial Architecture of Antigua Guatemala, Am Philos Soc, Philadelphia, 66; Colonial Central America, A Bibliography, Ariz State Univ Press, 77; Architecture and Urbanization in Colonial Chiapas, Mexico, Am Philos Soc Philadelphia, 83; Architecture & Urbanization in Colonial Central Am, Ariz State Univ Press, 93 & 94. *Mailing Add:* 919 Urban Ave Durham NC 27701-1503

MARKOWITZ, MARILYN
PAINTER, PRINTMAKER
b New York, NY. *Study:* Colo Col, BA, 63; Univ Colo, Boulder, MA, 71. *Work:* State of Colo Art in Pub Places, Univ Colo, Colorado Springs & Boulder. *Comn:* Painting, State of Colo, Colorado Springs, 81. *Exhib:* Solo exhibs, Brena Gallery, Denver, Colo, 75, Albatross Gallery, Boulder, Colo, 79, Carson-Sapiro Gallery, Denver, Colo, 80, Univ Colo, Colorado Springs, 82, Art Resources Gallery, Denver, 83, Western Nebr Art Ctr, Scotts Bluff & Reiss Gallery, Denver, 86; Hassel-Haesler Gallery, Denver, 92; Art of Craft, Denver, 93; Pinache, Denver, 94; Univ S NMex, 96; Nat Collage soc, Elyria, Ohio, 97; Curtis Ctr Arts & Humanities, Greenwood, Colo, 97; New World Art Ctr, NY, 98; Laura Knott Gallery, Bradford Col, Haverhill, Mass, 98; Alchemy, Nabisco Gallery, East Hanover, NJ, 200; plus many others. *Teaching:* Instr art, Dist No 11 Colorado Springs, 63-69 & Univ Colo, 70-71. *Awards:* Award, Boulder Fine Art Ctr, 71 & 72; Nat Asn Women Artists Award, 77, 79, 85 & 86; Art in Pub Places Award, State of Colo, 81. *Bibliog:* Am Artists Mag, 6/78; Very Important Women, Denver Mag; One Source: Sacred Journeys. *Mem:* Nat Asn Women Artists; Layerist Soc Am; Nat Asn Women Artists. *Media:* Acrylics, Oil; Sand. *Publ:* Contribr, La Revue Moderne, Paris, France, 80; Layering, an art of time and space, Empire Mag, 91; Very important women, Denver Post; One Source: Sacred Journeys, 97; Bridging Time and Space, 98. *Mailing Add:* 819 10th St Boulder CO 80302-7551

MARKOWSKI, EUGENE DAVID
PAINTER, SCULPTOR
b St Louis, Mo, Sept 16, 31. *Study:* Washington Univ Sch Fine Art, BFA, 60; Univ Pa Sch Fine Art, MFA, 61. *Work:* Minn Mus Art, St Paul; Lauren Rogers Mus Art, Laurel, Miss; Philip Morris Corp & First & Merchants Bank, Richmond, Va; NY Bank for Savings; Guaranty Savings & Loan, Charlottesville, Va. *Comn:* Chapel, Holy Comforter Roman Cath Church, Charlottesville, Va, 82; stained glass windows, St Mary's Roman Cath Church, Lovingston, Va, 83; sculpture (wood), St George's Roman Cath Church, Scottsville, Va, 83; painting, Civil War Trust, Washington, 92. *Exhib:* Northern Ill Univ Nat Drawing Competition, 71; Nat Drawing Competition, Minn Mus Art, 71; Int Print & Drawing Competition, Alta Col Art, 72; Regional Painting Competition, Montgomery Mus Fine Arts, 75; Novumn Gallery Ltd, Basel, Switz, 92; Frank Bustamante Gallery, NY, 91; and others. *Pos:* Art critic, Cablevision, Charlottesville, 72-; chmn, studio art dept, Univ Va, 86-; chmn Studio,Trinity Univ, Wash DC, 91-. *Teaching:* Asst prof painting, Univ Pa, 61-68 & Montgomery Col, Rockville, Md, 68-70; assoc prof painting, Univ Va, Charlottesville, 70-87; prof art, Trinity Univ, Washington, DC 88-. *Awards:* Drawing Award, Smithsonian Inst, 81; Sesquicentennial Associateship, Res Italy, Univ Va, 85; Fulbright Fel, research in India, Coun Int Exchange Scholars, 86. *Mem:* Col Art Asn Am; assoc mem Int Ctr Art Intelligence; Fullbright Asn. *Media:* Oil on Canvas; Wood. *Res:* Monuments and people of India, Fulbright to India, 87. *Specialty:* Painting; Schulpture. *Publ:* Auth, The Art of Photography: Image and Illusion, Prentice-Hall, 84; Art Fraud and authentication, Harry N Abrams, 2001. *Dealer:* Novumn Gallery Ltd Binningerstsrasse 82-88 Basel-Alischwil Switzerland; Artisans Gallery 4834 MacArthur Blvd NW Washington DC 20007; Voltz Gallery Poligono 2 Parcela 26 07340 Alaro Baleares Spain; Dist Fine Arts 1726 Wis Ave NW Wash DC 20007. *Mailing Add:* 4706 Foxhall Crescents NW Washington DC 20007

MARKS, LESTER
COLLECTOR
b June 53. *Pos:* Bd mem Cult Arts Council of Houston/Harris Co; patron, Seattle Art Mus; bd dir, Art League Houston, 2004-. *Awards:* Named one of Top 200 Collectors, ARTnews Magazine, 2004. *Mailing Add:* 2808 Rich Blvd Houston TX 77005-3046

MARKS, MATTHEW STUART
ART DEALER
b New York, NY, Nov 14, 62. *Study:* Columbia Univ 80-82, with Milton Resnick; Bennington Col, BA, 85. *Collection Arranged:* From the Collection of Matthew Marks, American Prints 1860-1960 (auth, catalog), Bennington Col, 85; British Modernist Prints 1900-1950 (auth, catalog), 85 & Je suis le cahier: The Sketchbooks of Picasso (auth, catalog), 86, Pace Gallery, NY. *Pos:* Consult, Pace Gallery, New York, 82-86; trustee, Bennington Col, Vt, 85-89; dir, Anthony d'offay Gallery, London, 87-89; pres, Matthew Marks, Inc, 81-89 & 90-; bd mem, Merce Cunningham Dance Co, 93-96. *Bibliog:* Rising Stars Under 40, Art News, 95; Portrait of the Dealer as a Young Man, Out, 11/97; and numerous articles in art mags. *Res:* 19th and 20th century European and American art; contemp Am art & European art. *Publ:* Auth, Henry Farrer's early etchings of New York, Imprint, 82; Provincetown prints, Print Collector's Newlett, 84; The graphic work of Lucian Freud, Print Quart, 86. *Mailing Add:* 523 W 24th St New York NY 10011

MARKS, ROBERTA BARBARA
SCULPTOR, COLLAGE PAINTER
b Savannah, Ga. *Study:* Univ Miami, Fla, BFA, 80; Univ S Fla, MFA, 81. *Work:* Victoria & Albert Mus, London, Eng; Galerie du Manoir, La Chaux-de-Fonds, Switz; AT&T Corp, Philip Johnson Bldg, NY; IBM Corp, Jacksonville, Fla; NMex Mus Fine Arts, Santa Fe; Ball State Univ, Ind; Mus of Arts & Scis, Santa Fe, NM; Notre Dame Univ, Ind; Rochester Inst Tech, NY; Smithsonian Instn, Washington; numerous others. *Exhib:* Craft Multiples, Renwick Gallery, Smithsonian Inst, Washington, DC, 75; 1976 Biennial Exhib, Mint Mus Art, Charlotte, NC, 76; A Painter and a Ceramist, Galerie Du Manoir, Switz, 78; 50 National Women in Art, Edison Community Col Mus Fine Art, Ft Myers, Fla, 82; The Primal Vessel, Garth Clark Gallery, Los Angeles, 83; Southeastern Ctr for Contemp Art, Winston-Salem, NC, 85; Key West Art & Hist Soc, E Martello Mus & Gallery, 85; New Gallery, Univ Miami, Fla, 87; Katie Gingras Gallery, Milwaukee, Wis, 87; Helander Gallery, Palm Beach, Fla, 88; Galerie Scapa, Bern, Switz, 88; Deux Femmes', East Martello Mus, Key West, Fla, 90; paintings, Roberta B Marks, Biel, Switz, 90; one artist exhib, Lucky Street Gallery, Key West, Fla, 87-2004, Barbara Gillman Gallery, Miami, Fla, 91 & 94, Galerie Arte Krone, Biel, Switz, 94 & Galerie Jones, Cortaillod-Neuchatel, Switz, 95, 98, 2003, Key West Mus Art & History, 2003; group exhib, Art Miami 95, Miami Beach, Fla, 95, Oxidation/Burial project, I/O Gallery, New Orleans, La, 97, Women's Art, Woodenhead Gallery, Key West, Fla, 98, Art in the Park, 98 & Fort Zachary Taylor, Key West, Fla, 98, Anderson Contemp Art, Santa Fe, 2004. *Collection Arranged:* Lake Superior Int Craft Exhib, Tweed Mus Art, Univ Minn, 72-75 & 77. *Pos:* Cur, The Valley of Oaxaca: The Zapotecs, Ceramic Sculpture, Univ S Fla, Tampa, 81; cur, Two-Dimensional Key West E Martello Mus, Key West, Fla, 85. *Teaching:* Vis artist ceramics, Univ SFla, Tampa, 76; instr ceramics, Rochester Inst Technol, NY, 76, Art Inst Chicago, 77, NC State Univ, Raleigh, 81, Nat Coun Educ for Ceramic Arts, Boston Univ, Mass, 84, Brookfield Craft Ctr, Conn, 85 & Univ Wis, Milwaukee, 87; Fla Key Comm Col, Key West, Fla, 96-; Armory Art Ctr, Palm Beach, Fla, 2002; Anderson Ranch Art Sch, Snowmass, Colo, 2004. *Awards:* Best in Show, Florida Craftsmen, Ceramic Monthly Publ, 73; Purchase Award, Am Crafts Coun, Am Bankers Insurance Co, 76; Merit Award, Ceramic League, Miami, Fla, 79; Lloyd E Herman Merit Award, Smithsonian's Renwick Gallery, Washington, DC, 81; Visual Artists Fel S Fla, 90. *Bibliog:* Judi Bradford (auth), Deux Artists, Solares Hill (pp 26-27), 3/90 & Letting go (pp 26-17) 11/92; Anita Geiser-Coref (auth),Neue Bilder, Ger, 93; Barbara Bowers (auth), Roberta Mark: Collages, Tropic Keys Mag, 1/94. *Mem:* Artists Equity Asn Inc; Am Crafts Coun; Nat Coun Educ Ceramic Arts; World Crafts Coun; Fla Craftsmen; Int Sculpture Ctr. *Media:* Assemblage, Collage. *Specialty:* Contemp Art. *Publ:* Auth, International Leaders of Achievement, Cambridge, Eng, 88-90. *Dealer:* Garth Clark Gallery 24 W 57th St New York NY 10019; Barbara Gillman Gallery, Miami, FL. *Mailing Add:* 1800 Atlantic Blvd Apt C-440 Key West FL 33040

MARKSON, EILEEN
LIBRARIAN
b New York, NY, Mar 13, 39. *Study:* Lewis & Clark Col, BA, 60; Ecole du Louvre, Institut de Phonetique, Paris, France, 62; New York Univ, MA, 64; Queens Col, MLS, 73. *Pos:* Dir lect prog, Archaeol Inst Am, 66-73, asst secy-treas, 68-73; head, Art & Archaeol Libr, Bryn Mawr Col, 73-96 & Rhys Carpenter Libr Art, Archaeol & Cities, 97-; copy ed, Art Documentation, 97-. *Mem:* Art Libr Soc N Am (exec bd, 85-86); Archaeol Inst Am. *Interests:* Classical archaeology; Dutch seventeenth century painting; Impressionism. *Publ:* Auth, Atlas of the Greek World (rev), Art Documentation, 2/82; co-auth, Archaeology resources in libraries: are they accessible?, Art Libr J, 12/87; auth, Raymond M Holt, Planning Library Building and Facilities: From Concept to Completion (review), Metuchen Scarecrow Press 89, Art Documentation, Winter issue, vol 9 no 4; Frances Van Keuren, Guide to Research in Classical Art and Archaeology, Chicago and London; Am Libr Asn 91 (review), Art Documentation, Summer issue, vol 11, no 2, 92; coauth, Claireve Grandjouan, Hellenistic Relief Molds from the Athenian Agora, Princeton, NJ: Am Sch Classical Studies at Athens, 89 (Hesperia: Supplement XXIII). *Mailing Add:* Rhys Carpenter Libr for Art Archaeology & Cities Bryn Mawr Col 101 N Merion Bryn Mawr PA 19010

MARKUSEN, THOMAS ROY
CRAFTSMAN, SCULPTOR
b Chicago, Ill, Jan 1, 40. *Study:* Univ Wis, Madison, BS, 65, MS, 66. *Work:* Am Craft Mus, NY; Lannan Found Art Mus, Palm Beach, Fla; Wustum Mus Fine Arts, Racine, Wis; Hand Workshop Gallery, Richmond, Va; Vatican Mus, Rome; and others. *Comn:* Sculpture Bed, Elson, Atlanta, GA, 80; Altar set, Newmen Oratory, Brockport, NY, 75-76; Altar set, First Univeralist Church, Syracuse, NY, 88. *Exhib:* Contemp Am Silversmiths & Goldsmiths, Corcoran Gallery, Washington, DC, 73; Int Goldsmiths & Weavers, Albright-Knox Art Gallery, Buffalo, NY, 74; 275 Yrs of Am Metalsmithing, Mus of Contemp Crafts, NY & Cranbrook Acad of Arts Mus, Bloomfield Hills, Mich, 75; one-man, Craft Company Sixth, Rochester, NY, 84; 41st Int Eucharistis Exhib of Liturgical Arts, Civic Ctr, Philadelphia, 76; Solid Wrought Iron, Southern Ill Univ Mus & Art Gallery, Carbondale, 76; Arts/Objects USA, Lee Nordness Gallery & Johnson Wax Found, NY, 76; and others. *Pos:* Dir & organizer metal exhib, Fine Arts Gallery, State Univ NY Col, Brockport, 71-78; guest lectr metalsmithing, Univ Wash, Mont State Univ, Va Commonwealth Univ, Syracuse Univ, State Univ NY Col, New Paltz, US Embassy-Mexico & Seventh World Craft Conf, Mex, 75-77; Chairman, 85. *Teaching:* Instr crafts, Univ Wis, Madison, 65-66; asst prof metalsmithing, Radford Col, Va, 66-68; assoc prof metalsmithing, State Univ NY Col, Brockport, 68-80, prof, 80-. *Awards:* Fac Res Fel, State Univ NY Res Found, 71 & 79; Craftsmen Fel, Nat Endowment for the Arts, 75; Tech Res Grant, Soc N Am Goldsmiths & Nat Endowment for the Arts, 77. *Bibliog:* Leon Nigrosh (auth), Forged iron today, Craft Horizons, 2/76; Jack O'Field (filmmaker), Hands: The Arts & Crafts of America, Raymond Lowry Int Productions, 76; Dona Z Meilach (auth), Decorative, Sculpture Ironwork, Crown, 77; Katherine Pearson (auth), American Carft, Stewart, Tabori Chang. *Mem:* World Crafts Coun; Am Craftsmen Coun; Artist & Blacksmiths Asn of N Am; Soc N Am Goldsmiths; NY State Craftsmen. *Media:* Metal, Wood. *Mailing Add:* 17218 Roosevelt Hwy Kendall NY 14476-9762

MARLATT, MEGAN BRONWEN
PAINTER
b Indianapolis, Ind, 57. *Study:* Memphis Col Art, Tenn, BFA, 81; Skowhegan Sch Painting & Sculpture, Maine, scholar, 85; Rutgers Univ, New Brunswick, NJ, State Coun Arts Grant, 85, MFA, 86. *Comn:* Site-specific asphalt & grass painting, Louisville Visual Art Asn, Ky, 91; fresco mural, Charlottesville City Hall Annex Bldg, Va, 91; site-specific asphalt & grass painting, Atlanta Arts Festival, Piedmont Park, 91; site-specific asphalt painting, Hillwood Mus, CW Post Campus, Long Island Univ, NY, 93; fresco mural, Emmanual Episcopal Church, Rapidan, Va, 96. *Exhib:* Solo exhibs, Gallery 201, Rutgers Univ, New Burnswick, NJ, 86, Fayerweather Gallery, Univ Va, Charlottesville, 90, Yvonne Rapp Gallery, Louisville, Ky, 91, Univ Ark, Little Rock, 91, DC Arts Ctr, 92, Art Nürnberg 8, Festival Arts, Ger, 93 & ARC Gallery, Chicago, 97; Va Mus Fine Arts, 90 & 93; Fresco, Elan Vital Gallery, Boston, 95; Picture This: artists interpret text, ACT Gallery, Detroit, Mich, 96; Spark Gallery, Denver, Colo, 96; Univ Calif, San Diego, 96. *Pos:* Adj fac, Ocean Co Col, Toms River, NJ, 87-88; assoc prof art, Univ Va, Charlottesville, 88-; panelist, Southeast Col Art Conf, Memphis, Tenn, 92 & Col Art Asn, NY, 94; juror, Asn Artists Winston-Salem, NC, 95. *Teaching:* Artist-in-residence, Watershed Ctr Ceramic Arts, North Edgecomb, Maine, 90, Cite Int Arts, Paris, 92 & Va Mus Fine Arts Affiliate Prog, 93; vis artist, Hampton Univ, Va, 92; vis artist & juror, Vanderbilt Univ, Nashville Tenn, 93. *Awards:* Fel Exchange Prog & Summer Res Grant, Univ Va, 90; Nat Endowment Arts Fel Painting, 95; Artist Fel, Va Comn Arts, 96. *Bibliog:* Ann Glenn Crowe (auth), Art papers, Objects Art, 2/91; Thomas Kliemann (auth), Nurnbergerer zeituing, Art Nurnberg 8, 4/24/93; Michael Becker (auth), Nurnberger nachrichten, Art Nurnberg 8, 4/24/93. *Publ:* Contribr & critic, Modern art, the individual vs the community, Arts Quart, spring 88. *Mailing Add:* 254 Belleview Ave Orange VA 22960

MARLOR, CLARK STRANG
HISTORIAN, COLLECTOR
b Camden, NJ, Nov 18, 22. *Study:* Carnegie-Mellon Univ, BFA, 45; Univ Mich, MA, 46; NY Univ, DEduc, 61. *Collection Arranged:* John Barnard Whittaker (with catalog), 68 & Eleanor C Bannister (with catalog), 71, Adelphi Univ; Benjamin Eggleston, Long Island Hist Soc, 75. *Teaching:* Prof, Adelphi Univ, 56-86. *Mem:* Salmagundi Club (mem, libr comt & bicentennial comt). *Res:* 19th century American artists. *Collection:* American artists of the 19th and early 20th centuries. *Publ:* John B Whittaker, Brooklyn artist, Antiques, 11/71; A quest for independence: the SIA, Arts & Antiques, 81; The Society of Independent Artists: Exhibition Record and History, 84; Salons of America, 1922-1936, 91; Brooklyn Index of Artists, 92; and others. *Mailing Add:* 35 Prospect Park W Apt 6C Brooklyn NY 11215

MARLOW, AUDREY SWANSON
PAINTER, DESIGNER
b New York, NY. *Study:* Art Students League, with Robert Brackman, Robert Beverly Hale & Raphael Soyer, 51-55. *Work:* NY Univ, City Hall, NY; Middle Island Pub Libr, Long Island; Sr Citizens Complex, Newark, NJ; Little Flower Childrens Servs, Wading River, NY. *Comn:* Millicent Fenwick, comn by Regency Housing Partners, Newark, NJ, 86; Harrison J Goldin, NY Comptroller, NY, 86; Monsignor John Fagan with 7 members of family, Quoque, NY, 88; Mother Katharine Drexel & 3 children, comn by Monsignor Fagan, Hanging at St Theresa of the child Jesus Convent, wading River, NY, 90; Mother Franceska Seidliska & 3 children, St Theresa of the Child Jesus Convent, 93. *Exhib:* Hudson Valley Artists, White Plains, NY, 79, 81, 83, 85, 88-90; Nat Acad Design, NY, 80 & 85; one-person show, Salmagundi Club, NY, 85; Parish Art Mus, Southampton, NY, 86; Pastel Invitational, Palais Rameau, Lisle, France, 88; Sumner Mus, Washington, 92. *Pos:* Package designer & illus, Prince Matchabelli Perfume Co (freelance), 57-68; textile designer, RS Assocs, New York, 60-72. *Teaching:* Design, Phoenix Sch Design, 72-73; demonstrs, pastel, Catharine Lorillard Wolfe Art Club, 85 & Hudson Valley Artists, 88. *Awards:* Five Awards, Salmagundi Club Shows, 78; Gold Medal, Nat League Am Pen Women, Cork Gallery, Lincoln Ctr, 85; Pastel Soc Am, Artists Professional League, 87. *Mem:* Am Artists Prof League; Knickerbocker Artists; Hudson Valley Artists; Pastel Soc Am; Nat League Am Pen Women (pres 80-82). *Media:* Multimedia. *Publ:* Illus, Breads of Many Lands, 66 & 4 H Club Bakes Bread, J Walter Thompson Advert Agency, 66; Anna Smith Strong and the Setauket Spy Ring, Peter Randall, 91. *Mailing Add:* 147 Northside Rd Wading River NY 11792

MARLOWE, WILLIE
PAINTER
b Whiteville, NC, Jan 17, 43. *Study:* Summer study, Pennsylvania Acad Fine Arts, 64; East Carolina Univ, BS, 65; Univ Idaho, MFA, 69; Post-graduate study, Mexican Culture and Civilization, Merida, Mex, Peace Col, Raleigh, NC, 93. *Work:* Wexford Arts Centre, Ireland; Albany Inst Hist & Art, NY; State Univ NY Art Mus, Albany; Schenectady Mus, NY; Greenville Mus Art, NC; Fondo del Sol, Visual Arts Centre, Washington, DC; Rocky Mount Art Center, Rocky Mount, NC. *Comn:* modular installation, Greenhut Gallery, Albany, NY, 93; modular paintings, Art Gallery Ltd, New Bern, NC, 2000. *Exhib:* Fire and Ice, Attleboro Mus, Mass, 98; Annual Juried Exhib, Nexus Gallery, New York City, 98 & 99; solo shows, Mint Mus Art, Charlotte, NC, 71, Schenectady Mus, NY, 75, Crosscurrents, Greenville Mus Art, NC, 82 & 97 & 10 Yr Retrospective, Wexford Arts Centre, Ireland, 98, Fonoo del Sol Visual Arts Center, Wash, DC, 2002, Barrett Art Center, Poughkeepsie, NY, 2002, Artemisia Gallery, Chicago, Ill, 2003, and others; group show, Int Art Expo, Masterpiece Art

Center, Taipei, Taiwan, 98 & Post Millennial Musings, Artemisia Gallery, Chicago, Ill, 2000; Reprize, Int Invitational Show, Wexford Arts Ctr, Wexford, Ireland, 2002; AIR Gallery, NY, 2001, 04 & 05. *Pos:* Partners of the Americas, Lectures at the US Embassy and at Colleges in Barbados, Bridgetown, Barbados, West Indies, 86; vis artist, Univ Ga Studies Abroad Program, Cortona, Italy, 89; vis artist, Wexford Arts Center, Wexford, Ireland, 98; artist-in-residence, The Millay Colony for the Arts, Austerlitz, NY, 99; International Artist Residency Program, Cill Rialaig, Ballinskelligs, Ireland, 2004. *Teaching:* prof, dept visual arts, Sage Col of Albany, NY, 77-87, chmn 79-87, 2004-; Sage at Oxford, Somerville Col, Oxford Univ, England, 92; Celtic Connections, Sage Col Int Studies abroad program, Trinity Col, Dublin, Ireland & Straithclyde Univ, Glasglow, Scotland, 2001; resident, The Emily Harvey Found, Venice, Itlay, 2006. *Awards:* Lewis Swyer Mem Award, 95; FJ Carlson Mem Award, 95; Purchase Award, Schenectady Mus, NY, 98; Fac Res Develop Grant, The Sage Cols, 78, 81, 84, 91 & 95; Spec Opportunity Stipend, The Art Ctr of Capital Dist, Troy, NY, NY Found for Arts, 91, 92, 93, 96, 98, 2002 & 2003. *Bibliog:* Nancy Norman, Arts panorama (interview), WMHT TV, 88; Bernice Steinbaum, The definitive American contemporary quilt (interview), Bernice Steinbaum Gallery, NYC, 91; Chuck Welch (auth), Eternal network, Univ Calgary Press, 95. *Mem:* WCA; Orgn for Women Artists; Fulton St Gallery; Artists' Equity; Albany Ctr Gallery (bd dir, 96-2000, chmn arts comt, 97, mem arts comt, 97-2000); Albany Inst Hist & Art, 99-; Artemisia Gallery, Chicago, Ill, 2001-03. *Media:* Miscellaneous Media. *Interests:* Travel, visual poetry. *Collection:* Indian and Persian miniatures. *Publ:* illusr, Healing, Color Cover Vol 2, Sacramento, Calif, 93; contribr, Reticular 44, Visual Poetry, Buchlabor, Germany, 93, Spinne - A Visual Poetry Publication, Dusseldorf, Germany & Common Sense, Almanac of Art & Literature, Kowalski & Tarlatt, 97. *Dealer:* Artforms Gallery 5 New Karner Rd Guilderland NY 12084; Lou Proctor Art Gallery Ltd 502 Pollock St New Bern NC 28508; Gallery C, Wade Ave, Raleigh, NC; Martinez Gallery, 3 Broadway, Troy, NY; Deborah Davis Fine Art, Inc, 345 Warren St, Hudson, NY. *Mailing Add:* 820 Cortland St Albany NY 12203

MARON, JEFFREY
SCULPTOR, PAINTER, COPPER ALLOY
b New York, NY, Feb 7, 49. *Study:* Washington Univ, St Louis, BA, 71, MFA, 73. *Work:* Mus Mod Art, Mexico City; Hakone Mus, Hakone, Japan; United States Embassy, Tokyo, Japan; The Lighthouse Pub Comn, NY, 94; Sumitomo Corp, Kobe, Japan. *Comn:* Oliver Carr Corp, Washington, DC; Philadelphia Sci Ctr, Pa; Koll Corp, Calif; Hartwell Bldg, Pittsburgh, Pa; The Lighthouse Inc, New York City. *Exhib:* Solo exhibs, Minami Gallery, Tokyo, Japan, 75, United States Info Serv, Am Cult Ctrs in Nagoya, Osaka, Fukuoka & Sapporo, Japan, 75, Alexander F Milliken Gallery, NY, 77-79, Martha White Gallery, Louisville, Ky, 81, Marisa del Re Gallery, NY, 83, 84, PS1 (Inst Art & Urban Resources), NY, 86 & Stephen Rosenberg Gallery, NY, 93; Art et Industrie, 10th Ann Exhib, 87; Lillian Heidenberg Gallery, NY, 88; Selected Sculpture, Kurts Bingham Gallery, Memphis, 94; ACA Gallery, NY, 96; Westwood Gallery, NY. *Awards:* Fulbright Hayes Grant to Japan, 74-75; Pollock Krasner Found Award, 89; Nat Endowment Arts, 74, 78 & 86. *Bibliog:* James Horwitz (auth), Olympic Tower of Power, Cosmopolitan Mag, 12/31/81; Susan A Harris (auth), Jeffrey Maron, Arts Mag, 11/84; Andrew Bill (auth), Chair Flair, Town & Country Mag, 5/87. *Media:* Copper Alloy. *Mailing Add:* 248 Lafayette St New York NY 10012

MARONEY, DALTON
SCULPTOR
b Greenville, Tex, July 9, 47. *Study:* E Tex State Univ, BS, 69; Univ Okla, MFA, 72. *Work:* Arco, Dallas, Tex & Anchorage, Alaska; Prudential, Newark, NJ; IBM, Washington, DC. *Exhib:* Solo exhibs, Dallas Mus Art, Tex, 83-84, D W Gallery, Dallas, Tex, 87, San Antonio Art Inst, Tex, 89 & Dalton Maroney Gallery, Pitsburg State Univ, Pittsburg, Kans, 96; Excellence '86 & '87, Tex Sculpture Asn, Dallas, Tex, 86 & 87; 2D/3D Frito Lay Corp, Plano, Tex, 87; Magic & Ritual Objects, Alexander Hoague Gallery, Univ Tulsa, 87; 10th Ann Exhib, Austin Vis Arts Asn, Tex, 87; Third Coast Review: A Look at Art in Texas, traveling exhib, Aspen Art Mus, Colo, 87-88; Renwick Gallery, Nat Mus Am Art, Washington, DC, 89; The Vessel, Dallas, Tex, 90; Woodworks, Arlington Mus Art, Tex, 90. *Pos:* Asst dir, John Michael Kohler Arts Ctr, Sheboygan, Wis, 72-73. *Teaching:* Asst prof art, Morningside Col, Sioux City, Iowa, 73-76; instr, Pittsburg State Univ, Pittsburg, Kans, 76-77; asst prof, Univ Tex, Arlington, 79-84, assoc prof, 84-. *Awards:* Visual Arts Fel, Nat Endowment Arts, 86-87. *Bibliog:* Jana Vander Lee (auth), article, Art Space, summer, 82; Susan Freudenheim (auth), Making art against the current, Tex Homes, 4/84 & Dalton Maroney at the Dallas Museum, Art Am, summer 84. *Mailing Add:* 2601 Burning Tree Ct Arlington TX 76014

MARQUIS, RICHARD
CRAFTSMAN
b Bumblebee, Ariz, 54. *Study:* Univ Calif, Berkeley, MA, 72. *Work:* Am Craft Mus & Corning Mus Glass, NY; Los Angeles Co Mus Art, Calif; Philadelphia Mus Art, Pa; Seattle Art Mus, Wash; Smithsonian Inst, Washington, DC; Auckland (New Zealand) Art Mus. *Exhib:* Am Glass Today, Oakland Mus, 79; one-person exhibs, Foster White Gallery, 86, Dowse Art Mus, Wellington, NZ, 87, Betsy Rosenfield Gallery, Chicago, 87, 89, 91, 93 & 94, Kurland/Summers Gallery, Los Angeles, 87, 88 & 91, Auckland Art Mus, NZ, 89, Louise Allrich Gallery, San Francisco, 89 & Sandra Ainsley Art Forms, Toronto, Can, 90 Ellery Brown Gallery, Seattle, 94, 99, 2001, Cafe Florian, Venice, 98, Galerie Rob Van Den Doel, The Hague, The Neth, 2000; New Glass, Gallery Nakama, Tokyo, 89; Craft Today: USA Int Touring Exhib, Am Craft Mus, 89-91; Chicago Int New Art Forms Expo, Betsy Rosenfield Gallery, 92; Elliott Brown Gallery, Seattle, Wash, 94, 96 & 98; Boston Mus of Fine Arts, 97; Los Angeles Co Mus of Art, 2000; Seattle-Tacoma Airport, Washington, 2001. *Awards:* Nat Endowment Arts Grants, 74, 78 & 84; Univ Calif-Los Angeles Research Grants, 79, 80, 81 & 82; Senior Fulbright Grants, NZ, 81 & 88; Distinguished Aliorvus award, Univ. Calif., Berkeley, 2000; Outstanding Achievement in Glass, Urban Glass, Brooklyn. *Bibliog:* Frantz, Susanne K. (auth) Marquis at the Caffe Florian, American Craft Magazine, 99. *Mem:* Fel Am Crafts Coun. *Publ:* Tina Oldknow (auth, monogr), Richard Marquis Objects, Univ Wash Press, 97

MARRERO, MARLO R
PHOTOGRAPHER, SCULPTOR
b Bristol, Conn, Nov 18, 69. *Study:* Univ Conn, with William E Parker, BFA, 92; Hartford Art Sch, with Mary Frey & Ellen Carey, MFA, 97. *Exhib:* Don't I Know You?, LACPS, Los Angeles, 94; The Ubiqustous Bead, Bellevue Mus Art, Wash, 96; Rebellious Bead, Mus of Southwest, Midland, Tex, 97. *Teaching:* instr photog, Central Conn State Univ, New Britan, 98 & Miss Porter's Sch, Farmington, Conn, 98-. *Awards:* Art Matters Fel, Art Matters Found, 95; Visual Arts Grant, Conn Comn of Arts, 2000. *Mem:* Col Art Asn; Soc Photog Educ; Circles, Ctr for Photog (dir, 98-99). *Media:* Fibers. *Publ:* contribr, Col Artists Visual Excess, Hartford Courant, 96, CT Student Wins Right to Reinstate Censored Artwork, Nat Campaign For Freedom of Expression, 96, Art Exhib Unites Three Artists, Hartford Courant, 98 & Marlo Marrero's Constellation, EL Extra News, 99

MARRIOTT, WILLIAM ALLEN
PAINTER, EDUCATOR
b Pontiac, Mich, July 17, 42. *Study:* Ctr Creative Studies, Col Art & Design; Wayne State Univ, BFA; Yale Univ, MFA; study with Lester Johnson, Irving Kriesberg, Nicholas Carone, Michael Goldberg, Robert Wilbert, David Mitchell, Gabor Peterdi & George Kubler. *Work:* Wayne State Univ, Detroit; The New Mus, NY. *Exhib:* Drawings USA 1975, Minn Mus Art, St Paul, 75; 5th Int Miniature Print Competition, Pratt Graphics Ctr, NY, 75; Nat Invitational Drawing Exhib, Southern Ill Univ, Carbondale, 75; 1977 Artists Biennial, New Orleans Mus Art, 77; 45th Southeastern Competition for Painting and Sculpture, Southeastern Ctr Contemp Art, 75. *Teaching:* Assoc prof painting, drawing & printmaking, Univ Ga, Athens, 67-. *Awards:* Purchase Awards, Appalachian Nat Drawing Competition, Appalachian State Univ, 74 & 45th Southeastern Competition for Painting & Sculpture, Southeastern Ctr Contemp Art, 77. *Media:* Drawing, Photography. *Mailing Add:* 588 Meigs St Athens GA 30601-2434

MARRON, DONALD BAIRD
COLLECTOR
b Goshen, NY, July 21, 34. *Study:* Baruch Sch Bus, 57. *Pos:* Mem Pres Comn, on The Arts and The Humanities, formerly; vchmn, Calif Inst for the Arts, formerly; vchmn, bd trustees, Mus of Modern Art, NY City, pres, formerly; Investment analyst, NY Trust Co, NY City, 51-56; Lionel D Edie Co, NY City, 56-58; mgr res dept George O'Neill & Co, 58-59; pres, DB Marron & Co Inc, NY City, 59-65, Mitchell Hutchins & Co Inc (merger with DB Marron & Co Inc 65), NY City, 65-69, pres, chief exec off, 69-77; co-founder, Data Resources, Inc, 69-79, chmn, formerly; dir, NYSE 74-81; gov, vchmn, Securities Industry Asn, 74-77; pres, PaineWebber Inc. (merger with Mitchell Hutchins & Co Inc 77), 77-80, Chief Exec Officer, 80-2000, chmn bd, 81-2000; gov, NASD 97-2001; chmn, Chief Exec Officer, founder, Lightyear Capital, LLC, NY City, 2000-; chmn, UBS Am, 2000-2003; bd mem, Fannie Mae 2001-, Shinsei Bank 99-; chmn, Collegiate Funding Serv's, 2004-; Chmn, Ctr for Study of the Presidency; mem adv bd, UBS Art Collection; mem bd overseers, and mgr's Mem Sloan-Kettering Cancer Ctr; trustee, Charles A Dana Found, Ctr for Strategic & Int Studies (private sector co-chmn, Nat Commission on Retirement Policy); bd dir, NY City Partnership; mem Gov's Sch & Bus Alliance Task Force, NY. *Awards:* Named one of Top 200 Collectors, ARTnews Mag, 2004-. *Mem:* Coun on Foreign Relations. *Collection:* Nineteenth and twentieth century European, modern & contemporary art. *Mailing Add:* Lightyear Capital LLC 11th Floor 375 Park Ave New York NY 10152

MARRON, JEAN See LaRue, Joan Marron

MARRON, PAMELA ANNE
PAINTER
b Hackensack, NJ, Nov 16, 45. *Study:* Parsons Sch of Design, AA, 1965-1968; Stanford Univ (postgrad), 1970. *Work:* Southern Vt Art Ctr Mus, Manchester, Vt; Yoder Brothers Int, Barberton, Ohio; Factory Point Bank, Manchester, Vt; Richard Heileman & Dr Abe Madkour, Manchester, Vt. *Comn:* Numerous Comns private collection, 1980-2005; Katharina Rich Perlow Gallery, New York City, 96-2004; Ole Moon Gallery, Breckenridge, Colo, 2004. *Exhib:* Hopkins Ctr, Dartmouth College, 77-85; Landscape Groups, Norwich Univ, Northfield, Vt, 1980; Berkshire Mus, Pittsfield Mass, 1981; AVA Gallery, Hanover, NH, 84; Castleton State College, 86; Pinder Gallery, New York City, 87; Landscape Solos, Nicholas Roerich Mus, NYC, 1990; Vt State House, Montpelier, Vt, 1992; Grayson Gallery, Woodstock Vt, 1999; Southern Vt Ctr, Manchester, Vt, 2006; Redux Gallery Dorset, Vt, 2006; Kerygma Gallery, Ridgewood, NJ. *Collection Arranged:* Omni Corp, New York City; Lotus Corp, Cambridge, Mass; Yoder Brothers Int, Barberton, Ohio. *Teaching:* Instr art, Southern Vt Col, Bennington, Vt, 1981-1982. *Awards:* Jay Conway Award, Jay Conway Fund, Southern Vt Arts Ctr, 87 & 90; Basin Harbor Artist Residency Prog, 97; Southern Vt Art Ctr Jurors Award, 98; Women Artist Calander, 99. *Bibliog:* Mary Hard Bort (auth) Art & Soul, Gallery Press LLC, 2000; Susan Sargent (auth) The Confort of Color, Manchester Vt & Bull Finch, 2003. *Mem:* Stratton Arts Festival (art comt), 1978-1980; Southern Vt Art Ctr (juror), 2005; Southern Vt Art Ctr (art comt), 2006; Nat Mus Women in the Arts, Washington DC, 2006; Cheffee Art Ctr, Rutland Vt; Vt Coun on Arts, S Vt Art Center (art comt, numerous art exhibs). *Media:* Oil. *Dealer:* The Redux Gallery Dorset Vt 05251. *Mailing Add:* PO Box 563 Dorset VT 05251

MARROW, JAMES HENRY
HISTORIAN, EDUCATOR
b New York, NY, Mar 27, 41. *Study:* Univ Minn, BA(magna cum laude), 63; Columbia Univ, MA, 66, PhD(with distinction), 75. *Teaching:* Assoc prof hist art, State Univ NY, Binghamton, 70-76 & Yale Univ, 76-80; prof, Univ Calif, Berkeley, 80-91, Princeton Univ, 91-. *Mem:* Col Art Asn Am. *Res:* Northern European art of the late Middle Ages and early Renaissance, with special interest in religious iconography, manuscript illumination and early prints. *Publ:* Coauth, The James A de Rothschild Collection at Waddesdon Manor: Illuminated Manuscripts, Office Livre, 77; coauth, Medieval and Renaissance Manuscripts at Yale: A Selection (exhib catalog), Yale Univ Press, 78; auth, Passion Iconography in Northern European Art of the Late Middle Ages and Early Renaissance, Van Ghemmert, 79; coauth, Hans Baldung Grien: Prints and Drawings (exhib catalog), Yale Univ Press, 78; auth, Simon Bening in 1521: A group of dated miniatures, Liebaers Festschrift, 84. *Mailing Add:* 104 Library Pl Princeton NJ 08540

MARSH, CHARLENE MARIE
FIBER ARTIST, OIL PAINTER
b Muncie, Ind, May 19, 56. *Study:* Ind Univ, Bloomington, BA, 79, BA, 86. *Work:* Evansville Mus Arts & Sci; Minnetrista Cult Ctr, Muncie; Harrison Steel Castings Co, Attica, Ind; Ind Orthopaedics & Sports Med, PSC, Indianapolis; Indianapolis Mus Art; The White House, Washington; Brown Co Community Found; Indianapolis Mus Art, Ind; Ind State Mus, Ind. *Comn:* Art in the Classroom, Purdue Univ, West Lafayette, Ind, 95; Tufled Tapestry, Minnetrista Cult Ctr, Muncie, Ind, 97 & Purdue Univ, West Lafayette, Ind, 98; West Baden Springs Historic Site, 2001; Brown Co Pub Libr, Nashville, Ind, 2002. *Exhib:* one-woman shows, Campus Community Art Ctr, Ind Univ, Bloomington, 91, Bellevue Gallery, Bloomington, Ind, 91 & 93, John Waldron Arts Ctr, Bloomington, Ind, 94, Univ Indianapolis, 95, Minnetrista Cult Ctr, Muncie, Ind, 97 & Ft Wayne Mus Art, 99; Northern Indiana Art Asn, Munster, IN, 94, 96, 98, 2000, 2001, 2002, 2004; 34th Mid-State Craft Exhib, Evansville Mus Arts & Sci, Evansville, Ind, 95-96; Nat Mus Women in Arts Ind Chap Exhib, Nat Women's Mus, Washington, DC, 99-2000; Gov's Residence, Indianapolis, 2002-03; Whispers to Shouts, Ind State Mus, Ind, 2005; Fiber Surfaces & Structure, Mobile, Ala, 2005; 42nd Ann Coconut Grive Arts Festival, Coconut Grove, Fla, 2005. *Pos:* Bd dir, Bellevue Gallery, 92-. *Teaching:* Instr oil painting, John Waldron Arts Ctr, Bloomington, Ind, 92-98. *Awards:* First Prize, Pittsburgh Ctr Arts, 95; Best of Show, Three Rivers Arts Festival, Pittsburgh, 96; Gold Medal Award, Westmoreland Arts & Heritage Nat Competition, Youngwood, Pa, 97; Past pres award, Northern Ind Arts Asn, 2002; Best of Show, 23rd Contemp Crafts, Mesa, Ariz, 2001; IAC prog grant, 1999-2000, 2002-03. *Bibliog:* Jean Robertson (auth), Infinity of Form: Indiana Fiber Art, Fiberarts Mag, 4/92; Steve Mannheimer (auth), Fiber art exhibits beg the questions, what's a female aesthetic, Ind Star, 1/17/93; Kathleen Mills (auth), Nature's soldier Marsh puts spirit into tapestries, Bloomington Herald Times, 7/29/92; Lydia Finkelstein (auth), Artists Marsh, Sage exhibiting to national audiences, Bloomington Herald Times, 6/23/96; film (producer-Ron Prickel), Continuing the Legacy of Art in Brown County, Emmy award winner; Laura Lane (auth), Angels Above, Bloomington Hoosier Times, 11/18/2001. *Mem:* Brown Co Arts Alliance; Brown Co Studio Tour; Brown Co Arts & Cult Comn; Indiana Artists Club; Hoosier Salon; Indiana Heritage Arts; Indiana Plain Air Painters Mus. *Media:* Hand Dyed Wool & Metallic Yarns Tufted onto Cotton Backing; Oil on Cotton on a Wood Panel. *Publ:* Auth, Celebration of hand hooked rugs, In: Raindrops on a Pond, 91, Rughooking magazine, In: Interconnections, 92, Celebration of hand hooked rugs II, In: Driftnels, 92 & Celebration of hand hooked rugs III, In: Season of Dread, 93, Stackpole Books; Portfolio, Arts Indiana, Ann M Stack, 93; Portfolio, American Craft, 95. *Dealer:* Charlene Marsh Studio & Gallery. *Mailing Add:* c/o Brown County Art Gallery One Artist Drive Nashville IN 47448

MARSH, DAVID FOSTER
EDUCATOR, PAINTER
b Salkum, Wash, Jan 24, 26. *Study:* Cent Wash Univ, BA; Univ Ore, MS. *Work:* Westminster Col, Fulton, Mo; Inst Mexicana-N Am, Guadalajara, Mex. *Exhib:* NW Watercolor Soc Exhib, 58, 62 & 77; NW Ann, 63 & 66. *Teaching:* Prof drawing & painting, Western Wash Univ, 57-92, dean, Fine and Performing Arts, 83-85, emer prof, 92-. *Mem:* Col Art Asn; Nat Art Educ Asn. *Mailing Add:* 101 Morey Ave Bellingham WA 98225

MARSH, GEORGIA
PAINTER
b Olean, NY, 51. *Study:* European Hon Prog, Rome, Italy; RI Sch Design, BFA, 72. *Work:* Boston Mus Fine Arts, Mass; Cleveland Art Mus, Ohio; Mass Inst Technol, List Visual Arts Ctr, Cambridge; Mus ée Nat d'Art Mod, Paris; Jane Voorhees Zimmerli Art Mus, Rutgers Print Archive, New Brunswick, NJ. *Exhib:* Solo exhib, McNell Gallery, Philadelphia, 87, A/D Gallery, NY, 91, Beth Urdang Gallery, Boston, 92 & 93 & Betsy Senior Gallery, NY, 94; Musée Nat de l'Art Mod, Paris, 75; Whitney Mus Am Art, Pa, 87 & 89; Aldrich Mus Contemp Art, 92; Re-Orientations: Looking East, Gallery at Takashimaya, NY, 94; The Source: A Dialogue with Trees & Wood, Art Complex Mus, Duxbury, Mass, 94; Themes & Variations, Condeso Lawler Gallery, NY, 94; Wall Paintings, Aldrich Mus, 95. *Awards:* Fel, Nat Endowment Arts, 87, 89 & 90; Int Fel, La Napoule Found, France, 90; Award, Pollock-Krasner Found, 92. *Bibliog:* Amei Wallach (auth), Immigrant Asian's Debut, New York Newsday, 3/11/94; Robert Taylor (auth), Provincetown's Magnetic Force, Boston Globe, 7/22/94; Charles Hagen (auth), The Print Fair, New York Times, 11/11/94. *Publ:* Contribr, David Deutsch: Interview, Bomb Mag, spring 86; Francesco Clemente: Interview, Art Preso, 4/87

MARSH, THOMAS A
SCULPTOR
b Cherokee, Iowa, May 7, 51. *Study:* Layton Sch Art, Milwaukee, Wis, BFA(painting), 74; Univ Southern Calif, aesthetics with John Hospers, 76-77; Calif State Univ, Long Beach, MFA, sculpture with Kenneth Glenn & Stephen Werlick, 77; also with Milton Hebald, Rome, Italy. *Work:* Univ San Francisco Rossi Libr, Calif; St Mary's Hosp Libr, San Francisco; Calif Mfrs Asn, Sacramento; Calif State Univ, Long Beach; Mus Tex Tech Univ. *Comn:* 6' Bronze figure in Santa Cruz, 91; 10 bronze panels, 3'x4' each, San Francisco, 91; bust, Richard M Lucas Ctr, Stanford Univ Med Sch, Palo Alto, Calif, 92; Goddess of Democracy (12' bronze monument), proj leader, Portsmouth Sq, San Francisco, 94; 7' bronze figure, Shrine St Joseph Church, Santa Cruz, Calif, 97; Bronze bust, St Mary's Church, Sacramento, Calif, 97; bust of Betty White & a figure of Dick Van Dyke, Acad Television & Scis Hall of Fame Sculpture Garden; 7' figure of John the Baptist at the Mission Church, San Juan Bautista Calif, 2000; 7' figure of St Joseph, Patron of the Unborn at Shrine of St Joseph Santa Cruz, Calif; 6 1/2 life size portrait bronze figure, Amgen, Inc Thousand Oaks Calif, 2002; bronze bust Sonoma State Univ Rohnert Park, Calif, 2003; 10' Crucifix 10' Cross, 6' Corpus St Joachim's Catholic Church, Madera, Calif, 2003; 7' bas reliefs. Resurrection Catholic Church, Aptos, Calif. *Exhib:* Solo exhibs, Civic Courtyard, Bracciano, Italy, 78, Alliance Francaise, San Francisco, 82 & Univ San Francisco, Calif, 85 & 87; Sioux City Connection, Sioux City Art Ctr, Iowa, 84; Interfaith Religous Art, Judah L Magnes Mus, Berkeley, Calif, 86; About Faces: A Celebration of the Portrait, Walnut Creek Civic Arts Gallery, Calif, 87 & Bay Area Bronze, 88; The Goddess of Democracy, 91; Yerba Buena Center, San Francisco. *Pos:* Bd dir, Chinese Democracy, Educ Found, San Francisco, Calif, 92- & Acad Art Univ, 92-. *Teaching:* Instr sculpture, Calif State Univ, Long Beach, 78-79 & San Francisco, 79-80, Calif; instr anatomy & Sculpture, Acad Art Univ, San Francisco, Calif, 81-2000, coordr MFA prog, 83-85. *Awards:* Elizabeth Greenshields Found Fel, 77; Outstanding Contrib Chinese Democracy Award, Serv Ctr Chinese Democracy, 91. *Bibliog:* Artweek (exhib rev), 2/21/91; San Jose Mercury News, 3/10/92; NY Times, 6/5/94. *Media:* Bronze, Wood. *Mailing Add:* 198 Peliso Ave Orange VA 22960

MARSHAK, ARTHUR
SCULPTOR, CERAMIST
b Brooklyn, NY, Apr 20, 27. *Study:* Venice School of Art, Venice, Calif, cert, 1968-69; S Fla Art Inst, Ft Lauderdale, Fla, cert, 1977-78; Fla Atlantic Univ, Boca Raton, Fla, cert, 1980-81. *Work:* The WIT Gallery, Lenox, Mass; Daniel D. Cantor Collection, Ft. Lauderdale, Fla; A. Smurfit Collection, London, Eng; Hans-Dieter Boegel Collection, Hamburg, Ger; Yves Chelly Collection, Montreal Can. *Exhib:* Ft. Lauderdale Mus of Mod Art, Hortt Exhibit, Fla, 1979; Art Expo, Jacob Javits Ctr, New York City, 1988-89; 8th Grand Prix Art de Paris, Salon du Vieu Colombier, City Hall, Paris, France, 1993; 2nd Flamboyance Exhib, Mus of Mod Art Unet, Bordeaux, France, 1993; 3rd Biennial of Aquataine, Mus of Mod Art Unet, Bordeaux, France, 1995; Opening Exhibit, Mus of Mod Art of Miami, Coral Gables, Fla, 1996. *Collection Arranged:* Steiner Gallery, Bal Harbor, Fla, Romance Collection, 81. *Bibliog:* Encyclopedia of Am Living Artists 7th Ed, Art Network, 93; Salon Du Vieux Colombier Paris Catalog, ane Chiroussor-Chambeaux, 93; Amy Ward (auth), Sculptor of Life, Forum Publisher, 2002; art, Local Sculptor Named in Who's Who in America, Forum Publ, 2004. *Mem:* Boca Mus Prof Artist Guild. *Media:* Clay, Metal, Cast, Metal, Welded, Miscellaneous Media. *Publ:* 10th Annual Art Expo NY Guide, Edgell Comm, 88; Turnberry Isle Yacht & Country Club, Turnberry Publ, 88; International Contemporary Collectors Magazine, 89; Decor Magazine Fine & Decorative Arts, Fall Guide, 89; Art & Antiques, 97; Florida Design Magazine, 2003. *Dealer:* Theodora Marshak Artist Representative 4960 Swans Ln Coconut Creek, FL 33073. *Mailing Add:* Marshak Sculpture Studio 4960 Swans Ln Coconut Creek FL 33073

MARSHALL, BRUCE
PAINTER, ILLUSTRATOR, WRITER
b Athens, Tex, Dec 23, 29. *Study:* Univ Ariz, Tucson; Southern Ariz Sch of Art (full scholar). *Work:* First Cavalry Mus, Ft Hood, Tex; Hill Coll History Complex, Hillsboro, Tex; San Jacinto Monument, Tex; The Alamo, San Antonio; Nat Infantry Mus, Ft Benning, Ga; Inst Tex Cultures, Univ Tex, San Antonio. *Comn:* Gen Achibald Gracie Jr (portrait), Gracie Mansion, NY, 63; Portrait of Dick Dowling, Dowling Sch, Houston, 70, comn by Sons of Confederate Veterans; paintings, Inst Texan Cult, Univ Tex, San Antonio, 70-75; Tex Citizen Soldier (mural), Tex Nat Guard for Nat Infantry Mus, Ft Benning, Ga, 76; Ten Historic Texans (cover painting), Southwestern Bell Telephone Co, 79-80; Tom Lubbock (portrait), W Tex Mus Asn, 83; Patriots, (painting), Dallas Baptist Univ, 92; plus many others. *Exhib:* Smithsonian Inst, Washington, DC, 54; First Cavalry Mus, Ft Hood, 72, Univ Ariz, 73, Llano Estacado Mus, 75; Rotunda, Tex State Capitol, Austin, 75, 76, 84 & 95; Chamizal Nat Mem, El Paso, Tex, 77; Mus of the Big Bend, Alpine, Tex, 77; Tex Navy Exhib, Tex State Archives & Libr, 78; Star of the Repub Mus Washington State Park, Tex, 78; The Alamo, 81; Le Musee de l'Historie de l'Homme, Brussels, Belg, 83; John E Conner Mus, Kingsville, Tex, 85-86; Cannan House Office Building, Wash, DC, 88; War Mem Mus, Va, 91-92. *Pos:* Auth & illusr, The Texas Star, 72-73; assoc ed, Military Hist Tex & South West, 72-88. *Awards:* Knighted by King Peter II, Yugoslavia, 66; Artist of the 65th Legislature, Tex, 77; Artist in Res, Tex Navy Asn, 90; National Artist, Confederate States of Am from Sons of Confederate Veterans. *Bibliog:* Margaret Taylor Dry (auth), article, Austin American Statesmen, 74; Robert St Johns (auth), article in Argosy Mag, 78; Frank Woods (auth), article in Austin Mag, 80; Bess Whitehead Scott (auth), article, Austin Homes & Gardens, 80; Ned Polk (auth), article, The Westerner, 87; Thomas W Knowles (auth), They Rode for the Lone Star-The Saga of the Tex Rangers, 99. *Mem:* Scots of Austin (pres); Hood's Tex Brigade Asn (past pres); Sons of Confederate Vets (past lt comdr & mem bd dirs Houston camp, Austin camp, Tex div, Trans-Miss dept); Confederate Hist Asn of Belgium (chargé d' affairs), 2001-; Tex Rangers Asn (formerly); Tex Navy Asn. *Media:* Watercolor, Oil. *Interests:* history & reading. *Publ:* Illusr, Military History of

Texas and the Southwest, Presidial Press, 71-78; The Texas Rangers: Their First 150 Years, Encino, 75; History of Hood's Texas Brigade, Hill Col, 78; Kent Biffles Texana Column, Dallas Morning News, 94-99 & 03; auth & illusr, Uniforms of the Republic of Texas, 98, Uniforms of the Alamo and the Texas Revolution, 2003; South Western Historical Quarterly, 05. *Dealer:* Westart PO Box 161616 Austin TX 78716. *Mailing Add:* 11204 Ranch Rd 1826 Austin TX 78737-3506

MARSHALL, JAMES DUARD
PAINTER, PRINTMAKER
b Springfield, Mo, Sept 29, 14. *Study:* Kansas City Art Inst, Mo, dipl painting, 40, with Thomas Hart Benton; Colo Col, BA(art), 45, with Boardman Robinson, Lawrence Barrett & Ricco Lebron; Univ Denver, MA(art), with Julio de Deigo & Ruth Reeves. *Work:* Libr of Cong, Washington, DC; Tex Fine Arts Asn, Austin. *Comn:* Murals, History of Missouri (7 ft x 30 ft), Pub Libr, comn by City of Neosho, Mo, 39; Children's Stories (500 ft long), Officer's Wives Nursery, Ft Worth, Tex, 52; Beginning of a New Day (two 4 ft x 6 ft mosaics), Jones Store, Prairie Village, Kans, 62. *Exhib:* San Francisco Mus of Art Ann, Calif, 38; Philadelphia Print Club Ann, Pa, 40, 45 & 52; one-man shows, Santa Fe Art Mus, NMex, 43 & Oklahoma City Art Ctr, 43; Carnegie Inst Int, Pittsburgh, 45; Denver Art Mus Ann, Colo, 45-47; Nat Acad of Design, NY, 46; Under the Influence, The Students of Thomas Hart Benton, Albrecht Kemper Mus Art, St Joseph, Mo, 93; Fifteen Colo Artists (Fifty Yr Reunion, 1998), Elizabeth Schlosser Gallery, Denver, Colo, 98. *Pos:* Chmn art dept, Ft Worth Children's Mus, Tex, 51-53; crafts dir, US Army, Ger, 54-60; asst to Thomas Hart Benton, Truman Libr & New York Power Authority Murals, 60. *Teaching:* Mem, Fed Teaching Prog, Fayetteville, Ark, 33-34; teacher summer & Saturday classes, Kansas City Art Inst, 36-40; asst prof drawing & painting, Univ Denver, Colo, 46-51; instr summer art sessions, Kansas City Univ, 63. *Awards:* Hon Mention, Denver Ann, Colo & Philadelphia Print Club, 46; Benedictine Art Awards, New York, 70-74. *Media:* Lithography, egg tempera painting; Woodcut. *Mailing Add:* 5927 Brookside Blvd Kansas City MO 64113

MARSHALL, JOHN
PAINTER, INSTRUCTOR
b St John's, Nfld, Oct 20, 57. *Study:* Univ of the South, study with Edward Carlos, 78-81; Mid Tenn State Univ, with David Le Doux, Jim Gibson, BFA, 83; Univ NC, Greensboro, with Walter Barker, MFA, 85. *Work:* Weatherspoon Art Gallery, Greensboro, NC; Meridian Mus Art, Miss; Nines Community Col District, Marie Hull Gallery. *Comn:* Sculpture, Campus of Meridian Community Col. *Exhib:* Art Wave, William Carey Col Gallery Gulfport, Miss, 88; Art on Paper, Weatherspoon Art Gallery, Greensboro, NC, 89; solo exhibs, General Art Gallery, 94, Miss Art Colony, 95, Jones Jr Col, 96, Horne-Marshall Gallery, 96, Sylvia Schmidt Gallery, New Orleans, 97, Marie Hull Gallery, Miss, 98 & Architectural Gallery, Miss State Univ, 98. *Collection Arranged:* 80's Images from North Carolina, 87, Visions of Flowers, 87, Southern Idiom: 3 Views, 88 & Stephanie Dinkins: Retro, 88, Meridian Mus Art, Miss; Jacob Drachler - Retrospective, Meridian Mus Art, 89; Homer Casteel: Early Figurative Years (essay, catalog), Meridian Community Col, 89; Casteel & His Students (auth, catalog), Meridian Mus Art, Miss, 98. *Pos:* Cur asst, Weatherspoon Art Gallery, 83-85, cur, 86; dir, Meridian Mus Art, 86-89. *Teaching:* Cur & instr, Meridian Community Col, 86-. *Awards:* Best of 3-D Design, Art Wave, 88; Art Education of the Year, 96; Lamplighter Award, Meridian Community Col, 96. *Mem:* Weatherspoon Art Asn; Col Art Asn; Meridian Coun Arts. *Media:* Oil, Mixed Media. *Dealer:* Sylvia Schmidt Gallery New Orleans LA, Horne-Marshall Gallery Meridian MS

MARSHALL, JOHN CARL
CRAFTSMAN
b Pittsburgh, Pa, Feb 25, 36. *Study:* Cleveland Inst Art, BFA; Syracuse Univ, MFA. *Work:* Everson Mus, Syracuse, NY; Chicago Art Inst, Ill; Am Craft Mus New; Syracuse Univ, NY; Mukhina Sch Art & Design, St Petersburg, Russia; and others. *Comn:* Gold Bowl, Hendricks Chapel, Syracuse, NY, 69; Series of 5 large silver sculptures, Patrick Lannan, 84; coffee tea service, Anne Gould Hauberg, Seattle, Wash, 87; eight flatware designs for Bloome Collection, Seattle, Wash, 88; star rose quartz sphere sculpture, White Rose Found, Calif, 91. *Exhib:* Masterworks of Am Jewelry since 1950, Victoria & Albert Mus, London, 85; Hong-ik Metalcrafts Asn Exhib, Walker Hill Art Ctr Mus, Seoul, Korea, 88; Craft Today USA, premiere opening Musee Des Art Decoratifs, Paris, France & toured major Europ cities, 89; Art that Works, The Decorative Arts of the Eighties Crafted in Am, toured maj US cities 2 yrs, 90; One man exhib, Nat Ornamental Metals Mus, Memphis, Tenn, 91; Fortunoff Silver Competition III, Silver New Forms & Expressions, New York, NY, 91. *Teaching:* Asst prof metalworking, design & enamel, Syracuse Univ, 65-70; Asst prof, Univ Wash, 70-75, prof, 75-. *Awards:* Nat Merit Award, Am Craftsmen Coun, Craftsmen USA, 66; Thomas C Thompson Prize 45th Ceramic Nat Competition, 68; Am Metalcraft Award, Nat Enamels Exhib, 70. *Bibliog:* C E Licka (auth), Sublime passages and other reflections: The work of John Marshall, Am Craft Mag, 85; John Marshall: A Conversation with Patterson Sims, Metalsmith Mag, 91. *Mem:* Am Craftsmen Coun; Soc N Am Goldsmiths; Soc Am Silversmiths; Fel Am Crafts Coun. *Media:* Gold, Silver. *Mailing Add:* 5618 75th Ct W University Place WA 98467-4512

MARSHALL, KERRY JAMES
DESIGNER, PAINTER
b Birmingham, Ala, Oct 17, 55. *Study:* Otis Art Inst, Los Angeles, Calif, BFA, 78. *Hon Degrees:* Otis Art Inst, D, 99. *Work:* Mus Contemp Art, Chicago, Ill; Whitney Mus Am Art, NY; San Francisco Mus Modern Art, Calif; Los Angeles Co Mus Art, Calif; Corcoran Mus Art, Washington, DC. *Exhib:* one-man shows, James Turcotte Gallery, Los Angeles, 83, Pepperdine Univ, Malibu, 84, Koplin Gallery, 85 & 91, Studio Mus Harlem, 86, Terra Incognito, Chicago Cult Ctr, 92, Jack Shainman Gallery, NY, 93, 95 & 99, Koplin Gallery, Santa Monica, Calif, 93, Cleveland Ctr Contemp Arts, 94, Addison Gallery Am Art, 97, Phillips Acad, Andover, Mass, 97 & Orlando Mus Art, Fla, 98; Drawings III, Koplin Gallery, Santa Monica, 93; Markets of Resistance, White Columns Gallery, NY, 93; 43rd Biennial of Contemp Am Painting, Corcoran Gallery Art, Washington, DC, 93; Bridges & Boundaries: Chicago Crossings, Spertus Mus, Chicago, 94; Saddlebrook Col Art Gallery, Mission Viejo, Calif, 94; About Place: Recent Art of the Americas, Art Inst Chicago, 95; No Doubt: African-Am Art of the 90's, Aldrich Mus Contemp Art, Ridgefield, Conn, 96; Whitney Biennial, Whitney Mus Am Art, NY, 97; The Corcoran Collects: Selections from the Permanent Collection, Corcoran Gallery Art, Washington, DC, 98; Postcards from Black Am: Contemp African-Am Art, De Beyerd, Breda, Amsterdam, 98; Collectors Collect Contemp: 1990-1999, Inst Contemp Art, Boston, 99; Trouble Spot: Painting, Mus Contemp Art Antwerp, Belgium, 99; Other Narratives: Fifteen Yrs, Contemp Arts Mus, Houston, Tex, 99; Age of Influence: Reflections in the Mirror of Am Cult, Mus Contemp Art, Chicago, 2000; Illusions of Eden: Visions of the Am Heartland, Madison Art Ctr, Wis, 2001. *Pos:* Production designer, Praise House & Hendrix Proj, 91; exhib comt mem, Randolf St Gallery, Chicago, Ill, 92-. *Teaching:* Art instr, Los Angeles City Col, 80-83; art fac, Los Angeles Southwest Col, 81-85; adj asst prof, Sch Art & Design, Univ Ill, Chicago, 93-94, assoc prof, 95-. *Awards:* Resident Fel, Studio Mus Harlem, 85; Fel, Art Matters Inc, 90; Nat Endowment Arts Visual Art Fel, 91; Ill Arts Coun Visual Arts Grant, 92; Tiffany Found Grant, 93; John D and Catherine T MacArthur Found, 97; Distinguished Artist Fellowship and Stillwater Found Grant, Col Fine Arts, Univ Tex, Austin, 2004. *Bibliog:* Gallery review, NY Times, 2/12/93; Art review, Los Angeles Times, 4/24/93; Up from the streets, Artweek, 4/28/93; Howard Halle, Portraits of the artists (the Whitney Biennial), Time Out NY, 3/20-27/97; Christopher Knight, Kerry James Marshall (Documenta), Art & Antiques, 9/97; Garrett Holg, Stuff your eyes with wonder, Art News, 3/98; Alan Artner, Broader canvas: painter Kerry James Marshall is finding new ways to say what he wants to say, Chicago Tribune, 5/3/98; Holland Cotter, In civil rights ferment, a conflicted nostalgia, NY Times, 10/2/98; Grace Glueck, Kerry James Marshall at Jack Shainman, NY Times, 4/9/99; Shaila Dewan, Too much for words, Houston Press, 6/10-16/99; Kenneth Baker, Through the past, mournfully: Marshall's art revisits civil rights era, San Francisco Chronicle, 11/23/99; Artist joins in students' search for their identities, Southampton Press, 1/3/2000; James Myer, Impure thoughts: the art of Sam Durant, Artforum, 4/2000; writer, dir, The Doppler Incident, 97. *Mem:* Ill Arts Coun. *Publ:* Auth, article, Visions Quart, fall 91; article, Los Angeles Times, 3/15/91; production designer, NUNU, 90; production designer, Prairie House, 91. *Mailing Add:* 4122 S Calument Ave Chicago IL 60653

MARSHALL, RICHARD DONALD
HISTORIAN, CURATOR
b Los Angeles, Calif, May 5, 47. *Study:* Calif State Univ, Long Beach, BA; Univ Calif, Irvine. *Collection Arranged:* Clay (auth, catalog), 74, Whitney Mus Am Art; Handmade Paper: Prints & Unique Works, 76, Mus Mod Art, NY; Calder's Universe (contribr, catalogs), 76-77, Robert Irwin (ed & contribr, catalog), 77, Art About Art (coauth, catalog), 78, New Image Painting (auth, catalog), 78, Biennial Exhib (coauth, catalogs), 79, 81, 83, 85, 87, 89 & 91, Isamu Noguchi (ed & contribr, catalog), 80, Louise Nevelson: Atmospheres and Environments (contribr, catalog), 80, Joel Shapiro (coauth, catalog), 82-83, American Art Since 1970 (auth, catalog), 84-85, Jonathan Borofsky (coauth, catalog), 84-85, Alex Katz (auth, catalog) 86, Robert Mapplethorpe (auth, catalog), 88, The New Sculpture: 65-75 (coauth, catalog) 89, Edward Ruscha (auth, catalog) 90, Jean-Michel Basquiat (auth, catalog), 92-93, Whitney Mus Art; Louise Bourgeois (auth, catalog), Mus Contemp Art, Monterrey, Mex, 96; Jean Michel Basquiat (auth, catalog), Serpentine Gallery, London, 96, Robert Mapplethorpel Mitsukoshi Mus Art, Tokyo; Joan Mitchell (auth, catalog), Mod Art, Valencia, Spain, 97; plus others. *Pos:* Consult, Art Adv Serv, Mus Mod Art, New York, 74-76; exhib coordr, Whitney Mus Am Art, New York, 74-76, asst cur exhib, 76-78, assoc cur, 78-88, cur, 88-93; art ed, Paris Rev Mag, 78-94; independent cur & consult, 94-. *Mem:* Calder Found/New York (adv bd); plus others. *Mailing Add:* 311 E 72nd St #6D New York NY 10021-4684

MARSHALL, ROBERT LEROY
EDUCATOR, PAINTER
b Mesquite, Nev, Dec 15, 44. *Study:* Brigham Young Univ, BA, 66, MA, 68; studies in Europe, primarily Spain & England. *Work:* Mus of the Southwest, Midland, Tex; Brigham Young Univ, Provo, Utah; Webster Oil Co, Springfield, Mo; Springville Mus, Utah; Shell Oil. *Exhib:* Watercolor West; Watercolor USA, Springfield, Mo; Utah Coun Arts, Salt Lake City; Am Watercolor Soc, NY; Butler Inst Am Art; Scottsdale Biennial, Ariz. *Teaching:* Prof painting & drawing, Brigham Young Univ, 69-, chmn dept art & design, 76-81. *Awards:* Purchase Award, Watercolor USA, Webster Oil Co. *Mem:* Nat Watercolor Soc; Nat Coun Art Adminrs; Springville Mus Art (mem bd dir, 77-). *Media:* Watercolor, Oil. *Mailing Add:* Dept Visual Arts Brigham Young Univ Provo UT 84602

MARSHALL, THOMAS E
EDUCATOR, PRINTMAKER
b Rocky Mount, NC, Jan 20, 41. *Study:* Va Commonwealth Univ, BFA, 63; Univ NC, Chapel Hill, MAT, 64. *Work:* Wilson Arts Coun, NC. *Comn:* Logo, Masthead, NC Humane Fedn, Chapel Hill, 81. *Exhib:* Faculty Painters, NC State Univ, Raleigh, 69; Only Prints and Drawings, Jacksonville State Univ, Ala, 70; Fayetteville Mus Art Invitational, NC, 75. *Pos:* Ed, Crucible Mag, 74-. *Teaching:* Instr painting, Rocky Mount Arts Coun, 64-65, assoc prof art, Atlantic Christian Col, 64-, chmn dept visual art, 83-88, chmn Fine art div, 88-. *Mem:* Southeastern Col Art Conf; NC Art Educ Asn; Nat Art Educ Asn. *Publ:* Illusr & auth, Image Mag, Va Commonwealth Univ, 62 & 63. *Mailing Add:* 1133 Kenan St W Wilson NC 27893

MARSTON, JD
PHOTOGRAPHER
b NY, Jan 30, 48. *Study:* Emerson Col, BS/SP, 70. *Work:* The Colo Col, Colo Springs; Ohio Wesleyan Univ, Deleware, Ohio; Sierra Club, San Francisco; MCI; Texaco; Lucent Technols; JD Marston Photography Gallery. *Comn:* This Land is Sacred, US Forest Service, Colo, 90; Healing Waters, Sisters of the Holy Redeemer, Pa, 99. *Exhib:* Creative Impulse, The Colo Col, 95; Homage to Ingmar Bergman, Birger Sandzen Gallery, Lindsborg, Kans, 97; L'Itimerances L'Art Fixe En Movement, Arles, France, 01; Recipients of the Ansel Adams Award, Sierra Club Gallery, Calif, 01. *Pos:* Artist in Residence, The Colo Col, Colo Springs, 93. *Teaching:* Vis Prof, The Colo Col, 94; Vis Prof, Ohio Wesleyan Univ, Delaware, Ohio, 95. *Awards:* Ansel Adams Award, Sierra Club, 92; Ernst Haas Scholarship, Anderson Ranch, 92. *Mem:* Am Soc Media Photogs. *Media:* Black and White, Silver Gelatin Photography. *Specialty:* photography of JD Marston. *Publ:* auth, Vince Bzdek, Meditations in Black & White, Denver Post, 92; The Waiting, Lenswork Quarterly, 94, Personal Themes, 99. *Dealer:* Joan Sapiro Art Consultants 4750 E Belleview Littleton Colo 80121. *Mailing Add:* PO Box 294 Crestone CO 81131

MARTEL, RICHARD
CONCEPTUAL ARTIST, EDITOR
b Bagotville, Provide, Que, July 7, 50. *Study:* Univ Laval, Que, BA, 75 & Hon MA, 79. *Exhib:* Workshop Art, Dokumeusa 7- OFAJ, Kassel, 82; Casscades, Galerie Du Musée, Que, 84; Europékunstruction in Memoriam Ugorugg Maciunas, Festival, Que, 84; La Pluie Au Nicaragua, La Lieu, Centre en Art Actuel, Oue, Can, 84; So Bor Dination, Galerie Donguy, Paris, France, 85; Mohouaec, Musée Du Que, Can, 86; Defrinazione, Centro Int Multimedia, Salerno, Italy, 86; Multimedia Exhib Musso del Sannio, Beneveito, Italy, 86. *Pos:* Pres, Editions Intervention, 78-; vpres, AEPOQ, 82-85. *Teaching:* Instr art, Univ Que, Chicicouimi, Can, 78-82. *Awards:* Soutien A La Création, Govt du Que, 82 & 85. *Media:* Performance Art. *Publ:* Illusr, 78-, auth, Activitiés Artisques, 1978-1982, 83 & Art Société Quebec, 1975-80, 82, Editions Intervention. *Dealer:* Le Lieu Centre Rn Art Actuel 629 St Jean Quebec PQ G1R 4P7 Canada. *Mailing Add:* 221 Lavingueur Quebec PQ G1R 1B1 Canada

MARTELL, BARBARA BENTLEY
PAINTER
b Trenton, NJ. *Study:* Philadelphia Col Art, Pa. *Work:* Mayor Watson Pharo's Collection, Borough Hall, Beach Haven, NJ; wall mural, Long Beach Island Hist Mus, Beach Haven, NJ. *Exhib:* Philadelphia Sketch Club Ann, 68-; Philadelphia Plastic Club, 71-72; Long Beach Island Found Arts & Sci; Long Beach Island Hist Mus, 79; NJ State Ann, 81 & 82. *Awards:* Second Prize for Oils, Willingboro Pa Art Alliance, 72; First & Third Awards, Manahawkin, NJ Arts Week Ann, Pine Shores Art Asn, 86. *Mem:* Ocean Co Artists Guild, Toms River, NJ. *Media:* Mixed. *Mailing Add:* 3225 Riverview Dr Triangle VA 22172-1421

MARTER, JOAN
HISTORIAN, CURATOR
b Philadelphia, Pa, Aug 13, 46. *Study:* Temple Univ, BA, 68; Univ Del, MA, 70, PhD(art hist), 74. *Collection Arranged:* Vanguard Am Sculpture 1913-1939 (guest cur & coauth, catalog), Rutgers Univ Art Gallery, 79; Design in America: The Cranbrook Vision 1925-1950, Detroit Inst Arts & Metrop Mus Art, 83; Beyond the Plane, American Constructions 1930-1965, NJ State Mus, 83; Alexander Archipenko Constructions (auth, catalog), Blum Art Inst, Bard Col, 85; Alexander Calder: Artist As Engineer, Mass Inst Technol, 86; Theodore Roszak: The Drawings, (auth, catalog), Elvehjem Mus Art, 92; Dorothy Dehner Retrospective, Katanoh Mus Art & Corcoran Gallery Art, 93-94; Women and Abstract Expressions (with catalog), Baruch Col & Guild Mus, 97; Off Limits: Rutgers & The Avant Garde 1957-63 (ed, catalog), Newark Mus, 99. *Pos:* Critic, Arts Mag, 77-82, Sculpture Mag, 90-, Art J 90-, Woman's Art J, 92-; ed, Woman's Art Jour, 2006-. *Teaching:* Prof art hist, Rutgers Univ, 77, disting prof art hist, 2000-; Prof art hist, Rutgers Univ, 77-& dir grad studies art hist, 94-97; dir curatorial studies prog, Rutgers Univ, 89-. *Awards:* Univ of Del Alumni Wall of Fame, 2004; Charles F Montgomery Prize, Decorative Arts Soc, 84; George Wittenborn Award, Art Libr Soc, 85; John Sloan Mem Found Grant, 89; Res Coun Grants, Rutgers Univ, 77-06; Pollock-Krasner Found/Stony Brook Res Fel, 2004-2005; Diamond Achievement Award, Temple Univ, 94; Best Exhibn Outside New York City, Int Asn Art Critics, 99; and others; Getty Rsch Inst Libr Grant, 2002; Grad Tchg Excellence Award, Northeastern Asn of Grad Schs, 99. *Mem:* Col Art Asn; Women's Caucus for Art; Int Asn Art Critics (mem USA sect); Art Table. *Res:* 20th century art; Am Sculpture; women studies. *Publ:* Auth, Jose De Rivera Construction, Madrid, 80; articles in Am Art J, Art J, Arts Mag & Sculpture, Woman's Art J; Alexander Calder, Cambridge Univ Press, 91 & 97; Theodore Roszak Drawings, Univ Wash Press, 92; Dorothy Dehner, Sixty Years of Art, Univ Wash Press, 93; Ed, Postwar Sculpture in Europe and America, Art J, winter, 94-95; auth, Off Limits: Rutgers University and the Avant-Garde 1957-63, Rutgers Univ Press, 99; co-auth, American Sculpture in the Metropolitan Museum of Art, Vol II, Metropolitan Mus Art, 2000; ed, Abstract Expressionism: The International Context, Rutgers Univ Press, 2007. *Mailing Add:* 220 Madison Ave New York NY 10016

MARTI, VIRGIL
PAINTER, SCULPTOR
b St Louis, Mo, 62. *Study:* Sch Fine Arts, Wash Univ, BFA (painting),84; Tyler Sch Art, Temple Univ, MFA (painting), 90; Skowhegan Sch Painting & Sculpture, 90. *Work:* Art Resources Transfer Inc, NY; Fabric Workshop & Mus, Philadelphia; Philadelphia Mus Art; Victoria & Albert Mus, London, Eng; The New Mus; The Fabric Workshop and Mus; Ctr Curatorial Studies at Bard Col; Art Resources Transfer, Inc; Whitney Biennial, Whitney Mus Am Art. *Exhib:* Solo exhibs, Paley Gallery, Moore Col Art & Design, Philadelphia, 92, Samuel S Fleisher Art Mem, Philadelphia, 94, White Columns, NY, 96, Thread Waxing Space, NY, 98, Holly Solomon Gallery, NY, 99, Ganser Gallery, Millersville Univ, Pa, 99, Ardmor Station, Pa, 2000, Habitat, London, 2000, Three Rivers Festival Gallery, Pittsburgh, 2001 & Morris Gallery, Pa Acad Fine Arts, Philadelphia, 2001; Energy Made Visible, Larry Becker, Philadelphia, 92; Gender Engendered, Community Educ Ctr, Philadelphia, 92; Shams, Southern Exposure Proj Artaud, San Francisco, 93; Dress Codes, Inst Contemp Art, Boston, 93; Color Theory, Vox Populi, Philadelphia, 94; Al Dente, Caren Golden Fine Art, NY, 94; Prison Sentences: The Prison as Site/The Prison as Subject (with catalog), Eastern State Penitentiary, Philadelphia, 95; Fake ID, 88 Room, Boston, 95; You talkin' to me? (with catalog), Inst Contemp Art, Philadelphia, 96; PhotoWORKS, Nexus, Philadelphia, 96; Patterns of Excess (with catalog), Beaver Col Art Gallery, Glenside, Pa, 96; Verso, Fabric Workshop & Mus, Philadelphia, 97; Apocalyptic Wallpaper (with catalog), Wexner Ctr Arts, Ohio State Univ, Columbus, 97; Pop Abstraction, Mus Am Art Pa Acad Fin Arts, Philadelphia, 98; Natural Dependency, Jerwood Gallery, London, 99; Gods and Monsters, McBean Gallery, San Francisco Art Inst, 99; Cardboard, Vinyl & Rhinestones, Expo/Sure at the Dowtown Arts Festival, NY, 99; Yard Sale, New York City Lab sch, NY, 2000; Gardens of Pleasure, John Michael Kohler Arts Ctr, Sheboygan, Wis, 2000; Biennial 2000, Del Art Mus, Wilmington, 2000; The Fabric Workshop & Mus, Philadelphie, au Centre d'Art Contemporaire, Ctr d'Art Contemp, Geneva, 2001; All of My Heart, Arte e Personae/Gallery Hotel Art, Florence, 2001; Philadelphia Selections 4: Brave/Smart, Levy Gallery, Moore Col Art and Design, Philadelphia, 2001. *Teaching:* lectr, Rosenbach Mus & Lib, Philadelphia, 98, Inst Contemp Art, Philadelphia, 99, Millersville U, 99 & Pa Acad Fine Arts, 99. *Awards:* Phila Mus Art Purchase Award, 94; Art Matters Fel, 95; Pa Coun Arts Fel, 97; Louis Comfort Tiffany Found Award, 97; others. *Bibliog:* Kristy Krivitsky (auth), Apocalyptic wallpaper, Art Papers, 11-12/97; Jan Estep (auth), Studio view, New Art Examiner, 5/98; Frances Richard (auth), rev, Artforum, 12/98; Michael Cohen (auth), rev, Flash Art, 10/99; Robert Fallon (auth), Sitting pretty, Philadelphia Weekly, 5/3/2000; Lori Wallace (auth), Commisions, Sculpture, 9/2000; other articles

MARTIN, ALEXANDER TOEDT
EDUCATOR, PAINTER
b Kinderhook, NY, Mar 11, 31. *Study:* Albright Art Sch, cert, 52; Univ Buffalo, BFA, 57; Tulane Univ, MFA, 63. *Work:* Neuberger Mus, State Univ NY Col, Purchase; Whitney Mus Am Art, Union Carbide Corp, Salomon Brothers, NY; Schenectady Mus, NY; Continental Transport Inc, White Plains, NY; Dow Jones, NY; Marist Col Collection, Poughkeepsie, NY. *Exhib:* Albright-Knox Art Gallery, Buffalo, 59; Southeastern Exhib, Delgado Mus, New Orleans, La, 63; Wadsworth Atheneum, Hartford Conn, 66; Convocation of Arts Exhib, State Univ NY, Albany, 69; Cooperstown Ann, NY, 75; Plaza Gallery, State Univ NY Central, Albany, 82; one-man show, Barrett House, Poughkeepsie, NY, 83 & Tom James Gallery, Westwood, NJ, 96; The New Response, Contemp Hudson River Painters Exhib, Albany, Poughkeepsie & NY, 86; James Cox Gallery, Woodstock, NY, 91-96; Maris Col, 2001. *Teaching:* Prof painting & drawing, State Univ NY Col, New Paltz, 63-96, emer prof, 96-. *Awards:* First Prize Painting, Schenectady Mus, 58 & Cooperstown Ann, 75. *Bibliog:* Hilton Kramer (auth), article in NY Times, 3/25/78; article, Am Artist, 5/82. *Media:* Oil, Watercolor, Pastel. *Publ:* Auth, Painting the Landscape, Watson Guptill, 85. *Dealer:* James Cox Gallery Woodstock NY. *Mailing Add:* 14 Watch Hill Rd New Paltz NY 12561

MARTIN, BERNARD MURRAY
PAINTER, EDUCATOR
b Ferrum, Va, June 21, 35. *Study:* Wake Forest Col, NC; Richmond Prof Inst, Va, BFA; Hunter Col, MA. *Work:* Va Mus Fine Arts, Richmond; Walter Rawls Mus, Courtland, Va; Chrysler Mus, Norfolk, Va; Nat Collection, Washington; First & Merchants Nat Bank, Richmond, Va. *Exhib:* Nostalgia and the Contemp Artist, Am Fedn Arts Traveling Exhib, 68; Am Painting 1970, Va Mus Fine Art, 70; Friends of the Corcoran, Corcoran Gallery Art, Washington, 71; one-man show, Gallery K, Washington, 78 & 80; 32nd Southeastern Exhib, Gallery Contemp Art, Winston-Salem, 72; Va Mus Fine Art, 96; Va Beach Art Ctr, 96. *Teaching:* Assoc prof painting, Va Commonwealth Univ, 61-98. *Awards:* Cert distinction, Va Artists Exhib, Va Mus Fine Arts, 64, 66, 68 & 70; First Prize, Southeastern Exhib, Gallery Contemp Art, 70 & 71; Nat Endowment Arts, 95; Va Mus, 98; State of Va, 99. *Media:* Oil. *Dealer:* Gallery K Washington DC 20013; Reynolds Gallery Richmond VA. *Mailing Add:* 1015 Francisco Rd Richmond VA 23229

MARTIN, BILL
PAINTER, SCULPTOR
b South San Francisco, Calif, Jan 22, 43. *Study:* Acad Art, San Francisco, Calif; San Francisco Art Inst, BFA, 68, MFA, 70. *Work:* San Francisco Int Airport; AT&T, NY; Owens Corning, Toledo, Ohio; Glenn C Janss Collection Boise Art Mus, Idaho; Levi Strauss, San Francisco, Calif; and others. *Exhib:* Baja, San Francisco Mus Mod Art, 75; Ninth Biennale de Paris, Musee d'Art Modern de la Ville, Paris, France, 75; University Show, State Univ NY, Postdam, 77; Triennial Invitational of India, 78; Painting and Sculpture Today, Indianapolis Mus Art, Ind, 78; New Am Painting (world traveling show), New Mus, NY, 79-80; Art in Bay Area 1945-1980, Oakland Mus, Calif, 85; Am Realism, San Francisco Mus Art, 85; one-person shows, Nancy Hoffman Gallery, NY, 82, 76 & 79-80, Joseph Chowning Gallery, San Francisco, 83, 85, 87, 89 & 92, Univ Nev, 88, Chabot Col, Calif, 90, Kabutoya Gallery, Tokyo, Japan, 91, Atrium Gallery, San Francisco, 92; Art of Fantasy & Science Fiction, Del Art Mus, 89; Watercolor USA Springfield Art Mus, Mo, 89; West Coast Works on Paper, Humbolt State Univ, Calif; Exhibition 48, Southern Utah State Univ, 89; Paper in Particular, Columbia Col, Mo, 90; From the Studio Oakland Mus, Calif. *Teaching:* Instr painting, Acad Art, San Francisco, Calif, Univ Calif, Berkeley, Univ Calif, San Jose, 73, Col of Marin, Kentfield, Calif, 75-78 & Col of Redwoods, Mendocino, Calif, 83-. *Awards:* Grant to Artists, Louis Comfort Tiffany Found, 70; Artist's Fel; Nat

Endowment Arts. *Mem:* Mendocino Art Ctr (bd of dir); Ft Braggs Ctr Art. *Media:* Oil, Bronze; Gouache, Watercolor. *Publ:* Contribr, Visions, 77, auth, 1969-1979 Bill Martin Paintings, 79; American Realism, Abrams; Arts of the San Francisco Bay Area, Univ Calif Press; auth, Joy of Drawing, Watson-Guptill Publ. *Dealer:* Joseph Chowning Gallery 1717 17th St San Francisco CA 94103. *Mailing Add:* 33611 Navarro Ridge Rd Albion CA 95410-9705

MARTIN, CAMERON
ARTIST
b Brooklyn, NY, 70. *Study:* Brown Univ, BA, 94; Whitney Mus Ind, NY, 96. *Work:* exhib in group shows at Home, Bellevue Art Mus, Wash, 1994 Whitney Biennial, Whitney Mus Am Art, 2004. *Exhib:* One-man shows, The Future Lasts Forever, Howard House, Seattle, 99, Future Views, Tate, NY, 99, Angstrom Gallery, Dallas, 2000, Three Pictures, Howard House, Seattle, 2001, New Paintings, Kevin Bruk Gallery, Miami, 2001, Standstill, Artemis Greenberg Van Doren Gallery, NY, 2002, Never Rider, Gallery Min Min, Tokyo, 2003, Clear Skies, Artemis Greenberg Van Doren Gallery, NY, 2004, A Turn Pale, Gallery Min Min, Tokyo, 2004; group shows, Home Northwest Ann, Ctr Contemp Art, Seattle, 95, Images Lost & Found, Chassie Post Gallery, NY, 96, Apartments, Artra, Milan, Italy, 97, Landscapes, Meyerson Nowinski Gallery, Seattle, 98, Open, Tate, NY, 98, Other Paintings, Huntington Beach Art Ctr, Calif, 99, Twice Born: Beauty, Mills Gallery, Boston, 2000, Flat File, Bellwether Gallery, Brooklyn, 2000, Three Painter, Lawrence Rubin Greenberg Van Doren Fine Art, NY, 2001, Guide to Trust No 2, Yerba Buena Ctr Arts, San Francisco, 2002, Linger, Artemis Greenberg Van Doren Gallery, NY, 2002 Everybody Knows This is Nowhere, Kevin Bruk Gallery, Miami, 2002, City Mouse/Country Mouse, Space 101, Brooklyn, 2003, How Come, Stux Gallery, NY, 2003, Nature Boy, Elizabeth Dee Gallery, NY, 2003, Giverny, Salon 94, NY, 2003, Colored Pencil, KS Art, NY, 2004, About the House, Howard House, Seattle, 2004, Stay Inside, Shoshana Wayne Gallery, Santa Monica, Calif, 2004. *Awards:* Samuel T Arnold Fel, 94; Recipient Pollock-Krasner Found Award, 2000; Artists Giverny Fel & Residency, France, 2001. *Mailing Add:* c/o Artemis Greenberg Van Doren Gallery 730 Fifth Ave 7th fl New York NY 10019

MARTIN, CHESTER YOUNG
PAINTER, MEDALIST
b Chattanooga, Tenn, Nov 2, 34. *Study:* Univ Chattanooga, BA, 61. *Work:* Smithsonian Inst; Brit Mus, London; Royal Swed Coin Cabinet, Stockholm; First Am NB Collection, State of Tenn, Nashville. *Comn:* Rose Inn (oil painting), Ga-Pac Corp, Crossett Div, Crossett, Ark, 73; Centennial mural, Chattem, Inc, Chattanooga, Tenn, 74; The Sixth Day (bronze relief sculpture), 81, Brookgreen Gardens Wildlife Medal, Brookgreen Gardens, Murrells Inlet, SC, 83; White House commemorative silver dollar, US Mint, Philadelphia, 92. *Exhib:* Medialia Gallery, New York City, Feb-April, 2005; Seaside Art Gallery Miniature Exhib, 2005. *Collection Arranged:* Smithsonian Brit Mus; Royal Swedish Coun Cabinet; ARt History Mus Vienna. *Pos:* Sculptor/engraver, US Mint, Philadelphia, 86-92. *Awards:* Purchase Award, Julius Wile Sons & Co, NY, 75; 16th Tenn All-State Artists' Exhib First Purchase Award, First Am Bank Nashville, 76; Medallic Sculpture Award, Am Numismatic Asn, 93. *Bibliog:* Ed Reiter (auth), World food day medal, New York Times, 84; George S Cuhaj (auth), Chester Martin: A life of art, The Numismatist, 93; George S Cuhaj (auth), Chester Y Martin: Painter and Sculptor, The Medal, Brit Art Medal Trust, 94. *Mem:* Fed Int de La Medaille; Am Medallic Sculpture Asn (vpres, 87). *Media:* Oil, Watercolor, Sculpture (including Medallic Art). *Interests:* modern languages. *Dealer:* Seaside Art Gallery Nags Head NC; Medialia Gallery, NYC. *Mailing Add:* 4110 Sunbury Ave Chattanooga TN 37411-5232

MARTIN, CHRIS
PAINTER
b Washington, DC, Oct 20, 54. *Study:* Yale Univ, 75. *Work:* Lannan Found; Progressive Corp. *Exhib:* Solo exhibs, Thread Bldg Gallery, NY, 80, Mary Delahoyd Gallery, NY, 85 & 87, Philippe Briet Gallery, NY, 88, John Good Gallery, NY, 90 & Jimenez & Algus Gallery, Brooklyn, NY, 91; Penultimate Salute, A Place Apart Gallery, Brooklyn, NY, 84; Twelve from New York, Yale Sch Art, Yale Univ, New Haven, Conn, 86; Brooklyn Mus, NY, 87; Words as Symbols, Aldrich Mus, Conn, 90; Visions/Revisions: Selections from the Contemp Collection, Denver Art Mus, 91. *Awards:* Am Acad & Inst Arts & Letts, Richard & Linda Rosenthal Award, 87; Nat Endowment Arts, 90. *Bibliog:* Chris Martin, NY Times, 4/27/90; Roberta Smith (auth), Chris Martin, NY Times, 4/27/90. *Mailing Add:* 284 Graham Ave Brooklyn NY 11211

MARTIN, DIANNE L
PAINTER, PRINTMAKER
b Boston, Mass, Apr 8, 40. *Study:* RI Sch Design with Robert Hamilton, BFA, 65; Univ Iowa, with Byron Burford, MA, 67. *Work:* Pepsico; Pfizer; JC Penney; Wilmington Trust Co; David Rockefeller Jr; Credit Suisse. *Comn:* watercolor painting, Spence Sch, NYC, 03. *Exhib:* Works on Paper, Brooklyn Mus, NY, 75; Juried Ann, Queens Mus, NY, 85; In Search of the Am Experience, Mus Nat Arts Found Nat Competition, 89; Fables of La Fontaine, Inst for Am Univ Aix En Prvance, Temple Univ, Rome, Md Inst, Univ Wash, 2003-04. *Pos:* Dir, Spence Gallery, 92-2005. *Teaching:* Chmn, Art Dept, Spence Sch, NY, 72-95. *Awards:* Resident fel, Va Ctr Creative Arts, 96. *Mem:* Nat Asn Women Artists; Manhattan Graphics Ctr. *Media:* Watercolor; Monotypes. *Collection:* David Rockefeller Jr, Pfizer Inc, Pepsico, JC Penney, Warburg Princess. *Dealer:* NoHo Gallery 530 W 25th St New York NY. *Mailing Add:* 27-15 41st Ave Long Island City NY 11101

MARTIN, DORIS-MARIE CONSTABLE
DESIGNER, SCULPTOR
b New York, NY, July 5, 41. *Study:* Miami-Dade Community Col, S Campus, Miami, Fla, AA, 71; Univ Miami; Univ NC, Asheville, BA, 76; Penland Sch Crafts, NC; Arrowmont Sch Crafts, MA, 81; Goddard Col, MA(sculpture), 80; Univ NC, Greensborough, MFA, 89. *Work:* Miami-Dade Community Col; Durham Art Guild, M Biddle Gallery for the Blind, NC State Mus, Raleigh; Chrysler Mus, Norfolk, Va; Miami Herald, Fla; Univ NC, Asheville; and others. *Comn:* Soft sculpture, Unitarian/Universalist Church of Asheville, 78. *Exhib:* Ann Painting & Sculpture Exhib, Mint Mus, Charlotte, 73 & 76; Marietta Col Int, Grover M Hermann Fine Arts Ctr, Ohio, 76 & 77; Springs Mills Traveling Show, Ft Mill, SC, 77 & 78; one-man shows, Chrysler Mus, 73 & Beyond Craft: Fiber-Form-Fabric, Univ NC, Asheville, 75; and many others. *Teaching:* Instr soft construction sculpture, Asheville Art Mus, 76-, instr beginning printmaking, 77-, instr watercolor, drawing & painting, currently; vis artist, Western NC & Ashville sch system, 70-. *Awards:* Best Sculpture, Craft Work 76, Am Crafts Coun, 76; Best Sculpture & One-Man Show, Durham Arts Guild, Inc, Allied Arts Ctr, NC, 76; Award for Sculpture, Springs Mills Traveling Show, 75 & 77. *Bibliog:* R Clermont (auth), Poloities & Expositions Diverses, Les Editions de la Revue Moderne Des Arts, Paris, France, 73; article, Miami Herald, 76. *Mem:* Am Crafts Coun; Fla Craftsmen, Miami; Western NC Fibers/Handweavers Guild; Handweavers Guild Am; NC Art Soc; and others. *Media:* Fiber. *Publ:* Contribr, Shuttle, Spindle & Dyepot, Handweavers Guild Am, 76. *Mailing Add:* 65 Woodland Rd Asheville NC 28804

MARTIN, DOUG
PAINTER
b Newton, Kans, Dec 10, 47. *Study:* Kans State Univ, BFA; Univ Nebr, MFA. *Exhib:* William Rockhill Nelson Gallery Art, Kansas City, 72; St Louis Art Mus, Mo, 72; Sheldon Art Gallery, Lincoln, Nebr, 75; Robert Hull Fleming Mus, Univ Vt, 81; solo exhibs, Oscarsson Hood Gallery, NY, 81 & Edward Thorp Gallery, NY, 82; Aldrich Mus Contemp Art, Ridgefield, Conn, 81; Herbert Johnson Mus, Ithaca, NY, 81; Krannert Art Mus, Univ Ill, Champaign, 86; Ruschman Art Gallery, Indianapolis, 87; Sherry French Gallery, NY, 88; The Hyde Collection, Glens Falls, NY, 90. *Pos:* Vis artist, Cornell Univ, Ithaca, NY, 81-, Colo Mountain Col, Vail, 75, 76 & 78-81, Univ Ill, Champaign, 86; asst to dir, Yaddo, Saratoga Springs, NY, 84-88. *Awards:* NY Found for Arts Grant in Painting, 89. *Media:* Oil. *Mailing Add:* Charles Cowles Gallery 537 W 24th St New York NY 10011

MARTIN, FLOYD W
HISTORIAN, EDITOR
b Gainesville, Ga. *Study:* Carleton Col, BA, 73; Univ Iowa, MA, 75; Univ Ill, Urbana-Champaign, PhD, 82. *Pos:* Mem bd dir, Southeastern Col Art Conf, 86-89, 2002-06; chair, Dept Art, Univ Ark, Little Rock, 94-95. *Teaching:* Prof art Hist, Univ Ark, Little Rock, 82-; inaugual prof, Univ Ark, Sch Pub Serv, Clinton, 2003-06. *Awards:* Award of Distinction, Little Rock Arts and Humanities Promotion Comn, 96; Exemplary Achievement Award, Southeastern Col Art Conf, 99; Pres's Award for Serv in Arts, Southeastern Col Art Conf, 2005. *Res:* Art history, esp British 1750-1850. *Publ:* Contrib, Art J, 83, Encyclopedia of Arkansas History and Culture, 2006; Contemporary Designers, Macmillan, 84; Victorian Britain, Garland, 88; Design for Arts in Education, 91; Encyclopedia of World Biography, 94; The Eighteenth Century: A Current Bibliography, 92; ed, Southeastern Col Art conf Rev, 91-98; Albion, 94, 2000 & 2001. *Mailing Add:* Univ Ark at Little Rock 2801 University Ave Little Rock AR 72204

MARTIN, FRED THOMAS
PAINTER
b San Francisco, Calif, June 13, 27. *Study:* Univ Calif, Berkeley, BA, 49, MA, 54; San Francisco Art Inst, with David Park, Clifford Still & Mark Rothko. *Work:* Whitney Mus Am Art, Mus Mod Art, NY; San Francisco Mus Mod Art; Oakland Mus of Calif; Fogg Art Mus, Cambridge, Mass. *Exhib:* one-man shows, MH DeYoung Mus, San Francisco, 54 & 64, San Francisco Art Inst, 72 & San Francisco Mus Mod Art, 58 & 73; San Francisco Mus Art Ann, 50-60; Whitney Mus Am Art, 70 & 73; Rena Bransten Gallery, San Francisco, 84; Frederick Spratt Gallery, San Jose, 96; Ebert Gallery, San Francisco, 97, 98, 99, 2000, 01, 03; Han Art, Montreal, 98; Oakland Mus of Calif, 2003. *Pos:* Dir, San Francisco Art Inst, 65-75, dean, 83-92; contrib ed, Art Week, 77-92. *Teaching:* Profr art hist, painting & drawing, San Francisco Art Inst, 79-. *Awards:* Nat Found Arts Artists Grant, 70-71. *Bibliog:* Dan Tooker (auth), article, Art Int, 11/75. *Media:* Miscellaneous. *Publ:* Auth, Beulah Land, A Book of Etchings, Hansen Fuller & Crown Press, 74; A Travel Book, Arion Press, San Francisco, 76; From an Antique Land, Green Gates Press, Oakland, Calif, 79. *Dealer:* Carlson Gallery Carmel CA; Han Art Montreal Que Can. *Mailing Add:* 232 Monte Vists Ave Oakland CA 94611-4922

MARTIN, JANE
PAINTER, DRAFTSMAN
b Montreal, Que, Mar 31, 43. *Study:* Bishop's Univ, Lennoxville, Que, BA(Hons), 65; Carleton Univ, Ottawa, Ont, MA, 66. *Work:* Nat Gallery, Ottawa; Can Coun Art Bank, Ottawa, Ont; City of Ottawa; Art Gallery Greater Victoria; Winnipeg Art Gallery. *Exhib:* Solo exhibs, Whitewater Gallery, North Bay, 85, Berkeley Castle Works 1984-1987, Toronto, 87, Gallery 101, Ottawa, 89, Gathie's Cupboard/Emblems/Transfigurations, Gallery 101, Ottawa, 89, Open Space, Victoria, 91, Rose Show, Toronto, 93, Ewen's Christmas Cabinet (and Rose Garden Tour), Toronto, 96; Wrapture, Ufundi Gallery, Ottawa, 90; Nat Gallery Can, Ottawa, 90; Eve's Eden: Problems in Paradise, Toronto, 94; The Four Show, Toronto, 95; Odd Bodies, Nat Gallery Can, Ottawa, Toronto & Calgary, 96-2000; and others. *Pos:* Artist-in-residence, Ont Arts Coun Project, 77; coordr, SAW Gallery, Ottawa, 78;

co-founder, Can Artists' Represention Copyright Collective, 88; founding bd, Can Reprography Collective, 88-93. *Teaching:* Lectr, UAAC Conf, Concordia Univ, Montreal, 81, Univ Ottawa, 81 & Powerhouse Gallery, Montreal, 81. *Bibliog:* Susan Crean (auth), Berkeley Castle Works 1984-1987, Can Art, fall 87, Body Language, 89; Lisa Rochon (auth), Portraits of suffering, Globe & Mail, 5/28/87; Joyce Nelson (auth), The Sacrament of the Flesh, Wrapture, Open Space, Victoria, 91. *Mem:* Can Artists Representation/Le Front Artistes Can (nat coun, 77-79, nat rep 89-91). *Media:* Oil, Prisma color. *Publ:* Illusr, 77 Best Canadian Stories, Oberon, 77; auth, Who judges whom, Atlantis, 79; illusr, Stories of Quebec, Oberon, 80; auth, Woman Visual Artists on Canada Council Juries, Can Artists Representation/Le Front Artistes Can, 81; illusr, Fat Woman, General, 82. *Mailing Add:* 21 Rose Ave Toronto ON M4X 1N7 Canada

MARTIN, JOHN RUPERT
HISTORIAN, LECTURER
b Hamilton, Ont, Sept 27, 16; US citizen. *Study:* McMaster Univ, BA, 38, DLitt, 76; Princeton Univ, MFA, 41, PhD, 47. *Teaching:* Instr art hist, Univ Iowa, Iowa City, 41-42; prof art hist, Princeton Univ, NJ, 47-. *Mem:* Col Art Asn Am (pres, 84-86); Am Philos Soc. *Res:* Northern baroque art (Rubens, Van Dyck, Rembrandt). *Publ:* Auth, The Farnese Gallery, Princeton Univ Press, 65; Rubens Ceiling Paintings for the Jesuit Church, 68 & Rubens: Pompa Introitus Ferdinandi, 72, Arcade, Brussels; Rubens: The Antwerp Altarpieces, Norton, 69; Baroque, Harper & Row, 77

MARTIN, KNOX
PAINTER, SCULPTOR
b Barranquilla, Colombia, Feb 12, 23; US citizen. *Study:* Art Students League, 4 yrs. *Work:* Corcoran Gallery Art, Washington; Mus Mod Art, Whitney Mus Am Art, NY; Mus Art, Austin, Tex; Univ Calif, Berkeley; Weatherspoon Art Gallery, Greensboro, NC; Mus Art, Baltimore, Md; Art Inst, Chicago, Ill; Mus Art, Dallas, Tex. *Comn:* 19 story wall painting, City Walls, Inc, West Side Hwy, NY, 71; wall painting, Mercor, Inc, Merritt Complex, Ft Lauderdale, Fla, 72; wall painting, Houston & McDougal Streets NY, 79; wall painting, Nieman Marcus, White Plains, NY, 80; John Wayne Mural, John Wayne Sch, Brooklyn, 82. *Exhib:* Whitney Mus Am Art, NY, 72; Int Sch Art, Italy, 90-92; many retrospectives, Art Students League, NY, 92; Tibor De Nagy, NY, 92; solo exhib, Gremillion Gallery, Houston, Tex, 93 & 95; Macon Fine Art Ltd, 95; Benny Smith Gallery, Nelsonville, NY. *Teaching:* Asst prof drawing & painting, Yale Univ, 65-70; instr, Art Students League, 72-; instr, Univ Minn & NY Univ. *Awards:* Nat Endowment Arts, 72; Creative Artists Pub Serv, 78; Pollack Krassner Award, 90; Goetlieb Award, 91. *Bibliog:* George Parrino (auth), Knox Martin, The Deadalian Work, 72; H Kramer (auth), rev, NY Times, 10/25/75; G Brown (auth), Knox Martin Retrospective, Arts, 12/75; G Henry (auth), review, Art News, 1/76; Vivian Raynor (auth), article, NY Times, 10/29/96; Arthur Danto (auth), Adventures in Pictorial Reason, 99. *Mem:* Visual Artists Group Asn; Nat Acad. *Dealer:* Janos Gat Gallery 1100 Madison Ave New York NY 10028. *Mailing Add:* 128 Ft Washington Ave Apt 8-J New York NY 10032

MARTIN, LARRY KENNETH
PAINTER, DEALER
b Anniston, Ala, June 7, 39. *Study:* Jacksonville State Univ, BS, 61; Tulane Univ, MS, 64, PhD, 70. *Work:* Off US Cong; US Senate Corp Collection; Gov's Mansion, Montgomery, Ala; White House. *Comn:* Archaeopteryx (painting), 80, Anniston Mus Natural Hist, Ala; In Pursuit (mural), US Dept Interior, Richard Russell Bldg, Atlanta, Ga, 80. *Exhib:* Ala Zoological Soc, Birmingham, 82-84; Fernbank Sci Ctr, Atlanta, 82-83; Southern Wildfowl Festival, Point Mallard, Ala, 82-88; Okla Wildlife Art Festival, Tulsa, 83-85; Southeastern Wildlife Expos, Charleston, SC, 84-88; Int Exhib Wildlife, Western & Am Art, Chicago, 84-85; Feature Artist, Fla-Nat Wildlife Art Show, 86; Nat Wildlife & Western Art Exhib, Minneapolis, Minn, 86-. *Pos:* Co-founder/co-owner, Nance's Creek Proj: Preserv Rustic Homes (pre-1860) & Hist Structures, 70-; cur, Anniston Mus Natural Hist, 76-79; owner/founder, Wren's Nest Gallery, Anniston, Ala, 78-. *Teaching:* Instr, Jacksonville State Univ, 82-84. *Awards:* Meritorious Serv Award, Nat Audubon Soc, 84; Living for Am Awards, Southeastern Wildlife Exposition, 88-. *Bibliog:* Kite (auth), cover story, Ala Purchasor, 9/82 & 10/83; Myers (auth), American characters: Eccentrics offer artist challenge and rewards, Art Bus News, 10/83. *Media:* Miscellaneous

MARTIN, LORETTA MARSH
CARTOONIST, CALLIGRAPHER
b Plymouth, Ind, Jan 22, 33. *Study:* Art Inst Chicago, BAE, 55; Univ Notre Dame, MA, 68; Famous Artists Schs, 68(cert com art). *Work:* Many pvt collections in US & other countries. *Comn:* Calligraphy for Granaderos de Galvez, (presented to the King of Spain) 86. *Exhib:* One-woman show, First Unitarian Church, South Bend, Ind, 62; Northern Ind Artists; Alumni Asn Art Inst Chicago; Artists 70 & 71, Citrus Co, Fla; El Paso Centennial Mus. *Pos:* Asst cur, El Paso Mus Art, 74-86. *Teaching:* Art instr, Grapevine Sch Art, Grapevine, Tex. *Mem:* Ft Worth Calligraphers Guild; Trinity Arts Guild. *Media:* All Media. *Interests:* Repair/restoration of objects d'arte: ceramic, porcelain, papier mache, etc. *Publ:* Graphic work included in Mangan Publ. *Mailing Add:* Martin Art Studio 1437 Simpson Hurst TX 76053

MARTIN, LUCILLE CAIAR
PAINTER, MURALIST
b Carlsbad, NMex, June 7, 18. *Study:* With La Vora Norman; Frederic Taubes Workshops, Cloudcroft & Ruidoso; Merlin Enabnit Art Sch, Chicago, dipl; workshop with Olaf Wieghorst, Puerto Vallarta, Mex, dipl, 75. *Work:* Carlsbad Libr & Mus, NMex; Houston Med Ctr, Tex; Univ Ariz, Tucson. *Comn:* Jordan River (mural), Hillcrest Baptist Church, Carlsbad, 62; Sacred River (mural), First Baptist Church, McCrory, Ark, 63; El Capitan (mural), Security Savings & Loan, Carlsbad, 64; NMex State Bird-Roadrunner, Young Democrats for Gov Off, State Capitol, Santa Fe, 64; roadrunner painting, comn by Gov Campbell for aircraft carrier Constellation, 64. *Exhib:* Fla Int Art Exhib, Lakeland, 52; Nat Palo Duro Art Show, WTex State Univ, Canyon, 64; Nat Sun Carnival Art Exhib, El Paso Mus Art, 64; one-man show, NMex State Univ, Las Cruces, 65; Boulder City Art Festival, Nev, 70; BPO Elks 385, Tuscon, 90-2000. *Pos:* Artist, Leanin' Tree greeting cards, reproduced by Boulder, Colo, 70-2000. *Teaching:* Workshops, Nev, Carlsbad, NMex & Tucson, Ariz. *Awards:* Grand Sweepstakes, Tri-State Art Exhib, El Paso, 57; First Place, Carlsbad Area Art Asn Exhibs, 64, 65 & 66; First Place, Nat Parks Show, 73, 75 & 76. *Bibliog:* Articles in NMex Newspapers & El Paso Times, 64 & 65; Elena Montes (auth), Lucille Martin's art, NMex Mag, 4/65 & 10/88. *Mem:* Charter mem Carlsbad Area Art Asn; Tucson Art Ctr. *Media:* Acrylic, Oil. *Publ:* Contribr, NMex Mag, 54 & 65 & Ariz Highways Mag, 3/70. *Dealer:* Two Coats Southwestern Gallery Tuscon AZ. *Mailing Add:* 5901 E Third St Tucson AZ 85711

MARTIN, LYS
PHOTOGRAPHER, CURATOR
b Lafayette, La, Mar 3, 57. *Study:* Univ Miss, Oxford, BA(summa cum laude), 79; Art Inst Chicago, BFA, 83, MFA, 86. *Work:* Art Inst Chicago; Mus Contemp Art. *Exhib:* Solo Exhibs, Artemisia Gallery, Chicago, 86; Moming Gallery, Chicago, 87; Vanitas, Chicago Pub Libr Cult Ctr, 90; Wade Wilson Gallery, Chicago, 90; Ross Wetzel Studios, Chicago, 93; Art Detour, Ojai, 96, 2000 & 2001; Ojai Art Stroll, Cherubs, 98; Trendz, 2000; Inner Alchemy, Ojai Creates! Ojai, Calif, 2006; Art Expo, 89, 90 & Selections, 90, Wade Wilson Gallery, Chicago; Personal Political: Sexuality Self-defined, Sch Art Inst Chicago, 90; Photo Projects, White Columns, NY, 90; Contrasts, John Michael Kohler Art Ctr, Sheboygan, Wis, 91; Still Alive: Contemp Still Life, Rockford Art Col, Ill, 91; Light, Milwaukee Inst Art & Design, Wis, 92; TRINE, Parkland Col Art Gallery, Champaign, Ill, 92; Picture This, Benefit Exhib & Auction, Renaissance Soc Chicago, Ill, 92; New Gallery, Houston, Tex, 92; Small Works, Hal Katzen Gallery, NY, 93; Artlantic City, Randolph St Gallery, Chicago, 93; Positive Images, Somism Found, Daley Ctr, Chicago, 93; Twenty Artists Under Twenty Four Inches, Hal Katzen Gallery, NY, 93; Is There Still Life in Chicago, Sazama Gallery, Chicago, 94; Art of Communication, Gallery Cafe, Chicago, 94; Women Photographers, New Gallery, Houston, 94; Camera Obscura/Obscura Camera, Betty Rymer Gallery, Sch Art Inst, Chicago, 94; Blast Exhib & Auction, 102 Greene St, New York City, 93, TZ Art & Co, NY, 94; Introductions, New Gallery, Houston, 93; Art Detour 2, Can Studio, Ojai, 96; The Visionary Show, Ojai Ctr for Arts, Ojai, Calif, 96; 11th Ann Hearts & Flowers Exhib, The Folk Tree Gallery, Pasadena, Calif, 98; Open a Book and Fall In, Ojai Ctr for Arts, 2000; Oak St Etalier, 2000; Touch of Light Gallery, 2001; Tula Hatti, Ojai Calif, 2001; Touch of Light Gallery, 2004. *Collection Arranged:* Polaroid & Polaroid Derived Imagery, 88, John Plouf & Howard Miller, 88 & Investigations, 90, MoMing Gallery, Chicago. *Pos:* Secy, Dept of Prints and Drawings, Art Inst Chicago, 84-87; co-cur, MoMing Gallery, 87-89; asst dir, Feigen Inc, 87-88; co-dir, Betsy Rosenfield Gallery, Chicago, 88-94. *Teaching:* Visiting Artist, Grad Critique Panelist, Sch Art Inst Chicago, 94; guest lectr, Col DuPage, Glen Ellyn, Ill, 94; artist in residence, Ragdale Found, Lake Forest, Ill; Life Drawing, San Antonio Sch, Ojai, CA, 2003. *Awards:* Unendowed Merit Scholar, Art Inst Chicago, 85 & 86; Spec Assistance Grant, Ill Arts Coun, 86; Community Arts Assistance Grant, Chicago Off Fine Arts, 90 & 91. *Bibliog:* Patricia C Johnson (auth), Galleries Host Their Annual Introductions, Houston Chronicle, 1 & 14, sec D, Friday, 7/9/93; Mark Frohman (auth), Home Shopping Art, Publ News, 7/28/93; Tina Wasserman (auth), Sense of Place (catalog, reproduc), Gahlberg Gallery Arts Ctr, Col DuPage, 94; Art Spirit Focus for Gallery Debut, Ojai Valley News, Pg A-8, June 18, 2004; Ojai Creates! hosts Lys Martin Show, Ojai Valley News, Pg A10, June 30, 2006 (photo); Arts Calendar, Ojai Valley News, Pg A8, July 7; Pg A10, July 14 (photo); pg A8, July 21 (photo); pg A10, July 28 (photo); pg A10, Aug 25, 2006. *Media:* Photography, Mixed Media. *Collection:* Gallery Mem show, BAT (Buenaventura Art Gallery), Ventura CA, 2002; Angels Around the World, Gardens of the World, Thousands Oaks CA, 2004. *Publ:* Contribr, Poetry, Seams, Vol 2, No 3, 86; Artist's Pages (collab), Primer, No 3, 89; Project Pages, WhiteWalls, No 26, fall & winter 90; Video Trine: Lys Martin, for Arts Sake, #22, 93; and many others. *Dealer:* Touch of Light 311 N Signal St Ojai CA 93023. *Mailing Add:* PO Box 82 Ojai CA 93024

MARTIN, MARGARET M
PAINTER, EDUCATOR
b Buffalo, NY. *Study:* Boston Univ, BFA; watercolor workshops with John Pike, Robert E Wood, John Pellew, Rex Brandt & Milford Zornes. *Hon Degrees:* Honorary Doctor of Fine Arts Degree, D'Youville Col, Buffalo, NY. *Work:* Burchfield Penny Art Mus & Adam's Mark Hotel, Buffalo, NY, Jacksonville & Daytona Beach, Fla; Oklahoma Christian Col, Oklahoma City; Taiwan Art Inst, Taipei; Hampton Inn, Buffalo. *Comn:* Painting, Lockport Savings Bank, NY, 90; paintings, Equity Savings Bank, Oklahoma Citym 91; Connors & Vilardo, Buffalo, NY, 94; paintings, Lancaster Opera House, NY, 96, 97; mural, D'Youville Col, Buffalo, 2001. *Exhib:* Am Watercolor Soc, 70-73, 78-79, 83, 86, 88-89, 94, 96, 2002; Nat Arts Club, NY, 74-97; Republic China/USA/Australia Watermedia Exhib, 94; Wet & Fresh: A Survey of Current Watercolor in Western NY, Burchfield-Penny Art Center, 2004; and others. *Collection Arranged:* Buffalo Seminary; Colby Art Collection, 20th Anniversary Exhib Coll, 04. *Pos:* Designer, Wagner Folding Box, Buffalo, NY, 62-64; art dir-designer, Manhardt-Alexander, Inc, Buffalo, NY, 64-77; freelance graphic designer & illusr, 77-80. *Teaching:* Watercolor classes & workshop sessions in many areas of US & Can. *Awards:* Hardie Gramatky Mem Award, Am Watercolor Soc, 83; Catherine Lorillard-Wolfe Gold Medal Honor Watercolor, 85; Transpararent Watercolor Award, Knickerbocker Artists, 90; Mary LaGreca Mem Watercolor Award, Hudson Valley Art Asn, 2006; and others. *Bibliog:* Splash, F&W Publ, 90 & 92; Watercolor 90, Am Artist, spring 90; The Best of Watercolor, Rockport Publ, 95. *Mem:* Am Watercolor Soc; Nat Transparent Watercolor Soc; Nat Watercolor Soc; Nat Arts Club; Catharine Lorillard Wolfe Art Club; and others. *Media:* Watercolor. *Specialty:* original paintings,

watercolors. *Publ:* Contribr, Painting with the White of Your Paper, F&W Publ, 95; The Best of Flower Painting, 96 & No More Wishy Washy Watercolor, F&W Publ; auth, Make a value judgement, Watercolor Magic, fall 96; contribr, AWS Isolating the Moment, Buffalo Spree, David Laurence Publ, fall 2005. *Dealer:* House Gallery, 4300 N Sewell Ste 201, Oklahoma City, Okla, 73119; Tidewater Gallery, 1038 Moore St, Swansboro, NC, 28584; Albright-Knox Art Gallery, Rental Sales Gallery, 1285 Elmwood Ave, Buffalo, NY, 14222. *Mailing Add:* 69 Elmwood Ave Buffalo NY 14201

MARTIN, MARY FINCH
PAINTER, GALLERY DIRECTOR
b Glens Falls, NY, Sept 7, 1916. *Study:* Pvt tutoring with Isabel La Freniere. *Exhib:* Rockport Art Asn, Mass, 71; Hamilton-Wenham Art Show, S Hamilton, Mass, 74; Newbury Art Asn, Mass, 75; Gloucester & Cape Ann Exhib, Gloucester, Mass, 72; N Shore Art Asn, Gloucester, Mass. *Pos:* Art dir, Harbor Gallery, Mass, 71-91. *Mem:* Rockport Art Asn; N Shore Art Asn. *Media:* Oil. *Mailing Add:* 730 SW Munjack Cir Fort Pierce FL 34986-3455

MARTIN, ROGER
PAINTER, WRITER
b Gloucester, Mass. *Study:* Boston Mus Fine Arts Sch (honors). *Hon Degrees:* Montserrat, DFA, 98. *Work:* pvt collections in New Eng, NY, the West Coast, Europe, Japan, Switz, S Africa; Cape Ann Hist Asn, Gloucester, Mass; Boston Pub Libr; Fogg Art Mus; Harvard Univ, Cambridge, Mass; Rubin & Rudman, Boston. *Comn:* Graphic art, D C Heath & Co, Allyn & Bacon, Beacon Press, 65-68 & United Church Teaching Pictures; designed cases & executed carvings, C B Fisk Pipe Organs, Harvard Univ & Pohick Church, Lorton, Va, 65-69; House of Hope Presby Church, St Paul, Minn, 79; Stanford Univ, 83; Presby Church, New Bern, NC, 85. *Exhib:* One-man shows, Trinity Col, Hartford, 61, Carl Siembab Gallery, Boston, 69, So Vermont Art Ctr, Manchester, 70, Rockport Art Asn, Rockport, Mass, 83, Orphanos Gallery, Boston Mass, 88, Montserrat Col Art, 90; Westend Gallery, Gloucester, Mass, 95; Acacia Gallery, Gloucester, Mass, 98; Cape Ann Hist Asn, 98. *Teaching:* Instr design & drawing & head freshman dept, New Eng Sch Art, Boston, 67-69; instr design & painting to chmn foundation prog dept, Montserrat College of Art, Beverly, Mass, 69-90, prof emer, 91, assoc prof, 90-, mem found fac, bd trustees, 92-93. *Awards:* Poet Laureate, Rockport, Mass, 90-98. *Bibliog:* Article, Gloucester Daily Times, 5/83. *Media:* Oil; Prints, Woodcut. *Res:* local history. *Interests:* gardening. *Publ:* Contribr, illus in New Yorker Mag, Atlantic Monthly & New York Times; articles & illus in Child Life Mag & textbks; contribr, Gloucester Daily Times, Mass, 89-98; contribr, Boston Sunday Globe, Mass, 92-94; Rockport Remembered: An Oral History, 97 & A Rockport Album: Photographs of Bygone Days, 98, Curious Traveller Press, Gloucester, Mass; Rockport Recollected, Real Stories From Real People, 2001. *Dealer:* David Hall Fine Art Dover Mass. *Mailing Add:* 29 Penryn Way Rockport MA 01966

MARTIN, YOUNGHEE CHOI
PAINTER, DRAFTSMAN, CURATOR
b Seoul, Korea, Aug 20, 54. *Study:* Brooklyn Mus Art Sch, 73; Yale Univ Summer Sch Music & Art, 76; RI Sch Design, Hon BFA, 77. *Work:* Norma Series, Salome Series, Poppea, The Magic Flute Series, The Waste Land Series, landscape paintings; The Aenied Series; In The Wilderness. *Exhib:* Creative Artists Pub Serv Prog Award Winners, Munson-Proctor Art Ctr, Utica, NY & Bard Col, 81; Operatic Themes by Two Artists, Alexandre Hogue Gallery, Univ Tulsa, Okla, 85, Inaugural Exhibit: Chronicling Time, Pastel Soc Am Art Showcase, NY, 93, Subjective Projections, 94, Art Showcase V, 95 & As Subjective as Possible, 97; Violent Nature, Gallery 28, New Eng Sch Art & Design, Boston, 94; 20th Century Oil Painting in Korea, Han Ga Ram Mus, Seoul, Korea, 94; 4th Nat Painting Competition, Cheekwood Mus Art, Nashville, Tenn, 94; Invitational Drawing Exhib, Smith Col, Northhampton, Mass, 96; 173rd Ann Exhib, Nat Acad Mus, NY, 98; Drew Univ, Madison, NJ, 98; one-woman show, Simon Gallery, Morristown, NJ, 98; Areum, Kyoto City Mus, Japan, 99; Voila! Le Monde Dans La Tete, Mus Art Modern Ville Paris, France, 2000; The Heart of Light, Nabi Gallery, Sag Harbor, NY, 2000; Donaldson Gallery, Miss Porter Sch, Farmington, Conn, 01; Florence Bienale, Italy, 02; Maurice Arlos Fine Art, NY, 02; Gallery Horikawa, Kobe, Japan, 02; Rich & Strange, Nobi Gallery, 2004; Bamidbar, 55 Mercer Gallery, 2005. *Collection Arranged:* Yonsei Univ, Seoul; Carpenter Design Group, NY; Bond Market Asn, NY; Bryn Mawr Col, Pa; Korea Merchant Bank, Seoul; Memorial Sloan Kettering, NYC. *Pos:* co-cur, Art Showcase, Bond Market Asn, 93-01; Full time Artist. *Awards:* Creative Artists Pub Serv Prog Painting Fel, 81; Nat Endowment Arts Painting Fel, 83; Vt Studio Ctr Award, 2000. *Bibliog:* Martica Sawin (auth), The drawings of Younghee Choi Martin, Visions and Revisions catalog, 97; Interview with painter: Younghee Choi Martin, Flora Mag, No 5, 12/99; Louis Finkelstein (auth), Women view: two generations of women artists from New York, Haverford Col, 2000; Eric Ernst (auth), Korean innovators on display at Nabi Gallery, SouthHampton Press, 5/25/2000; Joel Silverstein (auth) Oil Painting by Younghee Choi Martin, an Artist odyssey through the Waste Land, catalog, 2004. *Media:* Oil, Charcoal, Pencil. *Publ:* Oil Painting by Younghee Choi Martin an Artist Odyssey, Nobi Press. *Dealer:* Jeong Song Gallery Seoul Korea; Gallery horikawa, Kobe Japan; Nobi Gallery, NYC, NY. *Mailing Add:* 144 W 27th St No 9F New York NY 10001

MARTINEZ, ALFRED
PAINTER
b Ennis, Tex, Dec 24, 44. *Study:* Southern Methodist Univ, Dallas, BFA, 68; Syracuse Univ, MFA, 71. *Comn:* Invisible-Lips (painting), comn by Gerry Dorman, NY, 81; Electric Fans (painting), comn by William Maxwell, NY, 82; Mystery (painting), comn by Gray L Cooper, Austin, Tex, 85; painting, Venetian Blinds, SLS, comn by Jeff Russell; painting, Venetian Blinds, comn by Richard Pitts. *Exhib:* Dallas Mus Fine Arts Ann, 63; Artist-Initiate, Bronx Mus Arts, 78; Artists Books--Franklin Furnace, Walker Art Ctr, 81; History of Art Works Gallery Coop, Wadsworth Atheneum, 81; Prints Benefit, Ctr Inter-Am Arts, NY, 82; Appalachian Nat Drawing Competition, Appalachian Col, NC, 83; Movin-Light, Kamikaze Rock Club, NY, 84; Exploit/Expose, Kentler Int Drawing Space, Brooklyn, NY, 91; William Benton Mus, Storrs, Conn, 92; group exhib, Slater Mem Mus, Norwich, Conn, 93; one-person exhib, Sensate Light, Univ Gallery, Cent Conn State Univ, New Britain, 94; and others. *Teaching:* From assoc prof art to prof, Univ Conn, West Hartford, 73-86, dir, Campus Art Gallery, 81-86. *Awards:* Traveling Artist Fel, Syracuse Univ, 69; Res Grant, Univ Conn, 74; Vis Artist Grant, Castle Gallery, Col New Rochelle, Artists Space Inc, 80. *Bibliog:* Robyn Brentano & Mark Savitt (auths), One Hundred and Twelve Workshop, 112 Green Street, NY Univ Press, 81; Roger Winter (auth), Introduction to Drawing, Prentice-Hall, 83; Susanna Sheffield (auth), Alfred Martinez's Sensate Light, Cent Design/Cent Conn State Univ, New Britain. *Mem:* Film/Video Arts, NY. *Mailing Add:* 9 Chatham Sq Third Flr New York NY 10038-1027

MARTINEZ, DANIEL J
CONCEPTUAL ARTIST
b Los Angeles, Calif, 57. *Study:* Calif Inst Arts, BFA. *Comn:* Art work in bus shelters, Los Angeles, Calif, 90; Public art work, NY, 90. *Exhib:* Centro Cultural de La Raza, San Diego, Calif, 85; Trans Am Ctr Gallery, Los Angeles, Calif, 86; solo exhib, Abstraction Gallery, Los Angeles, 87; Arts Ctr, Boston, Mass, 87; performances, Barnsdall Music Mus series, Los Angeles, 88, Santa Monica Mus Art, Calif, 88, Los Angeles Festival premier, Los Angeles, 90. *Awards:* Rockefeller Found Grant Conceptual Performance, 87; Nat Endowment Arts, 89. *Mailing Add:* c/o Robert Berman/B-1 Gallery Bergamont Sta 2525 Michigan Ave Santa Monica CA 90404

MARTINEZ, ERNESTO PEDREGON
MURALIST, ARTIST
b El Paso, Tex, Feb 26, 26. *Study:* Self-taught. *Comn:* Mural, Pre-Columbian Mexico, Cafeteria Bowie High Sch, El Paso, Tex, 76; murals, Congressional Medal of Honor, Veteran's Clinic, El Paso, 77, 95; mural, The Resurrection, main altar, St Joseph's Catholic Ch, Houston; murals, Love of Country & Disabled Am Veterans, Veterans Hosp, NMex; mural, Labyrinth of the Americas, Univ of Tex, El Paso; mural, Desert Storm, Jr League of El Paso, 91-92. *Exhib:* One-man shows, NMex State Univ, 74, Univ Tex, El Paso, 74, Chamizal Nat Mus, 74-75 & Officer's Clubs, Univ Colo, 75; Exhib for First Ladies of US & Mex, Chamizal Nat Mus, El Paso, 77; Wight Gallery, Univ Calif, Los Angeles; Smithsonian Art Mus, Washington, DC. *Teaching:* Art consult, Boy Scouts Am, 60-; prof Mex-Am Art, El Paso Community Col, 74-; instr free classes for underprivileged & sr citizens; artist-in-residence, Chicano Studies dept, Univ of Tex, El Paso. *Awards:* Artist of Year, Lulac Coun, 74 & 79; City Coun Recognition, El Paso, 77; Tex Navy Admiral, Gov Tex; selected Tex State Artist in two-dimensional works of art, Senate of State of Tex, 97-98. *Bibliog:* Interview world television, Mexico City, 78; Art Diary, 82; Commander Veterans's of Foreign Wars. *Media:* Acrylics, Watercolors. *Publ:* Auth, articles on Pre-Columbian Art, El Paso Newspaper, 85-86; art articles, El Paseno Newspaper. *Mailing Add:* 7140 Villa Hermosa El Paso TX 79912-2221

MARTINEZ-CANAS, MARIA
PHOTOGRAPHER
b Havana, Cuba, May 19, 60. *Study:* Philadelphia Col Art, Pa, BFA, 82; Sch Art Inst Chicago, Ill, MFA, 84. *Work:* Int Ctr Photog, NY; Bibliotheque Nationale, Paris, France; Mus Latin Am Art Orgn Am States, Washington, DC; Los Angeles Co Mus Art, Calif; Ctr Creative Photog, Tucson, Ariz; Chrysler Mus, Norfolk, Va. *Exhib:* Solo exhibs, Chrysler Mus, Norfolk, 92, Southeastern Ctr Contemp Art, Winston-Salem, NC, 93, Cronologias: 1990-1993, Iturralde Gallery, Los Angeles, Calif, 94, Catherine Edelman Gallery, Chicago, Ill, 95, 99, 03, Piedras, Iturralde Gallery & Catherine Edelman, Los Angeles, Calif, 97, Mus Art, Fort Lauderdale, Fla, 02, Julie Saul Gallery, NY, 02; SFla Cult Consortium Fel Exhib, Ctr Fine Arts, Miami, 93; Tampa Mus Art, 93; Fac Exhib, Lowe Art Mus, Univ Miami, Fla, 93; Photog by Cintas Fellows, Art Mus, Fla Int Mus, Miami, 93; Fredric Snitzer Gallery, Miami, Fla, 99, 00, 02; and others. *Collection Arranged:* Bibliotheque Nat, Paris; Ctr for Creative Photog, Tucson, Ariz; Ctr Cult Art Contemp, Mex City; Chase Manhattan Bank; City of Orlando; Haverford Col, Pa; Int Ctr Photog, NY; Int Mus Photog, Rochester, NY; JP Morgan Bank, NYC; Lehigh Univ, Bethlehem, Pa; Light Work, Syracuse, NY; LA Co Mus Art; Miami Art Mus; Mus d'Art Mod de la villa de Paris; Mus Mod Art; Nat Mus Am Art, Smithsonian Inst; San Francisco Mus Mod Art; St Louis Art Mus; Prudential Insurance Co, NY; Whitney Mus Am Art, NY; Tampa Mus Art. *Awards:* Grant, Photog Fel, Nat Endowment Arts, 88-89; Artist-in-Residence, Light Works, Syracuse, NY, 90; Visual & Media Artists Fel, SFla Cult Consortium, 92-93; Grant, Metro-Dade Art in Pub Places Comn, Miami, 94; Grant, Nat Mus Women in the Arts, Washington, DC, 00. *Bibliog:* Cloe Cabrera (auth), Former Cuban artists form images in black and white, Tampa Trib, 7/13/93; Helen L Kohen (auth), Fellowship winners share their talents, Miami Herald, 7/24/93; Helen L Kohen (auth), Photos are linked by Cuban heritage, Miami Herald, 10/30/93; Elisa Turner (auth), Two Centuries of Latino Art, The Miami Herald, 12/9/2001; Elisa Turner (auth), Identity Crisis: Maria Martinez-Canas, The Miami Herald, 5/22/2002. *Dealer:* Catherine Edelman Gallery 300 W Superior Chicago IL 60610; Iturralde Gallery 154 N Brea Ave Los Angeles CA 90036. *Mailing Add:* 2011 SW 10th St Miami FL 33135

MARTINO, BABETTE
PAINTER
b Philadelphia, Pa. *Study:* L'Accademia di Belle Arti, Florence, Italy, dipl, 68; Temple Univ, Philadelphia, BA, 72; Inst Allende, Mex, MFA, 75. *Work:* Mohawk Valley Community Col, Utica; Subaru of Am, NJ; Blue Cross & Blue Shield, Philadelphia, Pa; Owensboro Nat Bank, Ky; New Music West, Calif; Villanova Univ, Pa; Am Col, Pa; Butler Institute Am Art, Ohio; Woodmere Art Mus, Pa; Art in the Embassies,

Washington, DC; Fell Pa Acad Fine Arts, Philadelphia, Pa; Price Waterhouse Collection, NJ. *Comn:* Paramount in the City, Las Vegas, Nev, 2003. *Exhib:* The Martino Family: A Legacy of Excellence in Painting, Shippensburg Univ, Pa, 88; Douglass Col Rutgers Univ, New Brunswick, NJ, 90; one-woman shows, Cudahy's Gallery, NY, 90, NY Univ, 95, Hahn Gallery, Phila, Pa, 01, Hoyt Inst, New Castle, Pa, 02, Salon Des Amis Gallery, Malvern, Pa, 03, Penn Coll, WIlliamsport, Pa, 05; Md Hall Creative Arts; Richard Stockton Col, NJ, 94; Classic traditions of oil painting, Am Col, Pa, 96; Butler Inst Am Art, Ohio and Woodmere Art Mus, Phila, Pa, 04-05; others. *Pos:* Independent lectr. *Teaching:* Instr painting & drawing, Munson-Williams-Proctor Inst, Utica, 78-80; instr drawing, Mohawk Valley Community Col, Utica, 78-81. *Awards:* Grumbacher Gold Medal, Allied Artists Am, NYC, 1990; Fel, Pa Coun Arts, 84, Nat Endowment Arts, 85, Pollack-Krasner Found, 92, Pew Fel in Arts, Phila, Pa, 00, 02, Pa Acad Fine Arts, 00; Everett award, Allied Artists Am, New York City, 1999 & 2001, Thompson award, 2001; Maxwell prize, Woodmere Art Mus, Pa, 2002; GAP Grant Fel Int Arts, Philadelphia, Pa, 2002; Young Hunter award, Allied Artists Am, NY, 03; and others. *Bibliog:* Babette Martino (auth), Composing urban landscapes, Am Art Mag, Vol 61, 36-41, 6/97. *Mem:* Fell Pa Acad Int Fine Arts; Col Art Asn; Allied Artists Am. *Media:* Oil painting. *Mailing Add:* 1435 Manor Ln Blue Bell PA 19422

MARTINO, EVA E
PAINTER, SCULPTOR
b Philadelphia, Pa. *Study:* Pa Acad Fine Arts, Philadelphia, Pa; Gwynedd Mercy Col; also with Giovanni Martino, La France Art Inst; hon degree, Diploma di Maestro d'Arte, Centro Artistico e Cultrale Int Napoli, Italia, 84. *Hon Degrees:* Cento Artistico e Cult Int, diploma di Maesto d'Arte, Napoli, Italy. *Work:* Butler Inst Am Art, Ohio; Woodmere Art Mus, Philadelphia, Pa; Villanova Univ, Pa; Am Col, Bryn Mawr, Pa; Milford Fine Arts Coun, Conn. *Exhib:* Pa Acad Fine Arts; Nat Acad Design, NY, 65; William Penn Mem Mus, Pa; Butler Inst Am Art, Ohio; Indiana Univ, Pa; The Martino Family, A Legacy of Excellence in Painting, Shippensburg Univ, Pa, 88; 4 Martinos 2 Generations, Villanova Univ, Pa, 93; In the Classic Tradition of Painting, Am Col, Pa, 96; Women Painters Pa, Shippensburg Univ, Pa, 97; Unique Perspectives, Hoppper House, Nyack, NY, 00; The Object Observed, Salon des Amis Gallery, Pa, 01; Martinos Women Painters, Atlantic City Art Ctr, NJ, 01, 03; Homenaje a la Familia Martino, Centro Cult, Mex, 02; The Martinos: A Falily Legacy, Butler Inst Am Art, Ohio and Woodmere Art Mus, Philadelphia, 04-05. *Collection Arranged:* Butler Inst Am Art; Woodmere Art Mus. *Awards:* Renee McNeely Award, Phillips Mill Art Asn, Pa, 91 & 98; Juror's Choice Award, Butler Inst Am Art, Ohio, 1994; Paul Mazza Award, 95 & Pilyna Sitarchuk Award, 96, Cheltenham Art Ctr; Catherine Gibbons Granger Award, Pa Acad Fine Arts, 98; Tobeleach Wechsler Founders Award, Cheltenham Art Ctr, Pa, 99; HV Hawley Award, Fellship of Pa Acad Fine Art, 01; Gold Medal Honor, Audubon Artists, NY, 03; Gibson Granger Award, Pa Acad Fine Arts, 03. *Bibliog:* The Best of Oil Painting, Rockport, Mass, 96. *Mem:* Nat Forum Prof Artists; Artists Equity Asn; Allied Artists Am; Fel Pa Acad Fine Arts. *Media:* Oil; Wood. *Mailing Add:* 1435 Manor Lane Blue Bell PA 19422

MARTINO, NINA F
PAINTER
b Philadelphia, Pa. *Study:* Temple Univ, Tyler Sch Art, BFA; Instituto Allende, Univ Guanajuato, Mex, MFA; L'Accademia di Belle Arti, Firenze, Italia (Embassy Scholar) Diploma; Pa Acad Fine Arts, Scholar; Moore Col Art, Philadelphia, Pa; Studied with Giovanni Martino, NA, AWS & Eva Martino. *Work:* Mex-NAm Inst, Mexico City; Utica Col, NY; Montgomery Col, Pa; Woodmere Mus, Chestnut Hill, Pa; Butler Inst Am Art, Ohio; Acad Fine Arts, Florence, Italy; Villanova Univ, Pa; Penn Wynne Sch, Philadelphia, Pa. *Comn:* Seascape (oil), Mercantil de Irapuato, Mex, 80; landscape (oil), Mercantil de Irapuato, Mex, 80; Watercolor: Bullfighter in Action, Corona Beer Co, San Miguel Agency, Mex; Portraits (2), Los Ricos Hacienda, San Miguel Allende, Mex; Murals (2), Corona Beer Co, Ocean Waves Breaking & Atotonilco Creek & Portrait Comn, Irapuato, Mex; Posters of Musicians incorporated in Landscapes, Tourism of Guanajuato, Mex. *Exhib:* Woodmere Mus, Pa; Audubon Artists, 79; Butler Inst Am Art, 79; Martino Family: A Legacy of Excellence in Painting, Mus Civic Center, Philadelphia, 80; 4 Martinos 2 Generations-Villanova Univ, Pa, 93; Solo Exhibs: Michelet Gallery, Zona Rosa, Mex City; Mexican-N Am Inst Cult Relations Gallery, Mex City; Whitfield Gallery, SMA, Guarajuato, Mex; Fne Arts Nat Inst, SMA, Guanajuato, Mex; Group: Traveling Instrs Exhib, Guanajuato & Queretero Mus, Mex; Exhib Profs/Instrs, Univ Guanajuato, Mex; 8 Women Instituto Allende, Gto, Mex. *Collection Arranged:* Woodmere Art Mus, Philadelphia, Pa; North Am-Mex Inst Cult Affairs, Mexico; Austin Coal Co, Ohio; Cervezas Modelo, S.A. de C.V., Mex. *Teaching:* Grad instr, painting & drawing, Inst Allende, Mex, 77-80. *Awards:* Antonio Cirino Mem Award, Allied Artists Am, 94; Klein Family Award, Cheltenham Ctr, 95; Joan & Thomas Holmes Award, Phillips Mill, 95; and others. *Mem:* Fel Pa Acad Fine Arts; Allied Artists Am, NYC; Audubon Artists Am, NYC. *Media:* Oil, Watercolor. *Dealer:* Schwarz Gallery 17th & Chestnut Sts Philadelphia, PA; Whitfield Galleries 5th Ave New York NY; San Francisco Street San Miquel de Allende Gto Mex. *Mailing Add:* 1435 Manor Ln Blue Bell PA 19422

MARTINOS, DINOS
COLLECTOR
Pos: Head, Thenamaris Ships Mgt, Athens, Greece. *Awards:* Named one of top 200 collectors, ARTnews Mag, 2004. *Collection:* Antiquities; modern & copntemp art. *Mailing Add:* Thenamaris Ships Mgmnt 16 Athinas & Verrou S Athens 166 71 Greece

MARTINSEN, IVAR RICHARD
PAINTER, EDUCATOR
b Butte, Mont, Dec 9, 22. *Study:* Mont State Col; Univ Ore; Univ Wyo. *Exhib:* Wyo Artists Traveling Exhib, Sheridan & Laramie; Scottsbluff, Nebr; Sheridan Inn Gallery, 75-76, 78 & 79. *Pos:* founder & bd mem, Martinsen Gallery, Sheridan Col; ret 85. *Teaching:* Prof art & chmn humanities div, Sheridan Col, formerly. *Awards:* Prizes, Wyo-Nebr Exhib, 58 & 59 & Wyo State Fair, 60. *Mem:* Sheridan Artist Guild; Wyo State Art Asn. *Mailing Add:* 452 Falcon Ridge Dr Sheridan WY 82801

MARTON, PIER
VIDEO ARTIST, EDUCATOR
US citizen. *Study:* Univ Calif, Los Angeles, BFA(cum laude), 76, MFA(film, video), 79; also in Paris. *Work:* Inst Contemp Arts, London, Eng; Nat Gallery Can, Ottawa; Long Beach Mus Art, Calif; Carnegie Mus, Pittsburgh; Mus Mod Art, NY. *Exhib:* Biennale de Paris, Mus Art Mod, Paris, France, 80; Mus Mod Art, NY, 85, 86 & 91; Video & Language, Am Mus Moving Image, NY, 89; The Eye and the I, Whitney Mus Am Art, NY, 89; Passage de l'Image, Beaubourg, Ctr George Pompidou, Paris, 89; Video Installations, Spertus Mus, Chicago, 90 & The Art Barn, Utah Arts Coun, Salt Lake City, 91; Performances for video, MOA Theatre/Video Gallery, Carnegie Mus Art, Pittsburgh, 94; JEW (video installation), part of Witness & Legacy (traveling), 95-2000. *Pos:* Dir, Found Art Resources, 81-83. *Teaching:* Asst prof film, video & photog, Occidental Col, 78-79 & 82-83; vis lectr video, Univ Calif, Los Angeles, 80-83 & Art Inst Chicago, 84; vis artist, Minneapolis Col Art & Design, 84-85; asst prof, Sch Art Inst Chicago, 85-90, chmn video area, 86-87; instr art hist & photog, Victor Valley Community Col, Calif, 91; vis assoc prof, Carnegie Mellon Univ, 93-95; fac editing, web & multimedia design & digital imaging, Pittsburgh Filmmakers, 95-97. *Awards:* Northwest Area Found Grant, 85; Media Arts Grant, 86 & Regional Fel Award, 87, Nat Endowment Arts; Ill Arts Coun, 87 & 90; Mem Found Jewish Cult Grant Award, 89. *Bibliog:* Lorri Zipay (ed), Artists' Video: An International Guide, EAI, Cross River Press, 91; Robert Raczka (auth), Pier Marton, The New Art Examiner, 5/94; Margot Lovejoy (auth), Post Modern Currents, Prentice-Hall, 96. *Mem:* Found Art Resources (bd dir, 81-82). *Media:* Digital Media, Installation. *Publ:* Auth, Ephemera No 3, U Carrion, Amsterdam, 79; Cahiers du cinema No 5, Cahiers, Paris, 81; Dreamwork No 4, Human Sci Press, 81; La Opinion, Los Angeles, 11/92-5/93. *Dealer:* Mus Mod Art New York NY; Electronic Arts Intermix New York NY. *Mailing Add:* 225 N Crescent Dr No 203 Beverly Hills CA 90210-4800

MARTON, TUTZI
PAINTER, SCULPTOR
b Bucharest, Romania, US citizen. *Study:* Acad Journalism, Budapest, grad, 71; silk screening, Salvator Fiume, Italy, 86; woodblock printing, Zhejiang Acad Fine Arts, Hangzhou, China, grad, 88. *Hon Degrees:* Fellow of American Biographical Inst; (hon fellow) Anglo-American Academy, Cambridge, 80. *Work:* Nat Arch, Washington, DC; Mus Art State Fla; Mus de Petit Format, Couvin, Belgique; Vatican, Rome; Mus Music & Ethnology, Haifa, Israel; private colls US, South Am, Australia, Austria, Belgium, Can, China, Ger, Greece, Hungary, Italy, Netherlands, others; Mus of History, Augustin Bunea, Romania, 2003. *Comn:* portrait His Holiness Pope John Paul II, Vatican, Rome; portrait Frank Sinatra, Hollywood, Calif; portrait Princess Redwing, RI. *Exhib:* one-person show, Kar Gallery Fine Art, Toronto, 78; Ann Show, Mus Art, Long Beach, NY, 79 & 81; Mus Petit Format de Papier, Exposition Int, Couvin, Belgique, 87; 6th Ann Int Exhib Miniature Art, Toronto, Can, 91; Mus of History, Augustin Bunea, Romania, 2003. *Collection Arranged:* (priv col) Romanian Library of NY, Foreign Press Association, NYC. *Pos:* Critic, 69-71. *Awards:* First Prize, Ann Show, Mus Art, Long Beach, 1981; Ioan & Maria Constantinescu Grant, Fondatia Cult Neth, 1981; I Passatore Award of Romana, Italy, 1982; Hon mention in Camerata Blajeana, Romania, 2003. *Mem:* Int Asn Art, UNESCO, Paris; Artists Equity Asn; For Press Asn, NY, 81; hon fellow Anglo-Am Acad. *Media:* Mixed Media, Oil; Precious Metal. *Res:* Bible, Art, Working with Metal. *Interests:* Art, music and museums. *Dealer:* Zois Shuttie Wallase Ave New York NY 10462. *Mailing Add:* 319 W 74th St Apt 3A New York NY 10023

MARTONE, MICHAEL
PHOTOGRAPHER
b New York, NY, Nov 8, 41. *Study:* Self-taught. *Work:* Mus Mod Art, NY; Fogg Mus, Harvard Univ; High Mus Art, Atlanta; Musee De L'Elysee Lausanne, Switz, 90; Major purchase of photogr, Musee De Elysee, Lausanne, Switz, 96. *Comn:* AIR Light Work, Syracuse Univ, NY, 78. *Exhib:* Die Welt Ausstellung der Photographie, Akad der Kunste, Berlin, 64; New Acquisitions, Mus Mod Art, NY, 70; Multiple Image Show, Mass Inst Technol, Cambridge, 72; New Acquisitions, Fogg Mus, Harvard Univ; solo exhibs, Hirshhorn Mus, Washington, DC, 79, photographs, Print Dept, Fogg Mus, Harvard Univ, 87 & Robert Menschel Gallery, Syracuse Univ, NY, 89; Fifth Vienna Biennale Contemp Photog, Austria, 81; The Foundation Select Collection, Musee De Elysee, Lausanne, Switz, 94. *Teaching:* Instr & artist in residence, Photo Dept, Tisch Sch Arts, New York Univ, 86. *Awards:* Purchase Awards, Art Festival Atlanta, 66 & 67; Photog Fel Grant, Nat Endowment Arts, 75; AIR Exhibitor & Lectr Grant for Light Work, Syracuse Univ, 78. *Bibliog:* A D Coleman (auth), Latent image, Village Voice, New York, 4/71 & article, New York Times, 3/74; Fred McDarrah (auth), Martone Show, Village Voice Rev, 85; A D Coleman (auth), Michael Martone Ripe for Rediscovery, Art News Mag, 11/96. *Publ:* Auth, Dark Light, Lustrum Press, 74; contribr, Creative Camera Mag, 74; The Grotesque in Photography, Summit Press, 78; Light Readings, Oxford Univ Press, 79; Altered photographs, Art News Mag, 81. *Mailing Add:* 342 E 15th St New York NY 10003-4028

MARTONE, WILLIAM ROBERT
PAINTER, INSTRUCTOR
b Wilmington, Del, Nov 30, 45. *Study:* Pa Acad Fine Arts, Cressen Traveling Scholar, certif, 68; Univ Pa, BFA, 69, MFA, 91; pvt study with Morris Blackburn, 65-73, Walter Stuempfig, 66-68, Franklin C Watkins, 69-72 & Julian Levi, 77-80. *Work:* Ronald Reagan Mus, Santa Barbara, Calif; US State Dept, Gen Serv Admin; White House, Washington, DC; Vatican Art Gallery, Vatican City; also many pvt collections. *Comn:* Portrait of Fredrick Joseph Kinsman, Third Episcopal Bishop, comn by Mr & Mrs Charles Proctor, Warren, Ohio, 72; San J Caleb Boggs, comn by Sen & Mrs J Caleb Boggs, Wilmington, 73; Joe Frazier (portrait), comn by Cloverlay, Philadelphia, 74; Joe Frazier & Family, 81; Portraiture & landscape, Poet Prodns, Disney Studios/Touchstone Pictures; M Lavoisier, Lavoisier Libr, DuPont Co; Dean A J Santoro, Widener Law Sch. *Exhib:* Ann Exhib, Nat Acad Design, NY, 67 & 75; Pa Acad Fine Arts, 75 & 79; Cottage Tour, Rehoboth Art League, Del, 75; solo exhibs, Grand Opera House, Wilmington, Del, 77 & Hardcastles, Wilmington, Del, 79; Rockwood Mus, Wilmington, Del, 81; Univ Delrs; Philadelphia Art Alliance; Philadelphia Mus Art; Butler Inst Am Art, Youngstown, Ohio. *Pos:* Account exec, Southam Assocs, 87-88 & Kimble & Melody Advertising & Media Features, 89-90; William Martone & Assocs, 90. *Teaching:* Instr, Howard Pyle Studios, Wilmington, Del, 69-85; instr portraiture, Pa Acad Fine Arts, 73-81; instr art & chmn upper sch dept, Wilmington Friends Sch, 74-77; instr adv/graphic design & typography, Art Inst Philadelphia, 86; instr vis arts & literacy & dir pre-intensive prog, Arts & Educ Intensive/Urban Educ Found, 90-91. *Awards:* First Prize, Philadelphia Watercolor Club, 72; First Prize, Chestertown Arts League, Wash Col, 77, 79 & 85; First Prize Oils, Soc NJ Artists, 79; and others. *Mem:* Del Archaeol Soc; Fel Pa Acad Fine Arts; Philadelphia Watercolor Club (bd dir, 72); Int Soc Artists; assoc Am Inst Conserv, Washington, DC. *Media:* Oil, Watercolor

MARUYAMA, WENDY
DESIGNER
b La Junta, Colo, July 11, 52. *Study:* San Diego State Univ, BA, 75; Rochester Inst Tech, MFA, 80. *Work:* Oakland Mus Art, Calif; Univ Art Mus, Univ Ariz, Tempe; Macy's, Miami, Fla; Am Craft Mus, NY; and many pvt collections. *Comn:* Linda Cohn, Phoenix, Ariz; Michael & Nina Zagaris, Modesto, Calif; Marion Lee, Portola Valley, Calif; Alice Zimmerman, Nashville, Tenn; Ronald & Anne Abramson, Washington; Don Thomas & Jorge Cao, NY. *Exhib:* One-woman shows, New Art Forms Expo, Joanne Raap Gallery, Chicago, 90, The Ingrained Image, Riverside Art Mus, Calif, 90, Signs of Support, John Michael Kohler Arts Ctr, Sheboygan, Wis, 90, Artists Design Furniture, Eve Mannes Gallery, Atlanta, 90, Gallery NAGA, Boston, Mass, 91, Peter Joseph Gallery, NY, 92 & 95, Margolis Gallery, Houston, Tex, 96, Virginia Breier Gallery, San Francisco, Calif, 97, Gallery NAGA, Boston, Mass, 97, Joanne Rapp Gallery, Scottsdale, Ariz, 98, Oceanside Art Mus, Calif, 99, Leo Kaplan Moder, NY, 2000 & Brad Grad Ctr Studies Decorative Art, NY, 2000; Pacific Rim: Japan, Calif Crafts Mus, San Francisco, Calif, 93; Hybridization: Contemp Northern Calif Craft, 1975-Present, Oliver Art Ctr, Calif Col Arts & Crafts, Oakland, 93; Functional Sculpture, Indigo Gallery, NY, 94; Masterworks Two, Peter Joseph Gallery, NY, 94, Breaking Barriers: Recent Am Craft, Am Craft Mus, traveling exhib, 95; World Urushi Cult Coun Exhib, Fujita Corp, Tokyo, 96; Talking to Myself: Cult, Fantasy and Domestic Condition, Porter Troupe Gallery, San Diego, Calif, 2001; Ariz State Univ Art Gallery, Tempe, 2001. *Pos:* Designer & maker contemp furniture, Comns & Speculative Work, 79-; artist-in-resident, Artpark, Lewiston, NY, 83, Carnegie-Mellon Univ, Pittsburgh, Pa, 84, Boston Univ, Mass, 84, Ind State Univ, Evansville, 84, La Napoule Art Found, France, 92, Buckinghamshire Col, High Wycombe, Eng, 94; bd trustees, Haystack Mountain Sch Crafts, 94-. *Teaching:* Instr metalworking & jewelry design, Crafts Ctr, San Diego State Univ, Calif, 73-75 & grad asst metalworking prog, 75; head, woodworking & furniture design prog, Appalachian Ctr Crafts, Tenn Technol Univ, Smithville, 80-85 & Calif Col Arts & Crafts, Oakland, 85-89; artist-in-residencies, Artpark, Lewiston, NY, 83, Carnegie-Mellon Univ, Pittsburgh, Pa, 84, Boston Univ, Mass, 84 & Ind State Univ, Evansville, 84; assoc prof, head, woodworking & furniture design prog, San Diego State Univ, Calif, 89-. *Awards:* Artists Fels, Nat Endowment Arts, 82, 84, 86, 90 & 92 & Tenn Arts Comn, 83; Metropolitan Home/Kraus Sikes Merit Award,89; Fulbright Grant, Eng, 94; Residency Grant, Nat Endoment Arts/Japan-US Friendship Comn, 95; Grants-in-Aid, San Diego State Univ, 96 & Rsch Scholar, Creative Activities Grant, 2000; Office Int Exchange Grant, 2000; Japan-US Friendship Comn Grant, 2000; Mini Grant, Adams Humanities, 2001. *Bibliog:* Daniel Mac Alpine (auth), Woodshop News, 12/93; Candice Miles (auth), Nothing Ordinary, Pheonix Home & Garden, 11/94; Barbara S Greene (auth), Peter Joseph Gallery an Art Furniture Affair, Woodshop News, 3/94; Candice Miles (auth), Nothing ordinary, Phoenix Home and Garden, 11/94; Stylemakers, San Diego Union Tribune, 8/11/96. *Mem:* Am Crafts Coun; World Urushi Cult Coun. *Media:* Furniture Design, Wood. *Publ:* Wendy's place, San Diego Union, 8/27/89; Crackerjack creations, Newsweek, 1/29/90; Art rev, Atlanta J & Constitution, 2/12/90; Back to the Past, Southern Accents Mag, 5/90; Contemporary Crafts for the Home, Kraus Sikes Inc, 90. *Mailing Add:* San Diego State Univ Sch Art Design Art Hist 5500 Campanile Dr San Diego CA 92182-4805

MARX, MADDY See Segall-Marx, Madeleine (Maddy Marx)

MARX, ROBERT ERNST
PRINTMAKER, PAINTER
b Northeim, Ger, 25. *Study:* Univ Ill, BFA, 51, MFA, 53; study & travel in Ger, Austria, Italy, Switz & France, 1 yr. *Work:* Mus Mod Art, NY; Philadelphia Mus Art; Dallas Mus Art, Tex; Seattle Art Mus; Hirschhorn Mus, Washington, DC; and many others. *Exhib:* Franz Bader Show, Baway Found, Vienna, Austria, 76; Art of Poetry, Nat Collection Fine Arts, Smithsonian Inst, 76; Premio Int Biella, l'Incisione, Italy, 76; Davidson Galleries, Seattle, Wash; US Embassy Gallery, Belgrade, Yugoslavia, 83; Davidson Gallery, Seattle, Wash, 95; Int Biennial Exhib Portrait Drawing, Tuzla, Yugoslavia; Int Exhib Graphic Art, Kustveilein, Zufrechen, WGer; Int Biennial Exhib Graphic Art, Ljubljana, Yugoslavia. *Pos:* Artist attached to USIA exhib in Prague & Bratislava, Czech, 65; dir, Flint Inst Art, 57 & Impressions Workshop, Boston, 69. *Teaching:* Instr, Univ Wis, 53; chmn dept art, Flint Jr Col, 56; instr, Sch Art, Syracuse Univ, 58; assoc prof art, State Univ NY Binghamton, 66-69; assoc prof, State Univ NY Col Brockport, 70-72, prof, 72-89, distinguished prof, 89, retired, 90; instr, Fulbright Sch Art, Delhi Univ, India, 84; lectr wkshp, Art Dept, Drake Univ, Des Moines, Iowa, 85. *Awards:* Grand Diploma Drawing, Third Int Biennial Exhib Portrait Drawings & Graphics, Tuzla, Yugoslavia, 84. *Bibliog:* Sebby Jacobson (auth), article, Times-Union, 11/22/85. *Media:* Etching; Oil on Canvas. *Dealer:* Davidson Galleries Inc 313 Occidental Ave S Seattle WA 98104; Arlene Bujese Gallery 66 Newton Lane East Hampton Long Island NY 11937. *Mailing Add:* 80 Nunda Blvd Rochester NY 14610-2840

MARZANO, ALBERT
PAINTER, DESIGNER
b Philadelphia, Pa, Aug 22, 19. *Study:* Philadelphia Graphic Sketch Club; Philadelphia Plastic Club. *Comn:* Murals, Dept Pub Health, Philadelphia, 67 & 69; portrait Riccardo Muti, Friends & Admirers Maestro Riccardo Muti, Philadelphia, 78; portrait Louis A DeSimone, Grand Lodge Pa, Order Sons Italy, Philadelphia, 81; portrait John Cardinal Krol, Archbishop Philadelphia, Grand Lodge Pa, Order Sons Italy, 84; portrait Rabbi Joshu Toledano, Congregation Mikveh Israel, 85. *Exhib:* Ann Mid-Year Show, Butler Inst Am Art, Youngstown, Ohio, 60; one man shows, St Joseph's Col, Philadelphia, 70, La Salle Col, Philadelphia, 71, Philadelphia Sketch Club, 74, Waldron Acad, 75 & Episcopal Acad, 77; plus others. *Teaching:* Instr drawing & painting, Sons Italy in Am, Philadelphia, 65-70. *Awards:* Gold Medals, Philadelphia Art Dirs Club, 54, 55 & 56; Gold Medal, Haddonfield Art Ctr, NJ, 59; Gold Medal, Nat Soc Painters in Casein, 61. *Mem:* Philadelphia Art Alliance. *Media:* Mixed. *Mailing Add:* 1949 Locust St Philadelphia PA 19103-5730

MARZIO, PETER CORT
HISTORIAN, MUSEUM DIRECTOR
b New York, NY, May 8, 43. *Study:* Juniata Col, BA, 65; Univ Chicago, MA, 66 & PhD, 69. *Pos:* Res asst to dir, historian Nat Mus Hist and Tech, Smithsonian Inst, 1969-73; Assoc cur, prints, Smithsonian Inst, 1977-78, chmn, dept cult hist, 1978; dir, Chief Exec Officer, Corcoran Gallery Art, Washington, DC, 1978-82; dir, Mus Fine Arts, Houston, 1982; Chmn, Fed Coun on Arts and Humanities, 1997-2000. *Teaching:* Instr, Roosevelt Univ, Chicago 1966-68. *Awards:* Smithsonian Fel, 68-69; Woodrow Wilson Sr Fel, Italy, 73. *Res:* Relationship of political democracy and fine art in America. *Publ:* Auth, Men and Machines of American Journalism, 73 & The Art Crusade, 76, Smithsonian Press; Rube Goldberg: His Life and Work, 75 & A Nation of Nations, 76, Harper & Rowe; The Democratic Art, David Godine, 79. *Mailing Add:* Mus Fine Arts 1001 Bissonnet PO Box 6826 Houston TX 77265

MARZOLLO, CLAUDIO
SCULPTOR
b Milan, Italy, July 13, 38; US citizen. *Study:* Columbia Col, BA. *Work:* Windsor Art Gallery, Ont; Neiman-Marcus Exec Off, Dallas, Tex; Mus Sci & Indust, Chicago; Ft Wayne Mus Art, Ind. *Comn:* Kinetic piece, ARCO Hq, Philadelphia, 74. *Exhib:* Loan Exhib, Everson Mus, Syracuse, NY, 72; One-man shows, Tafts Mus, Cincinnati, Ohio, 74, traveling exhib, Nat Acad Sci, Washington, DC, 77; Illum, Whitney Mus Am Art, NY, 74; New Acquisitions, Windsor Gallery Art, Ont, 75; The Logic & Nature of Color, Akron Art Inst, Ohio, 75; Hudson River Mus, Yonkers, NY, 76; One-man show, Virginia Beach Arts Ctr, 79. *Teaching:* Instr three-dimensional design, Sch Visual Arts, New York, 74 & Univ Bridgeport, Conn, 75-77; Mather vis scholar, Case Western Reserve Univ, Cleveland, 75; vis artist, US Military Acad, West Point, 78-. *Bibliog:* Joseph Horning (dir), Metamorphoses (film), Ohio Arts Comn, 75. *Media:* Plexiglas, Aluminum. *Mailing Add:* 437 Lane Gate Rd Cold Spring NY 10516

MASBACK, DENNIS
PAINTER, INSTRUCTOR
b Mar 3, 48. *Study:* Wash Univ, St Louis, BFA, 71, MFA, 73. *Work:* Mus Art, RI Sch Design; Fidelity Investments; Amerada Hess Co; Chemical Bank; AT&T Co; Champion Internat Corp. *Exhib:* Genovese Gallery, Boston, Mass, 91; Victoria Munroe Gallery, NY, 91; solo shows, 808 Penn Modern, Pittsburgh, Pa, 92 & Cynthia McCallister Gallery, NY, 94, K&E Gallery, New York City, 95, Radix Gallery, New York City, 97, Albertson-Peterson Gallery, Winter Park, Fla, 1998, Nancy Hoffman Gallery, New York City, 2000, Gail Severn Gallery, Ketchum, ID, 2001; K&E Gallery, New York City, 94; Nancy Solomon Galley, Atlanta, 95, 96, 97; Gail Severn Gallery, Ketchum, ID, 98,99, 2000. *Teaching:* Instr art, Parsons Sch Design, 90-; adj asst prof, Pratt Inst, 93-95, adj assoc prof, 95-. *Awards:* Nat Endowment Art Painting Fel, 91-92. *Bibliog:* Ann Fitzgibbons (auth), Portraits: Here's Looking at You (exhib catalog), Anchorage Mus Hist & Art, 88; Catherine Drillis (auth), rev, Art News, 4/94; Justin Spring (auth), Artforum, 2/96. *Dealer:* Dinberg Arts 49 W 24th St New York NY 10010; Gail Severin Gallery 620 Sun Valley Rd Ketchum ID 83340. *Mailing Add:* Six Varick St New York NY 10013

MASHECK, JOSEPH DANIEL CAHILL
HISTORIAN, CRITIC
b New York, NY, Jan 19, 42. *Study:* Columbia Univ, AB, 63, MA, 65, Dublin Univ (Trinity C), MLitt, 2001, Columbia, PhD, 73, study with Dorothea Nyberg, Meyer Schapiro & Rudolf Wittkower. *Exhib:* Dealers & Critics, Mo David Gallery, NY, 85; Smart Art, Carpenter Ctr Visual Arts, Harvard Univ, 85; Joseph Masheck Col Contemp Art, Rose Art Mus, Brandeis Univ, 86; Joseph Masheck & Peter Plagens, Emily Lowe Gallery, Hofstra, 89; Dan Devine: consumer Matrix & Joseph Masheck:

Dublin Paintings, Roseberg Gallery, Hofstra, 95; Critics as Artists, Andre Zarre Gallery, NY, 95; Makarevich's Second Level of Feeling: A Work of Perestroika Contextualized, Rosenberg Gall, Hofstra Univ, 2002; Photo-Archietecture: Diurnal/Nocturnal, Gallery Onetwenty-eight, NY, 2003. *Pos:* Ed & Chief Artforum Mag, 77-80; contrib ed, Art in Am Mag, 88-; ed consult, New Observations; bd dir, Crosby St Proj, 95-96; adv bd, Annals of Scholarship, 98-. *Teaching:* Lectr, Maidstone (Kent) Col Art, Eng, 68-69; preceptor art hist, Columbia Col, Columbia Univ, New York, 69-71; instr art hist, Barnard Col, 71-73, asst prof, 73-83; lectr visual studs, Harvard Univ, 83-86; vis prof art hist, Hunter Col, spr & fall 84; assoc prof art hist, Hofstra Univ, 87-94, prof, 94; vis prof art hist & Centennial fell, Edinburgh (UK) coll art, 2006. *Awards:* Samuel H Kress Found, fell, 68-69; NEA, fell, 72-73, 75-76; John Simon Guggenheim Mem Found, fell, 77-78; Soc fellos in the Humanities, Columbia Univ, 77-78; Edward Albee Found, Montauk, NY, residencies, 80 & 81; Reva & David Logan Grant for New Writing on Photography, Bost Univ, 85; Samuel Dorsky Found, Perennial Wisdom Award (medal), 2001; research grant, Malevich Soc, 2003. *Bibliog:* D. Carrier in Postmodernist Art Criticism Leodrdo 18, 85; Art Writing, Univ. Mass Press, 87. *Mem:* Am Asn Univ Profs; Col of Arms, London (hon armiger); Col Art Asn; Int Asn Art Critics; Royal Soc of Arts (fell); Soc Antiquaries of Scotland (fell); United Arts Club, Dublin. *Res:* Abstract modern and contemporary, art and architecture. *Interests:* Architecture of Adolf Loos, Painting of Kasimir Malevich. *Publ:* Historical Present: Essays of the 1970s, U M I Research Press, 84; Smart Art, Willis, Locker & Owens, 84; Modernities: Art-Matters in the Present, Penn State Press, 93; Building-Art: Modern Architecture Under Cultural Construction, Cambridge Univ Press, 93; Van Gogh 100, Greenwood Press, 96; ed, introd Arthur Wesley Dow, Composition 1899; 1913, Univ Calif Press, 97; Marcel Duchamp in Perspective, rev ed, Da Capo Press, 2002; C's Aesthetics, Slought Found and Bryn Mawr Coll., 2004. *Mailing Add:* 80 La Salle St 2H New York NY 10027-4712

MASIH, LALIT K
PAINTER - WATERCOLOR
b Almora, India, 32. *Study:* Syracuse Univ, 56-60; Long Island Univ, NY, MFA, 80-85; studied with Harold Stevens, Stan Brodsky, Arnold Siminoff & Milford Zornes. *Work:* Friends Nassau Co Mus; many pvt collections. *Exhib:* Salmagundi Club; Nat Watercolor Soc; Allied Artists Am; Audubon Artsts. *Teaching:* instr, watercolor workshops & demonstrations, currently. *Awards:* Winsor & Newton Award, Am Artists Prof League, 89; Silver Medal of Honor, Audubon Artists, 97; Jane Peterson Mem Award, Allied Artists of Am, 2000. *Mem:* Am Watercolor Soc; Nat Watercolor Soc; Am Artists Prof League; Salmagundi Club. *Media:* Watercolor. *Specialty:* Landscapes, street scenes & harbors. *Mailing Add:* 9 Old Rte 208 New Paltz NY 12561

MASNYJ, YURI
PAINTER, SCULPTOR
b Washington, 76. *Study:* Cooper Union, BFA, 98. *Exhib:* solo shows, On Our Black Rainbow, Sutton Lane, London, 2004, A World of Interiors, Metro Pictures, NY, 2004; 126a, Brooklyn Front Gallery, 2001; Ballpoint Inklings, Geoffrey Young Gallery, Mass, 2002; Shallow Interiors, Rivington Arms Gallery, NY, 2002; New Topography, 2003; From Here On, Guild & Greyskhul, NY, 2003; Drawings, Metro Pictures, NY, 2003; International Paper, Hammer Mus, Univ Calif, Los Angeles, 2003; Happy Days Are Here Again, David Zwirner, 2004; Radical Vaudeville, 2005; The Night Has a Thousand Eyes, 2005; Greater NY, PS 1 Mus Modern Art, Long Island City, NY, 2005; Landings, Susan Inglett Gallery, NY, 2005; Square Dance, Galerie Jacky Strenz, Frankfurt, Germ, 2005; Whitney Biennial: Day for Night, Whitney Mus Am Art, NY, 2006; NY Drawings, Travesia Cuatro, Madrid, 2006. *Mailing Add:* c/o Metro Pictures 519 W 24th St New York NY 10011

MASON, ALDEN C
PAINTER, EDUCATOR
b Everett, Wash, July 14, 1919. *Study:* Univ Wash, MFA. *Work:* Seattle Art Mus, Wash; San Francisco Mus Art; Denver Art Mus; Milw Art Mus; Oreg Mus Art. *Comn:* Mural, 80 ft, Senate Chambers, State Capitol, Olympia, Wash, 81. *Exhib:* One-man shows, Boise Art Mus, 49, Portland Ctr for Visual Arts, Ore, 73, Denver Art Mus, 73 & Chas Cowles Gallery, NY, 81; Allan Stone Gallery, NY, 74 & 78; 14 Abstract Painters, Frederick Wight Art Galleries, Univ Calif, Los Angeles, 75; Univ Art Galleries, Univ NDak, Grand Forks, 78; Mus Northwest Art, Laconner, Wash, 2000; and others. *Teaching:* Prof art, Univ Wash, 47-; retired. *Awards:* Purchase Award, 44th Northwest Ann, 63 & 54th Northwest Ann, 68, Seattle Art Mus; Regional Fel Visual Artists Award, 92; Kings Co Honors Comn Award. *Media:* Acrylic. *Dealer:* Woodside Brareth Gallery Seattle WA. *Mailing Add:* c/o Foster/White Gallery 1331 Fifth Ave Seattle WA 98101

MASON, EMILY
PAINTER
b NY City, 1932. *Study:* Bennington Col, 50-52; Cooper Union, NY City, BFA; Wheaton Col, Mass, DFA (hon), 2000. *Exhib:* Exhibs incl Grace Borgenicht Gallery New York City, Landmark Gallery New York City, Walker-Kornbluth Gallery Fairlawn NJ, Thomas Babeor Gallery San Diego, MB Modern New York City, Va Lynch Gallery Tiverton RI, Mugar Art Gallery Colby-Sawyer Col; rep in collections of Springfield (Mass) Mus, Rockefeller Group New York City, Ciba-Geigy Chemical Group Ohio; subject of Emily Mason: At the Heart of Abstraction, by David Ebony, 2002. *Teaching:* teacher, Hunter Col, New York City. *Awards:* Grantee Fulbright Fel, Acad delle Belle Arti, Venice, 56. *Mem:* Nat Acad (acad). *Mailing Add:* 263 Stark Rd Brattleboro VT 05301

MASON, FRANCIS SCARLETT, JR
ADMINISTRATOR, WRITER
b Jacksonville, Fla, Sept 9, 21. *Study:* St John's Col, Annapolis, Md, BA, 43; grad study art hist with Nikolaus Pevsner, Birkbeck Col, Univ of London, 61-64. *Pos:* Cult attache & exhibs officer, US Info Agency Foreign Serv, 54-64; chief US exhibs to Russia & E Europe, US Info Agency, 65-67; pres experiments in art & technol, New York, 68; asst dir, Pierpont Morgan Libr, New York, 75-87, acting dir, 88, consult on endowment campaign, 88-92. *Mem:* New York Studio Sch Drawing & Sculpture (chmn emer); Century Asn NY. *Publ:* Ed, Steuben, Seventy Years of Glassmaking, Praeger, 74; co-auth, Balanchine's Complete Stories of the Great Ballets, Doubleday, 77; 101 Stories of Great Ballets, Doubleday, 77; I Remember Balanchrine, Doubleday, 90; co-auth, I Remember Martha Graham, Doubleday, 97. *Mailing Add:* 46 Morton St New York NY 10014-4021

MASON, FRANK HERBERT
PAINTER, INSTRUCTOR
b Cleveland, Ohio, Feb 20, 21. *Study:* Nat Acad Design, New York, with George Nelson, 36-37; Art Students League, with Frank Vincent DuMond, 37-51. *Work:* Eureka Col Mus, Ill; Butler Inst Am Art, Youngstown, Ohio; Am Embassy, London; Hall of Governors, State Capitol, Albany, NY; US War Dept, Washington, DC; Mus of the City New York, NY; Anticoli Mus, Anticoli Corrado, Italy; Westmoreland Co Mus Art, Greensburg, Pa. *Comn:* Life of St Anthony of Padua (eight large canvases), 11th Century Church of San Giovanni di Malta, Venice, Italy, 64; Resurrection, Old St Patrick's Cathedral, NY, 72; San Rocco, Church of Santa Vittoria, Anticoli Corrado, Italy; 3 murals, King Faisel Naval Acad, Jidda, Saudi Arabia, 81. *Exhib:* Expos Intercontinentale, Palais des Congres, Monaco, 68; Nat Arts Club, NY, 73; Mood Gallery, Milan, Italy, 75; John Pence Gallery, San Francisco, 77 & 79; Metrop Mus Art, NY, 79; Union League Club, 88. *Teaching:* Instr fine arts, Art Students League, New York, 51-. *Awards:* Popular Prize, Asn Artists Pittsburgh, Carnegie Inst Mus Art, 46; Figure Composition-St Anthony, Penn-National, Ligonier, 68; Prix d'Amerique du Nord, Expos Intercontinentale, Monaco, 68. *Bibliog:* Condon Riley (auth), Frank Mason, painter, Am Artist, 6/64; Alexander Eliot (auth), Frank Mason: Allegiance to the old masters, Am Artist, 12/73; David L Bell (auth), Frank Mason, Artists of the Rockies and the Golden West, fall 83. *Mem:* Art Students League; Nat Soc Mural Painters; Int Inst Conserv of Hist & Artistic Works; Academician Nat Acad. *Media:* Oil, Graphics. *Mailing Add:* 385 Broome St New York NY 10013-3705

MASON, JOHN
SCULPTOR
b Madrid, Nebr, Mar 30, 27. *Study:* Otis Art Inst, Los Angeles, 49-52; Chouinard Art Inst, Los Angeles, 53-54. *Work:* Art Inst Chicago; Los Angeles Co Mus Art; San Francisco Mus Art; Mus Contemp Crafts, NY; Nat Mus Mod Art, Kyoto, Japan; and others. *Comn:* Ceramic relief, Palm Springs Spa, Calif, 59; ceramic relief, Tishman Bldg, Los Angeles, 61; ceramic doors, Sterling Holloway, South Laguna, Calif; and others; City of Biose, Idaho, 82; City of Sacramento, Calif, 82. *Exhib:* One-man shows, Pasadena Art Mus, Calif, 60 & 74; Whitney Mus Am Art, 64, 73 & 76; Kompas 4, Van Addemuseum Eindhoven, The Neth, 69; Nat Mus Mod Art, Kyoto, Japan, 71; and others. *Teaching:* Assoc prof art, Univ Calif, Irvine, 67-73, prof art & chmn dept studio art, 73-74; prof studio art, Hunter Col, New York, 74-85. *Awards:* Ford Found Award, 67th Am Exhib, Art Inst Chicago, 64; Univ Calif Award, Creative Arts Inst, 69-70; and others. *Bibliog:* John W Mills (auth), The Technique of Sculpture, Reinhold Corp, NY, 65; John Coplans (auth), John Mason--Sculpture, Los Angeles Co Mus Art, 66; Susan Peterson (auth) The Craft and Art of Clay, 00, 03. *Media:* Ceramics. *Dealer:* Frank Lloyd Gallery 2525 Michigan Ave B5B Santa Monica CA 90404. *Mailing Add:* 1521 S Central Ave Los Angeles CA 90021

MASON, LAURIS LAPIDOS
ART DEALER, WRITER
b New York, NY, Apr 21, 31. *Study:* Syracuse Univ, AB, 52; State Univ NY, New Paltz, MS, 55. *Pos:* Dir, Mason Fine Prints, 72-. *Specialty:* American & European original prints. *Publ:* Auth, Print Reference Sources: A Select Bibliography, 18th-20th Centuries, 75, second ed, 79; coauth (with Cecile Shapiro), Fine Prints: Collecting, Buying & Selling, co-ed (with Joan Ludman), auth, Print Collector's Quarterly: An Anthology of Essays of Eminent Printmakers of the World & coauth (with Joan Ludman), The Lithographs of George Bellows: A Catalogue Raisonne, KTO Press, rev ed 92. *Mailing Add:* Country Club Tower Apt 1112 10777 W Sample Rd Coral Springs FL 33065

MASON, MOLLY ANN
SCULPTOR, ENVIRONMENTAL ARTIST
b Cedar Rapids, Iowa, 53. *Study:* Univ Iowa Sch Art, BFA, 73, MA, 75, MFA, 76. *Work:* Univ Central Fla, Orlando; Univ Northern Iowa, Cedar Falls; City of Alexandria, La; City of W Palm Beach, Fla; City of Albuquerque, NMex. *Comn:* Stainless Steel/Copper Sculpture, City of Brisbane, Australia, 96; Bronze/Copper Sculpture, Royal Caribbean Cruise Lines, 96; Stainless Steel/Copper Sculpture, Michener Mus, Doylestown, Pa, 98; Stainless Steel/Copper Sculpture, Wyeth Labs, Pa, 2001; Bronze/Kiln-Formal Glass Sculptures, Northwest Valley Med Ctr, Tucson, Ariz, 2004. *Exhib:* Minneapolis Inst of Arts, Minn, 79; Soho 29 Gallery, NY, 87, 89, 92, & 95; Quietude Garden Outdoor Sculpture Gallery, NJ, 90 & 96; Elaine Benson Gallery, Bridgehampton, NY, 90 & 96; Gallery COM & Art Space Niji, Kyoto, Japan, 92; Sculpture Showcase Gallery, New Hope, Pa, 94-2002; Sculpture on the Grounds, Rockville Civic Ctr, Md, 95 & 96; James A Michener Mus Art (with catalog), Doylestown, Pa, 98-99; Johnson Atelier's Sculpture Mus, 99; Contemp Sculpture Chesterwood Mus, Stockbridge, Mass, 2000, 2001; and others. *Teaching:* Prof sculpture, Univ Minnesota, Morris, 76-78; instr, Southern Illinois Univ, Edwardsville, IL, 78-79; Asst prof sculpture, Univ NMex, 79-82 & Tulane Univ, New Orleans, La,

82-85; State Univ NY, Stony Brook, NY, 85-92. *Awards:* Am Asn Univ Women Found Fel, 84; Fel, Lilly Found, 87-88; Fulbright Fel, Japan, 91. *Bibliog:* Elizabeth Blair (auth), Scale, Spirit and Energy: Contemporary Sculpture thrives in Yugoslavia's Symposium, Int Sculpture Mag, 3-4/87; Jules Heller (auth), Twentieth Century North American Women Artists, Garland Press, 94; Stephen Paul Miller (auth), rev New York solo exhib, Cover Arts NY Mag, 95; Molly Mason: Sun and Shadow, James Michener Mus Art, 98-99; Virginia Watson Jones (auth), Contemporary American Women Sculptors, Oryx Press, 85; Jules Heller (auth), North American Artists of the Twentieth Century, Garland Press, NY, 95. *Mem:* Col Art Asn; Int Sculpture Ctr; Sculptors Guild, NY; Washington Sculptors Group, Washingon, DC. *Media:* Metal, Wood; Stone, Water Features; all Sculptural Media. *Dealer:* Tadu Contemporary Art, 940 E Palace Ave, Santa Fe, NM; Elaine Benson Gallery, 2317 Montauk Hwy, PO Box 3034, Bridgehamton, NY; Art 4 Business, 161 Leverington Ave, Philadelphia, PA, 19127; Art & Sculpture Consulting at: art and sculpture US; The Guild at guild.com; Contract Art, 11 Halls Rd, Old Lyme, CT, 06371. *Mailing Add:* 111 Beach St Port Jefferson NY 11777-1306

MASON, NOVEM M
SCULPTOR, EDUCATOR
b North Wildwood, NJ, Nov 22, 42. *Study:* NC State Univ Sch Design, BA(archit), 68; ECarolina Univ Sch Art, MFA, 74. *Work:* Relief sculpture, ECarolina Univ; Southern Univ, Shreveport, La; West Tex Mus, Lubbock, Tex. *Comn:* Sculptural screen, Southern Bank, Richmond, Va, 76; relief sculptures, Richmond Fredericksburg Petersburg Railroad, Richmond, Va, 77, Southern Univ, 80 & First Fed Savings & Loan, Lake Charles, La, 81; entrance sculpture, Mid-States Wood Preserving Inc, Simsboro, La, 82. *Exhib:* Anderson Gallery Summer Invitational, Richmond, Va, 76; Three Artists, Wyly Tower Gallery, Ruston, La, 81; Alumni Masonic Temple Studios, Anderson Gallery, Richmond, Va, 83; Canal Place/Art Place, Contemp Art Ctr, New Orleans, La, 86; Sculpture '86, Houston Mus Fine Arts, Tex, 86; The Red Clay Survey, Huntsville Mus Art, Ala, 88; Louisiana Artists, Louisiana Arts & Sci Ctr, Baton Rouge, 89; Art in Park, Lubbock, Tex, 90; Outstanding is Their Swamp, Sangre De Cristo Arts Ctr, Pueblo, Colo, 90. *Collection Arranged:* Drawing nude: Col of Faset I Seay, Atlanta, GA, 72; Painting still life: col of Augustus W Mason, Morehead City, NC, 73; Sculpture, Bust: Col of John J Armstrong, Glen Cove, NY, 73; Sculpture, Relief: col of sch of Art East Carolina Univ Greenville, NC, 74; Sculpture screen: col of Southern Bank, Richmond, VA, 75-76; Sculpture Relief: col of Richmond Fredrickburg Railroad, Richmond VA, 77; Sculpture abstract: col of A W Mason, Morehead City, NC, 77; Sculpture, screen: col of Woodsmith, Inc, Ruton, LA, 80; Sculpture Relief: col of First Federal Savings and Loan, Lake Charles, LA, 81; Sculpture Relief: col of AD Mazisys, Air, Ruston, LA, 82; Sculpture, Abstract: col of Mid States Woud Preservers, Inc, Simsboro, LA, 82; Sculpture, conceptual: col of Ken Willis, Glen Allen, VA, 84; Sculpture, Abstract: col of Dr Joseph Strother, Clayton, GA, 90; Sculpture, abstract col of Jack Lewis, Ruston, LA, 90; Sculpture abstract: col of West Texas Mus, Lubbock, TX, 91; Sculpture, abstract: col of Masuil Mus of Art Monroe, LA, 92. *Pos:* Partner, artist & designer, Design Collaborative, Richmond, Va, 74-79; designer & artist, Woodsmith, Ruston, La, 79 85. *Teaching:* Asst prof art, Va Commonwealth Univ, Richmond, 68-79; assoc prof art, La Tech Univ, Ruston, 79-88, prof, 88-90; prof, Univ NC, Greensboro, 90-. *Awards:* Summer Res Grant, La Tech Univ, 88; Juror's Choice Award, Huntsville Mus Art, 88; Design Educ of the Year Award, Carolina's Chap of Am Soc Interior Designers, 95; Sch Human Environ Scis Outstanding Teacher Award, 2002. *Mem:* Southern Asn Sculptors; Col Art Asn Am; Tex Sculpture Asn; Am Soc Interior Designers; Int Interior Design Asn; Interior Design Educators Coun. *Media:* Wood; Mixed. *Mailing Add:* Dept Interior Architecture 259 Stone Bldg Unc-G Greensboro NC 27412-5001

MASSAD, GEORGE DANIEL
PAINTER, EDUCATOR
b Oklahoma City, Okla. *Study:* Princeton Univ, BA in English, 1969; Univ Chicago, MA in English, 1977; Univ Kans, MFA in Painting, 1982. *Work:* Met Mus Art, NY; Art Inst Chicago; Philadelphia Mus Art; Smithsonian Am Art Mus; Milwaukee Art Mus; Philbrook Mus Art, Tulsa, Okla; Ark Art Ctr, Little Rock; and others. *Exhib:* Tatistcheff Gallery, New York City, 86; Pa Acad of the Fine Arts, Philadelphia, Pa, 91; Franklin & Marshall Col, Lancaster, Pa, 92; Allentown Art Mus, Allentown, Pa, 97; Forum Gallery, NY, 2001; Univ Richmond, 2002; Things Found Along the Way, Lancaster Mu Art, Lancaster, Pa, 2003; group exhib, Mid-Four, Nelson-Atkins Mus of Art, 83, Am Realism, San Francisco Mus of Modern Art, 85, Realism Today, Nat Acad of Design, New York City, 87, New Acquisitions, Nat Mus of Am Art, Wash, DC, 88, 20th Century Drawing & Sculpture, Cummer Mus of Art, Jacksonville, Fla, 89, Am Modern Still-Life, Snite Mus, Univ of Notre Dame, 98, Contemp Am Realist Drawings, Art Inst Chicago, 99, New Acquisitions, Philadelphia Mus of Art, 2000, About Face, Ark Arts Ctr, Little Rock, Ark, 2001; Representations: The Art of Drawing, Skidmore Col, 2002; Transforming the Commonplace, Susquehanna Mus Art, Harrisburg, Pa, 2003; solo exhib, Huntington Mus Art, WVa, 2003, Forum Gallery Ny, 2006, Philbrook Mus Art, Tulsa, 2006; Poem, Demuth Found, Lancaster, Pa, 2004; Graphic Masters, Highlights from the Smithsonian Am Art Mus, 2003-05. *Pos:* Artist-in-residence, Lebanon Valley Coll, Annville, Pa, 93-; trustee, Suzanne Arnold, Found, 97-. *Teaching:* adj prof, art & English honors prog, Lebanon Valley Col, Pa, 84-. *Awards:* Pa Council on the Arts; Pollock-Krasner Found; Nat Endowment for the Arts. *Bibliog:* Ronny Cohen (auth), G Daniel Massad, Artforum, summer 95; John Laughery (auth), Silent History, Forum Gallery & Univ Richmond Mus, 2001; Lynne Paricell (auth), The Meaning of Things, Am Artist, 10/2006. *Mem:* Col Art Asn. *Media:* Pastel. *Dealer:* Forum Galley 745 Fifth Ave New York NY 10151. *Mailing Add:* Art & Art History Dept Lebanon Valley College Annville PA 17003

MASSARO, KAREN THUESEN
CERAMIST, LECTURER
b Copenhagen, Denmark; US citizen. *Study:* State Univ NY, Buffalo, BSEd, 66; Univ Mass, Amherst, 67-68; Univ Wis, Maidson, with Don Reitz, MFA, 72. *Work:* Nat Gallery Art, Washington; Milwaukee Art Mus; Wustum Mus, Racine, Wis; Univ Wis, Madison; Decorative Arts Mus, Little Rock, Ark; Topeka & Shawnee Co Pub Libr Collection. *Exhib:* Solo exhibs, Kresge Art Gallery, Univ Mich, E Lansing, 79, Rochester Art Ctr, Minn, 80, Winfield Gallery, Carmel, Calif, 92, Porter Col, Univ Calif Santa Cruz, 95, Perimeter Gallery, Chicago, 2001, Pence Gallery, Davis, Calif, 2001, Artist of Yr Exhib, Co Gov Center, Santa Cruz, Calif, 2003; A Discerning Passion, Forum for the Visual Arts, Tex Tech Univ, Lubbock, 94; Ten Outstanding Women Ceramists, Univ Wis, Eau Claire, 96; Nat Coun Educ Ceramic Arts Ceramic Nat, Las Vegas, Nev, 97; The Common Object, Calif Col Arts & Crafts, Oakland, Calif, 97; Tea Bowl Invitational, San Francisco Craft & Folk Art Mus, San Francisco, Calif, 98; A Survey: Two Artists in Mid Career, Karen Thuesen Massaro & Joel Leivick, Mus Art Hist, Santa Cruz, 2000; Gallery Eight, LaJolla, Calif, 2003; Taking Measure: Am Ceramic Art in New Mellennium, World Ceramic Exposition, Yeoju, Republic of Korea, 2001; Sidney Myer Fund Int Ceramics Exhib & Competition, Shepparton Art Gallery, Australia, 2002. *Collection Arranged:* Guest Cur, Time & Place: Fifty Years of Santa Cruz Studio Ceramics, Mus of Art Hist, Santa Cruz, CA, Exhib 97, catalog pub 96 with same title; Revealing Influences: Conversations with Bay Area Artists, Mus of Craft & folk Art, San Francisco, CA, 2003; 21st Century Ceramics in the US & Can cur by Bill Hunt, Columus Col of Art & Design, OH, 2003; Fabrication, Bruce Gallery of Art, Edin Boro Univ of PA, 2004. *Pos:* Vis artist, Kohler Artist Ed, Kohler Co, Wis, 84-; guest cur, Mus Art Hist, Santa Cruz Co, Calif, 96-97. *Teaching:* Vis fac mem fine art & art hist, Beloit Col, Wis, 72-77; vis artist ceramic arts, Ohio State Univ, 77; vis fac mem, Scripps Col, Claremont, Calif, 80; lectr, Univ Calif, Santa Cruz Exten, 95. *Awards:* Purchase Prize, 51st Exhib Wis Crafts, Milwaukee Art Ctr, 72; Best in Ceramics & Outstanding Wis Craftsman, Beaux-Arts Designer-Craftsman 72 & Columbus Mus Fine Arts, 72; Honorable Mention & Patron Purchase, Wichita Nat All Media Crafts Exhib, 88; Santa Cruz Co Art of Yr, 2003; Viewpoint: Ceramics 2001, Grossmont Col, El Caton, CA, First Prize; Form Follows Function, Lill St Gallery, Chicago, Third Prize, 2004. *Bibliog:* Ceramic Art Taipei, Taiwan, profile by Lin Chen-Long, 70, 71, Spring 2003; The Craft Art of Clay by Susan Peterson, 2003; Making Marks, Robin Hopper. *Mem:* Nat Coun Educ Ceramic Arts (exhib chmn, 78-80). *Media:* Porcelain, Other Clay. *Res:* History of ceramic arts, studio ceramics by American women 1875-present. *Specialty:* Ceramics, painting, sculpture. *Interests:* Painting on abstract assemblage of 3-D ceramic forms. *Dealer:* Perimeter Gallery Chicago IL. *Mailing Add:* 617 Arroyo Seco Santa Cruz CA 95060

MASSEY, ANN JAMES
GRAPHIC ARTIST, PAINTER
b Evanston, Ill, Nov 9, 51. *Study:* Art Acad El Paso, 1970; Ramon Froman Sch Art, 1974; Univ Texas, El Paso, 70-71; Paris Am Acad, 78; Schuler Sch Fine Art, 90. *Work:* El Paso Mus Art, Huthsteiner Fine Arts Trust & Providence Mem Hosp, El Paso, Tex; Helen of Troy, LTD, El Paso. *Comn:* Portraits of Student of the Week, El Paso Electric Co, 82; Two Portraits, comn by Peter DeWetter (former Mayor), El Paso, 90; Portrait, Dr Reuben McDaniel, Austin, Tex, 1990; Tribute to Rob, comn by Robert Hoy, Jr, El Paso, Tex, 2005. *Exhib:* Carlsbad Mus & Art Ctr, NMex, 92; Am Drawing Biennial III, Muscarelle Mus Art, Williamsburg, Va, 92; retrospective, Chamizal Nat Mem, El Paso, Tex, 96; The Am Artist's Professional League 68th Grand Nat Exhib, Salmagundi Club, NY, 96; Expoarte 96, Fine Arts Mus Pronaf, Cuidad Juarez, Chihuahua, Mex, 96; Royal Scottish Acad 176th Ann Exhib, McLellan Galleries, Glasgow, Scotland, 2002; Catharine Lorillard Wolfe Art Club 107th Ann Open Juried Exhib, Nat Arts Club, NY, 2003; 3rd Worldwide Exhib Fine Arts in Miniature, Smithsonian Inst, Arts & Indust Bldg, Wash, DC, 2004; Ann Exhib, Mall Galleries, The Mall, London, UK, 2005. *Pos:* Owner, The Montwood Gallery, El Paso, Tex, 74-78 & Massey Fine Arts, Santa Teresa, NMex, 92-94; pres United Kingdon Coloured Pencil Soc, UK, 2004-. *Teaching:* Pvt drawing, instr, El Paso, 75-1994; Pvt consult & workshop instr, 1992-. *Awards:* Best Show, $6500 Purchase Prize, Ann EPAA Exhib, Sierra Med Ctr & El Paso Mus Art Asn, 91; First Place Drawing Pastel & Scrimshaw, Miniature Art Soc Fla 20th Int Miniature Art Show, Clearwater, Fla, 95; Barbara Tate Award, Soc of Women Artists 141st Ann Exhib, London, UK, 2002. *Bibliog:* Victor Martinez (auth), Pencil pusher opts for Paris, El Paso Times, 1/20/94; Sandra Angelo (auth), Colored pencil artists get it together, Am Artist Mag, 3/94; Deborah Martin (auth), Coming Home, El Paso Herald Post, 7/8/96; David Hockney (auth), book review on Secret Knowledge, Art Renewal Center, 2004. *Mem:* Signature mem Soc Women's Artists, Eng; Am Artists Prof League; signature mem Colored Pencil Soc Am & UK; Catharine Lorillard Wolfe Art Club. *Media:* Wax Pencil, Oil. *Publ:* Contribr, New things to expand your knowledge, Artists Mag, 9/93; Perfect Pencil Renderings, Artists Mag, 5/1993; The Best of Colored Pencil 1993-1995. *Dealer:* Don Waters Design Group 4120 Boy Scout La El Paso TX 79922; Adair Margo Gallery 415 E Yandell El Paso TX 79902. *Mailing Add:* 4 rue Auguste Chabrieres Paris 75015 France

MASSEY, CHARLES WESLEY, JR
PRINTMAKER, EDUCATOR
b Lebanon, Tenn, Aug 21, 42. *Study:* Mid Tenn State Univ, BS, 64; Univ Ga, MFA(honors), 72. *Work:* Pushkin Mus, Moscow, USSR; Bradford City Art Gallery, Eng; Libr of Cong, Washington, DC; Whitney Mus Am Art, NY; Corcoran Mus Art, Washngton; and 81 others. *Exhib:* Am Drawings III & IV, Smithsonian Traveling Exhib, 81-85; 1st & 2nd Int Print Exhibs, Seoul, Korea, 81-82; Boston Printmakers Nat Print Exhib, 81-84 & 86; Int Print Triennale, Cracow, Poland, 91, 94, 97 & 2000; curated exhib, Colorprint USA, 88, 91, 94, 98 & 2002; Nat Acad Design 177th Ann Exhib, NY, 2002; and approx 500 other int and nat exhibs since 1971. *Pos:* Univ prof art, Ohio State Univ, 74- & chairperson dept art, 82-88. *Teaching:* Instr art printmaking, Univ Ga, Athens, 72-74; prof printmaking, Ohio State Univ, 74-.

Awards: Ohio Arts Coun Fel Grant, 81 & 86-94; Purchase Awards, Philadelphia Print Club, 82 & 19th Oulin Nat, Knoxville, 87; Nat Endowment Arts Grant, 82; Nat Exhib Trenton, NJ, 88. *Bibliog:* Albert Christ-Janer (dir), Artist--Charles Massey, Jr, Printer (film), Univ Ga, 71. *Mem:* The Print Center, Philadelphia; Boston Printmakers; Col Art Asn; Columbus Art League (pres, 82-92); Southern Graphics Coun; Mid-Am Print Coun; Am Print Alliance. *Media:* Lithography, Drawing. *Publ:* Illusr, The Complete Screenprint & Lithography, Macmillan & Free Press, 74; Sing with Understanding, Broadman Press, 80; J Higher Educ, OSU Press, 83; Realizing the obvious: everything counts, Taipei Fine Art Mus, 12/2001; Prints and politics: everything counts, J of Am Print Alliance, Vol 10, Spring/2002. *Mailing Add:* 93 E Lincoln St Columbus OH 43215-1563

MASSEY, JOHN
COLLAGE ARTIST, CONCEPTUAL ARTIST
b Toronto, Can, July 6, 50. *Study:* Ont Col Art, AOCA, 74. *Work:* Ydessa Hendeles Art Found, Toronto; Stedelijk Mus, Amsterdam, Holland; Fonds Nat D'Art Contemporain, Paris; Nat Gallery Can, Ottawa; Mattress Factory, Pittsburgh. *Exhib:* Das Goldene Zeitalter, Wurttembergischer Kymstverein, Stuttgart, 91; Canada: Une Nouvelle Generation, Mus de Liabbaye, St Croix, France, 93; The Body/Le Corps, Kunsthalle Bielefeld, Ger, 94; Press Enter, Power Plant, Toronto, 95; La Luxure, Centre Georges Pompidou, Paris, 97; Biennale of Sydney, Artspace, Art Gallery NSW, Australia, 96; Ydessa Hendeles Art Found, 2000; New Photog, Olga Korper Gallery, Toronto, 2002; Canadian Centre for Contemp Photog, 2003. *Teaching:* asst prof fine arts dept, Toronto. *Awards:* Gershon Iskowitz award, 2001. *Bibliog:* Didier Ottinger (auth), The Jack Photographs, ou L'Ubiquite du Parachute Regard, 94; Terry Smith (auth), Invisible Touch, Power Publs, 97; Russell Keziere (auth), Digital being, reproduction in the age of art, Artbyte, 98. *Media:* Digital Photography. *Mailing Add:* 201/R Christie St Toronto ON M6G 3B5 Canada

MASSEY, OPHELIA BELL
PAINTER
b Atlanta, Ga, June 1, 24. *Study:* Shorter Col, Rome, Ga, 42-43; Samford Univ, Birmingham, 65-67; studied with Zolton Szabo, Doug Walton, Al Brouillette, Tom Lynch, George Shedd, Barbara Neichi & Katherine Chang Lu. *Work:* Bear Bryant Conf Ctr, Tuscaloosa, Ala; Arcadia Financial Ctr Riverchase, Southtrust Bank, Southern Gas Co, Birmingham, Ala; Emory Univ, Atlanta; pvt collections. *Comn:* City at Midnight, St Vincent's Hosp, Birmingham, 75; Spring Bouquet, Vestavia Pub Libr, Ala, 77; City View, Vestavia City Hall, Ala, 78; Fun Fair, Childrens Hosp, Univ Ala, Birmingham, 81; Diptych: Memories of Monet's Garden, Kirklin Clinic, Birmingham, 88. *Exhib:* 56 Nat Watercolor Exhib, Heritage Hall, Talledega, Ala, 56; solo exhib, Emory Univ, Atlanta, 75 & Jewish Community Ctr, Birmingham, 82; Food for Thought, Birmingham Mus Art, Ala, 75; 43rd Ann Watercolor Competition, Watercolor Soc Ala, Birmingham Mus Art, 83; Watercolor Soc Ala '96 Watercolor Gala, The Tutwiler, Birmingham, 93; Watercolor Gala Ann Exhib, Holland Smith Gallery, Huntsville, Ala, 95; Watercolor Soc Ala 54th Ann Nat Exhib, Ctr Cult Art, Gadsend, Ala, 95. *Teaching:* Instr, Cahaba Valley Art Asn, Trussville, Ala, 91; Studio By the Track, Irondale, Ala, 90. *Awards:* Merit Award, Watercolor Soc Ala, 96. *Bibliog:* Loretta Goodwin (auth), Ophelia Bell Massey, Lorettas Gallery Newsletter, Vol 2, No 1, June; Carolyn Featheringill (auth), Newsheet Jr League Birmingham, 83; Maggie Hall Walsh (auth), Birmingham News, 96. *Mem:* Mt Brook Art Asn (vpres, 86); signature mem Watercolor Soc Ala (pres, 93); Experimental Artists Ala. *Media:* Watercolor, Mixed Media. *Publ:* Illusr, aaction Mag, Atlanta Artists Club, 84; contribr, Southeastern Art Showcase, Douglas Kite, 87; Best of Watercolor, 95, Abstracts in Watercolor, 96, Rockport Publs. *Dealer:* Larry Atchison Gallery 2847 Culver Rd Birmingham AL 35223

MASSIE, ANNE ADAMS ROBERTSON
PAINTER
b Lynchburg, Va, 31. *Study:* St Mary's Col, Raleigh, NC, 1950; Randolph Macon Woman's Col, Lynchburg, Va, BA, 52, studied with Everett Raymond Kinstler, John Pike, Charles Reid, Rex Brandt & Alex Powers. *Work:* Randolph Macon Womans' Col; St John's Episcopal Church; Va Sch Arts; Hotel de Ville, Rueil-Malmaison, France; Lynchburg Col; Va Episcopal Sch. *Exhib:* Parkand Col Art Gallery; Nat Acad Design; Nat Arts Club; Butler Inst Am Art, 2001; solo exhib, Lynchburg Art Club, Joyce Petter Gallery, Saugatuck, Mich, Twentieth Century Gallery, Williamsburg, Va, Lynchburg Fine Arts Ctr, 2000. *Teaching:* EC Glass High Sch, Lynchburg, 55-59. *Awards:* Best in Show, Nat League Am Pen Women, 1994; Best in Show, Va Watercolor Soc, 1992 & 1997; M Graham & Co Award, Va; Watercolor Soc, 2000; Water Media Medal of Honor, Catherine Lorillard Wolfe Club,. *Bibliog:* Rachel Wolrd (ed), Splash 4, Splash 5; Chris Urwin (auth), The Artistic Touch; Christopher Schink (auth), Colorlight; The Best of Watercolor, Rockport Pub. *Mem:* Nat Arts Club; Allied Artists Am; Catharine Lorillard Wolfe Art Club; Fel, Va Ctr Ctreative Arts; Nat Watercolor Soc. *Media:* Watercolor, Acrylic, Oil. *Mailing Add:* 3204 Rivermont Ave Lynchburg VA 24504

MASSIE, LORNA
PRINTMAKER
b Milwaukee, Wis, Dec 27, 38. *Study:* Layton Sch Art, Milwaukee; Smith Col; Univ Calif, Berkeley, BA, 61; Marshall Glazier, New York, 67; Woodstock Sch Art, 74-76; Albert Handell Sch, 77; Art Students League, 78. *Work:* Woodstock Hist Soc. *Exhib:* Print Club Albany, 95; Allied Artists Am, 96; Audubon Artists, 96; Acad Artists, 96; Northeast Regional Exhib, 96; and others. *Awards:* Philip Isenberg Award for Graphics & Drawing, Knickerbocker Artists, 91; Nicholas Reale Mem Award Graphics, Allied Artists Am, New York, 93; Atlantic Papers Award, Audubon Artists, 96. *Bibliog:* Who's Who Am Women; Art Print Index; Art Network Encyl Living Artists. *Mem:* Woodstock Artists Asn; Albany Print Club; Women's Studio Workshop. *Media:* Serigraphs. *Mailing Add:* 452 Whitfield Rd Accord NY 12404

MASTELLER, BARRY
PAINTER, CRAFTSMAN
b Los Angeles, Calif, Apr 21, 45. *Study:* Studied painting & life drawing under Walter Titus, 62-64. *Work:* Monterey Mus Art, Monterey Conf Ctr, Calif; San Jose Mus Art, Calif; Gonzaga Univ, Seattle, Wash; Syntex Corp, Palo Alto, Calif; Bank of America, San Francisco, Calif; Santa Cruz Mus Art & History; Palm Springs Desert Mus; Crocker Mus. *Comn:* Paintings, Home Fed, Los Angeles, 85, Coldwell Banker, Philadelphia, 85, Pebble Beach Corp, Calif, Stouffer Corp, Los Angeles, 86 & Hyatt Regency, Chicago, 88. *Exhib:* Solo exhib, Monterey Conf Ctr Art Comn, 79 & 94, San Jose Mus Art, 82, Monterey Mus Art, 75, 83 & 94 & Shaklee Corp, San Francisco, 89 & 94, Patricia Rovzar Gallery, 2006, Trajan Gallery, Calif, 2006, Campton Gallery, NY, 2006; group shows include Newport Harbor Art Mus Invitational, 88 & 94; Bank of Am World Hq, San Francisco, 94; Lisa Parker Fine Art, NY, 96-97; Emmie Smock Gallery, San Francisco, 97; Tamara Bane Gallery, Beverly Hills, 97; Nelson-Rovzar Gallery, Kirkland, Wash, 99; Patricia Rovzar Gallery, 2001-2003; Caldwell/Snyder Gallery, New York, NY, 2000-2001, 2003-2005; Trajan Gallery, Carmel, Calif, 2003 & 2006; Mus of Southwest, Midland, Tex, 2005; Anderson Fine Art Ctr, Ind, 2005; Campton Gallery, NY, 2005-2006; Monterey Mus Art, Calif, 2006; Patricia Rovzar Gallery, Seattle, Wash, 2006. *Pos:* dir/cur, Pacific Grove Art Ctr, Calif, 81-83; owner, Masteller/Shadow Graphics, 80-89; owner/dir, Claypoole-Freese Gallery, 89-2003. *Awards:* Best of Show, Ann Monterey Mus Art; Best of Show, Members Exhibit Pacific Grove Art Ctr; First Place Award, Monterey Co Competitive; Best of Show, Beacon House Competitive. *Bibliog:* Michael Gardner (auth), Artists taps subconcious, San Jose Mercury, 81; Richard Reilly (auth), Mastellers dreamy strokes, San Diego Union, 81; Irene Lagorio (auth), Mastellers seriocomic paintings, Monterey Herald, 83; Rick Deragon (auth), Let There Be Light, 90; Dominique Nahas (auth), Ecstatic Reserve in the work of Barry Masteller; Kathleen Moody (auth), 2002 Catalog Essay. *Mem:* Artists Equity; Int Inst Conservation Hist Artistic Works; Santa Cruz Art League. *Media:* Watercolor, Oil; Drawing; Monotype. *Publ:* Exhibition Catalogs, Caldwell/Snyder, 2000-2002; Exhibition Catalogs, Campton Gallery, NY, Trajan Gallery, Carmel, Calif & Patricia Rovzar Gallery, Seattle, Wash, 2006. *Dealer:* Caldwell/Snyder Gallery San Francisco Calif; Patricia Rovzar Gallery Seattle Wash; Campton Gallery NY; Trajan Gallery Carmel Calif. *Mailing Add:* PO Box 397 San Juan Bautista CA 95045

MASTER-KARNIK, PAUL
MUSEUM DIRECTOR, CRITIC
b New York, NY, Nov 20, 48. *Study:* Rutgers Univ, BA, 70, MA, 71, PhD, 78; NY Univ, cert(mus studies), 79. *Collection Arranged:* Expressionism in Boston, 1945-85, DeCordova Mus, 85. *Pos:* Art critic, Staten Island Advan, Newhouse Publ, 76-81; dir, New Jersey Ctr for Visual Arts, 81-84; De Cordova Mus, 84-. *Teaching:* Adj prof cult & art hist, Rutgers Univ, New Brunswick, NJ, 71-78; adj prof mus studies, New York Univ, 80-84. *Awards:* Nat Endowment Arts Critics Fel, 80-81. *Mem:* Am Asn Mus; Asn Art Mus Dirs. *Res:* Methods and styles of contemporary art criticism; social history of the art museum; contemporary American art. *Publ:* Auth, Art criticism in the suburban context, Artview, Vol 3, No 1, 79; Philip Pearlstein: Progress of a Painter (exhib catalog), 82, American Realism 1930's/1980's: A Comparative Perspective (exhib catalog), 83 & William Zorach: Sculpture and Drawings (exhib catalog), 83, NJ Ctr Visual Arts. *Mailing Add:* DeCordova Museum and Sculpture Park 51 Sandy Pond Rd Lincoln MA 01773

MASTERFIELD, MAXINE
PAINTER
b Los Angeles, Calif, July 21, 33. *Study:* Cleveland Inst Art, grad 55. *Work:* First Chicago Trust of Ariz & St Joseph Children's Ctr, Phoenix; Nat Watercolor Soc; Bancohio Nat; Ohio Savings & Loan; Laguna Beach Mus Art; Chicago Bank of Ill; 3M Corp, Minneapolis. *Exhib:* Watercolor USA, Springfield Art Mus, Mo, 68 & 77; Nat Acad Design, 76; Aqueous Open, Arts & Crafts Ctr, Pittsburgh, Pa, 76-79; Butler Midyear Exhib, Butler Inst Am Art, Youngstown, Ohio, 77; Rocky Mountain Nat Watermedia, Foothills Art Ctr, Golden, Colo, 77-79; Nat Watercolor Soc, Los Angeles, 77-79; Ky Watercolor, Owensboro Mus Fine Arts, Ky, 78 & Mid-Am Art Exhib, 79; Sexton Gallery, Ft Lauderdale, 97-98. *Teaching:* Watercolor workshops, worldwide, 80-2000; pvt instr, Masterfield Studio, Sarasota, Fla. *Awards:* Purchase Award, Nat Watercolor Soc, 78; High Winds Medal, Am Watercolor Soc, 81; Grand Buckeye Leaf Award, 82, Silver Buckeye Leaf Award, 83 & Award of Excellence, 86, Ohio Watercolor Soc. *Mem:* Am Watercolor Soc, 76; Fla Watercolor Soc, 87; Ky Watercolor Soc, 76; Soc Experimental Artist; Int Soc Experimental Artist (found & lifetime mem, 92-2000, 06). *Media:* Watercolor, Enamel, Acrylic. *Publ:* Illusr, Watercolor Bold and Free, 80, Creative Seascape Painting, 81, auth, Painting the Spirit of Nature, Watson-Guptill; illusr, Exploring Color, North Light Bks; auth, painting in the Spirit of Nature, 83; Painting In Harmony with Nature, 90. *Dealer:* The Look Gallery Minneapolis MN. *Mailing Add:* 5075 Robinsong Rd Sarasota FL 34233-2249

MASTRANGELO, BOBBI
SCULPTOR; ENVIRONMENTAL ARTIST
b Youngstown, Ohio, May 16, 37. *Study:* State Univ NY, Buffalo, BS cum laude, 59; State Univ NY, Stony Brook, 69-79; studied printmaking with Dan Welden, John Ross, Clare Romano, Tim Ross & Gail Cohen Edleman. *Work:* Islip Art Mus, East Islip, NY; Baltimore Md Pub Works Mus; Suffolk Co Water Authority, Oakdale, NY; Nat Asn Women Artists Permanent Collection, Zimmerli Art Mus, Rutgers Univ, New Brunswick, NJ; Heckscher Mus, Huntington, NY; The Moscow Collection of World Manhole Covers. *Exhib:* City Views, Staller Ctr Arts, State Univ NY, Stony Brook, 92; Transformation of Matter into Art, NY, Acad Sci, 92; Group exhibs: Winners showcase Smithtown, NY Arts Council, 99; NY Collects Buffalo State, Burchfield Penney art Center; solo exhibs, NY Hall Sci, Flushing, 94, Baltimore Pub Works Mus, 96; Listen to the Earth, Hamilton Col, Clinton, NY, 95; Grateworks, Toast Gallery,

Port Jefferson, NY, 2003; Underfoot: Manhole and other covers, Attleboro Industrial Mus, Mass, 2004: Sewers of the World Unite! (Russia), 2006 http://sewers.artinfo.ru/archives. *Pos:* Judge, 11th Ann Cong Art Competition, Riverhead, NY, 92. *Teaching:* Paper making, Bd Coop Servs, Suffolk Co, NY, 87-94; Title One tutor, Smithtown, NY, 89-99; artist in residence, NY Middle Sch, Port Jefferson, 98; writing teacher, Smithtown, NY, 98 & 99. *Awards:* Spec Opportunity Stipend, NY Found Arts, 92 & 94; Eve Helman Award Work on Paper, Nat Asn Women Artists, NY, 92, Aida Whedon Mem Award, 97; Maryvale High Sch Hall of Fame for Achievement in the Arts and Environment, 94; Paul Harris Fel, Rotary Int, 96. *Bibliog:* Phil Mintz (auth), Going in circles, Newsday, 9/98; Sara Muller (TV reporter), Grate Works, News 12, 10/98; Michael Ollove (auth), Finding beauty in the grate beyond, Balt Sun, 9/2001; and others; Caryn Eve Murray (auth), Cover Girl, Newsday, 12/2002; Beauty under Foof, TV Park, Moscow, (auth), 2003; Stephen Koenig lauth, Maryvale Alumma Featured in Art Display, Buffalo, NY, Cheektowaga Times, 2004. *Mem:* Art & Sci Collabrs Inc, Staten Island, NY; Nat Asn Women Artists; Nat Mus Women Arts; Friends of Dard Hunter; NAWA Fla Chap; Solivita Artisans Guild. *Media:* Miscellaneous Media. *Specialty:* www.art-exchange.com. *Interests:* Sculpture, hand-made paper fiber art, A Novel Group, Poetry, creative writing walking exercise equipment; Singing. *Publ:* Auth, Grate works, Time Capsule; Manhole Covers, Oxymoron, The Fringe, Arts & Sci Ann, 98. *Mailing Add:* 747 Coronado Dr Poiniana FL 34759

MASUROVSKY, GREGORY
DRAFTSMAN, PRINTMAKER
b Bronx, NY, Nov 26, 29. *Study:* Art Students League, New York, study with Will Barnet; Parsons Sch of Design, New York; Black Mountain Col, NC, study with Ilya Bolotowsky. *Work:* Mus Mod Art, NY; Minneapolis Inst Art, Minn; Fogg Art Mus, Cambridge, Mass; Mus Nat Art Mod, Paris; Libr Cong, Washington. *Comn:* Decor, Costumes & Lighting, Ballet Theatre Contemp d'Angers, France, 75. *Exhib:* Estampe Contemp, Biblio Nat, Paris, 73; Minneapolis Inst Arts, Minn, 67; Mus de Pontoise, France, 82; 1ére Triennale des Ameriques, Maubeuge, France, 93; Nat Drawing Invitational, Ark Arts Ctr, 94. *Pos:* Graphics monitor to Will Barnet, Art Students League, New York, 52-53. *Teaching:* Vis prof drawing, Minneapolis Col Art & Design, Minn, 66-67; prof drawing, Am Ctr, Paris, 80-87; prof drawing, Atelier Elzevir, Paris, 87-94; Int Summer Acad, Salzburg, Austria, 89. *Awards:* Critics Prize, drawing, II Biennale de Paris, 61; Int Jury Prize, Etching III Biennial de Paris, 63; Fel, Tamarind Lithography Workshop, Los Angeles, 69; Djerassi Found Grant, 87. *Bibliog:* Michel Conil Lacoste (auth), Masurovsky, an American in Paris, Studio Int, 3/65; Michel Buter (auth), article, Opus Int, 71; Gregory Masurovsky (auth), A La Ligne, 94. *Mem:* Centre Georges Pompidou, Paris; Artists Equity Asn, NY; SPADEM, Paris. *Media:* Pen & Ink; Etching. *Publ:* Illusr, Litanie d'Eau, La Hune, Paris, 64; Western Duo, Tamarind Litho, Los Angeles, 69; Corps a Coeur, Urdla, Villeurbanne, France, 89; Ange De La Baie, J Matarasso, Nice, France, 92. *Dealer:* Galerie Daniel Varenne 8 Ave Toepffer 1206 Geneva Switzerland; Atelier Lambert 62 rue de la Boétie 75008 Paris France

MATARANGLO, ROBERT PATRICK
VIDEO ARTIST, MURALIST
b South Amboy, NJ, Mar 17, 47. *Study:* Montclair State Univ, MA, 1999; Vt Col, MFA, 2002. *Comn:* Exterior, Long Branch Chamber, West End LB, NJ, 2000; Interior, Siperstein's, Middletown, NJ, 2002; Exterior, Long Branch, NJ, 2006; Exterior, Health Farm, Middletown, NJ, 2003; Exterior, Herr Family Days Restaurant, Ocean Grove, NJ, 2004. *Exhib:* Solo, Monmouth Univ Gallery, Long Branch, NJ, 2003; Ion animation Festival, Culver City, Los Angeles, 2004; Mardi Gras Film Festival, Sidney, Australia, 2006; Monmouth Co Arts Coun, Monmouth Mus, Lincroft, NJ, 2006. *Pos:* Bd Dirs, Art Alliance, Red Bank, NJ, 2000-2004; Animation Club Adv, Monmouth Univ, Long Branch, NJ, 2002-2004; vpres, Shore Inst Contemp Art, Long Branch, NJ, 2003-2004. *Teaching:* Adj prof, art hist, Ocean Co Col, Toms River, NJ, 1999-2002; adj prof, art, Brookdale Community Col, Lincroft, NJ, 1999-; adj prof, Monmouth Univ, Long Branch, NJ, 2002, 2004. *Awards:* Best Local Animation Award, Garden State Film Festival, 2003, 04, 05; Champion of the Arts, Monmouth Co Arts Coun, 2004; Best Animation, Coney Island Film Festival, 2005. *Bibliog:* Steven Bove (auth), His Path to Joy, Asbury Park, Press, 2005; Linda DeNicola (auth), Video Mountain Arts Festival, The Hub, 2005; Robert Scott (auth), Tiny Tents, Cottage Style (mag), Harris Publs, 2005. *Mem:* ASIFA E, NYC; Black Box, Asbury Park, NJ; Freedom Film Soc, Red Bank, NJ; Monmouth Co Arts Coun, Red Bank, NJ (bd dirs 2002-2004); Shore Inst Comtemp Arts, Red Bank, NJ (vpres 2003-2004). *Media:* Video Animation. *Mailing Add:* 106 Lincoln Ln Avon By The Sea NJ 07717

MATEO, JULIO
PAINTER, PRINTMAKER
b Havana, Cuba, Apr 16, 51; US citizen. *Study:* Univ Fla, BFA, 73; Univ S Fla, MFA, 78. *Work:* NY Pub Libr; Univ S Fla, Tampa; The Printmaking Workshop, NY; Greenville Co Mus Art, SC; Chase Manhattan Bank, NY. *Exhib:* Brooklyn Mus, NY, 85; Mus Contemp Hispanic Art, NY, 86 & 88; Bronx Mus, NY, 87 & 90; PS 1, Long Island City, NY, 90; solo show, Cathedral St John the Divine, NY; and others. *Teaching:* instr art dept, Univ S Fla, 77; vis artist, guest lectr Eckerd Col, St Petersburg, Fla, 79; vis artist, guest lectr, St Petersburg Community Col, 78. *Awards:* Individual Artists' Grant, Arts Coun Fla, Tallahassee, 80; Artists Grant, Nat Endowment Art, Washington, DC, 89. *Bibliog:* Eastvillage 85, Pelham Press, 85; Ellen Handy (auth), Marks of Time, Arts Mag, 2/88; William Zimmer (auth), 50 Artists Reunited at Bronx Museum, NY Times, 8/5/90. *Media:* Oil; Intaglio. *Publ:* Contribr, Blast, Vol 1, No 12, Colab, New York, 87; Artextreme, No 8, Philadelphia, 89; Hoopoe, No 5, New York, 90. *Dealer:* James Baird Gallery; Pegasus Art Gallery. *Mailing Add:* 423 Marr St Truth or Consequences NM 87901-3380

MATHEWS, NANCY MOWLL
HISTORIAN, CURATOR
b Baltimore, Md, Feb 11, 47. *Study:* Goucher Col, BA, 68; Cleveland Mus Art, fel, 70-71; Case-Western Reserve Univ, MA, 72; NY Univ Inst Fine Arts, Goldwater fel, 73-74, PhD, 80. *Collection Arranged:* Mary Cassatt: The Color Prints (auth, catalog), 89-90; Maurice Prendergast (auth, catalog), Prestel, 90; Charles Prendergast (auth, catalog), 93; Maurice Prendergast: The State of the Estate, 98-99. *Pos:* Randolph-Macon Womans Col, 77-; Eugenie Prendergast cur, Williams Col Mus Art, currently. *Teaching:* Assoc prof, Randolph-Macon Womans Col, 77-87; lectr, Williams COl, 88-. *Awards:* Katherine Graves Davidson Award, 80; Smithsonian Postdoctoral Fel, 82; and others. *Mem:* Col Art Asn; IFA Alumni Asn; Am Asn Mus; Catalogue Raisonne Scholars Asn. *Res:* 19th & 20th century European and American painting; impressionism; Mary Cassatt; Maurice & Charles Prendergast; Gauguin; Women artists. *Publ:* Ed, Cassatt and Her Circle: Selected Letters, Abbeville Press, 84; Cassatt: A Retrospective, Levin, 96; auth, Mary Cassatt: A Life, Yale, 98; Maurice Prendergast: The Art of Leisure, 99. *Mailing Add:* Williams Col Mus Art Main St Williamstown MA 01267

MATHIAS, THELMA
CONCEPTUAL ARTIST, SCULPTOR
b New York, NY. *Study:* High Sch of Music & Art, NY; Univ Mich, BA; NY Univ, MSW. *Work:* Yeshiva Univ Mus, NY; Islip Art Mus, Long Island, NY; Stadtisches Mus, Kleve, Ger; Artists Mus, Lodz, Poland; Art/OMI, Ghent, NY. *Comn:* Bulgaria, NY, Elizabeth Found. *Exhib:* Stilte, Mus Silence, Amsterdam, 1999; Elements 2000, Here Art, New York City, 2000; Lugares Encantados, Islip Art Mus, Long Island, NY, 2000; Los Montanas, Ricardo Flores Ctr, Oaxaca, Mex, 1995; Under the Floorboards, BWA, Lublin, Poland, 1998; My Fathers List, Yeshiva Univ Mus, New York City, 1995; Pulling of the Threads, Newark Mus, NJ, 1999; Dumbo Double Deuce, New York City, 2001; The Puffin Room, New York City, 2001; Longview Mus Fine Arts, Texas, 2001; The London Biennale, Eng, 2000; Art Indust, Santa Fe, NMex, 2002. *Collection Arranged:* cur, Sculpture Addressing Social Issues, Artist Talk Panel, New York, 93, Bearing Witness, 94; cur, Repair Work, Deutsche Bank, New York, 94; cur, After 50 Years, City Hall, New York, 95; cur, Performance Night, Gallery 128, New York, 98; Analix Forever Galerie, Geneva, Hewlett Packard Corp, Palo Alto, Calif; Cabrini Hospice, NYC, Oppenheimer Capital Corp, NYC; Bank Am Corp, San Francisco, McDonalds Corp, Oakbrook, Ill; Blibliotheque d'Art et Archeololgie, Geneva, Poets House, NYC; Guggenhem Mus Library, NYC. *Pos:* Cur, Newark Mus, NJ, 99; guest speaker, Barnard Col, NYC, 2000, Islip Art Mus, Long Island, 2000, Cont Art Mus, Mexico City, 98. *Awards:* Nat Endowment for the Arts, 80; Puffin Found Grant, 93; Ctr Book Arts, Residency Grant, 98. *Bibliog:* Robert Morgan (auth) 4:45 AM, Art in America, 2/96; Dan Bishoff (auth), Pulling of the Threads, Newark Star Ledger, 4/99; Joel Silverstein (auth) Elements 2000, Review, 3/2000. *Mem:* Asn Video & Filmmakers; Orange Peel Pubs (pres 93-96); Artists Equity. *Media:* Video, Textual, Cultural Discards, Bronze, Cast Paper, Wax. *Specialty:* Contemp Art. *Interests:* Buddism, travel, semiotics, and much more. *Publ:* Contrib, Feminist Performance Art, R Wyler & Co, 93; co-auth, Repair Workbook, Orange Peel Press, 94, Mail Performance, Watermark Press, 98; auth, An Earth Shattering Experience, 2001. *Dealer:* Jurgen Richter Martin Luther Str 26 97616 Frankfurt, Germany. *Mailing Add:* PO Box 32106 Santa Fe NM 87594

MATHIS, BILLIE FRITZ
PAINTER, CONCEPTUAL ARTIST
b Lindale, Ga, Apr 16, 36. *Study:* Art Instruction Inc; studied with noted watercolorists, Paris for painting. *Work:* Promina; Cobb Bd of Educ Collection; Peachtree Ctr, Atlanta, Ga; Foster Higgons, Inc, Atlanta, Ga; also pvt collections. *Comn:* Plantation Resorts, Fla; Post Properties, Contel Corp, Pvt Collector, Germ; Reinhardt Col, Waleska, Ga. *Exhib:* Butler Inst Am Arts 53rd Nat, Youngstown, Ohio; Atlanta-Savannah Exhib, Visual Arts; Marietta Cobb Mus Art; Marietta/Cobb Collection Tours, Abstein Gallery; Gallery 300/SAGA; Celebrate the Arts, Marietta Cobb Mus Art; Marietta Cobb Mus Art; Across the Borders, Atlanta/Can, Md Fedn, New Orleans Int; one woman show, St Augustine, Fla; solo exhib, Cherokee Arts, Ga; group exhib, Metro Montage, I, II, & III, Marietta, Ga. *Awards:* Featured Artist, Marietta-Cobb Mus Arts Masterpiece Ball, 96. *Mem:* Nat Women in Arts; Asn Allied Artists; Atlanta Artist Soc; Asn Am Watercolor Soc; signature mem Ga Watercolor Soc (area dir); Visual Arts Coun; Cherokee Arts, Arts Alliance of Ga. *Media:* Mixed Media, Watercolor. *Publ:* Contribr, Georgia Artists, Mountain Prod, 88; artist, Am References; illustr, cover, AirBorne Mag; Break of Day, Lufrnint Publ, 11/97; Through My Window, Children's Poems, Lufraint Publs; Watercolor Video & DVD, Painting Loose, A Lesson in Watercolor. *Dealer:* Frame Works Gallery 1205 Johnson Ferry Rd, Marietta GA 30068; Artistic Frames, Jasper, Ga; Creations Gallery, Canton, GA. *Mailing Add:* 110 Cedar Ct No 3090 Waleska GA 30813-4604

MATHIS, EMILE HENRY, II
DEALER, COLLECTOR
b Superior, Wis, Feb 25, 46. *Study:* Dominican Col, Univ Wis, Superior, BFA, MFA. *Collection Arranged:* J A McN Whistler, (etchings & lithographs), 81; Rubber stamps by contemp Am artists, 81; 19th Century French Etching, 82; British printmakers of late 19th & early 20th century; Western Africa (sculpture), 91; Fibre & Utilitarian Objects, 92; Sir Francis Seymour Haden (etchings), 93; Whistler & Haden (etchings), 93; 5 Centuries of Printmaking; 19th & 20th century Am and European paintings, 99; Objects of ritual and reverence from various W African cultures, 2000; African objects of utility, 2002. *Pos:* Asst dir, La Porte Gallery, Racine, 70-71; dir, New Gallery One, Racine, 71-72; gallery owner, Mathis Gallery, Racine, 72-; Mem bd dir, Wustum Mus Fine Art. *Teaching:* Instr art, Sheboygan Sch Syst, Wis, 68-69. *Mem:* Racine Urban Aesthetics; Am Asn of Mus. *Specialty:* Old and modern masters; contemporary

graphics; paintings; fine prints and African sculpture. *Interests:* 18th Century Am furniture; Span Colonial Relig Art; Commemorative Medals & Medallions. *Collection:* American nineteenth and twentieth century contemporary drawings and paintings. *Mailing Add:* 328 S Main St Racine WI 53403

MATISSE, JACKIE (JACQUELINE) MATISSE MONNIER
PAINTER, SCULPTOR
b Neuilly-sur-Seine, France, July 12, 31; US citizen. *Exhib:* Drachen, Rhein Landesmuseum, Bonn, Ger, 81; Traveling exhib, Philadelphia Mus Art, 81; one-person exhibs, Fundacion Miro, Barcelona, Spain, 85, Magic Hair & Bottled Dream, Galerie Satellite, Paris, France, 93, Jacqueline Matisse Monnier, Kiallitasa, Bartok 32 Galeria, Budapest, Hungary, 98; Art that Flies, Dayton Art Inst, 90; Zero Gravity, 91; Les Artists Decident De Jouer, 91; Magic Hair & Bottled Dreams, Galerie Satellite, Paris, 93; Rolywholyover A Circus for Mus, Los Angeles, 94, Houston 94, NY, 94, Japan, 94-95, Philadelphia, 95; Happy End, Galerie Satellite, Paris, France, 96; 10 Jours d'Art Contemporain, Chateau de Nemours, Nemours, France, 97; From One Point to Another, L'Atelier Soardi, Nice, France, 97; Odeurs Une Odyssee, Passage de Retz, Paris, France, 97; Kitetail Cocktail, Goldie Paley Gallery, Philadelphia, PA, 99; Art that Soars, Mengei Int Mus, San Diego, Calif, 2000; Echigo Triennale, Art Front Gallery, Tokyo, Japan, 2001; Art Flying in and out of Spae, Va Tech, 2002; Art Volant dan l'Escape et Ailleurs, Virtual Reality Project, Chalon Sur Saone, France, 2003. *Bibliog:* Newman (auth), Kite Craft, Crown Publ Inc, 74; Jean-Michel Folon, Aquiloni, Alice Editions, Switz, 76; Suzi Gablik (auth), Cosmic kites, Art in Am, 11/80; Jackie Matisse (auth), The Blue Book, Ed de l'Onde, 97. *Media:* Miscellaneous Media. *Publ:* Art That Flies, 91; Eric et Marc Dumage (auth), Certs-Volants L'art en Ciel, Ed Alternatives, 96. *Dealer:* Jack Tilton Gallery 24 W 57th St New York NY 10019. *Mailing Add:* 23 Rue du Buisson Villiers-sous-Grez 77760 France

MATSUBARA, NAOKO
PRINTMAKER, ILLUSTRATOR
b Kyoto, Japan. *Study:* Kyoto Acad Fine Arts, BFA, 60; Carnegie-Mellon Univ, MFA, 62; Royal Col Art, London, 63. *Work:* Brit Mus, London; Mus Fine Arts, Boston; Tokyo Nat Mus Mod Art; Cincinnati Mus Art; Libr Cong; Royal Ont Mus, Toronto, Can. *Comn:* Mural, Kyoto Univ Hosp, 59; mural, Carnegie-Mellon Univ, Pittsburgh, 62; woodcut print, Smithsonian Inst, Washington, 67; woodcut print, Boston Winter Festival, 69; Solitude (portfolio), Aquarius Press, NY, 71; mural for new YMCA lobby, Oakville, Ont, 2002. *Exhib:* Takashimaya Art Gallery, Tokyo, Japan, 87; Vancouver Art Gallery, BC, 90; Hart House Gallery, Univ Toronto, 90; Oriental Mus, Durham, Eng, traveled to Ireland & Wales, 91-92; Japan Festival Prints Show, Spirit Sq, Charlotte, NC, 94; Davidson Galleries, Seattle, Wash, 95; Casa de la Cultura Oaxaquena, Mex, 95; World Artists for Tibet, Gallery at 678, NY, 98; Yamaso Gallery, Kyoto, Japan, 99; Through the Medium of Wood, Japan Found Gallery, 2001; Tree Spirit (with catalog), Royal Ont Cus, Toronto, Can, 2003. *Teaching:* Instr woodcut, Pratt Graphic Art Ctr, 65-67; instr woodcut, Univ RI, 67-68; asst prof woodcut, Univ Victoria, BC, summer 77; asst prof woodcut, Univ Guelph, Ont, 84; vis instr, Inuit Workshop, Cape Dorset, 85. *Awards:* Kegon Shou, Hangain Ten, Shiko Munakata, 63; Samuel Gold Award, Soc Am Graphic Artists, 68; Soc Am Graphic Artists Awards for Excellence, 84; CBC TV Documentary Video, 90. *Bibliog:* Fritz Eichenberg (auth), Naoko Matsubara, Xylon, Switz, 70; Joan Stanley-Baker (auth), The woodcuts of Munakata and Matsubara, Art Gallery Greater Victoria, 76; Franz Geirhaas (auth), The Creative Act Paths to Realization, Int Print Soc, 84. *Mem:* Soc Am Graphic Artists; Royal Can Acad Arts. *Media:* Woodcut; Watercolor, Collage. *Interests:* Hiking, Travel, Tai Chi, Meditation. *Publ:* Nantucket Woodcuts, 68, Boston Impressions, 70, Barre Publ, Kyoto Woodcuts, 78, Kodansha Int, Ltd, Tokyo; Hagoromo (porfolio), Pinetree Press, 86; Tibetan Sky, 30 color woodcuts on Tibet, Bayeux Arts, Can, 97; Tokonoma (ltd ed portfolio based on Eng haiku by James Kirkup), The Old Press, Eng, 99; Tales of Days Gone By, ALIS, Tokyo, Japan, 2003. *Dealer:* Gallery Tsutsui Tokyo Japan; The Tolman Collections Ltd Tokyo Japan & New York, NY. *Mailing Add:* 324 Coral Terr Oakville ON L6J 4C4 Canada

MATSUMOTO, ROGER
PHOTOGRAPHER
b Honolulu, Hawaii. *Study:* Self taught in primary medium. *Work:* Philadelphia Mus Art; Utah Mus Fine Art; Salt Lake City Int Airport; Libr Philadelphia; Buddy Holly Center, Lubbock, Tex. *Exhib:* Illuminance, Lubbock Fine Arts Ctr, Lubbock, Tex, 1997; Ann Photog Exhib, Phillips Mill, New Hope, Pa, 1998; Photog 18, Perkins Ctr Arts, Moorestown, NJ, 1999; Current Works 2000, Soc Contemp Photog, Kansas City, Mo, 2000; From the Collection/Philadelphia Area, Philadelphia Mus Art, 2000; Works on Paper, La Univ Union Art Gallery, Baton Rouge, La, 2002; Award Winners II, Biggs Mus Am Art, 2002; Alternative Process, Soho Photo Gallery, NY, 2004; Illuminince, Buddy Holly Art Ctr, Lubbock Texas, 2004; The Silver Garden, Philadelphia Mus of Art, 2005. *Pos:* Artist fellowship, Del Div Art, 2001. *Media:* Palladium prints. *Mailing Add:* 205 LaSalle Way Newark DE 19711

MATTEO, DOROTHY
PAINTER
b Summit, NJ, Dec 21 40. *Study:* Newark Sch of Fine & Indust Art, Cert, 1963; Ocean Co Col, Fine Art, 1974-1977; Sch of Visual Art, Silk Screen. *Work:* Hallmark, Meaning of Life (watercolor), Kansas City, Mo; Wonderful World of Oz (scarecrow sculpture), Los Angeles, Calif; Jesus Christ Superstar, Radio WABC (poster), NY. *Comn:* Private homes (murals, portraits & paintings), NJ; Tropicana Hotel, Atlantic City, NJ. *Exhib:* Solo shows, Ocean County Public Libr, 2006, Point Pleasant Libr, 2006, Georgian Court Col, 2006; Summit Art Ctr Members' Show, 65; New & Young Show, Ocean County Artists' Guild, 78; The Loft Gallery, Red Bank, NJ, 99; Women Artists of Ocean County, Jackson Public Libr, 2002; 20th State Juried Exhib, Ocean County Artists' Guild, 2005; 2005 Biennial, Noyes Mus, Brigantine, NJ, 2005. *Collection Arranged:* Summit Art Ctr, Summit, NJ; Loft, Red Bank, NJ; Ocean Co Col, Toms River, NJ; Pt Pleasant Libr, Pt Pleasant, NJ; Georgian Court Col, Lakewood, NJ. *Pos:* industrial designer, Lakewood, NJ, 89-2002; Art dir, nat marketing firm, 2001; exec asst, Ocean Co Artist Guild, Island Heights, NJ, 2006. *Teaching:* Instr, Spectrum Inst Sch of Art, 1970-1971, Toms River Adult Educ. *Awards:* Hallmark (student exhib), Hallmark Cards, 1958; Dynamic Graphics, 1978; Most Prominant Woman in Advertising, WABC Poster Contest, 89; Third pl Ocean Co Col Juried Show, 2005. *Mem:* Ocean Co Artists Guild (exec asst); Shore Inst of Contemp Art. *Media:* Oil; Mixed Media. *Mailing Add:* 123 Swan Blvd Toms River NJ 08753

MATTERNES, JAY HOWARD
PAINTER, ILLUSTRATOR
b Corregidor, Philippines, Apr 14, 33; US citizen. *Study:* Carnegie Mellon Univ Col Fine Arts, Mellon Found scholar & BFA, 55. *Work:* Cleveland Mus Natural Sci, Ohio; Carnegie Mus, Pittsburgh; Bedloe Island Mus Immigration, NY; Smithsonian Inst, Washington; Am Mus Natural Hist, NY, 93. *Comn:* Morristown Revolutionary War Mural, Nat Park Serv, NJ, 75; fossil primate murals & Paranthropus mural, Hall of Human Biology, Am Mus Natural Hist, 89-93; Reconstruction of fossil mammals, Hall of Fossil Mammals, Am Mus Natural Hist, 89-94; Homo habilis Utilizing Stone Tools (mural), Gunma Mus Nat Hist, Japan, 95; The Sculpting of the Clay Bison of Tuc d'Audoubert in France (mural), Gunma Mus Nat Hist, Japan, 96. *Exhib:* Art & the Animal, Royal Ont Mus, Ottawa, Can, 75; Nat Acad Western Art at Cowboy Hall Fame, Oklahoma City, 79; Leigh Yawkey Woodson Art Mus, Wausau, Wis, 80, 81 & 83; bird art, Royal Scottish Acad, Edinburgh; Brit Mus, London, 82; Ancestors, Mus Natural Hist, NY, 84; First Western Art Classic, Minnetonka, Minn, 84; Soc Illusrs, NY, 84, 86 & 88; Commonwealth Inst, London, Eng, 85 & 86; Game Conservation Int, San Antonio, Tex, 87; Australian Mus, Sydney, 88. *Pos:* Self-employed free-lance artist, 60-. *Awards:* Merit Award, 68 & Gold Medal, 82, Art Dir Club Wash; Award Merit, Soc Animal Artists, 79. *Bibliog:* Dr LB Leakey (auth), The Dawn of Man (film TV), 65 & Dr Clark Howell (auth), Man Hunters (film TV), 68, Nat Geographic Soc; John Heminway (auth), The Three Million Year Clue (film TV), Survival Anglia Ltd, 76. *Mem:* Artists Equity Asn; Soc Animal Artists; Nat Cowboy Hall Fame. *Media:* Oil, Acrylic; Charcoal, Pencil. *Publ:* Illusr, American Cowboy, 72 & Vanishing Wild Life of North America, 74, Nat Geographic Soc Bk Div; A New Look at Early Man in North America, World Yr Bk, 73; Lost Empires, Living Tribes, 82 & Peoples & Places of the Past, 83. *Mailing Add:* 4328 Ashford Ln Fairfax VA 22032-1435

MATTESON, IRA
SCULPTOR, DRAFTSMAN
b Hamden, Conn, June 6 1917. *Study:* Art Students League, with Arthur Lee, 1937-42, also with William Zorach, 1946-51; Nat Acad, with John Flanagan, 1946-47. *Work:* Akron Art Inst, Ohio; Cleveland Mus Art; Chrysler Mus, Provincetown, Mass; Norfolk Mus, Va; Akron Univ, Ohio. *Comn:* Figure-Bend, Cascade Plaza, Akron, 1977; Back, Case Western Reserve, Univ Cleveland, Ohio, 1981. *Exhib:* Kent State Univ; Akron Univ, 1988. *Pos:* Prof emer, 1985-. *Teaching:* Fac, Sch Art, Kent State Univ, Kent, 1968-87. *Awards:* Prix de Rome, Am Acad Rome, 53-55, Louis Comfort Tiffany, 56 & 60; Ohio Arts Coun Grant, 78. *Media:* Wood, Paper. *Publ:* Dialogue, 4/88. *Mailing Add:* PO Box 603 Thetford VT 05074

MATTHEWS, GENE (EUGENE) EDWARD
PAINTER, EDUCATOR
b Davenport, Iowa, Mar 22, 31. *Study:* Bradley Univ, 48-51; Univ Iowa, BFA, 53, MFA, 57. *Work:* Nat Mus Am Art, Washington, DC; Butler Inst Am Art, Youngstown, Ohio; Denver Art Mus, Colo; Nat Mus Poland; Chrysler Mus, Norfolk, Va. *Exhib:* Am Watercolors, Drawings & Prints, Metrop Mus Art, NY, 52; Antagonismes, Louvre, Paris, 60; One-man shows, James Yu Gallery, NY, 73 & 77, Dubins Gallery, Los Angeles, 81; Int Drawing Biennale, Middlesbrough Art Gallery, Eng, 77; Am Drawings, Smithsonian Inst, Washington, DC, 80-82; Galeria Wielka, Poznan, Poland, 82-83; Brena Gallery, Denver, Colo, 83, 86 & 88; Int Invitational, Galleria FMK, Budapest, Hungary, 85, 87 & 90; Int Invitational Exhib, Kyoto Int Art Ctr, Japan, 86, 88, 91 & 93. *Teaching:* Prof fine arts, Univ Colo, Boulder, 61-66, dir, vis artist prog, 66-81, prof emeritus. *Awards:* Univ Colo Fac Fel for Creative Res, Boulder, 66; Quartana Purchase Award, Int Watercolor Exhib, Baton Rouge, La, 73; Purchase Award, American Drawings IV, 82. *Bibliog:* Wendon Blake (auth), Acrylic Watercolor Painting, 70 & L C Goldsmith (auth), Watercolor Bold and Free, 80, Watson-Guptill. *Mem:* Fel Am Painting Acad, Rome; Watercolor USA Hon Soc. *Media:* Acrylic, Oil

MATTHEWS, HARRIETT
SCULPTOR, EDUCATOR
b Kansas City, Mo, June 21, 40. *Study:* Sullins Jr Col, Bristol, Va, AFA; Univ Ga, BFA & MFA; with Leonard DeLonga. *Work:* Univ Ga Art Mus; Colby Col Art Mus & Libr; Key Bank, Portland, Maine; Bristol K-8 Sch, Bristol, Maine. *Comn:* Designed awards for the Maine Arts & Humanities Comn, 69; outdoor sculpture, Kennebec Valley Vocational Tech Inst Per Cent for Art, 86; Univ Maine Law Libr, 93. *Exhib:* One-person shows, Vanderbilt Univ, 74, Treat Gallery, Bates Col, Lewiston, Maine, 79, Univ Southern Maine, Gorham, 82, Montpelier Cult Arts Ctr, Laurel, Md, 83, Colby Col Art Mus, 87, 92, 96 & 2001, Perspectives, Portland Mus Art, Maine, 90 & June Fitzpatrick Gallery, Portland, Maine, 97 & 2001; Payson Gallery, Westbrook Col, Portland, 85; Maine Coast Artist Gallery, 89; Dean Valentgas Gallery, Portland, Maine, 89; Anita Shapolsky Gallery, NY, 91; Frick Gallery, Belfast, Maine, 91-92; and others. *Teaching:* Vis instr sculpture, Univ Okla, 64-65; from instr to assoc prof sculpture & drawing, Colby Col, 66-85, prof, 85-. *Awards:* Colby Travel Grants, 71, 76, 78, 81, 85, 87 & 90; Colby Mellon Grant, 80; Ingram Merrill Grant, 80. *Bibliog:*

Virginia Watson-Jones (auth), Contemporary Women Sculptors; Arthur Williams (auth), Sculpture: Technique, Form, Content. *Mem:* Col Art Asn. *Media:* All. *Res:* Ancient cities and churches at various libraries and information centers. *Dealer:* Jamison Modern Portland ME. *Mailing Add:* Colby Col Dept Art Waterville ME 04901

MATTHEWS, WANDA MILLER
PRINTMAKER
b Barry, Ill, Sept 15, 30. *Study:* Bradley Univ, Peoria, Ill, BFA, 52; Univ Iowa, Iowa City, with Mauricio Lasansky, MFA, 57. *Work:* Libr of Cong; Philadelphia Mus Art; Los Angeles Co Mus; Boston Pub Libr; Portland Art Mus, Ore. *Exhib:* Solo exhibs, Am Ctr Gallery, US Info Agency, Belgrade & Piran, Yugoslavia, 82, A Decade of Intaglio Prints, Univ Colo, 85, House of Dreams Lost and Found, (monoprints), Jane Haslem Gallery, Washington DC, 90, The Printerly Image: Wanda Miller Matthews, 1951-1991, Arvada Ctr Arts & Humanities, Denver, Colo, 91, Wanda Miller Matthews Multiple Plate Color Intaglios, Mt St Mary's Col, Los Angeles, 2000; one-man retrospective, Prints: 1955-1982, Jane Haslem Gallery, Washington, 82; 3rd Int Biennial Print Exhib, Taipei, Taiwan, 87-88; CSP Exchange Show, Brandts Klaedefabrik Mus, Odense, Denmark, 89; Archit in Contemp Printmaking Traveling Exhib, Boston Archit Ctr, 94 & Am Inst Architects, Washington, 94; Am Prints: Last half of the 20th Century, Jane Haslem Gallery, Washington, 93; and others. *Pos:* Res assistantship printmaking, Univ Iowa, 56-57. *Awards:* Purchase Award, Soc Am Graphic Artists Nat Exhib, New York, 79; Stella Drabkin Award & Medallion, Am Color Print Soc Nat Exhib, Philadelphia, 81; Leila Sawyer Mem Award, Nat Asn Women Artists Exhib, New York, 86; Cash Award, Silvermine Guild, 96; Kathleen Caraccio Purchase Award, Soc Am Graphic Artists, NY, 97. *Bibliog:* Stanley L Cuba (auth), Wanda Miller Matthews, Southwest Art Mag, 11/90. *Mem:* Soc Am Graphic Artists, NY; Boston Printmakers; Calif Soc Printmakers. *Media:* Etching, Engraving. *Dealer:* Jane Haslem Gallery 2025 Hillyer Pl NW Washington DC 20004; The New Van Straaten Gallery 742 N Wells St Chicago IL 60610; Sandy Carson Gallery 760 Santa Fe Drive Denver CO

MATTHEWS, WILLIAM (CARY)
PAINTER
b NY, May 28, 49. *Study:* San Francisco Art Inst, 69. *Work:* Eiteljorg Mus, Indianapolis, Ind; Buffalo Bill Hist Ctr, Whitney Gallery, Cody, Wyo; Gene Autry Mus, Los Angeles, Calif; Nat Cowboy Hall Fame, Okla City, Okla; Denver Art Mus, Colo. *Comn:* Ann Bluegrass Festival poster, Telluride, Colo, 84-90 & 93-96; anniversary poster, WestFest, Copper Mountain, Colo, 92, 93 & 96; numerous designs, Warner Western Records, Nashville, Tenn, 92-96; Canyon de Chelly (commemorative post card), US Postal Serv, 94; twelve watercolors, Ritz-Carlton Hotel, Aspen, Colo, 94. *Exhib:* One-man shows, Am Quarter Horse Mus, Amarillo, Tex, 94, Nev Mus Art, Reno, 96; Prix de West, Nat Cowboy Hall Fame, Okla City, Okla, 95; Covering the West, traveling, 95-96; Great Am Artists, Cincinnati Mus Ctr, Ohio, 96; Buffalo Bill Invitational, Buffalo Bill Mus, Cody, Wyo, 96. *Pos:* Guest lectr, Nev Mus Art, Reno, 96-97. *Teaching:* Instr watercolor, Western Folklife Ctr, Reno, Nev, 96. *Awards:* William E Weiss Purchase Award, Buffalo Bill Hist Ctr, Cody, Wyo, 94; J Schram Prize, Schramsberg Vineyards, 92. *Bibliog:* M J Van Deventer (auth), William Matthews: A painter of cowboy images, Persimmon Hill, autumn 93; Dyan Zaslowsky (auth), William Matthews, Southwest Art, 3/95; Don Hagerty (auth), 100 Leading Contemporary Painters & Sculptors of the American West, Northland Publ (in press). *Media:* Watercolor. *Publ:* Auth, Buckaroo: Visions and Voices of the American West, Simon & Schuster, 93; Cowboys & Images: The Watercolors of William Matthews, Chronicle Books, 94. *Mailing Add:* c/o William Matthews Gallery 1617 Wazee St Denver CO 80202

MATTINGLY, JAMES THOMAS
PRINTMAKER, PAINTER
b Southgate, Calif, Mar 14, 34. *Study:* San Jose State Univ, with Fred Spratt, Terry Frost, Ken Auvil, Jeff Bowman, Robert Collins & Robert Freemark, BA, 63, MA(art), 66. *Work:* Montreal Mus Fine Arts; Honolulu Acad Arts; Coos Art Mus, Coos Bay, Ore; Wash State Arts Comn, Seattle; Gilkey Print Ctr, Portland Art Mus, Oreg. *Comn:* Box (wood sculpture), comn by Glenda Melton, Salem, Ore, 80; Theatrical Heartscape (mural), comn by Mid-Valley Arts Coun, Elsinore Theatre, Salem, Ore, 84; Coup Stick VI (sculpture), comn by Scott Casebeer, Salem, Ore, 97; Technicolor Coho Buck Salmon in the City (mixed media sculpture), Salem, Ore, 2005. *Exhib:* Northwest Prints 82, Portland Art Mus, Ore, 82; solo exhib, Renshaw Gallery, Linfield Col, Ore, 92, Monmouth Series, Hamersly Libr, Western Ore Univ, 2003, Focus Gallery, AN Bush Gallery, Salem Art Asn, Ore, 2002; NW Print Coun Group Show, Pierce Col Gallery, Los Angeles, Calif, 93; Hunterdon Art Ctr, Print Exhib, Clinton, NJ, 80 &93; Sitka Art Invitational, Jack Longman Forestry Ctr, Portland, 93, 94, 95 & 96; NW Print Coun Beyond Seeing, Interstate Firehouse Cult Ctr, Portland, 96, traveling exhib, 96; Cult Identity, Western Ore Univ, Monmouth, 2002; Beyond Seeing, Northwest Print Coun, Interstate Firehouse Cult Ctr, Portland, Ore, 96; Traveling exhib, Cooper Village Mus & Art Ctr, Anaconda & Custer Co Art Ctr, Miles City, Mont, 96; Election HQ, Seattle, Wash, 11/96; XXVII Fed Int Des Soc D'Amateur D'Ex Libris Congress, Boston, 2000; Cambridge Bookplate, Boston Pub Libr, Boston, Mass, 8/2000; Hamersly Libr, Western Ore Univ, Monmouth, Oreg, 12/2000-3/01; Pacific States Biennial Nat Print Exhib, Univ Hawaii, Hilo, 2002-03; Coos Art Mus, Coos Bay, Ore, 2003; Contemp Print Exhib, Univ Wollongong, Australia, 2003; Cascade Print Edition Exchange Exhib, Ore State Univ, Corvallis, Ore, 2005; solo exhib, Governor's Ceremonial Off, State Capital Building, Salem, Ore, 2005; Maryhou Zeck Gallery, Monmouth Series Landscapes, Salem, Ore, 2005; Retrospective Show, Salem Art Asn, Salem, Ore, 2005; From America, Mus Contemp Art, Minsk, Belarus, 2006. *Pos:* prof emer in art, Western Oregon Univ, Ore. *Teaching:* Asst art, San Jose State Col, 63-66; instr, Alta Col Art, Calgary, 66-68; prof, Western Ore State Col, 68-94, art dept head, 78-86 & 89-90. *Awards:* Reid Mem Award, Int Exhib Graphics, Montreal Mus Fine Arts, 71; Statewide Serv Travel Award, 74 & Visual Arts Resources Award, 77, Mus Art, Univ Ore; Fac Hon Award, Western Ore State Col, Monmouth, 85; All Ore Juried Art Ann, Salem, 89, 90, 91. *Mem:* Salem Art Asn, Ore (mem bd dir, 77-90); Northwest Print Coun (pres, 83-85, mem bd dir, 82-83, 85-); Hon Life Mem, Northwest Print Coun, Portland, Ore, 98. *Media:* Intaglio printmaking, painting, Mixed media. *Res:* Digital photog. *Collection:* Painting, original prints, drawing and mixed media objects. *Publ:* Auth, Professional Concerns, A Handbook for the Apprentice Professional Visual Artist, pvt publ, 96, Rev 98, 2003 & 2004; auth, Standing on the Water Like a Dragonfly, pvt publ, 2006. *Dealer:* Prints Arts Northwest, 416 NW 12th Ave, Portland, OR, 97209; May Lou Zeek Gallery, 335 State St. Salem, OR, 97301. *Mailing Add:* 15440 Strong Rd Dallas OR 97338

MATYAS, DIANE C
SCULPTOR, PRINTMAKER
b Pittsburgh, Pa, Nov 28, 61. *Study:* Cornell Univ, BFA, 84; Vermont Studio Sch, 86, Cornell, MFA, 89; Studies at Columbia Univ, Sch Bus, Ctr Non-Profit Mgt, 2006. *Work:* Sculpture, City of Mesa, Ariz; 2 murals, one interactive "puzzle" painting, Staten Island Children's Mus. *Comn:* Monkey Puzzle (sculpture), Philadelphia, Pa, 87; Water (mural, oil), Staten Island Childrens Mus, 92; Desert Pergola (sculpture), Mesa, Ariz, 93. *Exhib:* Alliance in the Park, Philadelphia, Pa, 87; New Visions Gallery, Ithaca, NY, 88; AIR Gallery, NY, 88; ARC Gallery, Chicago, Ill, 92; Columbus Circle, NY subway installation, 92. *Pos:* prog developer/instr, Homeless Art Proj, Queens Mus, NY; instr, Studio in a School Asn, NY, 91-92; Educ Dir, Noble Maritime Collection, 99-2002, prog dir, 2002-2005; Mus Dir of Exhib & Programs, Staten Island Mus, 2005-. *Teaching:* instr printmaking, Cornell Univ, 89-; instr painting & design, Wagner Col, 94. *Awards:* Cornell Fac Medal of Art, 84; Sculpture Grant, Pa Coun Arts, 87; Grant, The Greater New York Art Develop, 88. *Bibliog:* Helen A Harrison (auth), Young artist offers works of maturity, NY Times, 3/2/86; Karin Lipson (auth), Works of young & emerging artists, Newsday, 3/86; Thomas Hine (auth), The Philadelphia Inquirer, 7/27/87. *Media:* Terra Cotta, Intaglio; Pastel. *Publ:* Thoughts on Public Sculpture: The Work of Petah Coyne, 88 & The 1988 Venice Bennale, Q Mag, 88

MAUGHELLI, MARY L
PRINTMAKER, PAINTER
b Glen Lyon, Pa, Nov 20, 35. *Study:* Univ Calif, Berkeley, BA & MA; Pratt Graphic Ctr. *Work:* Fresno Art Mus, Calif; Helene Wurlitzer Found, Taos, NMex; Univ NMex Tamarind Prints, Albuquerque. *Exhib:* 85th Ann San Francisco Art Inst Exhib, San Francisco Mus Art, 66; Prints USA Malmo, Konstall, Sweden, 85; Beyond NY, AIR Gallery, NY, 89-2001; Condition: Human, AIR Gallery, 89-2003; Solo exhib, Silhouette Symbol & Spirit, Fresno Art Mus, Calif, 98, and many more; Female, Feminine, Feminist, Orlando Gallery, Tarzana, Calif, 2003; Persistent Image 2006, Tulare Historical Mus, Tulare, Calif; Explorations Gallery 25, Fresno, Calif, 2006. *Teaching:* prof art, Calif State Univ, Fresno, 62-98, prof art, emeritas, 98-; lectr design, Univ Calif, Berkeley, summer 63. *Awards:* Fulbright Fels, Italy, 59-61; Helene Wurlitzer Found Fel, Taos, NMex, summer 76, 77, 83, 86 & 91; artist-in-residence, Hambidge Ctr, Rabun Gap, Ga, 95 & 2006; artist-in-residence, Mishkenot Sha'ananim, Jerusalem, Israel, 96; Jentel artist-in-residence, Banner, Wyo, 2006. *Bibliog:* David Hale (auth), Her Free Floating Figures Defy Gravity, Convention, Fresno Bee, 5/31/98; David Hale (auth), Mary Maughelli: Her Style Remains Ageless, Fresno Bee, 3/11/90, Donald Munro (auth), Personal J, Fresno Bee, 11/13/03. *Mem:* Col Art Asn; Calif Soc Printmakers; Women's Caucus for Art; Southern Calif Women's Caucus for Art. *Media:* Mixed Media, Oil, Collage. *Dealer:* Fig Tree Gallery 644 Van Ness Ave Fresno Calif 93721; AIR Gallery 511 W 25th St New York NY 10001. *Mailing Add:* 1114 W Keats Ave Fresno CA 93711

MAURER, EVAN MACLYN
MUSEUM DIRECTOR
b Newark, NJ, Aug 19, 44. *Study:* Amherst Col, BA, 66; Univ Minn, MA, 68; Univ Pa, PhD, 74. *Collection Arranged:* The Native American Heritage (auth, catalog), Art Inst Chicago, 77; The Rising of a New Moon, 86; Visions of the People, Minneapolis Inst Arts, 92. *Pos:* Cur & asst to dir, Minneapolis Inst Arts, 71-73, dir & chief exec officer, 88-; cur art, Art Inst Chicago, 73-81; dir, Univ Mich Mus Art, 81-88. *Teaching:* Vis prof primitivism & mod art, Univ Chicago, 76; lectr primitivism, mod art & mus studies, Art Inst Chicago, 78-81, assoc prof, 81; prof art hist, Univ Mich. *Awards:* Recipient medal of Chevalier Order of Arts and Letters, French Govt, 2004. *Mem:* Col Art Asn; Am Asn Mus; Am Asn Mus Dirs. *Mailing Add:* Mpls Inst Arts 2400 3rd Ave S Minneapolis MN 55404-3506

MAURER, GILBERT CHARLES
PATRON
b New York, NY, May 24, 1928. *Study:* St Lawrence Univ, AB, 1950; Harvard Univ, MBA, 1952. *Pos:* With, Cowles Communications, Inc, 1952-71, Look Mag, 1952-62; publ, Venture mag, 1963-67; pres, Family Circle mag, 1967-69, vpres, dir corp planning, exec comt, 1969-71; sr vpres, dir, FAS Int, Inc, 1971-73; vpres mag div, Hearst Corp, 1973-74, exec vpres, 1974-76, 1985-98, pres mag div, 1976-90, chief operating officer, 1990-98, cons; mem NY adv bd, Salvation Army, 1979; trustee, Whitney Mus Am Art, 1983-, pres, 1994-98; trustee Norton Mus of Art, 1998-; mem vis com, Medill Sch Journalism Northwestern Univ, 1985-94, chmn, 1989-94; bd dir, Boys and Girls Club Am, 1986-, William Randolph Hearst Found, The Hearst Found; mem bd mgrs, NY Botanical Garden, 1989. *Mem:* Mag Publs Asn. *Mailing Add:* The Hearst Corp 959 8th Ave New York NY 10019-3795

MAURER, NEIL
PHOTOGRAPHER
b New York, NY, Jan 12, 41. *Study:* Brown Univ, BA, 62; RI Sch Design, MFA, 75. *Work:* Mus Mod Art, NY; Corcoran Gallery Art; San Antonio Mus Art; Mus Art, RI Sch Design; Libr Cong. *Exhib:* Solo shows, Marcuse Pfeifer Gallery, NY, 88, Art Forum Gallery, Quito, Equador, 91, New Gallery, Houston, Tex, 92, Martin-Rathburn Gallery, San Antonio, Tex, 96 & Silver Eye Ctr Photog, Pittsburgh, Pa, 96; Houston Ctr Photog, Tex, 95; Kobe Aid Fund, Tokyo, Japan, 96. *Teaching:* Asst prof, Div Art & Design, Univ Tex, San Antonio, 78-84, assoc prof, Div Visual Arts, 85-. *Awards:* Fulbright-Hays Grant, 75-76; Fulbright-Hays Sr Lectr Photog, Cent Univ, Quito, Equador, 91; Fel Award Photog, Mid-Am Arts Alliance/Nat Endowment Arts, 95. *Mailing Add:* 723 Woodlawn Ave San Antonio TX 78212-3136

MAURICE, ALFRED PAUL
PAINTER, PRINTMAKER
b Nashua, NH, 1921. *Study:* Univ NH, 40-42; Mich State Univ, BA, 47, MA, 49. *Work:* Libr Cong, Washington; Southern Ill Univ, Edwardsville; Anderson Art Ctr, Ind; Mus Contemp Art, Chicago; Portland Art Mus. *Comn:* Murals (with Raymond Pinet), Nat Youth Admin, Jr High Sch, Hudson, NH & Community Chest Bldg, Nashua, 39-40; Mural, Marshall Field Co, Chicago. *Exhib:* Butler Inst Ann, 81-83 & 90; one-man shows, Bradley Univ, 82, Mich State Univ, 83, Chicago Pub Libr Cult Ctr, 83, Anderson Art Ctr, 83, Joy Horwich Gallery, 85 & RH Love Galleries, 88 & 89 & Comus Gallery, 93; Paintings & Sculptures by Candidates for Art Awards, Am Acad Arts & Lett, 85; Archer Gallery, Clark Col, 97; Water Resources Ctr, Vancouver, BC, 98; and others. *Collection Arranged:* American Prints, Univ Ill, Chicago; Longview Foundation Collection, Kalamazoo Inst Arts, Mich; Executive Collection, Upjohn Pharmaceutical Co, Kalamazoo, Mich. *Pos:* Auth, Periodical Review, Art Educ, 57-59; dir art ctr, Kalamazoo Inst Arts, Mich, 59-65. *Teaching:* Instr printmaking, calligraphy & drawing, Macalester Col, 47-49; asst drawing, Mich State Univ, 49-50; from asst prof to assoc prof drawing, painting, printmaking & design, State Univ NY Col New Paltz, 50-57, actg chmn art dept, 55-56; exec dir, Md Inst Col Art, Baltimore, 57-59; chmn art dept, Univ Ill, Chicago Circle, 65-67, prof printmaking painting & drawing, 65-, assoc dean facs, 69-72, actg dean, Col Archit & Art, 75-77, prof emer, 88-; lectr, Clark Col, Vancouver, Wash, 2001-. *Awards:* Audubon Artists Medal Hon Graphics, 84; Richard Florsheim Art Fund Award, 97; A E S Peterson Award, 2001. *Bibliog:* New Art Examiner, 11/82; Chicago Sun-Times, 6/10/83; Mizue, Japan, Spring 88. *Mem:* Nat Soc Painters Casein & Acrylic; Pastel Soc Am; Soc Wash Artists; Print Arts Northwest; Southwest Wash Watercolor Soc. *Media:* Acrylic; Relief Printmaking, Colored Pencil. *Collection:* American women in printmaking from colonial times through 1950s; Fiske Boyde woodcuts; Winslow Homer wood engravings. *Publ:* Auth, Four Printmakers, 62; Miklos Suba, 64; Oliver Chaffee, 64; George C Miller & Son, Lithographic Printers to Artists Since 1917, Am Art Rev, Mar-Apr/76; and numerous exhib catalogs. *Dealer:* Print Arts Northwest 416 NW 12th Portland Ore 97209; Pike Arc Gallery 411 NE Dallas Camas Wash 98607. *Mailing Add:* 12515 SE McGillivray Blvd Vancouver WA 98683

MAURO, ROBERT F
EDUCATOR, PRINTMAKER
b Englewood Cliffs, NJ, Oct 2, 51. *Study:* Glassboro State Col, BA(art educ), 73; Pratt Inst, MFA(printmaking), 78. *Work:* Stedman Gallery Rutgers Univ, Camden, NJ; Univ Mich, Ann Arbor; Newark Pub Libr, NJ. *Comn:* 3-D serigraph, Subaru Am, Cherry Hill, NJ, 82; 3-D serigraph, Corning Glass, Philadelphia, Pa, 82; 3-D serigraph, PNB, Philadelphia, Pa, 83. *Exhib:* Korea Int Print Competition, Seoul, 80; Print Club Biennial Int, Philadelphia Print Club, Pa, 86; Artlink Prints, Artlink Contemp Space, Ft Wayne, Idaho, 8; Scan, Franklin Inst, Philadelphia, Pa, 93; Scan, Silicon Gallery, Philadelphia, Pa, 95. *Pos:* Chmn fine arts, Beaver Col, Pa, 78-. *Teaching:* Assoc prof printmaking, Beaver Col, Glenside, Pa, 78- & chmn, 93-. *Mem:* Philadelphia Print Club. *Media:* Computer Imaging. *Dealer:* Rosenfeld Gallery Arch St Philadelphia PA. *Mailing Add:* 805 Jamestown Rd Turnersville NJ 08012

MAURY, RICHARD
PAINTER
b Washington, DC, Nov 6, 35. *Study:* Corcoran Sch Art, Washington, DC; Art Students League, NY; Acad di Belle Arti, Florence, Italy. *Work:* Metrop Mus Art, NY; New Britain Mus Am Art, Conn; Arnot Mus Art, Elmira, NY; Flint Mus, Mich; rep in collections of Am Express Co, Arnot Art Mus Elmira NY, Mus Art NY City, New Britain (Conn) Mus Art, Fogg Mus Cambridge Mass. *Exhib:* The Figure in Am Art Since Midcentury, Silvermine Metro Ctr, Stamford, Conn, 88; New Britain Invitational, New Britain Mus, Conn, 89; Exquisite Painting, Orlando Mus Art, Fla, 91; Acad Inst Exhib of Painting & Sculpture, Am Acad & Inst of Arts & Letters, NY, 91; Midyear Invitational, Butler Mus Art, Youngstown, Ohio, 92; Ann Exhib, Nat Acad Design, NY, 92; Rerepresenting Representation, Arnot Mus Art, Elmira, NY, 93; one-man show, Greenville Co Mus, SC, 93; Forum Gallery New York City, 2001-03, Forum Gallery Los Angeles, 2003; Art Students League New York City, Flint (Mich); Uffizi Gallery Florence Italy. *Bibliog:* Margaret Matthews (auth), Richard Maury, Am Artist, 9/85; Jason Kaufman (auth), Realism rising, Atelier Mag Int Art; Thomas Hoving (auth), My eye, Connoisseur, 2/90. *Mem:* Nat Acad (acad). *Media:* Oil Colors, Charcoal. *Mailing Add:* c/o Forum Gallery 745 Fifth Ave New York NY 10151

MAUSSION, PIERRE EDOUARD See Edouard, Pierre Edward Maussion

MAVIGLIANO, GEORGE JEROME
ADMINISTRATOR, EDUCATOR
b Chicago, Ill, Oct 24, 41. *Study:* Western Ill Univ, BA, 64; Northern Ill Univ, MA, 67. *Pos:* Assoc Dean, Col Communications & Fine Arts, Southern Ill Univ, 86-. *Teaching:* Assoc prof art hist, Southern Ill Univ, 70-. *Awards:* Nat Endowment Arts Expansion Arts Grant, 77; Smithsonian Inst Fel, 81; Nat Endowment Humanities Summer Sem Award, 81 & 85. *Res:* New Deal art programs; art of the Capitol. *Publ:* Auth, A Matter of History: New Deal and the Arts (exhib catalog), 73; On Painting, Sculpture and Architecture, Stipes, 73; Fred Myers, Woodcarver, Southern Ill Univ, 80; The Federal Art Project: Holger Cahill's Program of Action, Art Education, Vol XXXVII, No 3, 5/84; The Chicago Design Workshop: 1939-1943, Journal of Decorative & Propaganda Arts, No 6, fall 87; The Federal Art Project in Illinois: 1935-43, Southern Ill Univ, 90. *Mailing Add:* 405 Marcia Carterville IL 62918-1555

MAVROS, DONALD ODYSSEUS
CERAMIST, SCULPTOR
b New York, NY, Mar 4, 27. *Study:* Mabel Claire Brady; Cooper Union; Columbia Univ. *Work:* Everson Mus Art, Syracuse, NY; Orange Cty Community Col-Heritage Collection, Middletown, NY; Warren Wilson Col, Swannanoa, NC. *Comn:* Sculptures, City of NY, 54; portrait, Nat Republican Club, NY, 55; architectural reliefs, Lanai Restaurant, NY, 63; medallion, Theodore Roosevelt Hist Site, NY, 64; sculpture, The Bank for Savings, NY, 65; eight sculptures, Road to Mecca, 90 production; Sculpture, Nat Archives, 88. *Exhib:* Ceramic Int, Everson Mus Art, Syracuse, NY, 58; Forms from the Earth, Mus Contemp Crafts, NY, 62; Greek-Am Artists, (sponsored by Embassy of Greece in conjunction with Search for Alexander Exhib) Grimaldis Gallery, Baltimore, Md, 81; I Love NY Ceramics, State Univ of NY, Albany, 83; Mt Aramah Exhib, Arden, NY, 86; Forty Yrs Retrospective, Hudson Guild & Lowe Art Gallery, NY, 88; Orange Co Art, Arden, NY, 90; Khoas Journey, Middletown Art Ctr, NY, 94. *Pos:* Vpres, Artists-Craftsmen NY, 55-69; founder/dir, Trias Gallery, NY, 65-77; founding mem/exec bd, Empire State Crafts Alliance, NY, 80-83; art reviewer, Times Herald Record, 85-86; cur, Orange Co Art, Orange Co Hist Soc, 90 & John Newton Howitt Retrospective Exhib, City Port Jervis, NY, 94 & 95; exec dir, Mus Village, Monroe, NY, 79-84, 97-99. *Teaching:* Dir/instr ceramics, Mavros Workshop, NY, 54-77; instr ceramics, New Sch Soc Research, NY, 60-77; dir/instr sculpture, Unionville Art Works, NY, 77-. *Awards:* Sculpture Award & Pottery Award, 5th Young Americans Exhib; Sculpture Award, 3rd Young Americans Exhib, Am Crafts Coun, 52; Hon memtion, 16th Nat Ceramic Exhib, Syracuse Mus Fine Art, 51. *Bibliog:* Audrey Hirsch (auth), It looks like a pot, it acts like a pot, and it floats, 77; Laurie Lisle (auth), A Passionate Life, Louise Nevelson, Summit Bks, 90; Eleanor Martin (auth), Mavros faces new sculptural challenge, Times Herald Record, 94. *Mem:* Artists Equity; Nat Sculpture Soc. *Media:* Clay. *Publ:* Auth, Getting Started in Ceramics, Macmillian, 70; contribr, 300th anniversary-Orange County, Publ, NY, 83; auth, Whither Mandeville, Orange Co Hist Soc, 89; Unionville-Diary of a Village, Royal Fireworks Press, 95. *Mailing Add:* 6190 Rte 9 Rhinebeck NY 12572-3628

MAVROUDIS, DEMETRIOS
SCULPTOR
b Thasos, Greece, Nov 18, 37. *Study:* Jersey City State Col, BA; Teachers Col, Columbia Univ, MA & EdD. *Comn:* Bronze sculptures, Bus Comt for Arts, Esquire, 73-76; sculpture, Lifestyles Mag, 77; ESG Enterprises, 86; mosaic of Madonna & Child in St Constantine & Helen's Greek Cathedral, Richmond, Va, 87. *Exhib:* Albright-Knox Art Gallery, Buffalo, NY, 70 & 71; Artists-in-Residence Traveling Exhib, Del Art Mus, Wilmington, 75 & 76; Sculpture in the Fields, Storm King Art Ctr, Mountainville, NY; one-man shows, Philadelphia Art Alliance, Pa, Anchorage Hist & Fine Arts Mus, Alaska & Alaska State Mus. *Pos:* Artist-in-residence, NJ Coun Arts, 71-73. *Teaching:* Asst prof sculpture, NY Univ, 69-71 & Teachers Col, Columbia Univ, 67-69 & 73-74; assoc prof sculpture & artist-in-residence, Univ Richmond, Va, 74-86. *Awards:* Dow Purchase Award, Columbia Univ, 69. *Mem:* Am Foundrymen's Soc; Nat Art Educ Asn; Col Art Asn. *Media:* Cast Metal, Wood. *Mailing Add:* 1808 Belleau Dr Richmond VA 23235-4214

MAWDSLEY, RICHARD
SILVERSMITH, GOLDSMITH
b Winfield, Kans, July 11, 45. *Study:* Emporia State Univ, BSE, 67; Univ KS, MFA, 69. *Work:* Am Crafts Mus, NY; Mus Fine Arts, Boston; Renwick Gallery, Smithsonian Inst, Washington; Yale Univ Art Gallery, New Haven, Conn. *Exhib:* Minn Mus Art, 70 & 78-80; Cocoran Gallery Art, 72; solo exhibs, Helen Drutt Gallery, Philadelphia, 77, Ornamental Metal Mus, Memphis, Tenn, 87 & Mobilia Gallery, Cambridge, Mass, 92; Vatican Mus, Italy, 78; Nat Mus Am Art, Smithsonian Inst, Washington, 81; Mus Fine Arts, Boston, 84-86 & 87-90; Oakland Mus, 84-86 & 87-90; Victoria & Albert Mus, 85; Philadelphia Mus Art, 86-87; Nat Mus Mod Art, Tokyo & Kyoto, 87-90; Grand Prix des Metiers d'Art, Int Invitational Exhib, Acad Royal Arts, Toronto & Salon des Metiers d'Art, Montreal, 88; 1988 Hong-iK Metalcrafts Asn Ann Exhib, Invitational Exhib, Walker Hill Art Ctr Mus, Seoul, Korea, 88; Explorations: The Aesthetic of Excess, Am Craft Mus, NY, 90; Stedlijk Mus, Amsterdam, The Neth, 95; America's Smithsonian (traveling), 96-98; Intl Invit Exhib, Brooching It Diplomatically: A Tribute to Madeleine K. Albright, Helen Drutt Gal, Phila, PA, Het Kruithuis, Mun Mus Contemp Art, 'sHertogenbosch, Netherlands, Mus Art & Design, Helsinki, Finland, Tarbekunstimuuseum, Tallin, Estonia, Am Craft Mus, NY, Villa Croce, Mus Contemp Art, Genova, Italy, Kunstgewerbemusuem, Berlin, Germany & Schmuckmusem, Pforzheim, Germany, 1998-2001; cur exhib, Attitude & Action! North American Jewelry, Univ Cent England, Birmingham Inst Art & Design, Eng & DESIGNyard Gal, Dublin, Ireland, 2000; Generating Connections Emerging Jewelry Artists & Mentors, Soc Arts & Crafts, Boston, Mass, 2002; A View From America: Contemporary Jewelry, Gold Treasury Mus, Melbourne, Australia, 2004; Think Small, Ill State Mus, Chicago Gallery, James R. Thompson Ctr, Ill State Mus, Springfield, & Ill State Mus, Lockport Gallery, 2005-06. *Pos:* Fellow, Am Craft Council, 98-; pres, Soc North Am Goldsmiths, 87-89. *Teaching:* Prof emeritus, Southern Ill Univ, Carbondale. *Awards:* Artist Fel in Crafts, Ill Arts Coun, 87-88, 97-98, 2000-01; Artist Fel Grant, Nat Endowment Arts, 77-78 & 94-95; Distinguished Alumni, Emporia State Univ, Kkansas, 93. *Bibliog:* Janet Koplas (auth), Richard Mawdsley Tubular Fantasies, Am Craft Mag, vol 43, no 2, April/May, 1983; Susan Barahal (auth),

Richard Mawdsley New Work: Architectural series, Metalsmith Mag, Vol 13, No 4, fall 92; Susan Grant Lerwin (auth), One of a Kind American Art Jewelry, Harry N Abrams, New York, 94; Helen W English Drutt (auth), Jewelry of Our Time: Art Ornament and Obsesion, Rizzoli, New York, 95; Howard Risatti (auth), Skilled Work: American Craft in the Renwick Gallery, Smithsonian Inst Press, Wash, DC, 1998. *Mem:* Soc NAM Goldsmiths (pres, 87-89). *Media:* Metals. *Mailing Add:* 204 Lynn Ln Carterville IL 62918

MAX, PETER
PAINTER, PRINTMAKER
b Berlin, Ger, Oct 19, 37; US citizen. *Study:* Art Students League; Pratt Inst; Sch Visual Arts. *Comn:* 12 environmental stamps, United Nations, 92; two murals (175'), Discovery, US Pavilion Expo 92; 108 portraits of Dali Lama, Hanson Gallery, 92; painting of the Nina, the Pinta & the Santa Maria, comn by Lady Pindling, 92; portrait, Gorby, comn by Mikhail Gorbachev, 92; The Better World, comn by Prince Rainier, 92; commemorative T-shirts, NY Harbor; and many others. *Exhib:* The Lady, created on the White House Lawn, 81; retrospective, Hermitage Mus, Russia, 91 & Acad Fine Arts, Moscow, 92; Flag (10' x 14'), Paints of Light Found, 92; Peter Max Paints Am 92, Richmond, Va; Recent Works, Palm Beach, 92; Statue of Liberty Collage, Presidential Libr, Simi Valley, Calif, 92; Decades of the Hearts, Beverly Hills, 92; Hartmann Gallery, Munich, Ger, 92; exhib, Sporting d'Hiver, Monte Carlo, 92; Pop to Patriotism, Tenn State Mus, 93 & Corcoran Gallery Art, Washington, DC, 94; and many others. *Pos:* Dir, Daly-Max Design Studio; designer, Gen Foods, Elgin Nat Industs, Takashimaya Ltd Japan, Van Heusen, UN & other major orgns; official artist, World Cup USA, Super Bowl & Grammy Awards. *Awards:* Celebrity Gala for Max, hosted by Don Johnson & Melanie Griffith, Aspen, Colo, 92; Official artist, Christopher Columbus Quincentenary, appointed by Congress, 92; Award, Int Poster Competition Poland; plus many others. *Bibliog:* Sal Manna (auth), Pushing it to the Max, Am Way, 6/25/85; Mark-Elliott Lugo (auth), Talent, enthusiasm hide behind Max's commercialism, 4/24/86; Maximum salute to the Statue of Liberty, 6/16/86 & Audrey Farolino (auth), Portrait of the artists-and his lady love, 6/23/86, New York Post. *Media:* Mixed. *Publ:* Auth, Peter Max Posterbook & Peter Max Superposterbook, Crown; Peter Max Japan Book; drawings & meditations syndicated in 176 papers in US & Can, two yrs; illusr, cover for TV Guide's Super Bowl issue, 92; and many others. *Mailing Add:* Via Max Enterprises 37 W 65th St New York NY 10023

MAXERA, OSCAR
PAINTER, ASSEMBLAGE ARTIST
b Buenos Aires, Arg, Jan 12, 30. *Study:* Acad Fine Arts, Arg, cert, 55. *Work:* Solomon R Guggenheim Mus (5 paintings), NY; Westport Mus, Conn, 77; Mus Mod Art, Buenos Aires, 82; Centro Argentino de Relaciones Internacionales, Buenos Aires, 79; Co-Art, New York, NY, 94; Solomon R Guggenheim Mus; Yale Univ Art Gallery, New Haven, Conn, 2003; and many more in pvt collections. *Comn:* Artists of the World, Meibner Edition, Lufthansa, Hamburg, 83. *Exhib:* One-man shows, Nice Gallery, 68, 70 & 71, Ctr Cult San Martin, 72, Lirolay Gallery, 73, Van Riel Gallery, Buenos Aires, 74, Westport Pub Libr, 77 & Sarmiento Gallery, Buenos Aires, 80; Mus Mod Art, Buenos Aires, 69-79; Mus Mod Art, Paraguay, 74; Solomon R Guggenheim Mus, 87 & 88; Ergane Gallery, NY, 90; La Mama Galleria, NY, 92; Silvermine Guild Arts Ctr, 95; New York Radiance, Lawrence Univ Art Ctr, Appleton, Wis, 95. *Teaching:* Acad Fine Art, Meeba, Buenos Aires, 57-60. *Awards:* First Prize, Salon for Newcomers Fine Arts, 68; First Prize, Vincente Lopez Munic Salon, 70; Second Prize, San Antonio de Areco Salon, 73; 2000 outstanding people of the 20th century, Int Biographical Ctr, Cambridge, Eng, 98. *Bibliog:* Arte D'Oggi (auth), Ultime Tendenze Nell, Gillo Dorfles, Italy, 74; Fifty Years of Collections: Painting Since World War II, Guggenheim Mus, 87; K G Saur (auth), Allgemeines Künstlerlexikon, Munchen Leipzig, 93. *Media:* Collage, Acrylic, Oil. *Publ:* Nueva Historia de la Pintura y Escultura en la Argentina, 3d ed, 99-2000. *Mailing Add:* 334 E 90th St No 3 C New York NY 10128-5185

MAXFIELD, ROBERTA MASUR
SILVERSMITH
b Chicago, Ill, Oct 30, 52. *Study:* Northern Ill Univ, with Eleanor Caldwell & Lee Peck, BFA, 74, MA, 75; Ind Univ, with Alma Eikerman, MFA, 77. *Work:* Ill State Mus, Springfield; Village Art Collection, Oak Park & River Forest High Sch, Ill. *Exhib:* Goldsmiths Show, Phoenix Art Mus, Ariz, 77; Ill Craftsmen, Ill State Mus, Springfield, 79; Everyday Metal Exhib, Nat Ornamental Mus, Memphis, Tenn, 80; Young Americans Metal, Am Crafts Mus, NY 81; Calso, traveling, 81; Alma Eikerman Retrospective Exhib, Ind Univ Art Mus, 85; Soc Arts Crafts Pa, 85; Scent Bottle Exhib, Signature Gallery, Mass, 85. *Awards:* Honorable Mention, Soc N Am Goldsmiths, 77; Purchase Award & Third Place, Village Art Fair, Village Art Comt, 79; Honorable Mention, Ill Crafts Exhib, Ill State Mus, 80. *Bibliog:* Craft Horizons, Am Coun Crafts, 4/77. *Mem:* Soc N Am Goldsmiths. *Media:* Sterling Silver. *Mailing Add:* 461 W Hillcrest Dr De Kalb IL 60115-2377

MAXIM, DAVID NICHOLAS
PAINTER, GRAPHIC ARTIST
b Los Angeles, Calif, May 11, 45. *Study:* Univ Calif Los Angeles, BA, 66, MA, 68. *Work:* San Francisco Mus Mod Art; Mus Fine Moderne Kunst, Frankfurt, Ger; British Mus, London,; Graphische Sammlung Albertina, Vienna; Brooklyn Mus, NY. *Exhib:* Bilder fur Frankfurt, Deutschen Architectur Mus, Frankfurt, Germ, 85; Ten Americans, Carnegie Inst Art, Pittsburgh, Pa, 88; Kunstverein, Heidenheim, Ger, 93; Painted Philosophy, Univ Calif, Berkeley Mus, Danville, 94. *Awards:* Grant, Judwig Vogelstein Found, 95. *Bibliog:* Jan Butterfield (auth), David Maxim (exhib catalog), Galerie Sander, 91; August & Dorothy Friedman (coauths), Maxim's paint machines, Downtown, New York, 4/8/92; Nicole Blunt (auth), Heroes and Giants, 96 & David Naxim: Drawings, Walsworth Publ, 98. *Media:* Acrylic & Mixed Media on Canvas; Drawing Media. *Publ:* Coauth, Painted Philosophy (exhib catalog), 94. *Mailing Add:* 224 Guerrero St San Francisco CA 94103

MAXWELL, ALLAN R
PHOTOGRAPHER
b New York, NY, Sept 18, 49. *Study:* Fla Atlantic Univ, BFA, 72; Kent State Univ, MFA, 77. *Work:* SE Mus of Photography, Daytona Beach; The Brevard Mus, Melbourne, Fla; The City of Orlando, Fla. *Exhib:* solo exhibs, Daytona Beach Community Col, Fla, 92, Atlantic Ctr for Arts, Fla, 92, Ormond Mem Art Mus, Ormond Beach, Fla, 93, Soc Contemp Photo, Kansas City, Mo, 94, Alexander Brest Mus, Jacksonville Univ, Fla, 94, Valencia Community Col, Orlando, Fla, 94, Hudson Valley Inst for Art & Photog, NY, 95, Truckee Meadows Community Col, Reno, Nev, 95, S Fla Art Ctr, Miami, 96; Amarillo Col, Southern Light Gallery, Tex, 96, Arts on Douglas Gallery, New Smyrna Beach, Fla, 97, Hugo de Pagano Gallery, New York City, 97, Camera Club of NY, New York City, 98, Univ Nev, Reno, 98, Pietra Di Luna Gallery, Hollywood, Fla, 2000, Minot State Univ, Northwest Art Ctr, NDak, 2000, Fla Dept State, Capitol Complex Exhib, Tallahassee, 2000, Univ Calif, Berkley, 00, Schacknow Mus Fine Art, Plantation, Fla, 02, Paulina Miller Gallery, Phoenix, 02; group exhibs, Fla State Univ, Tallahassee, 92, Virginia Miller Gallery, Miami, 93, Spacecase Gallery, New York City, 94, San Diego Art Inst, 95, Barrett House Galleries, Poughkeepsie, NY, 96, Toledo Mus Art, Ohio, 97, Univ Mobile, Ala, 98, Univ Louisville, Ky, 99, Fla Atlantic Univ, Boca Raton, 00, La State Univ, Baton Rouge, 01. *Collection Arranged:* Ctr for Photog at Woodstock, NY; Polaroid Corp, Cambridge, Mass; Southeast Mus Photog, Daytona Beach, Fla; Brevard Mus, Melbourne, Fla; City of Orlando, Fla; Valencia Community Col, Orlando, Fla; Maitland Art Ctr, Fla; N Am Biologicals, Inc, Miami. *Pos:* photo-journalist, The Atlantic Sun, Boca Raton, Fla, 70-72; photo lab tech, Fla Atlantic Univ, Boca Raton, Fla, 71-73; photo lab coordr, Kent State Univ, Ohio, 77; photog, Akron Art Inst, Ohio, 77-78; owner, operator, Allan Maxwell Photog, NY City, 83-89; owner, operator, Allan Maxwell Productions, Inc, Orlando, Fla, 91-. *Teaching:* photo instr, Akron Univ, Ohio, 77-78, Youngstown State Univ, Ohio, 77-78; asst prof art, Wilkes Univ, Wilkes Barr, Pa, 78-83; asst dean, NY Inst Photog, NY City, 86-88; adj asst prof photography, Tish Sch of Art, NY, 88; prof photography, SE Ctr for Photographic Studies, 90-91; adj prof, Univ Cent Fla, Orlando, 00; adj prof, Valencia Community Col, Orlando, 01-. *Awards:* individual artist fellowship, Pa State Arts Coun, 81, Fla State Arts Coun, 91, 03; hon mention, Fla State Arts Coun, 96. *Bibliog:* Nancy Howell Koehler (auth), Photo Art Processes, 80; Fla Mag, Orlando Sentinel, 12/22/91; Daytona Beach News Jour, 1/26/92, 3/13/94; Orlando Sentinel, 3/20/94; Ctr for Photog at Woodstock, Quarterly #58, NY, 5/1/94; Gary Monroe (auth), The Highwaymen, 01. *Publ:* Viewfinder #21, Allan Maxwell Photo, Photometro Vol 16, 98. *Mailing Add:* 1631 Crestwood Dr Orlando FL 32804-3430

MAXWELL, DAVID OGDEN
PATRON
b Philadelphia, Pa, May 16, 30. *Study:* Yale Univ, BA, 52; Harvard Univ, LLB, 55. *Pos:* insurance comnr to admin and budget secy, State of Pa, 67-70; gen counsel, HUD, Wash, 70-73; pres, Chief Exec Officer, Ticor Mortgage Insurance Co, 73-81; Chief Exec Officer, Fannie Mae, Wash, 81-91; bd dir, Centre Partners, LP, Fin Security Assurance Holdings, Ltd, currently; trustee, Nat Gallery Art, currently. *Mailing Add:* 5335 Wisconsin Ave NW Ste 440 Washington DC 20015-2052

MAXWELL, PETER
DESIGNER, ART DEALER
b Easton, Pa, May 2, 30. *Pos:* Pres, Maxwell & Maxwell, 60-75, Maxwell Communications, 75-80 & Maxwell's Business, 80-; owner, Dolan-Maxwell, Inc, Philadelphia, 84- & New York, 88-90; co-founder, Artist in Rural Ireland Fund, Pa & Ballinglen Arts Found, Co Mayo, Eire, 92-. *Mem:* Int Fine Print Dealers Asn. *Specialty:* Modern and contemporary works on paper. *Publ:* Publ, Susan Rothenberg, The Prints, A Catalog Raisonne, 87; Roger Vieillard, 88; The Sculpture of Bill Freelend, 89. *Mailing Add:* 2046 E Rittenhouse St Philadelphia PA 19138-3111

MAY, DANIEL STRIGER
DEALER
b Decatur, Ill, Sept 5, 42. *Study:* State Univ NY, Buffalo, BA, 64, MBA, 66 & MEd, 68. *Pos:* Dir, Jackson Hole Art Gallery, 70-72; owner & dir, May Gallery, Jackson, Wyo, 72-; owner, May Gallery, Scottsdale, Ariz, 78-. *Specialty:* Fine American paintings and sculpture; contemporary jewelry. *Mailing Add:* c/o Dan May & Assoc 4110 N Scottsdale Rd Suite 105 Scottsdale AZ 85251

MAYER, BILLY (WILLIAM) ROBERT MAYER
SCULPTOR
b St Paul, Minn, June 28, 53. *Study:* Univ Minn, BFA, 76; Pa State Univ, MFA, 78. *Work:* Frederick Weisman Collection, Los Angeles, Calif; Muskegan Art Mus, Mich; Univ Galleries, Univ Minn. *Comn:* Outdoor sculpture, Holland, Mich, 83; large-scale sculpture, Howard Miller Inc, Zeeland, Mich, 85; outdoor sculpture, Christ Community Church, Spring Lake, Mich, 88. *Exhib:* West Mich Art Exhib, Muskegon Mus Art, 86; Signs, Times and Writing on the Wall, Detroit Inst Art, Mich, 87; Appalachian summer sculpture competition, Appalachian State Univ Gallery, Boone, NC, 88; two-person exhib, Muskegon Mus Art, Mich, 88 & Rochester Art Ctr, Minn, 90; solo exhib, Grand Rapids Art Mus, Mich, 89; SW Tex State Univ, 90. *Pos:* Chmn art dept, Hope Col, Holland, Mich, 88-. *Teaching:* Instr ceramic/sculpture, Hope Col, 78-79, asst prof, 79-85 & assoc prof, 85-. *Awards:* Merit Award, Whirlpool Sculpture, Krasl Art Ctr, St Joseph, Mich, 85; Merit Award, W Mich Regional, Muskegan Mus Art, 88. *Media:* Clay, Welded Metal. *Mailing Add:* Hope Col PO Box 9000 Holland MI 49422-9000

MAYER, EDWARD ALBERT
SCULPTOR, EDUCATOR
b Union, NJ, Oct 30, 42. *Study:* Brown Univ, Providence, RI, BA, 64; Univ Wis, Madison, MFA, 66. *Work:* Milwaukee Art Mus, Wis; Huntington Galleries, WVa; Rose Art Mus, Waltham, Mass; Ohio State Univ; NMex State Univ; and others. *Comn:* Ohio Bldg Authority, Columbus, 74. *Exhib:* Sao Paulo Bienal, 85; Zolla Lieberman, Chicago, 85; Burchfield Art Ctr, Buffalo, 88; Pub Art Works, San Rafael, Calif, 89; Haenah Kent Gallery, NY, 93; Univ Albany, Mus 2005; Zabriskie, 2005. *Teaching:* Asst prof art, Carthage Col, Kenosha, Wis, 66-70; prof sculpture, Ohio Univ, Athens, 70-83; vis sculptor, Tyler Sch Art, Rome, Italy, 73-74; prof, Univ Albany, 83-; prof art, sculpture, chmn, currently. *Awards:* Nat Fel, Nat Endowment Arts, 78, 79 & 86; Ava Fel, 83; NYFA in Sculpture, 86; ISC Outstanding Educator, 2006. *Bibliog:* Helen Harrison (auth), review, New York Times, 3/28/93; Grace Glueck (auth), review, New York Times, 11/11/2005; Leigh Ann Miller (auth), review, Art in America, 2/2006; and others. *Media:* All. *Dealer:* Zabriskie Gallery, 41 E 57th St New York NY 10022. *Mailing Add:* State Univ NY Dept Art Albany NY 12222

MAYER, FREDERICK & JAN
COLLECTOR
Pos: Trustee, Denver Art Mus, 70-, vpres, 71-75, chmn bd trustees, 75-79, interim chmn bd tustees, 80-81; trustee, Am Fedn Art, 77-81, Nat Gallery, 83-; founders, JFM Found. *Awards:* Named one of Top 200 Collectors, ARTnews Mag, 2004, 2006. *Collection:* Colonial Latin American Art. *Mailing Add:* PO Box 481150 Denver CO 80248

MAYER, MONICA P
WRITER, CONCEPTUAL ARTIST
b Mexico City, Mex, Mar 16, 54. *Study:* Escuela Nacional de Artes Plasticas, BA(visual arts), 78; Goddard Col, MA(sociology of art), 80. *Work:* Mus de Arte Contemporaneo, Aguascalientes; Mus Int de Electrografia, Cuenca, Spain; Mus Nacional de la Estampa, Mexico City. *Exhib:* Novela Rosa o me Agarro el Arquetipo, Mus Carrillo Gil, Mexico City, 87; EMPA, Mus Univ del Chopo, Mexico City, 95; Binomio: Electrografia, Mus Casa Diego Rivera, Guanajuato, 96, Nat Gallery, Kingston, Jamaica, 96 & Casa Cultura Candido Mendes, Rio de Janeiro, Brazil, 97. *Bibliog:* Florisa Calderon (producer), La Casa de la tia Arte, Producciones Volcan, 96. *Mem:* Anglo Mex Cult Inst (bd mem, 95-98); Pinto mi Raya. *Media:* Performance. *Publ:* Auth, A Brief Story of Almost 10 Years of Applied Conceptual Art, Pinto mi Raya, 98; La Muestra (de performance), 98, Nunca ha visto un performance?, 98 & Concursus de arte sobre obesos y enanos, 98, El Universal. *Mailing Add:* Gonzales de Cosio 17 Mexico 03100 Mexico

MAYER, ROBERT ANTHONY
ADMINISTRATOR, PHOTOGRAPHER, WRITER
b New York, NY, Oct 30, 33. *Study:* Fairleigh Dickinson Univ, BA(magna cum laude), 55; New York Univ, MA, 67. *Work:* Plays: La Borgia, 71, Alijandru, 71, They'll Grow No Roses, 75. *Exhib:* Solo shows, South Wing Gallery, St Paul's Church, Cleveland Heights, Ohio, 95, Mayfield Jewish Community Ctr, Cleveland Heights, Ohio, 95 & Humphrey Atrium Gallery, Univ Hosps, Cleveland, Ohio, 96; Cleveland Inst Art Staff Show, 95; Cleveland Botanical Garden, 95; Park Synagogue Show, Cleveland Heights, Ohio, 96; Cleveland-Faces & Places, Great Northern Corp Ctr Art Gallery, North Olmstead, Ohio, 96; Chandler Pub Libr, Ariz, 2000; Schemer Art Ctr, Phoenix, 2001. *Collection Arranged:* Traveling Exhibs, Photographing the American Presidency (auth, catalog), 84, Blacks in America: A Photographic Record (auth, catalog), 86 & American Writers, Int Mus Photogr. *Pos:* Exec dir, NY State Coun Arts, 76-79; dir, Int Mus Photogr, George Eastman House, Rochester, NY, 80-89; vpres & bd trustees, Alliance Independent Col Art, 86-90; pres, Cleveland Inst Art, 90-97. *Mem:* NY State Asn Mus (pres); Nat Ctr Film & Video Preserv (adv bd); Asn Art Mus Dirs; NY State Motion Picture & Television Develop (adv bd); Mesa Art Ctr Found, (bd mem, currently). *Media:* Photography. *Publ:* Co-auth (with K C Hart), Patronage of the Arts in the United States, Funk & Wagnalls 1977 Yearbook; auth, New York: The State of Art, New York Affairs, 4/78; The Arts Debate: Elitism vs Populism, Grants Mag, 5/78; auth, The Local Arts Council Movement, NEA, 1980. *Mailing Add:* 2704 N 60th St Scottsdale AZ 85257

MAYER, ROSEMARY
SCULPTOR, GRAPHIC ARTIST
b Ridgewood, NY, Feb 27, 43. *Study:* State Univ Iowa, Iowa City, AB, 64; Brooklyn Mus Art Sch, 65-67; Sch Visual Arts, New York, 67-69. *Work:* Sidney Lewis Collection, Richmond, Va; Herbert Johnson Mus, Cornell Univ, Ithaca, NY; Allen Mem Art Mus, Oberlin Col, Ohio; Hartwick Col Collection, Oneonta, NY. *Comn:* Spell (temp outdoor work with weather balloons), Queens Coun Arts & Greater Jamaica Develop Coun, 77; Balloon, Rose Hill Property Assoc, NY, 78; plans for Orfeo, Soho Baroque Opera Co, NY, 82. *Exhib:* One-person shows, AIR Gallery, 73, Whitney Mus Am Art Resources Ctr, NY, 75, 55 Mercer St, NY, 79, Cornell Univ, 80 & Locrian Mode, Interart Ctr, NY, 80; Times Square Show, NY, 80; Moontent (outdoor installation), Lansing, NY, 82; Pam Adler Gallery, NY, 85; Long Island Univ, Brooklyn, NY, 93; and others. *Pos:* Art writer & reviewer, Arts Mag, 71-73 & Art Am, 74-75. *Teaching:* Vis artist painting, Art Inst Chicago, 74; vis artist painting & drawing, Hartwick Col, Oneonta, 76; Artist's Workshop Program, Nat Endowment Arts, 81-; lectr art, Baruch Col, City Univ NY, 87-91; adj prof, Brooklyn Eng, Long Island, Univ NY, 88-; lectr art, La Guardia Community Col, NY, 92-. *Awards:* Creative Artists Pub Serv Grant, NY State Coun Arts, 76-77, 80-81 & 82; Nat Endowment Arts Grant, 79-80; Pollock Krasner Found, 87 & 88. *Bibliog:* Bruce Kurtz (auth), Rosemary Mayer, Art in Am, 3-4/77; Valentin Tatransky (auth), Rosemary Mayer, Arts Mag, 4/78; Ballerini & Milazzo (eds), Pontormo's Diary/Rosemary Mayer, 82; Reagan Upshaw (auth), Rosemary Mayer, Art in Am, 10/85. *Media:* Fabric, Rag Vellum; Watercolor, Pencil. *Publ:* Auth, Those, White Walls, winter 80; Pontormo's Diary, Out of London Press, 82; Moontent, White Walls, winter 83; Luxe, Beauty and Critique, TSL Ltd, 83; Some of my stories, Heresies, no 23, 88. *Mailing Add:* 55 Leonard St New York NY 10013

MAYER, SONDRA ELSTER
ART DEALER
b New York, NY, July 12, 33. *Study:* Syracuse Univ, BA, 54; Columbia Univ, MA, 55; Mus Mod Art, 57-58; Pratt Inst, 68; Art Students League, 72. *Work:* Los Angeles Co Mus Art, Los Angeles; Syracuse Univ Lowe Gallery, NY; MacDowell Colony Collection, Peterborough, NH; Portland Art Mus, Ore; Crocker Nat Bank, San Francisco, Calif. *Comn:* Greeting card design, Mus Mod Art, NY, 76 & 78; design for Star & Snowflake Jewelry, Metrop Mus Art, NY, 77 & 81; greeting card design, UNICEF, 79 & 81; greeting card design, Cartier, 85. *Exhib:* Philadelphia Print Club; Boston Printmakers Ann, DeCordova Mus, Lincoln, Mass, 79; Current Works, Everson Mus, Syracuse, NY, 80; Heckscher Mus, Huntington, NY, 79-82; Int Miniature Show, Seoul, Korea, 80; Queens Mus, 81; and others. *Pos:* Asst dir, Printmaking Studio Sch, 75-84; rep Petersburg Press, 84-86; owner & dir, Sondra Mayer Fine Art. *Teaching:* Instr printmaking, Ruth Leaf Studio, Douglaston, NY, 76-90; instr, Great Neck Adult Ed prog, 2006. *Awards:* MacDowell Colony fel, Peterborough, NH, 78; Leila Sawyer Mem Prize in Graphics, Nat Asn Women Artists, 79; Graphics Award, Firehouse Gallery, Garden City, New York, 81. *Mem:* Artists Equity New York; Philadelphia Print Club; MacDowell Colony Fellows. *Media:* Etching, Intaglio. *Specialty:* Contemporary and modern art in all media with a special interest in master graphics. *Interests:* Contemporary ARt; Cosmology; Theatre and Literature. *Collection:* Contemporary Art; Books, art books, contemporary signed first editions, pop-up books. *Publ:* Illusr, Intaglio Printmaking Techniques, Watson-Guptill, 76; contribr, Graphis Ann, Graphis Press, 78-79; and others. *Mailing Add:* Six Wooleys Ln Apt A32 Great Neck NY 11023

MAYER, SUSAN MARTIN
EDUCATOR, MUSEOLOGIST
b Atlanta, Ga, Oct 25, 31. *Study:* Am Univ; Univ NC, BA(art); Univ Del; Ariz State Univ, MA(art educ); Atelier Grande Chaumier, Paris; Kans State Univ. *Exhib:* Earthly Delights: Garden Imagery in Contemp Art, Ft Wayne Mus Art, 88; solo show, Galveston Arts Ctr, 90; In the Beginning, Art Mus Beaumont, Tex, 93; Genesis Through Revelation, RH Love Contemp Art Gallery, Chicago, 93. *Teaching:* Coordr mus educ, Huntington Art Gallery, Univ Tex, 70- & art fac, 71-. *Awards:* Mus Educators Award, Nat Art Educ Asn, 83; Distinguished Serv Award, Nat Art Educ Asn, 91. *Mem:* Nat Art Educ Asn; Tex Art Educ Asn; Tex Asn Mus; Am Asn Mus. *Media:* Oil. *Publ:* coauth, (with B Reese & A Mayer), Texas, Trillium Press, 87; auth, Art Works, Holt Rinehart & Winston, 89; Museum Education: History, Theory & Practice, Nat Art Educ Asn, Reston, Va, 89; Museums & Art Education, In: Inside Art: culture, Theory, Expression, WS Benson & Co, Austin, Tex, 92; Educating the Public, Art Papers, 93. *Mailing Add:* Dept Art Univ Texas at Austin Austin TX 78712

MAYERI, BEVERLY
SCULPTOR
Study: Univ Calif, BA, 67; San Francisco State Univ, MA, 76. *Work:* Canton Art Inst, Canton, Ohio; Nat Mus of Hist, Taipei, Taiwan; Long Beach Parks and Recreation, Long Beach, Calif; Los Angeles Arts Comn, Los Angeles, Calif; Los Angeles Co Mus of Art, Decorative Arts Dept. *Exhib:* Solo exhibs, Ivory/Kimpton Gallery, San Francisco, Calif, 81 & 83, Garth Clark Gallery, NY, 85 & 87, San Jose Inst Contemp Art, Calif, 90, Dorothy Weiss Gallery, San Francisco, 90, 92, 94, 96 & 98 & Robert Kidd Gallery, Mich, 93, Robert Kidd Gallery, San Francisco, Calif, 2000, Dorothy Weiss Gallery, San Francisco, Calif, 2000 & Susan Cummins Gallery, Mill Valley, Calif, 2002; Renwick Gallery, Smithsonian Inst, Washington, DC, 81; Signet Arts Gallery, St Louis, Mo, 84; Robert L Kidd Gallery, Birmingham, Mich, 86 & 93; Fresno Arts Ctr & Mus, Calif, 87; Euphrat Gallery, De Anza Col, Cupertino, Calif, 88; Esther Saks Gallery, Chicago, 88 & 90; Dorothy Weiss Gallery, San Francisco, Calif, 90, 92 & 94; 500 Yrs Since Columbus (with catalog), Triton Mus Art, Calif, 92; The Clay Figure, Dorothy Weiss Gallery, San Francisco, 93; The Nude in Clay (with catalog), Perimeter Gallery, Chicago, 95; Beauty and the Beast, Sybaris Gallery, Mich, 96; and others; group exhibs, About Face, The Clay Studio, Philadelphia, PA, 2001, Figure It Out: A Ceramic Sculpture Invitational, Calif State Univ, Chico, CA, 2001, Head Ceramic Sculpture on a Heroic Scale, SSAC, San Antonio, Tex, 2002, Major Figures, Ferrin Gallery, lenox, MA, 2002. *Teaching:* invited lectr, Scripp's Col, Claremont, CA, 99; invited lectr & workshop, Cuesta Col, San Luis Obispo, CA, 2002; invited workshop, San Diego State Univ, San Diego, CA, 2002; invited speaker, CCACA, Natsoulas Gallery, Davis, CA, 2002; and others. *Awards:* Nat Endowment Arts, 82 & 88; Individual Artist Grant, Marin Arts Coun, 87; Recognition Grant, Virginia A Groot Fedn, 91; Grant, Marin Arts Coun Individual Artist, San Rafael, CA, 2002. *Bibliog:* Marcy Timberman (auth), Review shorts, Artweek, San Jose, Calif, Vol 21, 3/90; Victor Cassidy (auth), Beverly Mayeri, Am Ceramics, NY, Vol 8, No 4, 12/90; Stephen Luecking (auth), Beverly Mayeri, Am Crafts, NY, Vol 50, No 6, 12/90-1/91; Debra Koppman (auth), Beverly Mayeri, Artweek Previews, San Jose, CA, 2002; and others. *Publ:* Numerous articles in New Art Examiner, Artweek, Ceramics Mo, Am Craft, Am Ceramics, 88-90. *Mailing Add:* 201 Eldridge Ave Mill Valley CA 94941

MAYES, ELAINE
PHOTOGRAPHER, VIDEO ARTIST
b Berkeley, Calif, Oct 1, 38. *Study:* Stanford Univ, BA, 59; San Francisco Art Inst, with Paul Hassel, John Collier & Minor White. *Work:* San Francisco Art Inst; Mus Mod Art & Metrop Mus Art, NY; Minneapolis Inst Arts, Minn; Oakland Mus, Calif; and many others. *Exhib:* Photographs from Collection of Sam Wagstaff, Corcoran

Gallery Art, DC, Grey Gallery, NY Univ, St Louis Mus, Mo, Seattle Mus Art, Wash & Berkeley Mus Art, Calif, 78-79; Ft Wayne Ind Mus Art, 88; Sandra Berler, Chevy Chase, Md, 80, 82, 84, 88, 90 & 96; Friends of Photog, 97; Monterey Art and Hist Asn, 01; Contemp Mus, Honolulu, 2003-04; Metrop Mus, 05. *Pos:* prof Emer, Tisch Sch of Arts, New York City, currently. *Teaching:* Instr photog & filmmaking, Univ Minn, 68-70; assoc prof film & photog, Hampshire Col, 71-81 & Bard Col, 82-84; Chmn, Dept Photog, Tisch Sch Art, NY Univ, 84-2001, prof photog, prof emer, 2001-. *Awards:* Nat Endowment Arts, 71 & 78; CAPS, 82; Guggenheim, 91 & 92; Atherton Foun, 2002. *Mem:* Soc Photog Educ. *Media:* photography, video. *Collection:* Avon Collection, NY; Metropolitan Mus, NY; Getty Mus of Art, Calif; Boston Mus Fine Arts; Denver Mus Art; Philadelphia Mus Art; San Francisco Art Inst. *Publ:* Contribr, Faces: A History of Photographic Portraiture, Chanticleer Press, New York, 77; A Book of Photographs, by Sam Wagstaff, New York, 78; San Francisco Viewed, Chronicle Books, 85; The Cat in Photography, 90; Animal Attractions, Abrams, 94; and others; Leg, 88; It Happened In Monterey, 03. *Dealer:* Robert Burge New York NY; Sandra Berter 97950 Toner Ln Chevy Chase MD. *Mailing Add:* 97950 Toner Ln Brookings OR 97415

MAYES, STEVEN LEE
EDUCATOR, PRINTMAKER
b Los Angeles, Calif, Nov 7, 39. *Study:* Wichita State Univ, BFA & BAE, 62, MFA, 65. *Hon Degrees:* Tenesee tech unov, Crookville, TN; The Print Consortium, St Joseph, MO; Wichita Art Mus, Wichita, KS; Wichita State Univ, Wichita, KS. *Work:* SDak Mem Art Ctr, Brookings; Sioux City Art Ctr, Iowa; Wichita Art Mus, Kans; Tamarind Inst, Univ NMex, Albuquerque; Univ NDak, Grand Forks. *Exhib:* 15th Ann Fine Arts Competition, Greensboro Artists League, SC; Pattern: New Form, New Function, Arrowmont Sch Arts & Crafts, Gatlinburg, Tenn; 33rd Ann Chautauqua Nat Exhib Am Art, Chautauqua Art Asn Galleries, NY; High Tech/High Touch: Computer Graphics in Printmaking, Pratt Inst, Brooklyn & Manhattan, NY; The Second Emerging Expressions Biennial: The Artist & the Computer, Bronx Mus Arts, NY; Nat Computer Art/Electronic Media Exhib, Eastern Wash Univ, Spokane; 13th Midwest Biennial, Joslyn Mus, Omaha, Nebr, 72; 2nd Ann Rocky Mt Regional Juried Photography Exhibition, CO; Dos Hombres, Bradley Gallery, AK, State Univ, Jonesboro, AK. *Teaching:* Prof printmaking & drawing, SDak State Univ, Brookings, 71-77; prof printmaking & design, WTex State Univ, Canyon, 77-88; prof art, Ark State Univ, Jonesboro, 88-02. *Awards:* Purchase Awards, Fifth NDak Ann, Univ NDak, 61, 33rd & 35th Ann Fall Show, Sioux City Art Ctr, Iowa, 71 & 73. *Media:* Multi. *Mailing Add:* 676 Divide South Dr Divide CO 80814

MAYFIELD, SIGNE S
CURATOR
b Woodbury, NJ. *Study:* Univ Calif-Berkeley, BA(art hist), 65; George Washington Univ, MA Prog, Higher Education. *Collection Arranged:* Marriage in Form: Kay Sekimachi & Bob Stocksdale (tour), 93-96; David Park: Fixed Subjects, 94; Dominic DiMare: A Retrospective (tour), 97-99; Of Princely Courts & Pleasure Gardens: Indian Miniatures, 97-98; From the Philippines: Northern Tribal Art, 98-99; The Print is Cast, 99; Joseph Cornell: A Memoir, 99; The Thought of Things: Kiff Stemmons (tour), 2000; Big Idea: The Maquettes of Robert Arneson (tour), 2002; Creatures That Stir: Symbol & Satire in Animals of Imagination, 2003; Jim Campbell: Seeing Digital, 2004; The Gift: Surimo Prints from Bay Area Coll, 2005. *Pos:* Cur, Palo Alto Art Ctr, 89-; bd dir, Achenbach Graphic Arts Coun, 90-97. *Bibliog:* Merideth Tromble (auth), On The Future of Suburban Art Centers, Artweek, 12/95; Carolyn McMaster (auth), Inside the Museums, Four Young Curators at Work in California, Artweek. *Mem:* Am Art Study Ctr; Art Table. *Publ:* Coauth, Marriage in Form: Kay Sekimachi & Bob Stocksdale, Palo Alto Art Ctr, 93; Directions in Bay Area Printmaking: Three Decades; Christopher Brown: Works on Paper, 94; Dominic Di Mare: A Retrospective, 97; coauth, The Thought of Things: Jewelry by Kiff Slemmons, 2000; coauth, Big Idea: the Maquettes of Robert Arneson, 2002; Jim Campbell: Seeing Digital, 2004. *Mailing Add:* Palo Alto Art Ctr 1313 Newell Rd Palo Alto CA 94303

MAYHEW, RICHARD
PAINTER
b Amityville, NY, April 3, 34. *Study:* Art Students League; Brooklyn Mus Art Sch, studied with Edwin Dickinson and Reuben Tam, 51; Columbia Univ, New York, NY. *Work:* Whitney Mus Am Art; Nat Mus Am Art, Smithsonian Inst; Brooklyn Mus; Mus Mod Art; Nat Acad Design; and many others. *Exhib:* Butler Art Inst, Youngstown, Ohio, 61; Univ Ill, 63; Hamilton Col, Clinton, NY, 1974, Montclair State Col, NJ, 1975; retrospective, Studio Mus, NY, 78; solo exhibs, San Jose Mus Art, 80, Pa State Univ Mus, 83 & Young Gallery, San Jose, 85; Group shows: Brooklyn Mus, Whitney Mus, Nat Acad of Design, Carnegie Inst, Chicago Art Inst, San Francisco Mus Art, NY Cult Ctr, New York City, Gallery Modern Art, New York City, Butler Inst, Ohio, Chicago Art Inst, Am Acad Arts and Letters, New Sch Social Res, Smith Col, San Francisco Mus Art, Pa Acad Fine Arts, Hampton Univ Mus, Va, 1986; Midtown Galleries, NY, 82-87. *Teaching:* Instr art, Brooklyn Mus Art Sch, 63-68 & Art Students League, 65-71; instr, Smith Col, 69-70; asst prof, Hunter Col, 71-75; San Jose State Univ, 1975-76; prof, Pa State Univ, 77-. *Awards:* Recipient Macdowell Colony award, 58; recipient Childe Hassam purchase award, 1963-64, purchase award Ford Foundation, 62, Henry Ward Ranger purchase award, 64, National Inst Arts and Letters award, 65; Benjamin Altman Award, Nat Acad Design, 70; Butler Institute award, 74; Merit Award, Nat Acad Design, 77; Grumbacher Gold Medal, Nat Acad Design, 83. *Mem:* Nat Acad; MacDowell Colony Asn. *Media:* Oil, Watercolor. *Dealer:* Midtown Payson Galleries 745 Fifth Ave New York NY 10151; Braunstein/Quay Gallery 545 Sutter St San Francisco CA 94115. *Mailing Add:* c/o Alitash Kebede Contemp Art 1295 Ridley Dr Los Angeles CA 90019

MAYNARD, WILLIAM
PAINTER, EDUCATOR
b Brookline, Mass, Dec 31, 21. *Study:* Mass Col Art; Sch Mus Fine Arts, Boston, dipl, 50. *Work:* Boston Mus Fine Arts; Springfield Mus Fine Arts, Mass; Fairleigh Dickinson Univ; Fitchburg Mus Fine Arts; Tufts Univ; Mus Arts & Sci, Macon, Ga. *Exhib:* Shore Studio Galleries, Charles Childs Gallery & Vose Gallery, Boston; De Cordova Mus, Lincoln, Mass; Busche Reisinger Mus, Cambridge, Mass; J H Webb Gallery, Macon, Ga, 85. *Pos:* Chmn dept fine arts, New England Sch Art & Design, 74-. *Teaching:* Instr drawing & painting, Boston Mus Fine Arts, 60-67; instr painting, New Eng Sch Art & Design, formerly. *Mem:* New Eng Watercolor Soc; Provincetown Art Asn; Copley Soc; Brookline Soc Artists. *Media:* Watercolor, Acrylic. *Mailing Add:* 72A Commercial St Provincetown MA 02657

MAYNE, THOM
ARCHITECT
b Waterbury, Conn, Jan 19, 44. *Study:* Univ Southern Calif, BArch, 68; Harvard Univ, MArch, 78. *Work:* Archit one-man exhib incl Cheney Cowles Mus, Spokane, Wash, 1989, San Francisco Mus Modern Art, 1990, Laguna (Calif) Art Mus, 1991, G201 Gallery, Ohio, 1991, Mus of Contem Art, 1982 Mus Modern Art, San Francisco, 1983, Calif Mus Sci. and Indust, 1984 Cooper-Hewitt Mus, NY City, 1988 Deutsches Architektur Mus, Frankfurt, 1989. *Comn:* archit projs incl Sequoyah Educ and Res Ctr, Santa Monica, 1977 (Progressive Archit award 1974); Flores Residence, 1979 (Progressive Archit award 1980); Sedlak Residence, 1980 (Am Inst of Archits award 1981); Western Melrose Off Bldg, 1981 (Progressive Archit award 1982); Hermosa Beach Central Bus Dist (Progressive Archit award 1984); 72 Market St Restaurant, 1983 (Am Inst of Archits award 1985, CCAIA award 1986); Bergren Residence, 1984 (Am Inst of Archits award 1985, CCAIA award 1986, Nat Am Inst of Archits award 1986); Cedar Sinai Comprehensive Cancer Ctr, Los Angeles, 1988 (Progressive Archit award 1987, Am Ins of Archits award 1988, CCAIA award 1989),; Arts Park Performing Pavilion, 1988 (Progressive Archit award 1989); Leon Max Showroom, Los Angeles, 1988 (CCAIA award 1990, Archit Record Interior award 1990); Club Post Nulear, Laguna Beach, Calif, 1988; Berlin Wall Competition, 1988; Expo '90 Folly, Osaka, Japan, 1989; The Emery Ctr Performing Arts, 1989; Temple Univ Commodity Credit Corp, Philadelphia, 1989; Politix, 1990 (Am Inst of Archits award 1990); Salick Health Care Corp Hdqs, 1990 (Am Inst of Archits award 1992, CCAIA award 1993); Visual Performing Arts Sch at Thomas More Col, Crestview, NY, 1990; MTV Studios, Los Angeles, 1990, Higashi Azabu Tower, Tokyo, 1991; Disney Inst and Town Ctr Competition, Orlando, Fla, 1991; Cranbrook Acad Gatehouse Competition (Pilkington Planar prize 1993); Spreebogen Master Plan, Berlin, 1993, Check Point Charlie Off Bldg, Berlin, 1993. *Exhib:* one-man exhib, 2 AES Gallery, San Francisco, 88, Walker Arts Ctr, Minneapolis, 89, Gallery of Archit, Los Angeles, 89, Contemp Arts Ctr, Cincinnati, 89, Graham Found, Chicago, 90, Aedes Galerie and Archit Forum, Berlin, 90, Fenster Archit, Frankfurt, Ger, 90, Gallery MA, Toyko, 90, G201 Gallery, Ohio, 91, 1-Space Gallery, Chicago, 92, Sadock & Uzzan Galerie, Paris, 1992, Diane Farris Gallery, 93; group exhib, Umwelt Galerie, Stuttgart, Ger, 1978, The Archit Gallery, Venice, Calif, 1979, Inst Contemp Arts, London, 83, Archit Assoc, London, 83, Nat Acad of Design, New York City, 83, 88, G A Gallery, Tokyo, 85, 87, 90, Max Protech Gallery, New York City, 85, 86, IDC, New York City, 86, Axis Gallery, Tokyo, Milan, Paris, 88, Pacific Design Ctr, Los Angeles, 88, Australia Ctr for Contemp Arts, Victoria, 88, Aedes Galerie für Archit und Raum, Berlin, 88, Kirsten Kiser Gallery, 88, 89, Visual Arts Ontario, Toronto, 88, Gallery Functional Art, Santa Monica, Calif, 89, US Info Agency, Moscow, 89-90, Lameier Sculpture Park, St Louis, 89, Gwenda Jay Gallery, Chicago, 90, Sadock & Uzzan Galerie, 191, Bannatyne Gallery, Santa Monica, 91, ROM Galleri for Arkitektur, Oslo, 92, 65 Thompson St Gallery, New York City, 92. *Pos:* Mem fac, UCLA Sch Art and Archit, Santa Monica, Calif, 72-; bd dir, Southern Calif Inst Archit, 83-; archit Morphosis. *Teaching:* Vis fac, Calif State Col, Pomona, 71, Miami Univ, Ohio, 82, Wash Univ, St Louis, 84, Univ Tex, Austin, 84, Univ Pa, 85, Columbia Univ, New York City, 86, Harvard Univ, 88, Clemson Univ, 91, Yale Univ, 91, UCLA, 86, 92, Univ Ill, Urbana-Champaign, 92-93, Tech Univ, Vienna, Austria, 93, Berlage Inst, Amsterdam, 93, Hochschule für Andgewandt Kunst, Vienna, 91, 93; Adj prof, UCLA, 93; lectr in field. *Awards:* Rome Prize fel Am Acad Rome, 87; recipient Archit award Am Acad Arts and Letters, 92. *Mem:* Am Instit of Archit; Nat Acad. *Publ:* contributor articles to prof jour. *Mailing Add:* Morphosis 2041 Colorado Ave Santa Monica CA 90404-3415

MAYO, MARGARET ELLEN
CURATOR
b Charlottesville, Va, May 18, 44. *Study:* Randolph-Macon Womans Col, AB, 66; Rutgers Univ, PhD, 73. *Collection Arranged:* Ancient Portraiture: The Sculptor's Art in Coins and Marble, 80 & The Art of South Italy: Vases From Magna Graecia (auth, catalog), 82, Va Mus; Wealth of the Ancient World: The Nelson Bunker Hunt and William Herbert Hunt Collections (coauth, catalog), 83. *Pos:* Res assoc, Iconographical Lexicon, Rutgers Univ, 73-76; dir, Summa Galleries, Beverly Hills, 76-78; cur, Ancient Art, Va Mus, 78-. *Mem:* Archaeol Inst Am; Soc Promotion Hellenic Studies. *Res:* Greek art; Greek and south Italian vase-painting. *Mailing Add:* Va Museum Fine Art 200 N Blvd Richmond VA 23220-4007

MAYO, MARTI
MUSEUM DIRECTOR, CURATOR
b Bluefield, WVa, Oct 17, 45. *Study:* Am Univ, BA, 70, MFA, 74. *Collection Arranged:* Vernon Fisher Story Paintings & Drawings (auth, catalog), 80; The New Photography (auth, catalog), 80; Placements and Performances: Works for Washington, 80; Other Realities: Installations for Performance (auth, catalog), 81; 4 Painters: Jones, Smith, Stack, Utterback (auth, catalog), 81; Robert Morris: Selected Works 1970-1980 (auth, catalog), 81; Paintings by Pat Steir (auth, catalog), 83; Michael Tracy: Requiem Para Los Olvidados (auth, catalog), 83; Southern Fictions,

83; Recent works of Robert Helm, 84; Paintings by Mark Tansey, 85; Barbara Kruger: Striking Poses, 85; Robert Rauschenberg: Work from Four Series, 86; Works of Joseph Glasco, 86; Images on Stone: Two Centuries of Artists Lithographs, 87; 6 Artists: 6 Idioms, 88; Gael Stack: A Survey 1974-1989, 89; Reinventing Reality: Five Tex Photogrs, 90. *Pos:* asst dir, Jefferson Place Gallery, Washington, DC, 73-74; Coordr exhib, Corcoran Gallery Art, DC, 74-80; cur, Contemp Arts Mus, Houston, 80-86; dir, Blaffer Gallery, Univ Houston, 86-94, dir, chief cur, 94-; vpres Cultl Arts Coun Houston/Harris Co; mem rev panel Inst of Mus & Libr Servs; panelist Nat Endowment for Arts, Tex Comn on Arts. *Teaching:* Contemp art & criticism, Glassell Sch Art, Mus Fine Arts, Houston, 84-86; Art since 1960, Univ Houston, 86-91. *Mem:* Am Asn Mus; Col Art Asn; Asn Art Mus Dirs; Am Fedn Arts (bd trustees). *Publ:* Auth, Robert & Morris: Selected Works 70-80 (exhib catalog), 81; Robert Rauschenberg: A Chronology (exhib catalog), Contemp Arts Mus, Houston, 86; Joseph Glasco: 1948-1986 (exhib catalog), Contemp Art Mus, Houston, 86; Gael Stack (exhib catalog), Univ Houston, 88; Northwest x Southwest: Painted Fictions (exhib catalog), Palm Springs Desert Mus, 90; and others. *Mailing Add:* Contemp Art Mus 5216 Montrose Blvd Houston TX 77006-6598

MAYO, PAMELA ELIZABETH
CONSULTANT
b Richmond, Va, June 18, 59. *Study:* Longwood Col, BFA, 81. *Collection Arranged:* Lue Osborne & Cordray Simmons, Am Regionalists (auth, catalog), 80; America, the Sporting View, Sporting Art (ed, catalog), 85; The Art of Doris Spiegel (auth, catalog). *Pos:* Dir & appraiser, Gallery Mayo, Inc, Richmond, Va, 81-95; appraiser fine art, 86-. *Mem:* Int Soc Appraisers; Phi Kappa Phi. *Specialty:* Late 19th-early 20th century American art. *Mailing Add:* 710 Washington St Sewickley PA 15143

MAYO, ROBERT BOWERS
ART DEALER, COLLECTOR
b Phoenixville, Pa, 33. *Study:* Art Students League, 49; Chicago Art Inst, 51; Richmond Prof Inst (Va Commonwealth Univ), BA, 59. *Collection Arranged:* Thomas Sully & His Contemporaries, 78; Mrs Susan Waters, 19th Century Itinerant Painter, 79; American Paintings from Virginia Collectors, 81; America: The Sporting View (auth, catalog), 85. *Pos:* Cur, Jamestown Festival Park, Va, 59-61; exhibs designer, Arch Hist, Raleigh, NC, 61-66; dir, Valentine Mus, Richmond, 66-75; owner, Gallery Mayo Inc, currently. *Teaching:* Guest lectr, NY Hist Soc, Cooperstown, summer 72 & Longwood Col, Farmville, Va, 79. *Mem:* Am Asn Mus (nat coun, 73-77); SEastern Mus Conf Inc (pres, 74); Va Mus Fedn (vpres, 72-73); Antiquarian Soc Richmond (pres, 74-75); Collector's Circle, Va Mus Fine Arts. *Specialty:* 19th & 20th century art. *Interests:* Collector of early American Sporting Art - 19th & early 20th century. *Collection:* Am Sporting Art. *Publ:* Auth, Exhibit techniques for small museums, Mus News, 73; Painting collection of the Valentine Museum, Mag Antiques, 73; America: The Sporting View, 85. *Mailing Add:* 11758 River Crest Dr Gloucester VA 23061

MAYRS, DAVID BLAIR
PAINTER, EDUCATOR
b Winnipeg, Man, May 2, 35. *Study:* Vancouver Sch Art, dipl(hon), 57. *Work:* Vancouver Art Gallery; London Pub Libr & Art Mus, Ont; Etherington Art Ctr. *Exhib:* New Talent Show, Vancouver Art Gallery, 64; Young Contemporaries, London Art Mus, Ont, 65; Canadian Group of Painters, Montreal Mus Fine Art, 67; Nat Gallery Can Bi-Ann, 68; Young Vancouver Artists, Victoria Art Gallery, 68; H Marc Moyens Collection, Corcoran Gallery Art, 69; West Coast Artists, Sadie F Bronfman Ctr, Montreal, 75; BC Artists, Vancouver Art Gallery, 83; Mus Modern Art, Toyama, Japan, 87. *Teaching:* Instr painting & silkscreen, Emily Carr Col Art, Vancouver, 67-. *Awards:* Purchase Award, Burnaby Art Gallery Print Show, 71. *Media:* Acrylic. *Mailing Add:* 440 Ellis St North Vancouver BC V7H 2G6 Canada

MAYS, VICTOR
PAINTER, ILLUSTRATOR
b New York, NY, 1927. *Study:* Yale Univ, BA, 49. *Work:* De Grummond Collection of Children's Book Illus, Univ Southern Miss; Kerlan Collection, Univ Minn; Peabody Mus, Salem, Mass; Mystic Seaport Mus; Submarine Force Mus. *Comn:* Illusr for children's bks, major US publ, 55-. *Exhib:* Mystic Seaport, Conn, 79-82; Peabody Mus, 81; Mariners Mus, 85-86; Md Hist Soc, 89; Mystic Seaport Mus, 92-94; Frye Art Mus, Seattle, 97; Cummer Mus, Fla, 98; Cape Mus Fine Arts, Mass, 2001. *Awards:* Best in Show, Mystic Seaport Mus, Conn, 80, First & Second Prize Watercolor, 81 & Best in Show, Mystic Int Marine Art Exhib, 83, Award of Excellence, 86, 87, 97, 2000, 2002. *Media:* Watercolor. *Publ:* Auth & illusr, Fast Iron, 53, Action Starboard, 55, Dead Reckoning, 65, Bound for Blue Water, 2003. *Dealer:* Kirsten Gallery Roosevelt Way NE Seattle WA 98103; Mystic Maritime Gallery Mystic CT 06355. *Mailing Add:* 38 Groveway PO Box 207 Clinton CT 06413

MAYTHAM, THOMAS NORTHRUP
CONSULTANT
b Buffalo, NY, July 30, 31. *Study:* Williams Col, BA, 54; Yale Univ, MA, 56. *Exhib:* Alvan T Fuller Collection, Boston Mus Fine Arts; Eighteenth Cent Venetian painting, Boston Mus Fine arts; Hidden Treasures, Boston Mus; Ernst Ludwig Kirchner Retrospective, Seattle Art Mus; Great Am Paintings from the Boston and Metro Art Mus, Nat Gallery, Washington, St Louis and Seattle Art Mus. *Collection Arranged:* Ernst Ludwig Kirchner Retrospective (148 works), Seattle Art Mus, Pasadena Art Mus & Boston Mus, 68-69; Great American Paintings from the Boston & Metropolitan Museum (100 paintings, with catalog), Nat Gallery Art, City Art Mus, St Louis & Seattle Art Mus, 70-71; and others. *Pos:* Asst, Wadsworth Atheneum, summer 55; res asst, Prof Carroll L V Meeks, Yale Univ, summer 56; asst in dept paintings, Mus Fine Arts, Boston, 56-57; head dept paintings, Boston Mus, 57-67; assoc dir, Seattle Art Mus, 67-74; dir, Denver Art Mus, 74-83, consult, 83-. *Teaching:* Lectr, mus, clubs, groups & art asns, Boston, Seattle, Denver, Nat Gallery, Wash & Portland Art Mus, Maine & Ore. *Awards:* Governors Art Award, Seattle-Tacoma Airport Art Project. *Mem:* Am Asn Mus; Humanities Inst Univ Colo (bd mem); Asn Art Mus Dirs; Internat Exhib Found; Colo Coun on Arts and Humanities; United Arts Fund. *Publ:* Auth, articles in Boston Mus Bulletin, Antiques & Can Art; ed, American Painting in the Boston Museum & Metropolitan Museum of Art (catalog), Vols I & II, 68; auth, TV Prog for Nat Educ TV, produced by Boston Mus & WGBH-TV; Heritage Am Art (Slide/Tape) Publ Metro Mus Art, 77-present. *Mailing Add:* 3882 S Newport Way Denver CO 80237

MAZAL, RICARDO
PAINTER
b Mex, 50. *Work:* Museo de Arts Contemporaneo de Monterrey, Galeria Ramis Barquet, Mex; Galeria Maeght, Barcelona, Spain; Museo Palacio de Bellas Artes, Mex. *Exhib:* Pintura Mexicana de Hoy, Centro Cult Alfa y Galeria Arte Actual Mexicano, Monterrey, Mex, 90; Pinturerias: el Arte Taurino, Museo Palacio de Bellas Artes, Mex, 94; Premio MARCO (with catalog), Museo de Arte Contemporaneo de Monterrey, Mex, 95 & 96; Collective: Paintings on Cloth and Paper, Michael Dunev Gallery, San Francisco, 96; Red, Robin Rule Gallery, Denver, 96; Chicago Art Fair, 96. *Bibliog:* Guillermo Sheridan (auth), Mazal: Solo esta luz, en Ricardo Mazal: Pinturas (exhib catalog), Galeria de Arte Mexicano, 90; Elizabeth Ferrer (auth), Ricardo Mazal, Art Nexus, 5/91; Conrado Tostado (auth), Ricardo Mazal, Vuelta, 8/92. *Media:* Oil on Canvas. *Dealer:* Galeria Ramis New York/Mexico; Anne Reed Gallery 620 Sun Valley Rd Ketchum ID 83340

MAZER, MIKE
PAINTER, ARTIST
b Boston, Mass, May 17, 36. *Study:* Studied with Betty Lou Schlemm, AWS, DF, Robert Wade, AWS, John Stobart, Joseph Mcgurl. *Work:* New Bedford Free Pub Libr, MA; US Coast Guard, Washington, DC; Tabor Acad, Marion, MA; Mass Dept of Environmental Protection: MA Marion Art Center, Marion, MA. *Comn:* Painting art work for Festivale of Trees invitation, New Bedford Art Mus, Mass, 2006. *Exhib:* Watercolor USA, Springfield Art Mus, MO, 2003; Taos Nat, Watercolor Exhib, Taos Art Mus, 2004; 11th Ann Marine Art Exhib, Coos, Art Mus, Oregon, 2004; Am Soc Marine Artist, 13th Nat, Vero Beach Art Mus, Fl, 2004; Mississippi Grand Nat'l Exhib, Miss, Mus of Art, Jackson, 2004. *Pos:* Pres, New England Watercolor Soc, 2004-. *Awards:* Best in Show, Mississippi Grand Nat'l, 2003; Best in Show Rhode Island WC Soc, 2004 & 2006; Frank C Wright Mem Award, AAPL, 2004; 1st Place Canyon Art Assoc, Canton, MA, 2004; Best in Show, Stoughton Art Assoc, Mass, 2004; Special Recognition, 7th Ann Realism Internat'l Exhib, Upstream Gallery, Omaha, NE, 2005; Founder's Award, Phila, Pa, 2005; Best of Show, Arts Affair, Quincy, Mass, 2006; and over 65 other awards. *Bibliog:* The Standard Times, South Coast Today, Newpaper, Written by David B Boyce, 7/18/2001, 8/25/2004. *Mem:* New England Watercolor Soc Current Pres; Academic Artists Asn; Nat Soc Artists; The Salmagundi Club; Allied Artists Am; Watercolor USA, Honor Soc; Am Artists Prof League, Fellow. *Media:* Watercolor Painter. *Publ:* Splash 9 Tips & Techiques, North Light Books, F & W Pub, 2006; Contemporary American Marine Arts, 2002 & 2004. *Dealer:* Roger Gallery, Mattapoisett, MA; Trader Antiques Marion MA; Boat Meadow Gallery Dennis Mass. *Mailing Add:* 7 Holly Woods Rd Mattapoisett MA 02739

MAZUR, MICHAEL
PAINTER, PRINTMAKER
b New York, NY, Nov 2, 35. *Study:* Amherst Col, BA, 58, with Leonard Baskin; Yale Univ Sch Art & Archit, BFA, 59 & MFA, 61, with Gabor Peterdi & Bernard Chaet, Rico Lebrun. *Hon Degrees:* Art Inst of Boston, Lesley Col, 2001; Col of Creative Studies, Detroit, 2005. *Work:* Mus Mod Art, Whitney Mus Am Art & Metrop Mus Art, NY; Boston Mus Fine Arts; Fogg Art Mus, Harvard Univ; Art Inst Chicago; Libr Cong, Washington; Addison Gallery Am Art, Andover, Mass; Los Angeles Co Mus Art; Mus Fine Arts, Montreal, Can; plus others. *Comn:* Painting of Wassaw & Ossabaw Islands, Dept of Interior Bicentennial Exhib, 75-76; monotype murals, Mass Inst Technol, 83; Fed Reserve Bank, Boston; Swiss Bank, comn by Dillon Warburg, Stanford, Conn, 98. *Exhib:* one-man exhibs, Silvermine Guild Artists, New Canaan, Conn, 64, Barbara Krakow Gallery, Boston, 84, 86, 88, 90, 92, 94, 96, 98, 2000, Aldrich Mus Contemp Art, Ridgefield, Conn, 95, Univ Iowa Art Mus, 95, Boston Univ Art Gallery, 95 & Mary Ryan Gallery, NY, 91, 94, 95, 96, 97, 98, 2000. Zimerli Mus, Rutgers Univ, NJ, 2000-02, Mus of Fine Arts, Boston, Mass, 2000-02, Minneapolis Inst of Arts, Minn, 2000-02, Stanford Mus of Art, Calif, 2000-02; Contemp Realist Painting, Boston Mus Fine Arts, Mass, 83; Twentieth Century Am Drawings, traveling exhib, Whitney Mus Art, 84-86; Recent Prints, Brooklyn Mus, NY, 89; Group Invitational, Pa Acad Fine Arts, Philadelphia, 90; Albert Merola Gallery, Provincetown, Mass, 1994-2000; Artists Bouquets, Champion Int Corp, Stamford, Conn, 95; Barbara Krakow Gallery, Boston, 2002. *Pos:* Bd mem, Mass Coun on Arts & Humanities; bd mem, Artists Found; co-chmn bd, Fine Arts Work Ctr, Provincetown; mem Penell com, Libr Congress, 85-93; overseer, Mus of Fine Arts, Boston, 2003. *Teaching:* Instr prints & drawing, RI Sch Design, 61-64; asst prof prints & drawing, Brandeis Univ, 65-76; vis artist, Yale Sch Art & Archit, 71 & Harvard Univ, 76-78, 88, 90, 92, 94-95 & 97. *Awards:* Louis Comfort Tiffany Grant, 62; Nat Inst Arts & Lett Award, 64; Guggenheim Fel, 65. *Bibliog:* Grace Glueck (auth), article, NY Times, 81; William Corbett (auth), Mazur's recent work, Arts, 11-12/85; Michael Mazur (auth), The Prints, Hudson Hill Press, Trudy Hansen (ed), 99. *Mem:* Nat Acad. *Media:* Oil Painting, Printmaking. *Publ:* Auth, Prints by M Mazur, Artist Proof, 70; The Monoprints of Naum Gabo, Print Collections Newslett; The Prints of Michael Mazur, Hudson Hills Publ, 2000; The Inferno of Dante Electa Editions, Italy; and others. *Dealer:* Barbara Krakow Gallery 10 Newbury St Boston MA 02116; Mary Ryan Gallery 24 W 57 New York NY 10019. *Mailing Add:* 5 Walnut Ave Cambridge MA 02140-2706

MAZZE, IRVING
SCULPTOR, MEDALIST
b New York, NY. *Study:* With Beth Sutherland, 72; with Hermann Gass & Richard Hahn, 77. *Work:* Residenz Mus Munzsammlung, Munich; Cabinet Medailles, Bibliot Nat, Paris; Proust Mus, France. *Comn:* Citrine portrait, comn by Alice Whitfield, NY, 74; moonstone portrait, comn by Louise Benton, Chicago, 75; moonstone portrait Marcel Proust, comn by Mr & Mrs Milton Stern, Long Island, 75; crystal engraving, comn by James Van Aken, NY, 83; topaz engraving, comn by John Sinkankas for Smithsonian Inst, 84. *Exhib:* Sculpture Showcase Gallery, Pa, 95; Mus d'Art & d'Histoire, Neuchatel, 96; Residenz Mus, Munich, 96; Isao Gallery, Nara, Japan, 96; Gallery Heian, Kyoto, 96; Rock & Hamper Gallery, NY, 97; Mus Beelden aan Zee, The Neth, 98. *Pos:* Consult engraved gemstones, Dept Mineralogy, Am Mus Natural Hist, 79-. *Bibliog:* Beverly Philip Mazze (auth), The making of a gem engraver, Lapidary J, 6/73; John Sinkairkas (auth), Gem Cutting, Van Nostrand Reinhold, 84; Ingrid Weber (auth), Geschnittene Steine des 18, bis 20, Jahrhunderts, Deutscher Kunstverlag, 96. *Mem:* Am Medallic Sculpture Asn; Royal Soc Arts; Fedn Int Medaille. *Media:* Gemstone. *Mailing Add:* 332 W 83rd St Apt 6 New York NY 10024-4845

MCADOO, CAROL WESTBROOK
CERAMIST, PAINTER
b Colonial Heights, Va, Dec 28, 37. *Study:* Self taught. *Work:* Lauren Rogers Mus, Laurel, Miss; NCNB Art Collection, Charlotte, NC; P Hanes Collection, Winston-Salem, NC; AT&T Corp; Coca-Cola Corp. *Comn:* Mag cover, Brown's Guide to Georgia, Atlanta, 73. *Exhib:* Piedmont Painting & Sculpture, Mint Mus Art, Charlotte, NC, 71; 4th Realist Exhib, Southeastern Ctr Contemp Art, Winston-Salem, NC, 72; Rogers Mus Exhib, Lauren Rogers Mus, Laurel, Miss, 72; one-woman exhibs, Mint Mus Art, Charlotte, NC, 73 & Wilson Arts Coun, NC, 75; Soc Four Arts, Palm Beach, Fla, 73; Catherine Lorillard Wolfe, Nat Arts Club, NY, 80. *Teaching:* Private lessons. *Awards:* 3rd Place, Cape Coral Nat Exhib, 71; Purchase Award, Lauren Rogers Mus, 72; 1st Place Painting, 23rd Ann Poplar Lawn Art Festival, 81. *Mem:* Nat Soc Painters Casein & Acrylic; South Cobb Arts Alliance; SEastern Ctr Contemp Art. *Media:* Clay; Acrylic. *Publ:* Auth, Reflections of the Outer Banks, Island Publ House, 76. *Dealer:* Edward L Greene Box 265 Manteo NC 27954. *Mailing Add:* 5070 Sunset Tr Marietta GA 30068

MCALLISTER, GERALDINE E
GALLERY DIRECTOR
b Asher, Okla, Sept 22, 25. *Study:* Univ Calif, San Diego, BA, 72, MFA, 74. *Pos:* Dir, Mandeville Gallery, Univ Calif, San Diego, 75-. *Mem:* Nat Soc Arts & Lett; Univ Calif & San Diego Alumni Asn (pres). *Mailing Add:* 1705 Malden St San Diego CA 92109-2207

MCAULEY, SKEET
PHOTOGRAPHER, EDUCATOR
b Monahans, Tex, Mar 7, 51. *Study:* Sam Houston State Univ, BA, 76; Ohio Univ, MFA, 78. *Work:* Int Ctr Photog, NY; New York Pub Libr, NY; Mus Fine Arts, Houston, Tex; Rose Art Mus, Brandeis Univ, Waltham, Mass; Tyler Mus Art, Tex; Nat Mus Am Art, Washington, DC; Dallas Mus Art, Tex; Amon Carter Mus, Ft Worth, Tex; Ctr Creative Photog, Tucson, Ariz. *Comn:* San Francisco Mus Art, Calif. *Exhib:* The Art Elements, Dallas Mus Fine Art, Tex, 84; Views and Visions: Landscapes by Am Photogrs, Aldrich Mus, Ridgefield, Conn, 86; Recent Acquisitions, Houston Mus Fine Arts, Tex, 88; solo exhibs, Barry Whistler Gallery, Dallas, Tex, 89, Calif Mus Photog, Riverside, 91, Heard Mus, Amherst, Mass, 91, Moody Gallery, Houston, Tex, 92, Dallas Mus Art, Tex, 92, Christopher Grimes Gallery, Santa Monica, Calif, 95, 96, 97, Ibel Simeonou Gallery, Columbus, Ohio, 97, Feigen Contemp, New York City, 99, Mus Contemp Art, San Diego, 01; The Television Show, Dallas Mus Art, Tex, 89; The State I'm In, Dallas Mus Art, 91; Between Home and Heaven, Nat Mus Am Art, Washington, DC & Carnegie Mus Art, Pittsburgh, Pa, 92; This Sporting Life, High Mus Art, Atlanta, Ga, Sarah Campbell Blaffer Gallery, Houston, Tex, 92 & Albright-Knox Gallery, Buffalo, NY, 93; Souvenirs, Lawndale Art & Performance Ctr, Houston, Tex, 93; Wings of Change: Images of Contradiction and Consensus, Directors Guild, Los Angeles, 93; Seeing the Forest Through the Trees, Contemp Arts Mus, Houston, Tex, 93; Between Home and Heaven: Contemp Landscape Photog, Cleveland Mus Art, Ohio & Va Beach Ctr Arts, 94; The Am Lawn, Can Centre Archit, Montreal, Can; Expanded Visions, Addison Gallery Am Art, Andover, Mass; Perpetual Mirage, Whitney Mus Am Art, NY; Crossing the Frontier, San Francisco Mus Mod Art, Calif, 96; Feigen Contemp, New York City, 99, 01; Tyler Gallery, Philadelphia, 00. *Collection Arranged:* San Francisco Mus Mod Art; Nat Mus Am Art; Dallas Mus Art; Mus Fine Arts, Houston; NY Pub Libr; Int Ctr Photog, NYC; Price Waterhouse, NYC; 3M Corp, Houston. *Teaching:* Instr photog, Spring Hill Col, Mobile, Ala, 78-79 & Tyler Jr Col, Tyler, Tex, 79-81; assoc prof photog, Univ NTex, Denton, 81-93. *Awards:* Nat Endowment Arts Individual Artist Fels, 84 & 86; Polaroid Artist Support Grant, Polaroid Corp, 88. *Bibliog:* Charles Hagen (auth), Art in review: Skeet McAuley and Margaret Morton, Politics, NY Times, 8/27/93; Susie Kalil (auth), Lost in the woods, Houston Press, 9/9/93; Mark Frohman (auth), Travels far and near, Pub News, Houston, Tex, 12/22/93; Kay Koeninger, In a Tamed America, Gold Courses Could be Links to Wilderness, Columbus Dispatch, 6/8/1997; Herbert Muschamp (auth), Looking at the Lawn and Below the Surface, NY Times, 7/5/1999. *Publ:* Sign Language: Contemporary Southwest Native America, Aperture Press, 89. *Dealer:* Barry Whistler Gallery 2909-A Canton St Dallas TX 75226; Feiger Contemporary 535 W 20th St New York NY 10011

MCBRIDE, RITA K
SCULPTOR
b Des Moines, Iowa, Mar 28, 60. *Study:* Bard Col, BA, 82; Calif Inst Arts, MFA, 87. *Work:* Mus Contemp Art, San Diego, Calif; Los Angeles Co Mus Art; Witte DeWith Ctr Contemp Art, Rotterdam, Neth; Wake Forest Univ Col, NC. *Comn:* Glass mural, AT&T, NJ, 94. *Exhib:* Parts, Des Moines Art Ctr, 92; Watt, Witte de With, Rotterdam, The Neth, 94; Breakdown, San Diego Mus Contemp Art, 94; Critical Distance, Neuberger Mus, Purchase, NY, 95; Allergories of Site in Contemp Art, The Whitney Mus Am Art at Champion, Stamford, Conn. *Teaching:* adj prof sculpture, DeAteliers, Amsterdam, Holland, 97- & York Univ, 98. *Awards:* Rome Prize, Am Acad in Rome, 91-92; Penny McCall Found, NY, 98; DAAD, Berlin, Ger, 99. *Bibliog:* Michelle Kelly (auth), The Donkeys Way, Porto, Portugal, 97; Christian Rattemeyer (auth), Stage-Site-Situation, Arena, Rotterdam, Holland, 97; Catherine Ingraham (auth), Cahiers, Witte de With, Rotterdam, Holland, 98. *Mem:* Osmos, Belin, Ger. *Media:* All Media. *Dealer:* Margo Leavin Gallery 812 N Robertson Los Angeles CA 90069; Alexander and Bonin 132 Tenth Ave New York NY 10011

MCBRYDE, SARAH ELVA
PAINTER, PRINTMAKER
b Columbus, Ohio, July 2, 42. *Study:* Syracuse Univ, 60-61; Washington Univ, St Louis, Mo, BFA, 64, study with Fred Becker & Arthur Osver; Washington Univ scholar, Skowhegan Sch Painting & Sculpture; Am Univ, Washington, DC, MFA, 76. *Comn:* Mural on Hotel, San Blas Islands, Panama, Cent Am; paintings, Mr & Mrs Harry B Willis, Panama City, Cent Am, 67 & Mrs Hestlene Martin, Washington, DC, 71; mural, Transemantics, Inc, Washington, DC; and others; portraits of Giambattista Vico and others, Centro di Studi Vichiani, Naples, Italy; portrait on silk of G B Vico, NY Inst for Vico Studies, 89. *Exhib:* Batik Exhib, Martin Luther King Libr; Washington, New Archit, Washington, DC, 83; Potomac Craftsmen Gallery, Torpedo Factory Art Ctr, 83; Greenspring Gallery, Alexandria, Va, 86; Artists Equity Awards Exhib, 88; Concepts Gallery, Bethesda, Md, 90; Multimedia Exhib, Potomac, Md, 94. *Pos:* Gallery asst, Stuttman Art Gallery, Washington, DC, formerly; art division, Martin Luther King Libr, currently. *Awards:* Design Award, Am Libr Asn, 82. *Bibliog:* Paul Richard, Art Review, Washington Post, 10/77. *Mem:* Artists Equity; Am Soc Picture Prof. *Media:* Egg Tempera, Acrylic; Batik. *Publ:* Illusr (covers), Nat Educ Asn Publ, Sci & Children Mag; covers, Weekender Mag, Washington Star Newspaper, 76-78

MCCABE, MAUREEN M
COLLAGE ARTIST
b Quincy, Mass, June 12, 47. *Study:* RI Sch Design, Providence, BFA, 69; Cranbrook Acad Art, Bloomfield Hills, Mich, MFA, 71. *Work:* RI Sch Design; Wadsworth Atheneum, Hartford, Conn; Samuel Greenbaum & Kogod Collection, Washington, DC. *Exhib:* One-person shows, Gallery K, Washington, DC, 72, 75, 79, 82, 84, 87 & 95, Allan Stone Gallery, NY, 72, 75, 77, Phyllis Kind Gallery, Chicago, 78, Lyman Allyn Art Mus, New London, Conn, 81, Marianne Deson Gallery, Chicago, 84, Barry Friedman, Ltd, 85, Sackler Gallery, Stamford, Conn, 90, Cooley Gallery, Old Lyme, Conn, 95, Mattatuck Mus, Conn, 96, Perimeter Gallery, Chicago, 98, Network Gallery, Cranbrook Acad Art, Pontiac, Mich, 99, ALVA Gallery, New London, Conn, 2000, 2003, Kouros Gallery, New York City, 2001, 2003; Museo Tamayo, Mexico City, 85; Excavating Cult, Brattleboro Mus & Art Ctr, Vt, 96; Metaphor for Ireland, Boston Univ, Fuller Bldg Gallery, Mass, 97; Art Chicago 1998, Barry Friedman Ltd, Navy Pier, Chicago, 98; Allan Stone Gallery, New York City, 2000; 9th Int Exhib Contemp Collage, Paris, France, 2002. *Teaching:* Prof studio art, Conn Col, New London, 71-. *Awards:* Residence Grant, Cite des Arts, Paris, 77-78; Individual Artist Grant, Conn Comn Arts, 80; MacDowell Fel, 88; Rockefeller Fel, Bellagio, Italy, 88; John S King Fac Teaching Award, Conn Col, 97-98; named Joanne Toor Cummings prof studio art, 2001. *Mailing Add:* 50 Old Norwich Rd Box 346 Quaker Hill CT 06375

MCCAFFERTY, JAY DAVID
VIDEO ARTIST, PAINTER
b San Pedro, Calif, Feb 21, 48. *Study:* Los Angeles State Col, BA; Univ Calif, Irvine, MFA. *Work:* Los Angeles Co Mus Art; Long Beach Mus Art. *Exhib:* One-man shows, Grapestake Gallery, San Francisco, 78 & Cirrus Gallery, Los Angeles, 79, Mark Moore Gallery, Santa Monica, Calif, 2005; Baudoin Lebon, Paris, France, 80; Los Angeles Co Mus Art, 81; Cirrus Gallery, Los Angeles, 85 & 90; Works Gallery, Long Beach, Calif, 89; Mark Moore Gallery, Santa Monica, Calif, 94-96, 99. *Teaching:* Vis lectr art, World Campus Afloat, Chapman Col, 74; instr to prof, Los Angeles Harbor Col, Wilmington, Calif, 76-; instr, Claremont Col Grad Sch Art, 78; vis lectr, Univ Calif, Irvine, 80. *Awards:* New Talent Award, Los Angeles Co Mus Art, 74; Nat Endowment for Arts Fel, 76. *Bibliog:* Joseph Youth (auth), Los Angeles, Art Int, 1/75; article, Art News, 9/83; article, Rick Gilbert (auth), Art Week, 2004. *Media:* Sun, Paper. *Dealer:* Mark Moore Gallery Bergamot Station, 25 Santa Monica, CA 90404. *Mailing Add:* 1017 Beacon St San Pedro CA 90731

MCCALL, ANN
PAINTER, PRINTMAKER
b Toronto, Ont, Dec 12, 41. *Study:* McGill Univ, Montreal, BA, 64; Univ Pittsburgh, 71-73; Concordia Univ, Montreal, BFA, 78. *Work:* DeCordova Mus, Lincoln, Mass; Vancouver Art Gallery, BC; Winnipeg Art Gallery, Man; Can Coun Art Bank, Ottawa; Mus Lodz, Poland; McGill Univ, Rare Books Library, McGill Univ, La Bibliotheque National de Quebec, Montreal, Loto Quebec, Montreal. *Comn:* Edition (100) of Prints for Les Femmeuses Exhibition, Pratt & Whitney, Montreal. *Exhib:* Cracow Print Biennale: Cracow, Poland, 78, 80 & 88; Rockford Int, Ill, 79, 81 & 83; World Print III, San Francisco, 80; Norweigian Int Print Biennial, Frederikstad, Norway, 80, 82 & 84; Biennale Graphic Art, Ljubljana, 81 & 83; 7th & 8th British Int Print Biennial,

Bradford, Eng, 82 & 86; Listowel Int Print Biennale, Ireland, 86; Premio de Grabado Maximo Rames, Ferrol, Spain, 87 & 90; Int Print Bienale, LVIV, Russia, 90; McClure Gallery, Montréal, 99; M Gibson Gallery, London, Ont, 98-99, 00-01, 02; Montréal Mus Fine Arts Sales & Rental gallery, 02; Pratt & Whitney, Toronto, 88-90, 93-94, 97-99, 01, 02; Gallery 418, Montréal, 03; Galerie Clair-Obscur, Montreal, 2004; Time Remembered, Time Past, Boston printmakers Mems, 2004; Musee Pierre-Boucher, Trois-Rivieres, 2005; Galerie Jean-Claude Bergeron, Ottawa, 2005; Malaspina Printmakers, Vancouver, 2005. *Teaching:* Saidye Brontman Centre for the Arts, Montreal, Silkscreen Printing, 92-2005. *Awards:* Purchase Award, Burnaby Biennale, BC, 77; Merit Awards, Boston Printmakers Exhib, 77 & 83; Grant, Atelier de Ile, Val David, Québec, 02. *Bibliog:* Diana Nemiroff (auth), article, Vie des Arts, 78; Virginia Nixon (auth), article, The Montrealer, 82; CBC Radio Inteview, Exhibition at Gallerie Clair-Obscur, 2004. *Mem:* Boston Printmakers; Print & Drawing Coun Can; Visual Arts Ont; Royal Can Acad Arts; Conseil Québecois de L'Estampe; Print Consortium; Print Coun Australia. *Media:* Acrylic; Silkscreen; Collagraphy; Mixed Media. *Interests:* Incorporating weather patterns into works through imagery and symbols. *Dealer:* La Guilde Graphique, 9 St Paul Ouest, Montreal; Bordue Gallery-Montreal, 272 Laurier Ave, Montreal; Open Studio, Toronto and Richmond St, Toronto; Galerie Jean-Claude, 150 St Patrick St Bergeron, Ottawa

MCCALL, ANTHONY
FILMMAKER
b London, Eng, Apr 14, 46. *Study:* Whitgift Sch, Croydon, Eng, 56-64; Ravensbourne Col Art & Design, Bromley, Kent, Eng, 64-68, BA(first class hons), 68. *Work:* Royal Belgium Film Arch, Brussels; Arts Coun of Gt Brit, London; Mus of Mod Art, NY; Designing a Virtual Art Mus, 1996; Represented in permanent collections, Whitney Mus Am Art, Centres Georges Pompidou; Represented in permanent collections, Whitney Mus Am Art, Centres Georges Pompidou. *Exhib:* Documenta, Kassel, Ger, 77; Film as Film, 1910 to the Present, Kunstverein, Cologne, 78; Int Film Theory Conf 5, Univ Wis-Milwaukee, 79; Edinburgh Int Film Festival, 80; Berlin Film Festival, 81; and others. *Pos:* founder, Anthony McCall Assoc, 1979; founder, & managing partner Narrative Rooms LLC, 1996. *Teaching:* Instr, London Col Printing, 70-71; vis lectr avant-garde film theory, New York Univ Dept of Cinema Studies, 77. *Awards:* Marie-Josi Prize 5th Int Experimental Competition, Knokke, Belg, 75; Creative Artists Prog Serv Grant, 76; Film Production Grant, New York State Coun Arts, 81; and others. *Bibliog:* Annette Michelson & P Adams Sitney (coauth), A on Knokke and the independent filmmaker, Artforum, 5/75; Jane Weinstock (auth), The subject of argument, Downtown Rev, Vol 1, No 1; E Ann Kaplan (auth), Feminist approaches to history, psychoanalysis and cinema in Sigmund Freud's Dora, Millennium Film J, fall/winter 81; and others. *Publ:* Flim, Line Describing a Cone, 1973; author: (article) Visitors Online

MCCALL, ROBERT THEODORE
ILLUSTRATOR, PAINTER
b Columbus, Ohio, Dec 23, 19. *Study:* Scholar, Columbus Fine Art Sch, Ohio, two yrs; Columbus Col Art & Design, Hon Dr Visual Arts. *Hon Degrees:* Columbus Col Art & Design, Hon Dr Graphic Arts, 98. *Work:* Phoenix Art Mus, Ariz; Art Mus Univ NMex, Albuquerque; Collection of US Air Force, Col Smithsonian Inst Washington, DC; Ariz Indust Comn Bldg, Phoenix; Glendale Pub Libr, Ariz. *Comn:* Four Paintings for the film 2001 A Space Odyssey, MGM Film Corp, now in Nat Air & Space Mus, Washington, 68; Twenty-three commemorative stamps, US Postal Serv, 72-88; The Space Mural, A Cosmic View (2100 sq ft, in the Lobby), Smithsonian Inst for the Nat Air & Space Mus, Washington, DC, 76; Three Decades of Achievement (10 ft x 20 ft mural in visitors ctr), Nat Air & Space Admin, Hugh L Dryden Flight Res Ctr, Edwards, Calif, 77; Opening the Space Frontier--the Next Giant Step, mural, mus at Johnson Space Ctr, Houston, Tex, 78-79; The Prologue and the Promise (mural), Disney's EPCOT Ctr, Fla; Expanding the Frontiers of Flight (mural), VA Air & Space Str, Hampton, Va, 92. *Exhib:* Am Watercolor Soc, 65; Space Art, Nat Gallery Art, Washington, DC, 70; Air & Space, Grand Cent Art Galleries, NY, 78; One-man show, Space Artist Robert McCall, Phoenix Art Mus, Ariz, 71, Nat Air & Space Mus, Smithsonian Inst, 84, Ctr Space Educ, Kennedy Space Ctr, 94, Meadows Art Mus, Shreveport, 95, Aerospace Educ Ctr, Little Rock, 95, Space Ctr, Houston, 95, La Arts & Sci Ctr, Baton Rouge, 96 & Space & Rocket Ctr, Huntsville, 96; retrospective, Scottsdale Ctr Arts, Ariz, 81. *Pos:* Art dir, The Black Hole (motion picture), Walt Disney, 79; conceptual designer, Star Trek, The Motion Picture, Paramount Pictures, 79; bd dir Ariz Univ, Ariz Space Comn; bd advisors Rotary Nat Award Space Achievement. *Teaching:* Many speaking engagements. *Awards:* Soc Illusrs Hall of Fame, New York, 88; Honoree Award, Scottsdale Mem Hosp, 89; Stellar Award for Space Achievement, Rotary Club, Houston, Tex, 90; Inducted to Ariz Aerospace Hall of Fame, 2001. *Bibliog:* Joe Stacy (auth), Worlds Premier Aerospace Artist, Ariz Highways Mag, 73; Air & Space, Smithsonian, 90; City in the Stars (film), Imax-Ridefilm, 94. *Mem:* Soc Illusr, NY (Air Force art prog chmn, 63-64, secy, 66); Nat Space Soc. *Media:* Watercolor, Ink; Oil, Acrylic. *Publ:* Illusr many articles & covers for Life, Saturday Evening Post, Nat Geographic Mag, Popular Sci, Newsweek, Readers Digest, Colliers & others, 56-90; co-auth (with Isaac Asimov), Our World in Space, NY Graphic Soc, 74; A Vision of the Future, The Art of Robert McCall, Harry Abrams, 83; illusr, Pioneering the Space Frontier, Bantam Books, 86; The Art of Robert McCall, Bantam-Doublday, 92. *Mailing Add:* 4816 Moonlight Way Paradise Valley AZ 85253

MCCALLUM, CORRIE PARKER
INSTRUCATOR, PAINTER
b Sumter, SC, Mar 14, 14. *Study:* Univ SC, cert fine arts, 36; Boston Mus Sch, with Karl Zerbe. *Work:* La State Univ, Baton Rouge; SC Arts Comn, State Collection; Columbia Mus Arts, SC; Ford Motor Co; Mint Mus Art; and others. *Comn:* Mural, Home Federal Bank, 62. *Exhib:* Contemp Artists of SC (with catalog), Greenville Mus; one-man show, Concourse Gallery, State St Bank, Boston, Mass, 71; Art in Transition, Boston Mus Fine Arts, 77; Southeastern Contemp Art, Winston Salem, NC, 88; Gibbes Mus Art, Charleston SC, 89; Spoleto Festival USA, 91 & 92; solo retrospective, Gibbes Mus Art, 94. *Pos:* Emer printmaker, Southern Graphics Coun, 84. *Teaching:* Cur art educ for Charleston Co, Gibbes Art Gallery, 60-69; instr painting & drawing, Newberry Col, SC, 69-71; instr painting, drawing & printmaking, Col Charleston, 71-79. *Awards:* Purchase Prize for Drawing, Mint Mus Graphics Ann, 64; Painting Award, Guild SC Artists Ann, 65; Scientific Educ Found Grant for Travel & Study Around the World, 68. *Bibliog:* Jack Morris (auth), Contemp Artists of South Carolina, 70; Art in Transition, Boston Mus, 77. *Media:* All Media. *Publ:* Illusr, Dutch Fork Farm Boy, & 50 Years Along the Way, 68, Univ SC; coauth, A Travel Sketchbook, R L Bryan Co, 71; Corrie McCallum, A Life in Art, 94; Expressions: Images and Poems, Gibbes Mus Art, 97. *Dealer:* Kunstsalon Wolfsberg Bederstrasse 109 Zurich Switz; Halsey-McCallum Studio 20 Fulton St Charleston SC 29401. *Mailing Add:* c/o William Halsey Found 20 Fulton St Charleston SC 29401

MCCANDLESS, BARBARA ANN
CURATOR, HISTORIAN
b Plymouth, Mass, May 29, 49. *Study:* Syracuse Univ, BA, 71; Univ Tex at Austin, MA, 87. *Collection Arranged:* Photography in 19th Century America, Amon Carter Mus, Fort Worth, Tex, 91; New York to Hollywood: The Photography of Karl Struss, Amon Carter Mus, Fort Worth, Tex, 95. *Pos:* Asst cur photographs, Humanities Res Ctr, Univ Tex Austin, 84-88; cur photographs, Amon Carter Mus, Fort Worth, Tex, 88-. *Mem:* Soc Photog Educ; Tex Photog Soc (secy, 94-96). *Publ:* Coauth, Photography in Nineteenth Century America, Amon Carter/Abrams, 91; auth, Equal Before the Lens: Juotrica/Granger, Texas, Tex A&M Univ Press, 92; coauth, New York to Hollywood: Photography of Karl Struss, Amon Carter/Univ NMex Press, 95. *Mailing Add:* 2837 Ryan Ave Ft Worth TX 76110-3031

MCCANNEL, LOUISE WALKER
COLLECTOR
b Minneapolis, Minn, Nov 20, 15. *Study:* Smith Col, BA; Minneapolis Sch Art. *Pos:* Bd mem, Walker Art Ctr, Minneapolis, currently. *Collection:* Contemporary American sculpture and painting. *Mailing Add:* 1520 Waverly Pl Minneapolis MN 55403-1024

MCCARDWELL, MICHAEL THOMAS
GRAPHIC ARTIST, PAINTER
b Shelbyville, Ky, Aug 30, 49. *Study:* Murray State Univ, BFA, 71; Morehead State Univ, MA, 74; Univ Louisville, tchg cert, 76. *Work:* Evansville, Ind Mus Arts and Sci. *Exhib:* JB Speed Mus Eight State Show, JB Speed Mus, Louisville, 85, Ky Art Exhib, 86; 38th Mid-State Art Exhib, Evansville Mus Arts and Sci, Ind, 85, 38th Mid-State Art Exhib, 85, 5th Ann Realism Today, 87; July Juried Exhib, Floyd Co Mus, Ind, 86, 88, 89, 96; Brand Libr Art Galleries, Glendale, Calif, 87-88; Visions VI Int, Cathedral Found, Cincinnati, 96, 2000. *Teaching:* art teacher, Henry Co High Sch, 78-. *Awards:* Junta Woods Aiken Purchase Award, Evansville Mus, 85; First Place Drawing Award, Cathedral Basilica of the Assumption, 96; Al Smith grantee Ky Arts Coun, 98. *Media:* Pen, Pencil, Oil. *Mailing Add:* 579 Hinkle Lane Shelbyville KY 40065

MCCARRON, PAUL
ART DEALER
b Mason City, Iowa, June 15, 33. *Study:* Art Inst Chicago, BA, 58, MFA, 59. *Mem:* Int Fine Print Dealers Asn. *Res:* 16th to 20th century fine prints and drawings; Rembrandt; 16th century Italian prints; 17th century mezzotints; Martin Lewis. *Publ:* Auth, Martin Lewis: The Graphic Work (catalog) & Martin Lewis: Catalogue of the Retrospective Exhibit, Kennedy Galleries, 73; The Prints of Martin Lewis (catalog Raisonne), 95. *Mailing Add:* 1014 Madison Ave New York NY 10021

MCCARTHY, CHRISTINE M
DIRECTOR
b Hartford, Conn. *Study:* Providence Col, BA, 89; Syracuse Univ, MA, 92. *Pos:* ast dir, ICA, Boston, 94-98; dir admin plannin, ICA, 98-2001; exec dir, PAAM, Provincetown, Mass, 2001-; adj prof, Boston Univ, 2002-. *Teaching:* adj prof, Cape Cod Community Col, 2002-. *Mem:* AAM; New England Mus Asn; Consortium of New England Community Mus. *Specialty:* Am Art 1899-. *Collection:* Over 2,000 works, all media, from 1899-. *Publ:* George McNeil: Bather's, Dancer's, Abstracts, Provincetown Art Asn, 02; James Gahagan Hank Jenson, Provincetown Art Asn Mus, 02; Fine Arts Work Centers, Provincetown Arts, 02-03; American Art Review, 2006. *Mailing Add:* Provincetown Art Asn & Mus 460 Commercial St Provincetown MA 02657

MCCARTHY, DENIS
PAINTER
b New York, NY. *Study:* Cooper Union, 59-64; Yale Univ, BFA & MFA, 64-66. *Work:* Work in pvt collections only. *Exhib:* Stable Gallery, NY, 69; Painting Ann, 70 & Biennial Exhib, 73, Whitney Mus Am Art; Reese Palley, NY, 70; Exhib, O K Harris, NY, 72; Warren Benedek Gallery, NY, 73; Spring Exhib, Aldrich Mus, Ridgefield, Conn, 73; Paula Cooper Gallery, NY; Michael Wyman Gallery, Chicago, 74; Univ Maine Portland, 75; Automation House, NY, 76; Hundred Acres Gallery, NY, 77; NY Acad Sci, 78; One-man show, Stable Gallery, NY, 70, 55 Mercer Gallery, NY, 78 & NY State Col, Old Westbury, NY, 80; Times Square Gallery, NY, 96; Leubsdorf Gallery, NY, 97; Times Square Gallery, NY, 2000; Leubsdorf Gallery, NY, 2002. *Teaching:* Instr drawing, Sch Visual Arts, New York, 67-72 & New York Univ, 76-77; instr painting & printmaking, Hunter Col, 71-. *Mailing Add:* Hunter Col Dept Art 695 Park Ave New York NY 10021

MCCARTHY, DENNIS
SCULPTOR, EDUCATOR
b Chicago, Ill, Oct 27, 21. *Study:* Kansas City Art Inst, BFA, 49, MFA, 50; St Benedict's Col, Atchison, Kans, AB, 51; with Frederic Taubes, 66-70; with Elden Tefft, Kans Univ, 82-90. *Work:* St Theresa Convent, Decatur, Ill; St Benedict's Abbey, Muchnic Gallery & Maur Hill Prep Sch, Atchison, Kans; Allen Fieldhouse, Univ Kans, 87. *Comn:* Kansas Monk (bronze), 57 & mosaic murals, 58, St Benedict's Col, Atchison, Kans; mosaic mural, St Elizabeth Parrish, Kansas City, Mo, 60; corpus & cross, Maur Hill Chapel, 63 & entrance cross, Maur Hill Prep Sch, 83, Atchison, Kans; Portrait of a Nurse, VA Hosp, Leavenworth, Kans; The Frank & Buddy Award, Hill's Nutrition Inc, Topeka, Kans, 94. *Exhib:* Bronze Exhib, Kans Univ, Lawrence, 82; Kans Sculptor's Exhib, Johnson Co Community Col, Overland Park, 84; Sculpture Exhib, Wichita Art Mus, Kans, 85 & 86; Outdoor Sculpture Exhib, Lawrence, Kans, 87; Wyandotte Co Libr, Sculpture Show, 88, 89 & 90. *Pos:* Trustee, Kans State Art Exhib Serv, Manhattan, 58-60; treas, Kans Sculptors Asn, 84-85, pres, 85-86; vpres, Mokan Artists, 92-94. *Teaching:* Instr wood sculpture, Kansas City Univ, 53-54; instr art, St Benedict's Col, Atchison, 56-71; prof art, Benedictine Col, Atchison, 71-88. *Awards:* Purchase Award, River Bend Art Fair, Atchison, 86; Atchison Art Asn (charter mem, 64-). *Media:* All. *Mailing Add:* 435 East P St Atchison KS 66002

MCCARTHY, DORIS JEAN
PAINTER, INSTRUCTOR
b Calgary, Alta, July 7, 10. *Study:* Ont Col Art, 30; Cent Sch Arts & Crafts, London, Eng, 35, Univ Toronto, BA, 89, LLD, 2001, Univ Alberta & Trent Univ, 2002. *Hon Degrees:* Univ Calgary, LLD, 95; Nipissing Univ, LLD, 98. *Work:* Nat Gallery Ottawa; Art Gallery Ont, Toronto; London Art Gallery, Ont; Royal Art Collection, Windsor Castle, Eng; Ont Centennial Collection; McMichael Can Collection; and others. *Comn:* Mural, Toronto Pub Libr, 33; mem bk, Malvern Col, Toronto, 48; creche figures, Church of St Aidan, Toronto, 48; fabric banner Trinity, St James Cathedral, Toronto, 75; wall hangings, St Aidan's Church, Cana Place, Toronto. *Exhib:* Ont Soc Artists Ann, 33-; Royal Can Acad Ann, 34-; Can Soc Painters Watercolor, 38-; ann solo shows, Wynick/Tuck Gallery, 82-, Toronto; retrospective, Gallery Stratford, traveling, 91-94; and others. *Teaching:* Instr drawing, painting & hist art, Central Tech Sch Toronto, 33-, asst head, 68-72. *Awards:* Order of Can, 87; Fel Ont Col Art, 90-; Order of Ont, 92; William Kilbourn Award, toronto, 98; Julius Griffith Award, CSPWC, 2000. *Bibliog:* John Bentley Mays (auth), Portraits of the edge of the world, Globe & Mail, Toronto, 10/31/80; Doris McCarthy: Heart of a Painter (doc film), W Wacko Productions, Jasper, Alta; William Moore (auth), Feast of Incarnation (catalog); McMichael Canadian Art Collection, Celebrating Life - The Art of Doris McCarthy. *Mem:* Royal Can Acad; Ont Soc Artists (pres, 65-68); Can Soc Painters in Watercolor (pres, 56-57); Fedn Can Artists; Prof Artists Can (chmn, 67-69). *Media:* Oil, Watercolor. *Publ:* Contribr, Heart of a Painter (film), Wacko Prod, 83; A Fool in Paradise; Autobiography, 2 vols, Fool in Paradise & The Good Wine, McFarlane Walter & Ross, 90-91. *Dealer:* Wynick/Tuck Gallery 401 Richmond St W Suite 128 Toronto ON M5V 3A8 Canada. *Mailing Add:* One Meadowcliff Dr Scarborough ON M1M 2X8 Canada

MCCARTHY, MAURA
CRITIC, EDITOR
Pos: Visual arts critic and ed, WashingtonPost.com. *Mailing Add:* Washington Post 1150 15th St NW Washington DC 20071

MCCARTHY, PAUL
ARTIST
Study: Univ Utah, 66-68; San Francisco Art Inst, BFA, 69; Univ Southern Calif, MFA, 73. *Work:* Luhring Augustine Gallery, 97, 98, 2002. *Exhib:* New Mus Contemp Art, NY, 2000; Mus Contemp Art, Los Angeles, 2000; The Garden, Deitch Projects, 2000, 2001; Galerie Hauser & Wirth, Zurich, 2001; Tate Modern, London, 2003; Head Shop/Shop Head, Moderna Museet, Stockholm, 2006. *Mailing Add:* c/o 1301PE 6150 Wilshire Blvd 8 Los Angeles CA 90048

MCCARTY, LORRAINE CHAMBERS
PAINTER, INSTUCTOR
b Detroit, Mich. *Study:* Detroit Art Acad, Wayne State Univ, with G Alden Smith; Meinzinger Art Acad; Stephens Col, with Albert Christ-Janer, also with Glen Michaels, Emil Weddidge, Robert Wilbert & Adolph Dehn. *Work:* Butler Mus Am Art, Youngstown, Ohio; Smithsonian Nat Air & Space Mus, Fed Aviation Admin, Washington, DC; Northwood Inst, Midland, Mich; Int Women's Air & Space Mus, Ohio; and others. *Comn:* Painting, Bohn Copper & Brass, Detroit; painting, R L Polk Co Int Hq, Detroit, 73; painting, Wyandotte Paint Products, Troy, Mich, 74; murals, Int Women's Air & Space Mus, Ohio, 77 & Lear Siegler, 88; mural (24 x 52 ft), General Dynamics Landsystems, Mich. *Exhib:* Butler Mus Am Art Ann, 67 & 70-74; Womanart, Saginaw Mus Arts, Mich, 74; Fed Aviation Admin, Washington, DC, 77; Dayton Art Inst, Ohio, 78; Battle Creek Art Ctr, Mich, 78; Smithsonian Air & Space Mus, DC, 80-82; Flint Inst Traveling Exhib, 83; and 43 solo exhibs. *Pos:* Mem, Arts Cult Coun, Oakland Co, Mich, 75-; designer & adv, Int Women's Air & Space Mus, Ohio. *Teaching:* Instr painting, Flint Inst Arts, 70-; instr, Grosse Pointe War Mem, Mich, 70-79 & Birmingham Bloomfield Art Asn, currently; instr oil painting, Art Ctr, Pontiac, Mich, 75-; res artist, Stephens Col, Mo. *Awards:* 1st Place Educ Series, NFLCP Hometown USA, 84; 1st Prize, Poster Competition, Pontiac Gen Hosp, Mich, 89; MCA Grant, Design Consult, Oakland Tech Ctr, Mich, 90. *Bibliog:* Joy Hakenson (auth), Abstract artists focus on a real world, Detroit News, 79; Corinne Abatt (auth), Flight's romance captured, Birmingham Eccentric, Mich, 79; Cheryl Beller (auth), Take off just beginning, Royal Oak Daily Tribune, 79. *Mem:* Mich Acad Arts, Sci & Lett; Mich Watercolor Soc; Detroit Soc Women Painters & Sculptors; Scarab Club, Detroit; and others. *Media:* Acrylic, Oil. *Publ:* Dir, The Artist in You, 42 Show TV Series, aired nationally. *Mailing Add:* 1112 Pinehurst Ave Royal Oak MI 48073

MCCAULEY, ELIZABETH ANNE
HISTORIAN, WRITER
Study: Wellesley Col, BA, 72; Yale Univ, MA, 75, PhD, 80. *Pos:* Asst dir, Univ NMex Art Mus, 78-80. *Teaching:* Asst assoc prof art hist, Univ Tex, Austin, 80-88; assoc prof, Univ Mass, 88-94, prof, 95-. *Awards:* Mus Prof Grant, Nat Endowment Arts, 82-83; Getty Postdoctoral Fel, 85-86; Guggenheim Fel, 98-99. *Mem:* Col Art Asn. *Res:* History of photography; 19th & 20th century European art. *Publ:* contribr, Eakins and the Photograph: Works by Thomas Eakins and His Circle in the Collection of the Pennsylvania Academy of Fine Arts, Smithsonian Inst, 94; Olympe Aguado Photographe 1827-1894, Mus de Strasburg, 97; coauth, The Museum and the Photograph, Clark Art Inst, 98; auth, Geschickte Fotografen': Daguerreotypien und Portraits der Familie Bisson, Mus Folkwang, 99, Le realisme et ses detracteurs, Mus Carnavalet, 2000, Edward Steichen: Artist, Impresario, Friend & Auguste Rodin, 1908 & 1910: The Eternal Feminine, In: Modern Art & Am: Alfred Stieglitz and his New York Galleries, 2001. *Mailing Add:* Univ Mass Boston Dept Art Boston MA 02125

MCCAULEY, GARDINER RAE
ADMINISTRATOR, PAINTER
b Oakland, Calif, Aug 8, 1933. *Study:* Calif Col Arts & Crafts, studied with Hamilton Wolf, 48-51; Univ Calif, Berkeley, BA, 55, MA, 57, studied with Milton Resnick, David Park, Esteban Vicente, Erle Loran & Corrado Marca-Relli. *Exhib:* Ann Exhib of San Francisco Art Asn, San Francisco Mus Art, 55-57; Bay Area Invitational, Calif Palace of the Legion of Honor, San Francisco, 58; one-man shows, Berkeley Gallery, San Francisco, 64 & Columbia Art League Galleries, 81; Artists of Ore, 67, 70, 72; Spectrum, Portland Art Mus, Ore, 70; Stephens Faculty, Merril Chase Gallery, Chicago, 74; Marymount Manhattan Col, NY, 78; Area Painters, Art Gallery, Univ Mo-Columbia, 78; and others. *Pos:* Crafts dir, US Spec Serv, France & Ger, 59-62; exec dir, Montalvo Ctr Arts, Saratoga, 82-89. *Teaching:* Lectr drawing, Univ Calif, Berkeley, 62-65; instr art, Univ Santa Clara, Calif, 64; asst prof painting & drawing, Lewis & Clark Col, Portland, Ore, 66-72; head dept art, painting & drawing, Stephens Col, Columbia, Mo, 72-82; vis artist, Barnfield Col, Eng, 80. *Awards:* Juror's Prize, San Francisco Art Asn Ann, San Francisco Mus Art, 63; James D Phelan Found Award, Calif Palace of Legion of Honor, San Francisco, 65; Firestone-Baars Found Grant, 80. *Bibliog:* Joanna Magloff (auth), From the Berkeley Gallery, 12/63, Elizabeth Polley (auth), San Francisco: Gardiner McCauley & Howard Margolis, 3/64, Artforum; Anita Ventura (auth), Pop, Photo & Paint, Arts Mag, 4/64. *Mem:* Nat Coun Art Adminrs; Col Art Asn Am; Mid-Am Col Art Asn; Am Asn Univ Profs. *Media:* Acrylic, Oil. *Publ:* Auth, Introduction to Masayuki Imai: Ceramic Art, Saratoga Villa Montalvo, 85. *Mailing Add:* 14181 Gochine Dr Nevada City CA 95959

MCCHESNEY, CLIFTON
PAINTER, EDUCATOR
b Gary, Ind, Feb 8, 29. *Study:* Am Acad Art, dipl; Ind Univ, with Jack Tworkov, BS; Cranbrook Acad Art, with Zolton Sepeshy, MFA. *Work:* Detroit Inst Arts, Mich; Biwako Mus, Otsu, Japan; Wharton Ctr Performing Arts, Mich State Univ Campus, East Lansing; Cranbrook Mus, Bloomfield Hills, Mich; South Bend Art Mus, Jewish Community Ctr, Detroit, Mich. *Exhib:* One-man shows, Benni Gallery, Kyoto, 67 & Ginza Nova Gallery, Tokyo, Japan, 75; Western Mich Univ, 84; Cent Mich Univ, 85; Dennos Mus Arts, Traverse City, Mich, 90; Kresge Art Mus, East Lansing, Mich, 95; and others. *Collection Arranged:* SPX Corporation, Muskegon, MI; Troy Management Ctr, two 7x12 paintings, Troy, MI; Ingham Regional Medical Ctr, Lansing, MI; Physical Sci Bldg, MSU Campus. *Pos:* Guest artist, Kalamazoo Art Ctr, Mich, summer 64; Vis artist, State Univ NY Albany, fall 65; instr, Leland summer workshop, 65, 66, 80-89. *Teaching:* Prof painting & drawing, Mich State Univ, East Lansing, 60-91. *Awards:* Purchase Awards, Detroit Inst Arts, 61 & Purdue Univ, 70; Travel Grant to Japan, Ford Found, 74; Distinguished Faculty Award, Col Arts & Letts, Mich State Univ, 85. *Bibliog:* Spec American Issue, Arts Mag, Vol 39, No 7; article in, Geijutsu Seikatsu, No 4, 75; Studio Interview with Artist (film), Mich Bus Weekly, WKAR TV, East Lansing, 93-94. *Media:* Acrylic, Pencil. *Mailing Add:* 5301 Horstman Rd Williamston MI 48895

MCCHESNEY, MARY FULLER See Fuller, Mary (Mary Fuller McChesney)

MCCHESNEY, ROBERT PEARSON
PAINTER, MURALIST
b Marshall, Mo, Jan 16, 13. *Study:* Washington Univ Art Sch, with Fred Conway; Otis Art Inst, Los Angeles. *Work:* Whitney Mus Am Art; Art Inst Chicago; Oakland Art Mus; Nevada Mus Art; San Francisco Mus Mod Art; Fresno Art Mus, Calif; and others. *Comn:* Wall decoration, USS Monterey; mural, Social Serv Admin Bldg, San Francisco, Calif, 77. *Exhib:* Art Inst Chicago Ann, 47-61; Corcoran Gallery Art, 57; Expo 70, Osaka, Japan, 70; Retrospective, San Francisco Art Comn Gallery, 74, Nev Mus Art, Reno, 94; 19 Yrs, Calif State Univ, Hayward, 77; Calif Art Mus, Santa Rosa, Calif, 88; Solo exhib, 871 Fine Arts, San Francisco, 94 & Fresno Art Mus, Calif, 96, Phebe Conley Gallery, Calif State Univ, Fresno, Calif, 99, City Vision Gallery, Santa Rosa, Calif, 2000, Art Exchg, San Francisco, 2002. *Teaching:* Instr, San Francisco Art Inst, formerly. *Awards:* Purchase Prizes, San Francisco Art Comn, 50 & 69; Purchase Prize, Whitney Mus Am Art, 55; Prize, San Francisco Mus Art, 60. *Bibliog:* Robert McChesney: An American Painter, 96. *Media:* Acrylic. *Dealer:* Robert Green Fine Arts Mill Valley CA; Art Exchange Gallery San Francisco CA; Michael Rosenfeld NY; Dennis Calabi CA. *Mailing Add:* 2955 Sonoma Mountain Rd Petaluma CA 94952

MCCLAIN, ROBERT LEE
ART DEALER, GALLERY DIRECTOR
b Tokyo, Japan, Oct 24, 53; US citizen. *Study:* Kans State Univ, BA(journalism), 76. *Pos:* secy/bd dir, Houston Art Dealers Asn, 90; spec adv, Mayors Arts Task Force, Houston, 91-92. *Teaching:* Lectr, Glassell Sch Art, Mus Fine Arts, Houston. *Awards:* Nominee, Rhodes Scholar, 75. *Specialty:* Contemporary American & European paintings & sculpture

MCCLANAHAN, JOHN D
PAINTER, EDUCATOR
b Salina, Kans. *Study:* Bethany Col, Lindsborg, Kans, BFA; Univ Iowa, Iowa City, MFA. *Work:* Art Mus, Univ Iowa, Iowa City; Weatherspoon Art Gallery, Univ NC, Greensboro; Mint Mus Art, Charlotte, NC; Baylor Univ, Waco, Tex; Seguin Art Ctr, Tex. *Exhib:* One-man exhib, Mint Mus Art, 71; Mid-Am Art Exhib, Owensboro, Ky, 79, 82 & 86; Baylor Univ, 81 & 83; Art Ann Two, Okla Art Ctr, Oklahoma City, 81; Biennial Nat Small Painting Exhib, Mullaly-Matisse Galleries, Birmingham, Mich; Kans Nat Small Painting Exhib, Ft Hays State Univ, Kans, 84 & 87; 2nd Ann Int Exhib Miniature Art, Del Bello Gall, Toronto, Can, 87; 30th Ann Delta Art Exhib, Ark Art Ctr, Little Rock, Ark, 87; Retrospective Exhib, Baylor Univ, Tex, 95; 29th Ann Rocky Mountain Nat Watermedia Exhib, Foothills Art Ctr, Golden, Colo, 02; Vision Int Art Ctr of Waco, 02. *Pos:* dir, Allbritton Art Inst, 98-. *Teaching:* Instr painting, Stephen F Austin State Univ, Nacogdoches, Tex, 64-67; from asst prof to assoc prof painting, Queens Col, Charlotte, NC, 67-76, chmn dept art, 75-76; prof painting, Baylor Univ, Waco, Tex, 76-, acting dir visual arts, 85-89, chmn dept art, 89-; dir, Allbritton Art Inst, 98-. *Awards:* Purchase Prizes, Tex Painting & Sculpture Exhib, 77 & 82 & Fifth Biennial Five State Exhib, 79. *Mem:* Col Art Asn Am; Tex Fine Arts Asn. *Media:* Water Media, Collage. *Mailing Add:* Baylor Univ Sch Art Waco TX 76798-7263

MCCLEARY, MARY FIELDING
COLLAGE ARTIST, EDUCATOR
b Houston, Tex, Feb 27, 1951. *Study:* Tex Christian Univ, Ft Worth, BFA, 72; Univ Okla, Norman, MFA, 75. *Work:* Gihon Found, Santa Fe, NMex; San Antonio Mus Art, Tex; El Paso Mus of Art, El Paso, TX; Mus Fine Arts, Houston, Tex; Art Mus Southeast Tex, Beaumont. *Exhib:* One-man shows, Watson/de Nagy & Co Gallery, Houston, Tex, 80, 82, 83, 85, 86 & 89, Lynne Goode Gallery, Houston, 92 & 95, Adair Margo Gallery, El Paso, Tex, 93, 2000 & 2003, Scriptural References, Amarillo Mus Art, Amarillo, Tex, Moody Gallery, Houston, Tex, 2006; Works by Texas Woman, Nat Mus Women Arts, Washington, DC, 88; Establishment & Revelation, Dallas Visual Arts Ctr, Tex, 97; Word as Art; Contemp Pendings, Gallery at Am Bible Soc, NY 2000; A Broken Beauty, Laguna Mus of Art, Laguna Beach Calif; The Next Generation: Contemp Expressions of Faith, Mus Biblical Art, NY, 2005; I Love the 'Burbs, Katonah Mus Art, NY, 2006. *Pos:* Gallery dir, Stephen F Austin State Univ, 79-82. *Teaching:* regents prof art, Stephen F Austin State Univ, Nacogdoches, Tex, 75-2005, prof Emeritus. *Awards:* First Place Award, Houston Area Exhib, Blaffer Gallery, Univ Tex, 77; Awards, Assistance League Houston, Tex, 78, 93 & 2003; Mid-America Alliance/Nat Endowment Arts Fel, 88-89. *Bibliog:* Wayne Roosa (auth), A Fullness of Vision: The Collages of Mary McCleary, Image: J Arts & Religion, summer 99; Dana Friis-Hansen & Gregory Wolfe (auths), Mary McCleary: Beginning with the Word, Galveston Art Ctr, 2000; James Romaine (auth), Objects of Grace: Essays & Interviews on Creativity & Faith, Sq Halo Books. *Media:* Mixed Media on Paper, Collage. *Publ:* It Was Good; Making Art to the Glory of God, Square Halo Books, Baltimore, Md, 2006; After Paradise, Square Halo Books, Baltimore, Md, 2006. *Dealer:* Adair Margo Gallery 415 E Yandell El Paso TX 79902; Moody Gallery 2815 Colquitt Houston TX 72098. *Mailing Add:* 4005 Raguet Nacogdoches TX 75965

MCCLELLAN, DOUGLAS EUGENE
PAINTER
b Pasadena, Calif, Oct 10, 21. *Study:* Art Ctr Sch, Los Angeles, Calif; Colorado Springs Fine Arts Ctr, with Boardman Robinson & Jean Charlot; Claremont Grad Sch, MFA. *Work:* Los Angeles Co Mus Art; Los Angeles Co Fair Asn; Pasadena Art Mus. *Exhib:* Libr Cong, 48; San Francisco Mus Art, Calif, 49-52; Los Angeles Co Mus Art, 49-55; Metrop Mus Art, NY, 50; Pa Acad Fine Arts, Pa, 53; Corcoran Gallery Art, Washington, DC, 53; Pacific Coast Biennial, 55; Carnegie Inst of Technol, Pittsburgh, Pa, 55 & 57; Whitney Mus Am Art, NY, 57; One-man shows, Felix Landau Gallery, 53-59, Pasadena Art Mus, 54 & Univ Calif, Riverside, 55. *Teaching:* Instr, Chaffey Col, 50-59, Otis Art Inst, Los Angeles, Calif, 59-61, Scripps Col & Univ of Calif, Santa Cruz; prof art, Univ Calif, Santa Cruz, 70-. *Awards:* Painting Prize, Los Angeles Co Mus Art, 50 & 53; Nat Orange Show, 54. *Mailing Add:* 4150 Glen Haven Rd Soquel CA 95073-9580

MCCLELLAND, JEANNE C
PRINTMAKER, ASSEMBLAGE ARTIST
b Edmeston, NY. *Study:* Albright-Knox Sch Fine Arts, Buffalo, dipl; State Univ NY, Buffalo, BS(art educ); Munson-Williams-Proctor Inst, Utica, NY; Hartwick Col, Oneonta, NY; State Univ NY, Oneonta. *Work:* Mus Fine Arts, Springfield, Mass; St John Fisher Col, NY; Holyoke Mus, Mass; Munson-Williams-Proctor Inst, Utica, NY; Sidney Mem Pub Libr, NY. *Exhib:* Boston Printmakers, Mass; Studio Sch & Gallery, Int Mini Print Exhib, 86-88; Int Graphic Arts Found, Mini Print Exhib, NY; Nat Small Print Exhib; Three-person show, Kubiak Gallery, Oneonta, NY; and others. *Mem:* Munson-Williams-Proctor Inst; Cooperstown Art Asn; Roberson Ctr-Arts & Sci; Int Graphic Arts Found, Darien, Conn

MCCLENDON, MAXINE MCCLENDON NICHOLS
PAINTER
b Leesville, La, Oct 21, 31. *Study:* Univ Tex, Austin; Tex Women's Univ; Pan Am Univ. *Work:* Mus Int Folk Art, Santa Fe, NMex; IBM Collection; Lauren Rogers Mus Art, Laurel, Miss; Ark Arts Ctr, Little Rock; McAllen Int Mus, McAllen, Tex; Northwestern Univ Med Ctr, Chicago; Caterpillar Corp, Peoria, Ill; Tex Instruments, Dallas. *Comn:* Tex Instruments, Houston, 79; Union Bank of Switz, 80; Hyatt Regency Hotel, Ft Worth, Tex, 81; Continental Plaza, Ft Worth, Tex, 82; panels, Four Corners, Dallas, Tex, 86. *Exhib:* 16th Tex Crafts Exhib, Dallas Mus Fine Arts, 74; 8th & 9th Ann Southwestern Area Exhibs, Mus Southwest, Midland, Tex, 74 & 75; Fourth Nat Crafts Exhib, Marietta Col, 75; Invitational Biennial, Beaumont Art Mus, Tex, 76; 19th nat, El Paso Mus Art, Tex, 76; McAllen Int Mus, 76; SW Craft Ctr, Tex Designer/Crafts Ctr, San Antonio, 78; and others. *Pos:* Cur Mex Folk Art, McAllen Int Mus, 74-80. *Teaching:* Drawing Instr, McAllen Internat Mus, 89-91; Drawing Instr, Pvt Studio, 91-. *Awards:* Best in Exhib, 6th Ann Prints, Drawings & Crafts, Ark Art Ctr, 74; Judges Award, Fouth Marietta Nat, 75; Award of Excellence, Houston Designer/Craftsman, 76. *Mem:* Am Crafts Coun (state rep, 76-80); Tex Designer/Craftsmen (pres, 73-74). *Media:* Acrylic, Oil. *Dealer:* J Siegler 9410 Blue Jay Way Irving TX 75063 jsiegler.com. *Mailing Add:* 2018 Sharyland Rd Mission TX 78572

MCCLENNEY, CHERYL ILENE
ADMINISTRATOR
b Chicago, Ill, July 18, 48. *Study:* Art Inst Chicago, BFA, 69. *Work:* Solomon R Guggenheim Mus, NY. *Pos:* Cur coordr, Solomon R Guggenheim Mus, 70-74; asst prog dir, Mus Collab Inc, 74-76; asst comnr, New York City Dept Cult Affairs, 76-78; dir mus prog, Nat Endowment Humanities, 78-83; asst dir prog, Philadelphia Mus Art, formerly, vpres external affairs,currently. *Teaching:* Instr, Art Inst Chicago, 68-69. *Mem:* Am Asn Mus; Am Asn State & Local Hist; African-Am Mus Asn. *Mailing Add:* Philadelphia Mus Art PO Box 7646 Philadelphia PA 19101-7646

MCCLURE, CONSTANCE
PAINTER, EDUCATOR
b Huntington, WVa, Feb 12, 34. *Study:* Ringling Sch of Art, Sarasota, Fla; Skowhegan Sch of Painting & Sculpture, ME; Col of Mt St Joseph, BA; Univ Cincinnati, MFA. *Work:* Cincinnati Zoological Soc; Bell Telephone Co, Cincinnati; Cincinnati Art Mus; Federated Dept Stores, Cincinnati; Gennadeion Libr, Am Sch Classical Studies, Athens, Greece; Litton Industries, Hebron, Ky. *Comn:* Portrait of conductor, Cincinnati Symphony Orchestra, 70; 18 ft canvas mural, Ohio Nat Bank, Columbus, 76; portrait of pres, Mt St Joseph Col, Ohio, 77. *Exhib:* Ohio Women Artists: Past & Present, Butler Inst Am Art, Youngstown, Ohio, 76; 14 Cincinnati Artists, Tampa Bay Arts Ctr, Fla, Peachtree Ctr, Atlanta, Ga & Contemp Arts Ctr, Cincinnati, 76; Cincinnati Art Mus, 81; Daniel Brown's Collection, Middlebury Col, Vt, 81; Graphic Collection of Daniel Brown, Hunter Mus Art, Chattanooga, Tenn; Silverpoint Etcetera: Contemp Am Metalpoint Drawings, Ark Art Ctr, Huntsville Mus Art, Ala, Farnsworth Art Mus, Rockland, Maine & Phiadelphia Art Alliance, 92-93; Fresco: A Contemp Perspective, Snug Harbor Cult Ctr, Staten Island, Parsons Sch Design, NY & Boston Col Mus Art Gallery. *Collection Arranged:* Drawing & Print Awards Exhib, Cincinnati Art Mus, 75; Regional Proj, Contemp Arts Ctr, Cincinnati, 73; Frescoes: Working People, Arts Consortium, Cincinnati, 91. *Teaching:* Prof painting, Art Acad of Cincinnati, 74-98, prof emeritus, 98-. *Awards:* Best in Show, Cincinnati Zoo Arts Festival, 65-68 & 73; First Prize-Drawing, Exhib 180, Huntington Mus Art, 66; Purchase Prize, Jewish Community Ctr Invitational, 68. *Bibliog:* Sally Webster (auth), Regional project, Cincinnati Post, 10/73; Monica Geran (auth), Balancing the scales, Interior Design, 12/80; Jane T Stanton & Colleen M Wood (auths), Constance McClure, Frescoes-Working People (catalog), 91. *Mem:* Nat Soc Mural Painters. *Media:* Oil, Buon Fresco

MCCLURE, THOMAS F
SCULPTOR, EDUCATOR
b Pawnee City, Nebr, Apr 17, 20. *Study:* Univ Nebr, BFA, 41; Wash State Col, 41; Cranbrook Acad Art, MFA, 47. *Work:* Seattle Art Mus; Syracuse Mus Fine Arts, NY; Detroit Inst Arts; Wright Mem Ctr, Beloit Col, Wis; DeWaters Art Mus, Flint, Mich. *Comn:* Welded bronze relief, Victor Gruen Assocs, Eastland Shopping Ctr, Detroit, 56; cast bronze relief, DeWaters Art Ctr, 58; welded bronze free standing scultpure, Albert Kahn Assocs, Univ Mich Undergrad Libr, Ann Arbor, 59; ten cast bronze relief sculptures, Congregation Shaarey Zedek, Detroit, 69; large cast bronze sculpture, Mich Blue Cross Bldg, Detroit, 74; and others. *Exhib:* Pa Acad Fine Arts Ann, Philadelphia & Detroit, 58; Contemp Sculpture 1961, Cincinnati Art Mus & John Herron Art Inst, 61; Drawings USA, St Paul, Minn, 61; one-man exhibs, Gilman Galleries, Chicago, 68, 70 & 75, Arwin Gallery, Detroit, 76, Flint Inst Art, 78, Elaine Horwitch Gallery, Sedona, 87; Neon & Kinetic Art, Mus Neon Art, Los Angeles, 87. *Teaching:* Instr design, Sch for Am Craftsmen, Alfred, NY, 47-48; asst prof drawing & design, Univ Okla, 48-49; prof sculpture, Univ Mich, 49-79. *Awards:* Prize in Sculpture, 12th Nat Ceramics Ann, Syracuse, 47; Founders Prize in Sculpture, 45th Mich Artists Ann, Detroit, 54; Bicentennial Sculpture Competition Award, Pa State Col, 76. *Media:* Metal. *Specialty:* Painting; sculpture. *Publ:* Dennis Kowal (auth), Sculpture Casting, Crown Publishers, NY; Nicholas Roukes (auth), Plastics in Sculpture, Watson Guptill Pub; Lewis G Redstone (auth), Public Art-New Directions, McGraw Hill Book Co; Norman Gesky (auth), The American Painting Collection of the Sheldon Memorial Art Gallery. *Dealer:* Jordan Rd Gallery 395 Jordan Rd Sedona AZ 86336. *Mailing Add:* 5353 McAuley Dr Apt 328 Ypsilanti MI 48197-1019

MCCOLLUM, MIKE L
PAINTER, PRINTMAKER
b Hoquiam, Wash, June 22, 39. *Study:* Humboldt State Col, Arcata, Calif, BA, 67; Univ Calif, Berkeley, MA, 69, MFA, 73. *Work:* Bank of America, San Francisco Mus, DeYoung Mus & Security Pacific Bank, San Francisco; Brooklyn Mus, NY. *Comn:* Five paintings, Valley Bank, Nev, 80. *Exhib:* Solo exhib, De Young Mus, San Francisco, Calif, 73; Area X Gallery, NY, 84; World Print Coun, San Francisco, 85; Wenniger Gallery, Boston, Mass, 88; Allied Arts Gallery, Las Vegas, Nev, 90. *Teaching:* Dean col fine & performing arts, 89-95. *Awards:* Visual Arts Award, Nat Endowment Arts, 80. *Mem:* Int Coun Fine Arts; Deans Nat Coun Art Adminr. *Dealer:* Magnolia Editions Gallery 2527 Magnolia Oakland CA 94607

MCCONNELL, MICHAEL PATRICK
SCULPTOR
b Troy, Ohio, Dec 4, 48. *Study:* Ohio Univ, Athens, BFA(sculpture), 70, MFA(sculpture), 74. *Work:* Butler Inst Am Art, Youngstown, Ohio; Laguna Gloria Art Mus, Austin, Tex; Currier Gallery Art, Manchester, NH; Meadows Mus Art, Shreveport, La; Zanesville Art Ctr, Ohio. *Comn:* Sculpture, NH Comn Arts, 83. *Exhib:* Mainstreams, Marietta Col, Ohio, 75 & 76; Int Craft, Tweed Mus Art, Duluth, Minn,77; Drawing and Small Sculpture, Ball State Univ Art Gallery, Muncie, Ind, 77, 78, 79 & 81; Grand Prix Int d'Art Contemp de Monte-Carlo, Nat Mus Monaco, 80 & 82. *Teaching:* Assoc prof sculpture, Univ NH, 76-. *Awards:* Sculpture Award, Marietta Col, 76; Finalist, Int Competition, Johnson Atelier Inst, 79; Award of Merit, Saenger Nat, Univ Southern Miss, 78. *Media:* Welded Steel, Cast Bronze

MCCORISON, MARCUS ALLEN
LIBRARIAN
b Lancaster, Wis, July 17, 26. *Study:* Ripon Col, BA, 50; Univ Vt, MA, 51; Columbia Univ, MS, 54; Col Holy Cross, LHD, 92; Univ Vt, Hon DLitt, 92; Clark Univ, Hon LittD, 92. *Work:* Navy Federal Credit Union, US Coast Guard Hall of Heroes; The Florence Mus, SC; Marsh McLelland, Washington, DC; Nat Institutes of Health; Children's Nat Hosp, Washington, DC. *Collection Arranged:* A Society's Chief Joys (auth, catalog), Grolier Club, Newberry Libr, Univ Calif, Los Angeles, 68-70. *Pos:* Librn, Kellogg-Hubbard Libr, Montpelier, Vt, 54-55; chief rare bk, Dartmouth Col, Hanover, NH, 55-59; head spec collections, Univ Iowa, Iowa City, 59-60; librn, Am Antiq Soc, Worcester, Mass, 60-91, dir, 67-89, pres, 89-92, pres emer, 93; trustee, Fruitlands Mus, 80-89, Old Sturbridge Village, 81-92 & Historic Deerfield, 91, Newberry Libr, 92- & Am Printing Hist Asn, 98-2003; bd mgrs, Lewis Walpole Libr, Yale Univ, 95. *Awards:* Ripon Col, Distinguished Alumni Award, 89; Columbia Univ, Sch Lit Serv, Distinguished Alumni Award, 92; Laureate, Am Printing Hist Asn, 98. *Bibliog:* The 1764 Catalogue of The Redwood Library, Yale, 65; History of Printing in America, Isabela Thomas (auth), 70. *Mem:* Century Asn; Rare Bk Sect, Asn Col & Res Libr (chmn, 65); Independent Res Libr Asn (chmn, 72-73 & 78-80); Grolier Club (councillor, 79-84); Bibliog Soc Am (pres, 80-84); Washington Soc Landscape Painters. *Res:* History of American printing, publishing, book trades, including American prints. *Interests:* American prints in all media prior to year 1877. *Collection:* American prints of the 18th and 19th century. *Publ:* Auth, Vermont Imprints, 1777-1820, Am Antiq Soc, 63; 1764 Catalogue of the Redwood Library, Yale Univ Press, 65; ed, The history of printing in America, Imprint Soc, 70. *Mailing Add:* 3601 Knightsbridge Close Worcester MA 01609-1161

MCCORMICK, PAM(ELA) ANN
SCULPTOR
b Grand Rapids, Mich, Jan 7, 46. *Study:* San Jose State Univ, BA, 72, study with Sam Richardson, MA, 72; Stanford Univ, post-grad study in art hist, 76. *Comn:* Floating water sculpture, Artists Representing Environmental Art, NY, 84; Drawing Water from a Rock, Cent Park, NY, 84; World Win, water sculpture, Harbor Festival, NY, 85; Apollo Muses, sculpture, comn by Lila Tyng, NY, 86; Sculpture in the Mall, Corcoran Art Gallery & Wash Sculptors' Group, Washington, 86. *Exhib:* Aldrich Mus (with catalog), Ridgefield, Conn, 85; Ann Photo Auction, Ctr Photog, Woodstock, NY, 91; One-woman shows, Mus NY, 91, Unison Gallery & Learning Ctr, New Paltz, NY, 91 & Artopia Gallery, NY, 97; Blast Art Benefit, X-Art Found, 93; Children's Mus Manhattan, NY, 93; Atropia Gallery, NY, 95; Unison Gallery, New Paltz, NY, 96; Puffin Room, NY, 97; and others; Sculpture Symposium on the Mall, Corcoran Gallery & Wash Sculptors Group, 86. *Awards:* Nat Endowment Arts Fel, 74; Pollock Krasner Found, grant, 90; Lila Wallace Int Artist Grant, 94. *Bibliog:* Viboon Leesuwan (auth), Pam McCormick, Thai News, Bangkok, 10/21/94; Jon Kalish (auth), A work of art even fish love, NY Newsday, 8/13/94; Carter Ratcliff (auth), Art in Am, 2/96. *Mem:* Int Sculpture Soc; Artists Representing Environmental Arts; Artists Equity. *Media:* Water, Stone. *Publ:* Illusr, Palace Peeper, Gilbert & Sullivan Soc, New York, 12/85

MCCORMICK, ROD
SCULPTOR, CRAFTSMAN
b Battle Creek, Mich, 52. *Study:* Tyler Sch Art, Philadelphia, Pa, BFA, 74; RI Sch Design, Providence, MFA, 78. *Exhib:* Solo show, Owen Patrick Gallery, Philadelphia, 90, John Elder Gallery, NY, 98 & Design Arts Gallery, Drexel Univ, Philadelphia, 99; Contemp Philadelphia Artists, Philadelphia Mus Art, 90; Leo Kaplan Mod, NY, 92; Furniture - Sculpture, Md Art Place, Baltimore, 96; Pentimenti Gallery, Philadelphia, 96; and others; Univ Arts Fac Work, 2001; Rosenwald-Wolf Gallery, Univ of the Arts, Philadelphia, 2001; The Fine Art of Metal Invitational, Montgomery Col, Rockville, 2000. *Pos:* Owner, Mail & McCormick-Designers & Makers of Fine Jewelry, Philadelphia, 82-88. *Teaching:* Univ Arts, Philadelphia Col Art & Design, Pa, 81-, assoc prof, currently. *Awards:* Venture Fund Grant, Philadelphia Col Arts, 87, Univ Arts, 90 & 93, Pa; Nat Endowment Arts Fel, 90; Pa Coun Arts Fel, 91. *Bibliog:* Michael Dunas (auth), Rod McCormick-lamps, sculpture, lighted sculpture, Metalsmith, 41, fall 90; Tom Csaszar (auth), Review-Rod McCormick, New Art Examiner, 37, 2/91. *Mem:* Soc NAm Goldsmiths. *Media:* Steel, Bronze. *Mailing Add:* PO Box 29578 Philadelphia PA 19144

MCCOUBREY, SARAH
PAINTER
b New Haven, Conn, Sept 5, 56. *Study:* Univ Pa, BA, BFA, MFA, 81. *Exhib:* One-man shows, More Gallery, Philadelphia, Pa, 85, Leslie Cecil Gallery, NY, 89, Comfort Gallery, Haverford Col, Pa, 90, Robert Brown Contemp Art, Washington, DC, 90, Pa Acad Fine Arts, Philadelphia, 97 & Stone Quarry Art Park, Cazenovia, NY, 98; BAUhouse Gallery, Baltimore, Md, 90; Cheekwood Nat Contemp Painting Competition, Tenn, 91; Botanical Gardens & Fine Arts Ctr, Cheekwood, Nashville, Tenn, 91; Robert Brown Gallery, Washington, DC, 92, 93 & 97-98; Twilight Intervals, Patricia Shea Gallery, Santa Monica, Calif, 93; Border to Border, Larson Biennale Nat Drawing Exhib, Trahorn Gallery, Austin Peay State Univ, Clarksville, Tenn, 93; Matrilineage: Women, Art and Change, Altered Space, Syracuse, NY, 93; The Hill Becomes the Valley - Central New York Landscape Paintings, Eberson Mus, Syracuse, NY, 94. *Teaching:* Instr painting, Corcoran Sch Art, Washington, DC, Syracuse Univ, NY, 91-. *Awards:* Nat Endowment Arts Grant, 89; Artist's Colony Fel, Millay Colony, Austerliz, NY, 96; Saltomstall Found Award, 97. *Bibliog:* Washington Post, 12/18/93; New Art Examiner, summer 94; Art Papers, 3-4/94. *Media:* Oil. *Mailing Add:* c/o Robert Brown Gallery 2030 R St NW Washington DC 20009

MCCOY, ANN
MURALIST, DRAFTSMAN
b Boulder, Colo, July 8, 46. *Study:* Univ Colo, BFA, 69; Univ Calif, Los Angeles, MA, 72. *Work:* Metrop Mus Art, Whitney Mus Am Art, Mus Mod Art, NY; Hirshhorn Mus, Washington, DC; San Francisco Mus Mod Art, Calif; Art Inst Chicago; Nat Gallery Australia; Powis Art Gallery, Sydney, Australia; Dallas Art Mus, Tex; Denver Art Mus, Colo; Allen Mem Art Mus, Oberlin, Ohio; Des Moines Art Center, Iowa; New Orleans Mus Art, La; Honolulu Acad Art, Hawaii; Hunter Mus Art, Chattanooga, Tenn; Roy L Neuberger Mus, Purchase, NY; Indianapolis Mus Art, Ind; and others. *Comn:* Mural in pencil, Harris Bank. *Exhib:* 10 Yrs of Contemp Art Acquisitions, Los Angeles Co Art Mus, 73; Whitney Mus Am Art, NY, 73; 71st Am Exhib, Art Inst Chicago, 74; Solo shows, Fourcade, Droll, NY, 74, Inst Contemp Art, Boston, 77, Mus Ludwig, Cologne Ger, 77, Arts Club, Chicago, 79, Galerie Kornfeld, Bern, Switz, 83, Arnold Herstand Gallery, NY, 90 & Contemp Mus, Honolulu, 91, Cent Fine Arts, NY, 98; Am 1976, Corcoran Gallery Art, Washington, DC, Wadsworth Atheneum, Hartford, Conn & Fogg Art Mus, Cambridge, Mass, 76; 31st Ann Exhib, Brooklyn Mus, 78; Decade in Review, Whitney Mus Art, 79; Los Angeles Co Mus Art, 81 & 83; Second Sights, San Francisco Mus Mod Art, 86; Art & Alchemy, Venice Biennale, Italy, 86; La Jolla Mus Contemp Art, 89; High Mus Art, Atlanta, 89; Views from a Golden Hill, Equitable Gallery, NY, 96; Natural Selection, Z Gallery, NY, 97; Obcessed by Majic, ACA Gallery, NY, 97; Central Fine Arts, NY, 99. *Teaching:* Instr, Barnard Col, New York, 80-. *Awards:* Berliner Kunstler prog, DAAD, 77; Award Visual Arts, Prix de Rome, Nat Endowment Arts, 89; The Alice Barber Award, 90; The Pollock Krasner Award, 93; The Adolph and Esther Gottlieb Found, 96; The Pollock Krasner Found, 98. *Bibliog:* William Wilson (auth), Integrity fails to make shift from LA to NY, Los Angeles Times, 10/17/82; Mark Schipper (auth), Ann McCoy, Art Scene, 12/84; Michael Brenson (auth), They seek spiritual meaning in an age of skepticism, New York Times, 5/11/86. *Media:* Pencil, Bronze. *Publ:* Auth, Alice Baber: Light as subject, 9-10/80 & The daemon and the night sea, 11-12/80, Art Int; Maura Sheehan's urban artifacts, Arts Mag, 11/85

MCCOY, KATHERINE BRADEN
DESIGNER, EDUCATOR
b Decatur, Ill, Oct 12, 45. *Study:* Mich State Univ, BA, 67. *Comn:* Poster & catalog, Detroit Inst Arts, 73-76; archit signage & graphic design, Pontiac Silver Dome, Mich, 75-79; package design & signage, Tivoli Ltd, Birmingham, Mich, 77; environ design, Univ Mich, 78-79. *Exhib:* Commun Graphics Shows, Am Inst Graphic Arts Gallery, NY, 72, 76 & 79, Five Yrs of Posters, 79 & Covers Show, 79; Artists in Residence, Cranbrook Acad Art, Bloomfield Hills, Mich, 78; Station 100, Chicago, 78-81. *Collection Arranged:* Knoll and Herman Miller: The Development of Contemporary Furniture (auth, catalog), Cranbrook Acad Art, 75 & Design in Michigan (auth, catalog), 77; International Graphic Design Education, Icograda Chicago, 78. *Pos:* Designer, Unimark Int, Detroit, 67-68; sr designer, Chrysler Corp Identity Off, Detroit, 68-69; sr designer, Omnigraphics, Boston, 69-70; sr designer, Designers & Partners, Detroit, 70-71; partner, McCoy & McCoy, Detroit, 71-; bd ed, Indust Design Mag, 76-. *Teaching:* Co-chmn, Dept Design, Cranbrook Acad Art, 71-. *Awards:* Industrial Design Excellence Award, 80; I Award, Interiors Mag, 80; Showroom of the Year Award, Inst Business Designers, 80. *Bibliog:* Articles, Graphic Design Educ, 81, Interiors Mag, 82 & Novum Grebrauschgraphik, 82. *Mem:* Indust Designers Soc Am (pres, 83-84); Am Inst Graphic Arts; Soc Typographic Arts. *Publ:* Auth & ed, Projects and Processes, Cranbrook Acad Art, 76; Design in Michigan, Wayne State Univ Press, 78. *Mailing Add:* PO Box 2001 Buena Vista CO 81211

MCCOY, KEVIN & JENNIFER
EDUCATOR
b Kevin, Seattle, Wash, 67 b Jennifer, Sacramento, Calif, 68. *Study:* Kevin: Whitman Col, Walla Walla, Wash, BA(philosophy), 89; Univ Paris III, Dept Cinema & Audio-Visual Studies, Paris, France, 90; Rensselaer Polytechnic Inst, Troy, NY, MFA(electronic Arts), 94; Jennifer: Critical Studies Film Prog CIEE, Univ Paris III, Paris, France, 90; Cornell Univ, Ithaca, BA(theater arts), 90; Rensselaer Polytechnic Inst, Troy, NY, MFA(electronic arts), 94. *Exhib:* Solo exhibs, We Like to Watch, Postmasters Gallery, New York City, 2002, Love and Terror, Butler Art Inst, Youngstown, Ohio, 2002, We Like to Watch, Van Laere Contemp Art Gallery, Antwerp, Belgium, 2002, Stardust, San Jose State Univ Art Gallery, Calif, 2003, Soft Rains (FACT (catalog), Liverpool, UK, 2003, Galerie Guy Bartschi, Geneva, Switz, 2003, Soft Rains, Postmasters Gallery, NY, 2004, Learning to Watch, Sala Redkalde, Bilbao (catalog), 2004; group exhib, Cluster Images, Werkleitz Geselchaft, Tornitz, Ger (video screening), 96, Video Room Video Festival, Brooklyn, NY (video screening), 98, Tomorrow's Home Today, Mus Sci & Industry, Manchester, Eng, (inverative video installation), 98, Toys & Noise, OK Ctr Contemp Art, Linz, Aurtria, (interactive installation), 99, The 1999 Robert Flaherty Film Seminar, Durham, NC, 99, Airworld, Walker Art Ctr, Minneapolis, MN (web proj), 99, Viper Int Media Festival, Luceme, Switz, (interacative Installation), 99, Subject to Sound, Rotunda Gallery, Brooklyn, NY (electronic sculpture), 2000, Verbal 3, Kitchen, NY, (performance), 2000, Video Viewpoints, Mus Modern Art, NY, (screening), 01, New

Acquisitions, Dept Photographs, Metrop Mus Art, NY, 02, Am Dream, Ronald Feldman Gallery, NY, 02, Tag Team, White Box, NY, 03, Game Show, James Cohan Gallery, NY, 2004, Open House: Working in Brooklyn, Brooklyn Mus, NY, 04, Our Grotesque, Cur by Rob Storr, Fifth Int Biennial, SITE Santa Fe, NMex, 04. *Pos:* Kevin: Asst prof multimedia, art dept, City Col, NY, currently; Jennifer: Asst prof, computer graphics, Brooklyn Col, NY, currently. *Awards:* Kevin & Jennifer: Co-recipient Rave Award in Art, WIRED Mag, 2005. *Mailing Add:* c/o Postmaster Gallery 459 W 19th St at 10th Ave New York NY 10001

MCCOY, MICHAEL DALE
DESIGNER, EDUCATOR
b Eaton Rapids, Mich, Sept 16, 44. *Study:* Mich State Univ, BA, 66; Wayne State Univ, MA, 68. *Work:* Am Inst of Graphic Art, NY; Cranbrook Acad Art Mus, Bloomfield Hills, Mich; Cooper Hewitt Mus, NY; Philips Design Ctr, Neth; JIDA, Tokyo. *Comn:* Archit graphics, Pontiac Silverdome, Mich, 76; furniture, Knoll Int, NY, 78; Experimental dealership design, Chrysler Corp, Detroit, 78; interior design, Univ Mich, 79; furniture, Interior Ctr, Tokyo. *Exhib:* Commun Graphics, Am Inst Graphic Arts, NY, 74, 76 & 79; Cranbrook Art Mus, 77, 78 & 83; Cooper-Hewitt Mus Design, NY, 81; Progressive Archit Furniture Exhib, 81. *Pos:* Partner, McCoy & McCoy Design Consult, Bloomfield Hills, Mich, 71-. *Teaching:* Co-chmn design dept, Cranbrook Acad Art, Bloomfield Hills, Mich, 71-. *Awards:* Ann Design Rev Awards, Indust Design Mag, 71-80; Print Casebooks Award, Print Mag, 76-78; Design Excellence Award, Industrial Designers Soc Am, 80. *Bibliog:* Cranbrook comes back, 9/82 & Office of the year, 5/83, Interiors Mag. *Mem:* Indust Design Soc Am. *Publ:* Coauth, Problem Solving in the Man-Made Environment, Cranbrook Acad Art, 74. *Mailing Add:* PO Box 2001 Buena Vista CO 81211

MCCOY, PAT A
WRITER, CRITIC
b Seattle, Wash. *Study:* Ctr Mod Psychoanalytic Studies, cert; NY Univ with Ross Bleckner, Achille Bonito Oliva & Gillo Dorfles, 83; PhD candidate, Applied Linguistics, NY Univ. *Work:* Curated, The Inscribed Image, 1988, Specific Metaphysics, 1989, Body, Mind and Spirit, 1994, Into the Psychic Landscape, 1996. *Pos:* Art lectr to mus, univs & galleries, New Arts Prog, Pa & Atlantic area, 91-; ed text(s) journal, 93; vis artists, Pa Acad Fine Arts, 93, Moore Col Art, 94 & Mus Am Art, 95. *Teaching:* Lectr Engl, City Univ NY, 85-88 & John Jay Col Criminal Justice, 88-91; clinical spec educator, NY, 95-; NY Univ, 1998. *Awards:* Mid-Atlantic Grant, 92; Nat Endowment Art Grant, 92; Pew Charitable Trust, 93. *Bibliog:* Barry Schwabsky (auth), The Widening Circle: Consequences in Contemporary Art, 97. *Mem:* Asn Int Des Critiques D'Art; NY State Coun Humanities; Orthopsychiatry Asn. *Res:* Cultural study & analysis pertaining to art, psychoanalysis & aesthetics, "interior of individual" in post modern & modern eras; social & emotional learning in education. *Publ:* Auth, East Village: dead or alive, Artscribe Mag, 87; Disrupted narrative, 88 & Modern lexicon, 89, Arts Mag; Art Criticism Today (Round Table ed), M/E/A/N/I/N/G, 92; Innovations in Child Mental Health-rev, J Mod Psychoanalysis, 92. *Mailing Add:* 630 E 14th St Apt 3 New York NY 10009

MCCOY, T FRANK
PAINTER, EDUCATOR
b Wichita, Kans, Jan 27, 25. *Study:* Kans Univ, BFA, 1950, MFA, 52; Academie Des Beaux Arts, Liege Belgium, (summa cum laude), 51. *Work:* Columbia-Greene Community Col, Columbia-Greene, NY; Bank IV, Emporia, Kans; F & M Bank & Trust, Tulsa, Okla; Rennecote Corp, Stanford, Conn. *Exhib:* Silvermine Guild 9th Ann New Eng Exhib, Silvermine Guild, New Canaan, Conn, 38; All New Eng, Cape Cod Art Asn, Barnstable, Mass, 75, 86. *Teaching:* prof drawing, Univ of Mass, 58-91; prof painting, Dartmouth, formerly. *Awards:* Friends Award for a Seascape, Silvermine Guild 10th Nat Exhib, 59; First Prize in Oil, Audubon Artists 39th Ann Exhib, 81; Emily Lowe Found Award, Audubon Artists 44th Ann Exhib, 86. *Mem:* Audubon Artists. *Media:* Oil, Watercolor. *Mailing Add:* PO Box P56 Dartmouth MA 02748

MCCRACKEN, JOHN HARVEY
SCULPTOR, PAINTER
b Berkeley, Calif, Dec 9, 34. *Study:* Calif Col Arts & Crafts, BFA, 62, grad work, 64-65. *Work:* Mus Mod Art, Whitney Mus Am Art & Solomon R Guggenheim Mus, NY; Los Angeles Co Mus; Art Inst Chicago; Art Gallery Ont, Toronto; Honolulu Acad Art, Hawaii; Milwaukee Art Ctr, Wis; Mus d'Art Contemp de Montreal, Can; San Francisco Mus Art, Calif. *Exhib:* Primary Structures, Jewish Mus, NY, 66; Am Sculpture of the Sixties, Los Angeles Co Mus Art, 67; 5th Guggenheim Int Exhib, Guggenheim Mus, 67; Art of the Real, Mus Mod Art, NY, 69; 69th Am Exhib, Art Inst Chicago, 70; Mus Contemp Arts, Chicago, 70; one-man shows, Hoffman Borman Gallery, Santa Monica, Calif, 87, Newport Harbor Art Mus, Newport Beach, 87, Fine Art Gallery, Irvine, Calif, 87, The Sculpture of John McCracken, 1965-1986 (with catalog), PS 1, 89, La Louver, Los Angeles, CA, 2002, 2002 & Lisson Gallery, London, Eng, 2001, 2002; Carnegie Int (with catalog), 91; Carnegie Mus Art, Pittsburg, 91-92; Galerie Froment & Putman, Paris, 91; Galerie Xavier Hufkens, Brussels, 93; Galerie Art & Pub (with catalog), Geneva, 94; Lisson Gallery, London, 97; David Zwirner Gallery, NY, 97, 2004 & 2006; LA Louver Gallery, Los Angeles, 2000; Galerie Almine Rech, Paris, 2000; Zwirner & Wirth Gallery, NY, 2000 & 2004; S.M.A.K. (with catalogue), Ghent, Belgium, 2004; plus others; group exhibs, La Louver Gallery, Venice, Calif, 2001, I Love NY, Zwirner & Wirth, NY, 2001, Sammlung Hauser and Wirth/Part 2/Alternating Current, Sammlung and Wirth, St Gallen, Switz, 2001, Timewave Zero/The Polics of Ecstasy, Grazer Kuntsverein, Graz, Austria, 2001, Univ Md, Baltimore Co, Baltimore County, Baltimore, MD, 2001, St Mary's Univ Art Gallery, Halifax, Can, 2001, Painting Zero Degree, Fuller Mus of Art, Brockton, Mass, 2001, Painting Zero Degree, Cleveland Ctr for Contemp Art, Cleveland, Ohio, 2002, Ten Years, Galerie Hauser & Wirth, Zurich, Switz, 2002, Pieces of Collection/OEuvres Contemporaines, Ecole Supérieure des Beaux-Artsde Nîmes, France, 2002, The House of Fiction, Sammlung Hauser und Wirth in der Lokremise St Gallen, St Gallen, Switz, 2002 & Big Brown Bag, Gavin Brown's Enterprise, NY, 2002, A Minimal Future? Art as Objecy 1958-1968, Mus Contemp Art, Los Angeles, Calif, 2004, Los Angeles; Los Angeles 1955-1985: The Birth of an Artistic Capital, Centre Pompidou, Paris, France, 2006; Galrie Hauser & Wirth, Zurich, 99, 2005. *Teaching:* Asst prof sculpture & painting, Univ Calif, Los Angeles, 66-68; asst prof sculpture, Sch Visual Arts, New York, 68-69; asst prof sculpture & painting, Hunter Col, 71-72; asst prof sculpture & painting, Univ Calif Santa Barbara, Calif, 75-85; Univ Calif, Irvine, 65-66, 75-76; Univ Nevada, Reno, 72-73; Univ Nevada, Las Vegas, 73-75. *Awards:* Nat Endowment for Arts Award, 68. *Bibliog:* Essay Catalog, Carnegie Int, Vol 1, Carnegie Mus Art, Pittsburgh, 91-92; Essay, Remote viewing/psychic traveling, Frieze, June-July-Aug 97; Essay Catalog Exhib Galerie Almine Rech, Paris, Sept 2000; Essay, A Minimal Future?, Art in America, 9-10/2004; Essay Catalog, S.M.A.K., Ghent, Belgium, 2004. *Media:* Resin, Lacquer, Stainless Steel, Oils. *Dealer:* David Zwirner Gallery 525 W 19th St New York NY

MCCRACKEN, PHILIP
SCULPTOR
b Bellingham, Wash, 28. *Study:* Univ Wash, BA; sculpture with Henry Moore, Eng, 54. *Work:* LaConner School District, Wash; King County District Courthouse, Issaquah, Wash; City of Seattle, Wash; Bartlett Square, Tulsa, Okla; Anacortes Public Library, Wash. *Exhib:* One-man shows, Willard Gallery, New York City, 1960, 65, 68, 70, Seattle Art Mus, 61, Washington State Capitol Mus, Olympia, 1964, Victoria Mus, BC, 64, La Jolla Mus Art, Calif, 70, Anchorage Mus Art, 70, Tacoma Art Mus, 80, Kennedy Galleries, New York City, 85, Lynne McAllister Gallery, Seattle, 86, Valley Mus Northwest Art, LaConner, Wash, 93, Whatcom Mus, Bellingham, Wash, 94, Schneider Mus Art, Southern Ore State Col, Ashland, 97, Monterey Mus Art, 99, Port Angeles Fine Arts Ctr, 2001; Group: CSA Gallery, Christchurch, New Zealand, 96, Spanierman Gallery, New York, 98 & 2003, Seattle Art Mus, Wash, 2001, The Art & Culture Ctr, Fallbrook, Calif, 2002, Gordon Woodside/John Braseth Gallery, Seattle, Wash, 2005, and others. *Collection Arranged:* Univ Oreg Mus, Eugene; Whitney Mus Am Art, NYC; Int Minerals & Chemicals Corp, Skokie, Ill; Henry Art Gallery, Seattle; St Louis Art Mus; Sarah Werner, Aspen, Colo; Mr. & Mrs. Milton Trafton, Seattle; Mr. & Mrs. Langdon Simons, Seattle; Mr. & Mrs. Robert Sarkis, Seattle; Mr. & Mrs. Lawrence Martz, NYC; Anne Gould Hauberg, Seattle; Mr. & Mrs. Marshall Hatch, Seattle; Mr. & Mrs. William Haseltine, Gearhart, Oreg; Morris Graves, Lolita, Calif; Mr. & Mrs. Bill Gates, Seattle. *Awards:* Ruth Nettleton Award, 54; Univ Wash Art Prize, 54; Norman Davis Purchase Award, 57; Certificate for Superior Design & Execution, Am Inst Arch, 60; Governor's Award Washington State Artist of the Year, 64 & 94; Irene D Wright Memorial Award, 65; Cornish College of the Arts Lifetime Achievement Award, 99; and others. *Bibliog:* Dore Ashton (auth), Modern American Sculpture, Abrams, 67; James J Kelly (auth), The Sculptural Idea, Burgess Press, 70; Colin Graham (auth), Philip McCracken, Univ Wash Press, 80; Faith Medlin (auth), Centuries of Owls, Silverline; Donald W. Thalacker (auth), The Place of Art in the World of Architecture, 80; Reproductions - NY Times, Jeopardy Literary Mag, 87, NY Herald Tribune, Long Island Press, Seattle Times, Seattle Post-Intelligencer, Northwest Arts, Sat Review of Literature, Time Mag, Art News, Art in America. *Media:* All Media. *Dealer:* Winfield Gallery Carmel Calif; Gordon Woodside John Bronseth Gallery Seattle WA. *Mailing Add:* 5029 Guemes Island Rd Anacortes WA 98221

MCCRAY, DOROTHY WESTABY
PAINTER, PRINTMAKER
b Madison, SDak, Oct 13, 1915. *Study:* State Univ Iowa, BA (painting and art history) 37, MA, 39; Calif Col Arts & Crafts, MFA, 55; studies in Europe, 62-90. *Hon Degrees:* DHL, Western NMU, 01. *Work:* Smithsonian Inst; Worcester Art Mus, Mass; El Paso Mus, Tex; Western NMex Univ Gallery; Fine Arts Mus, Santa Fe, NMex; Governer Gallery, Santa Fe, Univ NM Art Gallery. *Exhib:* 20-21 Int Watercolor, Art Inst Chicago, 41-42; Dallas Print Soc, Dallas Mus, 60; US Off Info Traveling Show, Europe, 71-72; one-man show, Richard Levy Gallery, Albuquerque, NMex, 92; Printmaking in NMex, Mus NMex, Santa Fe, 92; one-man retrospective, Western NMex Univ, Silver City, 93. *Teaching:* From instr to emer prof art, Western NMex Univ, Silver City, 48-81. *Awards:* Purchase Awards, Print Drawing Ann, Mus NMex, 56 & 57; Francesca Wood Award, Am Color Print Soc, 60; NMex Gov Award for Excellence & Achievement in Art, 92. *Bibliog:* Clinton Adams (auth), Printmaking in New Mexico, Univ NMex, 91; David Acton (auth), The Stamp of Impulse: Abstract Expressionistic Prints, Worcester Art Mus. *Media:* Oil; Intaglio, Lithography. *Mailing Add:* PO Box 322 Silver City NM 88062

MCCREADY, ERIC SCOTT
ADMINISTRATOR, EDUCATOR
b Vancouver, Wash, Mar 14, 41. *Study:* Univ Ore, BS, 63, BA, 65, MA, 68; Univ Pavia, Italy, BA, 65; Univ Del, PhD(art hist), 72; Wintherthur Summer Inst. *Pos:* Dir, Huntington Art Gallery, Univ Tex, 79-89 & Portland Develop Prog, 92-. *Teaching:* Asst prof art hist, Bowling Green State Univ, 72-75; asst prof, Univ Wis-Madison, 75-79; assoc prof, Univ Tex, Austin, 79-89; assoc prof & vpres develop & pub affairs, Univ Ore, 96-97. *Awards:* Knight First Class, Order of St Olaf. *Mem:* Soc Archit Historians (mem decorative arts chap); Mid-West Art Hist Soc; Victorian Soc Am. *Res:* American art; decorative arts. *Publ:* Auth, The Nebraska State Capitol: Its Design, Background and Influence, Nebr State Hist Soc, 74; Tanner and Gilliam: Two American black painters, Negro Lit Forum, 74; Richard Taliaferro: 18th Century Virginia Architect, Univ Ore Press, 77; Bertram Goodhue: Master of many arts (rev), J Soc Archit Historians, 78; Huntington at 25, Univ Tex Press, 86. *Mailing Add:* c/o Univ Ore Portland Ctr 722 SW Second St Portland OR 97204

MCCUE, HARRY
PAINTER, PRINTMAKER
b New York, NY, Sept 27, 44. *Study:* Pratt Inst, with Romano, Blaustien & McNeil, BFA, 67; Univ Colo, Boulder, with Roland Ries & William T Wiley, MFA, 69. *Work:* Univ Colo, Boulder; Cornell Univ; Univ Pa, Edinboro; Maritime Mus, Ft Schuyler, NY; City of Ithaca, NY; Univ Maine; Ithaca Col, Sch Bus; Countess IngeVon Der Schulenberg, Hanover, Ger; Wichita Art Ctr, Wichita, Kans; The office of Senator Hilary Clinton, Washington, DC, 2004-. *Comn:* Set design (collabr, D Smyth), Cornell Dance Group, Ithaca, NY, 84; cart design & construction, Mystic Seaport Mus, Conn, 84; design carriage, NY State Hist Soc, Cooperstown, 85; design pastel drawings & prints, New Statler Hotel Complex, Cornell, Ithaca, NY. *Exhib:* one-man shows, Art Gallery, Adelphi Univ, 80, Schweinfurth Mus, Auburn, NY, 86 & Herbert F Johnson Mus, Cornell Univ, NY, 87 & Wells Col, Aurora, NY, 96; Elmira Col, NY; New Vision Gallery, Ithaca, NY, 86-90; Edinboro Univ, Pa, 87; Arnot Mus, Elmira, NY, 96; Parkside Nat Small Print Exhib, Univ of Wisc, 03; Wichita Art Ctr, Wichita, KA, 04; Purdue Univ, Lafayate, Ind, 04. *Pos:* Asst slide librn, Univ Colo, Boulder, 68. *Teaching:* Instr painting, drawing & printmaking, State Univ NY, Geneseo, 69-72; instr drawing, printmaking & painting, Ithaca Col, 73-77, chmn art dept, 78-, assoc prof 87-2000, prof 2001-. *Awards:* Lodestar Grant, Ithaca Col, 84; Grant, Horizon Bank, 85; Most Meritorious Fac, Ithaca Col, 95. *Bibliog:* Wellikof (auth), American Historical Supply Catalog, Schocken Press, 84; Sherry Chayat (auth), rev, Syracuse Herald Mag, 8/3/86; Patricia Morrisrow (auth), Robert Mapplethorpe, Random House, 95. *Mem:* Community Arts Partnership, Tompkins Co; Col Art Asn. *Media:* Intaglio Prints, Oil. *Specialty:* West end Gallery, Corning, NY. *Interests:* history, farming & carriages. *Collection:* prints by early 20th century artists. *Dealer:* West End Gallery Corning NY; Upstairs Gallery Ithaca NY; Ward/Pound Ridge Gallery Pound Ridge NY. *Mailing Add:* 2423 Skinner Rd Lodi NY 14860

MCCULLOCH, FRANK E
PAINTER, PRINTMAKER
b Gallup, NMex, Aug 24, 30. *Study:* Univ NMex, BA, 53; Princeton Univ, 53-54; MA, NMex Highlands Univ, 55; Inst Allende, Mex, MFA, 65. *Work:* Amarillo Art Ctr, Tex; Mus Albuquerque; Roswell Mus & Art Ctr, NMex; Mus Fine Arts, Univ NMex, Albuquerque; Inst Allende, San Miguel, Mex. *Comn:* Don Quixote Proj, One Percent For Arts Prog, Albuquerque, 82; acrylic, Cent Bank Cooperatives, Denver, 83; oils, Albuquerque Convention Ctr, City of Albuquerque. *Exhib:* Southwest Biennial, Mus NMex, Santa Fe, 63, 67, 74 & 76; one-man exhibs, Roswell Mus & Art Ctr, NMex, 79, Governors Gallery, State Capitol, Santa Fe, 81, Munson Gallery, Santa Fe 84, 88, RSV Gallery, Southampton, NY, 83, Dartmouth St Gallery, 88, 89, 91, 98, 2001, 02 & 03, Conrad Gallery, Galveston, Tex, 91, La Galleria del Carraresi (Civic Mus), Treviso (Venice) Italy, 91 & Cline Art Gallery, Santa Fe, 94, 2001, 04 & 05; Here & Now, Mus Albuquerque, 80; 46th Ann Midyear Exhib, Butler Inst Am Art, 82; Artists of Albuquerque, Mus Albuquerque, NMex, 90; and others. *Teaching:* Mem fac art, pub schs, Albuquerque, 56-85, Inst Allende, Mex, 63-65, Univ NMex, 70-73 & Southern Methodist Univ, 77, full time artist. *Awards:* Honoree of Year, Magnifico Show, Albuquerque, 94; Artist of Year, Albuquerque Arts Alliance, 1993; NMex Gov's Arts Award, 2001; Distinguished Alumnus of Year, NMex Highlands Univ, 2002. *Bibliog:* Sandy Ballatore (auth), article, NMex Mag; Mary Carrol Nelson (auth), article, Southwest Art; Frank McCulloch Colores feature, Pub Television, 1986, 1994. *Mem:* Albuquerque Arts Bd, 88; Capitol Arts Bd, Santa Fe, 1993; Mus Albuquerque (acquisition bd); Nat Hispanic Ctr (collections bd). *Media:* Acrylic, Oil; All Media. *Specialty:* Gen and Southwestern artist. *Interests:* Southwestern art history; musician and performer; res Hispanic folk music of NM and Mex. *Publ:* Auth, Raymond Jonson, Artspace, 81; Paranoid Dreams & Parallel Schemes (collected poems), 83; JD Robb (auth), Folk Music of New Mexico; Adams (auth), Printmaking in New Mexico; The Landscape (Dartmouth St Gallery). *Dealer:* Cline Fine Arts Gallery Santa Fe NM; Dartmouth St Gallery New Mexico; Scottsdale Arizonia. *Mailing Add:* 608 11th St Albuquerque NM 87102

MCCULLOUGH, DAVID WILLIAM
PAINTER, SCULPTOR
b Springfield, Mass, Dec 28, 45. *Study:* Boston Inst of the Arts, Mass, 63-64; Aspen Sch of Contemp Art, Colo, summer 68, with Wilbur Neiwald & Doris Cross; Kansas City Art Inst, Mo, BFA(printmaking, painting), 70; Univ Mich, 69, with printmaker, Emil Weddige; Calif Inst of the Arts, 70, with Allan Kaprow & Dick Higgins. *Work:* Continental Insurance Co, NY; Sony Corp, Parkridge, NJ; Joslyn Art Mus, Omaha; Indianapolis Mus Art; Kemper Insurance Co, Chicago. *Comn:* Sculptural fountain, Am Petrofina Oil Co, Dallas, 74; three monumental sculptures, Tex Comn Arts & Humanities, 74. *Exhib:* Dallas Mus of Fine Arts Bicentennial, 71; Okla Art Mus, Oklahoma City, 71; South by SW Exhib, Ft Worth Art Mus, 72; Tyler Mus of Art, 74; Beaumont Art Mus, Tex, 75; Joslyn Art Mus, Omaha, Nebr, 76; Amarillo Art Ctr, 77; and others. *Teaching:* Artist in residence video-audio, Western Wash State Col, Bellingham, 76; artist in residence painting & sculpture, Santa Fe Contemp Art Sch, NMex, 76; lectr, Kansas City Art Inst, 82, Minneapolis Sch Art & Design. *Awards:* First Prize, Painting/Sculpture Biennial, Dallas Mus of Fine Arts, 71; First Prize, Univ Tex, Arlington, 76; Best of Show, Meadows Art Mus, Shreveport Art Guild, La, 77. *Bibliog:* Museum People, KERA-TV film, 74; Victoria Melcher (auth), David McCullough, Arts Mag, 1/76; Sarah Burns (auth), David McCullough, Arts Mag, 1/82. *Media:* Acrylic; Sand, Mixed. *Dealer:* Virginia Miller Galleries 169 Madiera Ave Coral Gables Fla 33134; Patrick King Contemporary Art 427 Massachusetts Ave Fort Wayne Ind 46204. *Mailing Add:* c/o William Campbell Contemporary Art 4935 Byers Ave Ft Worth TX 76107

MCCULLOUGH, EDWARD L
SCULPTOR; INSTRUCTOR
b Danville, Ill, Sept 18, 34. *Study:* Ill State Univ, BS, 62, MS, 66. *Work:* Univ Iowa Mus Art, Iowa City; Fed Reserve Bank, Chicago; State of Ill Bldg, Chicago; Univ Notre Dame, South Bend, Ind; Luther Col, Decorah, Iowa. *Comn:* outdoor sculpture, Unified Schs, Watertown, Wis, 96; outdoor sculpture, Eastern Ill Univ, Charleston, 98; outdoor sculpture, Ctrl Ill Regional Airport, Bloomington, Ill, 2002; outdoor sculpture, Chicago Police Hdqr Bldg, 2002; outdoor sculpture, S Ill Univ, Sch Medicine, Springfield, 2005. *Exhib:* One-person shows, Loyola Univ, Chicago, 88, McLean Co Arts Ctr, Bloomington, Ill, 2001 & Spring Arbor Col, Mich, 2005; Sculpture Project, Nat Group Show, Univ Notre Dame, South Bend, Ind, 96; Pier Walk 98, Nat Group Show, Navy Pier, Chicago, 98; Second Biennial Nat Group Sculpture Show, South Bend Regional Airport, Ind, 2000-02. *Teaching:* Adj fac, 3-D design art Columbia Col, Chicago, Ill, 91-. *Awards:* Nat Endowment Arts Fel, 81-82; Tech Grant, Ill Arts Coun, 84. *Bibliog:* Tom Butler (auth), The Elegy Series, Mitchell Mus, 87; Alec Nicolescu (auth), Songs, Kean Col, NJ, 95. *Mem:* Chicago Artists Coalition. *Media:* Metal Welded. *Dealer:* Lee Hansley Gallery 225 Glenwood Ave Raleigh NC 27603; Heike Pickett Gallery 400 E Vine St Lexington KY 40507; Sculpture Site SF Convention Ctr Plaza 201 Third St Ste 102 San Francisco CA 94103. *Mailing Add:* 421 N First St Cissna Park IL 60924-9789

MCCULLOUGH, JOSEPH
ADMINISTRATOR, PAINTER
b Pittsburgh, Pa, July 6, 22. *Study:* Cleveland Inst Art, dipl, 48, Hon DA, 96; Yale Univ, with Lewis York, 49-50, BFA, 50, with Josef Albers, 50-51, MFA, 51; Univ Evansville, Ill, hon DFA, 80. *Hon Degrees:* Univ Evansville, Ind Dept Fine Arts, 80; Cleveland Inst Art, Dept Arts, 96. *Work:* Cleveland Mus Art; Ohio Univ; Syracuse Univ; Youngstown Pub Schs, Ohio. *Comn:* Stained glass windows, St Edmund Roman Cath Church, Warren, Mich, 69. *Exhib:* Corcoran Biennial Exhib, Washington, 55; Audubon Artists Ann Exhib, NY, 56; Contemp Am Painting & Sculpture, Univ Ill, 57; All Ohio Painting & Sculpture Show, Dayton Art Inst, 67; Cleveland Arts Prize Exhib, 71. *Pos:* Pres, Cleveland Inst Art, 55-89, pres, emer, 90; trustee, Minneapolis Col Art & Design, 88-98, Sculpture Ctr, Cleveland, 90-98; secy, Access to the Arts, Cleveland, 91-98. *Teaching:* trustee Lacoste Sch of the Arts, France, 86-88. *Awards:* Spec Award for Painting, Cleveland Mus Art, 58; Purchase Award for Painting, Dayton Art Inst, 67; Cleveland Arts Prize for Visual Arts, Women's City Club Cleveland, 71. *Mem:* Cleveland Art Asn (secy, 55-88); Nat Asn Schs Art (pres, 62-65); Col Art Asn (bd dir, 63-68); Osaka Univ Arts, Japan (hon trustee 76-89); Minneapolis Col Art and Design (trustee 88-98). *Media:* Acrylic, Watercolor. *Publ:* Contribr, Art in Cleveland Architecture, AIA Handbook to Cleveland Architecture, Reinhold, 58; The Enamelist, Kenneth Bates, World, 66. *Mailing Add:* 20101 N Park Blvd Shaker Heights OH 44118

MCCULLOUGH, LEE CATHERINE
PAINTER
b Greensburg, Pa, Jul 27, 38. *Study:* Univ Cincinnati, BS(educ, appl arts), 60; studies with Don Dennis, 75-85, Ed Betts, Frank Webb, Virginia Cobb & others. *Work:* Univ Cincinnati Col Med, Ohio; Univ Northern Ky, Highland Heights; Moorehead State Univ, Ky; Madison Co Libr, Jackson, Tenn; Opryland Hotel, Nashville, Tenn; Ky Fried Chicken Corp; Dinsmore & Shohl. *Exhib:* Capitol Art, Frankfort Capitol Bldg, Ky, 87; Ky Watercolor Aqueous, Owensboro Mus Fine Art, Ky, 88, The Experienced Eye Invitational, 88; Southern Watercolor Show, Fine Art Mus South Mobile, Ala, 89; All Ky Juried Womens Art Exhib, Headley Whitney Mus, Lexington, 91; Southern Watercolor Show, Strathmore Hall Arts Ctr, Bethesda, Md, 93; Ky Watercolor Aqueous, Ky Mus, Bowling Green, 94; Tenn Watercolor Show, Hunter Mus Am Arts, Chattanooga, 96; Southern Watercolor Show, Heritage Hall Mus, Talladega, Ala, 98; Germantown Performing Arts Ctr, 2000, 2002. *Awards:* Merit Award, Ky Watercolor Aqueous, 90, 96 & 98; Merit Award, Southern Watercolor Show, 1996, 2002; 57th Nat Watercolor Soc Award of Excellence, Ala, 98. *Mem:* Nat Asn Women Artists; signature mem Ky Watercolor Soc; signature mem Southern Watercolor Soc; Memphis/Germantown Arts League, Platinum Star Artist; signature mem Ala Watercolor Soc; signature mem Tenn Watercolor Soc. *Media:* Transparent Watercolor. *Interests:* Duplicate Bridge, Gardening. *Publ:* Watercolor Magic, 99; Artist Magazine 2001. *Dealer:* Argosy Gallery 110 Main St Bar Harbor Maine

MCCURDY, MICHAEL CHARLES
ILLUSTRATOR, WRITER
b New York, NY, Feb 17, 42. *Study:* Sch Mus Fine Arts, Boston; Tufts Univ, Medford, Mass, BFA, 64, MFA, 71. *Work:* New York Pub Libr; Boston Pub Libr & Mus Fine Arts, Boston; Univ Tex, Austin. *Comn:* Print, Lincoln Conserv Comn, Mass, 81; print, Art Soc, Cleveland Mus Natural Hist, 81; Albany Print Club, NY, 86; Rochester Print Club, 92. *Exhib:* Solo exhib, Michael McCurdy & Penmaen Press, Boston Athenaeum, Mass, 76; The Artist & the Book, Wenneger Graphics, Boston, 82; Int Exhib of Wood Engraving, Hereford City Art Gallery, Eng, 84; Univ of Mo Libr, 88; Elizabeth Stone Gallery, Birmingham, MI, 92; Club Odd Volumes, Boston, 99; and others. *Teaching:* Instr drawing, Boston Sch Mus Fine Arts, 66-67; instr drawing & graphics, Concord Acad, Mass, 72-75; instr fine printing, Wellesley Col, Mass, 76. *Awards:* Bronze Medal, Book Award, Die Schonste Bucher Aus Aller Welz, Leipzig, 83; Ten Best Illustrated Children's Books, New York Times, 86, 96; Literary Light, 2002, Boston Pub Libr. *Bibliog:* Fritz Eichenberg (auth), article, Illus 63 Mag, Ger, 76; Mary Peterson (auth), Penmaen Press, NAm Rev, 81; Eunice Agar (auth), Michael McCurdy and Penmaen Press, Am Artist, 84; Tamara Tragakiss (auth), Michael McCurdy, 2006. *Mem:* Soc of Printers, Boston. *Media:* Book Arts, Wood Engraving. *Publ:* Illusr, American Buffalo, Arion Press, 92; Giants in the Land, Houghton Mifflin, 93; ed & Illusr, Escape From Slavery: The Boyhood of Frederick Douglass, Alfred Knopf, 94; Singing America, Viking, 95; Trapped by the Ice, Walker, 97; An Alonquian Year,

Houghton Mifflin, 2000; The Signers: The 56 Stories Behind the Declaration of Independence, Walker, 2002; The Train They Call the City of New Orleans, Putnams, 2003; The Founders, Walker, 2005; Walden, Shambhala, 2004; Tale of Terror, Knopf, 2005; Knee-Deep in Blazing Snow, Word Song, 2005; Tales of Adam, Steerforth Press, 2005. *Mailing Add:* 66 Lake Buel Rd Great Barrington MA 01230

MCDANIEL, CRAIG MILTON
EDUCATOR, PAINTER
b Norfolk, Va, Sept 14, 48. *Study:* Univ Pa, BS, 70; Univ Mont, MFA, 75; Ohio State Univ, MFA(painting), 86. *Work:* Sheldon Swope Art Mus, Terre Haute, Ind; Southern Ohio Mus, Portsmouth. *Exhib:* Focus: Craig McDaniel, Gov Ohio's State Residence, Columbus, 87; In Indiana, Indianapolis Art Mus, 91, 95 & 2001; Craig McDaniel & Anita Bracalante, Ind Arts Comn, 91; two-person shows, South Bend Regional Art Mus, Ind, 93, New Harmony Gallery Contemp Art, Ind, 93 & Jan Cicero Gallery, Chicago, 95; solo exhibs, Ind Univ, 97 & Ft Wayne Mus Art, 99; Jan Cicero Gallery, Chicago, 99. *Collection Arranged:* Hurry Sundown: The 1930's (catalog with Jean Robertson), 79; Six Guns and Tomahawks (catalog with Jean Robertson), 81; The Last Laugh, 83; Object As Subject (exhib catalog), 89; Exploring Maps (catalog with Jean Robertson), 92; Native Streams (catalog with Jan Cicero), 96. *Pos:* Founding dir (with Jean Robertson), Southern Ohio Mus & Cult Ctr, Portsmouth, 78-84; dir progs dept, Columbus Mus Art, Ohio, 85-88; dir, Turman Art Gallery, Ind Stat Univ, 88-94. *Teaching:* Prof painting & mem fac, Sch Grad Studies, Ind State Univ, Terre Haute, 88-. *Awards:* Merit Award, Water Tower Ann, Louisville Visual Arts Asn, 91; Visual Artist Fel, Ind Arts Comn, 91 & 92; Award of Excellence, 48th Ann Wabash Valley Exhibit, Swope Art Mus, 92. *Bibliog:* Sarah Rogers Lafferty (auth), Selections: Six in Ohio, Contemp Arts Ctr, 82; Portfolio: Craig McDaniel, Arts Ind, 10/91 & 9/95; Portfolio: The Gettysburg Review, spring 96. *Media:* All. *Publ:* Auth, Under Intense Scrutiny (exhib catalog), Turman Gallery, 90; coauth, Artists Explore the Map, Midwest Quarterly, spring 96 & Painting as a Language: Materials, Techniques, Form, Content, Harcourt, 2000. *Mailing Add:* Ind State Univ Dept Art Fine Arts Bldg 108 Terre Haute IN 47809

MCDANIEL, RICHARD
PAINTER, INSTRUCTOR
b Berkeley, Calif, Aug 31, 48. *Study:* Calif State Univ, San Diego, BA; Art Students League; Univ Notre Dame, MFA. *Work:* New Britain Mus Am Art, Conn; Redding Mus Art & Hist, Calif; Newport Art Mus, RI; Hudson River Maritime Mus, Kingston, NY; McConnell Found, Calif. *Comn:* Northwestern Univ Hosp, Chicago, Ill, 99; St John's Med Ctr, Wash, 2000. *Exhib:* One-man shows, Lyman-Allyn Mus, Conn, 83, Northwestern Mich Col, 84, Post Col, Conn, 87, Univ Conn, 90, Schenectady Mus, NY, 91, NY Conserv Arts, 92 & Fairfield Univ, Conn, 93; Hudson River Maritime Mus, NY, 94; Reading Mus Art & Hist, 97; Sacremento Fine Arts Ctr, Calif, 98. *Pos:* Bd dir, Woodstock Sch Art, 89-97 & Pacifc Acad Fine Arts, 98-. *Teaching:* Instr painting & drawing, Woodstock Sch Art, 84-; instr drawing, Cent Conn State Univ, 85-87; vis artist art hist, Post Col, 87-88; instr painting, Pacific Acad Fine Arts, 98-. *Awards:* Residency Fel, Vt Studio Colony, 90; Residency Fel, Millay Colony, 96. *Bibliog:* Raymond J Steiner (auth), McDaniel at Woodstock, Art Times, 91; Philip Eliasoph (auth), Richard McDaniel: Winterlight, Fairfield Univ, 93; G Alexander Irving (auth), The interplay of shape, Am Artist, 94. *Mem:* Conn Acad Fine Arts; Pastel Soc Am; Pastel Soc WCoast; Oil Painters Am. *Media:* All Media. *Publ:* Auth & illusr, Catskill Mountain Drawings, Phantom Press, 90; Hudson River Drawings, Phantom Press, 94; The Drawing Book, Watson-Guptill, 95; Landscape, Watson-Guptill, 97. *Dealer:* John Pence Gallery 750 Post San Francisco CA 94109

MCDANIEL, WILLIAM HARRISON (HARRY)
SCULPTOR
b Wichita, Kans, Oct 29, 59. *Study:* Warren Wilson Col, 79; Col Atlantic, 80-81; Creative Arts Workshop, 85. *Work:* AD 2000, New Haven, Conn; Brevard Co Health Dept, Titusville, Gla; Fla Atlantic Univ, Boca Raton; UNLA-Kellogg Ctr, Hendersonville, Nebr; Robert Morgade Libr, Stuart, Fla. *Comn:* Sculpture, Md-Nat Capital Parks & Planning Comn, Redland, Md, 88; wooden wall sculpture, Fair Haven Woodworks, Fair Haven, Conn, 94; mobile, Moore Co Regional Hosp, Pinehurst, NC, 99; outdoor sculpture, Fla State Univ, Tallahassee, 2005; outdoor sculpture, New River Trail State Park, Pulaski, Va, 2003. *Exhib:* NC Fel Recipients 93/94, Southeastern Ctr Contemp Art, Winston-Salem, NC, 94; NC Artists Exhib, Fayetteville Mus Art, 95; Souvenirs from My Visit to Am, Urban Inst Contemp Arts, Grand Rapids, Mich, 95 & Spirit Sq Ctr Arts & Educ, Charlotte, NC, 96; Images of the Human Spirit, Asheville Art Mus, NC, 95; Am Artifacts, DC Arts Ctr, 2001; and others. *Pos:* Mgr, Highwater Studio Coop, Asheville, NC, 90-91; webmaster, www.tristatesculptors.org, 98-2003. *Awards:* Alternate Visions Proj Grant, Alternate Roots-Atlanta, 93; Visual Arts Fel, NC Arts Coun, 93 & 98; Award of Excellence, Roanoke Art Show, Art Mus WVa, 97. *Bibliog:* Susan Wadsworth (auth), Review: Connecticut circumscribed, Art New Eng, 10/86; Michela Oberlaender (auth), Review: Tri-State sculptures exhibition, Art Papers, 7/90; Tom Patterson (auth), McDaniel's "Souvenirs" scrutinize our US values, Charlotte Observer, 9/15/96. *Mem:* Tri-State Sculptors. *Media:* All Media, Wood. *Mailing Add:* 95 Cumberland Cir Asheville NC 28801

MCDARRAH, FRED WILLIAM
PHOTOGRAPHER, EDITOR
b Brooklyn, NY, Nov 5, 26. *Study:* New York Univ, BA(journalism), 54. *Work:* Albright Knox Collection. *Exhib:* Whitney Mus Am Art, NY, 74, 76-77 & 95; Dallas Mus Art, 74; San Francisco Mus Mod Art, 75; Wadsworth Atheneum, 75; Solo exhibs, Int Jack Kerouac Gathering, 58-60, Photographs of the Artists' World, 58-62, Musie de Quebec, Can, 87, Anita Shapolsky Gallery, NY, 88, The Power of Documentary Photog, Hartnett Gallery, Univ Rochester, 89, NY Sch Action Painters, Antioch Col, 89 & Rock 'n Roll Art & Artifacts, Mus Art, Sci & Indust, Bridgeport, 89; The Formative Decade: 1964-1974, G Ray Hawkins Gallery, Los Angeles, 89; Andy Warhol System-Pub-Pop-Rock, Found Cartier, Jouy-en-Josas, Paris, France, 90; Intellectual History of Greenwich Village, Pollock-Krasner Mus, E Hampton, 90; Jack Kerouac Traveling Writers, Saint-Malo Int Festival, France, 91 & 97; The Andy Warhol Show, Triennale di Milano, Milano, Ital, 2004-2005; Franz Kline-1910-1962, Castello di Rivoli, Torino, Ital, 2005; The Official Bob Dylan Exhib, Proud Galleries, London, Eng, 2005; and many others; Bayly Art Mus; J Paul Goitty Mus; Nat Portrait Gallery; Robert V Fullerton Mus; California State Univ, San Bernardino; The Official Bob Dylan Exhib, Proud Galleries, London, Eng, 2005. *Pos:* Writer, photogr & consulting picture ed, Village Voice, 59; bk reviewer, ASMP Infinity Mag, 72-73, Photo District News, 85-88, Picture Prof, 90-. *Awards:* Fel in Photogr, John Simon Guggenheim Mem Found Award, 72; Page One Award Best Spot News Photo, New York Newspaper Guild, 71 & 80. *Bibliog:* Profile Currents, Univ Rochester, 11/7/88; Village eye-fast track, New York Mag, 6/26/89; Jerry Tallmer (auth), Visions from the east village, New York Post, 7/23/89; The Still Photograph, Images Inc, Vol 4, Nos 2 & 3, 89; Carol Wheeler (auth), A Chronicler of the beats, E Hampton Star, 10/4/90; Assoc Press, 8/4/92. *Mem:* New York Press Photogr Asn; Am Soc Picture Prof; Nat Press Photogr Asn; Authors Guild, Inc; New York Press Club. *Publ:* Auth, Stock Photo & Assignment Sourcebook, Second Ed, 84; Kerouac & Friends: A Beat Generation Album, William Morrow, 84, new ed translated Japanese, Schichosha Ltd, Tokyo, 90; Museums in New York, 5th ed, St Martin's Press, rev ed, 90; Grennwich Village Guide, Accappela Ltd, 92; Gay Pride: Photographs From Stonewall to Today, Accappela Books, 94; contribr, New York Stories, Edizioni de Luca, Rome, Ital, 2001; contribr, Kerouac & Friends (2nd ed), Thunder's Mouth Press, 2002; contribr, Anarchy, Protest & Rebellion & the Counter Culture that Changed America, Thunder's Mouth Press, 2003. *Mailing Add:* 505 LaGuardia Pl New York NY 10012

MCDONALD, ROBERT HERWICK
WRITER, CRITIC
b Philadelphia, Pa, 33. *Study:* Univ Calif, Berkeley, BA, 54 & MA, 59, Mus Mgt Inst, 83. *Exhib:* Craig Kauffman, La Jolla Mus, 81; Morris Graves Art Mus of Santa Cruz Co, 84; Laguna Art Mus, 86A; Tom Savage, de Saisset Mus, 90; David Rankiu, de Saisset Mus, 92; plus others. *Pos:* Contribr ed, Artweek, 73-88; dir, Daniel Weinberg Gallery, San Francisco, 74-76; admin asst dir, Univ Calif Art Mus, Berkeley, 77-79; chief cur, La Jolla Mus Contemp Art, 79-82 & Laguna Art Mus, 84-85, Calif; dir, Art Mus Santa Cruz Co, Calif, 82-84; critic, Los Angeles Times (San Diego ed), 85-87; dir, de Saisset Mus, Santa Clara, Calif, 87-91; independent cur, critic & consult, 91-. *Teaching:* Instr, Europ cult hist, Univ Calif, Berkeley, 63-67, Riverside, 67-71, Calif State Univ, Hayward, 71-72 & 74, intro art hist & appreciation, Univ San Diego, 86-87. *Awards:* San Diego Press Club Award, 82; Silver Medal, Commonwealth Club of Calif, 95. *Mem:* Int Asn Art Critics (US). *Res:* Contemporary American art, California artists. *Publ:* DJ Hall Selected Works 1974-1985, Los Angeles Munic Art Gallery, 86; Sense of PLAce: DJ Hall, F Scott Hess, John Valadez (exhib catalog), Fisher Gallery, Univ S Calif, Los Angeles, 87; Morris Graves: Works of Fifty Years (exhib catalog), de Saisset Mus, Santa Clara Univ, 90; ed, The Unseen Peninsula, San Francisco: Oracle Publ, 94; auth, Local Color (di Rosa Preserve Collection), San Francisco: Chronicle Books, 99; Tom Holland Early Works, Mills Coll, 2000

MCDONALD, SUSAN STRONG
PAINTER, PRINTMAKER
b Rochester, NY, Aug 18, 43. *Study:* Sweet Briar Col, BA, 65; studied with Kathan Brown, 68-71; Yoshida Hanga Acad, 71-74. *Work:* Walker Art Ctr, Minneapolis Inst Art & Univ Minn Gallery, Minneapolis; Michael C Rockefeller Gallery, Fredonia, NY; Western Regional Post Off, San Francisco. *Comn:* YWCA Award Prints, St Paul, 89. *Exhib:* Photoetchings from Crown Point Press, Ames Gallery, Berkeley, 71; Oakland Mus Art, 74; Japan Printmakers Asn Ann Exhib, Tokyo, 75; Portrait of an Artist, Minneapolis Inst Art, 81; Five Minneapolis Artists, Tweed Mus Art, 82; WARM: A Landmark Exhib, Minn Mus Art, St Paul, 84; Women's Art Registry, 86; solo exhib, Soho 20, Invitational, 87, 4th Ann Minn Artists' Exhib, 87, Kew Studios, London, Eng, 88 & Hogarth Club London, 88, Out of Control: Artists Bks, ARC Gallery, Chicago, 90. *Pos:* Scientific illusr, Univ Calif, Berkeley, 69-71; muralist, Wall Painting Artists Inc, 78-81. *Teaching:* Instr, Int Sch Sacred Heart, Tokyo, Japan, 71-74, Metrop State Univ, Minneapolis, Minn, 79-90, North Hennepin Community Col, 83-90, Split Rock Arts Prog, Univ Minn, 84-89. *Awards:* CUE Award, City Minneapolis, 82; WARM Mentor Scholarships, 83, 86 & 89; One month residency fel for printmaking, Ucross Found, 87. *Bibliog:* Diane Hellekson (auth), Using the figure, 1/85 & Margot Kreil Galt (auth), Delving into the self and finding the bones of us all, 1/86, Artpaper; Sharon Zweigbaum (auth), Susan McDonald tackles Lay issues, Vol 3, No 5, FAN, 5/86. *Mem:* Founding mem Womens Art Registry Minn. *Media:* Acrylic, Oil; All Media. *Publ:* Auth, State: State of the art/art: Art of the state, Craft Connection, 75; Harmony Hammond: A ten year retrospective, 81, In the studio, 83 & Fitting into the fifties, 83, WARM J; Making art: Political and personal change, 84 & Mystery in art, 12/85, Exhibition or Carnival, 4/86 & Ritual & Tradition, Vol 6, No 8, 4/87, Art paper. *Dealer:* Asato Art Tokyo Japan

MCDONNELL, JOSEPH ANTHONY
SCULPTOR, PAINTER
b Detroit, Mich, Oct 20, 36. *Study:* Univ Notre Dame, with Ivan Mestrovic, BFA & MFA; Acad Belli Arte, Florence, Italy; Harvard Sch Design. *Work:* Milwaukee Pub Mus; Snite Mus, Univ Notre Dame; Art Inst for the Permian Basin, Odessa, Tex; Bruce Mus, Stamford, Conn. *Comn:* Sculpture fountain, Montgomery Co, Fenwick Park, Silver Spring, Md, 88; suspended sculpture, IBM, East Fishkill, NY, 89; sculpture, Nexus Properties Inc, Trenton, NJ, 90; wall sculpture, Durst Orgn, NY, 91; Univ Washington Campus, 2000; Foster White, Seattle, 2001. *Exhib:* Solo exhibs, McNay Art Inst, San Antonio, Tex, 64, Flint Art Inst, Mich, 64, Katonah Gallery, NY,

79, Century Asn, NY, 84 & Nardin Gallery, NY, 97; Snite Mus, Univ Notre Dame, 80; Nat Acad Design, 92; Andre Emmerich, NY, 93-95. *Pos:* Critic & asst ed, Artworld, 84-94. *Teaching:* Instr, Col New Rochelle, NY, 82-83. *Awards:* Award, New Eng Silvermine Exhib, 76 & 77; Sculpture Award, Jazz at Lincoln Ctr, New York, 96. *Bibliog:* Louis G Redstone (auth), New Directions in Shopping Centers and Stores, McGraw-Hill, 73; Vivian Raynor (auth), Westchester sect, NY Times, 10/9/94; Sean Simon (auth), Art Speak, NY, 12/97; Donald Kuspit & David Finn (auths), Joseph McDonnell, Univ Wash Press, 2004. *Mem:* Sculptors Guild; Century Asn. *Media:* Multi. *Publ:* Auth, monthly sculpture revs, Art World, 84-94. *Mailing Add:* 946 Federal Ave E Seattle WA 98102

MCDOUGAL, IVAN ELLIS
PAINTER, INSTRUCTOR

b Lometa, Tex, June 29, 27. *Study:* Schreiner Inst, Kerrville, 47; Trinity Univ, San Antonio, 48; Am Acad Art, Chicago, 49. *Work:* McNay Art Mus, San Antonio. *Exhib:* Western Fedn Watercolor Soc Ann, Albuquerque Art Mus, 76; San Antonio Art League, Koehler Cult Ctr, 78; Rocky Mountain Nat Watermedia Exhib, Foothills Art Ctr, Golden, Colo, 80; Southern Watercolor Soc, La Tech Univ Gallery, Ruston, 81; San Diego Watercolor Soc; and others. *Teaching:* Instr watercolor, Jewish Community Ctr, 78-92. *Awards:* Juror's Award, San Diego Watercolor Soc; Best of Show, 1st Western Fedn, Watercolor Soc, 76; Top 100 in Arts for the Parks Competition, 90 & 92; and others. *Bibliog:* Artist's Mag, 1/96; Channel 20, Paragon Cable, 2/96. *Mem:* San Antonio Art League; Tex Watercolor Soc; San Antonio Watercolor Group. *Media:* Watercolor, Acrylic. *Publ:* Contribr, The Texas hill country, interpretations of 13 artists, North Light Mag, Tex A&M Univ Press, 81; contribr, Pecos to Rio Grande, Tex A&M Univ Press, 83. *Dealer:* Nanette Richardson Fine Art 555 E Basse Rd San Antonio TX 78209; Sandra Canavan Fine Art Gallery 33 Scenic Loop Boerne Tex. *Mailing Add:* 14311 Ambleside San Antonio TX 78231

MCDUFF, FREDRICK H
PAINTER, PRINTMAKER

b Birmingham, Ala, Oct 20, 31. *Study:* Art Student's League, NY. *Work:* Pvt collections of Mrs Ronald Reagan, Burt Reynolds, former Gov & Mrs Pierre Dupont & Mrs Ethel Kennedy. *Exhib:* Catalog Raisonne 1982-1992 of Serigraphs, Va, 93. *Publ:* Cover illusr, Impressions, 10/88; cover illusr, Potomac Life, 3-4/91. *Mailing Add:* 2441 P St NW Washington DC 20007

MCEACHRON, (GENEVIEVE) ANN
PAINTER, INSTRUCTOR

b Los Angeles, Calif, Apr 14, 26. *Study:* Ariz State Univ, Col Fine Arts, 70-72; study with, Charles Reid, Katherine Liu, Frank Webb, Serge Hollerbach, Robert E Wood, and others, 81-95; Scottsdale Artists Sch, 91 & 95. *Work:* Col William & Mary, Williamsburg, Va; Govt Taiwan, Rep China, Taipei; Vice Mayors Ofc, City Glendale, Ariz; Glendale Pub Libr, Ariz; Thunderbird Samaritan Hosp, Glendale, Ariz. *Comn:* Watercolor paintings, The Wyatt Co, 86; triptych watercolor painting, Food Health Distribr Inc, 86; watercolor painting, Allied Aerospace Div, Garrette Corp, 88; Crim Dell (watercolor painting), comn by Dr Joyce Van Tassel Baska, Col William & Mary, Va, 92; 8 paintings, Armac Insurance Agency, Victorville, Calif, 2005 & 06. *Exhib:* Multiple Visions Invitational, Sun Cities Art Mus, Ariz, 92; Facets of Life/The Leading Edge, Ariz State Univ, Gammage Auditorium, Tempe, 95; Western Federation Watercolor Socs Traveling Exhib, Sun Cities, Mus, Ariz, 96; The Leading Edge Invitational, Union Galleries, Univ Ariz, Tucson, 97; Facets of Creativity in Watermedia/The Leading Edge Invitational, Sun Cities Art Mus/Great Gallery, Ariz, 97; Logan Gallery Invitational, Mid-Lothian, Va, 98; Univ Va Medical Ctr, Main Lobby, 2004; Va Watercolor Soc Ann, 2005 & 06. *Pos:* Juror, Dept Econ Security, State Capitol, Ariz, 85; Mesa Art League, 85; Epsilon Sigma Alpha Int, 93. *Teaching:* Watercolor, Shemer Art Ctr, City Phoenix Parks & Recreation Dept, 90-98; art forms, Talented & Gifted Prog, Col William & Mary, 91 & 93. *Awards:* Grumbacher Gold Medallion, Ariz Watercolor Asn Ann Exhib, Virginia Cobb, 87; First Place Watercolor, Ariz Artists Guild, 89; First Place, Matsuri Fine Art Competition, City of Phoenix, 91. *Bibliog:* Mary Jo Pitzl (auth), Paying dues, Ariz Repub, 87; Cory Silva (auth), Artist explores watercolor, Foothills Sentinal, 87; Jan Sitts (auth), Annual Ariz Watercolor Association show-juror, Red Rock News, 88. *Mem:* Hon Soc Ariz Watercolor Asn (former pres); signature mem Watercolor West; assoc mem Nat Watercolor Soc; assoc mem Am Watercolor Soc; Va Watercolor Soc. *Media:* Watercolor. *Specialty:* Watercolors, oils & pastels by local artists. *Interests:* Travel, painting, quilting and reading. *Publ:* auth, Picking Peaches, pvt publ, 90; various greeting cards & Christmas cards, Saga Inc, 93-; Pears, Scafa-Tornabene Inc, 96; cover, Natural Awakenings, 7-8/03; 100 Ways to Paint Landscapes, Vol I, Int Artists Mag, 2004. *Dealer:* Rich Wiseman 99 Alteza Santa Fe New Mexico 87508; Uptown Gallery 1305 W Main St Richmond Va 23220; Artisimo Gallery 4333 N Scottsdale Rd Scottsdale AZ 85251. *Mailing Add:* 3214 Shallowford Landing Terr Midlothian VA 23112

MCELHENY, JOSIAH G
SCULPTOR

b Boston, 66. *Study:* RI Sch Design, BFA, 88. *Comn:* Corning Mus Glass, NY, 2000. *Exhib:* One-man shows include Henry Art Gallery, Seattle, Isabella Stewart Gardner Mus, Boston, 99, Breant Sikkema, NY, 2000, 2003, Johnson Country CC, Overland Park, Kans, 2001, Art Inst Chicago, Centro Galego de Arte Contemporanea, Spain, 2002; Site Santa Fe, NMex; Whitney Biennial, Whitney Mus Art, NY, 2000; Saatchi Gallery, London; Nordic Inst Contemp Art. *Teaching:* vis faculty, Univ Nev, 2000; vis sculpture critic, Yale Univ Sch Art, 2001-2003. *Awards:* Louis Comfort Tiffany Found Award, 95; Bagley Wright Fund Award, Seattle, 98; MacArthur Fellow, John D and Catherine T MacArthur Found, 2006. *Media:* miscellaneous. *Mailing Add:* c/o Donald Young Gallery 933 W Washington Blvd Chicago IL 60607

MCELROY, JACQUELYN ANN
PRINTMAKER, EDUCATOR

b Rice Lake, Wis, June 28, 42. *Study:* Univ Minn; Univ Mont, BA, 65, MA, 66, MFA, 67. *Work:* Dulin Gallery Art, Knoxville, Tenn; Pillsbury Co, Minneapolis; Winnipeg Art Gallery, Man, Can; Plains Art Mus, Moorhead, Minn; Okla Art Ctr, Oklahoma City; and others. *Exhib:* Midwest Biennial Exhib, Joslyn Mus, Omaha, Nebr, 74; 62nd Ann Spring Salon, Springville Art Mus, Utah, 87; NJ Art Ctr Nat Show, 88; Critical Choices, Univ Art Galleries, Univ SDak, 90; Mid-Am Print Invitational, South Bend Art Ctr, Ind, 94; 35th Midwestern Invitational, Rourke Art Ctr, Moorhead, Minn, 94; Oscar Howe Art Ctr, Mitchell, SD, 94; On Common Ground, Oscar Howe Art Ctr, Mitchell, SD, Dahl Fine Arts Ctr, Rapid City, Sunset Mus, Gettysburg, SD Mus Art, Brookings, Old Courthouse Mus, Sioux Falls, Dakotah Prairie Mus, Aberdeen, 95; Midwestern Invitational, Rourke Gallery, Moorehead MN; Mind's Eye Gallery, Dickinson, ND, 99; Bismarck Art & Galleries Asso, ND, 2006; and others. *Teaching:* Prof art hist & printmaking, Univ NDak, Grand Forks, 68-2000, asst dean, 79-84 & 91-92, chmn visual arts, 86-2000; Retired prof emerita. *Awards:* Purchase Awards, Art & the Law, Minn Mus & Western Publ Co, 80, Challenge of the Land, Pillsbury Co, 81 & Tempo Gallery, Appleton, Wis, 83. *Bibliog:* Just Plain Art, Plains Art Mus Publ, Minn, 90. *Mem:* North Valley Arts Coun. *Media:* Serigraphy. *Dealer:* Rourke Art Gallery 523 S Fourth Moorhead MN 56560; Browning Arts 22 N 4th Grand Forks ND 58201. *Mailing Add:* 770 Ashley Ln NE Thompson ND 58278-9636

MCEVILLEY, THOMAS
WRITER, CRITIC

b Cincinnati, Ohio, July 13, 39. *Study:* Univ Cincinnati, BA, 63, PhD, 68; Univ Washington, MA, 65. *Exhib:* 84 Seasons, Oil and Steel Gallery, NY, 84; Cracked Transparency, Middelburg, The Neth, 10/84; Cracked Transparency II, Kunstmuseum, Bern, Switz. *Teaching:* chm, Dept Art Criticism, Sch Vis Arts, NY. *Awards:* Nat Endowment, Arts Critic's Grant, 84-85. *Res:* Contemporary art; art and philosophy; iconography; art theory. *Publ:* Auth, The Arimaspea, McPherson & Co, 93; Thornton Dial, The Tiger Paintings, Abrams, 93; Yves Klein, Conquistador of the Void, Schirmer-Mosel Verlag, 93; James Croak, Abrams, 98; Sculpture in the Age of Doubt, Allworth, NY, 99; Shape of Ancient Thought, Allworth, NY, 2002; Triumph of Anti-Art, McPherson, Kingston, NY, 2006. *Dealer:* c/o Artforum 65 Bleecker St New York NY 10012. *Mailing Add:* Tompkins Sq Sta PO Box 20725 New York NY 10009

MCEWEN, ADAM
SCULPTOR, PAINTER

b 1965. *Study:* Christ Church Col, Oxford Univ, BA, 1987 (english lit); Calif Inst of Arts, 1991. *Exhib:* Solo shows include Much Better, 17 Rosebery Ave, London, 2002, Sleeper, Edinburgh, Scotland, 2002, Alessandra Bonomo Gallery, Rome, 2003, The Wrong Gallery, NY, 2003, The McAllister Inst, NY, 2003, History is a Perpetual Virgin., Nicole Klagsburn Gallery, NY, 2004, Jack Hanley Gallery, San Francisco, 2006; group shows include Grapeshot Bullseye Harvest, Attache Gallery, London, 2001, Free Coke, Greene Naftali Gallery, NY, 2001, Art Transplant, British Consulate in NY, 2001, Yes We're Excerpts, Andrew Kreps Gallery, NY, 2002, Happy Birthday newspaper project, Gavin Brown's Enterprise, NY, 2002, I See A Darkness, Blum & Poe, LA, 2003, Melvins, Anton Kern Gallery, NY, 2003, A Matter of Facts, Nicole Klagsbrun Gallery, NY, 2003; I Love Music, Creative Growth Gallery, Calif, 2004, The Chaim Soutine: Tattoo Project, Frieze Art Fair, London, 2004, I'll Be Your Mirror: Hotel Project at Frieze Art Fair, 2004, Situational Prosthetics, New Langton Ctr. for Arts, San Francisco, 2005, Post Notes, Inst Contemp Art, London, 2005, in words and pictures, Murray Guy, NY, 2005, OK/OKAY, Swiss Inst Contemp Art, NY, 2005; Take it Furthur, Andrew Mummery Gallery, London, 2005, Bridge Freezes Before Road, Barbara Gladstone Gallery, NY, 2005, Drunk vs. Stoned 2, Gavin Brown Enterprise, 2005, Star Star: toward the center of attention, CAC Contemporary Arts Ctr, Cincinnati, 2005, Superstars, Kunsthalle Wien, Vienna, Austria, 2005. *Collection Arranged:* A Fete Worse Than Death, 2004; Couldn't Get Ahead, Independent Art Space, London, 2004; Power, Corruption and Lies, Roth Horowitz, NY, 2004; Interstate, Nicole Klagsburn Gallery, NY, 2005. *Mailing Add:* c/o Nicole Klagsbrun 526 West 26th St Room 213 New York NY 10001

MCFADDEN, DAVID REVERE
CURATOR

Study: Univ Minn, BA(magna cum laude), 72, MA, 78. *Collection Arranged:* The Education of Craftsmen: Silver, 75; Exotic Entrepreneurs:Trade with the Orient, 76; Cooper-Hewitt Collections of Decorative Arts (auth, catalog), 78-84, Scandinavian Modern: 1880-1980 (auth, catalog), 82, English Majolica, 82, Tiffany Studios Medalwork, 83, Design in the Service of Tea, 84 & Wine: Celebration and Ceremony, 85; L'Art De Vivre, 89; Flora Danica, 90. *Pos:* Cur, Minneapolis Inst Arts, 74-78 & Cooper-Hewitt Mus, 78-; Chief Curator & Vice Pres for Programs & Collections, Am Craft Mus, 97-. *Teaching:* Cooper-Hewitt/Parsons MA program, 82-. *Awards:* Knight First Class, Order of Lion of Finland, 84; Knight Commander, Order of Northern Star, Sweden, 88; Chevalier, Ordre des Arts et des Lettres, France, 89. *Mem:* Worshipful Co Goldsmiths; Decorative Arts Soc; Soc Silver Collectors; founder Decorative Arts Asn. *Res:* Nineteenth century decorative arts and ceramics; twentieth century design. *Collection:* Porcelain, 79, The Cooper-Hewitt Collection: Glass, 79 & The Cooper-Hewitt Collection: Furniture, 79. *Publ:* Auth, Recent Acquisitions in Silver: A Petrie and D Willaume, 75, An Aldobrandini Tazza: A Preliminary Study, 77 & Scandinavian Modern Design 1880-1980, 84, Minneapolis Inst Bull; L'Art De Vivre: Decorative Arts and Designs in France 1789- 1989, 89. *Mailing Add:* American Craft Mus 40 W 53rd St New York NY 10019

MCFADDEN, MARY
COLLECTOR, DESIGNER
b New York, NY, Oct 1, 38. *Study:* Columbia Univ: Traphagen Sch of Design; Int Fine Arts Col, Miami, Dr(fine arts), 84. *Work:* Lannan Found, Palm Beach, Fla; Metrop Mus Art Costume Inst, NY. *Exhib:* The Golden Eye, Cooper-Hewitt Mus, NY, 85. *Collection Arranged:* Biet Giorgis Trust, Lannan Found. *Pos:* Ed, Vogue Mag, S Africa, 65-68, US, 71-74; contribr, Rand Daily Mail, 69-70; pres & cur, Lannan Found, Palm Beach, Fla, 74-82; Chmn & chief exec officer, Mary McFadden Inc, 74- & Mary McFadden Jewels, 78-; chmn, Mary McFadden Collection. *Teaching:* Instr fashion, Fashion Inst of Technol, NY, 76; instr chic, Hunter Col, 77; instr style, Cooper-Hewitt Mus of Decorative Arts & Design, NY, 77; lectr, Smithsonian Inst, Archit League, NY, Syracuse Univ, Duke Univ, Brooklyn Mus, Metrop Mus Art, NY, Newark Mus, NJ, Sackler Mus, Wash DC, Polish Mus, Southampton, NY & Rubin Mus, NY; lectr, NY Univ Acad Medicine. *Awards:* First Living Landmark Excellency Design, NY Landmarks Conserv, 94; Women in Urban Leadership, Marymount Manhattan Col, 96; Designer of the Decade & Beyond, Philadelphia Breast Health Inst & Fashion Group Int. *Media:* Silk, Polester. *Collection:* Ancient artifacts Egypt, Greece & Madagascar; sculpture Africa; Oriental artifacts & furniture; contemporary American art, including painting by Tom Wudl, Robert Mangold, sculpture by Mark di Suvero, Kenneth Shores & Isamu Noguchi; Indian 16th-19th century miniatures, ancient textiles, 16th century Buddhist paintings & sculpture, Japan, Korea, Mongolia, China. *Publ:* Auth, var articles on Iran, Haiti, Madagascar, Ethiopia Burma, India, Kashmir, Usbzcistan-Tashkent & Easter Island, Vogue USA, 71; Mirabella, 89. *Mailing Add:* 525 E 72d St New York NY 10021

MCFARLAND, LAWRENCE D
PHOTOGRAPHER
b Wichita, Kans, Sept 1, 42. *Study:* Kansas City Art Inst, Mo, BFA(photog), 73; Univ Nebr, Lincoln, MFA(photog), 76. *Work:* Ctr Creative Photog, Tucson; Int Mus Photog George Eastman House, Rochester, NY; Mus Mod Art, NY; Amon Carter Mus, Ft Worth, Tex; Carpenter Ctr Arts, Harvard, Cambridge, Mass; Houston Mus Fine Arts; Nev Mus of Art, Reno; High Mus of Art, Atlanta; Los Angeles Co Mus of Art. *Exhib:* Solo shows, Int Mus Photog, Rochester, NY, 80, Etherton Gallery, Tucson, Ariz, 82, Lone Star Gallery, Austin, Tex, 83 & 85, Nexus Gallery Photog, Atlanta, Ga, 83, Gallery Milepost Nine, Ariz Western Col, 84, SRO Gallery, Tex Tech Univ, 88, Trans Avant-Garde Gallery, Austin, Tex, 90 & Fotofest Int, Col Mainland, Texas City, Tex, 94, Dragomanni Gallery, Coll of the Mainland, Tex City, Tex, 94, Dragomanni Gallery, Castiglion Florentino, Italy, 97, Blue Sky Gallery, Portland, Ore, 99; Road & Roadside, Chicago Art Inst, Ill, 87; Past/Present, Mus Fine Art, Houston, Tex, 92; 1992 New Orleans Triennial (catalog), New Orleans Mus Art, La, 92; Icons of the West, William Campbell Contemp Art, Ft Worth, Tex, 94; Real Vision/Photographs from the Southwest, Colo Gallery Arts, Arapahoe Community Col, 94; Canon Land Visions, Amon Carter Mus, Ft Worth, 95; Western Panoramas Städtisches Mus Simeon Trift Simeonslipfutz Trier, Ger, 95; Nev Mus of Art, Univ, Nev, Reno, 99; Visual Studies Workshop, Rochester, NY, 2000; Pine Manor Col, Chestnut Hill, Mass, 2001. *Pos:* Self-employed artist, 79-; co-dir, Etherton Ed, Tucson, Ariz, 83-. *Teaching:* Asst prof photog, Colo Mountain Col, Leadville, 78-79; assoc prof photog, Univ Tex, Austin, 85-. *Awards:* Nat Endowment Arts Fel, 78-79, 84-85 & 90-91. *Mem:* Soc Photog Educ. *Publ:* Contribr, Working papers, Am Photogr, 8/89; Memories carved in American west landscapes, Brutus, Tokyo, Japan, 8/15/89; Parting shots, Am Photogr, 11/89; Arizona Photographers: The Snell & Wilmer Collection, Ctr Creative Photog, Univ Ariz, 90; Amon Carter Museum Photography Collection (catalog), 93. *Dealer:* Ethenton Gallery 135 S Sixth Ave Tucson AZ. *Mailing Add:* 1702 Ravey St Austin TX 78704

MCFARREN, GRACE
PAINTER
b Philadelphia, Pa, Feb 6, 1914. *Study:* Sch Design for Women; Graphic Sketch Club; Pierce Jr Col, Philadelphia; study with Clayton Bachtel, Peter Dubaniewicz, Joseph McCullough, Marion Bryson & Doris Peters, Cleveland, Ohio; Del Art Ctr, Wilmington, with Robert McKinney, 60; study with Edgar Whitney, New York, 69. *Work:* Univ Del; Hagley Mus; DuPont de Nemours & Co; Nelson Rockefeller Collection; three Wilmington Banks; Mrs David Craven Collection; and others. *Exhib:* Ann May Show, Cleveland Art Mus; Dayton Art Mus Lending Libr of Paintings; Smithsonian Inst, Washington, DC; Am Watercolor Soc, Univ Del; Philadelphia Mus Art; Del Mus Art; Juror's Choice Exhib, Univ Del, 86; and others. *Teaching:* Lectr, Univ Del Days for Women Exten, four yrs; lectrs & demonstrations, studio group in Wilmington & univ women's group. *Awards:* Three Purchase Prizes, Univ Del Ann Regional Shows; First, Second & Hon Mention, Chester Co Art Asn; Best in Show, Nat League Am Pen Women Nat Show & Rehoboth Art League; and others. *Mem:* Am Watercolor Soc. *Media:* Watercolor, Acrylic. *Mailing Add:* 3 Winterbury Cir Wilmington DE 19808

MCFEE, JUNE KING
EDUCATOR
b Seattle, Wash, June 3, 17. *Study:* Whitman Col, 35-37; Univ Wash, BA, 39; Cent Wash Col, MEd, 54; Stanford Univ, EdD, 57; Archipenko Sch Art; Cornish Sch Art; also with Amede Ozenfant; Eastern Mich Univ, Hon Dr, 82. *Exhib:* Seattle Art Mus; Seattle Artists Summer Shows; Wash State Invitational; Stanford Art Gallery Fac Exhibs. *Pos:* Ed, Studies in Art Educ. *Teaching:* From instr to asst prof art educ, Stanford Univ, 55-63; vis assoc prof, Ariz State Univ, 64-65; from assoc prof to prof art educ & dir, Inst Community Art Studies, Univ Ore, 65-77, head, Dept Art Educ, 77-83. *Awards:* June King McFee Award, Nat Art Educ Asn, 75, Distinguished Serv Award, 83, Fel, 84, Presidential Citation for Life Work, 98; NAEA Art Educr Yr, Miami Univ, 81. *Mem:* Nat Art Educ Asn (pres, Pac Region, 67-69); Soc Res in Art Educ; Coun Policy Studies Art Educ. *Specialty:* Creative cultural diversity of Mexican Am children, nat study of middle and lower-income neighborhood children. *Publ:* Auth, Art, Culture & Environment, Kendall-Hunt, 80, rev ed 98; Cultural Influences on Aesthetic Experiences in Arts and Cultural Diversity, Holt Rinehart Winston, 80; Cultural dimensions in the teaching of art, in: The Foundations of Aesthetics, Art and Art Education, Praeger, 88; Change and the cultural dimensions of art education, in: Context, Content and community in art education: Beyond Post Modernism, Teachers Col Press, 96; Cultural Diversity and the Structure and Practice of Art Educaton, Nat Art Educ Asn, 98; A Position essay on art and culture in emerging art educ, Jour Multicultural and Cross-Cultural Art Educ, 99; plus numerous others articles and publs. *Mailing Add:* 750 Chorro No 9 San Luis Obispo CA 93401

MCGAHEE, DOROTHY BRAUDY See Braudy, Dorothy

MCGARRELL, JAMES
PAINTER, EDUCATOR
b Indianapolis, Ind, Feb 22, 30. *Study:* Ind Univ, AB, 53; Skowhegan Sch Painting & Sculpture, 53; Univ Calif, Los Angeles, MA, 55; Stuttgart Acad Fine Arts, Ger, Fulbright Fel, 56. *Work:* Whitney Mus Am Art, NY; Mus Mod Art, NY; Centre Georges Pompidou; Mus Hamburg, Ger; Metrop Mus Art, NY; Rose Art Mus, Brandeis Univ; and others. *Comn:* MCI Building, St Louis, 90. *Exhib:* Carnegie Inst Int, 58 & 82; New Images of Man, Mus Mod Art, NY, 59; Dokumenta III, Kassel, Ger; Americans, Art Inst, Chicago; Venice Biennale, 68; Art About Art, Whitney Mus, 78; The Human Figure in Contemp Art, Contemp Arts Ctr, New Orleans, 82; Five Whitney Mus ann & biennials; and others. *Pos:* Bd govs, Skowhegan Sch, 81-93. *Teaching:* Vis artist, Reed Col, 56-59; prof fine arts, Ind Univ, 59-80, Skowhegan Sch Painting & Sculpture, 64-68 & Wash Univ Sch Fine Arts, 81-93, emer prof, 93; artist-in-residence, Dartmouth Col, spring 93. *Awards:* Guggenheim Found Fel, 64; Nat Endowment Arts Award, 66, Fel 85; and othersJimmy Ernst Lifetime Achievement Award, Am Acad Arts & Letters; and others. *Bibliog:* Jean Lipman (coauth), Art About Art, EP Dutton, New York, 78; James Beasley, James McGarell, Ten Yrs of Big Paintings, Springfield Art Mus, MO, 94; Gerrit Henry (auth), James McGarell at George Adams, Art in America, 2003. *Mem:* Col Art Asn Am (bd dir, 70-74); Nat Acad. *Media:* Painting, Drawing. *Dealer:* George Adams Gallery 41 W 57th St New York NY 10019; The More Gallery Philadelphia PA; Galerie Simonne Stern, New Orleans, La; Printworks and Sonia Zaks Galleries, Chicago, Ill; Elliot Smith Contemp Art, St Louis, Mo; Jane Haslem Gallery, Wash, D.C. *Mailing Add:* PO Box 39 Newbury VT 05051

MCGEE, BARRY
PAINTER AND GRAFFITI ARTIST
b San Francisco, Calif, 1966. *Study:* San Francisco Art Inst, BFA (in painting and printmaking), 1991. *Exhib:* Solo shows: Maseu Lasar Segall, Sao Paulo, Brazil, 1992, Ctr for Arts, Yerba Buena, San Francisco, 1994, K&T Lionheart Ltd, Boston, 1995, Regards, Walker Art Ctr, 1998, Hoss, Rice Univ Art Gallery, Houston Tex, 1999, The Buddy System, Deitch Projects, NY, 1999, Alleged Galleries, Tokyo, 2000, UCLA Hammer Mus, 2000, Gallery Paule Anglim, 2002, Fondazione Prada, Milan, Italy, 2002; group shows include: Big Jesus Trashcan, Victoria Room, San Francisco, 1995, Post No Bills, Acme Gallery, Oakland, Calif, 1995, Degenerate Art, The Lab, San Francisco, 1995, City Folk, Holly Solomon Gallery, NY, 1996, Wall Drawings, The Drawing Ctr, NY, 1996, John Berggruen Gallery, San Francisco, 1997, Art From Around the Bay Area, San Francisco Mus Modern Art, 1998, Indelible Market, Inst Contemporary Art, Phila, 2000, Made in California, LA County Mus Art, 2000, Street Market, Deitch Projects, 2000, Widely Unknown, 2001, Venice Biennale, 2001, Liverpool Biennial, England, 2002, Drawing Now: Eight Propositions, Mus Modern Art, NY, 2002, Scribble and Scripture, Roberts & Tilton, LA, 2003, Outerspace Hillbilly, The Luggage Store, San Francisco, 2003, A Way With Words, John Berggruen Gallery, San Francisco, 2003, Surf Style, 111 Minna Gallery, San Francisco, 2003, Ten By Twenty, Yerba Ctr for Arts, 2003, Gallery Paule Anglim, 2004. *Awards:* Lila Wallace Readers Digest Travel Grant, 1994; SECA Art Award, San Francisco Mus Modern Art, 1996; Louis Comfort Tiffany Found Grant, 1999. *Mailing Add:* c/o Gallery Paule McGee 14 Geary St San Francisco CA 94108

MCGEE, CARRIE L
PAINTER
Study: Immaculate Heart Col, Los Angeles, Calif, BA, 76. *Exhib:* Solo exhibs, Penine Hart Gallery, NY, 89, Greater Nashville Arts Found, Tenn, 95, Cheekwood Mus Art, Nashville, Tenn, 96, Int Austausch Ateliers Regional Basel, Switz, 97 & Lowe Gallery, Atlanta, Ga, 98; Ten Abstract Painters, White Columns, NY, 89; Gallery Artists, Penine Hart Gallery, NY, 89 & 90 & Zeitgeist, Nashville, Tenn, 95 & 96; Bodily, Penine Hart Gallery, NY, 93; Reverent/Irreverent, Vanderbilt Univ, Nashville, Tenn, 93; Black/White, AKA Gallery, Nashville, Tenn, 93; Found Art, Gallery on Broadway, Nashville, Tenn, 93; On The Edge, Concrete Spaces, Nashville, Tenn, 93; Nat Contemp Painting Competition, Cheekwood Mus Art, Nashville, Tenn, 93; Invitational Exhib, Bell Gallery, Nashville, Tenn, 94; McGec, Hatlebert, Schatz, AKA Gallery, Nashville, Tenn, 94; Southeastern Ctr Contemp Art, Winston-Salem, NC, 97; Nat Endowment Arts/Southern Arts Fedn Regional, 97; Small Packages, Cumberland Gallery, Nashville, Tenn, 98. *Awards:* Fel, MacDowell Colony, NH; Southern Arts Fedn Visual Arts Fel, Nat Endowment Arts, 96; Int Austausch Ateliers Basel Exchange Artist, Christoph Merian Found, Basel, Switz, 97. *Bibliog:* Christine Kreyling (auth), Facing off, Nashville Scene, 7/95; Louis Lequire (auth), New York-Nashville, Nashville Life, 2-3/96; Susan Knowles (auth), article, Art Papers, 11-12/96. *Mailing Add:* 2033 Elliott Ave Nashville TN 37204

MCGEE, J DAVID
DIRECTOR, EDUCATOR
b Chelsea, Mass, Mar, 7, 45. *Study:* Ind Univ, MA & PhD (Kress Found Scholar) 80. *Pos:* From asst prof to assoc prof art hist, Ind-Purdue Univ, Ft Wayne, 80-87, chair dept, 84-87; chair dept, Grand Valley State Univ, 88-. *Mem:* Col Art Asn; Soc Archit Historians. *Res:* Medieval art and theory. *Publ:* Auth, Early Vaults of Saint-Etienne,

Beauvais, Soc Archit Historians, 86; John Scotor Erigena and Some Carolingian and Ottonian MSS, Mediavistik, 88; Iconograph, of Rose Window at Saint-Etienne, Beauvais, Grand Valley Review, 89. *Mailing Add:* Dept Art & Design Grand Valley State Univ 1 Campus Dr Allendale MI 49401

MCGEE, WINSTON EUGENE
PAINTER, EDUCATOR
b Salem, Ill, Sept 4, 24. *Study:* Univ Mo, BJ, 48 & MA, 49; Univ Wis; Ecole Superieure Beaux-Arts, 50-51; Atelier-M Jean Souverbie, French Nat Acad, 51; Fulbright Scholar to Paris, 51. *Work:* Whitney Mus Am Art, NY; Calif Palace of Legion of Honor, San Francisco; Philadelphia Mus Art; Smithsonian Inst, Washington, DC; Indianapolis Mus Art, Ind. *Comn:* Relief painting, Mo State Hist Soc, Columbia; mural, Trinity Cathedral, Cleveland, Ohio; mural, David Leach estate, Madison, Ohio; Sara Beck Mem, Lake Erie Col, 78; Calif Wall, ceramic mural, Turlock Centennial Found, Calif. *Exhib:* one-man show, Mitchell Mus, Mt Vernon, Ill, 74; 50th Yr Anniversary Traveling Show, Cleveland Mus, 68; Lincoln Fine Arts Ctr Dedication Exhib, 70; Atelier II, La Defense, Paris, France, 78; Calif State Univ-Stanislaus, Turlock, 78; Abante Fine Arts Gallery, Portland, Ore, 88, 92, 94 & 97; Craighead Green Gallery, Dallas, Tex, 98. *Pos:* Head, Dept Art, Lake Erie Col, 52-69; actg chmn art, Cleveland State Univ, 69-72, fac in painting, 72-76; prof & chmn art dept, Calif State Univ, Stanislaus, 77-93, prof emer, 98-. *Awards:* Cleveland Mus May Show Jury Award, 68; Annie McEntree Norton Award Painting & Graphic, Univ Mo; Gold Medal, Academie Italia delle Arti, 84; Res & Creative Grant, CSUS, 86. *Bibliog:* Articles, Graphic Artists, 72 & 75; article in Mo State Hist Soc Bulletin, 9/75; Materials & Techniques of 20th Century Artists, Cleveland Mus Art, 77. *Mem:* Cleveland Coun Arts; Cleveland Art Community; New Orgn for Visual Arts; fel Int Inst Arts & Lett (Switz). *Media:* Oil, Acrylic. *Publ:* Urban Crafts, PBS-TV, 76; Winston McGees Abstract Images, Art Seen, David Howard Production, San Francisco Ctr Visual Studies, 92; California Wall (film), Winsu Prod, 88; Winston McGee, Orchard Series, Abante Publ, Portland, Ore, 94. *Dealer:* Abante Fine Arts Gallery 204 SW Yamhill Portland OR; Craigheads Green Gallery 2404 Cedar Springs Dallas TX. *Mailing Add:* 1710 Smith St Turlock CA 95382-2825

MCGEEHAN, BETTY
SCULPTOR
b Passaic, NJ, Jan 27, 34. *Study:* Art Students League, with Jose deCreeft, 78; NY Sch Social Res, 84; Pratt Inst, New York, 86. *Work:* James A Michener Art Mus, Doylestown, Pa; Noyes Mus, Oceanville, NJ; Nabisco Food Group Inc, Parsippany, NJ; Overlook Hosp, Summit, NJ; Bristol-Myers Squibb, Princeton, NJ; and others. *Comn:* Bronze bas relief (5' x 3'), Deloite/Touch, Parsippany, NJ, 88; aluminum wall sculpture (6'), Toyota Motor Corp Hq, NY, 90; 2 wall sculptures (38" each), AT&T Capital Corp, Morristown, NJ, 92; aluminum wall sculpture (5'), Schering Plough Edison, NJ, 93; 2 wall sculptures (4' x 3' each), Coca Cola Corp, Atlanta, 93; and others. *Exhib:* One-woman shows, Fairleigh Dickinson Univ, Rutherford, NJ, 91, Phoenix Gallery, NY, 93, Gross McCleaf Gallery, Philadelphia, 93 & Drew Univ, Madison, NJ, 95; NJ Ctr Visual Arts Int, Summit, 91; Diversity & Vision, Snug Harbor Cult Ctr, Staten Island, NY, 92 & 93; Transformation of Matter into Art, NY Acad Scis, 92; Art NJ, Wm Paterson Col, Wayne, NJ, 93; and others. *Awards:* First Prize Ann Exhib, NJ Ctr Visual Arts, 86; Honorable Mention, Sculpture Exhib, Pen & Brush, New York, 88; Fel, Vt Studio Colony, Johnson, 88. *Bibliog:* Eileen Watkins (auth), Chatham sculptor, 84 & Explore interior scapes, 90, Star Ledger, NJ; William Zimmer (auth), Definitive decade show, New York Times, 10/30/94. *Mem:* Sculptors Asn NJ (pres, 83-84 & 90); Sculptors League (bd mem, 89-92); Nat Asn Women Artists; Allied Artists Am; Womens Caucus Arts. *Media:* Metal and Wood Assemblages. *Dealer:* Phoenix Gallery 568 Broadway Suite 607 New York NY

MCGHEE, JOHN GILMER
PAINTER
b Brooklyn, NY, May 21, 22. *Study:* Pratt Inst, Brooklyn, NY, 49; Sch Art Studies, New York, 51; studied with Edward Melcarth, 52. *Work:* Mus Art Mod, Toluca, Mex; Lowe Gallery, Univ Miami, Fla; Inst Politécnico Nac, Casa Cult San Angel, Mex. *Comn:* Village Life, Salon Helena, Mex, 56; Battle of Otumba (mural), Regional Preparatory Sch, Otumba, Mex, 88; Market Day (mural), Flores Meyer Dental Clinic, Mex, 89; Fall of Tlatlatzincatzin (mural), Casa Cult Gonzalo Carrasco, Otumba, Mex, 93. *Exhib:* City & Country, Galería Metrop, Univ Autónoma Mex, 90; The Mexico I Know, Mus Gonzolo Carrasco, Otumba, Mex, 91; Collective Exhib, Inst Politécnico Nac, Mex, 94; Panorama of Drawing in Mexico, Ctr Médico Nat Siglo XXI, Mex, 95; United States Artists in Mexico, Inst Estudios Educ Sindicales Am, Mex, 96. *Awards:* Emily Lowe Awards, NY, 51; ACA Gallery Competition, NY, 52. *Bibliog:* Merry MacMasters (auth), Nostalgia, El Nac, 12/86; Berta Taracena (auth), Recent works by John McGhee, Excelsior, 4/93; Salvador Pinoncelly (auth), The work of John McGhee, Obras, 7/95. *Mem:* World Coun Visual Artists (dir painting div, 95-96). *Media:* Oil, Pen & Ink. *Specialty:* figurative Mexican art. *Dealer:* Marisa Mataix Icacos 44-7 Mexico DF Mex CP 03020

MCGIBBON, PHYLLIS
PRINTMAKER, EDUCATOR
b Madison, Wis, 61. *Study:* Univ Wis, Madison, BFA, 83, MFA(printmaking, drawing & installation), 88. *Work:* Kohler Art Libr, Madison, Wis; Block Mus, Northwestern Univ, Evanston, Ill; Davidson Art Ctr, Middleton, Conn; Simmons Col, Boston, Mass; Achenbach Found, San Francisco, Calif. *Exhib:* Solo exhibs, JMKAC, Sheboygan, WI, 98, Sweet Briar Col, VA, 99, Orange Co Ctr Cotemp Art, Santa Ana, CA, 92, San Diego Univ, 94, Davis Mus & Cult Ctr, MA, 96; Bankside Gallery, London, 2000; DFN Gallery, New york, NY, 2000; Anchorgraphics, Chicago, Ill, 2001; New Art Ctr, Newton, MA, 2004; Univ No Iowa, Cedar Falls, IA, 2005; Rutgers Univ, 2005. *Teaching:* Numerous workshops, slide presentations & lectures at various locations worldwide, 83-97; artist-in-residence, Rijkscentrum Frans Masereel, Kasterlee, Belg, 84, Lowick House Printworkshop, Cumbria, Eng, 84, Bemis Ctr Contemp Art, Omaha, Nebr, 95 & Millay Colony Arts, Austerlitz, NY, 96; printmaker-in-residence, Peacock Printmakers, Aberdeen, Scotland, 84 & etching inst & vis artist, 86; asst drawing instr, Univ Wis, Madison, 85-88, instr life drawing, 88 & lectr drawing & life drawing, summer 89; guest artist lithography, St Michael's Printshop, St John's, Nfld, Can, 87; vis lectr grad liberal studies prog, Art Dept & Luther Gregg Sullivan Vis Artist, Wesleyan Univ, Middletown, Conn, 89-91; grad art fac painting & drawing, Claremont Grad Sch, Calif, 91-94; asst prof art drawing, Pomona Col, Claremont, Calif, 91-94; printmaker-in-residence, Kala Inst, Berkeley, Calif, 93; asst prof art printmaking, Wellesley Col, Mass, 94-97 & assoc prof, 97-. *Awards:* Art Matters Inc Grant, New York, 94; Works on Paper Individual Artist Grant, Nat Endowment Arts, 95; Fac Res Award, Wellesley Col, Mass, 96; Howard Found Grant, Brown Univ, 01. *Bibliog:* Christine Temin (auth), Wellesley's teachers go to the head of the class, 11/29/95 & Feathering the nest, 10/9/96, Boston Globe; Mary Kaye (auth), Radiant Brooder, New Art Examiner, 12-1/96-97. *Publ:* Illusr, Victory Over the Sun (Alexei Kruchenykh, auth), Isolde Press, Madison, Wis, 87; On Second Thought, Tiramisu Press, 88; A Chronology of Important Events, Isolde Press & Triangular Press Madison, Wis, 89; Carpe Diem, Tiramisu Press, 89; collabr, Shifting Grounds I, in prep. *Mailing Add:* Art Dept Wellesley College 106 Central St Wellesley MA 02481

MCGILVERY, LAURENCE
BOOK DEALER, PUBLISHER
b Los Angeles, Calif, May 21, 1932. *Study:* Pomona Col, BA, 54. *Pos:* Mem adv bd, Artbibliographs Mod, Santa Barbara, 73, Who's Who in Am Art & Am Art Dir, 78. *Mem:* Art Libr Soc of NAm; Antiquarian Booksellers Asn Am; San Diego Booksellers Asn. *Res:* Art periodical indexes and art bibliographies. *Publ:* Auth, Artforum, 1962-1968: A Cumulative Index to the First Six Volumes, McGilvery, 70; auth, The 21st Century Countdown Calendar, Countdown Enterprises, 98-2000; auth, The ArtForum Index (online version); coauth, several other bibliographies; The Frayed Knot and Other Sublime Tales, in press. *Mailing Add:* PO Box 852 La Jolla CA 92038

MCGINLEY, MARIBETH WILSON
GRAPHIC ARTIST, EDUCATOR, DIRECTOR
Pos: Pres, M Walton McGinley Design, 97-. *Teaching:* Art instr, Kidspace: A Participatory Mus, Pasadena. *Awards:* Recipient Grand Award, Los Angles Bicentennial Design Competition, 81; Gold Record for Art Direction for albums, Return of the Jedi & ET the Extra-Terrestrial, 83. *Mem:* Nat Coun on Arts; Nat Endowment for Arts; Best Friends Found (mem fin comt); Calif Art Club; Art Ctr Col Design (pres, alumni bd, currently). *Mailing Add:* 1001 E Mountain St Glendale CA 91207

MCGINLEY, RYAN
PHOTOGRAPHER
b Ramsey, NJ, 1977. *Study:* Parsons Sch Design, NY, BFA (photography). *Exhib:* Alleged, Space 1026, Phila, 2001; Raw: New York, New Work, Mamma Roma Ltd, 2001; Bystander, Andrea Rosen Gallery, NY, 2002; You're just a summer love, but I'll remember you when winter comes, Priska C. Juscha Fine Art, Brooklyn, 2002; K48 Teenage Rebel: The Bedroom Show, Johnm Connelly Presents, 2002; A New Scene: What About NY?, Galerie du Jour, 2003; Color Wheel Oblivion, Marella Arte Cotemporanea, Milan, 2004; Summer Solstice with Sam Gordon, Ryan McGinley and Collier Schorr, Ratio 3, San Francisco, 2004; Fresh: Youth Culture in Contemporary Photographs, The Ctr for Photography, Woodstock, NY, 2004; Greater NY, Mus Modern Art, Ny, 2005; one man shows: The Kids Are Alright, 420 W Broadway, NY, 2000, Mc Magma, Milan, 2002, Galerie Giti Nourbakhsch, Berlin, 2002, The Red Eye Gallery, Rhode Island Sch Design, 2003, Bailey fine Arts, Toronto, Canada, 2003, New Photographs, Mus Modern Art, NY, 2004; represented in permanent collections of San Francisco Mus Modern Art and Whitney Mus Am Art, NY. *Awards:* Photographer of Yr, Am Photo Mag, 2003

MCGINNIS, CHRISTINE
PAINTER, PRINTMAKER
b Philadelphia, Pa. *Study:* Pa Acad Fine Arts; Fleisher Art Mem. *Work:* Mus Nat Sci, Philadelphia; Civic Ctr Mus, Philadelphia; Free Libr Philadelphia; Am Embassy, Dublin, Ireland; Pa Acad Fine Arts. *Exhib:* Philadelphia Art Mus Regional Exhib, 64; Brooklyn Art Mus 14th Nat Exhib, NY, 65; Am Express Pavillion, NY World's Fair, 66; Libr Cong 20th Nat, Washington, DC, 67; Washington Art Mus, 77-81; Art Expo Traveling Show, 80-83; One-person shows, Roger LaPelle Galleries, 82, 84, 86, 89, 90, 93 & 97; Touchstone Gallery, Washington, DC, 88; Phoenix Gallery, NY, 88; Rose Lehrman Art Ctr, Harrisburg, Pa, 95. *Teaching:* Fleisher Art Memorial, Philadelphia; Sch Art League, Philadelphia; Wynne Art Ctr, Philadelphia. *Awards:* Award, Albany Print Club, 68; First Prize, Pa Acad, 74; Second Prize, Allentown Mayfair Festival, 92; Fellowship Prize, PAFA, 00. *Bibliog:* Margaret Holbern Ellis (auth), The Care of Prints and Drawings, 78; The Woodmere Art Museum: Index to the Permanent Collection, 86. *Mem:* Fel, Pan Am Festival Asn & Pa Acad Fine Arts. *Media:* Acrylic, Graphics. *Publ:* Illusr, Ctr City Mag, 63; Promenade Mag, 68; Audubon Mag, 70; Decor Mag, 78; Imfad Cat, 77-80. *Dealer:* Rodger LaPelle Galleries, Philadelphia. *Mailing Add:* 5929 Devon Pl Philadelphia PA 19138

MCGINNISS, JIM
SCULPTOR
b Bloomfield, NJ, 32. *Study:* self taught. *Work:* Stairway to Dedication, New Hope Fire Co, New Hope, Pa. *Comn:* replica model, New Hope CofC, New Hope, Pa, 2001; Fiddler on the Roof, Village Art Works, Lahaska, Pa, 2004. *Exhib:* solo exhib, Mary Anthony Gallery, SoHo, NY, 99; Trenton City, Mus NJ, 2000; Byer's Choice Limited Corp Ctr, Chalfont, Pa, 2001; Da Vinci Art Alliance Juried Exhib, Philadelphia, Pa,

2001; Ellarslie Trenton NJ City Mus, 2006; NOVA Gallery, 2005; Selma Burke Sculpture Show, 2005; Artsbridge at Phillip's Mill, 2006; Mary Anthony Galleries, New York, NY. *Awards:* First place Award, Metuchen Cult Arts Comn; First place Award, Plainfield Festival of Art; Second place Award, Franklin Arts Coun. *Mem:* Artsbridge, Lambertville, NJ; Art & Cult Coun Bucks Co, Pa. *Media:* Bronze, Kinetic Sculpture. *Specialty:* Early life. *Dealer:* Village Art Works 42 Street Rd Lahaska Pa 18931; Premiere Fine Arts Gallery Union Sq New Hope Pa 18938. *Mailing Add:* 103 Stoney Hill Rd New Hope PA 18938

MCGLAUCHLIN, TOM
SCULPTOR
b Beloit, Wis, Sept 14, 34. *Study:* Univ Wis, BS, 59, MS(art), 60; pottery with James McKinnell, Univ Iowa, 62; Oriental art hist, Univ Washington, 66-67. *Work:* Corning Mus Glass, NY; Toledo Mus Art, Ohio; Musee des Arts Decoratifs de la Ville de Lausanne, Switz; Nat Mus Mod Art, Kyoto, Japan; Kunst Mus, Dusseldorf, WGer; and others. *Comn:* Clouds of Joy (23' glass sculpture), Webstrand Ldt, Toledo, Ohio, 84; glass sculpture, Glass Capitol Columns, Crosby Gardens, Toledo, 86; glass & stainless steel sculpture, A Mountain for Toledo, Rotary Club Toledo, 88. *Exhib:* Glass Aus USA, Glasmuseum Frauenau, WGer, 79; Am Glass Now II, touring Japan, 80; Glass: Artist and Influence, Detroit Art Inst, 81; Nat Mus Mod Art, Kyoto, Japan, 81; Thirty Yrs of New Glass, 1957-1987, Corning Mus Glass, NY, 87; Int Exhib Glass 88, Kanazwa, Japan; and others. *Pos:* Chmn art dept, Cornell Col, Mt Vernon, 68-71. *Teaching:* Prof art, Cornell Col, Mt Vernon, Iowa, 61-71; prof & dir glass prog, Toledo Mus Art, 71-84. *Awards:* Ohio Arts Coun Grant, 79. *Bibliog:* Glass at Wagman, St Louis Globe Democrat, 4/23-24/82; Losken M Feuerzauber (auth), Glas aus USA, Kunst und Handwerk, WGer, 11-12/79. *Mem:* Glass Art Soc; Am Crafts Coun; Int Sculpture Ctr. *Media:* Glass; Steel. *Mailing Add:* 2527 Cheltenham Toledo OH 43606

MCGLOTHLIN, JAMES W
FINE ART COLLECTOR
Study: William & Mary Coll, B, Law. *Pos:* Chief Financial Officer, United Co, Big Rock, Va, 70-. *Awards:* Named one of Top 200 Collectors, ARTnews Mag, 2006. *Media:* miscellaneous. *Mailing Add:* United Company Inc PO Box 1280 Bristol VA 24203-1280

MCGLOUGHLIN, KATE
PRINTMAKER, PAINTER
b Kingston, NY. *Study:* Univ Ariz, with Robert Colescott, BFA(painting & drawing), 85; Woodstock Sch Art, with Robert Angeloch, 95. *Hon Degrees:* Master Printmakers, WSA. *Work:* Schenectady Mus, NY. *Comn:* Ann Membership Print Woodstock Artists Asn, 1992, 2000; Ann Collector's Prints, Friends of the Woodstock School Art, 1997. *Exhib:* Int Mini Print Expos, Juniper Gallery, Napa Valley, Calif, 92; Print Club Albany Nat Exhib, Schenectady Mus, 92; State of the Art 93, New Eng Fine Arts Inst, 93; National Works on Paper, Univ Tex, 93; Printworks 98, Barrett House Gallery, Poughkeepsie, NY, 98. *Collection Arranged:* Relief Prints in Woodstock, Kleinert James Gallery, Woodstock, NY. *Pos:* Bd dir, Woodstock Sch Art, 94-99, dir, 96-. *Teaching:* Instr monotype, Woodstock Sch Art, NY, 93-, instr lithography, 96-, head printmaking dept, 2003; instr watercolor, Il Chiostro d Toscana, Italy, 98-2001. *Awards:* Sidney Laufman Award, Woodstock Artists Asn, 95, Rudolph Galleries Award, 97, Frederick-Fiolic award, 97, Jacobs-Towbin award, 2001; Kuniyoshi Fund Award, Woodstock NY, 96. *Bibliog:* Bonnie Langston (auth), Woodstock's Next Generation, Kingston Freeman, 8/94; Raymond J Steiner (auth), 4 contemporary printmakers, Art Times, 9/94; Dakota Lane (auth), Bright rises and stark ramps, Woodstock Times, 4/98; Journal of Print World, Book Review, Winter 2003. *Mem:* Woodstock Artists Asn. *Media:* Relief printing, monotype, watercolor, oil. *Res:* 11 Century Mosgics of Torcello. *Publ:* A Walk in the Woods: Selected Etchings, Lithographs, and Block Prints 1991-1996, Precipice Publ, West Hurley, NY, 2002. *Dealer:* Sarah Stitham PO Box 1397 Olivebridge NY 12461. *Mailing Add:* Woodstock Sch Art 2470 Rte 212 PO Box 338 Woodstock NY 12498

MCGOUGH, CHARLES E
PRINTMAKER, EDUCATOR
b Elmhurst, Ill, Aug 2, 27. *Study:* Southwestern Univ; Ray Vogue Commercial Art Sch, dipl; Univ Tulsa, BA & MA; NTex State Univ; also with Hardin Simmons. *Work:* Boston Mus; Philbrook Mus; Dallas Mus Fine Arts; Little Rock Mus Fine Arts. *Comn:* Genre mural, Southern Hills Country Club, Tulsa, Okla, 56; mural, ETex State Univ, Commerce, 63; mural, Goodfellow AFB, San Angelo, Tex, 64; several graphic works, First Nat Bank, Dallas, Tex, 65; several graphic works, Southwestern Life Ins Co, Dallas, 67. *Exhib:* Nat Serigraph Ann, Brooklyn Mus Art, 63; Drawing USA, Walker Art Ctr, 66; Nat Print Ann, Boston Mus Fine Arts, 67; Southwest Print & Drawing Ann, Dallas Mus Fine Arts, 67, 68 & 70; Nat Print & Drawing Ann, Okla Art Ctr, 69-72. *Pos:* Owner, McGough Advert Co, 45-50; art dir, Crane Advert, Tulsa, 50-52. *Teaching:* Instr art, N R Crogier Tech High Sch, Dallas, 52-56; prof & head art dept, ETex State Univ, 56-. *Awards:* Graphic Purchase Award, Boston Univ Mus Show, 65; Southwest Print & Drawing Ann Award, Dallas Mus Fine Arts, 67; Graphic Purchase Award, Nat Print Ann, Okla Art Ctr, 71. *Mem:* Southwest Print & Drawing Soc; Tex Asn Schs Art. *Media:* Graphics. *Publ:* Auth, Print painting, Dallas Morning News, 67; Serigraphy, Dallas Times Herald, 68; Serigraph & the total image, Tex Trends Art Educ, 68. *Dealer:* Cushing Galleries 2723 Fairmount St Dallas TX 75201. *Mailing Add:* 1603 Walnut St Commerce TX 75428-3347

MCGOVERN, ROBERT F
PAINTER, SCULPTOR
b Philadelphia, Pa, Apr 1, 33. *Study:* Philadelphia Col Art, Pa, with Benton Spruance. *Work:* Mus Art, Free Libr, Philadelphia; Rare Bk Collection, Cornell Univ, Ithaca, NY; Marian Libr, Dayton Ohio; Georgetown Univ, Washington, DC. *Comn:* Portraits of Bishop Lorenz Grassel & Mathew Carey, Am Cath Hist Soc, Philadelphia, 76; carving of Bishop Neumann, Bishop Neumann High Sch, Philadelphia, 77; banner of St John Neumann, comn by Sister of St Francis for use at Canonization, Rome, Italy, 77; wood relief of St John Neumann for Daylesford Abbey, Paoli, Pa, 78; Suite of wood crarving, St Columba Church, Oxon Hill, MD, 85; Wood Carvings Mother of Sorrows Church, Tucson, Ariz, 87; Wood Carving St Mary Church, Jackson Tenn, 91; Wood Carving Albany Med Ctr, Albany NY, 93; Suite of Wood Carvings, St Charles Borromeo Church, Bensalem, PA, 93-2005. *Exhib:* Prints & Drawings, Philadelphia Art Alliance, 62; Print Club, Philadelphia, 63; Am Color Print Soc, Philadelphia, 73-77; Liturgical Arts, 41st Int Eucharistic Cong, 77; Solo shows, St Joseph Univ, Philadelphia, Pa, 80, Marian Libr, Dayton Ohio, 97, Villanova Univ, 2003; Group shows, Am Color Print Soc, 2000, Woodmere Art Gallery, Philadelphia, Pa, 2003. *Pos:* Co-chmn found prog, Univ Arts, 76-99; Prof Emertus, Univ of the Art, Philadelphia, Pa. *Teaching:* Prof drawing design & anatomy, Univ Arts, 56-99. *Awards:* Beitzel Distinguished Teaching Award, Univ of Arts 93; Stella Drabkin Mem Awards, ACPS, 97; Mother Teresa Award, St Bernadette Inst Sacred Art, 2006. *Bibliog:* Intro to Clay Vessels by Joseph Ferry; Essay in Exhib catalogue for Villanova Univ by Rev Msgr. Francis Carbine. *Mem:* Philadelphia Print Club; Artists Equity (pres, Philadelphia Chap, 64-65); Am Color Print Soc; Artist Equity; Am Color Print Soc; Asn Uniting Religion & Art (aura). *Media:* Wood Carving, Woodcuts; Oil, Printmaking. *Publ:* Auth, rev, Religious Art in 20th Century--An Understanding, Pax Romano, Fribourg, Switz, 65; coauth, Saturday Waiting, 60 Pen & Ink Drawings, Fortress Press, Philadelphia, 70; auth, A Re-emergence of religious art in the seventies, Dimension Mag, Philadelphia, 74; illusr, Uncommon Book of Prayer, Seabury Press, 78; Ten Woodcuts in Daniel by Daniel Berrigan, SJ Plough Publishing House, 98; Woodcuts in Clay Vessels, Poems by Rev, John MCNamee, Sheed & Ward, 95; Contemplation & The Artist, The Way, London England, 87; Nineteen Drawings in Wisdom by Daniel Berringan, SJ, Sheed & Ward, 2001; Frontispiece and Essay, Hopkins Variations, Saint Joseph Univ Press & Fordham Univ Press, 2002. *Mailing Add:* 120 Woodside Ave Narberth PA 19072-1930

MCGOWIN, ED (WILLIAM EDWARD)
PAINTER, SCULPTOR
b Hattiesburg, Miss, June, 2, 1938. *Study:* Univ Southern Miss, BS, 61; Univ Ala, MA, 64. *Work:* Whitney Mus Am Art & Guggenheim Mus, NY; Hirshhorn Mus, Nat Collection Fine Arts & Corcoran Gallery, Washington, DC. *Comn:* sculpture, Dallas Rapid Transit Authority, Tex, 94; NY Supreme Court, Queens, 98; sculpture, Socorro, NMex, 98; sculpture, NY MTA, 99; Univ Iowa, Cedar Falls, 2003. *Exhib:* Group shows, Whitney Mus Am Art, NY, 66 & 76; solo exhibs, Baltimore Mus Art (with catalog), 72, Mus Mod Art, Paris, 78, Cranbrook Acad Art Mus, Bloomfield Hills, Mich, 83, Boca Raton Mus Art, Fla, (catalog), 91, Paris, NY, Bangkok Gallery, Thailand, 94 & Anderson Gallery, Buffalo, NY, 94 & Silpakorn Univ, Bangkok, Thailand; Corcoran Gallery of Art, Washington, DC (catalog) 1975; Guggenheim Mus, NY, 83; Miss Mus Art, (catalog), 89; Art What Thou Eat, Edith Blum Gallery, Bard Col, NY (catalog), 90; Beyond Realism: Image & Inigma in Am Art, Southern Alleghenies Mus, Loretto, Pa (catalog), 92; In the Ring, Snug Harbor Cult Ctr, NY (catalog), 93; Thirty Something, Fine Arts Mus South Mobile, Ala (catalog), 94; PS1, Mus Modern Art Affiliate, Long Island City, NY, 2006; Mobile Mus Art, Ala, 2006. *Teaching:* Prof, State Univ NY, Old Westbury, 1976-2003. *Awards:* Grants, Nat Endowment Arts, 67, 76 & 80, Cassandra Found, 72; Miss Arts & Lett Award, Miss Arts & Lett Comt, 80. *Bibliog:* Jane Livingston Corcoran (auth), True Stories, Gallery Art, Washington, 1975; Susan Freudenhime (auth), The Southern Voice, Ft Worth Art Mus, Tex, 1981; Timothy Eaton (auth), Ed McGowin Painting, Boca Raton Mus Art, Fla, 1991; Ed McGowin, Namechange, Mobile Mus Art, Ala, 2006. *Mem:* Century Asn NY; Route 66 Comn, Santa Rosa, NMex, 2004; Ft. Lauderdale Fire Rescue Comn, Fla. *Media:* Mixed Media. *Publ:* auth, Artful Travelers still Making Magic after all these Years, The Gazette, Bethesda, MD; auth, Sculptures are Dramatic Visual Diaries, Richmond Times Dispatch, March, 1998. *Dealer:* Gracie Mansion Gallery 54 St Marks Pl New York NY 10009; Barbara Gillman Gallery Miami Fla; Osuna Gallery Bethesda Md. *Mailing Add:* 96 Grand St New York NY 10012

MCGRAIL, JEANE KATHRYN
PAINTER, PHOTOGRAPHER
b Minneapolis, Minn, May 1, 47. *Study:* Univ Wis, River Falls, BS, 70; Cranbrook Acad Arts, MFA, 72; Sch Art Inst, Chicago. *Work:* Univ Wis, Milwaukee; Miami-Dade Pub Libr, Fla; Univ Chicago; Nat Mus Women Arts, Washington, DC; Mus Sci & Indust, Chicago; Oakton Col. *Exhib:* Nat Mus Women in Arts, Washington; Mini Print Int Cadaques, Adogi Taller, Galleria Fort, Spain, 2000-2006; Blue, Northeastern State Univ Gallery, Chicago & Space 900 Gallery, Chicago; 14th Mini Print Int Exhib, Binghamton, NY, 2000; Visions Toward Wellness, Macy Gallery, NY, 2000; 24th Ann Invite Drawing, Norman R Eppink Art Gallery, Emporia, Kans; Red, Oakton Community Col; Ukrainian Mus, 2003; Lake Co Community Col, Ill, 2003; Chautauqua Natl Exhib, NY, 2004; Ukranian Mus Modern Art, Chicago, 2004; Rockford Col Art Gallery, 2006. *Pos:* Ed, CAG Newslett, Miami, Fla, 78-80; exec bd dir, CWCA, 92-95; adj fac, McHenry Co Col & Truman Col, 1992-, pres, photog adv. *Teaching:* Pvt instr. *Awards:* Award, Art Auction Exhib, N Miami, Fla, 80; Chicago Cult Arts CAAP Grant, 92; TCIA-art Institute of Chicago, 2004. *Bibliog:* Who's Who of Am Women, 1995-2005; Who's Who in the World, 1995-2005. *Mem:* Chicago Artists Coalition; Women's Caucus for Arts; Nat Asn Photoshop Profs; Col Art Asn; Chicago Prof Photogs Asn; Sierra Club (exec comt, sec prairie group). *Media:* Printmaker, Digital Imaging. *Publ:* Best of Printmaking, IBID Collections. *Dealer:* Space 900 Group 1040 West Huron LLW Chicago IL 60622. *Mailing Add:* 1S035 Euclid Ave Oakbrook Terrace IL 60181

MCGREW, BRUCE ELWIN
PAINTER
b Wichita, Kans, Oct 20, 37. *Study:* Wichita State Univ, Kans, BFA; Univ Ariz, MFA, 64. *Work:* Nat Park Serv, Three Rivers, Calif & Haleakala Nat Park, Maui, Hawaii; Univ Minn, Morris; Univ Kansai, Osaka, Japan; Univ Ariz, Law Sch. *Comn:* oil landscape, Georgetown Leather, Washington, DC, 77; watercolor, Pennie Edmonds Law Firm, NY, 77. *Exhib:* Kiosko del Arte, Hermosillo, Mex, 78; Maggie Kress Gallery, Taos, NMex, 79, Marion Locks, Philadelphia, 81; Colorado Springs Fine Arts Ctr, Colo, 81; Univ Ark, Fayetteville, 81; and others. *Teaching:* Instr painting & drawing, Univ Minn, Morris, 64-66; prof art, Univ Ariz, Tucson, 66-; artist-in-residence, Nat Park Serv, Sequoia & Kings Canyon Nat Park, Three Rivers, Calif, summer 75 & Haleakala Nat Park, Maui, Hawaii, summer 76; mem staff watercolor workshop, Summervail Art Workshop, Vail, Colo, summer 77; mem staff drawing & watercolor workshop, Univ Tex, El Paso, 4/78 & Guadalajara Summer Sch, Univ Ariz, 79. *Awards:* Fac Res Support in Humanities & Sociology, Univ Ariz, Tucson, 72-73; Purchase Awards, 13th Ann Cedar City Exhib, Utah, 74 & Ninth South Western Invitational Yuma Fine Arts Asn, Ariz, 75. *Media:* Watercolor, Oil. *Publ:* Contribr, Oracle: A Voluntary of Poems and Prints, Oracle Press, 74. *Dealer:* Marion Locks Gallery 1524 Walnut Philadelphia PA 19102. *Mailing Add:* PO Box 160 Oracle AZ 85623

MCGUIRE, MAUREEN
DESIGNER, STAINED GLASS ARTIST
b Flushing, NY, July 13, 41. *Study:* NY State Col Ceramics, Alfred Univ, BFA, 63; Pope Pius XII Inst, Florence, Italy (affil Rosary Col, Ill), Cardinal Spellman scholar & MA, 64; workshop, with Ludwig Schaffrath, Berkeley, Calif, 75. *Comn:* Design for large tapestry, La Casa De Cristo Lutheran Church, Paradise Valley, Ariz; leaded stained glass windows & laminated glass screen wall, St Matthew's United Methodist Church, Bowie, Md; faceted glass window, skylights, mosaic walls, exterior concrete bas relief sculptures, interior design, furniture design incorporating flower display system, St Francis Cemetery Resurrection Mausoleum; commercial installation: 15 faceted glass windows, Paradise Valley Mall, Paradise Valley, Ariz; residential installation: leaded glass window & light fixtures, Logan Van Sittert residence, Phoenix; and many others. *Pos:* Apprentice designer-craftsman, Glassart Studio, Scottsdale, Ariz, 64-69; independent artist-designer, Phoenix, 69-. *Awards:* Honor Awards, Nat Conf Relig Archit, 68 & Interfaith Forum Relig, Art & Archit, 79. *Bibliog:* Ann Patterson (auth), Stained glass: The art, Ariz Repub, 9/30/79. *Mem:* Stained Glass Asn Am; Interfaith Forum Relig, Archit & Arts; Am Craft Coun; Ariz Stained Glass Asn. *Media:* Leaded and Faceted Stained Glass; Mosaics in Glass. *Publ:* Auth-illusr, The case for the independent designer, Stained Glass Quart, 4/80. *Mailing Add:* 924 Bethany Home Rd E Phoenix AZ 85014-2147

MCGUIRE, RAYMOND J
PATRON
Study: Harvard Univ, AB, MBA, JD. *Pos:* Co-Head Global Investment Banking Citigroup, Inc; Managing dir, mergers & acquisitions group, First Boston Corp, Wasserstein Perella & Co Inc, Merrill Lynch, Morgan Stanley; trustee, Int Ctr Photog; trustee, Whitney Mus Am Art, mem investment comt; trustee, NY Presbyterian Hosp; chmn bd dir, Studio Mus; trustee, Lincoln Ctr; trustee NY Pub Libr, chmn bd, De La Salle Acad. *Mailing Add:* Citigroup 388 Greenwich St New York NY 10013

MCHAM, SARAH BLAKE WILK
HISTORIAN, EDUCATOR
b Boston, Mass. *Study:* Inst d'Art et Archéologie, Paris, France, 65-66; Smith Col, BA, 66; Inst Fine Arts, New York Univ, PhD, 77. *Teaching:* Asst prof art hist, Rutgers Univ, 78-84, assoc prof, 84-86, chmn, 86-90, prof, 92- & chmn, 96-99. *Awards:* Am Philoso Soc Grant, 81, 86 & 2000-01; Am Coun Learnd Soc, 84; Gladys Krieble Delmas Grant, 81, 2000 & Publ Subvention Grant, 93. *Mem:* Col Art Asn; Renaissance Soc Am; Ital Art Soc. *Res:* Italian Renaissance sculpture and painting. *Publ:* Donatello's tomb of Pope John XXIII, In: Life and Death in 15th Century Florence, Duke Univ Press, 89; The Chapel of St Anthony in Padua and the Development of Venetian Renaissance Sculpture, Cambridge Univ Press, 93; Looking at Italian Renaissance Sculpture, Cambridge Univ Press, 98, 2d ed, 2000; Donatello's bronze David and Judith as Metphors of Medici Rule in Florence, Art Bull, vol 83, 2001; The Role of Pliny's Natural History inthe Sixteenth-Century Redecoration of the Piazza San Marco, Diverse Approaches to the Representation of Classical Mythology in Art, Ikonographioche Repertorien zur Rezeption des antiken Mythos in Europa, III, 1, 2001; La scultura esterna di Santa Maria dei Miracoli, S Maria dei Miracoli, Istituto Veneto, 2002; and others. *Mailing Add:* Dept Art Hist Voorhees Hall Rutgers Univ 71 Hamilton St New Brunswick NJ 08901-1248

MCILVAIN, DOUGLAS LEE
EDUCATOR, SCULPTOR
b Mt Holly, NJ, July 26, 23. *Study:* Tyler Sch Fine Arts, Temple Univ, BFA & BS, Tyler Sch Fine Arts Rome; New York Univ, MA(art educ); also with Raphael Sabatini, Jose De Creeft & Bruno Lucchesi. *Work:* Monmouth Col; Merrill Lynch, Princeton, NJ; Tyler Sch Fine Arts Rome; Stanford, Conn Forum; Georvgin Ct Col. *Comn:* Four portraits, Health Hall of Fame, 80; Bell Tel Labs, 82; Portrait, Roosevelt Hosp, 89; Statue for ARC, NJ, 91; portrait, Mahatma Gandhi, 94; and others. *Exhib:* Pa Acad Art, 60; Morris Mus, NJ, 82; Art Expo, NY, 83; Monmouth Mus, NJ, 85-88, 92 & 94; Phoenix Gallery, NY, 92; Guild Creative Arts, 92; Lever House, NY, 95; and others. *Pos:* Art designer, Monmouth Mus, 78-79. *Teaching:* Assoc prof art, Georgian Ct Col, 68-86; instr sculpture, Longboat Key, Fla, 98-2000. *Awards:* First Prize, Jersey City Mus, 61; First Prize, Red Bank Festival Arts, 61-62, 64-65, 67, 69-71 & 73; First Prize, Guild of Creative Arts, 89; Best of Show Award, Longboat Key, Fla, 2000. *Mem:* Sculpture Asn NJ, vpres; Guild Creative Arts; Art Alliance; Am Asn Univ Prof; Int Sculpture Ctr. *Media:* Bronze, Wood

MCILVAIN, FRANCES H
PAINTER; INSTRUCTOR
b Newark, NJ, May 11, 25. *Study:* Tyler Sch Art, Temple Univ, BFA & BS, 47, Temple Univ Rome, with Charles LaClair, 65; Phildalephia Mus Sch Art, with W Emerton Heitland, 48; with Mario Cooper, 75, Nicholas Reale, 80, Marilyn H Phyllis, 89 & Louise Cadillac, 98. *Work:* Temple Univ, Philadelphia, Pa; Bell Laboratories, Holmdel, NJ; Continental Group Computer Hq, Conn; Firmenich Corp, Princeton, NJ; Nabisco Brands, E Hanover, NJ; Off of Senator John O Bennett, Majority Leader, State House, Trenton, NJ, 94-98. *Comn:* Mural of Noah's Ark, First Presbyterian Church, Red Bank, NJ, 60; paintings, Atchison Sch, Tinton Falls, NJ, 70 & 81; mural, Monmouth Mus, Lincroft, NJ, 80. *Exhib:* Garden State Watercolor Soc, Princeton, NJ, 81-2000; Art Expo, NY, 83; Ann Open Show, NJ Watercolor Soc, 85, 88-93, 88-89; Philadelphia Watercolor Soc, 94; Georgian Ct Univ, Lakewood, NJ, 2003; Longboat Roy Art Ctr State Show, 2003-06. *Pos:* Halsted & Van Vechten/Advert, 52-58. *Teaching:* Instr art, Rancocas Valley Regional High Sch, Mt Holly, NJ, 47-53; instr art, Tinton Falls Sch, NJ, 63-83, SCAN Learning Ctr, Eatmtnunor, NJ, 2003-06. *Awards:* Monmouth Arts First Prize, 83, Second Prize, 85; Best in Show, 88; Excellence Award, Garden State Watercolor, 93; Garden State 2000 Best in Show; Third Prize, Guild of Creative Arts, Shrewsbury, NJ, 2005; First Prize, Longboat Roy Art Ctr, Fla, 2005 & 06. *Bibliog:* Watercolors in a Weekend, Godsfield Press; Hazel Harrison (auth), Watercolores in a Weekend, David and Charles Publishers, London, 2000. *Mem:* Guild Creative Arts, (bd mem, 75-98); Am Watercolor Soc; NJ Watercolor Soc (1st vpres, 79-86, pres, 92-94); Garden State Watercolor Soc; Soc Experimental Artists. *Media:* Acrylic, Oil; All Media. *Publ:* Auth, Splash 3, North Light Books; Best of Watercolors, Rockport Press. *Mailing Add:* Sandy Cove Apt 612 Tinton Falls NJ 07753

MCILVANE, EDWARD JAMES
STAINED GLASS ARTIST, GLASSBLOWER
b New York, NY, July 5, 47. *Study:* St John's Univ, New York, BS(Art Educ), 75, RI Sch Design with Dale Chihuly & James Carpenter, MFA(Glass), 78. *Work:* Pilchuck Sch, Stanwood, Wash; Patrick Lannon Found, Palm Beach, Fla. *Comn:* Lobby windows, Temple Beth-El, Providence, RI, 82; chapel windows, Good Shepherd of Hills, Cave Creek, Ariz, 84; exec off windows, Bank of Boston, Mass, 85; two leaded glass skylight windows, Ctr Law & Soc, Stonehill Col, N Easton, Mass, 90; Lobby windows, Presby World Hq, Louisville, Ky, 92. *Exhib:* Young Americans in Clay & Glass, Mus Contemp Crafts, NY, 78; Das Bild in Glas (with catalog), Hessiches Landsmuseum, Darmstadt, W Ger, 79; Art in Craft Media: The Haystack Tradition, traveling exhib, 81; 3-Dimensions, Univ Tex, El Paso, 85; A History of Excellence, Newport Art Mus, RI, 87. *Teaching:* Instr stained glass, Haystack Mountain Sch Crafts, 77 & RI Sch Design, 78-; prog coordr, stained glass, Pilchuck Sch, 78. *Awards:* Crafts Fel, 80 & Design Fel, 86, RI State Coun Arts; Visual Artists Fel, Nat Endowment Arts, 83. *Bibliog:* K & F Breydert (auths), Ars Pro Deo, SMI, Paris, 86; Kemp & Perron (auths), Architectural Ornamentalism, Whitney Libr Design, 87. *Mem:* Am Crafts Coun. *Media:* Stained Glass. *Publ:* Contribr, artist's statement, In: Art in Craft Media, Bowdoin Col Press, 81; auth, New perspectives on glass in architecture, Glass Art Soc J, 87. *Mailing Add:* 329 Pomfret Rd Brooklyn CT 06234

MCINERNEY, GENE JOSEPH
PAINTER
b Easton, Pa, Jan 6, 30. *Work:* Miniature Art Soc NJ, Nutley; Fred Clark Mus, Carversville, Pa; Meadowbrook Sch, Philadelphia, Pa. *Comn:* Bicentennial Calendar, Northampton Co, Pa, Bicentennial Comn, 75. *Exhib:* Miniature Painters, Sculptors & Gravers Soc, Washington DC Arts Club, 72 & 73; Nat Soc Painters in Casein & Acrylic, NY, 72-75 & 98-2002; Mainstreams Int, Marietta, Ohio, 72 & 73; Butler Inst Am Art, Youngstown, Ohio, 84, 85 & 86; 20th Century Realism, Philip Desind Collection, Southbend Mus, 94. *Pos:* Adv panel, Winsor & Newton Artists, 93-95. *Awards:* Mainstreams Award of Excellence, Marietta Col, 72; Don Selchow Award, Northeast Watercolor Soc, 95; Howard Mandell Award, Nat Soc Painters in Casein & Acrylic, 2002. *Bibliog:* Art, Gene McInerney, La Rev Mod, 11/72. *Mem:* Nat Soc Painters in Casein & Acrylic. *Media:* Acrylic, Watercolor, Oil. *Publ:* Taking Advantage of Acrylics, Watercolor, An Am Artist Publ, fall 91; Maximum Impact, The Artist's Mag, May 99; Reproductions of Oil & Acrylic Paintings, Bruce Mcgaw Graphics, 2003; The Delicate Engineer, Am Artist, 10/2006. *Dealer:* Uptown Gallery 1194 Madison Ave New York NY 10128. *Mailing Add:* Gene McInerney Studio 315 Brodt Rd Bangor PA 18013-9236

MCINERNEY, SALLY LAIRD
SCULPTOR
Study: Pa Acad Fine Arts; Univ Pa, BFA (sculpture), 72. *Work:* The Noyes Mus Art; Art Mus Southern NJ. *Pos:* Sculpturer, Logan Clay Product Factory, 90-. *Media:* Wood, Metal, Stone and Clay. *Dealer:* Art Museum Southern NJ Lily Lake Rd Oceanville NJ 08231

MCINTOSH, GREGORY STEPHEN
PAINTER
b Ojai, Calif, May 7, 46. *Study:* Santa Clara Univ, BA, 68 & MA, 71. *Work:* Libr Cong, Washington, DC; Muskegon Mus Art, Mich; Calif Palace Legion Hon & San Francisco Mus Mod Art; Los Angeles Co Mus Art, Arco Ctr Arts, Calif Confed Arts & Cedar Sinai Med Ctr; Oakland Mus, Calif. *Comn:* Jazz at Ojai, Commemorative Fine Art Posters, 81 & 82; mural, US Post Off, 83; US Olympic Comt fine art commem poster, 84. *Exhib:* Solo exhibs, Ojai Art Ctr Gallery, Calif, 88, Park Gallery, Ft Lauderdale, Fla, 88, Jewish Community Ctr, Cleveland Heights, Ohio, 89, Waterstreet Gallery, Mystic, Conn, 89, Springfield Art Asn, Ill, 89 & Bernard's Township Libr, Basking Ridge, NJ, 89; Boca Raton Mus Art Festival, Fla, 88, 90, 91, 92, 96 & 97; Artist Show, Novometro Gallery, Cleveland, Ohio, 90; Miami Beach Festival Art, Fla,

91, 92, 97 & 98; Calif Gold Coast Watercolor Soc Ann Competition, Ojai Ctr Arts, 92; Art & Healing, Lipsett Gallery, Nat Ins Health, Bethesda, Md, 92; Oakbrook Ctr Invitational, Ill, 96 & 98; Old Orchard Invitational, Skokie, Ill, 96 & 98; Dreams & Visions, Ojai Ctr Arts, Calif, 96 & 97; Talking to the Creator, Appleton Art Ctr, Wis, 96; N Shore Art League Nat, North Brook, Ill, 97; Key Biscayne Art Festival, Fla, 97; Fort Lauderdale Mus Art Festival, Fla, 97 & 98; Arti-Gras 97, North Palm Beaches Fine Arts Bd, Fla, 97 & 98; The Big Little Show, Ojai Ctr Arts, Calif, 98; Open Spaces: The Ojai Landscape, Ojai Ctr Arts, Calif, 98; The Art of Healing Exhib, Lipsett Gallery, Nat Inst Health, Washington, 98; Ladislaus Gallery, Palm Desert, Calif, 2003. *Collection Arranged:* Calif Arts Coun; Aurora Pub Arts Commn, Ill; City of Miami Beach, Fine Art Commn, Fla; Ventura Co Historical Mus, Venice, Calif; Univ Art Mus, Univ Calif. *Teaching:* asst prof, ret. *Awards:* Various awards, City of Miami Beach Fest Art, Fla, 91, 92, 97 & 98; Drawing Award, 97 & Cur Award Recognition, 98, Ft Lauderdale Mus Fest Art, Fla; First Place Award, Ojai Ctr Arts, Calif & Miami Beach Fine Arts Bd, Fla, 98; First Place Award in Drawing, Scottsdale Ctr for Arts, Ariz, 2002; and many others; Comt Award, Hyde Park Art Exhib, Chgo, 2002. *Bibliog:* McIntosh sky scapes will be displayed at Maturango Museum during March, Daily Independent, 3/87; Beate Bermann-Enn (auth), In Search of Landscape Lost, Art Scene vol 8 no 4, 12/88; Best Pastel, Rockport Publ, Mass, 96. *Mem:* Pastel Soc Am (full mem, 90). *Media:* Gouache & Pastel on Paper, Oil on canvas. *Dealer:* Anca Colbert Fine Art Ltd. *Mailing Add:* PO Box 961 Ojai CA 93024

MCINTOSH, JERRY C
EDUCATOR, ADMINISTRATOR
b Kingstree, SC, Nov 4, 48. *Study:* Radford Univ, BS, 74, 75; Fla State Univ, PhD, 80. *Work:* Flossie Martin Gallery, Radford, Va; Elizabeth City State Univ Gallery, NC. *Pos:* Chair art, Elizabeth City State Univ, 78-. *Teaching:* Prof art, Elizabeth City State Univ, 78-. *Mem:* Nat Art Educ Asn; Nat Asn Schs Art & Design. *Res:* Multicultural art education; ancient art history, especially non-western. *Mailing Add:* Dept Art Elizabeth City State Univ ECSU Box 981 ECSU Sta 1704 Weeksville Rd Elizabeth City NC 27909

MCKAY, RENEE
PAINTER
b Montreal, Que; US citizen. *Study:* Inst Pedagogique, Montreal; McGill Univ, Montreal, BA, 41; studied with Ben Shahn, Morris Davidson & Joe Jones. *Work:* Slater Mem Mus, Norwich, Conn; Norfolk Mus, Va; Butler Inst Am Art, Youngstown, Ohio; Lydia Drake Libr, Pembroke, Mass. *Exhib:* Open Ann, Newark & Montclair, NJ; Nat Asn Women Artists Traveling Show, Butler Inst Am Art, Youngstown, Ohio; Nat Asn Women Artists Ann & Audubon Ann, Nat Acad Galleries, NY; Nat Asn Women Artists, Lever House & Union Carbide, NY; Weyhe Gallery, NY, 79. *Teaching:* Instr art, Peck Sch, Morristown, NJ, 55-57. *Awards:* Watercolor Award, 75 & Oil Award, 80, Audubon Artists; Acrylic Award, Nat Soc Painters Casein & Acrylic, 83; and others. *Mem:* Audubon Artists (pres, 79-80); Artists Equity Asn (vpres, 79-81); Nat Asn Women Artists (adv bd, 74-76); Nat Soc Painters Casein & Acrylic; Nat Arts Club; and others. *Media:* Acrylic, Watercolor. *Mailing Add:* 401 E 80th St Apt 22F New York NY 10021

MCKEE, DAVID MALCOLM
ART DEALER
b Cumbria, Eng, Oct, 8, 37. *Pos:* Dir, David McKee Gallery, currently. *Mem:* Art Dealers Asn Am. *Specialty:* Postwar and contemporary painting and sculpture, mainly American, including Philip Guston, Jake Berthot, Harvey Quaytman, Sean Scully & William Tucker. *Mailing Add:* McKee Gallery 745 Fifth Ave New York NY 10151

MCKEE, RENEE CONFORTE
DEALER
b Belgrade, Yugoslavia; US citizen. *Study:* Mt Holyoke Col, BA(magna cum laude); Univ Paris I, Sorbonne; Ecole du Louvre, Paris. *Pos:* Admin asst, Marlborough Gallery, New York, 68-72; dir & co-owner, David McKee Gallery, New York, 74-. *Specialty:* Contemporary American art. *Mailing Add:* c/o McKee Gallery 745 Fifth Ave 4th Fl New York NY 10151

MCKENNA, GEORGE LAVERNE
CURATOR
b Detroit, Mich, Dec 7, 24. *Study:* Univ Ore, 43-44; Univ Calif, 48-49; Univ Chicago, 50; Wayne State Univ, Mich, AB, 48, MA, 51. *Collection Arranged:* Repeated Exposure: Photographic Imagery in the Print Media (auth, catalog), 82; Posters and Modern Color Prints, 85; Expressionism in the Graphic Arts, 85; Art by Chance: Fortuitous Impressions (auth, catalog), 89. *Pos:* Registrar, Nelson-Atkins Mus Art, 52-82, cur prints & photogs, 60-96, cur drawings, 85-96, consult, prints, drawings & photogs, 97-. *Mem:* Print Coun Am; Am Asn Mus. *Publ:* Auth, 24 spec exhib brochures, 82-96, ed, Calendar of Events, 53-82 & co-ed, Handbook of Collections, 5th ed, 73, Nelson-Atkins Mus; The Collections of the Nelson-Atkins Museum: Prints, 1460-1995, 96. *Mailing Add:* Nelson-Atkins Mus Art 4525 Oak St Kansas City MO 64111-1873

MCKENZIE, ALLAN DEAN
EDUCATOR, HISTORIAN
b Pendleton, Ore, Aug 17, 30. *Study:* San Jose State Univ, BA(com art), 52; Univ Calif, Berkeley, MA(art hist), 55; Inst Fine Arts, NY Univ, PhD(art hist; Fulbright Scholar), 65. *Teaching:* Instr medieval art, NY Univ, 57-64; asst prof medieval & classical art, Univ Wis, Milwaukee, 64-66; assoc prof medieval art, Univ Ore, 66-74, prof, 74-90, emer prof, 90-. *Awards:* Consultation Grant, Icon Preservation Task Force, State Alaska & US Park Serv, 89; First Recipient of Earl L Hain Award for Distinguished Serv to Learning in Retirement (LIR) Prog, Univ Ore, 94; Outstanding Contributions to Learning in Retirement, 95. *Mem:* Col Art Asn, 57-86; Archeol Inst Am (Eugene Chap pres & secy, formerly); Int Ctr Medieval Art; Medieval Acad Am, 75-82; Am Asn Advan Slavic Studies. *Res:* Russian and Byzantine painting; Medieval art. *Publ:* Auth, Greek & Russian Icons, Northwest, 65; Russian Art: Old and New, Univ Ore, 68; Provincial Byzantine painting in Attica, Cahiers Arch, 82; Russian Icons in the Santa Barbara Museum of Art, 82; Mystical Mirrors, Icons of Russia, Maryhill Mus Art, 86; Sacred Images & The Millennium; Christianity & Russia (AD 988-1988), 88. *Mailing Add:* Univ Ore Dept Art Hist Eugene OR 97403

MCKENZIE, MARY BETH
PAINTER
b Cleveland, Ohio, July 30, 46. *Study:* Mus Fine Arts, Boston, 64-65; Cooper Sch Art, 65-67; Nat Acad Design, 69-74. *Work:* Hesse Collection; Danish Bank, Mus of City of NY, Metrop Mus, NY; Butler Inst Am Art, Youngstown, Ohio; Nat Mus Women in Arts, Nat Mus Am Art, Smithsonian Inst, Washington, DC; NY Hist Soc. *Exhib:* Solo exhibs, Nat Arts Club, 76 & FAR Gallery, 80, NY; Frank Caro Gallery, NY, 88; Joseph Keiffer Gallery, 91; Union Co Col, NJ, 98. *Teaching:* Instr painting, Nat Acad Design, 81-; Art Students League, NY, 96-. *Awards:* Greenshields Found Grant & Stacey Found Grant, 78; Thomas B Clarke Prize, Nat Acad Design Ann, 81; Isaac N Maynard Prize, Nat Acad Design, 90 & 97. *Bibliog:* Harvey Stein (auth), Artists Observed, Harry Abrams, 86. *Mem:* Nat Acad; Allied Artists; Audubon Artists; Pastel Soc Am. *Media:* Oil. *Interests:* theater, literaure. *Publ:* Auth, A Painterly Approach, Watson-Guptil, NY, 87. *Mailing Add:* 525 W 45th St Apt 3 New York NY 10036-3415

MCKIE, TODD STODDARD
PAINTER
b Boston, Mass, Apr 25, 44. *Study:* RI Sch Design, BFA(painting), 66. *Work:* Philip Morris, USA; Mass Inst Technol; Fogg Mus, Cambridge, Mass; Lincoln Ctr for the Performing Arts & Chase Manhattan Bank; Mus Fine Arts & Wellington Mgt Co, Boston, Mass. *Comn:* Mural (90ft x 40ft), City of Boston, 72; mural (7' x 60'), Mass Bay Transportation Authority, 96. *Exhib:* Eat Art, Contemp Art Ctr, Cincinnati, Ohio, 72; Boston Collects Boston, Mus Fine Arts, 73; Works on Paper, Fogg Art Mus, Harvard Univ, Cambridge, Mass, 74; Biennial Exhib, Whitney Mus Am Art, NY, 75; Painted in Boston, Inst Contemp Art, 75; Boston Watercolor Today, Mus Fine Arts, Boston, 76; Collectors Collect Contemp, Inst Contemp Art, Boston, 77; Rose Art Mus, Brandeis Univ, 90. *Awards:* Colman Award, Blanche E Colman Found, 72; Creative Artists Fel, Mass Arts & Humanities Found, 74 & 89. *Bibliog:* Carl Belz (auth), The grid and the buffet, Art Am, 3/72; David Greenberg (auth), Big art, Running Press, Philadelphia, 77. *Media:* Oil, Ceramics. *Dealer:* Gallery Naga 67 Newbury St Boston MA 02116; Victoria Munroe Fine Art 59 Beacon St Boston MA 02108. *Mailing Add:* 82 Holworthy St Cambridge MA 02138-4510

MCKIM, GEORGE EDWARD
PAINTER, GRAPHIC ARTIST
b Wilmington, NC. *Study:* Va Commonwealth Univ, BFA, 77; E Carolina Univ, MFA, 85; Skowhegan Sch Painting & Sculpture, study with Bell Jensen, Judy Pfaff, Peter Saul & Judith Shea. *Exhib:* NC Artist Triennial, NC Mus Art, 84, 87, 90, 93 & 96; Tampa Triennial, Tampa Mus Art, 85. *Media:* Acrylic, Oil on Canvas. *Publ:* Contribr, New American Paintings, Open Studio Press, 98. *Dealer:* Lee Hansley Gallery 16 W Martin St Suite 201 Raleigh NC 27601. *Mailing Add:* 2720 Wayland Dr Raleigh NC 27608

MCKINLEY-HAAS, MARY
PAINTER, DESIGNER
b St Louis, Mo. *Study:* Smith Col, BA; Studio & Forum Stage Design; Nat Acad Design: Art Students League with Norman Lewis. *Work:* Fontbonne Col, St Louis; Nat Mus Women Arts, Washington, DC; Northern Trust, Naples, Fla; Tari Women's Cult Ctr, New Guinea; Leon Templesman & Son, NY. *Exhib:* Solo exhibs, Tarlowe Gallery, Westhampton Beach, NY, 74, Fontbonne Gallery, St Louis, Mo, 77, Gallery Yssa (Ludlow-Hyland), NY, 79, Vered Gallery, East Hampton, NY, 81, The Neth Bankt Ludlow-Hyland Gallery, New York City, 81, Univ Tex, Austin, 88 & 92, RVS Fine Art, Southampton, NY, 90, TSS Gallery, NY, 92 & TAI Gallery, NY, 99; Design 70, Contemp Stage Design USA, Lincoln Ctr, NY, 74; Parish Art Mus, Southampton, NY, 75, 76, 78 & 81; Guild Hall, East Hampton, NY, 76, 78, 81, 85 & 96; Medeci-Berenson Gallery, Miami, Fla, 81; Water Mill Mus, Water Mill, NY, 83 & 92; Five Hampton Painters, Vered Gallery, East Hampton, NY, 85; Nabisco Brands Gallery, East Hanover, NJ, 89; Queens Col Art Ctr, NY, 91; Art by Design, Dorothy Chandler Pavillion, Los Angeles, 93; Stony Brook Univ Art Gallery, NY, 94; Elite Gallery, Moscow, Russ, 95; Nat Mus Women Arts, Washington, DC, 96; Soho 20 Gallery, NY, 98; Canajoharie Lib Art Ctr, Canajoharie, NY, 2000; Weill Cornell Med Libr, NY, 2002; Noho NY Art Walk, 2004-2005; Venezuelan Consulate 2006. *Pos:* Head, Costume Design Dept, ABC-TV, NY, 68-73; costume designer, CBS-TV, NY, 75-77. *Bibliog:* Helen Thomas (auth), Arts Reviews (review with black & white reproduction), Arts Mag, 9/79; Phyllis Braff (auth), From the Studio (review with black & white reproduction), East Hampton Star, 8/20/81; Jose Alaniz (auth), Nature's Growth through a Kaleidoscope (article with black & white reproduction), Daily Texan, 10/26/92; Scott Dietsch (auth) The Beauty and Danger of Lava on Exhibit, The Villager, 4/28/99; Art Pick, New York Post, 4/28/99; and several others. *Mem:* United Scenic Artists; Women Arts Found; NY Artists' Equity. *Media:* Oil, Mixed Media; Monotype. *Publ:* Auth, Designing Shadows, In: Dark Shadows Almanac (bk), Promegranate Press, 95. *Dealer:* Ezair Gallery 905 Madison Ave New York NY 10021. *Mailing Add:* 284 Lafayette St Loft 5B New York NY 10012

MCKINNEY, TATIANA LADYGINA
PAINTER, INSTRUCTOR
b Smolensk, Russia, 1909; US citizen. *Study:* Acad Vinogradov, Riga, Latvia, cert, 30; Escola Nacional de Belas Artes, Brazil, 45-48; New Col Fine Arts Inst, Sarasota, Fla, with Balcomb Greene, James Brook & Marca Relli, cert, 67. *Work:* Dartmouth Col, Hanover, NH; The Apostolic Delegation, Washington, DC; The Vatican Collection;

New Col Art Gallery & Fine Arts Soc, Van Wezel Hall, Sarasota, Fla; Holy Spirit Church, Venice, Fla, 90-93; painted mural hangings, Bishop Nevens, Venice, Fla, 97-2003; Appleton Mus, Ocala, Fla, 2003. *Comn:* Painted altar hanging, Chapel, St Francis Seminary, Milwaukee, Wis; painted mural hanging, comn by Archdiocese of Washington, DC and presented to Pope John Paul II; painted mural hanging, comn by Bishop Nevins, Venice, Fla; painted mural hanging, St Martha's Church, Sarasota, Fla; fixed panels, St Patrick's Church, Washington, 93-98. *Exhib:* Salão Nac Belas Artes, Mus Nac, Rio de Janeiro, Brazil, 55; Fla Arts Invitational, Cummer Gallery Art, Jacksonville, 66; Four Arts National Exhibit, Four Arts Soc, West Palm Beach, Fla, 66; Fla Arts Invitational, Lowe Art Mus, Univ Miami, Coral Gables, Fla, 68; XIII Salon Int, Mus d'Art Contemp, Clermont-Ferrand, France, 81; IXX Salon Int VF ACS, Palais des Beaux Arts, Charleroi, Belg, 86; Cyipros & Totaumtue, 92; Pioneers Show in Visual Arts, Sarasota, Fla, 98; Notable Venetians Gallery, Venice Art Ctr, Fla, 98; Oldtimers Invitational, Venice Art Ctr, 2002; plus others. *Teaching:* prog dir, Venice Area Art League, Fla, 68-71, instr art & painting, 68-; Instr, Paul VI Inst, Washington, 81-83 & St Boniface Acad, Siesta Key, Fla, 83-85; instr painting mountains, Burnsville, NC, 83-; panelist, New Col, Sarasota, Fla, 84; lectr, juror, Southwest Fla, 65-. *Awards:* Bronze Medal, Salão Nac Belas Artes, Mus Nac, Rio de Janeiro, Brazil, 55; Best of Show, Arts Coun Southwest Fla, Edison Col, 70; Capo D'Oro, Int Competition, Le Quartier Arts. *Bibliog:* Article, Tatiana McKinney at Interchurch, About Town Column, New Yorker Mag, 7/24/79; Father Thomas F Fait, Painting to be exhibited, Catholic Standard, 11/11/82; Monseignor Michael Farina, Tatiana McKinney, 11/82 & Tatiana McKinney does it again, 85, Paul VI Inst Lett. *Mem:* Artists Equity; Fla Artists Group; Venice Area Art League (vpres, bd mem, 65-70); Sarasota Fine Arts Coun (bd mem, 66-72); Nat Asn Am Pen Women. *Media:* Watercolor, Oil; Metal leaf. *Dealer:* Paul VI Inst Arts Washington DC 20036. *Mailing Add:* 8695 SW 205 Circle Dunnellon FL 34431

MCKINNICK, MARGARET I
PAINTER, PRINTMAKER
b Marlboro, Mass, Feb 2, 24. *Study:* Silvermine Guild Sch Art; lithography with Hiroshima Morimoto, Westbeth Workshop, NY. *Work:* Town Hall, Westport, Conn; City Hall & Norwalk Community Col, Norwalk, Conn; Gen Elec Co, Fairfield, Conn; Silvermine Ctr Arts; Dorems & Co, NY. *Comn:* Etching, Friends Silvermine Ctr Arts, 80. *Exhib:* One-man shows, Vassos Gallery, Silvermine Guild Calleries, New Canaan, Conn, 82 & 86, Art Place Gallery, Southport, 83 & 85, Fairfield Pub Libr, 84, Conn Gallery, Marlborough, 90 & Cast Iron Gallery, NY, 91-92; Hampshire Col Gallery, Amherst, Mass, 81; Works on Paper, Adelphi Univ, Garden City, Long Island, 81; New Eng Watercolor Soc Exhib, Mus of Art, Sci & Indus, Bridgeport, 82 & 89; Trustee's Choice, Aldrich Mus, 83; In the Family, Lyman Allyn Mus, New London, 84; Adelphi Univ Manhattan Ctr, NY, 90. *Teaching:* Instr art, Mus Mod Art, New York, 65-69, Calhoun Sch, New York, 70-75 & Sacred Heart Univ, 81-84. *Awards:* Print Award, Berkshire Mus, Pittsfield, Mass, 81. *Bibliog:* Russell Jinishian (auth), Artist lays it on the line, Bridgeport Sunday Post, 9/25/83. *Mem:* Silvermine Guild Ctr Arts (mem bd trustees, 78-81); Westport-Weston Coun Arts; Art Place, Southport, Conn. *Media:* Acrylic, Oil; Etching

MCKNIGHT, THOMAS FREDERICK
PAINTER, PRINTMAKER
b Lawrence, Kans, Jan 13, 41. *Study:* Wesleyan Univ, Middletown, Conn, BA(art); Columbia Univ. *Work:* Davison Art Ctr, Wesleyan Univ; NY State Mus, Albany; Smithsonian Inst, Wash; Metrop Mus Art, NY; White House, Wash; Clinton Libr, Little Rock, Ark. *Comn:* Poster & print, US Constitution Bicentennial, 89; prints, America's Cup, 92; paintings & prints, Urban Fair, Kobe, Japan, 93; White House Christmas card, Pres & Mrs Clinton, 94, 95 & 96. *Exhib:* One-man shows, Basel Art Fair, 75-77, Tomic Galerie, Dusseldorf, Ger, 76, Hartmann Gallery, Munich, Ger, 77 & Newport Art Asn, RI, 81; Seibu, Tokyo, Japan, 89; Davison Art Ctr, Weslyan Univ, 88; Kobe Munic Mus, Japan, 92; and many others. *Teaching:* Lectr, Crystal Cruise Lines. *Awards:* Distinguished Alumnus Award, Wesleyan Univ, 98. *Bibliog:* Thomas McKnight: Windows on Paradise, Abbeville Press, NY, 90; Annie Gottlieb (auth), Thomas McKnight: Voyage to Paradise A Visual Odyssey, Harper, San Francisco & Treville, Tokyo, 93; Francesco Colonna (auth), Thomas McKnight's Avoadia, Vendome Press, NY, 2006. *Media:* Casein; Serigraphy; Acrylics. *Interests:* Alchemy, neo-platonism, archety pal psychology, Venice and Greece. *Publ:* auth, Thomas McKnight, Scribners, 84. *Dealer:* Thomas McKnight LLC 30 Peck Rd Suite 2201 Torrington CT 06790; Polia Press 29 West St Litchfield CT 06759. *Mailing Add:* PO Box 98 Litchfield CT 06759

MCKOY, VICTOR GRAINGER
SCULPTOR
b Fayetteville, NC, Apr 21, 47. *Study:* Clemson Univ, BS(biology), 70, Sch Archit, two years. *Work:* Charleston Mus, SC; Ward Found Mus, Salisbury State Col, Md; Gibbes Art Gallery, Charleston, SC; Sanderling Inn, Duck, NC; Dover Corp, NY. *Exhib:* Birds of the Wood, Am Mus Nat Hist, 74; Expressions of Nature in Art, Greenville Mus Art, SC, 75 & Columbia Mus Art, SC, 75; Bird Sculpture Birmingham Mus Art, Ala, 76; One-man shows, Hammer Galleries, NY, 76, Gibbes Art Gallery, SC, 84, Coe Kerr Gallery, NY, 84, Brandywine River Mus, Chaddsford, Pa, 93 & Brook Green Gardens, 99; The Artist and the Animal, High Mus Art, Atlanta, Ga, 77; Wild Am, Kodak Gallery, NY, 78; Birds in Art, Leigh Yawkey Woodson Art Mus, 85. *Bibliog:* Margaret Pridgen (auth), When Wooden Birds Take Wing, Clemson World, fall 90; James Kilgo (auth), The Birds of Grainger McKoy, Georgia Rev, spring 93; Edward Sozanski (auth), The Real McKoy, Philadelphia Inquirer Mag, 7/23/93; James Kilgo (auth), The Sculpture of Grainger McKoy, Wyrick & Co, 99. *Media:* Wood, Bronze, Sterling. *Mailing Add:* 490 North Kings Hwy Sumter SC 29154-8655

MCLAUGHLIN, JEAN WALLACE
ADMINISTRATOR, CONSULTANT
b Charlotte, NC, Dec 19, 50. *Study:* Univ NC, Chapel Hill with George Kagergis, BA, 72, Calif Col Arts & Crafts, with Lia Cook, 83-85, Penland Sch with Diane Itter, 86, NC State Univ, MA(lib studies), 94. *Exhib:* Subtext, NC Mus Art, Raleigh, 89. *Pos:* Art educr, Charlotte Latin Sch, NC, 73-75; prog dir, Arts & Handicapped Prog, NC Dept Admin, 78-79; educ spec, NC Mus Art, Raleigh, 78; contrib ed, Sculptor's Int, 82-85; dir, Penland Sch Crafts, 98-. *Mem:* Am Crafts Coun; Nat Campaign Freedom Expression; NC Arts Advocates; Nat Asn Artists Orgn; Am Asn Mus. *Publ:* Auth, Art in the Churches & Synagogues of NC, NC Dept Cult Resources, 76; interview with Magdalena Abakanowicz & Understanding in contemporary craft movement, interview with Carl Djerassi, Sculpture Mag, 85; ed, New Works: A Public Art Project Planning Guide (Patricia Fuller, auth), Durham Arts Coun, 88. *Mailing Add:* Penland Sch Crafts Penland NC 28765

MCLEAN, JAMES ALBERT
EDUCATOR, PRINTMAKER
b Gibsland, La, Nov 25, 28. *Study:* Southwestern La Inst, AB, 50; Southern Methodist Univ, BD, 53; Tulane Univ, MFA with J L Steg, 61. *Work:* Seattle Mus Art, Wash; High Mus, Atlanta, Ga; Brooklyn Mus, NY; Olivet Col, Mich; Minot State Col, ND. *Exhib:* 33rd, 35th, 36th & 38th Northwest Printmakers Int, Seattle Mus, Wash, 62, 64, 65 & 67; 14th, 15th, 19th & 20th Nat Print Exhibs, Brooklyn Mus, 64, 66, 74 & 76; Nat Print & Drawing Exhibs, Minot State Col, 73-76; Colorprint, USA, Tex Tech Univ, Lubbock, 74-76; Spec Interest Group on Computer Graphics, 88; Postive/Negative Exhib, ETenn State Univ, 88; Small Print Exhib, Purdue Univ, 88; SIGGRAPH, 88, 89; Artware, Cebit, Hanover, WGer, 89. *Teaching:* Assoc prof gen art, LaGrange Col, Ga, 63-66; prof printmaking, Ga State Univ, Atlanta, 66-94. *Awards:* Purchase Award, Northwest Printmakers Int, 64, Western NMex Univ Nat Print Exhib, 73 & Minot State Col Nat Print & Drawing Exhib, 76; First prize, Glassboro State Col, 90. *Bibliog:* Illus in: Fritz Eichenberg (auth), The Art of the Print, Abrams, 76, Gene Baro (auth), 30 Years of American Printmaking, Brooklyn Mus. *Media:* Silkscreening. *Mailing Add:* 1256 Dunwoody Knoll Dr Atlanta GA 30338

MCLEAN, RICHARD
PAINTER
b Hoquiam, Wash, 34. *Study:* Calif Col of Arts & Crafts, Oakland, BFA, 58; Mills Col, Oakland, Calif, MFA; studied with Richard Diebenkorn. *Work:* Satin Doll, pvt collections, Oakland Mus, Calif; Smithsonian Inst; Whitney Mus Am Art, NY. *Exhib:* Whitney Mus Am Art, 70; Expo 70, Osaka, Japan; Documenta 5, Kassel, Ger, 72; This is Am, Aarhus Kunstmuseum, Aarhus, Denmark, 2001; Solo exhib, Valparaiso Univ, Ind, Univ Omaha, Neb. *Teaching:* instr, painting, drawing, San Francisco State Univ, 63-96. *Awards:* Nat Endowment for Arts, 85. *Media:* Acrylic, Oil, Watercolor. *Specialty:* Equine and canine subjects, landscapes. *Mailing Add:* 20530 Crow Creek Rd Hayward CA 94552

MCLEOD, CHERYL O'HALLORAN
PAINTER, INSTRUCTOR
b Nov 12, 44. *Study:* Indiana Univ, Pa, BS(art educ), 66; Boston Univ, Sch Fine Arts, 67; Mass Col Art, 83-84; studies with Daniel Greene, Albert Handel & Robert Cormier. *Work:* Delta Corp Services, Parsippany, NJ; Cogen Technol, East Brunswick, NJ; Libr Co-op Inc, Edison, NJ; Oklahoma City Allergy Clinic, Okla; Butler & Stein Attys, Tucson, Ariz; Farley & Bernathy, LLC Law Offices; plus others. *Exhib:* one-woman exhibs, Georgian Court Col, Lakewood, NJ, 94, Swain Gallery, Plainfield, NJ, 95, Barron Arts Ctr, 96, Union Co Arts Ctr, Rahway, NJ, 97, Lucca's Backroom Gallery, Metuchen, NJ, 98, Palmer Mus, Springfield, NJ, 98, Children's Specialized Hosp, Mountainside, NJ, 98, Aberjona River Gallery, Winchester, Mass, 2005; Arts Ctr Northern NJ, New Milford, 93; Winter Thoughts, Barron Arts Ctr, 93; Jersey City State Col, 93; Art Educators of New Jersey, Newark Mus, NJ, 94; Lever House Gallery, NY, 95; Exhib, Salmagundi Club, NY, 95 & 96; Catherine Lorillard Wolfe Art Club, NY, 95 & 97; Deleware Arts Alliance, Narrowsburg, NY, 2000. *Teaching:* Pvt & group instr, Studio-The Art Alcove, Wilmington, Mass & The Villages, Fla. *Awards:* HM Hulimann-Armstrong Award, Pastel Soc Am, 93; Paul Bransom Award, Grand Nat Shows, Am Artists Prof League, 93; Corp Award, Catherine Lorillard Wolfe Art Club, New York, 97; The Raymond Chow Memorial Award, Am Artist Prof League, 2003; Merit Award, Wilmington Arts Coun, 2006; and others. *Bibliog:* Constance Flavell Pratt & Janet Monafo (auths), The Best of Pastels, Rockport Publ, 96, Best of Pastels 2, 98; Landscape Inspirations (Quarry bk), Rockport Publ, 1/98. *Mem:* Pastel Soc Am; fel Am Artists Prof League; Allied Artists Am; Delta Phi Delta; signature mem, Pastel Society of America. *Media:* Pastel, Oil. *Interests:* Art educ, painting. *Publ:* The Best of Pastels 2, Rockport Pubs, 99; Landscape Inspirationa, Rockport Pubs, 88. *Dealer:* Swain Galleries 703 Watchung Ave Plainfield NJ 07060; The Art Alcove,162 Middlesex Ave., Wimington, MA 01887. *Mailing Add:* 162 Middlesex Ave Wilmington MA 01887

MCMANN, EDITH BROZAK
PAINTER - ALL MEDIA
b Totowa, NJ Mar 26, 29. *Study:* Sch Am Ballet, NY City, 1957; Art Students League, studied printmaking with Michael Ponce De Leon, NY City, 1977; State Univ of NY, studied painting with Roger Hendricks, BPA, 1984; Col of New Rochelle, NY, MA (Studio Art), 1989; George Balanchine's NYCB Westchester Art Workshop, 1976-84; Silvemine Col Art, 1989 (internship). *Work:* Nat Mus for Women in the Arts, Washington, DC; Libr & Mus for Performing Arts, Lincoln Ctr, NY; Harvard Theatre Collection, Dusey Libr, Cambridge, Mass; San Francisco Performing Arts Libr & Mus, San Francisco, Calif. *Comn:* Lawrence & Lee Theatre Research Inst, Columbus, OH; portrait, plaster sculpture, Trudy Paul, 1974; remembrance, dance sculpture,

Francesca Corkel, 1975; sectional abstract acrylic on canvas, Linda Rodregues, 1994. *Exhib:* one-man show incl: Dance in Art, Gutman Gallery, White Plains, NY, 1990; Hudson River Contemp Artists, Hammond Mus, Salem, NY, 1993; Mamaroneck Artsist 36th Juried, Westbeth Gallery, NY, 1994; Black, White, Shades of Gray, Townhouse Gallery, Stamford, Conn, 2001; Stamford Art Invitational, Tower Perrins Gallery, Stamford, Conn, 2002. *Awards:* Cert of Merit award, Dance in Art, Sen Nick Spano, 1989; Cert of Meit award, 17th annual Art Exhib, US State Assembly, Richard Brodsky, 1989; Letter of Appreciation, Green Burgh Art Exhib, US Sen Pat Moynihan, 1989-90. *Bibliog:* Articles: Reporter Dispatch, White Plains, NY, 5/73, The Enterprise, Westchester, NY, 11/89, Greenburgh Art & Culture, NY, 12/90, NYC Ballet Newsletter, NY, 3/2000. *Mem:* Mamaroneck Artist Guild, Inc (bd dir's, 1990-91); Stamford Art Asn; Allied Artists of Am, Inc; Nat Mus for Women in the Arts. *Media:* Painting, acrylic, oil, watercolors, sculpture. *Interests:* Interpreting dance into art works. *Dealer:* Wendy Porterfield Mamaroneck Artists Guild Gallery NY; Townhouse Gallery Stamford Art CT. *Mailing Add:* 10 Burkewood Rd Hartsdale NY 10530-2933

MCMANUS, JAMES WILLIAM
SCULPTOR, GALLERY DIRECTOR
b Glenwood Springs, Colo, Jan 1, 42. *Study:* Colo State Univ, BFA, 65; Univ Washington, MFA, 67. *Work:* Oakland Art Mus; San Diego Art Mus, Calif; Reading Art Ctr, Eng; Henry Art Mus, Univ Washington; 3M Corp, Chicago. *Comn:* Expo '74, Spokane, Wash; Admin Bldg, Wash State Hwy Comn, Olympia; Electro-Develop Corp, Seattle. *Exhib:* Six-man traveling exhib, Brit Art Coun, 73-75; Allrich Gallery, San Francisco, 77; Selected Works 1967-1977, de Saisset Mus, Univ Santa Clara, Calif, 77; Calif State Univ, Fresno, 77; Allrich Gallery, San Francisco, 79; Oakland Art Mus, 81. *Collection Arranged:* California Realism, 19th & 20th Century Comparison, 78; Mel Ramos, 79; Stanton Macdonald Wright, 80; Adja Yunkers, 80; Rodin's Burghers of Calais, 81; Alice Hutchins Survey, 82. *Teaching:* Teaching asst, Univ Wash, 67, instr art, 67-68; prof art & gallery dir, Calif State Univ, Chico, 68-; vis prof art, High Wycombe Col Art, Eng, 71-72. *Awards:* Fac Res Grant, Calif State Univ, Chico, 69; Fulbright-Hays Grant, Eng, 72. *Bibliog:* John Marlowe (auth), article, Current Art Mag, 6/75; James W McManus (30 min video tape), Calif State Univ, Chico, 77; Kevin Star (auth), article, San Francisco Examiner, 11/18/79; and others. *Media:* Bronze, Steel, Aluminum. *Dealer:* Allrich Gallery 251 Post St San Francisco CA 94133. *Mailing Add:* 5200 Trafalgar Sq Paradise CA 95969-6675

MCMILLAN, CONSTANCE
PAINTER, ILLUSTRATOR
Study: Bennington Col, painting with Karl Knaths & sculpture with Simon Moselsio, BA, 46; Mills Col, painting with William Gaw & ceramic sculpture with Antonio Prieto, fel, 53-55, MA, 55. *Exhib:* Slusser Gallery, Univ Mich, Ann Arbor, 80; Pindar Gallery, NY, 85; Il Mercate Galleria, Milan, Italy, 86; Galleria 9, Cologne & Spe-resta Del Carline, Bologna, Italy, 86; Solo exhibs, Cornerstone Gallery, Conn, 86-89, Atlantic Gallery, NY, 87 & Phoenix Gallery, NY, 89. *Teaching:* instr painting, design & art hist, Emma Willard Sch, Troy, NY, 52-53; instr painting & design, Angell Sch, Ann Arbor, 62-63. *Awards:* First Prize, Morris Gallery, New York, 56; Grad Fel, Mills Col, Calif. *Mem:* Ann Arbor Art Asn. *Media:* Oil, Gouache; Charcoal, Pastel. *Publ:* Illusr, Chikka, 62, Ponies for a King, 63, Reilly & Lee; illusr, Memory of a Large Christmas, Norton, 62; drawing reproduced record cover, Gateway Summer Sounds, Folkways Records, 82. *Dealer:* Phoenix Gallery 568 Broadway New York NY. *Mailing Add:* 2760 Heather Way Ann Arbor MI 48104

MCMILLAN, STEPHEN WALKER
PRINTMAKER, PHOTOGRAPHER
b Berkeley, Calif, Dec 21, 49. *Study:* Hornsey Col Art, London, Eng, 70-71; Univ Calif, Santa Cruz, AB, 72, BFA, 75. *Work:* Brooklyn Mus, NY; Achenbach Collection, San Francisco; Oakland Mus, Calif; Mem Mus, Petah-Tiqua, Israel; US Embassy, Tokyo, Japan; Portland Art Mus; Stanford Univ Libr, Palo Alto, Calif; and others. *Exhib:* 4th Int Biennial Print Exhib, Taipei Fine Arts Mus, Repub China; 21st Nat Print Exhib, Brooklyn Mus, 78; 17th Bradley Nat Print & Drawing Exhib, Lakeview Mus, Peoria, Ill, 79; 31st Ann Boston Printmakers Exhib, De Cordova Mus, Lincoln, Mass, 79; New Aquisitions, Achenbach Collection, San Francisco, 80; Prints from Kala Inst, Newcastle Art Gallery, NSW, Australia, 87. *Awards:* 4th Prize, 3rd Kochi Int Triennial Exhib Prints, Ino-cho Paper Mus, Kochi, Japan; Purchase Award, San Francisco Art Comn, 78, Davidson Gallery, Seattle, Wash, 78 & Los Angeles Printmaking Soc, 78; James D Phelan Art Award Printmaking, San Francisco Found, 95. *Mem:* Calif Soc Printmakers. *Media:* Etching, Lithograph. *Mailing Add:* 524 Joelle Heights Petaluma CA 94952

MCMILLEN, MICHAEL C(HALMERS)
ENVIRONMENTAL ARTIST, SCULPTOR
b Los Angeles, Calif, Apr 6, 46. *Study:* Calif State Univ, Northridge, BA; Univ Calif, Los Angeles, MA & MFA. *Work:* Australian Nat Gallery, Canberra; Art Gallery New South Wales, Australia; Los Angeles Co Mus Art; Oakland Mus, Calif; Guggenheim Mus, NY. *Exhib:* Eight Artists from Los Angeles, San Francisco Art Inst, Calif, 75; Sounds: Environments by Four Artists, Newport Harbor Art Mus, Newport Beach, Calif, 75; Biennial of Sydney, Art Gallery New South Wales, Australia, 76; Los Angeles in the 70s, Ft Worth Art Mus, Tex, 77; One-man shows, Inner City, Los Angeles Co Mus, Los Angeles, 77 & Whitney Mus Am Art, NY, 78; Eight Artists: The Elusive Image, Walker Art Ctr, Minneapolis, 79; Art in Los Angeles-The Mus as Site, Los Angeles Co Mus, 81; New Perspectives in Am Art: Exxon Nat Exhib, Guggenheim Mus, 83; 38th Corcoran Biennial: Exhibition of Am Painting, Corcoran Gallery Art, 83. *Teaching:* Lectr at var inst, 74-. *Awards:* travel grant, Biennale of Sydney, Australia Coun, 76; Nat Endowment Arts Fel, 78; Young Talent Award, Los Angeles Co Mus Art, 78. *Bibliog:* Melinda Wortz (auth), Inner City of the Mind, Art News, 2/78; Christopher Knight (auth), Some recent art and archit analogue, Los Angeles Inst Contemp Art J, 2/78; Christopher Knight (auth), Michael C McMillen, Arts & Archit, Fall 81. *Publ:* Auth, True confessions, Los Angeles Inst Contemp Art J, 75; contribr, Choke, Choke Publ, 76; auth, Special effects breakdown, Los Angeles Inst Contemp Art J, 77. *Dealer:* 45 N Venice Blvd Venice CA 90291. *Mailing Add:* c/o LA Louver Gallery 45 N Venice Blvd Venice CA 90291

MCMULLAN, JAMES BURROUGHS
ILLUSTRATOR, GRAPHIC ARTIST
b Tsingtao, China, June, 14, 34; US citizen. *Study:* Cornish Art Sch, Seattle, Wash; Pratt Inst, NY, BFA, 58. *Work:* Libr Cong, Washington. *Exhib:* Push Pin Retrospective, The Louvre, Paris, France, 70; Century of Am Illustration, Brooklyn Mus, NY, 72; Maps Show, Mus Natural Hist, NY, 77; Int Poster Biennale, Polish Mus, Warsaw, 84; World's Most Memorable Posters, UNESCO, Grand Palais, Paris, 86; Five Masters of the Contemp Poster, Lowell Gallery, NY, 87; solo exhibs, Giraffics Gallery, East Hampton, NY, 88 & Margo Feiden Gallery, NY, 88; Art of Illustration Show, Headley-Whitney Mus, Lexington, Ky, 88; Twenty Best Am Illustrators, Seoul, Repub Korea, 88. *Pos:* Illusr, Push Pin Studios, NY, 65-68. *Teaching:* Instr illus, Sch Visual Arts, NY, 71-84, instr drawing, 82-, master degree prof, 84-85. *Awards:* Gold Medal, 81, Hamilton King Award, 87 & Silver Medal, 88, Soc Illusrs; ANDY Award, Advert Club NY, 88. *Bibliog:* Richard Coyne (auth), James McMullan, Communication Arts Mag, 5-6/74; Michael Patrick Hearn (auth), The Art of the Broadway Poster, Ballantine Bks, 80; Ko Noda (dir), The Art of James McMullan, Van Gough Video, 83; S Chwast & S Heller (ed), The Art of New York, 84; S Heller (auth), Innovators of American Illustration, Van Nostrand Reinhold, 86; My life in the theater, Print Mag, 5/6/88. *Mem:* Am Inst Graphic Arts (dir, 74-76, vpres, 76-77); Soc Illusrs; Am Illus (adv bd, 85-); The Century Asn, 94. *Media:* Watercolor. *Publ:* Ed, Realism in illustration; auth, Revealing Illustrations, Watson-Guptill, 81; The Gant ad, How Mag, 1/85; High-Focus Drawing, Overlook Press, 95. *Mailing Add:* 207 E 32nd St New York NY 10016

MCNALLY, SHEILA JOHN
EDUCATOR, HISTORIAN
b New York, NY, Dec 10, 32. *Study:* Vassar Col, BA; Univ London; Univ Kiel; Univ Munich; Harvard Univ, PhD, 65. *Pos:* Prin investr, Excavations Diocletian's Palace, Split, Yugoslavia, 68-; dir, Excavations, Akhmim, Egypt, 78-. *Teaching:* Prof art hist, Univ Minn, Minneapolis, currently. *Awards:* Fulbright Res Grants, Ger, 53-54 & Yugoslavia, 67-68. *Mem:* Col Art Asn (bd dir, 75-79); Midwest Art Hist Soc; Archaeol Inst Am; Libyan Soc; Women's Archaeol Caucus. *Res:* Late Roman art. *Mailing Add:* 124 Bedford St SE Minneapolis MN 55414-3526

MCNAMARA, JOHN
PAINTER
b Cambridge, Mass, Feb 16, 50. *Study:* Mass Col Art, BFA(painting), 71, MFA(painting), 77. *Work:* Mus Fine Arts, Boston; Rose Art Mus, Brandeis Univ; Metrop Mus Art, NY; Honolulu Acad Fine Art; Visual Art Ctr MIT, Cambridge, Mass; Tucson Mus of Art; JB Speed Mus, Louisville, Ky. *Exhib:* Rose Art Mus, Waltham, Mass, 78; Boston Now, Inst Contemp Art, Boston, 81-83; one-man show, Exhib Space, NY, 82, Stavaridis Gallery, Boston, 83-85, 87 & 89, & Bess Cutler Gallery, NY, 84-86 & 88; Tucson Mus Contemp Art, Ariz, 92-96; Metrop Mus of Art, NY, 88; Painting in Boston 1950-2000, 2002-03; Clark Gallery, Lincoln, Mass, 2002; Bick Ebert Gallery, San Francisco, 2002. *Teaching:* Instr, sr lectr, Mass Col Art, San Francisco Art Inst & Univ Calif, Berkeley. *Awards:* Mass Arts & Humanities Grant, 80-83, 86, & 89; Nat Endowment Arts Fel, 81; Awards in Visual Arts II Fel, 82. *Bibliog:* Theodore Wolff (auth), The home forum, Christian Sci Monitor, 4/7/83; Nancy Stapen (auth), John McNamara, artforum, 1/88; David Bonetti (auth), John McNamara, Art News, 2/88. *Mem:* Berkeley Breakfast Club. *Media:* Oil on Canvas. *Mailing Add:* 171 Amherst St San Francisco CA 94134

MCNAMARA, MARY JO
HISTORIAN, EDUCATOR
b Troy, NY, Jan 23, 50. *Study:* Vassar Col, AB, 72; Stanford Univ, MA, 75, PhD, 83. *Pos:* Cur, Vassar Col Art Gallery, 76-78. *Teaching:* Instr art hist, Vassar Col, Poughkeepsie, NY, 76-78; lectr, Univ Wis, Milwaukee, 78-79; instr, Oberlin Col, Ohio, 79-80; acting asst prof, Univ Calif, Irvine, 80-83; vis asst prof, Univ Calif, Riverside, 84; asst prof, Wayne State Univ, 84-92 & State Univ NY, Potsdam, 93-. *Awards:* Cantor-Fitzgerald Res Grant, 75-76. *Mem:* Col Art Asn; Asn Historians 19th Century Art. *Res:* Modern Art. *Publ:* Coauth, Rodin's Burghers of Calais, Cantor-Fitzgerald Group, Los Angeles, 77. *Mailing Add:* 498 River Rd Potsdam NY 13676

MCNAMARA, WILLIAM PATRICK, JR
PAINTER, PRINTMAKER
b Shreveport, La, Sept 3, 46. *Study:* Centenary Col La, BA, 69; NMex Highlands Univ, MA, 72. *Work:* Centenary Col La; First Nat Bank, Shreveport, La; Ark Art Ctr, Little Rock; Springfield Art Mus; Phillips Petroleum Co, Tulsa, Okla. *Exhib:* Delta Art Exhib, Ark Arts Ctr, Little Rock, 80 & 84-88; Watercolor USA, 80 & 82-87 & A View from the Mountain, 89, Springfield Art Mus, Mo; Butler Inst Am Art, 82 & 83; Rocky Mountain Nat Watermedia Exhib, Foothills Art Ctr, Golden, Colo, 85; Watercolor West Nat, Riverside Nat Mus, Redlands, Calif, 85; Nat Watercolor Soc, Brea, Calif, 87 & 91; Watercolor Retrospective, Ark Arts Ctr, Little Rock, 89. *Teaching:* Instr drawing & composition, Centenary Col La, 73-76. *Awards:* Award Merit, Watercolor USA, Springfield Art Mus, Mo, 80; SMMA Purchase Award, The Monumental Image, Springfield Art Mus, Mo, 86; Binney-Smith Award, Nat Watercolor Soc, Brea, Calif, 87. *Bibliog:* M Stephen Doherty (auth), Watercolor today: Ten contemporary artists, Am Artist, 2/83; Elizabeth B Leonard (auth), Painting the Landscape, 84 & Mary

Suffudy (ed), Sketches Techniques, 85, Wastson-Guptill; Dan Morris (auth), McNamara Ventures into Monumentalism, Ark Gazette, 6/86; Donald Harrington (auth), Songs of sunlight & water, Ark Times, 7/89. *Mem:* Watercolor USA Honor Soc; Nat Watercolor Soc. *Media:* Watercolor. *Publ:* Auth, Watercolor page, Am Artist, 5/83. *Dealer:* Capricorn Galleries 4849 Rugby Ave Bethesda MD 20814; M A Doran Gallery 3509 S Peoria Tulsa OK. *Mailing Add:* HC-33 Box 52 Pettigrew AR 72752

MCNAMARA-RINGEWALD, MARY ANN THERESE
PAINTER, ILLUSTRATOR
b Hempstead, NY, April 11, 35. *Study:* Fordham Univ, BS, 1957; Adelphi Univ, MSA, 1972; Parsons School of Design (illus), 1973-75; Salve Regina Univ, 2003. *Work:* Fordham Univ, New York City; Adelphi Univ, Garden City, NY; St. Michaels Maritime Mus, Md; Yupo Corp, Chesapeake, Va & Japan; Doubleday, New York City. *Exhib:* one woman shows include Fordham Univ, 54, Andonia Gallery, Massapequa, NY, 74, Isis Gallery, Islip, NY, For the Birds, Salisbury, Conn, 78, Harguen Gallery, Port Jefferson, NY, 79, Adelphi Univ, Garden City, NY, 92, Wohlfarth Gallery, Washington, 94-95, SpanBauer Gallery, Naples, Fla, 96, Naples Philharmonic, Fla, 92, Gallery 44, Millbrook, NY, 97-98; group shows include Acad of Arts, Easton, Md, 93. *Collection Arranged:* Kennedy Gallery, Key West, Fla, 97-99; Chesapeake Col, Md, 98-99. *Pos:* owner, pres, South Shore Creative Arts Ctr, Massapequa, NY, 1975; illusr, Doubleday, Inc, NYC; art adv bd, Chespeake Col, Wye Mills, Md, 95-, lectr, 1998-99, 2000; symposium coord, Hofstra Univ, NY. *Teaching:* elem sch art tchr, Dept Educ, Freeport, NY, 1957-58, Farmingdale, NY, 1967; jr and high sch art tchr, Massapequa Sch Dist, NY, 1970-90; lectr, Naples Philharmonic, 1992. *Awards:* Outstanding Young Women of Am, Massapequa, NY, 1969; Nat Middle Sch Teachers Art, Massapequa, NY, 1988-89; Tobasco Book, Annapolis, St. Michael Mus, 1993; and others. *Mem:* Nat League of Am Pen Women, Wash, DC (pres Naples Fla bd 1996); Working Artist Forum, Easton, Md; Am Assoc Univ Women (pres Long Island, NY 1969); Annapolis Md Plein Air Painters; Bonita Springs Fla Art Asn. *Media:* Oil, Etching, Watercolor. *Res:* Analysis of East coast architecture, 88; Comparison of color theory, 98. *Interests:* Art, music, gardening & poetry. *Publ:* illusr, From a Lighthouse Window, Chespeake Maritime Mus, 92. *Mailing Add:* Marafour 5493 Anderby Dr Royal Oak MD 21662

MCNANY, TIM
PHOTOGRAPHER
b Newark, NJ, Dec 5, 55. *Study:* Boston Univ, BA, 79; Ctr Media Arts, New York, 89-90; New Sch, New York, with George Tice, 96. *Comn:* Landscapes & Location Portraits (black/white & color prints), comn by Tim Gill, Maplewood, NJ, 97. *Exhib:* Am Soc Media Photogr Fine Art Competition, Bergen Mus Art & Sci, Paramus, NJ, 94 & 95; Johnson & Johnson Nat Art Show (with catalog), Hunterdon Mus, Clinton, NJ, 94; Garden State Int, Watchung Art Ctr, NJ, 98; Montclair State Univ Nat Small Works, NJ, 98; one-man show, Presidents Gallery, Drew Univ, Madison, NJ, 98. *Teaching:* Instr photog, Ann St Sch, Newark, NJ, 98; invitational resident photogr, Paris, 99. *Awards:* Emmy Nomination, 94; Telly Award, 96; First Place, Am Soc Media Photogr, 98. *Bibliog:* Eye on TV, Star-Ledger, 10/31/92; Mitch Seidel (auth), Media lensmen's exhibition, Star-Ledger, 9/24/93; Susan Poor (auth), ASMP/NJ winners, Photo Distric News, 3/98. *Mem:* Int Ctr Photog; Advertising Photogr New York. *Media:* Black & White, Color. *Dealer:* Thistledown Gallery 1405-1 Third Ave Spring Lake NJ 07762. *Mailing Add:* 11 St Lawrence Ave Maplewood NJ 07040

MCNARY, OSCAR L
PAINTER, COLLECTOR
b San Antonio, Tex, Mar 23, 44. *Study:* San Antonio Jr Col, Tex; Tex Southern Univ; Southern Methodist Univ; Warren Hunter's Sch Art. *Work:* Univ Tex, Dallas; The McNary Collection, Dallas Visual Arts Ctr. *Exhib:* Ninth Biennial, Five State Art Exhib, Port Arthur, Tex, 87; Galerie Gorpal Invitational, Dallas, Tex, 88; 45th Ann Painting Competition, Abilene Fine Arts Mus, 89; Beverly Gordon Gallery Invitational exhib, 89 & 90; Tex Watercolor Soc Exhib, San Antonio, Tex, 86; and many others. *Pos:* Art consultant, 19th, 20th & 21st century Am & African Am art, currently. *Awards:* Emerging Artists from the Southwest, Studio Mus Harlem, 84; Purchase Award, Dallas City Hall, Tex, 85; Best of Show Award, Art Community Ctr, Corpus Christi, 78; and many others. *Bibliog:* Article, Art Voices South, 9-10/80. *Mem:* Irving Black Arts Coun; Tex Arts Alliance Bd Gov; Richardson Civic Art Soc (pres & bd gov); Tex Comn Arts/Visual Arts & Archit; Artists Coalition Tex, Dallas; and others. *Media:* Acrylic, Watercolor. *Collection:* 20th century contemporary ceramics; paintings, sculptures, graphics, collection loaned to various institutions; 21st century works. *Mailing Add:* PO Box 832627 Richardson TX 75083

MCNAUGHTON, JOHN W
SCULPTOR
b Winchester, Ind, 43. *Study:* Ball State Univ, BS(art educ), 65, MA, 69; Bowling Green State Univ, MFA, 70. *Comn:* Wooden sculpture, Welborn Hosp, Evansville, Ind, 89; walnut sculpture, Orr Ctr, Univ Southern Ind, 89; wooden sculpture, Citizens Nat Bank, Evansville, Ind, 90; sculptural cabinet, MCI Corp Hq, Washington, 92; Christmas ornament for President & Mrs Clinton, White House, 93; 3 wooden wall reliefs, St Mary's Hosp, Evansville, Ind, 99; 2 wooden wall reliefs, Meth Temple, Evansville, Ind, 99; corten steel/mild steel piece, Univ of So Ind, 2000. *Exhib:* Solo exhibs, Hokin/Kaufman Gallery, 89, Snyderman Gallery, Philadelphia, 90 & Mobilia Gallery, Cambridge, Mass, 90; Furniture of the Nineties, Hokin/Kaufman Gallery, Chicago, 91; Joan Robey Gallery, Denver, Colo, 91; Art Expo, Hokin/Kaufman Gallery, Chicago, Ill, 91; Katie Gingrass Gallery, Milwaukee, Wis, 91; Regional show, Owensboro, Ky, 2001; Nat show, Images Friedman Gallery, Louisville, Ky, 2001. *Pos:* Indust designer, General Motors, Warren, Mich, 65-68. *Teaching:* Prof art, Univ Southern Ind, Evansville, 70-; vis artist, Col Archit & Planning, Ball State Univ, 77-78, Art Acad Mexico City, 93. *Awards:* Nat Endowment Arts Grants, 76 & 92; Ind Artists Fel, 95. *Bibliog:* Fine Woodworking Mag, 11/86; Craft Today Poetry of the Physical, 86; The new art American craft, House Beautiful, 4/87; Furniture Studio, the Heart of the Functional Arts, 99; Evansville Crossroads of the Midwest, 2000. *Mailing Add:* 625 Marigold Ct Evansville IN 47712

MCNEIL, DEAN S
SCULPTOR, PHOTOGRAPHER
b Geneva, Ill, 57. *Study:* Antioch Col, Yellow Springs, Ohio, 75-79. *Work:* Metrop Mus, NY; Denver Art Mus; Brooklyn Mus. *Exhib:* One-man shows, Utopia/Dystopia, Scott Hanson Gallery, 88, Call & Talk, Paula Allen Gallery, 89, Sculpture for the Dead, Scott Hanson Gallery, 90 & Pioneers of Safety, Univ Art Mus, Univ Calif, Santa Barbara, 91; Getting to Know You, Kunfterhauf Bethanren, Berlin, 92; A Century of Silence, Univ Art Mus, State Univ NY, Binghamton, 93; Ctr Photog, Woodstock; Calif Mus Photog, Riverside; and others. *Awards:* Nat Endowment Arts, 88. *Bibliog:* Kim Levin (auth), The Village Voice, 5/16/86, 9/21/88. *Mailing Add:* 140 Sullivan St New York NY 10012

MCNEIL, WENDY LAWSON-JOHNSTON
PATRON
Pos: Vpres, Solomon R Guggenheim Found, currently; bd trustees Solomon R Guggenheim Mus, currently. *Mailing Add:* Solomon R Guggenheim Found 1071 Fifth Ave New York NY 10128

MCNICKLE, THOMAS GLEN
PAINTER
b New Castle, Pa, Oct 17, 44. *Study:* Edinboro Univ, BS(art), 66, MEd(studio), 72. *Work:* Butler Inst Am Art; Hoyt Inst Fine Art, New Castle, Pa; Vero Beach Mus of Art, Fla. *Comn:* US Air, Pitts, PA; Cox Comm, Atlanta, Ga; Bank of AM, Charlotte,NC; Pfizer Corp, Cleveland, Ohio; Price Waterhouse, Charlottle, NC. *Exhib:* Am Artists Prof League Grande Nat, NY, 82 & 83; Views of Youngstown, Butler Inst Am Art, 82; Audubon Artists Ann, Nat Arts Club, NY, 83, 84 & 85; Am Watercolor Soc Ann Exhib, 84; Watercolor USA, Springfield, Mo, 84 & 85. *Collection Arranged:* Forty Watercolors (auth, catalog), from collection Butler Inst Am Art, 82; Hoyt Nat Painting Show (auth, catalog), 84 & 85. *Teaching:* Instr art, Neshannock Twp Schs, New Castle, Pa, 66-98; private workshops watercolors, 79-. *Awards:* Award Excellence, Black Forest Inst, Exhib, 82; Second Prize Watercolor, Terrance Gallery Nat Exhib, 82; Ford Motor Co Fund Award, Mich Watercolor Soc Ann, 85; Outstanding Alumni Awards in the Arts, Edinboro Univ, 92. *Mem:* Nat Watercolor Soc; Pa Soc Watercolor Painters; Pittsburgh Watercolor Soc (bd dir, 83); Am Watercolor Soc. *Media:* Oil. *Dealer:* Thomas G McNickle 107 Fayette NF Road Volant PA 16156; Jerald Melberg Gallery Charlotte NC; David Findlay Fine Art, NYC; James Gallery, Pitt, PA. *Mailing Add:* RR 3 Volant PA 16156-9803

MCOWEN, C LYNN
ART DEALER, COLLECTOR
b Long Beach, Calif, July 12, 53. *Study:* Calif State Univ, BA, 77; studied with Master Painter, People Republic China, 85-86; pvt study with Calvin J Goodman in Art Marketing. *Pos:* Dir graphics & printing, East End Arts & Humanities Coun, Childrens Inst Res & Design Ctr, 77-79; graphic illusr, State Univ NY, Stony Brook, 79-84. *Mem:* UCLA Art Coun. *Specialty:* Contemporary paintings, prints & drawings from the People's Republic of China. *Collection:* Variety of paintings, prints, drawings & sculpture done by contemporary artists from the People's Republic of China. *Dealer:* Mayoon Fine Asian Art 6409 W 6th St Los Angeles CA 90048. *Mailing Add:* 934 N Holliston Ave Pasadena CA 91104-3012

MCOWEN, CAROL M
COLLECTOR
b Denver, Colo, Dec 23, 27. *Study:* Private study with Calvin Goodman (art marketing), 88; Calif State Univ, Long Beach, MA(Chinese art hist). *Pos:* Owner, MAYOON, Fine Asian Art, South Pasadena, Calif, formerly. *Mem:* Long Beach Art Mus (mem Friends Coun, 80-88); Los Angeles Co Art Mus (docent, 82-84); Univ Calif Art Coun, Los Angeles; Metrop Mus Art. *Res:* Contemporary landscape painting in the Peoples' Republic of China: 1976-1986. *Collection:* Variety of contemporary paintings, drawings & prints from China. *Mailing Add:* 111 S Orange Grove Blvd No 310 Pasadena CA 91105-1730

MCPHEE, SARAH COLLYER
HISTORIAN, EDUCATOR
Study: Harvard Univ, AB, 82; Columbia Univ, MA (art hist), 88; Columbia Univ, PhD (art hist), 97. *Pos:* Ed, writer, Metrop Mus Art, 84-86. *Teaching:* asst prof, Emory Univ, Art Hist Dept, 95-2001, assoc prof, 2001-; Vis assoc prof, Columbia Univ, Dept Art Hist & Archaeology, 2003-04. *Awards:* Fel Guggenheim Mem Found, 2004. *Mem:* Inst for Advanced Study. *Publ:* Co-auth: Drawings from the Roman Period 1704-1714, 99; auth: Bernini and the Bell Towers: Architecture and Politics at the Vatican, 2002. *Mailing Add:* Art His Dept Emory Univ 128 Carlos Hall Atlanta GA 30322

MCPHERSON, BRUCE RICE
EDITOR, PUBLISHER
b Atlanta, Ga, Oct 12, 51. *Study:* Brown Univ, AB, 73; Annenberg Sch Commun, Univ Pa, 75. *Pos:* Ed & publ, McPherson & Co (Documentext, Treacle Press), 74-. *Res:* Avant-Garde, 1958-present, principally United States, especially concerned with happenings, fluxus, performance art, cinematography and related areas. *Publ:* Ed, More than Meat Joy: Complete Performance Works and Selected Writings, by Carolee Schneemann, 79 & 97, Something Else Press: An Annotated Bibliography, by Peter Frank, 82, Documentext; Essential Brakhage: selected writings on filmmaking by Stan Brahage, 2001; Essential Deren: collect writings on Film by Maya Deren, 2005. *Mailing Add:* PO Box 1126 Kingston NY 12402-0126

MCPHERSON, CRAIG
PAINTER, PRINTMAKER
b Wichita, Kans, Sept 29, 48. *Study:* Univ Kans, BFA, 70. *Work:* Metrop Mus Art, & Whitney Mus Am Art, NY; Brit Mus London; Art Inst Chicago; Cleveland Mus Art; Fine Arts Mus San Francisco. *Comn:* Twilight: The Rivers & Bridges of Manhattan (mural), Am Express Co, NY, 85-86; Harbors of the World (mural), Am Express Co, NY, 87-92; paintings, Corp Lobby, World Financial Ctr. *Exhib:* Recent Acquisitions, Nat Gallery Am Art, Washington, 85; Recent Acquisitions, Metrop Mus Art, NY, 85; 162nd Ann Exhib, Nat Acad Design, NY, 87; Tradition & Innovation: 1500 to Present, San Francisco Mus Fine Arts, 89; Diamonds Are Forever, NY Pub Libr, Inst Contemp Art, Boston, Seiba Dept Store, Tokyo, Taipei Fine Arts Mus, Taiwan, Denver Art Mus, Albright-Knox Mus, Buffalo, Southeastern Ctr Contemp Art, NC, 90; NY, NY, The Fitzwilliam Mus, Cambridge, Eng, 94 & 98, Darkness into Light (retrospective), 98. *Pos:* Dir, Kans Cult Arts Comn Mobile Gallery, Wichita Art Mus, 71-73; mgr, Mich Artrain, Mich Coun Arts & Nat Endowment Arts, 73-74; cur, NY New Realism Gallery G Witchita, Kans, 75. *Awards:* Purchase Prize, Hassam & Speicher Fund Purchase Exhib, Am Acad & Inst Arts & Letters, 83, 41st Annual Acad Purchase Exhib, 89; Grant, Nat Endowment Arts, 84. *Bibliog:* John Arthur (auth), Craig McPherson (exhib catalog), Mary Ryan, 1/93. *Mem:* Nat Arts Club; Century Club. *Media:* Oil; Mezzotint. *Dealer:* Mary Ryan Gallery 24 W 57th St New York NY 10019. *Mailing Add:* 112 E 19th St Apt 3F New York NY 10003

MCPHERSON, LARRY E
PHOTOGRAPHER, EDUCATOR
b Newark, Ohio, 43. *Study:* BA, Columbia Col, Chicago; MA, Northern Ill Univ, 1978. *Work:* Mus Mod Art, NY; Art Inst Chicago & Exchange Nat Bank, Chicago, Ill; Int Mus Photog at George Eastman House, Rochester, NY; New Orleans Mus Art, La; Mus Fine Arts, Houston; Dayton Art Inst, Ohio; Birmingham Mus Art, Ala; Milwaukee Mus Art, Wisc; plus others. *Exhib:* One-man shows, Art Inst Chicago, Ill, 69, 78 & 81, Dayton Art Inst, Ohio, 92; Vision and Expression, George Eastman House, Rochester, NY, 69; Mirrors & Windows, Mus Mod Art, NY, 78; Farbwerke, Kunsthaus Gallery, Zurich, Switz, 80; Contemp Am Color, Galerie Rudolf Kicken, Koln, Ger, 80; Color as Form: A History of Color Photog, Corcoran Gallery & George Eastman House, 82; The Nature of the Beast, Hudson River Mus, Yonkers, NY, 89; 1992 Trienial, New Orleans Mus Art, 92; New Faces and Other Recent Acquisitions, Art Inst Chicago, Ill, 97; Visualizing the Blues, the Dixon Gallery and Gardens, Memphis, Tenn, 2000; plus others. *Teaching:* Assoc prof photog, Univ Memphis, Tenn, 78. *Awards:* Nat Endowment Arts Fel Photog, 75 & 79; Guggenheim Fel Photog, 80; Tenn Arts Commn Ind Artist Fel Photog, 96. *Bibliog:* Candida Finkel (auth), review, Afterimage, 10/78; Elaine King (auth), article, Camera Mag, 80; History of Photography, Spring 93; Wendy McDaris (auth) Visualizing the Blues, 2001. *Mem:* Soc Photog Educ. *Publ:* Memphis, Santa Fe, NMex, Center for American Places, 2002; Beirut City Center, Gottingen, Germany, Steidl, 2006. *Dealer:* Lisa Kurts Gallery 766 S White Station Rd Memphis TN 38117. *Mailing Add:* Univ Memphis Art Dept Jones Hall Rm 108 Memphis TN 38152

MCQUEEN, JOHN
CRAFTSMAN
b Champagne, Ill, 43. *Study:* Univ SFla, BA, 71; Tyler Sch Art, Temple Univ, Philadelphia, MFA, 75. *Work:* Cooper-Hewitt Mus, NY; Minneapolis Inst Art; Philadelphia Mus Art; Renwick Gallery, Smithsonian Inst, Washington, DC; Wadsworth Atheneum, Hartford, Conn; Detroit Inst of Art, Much. *Exhib:* Recent Acquisitions, Philadelphia Art Mus, 79; The Art Fabric Mainstream, San Francisco Mus Mod Art, Calif, 81; solo exhibs, Kansas City Art Inst, Mo, 83, Bellas Artes Gallery, Santa Fe, NMex, 87, Garth Clark Gallery, NY, 89, 92 & 94 & Los Angeles, 90, Nina Freudenheim Gallery, Buffalo, 91 & Smithsonian Mus, 92, Down the Line, Perimeter Gallery, Chicago, Ill, 2001, Elliot Brown Gallery, Seattle, Wash, Limbo, Perimeter Gallery, Chicago, Ill, 2002; Fiber R/Evolution Exhib, Milwaukee Art Mus, Wis, 85; Meeting Ground: Basketry Traditions and Sculptural Forms, The Forrum, St Louis, 90; Nat Objects Invitational, Ark Decorative Arts Mus, Little Rock, 91; Material Vision: Image and Object, Tarble Arts Ctr, Eastern Ill Univ, 91; Artists & Language, Soc Contemp Crafts, Pittsburgh, 93; Surface, Jan Weiner Gallery, Kansas City, 2003; Conscriptions, Mobilia Gallery, Cambridge, Mass, 2001, 03. *Awards:* Fels, Nat Endowment Arts, 77, 79, 86 & 92; NY Found Arts, 88; Louis Comfort Tiffany Found, 91; Artist's Fel, NY Found for the Arts, 2001. *Bibliog:* Victoria Geibel (auth), The Evolving Basket, Metropolis, pp 68-73, 6/89; Betty Freudenheim (auth), Can knots & netting be art?, New York Times, 12/3/89; Roxanne Orgill (auth), The gallery: boffo baskets, Wall Street J, 4/24/92. *Publ:* Auth, Interlacing the Elemental Fabric, Kudansha Int, Tokyo, 86; The Eloquent Object, Philbrook Mus Art, Tulsa, Okla, 87; The Tactile Vessel, Erie Art Mus, Pa, 88; Craft Today: Poetry of the Physical, Am Crafts Mus, 88; Crafts Symposium & Robert L Pfannebecker: Contemp Am Craft Exhib, Shippenburg Univ, Pa, 89

MCREYNOLDS, (JOE) CLIFF
PAINTER, INSTRUCTOR
b Amarillo, Tex, Jan 26, 33. *Study:* San Diego State Univ, BA, 59, MA, 60. *Work:* Chicago Art Inst; Music Corp of Am, Time Warner; Northern Trust Co, Chgo. *Comn:* Portrait of pres, Mesa Col, San Diego, Calif, 75. *Exhib:* Drawings USA Traveling Exhib, Minn Mus Art, St Paul, 75; Alternative Realities, Mus Contemp Art, Chicago, Ill, 76; Calif Painting & Sculpture--the Modern Era, San Francisco Mus Mod Art, 76; Juried Drawing Exhib, Chicago Art Inst, 77; Fourth Triennial--India Traveling Exhib, New Delhi, 78 & Tokyo, Japan, 79; For God's Sake--Cliff McReynolds, San Jose Mus Art, Calif, 83; Downey Mus Art, Calif, 87; Venice Arts Festival Venice, Calif, 88; Biola Univ La Mirada, Calif, 88; SDTYAE and traveling, Yukohama, Japan, 92; one-man show Taylor Libr, San Diego, 2001; others. *Pos:* Illusr, Psychol Today, 70-73, Esquire Mag, 73, Visions, 77 & Omni Mag, 78-79. *Teaching:* Instr drawing, Mesa Col, San Diego, 69-96. *Awards:* Best in Show, Del Mar Exhib, 63; Best in Show, All Calif Exhib, 63 & First Prize, Calif-Hawaii Regional, 72, Fine Arts Gallery, San Diego; First Prize, Small Images, Spanish Village, San Diego, 97, 98, 99. *Bibliog:* Marilyn Hagberg (auth), McReynolds--sharp satirist, San Diego Mag, 2/67; State of the Arts, Dr Gene Edward Veith Jr, 91; Karen L Mulder (auth), Inklings, The Art of Cliff McReynolds, 5/98. *Mem:* Christians in the Visual Arts. *Media:* Oil, Pencil. *Publ:* Auth, All Things New, Revelation Art, 80; Wonders of the Visible World, Critique of America 3/88; Making Art and Eating Too, The Forum, 93. *Mailing Add:* 6311 Dowling Dr La Jolla CA 92037

MCREYNOLDS, KIRK See St Maur, Kirk

MCROBERTS, SHERYL ANN
SCULPTOR
b Kalamazoo, Mich, Aug 14, 50. *Study:* Augsburg Col, BA(art), 73; St Cloud State Univ, MA(sculpture), 76; Ind Univ, MFA(sculpture), 78. *Work:* Missoula Mus Arts, Mont; Doane Col Art Gallery, Crete, Nebr; Normandale Community Col Art Collection, Bloomington, Minn. *Comn:* Fed Reserve Bank, Minneapolis, 90; Artstop, Powderhorn Park Neighborhood, Minneapolis, 91; St Cloud State Univ, Minn, 92; Fergus Falls Community Col, Minn, 93; Franconia Sculpture Park, Schafer, Minn, 99. *Exhib:* Wyoming: The Cowboy State, (traveling), 87; Sculpture to Touch, New Art Ctr, Washington, 87; Nicolaysen Mus, Univ Mont, 88; Forum Gallery, 91; MC Gallery, 92-94 & 96. *Teaching:* Asst prof sculpture, Doane Col, 80-84; Univ Wyo, 84-89; instr sculpture, Normandale Community Col, 89-. *Awards:* Ford Found Grant, 78; A Question of Scale Purchase Award, Missoula Mus Arts, 86; Fulbright Grant for Scholars, Fulbright Comn, 96. *Bibliog:* Karl Vokmar (auth), Review, Northern Lights Mag, 87; Mary Abbe (auth), Review, Minneapolis Star & Tribune, 89; Arthur Williams (auth), Sculpture Fundamentals, 89. *Mailing Add:* Normandale Community Col 9700 France Ave S Minneapolis MN 55431-4399

MCSHEEHY, CORNELIA MARIE
PRINTMAKER, PAINTER
b Floral Park, Long Island, New York, Aug 10, 47. *Study:* Mass Col Art, Boston, BFA, 69; State Univ NY, Albany, MA, 72. *Work:* Libr Cong, Washington, DC; Mus Fine Arts, Boston; State Univ NY, Potsdam; Art Inst Chicago, Ill; Tex Tech Univ, Lubbock; Univ Okla, and others. *Exhib:* Boston Printmakers, De Cordova Mus, Lincoln, Mass, 73; Print Exhib, Libr Cong, 75; Mus Fine Arts, Boston, 76; New Am Graphics 2 & 3, Madison Art Ctr, 82-84; Printed by Women, Port Hist Mus, Philadelphia, 83; Brit Int Print Biennial, WYorkshire, 86; Contemp Am Prints, US Consulate, Leningrad, Russia, 86; Wild, Wild Wit, Boston, 87; Cameron Univ, 88; SUNY-Albany, NY, 88; Printmakers, Anold Gallery, Newport, RI, 92; Fac Biennial Exhib, Mus Art, RI Sch Design, 92 & 95; Small Works Exhib, Woods-Gerry Gallery, RI Sch Design, 93; Colorprint USA 25, Tex Tech Univ, Lubbock, 94; Albany Alumni Artists, Univ Art Mus, State Univ NY, Albany, 94; Feminism in the Arts of the 70's, Univ Art Mus, State Univ NY, Albany, 95; Colorprint USA Spanning the States in '98, Tex Tech Univ, Lubbock, Tex, 98; Berkshire Comminuty col, Pittsfield, Mass, 99; Left/Right-Right/Left, Pacific Northwest Col Art, Portland, Oreg, 99; Art Bank Program Exhib, US Info Agency, Dept of State, Washington, DC, 2000. *Teaching:* Instr printmaking, Mass Col Art, Boston, 72-75; asst prof, Brown Univ, 76-77; prof, RI Sch Design, 77-, head printmaking prog, 78-89. *Awards:* Nat Endowment Arts Grant Printmaking, 75-76; Mellon Rac Res Grant, Polaroid Corp Grant, 85, 86, finaist, Mass Coun Arts, 87; John R Frazier Award Excellence in Teaching, RISD, 94. *Bibliog:* Nancy Stapen (auth), article, Boston Herald, Mass, 11/20/87; Christine Temin (auth), Boston Globe, MAss, 11/20/87; John Pantalone (auth), Newport This Wk, RI, 11/19/92. *Mem:* Boston Printmakers; MacDowell Colony Fel; Mus of Fine Arts Boston. *Media:* Printmaking; Painting, Mixed Media; Sculpture. *Publ:* The Collograph, Free Press, NY, 80. *Mailing Add:* 77 Barney St Rumford RI 02916

MCSHINE, KYNASTON LEIGH
CURATOR, CRITIC
b Port of Spain, Trinidad, Feb 20, 35. *Study:* Dartmouth Col, AB, 58; Univ Mich, 58-59; Inst Fine Arts, NY Univ, 60-64. *Collection Arranged:* Berlinart (auth, catalog), 61-87; Marcel Duchamp (auth, catalog), 73, Robert Rauschenberg, 77, Jackie Winsor (auth, catalog), 79 & Joseph Cornell, (auth, catalog), 80, Mus Mod Art, NY; Andy Warhol: A Retrospective (auth, catalog), 89; and others. *Pos:* Cur painting & sculpture, Jewish Mus, NY, 65-67, acting dir, 67-68; assoc cur painting & sculpture, Mus Mod Art, NY, 68-71, cur, 71-80, sr cur, 80-2001. *Teaching:* Asst prof art hist, Hunter Col, NY, 68-69; lectr art hist, Sch Visual Arts, NY, 69-76. *Mem:* Trustee Hopkins Ctr, Hood Mus Art, Dartmouth Col; Int Asn Art Critics; Col Art Asn; Am Asn Mus; Century Asn; and others. *Publ:* Auth, Josef Albers: Homage to the Square, 64 & Information, 70, ed & contribr, Marcel Duchamp, 73, The Natural Paradise: Painting in America 1800-1950, 76, An International Survey of Recent Painting and Sculpture, 84, Mus Mod Art, NY; Primary structures, Jewish Mus, 66. *Mailing Add:* c/o Mus Mod Art Chief Curator at Large 11 W 53rd St New York NY 10019

MCTWIGAN, MICHAEL
CRITIC, EDITOR
b Lincoln, Nebr, July 9, 48. *Study:* Lake Forest Col, Ill, BA(anthrop), 71; Columbia Univ, postgrad studies, 76-77. *Pos:* Ed asst, Craft Horizons Mag, New York, 72 & 74-78; asst ed, Art Quart, Metrop Mus, New York, 78-79; sr ed, Watson-Guptill Publ, New York, 79-81; ed, Indust Design, New York, 82-83; ed, Am Ceramics Mag, New York, 82-. *Awards:* Art Critics Fel, Nat Endowment Arts, 80. *Mem:* Decorative Arts Soc of Soc Archit Historians; Col Art Asn. *Res:* Post-World War II sculpture in the new craft media of clay, glass and fiber; architecture, decorative arts and portraiture. *Publ:* Auth, Heroes and Clowns (sculpture of Robert Arneson exhib catalog), Allan Frumkin Gallery, 79; William Daley: Duality in Clay, Am Craft, 80; First things first, 82 & The fruitful mysteries of Graham Marks, 82, Am Ceramics; An interior exchanges: Cynthia Carlson and Betty Woodman, Arts Mag, 82. *Mailing Add:* 51 Prospect Pl Brooklyn NY 11217-2801

MCVICKER, CHARLES TAGGART
PAINTER, INSTRUCTOR
b Canonsburg, Pa, Aug 31, 30. *Study:* Principia Col, BA, 52; Art Ctr, Col of Design, BPA, 57. *Work:* US Capitol, US Hist Soc & US Air Force, DC; Princeton Univ; Soc Illusr, NY. *Exhib:* NJ Artists, Newark Mus, 64; NJ Ann, NJ State Mus, Trenton, 70; Illusr Ann, Soc Illusr, NY; NJ Art Dirs Ann, Newark; Am Watercolor Soc Ann, Nat Acad, NY; Nat Audubon Artists; Watercolor, USA. *Collection Arranged:* Retrospective, Col of NJ. *Teaching:* Assoc prof illus, Pratt/Phoenix, New York, 79-84; asst prof art, Trenton State Col, 85-2005. *Awards:* Ralph Fabri Award, Nat Audubon Artists, 86 & Michael M Engle Award, 92, Nat Audubon Artists; Ralph Fabri Medal, NAPAC Exhib, 91; Merrill Lynch Award, GSWS, 96; Watercolor USA Awards, 98, 99, 2000, 02. *Mem:* Soc Illusr (pres, 76-78); Artists Alliance (pres 89-92); Am Watercolor Soc; Audubon Artists, 88-; Princeton Artists Alliance (founder); Garden State Watercolor Soc (pres). *Media:* Oil, Acrylic. *Interests:* Jazz Pianist. *Publ:* Illusr, Addie and the King of Hearts, Knopf Publ, 76; The Soccer Book, 76 & The Circus Book, 78, Random House; Guard of Honor, Franklin Libr, 78; Internat Artist, 03. *Dealer:* Artspan.com. *Mailing Add:* 26 Old Orchard Ln Princeton NJ 08540

MCWHORTER, ELSIE JEAN
PAINTER, SCULPTOR
b Laurel, Miss, Apr 5, 32. *Study:* Univ Ga, BFA, 54 & MFA, 56, with Lamar Dodd, Howard Thomas, Abbott Patterson, Joseph Di Martini, Ulfert Wilkie & Dan Lutz; Brooklyn Mus Art Sch, Max Beckmann scholar, 56-57, with Reuben Tam & Yonia Fain. *Work:* Gibbes Art Gallery, Charleston, SC; Brooks Art Gallery, Memphis, Tenn; Greenville Co Mus Art, SC; Arts Comn SC, Columbia; Miss Art Asn, State Coliseum, Jackson; and others; Cola Mus of Art, SC; Gibbs Art Gallery, Charleston Univ of SC; Columbia Col, SC; Univ SC Cola SC; Camden Post Office, Camden, SC; Richland Co Pub Libr, Columbia, SC. *Comn:* mural, US Post Off, Camden, SC, 67; mural, Baker Bldg, Southern Bell Tel Co, Columbia, 68; eight historic paintings, McDonald's Restaurant, Conway, SC, 76; life-size bronze relief, Sen Rembert Dennis, Dennis Bldg, Capitol Complex SC, 81; McNair Monument, SC State Capitol Complex; eleven wall hangings (paintings), Keenan Chapel Trinity Cathedral, Cola, SC, 89; Awards, Charter Day, Benedick Col, 90; seven foot relief Palmetto tree, Capitol Complex Gift Shop; Seven Paintings, Washington Street United Methodist Church, Cola, SC; Bronze plaque of Founding Fathers, Court yard, Washington St Meth Church, SC, 2004. *Exhib:* Mid-South Exhib, Memphis, Tenn, 62; Butler Inst Am Art Ann, Youngstown, Ohio, 63; Drawing USA, St Paul 2nd Biennial Competition, St Paul Art Ctr, Minn, 63; one-woman shows, Columbia Mus Art, Fine Arts Ctr, Univ Tenn, Chattanooga, 81, Hunter Mus, Chattanooga & Laurel Rogers Libr & Mus, Laurel, Miss; and others. *Teaching:* Asst prof art, Morningside Col, 58-61; instr drawing, painting & sculpture, Columbia Mus Art Sch, Columbia Mus Art, 61-84, supvr, 78-84; instr sculpture & design, Univ SC, 66-67; vis prof, Newberry Col, 82, asst prof art, Benedict Col, 85, emer, 94. *Awards:* First Prize Painting, Spartanburg Art Asn Ann, SC, 74; First Prize, Dutch Fork Art Asn Exhib, Cola, SC, 74; First Prize Sculpture, Art of the Carolinas, Spring Mills Ann, Lancaster, SC, 75; and many others. *Bibliog:* Jack Morris (auth), article, Contemp SC Artist, 70; 100 Years, 100 Artists: Views of the 20th Century, in South Carolina Art, SC State Mus. 2000. *Mem:* SC Artists (former mem); SC Craftsmen (former mem). *Media:* Painting, Sculpture. *Specialty:* Fine Arts. *Interests:* Drawing, painting, printmaking, sculpture & ceramics. *Dealer:* Cameo Fine Art Gallery 1213 Lincoln St Cola SC 29201. *Mailing Add:* 5419 Sylvan Dr Columbia SC 29206

MEAD, GERALD C, JR
COLLAGE ARTIST, EDUCATOR
b Hamburg, NY, Aug 16, 62. *Study:* State Univ Col, Buffalo, NY, BA (psychology), 85, BS (design), 86; Univ Buffalo, NY, 90-93. *Work:* Albright-Knox Art Gallery, Buffalo, NY; Castellani Art Mus, Niagara Falls, NY; George Eustman House, Int Mus Film & Photography, Rochester, NY; Burchfield-Penney Art Ctr, Buffalo, NY; Keran Ctr, Lookport, NY. *Comn:* poster design, Buffalo Ensemble Theatre, NY, 92; cover design, VOICES Mag, Buffalo, NY, 99; poster design, Buffalo United Artists, NY, 2000. *Exhib:* Rochester-Finger Lakes Exhibition, Rochester Mem Art Gallery, NY, 94; Western NY Exhibition, Albright-Knox Art Gallery, Buffalo, NY, 94; 72nd Ann Spring Show, Erie Art Mus, Erie, Pa, 95; World in a Match Box, Grand Central Art, Melbourne, Australia, 97; Three Rivers Arts Festival, Carnegie Mus Art, Pittsburgh, 2000; Regional 2000, Arnot Art Mus, Elmira, NY, 2000; SUNY Brockport, NY, 2002; Darmen Col, Amherst, NY, 2002; solo exhib, Custelleni Art Mus, Niagra Falls, NY, 2004, Cedar Arts Ctr, Corning, NY, 2006; Upstate Invitational, Rochester Contemp, NY, 2006. *Collection Arranged:* Roycroft Desktop (decorative art), 95; EB Green, Buffalo's Architect, 97; Buffalo's Grain Elevators (photography, painting), 97; James KY Kuo: A Retrospective (painting), 98; Art of the Chair: WNY Furniture Design (decorative art), 2000; Nancy Belfes: Textile Art, 2001; Wet & Fresh: A survey Current watercolor, 2004; Cindy Sherman, WNY collectins (photography), 2006. *Pos:* curator, Burchfield-Penney Art Center, Buffalo, NY, 87-2005; auditor, NY State Council on the Arts, New York City, 93-96; field reviewer, Inst Mus & Libr Serv, Washington, DC, 97-2005; Supervisor, Am Asn Mus, Washington DC, 2000-. *Teaching:* adj lectr design, State Univ Coll Buffalo, NY, 98-. *Awards:* First Place, Carnegie Art Ctr Nat Exhib, 93; Gold Medal, Seymour H Knox Found, 97; Silver Medal, 106th Buffalo Soc Artists Exhib, 2002. *Bibliog:* Elizabeth Licata (auth), Small and Smaller, Art Voice, 97; Robert Hirsch (auth), Exploring Color Photography, Brown & Benchmark, 97; John Valentino (auth), Photographic Possibilities, Focal Press, 2001. *Mem:* Buffalo Soc Artists (pres, 93-94); Big Orbit Gallery (bd pres, 95-); NY State Alliance Arts Educ (bd dir, 94-97); CEPA Gallery (adv bd 96-); Buffalo Arts Studio (bd mem, 2003-). *Publ:* editor, EB Green: Buffalo's Architect, Buffalo Sate Coll Found, 97, The Inanimate: 12 Artists on Still Life, 98, Craft Art from Western New York, 98; The Art of the Chair: Western New York Furniture Design, Buffalo State Coll Foun, 2000; editor, Wet & Fresh: A survey current watercolor in western New York, Buffalo state coll found, 2004. *Dealer:* Art Dialogue Gallery One Linwood Ave Buffalo NY 14209. *Mailing Add:* 209 Woodward Ave Buffalo NY 14214

MEADER, JONATHAN (ASCIAN)
PRINTMAKER, PAINTER
b Aug 29, 43; US citizen. *Work:* Whitney Mus Am Art, Metrop Mus Art, NY; Corcoran Gallery Art, Nat Collection Fine Art, Hirshhorn Mus, Washington, DC; and others. *Comn:* Serigraphs, Off Equal Employment Opportunity, 73; lithographs, Washington Printmakers' Workshop Proj, 74; serigraph, Washington Print Club, 75. *Exhib:* One-person shows, Corcoran Gallery Art, Dupont Ctr, 69, Green Panther Gallery, Frankfurt, Ger, 82, Fla Southern Col, 82, Seven Young Artists, Corcoran Gallery Art, Washington, DC, 72; Baltimore Mus, 72; Illumination, San Francisco, Calif, 80; Sylvia Ullman Gallery, Cleveland, Ohio, 80; Zenith Gallery, Washington, DC, 80; House of Artists, Moscow, USSR, 89; and many others. *Awards:* Stern Family grant, 70; Washington Printmaker's Proj, 74; Printmakers Grant, Nat Endowment Arts, 74. *Bibliog:* Dreamtime, The Washingtonian, 4/75; Paul Richard (auth), Making it as an artist, The Washington Post, 10/77. *Media:* Mixed. *Collection:* Fantasy and surrealism: Klinger, Milton. *Publ:* Auth, The Unicorn, Viking Press, 80; illusr, The Unicorn Calendar, Pomegranite Press, 80 & 82; Auth, The Wordless Travel Book, 10 Speed Press; In Praise of Women, Celestial Arts Press. *Mailing Add:* PO Box 97 Mill Valley CA 94942-0097

MEADOWS, PATRICIA B
CURATOR, CONSULTANT
b Amarillo, Tex, Nov 12, 38. *Study:* Univ Tex, BA, 60; additional studies with Ramon Froman, Julius Zsohar, William Henry Earle & Victor Armstrong. *Work:* Harlingen Court House, Tex; State Bar Tex Hq, Austin; Univ Tex Health Sci Ctr, Tyler. *Collection Arranged:* Presenting Nine (auth, catalog), Dallas, Tex, 84; Critic's Choice (auth, catalog), Dallas, Tex, 84-95; Texas Women (catalog), 88-89 & Texas: reflections, rituals (catalog), 90-91, Nat Mus Women Arts, Washington; Establishment Exposed (catalog), 96; Texas Sculpture Garden, Hall Off Park, Frisco, Tex. *Pos:* Co-founder & dir, D-Art Visual Art Ctr, Dallas, 81-99, pres bd dir, 82-85, cur, 90-97; bd dir, Arts Dist Management Asn, Dallas, Tex, 85-91, Tex State Comn, Nat Mus Women Arts, 86-98, Artists Sq Design Team, 88-90 & Mid-Am Alliance, Kansas City, Mo, 90-93; exhib dir, Texas Women, Nat Mus Women Arts, Washington, 87-89; acquisition comn, Dallas Mus Art, 88-92; founder & cur, The Collectors, Dallas, Tex, 89-96; adv bd, Univ Tex, Austin, Sch Fine Arts, 90-91; pres, Dallas Art Dealers Asn, 97-99; sr vpres, cur, Hall Financial Group, 99-. *Awards:* Serv to the Arts Award, Tex Fine Arts Asn, 84; Flora Award, 87; James K Wilson Award, 88; Legend Award, Dallas Visual Art Ctr, 96. *Mem:* Tex Sculpture Asn; Dallas Visual Art Ctr; Nat Mus Women Arts; Tex Fine Arts Asn Mus; Emergency Artists' Support League (co-founder, 92-); Dallas Mus Art. *Collection:* Art Shirer; Eliseo Garcia; Sherry Owens; Marty Ray; Randy Brodnax; James Watral; Karl Umlauf; Jerry Daniel; Margaret Ratelle; Heather Marcus; David Iles; Norman Kary; Andrea Rosenberg. *Mailing Add:* 2707 State St Dallas TX 75204

MEAGHER, SANDRA KREBS
PAINTER
b NY. *Study:* Smith Col, BA, 1958; Art Students League, 1973-1980. *Work:* Town of Fairfield, Conn. *Exhib:* Breaking the Rules, Katonah Mus, Katonah, NY, 2001; Art of the Northeast, Silvermine Guild Arts Ctr, New Canaan, Conn, 2003. *Awards:* First Prize (Breaking the Rules, Art of the Northeast), Katonah Mus, 2001; Carol Eisner Sculpture Award, 2003. *Bibliog:* Vivian Raynor (Auth), In Pelham, Artist Who Take to the Rd, NY Times, 1992. *Mem:* Silvermine Guild Art Ctr (chmn Inst Visual Artists, 1989); Art Place (pres, 2005). *Media:* Acrylic, Oil. *Publ:* auth, Nora, Cross Roads Press, 1991. *Mailing Add:* 8 Craw Ave Norwalk CT 06853-1603

MEARS, LINDA SHAW
PAINTER
b Los Angeles, Calif, Apr 23, 49. *Study:* Citrus Jr Col, LVN license, 72; Fresno State Univ, 74-76; Sacramento Col, AA, 87. *Work:* Galerie Je Reviens, Westport, Conn; Yvon Daigle Galerie Art Naif', Magog, Que; Galerie Pro Arte Kasper, Morges, Switz; Musee d'Art Int, Yvon M Daigle, Que; Musee d'Art de Bages, France. *Comn:* Oil paintings, comn by clients of Frank J Miele Gallery, NY, 87-; oil paintings, comn by Mr & Mrs Unger, Pioche, Nev, 91-; oil paintings, Niederhoffer & Niederhoffer, Inc, NY, 94-; oil paintings, comn by Steve Keeley, Westport, Conn, 95-96. *Exhib:* Small Works of Am Folk Artists, Galerie Pro Arte Kasper, Switz, 92; Celebrity Centre Int, Hollywood, Calif, 93; Uruguay Exhib Am Art, SAm, 97-. *Pos:* owner Linda Mears Studio, Hollywood Hills, Calif. *Bibliog:* Naive Art Gallery, (bk), Gakken Co Ltd, 91; Lia Kasper (auth), Gazette Galerie Pro Arte, Galerie Pro Arte, Kasper, 92; Yvon Daigle (auth), Naive Artists, Galerie Art Naif, 97. *Mem:* Am Folk Art Mus; Celebrity Ctr Int. *Media:* Oil or Acrylic on Canvas. *Specialty:* folk art. *Publ:* Illusr, Art Americana 1993, Golden Turtle Press, 91 & 93; Education of a Speculator, John Wiley & Sons, Inc, 96; 101 Adventures in Life & Times of Bo Keeley, 96; The Time Factory (calendars), 98-. *Dealer:* Horizon Art Productions, 2115 Arrow Route, Upland, Calif 91786

MECKSEPER, JOSEPHINE
SCULPTOR
b Lilienthal, Germ, 64. *Study:* Studies at Hochschule der Kunste, Berlin, 86-90; Calif Inst Arts, Valencia, MFA, 90-92. *Exhib:* Solo shows, Shine oder Jedem das Seine, Galerie Reinhard Hauff, Stuttgart, 2001; Lustgarten, Borgmann Nathusius Galerie, Cologne, 2002; Josephine Meckseper, Elizabeth Dee Gallery, 2003; IG Metall und die kunstlichen Paradiese des Politischen, 2004; %, 2005; The Bulletin Board, White

Columns, NY, 2005; Group shows, Tattoo Collection, Andrea Rosen Gallery, NY, 92; This Is Your Home, Stuyvesant Town, NY, 94; Wheel of Fortune, Lombard-Fried Fine Arts, NY, 95; Mixing Messages: Graphic Design in Contemporary Culture, Cooper-Hewitt, Nat Design Mus, NY, 96; Super Freaks: Post Pop and the New Generation, Part 1: Trash, Green Naftali, NY, 98; Overflow, D'Amelio Terras, Marianne Boesky Gallery & Anton Kern Gallery, NY, 99; Flea Market, Gavin Brown's Enterprise, NY, 2000; Wine, Women & Wheels, White Columns, NY, 2001; In the Public Domain, 2003; American Idyll, 2004; Girls on Film, Zwirner & Wirth, NY, 2005; Whitney Biennial: Day for Night, Whitney Mus Am Art, 2006; This Ain't No Fooling Around, Rubicon Gallery Contemporary Art, Dublin, 2006. *Mailing Add:* c/o Elizabeth Dee Gallery 545 W 20th St New York NY 10011

MEDEL, REBECCA ROSALIE
SCULPTOR, ENVIRONMENTAL ARTIST
b Denver, Colo, 47. *Study:* Ariz State Univ, Tempe, BFA(environ design), 70; Fiberworks, Ctr for Textile Arts, Berkeley, Calif, cert, 79; Univ Calif, Los Angeles, MFA, 82. *Work:* Mus des Arts Decoratifs, Lausanne, Switz; Mus de la Tapisserie, Aix-en-Provence, France; Art Inst Chicago, Ill; Longhouse Reserve, East Hampton, NY; Denver Art Mus, Colo. *Comn:* private collectors, Scottsdale, Ariz, St Louis, Mo, Chapel Hill, NC. *Exhib:* The 20th Century Textile Artist, Art Inst Chicago, Ill, 99; Contemp Art of Linear Construction (with catalog), Yokohama Mus Art, Japan, 99; Made in Calif 1900-2000, Los Angeles Co Mus Art, 2000; The Art of Containment, Hunterdon Mus, Clinton, NJ, 2002; Fibertart Int, Soc Contemp Arts, Pittsburgh, 2001; Small Works, Long House Reserve, East Hampton, NY 2002; solo exhib: Continuity & Change, Thirteen Moons Gallery, Santa Fe, NMex, 2003. *Teaching:* Asst prof fibers, Tenn Technol Univ, Smithville, 83-; assoc prof, Univ Calif, Los Angeles, 1989-91 & Tyler Sch Art, Philadelphia, 1995-. *Awards:* Bronze Medal, Fifth Int Triennal, Cent Mus Lodz, Poland, 85; Southern Arts Fedn Fel, 85; Nat Endowment Arts, 86 & 88; Pew fel in the Arts, 1999; Fel Pa Coun on the Arts, 2001; McRight Award for Contemp Art, Delaware Art Mus, 2000. *Bibliog:* Artweek, Oakland, Calif, 9/13/90; Nouvel Object III, Design House Publ, Seoul, Korea, 97; Article in fiber arts, Textile Plus & British Crafts, 98-99; Am Style, Baltimore, Md, Fall & Winter 2000. *Media:* Sized Linen & Cotton Thread, Fiber Optic Thread. *Dealer:* Brown Grotta Arts, 276 Ridgefield Rd, Wilton, Conn 06897; Thirteen Moons Gallery 652 Canyon Rd Santa Fe NMex 87501. *Mailing Add:* 2920 Meyer Ave Glenside PA 19038

MEDENICA, BRANKO
SCULPTOR
b Darmstadt, Ger, July 17, 50; US citizen. *Study:* Birmingham-Southern Col, BA, 72; Univ Miss, MFA, 75; Richard MacDonald Master Class, 98;. *Work:* Archives Am Art, Washington, DC; Univ Miss, Oxford. *Comn:* Duty Called (cast bronze), State of Ala, Montgomery, 85; Col Cullman (cast bronze), City of Cullman, Ala, 88; Aspirations (stainless steel), comn by Dr Sam Barker, Birmingham, 91; Centurion (cast bronze), Fraternal Order of Police, Birmingham, 92; Samuel Ullman (cast bronze), Univ Ala, Birmingham, 93; Jesse Owens (cast bronze), Oakville, Ala, 96. *Exhib:* Nat Sculpture '74 Traveling Exhib, 74; 1st Ala Sculpture Show, Mobile Mus, 80; Outdoor Sculpture Invitational, Univ Ala, Tuscaloosa, 82; The Fiery Furnace: Cast Metal Sculpture, Sloss Mus, Birmingham, 90; Chariscuro, Light & Dark, Montgomery Mus Art, Ala, 94; River Gallery, Chattanooga, 96; others. *Pos:* Co-founder, Birmingham Arts Comn, 80; chair long range planning comt, Bham Arts Comn, 81-83; chair visual arts adv panel, Ala State Coun Arts, 82-86. *Teaching:* Birmingham Southern Col, 95; Univ Ala Birmingham, 96. *Awards:* Addy Award, 71. *Bibliog:* George Inser (dir), Forging Art Through Friendship (film), City of Birmingham, 89; Mary Jean Parson (auth), Accessible art, Birmingham Mag, 89; Jesse Holland (auth), Gift honors UAB's aspirations, Post-Herald, 91. *Mem:* Nat Sculpture Soc; Int Sculpture Soc. *Media:* Cast Metal, Welded Metal. *Publ:* Auth, Old George: The Restoration Process by Branko Medenica. *Dealer:* Dale Chambliss Gallery Destin FL. *Mailing Add:* 2300 Peacock Ln Birmingham AL 35223

MEDRICH, LIBBY E
SCULPTOR
b Hartford, Conn. *Study:* NY Univ, 31; Vassar Col, 49 & 54; Silvermine Col Arts, 51; Art Students League, 52-55; White Plains Co Ctr, 57 & 58; also with John Hovannes, Domenico Facci, George Koras, Harold Castor & Helen Beling. *Work:* Univ Chicago; First Church Christ, Wethersfield, Conn; Bloomsburg Univ, Pa; Planned Parenthood, Los Angeles; numerous pvt collections in US & abroad; Claremont Manor, Calif; Univ Judaism, CA. *Exhib:* Mus Fine Art, Springfield, Mass, 66; Galerie Raymond Duncan, Expo Prix de Paris, 67; Wadsworth Atheneum Mus, Hartford, Conn, 72; Metrop Mus Art, NY, 77; Hudson River Mus, Westchester, Yonkers, NY, 77 & 82; Ward-Nasse Gallery, NY, 77; Silvermine Guild Arts Ctr, Conn, 82; Texaco Int Hqs, Purchase, NY, 83; Nelson Rockefeller Galleries, NY, 84; Allied Artists Am, Nat Arts Club, NY, 90; Solo exhib, Haas Gallery Invitational Bloomsburg, Pa, 92; and others. *Awards:* 31 including Int Women's Year Award Slide Exhib, 75-76; Am Soc Contemp Artists Sculpture Award Merit, 82; Audubon Artists Donors Sculpture Award, 82. *Bibliog:* Helen Harrison (auth), article, NY Times, 5/15/83; Joan Lentczner (auth), The Communige, Bloomsburg Univ, Pa, 7/30/92; Edith Landi (auth), Art in focus, Libby Medrich-sculptor, Tempo Mag, 5/94, Alta Loma, Calif; Libby Medrich The Wisdom of Age, Claremont Courier, 5/2/98. *Mem:* NY Artists Equity; Mamaroneck Artists Guild (pres, 68-70); Am Soc Contemp Artists; Hudson River Contemp Artists; Pomona Valley Art Asn. *Media:* Cast Bronze, Polymer Resin, Mixed Media. *Publ:* auth, Sculpture: From Conception to Birth, Manhattan Arts intl, Nov-Dec, 93. *Dealer:* Ward-Nasse Gallery 178 Prince St New York NY 10012; Mag Gallery 150 Larchmont Ave Larchmont NY 10538. *Mailing Add:* 650 W Harrison Ave Claremont CA 91711-4595

MEDVEDOW, JILL
DIRECTOR
b New Haven, Conn, Oct 4, 54. *Study:* Colgate Univ, BA, 76; NY Univ, Inst Fine Arts, MA, 78. *Hon Degrees:* Montserrat Col Art, Hon Dr, 1998. *Collection Arranged:* Honey, I'm Home, Midtown Art Ctr, Houston, Tex, 85; Outside New York: Seattle, New Mus, New York, 86; Dorit Cypis: The Body in the Picture (catalog), Isabella Stewart Gardner Mus, Boston, Mass, 93; Denise Marika: New Works (with catalog), Isabella Stewart Gardner Mus, Boston, 94; Juan Munoz: Potrait of a Turkish Nan Drawing (with catalog), Isabella Stewart Gardner Mus, Boston, 95. *Pos:* Artist-in-residence, Blue Mountain Ctr, 86 & 90; Prog developer, WGBH Educ Found, Boston, Mass, 89-92; freelance consult to museums regarding pub programming; consult, Nat Endowment Arts; dep dir progs & cur contemp art, Isabella Stewart Gardner Mus, Boston, Mass, 93-97; James Sachs Plaut dir, Inst Contemp Art, Boston, 98-. *Awards:* Writer in residence, Blue Mountain Ctr, NY, 84-86; Fel critical writing, Seattle Arts Comn, 85. *Mem:* Art Table; Am Asn Mus; Col Art Asn. *Publ:* Auth, A View from the outside: The art of Nancy Spero and Elaine Reichek, Cocafolio, Ctr Contemp Art, 85; coauth, Back to basics: media arts centers in the 80's return to their roots, Visions, spring 87; auth, Daniel Reeves, Video Currents, spring 87; coauth, Review of Hard Core: Power, Pleasure and the Frenzy of the Visible, The Independent, 91; ed, The Eye of the Beholder, Isabella Stewart Gardner Mus, 94. *Mailing Add:* Institute of Contemporary Art 955 Boylston St Boston MA 02115-3194

MEEK, A J
PHOTOGRAPHER, EDUCATOR
b Beatrice, Nebr, Aug 29, 41. *Study:* Art Ctr Col Design, Los Angeles, with Todd Walker, BFA, 70; Ohio Univ, Athens, with Arnold Gassan, MFA, 72; further study with Paul Caponigro. *Work:* New Orleans Mus Art, La; Inverness Mus & Art Gallery, Scotland & Royal Comn Ancient Monuments, Edinburgh; Mus Art, Houston, Tex; Int Mus Photo/George Eastman House; New Orleans Hist Collection. *Exhib:* Photog in La 1800-1980, New Orleans Mus Art, 80; Louisiana portraits, New Orleans Mus Art, 84; Am Photog Today, Invitational, Univ Denver, 84; Louisiana Photog 1884-1984, Corcoran Gallery Art, 85; Southern Arts Fedn, Atlanta Col Art, 88 & 94; Soc Contemp Photog Gallery, Kansas City, Mo, 90; Emerging Southern Photographers, Memphis Col Art, 92; Afterimage Gallery, Dallas, Tex, 94; and others. *Collection Arranged:* Spirit of Utah 1860-1976 (ed, catalog), Utah State Univ, 76. *Teaching:* Asst prof photog, Utah State Univ, Logan, 72-77; head photog film area, La State Univ, 77-. *Awards:* Nat Endowment for Arts Exhib aid, 76; Louisiana State Univ Coun Research Fel, 86 & 94; Purchase Award, Soc Contemp Photog, 87; Southern Arts Fedn/Nat Endowment Arts career enhancement grant, 87 & 93; La Div Arts Fel, 91. *Bibliog:* Review, Show we have seen, Popular Photography, 83; Nancy Barrett (auth), Louisiana Portraits, New Orleans Mus Art, 84; Herman Mhire (auth), A Century of Vision, Louisiana Photography 1884-1984, Univ Southwestern Louisiana Art Mus, 86. *Mem:* Soc Photog Educ; Friends of Photog. *Media:* Silver Prints, Alternative Processes. *Publ:* Contribr, The Highlands--Limited Edition Portfolio of Fine Prints, 80; monogr, Red Pepper Paradise: Avery Island, Louisiana, Audobon Park Press, 88; Aperture (monogr), Beyond Wilderness, summer, 90; Gardens of Louisiana, La State Univ Press, 95. *Dealer:* Gallery for Fine Photography 5423 Magazine St New Orleans LA; Afterimage Gallery the Quadrangle No 2502800 Routh St Dallas TX 75201

MEEK, J WILLIAM, III
DEALER, CONSULTANT
b Aberdeen, Md, Nov 8, 50. *Study:* Fla Southern Col, BA, 72. *Pos:* Asst dir, Harmon Gallery, Naples, Fla, 72-77; dir-owner, Harmon-Meek Gallery, 78-; bd mem, Richard Florsheim Art Fund, Tampa, Fla. *Awards:* Paul Harris Fel, Rotary Int; Contrib to Visual Arts Ann Award, Artists Equity Asn, 99. *Mem:* Fel Royal Soc Arts, London; Nat Arts Club, NY. *Specialty:* Paintings, drawings and sculpture by major American artists of the 20th century. *Collection:* Private collection of 20th century American art

MEEKER, BARBARA MILLER
EDUCATOR, PAINTER
b Peru, Ind, Dec 31, 30. *Study:* DePauw Univ, BA; also with Jack Pellew, Ed Betts, Edgar A Whitney, Claude Croney, Charles Reid, Ed Fitzgerald, Frank Webb, Millard Sheets, Robert E Wood, Miles Batt, Dong Kingman, Glen Bradshaw & Virginia Cobb. *Work:* DePauw Univ Art Ctr Print Collection, Greencastle, Ind; Purdue Univ, Calumet & Hammond Pub Schs, Ind; Tri-State Col, Angola, Ind; Oak Park River Forest High Sch, Ill; Lake Co Pub Libr; Ind Bell Telephone; Nat Easter Seal Soc. *Comn:* Viking Eng. *Exhib:* Ft Wayne Art Mus; Lafayette Art Mus; Artist Guild Chicago Watercolor Show, Rocky Mountain Nat Watercolor Exhib, Denver; Contemp Artists Ind, Indianapolis; Ind State Mus Invitational, Indianapolis; Nat Watercolor Oklahoma, Okla City; Watercolor USA; retrospective, NIAA, Munster, Ind. *Collection Arranged:* Calumet Collection, Purdue Univ; DePauw Univ Collection; Sand Ridge Bank Art Collection; Northern Ind Pub Svc Co Art Collection. *Pos:* Mem art comn, Ind State House, 63-65; bd dir, Midwest Watercolor Soc, 83-85 & VSA Arts, Ind, 2000-05; coordr, Very Special Arts, Ind, 88-89, 90 & 91; mem art com, Town of Munster, 2003-; bd dir, NIAA, 94-2000. *Teaching:* Emer prof freehand drawing & painting, Purdue Univ, Calumet, 65-86. *Awards:* Jury Prize Distinction, Indianapolis, 84; Nat Watercolor Okla, 87; Midwest Watercolor, 97. *Bibliog:* Hawkins & McClarren (auth), Indiana lives, Hist Rec Asn, 67; J L Collins (auth), Women Artists in America, Les Krantz. *Mem:* signature mem, Ky Watercolor Soc; life mem & signature mem, Midwest Watercolor Soc; Chicago Artists Coalition; N Coast Collage Soc; life mem Northern Ind Arts Asn (bd dir, 95-2001). *Media:* Watercolor, Collage, Acrylic. *Specialty:* Paintings, sculpture, prints. *Interests:* Gardening, traveling. *Collection:* Community Hospital, Munster, Ind; St. Catherine Hospital, E Chicago, Ind; Oak Park-River Forest HS, Oak Park, Ill; Hammond Public Schools, Ind; Whiteco Corp, Merrillville, Ind. *Publ:* Auth, Freehand Drawing, 72, 2nd ed, 75, 3rd ed, 80; contribr, Complete Guide to Creative Watercolor, 88. *Dealer:* Heart To Heart Gallery Munster IN; The Steeple Gallery St John IN. *Mailing Add:* PO Box 3204 Munster IN 46321

MEEKS, DONNA MARIE
ADMINISTRATOR, PAINTER
b Louisville, Ky, Jan 14, 60. *Study:* Univ Louisville, Kentucky, BA(honors, drawing), 82, MAT, 84; Univ Wis, Milwaukee, MFA(painting, sculpture), 86. *Work:* Hoyt Inst Fine Arts, New Castle, Pa; Wabash Col Art Dept; Kirkland Fine Arts Ctr, Millikin Univ; Cape Townsend Artists' Workshops, Algoma, Wis; Coca-Cola Bottling Co, Elizabethtown, Ky; Fundacion Torre Pujales, Corme, La Coruna, Galicia, Spain; Art Mus Southeast Texas, Beaumont; Brandywine Workshop, Phila, Pa. *Exhib:* Nat Works on Paper, Univ Gallery, St John's Univ, Jamaica, NY, 95; Nat Exhib, Denise Bibro Fine Art, Soho, 97; Nat Showcase Exhbn Alternative Mus, Soho, 99; Critics Choice Dallas Visual Art Ctr, Tex, 99; Beefcake/Cheesecake: Sex, Flesh, Money and Dreams, Orange Co Ctr for Cont Art, Santa Ana, Calif, 2001; Cerebral Candy, Lankershim Art Gallery, N Hollywood, Calif, 2004; Go Figure, Circle Gallery, Maryland Federation of Art, Annapolis, 2004; Oct Int Competition, Montgomery Art Ctr, West Palm Beach, Fla, 2004; 7th Ann All Media Exhib, Touchstone Gallery, Washington, DC, 2005; 19th Ann Int Juried Show, NJ Ctr Visual Arts, Summit, NJ, 2005. *Pos:* Cur educ, Tarble Arts Ctr, Eastern Ill Univ, Charleston, 87-93; dir educ, Am Acad Art, Chicago, 93-95; chmn, Art Dept, Lamar Univ, Beaumont, Tex, 95-. *Teaching:* Instr, Eastern Ill Univ, 87-93; prof, Dept Art, Lamar Univ, Beaumont, Tex, 95-. *Awards:* First Place Monetary Award, Works on Paper, Houston, 96; Provocative Symbolism Award, 2nd Annual Musky Nat, Muskingum Col, Ohio, 96; First Place, Small Works '98, Sam Houston State Univ, Huntsville, Tex, 98. *Bibliog:* Lois Michel (auth), Magical, mystical aura ect, Naperville Sun, 88; James Auer (auth), Gall exhib include kitchen sink, Milwaukee J, 89; Art symposium hailed a success, Leavenworth Times, Kans, 91; Cecelia Johnson (auth), Here & Hereafter: Artists explore questions of life, death and mortality in exhibit, Issue: The Arts Mag of the Art Studio Inc, 2003. *Mem:* Col Art Asn; Nat Asn Schs Art & Design; Nat Coun Arts Adminr; Tex Asn Schs Art. *Media:* Oil, Egg Tempera, Mixed. *Publ:* auth, The allegorical imperative (or why paint when the copy store is open twenty-four/seven), Visual Resources, Vol XV, No 2 fall 99; auth, Some Thoughts on Jesse Stuart and Emmanuel Kant: New Passageways in Men of the Mountains, Jack London Newsletter, Vol 16, No 1, Jan-Apr 1983; auth, Do We Know Our ABC's: Art, Bridges and Community, issue: The Arts Mag of the Art Studio Inc, Vol 9, No 9, 6/2003. *Mailing Add:* Lamar Univ Dept Art PO Box 10027 Beaumont TX 77710

MEHN, JAN (JAN VON DER GOLZ)
PRINTMAKER
b Chicago, Ill, Aug 26, 53. *Study:* Kansas City Art Inst, Mo, Calif Col Arts & Crafts, Oakland, BFA, 79, Ariz State Univ, Tempe, MFA, 87. *Work:* Auburn Arts Ctr, Ala; Univ Tex, San Antonio; Ariz State Univ, Tempe; Kansas City Art Inst, Mo; Calif Col Arts & Crafts, Oakland. *Exhib:* 31st Ann San Francisco Art Festival, Calif, 77; 13th Nat Print Exhib, Silvermine Guild Art, New Canaan, Conn, 80; 28th Nat Print Exhib, Hunterdon Art Ctr, Clinton, NJ, 84; 6th Miami Int Print Exhib, North Miami Mus, North Miami, Fla, 84; 37th Boston Printmakers, Rose Art Mus, Waltham, Mass, 85, Prints: Washington, The Phillips Collection, Washington, 88; Ariz State Univ Alumni, 99; Anchor Graphics, Ill, 99. *Pos:* Printers asst, De Soto Workshop, San Francisco, 79-80; Conserv aid, Nat Arch, Washington, 88-89; preparator, Sackler Gallery Art, Smithsonian, 89-90, Wash Proj Arts, Washington, 90; Studio Mgr, DePaul Univ, Chicago, 98-. *Teaching:* Instr drawing & printmaking, Ariz State Univ, Tempe, 84-87; instr monotype, Arlington Arts Ctr, Va, 88 & Pyramid Atlantic, Washington, 89; Va Mus, Richmond, 90-91; asst prof, Bradley Univ, Peoria, Ill, 91-92; DePaul Univ, Chicago, 98-00. *Awards:* Artist's Grant, District Columbia Arts & Humanities, 89; Artist's Grant, State Ill Arts Coun, 95; Change Found Grant, 00. *Bibliog:* JoAnn Lewis (auth), At the Phillips, Wash Post, 9/17/88; Daniel Barbiero (auth), Atlanta Art Papers, 1-2/89; Michael Welzenbach (auth), Wash Post, 4/7/90. *Mem:* Southern Graphics Conf; Mid-American Print Alliance. *Media:* Monotypes, Mixed Media. *Specialty:* Contemporary Art. *Dealer:* Chipp-D Gallery 2905 Broadway Long Beach Calif 90803. *Mailing Add:* 2711 S 59th Ct Cicero IL 60804

MEHRETU, JULIE
ARTIST
b Addis Ababa, Ethiopia, 70. *Study:* Univ Cheik Anta Diop, Dakar, Senegal, 90-91; Kalamazoo Col, BA, 92; RI Sch Design, MFA with hon, 97. *Exhib:* one-woman shows, Sol Kofler Gallery, Providence, RI, 95, Ancestral Reflections, Archive Gallery, NY, 95, Bombastic Righteous Passively Become Apparent Absurdities, Sol Kofler Gallery, Providence, RI, 96, Recent Work, Barbara Davis Gallery, Houston, 98, Module, Project Row Houses, Houston, 99; group shows, Ctr Curatorial Studies, Bard Col, Annandale-on-Hudson, 2000, Free Style, Studio Mus Harlem, 2001, The Americans, Barbican Gallery, London, 2001, Busan Biennale, Korea, 2002, 8th Baltic Triennial Vilnius, Lithuania, 2002, Drawing Now: Eight Propositions, Mus Modern Art, 2002, Painting at the Edge of the World, Walker Art Ctr, 2003, Carnegie Inter, Carnegie Mus Art, Pittsburgh, Pa, 2004, Sao Paulo Biennial, Sao Paulo, Brazil, 2004, Whitney Biennial, The Whitney Mus Am Art, New York City, 2004, Back to Paint, C&M Arts, New York City, 2004, Firewall, Ausstellungshalle Zeitgenössische Kunst, Munster, Ger, 2004; The Project, New York City, 2001, Art Pace, San Antonio, Tex, 2001, White Cube, London, 2002, Julie Mehretu: Drawing into Painting, Walker Art Ctr (traveling), 2003, REDCAT, Los Angeles, Calif, 2004, Albright-Knox Art Gallery, Buffalo, NY, 2004, Matrix, Univ Calif Berkeley Art Mus, 2004, earlier 1 gebauer, Berlin, Ger, 2004, Drawing, The Project, New York City, 2005, Current, St Louis Art Mus, 2005. *Awards:* Excellence Award, RI Sch Design, 96; Core Fels, Artist in Residence, Glassell Sch Art, Mus Fine Arts, Houston, 97-99; Penny McCall Award, 2001. *Mailing Add:* 3rd Floor 37 W 57th St New York NY 10019

MEIER, RICHARD ALAN
ARCHITECT
b Newark, NJ, Oct 12, 34. *Study:* Cornell Univ, BArch, 57; Univ Naples, Italy, Doctor (hon), 1991; The New Sch, NY City, Doctor (hon), 1995. *Hon Degrees:* Univ Naples; NJ Inst Tech; New Sch Social Res; Wheaton Col; Pratt Inst. *Work:* High Mus, Atlanta; Mus Contemp Art, Barcelona, Spain; Mus TV & Radio, Beverly Hills, Calif; US Fed Courthouse, Islip, NY; Neugebauer House, Naples, Fla, 97. *Comn:* High Mus Art, Atlanta, Ga; Douglas House; J Paul Getty Mus & Fine Arts Ctr, comn by J Paul Getty Trust, 84; Mus Decorative Arts; Frankfurt City Hall, The Hague; Des Moines Art Ctr additions; UCLA, vis design critic, 87, 88 & 89; Ara Pacis Mus, Rome, 2006. *Exhib:* Modernism Gallery, San Francisco, 80; Wadsworth Atheneum, Hartford, Conn, 80; High Mus Art, Atlanta, 80; Max Protetch Gallery, NY, 80; Harvard Univ, 80; Knoll Int, Tokyo, Japan, 88; October Gallery, London, Eng, 90; Royal Palace, Naples, Italy, 91; Galerie Nationale de Jeu de Paume, Paris, 99; Archit Inst, Rotterdam, 2001; Mus Applied Art, Frankfurt, Ger, 2003; High Mus Art, Atlanta, 2003-2004; Modena Forum, Italy, 2004. *Pos:* principal architect, Richard Meier & Assocs, NY, 1963-1980; mem adv coun, Col Art, Archit & Planning, Cornell Univ, Ithaca, NY, 71-; Resident architect, Am Acad in Rome, 73-74; juror, Int Competition, Convention Hall, Nara, Japan, 92. *Teaching:* Adj prof, Cooper Union, 64-73; William Henry Bishop vis prof, Yale Univ, 75 & 77; Eliot Noyes vis design critic, Harvard Univ, 80 & 81; vis design critic, Univ Calif, Los Angeles, 87, 88 & 89; vis prof, Cornell U, 2000-. *Awards:* Pritzker Archit Prize, 84; Royal Gold Medal, Royal Inst Brit Architects, 88; Gold Medal, Am Inst Architects, 97; Praemium Imperiale Award, Japan Art Assoc, 97; AIA Twenty five Year Award, 2000; World Archit Award, 2001; Legend Award, 2004. *Bibliog:* Richard Meier Architect, Rizzoli, 84; Wesner Blaser (auth) Richard Meier: Bldg for Art, 89; Gloria Gerace (ed), Getty Center Design Process, J Paul Getty Trust, 91. *Mem:* Nat Acad; fel Am Inst Architects; Int Acad Archit; Century Club New York; Am Acad & Inst Arts & Letts; hon fel Royal Inst Brit Architects. *Publ:* Coauth, Five Architects: Eisenman/Graves/Gwathmey/Hejduk/Meier, Wittenborn Co, 72; Richard Meier, Architect: Buildings and Projects 1966-1976, Oxford Univ Press, 76; Richard Meier, Architect, Rizzoll, 84; Richard Meir, Architect 2, Rizzoll, 91; and others. *Mailing Add:* Richard Meier & Partners 475 10th Ave 6th fl New York NY 10018-1120

MEISEL, LOUIS KOENIG
DEALER, HISTORIAN
b Brooklyn, NY, Sept 4, 42. *Study:* Tulane Univ; Columbia Univ; New Sch Social Res. *Collection Arranged:* Photo Realism 1973, Stuart M Speiser Collection (with catalog), Smithsonian Inst; Photo-Realism, Guggenheim Mus. *Pos:* Pres, Louis K Meisel Gallery, New York, currently. *Bibliog:* Les Levine (auth), New dealer, Arts Mag, 1/74; Judy Beardsall (auth), Louis Meisel, Art Gallery Mag, 9/73. *Res:* Photo realism. *Specialty:* Photo realism; abstract illusionism. *Publ:* Auth, 15 Years of Photorealism, Horizon Mag, 11/80; Richard E Estes, H N Abrams, 86; Clarice Cliff-The Bizarra Affair, H N Abrams, 88; Charles Bell, The Complete Paintings 1970-1990, H N Abrams, 91; Photo Realism Since 1980, H N Abrams, 93; The Great American Pin-up: Köln Germany, Benedikt Taschen Verlag, 95; auth, Photorealism, N H Abrams, Inc, 80; coauth, The Best of American Girlie Magazine, Benedikt Taschen Verlag, 97; coauth, The Edward Runci Collection: Pin Up Poster Book, Collectors Press, Inc, 97; co-auth, Gil Elvgren-All His Glamorous American Pin-Ups, Benedikt Taschen Verlag, 99; auth, Photorealism at the Millennium, N H Abrams, Inc, 2002. *Mailing Add:* 141 Prince St New York NY 10012

MEISEL, SUSAN PEAR
PAINTER, PRINTMAKER, PHOTOGRAPHER
b New York, NY, Apr 16, 47. *Study:* Barnard, 66; Parsons Sch Design, 68; Sch Visual Arts, 70; NY Univ, 2002-03. *Work:* Larry Aldrich Mus, Richfield, Conn; Ft Wayne Mus, Ind; State Dept, Washington, DC; numerous Am Embassies world wide. *Comn:* Libr Cong, Washington, DC; Smithsonian Inst, Washington, DC; Comsat Corp Hq, Washington, DC; Independence Hall, Philadelphia, Pa. *Exhib:* 10 yrs of Printmaking, Ft Wayne Mus, Ind, 80; 10 yrs of Printmaking, Tomasulo Gallery Union Col, NJ, 81. *Teaching:* Art teacher, UN Int Sch, 90-97. *Bibliog:* Judy Beardsall (auth), Susan Pear Meisel, Arts Mag, 5/78; Robert Voskowitz (auth), Susan Pear Meisel(catalog), Ft Wayne Mus. *Media:* Acrylic on Canvas. *Publ:* auth, The Hamptons, Harry N Abrams, 2000; auth, Hampton Pleasures, Harry N Abrams, 2004. *Mailing Add:* c/o Louis K Meisel Gallery 141 Prince St New York NY 10012

MEISELMAN, MARILYN NEWMARK See Newmark, Marilyn Newmark Meiselman

MEISSNER, ANNE MARIE
ADMINISTRATOR
Study: Oxford Univ, St Ann's Col, cert, 68; Univ Mich, Ann Arbor, MSW, 67; Univ Calif-Berkeley, BA, 79. *Pos:* Dir, San Francisco Art Comm Gallery, 87. *Mem:* Art Table (co-chair, prog comt, 91); Non-Profit Gallery Asn, San Francisco Bay Area (vprcs & bd dir); Art Span/Open Studios San Francisco. *Mailing Add:* 1673 Sacramento St San Francisco CA 94109-3718

MEISSNER, WALT
ADMINISTRATOR
Study: Texas A & M, BA; Boston Univ, MFA in theatre mgt & directing. *Pos:* Assoc dean-adminstr, affairs Boston Univ Col Fine Arts, 93-2001, acting dean, 2001-02, dean ad interim, 2002-. *Mailing Add:* Boston Univ Col Fine Arts 855 Commonwealth Ave Rm 230 Boston MA 02215

MEISTER, MARK J
INSTITUTE DIRECTOR, ART HISTORIAN
b Baltimore, Md, June 26, 53. *Study:* Washington Univ, AB (art & archeol), 74; Univ Minn, MA (art hist & museology), 76. *Pos:* Dir, Mus Art & Hist, Port Huron, Mich, 78-79, Midwest Mus Am Art, Elkhart, Ind, 79-81 & Mus Art, Sci & Indust, Bridgeport, Conn, 86-89; exec dir, Children's Mus, St Paul, Minn, 81-86; exec dir, Archaeol Inst Am, Boston, Mass, 89-. *Teaching:* Adj lectr museology, Kenyon Col, Gambier, Ohio, 77; lectr art hist, Ind Univ, South Bend, 80-81. *Awards:* Nat Endowment Humanities Museology Fel, 76-77; Kress Fel, 77; Bush Found Summer Fel, 83. *Mem:* Am Asn Mus; Am Coun Learned Socs; Archaeol Inst Am; Soc Am Archaeol; US Comt/Int Coun Monuments & Sites. *Publ:* Ed, Selections Art & Artifacts from the Kenyon College Collection (catalog), 77; auth, The man who painted Lake Gervais Tornado, Minn Hist Mag, 77; Midwest Photo 80 & 81, Midwest Mus Am Art; ed, American Artists Abroad (exhib catalog), 86 & Milton Avery (exhib catalog), Mus Art, Sci & Indust, 87; co-ed, Archaeology on Film, Kendall/Hunt Publ Co, 94. *Mailing Add:* Archaeological Inst of Am 656 Beacon St Boston MA 02215-2010

MEISTER, MICHAEL WILLIAM
HISTORIAN, EDUCATOR
b West Palm Beach, Fla, Aug 20, 42. *Study:* Harvard Col, BA, 64; Harvard Univ, MA, 71, PhD, 74; Univ Pa, Hon MA, 79. *Exhib:* Cooking for the Gods, Newark Mus, 95-96. *Pos:* Cur, South Asia Art Archive, 78-. *Teaching:* Asst prof art hist, Univ Tex, Austin, 74-76; asst prof, Univ Pa, 76-79, assoc prof, 79-88, grad chmn hist of art dept, 78-79 & 86-90, prof, 88- & chmn hist of art, 94-. *Awards:* Smithsonian Develop Grant, 81; Studies Awards, Am Inst Pakistan, 94 & 96; Interpretive Res Grant, J Paul Getty Trust, 96-98. *Bibliog:* SARAS Bull, No 3. *Mem:* Am Comt South Asian Art (mem bd dir, 76-79 & 83-86); Am Inst Indian Studies; Asn Asian Studies; Comt Art and Archeol; Col Art Asn. *Res:* South Asian art, particularly Hindu temple architecture, sculpture and iconology. *Publ:* Ed, Encyclopedia of Indian Temple Architecture, Vols 1 & 2, Princeton Univ Press, 83, 86, 88 & 91; Discourses on Siva, Univ Pa Press, 84; On the Development of a Symbolic Architecture: India, Res 12, 86; Making Things in South Asia, Univ Pa, SAsia Dept, 88; Coomaraswamy: Essays in Early Indian Architecture, 92; Essays in Architectural Theory, 95. *Mailing Add:* Hist Art Dept G-29 Meyerson Hall Univ Pa Philadelphia PA 19104

MEITZLER, NEIL (HERBERT)
PAINTER
b Pueblo, Colo, Sept 14, 30. *Study:* With Kenneth Callahan. *Work:* Seattle Art Mus, Wash; Washington Co Mus Art, Hagerstown, Md; Henry Gallery, Univ Wash, Seattle,; Safeco Collection & Seattle 1st Nat Bank; Mus Northwest Art, LaConner, Wash. *Exhib:* one-man show, Seattle Art Mus, Wash, 59; Artists of the Northwest, Japanese World's Fair, 71; Northwest Art from Corporate Collections, Seattle, Wash, 84; Artists of Washington Co, Hagerstown, Md, 85-87; Here to Horizon, Whatcom Mus Art, Bellingham, 99; To be Modern in Mid-Century, Henry Gallery, Univ Wash, 99; Iridescent Light, Mus Northwest Art, LaConner, Wash, 2002. *Pos:* Designer, Seattle Art Mus, 57-78. *Awards:* Katharine Baker Award, Seattle Art Mus, 58; Nat Coun Theatres Award, US Govt, 67. *Bibliog:* Art of Pacific NW, Portland Art Mus, 59; Albi & Peck (auths), Artists of Puget Sound, 61; Leo Lerman (auth), Mademoiselle Mag, 4/62; Dolores Ament Tarzan (auth), Iridescent Light, Univ Wash Press, Seattle, 2001; Kitty Harmon, Pacific Northwest Landscape, Sasquatch Books, Seattle, 2001. *Media:* Acrylic, Tempera, Watercolor, oil. *Dealer:* Foster-White Gallery 311 1/2 Occidental Ave S Seattle WA 98104. *Mailing Add:* 637 Pleasant St Walla Walla WA 99362-3367

MEJER, ROBERT LEE
PAINTER, EDUCATOR
b South Bend, Ind, Nov 8, 44. *Study:* SBend Art Ctr with Joseph Wrobel; Ball State Univ, BS; Miami Univ with Robert Wolfe, Jr, MFA; Kent State Univ with Nathan Oliveira & Milton Resnick, 73; Kalamazoo Art Inst with Harvey Breverman, 75; Oxbow Summer Sch Art with Leon Golub, Joe Wilfer & Richard Haas, 76-78 & 81; Notre Dame Univ with Michael Ponce de Leon, 79; Wash Univ with Ed Paschke & Sam Gilliam, 80; Univ Chicago with Vera Klement, 86. *Work:* Kemper Insurance Co, Chicago; Hallmark Cards, Mo; Quaker Oats Corp, Chicago; Neville Pub Mus, Wis; Shearson, Lehman, Hutton, NY. *Comn:* Serigraphs, AFA Press, Lakeside, Mich, 98. *Exhib:* Retrospective 1969-1979, Quincy Art Ctr, Ill, 79; 51st Nat Midyear Painting, Butler Inst Am Art, 87; Int One of a Kind: Monotypes, Sigma Gallery, NY, 90; 24th Bradley Nat Print & Drawing Competition, Ill, 93; Dakota's Int Artwork on Paper, Univ SDak Art Gallery, Vermillion, 94; Greater Midwest Int, Cent Mo State Univ, 96. *Pos:* Gallery asst, Ball State Art Gallery, Ill, 62-66; gallery cur, Quincy Univ, 68- & chair fine arts div; gallery asst, Quincy Art Ctr, Ill, 70- & chair exhibs comt, 76-80 & 89-95. *Teaching:* Instr painting & drawing, Ball State Univ, summers 66 & 67; instr drawing, Miami Univ, 66-68; prof art, Quincy Univ, 68-; instr, John Wood Community Col, 75-76; vis res fac, Skidmore Col, Summer Six II, NY, 82-96. *Awards:* City of Quincy Individual Artist Award, 90; Fel, Vt Studio Ctr, 96; Quincy Univ Serv Award, 97. *Bibliog:* Julia Ayers (auth), Monotypes, Watson-Guptill, 91; Helen Dobbyn (producer, dir & ed), Artscape: Bob Mejer, Quincy Univ, 1/28/96; Nita Leland (auth), Exploring Color, Watson-Guptill, 98. *Mem:* Life mem Quincy Univ Found; Quincy Art Ctr (bd dir, 76-80, vpres, 76 & 89-95); life mem Midwest Watercolor Soc; Watercolor USA Honor Soc. *Media:* Watercolor, Monotypes. *Specialty:* Contemporary artists. *Publ:* Illusr, Salt-Lick Mag, 68-71; illusr, Riverword Mag, Vols 1, 2, & 3, 77. *Dealer:* Miriam Perlman Gallery Chicago IL. *Mailing Add:* 619 Meadow Lark Quincy IL 62301-5943

MEKAS, JONAS
FILMMAKER
b Semeniskiai, Lithuania, 22. *Study:* Univ Mainz, Ger, Studied philos & romance lang,. *Exhib:* group shows at Whitney Biennial, Whitney Mus Am Art, 2004. *Pos:* Auth, Film Cult column Village Voice, 58-; co-founder, Filmmakers' Cooperative, 62; founder Filmmakers' Cinémathèque (later Anthology Film Archives), 64; Essential Cinema Collection, 70. *Publ:* Prodr.: (films) Guns of the Trees, 61, The Brig, 63, Walden, 69, Reminiscences of a Voyage to Lithuania, 72, Lost Lost Lost, 75, Zefiro Torna, 92; auth: (book of poetry) There is No Ithaca, 96. *Mailing Add:* Anthology Film Archives 32 Second Ave New York NY 10003

MELAMED, HOPE See Winter, Hope Melamed

MELAMID, ALEXANDER See Komar and Melamid

MELBERG, JERALD LEIGH
ART DEALER, COLLECTOR
b Minneapolis, Minn, Aug 17, 48. *Study:* Pillsbury Col, Owatonna, Minn; Bob Jones Univ, Greenville, SC. *Collection Arranged:* 1977, 1979 & 1981 Biennial Exhibition of Piedmont Painting & Sculpture (ed, catalog), 77, 1978, 1980 & 1982 Biennial Exhibition of Piedmont Crafts (ed, catalog), 78 & Romare Bearden 1970-1980 (ed, catalog), 80, Mint Mus Art, Charlotte, NC; Seymour Lipton: Sculpture (ed, catalog), 82; Herb Jackson: Drawings (ed, catalog), 83; Ed Buonagurio: Recent Paintings (auth, catalog), 83. *Pos:* Dir, Hampton III Gallery, Ltd, Greenville, SC, 73-74; exec dir, Anderson Co Arts Coun, SC, 75-76; cur exhib, Mint Mus Art, 77-84; owner, Jerald Melberg Gallery Inc, 84-. *Bibliog:* Wolf Kahn (auth), New Landscapes, 91; Arless Day (auth), Constructing the best of all possible worlds, Recent Collages, 93; Charles Basham (auth), View from the studio, New Pastel Landscapes, 94. *Mem:* Int Coun Mus; Am Asn Mus; assoc Smithsonian Inst, Washington, DC. *Res:* Herb Jackson, Wolf Kahn, Romare Bearden. *Collection:* Paintings, sculpture, graphics by United States artists, graphics by nationally known American artists, and early 20th century works. *Mailing Add:* c/o Jerald Melberg Gallery 625 S Sharon Amity Rd Charlotte NC 28211

MELBY, DAVID A
PAINTER, PHOTOGRAPHER
b Wichita, Kans, June 8, 42. *Study:* Kansas City Art Inst; Wichita State Univ, BFA, 67; Univ Nebr, MFA, 70. *Work:* Am Express Corp, Salt Lake City; McDonald Corp, Chicago; Mulvane Art Mus, Topeka, Kans; Sheldon Mem Art Gallery & Sculpture Garden, Lincoln, Nebr; Mus Nebr Art, Kearney; and others. *Comn:* Plains People, 78. *Exhib:* A Sense of Place, Joslyn Art Mus, Sheldon Mem Art Gallery, Mid-Am Arts Alliance & others, 73; Nat Small Works Exhib, York Univ, NY, 79, 80, 83 & 84; Gwenda Jay Gallery, Chicago, Ill, 89; Am Myth, Sioux City Art Ctr, Iowa, 90; Spirit of the Landscape: The Landscape of the Spirit, Mitchell Mus, Mt Vernon, Ill, 91; Western Ill Univ, Macomb, 94; St Mary Col, Leavenworth, Kans, 97; Leavenworth Mus Art, 2000; and others. *Collection Arranged:* Artists Behind Bars, Jewish Community Ctr, Kansas City, Mo, 76; In Respect of Space, 79, Groups: A Public Face, 79 & Gold Rush: Work of Hal Parker, 80, Swan River Mus; Points of View: Six Artists, St Mary Col, 81; Mixed Metaphors: Visual Affinities, 2000; Points of View, Leavenworth Mus Art, Leavenworth, Kans, 2001. *Pos:* Artist in residence, US Fed Penitentiary, Leavenworth, Kans, Nat Endowment Arts, 75-76; dir exhibs, Swan River Mus, Paola, Kans, 79-80; dir, Bedyk Gallery, Kansas City, Mo, 85-86; dir Leavenworth Mus Art, Leavenworth, Kans, 2000-01. *Teaching:* Instr drawing & painting, Iowa State Univ, Ames, 70-75; instr painting, drawing & photog, St Mary Col, Kans, 80-82; instr, Nelson Atkins Mus, Kansas City, 83-84 & Kansas City Art Inst, 90-91. *Awards:* First Prize, Kansas Two, Kans Arts Comn, 82; Award Merit, Mid-Four Exhib, Nelson Atkins Mus, 82; Fel (painting) Mid Am Arts Alliance, Nat Endowment Arts, 86. *Bibliog:* Knut Forsundrsund (auth), article, Fotografi, 11/77; Victoria Melcher (auth), Kansas City: Dizzying directions, Art News, 10/80; David Knaus (auth), article, Art Gallery, 4-5/84; Marilyn Propp (auth), article, New Art Examiner, 10/86. *Mem:* Kansas City Artists Coalition; Kans Grass Roots Arts Asn; Leavenworth Co Arts Coun (exec coun); and others. *Media:* Oil; Black & White Photo. *Specialty:* Painting, Photography. *Collection:* Nineteenth and twentieth century European, American and native American art, American folk art, Photography. *Publ:* Contribr, A Sense of Place: The Artist and the American Land, Mid-Am Arts Alliance, 73; co-dir, videotape, Artist in Residence Prog, US Bur Prisons, 76; contribr, Poets on Photography, Dog Ear Press, 81; The Kansas Landscape, Kansas Dept Econ Develop, 85; New York Art Review, 88; Forum, 1-2/90. *Dealer:* Hallar Gallery 4540 Main St Kansas City MO 64111. *Mailing Add:* c/o David Melby Fine Arts PO Box 508 Leavenworth KS 66048

MELCHERT, JAMES FREDERICK
SCULPTOR, EDUCATOR
b New Bremen, Ohio, Dec 2, 30. *Study:* Princeton Univ, AB; Univ Chicago, MFA; Univ Calif, Berkeley, MA; ceramics with Peter Voulkos. *Hon Degrees:* San Francisco Art Inst, Hon Dr; Col Art, Md Inst, Hon Dr. *Work:* Mus Mod Art, San Francisco; Mus Mod Art, Kyoto, Japan; LA Co Mus Art; Oakland Mus Art, Calif; Stedelijk Mus, Amsterdam. *Comn:* Ceramic tile mural, New Biology Bldg, Mass Inst Technol, Cambridge, 92; bronze wall sculpture, Biomedical Res Bldg, Case Western Reserve Univ, 94. *Exhib:* Abstract Expressionist Ceramics, Univ Calif, Irvine, 66; Contemp Am Sculpture, Whitney Mus Am Art, NY, 66, 68 & 70; Documenta 5, Kassel, Ger, 72; Solo exhibs, Galerie Fignal, Amsterdam, 78, San Francisco Art Inst, Calif, 81; Calif Painting & Sculpture, San Francisco Mus Mod Art & Nat Collection Fine Arts, Washington, 77; Words at Liberty, Mus Contemp Art, Chicago, 77; One Hundred Yrs of Am Ceramics, Syracuse Mus, NY & Renwick Gallery, Washington, 80; California Sculpture, San Francisco Mus Mod Art, 86; Holly Solomon Gallery, NY, 91; European

Ceramic Work Ctr, Denbosch, The Neth, 98; World Contemp Ceramics, Inchon, Korea, 2001; Contemp Am Ceramics, Nat Mus Mod Art, Kyoto, 2002; Secret History of Clay, Tate, Liverpool, 2004. *Pos:* Dir visual arts prog, Nat Endowment Arts, 77-81; dir, Am Acad Rome, 84-88. *Teaching:* Chmn dept ceramics, San Francisco Art Inst, 61-64; prof art, Univ Calif, Berkeley, 65-76 & 81-92; vis sculptor, Univ Wis-Madison, spring 71. *Awards:* Citation for Distinguished Serv Visual Arts, Nat Asn Schs Art & Design; Artist Fel, Nat Endowment Arts, 73; Award of Distinction, Nat Coun Art Adminrs, 89; Hon Doctorate, San Francisco Art Inst, 84; Disting Alumnus Award, Coll Environ Design, Univ Calif, Berkeley, 99. *Bibliog:* Nancy Princethal (auth), Jim Melchert at Holly Solomon, Art in Am Mag, 12/91; Marsha Miro (auth), Jim Melchert, Mister-In-Between, Am Ceramics Mag, Vol 12, No 2; Gerry Williams (ed), James Melchert: Conversations, Studio Potter Mag, 6/97. *Mem:* Century Asn. *Media:* Clay. *Dealer:* Gallery Paule Anglim, San Francisco; Revolution Gallery, Detroit. *Mailing Add:* 6077 Ocean View Dr Oakland CA 94618

MELIKIAN, MARY
PAINTER
b Worcester, Mass. *Study:* RI Sch Design, Providence, BFA, 55; Columbia Univ Teachers Col. *Work:* Worcester Mus Art, Mass; Mint Mus, Charlotte, NC; Yerevan Mus, Armenia; Vassar Col Art Mus; Art for US Embassies, State Dept; Centre Human Rights, UN, NY. *Exhib:* Nat Arts Club NY, 69 & 70; Galerie de Tours, San Francisco & Ankrum Gallery, Los Angeles, 70, Calif; Retrospective, Centenary Col, Hackettstown, 75; one-man shows, Bodley Gallery, NY, 78 & 81, Quadrangle Gallery, Dallas, 80 & Dorsky Gallery, NY, 86; Group show, Nicholas Gallery, Palm Beach, Fla, 79; Elaine Benson Gallery, Bridgehampton, NY, 91. *Pos:* Asst designer, Fuller Fabrics, NY, 56; asst dir, Grand Cent Moderns, New York, 60-61; dir pub rels, Grand Cent Art Galleries, New York, 61-67. *Teaching:* Instr art, Nutley High Sch, 57-60. *Awards:* First Prize, Kit Kat Club, 61, Armenian Student Asn, 61 & 62 & Women's Nat Repub Club, 70, 72, 73 & 75; Spirit of Art Award, 107th Artists Mem Exhib, Nat Arts Club, 2006. *Bibliog:* Colette Roberts (auth), article, France-Am; N Stepanian (auth), Paintings of Mary Melikian, Voice of Am, 68; Anna Avedisian (auth), The Heart Remembers, Ararat Mag, 92. *Mem:* Parrish Art Mus, Southampton, NY; Guild Hall, East Hampton, NY; Nat Arts Club, NY. *Media:* Watercolor, Oil. *Interests:* human rights, theology & music. *Publ:* Auth, articles, Ararat Mag. *Mailing Add:* 429 E 52nd St Rivercourt 27H New York NY 10022

MELL, ED (EDMUND) PAUL, JR
PAINTER, PRINTMAKER
b Phoenix, Ariz, Sept 17, 42. *Study:* Phoenix Col, AA, 63; Art Ctr Col Design, Los Angeles, BFA(advert illus), 67. *Work:* Scottsdale Ctr Arts, Ariz. *Comn:* Oil painting, Mary Kay Cosmetics, Dallas, 80; oil murals, Empire Bank, Denver, 82, Farm Bank Ctr, Denver, 82 & Courson Oil, Perryton, Tex, 83. *Exhib:* Ariz Invitational, Scottsdale Ctr Arts, 82; Artists of Arizona, Ctr Mod Art, Guadalajara, Mex, 82; solo exhibs, Art Resources Gallery, Denver, 82, Dewey-Kofron Gallery, Santa Fe, 83 & Long Beach Mus Art, Calif, 83. *Pos:* Art dir, Kenyon & Eckhardt Advert, 68-70; artist & co-dir, Sagebrush Studio, New York, 70-73. *Teaching:* Instr art, Bacavi Community Sch, Hotevilla, Ariz, summers 71 & 73. *Bibliog:* Article, Art Voices S, 80; Ed Mell--Mesas man made, Southwest Art, 82; A portfolio of regional landscape painting, Am Artist, 84. *Media:* Oil on Canvas, Pastel; Lithography

MELLMAN, MARGERY
PAINTER
Study: Skidmore Col, BA(art hist), 70. *Exhib:* Selections 37, Drawing Ctr, NY, 87; Margery Mellman-Paintings, Painting Ctr, NY, 94; solo exhib, Black & Herron, NY, 95 & Trans Hudson Gallery, NY, 96. *Pos:* Executor of Estate of Stewart Hitch. *Awards:* National Endowment Arts Award for Painting, 93-94. *Media:* Oil. *Mailing Add:* 255 Sixth Ave New York NY 10014

MELLON, MARC RICHARD
SCULPTOR, MEDALIST
b Brooklyn, NY, Oct 17, 51. *Study:* Brooklyn Col, BA (fine arts), 74; Art Students League, with Robert Beverly Hale, 75; Nat Acad Design, with Gaitano Cecere, 75. *Work:* Smithsonian Inst Nat Portrait Gallery, Washington DC; Nat Art Mus Sport, Indianapolis; Salmagundi Mus, NY; Elliot Mus, Jupiter, Fla; Brookgreen Gardens, Am Numismatic Soc; The British Mus. *Comn:* Alton Ochsner MD (statue), Ochsner Med Found, New Orleans; Kate Smith (statue), Spectrum Arena, Philadelphia; Generations, New Learning Ctr, Westport, Conn; The Planting (bas-relief), Glick Jewish Community Ctr, Indianapolis; Pres Bush (bust) Bush Sch Govt, College Station, Tex; Pred Lee Yeng-Hui (bust), Chi Mei Mus, Taiwan, 99; Pope John Paul II (bust), Vatican Collection, 2001; NCAA Centennial (sculpture), Indianapolis, 2006. *Exhib:* One-man shows Minds, Moods & Movement, Nat Arts Club, NY & The Figure in Motion, Elliot Mus, Stuart, Fla; Artists of Am, Colo Hist Mus, Denver, 2000; World Leaders, NSS, NY; Newington-Cropsey Mus Ann Exhib, Hastings-on-Hudson, NY. *Awards:* John Gregory Mem Prize, NSS, 84; Mod Art Prize, Salmagundi Club Ann Exhib, 98; Artist in Tribute, Hudson Valley Art Asn Ann Exhib, 98. *Biblio:* Adam Gopnick (arts ed), New Yorker Mag, 87; Steven Doherty (ed), Am Artist Mag, 91. *Mem:* Nat Arts Club; Salmagundi Club; Artists Fel Inc (pres 90-98); NSS; Audubon Artists; Am Renaissance for the 21st Century (adv bd); Nat Mus Am Illustration (adv bd); Portrait Soc Am (comt mem). *Media:* Bronze. *Publ:* auth, Art Ideas-Values & Achievement in Sculpture, 97; contribr, Art Ideas, 98. *Dealer:* Cavalier Galleries 405 Greenwich Ave Greenwich CT 06896. *Mailing Add:* 61 Pheasant Ridge Rd Redding CT 06896

MELLOR, MARK ADAMS
PAINTER, GALLERY DIRECTOR
b Chicago, Ill, Oct, 28, 51. *Study:* Univ Bridgeport, Conn, AA, 76; Illusr Workshop, Tarrytown, NY, cert, 83; Tony Van Hasselt Watercolor Workshop, 2001. *Work:* Quaker Oats Co, Chicago, Ill; Westport Town Art Collection & Stamford Town Hall, Conn; Aetna, Hartford, Conn; Pepsico, NY; Middlebank, Middletown, Conn. *Comn:* Historic watercolor painting, Westport, Conn, 80. *Exhib:* Conn Watercolor Soc Exhib, Wadsworth Athenaeum Hartford, 76-77; 112th Am Watercolor Soc, Traveling Exhib, Frye Mus, Seattle, Wash, Tweed Mus Art, Univ Minn, Duluth, & Springfield Art Ctr, Ohio, 79-80; New Haven Paint & Clay Ann, John Shade Ely House Gallery, Conn, 86; 5th New Eng Ann, Green Art Gallery, Guilford, Conn, 86; one-man shows, Max's Art Supplies, 90 & Fairfield Libr Gallery, 91; Conn Watercolor Soc Ann, Univ Hartford, 92; Conn Acad Fine Arts, Norwich Mus, Norwich. *Pos:* Illusr asst, Fred Otnes Illusr, W Redding, Conn, 76-96; Artist Gallery Owner, Oak St Gallery, Boothbay Harbor, Maine, 96-. *Teaching:* Watercolor demonstrations, Westport Nature Ctr Ann, Fairfield Adult Educ & Fairfield Pub Libr, 90-92. *Awards:* Art Friend Prize, Conn Watercolor Soc Mem Exhib, 80; Am Watercolor Soc Award, 112th Ann Traveling Exhib, 80. *Mem:* Conn Watercolor Soc; New Haven Paint & Clay Club, 85; Conn Acad Fine Arts, 90; Conn Classic Arts, Trumball (juror awards); Boothbay Region Art Found, 98-. *Media:* Watercolor. *Publ:* Auth, The watercolor page, Am Artist Mag, 1/84. *Dealer:* Oak Street Gallery, 35 Oak St. *Mailing Add:* 41 Oak St Boothbay Harbor ME 04538-1816

MELNICK, MYRON J
SCULPTOR, COLLAGE ARTIST
b Denver, Colo, Apr 28, 53. *Study:* Univ Colo, Boulder, BFA, 75; Univ Minn, Minneapolis, MFA, 78. *Work:* United Nations, NY; Columbus Gallery Fine Arts, Ohio. *Comn:* Cast paper wall construction, Denver Nat Bank, Colo, 80; wall relief, LA Law, NBC Studios, Burbank, Calif, 87; paper wall hanging, Pepsi Cola World Hq, NY, 88; paper wall hanging, Calvin Klein, NY, 89; paper wall hanging, Oprah Winfrey, Santa Fe, NMex. *Exhib:* Solo exhib, Rochester Art Ctr, 77, Hamline Univ, St Paul & Studio Arts Gallery, Univ Minn, 78, Tribeca Gallery, NY, 91, Laramie Community Col, Cheyenne, Wyo, 92 & Boulder Arts Ctr, 93 & Lincoln Ctr, Ft Collins, 94; Paper Surface Phenomena, Shoshana Wayne Gallery, Los Angeles, Calif, 84; Colo State Art, Colo Springs Fine Art Ctr, 89; Colo 1990, Denver Art Mus, 90; Paris Gibson Square Ctr Contemp Arts, Great Falls, Mont, 91; Nat Endowment Arts Fel Winners, Farrell Collection, Washington, DC, 91; Glen Green Gallery, Santa Fe, NMex, 92. *Awards:* Western States Art Fed Regional Fel, 89; Nat Endowment for the Arts Fel Grant, 90; Colo Visions Grant, Colo Coun Arts & Humanities, 94. *Media:* Hand Cast Paper, Monoprints. *Mailing Add:* c/o Madelyn Jordan Fine Art 40 Cushman Rd Scarsdale NY 10583

MELTON, TERRY R
ADMINISTRATOR, PRINTMAKER, PAINTER
b Gooding, Idaho, Nov 20, 34. *Study:* Idaho State Univ, BA, 58; Univ Ore, MFA, 64. *Work:* Portland Art Mus, Ore; Yellowstone Art Mus, Billings, Mont; Salt Lake Art Ctr, Salt Lake City, Utah; Mus Art, Univ Ore, Eugene; Boise Art Mus, Idaho; Colorado Springs Fine Arts Ctr, Colo. *Exhib:* 5 State Invitational, Univ Wyo Mus Art, Laramie, 66; solo exhib, Salt Lake Art Ctr, 70 & Univ Tex Pan Am, Edinburg, Tex, 95; Invitational, Idaho State Univ, Pocatello, 74; group show, Steinbaum-Krauss Gallery, NY, 93; Hallie Ford Mus, Salem, Ore, 2003. *Pos:* Regional rep, Nat Endowment for Arts, 75-84; exec dir, Western States Art Fedn, 84-90 & McAllen Int Mus, 93-96. *Awards:* Governor's Art Award, Mont Arts Coun, 91. *Media:* All Media. *Mailing Add:* 3860 Oak Hollow Ln SE Salem OR 97302

MELVIN, RONALD MCKNIGHT
MUSEUM DIRECTOR
b Regina, Sask, Oct 25, 27. *Study:* Univ British Columbia, BComm, 49. *Collection Arranged:* Important Western Art from Chicago Collections, 80; Five American Masters of Watercolor (auth, catalog), 81; American Naive Paintings from the Nat Gallery Art (auth, catalog), 82; Solitude--Inner Visions in American Art, 82; Woman, 84. *Pos:* Dir, Terra Mus Am Art, Evanston, Ill, 80-84; trustee, Berkshire Mus, 86-92; retired. *Mailing Add:* Black Birch 585 Norfolk Rd PO Box 278 Southfield MA 01259

MENDELSOHN, JOHN
PAINTER
b Topeka, Kans, Sept 12, 49. *Study:* Columbia Univ, BA, 71; Rutgers Univ, MFA, 74. *Work:* New Mus Contemp Art, NY. *Exhib:* Studio Program Exhib, Whitney Mus Am Art, NY, 71; Selections Edward R Downe Collection, Wellesley Col Mus, Mass, 86; Lukacs Gallery, Fairfield Univ, Conn, 94; Nuyorcian Poets Cafe, NY, 94; Separate Tables, Helen Harwood Gallery, NY, 96; Penny Liebman Contemp Art, Manhattan, 97; Harum-Scarum, MMC Gallery, NY. *Awards:* Nat Endowment Arts Fel, 87; Fairfield Univ Humanities Inst Grant, 95 & 96. *Bibliog:* Paul Krainak (auth), Compassionate Images (catalog), Herron Sch Art, 82; Marcia Tucker (auth), Paradise Lost, Paradise Regained (catalog), New Mus Contemp Art, 84; Robert Mahoney (auth), The Alice Paintings, rev, Arts Mag, 88. *Media:* Vinyl Paint on Jute. *Mailing Add:* 14 Harrison St New York NY 10013

MENDELSON, HAIM
PAINTER, PRINTMAKER
b Semiatich, Builsk, Poland, Oct 15, 23; US citizen. *Study:* Am Artists Sch, 36-40; Saul Baizerman Art Sch, 40-43; pvt study with Saul Baizerman, 43-52; Educ Alliance Art Sch, 46. *Work:* Contemp Drawing Collection, Minn Mus Art, St Paul; Print Collection of NY Pub Libr; Print Collection of St Vincent Col, Latrobe, Pa; Griffiths Art Ctr of St Lawrence Univ, Canton, NY; Edwin A Ulrich Mus, Wichita State Univ, Kans; Flint Inst Fine Arts, Flint, Mich. *Comn:* Dansk Designs, 80. *Exhib:* The Artist as Reporter, Mus Mod Art, NY, 40-41; Nat Acad of Design, NY, 65, 68, 75, 77 & 90; 10th Nat Exhib of Prints & Drawings, Okla Art Ctr, 68; Fedn of Mod Painters & Sculptors (traveling exhib), Gallery Asn NY, 76-78; Prints USA, Pratt Graphics Ctr Traveling Exhib, 82-85; Prominent Print Makers, Mo Western State Col, 88; East Coast Prints, Adrian Col, Mich, 88; Artists Proof, Arts Coun Gallery, Winston-Salem, NC, 88. *Pos:* Dir, Hudson Guild Art Gallery, New York, 71-72 & 73-94. *Teaching:*

Instr painting & drawing, City Col New York, 61-64; teacher, City & Country Sch, New York City, 64-91. *Awards:* Dr Maury Leibovitz Spec Merit Award, 87; Special Distinction Award, Graphics, Int Art Biennale Malta, 95; Award, Graphics, Audubon Artists New York Cent, 96; Florsheim Found Grant, 99. *Bibliog:* Article, The New Yorker, 6/70. *Mem:* Fedn of Mod Painters & Sculptors (pres, 74-); The Print Consortium; Audubon Artists; Am Soc Contemp Artists. *Media:* Oil, Acrylic; Intaglio. *Publ:* Auth, Mezzotint, Prize Winning Graphics Book III, Allied Publ, Ft Lauderdale, Fla, 65. *Dealer:* Susan Teller Art Gallery New York City NY. *Mailing Add:* 234 W 21st St New York NY 10011

MENDENHALL, JACK
PAINTER, INSTRUCTOR
b Ventura, Calif, Apr 7, 37. *Study:* Calif Col Arts & Crafts, BFA, 68 & MFA(painting), 70. *Work:* Univ Calif Art Mus, Berkeley; San Francisco Art Comn; Gallery Ostergren, Malmo, Sweden; Butler Inst of Am Art, Ohio; Va Mus of Fine Arts, Richmond; plus numerous pvt collections, individual & industrial, US & Europe. *Comn:* Rainbows, Waldo Tunnels, Calif Div Hwy, San Francisco, 70. *Exhib:* Amerikanske Realister, Panders Kunstmuseum, Sweden, 73; Tokyo Biennale 74, Japan, 74; New Photo Realism, Wadsworth Atheneum, Hartford, Conn, 74; one-man show, O K Harris Gallery, NY, 74, 79, 81, 83, 85, 88, 91 & 96; Realist Painting in California, John Berggruen Gallery, San Francisco, 75; Watercolors & Drawings, Am Realists, Meisel Gallery, NY, 75; plus others. *Teaching:* Prof painting & drawing, Calif Col Arts & Crafts, 70-. *Awards:* Purchase Award, San Francisco Art Comn, 70. *Bibliog:* William C Seitz (auth), The real and the artificial: Painting of the new environment, Art in Am, 12/72; Linda Chase (auth), Les hyperrealistes Americans, Paris, Ed Filipacchi, 73; Ellen Lubell (auth), article, Arts Mag, 2/75; and others. *Media:* Oil, Watercolor. *Dealer:* O K Harris Gallery 383 W Broadway New York NY 10012. *Mailing Add:* 5824 Florence Terr Piedmont CA 94611

MENIL, GEORGES & LOIS DE
PATRON, COLLECTOR
Study: Georges de Menil: AB Harvard, PhD Mass Inst Technol, 62/68; Lois de Menil: AB Wellesley, 60; Univ Paris (law), 62; Harvard Univ, PhD, 72. *Pos:* Lois de Menil: vis comt, Harvard Univ Art Mus, 75-, Int Coun, Mus Mod Art, NY, 75-, Nat Gallery Art, Washington, vchmn trustees coun, 78-97, trustee, vchmn, NY, Dia Ctr Arts, 84-96 & trustee, World Monuments Fund, 91-; chmn, Ctr for Khmer Studies. *Collection:* 20th century painting & sculpture, African Art. *Mailing Add:* Box 417 Fishers Island NY 06390

MENSCHEL, ROBERT BENJAMIN
PATRON
b New York, NY, Jul 2, 29. *Study:* Syracuse Univ, BS, 51; NYU, grad sch bus admin, 54. *Hon Degrees:* Syracuse Univ, LLD, 91. *Pos:* trustee, mem exec comt, Guild Hall, East Hampton, chmn bd, formerly; bd adv, Grad Sch Inst Int Bus Pace Univ, formerly; Mem, New York Stock Exchange, New York City, 50-51; specialist, HW Goldsmith & Co, 51-54; staff, Goldman, Sachs & Co, 54-66, general partner, institutional sales, 66-78, ltd partner, 79-2000, sr dir, 2000—; mem, Pres Clinton's comt on the arts & humanities; trustee, investment comt, Inst Advanced Study, Princeton, bd trustees, treas, Chess in the Sch, New York City; hon trustee bd, former bd pres, Dalton Sch, New York City; mem exec bd, NY chap Am Jewish Comt, NY; life trustee, former mem bd, exec comt, earned income comt, New York Pub Libr, New York City; bd dir, Parks Coun; bd trustees, mem investment comt, Human Rights Watch; vpres bd trustees, mem fin & exec comt, Temple Emanu-El, NY; mem bd trustees, NY Presbyterian Hosp; trustee, mem exec & investment comts, Syracuse Univ; former trustee, mem exec, investment & develop comts, Montefiore Hosp; managing dir, Horace W Goldsmith Found; bd dir assoc, YM-YWHA; chm bd trustees, former chmn photog comt, former pres, mem finance, investment, ann fund, maketing & exec comts, Mus Modern Art. *Awards:* Recipient George Arents medal Syracuse Univ, 84. *Mem:* Dunes Racquet Club (East Hampton), City Athletic Club (New York City), India House. *Mailing Add:* Goldman Sachs & Co 85 Broad St New York NY 10004-2456

MENSES, JAN
PAINTER, PRINTMAKER
b Rotterdam, Neth, Apr 28, 33; Can citizen. *Study:* Rotterdamse Kunst Akademie; hon degree, Univ Delle Arti, 81 & Accademia Bedriacense, 84. *Work:* Mus Mod Art & Guggenheim Mus, NY; Art Inst Chicago; Brooklyn Mus; Ryksmuseum, Amsterdam, Holland; Victoria & Albert Mus, London; Vatican Mus, Rome. *Comn:* Mural, Montreal Holocaust Mem Centre, Can. *Exhib:* Montreal Mus Fine Arts, 61, 65 & 76; 5th & 7th Biennial Can Painting, 63 & 68 & 1st & 2nd Biennial Can Watercolours, Drawings & Prints, 64 & 66, Nat Gallery Can, Ottawa; 20 New Acquisitions, Mus Mod Art, NY, 66; 9th & 11th Int Exhib Drawings & Engravings, Lugano, Switz, 66 & 72; Rotterdam Art Found, The Neth, 74; Univ British Columbia, Vancouver, 81; Mead Art Mus, Amherst, Mass, 83; Marywood Col, Scranton, Pa, 85; and others. *Teaching:* Vis lectr, var Can univs. *Awards:* Gold Medal, Accademia Italia Delle Arte, Italy, 80; Gold Medal, Int Parliament USA, 82; Gran Premio Delle Nazioni, Italy, 83. *Bibliog:* Jan Menses--Peintre et prophete, Johathan, 82; La peinture de Jan Menses: Kaddish, Klippoth Tikkoune, Tribune Juive, Montreal, 83; Jan Menses: Exile and Redemption (film), Can Broadcasting Corp, 85. *Mem:* Royal Can Acad Arts; Soc Artistes en Arts Visuels de Que; Accademia Italia Delle Arte, Italy; Accademia D'Europa; Accademia Delle Nazione; Jewish Am Acad Arts & Sci. *Media:* Tempera, Acrylic. *Dealer:* Galerie Don Stewart 1460 Sherbrooke St W Montreal PQ H3G 1K4 Can; Michel Tetreault Art Contemporain 4260 Rue Saint Denis Montreal PQ H2J 2K8

MENTHE, MELISSA
LIBRARIAN, PHOTOGRAPHER
b Hackensack, NJ, June 16, 48. *Study:* Montclair State Col, NJ, BA; Rutgers Univ, MLS. *Pos:* Reference librn, Art Dept, Newark Pub Libr, NJ, 71-76 & Rutgers Univ, New Brunswick, 76-82. *Awards:* Nat Endowment Arts Grant, 81. *Mem:* Art Libr Soc NAm; Asn Col & Res Libr, Am Libr Asn; Col Art Asn; Spec Libr Asn; Indust Photographers NJ. *Res:* Methodology in history of photography. *Interests:* History of photography, incunabula & fine printing, historic preservation. *Mailing Add:* PO Box 1246 Paramus NJ 07653-1246

MERFELD, GERALD LYDON
PAINTER, SCULPTOR
b Des Moines, Iowa, Feb 19, 36. *Study:* Am Acad Art, with William Mosby, 54-57. *Work:* Marietta Col, Ohio; McDonough Collection Am Art; US Navy Arch; John Deere & Co; Mus Contemp Impressionism, Conn. *Exhib:* Hope Show, Butler Inst Am Art, 72, 74, 76, 78, 80 & 82; Allied Artists Am Ann, NY, 75-77, 80; Hudson Valley Art Asn, 75, 81, 82, 86 & 90; Knickerbocker Artists, 75, 85, 86, 87 & 89; Civic Fine Arts Asn, Sioux Falls, SDak, 77; Vanishing Landmark Exhib, Springfield Art Mus, Mo, 77; Artists of the Rockies & Golden West Retrospective Exhib, Sangre de Cristo Arts Ctr, Pueblo, Colo, 83; Audubon Artists, NY, 73-90; Am Artists Prof League, NY, 89; Butler Inst Am Art, 81-83; Akron Soc Artists Grand Exhib, 91 & 92; North West Rendezvous Exhib, 96, 98, 99, 2000-06; Colo Gov Invitational, 97, 98 & 99. *Pos:* Studio asst, Dean Cornwell, New York, 57-60; combat artist, US Navy, Vietnam, 69 & Mediter, 71. *Awards:* Louis E Seley Gold Medal, Salmagundi Club, 71; Okla Mus Art Award, 75; First Prize, Hope Show Butler Inst Am Art, 80; First Prize, Drawing, Butler Inst Am Art, 83; Gold Medal of Hon, Am Artist Prof League, 89. *Bibliog:* Betty Harvey (auth), Gerald Merfeld, Artists of the Rockies & Golden West, fall 81; Ron Ranson (auth), Modern Oil Impressionists, 92; Betty Harvey-Manson (auth), Gerald Merfeld, Southwest Art, 7/96; Charles Movalli (auth), Gerald Merfeld's Teaching Tenets, Am Artist Mag, 12/78; Peggy & Harold Samuels (auth), Contemporary Western Artists; Fielding's Dictionary Am Painters, Sculptors & Engravers. *Mem:* Northwest Rendezvous Group (NWR). *Media:* Oil, Pastel. *Dealer:* Brookwood Gallery Westcliffe. *Mailing Add:* 2302 Muddy Rd Westcliffe CO 81252

MERIDA, FREDERICK A
ART DEALER, PRINTMAKER
b Indianapolis, Ind, Mar 10, 36. *Study:* Kansas City Art Inst, Mo, 54-57; Brooklyn Mus Sch, NY, 57-59; New Sch Social Res, New York, 57-59. *Work:* Columbia Mus Art, SC; Libr Cong, Washington; JB Speed Mus, Louisville, Ky. *Exhib:* 11th & 13th Ann Boston Printmakers, Boston Mus Fine Arts, 58 & 60; Pasadena Art Mus, Calif, 58; 15th Ann, Pa Acad Fine Arts, Philadelphia, 61; Prints 1962, State Univ NY, Potsdam, 62; 8 State Ann, JB Speed Mus, Louisville, Ky, 85, 87. *Collection Arranged:* Melville Price Retrospective 1920-1970, 70, Rookwood: A Historical Survey, 71, Biggest Show of Little Painting, 73 & Kentuckian Painters Invitational, 75, Frame House Gallery, Louisville, Ky; Black Artists Ann, 1980-1985, Nat Black Artists, Gallery One, 1st Nat Bank, Louisville, Ky. *Pos:* Dir, Frame House Gallery, Louisville, Ky, 69-75, dir bus art develop & asst to pres, 75-77; owner & dir, Merida Gallery, Louisville, Ky, 77-; cur corp art collection, Hilliard Lyons Ctr, Louisville, Ky, 88-92 & CSI, Paducah, Ky, 96-97, 2003-05. *Awards:* Pennell Purchase Prize, Libr Cong, Washington, 57; Purchase Awards, Nelson Gallery Art, Kansas City, Mo, 60 & JB Speed Mus, Louisville, Ky, 85, 87. *Bibliog:* Ira Simmons (auth), Art and money, Scene Mag, Louisville Times, 2/8/86. *Mem:* Am Soc Appraisers (chap pres, 85-86); Appraisers Asn Am. *Specialty:* Contemporary art; 19th century American and European paintings. *Publ:* Ed, Art Gallery Guide of Louisville, Merida Gallery, Inc, 68-69. *Mailing Add:* Merida Galleries PO Box 53 Farmington KY 42040-0053

MERIDA, MARGARET BRADEN
CRAFTSMAN, INSTRUCTOR
b Louisville, Ky, Jul 26, 37, Am Citizen. *Study:* Univ Louisville, Ky, BS (high honors), 59, MAT, 71; Nat Endowment Fel, George Wash Univ, 66. *Work:* Aetna Oil Collection, Louisville, Ky; CSI, Ky. *Exhib:* Quiltmaking Trends, Evansville Mus Art, Ky, 77; One man exhib, Appalachian Ctr, Smithville, Tenn, 2000; Womans Hands, Arts Coun, Berea, Ky, 2005. *Pos:* owner, Farmington Fiberarts, 98-. *Teaching:* Instr, Jefferson Co Publ Schs, Louisville, Ky, 64-90; instr, Gov's Scholars, Ky, 85-90; instr, Visual Arts Magnet Sch, Jefferson Co, Ky, 87-90; instr, Murray State Univ, Ky, 2000-. *Awards:* Purchase Award, Art Ctr Annual, Aetna Oil, 60; Best in Show, Louisville Craftsman Annual, 77; Best in Show, Ky Craft Marketing Prof, 2005. *Mem:* Ky Craft Marketing Prog, 98-; Ohio Designer's Craftsmen 2004-. *Media:* Fibers, Wearable art & quilted wall pieces. *Dealer:* Appalachian Fireside Gallery Main St PO Box 87 Berea Ky 40403; Ky Artisans Ctr Berea Ky 40403; Pear Tree Gallery 36840 Detroit Rd Avon Ohio; Rivers Bend Gallery First St Parksville Mo 64152

MERKEL, JAYNE (SILVERSTEIN)
HISTORIAN, CRITIC
b Cincinnati, Ohio, Sept 28, 42. *Study:* Simmons Col, with Wylie Sypher, BS, 64; Smith Col, with Henry-Russell Hitchcock, MA(art hist), 68; Univ Mich, with Leonard K Eaton, 66-68. *Collection Arranged:* Early Works: Alexander Calder (auth, catalog), Taft Mus, 72; Drawn by Cincinnati (auth, catalog), Collection of the Cincinnati Hist Soc, Contemp Arts Ctr, 80; 1930's Remembered, Part I, The High Style, Taft Mus, 82; In Its Place, the Architecture of Carl Strauss & Ray Roush, Contemp Arts Ctr, 85; Peter Eisenman: An Architecture of Absence, Contemp Arts Ctr, 86-87. *Pos:* Cur, Contemp Arts Ctr, Cincinnati, 68-69; dir educ, Taft Mus, Cincinnati, 69-74; archit critic, Cincinnati Enquirer, 77-88; reviewer, Artforum, 80-90; art & archit critic, WGUC-FM (pub radio), 83-88; contrib ed, Inland Archit, 84-93; ed, Oculus Mag, 94-02; contrib ed & mem ed bd, Archit Design Mag, London, 2000-. *Teaching:* Instr art hist, Art Acad Cincinnati, 73-78; vis instr art hist, Miami Univ, 78-79 & 81-82; asst

prof Eng (writing), Univ Cincinnati, 88-91; dir, grad prog archit & design criticism, Parsons Sch Design, New Sch, 92-96 & RISD; vis prof, Rhode Island Sch of Design, 99. *Awards:* Special citation for writing, ed & criticism from Am NY Chap, Am Inst Art, 98; Fellow Inst for Urban Design, New York, 99-; Harry B Rutkins Award, NY chap Am Inst Architects, 2001. *Mem:* Col Art Asn; Soc Archit Historians; Archit League; Century Asn. *Res:* Contemporary American architecture, art and criticism. *Publ:* articles & reviews, Am Inst Archit J, 78, Prog Archit, 80-82, 88-89, Artforum, 81-90, Inland Archit, 83-92, New Art Examiner, 83 & 88, Connoisseur, 84, Dialogue, 84-86, Amercraft 88, Art in Am, 86-94, Competitions, 92 & Design Book Review, 93-94; Intro to Kliczkowski's Hariri & Hariri, Casas Int 48, Asppan, Buenos Aires, 97; Pasanella + Klein Stolzman + Berg (an architectural monograph), Rockport Publ, 99; Chap, In: Modernism and Modernization in Architecture, Acad Ed, London, 99; Richard Dattner, Images Publishing, Malgrave, Australia, 2000; Bero Saarinen, Heroic Modern (monograph); and others. *Mailing Add:* 60 Gramercy Park N 7B New York NY 10010

MERKIN, RICHARD MARSHALL
PAINTER, PRINTMAKER
b Brooklyn, NY, Oct, 1938. *Study:* Syracuse Univ Sch Art, BFA, 60; RI Sch Design, MFA(teaching fel), 63. *Work:* Mus Art, RI Sch Design; Mus Mod Art, NY; Am Fedn Arts, NY; Rose Art Mus, Brandeis Univ; Mass Inst Technol; Pa Acad Arts, Philadelphia; Smithsonian Inst, Washington; Whitney Mus Am Art, NY. *Comn:* Seven murals, Blackstone Park Pub Sch, Boston, Mass, 75-76. *Exhib:* Whitney Mus Am Art, 67, 69 & 72; One-man exhibs, Terry Dintenfass Inc, NY, 73-74, 80-81, Eric Makler Gallery, Philadelphia, 81, 83, Karen Lennox Gallery, Chicago, 82, Susan Montezinos Gallery, Philadelphia, 84, Galleria Giulia, Rome, 84, Joe & Emily Lowe Art Gallery, Syracuse Univ, NY, 85, Foster-White Gallery, Seattle, Wash, 87, JRS Fine Art, Providence, RI, 88; Painting and Sculpture Today, Indianapolis Mus Art, 76; Alumni Artists Exhib, Syracuse Univ, 79; Nat Ann Midyear Show, Butler Inst Am Art, 79 & 82; Fiac 83, Paris, 83; I Love Paperino, Assessore alla Cultura de Commune di Roma, Rome, 84; The Music of Art, Artrain, Detroit, Mich, 85; The Grand Game of Baseball, Mus Borough Brooklyn, NY, 87; Diamonds Are Forever (traveling exhib), NY State Mus, Albany, in asn with Smithsonian Inst Traveling Exhib Serv, 87; Mod Am Realism, Sara Roby Found, Nat Mus Am Art, Washington, 87; New York, NY, Helander Gallery, NY, 91. *Pos:* Contribr ed, Vanity Fair, 86-. *Teaching:* Asst prof painting, RI Sch Design, 61-70, prof, currently; vis artist in residence, Syracuse Univ, 72. *Awards:* Purchase Award, Soc Washington DC Printmakers Show, Smithsonian Inst, 62; Tiffany Found Fel Painting, 62-63; Rosenthal Found Award, Nat Inst Arts & Lett, 75. *Publ:* Photog, Velvet Eden, Methuen Publ Co, 79; contribr, New Yorker Mag. *Dealer:* Jon Oulman Gallery Minneapolis MN; Gallery Camino Real Boca Raton; Gallery 444 444 Post Rd San Francisco CA 94102

MERKL, ELISSA FRANCES
PRINTMAKER, PAINTER
b Colorado Springs, Colo, July 2, 49. *Study:* Marymount Col, with Robert J Lee, John Hull & John Lotchtefeld, BA(fine arts), 71; NJ Ctr Visual Arts, with David Finkbeiner, 74. *Work:* Nabisco Hq, East Hanover, NJ; St Hubert's Giralda (Geraldine R Dodge Collection), Madison, NJ; Nat Bank Dtroit, Mich; America the Beautiful, Township Art Collection, Millburn, NJ; Fed Reserve Bank, Chicago. *Exhib:* Int Mini Print, Taller Galeria Fort & Trvl Cadaques, Spain, 86, 87 & 97; CL Wolfe Nat, Nat Arts Club, NY, 88 & 91; Animals in Art, La State Univ Sch Vet Med, Baton Rouge, 92; solo exhibs, Johnson & Johnson World Hq, New Brunswick, 96 & Childrens Specialized Hosp, Mountainside, NJ, 96, Monmouth Beach Cult Ctr, NJ, 02, Les Malamut Gallery, NJ, 02, The Show Bistro, NJ, 2000, Gallery 50, Bridgeon, NJ, 2006; We Love NY, Lever House, NY, 96; Int Mint Print, Taller Galeria Fort & Traveling Cadaques, Spain, 97; Small Pictures, Great Harmony Exhib, Nagano, Japan, 98; Small Works, Hopper House Art Ctr, Nyack, NY, 01; Northeast Prints, 01; William Paterson Univ, NJ, 01; Agora Gallery, Soho, 02; Open Juried Show, Pen & Brush, NY, 01; Int Juried Mini Show, Paper Mill Playhouse, NJ, 2003; Int Mini Print, Graphics Ctr, Conn, 2001-02; Take a Walk on the (not so) Wild Side, Wisner House, Summit, NJ, 2005; Juried: WomenArt, Summit Col Club, NJ, 2004; Monmouth Festival of the Arts, NJ, 2003, 2005; Nat Juried Miniature Print Exhibit, Arts Council of Creede, Colo, 2003; Int Juried Mini Show, Paper Mill Playhouse, NJ, 2001, 2003; Color, Gallery Petite, Clinton, NJ, 2004; Current Printmaking, Printmaking Currents, Old Church Cult Ctr, NJ, 2004; Wild for Wildlife, Columban Park Zoo, Lafayette, Ind, 2005; Prints 2005, Springfield Art Mus, Mo, 2005; Monmouth County Arts Coun Juried Show, Monmouth Mus, NJ, 2006. *Pos:* Publicity chair, NJ Ctr Visual Arts, 74 & 75; newslett ed, Art Gallery South Orange, 78-; co-chair/adv art fair, Millburn-Short Hills Chambers Com, 79-; art exhib chair, Millburn-Short Hills Arts Ctr, 88-90, pres, 98-2001; Ed, pub, Cult Events of NJ, 2001-; visual arts critiquer, Teen Arts Festivals, 95-; juror, judge area shows, 94-. *Teaching:* Demonstr serigraphy, Area Art Asn NJ, 72-, lectr marketing art, 94-; guest artist, Kids in Business, Newark Pub Schs, 2001-02. *Awards:* First Prize Graphics, Mamaroneck Art Guild Nat, 91; First Prize Prints, Nev Art Asn Nat Mini, 93; Award for Artistic Achievement, Art Fair 94 & 96, Millburn-Short Hills Chamber Com, 94; Awards of Merit, Old Church Cult Ctr, NJ, 01; Skylands Juried Show, NJ, 02; Jane Law Studio & Gallery Mini Show, NJ, 02; H M Caldwell Col Juried Show, NJ, 01; Awards of Merit, Millburn-Short Hills Arts Ctr Mems Show, Bedminster Libr, 2004, 2005; First Place Exterior/Architecture, Miniature Art Soc Fla Int Juried Show, 2006; Award of Merit, Carlisle Arts Learning Ctr Small Works Show, Carlisle, Pa, 2006. *Bibliog:* Mary La Motta (dir), Art al Fresco (video), TV 36, 91; Eileen Watkins (auth), New venue for representational art, Star Ledger, 94; Jean Galler (auth), Artists life work meshes together in exhibit: silk screen print process called lost art, Star Ledger, 1/96; Mary Windhorst (auth), Overlook Shows Work of Riv & Merkl, Independent Press, 2003. *Mem:* NJ Ctr Visual Arts; Westfield Art Asoc; Printmaking Coun of NJ; Milburn-Short Hills Art Ctr. *Media:* Acrylic; Serigraphy. *Publ:* Illus, Add a Little Love Cookbook, Pacelle Press, 74; auth, Bicentennial Coloring Book, private publ, 75; Color Images from Nikon, NJ Music & Arts, 75; contribr, Art Lovers Cookbook, NJ Ctr Visual Arts, 76. *Mailing Add:* 325 Morristown Rd Gillette NJ 07933

MEROLA, MARIO
SCULPTOR, PAINTER
b Montreal, Que, Mar 31, 31. *Study:* Ecole des Beaux Arts de Montreal, dipl, 52; Ecole Superieure des Arts Decoratifs de Paris, 53. *Hon Degrees:* diplome, Ecole Des Beaux-Arts, Montreal. *Work:* Mus d'Art Contemp & Mus Fine Arts, Montreal; Nat Gallery, Ottawa; Mus Munic, Brest, France; Mus Quebec; Carleton Art Gallery; Mus Fine Arts, Budapest. *Comn:* Mural, Mazenod Seminary, Ottawa, 65; fountain, Expo 67, Montreal, 67; two murals, Quebec Govt, Osaka, Japan, 70; stained glass, Montreal subway, 79; Monumental Door, Nagyiatad, Hungary, 89; plus over 100 comn. *Exhib:* Solo exhibs, Luminous Reliefs, Mus Fine Arts, Montreal, 65, Mus du Quebec, 71, Constructions, 1950-1976, Mus d'Art Contemp, Montreal, 76, Mus Munic, Toulouse, France, 77, Mus Munic, Brest, France, 78, Muvezsetek Hasa, Pecs, Hungary, 91 & Ady Endre Gymnazium, Nagyatad, Hungary, 92; Affect-Effect, La Jolla Mus, Calif, 68; New Tendency, Mus d'Art Contemp, Montreal, 78; Made in Canada, Nat Libr Can, Ottawa, 84; and many other group exhibs; Bibliotheque Nationale du Quebec, 02. *Teaching:* Prof fine arts, Ecole des Beaux Arts, Montreal, 60-69; prof drawing, Univ Que, Montreal, 69-91. *Awards:* First Prize, murals, Can Pavilion, Brussels, 57 & Inst d'Hotellerie, Can Govt, 73; First Prize, sculpture, Int Sculpture Meeting, St-Jean-Port-Jolie, 84; Hon Citizen, City Iri, South Korea. *Bibliog:* Jacques de Roussan (auth), Mario Merola, Ed Lidec, 70; L Letocha (auth), Mario Merola, Formart, 72; Robert Melancon (auth), L'espace de la ville, Liberté, 82; A Metchnikov (auth), Mario Merola, Fini-Infini, 92. *Mem:* Royal Can Acad Art; Conseil de la Sculpture du Quebec; hon mem Conseil de la Peinture du Quebec; Int Sculpture Ctr. *Media:* Polymer on Wood. *Publ:* Auth, UN Chef-D'Oeuvre Anonyme & Shadows Graphics, Figures, Dessiens (book of drawings), Ed Fini/Infini; Two Projects, Mayor's Hill Park, Queen Elizabeth Driveway, Integration, Ed A L'Oree, 84. *Dealer:* Galerie d'Art Contemp Montreal; Montreal Mus Fine Arts. *Mailing Add:* 216 Somerville Montreal PQ H3L 1A3 Canada

MERRILL, DAVID KENNETH
PAINTER, MURALIST
b Bridgeport, Conn, Oct 18, 35. *Comn:* Monroe Green, Town of Monroe, Conn, 72; ann report cover, William R Berkley Corp, NY, 73; IBM, Burlington, Vt, 74; 43 scenes of Southbury's past & present (mural), Southbury, Conn Town Hall Bldg Comt, 78; mural, Edmond Town Hall, Newtown, Conn, 83-85; Field Home, Yorktown Heights, NY. *Exhib:* Kent Art Asn, Conn, 69, 73 & 74; Northern Vt Artists Asn, 71-74; Mainstreams '74, Marietta, Ohio; Conn Acad Fine Art, 74; Douglas Gallery, Stamford, Conn, 74 & 75. *Teaching:* Instr art, Southbury Training Sch, Conn, 63-67. *Awards:* First Place, 72 & First & Second Place, 74, Northern Vt Artists Asn; First Prize Acrylic, Scan Art Exhib, 78 & 82. *Bibliog:* Randall E Christensen (dir), Newtown Mural (videotape). *Mem:* Kent & Washington Art Asns; Northern Vt Art Asn; New Haven Paint & Clay Club. *Media:* Acrylic. *Publ:* Auth, articles in This New England, Yankee Mag, Int Mag Marifacts, 10/78 & Connecticut's Child, 85; Business Digest, 94. *Dealer:* Douglas Gallery 1117 High Ridge Rd Stamford CT 06905; Warren ME

MERRILL, HUGH JORDAN
PRINTMAKER, PAINTER, PUB & COMMUNITY ARTS
b Olney, Md, Apr 28, 49. *Study:* Md Inst Col Art, BFA, 73; Yale Sch Art & Archit, MFA, 75. *Work:* Mus Mod Art, NY; Sackler Mus, Harvard Univ, Cambridge, Mass; Yale Univ Mus Art, New Haven, Conn; Davenport Mus Art, Iowa; Cranbook Mus Art, Mich. *Comn:* Nova Huta Rising, Works Festival, Edmonton, Alta, Can, 95; Sanford-Kimpton Health Facility, Columbia, Mo. *Exhib:* Lucky Dragon, Nelson Atkins Mus, Kansas City, Mo, 85; Palace Fine Arts, Krakow, Poland, 93; Life Cycles, Santa Barbara Contemp Art Forum, Calif, 93; Rosa Luxemberg Suite, Navy Pier Exhib, Chicago, Ill, 93; Transparent Motives, New Orleans Mus, La, 95; Portrait of Self (auth, catalog), Community Proj, Kemper Mus, Kansas City, Mo, 98; Collected Prints, Nelson-Atkins Mus, Kansas City, Mo, 98; Daum Mus, Sedalia, MO,; Touch, Morgan Gallery, KC, MO, 2005; Tides, Import Conference Pozan Poland. *Pos:* Pres, Southern Graphics Coun, 92-94; vpres, Mus Without Walls, Jewish Mus Fedn, 98-; Exec Dir Chameleon Arts & Youth Develop. *Teaching:* Prof paint & print, Kansas City Art Inst, 76-. *Bibliog:* Auschwitz Sky, New Letts Mag, 98; Lynn Allen & Phylis McGibbons (auths), Best in Printmaking, 98; Printmaking by Richard Noyce. *Mem:* Col Art Asn; Southern Graphics Counicl Berzinger Winery Collection, Donald Kuspit. *Media:* Mixed Media. *Publ:* Auth, Post Print Stacking Claim, Contemp Impressions, 94; coauth, Content as creativity, Printmaking Today, 95. *Mailing Add:* c/o Jan Weiner Gallery 3014 Eveningside Dr Topeka KS 66614

MERRILL, ROSS M
CONSERVATOR, PAINTER
b Abilene, Tex, 43. *Study:* Pa Acad Fine Arts; Oberlin Col, Ohio, MA; Intermus Conserv Asn, conserv cert. *Pos:* Admin head of conserv dept, Cleveland Mus Art, 74-81; head painting conserv, Nat Gallery Art, Washington, DC, 81-83, chief conserv, 83-; chmn bd trustees, Nat Inst Conserv Cult Property, currently. *Teaching:* Lectr mus conserv for var mus & conserv orgns. *Awards:* Halgarten Prize, Nat Acad Design, 96; Second Prize, Art League, Alex, Va, 96. *Bibliog:* Am Artist Mag, 4/96. *Mem:* Am Inst Conserv; Int Inst Conserv. *Media:* Oil, Watercolor. *Res:* modern and historical painting materials and techniques; American paintings. *Interests:* Early European paintings, American paintings. *Dealer:* Susan Conway Gallery Washington DC. *Mailing Add:* 3206 Norwood Terr Alexandria VA 22309-2130

MERRIN, EDWARD H
DEALER
b Brooklyn, NY, 28. *Study:* Tufts Col, BA, 50. *Pos:* Dir, Edward H Merrin Gallery, currently. *Mem:* Am Asn Dealers Ancient, Oriental & Primitive Art. *Specialty:* Classical and pre-Columbian antiquities. *Mailing Add:* Edward H Merrin Gallery 724 Fifth Ave 3rd Flr New York NY 10019

MERRITT, DAVID ROSS
ASSEMBLAGE ARTIST, SCULPTOR
b Sept 16, 55. *Study:* Univ Western Ont, BFA, 78; NS Col Art & Design, MFA, 82. *Work:* McMaster Mus Art, Hamilton, Ont. *Exhib:* Canope of Blue, McMaster Mus Art, Hamilton, Ont, 91; Unswept Room, Art Gallery Windsor, Ont, 92; Storyland, Walter Phillips Gallery, Banff, Alta, 95; solo show, Art Gallery Ont, Toronto, 96; Small as a Way of Working, Owens Art Gallery, Sackville, NB, 96. *Teaching:* Instr studio, NS Col Art & Design, 81-83; asst prof visual arts, Univ Western Ont, 87-. *Bibliog:* Gordie Rans (auth), Magic Voice/David Merritt, Vanguard, 88; Cyril Reade (auth), Unsweet Room, Parachute 68, 92; Christian Ritchie (auth), David Merritt/Present Tense, Art Gallery Ont, 96

MERTIN, ROGER
PHOTOGRAPHER
b Bridgeport, Conn, Dec 9, 42. *Study:* Rochester Inst Technol, BFA, 65; Visual Studies Workshop, MFA, 72. *Work:* Nat Gallery Can, Ottawa; Int Mus Photog & Visual Studies Workshop, Rochester, NY; Mus Mod Art, NY; Boston Mus Fine Arts; Libr Congress, Washington, DC. *Exhib:* Past into Present, Seattle Art Mus, Wash, 76; Great West: Real/Ideal, Univ Colo, Boulder, 77; Mus Mod Art, NY, 78 & 81; One-of-a-Kind Am Photog, Corcoran Gallery Art, Washington, DC, 79; Photog in the 70's, Art Inst Chicago, 79; Light Gallery, NY, 80; Friends of Photog, Carmel, Calif, 81; Solo exhibs, Living Evidence Presentation House, N Vancouver, BC, 90, O Tannenbaum, Nat Gallery Can, Ottowa, 91, The Library Project: Work in Progress, Athenqeum Mus & Arts Libr, LaJolla, Mus Contemp Art, San Diego, Calif, 93, Deck the Halls, Frederick R Weisman Art Mus, Univ Minn, Minneapolis, 95, Now & Then: Pedagoqic Problems, Minneapolis, 96, Rochester, NY, 1992-1996, Rush Rhees Art Libr Gallery, Univ Rochester, NY, 96, Libr Project: New Pictures, Meliora Gallery, Tucson, Ariz, 99; Magicians of Light: Photographs from the Collection of the Nat Gallery of Can (with catalog), Nat Gallery Can, Ottawa; San Francisco Camerawork, 93; Local Color: Recent Photog Works, Parts Gallery, Minneapolis, 94; Rituals and Transformation: An exhib of photog, Nat Gallery Can, Ottawa, 95; 11 Photographers, Col Vis Arts Gallery, St Paul, Minn, 96; Hot Lunch, Hartnett Gallery, Rochester, NY, 99. *Teaching:* Asst prof fine arts & photog, Univ Rochester, NY, 73-81, assoc prof, 81-91, prof art, 91-. *Awards:* Guggenheim fel photog, 74; Nat Endowment for Arts fel photog, 76; McKnight Artist fel photog, 99. *Bibliog:* Hungary Mind Review, No 19, St Paul, Minn, fall 91 & No 48, winter 98-99. *Mem:* Soc for Photog Educ. *Publ:* auth, Records 1976-78, Chicago Ctr Contemp Photog, 78. *Mailing Add:* c/o Univ Rochester Morey Hall 424 PO Box 270456 Rochester NY 14627-0456

MESA-BAINS, AMALIA
SCULPTOR
b Santa Clara, Calif, July 10, 43. *Study:* San Jose State Univ, BA (painting), 66; San Francisco State Univ, MA, 71; Wright Inst, MA, 80, PhD, 83. *Exhib:* Solo exhibs, INTAR Gallery, NY, 87, Artspace, Phoenix, 90, Whitney at Philip Morris, 93, William Col Mus Art, Williamstown, Mass, 94 & Steinbaum Krauss Gallery, New York, 95; Emblems of the Decade: Borders, La Reconquista: A Post Columbian New World Exhib, 3rd Int Biennial, Istanbul, Turkey, 92; Revelations: Hispanic Art of Evanescence, Cornell Univ, Ithaca, NY, 93; Queen of the Waters, Mother of the Land of the Dead: Homanje to Tonatzin/Guadalupe, Ante Am, Queens Mus Art, NY, 93; Venus Envy Chapter One, Whitney Mus Am Art at Philip Morris, 93; Grandmother Is That You, States of Loss: Migration, Displacement, Colonialism & Power, Jersey City Mus, NJ, 94; and others. *Pos:* Comnr of art, City of San Francisco, formerly; proj mgr, consent decree staff development, Div Integration, San Francisco Unified Sch Dist, 83-90; SPARC mural training proj, Los Angeles, 85-86; consult arts, INTAR-Hispanic Art Ctr, NY, 85-87, Ariz Comn Arts, 90, Tex Coun Arts, 90, Sci Educ Youth Found, Audubon Soc, 89-90; adv bd, Mex Mus, San Francisco, Calif, publ adv bd, Studio Mus Harlem, NY; producer/host, Community Affairs, Latin Tempo, KPIX-TV, Channel 5, San Francisco, 86-88; lectr/speaker, numerous mus, insts & exhibs, 88-93; sr res assoc, Far West Labs, San Francisco, 90-; dir, Bd Ctr Arts, Yerba Buena Gardens, San Francisco, Calif, 93-96, Galeria de la Raza, San Francisco, Mission Community Legal Defense, San Francisco & Visual & Pub Art Inst, Calif State Univ, 96-. *Teaching:* Bilingual, ESC & multicult educ, Elem Div, San Francisco Unified Sch Dist, 71-83; Univ Calif Regents Professorship, Irvine, 93. *Awards:* Golden Palm Award, INTAR Hispanic Arts Ctr, 91; Distinguished Serv Field Award, Asn Hispanic Arts, 91; Distinguished MacArthur Fel, John D & Catherine T MacArthur Found, 92. *Publ:* Auth, Grandma is that you, San Francisco Camerawork Quart, Photog & Belief, 91; Acts of Memory: The Alternative Chronicle of Mildred Howard, San Francisco Art Inst, 91; Chicano Chronicle & Cosmology: The Works of Carmen Lomas Garza, Laguna Gloria Mus, Austin, Tex, 91; The Real Multiculturism: A Struggle for Authority & Power in: Different Voices: A Social, Culture & Historical Framework For Change in the American Art Museum, New York, 92; Redeeming Our Dead: A Homanaje a Tenochtitlan, William Col, Williamstown, Mass, 92. *Mailing Add:* 326-A Capp St San Francisco CA 94110-1808

MESCHES, ARNOLD
PAINTER, EDUCATOR
b New York, NY, Aug 11, 23. *Study:* Art Ctr Sch; Chouinard Art Inst; Jepson Art Inst; self-taught in fine arts. *Work:* High Mus Art, Atlanta, Ga; San Francisco Mus Art; Nat Gallery Art, Washington, DC; Los Angeles Co Mus Art; Albright-Knox Gallery, Buffalo, NY; Metrop Mus Art, NY; and others. *Comn:* Murals, Temple Isaiah, Los Angeles, 73 & Bank of Am, Beverly Hills, Calif, 75; portraits, Frederick Weisman, Los Angeles; Gordon Hampton, Los Angeles; Billie Milam, Los Angeles; Richard Weisman & Vivien Lesnick, Seattle, Wash. *Exhib:* Civilian Warfare Gallery, NY, 84; Jack Shainman Gallery, Washington, DC, 87; Inst Contemp Art, Philadelphia, PA, 94; Jacksonville Mus Modern Art, Jacksonville, Fla, 2002; The Skirball Mus, Los Angeles, Calif, 2003; one-man shows: PS1 MOMA, Long Island City, NY, 2002-03, Jacksonville Mus Mod Art, Fla, 2004, Skirball Mus, Los Angeles, Calif, 2004, Univ Gall, Univ Buffalo, New Orleans Contemp Art Ctr, 2004, Harn Mus, Gainesville, Fla, 2005, Ogden Mus, New Orleans, 2006. *Pos:* Art dir, Frontier Mag, 54-60; Courtroom Artist, Walter Cronkite/CBS, 69-71; Master artist, Atlantic Ctr Arts, New Smyrna Beach, Fla, 2005. *Teaching:* Instr painting & drawing, Univ Southern Calif, summer 50; instr & dir, New Sch Art, Los Angeles, 55-58; instr, Otis Art Inst, 63-67, Otis/Parsons Art Inst, 75-84, Los Angeles; instr, Univ Calif Exten, Los Angeles, 72-77; guest prof, grad sch, Rutgers Univ, New Brunswick, NJ, 85- & vis lectr, 87-88; instr advan painting & drawing, Parsons Sch Design, NY, 86; instr grad painting, NY Univ, 88-; instr, NY Univ, 1988-2002; prof grad ptg, Univ Fla, Gainesville, 2003-. *Awards:* Nat Endowment Arts Grant, 82; NY Found Arts, 91; Artist Residence, Altos de Chavon, Dominican Republic, 94; Pollock-Krasner Found Grant, 2002; Art Critics of America, 2004. *Bibliog:* Eleanor Heartney (auth), Arnold Mesches, ARTnews, 92; Edward Sozanski (auth), Art in America, 97, Inst Contemp Art, Philadelphia Inquirer, 94; Willaim Zimmer (auth), Arnold Mesches: From Columbus to 2000, NY Times, 98; Eleanor Heartney (auth), Art in America, NY Times; Thomas McEvilley (auth), Neuberger Mus (catalog), Art in America; and others. *Media:* Acrylic, Collage. *Publ:* Coauth, Selections from the 80's, Buscaglia Castellani Art gallery & Burchfield Art Ctr Catalog, 88; coauth, Municipal Art Gallery Catalog, 83; coauth, Painting History, Inst Contemp Art, 94; Anomie: 1492-2000 (exhib catalog), Neuberger Mus Art, State Univ NY, Purchase, 98; Anomie: 1492-2000 (exhib catalog), Selby Gallery, Ringling Sch Art & Design, Sarasota, Fla, 98; Echoes: A Century Survey (catalog), Ore Jamsh Mus, 2000; Arnold Mesches A Painting History 1940-2003 (catalog), Jacksonville Mus Mod Art, 2003; auth, The FBI Files, Hanging Loose Press, NY, 2004. *Mailing Add:* 1602 SW 35th Pl Gainesville FL 32608

MESEROLE, VERA (VESSA) STROMSTED
PAINTER, PHOTOGRAPHER
b New York, NY, Aug 10, 27. *Study:* Wellesley Col, Mass, BA(hist art, painting), with A Abbot, B Swann & E Frisch & archit with J MacAndrew; Univ Vt, Burlington, adult educ with Francis Colburn; critique with Stan Marc Wright, Vt & father, Alf Stromsted, NY & NJ. *Work:* IBM, Montpelier, Vt; IBM, Essex Junction, Vt; Nat Life, Montpelier, Vt. *Exhib:* Northern New Eng Artists, Univ Vt, Burlington, 54; New Eng Artists, NY World's Fair, 64; Nat League Am Pen Women, Tulsa, Okla, 66, Salt Lake City, Utah, 70 & Atlanta, Ga, 82; Vt Pavilion, Expo, Montreal, 70; Fla Artists, Sarasota Art Ctr, 90, 92, 94, 95 & 96. *Pos:* Chmn, Ann State, Fleming Mus, Burlington, 66-73; supt art, Champlain Valley Expos, Vt, 67; auth, Newsletter Northern Vt Artists Asn, 67-73; mgr art ctr exhib, Burlington, 72-74. *Awards:* First Prize, Champlain Valley Expos, 60; First Prize Portraits, Nat League Am Pen Women, Vt, 66 & 70; First Prize Watercolor & Portrait, 81, & First Prize Photog, 84 & 85, Nat League Am Pen Women, Ga. *Bibliog:* Stuart Perry (auth), TV interview, WCAX, Burlington, 71; article, Burlington Free Press, 67 & 72. *Mem:* Northern Vt Artist Asn; Art Ctr Sarasota; Nat League Am Pen Women, Sarasota Fla Br; Sarasota Art Asn. *Media:* Watercolor, Photography, Color, Oil, Pen & Ink. *Mailing Add:* 8026 Midnight Pass Rd Sarasota FL 34242

MESIBOV, HUGH
PAINTER, PRINTMAKER
b Philadelphia, Pa, Dec 29, 16. *Study:* Fleischer Mem Art Sch, Philadelphia, 34-35; Pa Acad Fine Arts, Philadelphia, 35-37; Albert C Barnes Found, Merion, Pa, 36-40. *Work:* Metrop Mus Art & NY Univ Collection Contemp Am Art, NY; Philadelphia Mus Art & Nat Archives, Philadelphia; British Mus, London, Eng; Albert C Barnes Found, Merion, Pa; Whitney Mus Am Art. *Comn:* Mural design, Benjamin Franklin High Sch, 37-40 & Bennett Hall, Univ Pa, Work Progress Admin Art Proj, 37-40; mural, Steel Indust, US Treas, US Post Off, Hubbard, Ohio, 41; paintings & color lithograph, NY Hilton Art Collection, 62; acrylic on canvas mural, Job, Temple Beth El, Spring Valley, NY, 72. *Exhib:* Nabisco Brands Gallery, East Hanover, NJ, 91 & 98; Ellen Sragow Gallery, NY, 91-2006; Susan Teller Gallery, NY, 1991-2006; Krasdale Gallery, White Plains, NY, 93, 96, 2000, 2002; Baltimore Mus Art, Md, 2000; Fleisher Mus, Phila, 2001; Woodmere Mus Art, Phila, 2002; Reba and David Williams Collection, New York City, 2003; Cummer Mus & Gardens, Jacksonville, Fla, 2003; Blue Hill Cult Ctr, Pearl River, NY, 2003; Am Mural Studies 1935-1962, Teller Gallery, NY, 2004; Nat Acad Mus, NY, 2005; Phoenix Art Mus, Ariz, 2005. *Teaching:* Art therapist, Wiltwyck Sch Boys, NY, 57-66; prof art, Rockland Community Col, Suffern, NY, 66-88, prof emer, 93. *Awards:* Suny Fel Grant Research Award, 1967; Thornton Oakley Mem Prize, Philadelphia Watercolor Club, 68 & 76; Rockland Co Exec Arts Award, NY, 88; New York State Governor's Art Award, 90; Individual Artist Award, NY State Coun Arts, 95. *Bibliog:* Robert Delany & Richard Connely (dirs), Experience of the Artist--Hugh Mesibov (video tape), Rockland Community Col, NY; Five Artists from the 1930's and 1940's (catalog & monogr), Midtown Galleries, New York, 88; Linda Shopes (dir), audio tape & interview, Pa Hist & Mus Comn, Harrisburg, 90; Archives of American Art (video tape), Smithsonian Inst, Washington, 90. *Mem:* Rocklan Ctr Arts; Rockland Coun Arts; Artists Equity, NY; Whitney Mus Am Art; Fairlawn Art Asn, NJ; Hopper House Art Ctr, Nyack, NY. *Media:* Acrylic, Watercolor. *Res:* Pennsylvania Art Project, Painting, Printmaking and Mural Work; achieved national recognition for experimental work in printmaking. Co-inventor of Carborundum Print, and inventor of Color Carborundum Print. *Interests:* gardening. *Dealer:* Susan Teller Gallery 568 Broadway New York NY; Sragow Gallery 73 Spring St New York NY; Walker Kornbluth Gallery, 7-21 Fairlawn Ave, Fairlawn, NJ, 07410. *Mailing Add:* 4 Margetts Rd Chestnut Ridge NY 10952

MESSER, DAVID JAMES
DIRECTOR, MUSEUM DIRECTOR
b San Diego, Calif, Aug 25, 42. *Study:* Birmingham-Southern Col, BA; Purdue Univ, MS. *Pos:* Dir dept mus studies, Vincennes Univ, Ind, 76-79; cur exhibs, Beaumont Art Mus, Tex, 79-85; dir, Mus East Tex, Lufkin, 85-87 & Bergen Mus, Paramus, NJ, 87-. *Mailing Add:* Bergen Mus Art & Sci 327 E Ridgewood Ave Paramus NJ 07652

MESSER, THOMAS M
MUSEUM DIRECTOR, HISTORIAN
b Bratislava, Czech, Feb 9, 20; US citizen. *Study:* Thiel Col exchange student, Inst Int Educ, 39; Boston Univ, BA, 42; Sorbonne, Paris, France, 47; Harvard Univ, MA, 51; Spec Fel, Brussels, Belg, 53. *Collection Arranged:* First US mus shows, Egon Schiele & New Departures: Latin America, Inst Contemp Art; Solomon R Guggenheim Mus, NY. *Pos:* Dir, Roswell Mus, NMex, 49-52; dir, Am Fedn Arts, 52-56, trustee, 72-75; dir, Inst Contemp Arts, Boston, 57-61; dir, Solomon R Guggenheim Mus, 61-88, Solomon R Guggenheim Found, 80-88, dir emer, 90-; dir, Peggy Guggenheim Collection, Venice, Italy, 80-88; chief cur, Schirn Kunsthahe, Frankfort, 94-99. *Teaching:* Sr Fel advan studies, Wesleyan Univ Ctr Advan Studies, 66; prof, Hochschule fuer Angewandte Kunst, Vienna, Austria, 84, J W Goethe Univ, 91-, hon J W prof, 2000. *Awards:* Knight First Class, Order of St Olav, Norway, 66; Officer's Cross of Order of Merit, Fed Repub Ger, 75 & Goethe Medal, 90; Officer of Order of Leopold II, Belg, 78; Chevallier, Legion d'Honneur, France, 80, officer, 89; Cross of Hon, Science & Art, Austria, 80; Knight First Class, Order, Denmark, 83; Order Isabella Catolica, Spain, 84. *Mem:* Asn Art Mus Dir (pres, 74-75); Am Arts Alliance; Int Coun Mus (pres, 76-77); Am Asn Mus; Arts Int. *Publ:* Auth, The Emergent Decade: Latin-American Painters and Paintings in the 60's, Thames & Hudson, 66; Edward Munch, Library of Great Painters (series), Harry N Abrams Inc, 73; Vasily Kandinsky, Egon Schiele, Paul Klee, Joseph Beuys, Henri Michaux, Julius Bissier, Jiri Kolar and many others (catalogs); articles in Art News, Art in Am, Art Int, Am Scholar, Arts, Saturday Rev, World, Studio Int, Art Gallery, XX Siecle and others. *Mailing Add:* 205 E 77th New York NY 10021

MESSERSMITH, FRED LAWRENCE
PAINTER, EDUCATOR
b Sharon, Pa, Apr 3, 24. *Study:* Ohio Wesleyan Univ, BFA, 48, MA, 49. *Work:* Addison Gallery Am Art, Andover, Mass; Norton Mus Art, West Palm Beach, Fla; Butler Inst Am Art, Youngstown, Ohio; Springfield Art Mus, Mo; Stetson Univ & DeLand Mus Art; Mus Arts & Scis, Daytona Beach, Fla; many others. *Comn:* Hilton Hotel, Deland, Fla; Sun Banks, Fla; Volusia Co Court House, Deland, Fla. *Exhib:* Am Watercolor Soc, 57-; Mid-Year Show, Butler Inst Am Art, 65; Yale Univ, 71; World Bk Encyclopedia; Daytona Beach Mus Art & Sciences; Ringling Mus, Sarasota, Fla, 67; one man shows, Arno Gallery, Florence, Italy, 70, Old Sculpin Gallery, Edgartown, Mass, 83-86 & Michael Simpson, London, Eng, 92. *Teaching:* Chmn dept art, WVa Wesleyan Col, 49-59; chmn dept art, Stetson Univ, 59-89; instr, watercolor & drawing; artist-in-residence, Stetson Univ, 89; artist-in residence, Old Sculpin Gallery, Martha's Vineyard, Mass. *Awards:* First Award, Fla State Fair, 67 & Winter Park, 75; Ala Watercolor Soc Award, 75 & 81; Gold Award, Fla Watercolor Soc, 92; Bronze Medal, Southern Watercolor Soc, 2000; Award, Ala Watercolor Soc, 02. *Bibliog:* Norman Kent (auth), Fred Messersmith paints on rice paper, Am Artist Mag, 12/60; Edward Feit (auth), Fred Messersmith, taking risks with watercolor, Am Artist, 9/86. *Mem:* Am Watercolor Soc; Fla Artist Group (pres, 64-66); Ala Watercolor Soc; Fla Watercolor Soc; Watercolor Hon Soc; Southern Watercolor Soc. *Media:* Watercolor, Oil. *Publ:* Contribr, Artist and Advocate, Renaissance Ed Inc, 67; 100 Watercolor Techniques, 68; Acrylic Watercolor Painting, 70; Eyewitness to Space, 71; Best Watercolors, 95, 97 & 99, Landscape Inspirations, Rockport. *Dealer:* Old Sculpin Gallery 52 Dock St Edgartown MA 02539; Arts on Douglas New Smyrna Beach Fl 32168. *Mailing Add:* 726 N Boston Ave Deland FL 32724

MESSERSMITH, HARRY LEE
SCULPTOR, MUSEUM DIRECTOR
b Buckhannon, WVa, Aug 7, 58. *Study:* Stetson Univ, De Land, BFA, 81; Univ Fla, Gainesville, MFA, 83, Crealde Sch Art, Winter Park, Fla, 84-85, Penland Sch, NC, 2004; Atlantic Ctr for the Arts, New Smyrna Beach, Fla, 99. *Work:* Daytona Beach Justice Ctr, Fla; Volusia Co Public Sch, Fla; New Smyrna Beach Libr, Stetson Univ. *Comn:* Life size busts (four, bronze), Stetson Univ, De Land, Fla, 87-98; life size statue (bronze), Iverson Technol, Ellburn, Ill, 89; Volusia Co Coun, De Land, 90. *Exhib:* The Bronze Exhibit, Milan, Italy, 2000; Epcot & Disney World, Ann Int Garden Festival Sculpture Installation, 2000-05. *Collection Arranged:* De Land Nat Sculpture Exhib, Triennial juried competition, 91. *Pos:* Artist in educ, Volusia Co Schs, Fla, 86-89; exec dir, De Land Mus Art Fla Inc, 89-95, Lighthouse Gallery & Sch Art Inc, Fla, 95-96. *Teaching:* Artist in educ, traveling throughout Volusia Co, Fla, 86-89; instr art, Stetson Univ, De Land, Fla, 83-2005; instr ceramics, Daytona Beach Community Col, 88-89; Univ Ctrl Fla, 01-02. *Awards:* Best of Show Awards, Stetson Univ Homecoming, 78 & De Land Mus Art, 88. *Bibliog:* Margaret Linger Pearson (auth), Heroic Measures, Sch Arts Mag, Davis Publ Inc, 4/91. *Mem:* Int Sculpture Ctr; Col Art Asn; Fla Craftsman Inc; Fla Pyrotechnic Arts Guild. *Media:* Cast Bronze, Metals. *Mailing Add:* 726 N Boston Ave Deland FL 32724

MESSINA, CHARLES
ARTIST
b Wilmington, DE, Jan 6, 50. *Comn:* John A. Travalini, various, 78-2006; Albert Vitri, Landscape, watercolor, Greenville, DE, 98; Anthony Fusco, Portrait, oil, New Castl, DE, 99; John Adamson, Indian Setting, oil, Elsmere, DE, 2002; Mary Bensen, Row Homes, oil, Wilmington, DE, 2003; Diane Dufaj, Angels, oil, Wilmington, DE, 2004. *Exhib:* Federal Fel Exhibit, Federal Building, Wilmington, DE, 89; Local Artists Exhibit, Convention Ctr, Wilmigton, DE, 2003; Vendemmia da Vinci, sponsored by Societa da Vinci, Wilmington, DE, 2004. *Pos:* Owner, C Messina Art Studio, Wilmington, DE, 98-. *Bibliog:* Lex Bayard (auth), Mike Tyson (Boxing), Del Marva Beach Bull (from front page); Mus & Gall, The News Journal, 12/4/98; Berland Bruce, $1 Launched Artist's Brush with Fame, The News Journal, 5/12/99. *Publ:* Walkers Mill, Brandywine Deleware Today, 98; Little Italy, www.discoverlittleitaly.com, 2003; RE/Max Sunvest Michael A DiFonzo, 2004. *Mailing Add:* 1902 W 6th St Wilmington DE 19805

METCALF, BRUCE B
JEWELER, WRITER
b Amherst, Mass, Sept 30, 49. *Study:* Syracuse Univ, BFA, 72; Tyler Sch Art, Temple Univ, Philadelphia, MFA, 77. *Work:* La Mus Des Arts Decoratifs De Montreal, Quebec; Philadelphia Mus Art; Renwick Gallery, Nat Mus Am Art, Washington; Cooper-Hewitt Nat Mus Design, NY; Mint Mus Craft & Design, Charlotte, NC; Mus Arts & Design, NY; Nat Mus Scotland, Edinburgh; Mus Fine Art, Houston, Tex. *Exhib:* Forms in Metal - 275 Yrs of Am Metalsmithing, Mus Contemp Crafts, NY, 75; Good as Gold, Renwick Gallery, Smithsonian Inst, 81; Ohio Perspectives: New Work in Clay, Glass, Textiles, and Metal, Akron Art Mus, 88; Ornamenta 1: Int Exhib of Contemp Jewelry Art, Schmuck Mus, Pforzheim, Ger, 89; Jewelry Arsenals, Nat Mus, Zurich, Switz, 91; Modern Jewelry 1964-1991: The Helen Williams Drutt Collection, Mus Appl Arts, Helsinki, Finland, 92; Facet '93: International Biennial of Jewelry, Kunsthal Rotterdam, The Neth, 93; Jewelry in Europe & Am: New Times, New Thinking, Craft Coun Gallery, London; Jewelry Moves, Nat Mus Scotland, Edinburgh, 98; Defining Craft I, Am Craft Mus, NY, 2000; An Inaugural Gift: The Founders' Circle Collection, Mint Mus of Craft & Design, Charlotte, NC, 2000; Corporal Identity - Body Language, Frankfurt Mus für Angewandte Kunst, Ger, 2003. *Collection Arranged:* New Ohio Jewelry, Massillon Mus, Ohio, 90; Revising Classicism: The Language of Antiquity in Contemporary Furniture and Ceramics, Hicks Art Ctr, Newtown, Pa, 93; organizing cur, The Art of Gold, Exhibits USA, 2003. *Pos:* Soc NAm Goldsmiths, nominating comt chair, 87, bd dir & secy, 98-2002. *Teaching:* Temporary instr jewelry/metals, Colo State Univ, Ft Collins, 77-78; instr, Mass Col Art, Boston, 79-80; assoc prof, Kent State Univ, Ohio, 81-91; sr lectr, Univ Arts, Philadelphia, 94-95, 98-99. *Awards:* Ohio Arts Coun Crafts Fel, 83, 84 & 88; Fulbright Comn Teaching & Res Fel, Korea, 90; Pew Fel Arts, 96; PEW Fel Spl Opportunity Stipend, 2002. *Bibliog:* Cheryl White (auth), Focus: Bruce Metcalf, Am Craft, 10-11/90; C E Licka (auth), Focus: Bruce Metcalf between darkness and light, Metalsmith, winter 90; Ulysses Dietz (auth), Ohio Metals: A Legacy, Interalia/Design Books, 93. *Mem:* Am Crafts Coun; Soc NAm Goldsmiths. *Media:* Miscellaneous Media. *Publ:* Replacing the myth of modernism, Am Craft, 2-3/93; On the nature of jewelry, Metalsmith, winter 93; The Problem of the Fountain, Metalsmith, summer 2000; The Hand: At the Heart of Craft, Am Craft, 8-9/2000; Embodied Sympathy, Metalsmith, Summer 2002. *Dealer:* Charon Kransen Arts 456 W 25th St New York NY 10001. *Mailing Add:* 116 Leedom Ave Bala Cynwyd PA 19004

METCALFE, ERIC WILLIAM
VIDEO ARTIST
b Vancouver, BC, Aug 22, 40. *Study:* Univ Victoria, BFA, 70. *Work:* Art Bank Can, Ottawa; Nat Gallery Can; Akad Kunst, West Berlin; Univ Calgary, Alta; Art Gallery Ont. *Comn:* Multi-media performance, 78 & video performance, 83, Music Gallery, Toronto. *Exhib:* Chair Show, Art Gallery Ont, 74; From This Point of View, Vancouver Art Gallery, 77; Off the Wall, A Space, Toronto, 77; Chair Show, And/Or, Seattle, 79; Manner SM, Vancouver Art Gallery, 82; Okanada, Akad Kunste, West Berlin, 83. *Pos:* Dir & cur performance art, Western Front, 73-. *Awards:* Bursary, 73 & Video Production Award, 77, 80 & 83, Can Coun; JVC Corp Third Video Festival Award, 80. *Bibliog:* Balkind Shadbolt (auth), Visions, Douglas & McIntyre, 83; Peggy Gane (auth), Parachute, Colour Video, 83. *Media:* Video, Performance. *Mailing Add:* Western Front Soc 303 E Eighth Ave Vancouver BC V5T 1S1 Canada

METYKO, MICHAEL JOSEPH
CONSULTANT
b Port Arthur, Tex, Feb 27, 1945. *Study:* Houston Mus Fine Arts Sch; St Thomas Univ, Houston, with Dominique de Menil & Jermyne McAgy; Pratt Inst, Brooklyn; San Francisco Art Inst, MFA(printmaking). *Comn:* Tatto Parlor: Segment I (15 minute film) & Segment II (15 minute film with architect, Thomas Burke), David Gallery, Houston, 70; participation/doc event piece, Main St 76, Houston CofC, 76; installation piece, Houston Festival, 79. *Exhib:* The Bosch Show, Univ St Thomas, Houston, 76; Contemp Icons, Mus Mod Art, Houston, 76; Made in Houston, La Gallery, 78 & 79; group show, Art Ctr, Waco, Tex, 79; miniatures, Univ Houston Lawndale Gallery, 79; Univ Houston Thomas Gallery, 79; and many others. *Collection Arranged:* Texas Week in San Francisco, Festival & Exhib of Texas Art & The Artist's Archives, Exhib of Materials Collected by Artists, San Francisco Art Inst, 72; Main St/Houston Festival art & video exhibitions, 78 & 79; Texas Crafts touring exhibition (ed, contribr & illusr, catalog & producer media presentation), S C Blaffer Gallery, 78; Embroidery: Houston Emb Guild, Craft & Folk Arts Adv Comt, 79, Lone Star Sampler: Works by Texas Craftsmen, 79, Art/Craft: 6 Houston Craft Guilds, 79, Selected Works: Texas Designer Craftsmen, 79 & Dimensions in Glass, 79. *Pos:* Asst to chmn, Dept of Art, Rice Univ, 66-67; cur, Grad Print & Photo Gallery, San Francisco Art Inst, 71-72; asst to dir/cur, S C Blaffer Gallery, Univ Houston, 73-78; dir crafts events, Houston Festival, 79-80. *Awards:* Tex Comn Arts exhib support grant, 78 & Cult Arts Coun Houston proj support grant, 79. *Bibliog:* Niomi Berman (auth), Interview & article in Southwestern Craftsman Mag, 76; Charlotte Moser (auth), Review of Houston Artists, Art News, 76. *Mem:* Artists Equity Asn (pres chap, Houston, 75-77); Cult Arts Coun Houston; Tex Asn Mus; Am Coun Arts; Western Asn Art Mus. *Media:* Mixed. *Publ:* Contribr & illusr, 9th Congress of European Exchange Students Journal, Int Cult

Exchange Serv, 66; contribr & illusr, Conceptual Excerpts, Guano Mag, Univ Houston, 70; contribr & illusr exhib catalogues, S C Blaffer Gallery, 73-78; contribr introd, exhib catalogue for Donald Thornton, Col of the Mainland, 76; illusr, New Cultural Decision Makers in Houston, Art News, 77. *Mailing Add:* 1634 Branard St Houston TX 77006

METZ, FRANK ROBERT
PAINTER, DESIGNER
b Philadelphia, Pa, July 3, 25. *Study:* Philadelphia Mus Sch, with Ezio Martinelli; Art Students League, with Will Barnet. *Work:* Olsen Found, Guilford, Conn; Ball State Teachers Col, Muncie, Ind; Philadelphia Mus Art; Mass Inst Technol; Charles Pfizer Co; AT&T; Deutsche Bank. *Comn:* Col Tec Industries NC. *Exhib:* One-man shows, Alonzo Gallery, 74, 77 & 79, Haber Theodore Gallery, 84 & 85, Gross McCleaf Gallery, Philadelphia, Pa, 87 & Minor Mem Libr, Roxbury, Conn, 95, 2005; Monhegan Artists, Allentown Mus, Pa, 74; retrospective, Gross McCleaf Gallery, 85; From the Landscape, Washington Art Asn, Conn, 9g; Randall Tuttle Fine Arts, Woodbury, Conn, 99; Central High Sch Alumni Exhib, Woodmere Art Mus, Philadelphia, Pa, 2002; group show, Potter & Slack Gallery, Wash, CT, 2003, 2004; Frost Gully Gallery, 40th Anniversary Show, 2006. *Pos:* Art dir, Simon & Schuster, 50-95. *Awards:* Elisabeth Ball Purchase Award, Ball State Teachers Col, 64. *Bibliog:* Jules Perel (auth), Landscape drawings of Frank Metz, Am Artist, 5/62; Doreen Managan (auth), Landscape paintings of Frank Metz, Am Artists, 3/78 & Twenty Oil Painters and How They Work, Watson-Guptill, 78; Paul Bacon (auth), articles, Arts Mag, 3/84 & 4/85; Carl Little & Arnold Skolnick (coauths) Art of the Maine Islands, Down East Books; Landscapes & Inspiration, New Milford Times, 6/24/2005. *Media:* All Media. *Specialty:* Landscapes of Maine. *Interests:* Travel & Sketches. *Dealer:* Judith Selkowitz Art Advisory Services Inc 530 Park Ave New York NY 10021; Frost Gully Gallery Freeport ME; RVS Gallery, Southampton, NY. *Mailing Add:* 800 West End Ave Apt 6C New York NY 10025

METZ, MATTHEW J
CERAMIST
b Kendallville, Ind, Mar 16, 61. *Study:* Ball State Univ, BA; Edinburg Univ, MFA, 86. *Work:* Erie Art Mus, Pa. *Exhib:* Swidler Gallery, 91; Joann Rapp, Scottsdale, Ariz, 94 & 96; Little Street Studio, Chicago, Ill, 97. *Pos:* Studio potter, independent. *Awards:* Nat Endowment Arts, 91. *Dealer:* Lill St Studio 1021 W Lill St Chicago IL

METZGER, EVELYN BORCHARD
PAINTER, SCULPTOR
b New York, NY, June 8, 1911. *Study:* Vassar Col, AB, 32, with C K Chatterton; Art Students League, with George Bridgman & Rafael Soyer; also George Grosz, sculpture with Sally Farnham, Guzman de Rojas in Bolivia & Demetrio Urruchua in Arg. *Work:* Fine Arts Gallery San Diego, Balboa Park, Calif; Ariz State Mus, Tucson; Lyman Allyn Mus, New London, Conn; Univ Mo-Columbia; Butler Inst Am Art, Youngstown, Ohio; and others. *Exhib:* 19 One-man show, Galeria Muller, Buenos Aires, 50, Gallerie Bellechasse, Paris, 63, Washington Co Mus Fine Arts, Hagerstown, Md, 99- & Ann Norton Scultpure Garden, West Palm Beach, 2001; Norfolk Mus Art, Va, 65; Mex-Am Cult Inst, Mexico City, 67; Van Diemen-Lilienfeld Gallery, NY, 66; Bartholet Gallery, NY, 73; Arsenal Art Gallery, NY, 83; Nat Mus Women Arts, Washington, DC, 97, 02; Joan Whelan, NY, 97; Cornell Univ, 98; Curzon Gallery, Boca Raton, Fla, 2003. *Pos:* Hon dir, Vassar Art Gallery. *Bibliog:* Aymel Seghers (auth), New York News (and cover), Arts Rev, 4/63; M L D'Otrange Mastai (auth), An American flowering, 5/63 & Evelyn Metzger--recent works, 12/66, The Connoisseur; Nancy Heller & Brett Topping (auths), The Aged of Grandeur and a Woman Who Lived It, Nat Mus Women Arts, 95. *Mem:* Artists Equity Asn; Am Fedn Art; Arch Am Art. *Media:* Oil. *Mailing Add:* 815 Park Ave New York NY 10021

METZGER, ROBERT PAUL
CURATOR, DIRECTOR
b Detroit, Mich. *Study:* Wayne State Univ, BA, MA; Columbia Univ, with T Reff; Univ Calif, Los Angeles, with Fred Wight, PhD; Am Film Inst, with Jean Renoir. *Pos:* Cur, Lydia Winston Malbin Collection of Art, New York, 74-76; dir art, Stamford Mus, Conn, 76-; dir, Reading Mus, currently. *Teaching:* Asst prof art hist survey, Univ Detroit, Mich, 65-66; assoc prof Am art hist, Univ Bridgeport, Conn, 77-. *Awards:* Univ Calif Arts Coun Traveling Grant, 69; Mich State Univ Art Hist Res Grant, 74. *Mem:* Col Art Asn Am. *Res:* Biomorphism in the 20th century, American painting and sculpture 18th through 20th century, Reuben Nakian. *Publ:* Ed, Directory of American Periodicals, Oxbridge Press, 76; auth, Karl Struss, American Cinematographer, 76, Nakian's Place in History, 77 & The Case for Pop Art as Neo-Dada, 78, Stamford Mus. *Mailing Add:* c/o Reading Mus 500 Museum Rd Reading PA 19611

METZKER, RAY K
PHOTOGRAPHER, EDUCATOR
b Milwaukee, Wis, Sept 10, 31. *Study:* Beloit Col, BA, 53; Ill Inst Technol, MS, 59, with Aaron Siskind & Harry Callahan. *Work:* Mus Mod Art, NY; Art Inst Chicago; Smithsonian Inst; Bibliot Nat, Paris; Philadelphia Mus Art. *Exhib:* My Camera and I in the Loop, Art Inst Chicago, 59; One-man shows Mus Mod Art, NY, 67, Pa Acad Fine Arts, 80, Art Inst Chicago, 91, The Locks Gallery, Philadelphia, 96, Laurence Miller Gallery, NY, 96, 97, 98 & 99, Galerie Francoise Paviot, Paris, 97, Stephen Daiter Gallery, Chicago, 2000, The Philadelphia Mus Art, 2000; Milwaukee Art Ctr, 70; New Photog USA Traveling Exhibit, Mus Mod Art, NY, 70-72; Landscape/Cityscape, Metrop Mus Art, NY, 73; Philadelphia: Three Centuries of Am Art, Philadelphia Mus of Art, 76; From the Heart: The Power of Photography-A Collector's Choice, Art Mus South Texas, Corpus Christi, 98; Photog from the Martin Z Margulies Collection, The Art Mus, Fla Int Univ, Miami, 99; An Am Century of Photog, from Dry-Plate to Digital (The Hallmark Photog Collection), Phillips Gallery, Washington, DC, 99; The Century of the Body: Photoworks 1900-2000, Musee de l'Elysee, Lausanne, Switz, 99; Emerging Images: Selected Contemp Photog, Susquehana Art Mus, Pa, 99. *Teaching:* Prof photog, Philadelphia Col of Art, 62-81; assoc prof photog, Univ NMex, 70-72; adj photog, RI Sch Design, 77, Columbia Col, Chicago, 80-83; Smith Distinguished Vis Artist, George Wash Univ, 87-88. *Awards:* Guggenheim Fel, 66 & 79; Nat Endowment Arts Fel, 74 & 88; LaNapoule Art Found, La Napoule, France, 89. *Bibliog:* Peter C Bunnell (auth), Ray Metzker, Print Collector's Newslett, Vol IX, No 6, 79; Chuck Isaacs (auth), Ray K Metzker: An interview, Afterimage, 11/80; Andy Grundberg (auth), Ray K Metzker: form as expression, Mod Photog, 11/81; Anne W Tucker (ed), Unknown Territory; Ray K Metzker (monogr), Aperture/Mus Fine Arts, Houston, 84. *Publ:* Illusr, Razerol, Janus, 73; auth, Sand Creatures, Aperture, 79. *Mailing Add:* c/o Laurence G Miller Inc 20 W 57th St New York NY 10019

MEW, TOMMY
PAINTER, CONCEPTUAL ARTIST
b Miami, Fla, Aug 15, 42. *Study:* Fla State Univ, BS, MA; NY Univ, PhD. *Work:* Am Tel & Tel, NY; Jacksonville Art Mus, Fla; Moderna Mus, Stockholm; McDonald's Corp Collection; Macon Mus Arts & Sci; and others. *Exhib:* One-man shows, Montgomery Mus Fine Arts, Ala, 70 & Miss Mus Art, 79; Paintings, Mus Art, Macon, Ga, 72; Rockefeller Arts Ctr, NY; High Mus Art, Atlanta, 76; Nat Gallery Can, Ottawa, 77; Gallery 34, Kassel, Ger; and others. *Pos:* Dir, Fluxus West/South East. *Teaching:* Grad asst art, Fla State Univ, 64-65; asst prof art, Troy State Univ, Ala, 66-68 & Jacksonville Univ, Fla, 68-70; prof painting & chmn art dept, Berry Col, 70-; vis artist & lectr drawings, Nat Endowment Arts, 72 & Univ Tulsa, 81. *Awards:* Grant, Cowperthwaite Corp, 72 & Ga Coun Arts, 80. *Bibliog:* Annette Kuhn (auth), Scar art, Village Voice, 75; Peter Frank (auth), Auto-art-and how, Art News, 76; Alan Storey (auth), Tommy Mew, Art Voices S, 3/78. *Mem:* Col Art Asn; Southeastern Col Art Asn; Popular Cult Asn South; Nat Art Educ Asn; Am Fedn of the Arts. *Media:* Acrylic; Mixed. *Interests:* Running; Racing. *Publ:* Ed & contribr, Third Floor Love Poems, 66 & auth & ed, Le Voyage, 68, Troy State Press; ed & contribr, Dramatika, New York Press, 70; ed & contribr, Scartissue, Troy State Press, 76; auth, Ray Johnson, Col Art Asn J, 77; contribr, Intermedia Mag, Can, 77. *Dealer:* Marney Rhodes 111 Saddle Mt Rd Rome GA 30161. *Mailing Add:* PO Box 580-Art Mount Berry GA 30149

MEYER, EDWARD HENRY
PATRON
b New York City, Jan 8, 27. *Study:* Cornell U, BA, 1949. *Pos:* With Bloomingdale's div Federated Dept Stores, 1949-51; with, Biow Co, 1951-56; with, Gray Global Group, NYC,1956-, exec vpres 1963-68, pres 1968-, Chief Exec Officer, chmn,1970-; bd dir, Ethan Allan Interiors Inc, Harman Internat Industries Inc, Jim Pattison Group Inc,. *Mem:* Trustee, Solomon R Guggenheim Mus & NY Univ Med Ctr; bd mem, Am Mus Natural History & Film Soc fo Lincoln Ctr; Econ Club, Univ Club, Harmonie Club, Century Country Club, Atlantic Golf Club. *Mailing Add:* Grey Global Group Inc 777 Third Ave New York NY 10017-1401

MEYER, EL(MER) FREDERICK
PAINTER, WRITER
b Twin Falls, Idaho, May 24, 10. *Study:* Fed Schs Com Design, diploma, 29; Calif Sch Fine Arts, 30-31 & 54; studies with Eliot O'Hara, Rex Brandt, Millard Sheets, Tom Hill, Ken Potter, Morris Shubin, Barbara Nechis & Robert E Wood. *Work:* Santa Rosa City Hall, Calif; 1st Nat Bank Ariz & Tucson Realty & Trust Co, Tucson; Arts Coun, Phoenix. *Exhib:* California Art, State Fair Galleries, Sacramento, 80; Am Watercolor Soc, Nat Acad, NY, 81; Watercolor West, Riverside Art Ctr, 82; 35th Ann Soc Western Artists, Hall Flowers, San Francisco, 85; 22nd Ann Statewide Exhib, Santa Rosa Art Guild, Veterans Mem, Calif, 85. *Teaching:* Instr watercolor, on-location workshops, Forestville, Calif, 78-85; instr watercolor, Arts Guild, Arts Sch Belvedere, Calif, 80-81 & Wine Country Workshops, Calistoga, Calif, 82. *Awards:* Gerry Pierce Mem, 4th Ann Southern Ariz Watercolor Guild, 71; Special Award, 31st Ann Soc Western Artists, House of Hatch Covers, 78; Neva Rall Mem, 32nd Ann Soc Western Artists, 80. *Bibliog:* Watercolor Magic (film), Calif North, KFTY chan 50, Santa Rosa, Calif, 84. *Mem:* Art Workshop Western Sonoma Co; Soc Western Artists; Santa Rosa Art Guild (pres, 79-80). *Media:* Watercolor. *Publ:* Auth, Making Watercolor Work, pvt publ, 78; Watercolor Painting on Location, North Light Books, 84. *Mailing Add:* 5929 Van Keppel Rd Forestville CA 95436

MEYER, JAMES SAMPSON
WRITER, HISTORIAN
b Springfield, Mass. *Study:* Yale Univ, BA, 84; Inst Fine Arts, NY Univ, MA, 86; Johns Hopkins Univ, PhD, 95. *Collection Arranged:* What Happened to the Institutional Critique? (auth, catalog), Am Fine Arts, NY, 93. *Teaching:* Instr 20th century art, Sch Visual Arts, NY, 90-94; asst prof contemp art & criticism, Emory Univ, Atlanta, Ga, 94-. *Bibliog:* Christopher Reed (auth), Postmodernism & the Art of Identity, Concepts Mod Art, Thames & Hudson, 94; Barry Schwabsky (auth), Mel Bochner: thought made visible 1966-73, On Paper, 9-10/96. *Mem:* Col Art Asn. *Res:* American art 1955-1975; specifically mimimalism; conceptualism; institutional critique; contemporary art. *Publ:* Auth, AIDS & Postmodernism, Arts Mag, 92; The functional site, Platzwechsel, Kunsthalle, Zurich, 95; Ellsworth Kelly: Sculpture for a large wall, 1957, Matthew Marks Gallery, 98. *Mailing Add:* Art History Dept Carlos Hall Emory Univ Atlanta GA 30322

MEYER, JERRY DON
HISTORIAN, EDUCATOR
b Carbondale, Ill, Nov 19, 39. *Study:* Southern Ill Univ, Carbondale, BS, 62, MA(art hist), 64; New York Univ, Inst Fine Arts, PhD(art hist), 73. *Teaching:* Prof art hist, Northern Ill Univ, 68-2001 asst chair, 85-2001, prof emer, 2001-. *Mem:* Col Art Asn; Midwest Art Hist Soc; Am Acad Religion. *Res:* Late 18th & 19th century English &

American Art, 20th century art. *Publ:* Auth, Benjamin West's Chapel of Revealed Religion, Art Bull, 75; Benjamin West's St Stephen altar-piece, Burlington Mag, 76; Benjamin West's window designs for St George's Chapel, Am Art J, 79; The Woman Clothed with the Sun: Two Illustrations to St John's Revelation by William Blake, Studies in Iconography, Vol 12, 88; Profane and Sacred: Religious Imagery and Prophetic Expression in Postmodern Art, J Am Acad Relig, Vol 65/1, 97. *Mailing Add:* Sch Art Northern Ill Univ De Kalb IL 60115

MEYER, MELISSA
PAINTER
b New York, NY, 47. *Study:* New York Univ, BS, 68, MA, 75. *Work:* Mus Mod Art, Metrop Mus Art & Solomon R Guggenheim Mus, NY; Aldrich Mus Contemp Art, Ridgefield, Conn; Ark Art Ctr, Little Rock; Rose Art Mus, Waltham, Mass; Tampa Mus Art, Fla; Brooklyn Mus, NY. *Exhib:* Solo exhibs, J L Becker/East End Gallery, Provincetown, Mass, 88, Holly Solomon Gallery (with catalog), 91, 93 & 96, Miller Bloch Fine Art, Boston, Mass, 91, 94 & 96, Montgomery Glasoe Fine Arts, Minneapolis, Minn, 93 & 96 & Galerie Renee Ziegler, Zurich, 93; Painting, Nina Freudenheim Gallery, Buffalo, NY, 94; Embraceable You, Selby Gallery, Ringling Sch Art & Design, Sarasota, Fla, 94; About Color, Charles Cowles Gallery, NY, 94; Contemp Prints, Allez les Filles Gallery, Columbus, Ohio, 94. *Teaching:* Vis artist, Univ Iowa, 85, Syracuse Univ, 85 & 86, Art Inst Chicago, 85, Ft Hays State, Hays, Kans, 86, Middlebury Col, Vt, 86 & Univ Buffalo, 86; instr, Parsons Sch Design, New York, 82-91, Bennington Col, Vt, 82 & 85, Provincetown Art Mus, 85 & 86, Columbia Univ, 89, RI Sch Design, 92 & 94, Vt Studio Ctr, 92 & Sch Visual Arts, New York, 93-. *Awards:* CAPS Grant, 81-82; Grant in Painting, Nat Endowment Arts, 83-84 & 93; Grant, New York Found Arts, 92. *Bibliog:* Nancy Stapen (auth), Galleries/the vast canvas of abstraction, Boston Globe, 4/21/94; Joan Altabe (auth), Super-realism colors superb abstract show, Sarasota Herald-Tribune, 8/26/94; Mary Ann Marger (auth), A mission in abstract, Sarasota Times, 8/26/94. *Publ:* Illusr, Ms Mag, 12/73; coauth, Femmage, Heresies, spring 78; illusr, Parnassus: Poetry in Review, 83; Kimura at Ruth Siegel, Arts, 4/85; Provinceton Arts, fall 86, summer 87 & 88

MEYER, MILTON E, JR
PAINTER
b St Louis, Mo, Nov 26, 22. *Study:* Wash Univ, BSBA, 43; St Louis Univ, LLB, 50; NY Univ, LLM, 53; also studied with George Carlson, 83 & Daniel E Greene, 84. *Work:* Byron White Federal Courthouse, Denver; Cherry Hills Country Club, Denver, Colo; Roaring Fork Club, Basalt, Colo; Denver Zoo, Colo. *Comn:* Fed Court Appeals, 10th Circuit, Denver, Colo, 94. *Exhib:* Mem shows, Pastel Soc W Coast, 90, 91, 92, 93, 94 & 95 & Ann Open Exhib, 91, 92, 93, 94 & 95; 19th, 20th, 21st, 22nd, 23rd & 24th Ann Open Exhib, Pastel Soc Am, NY, 91, 92, 93, 94, 95 & 96; Denver Rotary's Artists Am Show, Colo, 2000. *Pos:* Chmn, Denver Rotary's Artists Am, Colo, 90-92; art consult, 10th Circuit Court of Appeals, Denver, 94. *Awards:* Second place (pastel) All-Media Competition, Artist's Mag; Award Merit, Pastel Soc Am, San Francisco, 96; Silver Award, Int Asoc Pastel Socs, Placerville, Calif, 2002; First place, Pastel Soc Colo, 2002; Master Circle, Int Asn Pastel Soc, 2005. *Bibliog:* Starr Yelland (auth), Work of Milton Meyer, CBS (TV), Denver, 7/89; Carole Katchen (auth), A Traveller's Mood, Focus, Santa Fe, 8/92; Carole Katchen (auth), Filling in the Blanks, The Artist's Mag', 7/94. *Mem:* Pastel Soc Am & W Coast; Knickerbocker Artists; Salmagundi Club. *Media:* Pastels. *Interests:* Foreign Travel and Subject matter. *Publ:* Auth, Approaching Photo Realism with Pastels, Am Artist, 11/92; Harnessing the spirit of water, The Artist's Mag, 12/98; contribr in various art publications of Quarto, Rockport Publishing and F&W Publications; auth, Picture perfect, Artist Int, 11-12/99; Selected pastels of Milton Meyer, Meyer, Meyer & McNeil, 2000. *Mailing Add:* 7123 W Belmont Dr Littleton CO 80123

MEYER, MORRIS ALBERT
PAINTER
b Lebanon, Pa, Oct 14, 36. *Study:* Pa State Univ, BSME, 58. *Comn:* Painting (3 children), comn by Mr & Mrs Harry Gardner, Dublin, Ohio, 94; painting (2 boys), comn by Elizabeth Coley, Dublin, Ohio, 96; painting (house 38 x 50), comn by Mr & Mrs Jon Tabor, Delaware, Ohio, 98; Rocky Mountain Nat Watermedia Exhib, 94, 97, Grand Exhib, 96, 97; Adirandacks Nat Exhib Am Watercolors, 96, 97. *Exhib:* Realism, Parkersburg Art Ctr, WVa, 95, 96, 97 & 98; Watercolor USA, Springfield Art Mus, Mo, 96 & 97; Taos Nat Exhib Am Watercolor, Taos Art Mus, NMex, 97; Ariz Aqueous, Tubac Ctr Arts, 98; Watercolor Ohio 98, 96, 97, 99, 2000, Canton Mus Art, 98. *Pos:* Artist, US Coast Guard, 94-. *Teaching:* Instr watercolor painting, pvt lessons, 98. *Awards:* Bloomsbury Award, Windsor Newton, 96; Award of Excellence, Trin Found, Strathmore, 96; Purchase/Gold Medallion, Brown Forman, 98; Best of Show, First Place. *Bibliog:* Betty Lou Schlemm (auth), People In Watercolor, Rockport Publ, 96; Webster Schlemm (auth), Best of Watercolor II, Rockport Publ, 97. *Mem:* Nat Watercolor Soc; Ohio Watercolor Soc; NW Watercolor Soc; Ala Watercolor Soc; Hon Soc, Watercolor USA; Watercolor USA. *Media:* Watercolor. *Publ:* Auth, Keeping clutter under control (art), Artist Mag, 4/98. *Mailing Add:* 8636 Gavington Ct Dublin OH 43017

MEYER, RUTH KRUEGER
HISTORIAN, ADMINISTRATOR
b Chicago Heights, Ill, Aug 20, 40. *Study:* Univ Cincinnati, Col Design, BFA, 63; Brown Univ, MA, 68; Univ Minn, PhD, 80. *Collection Arranged:* Proposals for Sawyer Point Park, 77; Arabesque (auth, catalog), 78; Walls, 80; The Pattern Principle, 81; Inner/Urban: How the Artist Saw the City in the 70's (auth, catalog), 81; New Epiphanies: Contemporary Religious Art; David Black, An American Sculptor (auth, catalog essay) Taft Mus, Cincinnati, 85; Sandy Rosen, Vestal Vases, Taft Mus, 86. *Pos:* Cur, Contemp Arts Ctr, Cincinnati, 76-80; dir, Ohio Found Arts, Columbus, 80-83. *Awards:* Kress Found Grant for Res, 67 & 76. *Mem:* Int Asn Art Critics; Col Art Asn. *Res:* Painters of French Barbizon School, Contemporary art, monumental and environmental sculpture. *Publ:* Auth, The Tafts of Pike St, Apollo, 12/88; ed & contribr, The modern art society: the center's early years, Contemp Arts Ctr, 79; contribr, A meeting place of humanistic experience, Natur Skulptur, Kunstverein, Stuttgart, 81

MEYER, SEYMOUR W
SCULPTOR
b Great Neck, NY. *Study:* With Louise Nevelson. *Work:* Arlen Industs, NY; Mus Mod Art, Rio de Janeiro, Brazil; Tel-Aviv Mus & Bat-Yam Mus, Israel; Temple Beth-El, Great Neck, NY; Fine Arts Mus, Long Island; and others. *Comn:* NY Inst Technol Libr, Old Westbury, NY; Isreal Tennis Ctr, Ramat Hashiron, Israel. *Exhib:* Metrop Mus Art, NY, 76; D Justin Lester Gallery, Los Angeles, Calif, 78-80; Royal Acad, London, Eng, 79; Galeria of Sculpture, Palm Beach, Fla, 79-80; Engel Gallery, Jerusalem, 81; Art in Embassies, US State Dept, 85-; Exec Mansion, Albany, NY, 94-2000. *Pos:* Bd Trustees, NY Inst Technol; fel, Am Col of Surgeons. *Awards:* First Place, National Physicians Art; Two Valentine Mott Medals. *Mem:* Am Fedn Arts; Mus Mod Art NY; Sculptors League of NY; Guggenheim Mus; Prof Sculptors Guild. *Media:* Bronze. *Dealer:* J Richards Gallery Eaglewood NJ 07631. *Mailing Add:* 495 E Shore Rd Great Neck NY 11024

MEYER, SUSAN E
EDITOR, WRITER
b New York, NY, Apr 22, 40. *Study:* Univ Perugia, 60; Univ Wis, BA, 62. *Pos:* Managing ed, Watson-Guptill Publ, NY, 63-70; ed in chief, Am Artist, NY, 71-79, retired; ed dir, Am Art & Antiques, NY, 78-80; ed dir, Am Artist, Art & Antiques & Interiors & Residential Interiors, NY, 79-80; treas, Art Table, 81-85; founder & pres, Roundtable Press, Inc, 81-92. *Teaching:* Adj prof, Empire State Col/Union Col, 76-78, NY Univ, currently. *Mem:* Artists Fel (trustee, 78-85); Art Table (treas, 81-85). *Publ:* Norman Rockwell's People, 81; Treasury of the Great Children's Books Illustrators, 83; Mary Cassatt, 90; Norman Rockwell's World War II, 91; Edgar Degas, 94. *Mailing Add:* 20 E Ninth St New York NY 10003

MEYER, TOBIAS
APPRAISER
Collection: Contemporary Art. *Mailing Add:* Sotherby's 1334 York Ave New York NY 10021

MEYERHOFF, ROBERT E
COLLECTOR
b Jan 24. *Hon Degrees:* Achievements include establishing Meyerhoff Scholars Prog at Univ Md Baltimore Co, 88. *Pos:* Pres, Henderson Webb Inc, Md; owner Fitzhugh Farm, Phoenix. *Awards:* Named Philanthropists of the Year (with wife Jane), United Way of Central Maryland, 2001; named one of Top 200 Collectors, ARTnews Magazine, 2004. *Mem:* Jockey Club, Thoroughbred Owners & Breeders Asn (Outstanding Md Owner-Breeder 99); Mem of corp Metrop Mus Art, New York City. *Collection:* modern & contemporary art, especially postwar Am abstraction; collection is pledged to Nat Gallery of Art, WA. *Mailing Add:* 3615 Blenheim Rd Phoenix MD 21131

MEYEROWITZ, JOEL
PHOTOGRAPHER
b New York, NY, Mar 6, 38. *Study:* Ohio State, BFA, 59. *Work:* Mus Mod Art, NY; Art Inst Chicago; Boston Mus Fine Arts; Philadelphia Mus; St Louis Art Mus. *Comn:* St Louis and the Arch, St Louis Art Mus, 80; Atlanta, IBM, 89; The Nutcracker Suite, Time/Warner, 92. *Exhib:* One-man shows, Art Forum Mus Modern Art, Tokyo, 91, James Danziger Gallery, NY, 92, San Jose Mus Art, 93, The Art Inst Chicago, Ill, 94 & 95, Bonni Benrubi Gallery, NY, 95; Street Photographs, NY, Turin Biennale, Italy, 99; Modern Starts, People, Places, Things, Mus Modern Art, NY, 99; Hope Photographs, Katonah Mus Art, NY, 2000; It's So Hot, Jackson Gallery, Atlanta, Ga, 2000. *Teaching:* Adj prof, Cooper Union, 71-78; lectr, Princeton Univ, 78 & New York Univ, 91-92. *Awards:* Guggenheim Fel, 71 & 79; Nat Endowment Arts Fel, 78; Photogr of Yr, Friends of Photog, 81. *Publ:* Auth, Redheads, Rizzoli, 91; Bay/Sky, Bluefinch, 93; Bystander/History of Street Photography, Bullfinch, 95; At the Waters Edge, Bullfinch, 96; Joel Meyerowitz, Phaidon, 2000. *Dealer:* James Danziger Gallery 851 Madison Ave New York NY. *Mailing Add:* 817 W End Ave New York NY 10025

MEYERS, DALE (MRS MARIO COOPER)
PAINTER, INSTRUCTOR
b Chicago, Ill, 22. *Study:* Corcoran Gallery Sch Art; Art Students League; watercolor with Mario Cooper; graphics with Seong Moy. *Work:* Space Mus, Smithsonian Inst; Palace of the Legion of Honor, San Francisco; Nat Air & Space Mus, Wash; Nat Acad Design, NY; Art Students League, NY; Portland Mus, Maine. *Comn:* Apollo 11 Moon Flight (painting), 69 & Project Viking (landing on Mars), 75, NASA, Nat Gallery Art, Washington; ecology paintings, Environ Protection Agency, Wash, 72; paintings, US Coast Guard, 84, 85 & 87. *Exhib:* Smithsonian Inst, Washington, 62-63; 200 Yrs of Watercolor Painting in Am, Metrop Mus Art, NY, 66; Nat Acad Design, 68-; Eyewitness to Space, Nat Gallery Art, 70; int watercolor exhib Can, US, Gt Brit, 1991-94, Chung Cheng Gallery, Taipei, 1994. *Pos:* Ed newslett, Am Watercolor Soc, 62-79, chmn awards, 67-79, chmn traveling exhibs & scholarships, 78-92; academician, Nat Acad Design, 79. *Teaching:* Instr watercolor, Kefauver Sch Art, Washington, DC, 61-62 & Art Students League, 79-; workshops in NMex, Calif, Maine, NY, Tex, Pa, Fla, Colo, Wyo, Ore, Ohio, Vt, Wis & Tenn, 70-77, 79, 81 & 88; lectr, Nat Acad & Parson's Sch Design, NY. *Awards:* Silver Medal, Allied Artists, 93;

Medal of Hon, Salmagundi Club, 94; Medal, Dolphin Fel, 2000. *Mem:* Allied Artists Am (pres, 75-78); Am Watercolor Soc (pres 1992-, hon mem Miami chpt); dolphin fel Am Watercolor Soc (pres, 92-); hon mem Soc Mex de Acuarelistas; fel Royal Soc Arts, Gt Brit; Nat Acad. *Media:* Watercolor. *Publ:* Contribr, Eyewitness to Space, Abrams, 71; Nat Sculpture Rev, 77; Watercolor Bold & Free & Let the Medium Do It, Watson Guptill, 80; auth, The Sketchbook, Van Nostrand Reinhold, 83; contribr, Exploring Color, North Light Publ, 85. *Mailing Add:* Art Students League 215 W 57th St New York NY 10019

MEYERS, MICHAEL K
PERFORMANCE ARTIST, PAINTER
b Chicago, Ill, Sept 28, 39. *Study:* Drake Univ, Des Moines, Iowa, BS, 61; Col Med, Univ Ill, cert, 65; Univ Iowa, MA(painting), 67. *Exhib:* Wattle and Daub Storefront and Street Theater, Int Performance Archives, Mus Mod Art, NY, 75; Short Plays for a Man on the Moon, Mus Mod Art, NY, 78; Cranbrook Acad Art, Bloomfield Hills, Mich, 81; An Illustrated History of the World, Joslyn Mus, Omaha, 82; Performance Space, Art Inst Chicago Sch, 83; Hefner Hall, Art Inst Chicago Sch, 84; Performance, Ind State Univ, 93; Drawing Exhib, Chicago Cult Ctr, 93; God's Brain, Chicago Cult Ctr, 93; Looking for Paradise, Pauline Oliveros Studio, Kingston, NY, 93; God's Brain, Dixon Place, NY, 93; and others. *Teaching:* Instr painting, Univ Iowa, Iowa City, 70-72; assoc prof art, Kansas City Art Inst, Mo, 72-83; prof performance/time arts & chair first year prog, Sch Art Inst Chicago, 83-. *Awards:* Nat Endowment Arts Individual Artist Fel, 80, 87 & 90; Sch Art Inst Chicago Fac Grant, 85-87, 90 & 91; Ill Arts Coun Individual Artist Grant, 86-88 & 91. *Publ:* Auth, Wasps and whales, Chouteau Review, Kansas City, 80; Scenes from an illustrated history of the world, 81, Teaching in the midwest, 81, High Performance Mag; Vacillation, Kans Quart, Manhattan, 85; Reconstructing the Temple from Memory, Whitewalls, Chicago, autumn, 86; Short pieces and performance fragments, J Dramatic Theory & Criticism, fall 90. *Mailing Add:* c/o Sch Art Inst First Yr Prog 37 S Wabash Chicago IL 60603

MEYERS, RONALD G
EDUCATOR, CERAMIST
b Buffalo, NY, Nov 4, 34. *Study:* State Univ NY, Col Buffalo, BS, 56, MS, 60; Sch Am Craftsmen, Rochester Inst Technol, with Frans Wildenhain, MFA, 65. *Work:* High Mus Art, Atlanta; Lamar Dodd Art Ctr, LaGrange, Ga; SC Arts Comn, Columbia. *Exhib:* Guild Prize Winners, Columbia Mus Art, SC, 71; Southeastern Crafts, Greenville Mus Art, SC, 74; 25 Southeastern Artists, High Mus, Atlanta, 75; Artist-Craftsmen Invitational, Southeastern Ctr Contemp Art, Winston-Salem, NC, 76; Tribute to Hands, Springfield Art Asn, Ill, 78; Drinking Companions, J M Kohler Art Ctr, Sheboygan, Wis, 79. *Teaching:* Asst prof ceramics, Univ SC, Columbia, 67-72; assoc prof, Univ Ga, Athens, 72-. *Awards:* Best of Show, Mid-South Ceramic & Crafts, 71 & SC Craftsmen, 71; Guild Purchase Award, Columbia Mus, 71. *Media:* Clay. *Mailing Add:* 180 Hidden Hills Ln Athens GA 30605-4202

MEZZATESTA, MICHAEL
HISTORIAN, MUSEUM DIRECTOR
b New York, NY, June 9, 48. *Study:* Columbia Col, BA, 70; NY Univ Inst Fine Arts, MA, 74, PhD, 80. *Collection Arranged:* Henri Matisse, Kimbell Art Mus, 84; Leonid Tishkov-Creatures (coauth, catalog), Duke Univ Mus Art, 93; Moscow Conceptualism, Duke Univ Mus Art, 95. *Pos:* Cur Europ art, Kimbell Art Mus, Ft Worth, 80-86; dir, Duke Univ Mus Art, 87-. *Teaching:* Adj prof art hist, Duke Univ, 87-. *Res:* Italian Renaissance; Baroque; 20th century. *Publ:* Auth, Dmitri Plavinsky, Ferzt, 95; Victor Hugo Irazabal, Art News, 95. *Mailing Add:* Duke Univ Museum Art PO Box 90732 Durham NC 27708

MHIRE, HERMAN P
MUSEUM DIRECTOR, CURATOR
b Lafayette, La, Nov 23, 47. *Collection Arranged:* Louisiana Bicentennial Exposition, Maison de Radio, France, Paris, 76; Henry Botkin: Paintings, Drawings & Collages 1928-1981 (coauth, catalog), 82 & Senegal: Narrative Paintings (coauth, catalog), 85, Univ Art Mus, Lafayette, La; A Century of Vision: Louisiana Photography 1884-1984 (auth, catalog), La State Mus, 84; Village Architecture in Jordan (contribr, catalog), Mus Anthrop, Univ Kans, 86; Baking in the Sun: Visionary Images from the South (contribr, catalog). *Pos:* Guest cur, Lafayette Natural Hist Mus, La, 75-84; dir, Gallery Sch Art & Archit, Univ Southwestern La, 77-83 & Univ Art Mus, 83-; founder and pres, Festival Int de Louisiane, 87-89. *Teaching:* Instr drawing & printmaking, Sch Art & Archit, Univ Southwestern La, 77-. *Awards:* Gold Medal Award, La Bicentennial Exposition, US Dept Com, 76. *Mem:* Am Asn Mus; Southeastern Mus Conf; La Asn Mus. *Publ:* Contribr, Contemporary Works on Paper, 84, Univ Art Mus, Lafayette, La, 84. *Mailing Add:* 1500 Myrtle Pl Lafayette LA 70506-2538

MICCOLI, ARNALDO
PAINTER, COLLAGE ARTIST
Study: Istituto d'Arte G Pellegrino Lecce, Italy, 60; Acad Fine Arts, Rome, Italy, 63; Univ Social Studies, Rome, 64; Acad Tiherina, Rome. *Work:* Mus Mod Art- Republica di San Marino, Italy; Pinacoteca Provinciale, Lecce, Italy; Webb & Athey Corp, NY; Bill Evans & Son Inc, Santa Monica, Calif; Kay Home Ctr, Lodi, NJ. *Exhib:* Nona Quadriennale Nazionale, Palazzo dell'Esposizioni, Rome, Italy, 65; Arnaldo Miccoli Paintings, Bergen Community Mus, Paramus, NJ, 68; NJ State Mus, Trenton Mus, 71; Int Art Show, Republica di San Marina State Mus, Italy, 74; Vereniging Volksuniversiteit Mus, Rotterdam, 86; Faces, Germanow Gallery, Rochester, NY, 87. *Awards:* Gold Medal, Citta di Mentana, Mentana City, 65. *Bibliog:* Toti Carpentiery (auth), Una storia Americana, Terzocchio, 83; Carlo Munari (auth), Metropolitan Apocalypse, Nuovo Sagittario, Milan, 85; A Sala & R Barletta (coauths), Arnaldo Miccoli, Capone Editore, 89. *Media:* Oil. *Mailing Add:* 107 Sunset Ln Tenafly NJ 07670-1612

MICHAEL, GARY
PAINTER, WRITER
b Denver, Colo, Apr 17, 37. *Study:* Denver Univ, BA; Colo Univ, MA; Syracuse Univ, with Sydney Thomas, PhD. *Work:* Denver Pub Libr Permanent Collection, Colo; Denver Art Mus; Mus Natural Hist, Denver; Colorado Springs Fine Arts Ctr, Colo; Miron Collection, Poughkeepsie, NY. *Comn:* Mural, Perlmack Corp, Regent Plaza, Denver, 75; bus panel design, Bill & Dorothy Harmsen Collection, Denver, 78 & Saks Gallery, Denver, 86. *Exhib:* One-man shows, First of Denver, Farraginous V, 76, United Bank, Denver, 75 & 76, The Fleeting Moment, Saks Gallery, Denver, 86, The Diamond and Other Wonders, Gary Michael Studio, 88 & Western Co Art Ctr, Grand Junction, Colo, 89; Northern Colo Invitational Art Exhib, 79; Pastel Soc Am, NY, 79; Faces and Places, Denver Nat Bank, 82; Of Lilies and Ladies, Kontny Studio, Englewood, Colo, 83; Visual Arts Ctr, Boulder, Colo, 90; Currents & Collossi, Huntsman Gallery, Aspen, Colo, 90. *Pos:* Demonstrating artist, Spree Arts Festival, 75-; lectr & demonstr, Grumbacher, New York, 77-; contribr ed, Southwest Art, 88; fac mem, Art Students League, 91-. *Teaching:* Prof humanities, Metrop State Col, Denver, 70-73; instr painting, Colo Univ, Denver, 75-76. *Awards:* Popular Vote Award, Pastel Soc Am Ann Exhib, 79; Merit Award, Colo State Fair, Pueblo, 79; cash award, Nat Pastel Exhib, Kans Pastel Soc; and others. *Bibliog:* Joan Gould (auth), Academician turned artist, Southwest Art, 5/75; Irene Clurman (auth), Farraginous artist, 11/76 & Marjorie Barrett (auth), Traditional artist with a rebellious streak, 11/79, Rocky Mountain News. *Mem:* Pastel Soc Am; Plein Ari Artists Colo. *Media:* Pastel, Oil. *Specialty:* American Art. *Publ:* Auth, Dorothy Mandel: Her woodcut magic, Am Artist, 1/79; The Art Institute of Chicago at 100, Denver Post, 8/26/79; Markings, Southwest Art, 3/81; Imagination in realist painting, Am Artist, 1/83; cover, Learning From the Pros, Watson-Guptill, Pastel Techniques, 2002. *Dealer:* Adamson-DuVannes Gallery 484 S Vicente Blvd Los Angeles CA 90048. *Mailing Add:* 3009 E Tenth Ave Denver CO 80206

MICHAELS, BARBARA L
HISTORIAN, WRITER
b New York, NY, Oct 4, 35. *Study:* Cornell Univ, BA, 57; NY Univ Inst Fine Arts, MA, 62; City Univ New York, PhD, 85. *Pos:* Gallery asst, Samuel M Kootz Gallery, NY, 58-63; asst cur, Mus Mod Art, NY, 73-76; guest cur, Gertrude Käsebier Traveling Exhib, 92-95. *Teaching:* Adj lectr art hist, NY Univ, 76-86. *Bibliog:* Gretchen Garner (auth), Gertrude Kasebeir & Helen Levitt, Art Journal, Winter, 92. *Mem:* Col Art Asn; Soc Archit Historians; Am Studies Asn; Authors Guild. *Res:* History of photography; modern art dealers. *Publ:* Auth, An introduction to the dating and organization of Eugene Atget's photographs, Art Bull, 9/79; Gertrude Käsebier: The Photographer and Her Photographs, Harry N Abrams Inc, 92; New light on F Holland Day's pictures of African Americans, Hist Photog, winter 94; Arthur Wesley Dow: His Art and His Influence, Spanierman Gallery, 99; catalog auth, On Cahrles Sheeler, The Camera Work that Wasn't, and Others that Might have Been, Camera Work: A Centennial Celebration, catalogue for Camera Work exhibition, James A Michener Art Mus, Published by, Phot Review, vol 26, 1 & 2, Doylestown, PA, 2003. *Mailing Add:* 336 Central Park W New York NY 10025-7111

MICHAELS, GLEN
ASSEMBLAGE ARTIST, PAINTER
b Spokane, Wash, July 21, 27. *Study:* Yale Sch Music, 50-52; Eastern Wash Col Educ, BA, 57; Cranbrook Acad Art, with Zoltan Sepeshy, MFA, 58. *Work:* Am Inst Archit, Detroit Chap; Kresge Found; Kirco Corp, Troy, Mich; Jacobson's, Birmingham, Mich; Univ Mich Alumni Ctr, Ann Arbor; Wall & Pool Floor, Wm Beaumont Hosp, Royal Oak, MI, 96; 20 ft Assemblage, tile, metal and wood, Shifman Library, Wayne State Univ, Detroit, Mich, 2002, Wayne State med Ctr, 2003, Tile, Metal & wood, Ford Hospital (lobby), Detroit, Mich, fused glass pool floor looby, Henry Ford Memorial Libr, Dearborn, Mich, 2004. *Comn:* fused glass pool, Mich State Mus, Archives & Libr, Mich, 90; Baldwin Pub Libr, Birmingham, Mich, 92-; Oil portrait, The Hon Avern L Cohn, Detroit Fed Court, Mrs Elmore Leanord, Glenn Davis, MD, Dean of Medicine, Mich State Univ, East Lansing, Mich, 2006; royal oak wall, Beaumont Hospital Imaging Center, 2000; portrait bust Ernest Goodman bronze, 2000; The Honorable John Feikens, US District Court, Detroit, Mich. *Teaching:* Supvr art for children, Cranbrook Acad Art, 59-65; asst prof sculpture, Wayne State Univ, 67-69 & Univ Windsor, 70-71. *Awards:* Kresge Grant, Detroit People Mover Station, 87; Artist of the Year Award, Mich Art Train, 90; Hon Affil Mem Fine Arts, Am Inst Archit, Mich Chap. *Bibliog:* Nordness (auth), Objects: USA, Viking Press, 70; The Confectioner's Art, Am Craft Coun, 89; Joann Lucktov (auth), The Art of Mosaic Design, Rockport Publ. *Media:* Bronze, Fused Glass, Oil. *Publ:* John Canaday (auth), NY Times, 62; Dorothy Rodgers (auth), A Chateau the sound of music built, Look Mag, 67; Art in Archit, Am Inst Archits, 80; Archit Rec, 80-81; Am Craft Mag, 6-7/92. *Dealer:* Robert Kidd Gallery, Birmingham, Mich. *Mailing Add:* 4800 Beach Rd Troy MI 48098

MICHAELS-PAQUE, J
PAINTER, SCULPTOR
b Menominee, Mich. *Study:* Layton Sch Art, Milwaukee, Wis, scholar, 55-57; Marquette Univ, 56-57; Milwaukee Inst Art & Design, 92. *Work:* Nat Mus Am Art & Nat Collection Fine Arts, Washington; Objects USA, Johnson Wax Co, Racine, Wis; Wis Elec Co, Einhorn Assocs Inc, Beck Carton Co & Unitarian Church, Milwaukee; Univ Mus, Ill State Univ, Normal; Arrowmont Sch Art, Gatlinburg; SCJ Insurance Serv, Pleasanton, Calif; St Norbert Col, De Pere, Wis; Golda Meier Collection, Univ Wis, 2006. *Comn:* Janis Salon, Pfister Hotel, Milwaukee, Wis, 92; Terry Hueneke, Milwaukee, Wis, 93; Beck, Chaet, Loomis, SC, Milwaukee, 96; H Arnold Arch Firm, Denver, 98; Mary Nohl Kohler Mus, 2006. *Exhib:* One-man shows, Australian Nat Univ Sch Art, Dayton Art Inst, 81, Ariel Gallery, Chicago, 83, Univ Notre Dame, 89, Cardinal Stritch Univ, 95 & Wis Lutheran Col, Milwaukee, 2000; The Third

Dimension Milwaukee Art Mus, 89; Antipodean Afterimages, Blatz Gallery, Milwaukee, 90; Inclinations, Godschalx Gallery, St Norbert Col, De Pere, Wis, 91; 50th Anniversary Fac Invitational, Arrowmont Sch Art, Gatlinburg, 95; Full of Herself, Cedarburg, Wis Cult Ctr; Int Expos Sculptural Objects & Functional Art, Chicago, Ill, 2000; Themselves, Schlueter Art Gallery, Wis Luth Col, Milwaukee, 2001-02; Sculptural Kinetic Books, JMP Gallery, 2005-06. *Pos:* Adv bd, Milwaukee Art Mus, currently & Artists Working Edn, Inc, 99-2006; cur, Internos Gallery Milwaukee, 95, Miad Milw Inst Art & Design, 93-98, 2001, 2003. *Teaching:* Vis artist, Miami Univ, Ohio, 81, Dayton Art Inst, 81, Kawashima Textile Sch, Kyoto, Japan, 83 & Bellas Artes, San Miguel de Allende, Mex, 85, Univ Queensland, St Lucia, Australia, 88, Univ Notre Dame, 89; instr art dept, Cardinal Stritch Col, 90-, workshops/seminars for Handweavers Guild Am, American Univ, Washington, 92; vis artist, Viterbo Col, La Crosse, Wis, 92, Australian Nat Univ, Canberra, Brisbane, Univ Tenn Arrowmont Sch Arts & Crafts, 90, 98, 2001, 03, 04, 05, 06; consult corp art, currently; Milwaukee Inst Art & Design, 93-96, 2003, 04, 05; The Clearing, Ellison Bay, Wis, 96, 2003, 04, 05, 06. *Awards:* Fac Develop Award, Cardinal Stritch Col, Milwaukee, 93 & 94; Nat Endowment Humanities & Wis Humanities Coun Grants, 95; Roundt's 45 Corp Grant, 2000; Gary Goberville Mem Fel, Ragdale Found, 2006; and others. *Bibliog:* Feature article, Herald, CNI Newspapers, 94; Louis Blinkhorn (auth), Art Imitates Life, Milwaukee J, 2/12/95; James Auer (auth), Relating through the Rhombus, Milwaukee Jour Sentinel, 5/3/2000; Milwaukee Mag, lifestyle sect, 2006. *Mem:* Am Crafts Coun; Int Guild Journalists, Auths & Photogrs; Wis Painters & Sculptors; Handweavers Guild Am; Int Sculpture Ctr. *Media:* Flexible Linear Material, Mixed Media. *Res:* Exploring the reclamation and transformation of unpretentious materials into lightweight, large scale reliefs and sculptures; published research paper ARS Textrina, Univ Manitoba, Winnepeg, Can, 88. *Publ:* Auth, reviews for Textile Fibre Forum, Australian Periodical, 92; Shuttle, Spindle & Dyepot (series of 4 articles), Art Approach to Bus, 93; Improvisation (article), Fiberarts, 94; Colored Threads, Fiberarts, 94; Lifecasting monograph, pvt publ, 96. *Dealer:* Snyderman Gallery 303 Cherry St Philadelphia PA 19106. *Mailing Add:* 4455 N Frederick Ave Milwaukee WI 53211

MICHAJLOW, EUSTACHY
PAINTER
b Jeziory, Poland, Apr 23, 30; US citizen. *Study:* Pvt studies with F Teogel, Ger, 48; S Selvanovski, Worcester, Mass, 54 J Glotzer, Vienna, 85; Cert Instr Art, 87 & 90; Sem with Helen Van Vyk, Rockport, Mass, 91. *Hon Degrees:* Col Han Munden, Germany, 50. *Work:* several pvt collections in US, Ger, France and Russia. *Comn:* 2 murals, Osnabruck, Ger, 48; 2 murals, Delmenhorst, Ger, 49; Mural (8' x 16)', Russ Orthodox Church, Worcester, Mass, 75. *Exhib:* Art League Exhib, Springfield, Mass, 86; Danielson Art Festival, Danielson, Conn, 86; one-man show, Fitchburg, Mass, 88, Glotzers Art Gallery, Cape Cod, Mass, 89 & NSB Fla, 91; Mitsukaido City, Japan, 93; Shared Visions Gallery, Delray Beach, Fla, 94; solo exhib, Fitchburg, Cape Cod, Mass & New Smyrna Beach, Fla. *Awards:* First Prize, Int Festival Art, 85; Purchase Prize, Int Art Show, Coca Cola, 85; Second Prize, Art Asn Exhib, 87. *Bibliog:* Encyl Living Artist Am, 92, 93 & 94; Int Artist Mag, 95; Southwest Art Mag, 95. *Mem:* Leominster Art Asn; Springfield Art League; Worcester Art Asn; Artists Workshop Inc. *Media:* Oil, Acrylic. *Mailing Add:* 2319 Travelers Palm Dr Edgewater FL 32141

MICHALS, DUANE
PHOTOGRAPHER
b McKeesport, Pa, Feb 18, 32. *Study:* Univ Denver, BA, 53. *Work:* Mus Mod Art, Metrop Mus Art; Nat Libr, Paris; Boston Mus Fine Arts; San Francisco Mus Mod Art; William Rockhill Nelson Gallery, Kansas City, Kans; and many others. *Exhib:* Frankfurt Kunstverein, 74; One-man shows, Galerie Watari, Tokyo, Japan, 83, Wellesley Col Art Gallery, Mass, 84, Sidney Janis Gallery, NY, 85, Studio 8 Gallery, Kalispell, Mo, 86, Art Ctr Col Design, Pasadena, Calif, 87, Ugo Ferranti, Rome, Italy, 88, Gallery for Fine Photog, New Orleans, 90; VA Mus Fine Arts, Richmond, 87 & 89; Musee d'Art Moderne, Paris, 88; Whitney Mus Am Art, 88; High Mus Art, Atlanta, Ga, 88 & 89; Fogg Mus, Cambridge, Mass, 89; Walker Art Ctr, Minneapolis, Minn, 89; Milwaukee Art Mus, Wis, 90. *Awards:* Nat Endowment Arts Grant, 76; Pa Coun Arts, 78; Carnegie Found Photog Fel, Cooper Union, 79. *Bibliog:* Carter Ratcliffe (auth), Duane Michals, Print Collector's Newslett, 9/75; Ronald H Bailey (auth), The Photographic Illusion, Alskog, 75; Stefan Mihal (auth), Take One and See Mt Fujiyama, 76; John H Lawrence (auth), Duane Michal's Recent Work, New Orleans Art Review, 1-2/90. *Publ:* The journey of the spirit after death, Winterhouse, 71; Things are queer, Wilde, Koln, 73; auth, Portraits, Twelvetrees Press, 88. *Dealer:* Sidney Janis Gallery 110 W 57th St New York NY. *Mailing Add:* 109 E 19th St New York NY 10003

MICHAUX, HENRY GASTON
EDUCATOR, SCULPTOR
b Morganton, NC, Jan 19, 34. *Study:* Tex Southern Univ, with John T Biggers, BFA, 59; Rochester Inst Technol, advanced design, 63; Pa State Univ, EdM, 60, EdD, 71. *Work:* NC State Mus, Raleigh; JB Speed Mus, Louisville, Ky; HC Taylor Gallery (A&T State Univ), Greensboro, NC; Univ Mus, Tex Southern Univ, Houston; BellSouth, Louisville, Ky; Tex Southern Univ, Houston, Tex; A&T State Univ, Greensboro, NC. *Comn:* Ceramic Mural on Medicine, comn by Dr & Mrs Carrol, Houston; coffee set (hand thrown), comn by John T Biggers, Houston; welded steel gift for Graduating High School, Houston Pub Sch, Tex, 69; stainless steel award, comn by James Oxygen & Welding, Hickory, NC, 75; ceramic sculptural representation of Justice, comn by atty Eddye L Lane, Columbia, SC, 94. *Exhib:* Houston Mus Art, Tex, 56; Competitive Invitational, Henri Studio Galleries, NY, 64; Afro-Am Artists, Denver Art Mus, Colo, 69; Afro-Am Artists: North Carolina USA, N Mus Art, Raleigh, 80; Dimensions and Directions: Black Artists of the South, Jackson State Col Mus, Miss, 80. *Pos:* Pres, Caldwell Arts Coun, Lenoir, NC, 75-76; organizer/planner, Ann Indoor/Outdoor Sculpture Competition, Lenoir, NC, 86; African Am monument com, State SC, 96-2000, adv com, selections recommendation com & designed prospectus adv com. *Teaching:* Prof sculpture, Tex Southern Univ, Houston, 68-70; prof ceramics, Appalachian State Univ, Boone, NC, 72-76; prof sculpture & ceramics, SC State Univ, Orangeburg, 78-96,retired, 96. *Awards:* Purchace Award, 9th Ann Black Artists' Exhib, Louisville Chap Links Inc, 88. *Bibliog:* Carolina Camera, feature story (film), WBTV Television, Charlotte, NC, 8/4/80; Biggers & Simms (coauths), Black Art in Houston, Univ Tex. *Mem:* Nat Asn Sch Art & Design; Am Crafts Coun; Nat Coun Educ Ceramic Arts; Sculpture Int; Nat Art Educ Asn. *Media:* Clay, Stainless Steel. *Publ:* Illusr, Folk Tales and Ghost Stories, Jourdan Atkinson, 57; auth, An Accommodational Esthetic: Precursor For One Legitimate Black Esthetic in African Rock Art Traditions, J Black Studies, 12/77; Black Art: Recognition, Nourishment, Celebration, Greensboro Asn Preservation Black Art, 78. *Mailing Add:* 310 Mulungu Pl NW Lenoir NC 28645-4234

MICHAUX, RONALD ROBERT
ART DEALER
b Springfield, Mass, Aug 8, 1944. *Pos:* Dir, Rolly-Michaux Galleries, Boston. *Specialty:* 20th century Europ masters & contemporaries, including paintings, sculpture & graphics; French Impressionists and Post-Impressionists. *Mailing Add:* c/o Rolly-Michaux Galleries LTD 290 Dartmouth St Boston MA 02116

MICHELS, ANN HARRISON
PAINTER, CONCEPTUAL ARTIST
b Newark, NJ. *Study:* Colby-Sawyer Col, AA, 51; Skidmore Col, BS (fine arts), 53. *Work:* IT&T Inc, NY; PNC Bank, Edison, NJ; Rollins Col, Fla; Skidmore Col, Saratoga Springs, NY; Prudential Securties Inc, Short Hills, NJ. *Comn:* mural, Landscape in Oil, comn by A Gary Shilling Inc, NY, 90-92. *Exhib:* N E Watercolor Soc-18th Ann Exhib, Trotter's Mus, Goshe, NY, 94; Ridgewood Art Inst First Grand Nat, Bergen Mus Art & Science, Paramus, NJ, 95-96; Catherine Corillard Woiff Open Show, National Arts Club, NY, 95-96; Audubon Artists Inc, Federal Hall, Wall St, NY, 96, Salmagundi Club, NY, 2000; AAPL (NJ) 60th Anniversary Show, Papermill Playhouse Gallery, Milburn, NJ 96; Nat Asn Women Artists Inc - The Heart of the Artists, Art Ctr Sarasota, Sarasota, Fla, 2000. *Pos:* pres, The Essex Watercolor Club, 94-96. *Teaching:* art instr, Cartaret Sch, W Orange, NJ, 53-54. *Awards:* Award of Merit, Essex Watercolor Club, 96. *Mem:* Fel Am Artists Prof League Inc; Audubon Artists Inc; Nat Asn of Women Artists Inc (newsletter editor, 98-99, bd mem, 96-2001); North Shore Art Asn, Gloucester, Mass; Garden State Watercolor Soc Inc. *Media:* Acrylic, Watermedia. *Publ:* Illus, Snowy Egret Greeting Cards, Audubon Inc, 75; auth, Member of the Issue, North Lights Mag, 93. *Dealer:* Chetkin Gallery 308 Morris Ave Spring Lake NJ 07762. *Mailing Add:* 6 Benson Ct Short Hills NJ 07078

MICHELS, EILEEN MANNING
EDUCATOR, ART HISTORIAN
b Fargo, NDak. *Study:* Univ Minn, BA, magna cum laude, 47, MA, 53, MA, 59, PhD, 71; Inst Fine Arts, NY Univ, 50-51; Sarbonne, Paris, 56-57; Am Sch Classical Studies, Athens, Greece, 80. *Collection Arranged:* Edwin Hugh Lundie, FAIA (auth, catalog), 72. *Pos:* art librarian, 1948-53, gallery curator & dir asst, 1954-56, Univ Minn; free-lance cur, Minneapolis Inst Arts, 73-74; Free-lance cur, Minn Mus Art, 72-73, assoc dir, 73-74. *Teaching:* Vis asst prof art hist, Stanford Univ, 72-73; assoc prof & chair dept, Univ St Thomas, 78-88, prof, 89-92, adj prof, 92 & prof emer, 92-. *Awards:* Fulbright, Paris, 56-57; Vincent Sully Jr Res Grant, Archit Hist Found, 94. *Mem:* Soc Archit Historians (dir, 76-79, secy 82-86); Col Art Asn. *Res:* Nineteenth and twentieth century architecture; American art. *Publ:* Auth, An Architectural View: Minneapolis Society of Fine Arts 1883-1974, Minneapolis Inst Arts, 74; A Landmark Reclaimed, Minn Landmarks, 77; Reconfiguring Harvey Ellis, Beavers Bond Press, 2004. *Mailing Add:* 2183 Hendon Ave Saint Paul MN 55108

MICHELSON, ERIC MICHAEL
PAINTER
b Manhasset, NY, 54. *Study:* State Univ, NY; Stony Brook, BA, 76; Art Student League, studied with Robert Phillipp, Ted Jacobs, Stanley Michelson. *Work:* Plaza Hotel, NY; Art Students League, NY; Hypernon Hotel, NY. *Exhib:* Art Students League, Main Street Gallery, Eva Monte Gallery, New York City, 1997; Weill Art Gallery, New York City, 2000; and others. *Awards:* Len Everett Mem Award, oils, Salmagundi Club, NY, 1999. *Mem:* Audubon Artists, NY, (vpres, currently). *Specialty:* Large figurative works, portraits and NY Living, 2001. *Mailing Add:* 32 Union Square East Rm 1216 New York NY 10003

MICHIE, MARY
SCULPTOR
b Ripon, Wis, Aug 8, 22. *Study:* Ripon Col, BA(cum laude), 43; Cent Sch Art, London, Eng, sculpture study, 50-52; Univ Wis, Madison, MA(art), 62. *Work:* Milwaukee Art Mus, Wis; Rahr-West Mus, Manitowoc, Wis; Madison Art Ctr, Wis; Ripon Col, Wis. *Comn:* Bronze, Marshall Erdman & Assoc, Marshfield, Wis, 75; bronze figure, Tomah Pub Libr, Wis, 81; bronze chalice & tray, St Paul's Cath Ctr, Madison, Wis, 83; bronze, Wis Sch Visually Handicapped, 83; limestone, Citi Arts & Dane Co Cult Comt, Madison, Wis, 92. *Exhib:* Midwest Juried Exhib, Walker Art Ctr, Minneapolis, Minn, 58 & 62; Nat Drawing & Sculpture, Ball State Univ Mus, Ind, 63; Sculptors at Wingspread, Wingspread Found, Racine, Wis, 63; solo exhibs, 68, 70 & TWA's Am Artists, 69, New Stanley Art Gallery, Nairobi, Kenya & Rahr-West Mus, Manitowoc, Wis, 88; XVIII Prix Internationale d'Art, Hall du Centenaire, Monte Carlo, 84; Nat April Salon, Springville Mus, Utah, 84 & 88. *Pos:* Grad asst sculpture, Univ Wis Madison, 60-61; proj asst, Univ Wis Exten Art Dept, 63-67; cur, Wis New Deal Art Exhib, 79-80. *Teaching:* Instr, Rhinelander Sch Art, Univ Wis, 79-80. *Awards:* Nat Endowment Arts Grant for bronze, 83. *Bibliog:* James Auer (auth),

Critical Review, Milwaukee J, 5/9/76; Virginia Watson-Jones (auth), Contemp American Women Sculptors, Oryx Press, 86. *Mem:* Wis Painters & Sculptors; Nat Asn Women Artists. *Media:* Bronze, Aluminum. *Publ:* Auth, Arts and Crafts in Kenyan Society, Univ Wis Exten, 72; Encounter with an African potter, Ceramics Monthly, 12/77; Lamu doors, Design Mag, winter 77; Search for a Kenyan craftsman, Christian Science Monitor, 11/28/78; An Artist's Eye View of Rural Wisconsin, Wis Acad Rev, 12/78. *Dealer:* Innovations Gallery Ft Collins CO

MICHOD, SUSAN A
PAINTER
b Toledo, Ohio, Jan 3, 45. *Study:* Smith Col; Univ Mich, BS; Pratt Inst, MFA. *Work:* Mus Contemp Art, Chicago, Ill; Ill State Mus, Springfield; Owens-Corning Fiberglass, Toledo, Ohio; Chase Manhattan Bank & Xerox Corp, NY. *Comn:* Shared Space (painted installation), Bronx Mus, NY, 83; painting with construction, Indust Trust & Savings Bank, Muncie, Ind, 84; mural, Regeneration, Rush-Pres St Luke's Hosp, Chicago, Ill, 91. *Exhib:* Painting and Sculpture Today, Indianapolis Mus Art, 76; Pattern Painting, PS1, Flushing, NY, 77; Jan Cicero Gallery, Chicago, 77-; Andre Zarre Gallery, NY, 78-79; Mus Contemp Art, Chicago, 79; Usable Art, State Univ NY, Plattsburg, 81; Susan Caldwell Gallery, NY, 81-83; The Chair Show, Thorpe Intermedia Gallery, Syracuse, NY, 82; Chicago Now, Brentwood Gallery, St Louis, Mo, 82; Wilson Galleries, Anderson Univ, Anderson, Ind, 92; Artemisia Gallery, Installation Show, Chicago, 93; Fragile Landscapes, Chicago Cult Ctr, 97; Stable Studios, Chicago, 2002; Florence Biennale, Ital, 2003; Andre Zorre Gallery, NY, 2003; Whitney Mus. Am. Art, NYC, 2006. *Teaching:* Instr painting, Chicago Acad Fine Arts, 69-74, Columbia Col Pougealis Apprentice Prog. *Awards:* Purchase Prize, Ill State Mus, 74; Purchase Prize, Carleton Col Exhib, 75. *Bibliog:* John Russell (auth), Art, New York Times, 7/10/81; Ronny Cohen (auth), rev, Art News, Vol 81, No 9, 11/82; Judith Kirschner (auth), rev, Artforum, 3/83. *Media:* Acrylic, Watercolor. *Mailing Add:* 1523 N Kingsbury St Chicago IL 60622-2533

MICKENBERG, DAVID
MUSEUM DIRECTOR, HISTORIAN
b Brooklyn, NY, Apr 24, 54. *Study:* Colgate Univ, BA, 76; Univ Wis, Milwaukee, MA(art hist), 79. *Collection Arranged:* Romantic Prints, Ind Mus Art, Indianapolis, 80; Ritual Power and Function (auth, catalog), 82, Winslow Homer: The Civil War Years, 83, Impressionism: Post-Impressionism (auth, catalog), 83 & Songs of Glory (auth, catalog), Okla Mus Art. *Pos:* Asst cur, Picker Art Gallery, Hamilton, NY, 74-76; coordr, Adult Educ Prog & asst dir, Indianapolis Mus Art, Ind, 79-81; exec dir, Okla Mus Art, Oklahoma City, 81-86; dir, Mary & Leigh Block Gallery Northwestern Univ, Evanston, Ill, 86-2001; dir, Davis Mus and Cult Ctr, Wellesley Col, Mass, 2001-. *Teaching:* Teaching asst, Univ Wis, 76-79. *Awards:* Dean's Scholarship, Ind Univ, 80-81. *Mem:* Col Art Asn; Am Asn Mus; Int Ctr Medieval Art. *Res:* Romanesque and Gothic architecture; contemporary prints; painting and sculpture. *Publ:* Maurice Prendergast (editor) (exhib catalogue) Large Boston Public Garden Sketchbook, 1981; editor, auth: (exhib catalogue) Songs of Glory: Medieval Art from 900 to 1500, 1985. *Mailing Add:* Wellesley Col Davis Mus and Cultural Ctr 106 Central St Wellesley MA 02481-8203

MICKISH, VERLE L
EDUCATOR, PAINTER
b Greeley, Colo, Sept 27, 28. *Study:* Colo State Col, BFA, 51; Univ Northern Colo, MAE, 55; Ariz State Univ, EdD, 70. *Hon Degrees:* Prof Emeritus, GA State Univ, 98. *Comn:* Acrylic painting, Great Moments in Music Corp, Atlanta, Ga, 83; Acrylic painting, Eastminster Presbyterian Church, 2000. *Exhib:* Georgia Ann Exhib, High Mus Art, Atlanta, 83-85; 3 one man shows; 32 national juried exhibs; 20 corporate collections; 28 private collections. *Pos:* Chmn, Int Cultural Arts, Nat Asn Partners of the Americas, 76-77; mem, Int Olympics Acad Comt, 78-80; mem Prof Standards Comt, Nat Art Educ Asn, Reston, Va, Southeastern mem 76-, vpres, 86-88. *Teaching:* Art dir K-12, Boulder Valley Pub Sch, Colo, 58-71; prof art, Ga State Univ, Atlanta, 71-; presentation of over 850 workshops throughout US, Canada, Europe & Brazil since 1961. *Awards:* Nat Art Educator of the Year, Nat Art Educ Asn, 83; Distinguished Ga Educator, Ga Univ Syst, 83 & 96; Nat NAEA Art Fellow, 93; Nat NAEA Distinguished Service Award, 2002; Verle L Mickish, W Robert Nix Award, 2002. *Mem:* Ga Art Educ Asn (pres, 79-81). *Media:* Watercolor, Acrylic. *Publ:* created over 140 illustrations used in magazines and books, 61-2005; Auth, Creative Art-Junior High Grades, Pruett Press, 62; illusr, Corn for the Palace, Prentice-Hall, 63; 16 cartoons in School Arts magazine, 2004-05; monthly cartoon in Emory Hospital Newsletter, 2004-05. *Mailing Add:* 5374 Pheasant Run Stone Mountain GA 30087-1235

MIDDAUGH, ROBERT BURTON
PAINTER
b Chicago, Ill, May 12, 35. *Study:* Univ Ill, 54-55; Art Inst Chicago, BFA, 64. *Work:* Art Inst Chicago; Boston Mus Fine Art; Los Angeles Co Mus; Phoenix Art Mus; Worcester Art Mus, Mass. *Comn:* Prehistoric Project (permanent educ display, with Martyl Langsdorf & Prof Robert Braidwood), Oriental Inst, Univ Chicago, 68. *Exhib:* Chicago & Vicinity Show, Art Inst Chicago, 64, 66 & 73-85; Ill Biennial Exhib, Krannert Art Mus, Urbana, 65; Ill Exhib, Ill State Mus, Springfield, 66, 68, 69 & 71; Am Painting Exhib, Va Mus Fine Arts, Richmond, 66; 162nd Ann Exhib, Pa Acad Fine Arts, Philadelphia, 67; solo shows, Kovler Gallery, Chicago, 65, 67, 69, Martin Schweig Gallery, St. Louis, 70, 72, 79, 83, Univ Wis, 76, 81-82, Fairweather Hardin Gallery, Chicago, 77, 80, 83, 85, Rockford Art Mus 87, Zaks Gallery, Chicago, 92093, 97, Printworks Gallery, Chicago, 2006. *Collection Arranged:* Coopers & Lybrand; Brinson Partners; Sonnenschein; Nath & Rosenthal. *Pos:* Asst cur, Art Collection First Nat Bank Chicago, 71-78, cur, 79-83; archivist, Chicago Park Dist, 98-2005. *Awards:* Purchase Prize, Am Acad Arts & Lett, 75. *Mem:* Arts Club Chicago. *Media:* All. *Publ:* Contribr, Buying Art on a Budget, Hawthorn, 68; contribr, Living World History, Scott Foresman. *Dealer:* Printworks 311 W Superior Chicago Ill 60610. *Mailing Add:* 1121 S Central Ave Burlington IA 52601

MIDDLEBROOK, DAVID A
SCULPTOR, EDUCATOR
b Jackson, Mich, May 1, 44. *Study:* Albion Col, BA, 66; Univ Iowa, with Jerry Rothman, Paul Soldner & Stuart Eddie, MA, 69, with Don Reitz, Byron Burford & Hans Braeder, MFA, 70. *Work:* Univ Wash Mus Art, Seattle; Koehler Mus, Sheboygan, Wis; San Jose Mus Art, Fresno Mus, Oakland Mus Art & San Francisco Mus Art, Calif; and others. *Comn:* Earth Sample (stone & marble), Thrust IV, Inc, Mt View, Calif, 85; Black Water, Bell Savings, San Jose, Calif, 85; Time Shadow, Sacramento Light Rail, 86-87. *Exhib:* Nine Calif Artists, Everson Mus Art, Syracuse, NY, 78; A Century of Ceramics in US, Smithsonian Mus, traveling, DC, 78-80; NCCR: Sculpture Now, San Francisco Mus Mod Art, 79; Joshua Wedgwood Invitational, Philadelphia Mus Art, 80; Illusionism in Am, Los Angeles Co Mus Art, Los Angeles, 80; Reconstructions, San Jose Mus Art, 81; Klein Gallery, Chicago, 81 & 82; one-person show, Fresno Mus, 83; RAU Sculpture Court, Johannesburg, 83; Asn Gallery, Capetown, 83; Ree Schonlau Galllery, Omaha, 85; Arvada Ctr Arts & Humanities, Colo, 85. *Teaching:* Asst prof art, Univ Ky, Lexington, 70-74; prof art, San Jose State Univ, 74-; vis prof art, Notre Dame Univ, 72 & 76, Mills Col, Oakland, Calif, 77; artist-in-residence, Darwin Community Col, Australia, 80, Shefield Polytechnic, Eng, 81; vis artist, SAfrica, 82. *Awards:* Westinghouse res award, Koehler Mus, Purdue Univ, 73; Nat Endowment for Arts artist grant, 77; Lucy Stern fel, Mills Col, 78; Environmental Improvement Award of Distinction, Assoc Landscape Contractors Am, 85. *Bibliog:* Elsbeth Wood (auth), Handbuilding, McGraw Hill, 78; Harvey Brody (auth), Low Fire Ceramics, 80; Susan Peterson (auth), Modern ceramic concerns, 81. *Mem:* Nat Conf Educ Ceramic Art; Col Art Asn; Am Crafts Coun. *Dealer:* Klein Gallery 356 Huron Chicago IL 60610. *Mailing Add:* 18404 Montevina Rd Los Gatos CA 95030-9105

MIDDLEBROOK, WILLIE ROBERT
PHOTOGRAPHER, ADMINISTRATOR
b Detroit, Mich, Aug 11, 57. *Study:* Communicative Arts Academy, cert, 75; Compton Community Col, AA, 78. *Work:* Los Angeles Co Mus Art, Calif; Art Inst Chicago; Light Works, Syracuse, NY; Compton Community Col, Calif; Golden State Mutual Life Insurance Co, Los Angeles. *Comn:* Painting, Co of Los Angeles-A C Bilbrew Libr, Los Angeles, 75; photog murals, Southern Calif Gas Co, Los Angeles, 92; design metro station, MTA-ART Prog, Los Angeles, 94. *Exhib:* One-man shows, Nexus Contemp Art Ctr, Atlanta, 93, Blue Sky Gallery, Portland, Ore, 94, Irvine Fine Arts Ctr, Calif, 94 & Art Inst Chicago, 95; Hale Wooddruff Mem, Studio Mus Harlem, NY, 94; New Photog II, Los Angeles Co Mus Art, 94; Issues and Identities, Art Inst Chicago, 94; East Coast/West Coast Photog Exhib, Memphis Col Art, Tenn, 94. *Pos:* Mem adv comt, Photo Dept, Compton Community Col, 83-; mem bd dir, Angels Gate Cult Ctr, 90-; dir, Watts Towers Arts Ctr, Los Angeles, 93-94; exhibs dir, Los Angeles Contemp Exhibs, 94-; mem nat bd, Soc Photog Educ, 94-. *Teaching:* Art instr photog, Watts Towers Arts Ctr, Los Angeles, 78-87; photog instr, Los Angeles Photog Ctr, 87-93; asst prof photog, Calif State Univ, Los Angeles, 88-91. *Awards:* Photog Fel, Nat Endowment Arts, 81-82 & 92-93. *Bibliog:* Amy Hufnagel (auth), Abstracted identities, Exhib Catalog - Light Works, 93; Deborah Willis Braithwaite (auth), Willie R Middlebrook, Nueva Luz, 93; Life in a day of black LA, Univ Calif Los Angeles Afro-Studies, 93. *Mem:* Soc Photog Educ. *Media:* Photographic, Mixed Media. *Dealer:* Schneider Gallery Inc 230 W Superior St Chicago IL 60610

MIDDLEMAN, RAOUL FINK
PAINTER
b Baltimore, Md, Apr 3, 35. *Study:* Johns Hopkins Univ, BA, 55; Pa Acad Fine Arts, 59-61; Brooklyn Mus Art Sch, 61. *Work:* Nat Acad Design; resp in permanent collections at ABC Network, Baltimore Mus Art, Corcoran Gallery, Frye Mus Art, Johns Hopkins Hosp Nat Acad of Design, Metrop Mus Art, NY Pub Libr, Syracuse Univ, Towson Univ, Univ, Md. *Exhib:* one-man show, Landscapes & Portraits of the Ardeche, Scott-McKennis Gallery, Richmond, Va, 80, Yale Norfolk Summer Sch, 80, Boston Univ, 81, Grimaldis Gallery, Baltimore, 81-84, 78, 79, 99 & 2001, Water Gap Art Gallery, Walpack Ctr, NJ, 82, William Capro Gallery, New Bedford, Mass, 83 & Swanston Fine Arts, Atlanta, 88; MB Modern, NY, 2000; Rodger LaPelle Galleries, Philadelphia, 2001, Bavarian Paintings, Murnau, Ger, 2001, Maryland Art Place, Baltimore, 2002; exhib in groups shows: Nat Acad Design, 1990, Md Inst, 1989-90, Gaumann Cicchino Gallery, 1989, Ingber Gallery, 1989, Bendann Gallery, 1989, Swanston Fine Arts, 1988, Haus der Kunst, 1986, Kornbluth Gallery, 1985, Steven Scott Gallery, and others; Kowos Gallery, NY, 2004; Roger Lapelle Galleries, Philadelphia, Pa, 2005; Grimaldis Gallery, 2005. *Pos:* pres, Nat Acad Design, 1998-01. *Teaching:* Chmn painting dept, Md Inst Col Art, Baltimore, 75-78; resident dir, summer landscape painting prog, Md Inst Col Art, 81-83; vis critic, Vt Studio Sch Summer Prog, 85; act dir, Hoffberger Sch Grad Painting, Maryland Inst, 98-99. *Awards:* Pres, Nat Acad Design, NY. *Bibliog:* Gerrit Henri (auth), rev in Art News, 72; Pat Mainardi (auth), rev in Art in Am, 7/74; H O Beil (auth), Arts Mag, 5/85. *Mem:* Nat Acad. *Media:* Oil, Watercolor. *Dealer:* MB Modern Gallery 41 E 57th St New York NY 10022; C Grimaldis Gallery 523 N Charles St Baltimore MD 21201. *Mailing Add:* 943 N Calvert St Baltimore MD 21217

MIECZKOWSKI, EDWIN
PAINTER
b Pittsburgh, Pa, Nov 26, 1929. *Study:* Cleveland Inst Art, BFA, 57; Carnegie Inst, MFA, 59. *Work:* Cleveland Mus Art; Robert Hull Fleming Mus, Vt. *Exhib:* One-man shows, Cleveland Inst Art, 65, Robert Hull Fleming Mus, 74, New Gallery, Cleveland, 74, Tyler Sch Art, Pa, 74, Mansfield Art Ctr, Ohio, 75, Ellen Myers Inc, NY, 76, Akron

Art Inst, Ohio, 77, Tanglewood Downtown, NY, 78, Cleveland Ctr Contemporary Art, 81, 85, 90, Kaber Gallery Ltd, NY, 82, Neo-Constructivism, Great Northern Corp Ctr, Ohio, 87, Brenda Kroos Gallery, Columbus, Ohio, 88, Scarab Gallery, Cleveland, 95, Visual Paradox: Transforming Perception, Lew Allen Contemporary, Santa Fe, N Mex, 2006; Vibrations Eleven, Martha Jackson Gallery, NY, 64; The Responsive Eye, Mus Modern Art, NY, 65; Inst Contemporary Art, London, England, 66; Second Arts Festival, Albright Knox Gallery, Buffalo, NY, 68; The Square in Painting, Am Federation Art, NY, 69; Grids, Inst Contemporary Art, Univ Pa, 72; Materials and Techniques of 20th Century Artists, Cleveland Mus Art, 76; Construction and Color, Myers Fine Arts Gallery, State Univ NY, Plattsburgh, 78; Visual Logic II, Parsons Sch Design, NY, 80; Kaber Gallery Ltd, NY, 83; American Purism Since 1945, Marylyn Pearl Gallery, NY, 84; Eight Sculptors, Cleveland Ctr Contemporary Art, 90; William Busta Gallery, Ohio, 97; Harmonic Forms on the Edge: Geometric Abstraction in Cleveland, Cleveland Fine Arts Found, Beck Ctr for Arts, 2001. *Mem:* Founding mem Anonima Group; Nat Organization Visual Artists, Cleveland. *Media:* Acrylic

MIEZAJS, DAINIS
PAINTER, INSTRUCTOR
b Kaucminde, Latvia, Mar 11, 29. *Study:* Ont Col of Art, 56. *Work:* Nat Gallery of Can, Ottawa, Ont; Art Gallery of Ont, Toronto; Mus Fine Arts, Montreal, Que; Art Gallery of Winnipeg, Man; Vancouver Art Gallery, BC. *Comn:* Series of 18 paintings, Trans-Can Pipeline, Toronto, Ont, 71. *Exhib:* Ann Can Soc of Painters in Watercolors, 61-78; Can Painters in Watercolor & Am Watercolor Soc Exchange Show, 73; Can Painters in Watercolor & Watercolor Soc of Japan, 77. *Collection Arranged:* Across Canada in Watercolor, Art Gallery of Ont, 69-71. *Teaching:* Instr drawing & painting, Ont Col of Art, Toronto, 60-, chmn fine art, 83-; dir landscape, Madawaska Valley Sch Art, Maynooth, Ont, 65-. *Awards:* Merit Award, Can Soc of Painters in Watercolor Ann; Purchase Awards, Can Soc of Painters in Watercolor. *Bibliog:* F Barwick (auth), Pictures from the Douglas Duncan Collection, Univ Toronto Press, 75. *Mem:* Can Painters in Watercolor (dir, 65-67); Latvia Soc Artists (vpres, 62-64). *Media:* Watercolor, Tempera. *Mailing Add:* c/o General Delivery Maynooth ON K0L 2S0 Canada

MIGLIACCIO, ANTHONY J
PAINTER, EDUCATOR
b Long Branch, NJ, Jan 24, 48. *Study:* Trenton State Col, BA (indust ed & tech), 1970; Kean Univ, MA (art educ), 1975. *Work:* EPA Bldg, Washington, DC. *Exhib:* Invitational Group Show, Milk Gallery, NY, 2005; MCAC State Juried Show, Monmouth Mus, Lincroft, NJ, 2005; Audubon Artists 64th Ann Nat Juried Exhibition, Salmagundi Club, NY, 2006; Invitational Group Show, Monmouth Mus, Lincroft, NJ, 2006; Nat Juried Exhib, Painters & Sculptors Soc, NY; solo shows, Guild of Creative Art, Shrewsbury, NJ, 2005, Frederick Gallery, Allenhurst, NJ, 2005, Brookdale Community Col, NJ. *Pos:* former pres, Art Administrators NJ, 97; former pres, Art Educators NJ, 98; delegate, NJ Eastern Regin Assembly, Nat Art Education Asn, 98; bd dirs, NJ Sch Arts, 99-2001; chm, NJ Core Curric Content Studies, Vis & Performing Arts, 2000; former pres, Alliance Arts Education, NJ, 2000. *Teaching:* art instr, Monmouth Regional High Sch, Tinton Falls, NJ, 70-82; printmaking instr, Monmouth Univ, W Long Branch, NJ, 86-88; supv, Vis Info Servs, Fort Monmouth, NJ, 88-91; art & music supv, Montville Pub Schs, NJ, 91-92, art & music supv, East Brunswick Pub Schs, NJ, 92-98; dir vis & performing arts, Red Bank Regional High Sch, Little Silver, NJ, 98-. *Awards:* Senate Citation, Contributions to the Arts, NJ, 2000; Governors Award, Arts Education, 2000; Geraldine R Dodge Found Painting Fel, 2002. *Mem:* Nat Art Education Asn; Art Educators NJ; Plein Air Painters, Jersey Coast; Art Administrators, NJ; Monmouth Co Arts Coun. *Media:* Landscape Oil Painting. *Mailing Add:* 580 Patten Ave Apt # 41 Long Branch NJ 07740

MIGNOSA, SANTO
CERAMIST, SCULPTOR
b Siracusa, Italy, Nov 14, 34; Can citizen. *Study:* Scuola d'Arte, Italy, Cert; Inst Statale d'Arte Firenze, Italy, Dipl: NY State Univ Alfred, MFA. *Work:* Univ Calgary Art Gallery, Can; Govt of Alta Art Found, Can; Govt of Tenn Ceramic Collection; Pall Mall of Can Art Collection; Art Centrum, Prague, Czech. *Exhib:* Smithsonian Inst, Washington, DC; Int Ceramic Exhib, Calgary, 73, Memphis Acad Art, 73; Tenn Int Ceramic Exhib, 73; Alta Govt Exhib, Atlanta, Ga, 75, Japan Tour, 79; Exhib of Miniatures Int Acad Ceramics, Kyoto & Tokyo, Japan, 80-81. *Collection Arranged:* Int Ceramic 73, Calgary, Can; Nat Ceramic 76, Calgary, Can. *Pos:* Co-chmn, Nat Ceramic Exhib, Calgary, Can, 75-76; Co-founder & vpres, Alta Potters, Asn, formerly; Co-founder, W Coast Clay Asn, Vancouver, BC, 93; bd dir & exhib comt & chmn, Seymour Art Gallery, North Vancouver, 93-94; dir, sculptor Soc BC, 94. *Teaching:* Instr ceramics & sculpture, Kootenay Sch of Art, Nelson, BC, 60-68; assoc prof ceramics, Univ Calgary, Alta, Can, 69-89 (ret). *Awards:* Gold Medal, Int Ceramic Exhib, Ostend, 58, Silver Medal, Prague, 61 & Second Prize Ex-Aequo, Calgary, 73, Int Acad Ceramics; Achievement Awards, Gov Alberta, 70 & 72. *Bibliog:* Al Riegger (auth), Featured Artist, Ceramic Mo, 63; article in, La Revue Mod des Arts et de la Vie, 67. *Mem:* Alta Potters' Asn (vpres, 70-71); Int Acad Ceramics, Geneva, Switz (coun mem). *Media:* Clay. *Mailing Add:* 571 N Dollarton Hwy North Vancouver BC V7G 1N3 Canada

MIHAESCO, EUGENE
PAINTER, ILLUSTRATOR
b Bucharest, Romania, Aug 24, 37, Switz citizen. *Study:* Fine Art Inst, Bucharest, BA, 59. *Work:* Cooper-Hewitt Mus, NY; Republic's Art Mus, Bucharest, Romania; Musee des Arts, Decoratifs de la Ville, Lausanne, Switz. *Exhib:* Bienal Sao Paulo, Sao-Paulo Mus, Brazil, 63; Art of the Times, Musee des Arts Decoratifs, Louvre, Paris, France; The Statue of Liberty, Ctr Pompidou, Beaubourg, Paris, France, 76. *Teaching:* Assoc prof illus, Pratt Inst, 81-82. *Awards:* Best Illus, 1977 Show, Am Inst Graphic Arts; Best Cover, News Paper Guild, 83; Gold Medal, Ann Show, Art Dirs Club, NY, 85. *Bibliog:* Deborah Phillips (auth), Eugene Mihaesco, Arts News, No 5, 81; Steven Heller (auth), Eugene Mihaesco, Arts, No 10, Vol 58, 84 & Graphis, No 238, 85. *Media:* Pastel; Pen & Ink. *Publ:* Ed artist, NY Times, 71-86; illusr, 12 covers, Time Inc, 78-86; 57 covers, New Yorker Mag, 72-86. *Mailing Add:* 25 Tudor City Pl No 1423 New York NY 10017-6819

MIHICH, VELIZAR See Vasa

MIKUS, ELEANORE
PAINTER
b Detroit, Mich, July 25, 27. *Study:* Art Students League; study in Cent Europe; Univ Denver, BFA & MA. *Work:* Mus Mod Art, Whitney Mus Am Art, NY; Victoria & Albert Mus, London; Los Angeles Co Mus Art; Indianapolis Mus Art, Ind; Nat Gallery Art, Washington, DC; and others. *Exhib:* Pace Gallery, New York City, 64; Columbus Mus Art, Columbus, Ohio, 71; Newark Mus, NJ, 72; Los Angeles Co Mus of Art, Los Angeles, Calif, 84; Solo exhibs, Mitchell Algus Gallery, Claudia Carr Gallery, OK Harris Gallery; Group show Indianapolis Mus & many others; Metropolitan mus, NY; Johnson Mus, Ithaca, NY; Ariz Mus Modern Art, Ariz. *Teaching:* Asst prof painting, Monmouth Col, 66-70; vis lectr painting, Cooper Union, 70-72; lectr painting, Cent Sch Art & Design, London, Eng, 73-77; assoc prof, Cornell Univ, 79-92, prof art, 92, emer prof, 94-; prof, Rome Prog, 89; prof emeritus, Cornell Univ, NY. *Awards:* Guggenheim Fellow, 66-67; Tamarind Fel in Lithogrpahy, 68; McDonell Fel in Painting, 69; Research Grant, Cornell Univ, 2001; Yaddo Grant in Drawing/Painting, 2004. *Bibliog:* Mark Daniel Cohen (auth), The Critical State of Visual Art in NY Paintings 1960's-1990's, Review Mag,; Mitchell Algus Cornell (auth), Eleanore Mikus Painting and Paperfolds, Cornell Alumni Mag, 2/01. *Mem:* Nat Asn Wanan Artists. *Media:* Oil, Paper Folds. *Publ:* Eleanore Mikus (auth), Shadows of the Real, Hobbs/Bernstock, Groton House, Itaca, in assoc with Wash Univ Press, Seattle & London, 91. *Dealer:* Mitchell Algus Gallery 25 Thompson St New York NY 10013

MILANT, JEAN ROBERT
DEALER
b Milwaukee, Wis, Dec 27, 43. *Study:* Univ Wis, Milwaukee, BA & BFA, 66; Univ NMex, Albuquerque, MA, 70; Lithography Workshop, Los Angeles. *Pos:* Dir & owner, Cirrus Ed Ltd, 70-; dir & owner, Cirrus Gallery Ltd, 70-; mem bd, Los Angeles Inst Contemp Art, 74-76; vpres, Los Angeles Visual Arts; vpres, Grunwald Ctr, UCLA, 2003-. *Teaching:* Instr UC Long Beach, 71-. *Awards:* Tamarind Master Printer, 69. *Bibliog:* Bruce Davis (auth), Made in LA the Prints of Cirrus, Lacma. *Mem:* LACMA; MOCA; LACE; MOMA. *Specialty:* Contemporary painting, sculpture, performance, environments of Southern California artists; publisher of lithographs and screenprints of noted California artists. *Publ:* ed, Artists/Prints 1976-1977, Contemp Art Publ Inc, 78. *Mailing Add:* 542 S Alameda St Los Angeles CA 90013

MILBOURN, PATRICK D
PAINTER, ILLUSTRATOR
b Omaha, NE, Sept 19, 50. *Study:* Self taught, Studied Aaron Shikler-David Levine painting group (mem), 1980-2000. *Comn:* Painting (feature articles), Time Mag, New Yorker, Sports Illus, Entertainment Weekly, House & Garden, Forbes, NY Mag, Bus Week, 1978-2006; Cover art (30 murder mystery novels), Putnam, Ballantine, Fawcett & Random House Publs, 1990-2002; Beaux Arts Ball posters, Green Co Coun on Arts, 1999-2006; portrait, Dir Soc Illustrators, NY, 2002; many other portrait comns, 90-2006. *Exhib:* Soc illusrs, NY, 1986, 1995; Nat Acad Design (juried), 1990, 1992; Salmagundi Club (juried), NY, 1992, 1993, 1995; Pastel Soc Am, NY, 1996, 1997,1999, 2001; Am Acad Arts & Letters (juried), NY, 1998. *Awards:* Master Pastelist, Pastel Soc Am, Nat Arts Club, NY, 94; Pastel Award, 21st Ann Juried Exhib, Salmagundi Club, 1998; Balin Award, 24th Ann Juried Exhib, Salmgundi Club, 2000; Strathmore Paper Award, 29th Ann Juried Exhib, Pastel Soc Am, 2001; and many more. *Bibliog:* Best of Pastel, Quarry Books of Rockport Publs, Gloucester, Mass, 1998; Best of Portrait Painting, North Light Books, F&W Publs, Cincinnati, Ohio, 1998; Best of Watercolor-Vol 3, North Light Books F&W Publs, Cincinnati, Ohio, 1999; Watercolor Expressions, Quarry Publs, Rockport Publ, Gloucester, Mass, 2000; Chronogram Magazine of Art, Culture & Spirit, Kingston, NY, 12/2005; Almanac Weekly, Ulster Publ, Kingston, NY, 10/27/2005; Art Times Journal, CSS Publ Inc, Patrick Milbourn at the M Gallery, 6/2006. *Mem:* Pastel Soc Am; Soc of Illusrs; Green Co Coun on the Arts; Thomas Cole Nat Hist Site; Olana Frederick Church Nat Hist Site. *Media:* Acrylic, Oil, Pastel, Miscellaneous Media. *Publ:* many publ, 93-2003. *Mailing Add:* 327 W 22nd St New York NY 10011

MILDER, JAY
PAINTER, SCULPTOR
b Omaha, Nebr, May 12, 34. *Study:* The Sorbonne; with Ossip Zadkine; with Andre L'Hote, Paris, France; Chicago Art Inst; study with Hans Hoffman, Provincetown, Mass. *Work:* Tel Aviv Mus, Israel; Chrysler Mus, Norfolk, Va; Skidmore Col, NY; Mint Mus, Charlotte, NC; Mus Puerto Rico, 60; Mus Fine Arts, Rio de Janeiro, Brazil. *Comn:* Sculpture, Sinai Temple, Los Angeles, Calif, 64; litho, Greenwich Light Opera, Conn, 70; etching, Rainbow Arts Found, NY, 77. *Exhib:* Mint Mus Art, Charlotte, NC; Joslyn Art Mus, Omaha, Nebr; Art for the Olympics, Mus Mod Art, NY; Retrospective 1958-91, (touring), Schick Art Gallery, Skidmore Col, Saratoga Springs, NY, Va Beach Ctr Arts, Va Beach, 91-92; one-man exhibs, Gallery Four, Charlotte, Va, 86, Richard Green Gallery, NY, 86, Sid Deutsch Gallery, NY, 86, Harcourts Contemp, San Francisco, 89, Missiah on the IND, Richard Green Gallery, NY, Gallery Jupiter, Little Silver, NJ, Anton Gallery, Washington, DC & Yares Gallery, Scottsdale, Ariz (catalog), 87-89; The Expanding Figurative Imagination, Anita Shapolsky Gallery,

NY, 90; Horace Richter Gallery, Jaffa, Israel, 90; Private Stories (catalog), Anderson Gallery, Va Commonwealth Univ, Richmond, 91; Alitosh Kebede Fine Art, Los Angeles, Calif, 91; "Retrospective," Mus of Fine Arts, Rio de Janerio, 2001 (solo); recent paintings, Andre Zarre, New York City, 2001 (solo); Mus of Modern Art, Bahia, Brazil, 2003- (solo). *Collection Arranged:* Rhino Horn Exhib, New Sch for Social Res, NY; Oakley Collection, Skidmore Col; 50 American Contemporary Drawings, Ann Arbor Mus, Mich. *Teaching:* Asst prof art, City Col, New York, 71-, assoc prof, 81-. *Awards:* Gutman Award, 60; First Prizes, All Ohio Artists, 64 & Am Figurative Artists, Bayonne, NJ, 77; Nat Endowment Art, 89-90. *Bibliog:* Leslie Judd Ahlander (auth), Miami art scene, Miami News, 11/18/88; Hilton Kramer (auth), art for art's sake show an apt finale for Ingber Gallery, NY Observer, 7/17-24/89; Barnaby Ruhe (auth), Ruhe views, Art World, summer 89. *Media:* Oil; Mixed. *Dealer:* Oscarsson Hood Gallery 41 W 57th St New York NY 10019

MILES, CHRISTINE M
MUSEUM DIRECTOR, ADMINISTRATOR
b Madison, Ind, Mar 2, 51. *Study:* Boston Univ, BA(fine arts), 73, George Washington Univ, MA, 82, Mus Mgt Inst, Berkeley, 85. *Pos:* Curatorial asst, Mus City New York, 73-75; dir, Mus Gallery, South St Seaport Mus, New York, 75-77, Fraunces Tavern Mus, New York, 80-86 & Albany Inst Hist & Art, New York, 86-. *Mem:* Am Asn Mus; Fedn Hist Serv (bd mem, 87-); Gallery Asn NY State (bd mem, 88-); Mus Asn NY. *Mailing Add:* Albany Inst History & Art 125 Washington Ave Albany NY 12210-2296

MILES, ELLEN GROSS
HISTORIAN, CURATOR
b New York, NY, July 28, 41. *Study:* Bryn Mawr Col, BA, 64; Winterthur Summer Inst, 67; Yale Univ Grad Sch, MPh, 70 & PhD, 76. *Pos:* Pub relations asst & registr, Corcoran Gallery Art, Washington, DC, 64-66; asst to dir, Nat Portrait Gallery, Washington, DC, 71-77, assoc cur, 77-84, cur, dept painting & sculpture 84-94 & chair dept painting & sculpture, 94-. *Mem:* Col Art Asn; Am Soc Eighteenth Century Studies; Walpole Soc London; Asn Historians Am Art. *Res:* Eighteenth and nineteenth century British and American portrait painting and drawing; profile portraits. *Publ:* coauth (with Richard H Saunders), American Colonial Portraits: 1700-1776, Smithsonian Press, 87; auth, Saint-Memin and the Neoclassical Profile Portrait, Smithsonian Press, 94; auth, American Paintings of the Eighteenth Century, Nat Gallery Art/Oxford Univ Press, 95; ed, The Portrait of Eighteenth-Century America, Univ Del Press, 93. *Mailing Add:* 5305 Glenwood Rd Bethesda MD 20814-1405

MILES, SHEILA LEE
PAINTER, CONSULTANT
b Indianapolis, Ind, Aug 10, 52. *Study:* Purdue Univ, West Lafayette, Ind, BA, 73, MA, 74; Hans Hoffman Sch Art, Provincetown, Mass, 74. *Work:* Purdue Univ, West Lafayette, Ind; Yellowstone Art Mus, Billings, Mont; Hockaday Ctr Arts, Kalispell, Mont; Mus Fine Art, Univ Mont, Missoula; Ray Graham Collection, Albuquerque, NMex; Deaconness Hosp, Billings, Mont. *Comn:* 2400 Sq foot ceiling, Maxines, Billings, Mont; Missoula Int Airport, Mont; Missoula in Motion, 5 paintings, Mssoula. *Exhib:* Provinctown Art Asn & Mus, Mass, 74-78; one-woman shows, Custer Co Art Ctr, Miles City, 84, Yellowstone Art Ctr (with catalog), Billings, 84, 99, Missoula Mus Arts, 86, 2003 & Paris Gibson Sq, Great Falls, 86, Mont; Coal Tax Collections, Yellowstone Art Ctr, Billings, Mont, 86; Owings-Dewey Fine Art, Santa Fe, NMex, 86, 87 & 88; retrospective (with catalog), Univ Mont, Missoula. *Pos:* Gallery dir, Provincetown Art Asn & Mus, 75-77 & Mont State Univ, 85-86; artist-in-residence, Mont Arts Coun-Custer Co Art Ctr, 83-84; cur, Yellowstone Art Mus, 86-90. *Teaching:* Instr drawing & painting, Mont State Univ, Billings, 80-82 & 85; instr painting, Mont State Univ, Bozeman, 85-86, Univ Mont, Missoula, 92-97; pvt instr art. *Awards:* Individual Artists Fel, Mont Arts Coun, 84; Purchase Award, Coal tax grant, Yellowstone Art Ctr, Mont Arts Coun, 84; Grant, Adolph and Esther Gottlieb Found, 2000. *Bibliog:* Chris Meyers (auth), Sheila Miles, Billings Gazette, 80-2002; Dan Rubey (auth), Artweek, San Francisco, Calif, 84; various auths, The Missoulian, Missoula, Mont, 86, 92-2005; Mus of Art & culture, UM, Simone Ellis, auth. *Mem:* Arts Advocacy. *Media:* Oil, gouache, drawings media. *Mailing Add:* Sheila Miles Fine Art 250 Main St Point Arena CA 95468

MILEY, LES
CERAMIST, EDUCATOR
b Petersburg, Ind, Nov 1, 34. *Study:* Purdue Univ, ceramics with Bill Farrell; Ind State Univ, BA & MA; Southern Ill Univ, with Nicholas Vergette & Brent Kington, MFA. *Work:* Ceramics Monthly Collection, Columbus, Ohio; Anner Pottery Inc, Oviedo, Fla; Sheldon Swope Mus, Terre Haute, Ind; NY Stock Exchange, NY; Evansville Mus Arts & Sciences, Inc; Jane B Owen Collection, Houston, Tex & New Harmony, Ind. *Comn:* Citizen's Bank, Evansville, Ind, 88; Archit ceramics, Robert L Blaffer Foundation New Harmony, Ind, 2005; Wall Plates, Old Nat Bank, IND, 2005, Sculptures. *Exhib:* solo exhibs, Sheldon Swope Mus, Terre Haute, Ind, 87, Harry Knohr Gallery, Platteville, Wis, 87,; Cambridge Salt Glaze Invitational, Wis, 96; Louisville, Ky Visual Art Assoc Invitational, 97; Paint the Town, Ind Mus Art, Evansville, 98; Mid-States Craft, Evansville, Ind, 98; Nat Tureen Exhib, R Bahr Gallery, New Albany, Ind, 99; Dinner Works, Louisville Visual Art Asn, 2000; The Regionalists, Mus Art, Owensboro, Ky, 2001; Capitol Arts Alliance Invitational, Bowling Green, Ky, 2002; 21st Century Ceramics Invitational Columbus, Ohio, 2004; Am Ceramic Soc Invitational Indianapolis, Ind, 2004; AMACO/BRENT NCECA Invitational Indianapolis, Ind, 2004. *Pos:* Dir, Blafter Foundation ceramic workshop, New Harmony, Ind, 67-. *Teaching:* Prof art, Univ Evansville, 61-, chmn dept, 65-66 & 69-99. *Awards:* Purchase Award, 44th Wabash Valley Art Exhib, Sheldon Swope Mus, 86; Artist of Yr, SW Ind Arts Coun, 96; Purchase Award, 35th Mid-States Craft Exhib, Evansville Mus, 97. *Bibliog:* Thomas Schafer (auth), Pottery Decoration, 75 & Jack Troy (auth), Salt-Glazed Ceramics, 77, Watson-Guptill; R Burkett (auth), Glen Nelson's Ceramics, A Potters Handbook, 12/90; Phil Rogers (auth), Ash Glazes, 91; Robin Hopper & Daniel Rhodes (auths), Clay and Glazes for the Potter, 2000; Robin Hopper (auth) Making Marks, 2004. *Mem:* Nat Coun Educ Ceramic Arts; Hoosier Salon, Ind. *Media:* Clay, Watercolor. *Mailing Add:* 1212 S Plaza Dr Evansville IN 47715-5145

MILHOAN, RANDALL BELL
PAINTER, DESIGNER
b Overton, Nebr, Feb 24, 44. *Study:* Kearney State Teachers Col, 64; Univ Nebr, Lincoln, BFA, 68; Univ Calif, Santa Barbara, Calif Regents Scholar, 70; Mont State Univ, 77; Arizona Western Col, 84-93. *Work:* Sheldon Mem Gallery, Lincoln, Nebr; Joslyn Mus, Omaha, Nebr; San Antonio Art Inst, Tex. *Comn:* Mural, Colo Arts Coun, Vail, 85; murals, Vail & Beaver Creek, Colo; mural, Town of Vail, Colo, 94; mural, Phillips '66, 96. *Exhib:* Joan Robey Gallery, Denver, Colo, 88; Cabrillo Gallery, Santa Cruz, Calif, 88; J Cotter Gallery, Vail, Colo, 88; Milhoan Studios, Vail, Colo; Santa Fe Pottery, Denver, 96; and others. *Collection Arranged:* Santa Fe Festival of Arts, NMex, 81; Colo Artists, Craftsman Asn Ann, Arvada, Colo, 85; Beaver Creek Arts Festival, 92. *Pos:* Dir, Colo Mountain Col, 70-84; founder & dir, Summervail Workshop for Art & Critical Studies, 71-85, pres & exec dir, Summervail Workshop Found, Inc, 84-85; dean, San Antonio Art Inst, 85-86; vpres, Int Marketing & Media, 86-88; owner/designer & pres, Milhoan Studios, Vail, Colo, 89-; exec dir, Vail Arts Coun, 93; Chm, Visioning Committee, Minturn, Colo, 2003-. *Teaching:* Instr advan studies & spec proj painting, Colo Mountain Col, Vail, 70-85; instr 2-dimensional studies, San Antonio Art Inst, 85-86. *Awards:* Purchase Award, Tenth Midwest Biennial, 68; Purchase Award, Crossroads Ctr, 94. *Bibliog:* Mark Huffman (auth), Milhoan's contribution to the local CMC, Vail Trail, 2/24/84; Irene Clurman (auth), Artists, teachers, converge at Vail workshop, Rocky Mountain News, 7/29/84; Paul Soderberg (auth), Little towns, Art-Talk, 8-9/91. *Mem:* Col Art Asn Am; Vail Valley Arts Coun; Art Pub Places (bd mem); Yuma Symp (adv bd). *Media:* Acrylic, Oil. *Specialty:* Contemp AM Paintings & Am Folk & Primitive Art. *Collection:* Contemporary American fine arts and crafts; primitive toys; masks from around the world. *Publ:* The American Painting Collection of the Sheldon Memorial Art Gallery. *Dealer:* J Cotter Gallery PO Box 385 Vail CO 81658. *Mailing Add:* 483 E Gore Creek Dr PO Box 1114 Vail CO 81658

MILLAR, ROBERT
CONCEPTUAL ARTIST
b Los Angeles, Calif, March 6, 58. *Study:* Cal State Univ, Northridge, BA, 80. *Work:* Newport Harbor Art Mus, Newport Beach, Calif; City & Co of San Francisco; Los Angeles Co Transportation Comn. *Comn:* Grand Ave Plaza, Pacific Atlas Corp, Los Angeles, 91; Waterfront Park, City of Santa Barbara, Calif, 91; Metro-Rail Sta, Los Angeles Co Transportation Comn, 91; Muni-Metro, San Francisco Public Utility Comn, 92; Rose Theatre Site, Imry Merchant, London, Eng, 92. *Exhib:* Robert Millar, Newport Harbor Art Mus, Newport Beach, Calif, 91; Systems, Los Angeles Munic Art Gallery, 91; Breaking Boundaries, Santa Monica Mus Art, Calif, 92; Rose, Rose Theatre Site, London, Eng, 92. *Bibliog:* Colin Gardner (auth), Robert Millar, Art Forum, 91; Susan Kandel (auth), Peculiarities of Perception, Los Angeles Times, 91; Peter Frank (auth), Robert Millar, Los Angeles Weekly, 91. *Dealer:* Thomas Solomon's Garage 928 N Fairfax Ave Los Angeles CA 90046

MILLARD, CHARLES WARREN, III
DIRECTOR, WRITER
b Elizabeth, NJ. *Study:* Princeton Univ, BA; Harvard Univ, MA & PhD. *Pos:* Asst dir, Dumbarton Oaks, 64-66; dir, Washington Gallery Mod Art, 66-67; cur 19th century European art, Los Angeles Co Mus Art, 71-74; art ed, Hudson Rev, 72-87; chief cur, Hirshhorn Mus & Sculpture Garden, 74-86; dir, Ackland Art Mus, NC, 86-93. *Teaching:* Adj prof art hist, Johns Hopkins Univ, 82-86 & Univ NC Chapel Hill, 86-93. *Mem:* Int Asn Art Critics; Assn Art Mus Directors (AAMD). *Res:* Nineteenth century French sculpture, particularly Degas and Preault; various topics in modern painting and sculpture. *Publ:* Auth, Sculpture of Edgar Degas, Princeton Univ, 76; and many other articles & rev in var periodicals, including Hudson Review, Jour Aesthetics and Art Criticism, others; Auguste Préault: Sculpteur Romantique 1809-1879, Gallimard, 97. *Mailing Add:* PO Box 811 Chapel Hill NC 27514

MILLEA, TOM (THOMAS) FRANCIS
PHOTOGRAPHER
b Bridgeport, Conn, Sept 30, 44. *Study:* Univ Western Conn, BA, 66; studied with Paul Caponigro & H Jonathon Greenwald, 67-73. *Work:* Mus Mod Art, NY; Victoria & Albert Mus, London, Eng; Ctr Creative Photog, Univ Ariz, Tucson; Oakland Mus; Philadelphia Mus Art; Australian National Gallery, Canberra; New Zealand National Mus, Wellington; and many others. *Exhib:* Solo exhibs, Friends Photog, Carmel, Calif, 78, DeSaisset Art Mus, Santa Clara, Calif, 80, Arco Ctr Arts, Los Angeles, 80, Camden Arts Ctr, London, 81, Galerie au Poisson Rouge, Praz, Switz, 81, Ctr Creative Photog, Tucson, 82 & The Malone Gallery, Rochester, NY, 86; New Orleans Mus Art, 84; Light Gallery, NY, 84; The Weston Gallery, Inc, Carmel, Calif, 84; Monterey Peninsula Mus Art, 85; The Platinum Print, NJ State Mus, Trenton, 86; The Western Landscape (traveling), Int Ctr Photog, NY, 86; Polaroid Int Collection Exhib, 86; and many others. *Pos:* Cinematographer, Robert Fulton Co, Danbury, Conn, 68; photographer, United Aircraft, Sikorsky, Stratford, Conn, 68-69. *Teaching:* Instructor & guest lecturer at many universities, workshops and galleries, 75-84. *Awards:* Ruttenberg Grant, 82 & Publ Workshop Grant, 83, Friends Photog; Polaroid Grant, 85. *Bibliog:* John Hafey & Tom Shillea (auths), The Platinum Print, Rochester Inst Technol, 80; interview, New Pictorialist Soc, 83; Alan Plone (auth), The Life and Work of Tom Millea, Vis Art Films Inc, 84; rev, Rochester City Newspaper & Democrat & Chronicle, Rochester, NY, 12/85. *Mem:* Friends Photog; Soc Photog

Educ. *Media:* Platinum, Palladium. *Publ:* Auth, The Technique of Platinum and Palladium, Platinum Workshops, 76; Death Valley Photographs (poster), Sunlight Graphics, 83. *Dealer:* Light Gallery 724 Fifth Ave New York NY; Weston Gallery Carmel CA. *Mailing Add:* c/o Winfield Gallery PO Box 7393 Carmel CA 93921

MILLER, ARTHUR GREEN
EDUCATOR, HISTORIAN
b New York, NY, May 19, 42. *Study:* Harvard Univ, PhD, 69. *Collection Arranged:* Maya Rulers of Time (auth catalog), Tikal Architectural Sculpture, Univ Mus, Univ Pa, 86. *Pos:* Dir, Maya Art prog, Univ Mus, Univ Pa, 79-82; dir of studies, Ecole des Hautes Etudes, Paris, 88-. *Teaching:* Instr, asst prof art hist, Yale Univ, 68-73; prof, Latin Am art hist & archeology, Univ Md, Col Park, 83-. *Awards:* Award, Guggenheim, 73; Grants, Nat Endowment Arts, 79, Nat Endowment Humanities 89-92. *Bibliog:* Esther Pasztory (auth), Mural painting of Teotihuacan J, Soc of Archit Hist, ArtBulletin, 74; Clemency Coggins (auth), On the Edge of the Sea, Am Antiquity, 83; William Fash (auth), Maya Rulers of Time, Am Antiquity, 88. *Mem:* Col Art Asn; Soc for Am Archeology. *Res:* Art history and archeology of pre-hispanic and early colonial Latin American; interaction between image and text communication systems. *Publ:* Auth, The Mural Painting of Teotihuacan Mexico, Dumbarton Oaks, 73; ed, The Codex Nuhall: A Picture Manuscript from Ancient Mexico, Dover Publ, 75; auth, On the Edte of the Sea, Dumbarton Oaks, 82; ed, Highland-Lowland Interaction in Mexiamerica: Interdisciplinary Approaches, Dumbarton Oaks, 83; auth, Maya Rulers of Time: Architectural Sculpture from Tikal, Guatemala, Univ Pa, 86. *Mailing Add:* Alfonso De Cossio 3 PO Box 41004 Sevilla Spain

MILLER, BARBARA DARLENE
PAINTER, PRINTMAKER
b Jarbidge, Nev. *Study:* Univ Wash, BA; Univ Hawaii, MEd; etching with Rudy Pozzatti & Gabor Peterdi; design with Clayton Rippey; painting with Tadashi Sato & Tseng Yu-Ho. *Work:* State Found Cult & Arts, Honolulu; Univ Hawaii Art Dept Etching Collection. *Comn:* Acrylic mural, KPOI Radio, Waikiki, Honolulu, 68; Christ with Thorns (acrylic painting), Church of Good Shepherd, Kahului, Maui, 70; Buddha (acrylic painting), Kahului Hongwanji Mission, Maui, 72; Mosaics (film), State Found & Maui Arts Coun, 72. *Exhib:* Walker Art Ctr Nat, Minneapolis, 65; Painters of Hawaii Circulating Exhib, 69; Etchings, Hawaii State Libr, 70; Regional Ethel Baldwin Mem, Wailuku, 72-81; Art Maui, Hawaii State Invitational Show, 81; plus others; Invitational Show, Honolulu Cult Plaza, 82. *Pos:* Artist, Logos Layouts, KPOI Radio, 65-67; art dir, KHVH Radio-TV, Honolulu, 67-68. *Teaching:* Art instr, Hilo High Sch, 57-60; elem art specialist, Kahului Elem Sch, 64-68; art instr & art program coordr, Maui Community Col, 68-95. *Awards:* Hawaii Artists Exhibs Awards & Prizes, 65-77; State Found Cult & Art Purchase Award, 72; Grand Prize, Best in Show, Hui Noeau Art Soc, 77. *Bibliog:* Eileen Webster (auth), Milady of the week--Barbara Miller, 68 & Darrell Neilson (auth), Works of Mrs Miller, 68, Maui News; Tim Mitchell (auth), Art news--Barbara Miller painter, Honolulu Mag, 69. *Mem:* Maui Arts Coun (visual arts chmn, 68-80); Hui Noeau Art Soc; Nat Art Educ Asn; Maui Mayors' Comt Cult and Art. *Media:* Acrylic, Intaglio. *Publ:* Illusr cover, Festival of Arts, 69; coauth, Grass Roots, Poetry & Art, 70; illusr cover, Our Changing Times, Univ Hawaii Div Continuing Educ, 70. *Dealer:* Village Gallery-Whalers Village Kaanapali Maui HI 96753

MILLER, BRAD
CRAFTSMAN, CERAMIST
Study: Univ Ore, BFA(ceramics & graphics), 74, MFA, 77. *Work:* Los Angeles Co Mus; Denver Art Mus; Brooklyn Mus, NY; Renwick Gallery, Smithsonian Inst, Washington; Southern Alleghenies Mus Art, Loretto, Pa. *Exhib:* Seattle Art Mus, 79; Nat Gallery Art, Renwick Gallery, Smithsonian Inst, Washington, 80; solo exhibs, Arvada Ctr Arts & Humanities, Colo, 88, Mill St Gallery, Aspen, Colo, 91 & 93, Anderson Ranch Arts Ctr, Snowmass Village, Colo, 91, Margo Jacobsen Gallery, Portland, Ore, 93, Robischon Gallery, Denver, 94 & Univ Nebr, Lincoln, 94, Margo Jacobsen Gallery, Portland Ore, 99, Robischon Gallery, Denver, Colo, 2000; Colorado Artists: Recent Acquisitions, Denver Art Mus, 96; Altered States, Ctr Visual Arts, Metrop State Col, Denver, 96; Current, Robischon Gallery, Denver, 96; LongHouse Foundation, East Hampton, NY, 96; New Visions in Clay, Mendocino Art Ctr Gallery, Calif, 96; Bellas Artes Santa Fe, NMex, 97; Rivers, the Foothills Art Ctr, Golden, Colo, 2000. *Pos:* Exec dir, Anderson Ranch Arts Ctr, Snowmass Village, Colo, 84-92. *Teaching:* Ceramics prog dir, Anderson Ranch Arts Ctr, Snowmass Village, Colo, 80-84, instr, 91, workshop, 94 & 96; vis artist, RI Sch Design, Providence, 87, Spring Island, Beaufort, SC, 93 & Univ Ore, Eugene, 95; workshop, Penland Sch Crafts, NC, 89 & Ore Sch Arts & Crafts, Portland, 95; vis prof ceramics, Univ Ga Studies Abroad, Cortona, Italy, fall 94. *Awards:* Artist Recognition Award, Colo Fedn Arts, 92; Visual Artists Fel, Nat Endowment Arts, 94. *Bibliog:* Laura Dixon (auth), Bradley Miller, Ceramics Monthly, 12/95; George Melrod (auth), Back to nature, Art & Antiques Mag, 2/96; Rose Slivka (auth), From the studio, East Hampton Star, NY, 6/6/96. *Dealer:* Robischon Gallery 1740 Wazee St Denver CO 80202. *Mailing Add:* 406 Twinning Flats Rd PO Box 89 Woody Creek CO 81656

MILLER, BRENDA
SCULPTOR, CONCEPTUAL ARTIST
b Bronx, NY. *Study:* Univ NMex, BFA, 65; Tulane Univ, MFA, 67. *Work:* Mus Boymans-Van Beuningen, Rotterdam, Holland; Haag Gemeente Mus, Holland; Hartford Atheneum, Conn; Univ Tex, Austin; Newport Harbor Art Mus, Newport Beach, Calif. *Comn:* A is for Anonymous, (pvt collection), Block Island, RI, 91. *Exhib:* solo exhib, Whitney Mus Am Art, 75; Portland Ctr Visual Art, 78; The Minimal Tradition, Aldrich Mus Contemp Art, 79; Cable Gallery, NY, 88; Dross to Art, Islip Art Mus, 89; The Fetish of Knowledge, Real Art Ways, Hartford, Conn, 91; AC Project Rm, NY, 92; Transparency, Luise Ross Gallery, NY, 92; Footfalls, Greenport, NY, 97 (coordr); Art Sites, Greenport, NY, 2000; PS 1, Long Island City, NY, 2000; Art Sites, Greenport, 2002. *Teaching:* Cooper Union, 67-68 & 80; State Univ NY, Stony Brook, 72-79, Old Westbury, 75. *Awards:* Creative Artists Pub Serv Grant, 75; Fels, Guggenheim Found, 78; Nat Endowment Arts, 76, 79 & 87-88. *Bibliog:* Susan Tower (auth), The object perceived, the object apprehended, Art Forum, Vol XII, No 5, 74; Lucy Lippard (auth), Brenda Miller: Woven stamped, Art in Am, Vol 64, No 3, 76; Ted Castle (auth), About Brenda Miller & her art, Mus J, Ser 22, No 1, 77. *Mem:* Am Abstract Artists; Greenport Arts & Culture Comt. *Media:* All. *Publ:* Auth, Vertical Alphabet SE, pvt publ, 90; Transparent Vertical Alphabet SE (26) pvt publ, 91

MILLER, DANIEL DAWSON
PRINTMAKER, SCULPTOR, PAINTER
b Pittsburgh, Pa, July 7, 28. *Study:* Lafayette Col, BA, 51; Pa State Univ, summers with Hobson Pittman; Univ Pa, MFA, 58. *Work:* Pa Acad Fine Arts, Philadelphia; Philadelphia Mus Art; Rutgers Mus, New Brunswick, NJ; Wilmington Soc Fine Arts, Del; Dickinson Col, Carlisle, Pa. *Exhib:* 11 Modern Am Artists, Rahr Mus, Manitowoc, Wis, 63; 158th-162nd Ann Exhib, Pa Acad Fine Arts, Philadelphia, 63-67; Artist's House, Philadelphia, 2001 & 2002; one-man shows, Peale House, Pa Acad Fine Arts, 67, Drexel Inst, 68, Rutgers Mus, Rutgers Univ, 70, Univ Maine, 72 & Rosenfeld Gallery, Philadelphia, Pa, 81, 84 & 92. *Pos:* Asst dean fac, Pa Acad Fine Arts, 83-86, actg dir, 84-85, head painting dept, 86-92, chmn grad sch, 98-. *Teaching:* Instr life painting, Pa Acad Fine Arts, 64-; instr art & head fine arts dept, Eastern Col, St Davids, Pa, 64-85; instr woodcut, Pa Acad Fine Arts, 83-. *Awards:* Prize for Oil, Del Ann, Del Soc Fine Arts, 60; May Audubon Post Prize, 61, Bertha M Goldberg Mem Award, 70 & 75, Leona Karp Brauerman Prize, 76 & Percy Owens Award, 86, Fel Pa Acad Fine Arts. *Mem:* Philadelphia Watercolor Club; Am Color Print Soc. *Media:* All. *Interests:* Travel. *Dealer:* Artist's House 57 2nd St Philadelphia Pa 19106. *Mailing Add:* PO Box 41 Christiana PA 17509

MILLER, DENISE
MUSEUM DIRECTOR, EDUCATOR
b Chicago, Ill. *Study:* St Xavier Univ, BA, 80, MBA, 86; Univ Chicago & Northwestern Univ. *Exhib:* Pub-Pvt, Works by Contemp Commercial and Fine Art Photogrs, incl Sheila Metzner, George Hurrell, Mary Ellen Mark, Victor Skrebneski, Robert Mapplethorpe, David Seidner, Burt Glinn, William Coupon & Barbara Karant, 86-87; Frank Gohlke: Landscapes from the Middle of the World-- Photographs 1972-1987, 87; Contemp Photographs from Japan, 88; Changing Chicago: Close Up, Photog Essays on Family and Community (co-ed, catalog), 89; Fire Sites--Defense-Deterrence-Bargaining Chips--Photogrpahs by Emmet Gowin, David Graham, David Hanson, Richard Misrach, Patrick Nagatani & Barbara Norfleet, 89; Linda Connor: Spiral Journey (auth, catalog), 90; Anthony Dyrek: Poland Under Martial Law, 90; Mus Contemp Photog, Columbia Col, Chicago, 92-98. *Collection Arranged:* Permanent Collection, Mus Contemp Photog, 59-. *Pos:* Dir, Mus Contemp Photog, Chicago, 86-; bd mem, Etant Donnes, Fr Am Fund Contemp Art, 97. *Teaching:* Instr mus & curatorial practices, Columbia Col, Chicago, 85-; instr bus admin, Graham Sch Mgt, St Xavier Col, Chicago, 86; principle prof mus studies, Columbia Col, Chicago, 86-. *Mem:* Am Asn Mus; Art Mus Asn Am; Col Art Asn; Soc Photog Educ; Int Coun Mus. *Res:* Contemporary art and photography, 59-. *Publ:* Auth & ed, Open Spain/Espana Abierta: Contemporary Documentary Photography in Spain, Lunwerg Editores, Barcelona & Madrid, 92; Within this Garden: Photographs by Ruth Thorne Thomsen, Aperture, NY, 93; auth, City of Secrets: Photography of Naples by Jed Fielding, Takarajima Bks, NY, 97; auth & ed, Photography's multiple roles: art, document, market, science, DAP Inc, 98. *Mailing Add:* Mus Contemp Photog 600 S Michigan Ave Chicago IL 60605-1901

MILLER, DOLLY (ETHEL) B
PAINTER, COLLAGE ARTIST
b Johnstown, Pa, June 14, 27. *Study:* Brooklyn Col, NY, BA(chemistry); NY Univ, MA(Fr lit); art hist, The Sorbonne & the Louvre, Paris, France; studied painting with Andre Lhote, Paris; Art Students League, with Julian Levi; also with Leo Manso, NY Univ. *Work:* Johnson & Johnson, Surgico, Inc, Piscataway, NJ; The Friends Acad, Locust Valley, NY. *Exhib:* One-person shows, Vt Conserv Arts, 84, Culinary Inst, Montpelier, 85, N Country Hosp Gallery, Newport, 85, Vt Coun Arts Montpelier, Cornelia St Cafe, Greenwich Village, NY; Northeast Open, Worcester, Mass, 86; N Country Hosp, Newport, Vt, 88; Wickwire Gallery, Lyndon State Col, Lyndonville, Vt, 90; The League at the Cape, Provincetown Art Asn, Mass, 93; Inaugural Invitational, Ctr Gallery, Newport, Vt, 94. *Awards:* Candidates for Art Award, Am Acad Nat Inst Art, New York, 76; Salmagundi Club Award, Nat Acad Galleries, 79; Vt Studio Sch Residency Grant, 86. *Mem:* Audubon Artists, Inc; Art Students League New York; Art Resources Asn Vt. *Media:* Oil. *Mailing Add:* 39 N Park St Apt 2E Lebanon NH 03766

MILLER, ELAINE SANDRA
PAINTER, PRINTMAKER
b Philadelphia, Pa. *Study:* Drexel Univ, BS, 51; Cheltenham Ctr for Arts, with G Noble Wagner, Jimmy Leuders & Paul Gorka, 71-84. *Work:* Siemens Corp Int; Rion Corp Ltd, Tokyo, Japan; Heritage Hall Mus, Tallageda, AL; Woodmere Art Mus, Philadelphia, Pa. *Exhib:* Solo Exhib, Philadelphia Art Alliance, 81; Nat Mus Am Jewish Hist, Philadelphia, 92; Nat Soc Painters in Casein & Acrylic, NY, 92; Am Color Print Soc; 2nd Worldwid Femenist Expo, Balt, MD, 2001; United Nations (UNIFEM) Women's History Month, NY, 2002; Permanent Millenium Collection (NAWA), 2000. *Teaching:* Teacher art, Forman Hebrew Day Sch, Pa, 80-82; Philadelphia Sch Sys, 81-82. *Awards:* Second Prize, Am Color Print Soc, 91; Beatrice Feldman Mem Award, Abington Art Ctr, Pa, 91; Third Prize, Philadelphia, Sketch Club, Pa, 91. *Mem:* Philadelphia Art Alliance; Nat Asn Women Artists; Am Color

Print Soc; Cheltenham Ctr Arts (bd mem, 82-90); Artists Cult Exchange (pres, 87-90); Nat Asn Women Artists, 2004. *Media:* Acrylic; All Media. *Specialty:* Fine Arts & Crafts. *Publ:* Auth, Best of Acrylic Painting, 97 & Creative Inspirations, 98, Rockport Publ. *Dealer:* Langman Gallery, Willow Grove, Pa. *Mailing Add:* 1003 Indian Creek Rd Jenkintown PA 19046

MILLER, F JOHN
PAINTER, MOSAIC ARTIST
b London, Eng, Apr 21, 29; Can citizen. *Study:* Ealing Sch Art, London, NDD, 50; Hornsey Col Art, London, ATD, 51; Emma Lake Workshops, Sask, with Clement Greenberg & Barnett Newman, 60-61. *Work:* Mus Quebec; Can Coun Art Bank, Ottawa, Ont; Concordia Univ, Montreal; Mus des Beaux Arts, Montreal. *Comn:* Mosaic murals, Govt Saskatchewan, Regina, 60-61, Catholic Church, Sask, 64 & Govt Nebr, 67. *Exhib:* Solo exhibs, Galerie Libre Montreal, 68 & Concordia Univ, 73 & 80, Espace 1428, Montreal, 88 Galerie Dan Delaney Westmount, Que, 88, Schorer Gallery, Montreal, 2001; Mus Art Contemp, Montreal, 67 & 69; Spring Show, Queen's Univ, Kingston, Ont, 69; Summer Show, Nat Gallery Art, Ottawa, 72; Recent Works with Rosemary Miller, Bishop's Univ, 94; John B Aird Gallery, Toronto, 95; Haskell Libr & Opera House, Derby Line, Vt, 96. *Collection Arranged:* Canadian Art Bank, Concordia Univ, Montreal. *Pos:* Dir design prog, NS Col Art, 63-65; vis prof art, Mount St Vincent Univ, NS, 63-65; prof painting, Concordia Univ, 65-96, chmn dept painting & drawing, 83-85. *Teaching:* prof fine arts, Concordia Univ, 65-96; prof emeritus, Concordia Univ, 96-. *Awards:* Prize Winner, Sask Arts Bd, 60; Prize Winner, Art Actuel au Quebec, Govt Que, 67. *Bibliog:* Guy Robert (auth), Art Actuel au Quebec, Iconia Press, 83. *Media:* Oil, Alkyd. *Interests:* Electronic Music. *Publ:* Illusr, Gammer Glover's Grammar, Fortune Press, London, 52. *Mailing Add:* 19 Mountainview St Stanstead PQ J0B 3E0 Canada

MILLER, (RICHARD) GUY
SCULPTOR
b Pittsburgh, Pa. *Study:* City & Guilds of London Art Coun, Eng, with Ennis Fripps, 58; Art Students League, New York, with Will Barnet & Robert Hale; Pratt Inst, Brooklyn, NY, with Calvin Albert, MFA, 65. *Work:* State Univ NY Col New Paltz; Pratt Inst, Brooklyn; New Sch, NY; Bennington Col, Vt; Long Island Hall Fame, Stony Brook, NY; and others. *Comn:* Stainless steel wall sculpture, New Sch, NY, 74; free standing stainless steel dual form, Sky Island Club, Plainview, NY, 79; free standing painted steel sculpture, Atrium, Jericho, NY, 85; free standing brass sculpture, Tower Apartment, Fort Lee, NJ, 87; brass wall sculpture, NY, 88; and others; free standing cast aluminum sculpture, Sedona, Ariz, 2000. *Exhib:* Cochise Col, Douglas, Ariz, 87; Copper Village Art Mus, Anaconda, Mont, 88; Missoula Mus Art, Mont, 88; Orr's Bailey Art Asn, Orr's Island, Maine, 89-92; Maine Arts Festival, Thomas Point, Maine, 92; AIDS Project, Ann Auction, 94-2000; and many others. *Pos:* Bd dir, Huntington Township Art League, 78; chmn, Orr's Bailey Art Assoc, 89-99. *Teaching:* Instr sculpture, Pratt Inst, Brooklyn, summer 64; prof art, Monmouth Col, West Long Branch, NJ, 64-65, prof sculpture, 66-69; artist-in-residence, Friends World Col, Lloyd Harbor, NY, 77-79. *Awards:* Tiffany Found Grant, 66; MacDowell Colony Found Fel, 68; Sculptor of the Year Award, Long Island Hall Fame, Sky Island Club, 79; and others. *Bibliog:* Discription of Sculpture, 11/86 & Clint Hagen (auth), Miller, 9/92, Time Rec; Brian Bixler (auth), Flotsam and jetsam, Fla Today, 1/91; Doug Hubley (auth), Art by Association, Times Rec, 7/98; and others. *Mem:* Art Students League, NY; Huntington Twp Art League, NY (bd dir, 78-81); Orrs Bailey Art Asn (chmn bd dir, 90-2000). *Media:* Stainless Steel; Lucite. *Res:* Sculptural habitat. *Dealer:* Marie Scott Palm Springs Calif. *Mailing Add:* 78 Prospect St New Paltz NY 12501

MILLER, HARVEY S SHIPLEY
PATRON
b Philadelphia, Pa, Sept 28, 48. *Study:* Swarthmore Col, BA, 70; Harvard Univ, JD, 73; Phi Sigma Kappa. *Pos:* Assoc, Debevoise & Plimpton, New York City, 73-75; mem, prints & drawings & photographs trustees adv comt, Philadelphia Mus Art, 74-, trustee, 85-, investment comt, 89-95, exec, develop & exhib comt, 93-96, chmn, 125th ann campaign, 99-2002; trustee, NY Studio Sch, 74-80, Univ the Arts, 79-86; bd dir, Once Gallery, Inc, 74-75, Wildlife Preserv Trust Int, Inc, 90-95; cur, dir, dept collections & spec exhib Franklin Inst, Philadelphia, 75-81; bd gov's Print Club, Philadelphia, 76-87; vis comt, on photog George Eastman House, Rochester, NY, 76-78; exec bd dir, Fabric Workshop, Philadelphia, 76-86; bd assoc, Swarthmore Col Librs, Philadelphia, 78-86; exec bd, Citizens for Arts in Pa, 80; treas, dir, Arcadia Found, Norristown, Pa, 81-; bd overseers, Univ Pa Sch Nursing, 81-, Edith C Blum Art Inst Bard Col, 84-87; assoc trustee, Univ Pa, 81-95; chmn adv bd, Inst Contemp Art Univ Pa, 82-84; vpres, Energy Solutions, Inc, New York City, 82-84; bd dir, mem corp, MacDowell Colony, New York City, 82-85; trustee, vchmn comt, on instruction Pa Acad Fine Arts, 82-91, trustee emer, 91-, chmn collections & exhib comt, 85-87; trustee, Milton & Sally Avery Arts Found, New York City, 83-, secy, 96-; pres, chief exec off, dir, Daltex Medical Scis, Inc, 83-86, dir exec comt, 83-94, chief operating off, vchmn, 86-91, pres, chief operating off, 91-93; mem, Mayor's Cult Adv Coun, Philadelphia, 87-91; mem collections comt, Hist Soc Pa, 91-93; chmn, Mayor's Art-in-City Hall Prog Philadelphia, 92-94; councilor trustee, 92-93; trustee, The Franklin Inst, Philadelphia, 93-95, Philadelphia Mus Art, 85-, exec comt, 93-96; trustees coun, Nat Gallery Art, Wash, 95-2000, 2001-; mem vis comt, photographs Metrop Mus Art, 96-, vis comt modern art, 98-; trustees' comt on drawings, Mus Modern Art, 96-, trustee, 2003-, Prints & Illustrated Books, 2001-; San Francisco Mus Modern Art, (mem photog accessions comt, 97-2002); mem photog accessions comt, San Francisco Mus Modern Art, 97-2002; mem vis comt, modern art Metrop Mus Art, 98-; adv bd The Highlands Hist Soc, 99-; arts adv comt, Fund for the Waterworks, 99-2001; founding mem, bd trustees, Maltz Jupiter (Fla)Theatre, 2001-; trustee, Arcadia Univ, 2002-; bd dir, Am Patrons of the Tate Gallery, 2003-; charter mem, The Drawings Group, Los Angeles Co Mus Art, 2003-; mem drawings comt, Los Angeles Mus Contemp Art, 2003-; bd trustees, Whitney Mus Am Art, 2004-, chmn comt, on drawings, 2004-; bd overseers, Hammer Jus, Los Angeles, 2004-; trustee, Ursinus Col, 2004-, Point Found, 2004-. *Awards:* Named 1st non-Russian recipient of Diploma of Merit, Russian Ministry of Culture, 2002. *Mem:* Fel The Pierpont Morgan Libr; Col Physicians Philadelphia; Am Bar Asn; Asn Bar of City of New York; Athenaeum, Libr Co Philadelphia; Am Philosophical Soc; Hist Soc Pa; Philadelphia Art Alliance; Union League of Philadelphia; Harvard Club New York City; Swarthmore Club Philadelphia. *Publ:* Auth, Milton Avery: Drawings and Paintings, 76, It's About Time, 79; auth, ed, New Spaces: Exploring the Aesthetic Dimensions of Holography, 79; coauth, Rapid Inactivation of Infectious Pathogens by Chlorhexidine-coated Gloves, 92; contribr, articles to prof jours. *Mailing Add:* 1110 Park Ave New York NY 10128-1201

MILLER, JOAN
PAINTER, COLLAGE ARTIST
b New York, NY, 30. *Study:* Brooklyn Mus with Gregorio Prestopino, 47; Parsons Sch Design; Tyler Sch Art Temple Univ, BFA, 52. *Work:* Butler Inst, Youngstown, Ohio; Slater Mem Mus, Norwich, Conn; Philadelphia Mus Art, Lending Libr, Pa; many private collections, US and abroad. *Exhib:* Group drawing shows, Cocoran Gallery, Wash, 53 & Brooklyn Mus, NY, 55; Nat Asn Women Artists, Nat Acad, NY, 65-80; 4-person invitational show, Port Wash Libr, NY, 70; solo exhibs, Graphic Eye Gallery, Port Wash, NY, 75 & 77 Phoenix Art Gallery, NY, 78, 81 & 83, Books & Co, 92, Donnell Libr, NY, 92, Southampton (NY) Col, 2002; Benson Gallery, Bridgehampton, NY, 86, 88, 90; Clayton-Liberatore Gallery, Bridgehampton, NY, 95; Parrish Mus, Southhampton, NY, 96; Gallery BAI, Soho, NY; group invitation show, Palazzo Vecchio, Florence, Italy; Gayle Willson Gallery, Southampton, NY, 2002. *Awards:* Cash award, Soc Painters Casein, Nat Arts Club, 69; Cash Awards, Ann Exhib, Nat Asn Women Artists; Award, Newyorkartists.net. *Mem:* Nat Asn Women Artists (graphic jury, 85-88); Painting jury. *Media:* Acrylic on Canvas, Collage on Paper. *Publ:* Reproduction of work in book Intaglio Printmaking Techniques by Ruth Leaf, Watson Guptill, 76. *Mailing Add:* 1192 Park Ave New York NY 10128

MILLER, JOAN VITA
MUSEUM DIRECTOR, ADMINISTRATOR
b New York, NY, Jan, 46. *Study:* Syracuse Univ, BA(art hist), MA(art hist); independent res in Italy. *Collection Arranged:* New York Eleven, 74; Louise Nevelson (auth, catalogue), 74; Gertrude Stein and Her Friends (auth, catalogue), 75; Wreck, 75; The Long Island Art Collector's Exhibit (auth, catalogue), 75; European Masters in Portraiture, 76; An Exploration of Photography 1839-1976 (auth, catalogue), 76; The Arts of China, 77; Marsden Hartley, 1877-1943, 77; Double Exposure: Alfredo Valente as Photographer and Collector, 78; The First 4000 Years: The Ratner Collection of Judaean Antiquities, 79; Realist Space, 79; African Sculpture: The Shape of Surprise, 80; Auguste Rodin, 80 & 81; Rodin: B Gerald Cantor Collection, Metrop Mus Art (auth, catalog), 86. *Pos:* Asst dir, Michael Rockefeller Arts Ctr, State Univ NY Col, Fredonia, 71-72; dir gallery & cur permanent collection, CW Post Art Gallery, CW Post Col, 73-80; dir, BG Cantor Sculpture Ctr, NY, 80-83, cur B G Cantor Collections, 83-89; mus & gallery mgr, CW Post Col, Long Island Univ, 76-80. *Mem:* Am Asn Mus; Col Art Asn. *Mailing Add:* c/o Dr Gary Marotta PO Box 41810 Lafayette LA 70504

MILLER, JOHN FRANKLIN
ADMINISTRATOR
b Hagerstown, Md, June 4, 40. *Study:* St Johns Col, Annapolis, BA, 62; Yale Univ, with Edgar Munhall, 65; Univ Md, with Ruth Butler, 69-72. *Work:* Hampton Nat Historic Site, Md; Stan Hywet Hall Foundation, Ohio. *Pos:* Resident cur, Hampton Nat Historic Site, Md, 72-75, admin, 76-79; cur of educ, Stan Hywet Hall Foundation, Akron, Ohio, 79-80, exec dir, 81. *Mem:* Am Asn Mus; Nat Trust for Hist Preserv; Am Asn State and Local Hist; Intermuseum Conserv Asn (trustee, 81). *Res:* European and domestic architecture of the late 17th and early 18th centuries and its influence in America. *Mailing Add:* Edsel & Elinor Ford House 1100 Lake Shore Rd Grosse Pointe MI 48236

MILLER, JOHN PAUL
JEWELER
b Huntingdon, Pa, Apr 23, 18. *Study:* Cleveland Inst Art, cert indust design; and with Baron Eric Fleming. *Work:* Cleveland Mus Art, Ohio; Mus Contemp Crafts, NY; The Fleischman Collection; Minn Mus, St Paul; Smithsonian Inst, Renwick Gallery, Washington, DC; Boston Mus of Art. *Exhib:* Int Jewelry Exhib, London, 61; Objects USA Traveling Exhib, US, Europe & Japan, 69; 15 Jewelers, Schmuck-Objekte, Mus Bellevive, Zurich, 71; Masterworks of Contemp Am Jewelry, Victoria & Albert Mus, London, 85; The Eloquent Object, Philbrook Mus, Tulsa, Okla, Traveling Exhib, 88; Am Craftsmen, Vatican Mus, Rome, Italy, 78. *Pos:* Gallery dir, Cleveland Inst Art, 60-81. *Teaching:* Instr design & jewelry, Cleveland Inst Art, 40-83. *Awards:* Gold Medal, Am Craftsman Coun, 94. *Bibliog:* Von Neumann (auth), Design and Creation of Jewelry, Chilton, 61; Graham Hughes (auth), Modern Jewelry, Crown; Wolters (auth), Die Granulation, Callwey, Ger, 83; Oppi Untracht (auth), Jewelry Concepts & Technol, Doubleday, 82. *Mem:* Fel Am Craftsmen Coun; Soc N Am Goldsmiths. *Media:* Gold, Enamel. *Mailing Add:* 9333 Highland Dr Brecksville OH 44141

MILLER, KATHRYN
PAINTER, PRINTMAKER
b Philadelphia, Pa, June 21, 35. *Study:* Univ NC, BA, 57; Ga Southern Col, 69; Savannah Col Art & Design, Ga, 79-80. *Work:* Waycross Junior Col, Ga; Savannah Col Art & Design; Marion Co Mus, SC. *Comn:* Delta Corp, Hilton Head Island, SC, 84 & 86; Mus Nat Hist, NY, 95. *Teaching:* Instr, Armstrong State Col, Savannah, Ga, 87-88 & Trenholm Artists Guild Workshop, 88. *Awards:* Second Place, Mandarin Art

Asn, 86; Award of Distinction, Tarpon Springs, 89; First Place Graphics, Atalaya Art Festival, 90 & 91. *Mem:* Ga Watercolor Soc; Southeastern Watercolor Soc; SC Crafts Asn; Savannah Art Asn; Hilton Head Art Asn. *Media:* Watercolor; Copper Etching, Oil. *Dealer:* Signature Gallery of Savannah 303 W Saint Julian St Savannah GA 31401. *Mailing Add:* 2 Stillwood Ct Savannah GA 31419

MILLER, LARRY
PAINTER, VIDEO ARTIST
b Marshall, Mo, 1944. *Study:* Southwestern Mo State Col, BFA, 68; Rutgers Univ, MFA, 70. *Exhib:* In the Spirit of Fluxus, Traveling Exhib, 94; The Multiple: From Duchamp to the Present, 871 Fine Arts, San Francisco, 95; The Gun, Icon of the Twentieth Century, Ubu Gallery, NY, 96; Fifteen Degrees from Rutgers, Rutgers Univ, NJ, 96; NEMO The Dream of New Man, Nikolaj, Copenhagen Contemp Art Ctr, 96; Dada Country: Duchamp and Friends in NJ, Hunterdon Mus Art, Clinton, 99; Off Limits: Rutgers Univ and the Avant Garde, Newark Mus, NJ, 99; Requiem, Living Artists Eulogize a Dying Century, Nexus Contemp Art Ctr, Atlanta, 99; and others. *Awards:* Creative Artists Prog Grant, 78; Nat Endowment Arts Artist's Fel, 79 & 89; NY State Found Arts Fel, 85. *Bibliog:* Jan van Toorn (ed), Fluxus Audio Issue, Slowscan Editions, Den Bosch, Holland, 92; Christel Schüppenhauer, Cologne, Ger, 92; Estera Milman (ed), Fluxus: A Conceptual Country, Visible Language, Vol 26, No 1/2, Providence, RI, 92; and others. *Publ:* Knives, 73; The Suitcase, 73; Discourse on All & Everything, 80; Accord, 81; Only One, 89; and others. *Mailing Add:* 107 W 28th St New York NY 10001

MILLER, MARC H
CURATOR, WRITER
b New York, NY, June 28, 46. *Study:* Univ Calif, Riverside, BA, 67; NY Univ, Inst Fine Arts, MA, 71, PhD, 79. *Collection Arranged:* Punk Art (auth, catalog) Wash Proj Arts, 78; Unforgettable Moments, ABC No Rio Gallery, 82; Television's Impact on Contemp Art (auth, catalog), Queens Mus, 86; Archit Models from the Last Decade (ed, catalog), Queens Mus, 87; Lafayette, Hero of Two Worlds (ed, catalog), Queens Mus, 89; Remembering the Future: The New York World's Fair From 1939 to 1964, Queens Mus (contrib catalogue), 89; Louis Armstrong: A Cultural Legacy, Queens Mus Art (ed Catalogue), 94. *Pos:* Prog dir, Art-New York, Inner Tube Video, 81-85; contrib ed, East Village Eye, New York, 82-86; cur, Queens Mus, NY, 85-91; mus consult, 91-. *Teaching:* Instr art hist, Sch Visual Arts, New York, 76-80; asst prof, St John's Univ, NY, 82-85. *Awards:* Smithsonian Inst Fel, 74 & 76. *Res:* 19th and 20th Century art reflecting broader political and social phenomenon. *Publ:* Auth, 25 years of Space Photog, Nieuwe Revu, Holland, 81; co-auth, ABC No Rio Dinero: the Story of a Lower East Side Art Gallery, Collaborative Proj, Inc, 85; The Panorama of New York City: A History of the World's Largest Scale Model, The Queens Mus, 90; Looking at Jazz, Cobblestone, 10/94. *Mailing Add:* 188 8th Ave Brooklyn NY 11215-2225

MILLER, MELISSA WREN
PAINTER
b Houston, Tex, Mar 3, 51. *Study:* Univ NMex, BFA, 74. *Work:* Mus Fine Arts, Houston; Mus Mod Art, NY; San Francisco Mus Mod Art; The Contemp Mus, Honolulu, Hawaii; Fort Worth Art Mus. *Exhib:* Solo exhibs, Melissa Miller: A Survey 1978-1986 (with catalog), Albright Knox Art Gallery, Buffalo, Contemp Art Mus, Houston, 81, Fort Worth Mus, Tex & Art Mus STex, Corpus Christi, 81; Whitney Biennial Exhib, Whitney Mus Am Art, 83; Biennial III, San Francisco Mus Mod Art, 84; Venice Bienniale, Italy, 84; Fresh Paint, Mus Fine Art, 85. *Pos:* Distinguished vis prof Art, SMU, 90. *Awards:* Nat Endowment Arts Grants, 79, 82 & 85; Anne Giles Kimbrough Award, Dallas Mus Fine Arts, 82. *Bibliog:* Susan Freuderheim (auth), Uniting art and allegory: The energetic paintings of Melissa Miller, Tex Homes, 82; Roni Feinstein (auth), Melissa Miller: The uses of enchantment, Arts, summer 84; Katherine Gregor (auth), Melissa Miller's Animal Kingdom, Artnews, 12/86. *Media:* Oil, Acrylic. *Mailing Add:* 167 N Tumbleweed Tr Austin TX 78733-3222

MILLER, MELVIN ORVILLE, JR
PAINTER
b Baltimore, Md, May 16, 37. *Study:* Md Inst Art, dipl, 59, Hon BFA, 96; studied under Jacques Maroger, Anne D Schuler & Earl F Hofmann. *Comn:* Paintings, Equitable Trust Co, Baltimore, 63-64; painting, Mercantile Bank & Trust, Baltimore, 82; 4 paintings, Transoceanic Cable Ship Co, 93; Floral Paintings for Collector Plates, Lenox Collection, 94-95; Baltimore City Hall, Baltimore City Coun; Warren Thomson, Newcort Capitol, Toronto, Ont, 98. *Exhib:* Corcoran Gallery, Washington, DC, 58; Butler Inst Am Art, Youngstown, Ohio, 63 & 98; Greenwich Workshop Gallery, Southport, Conn, 79-83; Kirsten Gallery, Seattle, 80-83 & 94-96; John Pence Gallery, San Francisco, 80-83; Foxhall Gallery, 83 & 94; Art in Embassies-25th yr exhib inclusion, Sierra Leone, Africa, 89; Foxhall Gallery, 96; 20 N Gallery, Toledo, Ohio, 97-98; Midwest Mus Am Art, 97-98; Evergreen House, John Hopkins Univ, Md, 98; Washington Co Mus Fine Arts, Md, 98. *Teaching:* Pvt classes, Conrad Miller Studios. *Awards:* Second Prize, John F & Anna Lee Stacey Scholarship Fund, 65. *Mem:* Assoc Oil Painters Am; Charcoal Club Baltimore. *Media:* Oil; Pen & Ink. *Dealer:* Foxhall Gallery 3301 New Mexico Ave NW Washington DC 20016; Bendann's Shops at Kenilworth 830 Kenilworth Dr Towson MD 21204. *Mailing Add:* 2001 Alto Vista Ave Baltimore MD 21207

MILLER, MICHAEL STEPHEN
PRINTMAKER, PAINTER
b Baltimore, Md, June 29, 1938. *Study:* East Carolina Univ, BS, 62; Pa State Univ, MA, 64. *Work:* Art Inst Chicago, Ill; Brooklyn Mus, NY; Philadelphia Mus Art, Pa; Springfield Art Mus, Mo; Joseph Heinz Corp, Pittsburgh, Pa. *Exhib:* Extraordinary Realities, Whitney Mus, NY, 75; solo exhib, Frumkin & Struve Gallery, Chicago, Ill, 83; 19 Print Biennial, 77 & 22nd Print Biennial, 80, Brooklyn Mus, NY; Site-Oriented Installations, Klein Gallery, Chicago, Ill, 83; Chicago Sculpture Int, Chicago Art Expo-Navy Pier, 83; Chicago Emerging Visions, Paine Art Ctr, Oshkosh, Wis, 85. *Collection Arranged:* VI Mostra De Gravura, Prints from Chicago, Curitiba, Brazil, 85. *Pos:* Chmn Grad Div & Prof Printmaking. *Teaching:* Instr printmaking, Middle Tenn State Univ, Murfreesboro, 64-67 & Southern Ill Univ, Carbondale, 68-69; asst prof printmaking, Univ Del, Newark, 69-73; prof printmaking, Art Inst Chicago, Ill, 73-. *Awards:* Artists Grant, Nat Endowment Arts, 79; DeWitt Award, 74th Chicago & Vicinity Exhib, Art Inst Chicago, 82; Visual Artists Grant, Ill Arts Coun, 86. *Mailing Add:* 1101 S Scoville Ave Oak Park IL 60304

MILLER, NANCY TOKAR
PAINTER
b Detroit, Mich, June 13, 41. *Study:* Chouinard Art Inst & Otis Art Inst, scholar, 56-59; Univ Calif, Los Angeles, AF, 64; Univ Ariz, MFA, 71. *Work:* Otis Elevator Co, Farmingdale, Conn; Nat Partnership, Los Angeles, Calif; Tucson Mus Art, Ariz; Pepsico, NY; TRW, Los Angeles, Calif; and others. *Comn:* Maui International Hotel, Hawaii, 75; Int Bus Machines Corp, Tucson, Ariz, 78; Western Savings, Tucson, 81. *Exhib:* Amarillo Art Ctr, 82; Stonewall Found Series, Yucson Mus Art, Ariz, 84; solo-exhibs, Elaine Horwitch Gallery, Scottsdale, Ariz, 81 & 83, Brooklyn Mus, NY, 86, April Sgro-Riddle Gallery Los Angeles, Calif, 87, Robischan Gallery, Denver, Colo, 89 & 93, Wade Gallery, Los Angeles, Calif, 91 & Etherton Gallery, Tucson Ariz, 92; and others. *Teaching:* Instr painting, drawing & design, Cambridge Ctr Adult Educ, Mass, 65 68; instr, Tucson Art Mus Sch, 72-78; vis artist, Ariz Western Col, 77. *Awards:* Purchase Award, Tucson Mus of Art, 78; Fel, Western States Arts Found, 75-76; Juror's Cash Award, Four Corners States Biennial, Phoenix Art Mus, 77. *Bibliog:* Sarah J Moore (auth), Arts Mag, 84; Contemporary Images I, Nancy Tokar Miller (catalog essay), Tucson Mus of Art, Ariz, 84; Robert M Quinn (auth), Fusion of East and West, Nancy Tokar Miller New Paintings, Art Week, 1/19/85; James Scarborough (auth), profile, Visions ARt Quart, fall 91; and others. *Media:* Acrylic. *Dealer:* Itherton Gallery 135 S 6th Ave Tucson AZ 85701. *Mailing Add:* c/o Robischon Gallery 1740 Wazee St Denver CO 80202

MILLER, NICOLE
ART COLUMNIST
Pos: "Arts Beat" columnist, Wash Post; visual arts columnist, for Sunday Source. *Mailing Add:* Wash Post 1150 15th St NW Washington DC 20071

MILLER, RICHARD KIDWELL
PAINTER
b Fairmont, WVa, Mar 15, 30. *Study:* Pa Acad Fine Arts; Am Univ, BA; Columbia Univ, MFA. *Work:* Edward Joseph Gallagher, III Mem Collection, Univ Ariz, Tucson; Hirshhorn Mus & Sculpture Garden, Washington DC; Rochester Mus Art, NY; Albrecht Gallery, St Joseph, Mo; Phillips Collection, Washington, DC; Watkins Gallery, Am Univ, Washington, DC. *Comn:* Painting, Plessey Corp, Gen Motors Bldg, NY, 71. *Exhib:* Pa Acad Fine Arts Ann, Philadelphia, 56-62; Whitney Mus Am Art Ann, NY, 60; Carnegie Inst, 62; One-man shows, Baltimore Mus of Art, 52, Graham Gallery, NY, 60, 62 & 63, Albrecht Kemper Mus Art, 1968, St Joseph, Mo, 69, Long Island Univ, 73, Westreth Gallery, 82, Aaron Berman Gallery, 83, John Jay Gallery, NY, 2000, 2 Westchester Gallery, White Plains, NY, 2000; Alternative Mus, NY, 81; 17th Ann Exhib, Nat Acad Design, 96; 47th Ann Exhib, Art of the Northeast, Silvermine Artists Guild, 96; and others. *Teaching:* Asst prof painting, Kansas City Art Inst, 68-69; adj prof painting & drawing, Westchester Community Col, 80-83. *Awards:* Gertrude Vanderbilt Whitney Scholar, Nat Inst Arts & Lett, 48-56; Washington Times-Herald Scholar, 47; Fulbright Fel, 53; Obrig Prize, Nat Acad of Design, 2004. *Bibliog:* Eunice Agar (auth), Richard Miller, Am Artist Mag, 88; Claude Marks (auth), Richard Miller, World Artists, 90; Theodore F Wolf (auth), Richard Miller, Christian Sci Monitor, 90. *Mem:* Nat Acad. *Media:* Oil, Acrylic. *Dealer:* Glass Art Gallery Inc New York NY. *Mailing Add:* 222 W 83rd St Apt 8C New York NY 10024

MILLER, ROBERT PETER
ART DEALER
b Atlantic City, NJ, Apr 17, 39. *Study:* Rutgers Col, BS & MFA; Cornell Univ. *Pos:* Exec vpres, Andre Emmerich Gallery Inc, NY, 75-77; pres, Robert Miller Gallery Inc, NY, 77-. *Awards:* Names one of Top 200 Collectors, ARTnews Mag, 2004. *Collection:* Collector of Art, especially old masters, 19th century painting; American abstraction. *Mailing Add:* c/o Robert Miller Gallery 526 W 26th St #10A New York NY 10001-5541

MILLER, ROBERT WARREN
COLLECTOR
Study: Cornell Univ, BS. *Pos:* Cofounder, Duty Free Shoppers, 60-97; founder, chmn, Search Group, Hong Kong, 74-; trustee, Asian Soc; co-chmn, Asian Fair, 97-. *Awards:* Named one of top 200 collectors, ARTnews Mag, 2004. *Collection:* Old masters, 19th Century painting, Am abstraction. *Mailing Add:* Search Group 909 Third Ave 5th Fl New York NY 10022

MILLER, RUTH ANN
PAINTER
b Columbia, Mo, Dec 7, 30. *Study:* Univ Mo, BA, 54; Art Students League, 55-56; studied with Esteban Vincente & Earl Kerkam, 55-58. *Work:* Dela Art Mus, Wilmington; Corcoran Gallery; Bryn Mawr Col, Philadelphia; Ndak Mus Art, 1993. *Exhib:* Ann-juried, Baltimore Art Mus, Md, 61; solo exhib, NY Studio Sch Gallery, 79 & 88; Vision and Tradition, Morris Mus, Morristown, NJ, 87; Colby Col Mus Art, Waterville, Maine, 88; Am Acad Inst Arts & Letts, NY, 89; Nat Acad Design, 167th

Ann, NY, 92, 93, 94 & 95. *Teaching:* Painting-drawing, NY Studio Sch, 73-; painting-drawing, Univ Hartford, Conn, 75-78; painting-drawing, Int Sch Art, Todi, Italy, 89; painting-drawing, Parsons, Grad Painting, NY, formerly; Parsons Sch Design, New York City, 1991-93. *Awards:* Ingram Merrill Grant, 81, 95. *Bibliog:* Robert Godfrey (auth), In Praise of Space, Art Dept Westminster, 76; Hearne Pardee (auth), Vision and Tradition, NJ State Coun Arts, 88; Andrew Forge (auth), On Ruth Miller's Still Life Painting, New York Studio Sch, 88. *Mem:* Bowery Gallery, NY; Wash Art Asn, Conn; Nat Acad (academician). *Media:* Oil, Watercolor

MILLER, TRACY A
VIDEO ARTIST
b Cincinnati, Ohio, May 23, 66. *Study:* Art Acad Cincinnati, BFA(painting), 90; Sch Art, Univ Cincinnati, MFA(electronic art), 93. *Exhib:* Interactive Experience, Inter CHI 93, RAI Cong Ctr, The Neth, 93; Mediatheque Lounge, ISEA 94, Helsinki, Finland, 94; Visual Surge, Studio San Guiseppe, Col Mt St Joseph, Cincinnati, Ohio, 94. *Teaching:* Instr media studios, Columbus Col Art & Design, Ohio, 94-; artist-in-residence media art, Southern Ohio Mus & Cult Ctr, Portsmouth, 95. *Awards:* Isabel Wolfstein Travel Grant, Univ Cincinnati, 93; Project Grant, Ky Found Women, 94; Individual Artist Fel, Ohio Arts Coun, 95. *Mem:* Int Animated Film Soc; Asn Independent Video & Filmmakers Inc; Col Art Asn. *Media:* Computer Based Interactive. *Publ:* Contribr, Multimedia CD-Rom, Siggraph 94, ACM Siggraph, 94; 1000 add One Frame, European Media Art Festival, Pool-Processing, 94. *Mailing Add:* c/o Columbia Col Art & Design 107 N 9th St Columbus OH 43215

MILLER, VIRGINIA IRENE
GALLERY DIRECTOR
b Tampa, Fla, May 29, 43. *Study:* Miami Dade Community Col, AA, 69; Univ Miami, BA in Psychology, 73. *Pos:* Art consultant, organizer, dir numerous art exhib for leading charities, financial instits, Dade Co, Fla, 69-73; owner, dir Va Miller Galleries, Inc, Coconut Grove, Fla, 74-84; pres, dir, MACH I, Metrop Mus and Art Ctr, Coral Gables, 79-80; owner, dir, ArtSpace/Virginia Miller Galleries, Coral Gables, Fla, 81-; guest lectr, Miami-Dade Community Col Ctr Continuing Educ of Women, 84, Univ Miami, 85, Fla Int Univ, 85. *Publ:* art writer Women's Almanac newspaper, 1978-79. *Mailing Add:* Artspace 169 Madeira Ave Miami FL 33134

MILLETT, CAROLINE DUNLOP
DESIGNER, ART DEALER
b Kansas City, Mo, Feb 14, 39. *Study:* Univ Edinburgh, 59-60; Univ Wis, BA, 61; Stanford Univ, MA, 63. *Collection Arranged:* Coordinator, US Contribution Sao Paulo Bienal, 73. *Pos:* Cult attache, Brasilia, 69-70; film dir, US Information Agency, 73; asst adv arts, Dept State, 74-80; adv arts, US Int Communication Agency, 81-; vpres, Philadelphia Col Art, 84-; pres, Millett Enterprises & Millett Design. *Teaching:* Assoc prof US cultural hist, Univ Sao Paulo, Brazil, 66-69; adj prof, Univ Pa, 92-2006. *Mailing Add:* 317 N 33rd St Philadelphia PA 19104-2549

MILLIE, ELENA GONZALEZ
CURATOR
b Greenwich, Conn. *Study:* Univ NC, BA, 64. *Collection Arranged:* Travel Then & Now, 70, The Paper Weapon (auth, catalog), 76, On View, 79 & American & European Posters (auth, catalog), 80; 19th Century American Book and Magazine Posters, 89. *Pos:* Cur, Libr Cong, 65-. *Publ:* Auth, Charlot, L'As des Comiques, 68, coauth, Tomorrow night, East Lynne, 80 & auth, Posters: A collectible art form, 82, Libr Cong Quart J; College poster art, Art J, 84; Jan Sawka, a Selected Retrospective (exhib catalog), Col New Paltz, NY, 89; The Polish Poster, 95; French Posters from World War I, 96. *Mailing Add:* Library of Congress First St & Independence Ave SE Washington DC 20540

MILLIKEN, GIBBS
PAINTER, EDUCATOR
b Houston, Tex, Dec 15, 35. *Study:* Scheiner Inst; Univ Colo; Trinity Univ, BSc; Cranbrook Acad Art, MFA. *Work:* Cranbrook Acad Art; Montgomery Mus Fine Arts, Ala; Serv League, Longview, Tex; Butler Inst Am Art. *Exhib:* San Antonio Artists, Witte Mus, 60-68; Tex Ann Painters & Sculptors, Witte Mus, Corpus Christi, Beaumont Mus & Dallas Mus Fine Arts, 62-66; Bucknell Univ, 67; Tex Fine Arts Comn, Hemisfair, San Antonio, 68; and many others. *Pos:* Asst, Univ Colo Mus, formerly; artist, photographer, asst cur, cur & head dept exhibs, Witte Mem Mus, San Antonio, formerly. *Teaching:* Instr painting & drawing, Cranbrook Acad Art, Bloomfield Hills, Mich, 64 & 65; instr art, Univ Tex, Austin, 65-69, asst prof, 69-73, assoc prof, 74-82, prof, currently. *Awards:* Grumbacher Award, Tex Watercolor Soc, Witte Mem Mus, 64, Naylor Award, 66 & Freeman Purchase Prize, 67; and many others. *Mem:* Am Fedn Arts; Am Asn Univ Prof; Men of Art Guild; Contemp Artists Group. *Mailing Add:* 434 Ridgewood Rd Austin TX 78746-5522

MILLOFF, MARK DAVID
PAINTER, SCULPTOR
b Miami, Fla, June 19, 53. *Study:* Conn Col, New London, BA, 75; Md Inst Col Art, MFA(painting), 77. *Work:* Fogg Mus, Harvard Univ, Cambridge, Mass; Minneapolis Art Inst; Atlantic Richfield, Los Angeles; Chase Manhattan Bank, NY; Prudential Insurance Co; Berkshire Mus, Pittsfield, Mass. *Exhib:* Aviary, Mus Mod Art, NY, 82; Fel Winners Exhib, Rose Art Mus, Brandeis Univ, Waltham, Mass, 82; Dogs, Chicago Mus Contemp Art, 83 & Hood Mus, Dartmouth Col, Hanover, NH, 84; Drawing, Minneapolis Art Inst, 83; Inaugural Exhib, Dog Mus Am, NY, 83; Contemp Drawing, Brockton Mus Art, Mass, 85; retrospective, Berkshire Mus, Pittsfield, Mass, 86; The Clocktower, NY, 86. *Awards:* Mass Coun Drawing Fel, 82; Nat Endowment Arts Fel Sculpture, 84. *Bibliog:* Jon Friedman (auth), Reinventing the heroic: The work of Mark David Milloff, 12/81 & Lisa Peters (auth), Mark Milloff, 5/83, Arts Mag; Christine Temin (auth), Perspective, Boston Globe, 10/10/85. *Media:* Pastels, Oils. *Dealer:* Stux Gallery 411 West Broadway New York NY

MILLS, AGNES
PRINTMAKER, SCULPTOR
b New York, NY. *Study:* Cooper Union Art Sch, dipl; Pratt Inst, BFA; NY Univ Sch Archit; Art Students League; Design Lab; studied with Raphael Soyer, Chaim Gross, Yasuo Kuniyoshi, Ruth Leaf, Harry Gottlieb, Krishna Reddy & Betty Holliday. *Work:* Libr Performing Arts, Friends Tampa Ballet; Univ Maine, Amhurst; Calif Sch Arts & Crafts, Oakland; C W Post Col; Lincoln Ctr Performing Arts; Boca Raton Mus Art. *Comn:* Mural, Wakefield Collection, Long Beach, Calif; Portraits Inc, NY; Family Portrait, Grand Collection, 92. *Exhib:* Seattle Art Mus Ann, 74; Friends Tampa Ballet, 82; Deja Vu Gallery, 90; Works in Progress, 92; Boca Raton Mus, 92; and others. *Pos:* Art dir, Mills Agency Inc. *Teaching:* Art coordr & art instr, NShore Community Art Ctr, Great Neck, NY, 57-82. *Awards:* First Prize in Printmaking, Washington Miniature Prints & Sculpture, 70; Purchase Prize, Hunterdon Co Art Mus, 72; Purchase Award, Nassau Community Col, 74; Purchase Prize, Nat Asn Women Artists, 81; Goldie Paley Award, 82. *Bibliog:* Article, Art News Mag, Oct, 81; New York Times, Mar, 81; Playbill, City Ctr Theatre, Mar, 81; Palm Beach Post, 3/91. *Mem:* Print Club; Nat Asn Women Artists; Artists Equity. *Media:* Color Etching, Cast Paper; Colograph, Monoprint. *Dealer:* Nuance Gallery Tampa FL 33609. *Mailing Add:* 1070 SW 22nd Ave No 3 Delray Beach FL 33445

MILLS, FREDERICK VAN FLEET
DESIGNER, EDUCATOR
b Bremen Fairfield, Ohio, June 5, 25. *Study:* Ohio State Univ, BS, 49; Ind Univ, MS, 51, EdD, 56. *Work:* City Vladimir, Russia; City Asahikawa, Hokkaido, Japan; Co of McLean; City of Bloomington; Town of Normal. *Comn:* Collectible ornament, State Farm Insurance Co Corp Hq & Northern Calif Regional Off; watercolor printed on VISA credit card, second watercolor, McLean Co Corp Off (limited ed), First Am Bank, Ill; collectible ornament, Easter Seal Asn, 90, 91 & 92; watercolor paintings, Diamond Star Motors Corp, 90 & 93; two watercolor paintings, Kemper Financial Securities/Kemper Financial Fund, 93. *Exhib:* One-man exhibs, McLean Co Arts Ctr, Bloomington, Lincoln Col, Ill & Ill Agriculture Asn Credit Union Art Exhib Series, Bloomington; permanent display, Wonderlin Gallery, Normal, Ill; Suzette Schochet Gallery, Newport, RI. *Pos:* Ed, Western Arts Bull, 58-62; mem res comt, Nat Sch Art & Design, Tenn Arts Comn, 67-78, Nat Alliance Arts Educ/Kennedy Ctr, 75-77; res reader humanities, HEW, 68-69; chmn, Major Gifts Comt, Normal Theater Restoration Proj, Normal, Ill, 68-; charter mem & sr res ed bd dir, Nat Coun Art Adminr, 73-81; instnl deleg, Nat Asn Sch Art, 74-84, res comt, 76-77; pres, Ill Alliance Arts Educ, 75-77, Ill Task Force Arts Educ Gen Educ, 76-77; resource person arts, Educ & Am Panel Rockefeller Report, Coming to our Senses, Am Coun Arts in Educ, 77-78; bd dir & vpres, McLean Co Arts Ctr, Bloomfield, 80-90; consult, Latin Am Scholar Prog in Brazil, Harvard Univ, 81-82; bd dir & co founder, Sugar Creek Arts Festival, Normal, Ill, 85-; charter mem & vpres bd trustees, Ill Summer Sch Arts, vpres Sch Found Bd, 88-94. *Teaching:* Prof art & art educ & chmn dept art educ, Ind Univ, Bloomington, 59-65; vis prof, Univ Tex, Austin, 65; chmn dept related arts, crafts & interior design, Univ Tenn, Knoxville, 66-68; prof art & chmn dept, Ill State Univ, 68-85, emer prof, 85-; prof art, Lincoln Col, Normal Campus, 86-. *Awards:* Outstanding Serv Award, Ill Alliance Arts Educ, 84; Excellence in Teaching Award, Lincoln Col, 88, 89, 90, 91, 92, 93 & 94. *Bibliog:* Featured in the Pontagraph, Bloomington, Ill, 1/16/94; featured in Hudson Pub Libr, 94; featured in IAA Credit Union League, 94. *Mem:* Nat Art Educ Asn (bd dir, 63-64); Col Art Asn Am; Western Arts Asn (pres, 62-64); Ill Art Educ Asn; Nat Coun Art Adminrs (res ed, 73-81). *Media:* Watercolor, Design. *Publ:* Coauth, Politics of the Visual Arts in Higher Education, Nat Coun Art Adminrs, 79; The visual arts, creative, intellectual & political, Res & Info Bull, Nat Coun Art Adminrs, 79; The Visual Arts in the Ninth Decade, Nat Coun Art Adminrs, 11/80; Art faculty update, Arts Res Bull, Ill State Univ, 82; Status of art faculty, schools & departments, Arts Res Bull, Ill State Univ, 83. *Mailing Add:* RR 2 No 60 A Hudson IL 61748-9802

MILLS, LEV TIMOTHY
PRINTMAKER, DESIGNER
b Wakulla Co, Fla, Dec 11, 40. *Study:* Fla A&M Univ, BA(art educ); Univ Wis, Madison, MA & MFA; Slade Sch Fine Art, Univ London, Eng; Atelier 17, Paris, France, with Stanley W Hayter. *Work:* High Mus Art, Atlanta; Victoria & Albert Mus, London; Libr of Cong, Washington, DC; Bibliot Nat, Paris; Mus Mod Art, NY. *Comn:* Three glass mosaic designs, Ashby St Subway Sta, City of Atlanta, Metrop Atlanta Rapid Transit Authority, 78; atrium floor design, City Hall, Atlanta, 88; mixed media work, Atlanta Pub Schs, 88. *Exhib:* Slade Centenary Exhib, Royal Col Art, London, 71; Artists in Ga, High Mus Art, Atlanta, 74, 20th Century Black Artist, San Jose Mus Art, 76; Retrospective, Studio Mus in Harlem, NY, 75; Miss Mus Art, Jackson; Birmingham Mus Art, Ala; and others. *Pos:* Art consult & mem bd trustees, Art Festival of Atlanta Inc, 77-. *Teaching:* Instr gen art, Everglades Jr High, Ft Lauderdale, Fla, 62-68; asst prof printmaking, Clark Col, Atlanta, 73-78; assoc prof art, Spelman Col, Atlanta, 79. *Awards:* Outstanding Postgrad Fel, Univ Wis, 69; Europ Study & Travel Fel, Ford Found, 70; Bronze Jubilee Award for Cult Achievement, City of Atlanta, 78. *Bibliog:* Pat Gilmour (auth), Lev Mills, Arts Rev, London, 72; Lewis & Waddy (coauth), Black artists on art, Contemp Crafts Inc, Calif, 76; Samella Lewis (auth), Graphic Processes, Art: African American, Harcourt, Brace Jovanovich Inc, New York, 78. *Mem:* Nat Col Art Asn; Black Artists Atlanta. *Media:* Mixed Media. *Publ:* Auth, I Do, A Book of Etchings & Poems, Cut Chain Press, 71. *Dealer:* Assoc Am Artists 663 Fifth Ave New York NY 10022. *Mailing Add:* 3128 Valleydale Dr SW Atlanta GA 30311-3064

MILNES, ROBERT WINSTON
SCULPTOR, EDUCATOR
b Washington, DC, April 1, 48. *Study:* Claremont Men's Col, BA(philosophy, fine arts), 70; Univ Wash, MFA, 74; Univ Pittsburgh, PhD, 87. *Work:* Smithsonian Inst, Renwick Gallery; Erie Art Mus, Pa; Seattle Arts Comn; Nelson Fine Arts Ctr, Ariz State Univ; San Jose Mus Art, San Jose State Univ. *Comn:* Sculpture, comn by Mr &

Mrs Warner Bacon, Erie, Pa, 81; sculptures & wall mounted plates, Aqui Restaurant, San Jose, Calif, 97, 2000. *Exhib:* Solo shows, Theo Portnoy Gallery, NY, 79 & 80, Erie Art Mus, Pa, 83, Tercera Gallery, Los Gatos, 2000; Richmond Art Ctr, 2004. *Pos:* Dir, Sch Art & Design, San Jose State Univ, 1990-2005; Dean, Sch Visual Arts, Univ N Tex, 2006-. *Teaching:* Instr ceramics, Penland Sch Crafts, NC, 72 & 79; prof, Edinboro Univ, 74-86, art dept chmn, 81-86; dir, Sch Art, La State Univ, Baton Rouge, 87-90. *Awards:* Juror Award, Erie Art Ctr, 83; Jurors award, Louisiana Festival of the Arts, Mazur Mus, Alexandria, La, 90; Bautzer Development Award, CSU, 2003; Global Studies Fel, SJSU, 2005. *Bibliog:* Leo Nigrosh (auth), Ceramic Sculpture, 91; Po Zhou (auth), American Ceramic Artists Today, 98; Susan Peterson (auth), The Craft & Art of Clay, 3rd ed, 99; Dan Tom (auth), Heads for Thought, Ceramics Monthly, Sept 2000. *Mem:* Col Art Asn; Nat Coun Arts Adminrs; Nat Asn Sch Art & Design. *Media:* Ceramics, Copper. *Res:* Higher educ accreditation; arts programs. *Specialty:* sculpture. *Interests:* mountainbiking. *Publ:* The Impact of State Governing Board Policies on Fine Arts Programs in Post-Secondary Education, (dissertation), Univ of Pittsburgh, Pa. *Mailing Add:* 1800 Palace Ct DENTON TX 76210

MILONAS, MINOS (HERODOTOS MILONAS)
PAINTER, SCULPTOR
b Heraklion, Crete, US citizen. *Study:* Los Angeles Pierce Col, Woodland Hills, Calif, AA, 68; Calif State Univ, Northridge, with Fritz Faiss, Hans Burkhardt, Walter Gabrielson, Robert Bassler, Donald S Strong & Dolores Yonkers, BA (art), 70 MFA (art with honors), 72; Univ Wash, Seattle, with George Tsutakawa & Everett Dupen. *Work:* Calif State Univ, Northridge; Hellenic Cult Ctr, Long Island City, NY; Cypriot Consultate, Young Broadcasting Inc & Girsberger Inc, NY. *Comn:* St Demetrios Cathedral, Seattle, Wash, 75; Int Drawing Biennale, Cleveland Eng, 82. *Exhib:* Solo exhibs, Kreonides Gallery, Athens, Greece, 84, Cypriote Consulate, NY, 90; Stockton Nat 85, Hagin Mus, Calif, 85-86; North Dakota Print & Drawing Ann, Univ of NDak, Grand Forks, 87; Paper in Particular, Columbia, Mo, 89; 35th Ann Drawing & Small Sculpture Show, Ball State Univ, Muncie, Ind, 89; Rethymnon Munic AA Gallery; Melina Merkouri Cult Ctr, Athens, Greece; and many others. *Teaching:* Teaching asst sculpture, Univ Wash, Seattle, 70-71, instr, 71-72. *Awards:* Poncho Sculpture Award, Univ Wash, Seattle, 71; 3 Merit Awards, 5th & 7th Ann Nat Greek Art Exhib, Springfield, Mass, 87 & 89; and others. *Bibliog:* Ball State Univ Art Gallery (producer), Artists Forum Video, 89; Minos Milonas-Art is: 500 Definitions, 90; George Agelides (auth), No to the commerciality of art, Nat Herald, 90; Abraham Ilein (auth), The message is more than the medium, Art Speak, 90; George Tomko (auth), Minos Milonas emerges as a major abstract painter, Manhattan Arts, 90; and others; Minos Milonas-Multimedia Artist-Video Art Seen-Center for Visual Studies, San Francisco. *Mem:* NY Artists Equity Asn Inc. *Media:* Oil; Gouache. *Publ:* The Small Caravan, collection of short stories, Athens, Greece, 62; An Ode to my Ancestors, The Greek-Am Rev, New York, 89; Sunset Over New Jersey, Nat Libr Poetry, Md, 96; Gaining and Losing - A Manifesto, Mod Poetry Soc, Fla, 96; Celestial Quest - Best Poems of the Nineties, Nat Libr Poetry, Md, 96; 12 books of poems, 1990-2003. *Dealer:* Kenneth Raymond Gallery 799 E Palmetto Park Rd Boca Raton FL 33432. *Mailing Add:* 790 11th Ave No 39A New York NY 10019

MILTON, PETER WINSLOW
PRINTMAKER
b Lower Merion, Pa, Apr 2, 30. *Study:* Yale Univ, with Josef Albers, BFA, 54, MFA, 62. *Work:* Mus Mod Art, Metrop Mus, NY; British Mus, London; Nat Gallery Art, Washington, DC; Tate Gallery, London. *Exhib:* Primera Bienal Americana de Artes Graficas, Mus La Tertulia, Cali, Colombia, 71; one-man shows, Corcoran Gallery Art, Wash, DC, 72 & Drawing Toward Etching, Brooklyn Mus, 80; Extraordinary Realities, Whitney Mus Am Art, 73; Norsk Internasjonal Grafikk Biennale, Gamlegyen, Norway, 74 & 92; 4th Int Exhib Original Drawings, Mus Mod Art, Rijeka, Yugoslavia, 74; Frank Kyle Gallery, London; Inter Exhib Found, Traveling Retrospective; Jack Rutberg Fine Arts, Los Angeles, 2001. *Teaching:* Instr drawing & basic design, Md Inst Col Art, Baltimore, 61-68; instr printmaking, Yale Univ Summer Sch Music & Art, 70; artist-in-residence, Dartmouth Col, winter 1983, Rockefeller Found, Bellagio, Italy, 1990, Pasadena (Calif) City Col, 1999, Weber State Univ, Ogden, Utah, 2004. *Awards:* Rockefeller Found Residency, Bellagio, Italy; Medal of Honor, Lvov, USSR, 90; Exequo Award, Graphic Triennial, Crakow, Poland, 91, 94, 2003; Commendary award Miniprint Exhib, Finland, 1998, Hon award Int Biennial, Varna, Bulgaria, 1997. *Bibliog:* Harriet Shapiro (auth), All realism is visionary: A reach into the ambiguous realm of Peter Milton, Intellectual Digest, 11/72; Piri Halasz (auth), The metaphysical games of Peter Milton, Art News, 12/74; Kneeland McKnulty (auth), Peter Milton: Complete Etchings 1960-1976, Impressions Workshop Inc, Boston, 77; Theodore F Wolff (auth), What Links Duper & Milton, The Many Masks of Modern Art, 89. *Mem:* Nat Acad. *Media:* Etching, Engraving. *Dealer:* Franz Bader Gallery 2124 Pennsylvania Ave NW Washington DC 20037; Impressions Workshop 27 Stanhope St Boston MA 02116

MIM, ADRIENNE CLAIRE SCHWARTZ
SCULPTOR, PAINTER
b Brooklyn, NY, Feb 4, 31. *Study:* Brooklyn Mus Art Sch & Brooklyn Col, NY, 50; Hofstra Univ, 65. *Work:* Mus Section, Guild Hall, East Hampton, NY; Sculpturesites, Amagansette, NY. *Comn:* Murals, Southampton Col, NY, 69; Robert & Joan Tausik-Pinto, East Hampton, NY. *Exhib:* Parrish Mus, Southampton, NY, 69; Heckscher Mus, Huntington, NY, 77; Wards Island, NY, 80; Brooklyn Mus, 81 & 84; Fordham Univ, Lincoln Ctr, NY, 81; Soho 20, NY, 85-88; Benton Gallery, Southampton, NY, 86, 89 & 90; and others. *Teaching:* Asst instr painting, Parrish Art Mus, 66-67; adj prof sculpture, Southampton Col, NY, 73-74. *Awards:* Fel, MacDowell Colony, 72-74; Helen B Ellis Mem Prize, Nat Asn Women Artists, 80; Silver Medal, Audubon Artists, 80. *Bibliog:* Carrie Rickey (auth), Stalking the wild sculpture, Village Voice, 7/1/80; Vivienne Wechter (interviewer), WFUV Radio, 6/81; Alexander Russo (auth), Profiles on Women Artists, Univ Pub of Am Inc, page 181-191, 85; Phillis Braff (auth), Messages in on the edge, NY Times, 6/90. *Mem:* Fedn Mod Painters & Sculptors; Nat Asn Women Artists; Sculptors Guild; Soho 20. *Media:* Fiberglass, Steel; Oil, Mixed Media. *Publ:* Auth, Helicomodmim, pvt publ, 79; illusr, Area Sculpture: Ward Island, Artists Representing Environmental Art, 80; Sculpturesites, Roger Wilcox, 81; Appearances, Independent Publ, 12/81; illusr, Appearances, Independent Publ, 12/81. *Dealer:* Roger Wilcox Sculpturesites Box 534 Amagansette NY 11930. *Mailing Add:* 69 Skimhampton Rd East Hampton NY 11937

MIN, YONG SOON
SCULPTOR, EDUCATOR
b S Korea, Apr 29, 53. *Study:* Univ Calif-Berkeley, BA, MA, MFA, 79; Independent Study Prog, Whitney Mus, 81. *Comn:* Sculpture, Pub Art Fund, 88; sculpture, Creative Time Inc, 90; sculpture, Jamaica Art Ctr; sculpture, Univ Southern Maine; sculpture, Real Art Ways, 93; Percent for Art, NY, 93. *Exhib:* Committed to Print, traveling, Mus Mod Art, NY, 88; Pub Art Fund, City Hall Park, NY, 88; Creative Time, Art in the Anchorage, Brooklyn, NY, 90; The Decade Show, New Mus, Mus Contemp Hispanic Arts & Studio Mus Harlem, 90; Across the Pacific, Queens Mus, NY & Kumho Mus, Seoul, Korea, 93-94; Asia/Am: Identities in Contemp Asian Am Art, The Asia Soc, NY, 94; solo exhib with Allan deSouza, Camerawork, London, 94; Plan: Photog Los Angeles Now, Los Angeles Co Mus Art, 95; Thinking Print, Mus Mod Art, 96; Crossing Over/Changing Places, Corcoran Gallery Art, Washington, DC, 97; Thinking Print: Books to Billboards, Henry Art Gallery, Seattle, Wash, 98; All You Can Eat, City Market, Los Angeles, 98; Not on Any Map, Betty Rymer Gallery, Sch Art Inst, Chicago, 99. *Collection Arranged:* Mus Modern Art, NYC. *Teaching:* Instr printmaking & drawing, Univ Ohio, 81-84; asst prof arts, Univ Calif, Irvine, 93-99, assoc prof studio art, 99-. *Awards:* Artists Fel Grant, Nat Endowment Arts, 89-90; Bellagio Res, Rockefeller Found, 97; Fac Res Award, Univ Calif, Irvine Sch Art, 97-98. *Bibliog:* Shirley Hune (ed), Asian Americans: Comparative & Global Perspectives, Wash State Univ Press; Arlene Raven (ed), New Feminist Criticism, HarperCollins, 94; Elaine Kim (ed), Writing Self Writing Nation, Third Women Press, 94. *Mem:* Asian Am Arts Alliance (bd mem, 87-); Artist Space (bd mem, 91-); Women's Caucus for Art (bd mem, 92-). *Media:* Glass, Mirror, Photo-based Imagery, Paper. *Publ:* Auth, DMZ XING (exhib catalog), Real Art Ways & Smith Col Mus Art, 94; Fermenting Kimchi (exhib catalog), Korean Am Mus, 98; Fermenting Kimchi (exhib catalog), Korean Am Mus, 98. *Mailing Add:* 8518 Saturn St Los Angeles CA 90035

MINDICH, ERIC
PATRON
Pos: Sr exec, ptrn, Goldman Sachs Group, Inc; founder, Eton Park Capital Mgt, 2005-; leadership coun, New Am Found; trustee, Whitney Mus Am Art. *Mailing Add:* Eton Park Capital Mgt 825 Third Ave New York NY 10022

MINEAR, BETH
WEAVER, TAPESTRY ARTIST
b Evanston, Ill, Aug 31, 39. *Study:* Skidmore Col. *Work:* Nat Inst Health, Bethesda, Md; Sulzer-Ruti Corp, Switz. *Comn:* Wall rug, Sulzer-Ruti Corp, Switz, 85, 87 & 96; wall rug, Scribner, Hall & Thompson, Washington, 88; and many pvt comns. *Exhib:* Philadelphia Craft Show, Pa, 87 & 89; Am Craft at the Armory, NY, 88 & 89; Washington Craft Show, 88 & 93; traveling mus show, Art that Works: The Decorative Arts of the Eighties, 90-93; Creative Arts Ctr Fiber Show, Chatham, Mass, 96; and others. *Awards:* Merit Award, Guild Am Crafts Awards, 87; Grant, DC Comn Arts & Humanities, 92. *Bibliog:* Bill Henry (auth), Artist profile, Hill Rag, 88; Maryann Ondovcsik (auth), Artist profile, Matter Mag, 90. *Mem:* Cape Mus Fine Arts, Dennis, Mass; Creative Arts Ctr, Chatham, Mass; Am Crafts Coun, NY. *Media:* Fiber. *Mailing Add:* PO Box 2165 Orleans MA 02653-6165

MINGWEI, LEE
PAINTER, ARTIST
b Taichung, Taiwan, 64. *Study:* Yale Univ, MFA. *Work:* Isabella Steward Gardner Mus, Boston, Cleveland Mus Art, Mus Modern Art, NY, Whitney Biennial, Whitney Mus Am Art, 2004. *Mailing Add:* c/o Lombard-Freid Fine Arts 531 West 26th St New York NY 10001

MINICK, ROGER
PHOTOGRAPHER, WRITER
b Ramona, Okla, July 13, 44. *Study:* Univ Calif, Berkeley, BA(hist), 69; Univ Calif, Davis, FMA, 86. *Work:* Mus Mod Art, Metropolitan Mus Art, NY; San Francisco Mus Mod Art; Los Angeles Co Mus Art; Houston Mus Fine Arts. *Comn:* Photo Survey, Nat Endowment Arts, 77, 78 & 80; Paramount Theater, Lancaster-Miller, Berkeley, 82. *Exhib:* Solo shows include Delta and Ozark Photographs, Friends of Photography, 71, Delta Photos, Int Ctr Photog, NY, 75, Ozark Photographs, Univ Art Mus, 75, Hunter Mus Art, Tenn, 75, Sightseers Series, Grapestake Gallery, San Francisco, Calif, 81, Jan Kesner Gallery, 97, 2000; Am Photogrs and National Parks, Corcoran Gallery, 81, Amon Carter Mus, Ft Worth, 82 & Los Angeles Co Mus Art, 83; Espejo: Photographs of the Mexican-American Community, Ctr Creative Photog, Tucson, 83; Photog in Calif: '45 to 80, San Francisco Mus Mod Art, 84 & Ctr Georges Pompidou, Paris, 85; Jan Kesner Gallery, LA, 96, 97, 98, 99; Yancey Richardson Gallery, NY, 98; LA County Mus Art, Calif, 2000; Friends of Photography, San Francisco, 2001; Oakland Mus, Calif, 2001; Mus Photographic Arts, San Diego, 85, 2004; George Eastman House, Rochester, NY, 2004. *Teaching:* Dir & instr photog, Asn Students Univ Calif Studio, Berkeley, 66-75; instr, Ansel Adams Workshop, Yosemite, 74, 75, 76 & 82, Owens Valley Workshop, Sacramento Delta, Calif, 79 & 81; instr photog, Acad Art Col, San Francisco, 86-. *Awards:* Am Inst Graphic Arts Award, New York, 70; Guggenheim Fel, 72; Nat Endowment Arts Grant, 77, 78, 80; Gyorgy Kepes Grant in

Photography, 88. *Bibliog:* A D Coleman (auth), Light Readings, Oxford Univ Press, 79; Hal Fischer (auth), article, Art Forum, summer 81. *Publ:* Auth, Delta West: Land and People of Sacramento-San Joaquin Delta, 69 & Hills of Home: Rural Ozarks of Arkansas, 75, Scrimshaw Press; contribr, American Photographers & the National Parks, Viking Press, 81; auth, Paramount Theater, Lancaster-Miller, 82; coauth, In the Fields, Harvest Press, 82

MINISCI, BRENDA (EILEEN)
SCULPTOR, CERAMIST
b Gowanda, NY, June 15, 39. *Study:* Study in Rome, Italy, 60-61, RI Sch Design, BFA, 61; Cranbrook Acad of Art, Bloomfield Hills, Mich, MFA, 64; Provincetown Fine Arts Workshop, with Harry Hollander. *Work:* Everson Mus, Syracuse, NY; Fitchburg Art Mus, Mass; Univ Mass, Amherst; Antonio Prieto Mem Collection, Mills Col, Oakland, Calif; N Adams State Col, Mass. *Comn:* Fiberglass fountain sculpture, Murray D Lincoln Campus Ctr & clear cast polyester resin sculpture, Hampden Dining Commons, Univ Mass, Amherst; ceramic relief panels, Burnside Bldg, Worcester, Mass, 62; welded steel sculpture, Mercantile Trust Co, St Louis, Mo, 65-66; and others. *Exhib:* Wit & Whimsey in Am Art, Cranbrook Art Mus, Bloomfield Hills, 63; Craftsmen of the East (traveling exhib), Mus Contemp Crafts, NY & Smithsonian Inst, Washington, DC, 64-65; Nat Ceramic Exhib, Everson Mus, Syracuse, 64 & 68; G W V Smith Mus Nat Exhib, Springfield, Mass, 70-72; Seven Sculptors, Boston City Hall Galleries, Mass, 74; and others. *Teaching:* Instr ceramics, Craft Ctr, Worcester, 61-62; instr ceramics & sculpture, Univ Mass, Amherst, 67-71; instr ceramics & sculpture, Williston-Northampton Sch, Easthampton, Mass, 71-; instr ceramics & sculpture, Summer Grad Sch, Wesleyan Univ, Conn, 75. *Awards:* First Prize for Bronze Sculpture, 52nd Nat Exhib, G W V Smith Mus & Springfield Art League, 71; Juror's Award for Sculpture, Providence RI Art Club, 71; Purchase Prize for Sculpture, 22nd Exhib Painting & Sculpture, Berkshire Mus, N Adams Col, 73. *Mem:* Am Crafts Coun, Northeast Assembly (treas, 73-75); Nat Coun on Educ for the Ceramic Arts; Boston Visual Artists Union; Int Sculpture Ctr. *Media:* Multimedia

MINKOWITZ, NORMA
SCULPTOR
b New York, NY, Oct 19, 37. *Study:* Cooper Union Art Sch, 58. *Hon Degrees:* Fel, Am Crafts Council. *Work:* Nat Mus Art/Renwick Gallery Smithsonian Inst, Washington, DC; Am Craft Mus & Metrop Mus Art, NY; Wadsworth Antheneum, Hartford, Conn; Erie Art Mus, Pa; Charles A Wustum Mus Fine Arts, Racine, Wis; Philbrook Mus Art, Tulsa, Okla; Mint Mus Art, Charlotte, NC; Kwan Ju Mus, Koroa, De Cordora; Contemp Mus, Honolulu, HI; Detroit Inst Art, Mich; Philadephia Mus Art, PA; Denver Art Mus, Colo. *Exhib:* The Tactile Vessel, Erie Art Mus, Erie, Pa, 88; Exploring the Figure in Sculptured Forms, Newport Art Mus, RI, 90; The Female Form in Contemp Art, Wadsworth Atheneum, 90; one-person show, The Body As Vessel, Bellas Artes Gallery, NY; Modern Design 1880-1990, Twentieth Century Art, Metrop Mus Art, NY, 92; 5th Int Shoebox Sculpture Exhib (catalog), Univ Hawaii, 94; Fiber Five Decades from the ACM, Am Craft Mus, NY, 95; Out on a Limb, Bellas Artes Gallery, Santa Fe, NMex, 96; 9th Int Triennial Tapestry, Lodz, Poland, 98; Weaving the World, Contemp Art of Linear Construction, Yokohama Mus Art, Japan, 99; Miniatures, Mus Art Design, Helsinki, Finland, 2000; US Dept State, Lome, Toga; Trienniala Form and Contents: Mus Für Angewandte Kunst, Frankfurt, ger, 03; Chicago Anthenaeum 2003, Mus Arts & Design, New York City; Fiber Art: Following the Thread, Smithsonian Archives Am Art, 02; Wadsworth Atheneum, Tradition/Transitions. *Collection Arranged:* Mus Art, RI Sch Design; M H DeYoung Mem Mus, Calif; Contemp Mus, Hawaii; Kwang Ju Mus, Korea; Mus Int Folk Art, Mass; DeCordova Mus Art, Mass; Detroit Inst Art. *Awards:* Artquest First Place Fiber, Artquest 86, Nat Competition, 86; Visual Arts Fel Grant, Nat Endowment Arts, 86; Purchase Award, Conn Comn Arts, 92; Named 100 Oustanding Conn Women, United Nations, 2000; Conn Comn on Arts Fellowship Grant, 02. *Bibliog:* Oral History Program Art News, Smithsonian Archives Am Art, 2002; Dottie Indike (auth), Nouvel Object IV, 9/2002; Portfolio Coll, Norma Minkowitz, Telos Art Publ, 2004. *Mem:* Am Crafts Coun (mem col fel); Conn Comn Arts. *Media:* Miscellaneous Media. *Res:* Smithsonian, Archives Am Art, Oral History Program, 2002. *Specialty:* fine arts. *Collection:* contemp art. *Publ:* contribr, Art News, Fiberarts, Surface Design; Sofa Catalog Essay, 2004; Sculpture Mag, 2005. *Dealer:* Bellas Artes Gallery 653 Canyon Rd Santa Fe NM 87501. *Mailing Add:* 25 Broadview Rd Westport CT 06880

MINSKOFF, EDWARD
ARCHITECTURAL FIRM EXECUTIVE
Study: Mich State Univ, undergrad; Univ Calif, MBA. *Pos:* Chief Financial Officer, Olympia & York; founder, chmn, Edward J Minskoff Equities Inc. *Awards:* Named one of Top 200 Collectors, ARTnews Mag, 2006. *Media:* miscellaneous. *Mailing Add:* 1325 Ave of Americas 53rd St New York NY 10019

MINSKY, RICHARD
BOOKBINDER, CONCEPTUAL ARTIST
b New York, NY, Jan 7, 47. *Study:* Brooklyn Col, BA(cum laude), 68; New Sch Social Res, 69-71; Brown Univ, MA, 70. *Work:* Victoria & Albert Mus; Hirshhorn Mus & Sculpture Garden; New York Pub Libr Rare Book Room; Nat Gallery Art; Getty Ctr; Metrop Mus Art; Yale Univ, Arts of the Book Coll, Art Inst Chicago. *Comn:* Leather & ivory binding for The Unicorn Tapestries, Metrop Mus Art, NY, 76; binding on Sha'arei Tefiloh, Donglomur Found, Villanova, Pa, 76; Program Book, White House, Washington, 77; binding for Buckminster Fuller's Tetrascroll, Universal Limited Art Ed, West Islip, NY, 77; Gracie Mansion regist, Gracie Mansion Conservancy, NY, 85; Brooklyn Mus Regist, 90. *Exhib:* one-man shows, Zabriskie Gallery, NY, 74 & 88, Allan Stone Gallery, 81 & Twining Gallery, NY 90, 25 Yr Retrospective, Harper Collins Gallery, NY, 92, Louis K Meisel Gallery, NY, 2002, Oberlin Col, 2002, Minn Ctr Book Arts, Minneapolis, 2003, Syracuse Univ, 2005; The Object as Poet, Renwick Gallery, 77 & Mus Contemp Crafts, NY, 77; The Artist and the Book, Dayton Arts Inst, Ohio, 78; Int Leather Arts Exhib, Sawtooth Ctr Visual Design, Winston-Salem, NC, 84; The First Decade, NY Pub Libr, 85; Bookworks by Photographers, Watson Libr, Metrop Mus Art, NY, 86; A Survey of Bk Arts, Queens Mus, Flushing, NY, 87; The Eloquent Object, Philbrook Mus, Tulsa, Okla, 87, Chicago Pub Libr Cult Ctr, Mus Fine Arts, Boston & Oakland Mus, Calif, 88, Va Mus Fine Arts & Orlando Mus Art, 89; Invitational Exhib, Benton Gallery, Southampton, NY; Book Making: Practical & Provocative, Painted Bride, Philadelphia; Completing the Circle: Artists' Books on the Environment (traveling exhib), Minn Ctr for Book Arts, 92; Redefing the Book, Brainstein/Quay Gallery, San Francisco, 95; Love, Arlene Bujeje Gallery, East Hampton, NY, 96; Legible Forms (traveling exhib); Legible Forms, Contemporary Art Ctr Va, 99; Not for Publication, Hillwood Mus, Long Island Univ, NY, 2001; Love and/or Terror, Univ Ariz Mus Art, Tucson, 2003; Beyond Reading: Contemporary Book Art, Ellipse Art Ctr, Arlington, Va, 2003; The Book at the Back of the Mind, Rutgers Univ, NJ, 2004; What's in a Book, Katonah Mus Art, 2004. *Collection Arranged:* Book Artchitecture, Watson Libr, Metrop Mus Art, New York, 85; The Bookworks of Tom Phillips, Ctr Bk Arts, New York, 86; The Effects of Time, Bookworks: London, Jean de Gonet, Ctr Bk Arts, NY, 87; Book Arts in the USA, Ctr Bk Arts, NY & nine venues in Africa & S Am under US Info Agency sponsorship, 90-92; Out of Bounds, Creative Arts Workshop, New Haven, Conn, 94; Open for Action, Ctr Book Arts, Minneapolis, Minn, 2003. *Pos:* Founder, Ctr Book Arts, 74, pres, 74-78, chmn, 74-82 & 2002-, cur, 85-86, pres, 90-98. *Teaching:* Instr book arts, Sch Visual Arts, New York, 77-. *Awards:* Nat Endowment Arts Fels, 77-81; Grant, Pollock-Krasner Found, 96. *Bibliog:* Ed McCormack (auth), From neo-conceptual to bodies, Artspeak, 4/21/81; Rose Slivka (auth), Richard Minsky, Arts Mag, 5/88; Caroline Seebohm (auth), Richard Minsky, At Home with Books, Clarkson Potter, 95. *Mem:* Ctr Bk Arts; Guild of Bookworkers. *Media:* Books; Gold, Gems. *Res:* Art & cognition; history of the bookArt movement. *Specialty:* BookArt. *Collection:* BookArt. *Publ:* Contribr, The decade: Change and continuity, Craft Horizons, 6/76; Innovation from Tradition in the Book Arts, Am Craft, 93; auth, Minsky in London, pvt publ, 80; Minsky in Bed, pvt publ, 96; American Decorated Publishers' Bindings 1870-1929, 2006. *Dealer:* Allan Stone Gallery 113 E 90th St New York NY; Zabriskie Gallery 41 E 57th St New York NY; Louis K Meisel Gallery, 141 Prince St NY. *Mailing Add:* 413 County Rte 22 Hudson NY 12534

MINTER, MARILYN A
PAINTER
b Shreveport, La, July 19, 48. *Study:* Univ Florida, BFA, 70; Syracuse Univ, MFA, 72. *Work:* Mus Mod Art, NY; Denver Mus, Colo; Deutsch Bank, NY; San Francisco Mus Modern Art, Calif; Mus Fine Arts, Boston, Mass; Mus Contemp Art, Los Angeles, Calif. *Exhib:* Solo shows at Tri Gallery, Los Angeles, Max Protetch Gallery, NY, 90, 92 & 95, PostMasters Gallery, NY, 95 & XL Gallery, NY, 97 & 98, San Francisco Mus Modern Art, Calif; group shows inlcude The Places of Art, Springel Mus, Hanover, Ger, 94; The Joy of Painting, Here, NY, 95; Thikning Print: Books to Billboard 1980-95, Mus Mod Art, NY, 96; Mona Hatoum, Lovett/Codagnone, Marilyn Minter, XL Xavier LaBoulbenne, NY, 96; Sex/Industry, Stephan Stux Gallery, NY, 97; Group Exhib #2, XL Xavier La Boulbenne, NY, 97; Alive & Well, Elizabeth Harris Gallery, NY, 97; Bathroom, Thomas Healy Gallery, NY, 98; Elbowroom, Third Link, Stockholm, 98; Photo Image, Mus Fine Arts, Boston, 98; Cloth-bound, Laure Genillard Gallery, London, 98; Salon 94, Fredericks Fraiser Gallery, NY; Whitney Biennial: Day for Night, Whitney Mus Am Art, 2006. *Teaching:* Instr painting, Sch Vis Arts, 87-. *Awards:* Nat Endowment Arts, 89; NY State Coun Arts, 92; Guggenheim Fel, 98. *Bibliog:* Pat McCoy (auth), Marilyn Minter: Disputed narratives, Arts Mag, 1/89; Bruce Hainley (auth), Solitary refinement, Art Forum, 1/96; Lisa Jane Young (auth), Cover Article, Art Review, 2005. *Mem:* Whitecolumns. *Media:* Enamel on Metal. *Dealer:* Salon 94 Thaddaus Ropac Paris; Baldwin Gallery Denver CO; Vogues & Partner Frankfort Germany; Adrehn-Schript Jenko Gallery Stockholm Sweden. *Mailing Add:* 152 Mercer St New York NY 10012

MINTICH, MARY RINGELBERG
SCULPTOR, CRAFTSMAN
b Detroit, Mich. *Study:* Albion Col; Ind Univ, BA; Queens Col; Univ Tenn; Univ NC, Greensboro, MFA. *Work:* Everson Mus Art, Syracuse, NY; Mint Mus Art, Charlotte, NC; RJ Reynolds; St Johns Art Mus, Wilmington, NC; Nations Bank; SC State Art Collection; Am Express. *Comn:* Sculpture, NC Arts Coun, Waterworks Gallery, Salisbury, 84; Capitol Ctr, Raleigh, NC; Cent Charlotte Asn, Charlotte, NC. *Exhib:* Mint Art Mus, Charlotte, NC; McKissick Mus, Columbia, SC, 81; Greenville Mus Art, SC, 81; Southeastern Ctr Contemp Art, Winston-Salem, NC; NC Mus Art, Raleigh; Clemson Univ; Columbia Mus, SC; Atlanta Arts Festival, Ashville Mus; SC State Mus. *Teaching:* Sacred Heart Col, 67-73; Penland Sch Crafts, 72; prof sculpture, design & metals, Winthrop Univ, 72-. *Awards:* Purchase Awards, Ceramics Nat & 8th Regional Piedmont Crafts Exhib; Purchase Award, SC, The State of the Arts, SC Arts Comn. *Mem:* Tri-State Sculptors; Int Sculpture Ctr; Piedmont Craftsmen Inc. *Media:* Multimedia. *Dealer:* Hodges Taylor Gallery 227 N Tryon St Charlotte NC. *Mailing Add:* PO Box 913 Belmont NC 28012

MION, PIERRE RICCARDO
ILLUSTRATOR, PAINTER
b Bryn Mawr, Pa, Dec 10, 31. *Study:* George Washington Univ; Corcoran Gallery Sch of Art, Montgomery Col, with Elliot O'Hara; also privately with Norman Rockwell. *Work:* Nat Geographic; Smithsonian Air & Space Mus; Smithsonian Mus Nat Hist. *Comn:* Team portrait of Apollo astronauts, Nat Geographic Soc; paintings of space futures, Look Mag, 69; mural, Antarctica, Nat Air & Space Mus, Washington, DC; stamp, Va Statehood, US Postal Serv; postcards incl Blairhouse, US Postal Serv, The Whitehouse, 89, Jefferson Mem, 89 & Washington, DC, Bicentenial, 91; and several other stamps. *Exhib:* Nat Ann Watercolor Exhib, Smithsonian Inst, 51 & 63; Robots to

the Moon, Hayden Planetarium, NY, 63; Artist & Space, Nat Gallery Art, Washington, 69; Space Art, Smithsonian Inst Air & Space Mus, 71 & Hudson River Mus, Yonkers, NY, 72; One-man shows, Acad of the Arts, Easton, Md, 72 & Metropolis Bldg Asn, Washington, 76; Int Space Art Show, Utrecht, The Neth, 86; Nat Geographic 100 Yrs Show, Soc Illusrs, NY, 88; Int Space Art Show, Madrid, Toledo, Seville, Barcelona, Spain, 90; Nat Geographic Art Show, Soc Illusr, NY, 2000; 5 Pieces in 100 Years of National Geographic Illustration, Norman Rockwell Mus, Stockbridge, Mass, Traveling thru the US. *Collection Arranged:* numerous one-man shows. *Pos:* Art dir illus, Creative Arts Studio, Washington, DC, 57-60; vpres art-design, Northern Sci Indust Exhibs, 64-66. *Teaching:* Instr illus, Marine Corps Inst, Washington, DC, 53-54; instr watercolor, Bethesda, Md, 81-82; instr watercolor, Pagosa Springs, Colo, 2002-2006. *Awards:* Award of Excellence, Int Edit Design Competition, 81; Award, Soc Publ Designers; Merit Award, Art Dirs Club; First Prize, Watercolor, Waterford Show, 86; Best Lodoun Co Artist, Waterford, 89, 90 & 95; 1st Place in Juried Exhib, Pagosa Springs, 2006; and others. *Bibliog:* Pierre Mion presents one-man show, Baltimore Sun, 72; Mary Runde (auth), Intensity brings detail to Mion's paintings, Star-Democrat, 72; Artist's cards get post office's stamp of approval, Washington Post, 89; and many others. *Mem:* Soc Illusrs; Int Asn Astronomical Artists. *Media:* Acrylic, Oil; Gouache, Watercolor. *Specialty:* Western Art. *Interests:* Travel; Model Railroading; Camping, 4x4 Wheeling. *Collection:* NASA, Smithsonian Nat Air & Space Mus; Nat Geographic. *Publ:* Illusr, The squalus is down, Reader's Digest, 68; All-girl team tests the habitat, 71 & First colony in space, 76, Nat Geographic; The Titanic, 86 & Mission to Mars, 88, Nat Geographic; Nile River Temples, 95; Populaton Supplement, Nat Geographic, 98; and many others. *Dealer:* Wild Spirit Gallery Pagosa Springs Colo. *Mailing Add:* 59 Cascade Ave Pagosa Springs CO 81147-9696

MIOTKE, ANNE E
PAINTER, EDUCATOR
b Milwaukee, Wis, Aug 31, 43. *Study:* Mount Mary Col, Milwaukee, BA, 65; Univ Wis-Milwaukee, with John N Colt & Laurence Rathsack, MS, 70 & MFA, 73. *Work:* Scripps, Howard Corp Hq, Cincinnati; Gilberts Commonwealth Asn, Reading, Pa; Deloitte, Haskins & Sells, Cincinnati; IBM, Los Angeles; and many others. *Comn:* Still life painting (publ as mus poster), Paine Art Ctr & Arboretum, Oshkosh, Wis, 92; Homage: Brooks Stevens painting and edited print, Milwaukee Chap, Young Presidents' Orgn, 93; Corporate Portrait (still life), The Jansen Group Inc, Milwaukee; Miller Art Mus, Sturgeon Bay, Wis. *Exhib:* J B Speed Art Mus, Louisville, 74; one-person shows, Dorothy Bradley Gallery, Milwaukee, 78, 81, 83, 85, 87, 89 & 91; Wustrum Art Mus, Racine, 69, 71-73, 93-2005; Yeiser Art Ctr, Paducah, Ky, 96; Tory Folliard Gallery, Milwaukee, Wis, 93, 95, 97, 99, 2001 & 2005; Charles Allis Art Mus, Milwaukee, Wis, 2004; and many other group and solo exhibs. *Pos:* Bd mem, Milwaukee Area Teachers of Art, 67-70; contrib ed, Midwest Art, 75-77. *Teaching:* Instr art, Mount Mary Col, Milwaukee, 70-72 & Layton Sch Art & Design, Milwaukee, 73-74; asst, Univ Wis-Milwaukee, 72 73; prof fine art, Art Acad Cincinnati, 74-92; adj prof, Milwaukee Inst Art & Design, 92-2005; adj prof, Mount Mary College, Milwaukee, Wis, 2005-. *Awards:* Nat Endowment Arts Vis Specialist Grant, Milwaukee Art Mus, 75-79; Nat Endowment Arts Guest Cur Grant, John Michael Kohler Arts Ctr, Sheboygan, Wis, 79; Ohio Arts Coun Fel, 80-81 & 88-89. *Mem:* Col Art Asn Am; Am Asn Univ Prof; Phi Kappa Phi. *Media:* Watercolor, Mixed. *Res:* Reverse glass painting research for the Milwaukee Art Mus & the Jon Michael Kohler Arts Ctr, Sheboygan, Wis. *Collection:* Am Bank, Beechwood, Ohio; IBM, Los Angeles, Calif; Miller Brewing Co, Milwaukee, Wis; The Univ Wis, Madison; The Charles A Wustum Mus Fine Arts, Racine, Wis. *Publ:* Contrib ed, Midwest Art, 75-77; contribr, Glass/Backwards (exhib catalog), John Michael Kohler Arts Ctr, Sheboygan, Wis, 79. *Dealer:* Tory Folliard Gallery 233 N Milwaukee St Milwaukee Wis 53202; Edgewood Orchard Galleries Peninsula Players Rd Fish Creek Wis 54212; Grace Chosy Gallery 1825 Monroe St Madison Wis 53711. *Mailing Add:* 4791 N Elkhart Ave Whitefish Bay WI 53211-1002

MIOTTE, JEAN
PAINTER
b Paris, France. *Study:* Ateliers Montparnasse. *Work:* Guggenheim Mus, NY; Cooper Hewitt Mus, Mus Mod Art, Smithsonian Inst, Nat Mus Design, NY; Bayrisch Staatsgoldesammlung, Munich; Mus D'Art Moderne, Paris; Ludwig Mus, Cologne; and others. *Comn:* Sculpture, Pub Sch Marcq-en-Baroel, France, 77; sculpture, Pub Sch, Orleans, France, 77; mural, rue Emile Zola, Paris, 91. *Exhib:* Kunstverein Cologne, 62; Kunst in Europe 1920-60, Cult Ctr Mechelen, 76; solo exhibs, N Mus, Singapore, 83, N Mus O/Hist, Taipeh, 83, Striped House Mus, Tokyo, Japan, 84, Seibu Mus, Tokyo, 90, Palais des Arts, Toulouse, 92, Mus Dunkirchen, 93 & Mus Les Cordeliers, Chateauroux, 94, Columbia Univ, Maison Francaise, NY, 1994, Mucsarnok Mus, Budapest, 1996, Wilhelm Hack Mus, Budapest, 1997, Nat Arts Club, NY, 1998, Mus d'Art Moderne et d'Art Contemp, Galeries Dufy et Mossa, Nice, France, 1998, Mus d'Art & d'Histoire, Fribourg, Switz, 1999, Jan van der Togt Mus, Amsterdam, 1999, Mus am Ostwall, Dortmund, Ger, 2000, Castle Prague, 2000, Mus Ludwig, Koblenz, Ger, 2000, Aboa Vetus Ars Nova Mus, Turku, Finland, 2000, Mus Contemp Art, Villa Heiss, Ger, 2000, Mus Brno, Czech Republic, 2002; Memoires de la Liberte, Ctr Poupidou, Paris, 91; Bard Col, Procter Art Ctr, NJ, 94; Musee d'Art Moderne et d'Art Contemporain, Nice; Wilhelm-Hack-Mus, Ludwighafen. *Teaching:* prof Tourcoing Beaux Arts, 1 yr. *Awards:* Ford Found Grant, 61. *Bibliog:* J L Chalumeau (auth), Fragment, Miotte Coll, Passeport, Paris, 90; M Pleynet (auth), Cercle d'Art, Miotte, Paris, 93; Karl Ruhrberg (auth), La Difference, Paris, 98; Himes, Pleynet, Tan Swie (auth), La Difference, Paris, 1988; M Pleynet (auth), Gimpel & Weitzenhoffer, 1988; C Himes (auth), SMI, Paris, 1977; A Verdet (auth), Keeser, Hamburg, 1996; C Morgan (auth), Guy Pieters, St Paul de Vence, 2000; Ingo Bartsch, Beate Reifenscheid (auth), Mus Ludwig, Coblence Mus am Ostwall, Dortmund, 2000; Kingsley (auth), Mus Turku, 2000; JC Lambert (auth), Mus Dunkerque, 1991; Mus Dunkerque, 1991; H Paalman (auth), Mus Amstelveen, 1999; J Yau (auth), Nat Arts Club, New York, 1998; H Gercke (auth), Mus Chateauroux, 1994. *Media:* Acrylic, Oil, Etching, Lithographic. *Dealer:* Chapel Art Ctr Cologne & Hamburg Ger; Galerie von Braunbehren Munchen Ger; Galerie Wild, Frankfurt; Galerie Helene Lamarque, Paris; Galerie Guy Pieters, St Paul de Vence; Galerie Walter Bischoff, Stuttgart. *Mailing Add:* 451 Broome St #6 New York NY 10013-2628

MIR, ALEKSANDRA
ARTIST
b Lubin, Poland, 67. *Study:* Schillerska/Gothenburg Univ, Commun & Media Studies, Gothenberg, 86-87; Sch Visual Arts, BFA in Media Arts, NY, 92; New Sch Social Res, Grad Faculty Cult Anthropology, NY, 94-96. *Work:* Whitney Biennial, Whitney Mus Am Art, 2004. *Exhib:* One-man shows, Life is Sweet in Sweden, Trixter, Gothenburg, 95, Pick UP (oh baby), Lyd/Galerie, Copenhagen, 97, City Forest (prototype), Tompkins Sq Park, NY, 98, Conspiracy Night, Swiss Institute, NY, 99, Gavin Brown's enterprise, NY, 2001, Corp Mentality, Lukas & Sternberg, NY, 2002, Naming Tokyo (part II), Swiss Inst, NY, 2003, Happy Holidays, The Wrong Gallery, NY, 2003, The Big Umbrella, NY, PS1 Contemp Art Ctr, NY, 2004, New Commission, Fundacion NMAC, Montenmedio, 2005; group shows, Empires without States, Swiss Inst, NY, 99, Democracy!, Royal Coll Art, London, 2000, COPY, Roth Horowitz Gallery, NY, 2002, The Twentieth Anniversary Show, Gavin Brown's enterprise, NY, 2003, Sandwiched, Jacob Fabricius, NY, 2003, Power, Corruption & Lies, Roth Horowitz, NY, 2004, Ca Earthquakes, Daniel Reich Gallery, NY, 2004. *Mailing Add:* c/o Andrew Roth 160 A E 70th St New York NY 10021

MIRAGLIA, ANTHONY J
EDUCATOR, PAINTER
b Militello Rosmarino, Sicily, Italy, Feb 10, 49; US citizen. *Study:* Cleveland Inst Art, BFA (painting), 73; Syracuse Univ, MFA (painting), 75. *Work:* Southern Alleghenies Mus Art, Loretto, Pa; Kenneth C Beck Center Visual/Performing Arts, Lakewood, Ohio; The Cabot Corp, Boston, Mass; Matsui Corp, Cleveland, Ohio; Nat City Bank Corp, Cleveland, Ohio. *Exhib:* The May Show, Cleveland Mus Art, Ohio, 72; Regional Juried Exhibition, Rochester Mem Art Gallery, NY, 75; Dedication & Inaugural Exhibition, Southern Alleghenies Mus Art, Loretto, Pa, 76; 40th Ann Mid-Year Show, Butler Inst Am Art, Loretto, Pa, 76; La Grange Nationa XV, La Grange, Ga, 90; Texas National 99, Austin State Univ, 99; National Juried Exhibition, Artforms Gallery, Philadelphia, Pa, 99; Concerning the Spiritual in Art, New Bedford Art Mus, Mass, 2000. *Pos:* acad adv Mediterranean studies, Univ Mass, 99-. *Teaching:* prof painting, Univ Mass, 75-. *Mem:* Mus Fine Arts. *Media:* Mixed Media. *Mailing Add:* 105 Gaffney Rd Dartmouth MA 02748

MIRAGLIA, PETER F
PHOTOGRAPHER
b Glen Cove, NY, July 11, 53. *Study:* Univ Rochester, BA (fine arts/photography), 76; Rochester Inst Tech, 73-75; George Eastman House, Rochester, NY, 73-75. *Work:* Baltimore Mus Art, Md; Calif Mus Photog; Dayton Art Inst, Ohio; The Print Center, Philadelphia; Villanova Univ, Pa; Phila Mus Art, Pa; PNC Bank; Lehigh Univ, Bethlehem, Pa; Rowan Univ, Glassboro, NJ; The Ctr for Photog, Woodstock, NY, Movavian Col, Bethelhem, Pa; many others. *Exhib:* Contemp Philadelphia Artists, Philadelphia Mus Art, 90; Beyond Aesthetics: Artworks of Conscience, Alternative Mus, NY, 91; Pennsylvania Photographers, Allentown Art Mus, 93; Focus 94, Ctr for Photog Art, Carmel, Calif, 94; Pittsburgh Filmmakers Gallery, 97; Biennial 98, Del Art Mus, 98; Int Competition, Print Center, Philadelphia, 2000; About Face, Del Ctr Contemp Arts, 2000; Pennsylvania Award Winners, Lancaster Mus Art, 2001; Krasdale Gallery, New York City, 2001; Phoenix Gallery, New York City, 2001; Print Center, Philadelphia, 2002; Univ of Arts, Philadelphia, 2002; Del Ctr for Contemp Arts, Wilmington, 2002; many others; JMS Gallery, Philadelphia, 2004; Allentown Art Mus, 2005; Villanova Univ Art Gallery, 2006. *Awards:* Artist Space Individual Artist Grant, NYC, 88; First Prize, Photo Review Nat Competition, 94; Nat Endowment Arts Visual Arts Fel, 98; Pa Coun on Arts Visual Arts Fel, 87, 97, 99, 2005; Finalist The Ctr for Documentary Studies/Honickman Book Prize in Photogr 2002, 2004. *Bibliog:* Anne d'Haroncourt (auth), Contemp Philadelphia Artists, Philadelphia Mus Art, 90; Jeanne Nugent (auth), Beyond Aesthetics: Artworks of Conscience, The Alternative Mus, NYC, 91; Burton Wasserman (auth), Peter Miraglia - A Photographer's Photographer, Art Matters, 2/94; Nela Principe-Nelson (auth), Portraits-interview with Peter Miraglia, Photographer's Forum, 2000; Helene Ryesky (auth), The Work of Peter Miraglia, The Photo Review, 2000; Dede Young (auth), About Face, Del Center for Cont Arts, 2000; D Dominick Lombardi (auth), Krasdale Exhibit Review, The Sunday NY Times, 5/27/2001; Victoria Donohoe (auth), Peter Miraglia, review with reproductions, The Phildelphia Inquirer, 2002; R B Strauss (auth), Peter Miraglia / DCCA, Art Matters, 2002; Edward Sozanski; (auth) Portrait of Kerala, The Philadelphia Inquirer (philly.com), 3/26/2004. *Media:* Gelatin silver prints, Chromogenic Prints. *Mailing Add:* 208 Catharine St Philadelphia PA 19147

MISHLER, JOHN MILTON
ARTIST
b Cairo, Ill, Sept 25, 46. *Study:* Orange Coast Col, Calif, AA, 1966; Univ of Calif, San Diego, AB, ScM, 1970-71; Univ of Oxford, Eng, Dphil, 1978. *Exhib:* Art of the State, State Mus of PA, Harrisburg, 1999, 2000; Annual Juried Exhib, Woodmere Art Mus, Philadelphia, Pa, 2000 & 2001; Ellarslie Open, Trenton City Mus, NJ, 2001; Non-members Exhib, Salmagundi Club, NY, 2002; Allied Artists Am, 2004; Nat Juried Exhib, Red River Valley Mus, Vernon, Tex, 2004; Ariz Aqueous XX, Tubac Ctr of the Arts, Tubac, Ariz, 2005; Nat Exhib, Calif Watercolor Assoc, San Francisco, Calif, 2005; Ann Exhibs: Audubon Artists, NY, Conn Acad of Fine Arts, 2005; Nat exhib, Okla Watercolor Asn, 2005; Nat exhibs: Acad Artists Asn, Mass, Chautauqua Center Visual Arts, NY, 2006. *Teaching:* Prof, Univ Mo, Kansas City, 1983-89; prof, Univ MD, East Shore, 1989-94; prof, Del Valley Col, PA, 1994-. *Awards:* Pres Award,

non-mem show, Salmagundi Club, NY, 2002; Best of Show, 18th Annual Juried Show, Louisville Art Assoc, Co, 2003; Winston Churchill Award Painting, Watercolor Soc, Mo, 2005; Ursus Abstract Award, Tubac Center Arts, Ariz, 2006. *Mem:* Mo Watercolor Soc (signature mem, 2005). *Media:* Watermedia. *Collection:* Robert Pierson private collection, 2004-2006. *Dealer:* Michelyn Galleries Doylestown PA. *Mailing Add:* 475 North St Apt 6F Doylestown PA 18901

MISRACH, RICHARD LAURENCE
PHOTOGRAPHER
b Los Angeles, Calif, July 11, 49. *Study:* Univ Calif, Berkeley, BA, 71. *Work:* Mus Mod Art, NY; Mus Mod Art, San Francisco; Metrop Mus, NY; Los Angeles Co Mus Art; Whitney Mus Am Art, NY; Nat Gallery Art, Washington; Mus Fine Arts, Houston. *Comn:* Photography, Am Tel & Tel, Washington, 78; Time Mag (cover), 7/4/88; High Mus Art, Atlanta, 98-99. *Exhib:* One-man shows, Ctr Georges Pompidou, Mus Art Mod, Paris, 79 & Mus Fine Arts, Houston (traveling), 96; Am Images, Corcoran Gallery Art & traveling, 79; Mirrors & Windows, Mus Mod Art (traveling), NY, 79-80; Beyond Color, San Francisco Mus Mod Art, 80; Whitney Biennial, Whitney Mus Am Art, NY, 81; Los Angeles Co Mus Art, 83; Honolulu Acad Arts, 84; 10-year retrospective, Friends Photog, Carmel, 84; Bravo 20: A National Park Proposal, Traveling exhib, Friends Photog, San Francisco, 90; Mus Contemp Art, Chicago, 97; San Jose Mus Art, 98. *Teaching:* Instr photog, Assoc Students Studio, Univ Calif, Berkeley, 71-77; vis lectr landscape archit, Univ Calif, Berkeley, 82; vis lectr, dept art, Univ Calif, Santa Barbara, 84 & Calif Arts, 91. *Awards:* Nat Endowment Arts Photog Fel, 73, 77, 84 & 92; Friends Photog Ferguson Grant, 76; Koret Israel Prize, 93. *Bibliog:* David Fahey (auth), Interview with Richard Misrach, G Ray Hawkins Newslett, 79; Carter Ratcliff (auth), Richard Misrach: Words and images, Print Collectors Newslett, 1-2/80; Irene Borger (auth), Richard Misrach, Exposure Mag, 80. *Publ:* Contribr, Graecism Portfolio, 83, Grapestake Gallery; auth, Desert Cantos, Univ NMex Press, 87; Richard Misrach: 1975-1987, Gallery Min, Tokyo, 88; Bravo 20: The Bombing of the American West, John Hopkins Univ Press, 90; Crimes and Splendors: The Desert Cantos of Richard Misrach, Bulfinch Press, 96; auth, The Sky Book, Arena Edits, 2000. *Dealer:* Fraenkel Gallery 55 Grant Ave San Francisco CA; Robert Mann Gallery 42 E 76th St New York NY 10021; Curt Marws Gallery, New York, NY; G Gibson Gallery, Seattle, Wash; Edelman Gallery, Chicago, IL; Jan Kesner Gallery, Los Angeles, CA. *Mailing Add:* 1420 45th St Emeryville CA 94608

MISS, MARY
SCULPTOR
b New York, NY, May 27, 44. *Study:* Univ Calif, Santa Barbara, BA, 66; Rinehart Sch Sculpture, Md Art Inst, Baltimore, MFA, 68. *Hon Degrees:* Washington Univ, St Louis, Mo, DFA, 2000. *Work:* Allen Mem Art Mus, Oberlin Col, Ohio; RI Sch Design Mus; La Jolla Mus Art; Louis Manilow Park, Governor's State Univ; Cincinnati Mus Art; Mus of Mod Art, NY; Guggenheim Mus, NY. *Comn:* Field Rotation, Governor's State Univ, Ill, 84; Laumeier Project, Laumeier Sculpture Park, Mo, 84; Study for an Entry, Danforth Mus, Framingham, Mass, 86; Southcove, Battery Park City, NY, 88; Art Ctr, Albright Col, Reading, Pa, 91; Des Moines Ctr, Iowa, 96; Univ Houston Athletic/Alumni Facility, 97; and others; Union Sq Subway Station, NY, 2000. *Exhib:* Sculpture Ann, Whitney Mus Am Art, NY, 70; 26 Contemp Women Artists, Aldrich Mus Contemp Art, Ridgefield, Conn, 71; Gedok-Am Women Artists, Kunsthaus, Hamburg, Ger, 72; Whitney Biennial, Whitney Mus Am Art, NY, 73; Waves, Cranbrook Acad Art, Bloomfield Hills, Mich, 73; Seven Artists, Inst Contemp Art, Boston, Mass, 74; Solo exhibs, Mus Mod Art, NY, 76, Fogg Art Mus, Harvard Univ, Cambridge, Mass, 80, Inst Contemp Art, London, 83, Danforth Mus Art, Framingham, Mass, 86, Archit Asn, London, 87, Harvard Univ Grad Sch Design, Cambridge, Mass, 90 & Freedman Gallery, Albright Col, Reading, Pa, 91; Women in Archit, Brooklyn Mus Art, NY, 77; Nine Artists: The Theodoran Awards, Solomon R Guggenheim Mus, NY, 77; Architectural Analogues, Whitney Mus Am Art, Downtown Br, NY, 78; The Minimal Tradition, Aldrich Mus Contemp Art, Ridgefield, Conn, 79; Drawings/Structures, Inst Contemp Art, Boston, Mass, 80; Whitney Biennial, Whitney Mus Am Art, NY, 81; Metamahattan, Whitney Mus Am Art, Downtown Br, NY, 84; The Artist as Social Designer, Los Angeles Co Mus Art, Los Angeles, Calif, 85; Making Their Mark: Women Artists Move Into the Mainstream 1970-85, Cincinnati, Ohio, New Orleans, La, Denver, Colo, Philadelphia, Pa, 89; New Photog 8, Mus Mod Art, NY, 92; The Second Dimension: 20th Century Sculptors Drawings From Brooklyn Mus, NY, 93; Art on Paper, Weatherspoon Art Gallery, Univ NC, Greensboro, 93; Differentes Natures, Art Defense Gallery, Paris, France, 93; Art as Machine, Artrax Gallery, NY, 95; More than Minimal: Feminism and Abstraction in the 70s, Rose Art Mus, Brandeis Univ, Waltham, Mass, 96; Laurance Miller Gallery, NY, 97; Mary Miss: An Artist Working in the Pub Domain, Roger Williams Univ, Bristol, RI, 2000; plus others. *Pos:* Adv bd, On View (J on pub art). *Teaching:* Sch Visual Arts, NY; Davenport vis prof archit, Yale Univ; Parsons Sch Design, NY; Cooper Union for Advancement Sci & Art, NY; Sarah Lawrence Col, Bronxville, NY; Hunter Col, NY; Pratt Inst, Brooklyn, NY; vis lectr, var univs, mus & art schs; resident artist, Am Acad Rome, spring 89; Univ RI, Kingston. *Awards:* Medal Hon, Am Inst Architects, 90; Philip N Winslow Landscape Design Award, Parks Coun, New York, 92; Urban Design Award (in collab with Studio Works), Progressive Archit Mag, 92. *Bibliog:* Ronald Onorato (auth), Illusive spaces: The art of Mary Miss, Artforum, 12/78; Deborah Nevins (auth), An Interview with Miss Mary Miss, Princeton, NJ, 85; Nancy Princenthal (auth), On the Lookout, Art Am, 10/86; Space exploration, Art News, 10/89; Karrie Jacobs (auth), Notes from underground, New York Mag, Issue: Portraits of the city, 12/96; Jan Garden Castro (auth), New territories: an interview with Mary Miss, Sculpture Mag, 7/99; Christian Zapatka (auth), An interview with Mary Miss, Quarterly Architectural Rev, 96, The Am landscape, Princeton Architectural Press, 95, Mary Miss, Molta Architettura, 96; Sandro Marpillero (auth), An interview with Mary Miss, Progres, Italy, 9/93, Pour projects by Mary Miss, A&U Mag, 12/96. *Mem:* Am Acad Rome (bd dir); Van Alen Inst (bd trustees). *Publ:* Auth, On a Redefinition of Public Sculpture, Yale Perspecta, 21, 84. *Mailing Add:* Box 304 Canal St Sta New York NY 10013

MISSAKIAN, BERGE ARTIN
PAINTER
b Alexandria, Egypt, Nov 6, 33; Can citizen. *Study:* Cornell Univ, BA, 59; Concordia Univ, BFA, 64; Bur Cartooning, dipl, 68. *Work:* Air Canada, Town of Montreal West City Hall, Can; Hamazkain Cult Asn, Toronto, Can; Mekhetariste Mus, Vienna, Austria; Inst Fur Armenische Fragen-Munchen, Munich, Ger; The Armenian Lib and Mus Am, Watertown, Mass. *Comn:* Painting, Comn by Town of Montreal West Centennial, 97. *Exhib:* Armenian Libr & Mus, Boston, Mass, 03; Un Printemps en Art, Musee Vaudreuil-Soulanges, Montreal, 93; Int Miniatures, Seaside Gallery, Nags Head, NC, 98; Winton Park, Fairfield, Conn, 95; Monty Stabler Galleries, Birmingham, Ala, 98, 04. *Pos:* Consult art show, Tekeyan Cult Asn, Montreal, 92-93. *Awards:* First Choice, Lambeth Art Fest, Ont, 89; Peoples Choice, Int Art Festival, London, Ont, 90; Seaside Gallery Hon Award, Int Miniature, 94. *Bibliog:* Sally MacDougall (auth), Ontario impressions, London Free Press, 88; Louis Bruens (auth), Qui Donc est Missakian?, La Palette, 92; Bernard Daoust (auth), The Fruit of Sharing, Parcours Arts, 95; Mary Ellen Riddle, Missakian - Jazz, The Coast - Art Beat, Nags Head, NC; James R Nelson (auth), Missakian puts energy in images, The Birmingham News, 2001; Nancy Snipper (auth), Artist jazzes up every canvas, The Chronicle, 2002. *Media:* Acrylic, Canvas. *Publ:* Auth, Paul Gaugin: Where do we come from?, Mag Art, 90; Group of seven-creators of Canadian art, Mag Art, 90; Clement: painter of time & space, Mag Art, 91; Henry Matisse: retrospective-Mus Mod Art, New York, Laurentian Mag, 93; Three Laurentians: three artists' view, Laurentian Mag, 93; auth, The Colors of Jazz, Art Bus Mag, summer 2005. *Dealer:* Seaside Art Gallery 2716 S Virginia Dare Tr Nag's Head NC 27959; Galerie Lamoureux Ritzenoff 1428 Sherbrooke West Montreal PQ Canada H3G 1K4. *Mailing Add:* 9 Northview West Montreal PQ H4X 1C8 Canada

MISSAL, JOSHUA M & PEGGE
ART DEALERS, CONSULTANTS
Mr Missal, b Hartford, Conn, Apr 12, 15; Mrs Missal, b Denver, Colo, Nov 25, 23. *Study:* Mr Missal, Univ Rochester, BM, 37, MM, 38; London Inst, Hon DM, 72; Mrs Missal, N Tex State Univ, BA, 44. *Pos:* Dirs & owners, Gallery M, Farmington, Conn, 70-76 & Missal Gallery Ltd, Scottsdale, Ariz, 76-85, Missal Art Assocs, Scottsdale, Ariz, 85-88 & Mesa, Ariz, 95-98. *Teaching:* Mr Missal, assoc prof interrelated arts, Wichita State Univ, 52-70. *Mem:* Am Fedn Art; Appraisers Asn Am. *Specialty:* Consultations. *Publ:* Mrs Missal, auth, On Collecting Art, Guest Informant, 76 & An Introduction to Printmaking for the Layman, 82; Mr Missal, auth, American art--the continuing boom, Art Talk, 12/81 & articles on art collecting, World Fine Art, 82-83. *Mailing Add:* 1742 W San Tan Chandler AZ 85224

MISSAL, STEPHEN J
PAINTER, INSTRUCTOR
b Albuquerque, NMex, Apr 23, 48. *Study:* Wichita State Univ, BFA, 70, MFA, 72; Marymount Col, 72. *Work:* New Britain Mus Am Art, Conn; Jefferson Federal Savings & Loan Gallery, Meriden, Conn; Ulrich Mus, Wichita, Kans; Ariz Pub Serv, Phoenix; and pvt collections. *Comn:* Packard Deli at the Borgata (mural), 89; Shakespeare Festival (mural), Scottsdale Ctr Arts, 82; Jed Nolans (mural), Scottsdale, 82. *Exhib:* 9th Ann Ark Competition, Pine Bluff, 76; Festival 8, Scottsdale Ctr Arts, Ariz, 85; Springfield Mus Art, Nat Competitive Exhib, Utah, 85; Wilde Meyer Gallery, Nat Competitive Exhib, Scottsdale, Ariz, 87; Nat Forest Serv Centennial Competitive Exhib (touring), 91; Wyoming Wildlife Stamp Contest Exhib, 94; CAC Regional Exhib, Tucson, Ariz, 97; Sterberg Mus Natural History, 99; Leprecon Regional Sci-Fi/Fantasy Art Show, 2001. *Pos:* Primary illusr, Scottsdale Progress, 79-, TSR-Wizards of the Coast, Call of Cihulhu; paintings, Raising Arizona, 20th Century Fox, Dino Discovery, Scholastic Books, and others. *Teaching:* Instr, White Mountain Sch, Littleton, NH, 72-74; instr, Northeast Mo State Univ, Kirksville, Mo, 74-77; vis instr painting, drawing & design, Scottsdale Community Col, Ariz, 79-87 & Phoenix Col, 84-; instr, Art Inst of Phoenix, 97. *Awards:* Purchase Awards, Tulsa Invitational, 72 & 14th Ann Midwest Exhib, 76; Best Drawing, Scottsdale Ctr Arts, 77; Nat Forest Serv Centennial Competition Touring Exhib, 91. *Mem:* Ariz Watercolor Soc; Ariz Artist's Guild. *Media:* Oil, Pen & Ink, Prismacolor, Acrylic. *Collection:* Frabk Sinatra; Director, Joshua Logan; Director/Producer, Samuel Arkoff; TV Personality, Gary Owens; Violinist, Itzhak Perlman; Sikorsky Family. *Publ:* Illusr, numerous periodicals & newspapers; Auth, Drawing for Animation, Delmar Publ, 2003; (auth) Exploring Character Design, Delmar Pub, 2005. *Dealer:* El Mundo Magico Gallery PO Box 186 Sedona AZ 86336. *Mailing Add:* 6255 E Earll Dr Scottsdale AZ 85251

MITCHEL, JULIO
PHOTOGRAPHER
b Havana, Cuba, 1942; US citizen. *Study:* Studied photog with Lisette Model. *Work:* Mus Mod Art, Int Ctr Photog, NY; Int Mus Photog/Eastman House, Rochester, NY; Musee de L'Elysee, Lausanne, Switz; Mus Mod Art, Valencia, Spain. *Exhib:* Solo exhib, Recontre Int, Arles, France, 89, Muse de L'Elysee, Lausanne, Switz, 90, Galerie Vier, Berlin, Ger, 90, Mus Mod Art, Valencia, Spain, 91; More Than One Photog, Mus Mod Art, 92. *Teaching:* Fac, Sch Visual Arts, Cooper Union Art Sch & New Sch, NY. *Awards:* Fel, NY State Coun Arts, 72; Fel, NY Found, 82 & 88; Fel, Nat Endowment Arts, 82 & 92. *Bibliog:* A D Coleman (auth), Light Readings, Oxford Univ Press, NY, 81; Ralph Quinke (dir), About Julio Mitchel, NDR TV Network, Hamburg, Ger, 90. *Publ:* Auth, Triptych, Parkett, 89; Do You Love Me?, IVAM, 91. *Mailing Add:* 161 Columbia Heights Brooklyn NY 11201

MITCHELL, ANN
PRINTMAKER, PAINTER
b Philadelphia, Pa, 27. *Study:* studied with Geza DVegh (oil painting), 60-65; studied with Ed Whitney (watercolor), 72-74; studied with Carl Molno, 76-80; Studied printmaking at Trenton State Col, 80-90 & Edison Community Col, 92-94. *Work:* John A Stewart, print pvt collection. *Comn:* A Tampa Bay Original, Westshore Plaza, Tampa, Fla. *Exhib:* Centennial Celebration, Ahemedabad Sanskar Kendia Mus, India, 89; Four Artists, Trenton City Mus, NJ, 89; Trenton Artists Workshop, Soviet Exchange Exhib, Moscow, Russia, 90; Knickerbocker Artists, Perry House Galleries, Alexandria, Va, 93; Mus Fine Arts, St Petersburg, Fla, 96; El Paso Art Asn, Int Exhib, Tex, 2003; Sun Bowl Art Exhib, Int Mus Art, El Paso, Tex, 2004. *Collection Arranged:* Nat Asn Women Artists, Slide Registry. *Awards:* Gehner Watercolor Award, Nat Asn Women Artists, 88; Graphics - Cert of Merit, 46th Audubon Artists Ann, 88; Joseph Bucciante Award, Fla Watercolor Soc, 92; Eve Helman Award, Nat Asn Women Artists, 99. *Mem:* Nat Asn Women Artists; NMex Watercolor Soc; Fla Watercolor Soc; Rio Bravo Watercolorist, El Paso, Tex; Nat Mus Women in the Arts. *Media:* All Media. *Publ:* The Best of Watercolor, 3-99; 2nd Best of Watercolor-Painting Composition, Rockport Publ, 97. *Dealer:* Nuance Gallery Tampa Fl; Inside-Out Designs El Paso TX. *Mailing Add:* 121 Cloud Song Santa Teresa NM 88008

MITCHELL, DEAN LAMONT
PAINTER
b Pittsburgh, Pa, Jan 20, 57. *Study:* Columbus Col Art & Design, BFA, 80. *Work:* Nelson-Atkins Mus Art, Kansas City, Mo; Margaret Harwell Art Mus, Poplar Bluff, Mo; St Louis Art Mus, Mo; Miss Art Mus, Jackson; Nat Parks Found, Jackson, Wyo. *Comn:* Jazz Mural (4 ft x 140 ft) Vista/Allis Plaza Hotel, Kansas City, Mo, 84-85; five historical Kansas City scenes, Mo Art Coun, 85. *Exhib:* Miniature Invitational, Tampa Mus Art, Fla, 89; Miniature Art Soc Fla 15th Intern Exhib, St Petersburg Mus, 90; Nat Acad Design, 165th Ann, NY, 90; Arts for the Parks, Wild Life Am West Art Mus, Jackson Hole, Wyo, 90; Artist of Am, Colo Hist Mus, Denver, 91-92; Gallery of Fine Art, New Orleans, 2006. *Teaching:* Instr, figure drawing, Kansas City Art Inst, 8-12/90. *Awards:* Hardie Gramatky Mem Award, Am Watercolor Soc, 90; Best in Show, June Baumgardner Geldart, Min Art Soc Fla, 90; Allied Artist Gold Medal, 91. *Bibliog:* James Edwards (auth), Dean Mitchell Artist, 90; Mike Smith (dir), Coming Home (film), Globalvision/Greenwich workshop, 92; Ann Saunders (auth), Coming Home, Bay Arts Alliance, 92. *Mem:* Am Watercolor Soc; Allied Artist Am; Nat Watercolor Soc; Knickerbocker Artists; Nat Soc Painters Casein & Acrylic. *Media:* Oil, Watercolors. *Publ:* Auth, article, Artist Mag, F & W Publs, 84; Am Artist, Billboard Publs, 89; US Art, Frank Sisser, 89; Southwest Art, CBH Publ, 91; Being An Artist, North Light Books, 92. *Dealer:* Strecker Gallery 332 Poyntz Manhattan KS 66502; Carol Siple Gallery 1401 17th St Denver CO 50202. *Mailing Add:* 101 S 12th St, #607 Tampa FL 33602

MITCHELL, DIANNE
PAINTER
b Joliet, Ill. *Study:* Univ Hartford, Conn, Art Sch, with Rudolph Franz Zallinger, 82-83; Florence Acad Art, Florence Italy, 2005-2006. *Work:* US Coast Guard Collection. *Comn:* Diamond T Trucks Inc, 96; Conneticut Transport Magazine Covers, 92-94; Thousand Oaks New West Symphony, 2002-2003. *Exhib:* Ann Exhib, Salmagundi Club, NY, 84; Nat Midyear Exhib, Butler Inst Am Art, Youngstown, Ohio, 84; 100 Nat Finalists, Grand Cent Art Galleries, NY, 85; Egg Tempera and Watercolor Exhibition, Esther Wells Collection Galleries, Laguna Beach, Calif, 86; Am Watercolor Soc, 87; one-woman shows, Lake Tahoe Visitors' Ctr, 88 & 89, & US Coast Guard Exhib, Governor's Island, NY, 90; Focus Gallery Group Show, Cambria, Calif, 99-2001; and others; Portrait Arts Ltd, Boston, MA, 87-88. *Teaching:* Egg Tempera Workshop, King's Beach, Calif, 92 & 97; painting on safari, Kenya, Africa, 92. *Awards:* Lo Manaco Studio Award, Pastel Soc Am, 82; 1st Prize Watercolor, 2nd Prize Watercolor & Best of Show, Emerald City Classic, Nepenthe Mundi Soc, 86; George Gray Award, US Coast Guard, 89; 1990 Commemorative Print Competition Winner, Lake Tahoe Summer Music Festival. *Mem:* Pastel Soc Am; Nat Mus Women Arts; Pastel Soc Am, 80-2005, signature mem. *Media:* Oil, Egg Tempera. *Publ:* Illusr, Spinning: Where to begin, Shuttle Spindle & Dyepot Mag, 85; illusr & auth, One Egg, Over Medium, Am Artist Mag, 86; US Coast Guard Recruiting Brochure & Poster, 90. *Dealer:* Esther Wells Collection 1390 South Coast Highway Laguna Beach CA 92651; Miden Lane Zantman Galleries San Francisco Carmel Palm Desert CA. *Mailing Add:* 677 Shamrock Dr Pismo Beach CA 93449

MITCHELL, JEFFRY
PAINTER, SCULPTOR
b Seattle, Wash, June 10, 58. *Study:* Univ Dallas, Irving, BA, 80; Tyler Sch Art, Temple Univ, Philadelphia, Pa, MFA, 88. *Work:* Fogg Mus Art, Boston; Philadelphia Mus Art; Seattle Art Mus; Mus Fine Arts, Boston; Contemp Mus, Honolulu. *Exhib:* Foreign Artists Working in Japan, Gallery R, Seto, Japan, 83; Northwest Ann, Ctr Contemp Art, Seattle, 89; Installation Socrates Proj, Long Island City, Queens, NY, 91; solo exhibs, Seattle Art Mus, 90 & My Spirit, Workspace Gallery, New Mus Contemp Art, NY, 92; The Art of Microsoft, Henry Art Gallery, Univ Wash, Seattle, 93; Garden of Delights, Tacoma Art Mus, 95. *Pos:* Vis artist, RI Sch Design, Providence, 97, Harvard Univ, Cambridge, 94 & Mont State Univ, Missoula, 98. *Teaching:* Instr drawing & printmaking, Cornish Col Arts, Seattle, 89-91; vis lectr ceramics, painting & drawing, Univ Wash, Seattle, 93-95 & 97. *Awards:* Artist Trust Grant, 94; Art Matters Inc Grant, NY, 94. *Bibliog:* Eric Frederickson (auth), Hello, I'm Sorry, The Stranger, 2/6/97; Frances DeVuono (auth), Jeffrey Mitchell, Artweek, 4/97; Jordan Biren (auth), Transgressive Prints, Reflex, spring 89. *Media:* Works on Paper, Ceramics. *Dealer:* Elliot Brown Gallery 619 N 35th St No 101A Seattle WA 98103

MITCHELL, JOAN ELIZABETH See Robertson, Joan Elizabeth Mitchell

MITCHELL, JOHN BLAIR
PAINTER, EDUCATOR
b Brooklyn, NY, Jan 30, 21. *Study:* Pratt Inst, cert, 39-43, Pratt Inst Sch Educ, 46-47; Columbia Univ Teachers Col, BS, 48, Univ, MA, 49; Pratt Graphic Arts Ctr, 60-61, with Edmondson, Rogalski & Ponce de Leon; NY Univ Sch Educ, PhD, 63. *Work:* Metrop Mus Art, NY; Libr Cong, Washington; Silvermine Guild Artists, Conn; Baltimore Mus Art; Georgetown Univ Libr, Notre Dame Col, Baltimore; Towson Univ, Baltimore, Md; and others. *Comn:* Mural, Baltimore City Hosp, 72. *Exhib:* Six shows, Corcoran Gallery Art, Washington, 54-63; Libr Cong 19th Nat Exhib Prints, 63; Silvermine Guild Artists 5th Nat, 64; one-man shows, Baltimore Mus Art, 64 & Towson State Univ, 64, 77, 85 & 88; Hochschild Kohn Md Artists Today Anniversary, 72; 15 Yr Survey of Baltimore Art, Artspace, 96; Works by Maryland Artists, Gov Mansion, 97. *Teaching:* Prof graphics drawing, painting & photog & coordr grad art prog, Columbia Univ Teachers Col, 49-80 & Towson State Univ, 49-96, instr art, summers 50, 53 & 54; chmn art dept, Towson State Col, 51-57 & 63-65; instr graphics, Baltimore Mus Art, 63-73; emer prof, 91. *Awards:* First Awards, Intercollegiate Art Exhib, Coppin State Col, 72 & Easton Acad Art, 75; Md State Arts Coun Works in Progress Grant, 80; President's Award for Distinguished Serv to the Univ, Towson State Univ, 86. *Bibliog:* Lincoln Johnson (auth), articles, Baltimore Sun, 12/71 & 2/24/77; Earl Arnett (auth), article, Baltimore Sun, 12/1/75; Marcella Sussman (auth), article, Sunday Sun Magazine, 10/12/80; Elisabeth Stevens, Baltimore Sun, 12/8/85. *Mem:* Artists Equity Asn; Baltimore Print Club; Md Printmakers; Baltimore Mus Art Print & Drawing Soc. *Publ:* Auth, Art Education, 52; coauth, Art in Our Maryland Schools, State Manual, State Dept Educ, 53; auth, School Arts, 2/57; auth, Eastern Arts Quart, 1-2/63; In Print, Md Printmakers Quart, 6/92 & 6/98

MITCHELL, KATHERINE
PAINTER
b Memphis, Tenn, Oct 25, 44. *Study:* Atlanta Col Art, BFA, 68; Tyler Sch Art, Rome, 68; Ga State Univ, MVA, 77. *Work:* Ark Art Ctr, Little Rock, Ark; JB Speed Mus, Louisville, Ky; High Mus Art, Atlanta; Michael C Carlos Mus, Atlanta; and others. *Exhib:* Avant-Garde: 12 in Atlanta (with catalog), 79 & Artists in Georgia, 80, High Mus Art; solo exhib, Notes on the Working Process, Atlanta Col Art Gallery, 81 & The NY Series and Beyond, Chastain Gallery, Atlanta, 83, Heath Gallery (with catalog), 86 & 87, Goodwyn Gallery, Auburn Univ, Montgomery, Ala, 90, Restrospective Chastain Gallery, Atlanta, 91, Galerie Stil und Bruch, Berlin, Germany, 93, Kiang Gallery, Atlanta, 2003, Atlanta Contemp Art Ctr, 2005, Labyrinthe, Kunstall Krems, Austria, 2006; 9 Women in Georgia (with catalog), Nat Mus Woman Arts, Washington, 96; Artists of Heath Gallery, MOCA GA, Atlanta, 2002. *Teaching:* Sr lectr drawing & painting, Emory Univ, 80-. *Awards:* Hassam Fund Exhib Purchase Award, Am Acad & Inst Arts & Lett, 79; Southern Arts Federation/Nat Endowment Arts Regional Fel Award, 92. *Bibliog:* John Howett (auth), Katherine Mitchell at Atlanta College of Art, Art in Am, 1/82; Katherine Mitchell: Paintings, Heath Gallery, Atlanta, Ga, 86; Amy Jinkner-Lloyd (auth), Katherine Mitchell at Chastain & Heath, Art Am, 2/92; Laura Lieberman (auth), Katherine Mitchell: A Retrospective and Recent Work, Art Papers, 2/92. *Media:* Acrylic, Miscellaneous Media. *Publ:* Contribr, Katherine Mitchell: A Retrospective (catalog), essay by John Howett, Atlanta, 91; 9 Women in Georgia, Nat Mus Women in Arts, 96. *Dealer:* Kiang Gallery Atlanta GA. *Mailing Add:* 80 Stratford Pl NE Atlanta GA 30342

MITCHELL, MACEO
PAINTER
Study: Wayne State Univ, Detroit, Mich, BFA; Univ IA, MA, 1969. *Exhib:* One-man show, Nine Arts, Gallery, Antwerp, Belgium, 1995, Bill Hodges Gallery, NY, 1998 & 2002, Galerie Michele Guerin, Limetz-Villez, France, 1999, Iandor Fine Arts, Inc, Newark, NJ, 1999; group exhib, Arnold Klein Gallery, Royal Oak, Mich, 1996; Pen & Brush Inc, Black Hist Celebration & Exhib, NY, 2002; Art in the Atrium, Morristown, NJ, 2003; Pastel Soc Ann, Nat Arts Club, NY, 2003; Flight, Mehu Gallery, NY, 2003. *Teaching:* instr, Pastel Soc Am, Nat Arts Club, New York City, currently; instr, elem to col level art, formerly. *Mem:* IA Print Group (IPG); signature mem, Pastel Soc Am (PSA). *Media:* Pastels. *Mailing Add:* 446 Central Park W New York NY 10025

MITCHELL, MARGARETTA K
PHOTOGRAPHER, WRITER
b Brooklyn, NY, May 27, 35. *Study:* Smith Col, BA(magna cum laude), 57; Boston Mus Sch, 58; Escuela de Bellas Artes, Madrid, Spain, 59; Univ Calif, Berkeley, MA, 85. *Work:* Int Ctr Photog, NY; Performing Arts Libr & Mus, San Francisco, Calif; Bannoft Libr, Univ Calif, Berkeley; Royal Print Collection, Windsor, Eng; Oakland Mus, Calif; San Francisco Mus Modern Art; NY Public Libr. *Comn:* Mural, Anixter Corp, San Francisco, Calif, 74; mural, Amax Corp, San Francisco, Calif, 74; mural, San Francisco Art Comn, Calif, 78; posters, Portal Publ, 90; Berkeley Symphony, 99; Chappelet Vineyard, St Helena, 90. *Exhib:* San Francisco Mus Mod Art, Calif, 78; Bouquet's to Art, Deyoung Mus, 91; Michael Shapiro Gallery, San Francisco, 89 & 94; Witkin Gallery, NY, 91 & 92; Pepper Gallery, Boston, 93; Scheinbaum & Russek, Santa Fe, 94; NY Pub Libr, 96; Nat Mus Women in the Arts, DC, 96; Akron Mus Art, Ohio, 97; Santa Barbara Mus Art, 97; Cheekwood, Nashville, 2001; Mechanics Inst Libr, San Francisco, 02; Univ San Francisco, 02. *Collection Arranged:* Recollections: Ten Women of Photography (auth, catalog), Int Ctr Photog, 79; Dance for Life (auth, catalog), Oakland Mus, Calif, 85. *Pos:* Pres, Am Soc Mag Photog, Northern Calif Chapter, 90-92, nat bd dir. *Teaching:* Instr photog, Univ Calif Extension, 76-78, 2003; instr photog, City Col San Francisco, Calif, 80-81; Calif Col Arts & Crafts, Oakland, 86, Univ Calif, summer session, 86; Friends Photog, summer workshop, 87, 88; workshop, Carleton Col, April, 88; Acad Art, San Francisco, 90-94; instr photog Univ

So Calif Extension, 2001-03; instr Acad of Art, San Francisco, 90-95; instr photog, Univ Calif, Santa Cruz Extension, 2001, 03-06. *Awards:* Nat Endowment Arts Mus Grant, 78-79; Calif Coun Arts Grant, Berkeley Art Ctr, 81-82; Grant, L J & Mary C Skaggs Found, 81. *Bibliog:* New Photography, Prentice-Hall, 83, 209-13; Encore Mag, fall 85; Focus Mag, April, 85; A History of Women Photographers, Abbeville Press, 94. *Mem:* Am Soc Mag Photog; Inst Hist Study. *Media:* Black & White, Color. *Res:* Photographers, particularly rediscoveries; Art and California history; dance. *Interests:* Photography, gardening, reading, traveling & yoga. *Publ:* Co-auth, To A Cabin, Grossman Publ, 73; introduction to: After Ninety, Univ Washington Press, 77; essays for Contemp Photogr, St Martin's Press, NY, 82; Dance for Life, Elysian Editions, 85; Flowers, Elysian Editions, 91; Introduction to The Eternal Body, Chronicle Books, 94; Ruth Bernard: Between Art and Life, 2000; Introduction to Under One Sky, Stanford Univ Press, 04; The Face of Poetry, 05. *Dealer:* Michael Shapiro 49 Geary St San Francisco CA. *Mailing Add:* 280 Hillcrest Rd Berkeley CA 94705

MITCHELL, N DONALD
ADMINISTRATOR, DEALER
b Mt Vernon, NY, Mar 5, 22. *Study:* Wichita State Univ; Abbe Inst, Monterey Peninsula Col, art hist, painting with George DeGroat & Fay Hopkins. *Pos:* Vpres, Universal Arts, Inc, Carmel, Calif, 60-; dir, Zantman Galleries, Ltd, Carmel, 60-; co-owner, Highlands Gallery, Carmel, 60-. *Specialty:* Quality works, mostly representational, in all media, styles and techniques. *Mailing Add:* 283 Heather CT Apt 1B Templeton CA 93465-9741

MITCHELL, ROBIN
PAINTER, EDUCATOR
b Los Angeles, Calif, Sept 29, 51. *Study:* Calif State Univ, Northridge, 68-70; Univ Calif, Los Angeles, 70-71; Calif Inst Arts, BFA, 72 & MFA, 74. *Work:* Security/Pac Corp Collection, Los Angeles, Calif; Flour Corp, Irvine, Calif; Kaufman/Broad-Paris Collection, France; Tuttle & Taylor Collection, Los Angeles, Calif. *Exhib:* solo exhibs, Comsky Gallery, Los Angeles, 74, Baum-Silverman Gallery, Los Angeles, 81, Jan Baum Gallery, Los Angeles, 83 & 84 & The Living Room, Santa Monica, Calif, 2001; Surface Tension, Santa Barbara Contemp Arts Forum, Calif, 95; Division of Labor: Women's Work in Contemp Art, Mus Contemp Art, Los Angeles, 95; Teeming, Post Gallery, Los Angeles, 96; Blessings & Beginnings, Skirball Cult Ctr, Los Angeles, 96; Feminist Directions 1970/1996 (catalog), Sweeney Art Gallery, Univ Calif, Riverside, 96; City of Los Angeles Exhib, Los Angeles Munic Art Gallery, 98; Ikon Gallery, 2000; Importance of Being Ernest, Occidental Col, 2001. *Teaching:* Vis artist studio art, Claremont Grad Sch, 79 & 83; lectr, Univ Southern Calif, 81- & Univ Calif at Irvine, 87- 92, Univ Calif, Santa Barbara, 93-95. *Awards:* Visual Artist Fel (painting), Nat Endowment Arts, 87; Visual Artists Award for Anonymous was a Woman, 96; City of Los Angeles Artist Grant, 97-98. *Bibliog:* Norma Broude & Mary Degarard (eds), The Power of Feminist Art, The American Movement of the 1970's, History & Impact, Abrams Publ, 94; Michael Duncan (auth), LA rising, Art Am, 12/94; Susan Muchnic (auth), The kindness of strangers, Los Angeles Times, 8/30/96. *Mem:* Col Art Asn. *Media:* All. *Publ:* AUth, Susan Rankaitis, spring, 91, Patrick Nickell & Michael Gonzalez, fall, 92 & Renee Petropoulos, summer 94, Visions. *Mailing Add:* 2614 Euclid Apt E Santa Monica CA 90405

MITCHELL, SHANNON DILLARD
CURATOR, ADMINISTRATOR
b Anchorage, Alaska, Oct 5, 58. *Study:* Colo Col, BA, 80; Southern Methodist Univ, MA(arts admin) & MBA, 84. *Collection Arranged:* Paintings by Clementine Hunter, Ark Colls, 93; Adrian Brewer: Arkansas Artist (contribr, catalog), 96; Edwin Brewer Retrospective, Univ Ariz, Little Rock, 96; 20th Century African American Art from the Darrell Walker Collection (contribr, catalog), 96. *Pos:* Dir, NS Haley Mem Libr & History Ctr, 81-82; asst to dir & cur asst, San Antonio Mus Art, 84-86; gallery cur, Univ Ark, Little Rock, 90-. *Teaching:* Adj asst prof mus studies, Univ Ark, Little Rock, 90-. *Mem:* Am Asn Mus; Southeastern Mus Conf; Ark Mus Asn. *Mailing Add:* Dept Art Univ Ark 2801 S University Little Rock AR 72204-1099

MITTY, LIZBETH J
PAINTER, PRINTMAKER
b New York, NY, Oct 28, 1952. *Study:* State Univ NY, Stony Brook, 69-71; Univ Wis, Madison, BS, 73, MFA, 75. *Work:* Metrop Mus Art, NY; Newark Mus, NJ; Mint Mus, Charlotte, NC; Nassau Mus, Roslyn, NY; Queensborough Community Col, Queens, NY; US State Dept, Va; Fidelity Investment, Boston; Greenpoint Bank, NY; Prudential Investments, NJ; NY Heart Found, NY; Blue Cross, Blue Shield, NY; Oak Park Bank, Chicago; Trierenberg Holdings, Traun, Austria. *Exhib:* Long Island Landscape Painting in the Twentieth Century, Mus Stonybrook, NY, 90; Nassau Mus, Roslyn, NY, 93; Steven Rosenberg Gallery, NY, 94; solo show, Cheryl pelavin Gallery, NY, 98, 2002 & 2005; and others. *Teaching:* Instr painting & drawing, Lake Erie Col, 75-76, Ohio State Univ, 76-77 & State Univ NY, New Paltz, NY, 91-; Hofstra Univ, 96-98. *Awards:* Best Show, Lyndon House, Athens, Ga, 78; Adolph & Esther Gottlieb Found Grant, 95. *Bibliog:* Grace Glueck (auth), rev, NY Times, 83; Edward Lucie-Smith (auth), American art now, Morrow, Inc, 85; Ronald Pisano (auth), Long Island Landscape Painting in the Twentieth Century, Little Brown Co, 90; NY Times weekend sect, Ken Johnson, 2001, Milwaukee Jour Sunday arts section, San Francisco Jour Sunday Arts section, NY Mag Art in Review, 2001. *Media:* Acrylic, Oil; Monoprint. *Dealer:* Cheryl Pelavin Fine Arts 13 Jay St New York NY 10013. *Mailing Add:* 165 Church St Apt 5N New York NY 10007-1830

MIYAMOTO, WAYNE AKIRA
PAINTER, PRINTMAKER
b Honolulu, Hawaii, Sept 6, 47. *Study:* Rensselaer Polytech Inst, 65-68; Univ Hawaii, BA & BFA, 70, MFA, 74. *Exhib:* Silvermine Int, 90, 92 & 94; 65th Nat Print Exhib, Soc Am Graphic Artists, NY, 93; Int Print Triennial, Cracow, Poland, 94; 3rd Bharat Bhavan Int Biennial Prints, Bhopal, India, 95; Inter-Kontakt-Grafik '95, Int Triennial Graphic Art, Prague, Czech Repub, 95; 45th N Am Print Exhib, Boston Printmakers, Duxbury, Mass, 95; Millennial Biennial Nat, Univ Richmond Mus, Va, 2000; VI Miedzynarodowe Triennale, Int Print Exhib, Majdanek 2000, Majdanek Mus, Lublin, Poland; Int Print Biennial, Varna, Bulgaria, 2001; Ecco Homo, 2000, Clemson Univ, SC; Prints USA, Springfield Mus Art, Mo, 2001; Int Biennial Cluj, Nat Mus, Cluj-Napoca, Romania, 2001; Biennial Int Print Comp, Edmonton, Alberta, Can, 2002; Global Matrix Int Exhib, Purdue univ, Indiana and Wright State Univ, Dayton, Ohio, 2002; 12th Space Int Print Biennial, Seoul, Korea, 02; Boston Printmakers N Am Biennial, Boston, 03; Honolulu Printmakers 75th Anniversary, Honolulu Acad Arts, 03; 4th Minn Nat Biennial, Univ Minn, 04; Boston Printmakers, Duxbury, Mass, 04; plus others. *Collection Arranged:* Univ Alaska, Fairbanks, Contemp Mus, Honolulu, State Found on Culture and the Arts, Hawaii Honolulu Acad of Arts, Fort Hayes State Univ, Kansas, Rutgers Univ, NJ, Portland Art Mus, Ore, Contemp Mus, Knoxville, Tenn, Univ Richmond Mus, Va, Nat Acad Fine Arts, Hangzhou, China, Assoc Premio Int Biella L' Incisione, Torino, Italy, Contemp Mus Asilah, Morocco, Int Print Triennial Soc, Cracow, Poland, State Mus Lublin, Poland, Nat Mus, Cluj-Napoca, Romania, Nat Mus, Hanoi, Vietnam; and many others. *Pos:* Visual art consult & acquisition comt, State Found Cult Arts, Island Hawaii, 81-; exec bd, Hawaii Alliance Arts Educ, Honolulu, 88-89; Friends of Univ Hawaii-Hilo Art, 81-, vpres, 85-88; artist-in-residence, 11th Asilah Int Cult Festival, Morocco, 88; artist-in-residence, The Printmaking Workshop, New York, 90. *Teaching:* Art Dept, Univ Hawaii, Hilo. *Awards:* Purchase Awards, State Found Cult Arts, Honolulu, 71, 74, 75, 87, 91 & 92; Juror's Award, Print Club, Philadelphia, Pa, 88; Purchase Awards, Honolulu Acad Arts, 92; Purchase Award State Found on Culture and the Arts, 97Pur; Purchase Award Univ Richmond Mus, Va, 2000. *Mem:* Honolulu Printmakers Asn (mem bd & treas, 71-72); Print Club, Philadelphia; Northwest Print Coun; Southern Graphics Coun; Col Art Asn; Boston Printmakers; The Print Consortium; Fla Printmakers Asn; Mid-Am Print Soc; Soc Am Graphic Artists. *Media:* Painting; Intaglio Printmaking. *Publ:* Auth, Unique art of Akaji, Honolulu Star Bull Advertiser, 76; Lee Chesney, 25 Years of Printmaking, Univ Presses Fla, Gainesville, 78; ed, Pacific States Regional Print Exhib (exhib catalog), Univ Hawaii, Hilo, 82; Pacific States Regional Print & Drawing Exhib, (exhib catalog), Univ Hawaii Hilo, 83, 84, 85 & 86; Pacific States Biennial Nat Print Exhib (exhib catalog), Univ Hawaii, Hilo, 88, 90 & 92. *Mailing Add:* Univ Hawaii Art Dept Office MC 395-1A 200 W Kawili St Hilo HI 96720-4091

MIYASAKI, GEORGE JOJI
PRINTMAKER, PAINTER
b Kalopa, Hawaii, Mar 24, 35. *Study:* Calif Col Arts & Crafts, BFA & BAEd, 57 & MFA, 58. *Work:* San Francisco Mus Art, Calif; Brooklyn Mus Art, NY; Mus Mod Art, NY; Art Inst Chicago; Pasadena Art Mus, Calif. *Teaching:* Prof art, Univ Calif, Berkeley, 64-. *Awards:* John Simon Guggenheim Fel, 63-64; Nat Endowment Arts, 80-81 & 85-86. *Bibliog:* Rudy Turk (auth), George Miyasaki, monograph, 81. *Mem:* Nat Acad. *Dealer:* Stephen Wirtz Gallery 49 Geary St San Francisco CA. *Mailing Add:* Magnolia Editions 2527 Magnolia St Oakland CA 94607

MNUCHIN, STEVEN T
PATRON
Study: Yale Univ, BA. *Pos:* Various mgt positions in tech div Goldman Sach, 85-2001, exec vpres, chief info off, 2001-2002; vchmn, Eng as Second Language Investments Inc, 2003; Chief Exec Officer, mem mgt comt, SFM Capital Mgt LP, 2003-04; chmn, co-Chief Exec Officer, Dune Capital Mgt LP, 2004-; Kmart (now Sears Holding Corp) (bd dir, currently). *Mem:* Yale Devel Board; Hirshhorn Mus & Sculpture Garden; Riverdale Co Sch, OCD Found; NY Presbyterian Med Ctr, (bd trustees, 2004-); Whitney Mus Am Art, (trustee, currently). *Mailing Add:* Dune Capital Mgt LP 888 Seventh Ave 28th fl New York NY 10106

MOBLEY, KAREN R
PAINTER, ADMINISTRATOR
b Cheyenne, Wyo. *Study:* Univ Wyo, BFA, 83; Univ Okla, MFA, 87. *Work:* NMex State Univ; Wyo State Mus; Nicolaysen Art Mus. *Comn:* Grandview Elementary Sch, Washington State Arts Comn; Bear Necessities, Spokaue, Ronald McDonald House. *Exhib:* New Am Talent, Laguna Gloria Art Mus, Austin, Tex, 92; Wyo State Mus, 94; Wyo Arts Coun Gallery, 95; Casper Col, Wyo, 95; Univ Wyo, 95; Mont State Univ, 96; N Idaho Col, 99; Spokane Art Sch, 2000; Whitworth Col, 04; Kress Gallery, 04. *Collection Arranged:* Ocho Inspiraciones, 89; Comics, 89; Painting Divergence (catalog), 90; The Computer Art Show, 91; The River, 2000. *Pos:* Dir, Univ Art Gallery, NMex State Univ, Las Cruces, NMex, 87-93; Nicolaysen Art Mus, Casper, Wyo, 93-97; Arts Dir, City of Spokane, Spokane Arts Comn, 97-. *Teaching:* Whitworth Col, Spokane, Wash, 2006. *Awards:* Best show, Sangre de Cristo Art Ctr, 89; Individual Artist Grant, Wyo Arts Coun, 94; Women of Achievement for Arts & Culture award, Spokane YWCA, 2000. *Bibliog:* Drawings, Puerto del Sol/NMex State Univ, 88; Drawings, Caldera, 94; Poems, Caldera, 96; Tom West, Catalog for Nicolaysen Art Mus, 98. *Mem:* Am Asn Mus; Col Art Asn; Washington State Arts Alliance; Rorary Club of Spokaue. *Media:* Mixed Media, Painting. *Dealer:* Art at Work Spokane WA; Good Works Spokane Wash. *Mailing Add:* 3515 S Lee Spokane WA 99203

MOCK, MARTHA L
CURATOR
b Chicago, Ill, Nov 3, 46. *Study:* Col Wooster, BA, 68; NY Univ, MA, 70; State Univ NY, Buffalo, MFA, 81. *Collection Arranged:* Ansel Adams: 100 Photographs, 79-80, August Sander: Photographs of an Epoch, 80, The Spirit of an American Place, 80-81, The New West: Photographs by Robert Adams, 81, American Frontiers: The Photographs of Timothy H O'Sullivan 1867-1874, 81-82, Danny Lyon: Pictures from the New World 1962-1982, 82, Frederick H Evans: The Desired Haven, 82, Minor

White, 83 & Tibet: The Sacred Realm, Photographs 1880-1950, 83, Philadelphia Mus Art; The Golden Age of British Photography 1839-1900, 84-85; All American, photogr by Burk Uzzle, 84-85; Twelve Photographers Look at Us, 87; Emmet Gowin photogr, 90. *Pos:* Assoc cur photogr, 85. *Awards:* Visual Arts Prog Critics Fel, Nat Endowment Arts, 79. *Mem:* Soc Photog Educ. *Publ:* Auth, Tibet: The Sacred Realm, Photographs 1880-1950, Millerton, 83; All American: Photographs by Burk Uzzle, St Davids, 84; Twelve Photographers Look at Us, Philadelphia Mus Art Bull, 84; Emmet Gowin Photographs, Philadelphia Mus Art, 90. *Mailing Add:* 406 E Main St Roaring Spring PA 16673-1353

MODE, CAROL A
PAINTER
b St Louis, Mo, Mar 27, 43. *Study:* Washington Univ, BFA, 65, Summer Art Inst, 80; Vanderbilt Univ, 81-82. *Work:* Tenn State Mus, Nashville; Hosp Corp Am, Nashville; Northern Telecom, Vanderbilt Hosp, Nashville; Nynex, Nat; Bell South, Nashville, Tenn. *Comn:* Billboard painting, IDS, Nashville; Tenn State Mus Collection, Nashville. *Exhib:* 47th Ann Nat Midyear Exhib, 83 & 50th Nat Am Midyear Show, 86, Butler Inst An Art; Clemson Nat Print & Drawing Exhib, Clemson Univ, SC, 85; solo exhibs, Transfigurations, Tenn Fine Arts Mus, Nashville, 85, Tenn Arts Comn Gallery, Nashville, 88 & 96, Leu Gallery, Belmont Univ, Nashville, Tenn, 91, & Cumberland Gallery, Nashville, 95; 21st Bradley Nat Print & Drawing Exhib, Biennial, Bradley Univ, Peoria, Ill, 87; 6th Ann Summer Lights Exhib, Metro Arts Comn, Nashville, 89-91; Christoph Merian Stiftung, Basel, Switz, 95; and others. *Awards:* Artist Residency/Christoph Merian Fel, 95-96; Individual Artist Fel, Tenn Arts Comn, 96. *Mem:* CAA. *Media:* Acrylic, Oil. *Dealer:* Cumberland Gallery 4107 Hillsboro Circle Nashville TN 37215. *Mailing Add:* 421 Moss Creek Ct Nashville TN 37205-2828

MODI-VITALE, LYDIA
MUSEUM DIRECTOR, CURATOR
b New York, NY, Jan 6, 17. *Study:* Scholar Award, Art Students League, New York; apprentice of Hans Hoffman, New York; internship, Museo Nac de Hist, 45-46 & Museo Nac de Antropologia, 58, Mexico City; studies in art conserv & restoration, Univ Calif, Davis, 70. *Collection Arranged:* Early American Folk Art, Nat Art Gallery, Washington, DC, 68; Art Nouveau, 68, 150 videotape exhibs, 70-78, Process Art, Wynn Bullock, 72, Six from Castelli's, 74, New Deal Art: California, 76, The Graham Nash Exhibit of Rare and Vintage Photography, 78, De Saisset Gallery, Univ Santa Clara, Calif; Bill Viola: An Instrument of Simple Sensations & The Vatican Collection with the De Young Mus, Mus Italo Americano, 83-84. *Pos:* Dir, Triton Mus, San Jose, Calif, 66-68 & De Saisset Mus, Univ Santa Clara, Calif, 68-78; consult, 78-; cur, Museo Italo Americano, 83-84; asst dir, Vorpal Gallery, San Francisco, 84, consult, 87-; bd dir, Archeoclub d'Italia, currently; proj dir, Soma Int Galleries, San Francisco, 95-; cur, Mus-Legion of Hon, 82. *Awards:* Adolph's Found Grant, 74, Calif Arts Comn Grant, 74; Nat Endowment for the Humanities Grant & exten, 74 & 75. *Mem:* Western Asn of Am Mus (exec secy, 69-71); Am Asn Art Mus; Bay Area Lawyers for the Arts; Archeoclub d'Italia. *Publ:* ed catalogs, Twenty Color Photographs: Light Abstractions, Wynn Bullock, 72, Fletcher Benton: Selected Works 1964-74, 74 & Scholder Collects Scholder 1965-75 Retrospective, 75, de Saisset Art Gallery & Mus; co-ed, James W McManus: Survey of Selected Works 1967-77, De Saisset Art Gallery & Mus, 77. *Mailing Add:* 100 Font Blvd Apt 3E San Francisco CA 94132

MODICA, ANDREA
PHOTOGRAPHER
b Jan 18, 60. *Study:* SUNY, BFA, Purchase, NY, 82; Yale Sch of Art, MFA, 85. *Work:* Metrop Mus Art, NY; Mus Modern Art, NY; Brooklyn Mus Art; Whitney Mus of Art, NY; San Francisco Mus of Modern Art. *Exhib:* Commonplace Mysteries Photos of Peter Hujar, Andrea Modica & Bill Owens, San Francisco Mus of Modern Art, 96; Andrea Modica: Minor League, Polk Mus Art, Lakeland, Fla, 96; Andrea Modica: Palazzo d'Accurso Museo Mirandi, Bologna, Italy, 97; Working/Still, Neuberger Mus, Purchase, NY, 97; Under the Dark Cloth, Mus of Photog Art, San Diego, 97; Andrea Modica: Treadwell, Cleve Mus of Art, 98; Hindsight, Whitney Mus of Art, New York City, 99. *Teaching:* assoc prof art, SUNY, Oneonta, 85-98; vis prof photography, Princeton Univ, NJ, 99. *Awards:* Fulbright-Hays Research Grant Scolar, Italy, 90-91; John Simon Guggenheim fel, 94-95; Spl Opp Stipend, NY Found for the Arts, 96. *Publ:* contribr, Women Photographers, Abrams, 90; auth, Minor League: Photographs by Andrea Modica, Smithsonian, 93; auth,Treadwell, Chronicle, 96; contribr, Hope Photographs, Thames & Hudson, 98; contribr, Brothers, Hyperion, 99. *Mailing Add:* 164 Clarksley Rd Manitou Springs CO 80829

MOEHL, KARL J
PAINTER, WRITER
b Oberlin, Ohio, June 24, 25. *Study:* Univ Colo, Boulder, BFA, 50; State Univ Iowa, Iowa City, MFA, 52. *Work:* Currier Mus Art, Manchester, NH; Ill State Mus, Springfield; Lakeview Mus, Peoria, Ill; Dirksen Research Libr, Pekin, Ill; Städt Bodensee-Mus, Friedrichschafen, WGer. *Exhib:* 15th Ann Int, Pa Acad Fine Arts, Philadelphia, 52; one-man shows, Lakeview Mus, Peoria, Ill, 75, Peoria Art Guild, 79, Ill Cent Col, East Peoria, 79 & Tower Park Gallery, Peoria Heights, Ill, 82; Ill Landscape Art, Lakeview Mus & traveling, 76; 31st Ill Invitational, Ill State Mus, Springfield, 79; Miss Corridor 1981, Davenport Art Gallery, Iowa, 81; two-man show with James Hansen, Bradley Univ, Peoria, Ill, 86. *Pos:* Contrib ed, New Art Asn, 80; Illnois ed, New Art Examiner, 81-95. *Teaching:* Instr studio, Univ NH, Durham, 53-55 & Brown Univ, Providence, RI, 56-57; prof art hist, Bradley Univ, Peoria, Ill, 57-95, prof emer, 95-. *Awards:* Purchase Award, Springfield Art Mus, Mo, 71; Merit Award, State Mus, Ill, 81; First Prize Painting, Ill Art League, 81 & 82. *Bibliog:* Dee Kilgo (auth), Karl Moehl Recent Work, New Art Examiner, 75. *Mem:* Chicago Art Coalition; Peoria Art Guild (bd mem, 72-81); Am Asn Univ Prof. *Media:* Acrylic, Graphite. *Publ:* Auth, 200 Years of American Painting, 65 & Edward Henry Pothast, 67, Lakeview Mus; Roger Annear Mem Exhib, Peoria Art Guild, 74; Metalsmith: Enamels' 87, Soc NAm Goldsmiths, 83; The Press of Primitivism, New Art Examiner, 85; Bradley University Print & Drawing Show, J Print World, 87- 89; Dow P Mitchell, Calder Lithos, 88. *Mailing Add:* 1700 W Ayres Ave Peoria IL 61606-1604

MOELLER, ROBERT CHARLES, III
CONSULTANT
b Providence, RI, Jan 22, 38. *Study:* Washington & Lee Univ, BA(hist art), 59; Harvard Univ, with John Beckwith, Dr Hanns Swarzenski, J M Delaisse & J H Plummer, MA(art hist), 63. *Collection Arranged:* Brummer Collection, Duke Univ Art Mus. *Pos:* Res assoc dept art, Duke Univ, 67-68, dir, Univ Art Mus, 68-69; asst cur dept decorative arts & sculpture, Mus Fine Arts, Boston, 70-71, cur decorative arts & sculpture, 71-80; private art dealer, 80-82; consult to private collectors, 82-94. *Teaching:* Teaching fel hist art, Harvard Univ, 64-65; instr art, Duke Univ, 68, asst prof, 68-69; instr sem medieval sculpture, Univ NC, Chapel Hill, spring 68. *Mem:* Int Coun Mus; Am Asn Mus; Am Ceramic Circle; Soc Silver Collectors; Int Ctr Medieval Art. *Res:* Study of mid-twelfth century sculpture in Burgundy concentrating on Narthex sculpture of Charlieu, seventeenth century sculpture and decorative arts. *Publ:* Contribr, The Brummer Collection at Duke University, Art J, 68; auth, foreword, The Graphic Art of Edvard Munch, Duke Univ Art Mus Exhib, 12/69; Sculpture from Brive & Sculpture from Savigny, RI Sch Design, 7/69; L'iconographie de la facade nord du narthex de Charlieu, Actes des Journees d'etudes d'histoire et d'archeologie, Charlieu, Soc Amis Arts, 73

MOFFITT, JOHN FRANCIS
HISTORIAN, PAINTER
b San Francisco, Calif, Feb 25, 40. *Study:* Calif Col Arts & Crafts, BFA, 62; Calif State Univ, San Francisco, MA, 63; Fac Lett & Philos, Univ Madrid, PhD, 66. *Exhib:* 13th Ann NC Artists Exhib, NC State Mus Art, Raleigh, 68; 1st Biennial 5-State Exhib, Gates Gallery, Port Arthur, Tex, 71; 12th Midwest Biennial, Joslyn Art Mus, Omaha, Nebr, 72; 21st Ann Exhib, Beaumont Art Mus, Tex, 72; 50th Regional Exhib, R S Barnwell Art Ctr, Shreveport, La, 72; plus others. *Pos:* dir, HMS Phake Potter Lit Found. *Teaching:* Asst prof art & art hist, E Carolina Univ, Greenville, NC, 66-68 & Sonoma State Col, Cotati, Calif, 68-69; vis prof landscape painting, Mendocino Art Ctr, Calif, 69; asst prof art hist, NMex State Univ, Las Cruces, 69-96, prof emer, 96-; vis assoc prof art, Fla State Univ, 78; vis prof art, Univ Valencia, Spain, 81; vis prof art hist, Univ Autonoma, Madrid, 85. *Awards:* many grants & scholarships. *Bibliog:* Articles, Art Bulletin, Art Hist, Archivo Espanol de Arte, Arte Lombarda, Artibus et Historiae & many others. *Mem:* Col Art Asn Am; Am Soc Hispanic Art Hist Studies; Renaissance Soc Am; Rocky Mountain Medieval & Renaissance Hist Asn; Hermetic Text Soc; many others. *Media:* Acrylic, Oil. *Res:* renaissance and modern art. *Interests:* Field of 16th and 17th century Spanish and Modern European art. *Publ:* Auth, El Caso de la Damade Elche: Cronica de una leyenda, Ediciones Destino, Barcelona, 96, 2nd ed, 97; coauth, El Caso de la Dama de Elche: Historia de una Falsificacion & O Brave New People: The European Invention of the American Indian, Univ NMEx Press, Albuquerque, 96; auth, The Arts in Spain: Prehistoric to Postmodern, Thames & Hudson, London & Viking, New York, 98; Alchemist of the Avant-Garde: The Case of Marcel Duchamp, State Univ NY Press, 2003; Picturing Extraterrestrials; Alien Imagery in Modern Culture, Prometheus Press, Buffalo, 2003; Our Lady of Guadalupe, McFarland, 2006; and many others. *Mailing Add:* 1104 Luna St Las Cruces NM 88001

MOGAVERO, MICHAEL
PAINTER
b Rochester, NY, Nov 4, 50. *Study:* Buffalo State Univ, BS, 73; Hoffberger Sch Painting, Md Inst Art, MFA, 75. *Work:* Rochester Mem Art Gallery, NY; Lowe Mus Art, Univ Miami, Fla; Minneapolis Mus Art, Minn; Prudential Insurance, Princeton, NJ; Artco Int, Geneva, Switz. *Exhib:* Md Biennial, Baltimore Mus Art, 74 & 75; Maryland Artists-A New Look, Baltimore Mus Art, 79; one person-exhibs, Gallery Six Friedrich, Munich, Ger, 83, Gallery Corinne Hummel, Basel, Switz, 85, Oscarsson Siegeltuch Gallery, NY, 86 & 87, Carol Getz Gallery, Miami, Fla, 88, Ruth Siegel Gallery, NY, 89, Lyons Matrix Gallery, Austin, Tex, 93 & Craighead-Green Gallery, Dallas, 95 & 97; San Francisco Mus Art, 87; Phizer Inc, Mus Mod Art, NY, 92; Fay Gold Gallery, Atlanta, Ga, 94; Eve Mannes Gallery, Atlanta, 94; New Works on Paper, Lyons Matrix Gallery, Austin, 95; Lynn Goode Gallery, Houston, 95; Valerie Miller Gallery, Palm Desert, Calif, 96; New Works by UT Faculty, Lyons Matrix Gallery, Austin, Tex, 96; Artspace, San Antonio, Tex, 96; Lyons Matrix Gallery, Austin, Tex, 98. *Teaching:* Assoc prof, Univ Tex, Austin, 84-. *Awards:* Individual Fel, NY Found Arts, 85. *Bibliog:* Kathryn Gregor (auth), Arts, Third Coast Mag, 85 & 88-89; Annette Carlozzi (auth), 50 Texas Artists, Chronicle Books, 86; John R Clarke (auth), Michael Mogavero at Lyons Matrix, Art in Am, 4/94. *Media:* Acrylic, Oil on Canvas. *Dealer:* Craighead-Green Gallery 2404 Cedar Springs Suite 700 Dallas TX 75201; Lyons Matrix Gallery 1712 Lavaca Austin TX 78701

MOGENSEN, PAUL
PAINTER, PRINTMAKER
b Los Angeles, Calif, Dec 3, 41. *Study:* Yale Univ, 62, Univ Southern Calif, BFA, 63. *Work:* Mus Mod Art, NY Pub Libr, NY; High Mus Art, Atlanta, Ga; Houston Mus Fine Arts, Tex; Wadsworth Atheneum, Hartford, Conn; Fogg Mus Art, Harvard Univ, Cambridge, Mass. *Exhib:* Modular Painting, Albright-Knox Art Gallery, Buffalo, NY, 70; A View of a Decade, Mus Contemp Art, Chicago, 77; Retrospective, Houston Mus Fine Arts, 78-79; Mary Boone Gallery, NY, 78; Edward Thorp Gallery, 87 & 88; Piccolo Spoleto Festival, Charleston, SC, 92; Reflex, Secession Mus, Vienna, Austria, 94; Art Et Industrie, NY, 97; Galerie Thomas Schulte, Berlin, 2002; A Minimal Future, Mus Contemp Art, Los Angeles, 2004. *Awards:* John Simon Guggenheim Mem Found

Fel, 76; Nat Endowment Arts, 80; Pollock-Krasner Found Grant, 88. *Bibliog:* Carter Ratcliff (auth), Paul Mogensen at Thorp, Art Am, 87; Klaus Kertess (auth), Painting Order, Secession Mus, Vienna, Austria, 94; Richard Kalina (auth), Paul Mogensen, Art Am, 97; James Mayer (auth), Minimalism, 2000. *Mailing Add:* 159 Mercer St New York NY 10012

MOHLE, BRENDA SIMONSON
ART DEALER
b Dallas, Tex, May 9, 59. *Study:* Univ Tex, Austin, BA, 80. *Pos:* Art adv, Newman Gallery, 81-84; art adv & gallery dir, Omni Art, 84-87; docent, Dallas Mus Art, 85-95; art consultant, (Art Appraiser & Pvt Dealer) Signet Art, 87-. *Awards:* Outstanding Member of the Year, 98. *Mem:* Int Soc Appraisers; Dallas Mus Art; Appraisers Asn Am. *Specialty:* Corporate work including late 19th century European work through contemporary American. *Mailing Add:* 2644 Newcastle Dr Carrollton TX 75007

MOHN, CHERI (ANN)
PAINTER, INSTRUCTOR
b Akron, Ohio, Aug 12, 36. *Study:* Akron Art Inst, Ohio; Youngstown State Univ, BA. *Work:* Butler Inst Am Art; Phoenix Gallery, Philadelphia; Johnny Artcher's Ghost Town Gallery, Mogollon, NMex. *Comn:* Portrait, Dean Miller, Busn Dept, Youngstown State Univ, 79; many other comns. *Exhib:* Solo exhibs, Village Art Gallery, 76, Gallery 732, Akron, Ohio, 85 & Butler Inst Am Art, 93; Peter Hurd Watercolor Show, Artesia, NMex, 68; Butler Inst Am Art Midyear Show, Youngstown & Guest Artist at Studio 09, Cleveland, 70; John Young Invitational, Youngston, 72-90; Paula Insel Gallery, NY, 73; Lynn Kottler Galleries, NY, 73; Trumbull Art Guild Art Show, 79-81; Mogollon Artists Mus, El Paso, Tex, 90. *Pos:* Art columnist, Niles Times, 58; auth & illusr, articles in Pigment & Form, 67-68; asst ed, writer & illusr, Paintin' Place News Inc, 72; illusr, Village Life Inc, 72; dir, Village Art Gallery, Village Market Place, Columbiana, Ohio, 76-77; ed & illusr, Theron's Country News, 86. *Teaching:* Dir & instr fine arts, Cheri Mohn Sch Arts, Youngstown, 63-67; instr fine arts, Cheri Mohn Studio, 68-90; instr fine arts, Butler Inst Am Art, 86-88. *Awards:* Watercolor Awards: Women--A Celebration, 84-90 & 93; Winners Show, Youngstown State Univ, 84, 85, 87; First in Show, In Praise of Arts, 93. *Bibliog:* Rakocy (auth), Artist of the month, Pigment & Form, 67; Yoder (auth), article, Paintin Place News, 74; feature in Grumbacher's Palette Talk, 86; New York Art Rev, 89. *Mem:* Copley Soc Boston; Soc NAm Artists; Friends Am Art; and others. *Media:* Oil, Watercolor. *Publ:* Auth, Art Features, Niles Times, 58; Art Editorials, Paintin Place News, 72. *Dealer:* Debora Altimus 2721 Heritage NW Canton OH 44718. *Mailing Add:* 12691 South Ave North Lima OH 44452

MOHR, MANFRED
PAINTER
b Pforzheim, Ger, June 8, 38. *Study:* Kunst & Werk, Schule, Pforzheim, 57-62; Beaux Art, Paris, 63-66. *Work:* Wilhelm-Hack Mus, Ludwigshafen, Ger; Mus D'Art Mod, Centre Pompidou, Paris,; Tel Aviv Mus, Israel; Stadt Mus Monchenglad Bach, Ger; Staats Galerie Stuttgart, Ger. *Exhib:* One-man shows, Mus D'Art Moderne, 71, Wilhelm-Hack Mus, 87, Reuchlin Mus, 88, Stuttgart Mus, 94; Printed Art-A View of 2 Decades, Mus Mod Art, NY, 80; Digital Vision, Everson Mus, 87; Josef Albers Mus, Bottrop Ger, 98. *Awards:* Golden Nica, Prix ARS Electronica, 90. *Bibliog:* Nadin, Keiner, Kurtz (monogr), Waser, Zurich, 94; M Dworschak (auth), Der Zeit, 10/31/96. *Mem:* NY Artists Equity; Am Abstract Artists. *Media:* Computer. *Dealer:* Teufel Cologne Germany; Mueller-Roth Stuttgart Germany. *Mailing Add:* 20 N Moore St New York NY 10013

MOIR, ALFRED
CURATOR, COLLECTOR
b Minneapolis, Minn, Apr 14, 24. *Study:* Harvard Univ, AM, 49, PhD, 53; Univ Rome, 50-51. *Collection Arranged:* Drawings by Seventeenth Century Italian Masters from the Collection of Janos Scholz, 74; European Drawings, Santa Barbara Mus Art, 76 & 96; Old Master Drawings from the Feitelson Collections, 83; Old Master Drawings from the Collection of John & Alice Steiner, 86; Van Dyck's Antwerp, 91. *Pos:* Chmn, Dept Art, Univ Calif, Santa Barbara, 63-69; art historian in residence, Am Acad Rome, 69-70 & 80; adj cur, Univ Art Mus, 74-, UCSB, 84-; dir, Univ Calif Educ Abroad Prog, Italy, 78-80; consult cur, Santa Barbara Mus Art, 97-. *Teaching:* From instr to assoc prof hist art, Newcomb Col, Tulane Univ, 52-62; from assoc prof to prof, Univ Calif, Santa Barbara, 62-91, prof emer, 91-. *Mem:* Soc Archit Historians; Renaissance Soc; Medieval Acad Am; Southern Calif Art Historians; Soc of Fels, Acad in Rome; Ateneo Veneto, Venice (Italy); and others. *Res:* Italian baroque art, particularly Caravaggio and his followers; drawings; Van Dyck. *Publ:* The Italian Followers of Caravaggio, Harvard, 67; Caravaggio & His Copyists, New York Univ Press, 77; auth, Caravaggio, Abrams, 82 & 89; Van Dyck, Abrams, 94; and others. *Mailing Add:* Univ Calif Dept Art Hist Santa Barbara CA 93106

MOJSILOV, ILENE KRUG
PAINTER
b St Paul, Minn, May 3, 1952. *Study:* Univ Minn, BFA, 74, MFA, 77; Ryusei Sch, Ikebana, studied with Kosen Otsubo, lic, 84. *Work:* Maki Gallery, Tokyo. *Exhib:* Tweed Mus Art, Duluth, Minn, 76; 37th & 38th Salon de Jeune Peinture, Grand Palais, Paris, 85 & 86; L'Ambiente Gallery, NY, 86 & 87; No Name Gallery, Minneapolis, 88; Bockley Gallery, 91; Wilensky Arts Gallery, 91-93; and others. *Pos:* Artist-in-residence, Asn Confluences, Paris, 84-85, La Vie des Formes, Chalon-sur-Sarbone, France, 90. *Teaching:* Instr painting, Tucson Mus Art Sch, 77-78; artist-in-residence, Minn State Arts Bd, 86-; instr, Walker Art Center, 88-. *Bibliog:* Yuri Akita (auth), New painting, Ikebana Soc, 8/83; Sandra Kwock-Silve (auth), From classical to avant-garde, Paris Free Voice, 4/85. *Mem:* Minn Alliance Arts in Educ; Minn Citizens for Arts. *Media:* Oil, Gouache. *Publ:* Auth, Performance and the mass media, Art Network (Japan issue), spring 84. *Mailing Add:* 4130 Blaisdell Ave S Minneapolis MN 55409-1513

MOKEME, OSCAR O
DIRECTOR
b Nigeria. *Study:* Southern NH Univ. *Work:* Atlanta Puppetary Mus; US Post Office, Portland, ME. *Exhib:* Spirit Masks of the Igbos, Mus of African Taibal Art, Portland, ME. *Collection Arranged:* Housing Spirits in Bronze, Mus of African Art, 2001; The Role Of Ancestors, Mus of African Art, 2002. *Teaching:* Instr, Me Coll of Art, 2000-02; Instr, Univ Southern Me, 2001-02; Instr, Barnad Coll, NY, 2002. *Awards:* Cultural Edn Award, River Rock Found, 2002; Cultural Diversity Award, Jefferson Award, 2000. *Mem:* Me Arts Comn; AAM; African Am Archives of Me. *Publ:* Kalshiah Redo, Cultivating Culture, Portland Press, 2002; Treasures of Me Pot, NY Times, 2002; Africa is not a Country, 2000; The Spirit Masks of the Igbos, Norman Pictures (DVD), 2002. *Mailing Add:* Mus African Tribal Art 122 Spring St #1 Portland ME 04101

MOLDENHAUER, SUSAN
MUSEUM DIRECTOR, CURATOR
Study: N IL Univ, BFA, 1974; Pa State Univ, MFA, 1982. *Pos:* Gallery mgr, Sch Visual Arts, Pa State Univ; exec dir, Second Street Gallery, Charlottesville, Va; cur mus progs, Univ Wyo Art Mus, Laramie, 1991-96, asst dir, 1996-2000, interim dir, 2000-02, dir, chief cur, 2002-. *Mailing Add:* Univ Wyo Art Mus Centennial Complex 2111 Willett Dr PO Box 3807 Laramie WY 82071-3807

MOLDROSKI, AL R
PAINTER, EDUCATOR
b Terre Haute, Ind, Aug 27, 28. *Study:* Ind State Univ, BS; Mich State Univ, MA; Southern Ill Univ, grant; Md Inst Art, Post Masters. *Work:* Continue to work on NY paintings & paper sculpture in Fla & NY. *Exhib:* Pa Acad Fine Arts; Detroit Mus Art; City Art Mus, St Louis; De Waters Art Ctr; Boston Festival Arts; and many others. *Pos:* Ill Spec Events Comn. *Teaching:* Lectr art, Southern Ill Univ, formerly; asst prof, Glenville State Col, formerly; from instr to prof art, Eastern Ill Univ, formerly, prof emer, currently; exchange prof, Portsmouth Polytech Fine Arts, Portsmouth, Eng & Wyzsza Szkola Roiniczo-Pedagogiczna w Siedlch, Poland. *Awards:* Tiffany Found Grant; Purchase Award, Pa Acad Fine Art; Mary Richart Mem Award in Painting & Art Directors Award, Detroit Mus Art; and many others. *Mailing Add:* 236 Mariner Ln Rotonda West FL 33947

MOLINARI, GUIDO
PAINTER, SCULPTOR
b Montreal, Que, Oct 12, 33. *Study:* Ecole Beaux-Arts, Montreal; Sch Art & Design, Montreal Mus Fine Arts. *Work:* Kuntsmuseum, Basel, Switz; Mus Mod Art, Guggenheim Mus & Chase Manhattan Bank, NY; Nat Gallery Art, Ottawa, Ont. *Comn:* Murals, comn by Dept of Pub Works, Ottawa for Vancouver Int Airport, BC, 68 & Dept Nat Defence Hq Bldg, Ottawa, 72. *Exhib:* 4th Guggenheim Int Exhib, NY, 64; The Responsive Eye, Mus Mod Art, 65; Canada: Art Aujourdui, Rome, Paris, Lausanne, Bruxelles, 68; Venice 34th Biennial, Italy, 68; Can 101, Edinburgh, Scotland, 68; Retrospective Exhib, Nat Gallery, Ottawa, Montreal, Toronto & Vancouver, 76; 15th Anniversary Paris Biennial, Mus Mod Art, Paris & Seibu Art Mus, Tokyo, Japan, 77-78; Contemp Can Painters Exhib, Dept External Affairs World Tour, 77-78. *Pos:* Founder & pres, L'Actuelle, 55-57. *Teaching:* Head painting sect, Sir George Williams Univ, 70-. *Awards:* Robertson Award, Montreal Mus Fine Arts, 65; Guggenheim Mem Found Fel, 66; Bright Found Award Painting, 68. *Bibliog:* Gros Plan (film), Radio-Can, Montreal, 71. *Mem:* Academician Royal Can Acad Arts; Soc Esthetique Experimentale, Paris; Soc Color Res, Nat Coun Res (dir, 72). *Publ:* Coauth, Debats sur la Peinture Quebecoise, Univ Montreal, 71. *Mailing Add:* 3288 Saint Catharine St E Montreal PQ H1W 2C6 Canada

MOLLER, HANS
PAINTER
b Wuppertal, Ger, Mar 20, 05; US citizen. *Study:* Kunstgewerbeschule Wuppertal-Barmen, 19-27; Acad Fine Arts, Berlin, 27-28. *Work:* Mus Mod Art & Whitney Mus Am Art, NY; Detroit Inst Art, Mich; Joseph Hirshhorn Mus, Washington, DC; Minneapolis Mus; and many others. *Comn:* Stained glass window, Am Fedn Arts, 53; tapestry, comn by Mr & Mrs Lawrence Buttenwieser, NY, 66; seven stained glass windows, comn by Mr & Mrs Neil Carothers, III, Washington, DC, 69. *Exhib:* Contemp Am Painting, Univ Ill, Urbana, 49-59; solo exhibs, Norfolk Mus, Va, 69, Midtown Galleries, NY, 70, 73, 76, 79, 81, 84 & 87, Allentown Art Mus, Pa, 96; Contemp Painting, Sculpture & Graphics, 69; Hobe Sound Gallery, Fla, 89; Allentown Mus Art, 93; Tooten Bröliau Galerie, Düsseldorf, Ger, 95. *Teaching:* Instr painting, Cooper Union Sch Art, 44-56. *Awards:* Carnegie Prize, Nat Acad, 85; Edwin Palmer Mem Prize, Nat Acad, 80 & 92; Gold Medal Prize, Audubon Artists NY, 92; and others. *Bibliog:* Abram Kampf (auth), Contemporary synagogue art, Union Am Hebrew Congregation, 66; Edward Betts (auth), Creative Landscape Painting, 78; 60 Years of Collecting American Art, Butler Inst, 79. *Mem:* Nat Acad. *Media:* Oil, Watercolor. *Publ:* Hans Moller: Works of the Fifties; Hans Moller: Sketchbook from the Forties. *Dealer:* Midtown Payson Galleries Hobe Sound FL; Gallery 424 Allentown PA. *Mailing Add:* 2207 Allen St Allentown PA 18104-4327

MOLNAR, MICHAEL JOSEPH
PAINTER, INSTRUCTOR
b Hazleton, Pa. *Study:* Luzerne County CC, studied comml art, 1968-70; Md Inst Col Art, BFA, studied under Joseph Sheppard, 1975; studies with Vincent Civiletti, 1977; studies with Joseph Sheppard, 1988; Schuler Sch Fine Art, Balt, studied with Ann Schuler, 1990-91. *Exhib:* Mid-West Mus Am Art, Elkhart, Ind, 1998; Evergreen House, Johns Hopkins Univ, Balt, 1998; Butler Inst Am Art, Salem, Ohio, 1998; invitational, Ea Sierra Art Found, Genoa, Nev, 1999; Allied Artists Am ann exhibn, Nat Arts Club, 2000; invitational, John Pence Gallery, San Francisco, 2002;

Rittenhouse Fine Art Gallery, 2003; Eleanor Ehinger Gallery, Tromp L'oeil Soc Exhib, 2003; Woodson Art Mus, Visual Deceptions Exhbns, 2003; Phoenix Art Mus, Fashion's Art of Illusion, 2003; Trompe L'Oeil: The Art of Illusion Traveling Exhib, 2006-2007; Legacy: A Tradition Lives On Traveling Exhib, 2006-2007; The Jule Collins Smith Mus of Art, Auburn, Ala, 2006-2007. *Pos:* asst to Leonard Bahr, Md Inst Col Art, 73; with commercial art dept, Luzerne Co Community Col. *Teaching:* pvt teaching & research Old Master techniques, 77-90; instr painting, drawing & sculpture, Luzerne Co Community Col, 80-2006. *Awards:* First Prize, Pa Col of Technol, 2002; 3rd Place-Portrait, Portrait Arts Festival Metrop Mus NY, 2003; Gary Erbe Award, Allied Artist of Am, 2005. *Bibliog:* Art Review, 2005; Legacy: A Tradition Lives On, 2005; American Artist Magazine, 2005. *Mem:* Am Soc Classical Realism; Allied Artists Am; Knickerbocker Artists; Scottsdale Art Sch; Am Soc Portrait Artists. *Media:* Oil. *Specialty:* realism. *Interests:* Painting. *Dealer:* John Pence 750 Post St San Francisco Calif 94109; Eleanor Ettinger Gallery 119 Spring St New York NY 10012; Robert Wilson Gallery, MA. *Mailing Add:* 1772 Hudson Dr Weatherly PA 18255

MOMENT, JOAN
INSTRUCTOR, PAINTER
b Sellersville, Pa, Aug 22, 38. *Study:* Univ Conn, BS, 60; Univ Colo, with Roland Reiss & William Wiley, MFA, 70. *Work:* E B Crocker Art Mus, Sacramento, Calif; Blue Cross of Southern Calif, Los Angeles; NY State Develop Corp, NY; Oakland Mus, Calif; Allen Mem Art Mus, Oberlin Col, Ohio; and others. *Comn:* City of Sacramento, Sacramento Metrop Art Comn, Calif, 90-97. *Exhib:* Contemp Am Art Biennial, Whitney Mus Am Art, NY, 73; One-person show, Whitney Mus Am Art, 74, Crocker Art Mus, Sacramento, Calif, 81, Quay Gallery, San Francisco, Calif, 82, Southeastern Ctr Contemp Art, Winston-Salem, NC, 84, Rena Branston Gallery, San Francisco, 85, Glass Gallery, Univ NC, Chapel Hill, 86 & Solomon Dubnick Gallery, Sacramento, 92; A Moment Becomes Eternity; Flowers as Image, Bergen Mus Art, NJ, 93; Building a Collection: Recent Acquisitions, Crocker Art Mus, Sacramento, 94; Choices: Recent Acquisitions, Oakland Mus, Calif, 94; Sexy: Sensual Abstraction in Calif Art, 1950's-1990's, Contemp Artists Collective/Temporary Contemp, Las Vegas, 95; and many others; Jay Jay Gallery, Sacramento, Calif, 2002; Cent Acad of Fine Art, Beijing, China, 2003. *Teaching:* prof art, Calif State Univ, Sacramento, 70-; vis artist, Univ Colo, Boulder, 75, Univ Mont, Missoula, 77, Diablo Valley Col, Pleasant Hill, Calif, 78, Bard Col, Milton Avery Grad Sch Arts, 85, Syracuse Univ, NY, 85, Univ NC, Chapel Hill, 86, Princeton Univ, NJ, 87 & Sonoma State Univ, Rohnert Park, CA; guest lectr, Eastern Wash State Col, Cheney, 73, Wash State Univ, Pullman, 74, Claremont Grad Sch, Calif, 80, Solano Community Col, Fairfield, Calif, 82, Univ of Reno, Nev, 83 & Cent Acad Beijing, China, 2003; vis assoc prof, East Carolina Univ, Greenville, 84; lectr, Crocker Art Mus, Sacramento, CA, 94. *Awards:* Rockefeller Artist-in-Residency Fel, 84; Meritorious Performance Award, Calif State Univ, Sacramento, 86. *Bibliog:* Kenneth Baker (auth), Studio, show a bright light in dark times, San Francisco Chronicle, 7/5/92; Jeff Kelly (auth), California dreaming: From the studio at the Oakland Museum, Art Week, Vol 23, No 22, 8/20/92; Randal Davis (auth), Hybrid hits & misses paintings by Joan Moment, Soonja Kim & Hideo Sakato, Sacramento News & Review, 11/12/92; and many others. *Media:* Acrylic on Wood Panel, Canvas & Arches Paper. *Dealer:* Jay Jay Gallery 2906 Franklin Blvd Sacrament CA 95818. *Mailing Add:* 1424 35th St Sacramento CA 95816

MOMIYAMA, NANAE
PAINTER, EDUCATOR
b Tokyo, Japan. *Study:* Bunka Gakuin Col, Tokyo; Tokyo Women's Col; Art Students League. *Work:* Nat Mus Mod Arts, Tokyo; Metrop Mus Arts, Tokyo; City Mus Kyoto, Japan; Munic Mus Osaka, Japan; Newberger Mus, Purchase, NY. *Exhib:* Mod Arts Asn Japan, 51-81; Grand Prix Humanitaire de France, 75; one-man shows, Seibu Gallery Tokyo, 74, 77, 79, 82, 84, 87 & 90, Ligoa Duncan Gallery, NY, 75 & Galeries Raymond Duncan, Paris, 75 & 76; plus many others. *Pos:* Permanent juror, Mod Art Asn, Japan, Nat Asn Women Artists, 68-77 & 90-92 & Salone Int di Pittura, Rome, 72. *Teaching:* Instr, State Univ NY Col, Purchase, 73-80; lectr, Nat Gallery Washington, DC, Philadelphia Mus, Brooklyn Mus, Pittsfield Mus, Columbia Univ, Pratt Inst, Japan Soc, NY & numerous other institutions in US & Japan. *Awards:* Madaille d'Argent, Grand Prix Humanitaire de France, 75; Charles Woodbury Mem Prize, Nat Asn Women Artists Ann, Nat Acad, NY, 78; Gold Medal, Accademia Italia delle Arti, 79; Golden Flame Prize, Accademia Italia, 85. *Bibliog:* Takachiyo Uemura (auth), Mizue, Bijitsu Shuppan-Sha, 54 & 74; Kaoru Yamaguchi (auth), Geijitsu Shincho, Shincho-Sha. *Mem:* Mod Arts Asn Japan; Japanese Artists Asn NY (pres, 78-79); Asn Int Artists Plastiques; Japanese Artist Asn; Nat Asn Women Artists; Contemp Artist Guild. *Media:* Oil, Mixed Media. *Publ:* Auth, Sumi-e, An Introduction to Ink Painting, 67; illusr, Makura-no-Soshi of Sei Shonagon, 67; Rev Paris, 68; cover design, The Asian, 85

MONAGHAN, KATHLEEN MARY
DIRECTOR
b Waterville, Maine, Sept 6, 36. *Study:* Univ Calif, Santa Barbara, BA, 78, MA, 81. *Collection Arranged:* Faces & Figures: European Drawings, Santa Barbara Mus Art, 81, American Modernism 1910-1945, 81, The Gloria & Donald B Marron Collection American Prints, 81, Rufino Tamayo-The Pre-Columbian, 82. *Pos:* Dir br mus, Whitney Mus Am Art, New York, 85-93, assoc cur, 92-93; dir, The Hyde Collection, Glen Falls, NY, 94-99; exec dir, Fresno Met Mus, 99-. *Awards:* Rubinstein fel, Whitney Mus Am Art, NY City, 78. *Mem:* Am Asn Mus Dir; Am Asn Mus; Int Comt Exhib Exchanges; Western Asn Art Mus; Southern Calif Art Historians Asn. *Res:* 19th-20th century American art; 18th century British art; Joseph Wright of Derby. *Publ:* contribr, Donald Marron Print Collection, SBMA, 80; The Stirling Morton Collection, SBMA, 81; auth, Elements, Whitney Mus Am Art, 87; Abstraction Before 1930, Whitney Mus Am Art, 91; Nature's Bounty, Whitney Mus Am Art, 93. *Mailing Add:* Fresno Metropolitan Museum Art 1555 Van Ness Ave Fresno CA 93721

MONAGHAN, WILLIAM SCOTT
PAINTER, SCULPTOR
b Philadelphia, Pa, Nov 1, 44. *Study:* Yale Univ, BA; Harvard Grad Sch Design, MA. *Work:* Addison Gallery Am Art, Andover, Mass; Brockton Fuller Mem Art Mus, Mass; Fed Reserve Bank, Boston; Hyatt Hotel, Boston; Aldrich Mus Contemp Art, Ridgefield, Conn. *Comn:* Sculpture, Boston 200 Bicentennial Art Collection, 76. *Exhib:* Sculptors' Workshop Show, Addison Gallery Am Art, 74 & Berkshire Mus, Pittsfield, Mass, 75; One-man show, Inst Contemp Art, Boston, 75; Contemp Reflections, Aldrich Mus Contemp Art, 76; Davidson Art Mus, Wesleyan Univ, Conn, 77; Two-man show, Soho Ctr for Visual Artists, NY, 77. *Mem:* Boston Visual Artists' Union. *Mailing Add:* 165 Perry St New York NY 10014-2382

MONAHAN, MATTHEW
ARTIST
b Eureka, Calif, 72. *Study:* Cooper Union, BFA, 90-94; Studies at Gerit Rietveld Accad, Amsterdam. *Exhib:* Solo shows, Anton Kern Gallery, NY, 97; Fools Gold, The Bank of Netherlands, 98; Artist is Proof, Buro Leeuwarden, Neth, 99; Gozaimas, Bur. Stedelijk, 2000; Nameless Man for Not-Even-Anywhere, Galeries Fons Welters, Amsterdam, 2002; Civilized Spl. Zone, Chinese European Art Ctr, Xiamen, 2002; Container, Art Basel Miami, 2003; Group shows, Night at Life, NY, 97; Exterminating Angel, Galerie Ghislaine Hussenot, Paris, 98; Subreal/The Human Condition, LA Int Biennial, Inmo Gallery, Los Angeles, 99; I Love NY, Anton Kern Gallery, 2001; Mean Mercy, Tent, Rotterdam, 2001; Free-Standing, Beaver Col Art Gallery, Philadelphia, 2001; To Be Recycled, Six Months, Los Angeles, 2004; Remembering, Univ Calif, Riverside Gallery, 2004; Whitney Biennial: Day for Night, Whitney Mus Am Art, 2006. *Awards:* Fel de Ateliers, Amsterdam, 94-96; Fonds BK Grant, Kitakysuhu, Japan, 2000; Chinese European Art, Ctr, Xiamen, 2002. *Mailing Add:* c/o Anton Kern Gallery 532 W 20th St New York NY 10011

MONCRIEF, RICHARD W
PATRON
Study: Univ Tex, BS. *Pos:* Principal, Moncrief Oil Interests, Ft Worth, owner Moncrief Oil Int, gen partner, Moncrief Oil Europe & Asia Holdings Partnership; bd trustees, US Azerbaijan CofC, Amon Carter Mus, William A & Elizabeth B Moncrief Found. *Mem:* All-Am Wildcatters. *Mailing Add:* Moncrief Oil 4920 Crestline Rd Fort Worth TX 76107

MONDALE, JOAN ADAMS
CRAFTSPERSON, CERAMIST
b Eugene, Ore, Aug 8, 30. *Study:* Macalester Col, St Paul, Minn, BA, 52. *Hon Degrees:* Barnard Col, 77, Manchester Col, 77, RI Sch Design, 78, Pomona Col, 79, Beloit Col, 81, Col New Rochelle, 81, San Francisco Inst Arts, 82, Corcoran Sch art, 83, Savannah Col Art & Design, 83, Alfred Univ, 89 & Minneapolis Col Art & Design, 90. *Work:* Boston Mus Fine Arts; Minneapolis Inst Arts; Nat Gallery Art, Washington. *Exhib:* Toad Hall Potters, Art Barn, Washington, 86. *Pos:* Bd mem, Macalester Col, 86-; US Postal Serv Citizen's Adv, Comm, 2005-. *Awards:* ArtTable Award for Distinguished Service to the Visual Arts, 97. *Mem:* Am Crafts Coun (bd mem, 80-87); Walker Art Ctr (bd, 87); Minnesota Orchestra (bd, 87-94); St Paul Chamber Orchestra (bd, 87-89), Nancy Hauser Dance Co (bd mem, 89-94); Hiawatha light Rail Transport Pub Art & Design com (chair 2000-). *Collection:* Japanese Pottery. *Publ.* Auth, Politics in Art, Lerner, 72; Letters from Japan, pvt publ, 98. *Mailing Add:* 2116 Irving Ave S Minneapolis MN 55405-2541

MONDINI-RUIZ, FRANCO
ARTIST
b San Antonio, Tex 61. *Study:* BA in English, St Mary's Univ, San Antonio, Tex, BA in English 1982; JD, St Mary's Univ, San Antonio, Tex, 1985. *Work:* group exhibs incl, Arlington Mus Art, 1991; Laguna Gloria Art Mus, Austin, 1997; Simply Beautiful, Contemp Art Mus, Houston, 1997; Collective Visions, San Antonio Mus Art, 1998; Material World, Austin Mus Art, 1998; Whitney Biennial, Whitney Mus Am Art, New York City, 2000; Mus Contemp Art, Helsinki, Finland, 2001; UCLA Fowler Mus Cult Hist, 2004-05. *Exhib:* Solo exhib incl, Infinito Botanica, ArtPace, San Antonio, 1996, Tableau Vivant, The Alamo, San Antonio, 1998, New Painting y Mas, Galeria Ortiz, San Antonio, 1999, Infinito Botanica: NY, Ctr Curatorial Studies, Bard Col, 1999, Mexique, El Museo del Barrio, New York City, 2000, Untitled Grid No 7, New Mus Contemp Art, New York City, 2001, Infinito Botanico: St Louis, Des Lee Gallery, Washington Univ, 2001, SHOP, Jessica Murray Projects, Brooklyn, 2001, Dust in the Wind, NY Pub Art Fund, 2002, Market Squared, Galeria Ortiz, San Antonio, 2002, Nacho de Paz (and Other TexMex Miracles), Frederieke Taylor Gallery, New York City, 2002, Pan in the Park, Laumeier Sculpture Park, St Louis, 2003, Infinito Botanico: Los Angeles, UCLA Fowler Mus Cult Hist, 2004-05. *Pos:* Atty USAA; owner Infinito Botanica and Gift Shop, San Antonio, 1995-98; ArtPace Artist in Residency Prog, 1996; Tryon Ctr Artist Residency Prog Charlotte, NC, 2003. *Awards:* New Forms Regional Initiative Grant, 1994, ArtPace General Grant, 1999, Pollock-Krasner Found Grant, 2000, Joan Mitchell Found Grant, 2001, Creative Capital Found Grant, 2001, Creative Capital Found Supplemental Grant, 2002, Penny McCall Found Fel, 2002, Jules Guerin Rome Prize Fel for Visual Arts, Am Acad in Rome, 2004-05

MONEO, JOSE RAFAEL
ARCHITECT
b Tudela, Navarra, Spain, 1937. *Study:* Madrid Univ Sch Archit, 61. *Comn:* Diestre Factory, Zaragoza, Spain, 65; Uremae Proj, San Sebastian, Spain, 68; Bankinter Office Bldg, Madrid Spain, 74; City Hall, Logrono, Spain, 74; Mus Roman Art, Merida, Spain, 80. *Exhib:* Prevision Espanoloa Budg, Seville, 82; Atocha Railway Station, Spain; San Pablo Airport, Seville, Spain, 90; Villahermosa Palace, Spain, 90; Diagonal

Bldg, Barcelona, Spain, 90; Kursaal Concert Hall & Cult Ctr, San Sebastian, Spain; Mus Art & Archit, Stockholm; Building in a New Spain: Contemp Spanish Archit, Art Inst Chicago, 92; Art Mus and Archit, Zmus Cantonale d'Arte, Lugano, Switz, 92; Ten Yrs of Spanish Archit 1980-90, Ministerio de Obras Publicas y Transportes, Madrid Spain, 92; Buildings and Projects 1973-1993, Arkitekturmuseet, Stockholm, Sweden, 93; Retrospective, Rafael Moneo, Building in the City, Adademie der Bildenden Kunste of Vienna, 93; Mus and Archit, Circulo de Bellas Artes, Madrid, Spain, 94; Mus Finnish Archit, Helsinki, Finland, 94. *Teaching:* Instr, Madrid Univ Sch Archit, 66, Cooper Union Sch Archit, New York, 76; vis prof, Princeton Univ, Harvard Univ & Univ Lausanne, Switz; chair prof, Sch Archit, Madrid, Spain, 80; chmn, Archit Dept, Harvard Univ Grad Sch Design, 84-90. *Awards:* Prince of Viana Prize, Govt Province of Navarra (Spain), 93; Schock Prize Visual Arts, Schock Found & Royal Acad Fine Arts, Stockholm, 93; Lauea ad Honorem, Sch Archit, Venice, 94; Pritzker Architecture Prize, 96. *Mem:* Am Acad Arts & Sci; Accademia di San Luca di Roma; hon fel Am Inst Archit; hon fel Royal Inst Brit Archit. *Mailing Add:* Harvard Univ Dept Archit 48 Quincy St Cambridge MA 02138

MONGRAIN, CLAUDE
SCULPTOR
b Shawinigan, Que, 1948. *Study:* Ecole des Beaux-Arts de Montreal, 66-69. *Work:* Mus des Beaux-Arts de Montreal; Can Coun Art Bank, Ottawa; Musee d'Art Contemporain de Montreal; Nat Gallery Can, Ottawa; Mus de Que. *Exhib:* Solo exhibs, Olga Korper Gallery, Toronto, Ont, 85, 90 & 93, Claude Mongrain; Deuvres Recentes, Concordia Art Gallery, Concordia Univ, Montreal, Que, 87, Art Gallery Windsor, Ont, 88, Galerie Christiane Chassay, Montreal, Que, 89, Accelerateur de particules, Galerie Obscure, Montreal, Que, 91, Deux Monuments a une etoile Filante, Toronto Sculpture Garden, Ont, 91 & Zapping, Galerie Aline Vidal, Paris, France, 92; Espaces Int, CREDAC, Centre d'Art Contemporain, Ivry-Sur-Seine, France, 90; L'art de l'installation, Mus d'Art Contemporain, Montreal, Que, 90; Singulier/Pluriels, Galerie de L'UQAM, Montreal, Que, 92; Ameriques, Centre Lotois d'Art Contemporain, FIGEAC, France, 92; Vues d'Ensemble, CIAC, Montreal, Que, 92. *Awards:* Materials Assts Grants, Can Coun, 71, 73, 76, 85 & 86; Work Grant, 80, Bourse de Que, 87, Que Ministry Cult Affairs. *Bibliog:* Trevor Gould (auth), Claude Mongrain, No 14, C Mag, Toronto, summer 87, 65-66; Jerry McGrath (auth), Art in the Soo, Sans Demarcation, Vanguard, 2-3/88, 10-13. *Publ:* Contribr, Le Dessin Errant (catalog), Dalhousie Art Gallery, Halifax, 88. *Mailing Add:* c/o Olga Korper Gallery 17 Morrow Ave Toronto ON M6R 2H9 Canada

MONK, NANCY
SCULPTOR, PHOTOGRAPHER
b Minneapolis, Minn. *Study:* Colo State Univ, BFA, 73; Univ Minn, MFA, 76. *Work:* Corning Mus Glass, NY; Mod Int Glaskunst, Ebeltoft, Denmark. *Exhib:* New Glass: A Worldwide Survey, Corning Mus Glass, NY, 79; Int Glas Exhib, Reria Int de Ceramica Vidrio, Valencia, Spain, 82; Int Glass Exhib, Mod Int Glass Mus, Elbeltoff, Denmark, 86; Long Beach Art Mus, 88; Handmade in Pasadena, Alfred Univ, NY State Col Ceramics, 91; Sam Francis Gallery, Crossroads Sch, Santa Monica, Calif; Site Specific, Armory Ctr for Arts, Pasadena, Calif; Part to the Whole, Lobend Gallery, Loyola Marymount Univ, Los Angeles; Solway-Jones Gallery, Los Angeles, 2003; The Brewery Project, Los Angeles, Calif, 2004; Irvine Fine Arts Center, 2004; one-person shows, Koplin Gallery, Los Angeles, Calif, 82, Los Angeles Junior Arts Ctr, Barnsdall Park, Calif, 84, NY Experimental Glass Workshop, Brooklyn, NY, 93, Clairemont Grad Sch East Gallery, 93 & Jan Kesner Gallery, Los Angeles, 96, Person and Thing, Craig Krull Gallery, Santa Monica, Calif, 99, Portraits, Craig Krull Gallery, 2001, Assorted Spring, Harris Gallery, Univ LaVerne, Calif, 2002; Craig Krull Gallery, Baroque, 2004; Santa Barbara Contemp Arts Forum, Syncopation, Santa Barbara, CA, Made in Pasadena, Craig Krull Gallery, 2006. *Teaching:* Instr, Minneapolis Col Art & Design, 76-77; instr, Pasadena City Col, 89-. *Awards:* Nat Endowment Arts, 86 & 89; City of Pasadena Artist Fel, 92; Emergency assistance grant, Adolf & Esther Gottlieb Found, 2001. *Bibliog:* K Moriyama (auth), Glassware Designed by Nancy Monk, Japan Interior Design; Suzanne K Frantz (auth), Contemporary Glass; Victoria Milne (auth), "Nancy Monk", Glass No 52, summer 94; Ingrid Calame (auth), "Nancy Monk", Art Issues No 43, summer 96; Christopher Miles (auth), The Part to the Whole, 2000. *Media:* Mixed Media. *Dealer:* Craig Krull Gallery 2525 Michigan Ave Bldg B3 Santa Monica CA 90404. *Mailing Add:* 444 S Euclid Apt 9 Pasadena CA 91101

MONK, ROBERT EVAN, JR
CURATOR
b New York, NY, Aug 20, 50. *Study:* Pratt Inst, Brooklyn, NY. *Collection Arranged:* Dimitry Merinoff, Paintings: 1950-1970, Clocktower, New York, 80. *Pos:* Cur, Merinoff Estate, 74-84 & Leo Castelli Gallery, 74-84; pres, Lorence Monk Gallery, New York, 85-92; sr vpres & dir contemp art, Sotheby's New York, 92-97. *Teaching:* Instr, Sotheby's Educ Prog. *Media:* Paintings, Drawings; Sculpture. *Mailing Add:* Gagosian Gallery 980 Madison Ave New York NY 10021

MONNIER, JACQUELINE MATISSE See Matisse, Jackie (Jacqueline) Matisse Monnier

MONROE, BETTY IVERSON
EDUCATOR
b Ames, Iowa, May 3, 22. *Study:* Iowa State Univ, BS, 44, MS, 50; Univ Mich, MA, 64, PhD, 73. *Collection Arranged:* Chinese Ceramics in Chicago Collections, 82-83. *Teaching:* Asst prof art hist, Wash Univ, St Louis, 66-67; asst prof, Northwestern Univ, 68-74, chmn dept, 74-78, assoc prof, 74-. *Mem:* Col Art Asn; Midwest Art Hist Soc; Am Comt S Asian Art. *Res:* Asian art history; Japanese painting. *Publ:* Ed & translr, Japanese Painting in the Literati Style, Weatherhill, New York & Heibonsha, Tokyo, 74; auth, Chinese Ceramics in Chicago Collections, Northwestern Univ Press, 82. *Mailing Add:* 325 College Ct Iowa City IA 52245-4403

MONROE, GERALD
PAINTER, EDUCATOR
b New York, NY, Aug 17, 26. *Study:* Art Students League; Cooper Union; NY Univ, BA, 67, MS, 68, EdD, 71. *Work:* NY Univ Collection; NJ State Mus; Newark Mus, NJ; Port Authority NY & NJ. *Exhib:* Solo exhibs, Cooper Union Art, New York City, 67, 69, Loeb Ctr, NY Univ, 71, Glassboro State Col, NJ, 71, William Paterson State Col, Wayne, NJ, 73, NJ State Mus, Trenton, 75, Wagner Col, Staten Island, NY, 76, Newark Mus, NJ, 78, Bell Gallery, Greenwich, Conn, 79, Elaine Benson Gallery, Bridgehampton, NY, 80, 82, 87, 92, 94, ETS Campus, Princeton, NJ, 83, Southampton Col, NY, 86, Benton Gallery, Southampton, NY, 86, 88, 93, Bologna-Landi Gallery, East Hampton, NY, 93, Donohue/Sosinski Art, New York City, 96, 98, 2001; Michael Steinberg Fine Art, 2005; Group exhibs, Aldrich Mus, Ridgefield, Conn, 74, Finch Col Mus, New York City, 73, NJ State Mus, Trenton, 73, Va Ctr Arts, Sweet Brair, 79, Parrish Art Mus, Southampton, NY, 81, 90, 98, 2000, Max Hutchinson Gallery, New York City, 83, Guild Hall Mus, East Hampton, NY, 87, Benton Gallery, East Hampton, NY, 89, Bergen Co Mus, NY, 93, Arlene Bujese Gallery, East Hampton, NY, 95, Vered Gallery, East Hampton, NY, 97. *Collection Arranged:* NJ State Mus; Newark Mus, NJ; NY Univ; Finch Coll Mus; Port Authority NY & NJ; Macalester Coll; Otis Elevator; Lanvin Corp; Best Products; Smith-Barney; mural, Glassboro High Sch, NJ. *Pos:* Assoc prof art, Glassboro State Col, 68-86; artist-in-residence MacDowell Colony, Va Ctr Arts, Ossabow Island Project. *Awards:* Nat Endowment for Humanities Fel, 73-74, Grant, 75; Ossabaw Island Proj, 77; Va Ctr Creative Arts, 78; and others. *Media:* Oil. *Res:* Influence of left-wing politics on art; strategies for drawing instruction; artists during the Great Depression. *Publ:* Auth articles in Art J, Arch Am Art J, Studio Int & Art in Am; illusr, Am Artist. *Dealer:* Michael Steinberg Fine Art, 526 26 St, New York, NY. *Mailing Add:* 463 West St New York NY 10014-2010

MONTANO, LINDA (MARY)
CONCEPTUAL ARTIST, VIDEO ARTIST
b Saugerties, NY, Jan 18, 42. *Study:* Villa Schifanoia, Florence, MA(sculpture), 66; Univ Wis, Madison, MFA(sculpture), 69; Hobart Welding School, 69. *Work:* Mus Mod Art. *Exhib:* How to Become a Guru, Womens Bldg, Los Angeles, 75; Learning to Talk, Univ Calif, San Diego, 76; Talking About Sex: For My Father, Kitchen, NY, 80; Mitchell's Death, Mus Mod Art, NY, 81; Palm Reading, Real Art Ways, Hartford, Conn, 82; Readings: Visual Collaborations, Chicago Art Inst, 83; Seven Yrs of Living Art: Wearing Only One Color Each Yr, Speaking in a Different Accent Each Yr, Listening to One Tone Seven Hours a Day (Doing Art-Life Counseling and Reading palms at the New Mus Once A Month), 84-91; Another Seven Yrs of Living Art: An Experience of the Seven Chakras with Seasonal Astral Visits to the Chagall Chapel, UN, 91-98. *Collection Arranged:* Schiffler Collection. *Teaching:* Instr performance, San Francisco State Univ, 78-79, San Francisco Art Inst, 79-80, Womens Bldg, 81 & Chicago Art Inst, 83, Univ Tex, Austin, 91-98. *Awards:* Fels, Nat Endowment Arts, 77 & 85; Women's Studio Workshop Grants, 82 & 83; Fel, NY State Found Arts, 86. *Bibliog:* Moira Roth (auth), Towards a history of college performance, Arts Mag, 12/78; Marcia Tucker (auth), Not just for laughs, New Mus, 11/81; Tony Whitfield (auth), Dressing up, acting out, Live Mag, 82. *Media:* Performance; Video; Books; Singing. *Collection:* Schiffler Collection. *Publ:* Contribr, High Performance, 77- & auth, Art in Everyday Life, 80, Astro Artz; co-ed, Fuse Mag, Franklin Furnace, 82; auth, Before and after art-life counseling, Women's Studio Workshop, 83; auth, Performance Artists Talking in the Eighties, 2000; Lett from Linda M Moutane, 2005. *Mailing Add:* The Art/Life Institute 185 Abeel St Kingston NY 12401

MONTEITH, CLIFTON J
CRAFTSMAN, SCULPTOR
b Detroit, Mich, July 8, 44. *Study:* Mich State Univ, BFA(painting & educ), 68, MFA (painting), 74. *Work:* Art Inst Chicago; Am Craft Mus, NY. *Exhib:* Art Expo, Carl Hammer Gallery, Chicago, Ill, 91; Preferred Seating, Wetsman Collection, Birmingham, Mich, 91; solo show, Miami Univ Mus, Oxford, Ohio, 92 & Interlochen Ctr Arts, Mich, 97; Of Tops and Bottoms, Ohio Designer Craftsman Traveling Exhib, 93; The Chair as Art, Gallery Functional Art, Santa Monica, Calif, 93; Carlm Hammer Gallery, 94; Tamarack Craftsman Gallery, Omena, Mich, 95; Hershey Mus, Pa, 96; Contemp NAm Furniture-A Survey of the Furniture Makers Art, Newberger Mus Art, Purchase, NY, 97; The Chair Show, Southern Highland Craft Guild, Asheville, NC, 97; Evolution in for Exhib, Arrowmont Sch Arts & Crafts, Gatlinburg, Tenn, 98. *Pos:* Owner furniture making bus, 84-. *Teaching:* Instr painting, drawing & sculpture, 68-84; guest lectr, Univ Mich Sch Art, Ann Arbor, 87, Calvin Col, Grand Rapids, 90 & Parnham Col, Dorset, Eng, 93; lectr, S Ohio Mus, 93, Takumi-Jyuku Wood Working Sch, Japan, 94, Far East Soc Architects & Engineers, Japan, 94, Osaka Designers' Col, Japan, 94, Int House Japan, 94 & Dennos Mus, Mich, 95; instr, Haystack Mountain Sch Crafts, Deer Isle, Maine, 96, Penland Sch Crafts, NC, 97, Anderson Ranch, Snowmass, Colo, 98 & Ore Col Arts & Crafts, Portland, 98. *Awards:* Nat Endowment Arts, 92; Fel, US-Japan Friendship Comn, 94; Fel, Japan Found, 99. *Bibliog:* Daniel Mack (auth), Making Rustic Furniture, Lark Books, Asheville, NC, 92; US News & World Report, 11/92; Ralph Kylloe (auth), Rustic Traditions, Gibbs Smith, 93. *Dealer:* Carl Hammer Gallery 200 W Superior St Chicago IL 60610. *Mailing Add:* 20341 Fowler Lake Ann MI 49650

MONTESINOS, VICKY
PAINTER, PRINTMAKER
b Mexico City, Mex. *Study:* Studied with Jose Bardasano, Mex; studied with Quinquella Martin, Buenos Aires. *Exhib:* Solo exhib, Galeria Rosana, Mexico City, Mex, 71; Espana Pintura Contemporanea Mex 77, Madrid, 77; Int Expos, Rotterdam; Int Expos, Tokyo; Clayton R Betts Gallery, San Francisco

MONTFORD, JAMES WEBSTER, JR
EDUCATOR
b New London, Conn, July 28, 51. *Study:* Brandeis Univ, AB, 74; Skowhegan Sch Painting & Sculpture, 75: Columbia Univ, MA 76; Hoffberger Sch Painting, 78; Md Inst Art with Grace Hartigan, MFA, 78. *Work:* Mus Nat Ctr Afro-Am Artists, Boston; De Cordova Mus, Lincoln, Mass; Slater Mus, Norwich, Conn; Contemp Inst Art, Scottsdale, Ariz. *Exhib:* Wall Installations, Wadsworth Antheneum, Hartford, 84; Praying Shoes/Preying Shoes, Nat Ctr Afro-Am Artists, Boston, 90; A Myth A Metaphor and More, Old State House, Hartford, 91; Immortal Words, Zone Art Ctr, Springfield, Mass, 92; Artist Dollars, Taft Mus, Cincinnati, 94; Subversive Images in Media, Art Space Gallery, New Haven, Conn, 94; Lost in the Myth of Am, Scottsdale Ctr Arts, 95; Paladia, Mobius, Boston, 96. *Pos:* Vis artist, Art All-State Worcester Art Mus, 92, Mass Col Art, Boston, 92 & RI Sch Design, Providence, 93; vis artist studio art, Hartford Art Sch, 92-94. *Teaching:* Fac, Univ Conn, 84-89; lectr, Univ RI, Kingston, 92-96. *Awards:* Yaddo Fel, 91, 93, 94 & 95; New Eng Found Arts, 93; Pollock-Krasner Found, 93; Nat Endowment Arts, 94; Art Matters, NY, 95. *Bibliog:* People for the American Way (auth), Artistic Freedom Under Attack, Art Save Proj, 92-94; Bill Rodriguez (auth), The language of hate, Providence Phoenix, 94; Robin Cembalest (auth), Sexist, racist or otherwise offensive, Art News, 94. *Mem:* Col Art Asn; New Eng Artist's Cong. *Dealer:* Howard Yezerski Gallery 11 Newbury St Boston MA 02116. *Mailing Add:* Howard Yezerski Gallery 14 Newbury St 3rd Fl Boston MA 02116

MONTHAN, GUY
PHOTOGRAPHER, EDUCATOR
b Tucson, Ariz, Apr 17, 25. *Study:* Syracuse Univ, BFA, 50; Calif State Univ, Los Angeles, MA, 67. *Exhib:* Los Angeles Co Mus Ann, 61; Southwestern Photog Exhibit, Dallas Mus Fine Arts, 73; Yuma Invitational, Ariz, 73-78; Coconino Ctr Arts Photog Show, Flagstaff, 89; 24th Southwestern Exhib, Yuma, 90; one man show, Northern Ariz Univ, 97. *Pos:* Advert design, Los Angeles, 50-68. *Teaching:* Assoc prof advert design, Northern Ariz Univ, Flagstaff, 68-90; Retired, 90. *Awards:* For Art and Indian Individualists, Rounce & Coffin Book Award, 76, Border Regional Libr Asn Southwest Book Award, 76, Bookbuilders W Award, 76 & For The Pueblo Storyteller, 86. *Publ:* Designer-illusr, Art and Indian Individualists, 75; designer-illusr, Nacimientos: Nativity Scenes by Southwest Indian Artisans, Northland Press, Flagstaff, 79; illusr, The Pueblo Storyteller, Univ Ariz Press, Tucson, 86. *Mailing Add:* PO Box 1021 Corrales NM 87048-9574

MONTI, JOHN
SCULPTOR, EDUCATOR
b Portland, Ore, Jan 8, 57. *Study:* Portland State Univ, Ore, BS, 80; Pratt Inst, Brooklyn, NY, MFA, 83. *Work:* Metrop Mus Art, Am Telephone & Telegraph, Chase Manhattan Bank, NY; Brooklyn Mus, NY; McNay Art Mus, San Antonio, Tex; Israel Mus, Jerusalem; Eli-Broad Family Found, Santa Monica, Calif; and others. *Comn:* Public Art Fund, NY City; New Berger Mus, NY. *Exhib:* Sculpture on the Wall, Aldrich Mus, Ridgefield, Conn, 86; one-person shows, Greg Kucera Gallery, Seattle, Wash, 90, White Room, White Columns, NY, 92, Sculpture Ctr, NY, 93, Ledisflam Gallery, NY, 93, Mus Art, Munson-Williams-Proctor Inst, Utica, NY, 93 & Inform Gallery, Kanazawa, Japan, 96 & Elizabeth Harris Gallery, 97 & 2000; Contemp Wood Sculpture, Brooklyn Mus, NY, 92; Art on Paper, Weatherspoon Art Gallery, Univ NC, 95; Sculpture Space: Celebrating 20 Yrs, Mus Art, Munson-Williams-Proctor Inst, Utica, NY, 95; Three Sculptors & Their Drawings, Grounds for Sculpture, Hamilton, NJ, 95; Changing Places, MetroTech Ctr, Brooklyn, NY, 96; Elizabeth Harris Gallery, NY, 98. *Teaching:* Prof, Dept Fine Arts, Pratt Inst, 88-, sculpture coordr, 95; vis asst prof, Parsons Sch Design, New York, 93-. *Awards:* NY Found Arts Fel Grant, 93; Louis Comfort Tiffany Found Grant, 93; Joan Mitchell Found Grant, 96. *Bibliog:* Jennifer Dunning (auth), Stories Told in Movement and Talk, NY Times, 1/21/92; Ken Johnson (auth), NY Times, 5/12/2000; Nancy Princenthal (auth), Art in Am, 10/2000. *Mem:* Artist Equity Asn; Found Community Artists. *Media:* Plastic, Rubber. *Dealer:* Elizabeth Harris gallery 529 W 20th St New York NY. *Mailing Add:* c/o Elizabeth Harris Gallery 529 W 20th St #6B New York NY 10011

MONTLACK, EDITH
PAINTER
b New York, NY. *Study:* Metrop Mus Art Sch, with Michael Jacobs, scholar; Nat Acad Design, with Louis Bouche; Art Students League. *Work:* Pvt collections of Shell Oil Co & Asiatic Petroleum; and others. *Comn:* Portraits of Martin Sheen; plus many others. *Exhib:* Nat Acad; Parrish Mus; Riverside Mus; Grand Central Art Gallery; Knickerbocker Artists; and many others. *Teaching:* Instruction in own studio. *Awards:* Emil Kohn Medal; St Gaudens Medal; First Prize Watercolors, Nat Asn Women Art. *Mem:* Life fel Royal Soc Art, London; Nat Asn Women Artists. *Media:* Oil. *Publ:* Auth, Paintings: A New Approach, Agni Press. *Mailing Add:* 90 Taymil Rd New Rochelle NY 10804-2802

MONTOYA, MALAQUIAS
ART EDUCATOR, ARTIST
b Albuquerque, June 21, 1938. *Study:* Univ Calif, Berkeley, BA, 70. *Pos:* Commerical artist, silkscreener, 62-68; foreman silkscreen dept Circo Inc, 63-66. *Teaching:* Art instr Laney Col, Berkeley, 69-70, Contra Costa Col, Richmond, Calif, 71; art workshop dir Alameda Co Neighborhood Arts Program, 74-81; lectr Chicano Studies Dept, Univ Calif, Berkeley, 60-74, full prof, 90-, cooperating faculty, 96-. *Mailing Add:* PO Box 6 Elmira CA 95625

MOODY, ELIZABETH C
DEALER, GALLERY DIRECTOR
b Memphis, Tenn, Nov 20, 44. *Study:* Univ Ky, Lexington, BFA, 66. *Pos:* Dir & owner, Moody Gallery, Houston, 75-. *Specialty:* Contemporary American: art, paintings, sculpture, photography, original works on paper. *Mailing Add:* Moody Gallery 2815 Colquitt Houston TX 77098

MOON, JIM (JAMES) MONROE
PAINTER, PRINTMAKER
b Graham, NC, June 7, 28. *Study:* Cooper Union, 45-48; Acad Vannucci, Italy, cert, 55; Richmond Prof Inst William & Mary, BFA, 57; grad study at Mexico City Col, 57; Boston Mus Sch 58-59; Columbia Univ, 66-67. *Work:* Mus Mod Art, NY; NC Mus Art, Raleigh; Peggy Guggenheim Mus, Venice, Italy; Winston-Salem Pub Libr, NC; Northwood Inst, Midland, Mich; Hamilton Mus, Can; Duke Univ & Cent NC Univ, Durham; and others. *Exhib:* Solo exhibs, Watkins/Fair Contemp Arts, NY, 80, la Gallerie, Am Col Paris, 81, Galleria Regina Cornaro, Asolo, Italy, 81, Alber Galleries, Philadelphia, 81, Calvert Collection, Washington, 83, Calvert Gallery, Palm Beach, Fla, 83 & Palm Beach Int Airport, West Palm Beach, Fla, 92; Mus Cuauhnahuac, Mex, 95; Skopje Macedonia, Nat Gallery, 2006. *Pos:* Pres Asolare Foundation. *Teaching:* Instr fine arts, Hofstra Univ, New York, 60-61; head dept visual arts, Barber Scotia Col, NC, 65-66 & NC Sch Arts, Winston-Salem, 67-71; pres, Asolare Fine Arts Acad, 96-. *Bibliog:* William E Ray (auth), ArtScene, coming to a theatre near you, 2-3/88 & Alice R Gray (auth), An artist for all seasons, Vol X, No 1, 1-3/92, Palm Beach Co Coun Arts, Fla; John Chapman (ed), Jim Moon, Five Essays on His Painting, 94; and others. *Mem:* Soc Leonaks, Repubic of Macedonia. *Media:* Egg Tempera, Oil; Serigraphy. *Mailing Add:* C/O Asolare Fine Arts Acad 687 Callahan Hill Rd Lexington NC 27292

MOON, MARC
PAINTER, INSTRUCTOR
b Middletown, Ohio, Apr 6, 23. *Study:* Appl Art Acad. *Work:* Canton Art Inst; Masillon Mus, Ohio; Richmond Mus, Va; Springfield Mus, Mo; Taylor Mem Libr, Cuyahoga Falls, Ohio. *Comn:* Mural, Canton Hall of Fame, Canton Hist Soc, Ohio, 70; mural, Lawson Milk Co, 75; McDonalds Restaurants, Akron, Ohio, 79. *Exhib:* Am Watercolor Soc, NY, 66-70; Nat Acad Design, 74; Watercolor USA, Springfield Mus, 74; Butler Art Inst, Youngstown, Ohio, 75; Nat Soc Painters Casein & Watercolor, NY, 81. *Teaching:* Instr watercolor, Hilton Leech Art Sch, Sarasota, Fla, 68-76, Marc Moon Gallery, Akron, Ohio, 82-84, Fort Meyers Branch Art Asn, 84. *Awards:* Mario Cooper Award, Am Watercolor Soc; Best in Show, Va Beach Art Asn; Purchase Award, Watercolor USA. *Bibliog:* R Fabri (auth), Medal of Merit, Todays Art, 66. *Mem:* Am Watercolor Soc; Ohio Watercolor Soc; Nat Soc Painters Casein & Acrylic; Rockport Art Asn; Allied Artist Am. *Media:* Watercolor, Acrylic. *Publ:* Auth, Watercolor page, Am Artist Mag, 74. *Mailing Add:* 731 Hunters Tr Akron OH 44313-8146

MOONELIS, JUDITH C
SCULPTOR, CERAMIST
b Jackson Heights, Queens, NY, May 30, 53. *Study:* Tyler Sch Art, Temple Univ, Philadelphia, BFA, 75; NY State Col Ceramics, Alfred Univ, MFA, 78. *Work:* Pa Acad Fine Arts, Philadelphia; Renwick Gallery, Smithsonian Inst, Washington, DC; NY State Col Ceramics, Alfred Univ, NY; Ill State Mus, Springfield; Everson Mus, NY; Am Craft Mus, NY. *Comn:* Sculpture, Heckscher Mus, NY, 83. *Exhib:* Solo exhibs, Heckscher Mus, Huntington, NY, 83, Rena Bransten Gallery, San Francisco, Calif, 85 & 88, Va Commonwealth Univ, 90, Swarthmore Col, PA, 92 & Hillwood Art Mus, Long Island Univ, NY, 93, John Elder Gallery, NY, 98; Sculpture, Pa Acad Fine Arts, Philadelphia, 86; A Passionate Vision: Daniel Jacobs Collection, DeCordova Mus, Lincoln, Mass, 84; Twenty Artists, Newport Harbor Art Mus, Calif, 85; Poetry of the Physical, Am Craft Mus, NY & traveling, 86-87; The Eloquent Object, Philbrook Art Mus, OK & traveling, 87-89; Am Figurative Ceramics, Art Gallery Western Australia, Perth & traveling, 89; The Nude, Perimeter Gallery, Chicago & Wustum Mus, Wis, 95. *Teaching:* Vis artist & lectr, numerous schs & institutions, 80-; instr ceramic sculpture, Parsons Sch Design, NY, 84-87 & Hunter Col, NY, 86-87; vis prof, Univ Hartford, 90 & RI Sch Design, 93, 94 & 97, Mass Col Art, 95 & 96. *Awards:* NY Found Arts Fel, 85 & 89; Virginia A Groot Found Grant, 91; Gottlieb Found Grant, 94. *Bibliog:* Gnossis Nos (auth), Judy Moonelis, Am Ceramics Mag, 5/86; Edward Sozanski, Rev, Philadelphia Enquirer, 2/21/92; Janet Koplos (auth), Judy Moonelis, Hillwood Art Mus, 94. *Mem:* Int Sculpture Ctr Am Craft Coun. *Media:* Clay, Mixed Media. *Dealer:* John Elder Gallery 529 West 20th St New York NY 10011. *Mailing Add:* 434 E 11th St Apt 3F New York NY 10009

MOONEY, MICHAEL J
PAINTER, ASSEMBLAGE ARTIST
b Albany, NY. *Study:* Empire State Col, Albany, BPS(arts), 80; State Univ NY, Albany, MA(painting), 82, MFA(painting), 83. *Work:* Center Galleries & State Univ, Albany; F D Rich Co, Stamford, Conn; State Univ NY, Albany; Paterson Mus, Paterson, NJ; Paco Das Artes, Sao Paulo; Museu Da Imagem Do Som, Sao Paulo. *Exhib:* East Village, NY, Galerie Knud Grothe, Copenhagen, Denmark, 83; Chicago Art Expo, Navy Pier, 84; Ruth Siegel Gallery, 83, 84, 86 & 91; solo exhibs, Sixth Sense Gallery, 85, Bridgewater Gallery, 86, EM Donahue Gallery, 86, 88, 89 & 93 & Landscape Antology, Grace Borgeniet Gallery, NY, 88; Grace Borgenicht Gallery (landscape anthology), 88; Albany Ctr Gallery, 94; Ctr Galleries, Albany, NY, 97; Schnectady Mus, 98; Rensselaer Co Coun Arts, Troy, NY. *Teaching:* Grad lectr painting, Col St Rose, Albany, NY, 92; instr drawing, State Univ NY Albany, 92. *Awards:* David Kroman Award, Discovery 78, Schenectady Art Group, 78; Albany Regional Painting Award, State Univ NY, Albany, Art Gallery, 81. *Bibliog:* Fred LeBrun (auth), Mooney at Center Gallery, Albany Times Union, 10/6/79; Peg Churchill-Wright (auth), Works Within Works, Schenectady Gazette, 10/11/79; James Lewis (auth), Art Forum, 12/89; William Jaeger (auth), Michael Mooney, How to Live in the World, Albany Times Union, 12/99; William Jaeger (auth), Michael Mooney, Life Reflections, Ctr Galleries, Albany, NY, 4/2000; Karen Bjornland (auth), Michael Mooney at Ctr Galleries, Schenectedy Gazette, 4/2000; Stacey Lauren (auth), Michael Mooney, Opposites Attract, Ctr Galleries, Metroland Magazine, 4/2000. *Media:* Oil. *Mailing Add:* 13 Belvidere Ave Albany NY 12203

MOONIE, LIANA
PAINTER, LECTURER
b Trieste, Italy. *Study:* Ist Magistrale G Carducci, Univ Trieste, BA(educ), 45; Art Student League, with Robert Brachman, 69; New York Univ; New Rochelle Col, 79 (printmaking). *Work:* State Assembly, Albany, NY; Salomon Inc, NY; Reference Libr, Nat Mus Arts, Washington; Pepsico Inc; Credit Anstalt Bank, Verein, NY; Natl Assn Women Artists Coll, Jane Vorhees Zimmerli Art Mus, NJ; Palm Beach intl Airport, West Palm Beach, FL. *Exhib:* Silvermine Artists Guild, New Canaan, Conn, 79 & 90-94; Hudson River Mus, NY, 79; traveling exhib, USA, 85-89; traveling exhib, India, 89; The Hurlbutt Gallery, Greenwich, Conn, 90-96; Greenwich Arts Ctr, Greenwich, Conn, 91; Art of the Northeast, USA, 95-96; UMA Gallery, NY, 2004; Interchurch Ctr, NY, 2004. *Pos:* Chair, Nat Asn Women Artists Collection, Jane Voorhees Zimmerli Art Mus, New Brunswick, NJ, 90-96 & 2003. *Teaching:* Private instruction, 79-81. *Awards:* Quinns Award, Greenwich Coun Arts, 92; Mary B Hathaway Award, Hurlbutt Gallery, 93; President's Award, A Celebration of Conn Art, CosCob, Conn, 94; The Owl Award, Nat League of Am Pen Women, 97; The Fred Krause Award for an Abstract Painting, Flinn Gallery, Greenwich, Conn, 2000. *Mem:* Mamaroneck Artists Guild (pres, 76-78); Hudson River Contemp Artists (pres, 81-83); Nat Asn Women Artists (vpres, 85-86; pres, 87-89); Silvermine Artists Guild; Greenwich Art Soc (pres, 90-91). *Media:* Watercolor, Oil. *Publ:* Contribr, article, Beaux Arts Mag, 74-76 & Philosophizing about art, 75. *Mailing Add:* 4 Lafayette Ct No PH Greenwich CT 06830-5320

MOORE, ALAN WILLARD
ART CRITIC, HISTORIAN
b Chicago, Ill, Oct 21, 51. *Study:* Univ Calif, Riverside, BA, 74; City Univ NY Grad Ctr, PhD, 2000. *Pos:* Intern writer, Art Forum, 73-74; writer, Art-Rite, 74-75 & Art Net Mag; co-founder, ABC No Rio, 80-83; dir MWF Video Distribution, 86-; co-ed, Part Mag. *Teaching:* vis asst prof, Kennesan State Univ; Adj Lectr, Ramapo Col, City Col, Col Staten Island; grad teaching fel, Bronx Community Col; instr, Pratt Inst. *Awards:* John Revald Disertation Fel. *Mem:* Col Art Asn. *Res:* History of Collaborative Projects, NY. *Publ:* Coauth (with Marc Miller), ABC No Rio Dinero: Story of a LES Art Gallery, NY, 83; ed, A Day in the Life: Tales from the Lower East, Semiotexte, 91; coauth (with James Cornwell), Local History: The Battle for Bohemia in the East Village, chap in: Alternative Art New York, 1965-1985, Univ Minn Press, 2002; auth, Political Economy as Subject & Form in Contemporary Art, Review of Radical Political Economics, Col 36, No 4, fall 2004; auth, General Introduction to Collectivity in Modern Art, Journal of Aesthetics & Protest, 8/2003, Spanish transl, 2005; coauth (with Debra Wacks), Being There: The Tribeca Neighborhood of Franklin Furnace, The Drama Review, Vol 49, No 1, spring 2005. *Mailing Add:* 123 Scribner Ave Staten Island NY 10301

MOORE, ANNE F
MUSEUM DIRECTOR, EDUCATOR, FINE AND DECORATIVE ART APPRAISER, ART DEALER
b Jackson, Tenn, Jan 6, 46. *Study:* Columbia Univ, BA, 69, MFA & MFAEd, 71; Hunter Col, MA, 82; Cert in Appraisal Studies, 2003. *Pos:* Lectr & res assoc, Kimbell Art Mus, 80-83; outreach dir, Dallas Art Mus, 86-88; cur ed & acad prog, Allen Art Mus, Oberlin Col, 88-91, from actg dir to dir, 91-96; dir Ctr for Book Arts, 2000; Proj Mgr, Peabody Essex Mus, 2000-2002. *Teaching:* Lectr mus studies, Oberlin Col, 88-95; lectr NYU, 99. *Mem:* Asn Art Mus Dirs; Col Art Asn; Intermus Conserv Asn (vpres, 92-95). *Publ:* Ed, Allen Memorial Art Museum Bull, 91-93 & AMAM Newslett, 91-, Oberlin Col. *Dealer:* Ancester Image. *Mailing Add:* 172 Pacific Ave Brooklyn NY 11201

MOORE, BENJAMIN POWELL
GLASS BLOWER, DESIGNER
b Olympia, Wash, Feb 5, 52. *Study:* Calif Col Arts and Crafts, BFA, 74; RI Sch Design, MFA, 77. *Work:* Corning Mus Glass, NY; Va Mus Mus Fine Arts, Richmond; J & L Lobmeyr Mus Collection, Vienna, Austria; Fravenau Mus, Bavaria, WGer; Glasmusem, Ebeltoft, Denmark. *Comn:* restaurant lighting, Lola Restaurant, NY, 84; restaurant lighting, Crescent Dining Club, Dallas, Tex, 85; restaurant lighting, Bravo Pagliacci, Bellevue, Wash, 85; law office lighting, Davis, Wright, Todd, Reise & Jones, Seattle, Wash, 86; private lodge lighting, Wright Runstad & Co, Blakely Island, Wash, 87. *Exhib:* Europeans in Glass, Nat Mus Mod Art, Tokyo/Kyoto, Japan, 80; New Glass; Worldwide Survey, Victoria & Albert Mus, London, 81 & Mus des Arts Decoratifs, Paris, France, 82; Am Glass Northwest, Essener Glasgalerie, Essen, WGer, 83; Poetry of the Physical, Am Craft Mus, NY, 86; Piuchuck Glass Northwest, US Embassy, Prague, Czech, 88; one-man shows, Recent Glass, Kurland Summers Gallery, Los Angeles, Recent Glass, Benjamin Moore, Traver Sutton Gallery, Seattle, Wash, 88 & 91. *Pos:* Designer glass, Fabbrica Venini Murano, Venice, Italy, 78-79 & J & L Lobmeyr, Vienna, Austria, 80-81; designer & owner, Benjamin Moore Inc, Seattle, Wash, 85-. *Teaching:* Grad instr glass, RI Sch Design, Providence, 75-77; interim prof glass, Mass Col Art, Boston, 80; admin glass, Pilchuck Glass Sch, Stanwood, Wash, 74-87. *Awards:* Young Am Award, Am Craft Mus, Am Craft Coun, NY, 78; Fragile Art Competition Award, Glass Art Mag, 83; NEA Grant, 90. *Bibliog:* Edie Lee Cohen (auth), Art Glass Lamps, Interior Design Mag, 5/85; Maureen Pickard (auth), The Light Touch, Restaurant & Hotel Design, 4/86; Lisa Hammel (auth), A Show of Hands, Metrop Home Mag, 11/88. *Mem:* Mem Am Craft Mus; Mem Glass Art Soc; Pilchuck Glass Sch (bd trustees). *Dealer:* William Traver Gallery 110 Union St Seattle WA 98101

MOORE, BRIDGET
GALLERY DIRECTOR
b York, Maine, Aug 22, 57. *Study:* Smith Col, Northampton, Mass. *Pos:* Co dir, Ledel Gallery, NY, 81-84; dir, Midtown Galleries, NY, 85-90 & Midtown-Payson Galleries, 90-95; Gallery owner/pres, DC Moore Gallery, NY, 95-. *Specialty:* Twentieth Century and Contemp Am art. *Publ:* The Reflective Image: Am Drawings 1910-1960, Midtown Galleries, 90. *Mailing Add:* DC Moore Gallery 724 Fifth Ave 8th Fl New York NY 10019-

MOORE, FAY
PAINTER, ADMINISTRATOR
b Cambridge, Mass. *Study:* Henry Hensche Sch, Provincetown; Boston Mus Sch; Phillips Gallery Sch, Washington, DC; Bennington Col, Vt, with Stephan Hirsch & Paul Feeley; Yale Grad Sch with Donald Oenslager. *Work:* NY Racing Asn; Nat Art Mus Sport, Indianapolis; Detroit Race Course, Mich; Univ Va, Charlottesville; Kentucky Derby Mus, Louisville; Georgetown Univ, Jacobs Col; Univ Ky Fine Arts Libr. *Comn:* Univ Va, Charlottesville, 67; Hockey Hall Fame, Can, 70; New York Giants, 71; Seven Murals, Kelso Rm, NY Racing Asn, 78; Murals, Rockwell Rm, Three Rivers Stadium, Pittsburgh, 76. *Exhib:* Saratoga Mus Racing, NY, 65; Pittsburgh Plan Art, Pa, 69; Nat Arts Mus Sport, NY, 70; Mus Contemp, Madrid, Spain, 72; retrospective, Headley Whitney Mus, Ky, 90; Modern Masters, Ky Derby Mus, 92; Nat Arts Club, NY, 93, 2001; and others; Butler Inst Amm Art, Ohio, 2001-03. *Teaching:* Instr, Univ Kansas City, Mo, 55-57, Carnegie-Mellon Univ, Pittsburgh, 57-59 & Yale Univ Grad Sch, New Haven, Conn, 59-60; workshops, Int Mus Horse, Lexington, Ky. *Awards:* Nat Arts Club Awards; Knickerbocker Artists Awards; Allied Artists Am Awards; Spirit Award, Pastel Soc Art. *Bibliog:* Creative painting with pastel, Katchen, Northlight Publ; The Best of Pastel, Rockport Publ, 96; L Price (auth), A Neo-Pointillist in Pastel, Amartist Mag, 97; Arboreal Attitudes Mag, 2006. *Mem:* Nat Soc Mural Painters; Nat Arts Club; Artists Fel (pres, emer); Nat Art Mus Sport (acquisitions); Allied Artists Am (vpres); Pastel Soc Am; Catherine Lorrilard Wolfe Art Club (bd dir); Pen & Brush; Am Acad Equinear (chmn bd). *Media:* Oil, Pastel. *Publ:* Equine Images, fall 90 & 97; The Artist's Mag, 11/90; Informart, 6/93; Am Artists, 12/97; Artists Mag, 7/99; Kentucky Derby Mag, 2006. *Dealer:* Heike Pickett Gallery 110 Morgan St Versailles, KY; The Sporting Gallery, Middleburg, VA. *Mailing Add:* Nat Arts Club 15 Gramercy Park S New York NY 10003

MOORE, INA MAY
PAINTER, INSTRUCTOR
b Hayden, Ariz, Feb 20, 20. *Study:* Univ Ariz, BA(educ, art & music); Ariz State Univ, MA(art educ). *Work:* First Interstate Bank, Valley Nat Bank, Ariz Bank & Thunderbird Bank, Phoenix; First Fed Savings & Loan Asn, Yuma; pvt collections. *Exhib:* Nat League Am Pen Women, Salt Lake City, Utah, 71; Nat Watercolor Exhib, Ctr Performing Arts, Scottsdale, Ariz, 77; Southwest Watercolor Fedn Exhib, San Diego, 83; Kerr Ctr, Scottsdale, Ariz, 83; Southwest Federation, Houston, Tex, 86; Univ S Dak. *Teaching:* Part-time instr art, Elem Pub Schs, 40-50; pvt classes, 50-64; instr watercolor, Phoenix Art Mus, 65-88; Phoenix Col, 78-97; juror & watercolor workshops; instr art, Paradise Valley Community Col, Phoenix, ret. *Awards:* Purchase Award, Empire Machinery Co, 77; Purchase Award, Thunderbird Bank, 79; Merit Award, Ariz Watercolor Exhib, 85; Grumbacher Award, 86 & 88; Merit Award, Ariz Artists Guild, 86 & 89. *Bibliog:* Women Artists of the American West, Univ Tex Press, 99. *Mem:* Ariz Watercolor Asn (pres, 66-68); Nat League Am Pen Women; Ariz Artist's Guild; Delta Kappa Gamma; Contemp Watercolor Asn (found). *Media:* Watercolor. *Publ:* Illusr, Junior League Calendar, 86. *Dealer:* Kachina Gallery, Taos NM. *Mailing Add:* 5718 N Tenth Ave Phoenix AZ 85013

MOORE, JOHN J
PAINTER, EDUCATOR
b St Louis, Mo, Apr 25, 41. *Study:* Washington Univ, Nat Found Arts & Humanities grant, Milliken foreign travel fel, BFA, 66; Yale Univ, MFA, 68. *Work:* Philadelphia Mus Art; Pa Acad Fine Arts, Philadelphia; Yale Univ Art Gallery, New Haven; Mus Fine Arts, Boston; Metrop Mus Art, NY. *Comn:* Lincoln Ctr, NY, 80; Fabric Workshop, Philadelphia, 81; Hancock Insurance, Boston, 85; Smith, Kline, French, Philadelphia, 86; Becton-Dickinson, NJ, 88. *Exhib:* Real, Really, Super Real, San Antonio Mus Art, Tex, 81; Contemp Am Realism Since 1960, Pa Acad Fine Arts, 82; Hirschl & Adler Mod, NY, 83, 86, 90 & 94; Am Realism: The Precise Image, Tokyo, Osaka, Yokohama, 86; Am Art Today: Night Paintings, Art Mus, Fla Inst Univ, 95. *Teaching:* Prof painting & drawing, Tyler Sch Art, Temple Univ, 68-88 & Sch Arts, Boston Univ, 88-99; artist-in-residence, Yale Summer Sch, 68 & 69; fac, Skowhegan Sch Painting & Sculpture, summers, 74, 80 & 84; vis prof painting, Univ Calif, Berkeley, 81-82; Gutman Prof Fine Arts, Univ Pa. *Awards:* Hassam Award, Am Acad Arts & Lett, 73 & 87; Vis Artist Fel Painting, Nat Endowment Arts, 82 & 92; Acad Award Painting, Am Acad Arts & Lett, 96. *Bibliog:* Carol Zemel (auth), Still Life and City View, Buscaglia-Castellani Art Gallery, 83; Laura Rath (auth), Uncommon Vistas, Boston Univ Art Gallery; Therese Dolan (auth), Inventing Reality: The Paintings of John Moore, Hudson Hills, 96. *Mem:* Univ Coun, Yale Univ 85-90; CIES (sr Fulbright comt, 89-92). *Media:* Oil, Watercolor. *Dealer:* Hirschl & Adler Modern 21 E 70th St New York NY 10021; Locks Gallery 600 Washington Sq S Philadelphia PA 19106

MOORE, JOHN L
PAINTER, CURATOR
b Cleveland, Ohio, Feb 2, 39. *Study:* Kent State Univ, BFA, 72, MA, 74. *Work:* Brookly Mus, NY; High Mus, Atlanta; New York Pub Libr; Montgomery Mus Fine Arts, Ala; New Jersey State Mus, Trenton; New York Pub Libr; Brooklyn Mus Art, NY; NJ State Mus; plus others. *Comn:* Ceiling Mural, Cleveland Pub Libr, Ohio, 96.

Exhib: One-man shows, Miami Univ Art Mus, 90, Indianapolis Ctr Contemp Art, Herron Gallery, 90, High Mus Art, Ga Pac Ctr, 90, Cleveland Ctr Contemp Art, 90, M-13 Gallery, NY, 92, 94 & 96, Amalie A Wallace Gallery, Col Old Westbury, 95, Montgomery Mus Fine Arts, 96; Slow Art: Painting in NY Now, Inst Contemp Art PS1, Long Island City, 92; Dream Singers, Story Tellers: An African-Am Presence, Fukui Fine Arts Mus, Japan, 92; Selections from the Collection, Brooklyn Mus, 94; Aspects of Abstraction, NJ State Mus, 96; Old Glory: The Am Flag in Contemp Art, Phoenix Art Mus, 96; After the Fall, Aspects of Abstract Painting Since 1970, Newhouse Ctr Contemp Art, Snug Harbor Cult Ctr, 97; Cleveland Collects Contemp Art, The Cleveland Mus Art, Ohio, 98. *Pos:* Asst cur dept educ, Cleveland Mus Art, 74-85; guest cur, Studio Mus Harlem, 86-87. *Teaching:* Adj asst prof, Queens Col, City Univ, 90; Adj prof, Parsons Sch Design, 92, La Guardia Community Col, 94-; vis prof, Rhode Island Sch Design, 92 &93, Univ Tex, Austin, 92; vis assoc prof, Skidmore Col, Saratoga Springs, 94-. *Awards:* Fel painting, Nat Endowment Arts, 87; fel painting, New York Found Arts, 89 & 94; Joan Mitchell Award, 99. *Bibliog:* Eleanor Heartney (auth), John L Moore: at M-13, Art in Am, 6/92; Marianne Doezema (auth), Painting Abstract, Mount Holyoke Univ, 96; Charlotta Kotiz (auth), John L Moore: Work of the Decade, Montgomery Mus Fine Art, 96. *Mem:* Art in Gen; Col Art Asn. *Media:* Painting. *Publ:* Coauth, The Contemporary Landscape: Five Views, Waterworks Visual Arts Ctr, 89; auth, New York City Works, One Penn Plaza, 88; dir, Bill Hutson, Paintings 1978-1987, Studio Mus Harlem, 88; auth, The Passion Pit, Anna Marie Arnold, for the Cleveland Ctr for Contemporary Art Ohio Selections, Dialogue Art J, 5/86; New Color Abstraction, Dialogue Art J, 1/85. *Dealer:* Howard Scott Gallery 529 W 20th St New York NY 10001. *Mailing Add:* 3515 84th St Apt 3G Jackson Heights NY 11372

MOORE, MARK TOBIN
PAINTER, COLLAGE ARTIST
b Washington, DC, Jan 19, 54. *Study:* Univ Charleston, WVa, BA(studio art), 83, MFA, (painting), 2000; Marshall Univ, MA(painting/printmaking), 85. *Work:* WVa Wesleyan Col; Marshall Univ; Univ Charleston; People's Col, City of Lich, Ger; Marshall Univ Grad Col. *Comn:* Large collageon canvas of sports cars, comn by Cdr Bill Biggs, USN, Charleston, WVa, 82; Rock & Roll 1964-1984 (painting), comn by Dr & Mrs Naz Abraham, Huntington, WVA, 84; Rock & Roll History/Social Commentary (mural), Gumby's Night Club, Huntington, WVa, 91; The Sheltering Sky (painting), comn by Robin Pauley, Charleston, WVa, 94. *Exhib:* Exhib 280, Huntington Mus Art, WVa, 84 & 92; Artista Vista, Lewis & Clark Gallery, Columbia, SC, 94; Showing Character, Governor's Mansion, Charleston, WVa, 94; Assemblages, WVa Wesleyan Col, Buckhannon, WVa, 95; Stories of the Heart, Sunrise Mus Downtown, Charleston WVa, 96; Collage Paintings 1991-1998, Fairmont State Col, WVa; Nat Collage Soc Exhib, Case Western Reserve Univ, Cleveland, Ohio, 98; Allied Artists WVa Exhib, Sunrise Mus, Charleston, 98; two group shows, Tamarack Gallery, Beckley, WVa, 98. *Collection Arranged:* Contemporary Art in WVa, WVa State Mus, 93, 94, 95 & 96; Juried Exhibition (auth, catalog), WVa State Mus, 93 & 95; June Kilgore: A Retrospective (co-auth & ed, catalog), WVa State Mus, 95; The Next Generation: Kilgore Alumni, WVa State Mus, 95; Contemp Works in Wood, WVa State Mus, 96. *Pos:* Dir, Giessen Arts & Crafts Ctr, US Army-Europe, Germany, 89-91; dir exhibs & cur contemp art, WVa State Mus, 93-98. *Teaching:* Instr art, Ohio Univ, Ironton, 85-87, WVa State Col, Institute, 93 94 & 96-, Univ Charleston, WVa, 95 & 96, grad teaching asst, 99-2000, vis adj instr, 2001, instr, Marshall Univ, Huntington, WVa, 98-. *Awards:* Award of Excellence, Allied Artists WVa Exhib, Sunrise Mus, 98; Merit Award, Nat Collage Soc Exhib, Cleveland, Ohio, 98. *Bibliog:* Bob Schwarz (auth), Face off: Mark Tobin Moore's portraits of pain, Charleston Gazette, 94; Beverly Rhoads (auth), Overly Personal/overly familiar, WV Wesleyan Col, 95; Andrea Bond (auth), Charleston artist's exhibit meets life head-on, Gazette-Mail, 96. *Mem:* Nat Collage Soc; Allied Artists, WVa. *Media:* Mixed Media. *Specialty:* abstract expressionism, pegboard collage. *Publ:* Numerous articles in Patterns Mag, 95-96

MOORE, MYREEN
PAINTER, CONSULTANT
b Norfolk, Va, June 2, 40. *Study:* William & Mary Col, 62; Chrysler Mus/Corcoran Gallery Art Sch, 64; Gibbes State Art Gallery, 68; Univ NC, MS, 71; Contemporary Art Ctr of Virginia, 73; with Charles Sibley, Wm Reimann & Ray Goodbred; Old Dominion Univ, MA, 97 with Linda McGreevy & others; additional graduate work, 98-05. *Work:* Old Dominion Univ, Norfolk, Va; Gibbes State Art Gallery, Charleston, SC; City of Chesapeake, Va, City of Hampton (Va) Devel. *Comn:* Statues, Child Study Ctr, Norfolk, 67; portrait, Founder of Friends, Kennedy Ctr; Statue Designs, St Mark's Church, 91; 70th Anniversary of Poetry Society (collage), Wren Bldg, 93. *Exhib:* Int Platform Asn, 89-97; Artists of Va 1996 Juried Art Show, Peninsula Fine Arts Ctr; Tidewater Artists Asn Portfolio Show, 96; Hampton Arts Comn Bay Days Juried Art Show, 96, 97, & 2002; Yorktown Virginia Heritage Show, 97 & 98; Suffolk Mus Invitational Artists & Writers Exhib, 96; Trinity Church Stations of the Cross, Portsmouth Mus, 97; Hermitage Mus Found Mini Show, 98; Nauticus Nat Maritime Ctr, 98, 2000; Norfolk (VA) Int Airport, 2001, 02, 03. *Collection Arranged:* Chrysler Mus Stud Art Show, 65; Charleston Pub Schs Permanent Print Collection, SC, 69; Original Art Collection, Norfolk Pub Libr Pub Lending, 72-75; W Ghent Arts Alliance Art & Literary Festival, 79; Life-Saving Mus Va Beach, 91; Crestar Bank, 91; Hermitage Mus, 92. *Pos:* Staff artist, William & Mary Col, 58-61; hearing reporter & secy, City of Norfolk Fine Arts Comt, 64-65; art librn & researcher, Norfolk Pub Libr, 70-90; contribr, Libr J, 73-76; ed, Poetry Soc Va, 90-93; bd dir, Dockside Art Review, D'Art Ctr, 91-92; writer art, Mid Atlantic Antique Mag, 94-2001; dir, W Ghent Arts, 97-; Art Appraiser, 99-2006. *Teaching:* Art teacher, Norfolk Pub Schs, 65-67; prof art, Palmer Jr Col, Charleston, SC, 67-68; W Ghent Arts Alliance, 78-83 & 98-. *Awards:* Nat Endowment Arts, 75; Tricentennial Alumni Award, William & Mary Col, 93; Gov Cert, Voluntary Contrib Arts Va, 94; Color Graphics Award, 96; IPA, First Place, Printmaking and Graphics, 98. *Mem:* Poetry Soc of Va (vpres, edit of newsletter, 84-93), 1984-; Tidewater Art Alliance (grants chmn, 90 & pres, 91-92), 2005; Irene Leache Soc, 91-2000, Hampton Arts League, 2005-; Va Writers Club, 1995-. *Media:* All Media. *Res:* The Sullys and the Poes, Norfolk, Va; 400th Anniversay of Jamestown, Va. *Publ:* Anthologies, Poetry Soc of Virginia, 85, 93, 2003; Poets Domain series, Live Wire Press, 95-2006; Articles published in Mid Atlantic Antiques Mag, 94-; and others. *Mailing Add:* 1404 Gates Ave Norfolk VA 23507

MOORE, MYRON NEIL
PAINTER, DRAFTSMAN
b O'Neill, Nebr, Feb 7, 63. *Study:* Kansas City Art Inst, with Wilbur Niewald, BFA, 86; Univ Nebr, Lincoln, with Martha Horvay & Keith Jacobshagen, MFA, 97. *Exhib:* Northern Nat Art Competition, LRC Gallery, Wis Campus, 97; 54th Juried Exhib, Sioux City Arts Ctr, Iowa, 97; Fourth Great Plains Nat, Moss-Thorus Gallery, Hays, Kans, 98; Nat Art Exhib, Charlotte Co Art Guild, Punta Gorda, Fla, 98; Art in the Woods, Nat Juried Exhib, Corp Woods, Overland Park, Kans, 98; 62nd Ann Midyear Nat, Butler Inst Am Art, Youngstown, Ohio, 98; NJ Ctr Visual Arts Int Show, Summit, 98; Sioux City Art Ctr 55th Exhib, 99; All Media Exhib, Touchstone Gallery, Washington, DC, 99; Nat Competition, First St Gallery, New York City, 99; 1st Nat Realism Show, Parkersburg, WVa, 99. *Awards:* Dori Brown Award, 10th Northern Nat Juried Art Competition, 97; Best of Show Award, 54th Juried Exhib, Sioux City Arts Ctr, Iowa, 97; Jurors Choice Award, Art in the Woods, Nat Exhib, Overland Park, Kans, 98

MOORE, PAMELA A
PAINTER, PRINTMAKER, MIXED MEDIA ARTIST
b Montclair, NJ, 1950. *Study:* San Francisco Art Inst, BFA, 73. *Work:* Smithsonian Inst, Washington; Lincoln Ctr, Sanyo Corp, Pepsico Corp, NY; Canon Corp, NJ. *Comn:* paintings as moveable set, Joyce Theater, Roz Newan & Dancers, NY, 85; 3' x 5' painting for fanfare, NY Philharmonic, 93; 18 paintings on film paper, Price Waterhouse, NY, 93; Am Inst For Studies, 99; Emcor Comn, 99; Thames Water, London, 2000; Am Inst Fgn Studies, 2000; United Airlines, 01; John Wiley & Sons, 02; Odyssey, 02; Castel Hill, 03; pvt comn by Congressman Bill Pascrell, 06; Time Warner Collection, 05; and many others. *Exhib:* New Talent, Castelli Graphics, NY, 85; solo exhibs, De Rotterdanse Schouburg, Rotterdam, The Neth, 85, Akad de Kunst, Berlin, Ger, 85, Gallerie Fenna de Vries, Rotterdam, The Neth, 87, Fay Gold Gallery, Atlanta, Ga, 92, Blue River Gallery, Jacksonville, Fla, 99, Walker/Kornbluth Gallery, 2000, Kathryn Markel Gallery, New York City, 03; Locus Gallery, St Louis, 99; Dillon Gallery, NY, 2000; White House Egg Display Representing NY State, 2001; Walker/Kornbluth Gallery, 03. *Pos:* manager, solo press shop, 80-85; owner, manager, Rhino Studios, 75-. *Teaching:* Queens Col, Printmaking Coun NJ, Pratt Graphic Ctr, Sch Queens Col, Printmaking Workshop, New York, Conn, Graphic Arts, Montclair Art Mus, Acad Art San Francisco & Viridian Print Studio. *Awards:* artist-in-residence, Oxbow Sch Art, 84 & Altos de Chavon Dominican Repub, Gulf & Western, 84; Dick Blick Arts Material Grant, 99; Artist Angel Grant, Vt Studio Ctr, 97; Pollock/Krasner Grant, 2006. *Media:* Acrylic, Oil; Miscellaneous Media. *Publ:* 8 Book Covers, Simon & Schuster, 99. *Dealer:* Kathryn Markel Gallery 529 W 20th New York NY; Walker/Kornbluth Gallery Fairlawn NJ. *Mailing Add:* 67 Vestry St New York NY 10013

MOORE, ROBERT ERIC
PAINTER
b Manchester, NH, Oct 13, 27. *Study:* Univ NH, 53; New Eng Sch Art, Boston, 51. *Work:* Farnsworth Mus, Rockland, Maine; Mus Fine Arts, Springfield, Mass; Headley Mus, Lexington, Ky; Colby Col Art Mus; Butler Mus Fine Arts, Youngtown, Ohio. *Exhib:* Centennial of Am Watercolor Soc, Metrop Mus Art, NY, 66; Maine Artists, US Embassy, Ottawa, Can, 79; Exchange Prog, Brazil, 79; Museo De La Acurela Mex, Mex City, 89; Int Waters, Int Travelex, Am Watercolor Soc, 91-92; Art of Maine: A Bounty of Woods & Water, Monmouth Mus, Lincroft, NJ, 92; and others. *Awards:* Pulsifer Award, Adirondacks Nat Exhib Am Watercolor, 87; Grumbacher Gold Medallion, Audubon Artists Ann Exhib, NY, 87; Adolph & Clara Obrig Prize, Nat Acad Designs 166th Ann Exhib, 91; and others; 1st Place Gold, Calif Watercolor Asn 35 Ann Exhib, 03; Am Pen Women Award, San Diego Watercolor Soc Internat Exhib, 02; HK HOlbein Inc Award, Tex Watercolor Soc, 03. *Bibliog:* Ed Betts (ed), Work reproduced in Creative Landscape Painting, Watson-Guptill Publ, 78; Louis Bartlett Tracy (auth), Adventuring in Art, Pineapple Press Inc, Sarasota, Fla, 90; Robert I C Fisher (auth), The Influence of the Masters, Watercolor '90, Am Artist Mag, 90; and others; History of American Watercolor Soc, The First 100 Yrs by Ralph Fabri & others. *Mem:* Am Watercolor Soc; Nat Acad; Audubon Artist, NY; Allied Artists Am; Miniature Artists Am, Clearwater, Fla. *Media:* Watercolor, Acrylic. *Publ:* Auth, Creative Seascape Painting by Edward Betts, Watson & Guptill Press, 81. *Dealer:* Firehouse Gallery Damariscotta Maine

MOORE, ROBERT JAMES
PAINTER, PHOTOGRAPHER
b San Jose, Calif, July 24, 22. *Study:* USAF Photo Sch, Lowry Field, Colo, grad; San Jose State Univ, BA; NY Inst Fine Arts, with Salmony, Schoenberger, Panofsky & Offner; Columbia Univ Teachers Col, MFA; Art Students League, with Brackman, Miller & Will Barnet. *Work:* NY Pub Libr Print Collection. *Exhib:* Pa Acad Fine Arts, Philadelphia, 50; James D Phelan Awards Competition, San Francisco Art Mus, 51; 11 Yr Retrospective of Prizewinners, Village Art Ctr, Whitney Mus Am Art, NY, 54; New York City Ctr Gallery, 59; Audubon Artists, Nat Acad Design, NY, 62; One-man shows, Ruth Sherman Galleries, NY, 64 & Adele Bednarz Galleries, Los Angeles, 65; Berkshire Mus, Pittsfield, Mass, 66; Art Students League & Ford Found Show, NY, 75; and others. *Teaching:* Assoc prof art, Goddard Col, 54-57; instr art & photog, Battin High Sch, Elizabeth, NJ, 59-64; instr art, Julia Richman High Sch, New York, 64-90. *Awards:* Second Prize, Village Art Ctr 7th Ann Graphic Art Show, Village Art

Ctr, New York, 52; Blue Ribbon, New Talent Show, Ruth Sherman Gallery, New York, 64; Berkshire Mus Award, 66. *Mem:* Artists Equity Asn of New York; life mem Art Students League; Visual Artists and Galleries Asn. *Media:* Oil, Graphics. *Mailing Add:* 246 E 51st St Apt 19 New York NY 10022-6515

MOORE, SABRA
ARTIST, CURATOR
b Texarkana, Tex, Jan 25, 43. *Study:* Univ Tex, Austin, BA(cum laude), 64; Brooklyn Mus Art Sch, 66; Centre WAfrican Studies Univ Birmingham, Eng, 67. *Work:* Mus Mod Art, Whitney Mus, Brooklyn Mus & Guggenheim Mus, NY; Nat Mus Women, Washington, DC. *Awards:* Fulbright Fel/Eng, 67; Helene Wurlitzer Found NMex, Artists Residency, 86 & 88; 2d Place, First Logan Biennal Nat Outdoor Sculpture, Utah State Univ, Logan. *Bibliog:* Deborah Wye (auth), Catalogue statement, Committed to Print, Mus Mod Art, New York, 88; Diane Armitage (auth), Sabra Moore - Place/Displace, The Mag, 3/97; and others; illusr, Aline Brandaven (auth), Fresco Fine Arts, Albuquerque, NM, 2004. *Mem:* Women's Caucus for Art (pres, 80-82); Heresies Collective. *Media:* Mixed Media. *Publ:* Illusr, Petroglyphs: Ancient Language/Sacred Art, Clearlight Publ, Santa Fe, 98. *Mailing Add:* PO Box 96 Abiquiu NM 87510

MOORE, SCOTT MARTIN
PAINTER, INSTRUCTOR
b Los Angeles, Calif, Oct 13, 49. *Study:* Calif State Univ, Long Beach, 67, 72 & 73; USMC, Hawaii, 70-72; John Pike Watercolor Sch, Woodstock, NY, 78. *Work:* Laguna Art Mus, Laguna Beach, Gibson, Dunn & Crutcher, Newport Beach, Rutaan & Tucker, Costa Mesa, Calif; Quaker Oats Co, Chicago. *Comn:* Four works oil & watercolor, Sedjwick James Insurance, 89-92. *Exhib:* Am Watercolor Soc Ann, Nat Acad, NY, 78, 80-84 & 86-87; Watercolor West, Riverside, Calif, 79-84 & 86-87; Nat Watercolor Soc, Los Angeles, 79-87; Allied Artists, Am Acad & Lett, NY, 80; Watercolor USA, 87. *Pos:* Illusr, USMC, Hawaii, 70-72; graphic designer, Scott Moore Studio, 73-78, painter, 78. *Teaching:* Instr transparent watercolor workshops, 76-92. *Awards:* First Awards, Watercolor West, 79 & 86; Walser S Greathouse Medal, 81 & Arjomari-Arches Paper Award, 86, Am Watercolor Soc. *Bibliog:* Julia P Chase (auth), Scott Moore: sheer color and light, Orange Co Illustrated, 8/79; Charles Dickens Phillips (auth), Gallery: Scott Moore, Westways Mag, 7/81; Jane Summer (auth), Familiar moments, Showcase Mag. *Mem:* Nat Watercolor Soc; Watercolor West; Am Watercolor Soc. *Media:* Transparent Watercolor, Oil. *Publ:* Auth, The drama of backlighting, The Artist's Mag, 12/84; Splash, American's Best Contemporary Watercolors, North Light Bks, 91. *Mailing Add:* 1435 Regatta Rd Laguna Beach CA 92651

MOORE, SUSAN
PAINTER
b Coco Solo, Panama, Mar 27, 53. *Study:* Yale Sch Art & Music, Norfolk, Conn, 76; Ind Univ, BFA, 77; Univ Calif, Davis, MFA, 79. *Work:* Aramark, Philadelphia, Pa; Pa Conv Ctr, Philadelphia Mus Art. *Exhib:* One-woman shows, Univ Mich, Ann Arbor, 85, Tyler Sch Art, Temple Univ, Rome, Italy, 86 & 98, Millersville Univ, 87, Charles More Gallery, Philadelphia, 89, Pa Acad Fine Arts, Philadelphia, 90, Janet Fleisher Gallery, Philadelphia, Pa, 92 & Locks Gallery, Philadelphia, 95 & 97; Art Now: Contemp Philadelphia Artists, Philadelphia Mus Art, Pa, 90; Language as Line: 11 Realists & Beyond Realism: Image & Enigma, Southern Alleghenies Mus, Loretto, Pa, 92; Mentors, Vox Populi Gallery, Philadelphia, 93; Figural Philadelphia, Woodmere Art Mus, Philadelphia, 93; Pa Coun Arts Fel Traveling Exhib, 94; Meet the Neighbors, Paley Design Ctr, Philadelphia Col Art & Textiles, Pa, 95; Women Mentoring Women, Westby Gallery, Rowan Univ, NJ, 97; The Face of Time: 75 Yrs of Time Magazine Cover Art, Nat Portrait Gallery, Smithsonian Inst Traveling Exhib, Nat Acad Mus, NY & Chicago Hist Soc, Ill, 98-99; Dal Volta al Rutratto, Temple Gallery, Rome, Italy, 98; Bizarro World, The Parallel Universes of Comics & Fine Art, Cornell Fine Arts Mus, Winter Park, Fla, 2000; Locks Gallery, Philadelphia, 95, 98, 2001. *Teaching:* Vis artist, numerous cols & univs, 82-91; instr, Tyler Sch Art, Philadelphia, Pa, 92-. *Awards:* Nat Endowment Arts, 88 & 89; Fel, Pa Coun Arts, 89, 92 & 95; Res grant, Temple Univ, 91; and others. *Bibliog:* Victoria Donahue (auth), Locks gallery scores again as talent scout, Philadelphia Inquirer, 7/17/81; Donald Chant Bohn (auth), Philadelphia stories, New Art Examiner, 12/91; Robert Baxter (auth), Her mentor, Courier-Post, Cherry Hill, NJ, 11/16/97. *Media:* Acrylic, Oil. *Dealer:* Locks Gallery. *Mailing Add:* c/o Locks Gallery 600 Washington Sq S Philadelphia PA 19106

MOORE, TODD SOMERS
PAINTER, EDUCATOR
b Oceanside, Calif, Nov 9, 1952. *Study:* Evergreen State Col, Olympia, Wash, BA, 75; RI Sch Design, MFA, 84. *Work:* Am Repub Insurance Co, Des Moines, Iowa; Hillhaven, Inc, Tacoma, Wash; Edwards & Angell, Boston, Mass; Princess House, Tavnton, Mass. *Comn:* Hist mural, RI State Coun Arts, E Providence, 84; mural, Princess House Corp, Taunton, Mass. *Exhib:* Wash Ann, Tacoma Art Mus, 77; Small Works, Wash Sq E Galleries, NY Univ, 80; Ann Exhib Am Art, Chautauqua Art Asn Galleries, 81 & 82; one-man show, Newport Art Mus, Newport, RI, 81; Nat Ann Show, Butler Inst Am Art, Youngstown, Ohio, 81 & 82; Untitled-without Theme (with catalog), Alternative Mus, NY, 82; The Real Thing, N Miami Mus, 85; Art of Northeast USA, Silvermine Galleries, New Cannan, Conn, 86; 1987: A Yr of the Arts, Newport Art Mus, RI, 87; two-man show, Wheeler Gallery, 91; Invitational Show, Bristol Art Mus, RI, 93; Todd Moore, 18 Views of Rumstick Point, White Gallery, Barrington, RI, 98; Somakatoligon, Fed Reserve Bank Gallery, Boston, 98; What's Really Real, Thoreau Gallery, Franklin Pierce Gallery, Rindge, NH, 99. *Pos:* actg dean, Div Found Studies, 2003. *Teaching:* Instr 2-D design & drawing, RI Sch Design, 84-93, assoc prof, 93-; curriculum coordr, Div Found Studies, 2000-04. *Awards:* 2-D Grant, RI State Coun of Arts, 79; Brown Mem Prize, Am Ann at Newport, Newport Art Mus, RI, 81; Juror's Spec Mention, Nat Ann Show, Butler Inst Am Art, 82. *Bibliog:* Bill van Siclien (auth), rev, Providence J, 7/88, 9/89, 3/93 & 4/93; Beth Gersh-Nesic (auth), Rev, Art New England, 12/91; Bill van Siclen (auth), rev, Providence 9/95, 9/97 & 7/98. *Mem:* RI Sch Design Faculty Asn (pres, 99-2003; treas, 2004-06). *Media:* Painting. *Mailing Add:* 991 Seapowet Ave Tiverton RI 02878

MOORE, WAYLAND D
PAINTER, PRINTMAKER
b Belton, SC, Sept 8, 1935. *Study:* Pvt art study, Belton, SC, 50-54; Ringling Sch Art & Design, Sarasota, Fla, cert, 54-57. *Work:* Headley Mus, Lexington, Ky; Nat Sports Hall Fame; corp & pvt collections. *Comn:* Ky Derby, Felicie, NY, 78; Maccabian Games of Israel, Horace-Richter Galleries, Old Jaffa, 79; medallion, 100th Anniversary Madison Sq Garden; 1984 & 1996 Olympics, Coca-Cola, USA, Atlanta, Ga, 84; Davis Cup, 98. *Exhib:* One-man exhibs, Studio 53, NY, 78, Quito, Ecuador, 78, Hermitage, La Braule, France, 80 & Gallerie Felicie, NY, 80; Cent Acad, Peking, China, 79; Tuscany One Man Show. *Collection Arranged:* Private Collection, Corp./Tennis Hall of Fame; Baseball Hall of Fame, US Olympic Hall of Fame, College, Etc. *Pos:* trustee, Ringling Sch Art & Design, Sarasota, Fla, formerly. *Teaching:* Instr art, Atlanta Fed Penitentiary, 70-76; instr art evening classes, Emory Univ, 83-; Instr Workshops. *Awards:* Pulitzer Prize nominee, Editorial Cartooning, 67; Teaching Commendation, The White House, 74. *Mem:* Int Soc Artists; New York Soc Illusr. *Media:* Watercolor; Acrylic, Serigraphy. *Res:* Each Yr travel to Europe on Painting locations adn workshops. *Specialty:* Landscape o Figures. *Interests:* sailing, tennis, adverture poetry, tall tales Festival. *Publ:* Articles in The Olympian Mag, Peachtree, Sports Illus, Braves Yrbk, Southwest Mag, Atlanta Mag; S.C. Education TV. *Mailing Add:* 2124 Azalea Cir Decatur GA 30033

MOORES, PETER
COLLECTOR
b Lancashire, England, April 9, 32. *Study:* Student, Oxford Univ, 54; Christ Church - Oxford, MA, 75. *Pos:* Dir, The Littlewoods Organization, Liverpool, England, 57-93, chairman, 77-80; director Singer & Friedlander, London, 72-92. *Awards:* Decorated medaglia d'oro (Italy); Commander Brit Empire; named One of the Top 200 Collectors, ARTnews mag, 2004, 2006. *Collection:* 15th to 20th century European art; Chinese archaic bronzes; contemporary British art

MOOS, WALTER A
DEALER
b Karlsruhe, Ger. *Study:* Ecole Superieure Com, Geneva, Switz, BA; New Sch Social Res, with Paul Zucker & Meyer Shapiro. *Pos:* Dir, Gallery Moos Ltd; vpres, Arts Mag, 77, pres, 82-83. *Awards:* TIAF Award Distinction, 2002. *Bibliog:* Paul Duval (auth), Ken Danby, 74; Paul Duval (auth), Ken Danby: The New Decade, 84. *Mem:* Prof Art Dealers Asn Can (pres, 71-74). *Specialty:* Contemporary Canadian, European and American paintings, sculpture and graphics. *Mailing Add:* Gallery Moos Ltd 622 Richmond St W Toronto ON M5V 1Y9 Canada

MOQUIN, RICHARD ATTILIO
PAINTER, SCULPTOR
b San Francisco, Calif, July 1, 34. *Study:* City Col San Francisco, AA; San Francisco State Col, with Seymour Locks, BA & MA. *Work:* Oakland Mus, Calif; Saks Fifth Ave, NY; Trans Am Bldg, San Francisco, Calif; San Francisco Mus Art; Mayor's Office, City Hall, San Rafael, Calif. *Exhib:* Solo exhibs, sculpture, Meyer-Breir-Wise Gallery, San Francisco, 80, sculpture, Gallery Paule Anglim, San Francisco, 84, sculpture & works on paper, Michel Dunev Gallery, San Francisco, 89 & 92, paintings, Select Art Gallery, Ariz, 97 & paintings, Ebert Gallery, Calif, 97; sculpture, Gallery Paule Anglim, San Francisco, 86; sculpture, James Calahan Gallery, Calif, 88; sculpture, Harleen-Allen Gallery, San Francisco, 95; paintings, Light and Spirit, Somar Gallery, San Francisco, 96; paintings, Omma gallery, Crete, Greece, 00 & 02; sculpture & paintings, Art Works gallery, San Rafall, Calif, 05. *Pos:* Vpres, Asn San Francisco Potters, 67-68. *Teaching:* Instr sculpture, City Col San Francisco, 69-. *Awards:* Purchase Awards, Sacramento State Fair, 68; M H de Young Mus, San Francisco, Calif, 66, 68 & 70; Clay and Glass, Oakland Mus, Calif, 74; sculpture, Col Marin, Kentfield, Calif, 75. *Bibliog:* Thomas Albright (auth), Art in the San Francisco Bay Area; Les Krantz (auth), articles in Am Artists, Calif Art Rev & NY Art Rev; Art News Mag, 7/97. *Media:* Acrylics, Oil; Oil bars. *Dealer:* Art Smart Gallery San Francisco CA; Ebert Gallery San Francisco CA. *Mailing Add:* 1745 Lovall Valley Rd Sonoma CA 95476

MORA, FRANCISCO
PAINTER
b Uruapan, Michoacan, Mex, May 7, 22. *Study:* San Nicolas de Hidalgo Univ, Mex, 40-41; Sch Painting & Sculpture, La Esmeralda, Mexico City, 41-45. *Hon Degrees:* Md Inst Col Art, Hon Dr Fine Arts, 99. *Work:* Nat Fine Arts Mus, Mex; Mus Mod Art, NY; Brit Mus, London; Zurich Art Mus, Switz; Nat Gallery, Prague, Czech; San Francisco Mus; Baltimore Mus. *Comn:* Freedom of the Press (mural), News el Sol de Toluca, Mex, 50; Folklore Map of Mexico (mural, with Covarrubuis), Hotel del Prado, Mex, 54; Education for the People (mural, with Pablo O'Higgins), Tarasquillo Schs, Mex, 56. *Exhib:* Exhib of Mex Art, Tate Gallery, London, 49; Exhib of Mex Art, Musee de Arte Moderne, Paris, 50; solo exhibs, Saxon Princes Summer Palace, Dresden, Ger, 73 & Old Mus, Berlin, 73; Unity and Variety, Palacio de Bellas Artes, Mex, 74-75; A Courtyard Apart, Miss Mus Art, Jackson, 90-91; A Courtyard Apart, Montgomery Mus Art, Ala, 91; Bronx Community Col, NY, 92; Inroads, Houston, Tex, 95; Third World Art Exchange, 96; Queens Col Art Ctr, Flushing, NY, 96; Stella Jones Gallery, New Orleans, La, 96; Mexican Prints, Brooklyn Mus, 99. *Pos:* Illusr, El Maestro Mexicano & Mag Capacitación, Secy de Ed Publica, 50-78. *Awards:*

Premium Award, Literacy Campaign, Pres of Mex, 43; Purchase Prize, Secy Hydraulic Resources, 51. *Bibliog:* Juan Mora (dir), Francisco Mora (video), 97 & Betty y Pancko (video), 98. *Mem:* Founding mem Salon de la Plastica Mex; Mex Acad Educ. *Media:* Watercolor, Oil. *Publ:* Illusr, Benito Juarez, El Hombre Ejemplar, 57 & Vicente Guerrero, El Insurgente Ciudadano, 57, Soc Libro Mexicano; The Mexicans, Little Brown Co, 70. *Dealer:* Isobel Neal 200 W Superior Chicago IL 60610; Sragow Gallery 73 Spring St New York NY 10012. *Mailing Add:* Tecolote 200 Lomas de Atzingo Cuernavaca Mor 62180 Mexico 62180

MORALES, ARMANDO
PAINTER, PRINTMAKER
b Granada, Nicaragua, Jan 15, 27. *Study:* Sch Fine Arts, Managua, Nicaragua; Pratt Graphic Art Ctr, NY. *Work:* Mus Mod Art, Guggenheim Mus, NY; Inst Art, Detroit; Mus Art, Philadelphia; Mus Fine Arts, Houston. *Exhib:* Bienal Mod Art, Sao Paulo, Brazil, 53, 55 & 59; Carnegie Inst, Pittsburgh, 58, 64 & 67; Arte Am y Espana, Madrid, Barcelona, Rome & Berlin, 61; Guggenheim Int, NY, 60; The Emergent Decade, Cornell Univ & Guggenheim Mus, 66. *Teaching:* Instr adv painting, Cooper Union, New York, 72 & 73. *Awards:* Ernest Wolf Award, V Bienal, Sao Paulo, Brazil, 59; Award, Arte Am y Espana, Madrid, 63; J L Hudson Award, Carnegie Int, 64. *Bibliog:* Dore Ashton (auth), Visual pleasure from austerity, Studio Int, London, 2/65; Heinz Ohff (auth), Anleitnung zum optimismus: Begegnung mit Armando Morales in Berlin, Der Tagespiegel, Berlin, 6/19/65; Esperanza Brault (auth), Armando Morales, El Sol Mex, Mexico City, 10/4/68. *Mailing Add:* Latin American Masters 264 N Beverly Dr Beverly Hills CA 90210

MORALES, RODOLFO
PAINTER
b Oaxaca, Mex, 1925. *Study:* Nat Sch Fine Art, San Carlos, BFA, 49, study with Rufino Tamayo. *Work:* Inst Polytecnico & Escuela Prep, Mexico City; Mus City Ocatlan, Oaxaca, Mex; Rincon de los Bosques, Bosques de las Lomas, Mex. *Exhib:* State Palace Malaga, Spain, 73; Mus Mex Art, San Francisco, Calif, 78; Mexico: The Next Generation, San Antonio Mus, Tex, 85; one-man exhib, Vorpal Gallery, NY, 85. *Teaching:* Instr art, Escuela Preparatoria No 5, 53-86. *Awards:* Medal, Oaxacan Culture House, Mexico, 86. *Bibliog:* Antonio Rodriguez (auth), Nostalgia accompanies solitude, Inst Politech Nat, Mex, 81. *Publ:* Auth, Rodolfo Morales (exhib catalog), Vorpal Gallery, New York & San Francisco, 88. *Mailing Add:* c/o Bond Latin Gallery 478 Post St San Francisco CA 94102

MORAN, KATE
PHOTOGRAPHER, SCULPTOR
b Langhorne, Pa, Dec 27, 58. *Work:* Mus Am Art, Pa Acad Fine Arts & CIGNA Mus & Art Collection, Philadelphia; Philadelphia Mus Art & Woodmere Art Mus, Pa; New Orleans Mus Art, La; Bryn Mawr Col Libr, Pa; State Mus Pa, Harrisburg. *Exhib:* Biennial 91, Del Art Mus, Wilmington, 91; 1992 New Orleans Triennial, New Orleans Mus Art, La; solo exhibs, Fleisher Art Mem, Philadelphia, Pa, 92, Philadelphia Art Alliance, Pa, 94, More Gallery, Philadelphia, Pa, 94, Lafayette Col, Williams Ctr Arts, Easton, Pa, 95, John Michael Kohler Arts Ctr, Sheboygan, Wis, 96, Univ NC, Chapel Hill, 97 & List Gallery, Swarthmore Col, Pa, 97; Acts of Delicacy (installation), Nexus Gallery, Philadelphia, Pa, 93; Works on Paper 1993, Beaver Col, Glenside, Pa, 93; Works on Paper, 3rd Biennial Exhib, Abington Art Ctr, Jenkintown, Pa, 93; Biennial 93, Del Art Mus, Wilmington, 93; Creative Artists Network, Stuart Levy Gallery, NY, 93; Recent Photographs, More Gallery, Philadelphia, Pa, 93; Art in City Hall (installation), City Hall, Philadelphia, Pa, 94; Works on Paper 1994, Beaver Col, Glenside, Pa, 94; Eros and Identity, Stuart Levy Gallery, NY, 94; NY Hot, K & E Gallery, NY, 95; Systemic Supports for Thin Wristed People, PS 122, NY, 95; In Three Dimensions, Women Sculptors of the 90's, Snug Harbor Cult Ctr, Staten Island, NY, 95; Del Art Mus Biennial, Wilmington, 96; A Woman's View, The Body as Form and Subject, Painted Bride Gallery, Philadelphia, Pa, 96; Telling Tales, SPACES, Cleveland, Ohio, 96; Creative Artists Network: Selections 1984-1996, Woodmere Art Mus, Philadelphia, Pa, 96; New Art on Paper No 2, Hunt Manufacturing Co Collection, Philadelphia Mus Art, Pa, 96; Vestiges, Suzanne H Arnold Art Gallery, Lebanon Valley Col Pa, Annville, 96; Objects and Souvenirs, Artists Multiples, Rosenwald-Wolf Gallery, Univ Arts, Philadelphia, Pa, 96; Hung Out To Dry, Steinbaum Krauss Gallery, NY, 97; Selections from Soho, Steinbaum Krauss Gallery, NY, 98; Ft Lewis Col Gallery Art, Durango, Colo, 98; Twenty Philadelphia Artists: Celebrating Fleisher Challenge At Twenty (with catalog), Mangel Gallery, Philadelphia, Pa, 98; Virtreous Humours, Philadelphia Mus Art, Pa, 98; Mus Am Art, Pa Acad Fine Arts, Philadelphia, Pa, 98; Steinbaum Krass Gallery, NY, 98; Four Hands for Two Pianos, Bernice Steinbaum Gallery, Miami 2000; Olin Gallery at Kenyon Col, Gambier Ohio 2000; and others. *Teaching:* MFA instr Pa Acadd of the Fine Arts, Phila, Pa. *Awards:* Visual Arts Fel, 92-93 & Interdisciplinary Arts Fel, 95-96, Works on Paper fellowship Pa Coun Arts; Leeway Found Grant for Excellence in Photog, 96-97; John Michael Kohler Arts/Indust Residency, 97. *Bibliog:* Mark Gallini (auth), Portfolio: Kat Moran, Seven Arts, 4/95; Edward J Sozanski (auth), Animated portrayals of soulless anonymity, Philadelphia Inquirer, 1/30/98; Richard Garfield (auth), Suffer the innocents, Sci, Vol 39, No 1, 1-2/99. *Media:* Photography, sculpture

MORCOS, MAHER N
SCULPTOR, PAINTER
b Cairo, Egypt, Feb 23, 46; US citizen. *Study:* Cairo Univ, BA(archit), 69; Leonardo de Vinci, Italy, 70. *Comn:* Bust Egyptian President Nasser, Ministry of Educ, Cairo, Egypt, 62; religious paintings, Heliopolis Cathedral, Cairo, Egypt, 64; mural, Valley Nat Bank, Scottsdale, Ariz, 84. *Exhib:* Charles Russell Show, Charles Russell Mus, Great Falls, Mont, 80 & 81; Am Inst Contemp Art, San Dimas, Calif, 80 & 81; Western Artists Am, Coliseum, Reno, Nev, 80 & 81; Western Heritage Show, Arapahoe Co, Littleton, Colo, 80 & 81; George Phippen Show, CofC, Prescott, Ariz, 80 & 81. *Awards:* Gold Medal, Death Valley Show, 80; Best of Show, Western Heritage Show, Arapahoe Co Asn, 81; Best of Show, Western Artists Am, City Reno, 81. *Bibliog:* William E Freckleton (auth), Guided by imagination, Southwest Art, 4/78; Scene, Tulsa Tribune, 78; Dick Spencer (auth), Western heritage, The Western Horseman, 80. *Media:* Bronze; Oil, Watercolor. *Mailing Add:* Eagle Art Gallery 1250 Prospect La Jolla CA 92037

MORENON, ELISE
PAINTER, INSTRUCTOR
b Paris, France, June 26, 39; US citizen. *Study:* Northwestern Univ, BS, 58-61; Sch Mus Fine Arts, Boston, 62 & 63; studied with Mario Cooper, Charles Reid & Edgar A Whitney, Yale Univ Grad Sch, 64 & 65. *Comn:* Portrait, comn by A Nisula, NJ, 89; double portrait, comn by G Barrow, NY, 90; portrait, comn by L S Craig, NY, 92. *Exhib:* Audubon Artists, Nat Art Club, NY, 82 & 91 & Salmagundi Club, NY, 1997-2005; Allied Artists Am, NY, 86-89, 97-2005; Two Artists-Natural Images, Fordham Univ, NY, 89; Watercolor USA, Springfield Art Mus, Mo, 91; Philadelphia Watercolor Club, Philip & Muriel Berman Mus Art, Collegeville, Pa, 92 & 94; Butler Inst Am Art, Youngstown, Ohio, 2001; Morris Mus, NJ, 2002-03. *Pos:* Scenic artist, designer, Berkshire Playhouse, Stockbridge, Mass, 62-64; display artist, Omega Watch Corp, New York, 66-86; lectr & juror, 78-. *Teaching:* Instr watercolor, Sch Visual Arts, New York, 78-84; instr, Teaneck Community Educ Ctr, NJ, 91-; instr, Hyatt Classic Residence, NJ, 94-. *Awards:* Juror's Special Choice Award, Nat Arts Club, 85; Nicholas Reale Mem Award, NJ Watercolor Soc, 91 & Audubon Artists, 97; June Sullivan Award, Northeast Watercolor Soc, 92; Winsor & Newton Award, Allied Artists Am, 97; Strathmore Award, Allied Artists Am, 2002. *Bibliog:* Beckwith (auth), Creative Watercolor, Rockport Publ, 95; Schlemm (ed), Watercolor Expressions, Rockport Publ, 99; Biographical Encylopedia of American Painters, Sculptors and Engravers of the US, Colonial to 2002, Dealers Choice Books, Inc. *Mem:* Am Watercolor Soc; Nat Asn Women Artists; Midwest Watercolor Soc; Allied Artists Am; Philadelphia Water Color Club; Audubon Artists; NJ Watercolor Soc. *Media:* Watercolor. *Interests:* Photography. *Collection:* Private Collections. *Mailing Add:* 420 Fairview Ave Fort Lee NJ 07024

MORGAN, ARTHUR C
SCULPTOR
b Riverton Plantation, La, Aug 3, 1904. *Study:* Beaux Arts Inst Design; also with Gutzon Borglum, Mario Korbel and others. *Work:* Centenary Col, Shreve Mem Libr & Civic Theater, Shreveport, La; Civic Ctr & Hist Libr, Thibodaux, La; plus numerous pvt collections. *Comn:* Heroic figure, Chief Justice Edward Douglass White, Edward Douglass White Mem Comn, US Capitol, Washington, DC, 55; Paul Geisler Mem, Comt Friends of Paul Geisler, Stadium Gounds, High Sch, Burwick, La, 65; Henry Miller Shreve Monument, City of Shreveport & Pub Subscription, River Pkwy, Shreveport, 66, A J Hodges Commemorative Bust, Trustees of Hodges Gardens, Hodges Gardens, Many, La, 72; monumental bust, Clyde E Fant, Clyde Fant Parkway, Shreveport, La, 76; Bust of Jean Despujols, Meadows Mus Art, 81; and others. *Exhib:* One-man shows, La State Univ, Baton Rouge, 27, La State Exhib Mus, Shreveport, 40 & 50; Philbrook Art Ctr, Tulsa, Okla, 52 & Centennial Mus, Corpus Christi, Tex, 57; Mem Exhib, Nat Arts Club, NY, 60-; Mem Exhib, Dartmouth House Club, London, 77. *Teaching:* Instr drawing, painting, sculpture & art hist & dir dept art, Centenary Col La, 28-34; dir sculpture & drawing, Southwestern Inst Arts, 34-74. *Awards:* Am Inst Archit Citations, 61 & 75, Shreveport Chap. *Bibliog:* Patsi Farmer (auth), Biographer in bronze, Shreveport Mag, 12/58; Mary Gray Morris Walker (auth), Portrait of an artist, NLa Hist Asn J, 7/65; Edwin Adams Davis (auth), Louisiana, the pelican state, La State Univ Press. *Mem:* Nat Arts Club; Dartmouth House Club, London, Eng. *Media:* Bronze, Marble. *Mailing Add:* 657 Jordan St Shreveport LA 71101-4748

MORGAN, CLARENCE (EDWARD)
PAINTER, EDUCATOR
b Philadelphia, Pa, May 21, 50. *Study:* Pa Acad Fine Arts, cert, 75; Sch Fine Arts, Univ Pa, MFA, 78; Temple Univ, summer 78. *Work:* Equitable Life Assurance Soc US, Washington, DC; Prudential Insurance Co Am, Jacksonville, Fla; Pa Acad Fine Arts, Philadelphia; Mem Union Gallery, Ariz State Univ, Tempe; General Mills Corp, Minneapolis, Minn. *Comn:* Large scale painting, comn by NC Gen Assembly, Raleigh, 83 & St Thomas Celebration Arts, Wilmington, 86, NC. *Exhib:* Seven Contemp Am Artists, Cleveland Mus Art, Ohio, 83; Portrait of the South, Palazzo Venezia, Rome, Italy, 84; Recent Works, Wake Forest Univ, Winston-Salem, NC, 84; Paradoxical Behavior, Hodges Taylor Gallery, Charlotte, NC, 85; Drawings & Paintings, Carleton Col, Northfield, Minn, 85; Southern Exposure, Alternative Mus, NY, 85; solo exhib, Harris Brown Gallery, Boston, Mass, 86. *Teaching:* Assoc prof painting & drawing, Sch Art, East Carolina Univ, 78-; artist-in-residence, Minneapolis Col Art & Design, 84-85. *Awards:* Fac Res Grant, East Carolina Univ, 79; Merit Award Painting, Fayetteville Mus Art, 82; Visual Arts Fel, NC Arts Coun, 82. *Bibliog:* Rubel Romero (auth), Universal language, Spectator, 84; Mason Riddle (auth), Midwest reviews, New Art Examiner, 84; Richard Maschal (auth), Abstractionist uses religous imagery, Charlotte Observer, 85. *Mem:* Col Art Asn Am. *Dealer:* Elizabeth Harris-Harris Brown Gallery 476 Columbus Ave Boston MA 02118; Dot Hodges-Hodges Taylor Gallery 227 N Tryon St Charlotte NC 28202. *Mailing Add:* c/o Marita Gilliam Gallery 912 Williamson Dr Raleigh NC 27608

MORGAN, DAHLIA
MUSEUM DIRECTOR, EDUCATOR
Study: McGill Univ, BA, 58; Sir George Williams Univ, Can, 68-69; Univ Miami, Fla, dipl col teaching, art hist, 74. *Pos:* Dir, Art Mus, Fla Int Univ, 80-96, Art in State Bldg Prog, Miami, Fla, 84-96. *Teaching:* Lectr art hist, Fla Int Univ, 75-96, creator/moderator, Critics' Lect Series, 80-. *Awards:* Maxie Award, Miami Arts

Exchange, 90; Excellence in Res Award, Fla Int Univ, 93. *Bibliog:* Michael Hayes (auth), Newsmakers: Dahlia Morgan, Miami Today, 12/7/89; Helen L Kohen (auth), Portraits, Miami Herald, 8/21/94; Sue Hearns (auth), Eyes on the Prizes, Miami Herald, 5/2/96. *Mem:* Fla Mus Dir Asn; Int Coun Mus; Fla Cult Action Alliance; Am Asn Mus; Asn Col & Univ & Galleries. *Res:* American modern and contemporary art. *Mailing Add:* c/o Fla Int Univ Art Mus Univ Park PC 110 Miami FL 33199

MORGAN, IKE EDWARD
PAINTER
Study: Self taught. *Work:* Mus African-Am Life & Culture, Dallas, Tex; San Antonio Mus Art, Tex. *Exhib:* Texas Black Folk Artists, Mus African-Am Life & Cult, Dallas, 93; Made in the USA, Collection de l'art brut, Lausanne, Switz, 93; Outside In, Laguna Gloria Mus, Austin, Tex, 93-94; Kelley Collection African Am Art, San Antonio, 94-95; African American Folk Art, Fine Arts Ctr, Taylor Gallery, Colorado Springs, 95-96. *Bibliog:* Denise Gamino (auth), Outsider art brings pride, Austin-Am Statesman, 89. *Media:* Pastel, Indian Ink

MORGAN, JAMES L
PAINTER
b Aug 7, 47. *Study:* Utah State Univ, BFA, 70. *Work:* Utah State Univ, Logan; Crecent Cardboard Co, Chicago; Leigh Yawkey Woodson Art Mus. *Comn:* 36 Paintings, Texaco, Washington, Iowa, 83-85; Merril Lynch, Salt Lake City, Utah, 87. *Exhib:* Nat Acad Western Art, Oklahoma City, Okla; NW Rendezvous Group, Park City, Utah; Landscape and Closer Views, CM Russell Mus, Great Falls, Mont; Birds in Art, Leigh Yawkey Woodson Mus, 82-83 & 86-94; Soc Animal Artists Exhib, 86; Birds Art Nat Tour, 88-91 & 92-2004. *Awards:* Red Smith Artists Choice Award, Nat Mus Wildlife Art, Jackson, Wyo; Artists Choice Award, Northwest Rendezvous Group, 93-94; Robert Lougheed Mem Award, Nat Acad Western Art, 94. *Bibliog:* Donald Hagerty (auth), Leading the West-100 Contemporary Artists, N Land Press; Modern Wildlife paintings, Yale Univ Press. *Mem:* Soc Animal Artists; Northwest Rendezvous Group; Nat Acad Western Art. *Media:* Oil, Watercolor. *Specialty:* Representational Western and Wildlife. *Publ:* Cache Mag, Herald J, 85; Fishes of the Great Basin, Univ Nev Press, 86; Art of the West Mag, 92-96, 2005; Southwest Art Mag, 92, 2005; Wildlife Art News Mag, 11-12/94-2005; and others. *Dealer:* Trailside Galleries Jackson WY; J N Bartfield Gallery New York NY; Simpson Gallagher Gallery Cody WY; Gerald Peters Galleries Santa Fe NM. *Mailing Add:* PO Box 331 Mendon UT 84325

MORGAN, NORMA GLORIA
PAINTER, ENGRAVER
b New Haven, Conn. *Study:* Art Students League, with Julian Levi; Hans Hofmann Sch Fine Art, New York; Atelier 17, New York, with Stanley W Hayter. *Work:* Nat Gallery Art & Pennell Collection, Libr of Cong, Washington, DC; Mus Mod Art, NY; Victoria & Albert Mus, London; Philadelphia Mus Art; Metrop Mus Art, NY; Art Inst Chicago; Lynd Ward Mem Collection, Portland, Ore Art Mus, 92; and others; Billups, Hatch Col, New York City; Storm Over Haworth Moor, Yorkshire (Eng) Col, Cliffe Castle Mus & Gallery, Keighley; Library of Congress, Wash DC included in Rob't Blackburn Collection-my Natural Stone Bridge, Adirondack Mtns-Engraving 2004. *Comn:* Engraving, Woodstock Artists Asn, 83; Moorland Sanctuary (oil mural), Old White Lion Inn, Haworth, Eng, 63; Grand Canyon (acrylic mural), Mary Ellen Pettee Collection, Salisbury, Conn, 80; Elk Lake (acrylic painting 7'x3 1/2') Adirondack Mountains, 92; Elk Lake (engraving), Adirondack Mountains, 92. *Exhib:* Group shows, Hillwood Mus, Long Island, 92, Audubon Artists Ann, NY, 92 & Paradox Gallery, Woodstock, NY; Soc Am Graphic Artists Ann Exhib, NY, 93; Woodstock Artists Ann Mem Show, NY; Shades of Grey, 96; and others; James E Lewis Mus Art, Morgan State Univ, Baltimore, Md, 2000. *Teaching:* Pvt lessons in drawing & watercolor painting. *Awards:* Blue Ribbon-First Prize for Graphics, Composers, Authors & Artists Conv, 69; Medal Honor-Gold Medal, Audubon Artists, New York, 76 & 90; 20th Century Award for Achievement Medal Honor, Int Biog Centre, Cambridge, Eng, 98. *Bibliog:* Fritz Eichenberg (auth), The Art of the Print, Abrams Publ, 76; Robert Henkes (auth), The Art of Black American Women, 93. *Mem:* Soc Am Graphic Artists (coun mem, 74-75); Audubon Artists, NY; Assoc Am Artists; Woodstock Artists Asn. *Media:* Acrylic, Watercolor; Copper Engraving. *Publ:* Woodstock Times, 11/11/99. *Mailing Add:* 595 Columbus Ave New York NY 10024

MORGAN, ROBERT COOLIDGE
ARTIST, CRITIC, WRITER
b Boston, Mass, July 10, 43. *Study:* Univ Redlands, BA, 64; Northeastern Univ, EdM, 68; Univ Mass, Amherst, MFA, 75; NY Univ, PhD, 78. *Work:* Mus Mod Art, NY; Clark Art Inst, Williamstown, Mass; NY Pub Libr; Chase Manhattan Bank Collection; Commodities Corp Collection, NJ; and many pvt collections. *Comn:* Painted Forms on Steel, Mayor's Off Cult Affairs, Boston, 72; Curved Curbs, Mass Coun on Arts, Boston, 74. *Exhib:* Interventions in Landscape, Hayden Gallery, Mass Inst Technol, Cambridge, Mass, 74; Performances: 4 Evenings, 4 Days, Whitney Mus Am Art, NY, 76; Erik Stark Gallery, 92; Daniel Newburg Gallery, 92; Galerie AB, Paris, 92; Construction in Process, Lodz, Poland, 93; Centro Espositivo della Rocca, Paolina, Italy, 94; Abraham Lubelski Gallery, NY, 98. *Collection Arranged:* Mus of Contemporary Art, Chgo; Commodities Corp Collection, Princeton, NJ; NY Pub Libr; Univ of SC, Columbia; U of Oldenburg, Germany; Mus of Modern Art Libr, NY. *Pos:* Bd adv, Art Omi, appt, 92; Gallery Committee, Pratt Inst. *Teaching:* prof emeritus, Rochester Inst Technol, NY, 81-2001; instr, Sch Visual Arts, Columbia Univ, NY, 90 & Barnard Col, 91-92; adj prof, Pratt Inst, 91-93. *Awards:* Nat Endowment Humanities Fel, 80, 87 & 88; Arcala award Salamanca, 99. *Bibliog:* David Craven (auth), article, Arts Mag, 9/83; Collins and Milazzo (coauth), article, New Observations, 87; Gary Nickard (auth), article, CEPA Quarterly, 87. *Mem:* Col Art Asn Am; Int Asn Art Critics. *Media:* Painting, Photog, Film, Installation. *Res:* Role of documentation in conceptual art; structural interactions, literal time and progressive sequence, often manifested in appropriation of swim images & TV images, recent photos of tondo paintings, art & criticism, critical theory. *Interests:* Swimming. *Publ:* After the Deluge: Thge Return of the Inner-Directed Artist, Arts, 3/2; Conceptual Art: An American Perspective, McFarland, 94; Art into Ideas: essays on conceptual arts, Cambridge Univ Press, 96; Between Modernism and Conceptual Art, McFarland, 97; auth The End of the Art World, Allworth Press, NYC 98; Gary Hill, ED, Johns Hopkins Univ Press, 2000; Bruce Nauman, Ed, Johns Hopkins Univ Press, 2002; Clement Greenberg, Ed, Univ of Minn Press, 2003; Vasarely, Geo, Braziller, 2004. *Mailing Add:* Pratt Inst Fine Arts Dept 200 Willoughby Ave Brooklyn NY 11205

MORGAN, ROBERTA MARIE
PAINTER, WRITER
b Baltimore, Md, Nov 24, 53. *Study:* Md Inst Col Art, BFA, 75, Univ Md, 91-92, Towson State Univ, 92. *Work:* City of Gaithersburg Coun Art, Md; Inst Notre Dame, Baltimore, Md. *Exhib:* Free State Three, Rockville Arts Place, Md, 93; Mamaroneck Artists Guild 36th Ann Exhib, Westbeth Gallery, NY, 94; 9th Ann Tallahassee Fla Nat Competition, Fine Arts Gallery & Mus Fla State Univ, 94; Art of Healing, E Campus Gallery, Valencia Community Col, Orlando, Fla, 95; Promising New Talent 1995-96, Mus Contemp Art, Washington, 96; Three Women Gallery Lumiere (with catalog), Savannah, Ga, 97; More Than Meets The Eye, Studio Gallery, Washington, DC, 98; Reflections of Humanity, Marlborough Gallery, Largo, Md; Brute Elegance, Mill River Gallery, Della, Md; Ancient Mother, Columbia Art Ctr, Columbia, Md. *Pos:* Gallery dir, Gaithersburg Coun Arts, 91-94, The Artists' Gallery, Columbia, Md, 95; co-cur, Watercolors of Belisario Contreras, 94; cur, Envelope, Rockville Arts Place & Visual Arts Exhib, Columbia Festival Arts, 2000. *Teaching:* Instr drawing & painting, Columbia Asn Ctr Arts, 94-. *Awards:* Coun Members Award, 75th Nat Exhib, George Walter Vincent Smith Art Mus, 94; Individual Artist Award, Md State Arts Coun, 95. *Bibliog:* Robin Z Goodstein (auth), Gaithersburg artist colors contemplation, Express Newspapers, 9/12/90; Mike Guiliano (auth), New at Slayton House, The Columbia Flyer, 1/23/92; George Howell (auth), Town meeting, Art Papers, 9-10/95; Marty Shooter (auth), The art of three women, Savanna News Press, 2/9/97; Marilyn Stevens (auth), Committment to a good co-op will reap rewards, Art Calendar, 6/97; Rima Shul Kind (auth), Roberta Morgan: more than meets the eye, Koan, 6/97; Phyllis Jacobs (auth), Envelope: Louis Roway, Jill Romanoke, Helga Thomson, Koan, 7/97; George Howell (auth), Wayne Edson Bryan: WEB/Roberta Morgan: more than meets the eye, Art Papers, 9/98; Included in Still Life in Oils edited by Theodora Philcox, published by Ava Publishing SA, this is a book about still life painting. *Media:* Oil. *Publ:* Auth, Creativity on display: Art center studios, 93 & Your local art critic, Art Calendar, 93; Elizabeth Friedman: Photographic explorations, Washington Review, 94; Separating the wheat from the chaff, 4/95 & Interview with Denee Barr: An emerging artist exhibits internationally (art calendar), 9/95; Do It On Your Desktop: Producing Your Own Color Catalog (art calendar), 11/97. *Dealer:* Sloane Jordan Gallery The Arboretum 10,000 Research Blvd Suite 257 Austin TX 78759. *Mailing Add:* Columbia Art Ctr and Gallery 61 Foreland Garth Columbia MD 21044

MORGAN, SUSAN
PAINTER, INSTRUCTOR
b Queens, NY, June 3, 53. *Study:* Art Students League, New York, 73-77. *Exhib:* Int Multimedia Exhib, Univ Sao Paolo, Brazil, 79; Tree Guards, Foundations Gallery, 82 & The Arsenal, 85, NY; Cloudworks, Stuart Neill Gallery, NY, 82; Ann Exhib, Queens Mus, Flushing, NY, 83; Solo exhib, South-Dade Libr, Miami, 84, Silpakorn Univ, Bangkok, US Info Serv, Chiang Mai, Thailand, 90; Off the Wall, Kamikaze Gallery, NY, 86; Second Ann Women's Exhib, Bangkok, Thailand. *Collection Arranged:* Community Cultural Center Annual Exhibitions, Brookings, SDak, 80. *Pos:* Co-owner, Nobe Gallery, NY, 77-79; asst to Jeanne-Claude Christo, NY, 82-84; co-owner, The Five & Dime, NY, 84-86. *Teaching:* Vis lectr, Silpakorn Univ, Bangkok, 90, Chaing Mai Informal Group, 92, Thailand; vis artist, Chaing Mai Univ, 90. *Bibliog:* Helen L Kohen (auth), article, Miami Herald, 84; Artists in the city, by Jenny Dixon, WNYC radio broadcast, 84; Ban Suan mag & several Thai newspaper articles, 90. *Media:* Oil Paint, Oil Pastel. *Publ:* Coauth, Tree Guards, with Holly O'Grady, silk screen edition, 80, Morgan/O'Grady publ, 82; For a Lahu Girl (video), 89. *Mailing Add:* c/o Joyce Morgan 324 Shore Dr E12 Highlands NJ 07732

MORGAN, WILLIAM
HISTORIAN, WRITER
b Princeton, NJ, June 13, 44. *Study:* Dartmouth Col, AB; Columbia Univ, MA & cert in restoration & preservation hist archit; Univ Del, PhD. *Work:* Portland Mus; Miami Univ; Univ Louisville. *Exhib:* JB Speed Mus, Louisville, Ky, 88. *Pos:* Chmn, Ky Hist Preservation Rev Bd, 75-90; archit critic, Courier-J, 75-80; bk rev ed, Landscape Archit Mag, 76-78; ed bd, Competitions, 90-; contrib editor, Art New Eng, 2000-2002. *Teaching:* Lectr art & archaeol, Princeton Univ, 71-74; asst prof fine arts, Allen R Hite Art Inst, Univ Louisville, 1974-76, assoc prof, 1976-81, prof, 1981-, distinguished teaching prof, 1995-99, vis prof, Roger Williams Univ, 1999-2001, vis. prof, Wheaton Col, 2002. *Awards:* Nat Collection Fine Arts Vis Res Fel, Smithsonian Inst, 71; Nat Endowment Humanities Res Fel, 84-85. *Media:* Photographer. *Res:* American art and architecture. *Publ:* auth, Louisville--Architecture and the Urban Environment, Bauhan, 79; Portals: Photographs by William Morgan, Bauhan, 81; The Almighty Wall: Architecture of Henry Vaughan, Archit Hist Found, 83; Collegiate Gothic: Architecture Rhodes Col, Mo, 89; Heikkinen & Komonen, Monacelli, 2000; American Counrty Churches, Abrams, 2004; Abrams Guide to American House Styles, Abrams, 2004; Cape Cod Cottage, Princeton Architectural Press, 2006. *Mailing Add:* 24 Orchard Pl Providence RI 02906

MORGANSTERN, ANNE MCGEE
HISTORIAN, EDUCATOR
b Morgan, Ga, Feb 5, 36. *Study:* Wesleyan Col, Ga, BFA, 58; Inst Fine Arts, NY Univ, MA, 61, PhD, 70. *Teaching:* Instr art hist, Vassar Col, Poughkeepsie, NY, 65-66; lectr art hist, Univ Wis, Milwaukee, 70-73; from asst prof to assoc prof, Ohio State Univ, 73-. *Awards:* Am Coun Learned Soc Grant-in-Aid, 73; Kress Sr Fel, 82-83; Kress Found Grant, 97. *Mem:* Historians Netherlandish Art; Medieval Acad Am; Col Art Asn; Int Ctr medieval Art (domestic adv, 83-86). *Res:* Gothic Sculpture in NEurope; Flemish painting of the 15th century. *Publ:* The rest of Bosch's Ship of Fools, Art Bull, 84; The Bishop, the Lion & the Two-headed Dragon: The Burghersh Memorial in Lincoln Cathedral, Acts of the XXIVth International Congress of the History of Art, 96; Gothic Tombs of Kinship in France, the Low Countries and England, 2000; Art and Ceremony in Papal Avignon: A Prescription for the Tomb of Clement VI, Gesta, 2001; Liturgical and Honorific Implications of the Placement of Gothic Wall Tombs, Hortus Artium Medievalium (Journal of the Intl Center for Late Antiquity and Middle Ages), 2004. *Mailing Add:* 70 Webster Park Columbus OH 43214

MORGANSTERN, JAMES
HISTORIAN, EDUCATOR
b Pittsburgh, Pa, Oct 16, 36. *Study:* Williams Col, BA, 58; NY Univ, MA, 64, PhD, 73. *Teaching:* Asst prof hist art, Univ Wis, Milwaukee, 70-73; asst prof, Ohio State Univ, Columbus, 73-80, assoc prof, 80-90, prof, 90-. *Awards:* Am Philos Soc Grant; Fulbright Research Award; Nat Endowment Humanities Collab Proj Grant. *Mem:* Col Art Asn; Soc Archit Historians; Archaeol Inst A; Medieval Acad; Soc Franc d'Arch. *Res:* Byzantine, architecture and archaeology; western medieval architecture. *Publ:* Auth, The church at Dereagzi: A preliminary report on the mosaics of the Diaconicon, Vols 23 & 24, 69 & 70, Dumbarton Oaks Papers; The church at Dereagzi: Its date and its place in the history of Byzantine architecture, Actes, XIV Congres Int Etudes Byzantines, 76; The Byzantine Church at Dereagzi and its Decoration, Ernst Wasmuth, 83; Working procedures in Byzantium: New evidence from southwestern Anatolia, Artistes, artisans et production artistique, Actes, II, Picard, 87; coauth, The fort at Dereagzi, and other material remains in its vicinity: From antiquity to the middle ages, Wasmuth, 93. *Mailing Add:* Dept Hist Art Ohio State Univ Columbus OH 43210

MORGENLANDER, ELLA KRAMER
PAINTER, INSTRUCTOR
b Bronx, NY, Aug 7, 31. *Study:* Brooklyn Col, 53; Brooklyn Mus Art Sch, with Reuben Tam, 60-70; New York Univ, 62; Barnes Found, Merion, Pa, 74-76; Art Students League, with Will Barnett, 78-79. *Exhib:* Ann Nat Asn Women Artists, Nat Acad Arts Gallery, NY, 71-81; Brooklyn Mus, NY, 76; one-woman show, Nicholas Roerich Mus, NY, 76; Artists Depicting the Humanities, Henry St Settlement, NY, 82. *Teaching:* Instr art, St George's Pre-Sch NY, 62-67; instr, Ethical Culture Sch, Brooklyn, NY, 63-66; instr art, Bank St Sch Childhood Educ, 68-72. *Awards:* Adelle M Schiff Award, 73; Ziuta & Joseph James Akston Found, 88th Ann Nat Asn Women Artists; Lillian Cotton Mem Award, 90; Hon Mention Award, Nat Asn Women Artists, 92. *Mem:* Artists Equity Asn, NY; Nat Asn Women Artists; Contemp Artists New York. *Media:* Oil, Watercolor. *Dealer:* Brooklyn Mus Community Gallery File 188 Eastern Parkway Brooklyn NY. *Mailing Add:* 210 Park Pl Apt 2C Brooklyn NY 11238-4324

MORI, MARIKO
PAINTER
b Tokyo, Japan. *Study:* Bunka Fashion Col, Tokyo, Japan, 86-88; Byam Shaw Sch Art, London, Eng, 88-89; Chelsea Col Art, London, Eng, 89-92; Whitney Mus Am Art Independent Study Prog, NY, 92-93. *Exhib:* Solo exhibs, Geneva Proj Room, NY, 93, Am Fine Arts Co, NY, 95, Shiseido Gallery, Tokyo, 95, Galerie Emmaneul Perrotin, Paris, 96, Ctr Nat D'Art Contemporain de Grenoble, 96 & Gallery Koyanagi, Tokyo, 97; Play With Me, Dallas Mus Art, Tex, 97; Contemp Projects 2: Mariko Mori, Los Angeles Co Mus Art, Calif, 98; Mus Contemp Art, Chicago, 99. *Mailing Add:* Deitch Projects 76 Grand St New York NY 10013

MORIMOTO, HIROMITSU
PHOTOGRAPHER
b Yokohama, Japan, 42. *Study:* St Joseph Col, 62; Calif State Univ, Long Beach, BA, 67; Art Students League, 67-68. *Work:* Baltimore Mus Art; Japan Found & Mus Mod Art, NY; Milwaukee Art Mus; Mus Fine Arts, Houston. *Exhib:* 20th Anniversary Show, Westbeth Gallery, NY, 90; XXI Sao Paulo Biennial (with catalog), Brazil, 91; Figureworks, Gomez Gallery, Baltimore, 95; Body Abstract, Korean Cult Serv, NY, 96; Diverse Visions//Photog Perspectives, Pittsburgh Ctr Arts, 97; one-man shows, Nishimura Gallery, Tokyo, 89-93, Past Rays Photo Gallery, Yokohama, Japan, 94, Alternative Mus, NY, 95, Sarah Morthland Gallery, NY, 97 & Hiromitsu Morimoto-Vellum & Rice Paper, Tokyo, 98. *Awards:* Creative Artists Pub Serv Grant, NY, 75 & 79; Nat Endowment Arts Grant, 80; Minister of Educ Prize, 11th Int Biennial Prints, Tokyo, Japan, 80. *Bibliog:* Vince Aletti (auth), Voice choices, Village Voice, 3/29/94; Caran-Maries Zambo (auth), Arts displays offers diversity, Daily News, McKeesport, Pa, 5/8/97; Mary Thomas (auth), Photography exposed to new processes, Pittsburgh Post-Gazette, 6/21/97. *Mailing Add:* c/o Jayne H Baum Gallery 26 Grove St Suite 4C New York NY 10014

MORIN, FRANCE
CURATOR
b Montreal, Que. *Study:* Montreal Univ, BA(art hist & film), 75. *Collection Arranged:* Canada-NY: From the Studios of Canadian Artists Living in NY, 84 & Icarus: The Vision of Angels, 86, 49th Parallel, Ctr Contemp Can Art, NY. *Pos:* Co-founder & co-ed, Parachute (comtepm art mag), 75-80; dir, Galerie France Morin, 80-83; dir & cur, 49th Parallel Ctr Contemp Can Art, 83-89; sr cur, New Mus Contemp Art, 89-95; independent cur, 95-. *Teaching:* Teacher art hist, grad prog, Concordia Univ, Montreal, 81-83. *Mailing Add:* One 5th Ave Apt 10A New York NY 10003

MORIN, JAMES CORCORAN
CARTOONIST, EDITOR
b Washington, DC, Jan 30, 53. *Study:* Syracuse Univ Sch Art, BFA, 75. *Work:* Mus Cartoon Art, Boca Raton, Fla; Emerson Col, Boston, Mass; Ohio State Univ, Columbus. *Exhib:* Art Collectors Gallery, Coral Gables, Fla, 93; Morin of the Herald, Mus Cartoon Art, Boca Raton, Fla, 96. *Pos:* Ed cartoonist, Beaumont Enterprise & J, 76-77, Richmond Times Dispatch, 77-78 & Miami Herald, 78-. *Awards:* H L Mencken Award; Berruman Award, 96; Pulitzer Prize, 96. *Bibliog:* Dick Comer (auth), A baker's dozen questions for one of America's brightest young cartoonists, Cartoonist Profiles, 9/79; David Finkel (auth), Etching political, Miami Mag, 8/79; David Astor (auth), Great Year for Ed Cartoonist, Ed & Publ, 10/96. *Mem:* Asn Am Ed Cartoonists; Nat Cartoonists Soc. *Media:* All Media. *Publ:* Contribr, Best Editorial Cartoons of the Year, Pelican, 78 & 79; America's Political System, Random House, 79; Famous Cats, William Morrow, 82; auth, Jim Morin's Field Guide to Birds, William Morrow, 85; James Morin's Line of Fire, Fla Univ Press, 92. *Mailing Add:* El Nuevo Herald One Herald Plaza Miami FL 33132

MORIN, THOMAS EDWARD
SCULPTOR, EDUCATOR
b Malone, NY; Sept 22, 34. *Study:* Mass Col Art, BS(educ), 56; Cranbrook Acad Art, MFA, 57; Brown Univ, cert(basic metal), 66, cert(plastics technol), 67. *Work:* Richmond Mus Art, Va; Brown Univ, Providence, RI; Barn Gallery Assoc, Ogunquit, Maine; NY Univ, Oneonta. *Comn:* Cast aluminum high relief, Brown Univ, 64; bronze sculpture & bronze screen, Am Tube, 72. *Exhib:* Inst Contemp Art Invitational, Boston, 60; Whitney Mus Am Art Ann, NY, 61; 11 New Eng Sculptors, Wadsworth Atheneum, Hartford, Conn, 63; Contemp Box & Wall Sculpture Invitational, RI Sch Design Mus Art, 65; Univ Conn Mus Art, Storrs, 70. *Teaching:* Head dept sculpture, Silvermine Guild Artists Col Art, 58-60; assoc prof sculpture & head sculpture grad prog, RI Sch Design, 61-. *Awards:* First Prize & Best in Show, Silvermine Guild Artists, 60; First Prize, RI Art Festival, 63; First Prize, New Haven Art Festival, 66. *Mem:* Union Independent Cols Art; Am Foundrymens Soc. *Mailing Add:* 15015 Woods Edge Minnetonka MN 55345-2900

MORIN-MILLER, CARMEN A
AUTHOR, CURATOR
b Montreal, Que. *Study:* Pvt studie, art & art history, 47-50 & 65-78. *Pos:* Writer, 55-74; dir & cur, Morin-Miller Galleries, New York, 86-90 & Collegeville, Pa, 90-99. *Publ:* Auth, Conspiration, Intrinseque, 77; Lumiere, Minerve, 88. *Mailing Add:* 233 Greenwood Ave Collegeville PA 19426-2707

MORISHITA, JOYCE CHIZUKO
HISTORIAN, PAINTER
b Newell, Calif. *Study:* Northwestern Univ, Evanston, Ill, BA(painting), 64, MA(painting), 65, PhD(art hist), 79. *Work:* Michael Reese Hosp & Med Ctr, Chicago, Ill; Rockford Art Mus, Ill. *Comn:* Oil-vaporous nudes, Michael Reese Hosp & Med Ctr, 72. *Exhib:* Rockford & Vicinity, Ill, 1983, 1985-86 & 1994; Her Works, Art Ctr, Sound Bend, IN, 1989 & 1992; New Horizons in Art, Evanston, IL, 1990; Aldo Castillo Gallery, 1996; Womens Work, 1996, 2000, 2002, 2003; and others. *Collection Arranged:* Third World Art Exhib, Gov State Univ, 76 & 77; Women's Suffrage documents (over 100). *Pos:* Mem adv comt, Renovation of Chicago Pub Libr, 73; bd trustees, Third World Conf Found, Chicago, 82-. *Teaching:* Prof art, painting & art hist, Gov State Univ, University Park, Ill, 73-. *Awards:* Artists & Lectrs Grant, 74 & Craftsman in Residence Grant, 75, Nat Endowment Arts; Acquisition Prog Grant, 76, Artist Grant, 84, Ill Art Coun. *Mem:* Col Art Asn Am; Chicago Artist Coalition; Turner Soc, London; Womens Caucus Art. *Media:* Oil, Mixed. *Res:* Study of J M W Turner at Petworth, 1802-1837. *Mailing Add:* 5000 S Eastend Ave Apt 6B Chicago IL 60615

MORISUE, GLENN TAKANORI
PAINTER, INSTRUCTOR
b San Francisco, Calif, Nov 22, 40. *Study:* Art Inst Pittsburgh (Willis Shook Scholar), dipl(advertising illus), 63; Cleveland Inst Art, BA, 65. *Work:* Hansen Mfg Co, Cleveland, Ohio. *Exhib:* 34th & 41st Ann Midyear Shows, Butler Mus Am Art, Youngstown, Ohio, 69 & 77; Butler Mus Am Art, 97, 98 & 99; Cleveland Inst Art, 2000. *Pos:* Illusr & photo retoucher, various Cleveland com art studios, 65-79, graphic designer & art dir, 81-91; product designer & creative dir, Copper K Indust, Cleveland, Ohio, 91-95. *Teaching:* Prof life drawing & airbrush, Cooper Sch Art, Cleveland, Ohio, 79-80, dean educ, 80-81. *Awards:* City of Geneva, Ohio, Best of Show & First Place Painting, Geneva Grape Jamboree Art Exhib, 94; Friends of Andover Best of Show, Andover Libr Art Exhib, 95, 99; 1st Place Painting, Bay Crafters Art Ctr, Bay Village, Ohio, 99 & Eastern Counties Show, Lake Erie Col, Painesville, Ohio, 99; National Prize Winner, American Artist Drawing Magazine, Sept, 04; others. *Bibliog:* Designers, illustrators, photogr show - Cleveland, Commun Arts, Mag, 68. *Mem:* Meadville Coun Arts, Pa; Am Soc Portrait Artists. *Media:* Graphite, Oil. *Publ:* featured artist, American Artists Drawing Magazine, Sept, 04. *Dealer:* Tulip Tree Gallery Ashtabula OH; Glenn Morisue Internet World Wide Web; Kada gallery Erie PA; Lakeview gallery Saybrook OH. *Mailing Add:* 6201 1/2 Lake Rd W Ashtabula OH 44004

MORITA, JOHN TAKAMI
PRINTMAKER, PHOTOGRAPHER
b Honolulu, Hawaii. *Study:* Chaminade Col, BA, 65; San Francisco Art Inst, BFA(photography), 74; San Francisco State Univ, MA(printmaking), 76. *Work:* Philadelphia Mus Art, Pa; San Francisco Mus Mod Art, Calif; Honolulu Acad Art, Hawaii; Cabo Frio Int Print Biennial, Brazil; Intergrafix, E Berlin, Ger; Honolulu Acad of Arts, Hawaii State Found on Culture & the Arts, Intergrafik, Berlin, Ger, San Francisco mus Modern Art. *Comn:* State of Hawaii's Comn on the Columbian

Quincentennial Observance, 92. *Exhib:* Solo exhibs, Honolulu Acad Arts, Hawaii, 77, San Francisco Mus Mod Art, 79, Recent Prints, Alternative Mus, NY, 87, Photo Etchings, Print Club, Philadelphia, 90, Radierungen USA (auth catalog), Intergrafik (auth catalog), 90, Berlin, Ger. *Teaching:* Lectr, Univ Hawaii, 82-84. *Awards:* Nat Endowment Arts Fel for Printmaking, 86; First Prize, Intergrafik '87, Ger; Selection Award, Print Club, 88; Individual Artist Fel Merit Award, Hawaii State Found on Cult & the Arts, 95. *Mem:* Honolulu Printmakers (vpres, 89); Northwest Print Coun. *Media:* Drypoint, Photo Etching, Etching, Video. *Interests:* Middle E Politics. *Publ:* Heirs, vol 6, no 1, winter, 75-76; John Morita: Journal by David Hett; Intergrafik 90; 9 Internationale engagieter Grafik inder DDR, Berlin 17, April bis 90; John Takami Morita Artist/Hawaii, Univ Hawaii Press, 96. *Dealer:* Valerie Harmon 1640 Ahihi St Honolulu Hawaii 96819. *Mailing Add:* 1640 Ahihi St Honolulu HI 96819

MORLEY, MALCOLM A
PAINTER, SCULPTOR
b London, Eng, 31. *Study:* Camberwell Sch Arts & Craft, 53; Royal Col Art, Assoc degree, 57. *Work:* Whitney Mus, Mus Mod Art & Metrop Mus Mod Art, NY; Wadsworth Atheneum, Hartford, Conn; Hirshhorn Mus Sculpture Garden & Corcoran Gallery Art, Washington, DC; Musee Nat d'Art Moderne, Paris; Walker Art Ctr, Minneapolis, Minn. *Exhib:* Contemp Am Painting, Whitney Mus, NY, 72; Documenta V, Kassel, 72, Projeckt & Cologne, 74, Ger; Retrospective exhib, Whitechapel Art Gallery, London, Kunsthalle Basel, Boymansvan Beuningen, Rotterdam, Cocoran Art Gallery, Washington DC, Mus Contemp Art, Chicago, Brooklyn Mus, NY, 83-84; one-man shows, New Work, Pace Gallery, NY, 88-89, Paintings, Sculpture and Watercolors, Anthony d'Offay Gallery, London 90, Recent Paintings and Sculptures, Pace Gallery, NY, 91, Watercolors, Tate Gallery, Liverpool, 91-92, Baumgartner Galleries, Washington DC, 94, 97, Galleria d'Arte Emillio Mazzoli, Modena, Italy, 98 & Hayward Gallery, 2001; Int Survey of Paintings & Sculpture, 84, Pop Art 1955-70, 85, Berlin Art 1961-1987, 87-88, Mus Mod Art, NY, 84; Portraits on Paper, Robert Miller, NY, 91; Images of the Era: Selections from the Permanent Collection, Mus Contemp Art, Los Angeles, 95-96; Arte Americana: Ultimo Decennio (catalog), Mus d'Arte della Citta di Ravenna, 2000. *Teaching:* Assoc prof, Ohio State Univ, 65-66, State Univ NY, Stony Brook, 72-74; instr, Sch Visual Art, NY, 67-69. *Awards:* First Ann Turner Prize, Tate Gallery, London, 84; Painting Award, Skowhegan Sch Painting & Sculpture, 92. *Bibliog:* Anthony Haden-Guest (auth), Portfolio: Four Drawings, Malcolm Morley, Paris Rev, spring 98; Ken Johnson (auth), Art in Review: Malcolm Morley, NY Times, 3/12/99; Grace Glueck (auth), A Rich Mix of Styles and Stimulations Under One Roof, NY Times, 2/25/2000. *Mem:* Nat Acad(academician). *Media:* Oil, watercolor. *Mailing Add:* c/o Gemini Gel at Joni Moisant Weyl 21B 58 W 58th St New York NY 10019-2509

MOROSAN, RON
PAINTER
b Detroit, Mich, Mar 25, 47. *Study:* Wayne State Univ, Mich, BFA, 71; Univ Iowa, Iowa City, MA & MFA, 73; Univ Mich, Ann Arbor, 74-75. *Work:* Univ Iowa Mus, Iowa City; Mus Contemp Art, Chicago; Detroit Inst Arts; The New Mus, NY. *Exhib:* Solo exhibs, Feigenson-Rosenstein Gallery, Detroit, 77 & 81, Robert Freidus Gallery, NY, 78 & Sheldon Ross Gallery, Birmingham, Mich, 90, Bemis Found, 93, Schloss Overhagen Gallery, Lippstadt, Ger, 94, New House Ctr Contemp Art, Staten Island, NY, 99 & Andre Zarre Gallery, New York City, 2003; Deaocónotation, Connotation, Implication, Eisner Gallery, City Col NY, 88; Snug Harbor Sculpture Festival, Staten Island, NY, 89; Art & Suitcase Will Travel, Gallery Gertrude Stein, New York City, 2000; Chánce of Meaning, Gallerie Schulgasse 18, Wiirzburg, Ger, 2001; Multi-Tasking, Islip Art Mus, 2005; Gallery Schulqasse 18, 2005; Case Studies, Katonah Art Mus, 2006; Head Up & Good Luck, Kunstwerk, Cologne, Germany, 2006. *Collection Arranged:* Martin Art Gallery, Muhlenburg, Col, Pa; NJ State Mus, Trenton; Mint Mus, Charlotte, NC; Mos Int, Japan. *Teaching:* Vis lectr, Frostburg State Col, Md, 77, Ill State Univ, Normal, 79 & Univ NC, Greensboro, 80; vis artist, Univ Nev, Reno, Univ Tex, Denton, Molloy Col, Rockville Centre, NY. *Awards:* Nat Endowment Arts Grant, 74; Grant in Sculpture, Louis Comfort Tiffany Found, 77; Ariana Found Grant, 83; Artists Fel Grant, 85; Residency: Bemis Found, Omaha, Nebr. *Bibliog:* New York Terminal Show, EVillage Eye, 83; Bill Zimmer (auth), Art & Siutcase Will Travel, NY Times, 1997; George Tysh (auth), Alley Culture, Metro Times, Detroit, 2000. *Mem:* Col Art Asn. *Dealer:* Gallery Gertrude Stein 56 W 57th St New York NY 10019. *Mailing Add:* 315 Eighth Ave Apt 16B New York NY 10001

MORPER, DANIEL
PAINTER, PRINTMAKER
b Ft Benning, Ga, Mar 26, 44. *Study:* Univ Notre Dame, BA, 66; Sch Arts, Columbia Univ; Corcoran Sch Art, Washington, DC. *Work:* Cleveland Mus Art; Minneapolis Art Inst; Indianapolis Mus Art; Ft Wayne Mus Art; Shite Mus Art, Notre Dame. *Comn:* Tulsa Panorama, Facet Corp, Okla, 86; South Bend Aerial View, St Joseph Bank, Ind, 86; Washington DC Panorama (mural), Mobil Oil, Merrifield, Va, 90; Grand Canyon diptich, Texaco, White Plains, NY, 92. *Exhib:* 19th Area Exhib, Corcoran Gallery Art, Washington, DC, 74; one-man show, Shite Mus Notre Dame, 86; 1987 Biennial, NMex Mus Art, Santa Fe, NMex, 87; Home Again, Colombus Mus, Ga, 90. *Media:* Oil, Gouache; Etching. *Mailing Add:* c/o Robischon Gallery 1740 Wazee St Denver CO 80202

MORPHESIS , JIM (JAMES) GEORGE
PAINTER
b Philadelphia, Pa, Aug 26, 48. *Study:* Tyler Sch Art, with Stephen Greene, with David Pease, BFA, 70; Calif Inst Arts, with Paul Brach, Miriam Schapirow & Allan Kaprow, MFA, 72. *Work:* Orange Co Mus Art; Phoenix Art Mus; Los Angeles Co Mus Art; San Francisco Mus Modern Art; Oakland Mus; plus others. *Comn:* painting, Broder-Kurland-Webb-Ufner Agency, Beverly Hills, 86; painting, Gannett Co, Inc, Washington, DC, 86; The Fall of Icarus (mural), Loyola Sch Law, Los Angeles, 83-84; painting, John Wayne Airport, Costa Mesa, Calif, 90; painting, Broder-Kurland-Webb-Uffner Agency, Beverly Hills, 86. *Exhib:* Los Angeles Artists, 76, Eight Artists, 76, Young Talent Awards: 1963-1983, 83, Los Angeles Co Mus Art; solo exhib, Tortue Gallery, Santa Monica, Calif, 83, 84, 86, 87, 90 & 92, Los Angeles Co Mus Art, Calif, 87, Deson/Saunders Gallery, Chicago, Ill, 87, 90 & 93 & Littlejohn/Sternau Gallery, NY, 92; Concerning the Spiritual, San Francisco Art Inst, 85; group exhib, Ancient Currents, Fisher Gallery, Univ Calif, Los Angeles, 86; Avant-Garde in the Eighties, Los Angeles Co Mus Art, Calif, 87; Abstract Expressionism & After, San Francisco Mus Mod Art, Calif, 87; Images of Death in Contemp Art, Haggerty Mus, Milwaukee, Wis, 90; Cruciformed: Images of the Cross Since 1980, Cleveland Ctr Contemp Art, Ohio, 92; Sanctuaries: Recovering the Holy in Contemp Art, Mus Contemp, Relig Art, St Louis, Mo, 93; Kardia, Tortue Gallery, Santa Monica, Calif, 94; Transformations: The Human Form in Diverse Contexts, Wignall Mus, Rancho Cucamonga, Calif, 94; Searching for the Spiritual, Hope Col, Mich, 98; Mod Odyssey, Queens Mus, NY; The One Chosen, Brauer Mus Art, Valparaiso, Ind, 2000; The Fate of Marsyas, Deep River Gal, Los Angeles, Caslif, 2000; Surreal, Jan Baum Gal, Los Angeles, Calif, 2000; Modern Odysseys, Queens Mus, NY, 2000; solo exhib, The Fate of Marsyas, Deep River, Los Angeles, Calif, 2001, Flora Lamson Hewlit Mus, Grad Theological Union, Berkeley, Calif, 2002, Cuts, Jan Baum Gallery, Los Angeles, Calif, 2005, Da Vinci Art Gallery, Los Angeles City College, Calif, 2006; invitational exhib, Representing LA: Pictorial Currents in Southern Calif Art, Frye Mus, Seattle, Wash, Art Mus S Tex, Corpus Christi, Tex & Laguna Art Mus, Laguna Beach Calif, 2001, Fourth Florence Int Biennial Contemp Art, Fortezza da Basso, Florence, Italy, 2003, On the Walls: Murals, Armory Ctr for the Arts, Pasadena, Calif, & Peace Tower 2006, Whitney Mus Am Art Biennial Exhib, Day for Night, New York, NY, 2006; plus others. *Teaching:* Instr painting, Calif Inst Arts, Valencia, 75, Immaculate Heart Col, 73-74, Los Angeles City Col, 74-79 & Otis Art Inst, 80-86, Claremont Grad Univ, 86-87, Art Inst of Southern Calif, 96, Pasadena City Col, 97-. *Awards:* Nathan Margolis Mem Award Painting, Tyler Sch Art, 70; Louis Comfort Tiffany Found Grant Award, 85-86; Artist-in-residence, Claremont Grad Sch, Claremont, Calif, 87, Fullerton Col, Fullerton, Calif, 93; first prize, Florence Intl Biennial Contemp Art, 2003. *Bibliog:* Robert L Pincus (auth), Art as Artifact, Flash Art, summer 85; J Morpliesis (auth), Terrence Dempsey (auth), The Tragic Sense of Life: J Morphesis, Image, spring 94; John Dillenberger, Theology of Artistic Sensibilities, 86; John Williams, Portraits of Passion, 99; Justin Spring (monogr), Jim Morphesis: Paintings, 91-92. *Mem:* Col Art Asn Am; Am Hellenic Inst. *Media:* Oil, Mixed Media. *Publ:* Justin Spring (monogr), Jim Morphesis: Paintings, 91-92. *Dealer:* Littlejohn Contemp Gallery 41 E 57th St New York NY 10022; Jan Baum Gallery, 170 S La Bred Ave, Los Angeles, Calif, 90036. *Mailing Add:* 708 1/2 S Santa Fe Ave Los Angeles CA 90021

MORREL, OWEN
SCULPTOR, PHOTOGRAPHER
b Amityville, NY, May 15, 50. *Study:* Colgate Univ, 68; Skidmore Col, BA, 70; Cranbrook Col, 72. *Hon Degrees:* NEA, 1980; CAPS, 1981. *Work:* Centre Nat d'Art Pompidou Mus, Paris, France; Artpark/Nat Heritage Trust, Lewiston, NY; Madison Art Center, Wis; Prudential Bache Co, New York City, NY; First Nat Bank Chicago, Ill; Fifth Ave, Flatiron Dist, NY, 97; Saint Paul Western Sculpure Park, Minn, 98; New Mus Building, NY, 99; and many pvt collections. *Comn:* sculpture, Pub Art Fund, NY, 84; sculpture, Natural Heritage Trust, Lewiston, NY, 80; sculpture Dresdner Bank, NY; sculpture Sithe Energy Group, Oswego, NY, 96; sculpture BPM assoc, NY, 99. *Exhib:* One man retrospective, Contemp Art Mus, Houston, 86, Madison Art Ctr, Wis, 88; solo shows, Walker Arts Center, Minneapolis, Minn, 88, Liz Galasso Fine Art, NY, 88, Jason McCoy, NY, 88, Philippe Staib Gallery, NY, 91. *Awards:* CAPS, NY State Coun Arts Grant, 79; Artists Fel, Nat Endowment Arts, Natural Heritage Trust, 80; CAPS, NY State Coun Arts Grant, 81. *Bibliog:* Michael McKinnon (auth), History of Western Art, London Visual Publ, 80; Tracking the marvelous, NY Times, 82; John Ash (auth) Morrel's Deleroius Structures, Art in Am, 91. *Media:* Steel, Aluminum. *Mailing Add:* 8 Greene St New York NY 10013

MORRELL, WAYNE (BEAM)
PAINTER
b Clementon, NJ, Dec 24, 23. *Study:* Philadelphia Sch Indust Art; Drexel Inst-Famous Artist Sch. *Work:* Sloan Kettering Cancer Res Ctr, NY; Clark Mus, Carversville, Pa; Lahey/Clinic, Burlington, Mass. *Exhib:* Expos Intercontinentale, Monoco, France; One-man shows, Washington Co Mus, Hagerstown, 73, Bliech Gallery Carmel, Calif, 82 & Golden Web, Santa Fe, NMex; Grand Cent Gallery, NY; Mont Crest Gallery, Chattanoga, Tenn; Dassin Gallery, Los Angeles; Newman Gallery, Philadelphia; many others. *Pos:* Art dir, John Oldham Studios, Conn, 55-61; owner & dir, Wayne Morrell Gallery, currently; designer, Paris & Brussel-World Fairs, currently. *Awards:* Jane Peterson Prize, 69 & 74 & Coun Am Art Socs Award, 71, Allied Artist Am; Gold Medal, 70, Mariboe Award, 80 & Harriet-Mattson Award, 80, Rockport Art Asn. *Bibliog:* R Kolby (auth), A stand for nature, Am Artist, 3/72. *Mem:* Allied Artist Am; Springfield Acad Artist (coun, 60-61); Hudson Valley-Am Soc Veteran Artists; Rockport Art Asn. *Media:* Oil, Watercolor. *Publ:* Illusr, Readers Digest, 67; Yankee Magazine, 8/80. *Dealer:* Newman Galleries 1625 Walnut Philadelphia PA 19103. *Mailing Add:* One Squam Hollow Rockport MA 01966

MORRILL, MICHAEL LEE
PAINTER, EDUCATOR
b Springfield, Vt, Oct 23, 51. *Study:* Alfred Univ, BFA, 73; Yale Univ, MFA, 75. *Work:* Carnegie Mus Art; Bayer Collection Contemp Art; Buchanan Ingersoll Prof Collection; Allda Corp; Mellon Financial Corp. *Comn:* Compass (site installation), Pittsburgh Int Airport, 93. *Exhib:* Solo exhibs, Siegfred Gallery, Ohio Univ, Athens, 80, Hewlett Gallery, Carnegie Mellon Univ, Pittsburgh, 81, Carnegie Mus Art

Entrance Gallery (Forum Gallery), 82, Mattress Factory, 83, Jus de Pomme Gallery, NY, 85 & 86 & Concept Art Gallery, Pittsburgh, 88, 89, 91 & 94; Ten Americans, Carnegie Mus Art, 88; Pittsburgh in Chicago, Deson Saunders Gallery, Chicago, 90; Five Artists at the Airport: Insights into Pub Art, Wood St Gallery, Pittsburgh, 92; Degrees of Abstraction: Eight Pittsburgh Artists, Three Rivers Art Festival, Pittsburgh, 93; 25th Anniversay Exhib, Concept Art Gallery, Phila, 97; Allegheny Col, Meadville, Pa, 2000; Artists Image Resourse, Phila, 2002; two-person show, Concept Art Gallery, Phila, 2000-01. *Teaching:* Assoc prof painting, Univ Pittsburgh, 76-. *Awards:* Ely Harwood Schless Mem Prize, Yale Univ, 75; Artists Fel, Pa Coun Arts, 81; Artist Residence Grant, Vermont Studio Ctr, Johnson, 96; Research Grant, Univ Phila, 2002. *Bibliog:* Kay Larson (auth), In brief, NY Mag, 11/86; Patrica Lowry (auth), Carnegie exhibit revives art of abstraction, Pittsburgh Press, 2/88; Mary Jean Kenton (auth), Lines, planes, colors & forms, new Art Examiner, 4/93. *Mem:* Col Art Asn. *Publ:* Contribr, Mattress Factory: Installation & Performance 1982-1989, 91; Bayer Collection of Contemporary Art, Bayer Corp, 95; Mike May (auth), Artists Present, Pitts Mag, 2000; Kurt Shaw (auth), Artistic Reproduction, Phitts Tribune Rev, 2002. *Dealer:* Sam Berkovitz. *Mailing Add:* 1031 S Braddock Ave Pittsburgh PA 15218

MORRIN, PETER PATRICK
MUSEUM DIRECTOR
b St Louis, Mo, Oct 31, 45. *Study:* Harvard Univ, AB, 68; Princeton Univ, MFA, 72. *Pos:* Dir, Vassar Col Art Gallery, 74-78; cur 20th century art, High Mus, 79-86; dir, J B Speed Art Mus, 86-. *Teaching:* Instr art hist, Vassar Col, 74-78, Emory Univ, 80-86 & Univ Louisville, 87-. *Awards:* Nat Collection Fine Arts Res Fel, Smithsonian Inst, 73-74; Res Fel, Smithsonian Mus of American Art. *Mem:* Asn Art Mus Dirs (pres, 2003-04). *Res:* modern art; American art; contemporary art; outsider art. *Publ:* Coauth (with Dr Eric M Zafran), Drawings from Georgia Collections: 19th and 20th Centuries (catalog), 81, auth, J J Haverty: The Taste of a Southern Collector (catalog), 81, 20th Century Paintings from the Collection of the Museum of Modern Art: A Viewer's Guide (catalog), 82, Chase Manhattan: The First Ten Years of Collecting, 1959-1969 (catalog), 82 & Content in Abstraction: The Uses of Nature (catalog), 83, High Mus Art, Atlanta; Advent of Modernism: Post Impressionism and North American Art (catalog), High Mus, 86. *Mailing Add:* Speed Art Mus 2035 S 3rd St Louisville KY 40208-1812

MORRIS, FLORENCE MARIE
DEALER
b Detroit, Mich, Apr 30, 28. *Study:* Wayne State Univ, BS. *Pos:* Dir, Donald Morris Gallery, Detroit & New York, 58-. *Mem:* Art Dealers Asn Am; New Detroit (mem visual arts comt, 77-); Detroit Art Dealers Asn. *Specialty:* 20th century painting, sculpture and drawings; African sculpture. *Mailing Add:* 25915 Salem Rd Huntington Woods MI 48070

MORRIS, GREGG
PAINTER, ACRYLIC
b Ann Arbor, Mich, Jan 21, 51. *Study:* Vanderbilt Univ, 68-69; Md Inst, BFA, 75; Syracuse Univ, MFA, 85. *Comn:* Sculpture, Nat Icee Corp, 90. *Exhib:* Soho Ctr Visual Art, 82; Smallworks 83, Univ Mass, 83; Rochester Finger Lakes Exhib, Rochester, NY, 84; 47th Ann Artists of Central NY, Muson-Williams-Procton Inst; Utica, NY, 84; Everson Biennial, Everson Mus Syracuse, NY, 84; Spectrum: The Generic Figure, Cororan Gallery Art, Washington, 86; McIntosh/Drysdale Gallery, Washington, 86; Case Gallery, Kennett Sq, Pa, 91; CCC Gallery, Philadelphia, 97. *Pos:* Owner, Hard Edge Art & Design, currently. *Awards:* MacDowell Colony Grant, 79; Artists Fel Grant, Nat Endowment Arts, 87. *Bibliog:* Ned Rifkin (auth), The Generic Figure (exhib catalog), Corcoran Gallery Art, 86. *Mailing Add:* 326 Delaware Cir Newark DE 19711

MORRIS, JACK AUSTIN, JR
MUSEUM DIRECTOR, ART DEALER
b Macon, Ga, Sept 29, 39. *Study:* Univ SC, AB, with Edmund Yaghjian, Augusta Wittkowski & Catherine Rembert; Univ SC; Harvard Univ Inst Arts Admin. *Collection Arranged:* Arnold H Maremont Collection (20th Century American & European Painting & Sculpture), 65; Ida Kohlmeyer (one-man exhib), 67; Jasper Johns Prints (with catalog), Harbor Town Mus, Hilton Head Island, SC, 71; Andrew Wyeth in Southern Collections, 78; Select Works by Andrew Wyeth: The Arthur and Holly Magill Collection, 79; Complete Serigraphs of Jasper Johns, 80; The John B Connally Collection, 88; The Robert Shelton Collection, 92; The John Bayer Collection, 2000; The John J. McMullen Collection, 2003. *Pos:* Curatorial assoc, Columbia Mus Art, 62-63, asst to dir, 63-65; exec dir, Greenville Co Mus Art, 65-80 & Greenville Co Art Asn, 75-80; mem exec bd, Metrop Arts Coun, 78-80; exec dir, Period Gallery West, 80-81; owner, Morris Fine Arts, 81-83; exec dir, Connally, Altermann & Morris Art Gallery, 83-87; co-owner, Altermann & Morris Galleries, Dallas & Houston, Tex, Santa Fe & Hilton Head Island, SC, 87-99; bd trustees, Mus Art Am West, Houston, 88; bd dir, Houston Art Dealers Asn, 90; owner, Worns & Whiteside Galleries, 99-; owner, Red Piano Art Gallery, 2002-; owner, Gallery at Palmetto Bluff, 2005-. *Teaching:* Lectr, Kress Collection, Columbia Mus Art, SC, 62-65; instr drawing & painting, Richland Art Sch, Columbia, 64-65. *Mem:* Guild SC Artists (pres, 68); founder, SC Fedn Mus (vpres, 71-72, pres, 73-74); SC Arts Comn (chmn exec comt, 72-73); SC Arts Found (pres, 75-80); Houston Art Dealers Asn (vpres, 91); Arts Ctr Coastal Carolina (bd mem 2000-06, chmn 2005-06); and others. *Res:* Contemporary American art; Art of the American West; Southern paintings & sculpture. *Specialty:* 19th & 20th Century American Art; Western and wild life, sporting art. *Publ:* Auth, Contemporary Artists of South Carolina (catalog), 70; William M Halsey: Retrospective (catalog), 72; Western Collectors, 84-96; American Art Classic, 1986-2005; Texas Renaissance, 1989-2004; and others. *Mailing Add:* 2618 Calibogue Club Hilton Head Island SC 29928

MORRIS, ROBERT
SCULPTOR
b Kansas City, Mo, Feb 9, 31. *Study:* Kansas City Jr Col; Kansas City Art Inst, 48-50; Univ Kansas City; San Francisco Art Inst; Reed Col, 53-55; Hunter Col, MA, 66. *Work:* Modern Museet, Stockholm, Sweden; Dallas Mus Fine Arts, Tex; Whitney Mus Am Art, NY; Tate Gallery, London, Eng; Wadsworth Atheneum; Detroit Art Inst; Nat Gallery Can, Ottawa; Nat Gallery Victoria, Melbourne, Australia; Walker Arts Ctr, Minneapolis, Minn; Pasadena Art Mus, Calif; Milwaukee Art Ctr. *Comn:* Earth Proj, Nat Planning Comn, Ottawa; Steam Piece, Western Wash Univ, Bellingham, 69; Grand Rapids Proj, City of Grand Rapids, Mich, 74; Observatory, Sonsbeek Unlimited, Oost-Flevoland, Holland, 77. *Exhib:* Guggenheim Int, Solomon R Guggenheim Mus, 67; The Art of the Real, Mus Mod Art, 68; One-man shows, Galerie Ileana Sonnabend, Paris, 71, Inst Contemp Art, Univ Pa, Philadelphia, 74, Mirror Works & Drawings, Wright State Univ, Dayton, Ohio, 79, Selected Works 1970-1981, Contemp Arts Mus, Houston, 81, Recent Felt Pieces, Galerie Nordenhake, Malmo, Sweden, 84, Sonnabend Gallery, NY, 85, Works of the Eighties, Mus Contemp Art, Chicago, 86 & Sonnabend Gallery, NY, 92; Whitney Mus Am Art, 72, 73, 75 & 76; Art Inst Chicago, 74, 76 & 77; Some Recent Am Art, Mus Mod Art, NY & traveling, 74; Galerie Ricke, Cologne, Ger, 74; Sculpture, Am Directions 1945-1975, Nat Collection Fine Arts, Smithsonian Inst, Washington, DC, 75; High Mus Art, Atlanta, Ga; NY State Mus, Albany, 77; Madison Art Ctr, Wis, 77; New Gallery Contemp Art, Cleveland, Ohio, 77; Kansas City Art Inst, Mo, 78; Mus Contemp Art, La Jolla, Calif, 78; A View from the Sixties: Selections from the Leo Castelli Collection and the Michael and Ileana Sonnabend Collection, Guild Hall Mus, East Hampton, NY, 91; Dessins d'Ameriques, Frac Picardie, Amiens, France, 92; plus many others. *Teaching:* Instr, Hunter Col, 67-. *Awards:* Prize, Guggenheim Mus, 67; Guggenheim Found Fel, 69; Sculpture Award, Soc Four Arts, 75. *Bibliog:* Annette Michelson (auth), Three notes on an exhibition as a work, Artforum, 6/70; Jack Burnham (auth), Robert Morris: Retrospective in Detroit, Artforum, 3/70 & Voices from the gate, Arts Mag, Vol 46 summer 72; Jeremy Gilbert-Rolfe (auth), Robert Morris: The complication of exhaustion, Artforum, 9/74. *Publ:* Auth, The art of existence, 1/71, Some splashes in the ebb tide, 2/73 & Aligned with Nazca, 10/75, Artforum; auth, The present tense of space, Art in Am, 1-2/78

MORRIS, ROGER DALE
PAINTER
b Huntington, WVa, Feb 23, 47. *Study:* Art instruction schs, illustrating, 68; workshop, with Albert Handell, 87. *Exhib:* Kentucky Artists Painting in a Southern Tradition, JB Speed Mus, Louisville, Ky, 84; Kentucky Artists Postcard Series, Barren River Arts Coun, Ky, 85; Oil Pastel Assoc Am, Pen & Brush Gallery, NY, 86; Miniature Painters, Sculptors, Gravers Soc, Arts Club, Washington, DC, 87; Pastel Soc Am, Nat Arts Club, NY, 87; SAF/Art Search, High Mus, Atlanta, Ga. *Awards:* Northlight Award, Oil Pastel Asn Am, Northlight Books, 86; Marie Devor Award, Pastel Soc Am, 87; Dow Corning Wright Award, Cent S Art Exhib, Nashville, 90. *Bibliog:* Betty Lowry MC (auth), The Art Scene, Murray Cable TV Network, 88. *Media:* Acrylic, Pastel. *Mailing Add:* The People's Bank 116 S Main St Marion KY 42064-1508

MORRIS, SARA See Swetcharnik, Sara Morris

MORRIS, WILLIAM
GLASS BLOWER
b Carmel, Calif, July 25, 57. *Study:* Studied at Calif Sate Univ & Cent Wash Univ. *Work:* Am Craft Mus, Metrop Mus Art, NY; Corning Mus Glass, NY; Hokkaido Mus Mod Art, Sapporo, Japan; Musee de Arts Decoratifs, Paris; Seattle Art Mus; Victoria & Albert Mus, London. *Comn:* Installation, SEA-TAC Int Airport, Seattle, 93. *Exhib:* Form & Light, Am Craft Mus, NY, 94; Breaking Barriers, Portland Art Mus, 95; Touch of Glass, Nat Geographic Mus, Washington, 95; Glass Now 17, Hokkaido Mus Art, Tokyo, 95; Graft at Gumps, San Francisco Craft & Folk Art Mus, 96; Holding the Past, Historicism in NW Glass Sculpture, Seattle Art Mus, 96; Studio Glass, Metrop Mus Art, NY, 96; Glass Today by Am Studio Artists, Mus of Fine Arts, Boston, 97; Int Movements in Glass, Auckland Mus, New Zealand, 98; Am Glass, Masters of the Art, Smithsonian Inst Traveling Exhib Serv, 98; solo shows, Riley Hawk Gallery, Columbus, Ohio, 98, Duane Reed Gallery, St Louis, 98, Friesen Fine Art, Sun Valley, Idaho, 98, Susan Duval Gallery, Aspen, Colo, 98, Foster/White Gallery, Seattle, 98, Marx Saunders Gallery, Chicago, 99, Imago Gallery, Palm Desert, Calif, 99, Lisa Sette Gallery, Scottsdale, Ariz, 99, Habatat Gallery, Boca Raton, Fla, 99, The Chrysler Mus of Art, Norfolk, Va (traveling), 99 & others. *Awards:* Individual Artists Grant, Nat Endowment Arts, 94; Outstanding Achievement in Glass Award, Urban Glass, New York, 97; Distinguished Alumni Award, Calif State Univ, Chico, 97. *Media:* Glass. *Mailing Add:* 220 3rd Ave S # 100 Seattle WA 98104-2608

MORRISEY, MARENA GRANT
MUSEUM DIRECTOR
b Va. *Study:* Va Commonwealth Univ, BFA (interior design); Va Commonwealth Univ, MA (art hist); Fel, Colonial Williamsburg, Post Grad Studies. *Collection Arranged:* Japanese Art from the Mary and Jackson Burke Collection; Gold of el Dorado; General Mills Art Collection; Westinghouse Art Collection. *Pos:* curator of educ, Orlando Mus of Art, Orlando, 70-76; exec dir, Orlando Mus of Art, Orlando, 76-. *Awards:* Fla State of the Arts Award; Women Who Mean Bus Award; Outstanding Women of the Year, Field of Art Award. *Mem:* AAM; Fla Asn Mus; Asn Art Mus Dirs; Fla Art Mus Dirs Asn. *Specialty:* vis art. *Mailing Add:* 2416 N Mills Ave Orlando FL 32807

MORRISON, BOONE M
ARCHITECT, PHOTOGRAPHER
b Berkeley, Calif, Jan 28, 41. *Study:* Stanford Univ, BA(archit), 62, BA(commun), 63; Yosemite Photog Workshops, with Ansel Adams, 71-73. *Work:* Honolulu Acad Art & Bishop Mus, Honolulu, Hawaii; State of Hawaii Collection; US Nat Park Serv; Nat Gallery Art, Washington, DC. *Comn:* Mural photographs, Kauai Mus, 71 & C Brewer & Co, 73; interior wall mural, State of Hawaii, Ka'u Hosp, 75. *Exhib:* Artists of Hawaii, 71-75; Mountains and the Shore, Honolulu Acad Traveling Exhib; Milolii, A Most Hawaiian Place Traveling Exhib, 75; Time on the Land Traveling Exhib, 76-77 & Am Photogrs and the Nat Parks, 81-83, Nat Park Serv. *Pos:* Owner-founder, The Foundry Gallery, Honolulu, 69-71; dir, Hawaii Photog Workshops, 71-; dir & founder, Volcano Art Ctr, Hawaii; pres & publ, Summit Press; principle & pres, Boone Morrison Archit, Inc, 88-; Fire Mountain Film, Producer, Pres. *Teaching:* Instr photog, Univ Hawaii, Manoa Campus, 69-71, instr archit, 70-72; instr photog, Hawaii Photog Workshops, 71-, State Hawaii Artists Schs, 74 & Kauai Community Col, 84; lectr, Univ Hawaii Ford Found, 80 & Art Dept, Univ Hawaii, Hilo, 82-84. *Awards:* Gold Medals For "Song of South Kona" San Francisco Int Film Festival, Houston Int Film Festival; Governor's Housing Comendation, 91; Preservation Honors Award, 93. *Bibliog:* Joan Murray (auth), Photography in Hawaii, Art Week, 73; Portfolio, 1979 Popular Photog Ann; The Photographers Eye (film), Hawaii, 80. *Mem:* Image Continuum Group; Am Inst Architects; Hist Hawaii Found; Nat Trust Hist Preserv. *Media:* Photography, Painting. *Publ:* Auth, Images of the Hula, Summit Press, 83; Song of South Kona (video), KHET Television & Hawaiian Air, 86; Legacy of Lia (video), 88; Mainstreet Hawaii (video), 88; articles, Hist Hawaii Mag, 93; columnist, Narrow Gauge Gazette mag, 95-; Sturgeous Sawmill, 2001; Video Caufornia Narrow Gauge, (video), 2003. *Mailing Add:* PO Box 131 Volcano HI 96785

MORRISON, EDITH BORAX
ARTIST, PAINTER
b New York, NY, July 14, 26. *Study:* Studies at Woodstock Guild of Craftsmen, Woodstock, NY, 1972; Empire State Col, Long Island, NY, BA, 1973; Long Island Univ, MA, 1976; Studies at Silvermine Guild Art Sch, 86-. *Work:* Purdue Univ; Bur Labor Statistics, NY; Beth El Synagogue, Long Island, NY; Finland's Del to UN; Town of Oyster Bay, NY. *Exhib:* Long Island Painters, Guild Hall, Mus Sect, Easthampton, NY, 1967; juried exhib, Morris Gallery, NY, 1967; solo shows, Morris Gallery, NY, Greenwich St Gallery, NY, Hillside Lib, NY & Picture This Gallery, Westport, Conn, 1999; Garden of Earthly Delights, invitational, Discovery Mus, Bridgeport, Conn, 1999; Hecksher Mus, NY; Silvermine Art Guild, New Caanon, Conn; Kehler Liddell Gallery, New Haven, Conn, 2006. *Teaching:* Guest lectr painting & sculpture, numerous clubs & orgns, 1965-75; grad asst fine art, Long Island Univ, 1975-76; pvt art tchr adult level, 1976-85; art tchr, Floral Park High Sch, Long Island, NY. *Awards:* Award, Nat Competition, Purdue Univ; award, Nat Art League, Douglastown, NY; award, Manhasset Art League, NY; Purchase award, Biennial Competition, Purdue Univ, 1969; 1st Prize, Ann Art Competition, Oyster Bay, NY, 1960's; numerous awards, regional exhibs, 1970-2002. *Mem:* Silvermine Artists Guild. *Media:* Pen & Ink, Acrylic, Mixed Media. *Interests:* Antiques, tribal art & Alaskan artifacts. *Mailing Add:* 6 Old Farm Rd Trumbull CT 06611

MORRISON, FRITZI MOHRENSTECHER
PAINTER, LECTURER
b Quincy, Ill. *Study:* Art Inst Chicago; Univ Chicago, with Edmund Giesbert, also with Charles W Hawthorne, Anthony Thieme, Karl Knaths, watercolor with Eliot O'Hara, John Pike & Dyke Remuller. *Work:* St Louis Art Mus, Mo; Western Ill Univ Art Mus, Macomb, Ill; Dartmouth Col Art Gallery, Hanover, NH; Whatcom Mus Hist & Art, Bellingham, Wash; Quincy Art Center, 6 watercolors, Ill; City Hall, Quincy, Mass; Am Savings; Huber Indust; Quincy Pub Libr; Blessing Hosp, Quincy, Ill; Gardner Mus, Quincy, Ill. *Comn:* Expedition Artist-Turkish Village, Anatolia, Turkey, 62. *Exhib:* retrospectives, Western Ill Univ Macomb, 80 & 89 & Quincy Art Ctr, Ill, 95; solo-shows (51), incl Elizabeth Sinnock Gallery Art Ctr, Quincy, Ill, 81 & 88, Lighthouse Gallery, Tequesta, Fla, 87, Quincy Soc Fine Arts, Ill, 92 & David Stawn Art Gallery, Art Asn, Jacksonville, Ill, 2000, Graint Bank Gallery, 2000, Spira, 2000, Inmam's Gallery of Art, 2001, 02, River Toad Show, Los Angeles, 2001, Quincy Art Ctr, 2002; Int Watercolor Exhib, Taiwan, 95; Int Watercolor Exhib, Korea, 96; Three Rivers Arts Festival, Pittsburgh, Pa, 96; Watercolor USA, 2002; Soc Diego Watercolor Soc, 2002. *Pos:* resident artist & vpres, Quincy Art Club, Ill, formerly. *Teaching:* Inst, Watercolor Classes, Quincy Art Club, Quincy Univ, Hannibal, Mo Art Club & other regional workshops. *Awards:* Hon Mention, Ill Watercolor Soc, 89; Quincy Art Club Awards: 5 first, in watercolor & 4 Best-in-Show; Women of Achievement Arts, YWCA, Quincy, 93; Hunmen Houston Watercolor Art Soc, 99. *Bibliog:* Krannert Mus Univ, Ill (auth), The George M Irwin Collection, 80; featured artist, Arts/Quincy, 12/84; Significant Architecture in Quincy, Ill from 1835-1915 (monogr), 85. *Mem:* Signature mem Am Watercolor Soc; signature mem Philadelphia Water Color Soc; signature mem Midwest Watercolor Soc Charter, Great River, Miss; signature mem Pa Watercolor Soc. *Media:* Transparent Watercolor. *Publ:* Contribr, Places in Watercolor, Rockport Publ, Mass; Facets of a Sparkling Medium, Palette Talk #46, 3/80; Alishar Remembered, Disappearing Ways of Life in a Turkish Anatolian Village, 99. *Dealer:* Inman's Art Gallery, Ill. *Mailing Add:* 1845 Jersey St Quincy IL 62301

MORRISON, KEITH ANTHONY
PAINTER, EDUCATOR
b Jamaica, West Indies, May 20, 42; US citizen. *Study:* Art Inst Chicago, BFA, 63, MFA, 65; Univ Ill; DePaul Univ; Loyola Univ. *Work:* Art Inst Chicago; Nat Mus Am Art, Washington; Corcoran Gallery Art, Washington; Philadelphia Acad Art. *Comn:* Painting for Liberian Govt, 64 & Dusable Mus Afro-Am Hist, 71; mural comn by Phyllis Kind Gallery for Main Bank, Chicago, 72; and others. *Exhib:* Biennial Chicago & Vicinity, Art Inst Chicago, 71; Corcoran Gallery Art, 83; Bronx Mus, 90; Alternative Mus, NY, 90; Alternative Mus, NY, 90; Cavin-Morris Gallery, NY, 92; Bomani Gallery, San Francisco, 96; Art in Chicago: 1945-95, Mus Contemp Art, Chicago, 96; and others. *Collection Arranged:* Toussaint L'ouverture (paintings of Jacob Lawrence, with catalog), DePaul Univ, Chicago, 69; Black Experiences in Art (exhib of painting & sculpture, with catalog), Bergman Gallery Univ Chicago, 71; Afro-Am Artists, Washington Proj Arts, 79; Wisconsin 80, Univ Wis, 80; Brandywine Workshop, 88; Smithsonian Inst, 89. *Pos:* Chmn art dept, DePaul Univ, Chicago, 69-71; assoc dean, Col Art & Archit, Univ Ill, Chicago, 71-75; prof & chmn, art dept, Univ Md Col Park, 88-92; dean creative art, San Francisco State Univ, 94-96; dean, Col Art & Humanities, Univ Md, College Park, 96-. *Teaching:* Instr art, Hyde Park Art Ctr, Chicago, 65-67; asst prof drawing, Fisk Univ, Nashville, Tenn, 67-68; assoc prof printmaking & chmn dept, DePaul Univ, 68-71; assoc prof, Univ Ill, Chicago Circle, 71-79; prof, Univ Md, College Park, 79-. *Awards:* Prize, Jamaica Inst, 59; Bicentennial Award Painting, City Chicago, 76; Int Painting Award, Orgn African Unity, Liberia, 79. *Bibliog:* Robin Glauber (auth), Keith Morrison at Black Hawk, Skyline, 9/70; Harold Hayden (auth), article, Chicago Sun-Times, 10/79; Paul Richard (auth), article, Washington Post, 83. *Mem:* Col Art Asn; Nat Conf Artists; Int Asn Art Critics. *Media:* Oil, Watercolor. *Res:* Role of black institutions in modern art of Washington, 1940-1970; contemporary black artists in America. *Publ:* Auth, art criticism: A Pan-American point of view, 79, guest ed, Afro-American Art, 81 & auth, Kitai: The sword of Don Quixote, 81, New Art Examiner; auth, 200 Years of Afro-American Women Art: A Critic's View, Ill State Univ, 80; auth, Poetic objects, New Art Examiner, 82. *Dealer:* Jan Cicero Gallery 437 N Clark St Chicago IL 60610

MORRISON, ROBERT CLIFTON
PAINTER, CALLIGRAPHER
b Billings, Mont, Aug 13, 24. *Study:* Carleton Col, BA; Univ NMex, MA. *Work:* Harvard Univ Libr Print Collection, Cambridge; Ministry Art & Culture, Ghana; Rocky Mt Col, Billings; Int Col Copenhagen, Denmark; Centre Medieval Studies, Oxford, Eng. *Comn:* Mosaic murals, Mont State Unemployment Comn, Helena, 61 & Lucerne Pub Schs Wyo; mural, Lockwood Pub Schs, Billings; Bicentennial mural, Yellowstone Co Courthouse, Billings; mural, Rocky Mountain Col, Billings. *Exhib:* Yellowstone Art Mus, 89; Pioneer Modernists of Mont Invitational, 90; CM Russell Mem Mus, 92. *Pos:* Ed, Rocky Mt Rev, 63-69; pres bd dir, Yellowstone Art Ctr, Billings, 64-65. *Teaching:* Dir art educ, Billings Pub Schs, 57-67; prof art, Rocky Mt Col, 67-90; artist-in-residence, Herning Folk Skole, Denmark, 83. *Awards:* Mont Artist-Teacher of Yr, Am Artists Prof League, 64; Best of Show Award, Landmarks Mont Exhib, 91. *Bibliog:* Montana Century, Falcon Press, 99; Writers Under the Rims, Parmly Libr Found Press, 2001. *Media:* Gouache, Oil. *Publ:* Translr & illusr, Maxims of LaRochefoucauld, 67. *Mailing Add:* 2815 Woody Dr Billings MT 59102

MORRISON, ROBERT J
SCULPTOR
Study: Calif State Univ Fresno, BA(art); Stanford Univ, MA(art); Univ Calif, Davis, postgrad. *Exhib:* Solo exhib, Foster Goldstrom Gallery, NY, 92; Architectural Commission, Sierra Nev Red Cross, Reno, 93; Triangle Artists Benefit, Lorraine Kessler Gallery, Poughkeepsie, NY, 93; Int Biennial, Mus Mod Art, Miami, 94; Luminous Impressions, Kala Inst, Berkeley, Calif, 94; Lake Worth Mus Mod Art, Fla, 98. *Teaching:* Univ Nev, Reno, 68-. *Awards:* Grant, Sierra Arts, Reno, Nev, 90; Nat Endowment Art Fel, 90; Individual Artist Award, Nev State Arts Coun, 94. *Bibliog:* Electric 34 oasis, High Performance, 4/88; Jeff Kelley (auth), Robert Morrison DICE (for the Development of Innovative Contemporary Exhibitions), 99; O Coeur, Artweek, 10/17/89. *Publ:* Cover, Foster Goldstrom Gallery, summer 92; Jules Olitski (exhib, catalog, essay), Salander-O'Rielly Galleries, New York, 94, New Gallery, Univ Miami, 94

MORRISROE, JULIA MARIE
MUSEUM DIRECTOR, PAINTER
b Chicago, Ill, Sept 26, 61. *Study:* Northern Ill Univ, Dekalb, BFA, 88; Univ Washington, Seattle, MFA, 90. *Work:* Appalachian State Univ, Charlotte Halpert Collection, NC; Cent Mich Univ, Mt Pleasant; WR Harper Col, Ill. *Exhib:* Halpert Biennial, Appalachian State Univ, 99, Saginaw Art Mus, 99; Fiber Art Int, 2002; one-women show, ACME Art Co, Ohio, 2002; traveling exhib, Comic Release: Negotiating a New Identity, Regina Miller Gallery & Carnegie Mellon Univ, 2003. *Collection Arranged:* Sari Khoury Retrospective (traveling exhib), 99; Home: A Reinterpretation, Ctrl Mich Univ, 99, Transformative Nature, 2000, Making a Mark, 2000, Natural Materials: Wood Fired Creamics, 2000, Subverting The Market: Art Work on the Web, 2001. *Pos:* pres, ARC Gallery, Chicago, Ill, 95-98; dir, Univ Art Gallery, Cent Mich Univ, 98-. *Teaching:* instr drawing/design, WR Harper Col, 91-98; instr curatorial practice Cent Mich Univ, 98-; instrnl asst prof, Ill State Univ, 2001-2002. *Awards:* Purchase Award, Halpert Biennial, 99; CMU Faculty Res Grant, 2000; Mich Coun for the Arts & Culture, 2000-01 & 2002-2003; Contemp Italian Art Faculty Res Grant, 2003. *Bibliog:* Chicago Tribune, 2001, Am Craft Mag, 2002, Fiber Art Mag, 2002, & Pittsburgh News, 2003. *Mem:* Col Art Asn; Women's Caucus For Art. *Media:* Mixed. *Res:* Comtemp Art, Media Art and Curatorial Studies. *Specialty:* Contemp Art. *Publ:* Wag, Wag, Wag (catalog essay), Univ Art Gallery, Central Mich Univ; Wood Sculpture, Encyclopedia of Sculpture, Fitzroy Publ; auth, review, Donald Sultan, New Art Examiner, 1-2/2002. *Mailing Add:* Cent Mich Univ Univ Art Gallery Wightman 132 Art Dept Mount Pleasant MI 48859

MORRISSEY, LEO
CONCEPTUAL ARTIST
b Philadelphia, Pa, Aug 22, 58. *Study:* Marietta Col, Ohio; Univ Fla, BFA, 83; Mason Gross Sch Arts, Rutgers Univ, MFA, 85. *Work:* Flight 93 Nat Mem Archive, Nat Park Serv, Somerset, PA; Mus of Modern Art/Franklin Furnace Book Collection, NY; Taiwan Mus of Art, ROC, Taiwan, Republic of China; The Jane Voorhees Zimmerli

Mus, New Brunswick, NJ; The Sharjah Art Mus, Sharjah, United Arab Emirates; Pilchuck Glass Sch Collection, Seattle, Wash; Boulder Mus of Contemp Art, A Sense of Place, Boulder, Colo; Brevard Mus of Art and Sci, Melbourne, Fla; Fulton Co Arts Council, Atlanta, GA; King Stephen Mus, Hungary; Glass Mus, Ebeltof, Denmark; Canadian Postal Mus, Ottawa, Can; The Noyes Mus, Educational Study Collection, Oceanville, NJ; The Ace Collection, Pvt Collection, NJ. *Exhib:* Jane Voorhees Zimmerli Art Mus, New Brunswick, 85; Experimental Art, Yamanashi Mus Art, Japan, 86; Sculpture Six, Bronx Mus Arts, NY, 86; New Yorkers in Spain, Togo Brunnes Gallery, Barcelona, 90; Gallery Vincent Bernat, Barcelona, Spain, 91; Z Gallery, NY, 91; Snapshot, Contemp Mus, Baltimore, Md, 2000; 6th Wexford Artist Books, The Workhouse Mus, Londonderry, Northern Ireland; The Non-informative Flyer Project, MH de Young Meml Mus, San Francisco, Calif, 99; The Sharjah Arts Mus, Sharjah, United Arab Emirates, 2000; plus others; Pierogi, Flat Files, Brooklyn, NY; Brent Sikkema Gallery, Postcards From the Edge, NY; Flight 93 Nat'l Memorial Design Competition, Somerset PA; Gallery Lelong, Visual AIDS Benefit, NY; Boulder Mus of Contemp Art, A Sense of Place, Boulder, Colo; Taiwan Mus of Art ROC11th Int Biennal Print and Drawing Exhib, Taiwan Republic of China; Monash Gallery of Art, Not Brick Chimmeys, Melbourne Australia; Exhib of Int Glass Art, Seattle WA; Gallery Lelong Postcards From The Edge, Visual AIDS Benefit, NY. *Collection Arranged:* Co-Curator w/Jackie Borsanyi, Book Art Show Scheduled for 2006, Brevard Mus of Art; in the eyes of the bewildered.(Things Printed), Brevard Mus of Art, 2005; Curator, Rutgers Sculpture, Rutgers Univ; Curator, Cuban Poster Show, Rutgers Univ. *Teaching:* teacher, Brevard Community Col, Melbourne, Fla; teacher, Indian River Community Col, Vero Beach, Fla. *Awards:* Pollock-Krasner Found Grant, 87. *Bibliog:* John Froonjian (auth), Noyes marks a year, 6/84 & Marjorie Donchey (auth), Morrissey self-portrait, 3/85, The Press, Atlantic City, NJ; Janson Kaufman, Watercolors and sculpture, Daily Tarqum, New Brunswick, NJ, 2/85; Art Smart, FLORIDA TODAY, Melbourne FL, August 30, 2002; Pilchuck Glass School, 24th Annual Auction, Catalog, Seattle, WA, 2002; This Glass has Class, FLORIDA TODAY, Melbourne, FL, May 28, 2003; Liberty Mus, Glass Now Auction, Catalog, 2004. Philadelphia, PA; Museletter, Brevard Mus of Art, Melbourne, FL, 2005; Mus Inside and Out, WMEL 920 AM, Radio Show Guest, 2005; American Art Collector, Book 4, Alcove Books, Berkeley, CA, 2005. *Mem:* Col Art Asn; Community Col Profs of Art and Art History. *Media:* All Media. *Publ:* Contribr, Books Build Bridges, Artist Bk, 86; The Search for Accidental Significance, Money for Food Press, 87. *Dealer:* Pierogi, Flat Files, Brooklyn, NY,

MORROW, TERRY
DRAFTSMAN, PRINTMAKER
b Austin, Tex, Oct 1, 39. *Study:* Univ Tex, BFA; Univ Wis; Ind Univ, MS, study with Rudy Pozzatti. *Work:* Univ Tex, Austin; Tex Christian Univ, Ft Worth; Western Tex Col, Snyder; Odessa Col, Tex. *Exhib:* Appalachian Nat Drawing Competition, Boone, NC, 78 & 79; two-person exhibs, Sch Galleries, Houston Mus Fine Arts, 71 & Art Dept Teaching Gallery, Univ Tenn, Knoxville, 77; one-person exhib, Clara M Eagle Gallery, Price Doyle Fine Art Ctr, Murray State Univ, 73; and many others. *Pos:* Consult in litho printing, Tex Christian Univ, Ft Worth, 69, Western Tex Col, Snyder, 74 & San Angelo Col, Tex, 78; guest artist, ETex State Univ, Commerce, 79. *Teaching:* Instr painting & printmaking, Univ Pa, Philadelphia, 65-66; asst prof drawing & printmaking, Univ Chattanooga, Tenn, 67-68; assoc prof drawing, printmaking, Tex Tech Univ, Lubbock, 68-, prof art, currently; prof, ETex State Univ, 85-. *Awards:* Cash awards, 16th Ann Drawing and Small Sculpture exhib, 70 & Tri-State Art Exhib, 76; 12th Ann Del Mar Drawing & Small Sculpture, 78. *Media:* Pen and Ink; Intaglio. *Mailing Add:* Tex Tech Univ Dept Art Box 42081 Lubbock TX 79409-2081

MORSE, BART J
PAINTER, PRINTMAKER
b Salt Lake City, Utah, Aug 16, 1938. *Study:* Brigham Young Univ, BS, 62; Univ Wash Sch Art, MFA, 64. *Work:* Latter Day Saints Mus Church Hist & Art, Salt Lake Co, Univ Utah, Salt Lake City; Wells Fargo Corp, Los Angeles; Provident Mutual Life Insurance Co, Philadelphia; Laguna Gloria Art Mus, Austin, Tex; Avon Software, Tucson, Ariz. *Comn:* I'm Going West to Go East, Col Fine Arts Grant Columbus Print, Univ Ariz, 92. *Exhib:* Nat Print Show, Moravian Col, Bethlehem, Pa & Hunterdon Art Mus, NJ, 81; Bradley Nat Drawing & Print Show, Peoria, Ill, 83; National Show, E Ky State Univ Mus, Richmond, 85; New Art in the West, Vorpal Gallery, San Francisco, 85; Contemp SW Art, Roland Gibison Gallery, NY; Watercolor USA, Springfield, Mo, 92-93. *Teaching:* Assoc prof studio art, Univ Ariz, Tucson, 70-; vis assoc prof studio art, Univ Del, Newark, 83-84. *Awards:* Award, Watercolor, USA, 92. *Mem:* Watercolor USA Hon Soc. *Media:* Watercolor, Woodcuts. *Publ:* Illusr, Dialogue: A Journal of Mormon Thought, Vol VII, No 2, Los Angeles, summer 72; auth, articles, The Ariz Daily Star, Tucson, Ariz, 75 & 81; articles, Salt Lake Tribune, Utah, 81 & 85; illusr, Brigham Young Univ Arts, Vol I, Brigham Young Univ Press, Provo, Utah, 77; auth, article, The Eastern Progress, Richmond, Ky, 85. *Dealer:* Phillips Gallery 444 E 2 South Salt Lake City UT 84111; Rosequist Galleries Tucson Az

MORSE, MARCIA ROBERTS
PRINTMAKER, WRITER
b Detroit, Mich, Mar 14, 44. *Study:* Radcliffe Col, BA(cum laude), 66; Stanford Univ, MFA, 74; with S W Hayter, Misch Kohn, Adela Akers, Leonore Tawney, Walter Nottingham & Ed Rossbach. *Work:* Honolulu Acad Arts & Contemp Arts Ctr, Honolulu, Hawaii; Smithsonian Inst, Div Graphic Arts, Washington, DC; Int Paper Co, NY; Greenville Co Mus Art, SC. *Comn:* Ann gift print, Honolulu Printmakers, Hawaii, 77; prints, Hawaii State Found Culture & Arts, Honolulu, 78. *Exhib:* Collectors' Choice, Joslyn Art Mus, Omaha, Nebr, 68; New Am Graphics, Madison Art Ctr, Wis, 75; one-woman show, Contemp Arts Ctr, Honolulu, Hawaii, 78; Textures, Contemp Artisans Gallery, San Francisco, Calif, 81; Nat Crafts, Greenville Co Mus Art, SC, 81; First Int Shoebox Sculpture, Univ Hawaii Art Gallery, Honolulu, 82. *Pos:* Freelance art writer, Artweek, 78-; art columnist, Honolulu Star Bulletin, Hawaii, 79-. *Teaching:* Instr printmaking, Univ Calif, Santa Cruz, 69-74; lectr printmaking & textiles, Univ Hawaii, 79-; instr papermaking, Honolulu Acad Arts, Hawaii, 80-. *Awards:* Craftsmen's Fel, Nat Endowment Arts, 81-82. *Mem:* Honolulu Printmakers (pres, 76-79, bd mem, 75-80); Hawaii Craftsmen (secy, 78); Surface Design Asn; Nat Soc Arts & Letters; Am Crafts Coun. *Media:* Handmade Paper. *Res:* Contemporary craft art; Japanese art both historical and contemporary. *Publ:* Illusr, Writing from the Inside, Addison-Wesley, 73; The Eight Rainbows of Umi, Topgallant Press, 76; auth, Nature distilled and distorted, 78 & auth, Language of materials, 81, Artweek; Filaments of the imaginagion, Fiberarts, 81. *Dealer:* The Source Gallery Folsom St San Francisco CA; Art Loft Honolulu HI. *Mailing Add:* Dept Humanities Honolulu Community Col 874 Dillingham Blvd Honolulu HI 96817

MORSE, MITCHELL IAN
DEALER, CONSULTANT
b Brooklyn, NY, Mar 10, 26. *Study:* Himeji Univ, 45-46; City Col New York, BBA, 47. *Pos:* Pres, Mann-Morse Graphics 68-69, Mitch Morse Gallery, Inc, 69-, M Morse Graphics, Inc, 69-91, Graphic Source I, 71-73; pres, Morse-Sun Art Assoc Inc, 72-75, Art Spectrum, 79-, China Spectrum Inc, 81-86, Art St Regis, 87-88; chief exec off, Morse Harris Art Group, Inc, presently; art consultant, 98-. *Awards:* Designer Official Seal, Village Lawrence, 67. *Specialty:* Artists agents, publishers of limited edition, original graphics; distributor painting, serigraphs on porcelain. *Publ:* Auth, Graphics as an original art form, Designer, 8/73. *Mailing Add:* 9 Fox Hollow Rd Woodstock NY 12498

MORTENSEN, GORDON LOUIS
PRINTMAKER, PAINTER
b Arnegard, NDak, Apr 27, 38. *Study:* Minneapolis Col of Art & Design, BFA; Univ Minn. *Work:* Nat Mus Am Art, Washington, DC; Honolulu Acad Art; Philadelphia Mus Art; Walker Art Ctr, Minneapolis; Brooklyn (NY) Mus; also pvt collections; and others. *Comn:* Green Giant Co, Cosgrove; Gov Karl Rolvag, Minn Hist Soc; membership print, Albany Print Club, NY, 1991. *Exhib:* Brooklyn Print Show, Brooklyn Mus, 76 & Eight West Coast Printmakers, 78; Plains Art Mus, Moorhead, Minn, 76 & 78; Boston Printmakers Nat Exhib, De Cordova Mus, 77, 79 & 83; Tokyo Cent Mus Art, Japan, 78; Ten West Coast Printmakers, RI Sch Design Mus; Rockford Int, Ill, 81; and others. *Teaching:* Minn Art Mus, St Paul, Minn, Rochester Art Ctr, Minn & Minnetonka Art Ctr, Wayzaya, Minn. *Awards:* Juror's Award, Rockford Int, Ill, 81; Purchase Award, Boston Printmakers 35th Nat Print Exhib, 83; Donna Jenssen Award, 21st Nat Print & Drawing Exhib, Bradley Univ, Peoria, Ill, 87; plus others. *Bibliog:* Robert McDonald (auth), Four West Coast woodcut artists, Graphics, 8-9/79; Karen Haber (auth), Gordon Mortensen, Southwest Art, 11/86 & Am Artist, 4/88; Karen Haber (auth), Am Artist, 4/88; Kathy Freise (auth), NDak Horizons, spring 91. *Mem:* Boston Printmakers; Philadelphia Print Club; Print Club of Albany; Los Angeles Printmaking Soc; Am Print Alliance. *Media:* Woodcut; Oil, Watercolor. *Dealer:* J Todd Galleries 572 Washington St Wellesley MA 02482; Concept Art Gallery 1031 S Braddock Ave Pittsburgh PA 15218; New Masters Carmel CA 93921; Davidson Galleries 313 Occidental Ave S Seattle WA 98104. *Mailing Add:* 4153 Crest Rd Pebble Beach CA 93953

MORTON, ROBERT ALAN
PUBLISHER, WRITER, EDITOR, CURATOR
b Jersey City, NJ, May 20, 34. *Study:* Dartmouth Col, BA, 55. *Exhib:* Matthieu Ricard: The Compassionate Eye, 2005. *Pos:* Series ed, Time-Life Libr of Art, New York, 66-70; ed dir, New York Graphic Soc, Inc, 70-73; ed in chief, Harry N Abrams, Inc, 76-78, dir spec proj, 78-98; editor-in-chief, Aperture Found, 2002-03. *Teaching:* Western Conn State Col, 80-81; Int Ctr Photog, 82-83; Santa Fe Ctr for Photog, 2003-05; Photolucida, 2005; Fotofest, Houston, Tex, 2006. *Awards:* Gold Medal, Soc of Illustrators, 98. *Res:* photography. *Publ:* Auth, Southern Antiques and Folk Art, Oxmoor House, 76; Mermaid and the Major, Abrams, 92; Leopold's Dream, Abrams, 93. *Mailing Add:* Box 16 Redding CT 00876

MOSBY, DEWEY FRANKLIN
MUSEUM DIRECTOR, HISTORIAN
b San Augustine, Tex, Jan 2, 42. *Study:* Lamar Univ, BS, 63; Univ Calif, Los Angeles, MA, 69; Harvard Univ, PhD, 74. *Hon Degrees:* Kendall Col Art & Design, PhD. *Collection Arranged:* French Painting 1774-1830: The Age of Revolution, 75; Cinco Siglos de Obras maestras de la pintura en colecciones norteamericanas cedidas en prestamo a Costa Rica, 78; The Second Empire: Art in France under Napoleon III, 1852-1870, Detroit, 79; Gods, Saints & Heroes: Dutch Paintings in the Age of Rembrandt, Detroit, 81; The Fodor Collection: Nineteenth Century French Drawing and Watercolors from Amsterdam's Historisch Museum, Hamilton, NY, 85; Abstraction, Non-objectivity and Realism: Twentieth-Century Painting from the Solomon R Guggenheim Museum, Hamilton, NY, 87; Across Continents & Cultures - The Art & Life of Henry Ossawa Turner - Nelson Atkins KC (traveling), 95. *Pos:* Cur Europ art, Detroit Inst Arts, 74-81; dir, Picker Art Gallery, Colgate Univ, Hamilton, NY, 81-2004, dir emeritus, 2004-. *Teaching:* Asst prof art hist, State Univ NY, Buffalo, 73-74; asst prof art hist, Harvard Univ, summer 74. *Awards:* Chevalier, Ordre des Arts et des Lettres, 79, Officer, 98; Silver Medal of Merit, Order of Costantiniano Di S Giorgio, 81. *Mem:* Col Art Asn Am; Am Asn Mus; Soc de l'Histoire de l'art Francaise; Int Comt Fine Arts. *Res:* 18th and 19th century art with an emphasis on Alexandre-Gabriel Decamps (1803-60); Henry O Tanner and other black artists working in France. *Publ:* Alexandre-Gabriel Decamps 1803-1860, 2 Vols, New York, 77; The Figure in Nineteenth-Century French Painting, Detroit, 79; Impressionist and Post-Impressionist Works from a British Collection, Hamilton, NY, 86; Henry Ossawa Tanner, New York, Rizzoli, 91; auth, Across Continents and Cultures: The Art and Life of Henry Ossawa Tanner, Nelson-Atkins Mus Art, 95. *Mailing Add:* 1738 Preston Hill Rd Hamilton NY 13346

MOSCATT, PAUL N
PAINTER, INSTRUCTOR
b Brooklyn, NY, July 9, 31. *Study:* Cooper Union Art Sch; Yale Univ Sch Fine Arts, BFA & MFA. *Work:* Univ Bridgeport, Conn; Yale Univ Art Gallery; Earlham Col, Richmond, Ind; Cincinnati Art Mus; Peale Mus, Baltimore, Md. *Comn:* Portrait, comn by Joseph Romano, 89; portrait, comn by Frank Toto, 89; portrait, comn by Fred Lazarus, 89; portrait, comn by Richard Kim Frank, 90; portrait, comn by S Reinholt; and others. *Exhib:* One-man shows, Portrait Drawings of the Am Indian, Md Inst Col Art, 73, Interiors & Nudes, C Grimaldis Gallery, Baltimore, Md, 78, Heads, Faces & Portraits, Blue Mountain Gallery, NY, 90 & Studio Nudes, Blue Mountain Gallery, 92; Hassam Exhib, Am Acad Arts & Lett, 79; Pinchard Gallery, 99; Resurgam Gallery, Baltimore, 2000. *Teaching:* Instr painting & drawing, Univ Bridgeport, 62-64; instr painting & drawing, Art Acad Cincinnati, 64-66; prof painting & drawing, Md Inst Col Art, 67-, chmn, painting dept, 77-79, acting chmn, 90-92. *Awards:* Mellon Fac Enrichment Grant, 84; AICA Grant, 86; Md State Arts Coun Award, 99. *Mem:* Artists Equity Asn. *Media:* Oil, Acrylic. *Publ:* Bernard Chaet (auth), The Art of Drawing. *Mailing Add:* 1300 Mt Royal Ave Md Inst Col Art Baltimore MD 21217

MOSCH, DEBORAH CHERRY
EDUCATOR, PAINTER
b Sunbury, Pa, May 24, 54. *Study:* Pa State Univ, BFA(painting), 77; Savannah Col Art & Design, MFA(illus), 91. *Work:* Savannah Col Art & Design Gallery, Ga. *Comn:* Mural, Miss Maggie's Morning Sch, Savannah, Ga, 92; mural, Garrison Elem Sch, Savannah, Ga, 93; cover, BellSouth Phonebook, Savannah, Ga. *Exhib:* Women's Works Exhib, Oglethorpe Ballroom, Savannah, Ga, 92; Traveling Exhib, South Gallery, Jacksonville, Fla, 93; Small Works Show, Exhibit A, Savannah Col Art & Design, Ga; Savannah Col Art & Design Fac Show, Bergen Hall Galleries, Ga, 98; Arts on the River, Ex Libris, Savannah, Ga, 98; Juries Alumni Show, Exlibris, 99; Small Works Exhib, Exhib A Gallery, 1999-2000; Mail Arts Exhibit, Lincoln Center, NY, 2000; Dog Days Exhibit, Atlanta, Ga, 2002; C.O.D. Traveling Exhibit, 2003; Ga Music Hall of Fame Exhibit, 2003; Nancy's in ATL & Worthwhile in Charleston, 2004; Design House Exhibit & Artisan Connection, 2005; Mutations, Starland Gallery, Savannah, Ga, 2006. *Pos:* juror, Coastal Carolina Art Fair, 99-. *Teaching:* Prof foundations, Savannah Col Art & Design, 92-. *Bibliog:* Skirt Magazine, 9/2005. *Mem:* Found Art Theory & Educ; Ganoskin Orchid; Am Craft Coun. *Media:* Thread, Gouache. *Res:* Color theory

MOSEMAN, M L (MARK)
PAINTER, COLLECTOR
b Oakland, Nebr, Jan 23, 45, USA. *Study:* Univ Nebr, BA, 69; Syracuse Univ, NY, MA, 72; Kans City Art Inst with M Monks & B Nichols, 78-89, pvt studio painting with Harry Fredman, 85 & with Phil Starke, 93. *Work:* Great Plains Art Collection, Univ Nebr, Lincoln; Nat Agr Hall Fame & Ctr Rural Art, Bonner Springs, Kans; Sioux City Art Mus, Iowa; Homestead Nat Monument, Beatrice, Nebr; Sprint Corporate Art Collection, Kansas City, MO. *Comn:* painting, Northwestern Mem Hosp, Chicago, Ill, 97. *Exhib:* Pastel Masters Int Exhib, Saks Gallery, Denver, 95; Grand Nat Exhib, Salmagundi Club, NY, 96; Pastels only, Nat Arts Club, NY, 97; Art for the Parks Top 100 (touring exhib), USA Mus, Wyo, Mo, Utah, Mass, NC, 97-98; Membership Exhib, Albrecht-Kemper Mus, St Joseph, Mo, 98; Keepers of the Land, Birger Sandzen Mem Gallery, Lindsborg, Kans, 98; Realism Today, John Pence Gallery, San Francisco, Calif, 2000; Australian Am Int Pastel Exhib, The Hughes Gallery, Fullerton, Australia, 2002; Am Art in Miniature, Gilcrease Mus, Tulsa, Okla, 2002, 2004 & 2006; Pastel Soc Am Exhib, Butler Inst Am Art, Youngstown, OH, 2003; Painting of My People, Dane Hansen Mus, Logan, KS, 2004; Great Plains Art Mus, Lincoln, NE, 2005. *Pos:* Artist in residence, Living Hist Farms, Des Moines, Iowa, 97, Konza Prairie, Manahttan, Kans, 2000. *Teaching:* Lectr archit design, Syracuse Univ, NY, 69-71. *Awards:* Pastel Soc Am Award, Allied Artists of Am, 11/95; Art for The Parks Top 100 Judges' Award Merit, Nat Park Acad Arts, 9/97; Am Artists Profl League Award, Hudson Valley Art Asn, 2000. *Bibliog:* Douglas Baughman (auth), Places in the Heartland, Am Artist, 12/98; Lewis Lehrman (auth) Master Painters of the World, International Artist, 2/99; Julie Osterman (auth) Artists to Watch, Southwest Art, 3/04. *Mem:* IAPS Master Circle; sig Mem Pastel Soc of America; Sig Mem America Artists Prof League; Sig Mem American Plains Artists; Master Pastelists, Mid America Pastel Soc. *Media:* Oil, Pastels. *Interests:* Donation of 35 Collected artworks to the Great Plains Art Collections, Center for Great Plains Studies, Univ of NE, Lincoln, NE; active supporting member of the friends of the Benton Home and Studio, Kansas City, MO. *Collection:* Great Plains artists; North American Indian art; oriental art; arts & crafts pottery. *Publ:* contrib, Art for the Parks Top 100, Nat Park Acad, 97; The Best of Portrait Painting, N Light Bks, 98; Beautiful Things, Guild Pub, 2000; Object Lessons, Guild Pub 2001, Paintings of My People, Univ NE Press, 2004. *Dealer:* Am Art Resources 3260 Sul Ross Street Houston Tex 77098; Streckton-Nelson Gallery 332 Poyntz Manhattan Kans; The Guild 931 East Main Street Madison Wis 53703

MOSENTHAL, CHARLOTTE (DEMBO)
PAINTER, PRINTMAKER
b Cleveland, Ohio. *Study:* Case Western Reserve Univ, BA; Cleveland Inst Art, studied with Donald Stacy, Mus Mod Art; Gregorio Prestopino, New Sch, NY. *Work:* Exxon Inc, Florham Park, NJ. *Comn:* Poster Designs, Gallery 9, Chatham, NJ 82, 84 & 86. *Exhib:* Nat Asn Women Artists, 89-2005, Audubon Artists, NY, 89-94, Nat Soc Painters in Casein & Acrylic, 92-2003; Silvermine Guild Arts Ctr, New Canaan, Conn, 96; Gallaria Le Logge, Assisi, Italy, 96; Saginaw Art Mus, Mich, 98; Nat Acad Design, New York City, 2000; Smithsonian Inst, Washington, DC, 2000; Venezuelan, Consillate, New York City, 2001 & 2003. *Collection Arranged:* West Side Printmakers, Broadway Mall Gallery, NY, 89; Exxon, Inc, Florham Park, NJ. *Pos:* Ed, Newslett, Westside Arts Coalition, NY, 86-91; serials libr technician, Cooper-Hewitt Nat Design Mus, NY, 90-2003; chmn, printmaking jury, Nat Asn Women Artists, 93-95, historian, 97-98. *Awards:* Elaine & Jas Hewitt Mem Award, Audubon Artists, NY, 89; Best Show, Visual Individualists, NY, 89; First Prize Prints, Housatonic Art League, Conn, 90; S Magnet Knapp Award, Nat Asn Women Artists, 94. *Mem:* Nat Asn Women Artists; Nat Soc Painters in Casein & Acrylic; Washington Art Asn, Conn; NY Artists Equity Asn. *Media:* Acrylic, Canvas; Woodcut. *Mailing Add:* 230 E 15th St #2K New York NY 10003

MOSER, BARRY
GRAPHIC ARTIST, PRINTMAKER
b Chattanooga, Tenn, Oct 15, 40. *Study:* Auburn Univ; Univ Tenn Chattanooga, with George Cress; also studied with Leonard Baskin & Jack Coughlin. *Work:* Brit Mus, London, Eng; Boston Athenaeum, Mass; Nat Gallery Art, Spec Collections, Washington, DC; Grolier Club, NY; Mus Fine Arts, Springfield, Mass; Newberry Libr, Chicago, Ill; Voices of Egypt, 2003; rep in permanent collections: Metrop Mus, British Mus, Harvard Univ, Princeton Univ, Libr. of Congress. *Comn:* principal works incl (illus) Alice in Wonderland, 1993 (Nat Book award for Design and illus, 1993) (publisher, illus) Moser-Caxton Bible, 1999. *Exhib:* Boston Printmakers, Waltham, Mass, 72; one-man shows, Berkshire Mus, Pittsfield, Mass, 73 & Boston Athenaeum, Mass, 76; Los Angeles Nat Print Show, Calif, 74; Libr Cong Nat Print Exhib, Washington, DC, 75-76; History of Printed Books, San Francisco Pub Libr, Calif, 76; 4th Int Exhibit of Botanical Art, Hunt Inst, Carnegie-Mellon Univ, Pittsburgh, Pa, 77-78; R Michelson Galleries, Northhampton, Mass, 85-96. *Collection Arranged:* New York Pub Libr; Swarthmore Col, Pa; Harvard Univ, Cambridge, Mass; Univ Iowa, Ames (collection of illus bks); Smith Col, 76. *Teaching:* Head studio art, Williston Northampton Sch, Easthampton, Mass, 67-82 & RI Sch Design, 90-. *Awards:* Second Prize, Cape Cod Ann, 71; Award of Merit, New Hampshire Int, 74; Am Bk Award. *Bibliog:* Worcester Sunday Telegram, 11/86; American Traditions in Watercolor, Abbeville Press, 87; The Art of Seeing, Prentice-Hall, 88. *Mem:* Am Printing Hist Asn; Nat Acad (academician 1994-). *Media:* Ink; Wood. *Publ:* Contribr, The Tinderbox, Little, Brown, 90; The Guild Shakespeare, Doubleday Bk Club, 90; The Holy Bible, Oxford/Doubleday, 90; Appalachia, HBJ, 90; Messiah, HarperCollins (in Prep); and others; Illustrator: Appalachia, the Voices of Sleeping Birds, 1991 (Boston Globe-Horn Book award); And Still the Turtle Watched, 1991; Tales of Edgar Allan Poe, 1991; Ali Jadhu Storybook, 1992; Ariadne, Awake!, 1994; Call of the Wild, 1994; Cloud Eyes, 1994; Farm Summer 1942, 1994; Pilgrim's Progress, 1994; What You Know First, 1995; When Birds Could Talk and Bats Could Sing, 1996; Shiloh Season, 1996; Earthquack!, 2002. *Mailing Add:* c/o Cove Gallery Commercial St Box 482 Wellesley MA 02667

MOSER, JOANN
CURATOR, HISTORIAN
b Chicago, Ill. *Study:* Smith Col, BA(art hist), 69; Univ Wis, Madison, MA(art hist), 72, PhD(art hist), 76. *Collection Arranged:* Atelier 17 (50 yr retrospective traveling exhib to five mus; auth, catalog), 77-78; Jean Metzinger in Retrospect, 85; Modernist Abstraction in American Prints, 89; The Drawings of Joseph Stella, 90. *Pos:* Cur of collections, Univ Iowa Mus Art, 76-86, actg dir, 80-83; sr head cur graphic arts, Nat Mus Am Art, Washington, DC, 86-. *Awards:* Ford Fel, Dept Art Hist, Univ Wis, 71-73; Kress Fel, Nat Gallery Art, Washington, 75-76. *Mem:* Col Art Asn; Print Coun Am; Am Asn Mus. *Res:* Prints and twentieth century art. *Publ:* Auth, The impact of Stanley William Hayter on post-war American art, Archives Am Art J, Vol 18, No 1; Jiri Anderle, 84; Visual Poetry: The Drawings of Joseph Stella, 88; Singular Impressions: The Monotype In America, 97; Singular Impressions: The Monotype in America, 97. *Mailing Add:* 5203 Benton Ave Bethesda MD 20814

MOSER, KENNA J
PAINTER
b Can, 64. *Study:* Queens Univ, Kingston, Ont, BFA, 88. *Work:* San Jose Mus Art, Calif; Wash State Arts Comn, Tacoma; 3M Corp, Minneapolis, Minn; Walker Richer Quinn, Seattle; Bellevue Club, Wash. *Comn:* Wine Label Imagery Series, Benziger Winery, Calif, 96; Playing Card-Game of Chance, Perimeter Gallery, Chicago, 97; installation, Swedish Hosp, Seattle, 99. *Exhib:* Icons in Contemp Art, Calif Craft Mus, San Francisco, 93; In the Spirit of Nature, San Jose Mus Art, Calif, 94; From the Land, Tacoma Art Mus, Wash, 95; Concept in Form, Palo Alto Cult Ctr, Calif, 95; Small Wonders, San Francisco Folk & Craft Mus, Calif, 96; drawings, Triton Mus Art, Santa Clara, Calif, 96; Series Series Series, Rockford Col Art, Ill, 97; The Idea of the Sacred, Ctr Arts & Religion, Washington, DC, 98. *Awards:* Painting Fel, Arts Coun Santa Clara Co, 92 & Nat Endowment Arts, 94. *Bibliog:* Kathryn Shields & Chris Bruce (auth), Within Sight, Nat Endowment Arts, 95; Joe Shannon (auth), Kenna Moser at Linda Hodges, Art News, 98. *Media:* Beeswax, Oil. *Dealer:* Gallery A 300 W Superior Suite 100 Chicago IL 60610

MOSES, BETTE J
PAINTER
b Blackwell, Okla. *Study:* Northwestern State Univ, Alva, Okla, BFA, 46; Inst Allende San Miguel, Guanajuato, Mex, with James Pinto, 74-75. *Exhib:* Smoky Hill, Ft Hays Univ, Kans, 74 & Women Aware Show, 75; Am Painters in Paris, Centre Int de Paris, France, 75-76; Kans I, Hutchinson Art Asn, Kans, 78; Kans Pub TV, Wichita, 78; Wichita Art Mus, 80; Kans Tri-state Watercolor Show, 84. *Collection Arranged:* Soc Prof Painters, West, State Capitol, Topeka, Kans, 78-80 & Wichita Art Mus, Kans, 79-81. *Pos:* Founder, Art Inc, Barton Co Community & Col, 70, pres, 71-72 & bd adv, 78-81. *Awards:* First & Second Prizes Mixed Media, Art Inc, Barton Community Col, 71-85; First Prize Prof Painters, Russell Original Art Revue, 73; Holliday Prize, Kans Tri-state Watercolor, 85. *Mem:* Kans Soc Prof Painters, West; Kans Watercolor Soc. *Media:* Mixed. *Mailing Add:* 20810 N Desert Sands Dr Sun City AZ 85375-5442

MOSES, ED
PAINTER
b Long Beach, Calif. *Study:* Univ Calif, Los Angeles, BA, 55, MA, 58. *Hon Degrees:* Otis Col Art & Design, hon PhD, 95. *Work:* Art Inst Chicago; Mus Mod Art & Whitney Mus Am Art, NY; Albright-Knox Art Gallery, Buffalo, NY; Walker Art Ctr, Minneapolis, Minn; San Francisco Mus Mod Art, Calif; Philadelphia Mus Art, Pa; Nat Mus Am Art, Corcoran Gallery Art, Smithsonian Inst, Washington, DC; Mus Contemp Art, Los Angeles Co Mus Art, Los Angeles, Calif; many others. *Comn:* lithography, Bernard Jacobson, Ltd, 71. *Exhib:* 32nd Biennial Exhib of Contemp Am Painting (with catalog), Corcoran Gallery Art, Washington, DC, 71; Robert Arneson and Edward Moses, San Francisco Mus Art, Calif, 74; 34th Biennial of Contemp Am Painting, Corcoran Gallery Art, Washington, DC, 75; Thirty Yrs of Am Painting, Mus Mod Art, NY, 76; Selections from the Frederick Weisman Co Collections of Calif Art, Corcoran Gallery of Art, Washington, DC, 79; Hist of Calif Arts, San Francisco Mus Art, Calif, 80; Am Drawings Since 1960, Los Angeles Co Mus Art, 92; solo exhibs, Zolla/Lieberman Gallery Inc, Chicago, 92, LA Louver, Venice, Calif, 92, 93, 94-95, 96 & 99, Louver Gallery, NY, 91 & 92, Tex Gallery, 92, Dennis Ochi Gallery, Sun Valley, Idaho, 93, 94 & 95, Drawings, Earl McGrath Gallery, Los Angeles, 93-94, Retrospective, Mus Contemp Art, Los Angeles, 96 & Peter Blake Gallery, Laguna Beach, 98; Elegant, Irreverent & Obsessive: Drawing in Southern Calif (catalog), Main Art Gallery, Calif State Univ, 93; Gallery Delaive BV, Amsterdam, The Neth, 94; Radical Past: Contemp Art & Music in Pasadena, 1960-1974, Norton Simon Mus Art, 98; 45th Biennial Corcoran Collects, 1908-1998, Corcoran Gallery Art, Washington DC, 98. *Pos:* fel, Tamarind Lithography Workshop, Los Angeles, 68. *Teaching:* Instr art, Univ Calif, Los Angeles, 68-72 & 75-76, Skowhegan Sch Painting & Sculpture, 83; Calif State Univ, Bakersfield, 77, Long Beach, 85-86. *Awards:* Nat Endowment Art Grant, 76; Guggenheim Fel, 80; Calif Arts Coun Comn, 84. *Bibliog:* Peter Plugens (auth), From school painting to a school painting in Los Angeles, Art in Am, 3-4/73. *Mem:* Nat Soc Literature & Arts Biographical Record. *Dealer:* LA Louver Gallery 45 N Venice Blvd Venice CA 90291. *Mailing Add:* 1233 Palms Blvd Venice CA 90291

MOSES, FORREST (LEE), JR
PAINTER, PRINTMAKER
b Danville, Va, May, 1934. *Study:* Washington & Lee Univ, BA, 56; Pratt Inst, 60-62. *Work:* Huntington Gallery, Univ Tex, Austin; Ill State Univ, Normal; Mus Fine Arts, Santa Fe, NMex; Citibank, NY; WR Grace & Co, Dallas; Mint Mus, Charlotte; Chicago Hilton, Ill; Roswell Mus, NMex. *Exhib:* Contemp Landscape Painting, Okla Art Ctr, Oklahoma City, 75; solo exhibs, Tibor de Nagy Gallery, 82 & 84, Marvin Seline Gallery, Austin, Tex, 85, Munson Gallery, 86, 87, 89 & 92, Peregrine Press, Dallas, Tex, 86, Sheldon Mem Mus Gallery, Lincoln, Nebr, 86, Watson Gallery, Houston, Tex, 86 & Gumps Gallery, San Francisco, Calif, 89; Am Artists as Print Makers, 23rd Nat Print Exhib, Brooklyn Mus, NY, 83; Contemp Western Landscape, Mus Art Am West, Houston, Tex, 84; Egypt, Munson Gallery, Santa Fe, NMex, 85; James Fisher Gallery, Denver, Colo, 85; Monotypes, James Robischon Gallery, Denver, Colo, 85; Contemp Am Monotypes, Chrysler Mus, Norfolk, Va, 85. *Teaching:* Instr drawing, Pratt Inst, 61-62; instr drawing & watercolor, Univ Houston, 69. *Awards:* Selected Juror's Award & Mus Purchase, Mus NMex Biennial, 74. *Media:* Oil; Monotype. *Dealer:* Clinc Lewallen Gallery 129 W Palace Ave Santa Fe NM 87501; Munson Gallery 225 Canyon Rd Santa Fe NM 87501. *Mailing Add:* 837 El Caminito St Santa Fe NM 87501-2842

MOSKOWITZ, IRA
PAINTER, PRINTMAKER
b Turka, Poland, March 15, 12; US citizen. *Study:* Art Students League, 30-33. *Work:* Metrop Mus Art & Whitney Mus Am Art, NY; Nat Gallery Art, Washington, DC; Biblioteque Nationale, Paris. *Exhib:* One-man shows, Bernhard Crystal Galleries, NY, 67, Waddington Galleries, Montreal, Can, 69, traveling show, Paris, Scotland, Ireland, 74 & Weintraub Gallery, NY, 79; Drawings of Ira Moskowitz, Haifa Mus, Israel, 69; 45 Yrs of Graphics (retrospective), Brooks Mem Art Gallery, Memphis, 75; John Davis Hatch Collection, Nat Gallery Art, Washington, DC, 79. *Pos:* Ed fine arts books, Shorewood Publ, New York, 55-62; dir publs, Am Art Collections Ltd, 83. *Awards:* Fel Creative Art, Guggenheim, 43; Am at War, Prize for Lithograph, 44; Libr Congress Award, Pennell Show, 45. *Bibliog:* John Davis Hatch (auth), The Drawings of Ira Moskowitz, Shorewood Publ, 66; Isaac Bashevis Singer (auth), Reaches of Heaven, Landmark Publ & Ferrar, Strauss & Giroux, 80; Joseph S Czestochowski (auth), 55 Years of Drawings of Ira Moskowitz, Alpine Fine Arts Collections Ltd, 84. *Media:* All Media. *Publ:* Auth, American Indian Ceremonial Dances, Crown Publ, 72; coauth, Hasidim, Crown Publ, 73; A Little Boy in Search of God, Doubleday, 76; (with Isaac Bashevis Singer), Satan In Goray, Sweetwater Eds, 82; auth, The Rites & Ceremonies of the Indians of the Southwest, Barnes & Nobles, 93. *Dealer:* Brewster Gallery 41 W 57th St New York NY 10019; J N Bartfield Galleries 30 W 57th St New York NY 10019. *Mailing Add:* 390 W End Ave New York NY 10024

MOSKOWITZ, ROBERT S
PAINTER
b New York, NY, June 20, 35. *Work:* Mus Mod Art & Whitney Mus Am Art, NY; Albright-Knox Art Gallery, Buffalo; Rose Art Mus, Brandeis Univ, Waltham, Mass; Wadsworth Atheneum, Hartford, Conn; Joslyn Art Mus, Omaha, Nebr; Kitakyushu Munic Mus, Japan; Philadelphia Mus Art; La Jolla Mus Contemp Art, Calif. *Exhib:* Art of Assemblage, Mus Mod Art, NY, 61; Whitney Mus Am Art Ann, 69 & New Image Painting, 78; One-man shows, Daniel Weinberg Gallery, San Francisco, 79, Margo Levin Gallery, Los Angeles, 79 & La Jolla Mus Contemp Art, Calif, 79; Great Big Drawings, Hayden Gallery, Mass Inst Technol, Cambridge, 82; Season's Greetings, Daniel Weinberg Gallery, Los Angeles, 83; Content: A Contemp Focus: 1974-1984, Hirshhorn Mus & Sculpture Garden, Washington, 84; Drawings and Sculpture, Manhattan Art Inc, NY, 85; Mus Mod Art, NY, 89; Joseph Hellman, NY, 95. *Awards:* Guggenheim Fel, 67; Award, NY State Coun Arts, 73; Award, Nat Endowment Arts, 75. *Bibliog:* Michael Compton (auth), Art and responsbility, Flashart, summer 80; Nan Freeman (auth), The magnitude of drawing, Art New Eng, 4/82; Ellen Schwartz (auth), What's New in Nueva York?, Artnews, 4/84; Robert Taylor (auth), Images endowed with layers of meaning at MIT, Boston Sunday Globe, 6/2/85. *Mailing Add:* 81 Leonard St New York NY 10013

MOSKOWITZ, SHIRLEY
PAINTER, COLLAGE ARTIST
b Houston, Tex, Aug 4, 20. *Study:* Mus Sch Art, Houston; Rice Univ, BA, 41; Oberlin Col, MA, 42; Philadelphia Col Art, 74-76; also with Morris Davidson, NY. *Work:* Mus Roma, Italy; Free Libr Philadelphia; Philadelphia Mus Art; Atwater Kent Mus, Philadelphia, Pa; State Mus Pa; Mus Fine Arts, Houston. *Exhib:* Juried shows of Pa Acad of Fine Arts, 53, 58, 61, 63 & 65; William Penn Mem Mus, 74-75; Univ Pa, Philadelphia, 81; Mus Philadelphia Civic Ctr; Port Hist Mus, Philadelphia; Philadelphia Art Alliance; Mus Fine Arts, Houston, Tex; Nat Acad Design, NY; Nat Mus, Wellington, New Zealand; Contemp Philadelphia, Artists, Philadelphia Mus of Art, 90; retrospective, A Half Century of Art, Univ Arts, Philadelphia, 96; Museo Epeo, Nocara, Italy, 2000; Ballinglen Arts Found, Repub Ireland, 2002; Mus Tarnow, Poland, 2002. *Teaching:* Instr art hist, Univ Tex, Austin, spring 43; lectr art, Houston Pub Schs, 43-46; dir art, Oberlin Pub Schs, 46-47. *Awards:* IBM Painting Prize, Expressions, Earth Art III, Philadelphia Civic Ctr, 79; Mid-Atlantic Regional Collage Show Prize, Univ Del, 79; Watercolor Prize, Artists Equity Triennial, Philadelphia, 81; and others. *Bibliog:* Gerald F Brommer (auth), The Art of Collage 1978, Print World, 81, 82; Samuel Gruber (auth), Shirley Moskowitz, A Half Century of Art, Borowsky Press, Univ Arts, Philadelphia, 96; Gerald F Brommer (auth), Collage Techniques, Watson-Guptill Publ, NY; Collage Transformed, Art Matters Mag, 97. *Mem:* Print Ctr. *Media:* Watercolor, Acrylic; Ink, Monotype, collage. *Specialty:* Graphic art. *Interests:* Succulent plant gardening. *Publ:* Contemp Philadelphia Artists, Philadelphia Mus Art, 90. *Dealer:* Philadelphia Print Ctr Gallery. *Mailing Add:* 1540 6th St #312 Santa Monica CA 90401

MOSS, BEN FRANK, III
PAINTER AND EDUCATOR
b Philadelphia, Feb 28, 1936. *Study:* Whitworth Col, BA, 59; Princeton Theological Seminar, postgrad, 60; Boston Univ, MFA, 63; studied with Walter Murch, Karl Fortess and Herman Keys. *Hon Degrees:* Dartmouth Col, MA, 93. *Exhib:* One man shows include Dartmouth Col, 89, 94, Susan Conway Galleries, 90, Tasis England Am Sch, 94, Queens Col, Univ Melbourne, 94, Houghton Col, 96 Gordon Col, 96, Kouros Gallery, NY, 2001, Augustana Col, Rock Island, Ill, 2002, Taylor Univ, Upland Ind, 2002, Bedford Art Mus, Mass, 2003, New England Col, Henniker, NH, 2003; group shows at Blair Acad, Blairstown, NJ, 96, Smith Col, North Hampton, Mass, 96, Pepper Gallery, Boston, 97-98, Spheris Gallery Fine Art, 97, Art Spirit Gallery Fine Art, Walpole, NH, 97, Coeur d'Alene, Ind, 98. *Teaching:* Instr Gonzaga Univ, Spokane, Washington, 64-65; assoc prof, dir MFA and vis artist program Fort Wright Col, 65-72; acting dean, cofounder Spokane Studio Sch, 72-74; prof painting and drawing Sch Art and Art History Univ, Iowa, 75-88; George Frederick Jewett prof art Dartmouth Col, Hanover, NH, 93-. *Awards:* Res and Travel Grant, Yaddo Found, 65, 72, Ford Found, 79-80; Travel Grant, Univ Iowa Found, 86; Distinguished Alumni Award, Boston Uni, 88; Development Grant, Univ Iowa, 80, 86. *Mem:* Col Art Asn; Nat Acad (acad, 94)

MOSS, JOE (FRANCIS)
SCULPTOR, PAINTER
b Kincheloe, WVa, Jan 26, 33. *Study:* WVa Univ, AB, 51, MA, 60. *Work:* Del Art Mus, Hercules Corp, Wilmington, Del; St Louis Art Mus, Mo; Sci & Cult Ctr, Charleston, WVa; Huntington Mus, WVa; and others. *Comn:* Sound Sculpture, Bloomsburg Col, Pa, 72; Sound sculpture, Shepherd Col, Shepherdstown, WVa, 78; Sound sculpture, Martin Fine Villa, Miami, Fla, 80; Sound sculpture, Cedar Crest Col, Allentown, Pa, 80; and others. *Exhib:* Members Exhib, Mus Mod Art, NY, 65; JB Speed Mus, Louisville, Ky, 77, Madison Square Park, NY, 80; Kunsthalle, Hamburg, Ger, 85; Monocle, Mass Inst Technol, 85 & 94; Boston Mus Sci, 87; Yeshiva Univ, NY, 88-89; and others. *Pos:* Fel, Ctr Advan Visual Studies, Mass Inst Technol, Cambridge, 73, 85 & 87-88. *Teaching:* Assoc prof art, WVa Univ, 60-70; vis prof, Univ Md, 67; prof sculpture, Univ Del, 70-98 & prof emeritus, 2001-. *Awards:* Prize for Environ Design, Three Rivers Arts Festival, Pittsburgh, 68; Sculpture Award, Appalachian Corridors Exhib, Charleston, WVa, 70; Fel, Nat Endowment Arts, 80-81. *Bibliog:* Alan Gerstle (auth), Joe Moss, Arts Mag; James Kelly (auth), The Sculptural Idea, Third Ed; Joe Moss, Sound Sculptor, CNN Sci Week, 88. *Media:* Metal, Miscellaneous Media; Oil, Acrylic. *Mailing Add:* 801 Valley Rd Newark DE 19711

MOSS, KAREN CANNER
PAINTER, EDUCATOR
b Boston, Mass, May 2, 44. *Study:* RI Sch Design, BFA, 66; Tufts Univ, Boston Mus Sch, MFA, 74. *Work:* Boston Mus Fine Arts, Mass; Addison Gallery Am Art, Andover, Mass; Vassar Col Art Gallery, Poughkeepsie, NY; Rose Art Mus, Brandeis Univ, Waltham, Mass; Bristol Community Col, Fall River, Mass. *Comn:* Outdoor mural, Mass Bay Transportation Authority, Boston, Mass, 77; ceramic tile mural, First Nat Bank Boston, 83. *Exhib:* Edinburgh Festival, Queens Col, Scotland, 74; Works on Paper, Fogg Mus, Harvard Univ, Cambridge, Mass, 74; Primitive Presence in the '70's, Vassar Col, Poughkeepsie, NY, 75; Boston Watercolor Today, Boston Mus Fine Arts, 76; one-woman show, Addison Gallery Am Art, Andover, Mass, 76; Contemp Issues: Works on Paper by Women, traveling show to Los Angeles, Salt Lake City & Houston, 77; Prints & Drawings, Mus Mod Art, NY, 78; one-woman show, Kathryn Markel Gallery, NY, 83; and others; 12th ann drawing show; Images of the New

World, Mus of Our Nat Heritage, Lexington, MA, 2000. *Pos:* Artist, trustee & rep, Boston Visual Artists Union, Inst Contemp Art, Boston, Mass, 71-73. *Teaching:* Instr drawing, Boston Mus Fine Arts Sch, 83. *Awards:* Blanche E Coleman Award, 72; First Prize for Watercolor, Silvermine Art Guild, 73; Finalist in State, Mass Arts & Humanities Found, 76-77; Bunting Finalist, 82. *Bibliog:* Wolf Kahn (auth), The subject matter in new realism, Am Artist, 11/79; Pam Allara (auth), Boston: shedding its inferiority complex, Art News, 11/79; Sarah McFadden (auth), Report from Boston, Art Am, 5/83. *Mem:* Boston Visual Artists Union. *Media:* Mixed Media Collage. *Publ:* New American Painting, Vol 26, 3/2000; Art New England, Apr/May 2001. *Mailing Add:* 14 Elm St Brookline MA 02445

MOSS, TOBEY C
ART DEALER, HISTORIAN
b Chicago, Ill, June 1, 28. *Study:* Univ Ill, Champaign-Urbana; Univ Calif, Los Angeles, AA, 47. *Collection Arranged:* Helen Lundeberg Since 1970, Palm Springs Mus, 83; Colorforms (auth, catalog), Gallery-Security Pacific, 85; Helen Lundeberg, Sesnon Art Gallery, Univ Calif, Santa Cruz, 88; Nora Eccles Harrison Mus of Art. *Pos:* Dir, Tobey C Moss Gallery, Los Angeles, currently; consult to cur & corp collections. *Teaching:* instr, series: print connoisseurship. *Mem:* Col Art Asn; Art Table; Women's Caucus Art; Los Angeles Co Mus Art Graphics Art Coun; Art Dealers Asn Calif; Int Fine Print Dealer Asn. *Res:* Modernist Californian artists working 1920-1960. *Specialty:* Modernism, Post-Surrealism, Hard-Edge; Lorser Feitelson, Helen Lundeberg, Peter Krasnow, Knud Merrild, Oskar Fischinger, S Macdonald Wright, Dorr Bothwell, Emerson Woelffer, Ynez Johnston, John McLaughlin, Palmer Schoppe, John Bernhardt, Gordon Wagner, Jean Charlot, William Dole, Jules Engel, David P. Levine, Lithography workshop of Lynton R Kistler. *Interests:* Tamarind lithography workshop. *Publ:* Auth, 2002 Gallery Catalog of Essays: Tobey C. Moss Gallery: Paintings, Sculptures; auth, Tobey C. Moss Gallery: Paper Passion, 2003. *Mailing Add:* Tobey C Moss Gallery 7321 Beverly Blvd Los Angeles CA 90036-2534

MOSS-VREELAND, PATRICIA
PAINTER, DRAFTSMAN
b New York, NY, July 26, 51. *Study:* Philadelphia Col Art, BFA, 73; Tyler Sch Art, Philadelphia, 73. *Work:* Norton Mus Art, West Palm Beach, Fla; Chicago Art Inst; Beaver Co Arcadia Univ, Glenside, Pa; Atlantic Richfield Co, Los Angeles; Bell Tel Labs, NJ; Fed Reserve, Philadelphia, Pa; Philadelphia Mus Art, Pa; Arcadia Univ, Glenside, Pa. *Comn:* Numerous private portrait commissions; mural, Philadelphia Mus Art, 89; handpainted ceramic mural, pvt residence, 91; Holocaust Mus, Houston, Tex, 96; Art in Science XIV Univ City Science Center, Esther Klein Gallery, Phil, PA. *Exhib:* Solo-shows, Marian Locks Gallery, Philadelphia, 79, 83 & 88 & Arronson Gallery, Univ Arts, Philadelphia, 93; Contemp Drawings (with catalog), Philadelphia Acad Fine Arts & Philadelphia Mus Art, 79; Made in Philadelphia III, Inst Contemp Art, Philadelphia, 80; Am Drawings: Black & White, Brooklyn Mus, 80; New Acquisitions, Philadelphia Mus Art, 86; Nat Group Invitational, Pindar Gallery, NY, 89; Contemp Women Artists Int Juried Exhib, Brussels, Belgium, 89; Julius Bloch Mem Exhib, Pertaining to Philadelphia, Philadelphia Mus Art, Pa, 92; Philadelphia Houston Exchange, Inst Contemp Art, Univ Pa; Memory Connections Matter (with catalog), Ester Klein Gallery, Univ City Sci Ctr, Philadelphia, Pa, 2000; Solo show, Univ of St Thomas Frey Libr, St Paul, MN, 2004. *Collection Arranged:* Milwaukee Mus of Art Stephens Collections Little Rock, AR; Library of Congress, Wash, DC. *Awards:* Drucker Painting Award, Cheltenham Ann Painting Exhib, Pa, 77; Purchase Award, Ann Juried Exhib, Arcadia Univ, Pa, 86; Philadelphia Mus Art Award, Ann Juried Show, Cheltenham Art Ctr, 86. *Bibliog:* Articles, Philadelphia Inquirer, 75, 77, 86, 88 & 2000, Archit Mag, 96, Sculpture Mag, 96, Houston, Chronicle, 97, Baltimore Sun, 2000; On tour in Philadelphia, Am Artist, 80. *Mem:* Col Art Asn. *Media:* Pencil, Oil, Mixed Media. *Mailing Add:* 2229 Bainbridge St Philadelphia PA 19146

MOSZYNSKI, ANDREW
PAINTER
b Eye, Suffolk, Eng. *Study:* Univ Nat de Buenos Aires, Argentina. *Work:* Metrop Mus Art, NY. *Exhib:* Solo exhibs, C Space, 80, J Walter Thompson Gallery, 83, Mission Gallery, 86, NY; Tweed Gallery, NJ, 82; Galeria Alberto Elia, Buenos Aires, Argentina, 83; PS1, Long Island City, NY, 84; Alternative Mus, NY, 85; Leonardo di Mauro Gallery, NY, 87. *Teaching:* Prof art & design, Fashion Inst of Technol, NY, 82-. *Awards:* Nat Endowment of Arts Grant, 85. *Bibliog:* Susana Torruella Leval (auth), Painting from under the volcano, Art News, 3/85; Elaine Louie (auth), Flat tops, NY Times, 4/90; John Howell White (auth), article, Artforum, 5/90. *Mailing Add:* 292 Lafayette St No 6E New York NY 10012

MOTTRAM, RONALD
ADMINISTRATOR, HISTORIAN
b Jersey City, NJ, Sept 27, 40. *Study:* Rutgers Univ, BS, 63; New York Univ, MA, 73, PhD, 80. *Collection Arranged:* D W Griffith Centennial Exhib, Mus Mod Art, New York & Danish Film Mus, 75; New Acquisitions Show (Danish Cinema), Mus Mod Art, 78; North Light (accompaning film series), Brooklyn Mus, 82; The Mystic North (accompaning film series), Art Gallery Ontario, 84. *Teaching:* prof, film hist, Sarah Lawrence Col, 78-83; prof, Illinois State Univ Art Dept, 83-, chair dept art, 91-. *Awards:* George C Marshall fels (study of Danish film mus), 73 & 75; Louis B Mayer Film Hist Prog (study of early sound film), 74-75; Fulbright Scholar Prog (teaching on American studies), UK, 90-91. *Mem:* Nat Coun Arts Admins; Soc Cinema Studies; Fulbright Asn; Ill Higher Edn Art Asn. *Res:* Film history (early cinema with specialization in Danish silent film). *Publ:* Auth, Inner Landscapes: The Theater of Sam Shepard, Univ Missouri Press, 84; contib, Schiavebianche allo specchio: le origini del cinema in Scandinavia, Edizioni Studio Tesi, 86; auth, The Danish Cinema Before Dreyer, Scarecrow, 88; auth, The great northern film company, Film History, 88; contrib, Questioning the Media: A Critical Introduction, Sage Publ, 90. *Mailing Add:* 402 Sycamore St Normal IL 61761-1773

MOULTON, SUSAN GENE
HISTORIAN, PAINTER
b Long Beach, Calif, June 7, 44. *Study:* Univ Calif, Davis, study with Wayne Thiebaud, BA(art), 66; Univ Padua, Italy, 64-65; Acad, Venice, Italy, with Prof Balest, 64; Stanford Univ, MA(art hist; Carnegie Found Fel), 69, PhD(art hist), 77. *Comn:* Glenn Ellen Winery. *Teaching:* Prof Renaissance & mod art, Sonoma State Univ, 71-, chairperson dept art, 75-79 & 81-83. *Awards:* Nat Endowment Humanities, 76-78. *Bibliog:* Susan Moulton, Sojourn, Spring 98. *Mem:* Col Art Asn; Women's Caucus Art; San Francisco Mus Soc; Nat Asn Schs Art & Design. *Media:* Mixed Media. *Res:* Sixteenth century Venetian painting, specifically Titian and the evolution of donor portraiture in Venice; 20th century American art, Aesthetics and Ecology; art of California; Neolithic Old Europe. *Publ:* Auth, Four From California, Edinburg, Scotland, 81; Works in Bronze; A Modern Survey, Sonoma State Univ, Calif, 85; Completing the Pictire: Native American, Mexican American, African American & Asian American Contributions to Twentieth Century American Art, Sonoma State Univ, Calif; Titan's Assunta as Hieros Gamos, From the Realm of the Ancestors, Kit, Manchester, Conn, 97; Venus envy, a sexual epistimology, Revision, winter, 98. *Mailing Add:* Dept Art Sonoma State Univ 1801 E Cotati Ave Rohnert Park CA 94928

MOUNT, MARSHALL WARD
HISTORIAN, ADMINISTRATOR
b Jersey City, NJ, Dec 25, 27. *Study:* Columbia Col, AB, 48; Columbia Univ, MA, 52, PhD, 66. *Pos:* Leader art study tours to Mali, Cameroun, India, Explorer Tours, Montreal, 69-77; dir art hist prog, Finch Col, San Marino, Italy, 73-75; cataloguer, Zim Collection of African Art, Children's Mus, Brooklyn, NY, 77 & 79; dir, L Kahan Gallery African Art, New York, 81-82. *Teaching:* Prof & chmn art hist dept, Finch Col, New York, 58-75; vis prof, Univ Iowa, Iowa City, summer 70 & Parsons Sch of Design, New York, 70-72; vis assoc prof, Hunter Col, New York, 72-73; prof and chmn creative arts dept, Univ Benin, Nigeria, 77-80; adj asst prof art hist, Fashion Inst Technol, New York, 82-; vis asst prof, Rutgers Univ, 87-88; adj instr, College Arts & Sciences, New York Univ, 2005-06. *Awards:* Rockefeller Found Fel, 61, 62 & 68; Fac Scholar Int Studies, Columbia, 66-67; Am Coun Learned Soc Grant, 73; George T Dorsh Fac Fel, Fashion Inst of Technol, 2004-05. *Mem:* Col Art Asn; fel African Studies Asn; Ctr for African Art. *Res:* Traditional and contemporary art of sub-Saharan Africa. *Publ:* Auth, African Art: The Years Since 1920, Ind Univ Press, 73, DaCapro Press, 89; African Art from New Jersey Collections, Montclair Art Mus, 83. *Mailing Add:* 74 Sherman Pl Jersey City NJ 07307

MOVALLI, CHARLES JOSEPH
PAINTER, WRITER
b Gloucester, Mass, Aug 20, 45. *Study:* Clark Univ, BA; Univ Conn, MA & PhD; spec study with Emile Gruppe, Roger Curtis, Zygmund Jankowski & Betty L Schlemm. *Work:* General Mills; High Voltage Engr; Hilton Hotel, Altamonte Springs; Exel Technol; Virginia Slims Collection; and others. *Exhib:* Rockport Art Assoc, 1979-; Guild of Boston Artists, 91,92; Judi Rutenberg Gallery, Boston, 95-2004; Old Lyme Art Assoc, 2002. *Collection Arranged:* Gloucester Historical Assoc. *Pos:* Contributing Ed, Am Artist, 1976-2004. *Awards:* Gold Medal, 82 & Silver Medal, 89, Rockport Art Asn; Gold Medal, Salmagundi Club, 85; Special Tribute, Hudson Valley Art Assoc, 2002. *Bibliog:* Numerous articles in American Artist Mag. *Mem:* Acad Artists; Guild of Boston Artists; Rockport Art Asn; N Shore Arts Asn. *Media:* Oil, Acrylic. *Res:* Contemporary and older painters working in plein-air tradition. *Publ:* Ed & coauth, Gruppe on Painting, 76; Brushwork, 77, Color in Outdoor Painting, 77 & Painting with Light, 78 & Art of Landscape Painting, 79, Watson-Guptill; auth, Croney on Watercolor, North Light, 82. *Mailing Add:* 237 Western Ave Gloucester MA 01930

MOWRY, ELIZABETH M
PAINTER, WRITER
b Kingston, NY, Mar 8, 40. *Study:* Alliance Col, BA(magna cum laude), 61; Carnegie Inst, 72-74; State Univ NY, MA, 83. *Work:* Am Cancer Soc, Kingston, NY; Merrill Lynch, Albany, NY; Mgt Compensation Group NY; Woodstock Hist Soc Permanent Collection, NY. *Comn:* Children's ward large painting, Suburban Gen Hosp, Pittsburgh, Pa, 74; mural landscape, Intercounty Bank, New Paltz, NY, 85; painting series, 87 & descriptive paintings 10 states, 88-92, Key Corp, Clcvcland, Ohio. *Exhib:* Solo exhib, Albany Inst Hist & Art, 86; Pastel Soc Am, Nat Arts Club, New York, 89-2000; Audubon Artists Am, Nat Arts Club, New York, 91; Allied Artists, Nat Arts Club, New York, 92; Knickerbocker Artists USA, Washington, 93. *Pos:* Sole Juror, Pastel Soc West Coast Nat Exhib, 98 & Pastel Soc NMex Nat Exhib, 98. *Teaching:* Instr painting & bd adv, Woodstock Sch Art, 87-. *Awards:* Pastel Soc Am, Landscape Award, Nat Arts Club, 89, 90 & 98; Excellence Award, Degas Pastel Soc, 91; Gold Medal Pastel & Most Innovative Use of Color, Knickerbocker Artists USA, 93; and others. *Bibliog:* Raymond J Steiner (auth), Profile: Elizabeth Mowry, Art Times, 4/86; John C Haviland (auth), Contemporary chronicle of HR, This Week NY, 6/86; Dennis Wepman (auth), Women's views of Woodstock, Artspeak, 11/87. *Mem:* Master pastelist Pastel Soc Am; Nat Asn Women Artists; Knickerbocker Artists USA; distinguished pastelist Pastel Soc W Coast; Woodstock Artists Asn (bd dir, 84-87). *Media:* Pastel. *Publ:* contribr, Best Pastel, Rockport Publ, 96; auth, The Poetic Landscape, 2001; auth, The Pastelists' Year, 2001. *Dealer:* Fletcher Gallery Woodstock NY

MOXEY, PATRICIO KEITH FLEMING
ART HISTORIAN
b Buenos Aires, Arg, Jan 4, 43; Brit & Arg citizen. *Study:* Univ Edinburgh, MA, 65; Univ Chicago, MA, 68, PhD, 74. *Teaching:* From instr to asst prof art hist, Tufts Univ, 71-74; from asst prof to assoc prof art hist, Univ Va, 74-86, prof, 86-, chmn art hist, 76-79 & actg chmn, 81-82; prof art hist, Barnard Col, 88-, chair art hist, 89-; prof art hist, Columbia Univ, 88-. *Awards:* Nat Endowment Humanities Fel, 78-79; sen fel, Ctr

Advan Study Visual Arts, Nat Gallery Art, 80-81; Humboldt Found Fel, 82-83; scholar, J Paul Getty Ctr Hist Art & Humanities, 91 & 92. *Mem:* Col Art Asn; Renaissance Soc; Hist Netherlandish Art; Sixteenth Century Soc. *Res:* Late medieval and Renaissance art in Northern Europe; critical theory & historiography. *Publ:* Auth, Peasants, Warriors & Wives, Popular Imagery in the Reformation, Chicago, 89; co-ed, Visual Theory: Painting & Interpretation, Polity, 91; the Practice of Theory, Cornell, 94; co-ed, Visual Culture: Images & Interpretations, Wesleyan/Univ Press New England, 94. *Mailing Add:* 39 Clarmont Ave New York NY 10027-6802

MOY, SEONG
PAINTER, PRINTMAKER
b Canton, China, Apr 12, 21; US citizen. *Study:* St Paul Sch Art, with Cameron Booth, 36-40; Art Students League, with Vaclav Vytacil, 41-42; Hofmann Sch, with Hans Hofmann, 41-42; Atelier 17, New York, 48-50. *Work:* Mus Mod Art; Brooklyn Mus; Metrop Mus Art; Pa Acad Fine Arts; NY Pub Libr; plus others. *Comn:* Three ed, Int Graphic Arts Soc; NY Hilton Hotel; mural, Bd Educ, PS-131, NY. *Exhib:* Metrop Mus Art, 50; Whitney Mus Am Art, 50; Univ Ill, 51, 53 & 54; Carnegie Inst, 52 & 55; NY World's Fair, 64-65; plus many other group & one-man shows. *Pos:* Dir, Seong Moy Sch Painting & Graphic Arts, Provincetown, Mass, summers 54-75. *Teaching:* Instr, Univ Minn, 51, Ind Univ, 52-53, Smith Col, 54-55, Univ Ark, 55, Vassar Col, 55, Cooper Union Art Sch, 57-70, Columbia Univ, 59-70 & Art Students League, 63-87; prof, City Col NY, 70-87. *Awards:* John Hay Whitney Found Grant, 50-51; Guggenheim Fel, 55-56; CAP, NY Arts Coun, 73-74; City Univ New York Research Found, 77-78. *Bibliog:* Saff & Sacilatto (auths), Printmaking--History and Process, Holt-Reinhart Winston Publ, 70. *Mem:* Art Students League; Am Fedn Arts; Artists Equity Asn; Col Art Asn Am; Fedn Mod Painters & Sculptors. *Media:* All Media. *Publ:* Five American Printmakers (film), USIA, State Dept, Washington, DC, 57; Seong Moy-A Print Artist of Today (film), US Military Acad, Westpoint, NY, 70. *Mailing Add:* 100 La Salle St New York NY 10027-4703

MOYA SOTO, ROBERTO
PAINTER, PRINTMAKER
b San Juan, PR, Oct 15, 35. *Study:* Eastern NMex Univ, 51-53; Pratt Graphics Art Ctr, 60-62, USC with Harry Sternberg, 80-82. *Work:* Mus Fine Art, Ft Lauderdale, Fla; Rutgers Univ; Jane Voorhees Zimmerli Art Mus; Rutgers Univ, Printmaking Studios; Duke Univ, Schaefer House, Raleigh, NC; and others. *Comn:* Schaefer House, Duke Univ, comm by Mr & Mrs Norb Schaefer. *Exhib:* One-man exhib, Series-Large Scale Paintings, Pratt Inst, NY, 89; Muestra Nac, 94; Olympic Comt PR Invitational, 94-95; El Santo en el Arte Puertorriqueno: devocion imagen y transcendencia, 96; Computer Graphics, Mus Barrio, 96; Retrospective, From Island to Island (with catalog), Hui No' eau Arts Sch, Hawaii; Images of Our Hispanic Heritage, The Newark Pub Libr, NJ, 01; Muestra Nacional, San Juan, PR, 02; Images of Our Hispanic Heritage, Newark Pub Libr, NJ, 2001 & 2006; Muestra Nacional, San Juan, PR, 02; La Ciudad Infinita, 00; and many others. *Pos:* Founder & pres, Galeria Palomas, 78-88. *Teaching:* Artist-in-residence, computer generated studies, Univ PR, 89-; sem, Hui No' eau Arts Sch, Hawaii, Spring, 98. *Bibliog:* E Ruiz de la Mata (auth), Roberto Moya Painter as Computer Whiz, 6/30/91; Sue Nash (auth), article, Island Currents; Retrospectiva de Roberto Moya en Hawaii, 6/10/98; La Ciudad Infinita, portfolio distributed to U.S. and European Mus; and others. *Media:* Oil & Acrylic on canvas

MOYER, LINDA LEE
PAINTER, EDUCATOR
b Niles, Mich, Feb 11, 1942. *Study:* Occidental Col, Calif, 59-61; Univ Calif, Los Angeles, BA, 64; Calif State Univ, Long Beach, MA, 77, MFA, 80, Univ Calif, Irvine, student, 84. *Work:* 24 paintings, Home Savings of America, Los Angeles; Greensburg Deposit Bank, Ashland, Ky; Univ Calif, Irvine. *Comn:* 6 paintings, Nat Bank of La Jolla, Calif, 85; Robert Danlap, Rolling Hills, Calif, 88; Mr & Mrs Keith Kelly, Alexandria, Va, 92. *Exhib:* Solo exhibs, Calif Contemp Artists IV, Laguna Beach Mus Art, Calif, 82, Louis Newman Galleries, 86, 88 & 90, Cerritos Col, Norwalk, Calif, 86, Westmont Col, Santa Barbara, Calif, 92 & Maturango Mus, Ridgecrest, Calif, 96; Am Watercolor Soc, Nat Acad Galleries, NY, 82; The Church of Jesus Christ of Latterday Saints Mus Art & Hist, Salt Lake City, Utah, 88 & 91; Watercolor: Contemp Currents, Riverside Art Mus, Riverside Calif, 89; Watermarks, Mt San Antonio Col, Walnut, Calif, 96; and others. *Teaching:* Part-time instr painting & drawing, Calif State Univ, Long Beach, 81-86; part-time instr painting, Saddleback Col, Mission Viego, Calif, 86-88, Goldenwest Col, Huntington Beach, Calif, 90 & Fullerton Col, Calif, 90 & 94; Nat workshops, currently. *Awards:* Gold Medal, 82, Walter S Greathouse Medal, 88 Am Watercolor Soc, Watercolor West Award, 99; Gold Medal for Watercolor, Allied Artists Am, 82; 2nd Ann Int Exhib Award of Merit, Church Jesus Christ Latter-Day Saints Mus Church Hist & Art, 91; Best of Show Award, Utah Watercolor Soc, 2000. *Bibliog:* Splash 2, North Light Book Co, 92; Phil Metzger (auth), Enliven Your Paintings With Light, North Light Book Co, 93; Carole Katchen (auth), Make Your Watercolors Look Professional, North Light Bk Co, 95. *Mem:* Nat Watercolor Soc; Watercolor West; West Coast Watercolor Soc; Watercolor W (pres, 99-01); Utah Watercolor Soc. *Media:* Transparent Watercolor. *Interests:* music, reading. *Publ:* Auth, Building vibrant color--layer by layer, Artist's Mag, 5/85; contribr (with Valerie Shesko), Finding your center of interest, Artist's Mag, 4/86; Auth, Making Use of Symbolism, Am Artist, 8/97. *Dealer:* Phillips Gallery Salt Lake city Utah; Louis Stern Galleries WestHollywood Calif. *Mailing Add:* 553 E Jade Park Ln Draper UT 84020

MOYER, ROY
PAINTER, ADMINISTRATOR
b Allentown, Pa, Aug 20, 21. *Study:* Columbia Col, BA, Columbia Univ, MA. *Work:* Fordham Univ, Lincoln Ctr, NY; Allentown Art Mus, Pa; Rochester Mem Art Gallery; Rockford (Ill) Art Inst; and others. *Exhib:* Nat Acad Design, NY, 77; Carl Battaglia Gallery, 80; Fordham Univ, 81; Rolly-Michaux Gallery, Boston, 81; Keen Gallery, NY, 93; Midtown Galleries, NY; and others. *Collection Arranged:* numerous others for Am Fedn Arts. *Pos:* Dir, Am Fedn Arts, 63-72; chief art & design, UNICEF, 72-86. *Teaching:* Lectr art hist, Univ Toronto, 53-55. *Awards:* First Prize, Butler Inst Am Art, 73 & Nat Acad Design, 77. *Bibliog:* An American Bestiary, Abrams, 78; Modern American Realism, Smithsonian Inst, 87. *Mem:* Nat Coun Arts (exec comt, 65-72); Am Soc Contemp Artists (pres). *Media:* Oil. *Res:* Byzantine art and architecture; sixteenth century painting and sculpture. *Interests:* Book illustration. *Publ:* Auth, Dogancay, 86; Nineteen films on visual perception with Rudolf Arnheim; editorials in Artspeak Mag, 88-97. *Mailing Add:* 440 Riverside Dr New York NY 10027

MOYERS, WILLIAM
PAINTER, SCULPTOR
b Atlanta, Ga, Dec 11, 1916. *Study:* Adams State Col, major fine arts; Otis Art Inst. *Hon Degrees:* Adams State Col, PhD in Fine Arts, 1992. *Work:* Gilcrease Inst, Tulsa, Okla; Nat Cowboy Fame, Oklahoma City; Adams State Col; Albuquerque Mus; Sangre Cristo Arts Ctr, Pueblo, Colo; Cowboy Artists Am Mus, Kerrville, Tex. *Comn:* Wind & Rain (life size sculpture), Albuquerque Mus, NMex & Adams State Col; Cowboy Artists Am Mus, Kerrville, Tex. *Exhib:* Cowboy Artist of Am Shows, Cowboy Hall Fame & Phoenix Art Mus, since 68; one-man shows, Adams State Col, Alamosa, Colo, 71 & Nat Cowboy Hall Fame, Oklahoma City, 73; group show, Mont Hist Soc, Helena, 72 & 73. *Awards:* Silver Medal sculpture, Cowboy Artists Am 1979 Exhib, Phoenix Art Mus, 79 & 80; Gold Medal-Sculpture, Cowboy Artists Am Exhib, 84; Silver Medal-Watercolor, Cowboy Artists Am Show, 89 & 91; and others. *Bibliog:* Ainsworth (auth), Cowboy in Art, World Publ, 68; Harmsen (auth), Western America, Northland, 71; Broder (auth), Bronzes of the American West, Abrams, 74. *Mem:* Cowboy Artists Am (vpres, 82-83, pres, 83-84 & 88-89). *Media:* Oil, Watercolor; Bronze. *Publ:* Illusr bks for nat publ, 45-62. *Dealer:* Taos Art Gallery Inc PO Box 1007 Taos NM 87571; Taos Gallery Scottsdale Ariz, 85251. *Mailing Add:* 1407 Morningside Dr NE Albuquerque NM 87110

MOZLEY, ANITA VENTURA
CURATOR, CRITIC
b Washington, DC, Aug 29, 28. *Study:* Northwestern Univ, Evanston, Ill, BA (hon art); Art Students League, with Morris Kantor. *Exhib:* Maine Coast Artists, Landscapes, (invit), 89; Figurative Painting, Palo Alto Art League, 98; Fulton Street Gallery, NY. *Collection Arranged:* Ansel Adams: The Portfolios, Stanford Univ Mus Art, Calif, 72; Eadweard Muybridge: The Stanford Years, 1872-1882 (ed & co-auth, catalog), 72; Mrs Cameron's Photographs from the Life (auth, catalog), 74; Freshwater (producer), 74; Monsen Collection of American Photography (auth, catalog), Seattle Art Mus, Wash, 76; Nadar: Portraits and Catacombs, from the coll of Samuel Wagstaff, 78; The Grand Tour: Mid-19th Century Photographs from the Leonard-Peil Collection, 79; Paintings by Joseph Raphael from San Francisco Coll (1869-1950), 80; Ansel Adams: Ski Experience, 83; Images of Hope and Despair: Robert Frank's Photographs, 85; Peter Stackpole, A photojournalist in Retrospect, 86. *Pos:* Reviewer, managing ed & West Coast corresp, Arts Mag, New York, 55-64; poster designer, Leo Castelli Gallery, New York, 55-62; film librn, Sextant, Inc, New York, 60-61; co-ed & publ, Scrap, a journal on the arts in NYC, 60-64; cur asst & ed, SEA Letter, San Francisco Maritime Mus, 64-67; registr, Stanford Univ Mus Art, Calif, 70-78; cur photog, 71-86. *Teaching:* Hist photogr, Stanford Univ, spring 81. *Awards:* Faricy Art Award, Northwestern Univ, 49; Out-of-Town Scholar, Art Students League, 50; First Prize Palo Alto Art League, 98. *Bibliog:* Reviews (monogr), Arts Mag, Studio International, 55-63, Arts Mag, San Francisco, 64-67, Photograph, Image, Afterimage, Print Collector's Newsletter, 73-85. *Mem:* Phi Beta Kappa. *Media:* Gouache, Watercolor, Oil, Collage. *Res:* Nineteenth and twentieth century photographers, particularly the works of Eadweard Muybridge, Julia Margaret Cameron, Thomas Annan, Imogen Cunningham, Peter Stackpole & Lorie Novak. *Interests:* History, Science, Cooking. *Collection:* Esta Kramer Damariscotta ME, Regina Rosenzweig San Francisco CA. *Publ:* Contribr to several art publ, 72-85; auth introduction, Thomas Annan, Photographs of the Old Closes & Streets of Glasgow, 1868-1877, Dover, 77; auth, The Bridge Builders, Pomegranate, 84; The Stanfords and Photography, Mus Builders in the West, Stanford, 86; Leo Holub's Photographs of Artists in the Collection of Mr and Mrs H W Anderson, Vol I, Atherton, Calif, 89; Joel Leivick's Photographs of Carrara (exhib catalog), auth essay, Joe Deal's The Fault Zone, Stanford, 90; contribr, Catalogue of the Drawing Collection, Stanford Mus, 93; auth essay, Explorations and Excavations in Joseph Zirker, Translucent Transformations, Santa Clara, De Saisset Mus, 2004. *Mailing Add:* 601 Laurel Ave Menlo Park CA 94025

MUCCIOLI, ANNA MARIA
PAINTER, SCULPTOR
b Detroit, Mich, Apr 23, 22. *Study:* Soc Art & Crafts; with Sarkis Sarkisian, Charles Culver & Jay Holland. *Exhib:* Butler Inst Am Art, Youngstown, Ohio, 69; Birmingham Mus Arts, 74; La Galleria, Ital Am Cult Soc, Warren, Mich, 86; Retrospective Watercolors, Lawrence Inst Technol, Mich, 86; Muccioli Studio Gallery, Detroit, Mich, 87; Art Ctr, Mt Clemens, 91; 3rd Ann CCS-CAD Alum Exhib, Scarab Club, Detroit, Mich, 93; Fine Arts Assoc, Dearborn Col, Univ Mich, 95; Women Artists Henry Ford Cmty Collage Sisson Gallery, Dearborn, Mich, 99; 34th Ea Mich Int Art Exhib, Port Huron Mus, 2000. *Pos:* Owner, Muccioli Studio Gallery. *Awards:* Third Place, Scarab Club, 71, Hon Mention, Silver Medal Exhib, 76 & 79; Second Place, Ford Motor Co Art Exhib, 76, First Place, 77, & Second Place, 79; Pallet Guild Juror award, Spring Art Show, Livonia City Hall, 2003. *Bibliog:* Impresario Mag Art Leisaure, 11/74; Leaders & Achievers, Detroit News, 1/20/83; Am Artists: An Illustrated Survey of Leading Contemporary Americans, 85; NY Art Rev, 88. *Mem:* Founders Soc Detroit Inst Arts; Friends Mod Art; Arts Crafts Ctr Studies Alumni, Col Art & Design, Detroit, Mich, 91. *Media:* Watercolor; Bronze, Stone. *Publ:* William T Noble (auth), The stockholder who told Henry how to build his new mustang, The Sunday News Mag, 9/73; Italian Tribune Paper, 1/98. *Mailing Add:* c/o Muccioli Studio Gallery 511 Beaubien Detroit MI 48266

MUCHNIC, SUZANNE
CRITIC, INSTRUCTOR
b Kearney, Nebr. *Study:* Scripps Col, BA, 62; Claremont Grad Sch, MA, 63. *Pos:* Ed, Artweek, Los Angeles, 77-78, contrib ed, 78-80; art critic & staff writer, Los Angeles Times, 78-; Los Angeles correspondent, Art News, 93-2004. *Teaching:* Instr art hist, Los Angeles City Col, 74-82; instr art criticism, Univ Southern Calif, 81 & Claremont Grad Sch, 83. *Awards:* Distinguished Alumna Award, Claremont Grad Sch, 82; Distinguished Alumna Award, Scripps Col, 87; Donald Pflueger History Award, Historical Soc of Southern Calif, 02. *Mem:* Int Asn Art Critics; Art Table; Col Art Asn. *Res:* Contemporary art, Norton Simon Museum. *Publ:* Auth, exhibition catalogue essays on Tim Nordin, Martha Alf, Mark Lere, Paul Darrow, Aldo Casanova & Barbara Strassen; essay on art, World Book Encyl Year Book, 93, 94, 95; Odd Man In: Norton Simon and the Pursuit of Culture, Univ Calif Press, 98. *Mailing Add:* c/o Los Angeles Times 202 W 1st St Los Angeles CA 90012

MUDFORD, GRANT LEIGHTON
PHOTOGRAPHER
b Sydney, Australia, Mar 21, 44. *Study:* Univ New South Wales, Australia, 63-64. *Work:* Mus Mod Art, NY; Int Mus Photog, George Eastman House, Rochester, NY; Victoria & Albert Mus; Australian Nat Gallery, Canberra; Nat Mus Am Art, Washington, DC; Mus Contemp Art, Los Angeles. *Comn:* Ten photog prints, Calif State Univ, Long Beach, 80 & CSR Ltd, Sydney, 81; Parliament House, Lewis comn, Canberra (under construct); Comprehensive Cancer Center Cedars-Sinai Medical Ctr, Los Angelas (under construction); Louis I Kahn: In The Realm Of Architecture, Moca, Los Angeles, 91. *Exhib:* The Land: 20th Century Landscape Photographs, Victoria & Albert Mus, 75-76; solo exhib, Hirshhorn Mus & Sculpture Garden, 79; Long Beach: A Photog Survey, Art Mus & Galleries, Calif State Univ, Long Beach, 80; Biennial Exhib, Whitney Mus Am Art, 81; Double Take: A Comparative Look at Photographs, Int Ctr Photog, NY, 81; Photog: A Sense of Order, Inst Contemp Art, Univ Pa, 81. *Teaching:* Instr, Art Ctr Sch Art & Design, Pasadena & Calif Inst Arts, Valencia. *Awards:* Nat Endowment Arts Photogr Fel, 80. *Bibliog:* Photographs by Grant Mudford, Interview Mag, 6/79; Celebrating the seldom-noticed, Los Angeles Times, 3/6/83; article, Artforum, summer 83; Availible Light, Mus Contemp Art, Los Angeles; Grant Mudford (auth), catalogue, Gallery Min, 86; California Photographers; catalogue, Gallery Min, 86. *Dealer:* Rosamund Felsen Gallery 2525 Michigaqn Ave B4 Santa Monica CA 90404. *Mailing Add:* 2660 Dundee Pl Los Angeles CA 90027-1328

MUEHLEMANN, KATHY
PAINTER
b Feb 9, 50. *Study:* State Univ NY, BFA, 79. *Work:* Ackland Art Mus, Univ NC, Chapel Hill; Cleveland Mus Art, Ohio; Contemp Mus, Honolulu, Hawaii; Calif Ctr Arts Mus, Escondido; Nelson-Atkins Mus Art, Kansas City, Mo; Milwaukee Art Mus, Wis; and others; Mus Contemp Art, Miami, Fla. *Exhib:* Solo exhibs, Oscarsson Siegeltuch Gallery, NY, 86, Lannan Mus (with catalog), Lake Worth, Fla, 88, Virginia Zabriskie Gallery, NY, 89, Contemp Mus Art, Honolulu, Hawaii, 91, Pamela Auchincloss Gallery, NY, 91 & 93-94, Nelson-Atkins Mus Art, Kansas City, Mo, 91 & Cedar Rapids Mus Art, Iowa, 94; Am exhib (with catalog), Am Acad Rome, Italy, 88; Nina Freudenhelm Gallery, Buffalo, NY, 90 & 93; Australian Print Workshop, Melbourne, 93; Jan Weiner Gallery, Kansas City, Mo, 93; Grey Art Gallery, NY Univ, 93; Fitchburg Art Mus, Mass, traveling, 93; Ackland Art Mus, Univ NC, Chapel Hill, traveling, 94; Maier Mus Art, Va, 95; The Hyde Collection Art Mus, NY, 98; and many others. *Teaching:* Assoc prof & chair art, Randolph-Macon Woman's Col, Va. *Awards:* Prix De Rome, 87-88; Nat Endowment Arts Award, 88; Fel, John Simon Guggenheim, 94. *Bibliog:* John Yau (auth), review, Art Forum, 3/92; Holland Cotter (auth), review, NY Times, 9/17/93; Kim Levin (auth), review, The Village Voice, 10/12/93; Paul Mattick (auth), review, Art in Am, 1/94; Alicia Faxon (auth), review, Art New Eng, 4-5/94; and many others. *Mem:* Fel Am Acad, Rome. *Media:* Oil. *Dealer:* Pamela Auchincloss Gallery 601 W 26th St 12th Floor New York NY 10001. *Mailing Add:* 5024 Inglewood Dr Lynchburg VA 24503

MUELLER, LOUIS ALBERT
SCULPTOR, CRAFTSMAN
b Paterson, NJ, June 15, 43. *Study:* Rochester Inst Technol, BFA, 69; RI Sch Design, MFA, 71. *Work:* RI Sch Design, Mus Art, Providence; Am Craft Mus, NY; Philadelphia Mus Art; Victoria & Albert Mus, London; Mus Fine Arts, Boston. *Comn:* Bronze sculpture, Philadelphia One Percent for Arts, 85; bronze medal, Philadelphia Mus Art, 85; three bronzes, Hyatt Hotel, Phoenix, 86; fences & gates, welded steel, Phoenix One Percent for Arts, 88; bronze & blown glass lighting, Port of Seattle, Wash, 91. *Exhib:* 1st Artist Soapbox Derby, San Francisco Mus Mod Art, 75; one-man show, NDak Mus Art, Grand Forks, 82; Design in the Service of Tea, Cooper-Hewitt, Nat Design Mus, NY, 84; Poetry of the Physical, Am Craft Mus, NY, 86; Modern Jewelry, Philadelphia Mus Art, 86. *Collection Arranged:* The Virgin (auth, catalog), Int Jewelry Exhib, 91-92. *Teaching:* Lectr metal art, Calif Col Art & Crafts, 71-75; prof jewelry & metal, RI Sch Design, Providence, 77-; lectr, Sch Mus Fine Arts, Boston, 78-79; lectr casting, Wellesley Col, Mass, 78-80. *Awards:* Fel Design, NY Found Arts, 85; Fel Sculpture, RI Coun Arts, 90, Fel Design, 96. *Bibliog:* Peter Dormer (auth), The New Furniture, Thames & Hudson, 87; Otto Kunzli (auth), Providence, Art Aurea, 89; Ralph Turner (auth), New Time - New Thinking, Int Crafts Coun-London, 96. *Media:* Bronze Constructed; Fabricated Sterling & Karat Gold. *Dealer:* Franklin Parrasch 20 W 57th St New York NY 10019. *Mailing Add:* 508 Lloyd Ave Providence RI 02906

MUELLER, STEPHEN
PAINTER
b Norfolk, Va, 47. *Study:* U Tex, BFA, 69, Bennington Col, MFA, 71. *Exhib:* Solo exhibs, Annina Nosei Gallery, NY, 82, 84, 86, 88, 90, 92 & 94, Fabian Carlsson Gallery, London, 85, 87 & 94, James Corcoran Gallery, Santa Monica, Calif, 92 & Baumgartner Galleries, Washington, DC, 93; Whitney Biennial, Whitney Mus Am Art, NY, 87; Isn't It Romantic?, On Crosby Street, NY, 94; In the Spirit of Things, Stux Gallery, NY, 94; Abstract Works on Paper, Robert Miller Gallery, NY, 94; Works on Paper: Selections from the Permanent Collection, Whitney Mus Am Art, 94; Works on Paper: Weatherspoon Gallery, Greensborough, NC, 94; Champions of Modernism - Art of Tomorrow/Art of Today, Castle Gallery, Col New Rochelle, NY, 96; and others; Bill Maynes, NY, 2000. *Awards:* Guggenheim Fel, 2000. *Bibliog:* Klaus Kertess (auth), Serendipitous elegance, Elle Decor, 4/94; Reviews in brief, NY Rev Art, 4/94; Lilly Wei (auth), Art in Am, 6/94. *Mailing Add:* 53 Little West 12th St New York NY 10014

MUELLER, OP, (SISTER) GERARDINE
CALLIGRAPHER, STAINED GLASS ARTIST
b Newark, NJ, 21. *Study:* Caldwell Col, BA; Univ Notre Dame, MA & MFA, with A Lauck, W Otto of Berlin & Albinas Elskus; Inst Cult, Guadalajara, Mex; Fordham Univ; Columbia Univ. *Work:* Illumination, Newark Pub Libr. *Comn:* Wall mural & glass panel, Dominican Sisters, Caldwell, NJ, 86; cloisonne enamel & wood tabernacle, windows, extended care facility, Newark, 87; stained glass stations, 89, life-size sculptures, 90 & 92, Dominican Sisters, Caldwell; 32 windows, Caldwell Col Theatre, 93-98; 3 windows, Summit Mausoleum, 94; chapel walls, Sacred Heart Sch, Newark, 96; 2 windows, St James Church, Newark. *Exhib:* Old Bergen Art Guild Tour, 79-86; NAm Calligraphers, Dallas, Tex, 74, Nat Miniature Art Soc, Fla, 75, 2001; Art by US Relig Women, Indianapolis, 81; Contemp Relig Art, Newark, 83-88; Barron Arts Ctr, Woodbridge, NJ, 86. *Pos:* Mem, Archdiocese Comm Div Worship (art & archit), 74-2003; dir art & design, Liturgy Conv, 81; ed bd, Word on Worship, 2005. *Teaching:* Lectr lettering & crafts, Fordham Univ, 61; prof art, Caldwell Col, 63-98, chmn art dept, 63-98, prof emeritus, 98. *Awards:* Nat Cath Educ Asn Award (glass), 86; Veritas Alumni Award, 91; Caldwell Col Cup, 2002. *Bibliog:* Articles in The NY Times, 11/77, New Jersey Music & Arts 12/77, Today's Art, 1/81, Newark Advocate, 10/81, Newark Star-Ledger, 11/81 & 1/86, Jersey J, 5/86, Suburban Life, 4/86 & New Community, Newark, 5/87; Channel 5 News Report, 10/93; Sunday Star Ledger, 5/1/94. *Media:* Stained Glass, Illuminator. *Res:* Pre-Columbian Art. *Interests:* Lettering, Pre-Columbia History. *Collection:* Caldwell Col, Univ Notre Dame. *Publ:* Auth, Yearbook production, Photolith Mag, 61; Art in Latin America & Art in Indian Mission of US, Cath Youth Encycl, McGraw-Hill, 62; New mosaic evolvement, Cath Fine Arts Soc, 68; contribr, Stained Glass Quart, summer 78; 2 articles, Word on Worship, 93 & 95; Dominican News, 11/2000. *Mailing Add:* 1 Ryerson Ave Caldwell NJ 07006

MUENZENMAYER, KENNETH JOHN
PAINTER
b Lakewood, Ohio, June 10, 50. *Study:* Ringling Sch Art & Design, BFA, 72; study with Calvin Goodman, 91-. *Work:* Mus Arts & Sci, Daytona Beach, Fla; Pensacola Mus Art, Fla; Fla Gulf Coast Art Ctr, Belleair, Fla; Lowe Art Mus, Coral Gables, Fla. *Exhib:* Fiesta, Laguna Gloria Art Mus, Austin, Tex, 87-98; Coconut Grove Art Festival, Miami, 89-98; Cain Park Art Festival, Cleveland Heights, Ohio, 91-98; Ann Arbor Street Art Fair, Mich, 94. *Awards:* Award of Excellence, Cent Pa Festival Arts, 89; Best in Show, Fiesta, Laguna Gloria Mus, 93; First in Painting, Naples Nat Art Festival, 95. *Bibliog:* Betty Rubinstein (auth), Exhibit illustrates the mystery of boundaries, Tallahassee Democrat, 4/27/90. *Mem:* Nat Asn Independent Artists. *Media:* Acrylic. *Dealer:* Coconut Grove Gallery 2790 Bird Ave Coconut Grove FL 33133

MUGAR, MARTIN GIENANDT
PAINTER
b Boston, Mass, Jan 23, 49. *Study:* Yale Univ, with William Bailey & Bernard Chaet, BA(cum laude), 71, with Al Held & Lester Johnson, MFA, 74. *Work:* Mass Inst Technol Mus, Cambridge; Boston Pub Libr, Mass; Fuller Mus, Brockton, Mass; Weatherspoon Art Gallery, Univ NC, Greensboro; Tufts Univ Mus, Medford, Mass. *Exhib:* One-man shows, Mass Inst Technol, Cambridge, 87, Hood Mus, Dartmouth, Hanover, NH, 88 & Bowery Gallery, NY, 91 & Creiger-Dane Gallery, Boston, 98 & 2000; Contemp Landscapes, Art Inst Boston, 91; Rising Tide Gallery, Provincetown, Mass, 93, 94 & 96; Bromfield Gallery, Boston, 93 & 95; Visions of Order, Mercury Gallery, 95; New Eng, New Talent, Fitchburg Mus, 96; New Eng Triennial, Fuller Mus, Brockton, Mass, 99; Picture Perfect, New Eng Sch Design, 2000; Montserrat Col Art Gallery, Wilderness of Sweets, 2001. *Teaching:* Asst prof painting, Univ NC, Greensboro, 80-86, Univ NH, Durham, 86-87, Dartmouth Col, Hanover, NH, 87-88 & Art Inst Boston, 88-99; instr, Univ NH, 94-95. *Awards:* John Courtney Murray Fel, Yale Univ, 71. *Bibliog:* Gail Kelley (auth), article, Boston Globe, 10/19/97; Cate McQuaid (auth), Boston Globe, 6/15/2000; Charles Givliano (auth), Arts Media, 6-7/2000. *Media:* All. *Dealer:* Joyce Crieger 33 Pond Ave Suite Brookline MA 02445. *Mailing Add:* 314 Durham Point Rd Durham NH 03824

MUHLBERGER, RICHARD CHARLES
WRITER, EDUCATOR
b Englewood, NJ, Jan 20, 38. *Study:* Calif Concordia Col, AA, 58; Wayne State Univ, BA(art hist), 64; Johns Hopkins Univ, Baltimore, MA(art hist), 67. *Pos:* Cur mus educ, Worcester Art Mus, Mass, 66-72; chmn educ, Detroit Inst Arts, 72-75; dir, Mus Fine Arts & George Walter Vincent Smith Art Mus, Springfield, Mass, 76-87; vice dir educ, Met Mus Art, 87-90; dir, Knoxville Mus Art, Tenn, 90-91. *Teaching:* Instr art history, Western New Eng Col, Springfield, Mass, 91-. *Awards:* Woodrow Wilson Nat

Fel, 65-67. *Mem:* Am Asn Mus; Asn Art Mus Dirs; New Eng Mus Asn (pres, 85). *Res:* Dutch seventeenth century bird painters. *Publ:* auth, What Makes a Picasso a Picasso, 1994, The Un-Seen Van Gogh, 1998, America Folf Marquetry, 1998, Charles Webster Hawthorne: Painting and Watercolors, 1999; contribr, video and book, Literature, Grade Seven, Prentice Hall, 2006. *Mailing Add:* 41 Smithfield Ct Springfield MA 01108-3129

MUHLERT, CHRISTOPHER LAYTON
PAINTER, PHOTOGRAPHER
b Brooklyn, NY, Mar 24, 33. *Study:* Case Western Reserve, BA, 64; Oberlin Col, MA, 66; Pratt Inst; Union Col; Cleveland Inst Art. *Work:* Cleveland Mus Art; Allen Mem Art Mus, Oberlin, Ohio; Phillip Morris Corp, Estate Joseph Hirshhorn, Washington, DC; Prudential Insurance Co, Merrillville, Ind; Brenton Bank of Cedar Rapids, Iowa; Alcon Lab, Ft Worth, Texas. *Exhib:* Black and White, Smithsonian Inst, 70-72; 19th Area Exhib, Corcoran Gallery Art, 74; two-person show, Barbara Fiedler Gallery, Washington, DC, 76; one-man shows, Davenport Munic Art Gallery, Iowa, 77, Barbara Fiedler Gallery, Washington, DC, 78, Carlin Gallery, Ft Worth, 83 & Graham Gallery, Houston, Tex, 84, Moudy Art Gallery, Texas Christian Univ, 87, William Campbell Contemp Art, 87-90 & Dutch Phillips & Co, 93-94. *Pos:* Preparator, Cleveland Mus Art, 60-64. *Teaching:* Instr design & painting, Oberlin Col, 66-68; instr found, Corcoran Sch Art, 70, asst prof drawing & design, 71-75. *Media:* Drawing, collage, photog. *Dealer:* William Campbell Contemporary Art Fort Worth TX. *Mailing Add:* 1108 Kay St Boalsburg PA 16827-1630

MUHLERT, JAN KEENE
MUSEUM DIRECTOR, HISTORIAN
b Oak Park, Ill, Oct 4, 42. *Study:* Neuchatel Univ; Inst European Studies, Paris; Sorbonne, with Andre Chastel; Inst de Phonetique; Acad Grande Chaumiere, 62-63; Albion Col, BA, 64; Oberlin Col, with Ellen H Johnson & Wolfgang Stechow, MA, 67. *Collection Arranged:* H Lyman Sayen (with catalog), Nat Collection Fine Arts, 70, Romaine Brooks, Thief of Souls (with catalog), 71 & William H Johnson 1901-1970 (with catalog), 71; The Ninth Level: Funerary Art from Ancient Meso America (with catalog), 78 & African Sculpture, The Stanley Collection (with catalog), 79, Mus of Art Univ Iowa. *Pos:* Asst cur collections, Allen Mem Art Mus, Oberlin Col, 66-68, asst cur contemp art, Nat Col Fine Arts, 68-73, assoc cur 20th century paintings & sculpture, 74-75; dir, Mus Art, Univ Iowa, 75-79; dir, Amon Carter Mus, Ft Worth, Tex, 80-95, Palmer Mus Art, Pa State Univ, 96-. *Teaching:* mus studies, Pa State Univ, 98-. *Awards:* Grant, Asn Art Mus Dir, 79. *Mem:* Asn Art Mus Dir; Am Asn Mus. *Res:* Charcoal drawings, 1900-1940; Arthur G Dove, 1880-1946. *Publ:* coauth, Tribute to Mark Tobey (catalog), Nat Collection Fine Arts, 74; contrib, Mauricio Lasansky, A Retrospective Exhibition, Univ Iowa, 76; contrib, American Paintings Selections from the Amon Carter Mus, 86; ed, proj mgr, An American Sculptor, Seymor Lipton, Palmer Mus Art, Pa State Univ, 99. *Mailing Add:* Pa State Univ Palmer Mus Art University Park PA 16802

MUIR, EMILY LANSINGH
PAINTER, SCULPTOR
b Chicago, Ill. *Study:* Art Students League, with Richard Lahey & Leo Lentelli; Univ Maine, LHD, 69. *Work:* Brooklyn Mus; Univ Maine; Margaret Chase Smith Libr. *Comn:* Designs & contracting of contemp summer & year round homes, mosaics & interior design, portraits and portrait busts for pvt owners. *Exhib:* Int Watercolor Soc; Maine Art Gallery; Univ Maine; Farnsworth Mus Art. *Pos:* Appointee, Nat Comn Fine Arts, 55-59. *Teaching:* Lectr art, Asn Am Cols, 50-60. *Awards:* Award in Archit, Maine Women in Arts; Maine Woman Yr, Westbrook Col; Mary A Vartman Award, UMO, Women in Arts, 94. *Bibliog:* Martin Dibner (auth), People of the Maine Coast, Doubleday; JR Wiggins (auth), article in Bangor Daily News; article in Maine Boats & Harbors, Island Inst; and others. *Mem:* Deer Isle Artists. *Media:* Oil, Mosaic; Clay, Wood. *Publ:* Auth, Small Potatoes, Scribner, 40. *Mailing Add:* Muir Studios PO Box 55 Stonington ME 04681

MUIRHEAD, ROSS P
KINETIC ARTIST, PHOTOGRAPHER
b Vancouver, BC, June 20, 56. *Study:* Emily Carr Inst Art & Design, dipl, 80; Univ BC, MFA, 89. *Exhib:* Solo exhib (contribr, catalog), Contemp Art Gallery, Vancouver, BC, 89; Un-Natural Traces: Contemp Art from Can (contribr, catalog), Barbican Art Gallery, London, Eng, 91; Working Truths/Powerful Fictions (contribr, catalog), MacKenzie Art Gallery, Regina, Sask, 91; Notions of Home (contribr, catalog), Edmonton Art Gallery, Alta, 92; Le Mois de la Photo a Montreal (contribr, catalog), Galerie Vox, Montreal, Que, 93; 69-94 Contemp Decades (contribr, catalog), Charles Scott Gallery, Vancouver, BC, 94. *Teaching:* Instr fine arts, Univ BC, 89. *Awards:* Proj Grant, Can Coun, 86 & B Grant, 91. *Media:* Photography. *Mailing Add:* 3096A Paisley Rd North Vancouver BC V7R 1C9 Canada

MULCAHY, KATHLEEN
GLASS ARTIST, SCULPTOR
b Newark, NJ, June 23, 50. *Study:* Kean Col NJ, Union, BA(art educ), 72; Alfred Univ, NY, MFA(glass sculpture), 74; Nat Endowment Arts Fel, 79; Individual Artist Fel, Pa Coun Arts, 81, 83 & 93; Lusk Meml Award Creative Artists, Fulbright Scholar, Italy, 84; Carnegie Mellon Univ Fac Res Grant, Italy & France, 86; Masterworks Fel, Creative Glass Ctr Am, Millville, NJ, 91. *Work:* Corning Mus Glass, NY; pvt collections, Westmoreland Co Mus Art, Pa; Carnegie Inst Mus Art, Pittsburgh; Am Craft Mus, NY; State Mus Pa, Harrisburg. *Comn:* Illuminated Glass Wall: Light Rail Transit, City Pittsburgh, 85, Donor Room, Rodef Shalom Congregation, 91 & Westinghouse Corp, Pittsburgh, 93; Centimark Corp, Wash, Pa, 96; Bayer Corp, 98; Pittsburgh Regional Alliance, 98; lobby installation, Pa Turnpike Comn Corp Hq, Harrisburg, Pa, 2001. *Exhib:* Corning Glass Ctr, 83, 87-88 & 93; one-person exhibs, Snyderman Gallery, Philadelphia, 86, Kimzey Miller Gallery, 91, Cleveland Ctr Contemp Art, 94, Kean Col, NJ, 95, Butters Gallery Ltd, Portland, Ore, 96 & Hodgell Gallery, Sarasota, Fla, 97; Crafts Today/USA traveling exhib, Am Crafts Coun, 89-92; Rosemont Col, Philadelphia, Pa, 99; Buy/By Women, Morgan Contemp Glass, Pittsburgh, 2000; Westmoreland Mus Art, Greensburg, Pa, 2000; and others. *Collection Arranged:* American Craft Mus; Renwick Galleries; Bayer Corporation; Carnegie Mus of Art; Westmoreland Mus of Art; State Mus of Penn; Corning Mus of Glass and More; Mus of American Glass at Wheaton Village. *Pos:* Vis artist, ArtPark, Lewiston, NY, 80; adv comt, Three Rivers Art Festival, Pittsburgh, 91-93; co-cur, In the Quest of Being, Three Rivers Art Festival Show, 93; artist-in-residence, Haystack Mt Sch Crafts, summer, 79 & 83, ArtPark, Lewiston, NY, summer, 80, Mid Atlantic Arts Fel, Studio Access to Glass, Corning, NY, 94 & Cité Int Arts, Paris, 97; artistic dir, Pittsburgh Glass Ctr, Pa, 1999-2002; co-founder, developer, Pittsburg Glass Ctr, Pa, 2001. *Teaching:* Head, glass prog, Bowling Green State Univ, Ohio, 75-76; dir & assoc prof art, glass sculpture prog, Carnegie-Mellon Univ, Pittsburgh, 76-89; lectr, Portcon Glass Conf, 82 & 83. *Awards:* Individual Artist Fel, Pa Coun Arts, 93; artist-in-residence, Mid Atlantic Arts Fel, Corning, NY, 95 & Cite Int des Arts, Paris, 97; Heinz Endowment Arts Award, 96; Distinguished Alumnus in the Arts, Kean Univ, 2005; and others. *Bibliog:* Graham Shearing (auth), "Regional Focus" takes art to another juror, 8/11/96, "His & Hers & Ours" at treat in a loft, 9/27/96, Tribune Rev & The Westmoreland Museum of American Art Launches A Survey, 2/20/2000; Michael Krumrine (auth), Kathleen Mulcahy: Lawrence Gallery at Rosemont, Glass Mag, winter 99; Mary Thomas (auth), Historic, Modern Glassworks Sparkle in Show, 4/8/2000; Sculpture Reference, Sculpture Books Publ, 2004; and others. *Mem:* Glass Art Soc (bd dir, 86-89), NY; Am Crafts Coun; Chartiers Valley Arts Coun, (bd dir, 89-90 & bd advisors, 91-), Carnegie, Pa. *Media:* Glass, Sculpture; Mixed Media. *Publ:* Profile, Glass Studio Mag, 11/81; Profile, Glass Mag, 1/95; critique, Glass Mag, winter 99; Lucartha Kohler: Women working in Glass, Schiffer,2003; catalog, 20/20 Vision, Susanne Frantz, 2003; review, Glass Mag, 2004. *Dealer:* Butters Gallery 520 NW Davis Portland OR 97209; 336 4th Ave Pittsburgh PA 15222. *Mailing Add:* 260 Whittengale Rd Oakdale PA 15071

MULHERN, MICHAEL
PAINTER
b Paisley, Scotland. *Study:* Newark Sch Fine & Indust Arts, Newark, NJ; Brooklyn Mus Sch, NY, 61-62; Sch of Visual Arts, New York. *Exhib:* One-person shows, Duane Street Gallery, 70, Adam Gimbel Gallery, 81, Exit Art Ringside Gallery, 85, Stephen Rosenberg Gallery, New York, 88, 90 & 93, Rosenberg & Kaufman Fine Art, NY, 95, 98, Salander-O'Reilly Galleries, NY, 2001; The Tenth Summer, Stephen Rosenberg Gallery, 93; The Inaugural Show, Painting Ctr, NY, 93; Presence & Absence (catalog), ES Vandam Gallery, NY, 93; Basic Marks: black & white paintings, Rosenberg & Kaufman Fine Art (auth catalog), 95; APC Galerie, Koln, Ger, 98; Salander O'Reilly Galleries, NY, 2001; Museo d'Arte Moderna, Gazoldo degli Ippoliti, Italy, 2002. *Awards:* Fel Grant, Nat Endowment Arts, 87; Painting Grant, Pollock-Krasner Found Inc, 89, 2000, Adolph & Esther Gottlieb Found, 2001. *Bibliog:* Peter Pinchbeck (auth), Incidence of Passage (exhib, catalog), 93; Alfred MacAdam (auth), Basic Marks, Art News, 3/95; Pepe Karmel (auth), Art in review, NY Times, 9/22/95; Maura Reilly (auth), Art in Am, 10/2001; Marid Naves (auth), The NY Observer, 1/2001; Karen Wikin (auth), Hudson Review, 2003. *Media:* Acrylic, Oil. *Dealer:* Salander-Oreilly, NY City; Spheris, Vt; Karolyn Sherwood, Des Moines. *Mailing Add:* 125 Cedar St 9N New York NY 10006

MULLEN, JAMES MARTIN
EDUCATOR, PRINTMAKER
b Altoona, Pa, May 14, 35. *Study:* Pa State Univ, BA, 57, MA, 63. *Work:* NJ State Mus, Trenton; Portsmouth Va Mus; Everson Mus, Syracuse, NY; Pa State Univ, Univ Park; Pushkin Mus, USSR. *Exhib:* Am Drawings III, Portsmouth Arts Ctr, Va, 80; World Print III, San Francisco Mus Mod Art, 80; 5th Nat Print, Honolulu Acad Art, Hawaii, 80; Small Works, Wash Sq Gallery, NY Univ, 80; Silvermine Guild Prints, New Canann, Conn, 80. *Pos:* Gallery dir, State Univ Col, Oneonta, NY, 76-. *Teaching:* Prof art, State Univ Col, Oneonta, NY, 63-. *Awards:* Chancellor's Award for Teaching Excellence, State Univ NY, 73; Chaning Hare Award, Soc Four Arts, Palm Beach, Fla. *Mem:* Soc Am Graphic Artist; Am Color Print Soc; Cooperstown Art Asn. *Media:* Watercolor. *Publ:* Auth, Subject matter, 66 & Student work, 69, Sch Arts Mag. *Dealer:* Miriam Perlman Inc Lake Point Tower Suite 1902 505 N Lakeshore Dr Chicago IL 60611. *Mailing Add:* 2 Brigham Rd Oneonta NY 13820

MULLEN, PHILIP EDWARD
PAINTER
b Akron, Ohio, Oct 10, 42. *Study:* Univ Minn, BA; Univ NDak, MA; Ohio Univ, PhD. *Work:* Guggenheim Mus, NY; Brooklyn Mus; Palm Springs Desert Mus; Denver Mus; Sonje Mus, Korea. *Exhib:* Biennial, Contemp Am Art, Whitney Mus Am Art, NY, 75; Smithsonian Inst Traveling Exhib; and many others. *Teaching:* distinguished prof emer, Univ South Carolina. *Bibliog:* Arts Mag, 2/76, 11/78, 3/82, 10/83 & 9/85; Art Voices S, 4/80; Art Am, 1/84; Artist's Mag, 4/85, 12/89, 5/90 & 6/91. *Media:* Acrylic. *Dealer:* David Findlay Galleries 984 Madison Ave New York NY 10021. *Mailing Add:* 5926 Marthas Glen Rd Columbia SC 29209

MULLER, DAVE
ARTIST
b San Francisco, Ca, 64. *Study:* Calif Inst Art, MFA, 93; Prog Sch Visual Arts, Fine Arts Grad, NY, 90-91; Univ Calif, B (chemistry and art). *Exhib:* One-man shows, Woo, Mint Gallery, Ca Inst Arts, 92, A Number of Ladders (Borrowed), Broad Studio #2, Calif Arts, 93, Studio 246, Kunstlerhaus Bethanian, Berlin, 96, Love Is All Around, Spanish Box, Santa Barbara, Calif, 97, LA, LA, LA, LA, LA, LA, Blum & Poe, Santa Monica, Calif, 98, here & now, Four Walls, San Francisco, 99, The

Approach, London, 2002, Blum & Poe, Los Angeles, 2003, 2006 San Francisco Mus Modern Art, 2003, Engholm Engelhorn, Vienna, 2004, The Approach, London, 2005, The Wrong Gallery, NY, 2005, Stars and Bars, Anthony Meier Fine Arts, San Francisco, 2005, Gladstone Gallery, NY, 2006; group shows, Sound Art erby, Beyond Baroque, Venice, Calif, 93, On the Eve of New Years: Eve A Cocktail Party, Three Day Weekend, Los Angeles, 94, Smells Like Vinyl, Roger Merians Gallery, NY, 95, Loves Labors Lost, SITE, NY, 96, Hot Coffee, Artist's Space, NY, 97, Three Day Weekend, P-House, Tokyo, 97, Los Angeles or Lilliput?, Long Beach Mus Art, Calif, 98, Standing Still and Walking in Los Angeles, Gagosian Gallery, Beverly Hills, Calif, 99, Subtle Occupation, Murray Guy, NY, 2003, For the Record: Drawing Contemp Life, Vancouver Art Gallery, British Columbia, Can, 2003, It Happened Tomorrow, 7th Lyon Biennale of Contemp Art, Lyon, 2003, Playlist, Palais de Tokyo, Paris, 2004, Whitney Biennial, Whitney Mus Am Art, 2004. *Pos:* founder, Three Day Weekend, LA

MULLER, JEROME KENNETH
ART DIRECTOR, PHOTOGRAPHER
b Amityville, NY, July 18, 34. *Study:* NY Univ; Marquette Univ, BS; Layton Sch Art; Brandt Painting Workshop; Calif State Univ, Fullerton; Nat Univ, MA; Newport Psychoanalytic Inst. *Work:* Univ Calif, Irvine; Portland State Univ, Ore; Marquette Univ, Wis; plus others. *Exhib:* Gallery 2, Santa Ana, 71; Souk Gallery, Newport Beach, Calif, 72; Cannery Gallery, Newport Beach, Calif, 74; Mus Graphics Gallery, Costa Mesa, Calif, 92; South Coast Art Gallery, Costa Mesa & Bistango, Irvine, Calif, 94; White Gallery, Portland State Univ, Ore, 96; Univ Calif, Irvine, 97; Nat Tel & Commun, Irvine, Calif, 98; Robert Mondavi Wine & Food Ctr, Costa Mesa, Calif, 2000. *Collection Arranged:* Cartoon Show, Original Works by 100 Outstanding American Cartoonists, Laguna Beach Mus Art, Calif, 72, Bowers Mus, Santa Ana, Calif, 76, EB Crocker Art Gallery, Sacramento, Calif, 77, Indianapolis Mus Art, Ind, 77, Tweed Mus Art, Duluth, Minn, 78, Everson Mus Art, Syracuse, NY, 78, Montgomery Mus Fine Arts, Ala, 78, South Bend Art Ctr, Ind, 79, Mem Art Gallery, Univ Rochester, 79, Neville Pub Mus, Wis, 79; Mickey Mouse: 1928-1978 (cur), Bowers Mus, 78; The Moving Image, art used in animated films, San Jose Mus Art, Calif, 80, Cooper-Hewitt Mus, New York, 81 & Nelson Gallery Art, Kansas City, 81, Mus of Sci & Industry, Chicago, 81; The Engravings of William Hogarth, Bowers Mus, 81; The American Comic Strip, Univ Tex, Arlington, 81, Univ Chicago, 83, Wichita Art Mus, Kans, 84 & Monterey Peninsula Mus Art, Calif, 85, Wash State Capitol Mus, Olympia, 85. *Pos:* Photogr, New York, 53-56; art dir, Orange Co Illus, 62-68, art ed, 70-79; dir, Mus Graphics, 79-; mng editor Country Beautiful, Milwaukee, 60-62. *Teaching:* Instr photog, Lindenhurst High Sch, NY, 53-54; instr, The Cartoon & the Comic Strip in Am, Univ Calif, Irvine, 79; instr design, Orange Coast Col, Costa Mesa, Calif, 97-02. *Awards:* Two Silver Medals, 20th Ann Exhib of Advert & Ed Art in the West, Los Angeles Art Dir Club, 64; Award of Merit, Illustration West, Los Angeles Illusr Club, 72-74; Inkpot Award, San Diego Comic Conv, 80. *Bibliog:* Steven Parker (auth), Comics are collectible, Acquire Mag, 7/77; Paul Maynard (auth), Collecting Can Be a Funny Business, Orange Co Illus, 11/1978; and others. *Mem:* Int Animated Film Soc; Art Mus Asn; Arts Orange Co; Cult Arts Com (City of Costa Mesa); Laguna Art Mus; Orange Co Fine Arts. *Media:* Oil, Photography. *Res:* Developed presentations, 20th century portraiture and Black & White Photogrpahy in NYC in 1950's. *Specialty:* Black & White Photog. *Interests:* 20th Century Am Painting. *Collection:* Cartoons, comic art and original animation art, exhibited in major museums throughout America. *Publ:* Auth, It's Rex Brandt, 10/73 & The comics: worth a second look, 11/73, SW Art; contribr, Mark Rothko, 74 & The Artist as Collector, 75, Newport Harbor Art Mus, Newport Beach, Calif, Mickey Mouse: 1928-1978, Bowers Mus, 78; Arts of Oceania, Shells of Oceania, Bowers Mus, 75; Publication Design & Production, 00. *Dealer:* Showcase Gallery S Coast Plaza Village Santa Ana Calif 92704. *Mailing Add:* Box 11155 Costa Mesa CA 92627

MULLER, MAX PAUL
PAINTER, INSTRUCTOR
b Dover, NJ, Sept 26, 35. *Study:* WVa Wesleyan, BA, 57; studied with Frank Webb, Valfred Thëlin & Fred Messersmith. *Comn:* Six paintings, comn by Dr Jack Corn, Sarasota, Fla, 89; two paintings, Handicapped Children's Ctr, Sarasota, 90. *Exhib:* Fla Watercolor Soc, Rollins Col Mus, Winter Park, 89; Grand Nat Watercolor Exhib, Miss Mus Art, Jackson, 90; Am Artist Prof League, NY, 93; Inst Soc Marine Painters Exhib, Kings Point, NY, 94; solo show, Sarasota Visual Art Ctr, 94; and others. *Pos:* Pres, M P Muller Gallery, Sarasota, Fla, 89- & Art Uptown Gallery, Sarasota, 90-; mem bd dir & exhib chmn, Sarasota Art Asn, Fla, 90; exec dir, Sarasota Visual Art Ctr, 90-96. *Teaching:* Instr watercolor, Sarasota Art Asn, 90-91 & Leach Studios, Sarasota, Fla, 91-; instr, Ringling Sch Art, currently; instr workshop, Epcot Ctr, Disney World, 95 & 96 & Samos, Greece, 96. *Awards:* Award of Merit, Orange Co Arts Coun, 78; Grumbacher Silver Medal, Sarasota Art Asn, 89; Grumbacher Gold Medallion Award, Sarasota Art Asn. *Bibliog:* Joan Altabe (rev), article, Sarasota Herald Tribune, 89; Srotff (auth), Profile, Sarasota Mag, 90; article, Artists Fla Mag, Vol II, Mountain Productions Inc, 90. *Mem:* Am Watercolor Soc; Fla Watercolor Soc; Miami Watercolor Soc; Fla Artists Group; Int Soc Marine Painters; and others. *Media:* Watercolor, Oil. *Specialty:* Original art; contemporary American artists

MULLER, PRISCILLA ELKOW
ART HISTORIAN, CURATOR
b New York, NY, Feb 15, 30. *Study:* Brooklyn Col, BA, 50; New York Univ, Inst Fine Arts, MA, 59, PhD, 63. *Collection Arranged:* Sorolla Paintings The Hispanic Soc Am, NY, 1988; Sorolla, An 80th Anniversary Exhib, NY, 1989; Ignacio Zuloaga in The Hispanic Soc Am, NY, 1991; Spain/Am, Circa 1840-1920, Small Oils by Am and Spanish Artists, NY, 1993; DeGoya a Zuloaga, La Pintura espanola de los siglos XIX y XX en The Hispanic Soc of Am, Madrid/Bilbao/Seville, 2000-01. *Pos:* Asst cur, Hispanic Soc Am, 64-68, cur paintings & metalwork, 68-, cur mus, 70-, cur emer, 95-; consult, Time-Life Bks, 68-69, Tree Publ, 81-82; adv bd, Master Drawings, Archivo Espanol de Arte, Int Found for Art Res. *Teaching:* Lectr, Brooklyn Col, 66. *Awards:* Fel Nat Endowment Arts, 77; Real Acad de Ciencias, Bellas Letras y Nobles Artes de Cordoba; Real Acad de Bellas Artes de San Fernando, Madrid; and others. *Mem:* Am Soc Hispanic Art Hist Studies; Int Comt Fine Arts; Int Coun Mus; Soc Jewelry Historians; Int Found Art Res; and others. *Res:* Spanish and Hispanic fine arts, 15th-20th centuries. *Publ:* contribr, Francisco Goya's Portraits in Paintings, Prints and Drawings, Richmond, 72; auth, Jewels in Spain 1500-1800, New York, 72; Goya's Black Paintings, Truth and Reason in Light and Liberty, New York, 84; and numerous articles in art-hist periodicals; De Goya a Zuloaga (exhib catalog), Madrid, 2000. *Mailing Add:* Hispanic Soc Am Mus Broadway & 155th St New York NY 10032

MULTHAUP, MERREL KEYES
PAINTER, SCULPTOR
b Cedar Rapids, Iowa, Sept 27, 22. *Study:* State Univ Iowa, with Phillip Guston, 42-43; Carnegie Tech, Pittsburgh, 45-49; Summit Art Asn, with Joe Jones, 51; Rice Univ, 72. *Work:* Madonna, Hosp, Montclair, NJ; paintings incl in over 200 pvt collections in US & Europe. *Comn:* Elizabeth Savage (portrait), comn by Francis Savage, London, Eng, 65; Marilyn Joy (portrait), comn by Marilyn Joy, London, Eng, 66; Molly Bing (portrait), comn by John Bing, Houston, Tex, 72; Betty Hittinger (portrait), comn by William Hittinger, Summit, NJ 78; Nancy Soderberg (portrait), comn by Lars Soderberg, Nantucket, Mass; and many other portrait commissions. *Exhib:* 1st Prize Juried Nat, Hartford Atheneum Mus, Conn, 61; Stamford, Mus, Conn, 62; Bridgeport Mus, Conn, 63; Artist's Equity, Newark Mus, NJ, 79; Nat Asn Womens Artists Mem & traveling exhib, 96-99; Nat Asn Women Artists Mem Show, Atelier 14 Gallery, NY, 2000; plus many others incl seven solo shows. *Pos:* Bd mem & chmn statewide exhibs, Summit Art Ctr, NJ, 51-59; bd mem, Silvermine Guild, New Canaan, Conn, 60-64; bd mem & chmn statewide shows, Artists Equity, NJ, 76-83; chmn statewide shows, Assoc Artists, NJ, 86-92; artists adv coun, Hunterdon Art Ctr, Clinton, NJ, 89-92. *Teaching:* Instr oil painting, Summit Art Ctr, NJ, 56-59 & Livingston Night Sch Prog, 57-58; fac, Hunterdon Art Ctr, Clinton, NJ, 84-92. *Awards:* Winsor Newton Award, Acad Design, Nat Asn Women Artists, NY, 58, Dorothy Seligsson Mem Award, 80 & Charlotte Winston Mem Award, 89; and many other awards in Iowa, Pa, NJ, Conn & NY. *Bibliog:* Michael Lenson (auth), Realm of art, Newark News, NJ, many critiques from 54-59. *Mem:* Nat Asn Women Artists Inc (juror); Albuquerque United Artists, NMex; charter mem Nat Mus Women Arts, 82-2004; Silvermine Nat Portrait Group, New Canaan, Conn. *Media:* Oil, Acrylic. *Dealer:* Blankley Gallery 1700 Mountain Ave NW Albuquerque NM. *Mailing Add:* 1321 Stagecoach Rd SE Albuquerque NM 87123

MUNCE, JAMES CHARLES
PRINTMAKER, DRAFTSMAN
b Sioux Falls, SDak, Aug 24, 38. *Study:* Minneapolis Sch Art, BFA, 66; Ind Univ, MFA, 71. *Work:* Brooklyn Mus, NY; Palace Legion Honor, San Francisco, Calif; Boston Printmakers, Mass; Univ Louisville, Ky; Mitsubishi Corp, Tokyo, Japan. *Exhib:* Los Angeles Printmakers 15th Biennial, 98; 43rd Exhib, Hunterdon Mus, NJ, 99; 75th Ann Int Competition, The Print Club, Philadelphia, Pa, 2001; Boston Printmakers, Paint Biennial, 2005; solo exhib, St Bonaventure, NY. *Teaching:* Instr prints, drawing, Univ Hawaii, Honolulu, 71-72; prof prints, drawing, Kans State Univ, Manhattan, 72-2003. *Awards:* Van Derlip Award, Minneapolis Sch Art, 66; Prints & Drawing Fel, Mid Am Arts Alliance, 84; Purchase Award, Boston Printmakers, 86; Chautauqua Inst Award, 92. *Bibliog:* Artists-A Kansas Collection, Rowley & Harper Artists Registry Inc. *Media:* Intaglio. *Dealer:* Strecker Gallery 332 Poyntz Manhattan KS 66502. *Mailing Add:* 1738 Fairchild Manhattan KS 66502

MUNDY, E JAMES
MUSEUM DIRECTOR, EDUCATOR
Study: Vassar Col, BA 74; Princeton Univ, MFA, 77, PhD, 80. *Collection Arranged:* The Draughtsman's Process, Milwaukee Art Mus, 86-87; Hidden Treasures, Milwaukee Art Mus, 87; Rookwood Pottery & the Arts, Milwaukee Art Mus, 87-88; Charting a New Frontier, Milwaukee Art Mus, 88; 1888: Frederick Layton & His World, Milwaukee Art Mus, 88; Renaissance & Baroque Bronzes, Milwaukee Art Mus, 89; Renaissance into Baroque, Milwaukee Art Mus & Nat Acad Design, 89-90; James Ensor Prints, Milwaukee Art Mus, 90. *Pos:* Chief cur, Milwaukee Art Mus, 86-91; dir, Frances Lehman Loeb Art Ctr, 91-. *Teaching:* Asst prof, Mt Holyoke Col, 79-85, assoc prof, 85-86; adj assoc prof, Univ Wis, Milwaukee, 87-91. *Publ:* Auth, Master Drawings Rediscovered, Mt Holyoke, 81; 1888: Frederick Layton and his world, Milwaukee Art Mus, 88; Renaissance into Baroque: Italian Master Drawings, Cambridge Univ Press, 89. *Mailing Add:* Vassar Col 124 Raymond Ave Box 23 Poughkeepsie NY 12601-6198

MUNHALL, EDGAR
CURATOR EMERITUS, EDUCATOR
b Mar 14, 33. *Pos:* Cur Emer, The Frick Collection, NY, 65-. *Teaching:* Instr art hist, Yale Univ, New Haven, Conn, 59-64, asst prof, 64-65; adj prof, Columbia Univ, 79 & 81-. *Awards:* Decorated Officer Ordre des Arts et des Lettres, 2001; Henry Allen Moe Prize, Frick Collection & NY State Hist Soc. *Interests:* 18th and 19th Century French Art. *Mailing Add:* 360 E 55th St Apt 5C New York NY 10022

MUNIOT, BARBARA KING
COLLECTOR
b New Orleans, La. *Study:* Sullins Col, Bristol, Va, art degree; Newcomb Col, spec study with Prof Franklin Adams. *Pos:* Asst dir, Orleans Gallery, 68-70, dir, 70-73; asst dir, Galerie Simonne Stern, 73-75, dir, 75-83. *Specialty:* Contemporary art. *Collection:* Paintings, drawings, prints, photographs & African art. *Mailing Add:* 5954 Laurel St New Orleans LA 70115-2140

MUNITZ, BARRY
ADMINISTRATOR, EDUCATOR, PATRON
b Brooklyn, NY, July 26, 41. *Study:* Brooklyn Col, BA, 63; Princeton Univ, NJ, MA, 65 & PhD, 68; Univ Notre Dame, Hon Dr Laws, 97; Hon Dr, Claremont Univ, Calif State Univ, Whittier Col. *Pos:* Chief Exec Officer & pres, trustee, J Paul Getty Trust, 98-2006; pres & Chief Operating Officer, Federated Develop Co, 82-91; vchmn, Maxxam Inc, LA, 82-91; acad vpres, Univ Ill Syst, 71-76; vpres, dean faculties, Cent campus Univ Houston, 76-77, chancellor, 77-82; chancellor, Calif State Univ system, Long Beach, Calif, 91-98; bd dir, KCET-TV, SLM Holdings, KB Home; trustee, Princeton Univ; chmn, Calif GovTransition Team, formerly. *Teaching:* Asst prof dramatic arts & lit, Univ Calif, Berkeley, 66-68; fac humanities, San Franciso Art Inst, Calif, 69-70; staff associate, Carnegie Comn Highter Educ, 68-70; trustee prof, English Dept, Calif Stae Univ, LA, 2006-. *Awards:* Alumnus award, Bklyn Coll, 79; Alumni Pres medal, Univ Houston, 81; fellow, Am Acad Arts & Sci; Woodrow Wilson fellow; Phi Beta Kappa. *Mem:* Am Asn Mus; art mus vis com, Princeton Univ & Harvard Univ. *Publ:* Auth, The Assessment of Institutional Leadership. *Mailing Add:* English Dept Calif State Univ Engineering and Technology A604 5151 State University Dr Los Angeles CA 90032

MUNIZ, VIK
PHOTOGRAPHER
b Sao Paulo, Brazil, 1961. *Work:* Metrop Mus Art, Mus Mod Art, NY; Mus Fine Arts, Boston; San Francisco Mus Mod Art; Art Inst Chicago. *Comn:* Equivalents (photographs & sculptures), SEI Investments Corp, Oaks, Pa, 98. *Exhib:* Multiples, Aldrich Mus Art, Ridgefield, Conn, 92; The Photog Condition, San Francisco Mus Mod Art, 95; Panorama da Arte Con't Brasileira, Mus de Art Mod, Sao Paulo, 95; Novas Aquisicoes, Mus de Arte Mod do Rio de Janeiro, Brazil, 96; Recent Acquisitions, Metrop Mus Art, NY, 96; New Photog XIII, Mus Mod Art, NY, 97; Beyond the Edges, Insider's Look at Early Photographs, NY, 98; Seeing is Believing, Int Ctr Photog, NY, 98. *Pos:* Ed, Blind Spot, Blind Spot Photog, 93-; contribr, Parkett, Parkett Pub, currently. *Teaching:* Instr drawing for photog, Sch Visual Arts. *Bibliog:* Andy Grundberg (auth), Sweet illusion, Art Forum, 9/97; Vince Aletti (auth), Organized confusion, Village Voice, 12/2/97; Vicki Goldberg (auth), It's a Leonardo? It's a Corot? Well, no, it's a chocolate syrup, NY Times, 12/25/98. *Dealer:* Tricia Collins Contemp Art 83 Grand St Ground Floor New York NY 10013. *Mailing Add:* 169 Bond Brooklyn NY 11217

MUNK, LOREN JAMES
PAINTER, COLLAGE ARTIST
b Salt Lake City, Utah, Sept 9, 51. *Study:* Idaho State Univ, 69-72; Univ Md, Ramstein Army Base, Ger, 73-75; Art Students League, 79. *Work:* Everson Mus, Syracuse, NY; Statue of Liberty Nat Monument; Chase Manhattan Bank, Sony Music Entertainment, Forbes Mag Collection, NY; Port Authority, NY & NJ; Mus City NY; Hood Mus Art, Dartmouth Col, Hanover, NH; numerous pvt colls including Vera List, NY, Dr & Mrs Donald Rubell, NY, Mrs Yitzhak Rabin, Jerusalem, Pierre Huber, Geneva, Tomas Wallin, Stockholm. *Comn:* Poster, Metrop Transit Authority, NY, 91-92; Montparnasse (wall mural), Mayors Office, Paris, 91-93; poster, C&C Vineyards, Bellville/Saone, France, 92; Litfass Design, Int Litfass Biennale, BMW, Munich, 92; mural, Independence Savings Bank, Brooklyn, NY, 95. *Exhib:* Solo shows, Galerie Svetlana & Hubner, Munich, 89, 90 & 92, Elisabeth Krief Galerie D'Art, Paris, 91 Andre Zarre Gallery, NY, 92 & 94 & in conjunction with BMW Introduction of 316i, Munich, 94, Amerikhaus, Munich, 95, Caesaria Gallery, Boca Raton, Fla, 96, Jeffrey Coploff Fine Art Ltd, NY, 97 & L'Antiquario, Sao Paulo, Brasil, 98, Am Contemp Art Gallery, Munich, Ger, 11/2000, 01, 02, MJ Wewerka Galerie, Berlin, Ger, 2002, Andre Zarre Gallery, NY, 2002, Mus Moderner Kunst, Passau, Ger, 2002; Prix de Peinture de Principal de Monaco, Monaco, Gallery Ruf, Munich, 92; Inaugural Exhib, J Claramunt Gallery, NY, 92; Through Thick & Thin, Andre Zarre Gallery, NY, 93; Blue, 450 Broadway Gallery, NY, 96; group shows, Summer Swelter, Gallery e49, NY, Basel Art Fair, Am Contemp Art Gallery, Munich; Mus City of NY, 99; Andre Zarre Gallery, NY, 2000; Am Contemp Art Gallery, Munich, Ger, 2000; many others. *Bibliog:* Robert Morgan (auth), Celebrating the American Vernacular (essay), 94; Hank Schlesinger (auth), Painting the town, Brooklyn Bridge, 12/95; Camila Viegas (auth), Cores vibrantes usadas por Munk establecem dialogo com o olhar, O Estado de S Paulo, 4/22/98; From the Mayors Doorstep, Halasz, Piri, 01/14/2003; New York Art Mag, 2002; Christopher Chambers (auth), Art Picks, Berliner Zeiturg, 9/21/2001. *Media:* Oil with Gold Leaf & Glass Tile. *Res:* Contemporary art. *Mailing Add:* 36 Tiffany Pl Brooklyn NY 11231

MUNO, RICHARD CARL
SCULPTOR, DIRECTOR
b Arapaho, Okla, July 2, 39. *Study:* Okla State Univ Sch Tech Training, cert com art. *Work:* Diamond M Mus, Snyder, Tex. *Comn:* Sculpture of Cavalry Man and Horse, Winchester Firearms, Hartford, Conn, 68; Western Heritage Awards Wrangler Trophy, Nat Cowboy Hall Fame, Oklahoma City, 68; Sculpture of a Lawman, Colt Firearms, Hartford, 73; Sculpture of Cowboy Branding Calf, Oklahoma City CofC, 75; Lifesize Sculpture of Pioneer Man, Bicentennial Comn of Clinton, Okla, 75; Promenade (sq dancers), Oklahoma City Fairgrounds, 89; Memorial (figures & fountains), Edmond Post Off, Okla, 89; Young at Heart (Johnny Kelley figures), Boston Athletic Assoc, Newton, MA, 93. *Exhib:* Philbrook Mus Art Exhib, Tulsa, Okla, 67; Sci & Arts Found Exhib, Oklahoma City, 68; Oklahoma City Zoological Exhib, 68; Okla Mus Art Five State Salon, Oklahoma City, 71-72; Solon Borglum Mem Sculpture Exhib, Nat Cowboy Hall of Fame, Oklahoma City, 75. *Pos:* Preparator, Gilcrease Inst Am Hist & Art, Tulsa, 60-64; cur, Nat Cowboy Hall Fame, Oklahoma City, 65-69, art dir, 70-77, dep dir, 77-78, managing dir, 78-85; sculptor, 85-. *Awards:* Numerous ribbons in various art shows. *Bibliog:* Marcia Preston (auth), Orbit Mag, Okla Publ Co, 68; Dean Krakel (auth), End of the Trail, Okla Univ Press, 73. *Media:* Bronze, Wood. *Collection:* Nat Acad Western Art Ann Exhibs, 73-75. *Publ:* Contribr, Persimmon Hill Mag, 72-75. *Mailing Add:* 6300 E Danforth Edmond OK 73034

MUNOZ, CELIA ALVAREZ
PHOTOGRAPHER
b El Paso, Tex, Aug 15, 37. *Study:* Univ Tex, El Paso, BA, 64; NTex State Univ, Denton, MFA, 82. *Work:* J Paul Getty Mus, Malibu, Calif; Fed Reserve Bank, & Atlantic Richfield Co, Dallas; Sackner Archives, Los Angeles; San Diego Mus Contemp Art, La Jolla, Calif; Longview Mus & Art Ctr, Tex; Mus Fine Art, Houston, Tex; Mus Contemp Art & Art Inst Chicago, Chicago, Ill; El Paso Mus Art, Tex; Carnnegie Mus; JC Penny Collection. *Comn:* Sentimental Journey (photog), Sky Harbor Int Airport Terminal, Pheonix, Ariz; Mind Games, NY Sch Construction Authority; If These Walls Could Speak, The Power of Place Embassey Bldg Proj. *Exhib:* Artist's Eye, Kimbell Art Mus, 89; traveling exhib, Chicano Art Resistance & Affirmation (with catalog), Denver Art Mus, Albuquerque Mus, San Francisco Mus Mod Art, Fresno Art Mus, Tucson Mus Art, Nat Mus Am Art, Washington, Bronx Mus, San Antonio Mus Art, 90; 1991 Biennial Exhib, Whitney Mus Am Art, 91; one-woman shows, San Diego Mus Contemp Art, La Jolla, Calif, 91, Ctr Fine Arts, Miami, 92, Ctr Contemp Art, Santa Fe, 93 Capp St Proj, San Francisco, 94, David Winton Bell Gallery, List Art Ctr, Brown Univ, Providence, RI, 94, Mex Fine Arts Ctr Mus, Chicago, 96 & Roswell Mus & Art Ctr, NMex, 96; traveling exhib, Mapping (with catalog), UTSA Art Gallery, Col Fine Arts & Humanties, San Antonio & NTex State Univ Art Gallery, 94; Diamonds R Forever, Arlington Mus Art, Tex, 94; Arrested Childhood (with catalog), Ctr Contemp Art, N Miami, 94; Mapping, Santa Barbara Contemp Arts Forum, 95; 1995 Triennial, New Orleans Mus Art, 95; AmericaFotoLatina (with catalog), Mus de la Artes, Guadalajara, Jalisco, Mex; Flatbed at Eleven: A Decade + of Collaborative Art, MAC, Dallas, Tex; Then and Now: Polemics of Change, Tyler Mus Art, Tex. *Teaching:* Visiting lectr, Sch Art Inst Chicago, Ill, 92. *Awards:* Grant, Nat Endowment Arts, 91-92; Honors Award, Women's Caucus for Art; Outstanding Centennial Alumnus, Univ N Tex; and many others. *Bibliog:* Lucy Lippard (auth), Slouching Towards 2000: The Politics of Gender, Women & Their Work, Austin, 92; Helen L Kohen (auth), rev, Miami Herald, 4/19/92; Janey Tyson (auth), rev, Ft Worth Star Telegram, 7/25/92; Texas: 150 Weeks from the Mus Fine Arts, Houston, Tex; The Lannan Collection: Modern and Contemporary Art, Art Inst Chicago; Lucy Wippard (auth), The Lure of the Local. *Publ:* auth, If These Walls Could Speak, The Power of Place, 91. *Mailing Add:* 5815 Arbor Valley Dr Arlington TX 76016

MUNOZ, RIE
PAINTER, PRINTMAKER
b Los Angeles, Calif. *Study:* Washington & Lee Univ; Univ of Alaska; pvt lessons. *Work:* Alaska State Mus; Anchorage Hist & Fine Arts Mus; Gov Off, Alaska; Frye Mus, Seattle, Wash. *Comn:* Alaska Coun Churches Mural, Univ Alaska Libr, Fairbanks, 67; Reindeer Round-Up, Reindeer Serv Bur Indian Affairs, 68; Ethnic People of Alaska Mural, Alaska State Libr, Juneau, 69; ChilKat Dancers (mural), Juneau Int Airport; Alaskan Children at Play (mural), Harborview Elementary Sch, Juneau. *Exhib:* Charles & Emma Frye Mus, Seattle, Wash, 73, 75, 81, 86, 89 & 92; Contemp Art from Alaska, Smithsonian Inst, Washington, DC, 78; Alaska Art Tour, 88; Washington Art Tour, 89 & 92; Ore Art Tour, 88, 90 & 94. *Pos:* Political cartoonist, SE Alaska Empire, 52-67; cur exhib, Alaska State Mus, Juneau, 68-72. *Awards:* Outstanding Alaska Artist, Anchorage Fine Arts Mus Asn, 77. *Bibliog:* Article, Artist in Juneau captures Alaska, Alaska Log, 73; Rie Munoz Alaskan Artist, Alaska Northwest Publ Co, 84; Article, Rie Munoz, Alaska Mag, 94. *Media:* Water-Base Colors; Silkscreen and Stone Lithography. *Specialty:* Lithographic prints by Alaskan artists; etchings; engravings; tapestries; Soapstone sculpture; baskets and pottery. *Publ:* King Island Christmas, Greenwillow Books, 85; Runaway Mittens, Greenwillow Books, 88; Andy, Cambridge Univ Press, 88; Rie Munoz Artist in Alaska, pvt publ, 87; Rie Munoz Portrait of Alaska, pvt publ, 95. *Mailing Add:* c/o Rie Munoz Gallery 2101 N Jordan Ave Juneau AK 99801-8047

MUNRO, ELEANOR
WRITER, CRITIC
b Brooklyn, NY, Mar 28, 28. *Study:* Smith Col, BA, 49; Columbia Univ, MA, 65; Sorbonne, Paris. *Pos:* Assoc ed, Art News, New York, 53-59; managing ed, Art News Ann, New York, 54-59. *Teaching:* Multiple vis-lectureships at Am Schs & Cols, 89-. *Awards:* Arts Prize, Cleveland, Ohio, 88; Woodrow Wilson Vis Fel, 89-; Medal, Smith Col, 94; Lifetime achievement award Women's Caucus for Art, 03. *Mem:* Am Asn Art Critics; Int Asn Art Critics; Authors Guild; PEN Am; Art Table. *Res:* American women artists; imagination and the creative process in the visual arts; pilgrimage in myth and art. *Publ:* Auth, Encyclop Art, Western Printing, 61; Originals: American Women Artists, Simon & Schuster, 79 & Touchstone Press, 82, enlarged edit, DA CAPO Press, 2000; On Glory Roads, Pilgrim book about pilgrimage, Thames & Hudson, 87; Memoir of a Modernist's Daughter, Viking, 88; Art in America: Essays by contemp Soviet and Am writers, Univ Wash Press, 90; and auth of essays, articles & reviews in collections, national magazines & newspapers. *Mailing Add:* 176 E 71 St New York NY 10021

MUNRO, JANET ANDREA
PAINTER
b North Reading, Mass, Dec 8, 49. *Study:* Self-taught artist. *Work:* The White House & Smithsonian Inst, Washington, DC; Am Mus, Bath, Eng; Jay Johnson Am Folk Heritage Gallery, NY; and others. *Exhib:* One-woman shows, Country Art Gallery, Locust Valley, NY, 80, Fowler Mills Galleries, Santa Monica, Calif, 80, Art World Gallery, Acton, Mass, 80-81 & America's Folk Heritage Gallery, NY, 81; Easter Egg Roll, White House, Washington, DC, 81; and others. *Bibliog:* Carolyn Norwood (auth), Mrs Munro paints for the White House, Islander Weekly, 81; Kevin Dean (auth), Mrs Munro, Art Voices, 11-12/81; Contemporary primitives, Colonial Homes Mag, 1-2/82. *Media:* Oil, Egg Tempera. *Mailing Add:* c/o Frank J Mick Gallery 1086 Madison Ave New York NY 10028

MUNRO, JP
ARTIST
b Inglewood, Calif, 75. *Exhib:* Ending is Better Than Mending, Sadie Coles HQ, London, 2002; Morbid Curiosity, I-20 Gallery, NY, 2002; Golden, Galerie Michael Jenssen, Cologne, 2003; Drawings, Metro Pictures Gallery, NY, 2003; 100 Artists See God, Inst Contemp Art, London, 2004; JP Munro, 2005; Contemp Art Ctr, Va, 2005; The Early Show, White Columns, NY, 2005; Whitney Biennial, Day for Night, Whitney Mus Am Art, 2006. *Mailing Add:* c/o China Art Objects Gallery 933 Chung King Rd Los Angeles CA 90012

MUNTADAS, ANTONIO
VIDEO ARTIST
b Barcelona, Spain, Sept 21, 42. *Study:* Escuela Technica Superior des Ingenieros Industriales of Barcelona; Pratt Graphic Ctr, NY. *Work:* Guggenheim Mus, NY; Palais de Beaux-Arts, Brussels; Nat Gallery, Ottawa, Can; Galerije Contemp Art, Zagreb; Mus de Arte Contemp, Caracas. *Exhib:* One man shows, Mus Mod Art, NY, 94, Atlanta Col Art, Ga, 96, Mus de Arte Mod, Buenos Aires, Arg, 97, 2000, Arad Mus, Arad, 98, Ludwig Mus, Budapest, Hungary, 98 and others; Mus d'Histoire Geneva, Switz, 99; Mus Art Contemp, Montreal, Can, 2000; Mus d'Arte Mod, Rio de Janeiro, Brazil, 2000; Univ Art Mus, Berkeley, Calif, 2001. *Teaching:* instr sems, Univ Calif, San Diego, Ecole des Beaux-Arts, Bordeaux, San Francisco Art Inst, Ecole Nat des Beaux-Arts, Paris & Univ San Paulo, Cooper Union, NY. *Awards:* Production Grant, Nat Endowment Arts, 91 & 95; Arts Electonica Prix for the File Room, 95; Premi Nac ce Arts Plastigues, Generalitat de Catalunya, 96. *Bibliog:* Susan Snodgrass (auth), Public domain, Muntadas and the file room, New Art Examiner, 10/94; Michael Tarantino (auth), Muntadas, Galerie de l'ancienne poste, Artforum, 2/95; Robert Atkins (auth), Art on line, Art in America, 12/95. *Media:* Mixed Media, Multimedia. *Dealer:* Kent Gallery 67 Prince St New York NY 10012. *Mailing Add:* 395 Broadway Apt 5C New York NY 10013-3540

MUNZNER, ARIBERT
PAINTER, EDUCATOR
b Mannheim, Ger, Jan 9, 30. *Study:* Syracuse Univ, BFA; Cranbrook Acad Art, MFA. *Exhib:* Nat & regional shows, 53-94. *Teaching:* Instr painting & design, Minneapolis Col Art & Design, 55-94, assoc prof painting, Div Fine Arts, 68-76, prof, 76-93, emer prof, 93-. *Mailing Add:* 2749 Bryant Ave S Minneapolis MN 55408-1249

MURAKISHI, STEVE
PRINTMAKING, SCULPTOR
b Honolulu, Hawaii, Dec 14, 49. *Study:* Mich State Univ, ELansing, BFA(sculpture), 72; Cent Mich Univ, Mt Pleasant, MA(printmaking),79; Univ Mich, Ann Arbor, MFA(printmaking), 81. *Work:* Mint Mus, Charlotte, NC; Brooklyn Mus, NY; Va Mus Fine Art, Richmond; Detroit Inst Art, Mich; Newport Harbor Mus Art, Newport Beach, Calif. *Exhib:* Cranbrook Acad Art Mus, Bloomfield Hills, Mich, 90; A Question of Purity, Hoffman Gallery, Ore Sch Arts & Crafts, Portland, 92; group show, Murder as Phenomena, San Francisco, Calif, 93; The Cult of Aesthetics, Ill Westleyan Univ, Bloomington, Ill, 94; Polemical Prints, Ctr Gallery, Detroit, 95; Clear Gravy, GMI, Flint, Mich, 96; Changing Media, Armory Ctr Arts, Pasadena, Calif, 97; A Place in Between, Steelhead Gallery, South Bend, Ind, 97; Re-cycling Ophelia, Site Installation-Cranbrook, Bloomfield Hills, Mich, 97; True Crime, Cranbrook Art Mus, Bloomfield Hills, Mich, 97; Postopia, Craft & Folk Art Mus, Los Angeles, 99. *Pos:* Head printmaking dept, Cranbrook Acad Art, Bloomfield Hills, Mich, 82-. *Teaching:* Instr, Toledo Mus Art Sch, Ohio, 81, Univ Mich, Ann Arbor, 84 & Mich State Univ, E Lansing, 90; instr, Univ Mich, Ann Arbor, 84, Mich State Univ, ELansing, 90. *Awards:* Visual Artists Fel Grant, Workson Paper, Nat Endowment Arts, 89. *Mem:* Col Art Asn. *Publ:* Auth, Morphability Inn America, New Art Examiner, 95

MURANAKA, HIDEO
PAINTER, PRINTMAKER
b Mitaka-shi, Tokyo, Japan, Feb 4, 46, nat US. *Study:* Tokyo Nat Univ Fine Arts & Music, BFA, 70, MFA, 72, cert, 74. *Work:* Brooklyn Mus; Achenbach Found, Calif Palace Legion Hon; Yergeau-Musee Int d'Art, Can. *Exhib:* One Hundred New Acquisitions, Brooklyn Mus, 78; Pacific Coast States Collection From the Vice President's House, Nat Mus Am Art, 81; IEEE Centennial Art Contest, NY, 83; Am Drawing Biennial, Muscarelle Mus Art, 88; Grand Prix de France Int, Chapelle de la Sorbonne, Paris Mus, France, 90. *Teaching:* Instr sumie, Acad Art Col, San Francisco, 74-75 & 84; teacher sumie & calligraphy, Acad Muranaka, San Francisco, 76-79; San Francisco State Univ, 84, 88 & 91-. *Awards:* Second Prize, Mus Hosio, Capranica-Viterbo, Italy, 84, first prize, 88; Hon Mention, San Bernardino Co Mus, Redland, Calif, 85; VJ's Artist Award, Palm Springs Desert Mus, 95. *Bibliog:* Tom Kent (auth), Visuals, City, 5/14/75; Thomas Albright (auth), Art, San Francisco Chronicle, 5/14/75. *Media:* All. *Publ:* auth Art of Japanese Writing and Calligraphy, 1st Books Library, 2000. *Mailing Add:* 179 Oak St No W San Francisco CA 94102

MURASHIMA, KUMIKO
EDUCATOR, TAPESTRY ARTIST
b Nishinomiya, Japan. *Study:* Women's Col Fine Arts, Tokyo, BFA(tfiber arts), 63; Serizawa Dyed Paper Inst, Tokyo, 63-67; Ind Univ, Bloomington, MFA(textiles), 70; Pasons Sch Design, New York, indust textile design cert, 91. *Work:* Evansville Mus Arts & Sci, Ind; Wills Eye Hosp, Philadelphia; Flour Corp Hq, Irvine, Calif; Hackensack Med Ctr, NJ; North Am Re-Insurance Co, NY; Chubb Insurance Corp Hq, NJ; Caxton Commodities, Princeton, NJ; AT&T Telecommuns, NJ; Marck, Sharpe & Dorne, Penn. *Comn:* Metrop design, Properties Inc, Birmingham, Ala, 74; mural (woven tapestry), Disneyland Hotel Convention Ctr, Anaheim, Calif, 75. *Exhib:* NJ State Mus, 78; Artists Equity Triennial Juried Exhib, Mus Philadelphia, Civic Ctr, 81; Oriental Influence in Contemp Am Crafts, The Craftman's Gallery, Scarsdale, NY, 81; Fairmount Inst, Philadelphia, 82; Henry Chauncey Conf Ctr, ETS, Princeton, NJ, 86; Art Alliance, Philadelphia, Pa; Stedman Art Gallery, Rutgers Univ, Camden, NJ, 2000. *Pos:* Freelance fiber artist, Izumi Archit Design, Co, Tokyo, 65-67 & Saphier, Lerner, Schindler, Inc, Environetics, Chicago, Ill, 7-71. *Teaching:* Instr fiber art, Rowan Univ, NJ, 71-75, asst prof, 75-82, assoc prof, 82-. *Awards:* Purchase Award, Mid-States Crafts Show, Malcolm Koch Mus, 69; Mr & Mrs Paul Arnold Merit Award, Mid-States Crafts Show, 70; Dorothy Grafly Mem Award, Artists Equity Triennial Juried Exhib, Philadelphia Civic Ctr Mus, 81. *Bibliog:* Dona Meilach (auth), Art Fabric: Form/Design, Crown Publ, 77; Eva Balassa (auth), article, Fibre Arts, 1-2/79; Burton Wasserman (auth), article, Artcrafts Mag, 8-9/80. *Mem:* Am Fed Col/Univ Fac; Art Educ NJ; Nat Educ Asn; Surface Design Asn; NJ Designer-Craftsmen Inc. *Media:* Tapestry Weaving, Japanese Paste-Resist Dyeing. *Publ:* Contribr, Pamela Scheiman's American Crafts, Am Crafts Coun, 78; Courier Post, Gloucester Times, Philadelphia Inquirer & Philadelphia Bull; Katazome, Altamonte Press, 94. *Dealer:* Dumont-Landis Fine Arts New Brunswick NJ; Faviana-Olivie-Galleria Manhattan Beach CA. *Mailing Add:* PO Box 515 Williamstown NJ 08094

MURCH, ANNA VALENTINA
CONCEPTUAL ARTIST, ENVIRONMENTAL ARTIST
b Dunbarton, Scotland, Dec 7, 48. *Study:* Leicester Polytech, BA, 71; Royal Col Art, London, MA, 73; Archit Asn, London, dipl, 74. *Comn:* If Wishes Were Fishes We Would All Cast Nets (suspended light sculpture Ferrucci Junior High Sch) Puyallup, Wash State Arts Comn, 87; Chaotic Chains, Exploratorium, San Francisco, 89; Railway Suite, outside waiting room, Cal Train Sta Santa Clara, Calif Arts Coun, 90; Everett Arbour (sculptural installation), Everett Community Col, Wash State Arts Comn, 92; Skytones, Seattle Arts Comn, 98; Cycles, The Courtyard, Queens Civic Ct, 97. *Exhib:* Voyages, San Francisco Mus Modern Art, 87; Staged Garden, San Francisco Arts Comn, 87; Memory Stateion, Art Park, Lewiston, NY, 88. *Teaching:* Lectr, Cal Polly Archit Dept, San Luis Obispo, 83, vis artist, 83-85; vis lectr, introd to sculpture, Univ Calif Berkeley, 84-86; vis lectr clay sculpture, San Mateo Community Col, 85; vis artist, East Carolina Univ, 87; vis lectr, San Francisco Art Inst, 87-89; vis artist, Mills Col, 91-92 & asst prof art, 92-. *Awards:* Pro Arts, 83; SECA Award, San Francisco Mus Mod Art, 87; Artist Fel, Calif Arts Coun, 92; and others. *Bibliog:* Francis Butler (auth), Shadow in the visual arts, installation by Murch, Berkeley Monthly, 9/87; A Study in Light & Shadow Landscape Archit, 1/88; Dorothy Burkart (auth), Three who broke barriers, cover story, San Jose Mercury News. *Mem:* San Francisco Art Inst (Artist Comt). *Media:* Multimedia, Sculpture. *Mailing Add:* 499 Alabama St Studio 306 San Francisco CA 94110-1353

MURCHIE, DONALD JOHN
WRITER, ARTIST
b Plainfield, NJ, Nov 23, 43. *Study:* Univ Colo, BA; Dalhousie Univ, MLS. *Exhib:* Dalhousie Art Gallery, 82; Eye Level Gallery & Owens Art Gallery, 95. *Pos:* Libr dir, NS Col Art & Design, Halifax, 72-90; assoc curator, Art Gallery NS, 95. *Awards:* Fel Nat Gallery Can, 95-96. *Mem:* Art Libr Soc/NAm (mem exec bd, 75-78, chmn, 76). *Media:* Mixed. *Res:* Contemporary art; Canadian art history. *Publ:* Auth, A Quiet Evening, 79; Opening, Open, Closed, Eye Level Gallery, 80; An Invitation; or One-Way Ticket, 83; Seven, 96; Anaesthetic, 96. *Mailing Add:* 178-Pond Shore Rd Sackville NB E4L 1K8 Canada

MURDOCH, JOHN
MUSEUM DIRECTOR
Pos: asst dir, collections Victoria and Albert Mus, London; gallery dir, Courtauld Inst, Univ London, 1993-2002; dir, Huntington Art Collections, San Marino, Calif, 2002-. *Mailing Add:* Huntington Art Collections 1151 Oxford Rd Pasadena CA 91108

MURDOCK, GREG
PAINTER
b Saskatoon, Sask, Can. *Study:* Univ Sask, BFA, 77; Inst Allende, San Miguel De Allende, Mex, 77-78; Emily Carr Col Art & Design, 79-81. *Work:* Osler-Hoskin, McMillan-Binch, Guaranty Trust, Midland-Doherty, Abols & Posthumous & Conwest Exploration Ltd, Toronto, Ont; Air Can & Maison Alcan Inc, Montreal, Que; Ring House Gallery, Edmonton, Alta; First City Trust, Vancouver, BC; Dept External Affairs, Ottawa; Microsoft Corp, Seattle; Disney Corp, Los Angeles; others. *Exhib:* Solo exhibs, 49th Parallel Ctr for Contemp Canadian Art (with catalog), NY, 85, Equinox Gallery, Vancouver, BC, 86, 88, 90, 92, 94 & 95 Tableaux (with catalog), 96, 98, 2000, Southern Alta Art Gallery, Lethbridge, 87, Olga Korper Gallery, Toronto, Ont, 87, 89, 91, 93, 96, 99, 2002, Littlejohn-Smith Gallery, NY, 87, Greg Murdock: On Paper, Kelowna Art Gallery, BC, 95 & Charles H Scott Gallery, Granville Island, Vancouver, BC, 95, Gail Harvey Gallery, Los Angeles, 97, 2001; Just a Taste of the Claridge Collection, Saidye Bronfman Centre, Montreal, Que, 92; A Taste of the Claridge Collection, Can Clay & Glass Gallery, Waterloo, Ont, 93; 64-94 Contemp Decades, Emily Carr Inst Art & Design, Vancouver, BC, 94; Hidden Values: Western Corporations Collect, Edmonton Art Gallery, Alta, 94. *Bibliog:* Elizabeth Godley (auth), review, Vancouver Sun, 9/14/88; Art Perry (auth), review, Province, Vancouver, 9/12/88; Monico Forestall (auth), review, Can Art Mag, spring 88. *Mailing Add:* c/o Olga Korper Gallery 17 Morrow Ave Toronto ON M6R 2H9 Canada

MURDOCK, ROBERT MEAD
CURATOR
b New York, NY, Dec 18, 41. *Study:* Trinity Col, BA, 63; Yale Univ, MA(hist art), 65; Mus Mgt Inst, Univ Calif, Berkeley, 80. *Collection Arranged:* Poets of the Cities: New York and San Francisco, 1950-1965, Dallas Mus Fine Arts, 74; Berlin/Hanover: The 1920s, Dallas Mus, 1977; Pioneers: Early 20th Century Art from Midwestern Mus, Grand Rapids Art Mus, 81; Richard Tuttle: Books and Prints, Trinity Col with NY Pub Libr (auth catalog), 96 & Lesley Dill, Trinity Col (auth catalog), 98; plus

others. *Pos:* Ford Found Mus Curatorial Training Prog interne, Walker Art Ctr, Minneapolis, 65-67; cur, Albright-Knox Art Gallery, Buffalo, 67-70; cur contemp art, Dallas Mus Fine Arts, 70-78; dir, Grand Rapids Art Mus, 78-83; chief cur, Walker Art Ctr, 83-85; program dir, IBM Gallery Sci & Art, New York, 85-87 & 90-93; dir exhib, Am Fedn Arts, New York, 88; independent cur, 93-. *Awards:* Nat Endowment for the Arts Fels for Mus Prof, 73. *Mem:* Int Asn Art Critics. *Res:* 20th century, especially constructivism, and recent American painting and sculpture. *Publ:* Variations on Geometry in Tyler Graphics: The Extended Image, Walker Art Ctr, 87; Gerald Murphy, Cole Porter and Within the Quota, Paris Modern, Fine Arts Mus San Francisco, 95; Jim Torok, Bill Maynes Gallery, New York, 99; Leland Bell, Swarthmore Col, 2001; Debra Bermingham, DC Moore Gallery, NY, 2002; intro, John Evans: Collages, The Quantuck Lane Press, 2004. *Mailing Add:* 202 First Ave No 14 New York NY 10009

MURPHY, CATHERINE E
PAINTER
b Cambridge, Mass, Jan 22, 46. *Study:* Skowhegan Sch Painting & Sculpture, with Elmar Bichoff, summer 66; Pratt Inst, BFA, 67. *Work:* Metrop Mus Art, Whitney Mus Art & Mus Mod Art, NY; Hirshhorn Mus & Sculpture Garden & Phillips Collection, Washington, DC; permanent collections Chase Manhattan Bank, NY City, Hirshhorn Mus & Sculpture Garden, Washington, Metrop Mus Art, New York City, Newark Mus, NJ Art Mus, Trenton, Phillips Collection, Washington, Va Mus Fine Arts, Richmond, Weatherspoon Art Gallery, Greensboro, NC, Whitney, Mus Am Art, New York City. *Exhib:* Whitney Mus Am Art Ann, NY, 71; Whitney Mus, NY, 73; Contemp Am Realism, Pa Acad Fine Arts, 81; Am Realism: Twentieth Century Drawings & Watercolors, San Francisco Mus Mod Art, 85; Am Acad Inst Arts & Lett, NY, 79, 87, 89, 90; The Window in Twentieth Century Art, Neuberger Mus, Purchase, 86; Making Their Mark: Women Artists Move into the Mainstream, Cincinnati Art Mus, 89; Solo exhib, Lennon, Weinberg Gallery, NY, 89, 92, 95 & 98; NY Realism-Past & Present, Tampa Mus Art, 94; Catherine Murphy: Paintings 1990-1994, Greenville Co Mus, 94; Inspired by Nature, Neuberger Mus Art, Purchase, NY, 94; Reality Bites, Kemper Mus Contemp Art, Kansas City, 95; Biennial, Whitney Mus Am Art, 95; Still-Life: The Object in Am Art 1915-1995 - Selections from the Metrop Mus of Art, Am Fed Arts, NY, 97-98; Whitney Mus Art, Philbrooke Mus, Ashville Art Mus, NC; Apex Art Curatorial Prog, New York City, 1997; DC Moore Gallery, New York City, 1999. *Teaching:* Senior critic, Yale Univ, 89-94. *Awards:* Purchase Award, Am Fedn Arts, 71; Nat Endowment Arts, 79 & 89; Guggenheim Fel, 82; Ingram Merrill Found Grant, 86; Art Award, Am Acad & Inst Arts & Letters, 90. *Bibliog:* John Gruen (auth), Catherine Murphy: The rise of a cult figure, ARTnews, 12/78; Gerrit Henry (auth), The Figurative Field, Art in Am, 1/94; Francine Prose (auth), Catherine Murphy, BOMB, fall 95. *Mem:* Nat Acad (academician). *Media:* Oil. *Dealer:* Lennon Weinberg Inc 560 Broadway Suite 308 New York NY 10012-3945. *Mailing Add:* c/o Lennon Weinberg Inc 514 W 25th St Apt 1 New York NY 10001-5585

MURPHY, DUDLEY C
EDUCATOR, GRAPHIC DESIGNER
b Danville, Ky, Apr 16, 40. *Study:* Univ Tulsa, BA, 65, MA, 69; Univ Okla, MFA, 71. *Exhib:* Okla Art Ctr, Oklahoma City, 70; Contemp Int Landscape Sculpture, traveling, Mo Arts Coun, 72; Nelson Gallery Art, St Louis, Mo, 74; Joslyn Art Mus, Omaha, Nebr, 74; SDak Art Ctr, Brookings, 75; Pittsburg State Univ, Kans, 79; and others. *Pos:* Design & layout artist, Litho Art Serv, Tulsa, Okla, 66-68; design & layout artist, Pub Relations Int Ltd, 68-69; owner & creative dir, Adworks, Springfield, Md, currently; ed, designer & publ, Nat Fishing Lure Collectors Mag, currently. *Teaching:* Instr design, SW Mo State Univ, Springfield, 69 70; cur educ, Springfield Art Mus, Mo, 71-78; assoc prof, Drury Col, Springfield, Mo, 78-. *Awards:* First Place, 80 & Merit Award, 82, Springfield Ad Club; Merit Awards, Springfield Ad Club, 89, 90 & 91. *Bibliog:* Edgar A Albin (auth), Dudley Murphy, Artcraft Mag, 80. *Mem:* Springfield Ad Club; Nat Coun Ceramic Arts. *Publ:* Auth, Straw, pvt publ, 71. *Mailing Add:* 1418 E Portland St Springfield MO 65804-1221

MURPHY, HASS
SCULPTOR, DRAFTSMAN
b Boston, Mass, Nov 1, 50. *Study:* Pratt Inst. *Exhib:* Romantic Abstraction, Brandeis Univ, Waltham, Mass, 71; Works on Paper, Logic Transformations, Contemp Arts Gallery, NY, 74; Biennial Exhib, Whitney Mus Am Art, NY, 75; New Drawings, NY, Grapestake Gallery, San Francisco, 75; Spare, Cent Hall Gallery, NY, 75. *Bibliog:* Interview, Seven Painters, Artrite, spring 75; Judy Rifka & Willy Lenski (dirs), Ten Studios (film), Basel Art Fair, 75. *Media:* Steel, Limestone. *Dealer:* Nancy Lurie Gallery 1632 N La Salle Chicago IL 60614; Nancy Lurie Gallery 230 E Ohio St Chicago IL 60611. *Mailing Add:* 8 Locust Ridge Cold Spring NY 10516-1902

MURPHY, MARILYN L
PAINTER, EDUCATOR
b Tulsa, Okla, Sept 22, 50. *Study:* Okla State Univ, BFA, 72; Univ Okla, MFA, 78. *Work:* Okla State Collection, Oklahoma City; State Univ NY, Potsdam; Boston Mus & Sch; Cheekwood Mus Art, Univ Wis, Parkside; Kemper Collection; Tenn State Mus. *Comn:* Shelter (color drawing), Prudential, Chicago; graphite drawing, Carroll Corp-Citi Corp, Nashville; Night Theatre, WDCN-PBS TV, Nashville; color drawing, Third Nat Corp, Nashville; Home (graphite drawing), Tenn Humanities Comn, Nashville. *Exhib:* San Diego Art Inst, Calif, 94; Nat Acad Design, NY, 96; Alexandria Mus Art, La, 98; Huntsville Mus Art, Ala, 2000; Armory Arts Ctr, West Palm Beach, Fla, 2000; One-woman show Artemisia Gallery, Chicago, Ill, 2000; Mid Career Survey, First Ctr for the Visual Arts, Nashville, Tenn. *Collection Arranged:* Dangerous Works, 82, Vanderbilt Univ, Nashville, Tenn; The Home Show, Tenn Arts Comn Invitational, 86; Dixie to Down Under, Perc Tucker Regional Gallery, Townsville, Australia & Sarratt Gallery, Vanderbilt, Univ, 92. *Pos:* Drafter Geophysical Archit Drafting Rm, Oklahoma City, Okla, 74-76; geological drafter, John A Taylor Petrol Exploration, Oklahoma City, 76-77. *Teaching:* Instr drawing & prints, Univ Okla, Norman, 78-80; prof painting & drawing, Vanderbilt Univ, 80-, chair Fine Arts, 97-99. *Awards:* Fel, Southern Arts Fed, 90; Fel Panelist Arts Midwest Works on Paper Grants, 94; Nat Painting Competition, Cheekwood Mus Art, Nashville, Tenn, 95. *Bibliog:* article, Southern Quart, Univ Southern Miss, spring 91; The Democratic Print (CD-Rom catalog), Wright State Univ, 97; Off the Wall Virtual Gallery (website), 97-; Lucy Lippard & Mark Scala (auth's), Suspended Animation: The work of Marilyn Murphy. *Mem:* Sinking Creek Film Festival (vpres, bd dir, 87-97). *Media:* Drawing, Painting. *Dealer:* Cumberland Gallery Nashville TN. *Mailing Add:* c/o Cumberland Gallery 4107 Hillsboro Circle Nashville TN 37215

MURPHY, MARY M
PAINTER, INSTRUCTOR
b Staten Island, NY, Mar 29, 58. *Study:* Tyler Sch Art, Philadelphia, 76-78, MFA(painting), 91; Columbia Univ, BA(eng & writing), 81; Va Ctr Creative Arts, 85-86; NY Studio Sch, 86-87; Skowhegan Sch Painting & Sculpture, Maine, 90. *Work:* Ark Art Ctr; Brooklyn Mus, NY; Wilmington Trust, Los Angeles; Am Express, NY. *Exhib:* Vibology, White Columns, NY, 92; 14 at 55, 55 Mercer St, NY, 94; Rhythm Bouquet, 558 Broome St, NY, 94; Current Abstraction, Tyler Sch Art, Philadelphia, 94; solo exhibs, SPACES, Cleveland, Ohio, 94 & Larry Becker Contemp Art, Philadelphia, 95, Fleisher Art Mem, Philadelphia, 95, Schmidt/Dean Gallery, Pa, 99 & DFN Gallery, NY, 99; Flirting From a Distance, Del Ctr Contemp Art, Wilmington, 97; Abstract Strategies, Philadelphia Art Alliance, Pa, 97; Collector's Choice, NJ Ctr Visual Arts, Summit, 98; Painting Pictures; rendering the (photo) real, Beaver Col, Pa, 99; and many others; Conceptual Abstraction, Univ of Arts, Phildelphia, 2000. *Teaching:* Instr, Fleisher Art Mem, Philadelphia, 92-98, Tyler Sch Art, 95; vis artist, Ohio State Univ, 93 & 97; instr artist, Inst Arts in Ed, Pa, 94 & 97; sr lectr, Univ Arts, Philadelphia, 96, asst prof, 2000-; lectr, Wash Univ, Mo, 98-; and many other lectures throughout US. *Awards:* Nat Endowment Arts Fel, 93-94; Fleisher Challenge Grant, Fleisher Art Mem, Philadelphia, 94; Indiv Fel Painting, Pa State Coun Arts, 98; and others. *Bibliog:* Robin Rice (auth), various articles in Philadelphia City Paper, 92-97; Victoria Donohoe (auth), various articles in Philadelphia Inquirer, 93-97; Edward Sozanski (auth), Making the Case for Abstraction as Natural, 11/4/94, Fleisher Art Memorial, 2/10/95, A Sampling of Abstraction From the Region, 1/98, Assesing Photography's Impact on Painting, 3/12/99 & Signaling Feeling with Deft Brushstrokes, 6/18/99; Liam Otten (auth), Campus Artists, Wash Univ Record, 2/25/99; Sid Sachs (auth), Conceptual Abstraction, Univ of Arts, 12/2000; and many others. *Mem:* Col Art Asn; Tyler Alumni (bd, 93-). *Media:* Oil. *Publ:* Auth, various articles in The New Art Examiner, 91-98; Drawing Rules (exhib catalog essay), 3/99. *Mailing Add:* 21 Whitemarsh Ave Erdenheim PA 19038

MURPHY, SUSAN AVIS MURPHY COLOMBINI
PAINTER
b New London, Conn, Sept 18, 1950. *Study:* Col New Rochelle, with William Maxwell, 78-79. *Work:* General Motors, US Gypsum, Int Harvester, Quaker Oats, Beatrice; FDIC; Mich Belle; Dataprompt. *Exhib:* Southern Watercolor Soc, 81-86, 90 & 93; Allied Artists Am, Nat Arts Club, NY, 81 & 82; Am Watercolor Soc, Nat Acad Design, NY, 82; Butler Inst Am Art Midyear Show, 82-88. *Pos:* Mgr, Falling Acorns Editions, 86-. *Teaching:* Instr watercolor, Falling Acorns Studio, Sandy Spring, Md, 86-. *Awards:* Gold Medal, Catharine Lorillard Wolfe Art Club 87th Ann, 79; Gold Medal, Baltimore Watercolor Soc Mid-Atlantic Exhib, 86; First Prize, Southern Watercolor Soc, 93. *Bibliog:* The Watercolor Page: Susan Murphy, Am Artist Mag, 3/86; Dream Studio, Am Artist Mag, 5/91. *Mem:* Watercolor Soc, Southern & Baltimore. *Media:* Watercolor. *Publ:* Orange Marmalade, Falling Acorns Editions, 91; Carnations and Lace & Dear Diary, Front Line Graphics, 92. *Dealer:* Miriam Perlman Inc Lake Point Tower Suite 5410 Chicago IL; McBride Gallery 215 Main Street Annapolis MD 21401. *Mailing Add:* 17520 Dr Bird Rd Sandy Spring MD 20860

MURRAY, ELIZABETH
PAINTER
b Chicago, Ill, 40. *Study:* Art Inst Chicago, BFA, 62; Mills Col, MFA, 64; Sch Art Inst Chicago, Hon Degree, 92; RI Sch Design, Hon Degree, 93. *Work:* Detroit Inst Arts; Guggenheim Mus, NY; Hirshhorn Mus, Washington; McCrory Corp, NY; Art Inst Chicago. *Exhib:* Solo shows include Pacewildstein, NY, 2006; group shows include Continuing Abstraction in Am Art, Whitney Mus Am Art, 74; Biennial Exhib, Whitney Mus Am Art, 77; Nine Artists, Solomon R Guggenheim Mus, 77; Biennial Exhib, Whitney Mus Am Art, 79; The Decade in Review: Selections from the 1970s, Whitney Mus Am Art, 79; Biennial Exhib, Whitney Mus Am Art, 81; Surveying the Seventies: Selections from the Permanent Collection of the Whitney Mus of Am Art, Whitney Mus Am Art, 82; Abstract Drawings, 1911-1981, Whitney Mus Am Art, 82; Some Contemp Acquisitions: Painting & Sculpture, Mus Mod Art, NY, 83; Minimalism to Expressionism: Painting & Sculpture Since 1965 from the Permanent Collection, Whitney Mus Am Art, 83; Some Contemp Prints, Mus Mod Art, NY, 83; The Am Artist as Printmaker: 23rd Nat Print Exhib, Brooklyn Mus, NY, 83-84; Am Art Since 1970: Painting, Sculpture & Drawings from the Collection of the Whitney Mus of Am Art, Whitney Mus Am Art, 84; Currents, Inst Contemp Art, Boston, 84; An Int Survey of Painting & Sculpture, Mus Mod Art, NY, 84; Contemp Installation, Mus Mod Art, NY, 84; Viewpoint 84: Out of Square, Cranbrook Acad Art Mus, 84; 1985 Biennial Exhib, Whitney Mus Am Art, 85; Pub & Pvt: Am Prints Today: The 24th Nat Print Exhib, Brooklyn Mus, NY, 86; Recent Acquisitions, Whitney Mus Am Art, 86; Philadelphia Collects: Art Since 1940, Philadelphia Mus Art, 86; 20th Century Drawings from the Whitney Mus of Am Art, Whitney Mus Am Art, 88; First Impressions: Early Prints by 46 Contemp Artists Traveling Show, Walker Art Ctr, 89; Whitney Biennial, Whitney Mus Art, 91; Timely & Timeless, Aldrich Mus Art, 93-94; One-person exhibs, Locks Gallery, Philadelphia, 93 & 95, Gemini GEL at Joni

Moisant Weyl, NY, 93, 94 & 96, Susanne Hilberry Gallery, Birmingham, Mich, 94, John Berggruen Gallery, San Francisco, 94, Paula Cooper Gallery, 94, Richard Feigen Gallery, Chicago, 95, Lafayette Col Art Gallery, Pa, 96, Va Commonwealth Univ, Anderson Gallery, Richmond, 98 & Susanne Hilberry Gallery, Birmingham, Mich, 2000, Pace Wildenstein, NY, 96, 97, 99, 2002, 2003; Evolutions in Expression: Minimal & Postminimalism from the permanent collection of the Whitney Mus of Am Art, Whitney Mus Am Art, 94; More Room for a View, Prints & Drawings Gallery, Brooklyn Mus, NY, 94; Jaffe-Friedet & Strauss Galleries, Hopki Ctr for the Arts, Dartmouth Col, Hanover, NH, 2002; IVAM, Inst Valencia d Art Modern, 2005; Mus Modern Art, NY, 2005; Maier Mus Art, Lynchburg, Va, 2005; Jaffe-Friede Strauss Galleries, Hanover, NH, 2005. *Collection Arranged:* Artist's Choice--Elizabeth Murray: Modern Women, Mus Modern Art, NY, 95; IVAM, Inst Valencia d'Art Modern, 05. *Teaching:* Instr painting, Bard Col, 74-75 & 76-77; vis prof painting, Calif Inst Arts, Valencia, 75-76; vis instr, Wayne State Univ, 75, Art Inst Chicato, 75-76 & Calif Inst Arts, 75-76; instr, Princeton Univ, NJ, 77, Yale Univ, New Haven, Conn, 78-79 & Sch Visual Arts, NY, 78-80; lectr, NY Studio Sch Drawing, Painting & Sculpture, NY, 87. *Awards:* Walter M Campana Award, Art Inst Chicago, 82; Skowhegan Prize Painting, 86; Larry Aldrich Prize Contemp Art, 93. *Bibliog:* Donald Kuspit (auth), Elizabeth Murray's dandyish abstraction, Artforum, 2/78; Jeff Perone (auth), rev in Artforum, 1/79; John Russell (auth), Elizabeth Murray's shaped canvases, NY Times, 6/9/81; Robert Storr (auth), Added dimension, Parkett, No 8, 86. *Mem:* Am Acad; Am Inst Arts & Lett. *Media:* Oil on Canvas. *Mailing Add:* c/o PaceWildenstein 32 E 57th St New York NY 10022

MURRAY, FRANCES
PHOTOGRAPHER

b Drugheda, Ireland, Sept 17, 47. *Study:* Self-taught. *Work:* Fine Arts Mus, Houston, Tex; Int Mus Photog at George Eastman House, Rochester, NY; Ctr for Creative Photog, Tucson, Ariz; Santa Barbara Mus Art, Calif; Okla Mus Art; Mus Photog Art, Belboa Park, San Diego, Calif; pvt collections include Laurence Miller, NY, Robert Taub, Mich, Mr & Mrs Woody Flowers, NY, Michael Stern, Tucson, Omar Claiborne, Tucson, Law Offices of Minnette Burges, Tucson, Desert Whale Jojoa Co Inc, Tucson, Presidio Grill, Tucson, John Richards, Tucson, Colistia Soble, Tucson, Marguerite & Sandy Mescel, Tucson, many others. *Exhib:* One-person exhibs, Univ Wis, Superior, 82, Etherton Gallery, Tucson, Ariz, 83, Neikrug Photographica Gallery, NY, 85, Univ Mo, St Louis, 87, Dinnerware Artists Coop Gallery, Tucson, Ariz, 89, Zeit Foto Gallery, Tokyo, Japan, 89, Temple Gallery/Etherton Stern, Tucson, Ariz, 92; Dinnerware Artists Coop Gallery, 85, 87, 89 & 90, Ctr for Creative Photog, Snell & Wilmer Collection, 90, New Acquisitions, Tucson, Ariz, 90, Tucson Mus Art/Fine Art for Fine Causes, 91; Etherton Stern Gallery, Tucson, 94; Luxarte Gallery, Canyon Rach, Tucson, 97; Etherton Gallery, Tucson, 96, 99; Dinnerware Contemp Gallery, Tucson, 99; Davis-Domingus Gallery, Tucson, 96; Mus Fine Arts, Houston, 93; Santa Barbara Mus Art, Calif, 89; and many others. *Pos:* Photogr & admin asst, Ariz Hist Soc. *Teaching:* lectr Saga Jr Col of Art, Kyoto, 88, Japan Photographic Col, Kyoto, 88, Internat House of Japan, Tokyo, 88, Ctr for Creative Photography, 90, Northlight Gallery, Ariz State Univ, 93. *Awards:* Nat Endowment Visual Artists, 86; Nat Endowment Arts US/Japan Exchange Fel, 87; Tucson Pima Arts Coun Visual Fel, 91. *Bibliog:* Photography for the Art Market, Watson Guphill Publ, 90. *Mailing Add:* 301 E Fourth St Tucson AZ 85705

MURRAY, IAN STEWART
SCULPTOR, CONCEPTUAL ARTIST

b Pictou, NS, Nov 4, 51. *Study:* NS Col Art & Design, BFA(fine art), 72. *Work:* Art Gallery Ont; Can Coun Art Bank, Ottawa; Nat Gallery Can; Banff Ctr Walter Phillips Gallery; Art Metropole. *Comn:* Changing Channels (3 color monos), Projections: Positions- Point of View (audio/video collage) & NOVA BOETIA-Another World, Halifax, Dartmouth & Sackville Community TV Stas, NS, 76; Tutorial: Radio by Artists, Fine Arts Broadcast Serv, Toronto, Ont, 80; DIET: Television by Artists, Fine Arts Broadcast Serv, Toronto, Ont, 80; The Lunatic of One Idea, Public Access Videowall series, Mississauga, Ont, 88. *Exhib:* Record as Art, Royal Col Art, London, 73; Audio Scene, Mod Art Galerie, Wein, Austria, 79; Books by Artists, 80-82; Biennale of Sydney, Australia, 82; Second Link, Banff Mus Art & traveling, 83; From Sea to Shining Sea, Power Plant, Toronto, 88; solo exhibs, Vancouver Art Gallery, 88, Definity Super, Thunder Bay, 89, White Water Gallery, NBay, Ont, 91, Macintosh Gallery, London, Ont, 93, Peterborough Art Gallery, 96 & Wynick Tuck Gallery, Toronto, 96 & 98; Art Gallery of Ontario, 99; Art Metropole, 2000, 2001, 2002; National Gallery of Canada, Ottawa, 2000; Univ Toronto, Blackwood Gallery, Edmonton Art Gallery, Edmonton Albonta, 2003. *Collection Arranged:* Attitudes Toward Photography (auth, catalog), Ann Leonowens Gallery, 72; Radio by Artists, 80. *Pos:* Bd govs planning & priority comt & chmn film/photog/video comt, Toronto Arts Coun, 86-92. *Teaching:* Instr, Media Arts Film & Video Courses & Film Tech Studies, Ryerson Polytech Inst, Toronto, 86-87. *Awards:* Can Coun Awards, 89; Medal Serv, City Toronto, 91; Ont Arts Coun Awards, 94; and others. *Bibliog:* Phillip Monk (auth), Television by artists, Can Forum, 81; Mary-Beth Laviolette (auth), Audio by artists, Vanguard Mag, 4/83; Jill Pollack (auth), Work rich in meaning, metaphor, Vancouver Courier, BC, 88. *Mem:* Artists Union; Can Artists Representation; Charles Street Video Soc (bd mem, 92-93); Toronto Arts Coun (bd dir, 86-92); Art Metropole (bd mem) 93-; Art Gallery Toronto (artist, life mem). *Media:* Multimedia; Collage. *Publ:* Auth, Twenty Waves in a Row, Straw Books, 71; Media Arts, Ontario Arts Council, 89; others. *Dealer:* V/Tapes Toronto Canada; Art Metropole Toronto Canada. *Mailing Add:* 10 Dora Ave Suite 807 Toronto ON M6H 4J2 Canada

MURRAY, JOAN
CRITIC, PHOTOGRAPHER

b Annapolis, Md, Mar 6, 27. *Study:* Calif Col Arts & Crafts, San Francisco Art Inst; Ruth Bernard Insight Studio; Univ Calif Exten; also studied with Wynn Bullock. *Work:* Int Mus Photog, Eastman House, Rochester, NY; San Francisco Mus Mod Art; Oakland Mus, Calif. *Exhib:* Male Nudes--One Man, Mind's Eye Gallery, Vancouver, BC, 73; 7 Visions, Heller Gallery, Berkeley, 89 & self portrait, 91; Children of Our Times, Steven Wirtz Gallery, San Francisco, 87; Joan Murray, Retrospective 1967-1992, Vision Gallery, San Francisco, 92; In Front of the Lens: Portraits of California Photographers, Oakland Mus, 96-97; A History of Women Photographers, NY Pub Libr, Smithsonian, Santa Barbara Mus & Akron Ohio Mus, 97-98; and others. *Pos:* Photog ed, Artweek, 69-; W Coast critic, Popular Photog, 75-77; contrib ed, Am Photogr, 78-81; consult, Photog Dept, Getty Mus, 86; mgr assoc, Art Studio, Univ Calif, 87-. *Teaching:* Instr photog, Univ Calif Exten, 70-82; instr photog, City Col San Francisco, 75-82; Friends of Photog Workshops, 90. *Awards:* Nat Endowment Arts Grant Art Criticism, 78. *Bibliog:* Naomi Rosenblatt (auth), A History of Women Photographers, Abbeyville Press, 94; Hisaki Kojima (ed), San Francisco Nude, Siskosa Publ, 95; Peter Palmquist (auth), Women In Photography, 96. *Mem:* Int Asn Art Critics; Soc Encouragement Contemp Art San Francisco Mus Art; San Francisco Mus Mod Art Foto Forum. *Dealer:* Vision Gallery 1155 Mission St San Francisco CA 94103. *Mailing Add:* 120 Blair Ave Piedmont CA 94611

MURRAY, JOHN MICHAEL
PAINTER

b Tampa, Fla, May 28, 31. *Study:* Univ Tampa, BA, 63; Ohio Univ, MFA, 65. *Work:* Staten Island Mus, NY; Bundy Art Mus, Waitsfield, Vt; NS Col Art, Halifax; NJ Mus. *Exhib:* Int Print Exhib, Crakow, 75; Langsam Gallery, Melbourne, Australia, 75; 19 Nat Print Exhib, Brooklyn Mus, 75; One-man shows, Dorsky Gallery, NY, 72, Halifax, 72, Blue Parrot, NY, 74 & Am Ctr, Belgrade, 81. *Teaching:* Chmn dept fine arts, New York Inst Technol, 66-. *Awards:* First Prize in Painting, Fla State Ann, 63. *Mem:* Am Asn Univ Prof; Col Art Teachers. *Publ:* Contribr, Art Work--No Commercial Value, Grossman, 72; Pratt Graphics Reprint, 74. *Dealer:* James Yu Gallery 393 W Broadway New York NY 10012. *Mailing Add:* 124 W Houston St No 4 New York NY 10012-2558

MURRAY, JUDITH
PAINTER

b New York, NY. *Study:* Pratt Inst, Brooklyn, NY, BFA, 62, MFA, 64; Acad Fine Arts, Madrid, Spain, 63. *Work:* Brooklyn Mus, NY Pub Libr & Chase Manhattan Bank, NY; Libr Cong; Nat Mus Am Art, Washington; Mus Modern Art, NY; Brit Mus. *Comn:* Poster & print, Mostly Mozart Festival, Avery Fisher Hall, Lincoln Ctr, NY, 81 & 86; poster & print, Mozart Bicentennial, Lincoln Ctr, 91 & 92. *Exhib:* Print Exhib, Brooklyn Mus, NY, 62; Solo exhibs, The ClockTower, Inst Art & Urban Resources, NY, 78, Dallas Mus Fine Arts, 82 & Bronx Mus Arts, 86; 1979 Biennial Exhib, Whitney Mus Am Art, NY, 79; traveling exhibs, Art in Our Time, 80-82, A Living Tradition-Selections from Am Art Asn (Eur, Can, Near East), 86, Lines of Vision, Drawings by Contemp Women (US & Eur), 89-91; The Persistence of Abstraction, Noyes Mus, NJ, 94; Conde Gallery, NY; Int Invitational Paintings & Sculpture, Am Acad Arts & Letts, NY; Newhouse Ctr Contemp Art, NY, 97; Solo shows, Schmidt Dean Gallery, Phila, 98, Ben Shahn Gallery, William Patterson Univ, Wayne, NJ, 99, Gibson Mus, SUNY at Potsdam, 2000, Mus Mod Art, Long Island City, NY, 2001, Sundaram Tagore Gallery, New York City, 2003; Two-person shows, Simon Gallery, Morristown, NJ, 99, 76 Varick St Gallery, NY, 99; Group shows, Subliminal View, Trans Hudson Gallery, NY, 99, Slight of Hand, Cummings Art Center, New London, Conn, 99, Reconstructing Abstraction, The Mitchell Algus Gallery, NY, 2000, Painting Abstraction II, NY Studio Sch, 2001, Newhouse Ctr. for Contemporary Art, 2003-2004, Am. Acad. Arts and Letters, 2005, Whitney Mus. Am. Art, 2006. *Teaching:* Artist-in-residence, USIA, Poland, 64-65; Long Island Univ, NY, 74-77; Princeton Univ, 94. *Awards:* Artist Fel Grant-Painting, Nat Endowment Arts, 83-84; Memorial fel John Simon Guggenheim Foundation, 2002-03. *Bibliog:* Judy Collischan Van Wagner (auth), Judith Murray: Interview, Long Island Univ Catalog, 11/85; Gail Stavitsky (auth), Three aspects of abstraction, Arts Mag, 4/86; Duane & Sara Preble (ed), Artforms, 5th ed, 94; Andrew Long (auth), Openings in Art & Antiques, 4/98; Lilly Wei (auth), Review Art in Am, 11/98; Barry Schwabsky (auth), Abstract introspection in two distinct styles, NY Times, 10/99; James Carroll (interview), New Arts Alive: Judith Murray, 2001. *Mem:* Am Abstract Artists. *Media:* Oil. *Dealer:* Sundaram Tagore Gallery 137 Greene St New York, NY 10012. *Mailing Add:* 429 W Broadway New York NY 10012

MURRAY, REUBEN
ADMINISTRATOR

Study: Univ NMex, BFA(theatre), 85, Univ Phoenix, MA, 91. *Pos:* Exec dir, SArk Arts Ctr, El Dorado, 91-. *Mailing Add:* c/o Nan McDonald 3301 Lousiana St Pine Bluff AR 71601

MURRAY, RICHARD NEWTON
MUSEUM DIRECTOR, CURATOR

b Bartlesville, Okla, Aug 7, 42. *Study:* San Jose State Univ, Calif, BA, 68; Univ Chicago, MA, 70. *Collection Arranged:* Art for Architecture: Washington DC 1895-1925 (auth, catalog), Nat Collection Fine Arts, Smithsonian Press, 75; America as Art, 76; Elihu Vedder (auth, catalog), 78; American Renaissance: 1876-1917 (auth, catalog), Brooklyn Mus, 79. *Pos:* Asst to dir, Nat Collection Fine Arts, Washington, DC, 76-79; dir, Birmingham Mus Art, Ala, 79-83 & Arch Am Art, Smithsonian Inst, 83-; cur, Nat Mus Am Art, Smithsonian Inst, 88-. *Publ:* Auth, Art of the American West, Birmingham Mus Art, 82; Murals of the American Renaissance, Influence on Am Art, 89; John Norton Mural Painter, In: John Norton, Ill Univ Press, 92; H Siddons Mowbray, Mural Painter; Murals in the Library of Congress. *Mailing Add:* 11300 Palisades Ct Kensington MD 20895

MURRAY, ROBERT (GRAY)
SCULPTOR, PAINTER

b Vancouver, BC, Mar 2, 36. *Study:* Univ Sask Sch Art, 55-58; Mex, 59; Art Students League, New York, 60; Emma Lake Artist's Workshops. *Work:* Whitney Mus Am Art, Metrop Mus Art, NY; Walker Art Ctr, Minn; Everson Mus, Syracuse; Hirshhorn Mus, Washington; Chase Manhattan Collection, NY; Detroit Mus Fine Arts, Mich; Univ

Toronto, Ont, Can; Del Art Mus; Art Gallery of Ont; Berkeley Mus; Joseph Hirshom Mus, Washington; Met Mus Art, NY; Nat Gallery of Canada, Ottawa; Whitney Mus Am Art, NY; Storm King Art Centre, Mountainville, NY; Grounds for Sculpture, Hamilton, NJ. *Comn:* Sculpture, Univ Mass, Amherst, 75; sculpture, Alaska Court Bldg, Juneau, 78; sculpture, Honeywell Inc, Minn, 79; sculpture, Univ Toronto, 83; sculpture, Can Nat Inst Blind, Toronto, 98; direct purchases as well as numerous commissions. *Exhib:* Nothing But Steel, The Lab, Cold Springs Harbor, LI, 87; The Opening Exhib, Nat Gallery Can, Ottawa, 88; Working Models & Other Sculpture, Del Art Mus, 90; Frank Martin Gallery, Muhlenberg Col, Allentown, 91; retrospective, Reading Pub Mus, Pa, 94; Solo-exhib, Andre Zarre Gallery, NY, 94, 95 & 96, Arno Maris Gallery, Westfield Col, Mass, 99, Moore Gallery, Toronto, Ont, Can, 99, Ericson Gallery, Philadelphia, 99, Art Gallery of Kelowna, BC, Can, 2000; The Factory as Studio, Nat Gallery Can, Ottawa, 99; Andre Zarre Gallery, NY, 2000; Appleton Mus, Ocala, Fla, 2000; Moore Gallery, Toronto, 2000. *Teaching:* Lectr, cols throughout US; instr, Sch Visual Arts, currently. *Awards:* Can Coun Bursary, 60 & Sr Grant, 69 & 83; Second Prize, X Sao Paulo Biennial, Brazil, 69; Nat Endowment Arts Grant, 69; Royal Archit Inst Can Allied Arts Medal, 77; Order of Canada, 2000. *Bibliog:* Krainin-Sage (auth), ArtIs (film), NY State Coun Arts, 71; Neil Marshall (auth), Robert Murray sculpture, Dayton Art Inst, 79; G Bellerby (auth), Robert Murray: Sculpture & Working Models, Art Gallery Greater Victoria, 83; Kim Rich (auth), Culture Shock (article), Anchorage Daily News, 10/9/88; Denise LeClerc, Barbara Rose (auth), Robert Murray, Factory as Studio, 99; Christine Finkelstein (auth), Robert Murray, 97, Grounds for Sculpture, Hamilton, NJ. *Media:* Steel, Aluminum. *Publ:* David Raskin (auth), Robert Murray: A Painter in Metal, Art in America, 9/99. *Dealer:* Andre Zarre Gallery 515 W 20th St New York NY 10011; Moore Gallery 80 Spadina Toronto ON Can M5V 2J3; Winchester Galleries Victoria BC Can. *Mailing Add:* 345 Lamborntown Rd West Grove PA 19390

MURRELL, CARLTON D
PAINTER
b Bridgetown, Barbados, WI, July 17, 45; nat US. *Study:* Art Student's League, 70; Pels Art Sch, 74. *Work:* Ctr Art Cult Bedford-Styvesant, Brooklyn; Barbados Mus, Bridgetown; Howard Univ, Washington, DC; Barbados Cent Bank; Medgar Evers Col, Brooklyn, NY; Schomburg Libr & Carver Fed Bank, NY; Prentice Hall, Sch Div, NJ. *Comn:* Prentice Hall, Div Simon & Schuster. *Exhib:* West Indian Artist, Brooklyn Mus, 76; Caribbean Connection, Nat Afro Am Mus Cult Ctr, Ohio Hist Soc, 86. *Teaching:* Instr drawing & painting, Brooklyn Truth Ctr & Fort Greene Sr Citizen Ctr, 88-; Children's Aid Soc, 99-. *Awards:* Second Prize, Flushing Art League; Fulton Art Fair Award, 82 & 87; Goddard Enterprise Award, Barbados. *Bibliog:* David Shirey (auth), Realism stands out in show by blacks, New York Times, 81; Will Grant (auth), To a Bajan beat, Art Speak, 88; Jude Schwendenwien (auth), Appealing, informative West Indian-American art exhibit, Hartford Courant, 88. *Mem:* Brooklyn Watercolor Soc. *Media:* Oil, Watercolor. *Publ:* Am Biog Inst Int Register Of Profiles, Cambridge, Eng, 11/88

MURRILL, GWYNN
SCULPTOR
b Ann Arbor, Mich, June 15, 42. *Study:* Univ Calif, Los Angeles, BA, 68, MA, 70, MFA, 72. *Work:* Bankers Life Co, Des Moines, Iowa; Bank Denver, Colo; Los Angeles Co Art Mus; Trans America, San Francisco, Calif; Security Pacific Bank, Los Angeles, Calif. *Comn:* Calif State Bldg, Los Angeles; Plaza Park Towers, Sacramento, Calif. *Exhib:* Los Angeles Eight, Painting & Sculpture, 76 & 20 Yrs of Talent Winners, Los Angeles Co Art Mus, Calif; Contemp Californians VIII, Laguna Beach Art Mus, Calif, 82; Wood Renditions, Security Pac Bank, Los Angeles, 84; Asher/Faure Gallery, Los Angeles, 87; John Berggruen Gallery, San Francisco; Gail Swerin Gallery, Ketchum, Idaho; and others. *Awards:* Prix Di Rome, Am Acad, Italy, 79; Nat Endowment Art Fel, 84 & Guggenheim Fel, 86. *Media:* All. *Dealer:* Asher Faure Gallery 612 N Almont Los Angeles CA 90069; John Berggruen Gallery San Francisco CA. *Mailing Add:* Patricia Faure Gallery 2525 Michigan Ave Suite B7 Santa Monica CA 90404

MURTIC, EDO
PAINTER, ENAMELIST
b Velika Pisanica, Croatia, 21. *Study:* Sch Applied Arts; Acad Fine Arts, 43. *Work:* Mus Mod Art, NY; Tate Gallery, London, Gt Brit; Nat Mus, Prague, Czech Repub; Nat Gallery, Berlin, Ger; Mus Mod Art, Seoul, Korea. *Exhib:* Nat Gallery Mod Art, Rome, Italy, 56; Tate Gallery, London, Gt Brit, 61; Mus Arts & Crafts, Zagreb, Croatia, 63; Mus Mod Art, Belgrade, Yugoslavia, 64; Palazzo Reale, Milan, Italy, 71; Grand Palais, Paris, France, 71; Pompidou Ctr, Paris, France, 81; Mus Mod Art, Seoul, Korea, 88. *Bibliog:* Paule Gauthier (auth), Edo Murtic, 50; Gerhard Wurzer (auth), Edo Murtic (exhibit catalog), Gerhard Wurzer Gallery, 81; Tonko Marovic/Chromos (auth), Murtic, Multigraf, 86. *Media:* Oil, Pastel; Enamel. *Mailing Add:* c/o Gerhard Wurzer Gallery 1217 S Shepherd Houston TX 77019

MUSGNUG, KRISTIN A
ARTIST
b Buffalo, NY, Nov 10, 59. *Study:* Williams Col, BA, 81; Pa Acad Fine Art, 83-85; Ind Univ, MFA, 88. *Work:* Mus of Fine Arts, Houston; Cavendish Col, Cambridge Univ, England; Center for Contemp Art, Prilep, Macedonia. *Exhib:* Tex Myths and Realities, Mus of Fine Arts, Houston, 95; Delta Exhib, Ark Arts Center, Little Rock, 99; MOAK 2000, Springfield Art Mus, Mo, 00; Landscape 2000, Merrimack Col, N Andover, Mass, 00; Hard Core, Galveston Arts Center, Tex, 02. *Teaching:* asoc prof painting & drawing, Univ Ark, Fayetteville, 91-. *Awards:* Artist Fel, Ark Arts Coun, 02. *Dealer:* Inman Gallery 1114 Barkdull Houston Tex 77006. *Mailing Add:* Fine Arts 116 Art Dept Univ Arkansas Fayetteville AR 72701

MUSGRAVE, SHIRLEY H
EDUCATOR, PHOTOGRAPHER
b Lexington, Ky, Nov 28, 35. *Study:* Miss State Col Women, BFA, 57; Colorado Springs Fine Arts Ctr, summer 56; Univ Kans, scholar, 57-58, MS, 63; Univ Ark, 64-65; Univ Iowa, 66-67; Fla State Univ, PhD(fel), 70. *Exhib:* One-artist photog exhib, Iowa City Civic Ctr, 65, Univ Ala-Huntsville, 72, Athens Col, Ala, 73 & Lambuth Col, Tenn, 74; Prof Women Artists of Fla, Lowe Art Mus, Miami, 76; Photograph, Huntsville Art League & Mus Asn Ann, Huntsville Art Mus, 79; and others. *Teaching:* Art supvr, Linwood Pub Schs, Kans, 58-60; assoc prof art educ, Memphis State Univ, 70-72 & Fla Int Univ; prof art educ & chairperson dept, Univ Ala, 78. *Awards:* Ark Artists Ann First Prize in Graphics, Little Rock Mus Fine Arts, 56; Fla Int Univ Found Grant, 76. *Mem:* Nat Art Educ Asn; Southeastern Col Art Conf; Ala Alliance Arts Educ; Ala Art Educ Asn. *Publ:* Coauth, Experiences in the Arts, 77; coauth, Annotated sources for Afro-American arts and the ancestral African background, Art Teacher, spring 80. *Mailing Add:* 1231 16th Ave Tuscaloosa AL 35401-3026

MUSGROVE, STEPHEN WARD
ADMINISTRATOR, CONSULTANT
b Pittsfield, Mass, Mar 28, 49. *Study:* Lenoir-Rhyne Col, BA(hist), 73; State Univ NY, Oneonta, 73-74, Cooperstown Grad Progs, MA(mus studies). *Pos:* Dir, Catawba Sci Ctr, Hickory, NC, 74-75; asst dir, Mint Mus of Art, Charlotte, NC, formerly; mus consult & writer, 92-. *Teaching:* Assoc prof, Univ NC, Charlotte, 90-. *Mem:* Am Asn Mus; Am Asn for State & Local Hist; Southeastern Mus Conf; NC Mus Coun. *Publ:* Auth & illusr, Making exhib labels: a mechanical lettering system, 76 & Electrifying exhibits: low voltage techniques, 78, Hist News; The alamanac: neglected witness of the American experience, 79 & For the fun of it, 80, Southeastern Mus Conf J

MUSSELMAN, DARWIN B
PAINTER
b Selma, Calif, Feb 16, 16. *Study:* Fresno State Col, AB, 38; Art Ctr Col Design, Los Angeles, 38-39; Calif Col Arts & Crafts, MFA, 50; Univ Calif, Berkeley, MA, 52; also with Lyonel Feininger, 37 & Yasuo Kuniyoshi, 49. *Work:* Oakland Art Mus, Calif; Fresno Arts Ctr, Calif; Sloan-Kettering Hosp, NY; Harvey Mudd Col. *Comn:* Mural of cotton indust, Prod Cotton Oil Co, Fresno, 54; portrait of former President, Calif State Univ, Fresno, 82. *Exhib:* 3rd Ann Legion of Honor Exhib, San Francisco, 48; Calif Artists Exhib, Los Angeles Mus, 49; Denver Mus Ann, Colo, 54; Butler Inst Am Art, Youngstown, Ohio, 56; Fresno Arts Ctr, 82; Wichita Art Asn, 82; and others. *Pos:* Artist & art dir, Thomas Advert, Fresno, 39-41 & 45-46. *Teaching:* Assoc prof painting & art educ, Calif Col Arts & Crafts, 48-53; prof painting & commercial art, Fresno State Univ, 53-78. *Awards:* First Prize Painting, San Joaquin Valley Art Contest, Rouze Gallery, Fresno, 47, Northern Calif Arts, Crocker Gallery, Sacramento, Calif, 56 & Ann Show, Fresno Arts Ctr, 61. *Bibliog:* Emil Kosa, Jr (auth), California painters, Am Artist Mag, 3/50; Barbara Cott (auth), Darwin Musselman, Fresno Arts Ctr, 62; Gordon T McClelland (auth), The California Style, 85; Directory of American Portrait Artists, Am Portrait Soc, 85. *Mem:* Am Watercolor Soc; Calif Nat Watercolor Soc; Am Portrait Soc; Am Soc Portrait Artists; Portrait Inst. *Media:* Oil, Egg Tempera. *Publ:* Illusr, Valley of the Yokuts, 40. *Mailing Add:* PO Box 3227 Apt 76 Lancaster PA 17604-3227

MYATT, GREELY
SCULPTOR
b Aberdeen, Miss, Mar 17, 1952. *Study:* Delta State Univ, Cleveland, Miss, BFA, 75; Univ Miss, Oxford, MFA, 80. *Work:* Masur Mus Art, Monroe, La; Univ Miss, Oxford; Miss Mus Art & Miss Craftsmen's Guild, Jackson; Ringling Sch Art & Design, Sarasota, Fla; Franklin Furnace Archives, New York, NY. *Comn:* Wood sculpture, Triangle Cult Ctr, Yazoo City, Miss, 79; wood sculpture, Prudential Insurance, Memphis, Tenn, 80; on site installation, Arts Festival Atlanta, 83 & 86. *Exhib:* Solo exhibs, Southeastern Ctr Contemp Art, Winston-Salem, NC, 84 & Kansas City Artists' Coalition, Kansas City, Mo, 88; solo installations, ARC/Raw Space, Chicago, Ill, 87 & Memphis Ctr Contemp Art, Tenn, 88; window installation, Franklin Furnace, NY, 88; Galveston Art Ctr, Tex, 89; Robinson Willis Gallery, Nashville, Tenn, 89; Memphis State Univ, Tenn, 90. *Teaching:* Instr art, Itawamba Jr Col, Fulton, Miss, 80-85; asst prof art, Ark State Univ, Jonesboro, 85-88, assoc prof, 88-89; asst prof art, Memphis State Univ, Tenn, 89. *Awards:* Merit Awards, Miss Exhib, Miss Mus Art, Jackson, 78, Gertrude Herbert Mem Art Inst Competition, Augusta, Ga, 83 & Sept Competition, Alexandria Mus, La, 85; Individual Artist Grant, Art Space, New York, 88; Installation Grant, Alexander Mus Art, La, 89; Site Grant, Arts in the Park, Memphis, Tenn, 89. *Mem:* Int Sculpture Ctr. *Media:* Mixed. *Dealer:* Robinson Willis Gallery Nashville TN. *Mailing Add:* 416 S Main St Memphis TN 38103-4441

MYER, PETER LIVINGSTON
KINETIC ARTIST, PAINTER
b Ozone Park, NY, Sept 19, 34. *Study:* Brigham Young Univ, BA, 56; Univ Utah, MFA, 59; summers with Harry Sternberg & Joseph Hirsch. *Work:* Springville Mus Art; Phoenix Art Mus, Ariz; Salt Lake City Art Ctr; Denver Art Mus; Las Vegas Art Mus; others; Nora Eccles Harrison Mus; Woodbury Art Gallery, UVSC. *Comn:* Sculpture, Mus Art, Brigham Young Univ. *Exhib:* One-man shows, Salt Lake Art Ctr, 80, Kimball Art Ctr, Park City, Utah, 85, Las Vegas Art Mus, 86, Brigham Young Univ Art Mus, 94, Nora Eccles Harrison Mus, Logan Utah 2000 & Bountiful Davis Art Ctr, 2002, Woodbury Art Gallery, UVSC, 2003 (One-Man Show); Light, Motion, Space, Walker Art Ctr, Minneapolis, 67; Some More Beginnings, Brooklyn Mus, 68; Art & Technology, High Mus Art, Atlanta, Ga, 69; Art of the 60's, Denver Art Mus, 70; Kinetic Light Show, Phoenix Art Mus, Ariz, 73; Utah Valley Sculptors Invitational Exhib, Springville Art Mus, 77; retrospective, Springville Art Mus, Utah, 79; AAPL Grand Nat Exhib, New York City, 2002; and others. *Teaching:* Assoc prof art & chmn

dept, Univ Nev, Las Vegas, 62-72; art gallery dir, Brigham Young Univ, 72-78, prof art, 72-, studio area head, 92-95, prof emer. *Awards:* Alcuin Fel, 96-99; Best of Show, Pastel Soc Utah, Salt Lake City, 2000; Col George J Morales Meml Award, Am Artist Profl League, NYC, 2002; The Newington Award-Best in Show 75th Grand National Exhibition AAPL- NYC-2003. *Bibliog:* Kranz (auth), Science and Technology and the Arts, Rheinhold, 74. *Mem:* Western Asn Art Mus; Am Asn Art Mus; Utah Mus Asn; Col Art Asn; Am Artists Profl League. *Media:* Kinetic Light Art, Pastels. *Publ:* Art: Do It!, Kendall/Hunt, 96. *Dealer:* New Amsterdam Art Exchange-Park City, Utah; Tivoli Gallery, Salt Lake City, Utah. *Mailing Add:* 1425 Oak Cliff Dr Provo UT 84604-3706

MYERS, DOROTHY ROATZ
PAINTER, CRITIC
b Detroit, Mich, March 24, 21. *Study:* Study with Yashuoe Kuniyoshi & Terrence Coyle; Antioch Col, Corcoran Gallery Art Sch; Art Students League. *Work:* US Coast Guard Collection, Washington. *Comn:* Painting, Texas Rose, Hess Oil Corp; painting, Main Course, Seafood Leader. *Exhib:* Mini Print Int, Cadaques-Taller Galeria Fort, Barcelona, Spain, Salmagundi Mus, Hellenic Inst, Athens, Greece, Tangentl, Liechtenstein; Festival Int, Paris, 88, Osaka, Japan, 89; Phoebus II, Athens, Greece, 90; Cornel Med Ctr, 92; Brookdale Col, 92; Ward-Nasse Gallery, 94; and others. *Pos:* Publicity, Montserrat Gallery. *Teaching:* Pvt critiques & art lecture programs. *Awards:* Diplome de Medaille d'Honneur Ligue d'Enseignement et Education Sociale, 87; Medialle Bronze Societe Academique d'education et d'encouragement (Paris) Arts, Sciences, Lettres, 88; Corresponding Academican, Accademia Internazionale Greci-Marino, Acad Off Knight, 2000. *Bibliog:* Anne Vanoli (auth), Roatz, La Cote des Arts, 10/84; feature article, Manhattan Arts Mag, 90. *Mem:* Life mem Art Students League; NY Artists' Equity; Salmagundi Club (dir, 88). *Media:* Oil, Watercolor; Monoprint. *Specialty:* contemp fine art. *Interests:* psychology. *Publ:* Freelance articles & reviews. *Dealer:* Ward-Nasse Gallery New York NY. *Mailing Add:* 1701 Ocean Ave Apt 23P Asbury Park NJ 07712-5629

MYERS, FORREST WARDEN
SCULPTOR
b Long Beach, Calif, Feb 14, 41. *Study:* San Francisco Art Inst. *Work:* Mus Mod Art & Whitney Mus Am Art, NY; Hirshhorn Mus, Washington, DC; Storm King Art Ctr, NY; Walker Art Ctr, Minneapolis; Aldrich Mus Contemp Art, Ridgefield, Conn; and others. *Comn:* Storm King Art Ctr, NY; Pepsi Cola, Osaka, Japan. *Exhib:* Philadelphia Mus Art, 68; Los Angeles Co Mus, 68; Whitney Mus Am Art, 68, 70 & 73; Unlimited Possibilities of Structure, Gallery 91, NY, 86; one-man show, Art et Industry Gallery, NY, 80-96; Katonah Mus, NY, 90; Brutus Gallery, Japan, 90; Grounds for Sculpture, Johnson & Johnson, Mercerville, NJ, 94; Art et Industry, NY, 98; PS 1, Queens, NY, 2000; and many others. *Teaching:* Instr sculpture, San Francisco Art Inst, 67; instr, Sch Visual Art, NY, 68; instr sculpture, Kent State Univ, 78, Parsons Sch Design, NY, 94. *Awards:* Guggenheim Fel, 73; Creative Artists Pub Serv Prog Grant, 77; Nat Endowment Arts Grant, 78; Design 100 Award, Metrop Home, 90. *Bibliog:* Interview with Billy Kluuer, Sculpture Mag, 5/91; Art in review, NY Times, 8/21/92; Sail Away, Samoa artist photo profile, Night Mag, 2/94. *Mailing Add:* 120 N Sixth St Brooklyn NY 11211

MYERS, FRANCES J
PRINTMAKER
b Racine, Wis, Apr 16, 1938. *Study:* Univ Wis, BA, 59, MA. 60, MFA, 65; San Francisco Art Inst. *Work:* Libr Cong & Nat Collection Fine Arts, Washington, DC; Victoria & Albert Mus, London; Metrop Mus Art, NY; Art Inst Chicago; Boston Mus Fine Arts; Brooklyn Mus. *Exhib:* 20th, 22nd & 24th Print Biennale, Brooklyn Mus, 76, 81 & 86; Perimeter Gallery, Chicago, 86, 88, 91, 93 & 97; Amerikahaus, Cologne, Ger, 91; Presswork: The Art of Women Printmakers, traveling exhib, Lang Communs Corp Collection; Portland Mus Art, Ore, 92; Duke Univ Mus Art, 94; Wis Acad Gallery, 97; and others. *Pos:* Cur, Printed by Women Exhib, Port Hist, Penn's Landing, Philadelphia, 83; cons Parsons Csh Art & Design, 2000. *Teaching:* Distinguished prof art, Mills Col, Oakland, Calif, 79; vis lectr, art dept, Univ Calif, Berkeley, 82; asst prof, Univ Wis, Madison, 86-88, assoc prof, 88-95, prof, 95-. *Awards:* Nat Endowment Arts Fel, 74 & 85; Wis Arts Bd Grant, 77-78; Romnes Fel, 91-92; Kellet Mid-Career Fel, 99-. *Mem:* Nat Acad. *Media:* Etching, Installations. *Dealer:* Perimeter Gallery Chicago IL. *Mailing Add:* 6641d Humanities Bldg Univ Wisc 455 N Park St Madison WI 53706

MYERS, JACK FREDRICK
PAINTER,
b Lima, Ohio. *Study:* Cleveland Art Inst, Ohio; Kent State Univ, MFA. *Work:* Butler Inst Am Art. *Exhib:* May Show, Cleveland Mus of Art, 49-54, 76-81; Freedson Gallery, Lakewood, Ohio, 69; Mid-Year Show, Butler Inst of Am Art, Youngstown, Ohio, 76, 78, 79 & 82; Nat Print Competition, San Diego State Univ, Calif, 80; Birke Art Gallery, Marshall Univ, Huntington, WVa, 81; Colorprint USA, Mus Tex Tech Univ, Lubbock, 83. *Pos:* Art dir, Premier Industrial Corp, 56-70. *Teaching:* Instr graphics & film, Cooper Sch Art, Cleveland, 70-80; prof art & dir commercial design, Univ Dayton, 82-87. *Awards:* First Prize (one minute animated film), ASIFA Festival, New York, 74; Purchase Prize, Mid-Year Show, Butler Inst of Am Art, 79; Special Mention, May Show, Cleveland Mus Art, 79 & 80; and others. *Media:* Oil, Various. *Publ:* The Language of Visual Art: Perception as a Basis for Design, Holt, Rinehart & Winston, 89; The Windy Side of Care, Llumina Press, 2002; The Greatest Gift, Llumina Press, 2002. *Mailing Add:* 22269 Country Meadows Ln Strongsville OH 44149-2000

MYERS, MARTIN
SCULPTOR, PAINTER
b Syracuse, NY, April 21, 51. *Study:* Va Commonwealth Univ, BFA, 73; Calif Col Arts & Crafts, MFA, 74. *Work:* Oakland Mus; San Francisco Mus Mod Art; Univ Art Mus, Berkeley, Calif; Newport Harbor Art Mus. *Comn:* Sculpture, IBM, 85. *Exhib:* Virginia Artists--1973, Va Mus Fine Arts, 73; Cityscapes, Fine Arts Mus San Francisco, 77; 35th Biennial Contemp Painting, Corcoran Gallery Art, 77; A Sense of Scale, Oakland Mus, 77; Viewpoint/77--Options in Painting, Cranbrook Mus, 77-78; Sculpture in California, 1975-1980, San Diego Mus, 80; New Bay Area Painting & Sculpture, Calif State Univ, Northridge, 82 & San Francisco Art Inst, 83; Constructions: Between Sculpture and Architecture, Sculpture Ctr, NY, 88; Redding Mus, Calif, 90; Sandra Gering Gallery, NY, 96, 98, 99, 2000; Reynolds Gallery, Richmond, Va, 99. *Pos:* Founder & dir, Artist For Nuclear War. *Bibliog:* Judith Dunham (auth), Sculpture as painting as sculpture, Artweek, 77; Morris Yarowsky (auth), article, Art in Am, 79; Richard Armstrong (auth), catalog, Modernism, 81. *Media:* All Media; Acrylic, Oil. *Dealer:* Sandra Gering Gallery Newxonu Rd #2 Box 236 Jefferson NY 12093. *Mailing Add:* 285 Grand St Brooklyn NY 11211

MYERS, PHILIP HENRY
PAINTER
b Jersey City, NJ, Aug 16, 22. *Study:* Art Students League, NY, studied with Reginald Marsh, 46-50, Robert Brackman, 50-52, Sidney Dickenson, 61-62. *Work:* Galleria de Bari, Bari, Italy; US Capitol, Washington, DC; Nat Inst Health, Bethesda, Md; Univ Miss Med Sch, State Col, Miss; Pollack Hosp, Jersey City, NJ. *Comn:* John McCormack portrait, Speaker of House, Washington DC, 65; Vpres Humphrey portrait, Toastmasters Int, Washington DC, 65; Sonny Jergensen portrait, Washington Redskins Football Team, Washington, DC, 66; Justice Thomas Stanton portrait, NJ Bar-John Stanton, Morristown, NJ, 67; Marchioness portrait, Marquis de Milfontes, Portugal, 77. *Exhib:* Salamagundi Club Nat Invitational, NY, 65; Southern Vermont Mus Nat Invitational, Manchester, 89; Schenectady Mus Nat Invitational, NY, 94. *Pos:* Partner, Portraits with Cortland Butterfield, New York City & Bucks Co, Pa, 59-76; resident artist, Werben Lang Gallery, NY, 63-65; resident artist, Legends Gallery, Saratoga Springs, NY, 96-98. *Awards:* NJ Performing Arts Prestige Award, Hudson Co Awards Comt, 76 & 77; Mulligan Award, Nat Juried Exhib, Southern Vt Mus & Art Ctr, 89; 1st Place Oil, Nat Juried Exhib, Atlantic City, NJ, 81. *Bibliog:* Washington Post, 3/65; Newark Star Ledger, Newark, NJ, 2/65; The Saratogian, 7/23/2000. *Mem:* Portrait Soc Am. *Media:* Oil. *Specialty:* 19th and 20th Century Am Art. *Dealer:* Legends 511 Broadway Saratoga Springs NY 12866; Saratoga Fine Art 15 Saddle Brook Dr Saratoga Springs NY 12866. *Mailing Add:* Philip Myers Fine Art 66 Meadowbrook Rd Saratoga Springs NY 12866

MYERS, RITA
VIDEO ARTIST
b Hammonton, NJ, Dec 10, 47. *Study:* Douglass Col, Rutgers Univ, New Brunswick, NJ, BA, 69; Hunter Col, City Univ New York, MA, 74. *Exhib:* Video and Ritual, Mus Mod Art, NY, 84; Solo exhibs, The Allure of the Concentric, Whitney Mus, NY, 85, Rift/Rise, Mass Col Art, Boston, 86, Alternative Mus, NY, 87, R H Love Mod, Chicago, 88, In The Drowning Pool, Long Beach Mus Art, Calif, 89, Berkshire Mus, Pittsfield, Mass, 90, Phantom Cities, Univ Gallery, Univ Mass, Amherst, 90, Carnegie Mus Art, Pittsburgh, Pa, 92 & Resurrection Body, Worldwide Video Ctr, The Hague, The Neth, 93; Am Landscape Video, Carnegie Mus Art, Pittsburgh, Pa, San Francisco Mus Mod Art, Calif, 88 & Newport Harbor Art Mus, Newport Beach, Calif, 89; Video-Sculptur Retrospektiv und Aktuell 1963-1989, Neuer Berliner Kunstverein, Berlin, 89 & Kolnischer Kunstverein, Koln, 89; Tenth Worldwide Video Festival, Kijkhuis, Hague, The Neth, 92; Video Int Festival, Sao Paulo, Rio de Janeiro, 94; ICI Benefit Exhib, 94; and other one-man & group exhibs. *Pos:* Mem, New York State Coun Arts, 85-88 & New York City Film/Video Prog, Jerome Found, 88-90; film/video artists panel, MacDowell Colony, 90-93. *Teaching:* Var lectures & screenings, 76-92; adj prof video, Cooper Union, NY, 95-. *Awards:* Nat Endowment for Arts, Inter Arts Grant, 84, Media Arts Grant, 87 & Visual Artist's Fel, 76, 80 & 87; NY State Coun Arts, Media Production Grant, 83, 85, 91 & 98, Media Distribution Grant, 93; First Prize, 10th Worldwide Video Festival, Kijkhuis, The Hagoo, Neth, 92. *Bibliog:* Lee Sheridan (auth), Rev, Art New Eng, 2/91; Tina Wasserman (auth), Rev, New Art Examiner, 9/91; Marita Sturken (auth), The moving image in space: Public funding and the installation form, Set in Motion, NY State Coun Arts, 94. *Mem:* Col Art Asn/Media Alliance. *Publ:* Auth, Directions/Questions: Approaching A Future Mythology, Illuminating Video; An Essential Guide to Video Art, Aperture with Bavc, 91. *Mailing Add:* 131 Spring St No 401E New York NY 10012

MYERS, TERRY R
CRITIC, CURATOR
b Ft Wayne, Ind, Jan 25, 65. *Study:* Depauw Univ, Greencastle, Ind, BA, 87; CUNY Grad Ctr, NY, 88-91. *Collection Arranged:* Kay Rosen: lifelike, Mus Contemp Art and Otis Gallery, Los Angeles, 98; Robert Overby: Parallel, 1978-1969, UCLA Hammer Mus, Los Angeles, Calif, 2000. *Pos:* Libr asst, Mus Mod Art, NY, 87-90; catalogue coord, Roy Lichtenstein Catalogue Raisonne, NY, 90-95; contrib ed Artext, Los Angeles, Calif; contrib ed New Art Examiner, Chicago, Ill; Ed bd Art Review, London, England. *Teaching:* Vis instr art criticism, Pratt Inst, NY, 90-94; assoc prof Otis Col Art and Design, Los Angeles, 94-99; adj Assoc Prof, Art Ctr Col Design, Pasadena, Calif, 95, 99-; vis fac Sch Art Inst Chicago, 2000-; vis prof, Royal Col Art, London, 2002-2004. *Mem:* Int Asn Art Critics; Col Art Asn. *Res:* Criticism & chronicling of contemporary art & its context. *Publ:* Sunshine & Noir: Art in LA, 1960-1997, Louisiana Mus Modern Art, Humlebaek, Denmark, 97; Peter Doig Blizzard Seventy-Seven, Kunsthalle Kiel, Kunsthalle Nurnberg, Whitechapel Art Gallery, London, 98; Kay Rosen: lifelike, Mus Contemp Art, Otis Gallery, Los

Angeles, Calif, 98; Standing Still & Walking in Los Angeles, Gagosian Gallery, Beverly Hills, Calif, 99; Robert Overby: Parallel, 1978-69, UCLA Hammer Mus, Los Angeles, Calif, 2000; Vitamin P: New Perspectives in Painting, Phaidon, London, 2002. *Mailing Add:* 4635 Finley Ave No 1 Los Angeles CA 90027

MYERS, VIRGINIA ANNE
PRINTMAKER; EDUCATOR
b Greencastle, Ind. *Study:* Corcoran Sch Art & George Washington Univ, Washington, DC, BA, 49 with Eugene Weisz, Richard Lahey & Jessalee Sickman; Calif Col Arts & Crafts, MFA, 51; Univ Ill, Champaign, printmaking with Lee Chesney; Univ Iowa, Iowa City, printmaking with Mauricio Lasansky; Atelier 17, Paris, printmaking with Stanley William Hayter. *Work:* San Francisco Art Mus; Nelson-Atkins Mus, Kansas City, Kans; Toledo Mus Art, Ohio; Nat Collection Women's Art, Washington, DC; US State Dept; Des Moines Art Center, Iowa; Union League Club, Chicago; Herbert Johnson Mus, Cornell Col, Ithaca, NY. *Exhib:* One hundred and eighteen one-women shows, 53-98; West '79/The Law Exhib, Minn Mus Art, St Paul; Seven Iowa Printmakers, Centro Internazionale della Graphica, Venice, Italy, 89-90; The Regilded Age, Newark Art Mus, NJ, 91; Ausstellung der Univ Iowa, Univ, Osnabruck, Ger, 2000. *Collection Arranged:* Natl Coll for Women in the Arts, Washington, DC; US State Dept; Iowa Art Center, Des Moines, IA; Fine Arts Coll, Cornell Univ, Ithaca, NY; Mus of Art, Davenport, IA; Univ Iowa Mus Art, Iowa City, IA. *Pos:* bd mem & treas, Elizabeth Found Visual Arts, NY; pres Iowa Foil Printer Corp. *Teaching:* Instr printmaking, Univ Iowa, Iowa City, 62-68, asst prof, 68-71, assoc prof, 71-80, prof, 81-. *Awards:* Fulbright Grant to Paris, 61; Develop Leave Award, Univ Iowa, 73, 78, 84, 89, 94-95 & 2000; Arts Endowment Grants, State Iowa Arts Coun & Nat Endowment Arts, 74, 82 & 85; Old Gold Summer Fel, Univ Iowa, 84 & 90. *Bibliog:* William Benson (auth), Foil stamping as an art form, J Print World, spring 93; Peter Alexander (auth), It all started as a Christmas card, Research, winter/spring, 98; Foil Stamping as a fine art, Hot Stamp News, spring 98; Elaine Lindgren (auth), Foil imaging.a new art form, book review, J Print World, Spring 2002. *Mem:* Soc Gilders; Foil Stamping & Embossing Asn; Mid-Am Print Coun; Mid-Am Col Art Asn; Iowa Foil Printer Corp (pres). *Media:* painting, drawing, printmaking. *Res:* Present, the definitive research & development to raise the craft of foil stamping, as pursued by the commercial printing industry, to the level of a fine art, 1986. *Interests:* reading; gardening; swimming. *Publ:* Auth & illusr, Owners Manual for the Iowa Foil Printer, Wenman Press, Iowa City, Iowa, 92; coauth & co-ed, Creating Original Prints with Hot Stamped Foil & the Iowa Foil Printer, Tenacre Print, Solon, Iowa, 93; auth Foil stamping program at the univ of Iowa expands, J Print World, Meridith, NH, spring 2000; auth, Foil Imaging.A New Art Form, WDG Communications, Cedar Rapids, Iowa, 2001; auth, Foil Imaging: The Original Editioned Prints, WDG Communications, Cedar Rapids, Iowa, 2006; and others. *Mailing Add:* 4244 NE 210th St Solon IA 52333

MYFORD, JAMES C
SCULPTOR, EDUCATOR
b Brackenridge, Pa, Aug 9, 40. *Study:* Edinboro Univ Pa, BS(art educ), 62; Ind Univ Pa, MEd(art educ), 66, MA(sculpture), 78. *Work:* Westmoreland Co Mus Art, Greensburg, Pa; Carnegie Libr, Pittsburgh, Pa. *Comn:* Outdoor aluminum sculptures, Aluminum Co Am, Pittsburgh, Pa, 75, First Nat Bank Pa, Erie, 78, Bloomsburg Univ, 80 & Manufacturing Data Systems Inc, Ann Arbor, Mich, 81; sculpture (stone & aluminum), City Pittsburgh, Pa, 83. *Exhib:* Assoc Artists Pittsburgh, Mus Art, Carnegie Inst, 70-83; 25th Ann Ball State Exhib, 79; Aluminum Sculpture, William Penn Mem Mus, Harrisburg, Pa, 79, Westmoreland Co Mus Art, Greensburg, Pa, 79 & Butler Inst Am Art, 83; Cast Aluminum Sculpture, Mus Art, Carnegie Inst, Pittsburgh, Pa, 80; Art Gallery Ont, 83; Sculptors Who Teach, Gov Mansion, Harrisburg, Pa, 83. *Teaching:* Assoc prof art, Slippery Rock Univ, 68-. *Awards:* Alcoa Award, Assoc Artist Pittsburgh, 78; Jurors Award, Pittsburgh Soc Sculptors, 80; Second Prize Sculpture, Great Lakes Art Exhib, 82. *Bibliog:* Richard Sutphen (producer), Preparation for Museum Show (videotape), 81; Marilyn Evert (auth), Discovering Pittsburgh's Sculpture, Univ Pittsburgh Press, 83. *Mem:* Int Sculpture Ctr; Pittsburgh Soc Sculptors (bd mem, 80-82); Asn Artists Pittsburgh. *Media:* Aluminum. *Mailing Add:* 320 Cranberry Rd Grove City PA 16127-4636

MYRON, ROBERT
HISTORIAN
b Brooklyn, NY, Mar 15, 28. *Study:* NY Univ, BA, 49, MA, 50; Ohio State Univ, PhD(fel), 53. *Teaching:* Prof art hist & art appraisal, Hofstra Univ, Hempstead, NY, 54-. *Awards:* Belgium-Am Found Awards, 53. *Mem:* Appraisers Asn Am. *Res:* Tribal arts; American-Asian and Western art. *Publ:* Auth, Prehistoric Art, 59 & Italian Renaissance, 61, Pitman; Mounds, Towns, Totems, 63 & Two Faces of Asia: India, China, 65, World; American Art, 2 vols, Crowell-Collier, 70. *Mailing Add:* 401 Garden Blvd Garden City NY 11530

N

NAAR, HARRY I
PAINTER, EDUCATOR
b New Brunswick, NJ, July 28, 46. *Study:* Philadelphia Col Art, BFA, 68; Ind Univ, with Robert Bailey, James McGanell, Robert Barnes, Marvin Lowe, Rudy Pozzatti, MFA, 70; stud under French Painter Jean Helion, Paris, France, 70-71; Printmaking Fel, Rutgers Univ Ctr Innovative Print & Paper. *Work:* Jane Voorhees Zimmerli Art Mus, Rutgers Univ; NJ State Mus, Trenton; Johnson & Johnson Corp, NJ; Bristol Myers Squibb Corp, Plainsboro, NJ; Am Coun on Edn, Washington; Morris Mus Art & Sci, Morristown, NJ; NJ State Mus, Trenton; Hunterdon Mus Art, Clinton, NJ; Montclair Art Mus, NJ; Newark Art Mus, NJ; Noyes Mus Art, Atlantic City, NJ; Jersey City Mus, NJ; plus others. *Exhib:* Nat Drawing Exhib, Corcoran Gallery Art, 70 & High Mus Art, 70; solo exhibs, Westby Art Gallery, Rowan Col, 94, Bowery Gallery, NY, 95, Gallery S Orange, NJ, 95, Lobby Gallery, NY, 96 & Woodrow Wilson Sch, Princeton Univ, NJ, 96; Beyond the Image, Rabbet Gallery, New Brunswick, NJ, 96; Fields of Vision, Lobby Gallery, NY, 96; Woodrow Wilson Sch, Princeton Univ, NJ, 96; Arts Works Trenton, NJ, 96; Hardcastle Gallery, Washington, DC, 97; Rider Univ Art Gallery, Laurenceville, NJ, 97; and others; Bristol Myers Squibb, Princeton, NJ, 98; New Jersey Landscapes, Rider Univ, NJ, 99; Holman Hall Art Gallery, The Col of NJ, 2000; The Considine Gallery, Stuart Co Day Sch, Princeton, NJ, 2000; Les Malaut Art Gallery, Union, NJ, 99; Sussex Co Col, Newton, NJ, 2000; Trenton City Mus, 2001, 2002; NJ State Mus, Trenton, 2001; Gallery South Orange, NJ, 2001; Blair Acad, Blairstown, NJ, 2001; Pringle Gallery, Princeton, NJ, 2002; Newark Mus, NJ, 2002; Mercer Co Community Col, Trenton, 2002; Acad Art Mus, Easton, Md, 2002; Bradley Univ, Prova, Ill, 2003; Eisenstranger, Howard Gallery, Univ Nebr, Lincoln, 2004; The Trenton City Mus, Trenton, NJ, 2004; Found for Hellenic Cult, NY, 2004; NJ State Mus, Trenton, NJ, 2005; A Sense of Place, Noyes Mus Art, Oceanville, NJ; Roman Gallery, Blair Acad, Blairstown, NJ. *Collection Arranged:* Joan Wortis-A Textile Journey, Thoughask & Monopront Col, 2000; Frederick Franck, Moments of Seeing, 2000; Marge Chavooshian, Drawings & Paintings From Here and Abroad, 2000; David Dewey-Past & Present, 2001; Leland Bell, Changing Phyths 1950's-1991, 2001; Michael Frechette, Malenel Life, 2002; Adolf Konrad, Moments of Vision, 2002; Michael Ramus, This & That, 2002; Altered Books: Spine Bonding Thrillers, 2003; Rosemaric Beck, Paintings, 2003; Louis Finklestein, paintings, 71-99; Judith k Brodsky, Mmemoir of an Assimilated Family, 2003; Joseph Fiore, 25 yrs Painting from Rock Fragments, 2004; Margaret Kennard Johnson, from Stone to Mesh, Sixty yrs, 2004; Diane Burke, Landscape: Paint/Pixel, 2005; Issac Witkin, Out of the Crucible: Images Born of Fire and Water, 2005; Aleksandr Manusov, The Tree of Life: Russian School Painting at the End of the Thirtieth Century, 2005; John Goodyear, The Elementary Series, 2005. *Pos:* Gallery dir, Rider Univ, Lawrenceville, NJ, 89-. *Teaching:* Instr painting & drawing, Beaver Col, Pa, 75-78 & Rutgers Univ, 78-80; assoc prof painting, drawing, printmaking & design, Rider Univ, Lawrenceville, NJ, 80-93, prof fine arts, 93-; vis artist, Philadelphia Col Art, 84; prof of art, Rider Univ, 93-. *Awards:* Summer Res Grant, Rider Col, 1982, 88, 99 & 2001; Dorothy Malloy Mem Award, Trenton City Mus, 92; best in show, Trenton City Mus, 2001 & 2002. *Bibliog:* Janet Purcell (auth), Bound to Open Eyes-State Museum Hosts Eyes on Trenton, The Times, NJ, 2/9/2001; Susan Van Dongen (auth), Sweptaway, The Times, Trenton, 10/4/2002; Nivcole Plett (auth), Line of Inquiry at Mercer County Community College, USI, Princeton, NJ, 12/1/2002; and others. *Mem:* Col Art Asn Am. *Media:* Oil, Acrylic, Watercolor, Drawing. *Publ:* auth, A Natural Thing, Jean Helion's Representational Paintings, Arts Mag, 4/84; auth, Reginald Neal, Works from 1958-Present, NJ, State Mus, Trenton, NJ, 89; auth, California Landscapes, Rider Col Art Gallery, NJ, 91; auth, Lois Dodd, Views of Windows and Doors, Rider Col Art Gallery, 92; auth, Louis Finkelstein, Paintings 71-99, Rider Univ Art Gallery, 99. *Mailing Add:* 4 Tracey Ct Lawrenceville NJ 08648

NADEL, ANN HONIG
SCULPTOR, CERAMIST
b San Francisco, Calif, May 9, 1940. *Study:* Univ Calif, Berkeley, 58-59; San Francisco State Univ, BA, 62, MA, 70. *Work:* VPres House, Washington; Frederick Weisman Found Art, Los Angeles; Hewlett-Packard Co. *Comn:* Paint-Stiks-Stoneware, Fireman Fund Insurance, San Marin Co, 83; Eden, bronze, Hewlett Packard Co, Palto Alto, 86; Kimono 88, bronze, comn by Marcia Weisman, Beverly Hills, Calif, 88; bronze, Rainbow Covenant Grad Theological Union, Berkeley, CA, 88, 94; Kimono, clay, comn by Pac Tel, 92. *Exhib:* Northern Calif Craft Exhib, Mendocino Art Ctr, 82; One-woman shows: Kimonos, Bluxome Gallery, San Francisco, 83-85, sculpture, Gallery 454 North, Los Angeles, Temple Emanu-El, San Francisco, 88, Graduate Theological Union, Flora Lamson Hewlett Libr, Berkeley, Calif, 88 & Earl McGarth Gallery, Los Angeles, 90 & 92; Earl McGrath Gallery, NY, 2000; Spacescapes, Contemp Jewish Mus, San Francisco, Calif, 94; Group Shows: Light Interpretations, Jewish Mus, San Francisco, Calif, 95; Judah L Magnes Mus, Berkeley, 87; By Womans Hand, JCC-Son, Rafael, Calif, 2002; Let There be Light, JCC, Baltimore, MD, 2004; Spice Box, Contemp Jewish Mus, San Francisco, Calif, 2005; L'Chaim, Jewish Mus, San Francisco, Calif, 97; Gates, Bradford Smock Gallery, 97; Meriam's Cups, Hebrew Union Col, NY, 97; Making Change, Contemp Jewish Mus, San Francisco, 2000. *Bibliog:* Leslie Katz (auth), Jewish Bulletin, San Francisco, 4/8/94; Dan Wakefield (auth), Expect a Miracle Miraculous Things that Happen to Ordinary People, Harper Collins, 95; Doug Adam (auth), Eyes to See Wholeness, Emi Press, 95. *Media:* Bronze, Clay. *Dealer:* Earl McGrath Gallery 20 W 57th St New York NY; Earl McGrath Gallery, 454 N Roberston, Los Angeles, CA. *Mailing Add:* 6 Starboard Ct Mill Valley CA 94941

NADOLSKI, STEPHANIE LUCILLE
PAINTER, PRINTMAKER
b Sacramento, Calif, Feb 21, 45. *Study:* San Jose State Col, 62-68; Sch Art, Bellevue, Nebr, 72; with Edgar Whitney, Robert E Wood & Glen Bradshaw, 78-83. *Work:* Univ Miss Libr, Oxford; Tex Commerce Bank, Scurlock Towers, Arthur Anderson & Co & Mus Art Am West, Houston; Bowne Corp, Detroit Mich and Chicago Ill; Wausau Insurance Co, Wausau, Wis; Kane Co Courthouse, St Charles, Ill; Stora Corp, Schaumburg, Ill; Towne Bank, Portsmouth, VA. *Comn:* Painting & offset lithographs, LeClub Condominiums, Galveston, Tex, 84; Mixed media painting, ACA Corp, Streamwood, Ill, 89; Handcast Paper wall relief, S McAllister, Palatine, Ill, 89; Paper wall relief, Unique Coupon Corp, Lake Barrington Shores, Ill, 91; Abstr monoprints, three, comn by Mr & Mrs Dilworth, Kenilworth, Ill, 92, abstract monoprints, comn by Mr & Mrs Michael Murray, Barrington, Ill, 94. *Exhib:* Allied Artists Am 80th Ann Exhib, NY, 93; Gallery West, Alexandria, VA, 2002; The Art League, Alexandria, VA, 2002; Nat Landscape, MD fedn of Art, Annapolis, MD, 2003; Making Your Mark,

Accad Art Mus, Easton, Md, 2003-2004; Md Fedn of Art, City Gallery, Baltimore, MD, 2004; Mid-Atlantic Regional Watercolor Exhib, Strathmore Hall, Rockville, Md, 2006; Water Works, Regional Exhib, Md Fed Art, Annapolis, Md; Solo exhibs, Gallery 18, Chesterton, Ind, 97; Claire E Smith Gallery, Barrington, Ill, 99; Chesapeake Ctr for the Creative Arts, Brooklyn, MD, 2002; Holley Gallery, Annapolis, MD, 2003; Acad Art Mus, Easton, MD, 2005; Artworks 2006, Annapolis Arts Alliance, 2006. *Pos:* Dir, Archway Gallery Houston, 76-87; dir, Barrington Area Arts Coun, 87-89; adv bd, Barrington Area Arts Coun, 89-94. *Teaching:* Instr watercolor, North Harris Co Col, 84-86; papermaking - mixed media monotypes, free lance workshops, 87-94; artist-in-residence, Virginia Lake Elem, Palatine, Ill, 90; Willow Grove Sch, Buffalo Grove, Ill, 93; instr experimental watermedia, Peninsula Art Sch, Fish Creek, Wis, 95, 96 & 98; artist in res, Chesterfield Co Public High Sch, Va, 2004. *Awards:* First Ann Flo Bash Award, Barrington Area Arts Coun, 89; Wausau Paper Found Award, Northern Nat Arts Competition, Rhine Lander, Wis, 94; Best of Category, Oconomowoc Festival of Arts, Wis, 97, Boston Mills Art Fest, Ohio, 2000; Award of Excellence, Geneva Lakes Art Fest, Wis, 98; 2nd Pl, Bel Air Art Festival Fine Art, MD, 2003; 3rd Place, Mixed Media, Mystic Outdoor Art Festival, Conn, 2004; 2nd Place, Mixed Media, Mystic Outdoor Art Festival, Conn, 2005. *Bibliog:* Sandra Dybal (auth), Portrait of an Artist, Daily Herald Paddock Publs, 87 & Chicago Art Rev, 89; Jodie Jacobs (auth), Art on the road, Chicago, Tribune, 94; Leeland & Williams (auth), Creative Collage Tech, 94; Collage in All Dimensions, NCS, 2005; The Art of Layering, Making Connections, 2005. *Mem:* Watercolor Art Soc, Houston (pres elect, 86); Barrington Area Arts Coun, (adv bd); assoc mem Chicago Artists Coalition (bd dir); assoc Allied Artists Am; signature mem Soc Layerists Multi Media; Colored Pencil Soc Am; Nat Collage Soc; Baltimore Watercolor Soc; Md Printmakers; Md Fed Art; NAIA. *Media:* Watercolor, Acrylic; Monoprint, Handmade Paper. *Interests:* Mayan history, travel, golf & scuba diving. *Publ:* Coauth, Mixed Media Gallery, Crafts Report, 84 & Shuttle, Spindle & Dyepot, 84; auth, Paintings, monotypes & paper, Town Mag, 85; The Business Side of Art, 97; cover art, New Visions Calendar, 99; Am Art Collector, North East Edition, 2005. *Dealer:* Benfield Gallery, 485 Jumpers Hole Rd., Severna Park, MD, 21146. *Mailing Add:* 4785 Idlewilde Rd Shady Side MD 20764-9765

NAEF, WESTON JOHN
CURATOR, HISTORIAN
b Jan 8, 42; US citizen. *Study:* Claremont Men's Col, BA, 64; Ohio State Univ, MA, 66; Brown Univ, PhD, 69. *Collection Arranged:* The Printerly Photograph, Metrop Mus Art, 73; Era of Exploration: Rise of Landscape Photography in the American West 1860-1880 (coauth, catalog), Metrop Mus Art, 75; The Collection of Alfred Stieglitz: 50 Pioneers of Modern Photography (auth, catalog), Metrop Mus Art, 78; The Truthful Lens, A Survey of the Photographically Illustrated Book, The Grolier Club, 80; Discovery and Invention (coauth, catalog), J Paul Getty Mus, 89; Arrows of Time, Arm & Hammer Mus, Los Angeles, 95; The Eye of Sam Wagstaff, J Paul Getty Mus, 97. *Pos:* Cur, Dept Prints & Photogs, Metrop Mus Art, 69-84; cur photogs, J Paul Getty Mus, 84-. *Publ:* Auth, Handbook of the Photgraphs Collection, J Paul Getty Mus, 95. *Mailing Add:* 844 Haurfrd Ave Pacific Palisades CA 90272

NAEGLE, MONTANA
PAINTER
b April 21, 40. *Study:* Univ Wyo, BFA. *Work:* First Interstate Bank Ariz, Tucson; Miller & Blau, Casper, Wyo; Fred Dowd & Co, Casper, Wyo; Hines Indust, Albuquerque, NMex; Williams, Porter & Day, Casper, Wyo; and others. *Exhib:* NMex Inter, Clovis, 85; solo exhib, Wyo State Art Mus, Cheyenne, 79, Nicolaysen Art Mus, Casper, 79 & 84, Casper Col Visual Art Ctr, 88; Watercolor USA, Springfield, Miss, 88; Univ NMex, Albuquerque, 88; Contemp Art in Cowboy State, Nicolaysen Mus, 9/88; and others. *Teaching:* Watercolor instr, Casper Col, Wyo, 83-84. *Bibliog:* Mary Carrol Nelson (auth), article, Southwest Art, 84; Montana Naegle-Report to Wyo, News Special, KTWO. *Media:* Watercolor. *Mailing Add:* 1540 Linda Vista Casper WY 82609

NAEVE, MILO M
CURATOR, HISTORIAN
b Ness Co, Kans, Oct 9, 31. *Study:* Univ Colo, BFA; Univ Del, Winterthur Prog Am Studies & MA. *Pos:* Mem staff, Winterthur Mus, Del & Colonial Williamsburg, Va; dir, Colorado Springs Fine Arts Ctr, Colo; Art Inst Chicago; ed bd, Am Art J; trustee, Showhegan Sch Painting & Sculpture, 91; dir, Libr Co Philadelphia, currently. *Awards:* Field McCormick Cur Emer Am Art, Art Inst Chicago, 91; Ill Acad Fine Arts Lifetime Achievement Award, 91; Robert C Smith Award, Most Distinguished Article, Decorative Arts Soc, 96. *Mem:* Brit Mus Asn; Royal Soc Arts; Am Asn Mus; Nat Trust for Hist Preservation; Victorian Soc Am; and others. *Res:* American painting, sculpture, architecture, and decorative arts from the seventeenth to present. *Publ:* Contribr, art mags & prof jour; ed, Winterthur Portfolio, Vol I-III & auth, The Classical Presence in American Art, Art Inst Chicago, 78; Identifying American Furniture: A Pictorial Guide to Styles and Terms, Am Asn State & Local Hist, 81, 3rd ed, 98; auth, John Lewis Krimmel: An Artist in Federal America, Univ Del Press, 87; 150 Years of Philadelphia Painters and Paintings, The Libr Co of Philadelphia, 99. *Mailing Add:* 24 Ingleton Cir Kennett Square PA 19348

NAGANO, PAUL TATSUMI
PAINTER, DESIGNER
b Honolulu, Hawaii, May 21, 38. *Study:* Columbia Col, BA, 60; Pa Acad Fine Arts, Philadelphia, 63-67. *Work:* Hawaii State Found of Cult & the Arts, Honolulu; William Rockhill Nelson Gallery, Kansas City, Mo; New Brit Mus Am Art, Conn; Boston Public Libr; Neka Mus, Bali. *Comn:* Lilac Sunday (watercolor), The Arnold Arboretum, Harvard Univ, 86; Sheraton Kauai Hotel, Hawaii, 90; mural, Campbell Estate, Hawaii, 93; The Tree (bronze sculpture) The Chapel, Hawaii Preparatory Acad, Waimea, 97. *Exhib:* Two Visions, Neka Mus, Ubud, Bali, 92; Nagano Variety Show, Somerville, Mass, 97; SymBALIst and Other BALI Views, Honolulu, 2000; Open Studio, Fenway Studios, 2001, 02; The SymBALIst Watercolors, Kupu-Kupu Gallery, Jakarta, Indonesia, 2002; Lotus Potpourri, Bibelot Gallery, Honolulu, Hawaii, 2003; Two decades: Nagano Watercolors of Bali, Jakata, Indonesia, 2005. *Pos:* Art dir, Pucker-Safrai Gallery, Boston, 67-89; trustee, Art Inst Boston, 93-98. *Awards:* First Prize Landscape with Figures, Popular Photog, 63; Packard Prize Drawing, 64 & Lewis S Ware Traveling Scholar, 67, Pa Acad Fine Arts; Grand prize, 16th Annual Shizuoka Friendship postcard Art Exhib, Honolulu, 2004. *Bibliog:* Nagano on Bali, 95. *Mem:* Fel Pa Acad Fine Arts; Asian Am Artists Asn Boston. *Media:* Watercolor, Acrylic; Photofusion, Sculpture. *Publ:* Contribr, Am Artist, 3/85; contribr, Watercolor Page, 5/78, 3/85. *Dealer:* Bibelot Gallery Honolulu HI. *Mailing Add:* Fenway Studio 406 30 Ipswich St Boston MA 02215-3615

NAGANO, SHOZO
PAINTER
b Kanazawa, Japan. *Study:* Kanazawa Fine Arts Univ, Japan, AB, BD; Art Students League, with Julian Levi; Pratt Inst, NY. *Work:* Allentown Art Mus, Pa; Berkshire Mus, Pittsfield, Mass; Citicorp, NY; Hudson River Mus, Yonkers, NY; State Univ NY Albany. *Comn:* It is Finished (painting), comn by Richard Hirsch, cur James Michener Collection, 71; Arts of Asia, NY, 85. *Exhib:* Nat Inst Arts & Lett, 72; Brooklyn Mus, 75, 77 & 78; one-man show, Squibb Art Ctr, 76; Japan Today, 79; Sindin Gallery, 82; Newark Mus, 83; and others. *Teaching:* Instr painting, Seibu Gakuen, Tokyo, 60-65. *Bibliog:* Alvin Smith (auth), article in Art Int, 5/72; David Shirey (auth), articles in New York Times, 9/75 & 3/76; article, Arts Mag, 6/85. *Mem:* Japanese Artists Asn NY (pres, 75). *Media:* Acrylic on Shaped Canvas, Human Future Subject. *Publ:* New American Paintings, Open Studios Press, Boston, Mass, 4/94; Endzeit Stimmung, Dumont Taschenbucher, Cologne, Ger, 5/94. *Mailing Add:* 39 Race St Jim Thorpe PA 18229

NAGATANI, PATRICK A
PHOTOGRAPHER
b Chicago, Ill, Aug 19, 45. *Study:* Calif State Univ, BA, 68; Univ Calif, Los Angeles, MFA, 80. *Work:* Baltimore Art Mus, Md; Denver Art Mus, Colo; Los Angeles Co Mus Art, Calif; Metrop Mus Art & Int Ctr Photog, NY; Mus Fine Arts, Houston, Tex; and others. *Exhib:* Studio Work: Photographs by Ten Los Angeles Artists (with catalog), Los Angeles Co Mus Art, 82; Photog Fictions, Whitney Mus Am Art, 86; Arrangements for the Camera: A View of Contemp Photog, Baltimore Mus Art, 87; The Photog of Invention: Am Pictures of the 1980's (traveling), Smithsonian Inst, Mus Contemp Art, Chicago & Walker Art Ctr, 89; In Close Quarters: Am Landscape Photog Since 1968, Art Mus, Princeton Univ, 93; solo exhibs, James & Meryl Hearst Ctr Arts, Cedar Falls, Iowa, 93, State Univ NY, 93, Royal Photog Soc, Bath, Eng, 93, Stanford Univ Mus Art, 93, Salathe Gallery, Pitzer Col, 94, Calif Mus Photog, Univ Calif, Riverside, 94, Alexandria Mus, Lafayette, La, 95, Amarillo Mus Art, Tex, 96, Isla Ctr Arts, Univ Guam, Mangilao, 97, The Albuquerque Mus, NMex, 98, Univ Art Mus, Univ NMex, Albuquerque, 99, Ctr Creative Photog, Univ Ariz, Tucson, 2000. *Collection Arranged:* The Ctr Creative Photography, Tucson, Ariz, 83-89. *Teaching:* Instr photog, Fairfax Community Adult Sch, 76-79, West Los Angeles Community Col, 80-83, Otis Art Inst, Parsons Sch Design, Los Angeles, 87; vis artist & instr, Art Inst Chicago, 83; artist residency, Calif Arts Coun, Los Angeles Theater Works, Juv Court & Community Schs, 86-87; asst prof art, Dept Art & Art Hist, Loyola Marymount Univ, 80-87; assoc prof, Univ NMex, Albuquerque, 87-. *Awards:* Leopold Godowsky Jr Color Photog Award, 88; Kraszna-Krausz Found Award, 92; Visual Arts Fel, Nat Endowment Arts, 92-93. *Bibliog:* Great photographers of New Mexico-Showcase 1993, Santa Fe Reporter, 8/25/93-8/31/93; Patrick Nagatani (auth), We Must make this world worthy of its children, Ilford Photo Instr Newsletter, fall 93; Phillip A Greenberg (auth), Dreams die hard, Sierra, 11/93. *Dealer:* Jayne H Baum Gallery New York NY

NAGIN, MARY D
PAINTER, EDUCATOR
b Amityville, NY, Dec 28, 53. *Study:* State Univ Col Plattsburgh, NY, BA, 75; Adelphi Univ, Garden City, NY, MA, 83, with Jeffrey R Webb. *Exhib:* Selections from the NDA, Hermitage Found Mus, Norfolk, Va, 88; Wichita Small Oil Competition, Wichita Art Asn, Kans, 88; Works on Paper Nat Exhib, Firehouse Gallery, NCC, Garden City, NY, 89; Allied Artists Ann, Nat Arts Club, NY, 90; Pastel Invitational, Mill Pond House STAC, St James, NY, 92; Solo Award Exhib, NY Paint Brush Club, NY, 96, East Meadow Libr, 98. *Pos:* Exhib chmn, Nat Drawing Asn, 88-89; cur gallery, Nassau Community Col, 89-90; art comt, Salmagundi Club, 90; exhib chmn, pastel div, Pen & Brush Club, 92. *Teaching:* instr drawing & painting, Art League of Long Island, 83-; instr watercolor, St John's Univ, NY, 91; guest art instr, Mill Neck Manor Sch for the Deaf, 98; art instr, Owl 57 Gallery, Hewlett, NY, 99-2000; art instr, North Shore Montesson Sch, 2000-01; art instr, Harbor Country Day Sch, St James, 2004. *Awards:* Beatrice Vare Award, Ann Pastels Only, Pastel Soc Am, 90; Philip Isenberg Award, Ann Pastel Exhib, Pen & Brush, 92; Pen and Brush Merit Award, 98; Pen & Brush Solo Show Award, 95. *Bibliog:* Phyllis Braff (auth), Show mixes the unusual and the traditional, NY Times, 1/22/86; NF Karlins (auth), Pastels front & center, Westsider, New York, 9/92. *Mem:* Art League of Long Island (fac mem, 83); Pastel Soc Am, New York, 88-; Salmagundi Club, New York (art comt, 90-); Pen & Brush, New York (exhib chmn, pastel div, 92). *Media:* Oil, Pastel. *Publ:* Tom Philbin (auth), The Everything Home Improvement Book, 97; Woman's Day Home Remodeling, Vol VIII, #4, 98; Tom Philbin (auth), The Irish 100, 99. *Mailing Add:* 280 Lowndes Ave Apt 307 Huntington Station NY 11746

NAGLE, RON
CERAMIST
b San Francisco, Calif, 39. *Study:* San Francisco State Col, BFA, 61. *Work:* Everson Mus Art, Syracuse, NY; Oakland Mus, Calif; Philadelphia Mus Art; San Francisco Mus Mod Art; St Louis Mus Art. *Exhib:* One-person exhibs, Currents 4, St Louis Art Mus, Mo, 79, Charles Cowles Gallery, NY, 81, 83, 85 & 89, Quay Gallery, San Francisco, Calif, 82 & 84, Greenberg Gallery, St Louis, Mo, 82, Delahunty Gallery, Dallas, Tex, 83, Betsy Rosenfield Gallery, Chicago, Ill, 84, Ron Nagle: Big Work, Rena Bransten Gallery, San Francisco, Calif, 88, Rena Bransten, San Francisco, Calif, 99, Revolution Gallery, Ferndale, Mich, 2000; Clay Revisions: Plate, Cup, Vase, Seattle Art Mus, Wash, 87; Building with Clay, Hoffman Gallery, Oregon Sch Arts & Crafts, Portland, 90; Vessels: From Use to Symbol, Am Craft Mus, NY, 90; Garth Clark Gallery, Los Angeles, Calif, 90, 95 & 96; retrospective, Carnegie Mus, Pittsburgh, 93; Franklin Parrasch Gallery, NY, 2001. *Teaching:* San Francisco Art Inst, Calif, 61-65, 76-78; Univ Calif, Berkeley, 62-73; Univ Calif Exten, San Francisco, 73-75; Calif Col Arts & Crafts, Oakland, 73-75; Calif State Univ, Hayward, 75; Univ Calif, Irvine, 75; Mills Col, Oakland, Calif, 78-. *Awards:* Fel, Nat Endowment Arts, 74, 79, 86; Adaline Kent Award, 78; Mellon Grant, 81 & 83; Visual Artists Award, Flintridge Found, 98; Fac Res Grant, Mills Col, 99. *Mailing Add:* c/o Garth Clark Gallery 24 W 57th New York NY 10012

NAHAS, DOMINIQUE FRANÇOIS
MUSEUM DIRECTOR, CURATOR
b Sallanches, France, Dec 27, 51; US citizen. *Study:* Univ Wis Madison, BA, 74; Sch Visual Arts, New York, BFA, 80; Inst Fine Arts, New York, MA, 85. *Collection Arranged:* Nancy Spero-Works since 1950, Everson Mus, traveled to Mus Contemp Art, Chicago & New Mus, New York, 87; Public Mind: Les Levine's Media Sculpture and Mass Ad Campaigns, 1969-1990, Everson Mus, traveled to Stedjek, Muka, Amsterdam, 90. *Pos:* Chief Cur Contemp Art, Everson Mus, Syracuse, NY, 85-89; dir, Neuberger Mus, State Univ NY, 90. *Teaching:* Vis fac, computer arts, Sch Visual Arts, New York, 89-90; Ed Dept, Metrop Mus Art, New York (lectr 90-). *Awards:* Grant, Luso Am Found, 89. *Mem:* Am Asn Mus, 85-92. *Publ:* Auth, Sacred Spaces, 87, coauth, Figures Form & Fiction, 88, Nancy Spero, works since 1950-Retrospective, 87 & auth, Public Mind: Les Levine's Media Sculpture & Mass Ad Campaigns, 69-90, Everson Mus; auth, Site: the recent work of Michel Gerard, Sculpture Mag, 5-6/92; Review Mag, NY, 96

NAIMAN, LEE
CONSULTANT
b Baltimore, Md, 26. *Study:* Goucher Col, BA; Sorbonne, Paris; Johns Hopkins Univ; NY Univ. *Work:* IBM, AT&T, MCI Corps; Philadelphia Nat Bank; Equitable Life Insurance; Consolidado Int Bank, NY. *Comn:* Etched glass, comn by B Gilsoul, NJ Supreme Court; Hillsborough Int Airport, Tampa; Lincoln Hosp, NY; Amwerst Subway Sta, Buffalo; Johnson & Johnson, NY. *Exhib:* Baltimore Mus Art; Manhattanville Col, Purchase, NY; Davison Art Ctr, Wesleyan Univ. *Collection Arranged:* Etchings of Gunter Grass, A G Becker Inc, NY; Equitable Life Insurance Co. *Pos:* Owner, Naiman Fine Art, 70-. *Teaching:* Instr, workshops, New Sch Social Res, NY & Glassboro Col. *Specialty:* Corporate collections, public sculpture

NAKAMURA, KAZUO
PAINTER
b Vancouver, BC, Can, Oct 13, 26. *Study:* Cent Tech Sch, Toronto. *Work:* Nat Gallery Can, Ottawa; Art Gallery Ont, Toronto; Mus Mod Art, NY; Brit Mus, London; Musee d'Art Contemporain, Montreal. *Comn:* Two sculptures, Toronto Int Airport, 63; mural panel, Queen's Park Complex, Toronto. *Exhib:* 2nd Bienniale Mus Art Mod, Paris, 61; Recent Acquisitions, Mus Mod Art, NY, 63; Can Artists 68, Art Gallery Ont, Toronto, 68; Nakamura 1951-1974, R McLaughlin Art Gallery, Can tour, 74-75; Ont Heritage Found Firestone Collection European Tour, 83-84; The 1950s - The Crisis of Abstraction in Canada, Nat Gallery Can, Ottawa, 92-93. *Awards:* Prizewinner, 4th Int Exhib Drawings & Engravings, Lugano, Switz, 56. *Bibliog:* Andrew Bell (auth), The Art of Nakamura, Can Art, 8/59; Selected Works, Art Gallery, Ont, 90; The Canadian Encyclopedia Hurtig Publ, 85 & 88. *Mem:* Ontario Col Art & Design (hon Fel); Christopher Cutts Gallery Toronto. *Media:* Oil, Watercolor. *Mailing Add:* 3 Langmuir Crescent Toronto ON M6S 2A6 Canada

NAKAZATO, HITOSHI
PAINTER, PRINTMAKER
b Tokyo, Japan, Mar 15, 36. *Study:* Tama Col Art, Tokyo, BFA(painting), 60, with Shosuke Oksawa; Univ Wis, MS(art, printmaking),64; Univ Pa, MFA(painting), with Piero Dorazio, 66. *Work:* Mus Mod Art, NY; Philadelphia Mus Art; Nat Mus Mod Art, Kyoto, Japan; Pa Acad Fine Arts, Philadelphia; Brooklyn Mus, NY. *Comn:* Mural, Furukawa Pavilion, Expo 70, Osaka, Japan. *Exhib:* Artists in Americas, Nat Mus Mod Art, Kyoto, 74; Three Hundred Yrs of Am Art, Philadelphia Mus, 76; Contemp Japanese Painting, Japan Art Festival 10th Anniversary, Tokyo, 77; Prints in Series: Idea into Image, Brooklyn Mus, NY, 77; One-man shows, Mercer Col, 78, West Chester Col, 79, Pa Acad Fine Arts, 79 Contemp Drawings: Philadelphia II, Philadelphia Mus Art, 79, One Eleven One, Tokyo Gallery, 89, Yaseido Gallery, Tokyo, 91, Gallery Kuranuki, Osaka, Japan, 92; Yokohama '92, First Int Contemp Art Fair, Japan, 92. *Teaching:* Asst prof painting, Tama Col Art, Tokyo, 68-71; asst prof printmaking, Grad Sch of Fine Arts, Univ of Pa, Philadelphia, 73-79, assoc prof, 79-. *Awards:* John D Rockefeller 3rd Grant, 66-67; Creative Artists Pub Serv Grant, 74-75. *Bibliog:* Joseph Love (auth), Tokyo Letter, Art Int, 3-12/71; Ruth Lehrer (auth), Three Hundred Years of American Art: Philadelphia, Philadelphia Mus, 76; Teruazu Suenage (auth), Art 78, Bijutsu Techo, 1/78. *Mem:* Am Color Print Soc. *Media:* Acrylic, Oil; All Media. *Mailing Add:* 361 W 36th St No 4A New York NY 10018-6408

NAKONECZNY, MICHAEL
PAINTER
b Detroit, Mich, Oct 30, 52. *Study:* Cleveland State Univ, Ohio, BFA, 79; Univ Cincinnati, MFA, 81. *Work:* Progressive Corp, Cleveland; Cincinatti Bell. *Comn:* Workbooks: Journal/Journeys, Columbia Col, Chicago Ctr for the Book & Paper Arts, Ill, 94. *Exhib:* 6 Artists Ohio/6 Artists Indiana, Cranbrook Acad Arts Mus, Bloomfield, Mich, 81; 39th Corcoran Biennial Exhibs Am Painting, Corcoran Gallery Art, Washington, DC, traveling, 85; solo exhibs, Zolla/Lieberman Gallery, Chicago, Ill, 86, 87, 90, 92 & 93, Eve Mannes Gallery, Atlanta, Ga, 91, Lew Allen Gallery, Santa Fe, NMex, 92 & 95, Cleveland Ctr Contemp Art, Ohio, 93, Evanston Art Ctr, Ill, 94, Purdue Univ, 95 & Columbia Col, Chicago, 96; AVA 7, Los Angeles Co Mus Art (with catalog), Calif, traveling, 87; USA Within Limits, Galleria De Arte, Sao Paulo, Brazil, 94; Tamarind into the Ninties (with catalog), Weatherspoon Art Gallery, Univ NC, Greensboro, traveling, 95; Witherspoon Art Gallery, Univ NC, 95; paintings, Horowitz-Lew Allen Gallery, Santa Fe, NMex, 96; and many others. *Teaching:* Artist-in-Residence, PS1, Long Island City, NY, 86, Bemis Found, Omaha, Nebr, 92; instr, Cuyahoga Community Col, Cleveland, Ohio, 87, Cleveland Inst Art, 88; vis artist, Herron Sch Art, Ind Univ, 90, Kansas City Art Inst, Mo, 91, Tamarind Inst, Albuquerque, NMex, 92 & 95 & Mont State Univ, 97-98; asst prof, Univ Alaska, Fairbanks, 2000-01. *Awards:* Fel, Awards in Visual Arts, 87; Individual Artist Fel, Ohio Arts Coun, 90; Fel, Arts Midwest, Nat Endowment Arts, 94-95; Fel, Ill Arts Coun, 95. *Mem:* Chicago Artist Collection. *Dealer:* Zolla Lieberman 325 W Huron Chicago IL. *Mailing Add:* 660 Rebecca St Apt 16 Fairbanks AK 99709-3563

NAMA, GEORGE ALLEN
PRINTMAKER, SCULPTOR
b Pittsburgh, Pa, Feb 23, 39. *Study:* Carnegie-Mellon Univ, BFA & MFA; Atelier 17, Paris, with Stanley William Hayter. *Work:* Philadelphia Mus Art; Smithsonian Inst, Libr Cong, Washington, DC; Brooklyn Mus; Butler Inst Am Art, Youngstown, Ohio; Carnegie Inst Mus Art; Biblioteque Nationale, Paris. *Comn:* Gulf Oil Co, Pittsburgh. *Exhib:* Original Prints, Calif Palace of Legion of Honor, San Francisco, 64; Pratt Graphic Art Ctr Serigraph Exhib, 65; Northwest Printmakers Int Exhib, 65-67; Contemp Am Prints, Gt Brit, 69-71; US Info Agency Exhibs, Japan Expo, 70; Nat Acad Design, 80-86. *Teaching:* Instr, Pratt Inst, 76-86, Sch Visual Arts, 79, The New Sch, 85-86 & Nat Acad Design, 80-86. *Awards:* David Berger Mem Prize, Mus Fine Arts, Boston, 67; Stuart M Egnal Prize, Philadelphia Print Club, 68; Stella Drabkin Mem Award, Am Color Print Soc, 71; Cannon Prize, Nat Acad Design, 85. *Bibliog:* Leonard Slatkes (auth), Printmakers on Exhibit, Art Scene, 68; Richard Shelton (auth), Journal of Return, Kayak, 69; S Hazo (auth), Poets & Prints, Artist Proof Mag, 71. *Mem:* Nat Acad. *Media:* Intaglio, Casting. *Publ:* Monuments, 71; Seascript, 71; Origin of Language, Nine Etchings, 79; Desert Water, 81; Grapes of Zeuxis, 87; and others. *Mailing Add:* Pratt Inst 144 W 14th St New York NY 10011

NANTANDY
PAINTER, MURALIST
b Abilene, Tex, Dec 22, 27. *Study:* North Tex State U, 45-47, Tex Univ, 48; Otis Art Inst, 61; Univ Southern Calif, BFA, 64; Calif State Univ, Long Beach, MA, 67; studied sculpture, painting with Judy Chicago and Peter Plagens. *Work:* Newport Harbor Mus, Calif; Laguna Beach Mus Fine Arts, Calif; Vay Adam Mus, Vajay, Hungary. *Comn:* History of San Bernardino Co from 1810-1927 (mural), Calif State Architect's Office, San Bernardo, 78-80. *Exhib:* Solo Retrospective, Jocob Javits Federal Bldg, NY, 85, Artist League of Tex, 89, Survival Art, Westbeth Art Gallery, NY, 93, Lifetime Achievement Exhib, 2005; Art Camp Invitees, Vay Adam Mus, Hungary, 98; Group Show (10 paintings), Mark Timmerman Studio, NYC, 2001; Group Drawing Show, Westbeth Gallery, NYC, 2002; On Becoming a Woman, Westbeth Holiday Show, 2004. *Pos:* owner/operator, Tanar Art Gallery & Studio, Calif, 62-81. *Teaching:* instr art La Quinta High Sch, Calif, 64-71; instr art Mt San Antonio Col, Walnut, Calif, 75-77. *Awards:* Tex Watercolor Soc Joske's of Tex Award, 51; Prix De Paris Award Ligoa Duncan Gallery, NY, 58; Honorable Mention Award Orange Co Art Asn, 68. *Bibliog:* Diana Reed (auth), Nothing Flat About Her Painting, Orange Co Evening News, 5/17/70; Patty Kelly (auth), Redlands Featured in New State Mural, Daily Facts, 8/27/80. *Mem:* Nat Soc Mural Painters (sec 83-88, 1st vp 97-99, exhib coordr, 92); Westbeth Visual Arts (exhib coordr 92). *Media:* Watercolor. *Publ:* auth, photogr, The Week, 7-14, 2002. *Dealer:* Tanar Art Gallery & Studio 463 West St New York NY 10014. *Mailing Add:* 55 Bethune St New York NY 10014

NARANJO, MICHAEL ALFRED
SCULPTOR
b Santa Fe, NMex, Aug 28, 1944. *Study:* Wayland Col, Plainview, Tex; Highland Univ. *Work:* Magee Womens Hospital, Pittsburgh, PA; Heard Mus, Phoenix, Ariz; Albuquerque Mus, NMex; Colorado Springs Fine Arts Ctr, Colo; Mus Fine Arts, NMex State Libr, Records & Archives, Santa Fe; Mercy Regional Medical Ctr, Durango, Colo, 2006. *Comn:* The Dancer, six ft bronze, Albuquerque Mus; Justice, Dennis Chavez Fed Bldg, Albuquerque, NMex, 94; Spirit Mother, Yale Park, Univ NMex, Albuquerque, NMex, 96; The Gift, Nonex State Libr, Records & Archives, Santa Fe, 98; Emergence, State Capitol, Santa Fe, NMex, 2001; All Things are Possible, City of Albuquerque, NMex, 2005. *Exhib:* Eiteljorg Mus Am Indian & Western Art, 92; Albuquerque Mus, NMex, 94; New Art of the West, 6th Ann Eiteljorg Mus Biennial, Indianapolis, Ind, 98; Veterans Admin Cent Off, Washington, DC, 98; Pfizer Gallery, NY, 98-99; United States Embassy, London, Eng, 2001; Inner Visions, the Sculpture of Michael Naranjo, The Heard Mus, Phoenix, Ariz, 2000-2001; The Works of Michael Naranjo & RC Gorman, The Governor's Gallery, Santa Fe, NMex, 2004; permanent, Michael Narangjo - Touching Beauty, Atrium Gallery, Bataan Bldg, Santa Fe, NMex, 2006. *Pos:* Bd mem, NMex Arts Comn, 71-73, NMex Very Spec Arts Festival, 83-, Access to Art, Mus Am Folk Art, 87; vis artist, Pojoaque High Sch, NMex, 96; Educ at Found for Blind Children, Phoenix, Ariz, 2001; panelist, Am Asn

Mus Annual Meeting, Dallas, Tex, 2002. *Awards:* Distinguished Achievement Award, Am Indian Resources Inst, 90; Clinton King Purchase Award, Mus Fine Arts, Santa Fe, NMex, 91; Outstanding Disabled Veteran of the Year, by the Disabled Am Veterans, 1999; Santa Fe Rotary Foundation, Distinguished Artist of the Year, NMex, 2004; and others. *Bibliog:* Bob Dotson (auth), In Pursuit of the American Dream, publ by Atherum, 85; Bodywatching, CBS Special produced by New Screen Concepts, 88; Mary Carroll Nelson (auth), Artist of the Spirit, Arcus Publ, 94; Teri Degler (auth), The Fiery Muse: Creativity & the Spiritual Quest, Random House, Can, 96; David Kirley (auth), An Artist Vision, Mod Maturity Mag, 3/2000-4/2000. *Media:* Bronze, Stone. *Publ:* Auth, Arizona highways, Ariz Dept Transportation, 5/86; Southwest Art Mag, 10/89; Colores, Pub Broadcast System documentary, 92; Article, Santa Fean Mag, 8/98. *Dealer:* Nedra Mastcucci Galleries, Santa Fe, NM. *Mailing Add:* PO Box 5803 Santa Fe NM 87502

NARDI, DANN
SCULPTOR
b Shelbyville, Ill, June 22, 50. *Study:* Ill State Univ, Normal, BS(art), 76, MS(painting), 78. *Work:* US Equities Inc, Chicago; State of Ill collection, State of Ill Bldg, Chicago; Saks 5th Ave & Prudential Ins Co, NY; Ill State Univ, Normal; Coca Cola Corp Collection, Atlanta, Ga. *Comn:* Outdoor site-specific sculptures, City of Mattoon, Ill, 82, State of Ill, Edwardsville, 85, Coe Col, Cedar Rapids, Iowa, 88-89 & Secy State, Springfield, Ill, 88-89; Rhone-Poulenc Rorer Inc, Philadelphia, Pa, 92; Eastern Ill Univ, Charleston, 92; Univ Ill, Chicago, 96; Bradley Univ, Peoria, Ill, 98; Ill State Univ, 99-. *Exhib:* One-man shows, Roy Boyd Gallery, Chicago, 85, 88, 90 & 92, Fay Gold Gallery, Atlanta, Ga, 89, Merwin Gallery, Ill Wesleyan Univ, Bloomington, 90 & Ill State Univ, Normal (with catalog), 95; Faculty & Alumni, Ill State Univ, Chicago, 88; Sculpture in the Landscape, Paine Art Ctr & Arboretum, Oshkosh, Wis, 88; Monuments and Memorials, State of Ill Gallery, 90; Chicago Sculptors, Klein Gallery, Chicago, 94; Ill Sculptors, Klein Gallery, Chicago, 94; and others. *Teaching:* Instr sculpture, Ill State Univ, Normal, 86-88. *Awards:* Grant, Ill Arts Coun, 83, 86 & 87; Fel, Nat Endowment Arts, 86 & 88. *Bibliog:* Alan Artner (auth), review, Chicago Tribune, 2/22/85; Claire Downey (auth), review, Artpapers, 12/86; Buzz Spector (auth), catalog essay, Dept Cult Affairs, 10/88. *Mem:* Int Sculpture Ctr

NARDIN, MARIO
COLLECTOR, SCULPTOR
b Venice, Italy, Mar 17, 40. *Study:* Acad Belle Arti, Venice, with Guido Manarin. *Work:* Hudson River Mus, Yonkers, NY; Fordham Univ; City of Santa Rosa, Calif; also in pvt collections. *Comn:* Actaeon Corp. *Exhib:* One-man shows, Fordham Univ, 69, Lesnick Gallery, 70, Sindin Galleries, 77, Village Gallery at Gallimafry, Croton-on-Hudson, NY, 78 & Soho Gallery-Herald Ctr, NY, 86; State Univ Plattsburgh, NY, 71; Sculpture in the Park, Loveland, Colo, 95; Garrison Art Ctr, 85, 86, 87, 89, 90; Meisner Gallery, Farmingdale, NY, 84; Howland Libr, Beacon, NY, 99; and others; Garrison Art Ctr Benefit Exhib, Tallix, 2004. *Pos:* Asst to Jacques Lipchitz, 64-71; asst mgr, Avent-Shaw Art Foundry, 64-75. *Awards:* New Rochelle Art Asn Award, 67; Greenburgh Arts & Cult Comt Award, 71 & 72; Mamaroneck Artist Guild Award, 73. *Bibliog:* Noel Frankman (auth), Nardin at the Hudson River Museum, Arts Mag, 3/72; Successo a Nuova York di uno scultore Veneziano, Gazzetino Venice, 72; David L Shirey (auth), Sculptor as master builder, New York Times, 3/78; Meg McConahey (auth), Sculptor Illuminates City Hall, The Press Democrat, 9/10/98. *Mem:* NY Artists Equity Asn. *Media:* Bronze. *Mailing Add:* 184 Warburton Ave Hastings-on-Hudson NY 10706-3706

NARDONE, VINCENT JOSEPH
PAINTER, COLLAGE ARTIST
b South Orange, NJ, Oct 19, 1937. *Study:* Newark Sch Fine and Indust Arts, NJ 55-56, Montclair State Col, NJ, BA, 61; Univ Southern Calif, Los Angeles, MFA, 66; Paris Am Acad Ecole De Beaux-Arts France, 78; Rosary Col Grad Sch Art, Florence, Italy, 81, with Genieve Secord, Joseph Domareki, Isa Petrozzani, Mildred Taylor, Paul Harris & Arnauld D'Hauterives, John Grabach, James Carlin. *Work:* Newark Mus & Newark Pub Libr, NJ; Collection Int, Paris Am Acad, France; Duncan Mus, Paris; Relais et Chateaux Inn, Lake Saranac, NY; Bristol-Meyers/Squibb Gallery, Princeton, NJ; Seton Hall Univ, NJ; Neurological Regional Assocs, Mapleshade, NJ; Dealers Choice Books Co, Land O' Lakes, Fla; Permanent Collection: Nat Mus of Fine Arts, Budapest, Hungary; The Noyes Art Mus, Oceanville, NJ, Kean Univ Mus, Union, NJ. *Comn:* exterior stone carving, Music & Art Corp, NJ, 70; original litho insert, NJ Music & Arts Mag, 72; watercolor alterpiece, Christ the King Parish, Ploughe, Sardinia, 72; mural, NJ Transit Sta, Maplewood, 92; Aqua Media Diptych (mural), Comn by Zanitsch Family, Bonita Springs, Fla, 98. *Exhib:* One-man shows, Ligoa Duncan Gallery, NY, 78, Luxembourg Mus, Paris, 78, Barron Arts Ctr, Woodbridge, NJ, 80, Il Centro Artistico, San Niccolo, Florence, Italy, 81, ITT Worldwide Commun Inc, NJ, 88, Robin Hutchins Gallery, Maplewood, NJ, 92-94, AT&T Corp, Basking Ridge, NJ, 93, Frederick Gallery, Allenhurst, NJ, 2006; Seoul Int Exhib Tour, Korea, 84-85; Audubon Artists Nat, 90-2006; La Watercolor Soc Int, New Orleans, 95; Soc Watercolor Artists Nat, Ft Worth, Tex, 95; Western Colo Watercolor Nat, Grand Junction, 95; Allied Artists of Am, 96-2006; Anchor and Palette Gallery, NJ, Jersey Five Group, 99; Atlantic City Art Center, NJ, 2001; The Morris Mus, NJ, The Art of Collecting Fine Art, 2002 & 2003; Ocean Co Artists Guild, NJ, 2003; Pastel Soc Am Int Juried Exhib, 2006; NJ State Juried Exhib, Artists Guild, Island Heights, NJ, 2006; Group show, Exposition Int d'Art de Mode, Pavillion du Val-de-Grace, Paris, 95; Ctr for Int Art & Cult Int Exhib, New York City, 2005; Taiwan Ctr, Flushing, NY Int Ann Pastels Juried Exhib, 2005-2006; Noyes Art Mus, 2006. *Pos:* Illusr & art consult, NJ Music & Art Mag, 69-73; art collector, 70; art adminr, NJ State Coun Arts Grant, Essex Co, NJ, 73; art dir, NJ Transit Mural Project, Maplewood, 92; nat nominating consultant, Biog Encyl Am Painters, Sculptors and Engravers: Colonial to 2002. *Teaching:* art specialist, South Orange/Maplewood Sch Dist, NJ, 61-89; instr painting adult sch, Maplewood, NJ, 66-70; adj art Prof, Seton Hall Univ, S Orange, NJ, 68-74; demo workshops, Monmouth Co, NJ, 96-2005. *Awards:* Raymond Duncan Medal, Prix de Paris, 79, Painting Award, Le Salon, Grand Palais, Paris, 78, Queen Fabiola, Prix Rubens Medal, Belg, 78; Medal of Artistic Merit, Rosary Col, Florence, Italy, 81; Silver Medallion, Int Arts Competition, Seoul, Korea, 84; Mid-Atlantic Regional Watercolor Award, Baltimore, 95; Louisa Melrose Gallery Painting Award, Frenchtown, NJ, 2002. *Bibliog:* Francois Perche (auth), critique, La Revue Moderne des Arts, Paris, 78; Viaczeslav Zavaliszen, Art Critic/Novoye Russkoye Slovo, NY, 78; Dorothy Hall (auth), critique, Park East, NY, 11/78; Lou Pessolano (auth), Artist of the month, NJ Artform, 82; Beth Fand (auth), Major Auction Review News Record of S Orange, Maplewood 8/91; and others. *Mem:* Audubon Artists, NY (vpres); Allied Artists Am, Dir; Manasquan River Group Artists, NJ; Guild Creative Art, Shrewsbury, NJ; Ocean Co Artists Guild, Island Heights, NJ; Monmouth Co Arts Coun, NJ; Salmagundi Art Club, NY. *Media:* Acrylics, Pastels, Watercolor, Mixed Media. *Publ:* Ecological Genesis (litho portfolio), Rubicon Graphics, NJ, 72; Contribr, Franklin & James Decade Review of Am Artists at Auction, 5/88 - 6/98; Davenports's Art Reference/Price Guide, 2003-2004; Art at Auction in America, Krex Press Publ Co, Silver Springs, Md, 91-95; Giclee Ltd Ed Print Series, Archive Print Inc, Brielle, NJ, 2002-2003. *Dealer:* Anchor and Palette Gallery 45 Mount St Bay Head NJ 08742; Frederick Galleries of Allenhurst & Spring Lake 401 Spier Ave Allenhurst NJ 07711; Tycoon Art Gallery 75 Main St Manasquan NJ. *Mailing Add:* 1218 Minnehaha Trail Manasquan NJ 08736

NARKIEWICZ-LAINE, CHRISTIAN K
MUSEUM DIRECTOR, WRITER
b Colorodo Springs, Colo, Jun 3, 52. *Study:* Université Strasbourg, Strasbourg, France, (archit), 70; Lake Forest Col, Lake Forest, Ill, (art hist), 75. *Hon Degrees:* Am Acad Rome, 80. *Exhib:* Art to Swatch, Pac Design Center, Los Angeles, Calif, 95; Wright in Chicago, Design Mus, London, Eng, 97; New Chicago Archit, Buenos Aires Biennale, Arg, 98; Children of Chernobyl, Thessaloniki Mus, Greece, 99; Nordic Visions, Cult Ctr of Cath Ch, Naxos Castle, Naxos, Greece. *Pos:* dir/pres, Chicago Athenaeum: Mus Archit and Design, Chicago and Schaumburg, Ill, 88-. *Teaching:* adj prof, Archit Ill Inst Technol, 86-89. *Awards:* Goldsmith Award, Indust Designers Soc Am, 93; Humanitarian Award, David K Hardin Generativity Trust, 97. *Publ:* auth, Distant Fires, 97, Baltic Hours, 99, Inspiration: Nature and Poet, 99 & Enemy of the People: Forty Belarusian Poets, 2001, Metrop Arts Press; Greenland, Metrop Arts Press, 2003. *Mailing Add:* Chicago Athenaeum 601 South Prospect St Galena IL 61036

NAROTZKY, NORMAN DAVID
PAINTER, PRINTMAKER
b Brooklyn, NY, Mar 14, 28. *Study:* Brooklyn Col, BA(cum laude), 49; Art Students League, 45-49; Cooper Union, 52, BFA, 79; Atelier 17, Paris, 54-56; Kunstakademie, Munich, 56-57; New York Univ, Inst Fine Arts, 57-58; study with Moses Soyer, Ad Reinhardt, S W Hayter, Morris Kantor, Nicholas Marsicano. *Work:* James A Michener Collection of 20th Century Am Painting, Univ Tex Art Mus, Austin; Philadelphia Mus Art; Mus Contemp Art, Madrid, Spain; Mills Col Art Gallery, Oakland, Calif; Cincinnati Art Mus, Ohio; Columbia Univ Rare Book & Manuscripts Libr, NY; John Hay Libr, Brown Univ, Providence, RI; Museu De L'Emorda, Figueres, Spain; Univ Iowa Libr, Iowa City; NY Public Libr, NY City. *Comn:* Mural, Banco de Guipuzcoa, San Sebastian, 63; ltd ed lithograph, Collectors Guild Ltd, 69 & Fine Arts 260, 72 & 76; ltd ed etchings, Galeria Fort, Barcelona, 75 & 83; Miquel Plana (ltd ed etching), Olot, 90. *Exhib:* Vi Bienal Sao Paulo, Brazil, 61; Mus Mod Art, 62; Whitney Mus Am Art Ann, NY, 62; Arte Am y Espana, traveling Europe, 63-64; San Francisco Mus Art, 68; Grosse Kunstler Ausstellung, Haus der Kunst, Munich, 71; Fundacion Joan Miro, Barcelona, 84, 85 & 86; Bienal d'Art, Barcelona, 85 & 87; L'Informalisme a Catalunya, Barcelona, 90; 40 Yr Retrospective, Museu de L'emporda, Figueres, Spain, 94; Retrospective, Centre D'art Santa Monica, Barcelona, Spain, 99; and 53 one-man shows. *Pos:* Staff, Collector's Guild Inc, 69-71 & Fine Arts 260, 71-80; dir art gallery, Cadaques, 73; dir painting workshop, Northern Mich Univ, summer 79. *Teaching:* Pvt studio, Cadaques, Spain, 59-69, Barcelona, 76-85; Northern Mich Univ, summer, 79. *Awards:* French Govt Fel, Paris, 55-56; Fulbright Fel, Ger, 57-58; Painting Grant, Generalitat de Catalunya, Spain, 83; Grand Prize, II Bienal d'Art, Barcelona, 87. *Bibliog:* Jose M, Moreno Galvan (auth), Spanish painting, the latest avant-garde, NY Graphic Soc, 69; Meilach & Ten Hoor (auth), Collage & Assemblage, Crown Publ, 73; Lourdes Cirlot (auth), La Pintura Informal en Cataluna, 1951-1970, Anthropos, 83. *Mem:* Art Students League; Cercle Artistic de Sant Lluc, Barcelona; Associacio D'Artistes Visuals De Catalunya. *Media:* Acrylic, Oil; Etching, Lithography; Collage. *Publ:* Auth, Spain: a disenchantment with materia, 9-10/65, Conversation with Cuixart, 3/66 & The Venice Biennale: pease porridge in the pot nine days old, 9-10/66, Arts Mag; Ibiza--from art refuge to art center, Art Voices, fall 65; Form & communication in my art work, Leonardo Mag, 7/69; The Raven, A Limited Edition Artists Book of Poe's Poem with 9 original color etchings & one embossed relief, Barcelona, 93. *Mailing Add:* Putxet 84 Barcelona 08023 Spain

NASGAARD, ROALD
CURATOR, HISTORIAN
b Denmark, Oct 14, 41; Can citizen. *Study:* Univ BC, BA, MA, 67; Can Coun Fels, 67-71; NY Univ Inst Fine Arts, PhD, 73. *Pos:* Cur contemp art, 75-78, chief cur & cur int contemp art, 78-, Art Gallery Ont; deputy dir and chief cur, 90-93; co-dir prog, Inst Mod & Contemp Art, Calgary, Alta, 95-00. *Teaching:* Asst prof art hist, Univ Guelph, Ont, 71-75; vis lectr, York Univ, Toronto, 76-78; vis lectr, Univ Toronto, 83-92; adj prof, Univ Toronto, 92-95; prof & chmn studio art, Fla State Univ, 95-2006, prof art history, 2006-. *Awards:* Can Coun PhD Fel, 67-68, 70-71; Rsch Fel Nt Gal Can, 02. *Mem:* Col Art Asn; Univ Art Asn Can; Int Art Critics Asn (Canadian secy-gen, 76-78);

Toronto Pub Art Comn, 86-88; Gershon Island Found (trustee, 91-). *Res:* Late 19th century to contemporary art. *Publ:* Auth, Structures for Behaviour, New Sculptures by Robert Morris, David Rabinowitch, Richard Serra and George Trakas, 78, Gary Neill Kennedy: Recent Works, 78, Yves Gaucher: Fifteen Year Perspective, 79 & 10 Canadian Artists in the 1970's, 80, Art Gallery Ont; The Mystic North: Symbolist Landscape Painting in Northern Europe and North America, 1890-1940, Art Gallery Ont, Univ Toronto Press, 84; Gerhard Richter: paintings, Thames & Hudson, London, Eng, 88; Individualtes: 14 contemporary Artists from France, 91 & Free Worlds: Metaphors and Realities in Contemporary Hungarian Art, 91, Art Gallery Ont, Toronto, 91; Concealing/Revealing, Voices from the Canadian Foothills, Mus Art, Fla State Univ, 97; Pleasures of Sight and States of Being: Radical Abstract Painting Since 1990, Mus Art, Fla State Univ, 01. *Mailing Add:* 2415 Winthrop Rd Tallahassee FL 32308

NASH, ALYCE LOUISE (SANDY)
CONSULTANT
b Mattoon, Ill. *Study:* James Millikin Univ, Decatur, Ill, 35-36; Heatherleys Sch Fine Art, London, Eng, 47-48; Atelier Zadkine, with Ossip Zadkine, Paris, France, 48-49; Chelsea Col Art, London Univ, with Henry Moore & Bernard Meadows, 49-51; Anglo-French Art Sch, London, 52. *Pos:* Exec secy, Edward MacDowell Assocs, 57-60; asst dir, Contemporaries Gallery, NY, 60-62; dir, Osgood Gallery, NY, 62-63; dir, Alice Nash Gallery, NY, 63-65; staff mem for exhibs & librn, Am Acad & Inst Art & Lett, NY, 65-72; assoc, Harmon Gallery, Naples, Fla, 78-84; dir, Friends of Art Mus Gallery, Naples, Fla, 84-89; assoc cur & registrar, Philharmonic Ctr Arts, Naples, Fla, 89-, actg cur, 91-, cur, 92-2000, cur, Naples Mus Art, 2000-; cur, Narhes Mus Art, 2000-03. *Mem:* Fel Royal Soc Arts, Eng; Naples Art Asn (bd mem 78-); Naples Mus Art (life). *Specialty:* Contemporary American and European paintings and sculpture. *Publ:* Auth, Collectors Handbook, Harmon-Meek Gallery, 82. *Mailing Add:* 6101 Pelican Bay Blvd Apt 302 Naples FL 33963

NASH, DAVID
SCULPTOR
b Eng, 45. *Study:* Kingston Col Art, BA (hons, fine art), 67; Chelsea Col Art, 69. *Hon Degrees:* Kingston Univ, Hon Dr in Fine Art, 98. *Work:* Walker Art Ctr, Minneapolis, Minn; Metrop Mus Art, NY; Laumeier Sculpture Park, St Louis, Mo; Mus Contemp Art, Los Angeles; Contemp Mus, Honolulu, Hawaii; Guggenheim Mus, NY; Tate Gallery, London; Kröler-Müller, Neth; Mus Wales; Louisiana Mus, Denmark. *Comn:* Sculpture, Grizedale Forest, Lake District, United Kingdom, 78; sculpture, DJ Erassi Found, Calif, 87; planted sculpture, General Mills, Minn, 94; sculpture, Nagoya City Mus, Japan, 94; sculpture, Towner Art Gallery, Eastbourne, United Kingdom, 96. *Exhib:* Otoineppu: Spirit of Three Seasons, Asahikawa Mus Art, Hokkaido, Japan, 94; Voyages and Vessels, Joslyn Art Mus, Omaha, Nebr, 94; Mes Enlla Del Bosc, Palaa De La Virreina, Barcelona, Spain, 95; Elements of Drawing, Leed City Art Gallery, Leeds, United Kingdom, 96; Line of Cut, Henry Moore Inst, Leeds, United Kingdom, 96; solo exhib, Mus Van Hendegasse Kunst, Antwerp, Belg, 96 & Aldrich Mus, NY, 98; Cincinnati Int Friendship Park, 2003; Six Noon Columns, Nat Forest, Eng, 2006. *Teaching:* vis prof, Univ Northumbria, UK, 98-; Master, masterclass, Atl Ctr Arts, Fla, 98 & masterclass, Northlands, Scotland, 2004. *Bibliog:* Marina Warner (auth), Forms into time, Acad ed; Julian Anderlis (auth) & Lund Humphries (coauth), The sculpture of David Nash; Graham Beal (auth) Voyages and Vessels, Joslyn Art Mus. *Mem:* Royal Academician. *Media:* Wood. *Res:* Environmental based research. *Publ:* Mes enlla del bosc, 95; Wood Primer, The Sculpture of David Nash, 87; David Nash Skulpturen, 97; David Nash, Spirit of Three Seasons, Hokkaido Asahikawa Mus of Art, 94-95; David Nash, Charwel Goed, Ctr for Visual Arts, Cardiff, 2000; The Return of Art to Nature, Schettel Galerie, Germ, 2003; Making & Placing, Tate Gallery, London, 2004. *Dealer:* Annely Juda Fine Art, London; Cheryl Haines 49 Geary San Francisco CA. *Mailing Add:* Capel Rhiw Blaenau Ffestiniog LL413NT Gwynedd United Kingdom

NASH, MARY
PAINTER, LECTURER
b Washington, DC, May 8, 51. *Study:* George Washington Univ, BA, 73; Wash State Univ, Pullman, MFA, 76. *Work:* San Antonio Mus Mod Art, Tex; Mus Contemp Art, Chicago, Ill; Whitney Mus Am Art, Mus Mod Art, NY; Cleveland State Univ; J Paul Getty Trust, Calif; and others. *Comn:* painting, Nat Hockey League, NY, 2000; painted sculpture, Birds I View, Public Art Proj, Prince George's Co, MD, 2003; sculpture, Raise the Roof, Public Art Proj, Prince George's Co, MD, 2005. *Exhib:* Corcoran Gallery Art, Washington, DC, 92; Stetson Univ, 94 & 97; Univ Ill, Chicago, 94; Anchorage Mus, Alaska, 94-95 & 96-97; New Orleans Mus Art, La, 95; Alexandria Mus, La, 95; one-person shows, Emerson Gallery, McLean, Va & Lincoln Ctr, Ft Collins, Colo, 97; Neighors, Art Mus Ams, Washington, 98; Dialogues, Gallery Korea, NY, 99; The Art is in the Cards II, Lake Co Mus, Ill, 2001; Sun Bowl Art Exhib, Int Mus Art, El Paso, 2002. *Pos:* Guest lectr, Mus Art, Wash State Univ, 76-, Second St Gallery, Charlottesville, Va, 78-, Univ Ala, Tuscaloosa, 81-, Southeastern Women's Studies Asn Conf, Univ Va, Charlotteville, 83, Arlington Arts Ctr, Va, 85 & 86 & Johnson State Col, Vt, 95; artist-in-residence, alkyd painting, Va Mus Fine Arts, 84-85 & Stetson Univ, Deland, Fla, 97; guest curator, 2001 New Orleans Triennial, New Orleans Mus Art, 2001. *Teaching:* guest lectr, Emerson Gallery, 1997. *Awards:* MacDowell Colony Fel, 77; Honorable Mention, Southeastern Ctr Contemp Art, 79; Purchase Award, Wash State Arts Comn, Olympia, 82. *Bibliog:* Artists' book beat, Print Collector's Newsletter, 5-6/88; Dan Cameron (auth), New Orleans Triennial, 95; Gordon Lubold (auth), Vienna Times, 95. *Mem:* Fel MacDowell Colony. *Media:* Acrylic, Ink. *Publ:* Auth, Skulls are Forever, Ichthys Books, 86; Auth, Eye on Washington, Eye Wash, Washington, 1992. *Mailing Add:* PO Box 307 Cora WY 82925-0307

NASH, STEVEN ALAN
HISTORIAN, CURATOR
b Wadsworth, Ohio, Apr 8, 44. *Study:* Dartmouth Col, BA; Stanford Univ, PhD. *Pos:* Res cur, Albright-Knox Art Gallery, Buffalo, 73-77, chief cur, 77-80; asst dir & chief cur, Dallas Mus Fine Arts, 80-88; assoc dir & chief cur, Fine Arts Mus San Francisco, 88-. *Teaching:* Adj prof, State Univ NY, Buffalo, 73-80. *Awards:* Mabel McCloud Lewis Found Fel, 71; Fr Govt Res Grant, 71; Prof Grant, Nat Endowment Arts, 81. *Mem:* Archives Am Art (adv panel); Am Asn Mus. *Publ:* Auth, Ben Nicholson: Fifty years of His Art, Buffalo Acad, 78; Albright-Knox Collection (catalog), 79; Naum Gabo: 60 Years of Constructivism, 85; A Century of Modern Sculpture: The Nasher Collection (exhib catalog), Dallas Mus Art, 87; 100 Years of Landscape Art in the Bay Area (exhib catalog), Fine Arts Mus San Francisco, 95. *Mailing Add:* Calif Palace of Legion Of Honor 100 34th Ave San Francisco CA 94121

NASHER, RAYMOND DONALD
COLLECTOR
b Boston, Mass, Oct 26, 21. *Study:* Boston Pub Latin Sch, 39; Duke Univ, BA, 43; Boston Univ, MA, 50; Phi Beta Kappa. *Hon Degrees:* Southern Methodist Univ, LLD(hon), LHD, 73. *Work:* Dallas Mus Art, Tex; Nelson-Atkins Mus Art, Kansas City, Mo; Nat Gallery Art, Washington, DC. *Exhib:* Sir Anthony Caro Retrospective, Trajan Market Pl, Rome, Italy, 92; TransForm, Kunstmuseum Basel, Switz, 92; Still Lifes by Picasso, Cleveland Mus Art, Philadelphia Mus Art, Pa & Musée Picasso, Paris, France, 92; and others. *Pos:* staff, US Comn to United Nations Educ, 62—65; chmn, Nat Comn Urban Develop, 64-65; US delegate to UN General Assembly, 67-68; staff, pres Comt, on Arts & Humanities, pres Comn, on Urban Housing (Kaiser Comn), 67-68, US Ger Cooperative Delegation, 67; bd dir, secy, chmn, Bus Comt Arts Inc, 88-; Ambassador cult affairs, City of Dallas, 88-93; chmn, Comerica Bank, Tex, Nasher Co, Dallas. *Awards:* Bus Arts Award, 76 & 87; Flora award, N Tex Univ, 94; Named one of Top 200 Collectors, ARTnews Mag, 2004, 2006; Am Inst Archit, Distinguished Serv to Visual Arts award; recipient Design of the Decade, 60's. *Bibliog:* Margaret Robinette (auth), Interview: Raymond and Patsy Nasher, Sculpture, 3-4/87; Joan Chatfield-Taylor (auth), The collectors: a passion for sculpture, Archit Dig, 10/87; Claire Frankel (auth), Collecting patterns, Art & Auction, 6/90. *Mem:* Pres Comt Arts & Humanities, 90-92; Dallas Mus Art (bd trustees, 92-); Nat Gallery Art (trustees coun, 88-91); InterCultura (bd trustees, 89-92); Dallas Mus Art (collections comt, 95-); Coun for Foreign Relations. *Interests:* Modern & contemporary art. *Collection:* Modern & contemporary sculpture, paintings & prints; Pre-Columbian art; Guatemalan textiles; Indonesian gold; Oceanic. *Mailing Add:* 4701 Miron Dr Dallas TX 75220-2018

NASISSE, ANDY S
SCULPTOR, WRITER
b Pueblo, Colo, Nov 1, 46. *Study:* Inst Allende, Mex, 69; Univ Colo, MFA, 73. *Work:* High Mus Art. *Comn:* Four Walls, City Altanta, 81. *Exhib:* Southeast Ctr Contemp Arts Exhib, Winston-Salem, NC, 79; Ga Artists, High Mus, 79, 80 & 83; More than Land or Sky, Nat Mus Am Art, 82; Southern Fervor, Anderson Gallery, Richmond, Va, 83; Birmingham Mus Biennial, 83; New Epiphanies, Univ Colo Mus, 83; New Talent, Nexus Space, Atlanta, 83; solo exhib, La Mar Dodd Ctr, La Grange, Ga, 84. *Teaching:* Assoc prof, Univ Ga, Athens, 76-, gallery dir, 82-83. *Awards:* Nat Endowment Arts Grant, 79; Creative Res Award, Univ Ga, 82; Ga Coun Grant, 84. *Media:* Ceramic. *Res:* Folk art. *Dealer:* Fay Gold Gallery 3221 Cains Hill Pl Atlanta GA 30305. *Mailing Add:* 160 Tracy St # 1A Athens GA 30601-1947

NATKIN, ROBERT
PAINTER
b Chicago, Ill, Nov 7, 30. *Study:* Art Inst Chicago, BA, 51. *Work:* Metrop Mus Art, Mus Mod Art, Solomon R Guggenheim Mus, Whitney Mus Am Art, NY; Albright-Knox Art Gallery, Buffalo, NY; Art Inst Chicago; Brooklyn Mus, NY; Fogg Mus Art, Harvard Univ, Cambridge, Mass; Los Angeles Co Mus Art; Mus Fine Arts, Houston, Tex; Hirshhorn Mus & Sculpture Garden, Smithsonian Inst, Washington, DC; Wadsowth Antheneum, Hartford, Conn; and others. *Comn:* Mural, Baxter Laboratories Corp Hq, Chicago, Ill, 75; mural, Rockefeller Ctr, NY, 92. *Exhib:* Whitney Mus Am Art, 60, 66 & 68; Int Biennale, Japan, 63; Mus Fine Arts, Houston, 63; retrospective, San Francisco Mus Art, 69, Charlotte Crosby Kemper Gallery, Kansas City, 76, Moore Col Art Gallery, Philadelphia, 76; one-man exhibs, Art Inst Chicago, 75, Andre Emmerich Gallery, NY, 70, 71, 73, 74, 76 & 78; Solomon R Guggenheim Mus, 73, 74, 75, 77, 79, 80; Gimpel & Weitzenhoffer Gallery, NY, 79, 80, 82, 84, 85, 87 & 89; Gimpel Fils Gallery, London, 80, 81, 84, 89, 90 & 92; Works on Paper, Springfield Mus, Mo, 90; Winchester Cathedral, Eng, 92; Eng & Co, London, 94; 45 yr retrospective, Butler Inst Am Art, Youngstown, Ohio, 97; and others. *Teaching:* Instr, Pratt Inst Art, NY, 63-65 & Cooper Union, NY, 68; vis artist, Kansas City Art Inst, 84; lectr, The Tate, London, 92. *Awards:* Emerging Artist Fel, 79 & Visual Artists Fel, 81 & 88, Nat Endowment Arts; Hon Chairperson Scholar Fund, Art Inst Chicago, 98. *Bibliog:* Peter Fuller (auth), Natkin, Abrams, 81; Gerald Nordland (auth), Robert Natkin: Art and Atists, London, 30-32, 12/74; Lawrence Campbell (auth), Color Coordinates: Natkins Recent Paintings & Drawings, Art Am, 188-193, 9/89. *Mailing Add:* 24 Mark Twain Ln West Redding CT 06896

NATZLER, OTTO
CERAMIST, SCULPTOR
b Vienna, Austria, Jan 31, 08; US citizen. *Work:* Mus Mod Art & Metrop Mus Art, NY; Art Inst Chicago; Mus Bellerive, Zurich, Switz; Victoria & Albert Mus, London; Nat Mus Am Art, Washington, DC; and others. *Exhib:* One-man exhibs, Art Inst Chicago, 63 & San Francisco Mus Art, 63; retrospective exhibs, Los Angeles Co Mus Art, 66, M H De Young Mem Mus, San Francisco 71 & Renwick Gallery, Smithsonian Inst, Washington, DC, 73 (coauth all catalogs). *Bibliog:* Article, Natzler

exhibition, Ceramics Monthly, 5/78; Sarah Booth Conroy (auth), article, Washington Post, 9/20/81; Florence Rubenfeld (auth), Otto Natzler--solo, Am Craft, 2-3/82. *Media:* Multimedia. *Dealer:* Louis Newman Galleries 322 N Beverly Dr Beverly Hills CA 90210; Susan Conway Gallery 1058 Thomas Jefferson St NW Washington DC 20007. *Mailing Add:* 7837 Woodrow Wilson Dr Los Angeles CA 90046

NATZMER VALENTINE, CHERYL LYNN
DEALER, HISTORIAN
b Detroit, Mich, May 14, 47. *Study:* Mich State Univ, BA, 69, MA, 99. *Collection Arranged:* Zuniga, Drawings, Graphics & Sculpture, 78; Sebastian-Geometric Transformables, steel sculpture, 79; A Tribute to Rufino Tamayo, Recent Works, 79; Dibujos/Drawings, survey of Latin Am drawings, 79; The New World and the Beast, Animal Imagery in Latin Am Art, 79; Tamayo's Mexico, 80; The Imaginary Surface, paintings by Manuel Felguerez, 81; El Zodiaco--Sculpture by Sebastian Traveling Exhib, 82-83; Images From Dream Myth and the Subconscious, 88; Artists Choose Artists, 89; First Ann Muraling Festival, 90. *Pos:* Dir & pres, Gryphon Galleries, Ltd, Denver, 71-78; dir & bd dir, Rutherford Barnes Collection, Ltd, Denver, Colo, 78-; adv Mex art, Denver, 82-; cur, Centerspace, Lansing, Mich, 88-90. *Teaching:* instr socio-cult diversity, dpet anthropology, Mich State Univ, 99-2000. *Mem:* Family Arts Network. *Res:* Creative Potential of Later Life. *Specialty:* Twentieth century Mexican and Latin American art; works of the Masters Tamayo and Cuevas. *Publ:* Co-producer, Columbian Art in the 80's (video). *Mailing Add:* 792 Knollwood Ct Saline MI 48176

NAUMAN, BRUCE
SCULPTOR, VIDEO ARTIST
b Ft Wayne, Ind, Dec 6, 41. *Study:* Univ Wis, Madison, BS, 64; Univ Calif, Davis, with William T Wiley, Robert Arneson, Frank Owen & Stephen Kaltenbach, MFA, 66; San Francisco Art Inst, 89; ArtsD (hon), Calif Inst Arts, 2000. *Hon Degrees:* San Francisco Art Inst, DFA, 89; California Inst Arts, 2000. *Work:* Whitney Mus, NY; Wallraf-Richartz-Mus, Cologne, Ger; Kunstverein, Aachen, Ger; Mus Mod Art, & Guggenheim Mus, NY; Los Angeles Co Mus Art, Calif; Fogg Art Mus, Cambridge, Mass; Australian Nat Gallery, Canberra, Australia; Art Inst Chicago; and many others, including pvt collections. *Exhib:* One-man exhibs, Nicholas Wilder Gallery, Los Angeles, 66, Leo Castelli Gallery, NY, 68 & 81, Art in Progress, Munich, Ger, 74, Minneapolis Inst Arts Col Gallery, Minn, 78, Hester van Royer Gallery, London, Eng, 79, Carol Taylor Art, Dallas, Tex, 83, Kunsthalle, Basel, Switz, 86, Drawings 1965-1986, traveling exhib to Europe & US, 86 & Sperone Westwater Gallery, NY, 88; Am Sculpture of the Sixties, Los Angeles Co Mus Art, Calif, 67; Corcoran Gallery Art, Wash, DC, 69; Anti-Illusion: Procedures/Materials, Whitney Mus Art, NY, 69; Solomon R Guggenheim Mus, NY, 69, 2004; Info, Mus Mod Art, NY, 71; Art & Image in Recent Art, Art Inst Chicago, 74; Mus Mod Art, NY, 75, 87 & 88; Whitney Mus Am Art, NY, 76, 87 & 88; Los Angeles Co Mus Art (also traveling), 82; Fogg Art Mus, Cambridge, Mass; one-man exhibs, Biennial Exhib, Whitney Mus Am Art, NY, 91, Mus Boymans-van Beuningen, Rotterdam, The Neth, 91, Fundacio Espai Poblenou, Barcelona, Spain, 91-92, Use Me (Graphics, Multiples, Videos and Installations), Inst Contemp Arts, London, Eng, 91-92, Neons, Anthony d'Offay Gallery, London, Eng, 92 & Ydessa Hendeles Found, Toronto, Ont, Can, 92, Walker Art Ctr, Minn, 93-95, Hayward Gellery, London, 97-99,Kunsthalle Wien Karisplatz, Vienna, 2000, Zwirner & Wirth, NY, 2001, Sperone Westwater, NY, 2002, Ludwig Mus, Cologne, Germany, 2003, PKM Gallery, Seoul, 2004, Tate Modern, London, 2004-2005, Tate Liverpool, 2006, Milwaukee Art Mus, 2006; retrospective, Galerie Hummel, Vienna, Austria, 91; Documenta IX, Kassel, Ger, 92; Transform BildObjektSkulptur im 20, Jahrhundert, Kunsthalle Basel, Switz, 92; Szenenwechsel, Mus Moderne Kunst, Frankfurt am Main, Ger, 92; Re: Framing Cartoons, Wexner Ctr, Ohio State Univ, Columbus, Ohio, 92, Both Art and Life: Gemini at 25, Newport Harbor Art Mus, Newport Beach, Calif, 92; Contemp Art Mus, Houston, 99; Retrospective, Mus Nacional Centro de Arte Reina Sophia, Madrid, Walker Art Ctr, Minneapolis, Mus Contemp Art, Los Angeles, Smithsonian Inst, Mus Mod Art, NY, others, 93-95; var exhibs at maj mus incl Whitney Mus Am Art, Mus Mod Art, Milwaukee Art Mus and others. *Teaching:* Instr, San Francisco Art Inst, 66-68; instr sculpture, Univ Calif, Irvine, 70. *Awards:* Nat Endowment Grant, Washington, DC, 68; Aspen Inst for Humanistic Studies Grant, Colo, 70; Aldrich Prize, Aldrich Mus, Ridgefield, Conn, 95; Praemium Imperiale Prize for Visual Arts, Japan, 2004; Named Best Internat Artist, Beaux-Arts Mag, Paris, 2004; many others. *Bibliog:* Robert Pincus-Witten (auth), Bruce Nauman: Another kind of reasoning, Artforum, 2/72; Brenda Richardson (auth), Bruce Nauman: Neons, Baltimore Mus Art, 82; Peter Schieldahl (auth), Profoundly Practical Jokes, The Art of Bruce Nauman, Vanity Fair, 83; many others. *Mem:* Fel Am Acad Arts & Scis; Akad der Künste, Berlin; Sagamore of the Wabash; Am Acad Arts and Letters. *Publ:* Auth, Pictures of Sculptures in a Room, Davis, Calif, 66; Clear Sky, San Francisco, 68; Burning Small Fires, San Francisco, 68; LA Air, Los Angeles, 70; Body Works, Interfunktionen, Cologne, Ger, 9/71. *Dealer:* Sperone Westwater New York NY; Donald Young Gallery Chicago IL. *Mailing Add:* c/o Sperone Westwater 415 W 13th St New York NY 10014

NAUMANN, FRANCIS M
HISTORIAN, CURATOR
b Albany, NY, Apr 25, 48. *Study:* State Univ NY, Buffalo, BA, 70; Sch Art Inst Chicago, MFA, 73; City Univ New York, PhD, 88. *Exhib:* Making Mischief: Dada Invades New York, Whitney Mus Am Art, 96-97; Beatrice Wood: A Centennial Tribute, Am Craft Mus, NY, 97; Man Ray: An American Surrealist Vision, Andre Emmerich Gallery, NY, 97 & Maria: The Surrealist Sculpture of Maria Martins, 98. *Pos:* Dir, Parsons Summer Prog Italy, 81-84. *Teaching:* Instr art hist, Art Inst Chicago, 72-73; adj prof, Queens Col, City Univ New York, 74-75; prof, Parsons Sch Design, 77-90. *Awards:* Nat Endowment Humanities Fel, 91-92; Best Show in a New York City Mus, Whitney Mus Am Art, Int Asn Art Critics, 96-97. *Mem:* Col Art Asn Am. *Res:* Dada and surrealism in Europe and America. *Publ:* co-ed, Marcel Duchamp: Artist of the Century, Mass Inst Technol Press, 89; New York Dada 1915-23, 94 & Marcel Duchamp: The Art of Making Art in the Age of Mechnical Reproduction, 99, Abrams; Making Mischief (exhib catalog), 97; Affectionately Marcel: The Selected Correspondence of Marcel Duchamp, Ludion, Ghent, 2000. *Mailing Add:* 1632 Hunterbrook Rd Yorktown Heights NY 10598

NAVARETTA, CYNTHIA
LECTURER, WRITER
b New York, NY. *Study:* Univ Wis; NY Univ; Columbia Univ, BA, 46, MA, 48. *Collection Arranged:* Women Choose Women (auth, catalog), Cult Ctr, New York, 73; Artists of Long Island (contribr, catalog), Guild Hall, East Hampton, NY, 79; Int Exhib Women Artists, Milan, Ital, 79; Int Festival Women Artists, Copenhagen, 80; A Lifetime of Art: Six Women of Distinction, Women's Caucus Art, New York, 82; American Women in Art; Works on Paper Africa & Europe (auth, catalog), 85. *Pos:* dir corp archit, 50-86; Ed, Women Artists News & dir, Midmarch Arts Press, 75-; ed adv, Art Press, 80-86. *Teaching:* lectr, 76-82; lectr, ann humanties sem, 78-82. *Awards:* Nat Orgn Women, 80. *Mem:* Coalition of Women's Art Orgns (chmn, 77-78); Nat Women's Caucus for Art (bd mem, 78-81); Found for Community of Artists (bd mem, 75-89); Women Artists Filmmakers (bd mem, 78-88); Artists Talk on Art (bd mem, 76-94); and many others. *Res:* Women artists; women's art groups; art and politics. *Publ:* Auth, Guide to Women's Art Organizations, 79; ed, Voices: Three on Three on Three, Midmarch Arts Press, 80; contribr, An Encyclopedia of 20th Century N Am Artists, 82; auth, Women Artists of the World, 85; auth, Whole Arts Dir, 86; auth, Artists and their Cats, 90; auth & ed, Women Artists in the US, 90; auth, Artists Colonies, Retreats & Study Centers, 95 & 98 (rev ed); auth, How to Publish Your Own Book, 2001; and many articles in nat publ. *Mailing Add:* 300 Riverside Dr No 8A New York NY 10025

NAVRAT, DEN(NIS) EDWARD
EDUCATOR, PAINTER
b Marion, Kans, May 15, 1942. *Study:* Kans State Univ, Manhattan, BA, 64; Wichita State Univ, Kans, MFA, 66; Univ Iowa, Iowa City, 69, with Virginia Myers; Photographer's Place, Derbyshire, Eng, 77, with Paul Hill & Ralph Gibson; Anderson Ranch Arts Ctr, Aspen, 83, with Catherine Reeve, Marilyn Sward, Bernie Vinzani, Katie McGregor and Terry Allen, Emma Lake, Sask, Can, 86, with Peter Bradley and John Link; Insel HombroiBh, Neuss, Ger, with Anatol Herzfeld, 96. *Work:* Mus of Fine Art, Houston, Tex; Atkinson Art Gallery, Metrop Bur of Sefton, Eng; Plains Art Mus, Moorhead, Minn; Sioux City Art Ctr, Iowa; ND Heritage Ctr, Bismarck; Mus Der Stadt Ratingen, Ger; Mus der Stadt Ratingen, Ger, 99. *Exhib:* solo exhibs, Paper Press, Chicago, Ill, 91 & Sud Dahcotah, Univ Art Gallery, Vermillion, SDak, 96; Am Embassy, Dakar Senegal, Africa, 94-96; Great Outdoors Invitational Exhib, SDak Art Mus, Brookings, 94; 53rd Ann Exhib, Sioux City Art Ctr, Iowa, 95; Summer Arts XVIII Regional Exhib, Univ Art Gallery, Vermillion, SDak, 95; Solo Imaging the Edge of Whirl, Den Navrat Retrospective, 1965-2005, Univ Art Galleries, Univ of South Dakota, Jan 11-31, 2005. *Collection Arranged:* Catalog, video. *Pos:* Visual consult, ASAAUM, Minneapolis, 81; COMPAS Artist Group, St Paul, Minn, 82; visual consult, Arts Midwest, Minneapolis/Des Moines, Iowa, 88; artist-in-residence, Sioux City Art Center, Iowa, 2001-2002; visitation team leader, Nat Asn Schs of Art and Design, 2002-. *Teaching:* Instr, Inst of Logopedics, Wichita, Kans, 65-66; from instr to asst prof art, Dickinson State Univ, 66-71, assoc prof art & chmn art dept, 72-79, prof art, 79-89; Fulbright-Hays Exchange prof art, Southport Col Art, Eng, 76-77; prof art & chmn, Univ SDak, 89-97; prof art & CFA Int Studies Coord, 97-2005, emeritus prof art, 2005. *Awards:* Grants for Creative Res, Paper Art, Off Res, Univ SDak, 1992, 1994, 2002; Purchase Award for Collection, Sioux City Art Ctr, Iowa, 93; Cash Award, 19th Biennial Nat Art Exhib, 2nd Crossing Art Ctr, Valley City, NDak, 95; Rsch Grante, Office of Rsch, USD, 97-99; Gov's Tech Awards, 2001, 2002. *Bibliog:* Sally Prince Davis (auth), The Fine Artist's Guide to Showing and Selling Your Work, North Light Bks, Cincinnati, Ohio, 89; Catharine Reeve (auth), Darkroom Photog Mag, 12/90; Sud Dahcotah: Art on/of Paper, (exhib catalog, illustr), Univ Art Galleries, Vermillion, SDak, 96. *Mem:* Col Art Asn; Fulbright Alumni Asn. *Media:* Mixed Media. *Res:* Internet website development of instructional materials; Handmade paper art at the Hummingbird mill/studio, Vermillion, SD. *Publ:* Auth, Images on Exchange, Mind's Eye Gallery, 78. *Mailing Add:* 32191 Ponderosa Dr Burbank SD 57010-7004

NAVRATIL, AMY See Ciccone, Amy Navratil

NAVRATIL, GREG ALLAN
ARTIST
b Denver, Co, Oct 14, 46. *Study:* Metrop State Col, BFA, 73. *Work:* Parkersburg Art Center, WV; Pikes Peak Community Col, Colo Springs; Rocky Mountain Nat Park Vis Center, Estes Park; Ouray Art Center, Colo; Kaiser Permanente, Lakewood, Colo. *Exhib:* The New West, Sangre de Cristo Fine Arts Center, Pueblo, Colo, 96; ANA 26, Holter Mus of Art, Helena, Mont, 97; Landscapes of the Wilderness, Univ Mont, Missoula, 96; Colo Landscapes, Lakewood Cult Center, Lakewood, Colo, 00; Our Beautiful Heritage, Lakewood Heritage Mus, 03-. *Awards:* Purchase Award, Am Realism, Parkersburg Art Center, 92; Top 100, Arts for the Parks, 97; Best of Show & Peoples Choice, Louisville Art Center, Colo, 98. *Media:* Acrylics. *Publ:* Jenny Phalzgraf (auth), Form from Abstraction, Artists Mag, 93; Leigh Duncan (auth), Greg Navratil Cover Artist, Sunshine Artist, 02; Gil Whiteley (auth), Greg Navratil, Colo Expression, 01. *Dealer:* William Havu Gallery 1040 Cherokee St Denver Colo 80204; Peggy Rice Gallery 7060 West 135th St Overland Park Kans 66223; Sumner & Dene 517 Central NW Albuquerque NM 87102. *Mailing Add:* PO Box 2346 Seaside OR 97138

NAWARA, JIM
PAINTER, EDUCATOR
b Chicago, Ill, Jan 25, 45. *Study:* Sch Art Inst Chicago, BFA, 67; Univ Ill, Champaign, MFA, 69. *Work:* Boston Mus Fine Arts; Detroit Inst Arts; Bradford City Art Gallery, Eng; Cleveland Mus Art; Nat Mus, Warsaw, Poland; Toledo Mus Art, Ohio; Butler Inst Am Art; and others. *Comn:* Screenprints, Western Mich Univ, Kalamazoo, 74; etchings, Mich Workshop Fine Prints, 75; wall drawing, Dept Recreation, 78; billboard, First Fed Savings, Detroit, 80. *Exhib:* Oakland Community Col, Farmington Hills, Mich, 94; Mich Gallery, Detroit, 95; Cary Gallery, Rochester, Mich, 98; Knoxville Mus Art, Tenn, 02; Wayne State Univ, Mich, 02; Parkland Col Champaign, Ill, 03; Austin Peay State univ, Clarksville, Tenn, 05. *Pos:* Acting chmn, dept art & art hist, Wayne State Univ, 88-89. *Teaching:* Prof drawing & painting, Wayne State Univ, 69-. *Awards:* Purchase Awards, Butler Inst Am Art Mid yr, 72 & Mich Printmakers, Detroit Inst Arts, 77; Res Awards, Wayne State univ, 77, 81, 84, 87-88 & 90-92, 93 & 94; Creative Artists Grants, Mich Co Arts, 81, 85 & 89. *Bibliog:* Simon Zalkind (auth), 30 yrs of American printmaking, Arts Mag, 2/77; Elizabeth Glassman & Marilyn Symmes (coauth), Cliche Verre: Hand-Drawn, Light-Printed, A survey of the medium from 1839 to the present, Detroit Inst Arts, 80; Gottfried Jager (auth), Bildgebende Fotografie, Fotografik-Lichtgrafik-Lichtmalerei, Dumont Buchverlag Cologne, 88. *Mem:* AAUP/AFT. *Media:* Oil. *Dealer:* Stewart and Stewart 5571 Wing Lake Rd Bloomfield Hills Mich 48301. *Mailing Add:* 30585 Vernon Dr Beverly Hills MI 48025-4944

NAWARA, LUCILLE PROCTER
PAINTER
b Oklahoma City, Okla, June 26, 41. *Study:* Smith Col, with Leonard Baskin, BA, 62; Boston Univ, Sch Fine & Applied Arts, with Walter Murch & Arthur Polonsky, BFA, 67; Univ Ill, Champaign, MFA, 69. *Work:* Mich Coun Arts & Detroit Inst Arts, Detroit; Springfield Col, Mass; Nat Endowment Arts, Washington; Univ Mich Art Mus, Ann Arbor; Kalamazoo Art Inst. *Comn:* Sea Squirts (intaglio), Oxbow Portfolio, Mich Coun Arts, Detroit, 73; Prisms (intaglio), Women's Portfolio, Nat Educ Asn & Mich Workshop Fine Prints, Detroit, 76; mural, Broken Symmetries, Fraser High Sch, Mich Coun Arts, 86. *Exhib:* San Francisco Mus Art, 70; Mid-Yr Ann, Butler Inst Am Art, Youngstown, Ohio, 75; two-man shows, Pontiac Art Ctr, 87 & Dennos Mus Ctr, Traverse City, Mich, 93, Padziewski Gallery, Ford Community and Performing Arts Ctr, Dearborn, Mich, 2002; The Unseen Landscape, 7 Artists, Community Art Gallery, Wayne State Univ, Detroit, 91-92; Expressive Visions & Exquisite Images: Part Two, Mich Artists, Meadowbrook Gallery, Rochester, Mich, 92; group exhib, Water, Mich Gallery, Detroit, 95; Out of Solitude, Mich Gallery, Detroit, 96; Art & Technology: The Polk Competition, Birmingham, Bloomfield Art Asn, Mich, 98; At the Water's Edge, APE Ltd, Northampton, Mass, 2000; Rivers and other Bodies of Water, River Gallery, Chelsea MI, 2004. *Pos:* Exhib coordr, Detroit Focus Gallery, 80; Artist-in-the-Schools Residency, Mich Coun Arts, Fraser Pub Schs, 83-86; dir, Nawara Gallery, Walled Lake, Mich, 86-88; co-pres bd, Detroit Focus Gallery, 91-92. *Teaching:* Asst prof drawing, Wayne State Univ, Detroit, 69-76; painting & design, Macomb Community Col, Mt Clemens, Mich, 77-84; instr drawing, Henry Ford Community Col, 82 & Ctr Creative Studies, 82-83; vis artist painting, Cranbook Acad Art, Bloomfield Hills, Mich, 92; Instr, Birmingham, Bloomfield Art Ctr, MI, 2004-05. *Awards:* Purchase Award Art & Tech, Birmingham Blomfield Art Asn, Mich, 1998; Art in the Villages, Livonia Art Comn, Mich, 1999; Our Town Community House, Birmingham, Mich, 2003. *Media:* Oil, Watercolor. *Interests:* violin, gardening. *Collection:* Detroit Inst. of Art; Butler Inst. of American Art; Oklahoma Art Ctr; Krannest Art Mus; Ford Motor Co; IBM. *Mailing Add:* 30585 Vernon Dr Beverly Hills MI 48025-4944

NAWROCKI, DENNIS ALAN
EDUCATOR, CURATOR
b Grand Rapids, Mich, Dec 29, 39. *Study:* Aquinas Col, Grand Rapids, Mich, BA, 62; Wayne State Univ, Detroit, Mich, MA, 64, MA 81. *Collection Arranged:* Kick Out The Jams, Detroit Inst Arts, 80; Dada & Surrealism in Chicago, Mus Contemp Art, 84; Grounded: Sculpture on the Floor, Univ Mich Mus Art, 90; Robt Farber & Hannah Wilke, Ctr Galleries, Ctr Creative Studies, 93 & Liza Lou: A Beaded Installation, 96; Up from the Streets: The Duffy Warehouse Collection, Wayne State Univ, Detroit, 2001. *Pos:* Cur educ, Detroit Inst Arts, 81-83 & Univ Mich Mus Art, Ann Arbor, 89-90; cur res & educ, Mus Contemp Art, Chicago, 83-88; dir, Ctr Galleries, Ctr Creative Studies, Detroit, 90-98. *Teaching:* Prof art hist, Coll for Ctr Creative Studies, Detroit, 90-; adj instr, Chicago Art Inst, 90-; adj fac, Wayne State Univ, Detroit, 93-. *Mem:* Col Art Asn; Midwest Art Hist Soc. *Res:* 20th century modernism; post-modernism; contemporary art and architecture. *Publ:* Coauth, Art in Detroit Public Places, Wayne State Univ Press, 80, rev ed, 99; Master Paintings in the Art Institute of Chicago, Art Inst Chicago, 88; auth, Gilbert & George: "Parked" in Nature, Detroit Inst Arts, 89; contribr, 20th Century Paintings & Sculpture from the Art Institute Chicago, Hudson Hills, 96; auth, Bill Viola: Intimations of Mortality, Bull Detroit Inst Arts, 2000. *Mailing Add:* Ctr Creative Studies 201 E Kirby St Detroit MI 48202

NAWROCKI, THOMAS DENNIS
PRINTMAKER, EDUCATOR
b Milwaukee, Wis, June 26, 42. *Study:* Univ Wis-Milwaukee, BFA, 64, MA, 65, MFA, 67. *Work:* Univ Wis-Madison; Northern Ill Univ; Brand Libr Art Galleries, Glendale, Calif; Montgomery Mus Art, Ala; Miss Art Asn, Jackson; Dulin Gallery Art, Knoxville, Tenn; Hunterdon Art Ctr, NJ; Univ Miss, Oxford. *Exhib:* Seattle Int Print Exhib, Seattle Art Mus, 68 & 71; Hawaii Nat Print Exhibs, Honolulu Acad Arts, 73, 75, 79, 82 & 84; World Print Competition, San Francisco Mus Mod Art, 77; Int Print Bienniale, Krakow, Poland, 78, 80, 84, 86, 88, 91 & 94; Wesleyan Int Exhib, 80; Rockford Int, Ill, 81 & 82; Bradley Univ Nat Exhib, Peoria, Ill, 81, 85, 89 & 91; 57th Ann Int, Print Club, Philadelphia, 81 & 83; Soc Am Graphic Artists, NY, 88, 89, 91 & 93; Boston Printmakers, 90; and many others. *Teaching:* Instr printmaking, Southwest Tex State Univ, 67-70; from asst prof printmaking & drawing to assoc prof, Miss Univ Women, 70-83, prof, 83-. *Awards:* Dixie Annual Print Competition Award, Montgomery Mus Art, 74; Purchase Award, Nat Print Competition, Edinboro State Col, Pa, 79; Okla Nat Print Award, Okla Art Ctr, 82; Purchase Award & Top Graphics Award, Nat Arts Festival, Tupelo, Miss, 83; Purchase Award, Dulin Nat Works on Paper Competition, Dulin Gallery Art, 85. *Mem:* Southern Graphics Coun; Los Angeles Printmaking Soc; Society of Am Graphic Artists, New York City; Fla Printmakers Soc; Graphic Arts Coun of New York; Kappa Pi (treas, mem exec bd). *Media:* Printmaking, Fiber Arts. *Res:* color collagraph prints. *Interests:* design and construction of art deco objects. *Collection:* Pratt Graphic Art Ctr, New York, Soc Am Graphic Artists, New York, No Ill Univ, DeKalb, Mississippi Mus Art, Jackson, miss, Dulin Gallery of Art, Knoxville, Tenn, others. *Publ:* contrib, Artists proof, Vol VI, no 9-10, Pratt Graphic Art Ctr, New York, 67; 1st National Invitational Color-Blend Print Exhibition, Univ Miss Press. *Mailing Add:* 147 Shane Cir Columbus MS 39702

NAYLON, BETSY ZIMMERMANN
PAINTER, MURALIST
b Buffalo, NY, Jan 27, 1934. *Study:* Rosary Hill Col, BA, 55; Daeman Col, 76; tutorial with William Paden, New York, 86. *Work:* Albright-Knox Members Gallery, Buffalo; Blue Cross of Western NY; NY State Univ Archives, Buffalo. *Comn:* Woodcut & drawing for play Men Should Weep, Studio Arena Theater, Buffalo, NY, 88; Integrated Waste Systems, 95; Milstones (5' x 11' acrylic mural), Niagara Falls Mem Hosp, 95, 35 sq ft mural, JNW Enterprises, Lewiston, NY, 97; Women Free (painting), Seneca Falls, NY, 98; 30 Sq Foot Triptych Mural for WTS, INC, Lewiston, NY. *Exhib:* 38th Western NY Exhib, Albright-Knox Gallery, Buffalo, 80; Art of the Printmaker, Burchfield Art Ctr, State Univ NY, Buffalo, 81; Eight Am Artists, O'Keefe Ctr, Toronto, Can, 82; Nat All on Paper Exhib, AAO Galleries, Buffalo, NY, 84; solo exhibs, Postcards from Italy, EW Brydges Pub Libr, Niagara Falls, 84, Woodcuts & Drawings, Chautauqua Inst Art Gallery, NY, 84, Woodcut Prints & Woods, Capen Hall, State Univ NY, Buffalo, 86, Paintings & Wood Cut Prints 94 works, 30 poems), Kans Ctr, Lockport, NY, 12/89 & Stella Niagara, 94-96; Nat League Am Pen Women, Inc, NY, 85-96; Buscaglia-Castellani Art Gallery, 85-90; Nat Asn Women Artists, Jacob K Javits Fed Bldg, NY, 86-96 & Soho, NY, 98; Nat Asn Women Artists Traveling Printmaking Show, Woodcut Print, 87-89; Response '87, Emerging Vision, Univ Wis Nat Art Exhib, 87; paintings & woodcut prints & drawings, PC Chelsea Art Gallery, Buffalo, NY, 88; Nat Asn Womwn Artists Traveling Painting Show to India, 89; Int Juried Exhib, Lockport, NY, 97; Int Juried Fine Arts Exhib, Fla, 97; Castellani Art Gallery, Niagara Univ, 2005. *Teaching:* Instr drawing, Daeman Col, Buffalo, 69-70; instr drawing & painting, State Univ NY, Buffalo, 74-79; Art Park, Lewiston, NY, 76, instr figure drawing, Adult Educ, Niagara Univ, 81-83; monotypes & painting, Trinity Adult Educ, Buffalo, 90-91; Teaching Adults in my Studio, 80-2004. *Awards:* Painting Award, Niagara Frontier Watercolor Soc, 90 & First Prize, 94; NLAPW Biennial Nat Juried Art Exhib, Washington, 96; Grumbacher Gold Medal Award, Spring Show, 96. *Bibliog:* Kathleen M DeLaney (auth), Updraft Sweeps You Away, Niagara Gazette, 6/24/86; E Comerford (auth) Niagara Gazette, 12/30/88, 12/8/89; Grace Banks (auth & judge), Niagara Guild Show, Union Sun J, 4/7/97; LCTV Channel 21, Interviews on Monotype with Acrylic. *Mem:* Niagara Coun Arts (bd mem, 83-84); National Women's Caucus for Art; Albright-Knox Art Gallery; Nat Asn of Women Artists; Nat League of Am Pen Women; Buffalo Soc Artists. *Media:* Acrylic, Watercolor. *Publ:* Special Editions, The Catalogue of Regional & Nat Art; Artistic Objective (article), Pen Women Nat Mag, 88; Related Possibilities (video, slides); Quadrant J, 9/90; ed, Les Krantz, NY Art Rev. *Mailing Add:* 33 Gates Cirlce 6F Buffalo NY 14209

NAZARENKO, BONNIE COE
PAINTER
b San Jose, Calif, Oct 26, 33. *Study:* San Jose State Col; Carmel Art Inst, under John Cunningham. *Work:* Mint Mus, Charlotte, NC. *Exhib:* Soc Animal Artists, Grand Cent Art Gallery, NY, 72, 74 & 75, Daytona Beach, Fla, 90, Mus Natural Hist, Cleveland, 91 & Tacoma, Wash, 93; Game Conservation Int, San Antonio, Tex, 80; Int Fish & Wildlife Expo, NY, 86; One Touch of Nature Gallery, Chicago, 95; Bennington Art Ctr; and others. *Awards:* Beaufort Art Festival Award, SC, 66; Mint Mus Purchase Award, 68. *Mem:* Soc Animal Artists; Am Artists Prof League. *Media:* Oil, Mixed Media. *Mailing Add:* 8314 Pocahontas St W Tampa FL 33615

N'COGNITA, VERNITA See Nemec, Vernita McClish N'Cognita

NEAL, ANN PARKER See Parker, Ann (Ann Parker Neal)

NEAL, (MINOR) AVON
WRITER, PUBLISHER
b Indiana, July 16, 22. *Study:* Long Beach Col; Escuela Bellas Artes, Mex, with Siquieros, MFA. *Work:* Metrop Mus Art, NY; Libr Cong & Smithsonian Inst, Washington, DC; Abby Aldrich Rockefeller Mus Am Folk Art, Williamsburg, Va; Winterthur Mus, Wilmington, Del. *Comn:* 500 original rubbings, 70, 250 original rubbings, 71 & ed 350 original rubbings, 74, Am Heritage; ed 100 original rubbings, 70 & ed 70 original rubbings, 74, for Arton Assocs (all with Ann Parker); ed 100 original rubbings, Mead Art Gallery, Amherst Col, 76; ed 475 original rubbings, Sweetwater Editions, NY, 82. *Exhib:* New Eng Gravestone Rubbings, Mead Art Gallery, 76; Gravestone Art, William Benton Mus Art, Univ Conn, 76; Molas, Art of the Cuna Indians, Alternative Ctr Int Arts, NY, 76; and others. *Pos:* Founder & pres, Thistle Hill Press, 78-. *Awards:* Ford Found Grants, 62-63 & 63-64; Fiction writing fellow Mass Arts Found, 79; Harriette Merrifield Forbes Award, Asn Gravestone Studies, 84; Mass Arts Coun Award, 96. *Bibliog:* M J Gladstone (auth), New art from

early American sculpture, Collector's Quart Report, 63 & Pedestrian art, Art in Am, 4/64; Stephen Chodorov (auth), Know Ye the Hour, Camera Three, CBS-TV, 11/68. *Mem:* The Artists Found, Mass Artists Fel Prog, 79; Am Antiquarium Soc. *Interests:* Stone rubbing and folk art. *Publ:* co-auth, Molas, Folk Art of the Cunas Indians, Barre, 77; auth, Scarecrows, Barre, 78; auth, Pigs & Eagles, Thistle Hill Press, ltd ed, 78; coauth, Early American Stone Sculpture, Sweetwater Editions, 82; auth, Los Ambulantes, the Itinerant Photographers of Guatemala, MIT Press, 82; auth, Hajj Paintings, Folk Art of the Great Pilgrimage, 95; auth, Die Kunst des Hadsch, 95; contribr to articles to profl jours. *Dealer:* Gallery of Graphic Arts 1603 York Ave New York NY 10028. *Mailing Add:* 126 School St North Brookfield MA 01535-1961

NEAL, FLORENCE ARTHUR
SCULPTOR, PAINTER
b Columbus, Ga, Nov 12, 54. *Study:* Auburn Univ, BFA, 76; Hunter Col, 77. *Work:* New York City Pub Libr, Mus Mod Art, NY. *Comn:* Four Winds (outdoor wind sculpture), Art Omaha, Nebr, 90; Dance of Life (outdoor wind sculpture), Univ Ala, 93. *Exhib:* Niagara Falls & Fossil Fuels, Bronx Mus Arts, NY, 86; 8 Women Sculptors, Erie Art Mus, Pa, 86. *Pos:* Founder, Everglade Press, Brooklyn, NY, 85-; dir, Kentler Int Drawing Space, Brooklyn, NY, 90-. *Awards:* Mid-Atlantic Arts Consortium, Erie, Pa, 87; Pollock-Krasner Found, 90; NY State Col Ceramics Alfred Univ Award, Prospect Park, 98. *Bibliog:* Voshiko Ebihara (auth), My art scene is a survival game, Brutus-Japan, 8/89; Kyle MacMillan (auth), Flaglike art gets feet wet, Omaha World-Herald, 11/5/90; Christine Stenstrom (auth), Florence Neal opens her studio, Brooklyn Woman, 7/94. *Mem:* Brooklyn Waterfront Artists Coalition. *Mailing Add:* 353 Van Brunt St Brooklyn NY 11231

NEAL, IRENE
PAINTER, SCULPTOR, JEWELRY DESIGNER
b Greensburg, Pa, May 14, 36. *Study:* Wilson Col, BA, 58; Sch Visual Arts, Rio de Janeiro, Cert, 76-77; Memphis State Univ, 79-80; Univ Bridgeport, 82-83; Triangle Art Workshop, (Sir Anthony Caro, organizer), Pine Plains, NY, 1985. *Work:* Planetarium, Rio de Janerio, Brazil; Westmoreland Mus Art, Greensburg, Pa; Newport Harbor Art Mus, Calif; Hoover Inst, Stanford Univ, Calif; Columbia Univ, NY; Int Paper, NY; Ft Lauderdale Mus; Nat Galerie of Prague; Denver Ctr of Performing Arts; Nat Mus Women in Arts; Appleton Mus Art, Ocala, Fla; Edmonton Art Gal, Can; Population Inst, Capital Hill, Wash, DC; Flint Inst Arts, Mich. *Exhib:* State Ten, NJ State Mus, Newark, 75; New Directions in Abstraction, Shippee Gallery, NY, 86; State of the Artist, Aldrich Mus Contemp Art, Ridgefield, Conn, 87; Eight Winners Exhib, Stamford Mus, Conn, 89; Outside NY, Univ Alta, Can, 90; Galerie Gerald Piltzer, Paris, France, 96; Fine Art 2000 Gallery, Stamford, Conn, 96 & 97; York Col, Queens, NY, 97; Mus Contemp Art, Palm Beach, Fla, 97; The Griffis Art Ctr, New London, Conn, 97; Flint Inst Arts, Mich, 99; Mus Contemp Art, Denver, Colo, 2000; Hotel de Ville, Brussels, Belgium, 2000; 69th Regiment Armory, NY, 2001; Nat Gallery, Prague, Czech Republic, 2002; Cooper Classics Collections, New York City, 2001-02; The Durst Organization, New York City, 2002-03; Musee du Bas-Saint Laurant Riviere de Lupe, Que, Can, 2002-03; Scope NY, Stevenson Fine Art, New York City, 3/2003; About Paint, Westpoint, Conn; Roultra, Cork, Ireland; Lurie Gal, Miami & Boca Raton, Fla, 2005; Lurie Gal, Los Angeles, Calif, 2006. *Teaching:* Guest speaker, Col Santa Fe, Albuquerque, NMex, 94. *Awards:* Special Mention of Honor, Brazilian Acad Arts & Letters, 77; Bronze Medal, Secy Brazilian Navy, 77; Tift award, Wilson Col, Chambersburg, Pa, 2003. *Bibliog:* Kenworth Moffett (auth), New New Painting, Nouvelles, Francaises, 92; William Zimmer (auth), A dozen new painters and a sculptor too, NY Times, 12/96; David Ebony (auth), article, Art Am, 4/97; Ken Carpenter (auth), With Honours in Prague, CA Art, Winter 2002; Jan H. Vitvar (auth), Barbansti malini 2 Ameriky dorazili do Prahy, Mlada Fronta Dnes, Prague, 4/18/2002; Jean Dumont (auth), Peinture: une voie nouvelle, New Painting Expositions Vie des Arts, Montreal. *Mem:* Nat Mus Women Arts. *Media:* Acrylic on Canvas, Wood, Lexan, Paper; Miscellaneous Media. *Collection:* A.N.E.W. Founcation Arts, Ft Lauderdale, Fla. *Publ:* Contrib, Abstract Painting, (Vicky Perry, auth), Watson-Guptill, 2005. *Dealer:* Kenworth W. Moffett Stamford CT; A.N.E.W. Foundation for the Arts Ft Lauderdale FL; Phthalo Gallery Miami FL; Gerald Piltzer Gallery, Paris, France. *Mailing Add:* 98 Maple Ave Old Saybrook CT 06475

NEAL, MICHAEL SHANE
PAINTER, INSTRUCTOR
b Nashville, Tenn, Nov 23, 68. *Study:* David Lipscomb Univ, BFA, 91; Santa Fe Inst Fine Arts, 94-95; Scottsdale Artist Sch; Everett Raymond Kinstler, 93-. *Work:* US Capitol, US Senate, Washington DC. *Comn:* Paul Nitze, former Secy the Navy, John Hopkins Univ, Sch Int Affairs, Washington DC, 2003; Sen Arthur Vandenberg (portrait), US Capitol, Washington DC, 2004; Marian McPartland (portrait), Nat Arts Club, NY; Whitney MacMillan (portrait), Cargill Corp, Minneapolis, Minn; The Architect of the Capitol Alan Huntman, US Capitol Hist Soc, Washington DC, 2004; Spencer Abraham, Secy Energy, Dept Energy, Washington DC, 2005; Justice Sandra Day O'Connor, Friends the Univ Ariz, Phoenix, Ariz, 2006. *Exhib:* Allied Artists of America, Nat Arts Club, New York, NY, 96-98, 2000 & 2004; Allied Artists Juried Exhib, Butler Mus Am Art, Youngstown, Ohio, 2000; Mentors & Proteges, Teaching the New Realism, Vose Gallery, Boston, Mass, 2004. *Collection Arranged:* Vanderbilt, Columbia, Johns Hopkins, Yale & Tulane Univs. *Teaching:* guest instr, Portraits, Acad Art Univ, San Francisco, Calif, 2006. *Awards:* Grand Prize, Portrait Soc America's Int Portrait Competition, 2001; Avalon Award for Creative Excellence, David Lipscomb Univ; Tara Fredrix Award, Audubon Artists Ann, 2004; Catherine Lorillard Wolfe Award, Nat Arts Club Ann, 2004; Artist's Mag Award of Excellence, Oil Painters of Am Nat Exhib, 2004. *Bibliog:* On the rise (article), Artist's Mag; Stephen Doherty (auth), The first 10 years, Am Artist, Mag, 2001; Jennifer King (auth), Commissioned portraiture, Fine Art Connoiseur, 2006; Sandra Carpenter (auth), Passing the torch, The Artist Mag, 2006. *Mem:* Nat Arts Club; Allied Artists of Am & Audobon Artists (full mem); Artist Fel of NY; Cumberland Soc of Painters; Portrait Soc of Am. *Media:* Oil on Canvas

NEAL, MO
SCULPTOR
b Houston, Tex, Oct 26, 50. *Study:* Wash State Univ, BA, 88; Va Commonwealth Univ, MFA, 91. *Work:* Bemis Ctr Contemp Arts, Omaha, Nebr; Pflum-Wolff, Vermillion, SDak; Yank-Hamon, Albuquerque, NMex; Ekedal & Marion, Muncie, Ind; also pvt collections of MA Doyle, Baton Rouge, La & Dennis & Susan Navrat, Vermillion, SDak. *Exhib:* Minn Mus Art, St Paul, 70; Sheldon Mem Art Gallery, Univ Nebr, Lincoln, 95; solo exhibs, AIR Gallery, NY, 95, Notre Dame Univ, Ind, 96, NW Mo State Univ, Marysville, 96, Murray State Univ, Ky, 96, Wayne State Univ, Nebr, 97, Buena Vista Univ, Storm Lake, Iowa, 97 & Univ Ill, Chicago, 97; Six Nebraska Women, Hillmer Gallery, St Mary's Col, Omaha, Nebr, 96; Fac Exhib, Univ Nebr, Lincoln, 97; Frogman Press, Beresford, SDak, 97; Bloomington Art Ctr, Minn, 97; Essence of Water, Fujiya Corp, Kyota, Japan, 98 & 99; Bemis Found Exhib, Omaha, Nebr, 98. *Pos:* Juror, Bemis Found, 94, Mid Am Col Art Asn, 95, SDak Arts Coun, 95 & Sioux City Art Ctr, Iowa, 96. *Teaching:* Grad asst, Va Commonwealth Univ, 90-91; instr sculpture, Univ SDak, Vermillion, 92-93; asst prof sculpture, Univ Nebr, Lincoln, 94-; lectr & vis artist at var univs, 95-97. *Awards:* Visual Arts Fel Sculpture, Nat Endowment Arts, 94; Res Coun Fac Develop Grant-in-Aid, Univ Nebr, 96-97; Nebr Arts Coun Fel, 98. *Bibliog:* Carol Toner Shane (auth), Dakota dreams, Tractor, Vol 1, No 3, winter 94; Kyle Macmillian (auth), Contemporary styles contrasting, but appealing, Omaha World Herald, 3/26/95; Leland E Warren (auth), Sculptor's works on view, Manhattan Mercury, 9/11/95. *Mem:* Col Art Asn; Mid Am Col Art Asn; SE Col Art Asn. *Media:* Wood. *Mailing Add:* 225 S University St Vermillion SD 57069

NEALS, OTTO
SCULPTOR, PAINTER
b Lake City, SC, Dec 11, 30. *Study:* Self-taught; studied briefly at Brooklyn Mus Art Sch with Isaac Soyer; printmaking workshop, studied with Bob Blackburn, Robert DeLamonica & Krishna Reddy. *Work:* Ghana Nat Mus, Accra; Prime Minister Forbes Burnham, Guyana Statehouse; Columbia Mus, SC; Medgar Evers Col. *Comn:* Earl Graves Publ Co; Prospect Park Alliance; Strivers Ctr Walk of Fame; Ezra Jack Keats Found; Herbert F Johnson Art Mus, Ithaca, NY, 2000; mural, Kings Co Hosp Ctr, 2001; Hampton Mus, Hampton, Va, 2002; St Joseph's Col, Brooklyn, NY, 2003; portrait, Yale Univ Divinity Sch, 2003; Bronze awards for Woodie King's New Fed Theatre. *Exhib:* Resurrection, Studio Mus, NY, 71; Millenium, Philadelphia Mus Art, Pa, 73; Selections 73, Brooklyn Mus, 74; 14 Black Artists, Pratt Inst Gallery, Brooklyn, 76; Migrations, Museo De Arte Moderno, Cali, Colombia, S Am, 76 & Caracas, Venezuela, 77; Columbia Mus of Art, Columbia, SC, 89; Brooklyn Mus, NY, 2004. *Pos:* former dir, Fulton Art Fair, Brooklyn, NY. *Awards:* Award for Excellence in Design, New York City Arts Comn; Award of Merit, Hampton Mus, 2002. *Bibliog:* Peter Bailey (auth), Ten Black artists depict Christ, Ebony Mag, 4/71; Diane Weathers (auth), Black artists taking care of business, New York Times, 8/19/73; Elton Fax (auth), Black Artists of the New Generation, Dodd/Mead & Co, 77. *Mem:* Nat Conf Artists; Asn Caribbean Am Artists; Fulton Art Fair. *Media:* Wood, Stone, Oil, Watercolor. *Publ:* Illusr, African Heritage Cookbook, Macmillan, 71; The Adventures of Tony David & Marc, Exposition Press, 76; Am Visions Mag, 8-9/94; Sculpture Mag, 2/98; Current Biography, 3/2003. *Dealer:* Dorsey's Gallery 553 Rogers Ave Brooklyn NY 11225. *Mailing Add:* 138 Sullivan Pl Brooklyn NY 11225

NECHIS, BARBARA
PAINTER, LECTURER
b Mt Vernon, NY, Sept 25, 37. *Study:* Univ Rochester, BA, 58; Alfred Univ, MS, 59; Parsons Sch Design. *Work:* Butler Inst Am Art; Slater Mem Mus, Conn; Banco de Crefisul, Sao Paulo, Brazil. *Comn:* Citicorp, NY; Int Bus Machines, NY; Westinghouse; NY Graphic Soc; Napa Valley Heritage Fund. *Exhib:* Am Watercolor Soc Exhib, Nat Acad Design, NY, 70-99; Mainstreams, Marietta Col, Ohio; Nat Acad Design Ann; Hudson River Mus; Tweed Mus, Minn; Bard Col, 2005; and others. *Pos:* dir, AWS, 85; Juror & dir, Am Watercolor Soc, 85; juror, New England Watercolor Soc Nat Exhib, Boston, 2000; juror, Nat Watercolor Soc Membership Exhib, Calif, 2000; juror, Transparent Watercolor Soc of Am (TWSA) 2005; juror, Watercolor West, 2006. *Teaching:* Fac mem, Parsons Sch Design 80-92; lectr workshops, currently; guest lectr, Pratt Inst, 94-97 & Can Soc Painters Watercolor. *Awards:* Lena Newcastle Award, Am Watercolor Soc, 85. *Bibliog:* AVP Video, 88; Watercolor 93, fall 93; Splash II, North Light Books, 93; Best of Watercolor, Rockport Pub, 97 (title page). *Mem:* Am Watercolor Soc; Artists Equity. *Media:* Watercolor, Mixed. *Interests:* photog, travel. *Publ:* Illusr, American Artists Group Reproduction, 73; auth, Watercolor, The Creative Experience, North Light/Van Nostrand Reinhold, 79; North Light, 6/79-92; Watercolor From the Heart, Watson-Guptill Publ, 93; auth Am Artist Mag Watercolor Page, Nov 2000. *Mailing Add:* 1085 Dunaweal Ln Calistoga CA 94515

NEEDLER, MABEL GLIDDEN See Howard, Linda

NEES, LAWRENCE
EDUCATOR, HISTORIAN
b Chicago, Ill, Aug 9, 49. *Study:* Univ Chicago, BA, 70; Harvard Univ, MA, 73, PhD, 77. *Teaching:* Vis lectr, Univ Victoria, BC, 76-77; lectr, Univ Mass, Boston, 77-78; from asst to prof, Univ Del, Newark, 78-. *Awards:* Mellon fel, 1982-82; Samuel H Kress sr fel, Ctr for Advanced Study in Visual Arts, 86; John Simon Guggenheim Mem fel, 2000-01; Am Acad award, Berlin, 2004. *Mem:* Int Ctr Medieval Art; Byzantine Studies Asn; Medieval Acad Am; Majestas; Col Art Asn Am. *Res:* Medieval manuscript illumination; Carolingian art. *Publ:* From Justinian to Charlemagne, G K Hall, 85; The Gundohinus Gospels at Autun, Medieval Acad Am, 87; A Tainted Mantle Hercules & the Classical Tradition at the Carolingian Court, Univ Pa, 91; ed, Approaches to Early-Medieval Art, Medieval Acad Am, 98, 2002. *Mailing Add:* Dept Art Hist Univ Del Newark DE 19716

NEFF, JOHN A
PAINTER, DESIGNER
b Lebanon, Pa, May 5, 26. *Study:* Whitney Sch Art, New Haven, Conn, cert; Paier Col Art, Hamden, Conn, with Herbert Gute. *Work:* New Brit Mus Am Art, Gtr Hartford Arts Coun & Mus Art, Sci & Indust, Bridgeport, Conn; Mus Fine Arts, Springfield, Mass; First Nat Bank Boston. *Exhib:* Am Watercolor Soc, NY, 98; RI Watercolor Soc, Pawtucket, RI, 98; Conn Watercolor Soc, 2002; Mystic Int, Maritime Gallery, Mystic, Conn, 2002; Modern Marine Masters, Maritime Gallery, Mytic, Conn, 2003. *Pos:* Sr graphic designer, Muirson Label Co, North Haven, Conn, 50-71; owner, Crossmark Assocs, Wallingford, Conn, 72-87. *Teaching:* Watercolor, privately. *Awards:* Esther Fay Mem Award, Conn Watercolor Soc, 98; 1st Prize Findlay Award, RI Watercolor Soc; Berets Award, Reed Marine Exhibit, Stamford, Conn, 99. *Bibliog:* T F Potter (auth), A proxy visit, Meriden Rec-J, Conn, 69; John Bickford (auth) Painting figures with impact, Artist's Mag, 5/97; Watercolor Expressions, Quarry Pub, 98. *Mem:* Am Watercolor Soc; Allied Artists Am; Conn Watercolor Soc (bd dir, 71-72); Whiskey Painters Am; Am Soc Marine Artists. *Media:* Transparent Watercolor. *Publ:* auth, Collected Best of Watercolor, Rockport Publs, 2002. *Mailing Add:* 17 Parkview Rd Wallingford CT 06492-3051

NEFF, JOHN HALLMARK
ART HISTORIAN, MUSEUM DIRECTOR
b Miami, Fla, Mar 28, 44. *Study:* Wesleyan Univ, Middletown, Conn, BA, 66; Harvard Univ, MA, 68, PhD, 74. *Collection Arranged:* 180 Beacon Collection (auth, catalog), Boston, Mass, 67, Great Ideas Prog, Container Corp, 78-80; First Nat Bank Chicago, 84-97; Am Medical Asn, Chicago, 89-90; John D and Catherine T MacArthur Found, 91-95; Holleb & Coff, 96. *Pos:* David E Finley fel, Nat Gallery Art, Washington, DC, 69-72; asst cur, Sterling & Francine Clark Art Inst, Williamstown, Mass, 72-73; cur mod art, Detroit Inst Arts, 74-78; dir, Mus Contemp Art, Chicago, 78-83; mem, adv comt for exhibs, Am Fedn of the Arts, 81-; mem, Nat Adv Comt, Art in Pub Places, Dade Co, Fla, 82-90; dir, art prog-art adv, First Nat Bank Chicago, 83-97; mem adv comt, Art & Ideas Prog, Sch Art Inst Chicago, 85-; Mus d'Art Am, Giverny, France, 97-99; Terra Mus Am Art, Chicago, 97-2001. *Teaching:* Teaching fel 19th & 20th century art hist, Harvard Univ, 67-69; asst prof 19th & 20th century art, Williams Col, Williamstown, Mass, 72-74, vis lectr, grad prog, 73-74; Matisse seminar, Grad Sch, Sch Art Inst Chicago, 94; Anselm Kiefer Seminar, Anderson Arts Ranch, Snowmass, Colo, 97. *Bibliog:* Hilton Kramer (auth), Rediscovering the genius of Henri Matisse, New York Times, 7/27/75; Robert Pincus-Witten (auth), Detroit notes, Arts Mag, 78; Anselm Kiefer (auth), A 'Gnostic' Triptych, NC Mus Art Bulletin, 97. *Mem:* Arts Club, Chicago; AAMD (bd mem, 83-94); Col Art Asn (bd dir, 96-2000); Renaissance Soc; Sculpture Chicago; ICOM. *Res:* Matisse scholar; Anselm Kiefer; public art, Kabbalistic imagery, corporate patronage. *Publ:* An Early Ceramic Triptych by Henri Matisse & Matisse's Forgotten Stained Glass Commission, The Burlington Mag, 12/72; Coauth, The Gott Impression of Pollaiuolo's Battle of Nudes, Nat Gallery of Art, Washington, DC, 73, Henri Matisse: Paper Cut-Outs, Abrams, 77; Some Thoughts on Barnett Newman, The Bulletin, Detroit Inst Arts, Spring, 78; Charles Simonds: Circles and Towers Growing, Mus Contemp Art, Chicago, 81; Contemporary Art from the Netherlands, Smithsonian Inst Traveling Exhib Service, 82; Anselm Kiefer, Bruch und Einung, Marian Goodman, New York, 87; contribr, Natural Light: Roger Ackling, Centre d'Art Contemp, Geneve, Switz, 91; Daring To Dream, Univ Chicago Press, 92; Hands On: Irwin and Abstract Expressionism (catalog essay), Mus Contemp Art, Los Angeles, 93; Kabbalistic Imagery in Negotiating Rapture, Mus Contemp Art, Chicago, 96

NEFFSON, ROBERT
PAINTER
b New York, NY, Dec 28, 49. *Study:* Art Students League, 64-67; Skowhegan Sch Painting, 69; Boston Univ, BFA(cum laude), 71, MFA, 73. *Work:* Roswell Mus, NMex; Boston Univ; Bristol Col, Mass; Charlestown Savings Bank, Boston. *Comn:* Arthur Anderson & Co; NY Life Insurance Co. *Exhib:* Butler Inst Am Art 45th Ann Midyear Show, 81; solo exhibs, Capricorn Gallery, Bethesda, Md, 83, Summer Remembered, Squibb Gallery, Princeton, NJ, 84 & Gallery Henoch, NY, 90, 92 & 97; Artists Studio 1840-1983, Allentown Mus, Pa, 83-84; OK Harris Works of Art, Birmingham, Mich, 93; 20th Century Am Realism, South Bend Reg Mus Art, Ind, 94; Evolution of a 20th Century Metrop, Pelham Art Ctr, NY, 94; and others. *Pos:* Artist-in-residence, Roswell Mus, NMex, 77-78. *Teaching:* Asst prof art, Ariz State Univ, 81-82, Pa State Univ, 82-88, Art Students League, NY, 95- & Pratt Inst, NY. *Awards:* Fulbright-Hays Fel, Rome, 76-77; Mass Coun Arts Grant, 76; Pa Coun Arts Visual Artists Grant, 83. *Bibliog:* Article, Survey of contemporary still lifes, Am Artist Mag, 2/86. *Mem:* Col Art Asn. *Media:* Oil. *Publ:* Auth, Using photographs to interpret the modern world, Am Artists Mag, 87. *Dealer:* Gallery Henoch 80 Wooster St New York NY 10012

NEGRON, JESUS
ARTIST
b Arecibo, Puerto Rico, 75. *Exhib:* Primero Auxillios, ARCO, 2002; M&M Proyectos, Viego San Juan, 2002; Art Basel Miami Beach, 2002; We Surrender, Venice, Italy, 2003; 24/7, NY, 2003; Colectivo La Rlexible, Biennial Caribe, Santo Domingo, 2003; Stray Show, Chicago, 2004; Galeria Comercial, San Juan, 2004; Whitney Biennial: Day for Night, Whitney Mus Am Art, 2006. *Pos:* res M&M, Proyectos, San Juan, Puerto Rico

NEGROPONTE, GEORGE
PAINTER
b New York, NY, Feb 11, 53. *Study:* Skowhegan Sch of Painting & Sculpture, 73; Yale Univ, BA, 75. *Work:* Chemical Bank, New York, NY; Bank of Am, San Francisco, Calif; Reader's Digest Asn, New York, NY; Metrop Mus Art, NY; Mus Art, Andros, Greece. *Comn:* Paintings, Olympia & York, 81 & TWA, 86, NY; IBM, NY. *Exhib:* Solo exhibs, Brooke Alexander Inc, NY, 81, 83 & 85, John Good Gallery, NY, 87-88, Real Art Inc, NY, 90 & Jason McCoy, 90-91, 95, 96 & 98, Jason McCoy, 03; New Drawing in Am, Mus Mod Art Ca'Pesaro, Venice, Italy, 83; An Int Survey of Painting & Sculpture, Mus Mod Art, NY, 84, 87 & 88; Recent Acquistions, Metrop Mus Art, 89; Yale Collects Yale, Yale Univ Art Gallery, New Haven, Conn, 93; Contemp Artists in NY, Edobori Gallery, Osaka, Japan. *Pos:* Consult, Drawing Ctr, NY, 82-84; visual arts panelist, NY State Coun Arts, 85-89, appeals panel, co-chmn Drawing Ctr, NY, 98-; co-chmn, Drawing Ctr, 98-02, pres, 2002. *Teaching:* Instr, Studio Sch, NY, 90- & Parsons Sch Design, 96-99, Princeton, 99-2000. *Awards:* Individual Artists Award, NY State Coun Arts, 88. *Bibliog:* Charles Hagen (auth), Art Forum, 10/87; Robet Edelman (auth), Art Am, 1/89; Jed Perl (auth), New Criterion, 3/89. *Media:* Oil. *Dealer:* Jason McCoy Inc New York NY; Charles Cowles Gallery New York. *Mailing Add:* 19 Hubert St New York NY 10013

NEHER, ROSS JAMES
PAINTER, WRITER
b Kingston, NY, June 5, 49. *Study:* Art Students League with Henry Billings & Fletcher Martin, 64-67; Sch Fine Arts, Wash Univ, BFA, 71; Pratt Inst, NY, MFA, 75. *Work:* Brooklyn Mus, NY; Mint Mus, Charlotte, NC; Sidney Lewis, Richmond, Va; Commonwealth Co, Lincoln, Nebr; Binney & Smith, Easton, Pa; Chase Manhattan Bank & Chemical Bank, NY. *Exhib:* Recent Abstract Painting, State Univ NY, Brockport, 76; The New Spiritualism, Robert Hull Fleming Mus, Burlington, 81; GRP Exhib, Albright Knox, Buffalo, 82; Newcastle Salutes NY, Newcastle-upon-Tyne Gallery, Eng, 83, 2 Smart Art Too, 55 Mercer, NY, 85; New Work, NY, Harvard Univ, Cambridge, 85; The New Response, Contemp Painters of the Hudson River, Albany Inst Art, NY, 86. *Teaching:* Prof grad painting, Pratt Inst, 80-. *Awards:* Tiffany Award, Tiffany Found, 86; Cité Des Arts, Paris Residency, Wash Univ, 86. *Bibliog:* Adrian Goddard (auth), Ross Neher: Painting Behavior, Artforum, 12/79; April Kingsley (auth), The New Spiritualism, Oscarrson Hood, 81. *Media:* Oil, Canvas. *Publ:* Auth, Bathysiderodromophobia, The Fox, 76; Dennis Masback's Paintings, 78 & Mentalism Versus Painting, 79, Artforum; The Death of Perception, Issue No 1, 84 & The Legacy of Picasso, Issue No 2, 85. *Dealer:* Howard Scott 72 Greene St New York NY 10012. *Mailing Add:* 545 Broadway New York NY 10012

NEIDHARDT, (CARL) RICHARD
PAINTER, SCULPTOR
b Chattanooga, Tenn, May 4, 21. *Study:* Ga Sch Tech, 39-41; Univ Tenn, Chattanooga, BA, 49; Univ Fla, MFA, 52; Rijksacademie, Amsterdam, Netherlands, 53-54; Ohio State Univ, PhD, 61. *Work:* Atlantic Richfield Oil Co; The Hall Group; Breed & Co; Pace Entertainment Group; Evin Thayer Studios; Chevy Chase Designs. *Exhib:* Dallas Mus Fine Arts, Tex, 63; Hunter Mus Art, Chattanooga, Tenn, 80; Houston Glassel Ann, Tex, 93; Green Mountain Sculpture Exchange, Crowley, Tex, 94; Houston Visual Arts Alliance, Tex, 94; Dallas Ctr Visual Arts, Tex, 94; Tex A & M Univ, 95; Mus of East Tex, 97. *Pos:* Chmn dept art, Hardin-Simmons Univ, Abilene, Tex, 60-65; dir dept art, Angelo State Univ, San Angelo, Tex, 65-66; chmn dept art, Austin Col, Sherman, Tex, 66-86, emer prof art, 86-. *Awards:* Fulbright Award to Netherlands, 53-54; Danforth Grant Res Painting, 58-59; Cullen Grant, 73; Richardson Grant, 75 & 82. *Media:* Acrylic on Canvas; Bronze. *Dealer:* Hooks-Epstein Galleries Inc 2631 Colquitt Houston TX 77098. *Mailing Add:* 321 N Grand Ave Sherman TX 75090

NEIDICH, BROOKE GARBER
PATRON
Study: NYU, BA. *Pos:* Founder, chmn, NYU Child Study Ctr, currently. *Awards:* Recipient Health Care Leadership Award, distinguished community serv, United Hosp Fund, 99. *Mem:* Trustee Chapin Sch, Mt Sinai - NY Univ Health Care Syst, NY Univ Medical Sch Found; bd dir, Lincoln Ctr Theater, Lubovitch Dance Co; adv council Children's Defense Fund - NY; vchmn, Whitney Mus Am Art. *Mailing Add:* c/o Whitney Mus Am Art 945 Madison Ave New York NY 10021

NEIL, J M
WRITER
b Boise, Idaho, June 2, 37. *Study:* Yale Col, AB, 59; Univ Wis, MS, 63; Wash State Univ, PhD, 66. *Collection Arranged:* Will James: The Spirit of the Cowboy (ed, catalog), 85-86 & Historic Ranches of Wyoming (with catalog), 86 & traveling, Nicolaysen Art Mus, Casper, Wyo. *Pos:* Dir, Idaho Bicentennial Comn, Boise, 72-76 & Nicolaysen Art Mus, Casper, Wyo, 83-89; city conservator, Seattle, Wash, 78-81. *Teaching:* Asst assoc prof Am studies, Univ Hawaii, 67-72; vis lectr art hist, Univ Victoria, BC, 76-77. *Mem:* Wyo Coun Arts (bd mem, 85-89); Natrona Co Pub Libr (bd mem, 88-89); Boise City Hist Preserv Comn. *Res:* Primarily in the history of American environmental design--architecture, landscape design, urban planning and others. *Publ:* Auth, Toward a National Taste: America's Quest for Aesthetic Independence, Univ Press Hawaii, 75; Saints & Oddfellows: A Bicentennial Sampler of Idaho Architecture, Boise Gallery Art, 76; The impact of the Armory Show, S Atlantic Quart, 80; Paris or New York? The shaping of downtown Seattle, 1903-1914, Pac NW Quart, 84. *Mailing Add:* PO Box 266-300 Straughan Ave Boise ID 83701

NEILSON, MARY ANN
PAINTER
b Springfield, Mass, May 16, 52. *Study:* Syracuse Univ, BFA, 74; Art Students League, studies with Diana Kan & TJ Clark. *Work:* New York Health & Hosp Corp, NY; Carnegie Hall Offices, NY. *Comn:* Vanderbilt Univ Med Center. *Exhib:* Solo show, Staten Island Botanic Garden, NY, 92; Ann Am Artists Prof League, Salmagundi Club, NY, 92; Autumn Showing, Newark Mus, NJ, 94; Focus on Nature, NY State Mus, Albany, 94; Nicholas Davies Gallery, NY, 95; Nature Ctr, Westport, Conn; Vogel Gallery, Ridgefield, Conn, 2002; Brick Gallery, Essex, Conn. *Pos:* Sr graphic designer, Cosgrove Assocs, New York, 76-82. *Teaching:* Instr botanical illus,

Brooklyn Botanic Garden, 90-96; pvt instr. *Mem:* Catherine Lorillard Wolfe Art Club; Westport Arts Center; Brooklyn Watercolor Soc (vpres, 91-94); Guild Natural Sci Illusr; Am Artist Prof League; Lyme Art Asn. *Media:* Watercolor, Alkyd. *Publ:* Contribr, Graphics International (Switzerland) Graphis, 85, Splash 6, Best of Watercolor, 2001. *Mailing Add:* 5 Daybreak Lane Westport CT 06880

NEIMAN, LEROY
PAINTER, PRINTMAKER, AUTHOR
b St Paul, Minn, June 8, 1927. *Study:* Art Inst Chicago; Univ Chicago; Univ Ill. *Hon Degrees:* Franklin Pierce Col, LHD, 76; St Johns Univ, Hon DFA; Iona Col, DFA, 85; Hofstra Univ, Hon Dr, 97; St Francis Col, Hon Dr, 98; St Bonaventure Univ, Hon Dr Art, 99; Inst Chicago, Sch of Art, Hon Dr Art, 2006. *Work:* Ill State Mus; Joslyn Art Mus; Wodham Col, Oxford, Eng; Hermitage, Leningrad, USSR; Art Inst Chicago; Mus de Bellas Artes, Caracas. *Comn:* comn work by NFL, Am's Cup, Baseball Hall of Fame, Belmont Stakes Horse Race, Buffalo NHL Hockey Team NBA Basketball Hall of Fame, Westchester Golf Classic, World Heavyweights Boxing Championships, Volvo Grand Prix Tennis Tournament, Newport Jazz Festival, New York Marathon, Masters Golf Tournament, NBA, Indianapolis 500 Auto Race, Ky Derby & others; album cover, Frank Sinatra Duets, Duets II & Classic Duets; Most Valuable Player annual painting, NY Mets, Cosmos, Jets, Knicks, Islanders, Rangers, Giants, '76ers and Pittsburgh Pirates. *Exhib:* Carnegie Pittsburgh Int Exhib Contemp Painting, 55; Am Exhib of Oil Painting, Corcoran Gallery Am Art, Washington, 57; Chicago Am Exhibit of Painting & Sculpture, Art Inst Chicago, 60; Hammer Gallery, 63-; Knoedler Gallery, London, 76; retrospective, Minn Mus Art, 76, Okla City Mus Art, 81; Neiman-Warhol, Los Angeles Inst Contemp Art, 81; New State Tretyakov Mus, Moscow, 88; Butler Inst, Youngstown, Ohio, 90; Salon d'Automne, Paris, 92 & 93; Galerie Marcel Bernheim, Paris, 93; Kentucky Derby Mus, Louisville, 97; Whitney Mus, NY; Art Inst Chicago; Baltimore Mus Fine Arts, Md; Duke Univ Mus Fine Art, Durham, NC; Hermitage Mus, Leningrad; others. *Collection Arranged:* Art Inst Chicago, Ill; The Armand Hammer Collection, Los Angeles, Calif; Hermitage Mus, St Petersburg, USSR; Indianapolis Mus Art, Ind; Joslyn Mus, Omaha, Nebr; Minneapolis Inst Arts, Minn; Univ Calif at Los Angeles; Archives Am Art, Smithsonian Inst, 2005. *Pos:* Off artist, ABC-TV, Munich, 72, Montreal, 76 & Olympics, Sarajevo & Los Angeles, 84; computer artist, Superbowl 78, CBS Sports Spectacular, 79, Good Will Games, Moscow, 86; 1st ofcl, Artist KY Derby, Louisville, 97; ofcl Artist Mardi Gras, New Orleans, LA, 2002. *Teaching:* Instr figure drawing, Art Inst Chicago, 50-60; instr painting, Winston-Salem Art Ctr, 64 & Atlanta Poverty Art Prog, 67-68; instr, master classes for high sch students, Art Inst Chicago, 2006. *Awards:* Art Inst Chicago; Univ Chicago; Univ Ill. *Media:* Oil, Enamel; Serigraphy, Etching. *Collection:* Art Inst Chicago; The Armand Hammer Collection, Los Angeles. *Publ:* paintings, Moby Dick or the Whale, Press of A Colish, New York, 1975; Horses, Harry N Abrams, Inc, New York, 1978 & 79, LeRoy Neiman Posters, 1980, Winners, 1983, Japanese transl, 1985, Big-Time Golf, 1992, An American in Paris, 1994 & LeRoy Neiman on Safari, 1997; Carnaval, Knoedler Publ, Inc, New York, 1981; Monte Carlo Chase, Alfred Van der Marck Edits, Inc, New York, 1988; Casey at the Bat, Deuce II Edits, Inc, New York, 2001 & Ecco Press, New York, 2001; The Prints of LeRoy Neiman, 91-2000; LeRoy Neiman, Five Decades, 2003; The LeRoy Neiman Sketchbook; 64 Liston/Clay; 65 Ali/Liston 2004. *Dealer:* Hammer Galleries 33 W 57th St New York NY 10022; Knoedler Publ Co 19 E 70th St New York NY 10021. *Mailing Add:* 1 W 67th St New York NY 10023

NEIMANAS, JOYCE
PHOTOGRAPHER
b Chicago, Ill, Jan 22, 44. *Study:* Art Inst Chicago, MFA, 69. *Work:* Mus Contemp Art, Chicago, Ill; San Francisco Mus Mod Art, Calif; Art Inst Chicago; Mus Fine Art, Houston; Int Mus of Photog, George Eastman House, Rochester, NY. *Exhib:* Solo exhibs, Recent Work, Ctr Contemp Photog, Chicago, 79, Color Construction, Oakland Mus, Calif, 79, Ctr Creative Photog, Tucson, Ariz, 84, Collisions, Presentation House, Vancouver, BC, 88, Ctr Photog, Woodstock, NY, 89 & Legends of Powerless, Gallery 954, Chicago, 93; BIG Pictures by Contemp Photog, Mus Mod Art, NY, 83; Signs of the Times: Some Recurring Motifs in Twentieth-Century Photog, San Francisco Mus Mod Art, Calif, 85; traveling exhib, Photog and Art: Interactions Since 1946, Los Angeles Co Mus Art, 87; Recorded and Revealed, Art Inst Chicago, Ill, 87; Photog Ill, State Ill Ctr Art Gallery, Chicago, 89; Am Photog since 1920: From the Collection of the Ctr for Creative Photog, Tucson, Ariz, 91; Past, Present, Mus Fine Arts, Houston, Tex, 92; Three Decades of Midwestern Photog, Davenport Mus Art, Iowa, 92; The Mediated Image, Univ Art Mus, Univ NMex, Albuquerque, 93; and others; Dog Show, Wood St Gallery, Chicago, 99; Am Perspectives: Photog from the Polaroid Collection, Tokyo Met Mus of Photog, Japan, 2000; Crossing the Line: Photog Reconsidered, Art Inst Chicago, 2000. *Pos:* Chairperson, Photog Dept, Art Inst Chicago. *Teaching:* Prof photog, Art Inst Chicago, 77-. *Awards:* Visual Arts Fel, Nat Endowment Arts, 79, 83 & 90; Artist Grant, Ill Arts Coun, 87; Computer Grant, Apple Corp, 92; Chicago Women's Caucus for Art Honoree. *Bibliog:* Poppy Evans (auth), Fresh Ideas in Photoshop, N Light Bks, 98; Floris Neussus (auth), Photo Poche Series: Photograms, Nathan Publ, Paris, 98; J Luciana & J Watts (auths), The Art of Enhanced Photography, Beyond the Photographic Image, Rockport Publ, 99; T Barrett (auth), Criticizing Photographs: An Introduction to Understanding Images, Mayfield Publ, 2000. *Media:* Collage, Digital Images. *Mailing Add:* Mus of Contemp Photog Columbia Coll Chicago 600 S Michigan Ave Chicago IL 60605

NELLIS, JENNIFRED GENE
SCULPTOR
b Lincoln, Nebr. *Study:* Univ Nebr, Lincoln, BFA, 70; Univ Iowa, Iowa City, MA, 76, MFA, 77. *Work:* Masur Mus, Monroe, La; Fine Arts Gallery, Univ Minn, Morris; Sprague Art Gallery, Joliet Jr Col. *Exhib:* Dahl Fine Arts Ctr, Rapid City, SDak, 89; three-person exhib, WARM Gallery, Minneapolis, Minn, 89; Icons made in Minnesota, AIR Gallery, NY 89; WARM Kansas City Artists Coalition, 90; Artemisia Gallery, Chicago, 90; plus many other group & solo shows. *Teaching:* Assoc prof sculpture, drawing, basic studio & ceramics, Univ Minn, Morris, 78-86, assoc prof, 86-. *Awards:* Sculpture Award, 29th Ann Iowa Artists, 77; Purchase Award, Monroe Nat, 79; Second Prize Award, Pyramid Art Ctr, Rochester, NY, 84. *Bibliog:* Mellissa Stang (auth), New Art Examiner, 5/87; Norita Dittberner (auth) Warm Journal, Vol 8, No 2, 87; Nancy Cohen (auth), Warming Up, Vinyl Arts, 1/12/88. *Mem:* Women's Art Registry Minn; Col Art Asn; Women's Caucus for Art. *Media:* Mixed Media. *Publ:* Auth, Geographies-Geologies, Milkweed Chronicle, winter 83; 1984 Calendar, Women in Art, 84. *Dealer:* Anderson & Anderson Gallery Minneapolis MN; Hamilton Frame & Gallery Independence MO. *Mailing Add:* 505 E 9th St Morris MN 56267-1027

NELSON, AIDA Z
PAINTER, WRITER
b New York, NY. *Study:* New York Univ, BA; Sorbonne, Paris; Art Students League. *Work:* Mus De San Miguel, Mex; Mus des Arts Decoratifs, Paris, france; Mus des Bellas Artes, Buenos Aires, Arg; Banff Ctr Arts, Can; Camac Center, France. *Exhib:* Contemp Group, Centre Culturel Am, Paris, 64; Salon de Jeune Peinture, Mus D'Art Moderne, Paris, 65 & Salon Interministeriel, 67; Art from 2 Americans, M Samtander Gallery, NY, 93; Love & Kisses, MBM Gallery, NY, 94; Pintoras Modernas, Galeria Juan Levy, Mex, 96; Aphrodites Revenge, Mus de San Miguel, Mex, 96; Song of Songs, Banff Ctr for Arts, Alberta, Can, 2000. *Teaching:* instr, Col New Rochelle, NY, 85-87, Sch Visual Arts, New York, 87-90 & New York Univ, 90-93. *Awards:* Emerging Excellence, Mus D'Art Moderne, 65 & Cezanne, 67; Originality in Concept, Mus de San Miguel, 96. *Media:* Acrylic, Mixed Media. *Mailing Add:* 444 Central Park West New York NY 10025

NELSON, HAROLD B
DIRECTOR
b Providence, RI, May 14, 47. *Study:* Bowdoin Col, AB, 69; Univ Del, MA, 72. *Collection Arranged:* Sounding the Depths: 150 Years of American Seascape, Am Fedn of Arts, 90-91; California Focus: Selections From the Collection of the Long Beach Mus Art, 96; New Visions: Selina Trieff (auth, catalog), 96-97; In Ye Grandest Manner and After Ye Newest Fashion (auth, catalog), 2000; Conjunction: The Melba and Al Langman Collection (auth, catalog), 2000; Imps on a Bridge: Wedgwood Fairyland and Other Lustres, (auth, catalog), 2001; The Enamels of Annemarie Davidson (auth catalog), 2004; The Modernist Jewelry of Claire Falkenstein (auth catalog), 2004; Port Visions, photographs by Tom Raiva (auth catalog), 2004; For the People, Am Folk Art (auth catalog), 2004. *Pos:* Cur mus art & archaeology, Univ Mo, 77-79; registrar, Solomon R Guggenheim Mus, 79-83; chief admin for exhibs, Am Fedn Arts, 83-89; dir, Long Beach Mus Art, 89-. *Awards:* Fel, Smithsonian Research, Nat Mus Am Art, 76. *Mem:* Col Art Asn; Am Asn Mus; Asn of Art Mus Dirs. *Res:* Ceramics, Decorative Arts. *Interests:* 20th Century Enamels. *Publ:* Auth, Sounding the Depths: 150 Years of American Seascape (catalog), Chronicle Books, 89. *Mailing Add:* Long Beach Mus Art 2300 E Ocean Blvd Long Beach CA 90803

NELSON, JAMES P
PAINTER
b Boston, Mass, 49. *Study:* Carnegie-Mellon Univ, BFA, 71. *Work:* Carnegie Mus Art; PNC Bank; Western Pa Hosp; Bayer Corp; plus others. *Exhib:* Solo exhibs, Westmoreland Mus Art, Greensburgh, Pa, 80, Hewlett Gallery, Carnegie Mellon Univ, 81, Pittsburgh Plan Art, 84, Carson Street Gallery, Pittsburgh, 87, 90 & 93, Pittsburgh Ctr Arts, 88 & Chatham Col Art Gallery, Pittsburgh, 94, The Univ Club Pittsburgh, 98; Ann Assoc Artists Pittsburgh, Carnegie Mus Art, Pittsburgh, 83-86, 88-89, 91-92 & 94-95; Pittsburgh in Chicago, Deson-Saunders Gallery, Chicago, 90; Pittsburgh X 7, Pittsburgh Ctr Arts, 93; Regional Focus, Pittsburgh Ctr Arts, 96; 42nd Chautauqua Nat, Chautauqua, NY, 99; Exquisite Surfaces, Concept Gallery, Pittsburgh, 2000, 2001 & 2002. *Teaching:* La Roche Col, Pittsburgh, Pa. *Awards:* Purchase Award & Juror's Award, Carnegie Mus Art, Pittsburgh, 87; Festival Award & Highlight Award, Three Rivers Arts Festival, Pittsburgh, 87; Nat Endowment Arts, 89; Painting Award 42nd Chautauqua Nat, Chautauqua, NY, 99. *Bibliog:* Cheryl Regan (auth), James P Nelson, Dialogue Mag, 36, 1-2/88; William Homisak (auth), Nelson's Pittsburgh: Moody City on the Mon, Tribune Rev, 4/21/89; Vicky Clark (auth), James P Nelson, 90; Murray Horne (auth) Pittsburgh X7 Cataloge, 93. *Mem:* Assoc Artists Pittsburgh. *Media:* Oil, Watercolor. *Dealer:* Concept Gallery Pittsburgh PA. *Mailing Add:* c/o Concept Art Gallery 1031 South Braddock Ave Pittsburgh PA 15218

NELSON, JANE GRAY
CURATOR
b Kankakee, Ill, Oct 10, 1928. *Study:* Univ Calif, Berkeley, MLS, 63, MA(classical archeol), 71. *Pos:* Librn, Fine Arts Mus, San Francisco, 71-89, asst cur, Dept Ancient Art, 74-76 & 89-. *Mem:* Am Inst Archeol; Soc Promotion Hellenic Studies; Brontë Soc; Jane Austen Soc; Calif Classical Asn. *Res:* Gnathia ware. *Publ:* Contribr, Three Centuries of French Art, 73, Claude Monet, 73, Africa, Ancient Mexican Art: The Loran Collection, 74, Two Early Hittite Theriomorphic Vessels of the Karum-Period, 82, Inside Wuthering Heights, 84 & Xylophones on Gnathia Vases, 86. *Mailing Add:* Calif Palace Legion of Honor 100 34th Ave San Francisco CA 94121

NELSON, JOAN
PAINTER
b Torrance, Calif, 58. *Study:* Wash Univ, St Louis, Mo, BFA, 81; Brooklyn Mus Sch, Max Beckman Mem Scholar, 81-82. *Work:* Mus Mod Art, Solomon R Guggenheim Mus, NY; Los Angeles Co Mus Art; Hirshhorn Mus & Sculpture Garden, Nat Mus Women Arts, Washington; Mus Fine Arts, Boston; Toledo Mus Art. *Exhib:* Solo exhibs, Contemp Arts Mus, Houston, Tex, 88, Freedman Gallery, Albright Col,

Reading, Pa, 91, Michael Kohn Gallery, 92, John Berggruen Gallery, San Francisco, 94 & Robert Miller Gallery, NY, 95; Currents 39, St Louis Arts Mus, 89; Biennial, Whitney Mus Am Art, NY, 89; Quotations, Aldrich Mus Art, Ridgefield, Conn, 92; 47th Ann Purchase Exhib, Am Acad Arts & Letts, NY, 95; The Small Painting, O'Hara Gallery, NY, 95-96; Changing Horizons: Landscape on the Eve of the Millennium, Katonah Mus, NY, 96; Cuenca Bienal of Painting, Ecuador, 96-97; Rediscovering the Landscape of the Americas (traveling), Gerald Peters Gallery, Santa Fe, NMex, 96-98. *Bibliog:* Michael Brenson (auth), Straightened landscapes of a post-modern era, NY Times, 1/13/89; Kay Larson (auth), Back to Nature, New York, 4/90; Michael Boodro (auth), Joan Nelson: Second Nature, Artnews, 9/90. *Media:* Oil, Wax on Wood. *Mailing Add:* c/o Robert Miller Gallery 526 W 26th St #10A New York NY 10001-5541

NELSON, JON ALLEN
CURATOR, HISTORIAN
b Omaha, Nebr, July 9, 36. *Study:* Univ Nebr, Lincoln, BFA, 59; museology, Univ Minn. *Collection Arranged:* Etchings of J Alden Weir (auth, catalog), 67, Thomas Coleman, Printmaker (auth, catalog), 72 & Sigmund Abeles: The First Twenty Years (auth, catalog), 79, Sheldon Mem Art Gallery, Univ Nebr, Lincoln; Great Plains 1930-1939 (auth, catalog), Ctr in Greater Plains Studies, Univ Nebr, 85. *Pos:* Pres, Nebr Mus Conf, 73; cur, Ctr Great Plains Studies Art Collection, Univ Nebr, formerly. *Teaching:* Adj asst prof, dept art & art hist, Univ Nebr, Lincoln, 91-. *Publ:* Auth, Art of Printmaking, Univ Nebr, Lincoln, 66. *Mailing Add:* 2300 Harwood St Lincoln NE 68502-3058

NELSON, MARY CARROLL
WRITER, PAINTER
b Bryan, Tex, Apr 24, 1929. *Study:* Barnard Col, BA(fine arts), 50, art hist with Julius Held & painting with Peppino Mangravite & Dong Kingman; Univ NMex, MA(art educ), 63, painting with Kenneth M Adams; art educ with Alexander Masley; grad studies art hist with John Tatschl, 69-70. *Exhib:* Art is for Healing, Tex, 92; Layering, NMex, 93; The Layered Perspective, Ark, 94; Celtic Connections, Mass, 98; Landscape Memory, Ariz, 2001; NMex Women in the Arts, Originals, Traces of the Journey, 2003; Masterworks, Miniatures, 2004; Art of Space, Rock, Paper, Scissors, Connections, We Are All One, Celebración, Yes, 2004. *Collection Arranged:* Layering: An Art of Time & Space, (auth, catalog), Albuquerque Mus, 85; Shrines & Sacred Places, NMex A & CF, Albuquerque, 88; Artists of the Spirit (auth, catalog), Walton Arts Ctr, Fayetteville, Ark, 94. *Pos:* cur, Layering, An Art of Time & Space, Albuquerque Mus, 85. *Awards:* Honoree Magnifico, Albuquerque, 97; Bravos Award, Albuquerque, NMex, 2004; Achievement Award, Masterwork, 2005. *Bibliog:* Something about the author, Vol XXIII, 81; Creative Collage: Techniques Leland, Williams North Light Books, 94; Collage: A Dynamic Medium of Experimentation, Bromer, Watson-Guptill, 94; Ann B Hartley (ed), Bridging Time & Space, Markowitz Publ, 98, Mary Todd (auth), Celebrate Your Creative Self Beam North Light, 2001; Rubinov, Jaconson (auth), Eyes of the Soul, Optimum Books, Druck, Germany. *Mem:* Soc Layerists Multi-Media (founder, 82, pres, 82-84, secy, 84-2002, hon, 2002). *Media:* Mixed Media. *Res:* American, Native American & Southwest artists; the relationship of artists' philosophy, spirituality and their technique. *Publ:* Coauth (with R Kelley), Ramon Kelley Paints Portraits, Figures, 77, Legendary Artists of Taos, 80 & auth, Masters of Western Art, 82, Watson-Guptill; auth, Connecting, the art of Beth Ames Swartz, Northland Press, 84; A Vision of Silence, The Art of Dons Steider, Alta Luz Ltd, 96; coauth, Bridging Time & Space, Weyrich Gallery, Albuquerque, NMex; co-auth, The Art of Layering/Making Connections, 2004. *Dealer:* Weyrich Gallery, Albuquerque, NM. *Mailing Add:* 1408 Georgia NE Albuquerque NM 87110

NELSON, PAMELA HUDSON
ASSEMBLAGE ARTIST, SCULPTOR
b Oklahoma City, Okla, Mar 25, 47. *Study:* Southern Methodist Univ, Dallas, Tex, BFA, 74. *Work:* MTV Collection, NY; Steak & Ale Collection, Dallas, Tex. *Comn:* Relief Animals, Dallas Zoo, Tex; Cotton Crown, Co Govt, Blytheville, Ark; Parkland Hosp, Dallas. *Exhib:* Tex Exhib, Nat Mus Women, Washington, DC, 88; Handmade in Texas, LTV Ctr, Dallas, Tex, 87; Tex Ann, Laguna Gloria Mus, Austin, 87. *Pos:* co-cur, Theatre Gallery, Dallas, 1985; workshops Dallas Mus Art, 1982, 85; created, produced award for Leadership Tex, 1993, Girls Club Am, Dallas, 1987, 89; superv, studio assts in mentor prog, 1988-91; juror DART Garland (Tex) Bus Transit Ct, 1992, Site Sculpture Competition, Municipal Ctr, Plano, Tex, 1993; Design Artist, Dallas Light Rail System. *Teaching:* Arlington Art Mus, Tex; pvt art tutor, 1987-93; Instr, Artlington Mus Art, 1991; guest lectr, Dallas Mus Art, 1993. *Awards:* Ron Gleason Award, Excellence 88, Tex Sculpture Asn, 88; Billboard Winner, Outdoor Art, Patrick Media Group, 88; Rec award Laguna Art Mus, 1982, Merit award Tex Christian Univ, 1984, Crystal award Dallas Cable Syst, 1985, Merit award Crescent Gallery, 1986, Merit award Alexandria Mus, 1987, Patrick Media Billboard award, 1988, Excellence '88 award Plz of Ams, 1988, Hon Mention award Longview Mus and Arts Ctr, 1990, Legend award, Dallas Visual Art Center, Merit award, Am Inst of Archits; named Artist-in-Residence, Connemara Conservancy, 1993. *Bibliog:* Judy Kelly (dir), Artseye (TV prog), KERA-Pub Television, Dallas, 87; Paul Nathan (auth), Texas Collects, Taylor Publ Co, 88; Sylvia Moore (auth), No Bluebonnets, No Yellow Roses, Midmarch Arts, 88. *Mem:* Tex Sculpture Asn. *Media:* Wood, Mixed Media. *Dealer:* Peregrine Gallery at the Crescent 2200 Cedar Springs Rd Dallas Tex 75201. *Mailing Add:* 312 S Harwood Dallas TX 75201-5602

NELSON, RUTH BASHA (BASHA RUTH NELSON)
SCULPTOR, PAINTER
b New York NY, July 1, 39. *Study:* Hunter Col, BA, 60; New York Univ, MA, 76. *Work:* Woodstock Hist Soc, NY; Inst Arts, Nassau, Bahamas; US Embassy, Nassau, Bahamas. *Exhib:* group exhib, Art & Cult Ctr, Hollywood, Fla, 82; Women in Art, N Miami Mus & Art Ctr, Fla, 82; Hudson Valley Artist, Mid Hudson Arts & Sci Ctr, Poughkeepsie, NY, 87; solo exhibs, Noho Gallery, NY, 90, 93, 96 & 2000; Woodstock Artists Asn, NY, 94; Biennale Int Dell' Arte Contemporarea, Florence, Italy. *Pos:* Dir, Summerwood Art Ctr, Lake Hill, NY, 85-87; arts coodr, Ulster Co BOCES, New Paltz, NY, 85-90. *Teaching:* Asst instr drawing, Metrop Mus Art, NY, 74-76; instr art, Col of Bahamas, Nassau, 78-80; adj instr art appreciation, Marist Col, Poughkeepsie, NY, 85-88. *Awards:* Welfred McGibbon, Norton Gallery & Mus, 80; Green Co Coun on Arts, The Artist at Play, 86; Lorenze Il Magnifico, 01. *Bibliog:* Tram Combs (auth), Basha Nelson's boxed colors, Woodstock Times, 6/25/87; New York Gallery Guide, Art Now, 5/88; Kingston Daily Freeman, Kingston, NY, 5/14/93; Woodstock Times, 9/95. *Mem:* Artists Equity; Woodstock Artists Asn. *Media:* Aluminum, Paper, Copper. *Dealer:* Noho Gallery 168 Mercer St New York, NY 10012

NELSON, SIGNE
PAINTER
b New London, Conn, Dec 3, 37. *Study:* Univ Conn, BA, 59; Yale-Norfolk Summer Art Sch, 59; Univ NMex, MA, 60; Univ Ore, sem with Ad Reinhardt, 63. *Work:* Tacoma Art Mus, Wash; Roswell Mus & Art Ctr, NMex; SDak Art Mus; Plains Art Mus, Minn; Sheldon Mem Art Gallery, Lincoln, Nebr; and others. *Comn:* Landwave (mural), Five Seasons Ctr, Cedar Rapids, Iowa, 77 & 78-79; Dakotaloft (painted relief), Convention Ctr, Aberdeen, SDak. *Exhib:* Solo exhibs, Sheldon Mem Art Gallery, 72, Montgomery Mus Art, 77, Plains Mus Art, 89, Civic Fine Art Ctr (with catalog), Sioux Falls, SDak, 89, NDak Mus Art, 90 & Kans State Univ, 91; Vessels and Paper, Minneapolis Art Inst, 82; Art for a New Century, SDak Art Mus, 89; Midlands Invitational, Joslyn Art Mus, 90; retrospective (with catalog), SDak Art Mus, 95 & 98; Taos, Santa Fe and Albuquerque: The City Series, Cedar Rapids Art Mus, 98; Albuquerque Mus. *Teaching:* Prof emer, Visual Arts Dept, SDak State Univ, 80-94. *Awards:* Fel Nat Endowment Arts 76, Art Pub Places, 78-79; U-Cross Found, residency, 90; and others. *Bibliog:* Jan Vander Marck (auth), The chromatic waves of Signe Nelson, Artscanada, 71; Mosaic: Interview with Signe Stuart (TV film), SDPTV, 77 & 86. *Media:* Acrylic on Canvas and Paper Constructions. *Dealer:* van de Griff Gallery Santa Fe NM; Anderson O'Brien Gallery Omaha NE. *Mailing Add:* 18 Gavilan Rd Santa Fe NM 87505

NELSON, STEVEN D
EDUCATOR
Study: Yale Univ, BA in studio art; Harvard Univ, MA, PhD(hist art & archit), 98. *Teaching:* Mem fac, Tufts Univ, Wellesley Col; assit prof, African and African Am art hist UCLA, 98-. *Awards:* Magalen O Bryant Int Fel, Radcliffe Inst for Advanced Study, Harvard Univ, 2004-05. *Mailing Add:* Dept Art Hist UCLA 351 Dodd Hall Box 951417 Los Angeles CA 90095-1417

NEMEC, VERNITA MCCLISH N'COGNITA
CONCEPTUAL ARTIST, CURATOR
b Painesville, Ohio. *Study:* Ohio Univ, BFA; New York Univ, MA; Naropa Inst; Performance writing with Simone Forti; Butoh movement with Noboru Kamita, Eiko, Kim Ito, Akira Kasai, Atsushi Takenouchi, Ko Murobushi, Yumiko Yoshioka & others, Japan Soc & The Cave, Williamsburgh, Bkly, NY. *Work:* Savaria Mus; Group Junij; Asian Am Arts Centre; Fairfax Hosp; Franklin Furnace; Mus Mod Art, NY. *Exhib:* Solo exhibs, Fiatal Muveszek Klubja, Budapest, 80, I Stood Without Moving, 10 on 8, 84, Private Places, Women's Bldg, Los Angeles & Franklin Furnace, NY, 85 & Surface Tensions, Experimental Intermedia Found, 86, South Eastern Mo State Univ Mus, 2001, Schacknow Mus, Plantation, Fla, 2006, Fountain St Gallery, Cape Girardeau, Mo, 2006; The Autumn of Her Descent (performance), AIR Gallery, 83, NY; Snug Harbor Cult Ctr, NY, 87; Casa del Lago, Mexico City, 88; Nat Inst Health, Washington, 95; Five Cities Project, Tokyo, Japan, 99; West Chester Community Col, 99; plus others. *Collection Arranged:* The Stories Exhib, Henry St Abrons Art Ctr, New York, 92; Recycling From Imagination Art from Detritus Metro (catalog), Portland, Ore, 94, Kansas City, Mo, 95, Pittsburgh, Pa, 96. *Pos:* Exhib coordr, Mus, A Project for Living Artists, NY, 69-70; contrib ed, Womanart, NY, 76-77; co-dir, Whitney Counterweight, NY, 77-81; dir, Floating Performance, 86; bd dir, Found New Ideas, 86-; pres & exec dir, Artists Talk on Art, 99-97; vpres, Heresies Collective Art & Politics, 92-96; dir, Viridian Artists, 98. *Teaching:* Prof art, City Univ NY, 73-79; vis artist, Univ Calif, Santa Barbara, 83; Studios in a Sch, NY, 86-87; vis artist Rutgers Univ, new Brunswick, 96; vis artist Mich State Univ, 2000; vis artist, Central Wyo College, 2005; vis artist, South Eastern Mo Univ, 2006. *Awards:* Exhib Grant, Artists Space, 79, 83, 85 & 86; Artist-in-residence, Millay Colony Arts, 81; Jerome Found Grant, 88; Kauffman Found, 1995; IACP Grant, The Field, NYC, 1997; Travel Grant, Performance Studies Int, Mainz, Gr; 7 Years of Living Art, Linda Montano, 2004-. *Bibliog:* Michael Fressola (auth), Staten Island Advance, 7/31/87; Kathleen Beckett (auth), NY Times, 3/17/91; Budapest Daily Courier, 3/93; Norma Bourde & M Garrard (eds) The Power of Feminist Art, 94; Lucy Lippard (auth), The Pink Glass Swan, 95. *Mem:* Am Asn Mus; Nat Mus Women Artists. *Media:* Mixed; Performance Art. *Publ:* Auth, Unmaled, pvt pub, 78; contribr, Re-View: Artists on art, Vered Lieb, 78; Tenth assembling, Richard Kostelanetz, 80; auth, Private Thoughts, Private Places, pvt publ, 84; The Red Pagoda, Modern Haiku Zasshi Zo, 88; Downtown Viewpoint, 94; plus others. *Dealer:* Gallery OneTwenty Eight, New York NY; Eleven East Ashland Phoenix AZ. *Mailing Add:* 361 Canal St New York NY 10013

NEMSER, CINDY
CRITIC, WRITER
b Brooklyn, NY, Mar 26, 37. *Study:* Brooklyn Col, BA, 58, MA, 64; Inst Fine Arts, NY Univ, with Walter Friedlander, Charles Sterling & Donald Posner, MA(art hist). *Exhib:* In Her Own Image, Fleisher Art Mem, Phila Mus Art, 1974. *Pos:* Curatorial intern, NY State Coun Arts, Mus Mod Art, 67; contrib ed, Arts Mag, 71-; ed, Feminist Art J, 72-77; theatre critic, NY Law J, 90-96, Our Town, 94-95, West Side Beat, 96, Town & Village, 96, City Search, 99. *Teaching:* Guest lectr, Pratt Inst, Md Inst, RI

Univ, NY Univ, Queens Mus, Brooklyn Mus; and others. *Awards:* Art Critics Fel, Nat Endowment Arts, 76; Commencement Speaker, Minneapolis Col Art, 77; semi-finalist, L Arnold Weisberger Playwrighting Competition, New Dramatists, 90; Veteram Feminists Am award. *Mem:* Founding mem Women in the Arts; Pen Am Ctr; Poets & Writers; Dramists Guild; Women's Cacus Art (adv bd mem, 75-78); Drama Desk Outer Critics Cir. *Res:* Position of women in the art world. *Interests:* Writing memoir about art world in 60's and 70's. *Publ:* Auth, Art Talk Conversations with 12 Women Artists, Scribners, 75; Eve's Delight, Pinnacle Books, 82; Ben Cunningham Monograph, 86; Art to Defy, Reveal and Heal, MS, Vol 3, 11 & 12, 12/92; auth, Art Talk Conversations with 15 Women Artists, HaperCollins, 1995. *Mailing Add:* 41 Montgomery Pl Brooklyn NY 11215

NERBURN, KENT MICHAEL
SCULPTOR, CRITIC
b Minneapolis, Minn, July 3, 46. *Study:* Univ Minn, BA, 68; Stanford Univ, 70; Grad Theological Union, PhD(with distinction), 80; training in wood technique, Marburg, WGer, 71; life drawing with Helmut Schmitt, 74-76; stone sculpture technique, Pietrasanta, Italy, 76; anatomy study with Herbert Shrebnik, Univ Calif, Berkeley, 76. *Work:* Greek Orthodox Diocese, San Francisco; Christ United Methodist Church, St Paul, Minn; Hiroshima Peace Mem Hall, Japan. *Comn:* Wood sculpture: pvt commissions, San Francisco, 74, Taylors Falls, Minn, 75 & Big Sur, Calif, 76; wood sculpture, Westminster Benedictine Abbey, Mission, BC, 80; bronze sculpture, New World Libr, San Rafael, Calif, 85; Humane Soc Hennepin Co, Minn, 91. *Exhib:* Spring Invitational Exhib, United Theological Seminary, New Brighton, Minn, 82; Religious Art, Lutheran Brotherhood Int Hq, Minneapolis, 83; Spiritual Forms, Hennepin Avenue Methodist Church, Minneapolis, 83; Religious Artifacts, Wesley United Methodist Church, Minneapolis, 85; Elegy-an installation in memory of victims of the holocaust, Bemidji State Univ, Bemidji, Minn, 88. *Pos:* Visual Arts Critic, St Paul Pioneer Press & Dispatch, 86, 87; sculpture writer, Art Mag, 86, 87, 88; founder & visual arts critic, Northern Arts Reviewers, Bemidji, Minn, 88; art criticism specialist, Minn Discipline - Based Art Educ Consortium, Minneapolis, 88-. *Teaching:* Instr, Grad Theological Union, 77-79 & Minneapolis Inst Arts, 85 & 86; J Paul Getty Found lect art criticism, Robbinsdale Sch Dist, 87, 88; Minn Humanities Comn visiting prof in Humanities & visual arts, Bemidji State Univ, Minn, 88. *Bibliog:* Adelheid Fischer (auth), The art of Kent Nerburn, Minn Monthly, 5/83. *Mem:* Soc Art, Religion & Cult; Soc Values in Higher Educ. *Media:* Wood. *Publ:* Auth, The age of bronze, Arts Mag, 86; Tribal masks evoke spirits of culture & Artists focus on Minnesota, St Paul Pioneer Press, 86; Peerless Perfection Polykleitos' Doryphoros, Arts Mag, 87; Henry Moore's Warrior with Shield, Arts Mag, 88; numerous reviews, critical articles & commentaries, currently. *Mailing Add:* 325 S Movil Lake Rd NE Bemidji MN 56601-8184

NERDRUM, ODD
PAINTER
Study: Art Acad, Oslo; study with Joseph Beuys, Dusseldorf. *Work:* Nat Gallery & Riksgalleriet, Oslo; Walker Art Ctr, Minneapolis; Hessisches Landes Mus, Darmstadt, WGer; Norsk Kultarrad, Norway. *Exhib:* Solo exhibs, Kunstnerforbundet, Oslo, 64, 67, 70, 73, 76 & 80, Gallery Tanum, Norway, 77 & 83, Martina Hamilton Gallery, NY, 84-87, Del Art Mus, Wilmington, 85 & Germans Van Eck Gallery, NY, 86; The Classic Tradition in Painting and Sculpture, Aldrich Mus, Conn, 85; Neo-Neoclassicism, Edith Blum Inst, Bard Col, Annandale, NY, 86; Second Sight: Biennial IV, San Francisco Mus Mod Art, San Francisco, 86; The Here and Now, Greenville Co Mus, SC, 86; Morality Tales: Hist Painting in the 1980s, Grey Art Gallery, NY Univ, 87; Univ Art Mus, Long Beach, Calif, 88; Mus Contemp Art, Chicago, 88; Madison Art Ctr, Wis, 88; Edward Thorp Gallery, NY, 88; Nelson-Atkins Mus, Kansas City, 89. *Bibliog:* Donald Kuspit (auth), Odd Nerdrum: The Aging of the Immediate, Arts Mag, 9/84; Eleanor Heartney (auth), Apocalyptic visions, arcadian dreams, Art News, 1/86; John Russell (auth), rev, in: New York Times, 5/16/86; Charles Jencks (auth), Postmodernism; and other art criticism. *Mailing Add:* c/o Forum Gallery 745 Fifth Ave New York NY 10151

NERI, MANUEL
SCULPTOR
b Sanger, Calif, Apr 12, 30. *Study:* San Francisco City Col, 49-50; Univ Calif, Calif Col Arts & Crafts, 52-57; Calif Sch Fine Arts, 57-59. *Hon Degrees:* San Francisco Art Inst Hon Dr, 90; Calif Col of Arts & Crafts Hon Dr, 92; Corcoran Sch Art Hon Dr Washington, DC, 95. *Work:* Oakland Mus, Calif; San Francisco Mus Mod Art; Corcoran Gallery Art, Washington, DC; Seattle Art Mus; Fine Arts Mus, San Francisco; Memphis Brooks Mus, Tenn; Portland Art Mus, Portland OR; San Jose Mus of Art, San Jose, CA. *Comn:* Marble sculpture, State Calif Gen Serv Admin, Bateson Bldg, Sacramento, 81-82 & Fed Bldg, Portland, Ore, 88. *Exhib:* Solo exhibs, The Corcoran Gallery Art, traveling exhib, Washington, DC, 96-98; Twentieth Century Am Sculpture at the White House, The White House, Washington, DC, 94-95; Beat Cult and the New Am, 1950-1965, Whitney Mus Am Art, NY, 95-96; San Jose Mus of Art, San Jose, Calif, 97; Manuel Neri: Artists' Books, Fine Arts Mus San Francisco, 2003; Manuel Neri: The Figure in Relief, Grounds for Sculpture, Hamilton, NJ, 2006-2007; Relief Sculptures, Portland Art Mus, Ore, 2007. *Teaching:* Instr, Calif Sch Fine Arts, 59-64; prof art, Univ Calif, Davis, 64-90; Mem fac, art Calif Sch Fine Arts, San Francisco, 1959—1965. *Awards:* Guggenheim Fel, 79; Nat Endowment Arts Fel, 80; Am Acad & Inst Arts & Lett Award, 82; award of merit in sculpture San Francisco Arts Comn, 1985; Lifetime Achievement Award, Int Sculpture Ctr, NY, 2006. *Bibliog:* Thomas Albright (auth), Manuel Neri, Bay Area Figurative Art, 89; Carolyn Jones (auth), Manuel Neri Plasters, Bay Area Figurative Art, 89; Jack Cowart (auth), Manuel Neri, Corcoran Gallery, Washington, DC, 95; Bruce Nixon (auth), Manuel Neri: Artists' Books, Fine Arts Mus of San Francisco, 2003; Bruce Nixon (auth), Manuel Neri: The Figure in Relief, Grounds for Sculpture, 2006. *Mem:* Nat Acad. *Media:* Marble, Plaster. *Dealer:* Ameringer & Yohe Fine Art, 20 W 57th St, New York, NY, 10019; Hackett Freedman Gallery, 250 Sutter St, San Francisco, CA, 94108; Riva Yares Gallery 3625 Bishop Lane Scottsdale AZ 95251. *Mailing Add:* c/o 115 Stonegate Rd Portola Valley CA 94028

NES, MARGARET ISABEL
PAINTER
b Paris, France, Sept 17, 50; US citizen. *Work:* Univ Tex Law Sch, Austin, Tex; Mt Sinai Med Ctr, NY; Mountain Bell Telephone Co, Denver; Mary Cabot Enterprises, Taos, NMex. *Exhib:* Solo exhibs, White Crane Gallery, Taos, NMex, 80, Gallery Sigala, Taos, NMex, 81-82, Varient Gallery, Taos, NMex, 85, Kyle Belding Gallery, Denver, Colo, 87-88 & E S Lawrence Gallery, Taos, NMex, 88-91; Another Great Love Affair, Denver Art Mus, 86; Right to Write, Opening Scene Gallery, Taos, NMex, 93 & 94; Indiana Collects the West, Eiteljorg Mus, Indianapolis, 94; 3rd Generation Show, Taos Art Asn-Stables Art Ctr, NMex, 94; and others. *Teaching:* Instr art, San Felipe Children's Home, San Cristobal, NMex, 82-83. *Awards:* Best in Show, Spirit in Art, Taos Spring Arts, 85; Rembrant Pastel Award, Md Pastel Soc Exhib, 89; Best of Show, Taos Invites Taos, 93. *Bibliog:* Sylvia Paine (auth), Secret lives of buildings, US Art Mag, 10/89; Simone Ellis (auth), Sante Fe Art, Random House, 93; Martha Longley (auth), Exploring the realm of the unknown, Focus Mag, 9/93. *Media:* Pastels, Monotype. *Dealer:* Edith Lambert Gallery Santa Fe NM; Collins-Pettit Gallery Taos NM. *Mailing Add:* c/o Michael McCormick Gallery 106-C Paseo del Puerto Norte Taos NM 87571

NESBITT, ILSE BUCHERT
PRINTMAKER, ILLUSTRATOR
b Frankfurt-Main, Ger, Sept 6, 32. *Study:* Univ Frankfurt, 53-54; Art Acad Hamburg, 54-56, with Richard von Sichowsky, 57-59; Art Acad Berlin, 56-57. *Work:* Deutsche Staatsbibliothek, Leipzig, Ger; Klingspor Mus, Offenbach, Ger; Hunt Botanical Libr, Pittsburgh; Houghton Libr, Harvard Univ, Cambridge, Mass; Newberry Libr, Chicago; State & Univ Libr, Hamburg, Ger; and others. *Comn:* Woodblock prints, Redwood Libr, Salve Regina Univ, Newport, RI, 90, 2002. *Exhib:* Int Book Exhib, Leipzig, Ger, 65 & 71; 20th Century Botanical Illust, Hunt Botanical Libr, Pittsburgh, Pa, 68-69; solo exhibs, Brown Univ Libr, Providence, 83, Rutgers Univ Libr, New Brunswick, NJ, 84, State & Univ Libr, Hamburg, Ger, 88 & Galerie Wolf-Buetow, Oberursel, Ger, 91 & 95 & Brown Univ Libr, Providence, RI, 96, 2006; NE Fine Arts Inst, Boston, Mass, 93; Reepschlagerhaus, Wedel, Ger, 98, 2006. *Pos:* Designer, illusr & printer, Third & Elm Press, Newport, RI, 65-. *Teaching:* Asst, typography & book design, RI Sch Design, Providence, 60-65. *Awards:* Hon Mention, Int Book Exhib, Leipzig, EGer, 65, Bronze Medal, 71; First Prize, Print, Newport Art Mus, RI, 83. *Bibliog:* William Flanagan (auth), The Third and Elm Press, Yankee Mag, 77; Walter Plata (auth), The Third and Elm Press, Philobiblon Quart, 85; Ronald Salter (auth), Ilse Buchert Nesbitt-eine deutsche Buchkuenstlerin in den USA, Illus, 63, 97. *Mem:* Boston Soc Printers; Newport Art Asn & Mus. *Media:* Woodcut; Book Design. *Interests:* Gardening. *Publ:* Coauth & illusr, Weathercocks and Weathercreatures, 70, illusr, The Wren and the Bear, 71, coauth & illusr, Sandy's Newport, 75, ed & illusr, The Best Tailor in the World, 83, auth & illusr, My Garden, 88, Third & Elm Press; ed, illusr, Steigendes, Neigendes Leben, 2000; illusr, Captured Views, 2006. *Dealer:* The Third & Elm Press. *Mailing Add:* c/o Third & Elm Press 29 Elm St Newport RI 02840

NESBITT, JACKSON LEE
PRINTMAKER
b McAlester, Okla, June 16, 13. *Study:* Univ Okla, 31-33; Kansas City Art Inst, 33-40. *Work:* Boston Pub Libr; Lib Cong & Corcoran Gallery, Washington, DC; Metrop Mus Art, NY; Cleveland Art Mus; Nelson-Atkins Mus, Kansas City; and others. *Comn:* 5 Editions, Asn Am Artists. *Exhib:* Stone & Press, New Orleans, 93; Univ Ga Art Mus, 99. *Teaching:* Instr etching, Kansas City Art Inst, 49-51. *Awards:* Eames Prize, Soc Am Etchers, 46. *Bibliog:* Earl Retif & Ann Salzer (auths), Jackson Lee Nesbitt, The Graphic Work (exhib catalog). *Media:* Etching, Lithography. *Dealer:* Stone & Press New Orleans LA 70130. *Mailing Add:* 238 C Chartres New Orleans LA 70130

NESIN, JEFFREY DAVID
EDUCATOR
Mailing Add: Memphis Coll Art Office of Pres 1930 Poplar Ave Memphis TN 38104-2756

NESSIM, BARBARA
PAINTER, ILLUSTRATOR, EDUCATOR
b Bronx, NY, Mar 30, 39. *Study:* Pratt Inst, BFA. *Work:* Smithsonian Inst, Wash; World Trade Ctr, NY; Libr Cong, Wash. *Comn:* Digital paintings, 600 Wash St Bldg lobby, NY City; Digital Paintings, Centria Bldg Lobby, New York City. *Exhib:* group exhib, Inaugural Show, Bitforms Gallery, Chelsea, NY, 01, A Teachers Legacy, Babbage Art Gallery Univ Conn, 02, 2003 Int Women Designers Exhib, Seoul Arts Ctr, Korea, 03, The Transparent Network, Somarts Gallery, 04; Ram 400, Colo State Univ, Ft Collins, Colo, 92; Ram 400, Ariz State Univ, Tempe, 93; Ram 400, Adams Landing Art Ctr, Cincinnati, Ohio, 94; Random Access Memories, Centro Colombo Americano, Bogota, Colombia, 95; Visual Solutions, Norman Rockwell Mus, Stockbridge, Mass, 99-; Black Truths/White Lies, Bitforms Gallery, Chelsea, New York City, 2003-. *Teaching:* adj prof visual concepts, Sch Visual Arts, NY, 67-87, adj prof computer art, 87-92; adj prof, Pratt Inst, Brooklyn, NY, 74-84; chairperson illus dept, Parsons Sch Design, NY, 92-2004, prof, Visual Concepts, Painting & Drawing, 204-; prof visual concepts, Painting & Drawing, Parsons Sch of Design, 92-2004-. *Awards:* Siggraph Grant, 90. *Bibliog:* Elinor Craig (auth), Barbara Nessim, Macweek, 5/88; Carol Olsen Day (auth), The art of Barbara Nessim, PC Computing, 10/88. *Mem:* Nat Computer Graphics Asn (bd mem & treas, Arts Sect, 87-); Asn Computer

Art & Design Educ; Graphic Artists Guild (treas, 88-); Siggraph. *Media:* Digital paintings, Digital installations, watercolor, etching. *Publ:* Auth, Barbara Nessim Sketchbook, pvt publ, 75; contribr, Living with Art, Alfred A Knopf, 87; Digital Visions, 87 & Varieties of Visual Experience, 87, Harry Abrams. *Dealer:* Bitforms Gallery

NESTOR, LULA B
PAINTER, ADMINISTRATOR
b Weirton, WVa. *Study:* WVa Univ, 55-56; West Liberty State Col, WVa, BAE; Eastern Mich Univ, MA(art), 73. *Work:* Pittsburgh Plate & Glass Co; Mt Lebonen Greek Orthodox Church, Pittsburgh; WVa Univ; Mich Educ Asn, State Collection Art; Ins Com & Galleries, Michalsons Gallery, Washington, DC. *Exhib:* Butler Inst Art, Butler Mus, Youngstown, Ohio, 73 & 75; Nat Soc Painter in Casien, Nat Gallery of Acad, NY, 76; Audubon Artist 35th Ann Exhib, Nat Acad Gallery, NY, 76; Nat Watercolor Soc 57th Ann, Calif State Univ, 77; one-woman exhibs, Univ Mich, 75, Univ WVa, Morgantown, 75, Constantine Grimaldis Gallery, 80 & 81 & Bowling Green State Univ, Ohio, 83; Univ Mich, 91. *Pos:* Dir, Hartland Regional Fine Arts Festival, 68-77; past pres & trustee mem, Hartland Art Show, Mich. *Teaching:* Instr, Richie Jr High Sch, Wheeling, WVa, 57-58, Elida High Sch, Elida, Ohio, 58-59 & South Lima Jr High Sch, Lima, Ohio, 60-62; art instr & dir art dept, Hartland High Sch, Mich, 68-81; instr adult educ classes, Hartland Consolidated Schs. *Awards:* First Place, Nat Pittsburgh Watercolor Aqueous Open Competition, 74 & 76; Int Artist in Watercolor Competition, London, 82; Award, Nat Watercolor Soc Ann, 82. *Mem:* Mich Watercolor Soc (mem bd); Midwest Watercolor Asn, Minn; Nat Watercolor Soc; Watercolor USA Honor Soc. *Media:* Watercolor; Casien. *Mailing Add:* 9865 Edward Dr Brighton MI 48116

NETSCH, WALTER
ARCHITECT
b Chicago, Feb 23, 1920. *Study:* Mass Inst Tech, 39-43. *Hon Degrees:* Lawrence Univ, Wis, D (hon), 68; Miami Univ, D (hon), 79; Northwestern Univ, DFA (hon), 80. *Comn:* Northwestern Univ Library, 64-70 (Superior Craftsman Award, Concret Contractors Asn of Chicago, 70); other projects for Northwestern Univ include Lakefill project, 62-68, Lindheimer Astronomical Res Ctr, 66, Rebecca Crown Ctr, 68, OT Hogan Biolgoical Sciences Bldg, 70, Frances Searle Bldg, 72, Regenstein Music Bldg, 77, Seeley G Mudd Library for Sci and Engineering, 77; US Air Force Acad Cadet Chapel, Colorado Springs, 54-63; Univ Ill, Chicago Campus, 61-65; Louis Jefferson Long Library, Wells Col, Aurora, NY, 68; Selby Public LIbrary, Sarasota, Fla, 78. *Exhib:* Transformations in American Architecture, Mus Modern Art, NY, 79; Late Entries to Chicago Tribune Competition, Mus Contemp Art, Chicago, 80; Zolla/Lieberman Gallery, Chicago, 81; Miami Univ Art Mus, Oxford, Ohio, 83, 91; Snite Mus Art, Univ Notre Dam, Ind, 84; Northwestern Univ Library, 2006. *Pos:* Architect for L Morgan Yost, 43; architect, Skidmore, Owings and Merrill, 47, design partner; pres bd dirs Chicago Park District, 86-87, commissioner, 86-89; established consulting practice, Chicago, 90-. *Awards:* R S Reynolds Award, 64. *Mem:* Fel, Am Inst Architects (Honor Award, 78, Bartlett Award, 78, Library Bldg Award, 78); Northwestern Univ (bd governors, life mem)

NETTLER, LYDIA K
PAINTER
b New York, NY, Aug 20, 47. *Study:* UCLA, BA, 68; Sch Social Work, MSW, 75; Univ Mass, Amherst, 76-78; Sch Mus Fine Arts, Boston, 78 79. *Work:* Sterling Drug Co, Philadelphia, Pa. *Comn:* paintings, Northampton Sch System, Mass, 97 & 98; mural, Hamshire City Long Term Care, Northampton, Mass, 99. *Exhib:* Drawing Show, Boston Ctr for Arts, 88, 89; one-woman shows, Hillyer Gallery, Smith Col, Northhampton, Mass, 88, Sarah Doyle Gallery, Brown Univ, Providence, RI, 92 & Student Union Gallery, Univ Mass, Amherst, 97; River Passage, Springfield Mus Fine Arts, Mass, 91; On the Verge, Eruus Gallery, Boston, 93; Collaboration, Albany Inst Art & Hist, 94. *Awards:* First prize, Women's Art Show, Mass, 77; Award, Greenfield Comn Col Show, 87 & 89; Finalist, Amherst Pub Art Competition, 90; Finalist, Mass Cult Comn Artist Grant, 2000. *Media:* Oil, Charcoal. *Collection:* Sterling Drulb, Private Collections. *Mailing Add:* 66 Washington Ave Northampton MA 01060

NETZER, NANCY
MUSEUM DIRECTOR
b Pittsburgh, Pa, Jul 25, 51. *Study:* Harvard Univ, MA, 1978; Harvard Univ, PhD, 1986; Univ Ulster, N Ireland, LittD (hon), 2000. *Pos:* Asst cur, Mus Fine Arts, Boston, 1982-90; prof fine arts, Boston Coll, 1990-; dir, McMullen Mus Art, 1990-; Board advs, Int Ctr Medieval Art, New York City, 1990-94; dir, Int Ctr Medieval Art, 1995-, Fragmented Devotion, 2000, Secular/Sacred, 2006. *Publ:* Auth: Medieval Objects in the Mus of Fine Arts, 1986, vol. II, 1991, Cultural Interplay in the Eighth Century, 1994, Memory and the Middle Ages, 1995. *Mailing Add:* McMullen Mus Devlin Hall #423 140 Commonwealth Ave Chestnut Hill MA 02467-3800

NEUBERGER, ROY R
COLLECTOR, PATRON
b Bridgeport, Conn, July 21, 03. *Study:* NY Univ; Univ Sorbonne; State Univ NY, Purchase, DFA, 82; Parson's Sch Design, New Sch Social Res, LHD, 85; Bar-Ilan Univ, Israel, DHL, 87. *Pos:* Bd dir, City Ctr Music & Drama, Inc, 57-74, finance chmn, 71-74, trustee, 74-; chmn adv coun arts, New York City Housing Authority, 60-68; trustee, Whitney Mus Am Art, 61-68, emer trustee, 69-; fine arts gifts comt, Nat Cult Ctr, 62-68; adv comt art, Mt Holyoke Col, 63-78; fine arts adv comt, Amherst Col, 63-70; hon trustee, Metrop Mus Art, 68-; pres coun, Mus City NY, 71-; benefactor, Newberger Mus Art, Purchase, NY, 74-. *Teaching:* Lectr art, Wadsworth Atheneum, Vassar Col, Brooklyn Mus, Detroit Inst Art, Mass Inst Technol Alumni Assocs, State Univ NY, Purchase. *Awards:* Gary Melchers Medal, Artist's Fel, Inc, NY, 84; Arts Award Coun for Arts Westchester, NY, 85; State Univ NY Purchase Award, Neuberger Mus Art; and others. *Mem:* Life fel Nat Acad Design; Benjamin Franklin Soc Arts; New Sch Social Res (trustee & mem exec comt, 67-78); Nat Gallery Art, Washington, (trustee, mem collector's comt, 78); Purchase Col Found (trustee, 71-85, chmn, 74-85); and others. *Collection:* Primarily American art. *Publ:* Contribr, Art in Am & var other art catalogs. *Mailing Add:* 605 3rd Ave 41st Flr New York NY 10158-3698

NEUHAUS, MAX
SCULPTOR, LECTURER
b Beaumont, Tex, Aug 9, 39. *Work:* Times Square, Metrop Transporation Authority, NY, 77; Collection Mus of Contemp Art, Chicago, 79; Collection Domaine de Kerguehennec, Locmine, France, 86; Three to One, AOK Building, Documenta 9, Kassel, 92; Collection CAPC Musee d'Art Moderne, Bordeaux, 93; Collection Castello di Rivoli, Museo d'Art Contemporanea Turin, 96; Collection Swisscom, Worblaufen-Bern, 99; Suspended Sound Line, Collection Kunst im offentlichen Raum die Stadt Bern; Collection Dia Art Found, NY, 2002; Promenade du Pin, Collection Fonds Contonal d'Art Contemporain, Geneva, 2002. *Comn:* Como Park, St Paul, Walker Art Ctr, Minneapolis, 80; Villa Celle, Pistoia, Italy, 83; River Grove, Roaring Fork River, Aspen, Int Design Conference, 88; Time Piece, Kunsthalle, Bern, 89; Lake Luzern, Geneva, Switz, 90. *Exhib:* Solo exhibs, Mus Mod Art, NY, 78, Stichting De Appel, Amsterdam, 78, Rive Russians, The Clocktower, NY, 79, ARC 2, Musee d'Art Moderne de la Ville, Paris, 83, Kunsthalle, Basel, 83, Bell Gallery, Brown Univ, Providence, 83, Sound Line, Centre Nat d'Art Contemporain, Grenoble, France, 88, A Bell for St Cacilien, Kolnischer Kunstverein, Cologne, 89, Two Sides of the Same Room, Dallas Mus Art, Tex, 90, Evoking the Aural, Drawings and their studies from the Place works, Villa Arson, Nice, 95, The Drawings from Three to One, Encore.Bruxelles and Found pour L'Architecture, Brussels, 97, Selected Drawings from the Sound Works: 1967-2000, Lisson Gallery, London, 2000, PS1 Contemp Art Ctr, NY, 2000 & Images from Eight Vectors 1953-2000, Christine Burgin Gallery, NY, 2000, Max Neuhaus, Three to One, Drawings from the sound work, Lawrence Markey, NY, 2002; group shows, Documenta 6, Kassel, Ger, 77, Time Piece Archetype, Whitney Biennial, Whitney Mus Am Art, NY, 83, Promenades, Centre d'Art Contemporain, Geneva, 85, Two Identical Rooms, Einleuchten, Deichtorhallen, Hamburg, 89, Three to One, Documenta 9, Kassel, Ger, 92 & Intersection I, Venice Biennale, Venice, 99. *Bibliog:* Carter Ratcliff (auth), Max Neuhaus: Aural Spaces, Art in Am, New York, 10/87; Calvin Tomkins (auth), Onward and upward with the arts-Hear, The New Yorker, 22, 10/88; Harald Szeemann (auth), Max Neuhaus, Kunstforum Int, vol 127, 94; Pier Luigi Tazzi (auth), Max Neuhaus: The Collection, Museo d'Art Contemporanea, 97 & Constructed Sound: Max Neuhaus, Carte d'Arte Internationale, 11/97; Doris von Drathen (auth), Gebaute Tone, Kritisches Lexikon der Gegenwartskunst, 98; Edward Leffingweil (auth), Max Neuhaus at Christine Burgin and PS1, Art in America, 4/2001; Marguerite Menz (auth), Ganf: Promenade du Pin Von Max Neuhaus, Kunst-Bulletin, 1/2003-2/2003. *Media:* Sound works. *Publ:* Auth, Sound Installation, (Ger, Eng) Kunsthalle Basel, 83; (Fr, Eng), Edition du Centre d'Art, Domaine de Kerguehennec, Locmine, France, 87; Two Sound Works 1989, (Ger, Eng), Kunsthalle Bern, Switz & Kolnischer Kunstverein, Cologne, Ger, 89; Elusive Sources and Like Spaces, (Ital, Eng), Giorgio Persano, Turin, Italy, 90; Sound Works vols 1-3 (Eng), Cantz, Stuttgart, Ger, 95; auth, The Place Works, Sound character and textures, The drawing after, The sound work for Castello di Rivoli, The Collection: Max Neuhaus, 97; Sound as a medium, Three to One, Brussels: La Lettre Volee, 97; Sound Art, PS1 Contemp Ctr, New York, 7/2000. *Mailing Add:* 350 Fifth Ave Suite 3304 New York NY 10118

NEUMAN, ROBERT S
PAINTER
b Kellogg, Idaho, Sept 9, 26. *Study:* Calif Col Arts & Crafts; Calif Sch Fine Arts, BAA, 50, MFA, 51; Univ Idaho, 44 & 46; studied with Max Beckman, Mills Col, James Budd Dixon & Hassel Smith, San Francisco Sch Fine Arts, Willi Baumeister, Statliche der Akademie der Bildenden Kunste, Stuttgart, Ger. *Work:* San Francisco Mus Art; Boston Mus Fine Arts; Fogg Mus Art, Harvard Univ; Mus Mod Art, NY; Farnsworth Mus, Rockland, Maine; plus others. *Exhib:* San Francisco Mus Art, 50; Oakland Mus Art, 50; Solo exhib, Gumps Gallery, San Francisco, 51 & 52, Galleria del Cavallino, Venice, Italy, 60, Allan Stone Gallery, NY, 72, Wingspread Gallery, Northeast Harbor, Maine, 80, Eliza Spenser Gallery, Newton, Mass, 91 & Alhambra Paintings, Lahey Clinic North, Peabody, Mass, 94; De Cordova & Dana Mus, 60-65; New Eng Art Today, 63 & 65; Allan Stone Gallery, NY, 63; Mus Mod Art, 64; Pace Gallery, Boston, 65; Sunne Savage Gallery, Boston, 79; Allan Stone Gallery, NY, 2006; Abbe Mus, Bar Harbor, ME; and many others. *Teaching:* Fac, San Francisco Sch Fine Arts, Calif Col Arts & Crafts, 52, Harvard Univ, RI Sch Design & Brown Univ; instr, State Univ NY, New Paltz, 55-57, Mass Col Art, Boston, 57- & Brown Univ, 61-63 & Carpenter Ctr Visual Arts, Harvard Univ, 63-72; prof art & chmn art dept, Keene State Col, NH, 72-90; guest lectr, Simmons Col, Boston, 65 & Univ Idaho, 69. *Awards:* Fulbright Grant, 53-54; Prize, San Francisco Mus Art; Guggenheim Fel, 56-57; and others; Bender Grant-in-Aid, San Francisco Art Asn, 1952. *Media:* Oils, Watercolor, Lithographs, Etchings, Drawing. *Publ:* Auth, Artists Book: Ship of Fools/Ship to Paradise, High Loft Press, Seal Harbor, Maine. *Dealer:* Allan Stone Gallery New York NY; Wingspread Gallery Northeast Harbor ME 04662. *Mailing Add:* 135 Cambridge St Winchester MA 01890

NEUMANN, ANDREW
EDUCATOR, PAINTER
Study: Emerson Col, BS. *Exhib:* Exhibs incl, FPAC Gallery, Boston, Gallery Bershad, ARCADE, DeCordova Mus, albums, No Fly Zone, Scramble: Lock: Combination. *Teaching:* Lectr, filmmaking Sch Mus Fine Arts, Boston; artist-in-residence, iEAR Studio, Rensalear Polytech Inst, Visual Studies Workshop. *Awards:* Fel Guggenheim Mem Found, 2004. *Mailing Add:* c/o Bitform Gallery 529 W 20th St New York NY 10011

NEUSTEIN, JOSHUA
PAINTER, CONCEPTUAL ARTIST
b Danzig, Poland, Oct 16, 40; US citizen. *Study:* City Col New York, 57-61, BA, 61; Art Students League, 59-61; Pratt Inst, Brooklyn, NY, 60-63. *Work:* Mus Mod Art, Whitney Mus Am Art, NY; Jerusalem Mus of Israel; Tel Aviv Mus of Art, Israel; Louisiana Mus, Copenhagen, Denmark. *Exhib:* Travel Art, Mus Mod Art, Oxford, Eng, 71; Documenta V, Kassel, Ger, 72; Photog in Art Camden Art Ctr, London, 72; Photog Triennale, Israel Mus, Jerusalem, 76; One-man shows, Mus Art, Wocester, Mass, 75 & Neutein-Ten Yrs, Tel Aviv Mus, Israel; With Paper About Paper, Albright-Knox Gallery, Buffalo, 80; Henri Onstad Art Ctr (catalog), Norway, 81; and many other solo & group exhibs. *Awards:* Willem Sandberg Prize, Jerusalem, 74; Guggenheim Fel, 87. *Bibliog:* R Pincus-Witten (auth), Sons of Light, 9/75, Six propositions, 12/75 & Neustein papers, 10/77, Arts Mag; Steven Kasher (auth), The substance of paper, 3/78 & Seven Artists of Israel, summer 79, Artforum Mag; Joseph Masheck (auth), Nothing not nothing something, Artforum Mag, 11/79 & Marking & Disclosure, H Johnson Mus, 83; Donald Kuspit (auth), Art with a moral mission, Flash Art, 87; Robert Morgan (auth), Neustein, Flash Art, 88; and many others. *Media:* Environment, Photo. *Res:* Art criticism. *Dealer:* Mary Boone 420 W Broadway New York NY 10012; B Urdang 23 E 74th St New York NY 10021. *Mailing Add:* 7 Mercer St New York NY 10013-2548

NEVELSON, MIKE
SCULPTOR
b New York, NY, Feb 23, 22. *Work:* Colby Col; Wadsworth Atheneum; Whitney Mus Am Art; Strater Mus; Stratford Col. *Exhib:* Staempfli Gallery; Whitney Mus; Grand Cent Moderns; Amel Gallery; Expo 68, Montreal; plus others. *Media:* All

NEVIA, JOSEPH SHEPPERD ROGERS
PAINTER
b Washington, DC. *Study:* Longfellow Sch with Theodora Kane and Berthold Schmutzart, 63; Greensboro Col, with Irene Cullis and Callie Braswell, BA, 67; Univ NC, Greensboro, with Will Insley, Peter Agostini, Walter Barker, Andrew Martin, Gilbert Carpenter & Stephen Antonagis, MFA, 69. *Work:* Maryland Collection, Univ Md. *Comn:* Mural, Bishop O'Connell Sch, Arlington, Va, 79; also pvt comns. *Exhib:* Artists of the 80's, Dallas, Tex, 85; Shelters '85, Zenith Gallery, Wash, DC, 85; The Art of Fantasy, Artspace, Raleigh, NC, 87; The Artful Chair, Target Gallery, Alexandria, Va, 90; Dream House, Peninsula Fine Arts Ctr, Newport News, Va, 92; Avien of Counter Vail, 2005; and others. *Pos:* Dir, Garfinckle's Art Gallery, Washington, DC, 72-74, Porcelaine Galleries, Baltimore, 74-75. *Teaching:* Instr art, Prince George Co Bd Educ, Upper Marlboro, Md, 69-70, Corcoran Sch Art & Col Inst Art, Columbia, Md, 70-71. *Bibliog:* Klim Caviness (auth), Renaissance and Joe Rogers, Alexandria Port Packet, Va, 84; Doris Miller (interviewer), Artist Nevia, Channel 10 Cable Station, Alexandria, Va, 84; Ann M Augherton (auth), Nevia's shadow boxes, Alexandria Gazette, Va, 84; and others. *Mem:* Am Asn Mus; Soc Archit Hist; and others. *Media:* Oil, Acrylic. *Mailing Add:* Beall's Pleasure PO Box 1268 Landover MD 20785

NEW, LLOYD H KIVA
EDUCATOR
Study: Sch Arts Inst, Chicago, BAE, 38; Harvard Univ, 73; Okla State Univ; Univ NMex; Univ Chicago. *Pos:* Co-dir, R & D Prog, Rockefeller Found; formerly arts dir, pres, Inst Am Indian Arts, 66-78, retired; interim pres, Inst Am Arts, Santa Fe, NMex, 89; sr adv, Nat Mus Am Indian, Smithsonian Inst, NY & Washington, DC. *Mem:* Indian Arts & Crafts Bd (comnr, chmn); Heard Mus of Anthropology & Primitive Art, Phoenix, Ariz (founding trustee, Nat Adv bd); Mus Am Indian, Heye Found, NY, Plains Indian Mus & Buffalo Bill Hist Soc, Cody, Wyo (Nat adv bd); Am Inst Interior Designers (hon mem); Am Crafts Coun (hon fel). *Mailing Add:* 706 Calle Vibora Santa Fe NM 87501

NEWBERG, DEBORAH
PAINTER, PRINTMAKER
b New York, NY, June 25, 61. *Study:* Oberlin Col, BA, 83; Univ NMex, 87. *Work:* State NMex Transportation Dept; Bernalillo Co Libr, Wyoming Br, Albuquerque, NMex; La Familia Clinic, Santa Fe, NMex. *Exhib:* SW 96 Biennial, Mus Fine Arts, Santa Fe, 96; solo exhibs, Mus of the Southwest, Midland, Tex, 2000. *Awards:* Fuller Lodge Art Ctr Second Place Award, Que Pasa?, Art in New Mexico, 92. *Media:* Oil, Monotypes. *Mailing Add:* PO Box 33184 Santa Fe NM 87594

NEWHOUSE, SAMUEL I & VICTORIA, JR
COLLECTOR
b 1928; Victoria: b Jan 27, 38. *Pos:* Samuel: chmn, Condé Nast Publs Inc, NYC, 1975-; chmn bd dir, chief exec officer, Advance Publs Inc, 1979-. *Awards:* Named one of Top 200 Collectors, ARTnews Mag, 2004, 2006. *Collection:* Modern and contemporary art. *Mailing Add:* 950 Fingerboard Rd Staten Island NY 10305

NEWICK, CRAIG D
ARCHITECT
b Feb 14, 60. *Study:* Lehigh Univ, Bethlehem, Pa, BA, 82; Yale Univ, New Haven, Conn, MArch, 87. *Comn:* Gallery Jazz, design for art gallery, New Haven, 85-86; interior renovation & exterior rehab, residence, 85-88; exhib display cabinet, Artspace, Inc, New Haven, 87; interior renovation & addition, residence, Florham Park, NJ, 88; Kroes Residence, 2000; Gallery & artists' studios, Eyebeam Atelier, NY, 2000; Harder & Co residence and video editing studio, 2002; Hamden Arts Commn Performance Space. *Exhib:* Home/Less: A Visual Dialogue, Artspace, New Haven, Conn, 92; The New Eng Holocaust Mem Competition: An Am Process, Gund Gallery Harvard Grad Sch Design, Cambridge, Mass, 92; Small Works Invitational, Artspace, New Haven, Conn, 93; The Visual Stage: Art in and Around the Theater, John Slade Ely House, 94; The African Burial Ground Memorial Competition, Munic Art Soc, NY, 94; Out of Bounds: Artists' Books, Creative Arts Workshop, New Haven, Conn, 94; and many others. *Pos:* Designer/draftsman, The Archit studio, Easton, Pa, 81 & 83-84 & 86; Centerbrook Architects, 86; Allan Dehar & Assoc, 88-90; partner, Lindroth & Newick, 88-; designer, Cesar Pelli & Assocs, 92; project archit, Tai Soo Kim Partners, 95-; prin, Newick Architects, 2001-. *Teaching:* Vis critic basic design, RI Sch Design, 88; vis critic archit design, Wesleyan Univ, 90-93; instr, drawing course in perspective, Creative Arts Workshop, New Haven, Conn, 91-92; vis critic archit design, Lehigh Univ, 93; vis critic, Yale, 2000-2006. *Awards:* New Eng Found Arts/Nat Endowment Arts, Fel in Sculpture, 93; Second Place, African Burial Ground Mem Competition, Munic Art Soc, NY, 94; First Prize, Out of Bounds, Artists' Books, 94; Hon Mention, Pub Space in the New Am City/Atlanta 1996 Design Competition, 94; Conn Comn Arts, Fel in Sculpture, 98; Design Award, AIA Conn, 2000; AIA Nat Award, 2006; and others. *Bibliog:* Annual Design Review, ID Int Design Mag, 7-8/90, 7-8/91 & 7-8/93; Reports, Storefront for Art & Archit, New York, summer, 91; AETNA Photography Series 4, catalog, 9/91. *Mem:* Am Inst Architects; Conn Soc Architects. *Mailing Add:* 219 Livingston St New Haven CT 06511-2209

NEWKIRK, KORI
ASSEMBLAGE ARTIST
b Bronx,. NY, 1970. *Study:* Sch Art Inst Chicago, BFA, 1993; Univ Calif, Irvine, MFA, 1997. *Work:* The World and the Way Things Are, 2001; Glint, 2005. *Exhib:* One man shows include BLOWOUT, Fine Arts Gallery, Univ Calif, Irvine, 1997, Higher Standard, Project Room, Rosamund Felsen Gallery, Santa Monica, Calif, 1998, Legacy, Deep River, LA, Calif, 1999, Midnight Son, Rosamund Felsen Gallery, Santa Monica, 1999, To See It All, Henry Art Gallery, Seattle, 2003, Bodybuilder & Sportsman Gallery, Chicago, 2004, Locust Projects, Miami, Fla, 2005, Art Gallery of Ontario, Toronto, Canada, 2005, The Project, NY, 2006, and others; group shows include Custom Complex, Helen Lindhurst Gallery, Univ Southern Calif, 1995, Just a Taste, Fine Arts Gallery, Univ Calif, Irvine, 1996, Five Emerging Black Artists, DAn Bernier Gallery, Santa Monica, 1997, Black is a Verb! WORKS, San Jose, Calif, 1997, The Comestible Compost, Galleyr 207 & Pavilion's, West Hollywood, Calif, 1998, Homeless in Los Angeles, The Mota Gallery, London, England, 1999, Frest Cut Afros, Watts Towers Arts Ctr, LA, Calif, 2000, Capital Art, Track 16 Gallery, Calif, 2001, Whippersnapper III, Vedanta Gallery, Chicago, 2001, Drive By, Reynolds Gallery, Richmond, VA, 2002, Loop, Gallery 400, Chicago, 2002, Hair Stories, Scottsdale Mus Contemporary Art, Ariz, Only Skin Deep, Int Ctr Photography, NY, 2003, Great Wghite, Ctr Curitorial Studies, Bard Col, NY, 2004, Eye of the Needle, Roberts and Tilton Gallery, Calif, 2004, Southern Exposure, Mus Contemporary Art, San Diego, 2005, Biennial, Whitney Mus Am Art, NY, 2006, Dakar Biennial, Senegal, 2006. *Teaching:* Artist-in-residence, Skowhegan Sch Painting and Sculpture, Maine, 1997. *Awards:* William H Johnson Prize, 2004. *Mailing Add:* The Project Gallery 37 West 57th St New York NY 10019

NEWLAND, JOSEPH NELSON
EDITOR, CONSULTANT
b Knoxville, Tenn, July 7, 53. *Study:* Univ NC, Chapel Hill, BA(hons), 75; Univ Wash, MA, 78. *Pos:* Asst dir, Diane Gilson Gallery, Seattle, 78-79; publ ed, Henry Art Gallery, Univ Wash, Seattle, 79-88; ed, Los Angeles Co Mus Art, 88-92; publ mgr, Asia Soc Galleries, 92-96; independent art bk packager, 96-. *Teaching:* Calif State Univ, Northridge, 89-92 of Art Collection, LACMA, 91. *Mem:* Am Asn Mus. *Interests:* East Asian influence on American art & culture. *Publ:* Edo: The Art of Japan, 1615-1868, Nat Gallery Art; Treasures of Asian Art: The Mr & Mrs John D Rockefeller 3rd Collection of Asian Art, TASG/Abbeville, 94; Worlds Seen and Imagined: Japanese Screens from the Idemitsu Museum of Arts, TASG/Abbeville, 95; Contemporary Art in Asia: Traditions/Tensions, TASG/Abrams, 96; Inside Out: New Art from China, San Francisco Mus Mod Art, 98

NEWMAN, ELIZABETH H
SCULPTOR
Study: Mich State Univ, BFA, 78; Sch Art Inst Chicago, MFA, 84. *Exhib:* One-woman shows, Marianne Deson Gallery, Chicago, 86, Galerie Eric Franck, Geneva, Switz, 89, Galerie Lelong, NY, 92, 95 & 98, Inst Contemp Art, Boston, Mass, Mus Contemp Art, Chicago, Ill, 92, San Diego State Univ Art Gallery, 95, Elizabeth Leach Gallery, Portland, Ore, 96, Zolla Lieberman Gallery, Chicago, 97, Van Every Smith Galleries, Davidson, NC, 98 & Galerie Lelong, New York City, 99; Resonance, Gibson Art Gallery, State Univ NY, 95; Art in Chicago: 1945-1995, Mus Contemp Art, Chicago, 96; Food for Thought, Kohler Arts Ctr, Sheboygan, Wis, 96; No Small Feat: Investigations of the Shoe in Contemp Art, Rhona Hoffman Gallery, Chicago, 97; Roots and Reeds: The Amazing Grace of the Gullah People, Bertha & Karl Leubsdorf Gallery, Hunter Col, NY, 98; Domestic Pleasures, Galerie Lelong, NY, 99; Welcome, Wave Hill, Bronx, NY, 2000; Almost Warm and Fuzzy: Childhood and Contemp Art (traveling exhib), Des Moines Art Ctr, Iowa, 99, Tacoma Art Mus, Washington, 2000, Scottsdale Mus of Contemp Art, Ariz, 2000, PS 1 Contemp Art Ctr, Long Island City, NY, 2001, Fundacio la Ciaxa, Barcelona, Spain, 2001. *Awards:* Nat Endowment Arts, 88; Ill Art Coun, 86, 87 & 89. *Bibliog:* Roberta Smith (auth), Also of note, NY Times, 3/17/95; Martha McWilliams (auth), Object lessions, Washington City Paper, 8/11/95; Robert L Pincus (auth), Childhood regained, San Diego Tribune, 11/30/95. *Mailing Add:* Samek Art Gallery Bucknell University Lewisburg PA 17837

NEWMAN, JOHN
SCULPTOR, DRAFTSMAN
b Flushing, NY, May 31, 52. *Study:* Independent Study Prog, Whitney Mus Am Art, 72; Oberlin Col, BA, 73; Sch Art, Yale Univ, MFA, 75. *Work:* Metrop Mus Art, Mus Modern Art, Whitney Mus Am Art, NY; Mus Fine Arts, Boston; Art Inst Chicago. *Comn:* Large scale sculpture-installation, City Univ New York, 77; large scale

wall-relief, Northrop Industs, Los Angeles, 84; large scale outdoor sculpture, Dept Transportation, Washington, 84; large scale outdoor sculpture, Gen Mills Outdoor Sculpture Park, Minneapolis, 89; large scale outdoor sculpture, Storm King Art Ctr, Mountainville, NY, 89. *Exhib:* Sculpture: Inside/Outside, Walker Art Ctr, Minneapolis, 88; Four Americans: Aspects of Current Sculpture, Brooklyn Mus, 89; Art in place, Whitney Mus Am Art, NY, 89; The Unique Print: 70s into 80s, Mus Fine Arts, Boston, 90; Singular and Plural, Recent Accessions: Drawing and Prints 1945-1991, Mus Fine Arts, Houston, 92; one-man show, Ft Wayne Mus Art, 93; New Acquisitions, NY Pub Libr, 94; Ideas and Objects: Selected Drawings and Sculptures from the Permanent Collection, Whitney Mus Am Art, 94. *Teaching:* Asst prof fine art, Grad Prog, Queens Col, City Univ New York, 80-82 & Sarah Lawrence Col, Bronxville, NY, 81-84; dir grad studies sculpture, Yale Sch Art, New Haven, 92-. *Awards:* Nat Endowment Arts Grant, 86; New York Found Arts Grant, 90; John S Guggenheim Found Fel, 92. *Bibliog:* Nancy Princenthal (auth), Beyond the Zero: John Newman's Recent Prints, Drawings & Sculpture, Mt Kisco: Tyler Graphics, Ltd, 90; Holland Cotter (auth), John Newman, New York Times, 92; Klaus Kertess, Angela Fritz & Emily Kass (auths), John Newman: Sculpture and Works on Paper (exhib catalog), Ft Wayne Mus Art, 93. *Mem:* Col Art Asn. *Media:* All Media. *Mailing Add:* 59 Franklin St New York NY 10013

NEWMAN, JOHN (BEATTY)
PAINTER, DRAFTSMAN

b Toronto, Ont, 33. *Study:* Ontario Col Art; Art Acad Cincinnati, scholarship. *Work:* Art Gallery Hamilton, Ont; Canadian Embassy, Washington, DC; Montreal Mus Fine Art; Art Bank, Can Coun; Canadian Embassy, Rome, Italy; and others. *Exhib:* Royal Acad, London, Eng, 72; Tokyo Metrop Gallery, Japan, 76; Art Gallery Ont, Toronto, Can, 76; Art Gallery of Hamilton, Ont, 76; Soc Int Beaux Arts, Grand Palais, Paris, France, 77; Palazzo Strozzi, Firenze, Ital, 77; Sichuan Fine Art Inst, Chongging, People's Repub China, 89; Seoul Watercolours Int, Seoul, Korea, 91; Centro Culturale Canadese in Roma, Italia, 92; Gallery/Stratford, 94. *Pos:* Exhib designer, Royal Ont Mus, Toronto, 58-63; mem gov coun, Ont Col Art, 73-76, 79-81 & 89-92, chmn fine arts dept, 79-83, Coord Off, Florence Prog, 76-77, 84-85, 92. *Teaching:* Instr figure painting, Ont Col Art, 63-. *Awards:* Int Painting Competition First Prize, Can Soc Graphic Art, 56, John Alfsen Award for Drawing, 73; Honor Award, Can Soc Painters Watercolor, 74; and others. *Bibliog:* Kay Kritzwiser (auth), A tender look at little girls, Globe & Mail, Toronto, 73; Peter Bell (auth), The transition to maturity, Evening Telegram, St John's, Nfld, 74; Robert Freeman (auth), Rites of Passage, 94. *Mem:* Royal Can Acad; Can Soc Painters Watercolor. *Media:* Oil, Watercolor. *Dealer:* Kinsman Robinson Galleries 112 Scollard St Toronto Can M5R 1G2; Galerie Walter Klinkoff 1200 West Ave Sherbrooke Montreal Can H3A1H6. *Mailing Add:* 40 Kinsman Robertson Galleries 112 Scollard St Toronto ON M5R 1G4 Canada

NEWMAN, LIBBY
PAINTER, PRINTMAKER

b Rockland, Del. *Study:* Univ Arts, BFA. *Comn:* Univ Pa Law Sch; Buchanan and Ingersoll Law Office; Dorfman Med Office; Newman Cosmetic Surgery Ctr. *Exhib:* Nat Watercolor & Drawing Exhib, Pa Acad Fine Arts, 64; Eastern Cent Drawing Exhib, Philadelphia Mus Art, 65; solo exhibs, Mangel Gallery, Philadelphia, 70-2004 & Philadelphia Art Alliance, 81; Twenty-Five Pa Women Artists, Southern Alleghenies Mus Art, Loretto, Pa, 79; Am Colorprint Soc Exhib, 79; Gov Thornburgh's Inaugural Art Comt--Cur of Contemp Sculpture Exhib, 79; Syria, Demasus, Syria, Baltimore Mus Art; Woodmere Art Mus, 2003. *Collection Arranged:* Philadelphia Mus Art; Israel Mus, Jerusalem; Nat Mus Belgrade; Tianjin Fine Art Col, Yugoslavia; Indus Valley Sch Art & Arch, Karachi, Pakistan; US Info Agy, SAm. *Pos:* Cur exhibs, Univ City Sci Ctr, 1975-2001. *Awards:* Best Picture of Year Award, Philadelphia Art Alliance, 65; National Print Award, Cheltenham Art Ctr, Pa, 70; Carl Zigrosser Award, Am Color Print Soc, 81; Distinguished Daughter of Pa, 92; Percy Owens Aeard, Pa Acad of Fine Arts, 95; The mayor's Citation for Artistic Merit, Mayor Ed Rendell, 95, Mayor John Street, 2001. *Bibliog:* Victoria Donohoe (auth), article, Philadelphia Inquirer, 72; Sheila Reid (auth), exhib catalog, Mus de Grand Palais; Edward Sozanski, Philadelphia Inquirer, 97-99. *Mem:* Artists Equity Asn (pres, Philadelphia Chap, 68-70, nat vpres, 71-75); Philadelphia Art Alliance; Am Color Print Soc; Philadelphia Watercolor Soc; and others. *Media:* Acrylic; Woodcut; Clay; Folding Screens. *Publ:* Auth, Obtaining art grants, Artists Equity Nat Newslett, 74; A City Sketched, a Guide to the Art & History of Philadelphia; Dr Burton Wasserman, Art Matters, 2003, 2001, 1997, 1992; R Buckminster Fuller Sketchbook, 1981. *Dealer:* Mangel Gallery 1714 Rittenhouse Sq Philadelphia PA 19103. *Mailing Add:* 2401 Pennsylvania Ave Apt 7B34 Philadelphia PA 19130-3029

NEWMAN, LOUIS
ART DEALER, COLLECTOR

b June 21, 47, US citizen. *Study:* Ariz State Univ, BA, 70; Univ Southern Calif, Los Angeles, MA, 74. *Collection Arranged:* The Richard Zahn Collection. *Pos:* Art dealer & dir, David Findlay Jr Fine Art. *Bibliog:* Louis Newman (auth/essay), Nine Artists from the 9th Street Show, David Findlay Jr Fine Art, 2006; Louis Newman (auth/essay), Robert Richenburg: The Richard Zahn Collection, The Nat Arts Educ Found, 2006. *Mem:* Nat Arts Club (lit comt), 96-; Municipal Arts Soc; Ctr Contemp Opera (bd mem), 97-2002; Nat Acad Design; NY Landmarks Conservancy, 96-; Fine Arts Fedn of NY city (bd mem, adv comt), 2000-; Encompass New Opera Theatre Bd (adv coun), 2001-. *Specialty:* Mid-twentieth century American paintings, prints, drawings & sculpture. *Publ:* Elie Nadelman: Selected Drawings, 87; Kurt Schwitters: Collages and Other Works on Paper, 88; Edward Hopper: Selected Drawings, 89; Reginald Marsh: Selected Works on Paper, 90; Thomas Hart Benton: Paintings and Drawings, 90; Calvin Goodman (auth), Art Marketing Handbook, 90 $ 2003; Molly Barnes (auth), How to Get Hung, 94; essay, Robert Richenburg: The Richard Zahn Collection, Nat Arts Educ Found, 2006; Calvin Goodman (auth), Nine Artists from the 9th Street Show, Antiques & the Arts Weekly, 7/2006; Robert Metzger (auth), Louis Newman: Bringing Artists to Light, Antiques & the Arts Weekly, 4/2006. *Dealer:* David Findlay Jr Fine Art 41 E 57th St 11th Fl New York NY 10022. *Mailing Add:* MB Modern 41 E 57th St New York NY 10022

NEWMAN, MARI ALICE MAE
PAINTER, SCULPTOR

b Esterville, Iowa. *Study:* Minneapolis Tech Col, 83-90; Minneapolis Community Col, 85-95; Minneapolis Center for Book Arts, 85-88; Minneapolis Col Art and Design, 89; Univ Minn (archit), 91-94. *Work:* Minn Mus Art, St Paul; Minneapolis Inst Arts, Minn; New Columbus Mus Art, Ohio; LeRoy Neiman, NY; New Orleans Mus Art, La; Pensacola Mus Art, Fla; Very Special Arts Mus, Washington, DC; Milwaukee Mus Art; MOBA Mus Art; Tampa Mus Art, Fla; Mennello Mus, Orlando, Fla. *Comn:* card designs, Anita Beck Cards, Minneapolis, 70-80, 98; train mobiles, Bruegger's Bagels, Minneapolis, 98; Alcoholics Anonymous 2000 (poster), Hazelden Found, Minneapolis, 2000; two extension murals, Dunn Brothers Inc, 02. *Exhib:* White Oak Gallery, Minneapolis, 88, 99, 2000, 01, 02, 03; Vaughan and Vaughan Gallery, Minneapolis, 89, 90, 92; Artlines, Minneapolis, 1990, 91, 93, 94, 95, 96, 97, 99, 2000; Sonia's Gallery, Minneapolis, 90, 92; No Name Gallery, Minneapolis, 92, 93, 94; Jack Wold Gallery, 92, 93, 94, 95, 96; Ice Box Gallery, Minneapolis, 99, 2000, 01, 02, 03; Gallery 360, 99, 2000, 01, 02, 03, 04; Sister Kenny, Minneapolis, 2002, 03, 04; and many others. *Awards:* Abbey Weed Gray Scholar, Minneapolis Col of Art & Design, 89; Best Minn Self-Taught Artists, City Pages, 2000; Sister Kenny Inst Int Juried Show, Best of the Show Award, 01, First Place Award, 02, Snyder Calendar Award; Artist Reconization Grant, Jerome Foundation, 98; Puffin Found Grant Award, 2002; First Place, APH In Sights, 2006. *Bibliog:* Mark Engebretson (auth), Do Artist's Offensive Symbols Stir Hate on Reflection, Southwest Journal, 3/24/98; Michael Fallon (auth), The Outsiders, City Pages, Arts, 9/13/2000; Richard Chin (auth), Artists in Residence, St. Paul Pioneer Press, Express, 9/24/2000; Doug Grow (auth), Eyes of Beholder See No Art In Home, Artist's Neighbors Don't Lack For Opinions of Her House Work, 3/16/98; Full color with Mari Newman, Industry Mag #2, 9-10/2004; Mari Newman's Sculpture Garden - art or obstruction, Raw Vision #48, Autumn-Fall 2004; Michael Metzger (auth), Are you an antlaw, Southwest Journal, 6/24/2004; Mary Abbe (auth), One of the Twin Cities most authentic and original artists, Minneapolis Star Tribune News, 5/30/2003. *Mem:* Minn Soc Children's Book Writers & Illusr; Nat Sculpture Soc; Nat Asn Women Artists; Guild Metalsmiths Pastel Soc; Minn Wood Workers Guild; Nat Watercolor Sco; Am Watercolor Soc; Am Soc Contemp Artists. *Media:* Tempera, crayon, found materials. *Publ:* Illusr, All Hearts with Bubbles, Raw Vision Mag, NY; Self Portrait of Polka Dot House, Readers Digest Inc, NY; Turkey of the Rainbow, Star Tribune, Minneapolis, Minn; Art News Mag (summer), Artists Directory, NY, 2001; Jambalaya Mag, Houghton Mifflin Co, 95; Raw Vision Mag, Raw Classics, England, 97; West 81 Art & The Law, West Publ, St Paul, Minn, 81; New Art Internat edition, 2001-, Book Art Press, NY, 2001. *Mailing Add:* 5117 Penn Ave South Minneapolis MN 55419

NEWMAN, RICHARD CHARLES
SCULPTOR, PHOTOGRAPHER

b North Tonawanda, NY, Dec 29, 38. *Study:* Cleveland Inst Art, dipl painting, 60; Cranbrook Acad Art, BFA, 62; Cornell Univ, MFA, 64. *Work:* Addison Gallery Am Art, Phillips Acad, Andover, Mass; Middle Tenn State Univ, Murfreesboro; Herbert F Johnson Mus Art, Ithaca, NY; Univ Ore Mus Art, Eugene; Robert Lehman Art Ctr, Brooks Sch., N Andover, Mass. *Exhib:* Birth of Wisdom, St John's Col, Santa Fe, 2000; Icons and Altars, New Art Ctr of Newton, Newtonville, Mass, 2000 & 20001, Gallery of Contemp Art, Univ Colo, 2001; Landscape and Memory, Sedona Art Ctr, Ariz, 2002; New Bedford Art Mus, Mass, 2003; No AM SC Exhib Foothill Art Ctr, Golden, CO, 2004; 38th LaGrange Nat Biennial, Lamar Dodd Art Ctr, LaGrange Coll GA, 2004; On the Edge, Peeninsule Fine Art Ctr, Newport, Va, 2005; Digital art, Owen Smith Sheeman Gallery, Groton, Mass, 2006; Nat Collage Soc 21st Nal Butler Inst Ame Art, Ohio, 2006. *Pos:* Juror, Marblehead Art Asn, Mass, 78: Ann Spring Art Exhib, Newton Art Asn, Mass, 80, Boston Globe Scholastic Art Awards, State Finals, Mass, 87, 88 & 89; guest speaker, Artists on Art (lectr ser), Addison Gallery/Phillips Acad, Andover, Mass, 78, Artists Series, Boston Visual Artists Union, Mass, 80; panelist, T W MacKesey Seminar Ser, Col Archit, Art & Planning, Cornell Univ, Ithaca, NY, 82; cur, Sculpture As Monument Exhib, Boston Visual Artists Union Gallery, Mass, 84, The Healing Experience, Soc Layerists, Bradford Col, 91 & Crossings Exhib, 94; keynote speaker, Reflection of Life & Death: The Arts and Thanatology Symp, Found Thanatology, New York, 89; speaker, Art and Healing Conf, New Harmony, Ind, 90, Affirming Wholeness Conf, San Antonio, Tex, 92 & Artists of the Spirit Symp, Walton Arts Ctr, Fayetteville, Ark, 94, numerous other confs; pres, Soc Layerist in Multi-Media, 86-2003; artist-in-residence, Merrimack Col, N Andover, Mass, 2000. *Teaching:* Instr art, Univ Wash, Seattle, 64-65; asst, Sch Archit, Cornell Univ, 63-64; prof & chmn Creative Arts Div, Bradford Col, 65-99, prof emer, 99-; Adjunct Prof Merrimack College No Andover, MA. *Awards:* Finalist in Sculpture, Mass Artists Found Grant, 77; Jubilee Celebration Showcase Artist for window proj, City Hartford, Conn, 86; Jane Walker Kopf Chair (art hist & theory), Bradford Col, Mass, 92-98. *Bibliog:* Rochelle Newman & Donna M Fowler (auths), Space, Structure & Form, Pythagorean Press & Brown & Benchmark, 95; Nicholas Roukes (auth), Humor in Art, Davis Publ, Mass, 96; M C Nelson (auth), Bridging Time and Space, Markowitz Publ, 98; Rochelle Newman (auth) Malleable Matter/Stretchable Space, Pythagorean Press, Bradford, Mass, 2000; and others. *Mem:* Soc of Layerists in Multi-Media, Albuquerque, NMex (pres, 86-2004); Boston Mus Fine Arts, Mass; Pythagorean Press, Bradford, Mass; New Eng Sculptors Asn. *Media:* Mixed Media. *Interests:* Photography. *Publ:* Contribr, Collage: Critical Views, Univ Mich Press, 89; Am Craft Mag, 8-9/90 & 4/91; Artists of the Spirit, Arcus Publ, 94;

Humor in Art, Davis Publ, Worchester, Mass, 97; Artful Jesters, Ten Speed Press, 2004, by Nicholas Roukes; The Sculpture Reference, Sculpture Books Pub, by Arthur Williams, 2004; The New Creative Artist, Nita Leland, North Light Books, 2006; and others. *Mailing Add:* PO Box 5162 Bradford MA 01835

NEWMAN, WALTER ANDREWS, JR
ART DEALER, GALLERY DIRECTOR
b Philadelphia, Pa, May 16, 30. *Collection Arranged:* Daniel Garber Meml Exhib, 65; Edward W Redfield, Retrospective Exhib, 68; Joe Brown, Bronzes, Retrospective Exhib, 87; John Fulton Folinsbee, Following His Own Course, 90; The Folinsbee Legacy, 05. *Pos:* Pres, Newman Galleries, Philadelphia, Pa, 69-. *Specialty:* Early 20th century impressionists; Pennsylvania landscape school. *Dealer:* Newman Galleries, 1625 Walnut St, Philadelphia PA. *Mailing Add:* 1625 Walnut St Philadelphia PA 19103

NEWMAN-RICE, NANCY
PAINTER, CRITIC
b New York, NY, Mar 28, 50. *Study:* Cornell Univ; Washington Univ, BFA, 72, MFA, 74. *Exhib:* Drawing & Sculpture, Ball State Univ, Ind, 76; St Louis Artists, Cervantes Convention Ctr, St Louis, 78; Painting Invitational, Salisbury State Univ, Md, 79; Mississippi Corridor, Davenport Art Gallery, Iowa, 80; Works On-Of Paper, Bixby Gallery, Washington Univ, Landscapes 88 BZ Wagman, 80; solo exhibs, Currents 2, St Louis Art Mus, 79 & Brentwood Gallery, St Louis, 85 & 86, Sazama/Braver Gallery, Chicago, 87 & 89. *Pos:* Ed in chief, St Louis Seen, Newspaper for Visual Arts, 75-77; St Louis ed & critic, New Art Examiner, 78-; Critic, St Louis Post Dispatch. *Teaching:* Asst painting, Washington Univ, 72-74; assoc prof, Maryville Col, 74-. *Awards:* Midwest Art Alliance-Nat Endowment Arts Grant. *Bibliog:* Sidra Stitch (auth), Nancy Rice & Yvette Woods, New Art Examiner, 79; Mary King (auth), Rice's floating lattice spheres, St Louis Post Dispatch, 80; P Desmer (auth), Nancy Rice's work dazzles, St Louis Post Dispatch; Herb Gralnick (auth), Nancy Rice, St Louis Globe Democrat; Betsy Goldman (auth), Nancy Rice, New Art Examiner. *Mem:* Col Art Asn; Midwest Col Art Asn; Women's Caucus for Art (bd dir, 76-77); Artspace. *Media:* Acrylic, Oil. *Dealer:* Sazama/Braver Gallery 361 West Superior Chicago Ill 60610; BZ Wagman Gallery Galleris St Louis Mo 63117. *Mailing Add:* 0 E 4th St Richmond VA 23224

NEWMARK, MARILYN NEWMARK MEISELMAN
SCULPTOR, INSTRUCTOR
b New York, NY, July 20, 28. *Study:* Adelphi Col; Alfred Univ; also with Paul Brown, Garden City, NY. *Work:* Nat Mus of Racing, Saratoga, NY; Nat Art Mus of Sport, Indianapolis, Ind; Am Saddle Horse Mus, Lexington, Ky; Int Mus Horse, Ky Horse Park, Lexington, Ky; Firestone; Phipps; Galbreath; Dupon T III; Brookgreen Gardens, NC; and others. *Comn:* Bronzes of Majestic Light, comn by Ogden Phipps Jr, 76; Man o' War, Franklin Mint, 77; Affirmed, Thoroughbred Racing Asn, 78; Ruffian, 83 & Genuine Risk, 84, Int Mus Horse; Race Horse, Japan Racing Assoc, Japan, 97; and others. *Exhib:* Nat Acad Design, NY, 71-72, 74-82, 86-94, 95, 97, 99, 2001 & 2003; Int Mus Horse, Ky, 92-2002; Palazzo Mediceo di Seravezza, Italy, 94; Old Algonquin Mus, Can, 95; Fleisher Mus, Ariz, 99-; Butler Inst Am Art, Ohio, 2001. *Pos:* Vpres, Soc Animal Artists; coun, Nat Scot Soc; founder, Am Acad Equine Art. *Awards:* Ellin P Speyer Award, Nat Acad Design, 74, 93 & 99; Gold Medal, Allied-Artist Am, 81 & 93; Leonard Meiselman Mem Award, Nat Sculpture Soc & Audabon Soc, 2003. *Bibliog:* Horsewoman & Artist Extraordinaire, Horse of Course, 77; She Wanted Horses, Equine Images, 92; Masters of American Sculpture, 93. *Mem:* Nat Acad; Nat Sculpture Soc; Allied Artists Am; Soc Animal Artists; Pen & Brush; Am Acad Equine Art. *Media:* Bronze Cast, Clay. *Specialty:* Animal Art. *Publ:* Contribr, Equine Sculpture, A Mixed Medium, Morning Telegraph, 8/9/71; Equine Sculpture, Chronicle of the Horse, 9/10/71; Horse in sculpture, Am Horseman, 12/72; From the love of horses, Catasus, spring 89. *Dealer:* The Sportsman's Gallery 309 E Paces Ferry Rd Atlanta GA 30305. *Mailing Add:* #22 Woodhollow Rd East Hills NY 11577

NEWSOM, BARBARA YLVISAKER
ADMINISTRATOR, WRITER
b Madison, Wis, July 14, 26. *Study:* Bethany Lutheran Col, Mankato, Minn, AA; Univ Minn, BA; Hunter Col, MA. *Pos:* Pub affairs consult to 100th Anniversary Comt, Metrop Mus Art, New York, 67-70, consult to vdir for educ, 70-71; study dir, Coun Mus Educ, 71-73; proj dir, Coun Mus & Educ in Visual Arts, New York & Cleveland, Ohio, 73-78; staff assoc, Rockefeller Brothers Fund, 73-80, consult, 80-. *Mem:* Am Asn Mus (coun mem, 75-78). *Res:* Art museum education and urban aesthetics. *Publ:* Auth, The museum as the city's aesthetic conscience, Metrop Mus Bull, 68; The Metropolitan Museum as an Educational Institution, 70; ed, The Art Museum as Educator, 78

NEWTON, JOHN NEIL
PHOTOGRAPHER, PRINTMAKER
b Montreal, Que, Can, Oct 30, 33. *Study:* St Martins Sch Art, London, England, 53-55; Open Studio, 72-73; Visual Studies Workshop, Rochester, NY, with Nathan Lyons, 73. *Work:* Nat Gallery Can; Nat Film Bd Can, Can Coun Art Bank, Pub Arch Can, Ottawa; Mod Mus, Stockholm. *Exhib:* Solo exhib, Shaw Rimmington Gallery, Toronto, 74; Exposure--Canadian Contemp Photog, Art Gallery Ont, 75; Photographs From the Permanent Collection, Nat Gallery Can, 75; 1001 Photographs, Mod Mus, Stockholm, 78; Retrospective, Can House Exhib Ctr, London, Eng, 80; Academic Images, Can Ctr Photog, Toronto, 82; Art Forms, Kitchener-Waterloo Art Gallery, Ont, 83. *Pos:* Founding dir, Photog Gallery, Bowmanville, Ont, 71-78 & Newcastle Visual Arts Ctr, Bowmanville, Ont, 74-76. *Teaching:* Lectr photog, York Univ, Toronto, 70-72 & Ryerson Polytech Inst, Toronto, 77-78. *Bibliog:* Annette Snowdon (auth), Holdouts, Can Mag, 7/22/78; Joan Murray (auth), Neil Newton Retrospective (exhib catalog), Robert McLaughlin Gallery, Oshawa, 4/78. *Mem:* Royal Can Acad Arts (coun mem, 83-85); Visual Arts Ont; Can Artists Rep. *Media:* Silver and Non-Silver Printmaking. *Mailing Add:* 9738 Willow St Box 748 Chemainus BC V0R 1K0 Canada

NEWTON, RICHARD EDWARD
CONCEPTUAL ARTIST, FILMMAKER
b Oakland, Calif, Feb 29, 48. *Study:* Univ Calif, Irvine, study with Ed Moses, John Mason, Vija Celmins, Tony Delap, Barbara Rose & Phillip Leider, MFA, 73. *Comn:* Mural, comn by John Mason, Los Angeles, 72; mural, comn by Mark Finkelstein, Corona del Mar, 74; theater piece, Los Angeles Theatre Ctr, 86. *Exhib:* Calif Suite, Los Angeles Co Mus Art, 77; Re: Pages traveling exhib, New Eng, 81; Space Invaders, PS 1, NY, 82; 26th Chicago Int Film Festival, 90; Anthology Film Archives, NY, 91; ARCO '91 & ARCO '92, Exhib of Experimental Cinema, Madrid, Spain, 91 & 92; Melbourne Int Film Festival, Australia, 91; 20th Int Festival of Short Films, Huesca, Spain, 92. *Pos:* Assoc ed & designer, High Performance, Los Angeles, 77-80. *Awards:* Best First Film & Runner-up as best film in festival, 19th Festival Int de Cinema, Portugal, 90; Third Prize, Exhib of Experimental Cinema, Spain, 91; First Prize, Cetamen Int de Cine Ciutat D'Igualada, Spain, 91. *Bibliog:* Jorge Castilho (auth), Richard Newton: um underground com bisavo portugues, J de Coimbra, 9/90; Manohla Dargis (auth), National Obsessions, Village Voice, 1/91; David E Williams (auth), underground, Film Threat, 10/92. *Media:* Live Performance

NG, NATTY (YUEN LEE)
PAINTER, GRAPHIC DESIGNER
b Hong Kong, May 14, 48; Can citizen. *Study:* Poly Tech Col, 67; Sir Robert Black Col Educ, 68; Grantham Col Educ, Hong Kong, 86, Kwantlan Col, Vancouver, Can, 91. *Comn:* oil on canvas painting, Can Brass Hardware, 2000; 2 oil & mixed media paintings, Intra Corp, Can, 2001; oil on canvas painting, Internat Language Sch Can, 99, 2002; 2 oil & mixed media paintings, Progressive Wireless Co, Can, 2004. *Exhib:* Project E '88, Hong Kong Art Show, Art Ctr, 88; Mind & Matter Festival of the Art, Mind & Matter Gallery, Vancouver, BC, Can, 91; Victoria Regional Art Show, BC, Can 91; Ninth Ann Art Exhib, Community Art Coun, Vancouver, BC, Can, 91; Images '92, Burnaby Arts Coun & Arts Coun New Westminster, Can, 92; one-person art show, We "B" Art Gallery Seattle, Wash, 92; The Grind Gallery, Vancouver, BC, Can, 93-94; Biennale Internat Dell 'Arte Contemporanea, 2005. *Pos:* Graphic designer, Imageworks, Port Coquitlam, BC, Can, 91-. *Teaching:* Art & design, Kwun Tong Govt Sec Sch, Hong Kong, 86-90. *Awards:* First Place Honors Oil Painting, All Cols & Univ Art Show, 86; and others; Hon Mention Image 92, Burnaby Arts Coun, Arts Coun of New Westminster, Can, 92. *Media:* Oil, Mixed Media. *Publ:* Preview of Visual Arts, Alberta, BC, Oreg and Wash, 93; Quinta Edizione - Biennale Internat. Dell 'Arte Contemporanea, 2005. *Mailing Add:* 107-2109 Rowland St Port Coquitlam BC V3C 6J4 Canada

NIBLETT, GARY LAWRENCE
PAINTER
b Carlsbad, NMex, Jan 9, 43. *Study:* Art Instruction Inc, Minneapolis, Minn; Eastern NMex Univ, Portales; Art Ctr Col Design, Los Angeles, Calif. *Comn:* Albuquerque Munic Airport, 88; Carlsbad Mus Fine Art, NMex, 88; Sunwest Bank Hist Collection, Santa Fe, NMex; NMex State Capitol Bldg; calendar artist, NMex Mag, 90; and others. *Exhib:* Grand Palais Paris, France, 75 & 76; Cowboy Artists Am, Phoenix Art Mus, Ariz, 77-91; Artists of Am, Colo Hist Mus, Denver, 82-91; Royal Watercolor Soc, London, 90-91; A New Mexico Tradition: Southwestern Realism, Taiwan Mus Art, Taichung, 91; and others. *Teaching:* Cowboy Artist Am Mus, 86 & 88. *Awards:* Silver Medals, Cowboy Artists Am Show, Phoenix Art Mus, 77, 82, 83 & 86 & Gold Medal, 91; Artist of Year, Tucson Festival Soc, 86; Hubbard Award Excellence, Hubbard Mus, Ruidoso, NMex, 90-91; and others. *Bibliog:* Vicki Stavig (auth), Art of the West, 9-10/89; Mary Terrence McKay (auth), Gary Niblett: A New Look at the Old West, Actian Press, 90; Neirdra Jane Almjer (auth), A new look at the old west, Int Fine Art Collector, 8/91. *Mem:* Cowboy Artist Am; charter mem Santa Fe Watercolor Soc. *Media:* Oil. *Publ:* Cowboy Artist of Am, Desert Hawk Publ, El Paso, Tex, 88. *Mailing Add:* 308 Vistoso Pl Santa Fe NM 87501

NIBLOCK, PHILL
FILMMAKER, VIDEO ARTIST
b Anderson, Ind, Oct 2, 33. *Study:* Ind Univ, BA, 56. *Work:* Carpenter Ctr Visual Arts, Harvard Univ. *Comn:* NY Found Artists, 87; New Works Prog, Mass Coun Arts, 88; Found Contemp Performance Arts, 94. *Exhib:* Cineprobe, Films and Music, Mus Mod Art, NY, 73; Sur, Wadsworth Atheneum, Hartford, Conn; Trabajando, Herbert F Johnson Mus, Cornell Univ, 76; Carpenter Ctr Visual Arts, Harvard Univ; Inst Contemp Arts, London; Contemp Arts Forum, Santa Barbara, Calif; and others. *Pos:* Dir, Experimental Intermedia Found, New York, 70-. *Awards:* NY State Coun Arts Grant, Kirkland Art Ctr, 70, Exp Intermedia Found, 72-74; Nat Endowment Arts Pub Media Prog, 75-76; Guggenheim Fel; and others. *Bibliog:* Tom Johnson (auth), Music reviews, Village Voice, 72, 73 & 74; John Rockwell (auth), What's new, High Fidelity/Musical Am, 5/74; Abigail Nelson (auth), Who's Who in Film, Sight Lines, winter 74. *Mem:* Experimental Intermedia Found. *Mailing Add:* 224 Centre St New York NY 10013

NICE, DON
PAINTER
b Visalia, Calif, June 26, 1932. *Study:* Univ Southern Calif, BFA, 54; Yale Univ, MFA, 64. *Work:* Del Art Mus, Wilmington; Minneapolis Inst Art; Mus Mod Art & Whitney Mus Am Art, NY; Walker Art Ctr; Julius Bar Bank, Zurich, Switz; and many others. *Comn:* Wall murals, Nat Fine Arts Comn, Lake Placid, NY; Art in Archit Prog, Vets Admin, White River Junction, NY; participant bicentennial exhib, America, 76, US Dept Interior; Mostly Mozart Festival, 78 & 18th Ann Holiday Festival, Lincoln Ctr Posters, 88. *Exhib:* A Feast for the Eyes, Mus Mod Art, 84; The New Expressive Landscape, Sordoni Art Gallery, Wilkes Barre, Pa, 85; solo exhibs, John Berggruen Gallery, San Francisco, 89, Frederick Gallery, Washington, 89, Sun Valley Ctr Arts & Humanities, Idaho, 90, Images Gallery, Toledo, Ohio, 91, Albany Inst Art, NY, 92,

Huntington Art Mus, WVa, 95 & Hudson River Mus, Yonkers, NY, 95; Common Objects, Pfizer Inc Loan, Art Adv Servs, Mus Mod Art, NY, 91; The Unique Print, Pace Prints, NY, 91; The Art of Advocacy, Aldrich Mus Contemp Art, Ridgefield, Conn, 91; On Rivers Edge, Hudson River Mus, Yonkers, NY, 95; solo exhib, Huntington Art Mus, WVa, 95. *Teaching:* Instr, Minneapolis Sch Art, 60-62; instr, Sch Visual Arts, New York, 63-, dean, 64-66; artist-in-residence, Dartmouth Col, New Hampshire, 82. *Awards:* Ford Found Purchase Award, 63. *Bibliog:* Todd Strasser (auth), interview, Ocular, fall 79; Suzanne Muchnic (auth), Really big show in Newport, Los Angeles Times, 80; Donald B Kuspit (auth), What's real in realism, Art in Am, 81. *Mem:* Nat Acad. *Dealer:* Babcock Galleries 724 5th Ave New York NY 10019. *Mailing Add:* Tandem Press Univ Wisc 201 S Dickinson St Madison WI 53703

NICHOLAS, DONNA LEE
CERAMIST, SCULPTOR
b South Pasadena, Calif, Mar 30, 38. *Study:* Pomona Col, BA(cum laude), 59; apprentice with Hiroaki Morino, Kyoto, Japan, 60-62; Claremont Grad Sch & Univ Ctr, with Paul Soldner & MFA, 64-66. *Work:* Flint Inst Arts, Mich; Edinboro Univ, Pa; Lowe Gallery, Miami; Calif Polytechnic Univ; Plains Art Mus, Moorhead, Minn; St Petersburg Univ Art, Russia; Erie Art Mus. *Exhib:* Salt Glaze Ceramics, Mus Contemp Crafts, NY, 72; Object as Poet, Renwick Gallery, Smithsonian Inst, Washington, DC & Mus Contemp Crafts, NY, 76; Clay, Fiber, Metal, Women Artists, Bronx Mus, NY, 78; A Century of Ceramics in the US 1879-1979, Everson Mus, Syracuse, NY, 79; one woman exhib, Canton Art Inst, Canton, Ohio, 88; Fragile Blossoms, Enduring Earth, Everson Mus Art Syracuse, NY, 89; AC Delegates Exhib, Scottish Gallery, Edinburgh, Scotland, 90; and other group & one-woman shows. *Teaching:* Instr ceramics, Mott Community Col, Flint, 66-69; prof ceramics, Edinboro Univ, 69-96; vis artist-instr, Penland Sch Crafts, NC, 71, Scripps Col, 74 & Moore Col Art, Philadelphia, 75. *Awards:* Outstanding Educators Am Award, 75; Distinguished Teaching Chair, Commonwealth of Pa Teachers, 81. *Bibliog:* Susan Wechsler (auth), Low Fire Ceramics, Watson-Guptill, 81; Elsbeth Woody (auth), Handbuilding Ceramic Forms, Farrar Strauss & Giroux, 78; John Byrum (auth), New Art Examiner, 88; Richard Zakin (auth), Ceramics, Mastering the Craft, Chilton, 90. *Mem:* Am Craftsmen's Coun (Pa rep to Northeast Assembly, 75-78); Northwest Pa Artists Asn; Assoc Artists of Pittsburgh; Nat Coun Educ Ceramic Arts; Am Crafts Coun. *Media:* Clay. *Publ:* Auth, 27th Syracuse Nat, Craft Horizons, 12/72; Nat Coun on Educ for Ceramic Arts J, Vol 9, No 1, fall 88; Gai Jin, Studio Potter, 12/92; Japanese Women Ceramists-Part I, Studio Potter, 12/94. *Mailing Add:* 119 Valley View Dr Edinboro PA 16412-2316

NICHOLAS, THOMAS ANDREW
PAINTER
b Middletown, Conn, Sept 26, 34. *Study:* Studied with Ernest Lohrmann, Meriden, Conn, 50-53; Sch Visual Arts, NY, scholar, 53-55. *Work:* Butler Inst Am Art, Youngstown, Ohio; Ga Mus, Athens; Farnesworth Mus, Rockland, Maine; Hispanic Soc Am, NY, NY; Peabody Mus, Salem, Mass; and others. *Comn:* Four ten-colored lithographs, Franklin Mint, 77. *Exhib:* Major exhibs, NY, New Eng, Wash & Calif, 2005. *Teaching:* Instr, Famous Artists Schs, Westport, Conn, 58-61, summer workshops, Rockport, Mass, 62-65, etc, Jade Fon Watercolor Workshop, Carmel, Calif, 78-2000. *Awards:* Elizabeth T Greenshields Mem Found Grants, 61 & 62; Gold Medal Honor, Allied Artists Am, 68; Gold Medal Honor, Am Watercolor Soc, 69; recipient Gold medal of Hon New Eng Watercolor Soc, Boston, 1985; Acad Artists Asn, 1985; named Knickerbocker Honoree Artist of Yr, 1989; recipient Grumbacher award watercolor, Acad Artists Asn, 1990; Grumbacher Gold medal Gouache New Engl Watercolor Soc, 1992; Gouache Transparent Watercolor, 1995; 40 Medals of Honor 1962-2004. *Bibliog:* Articles in Am Artist, 3/60 & 8/72; article in North Light Mag, fall 70; John L Cooley (auth), article in The Old Watercolor Soc, Eng, 71; plus others. *Mem:* Nat Acad; Am Watercolor Soc; Allied Artists Am; New Eng Watercolor Soc; Boston Guild Artists (Grumbacher Gold medallion award watercolor 1988, No Shore Arts Asn award oil 1991); Rockport Art Asn (Silver medal 1988, 94, Darrand award oil 1992, Cirino award 1st prize Gouache 1992, Clark Polupar award Gouache 1992, Cooley award graphics 1995, Clark Popular award Gouache 1995, Cirino award Gouache 1995, Davis Mem award watercolor 1996, Mills Mem award Gouache 1996); Hudson Valley Artists (Gold medal 1974, 85, 94, Huntington Mem award oil 1995, Bohnert Mem award oil 1996). *Media:* Oil, Watercolor. *Publ:* Auth, article, SW Art, 12/82; Creative Watercolor, Rockport Pub Inc, 95; A Gallery of Marine Art, Rockport Pub Inc, 98. *Dealer:* Tom Nicholas Gallery 71 Main St Rockport MA 01966; Di Tomasso Gallery Jackson Hole WY and Scottsdale AZ; Vermont Fine Art, Stowe, Vermont. *Mailing Add:* 7 Wildon Heights Rockport MA 01966

NICHOLS, EDWARD EDSON
PAINTER, EDUCATOR
b Chicago, Ill, 20. *Study:* Univ Kans, BFA, 57, MFA, 59; Huntington Hartford Found, 60, 64. *Work:* Miss Art Asn, Jackson; Tex Instruments Collection, Dallas; McAllen Int Mus, Tex; Univ Tex-Pan Am, Edinburg. *Comn:* Painting, Hidalgo Co Hist Mus, 92; TWS 50th Ann Exhib, 99. *Exhib:* Tenth Washington Area Show, Corcoran Gallery Am Art, 56; 22nd Ann, Butler Inst Am Art, 57; 154th Ann, Pa Acad Fine Arts, 59; Third Ann Delta Exhib, Ark Arts Ctr, Little Rock, 60; 23rd Am Drawing Biennial, Norfolk Mus Art, Va, 65; Art Mus STex Ann, Corpus Christi, 70; Tex Painting & Sculpture, Dallas Mus Fine Art, 71; Tex Watercolor Soc Travel Award Exhib, San Antonio, 80, 2002. *Teaching:* Assoc prof to full prof Art, Univ Tex Pan-Am, Edinburg, Tex, 65-99, retired, 99. *Awards:* Winsor Newton Award, Tex Watercolor Soc Exhib, 80, Patron's award, 2002; Del Mar Col Drawing Award, Ann Nat Drawing Competition, 84; Juror's Choice Award, Tip o' Texas Exhib, 91. *Mem:* Tex Watercolor Soc. *Media:* Watercolor, Oil. *Publ:* Riversedge, Univ Tex Pan-Am, Edinburg, Tex, 92; Fifty Years of Excellence, Tex Watercolor Soc, 99. *Dealer:* www.jsiegler.com. *Mailing Add:* 2018 Shary Rd Mission TX 78572

NICHOLS, FRANCIS N, II
PRINTMAKER, EDUCATOR
Study: Wichita State Univ, MFA; also with David Bernard & Robert Kiskadden. *Work:* Anderson Fine Art Ctr, Ind; Univ Miss; Wichita State Univ, Wichita Art Mus; Deines Cult Arts Ctr, Kans. *Exhib:* Kans 17th Ann Small Painting, Drawing & Print Exhib, 91; Print Types Consortium Exhib, Ind Univ, 91; Cimarron Nat Works on Paper, Okla State Univ, 91; 8th Ann Nat Works on Paper, Berkeley, Calif, 92; and others. *Teaching:* Fel, Wichita State Univ, 65-67; prof printmaking, Ft Hays State Univ, 67-. *Awards:* Merit & Purchase Award, Anderson Winter Show, Ind, 89; Best of Show, 15th Ann Prairie Art Exhib, Sterling, Kans, 89; First Place, Carrier Found Nat Competition, Belle Meade, NJ, 91. *Mem:* Kans Art Educ Asn; Print Consortium; Nat Educ Asn; Nat Art Educ Asn; Kans Art Educ Asn. *Media:* Intaglio, Lithography. *Dealer:* Rueben Saunders Gallery Wichita KS. *Mailing Add:* 1100 Amhurst Hays KS 67601

NICHOLS, MAXINE MCCLENDON See McClendon, Maxine McClendon Nichols

NICHOLS, WARD H
PAINTER
b Welch, WVa, July 5, 30. *Study:* WVa Univ. *Work:* Integon Corp & R J Reynolds Co, Winston-Salem, NC; Gutenberg Mus, Mainz, Ger; Huntington Gallery Art, WVa; Springfield Mus Art, Mass; Lowes Corp, North Wilkesboro, NY; BankAmerica, Charlotte, NC. *Comn:* Oil painting, Integon Corp, Winston Salem, NC, 75; oil painting, Printing Indust Carolina, Charlotte, NC, 81, 83 & 92; oil painting, NC State Beekeepers Asn, Raleigh, 82. *Exhib:* Allied Artist Exhib, Nat Acad Galleries, NY; El Paso Mus Art, Tex; Russell Centenary Exhib, Nottingham, Eng; NC Mus Art, Raleigh; Mainstreams, Fine Arts Ctr, Marietta Col, Ohio; and others. *Pos:* Artist-in-residence, Univ Ind, Terre Haute, Ind, Greenbrier, White Sulphur Springs, WVa & W Liberty Col, West Liberty, WVa. *Teaching:* Guest lectr, many cols in eastern US. *Awards:* Grumbacher Award Merit, El Paso Mus Art, 70; Jurors Merit Award, Miss Mus Art, 71; PICA Award, Printing Indust Carolinas, 75-90. *Bibliog:* Article, Pace Mag, Piedmont Airlines, 78; article, Todays Art, 80; Invitation to a Country Walk (film), Assoc Images, 80. *Mem:* Wilkes Art Guild. *Media:* Oil. *Publ:* Contemp Graphic Artists, 87; New York Art Rev, 90; Dict Int Bio, 91; Country J, 2/92. *Dealer:* Top Drawer 209 W Third St Winston-Salem NC 27101. *Mailing Add:* 734 Beaumont Elm St Wilkesboro NC 28659

NICHOLSON, MYREEN MOORE See Moore, Myreen

NICHOLSON, NATASHA
ASSEMBLAGE ARTIST, SCULPTOR
b St Louis, Mo, May 29, 45. *Study:* Ringling Sch Art, 64-65. *Work:* Oakland Mus Art, Calif; Addison Gallery Am Art, Phillips Acad, Andover, Mass; Los Angeles Co Mus Art; Madison Art Ctr, Wis. *Comn:* Sculpture, Rayovac Corp, Madison, Wis, 86. *Exhib:* Solo exhibs, Addison Gallery Am Art, 74, Asher-Faure Gallery, Los Angeles, 81 & 83 & Perimeter Gallery, Chicago, 83; Collage and Assemblage in Southern Calif, Los Angeles Inst Contemp Art, 75; A Sense of Space, Oakland Mus Art, 77; Global Space Invasions, San Francisco Mus Mod Art, 78; Our Own Artists: Art in Orange Co, Newport Harbor Art Mus, 79; Tableau, Middendorf-Lane Gallery, Washington, DC, 80; Forgotten Dimension: A Survey of Small Sculpture in Calif Now, Fresno Art Ctr, traveling, 82; Chicago & Vicinity Exhib, Chicago Art Inst, 84; and others. *Collection Arranged:* The Other Things That Artists Make, San Francisco Mus Mod Art, 76; Useable Art, Decorative Arts, Quay Gallery, San Francisco, 77; Decorative Arts of Dane Co, Madison Art Ctr, Wis, 82. *Pos:* Dir, Natasha Nicholson/works of Art, Madison, Wis, 87-90. *Awards:* Individual Artist Grant, Nat Endowment Arts, 77; Artists Fel, 83 & Proj Grant, 83, Wis Arts Bd. *Bibliog:* Alfred Frankenstein (auth), For the magical love of oddities, San Francisco Chronicle, 77; Melinda Wortz (auth), Los Angeles, Art News Mag, 12/79; Vivien Raynor (auth), Anxious interiors, NY Times, 9/85. *Media:* Mixed. *Mailing Add:* 1962 Atwood Ave PO Box 3493 Madison WI 53704

NICHOLSON, ROY WILLIAM
PAINTER, EDUCATOR
b Cambridge, Eng, Mar 21, 43. *Study:* Hornsey Col Art, London, Eng, with John Hoyland, NDD, 65; Brooklyn Mus Sch Art, Max Beckmann Mem Scholar, 66; Vermont Col, Norwich Univ, MFA, 95. *Work:* Guild Hall Mus; State Univ Stony Brook; Heckscher Mus, Huntington, NY; Royal Col Heralds & Abbot Hall Art Gallery Mus, Eng; Fed Reserve Bank Atlanta, Ga; Long Island Mus Am Art; Yale Univ Art Gallery, New Haven CT. *Comn:* Count Robin De Lanne-Mirrles (portrait), 64; Met Transportation Authority, Arts for Transit, 2 glass mosaics, 2002; Holder Properties, Post Meridian; Twilight in the Garden, Columbia, SC, 2004; Los Angeles MetroArt, Union Station, Goldline, 3 glass mosaics, 2006. *Exhib:* US Consulates, Brazil, 87; Katharina Rich Perlow Gallery, NY, 91; 18 Suffolk Artists, Univ Art Gallery, State Univ NY, Stonybrook, 95; 52 Weeks, Heckscher Mus, Huntington, NY, 98; Rathbone Gallery, Sage Col, Albany, NY, 99; Lizan Tops Gallery, East Hampton, NY, 2000; Dunedin Art Ctr, Fla, 2000; Gloamings, Avram Gallery, Southampton Col, NY, 2002; and many others. *Collection Arranged:* The Art of Claude Lorrain, Newcastle & London, 69; The Art of Paul Nash, Newcastle, 71; Alan Davie/David Hockney: Watercolors & Drawings, touring, 71; The Craftsman's Art, Victoria & Albert Mus, London, 73; Watercolor & Pencil Drawings by Paul Cezanne, Hayward Gallery, London & Newcastle, 73; many one person & group exhibs organized at Long Island Univ, Southampton Fine Arts Gallery, 86-93, including photography of Peristroika, 91 & Betty Parsons, 92. *Pos:* Asst dir, Brook Street Gallery, London, 66-68; visual arts officer, Northern Arts, Newcastle, Eng, 68-74; bd gov, Lancaster Col Art, Eng, 72-74; dir, art gallery, Long Island Univ Southampton Campus, 86-93. *Teaching:* Vis artist,

State Univ NY, Stony Brook, 78-79; adj assoc prof art, Long Island Univ Southampton Campus, 81-86, asst prof art, 86-93 & assoc prof art 93-2001, prof art Emeritus, 2005; prof art, Victor d'Amico Art Inst, Easthampton, NY, 89-94. *Awards:* Max Beckmann Mem Scholar; LI Univ Trustees Award, Scholarly Achievement, 2000. *Bibliog:* several articles, reviews, New York Times between 83 & 2001; Marion Wolberg Weiss (auth), article, Country Mag, 95; Ariella Budick (auth), Article, Newsday, 98; Becker and Colacello (auths), Studios by The Sea Abrams, 2002; John Eston, Hampton Gardens; A 350 Year Legacy, New York, Rizzort, 2004. *Media:* Oil, Acrylic; Lithography, Etching. *Dealer:* Suzanne Randolph Fine Art, 234 5th Ave Ste 301, New York, NY, 10001; Alpan Gallery 2 W Carver Huntington NY. *Mailing Add:* 760 E Hampton Tpke Sag Harbor NY 11963

NICK, GEORGE
PAINTER, EDUCATOR
b Rochester, NY, Mar 28, 27. *Study:* Cleveland Inst Art, with Frank Wilcox; Brooklyn Mus Art Sch; Art Students League, with Edwin Dickinson; Yale Univ, BFA & MFA. *Work:* Hirshhorn Mus, Washington, DC; Boston Mus Fine Arts; Joslyn Art Mus, Omaha, Nebr; Rose Art Gallery, Brandeis Univ, Waltham, Mass; Metro Mus, NY; group exhibs: Corcoran Gallery, Mus Baltimore, Boston Mus Fine Arts; rep in permanent collections: Boston Mus Fine Arts, Metrop Mus Art, Folks Mus, Essen, Ger, Nat Mus, Johannesburg, Southern Africa, Hirshorn Mus and Sculpture Garden, Wash, John Updike, Bob Dylan, Governor Michael Dukakis. *Exhib:* Md Artists Ann Exhib, Baltimore, 66; Pa Artists Ann, Philadelphia Acad Fine Arts, 67; One-man exhibs: Schoelkolpf Gallery, Tibor de Nagy Gallery, Fischbach Gallery; group exhibs: Corcoran Gallery, Pa Acad Fine Arts, Butler Inst Am Art, Flint Inst, Nat Acad of Design. *Teaching:* Assoc prof drawing, Carnegie-Mellon Inst, 64-65; assoc prof painting, Univ Pa, 66-69; assoc prof painting, Mass Col Art, Boston, formerly, prof two-dimensional art, currently; Fac Hollins Univ, Va, Mass Col of Art, 1969-1994; now fac NY Studio Sch. *Awards:* Mass Coun Arts Grant, 74; Nat Endowment Arts Award, 76; Am Acad Arts & Lett Award, 76; Dept of Interior Bicentennial grant. *Mem:* Nat Acad. *Media:* Oil. *Mailing Add:* c/o Concord Art Assn 37 Lexington Rd Concord MA 01742

NICK, LLOYD
MUSEUM DIRECTOR, PAINTER
b Rochester, NY, Mar 11, 42. *Study:* Yale, Norfolk, with William Bailey, 65; Hunter Col, with Tony Smith, BFA, 66; Skowhegan Sch Painting & Sculpture, with Philip Pearlstein, 67; Univ Pa, with Neil Welliver, MFA, 68. *Work:* Princess Grace de Monaco; Baron & Baroness Guy de Rothschild, Monaco; AT&T, Bank South, Atlanta; Barclays Bank, Charlotte, NC & Eng. *Comn:* Four color lithograph print, Hurt Building's 50th Anniv, 86; Colored pencil drawing, Petainer Inc, Atlanta & Stockholm, Sweden, 87; Drawing for book, Your Fondest Dream, The Power of Creativity, 89. *Exhib:* Philadelphia Mus Art, Nicholas Roench Mus & Automation House, NY; Gallery Contemp Art, Philadelphia, Pa; Fayetteville Mus Art, NC; Gallerie Monte Carlo, Monaco; Gallery Mod Art, Fredericksburg, Va; and others. *Collection Arranged:* The Family Photographs of Claude Monet (auth, catalog), Oglethorpe Univ Mus, 86; Black Artists from South Africa (auth, catalog), Oglethorpe Univ Mus, 89; Four from Madrid: Contemp Spanish Realism Oglethorpe Univ Mus, 94; The Spirit & the Flesh: Contemp Am Realism, Oglethorpe Univ Mus, 95; The Mystical Artists of Tibet, Oglethorpe Univ Mus, 96. *Pos:* Art gallery dir, Oglethorpe Univ, Atlanta, Ga, 83-92, mus dir, 92-. *Teaching:* Chair & prof art, Am Col Monaco, Monte Carlo, 69-70; prof painting, Guilford Col, Greensboro, NC, 73-76; chair & prof painting & art cult, Oglethorpe Univ, Atlanta, 84-. *Awards:* Nat Endowment Humanities Grant, 74; Int artist-in-residence, Ljubljana, Slovenia, Yugoslavia, 77; Fac Develop grants, Guilford Col, 74 & Oglethorpe Univ, 90 & 94. *Bibliog:* Atlanta J/Constitution, Atlanta, 86; Aesthetics & Philosophy, Sofia, Bulgaria, 91; Interview, Bulgarian Nat Radio, 91. *Mem:* Am Asn Mus; Asn Col & Univ Mus & Galleries; Ga Asn Mus & Galleries; panelist, Asian Art Conf, Int East-West Ctr, Atlanta, 98. *Media:* Oil. *Publ:* Ed, The Family Photographs of Claud Monet, 86, The Many Faces of Buddha, 86, Oglethorpe Univ; contribr & ed, Four from Madrid: Contemporary Spanish Realism, 94, The Spirit & the Flesh: Contemporary American Realism, 95, Oglethorpe Univ Mus; contribr, The Mystical Arts of Tibet, featuring the Personal Sacred Objects of the Dalai Lama, Longstreet Press, 96; and many others. *Mailing Add:* Oglethorpe Univ Mus 4484 Peachtree Rd NE Atlanta GA 30319

NICKARD, GARY LAURENCE
PHOTOGRAPHER, CURATOR
b Toronto, Ont, June 14, 54. *Study:* State Univ NY, Buffalo, BFA, 78, MA, 82, MFA, 86. *Work:* Albright-Knox Art Gallery, Buffalo; Burchfield Art Ctr, Buffalo; Capen Gallery, State Univ NY, Buffalo; Castellani Art Mus. *Exhib:* Mod Sci, CEPA Gallery, Buffalo, 82; 40th Western NY Exhib, Albright-Knox Art Gallery, Buffalo, 84; Alien Art, Artists Gallery, Buffalo, 85; Insidious Protocols, Artmart, Buffalo, 86; Insidious Protocols, Dana Art Ctr, Colgate Univ, 87; Soc Studies, YYZ Gallery, Toronto, 87; Dislocations, Alternative Mus, NY, 87; 42nd Western NY Exhib, Albright-Knox Art Gallery, Buffalo, 88; Science as Spectacle, Burchfield Art Ctr, Buffalo, 91. *Collection Arranged:* Riding First Class on the Titanic, Nathan Lyons (catalog), 87, Crocodile Tears, Douglas Huebler (catalog), Albright-Knox Art Gallery, 85; Sharp Rocks, Edgar Heap of Birds (catalog), 86, Tableau Morte, Akin/Ludwig, 87, Stereo Views, Jim Pomeroy (catalog), 88, On Britain's Doorstep, Stephen Shortt, 88, CEPA Gallery; Belfast/Beirut, Alternative Mus, 90; Photostroika: New Soviet Photography, The Body in Question, Enfleshings: Helen Chadwick, Aperture Burden Gallery, 90 & 91; Light Images, Chrysler Mus, 90; Ireland: A Troubled Aperture, A Terrible Beauty, Artists Space, 94. *Pos:* Exec dir & cur, CEPA Gallery, Buffalo, 82-88; consult, Nat Endowment Arts, 84-90 (panelist, 88-90); NY State Coun Arts, 88-90 & NJ State Arts Coun, 90-94; assoc cur, Alternative Mus, NY, 88-90; dir & cur, Aperture Burden Gallery, NY, 90-91; dir prog & cur, Artists Space, NY, 92-94. *Teaching:* Instr photog, State Univ NY, Buffalo, 85-88; vis asst prof photog, State Univ NY, Buffalo, 95-. *Awards:* Grant, NY State Coun Arts. *Bibliog:* Robert C Morgan (auth), Gary Nickard, 1/88, Arts Mag; Richard Huntington (auth), Art & science, ambivalence in the middle, Buffalo News, 2/17/91; Elizabeth Licata (auth), Gary Nickard, Burchfield Art Ctr, Artforum Mag, 5/91. *Mem:* Soc Photog Educ. *Media:* Installation. *Res:* postmodern photography. *Publ:* Contribr, Buffalo Arts Rev, Center Quart (Catskill Ctr Photog) & Cepa Quart, 86; High performance, Buffalo News, 88; Afterimage, Border Crossings, 91; Exposure, 97

NICKEL, DOUGLAS ROBERT
CURATOR, CRITIC
b Williamsport, Pa, Apr 24, 61. *Study:* Cornell Univ, BA, 83; Princeton Univ, MFA, 89, PhD, 95. *Collection Arranged:* Picturing Modernity, 94-; Nature/Culture, 94; The Photographic Condition, 95; Snap Shots: The Photography of Everyday Life, 1888-The Present (with catalog), 98; Carleton Watkins: The Art of Perception (with catalog),1999; Stranger Passing: Collected Portraits by Joel Sternfeld (with catalog), 2001; Dreaming in Pictures: The Photography of Lewis Carroll (with catalog), 2002. *Pos:* cur photog, San Francisco Mus Art. *Teaching:* Instr studio art & photog, Cornell Univ, 84; adj asst prof art hist, Univ Calif, Berkeley, 95; adj prof art history, Stanford U, 1999, 2002. *Mem:* Col Art Asn. *Publ:* Auth, American photographs revisited, Am Art, spring 92; Nature's supernaturalism, Tamarind Papers, Univ NMex, 96; Francis Frith in Egypt and Palestine, Princeton Univ Press, 2003. *Mailing Add:* 151 Third St San Francisco CA 94103

NICKERSON, SCOTT A
PAINTER
Study: Sch Visual Arts, NY, BA, 96; Art Students League of NY, 2000-; studied with Nelson Shanks, Art Students League, NY. *Comn:* Friends of Akim. *Exhib:* solo exhib, Thompson Park Art Exhib, Lincroft, NJ, 98, Orchid Island Golf & Beach Club, Vero Beach, Fla, 98, JW Ross Sea Bright Libr, NJ, 98; Annual Scholarship Competition, Soc of Illustrators, NY, 96; Open State Juried Exhib, Am Artists Prof League, Toms River, NJ, 98; Nat Exhib, Acad Artists Asn, Springfield, Mass, 99; group exhib, Frederick Gallery, Allenhurst, NJ, 99, Cork Gallery, Avery Fisher Hall Lincoln Ctr, NY, 2000; Open Portrait Exhib, The Portrait Soc Atlanta, Ga, 2000; Juried Children's Portrait, The Portrait Soc Atlanta, Ga, 2001. *Pos:* Portrait artist, currently. *Teaching:* instr, figure drawing & oil painting, Guild of Creative Art, Shrewsbury, NJ, currently. *Awards:* Hon Mention, Monmouth Co Arts Coun, Lincroft, NJ, 98; Best Portfolio Award, Am Soc Portrait Artists, NY, 2000; Peoples Choice Award, Portrait Soc of Atlanta, Roswell, Ga, 2001. *Bibliog:* illustr, Artist's Mag, 12/97; article, NJ Savvy Living Mag, winter, 2000. *Mem:* Portrait Soc Am; Am Soc Classical Realism; Am Soc Portrait Artists, Montgomery, Ala; Guild Creative Art, Shrewsbury, NJ. *Media:* Oil & Pencil. *Mailing Add:* 56 Phoenix Ct Asbury Park NJ 07712

NICKSON, GRAHAM G
PAINTER, EDUCATOR
b Knowle Green, Lancashire, Eng, 46. *Study:* Camberwell Sch Arts & Crafts, London, BA, 69; Royal Col Art, London, MA, 72; Prix de Rome (scholarship) RS, 72-74; Yale Univ Sch Art, Harkness Fel, 1976. *Work:* Metrop Mus Art, NY; Neuburger Mus, Purchase, NY; Albright-Knox Gallery & Mus, Buffalo, NY; La Jolla Mus Contemp Art, Calif; William Benton Mus Art, Univ Conn; Rep in permanent collections Metrop Mus Art, NY City, Neuberger Mus, NY, La Jolla Mus Contemp Art, Calif, Israel Mus; exhibs incl Art Mus, Fla Inter, 1996. *Comn:* Painting, Skidmore Owings & Merrill, San Francisco, 85. *Exhib:* One-man exhib, William Benton Mus, Storrs, Conn, 82, Northern Ctr Contemp Art, Sunderland, Eng, 88, Warwick Arts Ctr, Mead Mus, Eng, 89 & Weatherspoon Art Gallery, Univ NC, Greensboro, 91; 30 Painters: New Acquisitions, Metrop Mus Art, NY, 82; New Drawing in Am, Drawing Ctr, NY, 82; Motion-Arrested Motion, Chrysler Mus, Norfolk, Va, 87; London-Glasgow-NY, Metrop Mus Art, NY, 88; exhibs incl Terry Dintfass Gallery, NY, 1996, Lizan-Tops Gallery, E Hampton, NY, 1996, Nat Acad of Design, New York City, 1996, Ark Art Ctr, Little Rock, 1997; One-man shows incl Salander O'Reilly Galleries, New York City, 1997, 1998, Adelaide Central Gallery, Australia, 1995, Camino Real Gallery, Boca Raton, Fla, 1996, Glenn Horowitz Gallery, E Hampton, NY, 1996; Represented in permanent collections Albright Knox Art Gallery, NY. *Pos:* Head, first-year diploma studies Byam Shaw Sch Art, London, 1974; Dean, NY Studio Sch Drawing Painting & Sculpture, 88-. *Teaching:* painting fac Rome Scholarships, British Sch, Rome, 1975; lectr, drawing Philadelphia Sch Art, 1980; fac New York Studio Sch, New York City, 1981-88. *Awards:* Harkness Fel, Commonwealth Fund, 76; Howard Found Fel, Brown Univ, 80; Howard Found Fel in Fine Art, 80; Guggenheim Fel, 89; Ingram Merill Fel in Painting, 93. *Bibliog:* Jack Flam (auth), Graham Nickson: Drawing into color, William Benton Mus, 82; John Russell (auth), Painter of beach life, Nickson's Beaches, New York Times, 82; Andrew Forge/Jack Flam/Bob McDaniel (coauths), Graham Nickson paintings & drawings, Northern Ctr Contemp Art, 88. *Mem:* Nat Acad. *Media:* Oil, Acrylic. *Dealer:* Salander-O'Reilly Galleries Inc 20 E 79th St New York NY 10021. *Mailing Add:* Dean NY Studio Sch 8 W 8th St New York NY 10011

NICOTRA, JOSEPH CHARLES
PAINTER, MURALIST
b Corona, NY, Aug 9, 31. *Study:* Art Students League, New York, 55-60 & Woodstock, 60; Am Art Sch, New York, 61. *Hon Degrees:* Numerous hon degrees from foreign univ. *Work:* Mayor O'Dwyer, DAV Comn, 55; John F Kennedy Libr & Nat Arch Collection, 76; African Methodist Escopalian Church, 77; Queens Mus, 81; Burough of Queens, 92-93. *Comn:* ARC de Triomphe-Walk Through Mural (two sided, free standing, 688 sq ft), Moulin-Rouge Ball, LI Philamonic, Huntington Town House, 87; Even So Amen from Revolations (painting), comn by actor James Russo, 88-91; sculpture, LIJ Hosp, 94; Cancer Surgery Proceedure (four progressive illus),

comn by Dr Robert Weiss, LIJ Hosp, 96; series of 5 anatomical studies for presentation to the Chicago Med Bd, comn by Dr Robert Weiss, 97. *Exhib:* Solo mural exhibs, Armstrong Gallery, Flushing, NY, 68, Roma Gallery, Miami, Fla, 73, LBAA Galleries, NY, 78, Long Beach Pub Libr Art Gallery, 79 & St Pauls Church, 92; Art Students League Gallery, Bayside, 57 & Woodstock, NY, 61; 32nd Nat Competition, 62; Am Artist Gallery's Stable, NY, 63; Roma Gallery, Miami Beach, Fla, 73; La Galerie Mouffe, Paris, France, 76; Nudes, LBAA Gallery, NY, 78; 29th Ann, Comn Arts, Long Beach Mus, 79; Moe's Pit, Queens Mus 80 & Invitational Show, 82, 83 & 84; Western Views and Eastern Visions Nat Traveling Show, Queens Mus, Smithsonian Inst & Kennedy Gallery, 81; CAM Art Ctr, 82; Pricilla Redford Roe Gallery, Suffolk NY, 82; Artist Contemporanei, Academia, Italy, 82; Palazzo del Malfestazione, Italy, 83; 6th Int Biennial, Garbo, Bulgaria, 83; Flushing Coun Cult & Arts, 86; AMMO Gallery, 86. *Pos:* painter, muralist, Fine Arts Easel, currently. *Teaching:* Lectr, demonstrations, workshops, drawing & painting. *Awards:* Gold Medal, Intl Parliment Safety & Peace Artistic Merit, 83; Gold Plaque Award, Italia Accadermia, 86; Primo Milano Gold Medal, 88. *Bibliog:* Getting to know Joe Nicotra (feature story & photo), Queens Mus First News, 89; Nicotra (video art bio), 93; QMA, Queens Mus, 97. *Mem:* Life mem Art Students League; Orgn Independent Artists; Queens Coun Arts, life time mem; Int Platform Asn; Queens Coun Arts. *Media:* Oil, Acrylic. *Res:* Continually Ferie Artist. *Specialty:* Emotional Realism. *Interests:* To say I feel through Ferie Art. *Collection:* My personal body of work. *Publ:* Auth, Golden Pictures by Contemp Masters, 84; Am Ref Publ, 90; Anatomy of the Jugular Forsa, Med J, 97. *Mailing Add:* 59-32 156th St Flushing NY 11355

NIEDERER, CARL
PAINTER
b Portland, Ore, Mar 14, 27. *Study:* Univ Ore, Eugene, with Jack Wilkinson, BS, 49; Atelier Fernand Leger, Paris, France, 51; New Sch, New York, with Alexi Brodovitch, 53. *Work:* Univ San Francisco Collection & City of San Francisco Collection, Calif; Univ Wyo Mus, Laramie; Peace Harbor Hosp, Florence, Ore. *Comn:* Bronze facia frieze, Bank Calif Hq, San Francisco, 63; polychrome ceiling stabile, Univ Calif, Berkeley, 74; enamel entryway panels, Pac Bell, San Francisco, Calif, 75; elevator door murals, Chevron, 75 & AT&T, 77, San Francisco, Calif. *Exhib:* Pac Int, Perc Tucker Gallery, Townsville, Australia, 82; Australian Observations, Nicolaysen Art Mus, Casper, Wyo, 82; Wyo Biennial, traveling exhib, Cheyenne, 86 & 88; Wyo Fel Show, 88; solo shows, Citicorp Plaza, Los Angeles, Calif, 91, Triad Gallery, Seal Rock, Ore, 96; and others. *Pos:* Prof emer, Univ Wyo, Laramie, 91. *Teaching:* Assoc prof design, Univ Ore, Eugene, 68-70; head dept painting, Univ Wyo, Laramie, 77-82, prof art & watercolor, 82-89. *Awards:* Purchase Award, San Francisco Arts Festival, 64; Second Prize, Laramie Art Guild Show, 86; Best of Show, Wyo Watercolor Soc Show, 87; Wyo Coun Arts Fel, 88. *Bibliog:* Francis H Hoover (auth), San Francisco Gallery Guide, 75. *Mem:* Laramie Art Guild; Wyo Watercolor Soc. *Media:* Miscellaneous Media, Watercolor. *Mailing Add:* PO Box 2833 Florence OR 47439-0163

NIEDZIALEK, TERRY
SCULPTOR, ENVIRONMENTAL ARTIST
b July 10, 56. *Study:* Univ Colo, Boulder, 78-80; NY Inst Technol, Old Westbury, NY, BFA, 81. *Work:* Galerie Alain Oudin, Paris; NY Inst Technol, Old Westbury; Galerie Il Diaframma, Milan, Italy. *Exhib:* Long Island's Alternative Spaces, Islip Mus, NY, 85; Fashion & Surrealism, Fashion Inst, NY, 87 & Victoria & Albert Mus, London, 88; The Political Landscape, Hillwood Art Mus, Greenvale, NY, 90; Hair Sculpture & Its Roots, Lehigh Univ Mus, Bethlehem, Pa, 91; and others. *Teaching:* Fac sculpture, Pa Govs Sch Arts, Erie, 92. *Awards:* Nat Endowment Arts Grant, 88; Individual Artists Award, Pollock-Krasner, 89; Cross Disciplinary Award, Performance, Pa Counc Arts, 91. *Bibliog:* Julius Vitali (auth), Hair Sculpture, Domus, Italy, 85; Andrienne Redd (auth), Hair Sculpture & Its Roots, Lehigh Univ Mus, 91; Dan Friedman (auth), Terry Niedzialek Hair Sculpture, Fiber Arts, 91. *Media:* Miscellaneous Media. *Publ:* Illus, Italian Vogue, 86; Epoca, Mondadori, Italy, 86; New look, Filipachi, France, 86; contribr, The Costume Maker's Art, Lark Bks, 92; Earth Journal, Buzzworm Bks, 92. *Mailing Add:* PO Box 506 Kutztown PA 19530-9439

NIELSEN, NINA I M
DEALER
b Riverdale, NY, Nov 5, 40. *Study:* Bucknell Univ, BA, 62; Univ Vienna. *Pos:* Owner, Nielsen Gallery, Boston, currently; vis comt mem, Boston Mus Sch, 79-80. *Specialty:* Modern and contemporary paintings, drawings and sculpture. *Mailing Add:* c/o Nielsen Gallery 179 Newbury St Boston MA 02116

NIEMANN, EDMUND E
PAINTER, SCULPTOR
b New York, NY. *Study:* Nat Acad Design; Art Students League. *Work:* Slater Mus, Norwich, Conn; Butler Inst Am Art, Youngstown, Ohio; Syracuse Univ Art Mus; Swarthmore Col. *Exhib:* Directions of Am Painting, Carnegie Inst, Pa, 41; Nat Acad Design Ann, 62-68; Pa Acad Fine Arts Watercolor & Drawing Ann, 64; Butler Inst Am Art Painting Nat, 68, 74, 77 & 80; Watercolor USA, 72. *Awards:* New Eng Ann Lyon Award, 77; Audubon Artist Ann Hirsch Mem Award, 78; Young-Hunter Mem Award, Allied Artists, 80; and others. *Mem:* Audubon Artists; Am Watercolor Soc; Allied Artists Am; Nat Soc Painters Acrylic & Casein. *Publ:* Contribr, Todays Art, 7/68 & 8/73; auth, Drawing with unusual tool, Am Artists, 1/70. *Mailing Add:* 327 Central Park W #47 New York NY 10025-7631

NIERMAN, LEONARDO M
PAINTER, SCULPTOR
b Mexico City, Mex, Nov 1, 32. *Study:* Nat Univ Mex, BA. *Work:* Ft Worth Art Mus, Tex; Mus Arte Mod, Mexico City; The Wave, Detroit Inst of Arts; Bird in Flight, Acad Fine Arts, Honolulu; Genesis, Israel Mus, Jerusalem; and others. *Comn:* Murals Sch Com, Univ City, Mex, 56; mural, Golden West Savings, San Francisco, 65; stained glass windows, two temples, Mexico City, 66-67; Cosmic Meditation (mural), Physics Bldg, Princeton Univ, NJ, 68; Eagle (bronze sculpture), Toronto, Can, 72. *Exhib:* Paris Biennale, Mus Mod Art, France, 61; Marlborough-Gerson Gallery, NY, 64; Pittsburgh Int, Carnegie Inst, Pa, 64 & 67; El Paso Mus Art, Tex, 64 & 71; Mus Arte Mod, 72; and many one-man shows. *Awards:* First Prize, Art Inst Mex, 64; Palm D'Or Beaux Arts, Monaco, 69; Gold Medal, Tomasso Campanella Found, Italy, 72. *Bibliog:* Enrique Gual (auth), Leonardo Nierman, Ed Monterrey, 64; Jose Gomez Sicre (auth), Nierman, Artes Mex, 71; Julio Cortazar & Max Pol Fouchet (auth), Leonardo Nierman, A Capell & A Elmayan Ed, Paris, 75. *Mem:* Royal Soc Arts, London; Int Biog Asn: UK; Int Arts Guild, Monte Carlo; Salon Plastica, Mex. *Media:* Acrylic; Onyx, Bronze

NIESE, HENRY ERNST
ENVIRONMENTAL ARTIST, PAINTER
b Jersey City, NJ, Oct 11, 1924. *Study:* Cooper Union, cert, with Robert Gwathmey & Morris Kantor; Acad Grande Chaumiere, cert, with Othon Friesz; Columbia Univ, BFA, with Leo Manso, John Heliker & Meyer Schapiro. *Work:* Whitney Mus Am Art, NY; Corcoran Gallery, Washinton; Nat Mus Am Art, Washington; Filmkundliches Arkiv, Cologne, WGer; Chrysler Mus, Norfolk; and others. *Exhib:* Young Am, Whitney Mus Am Art, 62 & 40 Artists Under 40, 64; 4th Int Exp Film Festival, Brussels, Belg, 69; NY Avant Garde Festivals, 69-78; Six Nations Mus, NY & Corcoran Gallery, 76; Foundry Gallery, Washinton, 80; also numerous on-site ceremonial structures and performances in New York City, Mass, Vt, Md & SDak, 78-. *Pos:* leader/participant, 36 Sundances, 1976-2000; Univ Hons Program, Univ Md Col Park (UMCP), 1982-1995; Md Inst Col Art, 2003-2006; Dir, Traditional Wisdom Prog, Eagle Voice Ctr, Glenelg, Md, currently; guest lectr, Va Tech. *Teaching:* Spec lectr grad humanities, NY Univ, 65-69; asst prof studio art, Ohio State Univ, 66-69; assoc prof studio art, Univ Md, 69-95; vis artist, Univ Calif, Santa Barbara, 75; guest fel, Yale Univ, 79. *Awards:* Pulitzer Found Traveling Fel, 55; Int Cinema Prize, Mus Arte Mod, Vitoria, Brasil, 69; Creative & Performing Arts Grant, Univ Md, 71 & 73. *Mem:* Sioux Nation Sundance. *Media:* Multimedia. *Interests:* ceremonial structures based on Native Am tradition. *Publ:* auth, The Man Who Knew the Medicine: Bill Eagle-Feathers Teaching, Bear & Co, 2002. *Mailing Add:* Box 44 Glenelg MD 21737

NIETO, JOHN W
PAINTER, SCULPTOR
b Denver, Colo, Aug 6, 36. *Study:* Pan Am Univ, 55-56; Southern Methodist Univ, 57-59; Dallas Mus Fine Arts, 60. *Work:* Heard Mus, Phoenix, Ariz; Smithsonian Inst, Washington, DC; NMex Mus Fine Arts, Santa Fe; Wagner Corp Collection, Austin, Tex; Goldwaters Pvt Collection; The White House, Washington, DC; Marine Corp Mus. *Comn:* Murals, Lakewood State Bank, Dallas, 61; bronze bust of chmn of bd, Tex Power & Light, Dallas, 80; portrait of Barry Goldwater, Goldwaters, Phoenix, Ariz, 83; Plains Prayer (poster), comn by ABC. *Exhib:* 20th Century Am Indian Artist, Kimball Art Mus, Park City, Utah, 81; Am Indian Contemp Art, Smithsonian Inst, Washington, DC, 82; Night of the First Am, John F Kennedy Ctr, Washington, DC, 82; Salon d'Automne, Grand Palais, Paris, 82; one-man shows, US Embassy, Barbados, 82 & Wheelwright Mus, Santa Fe, 86; Images of Ranchos de Taos Church, NMex Fine Arts Mus, Santa Fe, 83; Native Am Works, Pensacola Mus Art, Fla; The Art of the Native Am, Owensboro Mus Fine Art, Ky; Le Salon Des Nations A Paris, Centre Int D'Art Contemporain, 86. *Pos:* Bd dir, Wheelwright Mus, Santa Fe, NMex, 84. *Teaching:* Art, NTex State Univ, Denton, 64-65 & Southern Methodist Univ, Dallas, 74-75. *Awards:* Blue Ribbon Award, Arts & Crafts Show, Heard Mus, Phoenix, 81; Artist of Year, Santa Fean Mag, 82; Featured Artist, Festival Arts & Pageant of Masters, Laguna Beach, Calif; Feather Dancer Poster Piece, 65th Inter-Tribal Indian Ceremonial, Gallup, NMex, 86. *Bibliog:* Erica Benis (auth), John Nieto Artist, Voice Am, US Int Commun Agency, 81; Ms Goldman (auth), Artist in Santa Fe, Nat Pub Radio, Washington, DC, 82; William Carpenter (auth), Profile of John Nieto, Carpenter & Assoc, 83. *Media:* Oil, Watercolor; Clay. *Dealer:* J2 Cacciola Galleries 125 Wooster St New York NY. *Mailing Add:* c/o Ventana Fine Art 400 Canyond Rd Santa Fe NM 87501

NIEWALD, WILBUR
ARTIST
b Kansas City, Mo, 25. *Work:* Rep in permanent collections Metrop Mus Art, NY City; Albrecht-Kemper Mus Art, 2004, Marianna Kistler Beach Mus Art, 2004. *Exhib:* Rep in permanent collections Moffett Family Collection, Heartland Spine & Specialty Hosp, Kansas City; exhib incl (selected) Wright State Univ Art Galleries, 1996, Rider Univ, 2004. *Pos:* Vis artist, Vt Studio Ctr. *Teaching:* instr to chrmn, sr prof, painting Kansas City Art Inst, 49-92, prof, emer, 92-. *Awards:* Recipient Distinguished Teaching of Art award, Col Art Assoc, 88; Charlotte Street Lifetime Achievement award, 99. *Mem:* Nat Acad. *Mailing Add:* Albrecht-Kemper Mus Art 2818 Fredrick Ave Saint Joseph MO 64506

NIGROSH, LEON ISAAC
CERAMIST, WRITER
b Cambridge, Mass, Aug 7, 40. *Study:* Carnegie Inst Technol, 58-59; RI Sch Design, BFA, 63; Rochester Inst Technol, MFA, 65. *Comn:* Ceramic sculpture, Temple Shalom Emeth, Burlington, Mass, 83; porcelain wall panel, comn by Mr & Mrs Joseph Epstein, Carlsbad, Calif, 83; porcelain signature wall, Holden District Hosp, Barre, Mass, 84; porcelain mural, Worcester Historical Mus, Mass, 86; ceramic mural, JCC Springfield, Mass, 94. *Exhib:* Artworks, Worcester, Mass, 81; Mirage Collectables, Miami, Fla, 82; Ely Art Gallery, Westfield, Mass, 83; Benchmarks Gallery, Washington, DC, 84; Signature, Boston, 85, 93-96; Cambridge Gallery, Worcester, 88 & 91; Higgins Armory Mus, Worcester, Mass, 98; ARTS Worcester, 00-02. *Collection Arranged:* Bay State Clay, Fitchburg Art Mus, Mass, 93. *Pos:* Comnr, Worcester Cult Comn, 86-88. *Teaching:* Instr ceramics, Auburn Community

Col, 64-65; instr ceramics & studio mgr, Greenwich House Pottery Sch, New York, 65-66; instr ceramics & head dept, Craft Ctr, Worcester, 67-78; vis prof, RI Col, 78-79; lectr art, Clark Univ, Worcester, Mass, 81-89; adj prof art, Quinsigamond Community Col, 99-. *Awards:* Mass Arts Lottery Coun Grant, 82, 84, 89, 92, 95 & 97; Third Prize, Arts Worcester, 85; Award for Sculptors, Higgins Armory Mus, Worcester, 91; Artsworcester Biennial, 97; Artist Fel, Worcester, Cult Comn, 2004. *Bibliog:* Articles, Moment Mag, 84 & Worcester Mag, 85; Worcester Telegram and Gazette, 91. *Mem:* Arts Worcester; Am Crafts Coun; Nat Asn Educ in Ceramic Arts. *Media:* Ceramic. *Publ:* Auth, Claywork, 75 & Low Fire, 80, Davis; five articles in Sch Arts, 76-77; Claywork, second ed, 86; Sculpting Clay, 1991, Claywork, 3rd ed, 94, Art Critic-Worcester Phoenix, 93-2001; Art Critic, Worcester Mag, 2000-05; contri ed, Arts Medica, 2002. *Mailing Add:* 11 Chatanika Ave Worcester MA 01602

NIKKAL, NANCY EGOL
COLLAGE ARTIST
b New York, NY, 44. *Study:* Syracuse Univ Sch Fine Arts, 62-64; Hunter Col, City Univ New York, 73; Pratt Graphics, Manhattan, 80. *Work:* Exec offs, Sun Chemical, NY; exec offs, Dainippon Ink & Chemical, Tokyo, Japan; Kawamura, Mus Mod Art, Tokyo, Japan; exec offs, St Paul Reinsurance Mgt, NY; Cong Off, Cong Dioguard, Washington, DC. *Exhib:* 9th Small Works Exhib, Wash Sq Galleries, NY, 85; New Art USA, Isis Gallery, Long Island, NY, 86; Ann Exhibs, Bergen Mus Arts Sci, Paramus, NJ, 87 & 89; Metro Show, City Without Walls Gallery, Newark, NJ, 88; Other Realities, Jadite Gallery, NY, 88; solo exhib, William Carlos Williams Ctr Performing Arts, Rutherford, NJ, 88; Centennial Exhib, Jehangir Gallery, Bombay, India, 89. *Awards:* Fourth Prize, New Art USA, Isis Gallery, 86; Irwin Z Lowe Mem, Fed Plaza, Nat Asn Women Artists, NY, 88; Contemporary Art/Painting Award, Westbeth Galleries, Am Soc Contemp Artists, 90. *Bibliog:* Helen A Harrison (auth), Winners in a juried show whose novelty is in its concept, NY Times, 4/13/86; John Zeaman (auth) A clearer picture at Bergen Museum, Record, 1/3/88; Jerry Tallmer (auth), Art's sexism gets a good once-over, NY Post, 8/4/89. *Mem:* Am Soc Contemp Artists; NJ Women's Caucus Art; Nat Asn Women Artists (foreign exchange co-chmn, 88-89); Salute Women Arts (regional, pres, 90-92). *Media:* Collage, monoprint, mixed media. *Mailing Add:* PO Box 455 Hastings On Hudson NY 10706-0455

NIKOLIC, JEAN
PAINTER, GRAPHIC ARTIST
b Jackson, Miss, Sept 6, 32. *Study:* Columbia Univ, New York, with John Heliker & Andre Racz, 59; Mus Mod Art, New York, cert, 58; Miss Univ Women, BFA & teacher's lic, 57; La State Univ, Baton Rouge, with Caroline Durrieux, 53-55. *Work:* Sydney & Frances Lewis Contemp Art Collection, Va Mus Fine Arts; Va Mus Fine Arts, Richmond; Grey Art Collection, NY Univ; also pvt collection of Her Majesty, Queen Elizabeth II, Buckingham Palace, London; La State Univ, Baton Rouge. *Exhib:* Va Mus Fine Arts, Richmond, 71, 72, 73 (2), 78 (2), 79 & 80; Chrysler Mus, Norfolk, Va, 75; Nat Collection Fine Arts, Washington, DC, 76-77; Int Women's Arts Festival, NY & USA Tour, 76; Smith Col, Northampton, Mass, 77; James Ctr Gallery, Richmond, Va, 90; Eyeclopes Gallery, Fredericksburg, Va, 99, 2000-03. *Pos:* former dir, Gallery of Mod Art, Fredericksburg, Va. *Teaching:* Guest lectr, Col William & Mary, Pace Univ, NY & Gallery Mod Art, Fredericksburg, Va. *Bibliog:* Linda Evans (auth), article, Free Lance-Star, Fredericksburg, Va, 11/72; The Lewis Contemporary Art Fund Collection, Va Mus Fine Arts, 80; S B Hitz (auth), article, Stafford Sun, 5/26/2000. *Mem:* Washington Proj Arts/Corcoran Mus Art; charter mem, Nat Mus Women Arts. *Media:* Liquitex Acrylic; Ink. *Publ:* Contribr, The Art of Poetry, National Collection of Fine Arts, Smithsonian Paperworks (exhib catalog), Washington Gallery, Washington, DC. *Dealer:* Eyeclopes Gallery 810 Caroline St Fredericksburg VA 22401. *Mailing Add:* 12 Winston Pl Fredericksburg VA 22405

NILSSON, KATHERINE ELLEN
PAINTER
b Sept 12, 66. *Study:* Conn Col, BA, 93. *Work:* US Trust Co, Essex, CT. *Exhib:* 21st Juried Show, Soc Watercolor Artists; 62nd Ann Juried Show, Conn Watercolor Soc; Art of New Eng, Old Lyme Art Asn, CT; 22nd Juried Show, Soc Watercolor Artists. *Awards:* Chairmans Award, Soc Watercolor Artists, 2002; Judges Award, Ann Artists Show, Essex Art Asn, 2001. *Mem:* Old Lyme Art Asn; Essex Art Asn. *Media:* Watercolor, Acrylic, Oil

NIND, JEAN
PAINTER, PRINTMAKER
b Miri, Sarawak, Borneo, June 17, 30; Can citizen. *Study:* Chelsea Art Sch, London, Eng; Univ Sask, Can, studied with Otto Rogers & Eli Bornstein. *Work:* Sask Power Corp, Regina; Esso Can Ltd, Vancouver, BC; Trent Univ, Peterborough, Ont; Volvo Corp, Halifax, NS; Art Gallery Peterborough, Ont. *Comn:* Symphony (oil), comn by mem bd, Saskatoon Symphony, Sask, 64; five serigraphs (for presentation to guest speakers), Trent Univ, Peterborough, Ont, 69. *Exhib:* Kingston Spring Exhibs, Agnes Etherington Art Ctr, Ont, 69; one-person shows, Artspace, Ont, 75, 77, 78 & 88, Bau-xi Gallery, Toronto & Vancouver, 78 & 79 & Williamson House Gallery, Peterborough, Ont, 88 & 90; Art Gallery Peterborough, 81 & 89; Lindsey Gallery, Ont, 89; Magic Image Gallery, Pickering Village, On, 92; Russell Gallery, Lindsay, 93; and others. *Teaching:* Instr child art classes, Mendel Art Gallery, Saskatoon, Sask, 65-66; instr early childhood art, Sir Sandford Fleming Col, Peterborough, Ont, 69-71, painting instr art admin, 73-77. *Awards:* Merit Award, Ont Arts Coun, 74, 75, 89 & 90; Award Winner, Juried Show, The Lindsay Gallery, 87; Award Winner, Juried Show, Art Gallery Peterborough, 94. *Bibliog:* Harry Underwood (auth), Spirit in the Art of Jean Nind, Globe & Mail, Toronto, 76; Colin Macdoneld (ed), Dictionary of Canadian Artists, Vol 5, Can Paperbacks, Ottawa, 77; Hennie Wolff (auth), The index of Ontario artists, 77; Printworld Inc, Bala Cynwyd, Pa, 87; Marketa Newman (auth), Biographical Dictionary of Saskatchewan Artists, Women, 90. *Mem:* Art Gallery Peterborough (mem bd, 72-78); Artspace, Peterborough, Ont (mem steering comt, 75); Visual Arts Ont; Art Gallery Ont, Toronto. *Media:* Oil on Canvas; Serigraphy. *Dealer:* Russell Gallery Peterborough Ont. *Mailing Add:* 29 Merino Rd Peterborough ON K9J 6M8 Canada

NISSEN, CHRIS (JOHN CHRISTIAN NISSEN), III
PAINTER
b Patterson, NJ, May 25, 49. *Study:* Univ Va, BA, 71; Pa Acad Fine Arts(Fel, 4 yr cert), 80. *Work:* Cleveland Mus Art; Va Mus Fine Art, Richmond; Pa Acad Fine Arts, CIGNA Mus & Art Collection, Woodmere Art Mus, Philadelphia. *Comn:* Large paintings, Northwestern Univ, Chicago, Ill, 99; painting, Coopers Lybrand Inc, Philadelphia, 88; painting, Firestone Country Club, Akron, Ohio, 91; painting, comn by E I Dupont de Nemours, Wilmington, Del, 93; painting, Manufacturers Hanover Trust, Wilmington, Del, 93. *Exhib:* The Art of Business, Del Art Mus, Wilmington, 86; 2nd Ann Nat Juried Show, First Street Gallery, NY, 89; Evening Skies, Noyes Mus, Oceanville, NJ, 89; Contemp Philadelphia Artists (with catalog), Philadelphia Art Mus, 90; Marcel DuChamps Mothers Potato Masher & Other Works of Art, Va Mus Fine Art, Richmond, 90; 91st Ann Exhib, Woodmere Mus Art, Philadelphia, 92; US Artists '98, Pa Acad Fine Arts, Philadelphia, 98. *Teaching:* Adj asst prof drawing & design, Temple Univ, Philadelphia, 88-95. *Awards:* Purchase prize, Pa Acad Fine Arts, 80-81; Gifunni Brothers Purchase Prize, Pastel Soc Am, 84. *Bibliog:* Victoria Donohoe (auth), The arts, Philadelphia Inquirer, 92; Atlas of Florida, Fla State Univ Press, 93. *Media:* Oil, Pastel. *Dealer:* Carspecken Scott Gallery 1707 N Lincoln St Wilmington DE 19806. *Mailing Add:* 67 E Mermaid Ln Philadelphia PA 19118

NISULA, LARRY
PAINTER, SCULPTOR
b Phoenix, Ariz, Oct 10, 60. *Study:* Glendale Community Col, 83; self-taught painting. *Work:* Tavan Sch Masterpiece Collection, Phoenix; Nott Corp, Irving, Tex; Mus Northern Ariz, Flagstaff; Merchants Press, Poughkeepsie, NY; Ariz State Univ West. *Comn:* Abstract painting, comn by John Gibney Med Ctr, Scottsdale; sculpture, comn by Mr & Mrs Augustus Boss, Ramada Corp, Scottsdale; sculpture, comn by Glendale Community Col, Glendale, Ariz; paintings, Valley Nat Bank, Phoenix, Ariz; prints, Designology, Scottsdale, Ariz. *Exhib:* Solo exhibs, Phoenix Col, 85, Fagen-Peterson Fine Art, Scottsdale, Ariz, 87-98 & Glendale Community Col Art Mus, Ariz, 92 & 95; Mars Gallrey, Phoenix, Ariz, 86, 93 & 96; Bell-Ross Gallery, Memphis, Tenn, 87; Bristol Gallery, Denver, Colo, 95; West Valley Art Mus, 98-. *Awards:* Third Place Sculpture, Glendale Festival of Art, 82 & 84, First Place, 83. *Bibliog:* Barbara Cortright (auth), Profile Larry Nisula, Zone Mag, spring 91; Jesse Evans Gray (auth), Larry Nisula, From the Ashes, 2/93. *Mem:* Phoenix Blues Soc. *Media:* Acrylic; Ceramic. *Publ:* Barbara Cortright (auth), Profile Larry Nisula, Zone Mag, spring 91. *Dealer:* MARS Artspace 126 S Central Ave Phoenix AZ 85004; The Bell Gallery 6150 Poplar Ave Memphis TN 38119. *Mailing Add:* 1506 W Fillmore Phoenix AZ 85007

NIX, NELLEKE LANGHOUT
WRITER, PUBLISHER
b Utrecht, Netherlands, Mar 27, 39. *Study:* Royal Acad Visual Arts, MFA, 58, The Hague, Netherlands. *Hon Degrees:* Certificate Degree, Stanford Calif Prof Publ, 94. *Work:* Nat Mus Women in the Arts, Washington, DC; Mus of the Holocaust, Providence, RI; Victoria and Albert Mus, London; Allen Libr Univ Washington, Seattle. *Comn:* The Inadvertent Garden Mural, NY, 1999; Zones of Time Sand & Rain, Libr Tellows Nat Mus of Women in the Arts, Washington, 2000. *Exhib:* Book as Art XIV, Nat Mus Women in Arts, Washington, 02; Northwest Ann, Bellevue Art Mus, WA, 95; Dutch Contribution, Nordic Heritage Mus, Seattle, 94; Noble Maritime Coll, Staten Island, NY, 2005. *Pos:* Artist in Residence, Fairhaven Coll, Bellingham, WA, 74; Owner Nelleke Nix Studio, 75-. *Teaching:* Artist in Residence, Boyer Childrens Clin, Seattle, 99; Head Art Dept, Bush Sch, Seattle, 69-72; Artist in Residence, Noble Maritime Mus, Staten Island, 2002. *Awards:* 2000 Libr Fel Grant Award, Nat Mus Women in Arts, 2000. *Bibliog:* Lee Goss (auth), Time is on her side, Eastside Week, 10/14/1992; Mary McCoy (auth), Women in the arts: recreating a medium to send their messages, The Washington Post, 12/24/1992; Barbara Brachti (auth), For the love of art, The Journal American, 2/1993; Ted Lindberg (auth), A Dutch contribution, Nordic News, 4/1994; Marjorie Hack (auth), Hauntingly good taste, Staten Island Advance, 10/26/1995; Krystyna Wasserman (auth), Artists on the Road, Travel as Inspiration, The Nat Mus of Women in the Arts, 1997; Painters put imagination first, The Seattle Times, 4/24/1997; and many others. *Mem:* Nat Mus Women in Arts; Women in the Arts; Artist Trust; Mus Modern Art; Soho20 Gallery. *Media:* Mixed Media, Digital, Sculpture, Photography, Painting. *Res:* women's art cross culturally. *Specialty:* women's art. *Collection:* Frida Kahlo & Friends; Women's Art. *Publ:* auth, The Magic of Remedios Varo, Brochure Annual Gala Nat Mus Women in the Arts, Spring 2000. *Dealer:* Sohozo Gallery 511 25 Street #605 NY NY 10001. *Mailing Add:* PO Box 375 Mercer Island WA 98040

NIX, PATRICIA (LEA)
SCULPTOR, PAINTER
b US citizen. *Study:* NY Univ, BA; New Sch Soc Res, with Anthony Toney; Art Students League, with Vaclav Vytlacil. *Work:* Nat Mus Am Art, Smithsonian Inst, Washington, DC; Heckscher Mus, Huntington, NY; Univ Windsor, Can; Staten Island Mus, NY; Newport Harbor Mus, Calif; Credit Svisse, NY; San Antonio Mus Art; Santa Fe Mus Fine Art; Texa tech Mus. Lubbock, 2000; rep in numerous permanent collections, designer sets and costumes (ballets) Petrushka, Pulcinella, Jeu de Cartes, 2002. *Comn:* Sets & Costumes for 3 Stravinsky Ballets, Carolina Ballet. *Exhib:* One-woman show,NY Univ Contemp Arts Gallery, 80, Am Embassy, Nambia, 99, Slovenia, 99, Merrill Chase Gallery, Chicago, Ill, 99, Tex Tech Mus, 2000, San

Angelo Mus Art, 2000, Evelyn Siegel Galleries, Ft Worth & Dallas, Tex, 2000, Hilligoos Gallery, Chicago, Ill, 2000, 2002; Dillon Gallery, NY, 94, 95, 96 & 97; Boxes, Fatoui-Cramer Gallery, 95; Magic & Mystery, Austin Mus Art, Tex, 95; Galerie Donguy, Paris, France, 94; Nat Acad Mus, NY, 77, 79, 81, 83, 85, 87, 89, 91, 92, 93, 95, 97 & 99; Hilligoss Galleries, 2000-03. *Collection Arranged:* Totem Aitar, St Peters Church, NYC, 2004; Gallerie Marie Claude Goinnard, Paris, France, 2005. *Awards:* Salzman Prize, Nat Arts Club Ann, 78 & 88 & 1st Prize, 86; Cert of Hon for Oil Painting, Nat Acad Design, 87; First Prize Gold Medal City Paris, Fedn Internationale Culturelle Fe'Minine, 93. *Bibliog:* Patricia Nix, Dillon Press, 96; Icons & Altars, Dillon Press. *Mem:* Nat Acad; New York Artists Equity. *Media:* Oil, Found Objects; Mixed. *Publ:* Cover illusr, The Family, Random House, 97; Readers Dig, 97; Meninger Foundation Journal. *Dealer:* Hilligoos Galleries Chicago Ill 60611; Evelyn Siegel Gallery 3700 W 7th St Ft Worth Tex 76107; Dillon Gallery Oyster Bay NY. *Mailing Add:* 115 E 35th St New York NY 10016

NIXON, NICHOLAS
PHOTOGRAPHER
b Detroit, Mich, 1947. *Study:* Univ Mich, BA(english), 69; Univ NMex, MFA, 74. *Work:* Mus Mod Art, NY; Fogg Art Mus, Harvard Univ, Mass; Australian Nat Gallery, Canberra; San Francisco Mus Mod Art; Detroit Art Inst, Mich; Philadelphia Mus Art, Pa; and others. *Exhib:* One-man exhibs, Fraenkel Gallery, San Francisco, 80, 82, 84, 86, 88, 90, 92, 93, 95, 97, 98 & 2001, Zabriskie Gallery, NY, 88, 90, 92, 94, 97, 98 & 2000, San Diego Art Mus, 91 & 2000, Paul Kopeikin Gallery, Los Angeles, 92, Sprengel Mus (with catalog), Hannover, Ger, 94 & 2000, Musee de L'Art Moderne, Paris, 95 & Barbara Krakow Gallery, Boston, 96; Am Photog in the 70's, Chicago Art Inst, 80; Variants, Mus Mod Art, NY, 86; Santa Barbara Mus Art, Calif, 86; Photographs from the Last Decade, San Francisco Mus Mod Art, 87; Twelve Photographers Look at US, Philadelphia Mus Art, 87; Honolulu Acad Arts, 89; Photog Until Now (catalog), Mus Mod Art, NY, 90; Fables of the Visible World, Mass Col Art, 92; Addison Gallery Am Art, 92; Pleasures and Terrrors of Domestic Comfort (catalog), Mus Mod Art, 92; Hidden Faces, Paul Kopeikin Gallery, Los Angeles, 94; Visions of Childhood, Bard Col, 95; About Faces: The History of the Portrait in Photog, Fogg Art Mus, Boston, 97. *Teaching:* Part-time prof photog, Mass Col Art, Boston, currently. *Awards:* Photog Fels, Nat Endowment Arts, 76, 80 & 87; Fels, Guggenheim Mem Found, 77 & 86; Friends of Photog Peer Award, 88; Fel, George Gurd Found. *Bibliog:* John Szarkowski (auth), 20th Century Photographs from the Museum of Modern Art, New York, 84; Peter Galessi (auth), Nicholas Nixon: Pictures of People, Mus Mod Art, New York, 88; Family Pictures: Photographs by Nicholas Nixon, Smithsonian Press, Washington, DC, 91. *Publ:* auth, Photography Until Now, John Szarkoswki, Mus Modern Art, NY, 90; auth, People with AIDS, Bebe Nixon, David R. Godine, Boston, 91; auth, Familienbilder: Nicholas Nixon, Sprengel Mus, Hannover, 94; auth, School, Photrographs from Three Schools, Nicholas Nixon, Bulfinsh Press/Little Brown, NY, 98; auth, The Brown Sisters, Mus Modern Art, NY, 99. *Mailing Add:* 25 Waverly St Brookline MA 02146

NOBLE, HELEN (HARPER)
PRINTMAKER, PAINTER
b Northville, Mich, Mar 27, 22. *Study:* Wayne State Univ, 39-41; Western Reserve Univ, 42-43; Santa Barbara Art Inst, 70-72; Douglass Parshall, Nat Acad, 75. *Exhib:* Small Works National 81, Rochester, NY; Second Nat Print Exhib, Springfield, Ill, 82; 24th Ann Exhib Prints & Drawings, Oklahoma City, 82; Third Women in Art Exhib, Springfield, Ill, 83; Arts Festival, Santa Barbara, Calif, 85; 40th Ann Nat Juried Print Competition, Clinton, NJ, 96; Stone Metal Press, San Antonio, Tex, 12/2005-1/2006. *Awards:* Eight Awards, Santa Barbara Art Asn, 71-79; Third Place, 41st Ann Minature Art Soc, Washington, 74; Hon Mention Seventh Annual Exhib Miniature Art Soc, NJ, 77. *Media:* Oil, Wood. *Collection:* numerous private collections. *Dealer:* Ward-Nasse Gallery 178 Prince St New York NY 10012. *Mailing Add:* 1702 Cliff Dr Santa Barbara CA 93109

NOBLE, KEVIN
PAINTER, PHOTOGRAPHER
b Brooklyn, NY, 52. *Study:* State Univ Col, Buffalo, NY, BA, 75; State Univ NY, Buffalo, MFA, 78. *Work:* Burchfield-Penny Art Ctr & Albright-Knox Art Gallery, Buffalo, NY. *Exhib:* Solo exhibs, Artists' Space, NY & Cepa Gallery, Buffalo, 80, The Kitchen, NY, 81, White Columns, 86, Mednick Gallery, Philadelphia, 87, Frank Bernaducci Gallery, NY, 87 & Panopticon, Irish Art Ctr, NY, 91; A Decade of New Art, Artists' Space, NY, 84; Photo-Syntheseis, Frank Bernaducci Gallery, NY, 87; Belfast/Beirut, A Tale of Two Cities, Alternative Mus, NY, 89; Images of War, El Bohio, NY, 91; Bloody Sunday Show, Irish Arts Ctr, NY, 92; Cepa Gallery, Buffalo, NY, 99. *Awards:* Artists Fel, Nat Endowment Arts, 79 & 87. *Mailing Add:* 227 DeWitt Rd Olivebridge NY 12461-5223

NOCHLIN, LINDA (POMMER)
HISTORIAN, EDUCATOR
b New York, NY, Jan 30, 31. *Study:* Vassar Col, BA; Inst Fine Arts, NY Univ, PhD; Colgate Univ, Hon Dr, 87. *Teaching:* Mary Conover Mellon prof art, Vassar Col, 63-80; distinguished prof art hist, City Univ New York Grad Ctr, 80-90; prof art hist, Yale Univ, 90-92; prof mod art, New York Univ Inst Fine Arts, 92-. *Awards:* Frank Jewett Mather Prize Critical Writing, 77; Scholar of Year Prize, New York State Coun Humanities, 97; Ann Recognition Award, Col Art Asn Comt Women Arts, Toronto, 98. *Res:* Painting and sculpture of 19th and 20th century. *Publ:* Auth, Realism and Tradition in Art, 1848-1900, 66 & Impressionism and Post-Impressionism, 1874-1904, 66, Prentice-Hall; Realism, Penguin, 72; Gustave Courbet: A Study of Style & Society, 76; contribr, Art Bull, Art News, Art News Ann & Artforum; Woman Artists: 1550-1950, Alfred Knopf, 76; ed, Art & Architecture in the Service of Politics, Mass Inst Technol Press, 78; Courbet Reconsidered, Yale Univ Press, 88; Women, Art, Power & Other Essays, Harper & Row, 88; The Politics of Vision, Harper & Row, 90; Representing Women, Thanes & Hudson, 99; Self & History: A Tribute to Linda Nochlin, Thames & Hudson, 2000; Bathers, Bodies, Beauty: The Visceral Eye, 2006. *Mailing Add:* 875 West End Ave New York NY 10025

NODA, MASAAKI
PAINTER, PRINTMAKER
b Hiroshima, Japan, Dec 19, 49. *Study:* Osaka Univ Art, Japan, BFA, 72; Art Students League, NY, 80. *Work:* Brooklyn Mus; Albright Knox Mus, Buffalo, NY; Philadelphia Mus Art; Hofstra Mus, Hemstead, NY; Portland Art Mus, Ore. *Comn:* stained glass, Keihan Rail Road, Kyoto, Japan, 97; sculpture & monument, Shinichi Lions Club, Hiroshima, Japan, 2000. *Exhib:* Int Biennial of Graphic Art, Mus Mod Art, Ljubjana, Yugoslavia, 85, 89, 91 & 95; National Triennial Print Exhibition, Schenctady Mus, NY, 95; Int Print Triennial, Nat Mus, Cracow, Poland, 84 86, 88, 94 & 96; The Boston Printmakers, Duxbury Art Complex Mus, Boston, 97; Stockton National Exhibition, Haggin Mus, Calif, 98; Surface and Diversity, Housatonic Mus Art, Bridgeport, Conn, 98; 20th National Print, Schenectady Mus, NY, 98; White and Black, Fukoyama Mus Art, Hiroshima, Japan, 99. *Pos:* Printmaker & painter, self employed. *Teaching:* vis artist, Univ Pennsylvania, 83-89, New School, NYC, 94. *Awards:* First Award, 1st Internat Art Show, Ga Art Soc, 86; First Award, 16th Internat Dogwood Art Show, Atlanta, 89; Purchase Award, Audubon Artist, NY, 2000. *Bibliog:* Robert S Bianch (auth), Art-Phitheater, PT Efstathiou Fine Art, 94; Srdan Markovic (auth), Leskovac International Biennial, Gallery Sunre, 98; Pam Koob (auth), 30/30, Art Students League, 2000. *Mem:* Audubon Artist Inc (dir, 98); Soc Am Graphic Artist (coun, 96); Boston Printmakers; Print Club Albany; Graphic Art Coun NY. *Media:* Serigraphy, Silkscreen. *Publ:* auth, Masaaki Noda Works in New York 1980-91, Abe Publ Company, 91; auth, Abstract Expression, 94 & Twisted Circulation, 95, Les Cyclades; auth, Breeze From New York, PT Efstathiou Fine Art, 2000. *Dealer:* 12 East 86th St #609 New York, NY 10012. *Mailing Add:* 393 W Broadway Apt 5WM New York NY 10012

NODA, TAKAYO
COLLAGE ARTIST, PRINTMAKER
b Tokyo, Japan. *Study:* Gakushuin Univ, Tokyo, Japan; Art Students League, studied printmaking with Michael Ponce de Leon and Seong Moy, 79-83; Pvt Study with Leo Manso. *Work:* Honolulu Acad Arts, Hawaii; NJ State Coun Arts, Trenton; Hawaii State Found Cult & Arts; Jane Voorhees Zimmerli Art Mus, New Brunswick, NJ; Portland Art Mus, Ore; The Nat Arts Club, New York City; Art Students League, New York City; New Orleans Mus Art, La. *Comn:* Subway Poster Proj, Metrop Transportation Authority, NY, 98; Subway station window design, Metrop Transportation Authority, NY, 2006. *Exhib:* Nat Print Exhib, Honolulu Acad Arts, Hawaii, 85; Wenniger Graphics, Boston, MA, 88; Nat Acad Design, NY, 90 & 96; Nat Asn Women Artists, Bergen Mus Art & Sci, NJ, 91; Portland Art Mus, Ore, 92; Mus Provincetown Art Asn, Provincetown, Mass, 93; Nat Asn Women Artists Collection, Rutgers, Zimmerli Art Mus, New Brunswick, NJ, 94; Alexandria Mus, La, 96; Newark Mus, NJ, 99; solo show, Interchurch Ctr, NY, 94; Tiffany Windows, NY, 95; Port Washington Pub Libr, Port Washington, NY, 98; Donnell Libr, NY, 2003; Wolcott Libr, NY, 2003; Austin Pub Libr, Tex, 2003; Hartford Co Libr, Mo, 2003; Phoenix Pub Libr, Ariz, 2004; Zimmerli Art Mus, NJ, 2005; Donnell Libr, NY, 2006. *Awards:* Gold Medal Hon Graphics, 50th Ann Exhib, Audubon Artists, 92; Nat Print Exhib Acquisition Award, Univ Hawaii, 94; Nat Arts Club Award for Graphics, Allied Artists Am, 2003. *Bibliog:* Geraldine E Rhoads (ed), It's all in a woman's day, Woman's Day Mag, Fawcett Publ, 3/70; Helen A Harrison (critic), Hard-Edged imagery but surprisingly sensuous, New York Times, 5/10/98; John Edward Peters (auth), Deeply Engaging Visual and Thematic Currents, Kirkus Review, 2003. *Mem:* Nat Arts Club; Boston Printmakers; Soc Am Graphic Artists; Audubon Artists; Nat Asn Women Artists; Lotos Club; Authors Guild; Acad of Am Poets; Allied Artists of Am. *Media:* Graphics, Dimensional-Collage. *Publ:* contbr, At Grandmother's Table, Fairview Press, 2000; Dear World, Penguin Young Readers Group, 3/2003; Song of the Flowers, Penguin Young Readers Group, 4/2006. *Mailing Add:* Five Charles St New York NY 10014

NODIFF, JACK
PAINTER
b New York, NY, May 2, 22. *Study:* New York Univ, BA, 45; Long Island Univ, BS, 51; Art Students League, 55; New York Dept Cult Affairs, artist cert, 87. *Exhib:* Solo exhibs, East Rockaway Libr, NY, 78 & 89, Village Gallery, Hewlett, NY, 80, Malverne Gallery, NY, 82, Welles Gallery, Lenox, Mass, 91, Becket Art Ctr, Mass, 97 & Hewlett-Woodmere Libr Downstairs Gallery, NY, 2000; group exhibs, Int Art Festival, East Rockaway, NY, 83, Salmagundi Club, NY, 83 & 87, Chung-Cheng Art Gallery, Queens, NY, 84, Shelter Rock Libr, Albertson, NY, 85, Freeport Mem Libr, NY, 86 & 87, Nassau Co Mus Fine Arts, Roslyn, NY, 86 & 94, Garden City Pub Libr, Garden City, NY, 86, Syosset Pub Libr, NY, 87, Sheffield Art League, Mass, 92, 93, 95 & 96, Chelsea Art Ctr, Muttontown, NY, 92, Owl Gallery, Woodmere, NY, 96, Becket Art Centre, Becket, Mass, 96; E Rockaway Libr, NY, 97-98; Nassau Co Mus, Roslyn, NY, 97-98; downstairs Gallery, Hewlett Wood Mere Pub Libr, Hewlett, NY 2000; Sheffield Art League, Mass, 97-2005. *Awards:* Grumbacher Silver Award, Freeport Mem Libr, 87; First Prize, Sheffield Art League, 96, 97 & 99; Merit Award, Nassau Co and LI Partnership Fine Art Exhib, 2001. *Bibliog:* Valley Stream, Malverne J, 82; Long Island Local News, 82; Nassau Herald, 83. *Mem:* Tri Co Artists; Housatonic Valley Art League (2006); Becket Art Ctr; Communities Art League (CAL). *Media:* Oil. *Mailing Add:* 6 Emmet Ave East Rockaway NY 11518

NODINE, JANE ALLEN
PAINTER, SCULPTOR
b Spartanburg, SC, Mar 14, 54. *Study:* Western Carolina Univ, Cullowhee, 72-73; Univ SC, Columbia, BFA, 76, MFA, 79; Kent State Univ, 78. *Work:* Equitable Life, NY; Palmetto Bank & Trust, SC; two Stouffers Hotels, NC; Capital South Inc, SC; Buyers Communs Systems, Atlanta, Ga; SC State Collection. *Exhib:* Americas 2000: Works on Paper, Minot State Univ, ND, 93; The Wichita Nat, Wichita Ctr Arts, Kans, 93; Dakotas Int Exhib of Artwork on Paper, Univ SD, 94; Visual Voices; The Female, Univ WFla, Pensacola, 94; LaGrange Nat Biennial XVIII, LaGrange, Ga, 94; 28th Nat Drawing & Small Sculpture Show, Del Mar Col, Corpus Christi, Tex, 94; and others; Traces, traveling exhib, 2002-04. *Pos:* Gallery dir, Univ SC, Spartanburg, 94-95. *Teaching:* Instr, Greenville Mus, SC, 79-80, Presby Col, Clinton, SC, 80-, Wofford Col, Spartanburg, SC, 81 & 83 & Sacred Heart Col, Belmont, NC, 82-; Converse Col, Spartanburg, SC, 90-95; Dir Univ of SC Art Gallery; assoc prof art, Univ SC, Spartanburg. *Awards:* Individual Artist Fel, NEA/SECCA Southeast Seven IV, 80; Artists Fel, SC Arts Comn, 81-82 & 90-91; Belle W Baruch Scholar, 2002-03. *Mem:* Col Art Asn; Am Crafts Coun. *Media:* Metal, photo-based two and three dimensional work. *Dealer:* Mary Praytor Gallery 26 Main St Greenville SC; Hodges Talor, Charlotte, NC; Zone One, Asheville, NC. *Mailing Add:* 113 Rockwood Dr Spartanburg SC 29301-3822

NOE, JERRY LEE
SCULPTOR, EDUCATOR
b Harlan Co, Ky, Sept 27, 40. *Study:* Univ Ky, BA; Art Inst Chicago, Ford Found Scholar, MFA. *Exhib:* Sculpture 70, Art Inst Chicago, 70; Forty Yrs of Am Landscape, Gimpel-Wietzenhoffer Gallery, NY, 73; Nat Sculpture Traveling Exhib, 73-75; Contemp Reflections, 1973-74, Aldrich Mus Art, Ridgefield, Conn, 74; Southeast 7, Southeastern Ctr Contemp Art, Winston-Salem, NC, 77; one-man shows, Henri Gallery, 77 & Mercer Gallery, 77. *Teaching:* Sculptor, Young Artists Studio, Art Inst Chicago, 69-71; vis lectr sculpture, Wis State Univ, Whitewater, 70-71; assoc prof art, Univ NC, Chapel Hill, 71-. *Awards:* John Quincy Adams Traveling Fel, 71; First Place, 73 & Third Place, 75, Southern Asn Sculptors; Nat Endowment Arts Grant, 77; and others. *Bibliog:* B J Ott (auth), Artist builds bridge, Buffalo Courier Newspaper, 75; Fun & games at art park, New York Times Sunday Ed, 75; and others. *Mem:* Southern Asn Sculptors (mem bd dir, 74-75, conf chmn, 75, exhib chmn, 75); Col Art Asn; Southeastern Col Art Conf; Southeastern Ctr Contemp Art. *Media:* Neon, Mixed. *Publ:* Coauth, Neon--The Artist (film), Res Coun, Univ, NC, 75. *Dealer:* Henri Gallery 1500 21st St NW Washington DC 20036. *Mailing Add:* 2008 Ridgewood Rd Chapel Hill NC 27516-9310

NOEL, DONALD CLAUDE
SCULPTOR, MOSAIC ARTIST
b Blue Island, Ill, Aug 2, 30. *Study:* St Norbert Col, De Pere, Wis, BA(philos), 57; Univ Wis, Madison, MA(libr sci), 63; Rosary Col, Grad Sch Fine Arts: Villa Schifanoia, Florence, Italy, MFA(sculpture), 83. *Work:* Inter Sculpture Garden, Marusici, Yugoslavia; The Leo House, NY. *Comn:* Norbert of Xanten, St Norbert Col, DePere, Wis, 84; James Kenneth Allen (7' bronze), Morris, Ill, 88; The De Pere History Walk, De Pere Hist Walk Trust, Wis, Forthcoming. *Exhib:* One-man show, Galerija di Villa Schifanoia, Florence; Ten Pietrasanta Pieces, The Tree Studios, Chicago, Ill, 83; Matter Over Mind, Fermi Lab Nat Atomic Accelerater, Batavia, Ill, 91; retrospective, O'Connor Gallery, Rosary Col, Ill, 95. *Pos:* Sculptor & owner, The Open Sea Sculpture Studio, Green Bay, Wis, 83-. *Awards:* Best of Show, Northeast Exhib, Waupaca, Wisc, 98; Sculpture Award, Milwaukee Inst Art & Design, 97. *Mem:* Int Sculpture Ctr, Washington, DC; assoc mem Nat Sculpture Soc, NY; Chicago Artists Coalition; Wis Painters & Sculptors; Am Monument Asn. *Media:* Bronze, Marble. *Mailing Add:* 1016 N Broadway De Pere WI 54115

NOEL, GEORGES
PAINTER, SCULPTOR
b Beziers, France, Dec 25, 24. *Study:* Studied in France. *Work:* Albright-Knox Art Gallery, Buffalo, NY; Chase Manhattan Bank, NY; Aldrich Mus of Contemp Art, Ridgefield, Conn; Centre Nat d'Art, Contemporain, Paris; Mus Mod Art, NY; Schlumberger Co, Paris; Guggenheim Mus, NY; National Galerie, Berlin. *Comn:* Painting, Cité de la Musique, Paris. *Exhib:* Galerie Municipale d'Art Contemporain, Saint-Priest, Musee de Brou, Bourg en Bresse-Centre National des Arts Plastiques, Paris/NY, Arnold Herstand Co, 88 & 90; Galerie Nothelfer, Berlin, Ger, 89 & 92; Arnold Herstand Co, NY, 88 & 90; Denis Hotz Fine Art Ltd, London, 90; Lorenzelli Arte, Milan, Italy, 90; Galerie Sander, Darmstadt, Ger & Zurich, Switz, 91; Galerie Baumgarten, Freiburg, Ger, 91; Base Gallery, Tokyo, 91 & 92. *Teaching:* Instr, Minneapolis Sch Arts, 68-69. *Media:* Multi. *Dealer:* Arnold Herstand 24 W 57th St New York NY 10019. *Mailing Add:* Haim Chanin Fine Arts 2nd Floor 210 Eleventh Ave New York NY 10001

NOEL, JEAN LAMBERT
SCULPTOR
b Montreal, Que, Can, 1940. *Study:* Assumption Col, Worcester, Mass, 60; Ecole des Beaux-Arts, Montreal, Que, 63. *Work:* Assumption Col, Worcester, Mass; Musee des Beaux-Arts, Montreal; Galerie Nationale du Can, Ottawa; Musee nat D'Art Moderne, Paris; Rose Hart Mus, Waltham, Mass; and others. *Comn:* Nat Research Council, Ottawa, Setauroute Bldg, Guyancourt, France; Univ Montreal, Can. *Exhib:* Group; Musée de Toulon, France, 82; Art Bank, Can Coun, Montreal & Vancouver, 82; Photosequences, Art Gallery Peterborough, Ont, 83; Avec Plastiques et Plasticiens, Musee de Martiques, Centre Georges Pompidou, Paris, 84; Musee Joliette, Canada, 2003; Galerie Pixi, Paris, 2006; solo exhib, Musee de Martiques, 84, Musee de Rochechouart, France 85, Found Cartier, Paris, 85, Musee de Valence, France, 87, Galerie Michel Tetreault, Montreal, 85-88, Musee de Maubeuge, France, 91, Galerie Krief, Paris, 86, 89 & 94. *Teaching:* Instr, Parsons Sch Design, Paris, France, 82-88. *Media:* Wood, Fiberglass, Steel. *Interests:* Architecture, History, Archeology. *Dealer:* Pink Gallery Montreal Can; Gallery Pixi, Paris, Gallery Krief, Paris. *Mailing Add:* 5 Cite Griset Paris 75011 France

NOFFKE, GARY L
GOLDSMITH
b Decator, Ill, Aug 27, 43. *Study:* Southern Ill Univ, MFA, 69. *Work:* Am Craft Mus, NY; Mint Mus, Charlotte, NC; Nat Ornamental Metal Mus, Memphis, Tenn; Melbourne State Col, Victoria, Australia; McDougal Art Gallery, Christ Church, NZ; John Michael Kohler Arts Ctr, Sheboygan, Wis; and others. *Exhib:* Masters in Am Metalsmithing, Nat Ornamental Metal Mus, Memphis, 89; Silver-New Forns & Expressions, Fortunoff's Silver Co, NY, 90; Vessels: From Use to Symbol, Am Craft Mus, NY, 90; Chasing the Runicible Spoon, retrospective, Kohler Arts Ctr, Sheboygan, Wis, 91; plus over 200 pub exhibs, regional & national competitive & invitational; one man exhibs Univ Ga Visual Arts Gallery, Athens, 70, Humboldt Sate Univ, Arcata, Calif, 71, Nat Ornamental Metal Mus, Memphis, 79, 88 & Western Carolina Univ, Cullowhee, NC, 81; L'Chaim, Int Invitational Exhib Multi-Media Kiddush cups, The Jewish Mus, San Francisco, 97-98; The Functional Vase Project: 1998, SOFA, NY & Yaw Gallery, Birmingham, Mich, 98; Handmade: Shifting Paradigms, The Singapore art Mus, 99; 1999 Seoul Int Metal Artists Invitational Exhib, Seoul Arts Ctr, Korea, 99. *Teaching:* Prof art, Univ Ga, Athens, 71-. *Awards:* NEA Fel, 90; The Delta Prize, Delta Airline & Univ Ga. *Bibliog:* Jim Buonaccorsi & LeeAnn Mitchell (auths), American masters of hollowware in the late 20th Century, Metalsmith Jour, Fall, 97; Ben Mitchell (auth), The jewelry of Ken Cory - Play Disguised, Univ Wash Press, 97; Bruce Metcalf (auth), Ken Corey: small monuments to a big imagination, Am Craft, Jour Am Craft Coun, Vol 58, No 3, 6-7/98. *Mailing Add:* PO Box 776 Farmington GA 30608

NOGALES, LUIS GUERRERO
PATRON
b Madera, Calif, Oct 17, 1943. *Study:* San Diego State Univ, BA, 1966; Stanford Univ, JD, 1969. *Pos:* Asst to pres, Stanford Univ, Calif, 1969-72; White House Fellow, asst to sec US Dept Interior, Washington, 1972-73; exec vp, dir, Golden West Broadcasters, Los Angeles, 1973-80; pres, Nogales, Bermudex, Chase and Tamayo, LA, 1981-82; chmn, Chief Exec Officer, UPI, Washington, 1983-86; pres, ECO Int News Serv, 1987, Univision, 1987-88; gen partner, Nogales Castro Partners, 1989-90; pres, Nogales Investors, La, 1990-. *Mem:* Bd dir, The Bank of Calif, San Francisco, Stanford Univ Ctr for Pub Serv, The Ford Found, State of Calif Bd Higher Educ, Sacramento, 1973-79, Los Angeles Redevelop Agency, 1973-76, United Way Am, Va, 1984-88; trustee, J Paul Getty Trust, 2000-, Claremont Univ Ctr and Grad Sch, 1987, Stanford Univ. *Mailing Add:* Nogales Investment Mgmt Inc 9229 W Sunset Blvd Ste 900 Los Angeles CA 90069

NOLAND, KENNETH
PAINTER, PRINTMAKER
b Asheville, NC, Apr 10, 1924. *Study:* Black Mountain Col, 46-48 & 50; also with Ossip Zadkine, Paris, 48-49. *Work:* Guggenheim Mus, Mus Mod Art, Metrop Mus Art & Whitney Mus Am Art, NY; Mus Fine Arts, Boston; Art Inst Chicago; Los Angeles Co Mus Art; Nat Gallery Art, Washington; Theatre Mus, London, Eng; Australian Nat Gallery, Canberra. *Exhib:* Baltimore Mus Art, Md, 52 & 70; Corcoran Gallery Art, Washington, 59 & 75; Whitney Mus Am Art, NY, 62, 71-73; Los Angeles Co Mus Art, 64; Walker Art Ctr, Minneapolis, Minn, 64 & 84; Mus Mod Art, NY, 65 & 85; Solomon R Guggenheim Mus, NY, 66; Albright-Knox Art Gallery, NY, 70; Art Inst Chicago, Ill, 76; one-person exhibs, Gallery One, Toronto, Can, 88, Hokin Gallery, Bay Harbor Islands, Fla, 89, Heath Gallery, Atlanta, Ga, 89, Salander-O'Reilly Galleries Inc, NY, 89, 90, 91 & 92; Salander-O'Reilly Galleries Inc, Beverly Hills, Calif, 90; Baltimore Collects: Paintings & Sculpture Since 1960, Baltimore Mus Art, 90; Geometric Abstraction, Marc Richards Gallery, Santa Monica, Calif, 90; Inaugural Exhib, Salander-O'Reilly Galleries, Berlin, Ger, 91; Slow Art: Painting in NY Now, PS 1 Mus, Long Island, NY, 92; Metrop Mus Art, NY; Nat Gallery Art, Washington. *Pos:* Bd of trustees, Bennington Col, 85-. *Teaching:* Inst Contemp Art, Washington, DC, 49-51; Cath Univ, Washington, DC, 51-60; Washington Workshop Ctr for Arts, 52-56; Milton Avery Prof Arts, Bard Col, Annandale-on-Hudson, NY, 85; First artist-in-residence, Computer Video Arts, Pratt Inst, NY, 86-87. *Bibliog:* Artist's dialogue: Kenneth Noland, Archit Digest, 3/88; Elizabeth Hayt-Atkins (auth), Kenneth Noland at Salander-O'Reilly, ARTnews, 1/90; Ann E Berman (auth), Two of a Kind, Art & Auction, 4/90. *Dealer:* Salander-O'Reilly Galleries Inc 20 E 79th St New York NY 10021. *Mailing Add:* Park St PO Box 359 Port Clyde ME 04855-0359

NOLAND, WILLIAM
SCULPTOR, PHOTOGRAPHER
b Washington, DC, May 13, 1954. *Study:* Hampshire Col, with Gary Hudson & Leonard Delonga, 72-74; Sarah Lawrence Col, with Lou Sgroi & Mary Miss, BA, 77. *Exhib:* Solo exhib, Va Polytechnic Inst Art Gallery, 81; New Works in Clay III, Everson Mus Art, 81; Sculpture Invitational, Tibor de Nagy Gallery, NY, 81; Contemp Art in Detroit Collections, Detroit Inst Arts, 82; Five Am Artists, Galeria Joan Prats, NY, 83; Am Cult Ctr, Taipei, Taiwan, 99; McAllen Int Mus, Tex, 2000. *Bibliog:* Gene Baro (auth), article, Art Int, 8-9/81; Jo Ann Lewis (auth), article, Washington Post, 11/5/81; Valentin Tatransky (auth), article, Arts, 1/84. *Media:* Metal. *Mailing Add:* 231 Forrest Wood Dr Durham NC 27707-2235

NOLD, CARL R
MUSEUM DIRECTOR, HISTORIAN
b Mineola, NY, Nov 26, 55. *Study:* St Johns Univ, Jamaica, NY, BA(hist), 77; Cooperstown Grad Prog, MA(mus studies), 82. *Pos:* Registr, NY State Hist Asn, Cooperstown, 78-80; dir, Gadsby's Tavern Mus, Alexandria, Va, 80-84, State Mus Pa, 84-91 & Mackinac State Hist Parks, 92-; bd mem & treas, Midwest Mus Conf,

98-2000; pres, Asn Midwest Mus, 2001-. *Teaching:* Lectr, Cooperstown Grad Prog, 78-80 & George Washington Univ, Washington, DC, 82-84. *Mem:* Am Asn Mus (chair coun regions, 2000); Am Asn State & Local Hist; Mid Atlantic Asn Mus (bd mem, 87-88); Cooperstown Grad Asn (bd mem, 85-88); Mich Mus Asn (bd mem, 95-98, 99-, bd sec, 99-2001). *Publ:* Auth, Co-op docents: Volunteer management, Hist News, Am Asn State & Local Hist, 84; coauth, Gadsby's Tavern Museum Interpretive Master Plan, Alexandria, Va, 85. *Mailing Add:* c/o Mackinac Island State Park Commission Box 30028 Lansing MI 48909-7528

NONAS, RICHARD
SCULPTOR
b New York, NY 36. *Work:* Mus Contemp Art, Los Angeles, Calif; Mus Mod Art, NY; Moderna Museet,Stockholm, Sweden. *Exhib:* One-man exhibs, Ink, Zurich, Switz, 79, Oil & Steel Gallery, NY, 80, Hudson River Mus, Yonkers, NY, 81 & Univ Mass, Amherst, 82; Ace Gallery, Los Angeles, Calif, 93; Xibbos, Paris, 94; Gallery 1-5, Brussels, Belg, 94; Ace Gallery, Denmark, 95. *Bibliog:* Jonathan Crary (auth), Richard Nonas: Boundary works, Artforum, 4/78; Donald Kupsit (auth), rev, Art in Am, 3/81; Grace Glueck (auth), An art blackout in Poland, 1/24/82. *Publ:* Auth, Summer 1906, 73, My Life on the Floor, 75 & Lost in Spoleto, 76, Buffalo Press; Hotel, 80, Boiling Coffee, 80 & Goats Itch (sound tape), 82, Tanam Press; auth, Richard Nonari Sculpture 1970-1988, Ace Contemp Exhibits, 88. *Dealer:* Ace Contemporary Exhibitions 5514 Wilshire Blvd Los Angeles CA 90036. *Mailing Add:* 14 Harrison St New York NY 10013

NOONAN, TOM
FILMMAKER
Exhib: What Happened Was, Sundance Film Festival, 94 & The Wife, 95; and numerous other movies and plays. *Pos:* Founder & artistic dir, Paradise Theater, 82-; pres, Genre Pictures. *Awards:* Nat Endowment Arts Grant for Narrative Filmmaking, 94 & 95; Screenwriting/Playwriting Fel, NY Found Arts, 98; Guggenheim Filmmaking Fel, 98. *Mailing Add:* Paradise Theater 64 E Fourth St New York NY 10003

NORDAN, ANTOINETTE SPANOS JOHNSON
CURATOR, HISTORIAN
b Birmingham, Ala, June 27, 53. *Study:* Univ Ala, Birmingham, BA, 75; Vanderbilt Univ, MA, 85. *Work:* Digital Manipulation-Contemp Printmaking, 2000; Contemp computer Photography, 2000; 2 Views: Photographs by Dan Budnik and Paintings by Bernard Williams, 2001; Paintings by Mark Messersmith, 99; Works from the Paula Cooper Gallery, 98. *Collection Arranged:* Ed Willis Barnett: Photographs, 86; Vision of the West: The Art of Will Crawford (auth, catalog), Birmingham Mus Art, Ala, 86; Post-Industrial Steel Town (auth, catalog), 88; Birmingham/Hitachi: An Exhib of Contemp Birmingham Artists (auth, catalog), Hitachi, Japan, 89; Michael Ponce de Leon: Prints and Plates (auth, catalog), 90; Prints and Preparatory Drawings of Felix Vallotton (auth, catalog), 93; Ferrously Yours: Contemporary Cast Iron Art (intro & ed, catalog), 94; Hans Grohs, Prints, Painting & Watercolor, 97; A Collectors Eye, SB Barker Collections, 98; catalog, UpSouth, 99; Perspectives on HIV & Women, 99; Paintings by Mark Messersmith, 99; catalog, 2 Views-Photographs by Dan Budnick & Paintings by Bernard Williams, 2001. *Pos:* Ed, Visual Arts Gallery Papers, 80- & contribr, 85-, Univ Ala, Birmingham; instr art hist, 84-90; cur, Visual Arts Gallery, 85-01, admin dir, 9-01, cons 2001-. *Teaching:* Instr art hist, Univ Ala, Birmingham, 83-. *Awards:* ARLIS-SE Award, 94; Ferrously Yours: Contemp Cast Iron Art, 95. *Mem:* Col Art Asn; Southeastern Col Art Asn. *Res:* 19th and 20th Century drawing and illustration. *Publ:* Auth, Vision of the West: The Art of Will Crawford, Birmingham, 86; Birmingham/Hitachi: An Exhibition of Contemporary Birmingham Artists, Birmingham/Hitachi, Japan, 89; Ferrously Yours: Contemporary Cast Iron Art, 94; Felix Vallotton (auth), Prints and Preparatory Drawings, 93; Up South, 99. *Mailing Add:* 2907 Virginia Rd Birmingham AL 35223-1253

NORDIN, PHYLLIS E
SCULPTOR, PAINTER
b Chicago, Ill. *Study:* Beloit Col & Wayne State Univ, 54-56; Univ Toledo, BS, 63, BA(cum laude), 74; Toledo Mus Art, grad, 74, Univ Toledo, MLS Grad Degree, 92. *Work:* Ronald McDonald House, Toledo, Ohio; Town Ctr Mall, Port Charlotte, Fla; Univ Toledo; Beloit Col, Wis; Lucas Co Main Libr & Lucas Co Courthouse, Toledo, Ohio; Ft Defiance Park, Defiance, Ohio. *Comn:* Playmates (bronze), Treasure Coast Mall, Stuart, Fla; Beloved Son (bronze), Christ Presby Church, Toledo; Time Out (bronze), Ore, Ohio Branch Libr; Discovery (bronze), Port Clinton, Ohio Libr; Spiritus (ferro-cement), Flower Hosp, Sylvania, Ohio; and others. *Exhib:* Ann Sculpture & Ceramic Show, Butler Inst Am Art, 68-78; Liturgical Arts Nat, McFall Gallery, Bowling Green State Univ, 81 & 83; Liturgical Art Guild Ohio Ann, Schumacher Gallery, Capital Univ, 81 & 83; Allied Artists Am Ann, Nat Acad Galleries, NY, 84; N Am Sculpture Exhib, Far Hills Gallery, Golden, Colo, 84; Salmagundi Club & Audubon Artists Ann Exhib, Nat Arts Club, NY, 87; and others. *Pos:* former trustee, Toledo Mod Art Group; bd mem, Toledo Arts Comn & Toledo Artist's Club. *Teaching:* Instr, Lourdes Col, Sylvania, Ohio, Univ Toledo; instr ceramics & sculpture, home studio. *Awards:* First Prize, 43rd Ann Nat Art Exhib, Cooperstown Art Asn, NY, 78; Alpha Award, Best of Show, Energy Art Nat Exhib, Foothills Art Ctr, Golden, Colo, 83; Named to Lyons Twp High Sch Hall of Fame, La Grange, Ill, 96. *Bibliog:* Louise Bruner (auth), Toledo, city of sculptures, Blade, 80; M Biedron (ed), On the Cover, Radio Listener, WGTE Pub Radio, 80; J Hayes (auth), Contemporary sculpture alive, Columbus Dispatch, 82. *Mem:* Nat Asn Women Artists; Ohio Designer Craftsmen; NW Ohio Watercolor Soc; Liturgical Art Guild Ohio; Athena Art Soc; Catharine Lorillard Wolfe Art Club. *Media:* Bronze, Welded Steel. *Publ:* Auth, Downtown churches house treasures, Accent Arts, 80; contribr, Centennial Mall's crowning jewel, Alumnus, Univ Toledo, 80; Auxiliary presents sculpture, Toledo Hosp News, 81; Gallerie Women Artists, 90; Liturgical Art Guild Ohio, newsletter, 92. *Mailing Add:* 4035 Tantara Rd Toledo OH 43623

NORDLAND, GERALD JOHN
GALLERY DIRECTOR, CRITIC
b Los Angeles, Calif, 27. *Study:* Univ Southern Calif, AB & JD. *Collection Arranged:* Gaston Lachaise (with catalog), Los Angeles Co Mus Art & Whitney Mus Am Art, 63-64; Richard Diebenkorn Retrospective, 64, Josef Albers, 65, Washington Color Painters, 65, Washington Gallery Mod Art, Washington, DC; John Altoon, Julius Bissier (with Guggenheim Mus), Robert Natkin, Al Held, Fritz Glarner, Paul Jenkins, Peter Voulkos Bronzes, and others, San Francisco Mus Art; Gaston Lachaise Retrospective (with Cornell Univ; catalog), 74, Alberto Burri (with Guggenheim Mus; catalog), 77, and others, Frederick S Wight Art Gallery, Univ Calif, Los Angeles; Richard DeVore 1972-1982, 83, Controversial Public Art (with catalog), 83, and others, Milwaukee Art Mus. *Pos:* Dean, Chouinard Art Sch, Calif Inst Arts, 60-64; dir, Washington Gallery Mod Art, 64-66, San Francisco Mus Art, 66-72, Frederick S Wight Galleries, Univ Calif, Los Angeles, 73-77 & Milwaukee Art Mus, 77-85; art consult, Chicago, 86-. *Awards:* Lachaise Found Grant, 73; Guggenheim Found Fel, 85-86. *Res:* More than forty museum publications on twentieth century artists and movements, emphasizing American painting, sculpture and photography. *Publ:* Auth, Richard Diebenkorn / Graphics 1981-88, Yellowstone Art Center, 1989; In the Spirit of the Times, Nora Eccles Harrison Museum of Art, Utah State Univ., 2003; Emerson Woelffer, RedCat, CA Inst, of the Arts, 2003; Reuniting an Era: abstract expressionists of the 1950's, Rockford Art Museum IL, 2004; ed, Richard Diebenkorn, Rizzoli Int, 87 (2nd ed, 2001), Frank Lloyd Wright: In the Realm of Ideas, SIU Press, 88; Zhou Brothers, Chicago: East-West Ltd Ed, 94; Ynez Johnston, Grassfield Press, Univ Ohio, 96; Twentieth Century American Drawings,Arkansas Arts Center, Little Rock, AR 98; Jon Schueler: To The North (with Richard Ingleby), London Merrell, 2002; Emerson Woelffer: A Solo Flight Los Angeles, RedCat, 2003; and others. *Mailing Add:* 645 W Sheridan Rd No 3FL-2 Chicago IL 60613-3316

NORDSTROM, ALISON DEVINE
ADMINISTRATOR, CURATOR
b Boston, Mass, Jan 17, 50. *Study:* Boston Univ, BA; Univ Okla, MLS. *Work:* New Work Japan (sculpture), 87. *Collection Arranged:* Robert & Frances Flaherty (film & photographs; auth, catalog), 83; Pro Femina (photographs of women by women), 93; Nervous Landscapes (7 photogr; auth, catalog), 94; Colonial Photography of Somoa (auth, catalog), 94. *Pos:* Dir, Brattleboro Mus, Vt, 83-88; res assoc, Peabody Mus, Harvard Univ, 89-91; dir, Southeast Mus Photog, 91-. *Awards:* Darrah Award, 89; Nat Endowment Humanities Fel, 91. *Mem:* Am Asn Mus; Fla Asn Mus (trustee, 90-91); Soc Photog Educ; Oracle; Vt Mus & Gallery Alliance (trustee, 88-90). *Publ:* Auth, Early photography in Samoa, Hist Photog, 91; Imag(in)ing the Seminoles, SEMP, 93; Persistent images: photographs in ethnographic collections, Continuum, 93. *Mailing Add:* 205 Tarragona Way Daytona Beach FL 32114

NORELLI, MARTINA ROUDABUSH
CURATOR
b Washington, DC, Oct 2, 42. *Study:* Mary Washington Col, Fredericksburg, Va, 60-62; George Washington Univ, DC, BA(art hist), 69, MA(museology), 72, PhD(art hist),99. *Collection Arranged:* Artist-Naturalists: Observations in the Americas (auth, catalog), 72, Birds (auth, catalog), 80, An American Perspective: Selections from the Bequest of Frank McClure (auth, catalog), 81, Werner Drewes, Sixty-five Years of Printmaking (auth, catalog), 84, Art, Design and the Modern Corporation (auth, catalog), 85, Symbols and Ceremonies: Pueblo Indian Watercolors, 86, Figure Prints: Washington Print Club 11th Biennial Members' Exhibition (auth, catlog), 86, Close Focus: Prints, Drawings, & Photographs, 87, Nat Mus Am Art, Smithsonian Inst, Washington; East Meets West: Chen Chi Watercolors (auth, catalog), Columbus Mus Art, Ga, 89; Naturally Drawn: Drawings from the Collection (auth, catalog), Leigh Yawkey Woodson Art Mus, Wausau, Wis, 92. *Pos:* Curatorial asst, Dimock Gallery, George Wash Univ, 68-69; secy, Dept Graphic Arts, Nat Mus Am Art, Smithsonian Inst, Washington, DC, 70-71, mus technician, 71-74, asst cur, 74-78, assoc cur, 78-91; independent cur, 91-. *Awards:* Serv Award, Leigh Yawkey Woodson Art Mus, Wausau, Wis, 86; David Lloyd Kreeger Prize in Art History, George Wash Univ, 88; Univ Fel, George Wash Univ, 88-92. *Mem:* Print Coun Am. *Res:* American prints and drawings; Estonian 19th & 20th art; Franz Marc German expressionism; Wildlife art. *Publ:* Auth, The Watercolors of Antoine-Louis Barye, Antione-Louise Barye, Corcoran Collection, Washington, 88; John James Audubon, John Woodhouse Audubon, Vincent Gifford Audubon, 92; Drawing on Nature, Geelong Art Gallery, Melbourne, Australia, 92; Thoughts on Smallness, essay in Natural Wonders: John & Alice Woodson Forester Miniature Collection, Leigh Yawkey Woodson Art Mus, Wausau, Wis, 93; Mark Catesby, William Clutz & Ford Crull, Werner Drewes, Eleanor Dickinson, Harald Eelma, Sirje Eelma, Onne Eelma, Kenneth Engblom, Oriole Farb Feshbach, Janet Fish, Susan Fishgold, SV, Allgemeines Kunstlerlerlexikon, Saur Verlag, Leipzig, 96-2006. *Mailing Add:* 11219 S Shore Rd Reston VA 20190

NORFLEET, BARBARA PUGH
CURATOR, EDUCATOR
b Lakewood, NJ. *Study:* Swarthmore, BA, 47; Harvard-Radcliffe, MA, 50 & PhD, 51. *Hon Degrees:* New Hampshire Inst of Art, 97. *Work:* Mus of Mod Art, NY; Mus Fine Arts, Boston; Corcoran Gallery Art; Whitney Mus Am Art; Houston Mus Fine Arts. *Comn:* Writers & The American Photogr Scene, 99. *Exhib:* Boston Mus Fine Arts Arch, 83; Inst Contemp Art, Boston, 83 & 91; Mass Col Art, Boston, 85; Mus Art, Eugene, Ore, 86; Int Ctr Photog, NY, 87 & 93; Philadelphia Mus Art, Philadelphia, 87; Mus Mod Art, NY, 87; George Eastman House, 89; Houston Mus Fine Arts, 93; Davo Mus, Wellesley Col, 96; Whitney Mus Am Art, 96; San Francisco Mus Mod Art, 96; St Louis Art Mus, 97; Traveling exhib, 97-98. *Collection Arranged:* The Photography Archive on the Photographic Social History of the US; The Social Question: Social Reform at the Turn of the Century, Harvard & Mus Mod Art, 73; Richard Misrael, 80; Joseph Kondelka, 90; When We Liked Ike, 2001; Line of Ascent- Blue Sky, 2003.

Pos: Cur, Harvard Univ, 72-2001; consult on art, numerous orgns, 73-. *Teaching:* Sr emer lectr photog, Harvard Univ, Cambridge, 70-96. *Awards:* Nat Endowment Arts, 75, 79, 81, 83 & 84; MA Artists Fel, 82; Nat Endowment Arts Fel, 82; John Simon Guggenheim Fel, 84; MA Artists Fel in Photog, 87. *Mem:* Col Art Asn. *Media:* Photography. *Res:* Have compiled an archive of over 30,000 negatives and prints on the social history of the US from 1900-1970. *Interests:* American History & Photogr. *Publ:* Auth, The Head and the Heart, Harvard Press, 78; The Champion Pig, 79 & Killing Time, Godine, 83; All the Right People, New York Graphic-Little Brown, 86; Manscape with Beasts, New York, Harry Abrams, 90; Looking At Death, Godine, 94; and others

NORGARD, KAREN-SAM
SCULPTOR, EDUCATOR
b Plainfield, NJ, June 6, 52. *Study:* Univ NC, Greensboro, BFA, 74; Univ Cincinnati, MFA, 76. *Work:* Ga Southwestern Univ, Americus; Savannah Col Art & Design, Ga. *Comn:* Blue Moon Experience (collab series), 99, 20 Dresses in Celebration (paper relief constructs), 99, Provost Comn, Savannah Col Art & Design, 99. *Exhib:* Ten Artists, Gallery in Cork St, London, Eng, 96; Arts on the River, City of Savannah, Ga, 97; Women at Work, Univ Wis-Whitewater, 97 & 98; 20 x 10, Fleischer Art-Philadelphia Mus, 98. *Pos:* Chair visual arts, Metrop Sch Arts, 93-94. *Teaching:* Prof foundations, Savannah Col Art & Design, Ga, 94-99; asst prof, Univ Wis, Whitewater, 99-. *Awards:* Chancellor's Award, Univ Wis-Whitewater, 98. *Mem:* Found Art Theory & Educ; Coalition Active Sculptors Teaching. *Media:* Mixed Media. *Dealer:* Peltz Gallery 1119 E Knapp St Milwaukee WI 53202-2828. *Mailing Add:* 417 N Center Ave Jefferson WI 53549-1207

NORRIS, ANDREA SPAULDING
HISTORIAN, MUSEUM DIRECTOR
b Madison, Wis, Apr 2, 1945. *Study:* Wellesley Col, BA, 67; NY Univ, MA, 69, cert(mus training), 70, PhD, 77; Mus Mgt Inst, Univ Calif, Berkeley, 80. *Exhib:* The Sforza Court, Milan in the Renaissance, 1450-1535, 88-89; Hopi Pottery, 96; Am Indian Traditions Transformed: Contemp Pottery, 2000; Four Photographers, 2002. *Pos:* Asst to dir, Yale Univ Art Gallery, 77-80; chief cur, Archer M Huntington Art Gallery, Univ Tex, Austin, 80-88; dir, Spencer Mus of Art, Univ Kans, Lawrence, 88-. *Teaching:* Lectr art hist, Queens Col, City Univ NY, 73-74, Yale Univ, 78-79 & Univ Tex, Austin, 84-88; adj instr art hist, NY Univ, 76-77; adj prof art hist, Univ Kans, Lawrence, 88-. *Awards:* Ford Found Mus Training Grant, 69-72. *Mem:* Col Art Asn Am (bd dir, 2000-, vpres comt, 2002-); Renaissance Soc Am; Asn Art Mus Dirs. *Res:* Italian Renaissance painting and sculpture; medals; Gian Cristoforo Romano; Lombard Renaissance sculpture; art patronage in America; America Indian Art. *Publ:* Coauth, Medals and Plaquettes from the Molinari Collection at Bowdoin Col, 76; contribr, Dizionario Biografico degli Italiani, Treccani, 77-81; auth, New-Found Works and Pollock's Career, In: Jackson Pollock: New-Found Works, Yale Univ Art Gallery, 78; Gian Cristoforo Romano: The courtier as medallist, In: Studies in the History of Art, 88; The Sforza of Milan, In: Schifanoia, 91; Sanford Gifford: A Discovery Joins a University Collection, In: Am Art Rev, 96. *Mailing Add:* Spencer Mus Art Univ Kans 1301 Mississippi St Lawrence KS 66045

NORRIS, MERRY
CONSULTANT, COLLECTOR
b Rochester NY. *Study:* Univ Calif, Berkeley, AA, 59; Univ Calif Los Angeles, 80. *Work:* Cerritos Ctr Performing Arts, 93; Hon AIL/LA; Hon SDSA, Set Decorators Soc of Am. *Comn:* BMC Software, Houston, 98; Los Angeles Ctr Studios, 99; Universal City Walk; Hollywood Athletic Club, 94. *Exhib:* Cool Dogs, Hot Digs, 94 & 96; Calif Grown: Kenny Scharf. *Collection Arranged:* Community Redevel Agy, Los Angeles, 1984; LACRA (community Redevelop Agency), 81-87; Cedars- Sinai Comprehensive Cancer Ctr, 87; Gonda Neuroscience & Genetics Res Ctr, UCLA, 98; Ernst & Young LLP Hq, 99; Heller, Ehrman, White & McAuliffe, Los Angeles, 92. *Pos:* Exec Dir, Gateway to LA, PBID, 97-2001; Vpres Bus Develop, Pacific Design Ctr, 95-96; Pres, Los Angeles Cult Affairs Comn, 86-90; Found & Co-Chmn Major Gifts Com, MOCA, 79-84. *Awards:* AIA/CC Pub Serv Award, 93; Women in Leadership, Exec Bus, West Hollywood CofC, 96; AIA/Los Angeles Design Award in Asn with Johnson Favaro Archit & Urban Design, 98; Inaugural Honoree, Los Angeles Forum for Arch and Urban Design, 2002. *Bibliog:* The Art Newsletter, 5/95; Los Angeles Times Mag, 7/30/96 & 10/18/93; Access Los Angeles, 91 & 93; cover story, House of Business, 11/2000; Los Angeles Times, Concrete Canvas, 7/10/04; House of Bus, Mark Stock Paintings, 2000; Home Across Am, HG-TV, 98; Artful Lodger, Los Angeles Times Mag, 7/30/05. *Mem:* AIA (bd dir, 95-); Southern Calif Inst Architects; hon mem AIA (LA chap); hon mem, Set Decorator Soc Am; Current Mem, Bd of Dir: SCI-Arc (Southern Calif Inst of Archit; AIA (Am Inst of Archit) Los Angeles Chap; Pasadene Mus of Calif Art; Col Dance Theatre; Los Angeles Conservancy; ArTable, 83-98. *Interests:* Contemp & Archit; Urban Design. *Collection:* Young and emerging artists. *Publ:* Auth, Daniel Weinberg, Galeries Mag, 12/89-1/90. *Mailing Add:* 1473 Oriole Dr Los Angeles CA 90069

NORRIS, WILLIAM A
COLLECTOR
b Turtle Creek, Pa, Aug 30, 27. *Study:* Princeton Univ, BA, 51; Stanford Univ, JD, 54. *Collection:* Contemporary California paintings and sculpture. *Mailing Add:* Akin Gump Strauss Hauer & Feld LLP 2029 Century Park E Ste 2600 Los Angeles CA 90067

NORSTEN, TODD
ARTIST
Study: Yale Univ, Norfolk Prog, 1989; Minn Col Art & Design, BFA, 1990. *Exhib:* One-man shows: Paintings & Drawings, Willmar Community Col, Minn, 1992; Vermillion Gallery, Minn, 1992; Montgomery Glasoe Fine Art, Minn, 1994; New Paintings, 1996; Paintings & Drawings, Jennifer Armetta Fine Art, Chicago, 1997; Sighting, Weinstein Gallery, Minn, 1998; Paintings, Stephen, Wirtz Gallery, San Francisco, 1999; Recent Paintings, Finesilver, San Antonio, 1999; TrueFalse, 2001; Allsomenone, High Point Center Printmaking, Minn, 2003; Happy Happy Happy, Franklin ArtWorks, Minn, 2004; Treasures from the Upper Midwest, Cohan & Leslie, 2006; Safety Club, Midway Contemp Art, Minn, 2006; Group shows: Marks & Lines, Montgomery Glasoe Fine Arts, 1993; Brown Whiskey Club, 1995; Composing a Collection, Walker Art Center, Minn, 1996; Vistor's Voices: Recomposing the Collection, 1996; Dialogues, 1997, 1998; Elizabeth Dee Gallery, NY, 1998; Five McKnight Artists, MCAD Gallery, Minn, 1999; Summer Show, Margaret Thatcher Gallery, NY, 2000; Uncanny Visions, Plains Art Mus, Fargo, 2004; Abstract Painting in Minnesota, Minn, Mus Am Art, 2005; Young Am, Arario Mus, Seoul, 2006; Whitney Biennial: Day for Night, Whitney Mus Am Art, NY, 2006. *Mailing Add:* c/o Cohan and Leslie 138 Tenth Ave New York NY 10011

NORTH, JUDY K RAFAEL
PAINTER
b Los Angeles, Calif, June 24, 37. *Study:* Otis Art Inst, 55-58; San Francisco Art Inst, 58-59. *Work:* Los Angeles Co Mus, Security Pac Bank, Los Angeles; Mus Contemp Art, Chicago; Oakland Mus, Calif; Opera Plaza Restaurant, San Francisco, Calif; Boise Art Mus, Idaho; Madison Art Ctr, Wis. *Comn:* Stained Glass, Northbrae Community Church, 59; stained glass, Holy Name Jesus Christ, 63; stained glass, Salvation Army, 72; Portrait of Dean of Law Sch, Stanford Univ, 77. *Exhib:* Pilchuck Fac Exhib, Seattle, Wash, 85; Am Realism, 20th Century Drawings & Watercolors, 85; Prichard Gallery, Idaho, 86; Monumental Image, Springfield, Mo, 86; solo shows, Contemp Arts Forum, Santa Barbara, Calif, 90, Lidija Grzac Gallery, San Anselmo, Calif, 90, Portland Community Col, Ore, 91, Calif Mus Art, Santa Rosa, 91, Gallery Stevenson Union S Ore State Col, Ashaldn, 92, Slanted Door, San Francisco, Calif, 95, Immortal-Eye Your Pet, San Francisco Mus Mod Art Gallery, Ft Mason, Calif, 96; Liberation By Seeing, Gold Ridge Sangha, Am Sch Japan Arts, Santa Rosa, Calif, 94; No More Scapegoats, Anne Frank and the World Today, Corte Madera, Calif, 95; East Meets West, Bolinas Mus, Calif, 95; Animal Portraits, 3Com Corp-Great Am Site, Santa Clara, Calif, 96; Animal Portraits in Executive Ctr, Hitatchi Data Systems, Los Altos, Calif, 96. *Pos:* Staff designer, Actors Workshop, 60-64 & Cummings Stained Glass Studio, 63-65; designer, Bennington Col, 66-69. *Teaching:* Instr theatre design & stained glass, Bennington Col, 66-69; instr theatre design, Actors Workshop, San Francisco, 60-64; instr, Univ Calif, Davis, 83-86, Acad Art, San Francisco, 85 & Pilchuck Glass Sch, 85-88. *Awards:* Marin Arts Coun Grant, San Rafael, Calif, 90. *Bibliog:* Joseph Woodard (auth), Iconography of sacred and protane, Artweek, 90; Thomas Garver (auth), Regarding Art: Artworks about art, 90; Wayman R Spence (auth), Celebration of life, The Art of Medicine, 94. *Media:* Watercolor; Mixed. *Dealer:* Marion Parmenteer San Francisco Mus Gallery Ft Mason San Francisco CA. *Mailing Add:* PO Box 425 San Geronimo CA 94963

NORTON, MARY JOYCE
PAINTER, JEWELER
b Tampa, Fla. *Study:* Akron Univ; Ariz State Univ; color theory with Dorothy Fratt. *Work:* Honeywell Corp, Minneapolis, Minn; First Nat Bank, Phoenix; Houston Oil & Mineral Corp, Tex; IBM, Endicott, NY; Drexel, Burnham, Lambert, Scottsdale, Ariz. *Comn:* Gateway Hotel, Phoenix, 85. *Exhib:* Watercolor Biennial, Phoenix Art Mus, 70-72, Four-Corners Biennial, 71-73; 8 West Biennial, Colo Ctr Arts, 72-74; Southwestern Fine Arts Biennial, Mus NMex, 72-74; Joslyn Mus, Omaha, Nebr, 74; and others. *Awards:* Southwestern Purchase Prize, Yuma Fine Arts Ctr, 67 & 73; 19th Nat Sun Carnival Exhib, El Paso Mus Art, 77; Ariz Painting Nat Competition, Scottsdale Ctr Arts, Ariz, 77. *Bibliog:* Barbara Cortright (auth), Meet the circle, Phoenix Mag, 2/75 & The look of nature, the flow of paint, Artweek, 5/75; Rosemary Holusha (auth), Mary Joyce Norton, Art Voices S, 5-6/79. *Mem:* Nat Women's Caucus Art. *Media:* Acrylic; Mixed. *Mailing Add:* 10648 N 100th St Scottsdale AZ 85260-6334

NORTON, PAUL FOOTE
HISTORIAN, EDUCATOR
b Newton, Mass, Jan 23, 1917. *Study:* Oberlin Col, BA, 38; Princeton Univ, MFA, 47, PhD, 52. *Pos:* Mem, Amheart Hist Com, 1970-74, 2002-06 & Mass State Hist Comn, 80-83; asst nat dir, Census Stained Glass Am. *Teaching:* From asst prof to assoc prof hist art, Pa State Univ, University Park, 47-58; from assoc prof to prof hist art, Univ Mass, Amherst, 58-93, chmn art dept, 58-71, chmn art history, 82-85 & 89-93, emer prof, 93-. *Awards:* Fulbright Sr Res Fel, 53-54; Nat Endowment Humanities Sr Fel, 71-72; Fel, JN Brown Ctr Study Am Cult, 93-95; Rhode Island Com Humanities Grant, 95-96; Merit Award, Am Asn State and Local History, 2002. *Mem:* Soc Archit Historians (dir & ed jour, 59-64); Soc Archit Historians Gr Brit; Archeol Inst Am; Soc Preserv NEng Antiquities; Ctr Int Vitrail; Pioneer Am Soc; Victorian Soc; Mountain View Country Club; US Tennis Asn; others. *Res:* History of architecture; England and America in the 18th and 19th centuries; survey of stained glass windows in Mass & Vermont; architecture in Amherst. *Publ:* auth, Amherst: A Guide to its Architecture, 75; Latrobe, Jefferson and the National Capitol, 77; auth, articles in J Soc Archit Historians, Art Bull, Britannica Encycl Am Art, Stained Glass Quart & Encycl World Biog; ed, Jour Soc Archit Historians; The Mountain View Country Club: Centennial 1898-1998, 98; auth, Rhode Island Stained Glass, 2001. *Mailing Add:* 57 Woodside Ave Amherst MA 01002

NORTON, PETER K
COLLECTOR & PATRON
b Aberdenne, Wash, Nov, 14, 43. *Study:* Programmer, Norton Utilities (sold business to Symantec). *Comn:* Trustee Mus Modern Art, New York City. *Pos:* Prog, Norton Utilities (sold bus to Symantec), formerly; trustee, Mus Modern Art, New York City, currently; Coauth (with David Wild): Peter Norton's Computing Fundamentals, 95;

Coauth: (with Arthur Griffith) Peter Norton's Complete Guide to Linux, 99; coauth: (with Scott Clark) Peter Norton's New Inside the PC, 2002, and several others; contributor articles to professional journals. *Awards:* Named one of Top 200 Collectors, ARTnews Mag, 2004, 2006. *Collection:* Contemporary art. *Publ:* Coauth (with David Wild) Peter Norton's Computing Fundamentals, 95; coauth (with Arthur Griffith) Peter Norton's Complete Guide to Linux, 99; coauth (with Scott Clark) Peter Norton's New Inside the PC, 2002; contribr, articles to prof jour. *Mailing Add:* 225 Arizona Apt 350 Santa Monica CA 90401-1244

NORVELL, PATSY
SCULPTOR, ENVIRONMENTAL ARTIST
b Greenville, SC, July 13, 42. *Study:* Bennington Col, Vt, BA; study with David Smith; San Francisco Art Inst; Hunter Col, MA. *Work:* Orlando Mus, Fla. *Comn:* Cooperheads, outdoor sculpture, Fed Courthouse, Bridgeport, Conn, Gen Serv Admin, 83-84; Glass Jungle, environ glass installation, 4600 East-West Hwy, 84-88; Glass Passage, environ glass installation, Home Savings Am Tower, 87-88; New York Newsstand, collab with Frances Halstand, AIA Pub Art Fund, 88, installation, NY, 93; renovation & art installation, Metrop Transportation Authority, Beverly & Courtelyou Subway Sta, 92-94; and others. *Exhib:* Solo exhibs, AIR Gallery, NY, 73, 75, 78, 80, 82, 87 & Matthew Hamilton Gallery, 84; retrospective exhib, Barrett House & Vassar Col Art Mus, 79; The Folding Image, Nat Gallery Art, Washington & Yale Univ Art Gallery, 84; Gallery Artists, Max Protetel Gallery, NY, 87-88; Gardens Real and Imagined, Nat Mus Tour, 90-93; Artists Gardens, Noyes Mus, NJ, 90; Midtown Flower Show, Midtown-Payson Gallery, 92; Am Artist's Ode to Gardens & Flowers, Nassau Ctr Mus, 92; and many others. *Teaching:* Instr sculpture & drawing, Rutgers Univ, Newark, NJ, 69-70; instr materials & printmaking, Montclair State Col, Upper Montclair, NJ, 70-74; panelist, lectr & instr workshops, Nassau Co Mus, Aldrich Mus, Sarah Lawrence Col, City Univ New York, Skidmore Col, Mt Holyoke Col, Grad Sch Sculpture, Yale Univ & Wooster Col, Ohio, 71-79; assoc sculpture, Columbia Univ, New York, 77; adj instr, Queens Col, NY, 77-78; adj & vis prof sculpture & drawing, Hunter Col, NY, 78-; vis artist & lectr, pub art, Okla Arts Inst, 91. *Awards:* Nat Endowment Arts Grant, 76-77; Pollick-Krasner Artist Grant, 96; Elixir-Napenthe Grant, 96-97. *Bibliog:* Paul Tschinkel (dir), video interview, Manhattan Cable TV, 78; Michael Komanecki & Virginia Fabri Butera (auths), The Folding Image, Nat Gallery Art & Yale Univ (catalog), 84; Grace Glueck (auth), The screen comes into its own, NY Times, 9/19/82. *Media:* Glass, Natural & Man-made Materials. *Publ:* Contribr, Six Years, Lucy Lippard, Praeger, 69; auth, Patsy Norvell, Artists Discuss Their Work, Glass Art Soc J, pp 55-57, 84-85; Patsy Norvell (auth), Recording Conceptual Art, Univ Calif Press, 2001. *Mailing Add:* 78 Greene St New York NY 10012

NORWOOD, MALCOLM MARK
PAINTER, EDUCATOR
b Drew, Miss, Jan 21, 28. *Study:* Miss Col, BA & MEd; Univ Ala, MA; Univ Colo, painting with Mark Rothko. *Work:* Miss Mus Art, Jackson; Miss Collection, Trustmark Bank, Jackson; Miss Col; Belhaven Col; Jackson Country Club. *Comn:* Landscapes & watercolors, First Nat Bank, Cleveland, Miss, 64 & 66; Rosalie (painting), comn by Daughters Am Revolution for USS Miss, 78; 5 Mile Run, comn by Gov's Coun on Physical Fitness, 81; and others. *Exhib:* Southern Methodist Univ Invitational, Ft Worth, Tex, 62; Washington Watercolor Asn, Smithsonian Inst, 63; Contemp Southern Art Exhib, Weatherspoon Art Gallery, Univ NC, 66; Artists Registry Exhib, Brooks Art Gallery, Memphis, Tenn, 69; La State Art Comn, Baton Rouge, 69. *Pos:* Bd dir, Miss Mus Art, Jackson; dir festival, Crosstie Arts Coun, 70-75, pres 79-80; mem bd dir, Miss Arts Comn, 80-85. *Teaching:* Prof & chmn dept art, Delta State Univ, 62-90, emer prof, 90-. *Awards:* Painting Award, Holiday Inns Am Arts Festival, 69; First Prize in Drawing, Edgewater Merchants Asn Ann, 71; Miss Governors Award for Excellence in Arts, 92. *Mem:* Miss Art Asn; Cross-Tie Arts Couns. *Media:* Watercolor, Oil. *Publ:* Auth, article in Jackson Daily News/Clarion Ledger, 64; illusr, 64 & cover, 68, Delta Rev; coauth, The Art of Marie Hull, 75; auth, Guide to the Roberts Library Art Collection, 77; The Garrard Collection, 94. *Mailing Add:* 600 Canal Ave Cleveland MS 38732-3016

NOTARBARTOLO, ALBERT
PAINTER, ENVIRONMENTAL ARTIST
b New York, NY. *Study:* Nat Acad Fine Arts, scholar, 50; apprenticeship to mural painter Ignacio La Russa, 51-53. *Work:* Ft Bragg, NC; Aldrich Mus Contemp Art, Ridgefield, Conn; Nat Gallery Art, Washington, DC. *Comn:* Series of paintings, comn by Larry Aldrich, NY, 67; painting, Radio Corp Am, NY, 71; drawing, Newsweek, 72; tapestry, Aubusson, France. *Exhib:* Corcoran Gallery Art, Washington, DC, 68; Mus Mod Art, NY, 68-70; 21 Am Artists, Del Art Mus, 70; Aldrich Mus Contemp Art, 72; Aubusson Tapestry Exhib, Norton Gallery Mus, Fla; Nat Gallery Art, Washington, DC, 76; plus others. *Awards:* First Prize, New York Intercult Soc, 53; Dept Housing & Urban Develop Nat Community Art Competition Award, Washington, DC, 73; Nat Award, New Glory Bicentennial Flag Design Competition (for flag for first lunar colony), Santa Barbara Mus of Art, 76. *Mem:* Nat Soc Lit & Arts. *Media:* Oil, Mixed Media. *Publ:* Contribr, Art Workers News, 4/74; Leonardo Mag, spring 75; Art-World newspaper, 1-2/78; Pen World Mag, 1-2/96

NOTESTINE, DOROTHY J
INSTRUCTOR, PAINTER
b Udall, Kans, Dec 3, 21. *Study:* Univ Houston, 62-63; study with John Pike, Zolten Szabo, Edgar Whitney and others, 76-85. *Exhib:* Ann Art Show, Hill Country Arts Found, Ingram, Tex, 77; Art of Dorothy/Tom Notestine, Univ Tex Sci Ctr, San Antonio, 79; Carrizo Art Inst Show, Ruidoso, NMex, 85 & 86; Artists of Tex, Dallas Creative Arts Bldg, 86; Art of Travel, Love Gallery, Int Airport, San Antonio, 88. *Collection Arranged:* Watercolors of the World (with catalog), Northside Bank, San Antonio, 76; Collection Int Known Artists (with catalog), Kerrville, Tex, 77. *Pos:* Co-ed, monthly pub, San Antonio Watercolor Group, 76-78; bd-mem, Coppini Acad Fine Arts, San Antonio, 80-82. *Teaching:* Instr watercolor, Carrizo Art Ctr, Ruidoso, NMex, 85-86, Artists of SW Cruise Art, 86, San Antonio Col, 70-86; art instr, SS Star Princess, cruising Mediterranean & Europe, 92 & SS Dawn Princess, cruising Mex Riviera, Panama Canal & Caribbean, 93. *Bibliog:* Pat Breedlove (auth), Artists of Texas, Mountain Productions Inc, 86; Carla Tam (auth), Carrizo Art Mag, 86; Skip Singleton (auth), Ruidoso Life Style, Sunrise Productions, 87. *Mem:* San Antonio Watercolor Group (co-founder); River Arts of San Antonio; Colonial Hills Watercolor Artist Asn. *Media:* Watercolor. *Publ:* Coauth, Oklahoma Artists of Distinction, Paint Spree Publ, 89; many articles in daily and monthly publ. *Mailing Add:* 358 Ave Maria Ave San Antonio TX 78216-7143

NOTKIN, RICHARD T
SCULPTOR, CERAMIST
b Chicago, Ill, Oct 26, 48. *Study:* Kansas City Art Inst, with Dale Eldred & Ken Ferguson, BFA, 70; Univ Calif, Davis, with Robert Arneson, MFA, 73. *Work:* Stedelijk Mus, Amsterdam, Holland; Nat Collection Fine Arts, Smithsonian Inst, Washington DC; Los Angeles Co Mus Art; Victoria & Albert Mus, London, Eng; Met Mus Art, NY; and others. *Exhib:* One-man shows, Garth Clark Gallery, NY, 88, 89, 91, 93, 95, 97, 2000 & 2003, Seattle Art Mus (catalog), 90, Everson Mus, 91, Newark Mus, NJ, 91, Crocker Art Mus, Sacramento, 91, Margo Jacobsen Gallery, Portland, Oreg, 2001; Contemp Ceramics: Sels from the Met Mus Art, NY; Int Ceramics Exhib, Hovikodden Art Ctr, Oslo, Norway, 90; Metamorphosis of Contemp Ceramics: The Int Exhib Contemp Ceramics, Shigaraki Ceramic Cult Park, Shigaraki, Japan, 91; Color and Fire: Defining Moments in Studio Ceramics 1950-2000, Los Angeles Co Mus Art, 2000; Contemp Am Ceramics 1950-1999, Nat Mus of Modern Art, Kyoto, Japan, 2002; Elizabeth Leach Gallery, Portland, Ore, 2006. *Pos:* Artist-in-residence, Kohler Co, Wis, 76 & 78; artist-in-residence, Archie Bray Found, Helena, Mont, 81; guest artist, Shigaraki Ceramic Cult Park, Shigaraki, Japan, 02. *Teaching:* Vis asst prof sculpture & ceramics, Univ Utah, Salt Lake City, 75; acting chmn & vis lectr ceramics, Md Inst Col Art, Baltimore, 77; vis artist/lectr, Ohio State Univ, 82; vis artist, Found Dept, Kansas City Art Inst, 84 & 95; vis artist, Bezalel Acad Art & Design, Jerusalem, Israel, 90. *Awards:* Visual Arts Fel, Nat Endowment Arts, 79, 81 & 88; Guggenheim Found Fel Sculpture, 90; Louis Comfort Tiffany Found Fel, 91; Jerry Metcalf Found Award, 2000 & 2006. *Mem:* Nat Coun Educ Ceramic Arts; Am Crafts Coun; Archie Bray Found, Helena, Mont. *Media:* Ceramics, Mixed. *Mailing Add:* PO Box 698 Helena MT 59624

NOTTEBOHM, ANDREAS
PAINTER
b Eisenach, Ger, Oct 13, 44. *Study:* Acad Fine Arts, Munich, Ger, 65-68. *Work:* Nat Air & Space Mus, Smithsonian Inst; Bundestag Cong Ger, Bonn; Asn Friends House Arts, Munich Ger; NASA Art Col, Kennedy Space Ctr, Fla; Lily of Salzburg, Austria. *Exhib:* Ann Shows, Haus der Kunst, Munich, Ger, 66 & 67; Halley's Comet Commemorated, State of the Universe & Calling All Stars, Nat Air & Space Mus, Washington. *Media:* Acrylic on Aluminum. *Publ:* Auth, Astropoeticon, Jurhot, Munich, Ger, 79. *Dealer:* Weinstein Gallery Geary St San Francisco CA 94102. *Mailing Add:* 17496 7th St E Sonoma CA 95476-4727

NOVA, RES See Yarotsky, Lori

NOVINSKI, LYLE FRANK
PAINTER, EDUCATOR
b Montfort, Wis, June 23, 32. *Study:* Univ Wis/Platteville, BA; Univ Wis, MS & MFA; Marquette Univ. *Comn:* Major leather wall construct, Amarillo & Dallas, Tex, 77; Chapel of the Incarnation, Univ Dallas, 85; St Joseph Church, Moulton, Tex, 94; Major stained glass installations, St Rita, Dallas, 86 & St Joseph's, Arlington, Tex., 97; Perkins and Neuhoff Chapel appointments, Southern Methodist, Dallas, 99; Bronze Relief, Mahquette Univ, Milwalkee, 2000; Sacred Heart Church, Spearman, Tex, 2000. *Exhib:* Tex Gen, 64 & 72; Okla Eight State Exhib, 68; Okla Invitational, 70; Ft Worth Art Ctr, 71; Nat Interfaith Conf on Relig & Archit, 75; Tex Wesleygon, 2002; CIVA, 2001. *Teaching:* Prof art & dir dept art, Univ Dallas, 60-; fel, Dallas Inst Humanities & Cult, 80-. *Awards:* Purchase Award, Okla Eight State, 68; Top Award, Tex Gen, 72; Distinguished Alumni, Univ Wis Platteville, 95; Novinski Art Found Bldg, Univ Wis, 2001. *Bibliog:* Articles, Christian Arts, 68, Liturgical Arts, 70 & Art Gallery, 71-72. *Mem:* Interfaith Forum Relig, Art & Archit; Col Art Asn; CIVA; Kimball; Christians in Visual Arts. *Media:* Leather, Oil, Ceramic, Bronze, Stained Glass. *Res:* Liturgical Art and Design. *Dealer:* Valley House Gallery 6616 Spring Valley Rd Dallas TX 75240. *Mailing Add:* 1101 Owenwood Dr Irving TX 75061-5536

NOVROS, DAVID
PAINTER
b Los Angeles, Calif, 41. *Study:* Univ Southern Calif, BFA, 63. *Work:* Mus Mod Art, Whitney Mus Art, NY; Atlantic Tower (Philip Johnson Bldg), Ga; Doumani House, Marina Del Ray, Calif; Menil Found Collection, Houston; Charleston Col, SC; and others. *Exhib:* Systemic Painting, Solomon R Guggenheim Mus, NY, 66; Whitney Mus Am Art, 67, 69 & 73; The Structure of Color, Whitney Mus Am Art, 71; Corcoran Biennial, Washington, 71; White on White, Mus Contemp Art, Chicago, Ill, 71-72; Art Inst Chicago, 72; one-man exhibs, Sperone Westwater Fischer Inc, NY, 76 & 78, Picollo Spoleto, Charleston, SC, 92 & Int Mus Mod Art, Dublin, Ireland, 92; Hoffman Borman Gallery, Santa Monica, Calif, 88; Abstraction Geometry painting, Albright-Knox Art Gallery, Buffalo, NY, 90; Inaugural Exhib, Mus Contemp Art, Dublin, Ireland, 91; Lafrenz Collection, on loan to Nat Gallery, Dublin, Ireland & Bremin, Ger, 91; Gross Bldg, Winslow, Ariz, 96. *Awards:* Fel, Guggenheim Found, 70. *Bibliog:* Frances Colpitt (auth), The Shape of Painting in the Sixties, Art J, Vol 50, No 1, spring 91; Loic Malle (auth), Virginia Dwan Art Minimal-Art Conceptuel Earthwork, Gallerie Montaigne, 92; Michael Phillip's, Painting Self Evident, 92. *Mailing Add:* 433 Broome St New York NY 10013

NOWYTSKI, SVIATOSLAV
FILMMAKER, PHOTOGRAPHER
b Oct 19, 34; Can & US citizen. *Study:* Pasadena Playhouse Col Theatre Arts, BA(theatre), 58; Columbia Univ, MFA(motion pictures), 64. *Work:* Educ Film Libr Asn, NY; Libr Cong; Dept Tourism, Recreation & Cult Affairs, Govt Man; Fedn Asn Arts, Man; Ont Ministry Educ, Toronto. *Comn:* Reflections of the Past (film), Ukrainian Cult & Educ Ctr, Winnipeg, 74; Last of the Jacks (film), Minn Hist Soc, 76; Immortal Image (film), Filmart Prod, 78; Grass on the Roof (film), Underground Space Ctr, Univ Minn, 79; The Helm of Destiny (film), UNA, NJ, 81; Harvest of Despair (film), UCRDC, Can, 84; We're Not Robots, You Know (video), Synergenesis Corp, 88. *Exhib:* Sheep in Wood (film), Am Film Festival, NY, 71; Reflections of the Past (film), Can Film Awards, Niagara on the Lake, Ont, 75 & 11th Int Chicago Film Festival, Ill, 75; Pysanka: The Ukrainian Easter Egg (film), Chicago Int Film Festival, 76; 1 hr feature documentary for UCRDC (Toronto): Between Hitler and Stalin, Ukraine in WW II - The Untold Story (prodr/dir), narration by Jack Palance, 01. *Pos:* Ed, Ukrainian, Polish & Russian Sect, Cinema & TV Digest, 63-; ed, Filmart Prod, St Paul, Minn, 71-82; freelance prodr/dir Slavko Nowytski & Assocs, 82-93; internat TV broadcaster & video journalist Voice of America TV, Window on America weekly program on UT-1 nat TV network, Ukraine, 93-. *Awards:* Blue Ribbon Award for Sheep in Wood, Am Film Festival, 71; Gold Hugo for Pysanka: The Ukrainian Easter Egg, Chicago Int Film Festival, 76 & Silver Venus Medal, Virgin Islands Int Film Festival, 77; Bronze Medal for Immortal Image, Int Film & TV Festival, NY, 78. *Mem:* Minn Soc Fine Arts; Twin Cities Metrop Arts Alliance; Intermedia Arts. *Media:* Film; TV. *Interests:* Prodn of historical and cultural films & programs

NOYES, SANDY
PHOTOGRAPHER
b New York, NY, Dec 18, 41. *Study:* Yale Univ, with Bud Leak, BA, 63; workshop with Paul Caponigro, 73 & Minor White, 74; New Sch Soc Res, with George Tice, 74. *Work:* Metrop Mus Art, NY; Bibliot Nat, Paris; Addison Gallery Am Art; High Mus Art; Amon Carter Mus, Ft Worth, Tex; Int Mus Photog at George Eastman House, Rochester, NY. *Exhib:* NJ State Mus, Trenton, 79; Contemp Platinotype, Rochester Inst Technol, NY, 79; Intervals, 22 Wooster St Gallery, NY, 82; Nikon House, NY, 84; Albany Inst Hist & Art, 89. *Teaching:* Instr, Int Ctr Photog, New York, 76-81. *Awards:* Proj Grant (co-recipient), Seven Photogrs, Del Valley, Nat Endowment Arts, 77; Ossabaw Island Proj Fel, Ga, 79; Creative Artists Prog Serv Grant, NY, 83. *Mem:* Albany/Schenectady League Arts; Soc Indust Archeol. *Mailing Add:* Sandy Noyes Photography 745 Dugway Rd Chatham NY 12037-2214

NOZKOWSKI, THOMAS
PAINTER
b Teaneck, NJ, 44. *Exhib:* Solo shows include Max Protetch Gallery, NY City, 90, 91, 93, 95, 97, 2000, 2001, 2003,; group shows include From Earth to Archetype, Ledisflam Gallery, NY, 90; 10 Abstract Painters, Baumgartner Galleries, Washington, 91; Shades of Difference, Sandra Gering Gallery, NY City, 92; Return of the Cadavre Exquis, The Drawing Ctr, NY City, 93; A Hundred Hearts, The Contemp, NY City, 94; Re-Picturing Abstraction, 1708 Gallery, Richmond, Va, 95; New Narrative Abstraction, Brooklyn Col, 96; Purely Painting, Elizabeth Harris Gallery, NY City, 97; Pertaining to Painting, Contemp Arts Mus, Houston, 2002; group shows include Michael Berger Gallery, Pitts, 2003; Nat Acad Mus, NY City, 2006; represented in public collections of Whitney Mus Am Art, NY City, San Francisco Mus Modern Art, Orlando Mus Art, Fla, Mus Modern Art, NY City, Metrop Mus Art, Hirshhorn Mus and Sculpture Garden, Washington, DC, High Mus Art, Atlanta, Corcoran Gallery Art, Washington, DC, Brooklyn Mus Art. *Teaching:* Assoc prof Mason Gross Sch Arts, Rutgers Univ, NJ, 2000-. *Awards:* Purchase Prize, Am Acad Arts and Letters, 98, 99; Am Acad Arts and Letters Award in Painting, 99; Individual Artist Grant, Nat Endowment Arts, 84; NY State Creative Artists Public Serv Grant, 85; NY State Found Arts Fellowship, 89; John Simon Guggeheim Memorial Found Fellowship, 93. *Mailing Add:* c/o Max Protetch Gallery 511 W 22nd St New York NY 10011

NUCHI, NATAN
PAINTER, PRINTMAKER
b Nahalal, Israel, Feb 8, 51; US & Israeli citizen. *Study:* Self educated. *Work:* Jewish Mus, NY; Mus RI Sch Design; Nat Jewish Mus, Washington; Haifa Munic Mus Mod Art, Israel; Israel Mus, Jerusalem. *Exhib:* One-man shows, Haifa Mus Mod Art, Israel, 93, Nat Jewish Mus, Washington, 95 & Digital Drawings, Ramat Gan Mus Israeli Art, 97; Acquisitions, RI Sch Design, Providence, 94; After Auschwitz: Responses to the Holocaust in Contemp Art, Royal Festival Hall, London, Manchester City Art Gallery, United Kingdom, 95-96; Windows: Seven Subjects in Contemp Art, Israel Mus, Jerusalem, 96. *Bibliog:* Donald Kuspit (auth), The Abandoned Nude, Klarfeld Perry, 92; Gerrit Henry (auth), Review one-man show, Art in Am, 93; Matthew Baigell (auth), The Persistence of Holocaust Imagery in American Art, Minn Art Mus, 95 & Jewish American Artists and the Holocaust, Rutgers Univ Press, 97. *Mailing Add:* 5 E 3rd St New York NY 10003

NUGENT, BOB L
PAINTER, PRINTMAKER
b Santa Monica, Calif, Aug 15, 47. *Study:* Col Creative Studies, Univ Calif, BA, 69; Univ Calif, Santa Barbara, MFA, 71. *Work:* Bank Am Headquarters, San Francisco, Calif; Washington State Art in Public Places, Spokane; Indianapolis Mus Art, Ind; Ariz State Univ, Tempe; Brooklyn Mus, NY; Oakland Mus Art; Philadelphia Mus Art; Mus Art Sao Paulo. *Comn:* Hyatt Hotel, Phoenix, Ariz, 99; Westin Hotel, Indianapolis, Ind, 99. *Exhib:* One-man shows, Antiscope, Brussels, Belgium, 79, Kathryn Markel Fine Arts, NY, 80, Los Angeles Munic Art Gallery, Calif, 80 & Tucson Mus Art, Ariz, 81, Dan Galleria, Sao Paulo, Brazil, 99, Robert Kidd Gallery, Birmingham, Mich, 2000; Paper Art, Smithsonian Inst, Washington DC, 80; Painting & Sculpture Today, Indianapolis Mus Art, Ind, 80. *Collection Arranged:* California Collage (auth, catalog), 81; California Clay (auth, catalog), 81; Sculpture 82 (auth, catalog); Chicago Abstract Painting (auth, catalog). *Teaching:* Prof art painting, Pepperdine Univ, Calif, 73; prof art painting, Col Siskiyavs, Calif, 73-81; prof art, Sonoma State Univ, Rohnert Park, Calif, 81-2005; prof emeritus, Sonoma State Univ, 2005. *Awards:* Individual Artists Fel, Nat Endowment Arts, 79; Fulbright Travel Grant to Brazil, 86; Fel, Calif Arts Coun Artist, 90; Gourmand Award, 2005. *Media:* Mixed. *Publ:* Contribr, Paper Art, E B Crocker Art Mus, 80; auth, Imagery Art for Wine, Wine Appreciation Guild, San Francisco, Calif, 2005. *Dealer:* Elins Eagle Smith San Francisco Calif; Cumberland Gallery Nashville Tenn. *Mailing Add:* 5115 Middlebrook Ct Santa Rosa CA 95404-1959

NUNN, ANCEL E
PAINTER, PRINTMAKER
b Seymour, Tex, Apr 27, 28. *Work:* Univ Tex, Austin; Tyler Mus Art, Tex; Tex A&M Univ, Col Station; Baylor Univ, Fine Arts Ctr, Waco, Tex; E Tex Mus, Lufkin. *Exhib:* Fire, Contemp Arts Mus, Houston, 79; Making of a Lithograph, Mus E Tex, Lufkin, 83; Carousel Fantasia, Mich State Univ Mus, E Lansing, 86; The McDonald Collection, Mus Abilene, Tex, 92. *Bibliog:* Bob Bowman (auth), The Best of East Texas, Lufkin Printing Co, 79; Smithsonian, Texas Project, Archives Am Art J, 84. *Media:* Acrylic; Pencil. *Mailing Add:* c/o Gerhard Wurzer Gallery 1217 S Shepherd Houston TX 77019

NUNNELLEY, ROBERT B
PAINTER
b Birmingham, Ala, Sept 5, 29. *Study:* Univ Ark, BA(art), 51, with David Smith, MFA(painting), 56; Boston Mus Sch, with Karl Zerbe & David Aronson, 51-52; Colo Springs Fine Arts Ctr, with Robert Motherwell, 54. *Work:* Rockhill Nelson Gallery, Kansas City, Mo; Des Moines Art Ctr, Iowa; Meml Sloan-Kettering Cancer Ctr; pvt collections. *Exhib:* Solo exhibs, Hudson River Mus, Yonkers, 67 & Schenectady Mus, NY, 79, Rensselaer Co Coun Arts, NY, 80, Fairleigh Dickinson Univ, Madison, 82, Besides Myself Gallery, Arlington, 83 & 88, Univ Col Gallery, Jeaneck, 94 & Blue Mountain Gallery, NY, 97, Gallery 668, Battenville, NY, 2000 & 2003; Focus on the Arts, Bergen Community Mus, Paramus, NJ, 82; Nat Competion 2 Dimensional Work, Bowery Gallery, NY, 91; Nat Drawing, Newark Mus, Trenton State Col, NJ, 92; The Contemp Am Landscape, Yale Univ Art Gallery & Erector Square Gallery, New Haven, Conn, 92; Works on Paper, Fairleigh Dickinson Univ Col Gallery, Teaneck, San Jacinto Col S, Houston & The Drawing Ctr, NY, 93. *Pos:* Dir, Maples Gallery, Farleigh Dickinson Univ, Teaneck, NJ, 82-87. *Teaching:* Prof painting-drawing-design, Fairleigh Dickinson Univ, Teaneck, NJ, 66-95. *Awards:* Purchase Award, Mid-Am Col Art Asn, 55; Research Grant, Fairleigh Dickinson Univ, 67 & 77; Prize, Nat Competition Works on Paper, San Jacinto Col South, 93. *Mem:* Nat Asn Sch of Art & Design; Col Art Asn. *Media:* Oil. *Specialty:* Still Life and Landscape. *Interests:* Reading, 18th Century Am Furniture. *Publ:* Rev, Arts News, 3/57 & 10/59; France-Amerique, 10/59; Arts Mag, 9/59 & 1/68. *Dealer:* Solange Herter Greenwich NY 12834. *Mailing Add:* 2850 State Route 29 Greenwich NY 12834

NUSS, JOANNE RUTH
SCULPTOR, PAINTER
b Great Bend, Kans, May 2, 51. *Study:* Studied Univ Kans, 72-73, Univ Copenhagen, Denmark, 74; Ft Hays State Univ, Kans, BA, 75; studied with The Henry Moore Found, 80; Santa Fe Inst Fine Arts, M, 91; special study with world renowned sculptor Beverly Pepper. *Work:* The Am Legation Mus, Tangiers, Morocco; The Univ Gallery, Ft Hays State Univ, Kans; The Lawrence Arnott Art Gallery, Tangiers, Moroco; The Royal Train, King Hassan of Morocco, Rabat; The Royal Palace, The Prince of Borneo, Brunei; many other pvt collections in the US, Europe, Morocco & Malaysia, 84-. *Comn:* bronze sculpture, Sherman Dreiszun Develop, Inc, Overland Oark, Kans, 83; bronze sculpture, The Royal Palace, Brunei, 85; painting, Mimoun Mokhtar, Morocco, 88-90. *Exhib:* Mid-West Regional Artist, Spiva Art Ctr, Joplin, Mo, 81; North Am Sculpture Show, Art Ctr Gallery, Golden, Colo, 84; Joanne Nuss: Bronze Sculptures, Univ Gallery Ft Hays State Univ, Kan, 85, Agora Gallery, NY, 2001; Joanne Nuss: Sculpture in Bronze, Inma Gallery, Saudi Arabia, 94; Gallery Artists, Shidoni Gallery, Tesuque, NMex, 99, 2000; Influences, The Birger Sandzen Meml Gallery, Kans, 2000; Attleboro Mus, Attleboro, Mass, 2002; Laboratorio del Galileo restaurant, DC, 2002; Jeanette Hare Art Gallery, West Palm Beach, Fla, 2002; 12th Ann Benefit Auction, Attleboro Mus, Mass, 2002; Amsterdam-Whitney Int Fine Art Inc, NY, 2003; 114th Ann Exhib, Nat Asn Women Artists, Fifth Ave Gallery, NY, 2003; Attleboro Mus, Mass, 2003; Baker Arts Ctr, 7th Nat Juried Art Exhib, 2004; Carolina Exhibs, McDowell Arts and Crafts Asn; Shelby Arts, Ashe Co Arts, 2004-05; Ann All Media Int Juried Online Exhib, Upstream People Gallery, Omaha, 2005-06. *Teaching:* instr drawing, Nelson-Atkins Mus, Kansas City, Mo, 79-81; lectr, instr Brookside Elem Sch, 81-82; lectr, Barton County Community Col, Great Bend, Kans, 84; lectr, Nelson-Atkins Mus, Kansas City, Mo, 84. *Awards:* 3-D Work Award, Kans Artist Craftsmen Asn, Wichita, Kans, 83; Artist in Residence Grant, The Helene Wurlitzer Found, Taos, NM, 84 & 90; Purchase Award, Kans Profl Artists Collection, Ft Hays, 85; First Place, cash award, Univ Northern Iowa, Cedar Falls, Iowa, 2001; Excellence Cash Award, Period Gallery, Omaha, Nebr, 2002; Award of Excellence, 7th Ann All Media Internat Juried Online Exhib, Upstream People Gallery, Omaha, 2004; Int Visual Artist Year, Int Biographical Ctr, Cambridge, Eng, 2005; Women Achievement Award, Am Biographical Inst, Raleigh, NC, 2006. *Bibliog:* Jennifer Schartz (auth), Bronze Work Shown First In Hometown, Great Bend Tribune, Kans, 4/4/80; Rick Dunway (auth), Artists Gets Her Chance With Borneo Commision, The Hutchinson News, Kans, 3/25/85; Alexander McCormick (auth), Joanne Nuss, ArtisSpectrum Magazine, Agora Gallery, New York, Vol 8, 2001. *Mem:* Nat Asn Women Artists; Nat Sculpture Soc; Internat Sculpture Ctr; Nat Mus Women in Arts;

Am Craft Coun; NMex Women in Arts; Kans Sculptors Asn. *Media:* Bronze, Stone. *Interests:* Working with other artists, creating a sculpture garden. *Publ:* Louisa Abernathy (auth), Kansas City's Single Professionals: Woman and Men, Sher, Jones, Shear & Assocs, 81; Glenn B Optiz (auth), Dictionary of American Sculptors 18th Century to the Present, Apollo Book, 84; Philip Martin (auth), Artists Working in Morocco/BBC Radio Network, London, 86. *Dealer:* Amsterdam Whitney International Fine Art Inc New York NY; The Lawrence-Arnott Art Gallery, Tangiers & Marrakech, Morocco. *Mailing Add:* 152 E Lupita Rd Santa Fe NM 87505

NUTT, CRAIG
CRAFTSMAN, SCULPTOR
b Belmond, Iowa, Apr 13, 50. *Study:* Univ Ala, BA, 72. *Work:* Birmingham Mus Art; Mobile Mus Art; High Mus Art; Huntsville Mus Art; Hawaii State Found Cult & Arts; Renwick Gallery, Smithsonian's Am Art Mus; Corcoran Gallery Art; Tenn State Mus; Columbus Mus, GA. *Comn:* Many comns for pvt collections; sculpture, Schering-Plough Corp, 93; sculpture, Birmingham Int Airport, 93; Hartsfield Atlanta Int Airport. *Exhib:* Solo exhibs, Dinosaurs & Flying Vegetables, Kentuck Mus, Northport, Ala, 87, Huntsville Mus Art, 89, Meredith Gallery, Baltimore, 93, Southeastern La Univ, Hammond, 94 & 95 & Univ N Ala Art Gallery, Florence, 97; Red Clay Survey, Huntsville Mus Art, 88; Nat Objects Invitational, Ark Arts Ctr, Little Rock, 89; Focus: Four Alabama Artists, Birmingham Mus Art, 90; Signs of Support: Furniture Forms in Contemp Am Art, Kohler Arts Ctr, Sheboygan, Wis, 90; Contemp Works in Wood, Southern Style, Huntsville Mus Art, 90; Artists, Archits & Designers: Furniture of our Century High Mus Art, Atlanta, Ga, 92; Seeds of Change, Smithsonian Inst, 91; Contemp Crafts: The National Scene, Ky Art & Craft Found, 93; Please be Seated: Masters of the Art of Seating, Flagler Mus, Palm Beach, Fla, 95; Alabama Impact, Mobile Mus Art & Huntsville Mus Art, 95; On the Surface: The Spirit Revealed, Am Craft Coun SE Region Conf, Louisville, Ky, 96; Craig Nutt: Furniture With a Flair, Huntsville, Ala, 97; By Heart and Hand: Collecting Southern Decorative Arts, Art Mus WVa, Roanoke, 98; Craig Nutt: Furniture & Sculpture, Joan Derryberry Art Gallery, Tenn Tech Univ, Cookeville, Tenn, 99; Studio Furniture: A Fine Art Invitational, Memphis, Coll Art, Tenn, 2000; Objects for Use: Handmade by Design, Am Craft Mus, New York City, 2002; Studio Art Furniture Invitational, Ark Art Ctr, Little Rock, 2002; Southeastern Craft Innovations, Knoxville Mus Art, Tenn, 2002; Materials & Contemp Illusions: Innovations in Lathe Turning, Brookfield Craft Ctr, Conn, 2002; Wood Turning Ctr, 2001; Yale Univ Art Gallery, 2001, 02; Minneapolis Institute Art, 2001; Renwick Gallery, 2001. *Pos:* Artist-in-residence, Appalachian Ctr Crafts, Smithville, Tenn, 97-98; artist lectr, Univ N Ala, Florence, 97; bd trustees, Furniture Soc, 97-, chmn, Web Site Comt 96- & Steering Comt, 96-97, fin coord, 99. *Teaching:* guest lectr, SUNY, NY, 2000. *Awards:* Gov Art Award, Ala State Coun Arts, 85, fel, 88 & 95; Nat Endowment Arts Fel, 89; Tenn State Arts Com Fel, 98; Alumnus Arts Award, Univ Ala, 97. *Bibliog:* Craig Nutt (auth), article in Am Craft, 87 & From furniture to flying vegetables, Southern Accents Mag, 88; Craig Nutt: Combining Humor and a Bit of Cayenne, Fine Woodworking, 91. *Mem:* Ala Crafts Coun (trustee, 80-86); Am Craft Coun, SE Region (bd dir, 82-89). *Media:* Wood. *Publ:* Auth, Lathe turned, woodturners gather at Arrowmont, Am Craft, 86; A partnership, The Guild, 87; Ed, Spotlight 88, SE/SW Crafts Exhib Catalog, Am Craft Coun, SE Region, 88; Turners in Texas, Am Craft, 91; auth, Craft and ethics, Am Craft, 94, Keyboard Instruments by Anden Houben, 98. *Mailing Add:* 1305 Kingston Springs Rd Kingston Springs TN 37082-9282

NUTT, JIM
PAINTER, DRAFTSMAN
b Pittsfield, Mass, Nov 28, 38. *Study:* Wash Univ, St Louis, 58-59; Art Inst Chicgo, with Whitney Halstead & Dominic DiMeo, dipl, 65. *Work:* Whitney Mus Am Art, Mus Mod Art, Metrop Mus Art, NY; Mus Contemp Art, Chicago; Mus Mod Kunst, Vienna; High Mus, Atlanta, Ga; Philadelphia Mus Art; Scotish Nat Mus, Glasgow; Hirshhorn Gallery/Mus, Washington, DC; Mem Art Gallery, Univ Rochester, NY. *Exhib:* Am Exhib, Art Inst Chicago, 72 & 76 (group); solo exhibs, Phyllis Kind Gallery, Chicago, 82, 85 & 91, Phyllis Kind Gallery, NY, 80, 84, 88, 91, Galerie Bonnier, Geneva, Switz, 92, Mus Contemp Art, Chicago, 99 & Nolan Eckman Gallery, NY, 99, Nolan/Eckman Gallery, NY, 2003; 39th Biennial Exhib Contemp Am Painting, Corcoran Gallery Art, 85; Word As Image: Am Art 1960-1990, Milwaukee Art Mus(solo), Wis & traveling to Oklahoma City Art Mus & Houston, 90-91; Parallel Visions: Modern Artists & Outsider Art, Los Angeles Co Mus Art traveling to Madrid & Tokyo, 92-93; From America's Studio: Twelve Contemp Masters, Art Inst Chicago, 92; traveling exhib, Milwaukee Art Ctr, Henry Art Gallery, Seattle, Mus Am Art, Washington & Contemp Art Ctr, Cincinnati, 94-95; Printmaking in Am, Collaborative Prints & Presses 1960-1990 (traveling), incl Mus Fine Arts Houston, 95-96; Am Acad Invitational Exhib Painting & Sculpture, NY, 96; Second Sight: Printmaking in Chicago 1935-1995, Northwestern Univ, 96; Art in Chicago 1945-1995, Mus Contemp Art, Chicago, 96; solo exhibs, Mus Contemp Art, Chicago, Ill & Nolan Eckman Gallery, NY, 99; 117th Ann, Nat Acad of Design, NY, 2002. *Teaching:* Assoc prof painting & drawing, Calif State Univ, Sacramento, 68-75; adj assoc prof, Sch Art Inst Chicago, 90-. *Awards:* Nat Endowment Arts Grant, 89; Acuff Chair Excellence, Austin Peay State Univ, Clarksville, Tenn, 94; Acad Award in Art, Am Acad Arts & Lett, New York, 96. *Bibliog:* Russell Bowman (auth), Jim Nutt (exhib catalog), Rotterdam Kunststichting Lijnbaan Centrum, 80; John Yau (auth), Jim Nutt: Recent Works, Mayor Gallery, London, Eng; Russell Bowman, Linda Hartigan & Robert Storr (auths), Jim Nutt (exhib catalog), Milwaukee Art Mus, 94. *Dealer:* Nolan/Eckman Gallery 560 Broadway New York NY. *Mailing Add:* 1035 Greenwood Ave Wilmette IL 60091

NUTZLE, FUTZIE (BRUCE) JOHN KLEINSMITH
CARTOONIST, PAINTER
b Lakewood, Ohio, Feb 21, 42. *Study:* Self-taught. *Work:* Mus Mod Art, NY; San Francisco Mus Mod Art; Oakland Mus, Calif; Santa Cruz City Mus, Calif; Whitney Mus Am Art, NY. *Exhib:* Corresp Sch Art, Whitney Mus, NY, 70; Empty Canoes, Lithographs, San Francisco Mus Mod Art, 72; Opening, Santa Cruz Artists' Mus Proj, 73; Twin Rocker Paper Exhib, Indianapolis Mus Art, Ind, 75; Laica, Los Angeles, 78; one-man shows, Santa Barbara Mus Art, 80; Univ Col Santa Cruz, Retrospective, 90; Prague Eco-Fair, 91. *Teaching:* Artist-in-residence, Victor Valley Col, 83; instr, adult classes, cartooning & drawing, Art Sch Santa Cruz, fall, 88. *Bibliog:* My art belongs to Dada, Esquire Mag, 8/74; feature article, Quest, 6/79. *Media:* Pen and Ink, Wash on Paper; Oil on Canvas. *Publ:* Contribr, Balloon Newspaper, 68-72, Rolling Stone, 75-80, Quarry West, 77 & San Francisco Bay Guardian, 81-83; Japan Times/current; auth, Modern Loafer (cartoons & drawings) Thames & Hudson, Inc, 81; Futzie Nutzle, Jazz Press, 83; Run the World: 50 cents, Chronicle Bks, 91; Bob Brozman, Devil's Slide, Rounder Records; Twenty-Fifth Int Salon of Cartoons, 88; Int Pavilion of Humour, Man and His World, Montreal, Can. *Dealer:* Fools Gold 34A Polk St San Juan Bautista CA 95045. *Mailing Add:* PO Box 325 Aromas CA 95004

NYAMBI, OBAJI A
PAINTER, PRINTMAKER
b Ikom, Nigeria, Mar 6, 60. *Study:* Okla Univ, BFA(graphic design), 84; Sch Art Inst Chicago, MFA (printmaking & drawing), 87. *Work:* McCormick Place, Chicago Expo & Conv Ctr; Chicago Mag; Fred Jones Art Ctr, Okla Univ; SAP Am; Cosmopolitan Bank, Chicago; and several pvt collections. *Comn:* Hyatt Develop Corp; Mr & Mrs L Piannetto (painting), Chicago; Lettuce Entertain You Inc, Chicago. *Exhib:* Portraits, Fed Reserve Bank Chicago, 93; Chicago Ill Mid West Pastel Soc Ann Exhib, James Thompson Art Ctr, 94; Chop Marks, Morain Valley Community Col Fine & Performing Art Ctr, Palos Hills, Ill, 94; Go Figure, Chicago, Printmakers Collab, 94; Anchor Graphics, Chicago, Ill, 94; Naked Truths (figure representations), Univ Hawaii Art Gallery, Honolulu, 96; The African Am Presence at the Sch, Gallery 2, Art Inst Chicago, 96; Satori Fine Art Gallery, 97 & 98; Designer Show Vol 2, Beret Int Gallery, Chicago, 97; Chicago Printmakers Collab, Mars Gallery, 97; Satori Fine Art Gallery, Chicago, 98; Around the World, Pentimenti Gallery, Philadelphia, 98; Flash of Spirit (traveling), Libreria Pegaso en Casa Lamm, Mexico City, & Del Centro Cult del Nigromante, SMA, Gto, Mex, 98; John G Blank Ctr for Arts, 2001 (group); Geoscapes, Union League Club, Chicago, 2000 (solo); Obaji Nyambi at Guild Complex, 1999. *Collection Arranged:* Hyatt Dev Corp, Chicago; S.A.P. Am Corp; Planet Grp, Chicago; Estacion Internet of SMA, Gto, Mexico; McCormick Conv Comp Art Coll; Metro Pier and Expo Auth, Chicago; Cosmo Bank, Chicago. *Pos:* Pub art adv panelist, Chicago Pub Art Prog, 93-94; mus tech, art installation & Asian art dept, Art Inst Chicago Mus, 96-97; dir, Pi Gallery, Chicago, 98. *Teaching:* Vis artist, Okla Univ, 87, Am Acad Fine Art, Chicago, 92 & Governor's State Univ, University Park, Ill, 92; instr life drawing, Near North West Arts Coun, Chicago, Ill, 92; vis artist & instr, Sch Art Inst Chicago, 93-95; pvt instr lithography, Chicago PrintMakers Collab, 94. *Awards:* Artist Fel Grant in Visual Arts, Nat Endowment Arts, 93; Award of Distinction, Mid West Pastel Soc, 94; Artist Fel Grant, State Ill Arts Coun, 94; Artist Fel Grant, Readers Digest Fund for Artist at Giverny, 1995. *Bibliog:* Mitchell Stevens (auth), Myth & decay, Chicago Reader, 5/92; Road to Morocco, Tribune Mag, 10/95; Leatha S Mitchel (auth), FreshPaint, rev, Int Rev African Am Art, winter 97. *Mem:* Col Art Asn Am; Near North West Arts Coun; Chicago Printmakers Collab; Hyde Park Arts Ctr; Chicago Artists' Coalition. *Dealer:* Pentiment Gallery

NYDORF, ROY HERMAN
PAINTER, PRINTMAKER
b Port Washington, NY, Oct 1, 52. *Study:* Art Students League NY, 69; State Univ NY, Brockport, with Robert Marx, BA, 74; Yale Univ Sch Art, with Peterdi, Bailey & Johnson, MFA, 76. *Work:* Hirshhorn Mus & Sculpture Garden & Smithsonian Am Art Mus, Washington; Honolulu Acad Art, Hawaii; Weatherspoon Art Mus, Greensboro, NC; Yale Art Gallery, New Haven, Conn; Nelson Atkins Mus Art, Kansas City, Mo; Huntsville Mus Art, Ala; Georgetown Univ, Washington, DC; Ark State Univ, Ark. *Comn:* Wall mural, comn by Garret Trudeau, New Haven, Conn, 77; portrait pres, Guilford Col, Greensboro, NC, 81; etchings, NC Nat Bank, Charlotte, 87; etchings, United Arts Coun Greensboro, NC, 87; pres portrait, Guilford Col, Greensboro, NC, 96. *Exhib:* 27th Bradley Nat Print & Drawing Exhib, Bradley Univ, Peoria, Ill, 98; Red Clay Survey: Biennial Exhib of Contemp Southern Art, Huntsville Mus Art, Al, 98; About Memory: A Selection of 20th Century Portraits, Ball State Univ Mus, Munice, Ind, 97; Pablo Picasso: Homage to a Modern Icon, Fraser gallery, Washington, DC, 98; Roy Nydorf: Painted Realms, Christel De Haan Fine Arts Ctr, Univ Indianapolis, Ind, 99; Monothon, SITE Sante Fe, 2001; Lean on Me, Wharton Eshrick Mus, Pa, 2001; Celebrating the Legacy of Romare Bearden, Mint Mus of Art, Charlotte, NC, 2002; Roy Nydorf & Turner McGehee, Haydon Gallery, Lincoln, Nebr, 2002; Art on Paper, Maryland Federation of Art, Annapolis, MD, 2004; solo exhib, Gallery, 55, Natick, MA, 2005. *Teaching:* Instr design, Univ New Haven, Conn, 77; asst prof art & art hist, Guilford Col, Greensboro, NC, 78-86, assoc prof, 86-96, prof, 96-, chmn, Art Dept, 83-85 & 88-91, 96-99. *Awards:* Robert Donaldson Award for drawing, Govs Bus Coun Arts & Humanities, Raleigh, NC, 95; Purchase Award, Delta Nat Small Print Exhib, 96; ARText 98 Best in Show, Asn Artists Winston-Salem, NC, 98; and others. *Bibliog:* Tom Patterson (auth), South Passion for Racing Gets Artistic, Atlanta J Constitution, 9/6/99; Lisa Skeen (auth), Roy Nydork, Living the Art, Northwest Observer, 11/16/01; Cathy Gant-Hill (auth), Paperwork, Greensboro News & Record, 11/22/02. *Mem:* Southeastern Ctr Contemp Art; Green Hill Ctr NC Art; Southern Graphics Coun. *Media:* Oils, Gouache; Etching, Monotype. *Dealer:* Somerhill Gallery 5504 Chapel Hill Blvd Durham NC 27707. *Mailing Add:* 1815 Oak Ridge Rd Oak Ridge NC 27310

NYERGES, ALEXANDER LEE
MUSEUM DIRECTOR, HISTORIAN
b Feb 27, 1957. *Study:* George Washington Univ, BA(Am studies & anthrop), 79, MA(mus studies), 81. *Exhib:* auth, In Praise of Nature, (catalog) 99. *Collection Arranged:* Southeastern Watercolorist I-III (auth, catalogs), 83-85 & Piranesi: 18th Century Etchings (ed, catalog), 84, DeLand Mus Art, Fla; Collector's Choice 1985 & French and American Impressionism 1855-1912, 85, The American Landscape 1850-1910, 86, Miss Mus Art, Jackson; Norman Rockwell: The Great American Story teller, 88. *Pos:* Exec dir, Deland Mus Art, Fla, 81-85 & Miss Mus Art, Jackson, 85-92; southeast regional rep, non-print media comt, Am Asn Mus, 83-85, legislative comt, 86-; dir & chief exec officer, Dayton Art Inst, Ohio, from 92; dir, Virginia Mus Fine Art, 2006-. *Awards:* Phi Beta Kappa, 79. *Mem:* Miss Inst Arts & Letts (bd trustee); Southeast Mus Conf (bd trustee); Art Mus Asn Am (regional rep); Am Asn Mus; Asn Am Govt Affairs Comt; Asn Art Mus Dirs; and others. *Res:* South American, Pre-Columbian Art; Photography; American & European 20th Century Photography. *Publ:* The Ages of Mexico (exhib catalog), DeLand Mus Art, No 4, 83; auth, In Praise of Nature: Ansel Adams and Photographers of the Am West (catalog), 99; Pre Columbian Treasures, 2003, Edward Weston; A Photogr's Love of Life, 2004; A Photographers Love of Life, 2004-05, Edward Weston. *Mailing Add:* Virginia Mus Fine Arts 200 North Boulevard Richmond VA 23220

NYMAN , GEORGIANNA BEATRICE ARONSON
PAINTER
b Arlington, Mass, June 11, 30. *Study:* Boston Mus Fine Arts Sch, study with David Aronson & Karl Zerbe, dipl, 52, cert, 54; Longy Sch Mus, 65-75; McClosky Voice Inst, 75-81; Boston Acad Mus, with Richard Conrad, 91-95. *Work:* Rose Art Mus, Brandeis Univ, Waltham, Mass; New Eng Sch Law, Boston, Mass; Sch Med, Univ Pittsburgh; Milton Acad, Mass; US Supreme Court; State House, RI. *Comn:* portrait, Justice Sandra Day O'Connor, New Eng Sch Law, 91; portrait, Justice Harry Blackmunn, New Eng Sch Law, 93; portrait, Justice Clarence Thomas, New Eng Sch Law, 96; portrait, Anthony Kennedy, New Eng Sch Law, 2005; portrait, Justice Antonin Scalia, New Eng Sch Law, 2006; portrait, Justice Anthony B Kennedy, New Eng Sch Law, 2005. *Exhib:* Boston Arts Festival And Juried Exhibs, 54 & 61; Shore Studio Galleries, Boston, 63; Group Show, Lee Nordness Galleries, NY, 65; Nat Acad Design, NY, 90; solo exhib, Nancy Lincoln Gallery, Chestnut Hill, Mass, 90; group show, Alter & Gil Galleries, Beverly Hills, Calif, 99. *Teaching:* Instr drawing & painting, Boston Ctr Adult Educ, 52-54; instr painting, Boston Univ Sch Continuing Educ, 58-59. *Awards:* Boit Prize, Boston Mus Sch, 51; Kate Morse Prize, Boston Mus Fine Arts, 53; Cert Merit, Nat Acad Design, NY, 92; Medal for Excellence, awarded by Advutant Gen of RI, 2003. *Bibliog:* Darlene Arden (dir), Creatively Speaking (film). *Mem:* Boston Acad Music; life mem Women's Indust Inst. *Media:* Pastel, Oil. *Specialty:* fine art, painting, portraiture, sculpture, drawing. *Publ:* Contribr, Native Island (Gerta Kennedy), Houghton-Mifflin, 56; Art of Karl Zerbe (film), 88. *Dealer:* Galerie Yorem Gil 319 No Canon Dr Beverly Hills CA 90210; Pucker Gallery 171 Newbury St Boston MA 02116. *Mailing Add:* 137 Brimstone Ln Sudbury MA 01776

NYREN, EDWARD A
PAINTER
b Boston, Mass. *Study:* Boston Mus Fine Arts Sch; Art Students League; Frank Reilly Sch, NY. *Work:* Reader's Digest Asn Inc, NY; Lynden Air Freight, Seattle; Key Bank, Seattle; Rainier Bank, Seattle; Shawmut Bank, Boston; Raymond James Financial, Inc, St Petersburg, Fla. *Exhib:* NJ Watercolor Soc, Morris Mus Arts & Sci, 70; Conn Watercolor Soc, Wadsworth Atheneum, 72; Grand Nat, Am Artists Prof League, 73, 79, 80, & 81; one-man show, Newport Art Mus, RI, 81; Major Fla Artists Show, Foster-Harmon Galleries Am Art, Sarasota, Fla, 90; Art Encounter State Competition, Naples Art Asn, Fla, 90; Fla Artists Group, Mus Arts & Sci, Daytona, Fla, 94; Uncommon Ground, Pinellas Co Art Coun, Fla, 99; Nat Park Acad Arts, 2001. *Awards:* Second Prize (aquamedia), Art Encounter State Competition, Naples, Fla, 90; Best in Category (pastel), Sarasota Visual Arts Asn, Fla, 96; Purchase Award, Univ South Fla, 2001; and others. *Bibliog:* Edward J Sozanski (auth), Masculine hand led by mind with vision, Providence J, 81; Chuck Twardy (auth), Nyren's pastels, richly done and highly appealing, Orlando Sentinel, 12/16/90; Mary Ann Marger (auth), Art by Mellow Masters, St Petersburg Times, 9/30/94; and others. *Media:* Pastel, Watercolor. *Mailing Add:* PO Box 22784 Saint Petersburg FL 33742-2784

O

OAKES, JOHN WARREN
EDUCATOR, PAINTER
b Bowling Green, Ky, Feb 26, 41. *Study:* Art Instr Sch Minneapolis; Art Students League, New York, Albert Dorne Scholar; Western Area Voc Sch; Western Ky Univ, AB, 64; Univ Iowa, MA, 66, MFA, 73; Harvard Univ, cert arts admin, 75. *Work:* Numerous works in pub and pvt collections in AL, CA, CO, FL, GA, IN, IA, IL, Ky, MA, ME, MD, MI, MS, NV, NJ, NY, NH, SD,TN, TX, VA, England, Ireland, Japan, Romania, Belgium, Australia, Brazil, Canada, Germany, Turkey, Czechoslovakia, Italy, Netherlands, Norway, Poland, Spain, West Indies. *Exhib:* Forty solo exhibs. *Pos:* Gallery dir, Western Ky Univ Gallery, 66-85, staff asst, off dean, Potter Col Arts & Humanities, 73-75, asst dean admin, 75-85. *Teaching:* Instr art, Western Ky Univ, 66-71, asst prof art, 71-76, assoc prof art, 76-87, prof art, 87-. *Bibliog:* Joseph G Rosa (auth), The West of Wild Bill Hickok, Daily News 6/82 & Univ Okla Press, 83. *Mem:* Ky Arts Admin (pres, 82-83); Ky Citizens for Arts; Southern Ky Photog Soc (pres, 86-89); Kappa Pi. *Media:* Painting, Computer Graphics. *Res:* Influences of Pablo Picasso's work that have been overlooked; minimum aperture photography; The Role of Gender in art production and criticism. *Publ:* Auth, Camera Blending, Instant Projects, Polaroid Corp Publ, 86; Photography Using Pinhole Cameras, Univ Press of Am, 86; Action Amiga: Computer Graphics, Animation and Video Production, Univ Press of Am, 88; Art by Computer, Acorn Press, 90; contribr, Electronic Art Lab Manual, Acorn Press, 98; Kentucky Women Artists 1850-1970 pub in Arts Across Kentucky, 2001; Catalog Contribor Kentucky Women artists 1850-1970 Owensboro Art Mus KY 2002; auth, The Servicemen's Readjustment Act of 1944: How it Affected the Education of Women Artists, Int Jour Vis Culture & Gender, 2006. *Dealer:* Capitol Arts Ctr Main St Bowling Green KY 42101. *Mailing Add:* 1315 Lois Ln Bowling Green KY 42104-4673

OAKES, WILLIAM LARRY
PAINTER, SCULPTOR
b Richmond, Va, Apr 16, 44. *Study:* Univ Md, 69-70; Cornish Sch Allied Art, 64-65; Burnly Sch Art, 65-67; Univ Mass, MA, 84-88. *Work:* US Navy Fine Art Collection, US Info Agency & Libr Cong, Washington, DC; Franklin Mint, NY; US Naval Acad, Annapolis, Md. *Comn:* Portrait, Secy of Navy, US Naval Mus, Washington, DC, 69; Court Art, Watergate Hearings, Washington Post, ABC News, Nat Geographic & Christian Sci Monitor, Washington, DC & Boston, 74. *Exhib:* Imaginations, Corcoran Gallery Art, DC, 71; Naval Hist, Navy Mus, DC, 71; Illusr 13, traveled, NY, 72 & Art Dirs' Show 50, 72; Combat Art, Salmagundi Gallery, NY, 72; Painter as Illusr, Old Town Hall Gallery, Salem, Mass, 79-80; The Power of a Tiny Light, Newburyport Cult Ctr, 92. *Teaching:* Instr art, Comt for Community Improvement, Washington, DC, 68-71; instr drawing & painting, pvt classes, Washington, DC & Boston, 71-76; dean freshman found & illus, New Eng Sch Art & Design, 76-80; instr, Art Inst Boston, 80-. *Awards:* Scholar Award, Salmagundi Club, New York, 70; Award of Merit, Soc Illusr, New York, 71; Award of Excellence, Art Dirs Club, New York, 71. *Bibliog:* Peggy Thompson (auth), Pick a dot, Am Mag, 72; David Windor (auth), Morocco: A visual documentary by Bill Oakes, Christian Sci Monitor, 78; David Wiegand, (auth), Bill Oakes, Illustrator Extraordinaire, Divisions, 79. *Mem:* Soc Children's Bk Writers. *Media:* All. *Publ:* Auth, The Lesson Sketcher, 78, Imagination 2, Cowleybinder, 80 & Art by Design, 81, Acorn Press; illusr, Sound and the Fury, by Faulkner, 77 & The Plays of Shakespeare, 78-79, Franklin Libr; Numblers, 88, Dial Books 88 & 89, Puzzlers, 89 & Once Upon Another Dial Books, 90. *Dealer:* Intuit Art Gallery 861 Lafayette Rd Hampton NH 03842. *Mailing Add:* 861 Lafayette Rd Unit No 7 Hampton NH 03842

O'BANION, NANCE
ASSEMBLAGE ARTIST
b Oakland, Calif, June 7, 49. *Study:* Univ Calif, Berkeley, BA, 71, MA, 73. *Work:* Seattle Art Mus; Mus Arts Decoratifs Ville Lausanne, Switz; Am Craft Mus, NY; London Inst, Victoria & Albert Mus, London, Eng; Cleveland Art Mus; Bellerive Mus, Zurich, Switzerland; Co of Los Angeles; Getty Mus, Los Angeles; Ghent Mus, Belgium; Haderslev Mus, Jutland, Denmark; Harvard Univ, Cambridge, Mass; Kaho-Machi Mus, Kyushu, Japan; Mills Col, Oakland, Calif; RI Sch Design, Providence; San Francisco Mus; Univ Alta, Edmonton, Can; Univ Ga Art Mus, Athens; Univ Wis, Madison; Victoria & Albert Mus, London; Va Commonwealth Univ; Yale Univ, New Haven. *Comn:* Large wall construction (paper & bamboo), Sheraton Hotel, Tokyo, Japan, 87; painting (paper & bamboo), Bishop Ranch, Calif, 87; construction (paper & bamboo), Cranston Securities; well construction, pair (paper & bamboo), Ballston, Va, 88. *Exhib:* One-woman shows, Kauffman Galleries, Houston, 83, Hestkobgaard-Birkerod, Denmark, 84, BZ Wagman Gallery, St Louis, 84, Allrich Gallery, 80-85, 87-88 & 91, Monterey Art Mus, Calif, 89, Day Dreams for the Heart, Oakland Mus, Calif, 98, Breaking the Sorface: Telling Stories, JFK Univ Art Gallery, Berkeley, Calif, 2001; Mythical Figures & Fantastic Facades: O'Banion and Winter, San Francisco Folk & Craft Mus, 91; Eleven at 1111, Oakland Mus, Calif, 91; Works on Paper: The Craft Artist as Draftsman, Renwick Gallery Nat Mus Am Art, Washington, DC, 92; Craft Today USA, Zappeion Mus, Athens, Greece, 92; Self-Portraits in Black and White, Edith Caldwell Gallery, San Francisco, 93; Contemp Crafts and the Saxe Collection, Newport Harbor Mus, Calif, 94; The Chair, Oakland Mus, Calif, 96; Re-Incarnation, Oakland Mus, Calif, 96; The Paper Path, Haderslev Mus, Jutland, Denmark, 96; Fiberarts, Cult Centrum Mus, St Truiden, Belg, 96; 25 Yrs of Book Arts at CCAC, San Francisco Ctr for Book, 97; Out West: The Artist's Book in Calif, Ctr for Book Arts, New York City, 98; Hypnoponia, Int Asn for Study of Drams, Univ Calif Art Gallery, Santa Cruz, 99; Making Change, Jewish Art Mus, San Francisco, 99; Book as Object as Book, Fla Atlantic Univ Art Mus, Miami, 2000; Reading the Cards, San Francisco Ctr for the Book, 2001. *Teaching:* Instr, Univ Calif, Davis, 72-79; assoc prof textiles, Calif Col Arts & Crafts, 74-84, prof printmaking, 74--; vis artist & lectr, Hestkobgaard-Birkerod, Denmark & Carnegie Mellon Inst, Pittsburgh, Pa, 84, Chicago Art Inst, 87, San Francisco Craft Folk Art Mus & San Luis Obispo Art Asn, 89 & many others. *Awards:* Arthur Jacobsen Mem Award for Excellence in Arts, 75; Vis Art Fel, Nat Endowment Arts, 82-83 & 88-89; Juror, Calif Arts Coun Fel, 90. *Bibliog:* Charles Talley (auth), Nance O'Banion: Lines of energy, Artweek, 11/15/88; Robert Atkins (auth), Artspeak: A Guide to Contemporary Ideas, Movements and Buzzwords, Abbeville Press, New York, 69; Claire Campbell Park (auth), Finding the Link Between Fiber and Mixed Media: Nance O'Banion, Fiber Arts, summer 91. *Media:* Handmade Paper and Bamboo. *Publ:* Contribr, Contemporary American Craft Art: A Collector's Guide, Peregrine Bks, 88; auth, Comestic Science: Pop-up Icons and Idioms, Flying Fish Press, 90; auth, Design for Utopia, Col Environ Design Alumni Newsletter, Univ Calif, Berkeley, 92; Correspondence Course, Flying Fish Press, 93; Commentary: Intersections of Thought, Fiberarts, Vol 21, No 1, summer 94; Magic Door, Permanent Press, 95; Collaboratoor, Two-Sided Rochochet: Angelita Surmon and Nancy O'Banion, Southwest Craft Ctr, San Antonio, 90, Handwriting: Thomas Wojak and Nance O'Benion, Calif Craft Mus, San Francisco, 93, Lines of Correspondence: Angelita Surmon and Nance O'Banion, Hoffman Gallery, Oreg Sch Arts & Crafts, Portland, 94. *Mailing Add:* 5756 Ivanhoe Rd Oakland CA 94618

O'BEIL, HEDY
PAINTER, CRITIC
b New York, NY. *Study:* Art Students League, 53; Brooklyn Mus Art Sch, 58 & 59; Skowhegan Sch Art, 59; Empire State Col, State Univ NY, BS, 77; Goddard Col, MFA, 79. *Exhib:* One-person exhibs, Guild Hall, Easthampton, NY, 70, Heckscher Mus, Huntington, NY, 72, Landmark Gallery, 79, Barbara Ingber Gallery, 83 & Sunnen Gallery, 92; Elayne Benson Gallery, Bridghamton, 96; Katherine Perlowe Gallery, 98; New York City Andre Zarre Gallery, 01; New York City Studio 18 Gallery, 03; Westbeth Art Gallery, 2004; Art League of Long Island, 2005. *Collection Arranged:* The Symbolic View, Soho 20 Gallery, 82; Revelations, Pleiades Gallery, 84; Costumes, Masks & Disguises, The Clocktower Gallery, 86, Painting-Yes, 98 & The Gesture & The Brush, 99; NYC Broome St Gallery, Abstraction-5, 1903. *Pos:* Critic, Arts Mag, 76-86, Manhattan Arts Mag, 89-, West Side Beat, 96 & 97, The Proof, 95-. *Teaching:* Instr art, Nassau Community Col, 74; lectr, Art Ctr Northern NJ, 76-; lectr art hist, 92nd St Y, NY, 81-82. *Awards:* Heckscher Mus, 69; Fel, Cummington Community Arts, 80, YADDO, 84, Printmaking Workshop, 92. *Bibliog:* William Zimmer (auth), article, Soho News, 79; Elaine Wechsler (auth), article, Arts Mag, 83; Jennifer Dunning (auth), article, New York Times, 86; Diana Roberts (auth), Manhattan Arts, 90; Artspeak, 90; and others. *Mem:* Women's Caucus Art; Am Inst Critics Asn; Yaddo; NY Artists Equity; and others; Am Soc Contemp Artists; Contemp Artists Guild. *Media:* Acrylic, Ink. *Res:* Classical and modern art history with emphasis on surrealism; Minoan Cubismand. *Publ:* NY Times; Newsday; Soho News; Studio & Gallery; Arts Mag. *Dealer:* Get Real Art Gallery 156 Fifth Ave New York New York 10010. *Mailing Add:* 463 West St Apt 1103A New York NY 10014

OBERING, MARY M
PAINTER
b Apr 3, 37. *Study:* Hollins Col, Va, BA, 58; Radcliffe Col, Boston, 59; Univ Denver, MFA, 71. *Work:* Aldrich Mus Contemp Art, Ridgefield, Conn; Museo de Arte Costariccense, San Jose, Costa Rica; Wadsworth Atheneum, Hartford, Conn; Detroit Inst Art; Mus Fine Arts, Boston; Whitney Mus, NY. *Comn:* Painting, Norfolk & Southern Corp, Roanoke, Va, 94. *Exhib:* Whitney Mus Am Art Biennial, NY, 75; one-woman shows, Ben Shahn Galleries, Wayne, NJ, 81 & Museo de Arte, San Jose, 88, Am Abstr Artists, Ulrich Mus, Wichita, 92; Abstraction, Mus Fine Arts, Boston, 95; Tribute to Julian Pretto, Wadsworth Atheneum, Hartford, Conn, 96; Painting, Mus de Arte Costaricense, Costa Rica. *Teaching:* Fel basic design & art hist, Univ Denver, 70-71; spec sem egg tempera & gold leaf, Princeton Univ, 94. *Mem:* Am Abstr Artists. *Media:* Egg Tempera, Gold Leaf. *Dealer:* Little John Contemp 41 E 57th St New York NY 10028. *Mailing Add:* 69 Wooster St New York NY 10012

OBLER, GERI
PRINTMAKER, COLLAGE ARTIST
b New York, NY, May 1, 42. *Study:* Pratt Inst, with Richard Lindner & Fritz Bultman, BFA, 63; Hunter Col, with Ron Gorchov, MA, 66; Columbia Univ, with Peter Golfinopolis, EdD(fine arts & fine arts educ), 74. *Work:* Berkshire Mus, Pittsfield, Mass; Univ Wyo Art Mus, Laramie; US Embassy, Nairobi, Kenya; Conf Bd, Scottish Develop Agency, NY. *Exhib:* Nat Asn Women Artists, NY Dept Cult Affairs, 81 & Traveling Graphics Exhib, 92; 67th Hudson River Mus Ann, Yonkers, NY, 82; Jesse Besser Mus, Alpena, Mich, 83; Pratt Graphics Ctr Ann, NY, 83; Hunterdon 27th Nat Print Exhib, Wallingford Art Ctr, Pa, 83; Sarah Lawrence Col, Bronxville, NY, 92; and others. *Bibliog:* Malcolm Preston (auth), Three printmakers on display, Newsday, 6/18/79; Helen Harrison (auth), Many shades of white, New York Times, 1/11/81; Jeanne Paris (auth), A showing of Long Island's best graphics, Newsday, 10/6/81; Phyllis Braff (auth), Bending Paper into a Complex Modern Medium, New York Times, 3/16/86. *Mem:* Nat Asn Women Artists; Philadelphia Print Club; Graphic Eye Artists (pres, 78-80, bd dir, 81). *Dealer:* Henry Howels Gallery 164 Thompson St New York, NY 10012. *Mailing Add:* 26 Brokaw Ln Great Neck NY 11023

OBRANT, SUSAN ELIZABETH
PAINTER, ILLUSTRATOR
b Phildaelphia, Pa, Aug 24, 46. *Study:* State Univ NY, Buffalo, 66; Parsons Sch Design, 68; Spec studies in Louvre, Paris, 83. *Work:* Palace Mus, Isle of Malta; Mus of Modern Art, Caracus, Venezula; The Hapsburg Found, Vienna; Knights of the Teutonic Order, NYC. *Comn:* Oil on Canvas, The Hackley Sch, Tarrytown, NY, 95; Oil on Canvas, The Dominican Sisters, Ossining, NY, 96. *Exhib:* Hudson River Mus, NY, 76; Hammond Mus, NY, 97; Invitational Exhbn, Nat Arts Club, Pastel Soc of Am, New York City, 76; Mcnay Inst, Tex, 97; World Futurists Soc, NY, 86; Columbia Univ, New York City, 87; Santa Fe Weaving Gallery, 2004; Katonak Mus, NY, 2004. *Pos:* Artist in Residence, Eastview Tech Ctr, 96-99; judge, Soc Illusr, NYC, 73; artist in residence, Pace Univ Law Sch, 97. *Teaching:* Instr, Sch of Visual Arts, NY, 74; Lectr, Syracuse Univ, NY, 2002. *Awards:* Grammy Nomination, Through A Looking Glass, Nat Acad of Recording Arts & Scis, 71; Award of Excellence, Melanie, Soc of Illustrators, NY, 72. *Bibliog:* Lynn Roessler, Visions & Voices, Half Moon Press, 97; Teresa Lawrence, Cyberspace Maelstrom, Curio Mag, 98. *Mem:* Westchester Arts Coun; Ossining Arts Coun. *Media:* Oil, Pastel; Pen & Ink, Watercolor, Wearable Art. *Publ:* Visions and Voices of Westchester, London, 97; Journeys I: The Southwest, London, 98; A Visual Suite, London, 2002. *Dealer:* Julian Von Heisermann, 1150 Fifth Ave, NY, 10028. *Mailing Add:* 341 Furnace Dock Rd #8 Cortlandt Manor NY 10567

OBUCK, JOHN FRANCIS
PAINTER
b Detroit, Mich, Aug 20, 46. *Study:* Wayne State Univ, BFA, 68; Sch of Art Inst Chicago, MFA, 72. *Work:* Mus Contemp Art, Chicago; Cincinnati Mus Art; Chase Manhattan Bank. *Exhib:* Chicago and Vicinity Show, Art Inst Chicago, 80; solo shows, Delahunty Gallery, Dallas, 82, Barbara Gladstone Gallery, NY, 82, Young/Hoffman Gallery, Chicago, 83, Hanes Art Ctr, Univ NC Chapel Hill, 87, Am Acad, Rome, Italy, 89, Feigenson/Preston Gallery, Birmingham, Ala, 90 & 92 & Jack Hanley Gallery, San Francisco, 91, OHT Gallery, Boston, Mass, 2004 & 06; New Abstraction, Milwaukee Art Ctr, 85; The Persistence of Abstraction, Edwin A Ulrich Mus, Wichita State Univ, Kans, 92; Basic Marks: Black & White Paintings, Rosenberg/Kaufman Fine Art, NY, 95; 60th Anniversary Exhib, Westbeth Gallery, NY, 96; Affinities: Contemp & Historic Art, Snyder Fine Art, NY, 96; Thing, Deven Golden Fine Art Ltd, NY, 96; Mus Contemp Art, Chicago; Cinn Art Mus; Herbert F Johnson Mus Art, Cornell Univ, Ithaca, NY; Harry Ranson Ctr, Univ Tex. *Teaching:* Instr, Univ NC, 87, Univ Tex, Austin, 87, 90-91, Tyler Sch Art, Philadelphia, 92 & Princeton Univ, NJ, 92-93, 94-97, Harvard Univ, 2003. *Awards:* NY State Coun on the Arts, 88; Rome Prize Fel Painting, 88-89; Pollock-Krasner Grant, 92. *Bibliog:* Judith Kirshner (auth), rev, Art Forum, 83; Grace Glueck (auth), NY Times, 11/16/84; Kim Levin (auth), rev, Village Voice, 85. *Mem:* Am Abstract Artists; fel Am Acad Rome. *Media:* Oil Paint, Watercolor. *Dealer:* Feigenson-Preston Gallery 796 N Woodward Birmingham MI; Jack Hanley Gallery, 2610 Jackson St, San Francisco, CA; OH&T Gallery 450 Harrison Ave Boston MA 02118. *Mailing Add:* 20 Murray St #5S New York NY 10007

OCAMPO, MANUEL
PAINTER
b Quezon City, Philippines, 65. *Study:* student, Univ Phillipines, Quezon City, 84; student, Calif State Univ, 85. *Work:* Heridas de la Lengua. *Exhib:* Corcoran Biennial, 1993, Kwangju Biennial, 1997, Biennale d'art Contemporain de Lyon, 2000, Berlin Biennale, 2001, Venice Biennale, 2001, Seville Biennale, 2004, Casa Asia, Barcelona, 2005, Lieu d'Art Contemporain, Sigean, France, 2005; exhibited in group shows at Asia Society, NYC, 1994, Setagaya Art Mus, Tokyo, 1997, Aldrich Mus Art, 1998, LA County Mus Art, 2000. *Collection Arranged:* Pvt collections. *Awards:* Rome Prize, Am Acad, 1995, award, Nat Endowment for the Arts, 1996, Pollock-Krasner Found, 1995. *Media:* Acrylic, Oil. *Specialty:* Social and Political themes. *Mailing Add:* 2649 34th St Apt B Santa Monica CA 90405-3151

OCAMPO, MIGUEL
PAINTER
b Buenos Aires, Arg, Nov 29, 22. *Study:* Archit. *Work:* Albright-Knox Collection, Buffalo, NY; Mus Mod Art, NY; State Collection, France; Mus Fine Arts, Montevideo, Uruguay; Mus Fine Arts, Buenos Aires. *Exhib:* Stedelijk Mus, Amsterdam, 53; one-man shows, Mus Mod Art, Rio de Janeiro, 59, Galeria Aele, Madrid, 74 & Jacques Kaplan Gallery, NY, 75; Mus d'Art Mod, Paris, 73. *Media:* Acrylic, Oil. *Dealer:* Jacques Kaplan 19 E 71st St New York NY 10021

OCEPEK, LOU (LOUIS) DAVID
PRINTMAKER, PAINTER
b Detroit, Mich, Aug 27, 42. *Study:* Wayne State Univ, BFA, 64; Univ Iowa, Iowa City, with Lasansky, MA, 67. *Work:* Portland Art Mus, Ore; Portland State Univ, Ore; San Diego State Univ; State Univ NY, Oswego; Western Mich Univ, Kalamazoo. *Comn:* Paintings, Metrop Arts Comn, Portland, Ore, 78 & Art Advocates Inc, Portland, Ore, 78; prints, Clairmont Hotel Collection, Berkeley, 78, Seattle Arts Comn, 80 & Wash Arts Comn, Olympia, 81. *Exhib:* Northwest Printmakers Int, Seattle Art Mus, 70; Testimony to a Process, 74 & Constructions, Drawings and Prints, 76, Portland Art Mus; 12 Northwest Artists, 77 & A Directors Choice, 81, Portland Ctr Visual Arts, 81. *Teaching:* Prof design & printmaking, Portland State Univ, 71-83; prof design & illus, Mont State Univ, Bozeman, 83-; instr graphic & art design, NMex State Univ. *Awards:* Purchase Awards, The Artist Teacher Today, State Univ NY, 68, San Diego State Print Exhib, 69 & Multiples USA, Western Mich Univ, 70. *Bibliog:* David Stewart (producer), Lou Ocepek, artist, teacher, eckist, ECK World News, 78. *Mem:* Northwest Print Coun (bd dir, 83). *Media:* Silkscreen; Gouache, Acrylic. *Mailing Add:* 1761 Pomona Dr Las Cruces NM 88011-4919

OCKENGA, STARR
PHOTOGRAPHER, EDUCATOR
b Boston, Mass, June 14, 38. *Study:* Wheaton Col, Ill, BA, 60; RI Sch Design, with Harry Callahan & Aaron Siskind, MFA, 74. *Work:* Sheldon Art Gallery, Univ Nebr; Bibliot Nat, Paris; Mus Mod Art, NY; Addison Gallery of Am Art, Andover, Mass; Albert O Kuhn Gallery, Univ Md; Polaroid Collection, Cambridge, Mass; Univ Md, Baltimore. *Exhib:* Univ Bridgeport, Conn, 83; Ga State Univ, Atlanta, 83; Currents, Inst Contemp Art, Boston & Baskerville & Watson, NY, 84; Boston Now, Inst Contemp Art, Boston & Contemp Arts Ctr, New Orleans, 85; Catskill Ctr Photog, Woodstock, NY, 86; Albert O Kuhn Gallery, Univ Md, 87; The Ark in the Attic, Children's Mus Boston, Mass, 87; Starr Ockenga, Film in the Cities, St Paul, Minn, 87; Mothers & Daughters, Aperature Found, NY, 87; Photog: A Child's World, Michael Shapiro Gallery, San Francisco, Calif, 88; Am Color, Slatell Art Gallery, Los Cruces, NMex, 88; Photog in Boston: 1955-1985, Lincoln, Mass, 2001. *Pos:* Dir, Creative Photog Lab, Mass Inst Technol, 76-82; pres, Stone Wall Studio, Inc, currently. *Teaching:* Assoc prof photog, Mass Inst Technol, 76-82; vis prof, Bennington Col, 84. *Awards:* Nat Endowment Arts Photog Fel, 81; Mass Artist Photog Fel, 83; Am Horticultural Soc Book Award, 99. *Bibliog:* Parish Dobson (auth), Views, PRC Boston, Vol 2 & 3, 81; article, Mass Rev, Vol XXIV, No 1; Kelly Wise (auth), Boston Globe review, 2/27/84; John Dorsey (auth), Baltimore Sun review, 3/9/87; Steve Purchase (auth), Baltimore Sun review, 3/26/87. *Media:* Polaroid & Fresson Prints. *Publ:* Auth, The Ark in the Attic, Godine, 87; World of Wonders, Houghton Miffin, 88; coauth, A World of Wonders, A Trip Thru Numbers, 89 & Then & Now, a Book of Days, 90, Houghton & Mifflin; On Women and Friendship, Stewart, Tabori and Chang, 93; Earth on Her Hands: The American Woman in Her Garden, Clarkson Potter Publ, 98; Eden on Their Minds: American Gardeners with Bold Visions, 10/2001. *Mailing Add:* 68 Laight St New York NY 10013

OCKERSE, THOMAS
DESIGNER, EDUCATOR
b Holland, Apr 12, 40; US citizen. *Study:* Ohio State Univ, BFA, 63; Yale Univ, MFA, 65; with Norman Ives, Herbert Matter, Walker Evans, Paul Rand & Alvin Eisenman. *Work:* Mus Mod Art, NY; Stedelijk Mus, Amsterdam; Jean Brown Arch; Richard Demarco Gallery, Edinburg, Scotland; Indianapolis Mus Art. *Exhib:* Solo exhibs, Gallery Sch Art, Sheffield Polytechnic, Sheffield, Eng, 75, Richard Demarco Gallery Ltd, Edinburgh, Scotland, 75, Wheeler Gallery, Providence, 75, Lit Gallery, Md Writers' Coun, Baltimore, 76, other Bks & So Gallery, Amsterdam, The Neth, 77, Swain Sch Design Gallery, New Bedford, Mass, 79 & Feren's Art Gallery, Hull, Eng, 81; Faculty Biennial, RI Sch Design Mus, 88; Decade of the Eighties, Belk Bldg Art Gallery, Western Carolina Univ, Cullowhee, NC, 88; Kopie Als Origineel, Mus Photogr, Antwerp, Belg, 88; Universal/Unique, Rosenwald-Wolf Gallery, Univ Arts, Philadelphia, 88; Artist's Books: An Investigation of Time/Sequence Manipulation, Western Carolina Univ, Bell Gallery, 90; and many other one-man & group exhibs. *Pos:* Vpres bd, Am Inst Graphic Arts, 80-85, chmn educ comt, currently; consult graphic design, United Nations Development prog, 86; expert graphic design, Nat Inst Design, Ahmedabad, India, 86; Janvaneyck Acad, Neth, 92-. *Teaching:* Asst prof graphic design, Ind Univ, Bloomington, 67-71; prof graphic design, RI Sch Design, Providence, 71-, head graphic design dept, 73-93, prog head grad studies, 76-. *Awards:* Fac Develop Fund Grant, RI Sch Design, 85; Nominated, John Frazier Award Excellence in teaching, RI Sch Design, 85-; Educ Award, Am Ctr Design, Chicago, 91; and many others. *Bibliog:* J Bowles (auth), This Book is a Movie, Dell, 71; Kostelanetz (auth), Breakthrough Fictioneers, Something Else Press, 72; Camera Three (NY TV prog), 74. *Mem:* Semiotic Soc Am; Am Inst Graphic Arts; Indust Designers Soc Am; Soc Typographic Arts; Am Ctr Design; and others. *Publ:* Auth, Professional degrees for graphic design, proposed progs, RI Sch Design, 81; Aperture 93, Aperture Inc, Millerton, NY, 83; Design education theory vs practice, Am Inst Graphic Arts J, Vol 2, No 4, 84; De-sign/super-sign, Semotica 52-3/4, Mouton Publ, 84; Chaoni CE (or chance/choice), Providence, RI, 88; and many others. *Mailing Add:* 37 Woodbury St Providence RI 02906

O'CONNELL, ANN BROWN
PRINTMAKER, COLLECTOR, PRINTMAKER - MISC MEDIA
b Worcester, Mass, June 3, 31. *Study:* Bradford Col, AA; Boston Univ Exten; George Mason Univ, BA(art hist); Sumi-e with Evalyn Aaron, Port Washington, NY; Chinese brush painting with Audrey Nossal, Potomac, Md; also with Roddy McLean, Annandale, Va; etching, monotype, watercolor, Art League Sch, Alexandria, Va; monotype with Joyce Zavorskas & Beverly Edwards, Cape Cod, Mass. *Exhib:* Sixth Ann Exhib, Bank of Tokyo Trust Co, NY, 69; 7th Ann Exhib, Nippon Club, NY, 70; Am Inst Architects, 79 & 80; Open Ann Art Exhib Anthenaecen, Mid-Atlantic Regio, 92 & 94; Art League Juried Exhibs, 92, 93 & 94; juried exhibs, Cape Cod Art Asn, 95-98, 99, 2000 & 2001-03; and others. *Awards:* First Prize Mixed Media Graphics, Cape Cod Art Asn, 95, 96 & 97, Jurors Award, 98. *Mem:* Sumi-e Soc Am, Inc (mem secy, 71-73, founder, Wash Chap, 72, nat vpres, 72-73, nat pres, 74-78); Cape Cod Art Asn; Creative Arts Ctr; Bd mem, Printmakers Cape Cod & Monotype Guild, New Eng; Bd mem, Cape Cod Mus Art. *Media:* Monotype. *Collection:* Print collection specializing in early 20th century American printmakers; 19th and early 20th American and European paintings. *Publ:* Coauth (with Brian O'Connell), Volunteers in Action, Found Press, New York, 89. *Dealer:* Fresh Paint Gallery 143 Route 6A Yarmouth Port MA 02675. *Mailing Add:* 50 Chase St Chatham MA 02633

O'CONNELL, DANIEL MOYLAN
MURALIST, ADMINISTRATOR
b Springfield, Mass, Aug 24, 49. *Study:* Univ Iowa, Iowa City, BFA, 72, MA, 75. *Work:* Berkshire, Pittsfield, Mass; Univ Iowa; Air Gold, NY; City of Pittsfield, Mass; Canyon Ranch of Berkshires, Lenox, Mass. *Comn:* Mural, Nichols Brothers Inc, 87; Vietnam Vets Mem Mural, 90 & 91; mural, Capitol Theatre, Pittsfield, Mass, 92-93; Dedicated to Those Who Serve, firefighters mural, 96; mural, To Serve and Protect-Together, Pittsfield Police Dept, Mass, 98; Transitions, Pittsfield Boys & Girls Club 100th Anniversary, Mass, 02; Intermodel Transportation Ctr mural, Pittsfield, Mass, 03-. *Exhib:* Abstract Landscapes, Berkshire Artisans, Pittsfield, Mass, 76; Berkshire Art Asn Exhib, Berkshire Mus, Pittsfield, 80 & 81; Artists Living in the Berkshires, Clark Whitney Gallery, Lenox, Mass, 86; Collection of Mort Cooperaman, The Studio, 96. *Pos:* Comnr Cult Affairs, Pittsfield, Mass, 76-; regional consult, Nat Endowment Arts, 80-82. *Teaching:* Prof watercolor, Berkshire Artisans, 78-80, 81-, mural painting 86-. *Awards:* Gov's Award, Design in Mass, 82; Arts Inter-Arts Grant, Nat Endowment, 85; Nat Endowment Arts Int Exchange Grant, 96. *Bibliog:* Rosalyn Wilder (auth), Arts and Older Americans, Harcourt Press, 82; Vietnam Muralist, Am Vet, 12/91. *Mem:* Consortium of Local Arts Agencies in Mass; Berkshire Arts Alliance; Nat Alliance Local Arts Agencies; Lichtenstein Found Music & Art (assoc dir, 82-88); Pittsfield Cult Comn (assoc dir, 85-86, comnr 87-, chair, 98-); Pittsfield Cult Coun. *Dealer:* Diane Marchal Fine Art, Telluride, Colo. *Mailing Add:* Berkshire Artisans/Lichtenstein Ctr Arts 28 Renne Ave Pittsfield MA 01201

O'CONNELL, EDWARD E
PHOTOGRAPHER, PRINTMAKER
b New York, NY. *Study:* Hofstra Univ, BS; Pratt Inst, MFA. *Work:* Metrop Mus Art, NY; Brooklyn Mus, NY; Philadelphia Free Libr, Pa; Univ Mass, Amherst; Univ Tenn, Knoxville; plus others. *Exhib:* Photog into Sculpture, Mus Mod Art, NY, 70; 17th Nat Print, Brooklyn Mus, 70; US Pavilion, World's Fair, Osaka, Japan, 70; New Talent in Printmaking, Am Artists, NY, 70; Oversize Prints, Whitney Mus, NY, 71; Michael Ingbar Gallery, Soho Gallery, NY, 96. *Teaching:* Asst prof photog & graphics, Montclair Sch Visual Arts, New York, 69-71; asst prof photog & printmaking, Fordham Univ, 70-. *Awards:* Found Grant in Printmaking, Louis Comfort Tiffany Found, 66; Purchase Award, Brooklyn Mus, 70. *Bibliog:* James R Mellow (auth), Contemporary prints, the medium is not the message, NY Times, 6/28/70. *Mem:* Col Art Asn Am. *Media:* Silkscreen; Acrylic. *Dealer:* Assoc Am Artists Gallery 663 Fifth Ave New York NY 10022

O'CONNELL, GEORGE D
PRINTMAKER, EDUCATOR
b Madison, Wis, Oct 16, 26. *Study:* Univ Wis, BS, 50, MS, 51; Ohio State Univ; Rijksakademie Van Beeldende Kunsten, Amsterdam, Netherlands, Fulbright fel, 59-60. *Work:* Smithsonian Inst, Washington, DC; Libr Cong, Washington, DC; Gemeentemuseum Van Schone Kunsten, The Hague, Neth; Brit Mus, London, Eng; Archives of Am Art. *Comn:* Volunteer artist prog, Dept Hist Army, 71; presentation print ed, Rochester Print Club, 83. *Exhib:* Am Embassy, Dublin, Ireland; Baltimore Mus; John & Mabel Ringling Mus Art; Contemp Am Graphic Art, Corcoran Gallery Art, Washington, DC; US Info Agency Traveling Exhib Contemp Prints; Miriam Perlman Gallery, Chicago, 84; one man show, The Jazz Series, Oswego Art Guild, NY, 88; Retrospective (auth, catalog), All that Jazz, 54-92, SUNY Oswego, Tyler Gallery, NY, 92. *Pos:* Dir, Master Printer, Grey Heron Press, Oswego, NY. *Teaching:* Assoc prof printmaking, Univ Md, 61-68; prof printmaking, State Univ New York Col, Oswego, 69-91, prof emer, 91-; vis artist, Tamarind Inst, Univ NMex, 79. *Awards:* Creative Art Award, State Univ NY, Oswego, 86; Soc Am Graphic Artists Award, 89; Juror's Commendation, Boston Printmakers, Mem Exhib, 92. *Mem:* Boston Printmakers; Soc Am Graphic Artists; Int Soc Graphic Artists. *Media:* Relief, Lithography. *Dealer:* Oxford Gallery 267 Oxford St Rochester NY. *Mailing Add:* 14 Baylis St Oswego NY 13126

O'CONNELL, KENNETH ROBERT
FILMMAKER, ADMINISTRATOR
b Ogden, Utah, Jan 22, 45. *Study:* Univ Ore, BS, 66, MFA, 72. *Work:* Sinking Creek Film Collection, Nashville; Univ Ore Film Libr, Eugene; Uncross Found Collection, Wyo; Northwest Film Study Ctr, Portland; Charles Samu Int Prod, NY; Int Animation Libr, Tokyo, Japan. *Exhib:* USA Film Festival, Cult Ctr Hall, Dallas, 80; Athens Int Festival, Univ Theater, Athens, Ohio, 81; Hong Kong Film Festival, Exhib Hall, Hong Kong, 81; Ore Biennial, Portland Art Mus, 83 & 87; NY Film Festival Exposition, Metrop Mus Art, NY, 85; Bumbershoot '85, Seattle Art Comn, 85; Hiroshima '85, Peace Park, Japan, 85; Zagreb '86 World Animation Festival, Yugoslavia, 86; Stuttgart '90 Animation Festival, Int Festival of Children's Films, Chicago, 90; Medicine Wheel Animation Festival, Groton, Mass; Univ Ore Mus of Art, 99; Portland State Univ Gallery, 2000. *Collection Arranged:* Computers in the Creative Process (traveling exhib), Univ Ore Mus Art, 86-89; Computers in the Creative Process II, 89-91; Jack Wilkinson; Artist, Philosopher 1914-1973, Univ Ore Mus Art, 90. *Pos:* Co-dir, Comput Graphics Conf, Univ Ore, Eugene, 81-82; steering comt mem, Pac NW Comput Graphics Conf, Eugene, Ore, 82-90; Electronic Theather Comt, ACM/SIGGRAPH, Chicago, Ill; dir Internat Media Design Lab. *Teaching:* Prof film & visual thinking, Univ Ore, Eugene, 78-83, assoc prof comput art & head dept, 83-; adj prof slides & film, Goddard Col, Vt, 80-81. *Awards:* Cash Award, Ann Arbor Film Festival, 80; Third Place, USA Film Festival, 80; Selection Award, New York Film Expos, 85; First Place, Eugene Celebration Film & Video Festival. *Bibliog:* Cathy Goethals (auth), Painting at the Speed of Thought, Venture, 84. *Mem:* Col Art Asn; Found Art, Theory & Educ; Soc Animation Studies (SAS); Assoc Computer Machinery (ACM-SIGGRAPH). *Media:* Computer Graphics, Drawing. *Publ:* Auth various articles in Sch Arts Mag, 84-90; ed Jack Wilkinson: Artist/Philosopher, 89. *Dealer:* Film Distributor: Picture Start 221 E Cullerton 6th Fl Chicago IL 60616; Chicago Filmmakers 1229 W Belmont Chicago IL 60657; Internat Film Libr Tokyo Japan. *Mailing Add:* Univ Ore 220 W 23rd Ave D Eugene OR 97405-2856

O'CONNOR, CHUCK
PAINTER
b Buffalo, 1943. *Study:* Pratt Inst, Brooklyn, 61-64; NY Studio Sch, 64-66. *Exhib:* Celebration, Lohin Geduld Gallery, NY, 2005; Nat Acad Mus, NY, 2006. *Awards:* Fulbright fellow. *Mailing Add:* c/o Lohin Geduld Gallery 531 W 25th St New York NY 10001-5501

O'CONNOR, FRANCIS VALENTINE
HISTORIAN, CONSULTANT
b Brooklyn, NY, Feb 14, 37. *Study:* Manhattan Col, New York, BA, 59; Johns Hopkins Univ, MA, 60, PhD(art hist), 65. *Pos:* Sr vis res assoc, Nat Collection of Fine Arts, Smithsonian Inst, Washington, DC, 70-72; ed & publ, Fed Art Patronage Notes, 74-86; dir, Raphael Res Enterprises, 79-; editor, publ, O'Connor's Page http://members.aol.com/FVOC. *Teaching:* Lectr art hist, Univ Md, 64-66, asst prof, 66-70; Robert Sterling Clark, vis prof art hist, Williams Col, 90; vis prof art hist, George Washington Univ, 93. *Awards:* Grant, Nat Endowment Arts, 67-68; Independent Scholars Fel, Nat Endowment Humanities, 87-88; Rockefeller Resident Fel, Inst Med Humanities, Univ Tex, Med Br, Galveston, 91; Fel, Nat Humanities Ctr, 94-95. *Mem:* Soc for the Arts, Relig & Contemp Cult (mem bd, 74-80); Col Art Asn; Founder Asn Independent Hist Art (pres, 83-87). *Res:* Twentieth century American art; New Deal Art Projects; abstract expressionism; projected history of American mural; psychodymanics of creativity. *Publ:* auth, Jackson Pollock, New York: The Mus Modern Art, NY, 67; ed, Art for the Millions, The New York Graphic Soc Ltd, Greenwich, CT, 73; co-ed & co-auth, Jackson Pollock: A Catalogue Raisonne of Paintings, Drawings and Other Works, Yale Univ Press, New Haven, 78; auth, Charles Seliger: Redifining Abstract Expressionism, Hudson Hills Press, New York, NY, 2003. *Mailing Add:* 250 E 73rd St 11C New York NY 10021-4310

O'CONNOR, JOHN ARTHUR
PAINTER, EDUCATOR
b Twin Falls, Idaho, Jan 23, 40. *Study:* Univ Calif, Davis, AB(with hon & scholar), 61, with Wayne Thiebaud & William T Wiley, MAA, 63; San Francisco Art Inst(scholar), with James Weeks, 61. *Work:* Ringling Mus Art, Sarasota, Fla; State Calif Collection, Sacramento; Kemper Gallery, Kansas City Art Inst, Mo; IBM Corp; Cornell Fine Arts Mus, Rollins Col, Winter Park, Fla. *Comn:* Carr Van Anda Award for NY Times, Ohio Univ, 68; triptych, comn by Mr & Mrs George Varian, Palo Alto, Calif, 71. *Exhib:* Reality of Illusion, Denver Art Mus & traveling; Ann Exhib Am Painting, 82 & Mainstream Am: The Collection of Phil Desind, 87, Butler Inst Am Art, Youngstown, Ohio; 52nd Ann Nat Exhib Contemp Paintings, Soc Four Arts, Palm Beach, Fla, 90; 1991 Cheekwood Nat Painting Exhib, Nashville, Tenn, 91; Art Cult Technol at Rio, Summer Olympic Games, Atlanta, Ga, 96; Int Sculpture Garden & Park, Chelsea Pier, NY, 96; Fla Int Univ, Miami, 96; retrospective exhib, Cornel Fine Arts Mus, Winter Park, Fla, 98; Univ Fla Ctr Atrs, 2000; Retrospective Exhib, Pensacola Mus of art, Univ WFla, 2003; The Art Gallery, Univ of Fla, 2005; Thomas Ctr Main Gallery, 2005. *Pos:* Dir, Art Gallery, Univ Calif, Davis, 62-63, Art Gallery, Ohio Univ, 67-68 & Appalachian Ctr Crafts, Smithville, Tenn, 81-; sr investr, Ctr Creative & Optimal Design, Univ Fla, 72-, dir dept art gallery, 79-80, dir, MBA degree prog arts admin, 91-; artist-in-residence, Col Creative Studies, Univ Calif, Santa Barbara, 74; fac prog consult, Bd Regents, State Univ System, Fla, 83-95; exec dir, Fla Higher Educ Arts Network, 85-; dir, Ctr Arts & Pub Policy, Univ, Fla, 88-. *Teaching:* Inst painting & drawing, Univ Calif, Santa Barbara, 63-64 & Ohio Univ, 65-69; asst prof art, Univ Fla, 69-75, assoc prof, 75-85, prof, 85-. *Awards:* State of Fla Individual Artist's Fel, 91, 92 & 2003; Southern Arts Fedn, Nat Endowment Arts Regional Fel, 92-93; Lifetime Achievement Award, Fla Higher Educ Arts Network, 2005. *Bibliog:* Peter Frank (auth), John O'connor, How you see it, How you Don't; Conceptual Realism68-2003, Pensacola Mus of Art & Univ of FL, 2003, 2005. *Mem:* Col Art Asn Am; Fla Cult Alliance; Fla Higher Educ Arts Network (exec dir, 85-). *Media:* Acrylic, Watercolor. *Publ:* Ed, Graphics 1968-Ultimate Concerns, 68; coauth, Unbottle Your Creative Ideas-A Cooperative Venture of Engineering and Art, 72; contribr, A Pictorial History of the World, 75; Florida Arts Celebration and the Art in Public Places Initiative, Int Conf Sculpture, Dublin, Ireland, 89; auth, The public art process in Gainesville: a case history, J Arts Mgt, Law & Soc, fall 92. *Dealer:* Art South/Art4buriness, 161 Leverington Ave, Phila, PA 19127. *Mailing Add:* P O Box 14652 Gainesville FL 32604

O'CONNOR, STANLEY JAMES
HISTORIAN, EDUCATOR
Study: Cornell Univ, BA, 51, PhD, 64; Univ Va, MA, 54. *Pos:* Chair Dept Asian Studies, Cornell Univ, 1966-70, chair Dept Art History, 1971-76, Dir, Southeast Asia Program, 79-84; bd, Wells Col, Studies in SE Asia; editorial, Book Art & Ctr. *Teaching:* Prof art hist, Cornell Univ, 64-. *Awards:* Fellow, Explorers Club. *Mem:* Asn Asian Studies (SE Asia Coun, 78-81), Malaysian Br, Royal Asiatic Soc; Am Comt South Asian Art; Siam Soc. *Res:* Early trade of Southeast Asia; Buddhist and Hindu art. *Publ:* Auth, Hindu Gods of Peninsular Siam, Artibus Asiae, 72; contribr, Buddhist Votive Tablest & Caves in Peninsular Siam, Nat Mus Bangkok, 74; Iron working as spiritual inquiry in Indonesia, Hist of Relig, 75; Tambralinga and the Khmer Empire, Siam Soc J, 75; coauth, Dyer's Art, Weaver's Hand: Textiles from the Indonesian Archipelago, 85; coauth, Excavations of the Prehistoric Iron Industry in West Borneo, 69; coauth, Gold and Megalithic Activity in West Borneo, 70; Critics, Connoisseurs in the Southeast Asian Rainforest, Asian Art and Culture, 91; Humane Literacy and Southeast Asian Art, Jour of SE Asian Studies, 95; Tuye res and the Scale of the Santubong Iron Industry, Living a Life in Accordance with Dhamma, Bangkok, 97. *Mailing Add:* 617 Highland Rd Ithaca NY 14850-1411

O'CONNOR, THOM
PRINTMAKER
b Detroit, Mich, June 26, 37. *Study:* Fla State Univ, BA; Cranbrook Acad Art, MFA; Tamarind Printery Fel, 64; State Univ NY Res Found Fel, 65 & 72. *Work:* Mus Mod Art, Whitney Mus Am Art, NY; Brooklyn Mus; Philadelphia Mus Art; Pushkin Mus, Moscow; Hermitage, St Petersburg; Nat Collection of Fine Arts, Washington, DC; Smithsonian Instn, Washington, DC; Baltimore Mus Art; Boston Pub Libr; San Diego Art Mus; Santa Barbara Art Mus, Calif; NY Pub Libr; Rochester Meml Mus, NY. *Comn:* Witches of Salem (suite), State Coun Arts, NY, 72. *Exhib:* solo exhibs, Am Ctr, Belgrade, Yugoslavia, 80, Univ Art Mus, Univ Albany, 82, 99, Kalundborg Art Ctr, Denmark, 83, Gallery Strindberg, Helsinki, Finland, 84, Mus Mod Art, Belgrade, Yugoslavia, 87, Taidegraphik, Helsinki, Finland, 87, 90, Sarajevo Acad Gallery, 88, Albany Ctr Galleries, NY, 91, Haenah-Kent Gallery, NY, 92, 93, Raleigh Contemp Gallery, NC, 98, WDO Gallery, Charlotte, NC, 98, Mus Art Espirito Santo, Vitoria, Brazil, 2000; group exhibs, Detroit Print Symposium, Cranbrook Acad Art, Bloomfield Hills, Mich, 80; Int Biennial, Ljubljana, Yugoslavia, 85, 86; Joensuu Mus, Finland, 95; Ark State Univ, Fayetteville, 96; Richmond Art Ctr, Calif, 96; Union Col, Schenectady, NY, 99; Wexford Art Ctr, Ireland, 2001; Rice Gallery, Albany Inst Hist & Art, NY, 2002; Lessedra World Art Print Ann, Sofia, Bulgaria, 2003, 04; Boston Printmakers, 2005; Mus Contemp Art, Liege, Belgium, 2005; and many others. *Teaching:* Prof lithography, Univ Albany, 62-; vis artist, Swedish Acad Fine Arts, 78 & Cranbrook Acad Art, 81. *Awards:* Rissanen Prize, Kuopio, Finland, 83; Fulbright Award, Yugoslavia; Nat Endowment Arts Grant. *Publ:* auth, Wizards, Cabalists, Mystics and Magicians, 66; auth, Witches of Salem, 72; auth, Daydreams, 83; auth, Dreams of Kuopio, 84; auth, Night Dreams, 85. *Dealer:* Hanna-Kent Gallery, New York NY. *Mailing Add:* Moss Rd Voorheesville NY 12186

O'CONNOR-MYER, ROSE ANN
ART DEALER, LECTURER
b New York City, NY, Nov 14, 60. *Study:* SUNY at Buffalo, Buffalo, NY, BA, 82; NY Univ, New York City, NY, 94. *Collection Arranged:* Charles Hoffbauer (1875-1957), Comenos Fine Arts, 87; Paintings of Trav Niedlinger, Moonstruck, 2000; Mid Century Masters, Moonstruck, 2001; New Yorker Cartoonist: Barbara Shermund, Corner Joint, 2002; A NJ Artist: Alex Cotler, Fredrick Gallery, 2005; and others. *Pos:* Dir, Comenos Fine Arts, Boston, Mass, 82-93; Pres, Art Research Assocs, Allenhurst, NJ, 93-. *Teaching:* Identifying Fine Art Prints, Cambridge Ctr for Adult Educ, 88-90. *Mem:* Appraiser Asn Am. *Specialty:* Am & Europ 18th, 19th, & early 20th century paintings, drawings, sculptures & prints. *Mailing Add:* 44 Ocean Ave Allenhurst NJ 07711

OCVIRK, OTTO G
SCULPTOR, PRINTMAKER
b Detroit, Mich, Nov 13, 22. *Study:* State Univ Iowa, BFA & MFA. *Work:* Dayton Art Inst, Ohio; Detroit Inst Art; Dayton Co, Minneapolis. *Comn:* Sculpture, Bowling State Univ, 69. *Exhib:* Walker Art Ctr, Minneapolis, 47-49; Brooklyn Nat Print, NY, 49; Northwest Printmakers, Seattle, Wash, 49; San Francisco Ann Print & Drawing, 49-50; Libr Cong Nat Print Show, Washington, 50. *Teaching:* Prof emer art, Bowling Green State Univ, 50-85. *Awards:* Sculpture Exhib, Walker Art Ctr, Minneapolis, 47; Mich Artist Exhib, Hal H Smith, Detroit, 50; Broadcast Media Award, WBGU-TV, 19th Ann Broadcasters, San Francisco. *Media:* Stone; Intaglio. *Publ:* Coauth, Art Fundamentals, Theory and Practice, Brown, 60, 68, 75, 81, 85, 90, 94, 97, 2001 & 05. *Mailing Add:* 231 Haskins St Bowling Green OH 43402

ODA, MASAYUKI
SCULPTOR
b Tokyo, Japan, Jan 27, 50. *Study:* Cranbrook Acad Art, Mich, 76; Univ Calif Los Angeles, MA, 78, MFA, 79. *Work:* Univ Calif Los Angeles Career Planning & Replacement Ctr, Security Pac Bank, Keye/Donna/Pearlstein Inc, Robert Ross Inc, Yasuda Bank and Trust, & Kajima Int, Los Angeles, Calif; Citizen Corp, Santa Monica, Calif; Detroit Art Inst, Mich; Merchant Bank of Beverly Hills, Calif; Cranbrook Acad Art, Bloomfield Hills, Mich. *Comn:* Sculpture plaza, Mazda, Flatrock, Mich, 87-87, comn by Frederick Weisman Virginia Beach, 90; environ sculpture, Osaka Expo, Japan, 90. *Exhib:* Solo exhibs, Krygier/Landau Contemp Art, Los Angeles, Calif, 86, Virginia Beach Ctr for the Arts, Va, 90, Galerie Hubertus Wunschik, Dusseldorf, Ger, 93, Kunstpalastim Ehrenhof Mus, Dusseldorf, Ger, 93, Hunsaker/Schlesinger Fine Art, Santa Monica, Calif, 96 & 98; Malibu Int Sculpture Exhib, Calif, 93; Grobe Kunsstausstellung NRW, Dusseldorf, Ger, 93; Illusion-Trompe l'oeil and Slight of Hand, The Riverside Art Mus, Calif, 98; Summer Exhib, Hunsaker/Schlesinger Fine Art, Santa Monica, Calif, 2000; Floats, Sam Francis Gallery, Crossroads Sch, Santa Monica, Calif, 01; and others. *Awards:* Grant, Nat Endowment Arts, 88; Grand Prize, Int Environ Art Exhib, Osaka, Japan, 90; German Award, Osaka Triennale, 92. *Publ:* Illusr, Review, New Art Times, 6/11/90; Los Angeles Times, 5/1/93; Westdeutsche Zeitung, 8/13/93; Westfalischer Anzeiger, Mittwoch, 8/18/93; APEX Mag, No 18, Cologne, Ger, 93. *Mailing Add:* 441 N Croft Ave Los Angeles CA 90048

ODA, MAYUMI
PAINTER, PRINTMAKER
b Tokyo, Japan, June 2, 41. *Study:* Tokyo Univ Fine Art, BA, 66. *Work:* Mus Mod Art, NY; Mus Fine Arts, Boston; Libr Cong, Washington, DC; Honolulu Acad Art; Cincinnati Art Mus; Cleveland Mus; Portland Art Mus. *Comn:* Poster, Rainbow Art Found, NY, 77; Goddess of Hawaii, East West Ctr, Honolulu, 85; poster, Hawaiian Int Film Festival, Honolulu, 85. *Exhib:* 22nd Nat Exhib Prints, Libr Cong, Washington, DC, 71; solo exhibs, Goddesses: Visions of Women, Univ Hawaii, Honolulu, Tucson Art Mus, Ariz, 82 & Expression of Yin, Mills Col, Oakland, Calif, 86; retrospective, East West Ctr, Honolulu, 85; Honolulu Acad Art 87; Cathedral St John the Divine, NY; Centro Int della Grafica, Venice, Italy, 90; and others. *Teaching:* Artist-in-residence, Inst Cult & Communication, East West Ctr, Honolulu, 85-86. *Awards:* Lindisfarne Fel. *Bibliog:* Martha Gressing (producer), Women Artists, KQED-TV, San Francisco, 78; Mary & Norman Tolman (auths), People who make Japanese prints, Sobunsha, 83; Pauline Sugino (auth), Goddesses, vision of women, Bridge Mag, 84; Connecting Conversations, Eucalyptus Press; Womens Culture, Bettina Aptheker Galleries, 88; Mary Ann Lutzker (auth), Goddess Banners, Orientation, 2/90. *Media:* Acrilic; Silkscreen, Etching. *Publ:* Collabr, Goddesses, Lancaster Miller, 84; Song of Vegetables, Koguma Sha, Tokyo, 86; Goddesses, Volcano Press, 88; Happy Veggies, Parallex Press, 88; Random Kindness and Senseless Acts of Beauty, Volcano Press, 93. *Dealer:* The Tolman Collection New York; Ren Brown Collection CA. *Mailing Add:* 1795 Shoreline Hwy Sausalito CA 94965-9724

ODATE, TOSHIO
CONCEPTUAL ARTIST, EDUCATOR
b Tokyo, Japan, July 9, 30. *Study:* Art Sch, Tokyo, 50-54; Nat Chiba Univ, 57-58. *Work:* Rochester Mem Art Gallery, NY; Bundy Art Gallery, Waitsfield, Vt; Great Southwest Atlanta Corp, Atlanta, Ga; Mus Wis; Hirshhorn Mus, Washington. *Exhib:* Waning Moos and Rising Sun--Japanese Artists, Houston Mus Art, Tex, 59; Joseph H Hirshhorn Collection, Solomon R Guggenheim Mus, NY, 63; The Artists Reality, New Sch Social Res, NY, 64; Whitney Mus Am Art Sculpture Ann, 65-66; Attitudes, Brooklyn Mus, 70; Md Inst Col Art, Baltimore, Md, 87; Brattleboro Mus, 89; Matters of the Heart, Mattatuck Mus, 92. *Teaching:* Instr sculpture, Brooklyn Mus Art Sch, 61-; prof, Pratt Inst, currently; guest lectr, Denver Mus Art, 67, Univ Wis, Wausau, 68 & Univ Ky, 69, Cooper Union, 72, Cooper-Hewitt Mus, 77, Harvard Univ, 88, Yale Univ Art Gallery, 89, Carnegie-Mellon Univ, 95-96. *Media:* Mix. *Publ:* Contribr,

Modern sculpture from the Joseph H Hirshhorn Collection, 62; Modern American sculpture, 67; auth, Japanese Woodworking Tools Their Tradition, Spirit & Use, 84; Asian Art-Soul of the Tool, Arthur M Sackler Gallery, Smithsonian Inst, Oxford Univ Press, 91; Am Woodworker, 1/91, 10/92, 9-10/93, 2/95 & 10/95. *Mailing Add:* 63 Pomperaug Rd Woodbury CT 06798-3714

O'DELL, ERIN (ANNE)
PAINTER, DESIGNER
b Phoenix, Ariz, Dec 7, 1938. *Study:* Moore Col Art, BFA (textile design); Ariz State Univ; with John Pike in Mex, Jamaica, Ireland, Italy & Guatemala. *Work:* Ariz Bank, Phoenix; Colo Nat Bank, Colorado Springs; First Nat Bank, Mesa, Ariz; Valley Nat Bank, Scottsdale & Mesa, Ariz. *Exhib:* Two Flags Festival Arts, Douglas, Ariz, 73-79; Laramie Nat Miniature Show, 78 & 79; Ariz State Fair, 81; La Galeria Group Show, Casa Grande, 85; Solo exhibs, Scottsdale Methodist Church, Ariz, 86 & Phoenix Women's Club, 88; and others. *Pos:* Designer, Henry Cantor, Inc, Philadelphia, Pa, 61-64; freelance designer, C A Reed Co, Williamsport, Pa & Beach Prod, Kalamazoo, Mich, 64-75; artist, Modern Color Printing, Mesa, 69-74. *Teaching:* Instr hist textiles, Moore Col Art, 63-65. *Awards:* Mesa Artist of the Year, Mesa Art League, 73 & 79; Watercolor Award, Douglas Art Asn, 73; Artist of the Year, Ariz Saguaro Artists League, 77. *Mem:* Southwestern Watercolor Soc; Scottsdale Artists League; Midwest Watercolor Soc; Ariz Artists Guild; Watercolor West. *Media:* Watercolor. *Mailing Add:* 1310 E Grandview Mesa AZ 85203

O'DOUGHERTY, WINNIE
PAINTER
b Brooklyn, NY, Jan 11, 28. *Study:* Pratt Inst; Brooklyn Col. *Work:* Admin building, Sussex, NJ; Our Lady of Fatima Church. *Comn:* Warwick Valley Telephone Commun, 88, 92, 96 & 98; House portraits, by pvt comn; Restoration calendar, Goshen, NY, 90. *Exhib:* Morris Mus, NJ; Hudson Valley Art Asn, Newington-Cropsey Mus, NY; Audubon Artists, Salmagundi Club; NJ State Fair, 2004. *Collection Arranged:* Bank of NY; Tunnell Advert Agency, Warwick; NY Savings Bank. *Pos:* Com Illusr, newspaper advertising Co, formerly. *Teaching:* instr, art, Pvt NY & NJ Schs, formerly. *Awards:* First place Award, Northeast Pastel Artists, 95; Dick Blick Merit Award, Audubon Artists, Inc, 99; Friede Stroble Mem award, 2000. *Mem:* Audubon Artists; Northeast Watercolor Soc (pres, 2003-2004); Am Artist Prof League; Hudson Valley Art Asn (bd dirs). *Media:* Watercolor, Oils & Pastels. *Interests:* Historic Buildings, landscapes & animals. *Mailing Add:* 699 Canistear Rd Highland Lakes NJ 07422

OESTREICH, JEFFREY
CERAMIST
b St Paul, Minn, 1947. *Study:* Univ Minn, studied with Warren MacKenzie, 67; Bemidji State Univ, BA, 69; studied with Bernard Leach, Eng, 69-71. *Work:* Everson Mus Art, Syracuse; Victoria & Albert Mus, London; Taipei Fine Arts Mus, Taiwan; Nottingham City Mus, Eng; Smithsonian Mus; and others. *Exhib:* Garth Clark Gallery, NY, 91; Pro-Art, St Louis, Mo, 92; CPA, London, Eng, 98; Ceramic Art Gallery, Sydney, Australia, 99; Gallery, Munich, Ger, 2001. *Teaching:* instr, artist-in-residence, Col William and Mary, Williamsburg, Va, 2001. *Awards:* Fel, Nat Endowment Arts, 86; Minn State Arts Board Fel Grant, 90; McKnight Fel, McKnight Found, Minn, 98; Jerome Found Travel Grant, Minn, 98; Minnesota State Arts Board Fel, 99. *Mailing Add:* 36835 Pottery Tr Taylors Falls MN 55084

OFFNER, ELLIOT
SCULPTOR, PRINTMAKER
b Brooklyn, NY, July 12, 31. *Study:* Cooper Union; Yale Univ, with Josef Albers & Rico Lebrun, BFA & MFA. *Hon Degrees:* Converse Col, Spartanburg, SC, Hon Dr Art, 2004. *Work:* Brooklyn Mus; De Cordova Mus, Lincoln, Mass; Lowe Art Mus, Syracuse Univ; Smith Col; Hirshhorn Mus and Sculpture Garden, Washington, DC. *Comn:* three bronze sculptures, Nat Asn Letter Carriers, Milwaukee, Wis, 89; The Welcoming, bronze, Children's Inn, Nat Inst Health, Bethesda, Md, 90; Fountain and Sculptures (granite & bronze, 20' x 30' x 17'), Downtown Minneapolis, 92; Heron, Gouse and Loon, Fountain and Bronze Sculptures, Brookgreen Gardens, Pawley's Island, SC, 2002; Historic Am Women, project dir, 10 over life-size sculptures by leading Am sculptors, Converse Col, Spartanburg, SC, 2003-2006. *Exhib:* One-man shows, Forum Gallery, NY, 64, 67, 72, 79, 84, 93 & 99 Int Fine Arts Galleries, Wash, 68, 73 & 79, Slater Mem Mus, Norwich, Conn, 76, Boston Atheneum, 79, Jorgensen Gallery, Univ Conn, 80 & Springfield Mus Fine Arts, 84 & Franz Bader Gallery, Wash, 86 & 92, WM Baczek Fine Arts, Northampton, Mass, 99 & Leigh Yawkey Art Mus, Wausau, Wis, 2003; group shows, Birds in Art, Leigh Yakley Woodson Art Mus, Wausau, Wis, 91, 1996-2003, Nat Sculpture Soc (Ann), 89-2003; 175th Ann Exhib Nat Acad Design, NY, 2000. *Pos:* Dir, Rosemary Press, 67-; printer, Smith Col, 75-; curator, Chesterwood Ann Sculpture Exhib, 95-2004. *Teaching:* Instr art, Univ Mass, 59-60; prof art, Smith Col, 60-74, Andrew W Mellon prof humanities, 74-; vis lectr, Royal Col Art; Yale Univ, Boston Univ, Cambridge Univ, & others. *Awards:* Mary Amelia Cummins Harvey Fel, Girton Col, Cambridge Univ, 90; Gold Medal, Nat Sculpture Soc, 92 & 05; Ellin P Speyer Prize, Nat Acad Design, 96; Vis fel, Trinity Coll, Cambridge, 99; Harry Watrous Gold Medal & Prize, Nat Acad Design, 2000; Ruch Nickerson Prize, Nat Sculpture Soc 67th Ann, 2000; Master Wildlife Artist, Leigh Yawkey Woodson Art Mus, Wausau, Wis, 2003. *Bibliog:* Cathedral's death camp sculpture, One World, 9/78; The sculpture of Elliot Offner, Hampshire Life, 5/26/79; The Fowl of the Air, the Fish of the Sea & the Beasts of the Field: The Animal Sculptures of Elliot Offner, Mus Fine Arts, Springfield, Mass, 84; Justina and Patrick Gregory, Marry Wonders: The Sculpture of Elliot Offner. *Mem:* Printing Hist Soc; William Morris Soc; Am Printing Hist Asn; Bibliog Soc; Sculptors' Guild; Fel, Nat Sculpture Soc; Nat Sculpture Soc (vpres 93-99, pres 1999-2003). *Media:* Wood, Bronze; Mixed. *Specialty:* figurative art. *Collection:* Hirshhorn Museum and Sculpture Garden, Washington, D.C.; Smith College Museum of Art, North Hampton, Mass; Brooklyn Museum, New York; Oberlin College Museum of Art, Ohio; Detroit Institute of Arts, Michigan; Springfield Fine Arts, Mass; Milwaukee Museum Fine Arts, Michigan; Sculpture Garden, Brookgreen Gardens, Murrills Inlet, South Carolina. *Publ:* Auth & illusr, The Granjon Arabesque, Rosemary Press, 69; Elliot Offner Recent Sculpture, exhib catalogue, Forum Gallery, NY, 99. *Dealer:* Forum Gallery 745 Fifth Ave New York NY 10151. *Mailing Add:* 74 Washington Ave Northampton MA 01060-2825

OGINZ, RICHARD
SCULPTOR, DRAFTSMAN
b Philadelphia, Pa, Feb 7, 44. *Study:* Tyler Sch Art, Temple Univ, BFA, 66; Univ Wis-Madison, MA, MFA, 68. *Work:* Los Angeles Co Mus Art; Arts Coun Gt Brit, London; Bradford Mus, Yorkshire; Leeds City Art Mus, Madison, Wis; Madison Art Mus, Wis. *Comn:* Elevator Doors lobby, Junipero Serra State Office Bldg, Los Angeles, Calif, 98. *Exhib:* Artists Chairs, Santa Monica Mus Art, Calif, 95; Drawn From Los Angeles, Armory Ctr Arts, Pasadena, Calif, 96; Containers, Los Angeles Co Mus Art, 96; Grins: Humor and Whimsy in Contemp Art, Millard Sheet Gallery, Los Angeles Co Fair, Pamona, Calif, 97; Mechanical Wonders, Craft & Folk Art Mus, Los Angeles, 2001; Sculptors Draw Art Gallery, Glendale Community Col, Calif, 2001; Raw Draw, Pasadena City Col Art Gallery, Calif, 2002; Solo exhibs, Recent Sculpture, Glendale Community Col, Calif, 92, Ruth Bachofner Gallery, Santa Monica, Calif, 91 & 93, Worlds-Bodies-Machines, Sam Francis Gallery, Crossroads Sch, Santa Monica, Calif, 95, Richard Oginz, Drawing from a Sculptor's View, Los Angeles Co Mus Art, Calif, 97, New Work: Gallery of Functional Art, Santa Monica, Calif, 99, Richard Oginz, Jan Baum Gallery, Calif, 2001; New Work Gallery of Functional Art, Santa Monica, Calif, 2005. *Pos:* bd dir, Los Angeles Contemp Exhibs (LACE), 1983-1987. *Teaching:* Principal lectr sculpture, Middlesex Polytech, London, 74-76; sculpture fac, Otis Art Inst, Los Angeles, 76-95; Pierce Community Col, 2002-04; Glendale Communiy Col, 2003; UCLA World Arts and Cultures, 2005-06. *Awards:* Ford Found Grant, 78-79; Young Talent Award, Los Angeles Co Mus Art, Calif, 79; Nat Endowment Arts Visual Artists Forum Grant Figurative Sculp, Otis Arts Inst, Calif, 84; Gregory Fel, Leeds (Eng) Univ, 1971-1973. *Bibliog:* Pamela Hammond (auth), Narratives of isolation, Artweek, 11/10/84; Peter Plagens (auth), Bee-Bop Da Reebok in LA, Art in Am, 4/85; Peter Clothier (auth), Richard Oginz Sculpture, Art News, 5/91. *Media:* Mixed. *Publ:* Illusr, Drawing A contemporary Approach, Holt Rhinehart & Winston, 87; Joseph Campbell, Maurice Tuchman (auths), Masquerade, Chronicle Books, 1993; Budd & Arloa Goldston (auths), Watts Towers, The Getty Conservation Inst, 1997; Barbara Tober (auth), Object Lessons, Guild Inc, 2001. *Mailing Add:* 21393 Encino Rd Topanga CA 90290

O'GORMAN, JAMES FRANCIS
EDUCATOR, WRITER
b St Louis, Mo, Sept 19, 33. *Study:* Washington Univ, Mo, BA(arch); Univ Ill, Urbana, MA(arch); Harvard Univ, PhD. *Teaching:* Grace Slack McNeil Prof Emer of Am Art, Wellesley Col, 75-. *Awards:* NEH fel, 88-89 & 96; Mellon Foundation Fellow, 2005-06. *Mem:* Soc Archit Historians (pres, 70-72); Col Art Asn; life fel Philadelphia Athenaeum; Am Antiquarian Soc (chmn, Maine); Historic Preserv Com, 2006-. *Res:* American art and architecture. *Publ:* Auth, The Architecture of the Monastic Library in Italy, New York Univ Press, 72; coauth, The Architecture of Frank Furness, Philadelphia Mus of Art, 73; auth, H H Richardson and His Office: Selected Drawings, Harvard Col, 74; This Other Gloucester, pvt publ, 76; H H Richardson, Architectural Forms for an American Society, Univ Chicago Press, 87; Three American Architects: Richardson, Sullivan and Wright, 1865-1915, Univ Chicago Press, 91; Living Architecture: A Biography of H.H. Richardson, Simon and Schuster, 97; ABC of Architecture, Univ Pennsylvania Press, 98; Accomplished in All Departments of Art: Hammatt Billings of Boston, Univ Mass Press, 98; Connecticut Valley Vernacular, Univ Pennsylvania Press, 2002; coauth, The Maine Perspective: Architectural Drawings, 1800-1980, Portland Mus Art, 2006; and others. *Mailing Add:* 81 Nash Road Windham ME 04062

O'HAGAN, DESMOND BRIAN
PAINTER
b Wiesbaden, Ger; US citizen/Irish citizen, 59. *Study:* Univ NMex 77-79; Colo Inst Art, AA, 82. *Work:* Denver Pub Libr Art Collection, Colo; City of Loveland, Colo; and many pvt corp collections. *Exhib:* Pastel Soc Am Show, NY, 87,88, 97 & 98, 99; Artists of the West Exhib, Pioneers Mus, Colorado Springs, 93; Artsts of Am Exhib, Colo Hist Mus, Denver, 96-98; Pastel Soc Am China Exhib, Xian, China, 97; Galleria Prov, Tokyo, Japan, 98; Int Asn Pastel Soc Exhib, Albuquerque, 99; solo show, E.S. Lawrence Gallery, Aspen, Colo, 2005. *Pos:* master pastelist, Pastel Soc Am Asn. *Teaching:* workshop instr, various art socs and schs. *Awards:* George Innes, Jr Mem Award for a pastel, Salmagundi Club, 96; Conn Pastel Soc Asn Show Award, 9/97; Mrs Pearl Kalikow Award, Pastel Soc Asn Show, 9/98; Prix'd Pastel Award, Best of Show Int, Asn Pastel Soc, 99; Hudson Valley Art Asn Award, PSA Open Show, 99. *Bibliog:* M Stephen Doherty (auth), Stirring the viewer's imagination, Am Artist Mag, 12/89; Desmond O'Hagan, United Airlines Hemispheres Mag, 1/96; Gekkan Bijyutsu Art Mag, Japan, 5/98. *Mem:* Pastel Soc Am; Pastel Soc Colo Asn; Int Asn Pastel Soc (masters circle). *Media:* Pastels, Oils. *Specialty:* Contemporary Representational. *Interests:* The Study of Light on the Urban Landscape. *Publ:* auth, Light on the subject, Artists & Illusrs Mag, 10/98; A sense of place, Artist's Mag, 9/01; Desmond O'Hagan, Pastel J, 5/03; Contrasting Color, Contrasting Mediums, Int Artist Mag, 2/01. *Dealer:* ES Lawrence Gallery 516 East Hyman Aspen CO 81611; Saks Galleries 3019 E 2 Av Denver CO 80206; The Gallery 329 Primrose Rd Burlingame CA 94010. *Mailing Add:* 2882 S Adam St Denver CO 80210

O'HARA, MORGAN
PAINTER, CONCEPTUAL ARTIST
b Los Angeles, Calif, Jan 7, 41. *Study:* Immaculate Heart Col, Los Angeles, Calif, BA(art), 69; Calif State Univ, Los Angeles, MA(art), 71. *Work:* Stedelijk Mus, Amsterdam, Holland. *Comn:* Frieze (175 Ft), comn by Eugene Burgur Corp, Larkspur, Calif, 83. *Exhib:* Solo exhibs, Musée Cantonal des Beaux Arts, Lausanne, Switz, 80 & Univ Calif, Berkeley, 82, Gracie Mansion Gallery, NY, 97 & Galerie Dobreho Pastyre, Czech Repub, 97; Elegant Miniatures from San Francisco & Kyoto, San Francisco Mus Mod Art, Calif, 83; 8th Floor Gallery, NY, 96; Galerie Singel 74, Amsterdan, The Neth, 96; New Langton Arts, San Francisco, Calif, 97. *Teaching:* Instr, San Francisco Art Inst & Ecole des Beaux Arts. *Awards:* Interarts Grants, Nat Endowment Arts, 85, Echoes from the Moon, Mobius, Boston, 86 & Time-Geography Studies, Fessenden Found, 86. *Bibliog:* Kristie Stiles (auth), Introduction to the Art of Morgan O'Hara, Musée Catonal des Beaux Arts, Lausanne, Switz, 80; Ron Gagnon (auth), Six Portraits, Action Image, 84. *Media:* Ideas, Time & Space. *Publ:* Auth, Zeit und Raumbilder, Feministisches Studien, Weinheim, Ger, 82; coauth, Formal records of time and movement through space: A conceptual & visual series of artworks, Leonardo J, 83; Interviews with Artists, 86; auth, Geographical self portraits, Corona 4, 86; Time out of mind, The Act, New York, 86. *Mailing Add:* 106 MacDougal St New York NY 10012-1268

O'HARA, PAUL
PRINTMAKER, SCULPTOR
b Indiana, Pa, Sept 16, 38. *Study:* Endinboro Univ, BS, 61; Pa State Univ, MA, 65; studies with George Zoretich, Hobson Pittman, Hugo Weber & Lynwood Thompson; Univ Pittsburgh, printmaking with George Nama; Calif Univ, Pa (photog). *Work:* Meri Portfolio, 2002; Cape Cod Community Col; Thomas Hosp, Fair Hope, Ala; DuBois Regional Med Ctr, Pa; Am Print Alliance. *Exhib:* One-man exhibs, St Francis Col, Ft Wayne, Ind, 68, Univ Iowa, Iowa City, 68, Univ Pittsburgh, Pa, 69, Pa State Univ, University Park, Pa, 72, Adams Art Bellefonte, Pa, 94, Frank L Melega Art Mus, Brownsville, Pa, 2000, Fayette campus Pa State Univ, 2001; Pratt Int Miniature Print Show, 71-74; Ann Drawing & Small Sculpture Show, Ball State Univ, Muncie, Ind, 73-74; Delmar Col Ann Drawing & Small Sculpture Show, Corpus Christie, Tex, 73; Butler Inst Am Art, Youngstown Ohio, 87; Mini Print Int, Cadaques, Spain, 89-98, Wingfield Art & Music Festival, Eng, 92-2000; L'Etang d'Art, Bages, France, 95-2000; Soc Am Graphic Artists at the Print St Gallery, NY, 99, at Stephen Gang Gallery, NY, 2000; Nemacolin Woodlands Resort, Farmington, Pa, 2000; Soc Am Graphic Artists 67th Nat Members Exhib, Prince St Gallery, NY, 99, 68th Nat Members Exhib, & 69th Nat Members Exhib, 2002; Soc Sculptors, Pitts, 63-66, 68-84; Assoc Artists, Pitts, 62-63, 66-67, 68, 70, 72-73, 75-79, 81, 84, 86; and numerous others. *Pos:* photographer, Pa State Univ, University Park, 77-78. *Teaching:* Ret art teacher, Chartiers Valley Schs, 61-94. *Awards:* Print Award, Assoc Artists Pittsburgh, 67; Soc Sculptors Prize, 68, 74 & 83; Sculptor Award, Three Rivers Art Show, Pa, 76-77. *Bibliog:* Brenda Joyce (dir), Interview Week-End 1, KDKA TV, 64. *Mem:* Am Print Alliance; Soc Am Graphic Artists; Int Sculpture Ctr; Int Asn for Diffusion of Graphic Arts Print Group; Erie Mus. *Media:* Woodcut; Wood and Metal Cast. *Res:* The emersion of the human figure in sculpture. *Publ:* Contribr, Supermud Conference - Pennsylvania State University, Ceramics Monthly, Spencer L Davis, 75 & 77. *Mailing Add:* PO Box 132 Roscoe PA 15477

OHE, KATIE (MINNA)
SCULPTOR, INSTRUCTOR
b Peers, Alta, Can, Feb 18, 37. *Study:* Alta Col Art, dipl(fine arts); Montreal Sch Art & Design, with Dr Lismer; Sculpture Ctr, New York, with Sahl Swarz & Dorothy Denslow, Fonderia Fabris, Verona, Italy. *Hon Degrees:* U Calgary, LLD, 01. *Work:* Can Coun Art Banks, Ottawa, Ont Alta Art Found, Edmonton; Visual Arts, Cult Activities, Edmonton; Shell Can Art Collection, Calgary; Alta Col of Art; Glenbow Mus, Calgary, Alberta, Can. *Comn:* chromed steel sculpture, Univ Calgary, 67 & 75; cast stone sculpture relief, Fed Western Regional Bldg, Calgary, 67; bronze sculpture, Sch Bd, City of Calgary, 75; Esso: Imperial Oil, Res Ctr, Calgary, 90; Univ Calgary, 96. *Exhib:* Sculpture Ctr, NY, 62-70; Brit Int Print Show, London, Eng, 71; Venice Biennial, Italy, 72; Alta Art Found Traveling Exhib, Can House Gallery, London, Brussels, Paris & NY, 75-76; Changes: 11 Artists Working on the Prairies Traveling Exhib, 75-76; retrospectives, Alta Col Art, Calgary, 91, Edmonton Art Gallery, 97-98 & Nickle Art Mus, Univ Calgary, 96; solo exhibs, Glenbow Mus, Calgary; and many other group exhibs. *Collection Arranged:* Edmonton Art Gallery, Glentow, Calgary, Alberta, Can. *Pos:* cur, Triangle Gallery Visual Arts. *Teaching:* Instr sculpture, Mt Royal Col, Calgary, 70-, Alta Col Art, Calgary, 70-03 & Univ Calgary, 79, Calgary Allied Art Ctr. *Awards:* Nat Gallery Study Grant, 58; Can Coun Grants, New York, 63, Europe, 68 & Verona, Italy, 74; Allied Arts Award Medal, Royal Archt Inst of Can, 84. *Bibliog:* Clement Greenburg (auth), View of art on the prairies, Can Art, 63; Anita Aarons (auth), Allied Art Catalogue, Vol 2, Arts and Architecture, Royal Archit Inst Can, 68; Barb Kwasney (auth), Canadian Golden West, Western Artist, spring 76. *Mem:* Royal Can Acad Arts; Alta Soc Artists. *Media:* Multimedia. *Publ:* Canadian Art; Encyclopedia of Twentieth Century North Am Women Artists. *Mailing Add:* Alberta Col Arts 1407 14th Ave NW Calgary AB T2M 4R3 Canada

OHLSON, DOUGLAS DEAN
PAINTER, EDUCATOR
b Cherokee, Iowa, Nov 18, 36. *Study:* Univ Minn, BA, 61. *Work:* Corcoran Gallery Art, Washington, DC; Minneapolis Inst Art; Dallas Mus Fine Art; Metrop Mus Art, NY; Mus Mod Kunst, Frankfurt, Ger; Brooklyn Mus, NY; and others; Lowe Art Mus, Miami, Fla; Karl Ernst Osthaus Mus, Hagen, Ger; Albright-Knox Gallery, Buffalo, NY; Whitney Mus, New York City; Harvard Art Mus, Cambridge, Mass. *Exhib:* Art of the Real: USA 1948-1968, Mus Mod Art, NY, 68-69; Structure of Color, Whitney Mus Am Art, NY, 71; Am Art Since 1960, Art Mus, Princeton Univ, 70; The Way of Color, 33rd Biennial Exhib, Corcoran Gallery Art, Washington, DC, 73; 14 Abstract Painters, Wight Gallery, Univ Calif, Los Angeles, 75; Am Acad Arts, 92, 94, 96-97, 2002; Elaine Baker Galleries, 96, 2003; and others. *Teaching:* Prof art, Hunter Col, fomerly. *Awards:* Guggenheim Fel, 68; Nat Endowment Arts, 76. *Bibliog:* G Battcock (ed), Minimal Art (critical anthology), Dutton, 68; Britannica Encyl Am Art, Simon & Schuster, 73; Carter Ratcliff (auth), Doug Ohlson's color condensations, Art in Am, 5-6/78; and others; Carter Ratcliff(auth), Doug Ohlson's fields of Meaning, Art in AM, 2003. *Media:* Acrylic, Oil. *Dealer:* Andre Zarre Gallery 529 W, 20St, New York NY 10011. *Mailing Add:* 35 Bond St New York NY 10012

OHNO, MITSUGI
GLASSBLOWER
b Tochigi, Japan, June 28, 26; US citizen. *Work:* US Capitol replica, Smithsonian Inst, Washington; Independence Hall, White House, 72; US Capitol, 75; Anderson Hall, Kans State Univ, 77; Dwight D Eisenhower Libr; Chemistry Bldg, Tokyo Univ, Japan; Royal carriage & harp replica (given to Crown Prince of Japan), 87. *Comn:* Ohno Klein Bottle, Smithsonian Inst, Washington, 75, given to Emperor of Japan, 79; Nikko Toshogu Shrine, 86 & 88, Tochigi Prefecture, Japan; Nippon-Maru, given to Emperor of Japan, 94. *Exhib:* Smithsonian Inst, 75; Tochigi Mus, Japan, 88; Hyogo History Mus, Japan, 93; Imperial Palace, Japan, 94; Aircraft Carrier USS Nimitz, Battleship USS Mo & USS Constitution (Old Ironsides), Kans State Univ, 96; HMS Victory, Kans State Univ, 98. *Pos:* Sr master sci glassblower, Kans State Univ, retired. *Teaching:* Prof, Scientific Glassblow, 94; adj prof, Kans State Univ, 94. *Awards:* Yoshikawa-Eiji Prize for Cult Merit, Tokyo, Japan, 79; Walter E Morrison Award, Kans State Univ, 79; University Medallion of Excellence, Kans State Univ, 98. *Media:* Glass. *Publ:* The Life of Japanese Man living in Kansas; Japan (A man captivated by glass), 90. *Mailing Add:* 2808 Nevada St Manhattan KS 66502

OJI, HELEN SHIZUKO
PAINTER
b Sacramento, Calif, Aug 27, 50. *Study:* Yuba Col, Marysville, Calif, AA, 70; Calif State Univ, Sacramento, BA(art), 72, MA(art), 75. *Work:* Jacksonville Art Mus, Fla; Mus S Tex, Corpus Christi; Gen Elec Corp, Fairfield, Conn; Mus Mod Art, NY; Jane Voorhees Zimmerli Art Mus, Rutgers State Univ, New Brunswick, NJ. *Comn:* Calendar-poster, Asian Cinevision, NY, 84; Monoprint etching, The Jane Voorhees Zimmerli Art Mus, New Burnswick, 85. *Exhib:* Solo exhibs, Fine Arts Ctr/Wake Forest Univ, Winston-Salem, NC, 80, Monique Knowlton Gallery, NY, 81 & 82, Nelson Gallery, Univ Calif, Davis, 82, Real Art Ways, Hartford, Conn, 84 & Intar Gallery, NY, 86; Mus Mod Art, NY, 81 & 88; Corcoran Gallery Art, Washington (traveling), 93; Zimmerli Art Mus, NJ, 96; A Woman's Place, Monmouth Mus, Randolph, NJ, 96; Would You Mind Repeating That Again?, Broadway Gallery, NY, 96; If the Shoe Fits, FAO Gallery, NY, 96; plus many others. *Pos:* Panelist, NY Found Arts, 86-87, Mass Artists Fel Prog, 87, NY State Coun Arts, 89-91 & New Langton Arts, 90; guest panelist, Soho 20 Gallery, WCA, NY, 88, Chinatown Hist Proj, NY, 88 & Prowess Interarts Inc, NY, 92. *Teaching:* Instr beginning painting & printmaking, Yuba Col, Marysville, Calif, 76; guest lectr, Women's Caucus Arts, NY, 81, Asian Am Art Ctr, NY, 85, Parsons Sch Design, NY, 89 & Alternative Mus, NY, 92; instr visual art workshop, Hospital Audiences Inc, 87-89 & Bergen St Residence, Brooklyn, NY, 92-; guest artist Penn State Univ, 92, State Univ NY, New Paltz, 93 & Columbia Univ, 94; substitute instr art dept, St Ann's Sch, Collegiate Sch, grades K-12, 96; adj instr, Fashion Inst Technol, NY, 96-. *Awards:* Ariana Found Arts Inc Mixed Media Grant, 84; Artists Space Mat Grant, New York, 86; Vis Artist Fel, Brandywine Workshop, Philadelphia, 95. *Bibliog:* Arlene Raven & Cassandra L Langer (auths), positions, NYFAI, New York, 89; The Return of the Cadavre Exquis (exhib catalog), Drawing Ctr, 94; Alice Yang (auth), Haenah-Kent, Asian Art News, 3/94. *Media:* Painting. *Mailing Add:* 360 W 36th St Apt 5NW New York NY 10018

OKAMURA, ARTHUR
PAINTER
b Long Beach, Calif, Feb 24, 32. *Study:* Art Inst Chicago(scholar), 50-54; Univ Chicago, 51 & 53; Yale Univ Summer Art Sem, 54; Edward L Ryerson Travel Fel, 54; Univ Chicago, 57. *Work:* Corcoran Gallery Art, Washington, DC; Nat Collection Fine Arts, Smithsonian Inst; Nat Inst Arts & Lett; Hirshhorn Mus, Washington, DC; San Francisco Mus Art, Calif; and others. *Exhib:* Painters Behind Painters, Calif Palace Legion Honor, San Francisco, 67; one-man shows, San Francisco Mus Art, 68, Calif Col Arts & Crafts, 72, Southern Idaho Col, 72, Kent State Univ, Ohio, 73 & Honolulu Acad Arts, 73; Takashima 1970 Expos, Osaka, Tokyo, Japan, 70; Asian Artists, Oakland Mus, 71; and others. *Pos:* Dir, San Francisco Studio Art, 58. *Teaching:* Instr, Cent YMCA Col, Chicago & Evanston Art Ctr, Ill, 56-57, Art Inst Chicago, N Shore Art League, Winnetka, Ill & Acad Art, San Francisco, 57, Saugatuck Summer Art Sch, Mich, 59 & 62; prof, Calif Col Arts & Crafts, 58-59 & 66-97; guest lectr, Univ Utah, 64 & 75. *Awards:* Schwabacher-Frey Award, 79th Ann, San Francisco Mus, 60; Neysa McMein Purchase Award, Whitney Mus Am Art, 60; Purchase Award, Nat Soc Arts & Lett; plus many others. *Bibliog:* Lee Nordness (ed), Art: USA: Now, C J Bucher, 62; Art Trek Watercolor Workshop, Univ Calif, 89 & 92. *Mem:* Am Fedn Arts. *Dealer:* Ruth Braunstein Gallery 254 Sutter St San Francisco CA 94108. *Mailing Add:* 210 Kale St Bolinas CA 94924

O'KEEFE , MICHAEL
ADMINISTRATOR
b Mc Cloud, Minn. *Study:* Marquette Univ, BS in Physics, Mathematics & Philos; Univ Pittsburgh, MS in Nuclear Physics & Mathematics; Hamline Univ, LittD (hon). *Pos:* Pres, Consortium for Advan of Pvt Higher Educ, Wash, 83-89; exec vpres & Chief Exec Officer, McKnight Found, Minneapolis; asst secy, Fed Dept Health, Educ & Welfare; pres, Minneapolis Col Art & Design, 2002-; human serv comnr State of Minn, 99-2002. *Mailing Add:* Minneapolis Col Art & Design Off of Pres 2501 Stevens Ave S Minneapolis MN 55404

OKOSHI, E SUMIYE
PAINTER, COLLAGE ARTIST
b Seattle, Wash. *Study:* St Margaret & Futaba Col, Tokyo; Seattle Univ, with Fay Chang & Nicholas Damascus; Henry Frye Mus Sch & New Sch Workshop, with Jacob Laurence. *Work:* Zimmerli Art Mus, Rutgers Univ, NJ; Hammond Mus, North Salem, NY; Palace Hotel, Guam Island; Ikue Gakuen, Japanese Children Sch, NJ; Nagoya Bank of NY; plus many others. *Exhib:* Metrop Mus Art, NY, 77; Newark Mus, NJ, 83; Bergen Mus Art & Sci, NJ, 83; Nat Acad Sci, Washington, DC; Port Washington Pub Libr; Viridian Gallery, NY; Hammond Mus, NY; and others. *Awards:* Belle Cramer Mem Award; Ziuta & Akston Found Award; Bertha P Greenblatt Mem Award for abstract painting, 2000. *Bibliog:* Articles in Wash Post, NY Times & OCS News, NY; Gerald Brommer (auth), Collage Techniques. *Mem:* Nat Asn Women Artists. *Media:* Acrylic; Etching. *Publ:* Contribr, Int Economy Mag, Yomiuri News, Manhattan Art & NY Times. *Mailing Add:* Westbeth Studio G226 55 Bethune St New York NY 10014

OKUHARA, TETSU
PHOTOGRAPHER, CONCEPTUAL ARTIST
b Los Angeles, Calif, 40. *Study:* Univ Chicago, 58-61; Cooper Union, New York, 70. *Work:* Los Angeles Co Mus of Art; Hasselblad Collection, Sweden; Mus Mod Art, NY; Nat Gallery of Australia, Melbourne; Tokyo Metrop Mus Photography, Japan. *Comn:* B&W photo Tryptch, Greater Hartford Comm Col, Conn, 82; Photographic mural, Automated Data Processing, Chicago, 88. *Exhib:* Mirrors & Windows, Mus Mod Art, NY, 78; Big Pictures, Mus Mod Art, NY, 84; Grupa Junij 85, Belgrade Hilton, Yugoslavia, 85; Art In Gen, NY, 90; AAAC, NY, 91; Chicago Art Inst Ill, 91-92; San Francisco Cameraworks, Calif, 94; Art Inst Boston, 94; Chicago Cult Ctr, Ill, 98. *Awards:* Guggenheim Found, 75; NY Found for Arts, NY State, 87-88, 2000; Nat Endowment Arts, 88-89; James D Phelan Award, Nat Endowment Arts, 94. *Bibliog:* Marjorie Bevlin (auth), Design Through Discovery, HR&W, 77; Ralph Gibson (auth), Contact: Theory, Lustrum Press, 80; Article in Contact Sheet, 90, Light Work, 97, Christies Mag, 99. *Publ:* Auth, Foto, Sweden, 88; Nueva Luz, 88; New York Mag, 88; 100 Nudes, Sun Mag, Tokyo, Japan, 91; Intuitive Eye, Chicago Art Inst, 92. *Dealer:* Freddie Fong Gallery 760 Market St San Francisco, Calif. *Mailing Add:* 202 E 42nd St New York NY 10017

OKULICK, JOHN A
SCULPTOR
b New York, NY, 47. *Study:* Univ Calif, Santa Barbara, BA, 69; Univ Calif, Irvine, MFA, 74. *Work:* Hawaii Mus Contemp Art, Honolulu; Fogg Art Mus, Harvard Univ, Cambridge, Mass; Smithsonian Inst, Washington; Va Mus Fine Arts, Richmond; Power Gallery, Contemp Art, Univ Sydney, Australia; Phoenix Mus Art; and many others. *Comn:* Los Angeles State Off Bldg, Van Nuys; Ronald Reagan State Off Bldg, Los Angeles, 90; Port of Los Angeles, Harbor Con Multiuse Bldg, San Pedro, Calif, 92; City of Reno, Nev, 92; Chatsworth Metrolink Sta, Los Angeles Co Transportation Authority; Mus Sci and Industry, LA; Culver City Police Dept, Calif; Van Nuys State Off Bldg, Calif. *Exhib:* New Am Graphic Art, Fogg Art Mus, Harvard Univ, 73; one-man exhibs, Asher/Faure Gallery, Los Angeles, 80, 81, 83, 85 & 87, John Berggruen Gallery, San Francisco, 83, 85, 88 & 90, Richard Gray Gallery, Chicago, 86, 89 & 92, Del Art Mus, 91, Fay Gold Gallery, Atlanta, 92, 95 & 97, Nancy Hoffman Gallery, 94, 96 & 98, Gallery at 777, Los Angeles, 99, Nancy Hoffman Gallery, New York City, 00, 01, Imago Gallery, Palm Desert, Calif, 01, Fay Gold Gallery, Atlanta, 01; Frederick and Marcia Weisman Collection of California Art, Corcoron Gallery, 79; Young Talent Awards 1963-83, Los Angeles Co Mus Art, 83; Intermedia: Between Painting and Sculpture, Aldrich Mus, 84; Relief Sculpture, Selections from the Mus Collection, Hirshhorn Mus & Sculpture Garden, 86; Sculpture on the Wall, Aldrich Mus Contemp Art, 86-87; Selections from the Frederick R Weisman Collection, Frederick R Weisman Mus Art, Pepperdine Univ, 95; Light Interpretations, Jewish Mus, San Francisco, 95; From Behind the Orange Curtain, Muckenthaler Cult Ctr, Fullerton, Calif, 95; Collector's Choice, Ctr for Arts, Vero Beach, Fla, 95-96; Nancy Hoffman Gallery, NY, 96, 97 & 98; Flanders Contemp Art, Minneapolis, Minn, 97; LA Current: A Media Fusion, Armand Hammer Mus Art, Univ Calif, Los Angeles, 97; Collector's Show, Ark Arts Ctr, Little Rock, 97-98; Illusion: Tromp l'Oeil and Sleight of Hand, Riverside Art Mus, Calif, 98; group exhibs, Nancy Hoffman Gallery, New York City, 99-00, 01, Flint Inst Arts, Mich, 99-00, Ark Arts Ctr, Little Rock, 00; and many others. *Collection Arranged:* Fogg Art Mus, Harvard Univ, Cambridge, Mass; Los Angeles Co Mus Art; Memphis Mus Art; Oakland Mus, Calif; Phoenix Art Mus; San Francisco Mus Modern Art; Smithsonian Inst; Va Mus of Fine Arts, Richmond. *Bibliog:* Michele Hunevan (auth), A way with wood, Angeles Mag, 3/89; Alan G Arther (auth), Chicago Tribune, 3/89; Michael Webb (auth), Concrete dreams, LA Style Mag, 7/89. *Mailing Add:* c/o Nancy Hoffman Gallery 429 W Broadway New York NY 10012

OKUMURA, LYDIA
PAINTER, SCULPTOR
b Sao Paulo, Brazil. *Study:* Fac Plastic Arts, Armando Alvares Penteado Found, Sao Paulo, Brazil, BFA, 73; Pratt Graphics Ctr, New York, 74-77. *Work:* Hara Mus Contemp Art, Tokyo; Pinacotheca of State & Mus Contemp Art, Sao Paulo, Brazil; Mus Mod Art, Bogota, Colombia; Mus Contemp Art, Caracas, Venezuela; Mus Modern Art, Sao Paulo, Brazil; Itamaraty Palace, Ministry of For Affairs, Brazil; Mario de Andrade Pub Libr, Sao Paulo. *Exhib:* Solo exhibs in Sao Paulo, Tokyo, Osaka, NY & Ottawa, 68-2004; Biennial Art, Medellin, Colombia, 81; Atlantic Capital Corp, NY, 81; Nat Mus Osaka, Japan, 81; Hara Mus Contemp Art, Tokyo, 85; Mus Mod Art, Sao Paulo, 88; and others. *Awards:* Creative Artists Pub Serv Prog Graphic Grant, 78; Japan Found Fel, 79; Norway Graphic Biennial, 80; Int Biennial Sao Paulo Prize, 1973, 1977. *Bibliog:* I L Brandao (catalog), Galeria Sao Paulo, Brazil, 4/84; A Amaral (auth), Today's Art of Brazil (catalog), Hara Mus Contemp Art, Tokyo, Japan, 11/85; William Zimmer (auth), NY Times, 90; and others. *Media:* Acrylic, Oil. *Publ:* Coauth, Fujieda, Akio Dialogue with the contemporary, Mizue Mag, No 904, Tokyo, 80; John Mendelson (exhib catalog), Pinacoteca, Sao Paulo, Brazil, 9/95; Ichiro Hariu, Takeshi Kanazawa (catalog), Kate Art Gallery, Sao Paulo, 1991. *Dealer:* Onetwentyeight Gallery, New York. *Mailing Add:* 32 Union Square E 513 New York NY 10003

OKUN, BARBARA-ROSE
ART DEALER, GALLERY DIRECTOR
b New Rochelle, NY, July 29, 32. *Study:* Mt Holyoke Col, S Hadley, Mass, BA, 54; Lindenwood Col, St Charles, Mo, 86. *Collection Arranged:* Ceramics & Social Commentary (auth, catalog), Laumeier Sculpture Park Gallery, 85. *Pos:* Owner, Okun Gallery, Sante Fe, NMex, currently; friends bd, St Louis Art Mus, Mo, 84-86; trustee, Laumeier Sculpture Park, St Louis, Mo, 84-86 & Am Craft Coun, New York, 86-89; Santa Fe Inst Fine Art, NMex, 89-93. *Teaching:* Inst, Educ Ctr, Longboat Key, Fla, 91 & 94. *Mem:* Am Craft Coun; Collectors Circle; Friends of Contemp Art; NMex Mus Fine Arts. *Specialty:* 20th Century American art & craft and The Art of the Basketmaker, Blacksmith and Ceramist. *Publ:* Auth, Five Colorado Potters, Colo Art, summer 83; Auction house activities; The secondary market for contemporary art, Am Soc Appraisers Personal Property News, spring & summer, 86. *Dealer:* Lew Allen Contemporary 129 W Palace Ave Santa Fe NM 87501; R Duane Reed Gallery 7513 Forsyth Blvd St Louis Mo 63105. *Mailing Add:* PO Box 665 Tesuque NM 87574

OKUN, JENNY
PHOTOGRAPHER
b NJ, Oct 3, 53. *Study:* Wimbledon Sch Art, London, found degree, 71; Chelsea Sch Art, London, BA & MA, 75; Slade Sch Art, postgrad degree, 77. *Work:* Victoria & Albert Mus, London; Brooklyn Mus; Herbert F Johnson Mus, Cornell, NY. *Comn:* 18 60″ photographs, Baker & Daniels, Indianapolis, 89; 6 x 120″ photographs, Bournemouth, Gen Hosp, England, 89; 8 x 80″ photographs, JP Morgan, London, 91; 78 CD covers, Decca Records/London Records, 93. *Exhib:* Film/London, Nat Film Theatre, London, 84; Royal Inst Brit Architects, London, 85; Dining Room, Albright Knox Mus, 89; 25 Yrs of British Avant Garde Film, Tate Gallery, London, 91; LA Current: UCLA Armand Hammer, 96. *Teaching:* Teacher found art/painting, Cent Sch Art, London, 77-80, Chelsea Sch Art, London, 80-84. *Bibliog:* Max Wykes-Joyce (auth), Jenny Okun Galerie Zabriskie, Herald Tribune, 80; Summer 1992 reviews, Art News, 92; William Packer (auth), The art of wrapping up, Financial Tunes, London, 95. *Dealer:* Craig Krull Gallery Bergamont Sta 2525 Michigan Ave Bldg B Santa Monica CA 90404. *Mailing Add:* 942 N Alpine Dr Beverly Hills CA 90210

OLDENBURG, CLAES THURE
SCULPTOR
b Stockholm, Sweden, Jan 28, 1929. *Study:* Yale Univ, BA, 51; Art Inst Chicago, 1952-54; studied Oberlin Col, 1970, Art Inst Chicago, 1979, Bard Col, 1995, Royal Col Art, London, 1996, with Losie van Bruggen, Nova Scotia Col Art and Design, 2005. *Work:* Albright-Knox Art Gallery, Buffalo; Mus Mod Art, Whitney Mus Am Art, Guggenheim Mus, NY; Art Gallery Ont, Toronto; Art Inst Chicago; Walker Art Ctr; plus many others. *Comn:* Clothespin, Center Sq, Philadelphia; column, HW Social Security Ctr, Chicago; stake, Dallas Mus Art; sculptor, Parc de la Villette, Paris; Piazzale Cadorna, Milan; and others. *Exhib:* solo exhibs Reuben Gallery, NY, 60, Green Gallery, NY, 62, Sidney Janis Gallery, NY, 64-70, Galerie Ileana Sonnabend, Paris, 64, Robert Fraser Gallery, London, 66, Moderna Mus, Stockholm, 66, 77, Mus Contemp Art, Chicago, 66, 77, Irving Blum Gallery, Los Angeles, 68, Mus Modern Art, NY, 69, Stedelijk Mus, Amsterdam, 70, 77, Tate Gallery, London, 70, Pasadena Art Mus, 71, Nelson-Atkins Mus, Kansas City, 72, Art Inst Chicago, 73, Leo Castelli Gallery, NY, 74, 76, 80, 90, Margo Leavin Gallery, Los Angeles, 75, 76, 78, 88, 89 and others; Metrop Mus Art, NY, 69; retrospective, Mus Mod Art, NY, 69, Pasadena Art Mus, Calif, 71, Walker Art Ctr, 75 & Kunsthalle, Tubingen, WGer, 75; Los Angeles Co Mus Art, 71; Seattle Art Mus, Wash, 73; Am Pop Art, Whitney Mus Am Art, 74; Mus Mod Art, NY, 87, 88, 90 & 91; Whitney Mus Am Art, 88; The Art of Assemblage, Locks Gallery, Philadelphia, 94; Aldrich Mus Contemp Art, 94; Marian Goodman Gallery, NY, 94; Drawing on Sculpture, Cohen Gallery, NY, 94; White Works, Pace Wildenstein, NY, 94; Worlds in a Box (traveling), City Art Centre, Edinburgh, 94-95; and many others. *Awards:* Creative Arts Award for Lifetime Artistic Achievement, Brandeis Univ, 93; Lifetime Achievement Award in Contemp Sculpture, Int Sculpture Ctr, Washington, 94; Rolf Shock Prize, Stockholm, Sweden, 95; Nat Medal of Arts, 2000. *Mem:* Am Acad Inst Arts & Lett; Am Acad Arts & Sci; Nat Acad. *Publ:* Auth, Notes in Hand, Dutton & Petersburg, 71; Object into monument, Pasadena Art Mus, 71; Raw Notes, Nova Scotia Col Art & Design Press, 73; coauth (with Coosje van Bruggen), Sketches and Blottings Toward the European Desk Top, Milan and Turin: Galleria Christian Stein; and Florence: Hopeful Monster, 90; Multiples in Retrospect, Pizzoli Int, 1990; and others. *Dealer:* PaceWildenstein 32 E 57th St New York NY 10022; Paula Cooper Gallery NY

OLDENBURG, RICHARD ERIK
MUSEUM DIRECTOR
b Stockholm, Sweden, Sept 21, 33; US citizen. *Study:* Harvard Col, AB, 54. *Pos:* Dir publ, Mus Mod Art, New York, 69-72, dir mus, 72-94, dir emer, 95-; chmn, Int Comt Mus Collections Mod Art, Int Coun Mus, 83-86, exec bd; chmn, Sotheby's North & South Am, 95-. *Awards:* Order of North Star, Sweden; Order of Isabel la Catolica, Spain; Order of Arts & Lett & Chevalier of Legion d'honneur, France. *Mem:* Asn Art Mus Dirs (1st vpres, 86-87, pres, 87-88). *Mailing Add:* 11 W 53rd St New York NY 10019

OLDMAN, TERRY L
MUSEUM DIRECTOR
Study: Univ Kans, BS; Univ Kans, MA(art mus educ); Univ Hawaii, MS(bus admin). *Pos:* Interim assist dir, Spencer Mus, Lawrence, Kans; dir/cur educ Mus Art, Tallahassee; dir Albrecht-Kemper Mus Art, St Joseph, Mo, 99-. *Awards:* Decorated Distinguished Flying Cross, Bronze Star, Aerial Achievement Medal. *Mailing Add:* Albrecht-Kemper Mus Art 2818 Frederick Ave Saint Joseph MO 64506

OLEA, HECTOR
CURATOR
Work: Co-cur (with Mari Carmen Ramirez) (exhib) Inverted Utopias: Avant-Garde Arts in Latin America, 2004 (Award for Best Thematic Mus Show Nationally, Int Asn Art Critics/USA, 2005). *Pos:* Independent cur, writer, translator. *Publ:* co-auth (with Mari Carmen Ramirez): (book) Inverted Utopias: Avant-Garde Arts in Latin America, 2004

O'LEARY, DANIEL
MUSEUM DIRECTOR
Study: Princeton Univ, PhD in art Hist; Univ Mich, MBA in mktg and mgt. *Pos:* Dir Minn Inst Arts, Portland Mus Art, Maine, 1993—. *Mailing Add:* Portland Mus Art 7 Congress Square Portland ME 04101

OLENICK, DAVID CHARLES
ADMINISTRATOR, DEALER
b Rockville Centre, NY, Apr 21, 47. *Study:* NY Univ; Hofstra Univ; New Sch Social Res; State Univ NY. *Pos:* Co-dir, Mansight Educ, Full Circle Assocs, 68-69; owner & dir, Park Gallery, Brooklyn, 69-71; ed consult & field prog coordr, Proj Am Develop, US AID State Dept, 69-70; asst dir, Brooklyn Mus Art Sch, 74-77, admin head, 77-81, adminr educ & prog develop, 78-81; gallery dir, Adam L Gimbel Gallery, New York, 81-83; cur contemp art, Saks Fifth Ave, New York, 81-83; owner & dir, David Olenick Fine Art, New York, 85-. *Specialty:* Contemporary paintings and sculpture; tribal art; asian art. *Mailing Add:* 120 Park Pl Brooklyn NY 11217

OLESZKO, PATRICIA
VISUAL ARTIST, PERFORMANCE ARTIST
b May 19, 47. *Study:* Univ Mich, BFA, 70. *Exhib:* Performances, Taxidermis, 76, Pat Oleszko-Sew What, 76 & The Three Musicians Pats Picasso, 77, Mus Mod Art, NY, Clothe Your Eyes (Review), Los Angeles Co Mus, Calif, 77, Dots What's Happening, 80 & The Tool Jest-Tooth & Consequences, 81, Metrop Mus Art, NY, All the World's a Stooge, 80 & Revel Without a Claus, 88, Whitney Mus, NY, The Pats to Suckcess, 85 & Inflation: The Air Apparent, 87, Cranbrook Acad Art, Mich; Guise on Dolls: Signatures at an Exhib, Ctr Contemp Art, Santa Fe, NMex, 91, Nat Mus Women Arts, Washington, DC, 92, Bass Mus, Miami Beach, Fla & Neuberger Mus, State Univ, NY, Purchase, 93 & Nexus, Atlanta, Ga, 94; USA Today (Udder De Light), Textile Mus, Antwerp, The Neth, 93; Outside the Frame, Performance & the Object (Udder De Light), Cleveland, Contemp, Ohio, 93; Blowhard, Anchorbat & Jug-lure, Buskers Fest, World Trader, 93; To Air is Human, Southern Exposure, San Francisco, Calif, 93; The Errant Space Mus, Wesleyan U, Middletown, Conn, 99; Roamin' Holiday: A View from A Broad, Am Acad Rome, 2000; The Clothes Lines, The Kitchen & PS 122, NY, 2000; Five Easy Pieces (Lighten Up: Art with a Sense of Humor), De Cordova Mus and Sculpture Park, Lincoln, Mass, 2000; and other exhibs and performances. *Teaching:* SUNY, Purchase, 99, Kansas City Art Inst, Kans, 2000 & San Francisco Art Inst, 2001. *Awards:* NY State Coun Arts Grant, 73, 80, 87 & 91; Nat Endowment Arts Fel, 78, 85, 87 & 93; Mass Coun Arts, New Works, 88; Guggenheim Fel, 90; First Prize, Fourth of July Parade, Aspen, Colo, 93; Rome Prize, Am Acad, Rome, 98-99; Gladys Krieble Delmas Found, 99; Best Show of an Underknown or Emerging Artist, 2nd Place, Asn Int Art Critics, 2000; Yaddo, 2001; MacDowell Colony, 2001; New York Found Arts Award, 2001. *Bibliog:* Articles in Art Am, 82 & 91, Art Express, 82, Portfolio, 83, High Performance, 83 & 84, Arts & Antiques, 84 & Artforum, 86, New Yorker, 90; numerous articles in Penthouse, Oui, Ms, Artforum, Sesame Street & others. *Publ:* Films, Not a Pretty Sight: The Wurst is Yet to Come, 86; Little Red Writing: The Free Little Pig; producer, 26 short films, videos. *Mailing Add:* 190 Duane St New York NY 10013

OLIN, FERRIS
HISTORIAN, CURATOR
Study: Douglass Col, BA, 70; Rutgers Univ, MLS, 72, MA, 75, PhD, 98. *Work:* Hopewell Mus, NJ. *Collection Arranged:* Architecture of New Brunswick and its Environs, 79; Women in the Community, series exhibs, 82; Artists Books: From the Traditional to the Avant-Garde, 82; Women's Spheres (co-ed, catalog), 83; Baroness Hyde de Neuville, Sketches of America, 1807-22, 83; Representative Works and Focused Fragments, 84; Past and Promise: Lives of New Jersey Women, 90; Mary H Dana Women Artists Series, 94-; 25 Years of Feminism, 25 Years of Women's Art, 96. *Pos:* Dir, Rutgers Art Libr, 76-85; res-consult, New York Feminist Art Inst, 77-78; bk reviewer, Leonardo, 77-82; ed prof lit column, Art Libr Soc NAm Newslett, 80-84; exec officer, Inst Res on Women, Rutgers & Laurie NJ Chair in Women's Studies, 85-94; Librn, Douglass Col Libr, 94-; cur, Mary H Dana Women Artists Series, 94- & Women's Arch, 94; head Margery Somers Foster Ctr, 2000-. *Teaching:* Dir & art librn, Rutgers Univ, New Brunswick, 76-85, assoc prof, 80-. *Awards:* Rhoda Freeman Recognition Award, NJC & UCWE, 88. *Mem:* Am Studies Asn; Womens Caucus for Art; Col Art Asn; Art Table. *Res:* Contributions of women artists to art history; regional history and material culture; 20th century American woman art collectors. *Interests:* 19th & 20th Century Europ & Am art & archit; women's art history. *Publ:* Contrib, Dictionary of Women Artists Born Before 1900, GK Hall, 85; coauth, Making Their Mark: Women Artists, 1970-85, 89; auth & co-ed, The New Jersey Project: Integrating the New Scholarship on Gender, 1986-90, 90; Past and Promise: Lives of New Jersey Women, 89 & 96; 25 Years of Feminism, 25 Years of Women's Art, 96. *Mailing Add:* 54 McComb Rd Princeton NJ 08540

OLIN, LAURIE DEWAR
ARCHITECT, EDUCATOR
Work: Los Angeles Co Mus Art, 1987, Toledo Mus Art, 1995. *Comn:* Prin works incl ARCO Hdqs, Newtown Sq, Pa, 1976, Johnson & Johnson Hdqs, Denver, 1977, Canary Wharf, London, 1985, Vila Olimpica, Barcelona, Spain, 1991, Independence Nat Historic Park, Philadelphia, 1997, Beringer Vineyard and Chateau St Jean Winery, Calif, 1998, site design, Washington Monument, 2002. *Exhib:* Nat Gallery Sculpture Garden, Washington, DC, 1993. *Pos:* chr, landscape archit dept, grad sch design Harvard Univ, 82-86; prin, Hanna/Olin Ltd landscape archits, Philadelphia, 76-96. *Teaching:* Lectr, to practice prof landscape archit, regional planning Univ Pa, 76-; Olin Partnership, Philadelphia, 96-. *Awards:* Recipient Bradford Williams medal for writing on landscape archit, 91. *Mem:* Fel, Am Acad Arts & Sci's; Am Soc Landscape Archits; Am Inst Archits (hon); Nat Acad. *Mailing Add:* Olin Partnership Public Ledger Bldg 150 S Independence Mall W Ste 1123 Philadelphia PA 19106

OLIPHANT, PATRICK
POLITICAL CARTOONIST, SCULPTOR, PAINTER
b Adelaide, Australia, July 24, 35; US citizen. *Hon Degrees:* Dartmouth Col, DHL. *Work:* Nat Portrait Gallery, Nat Archives, Presidential Libr, Libr Cong & Nat Mus Am Hist, Washington, DC; Detroit Inst Art, Mich. *Exhib:* Gallery Exhibs, Susan Conway Gallery, Washington, DC, 88, 89, 90, 91, 92, 93 & 94, Lotos Club, NY, 92; one-person exhibs, Gerald R Ford Pres Mus, Grand Rapids, Mich, 91, Fullerton Mus, Calif, 91, Kiplinger Collection, Ronald Reagan Pres Libr, Simi, Calif, 91, Columbia Mus Art, SC, 91, Lyndon Baines Johnson Pres Libr, Austin, Tex, 92, Nelson Atkins Mus, Kansas City, Mo, 93, Detroit Inst Arts, Mich, 94 & traveling exhib, Prague, Czech Republic, Warsaw, Poland, Budapest Hungary, Bratislava Slovakia, Nitra Slovakia, 94-95; group show, Nat Archives, Washington, DC, 91-92, Princeton Club, NY, Century Asn, NY, 92, 93 & 94, Princeton Univ Libr, NJ, 93, Libr Congress, Washington, DC, 98, Mus Fine Arts, Sante Fe, NMex, 2000. *Pos:* Copyboy, press artist, Adelaide Advertiser, 53-55, ed cartoonist, 55-64; ed cartoonist, Denver Post, 64-75, Washington Star, 75-81; syndicated cartoonist, Los Angeles Times Syndicate, 65-79 & Universal Press Syndicate, 79-. *Awards:* Pulitzer Prize for Editorial Cartooning, 67; Reuben Award, Nat Cartoonist soc, 68 & 72; Nat Headliner Asn Award, 79; and others. *Mem:* Int Salon Cartoons (jury chmn). *Media:* Oil. *Specialty:* Contemporary Am. *Publ:* Fashions for the New World Order, 91, Just Say No, 92; Why Do I Feel Uneasy?, 93; Oliphant-Cartoon for the New World Order (1983-1993) Traveling Exhib (with catalog), 93; Waiting for the Other Shoe to Drop, 94; and others. *Dealer:* Susan Conway Gallery

OLITSKI, JULES
PAINTER, SCULPTOR
b Snovsk, Russia, Mar 27, 22. *Study:* Nat Acad Design, NY, 39-42; Beaux Arts Inst, NY, 40-42; Acad Grande Chaumiere, Paris, France, 49-50; NY Univ, BS, 52, MA, 54. *Hon Degrees:* Univ Hartford, DA (hon), 97; Keene State Col, Univ NH, DA (hon), 98. *Work:* Art Inst Chicago; Corcoran Gallery Art, & Nat Gallery, Washington; Whitney Mus Am Art, Mus Mod Art, Guggenheim Mus, Metrop Mus, NY; Nat Gallery Australia, Canberra; Israel Mus, Jerusalem; and others; Art Gallery of Ontario, Beth Tzedek Congregation, Toronto; Mus of Fine Arts, Boston, Mus of Modern Art, New York City, Mus of Fine Arts, Houston, Guggenheim Mus, New York City. *Comn:* Welded steel sculpture, Gallaudet Col for the Deaf, Washington, 79. *Exhib:* Solo shows, Gallery One, Toronto, 90 & 91, Salander O'Reilly Galleries, Berlin, Ger, 92 & 93, Thorne-Sagendorf Gallery, Keene State Col, NH, 93, Gallery Camino Real, Boca Raton, Fla, 94 & Univ Miami, Fla, 94, Portland (Maine) Mus, Virginia Lynch Galleries, Tiverton, RI, 98, Galeria Metta, Madrid, Bernard Jacobsen Gallery, London, Drabinsky Friedland Gallery, Toronto, 99, Butler Inst Am Art, Amringer/Howard Fine Art, New York City, 2000, Bonington Gallery Nottingham Trent Univ, Nottingham, Eng, Virginia Lynch Gallery, Tiverton, RI, 2001; Strategies for the Next Painting, Wolff Gallery, NY, 91; Gallery Selections, Salander-O'Reilly Galleries Inc, NY, 91; 168th Ann Exhib, Nat Acad Design, NY, 93; The Brushstroke and its Guises, NY Studio Sch, 94; Nat Acad Design, New York City, 93; Galerie Gerald Piltzer, Paris, 94; Annandale Galleries, Sydney, Australia, 2000. *Teaching:* Asst prof, State Univ NY, New Paltz, 54-55; prof & chmn dept fine arts, CW Post Col, Long Island Univ, 56-63; instr art, Bennington Col, 63-67. *Awards:* First Prize for Painting, Corcoran Gallery Art, 67; Milton & Sally Avery Distinguished Professorship, Bard Col, 87; Assoc Nat Academician, Nat Acad Design, 93; Named Disting Artist, Ark Celebration of Arts, Hot Springs, 96. *Bibliog:* Hovey Brock (auth), Jules Olitsky, ARTnews, Summer 92; Peter Schjeldahl (auth), The death of painting, Village Voice, 3/31/92; Sue Scott (auth), review, Artnews, summer 93; Stephen Hodeker (auth) A Conversation with Jules Olitski, New Hampshire Images, Summer, 97; Artists Portraits- A Gallery of the Century's Brightest Talents, Architctural Digest, Apr., 99; Donald Kuspit (auth) Jules Olitski, Ameringer /Howard Fine Art, Artforum, Dec., 2000. *Mem:* Fel Am Acad Arts & Sci, Boston; Amer Acad Arts and Letters; Nat Acad. *Publ:* Auth, First Chapter (a short story), Partisan Rev, Vol II, 78; The Courage of Conviction, Dodd Mead & Co, Ballantine Books, 86; How I Got My First New York Show, Partisan Rev, 1/89. *Mailing Add:* PO Box 440 Marlboro VT 05344

OLIVEIRA, NATHAN
PAINTER
b Oakland, Calif, Dec 19, 28. *Study:* Mills Col, 50; Calif Col Arts & Crafts, MFA, 52, DFA, 68. *Work:* Hirshhorn Mus & Sculpture Garden, Smithsonian Inst, Washington, DC; Mus Mod Art, NY; San Francisco Mus Mod Art; Solomon R Guggenheim Mus, NY; Acad Art, Honolulu; and many others. *Exhib:* The Contemp Monotypes, Edith C Blum Art Inst, Annandale-on-Hudson, NY, 85; John Berggruen Gallery, San Francisco, 85; Recent Acquisitions, John Berggruen Gallery, 91; Contemp Monotypes: Six Masters, De Saisset Mus, Santa Clara Univ, Calif, 85; solo exhibs, Sites and Related Works, 1957-86, Stanford Univ Art Gallery, Palo Alto, Calif, 86, Ital Sites,

Monotypes, Richard Gray Gallery, Chicago, 86, John Berggruen Gallery, San Francisco, 87, 89, 90 & 93, Nathan Oliveira, 1957-1977, Campbell-Thiebaud Gallery, 91, Paintings and Works on Paper, 1959-1991, Salander-O'Reilly Galleries, 91 & New Mexican Sites: Hand Painted Monotypes executed at Hand Graphics, Santa Fe, John Berggruen Gallery, Santa Fe, 91; Large Scale Works on Paper, John Berggruen Gallery, San Francisco, 91; and many other one-man & group exhibs. *Teaching:* Prof art, San Francisco Art Inst, Calif Col Arts & Crafts, 55-56, Univ Ill, 61-62, Univ Calif Los Angeles, 63-64, Cornell Univ, 64, Stanford Univ, 64-, Univ Colo, 65, Univ Hawaii, 71, Cranbrook Acad Art, Bloomfield Hills, Mich, 72, Baltimore Art Inst, 72, John Herron Art Inst, Indianapolis, Ind 72 & Kent State Univ, 73; artist-in-residence, Univ Ill, Urbana, 61-62, Univ Calif, Los Angeles, 63, Santa Rosa Jr Col, Calif 78 & Harvard Univ, Cambridge, Mass, 78; vis artist, San Antonio Art Inst, Tex, 61-62, Univ Colo, Boulder, summer 65, Univ Hawaii, Honolulu, 71, Cranbrook Acad Arts, Bloomfield Hills, Mich, 72, Fullerton Col, Calif, 72, Herron Sch Art, Indianapolis, Ind, 72, Md Inst Col Art, Baltimore, 72, Kent State Univ, Ohio, 72, Ft Wright Col, Wash, 73, Wichita State Univ, Kans, 76, Centrum, Port Townsend, Wash, summer, 77. *Awards:* Grant, Nat Endowment Arts, 74; Award, Am Acad & Inst Arts & Lett, NY, 84; Academician, Graphic Arts, Nat Acad Design, NY, 85. *Bibliog:* Thomas Albright (auth), Art in the San Francisco Bay Area, 1945-1980: An Illustrated History, Univ Calif Press, 85; Marc Harrison (auth), Nathan Oliveira, Peninsula, 2/91; Eugenia Parry Janis (auth), Nathan Oliveira, rapture & release, Artspace, summer 91. *Mem:* Nat Acad; Am Acad Arts & Sci; Am Acad & Inst Arts & Lett. *Mailing Add:* John Berggruen Gallery 228 Grant Ave San Francisco CA 94108-4612

OLIVER, BOBBIE
PAINTER
b Canada, June 17, 49. *Study:* Ctr Creative Studies, Detroit, 66-68; St Albans Sch Art, Eng, 68. *Work:* Robert McLaughlin Gallery, Oshawa, Can; Nuffield Found, Eng; Can Coun Art Bank, Can; Glenbow Mus, Alta, Can; pvt collections. *Exhib:* Art Gallery Ont, Toronto, 78; solo exhibs, Wolfe Gallery, 85, Olga Korper Gallery, Toronto, 86-88, 88, 91, 94, 96 & 99, Lenore Gray Gallery, Providence, RI, 95 & 98, Univ Waterloo, Can, 99, Thompson Gallery, Owen Sound, Can, 99 & Nature Morte Gallery, India, 99, West Space, NY, 2002, Olga Korper, 2003 & 2006. *Teaching:* Prof, RI Sch Design, Princeton Univ, Sch Visual Arts, New York & Banff Sch Fine Arts, Can; chair, painting dept, RI Sch Design, 2006. *Awards:* Ont Arts Coun Grant, 80; Pollock-Krasner Grant, 86; Can Coun Arts Grants, 80, 83, 85 & 96; and others. *Bibliog:* J Zinsser (auth), Bobbie Oliver at Wolff, East Village Eye, 5/85; John Bentley Mays (auth), Invoking a sense of place, Globe & Mail, 3/89; John Kissick (auth), A tale of two painters, Can Art; James Campbell (auth), Nameless Waters, 99; Ken Johnson (auth), NY Times, 99. *Media:* Acrylic. *Dealer:* Olga Korper Gallery Toronto Canada. *Mailing Add:* 140 W Broadway New York NY 10013

OLIVER, JULIE FORD
PAINTER, INSTRUCTOR
b Manchester, Eng, Nov 23, 42, US citizen. *Study:* Manchester Sch Art, Eng, 57-60; Art Students League, Denver, Colo, 85-89. *Work:* Pronof Mus Art, Juarez, Mex; Int Mus Art, El Paso, Tex; Americana Mus, El Paso, Tex. *Comn:* Children's Ward, Thomason Hosp, El Paso, Tex, 98. *Exhib:* solo exhib, Americana Mus, El Paso, Tex, 97, Charmizal Nat Mem, El Paso, Tex, 2003; Exchange, Pronof Mus Cuidad Juarez, Chihuahua Mex, 98; Divas, Charmizal Nat Mem, El Paso, Tex, 2000; Desert Echo, Women's Mus Dallas, Tex, 2001; Border Artists, Mus Fine Art & Cult, Las Cruces, NMex, 2002; Curators Invitational, Int Mus Art, El Paso, Tex, 2004; Along the Rio Grande, Mus Dept Interior, Washington DC, 2005. *Pos:* illusr & graphic design, Banker & Bris Bois, Grand Rapids, Mich, 85-90; illusr, E & J Distributing, Las Cruces, NMex, 90-97. *Teaching:* teacher, painting, Monday Studio, Las Cruces, NMex, 2004-2006. *Awards:* Grumbacher Gold Medal, El Paso Mus Art, Sierra Medical Ctr, 82-83. *Mem:* El Paso Art Asn; Las Cruces Art Asn. *Media:* Oil, Egg Tempera. *Publ:* contribr, Desert Echo, Woman's Mus, Dallas, 2000; contribr, The New Creative Artist, N Light, 2006. *Dealer:* Joseph Bender Art & Antiques 100 Executive Center Blvd El Paso Tex 79902; C Bunch Patio Art Gallery 655 Univ Las Cruces NMex 88005. *Mailing Add:* 1590 Imperial Ridge Las Cruces NM 88011

OLIVER, MARVIN E
CRAFTSMAN
b Seattle, Wash, 1956. *Study:* San Francisco State Univ, BA, 70; Univ Wash, MFA, 73. *Comn:* Bronze, glass & concrete sculpture, Spirit of Washington, 92; 40 ft bronze sculpture, Spirit of Our Youth, 92-93; River of Life, South Puget Sound Col, Olympia, Wash, 93; Red Wolf, Cedarcrest High Sch, Duvall/Carnation, 94; Arctic Lights (steel & glass sculpture), Arctic Light Elem Sch, Fairbanks, Alaska, 94. *Exhib:* Salmon: Ritual & Resource, Stonington Gallery, Seattle, 92; From the Woods, Bellevue Art Mus, Wash, 92; Unending Journey: A Selection of Contemp Native Am Crafts, Sch Visual Arts Mus, NY, 92; Traditional & Contemp Trends in Native Arts, Western Gallery, Western Wash Univ, Bellingham, 93; Signals in Sculpture, Inst Am Indian Arts Mus, Santa Fe, NMex, 93; and many others. *Pos:* Bd pres, Inst Am Indian Arts, 83-87; artists, Elders Forum, 86; comt mem, Wash State Centennial, 89; instr, Pratt Fine Arts Ctr, 91; lectr, Seattle Art Mus, 92. *Teaching:* Assoc prof, Univ Wash. *Awards:* Nat Endowment Arts, 88; Fel Glass Casting, Pratt Fine Arts Ctr, 90; Artists Guest Hosts' Honor, Northwest Visionaries, Seattle Art Mus, 94. *Bibliog:* Ten Artists From Washington State (film), Tacoma Art Mus, Wash, 90; Mayumi Nakazawa (auth), Native American arts, Elle Deco, Japan Mag, No 3, winter 91; Robin K Wright (auth), A Time of Gathering: Native Heritage in Washington State, Burke Mus, Univ Wash Press, Seattle, 91. *Mem:* Asn Nat Humanities Fac, 78-88; pres, Inst Am Indian Arts, 84-86. *Publ:* Illusr, cover & book, Shamans & Kushtakas, Mary Beck, 91; Potlatch, Mary Beck, 93; front cover, Wash State Treasurer's Report, 94; Reaching Home, Fobes, Jay & Matsen. *Mailing Add:* Univ Wash Am Indian Studies Ctr Box 354305 Seattle WA 98195

OLIVER, ROBERT S
PAINTER, ARCHITECT
b Anaconda, Mont, Nov 11, 19. *Study:* U Calif, Berkeley, BA, 43, MFA, 48; Inst Allende, San Miguel de Illende, Mex, MFA, 68. *Work:* Phoenix Art Mus, Ariz; City of Phoenix, Ariz; An Inst Archit Arch, Washington, DC; Glendale Community Coll, Ariz; St Joseph's Hosp, Phoenix, Ariz. *Comn:* painting, City of Phoenix, Ariz, 70; painting, Western Savings & Loan, Phoenix, Ariz, 73, 95; painting, Ariz Bank, Sun City, 74. *Exhib:* Phoenix Art Mus, Ariz, 72, 73; Am Watercolor Soc, NY, 73, 75, 80, 84, 95; Nat Watercolor Soc, Brea, Calif, 83, 94, 97; Rocky Mountain Nat Watercolor Soc, Golden, 87; Festival VII, Scottsdale Ctr for Arts, Scottsdale, Ariz, 76. *Pos:* archit, 48-63. *Teaching:* prof archit design/delineation, Ariz State Univ, Tempe, 63-87. *Awards:* Best of Show, Four State Watercolor Biennial, Phoenix Mus, 73; Ciel Ellwanger award, Am Watercolor Soc, 73; Hal and Fran Larsen award, Western Fed Watercolor Socs, 84. *Bibliog:* Other Arts by Architects, Ariz Archit, 71; Dr Horry Wood, Oliver Splashes Color for Experience, Scottsdale Daily Progress, 74; Spotlight on the Artist, Southwestern Watercolor Soc, 75. *Mem:* Am Watercolor Soc; Nat Watercolor Soc; Southwestern Watercolor Soc; Ariz Watercolor Asn; Ariz Artists Guild. *Media:* Watercolor, Acrylic. *Publ:* auth, The Sketch, 79, The Sketch in Color, 83 & The Complete Sketch, 89, Van Nostrand Rheinhold; auth, Fabrig Zeichnan, Bauveriat Gmbh, 86; contribr, The Best of Watercolor, Rockport Press, 86, 87. *Mailing Add:* 4111 E San Miguel Phoenix AZ 85018

OLIVER, SANDRA (SANDI)
ART DEALER, PAINTER
b Bronxville, NY, Apr 2, 41. *Study:* Marymount Col, Tarrytown, BA, BFA, 63. *Hon Degrees:* New England Fine Arts. *Work:* Hammer Mus Gallery, Conn; Lilco Gallery, Long Island; McKlean-Grove Mus, Greenwich. *Comn:* Productions & prom, ABC & NBC TV, 80; USA space production, United Tech-Norden, 80; St Mary's, 98. *Exhib:* Westport Merchants Show, Conn, 78, 86, 87 & 92-2001; Waveny Barn Mus, New Canaan, 85, 86 & 87; Westport Art Ctr Mus, 86 & 87; Wilton Historical, Soc Am Craftsmanship Show, Conn, 91 & 92. *Pos:* Commercial artist rep, Sandi Oliver Inc, Weston, 79-84; pres, Sandi Oliver Fine Art Inc, 82-; dir, Sandi Oliver, 91-. *Teaching:* Art & art hist teacher, New York City Sch System, 63-65 & Westchester Diocese Cath Sch, 64-67. *Awards:* First Prize, Christmas Show, Pelham Chamber of Com, 60; Revlon Bravo Award, Revlon Corp, 80; First Prize, Casa D'Oliver Garden Show, Conn, 91. *Bibliog:* Contribr, Vision of flowers (article), Your Family, 3/90. *Mem:* NEAA; AAA Inc; AFA. *Media:* Oil. *Specialty:* American impressionist painting & sculpture. *Interests:* Walking, raising dogs, collecting antiques. *Publ:* Auth, American Impressionist Paul Alan Williams His Garden & His Oil Paintings, 91, 92 & 93. *Mailing Add:* Sandi Oliver Fine Art PO Box 1203 Weston CT 06883-0203

OLIVERE, RAYMOND
PAINTER, ILLUSTRATOR
b Wilmington, DE. *Study:* Wilmington Acad Art studied with NC Wyeth, Frank Schoonover; Art Student League NY with Ivan Olinsky, 1947-1950. *Work:* NY Co Lawyers Asn, NY; Lasell Col, Newton Mass; Pernod Ricard Inc, Lewisburg, Ky. *Comn:* Illus (painted approx 250 book covers for paperback books), Harlequin, Bantan, Dell, Jove, Ace, 1981-1994. *Exhib:* Nat Acad Ann, Nat Acad of Art, NY, 1973; Provincetown Art Asn Show, Provincetown Art Mus, Provincetown, Mass, 1974; Allied Artist Ann, Nat Arts Club, NY, 2000-2003; 67th Midyear Exhib, Butler Mus Am Art, Butler Inst, Youngstown, Ohio, 2003; Audubon Artists Ann, Salmagundi Club, NY, 2004-2005. *Awards:* First Prize & Cover winner, North Light Mag, 2001; Finalist & Certificate of Merit winner, Am Soc Portrait Artists, 2002; Tara Fredix Artist Award, Audubon Artists Show, Tara Fredix Co, 2005. *Bibliog:* Libby Fellerhoff (auth), North Light Mag, Artists Mag, 2001-2003. *Mem:* Allied Artists Am; Audubon Artists (corresp secy 2001-); Soc Illusrs. *Media:* Acrylic, Oil, Portrait. *Dealer:* Kathryn Wakefield 1435 Lexington Ave NY 10128. *Mailing Add:* 1435 Lexington Ave New York NY 10128

OLKINETZKY, SAM
COLLAGE ARTIST, CONSULTANT
b New York, NY, Nov 22, 19. *Study:* Brooklyn Col; Inst Fine Arts, NY Univ. *Work:* Philbrook Art Mus, Tulsa, Okla; Okla Art Mus, Oklahoma City; Mus Art, Univ Okla, Norman; Sch Bus, Okla State Univ, Stillwater; Lawton Munic Collection, Okla; and others. *Exhib:* Philbrook Art Ctr Ann, 50-70; Int Painting & Sculpture Exhib, Mus Non-Objective Art, NY, 51-52; Recent Drawings, USA, Mus Mod Art, NY, 55; Momentum Midcontinental, Chicago Inst Design, 55; Southwestern Painting and Sculpture Ann, Okla Art Ctr, 60-70; Artsplace II, Oklahoma City, 79; 50 Yr Retrospective 1942-1992, Norick Art Ctr, Oklahoma City, 92. *Pos:* Dir, Mus Art, Univ Okla, 59-83; art consult, Kerr-McGee Indust, 64-; art consult, Okla Art Ctr, 72-. *Teaching:* Asst prof art, Okla State Univ, 47-57; prof art, Univ Okla, 57-83; vis prof art & humanities, Univ Ark, 62-67; lectr humanities, Langston Univ, 69-70. *Awards:* St Gaudens Medal for Draughtsmanship, City New York, 37; Purchase Award for Painting, Philbrook Art Ctr, 51; Purchase Award for Drawing, Okla Art Ctr, 65; Gov's Art Award, 81. *Mem:* Am Asn Mus; Okla Mus Asn; Art Mus Asn. *Media:* Collage, Drawing. *Publ:* Auth, Oklahoma Designer Craftsman Exhibition, Craft Horizons, 71; contribr, The Art of Douglas Warner (catalog essay), 80; Cross Currents, Okla Visual Arts Coalition, Oklahoma City

OLLMAN, ARTHUR L
PHOTOGRAPHER, MUSEUM DIRECTOR
b Milwaukee, Wis, Mar 6, 47. *Study:* Univ Wis-Madison, BA, 69; Visual Studies Workshop, Rochester, 72; San Francisco Art Inst, 74; Lone Mountain Col, MFA, 77. *Work:* Mus Mod Art, NY; Bibliot Nat, Centre Georges Pompidou, Mus Nat d'Art, Paris, France; Mus Mod Art, San Francisco; Mus Fine Arts, Houston; Tokyo Inst Polytech. *Exhib:* Mirrors & Windows, Mus Mod Art, NY, 78; Grapestake Gallery, San

Francisco, 79; Beyond Color, San Francisco Mus Mod Art, 80; Biennial, Whitney Mus, NY, 81; one-man shows, Contemp Art Ctr, New Orleans, 80, Photog Gallery, NY, 81; Centre Georges Pompidou, Mus Nat d'Art, Paris, France; Tower of David Mus, Jerusalem, 96. *Collection Arranged:* Oversaw Building of 9,000 item Collection, Mus photog Art, San Diego, CA. *Pos:* Dir, Mus Photog Arts, San Diego, 83-. *Awards:* Special Proj Award, Calif Arts Coun, 77; Nat Endowment Arts Fel, 79. *Bibliog:* Charles Whitin (auth), Arthur Ollman, Am Photog Image Nation, 11/78; Arnaud Claass (auth), Arthur Ollman, Zoom/Publicness, 6/79; Arthur Ollman, Time-Life Photog Yr, 79. *Mem:* Am Asn Mus; Oracle. *Media:* Photography; Writing. *Publ:* Other Images, Other Realities, Rice Univ Press, 89; Revelaciones, Art of Manuel Alvarez Bravo, Mus Photog Arts, 90; Persona, Mus Photog Arts, 92; Seduced By Life: The Art of Lou Stoumen, Mus Photog Arts, 93; Points of Entry: A Nation of Strangers, Mus Photog Arts, 95; The Model Wife: 1999, Bullfinch Press; First Photographs: The Art of Wm Henry Fox Talbot, 2004, Mus of Photog Arts. *Mailing Add:* 4310 Goldfinch St San Diego CA 92103

OLPIN, ROBERT SPENCER
HISTORIAN, ADMINISTRATOR
b Palo Alto, Calif, Aug 30, 40. *Study:* Univ Utah, BS, 63; Boston Univ, AM, 65, PhD, 71. *Collection Arranged:* Alexander Helwig Wyant, 1836-1892 (with catalog), 68, Mainstreams of American Architecture-Reflections on Salt Lake City (with catalog), 73 & Am Painting Around 1850, 76, Utah Mus Fine Arts; Contemporary Utah Artists Exhibition, Billboard Art, Tracy Collins Bank (with catalog), 74 & The Art Life of Utah, 1776-1976 (with catalog), 76, Salt Lake Art Ctr; A Retrospective of Utah Art (with catalog), Utah Arts Coun, Utah Mus Fine Arts, 81; Waldo Midgley Retrospective (with catalog), Utah State Univ, Univ Utah & Springville Mus Art, 83; Salt Lake Co Fine Art Collection (with catalog), 87; Jos A F Everett (1883-1945), Springville Mus Art & Salt Lake Art Ctr, 89; George Dibble Paintings, 1928-1988, Utah Mus Fine Arts, 89; Mary Kimball Johnson, Gittins Gallery, U Utah, 90; Art at the Univ Utah, First 150 Yrs, Utah Mus Fine Arts, 2000; Utah Art / Utah Artists, 150 Year Survey, Springville Mus Art, 2002. *Pos:* Chmn art hist prog, Univ Utah, 68-71, 82-87, 99-, chmn art dept, 70-72, 75-82, 99-2000; consult cur Am art, Utah Mus Fine Arts, Univ Utah, 73-99, cons cur collections, Springville Mus Art, 2000-; dean, Col Fine Arts, 87-97; co-chmn, Utah Fine Arts Inst, 97-. *Teaching:* Lectr art hist, Boston Univ, 65-67; from asst prof to assoc prof art hist, Univ Utah, 67-77, prof, 77-. *Awards:* Utah Hist Media Award, Utah State Hist Soc, 92; Honor in Arts Award, Salt Lake Area C of C, 93; Thomas D Dee Fellowship, 97; Utah State Gov's Mansion Libr Outstanding Book Award, 98. *Mem:* Col Art Asn Am; Utah Arts Coun; Historians of Am Art/Western States Arts Found. *Res:* Nineteenth and 20th century American art, with special emphasis on 19th century American landscape painting and the regional art and architecture of Utah. *Interests:* Collecting. *Collection:* Eighteenth and 19th century European and American prints. *Publ:* Co-auth, Utah, State of the Arts, Meridian Int, 93; Painting & Sculpture, Utah Hist Encycl, 94; Dutch Influence on American Art & Architecture, Garland's Dutch Art Encyl, 96; A H Wyant, T F Murphy, Dwight Tryon, Macmillan's Dictionary of Art, 96; Utah Painting & Sculpture, Peregrine Smith, 97; William H Gerdts, Art Across Am, Abbeville, 90; Linda Jones Gibbs, 150 Years of American Painting, Brigham Young U, 94; Mary Francey/The Affable Mr Utah Art, Continuum, 97; co-auth, Utah Art / Utah Artists, Springville Mus, Peregrine Smith, 2002. *Mailing Add:* Dept Art & Art History Univ Utah 375 South 1530 East Salt Lake City UT 84112

OLSEN BERGMAN, CIEL (CHERYL) BOWERS
PAINTER, ENVIRONMENTAL ARTIST
b Berkeley, Calif, Sept 11, 38. *Study:* San Francisco Art Inst, MFA(with honors); Univ Calif, Berkeley with Fred Martin, Bob Hudson, Peter Voulkos, Harold Paris & Peter Plagens. *Work:* New Port Harbor Art Mus; Arts Coun Gt Brit; Oakland Mus; San Francisco Mus Mod Art; Metrop Mus Art, NY. *Comn:* Painting Solar Screen, Gildea Ctr, 87; Paseo Nuevo (136 Ceramic Form), Gildea Ctr, 90. *Exhib:* Women From Permanent Collection, Univ Mus, Berkeley, 73; Biennial, Whitney Mus Am Art, NY, 75; San Francisco Mus Art, 75; 18 Bay Area Artists, Los Angeles Inst Contemp Art, 76; New Work, Oakland Mus, 76; Hamilton Gallery Contemp Art, NY, 79; Ruth Schaffner Gallery, Los Angeles, 79; Ian Birksted, London; Fresh Paint--15 Calif Artists (auth, catalog), San Francisco Mus Mod Art, 82; Revelations, The Transformative Impulse in Recent Art, Aspen Art Mus, (catalog), 89; Flora: Contemp Artists & The World Of Flowers, traveling exhib (catalog), 95; Ciel Bergman: Before New Mexico, After California, Richard L Nelson Gallery & Fine Arts Col, Univ Calif, Davis, 98; Antidote, Linda Durham Contemp Art, NMex, 2000; The Last Sunset of the 20th Century, RB Steveson Gallery, Calif, 2000; The Alchemy of Devotion, RB Steveson Gallery, San Diego, 2002. *Teaching:* Lectr painting, Calif State Univ, Hayward, 75; vis lectr painting, Univ Calif, Berkeley, 75-79; assoc prof painting & drawing, Univ Calif, Santa Barbara, 79, prof 80-94, emer prof, 94. *Awards:* Tamarind Lithographic Inst Fel, 72; SECA Award, Soc Creative Arts, San Francisco, 75; Louis Comfort Tiffany Award, 80. *Bibliog:* Sylvia Moore (auth), Yesterday & Tomorrow Calif Woman Artists; Dr Elinor Gaddon (auth), The Once & Future Goddess; Suzi Gablik (auth), The Reenchantment of Art, 91; Sandy Ballatore (auth), Ciel Bergman Reconnecting Art, Crosswinds, 9/93. *Mem:* Santa Barbara Contemp Art & Art Forum, New Mus, NY. *Media:* Oil, Watercolor Sculpture. *Dealer:* Laura Carpenter Fine Art 309 Read St Santa Fe NM 87501. *Mailing Add:* PO Box 95 Coyote NM 87012

OLSHAN, BERNARD
PAINTER, PRINTMAKER
b New York, NY, Jan 31, 21. *Study:* Am Artists Sch, NY, 37-40; Ozenfant Sch Fine Arts, NY, 47; Acad de la Grande Chaumiere, Paris, 48-51. *Work:* Emily Lowe Mus, Coral Gables, Fla; New York City Community Col & Health & Hosp Corp, NY; Nat Acad Design, NY; Emily Lowe Gallery, Coral Gables, Fla; Health & Hosp Corp NY. *Comn:* Mural, Theodore Roosevelt High Sch & WPA, NY, 39-40. *Exhib:* Camp Maxey Art Exhib, Dallas Mus Fine Arts, 43; Whitney Mus Am Art, NY, 48; Art USA, Madison Sq Garden, NY, 58; 144th Ann Exhib, Nat Acad Design, NY, 69; Hudson River Mus, NY, 71; Seven Bronx Artists, Herbert H Lehman Col, NY, 74; GCCA Mountain Top Gallery, Windham, Vt, 84; Bronx Mus Arts, 86; Lehman Col Art Gallery, 86; solo shows Greenberg Pub Libr, NY, 96, Bronx Mus of the Arts, 91-92, Grace Gallery, NY, 89, others; Nardin Gallery, Somers, NY, 97; Beatrice Conde Gallery, NY, 2000. *Pos:* Chmn visual arts comt, Amalgamated Houses, NY, 80-; cultural arts dir, Mosholu Montefiore YM-YWHA, NY. *Teaching:* Instr, Crafts Students League, 53 & New York City Community Col, 65-69; teacher & dir, Cult Arts Dept, Mosholu-Montefiore Community Ctr, NY, 66-79; instr, Nat Acad Design Sch Fine Arts, 98. *Awards:* Inter-city Mural Award, Theodore Roosevelt High Sch & Works Progress Admin, 39-40; Emily Lowe Award 1st Prize, 2nd Ann, 50; Ralph Mayer Mem Award, 84, 87; Andrew Carnegie Award, Nat Acad Design, 99. *Bibliog:* Dr Lawrence J Hatterer (auth), The Artist in Society, Grove Press, New York, 65; Barry Schwartz (auth), The New Humanism in Time of Change, Prager Publ, 74; articles in New York Times, Art News, Herald Tribune, Art Digest & others; Riverdale Press. *Mem:* New York Artists Equity Asn; Am Soc Contemp Artists (treas); Bronx Soc Sci & Lett; Nat Acad; Fedn of Modern Painters & Sculptors. *Media:* Oil, Watercolor, Pastel, Pen & Ink, Etching. *Mailing Add:* Nat Acad Sch 5 E 89th St New York NY 10128

OLSON, BETTYE JOHNSON
PAINTER, INSTRUCTOR, LECTR
b Minneapolis, Minn, Jan 16, 1923. *Study:* Univ Minn, BS(art educ), 45, MEd, 49; Univ NMex, Taos, summer 47; Cranbrook Acad Art, Mich, 48; Sante Fe NMex Workshop, 2000. *Work:* Vaxjo, Sweden; Pillsbury World Hq, Minneapolis; Augsburg Col; Luther Col, Decorah, Iowa; St Paul Co's; Lutheran Brotherhood, Lutheran Seminary, St Paul; 3 M, Minn Mining & Manufacturing; Luther Seminary Thrivent Co; Kuopio, Finland; and numerous others. *Comn:* Radisson Hotel, Fla, 83. *Exhib:* Walker Art Ctr Biennial, 47 & Minneapolis Art Inst Biennial, 48; Metamorphose One, Minn Mus Am Art, 76; Mid Yr Show Ann, Butler Inst Am Art, 77; Watercolor USA, Springfield, Mo, 77; Minn Artists Selected for Kuopio, Finland, Univ Minn Gallery, 81; Artists, Looking Back: Minn Mus Am Art, 88; Mentor-Protogee Show, Macalester Col, 92, Univ Minn, Nash Gallery, 94; Augsburg Col Retrospective 96, Hill House Swed Am Artists, 96; and many others; solo exhibs, St Olaf Col, 77, Augsburg Col, 79, Luther Col, Decorah, Iowa, 80, Am Swedish Inst, Minneapolis & Smaland Mus, Vaxjo, Sweden, 82, Westlake Gallery, Minn, 64-82, Lutheran Brotherhood Co, 83, Augsburg Col, Minneapolis, 1996, Luther Seminary, St Paul, 1998, Berge Gallery, Stillwater, 2001, Sosin Gallery, 2002, Johnson Heritage Gallery, Grand Marais, 2002; Col St Catherine, St Paul, Minn, 2006. *Pos:* Art fac, Univ Minn, 47-49, Lutheran Cols, Concordia Col, 78-79, Augsburg Co, 88-89; judge, Univ Minnesota Student Show, 56; Juried Women, Warm Gallery, Minneapolis, 1990 & Mentor Prog, 1991-94, Minn State Fair Exhib, 2000, Minn Watercolor Soc, 1988. *Teaching:* Instr, Summit Sch Girls, 45-47 & Univ Minn, 47-49; artist-in-residence, Holden Village Lutheran Retreat Ctr, Chelan, Wash, 67-79 & 86-88; instr painting & design, Concordia Col, St Paul, 75-78, 83-84 & Augsburg Col, summer 84-86 & 87-; instr painting & printmaking, Augsburg Col, Minneapolis, 87-88; mentor proj, Womens Art Registry of Minn, 19 91-92, bd mem, elder Learning Inst, Univ Minn, 2001-2003; Faculty, 2004-2006. *Awards:* Merit Award, Twin City Show, Minn Mus Art, 61; 3rd Prize, Merit Award, Minn State Fair, 76 & 77-93; Grand Prize, Purchase Award, Northern Lights Show, White Bear Arts Coun, Lakewood Col, 77; Am Asn Univ Women Arts Award, St Paul, 85; Best of Show, St Matthews Community Show. *Bibliog:* Two Women Artists Sweden (video interview), Video Team Westover, 93-94. *Mem:* Delta Phi Delta (pres, 46); Artists Equity Asn (secy, 74); Art Caucus: Women; Womens Art Registry of Minn Monotypes. *Media:* Watercolor, Acrylic. *Publ:* Crisp Pine, Poetry Sketches, AAUW Press, St Paul, 90; Creativity in Aging Art (video), Minn Arts, 94; Minnesota Artists (video), 95 & 96; Retrospective brochure, Augsburg Col, 1996. *Mailing Add:* 1721 Fulham St Unit H Saint Paul MN 55113-5152

OLSON, CHARLES
PAINTER, INSTRUCTOR
Study: Ind Univ Pa, BS, 74, MA, 76; Tyler Sch Art, Temple Univ, 81. *Work:* Carnegie Inst Mus Art, Pittsburgh, Pa; Osaka Mus Mod Art, Japan; Charleston Mus Art, WVa; Gallery Liilebonne, Nancy, France; S Alleghenie Mus Art, Loretto, Pa. *Exhib:* Springfield Nat Exhib, Mass, 82; Seven New Artists, Carnegie Mus Art, Pittsburgh, Pa, 84; Artist Educator Exhib, 84, William Penn Mus, Harrisburg, Pa & Art of the State, 89; Invitational Exhib, Del Mus Art, Wilmington, 90; Winterlude Invitational, W Moreland Mus, Greensburg, Pa, 93; Am Abstraction, Alleghenies Mus, Loretto, Pa, 94; Pittsburgh Ctr Arts Biennial, Pa, 98. *Teaching:* Assoc prof art & chmn fine arts dept, St Francis Col, Loretto, Pa, 76-. *Bibliog:* Rachel Youeng (auth), Naturilized depth, Cover Mag, NY, 96; Graham Shearing (auth), Abstract Olson rooted in real, Tribune Rev, Pa, 96; Mary Thomas (auth), Olson & work paints enticing landscape of Shaker experience, Pittsburgh Post Gazette, 97. *Media:* Acrylic on Canvas & Paper. *Dealer:* Denise Bibro Fine Art 529 W 20th 4th Flr New York NY 10011. *Mailing Add:* 427 S 7th St Indiana PA 15701

OLSON, DOUGLAS JOHN
EDUCATOR, PHOTOGRAPHER
b Wausau, Wis, Aug 26, 34. *Study:* Layton Sch Art, BFA; Univ Cincinnati, MFA. *Work:* Montgomery Mus Fine Arts, Ala; Pope & Quint Corp; Gallery S; First Nat Bank Ala; South Central Bell, Birmingham, Ala; and others. *Exhib:* One-man shows, Southeastern Ark Univ, Magnolia, 99, Kans Wesleyan Univ, Salina, 2000, Quincy Univ, Ill, 2001; Emeritus Faculty Exhib, Auburn Univ, 2003; Glacial Rocks Exhib, Cedar Grove, Wis, 2005 & Plymouth, Wis, 2006. *Teaching:* Instr drawing, Univ Cincinnati, 67-68; prof drawing, design & photog, Auburn Univ, 68-2003. *Awards:* Best of Show, LaGrange Nat X, Chattahoochee Valley Art Gallery, 85; Res Awards,

Auburn Univ, 85-2000, Photog, 99; 1st Place, Tenn Valley Art Ctr, 99; and others. *Media:* Black & White Photography; Electronic Imaging. *Publ:* The Civil War News (3 photos & captions), Tunbridge, Vt, 12/97, 12/98; The Civil War News (5 photos & article), Tunbridge, Vt, 6/99; The Civil War News (3 photos & article), Tunbridge, Vt, 2-3/2000; many others. *Mailing Add:* 302 E Thach Ave Auburn AL 36830

OLSON, GENE RUSSELL
SCULPTOR, TAPESTRY ARTIST
b Lake City, Minn, Mar 1, 49. *Study:* Univ Minn, 67-72. *Work:* Pac Gas & Elec, San Francisco, Calif; Univ Wis, River Falls, Anodized Aluminum, Univ Wis, River Falls, 88-89. *Comn:* Steel Painted Welded Kinetic, Childrens Mus, Minneapolis, Minn, 83; Cast Bronze, City of Minneapolis, Minn, 85 & Minneapolis Pub Libr, 87; Woven Bronze & Copper, Jostens Inc, Minneapolis, 86; Anodized Aluminum, Univ Wis, River Falls, 88-89; Woven Copper wall relief, Fountains Country Club, Lake Worth, Fla, 90; Bronze & Slate Fountain, River Falls Area Hosp, Wis, 94. *Exhib:* A Feast of Function, Gallery Functional Art, Santa Monica, Calif, 88; Adventures in the Art Zone, Minn Mus Art, St Paul, 95-96; Artists who Collaborate with Architects, Phipps Art Ctr, Hudson, Wis, 96. *Awards:* Second Honor, 74th Fine Arts Show, Minn State Fair, 85; Cover Background Artist, The Guild, Kraus Sikes, 88; 1st Peer Award & Artist's Choice Award, Minn Fiber/Metal, 93. *Bibliog:* Robert T Smith (auth), column, Minneapolis Start Tribune, 81; Gary Gillson, TV review interview, KTCA Channel 2, Minneapolis/St Paul, 83. *Mem:* Int Sculpture Ctr. *Media:* Bronze. *Mailing Add:* c/o The Mettle Works 8600 NE Odean Elk River MN 55330-7167

OLSON, LINDA A
SCULPTOR, EDUCATOR
b Harvey, NDak, Aug 14, 56. *Study:* Minot State Univ, NDak, BS(cum laude, Gertrude M Eck Scholar), 84; Univ Mont, Missoula, MA(ceramic sculpture, magna cum laude), 87; Univ NDak, Grand Forks, MFA(ceramic sculpture, magna cum laude, NDak Bd Higher Educ Scholar, Grad Res Grant & Ethel, Harriet & Stella Haugan Art Scholar), 90. *Work:* Univ NDak, Grand Forks; Minot State Univ, NDak; Bemidji State Univ; plus many pvt collections. *Comn:* Archaeol recs, Bur Land Mgt, Billings Resource Area, Mont, 92; archaeol recs, Bur Land Mgt, Worland, Wyo, 92; illustrations, Indian Cultures on the Great Plains, AD 500-1500: Prehistory to History, Karl H Schlesier (ed), 93; cover art, University 101: An Orientation Textbook for Freshman Students, Midcontinent Inst, Minot State Univ, NDak, 93; cover illus, Connections Mag, Develop Asn, Minot State Univ, 93. *Exhib:* Midwestern Invitational, Rourke Gallery, Moorhead, Minn, 89, 90, 93, 94 & 96; Tribal & Western Art of the Great Plains, Oscar Howe Art Ctr, 95; Minot State Univ Fac Biennial Exhib, Hartnett Hall Gallery, Minot State Univ, 96; North Am Rock Art, Minds Eye Gallery, 96, James Mem Preserv Soc, 96, Bismarck Art Gallery, 97 & Jamestown Art Ctr, 98; Womens Self Images, Tallery Gallery, 96, Libr Gallery, Minot State Univ, 97. *Pos:* Gallery asst, Hartnett Hall Gallery, Minot State Univ, NDak, 80-83; rock art recording artist, proj mgr & instr, 89-; dir, NW Art Ctr, Minot State Univ, 91-; NDak Art Gallery Asn, 94-. *Teaching:* Art asst, Minot State Univ, 80-84, instr art dept, 90-95, asst prof, 95-; grad teaching asst, Univ NDak, formerly. *Awards:* Grants, NDak Coun Arts, 93-96; Artworks Fund Grant, NW Art Ctr, 95; Woman of Distinction Nominee, YWCA, 95. *Bibliog:* Rock Artist Brings Work to Hazen Kids, Hazen Star, 11/3/94; Artist Encourages Kids to Create, Hazen Star, 11/17/94; Capturing the Native Image, Resident artist teaches children/adults, Foster Co Independent, 3/20/95. *Mem:* Minot Area Coun Arts; Minot Art Gallery (vpres, 92-94 & comt chair, 93, 95 & 96); Minot Art Asn; NDak Coun Arts; NDak Art Galleries Asn (pres, 92-94). *Media:* Ceramic. *Res:* North American rock art; archaeological recording. *Publ:* Auth, Secondhand Storytellers, Mont Writing Proj, 86; Rock Art Study Yields New Evidence of Bear Ceromonialism, Am Rock Artist Asn, 5/91; Ideas for drawing development, Ideas: Mid Continent Inst Newsletter, 10/93. *Mailing Add:* 412 Nineteenth Ave SW Minot ND 58701-6420

OLSON, MAXINE
PAINTER, INSTRUCTOR
b Kingsburg, Calif, June 29, 31. *Study:* Otis Art Inst, Los Angeles, Calif, 71 & 72; Inst Allende, San Miguel, Mex, 73; Calif State Univ, Fresno, BA, 73, MA, 75; Univ Calif, Santa Barbara; Bennington Col, Vt, 97. *Work:* Mural Design for Friends of Library, Kingsburg San Francisco Mus Mod Art/Artist Gallery, 2002; Lost in Translation, Fresno Art Mus, 2006. *Comn:* Mural painting, Fresno Arts Mus, Fresno, Calif, 93-94; Cross Church (mural), Fresno, Calif; Calif Dept FIsh and Game, Fresno, 2002; 12 Portraits of Farmers for the Fed Land Bank, Hanford, Calif, 2002. *Exhib:* Am Realism, William Sawyer Gallery, San Francisco, Calif, 85; Palazzo Vagnotti, Cortona, Italy, 87; Nexus Contemp Gallery, Atlanta, Ga, 88 & 90; Church of San Stae, Venice, Italy, 89; Archival Gallery, Sacramento, Calif, 93; Seybold, San Francisco, Calif, 98; San Francisco Mus Modern Art, 2001; The Great S. Patterson Bldy, Fresno, Calif, 2005; Chait Galleries, Iowa City, Iowa, 2005; and others. *Collection Arranged:* About Women, Orange Co Ctr Contemp Art, 82; Symposium on Portuguese Traditions, Univ Calif, Los Angeles, 85; Fresno Arts Mus, 85. *Teaching:* Instr, Calif State Univ, 76-85; asst prof painting & drawing, Univ Ga, Athens, 86-89; asst prof, Univ Ga Studies Abroad Prog, Cortona, Italy, 86-87 & 93. *Awards:* IDN Design Awards, Wanchai, Hong Kong, 97-98. *Bibliog:* David Hale (auth), Art in California Awards, The Fresno Bee; Ageing The Process: The Perception (catalog), Forum Gallery, Jamestown, New York, 90; Susan R. Ressler (auth), Women Artists of the American West, Mc Farland & Company, 2003; Rosa Maria Neves Simes (auth), Women in the Azores and Immigrant Communities (A Mulher Nos Acores E Nas Communidades), Universidade dos Azores, San Miguel, Azores; and others. *Mem:* Fresno Art Mus; Nat Women's Mus Art, Washington, DC. *Media:* Oil, Pencil; Computer Art. *Publ:* Art in Calif, 12/92; Computer Artist Mag, 10/94. *Dealer:* Spectrum Gallery Fresno CA. *Mailing Add:* 1555 Lincoln St Kingsburg CA 93631

OLSON, RICHARD W
PAINTER, EDUCATOR
b Rockford, Ill. *Study:* Univ Wis, Madison, BS & with R Knipschild, Leo Steppat & Italo Scanga, 60, MS(studio art-painting & graphics) 61 & MFA with Warrington Colescott, 62. *Work:* Mus Contemp Art, Chicago; Nat Gallery; Albright-Knox Gallery; Walker Art Ctr; Mus Mod Art, NY; and others. *Exhib:* 25th Print Nat, Intaglio, Nat Collection Fine Arts Div, Smithsonian Inst, Washington, 64; Book as Object, Visual Studies Workshop, 79; Artists Books Permanent Collection, 82 & Artists Books & Recordings, 85, Mus Contemp Art, Chicago; Less is More, Pratt Manhattan Ctr, NY, 83; Artifacts at the End of a Decade, Franklin Furnace, NY, 83; Artists Books, Univ Ore, Eugene, 88; Arts of the Book, Philadelphia Col Art & Design, 88; Retrospective, Wright Mus, Beloit, Wis. *Teaching:* From asst prof to assoc prof, Beloit Col, Wis, 63-77, chmn dept art, 69-76, 80-82, 84-85, 87-88, 96-99, prof art drawing, printmaking, painting, 77-. *Awards:* Gimbels Award, Wis Painters & Sculptors, Gimbels-Milwaukee, 62; Gimbels-Schusters Award, Wis Salon Art, Gimbels-Schusters, 68; Cullister Awards, 78-85; Hewlitt Mellon Award, 83; Wis Artists Biennal Cash Award, 87; Cullister Grant, 86-99. *Bibliog:* Books in an expanded context, Artweek, 7/81; Fluxus and friends, Milwaukee J, 11/84. *Publ:* Illusr covers, Beloit Poetry J, 64 & 69; Artifacts at the End Decade, Watson & Heubner, 81. *Dealer:* Printed Matter 77 Wooster St New York NY 10013. *Mailing Add:* Dept Art Beloit Col 700 Col St Beloit WI 53511

OLSON, RICK
PAINTER
b Mayville, NDak, Mar 15, 50. *Study:* Moorhead State Univ, Minn, 68-72. *Work:* Mus Art, Ft Lauderdale, Fla; Minneapolis Inst Arts, Minn; Canton Art Inst, Canton, Ohio; Nat Portrait Gallery, Smithsonian Inst, Washington; Butler Inst Am Art, Youngstown, Ohio. *Comn:* Five portraits, Joseph H Hirshhorn, Washington, 79; 1st pres Patty Berg (portrait), Ladies Prof Golf Asn, Fla, 98. *Exhib:* Butler Inst Am Art, Youngstown, Ohio. *Media:* Pastels, Oil On Canvas. *Mailing Add:* 32929 135th St Dalton MN 56324

OLSON, ROBERTA JEANNE MARIE
HISTORIAN, CURATOR
b Shawano, Wis, June 1, 47. *Study:* St Olaf Col, BA, 69; Univ Iowa, MA, 71; Princeton Univ, MFA, 73, PhD(Kress Fel, 73-74, Whiting Fel, 74-75), 76. *Collection Arranged:* Forty Drawings:Graphic Gaudier-Brzeska, Art Mus, Princeton, Univ, 74; An Album, Italian 19th Century Drawings & Watercolors (auth, catalog), Shepherd Gallery, NY; Sixty Italian 19th Century Drawings (auth, catalog), San Jose Art Mus, 76; Italian Drawings 1780-1890 (auth, catalog), (traveling), Nat Gallery of Art, Washington, 80-81; Disegni di Tommaso Minardi (auth, catalog), Galleria Nazionale d'Arte Moderna, Rome, 82-83; Fire & Ice: A History of Comets in Art (auth, catalog), Nat Air & Space Mus-Smithsonian Inst, 85-86; Thomas Jefferson Bryan Gallery: Changing Attributions, NY Hist Soc, 90; Ottocento: Romanticism and Revolution in Nineteenth Century Italian Painting, (traveling) Walters Art Gallery, Baltimore, 92-93; The Art of Drawing; Selection from The Wheaton Col Collection, Watson Gallery, Norton MA, 97; Manhattan Unfurled, NY Hist Soc, 2002; Building of the Flation: The Centenary of a NY, Icon, 1902-2002; NY Hist Soc, 2002; Seat of Empire Napolean's Armchair from Malmaison to Manhattan, NY Hist Soc 2003; Petropolis: A Social Hist of Urban Animal Companions, NY Hist Soc, 2003; Birds of Central Park: Auduborks Watercolors, NY Hist Soc, 2004; Audubon's Aviary, NY Hist Soc, 2005 & 06; The Hudson River Sch at the NY Hist Soc; Nature and the Am Vision, NY Hist Soc, 2005. *Pos:* Contrib ed, Arts Mag, 73-75; art news ed, Soho Weekly News, 76-78; bd dir, The Drawing Soc, 84-94, The Friends of Art; consult, Smithsonian Inst, 84-86; bd adv, Halley's Comet Soc, 86-; mem vis comt drawing and print dept, Metrop Mus Art, NY, 93-; guest curator, Art Mus Princeton Univ, 74, Nat Gallery Art, 80; The NY Hist Soc 89-90; assoc curator of Drawings, The NY Hist Soc, 90-; mem col comt drawing dept, Fogg Art Mus, Harvard Univ, 97-; Art Table, 2003; mem vis comt paper conservation Metrop Mus Art, 2004. *Teaching:* From instr to prof art hist, Wheaton Col, 75-88, prof, 88-2000, chmn, Art Dept, 87-89 & 92-93, 97-98, A Howard Meneely chair, 90-92, Mary L Heuser fac chair arts, 97-2000. *Awards:* Fel, Whiting Found for Humanities, 74-75, NEH 82-83; Phi Beta Kappa Cpres, Kappa Chapt 80-82; 87-88; Am Philos Soc Grant, 89; Am Coun Learned Soc Grant, 90-91; Sr Res Grant, Getty Found, 94-95; Samuel H Kress Fel, 73-74; 2001-02; Grantee, 96, 99, 2000; Getty Grantee, NY Hist Soc 2003-05. *Bibliog:* One of the Best--Kept Secrets: The Drawings Collection of the New-York Historical Society, 2004; John Singer Sargent and James Carroll Beckwith (auth), Americans in Paris: A Trove of their Unpublished Drawings, 2005; The Biography of the Object in Medieval and Renaissance Art, Blackwell Publishing, 2006. *Mem:* Col Art Asn Am; Drawing Soc (bd dir, 84-94); Halleys Comet Soc (bd adv, 86-); Italian Art Soc; Asn Univ Porfs Italian; Ren Soc Am. *Res:* Italian renaissance; 19th century Italian painting, sculpture and drawings aimed at illuminating cultural backgrounds and interconnections across disciplines; astronomical images in art; American and European drawings. *Publ:* Contribr to many magazines from 73-2006; Italian Drawing, 1780-1290, 80; Fire & Ice A History of Comets in Art Walker & Smithsonian Institions, 85; Historical Comets Over Bavaria: The Nuremberg Chronicle and Broadsides, Comets in the Post-Halley Era, 91; The 1816 solar eclipse and comet 1811 in John Linnell's astronomical album, J Hist Astronomy, 92; Italian Renaissance Sculpture, Thames & Hudson, 92; Lost and partially found: The Tondo, a significant Florentine art form, in documents of the Renaissance, Artibus et Historiae, 93; Officento; Romanticism & Revolution in the 19th Century Italian Painting, AFA and Centrto Di, 93; An Old Mystery Solved: The 1947 Payment Document to Botticelli for a Tondo, Mitteilungen des Kunsthistorichen Inst Florenz, 95; Fire in the Sky: Comets and Meteors, the Decisive Centuries in British Art and Science, Cambridge Univ Press, 98; The Florentine Tondo, Oxford Univ Press, 2000; Seat of Empire, 2002; plus others. *Mailing Add:* 1220 Park Ave 3C New York NY 10128-1733

OLYNYK, PATRICIA J
PRINTMAKER, EDUCATOR
b Regina, Saskatachewan, Can, Oct 4, 61. *Study:* Alberta Col of Art and Design, Can, 79-83; Calif Col of Arts and Crafts, MFA, 85-88; Osaka Nat Univ of Foriegn Studies, 89; Kyoto Seika Univ, Kyoto, Japan, 90-93. *Work:* East Tenn State Univ, Johnson City; Athabasca Univ, Calgary, Alberta, Can; Can Western Nat Gas, Calgary, Alberta, Can; Fogg Mus, Harvard Univ; Life Sci Inst, Univ Mich; Am Council on Educ, Washington, DC. *Comn:* Hewlett Packard Corp Hq, Palo Alto, Calif; Fairmont Moter, Dallas, Tex; Schultz Law Offices, Sacramento, Calif, 2000. *Exhib:* Los Angeles Int Biennial Invitational, Toby Moss Gallery, Calif, 95; Paper in the Millennium, RC Williams Am Mus Papermaking, Atlanta, Ga, 2000; Int Artists Book Triennial, Gallery Iarkai, Vilhus, Lithuania and Galerie 5020, Salzberg, Austria, 2000; Paper Road, Mused Del Croso, Rome, Italy, 2001; Print Nat, Brooklyn Mus, NY, 2001; Gallerie Grafica Tokyo, Japan, 2002; North Am Print Biennial, Gallery 808, Boston, Mass, 2003; solo show, Transfigurations/Transmutations, Art Life, Mistuhashi, Kyoto, Japan, 2003; solo show, Material Shadows, Ufer! Gallery, Kyoto, Japan, 2003; group show, Transitions Int, Trends in Contemp Printmaking, Int Gallery Contemp Art, Anchorage, AK; group show, Sculpture Prints, Print Ctr, Philadelphia, PA, 2003; group show, 2003 Contemp Art Festival Exhib, Saitama Modern Art Mus, Saitama, Japan, 2003; group juried show, Lessedra 3rd World Art Print Ann, Nat Palace of Cult, Sofia, Bulgara; solo show, Nat Accad Sciences, Washington, DC, 2006; solo show, Life Sciences Inst, Univ Mich, 2006. *Pos:* adminr, Headland's Ctr for Arts, Sausalito, Calif, 87-89; coordr internships, Calif Col Arts & Crafts, San Francisco; vis scholar, Kyoto Seika Univ, Kyoto, Japan, 90-93. *Teaching:* instr dept printmaking, Seika Univ, 91-93; asst prof, Univ Neb, 99; dir of Stamps Disting Visitors Prog; asst prof, Univ Mich, 99-2005; assoc prof & res assoc prof, Sch Art & Design, Univ Mich, 2005-. *Awards:* Purchase Award, East Tenn State Univ, 89; Rakuyo Exhibition Prize Award, Mus of Kyoto, 92, 93; Juror's Award, Works on Paper Nat Juried Exhib, 99; North Am Print Biennial Award, 2003; First Prize Award, Lessedra 3rd World Art Print Ann, Intl Juried Show, 2004. *Bibliog:* Akira Kurosaki (auth), New directions in print, Hangwa Geijutsu, 93; Michael Anderson (auth), Shinpei Sakakura, Akira Nagasawa & Patricia Olynyk, Art Issues, 95; Glenn Kurtz (auth), The art of digital technology, Artweek, 98; John Carlos Cantu (auth), Olynyk's Sticks, Pods, Bones, Ann Arbor News, 11/2000; Jeanette Wenig Drake (auth), Dialogue, 2001; Mariane Rzepka (auth), Printmaking Merges Art & Science, Ann Arbor News, Sept 2, 2004. *Mem:* Am Print Alliance; Southern Graphics Coun; Mid Am Print Coun; Col Art Asn; Women's Caucus for the Arts; Boston Printmakers; Inter Soc for Electronic Arts; Art & Science Collaborations Inc. *Media:* Installation, Sculpture, Sound, Mixed Media. *Specialty:* Modern and Contemp. *Interests:* Art and Sci. *Publ:* ROC Internat Print Biennial (exhib catalog), 85; Stonemetal Press (exhib catalog), 2000; Mid Am Print Coun (exhib catalog), 2000; Paper Road (exhib catalog), 2000; Transfigurations, 2002; American Print Alliance, 2002. *Dealer:* Michael Himovitz Gallery 1616 Del Pasi Blvd Ste 3 Sacramento CA 95815. *Mailing Add:* c/o Univ Mich 2000 Bonisteel Blvd Ann Arbor MI 48109

OMAR, MARGIT
PAINTER, EDUCATOR
b Berlin, Ger, May 17, 41; US citizen. *Study:* Univ Colo, Boulder, MFA, 71. *Work:* Los Angeles Co Mus Art, Mus Contemp Art & Polygram Pictures, Los Angeles; Atlantic Richfield Co, Denver; Turtle Creek Mansion, Dallas; and others. *Comn:* Aerojet Gen, La Jolla, Calif, 82; Robinson's, Newport Beach & Santa Monica, Calif, 82. *Exhib:* New Abstract Painting in Los Angeles, Los Angeles Co Mus Art, 76; solo exhibs, Janus Gallery, Venice, Calif, 77, 78, 80, 82 & 84, Univ Southern Calif, Los Angeles, 86 & Calif State Univ, Long Beach, 87; Fresh Paint, San Francisco Mus Mod Art, 82; Drawings by Painters, Oakland Mus Art, 83; Young Talent Awards 1963-1983, Los Angeles Co Mus Art, 83. *Teaching:* Assoc prof graduate studies & painting, Univ Southern Calif, Los Angeles, 73-. *Awards:* Young Talent Award, Los Angeles Co Mus Art & Contemp Art Coun, 77; Individual Artists' Grant, Nat Endowment Arts, 80. *Bibliog:* Susan C Larsen (auth), Margit Omar's California Suite, Arts Mag, 9/78; Water Gabrielson (auth), Pasadena pluralism: The painting Seventies, Art Am, 5/81; Ruth Weisberg (auth), Margit Omar at Janus, Images & Issues, 10/82. *Mem:* Los Angeles Contemp Exhibs. *Media:* Acrylic; Mixed Media. *Mailing Add:* Univ Southern Calif School of Fine Arts Watt Hall 104 Los Angeles CA 90089

ONDISH, ANDREA
PRINTMAKER, EDUCATOR
b Scranton, Pa, Apr 29, 60. *Study:* Marywood Univ, BFA, 85; Eastern Ill Univ, MA, 86; Ind State Univ, MFA, 92. *Work:* Ind Hist Soc, Indpls; Ind State Univ, Terre Haute, Ind; Acad Fine Arts & Design, Bratislava, Slovakia; Univ Manitoba, Winnipeg, Man, Can; Julian Ctr, Indpls. *Exhib:* Contract on Am, Artemesia Gallery, Chicago, 95; Isn't It a Pretty World, ARC Gallery, Chicago, 95; Conflict/Resolution, Woman Made Gallery, Chicago, 99; Pressing Forward, Hoosier Salon Gallery, Indianapolis, 01; INdiana and Beginnings, Ind Hist Soc, Indianapolis, 01; INjoy, Ind Univ-Kokomo Art Gallery, Kokomo, Ind, 02; INtouch and INdigenous, Indianapolis Art Ctr, Ind, 04; Beginnings, Muncie Art Ctr, Zionsville, Ind, 03. *Pos:* preparator permanent collection, Ind State Univ, 89-92; prog & exhibs coord, Swope Art Mus, Terre Haute, Ind, 97-01; cur educ, interim dir, Marshall Fredericks Sculpture Mus, Univ Ctr, Mich, 01-. *Teaching:* instr, screenprinting, Indianapolis Art Ctr, 98; adj instr, art appreciation, Saginaw Valley State Univ, 02-; adj lectr, Art Hist, Saginaw Valley State Univ, 03-. *Bibliog:* Regina Grady Schieffer (auth), Fresh Targets, Spectrum Weekly, Little Rock, Ark, 11/1991; Patty Poremba (auth), 50th Wabash Valley exhibit at Swope., Indiana Statesman, 3/18/1994; Roger Green (auth), Exhibit of comics is ambitious., The Grand Rapids Press, 1/2/1996. *Mem:* INprint (founding mem); Mid-Am Print Coun; Am Print Alliance; Am Asn of Mus. *Media:* All Media. *Mailing Add:* PO Box 5146 Saginaw MI 48603

O'NEAL, ROLAND LENARD
ILLUSTRATOR, GRAPHIC ARTIST
b Meridian, Miss, Feb 1, 48. *Study:* Meridian Mus Art, Miss, 68; Jackson State Univ, BS(art educ), 72, studied with Hale Woodruff, New York, 76. *Work:* Wyo Univ Art Mus, Laramie; Idaho Univ Art Mus, Moscow; Sch Archit, Univ Southern Calif; Family Serv Ctr, W A Reed Jr Vocational & Tech Bldg, Meridian Community Col, Meridian, Miss; Retired Sr Vol Prog, Meridian; and others; Belhaven Col, Jackson, Miss; Family Service Ctr, Meridian Naval Air Sta; Meridian Lauderdale Co Pub Libr; Meridian City Hall; W A Reed Jr Vational & Tech Bldg, Meridian Cmty Col, Miss. *Exhib:* Ball State Univ Drawing & Sculpture Exhib, 74; Colo Print & Drawing Exhib, Sch Art, Univ Colo, Boulder, 75; Wind River Nat, Wind River Artist Guild, Ladner, Wyo, 76; Meridian Pub Libr, 77. *Teaching:* Miss Action For Progress Volunteer Arts and Crafts, 69-79; substitute teacher art educ, Meridian Pub Schs, Miss, 72-79. *Mem:* Wind River Valley Artist Guild; Athenian Art Club, Jackson State Univ. *Media:* Pencil, Charcoal; Watercolor, Mixed Media. *Mailing Add:* 506 Front St Ext Apt D-10 Meridian MS 39301-4568

O'NEIL, ROBYN
PAINTER
b Omaha, 77. *Study:* Kings Col London, 97; Tex A & M - Com, BFA, 2000; Univ Ill, 2000-01. *Exhib:* One-woman shows incl: These Are Pictures of Boats & Dinosaurs, Angstrom Gallery, Dallas, 2002, Even If It Shall Break Them: Prelude to a Solid Hope for Something Better, Clementine Gallery, NY, 2003, New Works, ArtPace, San Antonio, 2003, Bodybuilder & Sportsman, Chicago, 2004, Clementine Gallery, NY, 2005; exhib in group shows at Bad Touch, Ukrainian Inst Modern Art, Chicago, 2002, Drawn II, Barry Whistler Gallery, Dallas, 2002, Summer Drawings, Mixture Gallery, Dallas, 2002, Super Nature, Inman Gallery, Houston, 2002, The Co We Keep, 2003, Come Forward, Dallas Mus Art, 2003, Am Dream, Ronald Feldman Fine Arts, NY, 2003, Whim?, Angstrom Gallery, Dallas, 2003, Young Am, Galerie Hof & Huyser, Amsterdam, The Neth, 2004, The Drawn Page, Aldrich Mus Contemp Art, Ridgefield, Conn, 2004, It's a Wonderful Life: Psychodrama in Contemp Painting, Spaces, Cleveland, 2004, Whitney Biennial, Whitney Mus Am Art, 2004. *Awards:* Artadia Grant, Fund Art & Dialogue, NY, 2003; Tex Int Artist in Residence, ArtPace Found Contemp Art, San Antonio, 2003. *Mailing Add:* c/o Whitney Mus Am Art 945 Madison Ave New York NY 10021

ONO, YOKO
CONCEPTUAL ARTIST
b Tokyo, Japan, Feb 18, 33; US citizen; arrived in Calif, 35. *Study:* Peers' Sch, Gakushuin Univ, Tokyo; Sarah Lawrence Col, New York; Harvard Univ, Cambridge, Mass. *Hon Degrees:* Art Inst Chicago, PhD (hon), 97; Liverpool Univ, PhD (hon), 2001; Bard Col, PhD (hon), 2002. *Exhib:* Solo exhibs, Alchemical Wedding, Albert Hall London, 67, Evening with Yoko Ono, Birmingham, 68, Event, Univ Wales, 69, & Everson Mus, Syracuse, NY, 71, Objects, Films, Whitney Mus Am Art, 89, A Piece of Sky, Galleria Stefania Miscetti, Rome, 93, Endangered Species, Wacoal Art Ctr/Spiral Garden, Tokyo, 93, Fluxus, Royal Festival Hall, South Bank Centre, London, 97, Have You Seen the Horizon Lately? Mus Modern Art, Oxford, 97, Open Window, Umm El-Fahem, Israel, 2000, Yes Yoko Ono, Japan Soc, 2001, My Mommy Was Beautiful, Shoshana Wayne Gallery, Santa Monica, 2002, Yoko Ono Women's Room, Mus d'Art Moderne de la Ville de Paris, 2003, Odyssey of a Cockroach, Inst Contemp Arts, London, 2004, Heal, 2006; group shows include Fluxshoe, Sch Art, Falmouth, Cornwall, Eng, 72; Liverpool Biennial Contemp Art, 2004; Techniques of the Visible, Shanghai 5 Biennial, 2004; Do You Believe in Reality? Taipei Biennial, 2004; At the Mercy of Others: The Politics of Care, Whitney Mus Am Art, 2005; Experiencing Duration, Biennale de Lyon, 2005; Looking at Words, Andrea Rosen Gallery, NY, 2005; To the Human Furture, Flight from the Dark Side, Art Tower, Mito ATM, Mito; The Expanded Eye, Kunsthaus, Zurich, 2006. *Pos:* Established the Lennon Ono Grant for Peace in 2002 given to artist living in regions of conflict. *Awards:* Helen Caldicott Leadership Award. 87; Showhegan Award, 2002; Lifespire Award, 2002; MOCA Award, 2003. *Bibliog:* P Devlin (auth), Yoko Ono, Vogue, New York, 12/71; Michael Benedikt (auth), Yoko notes, Art & Artists, London, 1/72; E Wasserman (auth), This is not here: Yoko Ono at Syracuse, Artforum, New York, 1/72. *Publ:* Auth, Six Film Scripts, Tokyo, 64; Thirteen Film Score Scores, London, 67; John & Yoko Calendar, New York, 70; Grapefruit, London, 70 & A Hole to See the Sky Through, New York, 71 Just Me! (Tada No Atashi), 86, Sometime in New York City, 95, Acorns, 96

ONORATO, RONALD JOSEPH
HISTORIAN, CURATOR
b Jersey City, NJ, Jan 26, 49. *Study:* Rutgers Col, AB, 70; Brown Univ, MA, 73, PhD(Kress Found Grant), 77. *Collection Arranged:* Labyrinths, 75; Watson Gallery, Wheaton Col, 75-77; Mary Miss Interior Works, 82; Sailing Design Today, 86; Vito Acconci Domestic Trapping, 87; The Art of Douglas Huebler, 88. *Pos:* Asst cur, NY Cult Ctr, 73-74; dir exhib, Univ RI, 77-82; sr cur, La Jolla Mus Contemp Art, 85-88; trustee, Newport Hist Soc, 92- & Newport Art Mus, 92-; bd mem, RI Comt Humanities, 93. *Teaching:* Vis lectr art hist, Wheaton Col, 75-77; chmn & prof, Univ RI, 77-; adj prof criticism & art hist, RI Sch Design, 81-. *Awards:* Nat Endowment Humanities Grant, 83; Nat Endowment Arts Exhib Grants, 86 & 87; Grants, Champlin Found, 92, CLG, 95-96 & Prince Found, 97. *Mem:* RI Hist Preserv Comn; Nat Regist Rev Board. *Res:* Nineteenth century American art, and architecture; contemporary art criticism; public sculpture. *Publ:* Auth, Douglas Huebler, 88; Richard Fleischner's St Louis Project (catalog), 90; Selections: Permanent Collection, San Diego Mus Contemp Art, 90; Blurring the Boundaries, 25 Years of Installation Art, 96; Outdoor Sculpture of Rhode Island, 98; and others. *Mailing Add:* Dept Art Univ RI Upper College & Bills Rd Kingston RI 02881-0820

OPIE, CATHERINE
PHOTOGRAPHER
b Sandusky, Ohio, 1961. *Study:* San Francisco Art Inst, BFA, 85; CalArts, Valencia, Calif, MFA, 88. *Work:* Whitney Mus Am Art, NY; Mus Mod Art, San Francisco; Mus Contemp Art & Los Angeles Co Mus Art, Calif; Mus Fine Arts, Boston, Mass; plus many others. *Exhib:* Camerwork Gallery, San Francisco, Calif, 85; Guggenheim Gallery, Orange Co, Calif, 87; Los Angeles Art Fair, Los Angeles Convention Ctr, Calif, 88; Young Calif Artists, Southcoast Mus, Costa Mesa, 89; Someone or Somebody, Meyers/Bloom Gallery, Los Angeles, Calif, 91; Wasteland, Fotografie Biennale Rotterdam III, The Neth, 92; I am the Enunciator, Thread Waxing Space, NY, 93; Dress Codes, Inst Contemp Art, Boston, Mass, 93; Persona Cognita, Mus Mod Art Heide, Melbourne, Australia, 94; Feminin-Masculin: The Sex of Art, Mus Nat d'Art Mod, Ctr Georges Pompidou, Paris, France, 95; Whitney Mus Am Art Biennial, NY, 95; Campo, Corderie, Venice, Italy, 95; Images of Masculinity, Victoria Miro Gallery, London, Eng, 95; solo exhibs, Richard Fonke Galerie, Ghent, Belg, 95, Richard Feigen Gallery, Chicago, Ill, 96, Jay Gorney Mod Art, NY, 96 & 98, Regen Projs, Los Angeles, Calif, 96, Ginza Art Space, Shiseido, Tokyo, Japan, 97, Suzanne Hilberry Gallery, Birmingham, Ala, 97, Mus Contemp Art, Los Angeles, Calif, 97, Stephen Friedman Gallery, London, Eng: Wall Street, 2001, Regen Projects, Los Angeles, Calif,: Icehouses, 2002; Just Past: The Contemp in MOCA's Permanent Collection, 1975-96, Mus Contemp Art, Los Angeles, Calif, 96; Art at the End of the 20th Century, Nat Gallery, Athens, Greece, 96, Museu d'Art Contemporani, Barcelona, Spain, 96-97 & Kunstmuseum, Bonn, Ger, 97; Evident: Joseph Bartscherer, Martin Cole, Stefan Gec, Axel Hutte, Catherine Opie, James Welling, Photogr Gallery, London, Eng, 96; Inbetweener: Jeanne Dunning, Yasumasa Morimura, Catherine Opie, Inez van Lamsweerde, Collier Schorr, Ctr Contemp Arts, Glasgow, Scotland, 96-97; Fabrications: Hamish Buchanan, Catherine Opie, David Rasmus, Vancouver Art Gallery, BC, Can, 97; Rrose is a Rrose is a Rrose: Gender Performance in Photog, Guggenheim Mus, NY, 97; Defining Eye: Women Photogs of the Twentieth Century (with catalog), Saint Louis Art Mus, Mo, 97; Sunshine & Noir: Art in LA, 1960-1997 (with catalog), Castello di Rivoli, Mus d'Arte Contemporanea, Italy & Univ Calif Los Angeles at Armand Hammer Mus Art & Cult Ctr, Calif, 97; Nirvana: Capitalism and the Consumed Image, Ctr Contemp Art, Seattle, Wash, 97; Cruising LA: Paul McCarthy, Martin Kersels, Catherine Opie, Lari Pittman, Jason Rhoades, Galeria Soledad Lorenzo, Madrid, Spain, 97; Kunst, Arbeit, Sudwestdeutsche Landesbank Forum, Stuttgart, Ger, 97-98; Am Vernacular, Mus Contemp Art Los Angeles, Calif, 98; Babes: Lutz Bacher, Mark Bennett, David Levinthal, Catherine Opie, Mel Ramos, Andy Warhol, Mark Moore Gallery, Santa Monica, Calif, 98; Where: Allegories of Site in Contemp Art, Whitney Mus Am Art Champion, Stamford, Conn, 98; From the Corner of the Eye, Stedelijk Mus, Amsterdam, The Neth, 98; one-women shows, Wood St Galleries, Pittsburgh, 99, Regan Projects, Los Angeles, 99, Susan Inglett, NY, 2000, Gorney Bravin + Lee, NY, 2000, ArtPlace Found Contemp Art, San Antonio, Tex, 2000, Thread Waxing Space, NY, 2000, The Photographers Gallery, London, 2000, St Louis Art Mus, 2000 & Walker Art Ctr, Minneapolis, 2001; Collectors Collect Contemp: 1990-1999, Inst Contemp Art, Boston, 99; The Am Century: Art & Cult 1950-2000, The Whitney Mus Am Art, 99; Beyond Boundaries: Contemp Photog in Calif, Univ Art Mus, Calif State Univ Long Beach, 2000; Juvenilia, Yerba Buena Ctr for Arts, San Francisco, 2000; Driving Women, Castle Gallery, Col New Rochelle, NY, 2001; Mask or Mirror?, Worcester Art Mus, Worcester, Mass, 2002-03; plus many others. *Teaching:* instr photog, Univ Calif, Los Angeles, 90, Cross Roads Sch, 91, Chapman Univ, 91-93; letc photog, Univ Calif, Irvine, 95-99; asst prof photog, Yale Univ, 2000-01; prof photog, Univ Calif, Los Angeles, Calif, 2002 (tenure); plus many pub lectures throughout US. *Awards:* Citibank Private Bank Emerging Artist Award at MoCA, Los Angeles, 97; Henry and Natalie Freund Fel, 99; Photog Fel, Houston Ctr Photog, 2000; Calumet Finalist, 2000. *Bibliog:* Leah Ollman (auth), A Multi-Sided Look at Lone Women, 10/2/98; Celia Lyttelton (auth), The Now Art Book, Shiseido & Korinsha Press & Co Ltd, Toyko, 96; Colette Dartna; (auth), exhib catalog, Mus Contemp Art, Los Angeles, 97; Frances Borzella (auth), Seeing Ourselves: Women's Self-Portraits, Thames & Hudson, London, 98; Alexandre Melo (auth) exhib catalog, Lost Paradise: Catherine Opie, Joachim Koester, Ellen Cantor, Presenca Gallery, Porto Portugal, Ill, 98; Rochelle Steiner (auth), Catherine Opie: Inbetween here and there, St Louis Art Mus, Ill, 2000; Cherry Symth (auth), Art Monthly, 11/2000; Michael J McAuliffe (auth), Collector's Choice at Exit Art, Reviewny.com, 12/2000; Raymond Ryan (auth), Urban Generations, Tate (London), Spring 2001; Roberta Simth (auth), Before They Became Who They Are, NY Times, 2/9/2001; Susan Wiegand (auth), Photography and the Human, Art (Kansas City), 4/2001; plus many others. *Dealer:* Gorney Bravin + Lee 534 W 26th St New York NY 10001; Regen Projects 629 N Almont Dr Los Angeles CA 90069. *Mailing Add:* c/o Gorney Bravin & Lee 534 W 26th St New York NY 10001-5515

OPIE, JOHN MART
PAINTER
b Sandusky, Ohio, Dec 10, 36. *Study:* Kent State Univ, BFA, MA. *Work:* Allentown Art Mus, Pa; Akron Art Inst, Ohio; Fordham Univ, NY; New Orleans Art Mus, La; St Lawrence Univ, NY. *Exhib:* one-man shows, New Orleans Art Mus, 68, Galerie Simonne Stern, New Orleans, 69, 70, 72, 75, 80 & 83, Bowery Gallery, NY, 73, 76 & 79 & Allentown Art Mus, Pa, 84; The More Gallery Inc, Philadelphia, 81, 82, 87-89; Award Winning Artists, Witte Mem Mus, San Antonio, Tex; Art Now, Philadelphia Mus Art, 90; East Stoudsburgh Univ, PA, 2003. *Teaching:* Instr painting, Pasadena City Col, Calif, 63-65; assoc prof painting, La State Univ, Baton Rouge, 65-70. *Awards:* Natl Endowent for the Arts, 67, 89; Nat Endowment Arts Award, 67; Best of Show, 21st Ann Juried Exhib, State Mus Pa, 88. *Bibliog:* Leonard Edmondson (auth), Etching, Van Nostrand Reinhold, 73. *Media:* Acrylic and Oil on Panel. *Mailing Add:* 1765 State Rd Quakertown PA 18951-3338

OPPENHEIM, DENNIS A
SCULPTOR
b Mason City, Wash, Sept 6, 38. *Study:* Calif Col Arts & Crafts, BFA, 65, Univ Hawaii; Stanford Univ, MFA, 66. *Work:* Mus Mod Art, Whitney Mus Am Art, NY; Stedelijk Mus, Amsterdam, Neth; Centre Georges Pompideau, Paris; Kunsthaus, Zurich, Switz; Detroit Art Inst, Cranbrook Acad Art, Bloomfield Hills, Mich; Everson Mus Art, Syracuse; plus many others. *Comn:* sculpture, Fattoria di Celle, Pistoia, Italy, 83; sculpture, Olympic Park, Seoul, Rep Korea, 88; sculpture, Principality of Andorra, 92; sculpture, Balllerup Kommune, Copenhagen, Denmark, 95; sculpture, Europos Parkas, Vilnius, Lithuania, 95. *Exhib:* Whitney Mus Am Art, NY, 86; Pierides Mus, Athens, Greece, 90; Le Chanjour, Nice, France, 90; Berndt & Krips, Kolin, Ger, 90; one man exhibs, Musee d'art Moderne Villeneuve d'Ascq, France, 94, Palazzo Delle Exposizioni, Rome, Italy, 96, 2nd Johannesburg Biennale, SAfrica, 97, Museo de Arte Alvar, Mexico City, Mex, 98 & Palais Lichtenstein, Vienna, Austria, 99; Mus Contemp Art, Los Angeles, 95 & 96; Musee d'art moderne et d'art contemporain, France, 96; Mac Galeries Contemporaines des Musees de Marseille, France, 96; Inst Contemp Art, PS1 Mus, NY, 97; Centre Georges Pompidou, Paris, France, 97; and others. *Teaching:* Guest artist sculpture, Yale Univ, 69; guest artist, Pratt Inst Art, Brooklyn, 69, Calif Col Arts & Crafts, 70, RI Col Design, 70 & Univ Wis, Whitewater, 70; guest artist sculpture, Art Inst Chicago & NS Col Art, 71-72. *Awards:* Newhouse Found Grant, Stanford Univ, 65; John Simon Guggenheim Found Fel, 71-72; Grant, Nat Endowment Arts, 74 & 81. *Dealer:* Sonnabend Gallery New York NY. *Mailing Add:* 54 Franklin St New York NY 10013

ORDUNO, ROBERT DANIEL
PAINTER, SCULPTOR
b Ventura, Calif, Sept 5, 33. *Study:* Los Angeles Art Ctr, 60. *Work:* Buffalo Bill Hist Ctr, Cody, Wyo; Red Cloud Indian Sch, The Heritage Ctr, Inc, Pine Ridge, SDak. *Comn:* Lewis & Clark, mural, City of Great Falls, Mont, 83. *Exhib:* Colo Indian Market, Denver, 87; Mont Indian Nations Art Rendezvous, Gov's Residence, Helena, 87; The New West, Buffalo Bill Hist Ctr, Cody, Wyo, 90; Life Death Rebirth, Paris Gibson Sq Mus Art, Great Falls, Mont, 93; and others. *Teaching:* Lectr native Am Indian art, Australian Asn Adult & Community Educ, Coun Adult Educ, Australia, 93. *Awards:* 5th Ann Native Am Art exhib, artists choice, best painting, merit award, Great Falls, Mont, 87; Special Merit Award, 7th Ann Native Am Art Exhib, 89; Jurors Choice & Best Show Award, 11th Ann Native Am Art Exhib, 93. *Bibliog:* Featured Artist & Cover Image, InformArt Mag, 7-8/94; Native America calling (interview), KUNM Radio, 1/16/96; Trophies of honor, art chronicles of indigenous peoples, Fineart Online, 8/96. *Mem:* Nat Serv Orgn Native Arts. *Media:* Oil. *Collection:* Charlie Russell Museum, Buffalo Bill Historical Center, Cody Wyoming. *Publ:* Southwest Art Mag, 6/90; Shamons Drum. Int Fine Art Collector, 2/92; Inform Art Mag, 7-8/94. *Mailing Add:* 153 Calle Don Jose Santa Fe NM 87501

O'REILLY, JOHN B
PHOTOGRAPHER, COLLAGE ARTIST
b Orange, NJ, Feb 22, 30. *Study:* Syracuse Univ, BFA, 52; Art Inst Chicago, MFA, 56. *Work:* Mus Mod Art, NY; Addison Gallery Am Art, Andover, Mass; San Francisco Mus Mod Art, Calif; Fogg Art Mus, Cambridge, Mass; Mus Fine Arts, Boston, Mass. *Exhib:* 4 Rooms-4 Artists, Addison Gallery Am Art, Andover, Mass, 83; The Photographers Persona 1840-1985, Mus Mod Art, NY, 85; Legacy of Light, Int Ctr Photog, NY, 87; Photog Truth, Bruce Mus, Greenwich, Conn, 88; Assembled, Wright State Univ Art Gallery, Dayton, Ohio, 91; Cannibal Eyes, Mass Inst Technol, List Visual Arts Ctr, Cambridge, 92; Biennial, Whitney Mus Am Art, NY, 95; Photog in Boston: 1955-85, Decordova Mus, Lincoln, Mass, 97; Transcience and Sentimentality, Inst Contemp Art, Boston, Mass, 97; Nude in Contemp Art, Aldrich Mus Contemp Art, Ridgefield, Conn, 99; John O' Reilly: Assemblies of Magic (auth, catalog), Addison Gallery Am Art, Andover, 2002. *Awards:* Fel Mass Art Fdn, 86; Fel Nat Endowment Arts, 88. *Bibliog:* Koslow Miller (auth), O'Reilly's Miniature Polaroid Collages, Print Collectors Newsletters, Vol 26, 95; Hawkey & Forman (auths), John O'Reilly Interview & Portfolio, Jubilat, #2, 2000; Greater Boston Arts (film), PBS, John O'Reilly Show 701, 2002. *Media:* Photographic Collage. *Publ:* John O'Reilly Self-Portraits 1977-1995, Howard Yezerski Gallery, 96; auth, Occupied Territories, 99; auth, Asemblies of Magic, Twin Palms Publ, 2002. *Dealer:* Howard Yezerski Gallery 186 South St Boston MA 02111; Julie Saul Gallery 535 W 22 St New York NY 10011; Hosfelt Gallery 430 Clementina San Francisco CA 94103. *Mailing Add:* 1168 Grafton St Worcester MA 01604

ORENSANZ, ANGEL L
SCULPTOR, CERAMIST
b Larues, Spain, Feb 11, 41. *Study:* San Jorge Royal Fine Arts Sch, Barcelona, MA(fine arts), 64; Ecole Nat Beaux Arts, Paris, dipl(advan studies), 67; Royal Sch Fine Arts, London, dipl(advan studies), 68. *Work:* Calif Mus Sci & Indust, Los Angeles; Mus Art Mod Ville Paris; Mus Arte Contemp, Madrid, Spain; Univ Madrid, Spain; Univ Bunka Gakuin, Tokyo, 90. *Comn:* American Landscapes, IBM Corp, Boca Raton, Fla, 81; Purple Environment, comn by Martin Gelber, Los Angeles, 82; South Music, Atlanta, 85; Sun Screen & Sea Island, Ga, 86; World Fair, Seville, Spain, 92; and others. *Exhib:* Roppongy Park, Heartland Gallery, Tokyo, 90-91; Tallinn Arts Ctr, Etonia, 91; Metrop Mus Art, Tokyo, 92; Sculptor's Soc Canada Gallery, 95; Galerie Vouguorde, Wroclow, Poland, 95; Charles Luckmon Gallery, Calif State Univ, Los Angeles, 95; Central Recoleta, Buenos Aires, Argentina, 96; Westchester Art Gallery, State Univ NY, 97; Galerie CA D'oro, Rome, 98; Siedfried Blou Gallery, Dusseldorf, 98. *Awards:* Gold Medal, City Saragossa Bienale, 76; Arts, Sci, Lett, City Paris, 77; Academie Internazzionale Arte Moderne, Rome, 97; and others. *Bibliog:* James Sweeney (auth), Orensanz's sculpture, 81 & Pierre Restany (auth), The great

interplay, 81, Sculpture & Environment; Mario A Marrodan (auth), Escultoevaluacion de Angel Orensanz, 90; Thomas McEvilley (auth), Donald Kuspit, Installation Art, NY, 95 & Angel Otensaz's Sculptures, NY 96. *Mem:* Royal Acad St Louis, Saragossa; Asn Artists & Ecrivains, Paris; Artists Social Responsibility, NY. *Mailing Add:* 172 Norfolk St New York NY 10002

ORENSTEIN, GLORIA FEMAN
EDUCATOR, HISTORIAN
b New York, NY, Mar 8, 38. *Study:* Brandeis Univ, BA(romance lang & lit), 59; Radcliffe Col, MA(Slavic lang & lit), 61; NY Univ(Danforth Grad Fel for Women), 66-71, PhD(comp lit), 71. *Pos:* Contrib ed, Womanart, Chrysalis Mag & Feminist Art J; co-founder, The Woman's Salon; dir, cult prog for hon students & fac-in-residence, Pac Apartments, Univ Southern Calif, 81-85; coord & dir, UN End of Decade Conf on Women, Nairobi, 85; Contr Ed, FemSpec; Coordr Reberon Festivities America, Salute to Women Artists. *Teaching:* Lectr women of surrealism, Cornell Univ, 73, Pa State Univ, 74, Inst 20th Century Studies, Univ Wis, 75, Sheridan Col, 75 & Artists Space, New York, 75; asst prof women in contemp arts, Douglass Col, 74-, asst prof Eng, 75-, chairperson women's studies prog, 76-78; dir, Rutgers Jr Yr in France, 78-79; assoc prof comparative lit & prog for study of women & men in soc, Univ Southern Calif, Los Angeles, 81-82. *Bibliog:* Article in Female Artists: Past & Present, Women's Hist Res Ctr, 74; coordr panel, Women Artists: Preparing for Changing our Future, Centre Cult Am, Paris, 79; articles in: WomanArt, Feminist Art J, Fireweed, Chry Salis, Heresies, The Power of Feminist Art. *Mem:* Mod Lang Asn; Jewish Women Fac Group; Nat Women's Studies Asn; Int Comparative Lit Asn; Int Asn Study Dada & Surrealism; Veteran Feminists of America. *Res:* Surrealism; women's art history; women in the arts; re-emergence of the goddess in contemporary art and literature. *Specialty:* Ecofeminists Art, Shamanism & the Arts, Jewish Women Artists. *Publ:* Auth, A renaissance of goddess-culture art, Fireweed: A Woman's Lit & Cult J, No 1, 78; coauth (with Miriam Brumer), Americans in Paris revisited, Women Artists News, 79; The goddess in art by contemporary women, Women's Resource & Res Ctr, London, Eng, 79; Reclaiming the great mother: A feminist journey to madness and back in search of a goddess heritage, Symposium, spring 82; Towards a bifocal vision in surrealist aesthetics, Trivia, fall 83; A World in words, in: Women Artists of the World, Midmarch Arts, NY, 85; The Theatre of the Marvelous: Surrealism & the Contemporary Stage, NYU Press, 75; The Re-Flowering of the Goddess, Perganon Press, Athene Series, 90; Re-Weaving the Word: The Emergence of Eco-Feminsim, Sierra Club Books, 90. *Mailing Add:* Dept Comp Lit & Sociology Univ Southern Calif Univ Park Los Angeles CA 90089

ORENTLICHER, JOHN
VIDEO ARTIST, SCULPTOR
b Roanoke, Va, June 7, 43. *Study:* Goddard Col, BA, 68; Art Inst Chicago, MFA, 70. *Work:* Everson Mus, Syracuse, NY; Video Collection, Long Beach Mus, Calif; V-tapes, Toronto, Ont; Montevideo, Amsterdam; London Video Arts, London. *Exhib:* Outrageous Film, Whitney Mus Am Art, NY, 74; one person exhibs, Art Metropole, Toronto, 82, Ctr Art Tapes, Halifax, NS & Hallwalls (video), Buffalo, NY, 82 Festival AFI, Los Angeles, 88; Dutch Film Mus, Amsterdam, The Neth; Bienal de Video Santiago, Chile, 94; Worldwide Video Festival, Amsterdam, The Neth, 97; Ovni 2000, Barcelona, Spain; De Sendungen Zum, Int Media Competition, 2000; Athens Int Film Video Festival, 2000; and others. *Pos:* Peace Corps, Chile, 64-66; bd trustees, Synapse Video, Syracuse, NY, 78-81. *Teaching:* Prof video, Col Visual & Performing Arts, Syracuse Univ, 76-81, chmn dept experimental studios, 81-85, chmn art media studies, 83-85 & 87-89; Fulbright lectr video, Bogota, Colombia, 85 & Santiago, Chile; chmn, Art Media Studies, 81-85 & 87-89, chair, 98-2004, chair dept transmedia, 2004-. *Awards:* Nat Endowment Arts, 76; Fulbright, 85 & 94; Rockefeller, 88. *Bibliog:* Sherry Chayat (auth), America on video, Syracuse Herald Am, 9/4/88; Vidiesta John Orentlicher El Mecurio, 9/18/93; Kathy High (auth), Felix, vol 2 no 2, 1999; and others. *Mem:* Media Alliance, NY; Am Independent Video Film Univ Asn. *Media:* Video. *Specialty:* V-Tape, Toronto. *Dealer:* V-Tape Toronto; The Kitchen New York NY. *Mailing Add:* Dept Transmedia Syracuse Univ 102 Shaffer Syracuse NY 13244

ORLAND, TED N
PHOTOGRAPHER, WRITER
b San Francisco, Calif. *Study:* Univ Southern Calif, BS(industrial design), 63; San Francisco State Univ, Calif, MA(interdisciplinary arts), 74. *Work:* Corcoran Gallery Art, Washington, DC; San Francisco Mus Mod Art, Calif; Amon Carter Mus, Tex; Boston Mus Fine Art, Mass; Univ Ariz Ctr Creative Photog, Tucson. *Exhib:* New Acquisitions, Corcoran Gallery Art, Washington, DC, 81; Am Photog & Nat Parks, national tour, 81-83; Univ Ore Art Mus, Eugene, 82; Monterey Art Mus, Calif, 86; Nat Mus Mod Art, Kyoto, Japan, 87; Crocker Art Mus, Sacramento, Calif, 90; Fresno Metrop Mus, Fresno, Calif, 93; Ansel Adams Gallery, Yosemite, Calif, 94. *Pos:* Apprentice, Saul Marks, Los Angeles, Calif, 62-63; asst, Charles Eames, Venice, Calif, 68-71; asst, Ansel Adams, Carmel, Calif, 72-75; ed, Image Continuum Press, 74-. *Teaching:* Asst prof & dir undergrad and grad prog, Univ Ore, 81-84; dir, Ansel Adam's Gallery Photog Workshops, 84-86; resident fac, Maine Photog Workshops, 85-90; Roy Acuff Chair of Excellence in the Creative Arts, Austin Peay State Univ, Tenn, 89. *Awards:* Artist-in-residency, Volcanoes Nat Park, Volcano Arts Ctr, Hawaii, 76; Individual Artist's Fel, Ore Arts Comn, 82; Artist-in-residency, Yosemite Nat Park, 2000. *Bibliog:* Joel Pickford (auth), Ansel Adams & Ted Orland: A critical comparison, Image Continuum J, 79; David Robertson (auth), The Art & Literature of Yosemite, Yosemite Nat Hist Asn, 82. *Mem:* Ctr Photog Art, Carmel, Calif. *Media:* Hand-colored Silverbase Prints, Electronic Imaging. *Publ:* Illusr, Yosemite Reflections, Flying Spur Press, 77; auth, T Orland's Compendium of Photographic Truths, Image Continuum Press, 81; Man and Yosemite: A Photographer's View of the Early Years, Image Continuum Press, 85; Scenes of Wonder & Curiosity: The Photographs and Writings of Ted Orland, David R Godine Publ, 88; coauth, Art & Fear: Observations on the Perils (and Rewards) of Artmaking, Capra Pub, 94. *Dealer:* Ansel Adams Gallery PO Box 455 Yosemite CA 95389. *Mailing Add:* 1017 Seabright Ave Santa Cruz CA 95062

ORLYK, HARRY V
PAINTER
b Troy, NY, Jan 8, 47. *Study:* New York State Univ Col, New Paltz, BS, 70; Univ Nebr, Lincoln, MFA, 74. *Work:* Springfield Mo Art Mus; Albany Inst Hist & Art, NY; Sheldon Art Mus, Lincoln, Nebr. *Exhib:* Candidates for Art Awards, Am Acad & Inst Arts & Lett, NY, 87; Contemp Landscape Photographs & Paintings, Mem Art Gallery, Univ Rochester, 88; Artists of the Mohawk-Hudson Regional Invitational, Ctr Galleries, Albany, NY, 90; Truth & Beauty, Loyola Marymount Univ, Los Angeles, Calif, 92; Under the Influence, Tatistchiff, Santa Monica, Calif, 92; Venable/Neslage Gallery, Washington, DC, 92. *Awards:* L A Sawyer, Mohawk-Hudson Regional, 89; Albany Inst Purchase Award, 89; Purchase Award, Albany Inst Hist & art, 92. *Bibliog:* Thomas Bolt (auth), Harry Orlyk, Arts Mag, 11/86; Margaret Mathews Berenson (auth), Am Artist, 7/87; Timothy Cahill (auth), Working the Land, Metroland, 12/88. *Dealer:* Tatistcheff 50 W St New York NY 10019. *Mailing Add:* Blind Buck Rd Salem NY 12865

ORNSTEIN, JUDITH
PAINTER
b Newark, NJ, May 4, 51. *Study:* Wimbledon Sch Art, Eng, 70-71, Philadelphia Col Art, BFA, 73, Yale Univ, MFA, 75. *Work:* Albright Knox Mus, Buffalo, NY; Cooper Hewitt Mus, NY; Vassar Col Mus, Poughkeepsie, NY. *Exhib:* One-person shows, Willard Gallery, NY, 77, 79, Cirruss Gallery, Los Angeles, 83, V Levy Fine Arts, NY, 84. *Awards:* Nat Endowment Arts Fel. *Mailing Add:* 28 Tiffany Pl Brooklyn NY 11231-2917

OROPALLO, DEBORAH
PAINTER
b Hackensack, NJ, Nov 29, 54. *Study:* Leo Marchutz Sch Drawing & Painting, Aix-en-Provence, France, 75; Alfred Univ, New York, BFA, 79; Univ Calif, Berkeley, MA, 82, MFA, 83. *Work:* Whitney Mus Am Art & Lang Commun, NY; San Francisco Mus Mos Art, San Francisco Pub Libr, Robertson Stephens & Co, Palace Legion Hon, San Francisco; Baltimore Mus Art; Mus Fine Arts, Boston; Milwukee Art Mus, Wis; and others. *Exhib:* 4th Western Drawing Exhib, Albright Knox Mus, Buffalo, 80; New Acquisitions, Achenbach Found Graphic Arts, MH De Young Mem Mus, San Francisco, 89; Biennial Exhib, Whitney Mus Am Art, NY, 89; Words as Symbols, Aldrich Mus Contemp Art, Ridgefield Conn, 90; traveling exhib, Word as Image, Milwaukee Art Mus, Okla Mus Art, Contemp Art Mus, Houston, 90-91; one-woman shows, Stephen Wirtz Gallery, San Francisco, 86, 88, 90, 93, 95, 97 & 98, Weatherspoon Gallery, Univ NC, Greensboro, 92, Kate Block Fine Arts, Boston, 93, San Jose Mus Art, 94 & Zolla/Lieberman Gallery, Chicago, 96, Pasadena City Col, Calif, 97 & Maine Col Art, Portland, 97, Oropallo on Paper: 1990-2001, Montalvo Gallery, Calif, 2002, How-To: The Paintings of Deborah Oropallo, San Jose Mus of Art, Calif, 2001-03, Material Handling, Stephen Wirtz Gallery, San Francisco, Calif, 2001-03, General Purpose, Weinstein Gallery, Minneapolis, Minn, 2002; traveling exhib, Cruciformed, organized by Cleveland Ctr Contemp Art, Mus Contemp Art, Wright State Univ, Dayton, Western Gallery, Western Wash Union, Bellingham, Wash, MacDonald Stewart Centre, Guelph, Ontario, Can, 91-92; Her Story, Oakland Mus, 92; traveling exhib, The Return of the Cadavre Exquis, Drawing Ctr, NY, Corcoran Gallery Art, Washington, Found Contemp Art, Mex, Santa Monica Mus, Los Angeles & The Forum, St Louis, 93; Blue, Stephen Wirtz Gallery, San Francisco, 95; Trillium's Graphics, Artists Contemp Gallery, Hyatt Regency Plaza, Sacramento, 95; Artist/Books, Oropallo & Saunders, City Col San Francisco, 96; Foster Gallery, Univ Wis, Eau Claire, 96; Am Kaleidoscope: Themes and Perspectives in Recent Art (with catalog), Nat Mus Am Art, Washington, 96; Five Fine Arts Presses, Emmie Smock Gallery, San Francisco, 97; Heart, Body, Mind, Soul, Whitney Mus Am Art, NY, 97; Weinstein Gallery, Minneapolis, Minn, 97; Masterworks on Paper from the Collection of George Hopper Fitch, MH de Young Mem Mus, Fine Arts Mus, San Francisco, 98; Calif Current, RARE Gallery, NY, 98; Art from Around the Bay: Recent Acquisitions, San Francisco Mus Mod Art, Calif, 98; Paper Thin & Works on Paper, Stephen Wirtz Gallery, San Francisco, 98; In Over Our Heads: The Image of Water in Contemp Art, San Jose Mus Art, Calif, 98; group exhibs, The Not-so Still Life: A Century of California Painting and Sculpture, San Jose Mus of Art, Calif, 2003-04. *Teaching:* Asst sculpture, Alfred Univ, NY, 79; asst beginning drawing, Univ Calif, Berkeley, 82; beginning painting, San Francisco Art Inst, 84-85, vis prof, 93; advan painting, San Francisco Art Acad Col, 86-87. *Awards:* Art Space Grant, San Francisco, Calif, 88 & 90; Calif Arts Coun Grant, 90; Nat Endowment Arts Award, 91; Fleishhacker Award, 93. *Bibliog:* Kenneth Baker (auth), Deborah Oropallo, Art News, 9/97; David Bonetti (auth), Succeeding by resisting early success, San Francisco Examiner, 4/25/97; Mason Riddle (auth), Berkeley artist's show is on the house, St Paul Pioneer Press, 6/2/98. *Media:* Oil. *Publ:* 1991 Art on Paper, Weatherspoon Art Gallery, Univ NC, Greensboro, 91; Her Story: Narrative by Contemporary California Artists, Oakland Mus, 91; Corollaries of Apprehension, Calif Col Arts & Crafts, Oliver Arts Ctr, 92; The Rutgers Archives for Printmaking Studios, Jane Voorhees Zimmerli Art Mus, Rutgers State Univ, NJ, 92; 43rd Biennial Exhibiton of Contemporary American Painting, Corcoran Gallery Art, Washington, DC, 93. *Mailing Add:* c/o Stephen Wirtz Gallery 49 Geary 3rd Flr San Francisco CA 94108

OROZCO, GABRIEL
SCULPTOR
b Jalapa, Veracruz, Mex, 1962. *Study:* Escuela Nac de Arte Plastica, UNAM, Mex, 81-84; Circulo de Bellas Artes, Madrid, 86-87. *Exhib:* Video DF, Bronx Mus Arts, NY, 90; Another Mexican Art, Pasadena Art Ctr, 91; Cuerpos Encontrados, Mus de la Alhondiga de Granaditas, Guanajuato, 91; Am, Bride of the Sun, Koninklijk Mus voor Schone Kunsten, Antwerpen, 92; In Transit, New Mus Contemp Art, NY, 93; solo exhibs, Mus Mod Art, NY, 93, Mus Contemp Art, Chicago, 94, Mus d' art Mod de la Ville de Paris, France, 95, Inst Contemp Art, London, Eng, 96, St Louis Mus Art, Mo, 98, Galerie Chantal Crousel, Paris, France, 99, Philadelphia Mus Art, Pa, 99, Mus Contemp Art, Los Angeles, Calif, 01, Mus Internac Rufino Tamayo, Mexico City, 01, Museo de Arte Contemporaneo de Monterey, Mexico, 01, Marian Goodman Gallery, New York City, 01, 02; Real Time, Inst Contemp Arts, London, Eng, 93; The Epic and the Everyday: Contemp Photog Art, Hayward Gallery, London, Eng, 94; Realite Decalee, Fonds Regional d' Art Contemporain Bretagne, Chateaugiron, 95; Where is Abel, Thy Brother?, Zacheta Nat Gallery Contemp Art, Warsaw, Poland, 96; Site of Being, Inst Contemp Art, Boston, Mass, 96; Das Americas, Mus Art Sao Paolo, Brazil, 96; New Acquisition Display, Metrop Mus Art, NY, 96; Kwangju Biennial, Seoul, Korea, 96; Drawing on Chance: Selections from the Permanent Collection, Mus Mod Art, NY, 96; Everything That's Interesting is New, Dakis Joannou Collection, Deste Found & Mus Mod Art, Copenhagen, 96; Gabriel Orozco, Rirkit Tiravanija og, Living Art Mus, Reykjavik, 96; Whitney Biennial, Whitney Mus Am Art, NY, 97; Galerie Micheline Szwajcer, Antwerpen, 97; Sao Paulo Biennal, 98; Berlin Biennal, Ger, 98; Breaking Ground, Marian Goodman Gallery, NY, 98; Carnegie Int, Carnegie Mus Art, Pittsburgh, Pa, 99; La Casa, il corpo, il cuore, Mus Moderner Kunst Stiftung Ludwig Wien, Vienna, Austria, 99; Economia de Mercado, Galeria Kurimanzutto/Mercado de Medellin, Mexico City, Mex, 99; Let's Entertain, Walker Art Center, Minneapolis, Minn, 2000; A Celebration of Contemp Art, Va Mus Fine Arts, Richmond, 2000; Orbis Terrarum, Mus Plantin-Moretus, Atwerp, Belgium, 2000; Sabrosa, El Inst de Cultura de Morelos, Cuernavaca, Mex, 2000, 01; Nothing, Northern Gallery for Contemp Art, Sunderland, Eng, 01; ARS 01, Mus Contemp Art, Helsinki, Finland, 01; Mus Modern Art, 02, Serpentine Gallery, London, 02, Guggenheim Mus, New York City, 02, Marian Goodman Gallery, New York City, 03, Baltimore Mus Art, 03; Inst Contemp Arts, Philadelphia, 2004; Venic Biennial, 2005; Speaking wtih Hands, Mus Folkwang Essen, 2006; and others. *Awards:* Hon Men, Salon Nac de Artes Plasticas, Drawing sect, Inst Nac de Bellas Artes, Mex City, 83; Hon Men, III Encuentro Nac de Arte joven, Inst Nac de Bellas Artes, Aquascalientes, 83; Mus de Arte Mod, Mex City, 87. *Mailing Add:* c/o Marian Goodman Gallery 124 W 57th St New York NY 10019

ORR, JOSEPH CHARLES
PAINTER
b Tokyo, Japan, Oct 31, 49; US citizen. *Study:* With Anthony Allison, 71; Univ Mo, Columbia, with Frank Stack, 77-78. *Work:* State Mo Hist Soc, Columbia; Nat Collegiate Athletic Asn, Kansas City, Mo; Osage Co Hist Soc, Linn, Mo; Dunnegan Mus Art, Bolivar, Mo; Fed Reserve Bank, Kansas City, Mo. *Comn:* Paintings, Community Fed Savings, Mexico, Mo, 80 & Mercantile Bank, Eldon, Mo, 81; centennial painting, City Eldon, Mo, 82. *Exhib:* Arts for Parks Top 100, Jackson Hole, Wyo, 90, 93, 94, 2002, 2003 & 2006; Miniatures 94 & 98, Albuquerque Mus, NMex; Am Art in Miniature, Gilcrease Mus, Tulsa, Okla, 94, 99, 200, 2001, 2004 & 2006; Akron Soc Artists, Ohio, 96; Ashby-Hodge Gallery Am Art, Fayette, Mo, 97; Margaret Harwell Art Mus, Poplar Bluff, Mo, 99 & 2006; and others. *Awards:* First Prize, Nat Wildlife Collectors Soc Ann Exhib, Minneapolis, Minn, 84; Winsor & Newton Award, 14th Salmagundi Club Exhib, NY, 91; Arts for Parks Top 100 Hist Art Award, Jackson, Wyo, 93. *Bibliog:* Rita Mathews-Orr (auth), My husband the artist, Mo Life, 75; Hope Mathews (auth), Rural scenes with an Ozark Flavor, Midwest Art, 10/84; Franz Brown (auth), Joseph Orr, Southwest Art, 4/97; Nancy Gillespie (auth), Wonderful Wanderlust, Art of the West, 2003; Stephen Doherty (auth), Joseph Orr, Workshop Magazine, 2005. *Mem:* Nat Soc Painters Casein & Acrylic; co-founder, Nat Oil & Acrylic Painters' Soc, Osage Beach, Mo. *Media:* Acrylic on Masonite & Canvas, Watercolor. *Publ:* Auth, Painting in acrylic, Am Artist, 3/86; auth, Lighting your way to stronger landscapes, The Artists, 1/96; Acrylic Painting Techniques, 95, Northlight Artists Guide to Materials & Techniques, 96 & Acrylic Painting, Styles and Techniques, 97, North Light Bks. *Dealer:* Morris & Whiteside Galleries, 807 Wm Hilton Pkwy, Hilton Head, SC 29928; American Legacy Gallery, 5911 Main St, Kansas City, MO 64113; New Masters Gallery, Dolores Btwn Ocean & 7th, Carmel, CA 93921. *Mailing Add:* 1405 Hwy KK Osage Beach MO 65065

ORR, LEAH
SCULPTOR
b Hammond, Ind, Aug 16, 37. *Study:* John Herron Sch Art, Indpls/ St Mary of the Woods, Ind, BS (educ), 61; St Mary of the Woods, Ind, BS (art), 69; Ind Univ, Bloomington, MS (art), 72. *Comn:* wirework, Ameritech, Indianapolis, Ind, 88; wirework, Am Red Cross, Indianapolis, Ind, 91; wirework, Kendrick Mem Hosp, Mooresville, Ind, 93; wirework, Health pointe, Jasper, Ind, 96; wirework, Horizon Bank, Mich, Ind, 97. *Exhib:* 68th & 69th Ann Ind Artists Show, Indianapolis, 81 & 83; Bonnie Stahlecker and Leah Orr: The Creative Process, Indianapolis Artsgarden, 2000. *Pos:* asst cur, Indianapolis Mus Art, 73-76. *Teaching:* private lessons throughout Ind, 57-73; summer sch, St Mary of the Woods, 61-63. *Awards:* First Place Sculpture, Am States, 94; Creative Renewal Fel Arts Coun of Indianapolis. *Bibliog:* Pat Pickett (auth), Capture the vision, The Indianapolis Register, 93; Leah Orr (auth), Am states exhib, Fiberaris Mag, 95. *Media:* Wireworks, Miscellaneous Media. *Mailing Add:* 926 Alabama St Indianapolis IN 46202-3319

ORR-CAHALL, ANONA CHRISTINA
CURATOR, HISTORIAN
b Wilkes-Barre, Pa, Jun 12, 47. *Study:* Mt Holyoke Col, BA; Oxford Univ; Ecole du Louvre; Yale Univ, MA, MPhil, PhD. *Collection Arranged:* Am Drawing 1970-1973, Yale Univ Art Gallery, 73; Addison Mizner Architect of Dreams and Realities, Norton Gallery Art, 77; Charles Griffin Farr: A Retrospective, 84 & Gordon Cook: A Restropective, 87, Oakland Mus. *Pos:* Chief cur art, Oakland Mus, formerly; dir, Corcoran Gallery Art, Wash, formerly; dir, Norton Mus Art, currently; dir art div, chief cur, Oakland (Calif) Mus, 1981-88; chief exec off Corcoran Gallery Art, Wash, 1988-90; dir, Norton Mus Art, West Palm Beach, 1990-. *Teaching:* Asst prof art hist & mus studies, Calif Polytech State Univ, San Luis Obispo, 78-81, distinguished pro, 1981. *Res:* California art 1925-present. *Publ:* Auth: Addison Mizner: Architect of Dreams and Realities, 1974, 2d printing, 1993, Gordon Cook, 1987, Claude Monet: Am Impression, 1993; editor: The Art of Calif, 1984, The Am Collection at the Norton Mus of Art, 1995. *Mailing Add:* Norton Mus Art 1451 S Olive Ave West Palm Beach FL 33401

ORTEGA, TONY (ANTHONY) DAVID
PAINTER, PRINTMAKER
b Santa Fe, NMex, Feb 24, 58. *Study:* Univ Colo, BA, 80; Rocky Mountain Sch Art, AA, 82; Univ Colo, MFA, 95. *Work:* Denver Art Mus; Museo Estudio Diego Rivera, Mexico City; Los Angeles Co Art Mus; Mus del Barrio, NY; Laguna Art Mus, Calif. *Comn:* Mosaic mural, City & Co of Denver, Colo. *Exhib:* Los Three, Millicent Roger Mus, Taos, NMex, 92; First Sighting: Recent, Modern & Contemp Aquisitions, Denver Art Mus, Colo, 93; Chicano Expression, Musee du Nouveau Monde, La Rochelle, France, 95; Pasion por Frida, Centro Cult Neco Leta, Buenos Aires, 96; The View from Denver, Mus Mod Art, Vienna, Austria, 97; Prints from Self-Help Graphics, Los Angeles Co Mus Art, Calif, 97; Paraiso, Mus Nacional de Bellas Artes, Santiago, Chile, 98; La Guadalupana, Tacoma Art Mus, Wash, 98. *Awards:* Alliance Contemp Art Award, Denver Art Mus, 91; 1998 Artist Fel, Colo Coun Arts, 98; Mayor's Award for Excellence in the Arts, City & Co of Denver, 98. *Bibliog:* Carol Ketchum (auth), Painting in two stages, Artist Mag, 12/86; Carol Dickerson (auth), Tony Ortega, Southwest Art, 7/89. *Media:* Pastel, Acrylic. *Publ:* Illusr, A Migrant Child's Dream, CU Bouller, 93; coauth, Focus, 94; with Donald J Hagerty, Leading the West: 100 contemporary Painters & Sculptors, Northland Publ, 97; illusr, Days of the Dead: Aztec Adventures of Chalo, Vato & Paro, CU Bouller, 98. *Dealer:* William Haku Gallery 1040 Cherokee St Denver CO 80204. *Mailing Add:* 3650 Eliot Denver CO 80211

ORTIZ, GEORGE
COLLECTOR
Awards: Names one of Top 200 Collectors, ARTnews Mag, 2004. *Collection:* Greek Art-Neolithic to Byzantine; tribal art; 15th Century Italian & 18th Century European arts. *Mailing Add:* Chougny Fontaine Vandoeuvres CH 1253 Switzerland

ORTIZ, RAPHAEL MONTANEZ
CONCEPTUAL ARTIST, EDUCATOR
b New York, NY, Jan 30, 34. *Study:* Brooklyn Mus Art Sch; Art Students League; Pratt Inst, BS & MFA; Columbia Univ, EdD, 82. *Work:* Whitney Mus Am Art, Finch Mus, Mus Mod Art, NY & Museo del Barrio, NY; Syracuse Mus Contemp Art, NY,; Ludwig Mus, Cologne, Ger; Mus Mod Art, Brussels, Belg; Friedricheshof Mus, Zurndorf, Austria; and many others. *Exhib:* Traveling Assemblage Exhib, Mus Mod Art, NY, 63; Young Am Exhib, Whitney Mus Am Art, NY, 65; retrospective, sculpture, performance, computer-laser-video, Museo del Barrio, NY, 88; Computer-Laser-Video, Selected Works, Berlin Video & Film Festival, Ger, 91; performance, Rites of Spring, Alternative Mus, Soho, NY, 92; exhib, Artists of Conscience, Alternative Mus, Soho, NY, 92; performance, Ritual and Installation, Kunst, Vienna, Austria, 92; performance, Utilizing Video Conference Syst Between Kôln & Kassel Ger, Documenta, Electronic Cafe, 92; plus numerous one-man & group shows & performances. *Pos:* Founder, dir & cur, Museo del Barrio, NY, 69-; comt mem, Ghetto Arts Panel, NY State Coun Arts, 70-71; vchmn, Planning Corp Arts, NY, 71; chmn bd, Fondo Del Sol, Washington, DC, 79-81; founder & pres, Mus Computer Art, NJ, 84. *Teaching:* Full prof visual arts, grad & undergrad fac, Mason Gross Sch Arts, Rutgers Univ, 72-. *Awards:* John Hay Whitney Fel Grant, 65; Nat Endowment Arts Grant, 72; NJ Coun Arts, 87. *Bibliog:* Dr Kristine Stiles (auth), Work discussed in Out of Control, ARS Electronea, Duke Univ, 91; Dr Kristine Stiles (auth), Survival ethos and destruction art (discourse), J Theoretical Studies Media & Culture, Duke Univ, spring 92. *Mem:* Col Art Asn of Am; Mus Computer Art (founder & pres, 84); Hispanic Asn Higher Educ, NJ; Asn Res & Enlightenment. *Media:* Mixed Media, Technology. *Publ:* Auth, Disassemblage, Art & Artists, 66; ed & auth, Ritual theatre, Aspen Mag, 69; auth, Culture and the people, Art in Am, 71; Towards an Authenticating Art, Univ Mich, Dissertation Serv, Ann Arbor, 82. *Mailing Add:* Rutgers Univ Visual Arts Dept PO Box 5062 New Brunswick NJ 08903-5062

ORTLIP, PAUL DANIEL
PAINTER
b Englewood, NJ, May 21, 26. *Study:* Houghton Acad; Art Students League; with Louis Bouche, 47, Reginald Marsh, 48, Robert Brackman & Edwin Dickinson, 49; Acad Grande Chaumiere, 50; Houghton Col, Hon DFA, 88. *Work:* US Navy Art Collection, Pentagon, Washington, DC; Air & Space Mus, Smithsonian Inst, Washington, DC; Am Col Clin Pharmacology, NY Acad of Med, NY; Hist Mural, Vistors Ctr Palisades Interstate Park, Ft Lee, NJ; Bush Presidential Libr col Station, Tex. *Comn:* Mem portrait of JFK, Fairleigh Dickinson Univ Libr, 64; Gemini 5 Astronauts, Off Info, USN, 65, Vietnam (painting), 67, Apollo 12 Astronauts, 69 & Apollo 17 Astronauts, 72; and others. *Exhib:* Salon L'Art Libre Ann, Paris, France, 50; Allied Artists Am Ann, 60-71; Collection of Fine Arts, Smithsonian Inst, Wash,

DC; Galerie Vallombreuse, Biarritz, France, 74; La Galerie Mouffe, Paris, 75; James Hunt Barker Galleries, NY, Palm Beach & Nantucket, 83; retrospective, Houghton Col, NY, 01. *Pos:* Off US Navy artist, Off Info, Washington, DC, 63-; art cur, Fairleigh Dickinson Univ, 67-70. *Teaching:* Instr painting, Montclair Acad, NJ, 57-58; artist in residence, Fairleigh Dickinson Univ, 57-67; instr painting, Montclair Mus, 58-59 & 76-80. *Awards:* First Prize, US Armed Forces Exhib, Far East, 46; First Prize, Am Artist Prof League, State Exhib, NJ Chap, 60; Outstanding Achievement Award, Oil Painting, USN, 68; Artist of Year Award, Hudson Artists, Jersey City Mus, NJ, 70. *Bibliog:* Marg Dulac (auth), Odyssey of an artist, NJ Mus & Arts, 5/71; Luc Elyse10e10 Serraf (auth), Paul Ortlip, Artiste American, La Cote des Arts, cover Marseil, France; M Stephen Doherty (auth), Paul Ortlip, His Heritage and His Art, Phoenix Pub, 83. *Mem:* Life mem Art Students League NY; Allied Artists Am; Salmagundi Club; Nat Soc Mural Painters; Artists Fel, Inc; Portrait Soc Am. *Media:* Mixed. *Interests:* Travel, classical music. *Dealer:* Four Generations Art Gallery 517 SR PO Box 4150 Vineyard Haven MA 02568. *Mailing Add:* 2917 S Ocean Blvd #703 Highland Beach FL 33487-1836

ORTMAN, GEORGE EARL
PAINTER, SCULPTOR
b Oakland, Calif, Oct 17, 26. *Study:* Ariz State Univ; Calif Col Arts & Crafts; Atelier 17, NY; Acad Andre Lhote, Paris; Hans Hofmann Sch, NY. *Work:* Guggenheim Mus & Mus Mod Art, NY; Walker Art Ctr, Minneapolis, Minn; Albright-Knox Art Gallery, Buffalo; Milwaukee Art Ctr; Nat Gallery Art; Smithsonian Mus Am Art; Mus Mod Art, NY; plus others. *Comn:* Mural, comn by Bd Educ, PS 192, NY, 67; Reredo, Unitarian Church, Princeton, NJ, 68; banners, Ind Univ Opera House, 71; Oracle (three panels), Mfrs Hanover Trust, 71; Albert Kahn & Assoc Inc, 81; Wharton Ctr Performing Arts, Mich State Univ. *Exhib:* Carnegie Inst Int, Pittsburgh, 60, 64 & 70; Toward a New Abstraction, Jewish Mus, NY, 63; Tokyo Biennial, Japan, 64; 100 Yrs of Am Art, 64 & Two Decades of Geometric Abstraction, 65, Whitney Mus Am Art. *Teaching:* Sr fel painting, Princeton Univ, 66-69; head painting dept, Cranbrook Acad Art, 70-91; co-dir Sch Visual Art, 60-65, NYU, New York, 64-65. *Awards:* Guggenheim Fel, 65; First Prize Religion Art, Birmingham Mus Art, 66; First Prize, NJ State Mus Second Ann, 67; LCR Krasner Award, 2004. *Bibliog:* J Borgzingler (auth), Analytical art, Time Mag, 4/64; Martin Friedman (auth), Symbols, Art News, 10/65. *Mem:* Nat Acad. *Media:* Oil, Mixed Media. *Collection:* Mus Modern Art; Whitney Mus of Am Art; Guggenheim Mus; Cleveland Mus; Dallos Mus; Tate Mus; Los Angeles County Mus; Portland Mus; Walker Art Ctr. *Dealer:* Hill Gallery 163 Townsend Birmingham MI 48009. *Mailing Add:* Box 192 Castine ME 04421

ORZE, JOSEPH JOHN
ADMINISTRATOR, SCULPTOR
b Exeter, Pa, Dec 11, 32. *Study:* Syracuse Univ, BFA(magna cum laude), 55, MS, 56; George Peabody Col, EdD, 70. *Work:* Munson, Williams, Proctor Inst, Utica, NY; Sch Benedictine Fathers, Rome, Italy; Mass Maritime Acad, Buzzards Bay. *Exhib:* One-man & two-man shows, J B Speed Art Mus, Louisville, Ky, 65, Dana Arts Ctr, Colgate Univ, Hamilton, NY, 69; Brooks Mem Gallery, Memphis; Hunter Gallery, Univ Chattanooga; Syracuse Univ, NY; Conn Acad Fine Arts, Wadsworth Atheneum, Hartford; Everson Mus Fine Art, Syracuse; and others. *Pos:* Vpres & dir, Southern Asn Sculptors, 64-66; chmn, Conn Col Coun Arts, 67-69; vpres & dir, Marion Art Ctr, Mass, 73-75; dir & treas, Pub Art Proj, Inc, New Bedford, Mass, 74-. *Teaching:* Instr art & educ, Syracuse Univ, 56-59; assoc prof sculpture & art educ, State Univ NY Col New Paltz, 59-61; assoc prof art & head dept, Middle Tenn State Univ, 61-66; prof art & chmn dept, Southern Conn State Col, 66-69; dean, Col Fine & Applied Arts, Southeastern Mass Univ, 69-75; pres, Worcester State Col, 75-, Northwestern La State Univ, currently. *Awards:* Purchase Award for Sculpture, Munson, Williams, Proctor Inst, 58; R A Rathbone Best in Show Award, New Haven Print & Clay Club, 66; First Prize in Sculpture, New Eng Arts Festival, Waterbury, Conn, 67 & 68. *Mem:* Col Art Asn; Nat Art Educ Asn. *Publ:* Auth, Understanding children's art, Instr Mag, 5/64; Enigma of modern art, Peabody Reflector, 5/66; Role of the Fine Arts in the University, Middle Tenn State Univ, 69; Visual arts in higher education, Mass Art Educ Asn, 70; co-auth, Art From Scrap, Davis, 2nd ed, 73. *Mailing Add:* 921 Cypress Way Boca Raton FL 33486

OSBORN, KEVIN RUSSELL
BOOK ARTIST, PRINTMAKER
b Boston, Mass, July 3, 51. *Study:* Ecole Nat Arts Decoratifs, Nice, France, 71-72; Univ Vt, Burlington, BA(cum laude), 73; Visual Studies Workshop, State Univ NY, Buffalo, MFA, 77. *Work:* Mus Mod Art, NY; Mus Nat Art Mod, Paris; Whitney Mus; Art Inst Chicago; DeYoung Mus, San Francisco. *Comn:* Parallel (artist book), Ga State Arts Coun, Atlanta, 80. *Exhib:* Words and Images, Philadelphia Art Alliance, 80; solo exhib, Washington Proj Arts, 80; Ex Libris, Traction Gallery, Los Angeles, 81; Re/pages, New Eng Found Arts Touring Exhib, 81-82; Cent Livres d'Ailleurs, Ed Jean-Michel Pl, Paris, 82; 12th Biennale Paris, Mus Mod Art, Paris, 82. *Pos:* Dir, Bookworks Prog, Writer's Ctr, Bethesda, Md, 77-. *Teaching:* Instr workshops, Calif Col Arts & Crafts, 80, Va Commonwealth Univ, 83 & State Univ NY, Purchase, 83. *Awards:* Grant Vector Rev (artist book), Found Todays Art, 83; Va Mus Fel, 83; Nat Endowment Arts Fel, 84. *Bibliog:* Clive Phillpot (auth), Real lush, Artforum, 5/82; Paul Zelevansky (auth), Visual literature, Am Book Rev, spring 83; Nancy Solomon (auth), The layered look, Afterimage, summer 83. *Media:* Artists Books; Experimental Offset. *Mailing Add:* 3411 15th St N Arlington VA 22201-4911

OSBORNE, CYNTHIA A
PRINTMAKER, EDUCATOR
b New Milford, Conn, Dec 13, 47. *Study:* Conn Col, New London, BA, 69; Univ Wis-Madison, MFA, 73. *Work:* Bradley Univ, Peoria, Ill; Davidson Col, NC; Security Pac Nat Banks, Calif; State Univ NY Buffalo; US Info Agency, Selected US Embassies. *Exhib:* Miami Graphics Biennial, Metrop Mus, Fla, 76 & 80; Current Directions in Southern Calif Art, Los Angeles Inst Contemp Art, 77 & 78; Nat Print Exhib, Soc Am Graphic Artists, NY, 77 & 79; Drawings & Prints, Space, Los Angeles, 79; Paper in Particular, Columbia Col, Mo, 80; and many others. *Pos:* Vis artist, Nat Print Symp, Cranbrook Acad Art, Detroit, spring 80. *Teaching:* Assoc prof printmaking, Calif State Univ, Long Beach, 75-82, assoc prof art, currently; lectr printmaking, Otis Art Inst, Los Angeles, 77. *Awards:* Purchase Awards, Griffin Press Co, Oakland, Calif, 75 & Los Angeles Printmakers Nat Exhib, Graphic Chemical, Chicago, 77. *Mem:* Los Angeles Printmaking Soc (bd mem, 77); Soc Am Graphic Artists; World Print Coun, San Francisco. *Media:* Printmaking; Lithography. *Mailing Add:* Dept Art Calif State & Long Beach 1250 Bellflower Long Beach CA 90840

OSBORNE, ELIZABETH
PAINTER, CRITIC
b Philadelphia, Pa, June 5, 36. *Study:* Pa Acad Fine Arts, cert(Schiedt Traveling Scholarship), 58; Univ Pa, BFA(with hons), 59. *Work:* Chase Manhattan Bank, NY; Philadelphia Mus Art, Pa; Pa Acad Fine Arts, Philadelphia; Del Art Mus, Wilmington; McNay Art Mus, San Antonio, Tex; Am Re-Insurance, New York, NY; Am Telephone & Telegraph, New York, NY; Brown, Wood, Ivey, Mitchell, and Petty, New York, NY; Chemical Bank, New York, NY; CIGNA, Philadelphia, PA; Commerce Bancshares, Inc, Kansas City, MO; Dechert, Price and Rhoads, Philadelphia; Duane, Morris, and Heckscher, Philadelphia, PA; First Pennsylvania Bank, Philadelphia, PA. *Comn:* Etching Edition 100 Prints, Philadelphia Print Club, Pa, 81; Lithograph Ed 125 Prints, Friends of the Philadelphia Mus Art, Pa, 79. *Exhib:* Philadelphia: Three Centuries of Am Art, Philadelphia Mus Art, Pa, 76; Painting & Sculpture Today, 1978, Indianapolis Mus Art, 78; The New Am Still Life, Westmoreland Co Mus, Pa, 79; Contemp Am Realism Since 1960, Pa Acad Fine Arts, 81; Collectors Gallery, McNay Art Inst, San Antonio, Tex, 82; Realist Watercolors Fla, Univ Miami, 83; Mainstream Am, Butler Art Inst, 87; Janss Collection, Boise Art Mus, 88; Utopian Visions, Mus of Mod Art, NY, 88; solo exhibs, Old Main Art Mus, Northern Ariz Univ, Flagstaff, Ark, 98, Vantage, Locks Gallery, Philadelphia, 2000, Elizabeth Osborne: Thirty Yrs, Works on Paper, Locks Gallery, Philadelphia, 2002, State of the Art 2003 & Biennial Sienna Univ, Mich, 2003; group exhib, Am Watercolors at the Pa Acad, Pa Acad Fine Arts, Philadelphia, 2000; group exhib, Bruce McGrfew, Murray Dessner & Elizabeth Osborne, Davis Dominguez Gallery, Tucson, Ariz, 2002; group exhib, Biennial Watercolor invitational, Parkland Col, Champaign, Ill, Siena Heights Col, Adrian, Mich, 2003. *Pos:* Critic & chairperson, Pa Acad Fine Art, Philadelphia, 61-. *Awards:* Fulbright Scholar, Paris, 63; Rosenthal Found Award, Nat Inst Arts & Lett, 71; MacDowell Fel, Pa Acad of Arts, 83; Percy M Owens Award for a Distinguished Pa Artist, 92nd Ann Juried Exhib, Am Col, Bryn Mawr, 89. *Bibliog:* Eve Medoff (auth), article, Am Artist, 77; Christine Hopf (dir), In Praise of Women Artists (film), Bo-Tree Productions, 79; Frank Goodyear (auth), Contemporary Realism Since 1960; Charles LeClair (auth), The Art of Watercolor; M Martin (auth), American Realism: 20th Century Drawings and Watercolors from the Janss Collection; Donna Gustafan (auth), Elizabeth Osborne: Vantage, Locks Gallery Publ, Philadelphia, 2000; David A Lauer & Stephen Pentak (auths), Design Basics, Harcourt Brace Col Publ, NY, 2000. *Mem:* Philadelphia Print Club. *Media:* Oil, Watercolor. *Publ:* AColor-conscious, The Pennsylvania Gazette, 1/2001-2/2001. *Dealer:* Locks Gallery 600 Washington Sq S Philadelphia PA 19106

OSBORNE, FREDERICK S
EDUCATOR, ADMINISTRATOR
b Philadelphia, Pa, Sept 10, 40. *Study:* Tyler Sch Fine Arts, Temple Univ, BFA, 63; Yale Univ, MFA, 65. *Exhib:* Woodmere Gallery, 59, 60 & 63; Makler Gallery, 61-62; Haverford Col, 62; Pa Acad Fine Arts, 62, Smith Col, 66; Temple Univ, 76; Girard Bank, 84. *Pos:* Dir continuing educ, Philadelphia Col Art, 77-85; co-founder, co-dir & trustee, Vt Studio Ctr, Johnson, 83-89; dean & dir, Pa Acad Fine Arts, Philadelphia, 85-; consult, Inst Int Educ, New York, 84; Jury, Korean War Vet Mem, Washington, DC, 89; vpres external & alumni affair, dir edn program Violette de Magia Trust, 99-. *Teaching:* Univ of the Arts, Philadelphia, 76-85 & Pa Acad Fine Arts, Philadelphia, 91-; From instr sculpture to asst prof, Grad Sch Fine Arts, Univ Pa, 66-77; lectr, Smith Col, 66 & Univ Maine, 80; lectr, Violette de Magia Trust, Barnes Found. *Mem:* Nat Asn Schs Art & Design (bd dir, 89-96); Asn Independent Cols Art & Design (trustee, 91-95); Col Art Asn; Am Coun Arts. *Publ:* Auth, The Classical Education of an Artist: Another View from a Contemporary Window, Art J/Col Art Asn, 94. *Mailing Add:* Pa Acad Fine Arts 118 N Broad St Philadelphia PA 19102

OSBORNE, JOHN PHILLIP
PAINTER, INSTRUCTOR
b Paterson, NJ, July 9, 51. *Study:* Pratt Inst, cum laude BFA(art educ & environ design), 73. *Work:* NY Life; Union Labor Life, Washington, DC; Metrop Life & Int Telephone & Telegraph Hq, NY; First Common Wealth Saving Bank, Washington, DC. *Comn:* 4 Landscapes of each season, comn by pvt collector, Kinnelon, NJ, 85-86; Portrait, comn by pvt collector, Saddle River, NJ 92. *Exhib:* Invitational Exhib, Nat Arts Club, NY, 88; Invitational Exhib, US Embassy, Moscow, 91-93, Harare, Zimbabwe, 92-94, Jarkarta, Indonesia, 93-95, Columbia, South Am, 94-96 & Reykjavik, Iceland, 99-2000; Invitational Exhib, pvt gallery, Taiwan, 92; Bergen Mus Art & Sci, NJ, 96; Nat Park Acad Arts, USA Tour, 98; The Legacy of Frank Vincent Du Mond, Belmont Univ, Nashville, Tenn, 2002. *Pos:* Illustr, Rudolph, Russell & Fluery Assoc, New York, 72; art restorer & conserv of oil paintings, Frank Moratz, Wyckoff, NJ, 79-84; gallery partner, Albert, Schlenz & Osborne Studio-Gallery, Midland Park, NJ, 81; pres & owner, Artists on Location-J P Osborne, Inc, Ringwood, NJ, 85-. *Teaching:* Dir oil painting, Artists on Location-J P Osborne Inc, Ringwood, NJ, 85-; sr instr oil painting, Ridgewood Art Inst, NJ, 86-; instr, Plein-air workshop, Nantucket, Mass, 89-2004; instr oil painting, Hilton Head Art League, SC, 94. *Awards:* Gold Medal Honor, Hudson Valley Art Asn, 86; Nat Achievement Award, Teacher Oil Painting, Am Artist Mag, 92; Inaugural Inductee, Masterdon Artists Soc,

Bergen Mus Art & Sci, 97. *Bibliog:* Art on tour, NJ Monthly, 92; Review of one man show at Mongerson-Wunderlich, ARTnews, 94. *Mem:* Ridgewood Art Inst (trustee, 87-); Am Artists Prof League; Allied Artists Am; Hudson Valley Art Asn (trustee, 93-99); Knickerbocker Artists, NY; Kent Art Asn (life mem). *Media:* Oil. *Interests:* Classical music & gardening. *Publ:* Auth, Romancing the Light, Am Artist, 91; Critical Initial Lay-In, Palette Talk, Grumbacher, 91; The Joy of Painting Large, Am Artist, 95; American Artist Summer Workshop, 2006. *Dealer:* The John Pence Gallery 750 Post St San Francisco CA 94109; The Gallery at Four India St Nantucket MA 02554; Eleanor Ettinger Inc 119 Spring St New York NY 10012; GC Lucas Gallery 4930 N Pennsylvania St Indianapolis IN 46205; and others. *Mailing Add:* 325 Lakeview Ave Ringwood NJ 07456

OSBY, LARISSA GEISS
PAINTER
b Artemowsk, Russia, June 7, 28; US citizen. *Study:* Lyceum & Univ Goettingen, Ger; Univ Munich; Acad Fine Arts, Munich, Ger. *Work:* Carnegie Inst, Pittsburgh; Alcoa Collection; US Steel Collection; Westinghouse Elec Co Collection; plus others. *Comn:* Am for Democratic Action, 69; Koppers Co & First Fed Savings & Loan Asn, Pittsburgh, 72; United Steelworkers of Am, 73; Nat Steel Corp, 77. *Exhib:* Mid-Yr Nat, Butler Inst Am Art, Youngstown, Ohio, 58, 59 & 79; Guest of Hon Exhib, Birmingham Arts Festival, Mich, 61; Drawings USA, St Paul Art Ctr, Minn, 63; Chautaugua Art Ctr Ann, NY, 64; Walker Art Ctr Biennial, Minneapolis, 66; one-man shows, Carnegie Inst Mus Art, 72 & Pa State Unit, New Kensington, 73; Am Artists in France, Palais des Congres, Paris, 75-76; solo exhib, Pittsburgh Ctr Arts, 83-; Dunfermline, Scotland, 84; Women in Art, Youngstown, Ohio, 95-96; Art in SW Pennsylvania, Westmoreland Co Mus Art, Greensburg, Pa, 96. *Teaching:* Instr art, Pittsburgh High Sch Creative & Performing Arts & Pittsburgh Ctr Arts. *Awards:* Jury Award of Distinction, Mainstreams Int, 68 & Assoc Artists Pittsburgh Ann, 58-59, 60-61 & 69; Pittsburgh Artist of the Year, 83; and others. *Mem:* Asn Artists Pittsburgh. *Media:* Oil, Collage. *Mailing Add:* 2665 Hunters Point Dr Wexford PA 15090

OSCARSSON, VICTORIA CONSTANCE GUNHILD
ART DEALER, CONSULTANT
b Stamford, Conn, Dec 18, 51. *Study:* The Sorbonne; Trinity Col, Hartford, Conn, BA(art hist & languages), 73; Sotheby's Works of Art Course, London, 74. *Pos:* Researcher, Guggenheim Mus, New York, 73; asst, Richard Nathanson, pvt dealer, London, 74-76; dir, Noonday Graphics, London, 76-77; Landmark Gallery, New York, 77-80; art consult, Boston Mutual Life Insurance Co, 78-79; dir, Oscarsson-Hood Gallery, New York, 80-87; pres, Oscarsson Mod & Contemp, 87-. *Mem:* Art Table; Drawing Soc. *Specialty:* Modern and contemporary art, American and European; 17th European Antiques. *Mailing Add:* Schreyvogelgasse 3/12 Vienna 1010 Austria

OSGOOD, JERE
CRAFTSMAN
b Staten Island, New York, 1936. *Study:* Univ Ill, 55-57; Rochester Inst Technol, Sch Am Craftsmen, BFA, 60. *Work:* Mus Contemp Crafts; Rochester Inst Technol; Mus Fine Arts, Boston. *Exhib:* Am Chairs, Kohler Arts Ctr, 78; Wood Traditions & Motivations, Kagain Gallery, Philadelphia, 78; New Hampshire Furniture, Mus Contemp Crafts, 79; Brockton Mus Show, 81; Studio Craft Furniture at Work, Pritam & Eames Gallery, Easthampton, NY, 83; Brentwood Today, RI Sch Design, 84; Elegant Wit, Gallery Naga, Boston, 85; Cuttier Gallery, Manchester, NH; Am Craft Mus, NY; Renwick Gallery, Smithsonian Inst, Washington, DC. *Teaching:* Instr woodworking & furniture design, Craft Students League, New York, 62-70; Philadelphia Col Art, 70-72; Rochester Inst Technol Sch Am Craftsmen, 72-75; lectr, RI Sch Design, Va Commonwealth Univ, 75-77; workshop, NH League of Craftsmen, 77; assoc prof, Prog Artisanry, Boston Univ, 75-85; instr, Penlands Sch, NC & Peters Valley Craft Sch, Layton, NJ, 2001. *Awards:* Nat Endowment Arts, 80. *Bibliog:* Dona Meilach (auth), Creating Modern Furniture; Pat Conley (auth), Art for Everyday, 91. *Mailing Add:* 626 Abbott Hill Rd Wilton NH 03086

O'SHEA, TERRENCE PATRICK
PAINTER, SCULPTOR
b Los Angeles, Calif, Sept 8, 41. *Study:* Holy Cross Col; Boston Mus Sch; Chouinard Art Inst. *Work:* Los Angeles Co Mus Art; Patrick Lannan Mus, Palm Beach, Fla; AT&T Collections, Chicago; Metromedia Collection; Laguna Mus Art, Laguna, Calif. *Exhib:* A Plastic Presence, Jewish Mus, NY, 69-70; Permutation, Light & Color, Mus Contemp Art, Chicago, 70; Pierres de Fantaisie, Oakland Mus, 70; Temple Street, Long Beach Mus, 71; First Int Biennial Small Sculpture Show, Budapest, Hungary, 71. *Teaching:* Instr, Otis Art Inst, Los Angeles, 76 & Art Ctr Col Design, Pasadena, 80-81. *Awards:* Contemp Art Coun Purchase Award, Los Angeles Co Mus Art, 65. *Bibliog:* Jerry Rosen (auth), Terry O'Shea (video taped interview), 74. *Mem:* Artist Equity Asn (bd dir, 80-81). *Media:* All. *Mailing Add:* 1533 Yale St Apt D Santa Monica CA 09040-3625

OSHIMA, MARI
SCULPTOR
b Troy, NY, May 31, 58. *Study:* Giovanni Cusa Art Inst, Nuoro, Italy, 80; State Univ NY, Albany, BA(fine arts), 83; Empire State Col, NY, Studio Prog, 86; NY Univ, 88; Parsons Sch Design, NY, MFA(sculpture), 88. *Exhib:* Solo exhibs, Losing of Home, installation, NY Univ, 86, Buddha's Birthday, installation on 13th St, NY, 87, Keiko Space, NY, 89, Baca Downtown, Brooklyn, NY, 90, Soho 20, NY, 90, Gallery Shimada, Yamaguchi, Japan, 90 & 92; Keyaki Hall, Tanto, Hyogo, Japan, 90 & 92; JAA at Consulate Gen of Japan, NY, 91; Pelham Art Ctr, NY, 92; Pacifico Yokohama Plaza, Japan, 92; Infused with the Spirit, Police Bldg, NY, 93; Bevier Gallery, Rochester Inst Technol, NY, 93; Dana Room Gallery, Franklin & Marshall Col, Lancaster, Pa, 94. *Teaching:* Lectr, Ako Pub Sch, Hyogo, Japan, 89, Global Study, Japan, 89, Vis Arts Prog, State Univ NY, Albany, 91. *Awards:* Artists Grant, Artist Space, NY, 88-89, 89-90 & 90-91; Visual Arts Fel, Nat Endowment Arts, 90; Artist Grant, NY Found Arts, 91. *Bibliog:* Randolph Williams (auth), The Trend Gallery, Brooklyn Trend, 11/87; Roberta Smith (auth), NY Times, 3/23/90; Mikio Takada (auth), Contemp Art Info, No 15, 1/91

OSHITA, KAZUMA
SCULPTOR
b Hiroshima, Japan, Oct 17, 49. *Study:* Nat Tokyo Univ Arts Grad Sch, 74. *Work:* Am Express Co, NY; J B Speed Mus, Louisville, Ky. *Comn:* Forbes Mag, NY, 88; Hiroshima Univ Libr, Japan, 93; Biwako Hotel, Kyoto, Japan, 98; IS 125, NY. *Exhib:* Solo exhibs, Kanuma Gallery, Tokyo, 76, Alexander F Milliken Inc, NY, 83, 87 & 90, Hokin Kaufman Gallery, Chicago, 89 & 92, Hiro Chikashige Gallery, Okayama, 92, Suzukawa Gallery, Hiroshima, 92 7 96, Ryoko Art Corp, Kyoto, 92 & Yamamoto-Tarpin Gallery, Kyoto, 93, Arden Gallery, Boston, 94, Suzukawa Gallery, Hiroshima, Japan, 96, Humanite Gallery, Nagoya, Japan, 97; Arden Gallery, Boston, 88, 93-95; Fall Exhibition-Gallery Artists, Alexander F Milliken Inc, 88; On Paper, Hokin Kaufman Gallery, Chicago, 90; Metal Work and Sculpture, Gallery Art, Univ Northern Iowa, Cedar Rapids, 93; Art in Metal, Hamanite Gallery, Nagoya, 97; Int Art Fair NiCAF, Toyko, 97; two-person show, Ryoko Art Corp, 97; New Works by Contemp Artists and Selections from Our Archives, Gerald Peters Gallery, Santa Fe, 98; Pub collections: Am Express, New York City, Forbes Mag, New York City, The Speed Mus, Louisville, Hiroshima (Japan) Univ Libr. *Awards:* Salon de Printemps Prize, Nat Tokyo Univ Arts, 72; Fel, Nat Endowment Arts, 86-87. *Bibliog:* Therise Lichtenstein (auth), article, Arts Mag, 1/84; Lynn Nesmith (auth), The arts-metal fragments of reality, Archit, 11/84; Christiana DePaul (auth), Kazuma Oshita: The Art of Metal Hammering, Metalsmith, Spring 88. *Media:* Hammered Metal. *Dealer:* Arden Gallery 129 Newbury St Boston MA 02116; Gerald Peters Gallery 1011 Paseo De Peralt Santa Fe NM 87501. *Mailing Add:* 511 S Mountain Rd Gardiner NY 12525-5030

O'SICKEY, JOSEPH BENJAMIN
PAINTER, EDUCATOR
b Detroit, Mich, Nov 9, 18. *Study:* Cleveland Sch Art, with Paul Travis, Henry G Keller, Carl Gaertner, Frank N Wilcox & Hoyt L Sherman, cert. *Work:* Cleveland Mus Art; Cleveland Arts Asn; Canton Art Inst, Ohio; Westmoreland Art Mus; Butler Inst Am Art, Youngstown, Ohio. *Exhib:* Two-person show, Butler Inst Am Art; Pa Acad Fine Art, Philadelphia; one-man shows, Akron Art Inst, Canton Art Inst, Butler Inst Am Art, Youngstown, Ohio, seven shows, Jacques Seligman Galleries, NY, 64-78, Cleveland Inst Art, 82, Kennedy Galleries, NY, 88, 91 & 94 & Philharmonic Ctr Arts, 90; and others. *Pos:* Art dir & graphic designer, pvt co, 49-64. *Teaching:* Instr art, Ohio State Univ, 46-47 & Akron Art Inst, 49-52; lectr art, Case Western Reserve Univ, 56-64; prof art, Kent State Univ, 64-88, coordr painting & sculpture, 68-73; retired. *Awards:* Cleveland Arts Cash Prize for Outstanding Achievement in the Arts, 74; Medal, Cash Award & Purchase Award, Butler Inst Am Art, Ohio, 74; First Prize Cash Awards, All-Ohio Exhibs, 74 & 77 & Best in Show Cash Prize, 74; Purchase Award, Am Acad and Inst Art and Letters, 11/88. *Media:* Oil, Watercolor. *Mailing Add:* 7308 SR 43 Kent OH 44240

OSORIO, PEPÓN
PAINTER
b Santurce, PR, 55. *Study:* Univ Inter-Americana, Rio Pedras, PR, 74; Herbert H Lehman Col, BS, 78; Columbia Univ, MA, 85. *Work:* El Mus del Barrio, NY; Nat Mus Am Art, Washington, DC; Walker Ctr for Arts, Minneapolis; Wadsworth Atheneum, Hartford, Conn; Whitney Mus Am Art, NY; Rhode Island Sch Design, Providence, RI; Bronx Mus Arts, NY; Newark Mus, Newark, NJ. *Comn:* Café America, (traveling show), Joyce Theatre, NY, 90; The Warrior of Gringostroika, Brooklyn Acad of Music, Brooklyn, NY, 91. *Exhib:* Solo exhib, Cleveland Inst Art, 93, Otis Gallery, Otis Col Art & Design, Westchester, Calif, 97, Mus Alejandro Otero, Caracas, Venezuela, 98 & Espacio Uno, Mus Nac Centro de Arte Reina Sofia, Madrid, 98, RI Sch Design Mus, Providence, 99 & Pepon Osorio: Door to Door (with catalog), Escuela de Artes Plasticas, Mus de San Juan, Mus de Arte Contemp de Puerto Rico, Mus de Arte de Puerto Rico, 2000, Lehman Col Art Gallery, Bronx, NY, 2002 & Bernice Steinbaum Gallery, Miami, Fla, 2003; Biennial, Whitney Mus Am Art, NY, 93; Art at the Edge: Social Turf, High Mus Art, Atlanta, 95; Archaeological Urban Data, Whitney Mus Am Art at Champion, 95; Am Kaleidoscope: Themes & Perspectives in Recent Art, Mus Am Art, Smithsonian Inst, Wash, DC, 97; VI Cuban Bienniale, Havana, 97; As Time Goes By: History, Memory and the Sentimental, Whitney Mus Am Art at Champion, Stamford, Conn, 97; Am Stories - Amidst Displacement & Transformation, Setagaya Art Mus, Tokyo, 97; Asi esta la Cosa: Instalacion y Arte Objecto en Am Latina, Centro CultArte Contemporaneo Mexico City, Mex, 97; 2nd Johannesburg Bienniale, Africus Inst Contemp Art, S Africa, 98; Other Narratives, Contemp Arts Mus, Houston, 99; The Rescue: Eight Artists in an Archive, Int Ctr Photog, NY, 99-2000; group exhibs, RISD Mus, Providence, RI, 2002, Contemp Arts Centemp Arts Ctr, Cincinatti, Ohio, 2003; Historias, Univ of Arts, Samuel S Fleischer Art Mem, Philadelphia, PA, Jacob's Pillow Dance Festival, Lee, MA, 92; Familias, Hostos Ctr for the Arts and Cult, Hostos Community Col, Bronx, NY, 95; Retrospective (with catalog), Whitney Mus of Art & Harry N Abrams, Inc, NY, 93, VI Cuban Bienniale, 97. *Pos:* artist in residency, Manchester Craftsmen's Guild, Pittsburug, PA, 97; vis artist, Univ of Hawaii, Honolulu, Skowhegan Sch of Painting and Sculpture, ME, 98. *Teaching:* keynote panel mem, SUNY sch of fine & performing arts, SUNY New Paltz, New Paltz, NY, 2001; host, inst of contemp art, Univ of Pa, Philadelphia, 2002. *Awards:* Grant, Joan Mitchell Found, 96-97; Nat Endowment for Arts Artist Fel, Sculpture, 88; MacArthur Found Fel, 99; Cal Arts Alpert Award for visual arts, 99; Skowhegan Medal for sculpture, 2001. *Bibliog:* William Zimmer (auth), A meditation on masculinity wrapped up in a barbershop, New York Times, 8/14/94; Berta Sichel

(auth), Pepon Osorio: Interviewed by Berta Sichel, Atlantica, No 12, winter 95-96; Amei Wallach (auth), Roving taxis with a message told through art, New York Times, 2/16/97; Lesli Camhi (auth), Pepón Osorio, Thye Village Voice, 10/22/2002; Graciela Kartofel (auth), Pepón Osorio, Art Nexus, Vol 1, 2003. *Mem:* Centro de Estudios Puertoriqueños (mem advisory bd, 96-98); The New Mus, NY (mem advisory bd, 96-98); Performance Space 122 (mem advisory bd, 89-93). *Mailing Add:* c/o Ronald Feldman Fine Arts 31 Mercer St New York NY 10013

OSTENDARP, CARL
PAINTER
b Amherst, Mass, Nov 15, 61. *Study:* Boston Univ, BA, 83; Yale Univ, MFA, 96. *Work:* Whitney Mus Am Art; Wadsworth Atheneum; Art Inst, Chicago; Fogg Art Mus, Harvard Univ; Mus Moderne Kunst, Frankfort, Germ; Mus Contemp Art, Los Angeles; San Francisco Mus Mod Art. *Exhib:* Altered States-USA Art of 90's, Forum Contemp Art, St Louis, Mo, 95; Pittura-Immedia, Landesmuseum Joanneum, Guaz, Austria, 95; Transformed, Weiner Secession, Vienna, 96; Carl Ostendarp 189 Drawings, Aldrich Mus Contemp Art, Ridgefield, Conn, 2003. *Teaching:* Adj prof painting, NY Univ, 92-96; instr drawing, Sch Visual Arts, NY, 94-95, Tyler Sch Art, Temple Univ, Philadelphia, 97, Rutgers State Univ, NJ, 98 & Cornell Univ, 2000-2006. *Bibliog:* Anthony Ianacci (auth), Ostendorp/Weinstein, Studio Citta-Verona, 96; John Waters & Bruce Hainley (co-auths), Art-A Sex Book, New York, Thames & Hudson, 2003; Udo Kittelmann & Klaus Görner (co-auths), What's New Pussycat? Recent Acquisitions 2002-2005, Museum Modern Kunst, Frankfurt, Germ, 2006. *Media:* Acrylic. *Dealer:* Rolf Picke Galerie Koln Ger; Elizabeth Dee Gallery New York NY

OSTENDORF, (ARTHUR) LLOYD, JR
PAINTER, INSTRUCTOR
b Dayton, Ohio, June 23, 21. *Study:* Dayton Art Inst; Lincoln Mem Univ, Lincoln Dipl Hon, 66, hon ArtD, 74; Lincoln Col (Ill), LittD, 68. *Work:* Gov William Lee De Ewing (oil portrait) & Speaker W Robert Blair (oil portrait), Ill State Capitol, Springfield; Msgr Harry Ansbury (oil portrait), Parish Recreation House, Corpus Christi; Msgr Joseph D McFarland (oil portrait), Holy Angels Sch, Dayton, Ohio; Dr Herbert Y Livesay (oil portrait), Lincoln Mem Univ; Gen George Rogers Clark (oil), Restored Gov Mansion, Springfield. *Comn:* The Jesuit Martyrs (oil), Jesuit Retreat Chapel, Milford, Ohio, 49; six religious oil paintings, Hoyne Funeral Chapel, Dayton, 55. *Exhib:* Dayton Art Inst, 41. *Pos:* Art ed, Lincoln Herald, 57-. *Teaching:* Instr com art & painting & dir, Ostendorf Art Acad, 69-. *Awards:* Winner in Design for Chicago Lincoln (statue), Lincoln Sq C of C, 58. *Mem:* Montgomery Co Hist Soc (vpres, 56); Civil War Round Table of Dayton (pres, 55-56 & 58-59). *Media:* Watercolor, Oil. *Publ:* Auth, Mr Lincoln Came to Dayton, 59; auth & illusr, A Picture Story of Abraham Lincoln, 62; co-auth, Lincoln in Photographs, An Album of Every Known Pose, 63; auth, The Photographs of Mary Todd Lincoln, 69; coauth, Lincolns Unknown Private Life, 96. *Mailing Add:* 225 Lookout Dr Dayton OH 45419

OSTERMILLER, DAN
SCULPTOR
b Cheyenne, Wyo, 56. *Comn:* Fuente de Los Osos, Quail Run, Santa Fe, NewM; Fleischer Mus, Scottsdale, Ariz; Trammel Crow, Chicago, Ill; Wyoming State Capital, Cheyenne, Wyo; Brookgreen Gardens, Murrells Inlet, SC; Dupont Corp. *Pos:* pres, National Sculpture Soc, New York, 2005-. *Mem:* Soc Animal Artists; Allied Artists of Am; Fel Nat Sculpture Soc. *Dealer:* Nedra Matteucci Gallery and Medra Matteucci Fine Art Gallery Santa Fe NewM; Claggett-Rey Gallery Vail Colo; Spanierman Gallery New York NY. *Mailing Add:* 100 W First St Loveland CO 80537

OSTIGUY, JEAN-RENE
PAINTER, ART HISTORIAN
b Marieville, PQ, Aug 14, 25. *Study:* Univ Montreal, BA; Ecole des Beaux-Arts, Montreal; Sch Art & Design, Montreal, dipl. *Work:* Carleton Univ, Ottawa; Ottawa Univ. *Exhib:* Montreal Spring Exhib, 51 & 52. *Collection Arranged:* Leon Bellefleur, 68, Adrien Hebert, 71 & Ozias Leduc, 74, Nat Gallery Can. *Pos:* Cur Can art, Nat Gallery Can, 64-85. *Teaching:* Prof, Ecole des Beaux-Arts, Montreal, 53-55; prof Can art, Ottawa Univ, 66-71; vis prof Can art, Laval Univ, 71-72. *Awards:* Chriss Award, 62. *Mem:* Can Mus Asn (councillor, 63-65); Int Comt Mus. *Res:* Nineteenth and early twentieth century Canadian art. *Mailing Add:* 21 Rue Thibault Hull PQ J9A 1H4 Canada

OSTROM, GLADYS SNELL
WRITER, EDUCATOR
b Schenectady, NY, Nov 1, 35. *Study:* Famous Writers School,Westport, Conn, cert, 70, 79; Beacon Col, Washington, MA, 83; Nat Inst Expressive Therapy, Hon PhD, 92; Summit Univ La, Hon PhD, 94. *Work:* Arts-In-Education Showcase, Albany/Schenectady League of Art, Glenville, NY; Ecosynthesis, Yale Univ Conf Ctr. *Comn:* Irene Balas: Portrait Painter, Nat Asn Creative Child & Adult, Toronto, 77; Imagery and Intuition, Am Imagery Asn, NY, 81; Imagery and Magic Island, Am Asn Art Therapy, Cambridge, Mass, 82; Ecosynthesis, Am Imagery Inst, Toronto, Can, 87; Ecosynthesis, Nat Asn Creative Child & Adult, Terrytown, NY, 87. *Exhib:* Creative Artistic Training, Univ Utah, Salt Lake City, 89; Creative Artistic Training, Fort Mason Conf Ctr, Fort Mason, Calif, 91. *Pos:* Vpres, Zonta Club Schenectady, 83-. *Teaching:* Fac, Creative Artistic Training, Nat Inst Expressive Therapy, 92-; provost, Summit Univ La, 94-; part-time fac, Empire State Col, State Univ NY, 94-. *Awards:* Key Award, Am Biog Inst, 95; Order Int Ambassador, 20th Century Award for Achievement, Int Biog Ctr, 96. *Mem:* Nat Asn Creative Children & Adults (exec secy & vpres, 74-); Nat Sch Art & Design; Am Inst Graphic Artists; Int Platform Asn. *Res:* Self-realization training for artists & writers using imagery, music & realization. *Publ:* Auth, Ecosynthesis: Creative parenting, Mensa 28 Res J, 90; Creative Artistic Training, Vantage Press, 95; ed, Marcel Vogel Workbook, CATCO Publ, 96; auth, Leggys in Letter-Land, 97 & Leggys in Number Land, 97, Commonwealth Publ. *Mailing Add:* c/o Creative Artistic Training 2887 Shaw Rd Middle Grove NY 12850

OSTROW, SAUL LIEB
GALLERY DIRECTOR, CRITIC
b Brooklyn, NY, Aug 3, 48. *Study:* High Sch Art & Design, 62-66; Sch of Visual Arts, cert, 70; U Mass, Amherst, MFA, 72. *Collection Arranged:* Painting All-over again, Munic Gallery, Zargosa, 97; Domesticit, Nostalgia & Domesticity, Gallery 1708, 97; Divergent Models, KunstVerien, Weisbaden, Ger, 97; Mug Shots, Ctr for Visual Art & Culture, 99; Working Digitally, Ctr for Visual Art & Culture, 2000; Painting Function, Spaces, Cleveland, Ohio, 2000. *Mem:* Int Asn Art Critics (bd dir, 99-2000); Col Art Asn. *Publ:* Contribr/author, Routledge Encyclopedia of Post Modernism, Routledge, 2000; contribr book, Exhibition Catalog for Wlod Ksiazek, Col Arts, London, 2000; editor, Mug Shots/Performing Persona, New Observations, 2000; editor/book, Aby Warburg: Art as Cultural History, G&B Arts Int, 2001, Alois Riegl: Framing Formalism, 2001; ed bd, Art Jour. *Mailing Add:* 162 W 21 St New York NY 10011

OSTROW, STEPHEN EDWARD
ADMINISTRATOR, CURATOR
b New York, NY, May 7, 32. *Study:* Oberlin Col, BA, 54; NY Univ Inst Fine Arts, MA, 59, PhD, 66. *Collection Arranged:* Baroque Painting: Italy and Her Influence (with catalog), 68; Visions and Revisions (with catalog), 68; Raid the Icebox I, with Andy Warhol, (with catalog), 69-70. *Pos:* Cur collections, Herron Mus Art, 66-67; chief cur, Mus Art, RI Sch Design, 67-71, dir, 71-78; dean Sch Fine Arts, Univ Southern Calif, 78-, dir mus studies prog, 79-82; exec dir, Portland Art Asn, 82-84; chief, Prints & Photog div, Libr Congress, 84-96; guest cur, Nat Gallery Art, Washington, DC, 99-. *Teaching:* asst prof art hist, Univ Mo-Columbia, 62-66; vis lectr art hist, Brown Univ, 70, 71, 74, 76 & 77; prof art hist, Univ Southern Calif, 78-82. *Awards:* Stephen E Ostrow Distinguished Visitor Prog, Reed Col, Portland, endowed by Sue Cooley and Betty Gray, 96. *Mem:* Print Coun Am (exec bd, 86-89). *Publ:* Auth, Annibale Carracci and the Jason frescoes: Toward an internal chronology, Art Bull, 64; Diana or Bacchus in the Palazzo Riario, Marsyas, 65; A drawing by Annibale Carracci for the Jason frescoes and the S Gregorio baptism, Master Drawings, 70; prefaces and introductions, In: The Selection Series & Classical Collection (10 catalogs), Mus Art RI Sch Design, 72-77; Digitizing Historical Pictorial Collections for the Internet, CLIR, 98. *Mailing Add:* 3801 Inverness Dr Chevy Chase MD 20815

O'SULLIVAN, DANIEL JOSEPH
PAINTER
b Brooklyn, NY, Aug 18, 40. *Study:* Fordham Col; Brooklyn Mus Art Sch; Pratt Graphics Ctr. *Work:* Commerce Trust Co, Kansas City, Mo; Wichita Art Mus; Mus of Albuquerque, NMex; also in pvt collections of Hirshhorn, Neuberger & West; Tobin Collection, San Antonio, Tex. *Comn:* Portraits, Brooklyn Bar Asn & Pace Univ, Adelphi Univ & Cox Enterprises. *Exhib:* US Dept State Art in Embassies Prog, Korea, 75; Am Acad Arts & Lett, NY, 75 & 76; one-man show, Kraushaar Galleries, NY, 75 & 79, 82 & 86; Food, Bronx Mus Art, NY, 87; Narrative Art, Fla Int Univ, Miami, 88; Newspapers, Amherst Col Mus, 88, Art & Law, 90, David Adamson, Washington, 93; Hampton Sq Gallery, W Hampton Beach, NY, 94; Krasdale Galleries, White Plains, NY, 95; Heckscher Mus, Huntington, NY, 97. *Awards:* Purchase Award, Am Acad Arts & Lett, New York, 76; Art & Law Purchase Award, West Publ Co, 90. *Media:* Oil, Acrylic. *Mailing Add:* c/o Kraushaar Galleries 724 Fifth Ave New York NY 10019

O'SULLIVAN, JUDITH ROBERTA
MUSEUM DIRECTOR, PAINTER
b Pittsburgh, Pa, Jan 6, 42. *Study:* Carlow Col, BA, 63; Univ Md, MA, 67, PhD, 76, JD, 96. *Pos:* ed, Am Film Inst, 74 77; assoc prog coordr, Smithsonian Assocs, 77-78, dir develop Nat Arch, 78-79; exec dir, Md State Humanities Coun, 79-84 & Ctr for Bk in Libr of Congress, 81-82; Deputy asst dir, Smithsonian Inst, Nat Mus Am Art, 84-89; pres & Chief Exec Officer, Mus Stony Brook, NY, 89-92. *Teaching:* Smithsonian Assocs For Studies, Trinity Col & Univ Md. *Mem:* Am Asn Mus; Mid Atlantic Mus Conf; Smithsonian Women's Coun (chair, 88-89). *Media:* Landscape Painting. *Interests:* southwestern landscape painting. *Publ:* Auth, The Art of the Comic Strip, 71 & Workers and Allies, 75, Smithsonian; ed, Am Film Inst Catalog, R R Bowker, 76; coauth, The Complete Prints of Leonard Baskin, 84 & auth, The Great American Comic Strip, 90, Little Brown

OSVER, ARTHUR
PAINTER
b Chicago, Ill, July 26, 1912. *Study:* Northwestern Univ, 30-31; Art Inst Chicago, with Boris Anisfeld, 31-36. *Work:* Mus Mod Art; Whitney Mus Am Art; Metrop Mus Art, NY; Peabody Mus, Salem, Mass; plus many others. *Comn:* Cover, Fortune Mag, 60. *Exhib:* Solo exhibs, St Louis Art Mus, 73, Nelson Gallery-Atkins Mus, Kansas City, 73, Terry Moore Gallery, St Louis, 75 & 77, Timothy Burns Gallery, St Louis, 81 & 84, Art Expo 85, Navy Pier, Chicago, 85 & BZ Wagman Gallery, St Louis, 87; Am Acad & Inst Arts & Letts; Art Inst Chicago; Corcoran Gallery; Galeria Naz Roma; Gallery Mod Art, Tokyo; Mus Mod Art, Rio de Janeiro; Venice Biennale; and others. *Teaching:* Instr painting, Brooklyn Mus Art Sch, 49-51; instr, Columbia Univ, 52 & Univ Fla, 54-55; instr painting, Cooper Union Art Sch, 55 & 58; vis critic painting, Yale Univ, 56-57; painter-in-residence, Am Acad Rome, 57-58; instr, Washington Univ, 60-, prof emer, 81-. *Awards:* Medal, Art Dirs Club, Chicago, 61; J Henry Schiedt Mem Prize, Pa Acad Fine Arts, 66; Sabbatical Grant, Nat Endowment Arts, Washington, DC, 66; plus many others. *Bibliog:* Ray Bethers (auth), How Paintings Happen, Norton, 51; Lee Nordness (ed), Art: USA: Now, C J Bucher, 62. *Mem:* Nat Acad. *Mailing Add:* 465 Foote Ave St Louis MO 63119

OSYCZKA, BOHDAN DANNY
PAINTER
b Herkimer, NY, May 18, 21. *Study:* Vesper George Sch Art; Col Fine Arts, Syracuse Univ, BFA; Art Students League. *Work:* Prudential Insurance Co Am, Mass; Pfizer Learning Ctr, Ryebrook, NY; AT&T, NY; IBM, NY; Monhegan Cult Hist Mus. *Comn:* Religious murals, St Peter & Paul Ukranian Orthodox Church, Utica, 48; Pepsico

World HQ, Purchase, NY, 76. *Exhib:* One-man shows, Katonah Gallery, NY, 71, 76 & 82, Silvermine Guild Artists, New Canaan, Conn, 71 & 78 & Nicolaysen Art Mus, Casper, Wyo, 79, Nardin Galleries, Somers, NY, 95, Howland Ctr, Beacon, NY, 96, Flat Iron Gallery, Peekskill, NY, 2000, Katonah Mus Art, Katonah, NY, Hollis Taggart Galleries, NYC, 2005, Gallery at Sixth & Sixth, Tuscon, Ariz, 2006 plus others; Osaka Munic Mus Art, Japan, 94-96; Katonah Mus Artist Asn, Kisco, NY, 2000; Bates Col Mus, Maine, 2001; Gary Snyder Fine Arts, NY, 2002; The Katonah Mus Art, NY, 2005; The Studio Armonk, NY, 2004. *Pos:* Lectr-demonstr, Katonah Gallery, 71-84, Kirkland Col, Clinton, NY, 74 & Hudson River Mus, Yonkers, NY, 74; juror of selection, 86, juror of awards, 89, Cooperstown Art Asn. *Teaching:* Instr, Parsons Sch Design, NY, 70-94. *Awards:* Watercolor Award, Westchester Art Soc, 67-70; Sindin Harris Gallery Award, 74 & Mus Purchase Award, 76, Hudson River Mus, Yonkers, NY; Hon Award, Osaka Mus, Japan, 94. *Bibliog:* Fay Ellis (auth), Enter the Artist's Studio, Art News, Westchester Art Coun, 94; Kathy Grantham (auth), Nardin exhibits the pure watercolor of Bohdan Osyczka's interior world, N Co News, NY, 95; Virtuosity (3-CD CD-ROM), Art Communication Int, Park Ave Armory, New York, 95. *Mem:* Japan Mod Fine Art Asn, Osaka; Katonah Mus Art Asn, NY; Artist Equity Asn, NY; Westchester Arts Coun, White Plains, NY; Visual Artists & Gallery Asn, NY. *Media:* Watercolor. *Publ:* Contribr, Am Artist, 9/65; NY Art Rev, Am Reference, 88 & 89; coauth with Robert Ayers, Art News, summer 2005. *Mailing Add:* 1450 Summit Ave Peekskill NY 10566

OTANI, JUNE
ILLUSTRATOR, PRINTMAKER
b Santa Paula, Calif, July 7, 34. *Study:* Pasadena City Col, Calif, AA, 54; Art Ctr Col Des, BFA, 56; Pratt Graphic Ctr, 76-85. *Exhib:* Solo exhib, Palisades Gallery of Hudson River Mus, Yonkers, NY, 87. *Awards:* Printmaking Award, Gallery at Hastings-on-Hudson, 78; Mamaroneck Artist Guild Award, ann show, 80; Dr & Mrs I C Gaynor Award, Nat Asn Women Artists, ann show, 87. *Mem:* Nat Asn Women Artists; Silvermine Guild. *Media:* Etching, Oils. *Publ:* Illusr, The Poodle Who Barked at the Wind, 87, Ten Potatoes in a Pot, 90 & Oh Snow, 91, HarperCollins; Peach Boy, Bantam, 92; If You Lived in Colonial Times, Scholastic, 92. *Mailing Add:* 47 Calumet Ave Hastings-on-Hudson NY 10706

O'TOOLE, JUDITH HANSEN
MUSEUM DIRECTOR, WRITER
b Minneapolis, Minn, Sept 24, 53. *Study:* Univ Minn, BA(art hist), 75; Pa State Univ, MA(art hist), 80; Mus Mgt Inst, Boulder, Colo, 89. *Collection Arranged:* Pennsylvania Prints (auth, catalog), Mus Art, Pa State Univ, 80; Carl Sprinchorn: Realist Impulse & Romantic Vision (auth, catalog), Sordoni Art Gallery, Wilkes Col, 83; George Luks: An American Artist (auth, catalog), Sordoni Art Gallery, Wilkes Col, 87; Valley of Work: Scenes of Industry in Western Pennsylvania, Westmoreland Mus Am Art, 93; George Luks-Expressionist Master of Color: Watercolors Rediscovered (auth, catalog), Canton Mus Art, 95. *Pos:* Dir, Sordoni Art Gallery, Wilkes Univ, 82-93; dir & chief exec officer, Westmoreland Mus Am Art, 93-. *Teaching:* Assoc prof, Art Dept, Wilkes Univ, 90. *Mem:* Am Asn Mus; Asn Col & Univ Art Mus; Asn Historians Am Art; Col Art Asn; Middle Atlantic Asn Mus. *Publ:* Auth, Severin Roesen (catalog), Bucknell Univ Press/Assoc Univ Presses, 92; contribr, Essay George Luks (catalog), Mus Fine Art, St Petersburg, Fla, 94; George Luks-expressionist master of color: the watercolor rediscovered, Canton Mus Art, 95; A collaboration in limbo, In:Institutional Trauma, Am Asn Mus, spring 95; Valley of work: scenes of industry in western Pennsylvania, Am Art Rev, 3/96. *Mailing Add:* Westmorel Mus Art 221 N Main St Greensburg PA 15601

OTT, WENDELL LORENZ
MUSEUM DIRECTOR, PAINTER
b McCloud, Calif, Sept 17, 42. *Study:* San Francisco Art Inst, 60-61; Trinity Univ, San Antonio, Tex, BA, 68; Univ Ariz, Tucson, MFA, 70. *Work:* Witte Mem Mus, San Antonio, Tex. *Exhib:* Tex Painting & Sculpture, Dallas Mus Fine Arts, 66; 11th Ariz Ann, Phoenix Art Mus, 69; Yuma Fine Arts Asn, Ariz, 69; Juarez Mus Art, Mex, 73; one-man shows, George Walter Vincent Smith Art Mus, Springfield, Mass, 73 & Eastern NMex Univ, Portales, 74. *Pos:* Dir, Roswell Mus & Art Ctr, NMex, 70-86; dir, Tacoma Art Mus, Wash, 87-92; pres, Wash Art Consortium, 89-90; pres, Mus Southwest, 92-94; pres, Tyler Mus Art, 95-. *Teaching:* Instr painting, NMex Mil Inst, Roswell, 74-80. *Awards:* Onerdonk Award, Witte Mem Mus Ann, 68; Purchase Award, 11th Ariz Ann, Phoenix Art Mus, 69; Nat Mus Act Travel Grant, 73. *Mem:* Am Asn Mus; NMex Asn Mus (chmn, 73-75). *Media:* Oil. *Mailing Add:* Tyler Mus of Art 1300 S Mahon Tyler TX 75701

OTTERNESS, TOM
SCULPTOR
b Wichita, Kans, June 21, 52. *Study:* Art Students League, New York, 70; Independent Study Prog, Whitney Mus Am Art, 77. *Work:* Brooklyn Mus; Whitney Mus Am Art, Mus Mod Art & Solomon R Guggenheim Mus, NY; Israel Mus, Jerusalem. *Comn:* The Real World, Battery Park City Authority, NY, 92; Die Uberfrau, Munster State Libr, Ger, 93; Eli Broad Family Found, Santa Monica, Calif, 95; Dreamers Awake, Wichita Art Mus, Kans, 95; The Music Lesson, Music Bldg, Univ NC, Greensboro, NC Arts Coun, 99. *Exhib:* New Art at the Tate Gallery, London, 83; An Int Survey of Recent Painting & Sculpture, Mus Mod Art, NY, 84; The Human Condition: Biennial III, San Francisco Mus Mod Art, 84; Biennial Exhib, Whitney Mus Am Art, 85; The Classic Tradition in Recent Painting & Sculpture, Aldrich Mus Contemp Art, Conn, 85; Working in Brooklyn, Brooklyn Mus, 85; Spectrum: The Generic Figure, Corcoran Gallery Art, Washington, 86; solo shows, Mus Mod Art, NY, 87, 90, IVAM Centre Julio Gonzalez, Valencia, Spain, 91, Portikus/Senckenbergmuseum, Frankfurt am Main, 91, Haags Gemeentemuseum, The Hague, The Neth, 91, Carnegie Mus Art, Pittsburgh, 93, Wichita Art Mus, Kans, 95 & Galeria Marlboro, Madrid, Spain, 99; Sounding the Depths, 150 Yrs of Am Seascape, Butler Inst Am Art, 89; Allegories of Modernism, Mus Mod Art, NY, 92; The Elusive Object: Selections from the Permanent Collection, Whitney Mus Am Art, 93; Eleventh Biennial Benefit, San Francisco Mus Mod Art, 94; Marlborough Gallery, NY, 95-96; Imaginary Beings, Exit Art, NY, 95-96; The Gun, Icon of the Twentieth Century, Ubu Gallery, NY, 96; A Century of Am Drawing from the Collection, Mus Mod Art, NY, 96; Contemp Sculpture: The Figurative Tradition, Woodson Art Mus, Wasau, Wis, 97; Alternating Currents: Am Art in the Age of Technology, San Jose Mus Art, Calif, 97-98; Pop Surrealism, Aldrich Mus Contemp Art, Ridgefield, Conn, 98; An Exhibition for Children, 242, NY, 98; Free Money and Other Fairy Tales, See No Evil, Marlborough Gallery, NY, 2002; What the Hay, Utica, Mont, 2002; Free Money on Park Avenue, NY, 2003; Bombeater, Skoto Gallery, NY, 2003; Navy Pier Walk 2002, the Chicago Int Sculpture Exhib, Ill, 2002. *Bibliog:* Tony Kushner (auth), Four artists on dreams: Egos and the learning process, NY Times, 5/26/96; Holland Cotter (auth), Sculpture that basks in summer sunlight and air, NY Times, 8/9/96; Jill Kopelman (auth), Tom's treat, Interview, 8/96. *Mem:* Nat Acad. *Mailing Add:* c/o Marlborough Gallery Inc 40 W 57th St New York NY 10019

OTTMANN, KLAUS
CURATOR, CRITIC
b Nuremburg, Ger, 1954. *Study:* Free Univ Berlin, Ger, MA(philos, art hist), 80. *Pos:* Ed, J Contemp Art, 90-; cur, Am Fedn Arts, New York, currently. *Mem:* Am Asn Mus; Int Asn Art Critics. *Res:* Twentieth century art. *Publ:* Auth, Painting in the age of anxiety, Flash Art Mag, 84; The re-invention of painting, Arts Mag, 89; The new spiritual, Arts, 90; L'activite fractale, Art Press, Paris, 90; Heidegger, Bevys & the consequences, Flash Art, 10/90. *Mailing Add:* c/o Ezra & Cecile Zilkha Gallery Center for the Arts Wesleyan Univ Middletown CT 06459-0442

OUBRE, HAYWARD LOUIS
SCULPTOR, PAINTER
b New Orleans, La. *Study:* Dillard Univ, BA; Univ Iowa, MFA; also with Hale Woodruff, Nancy E Prophet, James Lechay, Mauricio Lasansky & Humbert Albrizio. *Work:* Univ Iowa Gallery, Iowa City; Atlanta Univ Gallery, Ga. *Comn:* Ram (wire sculpture), Winston-Salem State Univ Libr, 65; two paintings, Bakker Auction, Cambridge, Mass, 5/92. *Exhib:* Six States Exhib, Joslyn Mem Mus, Omaha, Nebr, 47; Northwest Printmakers, Seattle Art Mus, Wash, 48; John & Mable Ringling Mus, Sarasota, Fla, 48; Ball State Ann Exhib, Muncie, Ind, 60-62; Madison Gallery Exhib, NY, 62; Lenexa Nat Three-Dimensional Art Show, Kans, 85. *Collection Arranged:* Installed Dr Selma Burke's Art collection, Selma Burke Gallery, Winston-Salem State Univ, 83. *Pos:* Arranger & cur, Selma Burke Gallery, Winston-Salem State Univ, NC, 83-84, cur, 84-90. *Teaching:* Chmn painting & sculpture, Fla A&M Univ, Tallahassee, 48-49; chmn drawing & painting, Ala State Univ, Montgomery, 49-65 & Winston-Salem State Univ, 65-81. *Awards:* First Prize for Trailerview (oil), Iowa State Fair, 47; First Prize for Crown of Thorns (wire), 58 & Second Prize for Equivocal Fox (painting), 68, Atlanta Univ; and many others. *Bibliog:* Art of wire sculpture, Design Mag, 62, 68 & 71. *Mem:* Southeastern Art Asn; Nat Conf Artists. *Media:* All; Acrylic. *Res:* Designed & copyrighted Colorwheel with Four Intensity Bands, 62 & Colorchart with Three Intensity Bands, 66; corrected color triangle devised by Johann Wolfgang Von Goethe, 75; designed Four Intensity Band Color Wheel, 77. *Publ:* Auth, Directions of modern art, Art Rev Mag, 66. *Mailing Add:* 2422 Pickford Ct Winston-Salem NC 27101

OURSLER, TONY
VIDEO ARTIST
b New York, NY, May 19, 1957. *Study:* Calif Inst Arts, BFA, 79. *Work:* Whitney Mus Am Art; Mus Mod Art; Saatchi Collection; Tate Gallery, London; Cincinnati Art Mus. *Comn:* L-7, L-5, The Kitchen, NY, 84; EVOL, CAT Fund, Boston, Mass, 84; Spheres of Influence, Centre Georges Pompidou, Paris, France, 85-86; Constellation: Intermission, Serious Fun Festival, NY, 88. *Exhib:* Solo shows at Lisson Gallery, London, 96, Metro Pictures, NY, 96, Mus Contemp Art, San Diego, 96, Kasseler Kunstverein, Kassel, Ger, 96, Jean Bernier Gallery, Athens, Greece, 96, Inst Contemp Art, Philadelphia, 97 & Margo Leavin Gallery, Los Angeles, 97; group shows include Video Viewpoints, Mus Mod Art, NY, 81; Binational, Inst Contemp Art, Boston, Mass, 88; Film Video Arts--17 yrs, Mus Mod Art, NY, 88; Whitney Biennial, Whitney Mus Am Art, NY, 89, 97, 2006; Scream & Scream Again, Mus Mod Art, Oxford, 96; Being & Time: The Emergence of Video Projection, Albright-Knox Art Gallery, 96; New Persona/New Universe, Biennale di Firenze, Florence, Italy, 96; Philadelphia Mus Art, 96; The Red Gate, Whitney Mus Am Art, 96; The Scream, Nordic Arts Ctr, Helsingfors, Finland, 96; Anatomy of Space/Time, Kobe Fashion Mus, Japan, 97; Studio and Climaxed, Metrop Mus Art, NY, 2005; Blue Invasion, Sydney Festival, Australia, 2005; Perfect Partner (with Kim Gordon) Barbican, London, 2005; Thought Forms, Metro Pictures, NY, 2006; Sound Digression in Seven Colors, Nyehaus Gallery, NY, 2005; Galerie Faurshou, Copenhagen, 2006; Galeria in Acro, Torino, Italy, 2006. *Teaching:* Vis lectr art, Art Inst Chicago, 82; Univ Calif, San Diego, 85; asst prof art, Mass Col Art, 88-. *Awards:* Fel, Nat Endowment Arts, 84; Production Grant, NY State Coun Arts, 84; Video Fel, NY Found Arts, 87. *Bibliog:* Holland Cotter (auth), Optic nerve, Art in Am, 6/96; Leah Ollman (auth), Art that talks back: the shrink is in, Los Angeles Times, 6/30/96; Caryn James (auth), Art flickers from video screens, NY Times, 7/26/96. *Publ:* Auth, Vampire, Communications Video, 88; contribr, Illuminating Video: An Essntial Guide to Video Art, Apterture Found, 90; Triune: A work in progress, Visions, summer 91; Dummies, Flowers and Altars, In: Grand Street: Games, Jean Stein & Torsten Weisel, New York, 95; The Warped vision of Bruce Nauman, Paper, 5/95

OUTLAND, WENDY HELEN
CONSULTANT, LECTURER
b St Petersburg, Fla, Jan 9, 53. *Study:* Ringling Sch Art & Design, Cert, 79, BFA, 84. *Collection Arranged:* Images of the Everglades, Gov office, Tallahassee & traveling, 86; Maggie Davis, 87, The Ten: Women in Art, 88, Akiko Sugiyama, 89, selected exhibs from Capitol Complex Exhib Prog, Tallahasee; The Three Graces: Janet Mauney, Dawn McMillan & Yvonne Tucker, 90. *Pos:* Cur asst & asst registr, Ringling Mus Art, Sarasota, Fla, 81-85; arts adminstr, Fla Arts Coun, Tallahasee, formerly; gallery mgr Blue Spiral 1, Asheville, NC, 95-96; pres, Who Knows Art, cons Visual Artists & Arts Org, 2004-. *Awards:* Fla dept of State Service Award, 89. *Mem:* Am Asn Mus; Am Craft Coun. *Interests:* contemporary art, fine craft. *Publ:* Asst Ed, Ringling MoA Jour, Ringling Mus Art, 82; contribr, Art museums of the world, Greenwood Press, 87; ed, Blue Spiral 1, Rbt Johnson: The Nature Conservancy Series; Mus Fine Arts, St Petersburg, Fla, Figures from Life: Porcelain Sculpture from Met Mus Art c 1740-1780, 92. *Mailing Add:* PO Box 1382 Asheville NC 28802

OUTTERBRIDGE, JOHN WILFRED
SCULPTOR, ADMINISTRATOR
b Greenville, NC, Mar 12, 33. *Study:* Agr & Tech Univ, Greensboro, NC; Am Art Acad, Chicago, with Vernon Stakey; Otis Col Art & Design, Calif, hon, DFA, 94. *Work:* Oakland Mus, Mills Col, Oakland, Calif; Calif State Col, San Jose; Compton Community Col, Calif; Watts Health Found, Univ Southern Calif, Los Angeles; Calif African Mus Art, Los Angeles; Co Art Mus, Los Angeles. *Comn:* Mural collages (mixed-media), Communicative Arts Acad, Compton, 70; Ethnic Heritage Doll Ser (five units), Studio Watts Endowment Fund, 77; CHG Architec Bldg, Old Town, Pasadena, 91; The Avalon/Imperial Green Station Plaza, Los Angeles, 94; El Central Cult Onsite Collaboration & Sculpture, Tijuana, Mex, 94; Staples Ctr Grounds, Los Angeles, 98. *Exhib:* Oakland Mus, 67; 6th & 9th Southern Calif Ann, Long Beach Mus Art, 68 & 70; Los Angeles Co Mus Art, Los Angeles, 69; Dimensions in Black Art, La Jolla Mus Contemp Art, Calif, 70; St Art by Black Am, Merabash Mus, Willingboro, NJ, 75; W Coast Artists, Studio Mus of Harlem, NY, 77 & 95; Made in Calif, 1900-2001, Los Angeles Art Mus Commn & Exhib, 2000-; 22d Biennial, Sao Paulo, Brazil, 94; 1st Biennial Under Mandela, South Africa, 94. *Pos:* Painter/designer, Art Craft, Div Traid Corp, Burbank, 64-68; artistic dir, Communicative Arts Acad, Compton, 69-75, mem bd dir, presently; dir, Watts Towers Arts Ctr, Cult Affairs Dept, Los Angeles, 75-92; US Rep, Sao Paulo Biennal, Brazil, 94, Johannesburg, 1st Biennal, South Africa, 94; Flint Ridge Found Adv Panel, 98-99. *Teaching:* Instr assemblage & sculpture, Pasadena Art Mus, 67-70; lectr art hist, Calif State Col, Dominguez Hills, 67-71; Univ Calif, Irvine, Claremont Col, Calif, Dillart Univ, New Orleans, 2001. *Awards:* Fulbright Fel, Nat Conf Maori Artists, 88; Nat Conf Art Educ Award, 87; Cola Grant, Visual Arts Fel, 2001; Getty Inst Visual Arts Fel, 94; Visual Arts Fel, Nat Endowment Arts, 94; JR Hyde Vis Artists Fel, 94; Residency Program, Getty Inst, Los Angeles, 2001; US Rep to Sao Paulo, Brazil 22nd Biennial, 94. *Bibliog:* article, Wilson Libr Bull, 4/69; Elton C Fax (auth), Black Artists of the New Generation, Dodd, Mead & Co, 77; interview, Am Oral History, Univ Calif, Los Angeles, 93; Steven Harris, D Burke (ed) Architecture of the Everyday, Princeton Archit Press & Yale Publ on Archit, 98; Barbara Isenberg (auth) State of the Arts, Wm Morrow, Harper Collins Publ, 2001; catalog, Made in California, 1900-2000, 2001. *Mem:* Calif Confedn of Arts, Los Angeles; Advocates for the Arts; Mus African Am Art; Nat Conf Artists, Va Commonwealth Univ. *Media:* Welded Metal, Wood. *Publ:* Letters Documents, American Archives, Huntington Library, Smithsonian Inst, San Marino, Calif, 94; catalog, 22nd Biennale, Sao Paulo, 94; catalog, 1st Bienale Under New Adminstrn, South Africa, 94; African Am Art Mus, 94. *Mailing Add:* 5838 W Woodlawn Ave Los Angeles CA 90003

OVERLAND, CARLTON EDWARD
CURATOR, HISTORIAN
b Stoughton, Wis, Feb 28, 42. *Study:* St Olaf Col, BA; Univ Wis-Madison, MA. *Collection Arranged:* 20th Century Graphics: The Hollaender Collection, 74. *Pos:* Cur prints & drawings, Elvehjem Art Ctr, Madison, Wis, 72-77, cur collections, 77-. *Teaching:* Instr art hist, Univ Northern Iowa, Cedar Falls, 68-70. *Mem:* Am Asn Mus. *Mailing Add:* 5113 Sherwood Rd Madison WI 53711-1019

OVITZ, MICHAEL S
COLLECTOR, PATRON
b Dec, 14, 46. *Study:* Univ Calif, Los Angeles, 68. *Comn:* Trustee Mus Modern Art, New York City; bd governors Cedars-Sinai Hosp, Los Angeles; mem exec adv bd Pediatric AIDS Found; bd dir, DARE Am; nat bd adv, Children's Scholarship Fund. *Pos:* Co-founder & chmn, Creative Artists Agency, Los Angeles, 75-95; pres, Walt Disney Co, Burbank, Calif, 95-97; trustee, Mus Mod Art, NY; bd dir, Calif Inst Arts & Sundance Inst; Chmn exec bd dir, UCLA Hosp and Med Ctr; bd adv Sch Theater, Film and TV UCLA; bd dir, Livent, Inc, Gulfstream Aeronautical Corp, J Crew Group, Inc, Opsware, Inc, Yankee Candle Corp; Exec prodr: Gangs of NY, 2002; exec prodr: Timeline, 2003. *Awards:* Named one of Top 200 Collectors, ARTnews Mag, 2004, 2006. *Mem:* Council Foreign Relations, Zeta Beta Tau. *Mailing Add:* 2601 Colorado Ave Santa Monica CA 90404-3518

OWEN, FRANK (FRANKLIN) CHARLES
PAINTER
b Kalispell, Mont, May 13, 39. *Study:* Antioch Col; Calif State Univ Sacramento; Univ Calif, Davis, BA & MA. *Work:* Corcoran Gallery of Art, Washington, DC; Albright-Knox Art Gallery, Buffalo, NY; St Louis Art Mus, Mo; Des Moines Art Ctr, Iowa; Madison Art Ctr, Wis; plus others. *Exhib:* 32nd Corcoran Biennial, Washington, DC, 71; Madison Art Ctr Exhib, 73; 15th Nat Exhib of Contemp Am Painting & Sculpture, Univ Ill, 74; 71st Ann Exhib, Art Inst Chicago, 74; Soho in Berlin, Berlin Kunstmuseum, WGer, 76; one-man shows, Leo Castelli Gallery, 72, 75 & Sable-Castelli Gallery, Toronto, 77. *Teaching:* Instr painting, Calif State Univ, Sacramento, 67-68; instr fine arts, Sch Visual Arts, New York, 70-. *Bibliog:* Peter Schedjahl (auth), Six painters of the 70s, Ackland Art Ctr, NC, 73; Douglas Davis (auth), Painter's painters, Newsweek, 5/13/74. *Mailing Add:* Atea Ring Gallery Sam Spears Rd Westport NY 12993

OWENS, GWENDOLYN JANE
ADMINISTRATOR, CURATOR
b Baltimore, Md, July 8, 54. *Study:* Tufts Univ, BA, 76; Williams Col, MA, 79. *Collection Arranged:* Watercolors by Maurice Prendergast from New England Collections (auth, catalog), 78 & Master Drawings from the Collection of Ingrid and Julius Held (co-auth, catalog), 79, The Dr and Mrs Milton Lurie Kramer Collection (auth, catalog), 81; Golden Day, Silver Night, Perceptions of Nature in American Art, 1850-1910 (coauth, catalog), 82; The Watercolors of David Milne (auth catalog), 84; Nature Transcribed: The Landscapes and Still Lifes of David Johnson, 1827-1908 (auth, catalog), 88; Viewing Olmsted (proj dir) 96; Departure for Katsura (proj dir) 98. *Pos:* Ed asst, Am Asn Mus, Washington, DC, 76-77; registr, Williams Col Mus Art, Mass, 78-79; asst cur, Herbert F Johnson Mus, Cornell Univ, Ithaca, NY, 79-81, assoc cur, 81-85, cur, 85-86; Prendergast Fel, Williams Col Mus Art, 86-88; dir, The Art Gallery, Univ Md, 88-91; affiliated fac, 88-91; asst dir, Can Ctr Archit, Montreal, 91-2003; Consulting Cur, Canadian centre for Archit, Montreal, 2003-. *Teaching:* Affiliated fac, Univ Md, dept art hist, 88-91. *Mem:* Col Art Asn; Am Asn of Mus; Am Studies Asn; Can Mus Asn; Soc Archit Historians. *Res:* 19th and 20th century American art and architecture. *Publ:* Contribr, Pioneers in American Museums: Bryson Burroughs, Mus News, 79; H Siddons Mowbray, Easel Painter, Art & Antiques, 80; Alive, Well and Prospering, Cooperative Conservation Centers Come of Age, Mus New, 82; coauth, Maurice & Charles Prendergast; A Catalogue Raisonne, Prestel, 90; contribr, Painters of a New Century: The Eight, Milwaukee Art Mus, 91; American Women Modernists The Legacy of Robert Henri, 2005. *Mailing Add:* Can Ctr Archit 1920 Rue Baile Montreal PQ H3H 2S6 Canada

OWENS, LAURA
PAINTER
b Euclid, Ohio, 1970. *Study:* RI Sch Design, BFA, 92; Calif Inst Arts, Valencia, MFA, 94. *Work:* Original Language, Mus Contemp Art, Chicago, 2001; New Work, Isabella Stewart Gardner Mus, Boston, 2001; Urgent Painting, Musée d'Art Moderne de la Ville de Paris, 2002; Laura Owens, Milwaukee Art Mus, 2003; The undiscovered country, UCLA Hammer Mus, Los Angeles, 2004; Whitney Biennial, Whitney Mus Am Art, 2004; Rep in permanent collections, Guggenheim, NY, Centre Georges Pompidou, Paris. *Exhib:* Rosamund Felsen, Santa Monica, Calif, 95; Painting Show, Regen Projects, Los Angeles, 95; Palace, Beret Int Gallery, Chicago, 97; Sadie Cole's Headquarters, London, 97; Young Americans II, Saatchi Collection London, 98; Galerie Gisela Capitain Köln, Ger, 99; Examining Pictures, Whitechapel Art Gallery, London, 99. *Mailing Add:* c/o Acme 6150 Wilshire Blvd #1 Los Angeles CA 90048

OWENS, TENNYS BOWERS
DEALER
b Washington, NC, June 25, 40. *Study:* St Mary's Jr Col, Raleigh, NC; Univ NC. *Pos:* Pres & owner, Artique Ltd, 71-. *Specialty:* General art merchandise, prints, paintings, sculpture and pottery, traditional and contemporary. *Mailing Add:* c/o Artique Ltd 314 G St Anchorage AK 99501

OWENS, WALLACE, JR
ADMINISTRATOR, PAINTER
b Muskogee, Okla. *Study:* Langston Univ, BA(art educ), 59; Cent State Univ, Edmond, Okla, Masters(teaching), 65; Inst Allende, San Miguel de Allende, Mex, MFA(painting), 66; Doctorial Studies, NTex State Univ, 70-71. *Work:* Okla State Permanent Collection, Oklahoma City; Gainesville Col, Ga; Okla Univ. *Comn:* 20 ft tall metal sculpture, from Langston Univ to the Universe, Langston Univ. *Exhib:* Cent State Univ, Edmond, 65; Univ Okla, Norman, 69; Retrospective Show, Kirkpatrick Ctr, Oklahoma City, 2003. *Pos:* dir, Owens Arts Place Mus (Fine Arts Mus), Guttrie, Okla. *Teaching:* Dept chmn visual arts, Langston Univ, Okla, 66-; dept art, Edmond, Okla, 80-87; retired. *Awards:* Fulbright Scholar Italy, Univ Rome, 70; Study Tour Award, African Am Inst, New York, 74. *Mem:* Okla Art Ed Asn; Nat Conf Artist (charter mem, 60). *Media:* Acrylic, Metal. *Collection:* Contemporary paintings in acrylic and oil; fine prints in lithography woodcuts and etching; concentrating on metal sculpture. *Publ:* Status of Art Education in State of Oklahoma, 68. *Mailing Add:* 3374 Sunny Acres Ln Guthrie OK 73044

OWSLEY, DAVID THOMAS
CONSULTANT
b Dallas, Tex, Aug 20, 29. *Study:* Harvard Col, AB, 51; Inst Fine Arts, NY Univ, MFA, 64. *Hon Degrees:* Ball State Univ, Muncie, Ind, LHD, 2005. *Collection Arranged:* Carnegie Inst Mus Art; Ailsa Mellon Bruce Collection Decorative Arts; Hovey Collection Islamic & Chinese Art. *Pos:* Fel, Am Wing, Metrop Mus Art; asst cur decorative arts & sculpture, Mus Fine Arts, Boston; visitor, Victoria & Albert Mus, London, Eng; cur antiquities, Oriental & decorative arts, Carnegie Inst Mus Art. *Teaching:* Decorative arts, Univ Pittsburgh Ext. *Awards:* Cert Appreciation, Am Soc Appraisers, 83. *Mem:* Knickerbocker Club. *Publ:* Auth, article, Antiques, 12/72 & 4/73 & Apollo, 8/73; coauth, Wendy and Emery Reves Collection (exhib catalog), Dallas Mus Art, 85. *Mailing Add:* 116 E 68th St New York NY 10021

OX, JACK
PAINTER, CONCEPTUAL ARTIST
b Denver, Colo, Feb 4, 48. *Study:* San Francisco Art Inst, BFA, 69; Yale Univ, 73-74; Univ Calif, San Diego, MFA, 77; Manhattan Sch Music 11, NY, postgrad, 80-82. *Work:* Univ Iowa Collections, Iowa City; Atlantic Richfield Corp, Dallas, Tex; Gen Electric Corp, Ridgefield, Conn; Hood Mus Art, Dartmouth Col, Hanover, NH;

Nordstern Versicherung, Cologne; and others. *Exhib:* On the Wall, On the Air, Hayden Gallery, Mass Inst Technol, Cambridge, 84; solo exhibs, Galerie Inge Baecker, Cologne, Ger, 88 & 91, Univ Calif, Irvine, 88 & 91, Meyers/Bloom Gallery, Santa Monica, Calif, 88 & 91 & Kunsthalle Bremen, Ger, 90; Das Bruckner-Bild im Wandel, Bruckner Fest, Würzburg, Ger, 93; Kleine Formate II, Galerie der Spiegel, Cologne, 93; Am Asn Advan Sci, Washington, 94. *Pos:* Ed adv, Leonardo Mag, 87-. *Teaching:* Vis assoc prof, Univ Calif, Irvine, 86. *Awards:* Juror's Choice Award, The Moment Redefined Exhib, 82. *Bibliog:* Petra Runge (auth), Raubkopie bewahrte stimme des merz-künstlers, Art, 10/93; Christopher Phillips (auth), Scwitters greatest hit resurfaces, Art in Am, 5/94; Maria Porges (auth), Jack Ox at Catharine Clark Gallery, Art Forum, summer 96. *Mem:* Col Art Asn Am. *Media:* Oil, Drawing. *Publ:* Coauth, The systematic translation of musical compositions into paintings, Leonardo Mag, fall 84; auth, Editorial: intellectual versus property right, Leonardo, MIT Press, 1/93; Bilder nach Kompositionen, Positionen, 11/93; Creating a visual translation of Kurt Schwitter's URSONATE, Leonardo Music J, 93. *Dealer:* Galerie Chobot Domgasse 6 1010 Vienna Austria

OXMAN, KATJA
PRINTMAKER
b Munich, Ger; US citizen. *Study:* Pa Acad Fine Arts, Philadelphia, cert, 65; Acad Munich, 65-66; Royal Col Art, London, Eng, cert, 67. *Work:* Philadelphia Mus; Smithsonian Inst, US State Dept, Washington; Pa Acad Fine Arts; Southern Alleghenies Mus Art; Art Complex Mus, Duxbury, Mass; and others. *Exhib:* Solo exhibs, Jane Haslem Gallery, Wash, 81 & 2006, Assoc Artists, NY & Philadelphia, 83, The Print Club, 86, David Adamson Gallery, 87, 89 & 93, Marcus Gordon, Pittsburgh, Pa, 89, Randal Beck Gallery, Boston, Mass, 89, 90 & 94, Locus Gallery, St Louis, Mo, 95, Hollins Col, Roanoke, Va, 97, Esmay Fine Arts, Rochester, 97, 2000, Chautaugua Inst, NY, 2005, Steven Scott Gallery, Owings Hills, Md, 2006; Steven Scott Gallery, Baltimore, MD, 91-2002; Women in Print: Prints from 3M by Contemp Women Printmakers Traveling Exhib (with catalog), 95-; Nat Acad Mus, New York City, 96, 98, 2000, 2002; Susan Conway Gallery, DC, 99-2000; Nat Mus of Women in Arts, DC, 2000; MidAmerican Print Coun Conf, Univ Dallas, 2002. *Teaching:* Adj prof printmaking, Am Univ, 76-85; vis lectr, Univ Mass, 75; vis critic, Pa Acad Fine Art, Philadelphia, 96-2000. *Awards:* Purchase Prize, Bradley Univ, Peoria, Ill, 95; Awards in the Visual Arts, 2000 Md State Arts Coun; Purchase Prize, 28th Annual Bradley Nat Print Exhib, Bradley Univ Peoria K, 2001. *Bibliog:* Ann Evry (dir), Art Strokes, Blue Cow Productions, Sandy Spring, Md, 94; Carol Ferring Shepley (auth), Works in mixed media and works on paper, Get Out Corresp, St Louis, Mo, 6/95; Ferdinand Protzman (auth), Galleries, Wash Post, 7/6/96; Lynne E Moss (auth), Daily life in still life, Am Artist, 5/98; plus others. *Mem:* Boston Printmakers; Print Club of Philadelphia. *Media:* Etching, Aquatint. *Dealer:* Station Gallery Greenville DE; Steven Scott Gallery Owings Mills MD; WM Baczek North Hampton MA; The Print Center Philadelphia PA; Esmay Fine Art Rochester NY. *Mailing Add:* 620 Gist Ave Silver Spring MD 20910

OXMAN, MARK
SCULPTOR, EDUCATOR
b New York, NY, Mar 9, 40. *Study:* Adelphi Univ, Long Island, NY, 58-61; Pa Acad Fine Arts, Philadelphia, 61-65; Showhegan Sch, summer 65; City & Guilds London, 65; Art Sch, London, 67. *Comn:* Large sculpture relief, Bellmore Mem Libr, Long Island, NY, 73; large sculpture relief, Queens Plaza Complex, NY, 76. *Exhib:* one-man shows, Wash Co Mus Fine Arts, Hagerstown, Md, 88, Fountains & Figures, Am Univ, 90, Western Md Col, 92, Arts Alive, Montgomery, Md, 93, West Chester Univ, Penn, 94, Watkins Collection, Wash, DC, 98 & Hobart & William Smith Col, Geneva, NY, 99, Wash & Jefferson Col, 2000, Harmony Hall Gallery, Ft Wash, Md, 2001, Notre Dame Univ, 2002, Thiel Col, Pa, 2003, The Gallery at Quiet Waters, Annapolis, Md, 2004, Marlboro Col, Vt, 2004, Rosemont Col, Pa, 2005, Southern Md Col, La Plata, Md, 2005; 21st Area Show Sculpture, Corcoran Mus, Wash, 78; Sculpture On & Off the Wall, A Salon Ltd, Wash, 95; Washington Figurative Sculptors, Md Sch Art & Design, 95; 16 Sculptors, Watkins Gallery, Wash, 95; Artist to Artist, Art Barn, Wash, 95. *Pos:* Dean students, Skowhegan Sch, 69 & 72. *Teaching:* Lectr art, Haverford Col, Pa, 67-70; asst prof art, Amherst Col, Mass, 70-76; assoc prof sculpture, Am Univ, Washington, DC, 76-94, prof, 94-. *Awards:* Travel Res Grant, Amherst Col, 75; Mellon Fac Develop Grant, Am Univ, 80 & Curric Develop Award, 88; CAS Course Release, 93 & 94. *Media:* Bronze, Plastic. *Mailing Add:* Dept Art American Univ 4400 Massachusetts Ave NW Washington DC 20016

OYUELA, RAUL M
MUSEUM DIRECTOR, CURATOR
b Buenos Aires, Argentina, Nov 7, 35. *Study:* Univ Buenos Aires, PhD, 59; Fedn Int D'Art Photographique, AFIAP, 72. *Work:* Fla Mus Hispanic & Latin Am Art, Miami; San Francisco Mus Contemp Hispanic Art, Calif. *Collection Arranged:* Orlando Agudelo Botero, One Woman Show, 93; From Africa to Cuba, 34 Artists, 96; Women in the Arts, 52 Women Artists, 96; Hispanic Heritage in Am, 29 Artists, 96; Romero Britto, One Woman Show, 96. *Pos:* Dir, Mediterranean Art Ctr, Barcelona, 85-88, San Francisco Mus Hispanic Art, 88-90, dir & pres, Fla Mus Hisp Art, Miami, 91-96; dir, Fla Mus Hispanic & Latin Am Art, currently. *Teaching:* Prof photog, Argentine Fedn Photog, 74-76. *Awards:* Gold Medal, Sao Paulo Biennial, 64; Bronze Medal, Govern of Romania, 64; Gold Medal, Kaiser Corp, 66. *Mem:* Int Coun Mus; Am Asn Mus. *Res:* Latin American and Spanish Art. *Publ:* Auth, Street Sculptures in Chicago, Batik, 89; Tibet: The Forgotten Land, Bohemia News, 89; Los Falsos (The Flakes), La Bohemia, 94. *Mailing Add:* c/o Museum of the Americas Ste 104 2500 NW 79th Ave Doral FL 33122-1071

OZONOFF, IDA
PAINTER, COLLAGE ARTIST
b La Crosse, Wis, July 27, 04. *Study:* State Teachers Col, Milwaukee, grad, 24; Milwaukee Downer Col, 58 & 59; Univ Wis-Milwaukee, 60-64 & 69-70. *Work:* Print Div, Smithsonian Inst, Washington, DC; Milwaukee Pub Schs; Univ Wis, Fond du Lac Campus; Abilene Fine Arts Mus, Tex; Carleton Col, Northfield, Minn. *Exhib:* Nat Acad Design Exhib, NY, 68 & 69; Allied Artists Am Exhib, NY, 70; West Bend Gallery Fine Arts, Wis, 76 & 77; Univ Wis Alumni Exhib, 78; Kohler Art Ctr, Sheboygan, Wis, 88-90. *Awards:* Purchase Award, Western Publ, 66; Benjamin Altman First Prize, Nat Acad Design, 68; Carleton Col Purchase Award, Charles E Merrill Trust Fund, 75. *Bibliog:* Gerald F Brommer (auth), The Art of Collage, 78; Wis Acad Rev (spec ed), Wis Painters & Printmakers, 3/83; and others. *Mem:* Wis Arts Coun. *Media:* Acrylic, Oil. *Dealer:* Bradley Galleries 2639 N Downer Milwaukee WI 53211. *Mailing Add:* 1414 N Prospect Ave Rm 2219 Milwaukee WI 53202

P

PABLO
PAINTER, EDUCATOR
b Moulton, Iowa, 34. *Study:* Iowa Wesleyan Col, with S Carl Fracassini, BA, 55; Wichita State Univ, with Robert Kiskadden, MA, 59. *Hon Degrees:* Washington & Jefferson Col, DFA, 97. *Work:* Iowa Wesleyan Col Art Dept; Wichita State Univ Art Dept & Wichita Art Mus, Kans; Citizens Libr, Washington, Pa. *Comn:* Mosaic mural, Halstead Hosp Lobby, 59; mural, Tosco Mining Co, Washington, Pa, 78. *Exhib:* Ann Nat Graphics Art Show, Wichita Art Asn, 60; Ann Juror's Award Show, Huntington Gallery, WVa, 65; Ann Nat Decorative Arts Show, Wichita Art Asn, 66; Max 24, Nat Small Painting Show, Purdue Univ, 66; 2nd Nat Polymer Exhib, Eastern Mich Univ, 68; Art in the Garden, Washington, Pa, 94-96. *Collection Arranged:* Washington & Jefferson Col Nat Painting Show, 67-96; Malcolm Parcell-Retrospective, Olin Art Gallery, 82; 100th Anniversary-Malcolm Parcell Retrospective (auth, catalog), 96. *Pos:* Co-dir, Bottega Art Gallery, Wichita, 60-62; pres, Wichita Artists Guild, 61-62; dir, Gallery 319, Wichita, 62-63 & Olin Art Gallery, 80-97; bd dir, Malcolm Parcell Found. *Teaching:* Instr ceramics, Wichita State Univ, summer 62; asst prof sculpture & ceramics, WLiberty State Col, 63-66; prof art & chmn art dept, Washington & Jefferson Col, 66-97. *Awards:* Aim is best Parcell exhibit in history, Post-Gazette, 9/8/96; Washington's finest, Observer-Reporter, 9/13/96; Juror's Best of Show Award, Huntington Gallery, 65. *Bibliog:* Aim is best Parcell exhibit in history, Post-Gazette, 9/8/96; Washington's finest, Observer-Reporter, 9/13/96; Malcolm Parcell (auth), His Life and Work. *Mem:* Wash Co Hist Soc. *Media:* Acrylic, Oil. *Publ:* Paul Burgess Edwards (auth), The Life and Work of Malcolm Parcell, 2003. *Mailing Add:* 65 Dewey Washington PA 15301

PACE, JAMES ROBERT
COLLAGE ARTIST, PRINTMAKER
b Tahlequah, Okla, Feb 19, 58. *Study:* Univ Okla, BFA, 81; Ariz State Univ, MFA, 84. *Work:* Fogg Art Mus, Harvard Univ; Nelson-Atkins Mus Art; Scottsdale Mus Contemp Art; Okla State Art Collection; St John's Mus Fine Art; many others. *Exhib:* 13 Parkside Nat Print Exhib; The Song of Images, New Delhi, India; Centerfold, Leslie Powell Found Gallery; Snapshot (int); Another View: Selected Works from Contemp Am Printmakers; many others. *Teaching:* Grad asst drawing, Ariz State Univ, Tempe, 82-83; art instr drawing & design, S Mt Community Col, Phoenix, Ariz, 85; assoc prof drawing & printmaking, Univ Tex, Tyler, 85-, prof art, Oge prof, 98-. *Awards:* HL Gully Res Award, Ariz State Univ, 84; Juror's Choice Award, New Art: Painting from NY, Calif & Tex; Nat Endowment Arts, 92; and many others. *Mem:* Col Art Asn. *Media:* Mixed; Drawing, Collage. *Publ:* Beyond Ourselves, X-Press, 96. *Mailing Add:* 14688 County Rd 2337 Tyler TX 75707

PACE, STEPHEN S
PAINTER, PRINTMAKER
b Charleston, Mo, Dec 12, 18. *Study:* Inst Arte, San Miguel Allende, Mex; Acad Grande Chaumiere, Paris; Inst Arte Statale, Florence, Italy; Art Students League, with Cameron Booth & Morris Cantor; Hans Hofmann Sch. *Hon Degrees:* Univ So Ind, DFA; Maine Col Art, DFA. *Work:* Boston Mus Fine Art; Univ Calif, Berkeley; James Michener Found, Univ Tex, Austin; Walker Art Ctr, Minneapolis; Metrop Mus; Whitney Mus. *Exhib:* Int Watercolor Exhib, Brooklyn Mus, 53 & 55; Whitney Mus Am Art Ann, 53-54, 57-58 & 61; Int Biennial, Japan, Selected by Mus Mod Art, NY, 57; one-man shows, Howard Wise Gallery, NY, 60-61 & 63-64 & A M Sachs Gallery, NY, 74, 76 & 78-79, 81, 83 & 85; Walker Art Ctr, 62; Abstract Watercolors by 14 Americans, Mus Mod Art, tour of Europe, Asia & Australia, 64-66; 10-Yr Retrospective, Des Moines Art Ctr, 70; Univ Tex Art Mus, 70; Katharina Rich Perlow Gallery, NY, 87, 89, 91, 94, 97-98, 2000, 2002 & 2004; Vanderwoude Tananbaum, NY, 91; Univ NC, Greensboro, 91; Evansville Mus Arts Sciences, Ind, 92; Maine Coast Artists, Art Gallery, Rockport, 94; Bates Col Mus Art, Lewiston, Maine, 94; Union Col, Schenectady, NY, 99; AJ Bueche Gallery, Northeast Harbor, Maine, 2002; The Farnsworth Mus, Rockland Maine, 2004; Portland Mus, Maine, 2004. *Teaching:* Artist-in-residence, Washington Univ, spring-summer 59; instr art, Pratt Inst, 61-68; instr art sem, Univ Calif, Berkeley, spring 68; prof art, Am Univ, 75-83. *Awards:* Guggenheim Fel, 80-81; Benjamin Altman Award, 93; Edwin Palmer Prize, 2001; Jimmy Ernst Award. *Bibliog:* Hubert Crehan (auth), A change of pace, Art News, 4/64; Russell Arnold (auth), Paintings by Stephen Pace, Crucible, fall 65; Denver Lindley (auth), In a landscape (film), 69-71; Martica Sawin (auth), Stephen Pace: Action Painting in Two Modes, Arts, 4/87. *Mem:* Nat Acad. *Media:* Oil, Watercolor; Monotype, Prints. *Specialty:* Paintings, photog, drawings, prints & sculpture. *Publ:* Martica Sawin (auth), Stephen Pace: Hudson Hills Press. *Dealer:* Katharina Rich Perlow Gallery, New York NY. *Mailing Add:* 90 Indian Point Rd Stonington ME 04681-3408

PACHNER, WILLIAM
PAINTER
b Brtnice, Czech, Apr 7, 1915; US citizen. *Study:* Acad Arts & Crafts, Vienna, Austria; Univ Tampa, DFA AC, 81. *Work:* Whitney Mus Am Art, NY; Butler Inst Am Art, Youngstown, Ohio; Ft Worth Art Ctr, Tex; Hirshorn Mus, Washington, DC; also pvt collections of Lee A Ault and Walter P Chrysler; Delgado Mus, New Orleans; Detroit Inst Am Art; Ein-Herod Mus, Israel; and others. *Exhib:* Carnegie Inst Int, Pittsburgh; Whitney Mus Am Art Ann; Corcoran Gallery Art Biennial, Washington, DC; Pa Acad Fine Arts, Philadelphia; US Fine Arts Pavilion, NY World's Fair, 65; Gallery Mod Art, NY, 69; Univ Tampa, 81; Detroit Inst Fine Arts; one-man show, Pachner Landscapes (with catalog), Mus Fine Arts, St Petersburg, Fla, 83; more than twelve one-man shows in NY; Affirmations--1936-1986, 50 yr retrospective (with catalog), Tampa Mus Art, Fla, 86; black & white drawings, Univ S Fla, 86 & Art Ctr, St Petersburg, Fla, 87; Retrospective, Holocaust Mus, St Petersburg, 2005. *Collection Arranged:* Delgado Mus, New Orleans, La; Detroit Inst Am Art, Mich; Ein-Herod Mus, Israel; Gulf Coast Mus Art, Largo, Fla; Holocaust Mus, St Petersburg, Fla. *Teaching:* Instr painting & drawing, Art Students League, 69-70. *Awards:* Am Acad Arts & Lett Award, 49; Ford Found Awards, 59-64; Guggenheim Fel, 60. *Bibliog:* Kenneth Donahue (auth), William Pachner, NY, The Am Fed Arts, 1959; Robert Martin (auth), Pachner Landscapes, Mus Fine Arts, St. Petersburg, Fla, 2/1987; Lennie Bennett (auth), Season in the Sun, St. Petersburg Times, 5/16/2004. *Media:* Oil, Watercolor, Collage. *Dealer:* Brad Cooper Gallery 1712 E 7th Ave Tampa FL 33605. *Mailing Add:* c/o Brad Cooper Gallery 1712 E 7th Ave Tampa FL 33605

PACHTER, CHARLES
PAINTER, PRINTMAKER
b Toronto, Ont, Dec 30, 42. *Study:* Sorbonne, Paris, dipl de L'ESPFE, 63; Univ Toronto, BA, 64; Cranbrook Acad Art, Mich, MFA, 66. *Work:* Nat Libr, Ottawa; Art Gallery Ont, Toronto; Mus d'Art Contemporain, Montreal; Can Embassy, Washington, DC; Centre d'Art Présence Van Gogh, St Rémy de Provence, France. *Comn:* To All In Tents (35th anniversary painting & commemorative poster), Stratford Shakespearean Festival, Stratford, Ont; Hockey Knights in Canada (subway mural), Toronto Transit Comn, 85. *Exhib:* One-man retrospectives, Centre d'Art Présence Van Gogh, St Rémy de Provence, France, 91 & Haus an der Redoute Bonn, Ger, 92; Esler/Pachter ESP, Nat Gallery Can, Ottawa; Color Prints of the Americas, NJ State Mus; Int Print Biennale, Mus Mod Art, Tokyo; Vestiges of Empire, Camden Centre, London; one-man show, Royal Ont Mus, Toronto, 94. *Bibliog:* Charles Pachter (monogr), B Welsh-Ovcharov, McClelland & Stewart, Toronto; 30/50 Pachter (film), Nat Film Bd Can; Private Presses, Can Encyl, Hurtig, page 1488. *Publ:* Auth & illusr, The Queen of Canada Colouring Book, Anansi, Toronto, 76; illusr, J Susanna Moodie, Margaret Atwood, 80; illusr & contribr, Soho Square III, pages 89-90, Bloomsbury Publ, London, 90; illusr, How We Are Governed, Harcourt-Brace, Toronto, 94. *Mailing Add:* 2 Grange Pl Toronto ON M5T 1Z5 Canada

PACHTER, MARC
GALLERY DIRECTOR
Study: Univ Calif Berkeley, summa cum laude. *Pos:* Chief historian and asst dir, Nat Portrait Gallery, Smithsonian Inst, Washington, DC, 1974, dep asst sec external affairs, 1990-94, counselor to sec, 1994-2000, dir, 2000 ; acting dir, Nat Mus Am History, Smithsonian Inst, Washington, DC, 2001-02; consult, Smithsonian World (PBS); frequent commentator, Nightwatch, CBS, the Voice of America, and C-SPAN; faculty mem, Salzburg Seminar Session 212, Contemporary American Literature, 1982, chair, Salzburg Seminar Session 387, Museums in the 21st Century, 2001; sr cultural adv, US Info Agy, 1985-90. *Teaching:* Tchr colonial history, Harvard Univ, tutor honors program. *Awards:* Woodrow Wilson Fellow; Five Yr Prize Fellow in Am History, Harvard Univ. *Publ:* Editor, Biography jour; editor, Telling Lives: The Biographer's Art. *Mailing Add:* National Portrait Gallery Smithsonian Inst PO Box 37012 Victor Bldg Ste 8300 MRC 973 Washington DC 20013-7012

PADOVANO, ANTHONY JOHN
SCULPTOR, DRAFTSMAN
b Brooklyn, NY, July 19, 33. *Study:* Carnegie Inst Technol; Pratt Inst; Columbia Univ, with Oronzio Maldarelli; Hunter Col, MA, 80. *Work:* Whitney Mus Am Art; Nat Collection Fine Arts, Washington, DC; Univ Ill; John Herron Art Inst; Storm King Art Ctr, NY. *Comn:* Sculpture In The Park, Parks Dept, NY, 68; design, NY State Art Awards, NY State Coun Arts, 69; sculpture, World Trade Ctr, Port Authority NY & NJ, 70; three arcs, donated by Trammel & Crow Co for City of Dallas, 72; sculpture, Nebr Bicentennial Sculpture Corp, 76. *Exhib:* 3rd Mostra Arte Figurative Int, Rome, Italy, 61; Young Am, Whitney Mus Am Art, 65; Am Sculpture, Mus Mod Art, 66; Am Express Pavilion, NY World's Fair, 66; Inauguration of Nat Collection Fine Arts, Washington, DC, 67. *Pos:* Adv mem, NJ State Coun Arts, 65-67. *Teaching:* Asst prof sculpture, Columbia Univ, Univ Conn, 72 & Kingsborough Community Col, 83; adj asst prof sculpture, Queens Col, City Univ NY, 72; instr, Dept Art, Art Students League, NY; assoc prof, Kingsborough Community Col, 83-. *Awards:* Guggenheim Found Fel, 64; Ford Found Purchase Award, 66; Inst Arts & Lett Award, 76; Prix de Rome, 60 & 61. *Bibliog:* Young talent, Art Am, 65; James Mellow (auth), article in New York Times Sun Rev, 4/70. *Mem:* Sculptors Guild (vpres, 68-69); Silvermine Guild Artists; Nat Acad. *Media:* Metal, Stone. *Publ:* Auth, Process of Sculpture, Doubleday Co, 81. *Dealer:* Vorpal Gallery 411 W Broadway New York NY 10012

PADULA, FRED DAVID
FILMMAKER, PHOTOGRAPHER
b Santa Barbara, Calif, Oct 25, 37. *Study:* Univ Calif, Santa Barbara; Calif State Univ, San Francisco, BA(music), with Jack Welpott, Don Worth & Wynn Bullock, MA(art). *Work:* George Eastman House, Rochester, NY; San Francisco Mus Art; Oakland Mus Art; Kalamazoo Art Ctr, Mich; Crocker Mus Art, Sacramento, Calif; and many pvt collections. *Comn:* Children's Letters to God (film), Lee Mendelson, San Francisco, 68; Navaho (film), Pub Broadcast Lab, KQED-TV, San Francisco, 68; S F Mix (film), Ford Found, 70; film, Am Film Inst. *Exhib:* 30 Photographers Nat Exhib, Buffalo, NY, 64; one-man shows, San Francisco Mus, 64, George Eastman House, 68 & DeYoung Mus, San Francisco, 69; Mus Mod Art, NY, 67; completion & premiere showing of El Capitan (film), San Francisco Mus of Mod Art, 78; and others. *Pos:* Mem Selection comt, US Art in the Embassies, 68; mem bd dir, Canyon Cinema Coop, 71-. *Teaching:* Lectr photo & film making, San Francisco State Univ, 63- & Univ Calif, San Francisco, 66-71; resident artist, Univ Minn, Minneapolis, 70. *Awards:* Awards for film El Capitan: Grand Prize, Banff Festival Mountain Films, Can, 79, Gold Medal, Festival Int Film Alpin, Les Diablertets, Switz, 79 & Silver Medal, Int Bergfilm Munchen, Munich, Ger, 79; and others. *Bibliog:* Callenbach (auth), Ephesus, Film Quart, Univ Calif, winter 66-67; Winston (auth), American film maker, Melbourne Art Rev, fall 68; Hoffmann (auth), Ephesus, Weg Zum Nachbarn, Oberhausen, Ger, 68. *Dealer:* Canyon Cinema Coop San Francisco, CA. *Mailing Add:* PO Box 254 Mill Valley CA 94941

PAGE, CASEY (VIVIAN)
SCULPTOR, CURATOR
b Cookville, Tenn, Mar 11, 57. *Study:* St Mary's Col, Md, BA (cum laude, art, Individual Artist Grant), 97. *Work:* St Mary's Col Teaching Collection Art, Md. *Comn:* Fantasy Habitat, Am Chestnut Land Trust, Lexington Park, Md, 2000. *Exhib:* Warriors Rest, Calvert Marine Mus, Solomons Island, Md, 97; Sculpture Now, Wash Sq, Wash DC, 98; The Figure, Montgomery Col, Md, 99; Form and Figure, Glen Echo Gallery, 99; Fantasy habitat, Anne Marie Sculpture Gallery, Solomons Island, 2000. *Collection Arranged:* Quiet Movements, Boyden Gallery, St Mary's City, Md, 97; Reclamation, Boyden Gallery, 99; Sticks & Stones, Boyden Gallery, 99; Russian Dissident Art, Boyden Gallery, 99; Presence: Moe, Silberman & Venn, Boyden Gallery, 2000; Totem, Boyden Gallery, 2000. *Pos:* freelance art consult, 80-92; asst dir Boyden Gallery, St Mary's Col Md, 93-97, gallery dir, 97-; program dir Maryland Art Place, Baltimore, 2001-. *Awards:* Senior Purchase Award, St Mary's Col Md, 97; Individual Artists Grant, St Mary's Co Arts Coun. *Mem:* Md Arts Pl; Wash Sculptors Group; St Mary's Col Arts Alliance; WPA, Corcoran. *Media:* Stone, Bronze, Mixed Media

PAGE, JEAN JEPSON
COLLECTOR, HISTORIAN
b Minneapolis, Minn, Aug 22, 24. *Study:* With Walter S Baum; Minneapolis Inst Arts; San Francisco Inst; Smith Col, BA, 46. *Pos:* Comnr, Dist Columbia Comn Arts & Humanities, 76-80; dir, Am Painting Info Serv; Am painting appraiser. *Res:* American painting, particularly 19th century; political aspects of art patronage; Frank Mayer. *Collection:* American paintings. *Publ:* Auth, Francis Blackwell Mayer, Antiques, 2/76; Frank Blackwell Mayer: Painter of the Minnesota Indian, Minn Hist, 78; Notes on the contributions of Francis Blackwell Mayer and his family to the cultural history of Maryland, Md Hist Mag, 81; James McNeill Whistler, Baltimorean, and The White Girl, Md Hist Mag, 89. *Mailing Add:* 3219 Chesapeake St NW Washington DC 20008

PAIGE, WAYNE LEO
PAINTER, DRAFTSMAN
b Chicago, Ill, Mar 5, 44. *Study:* Univ Ill, Urbana, BFA, 68; George Washington Univ, MFA, 71. *Work:* George Washington Univ; Western Mich Univ; Danville Mus Art & Hist, Va. *Exhib:* Solo exhibs, Gallery K, Washington, DC, 78, 82, 84, 88, 91, 93 & 95, Washington Co Mus, Hagerstown, Md, 85 & Zaks Gallery, Chicago, 85 & 91, Western Mich Univ, 90 & Danville Mus Art & Hist, 91; Works on Paper, Corcoran Gallery, Washington, DC, 80; Southern Fervor, Anderson Art Gallery, Richmond, Va, 83; Emergency, Md Art Place, Baltimore, 83 & Arlington Arts Ctr, Va, 94. *Teaching:* Instr drafting, Eastern High Sch, Washington, DC, Md Drafting Inst, 79-. *Awards:* Cecille Hunt Award, George Washington Alumni Competition, 88; Va Comn on the Arts (print & drawing category), 89. *Bibliog:* Jo Ann Lewis (auth), Galleries: Paintings by Wayne Paige, Washington Post, 2/13/82; Judith Cox (auth), East Coast Review: Wayne Paige, New Art Examiner, 4/82; Miller Leonore (auth), Wayne Paige Drawings Gallery K, Washington Rev, 88. *Media:* Miscellaneous. *Dealer:* Gallery K 2010 R St NW Washington DC 20009; Zaks Gallery 600 N Michigan Ave, Chicago IL 60611. *Mailing Add:* 617 Zachary Taylor Hwy Flint Hill VA 22627

PAIK, NAM JUNE
VIDEO ARTIST
b Seoul, Korea, 32. *Study:* Univ Tokyo, BA, 56; Pratt Inst, Hon DFA, 98. *Exhib:* The Machine as Seen at the End of the Mechanical Age, Mus Mod Art, NY, 68; Vision & Television, Rose Art Mus, Brandeis Univ, Waltham, Mass, 69; solo exhibs, Mus Mod Art, NY, 71 & 77, Everson Mus Art, Syracuse, NY, 74, Whitney Mus Am Art, NY, 80 & 82, Holly Solomon Gallery, NY, 86, 88, 89, 90, 92, 93 & 95, Seville World Expo, Korean Pavilion, 92, Ft Lauderdale Mus Art, 94 & Nelson-Atkins Mus Art, Kansas City, Mo, 97, Butler Inst Am Art, Youngstown, Ohio, 99, James Goodman Gallery, NY, 00, Santa Barbara Mus Art, Calif, 00, Mus Gegenwartskunst, Basel, Switz, 00, Solomon R Guggenheim Mus, NY, 00; Circuit: a Video Invitational, Everson Mus Art, Syracuse, NY, 73; Open Circuits: The Future of Television, Mus Mod Art, NY, 74; Computers & Art, Everson Art Mus, Syracuse, 87; Biennial Exhib, 87 & Video Art: Expanded Forms, 88, Whitney Mus Am Art, NY, 88; The Arts for Television, Mus Mod Art, NY, 89; Whitney Mus Art, Stamford, Conn, 89; Mediascape, Guggenheim Mus Soho, NY, 96; Neo-Dada: Redefining Art, 1958-1962, Scottsdale Ctr Arts, 96; Landscape Reclaimed: New Approachhes to an Artistic Tradition, Aldrich Mus Contemp Art, 96; Portraits, James Graham & Sons, NY, 96; Freedman Gallery (with catalog), NY, 96; It's Only Rock & Roll, Bedford Gallery, Walnut Creek, Calif, 96; Holly Solomon Gallery, NY, 97; Pioneers of Digital Photog, Open Space Gallery, Allentown, Pa, 98; The Aldrick Mus Contemp Art, Ridgefield, Conn, 00. *Teaching:*

Artist-in-residence, WGBH-TV, Boston, 69 & GNET-TV, New York, 71. *Awards:* Kyoto Prize, 98. *Bibliog:* Doris Athineos (auth), O, brave new world, Forbes Mag, 9/23/96; Dick Kagan (auth), Another side of Soho, Art & Antiques, 10/96; Kathleen Vanesian (auth), Dada's got a brand-new bag, New Times, 11/24/96

PAIKOWSKY, SANDRA R
CURATOR, HISTORIAN
b St John, NB, Can, Dec 29, 45. *Study:* Sir George Williams Univ, BA(art hist), 67; Univ Toronto, MA(art hist), 70. *Collection Arranged:* Eric Fischl: Painting (auth, catalog), 83, The Non-Figurative Artist's Association of Montreal (auth, catalog), 83, Goodridge Roberts: The Figure Works (auth, catalog), 84, Betty Goodwin: Passage (auth, catalog), 86, Ron Shuebrook: Recent Work (auth, catalog), 86, David Craven: Recent Work (auth, catalog), 86, Concordia Art Gallery, Montreal, Que; Rita Letendre: The Montreal Years (auth, catalog), 89. *Pos:* Cur, Concordia Univ Art Gallery, Montreal, Que, 81-. *Teaching:* Assoc prof art hist, Concordia Univ, 69-. *Publ:* Publ & co ed, The Journal of Canadian Art History, Owl's Head Press, 76. *Mailing Add:* Concordia Univ Art Gallery 1455 W de Maisonneuve Blvd W-VA432 Montreal PQ H3G 1M8 Canada

PAINE, ROXY
SCULPTOR, CONCEPTUAL ARTIST
b New York, Sept 20, 66. *Study:* Pratt Inst. *Work:* New Sch Social Res, NY. *Exhib:* one-man shows, Herron Test Site, NY, 92, Ronal Feldman Fine Arts, NY, 95; The Nature of the Machine, Chicago Cult Ctr, Ill, 93; Out of Town, Krannert Art Mus, Champaign, Ill, 93; Human/Nature, New Mus Contemp Art, NY, 95; Inside, Calif Ctr Arts Mus, Escondido, 96. *Bibliog:* Jonathan Fineberg (auth), Art Since 1940, Prentice-Hall, 95; Elizabeth Hess (auth), Cross hatching, Village Voice, 5/16/95; Eleanor Heartney (auth), Roxy Paine at R Feldman, Art in Am, 11/95

PAISNER, CLAIRE
PAINTER
b Boston, Mass. *Study:* Cornell Univ, BA; Harvard Univ, MA. *Exhib:* Various juried Exhib, New York City. *Awards:* Pastel Soc Am Award, (PSA); Alliance Queens Artists Award; Nat Art League, The Salmagundi Club. *Bibliog:* Best of Pastel 2, Rockport Publ, 98; L'Art du Pastel, France, 2005. *Mem:* Pastel Soc Am (PSA), (sig mem, bd mem, currently). *Media:* Pastel. *Publ:* Co-ed, Pastelagram, Publ by Pastel Soc Am. *Dealer:* J Lippmann Fine Arts Gallery 8 N Dutcher St Irvington on Hudson NY 10533. *Mailing Add:* 102-30 66th Rd Flushing NY 11375

PAL, PRATAPADITYA
CURATOR, HISTORIAN
b Sylhet, Bangladesh, Sept 1, 35. *Study:* Delhi Univ, BA(hons), 56; Calcutta Univ, MA, 58, DPhil, 62; Cambridge Univ, PhD, 65; Getty Scholar 95-96. *Collection Arranged:* The Sensuous Line (with catalog), 76; The Sensuous Immortals (with catalog), 77; The Divine Presence (with catalog), 78; The Classical Tradition in Rajput Painting (with catalog), 78; The Ideal Image (with catalog), 78; Elephants and Ivories (catalog), 81; Light of Asia (with catalog), 84; From Merchants to Emperors (with catalog), 86; Romance of the Taj Mahal (with catalog), 89; Art of the Himalayas (with catalog), 91; The Peaceful Liberators (with catalog), 94; A Collecting Odyssey (with Catalog), 1997; Tibet Change and Tradition (with catalog) 97; Desire & Devotion (with catalog), 2001; Himalayas: An Aesthetic Adventure (with catalog), 2003; Painted Poems (with catalog), 2004. *Pos:* Sr res assoc, Am Acad Benares, 66-67; keeper of Indian collections, Mus Fine Arts, Boston, 67-69; curator Indian & Southeast Asian art, Los Angeles Co Mus Art, 70-; Fel for Research, Norton Simon Mus, Pasadena, Calif, 96-; vis cur, Art Institute, Chicago, Ill, 97-2003; ed MARC publ, Mumbai, 1993-. *Teaching:* Lectr Indian art, Harvard Univ, 68-69; lectr Nepali art, Univ Calif, Los Angeles, 70; adj prof SE Asian art, Univ Southern Calif, 70-89; fac, Univ Calif, Irvine, 92-94; teacher, courses on hist of Indian, Himalayan, SE Asian and Islamic Arts. *Awards:* Most Distinguished Indian (fine arts award), Fed Indian Asn NAm, 80; BC Law Gold Medal 1993; RP Chanda Contemp Medal, Asiatic Soc, Calcutta, India, 2003. *Mem:* Hon fel Asiatic Soc; Am Comt South Asian Art; Asia Soc, Calcutta; Tantric Soc; Burma Soc; Asia Soc, NY. *Res:* Arts, architecture and cultural history of India, Islamic countries, Nepal, Tibet & Southeast Asia. *Publ:* Divine Images Human Visions, 97; (auth) Catalogue of the Indian Coll, LACMA, Vol. I, Sculprture 1986, Vol. II, Sculpture, 1988; (auth) Indian Painting, 93. *Mailing Add:* 10582 Cheviot Dr Los Angeles CA 90036

PALAIA, FRANC (DOMINIC)
PHOTOGRAPHER, MURALIST
b New Rochelle, NY, Sept 18, 49. *Study:* Newark State Col, Union, NJ, BA(fine arts), 71; Univ Cincinnati, Ohio, MFA(scholar, teaching asst), 73. *Work:* Newark Mus, NJ; Stedelijk Mus, Holland; McDonald Corp; Smithsonian, Washington, DC; Polaroid Corp; and others. *Comn:* Painting, comn by Richard Ekstract, NY. *Exhib:* Alternative Mus, NY, 81; Fashion Moda, NY, 84; Metrop Mus Art, NY, 84; New Mus, NY, 85; Hal Bromm Gallery, NY, 85; Sidney Janis Gallery, NY, 88; Morris Mus, 95; Exit Art, 96; and others. *Teaching:* Instr art hist, Essex Co Col, Newark, NJ, 76-77; instr sculpture, Upsala Col, East Orange, NJ, 76; instr painting, Kean Col, NJ, 78-82. *Awards:* Grant, Louis Tiffany Found, New York, NY, 84; Rome Prize (Painting), Am Acad in Rome, Italy, 85; Sponsorships, Polaroid Corp, Boston, Mass, 86 & 87. *Bibliog:* Peter Frank (auth), article, Village Voice, 78; John Caldwell (auth), review, New York Sunday Times, 81; Precious, Grey Art Gallery, Art in Am, 85. *Media:* All. *Publ:* Contribr, Art Am, Appearances Mag, Umbrella Mag, NJ, Monthly Mag, 83, New Look Mag, 85 & Street Art, Dial Press, 85; Great Walls of China, Eastview Eds, 74. *Mailing Add:* 371 Fourth St Jersey City NJ 07302

PALAU, MARTA
ENVIRONMENTAL ARTIST, SCULPTOR
b Albesa, Lerida, Spain, July 17, 34; Mexican citizen. *Study:* La Esmeralda, Inst Nat Bellas Artes, Mex; San Diego State Univ, Calif; Grau Garriga's Atelier, Barcelona, Spain. *Work:* Secretaria Relaciones Exteriores, Mexico City; Mus Mod Art, Mexico City; Mus Mod Art Latinamerica, Washington; Tamayo Mus, Mexico City; Mus Mod Art, Univ Sao Paulo, Brazil. *Comn:* Purépecha, Metal Sculpture 18 meters, Morelia, Michoacan, 85; 19 Biennial of Sao Paulo, Brazil, Recinto de Chamanes installation, 87; Aztlan, Exterior Mural, MAM Mexico City, 88; Art Museum of the Americas, Naualli Circulo de Sal, installation, Washington, 90; Genova 92, Naualli Centinelas, installation, Genova, Italy, 92. *Exhib:* Americas-Japan, MAM, Tokyo, Japan and MAM Kyoto-Japan, 77; 8th Int Biennial of Tapestry, Laussana, Suiza, 77; Mus de Arte Mod, Mexico City, 78, Sala Nac, Palacio de Bellas Artes, Mexico City, 85, Fisher Gallery, installation, Los Angeles, Calif, 91 & Galeria de Arte Mexicano, Mexico City, 93; Mücsarnok Palace of Exhibitios Kunsthalle, Budapest, Hungary, 92; Naualli-Centinelas, Nexus Contemp Art Ctr, Atlanta, Ga, 93; and others. *Teaching:* Artist-in-residence, Casa Americas & Inst Superior de Arte, Havana, Cuba. *Awards:* Installation Award, Second Biennial, Havana, Cuba, 86; Burgerpreis, 5th Triennial, Fellbach, Ger, 92; Artistic Creator, Conacult Fel, Mexico City, 93. *Bibliog:* Juan Acha (auth), Fiber Works, Americas-Japan, Mus Mod Art, Kyoto, Japan, 78; Rita Eder (auth), Marta Palau, La Intuicion in y la Tecnica, CEGM, 85; Margaret Sayers Peden (auth), Out of the Volcano, Smithsonian Inst Press, 91. *Publ:* Auth, Lo Mas Antiguo y Lo Mas Moderno en el Arte de Marta Palau, Antonio Rodriguez, 73. *Dealer:* Galeria de Arte Mexicano Gob Rafael Rebollar 43 Mexico 11850 DF. *Mailing Add:* Galileo 16-6 Mexico DF 11560 Mexico

PALAZZOLO, CARL
PAINTER
b Torrington, Conn, 45. *Study:* Boston Mus Sch, 65-69; Tufts Univ Mus Sch Prog, 66-68; Boston Mus Sch (independent grad prog), 69-70. *Exhib:* Whitney Mus Am Art, 75; Inst Contemp Art, Boston, 75; Mus Fine Arts, Boston, 85 (two exhibs); solo exhibs, Bette Stoler Gallery, 86, Harcus Gallery, Boston, 88, Lennon, Weinberg Inc, NY, 90 (with catalog) & 92, Marguerite Oestreicher Fine Arts, New Orleans, 91 & 93, Thomas Babeor Gallery, La Jolla, Calif, 92 & Carl Palazzolo: Private Viewing, AN Exhibition of Recent Watercolors, Miller Block Gallery, Boston, MA, 99 & Recent Work, Rebecca Ibel Gallery, Columbus, Ohio, 99& Recent Work, Robert Bowman Ltd, London, Eng, 2001; Truth Be Told: It's All about Love, Lennon, Weinberg Inc, NY, 94; Novices Collect: Selections from the Sam & May Gruber Collection, Currier Gallery Art, Manchester, NH, 94; Works on Paper, Allez les Filles, St Louis, 94; Lennon, Weinberg Inc, NY, 95; group exhibs, Drawing Rooms: Carl Palazzolo, Denyse Thomasos, Robin Hill, NY, Lennon, Weinberg, Inc, 2000, Reflection, Rebecca Ibsl Gallery, Columbus, Ohio, Underfoot, Dan Galeria, Sao Paulo, 2001; Retrospective (with catalog), Weinberg, Inc, NY, 90; retrospective, Miane Coast Artists, 92. *Teaching:* Dean, Boston Music Sch, 92-; instr advanced painting seminar, Sch of Boston Mus of Fine Arts, 96; vis lectr slide presentation, Boston Col, 96; vis lectr slide pesentation, Bates Col, 99. *Awards:* Bicentennial Traveling Exhib Grant, Mass Coun Arts, 75; Clarissa Bartlett Traveling Scholar Alumni Award, Sch Boston Mus Fine Arts, 85; Nat Endowment Arts & Humanities, 87; Grant, Nat Endowment for the Arts and Humanities, 87. *Bibliog:* Robert L Pincus (auth), Visual arts: Critics choice, San Diego Union-Tribune, 3/12/92; Jonathan Saville (auth), Hovering at the edge of meaning, San Diego's Weekly Reader, 2/20/92; George Melrod (auth), Openings: Carl Palazzolo, Art & Antiques, 11/94. *Publ:* Carl Palazzolo at Lennon, Weinberg, Art in America, 11/90; About town: art, The New Yorker, 6/4/90. *Dealer:* Lennon-Weinberg Gallery 560 Broadway Ste 308 New York NY 10012-3945. *Mailing Add:* 35 Two-Dog Ln Georgetown ME 04548

PALERMO, JOSEPH
PAINTER, SCULPTOR
b Pittsburgh, Pa. *Study:* Ecole des Beaux Arts, Paris, cert des arts, 1964; Univ Complutense de Madrid, dipl de coupletacion, 1978. *Work:* USAF Mus, Dayton, Ohio; Air and Space Mus, Washington, DC; Sumter Co Historical Soc, SC; Libr Congress, Washington, DC; Banco Hispano Americano, Madrid, Spain; So NV Mus Fine Art. *Comn:* 20 foot stainless steel sculpture, Banco Hispano Americano, Madrid, Spain, 76; 18 foot stainless steel sculpture, Ameribank, Madrid, Spain, 76; 20x30 foot oil mural, Massaro Corp, Pittsburgh, Pa, 94; 12 foot stainless steel sculpture, McCarran Corp Plaza, Las Vegas, Nev, 99; 20 foot stainless steel sculpture, DAVRIC Corp, Henderson, Nev, 2000; Clark Co Parks and Recreation, NV. *Exhib:* 34th Biennial Contemp Am Painting, Corcoran, Washington, DC, 1975; Sixto Exposition de Arte, Galleria de Arta Int, Madrid, Spain, 1976; Biennial, Ministrario de cultura Espagna, Samora, Spain, 1976; Secundo, Exposition National de Arte Contemporaneo, Madrid, Spain, 1976; Biennial, Musei Espanole de Arte Contemporaneo, Madrid, Spain, 1977; Assoc Artists, Carnegie Mus, Pittsburgh, Pa, 1990; Annual Juried, Pittsburgh Cen Arts, 1992; Annual Juried, Assoc Artists Pittsburgh, 1993; Retrospective Las Vegas Art Mus. 2005. *Pos:* exec dir, Las Vegas Art Mus, 1997-2004; consult exec dir, S Nev Mus Fine Art, 2005-. *Awards:* Secunda Medalla, Bellas Artes, Musei Epsanole, 1977; Medalla de Oro, Biennial de Artistas plasticos, Samora, 1977; Spain ARTV Award, 2003; 2 ARTV Awards, Artist of the Year and Printmaking 2005. *Bibliog:* Emilio Delgado Espenosa (auth), Escultures, Esculture de Madrid, 1975; Antonio Vivas (auth), Ceramica, Nuavo, Ceramica Espagna, 1985; James Mann (auth), International Dictionary of Modern & Contemporary Art, 1999-2000, rev ed, 2001-2002. *Mem:* Las Vegas Art Mus (pres 1996-97); Contemp Arts Collective; Desert Sculptors; Asn Artistsas Plasticos Madrid; Henderson Art Asn (co-founder). *Media:* Oil, Acrylic, Steel, Clay, Stainless. *Interests:* The direction of art & artist for the 21st century & art beyond post-modernism. *Collection:* Marc Chagall, 2000; Dali Retrospective, 2000; Dale Chihuly, 2001. *Publ:* Art Scene, Pittsburgh Post Gazette, 1993; Viva Las Vegas, Creative Loafing, Arts Around the World, Dr James Mann, 1996; Internet Gambling Report and II Cover &

Bio, Anthoy Cabot, 1997-98; Distinguished Men of Nev, Distingsuished Pub Co, 2000-; International Dictionary of Modern & Contemporary Art, Casaeditrice Alba, 1999, rev ed, 2000-2002; Las Vegas Review Jour., Ken White, 2005. *Dealer:* Timeless Treasures 982 American Pacific Ste 204 Henderson NV; Southbank Galleries, Pittsburgh, PA 15203; Gallery P, Las Vegas, NV 89102

PALEY, ALBERT RAYMOND
GOLDSMITH, DESIGNER
b Philadelphia, Pa, Mar 28, 1944. *Study:* Tyler Sch Art, Temple Univ, BFA, 66, with Stanley Lechtzin, goldsmithing, MFA, 69; Univ Rochester, Hon Dr, 89. *Work:* Metrop Mus Art, NY; British Mus Art; Philadelphia Mus Art; Smithsonian Inst, Renwick Gallery, Washington, DC; Victoria & Albert Mus, London. *Comn:* Wrought iron portal gates, Renwick Gallery, Smithsonian Inst, Washington, DC, 74; Stairway sculptures & door pulls, Wortham Theatre Ctr, Houston, Tex, 87; Sculpture, Adobe Systems, Inc, San jose, Calif, 98; Sculpture, Bausch & Lomb Corp, Rochester, NY, 96; Sculpture, Fed Bldg, Asheville, NC, 95. *Exhib:* Art to Art, Paley, Dine, Statom, Toldeo Mus Art, Ohio, 96; Age of Steel: Recent Sculpture, Brigham Young Univ, Provo, Utah, 96; Sculpture, San Antonio Art Inst, Tex, 93; Sculpture, Samuel P Harn Mus Art, Univ Fla, Gainesville, 92; Nat Mus Wales, Cardiff, 89; Towards a New Iron Age, Victoria & Albert Mus, London, 93; Zonju Int Biennial, Comju City, Korea, 99. *Pos:* pres, founder, Paley Studios Limited, Rochester, NY, 72. *Teaching:* prof, State Univ NY Col, Brockport, 72-84; prof & artist in residence, Sch Am Craftsmen, Rochester Inst, 84-. *Awards:* Master of New Medium Award, Smothsonian Inst, 97; Lifetime Achievement Award, Am Inst Archit, 95; Citation Distinguished Svc in Visual Arts Award, Nat Asn Schs Art & Design, 95. *Bibliog:* Edward Lucie-Smith (auth), The Art of Albert Paley, 96. *Mem:* Internat Sculpture Ctr. *Media:* Forged and Fabricated Mild Steel. *Mailing Add:* Paley Studios Ltd 25 N Washington St Rochester NY 14614

PALKO KOLOSVARY, PAUL
COLLAGE ARTIST, PRINTMAKER
b Bekescsaba, Hungary; US citizen. *Study:* Atelier Art Sch, Budapest, dipl, 40; Acad Fine Art, Budapest, dipl, 52. *Work:* Mus Fine Arts, Budapest, Hungary; Norton Simon Corp, Fullerton, Calif; Downey Mus Art, Calif; Huntsville Mus Art, Ala; Tex Tech Univ, Lubbock. *Exhib:* Retrospective, Huntsville Mus Art, Ala, 80; Recent Am Works on Paper, Smithsonian Inst, 85-87; 4 Contemp Printmakers, Downey Mus Art, Calif, 88; juried, Royal West Eng Acad, Bristol, Eng, 89; invitational, Salford Mus, Salford, Eng, 89; Int Survey, Stamford Mus, Conn, 90. *Awards:* Nat Munkacjy Prize, Mucsatlnok, Budapest, 52; Int Art Contest Gold Medal, Los Angeles, 84; Art Quest Nat 1st Prize, Boston/Los Angeles, 87. *Bibliog:* Michael Preble (auth), Paul & Eva Kolosvary, Walnut Col, 75. *Mailing Add:* 30211 Via Rivera Rancho Palos Verdes CA 90274

PALLADINO-CRAIG, ALLYS
DIRECTOR, CURATOR
b Pontiac, Mich, Mar 23, 47. *Study:* Fla State Univ, BA, 67, MFA, 78, PhD, 96; Univ Toronto, 68-69; Univ Va, 75-76. *Work:* Fla House of Rep. *Pos:* Dir contemp art, Four Arts Ctr, Tallahassee, 79-82; ed, Athanor, Fla State Univ, Ann Jour Art Hist, 80-; dir, Fla State Univ Mus Fine Arts, Tallahassee, 82; ed-in-chief, Fla State Univ, Mus Fine Arts Press, currently. *Teaching:* Mus Practices and studio. *Awards:* Individual Artist Fel, Fla Arts Coun, 79; and over 75 grants from Fla State Univ, Mus Fine Arts. *Mem:* FAMDA; FAM. *Publ:* Chroma, Fla State Univ Mus Fine Arts, 94; Body Language, Fla State Univ Mus Fine Arts, 96; auth, Mark Messersmith: new mythologies, Fla Gulf Coast Art Ctr, 96; Alexa Kleinbard (auth), Talking Leaves, Gulf Coast Mus Art, 99; Jake Fernadez (auth), Ethereal Journeyman, Ft Lauderdale Mus Art, 2000; Jim Roche (auth), Sense of place, Gulf Coast Mus Art, Largo, Fla, 2003; contribr ed, Terrestrial Forces, Fla State Univ, Mus Fine Arts, 2004; contribr ed, High Roads & Low Roads, Fla State Univ, Mus Fine Arts, 2006. *Mailing Add:* 1410 Grape St Tallahassee FL 32303

PALMER, A LAURE
SCULPTOR, WRITER
b Albany, NY. *Study:* Williams Col, BA(eng & art), 81; Art Inst Chicago, MFA(art), 88. *Work:* Artists Books Collection, Mus Contemp Art, Chicago. *Comn:* Outdoor sculpture, Krasl Art Ctr, St Joseph, Mich, 92. *Exhib:* Occupied Territory: Art at the Armory, Mus Contemp Art, Chicago, 92; Collection of Wilhelm Shurman, Ludwig Forum, Aachen, Ger, 92; Young Curators Group Show, Magasin, Grenoble, France, 92; Porgetto Cuspide Sardegna, ASPIS, Caglian-Pirri, Italy, 92; Hothouse: The Orchid Room, Hewett Gallery, Carnegie Mellon Univ, Pittsburgh, Pa, 92. *Teaching:* Asst prof sculpture, Univ Calif, Santa Barbara, 89-90; asst prof sculpture, Carnegie Mellon Univ, 91-92. *Awards:* Art Matters Fel, 89; Arts Midwest, Nat Endowment Arts Fel, 89; Ill Arts Coun Artists Fel, 90. *Res:* Contemporary art and sculpture installation. *Publ:* Contribr, Artforum, 89-91; Jeanne Dunning (catalog), Ill State Univ, 91

PALMER, HERBERT BEARL
DEALER, COLLECTOR
b New York, NY, June 23, 15. *Study:* NY Univ Inst Fine Arts, with A P McMahon, BA(Carnegie Scholar), MA(Michael Friedsam Scholar, Charles Hayden Scholar); Univ Southern Calif; Univ Calif, Los Angeles. *Collection Arranged:* The Film and Modern Art (auth, catalog), Los Angeles Munic Art Gallery, 69; Tantric Art, Twentieth Century Masters & many solo exhibs incl Bridget Riley, Allen Jones & George Grosz, Herbert Palmer Gallery; Calder, Red Grooms, Henry Moore. *Pos:* Western ed, Minicam Photogr, Cincinnati, 46-50; mgr, Feigen Palmer Gallery, Los Angeles, 63-68; owner & pvt art dealer, Herbert B Palmer & Co, Los Angeles, 68-75 & 81- & Beverly Hills, 75-81. *Teaching:* Lectr collecting & investing in art, Univ Calif, Los Angeles Exten. *Mem:* Am Asn Mus; Col Art Asn; Ethnic Arts Coun Los Angeles (bd dir, 69-71); Int Coun Mus; Art & Antique Dealers League Am. *Specialty:* Modern and contemporary painting, sculpture and drawings. *Collection:* Twentieth century abstract American painting. *Publ:* Auth, Art museums face crisis of identity, Los Angeles Times; Anti-educational influence of pictorial communication, J Sec Educ; Perspective and optical illusions, Design; The mollusk in art, Nature Mag; and others. *Mailing Add:* 9003 Melrose Ave Los Angeles CA 90069-5609

PALMER, KATE (KATHARINE) A
PAINTER
b Oklahoma City, Okla, July 28, 48. *Study:* Okla City Univ, BA (Eng lit), 70, BA (art), 74; Studio classes with Richard Goetz, 79-81, David A Leffel, 83-84; Workshops with William Reese, 88, Mark Daily, 90, Michael Lynch, 97-98. *Exhib:* Wichita Ctr Arts, Kans, 96; Butler Inst Am Art, 97; Allied Artists Am at the Butler, Butler Inst Am Art, 2000; Am Women Artists, The Cloisters, Sorrento, Italy, 2000; Am Artists Prof League Grant Int, Salmagundi Club, NY, 2000; Oil Painters Am Nat, Gallery Americana, Carmel, Calif, 2000; Allied Artists Am Ann, Nat Arts Club, NY, 2000; among others. *Pos:* cons art restoration, Mabee-Gerrer Mus, Shawnee, Okla, 85-86; workshop asst, Albert Handell, 94-95. *Awards:* Alfred C Crimi Mem Award, Audubon Artists, 97; Gamblin Artists Colors Award Excellence, Oil Painters Am, 97; First Prize Medal of Honor, Catharine Lorillard Art Club, 98; Frank C Wright Best in Show Medal, Am Artists Prof League, 2000; Jack Richeson First Prize Best Artist Products Award, Salmagundi Club, 2000; Grumbacher Gold Medal, Allied Artists Am 87th Ann, 2000. *Bibliog:* Christina Adams (auth), Oil Painters of America, Southwest Art, 5/98; Jim Lynch (auth), Making the Landscape Your Own: Kate Palmer, Am Artist Mag, 11/99; Gussie Fauntleroy (auth), Women in the Arts, Southwest Art, 6/2000. *Mem:* Allied Artists Am Inc; Am Women Artists (chair exec bd); Audubon Artists; Catharine Lorillard Wolfe Art Club; Salmagundi Club. *Media:* Oil, Pastel. *Dealer:* Joe Wade Fine Arts 102 E Water St Santa Fe NM 87501; Dragonfly Gallery Chapel Sq Avon CO 81620. *Mailing Add:* 103 Vista Redonda Santa Fe NM 87506

PALMER, LAURA HIGGINS
ARTIST
b Kansas City, Mo, Mar 16, 55. *Study:* Corcoran School Art; Cornell Univ, with Freidel Dzubas, BFA, 75; George Washington Univ, History of Art, MA, 78. *Work:* Md Artists Col, Univ Md, College Park, MD, 85-2005. *Comn:* Dianne Hurit Dance Ensemble, Takoma Park, 80-81; Numerous props, sets, etc, Ballet Theatre Maryland, Annapolis, MD, 85-2005. *Exhib:* Three Rivers Arts Festival, Carnegie Mus Art, Pittsburgh, Pa; Area 86, Hirschorn Mus, Washington, DC; New Artists, Madison Square Garden, NY. *Pos:* Coll mgr asst, Smithsonian Nat Mus Am Hist, 78-80; Slide Librn, Howard Univ Sch of Art, 80-82. *Teaching:* Instr, Drawing & Painting, Mt Holyoke Coll, 78; Instr, Drawing, Painting Design, Md Hall, Annapolis, MD, 86-94. *Awards:* Faculty scholarship, George Washington Univ, 77-7; Md fedn Art, 85; painters choice, Wall to Wall. *Bibliog:* The Art of Dance, Baltimore Sun Newspaper, 4/5/91; Mike Driscoll (auth), Impressions of Ballet, Capitol, Annapolis, 92; Artist in Step with Dance, Washington Post, 4/8/2004. *Mem:* Col Art Asn; Ballet Theatre Md Bd of Trustees, secy, 2002-2003; Cult Arts Found of Anne Arundel Co. *Media:* Brush & Ink, Oil

PALMER, MEREDITH ANN
ART DEALER
b Los Angeles, Calif, July 7, 51. *Study:* Radcliffe Col, Harvard Univ, with Rudolf Arnheim, BA, 73; Harvard Bus Sch, Owner/Pres Prog, 84. *Collection Arranged:* Chinese Archeol Exhib, US Dept State, 74-75; Print Publishing US Info Agency (overseas exhibs), in America, 79-80, Sam Francis: Works on Paper, 80-81, American Paintings from the Boston Mus Fine Arts in China, 81 & The New American Realism 1960-80, 82; Shoichi Ida, 86 & 89; Figurative European Moderns, 87; Bunka-Viewing: Sculptors & Their Drawings from Japan (auth, catalog), 90; George Peck: Composite Pictures, 94-95. *Pos:* Foreign serv reserve officer (art specialist), US Dept State, 73-76 & US Info Agency, 76-82; dir & partner, Herbert Palmer Gallery, Los Angeles, Calif, 82-91; pres, Meredith Palmer Gallery Ltd, New York, 91-. *Awards:* Grant, Nat Endowment Arts, 73. *Bibliog:* Susan Bidel (auth), Like Father, Like Daughter, Success: The Next Generation, Angeles Mag, 6/91. *Mem:* Am Asn Mus; Col Art Asn; Art Table, Inc; Curators Coun; Mus Contemp Art Los Angeles; and others. *Res:* Influence of traditional Asian arts on contemporary American and European art; Legislation and issues concerning illict trafficking in cultural properties; cross-cultural exchange and public diplomacy. *Specialty:* 20th century Modern masters and Contemporary art, painting, sculpture and drawings, includes American, European and emerging Asian artists. *Publ:* Auth, The Plundered Past, J Int Law, 4/74; China Premiers Art, US Dept State Exchange Mag, spring 75; Monet to Matisse Exhibition: A look at its positive elements, Los Angeles Times, 8/26/91. *Mailing Add:* 40 E 94th St 22D New York NY 10128-0375

PALMER, MICHAEL ANDREW
PAINTER, ART DEALER
b Mt Sterling, Ky, Dec 8, 42. *Study:* Univ Ky; Univ Hawaii; Univ NH, BA, 70. *Work:* Ogunquit Mus Art, Maine; DeCordova Mus Art, Lincoln, Mass; Colby Col Mus, Waterville, Maine; Elliott Mus Art, Stuart, Fla; Univ Maine, Orono. *Comn:* Auburn (portrait of city), Scammon & Gould, Inc, Maine, 78. *Exhib:* Nat Drawing & Small Sculpture, Ball State Col, Muncie, Ind, 72; Artists of Our Time, Ogunquit Mus Art, Maine, 75, 76 & 78; Am Artists Paris, State Dept, France, 76; one-man shows, Hobe Sound Galleries, Fla, 73, 74 & 81, Bates Col, Lewiston, Maine, 78, Elsa London, Montreal, Can, 80, 83 & 85, Art Ctr, Spartanburg, SC, 85 & PS Lane Gallery, Key West, Fla, 90-92 & 93; Arts Exclusive, Simsbury, Conn, 85-92; Button Gallery, Douglas, Mich, 94 & 95. *Pos:* Dir, Bray-Hampton Gallery, Atlanta, Ga, 65-67; co-owner & dir, PS Galleries, Ogunquit, Maine, 78- & Dallas, Tex, 81-86; bd dir, Keywest Art & Hist Soc, 93-96. *Awards:* Dr Morton M Shur Mem Award, Nat Soc Painters Casein & Acrylic, 75; Purchase Award, DeCordova Mus, 76; First Prize,

Bankers Int Collection, Orlando, Fla, 78. *Bibliog:* A young artist in Georgia, Southern Living, 68; Kathleen Hawk (auth), Michael A Palmer in Dallas, Art Voices, 81; Betty Joyce (auth), Maine in Transition, Phoenix Press, Kennebunk, Maine, 92; Betty Joyce (auth), Maine Remembered, Phoenix Press, 92. *Mem:* Nat Soc Painters Casein & Acrylic; Ogunquit Art Asn (pres, 74-77). *Media:* Ink, Acrylic. *Specialty:* Primarily representational contemporary artists as well as late 19th and early 20th century American artists. *Dealer:* PS Galleries Rte 1 Ogonquit ME 03907

PALMGREN, DONALD GENE
PAINTER, PHOTOGRAPHER
b Moline, Ill, Nov 22, 38. *Study:* Augustana Col, BA; Lutheran Sch Theol, Chicago, MDiv; Detroit Soc Arts & Crafts; Cranbrook Acad Art, with George Ortman, MFA. *Work:* St John's Univ; Anoka-Ramsey Col; Gustavus Adolphus Col; 3 M Corp. *Exhib:* Drawings USA, 73; Appalachian Nat Drawing Competition, Appalachian State Univ, Boone, NC, 77; Rutgers Nat Drawing, 79; Talent at Allan Stone Gallery, NY, 89; Hamline Univ, 89; Mankato State Univ, 89; plus many others. *Teaching:* Vis asst prof drawing & design, Murray State Univ, 72; assoc prof drawing & photog, Gustavus Adolphus Col, 72-. *Awards:* Res grants, Gustavus Adolphus Col, 73, 75 & 76. *Media:* Charcoal, Pastel Oil; Black & White Film. *Publ:* Auth, Space Upon Space: The Liberal Connection, Art and Academe, spring 89. *Dealer:* Jane Haslem Gallery Washington DC; Groveland Gallery Minneapolis MN. *Mailing Add:* 1309 S Washington Ave Saint Peter MN 56082-1524

PALOMBO, LISA
PAINTER
b Providence, RI, Mar 1, 65. *Study:* RI Sch of Design, BFA, 87. *Work:* MD Anderson Hosp, Houston; Cenavra Bank, Rocky Mount, NC; Hilton Garden Inn, Washington, DC. *Exhib:* Oil Painters of Am Regional Exhib, Brazier Fine Art, Richmond, Va, 02; Hudson Valley Art Asn, Found of Art, Hasting on the Hudson, NY, 02; Pen & Brush Regional Open Exhib, NY, 2003; Best of Am, The Nat Oil & Acrylic Painter's Soc Ann, Nat Exhib, Bolivar, MO, 2004; Conn Acad Fine Arts Ann Exhib, Mystic, Conn, 2004. *Awards:* Award of Merit, Am Artist Prof League, 02; Showcase Award Winner, Manhattan Arts Internat Competition, 96; Finalist, Artist Mag Ann Art Competition, 02. *Mem:* Oil Painter of Am; Am Artists Prof League; Southern Vermont Art Ctr. *Media:* Oil. *Publ:* Best of Oil Pianting, Rockport Pub, 96; Exploring Color, NorthLight Books, 98. *Mailing Add:* c/o Palombo Studios 55 Mountain Ave Caldwell NJ 07006

PALUMBO, JACQUES
PAINTER, SCULPTOR
b Philippeville, Algeria, Sept 16, 39; Can citizen. *Study:* Sch Fine Arts, Algiers, Algeria, BA, 60; Sch Fine Arts, Paris, France, MA, 65; Educ Technols Univ Montreal, PhD, 87. *Work:* Mus Contemp Art, Mus Fine Arts, Montreal, Que; Nat Gallery, Ottawa, Ont; Sincron Cult Ctr, Brescia, Italy; Found IDC, Zoetermeer, Neth. *Comn:* Monumental sculpture, City Hall, Trois-Rivieres, 92. *Exhib:* Konkret Acht, Kunsthaus, Nuremberg, 88; Systematic & Constructive Art, Villa de Madrid, Spain, 88; Europa 90, Sincron Cult Ctr, Brescia, Italy, 90; De L'Abstraction Geometrique, Mus Fine Arts, Montreal, 91; Propos D'Art Contemp, Mus Contemp Art, Montreal, 91; and others. *Bibliog:* Peter Perrin (auth), Icon and Numbers, Arts Can, 78; Gianguido Fucito (auth), Dualita, catalogue, 89; Leo Rosshandler (auth), Vers un Art Exact, Vie Des Arts, 90. *Mem:* Soc des Artistes Profs du Que, Montreal, 71; Conseil de la Peinture, Montreal, 91. *Media:* Acrylic, Oil; Metal, Cast. *Dealer:* Galerie Bervard, 90 rue Laurier Ouest, Montreal, Quebec, Canada, H2T 2N4. *Mailing Add:* 467 Ave Wiseman Montreal PQ H2V 3J9 Canada

PANCZENKO, RUSSELL
MUSEUM DIRECTOR
b Frille, Ger, Mar 23, 47. *Study:* Fairfield Univ, BA, 69; Universita degli Studi di Firenze, Italy, Dottore in Lettere, 79. *Pos:* Asst dir, Williams Col Mus Art, 80-84; dir, Elvehjem Mus Art, Univ Wis, Madison, 84-. *Teaching:* Mus studies & connoiseurship. *Awards:* Mus Fel, Nat Endowment Arts. *Mem:* Asn Art Mus Dirs; Am Asn Mus; Col Art Asn; Int Coun Mus; Wis Fedn Mus. *Res:* Early Italian Renaissance; late 19th Century and 20th Century Art. *Publ:* Auth, Gentile da Fabriano and classical antiquity, 80 & Umanesimo di Gentile da Fabriano, 83, Artibus et Historiae; Florence in Italian Paintings, 1850-1910, Clark Inst, Williamstown, Mass, 82; Richard Artschwager: PUBLIC/public (exhib catalog), 91. *Mailing Add:* 160 N Prospect Ave Madison WI 53705-4073

PANDOZY, RAFFAELE MARTINI
CONCEPTUAL ARTIST, LECTURER
b Rome, 1937. *Study:* Accademia Belle Arti Roma, 63; Univ Dallas, Tex, MA(sculpture), 74; New York Univ, NY, PhD, 85. *Work:* Dallas Mus Fine Arts, Tex; Ft Worth Mus Mod Art, Tex; San Francisco Mus Art, Calif. *Comn:* Pubsculpture, Eastfield Col, Dallas, Tex; indoor sculpture, Univ Tex, Dallas. *Exhib:* Tarrant Co Exhib, Ft Worth Mus, Tex, 72; Dallas Artist, Dallas Mus Fine Arts, Tex, 75; Twelve Texas, Mus Contemp Art, Houston, Tex, 76; 25 Contemps, Ft Worth Mus, Tex, 76; Texas Art, Univ Tex Campus, Dallas, 78; Dallas-San Francisco Exchange, San Francisco Mus Art, Calif, 78; Epigraphs, Hunter Col Gallery, NY, 80; Earth & the Environment, DCAM, Dallas, 94. *Awards:* Campbell Found Award for Sculpture, 75; First Place Award, Dallas City Hall, 78. *Bibliog:* Janet Kunter (auth), The art of hole making, Art News, 76; Janet Kunter (auth), Phenomenology, Dallas Morning News, 81. *Mem:* Col Art Asn; Nat Art Educ Asn; Nat Comt Hist Art; Am Soc Aesthetics; Int Asn Philos & Lit. *Media:* Earth Pigment. *Publ:* Of Arteology, Artimes Ed. *Dealer:* Art for the 90's 65 S 11th St Brooklyn NY 11211

PANTELL, RICHARD KEITH
PAINTER, PRINTMAKER
b Bronx, NY, May 2, 51. *Study:* Univ Bridgeport, Conn, 69-71; Art Students League, with David Leffel, Frank Mason & Earl Mayan, 74-75. *Work:* Butler Inst Am Art, Youngstown, Ohio; Wichita Art Mus, Kans; New York Pub Libr; Jewish Mus, Stokholm, Sweden; British Mus, London. *Comn:* mural Saugerties Timescape, Saugerties Cent Schs, NY, 93. *Exhib:* Butler Inst Am Art, 81-83, 2001; Ann Allied Artists Exhib, Nat Arts Club, NY, 83-2000; solo exhibs, Gallery Roundout, Kingston, NY, 83 & Gallery Luciano, Uppsala, Sweden; Bernard & S Dean Levy Gallery, NY, 84; Soc Am Graphic Artists, NY, 86-2000; Old Print Shop, NY, 94; and others. *Teaching:* Instr painting & drawing, Continuing Educ, Univ Uppsala, Sweden, 76-77 & Woodstock Sch Art, NY, 79-93; instr printmaking, State Univ NY, Col New Paltz, 89-91 & Art Students League, NY, 96-. *Awards:* Ben & Beatrice Goldstein Found Purchase Prize, Soc Am Graphic Artists, New York Pub Libr, 86; NY State Found Grant, 92; Grumbacher Gold Medal, Allied Artists Am, 96 & 98. *Bibliog:* Palmer Paroner (auth), The art of Richard Pantell, 7/23/81 & A transplanted New Yorker, 7/7/83, Artspeak; Tram Combs (auth), Pantell's luminous urbanities, Woodstock Times, 7/21/83; Fridolph Johnson (auth), Richard Pantell, Am Artist, 2/87. *Mem:* Allied Artists Am; Art Students League, NY; Woodstock Artists Asn (bd dir, 79-80 & 82-83); Soc Am Graphic Artists (coun mem, 89-94). *Media:* Oil; Etching. *Dealer:* Old Print Shop 150 Lexington Ave New York NY. *Mailing Add:* 37 Cooper Lake Rd Bearsville NY 12409

PANZA , GIUSEPPE
COLLECTOR
b Milan, Mar 23, 23. *Study:* State Univ, Milan, 48. *Pos:* Art collector, mgr Panza Collection, Lugano, Italy. *Awards:* Names one of Top 200 Collectors, ARTnews Mag, 2004. *Collection:* Contemporary Art, especially 1960's & 1970's. *Mailing Add:* Sentiero Vinorum Massagno 2 CH 6900 Switzerland

PANZERA, ANTHONY
ARTIST
Study: State Univ NY, New Paltz, BS; Southern Ill Univ, Carbondale, MFA. *Work:* Ariz State Univ Mart Mus, Tempe, NJ State Mus, Trenton, Jane Voorhees Zimmerly Art Mus, New Brunswick, NJ. *Exhib:* One-man shows incl Bates Col, Lewiston, Maine, Marsh Art Gallery, Richmond, Va, Colgate Univ Art Gallery, Hamilton, NY; group exhib, Nat Acad Ann, Century Assoc, Leubsdorf Gallery, Laurel Tracy Gallery, Red Bank, NJ, Robert Wilson Gallery, Nantucket, Rep in permanent collections Bristol-Myers Squibb Collection, Princeton. *Pos:* Mem Abbey Mural Comt Nat Acad. *Teaching:* Teacher, fine arts, Hunter Col, City Univ of NY, 68-, Brooklyn Col, New York Acad of Art; co-dir, Art in Florence/Rome Summer prog; fresco instr, RI Sch of Design; now fac Nat Accad, New York City. *Publ:* contribr articles on art hist to Art World Mag. *Mailing Add:* Hunter College Dept Art 11th Floor North Bldg 695 Park Ave New York NY 10021

PAONE, PETER
PAINTER, PRINTMAKER
b Philadelphia, Pa, Oct 2, 36. *Study:* Philadelphia Col Art, BFA, 58. *Work:* Libr Cong; Philadelphia Mus Art; Mus Mod Art; Art Inst Chicago; Victoria & Albert Mus, London, Eng; and others. *Exhib:* Brooklyn Mus, 62 & 64; Butler Inst Am Art, 65; Forum Gallery NY; Otis Art Inst, Los Angeles, 64 & 66; Kennedy Galleries, 70-74; one-man shows, Contemp Art Mus, Houston, 76, Roswell Mus, NMex, 77 & Hooks-Epstein Galleries, Houston, 78-88; Pa Acad Fine Arts, 83; Merlin Verlact, Ger, 97-98; 12 Anonymous Poets, Nat Acad Design Mus; and many others. *Teaching:* Instr, Philadelphia Col Art, 59 & Pratt Inst, 59-66; instr art hist, Positano Art Sch, Italy, 61; prof drawing & chmn graphics dept, Pa Acad Fine Arts, 78-. *Awards:* Guggenheim Fel, 65-66; Tiffany Grant, 65-67; Print Club Award of Merit, Philadelphia, 83; MidAtlantic Grant, 98; and others. *Bibliog:* Selden Rodman (auth), The Insiders, La State Univ, 60. *Mem:* Soc Am Graphic Artists; Nat Acad. *Media:* All. *Res:* Bernarda Bryson Shahn. *Publ:* Auth & illusr, Paone's Zoo, 61, Five Insane Dolls, 66 & My Father, 68; auth, Kachina--Paone, 76; and others. *Mailing Add:* 1027 Westview St Philadelphia PA 19119

PAPAGEORGE, TOD
PHOTOGRAPHER
b Portsmouth, NH, Aug 1, 40. *Study:* Univ NH, BA. *Hon Degrees:* Yale Univ, Hon MA. *Work:* Mus Mod Art, Seagrams Inc, NY; Art Inst Chicago; Bibliot Nat, Paris; Boston Mus Fine Arts; Dallas Mus Fine Art. *Comn:* The American Courthouse Bicentennial Doc, Seagrams, Inc, 75; American Images, AT&T, 78; The Acropolis, Warner Commun Inc, 83. *Exhib:* Recent Acquisitions, Mus Mod Art, 71, 73, 74 & 79, Pub Landscapes, 74 & Mean Streets, 91; 14 Am Photogr, Baltimore Mus Art, 75; Mirrors & Windows, Mus Mod Art, 78; one-man exhibs, Art Inst Chicago, 78, Galerie Zibriskie, Paris, 80, Daniel Wolf Gallery, NY, 81 & 85, Akron Art Mus, 81, Galerie Lange-Irschl, Munich, WGer, 81, Sheldon Mem Art Gallery, Lincoln, Nebr, 81 & Franklin Parrasch Gallery, NY, 91; California Dreaming, Franklin Parrasch Gallery, NY, 92; Summer Pastimes, Joseph Seagrams & Sons, NY, 92; Art in the Machine Age, Worcester Art Mus, Mass, 94; Varied Viewpoints, Seagram Gallery, NY, 95; The Permanent Collection, Mus Mod Art, NY, 95; DeCordova Mus, Lincoln, Mass, 96. *Teaching:* prof photography and dir grad study, Yale Sch Art, 79-; teacher Parson Sch, 69-72, Pratt Inst, Cooper Union, 71-74; instr Queens Coll, 72-74, MIT, 75, Harvard, 76, Yale Sch Art, 78-. *Awards:* Guggenheim Found Fel Photog, 70 & 77; Nat Endowment Arts Fel Photog, 73 & 75. *Bibliog:* Leo Rubinfien (auth), Love-hate relations, Artforum, summer 78; Ben Lifson (auth), Clothed in possibilities, Village Voice, 12/12/79; Maren Stange (auth), Tod Papageorge, In: Contemporary Photographers, St Martin's Press, 82. *Publ:* Contribr, articles, Aperture, Vol 19, No 1

& No 85, 81; auth & ed, Public Relations, The Photographs of Garry Winogrand, Mus Mod Art, 77; auth, Walker Evans and Robert Frank: An Essay on Influence (catalog), Yale Art Gallery, 81; auth, What We Brought, The Photographs of Robert Adams, Yale Art Gallery, 2002; and others. *Mailing Add:* 122 Cottage St New Haven CT 06511-5652

PAPIER, MAURICE ANTHONY
EDUCATOR, PAINTER
b Ft Wayne, Ind, Apr 14, 40. *Study:* Ball State Univ, Muncie, Ind, BS, 63; St Francis Col, Ft Wayne, Ind, MS, 67; Bowling Green State Univ, Ohio, MA, 78. *Work:* Lincoln Life Insurance Co; Gen Tele Co; First Nat Bank; North Am Van Lines; Warner Commun, NY. *Exhib:* Ball State Drawing & Small Sculpture, Ball State Univ, Muncie, Ind, 68; Northwestern Indiana Artists, Hammond Mus, Ind, 76; Paper Chase, Artlink Gallery, Ft Wayne, Ind, 83; Tri-Kappa Regional Artists, Ft Wayne Mus Art, Ind, 83; Rental Gallery, Ft Wayne Mus Art, Ind, 83. *Teaching:* Instr art, Ft Wayne Community Sch, 63-72; dept head art, St Francis Col, 72-. *Awards:* Third Prize Sculpture, Van Wert Regional, 70; Tri-Kappa Regional Artists Exhib, several awards; Outstanding Professor of Year, St Francis Col, 92. *Mem:* Artlink Alternative Artists' Space (panel mem); Mayor's comt Pub Art Works; Col Art Asn. *Media:* Acrylic, Collage. *Dealer:* Sharon Eisbart 3601 N Washington Rd Ft Wayne IN 46808. *Mailing Add:* Dept Art St Francis Col 2701 Spring St Fort Wayne IN 46808

PAPO, ISO
PAINTER
b Sarajevo, Yugoslavia, May 2, 25; US citizen. *Study:* Polytech Milan; Brera Acad Fine Arts, Milan, Italy, grad, 51; Boston Mus Sch; also with Carlo Carra. *Work:* Boston Pub Libr; Danforth Mus Art, Framingham, Ma. *Comn:* Paintings for films & posters, United Church of Christ, 64-65. *Exhib:* Inst Contemp Art, Boston, 68; one-man shows, Boston Athenaeum, 73 & Boston Psychoanal Soc & Inst, 75 & 86; Boston Visual Artists Union, 78; Helen Bumpus Gallery, Duxbury, 80 & 94; Hess Gallery, 86, 88, 91, 95 & 98; Allon Gallery, Brookline, 90; Art of Corea, Ellsworth, 95; Wiggins Gallery, Boston Pub LIbr, 2000i; Danforth Mus, 2001; and others. *Teaching:* Instr art, Kirkland House & Quincy House, Harvard Univ, 64-69; assoc prof painting, Boston Univ, 67-75; assoc prof & chmn, Arts and Commun Div, Pine Manor Col, 68-89, prof emer currently. *Awards:* Nat Scholastic Competition First Prize, Govt Italy, 50; Camargo Found Fel, 86. *Mem:* Boston Visual Artists Union. *Media:* Watercolor, Oil, Pen, Ink, Pastel. *Publ:* Illusr, The Art of Responsive Drawing & Figure Drawing, Prentice-Hall; Artistic Anatomy and Figure Drawing, Van Nostrand Reinhold; Catalogue of Boston Public Library's Collection. *Mailing Add:* 212 Aspinwall Ave Brookline MA 02146

PAPPAJOHN, JOHN & MARY
COLLECTOR, PATRON
Study: John: Univ Iowa, BSc, 52; Mary: Univ Minn, BS, 55. *Pos:* Owner, Pappajohn Insurance Agency, Mason City, Iowa, 53-59; pres, founder Guardsman Life Investors, Inc, Des Moines, 62-69; co-founder, vpres, Guardsman Life Insurance Co, West Des Moines, Iowa, 62-69; pres, Equity Dynamics Inc, Des Moines, 69-, Pappajohn Capital Resources, Inc, Des Moines, 69-; dir, Allion, Inc, HAQ, Am Care Source, Inc, Patient Inforsystems, Horatio Alger Asn, Leadership 100. *Awards:* Recipient Spec Achievement award Big Brothers, 72, Big Brother of Yr award, 74, Oscar D Schmidt Iowa Bus Leadership award, Univ Iowa Col Bus, 93, Horatio Alger award, Horatio Alger Association, 95, Brotherhood award, Iowa Region Nat Conference of Christian and Jews, 97, Beta Gamma Sigma Mediallion for Entrepreneur of Yr, 97, Hellenic Hertiage Achievement award, 97, Meredith Willson Heritage award, 98, Ellis Island Medal of Honor, 2000, Greek Orthodox Archon award, 2000, Univ Iowa Homecoming Honored Guest, 2002; Finkbine award, Univ Iowa Bus Sch, 2004; named Iowa Bus Leader of Year, 1993; named to Iowa Hall of Fame, 1996, Central Iowa Bus Hall of Achievement, 1999; named to of Top 200 Collectors, ARTnews Mag, 2004. *Mem:* Collector's Comt Nat Gallery Art, Washington, DC, trustee's coun; Collector's Comt Whitney Mus Am Art, NY; Nat Comt John F Kennedy Ctr Performing Arts; trustee Des Moines Art Ctr; Mem Univ Iowa Alumni Asn (pres' club), Des Moines Club, Embassy Club, Univ Club, Order AHEPA, Masons, Shriners, Phi Gamma Delta. *Collection:* Modern and Contemporary Art

PAPPAS, GEORGE
PAINTER
b Boston, Mass, Jan 25, 29. *Study:* Mass Col of Art, BS, 52; Harvard Univ, MA, 53; Mass Inst of Technol, with Gyorgy Kepes, 52-53; Pa State Univ, PhD(educ), 57. *Work:* De Cordova Mus, Lincoln, Mass; St Paul Gallery of Art, Minn; Tampa Bay Art Ctr, Fla; Pa State Univ, Univ Park; Nat Gallery Art, Washington, DC; First Fla Bank, Tampa; McDonald Corp, Chicago, Ill; Neiman Marcus, Dallas. *Exhib:* Corcoran Biennial, Washington, DC; De Cordova Mus Art, Lincoln, Mass; Ringling Mus Art, Sarasota, Fla; Detroit Inst of Art, Mich; Boston Mus Fine Arts, Mass; Kanegis Gallery, Boston; Nordness Gallery, NY; Stein Gallery, Tampa, Fla; Fla Gulf Coast Art Ctr; Univ S Fla Mus. *Teaching:* Asst prof painting & art educ, Pa State Univ, 55-56; chmn dept art, Univ S Fla, 66-83, prof art, 66-93, chair, prof emer, 93-. *Awards:* Purchase Awards, Drawing USA, St Paul Gallery of Art, Chautaqua Nat, Chautaqua Art Asn & Tampa Bay Art Ctr, Fla; Indiv Artists Grants, Fla, 83 & 96. *Mem:* Col Art Asn; Nat Conf of Art Adminr; Nat Art Educ Asn; Sarasota Arts Coun. *Media:* Oil. *Res:* Painting with artificial light, 1971; tracing the Odyssey in Greece & Turkey, 1990; Study of William Turner landscapes, London, 1991; Greek archeological sites, 1993. *Collection:* Contemp prints: works by Barnett Newman, James Rosenquist, Philip Perlistein, Ed Ruscha, Ed Paschke & others. *Publ:* Co-auth, Design, It's Form and Function, Pa State Univ, 65; Concepts in Art & Education, Macmillan, 70. *Dealer:* Clayton Galleries Tampa FL; Allen Gallup Contemporary Art, Sarasota FL; Arts on Douglas New Smyrna FL. *Mailing Add:* 924 Indian Beach Dr Sarasota FL 32168

PARAVANO, DINO
PAINTER
b Rome, Italy, Nov 9, 35. *Study:* Johannesburg Art Col, S Africa, 1954-1955. *Work:* Leigh Yawkey Woodson Art Mus, Wausau, Wis; The Wildlife Experience, Parker, Colo; Hiram Blauvelt Art Mus, Oradell, NJ; Bennington Ctr Arts, Bennington, Vt. *Comn:* Paintings of Nat Parks, S African Prks Bd, Pretoria, Johannesburg, 1983. *Exhib:* Birds in Art, Leigh Yawkey Woodson Art, Wausau, Wis, 1985-2006; Birds in Art, Beijing Mus Nat His, Beijing, China, 1986; Art and the Animal, Old Algonquin Mus, Algonquin, Ont, 1995; Visions of the Veld, Nat Mus Wildlife Art, Jackson, Wyo, 1996; Art & the Animal Kingdom, Bennington Ctr Arts, Bennington, Vt, 1996-2006; Feline Fine Art of Cats, Arts & Sci Ctr S Ark, Pine Bluff, Ark, 2002; American Art in Miniature, Gilcrease Mus, Tulsa, Okla, 2005. *Awards:* Award of Excellence, Art & the Animal, Soc Animal Artists, 1990; Master Wildlife Artist, Birds in Art, Leigh Yawkey Woodson Art Mus, 1993; First Place Winner, Pastel 100 Competition, Pastel J, 2005. *Bibliog:* Ruth Summer (auth), Painting Wildlife & Wild Scenes, Pastel J, 2000; Devon Jackson (auth), Out of Africa, Southwest Art, 2005; Michael Scott-Blair (auth), A Virtuoso in Light Shadows, Wildlife Art, 2005. *Mem:* Soc Animal Artist (signature mem 1979-2006); Pastel Soc Am (signature mem 1992-2006); Oil Painters Am (2004-2006). *Media:* Pastel, Acrylic, Oil, Miscellaneous Media. *Publ:* Illusr, Last Horizons, St Martins Press, 1989; Contribr, African Wildlife in Art, Clive Holloway Books, 1991; Illusr, Hunting in Botswana, Safari Press, 1994; Contribr, Drawing and Painting Animals, Watson Guptill, 1998; Contribr, Best of Wildlife 2, North Light Books, 1999. *Mailing Add:* 9030 E Chof Ovi Dr Tucson AZ 85749

PARDEE, WILLIAM HEARNE
PAINTER, EDUCATOR
b Pittsburgh, Pa, Aug 25, 46. *Study:* Yale Univ, with Sewell Sillman, BA, 69; New York Studio Sch, with Philip Guston, George McNeil & Leland Bell, 69-73; Columbia Univ, with Meyer Schapiro, MFA, 75. *Work:* Maine Savings Bank; Blue Cross/Blue Shield of Maine; Yosemite Mus. *Exhib:* Bowery Gallery, 85, 86, 89, 92 & 95; Jersey City Mus, NJ, 86; Maine Coast Artists, Rockport, 87; Bowery Gallery, 89, 92, 95 & 98; Congress Square Gallery, Maine, 92; and others. *Collection Arranged:* Linens, Wall-Clothing and Straw Sculpture, sculptures by Maureen Connor, 82; Aspects of Abstraction, sculpture by Deborah de Moulpied, Gerald DiGiusto & Lawrence Fane, 83; Landscape and Abstract Art: A Continuing Dialogue, 85, Inner Images, 86 & Clear Perceptions, 88, Colby Mus Art, Maine; Meyer Schapiro's Semiotics of Painting, New York Studio Sch, 89; Joan Mitchell, Maier Mus Art, Lynchburg, Va; Reinterpreting Landscape, Maier Mus Art, 96. *Pos:* Consult contemp art, Colby Col Mus Art, Maine, 82-88; asst prof painting & design, Colby Col, Maine, 82-90; adj cur, Maier Mus Art. *Teaching:* Vis asst prof, Col William & Mary, 83; asst prof painting & design, Colby Col, Maine, 82-90; painting & drawing, Univ Va, 92, Rice Univ, 97-98 & Univ Conn, 98-99. *Awards:* Residency, Djerassi Found, 86, Yosemite Nat Park, 93. *Bibliog:* Gerrit Henry (auth), Hearne Pardee, Artnews, 12/92; Jonathan Goodman (auth), Hearne Pardee, Artnews, 4/95; Valerie Gladstone (auth), Hearne Pardee, Artnews, 6/98. *Mem:* Col Art Asn Am. *Media:* Oil, Collage. *Publ:* Auth, Proust's visual imagery, Yale French Studies, 65; A reading of Marsden Hartley, 83, Six painters at the Hudson River Museum, 83, Landscape and the language of abstraction, 9/85, Inner Images, 11/86 & Peter Campus, 11/88, Arts Mag; short reviews, Artnews, 87-94. *Dealer:* Bowery Gallery 121 Wooster St New York NY 10012. *Mailing Add:* 2855 Mallorca Ln Davis CA 95616-6579

PARDINGTON, RALPH ARTHUR
CERAMIST, SCULPTOR
b Highland Park, Mich, June 14, 38. *Study:* Albion Col, BFA, 60; Alfred Col Ceramics, summers 61 & 65; Cranbrook Acad Art, MFA, 62; with Hal Reiger & Palo Soleri, 64 & Dominic Labino, 67. *Work:* Inst Contemp Arts, Washington, DC; Mus Int Folk Art, Santa Fe; Mus Fine Arts, Div Mus NMex, Santa Fe; Mus Albuquerque; Mus Fine Art, Univ Okla. *Comn:* Bas-relief wall sculpture of patron saint, 69, holy water fountain, 69, Christ Desert Monastery, Albuquerque; sculpture, comn by Fritz Scholder, Galisteo, NMex, 70; outdoor planters, comn by A J O'Brien, Harbor Springs, Mich, 73; two large punch bowls, Int Folk Art Mus, Santa Fe, 73. *Exhib:* 25th Ceramic National, Syracuse, NY, 68; Object Makers, Univ Utah, 71; Inst Am Indian Arts Fac Exhib, Smithsonian Inst, Washington, DC, 73; Christmas Exhib, ACC Gallery, NY, 74; NMex Exhib, Univ Albuquerque, 74; and others. *Teaching:* Prof emer, Inst Am Indian Arts, 62-90; instr ceramics, Penland Sch Crafts, summers 67 & 69. *Awards:* First Prize, Int Folk Art, 68; Outstanding Work Award, Mus Albuquerque, 70; Commission Prize, Mus NMex, 71. *Bibliog:* Article in NMex Mag, winter 71. *Mem:* NMex Potters Asn; Am Crafts Coun; NMex Designer Craftsmen (pres, Santa Fe Chap, 64-65, state pres & vpres, 65-66). *Media:* Clay, Wood. *Publ:* Auth, 30-minute demonstration prog, KNME TV, 66. *Mailing Add:* 12 Elk Cir Santa Fe NM 87501-8510

PARE, RICHARD
PHOTOGRAPHER, CURATOR
b Portsmouth, Eng, Jan 20, 48. *Study:* Brighton Col, Eng, 60-65, Winchester Sch Art, Eng, 66-67, Ravensbourne Col Art & Design, Eng, BFA, 70, Art Inst Chicago, MFA, 73. *Work:* Mus Mod Art, NY; Stedelijk Mus, Amsterdam, Neth; Victoria & Albert Mus, London; Art Inst, Chicago; Mus Fine Arts, Houston; Can Ctr Archit, Montreal; Toledo Mus Art. *Comn:* Musee du Nouveau Monde, La Rochelle, France, 80; Casa Pilatos, comn by Duque de Segorbe, Seville, Spain, 83; Japanese Gardens, Can Ctr Archit, Montreal, 86-90; Comune di Venezia Marghera Proj. *Exhib:* Court House, traveling exhib in US & Eng (cur & ed catalog), Mus Mod Art, NY, Art Inst, Chicago, San Francisco Art Inst, Atlanta Hist Soc, Ctr Creative Photog, Tucson, Old Court House, St Louis, Mo, 76-80, Chiswick House, La Montreal, Carnegie Mus, Pittsburgh, Royal Acad London, 94-95; solo exhibs, Art Inst, Chicago, 81 & 85, Corcoran Gallery Art, Washington, DC, 87, Camera Obscura Thessaloniki, 95, Max Protech Gallery,

NY, 97, Ctr Archit, Montreal, Can, 97, Heinz Ctr, Pittsburg Mus Art, 97 & Querini Stampalia Venezia, 98; SK Josefsburg Studio, Portland, Ore; Berlin Art Fair, Rudolf Kicken Galerie. *Collection Arranged:* Robert Macpherson, 1811-1872 (auth catalog), Can Ctr Archit, 82-84; Photography & Architecture, 1839-1939 (auth catalog), Can Ctr Archit, 82-84. *Pos:* Cur photog, Can Ctr Archit, Montreal, 74-90; consult cur, Seagram Collection, 74-90, Can Ctr Archit, 90-. *Teaching:* Prof photog & photog hist, Columbia Col, Chicago, 73-75; Mellon Found vis lectr photog hist, Cooper Union, NY, 77. *Awards:* Fel, John Simon Guggenheim Mem Found, 87; Europe AW Regional Design Ann Award for Colours of Light, 98; AIA Monogr Award, 98. *Res:* Russian modernist architecture 1922-32; Felice Beato & Roger Fenton for major retrospectives. *Publ:* Auth, Courthouse a Photographic Document, Horizon Press, 78; Photography and Architecture 1839-1939, CLA/Mass Inst Technol, 83; Egypt: Reflections on Continuity, Timken Publ, 90; The Colours of Light, The Architecture of Tadao Ando, Phaidon Press, London, 95. *Dealer:* Max Protech 511 W 22nd New York NY 10021-1104. *Mailing Add:* 174 Park St Montclair NJ 07042

PARFENOFF, MICHAEL S
EDUCATOR, LITHOGRAPHER
b Gary, Ind, Aug 8, 26. *Study:* Art Inst Chicago, with Boris Anisfeld & Max Kahn, BFA & MFA. *Exhib:* Print Exhib, Libr Cong, Washington, DC; Momentum, Art Inst Chicago; Philadelphia Print Club. *Pos:* Pres, Blackhawk Mountain Sch Art, 63-. *Teaching:* Instr lithography, Art Inst Chicago, 58-65; prof art, Chicago City Col, 58-. *Mem:* Am Asn Univ Prof; Ill Art Educators. *Media:* Stone. *Mailing Add:* 453 W Roslyn Pl Chicago IL 60614-2712

PARIS, JEANNE C
CRITIC, CONSULTANT
b Newark, NJ. *Study:* Newark Sch Fine Arts; Tyler Sch Art, Temple Univ; Columbia Univ; NY Univ. *Collection Arranged:* Organized & directed The Artist of the Month, providing lecturers & demonstrators in all the arts for organizations & schools; organized exhibs of American art for Latin America, Italy & USA. *Pos:* Assoc dir, Valente Gallery, New York, currently; art critic, Long Island Press, 63-; art critic, Newsday, 77-. *Teaching:* Lectr art, univs, cols, art leagues, women's clubs, mus asns, radio & NBC-TV series, You're a Part of Art. *Mem:* Glen Cove Pub Libr; Coun Arts North Shore; New York Reporters Asn; Newspaper Women's Club; and others. *Collection:* Twentieth century painting & sculpture. *Publ:* Auth articles for Weekly Newspaper Chain, Record Pilot & Newsday; article, Cue Mag, 7/72. *Mailing Add:* 94 School St Glen Cove NY 11542

PARISH, NORMAN
GALLERY DIRECTOR
b New Orleans, Aug, 26, 37. *Study:* Sch of Art Inst of Chicago, BA(painting), 60. *Exhib:* Contribr to Wall of Respect, Chicago, 1967. *Pos:* Draftsman, to asst proj leader, to proj leader to supervisor of computer-aided drafting; found, dir, Parish Gallery, Wash, 91—. *Mailing Add:* Parish Gallery 1054 31st St Washington DC 20007

PARISI, MARTHA
GRAPHIC ARTIST, PRINTMAKER
b July 29, 46. *Study:* Sir Wilfred Laurier Univ, BA, 68; Univ Toronto, MED, 69, specialist, 78. *Work:* NY Mus, Albany. *Comn:* Drawing, Northeastern Wildlife Expo, Albany, 88; cover design, Saugerties Cent Schs, NY, 90; cover design, Smithsonian, Nat Zoological Park, Washington, 91; portrait, Marc Curtrone, Jupiter, Fla, 96. *Exhib:* The Arts, Schenectady Mus, NY, 86; The Arts, NY State Mus, Albany, 87; Northeastern Wildlife Expo, NY State Mus, Albany, 87; solo exhibs, Stedman Gallery, Colonie, NY, 87, Town Hall, Saugerties, NY, 90, Sundancer Gallery, Cocoa Village, Fla, 96; group exhibs, Amrita Gallery, Poughkeepsie, NY, 95, Signature Gallery, San Diego, Calif, 95. *Pos:* Owner, Nature Art Gallery, 87-. *Awards:* Art in DC Award, Ulster Arts Alliance, 96; Best of Show, Art League, 95; First Place: Drawing, Mandarin Arts Coun, 96. *Bibliog:* Kevin Geoghan (auth), A festival of art, ESCA, Chemung Valley, 8/22/92; James G Shine (auth), Art beat, Daily Freeman, 10/28/94; Tribute to Women, YWCA Arts Coun, 95. *Mem:* Southern Utah Art Ctr; Nat Mus Am Indian; Empire State Crafts Alliance. *Media:* Drawing, Pencil; Printmaking. *Publ:* Illusr, International Cheetah Studbook, Smithsonian Inst, 91. *Mailing Add:* PO Box 597 Worcester NY 12197-0597

PARK, LEE
PAINTER
b Seoul, Korea, Oct 25, 38; US citizen. *Study:* Fla State Christian Univ, MA, 86. *Work:* Bridgeport Univ, New York City; YWCA HQ, Los Angeles; Los Angeles City Councilman 10th Dist Office, Los Angeles; Christian Children's Fund Inc, Beverly Hills, Calif. *Exhib:* Pacific Asia Mus, Pasadena, Calif, 86; Asia Art Exhibition, Metro Politan Mus Art, Seoul, Korea, 93; Musee d'Art Moderne de la Commanderie d'Unet, Paris, France, 94; Biennale Int de Paris, City Hall of Paris, France, 94; Art Addiction Int, Stockholm, Sweden, 97; Prima Biennale Int di Art Contemporanea, Perugia, Italy, 98; World Peace Art Exhibition, Saejong Center, Seoul, Korea, 99; 50th Commemoration Nat Found China, Beijing, 99. *Teaching:* instr oriental art, K-A Art Inst, Los Angeles, 93. *Awards:* Bronze Discovery Award, Art Calif Mag, 93; Gold Medal, Art Addiction, 97; Art Addiction Int Prize, Organizing Comt, Stockholm, 97. *Mem:* World Artist Asn; Korea Modern Art Asn; Asia Art Invitational Asn; Korea-Japan Art Exchanging Asn; Art 2000 Inst. *Media:* All media. *Publ:* contrib Art of California Magazine, Artweek Magazine, Art Exposure, Art Diary, Encyclopedia of Living Artists Magazine, Internat Encyclopedic Dictionary of Modern and Contemp Art, Ferrara, Italy. *Dealer:* Simon Kim Gallery 8643 Wilshire Blvd Beverly Hills CA 90211. *Mailing Add:* 1935 S La Salle Ave Ste 31 Los Angeles CA 90018

PARKER, ANN (ANN PARKER NEAL)
PHOTOGRAPHER, WRITER
b London, Eng, Mar 6, 34; US citizen. *Study:* RI Sch of Design; Yale Univ, BFA. *Work:* Metrop Mus Art, NY; Smithsonian Inst, Washington, DC; Mus Mod Art, NY; Boston Pub Libr, Mass; Ctr Creative Photog, Tucson, Ariz. *Comn:* Arton Assoc, 70 & 74; Mead Art Gallery, Amherst, Mass, 76; Sweetwater Eds, 82; Thistle Hill Press, 83-85. *Exhib:* One-man exhibs, Nat Mus Art, La Paz, Bolivia, 85, Princeton Univ Libr, NJ, 86, Inst Dominicano de Cultura Hispanica, Santo Dominican Republic, 87, Maxwell Mus, Univ NMex, Albuquerque, 88. *Awards:* Ford Found Grant in Arts & Humanities, 62-64; First Prize in Photog, Americana Bicentennial Photog Contest, 76 & Mass Open, 77. *Bibliog:* Stephen Chodorov (producer), Know Ye the Hour, Camera Three, CBS-TV, 11/68; Vicki Goldberg (auth), Am Photogr, 1/83; Lois Parkinson Zamora (auth), Spot, Houston Ctr Photog, fall 89. *Mem:* Friends of Photog; Photog Resource Ctr, Boston Mass; Asn Gravestone Studies. *Media:* Cibachrome, Silver Prints; Non Fiction. *Publ:* Photogr, Ephemeral Folk Figures, Clarkson Potter, New York, 69; Molas Folk Art of the Cuna Indians, Barre Publ, New York, 77; Scarecrows, Barre Publ, New York, 78; Early American Stone Sculpture, Sweetwater Eds; Los Ambulantes, the itinerant photographers of Guatemala, Mass Inst Technol, Cambridge, Mass, 82; coauth, Folk Art of the Great Pilgrimage, Smithsonian, 95. *Dealer:* Gallery of Graphic Arts 1603 York Ave New York NY 10028. *Mailing Add:* 126 School St North Brookfield MA 01535-1961

PARKER, GERTRUD VALERIE
SCULPTOR
b Vienna, Austria; US citizen. *Study:* Univ Calif, Berkeley, BA(political sci); San Francisco State with Alexander Nepote, Pac Basin Sch Textiles with Lillian Elliott. *Work:* NY Times Offices, NY; Oakland Mus, Oakland, Calif; Smithsonian Archives, Washington; Prefecture of Gunma Gun, Japan. *Exhib:* Innerskins/Outerskins Gut & Fishskins, Anchorage Mus, State Mus Juneau & Univ Alaska Mus, Fairbanks, Alaska, 88; Mixing It Up, Coos Art Mus, Ore, 88; solo show, Art Exhib Galleries, Manu Co Civic Ctr, San Rafael, Calif, 88 & SE Craft & Folk Art Mus, 93; Image of the Horse, Redding Mus, Calif, 90; 1993 Crocker-Kingsley Ann Art Show, Crocker Mus, Sacramento, Calif, 93; solo shows incl Galerie Haasner, Wiesbaden, Ger, 2000, Vernissage & Kolloquium, Gundes institut, St Wolfgang, Austria, 2000, Spertus Mus, Chicago, 2000, Laguna Art Mus, Laguna Beach, Calif, 99, Toyamura Int Schulpture Biennale, Hokaido, Japan, 99, plus others. *Pos:* Co-founder & chmn bd, San Francisco Craft & Folk Art Mus, Calif, 82-89. *Awards:* Cert Excellence Outstanding Archit Fiber, Int Art Competition, New York, 88; Discovery Award-Bronze Medal, Art Calif Mag, 92; Richard A Florsheim Art Fund Grant, San Francisco Craft & Folk Art Mus Solo Show, 93; Gold Medal Iser Int Exhib, Stockholm, Sweden, 97; Ornament for the White House Tree, Washington, 98. *Bibliog:* Wayne Freedman (producer), Inside Art, KRON-TV, 88; Doromay Keasbey (auth), Sheer Delight-Handwoven Transparencies, Stella Publ House, 90; Jeanna Haney (auth), Gertrude Parker-Metamorphosing a humble material, Fiber Arts, 91; Gertrud Parker: Sheer Artistry, Woman's Art Jour, 99; Toyamura Int Sculpture Biennal, Japan (catalog), 99; The Biennale Shoebox Show, Univ Hawaii, (catalog) ArtWeek, 2000. *Mem:* Marin Arts Coun (bd dir, 83); Marin Soc Artists; Pacific Rim Sculptors Group. *Media:* Metal, Miscellaneous Media. *Dealer:* B Haasner Gallery Wiesbaden Germany. *Mailing Add:* 2 Tara Hill Rd Tiburon CA 94920-1523

PARKER, HARRY S, III
MUSEUM DIRECTOR
b St Petersburg, Fla, Dec 23, 1939. *Study:* Harvard Univ, BA; Inst Fine Arts, NY Univ, MA. *Pos:* Asst to dir, Metrop Mus Art, New York, 63-67, vdir educ, 68-73; dir, Dallas Mus Art, 74-87; dir, Fine Arts Mus San Francisco, 87-05. *Teaching:* Lectr mus educ. *Mem:* Am Asn Mus; Am Fedn Arts; Int Coun Mus; Asn Art Mus Dirs

PARKER, JAMES VARNER
DESIGNER
b Senath, Mo, June 27, 25. *Study:* Phoenix Community Col, AA; Ariz State Univ, BFA & MA. *Work:* Southeast State Teachers Col; City of Phoenix Civic Art Collection; Malaysian Embassy, Washington, DC; Scottsdale Art Collection; Pres Ronald Reagan. *Comn:* Carl Hayden High Sch Student Body, Phoenix, 60; Greater Ariz Savings Bank, Tucson; Heard Mus; Cape Girardeau Pub Libr. *Exhib:* Tucson Art Ctr, 66; Phoenix Art Mus, 66; Stanford Res Inst, Palo Alto, Calif, 66; Yuma Art Asn, Ariz, 70; plus others. *Collection Arranged:* Indian Art Collection, 68 & 72; African Art, Heard Mus, 6/72 & 9/72; Indian Art of the Americas; Missouri Mills, 77; Beckwith Collection, 77; William Faulkner, 80. *Pos:* Cur educ, Heard Mus, 58-68, illusr, 58 & 71, cur art, 68-75; consult adminr, Phoenix Mus Hist, 75-77; mus dir, Southeast Mo State Univ Mus, 77-90, retired. *Teaching:* Instr art, Phoenix Col, 68-70; instr art, Glendale Community Col, 71-72; instr, Southeast Mo State Univ, 76-90. *Awards:* Nat Vet Award, Santa Monica Recreation Dept, 53; O'Brien Art Award, Ariz State Fair, 60; UNICEF Award, 68. *Bibliog:* Design-Crafts-Education (film), KAET TV, Ariz State Univ, 60. *Mem:* Ariz Watercolor Asn (found & pres, 59); Ariz Art Asn (pres & secy, 60); Nat Art Educ Asn; Am Mus Asn. *Publ:* Illusr, The Story of Navaho Weaving, 61; Pima Basketry, 65; The Dennis Collection, Egyptian Antiquities, 79; The Art of Collage, 79. *Mailing Add:* 445 Marie Cape Girardeau MO 63701

PARKER, JONI Y
PAINTER, INSTRUCTOR
b Tokyo, Japan. *Study:* Butler Inst of Am Art, 1972; Kent State Univ. *Work:* Hoyt Inst of Art, New Castle, Pa. *Exhib:* All-Ohio Competition, Canton Art Inst, Canton, Ohio, 1979, 1981, 1984; Midyear Show National, Butler Inst of Am Art, Youngstown, Pa, 1980-1981, 1983-1984, 1998, 2004; Allied Artists Ann, Nat Arts Club, NY, 1982-1983, 1985, 1987, 1990, 2001, 2003-2004; May Show, Cleveland Mus of Art, Cleveland, Ohio, 1983, 1985; Solo Exhibs, Butler Inst Am Art, 1987 & Kent State

Univ 1989; Allied Artists Mem Show, Butler Inst Am Art, Youngstown, Ohio, 2000; Traveling Show, Allied Artists, 2003-05. *Teaching:* pvt instr. *Awards:* Area Artists Ann, Butler Inst of Art, Friends of Am Art, 1980, 1985; All Ohio 2nd Place, All Ohio Competition, Canton Art Inst, 1981; John McCrady Award, Allied Artists of Am Ann, John McCrady Mem Fund, 1983. *Mem:* Allied Artists of Am. *Media:* Oil. *Mailing Add:* 8285 Kincross Dr Boulder CO 80301

PARKER, JUNE
PAINTER
b Bryn Mawr, Pa, 28. *Study:* Student Shelly Fink (drawing), 1970; student Charles Movalli, 1991; student Constance Flavell Pratt, 1995; student Frank Federico, 2000-02. *Comn:* numerous commns for portraits, pvt homes, and landmarks. *Exhib:* Berkshire Art Asn Juried Exhbn, Berkshire Mus of Art, Pittsfield, Mass, 1970; Pittsfield Art Asn Juried Exhbn, Berkshire Mus, 1988; NB Juried Members Show, New Britain Mus of Am Art, New Britain, Conn, 2000-02; Renaissance in Pastel, Slater Meml Mus, Norwich, Conn, 2002-03. *Collection Arranged:* Fox Valley Corp, Appleton, Wis; Berkshire Bank, Pittsfield, Mass; Canaan Nat Bank, Egremont, Mass; Wyantenuck Co Club, Gt Barrington, Mass. *Pos:* chair, Egremont Arts Lottery, Cult Coun, Mass, 88-91. *Teaching:* teacher pastels Art Sch of Berkshires, 2003; instr workshops, Norman Rockwell Mus, Sheffield Art League, Becket Art Center. *Awards:* Dianne Bernhard Silver Medal, Hudson Valley Art Asn, Hastings-on-Hudson, NY, 2001; Award for Excellence, Renaissance in Pastel, Conn Pastel Soc, 2001; Honor Award-Pastel, Acad Artists Asn, Springfield, Mass, 1993; Best of Show Awards Sheffield Art League, Mass, 1992, 2000, 2001, others; 1st Prize Juried Members show, New Britain Mus Am Art, Conn, 2000-02. *Mem:* Acad Artist Asn; Hudson Valley Art Asn; Conn Pastel Soc; Kent Art Asn (Conn); sheffield Art League (Mass); Housatonic Valley Art League. *Media:* Pastel. *Publ:* contbr, Portraits of an Artist, Berkshire Eagle, July 75; contbr, Profile June Parker Artists, Berkshire Courier, Mar 79; contbr-ilus, cover art, Only in Berkshires, Berkshire Courier, 85; contbr, June Parker Artists in Many Media, Berkshire Media Group Publ, Sept 85; ilus, Artwork for Cancer Control Journal, Moffett Cancer Ctr at Univ S Fla, Mar 2003, 2004; contbr, Art & the River (bk), Sheffield Art League, 2004. *Dealer:* Gallery on the Green S Egremont MA 01258; Jack Wood Berkshire Art Gallery. *Mailing Add:* 1 Village Green South Egremont MA 01258-0097

PARKER, NANCY WINSLOW
ILLUSTRATOR, WRITER
b Maplewood, NJ, Oct 18, 30. *Study:* Mills Col, Calif, BA, 52; Art Students League & Sch Visual Arts, NY. *Exhib:* Audubon Artists 29th Ann Exhib, NY, 71; Webb & Parsons, Bedford Village, NY, 76; Master-Eagle Gallery, NY, 80, 83, 85 & 87; Webb & Parsons, New Canaan, Conn, 83; Jane Vorhees Zimmerli Art Mus, Rutgers Univ, NJ, 86; Bay head Hist Soc Mus, NJ, 2004. *Pos:* Art dir, Appleton, Century, Crofts, New York, 68-70; graphic designer, Holt Rinehart & Winston, New York, 70-72. *Awards:* My Mom Travels A Lot, New York Times Ten Best Illustrated Books, 81; Christopher Award, 76 & 81; AIGA Book Show, 76 & 81. *Mem:* Authors Guild. *Media:* Watercolor, Wood. *Publ:* The President's Cabinet (rev), Harper Collins, 91; Barbara Frietchie (Whittier), 92, Working Frog, 92, The Dress I'll Wear to the Party (Neitzel), 92 & Sheridan's Ride (Read), 93, Greenwillow; Money, Money, Money: The Meaning of the Art and Symbols on United States Paper Currency, Harper/Collins, 95; Locks, Crocs and Skeeters: The Story of the Panama Canal, Greenwillow, 96; Land Ho! Fifty Glorious Years in The Age of Exploration with 12 Important Explorers, Harper Collins, 2001. *Dealer:* Webb & Parsons Burlington Vt. *Mailing Add:* 51 E 74th St New York NY 10021

PARKER, OLIVIA
PHOTOGRAPHER
b Boston, Mass, June 10, 41. *Study:* Wellesley Col, BA, 63. *Work:* Victoria & Albert Mus, London; Boston Mus Fine Arts; Mus Mod Art, NY; Art Inst Chicago; Int Mus Photog, Eastman House, Rochester; and others. *Comn:* Photographic Resource Ctr, Boston, 81. *Exhib:* 14 New Eng Photogr, Boston Mus Fine Arts, 78; Loans to the Collection, Art Inst Chicago, 78; One of a Kind Traveling Exhib, Mus Fine Arts, Houston; 20 x 24, Light Gallery, NY, 79; one-person shows, Friends Photog, Carmel, Calif, 79 & 81, Eastman House, Rochester, 81, Mus Art, Univ Ore, 82, Catskill Ctr Photog, Woodstock, 82 & Art Inst Chicago, 82; and others. *Awards:* Artists Found fel, 78; Cert of Excellence, Am Inst of Graphic Arts Bk Show, 79; Ferguson Grant, 81. *Bibliog:* Owen Edwards (auth), The clear Yankee eye, Saturday Rev, 79; Vicki Goldberg (auth), Signs of (still) life, Am Photogr, 79; David Featherstone (auth), Olivia Parker, Mod Photog, 80. *Mem:* Soc for Photog Educ; Friends Photog. *Media:* Photography. *Publ:* Auth, Signs of Life, 78 & contribr, One of a Kind, 79, David Godine; contribr, Darkroom Dynamics, Curtin & London, 79; auth, Under the Looking Glass, New York Graphic Soc, 83. *Mailing Add:* 3901 Elm St Sacramento CA 95838-3614

PARKER, ROBERT ANDREW
PAINTER
b Norfolk, Va, May 14, 27. *Study:* Art Inst Chicago, BAE, 52; Skowhegan Sch Painting & Sculpture; Atelier 17, New York, 52-53. *Work:* Los Angeles Co Mus; Metrop Mus Art; Morgan Libr, NY; Mus Mod Art; Whitney Mus Am Art; plus others. *Comn:* Designer sets, William Shuman Opera, Mus Mod Art, 61. *Exhib:* Brooklyn Mus, 55; Mus Mod Art, 57; Laon Mus, Aisne, France, 56; New Sch Social Res, 65; Sch Visual Arts, NY, 65; and many others. *Teaching:* Instr, Parson Sch Design, 80-85, RI Sch Design, 84 & Pratt Inst, Brooklyn, NY, 85. *Awards:* Rosenthal Found Grant, Nat Inst Arts & Lett, 62; Tamarind Lithography Workshop Fel, 67; Guggenheim Fel, 69-70; plus others. *Mem:* Nat Acad. *Media:* Watercolor, Etching. *Publ:* Illusr, hand-colored ltd ed poems, Mus Mod Art, 62; illusr poetry, The days of Wilfred Owen (film), 66. *Dealer:* Doris Longdale 231 E 60th New York NY 10022. *Mailing Add:* c/o Flinn Gallery Greenwich Library 101 W Putnam Ave Greenwich CT 06830

PARKER, SAMUEL MURRAY
PAINTER
b Madison, Wis, Aug 6, 36. *Study:* Wis State Univ, Eau Claire, BA(art), 63; Univ Wis, MS(painting & drawing, 64, MFA(painting), 65. *Work:* Springfield Mus; Playboy Club; Laura Musser Mus, Muscatine, Iowa; Container Corp Am. *Comn:* Serigraphy, Ill Print Comn, Ill Arts Coun, 73. *Exhib:* Univ Pac Nat Small Painting Show, 71; 3rd Nat Drawing Show, Oshkosh, Wis, 71; New Talent: Midwest USA, Gallery 1640, Montreal, Que, 72; Dong a Ibo Korean Int Print Show, Seoul, 72; Nat Print Invitational, Artists Contemp Gallery, Sacramento, Calif, 73. *Teaching:* Assoc prof painting & drawing, Western Ill Univ, 65-78, prof, 78-. *Awards:* First Prize for Painting, Ill State Fair Show, 72, 25th Ill Invitational, Ill State Mus, 72 & Laura Musser Mus, 73. *Media:* Acrylic Polymer. *Mailing Add:* 216 E Jefferson St Macomb IL 61455-2204

PARKER, WILMA
PAINTER
b Springfield, Mass, 41. *Study:* RI Sch Design, BFA, 63; Art Inst Chicago, MFA, 66. *Work:* Nat Mus Naval Aviation, Pensacola, Fla; Palm Springs Desert Mus, Calif; de Saisett Mus; Laguna Gloria Mus Austin, Tex; Mesa Southwest Mus, Mesa, Ariz; and others. *Comn:* IBM, Tucson, 81; IBM, Poughkeepsie, NY, 85; Sonora Cafe, Los Angeles, 86; Presidental Suite, Fairmont Hotel, Calif, 88; Launch of the Springfield, US Navy, 92; Legacy Painting, Officers Club, Alameda, Calif; US Coast Guard; US Navy. *Exhib:* Salmagundi Club,NY; Lyman Allyn Mus, New London, 92; Nautilus Mus, Groton, Conn, 92; Am Soc Marine Artists, Frye Art Mus, Seattle, 97; Rotunda, House Rep, Washington, DC, 97; Cummer Art Mus, Jacksonville, Fla, 97; Int Soc Marine Artists, Camsen, Maine, 98; Arnold Gallery, Newport, RI, 98; and others. *Collection Arranged:* Palm Springs Desert Mus, Palm Springs, Calif; Yergeau Musee d'Art Int, Montreal, Can; De Saisset Mus, Santa Clara, Calif; Mus Fine Arts, Springfield, Mass; Nat Air and Space Mus, Wash, D.C.; Mesa Soutwest Mus, Mesa, Ariz; Laguna Gloria Mus, Austin, Tex; Springfield Pub Libr, Aston Collection of Wood Engravings, Mass. *Pos:* painter, owner, Wilhelmina Cruz Fine Art, currently. *Teaching:* dean, Clara St Studio Sch, currently. *Awards:* COGAP Award, Salmagundi Club, NY, 94. *Bibliog:* Art Talk, Scottsdale, Ariz, 10/89; Calif Art Rev, 91; Am Artists, Am Ref Publ Group, 91. *Mem:* COGAP; Salmagundi Club, NY; Am Soc Marine Artists; Int Soc Marine Painters; Tailhook Asn. *Media:* Oil on Canvas, Paper, monoprints. *Specialty:* The work of Wilma Parker and Parker Watercolor Artists. *Interests:* Art Hist, Saux Effects. *Collection:* The Marquis of Bath, Longleat House, GB; Embassy of US, Kazalcatan, Lesotho, Bangladesh; USS Wornet, Alameda IBM Corp. *Publ:* Auth, Wilma Parker, an interchange in life, SW Art Mag, 81; Mono No Sono, SF Tea Poetics Soc, 91; Arts & Entertainment, Union News, NH, 10/94. *Dealer:* Arnold Gallery Newport RI; Amsterdam/Whitney NYC. *Mailing Add:* 222 Clara St San Francisco CA 94107

PARKERSON, JOHN E
ART DEALER, GALLERY DIRECTOR
Study: Rice Univ, BA, 60; Univ Va, MA (art hist), 70. *Pos:* vpres, Sotheby's USA, 70-80; head painting dept, Sotheby's Los Angeles, 76-80. *Mem:* cert mem Appraisers Asn Am, Inc (76-); Cult Arts Coun Houston (vpres, 95-). *Specialty:* 19th & 20th century American and European art. *Mailing Add:* Parkerson Gallery 3510 Lake St Houston TX 77098

PARKHURST, CHARLES
EDUCATOR, CURATOR
b Columbus, Ohio, Jan 23, 13. *Study:* Williams Col, BA, 35; Oberlin Col, MA, 38; Princeton Univ, MFA, 41. *Pos:* curatorial asst, Nat Gallery Art, 41-43, asst dir & chief cur, 71-83; Asst to dir, Albright Art Gallery, Buffalo, 45-47; dir, Allen Mem Art Mus, Oberlin Col, Ohio, 49-62 & Baltimore Mus Art, Md, 62-70; co-dir, Williams Col Mus Art, 83-84, actg dir, Graduate Prog Hist Art, 86-87; interim dir, Smith Col Mus Art, 91-92 (dir emer). *Teaching:* Asst prof art & archaeol, Princeton Univ, 47-49; prof hist & art & head art dept, Oberlin Col, 49-62; vis lectr, Univ Minn, Univ Calif, Los Angeles, Johns Hopkins Univ & Univ Wis; vis prof & lectr, Williams Col, 85-92. *Awards:* Chevalier, Legion of Hon, Fr Govt, 47; Ford Found Fel, 52-53; Fulbright Res Fel, Univ Utrecht, 56-57. *Bibliog:* H Matile (auth), Die Farbenlehre PO Runges, Munich, 79; M Kemp (auth), The science of art, Yale Univ Press, London, 90; AE Shapiro (auth), Artists' colors and Newton's colors, Isis, 12/94. *Mem:* Col Art Asn Am (past pres); Intermus Conserv Asn (co-founder & past pres); Asn Art Mus Dirs (past vpres); Am Asn Mus (past pres & founder Accreditation Comn). *Res:* History of scientific color theories in the visual arts; Giotto's color & light; Giotto & sacred theater of his day; Duccio & the tableau vivant 1285. *Publ:* Auth, Aquilonius' Optics and Rubens' Color, Nederlands Kunsthistorisch Jaarboek, 61; coauth (with RL Feller), Who invented the color wheel?, Color Res & Application, 82; Color In Renaissance Painting: Alberti's Place in the History of Color Schemes, JJ Augustin, Locust Valley, NY, 87; Roger Bacon on Color: Sources, Theories and Influence, In: Essays in Honor, WS Heckscher, Italica Press, NY, 90. *Mailing Add:* 33 Dana Pl Amherst MA 01002

PARKHURST, VIOLET KINNEY
PAINTER, WRITER
b Derby Line, Vt, Apr 26, 26. *Study:* Studied at Sch Practical Arts, Boston, 42, Baylor Col, 45, Mus Rio de Janeiro & scholar to Mus Arts, Worcester, Mass. *Work:* Los Angeles Maritime Mus, San Pedro, Calif; Stockholm Mus, Sweden; Kans Mus & seven mus worldwide; also pvt collections of Presidents Nixon, Bush, Reagan & others. *Comn:* History of the Peninsula (painting), Palos Verdes Hist Mus, 97. *Exhib:* Parkhurst on the Sea, Maritime Mus, San Pedro & Toured Europe for the Cult Exchange. *Pos:* Owner, Parkhurst Enterprises Art Galleries, 85-. *Teaching:* Prof emer Jilin Col, Chanchung, 2002. *Awards:* Best in Show, Santa Monica Art Asn, Calif.

Mem: Coast Guard Auxiliary; Elks. *Media:* Acrylic, Oil. *Publ:* Auth, Parkhurst on Sunsets, Walter Foster, 70-; Painting at the Sea Shore, No 122; Painting the Ocean from Slides, No 146; Parkhurst on Seascapes, Art Made Famous, 80. *Mailing Add:* 2300 Daladier Dr Rancho Palos Verdes CA 90275

PARKS, CARRIE ANNE
CERAMIST, EDUCATOR
b Chattanooga, Tenn, Jun 9, 55. *Study:* Wesleyan Col, BFA, 76; apprentice to Takeo Sudo, Mashiko, Japan, 77-78; Va Commonwealth Univ, Richmond, MFA, 81. *Work:* Clemson Univ, Clemson, SC; Rutgers Univ, Camden, NJ; Auburn Univ, Ala; Austin Peay State Univ, Clarksville, Tenn; Saginaw Valley State Univ, University Center, Mich. *Comn:* Ceramic tile murals, Alma Col, Alma, Mich, 87 & 90; Pine Ave Sch, Alma, Mich, 97. *Exhib:* Figurative Clay: Nat Juried Exhib, Ga State Univ, Atlanta, 91; Form from Fragment: Four Contemp Tilemakers, SW Crafts Ctr, San Antonio, Tex, 97; NCECA Clay Nat RJ Stevenson Gallery, San Diego, Calif, 2003; 2nd Cheongju Int Craft Competition, Cheongju Arts Hall, Korea, 2001; Spaces: Interior & Exterior, The Clay Studio, Philadelphia, 2000; Figure/Figurine, Pewabic Pottery, Detroit, 2001. *Teaching:* Adj fac ceramics, Va Commonwealth Univ, Richmond, Va, 81; prof art, Alma Col, Mich, 82. *Awards:* Second Place, Lill Street Gallery, 91; First Place, Wichita Falls Mus, 91; Regional Visual Arts Fel Award, Arts Midwest/Nat Endowment Arts, 93-94; Award of Excellence, Rosewood Gallery, 2002; Special Selection award, Cheongju Arts Hall, Korea, 2001. *Bibliog:* Amy Brower Gleason (auth), 7th Wichita Falls National, Ceramics Monthly, Vol 40, 92; Frank Giorgini (auth), Handmade Tiles, Lark Bks, 94; Kathy Triplett (auth), Handbuilt Ceramics, Lark Bks, 97; Peter King (auth), Architectural Ceramics for the Studio Potter, Lark Bks, 1999; Lynn Peters (auth), Surface Decoration for Low Fire Ceramics, Lark Bks, 1999; Chris Rich (auth), The Ceramic Design Book, Lark Bks, 1998. *Mem:* Nat Coun Educ Ceramic Arts; Am Crafts Coun; Mich Potters Asn; Tile Heritage Found. *Media:* Clay, Pencil. *Dealer:* Ann Nathan Gallery 210 W Superior Chicago IL 60610; Ariana Gallery 119 S Main St Royal Oak MI 48067. *Mailing Add:* 9667 Van Buren Rd Riverdale MI 48877-9707

PARKS, CHARLES CROPPER
SCULPTOR
b Va, June 27, 22. *Study:* Pa Acad Fine Arts, 47-51; Wemy Found Travel Grant, Greece, 65-66, Widner Univ, LHD, 88. *Work:* Del Art Mus, Wilmington; Brookgreen Gardens, Murrells Inlet, SC; Mystic Seaport, Mystic, Conn; Blount Corp, Montgomery, Ala; Amway Corp, Ada, Mich. *Comn:* Boy with Dogs, H B du Pont, Wilmington, Del, 69; James F Byrnes, Byrnes Found, Columbia, SC, 70; Boy with Hawk, Brandywine River Mus, 73; Boy with Gulls, Mystic Seaport Mus, 75; Pres Gerald Ford as an Eagle Scout, Boy Scouts Am, Grand Rapids, Mich, 97. *Exhib:* Nat Sculpture Soc Ann, 62-77; Nat Acad Design, 65-77; six-city tour, Equitable Life Assurance Soc, 76-77. *Pos:* Mem adv comt, John F Kennedy Ctr, 68-; pres, Nat Sculpture Soc, New York, 76-78; trustee, Brookgreen Gardens, SC, 79-. *Awards:* Am Artists Prof League Gold Medal, 70; Nat Sculpture Soc Gold Medal, 71; Watrous Gold Medal, Nat Acad Design, 80. *Bibliog:* Nancy Mohr (auth), The Parks Family, Del Today Mag, 72; Donald M Reynolds (auth), Masters of American Sculpture, 93; Wayne Craven (auth), American Art: History and Culture, 94. *Mem:* Fel Nat Sculpture Soc (pres, 76-78); Pa Acad Fine Arts; Del Ctr for Contemp Arts, Artists' Fel; Nat Acad. *Media:* Cast Bronze, Welded Steel. *Publ:* Contribr, Sights and Sounds of Easter (film), Wilmington Co Churches

PARNESS, CHARLES
PAINTER
b Staten Island, New York, Jan 1, 45. *Study:* Parsons Sch Design, 65; New York Univ, Sch Educ, BS, 66; Pratt Inst Grad Sch, MFA, 69. *Work:* Oakleigh Collection, Pleasantuxle, NY; Reader's Dig, Westchester, NY; Butler Inst, Youngstown, Ohio; Ruhrwest Mus, Wis; Reader's Digest, NY. *Exhib:* one-man shows, GW Einstein Gallery, NY, 94, Univ Wis Art Mus, Milwaukee, 94, Rockport Art Mus, Ill, 95, Vt Wax Works & Mus Store, Manchester, 95, Hebrew Home Aged Riverdale, Bronx, NY, 96 & Rahr-West Mus, Manitowoc, Wis, 97 & Krasdale Gallery, White Plains, NY, 98, Anne Dean Terk Fine Art Center, Kilgore Col, Kilgore, Tex, 2002, Lewallen Contemp Gallery, Santa Fe, NMex, 2004; Positive ID, Southern Alleghenies Mus, Lovetto, Pa, 89; Marian Graves Mugar Art Gallery, Colby-Sawyer Col, NH, 96; Self Relevation: Artist Confrontation, George Sherman Union Gallery, Boston Univ, 98; MB Mod Gallery, NY, 99; Weil Gallery, Tex A&M Univ, Corpus Christi, 2001; Recent Am Portraits; Fischbach Gallery, 2000; Am Acad Arts & Letters, 2001; Nat Accad Art Design; Nat Biennial Watercolor Invitational, Parkland Art Gallery, Champaigne, Ill, 2005; Artful Jesters, The Painting Ctr, NY, 2006. *Teaching:* Vis artist painting, Marie Walsh Sharpe Found, 89-2001; Vt Studio Sch, 91, 93, 2002. *Awards:* Vis Artist Fel, Brandywine Workshop, Philadelphia, Pa, 88; Carnegy Award, Nat Acad, 2002; Purchase Award, Am Acad, 2001. *Bibliog:* Sasha Brodsky (auth), rev, Villager, 3/16/94; Grace Gleuck (auth), rev, NY Observer, 3/21/94; Edmund Lietes (auth), rev, Cover Mag, 5/94; Nicholas Roukes (auth), Artful Jesters, Ten Speed Press; & many others. *Mem:* Artist Equity. *Media:* Oil. *Mailing Add:* 68 Greene St New York NY 10012

PARRA, CARMEN
PAINTER, PRINTMAKER
b Mexico City, Mex, Nov 12, 44. *Study:* Escuela Nac Antropologia e Hist, Mexico City, BA, 64; Acad Belles Artes, Rome, BFA, 67; Esmeralda, 67; Royal Col Art, London, 70. *Work:* Mus de Arte Mod, Mexico City; Univ Nac Autonoma Mex. *Comn:* XIV Anniversary of Tabamex Libr, 84-; Mural Libr of Justice Dept, Mexico City. *Exhib:* Decima Bienal Paris, Mus D'Art Mod, France, 77; Las Ventanas, Mus Art Mod, Mexico City, 79; Mexico de Manana, Mus Bibliot Pape, Monetove, Coahuila, 79; La Creacion Femenina, Kunstler Haus Bethanien, Berlin, 80; Musica y Angeles, Metrop Cathedral Mex, Mexico City, 83; La Catedral de Mexico, Temps Captif, Orangerie in the Sully Hotel, Paris, France; Hojas Transfiguradas, Palacio de Minieria of the Nat Univ Mex, Mexico City, 86; Eternidad de lo Efimero, Mus de Arte Mod, Mexico City, 87; Museo Nacional de la Estampa, 91. *Pos:* Stage & wardrobe designer; film art dir, Frida, Naturaleza Viva, 88. *Awards:* Fiesta Primavera Otono, Mexico City, 81. *Bibliog:* Imagenes (Videotape) Carton y Papel de Mex, 82; La Mujer Mex en el Arte, ed Bacreser, 87. *Mem:* Soc Amigos del Centro Hist de la Ciudad de Mexico; Soc Amigos de la Catedral Metropolitana. *Media:* Acrylic, Oil; Lithography. *Publ:* Illusr, La Grafostatica u Oda a Eiffel, Talleres Graficos Nacion, 78; Tiempo Cautivo, La Cathedral de Mexico, Ed Arvil, 80; De la Pluma al Angel, Ed Nayaqui, 83; Templo Mayor, Ed Multiarte, 83; La Eternidad to lo Efimero, Miquel Angel Porrua, 83; Via Crucis, Multiarte, 91. *Dealer:* Lourdes Chumacero Gallery Estocolmo 34 Mexico DF Mex 06600; Sloane Arcotta Gallery. *Mailing Add:* Primera Cerrada de Galeana 13 San Angel Mexico DF 01000 Mexico

PARRINO, GEORGE
PAINTER, EDUCATOR
b New York, NY, Sept 25, 42. *Study:* Cooper Union Art Sch, BFA, 64; Yale Univ Art Sch, MFA, 70; Acad Fine Art, India, Fulbright Res Fel Painting, 71-72. *Work:* Metrop Mus Art & Guggenheim Mus, NY; Brooklyn Mus, NY; Marion Koogler McNay Art Mus, San Antonio, Tex. *Exhib:* Fac Exhib, Brooklyn Mus, NY, 73; solo exhibs, Ingber Gallery, NY, 74 & 76, Univ Tex, San Antonio, 79; Fulbright Artists, Inst Int Educ, NY, 77; Cubist Syntax in the 70's, Ingber Gallery, 78; Artists' Kites, Danforth Mus, Conn, 78; and others. *Awards:* Residence Fels, Yaddo, 75 & 76. *Bibliog:* Phyllis Derfner (auth), New York letter, Art Int, 1/75; Modris Ramans (auth), George Parrino, Arts Mag, 11/76; Lawrence Alloway (auth), Cubist syntax in the 70's, Nation, 78. *Mem:* Col Arts Asn; Nat Coun Art Adminr; Nat Asn Sch Art & Design; Tex Arts Alliance (bd mem). *Media:* Acrylic. *Mailing Add:* Vis Arts Div State Univ 735 Anderson Hill Rd Purchase NY 10577-1400

PARRIS, NINA GUMPERT
EDUCATOR, PHOTOGRAPHER
b Berlin, Ger, Sept 11, 27; US citizen. *Study:* Bryn Mawr Col, BA (art hist); Woodrow Wilson Fel, 68; Univ Pa, MA (art hist), 69, PhD (art hist), 79; Vt Col Union Inst, MFA (visual arts), 2005. *Exhib:* Cameo Gallery, Univ Vt, Columbia, SC; St Michael's Col, Vt; Colburn Gallery, UVM; Burlington Col; Wood Gallery, Montpellier, VT. *Collection Arranged:* Prints & Paintings in Permanent Collection (auth, catalog), Robert Hull Fleming Mus, 71; The South Carolina Collection of the Columbia Mus Art, 76. *Pos:* Cur, Robert Hall Fleming Mus, Univ Vt, 71-79; chief cur, Columbia Mus Art, 79-90; fac residence visual cult, Vt Col. *Teaching:* Lectr art hist, Philadelphia Col Art, 70-71, Univ Vt, 71-80; lectr mus studies, Univ SC, Columbia, 80-90; fac, MFA Visual Arts, Vt Col, 92-2005. *Awards:* Woodrow Wilson Fel, 68. *Mem:* Am Asn Mus; Col Art Asn; Soc for Photog Educ. *Media:* Photography. *Res:* Late 19th and 20th century art including contemporary art. *Publ:* Prints & Paintings the Collection of the Robert Hull Fleming Mus, 76; Auth, Van de Velde, Obrist, Hoelzel: The Basic Course at the Bauhaus, McMaster Colloquium, 81; The South Carolina Collection, Columbia Mus Art, 86; numerous exhib catalogs. *Mailing Add:* 17 S Union St Burlington VT 05401

PARRISH, DAVID BUCHANAN
PAINTER
b Birmingham, Ala, Jun 19, 39. *Study:* Washington & Lee Univ, Lexington, Va, 57-58; Univ Ala, with Melville Price & Richard Brough, BFA, 61. *Work:* Wadsworth Atheneum, Hartford, Conn; Birmingham Mus Art, Ala; Everson Mus Art, Syracuse, NY; Montgomery Mus Fine Arts, Ala; Tenn Art League, Nashville; Rose Art Ctr, Braindeis Univ, Waltham, Mass; Huntsville Mus Art, Ala. *Exhib:* Southeastern Ann Exhib, High Mus Art, 63, 67-68 & 68-69; Annual Jury Exhibition, Birmingham Mus Art, Ala, 63-71; Butler Inst Am Art, 69; 15th Ann Mid-South Exhib, Brooks Mem Art Gallery, 70; one-man show, Galerie Andre Francois Petit, Paris, 73, Sidney Janis Gallery, 75, Huntsville Mus Art, Ala, 77 & 81, Nancy Hoffman Gallery, NY, 81, Greenville Co Mus Art, NY, 90-95, Louis K Meisel Gallery, NY, 90-95 & 2003 & Westpac Gallery, Victorian Arts Ctr, Melbourne, Australia, 96; New/Photo Realism, Wadsworth Atheneum, Hartford, Conn, 74; Super Realism, Baltimore Mus Art, Md, 75; Some Faces, Louis K Meisel Gallery, NY, 92; Am Realism: The Urban Scene, Selections from the Glenn C Janss Collection Traveling Exhib, Redding Mus & Art Ctr, 93-94; The Detailed Image: Realism Here and Abroad, Harcourts Contemp, San Francisco, 86; Photorealists, Savannah Col Art & Design, Ga, 97; The Photorealists, Ctr for Arts, Holmes Gallery, Vero Beach, Fla, 2000; This is Am, Aarhus Kunstmuseum, Copenhagen, Denmark, 2001. *Awards:* Award of Merit, 23rd Southeastern Ann Exhib, High Mus, Atlanta, 68; Top Award, 61st Ann Exhib, Birmingham Mus Art, 69; Top Award, Mid-South Ann, Brooks Mem Art Gallery, 70. *Bibliog:* John L Ward (auth), American Realist Painting 1945-1980, UMI Res Press, 86; Ann Marie Martin (auth), The World of David Parrish-Huntsville artist transforms ordinary items into vibrant images, Huntsville Times, 5/10/89; Stephanie Hanor (auth), Review of Photorealism since 1980, Tulanian, New Orleans, 93. *Media:* Oil. *Publ:* Ed, The South: A Treasury of Art & Literature, Lisa Howorth, Hugh Lauter Levin Assocs, New York, 93; The Fine Art Index, Vol I, Int Art Reference, Chicago, 94; New art in an old city/2 (essay), Edward Lucie-Smith, Virlane Found & K&B Corp Collections, New Orleans, 94. *Dealer:* Louis K Meisel New York NY 10012. *Mailing Add:* 700 Cleermont Dr SE Huntsville AL 35801-1842

PARRY, ELLWOOD COMLY, III
HISTORIAN
b Abington, Pa, Aug 9, 41. *Study:* Harvard Univ, AB, 64; Univ Calif, Los Angeles, MA, 66; Yale Univ, PhD, 70. *Teaching:* Asst prof, Dept Art Hist & Archaeol, Columbia Univ, 69-75; assoc prof, Sch Art & Art Hist, Univ Iowa, 76-81; prof, Dept Art, Univ Ariz, Tucson, 81-. *Awards:* Nat Endowment Humanities Fel, 75-76;

Huntington Libr Fel, 88. *Mem:* Col Art Asn; Asn Historians Am Art. *Res:* Iconography of American art and the interaction between 19th-century painting, the popular arts, photography, and science. *Publ:* Auth, The Image of the Indian and the Black Man in American Art, 1590-1900, George Braziller, 74; coauth, Reflections of 1776: The Colonies Revisited, Viking Studio, 74; auth, Thomas Eakins's "Naked Series" reconsidered: another look at the standing nude photographs made for the use of Eakins's students, Am Art Journal, vol 20, no 2, 88; The Art of Thomas Cole: Ambition and Imagination, Univ Del Press, 88; Cooper, Cole and The Last of the Mohicans, Papers in Art History, Art and the Native American: Perceptions, Reality and Influences, Vol X, Pa State Univ, 2001. *Mailing Add:* Univ Ariz Dept Art Tucson AZ 85721

PARRY, EUGENIA
WRITER
b July 28, 40, US citizen. *Study:* Univ Mich, with Marvin Eisenberg, BA, 61; Harvard Univ, with Agnes Mongan & Jacob Rosenberg, MA, 63, PhD, 71. *Teaching:* Prof art hist, Wellesley Col, Mass, 68-86 & Univ NMex, Albuquerque, 87-94. *Awards:* Guggenheim Fel, 74; Decorated Chevalier des Palmes Academiques, Fr Gov, 87; Award in lit, Nat Endowment Arts, 93. *Res:* Graphic arts of the 19th century; monotypes of Edgar Degas; early artistic photographers in France, the Calotypists; contemporary photographers. *Publ:* Coauth, The Art of French Calotype, Princeton Univ Press, 83; auth, The Art of a Collector: Henri Le Secq Photographer, Musee des Arts & Decoratifs & Flammarion, 86; The Photography of Gustave LeGray, Univ Chicago Press, 88; contribr, Nuclear Enchantment, Photographs of Patrick Nagatani, Univ NMex Press, 91; Joel Peter Witkin, Centre Nat de la Photog, Paris, 91; and others. *Mailing Add:* 815 E Palace Ave No 16 Santa Fe NM 87501

PARRY, MARIAN
ILLUSTRATOR, PRINTMAKER
b San Francisco, Calif, Jan 28, 24. *Study:* Univ Calif, BA, 46; Contemporaries Gallery, etching & lithography with Michael Ponce de Leon, stone engraving with Ben Shahn. *Work:* Boston Pub Libr Print Collection, Mass; Metrop Mus Art Print Collection, NY; Smith Col Rare Bk Collection; Wellesley Col Rare Bk Collection; Univ Mass Rare Bk Collection, Northampton; Boston Mus Fine Arts Rare Bk Collection. *Exhib:* Boston Visual Artists Union, 74; Cambridge Art Asn, 2001-2003; one-man show, Smith Col Rare Bk Rm, 77 & Wendell St Gallery, Cambridge, Boston Pub Libr Wiggin Gallery, 96; Los Angeles Inst Contemp Art, 78; Matrix Gallery, Provincetown, 93; Cambridge Artists Cooperative, 97, 99, 2001, 2003; Boston Pub Libr 97, 99, 2001. *Teaching:* Lectr, Radcliffe Sem Prog, 74- & Emmanuel Col, 74-; lectr, Lesley Univ. *Awards:* Scholar, Radcliffe Inst, 65-67; Best Illus Bk Award for Birds of Basel, New York Times Bk Panel, 69; One of 50 Bks of the Yr (Birds of Basel), Am Inst of Graphic Arts, 69. *Mem:* Soc Children's Bk Writers; New Eng Authors & Illusrs Children's Bks; New Eng Poetry Soc; Soc Printers. *Media:* Pen and Ink, Watercolor; Printmaking with Linoleum, Xerox Watercolor. *Res:* history of watercolor, waterclor techniques. *Publ:* Auth & illusr, Birds of Basel, Pharos Verlag, 67 & Knopf, 69; Roger & the Devil, Knopf, 72; King of the Fish, MacMillan, 77; I Am a Big Help, Greenwillow, 80; illusr, The Education of a Mouse, Countryman Press, 83; and others. *Dealer:* Wendell Street Gallery 17 Wendell St Cambridge MA 02138; Galerie Caroline Corre 14 rue Guenegaud 75006 Paris France. *Mailing Add:* 60 Martin St Cambridge MA 02138

PARRY, PAMELA JEFFCOTT
LIBRARIAN, ADMINISTRATOR
b New York, NY, Mar 6, 48. *Study:* Univ Ariz, BA, 69; Columbia Univ, MA(art hist & archaeol), 72, MLS, 73. *Pos:* Asst fine arts librn, Columbia Univ, NY, 72-76; ed, Art Reference Collection, 78-82 & Art Doc, 82, 85-86; ed, Art Libr Soc NAm, 78-81, exec secy, 80-83, exec dir 83-93; librn, Int Dada Arch, Univ Iowa, 79-81. *Awards:* Distinguished Serv Award, Art Libr Soc, 00. *Mem:* Visual Resources Asn; Soc Am Archivists; Am Soc Asn Execs; and others. *Publ:* Contribr, From Realism to Symbolism: Whistler and His World, Columbia Univ/Philadelphia Mus Art, 71; auth, Contemporary Art and Artists, 78, Photography Index, 79 & Print Index, 83, Greenwood Press. *Mailing Add:* 3775 Bear Creek Cir Tucson AZ 85749-9454

PARSLEY, JACQUE (CARTER)
COLLAGE ARTIST, GALLERY DIRECTOR
b Memphis, Tenn, Jan 10, 47. *Study:* Louisville Sch Art, Ky, BFA, 80; Univ Louisville, Ky, MA(creative arts), 90; Univ Ky, Lexington, MFA, 94. *Work:* Evansville Mus Arts & Sci, Ind; Alabama Power & Light, Huntsville; US Office Comptroller of Currency, Cincinnati, Ohio; Ky Ctr Arts, Home of Innocents, Benefit Actuaries, Creative Alliance & Hillard Lyons Kentucky Art Collection, Louisville; Owensboro Mus Fine Art, Ky. *Comn:* Collage Assemblage, Home of the Innocents, Louisville, 88; many pvt comms. *Exhib:* Under a Foot, Galeria Mesa, Ariz, 88; Exhib 280 Works on Walls, Hunting Mus Art, WVa; Worlds Women On Line Exhib, United Nations Fourth World Conf, Beijing, China, 96 & Nat Mus Women Arts, Washington, 96; Aspects of Love, Objects of Desire Gallery, Louisville, Ky, 96; Bags & Baggage Nat Competition, New Form/New Function, Arrowmont Sch Arts & Crafts, Gatlinburg, Tenn, 96; two person exhib, Ky Art & Craft Found, 96; River Sticks, Louisville Vis Art Asn, Ky, 97; Exhib 280: Works on Walls, Hunting Mus Art, WVa, 97; Festival of Artisans, Int Exhib with Louisville Sister Cities Prog, Mainz, Ger, 98; Born Again, Art Walk, Atlanta, Ga, 98; Alliance Women Artists 2nd Int Exhib, Ft Mason, San Francisco, 98; one person show, Found Object Assemblages, Chapman Gallery, Shelbyville, Ky, 98. *Collection Arranged:* 50 Local & Regional shows, Bank One Gallery, 80-92; Flowers & Gardens, Louisville Visual Art Asn, 83; Kentucky Baskets, Louisville Craftsman Guild, Kentucky Art & Craft Fedn, 85; Scholastic Art Awards, 85, 86, 87 & 90. *Pos:* Dir, WHAS Gallery, 80-81, Bank One Gallery, 80-. *Teaching:* Adj prof, Univ Ind SE, spring & fall, 95 & spring 96, Univ Louisville, Fiber Dept, spring, 88 & fall, 89. *Awards:* Merit Award, Water Tower Ann, Water Tower Art Asn, 84 & 89; First Place, NY Nat Competition, Amos Eno Gallery, NY, 89; First Place, National Art Competition, Cleveland State Univ, Ohio, 90. *Bibliog:* Lynn Lewis Young (auth), article, Surface Design J, winter 94; Ann Hottelet (auth), Flying Needle, Mag of the Embroiders Guild Am, 2/94; Informed Sources, Surface Design J, fall 95; and many others. *Mem:* Ky Art & Craft Found (bd dir, 82-88); Louisville Visual Art Asn (bd dir, 84-87); Am Crafts Coun, Ky (rep SE Reg Asn 87-90); Surface Design Asn (Ky rep, 91-95); exhib mem, Ky Guild Artists & Craftsmen. *Media:* Collage, Mixed Media. *Publ:* Auth, Avalon Series, Fiberarts Mag, 82; Exposure, Surface Design J, winter 87; Gamut, Cleveland State Univ, Ohio, 90; and many others. *Dealer:* Kentucky Art & Craft Gallery Louisville KY

PARSONS, CYNTHIA MASSEY
PAINTER, WRITER
b Birmingham, Ala, Oct 29, 46. *Study:* Fla State Univ, Tallahassee, with William Walmsley (lithography) & Arthur Deshaies (etching), BA, 68. *Work:* Frederick Co Judicial Ctr, Winchester, Va; William B Bunker Bldg, Redstone Arsenal, Ala; US Olympic Mus, Phoenix, Ariz; Florence Conf Ctr, Ala; Huntsville Mus Art, Ala. *Comn:* President James Davis (painting), Shenandoah Col Conserv, Winchester, Va, 90; Montage of Huntsville, Madison Co Chamber Com, Ala, 96; Pope John Paul II (painting), Archdiocese of NY, 98; Gen Hamilton H Howze (painting), Aviation-Bunker Bldg, Redstone Arsenal, Ala; Sen Howell Heflin (painting), Howel T Heflin Complex, Redstone Arsenal, Ala, 98. *Exhib:* Birmingham Mus Art Ann Exhib, Ala, 68; Ala Contemp Women Artists Exhib, Ala State Coun Arts, Montgomery, 93; Printworks: Images & Words Tell a Story, Mus ETex, Lufkin, 95; one-woman exhib, Kennedy-Douglas Art Ctr, Florence, Ala, 95; 18th Ann Mini Works Exhib, Jacksonville State Univ, Ala, 96; Watercolor Soc Ala Exhib, Birmingham Pub Libr, 96; New Works: Opulence & Frivolity Invitational, Loft Gallery, Huntsville, Ala, 98; Billboard, Mass Mus Contemp Art, North Adams, 99. *Awards:* Ala Outdoor Billboard Prog Grant, Ala State Coun Arts, 93; Proclamation of Recognition of Artistic Contrib, State of Ala Legislature, 97. *Bibliog:* Kathy Holland (auth), Taking Art to the Streets, Ala Arts Mag, Vol III, No 1, Ala State Coun Arts, spring 94; Melissa Ford Thornton (auth), Art for Sake, Hometown Press Mag, Vol 8, No 1, Hometown Press, spring 94; Charles Groover (auth), Artist 2 Artist, Ala Art Monthly, Vol I, Issue 10, Agnes, 4/95. *Mem:* Watercolor Soc Ala (publicity chmn, 95-96); Nat League Am Pen Women; Nat Artist Slide Registry, Washington, DC. *Media:* Oil, Watercolor; Mixed Media. *Res:* Leonardo da Vinci love letters. *Publ:* Illusr, Stars of Alabama-Official Commemorative Poster of Alabama, 175 Years of Statehood, Ala Bureau Tourism & Travel, 94; Pride Runs Deep-Official Coach Gene Stallings, '96 Iron Bowl Poster, 96 & auth/illusr, Impressions-Men's Summer Soccer '96, 96, ArtSouth Enterprises; contribr, Annual Maple Hill cemetary walking tour, Hist Huntsville Quart, Huntsville Hist Found Inc, spring 98; illusr, The unsung heroine & glutenous gofer, Right Road Mag, Vol I, Right Road Ministry, 11/98. *Dealer:* Carlisle Gallery 601 Pratt Ave Huntsville AL 35801; The Loft 1201 Meridian St N Huntsville AL 35801. *Mailing Add:* 412 Newman Ave SE Huntsville AL 35801

PARSONS, MERRIBELL MADDUX
MUSEUM DIRECTOR, CURATOR
b San Antonio, Tex. *Study:* Newcomb Col, BFA; Ecole du Louvre, cert; Inst Fine Arts, NY Univ, MA; Metrop Mus & Inst Fine Arts, dipl(mus training). *Pos:* Bell mem cur decorative arts, Minn Inst Arts, 69 74, chief cur & cur sculpture & decorative arts, 74-79; chmn & curatorial liaison for educ, Metrop Mus Art, 79-80, vice dir, 80-87; dir, Columbus Mus Art, 87-94 & Glen Burnie Found, 94-98; pres, Parsons & Assocs, cons to mus, 98-; adj curator of decorative arts, San Antonio Mus Art, 2004. *Teaching:* adj prof, Inst Fine Arts, NY Univ, 80-87; adj prof, Ohio State Univ, 87-93. *Awards:* Longhi Fel; Ford Found Fel; Nat Endowment Arts Fel. *Mem:* Am Asn Mus; Asn Art Mus Dirs. *Res:* European sculpture, 1600-1900. *Specialty:* Decorative Arts, 1600-1900. *Publ:* Auth, Sculpture in the David Daniels collection, Minn Inst Arts Bull, 69-74. *Mailing Add:* 486 E Olmos Dr San Antonio TX 78212

PARSONS, RICHARD DEAN
PATRON
b NY City, Apr, 4, 48. *Study:* Univ Hawaii, 68; Univ Ala Law Sch, JD, 71. *Hon Degrees:* Adelphi Univer, LLD, 90; Medgar Evers Col, NY City, LLD, 91; Univ Hawaii, LHD, 2003. *Pos:* gen counsel, assoc dir, domestic coun White House, 75-77; partner, Patterson Belknap Webb & Tyler, New York City, 79-88; pres, Chief Operating Officer, Dime Savings Bank NY, 88-90, chmn, Chief Exec Officer, 90-94; dir, Time Warner, 91-, pres, 95-99, Chief Exec Officer, Time Warner Inc, 2002-, chmn, 2003-; co-Chief Operating Officer, AOL Time Warner, Inc, 99-2002; Mus Modern Art, Howard Univ; Met Mus Art. *Awards:* Recipient Distinguished Alumnus Award, Univ Hawaii, 2003. *Mem:* Apollo Theatre Found (chmn, currently); Pres Drug Task Force; Wildcat Serv Orgn, New York City Econ Develop Corp (chmn, currently); NY Zoological Soc (bd dir, currently); Howard Univ, Metrop Mus Art (trustee, currently). *Collection:* Owns winery in Tuscany, Italy. *Mailing Add:* Time Warner Inc 75 Rockefeller Plaza New York NY 10019-6990

PARTIN, ROBERT
PAINTER, EDUCATOR
b Los Angeles, Calif, June 22, 27. *Study:* Univ Calif, Los Angeles, with Clinton Adams, Gordon Nunes & S Macdonald-Wright, BA, 50; Yale-Norfolk Art Sch, fel & study with Conrad Marca-Relli, 55; Columbia Univ, with Andre Racz, John Heliker, Meyer Shapiro, Paul Tillich, MFA, 56; Tamarind Lithography Workshop, Herron Art Sch, fel & study with Garo Antreasion, 63. *Work:* Solomon R Guggenheim Mus Art, NY; Nat Gallery Art, Washington; NC Mus Art, Raleigh; Jonson Gallery, Univ NMex; Weatherspoon Art Gallery, Univ NC. *Exhib:* Whitney Mus Am Art Ann, NY, 63; San Francisco Art Asn Centennial Exhib, De Young Mus, 71; West Hills Col, Coalinga,

Calif, 82; Orange Co Ctr Contemp Art, Santa Ana, 85; Art Angles Gallery, Orange, Calif, 89; McPhee Gallery, Cal Poly, San Luis Obispo, 95; World Works Gallery, Pismo Beach, 96; and others. *Teaching:* Assoc prof art, Univ NC, Greensboro, 57-66; vis assoc prof art, Univ NMex, 63-64; prof art, Calif State Univ, Fullerton, 66-89. *Awards:* Ford Found Purchase Prize, Whitney Mus Am Art Ann, 63; Purchase Award, Viewpoints Five, Colgate Univ, 71; 10 Prints from Tamarind Litho Workshop to Nat Gallery Art, Washington, 84. *Bibliog:* Van Deren Coke (auth), Robert Partin, The Painter and The Photograph, 65; Robert Ewing (auth), Reticence clarified, Artweek, 4/80; Suzanne Muchnic (auth), The valley, Los Angeles Times, 1/81; and others. *Media:* Oil, Pastel. *Dealer:* World Works Gallery PO Box 145 Pismo Beach CA 93448

PARTON, NIKE
PAINTER, ENVIRONMENTAL ARTIST
b New York, NY, June 23, 22. *Study:* Ringling Sch Art, fine art cert; also sculpture with Lesley Posey & painting with Jay Connaway. *Work:* Univ Fla; Stetson Univ; SFla Mus, Bradenton. *Exhib:* One-man shows, Sarasota Art Asn, 69; Art League Manatee Co, 73; Beaux Arts Gallery, Pinellas Park, Fla, 80; Friends Art & Sci, Sarasota, Fla, 86; Golden Apple Gallery, Sarasota, Fla, 91; and others. *Teaching:* Instr painting, Art League Manatee Co, 54-74; instr pvt studio, 63-90. *Awards:* Second Prize, Sarasota Art Asn, 89; Best Show, Fla Suncoast Watercolor Soc, 94; Top Three Winner, Peticoat Painters Show, Leech Gallery, 96. *Mem:* Fla Artist Group; Sarasota Art Asn; Art League Manatee Co; Fla Suncoast Watercolor Soc; Longboat Key Art Ctrs, Fla. *Media:* Watercolor, All Media. *Dealer:* Art Uptown Inc 1367 Main St Sarasota FL 34236. *Mailing Add:* 840 Edgemere Ln Sarasota FL 34242

PARTON, RALF
SCULPTOR, EDUCATOR
b New York, NY, July 2, 32. *Study:* Albright Art Sch, Buffalo, dipl, 53; NY Univ Col, Buffalo, BS(art educ), 54; Columbia Univ, MA(art), 55. *Work:* Civic Ctr, Turlock, Calif; City Hall, Turlock, Calif; Northwestern Mich Col Gallery, Traverse City, Mich; Our Lady of Fatima, Modesto, Calif. *Comn:* Tree of Life (steel sculpture), Beth Shalom Synagogue, Modesto, Calif, 79; and many pvt commissions. *Exhib:* one man show, Galerie de la Maison des Beaux-Arts, Paris, 82, Artists Forum, Los Angeles, Calif, 85; San Francisco Mus Art, San Francisco, Calif, 72; Art Fac Exhib, Calif State Col Stanislaus, Turlock, Calif, 73; Calif State Col Stanislaus Art Fac Exhib, Univ of Pac, Calif, 76; McKissick Mus, Columbia, SC, 88. *Pos:* Dir, Art tours around the world, 90-; tour dir, Art Tours Around the World, 94-. *Teaching:* Chmn dept painting & sculpture, Northwestern Mich Col, 58-62; prof sculpture, Calif State Univ, Stanislaus, 63-96, chmn dept art, 63-70, prof emer, 96-. *Awards:* Horohoe Prize Originality Sculpture, Sisti Gallery, Buffalo, NY, 57; Reynolds Prize Sculpture, Stockton Art Show, Calif, 66. *Bibliog:* David Otth (auth), Monoliths to miniatures, Toy Train Operating Soc Bulletin, Vol 2, No 2; Dr H Werness (auth), Calif Landscapes, catalog, 86; Dictionary of Am Sculptors, 87. *Mem:* Diablo Reg Art Asn; Rossmoor Art Asn (bd trustees). *Media:* Bronze, Vacuum Formed Styrene. *Publ:* Auth, Art lovers tour, Artsline, 1/93; A Professorial Trip, Contra Costa Times, 1/2/94; Mask Making, Rossmoor News, 1/18/95; auth, Parton's Art Tours, Artsline, 11-12/2000, Rossmoor News, 11/15/2000 & Contra Costa Times, 3/11/2000. *Mailing Add:* 1122 Skycrest Dr No 8 Walnut Creek CA 94595

PARTRIDGE, DAVID GERRY
PAINTER, SCULPTOR
b Akron, Ohio, Oct 5, 19; Can citizen. *Study:* Univ Toronto, BA; Queen's Univ, Kingston, Ont; Art Students League; Slade Sch, London; Atelier 17, Paris, with WS Hayter. *Hon Degrees:* DSLitt, Order of Can. *Work:* Tate Gallery, London; Nat Gallery Can, Ottawa; Libr Cong, Washington; Art Gallery Ont, Toronto; Gallery NSW, Sydney, Australia. *Comn:* Nail murals, York Univ, Toronto, 70, Westminster Cathedral, London, 71 & foyer, Toronto City Hall, 77, Bell Trinity, Toronto, 83 & Can Capital Cong Ctr, Ottawa, 83; and others. *Exhib:* Montreal Mus Fine Arts Spring Show, 62; Art of the Americas & Spain, Madrid & Barcelona, 63; Carnegie Int, Pittsburgh, 65; Sculpture '67, Toronto; Art Gallery Windsor, 79; Circa 1996, Toronto, 96. *Teaching:* Art master, Ridley Col, St Catharines, Ont, 46-56; instr art, Queens Univ, Ont, summers 56-60 & Ont Col Art, 74-75. *Awards:* Brit Coun Scholar to Slade Sch, 50-51; Sculpture Prize & Purchase Award, Montreal Mus Fine Arts, 62. *Bibliog:* Kenneth Coutts-Smith (auth), David Partridge, Quadrum, 65; Jim Tiley (auth), Vanguard Vol 2, No 3, David Partridge, Art in Archit, Visual Arts, Ont, 82; Modern Mosaic Techniques/Lovoos Paramoore, David Partridge, Nail Mosaics, Watson Guptill. *Mem:* Fel Royal Soc Arts; Royal Can Acad. *Media:* Acrylic on Canvas; Wood, Nails. *Dealer:* Moore Gallery Ltd 80 Spadina Ave Suite 404 Toronto M5V 2J3 ON Canada; The Russell Gallery Peterborough Ont Canada. *Mailing Add:* 77 Seaton St Toronto ON M5A 2T2 Canada

PARTRIDGE, LOREN WAYNE
EDUCATOR, HISTORIAN
b Raton, New Mex, Apr 11, 36. *Study:* Yale Univ, Ba in Eng Lit, 58; Univ Buenos Aires, Cert in Latin Am Lit, 59; US Army Language Sch, Monterey, Calif, Diploma in Russian, 61; Harvard Univ, MA in Fine Arts, 65; Harvard Univ, PhD in Fine Arts, 69. *Pos:* Reviewer Art Bull, 72, 78, 80, 83, Renaissance Quarterly, 84, 87, 90, 99, Design Book Rev, 87, Master Drawings, 87, Am Hist Rev, 93, Apollo, 96; chmn, dept hist of art, 78-87, 90-93; chmn dept art practice, 2004-. *Teaching:* Teaching, fel Harvard Univ, Cambridge, Mass, 64-66; lectr, Univ Calif, Berkeley, 68, acting asst prof, 69-70, asst prof, 70-76, assc prof, 76-80, prof, 80-; resident, in art hist Am Acad in Rome, 85. *Awards:* Scholar Yale Univ, 1955-58; Fulbright fel, 1958-59, 75; Harvard Univ, 1964-66; Am Acad in Rome fel, 1966-68; grantee Kress Found, 1968-69, 71-72; Univ Calif, 72, 77, 82, 85, 93-94, 99-2000, 2003-2004; Kress fel Inst for Advanced Studies, 1974-75; Guggenheim fel, 1981-92; Getty sr res grantee, 1988-89. *Publ:* Auth: John Galen Howard and the Berkeley Campus: Beaux-Arts Archit in the Athens of the West, 1978, Caprarola, Palazzo Farnese, 1988, (with Randolph Starn) A Renaissance Likeness: Art and Culture in Raphael's Julius II, 1980 (with Randolph Starn), Arts of Power: Three Halls of State in Italy 1300-1600, 1992, The Art of Renaissance Rome, 1400-1600, 1996, Michelangelo: Michelangelo Last Judgment: A Glorious Restoration, 1997; contribr auth: Encycl of Italian Renaissance, 1981, Int Dict Art and Artists, 1990, Dict of Art, 1994; contribr articles to prof jour. *Mailing Add:* U Calif Dept Hist of Art 6020 416 Doe Library Berkeley CA 94720-6020

PAS, GERARD PETER
PAINTER, SCULPTOR
b Valkenswaard, North Brabant, Neth; Can citizen. *Study:* H B Beal Tech Sch, London, Can, Spec Art, 73-74; assisted artist-inventor Murray Favro in Art Fabrication, independent study, 74; L'Abri, Eck En Wiel, Neth, independent study, 75-81. *Work:* De Appel, Amsterdam, Neth; Middelburg Archieven, Rotterdam, Neth; McIntosh Gallery, Univ Western Ont, London, Can; Ont Arts Coun, Toronto, Can; London Regional Art Gallery, Can. *Comn:* The Public Crutch in the Private House, Filmworks Inc, London, Can, 87. *Exhib:* This Is Information, Gallery T'Venster, Rotterdam, The Neth, 80; Solo shows, Päs Plus-Päs Moins, Walter Phillip Gallery, Banff Ctr Arts, Can, 88 & Red-Blue Works, Mercer Union Ctr Contemp Arts, Toronto, 89; Hommage-Demontage, group show, Neve Galerie-Sammlung Ludwig, Aachen, Ger, 88-89; Hommage-Demontage, traveling exhib, Wilheim Hack Mus, Ludwigs Hafen, Ger, 88-89 & Mus Moderner Kunst, Vienna, Austria, 88-89; The Place of Work, traveling exhib, Royal Archit Inst Can, Winnipeg, 89-90. *Pos:* Mem bd dir, Forest City Art Gallery, London, Can, 75-79 & Embassy Cult House, London, Can, 89-91; writer & critic, Art Zien Mag, Amsterdam, Neth, 78-79. *Teaching:* Lectr performance art, Academisch Kunst Institute, Enschede, Neth, 79; instr drawing figure, London Regional Art Gallery, Can, 86-88; prof drawing & painting, Redeemer Col, Ancaster, Can, 89-. *Awards:* Travel Award, Ministry Cult Neth, 79; B Grant Award, Can Coun, 90; Proj Grant, Ont Arts Coun, 79. *Bibliog:* Dr Uli Bohnen (auth), Pas: Less & More-More of Less, McIntosh Gallery, V W O, Can, 87; Linda Genereux (auth), Toronto-Gerard Pas, Art Forum, New York, 89; Dr Graham Birtwistle (auth), Pas: The Modular Ambulant, Ctr Art Gallery-Calvin Col, 91. *Media:* Mixed. *Publ:* Contribr, L'Arte Di Gerard P Päs, Domus Mag, 88; The Living Meridian, Visual Aids London Life/AIDS Comt, 88; Typographie, Rotis Inst, Druckhaus Mack, 88; A Re-invented Object, Can Art, 90; Untitled Legs, Banner Publ, 91. *Mailing Add:* 631 Wallace St London ON N5Y 3R8 Canada

PASCHALL, JO ANNE
PRINTMAKER, LIBRARIAN
b Murray, Ky, Mar 9, 49. *Study:* Memphis State Univ, BFA, 71; Univ GA, MFA, 74; Art Studies Abroad, Cortona, Italy, Dodd-Carnegie scholar, 73-74; Univ Ala, 76-77; Atlanta Univ, MLS, 81. *Work:* Huntsville Mus Art, Ala; Memphis State Univ Collection; Univ Ga Collection. *Exhib:* Eleven Printmakers, Southeastern Ctr Contemp Art, Winston-Salem, NC; Invitational Exhib, Atlanta Artworkers Coalition Gallery, Ga; Invitational Print Exhib, Huntsville Mus Art, Ala; one-person exhib, Memorabilia, Univ Ala Gallery, Huntsville; Inst Prof Femminnile di Stato Gino Severini, da Cortona, Italy. *Pos:* Grad asst printmaking, Univ Ga Art Dept, 73-74; intern, Art for Exceptional Children, Ga Retardation Ctr, 77; cur, Visual Collections, Atlanta Col Art Libr, 78-79, head librn, 79-86; orgn consult, High Mus Art, 83-85; asst dir, Nexus Press, 86-93, dir, 93-. *Teaching:* Assoc instr printmaking, Art Studies Abroad, Cortona, Italy, 74; div head printmaking dept, Univ Ala, Huntsville, 75-77 & Atlanta Col Art, 80-85. *Awards:* Third Place, painting, Tenn All-Artists Exhib, Nashville, 71; Special Purchase Award, Inst Prof Femminnile di Stato Gino Severini da Cortona, Italy, 74. *Mem:* Art Libr Soc NAm; Anarchist Librns Group Am. *Media:* All Media. *Interests:* 20th century; contemporary issues; artists books and publications, bookworks; developed the Atlanta Col Art artists books collection. *Publ:* Contribr, Macmillan Encycl Archits, Macmillan Publ Co, 82. *Dealer:* Heath Gallery 416 E Paces Ferry Atlanta GA 30305. *Mailing Add:* 733 Sherwood Rd Atlanta GA 30324-5279

PASHGIAN, M HELEN
PAINTER, SCULPTOR
b Pasadena, Calif. *Study:* Pomona Col, BA; Columbia Univ; Boston Univ, MA(fine arts). *Work:* Andrew Dickson White Mus Art, Cornell Univ; Security Pac Bank, Los Angeles & Singapore; Seattle First Nat Bank, Wash; Atlantic Richfield Co, Dallas, Tex; Los Angeles Co Mus Art. *Comn:* painting, Home Savings & Loan World Hq, Irwindale, Calif, 88. *Exhib:* Solo exhibs, Stella Polaris Gallery, Los Angeles, 81, Kaufman Galleries, Houston, 82, Modernism Gallery, San Francisco, 83, The Works Gallery, Long Beach, Calif, 87-88, The Works Gallery South, Costa Mesa, Calif, 90, 91 & 92 & Malka Gallery, Los Angeles, 97; San Francisco Mus Art, 69-70; A Plastici Presence, Milwaukee Art Ctr, 69-70; Welton Beckett, Architects, 84; Selections from Security Pacific Bank Collection, Laguna Art Mus, 87; Town Hall, Paris, France, 88; Hotel de Ville Mus, Paris, France, 89; and others. *Pos:* Trustee, Pomona Col, Claremont, Calif, life-term; bd dir, Los Angeles Master Chorale, Los Angeles Music Ctr. *Awards:* Phelan Award, Calif State Painting Exhib, 78; Fel, Nat Endowment Arts, 86. *Bibliog:* Gaye Anne Mueller (auth), Cast Resin Sculpture: Five Los Angeles Artists, 1965-1972, Calif State Univ, 79; (auth), Blowing in the wind, Art News, 3/82; Merle Schipper (auth), Light/energy/radiance: the epoxy paintings of Helen Pashgian, Images & Issues, spring 82; and others. *Media:* Miscellaneous Media; Epoxy. *Mailing Add:* 731 S Grand Ave Pasadena CA 91105

PASKEWITZ, BILL, JR
PAINTER, EDUCATOR
b Brooklyn, NY, Aug 5, 53. *Study:* Cooper Union, with Deborah Remington, BFA, 75; Queens Col, City Univ, New York, with Louis Finkelstein, MFA, 78. *Work:* KUB Res, Irvine, Calif; also pvt collections of Mr & Mrs Herbert Brownell, Laguna Beach, Calif, Mr James Rush, New York, NY, Dr & Mrs Michael Moses, Newport Beach &

Mr Jules Marine, Newport Beach, Calif. *Comn:* Mural, comn by Henry Seger Strom, Costa Mesa, Calif, 86. *Exhib:* Solo exhibs, Contemp Art Gallery, NY, 72, Jacques Seligmann, NY, 78, West Coast Gallery, Newport, Calif, 80, James Turcotte Gallery, Los Angeles, 84, Orange Coast Col, Costa Mesa, Calif, 87 & Merging One Gallery, Santa Monica, 96; NY Painters, Columbus Mus Art, Ohio, 78; Art in Orange Co, Newport Harbor, Newport Beach, Calif, 79; Triton Mus of Art, Santa Clara, Calif, 1998, 2000. *Pos:* Dir, Art Squad, Bayside, NY, 73-75. *Teaching:* Instr printmaking, Newport Harbor Art Mus, 79-81; instr painting, Irvine Valley Col, Irvine, Calif, 79-; adj lectr fine arts, Golden West Col, Huntington Beach, 80-; Visual Arts Dept coord & instr painting, drawing, art hist & art appreciation, Las Positas Col, Livermore, Calif, currently. *Awards:* Harvey Medal, 71, Sch Art League; Gold Metal Scholastic Award in Printmaking, 72; Anna E Meltzer Soc Award for Creativity in Painting, 75. *Bibliog:* Barbara Cavaliere (auth), Newcomers, 9/77 & Bill Paskewitz, 9/78, Arts Mag; Ralph Bond (auth), Texture image diversity, Artweek, 81. *Mem:* Col Art Asn Am. *Media:* Watercolor, Pastel, Oil. *Specialty:* Watercolor, oil. *Interests:* Inspiring through brushstrokes. *Collection:* Armorall, Inc. Los Angeles, Calif; KUB Res, Irvine, Calif; Mr & Mrs R. Altman, NY; Barbara Cavaliere, NY; Mr & Mrs H Brownell, Laguna Beach, Calif. *Publ:* Auth, Art connections, Orange Co Arts Comn, 74; Art in Orange County, Newport Harbor Art Mus, 79; Carving out an artistic lifestyle, Branding Iron, 4/12/84; The why and how of making your own pastels, Inksmith, 9/85. *Dealer:* www.bpaskewitz.com. *Mailing Add:* 115 Hillside Rd Antioch CA 94509

PASQUINE, RUTH
CURATOR, LECTURER
b Newark, NJ, Jan 21, 48. *Study:* Franconia Col, BA, 70; Clark Art Inst, MA, 81; Grad Ctr, City Univ NY, PhD, 2000. *Pos:* Res asst, Nat Acad Design, New York, 86-89; cur educ, Norton Art Gallery, West Palm Beach, 89-91; cur collections, Ark Arts Ctr Little Rock, 91-97. *Teaching:* lectr visual arts, Pulaski Tech Col, 2000; asst prof, gallery dir, Univ Ark, Pine Bluff, 2001-03, Univ Cent Ark, 03-04. *Mem:* Am Asn Mus; CAA. *Res:* American art, 20th century. *Publ:* Poetry in Drawing & Hollis Sigler, Ark Arts Ctr, Little Rock, 96. *Mailing Add:* 1850 S Gaines St Little Rock AR 72206

PASSANTINO, GEORGE CHRISTOPHER
PAINTER, INSTRUCTOR
b New York, NY. *Study:* Art Students League, 48-53. *Work:* Adelphi Univ, Garden City, NY; Metrop Opera Guild, NY; and many others. *Comn:* comn by Hanes Family, Rockefeller, Roosevelt. *Exhib:* Conn Acad Fine Arts, Wadsworth Antheneum, Hartford, 75-76; Audubon Artists, Nat Acad, NY, 76; 49th Ann Exhib, Hudson Valley Art Asn, White Plains, NY, 77; Silvermine Guild, New Canaan, Conn; Stamford Mus, Stamford, Conn; one-man show, Idyllic Impressions, Southport Harbor Gallery, Conn, 2003. *Teaching:* Instr drawing, painting & compos, Famous Artists Sch, Westport, Conn, 57-63, supervisor, 63-74; instr, Univ Bridgeport, Conn, 74-75; instr drawing & painting, Art Students League, 78-; instr, landscape workshops, New York, 91, France, 93 & Vero Beach, Fl; instr, portrait & landscape, Silvermine Guild, New Canaan, Conn, 95 & Valdes, Santa Fe, NMex. *Awards:* Charles Noel Flagg Mem Prize, Conn Acad Fine Arts, 76. *Mem:* Life mem Art Students League; Allied Artists Am. *Media:* Oil, Watercolor. *Publ:* Coauth, Six artists paint a portrait, Northlight, 74; The Portrait and Figure Painting Book, Watson-Guptill, 79. *Dealer:* Portraits Inc 985 Park Ave New York NY 10022; Portrait Brokers of America 36B Church St Birmingham AL. *Mailing Add:* 484A Commanache Ln Stratford CT 06614-8261

PASSLOF, PAT
PAINTER, EDUCATOR
b Brunswick, Ga, 28. *Study:* Queens Col, 46-48, Black Mountain Col, 48; studied with Willem de Kooning, 48-50; Cranbrook Acad Art, BFA, 51. *Work:* Milwaukee Art Ctr & Mus; Corcoran Mus, Washington; Birla Mus, Calcutta, India; Mrs Harry Lynde Bradley Collection; Weatherspoon Mus, Greensboro, SC; Roswell Mus, NM; Maier Mus Art, Lynchburg, Va; and others. *Exhib:* solo exhibs, Circle Gallery, Detroit, Mich, 52, Greene Gallery, NY, 61, Globe Gallery, NY, 62 & 63, Feiner Gallery, NY, 64 & 65, Forrest Gallery, Milwaukee, 1973, Landmark Gallery, NY, 1974 & Elizabeth Harris Gallery, NY, 93, 96, 98, 2000, 02 & 05 & Col Staten Island, NY, 2001; group exhibs; Jack Tilton Gallery, NY, 1989; Figuration 93, 55 Mercer Street Gallery, NY, 1993; Spellbound, Blondies Contemp Art, NY, 1994; Am Acad of Arts & Letters, NY, 1997; Crossing the Threshold (traveling), Steinbaum Krauss Gallery, NY, 1997-98; Material Abstraction, Elizabeth Harris Gallery, NY, 1999; Painting Ctr, 2000; Artist Couples, Katherina Rich Perlow Gallery, 2000; Generation III, 2002; Generation IV, 2003; Black Mt, Reina Sofia Mus, (with catalog), Madrid, 2002-03; 181st Ann: An Invitational Exhib Contemp Art, Nat Acad Mus, NY City, 2006. *Pos:* mem panel, Artlab, Snug Harbor, Staten Island, 2002. *Teaching:* Prof art, Col Staten Island, City Univ NY, 72- & State Univ NY, New Paltz, 73-74; lectr, MFA prog, Brooklyn Col, 2002, NY Studio Sch, 2002; lectr expressionism, panel moderator, Joel Siverstein at ATOA, 2002. *Awards:* Staten Island Coun Arts award; Purchase Award, Hassam Speicker Bells and Symons Fund, 2002; Edwin F Palmer Award, Nat Acad, 2006. *Bibliog:* Joseph Walentini (auth), Pat Passlof at Elizabeth Harris Gallery, Abstract Art Online, 2/15/2005; Ken Johnson (auth), Pat Passlof, NY Times, 3/04/2005; Ben LaRocco (auth), Pat Passlof, Brooklyn Rail, 3/2005; and others. *Media:* Oil on Linen, Gouache and Acrylic on Rag Paper. *Publ:* Gretna Campbell, 4/76, Claire Moore, 12/78 & Arthur Levine, Arts; Nostalgia, Issue 5, winter 86; 1948, Art J, 12/89; Painting, The Painters Series, Green Hill Ctr for NC Art, 2000; Out of the Picture, Milton Resnick - Passlof Remembers, pp 274-312, 3, 02/03. *Dealer:* Elizabeth Harris Gallery 529 West 20th St 6E NY 10011

PASSUNTINO, PETER ZACCARIA
PAINTER, PRINTMAKER
b Chicago, Ill, Feb 18, 36. *Study:* Art Inst Chicago, scholar, 54-58; Oxbow Sch Painting, Mich, summer 58; Inst Art Archeol, Paris, 63-65. *Work:* Walter P Chrysler Mus; Hirshhorn Mus, Washington, DC; Norfolk Mus, Va; Titan Steel Corp; Provincetown Art Asn & Mus; also pvt collections of Joseph H Hirshborn, Walter P Chrysler, Henry Geldzahler and others. *Exhib:* Art Inst Chicago, Ill, 57; Corcoran Gallery Art, Washington, DC, 74; one-man exhibs, The White Room, Belg, 81, Yvonne Seguy Gallery, NY, 82 & 84, Fordham Univ at Lincoln Ctr, NY, 86, Terne Gallery, NY, 86, Pike St Art Ctr, Pt Jervis, NY, 91, Lakin Jones Gallery, Omaha, Nebr, 96 & Nat Arts Club, NY, 99; AIR Invitational Exhib, NY, 83-84; Trisolini Gallery, Ohio Univ, Athens, 84; Expressionism an Am Beginning, Provincetown Art Asn & Mus, RI, 85; Kisker Gallery, Scottsdale, Ariz, 86; Daedal Fine Arts, Fallstown, Md, 88; Frankel Estate, Mus Contemp Art, Chicago, Ill, 88; Arts Club of NY, 99; Broome St Gallery, NY, 99. *Pos:* Chmn, Momentum, Chicago, 57-58. *Teaching:* Instr, Rutgers-Livingston Col, Bayonne Jewish Community Ctr, NJ & Greenwich Art Soc, Conn. *Awards:* Fulbright Fel, 63-64; Guggenheim Fel in Graphics, 71; Nat Endowment Arts Grant, 83. *Bibliog:* Articles in Art News, summer 76 & 9/84, Art in America, 5/75 & 9/84, Soho News, 4/76 & 3/79, Arts Mag, 3/76 & 6/76. *Mailing Add:* 530 La Guardia Pl New York NY 10012

PASTINE, RUTH
PAINTER, LECTURER
b New York, NY, Dec 10, 64. *Study:* SUNY Col Purchase, 82-84; Cooper Union for Advan Sci & Art, BFA, 87; The Rietveld Akademie, Amsterdam, 87-88; Hunter Col, City Univ of NY, MFA, 93. *Exhib:* Group Exhib, Metrop Mus Art, NY, 82; Nat Arts Club Ann Exhib, NY, 87; East Meets West, Claremont Grad Univ, Calif, 96; Presentational Painting II, Bertha & Karl Leubsdorf Art Gallery, NY, 97; Current Expressions in Contemp Art, TIAA/CREF, NY, 97; Sudden Incandescence, Bemis Ctr for Contemp Arts, Omaha, Nebr, 99; Abstraction & Immanence, Hunter Col Times Sq Gallery, NY, 2001; Monochrome/Monochrome?, Florence Lynch Gallery, NY, 2001; Solo exhibs, Arc Paintings, Houghton Gallery, Cooper Union, NY, 87, Diffusion Paintings, Times Square Gallery, Claremont, Calif, Ray Paintings: Blue-Orange-Violet, Brian Gross Fine Art, San Francisco, 98, New Paintings, Quint Contemp Art, La Jolla, Calif, Numinous Duochrome, Yellow Magenta-Violet Paintings, Bentley Gallery, Scottsdale, Ariz. *Teaching:* asst prof painting, Hunter Col, New York, 92-93; guest artist & lect, Dept Art, UCLA, Los Angeles, 4/96; vis prof, Ariz State Univ, Phoenix, 11/97. *Awards:* Alexander Medal, Metrop Mus Art Hon Awards, 82; Grumbacher Artist Award, 86; Elizabet Found for Arts Grant, 99. *Bibliog:* Robert L Pincus (auth), Color Guard: Ruth Pastine Revels in the Art, San Diego Union Tribune, 4/1/99; Kenneth Baker (auth), Paintings Colored by Illusion, San Francisco Chronicle, 8/12/2000; Ken Johnson (auth), Ruth Pastine, NY Times, 10/6/2000; Ken Johnson (auth), Abstraction and Immanence, Hunter Col, Times Square Gallery, NY Times, 3/23/2001. *Media:* Oil. *Dealer:* Margaret Thatcher Projects 529 W 20 St New York NY 10011; Haines Gallery 49 Geary St San Francisco CA 94108. *Mailing Add:* 11225 Creek Rd Ojai CA 93023

PASTOR, JENNIFER
SCULPTOR
b Hartford, Conn, 1966. *Study:* Sch Visual Arts, New York, BFA, 88; Univ Calif, Los Angeles, MFA(sculpture), 92. *Exhib:* Invitational 93, Regen Projs, Los Angeles, 93; Surface De Reparation (with catalog), FRAC Bourgone, Dijon, France, 94; Richard Telles Fine Art, Los Angeles, 94; solo exhibs, Richard Telles Fine Art, Los Angeles, 94, Studio Guenzani, Milan, 95, Mus Contemp Art, Chicago, 96 & Mus Contemp Art, Los Angeles, 96; Universalis (with catalog), 23rd Biennial, Sao Paulo, Brazil, 96; Contrafigura, Studio Guenzani, Milan, 96; Sunshine & Noir: Art in Los Angeles 1960-1997 (with catalog), Los Angeles Mus Mod Art, Humbleback, Denmark, 97; Biennial Exhib, Whitney Mus Am Art, NY, 97; Present Tense, Mus Mod Art, San Francisco, 97; New Work: Drawing Today, San Francisco Mus Mod Art, 97. *Awards:* Louis Comfort Tiffany Grant, 95. *Bibliog:* Mario Cutjar (auth), rev, LA Weekly, 2/7-13/97; Dennis Dahlquist (auth), rev, Expressen, Stockholm, 4/12/97; Brooks Adams (auth), Turtle derby, Art Am, 6/97. *Mailing Add:* c/o Richard Telles Fine Art 7380 Beverly Blvd Los Angeles CA 90036

PATERNOSTO, CESAR PEDRO
PAINTER, SCULPTOR
b La Plata, Buenos Aires, Arg, Nov 29, 31; US citizen. *Study:* Nat Univ La Plata, Sch Fine Arts, 57-59, Inst Philos, 61. *Work:* Mus Mod Art, NY; Nat Fine Arts Mus, Buenos Aires; Albright-Knox Gallery, Buffalo; Hirshhorn Mus, Washington; and others. *Exhib:* The 1960's, Mus Mod Art, NY, 67; one-man shows, Dusseldorf, WGer, 72, NY, 73, Paris, 74 & Tokyo, 82; Painting Since WWII, Guggenheim Mus, NY, 87; Am, Bride of the Sun, Royal Fine Arts Mus, Antwerp, Belg, 92; Lat Am Artists of Twentieth Century, Mus Mod Art, NY, 93; and others. *Awards:* Guggenheim Fel Painting, 72; Pollock-Krasner Found Grant, 90; Gottlieb Found Grant, 91. *Bibliog:* Sam Hunter (auth), The Cordoba biennial, Art Am, 4/67; Lucy R Lippard, Overlay, 83; Barbara Braun (auth), Pre-Col Art in Post-Col World, Abrams, 93. *Media:* Acrylic & Oil on Canvas; Cast Cement, Wood. *Publ:* Auth, Piedra Abstracta, Mexico-Buenos Aires, 89; English translat, The Stone and The Thread, Univ Tex Press, 96. *Mailing Add:* 135 Hudson St New York NY 10013

PATERSON, ANTHONY R
SCULPTOR, EDUCATOR
b Albany, NY, Dec 17, 34. *Study:* Sch of Mus Fine Arts, Boston, dipl & grad dipl; study with Harold Tovish, Ernest Morenon, Peter Abate; La Grande Chaumiere Sch Drawing, Paris; Mass Inst Technol, welding; Univ Guadalajara, Mex. *Work:* Rose Art Mus, Brandeis Univ, Waltham, Mass; Univ Art Gallery, Univ Pittsburgh, Pa; San Bernardino Fine Arts Mus, Calif; Eastman Sch of Music, Rochester, NY; Juliard School of Music, NY. *Comn:* Portrait of Seymour H Knox (bronze torso), comn by Buffalo Found, 78-79, life-size portrait of Charles Darwin, Centennial Conf on Darwin, 82; portrait of composer Samual Adler, 94; Univ Rochester, Rochester, NY; Phillipe Elliot, Univ Buffalo, Buffalo, NY; Gregory Jarius, Astronaut, Univ Buffalo 1993. *Exhib:* NAm Sculpture Exhib, Denver, Colo, 86, 88 & 90; Dimensions 88--3D

Art Show, Lenexa Ann Nat, Kans, 86, 88 & 90; 63rd Ann Nat Exhib, Nat Acad Design, NY, 88; solo exhib, Andrews Gallery, William & Mary Col, Williamsburg, Va, 88; Metal Media, Sawtooth Ctr Visual Arts, Winston-Salem, NC, 90; and others; The Am Way, Mobile Mus of Art Invitational Exhib, 2002-04. *Pos:* Restorer 1968-2003. *Teaching:* Instr sculpture, Sch Mus Fine Arts, Boston, 62-65 & Mt Ida Jr Col, Newton, Mass, 64-68; assoc prof sculpture & head of sculpture, State Univ NY, Buffalo, 68-2003; dir, Casting Inst, Univ Buffalo, 2003; prof emer, 2003-. *Awards:* Festival Award, Three Rivers Art Nat Festival, 89 & 90; Elliot Lisken Award for Sculpture, Audubon Artists Nat Soc, 89; Acad Artist Asn Nat Award, Springfield, Mass, 90. *Mem:* Artists Comt, Buffalo; Nat Sculpture Soc Can, NY; Int Sculpture Soc, Washington; N Am Sculpture Soc, Denver, Colo. *Media:* Metal, Cast. *Res:* Connections: A study of the interrelatedness of native american art and architecture of the North American continent, 98. *Interests:* Restoration, photography, archaeology. *Publ:* auth, Portrait Sculpture: Contemporary Points of View, Univ Buffalo publ, 83. *Mailing Add:* 530 Norwood Ave Buffalo NY 14222-1319

PATINA, REY
COLLAGE ARTIST, SCULPTURE, LECTURER
b Newark, NJ, Jan 14, 62. *Study:* Harvard Univ, BA, 74; Rutgers Univ, MA 82. *Hon Degrees:* Harvard Univ, LLD, 74. *Exhib:* One woman show, Paper & Collage Exhib, NJ, 99, Collage Mess, Artist Gallery World, NY, 2001, Sculpture Art, Peanut Gallery, Mich, 2003, Art Exhib, Jimbo World Gallery, 2005; Seashore Exhib, 17th Ann Seashore Arts & Crafts Show, LBI Gallery, 2000. *Pos:* Cur, Long Beach Island Gallery, NJ, currently; collage artist, currently. *Teaching:* Teacher am hist, John P Stevens High Sch, Edison, NJ, 85-88; asst prof hist, Rutgers Univ, New Brunswick, NJ, 88-94; prof am art, Rowan Col, NJ, 96-. *Awards:* third place prize, Paper & Collage Exhib, Raritan Ctr Arts & Craft Exhib, NJ, 2000; Best of Show, 15th Ann Sculpture & Collage Exhib, Surf City, NJ, 2001; NJ State Fel Award, 98, 99 & 2003. *Mem:* Guild of paper makers (bd dir, currently); Am Artist Asn; Nat Collage & Sculpture Asn; Am Women's Artist Asn. *Media:* Paper, Clay & Sand. *Res:* Ocean depth and the coral reefs. *Specialty:* Collage of Flowers, fish and other pretty scenes. *Interests:* Sailing, Snorkeling and travel. *Collection:* Disney and other cartoonist portraits. *Dealer:* Peanut Gallery 1111 Sissy Dr Newport RI 22222. *Mailing Add:* 151 W Park St Lee MA 01238-1714

PATKIN, IZHAR
PAINTER, SCULPTOR
b Israel, 55; US citizen. *Study:* Corcoran Sch Art, Washington, BFA, 79; Whitney Independent Study Prog, New York, 79-80. *Work:* Mus Mod Art, Brooklyn Mus, Whitney Mus Am Art, Solomon R Guggenheim Mus, NY; Contemp Mus, Honolulu, HI; Mus Contemp Art, Los Angeles; Ringling Mus Art, Sarasota, Fla; Palais Liechtenstein, Vienna; and others. *Comn:* Don Quixote (monument), VMS, NY, 88. *Exhib:* Solo exhibs, Holly Soloman Gallery, NY, 83-85, 87 & 89-90, 93-94 & 98, Winnipeg Art Mus, Manitoba, Can, 88, John & Mable Ringling Mus Art, Sarasota, Fla, 89, Stedelijk Mus, Amsterdam, 90, Venice Bianale, 90, Kalisher Five, Tel Aviv, Israel, 91 & Blancpain Stepozynski Galerie d'Art, Contemporain, Geneva, Switz, 92, Holly Solomon Gallery, NY, 93, 94, 98; Biennial, Whitney Mus, NY, 87; AnniNovanta: The Nineties, Galleria Comunale d'Arte Mod, Bologna, Italy, 91; Rope, Fernando Alcolea Gallery, Barcelona, Italy, 91; Das Goldene Zeitalter(with catalog), Wurttembergischer Kunstveren Stuttgart, Ger, 91; Am Art Today: Surface Tension (with catalog), Art Mus Fla Int Univ, Miami, 92; Walls, Windows, Doors, Holly Solomon Gallery, NY, 93; Masters of the Masters: MFA Faculty of the Sch of Visual Arts, NY, 1983-98; Butler Inst Am Art (catalog), Youngstown, Ohio, 98; Remix, Holly Solomon Gallery, NY, 98, 99; and others. *Teaching:* Sch Visual Arts, NY. *Awards:* Fel, Nat Endowment Arts, 87. *Bibliog:* Robert Morgan (auth), Walking through spaces (uptown and downtown), Cover, 5/94; Margaret Moorman (auth), Izhar Patkin at Hooly Solomon, Art News, 9/94; Julie V Louine, One artist's porcelain period, NY Times, Home Section, 4/30/98. *Media:* Acrylic, Oil; All

PATNER, ANDREW
CRITIC, WRITER
Study: Univ Chicago; Univ Wis, Madison. *Teaching:* Lectr and teacher in Chicago and Eastern Europe. *Awards:* Recipient Peter Lisagor award. *Mem:* The Cliff Dwellers, Asn of Literary Scholars and Critics; Chicago Art Critic Asn; Arts Club Chicago (co-chmn,interarts coun, currently). *Publ:* Former editor, staff writer Chicago Mag; staff reporter Wall St Jour; former art critic. program host, producer WBEZ-FM, critic-at-large, interviewer WFMT Fine Art Radio, contrib Chicago Sun-Times, 91-, contrib editor Art & Antiques, The Art Newspaper (London), The New Yorker, German GEO, Jewish Forward, New Art Examiner, Die Opernwelt, The Christian Science Monitor, High Performance, and other publications; auth: IF Stone: A Portrait, 88; editor: Alternative Futures: Challenging Designs for Arts Philanthropy, 95; dir: "Democratic Vistas: Towards a New Am Arts Policy", Columbia Col Chicago sponsored by John D and Catherine T. MacArthur Found. *Mailing Add:* 2175 W Leland Chicago IL 60625

PATNODE, J SCOTT
EDUCATOR, MUSEUM DIRECTOR
b Seattle, Wash, Oct 19, 45. *Study:* Gonzaga Univ, AB, 68; Pratt Inst, fel, 68, MFA, 70; also with George McNeil, Walter Rogalski & Clare Romano. *Work:* Cheney Cowles Mem Mus, Spokane; Kalamazoo Inst Arts, Mich; Evergreen State Col, Olympia, Wash; Pac Nat Bank of Wash, Seattle; Honolulu Acad Art, Hawaii. *Exhib:* Hawaii Nat Print Exhib, Honolulu Acad Art, 71 & 73; CCAC World Print Competition, San Francisco Art Mus, 73; New Generation Drawings Exhib, circulated by Western Asn Art Mus, 73-75; 59th Ann Exhib Northwest Artists, Seattle Art Mus, 74; Gov Invitational, 78; Northwest Juried Art, 83; Cheney Cowles Mem Mus, Spokane, Wash, 83. *Pos:* Dir, Ad Art Gallery, Gonzaga Univ, 71-94, Jundt Art Mus, 95-. *Teaching:* Prof art, Gonzaga Univ, 70-, chmn dept art, 79-82. *Awards:* Print Purchase Award, Honolulu Acad Art, 71; Fremont Lane South Award for Painting, Spokane Art Mus, 72. *Mem:* Am Asn Mus. *Mailing Add:* Jundt Art Mus Gonzaga Univ East 502 Boone Ave Spokane WA 99258-0001

PATNODE, MARK WILLIAM
PAINTER, DESIGNER
b Ilion, NY, Apr 29, 56. *Study:* State Univ New York, Purchase, BFA, 78. *Work:* The Price of Freedom, New London Harbor, Julia "Susette Kelo's House". *Exhib:* Neuberger Mus, 78, Lyman Allyn Art Mus, New London, Conn, 89, Artist Sees New London, 91; Conn Open, Real Art Ways, Hartford, Conn, 95; Faber Birren Nat Color Award Show, Stamford Art Asn, Conn, 95, New London Art Soc, 99; Chelsea Groton Savings, mindsisland.com; Latin Views, Conn, 2006. *Collection Arranged:* Mitchell Col, New London, Conn. *Pos:* CT Comn on Cult & Tourism, Master Teaching Artist; Adjunct Prof, painting on the beach, Mitchell Col; 2 hon mentions MAC; Selected for int artist res cu (Bulgaria); Urban Artists Initiative Fel Grantee; CT Comn on Cult & Tourism Award, residencies to VT Studio Ctr; mem Am/Bulgarian Exchange. *Bibliog:* United States Submarines, Hugh Lauter Levin, 2002. *Mem:* Mystic Art Asn elected (assoc); Lyme Art Asn (assoc). *Media:* Oil, Watercolor, Drawing, Pastel. *Interests:* Weight training, sking. *Collection:* Chelsea Groton Bank, Mitchell Col; Radek Assocs, Babson Capital. *Publ:* Auth, Art Folio; Am Artist Mag. *Dealer:* www.mindsisland.com. *Mailing Add:* 33 Granite St New London CT 06320-5944

PATRICK, ALAN K
CERAMIST, PAINTER
b Richmond, Ind, June 16, 42. *Study:* Ball State Univ, with Byron Temple, BS, 64, MA, 66. *Work:* Ball State Univ Art Gallery; Earlham Col & Richmond Art Mus, Ind; Minnetrista Cul Ctr, Muncie, Ind; City of Muncie, Ind. *Comn:* Painting, Minnetrista Cult Ctr, Muncie, Ind, 96; painting, Alltrista Corp, Muncie, Ind, 97. *Exhib:* Hoosier Salon, Indianapolis, 90-2006; Ind Artist Club Juried Exhib, Indianapolis, 92-2006; The Bethel Pike Pottery: The First Thirty Yrs, Minnetrista Cult Ctr, 96; Eds Ltd Gallery, Indianapolis, 96; Richmond Art Mus, Ind, 98-2005. *Awards:* Best of Show, Hoosier Salon, Indianapolis, Ind, 91-; Best of Show, Minnetrista Regional Exhib, Muncie, Ind, 92-; Best Landscape, Hoosier Salon, Indianapolis, Ind, 92-; Best of Show, Ind Artists Club, Indianapolis Mus Art, 2000. *Bibliog:* Kathleen R Postle (auth), Bethel Pike Pottery, Spinning Wheel, 6/79; Gerry Williams (auth), Conversations with Indiana Potters, Studio Potter 19:2, 6/91; Ned H Griner (auth), The Bethel Pike Pottery, the First Thirty Years, Minnetrista Cult Found Inc, Muncie, Ind, 96. *Mem:* Hoosier Salon; Ind Heritage Arts; Ind Artists Club. *Media:* Stoneware, Porcelain; Oil. *Collection:* McGraw Hill Publ, NY, Driehaus Capital Mgt, Chicago, Ill, First Merchants Corp, Muncie, Ind; Ball State Univ, Muncie, Ind; Richmond Art Mus, Richmond, Ind. *Dealer:* Gordy Fine Arts, Muncie, Ind; Patrick Gallery, Albany, Ind. *Mailing Add:* 5809 E Pottery Rd Albany IN 47320

PATRICK, DARRYL L
HISTORIAN
b Havre, Mont, Oct 5, 36. *Study:* Northern Mont Col, BS, 62; Univ Wash, MA, 70; N Tex State Univ, PhD, 78. *Teaching:* Instr art hist, Factory of Visual Arts, Seattle, Wash, 69-71; Assoc prof, Sam Houston State Univ, Huntsville, Tex, 71-79, dir dept art, 78-84, asst prof, 79-80 & prof, 91-. *Mem:* Col Art Asn. *Res:* Late 19th century Europe, 19th and 20th century American art. *Mailing Add:* Sam Houston State Univ Dept Art Huntsville TX 77340

PATRICK, GENIE HUDSON
PAINTER, INSTRUCTOR
b Fayetteville, Ark, Nov 25, 38. *Study:* Miss State Col Women, 56-58; Univ Ga, BFA, 60; Univ Ill, Urbana-Champaign, 60-61; Univ Colo, MA, 62. *Exhib:* Walker Ann, Minneapolis, 66; Mid-Miss Invitational, Davenport Munic Art Gallery, 79; two-man exhib, Drawing & Painting, Coe Col Galleries, Cedar Rapids, Iowa, 71, Laura Musser Mus, Muscatine, Iowa, 72 & 77, Fine Art Ctr, Univ Mo-Columbia, 75 & Myers Fine Art Gallery, State Univ NY, Plattsburgh, 76; and others. *Pos:* Fel-in-Residence, Huntington Hartford Found, Pacific Palisades, Calif, summer 64. *Teaching:* Instr art, Northeast Miss Jr Col, Booneville, 62-64; instr art, Radford Col, Va, 64-65; instr children's art classes, Cedar Rapids Art Ctr, Iowa, 65-70; instr drawing & painting, Univ Iowa Exten, 74-, instr drawing, Sch Art & Art Hist, Univ Iowa, Iowa City, 74 & 80. *Media:* Oil, Drawing. *Mailing Add:* 1190 E Court St Iowa City IA 52240-3232

PATRICK, JOSEPH ALEXANDER
PAINTER, EDUCATOR
b Chester, SC, Feb 10, 38. *Study:* Univ Ga, BFA, 60; Univ Colo, Boulder, MFA, 62. *Work:* Keokuk Art Asn, Iowa; Luther Col, Iowa; SDak Mem Art Ctr, Brookings; Laura Musser Mus, Muscatine, Iowa; Univ Mo Alumni Collection, Columbia. *Exhib:* One-man shows, Augustana Col, SDak, 72, Univ Iowa Mus Art, 73, Iowa State Univ Design Ctr, Ames, 74, Kans State Univ, Manhattan, 75, Northwest Mo State Univ, Maryville, 77 & Friends Gallery, Minneapolis Inst Arts, Minn, 77; and others. *Pos:* Mus asst, Univ Ga Mus Art, Athens, 58-60. *Teaching:* Asst art, Univ Colo, Boulder, 60-62, instr drawing & painting, 61-62; instr & head dept, Northeast Miss Jr Col, Booneville, 62-64; instr, Radford Col, 64-65; instr, Univ Iowa, 65-68, asst prof drawing & painting, 68-71, assoc prof drawing, 71, head dept drawing, 79-. *Awards:* Residence Fel, Huntington Hartford Found, 64; Summer Fac Fel, 69 & Fac Grants, 73, 77 & 78-79, Univ Iowa Found. *Mem:* Mid-Am Art Asn; Col Art Asn Am. *Media:* Oil, Watercolor. *Mailing Add:* 1190 E Court St Iowa City IA 52240-3232

PATTERSON, CLAYTON IAN
SCULPTOR, VIDEO ARTIST
b Calgary, Alta, Oct 9, 1948. *Study:* Univ Alta, BEd, 73; Nova Scotia Col Art, BFA, 77. *Work:* Brooklyn Mus, NY; New York Pub Libr; Libr Cong, Washington; Rutgers Mus, New Brunswick, NJ; Flint Mus, Mich; Matt Dillon, also pvt collections of Mick Jagger & Jack Nicholson. *Exhib:* Sacred Artifacts and Objects of Devotion,

Alternative Mus, NY, 82; Works on Paper, NC Mus, Greenville, 84; Australian Invitational Traveling Print Show, 84-85; Works on Paper, Bronx Mus, 85; Tiffany Collection, Brooklyn Mus, 85; Beauty and the Beast, Pratt Inst, NY, 85; Am Collections Pvt & Publ, Brooklyn Mus, 86; Rock and Roll Hall of Fame Archives, 95; and others. *Teaching:* Instr art, Alta Col Art, 78. *Awards:* Justice Orgn Award, 92; Manhattan Cable Access Awards, 92; Manhattan Neighborhood Network Proj Grant, 95; and others. *Bibliog:* Richard Merkin (auth), The discreet charm of the baseball cap, Gentleman's Quart, 89; Mark Rose (auth), Top hat, New York Press, 91; Richard Kostelanetz (auth), Dictionary of the Avant-Gardes, A Cappella Books, 93. *Mem:* Tattoo Soc New York (pres). *Media:* All. *Publ:* Lower East Side, New York (video), 87-88; Tompkin Square Park Police Riot (video), 88. *Dealer:* Arborite Art 161 Essex St New York NY 10002-1507. *Mailing Add:* Prince St Sta PO Box 103 New York NY 10012-0103

PATTERSON, CURTIS RAY
SCULPTOR, INSTRUCTOR
b Shreveport, La, Nov 11, 44. *Study:* Grambling State Univ, BS, 67; Ga State Univ, MVA, 75. *Comn:* mild steel, Atlanta Rapid Transit Authority, 78; David Franklin Assoc, Atlanta, 89; Roy Wilkins Bond, St Paul, Minn, 92; Rapid Transit, Cleveland, Ohio, 94; Hartsfield Int Airport, Atlanta, Ga, 99. *Exhib:* Thirty-five Artists in the SE (contribr, catalog), High Mus Art, Atlanta, Ga, 76; 35 Artists in the SE Traveling Show, 77-78; Festival of Arts & Cult, Lagos, Nigeria, 77; Fourteen Sculptors, High Mus Art, Atlanta, 77; Nexus Contemp Art Ctr, Atlanta, Ga, 93; Middle Tenn State Univ, 94; Spaces Gallery, Cleveland, Ohio, 96. *Pos:* Vpres, Thirteen Minus One, 76-77. *Teaching:* Teacher sculpture & pottery, Therrell High Sch, Atlanta, 70-76; instr sculpture, Atlanta Col of Art, 76-. *Awards:* City Atlanta Bur Cult Affairs Award, 93; Fulton Co Arts Coun Award, Atlanta, 93; Nat Endowment Arts, 94-95. *Mem:* Black Artist of Atlanta; Thirteen Minus One. *Media:* Metal, Clay. *Mailing Add:* 1091 Flamingo Dr SW Atlanta GA 30311

PATTERSON, PATRICIA
FILM CRITIC, PAINTER
b Jersey City, NJ, Mar 17, 41. *Study:* Parson's Sch of Design, grad cert. *Exhib:* Houston Mus Contemp Art, Tex, 77; La Jolla Mus Contemp Arts, Calif, 78; Inst for Art & Urban Resources, PS1, NY, 78; Cleveland Mus Art, Ohio, 78; Fine Arts Gallery, Univ Calif, Irvine, 78; and others. *Pos:* Contrib writer, Film Comment Mag, New York, 75-. *Teaching:* Asst prof painting, drawing & art criticism, Univ Calif, San Diego, 76-. *Media:* Casein, Enamel; Watercolor. *Publ:* Coauth, Werner Herzog, The cinema of Fata Morgana, 75 & The new breed of filmmakers: A multiplication of myths, 75, City Mag; auth, Fassbinder, 75 & coauth, Gun crazy--Part II, 76 & Beyond the new wave: I (Kitchen without Kitsch), 77, Film Comment; auth, Aran kitchen, aran sweaters, Heresies, 78. *Dealer:* Ellie Blankfort Gallery 2341 Ronda Vista Dr Los Angeles CA 90027. *Mailing Add:* 467 La Costa Levcadia CA 92024

PATTERSON, SHIRLEY ABBOTT
PAINTER, INSTRUCTOR
b Buffalo, NY, Dec 13, 23. *Study:* Albright Sch Fine Art, Buffalo, NY, dipl, 44; New York State Univ, Buffalo, BS(art educ), 45. *Work:* E I Dupont deNemours & Co, Del Trust Co, Sun Oil Co & Blue Cross-Blue Shield, Wilmington, Del; Widener Col Mus, Chester, Pa; State Del Div Libr, Dover. *Exhib:* Regional Art Echib, Univ Del, Newark, 75-77, 79 & 81; Regional Art Exhib, Del Art Mus, Wilmington, 75, 78-79 & 81; Am Watercolor Soc, Nat Acad Galleries, NY, 79; Pa Soc Watercolor Painters, Harrisburg, 79 & 85; Ky Watercolor Soc, Louisville Water Tower Mus, 80-81; Mattatuck Mus, Waterbury, Conn, 90, 91; Conn Women Artists, New Haven, Conn, 91; solo exhib, S Windsor Pub Libr, 91. *Collection Arranged:* Mid-Atlantic Regional Exhib Collage, Univ Del, 79; Charter Oak Temple Annual Exhib, Hartford, Conn, 91. *Pos:* Juror, Delaware Camera Club, 86, 87, 88; Radio Talks, WXDR, 86, 87, 88; WDEL, 76, 79, 81. *Teaching:* Instr art, Griffith Inst Cent Sch, Springville, NY, 45-46; critic instr art, Kenmore Pub Sch, NY, 46-49; instr art, privately, 58-70. *Awards:* Artist of the Year, Hotel DuPont, Wilmington Christmas Comt, 76; First Prize, Del State Biennial, Nat League Am Pen Women, 77, 79, 81, 83 & 85. *Bibliog:* Lise Monty (auth), feature in Sunday News J, 4/8/79; article in Artists register, Del Artline, 7/79; Delaware Artists Series (slides), Univ Del, 83, 86. *Mem:* Nat League Am Pen Women, Diamond State Branch (pres, 78-80); Studio Group Inc, Wilmington, Del (pres, 78-80); Pa Watercolor Soc; Ky Watercolor Soc. *Media:* Watercolor, Mixed Media. *Mailing Add:* 15 Wedgewood Ln South Windsor CT 06074

PATTI, TOM
SCULPTOR
b Pittsfield, Mass, 43. *Study:* Pratt Inst Sch Art & Design, BID, 67, Grad Sch Art & Design, MID, 69; New Sch Social Res, with Rudolph Arheim, 69. *Work:* Metrop Mus Art & Mus Mod Art, NY; Toledo Mus Art, Ohio; Kunstmuseum Dusseldorf, WGer; Victoria & Albert Mus, London. *Comn:* Plastics Technol Ctr, Gen Elec Plastics Genic Doron Divider (atrium), 84; Gen Elec Co, Plastics Group Awards Comn, 86. *Exhib:* Art & Relig, Vatican Mus, Rome; Mex-NAm Cult Inst, Mexico City, 82; Recent Aquisitions: Archit & Design, Mus Mod Art, NY, 79; New Glass: A Worldwide Survey, Corning Mus Glass, 79. *Awards:* Nat Endowment Arts, 79; 1st Prize, Glaskunst 81, Kassel, WGer. *Media:* Glass. *Publ:* Auth, articles, Neues Glas, 3/81 & Art News, summer 81. *Dealer:* Ute Stebich Gallery 69 Church St Lenox MA 01240. *Mailing Add:* Tom Patti Studios 10 Federico Dr Pittsfield MA 01201

PATTON, ANDY (ANDREW) JOHN
PAINTER
b Winnipeg, Man, Feb 25, 52. *Study:* Univ Man, BA, 72. *Work:* Nat Gallery Can, Ottawa; Art Gallery Ont, Toronto; Univ Lethbridge, Alta. *Exhib:* Fifth Bienniale Sydney (with catalog), Art Gallery New SWales, Australia, 84; Toronto Painting 84 (with catalog) & Art Gallery Ont, 85, Toronto; Fire & Ice (with catalog), Gallery Walcheturm, Zurich, 85; Late Capitalism (with catalog), Harbourfront, Toronto, 85; Allegorical Image (with catalog), Agnes Etherington Arts Ctr, Kingston, Ont, 85; Songs of Experience (with catalog), Nat Gallery Can, Ottawa, 86; Day After Day: A Wall Painting, Winnipeg Art Gallery, Winnipeg, 92; The Whole Light of the Sky, Oboro, Montreal, 94; and others. *Teaching:* Painting instr, Univ Western Ont, London, 95-. *Awards:* Canada Coun B Grants, 84 & 85. *Bibliog:* David Craven, (auth), Toronto, Bomb Mag, NY, Spring, 88; Myron Turner (auth), The Indescribable Blueness of Being, Border Crossings, Winnipeg, spring 93. *Mem:* YYZ Artists Outlet (bd mem, 82-); Independent Artists Union. *Media:* Oil on Canvas, Oil on Linen. *Publ:* Auth, Poems and Quotations, Four Humours Press, 75; The Real Glasses I Wear, A Space, Toronto, 81; Civil space, Parachute Mag, Montreal, 83; Buchloh's history, C Mag, Toronto, 85; coauth, The Interpretation of Architecture (exhib catalog), YYZ, Toronto, 86; Sorrow at the End of the Canal, Stride Gallery (exhib catalogue), 90; No Communication between the living and the dead (in Wanda Koop, exhib cat), Southern Alberta Art Gallery, Lethbridge, 92; Introduction to the Introduction to Wang Wei, Brick Books, 2000. *Mailing Add:* 243 Macdonell Ave Unit 2 Toronto ON M6R 2A9 Canada

PATTON, KAREN ANN
PAINTER
b New York, NY, Oct 27, 37. *Study:* studied with Wolf Kahn, Nat Acad of Art, New York, 2000, Polly Hammett, AWS, Skip Lawrence, AWS, Glen Bradshaw, AWS, 99. *Work:* Watercolor Olympus Corp of Am. *Comn:* Watercolor, Am Automobile Asn, Garden City, NY, 85. *Exhib:* HTAL Open Juried Show, Heckscher Mus, Huntington, NY, 81 & 85; Nassau Co Mus Fine Arts, Roslyn, NY, 88; 57th Treasury Gallery, St Augustine Art Asn, 03; Atlantic Ctr Art, Harris House, New Smyrna Beach, Fla; Ormond Beach, Fla, 2004; Ormond Mem Mus & Gardens, Ormond Beach, Fla, 2006; Casements, Ormond Beach, Fla, 2006. *Pos:* also art judge/juror & teacher, Plantation Bay, Ormond Beach, Fla. *Awards:* Award of Excellence, Malverne Artists of Long Island, 83, Art League Nassau Co, 85; Grumbacher Silver Medal, Tri-Co, 88; Best of Show, Artists Workshop, New Smyrna Beach, Fla; Award of Merit, Island Art, St. Augustine, Fla, 2006. *Bibliog:* Malcolm Preston (auth), articles in Newsday, 83 & 85; Laura Stewart (auth), News Journal, 2003. *Mem:* Plein Aire Painters; Daytona Beach Art League; Plein Air Fla. *Media:* Watercolor, Pastel. *Interests:* plein air painting. *Publ:* The Best of Flower Painting, 12/96, North Light Publ. *Dealer:* Rachel Thompson Gallery St Augustine Fla; Metropolitan Gallery Ormond Beach Fla. *Mailing Add:* 91 Bridgewater Ln Ormond Beach FL 32174

PATTON, SHARON FRANCES
ART HISTORIAN, MUSEUM DIRECTOR
b Chicago, Ill. *Study:* Roosevelt Univ, BA(studio art) with Don Baum, 66; Univ Ill, Urbana, MA, 69; Northwestern Univ, (African art) with Frank Willett & Ivor Wilks, PhD(art hist), 80. *Work:* Print, Black Am Art Collection, Johnson Publ Co, Chicago. *Exhib:* Contemp Afro-Am Arttists, Lake Forest Col, 72; Traditional Forms & Modern Africa: W African Art at the Univ MD, Col Park (auth, catalog), 83, E-W Contemp Am Art, Calif Afro-Am Mus Los Angeles (auth Catalog), 84; The Decade Show Studio Mus New Mus Contemp Art, 90; Home: Contemp Urban Images by Black Photogrs, Studio Mus in Harlem, NY, 90; Memory & Metaphor, Art of Romare Bearden (traveling exhib) The Studion Mus in Harlem, 91; African Art: A Celebration, Univ Mich Mus Art, 93; Ralph T Coe Collection of African Art; Treasures, Allen Art Mus, 2002; Nat Mus African Art, 2004. *Collection Arranged:* Contemporary Afro-American Artists, Lake Forest Col, 72; Traditional Forms & Modern Africa: West African Art at the Univ Md, College Park (auth, catalog), 83; East-West Contemp Am Art, Calif Afro-Am Mus, Los Angeles (auth catalogue), 84; The Decade Show, Studio Mus New Mus Contemp Art, 90; Home: Contemp Urban Images by Black Photographers, Studio Mus in Harlem, NY, 90; Memory & Metaphor, Art of Romare Bearden, (traveling exhib) The Studio Mus in Harlem, 91; African Art: A Celebration, Univ Mich Mus Art, 93. *Pos:* Mem Collections Comt, Baltimore Mus of Art, 83, 84; dir, The Art Galleries, Montclair State Univ, 86-87; chief cur, The Studio Mus in Harlem, NY, 88-91; John GW Cowels dir, Allen Mem Art Mus Oberlin Col, Ohio, 98-; dir, Ctr for Afroamerican and African Studies, 1996-98; mem adv bd, Nat Mus African Art, Wash, 2000-, dir, 2003-; mem adv. board, Nat Mus African Art, Wash, 2000-; dir, 2003-; African Am Advisory Committee, Cleveland Mus of Art, 2001-2003. *Teaching:* Instr, Mankato State, Minn, 68-70 & Lake Forest Col, Ill, 71-72; asst prof art hist, Va Commonwealth Univ, Richmond, 72-73; instr, African-Amm & African art, Univ Houston, 76-79; asst prof, African art hist, Univ Md, Col Park, 79-85; assoc prof art hist, Univ Mich, Ann Arbor, 91-98; prof art Oberlin Col, 1998-2000. *Awards:* FAC Rsch fel Smithsonian, 85; Outstanding Academic Book African Art Award, Choice Mag, 98. *Mem:* African Studies Asn; Arts Coun African Studies Asn; Nat Conf Artists; charter mem African & African-Am Hist Soc; Art Table; Leadership Cleveland, 2000. *Res:* Sub-Saharan west Africa, especially Asante; African art as Political & Prestige emblem; antebellum Louisiana African-American art; Contemporary African American Art. *Publ:* auth, Asante umbrella, African Arts, 84; Vincent D Smith, Riding on a Blue Note, Louis Abrons Art Ctr, 90; auth, Andebellum Louisiana artisans, Int Rev African Am Art, 95; Sharon Patton (auth), Home: Contemp Urban Images by Black Photogr, Studio Mus, 90; Sharon Patton (auth), Memory & Metaphor, Art of Romare Beardon, Oxford Press, 91; Sharon Patton (auth) African Am Art, Oxford Univ Press, 98; Treasures, 2004; Romare Bearden, Narrations, Neuberger Mus, 2002; Emma Amos, Art Matters, NICA Journal of Contemp Art, 2002. *Mailing Add:* Nat Mus African Art Smithsonian Instn MRC 708 PO Box 37012 Washington DC 20013-7012

PATTON, TOM
PHOTOGRAPHER, CURATOR
b Sacramento, Calif, May 17, 54. *Study:* San Francisco Art Inst, BFA, 76; Univ NMex, MA, 77, MFA, 82. *Work:* San Francisco Mus Mod Art; Australian Nat Gallery, Canberra; St Louis Art Mus; Oakland Mus, Calif; Art Mus, Univ NMex, Albuquerque; and others. *Exhib:* Recent Acquisitions, San Francisco Mus Mod Art, 79; Highlights:

Aspects of the Collection, Mus Photog Art, San Diego, 85; The Isolation & Intrusion Series, Developed Image, Adelaide, Australia, 85; New Landscapes (auth, catalog), Tasmanian Sch Art & Australian Ctr Photog, Hobart, Sydney, Australia, 85; Night Light: A survey of 20th century night photog (traveling exhib), Nelson-Atkins Mus Art, Kansas City, Evansville Mus Art, Ind, Lowe Art Mus, Coral Gables, Fla, 89; Kansas City Art Inst, 94; Technol Cult, Erie Art Mus, 98; Feed, San Francisco Camerawork Gallery, 98; Snapshot, Contemp Mus, Baltimore, Md, 2000. *Collection Arranged:* New Views: Landscape Photographs From Two Continents, Univ Mo, St Louis, 86. *Teaching:* Instr photog, Skidmore Col, Saratoga Springs, NY, 82-83; prof photog, Univ Mo, St Louis, 83-, dept chair, dir, Gallery 210, 84-86; vis lectr, Univ Tasmania, Australia, 85. *Awards:* Visual Artists Fel, Nat Endowment Arts, 90-91. *Bibliog:* James Jacobs (auth), Prelude 1976, Artweek Mag, 1/31/76; Joan Murray (auth), Books: The individual and history receive recognition, Artweek, 9/15/79; Michael Costello (auth), Space invaders, Afterimage (visual studies workshop), Rochester, NY, 4/9/80. *Mem:* Soc Photog Educ. *Media:* Digital Imaging. *Mailing Add:* Art Dept Univ Mo 8001 Natural Bridge Rd St Louis MO 63121

PAUL, ART(HUR)
DESIGNER, PAINTER
b Chicago, Ill, Jan 18, 25. *Study:* Art Inst Chicago, 41-43; Inst Design, Chicago, 46-50. *Comn:* Playboy Magazine. *Exhib:* Kunstverein Munchen, Munich, WGer, 72, mus des Art Decoratifs, Lausanne, Switz, 72, Lowe Mus Art, Coral Gables, Fla, 73, Munic Art Gallery, Los Angeles, 74, NY Cult Ctr, 74, Columbia Col, 81 & Bowling Green Univ, 88; traveling exhibs, Beyond Illus-the Art of Playboy, Royal Col Art, London, 71, The Art of Playboy-the First 25 Yrs, Chicago Cult Ctr, 78; Chicago Art Inst, Betty Rymer Gallery, 92; one-man shows, Chicago Cult Ctr, 97-98 & Parkland Col, Ill, 98; group show, The Manuscript Illuminated, Columbia Col, Chicago, Ctr for Book & Paper Arts, 2001; NY Art Directors Club Mus, 2002. *Pos:* Self-employed freelance designer, 50-53; art dir, Playboy Mag, 53-82, vpres corp art & graphics dir, Playboy Enterprises, Inc, 78-82. *Teaching:* Guest lectr mag design & illus, Art Inst Chicago, 78, Syracuse Univ, NY, 79, summer designers course 83 & hon teacher, Tokyo Design Sch, Japan, 81, Art Center, Pasadena, 86 & Univ Ill, Chicago, 87. *Awards:* Trademark, Soc Typographic Arts, 64; Gold Medal, City Milan, Italy, 72; Polycube Award, Art Dirs Club Philadelphia, 75; Gold Medal, Poster Design, NY Acad Club, 80; IIT Alumni Assoc Professional Achievment Award, 83; Art Directors Hall Fame, 86; The Soc Publ Designers Herb Lubalin Award fir Lifetime Achievment, 2006; Gov Appointment Charter Trustee to Ill Summer Sch the Arts, 6 yr term, Post Playboy. *Bibliog:* Sarah Bodine (auth), Contemporary Designers, 90; Mark Hawkins-Dady (auth), Contemporary Master Work, 91; Koichiro Inagaki (auth), Visual Identity in Chicago, 91; Aomando Milani (auth), A Double Life of 80 Agi Designers (Creativity and Sense of Humor), 96; The Art (Paul) of Playboy, Print Mag, Jan-Feb/2000. *Mem:* Alliance Graphique Int; Mus Contemp Art (bd trustees, 71-86); Am Ctr Design; NY Art Dir Club. *Media:* Acrylic, Mixed. *Interests:* Prismacolor. *Publ:* The high art of low art, Print Mag, 72; The world of work: An artists-design view, In: National Art Education Association Career Education Handbook, Purdue Univ; Vision, Art Paul, Japan Publ, 81; The Art of Playboy, Alfred Van Dermark Publ, 85; 1950s-60s Transition of Modern Typography Europe & America, 96; Sex Appeal: The Art of Allure in Graphic and Advertising Design (edited by Steven Heller), 2000; auth, Graphis # 353, 2005. *Mailing Add:* 175 E Delaware Pl Chicago IL 60611

PAUL, BILL See Paul, William D, Jr

PAUL, KEN (HUGH)
PRINTMAKER, PAINTER
b Ogden, Utah, Apr 24, 38. *Study:* Univ Utah, 58-59; Univ Wyo, BA(with honors), 61, MA, 65. *Work:* Art Gallery SAustralia, Adelaide; Univ Ore Mus of Art, Eugene; Portland Art Mus, Ore; Cheney Cowles Mus, Spokane, Wash. *Comn:* Translucent painting, Adelaide Arts Festival, 67; ceiling panel restoration, Sacred Heart Chapel, Geelong, Australia; Directors' Print Portfoloio, Northwest Print Coun, Ore, 92. *Exhib:* First Springfield Col Nat Print Exhib, Mass, 65; Denver Art Mus Nat Show, 65; Calif Soc Printmakers Ann, Richmond, 71; Seattle Print Int, 71; Ore Artists Ann, Portland, 72-73 & 75; one-man show, Cheney Cowles Mus, Spokane, 79; Univ Ore Mus Art, Eugene, 81; Ore State Univ, Corvallis, 94. *Teaching:* Lectr art, Gordon Inst Technol, Geelong, 66-67; lectr printmaking, SAustralian Sch Art, Adelaide, 67-69; assoc prof printmaking, Univ Ore, 70-; vis instr, M I Kerns Art Ctr, Eugene, Ore, summer 71; vis instr, Pac Northwest Graphics Workshop, Cheshire, Ore, 74; vis assoc prof, Univ Calgary, Alta, 89. *Awards:* Prize for Painting, Ore Col Educ, Monmouth, 72; Graduate Sch Summer Res Grant, Univ Ore, 73 & 83; Purchase Award, Printmakers Ore, 75. *Mem:* NW Print Coun (bd/secy, 82-). *Media:* All Print Media; Oil, Acrylic. *Mailing Add:* 3837 Potter St Eugene OR 97405

PAUL, RICK W
SCULPTOR
b 45. *Study:* Univ Fla, Gainesville, BFA, 67; Pa State Univ, Univ Park, MFA, 69. *Work:* McDonalds Corp, Chicago, Ill; Blakley Corp, Ind State Mus, Young & Laramore, Mansur Develop Corp & Indianapolis Art League, Ind; Univ NDak, Grand Fork; Miami Univ, Oxford, Ohio; Owensboro Mus Fine Art, Ky; plus numerous others in pvt collections. *Exhib:* Ohio & Indiana Artists & Viewpoints 1980, Cranbrook Acad Art, Detroit, Mich, 81; solo exhibs, Huntsville Mus Art, Ala, 87, Ft Wayne Mus Art, Ind, 89, Shepherd Col, Shepherdstown, WVa, 89, Portland Sch Art, Orem 89, Patrick King Contemp Art, Indianapolis, Ind, 91, Gallery uno, Univ Nebr, Omaha, 94, Artlink, Ft Wayne, Ind, 94, Albion Col, Mich, 98, Purdue Univ, Lafayette, Ind, 99; Computer Artists Invitational, Augusta Col, Ga, 88; Ann Marie LeBlanc and Rick Paul, Eastern Ky Univ, Richmond, Ky, 89; Curator's Choice, Northern Ind Arts Asn, Munster, 89; Sculpture Invitational, Greater Lafayette Mus Art, Ind, 91; Group Exhib, Wabash Col, Crawfordsville, Ind, 94; plus many others. *Pos:* Vis artist & speaker at numerous Univs & orgns, 81-89. *Teaching:* Asst prof art, Eastern Ky Univ, Richmond, 69-74; assoc prof art & design, Purdue Univ, W Lafayette, Ind, 74-; co-instr, Univ Mich, Ann Arbor, 86; computer workshop, Huntsville Mus Art, Ala, 87; lectr, Univ Mass & Augusta Col, Ga, 88; computer graphics workshop, Wabash Col, Ind, 94. *Awards:* Individual Artist Fel, Ind Arts Coun, 87; Master Fel Sculpture, Nat Endowment Arts, 90; Creative Endeavors Fel, Purdue Univ, 97. *Bibliog:* Stephen Sylvester (auth), Dialogue, Columbus, Ohio, 87; Sharon L Calhoon (auth), New Art Examiner, Chicago, Ill, 90; Carl Brentengani (auth), Dialogue, Columbus, Ohio, 94; plus many others. *Dealer:* Patrick King Contemp Art Inc 427 Massachusetts Ave Indianapolis IN 46220-1610. *Mailing Add:* Purdue U Div Arts & Science 701 W Stadium Ave Purdue University IN 47907-2045

PAUL, WILLIAM D, JR
PAINTER, PHOTOGRAPHER
b Wadley, Ga, Sept 26, 34. *Study:* Atlanta Col of Art, BFA; Univ Ga, AB & MFA; Emory Univ; Ga State Col; Univ Rome, Italy. *Work:* General Mills, Inc, Minneapolis; Hallmark Cards, Kansas City, Mo; Little Rock Art Ctr, Ark; Univ Ga, Ga Mus Art, Athens; Kinsey Inst, Univ Ind; and others. *Exhib:* Va Intermont Col, Bristol; Birmingham Ann, Ala; Corcoran Gallery Art, Washington, DC; Art of Two Cities, Nat Traveling Exhib, Am Fedn Arts; USA-Volti del Sud, Palazzo Venezia, Rome, Italy; solo shows, Gasperi Gallery, New Orleans, La, 93 & Contemp Arts Ctr, New Orleans, La, 94; and many others. *Collection Arranged:* Sixty small original exhibs, Charlotte Crosby Kemper Gallery, Kansas City Art Inst, 61-65; Art of Two Cities, Am Fedn Arts Traveling Exhib, 65; The Visual Assault, 67, Drawings by Richard Diebenkorn, Selections: The Downtown Gallery, Drawing and Watercolors by Raphael Soyer, Recent Collages by Samuel Adler, 20th Anniversary Exhibition & Art of Ancient Peru, The Paul Clifford Collection, Ga Mus Art; American Painting: the 1940's, 68; American Painting, the 1950's, 68; American Painting: the 1960's, 69; Philip Pearlstein, Retrospective Exhibition (auth, catalog), 70; Alice Neel, Retrospective Exhib (auth, catalog), 75; and many others. *Pos:* Dir exhibs & cur study collections, Kansas City Art Inst, 61-65; cur, Ga Mus Art, 67-69; dir, Ga Mus Art, 69-80. *Teaching:* Instr art & art hist, Kansas City Art Inst, 59-64; asst prof, Univ Ga, 65-69, assoc prof, 69-97, prof, 97-; prof, Gen Sandy Beaver, 2000-03. *Awards:* Macy's Ann, Kansas City, 59, 61, 63 & 64; Atlanta Paper Co Ann, 61; Hallmark Award, Mid-Am Ann, 62; Outstanding Undergrad Mentor Award, Univ of Ga; and others. *Bibliog:* Michael McLeod (auth), Portrait of a daring artist, The Orlando Sentinel, 6/16/91; Peek Photographs from the Kinsey Institute, Arena Editions, 2000; and others. *Mem:* Am Fedn Arts (trustee, 69-80); Col Art Asn; Southeastern Mus Conf; Am Asn Mus; Arts Festival Atlanta (vpres, 82-85). *Media:* Collage, Installation; Painting. *Res:* Gender identity issues in visual arts. *Interests:* constitutional rights, censorship, ecosystem protection. *Publ:* Auth foreword, Alice Neel, Harry N Abrams, 83; and others. *Dealer:* Independent Gallery 4900 Barnett Shoals Rd Athens GA 30605. *Mailing Add:* 150 Bar H Ct RR 9 Athens GA 30605

PAULEY, EDWARD E
ADMINISTRATOR
b Huntington, WVa. *Study:* Marshall Univ, BFA; OH Univ, MFA in painting. *Pos:* Dir educ, Huntington Mus Art, WVa; exec dir Black Mountain-Swannanoa Ctr for Arts, NC, Cult Ctr Fine Arts, Parkersburg, WVa; pres, Chief Exec Officer, Plains Art Mus, Fargo, ND, 2003-. *Teaching:* instr, Marshall Univ, Huntington, Univ NC, Asheville. *Mailing Add:* Plains Art Mus 704 1st Ave N Fargo ND 58102

PAULOS, DANIEL THOMAS
PRINTMAKER, WRITER
b Sioux City, Iowa, Dec 16, 49. *Study:* Studied paper-cutting under Sister Mary Jean Dorcy; studied iconography under Robert Lentz; studied oil painting under Grieg Chapian; studied calligraphy under Sister M DeLourdes Bragg. *Work:* La Salle Univ Fine Art Mus, Philadelphia, Pa; Billy Graham Sacred Art Mus, Wheaton, Ill; Biblical Arts Mus, Dallas, Tex; Libr Contemp Art, Vatican. *Comn:* Profile-portrait, Cardinal Cooke Guild, 87; paper-cuts illustrating book, He's Put The Whole World in Her Hands; paper cut, Santa Maria de la Paz Church, Santa Fe, NMex, 92; granite etched designs, St Mary's Prayer Garden, Pueblo, Colo, 93. *Exhib:* Butler Inst Am Art, Youngstown, Ohio; Biblical Arts Mus, Dallas, Tex; Villanova Univ Fine Arts Gallery; Marian Libr, Dayton, Ohio; Billy Graham Sacred Arts Mus, Wheaton, Ill; Paul VI Inst Arts, Washington; El Santuario De Guadlupe, Santa Fe; Visions Gallery, Albany, NY. *Pos:* Dir, St Bernadette Inst Sacred Art. *Awards:* AURA Ann Arts Award, 91; First Place Journalism Award for Best Cover, 93; Juror's Award, Fontbonne Fine Arts Gallery, 96. *Bibliog:* Raymond Carrillo & Daniel Kopald (dirs), A Seeing Heart, 92; Bernadette, 97; Guadalupita, 98. *Mem:* Cath Artists Am; Cath Fine Arts Soc; Asn Uniting Relig & Art; Christians Visual Arts; Escribiente-Calligraphy Soc NMex. *Publ:* Contribr, Spring Comes to the Hill Country, Roman, Inc, 84; He's Put The Whole World In Her Hands, Roman, Inc, 89, Ignatious Press, 93; A Living Love Hurts, Don Bosco Press, Tokyo, Japan, 90; Dio Ha Posto Il Mondo Intero Nelle Mani Di Maria, Vatican Press, 92; Behold The Women, St Bernadette Inst, 97. *Mailing Add:* c/o St Bernadette Inst Sacred Art PO Box 8249 Albuquerque NM 87198-8249

PAULSEN, BRIAN OLIVER
PAINTER, PRINTMAKER
b Seattle, Wash, Mar 29, 41. *Study:* Univ Wash, BA, 63; Wash State Univ, MFA, 66. *Work:* Western Ill Univ; S S Kresge Inc, Detroit, Mich; Wesleyan Univ, Lincoln, Nebr; Kemper Insurance Co, Ill; Sioux City Art Ctr, Iowa; and others. *Comn:* 3 Wall murals, Nat Endowment Arts, 77. *Exhib:* San Francisco Art Int Centennial Exhib, San Francisco Mus Art, 70; Extraordinary Realities, Whitney Mus Am Art, NY, 73; Smithsonian Traveling Drawing Exhib, 79-80; solo exhib, Rochester Art Ctr, Minn, 80; New Am Graphics 82-83, Butler Inst Am Art, 82; Shelby, NC, 87; Colorprint USA, 88; Springfield Art Mus, Mo, 91; Washington-Jefferson, Pa, 94; Baylor Univ,

98. *Teaching:* Asst prof printmaking & drawing, Calif State Univ, Chico, 66-71; asst prof painting & drawing, Univ Calgary, 71-73; prof, Univ NDak, 73-. *Awards:* Purchase Awards, Lagrange, Ga, 78, Owensboro Mus, Ky, 79 & Masur Mus, La, 79; Watercolor USA, 77, 80-85; Nat Endowment Arts Fel, 81-82; SWTSU San Marcos, 85; Print Club, 85; Hoyt Inst, 87. *Bibliog:* Article, Art Express Mag, 1-2/82; Article in Am Artist, 10/86. *Mem:* Nat Acad. *Media:* Watercolor; Engraving. *Publ:* Auth, Watercolor, 94. *Mailing Add:* 320 N 16th St Grand Forks ND 58203

PAVLOVA, MARINA
DIRECTOR, EDUCATOR
b Gottingen, WGer, Sept 29, 52; US citizen. *Study:* Rutgers Univ; Broward Community Col; Fla Atlantic Univ, BFA, 83; Univ Miami (scholar); MS, Fla Int Univ, Miami, 92. *Work:* Mus Discovery and Sci, Ft Lauderdale, Fla; and other pvt collections. *Exhib:* Andrews Ave Gallery, 94; BAG Gallery, Fort Lauderdale, Fla, 85-90. *Collection Arranged:* Ann Exhib (with catalog), 85-90; Human Image Exhib, 85-90; Membership Exhib (with catalog), 85-90; Riverwalk Art Festival (with catalog), 87-90; Salon des Refuse (with catalog), 87-90. *Pos:* Exec dir, Broward Art Guild, Ft Lauderdale, Fla, 85; community adv bd, WXEL; pres, Fla Asn Nonprofit Organizations Inc, currently; asst exec dir, Miami-Dade Co League of Cities; ed bd, ASPM Pub. *Teaching:* Artist-in-residence weaving, Discovery Ctr Mus, 78-86, Univ Miami, 86-87, Broward Community Col, 90-93, 2000-, Fla Int Univ, 92-2000. *Awards:* Moretti Award, Community Achievement Comt, 88 & 89; Outstanding Community Service, Junior League, Ft Lauderdale, 88. *Mem:* Broward Co Teachers Art Guild; Women's Caucus Art; Coalition Women's Art Orgn (vpres corresp S states, 91-93); Nat Coun Nonprofit Asn (dir, 98, ind sector Washington DC). *Media:* Mixed Media. *Mailing Add:* 7480 Fairway Dr Suite 206 Miami Lakes FL 33014

PAYNE GOODWIN, LOUIS (DOC)
CARTOONIST, PAINTER
b Flintville, Tenn, Oct 9, 22. *Study:* Ark Polytech Col, 41-42; Univ Chattanooga, BA, 48; Ohio State Univ, 74. *Pos:* Advert & ed cartoonist, Dispatch Printing Co, Columbus, 52-62; ed cartoonist, Columbus Eve Dispatch, 62-87. *Awards:* Cartoon Award, Freedoms Found, 62-69, 71, 73 & 79; Cartoonists Award, Hwy Safety Found, 66. *Mailing Add:* 5158 Woodside Dr Columbus OH 43229-5128

PAYSON, JOHN WHITNEY
ART DEALER, COLLECTOR
b New York, NY, Aug 7, 40. *Study:* Pepperdine Univ, BA, 66. *Pos:* Founder, Joan Whitney Payson Gallery Art, Westbrook Col, Portland, Maine; bd trustees, Skowhegan Sch Painting & Sculpture, currently; mem, bd trustees, St Gaudens Mem, Cornish, NH, currently; pres, Payson Enterprises, Inc; pres, Hobe Sound Galleries & Hobe Sound Galleries, North; pres, Midtown Galleries, Inc; bd mem, Spoleto, 87. *Awards:* Maine Patrons Award, Skowhegan Sch Painting & Sculpture, 77. *Bibliog:* David Patillo (auth), The real Hobe Sound, Palm Beach Life Mag, 7/86. *Mem:* Martin Co Coun Arts (mem, adv bd); fel Portland Mus Art; Salmagundi Club, NY; Barn Gallery Assocs; Penobscot Marine Mus. *Specialty:* Contemporary American art. *Publ:* Auth, forward to catalog, Expressions from Maine, 76; forward to catalog, From Goya to Wyeth, The Joan Whitney Payson Collection, 80; forward to catalog, Bernard Langlais, The Middle Years, 86; forward to catalog of the permanant collection, Joan Whitney Payson Gallery Art, Westbrook Col, Portland, Maine. *Mailing Add:* Midtown Payson Galleries Exec Offices 11870 SE Dixie Hwy Hobe Sound FL 33455

PAYTON, CYDNEY M
MUSEUM DIRECTOR, CURATOR
Pos: Asst, K Phillips Gallery, 1984; owner, Cydney Payton Artfolio, 1985-90; co-owner, Payton-Rule Gallery, 1990-92; dir, Boulder Mus Contemp Art, Colo 1992-2000; dir, cur, Mus Contemp Art/Denver, 2001-. *Mailing Add:* Mus Contemp Art/Denver 1275 19th St Denver CO 80202

PAZ, BERNARDO
COLLECTOR
Awards: Named one of Top 200 Collectors, ARTnews Mag, 2004. *Collection:* Contemporary Art, especially Brazilian. *Mailing Add:* Instituto Horizontes Salas 304-305 Rua da Bahia 1598 Belo Horizonte MG 30160-011 Brazil

PEACE, BERNIE KINZEL
PRINTMAKER, COLLAGE ARTIST
b Williamsburg, Ky, Oct 20, 33. *Study:* Berea Col, AB(art), 54; Ind Univ, MFA(painting), 57. *Work:* Fed Reserve Bank, Richmond, Va; Ind Univ; WVa Univ; State WVa, Charleston; Wash & Jefferson Col; and others. *Comn:* Painting, WVa Arts & Humanities Coun, Charleston, 72. *Exhib:* Retrospective (catalog essays) Charleston Art Mus, WVa, 78, Delf Norona Mus, WVa, 80 & (catalog essays), Liberty State Col, 95; 12th Nat Painting Show, Wash & Jefferson Col, Pa, 80; 14th Ann Nat, Marietta Col, Ohio, 81; W&J Nat Painting Show, 87 & 91; Erie Art Mus, Erie, PA; solo exhibs, Northeast Mo State Univ, Kirksville, 87, WVa Juried Exhib 87, 89, Oak Ridge Mus Fine Art, Tenn, 88, Art Store Gallery, Charleston, WVa, 92, Ohio Univ Ea Campus, St Clairsville, Ohio, 99; and others. *Teaching:* Prof drawing & painting, West Liberty State Col, 60-95, emer prof art, 95. *Awards:* Grumbacher Medal Merit, 89, 92; Best Show, Bethany Col, Fall, 91; Grumbacher Gold Medallion, Wash & Jefferson Col Nat Painting Show, 95; Disting Alumnus Award Berea Col, Berea, KY, 98; plus others. *Mem:* Wheeling Area Photog Club; Allied Artists WVa; WVa Art & Craft Guild. *Media:* Woodcuts, Photo Collage. *Dealer:* The Art Store Charleston WVa. *Mailing Add:* 1214 Washington Farms Wheeling WV 26003

PEACOCK, CLIFFTON
PAINTER
b Chicago, Ill, Oct 21, 53. *Study:* Boston Sch Fine Arts, Boston Univ, BFA, 75, MFA, 77, with Philip Guston. *Work:* Mus Fine Arts, Boston; Hood Mus, Dartmouth Col, Dartmouth, NH; Carnegie-Mellon Univ Art Gallery, Pittsburgh, Pa; Rose Art Mus, Brandeis Univ, Waltham, Mass; Mass Inst Technol, Cambridge. *Exhib:* Boston Now: Figuration, Inst Contemp Art, Boston, 82, 83; solo exhibs, Thomas Segal Gallery, Boston, 83, 86 & 90, Germans Van Eck, NY, 89 & 90, Jan Baum Gallery, Los Angeles, 91, William Halsey Gallery, Col Charleston, SC, 91, Greenville Co Mus Art, SC, 91 & 93, Southeastern Ctr Contemp Art, NC, 92, Germans van Eck Gallery, NY, 93; Boston Collects, Mus Fine Arts, Boston, 86; Awards in the Visual Arts, Los Angeles Co Mus Art, 88; AVA 7, Va Mus Fine Arts, Richmond, 89; Nuclear Solstice, Boston Ctr Arts, 91; Germans Van Eck Gallery, 91 & 92; Thomas Segal Gallery, Boston, 91 & 92; Drawing Ctr, NY, 92; and others. *Pos:* Vis artist painting & drawing, Monserrat Col Art, Beverly, Mass, 85 & 87. *Teaching:* Instr painting & drawing, Boston Mus Sch Arts, Mass, 88-91; adj prof, Dept Art, Col Charleston, 91-93, asst prof, 93-. *Awards:* Nat Endowment Arts Grant, 81, 83 & 87; Louis Comfort Tiffany Grant, 89; Rome Prize Fel, Am Acad Rome, 93. *Bibliog:* David Hornung (auth), Artnews, 12/90; Richard Kalina (auth), Art in Am, 12/90; Ingrid Shaffner (auth), Arts, 12/90. *Mailing Add:* c/o Art Dept Col Charleston Charleston SC 29424

PEARL, MARILYN
ART DEALER
b Akron, Ohio. *Study:* Hunter Col, BA; Columbia Univ, MA. *Pos:* Dir & pres, Marilyn Pearl Gallery, 76-. *Teaching:* Asst prof hist, New York Inst Technol, New York & Old Westbury, NY, 68-74. *Mem:* Art Dealers Asn. *Specialty:* Contemporary American painting, sculpture, drawing

PEARLMAN, E(TTA) S
PAINTER
b New York, NY, Mar 30. *Study:* Brooklyn Col, BA, 60; Brooklyn Mus Art Sch. *Work:* Power Gallery Contemp Art, Univ Sydney, Australia; Brooklyn Mus; Temple Univ, Pa; Mus Mod Art, NY; Metrop Mus Art, NY. *Exhib:* One-person shows, Brooklyn Mus Little Gallery Series, 73 & 74 & Pleiades Gallery, 75-76, 78-80 & 82; Brooklyn Mus Art Sales & Rental Gallery, 75; Fine Arts Mus Long Island, NY, 88; Artists at Work, Nassau Co Mus Fine Arts, 90. *Awards:* Curatorial Award for solo shows in Little Gallery Series, Brooklyn Mus. *Mem:* Ctr Book Arts, NY; Dieu Donne Papermill, NY; Int Soc Copier Artists, NY; Orgn Independent Artists, NY; Art Initiatives, NY. *Media:* Mixed Media Painting, Artist Books. *Publ:* The Art of Collaging, GF Brommer, Davis Publ, 78 & 94; Int Soc of Copier Artists, Original Art Publ, 93 & 94. *Dealer:* Contact Studio 2934 Clubhouse Rd Merrick NY 11566. *Mailing Add:* 10044 Brandon Cir Orlando FL 32836-3714

PEARLMAN, GEORGE L
CERAMIST
b Brooklyn, NY, Oct 06, 61. *Study:* Syracuse Univ, BS, 83; NY Sch Visual Arts, 84; Pa State Univ, MFA, 94. *Exhib:* one-man show, The Clay Studio, Philadelphia, 88, 91; Fletcher Challenge, Auckland Center, New Zealand, 94; Monarch Clay Nat, Kennedy-Douglas Center, Ala, 97; Eleven Me Arts Comn Fel, Univ Me Farmington, 2002; Pearlan Current Work, St George Pottery, ME, 2002; St George Pottery, 05; La Coste Gallery, Mass, 05; Firehouse Gallery, Maine, 05. *Pos:* artist in residence, The Clay Studio, Philadelphia, 88-92; artist in residence, Watershed Ctr for Ceramic Art, Me, 94-96; owner, St George Pottery, Me, 99-. *Teaching:* adj instr ceramics, Pa State Univ, 92-94; adj instr, Univ Me, 96; head of ceramics, Hope Coll, Holland, Mich, 97-98. *Awards:* Artist Fel 2002, Me Coun Arts, 2002; McKnight Fel, 3M Corp, 2002; Good Idea grant, Maine Coun Arts, 05. *Mem:* Center fro Me Contemp Art; ACC; Nat Coun Educ Ceramic Art. *Media:* Ceramics, Porcelain. *Specialty:* ceramics. *Dealer:* St George Pottery 1012 River Rd St George ME 04860. *Mailing Add:* St George 1012 River Rd Saint George ME 04860

PEARLSTEIN, ALIX
VIDEO ARTIST
b New York, NY, 1962. *Study:* Cornell Univ, BS, 83; SUNY Purchase, MFA, 88. *Work:* Commodities Corp, Princeton, NJ. *Exhib:* Solo exhibs, White Columns, NY, 88, Laurie Rubin Gallery, NY, 90, Tom Solomon's Garage, Los Angeles, 91, Elizabeth Koury Gallery, Project Room, NY, 92, Postmasters Gallery, NY, 92, 94, 96 & 99 & Johan Jonker Galerie, Video Room Project, Amsterdam, 93; Blast 4: Bioinformatica, Sandra Gering Gallery, NY, 94; Use Your Allusion: Recent Video Art, Mus Contemp Art, Chicago, 94; Simply Made in Am, Aldrich Mus, Conn & Contemp Arts Ctr, Cincinnati, Ohio, 94; Lauren Whittles Gallery, NY, 95; Postmasters Gallery, NY, 96; Up Close and Personal, Philadelphia Mus Art, Pa, 98; Yound and Restless, Mus Mod Art, NY, 98; Video Lisboa 99, Lisbon, 99; In Video Festival, Milan, Italy, 99; TransMediale Festival, Berlin, Ger, 99; Galleria Marabini, Bologna, 99; and many others. *Teaching:* Instr, State Univ NY, Purchase, 87, Rockland Community Col, 90-91, Brooklyn Col, NY, 91, Sch Visual Arts, NY, 91-93, 94 PSI, Youth Arts Prog, NY, 93-94, Cornell Univ, 93 & NY Univ, 93; guest lectr, Montclair State Col, NJ, 91, Parsons Sch Design, 99, Rugers Univ, 99 & Tyler Sch Art, 99; vis artist, NY Univ, 94. *Awards:* Nat Endowment Arts, 89; Fel, Edward F Albee Found, 92; Art Matters Inc Fel, 96. *Bibliog:* Kim Levin (auth), Art/Choices, Alix Pearlstein at Postmasters, Village Voice, 5/3/94; Claire McConaughty (auth), SIB, Pretty Decorating, 9/94; Working Conditions: A Forum on Art & Everyday Life, Meaning, no 16, fall 94; and many others. *Dealer:* Postmasters Gallery 459 W 19th St New York NY

PEARLSTEIN, PHILIP
PAINTER, EDUCATOR
b Pittsburgh, Pa, May 24, 1924. *Study:* Carnegie Inst, with Sam Rosenberg, Robert Lepper & Balcomb Greene, BFA, 49; Inst Fine Arts, New York Univ, MA, 55. *Work:* Boston Mus Fine Arts; Metrop Mus Art, Whitney Mus Am Art & Mus Mod Art, NY; Corcoran Gallery Art, Hirshhorn Mus & Sculpture Garden, Washington; Philadelphia Mus Art; Art Inst Chicago; also in pvt collections. *Exhib:* Ann Exhib, Whitney Mus Am Art, 55-56, 56-57, 58-59, 62-63, 67-68 & 69-70; Recent Acquisitions, Whitney Mus Am Art, 58 & 70; Biennial Exhib, Corcoran Gallery Art, Washington, 67, 71, 75;

Return to the Figure, Pa Acad Fine Arts, Philadelphia, 71-72; Hayden Gallery, Mass Inst Technol, 71; Biennial Exhibs, Whitney Mus Am Art, 73, 79 & 91; Am Drawings, Whitney Mus Am Art, 73; Seventy-First Am Exhib, Art Inst Chicago, 74; New Portraits, Whitney Mus Am Art, 74; Twelve Am Painters, Va Mus Fine Arts, Richmond, 74; Seventy-Second Am Exhib, Art Inst Chicago, 75; Am 1976 (traveling), Corcoran Gallery Art, 76; Eight Contemp Realists, Pa Acad Fine Arts, 77; Nothing but Nudes, Whitney Mus Am Art, 77; The Human Form, Contemp Am Figure Drawing and the Academic Tradition, Corcoran Gallery Art, 80; Am Drawing in Black and White, Brooklyn Mus, NY, 80-81; solo exhibs, Weatherspoon Art Gallery, Univ NC, Greensboro, 81, Brooklyn Mus, NY, 89, Butler Inst Am Art, 92, Honolulu Acad Art, 94, Springfield Art Mus, Mo, 95, Robert Miller Gallery, NY, 86, 95; New Dimensions in Drawing, Aldrich Mus, Ridgefield, Conn, 81; 45th Ann Nat Painting Exhib, Butler Inst Am Art, 81; American Prints: Process and Proofs, Whitney Mus Am Art, 81-82; Contemp Am Realism since 1960 (traveling), Pa Acad Fine Arts, 82; Homo Sapiens: The Many Images, Aldrich Mus Contemp Art, 82; Perspectives on Contemp Am Realism, Pa Acad Fine Arts, 83; Viewpoint: Painting and the Third Dimension, Cranbrook Acad Art Mus, 86-87; From the Model, Whitney Mus Am Art at Philip Morris, NY, 89; The Body Human, Nohra Haime Gallery, NY, 94; NY Realism Past and Present (traveling), Odakyu Mus, Tokyo, 94-95; Embody, Proctor Art Ctr, Bard Col, 94; Am Art Today: Night Paintings, Art Mus, Fla Int Univ, Miami, 95; plus many others. *Pos:* Vis critic, Yale Univ, 62-63; artist-in-residence, Am Acad Rome, 82. *Teaching:* Instr, Pratt Inst, 59-63; from asst prof to prof art, Brooklyn Col, 63-88, distinguished prof art emer, 88-. *Awards:* Fulbright Fel to Italy, 56-59; Nat Endowment Arts Fel, 68; Guggenheim Fel, 69. *Bibliog:* Jerome Viola (auth), The Paintings and Teachings of Philip Pearlstein, Watson & Guptill, 82; Mark Strand (ed), Art of the Real: Nine American Figurative Painters, Clarkson N Potter, Inc, 83; Russell Bowman (auth), Philip Pearlstein: The Complete Paintings, Alpine Fine Arts Collection, 83; Philip Pearlstein draws the artist's model, Interactive laserbeam videodisc or videocassette, Interactive Media Corp, New York, 85; John Perreault (auth), Philip Pearlstein Drawings and Watercolors, Harry N Abrams Inc, 88. *Mem:* Amer Acad Arts and Letters (pres 2003-06), Nat Acad. *Media:* Oil, water color, graphics. *Publ:* Auth, Figure paintings are not made in heaven, Art News, 62; Whose painting is it anyway? Arts Yrbk 7, 64; A Concept of New Realism: Real, Really Real, Superreal, San Antonio Mus Asn, 81; When paintings were made in heaven, Art in Am, 2/82. *Dealer:* Betty Cunningham Gallery, 541 E 25th Street, New York, NY, 10001. *Mailing Add:* 361 W 36th St New York NY 10018

PEARLSTEIN, SEYMOUR
PAINTER, EDUCATOR
b Brooklyn, NY, Oct 14, 23. *Study:* Pratt Inst; Art Students League; also pvt study with Jack Potter, NY. *Work:* Mus NMex, Santa Fe; Mint Mus Art, Charlotte, NC; Nat Acad Design & Queens Mus, NY; Fine Arts Gallery San Diego, Calif; Munson-Williams-Proctor Inst, Utica, NY. *Exhib:* Butler Inst Am Art, Youngstown, Ohio, 75; US Dept State Art in Embassies Prog, 76-78; Am Watercolor Soc, NY, 77; Nat Arts Club 78 & 90, Nat Acad Design, 90 & 92 & Queens Mus, NY, 78; NY Hist Soc, 81; Colo Heritage Ctr Mus, Denver, 81; Grace Gallery, Brooklyn, NY, 96, 98 & 99; and many one-man shows; Audubon Artists at Nat Arts Club, 02. *Teaching:* Prof, dept art & advert design, New York City Tech Col, City Univ New York, Brooklyn, 70-96, chmn dept, 85-88, prof emer, 93-. *Awards:* Childe Hassam Purchase Award, 77 & Grant, 75, Am Acad of Arts & Lett; Henry Ward Ranger Purchase Award, Nat Acad of Design, 82 & W H Leavin Prize, 85; George Tweed Mem Award-Allied Artists of Am, 89. *Bibliog:* Malcolm Preston (auth), Seymour Pearlstein Newsday, 5/4/79; David L Shirey (auth), Seymour Pearlstein, New York Times, 5/13/79; Lawrence Campbell (auth), Seymour Pearlstein, Art in Am, 11/92. *Mem:* Alliance of Figurative Artists (chmn, 76-77); Allied Artists of Am (dir, 76-78); Am Watercolor Soc (dir, 78-80); Audubon Artists (dir, 90-93); Nat Acad (bd dir, 80-84). *Media:* All. *Publ:* Auth, Acrylics, Am Artist Mag, 2/79; New York Silence, 92 & F Train Series-Subway Drawings, 99, Perspectives, a Journal, City Tech Press,; auth, F Train Series-Subway Drawings, Perspectives, a Journal, City Tech Press, 99. *Mailing Add:* 52 Dartmouth St Forest Hills NY 11375

PEARMAN, SARA JANE
HISTORIAN, LIBRARIAN
b Dallas, Tex, Sept 6, 40. *Study:* Univ Wichita, BAE; Univ Kans, MA(art hist); Case-Western Reserve Univ, PhD(art hist). *Collection Arranged:* Glass Collection of the University of Kansas (auth, catalog); The Fine Art of Graphic Design, 85 & The Fine Art of Graphic Design (auth, catalog), 86, Beck Fine Arts Ctr, Cleveland Mus Art. *Pos:* Slide librn, Cleveland Mus Art; Bk reviewer, Art Documentation, 80- & Visual Resources, 85. *Teaching:* Instr art hist, Kearney State Col, 64-66; lectr, Akron State Univ, 68-, Cleveland State Univ, 77- & Kent State Univ, currently; adj asst prof, Kent State Univ, currently. *Mem:* Col Art Asn; Midwest Art Hist Asn; Cleveland Medieval Soc; Art Libr Soc NAm; Mid-Am Col Art Asn; Visual Resources Asn; Hist Netherlandish Art. *Res:* Iconography of all periods; Late Medieval and northern Renaissance wood sculpture; slide classification systems and visual resources; history of graphic design. *Publ:* Auth, Mirror of Art, Ralph, Vol 4, 77; Otto Dix, A Self Portrait (exhib catalog), Univ Kans; A Netherlandish Saint Andrew from Cleves, Bull Cleveland Mus Art, 12/80. *Mailing Add:* c/o Ingalls Library Cleveland Museum of Art 11150 E Blvd Cleveland OH 44106

PEARSON, BRUCE
PAINTER
Exhib: Out of Town, Krannert Art Mus, Univ Ill, Urbana-Champaign, 92; Working: 4 Walls in Munich, Munich Kunstverein, Ger, 94; Faux, Ronald Feldman Fine Arts, NY, 94; NY State Biennial, Albany Mus, 96; Redefinitions, A View from Brooklyn, Calif State Univ, Fullerton, 97; Current Undercurrent: Working in Brooklyn, Brooklyn Mus, 97; Project 63 (with catalog), Mus Mod Art, NY, 98; Wild, Exit Art, NY, 98; Univ Galleries, Ill State Univ, Normal, 99; Shaheen Mod and Contemp Art, 00; Robert V Fullerton Art Mus, Calif State Univ, 01; Palm Beach Inst Contemp Art, Lake Worth, Fla, 01; Rose Art Mus, Brandeis Univ, 01; Locks Gallery, Philadelphia, 02; Times Sq Gallery, Hunter Col, New York City, 03; Schroeder Romero, Brooklyn, NY, 03; solo exhib, Peirogi 2000, NY, 98, Ronald Feldman Fine Arts, NY, 99, 01. *Collection Arranged:* Karl Ernst Haus Mus, Hagen, Ger; Mus Mod Art; Rose Art Mus, Brandeis Univ; Sprint Corp; Whitney Mus Am Art. *Awards:* 1997 Biennial Competition Award Winner, Louis Comfort Tiffany Found, 97; Skowhegan Residency Prog for Advanced Vis Arts, 01. *Bibliog:* Museum of Modern Art, The New Yorker, 6/15/98; David Clarkson (auth), When words fail: the psychedelic solution of Bruce Pearson, BOMB, winter 98; Donna Desrochers (auth), The Alchemies of the Sixties' and Bruce Pearson at the Rose, 9/99; Andras Szanto (auth), A Business Built on the Hard-to-Sell, NY Times, AR 35, 37, 10/6/2002. *Mailing Add:* c/o Ronald Feldman Fine Arts 31 Mercer St New York NY 10013

PEARSON, HENRY C
PAINTER, INSTRUCTOR
b Kinston, NC, Oct 8, 14. *Study:* Univ NC, BA, 35; Yale Univ, MFA, 38; Art Students League, 53-56. *Work:* Mus Mod Art, Metrop Mus Art & Whitney Mus Am Art, NY; Albright-Knox Art Gallery, Buffalo; NC Mus Art, Raleigh. *Comn:* World University Service (poster), List Art Posters, 65; 6th New York Film Festival--Lincoln Center (poster), List Art Posters, 68;. *Exhib:* The Responsive Eye, Mus Mod Art, NY, 65; 29th Biennial Exhib, Corcoran Gallery Art, Washington, DC, 65; Drawings USA, Minn Mus Art, St Paul, 71-73; Art Students League Centennial Exhib, 75; Truman Gallery, NY, 76-79; Marilyn Pearl Gallery, NY, 79-; Dissent: The Issue of Modern Art, Inst Contemp Art, Boston, Mass, 86; Retrospective, Columbia Mus Art, SC, 88; Henry Pearson & Friends, Comm Council Arts, Kinston, NC 93; Native Son: The Works of Henry Pearson, Grey Gallery, ECarolina Univ, Greenville, NC, 98; By Am, Yale Univ Art Gallery, New Haven, Conn, 98; and others. *Teaching:* Instr painting, New Sch Social Res. *Awards:* Kreeger Purchase Prize, Corcoran Gallery Art, 65; J Henry Scheidt Award, Pa Acad Fine Arts, 69; NC Governor's Gold Medal Achievement Fine Arts, Raleigh, 70. *Bibliog:* Lippard (auth), Henry Pearson, Art Int, 65. *Mem:* Am Abstract Artists; Century Asn. *Media:* Oil, Watercolor. *Publ:* Illusr, Five Psalms, Brandeis Univ, 69; Poems and a Memoir (auth, Seamus Heaney), The Limited Editions Club, New York, 81; Sweeney Praises the Trees (auth, Seamus Heaney), Kelly/Winterton Press, New York, 81. *Dealer:* Marilyn Pearl Gallery 710 Park Ave New York NY 10012. *Mailing Add:* c/o Marilyn Pearl Gallery 710 Park Ave New York NY 10021

PEARSON, JAMES EUGENE
INSTRUCTOR, SCULPTOR
b Woodstock, Ill, Dec 12, 39. *Study:* Northern Ill Univ, BS(educ), 61, MS(educ), MFA, 64; Tyler Sch Art, Temple Univ; Ithaca Col. *Work:* Northern Ill Univ, DeKalb; Palais des Beaux Arts, Charleroi, Belg; Taft Field Campus, Northern Ill Univ, Ore; Dixon State Sch, Ill; Sch Dist 15, McHenry, Ill. *Comn:* Lorado Taft, Taft Field Campus, Northern Ill Univ, 67; Vicki Unis, Sarasota, Fla, 69; Mae Stinespring, Harry Stinespring, McHenry, Ill, 69; portraits in oils of Mr & Mrs Francis Hightower, comn by Mrs Nancy Langdon, Woodstock, Ill, 71; Civil War Monument, Greenwood Cemetery, Ill, 77; AG Edwards & Sons, Murals, Woodstock, Ill, 88. *Exhib:* 21st Am Drawing Biennial, Norfolk Mus Arts & Sci, Va, 65; 54th Ann Exhib, Art Asn Newport, RI, 65; 2 eme Salon Int de Charleroi, Palais des Beaux Arts, Belg, 69; 5th Int Grand Prix Painting & Etching, Palais de la Scala, Monte Carlo, Monaco, 69; one-man show sculpture, Mitchell Art Mus, Mt Vernon, Ill, 75. *Pos:* Editorial cartoonist, The Woodstock Independent, 1994-. *Teaching:* Instr art, Woodstock High Sch, Ill, 61-94; instr art, McHenry Co Col, Crystal Lake, Ill, 62-78. *Awards:* Best of Show Award, William Boyd Andrews, 61; Purchase Prize, Mr & Mrs Allen Leibsohn, 63; Mary E Just Art Award, Waukegan News-Sun, 69; First Prize, Ill Press Asn, 98, 01 Northern Ill Press Asn, 96, 97, 98 & 02; Recognized by Nat Newspapers Asn 98 & 99. *Bibliog:* F Tramier (auth), James E Pearson, La Rev Mod, 65; Sally Wagner (auth), Volume tells McHenry history, Chicago Tribune, 69. *Mem:* Col Art Asn Am; Ill Art Educ Asn; Ill Craftsmen's Coun; Am Fedn Arts; Centro Studi E Scambi Internazionali, Rome. *Publ:* Illusr, McHenry County 1832 1968, 68; auth, A dream never realized, 69 & Eagle's nest colony, 70, Outdoor Ill; Perspective: outdoor education from an artists point of view, J Outdoor Educ, 71; illusr, The rectangle, 72. *Mailing Add:* 5117 Barnard Mill Rd Ringwood IL 60072

PEARSON, JOHN
PAINTER, EDUCATOR
b Boroughbridge, Yorkshire, Eng, Jan 31, 40. *Study:* Harrogate Col Art, Yorkshire, nat dipl design, 60; Royal Acad Schs, London, cert, 63; Northern Ill Univ, MFA, 66. *Work:* Mus Mod Art, NY; Bochumer Mus, Stuttgart, WGer; Pasadena Mus Fine Art, Calif; Kleye Collection, Doertmund, WGer; Kunstverien, Hanover, WGer; Art Inst Chicago; Cleveland Mus Art. *Exhib:* Am Drawing 1963-73, Whitney Mus Am Art, NY; one-man shows, Gray Gallery, Chicago, 67, 68 & 82, Paley & Lowe Gallery, 71, Fischbach Gallery, 74 & 76, NY & Akron Art Mus, 83. *Teaching:* Instr painting, Univ NMex, 66-68; assoc prof painting & head dept, NS Col Art & Design, Halifax, 68-70; int artist-in-residence, Cleveland Inst Art, Ohio, 70-72; prof art & chmn dept art, Oberlin Col, 72-. *Awards:* Can Coun Grant, 70; Cleveland Arts Prize, 75; Nat Endowment Arts, 76. *Bibliog:* Jock Wittet (auth), Editorial, Studio Int, 3/68; Harry Borden (auth), John Pearson, Artforum, 2/72; James R Mellon (auth), article, New York Times, 2/3/75; Edward Henning (auth), The art of John Pearson: An analogy of works of art & general systems, Art Int, 4-5/77. *Publ:* Contribr, Art: The measure of man, Directions 66/67; article in Mus Educ J, 66. *Dealer:* Bertha Urdang Gallery 23 W 74th St New York NY 10021; Richard Gray Gallery 620 N Michigan Ave Chicago IL 60611. *Mailing Add:* 35 E College St Oberlin OH 44074-1612

PEART, JERRY LINN
SCULPTOR
b Winslow, Ariz, Feb 26, 48. *Study:* Ariz State Univ, BFA(sculpture); Southern Ill Univ, Carbondale, MFA(sculpture). *Work:* Mus Contemp Art, Chicago; Palm Springs Desert Mus, Calif; Ill State Mus, Springfield; Mus NMex, Santa Fe; Univ Ariz Mus, Tucson. *Comn:* Sculpture, Hyatt Regency Peachtree Ctr, Atlanta, 90; sculpture, Boulevard Towers, Michigan Ave, Chicago, Ill, 86; sculpture, The Promontory, Rancho Barnardo, Calif, 90; sculpture, Carill on Building, Hesta Corp, Charlotte, NC, 91; sculpture, Bradley Univ, Peoria, Ill, 94. *Exhib:* Art in Chicago, 1945-95, Mus Contemp Art, Chicago; one-man shows, Richard Gray Gallery, Chicago, 88 & 92, Jean Art Ctr, Seoul, 95; 3 person show, Coast to Coast to Coast, Marqulis-Taplin Gallery, Miami, Fla, 93. *Teaching:* Vis prof sculpture, Ariz State Univ, spring, 84. *Awards:* Jeannette Sacks Art Achievement Medal, Ariz State Univ, 70; First Chicago Art Awards for Best Body of Work Over the Yr, Chicago Art Asn, 76-77. *Mem:* Sculpture Chicago (comt mem, 85-); City of Chicago, Percent for Art (mem pub art comt, 86-90). *Dealer:* Richard Gray Gallery 620 N Michigan Chicago IL 60611. *Mailing Add:* 1544 N Sedgwick St Chicago IL 60610-1223

PEASE, DAVID G
ADMINISTRATOR, PAINTER
b Bloomington, Ill, June 2, 32. *Study:* Univ Wis, Madison, BS, 54, MS, 55, MFA, 58. *Work:* Whitney Mus Am Art, NY; Philadelphia Mus Art; Pa Acad Fine Arts, Philadelphia; Power Gallery, Univ Sydney, Australia; Des Moines Art Ctr, Iowa. *Exhib:* Carnegie Int Exhib Painting & Sculpture, Carnegie Inst, Pittsburgh, 61; Corcoran Biennial Painting, Corcoran Gallery Art, Washington, 61 & 63; Whitney Ann Exhib Painting, Whitney Mus Am Art, NY, 63; Nat Drawing Exhib, San Francisco Mus Art, Calif, 69; Drawings USA, Minn Mus Art, St Paul, 71, 73 & 75. *Pos:* Dean, Tyler Sch Art, Temple Univ, 77-83; dean, Sch Art, Yale Univ, 83-96. *Teaching:* Prof painting dept painting & sculpture, Tyler Sch Art, Temple Univ, 60-83; prof painting, Yale Univ, 83-. *Awards:* William A Clark Award, Corcoran Gallery Art, 63; Guggenheim Fel, 65-66; Childe Hassam Fund Purchase Award, Am Acad Arts & Lett, 70. *Mem:* Col Art Asn Am; Nat Coun Arts Adminr (bd dir, 88); Nat Asn Sch Art & Design; Alliance Independent Cols Art (bd dir, 88-95); Louis Comfort Tiffany Found (bd trustees, 88-). *Media:* Acrylic, Gouache. *Mailing Add:* 95 Thankful Stowe Rd Guilford CT 06437-2529

PECCHENINO, J RONALD
PAINTER, EDUCATOR
b Murphy, Calif, Apr 3, 32. *Study:* Col Pac, BA, 56; Calif Col Arts & Crafts, MFA, 69. *Work:* Univ Calif, Chico; Univ Pac; Crocker Art Gallery. *Comn:* Acrylic lacquer paintings, Hilton Hotel, Stockton, Calif, 81; Sheraton Hotel, Boston, 83; Cruise Ships, MS Skyward, 85 & Song of Norway, 86. *Exhib:* Third Ann Art Invitational, Pleasant Hill, Calif, 69; Northern Calif Arts Exhib, Crocker Mus Art, Sacramento, 72; solo exhib, Lyon Art Gallery, San Francisco, 79 & 81. *Pos:* Mem, Art Adv Panel, Calif State Comn, 71-80. *Teaching:* Instr art, Manteca Unified Sch Dist, Calif, 56-70; prof painting, Univ Pac, 70-, chmn art, 83-. *Awards:* Purchase Awards, Lodi Ann Exhib, M Neufield & Sons, 68, Third Ann Art Invitational, City Pleasant Hill, 69 & Northern Calif Arts Exhib, Crocker Art Gallery, 72. *Media:* Acrylic Lacquer, Air Brush. *Dealer:* Contract Art Inc Falls River Offices PO Box 520 Essex CT 06426. *Mailing Add:* Dept Art Univ of the Pacific 3601 Pacific Ave Stockton CA 95211

PECH, ARLETA
PAINTER, INSTRUCTOR
b Princeton, IL, July 30, 1950. *Work:* Petro Lewis Inc, Denver, Colo; Greeley Nat Bank, Greeley, Colo. *Exhib:* One man shows, Cardinal Art Gallery, 1999, 2001, 2003; Gallery One, Mentor, Ohio, 2000, 2002, 2004, 2005; Germanton Art Gallery, 2001, 2003; Realism Today (invitational), John Pence Gallery, San Francisco, Calif, 2000; Birds in Art (traveling), Woodson Art Mus, Wasau, Wis, 2004, 2005; Best of Realism (invitational), Winstanley-Roark, Cape Cod, Mass, 2006; Int Realism Guild Exhib, Manitou Galleries, Santa Fe, NMex, 2006. *Teaching:* Instr (artist) watercolor, Foothills Art Center, Golden, Colo, 1980-2005; instr (artist), Vancouver Art Acad, 1998-2004; instr (artist), The Rankin Art Center, Columbus, Ga, 2006. *Mem:* Int Realism Guild; Rocky Mountain Nat Watermedia Soc. *Media:* Oil, Egg Tempera, Watercolor. *Publ:* Coauth, Keys to Commanding Light, Arttist Mag, 1995; coauth, Using Glazes to Paint Dramatic Watercolors, Artist Mag, 2000; coauth, Fixing 4 Common Floral Problems, Australian Artist, 2000; auth, Arleta Pech & Jane Jones, Friends Who Paint Flowers, InformArt Mag, 2002; auth, Harnessing the Power of Light, Int artist Mag, 2004. *Dealer:* Mary Martin Gallery of Fine Art 39 Broad St Charleston, SC 29401. *Mailing Add:* 6024 Pierson St Arvada CO 80004

PECK, JOHN See Banning, Jack, Jr

PECK, JUDITH
SCULPTOR, WRITER
b New York, NY, Dec 31, 30. *Study:* Adelphi Col, BA; Art Students League; Sculpture Ctr, New York; Columbia Univ, MA & EdM; New York Univ, EdD. *Work:* Yale Univ; Ghetto Fighters Mus, Acco, Israel; Teaneck Pub Libr, NJ; West Palm Beach Libr, Fla; Citizens for Pub Art, Ridgewood, NJ. *Comn:* Monuments, Temple Beth El, Spring Valley, NY, 71, James Richard Elster Mem Courtyard, Tenafly High Sch, NJ, 72 & Temple Oheb Sholom, Baltimore, Md, 75; Annual Partners Award Sculpture, Art Coun Rockland, 83, 84 & 85; Rockland Ctr Holocaust Studies, Spring Valley, NY, 88; North Shore Synagogue, Syosset, NY, 92; Teaneck Centennial, NJ, 95. *Exhib:* Solo sculpture shows, Unicorn Gallery, NY, 75 & 76, NJ State Mus, Trenton, 78, Reyn Gallery, NY, 81-83, Col Misericordia, Dallas, Pa, 85 & Lincoln Ctr Campus, Fordham Univ, NY, 90 & 2000, Dag Hammarskjold Plz, New York City, 2001-2002; Blue Hill Cult Ctr, Pearl River, NY, 84-85; Edward Hopper House, Nyack, NY, 84; Montclair State Col, 92; Adelphi Univ, 92; Int Biennial Art, Malta, 95; Bergen Mus Art & Sci, 2005. *Pos:* Prof of Art, Ramapo Col of NJ. *Teaching:* Prof art, Ramapo Col, NJ, 71-; Rutgers Grad Sch Educ, 94; Ramapo State Col of NJ; Prof Art, Ramapo Col of NJ, 71-. *Awards:* Grants, Art on the Outside, NJ Dept Higher Educ, Title I, 75, 76 & 77; Distinguished Serv Award, Rockland Co Legislature, 88. *Mem:* Int Sculpture Soc; Am Art Therapy Asn. *Media:* Bronze, Fiberglass. *Publ:* Auth, Leap to the Sun: Learning through Dynamic Play, Prentice-Hall, 79; Sculpture as Experience: Working with Clay, Wire, Wax, Plaster, Foil and Found Objects, Chilton Publ, 89; Art & Interaction, Ramapo Col, 90; Art Activities for Mind & Imagination, Imagination Arts Pub, 2004; Artistic Crafts, Imagination Arts Publications, Mahwah, NJ, 2004. *Mailing Add:* 57 Thunderhead Pl Mahwah NJ 07430

PECK, LEE BARNES
JEWELER, EDUCATOR
b Battle Creek, Mich, Sept 21, 42. *Study:* Kellogg Community Col, AA, 63; Western Mich Univ, BS(art educ), 65; Univ Wis, MFA(art metal), 69. *Work:* Johnson Wax Co. *Exhib:* The Goldsmith, Renwick Gallery, Smithsonian Inst, Washington, DC, 74; Am Goldsmiths Now, Washington Univ, St Louis, 78; Sangree De Cristo Art Ctr, Pueblo, Colo, 78; Northeast Mo State Univ, Kirksville, 78; Visual Arts Ctr Alaska, Anchorage, 78; one-man show, Mich Tech Univ, Houghton, 78; Objects 79, Western Colo Arts, 79; and many others. *Teaching:* Assoc prof jewelry & metalwork, Northern Ill Univ, 70-82, prof art, currently; lectr in jewelry, Rosary Col, 72-. *Awards:* Lakefront Festival Art Prize, Milwaukee Art Ctr, 75; The Metalsmith Award, Phoenix Art Mus, Ariz, 77; First Prize in Metal, Cooperstown Art Asn, NY, 77. *Mem:* Am Crafts Coun (Ill rep, 72-74); Wis Designer Craftsman; Soc NAm Goldsmiths. *Media:* Precious Metals. *Publ:* Auth & illusr, Jewelry Making, Vol 3, In: Illustrated Libr of Arts & Crafts, 74. *Mailing Add:* 121 Mason Ct Sycamore IL 60178-1314

PECK, WILLIAM HENRY
HISTORIAN, CONSULTANT
b Savannah, Ga, Oct 2, 32. *Study:* Ohio State Univ, 50-53; Wayne State Univ, BFA, 60, MA, 61. *Collection Arranged:* Mummy Portraits from Roman Egypt (with catalog), 67, Detroit Collects: Antiquities, 73 & Akhenaten & Nefertiti, 73-74; Cleopatra's Egypt, 89; Splendors of Ancient Egypt, 97; plus many others. *Pos:* Jr cur educ, Detroit Inst Arts, 60-62, asst cur educ, 62-64, assoc cur, 64-68, cur ancient art, 68-2004, sr cur, 88-2004; mem, Brooklyn Mus Theban Exped, 78-, assoc field dir, 80-. *Teaching:* Lectr art hist, Cranbrook Acad Art, 63-65; adj prof art hist, Wayne State Univ, 66-; vis lectr classics, Univ Mich, 70 & lectr art history, 2005-; Lectr Col for Creative Studies, 2004, history, Univ. Windsor, Ont, 2006. *Awards:* Travel Grant, Ford Motor Co, Eng, 62, Am Res Ctr Egypt Fel, 71 & Smithsonian Inst, 75; Arts Achievement Award, Dept Art & Art Hist, Wayne State Univ. *Bibliog:* Who's Who in America; Who's Who in the Mid West. *Mem:* Soc Study Egyptian Antiques; fel Am Res Ctr Egypt; Cranbrook Acad Art (mem bd gov, 74-85); Archaeol Inst Am; Int Asn Egyptologists; Oriental Inst, Univ Chicago; Asn Study of Travel in Egypt and Near East. *Res:* Ancient Near East and classical world with a particular specialty in Egyptology & Egyptian Art. *Interests:* Origanni, Early Music, TE Lawrence. *Publ:* Auth, The present state of Egyptian art in Detroit, 12/70 & The arts of the Ancient Near East in Detroit, 7/73, Connoisseur; Drawings From Ancient Egypt, Thames & Hudson, 78, German transl, 79, French transl, 80, Arabic transl, 87; The constant lure, chapter In: Ancient Egypt: Discovering its splendors, Nat Geographic, 78; The Detroit Institute of Arts: A Brief History, 91; Splendors of Ancient Egypt, 97; Many Articles, Book reviews and Contributions to Everydopcelias. *Mailing Add:* 1901 Orleans Detroit MI 48207

PECKHAM, NICHOLAS
ARCHITECT, EDUCATOR
b Teaneck, NJ, Apr 11, 40. *Study:* US Merchant Marine Acad, BS, 62; Univ Calif, Berkeley, 63; Univ Pa, BArch, 67, MArch, 73, with Louis Kahn, PhD cand with R Buckminster Fuller. *Pos:* Pres, Peckham & Wright Architects, Columbia. *Teaching:* Prof design, Stephens Col, Columbia, 75-. *Awards:* Cycle-4 Solar Award & Passive Cycle Award, Dept Housing & Urban Develop; Com Solar Award, Dept Energy. *Mem:* Construct Specifications Inst; Am Inst Architects; Int Solar Energy Soc. *Res:* Optimization in architecture. *Publ:* Auth, Evolution in architecture, Pass-Age, summer 75. *Mailing Add:* 3151 W Rte K Columbia MO 65203-9613

PEDEN WESLEY, DONALEE
PAINTER
b Syracuse, NY, Apr 1, 52. *Study:* Syracuse Univ, BFA, 76, MFA, 92. *Work:* Everson Mus, Syracuse, NY; Munson-Williams-Proctor Mus, Utica, NY. *Exhib:* Solo exhibs, Munson-Williams-Proctor Inst, Utica, NY, 86, Gertrude Thomas Chapman Art Gallery, Cazenovia Col, NY, 86 & 87, Colgate Univ, Hamilton, NY, 88 & Tyler Art Gallery, Oswego, NY, 90, The Drawing Room, Schaffer Art Bldg, Syracuse, NY, 2006, Made in NY, Schweinfurth Art Center, 2006; New Visions Gallery, Ithaca, NY, 88; group shows, NY Women Artists, NY State Mus, Albany, 89-90, Burchfield Art Ctr, Buffalo, NY, 90, Ariel Gallery, NY, 90, Syracuse State, 90, Gertrude Thomas Chapman Art Gallery, Cazenovia Col, NY, 90-91, Colgate Univ, Hamilton, NY, 91 & Cooperstown Art Asn, NY, 95, SUNY, Oswego, Sydney Col Gallery, Sydney Col of the Arts, Kozelle, Australia, Contemp Realism III Gallery Alexy, Philadelphia, Pa, 25th Anniversary Exhib, ARC Gallery, Chicago, Ill, Four Artists Drawing, Kirkland Arts Ctr, Clinton, NY, State Univ Plaza, Albany, NY; Derecci Gallery, Edgewood Col, Madison, Wis, 93; Rome Art Ctr, NY, 96; ARC Gallery, Chicago, Ill, 98-99; Drawing Lives, Invitational Show, Emily & Lowe Mus, 2005; Delevan Art Ctr, Group Show, 2004, 10 from OCC, 2004; Fac Show, Syracuse Univ, 2004; Fac Show, Syracuse Univ & OCC, NY, 2004-2006; Biennial Rochester Mem Art Gallery, 2006. *Teaching:* Instr watercolor & figure drawing, Syracuse Univ, 83-, material & techniques, 89, 90 & 91; instr drawing, Cazenovia Col, 86-87, Hamilton Col, 89 & Univ Madison, Wisc, 93;

instr drawing I & figure drawing, Syracuse Univ, NY; vis artist, Oswego, NY-SUNY, 96; asst prof, SUNY, Oswego; Onondaga Community College, 2003-; instr figure & drawing watercolor, Syracuse Univ, NY, 2003-2006. *Awards:* New York Found Arts Fel, Drawing, 86; Nat Endowment Arts Grant, Drawing, 87; Jacob Javits Fel, 90; Best of Show, Anderson Arts Ctr, Kenosha, Wis, 95. *Bibliog:* Arthur Williams (auth), The Sculpture Reference Illustrated, 2004. *Dealer:* Delavan Art Gallery, Syracuse, NY. *Mailing Add:* 8225 Vicksburg Pl Baldwinsville NY 13027-8303

PEDERSEN, CAROLYN H
PAINTER
b Dec 12, 42; US citizen. *Study:* Syracuse Univ, BS, 64; Rockland Ctr for Arts, W Nyack, NY, studied printmaking with Roberta De Lamonica, 86-91, studied watercolor with Edgar A Whitney; studied printmaking with Roberta DeLamonica, 86-91, painting and collage with Bruce Dorfman, 90, watercolor with Edgar A Whitney. *Work:* Art Pub Places, Rockland Co, New City, NY; Gallery Mus Hebrew Home for Aged, Riverdale, NY; G C Hanford Mfg Co, Syracuse, NY; Pub Serv Elect & Gas, NJ; Katz Commun, San Francisco, Calif. *Exhib:* Watercolor USA, Springfield Mus, Mo, 85; Am Watercolor Soc, Salmagundi Club, NY, 84; Nat Watercolor Soc, Los Angeles, Calif, 84, 85, 87; Audubon Artists Ann, Nat Arts Club, NY, 85, 86, 88. *Pos:* Pres, Art Craft Asn Rockland Co, NY, 79-80; mem chmn, Northeast Watercolor Soc, NY, 87-89; exhib comt mem, Rockland Ctr Arts, NY, 88-91; asst treas, Catharine Lorillard Wolfe Arts Club, 90-92; founding mem, Piermont Fine Arts Gallery, NY, 93. *Teaching:* Instr watercolor (workshops & demonstrations) Rockland Ctr Arts, West Nyack, NY, 85-91, int workshops; adj prof, Col New Rochelle, NY & Seton Hall Univ, 96-99. *Awards:* Am Watercolor Soc Traveling Award, 84; travel award, Ky Watercolor Soc, Aqueous 86, 86. *Bibliog:* Adam Pfeffer (auth), On the arts, Spotlight Mag, 2/88. *Mem:* Nat Watercolor Soc; Nat Asn Women Artists; Audubon Artists; Catherine Lorillard Wolfe Arts Club; Midwest Watercolor Soc. *Media:* Watermedia, Collage. *Publ:* Auth, Splash, America's Best Contemporary Watercolors, 90 & Splash 6, 2000, Northlight; Best of Watercolor, watercolor book, 95 & Floral Inspirations, 97, Rockport Publ; The Artistic Touch 3, Creative Press, 98. *Mailing Add:* PO Box 99 Cerrillos NM 87010

PEEPLES-BRIGHT, MAIJA GEGERIS ZACK WOOF
PAINTER
b Riga, Latvia, Nov 21, 42. *Study:* Univ Calif, Davis, BA, 64, MA, 65; also with William T Wiley, Robert Arneson & Wayne Thiebaud. *Work:* Crocker Art Gallery, Sacramento, Calif; La Jolla Mus Art, Calif; Matthews Art Ctr, Tempe, Ariz; San Francisco Mus Art; Norman MacKenzie Art Gallery, Regina, Sask. *Comn:* Beast rainbow painting, City San Francisco, Civic Ctr, 67; rainbow house, pvt party, San Francisco, 67-68; ceiling murals, Rainbow House, San Francisco, 67-68; crocheted, woven & sewn beast curtains, Univ Calif Art Bldg, Davis, 71; Sun of Alion, Fiberglass Sculpture for pride of Sacramento, 2004. *Exhib:* San Francisco Art Mus, 73-75; Rainbow Show, De Young Mus, San Francsico, 74-75; one woman show, Iris Upon a Star, J'Nette Gardens, Oakland, Calif, 87-88, Maija's Flowers, Candy Store Gallery, Folsom, Calif, 90, Life Is Just a Bowl of Terriers, Nev Mus Art, Reno, 91 & Paintings & Ceramics, Solomon/Dubnick Gallery, Sacramento, Calif, 95; All Creatures Great & Small, Natsoulas Gallery, Davis, Calif, 92; My Plezoores, Anya Horvath Gallery, Sacramento, Calif, 93 & 94; Small Wonders, I Wolk Gallery, St Helena, Calif, 93-94; Form and Fire, 2000; Regina Clay Worlds In the Making, MacKenzie Gallery, 2006-06; Woof's Heroes, Explodinghead Gallery, Sacramento, Calif, 2005; Laughing Owl the Way, Canadian Clay & Glass Gallery, Waterloo, Ontario, 2006. *Collection Arranged:* The Nut Show, for Kaiser-Aetna, Tahoe Verdes, Calif, 72. *Teaching:* Instr art, Laney Col, Oakland, 68-69, Univ Calif, Davis, 71-72 & Sierra Col, Rocklin, Calif, 71-73; painting workshop, Sierra Oaks Sch, Sacramento, Calif, 93. *Awards:* Award, Ceramics Excellence, Calif State Fair, 74. *Bibliog:* Ellen Schlesinger (auth), As Fate would have it, Peeples is an artist, Sacramento Bee, 7/4/82; Ronnie Cohen (auth), Maija's Zoo, Neighbors Mag, 2/84; Rachel SAvage (auth), Always Merry and Bright, Inside the City Mag, 9/2005; Dawn Blunk (auth), At the Heart fo the Art, Sacramento Mag, 4/2004. *Media:* Multi. *Dealer:* Exploding head gallery, 925-12th St., Sacramento, CA 95814

PEEPS, CLAIRE
CURATOR, PHOTOGRAPHER
b Vancouver, BC, Oct, 24, 56. *Study:* Stanford Univ, BA, 78; Univ NMex, MA, 82. *Exhib:* Houston Art Ctr, Tex, 83; San Francisco Camera Works, Calif, 84. *Pos:* Assoc art dir, cur performing & visual arts, Los Angeles Arts Festival, Calif, 89-96; exec dir, Durfee Found, Santa Monica, Calif, currently. *Awards:* Purchase Award, Univ Ariz, 82. *Mem:* 18th St Arts Complex (bd mem, 88-94); Arts Inc (bd mem, 89-93); Calif Coun Humanities. *Publ:* Cycles: The Photography of Judith Golden, 87; Mario Giacomelli, 83. *Mailing Add:* c/o Durfee Found 1453 3rd St Suite 312 Santa Monica CA 90401

PEI, I M
ARCHITECT, DESIGNER
b Canton, China, Apr 26, 1917; US citizen. *Study:* Mass Inst Technol, BArch, 40; Harvard Univ, MArch, 46; Hon DFA degrees from New York Univ, Univ Pa, Rensselaer Polytechnic Inst, Brown Univ, Carnegie-Mellon Univ, Northeastern Univ, Dartmouth & Univ Rochester; DHL degrees from Columbia Univ, Univ Hong Kong, Am Univ Paris & Univ Colo; Chinese Univ, Hong Kong & Pace Univ, DL. *Comn:* JFK Library, Boston, 79; West Wing, Mus Fine Arts, Boston, 81; Fragrant Hill Hotel, Beijing, China, 82; New York Expos & Conv Ctr, NY, 86; Bank China, Hong Kong, 89; Dallas Symphony Hall, 89; Grand Louvre, Paris, 89 & 93; Miho Mus, Shiga, Japan, 91; Kirklin Clinic, Univ Ala, Birmingham, 92; Rock and Roll Hall of Fame, Cleveland, Ohio, 95; Friend Ctr for Engineering, Princeton Univ, 2001; extension to Deutsches Historisches Mu, Berlin, Germany, 2003; Ferguson Ctr Performing Arts, Christopher Newport Univ, Va, 2005; Martha Stewart Ctr for Living, Mt Sinai Hosp, NY, 2005. *Pos:* Dir archit, Webb & Knapp Inc, New York, 48-55; archit, New York, 55-; mem, Nat Coun Humanities, 66-70; mem, Urban Design Coun, New York, 67-72. *Teaching:* Instr, Harvard Grad Sch Design, 45-48. *Awards:* Gold Medal, Univ Calif, Los Angeles, 90; First Award for Excellence, Colbert Found, 91; Excellence 2000 Award, 91; Medal of Freedom, 93; NY State Gov's Arts Award, 1994; Munic Art Soc, Jacqueline Kennedy Onassis Medal, NY, 1996; Hist Landmarks Preserv Ctr, Cult Laureate, 1999. *Bibliog:* Bruno Suner (auth), Ieoh Ming Pei, Hazan, Paris, 88; Carter Wiseman (auth), I M Pei, A Profile in American Architecture, Abrams, New York, 90. *Mem:* Corp mem Royal Inst Brit Archit; fel Am Inst Architects; Am Acad & Inst Arts & Lett (chancellor, 78-80); hon fel Am Soc Interior Designers; Am Acad Arts & Sci; Nat Coun Arts; and others; Nat Acad (assoc, 63, acad, 65)

PEI, IEOH MING See Pei, I M

PEIPERL, ADAM
VIDEO ARTIST, KINETIC ARTIST
b Sosnowiec, Poland, June 4, 35; US citizen. *Study:* George Washington Univ, BS, 57; Pa State Univ, 57-59. *Work:* Nat Mus Am Hist, Hirshhorn Mus & John F Kennedy Ctr Performing Arts, Washington, DC; Pa Acad Fine Arts, Philadelphia; Boijmans Van Beuningen Mus, Rotterdam, Holland. *Comn:* Video shorts, WETA TV Channel 26, Washington, DC, 84; dance collaboration with Maida Withers, Lincoln Ctr Out-of-Doors, 96. *Exhib:* Corcoran Gallery Art, 68; one-man shows, Baltimore Mus Art, 69, Pa Acad Fine Arts, 69, Nat Mus Am Hist, 72-73, Philadelphia Art Alliance, 78, Nat Mus Am Art, 81; Kent State Univ, 69; Mem Art Gallery, Univ Rochester, 78; Pa Acad Fine Arts, 86 & 2004; Art of the Sixties, Fred Jones Jr Mus Art, Univ Okla, 2002; Radicals and Conservatives: Abstraction 1945 to Present. *Awards:* Int Platform Asn Art Show Silver Medal, 83, Gold Medal, 84. *Bibliog:* Frank Getlein (auth), He defied tradition and made it work, Sun Star, 7/21/68; Diane Chichura & Thelma Stevens (auths), Super Sculpture, Van Nostrand-Reinhold, 74; Victoria Donohoe (auth), Kinetic art lives on, Philadelphia Inquirer, 10/27/78; George Washington Univ Mag, spring 92 & winter 2002. *Media:* Miscellaneous. *Publ:* image, Time/Life Book-of-the-Month Club, 95-96. *Mailing Add:* 1135 Loxford Terr Silver Spring MD 20901

PEKAR, RONALD WALTER
PAINTER, SCULPTOR
b Cleveland, Ohio, Oct 9, 42. *Study:* Cleveland Inst Art; Wash Univ, BFA, fel, 66-67, MFA. *Work:* Memphis Brooks Mus Art; Mississippi Mus Art; Carroll Reece Mus, Tenn; Cheekwood Mus Art, Tenn; St Jude Children's Res Hosp; painting series, Federal Express Corp; represented in more than 200 corporate and mus collections worldwide. *Comn:* Mural series, Memphis Convention Ctr Complex; sculptural environments, Holiday Inns, Inc (nationwide); illuminated painting, Gen Pub Utilities, Pa; two 3-story illuminated sculptures, Lemoyne-Owen Col. *Exhib:* Solo shows: Memphis Brooks Mus, Miss Mus Art, Rhodes Col, Univ Tenn, Memphis Col Art & Ark State Univ; 10 in Tennessee, Statewide-Traveling Bicentennial Exhib; Mid South Artists Traveling Exhib; Memphis Pink Palace Mus Commemorative Painting; Spirit of the River (audio-visual environment), Memphis Brooks Mus, 77-81. *Pos:* Found div chair, Memphis Col Art, currently; lectr & critic, Univ Tenn, ETex State Univ, Ark State Univ; former cons The Walt Disney Co, Worldwide. *Teaching:* Prof, 2-D and 3-D design, drawing and painting, Otis Col Art and Design & Calif State Univ, Northridge. *Awards:* Cult Contribution Award, State of Tenn; Tenn Valley Authority Monumental Sculpture Award. *Bibliog:* Man of steel and crayon, Mid South Mag Commercial Appeal; profile, Memphis Mag. *Mem:* Calif Art Club. *Media:* Acrylic, Oil; All, Bronze, Steel. *Publ:* Illusr, Air poster, Memphis Acad Arts, 69; illusr rec label, Ardent Rec, 72; ed & illusr, Homage to the Land and Sky, 73; illusr rec label, Privilege Rec, 74. *Dealer:* Tirage Gallery 1 West California Blvd Pasadena CA 91105. *Mailing Add:* 1426 Highland Ave Glendale CA 91202

PEKARSKY, MEL(VIN) HIRSCH
PAINTER, EDUCATOR
b Chicago, Ill, Sept 18, 1934. *Study:* Art Inst Chicago; Northwestern Univ, BA, MA. *Work:* Corcoran Gallery Art, Washington; Minneapolis Inst Arts; Cleveland Mus Art; Weatherspoon Mus, Univ NC; Fogg Mus Art, Harvard Univ; Yale Univ Art Mus; Indianapolis Mus Art; Nev Mus Art; Roswell, NMex, Mus Art; Notre Dame Univ Art Mus; and many others. *Comn:* Exterior mural, City Walls Inc: Kaplan Fund, 70; exterior mural, Nat Endowment Arts, 72; exterior mural, US Dept Housing & Urban Develop, 74. *Exhib:* New Editions 74-75 & NY Cult Ctr, 75; Drawings by Seven Am Artists, Cleveland Mus, 78; The Am Landscape: Recent Developments, Whitney Mus Am Art, NY, 81; Selected Am Drawings, Noyes Mus Art, NJ, 96; New Acquisitions, The Fogg Mus of Art, Harvard Univ, 2000 & 2006; Albright Knox Gallery, Buffalo, NY, 2002-2003; Nielsen Gallery, Boston, 2001, 02, 03, 04; Am Acad Arts and Letters, 2001; Nat Acad Design, 2001; Kuznetsky-Most Gallery, Moscow, 1989; Musées Royeaux de Beaux-Arts de Belgique, 1978; others; one-man shows, G W Einstein, NY, 75, 77-78, 80-81, 84, 86, 88, 91 & 95, Gallery 112 Greene St, NY, 80, Butler Inst Am Art, 90 & Mus Stony Book, NY, 93, Nev Mus Art, 2001, Nielsen Gallery, Boston, 2002-2003. *Collection Arranged:* curator, Reuben Radish, Julius Tobias, Gladys Nielson, Jim Nutt, Lucio Pozzi. *Pos:* Founding mem & mem bd, City Walls, Inc, 69-75, vpres, 70-75; bd dir, Reuben Kadish Found Arts, currently; adv bd, Gallery North, currently. *Teaching:* From asst to assoc dean art, Sch Visual Arts, New York, 67-69; fac, New York Univ Grad Sch Art, 70-71; prof art, State Univ NY, Stony Brook, 75-, chmn, 76-78 & 84-89, dir studio progs, 75-2003, dir, MFA Prog, 89-2003, chm, 2005-. *Awards:* grants, NY State Coun Arts, Nat Endowment for Arts, Kaplan Fund, Bernhard Found, US Dept Housing & Urban Devel. *Bibliog:* Donald Kuspit (auth), Mel Pekarsky, catalog, 10/84 & Pekarsky's Desert Tundra, catalogue, 10/88; Robert G Edelman (auth), The Transformative Vision: Contemporary Am Landscape

Painting, Pittsburgh Carnegie Mus, 89; John Driscoll & Arnold Skolnick (auths), The Artist and the American Landscape, San Francisco, 98; Printworld Directory. *Mem:* Col Art Asn; Pub Art Fund. *Media:* Oil, Mixed Media. *Specialty:* paintings & drawings. *Publ:* Illusr, The Curious Cow, 60, Little Quack, 61, The Three Goats, 63 & The Little Red Hen, 63, Follett; Handbook of Gestures, Mouton, The Hague, 72. *Dealer:* Nielsen Gallery, 179 Newbury St, Boston, Mass, 02116; GW Einstein Co Inc New York. *Mailing Add:* Box 1575 Stony Brook NY 11790

PELADEAU, MARIUS BEAUDOIN
WRITER, MUSEUM DIRECTOR
b Boston, Mass, Jan 27, 35. *Study:* St Michael's Col, Winooski Park, Vt, BA(cum laude), 56; Boston Univ, Mass, MS, 57; Georgetown Univ, Washington, DC, MA(fel), 61. *Pos:* Dir, Maine League of Hist Soc & Mus, 72-76; dir, William A Farnsworth Libr & Art Mus, 76-87, consult & writer, 87-; managing dir, The Theater, Monmouth, ME, 88; cur, LC Bates Mus, 93-2001. *Teaching:* guest lectr, Univ Maine. *Mem:* VT Hist Soc, Co of Military Hist. *Media:* Print media. *Res:* American art and the decorative arts; 18th and 19th century American Art, folk art & decorative arts. *Publ:* The Prose of Royall Tyler, Vt Hist Soc, 72; Adventures in Maine History, Maine League of Historical Socs, 76; auth, Chansonetta: The Photographs of Chansonetta Stanley Emmons, 1858-1937, Morgan & Morgan, 77; Charles Daniel Hubbard: American Impressionist, 1876-1951, LC Bates Mus, 96; Looking at Katahdin: Maine Artists' Inspiration, LC Bates Mus, 99. *Mailing Add:* 158 Thorp Shores Rd Readfield ME 04355

PELLETTIERI, MICHAEL JOSEPH
PRINTMAKER, PAINTER
b New York, NY, Nov 25, 43. *Study:* The New School, 62; Art Students League New York, with Robert B Hale, Edwin Dickinson, Harry Sternberg & Joseph Hirsch, 63-66; City Col New York, BA, 65; City Univ New York, MA, 69. *Work:* De Cordova Mus, Lincoln, Mass; Taz Gallery & Co, Boston; Newark Art Libr, NJ; Ben Goldstein Collection, NY; Columbia Mus Art, SC; NY Pub Libr; Libr Congress; Dave and Reba Williams Collection; NDak Univ; Art Students League of NY; Franz Grierhass Collection; Wallace Found; Amity Arts Found; NY Hist Soc; and others. *Exhib:* Boston Printmakers 32nd Nat, DeCordova Mus, Lincoln, Mass, 79; Hunterdon Art Ctr 23rd & 25th, Newark Art Libr, NJ, 79 & 81; Nat Acad & Inst Arts & Letts, 80; Charlotte Printmakers, NC, 81; Columbia Univ, NY, 87, 93; Landmark Gallery, Kingston, NY, 88; New Renaissance Gallery, NY, 91; City Views Decordova Mus, Lincoln, Mass, 98; Seaton Hall Univ, Ital Am Printmakers, NJ, 01; Up on the Roof, NY Hist Soc, 01; NY Etchers Soc Inaugural Exhib, 2000; Old Print Shop, NY, 01; A Message from NY, The Sky Gallery, Umeda Sky Building, Osaka, Japan, 02; NY Soc of Etchers, Mus of City of NY, 02; PaineWebber Galleries, A Century on Paper, Prints by Art Students League Artists, 125th Anniversary, 02; Retrospective, Paintings and Prints, Art Students League of NY, 02, Durst Gallery, A Message from NY, 03; Gallery of Graphic Art, Printmaking A to Z, NY, 03; Old Print Shop, Prints and Watercolors, NY, 2004; NY Hist Soc, Impressions of NY, 2004; NY Hist Soc, Around Town Underground, From the Coll of Dave and Reba Williams, NY, 2004; Boston Printmakers, Nat Exhib, 2005. *Collection Arranged:* Exhibition advisor, A Century on Paper, Prints by Art Students League Artists, 125th anniversary exhibition, PaineWebber Galleries, 02; coord, Twenty-first-Century Print Portfolio, Commemorative Print Portfolio Celebrating 125th Anniversary of the Art Students League of New York, 02; juror, Inaugural Exhibition of New York Etchers Society Exhibition, 2000; coord, Portfolio 2000, The Graphics Workshop of the Art Students League, 2000. *Teaching:* Instr lithography, Art Students League New York, 77-79, instr graphics, 79-, instr intaglio, Summit Art Ctr, 82-88; instr printmaking, Columbia Univ, Teachers Col, 87-. *Awards:* Mitchell Fund Award, 86; Mac Dowell Colony Fel, 88; Purchase Prize, Nat Works Paper, Univ Miss, 91; and others; Ben and Beatrice Goldstein Found Award, 91; Robert Conover Mem Award, 2000; Burr Miller Award for litography, SAGA, 02. *Bibliog:* Garry Simpson (auth), Currier & Ives (film for television), Univ Vt, 76; In Honor of low tech printmaking, The Record, NJ, 2002; Portfolio, Old Print Shop, 20th Century Prints, 95. *Mem:* Artist Equity NY; Art Students League NY (bd control, 65, treas, 66-67); Audubon Artists (dir graphics 82-84, vp 1985); Boston Printmakers. *Media:* Intaglio, Lithography; Oil. *Specialty:* American Prints. *Publ:* Contribr, Print Review Ten, Pratt Graphic Art Ctr, 79; Linea, What Are the Greatest Obstacles to Developing as an Artist, 1998; New York Society of Etchers, Harry Stenberg, A Life Celebrated, 2000; Auth, A Retrospective, Michael Pellettieri, 2002; New York Soc Etchers, Catalogue Forward, Inaugural Exhib, 2002; Linea, Interview with Will Barnet on the Life of Bob Blackburn, 2004. *Dealer:* The Old Print Shop 150 Lexington Ave New York NY 10016; Gallery of Graphic Art 1610 York Ave New York NY 10028. *Mailing Add:* 325 W 77th St New York NY 10024

PELLI, CESAR
ARCHITECT
b Tucuman, Arg, Oct 12, 26; US citizen. *Study:* Univ Tucuman, Dipl in Archit (cum laude) 49; Univ Ill, MS (archit), 54. *Comn:* Mus Mod Art, NY; World Financial Ctr, NY; Herring Hall, Rice Univ, Houston, Tex; North Terminal at Wash Nat Airport; Petronas Twin Towers, Kuala Lumpur, Malaysia. *Exhib:* One-man exhibs, Current Work, Schindler House Gallery, Los Angeles, 86, Architecture of Response, Delphi Res Inc, Tokyo, Japan, 94 & Current Works, Biennale, Mus Nac Bellas Artes, Buenos Aires, Argentina, 95; Lieux? de Travail, Centre Georges Pompidou, Centre de Cretion Industrielle CCI, Paris, France, 86; Monumental Arches, Arches for Galveston, Cooper-Hewitt Mus, NY, 87-88; New Chicago Projects, Chicago Athenaeum: Ctr Archit, Art & Urban Studies, Chicago, Ill, 89; retrospective, Col Archit Gallery, Univ NC, Charlotte, 92 & Pattern and Context, 92; City Metropolis: New Directions in Italy, Soviet Union, United States, Columbia Univ, NY, 93; Mus Designs by Distinguished 20th Century Architects, Jacksonville Art Mus, Fla, 94; Shoe Exhib, Conn Hist Soc, 95; Works in Progress, Boston Soc Architects, 95; Am Inst Architects, Queens West, 95; Architecture of Response, Vente Mus, 95, Am Inst Architects Nat Conv, Atlanta, 95, Hurlbutt Gallery, Greenwich, Conn, 96, Artspace, New Haven, Conn, 97; Middfest Int, Aronoff Ctr Arts, 96; The Petronas Towers, Skyscraper Mus, 97; Democratic Design: A New Era of Federal Architecture, Chicago Atheneaum, 97; City, Space and Globalization, Col Archit & Urban Planning, Univ Mich, 98. *Pos:* Designer, Eero Saarinen & Assoc, 54-64; dir design, Daniel Mann, Johnson & Mendenhall, 64-68; partner design, Gruen Assoc, Los Angeles & New York, 68-76; prin, Cesar Pelli & Assoc, New Haven, 77-. *Teaching:* Dean, Sch Archit, Yale Univ, 77-84, vis lectr, currently. *Awards:* CSA/AIA Unbuilt Project Award, 88; Design Awards, Am Inst Architects, Conn, 91, 96, 97 & 98; Bard Award, 92; Gold medal, AIAA, 95; Numerous archit. awards from govts, prof soc, educ inst, publ, 1966-. *Bibliog:* Cesar Pelli Special Ed atu (Japan), 7/85; Cesar Pelli: 1965-1990, Rizzoli Int Publs, 90; Cesar Pelli Selected and Current Works, The Master Architect Series No 1, The Images Publ Group, 93. *Mem:* Fel Am Inst Archit; Am Acad & Inst Arts & Lett; Nat Acad; trustee, Wadsworth Atheneum; Int Acad Archit; Acad d' Arch de France; Russian Acad Archit and Constuction Scis; Soc Arquitectos de Cordoba. *Publ:* Auth, Architectural Form & the Tradition of Building, VIA, 83; Skyscrapers, Perspecta No 19, 81; Pieces of the City, Archit Digest, Aug, 88; Cesar Pelli: The Megabuilding in Context, Archit Design, 11/12/88; Auth. Observations for Young Artists, Monacelli Press, 99. *Mailing Add:* c/o Cesar Pelli & Assoc Inc 1056 Chapel St New Haven CT 06510

PELUSO, MARTA E
PHOTOGRAPHER, ART INSTRUCTOR
b New Brighton, Pa, Apr 30, 51. *Study:* Allegheny Col, Meadville, Pa, BA, 73; Panopticon Photo Workshop with Garry Winogrand, Greece, 77; Univ Calif, Davis, MFA, 82. *Work:* Univ Calif, Davis/Nelson Gallery; Mercyhurst Col Libr, Erie, Pa. *Exhib:* Solo exhib, Photographs, Pittsburgh Filmmakers Gallery, Pa, 81; The Guiding Light, Eye Gallery, San Francisco, Calif, 90 & Santa Barbara Contemp Arts Forum, Calif, 91; Scarred Texts/Sacred Territories, Scarlet Palette, Cambria, Calif, 92; Memorie, Arternatives, San Luis Obispo, Calif, 95. *Pos:* Photograph proj coord, Ethnic Impressions, Erie, Pa, 75-79; Gallery dir, Cuesta Col, San Luis Obispo, Calif, 86-2001; exec dir, ARTS Obispo, San Luis Obispo, Calif, 2006-. *Teaching:* Lectr photog, Cal Polytech State Univ, San Luis Obispo, 83-87; instr studio art, Cuesta Col, San Luis Obispo, Calif, 86-2007. *Bibliog:* Les Krantz (auth), California art review, Am References, 89. *Mem:* Soc Photog Educ (W Region chmn, 89); San Luis Obispo Co Arts Coun (bd mem, 90-93). *Media:* Photography, Assemblage. *Publ:* Marta Peluso's quest for the best, The Tribune, San Luis Obispo, 10/31/99; Art Rag, San Luis Obispo, Calif, 11/99 & fall 2000; Iris, Univ Va, Charlottesville, winter/spring 99; Rethinking the Natural (catalog) Austin Mus Art at Laguna Gloria, Austin, Tex, 95. *Mailing Add:* 557 Stoneridge Dr San Luis Obispo CA 93401-5671

PENA, AMADO MAURILIO, JR
PAINTER, ILLUSTRATOR
b Laredo, Tex, Oct 1, 43. *Study:* Tex A&I Univ, BA(art), 65, MA (art & educ), 71. *Work:* Tex A&I Univ; Inter-Am Develop Bank, Washington; Univ Tex, Austin; Juarez-Lincoln Univ, Austin; Los Pinos, Pres Palace, Mexico; and others. *Comn:* Mural, Laredo Independent Sch Dist, Serv Ctr, 70; mural, City Hall, Crystal City, 72; painting, City Coun Crystal City, 72; centennial poster, Univ Tex, Austin, 83; Amarille Art Ctr, Tex, 83; and others. *Exhib:* Chicago Art Exhib, Nat Lulac Conf, Washington, 73 & Univ Tex Student Ctr, 74; Chicano Artists of the Southwest, Inst Mex Cult, San Antonio, 75; one-man retrospectives, Mus Nuevo Santander, Laredo, Tex, 83 & Laguna Gloria Art Mus, Austin, Tex, 83; and others. *Teaching:* Teacher art, Laredo Independent Sch Dist, 65-70, Crystal City Independent Sch Dist, 72-74, LC Anderson High Sch, Austin, 74-80 & Idyllwild Sch of Art, 88; artist in residence, instr Austin Community Coll, 90-92, Laredo Community Col, 97; founder, artist in residence, Studio Art Prog at Alexander High Sch, Laredo, 94-. *Awards:* Best of Show Award, First Place Award Painting & People's Choice Award, Southwest Arts Festival, Indio, Calif, 2000; First Place Award Painting, Bayou City Arts Festival, Houston, 2000; First Place Award Painting & First Place award Printmaking, Castle Rock Arts Festival, Colo. *Bibliog:* Amado M Pena to speak at graduation ceremony, The PAN AMERICAN, 97; Noted artist likes Alton enough to come back, The Telegraph, 97; Pena conversation starts Speaker Series, Laredo Morning Times, 97. *Mem:* Laredo Art Asn (pres, 68-69); Austin Art Teachers Asn (treas, 74-75). *Media:* Serigraphy; Watercolor. *Publ:* Contribr & auth, Chicano Art of the Southwest, Chicano Slide Collection, 73; contribr, Tejidos, Magazin & Calendario Chicano; illusr, Cuenots, 75. *Dealer:* El Taller Gallery 723 E Sixth St Austin TX 78701; Gallery Mack Seattle WA. *Mailing Add:* Pena Studio Gallery 235 Don Gaspar Santa Fe NM 87501

PENCE, JOHN GERALD
DEALER, PATRON
b Ft Wayne, Ind, Feb 8, 36. *Study:* Wabash Col, BA, 58; Am Univ, MA, 63. *Collection Arranged:* Douglas Fenn Wilson, Worcester Mus, Dartmouth Col, Janus Gallery, Santa Fe, San Francisco Mus, Hibernia Bank, San Francisco & Deloitee, Haskins & Sells, NY; Michael Bergt, Pence Gallery, San Francisco & San Francisco Mus; Frank Mason, Clorox Co & Pence Gallery, San Francisco; Robert Maione, Pence Gallery, San Francisco, Clorox Co, Standard Oil of Calif, Hering & Assoc, Portland & Allen-Pacific Co, San Francisco; Gillian Wiles, Pence Gallery, San Francisco & URS Corp, Dallas; Donald Davis, Cellocon Inc, San Francisco, Deloitee, Haskins, Sells, NY & James Malott Architects; Will Wilson, Buckeye Petroleum, NJ & Butler Inst Am Art; McKenzie Family Found, Conn. *Teaching:* Instr, US Naval Acad, Annapolis, Md. *Mem:* San Francisco Art Dealers Asn (pres, 61-63). *Interests:* American contemporary realists--advance support prior to initial presentations. *Publ:* Auth, Will Wilson, Am Artist Mag, 5/83. *Mailing Add:* Pence Gallery 750 Post St San Francisco CA 94109

PENCZNER, PAUL JOSEPH
PAINTER
b Hungary, Sept 17, 16; US citizen. *Study:* In Hungary. *Work:* Vatican, Rome; Capitol Bldg, Jefferson City; Univ Tenn, Memphis; Univ Mo, Cape Girardeau; Fla State Univ, Tallahassee. *Exhib:* Pa Acad Fine Arts, Philadelphia; Brooks Mem Art Gallery, Memphis; Jersey City Mus; Smithsonian Inst, Washington, DC; El Delgado Mus, New Orleans; Tenn Botanical Gardens & Fine Art Ctr, Nashville. *Pos:* Owner, Penczner's Fine Art Studio & Gallery, Memphis, Tenn. *Awards:* Distinguished Achievement Award, Modern Maturity, 86; Best Of Show, Southern Biannual, 84. *Mem:* Nat Soc Painters Casein; Tenn Watercolor Soc; Am Artist Prof League; Southern Watercolor Soc. *Media:* Multimedia. *Res:* Originator, Time Expressionism by using three dimensional or cylinderical surfaces to express continuous and repetative time and space; originator a new variation of impressionism called Oil Graphics by using wax panels into a wet oil paint combining the ground color, surface colors and drawn colors rather than the French impressionists juxtapostion of colors. *Dealer:* Laurelwood Gallery 404 Perkins Ext Memphis TN 38117. *Mailing Add:* 2383 S Stratmore Cir Memphis TN 38112-3221

PENDERGRAFT, NORMAN ELVEIS
MUSEUM DIRECTOR, HISTORIAN
b Durham, NC, Mar 4, 34. *Study:* Univ NC, Chapel Hill; Conservatorio di Musica G Rossini, Pesaro, Italy, with Maestra Raggi-Valentini; Ohio Univ, Athens; Mus Mgt Inst, Univ Calif, Berkeley; Nat Endowment Humanities Sem, Rome, Italy. *Pos:* dir art mus, NC Cent Univ, Durham, 76-96, emer; art consult, 96-. *Teaching:* Prof art hist, NC Cent Univ, Durham, 66-96, emer. *Awards:* Outstanding contrib to Art Educ Award, NC Art Educ Asn, 84; Prof Serv Award, NC Mus Coun, 95. *Bibliog:* OM Foushee (auth), Art in North Carolina: Episodes & Developments, Chapel Hill, NC, 72; LM Igoe (auth), 250 yrs of Afro-American Art: An Annotated Bibliography, RR Bowker, 81. *Mem:* Am Asn Mus; Southeastern Mus Coun; Col Art Asn; Am Asn Univ Prof; NC Mus Coun. *Res:* Italian Renaissance, Afro-American and American art. *Publ:* Auth, Heralds of Life: Artis, Bearden & Burke, 77 & Duncanson: A British American Connection, 84 & Geoffrey Holder: Painter, 86, & Gullah Life Reflections, 88, NC Cent Univ Art Mus; Joy of Living: Romare Beardons Late Work, NC Cent Univ Art Mus, 94; Artistic Legacy: Collection of Art from CIAA schools, Diggs Gallery, Winston-Salem State Univ, NC, 94; A Gift of Art, Herald Sun, Durham, NC, 98. *Mailing Add:* 807 W Trinity Ave Apt 258 Durham NC 27701

PENDERGRASS, CHRISTINE C
CERAMIST, SCULPTOR
b Detroit, Mich, Jan 5, 52. *Study:* Stanford Univ, BA(studio art), 73. *Work:* State Art Collection, Dept Motor Vehicles, Salem Ore; State Art Collection, Badger Rd Sch & 2 Rivers Sch, Fairbanks, Alaska; Municipal Art Collection, Lynnwood, Wash. *Comn:* 4 ceramic wall sculptures, Mid-Columbia Med Ctr, The Dalles, Ore, 93 & 96; 4 ceramic wall sculptures, Mass Gen Hosp, Boston, 94; 2 ceramic wall sculptures, Wells Fargo Bank, Portland, Ore, 95; 3 ceramic wall sculptures, St Charles Med Ctr, Bend, Ore, 95; 2 outdoor artworks, Downtown Eugene Inc, Ore, 2002, 03. *Exhib:* Solo shows, Stanford Univ, 92, Reno City Hall Gallery, Nev, 93, Russell Senate Bldg, Washington, 95, Chico Art Ctr, Calif, 96 & Sun Cities Mus Art, Ariz, 97. *Teaching:* pvt tchr. *Awards:* Grant, Ludwig Vogelstein Found, New York, 84; Artist Award, Earthwatch, Watertown, Mass, 94; Internet Art Connection Award, 94. *Bibliog:* Danielle C Malka (auth), Merged realities-artists & scientists borrow from one another, Ariz Daily Star, 95; Larry Savadove (auth), Function follows form in found show, Sandpaper, Loveladies, NJ, 98; Morley Young (auth), A Sense of Humor, and Beauty, The Ruralite, 2004. *Media:* Ceramics. *Publ:* contribr, Body of Art, Willoughby & Baltic Fine Arts, Cambridge, Mass, 2006; auth, Ceramics Monthly Mag, 86, 90 & 93; auth, Fans-The Bulletin of the Fan Circle Int, London, 90; contribr, Art Calendar-The Bus Mag for Visual Artists, 94; auth, Ceramics in Healthcare, Fine Art Ceramics, Welches, Oreg, 2002; contribr, The Hastings Ctr Report, Garrison, NY, 2004. *Dealer:* Art Factors 7035 SW Macadam Portland OR. *Mailing Add:* 92130 Sharewater Ln Cheshire OR 97419-9704

PENKOFF, RONALD PETER
EDUCATOR, PAINTER
b Toledo, Ohio, May 18, 1932. *Study:* Bowling Green State Univ, BFA, 54; Ohio State Univ, MA, 56; Stanley William Hayter's Atelier 17, Paris, 65-66; Univ Kans, 80 & 81. *Work:* Libr Cong, Washington; Columbus Gallery Art, Ohio; Munson-Williams-Proctor Inst, Utica, NY; Montclair Mus, NJ; Ball State Art Gallery, Muncie, Ind. *Comn:* Frank Lloyd Wright-Wyoming Valley (paintings), VW Col, 94-98. *Exhib:* Pennell Int Exhib Prints, Libr Cong, Washington, 55-57; Notre Dame Mus, 70; Skylight Gallery, 73; Madison Art Ctr, 75; Alvehjem Mus, 77 & 83; Milwaukee Art Mus, 78; Crossman Gallery, Univ Wis, Whitewater, 90. *Teaching:* Asst prof art, State Univ NY, Oneonta, 56-59; asst prof, Ball State Univ, 59-67; vis prof, Bath Acad Art, Corsham, Eng, summer 66; prof, Univ Wis, Waukesha, 67-87, Richland Ctr, 87-98, chmn, Ctr Syst Art Dept, 70-89 & 95-98, prof emeritus. *Awards:* Munson-Williams-Proctor Inst Award, Cent NY Artists, 58-59; First Award Painting, Eastern Ind Artists, 64; Nat Endowment Humanities Grant, 78. *Bibliog:* W Fabricki (auth), Prints and drawings of Ronald Penkoff, Quartet, 63; ME Young (auth), Profile, Wis Acad Rev, 69; Donald Key (auth), Color printing is an elusive endeavor, Milwaukee J, 71. *Mem:* Col Art Asn. *Media:* Intaglio. *Publ:* Auth, The eye and the object, Forum, 62; Roots of the Ukiyo-E, 65; Sign, Signal, Symbol, 70; The Japanese Print & the Grounding of Frank Lloyd Wrights' Architecture, 90; The Woodblock Prints of Andrea Rich, 2006. *Dealer:* Red Door Gallery Richland Ctr WI 53581. *Mailing Add:* 420 East Court Richland Center WI 53581

PENN, IRVING
PHOTOGRAPHER
b Plainfield, NJ, 1917. *Study:* Philadelphia Mus Sch Indust Art, 34-38. *Work:* Mus Mod Art & Metrop Mus Art, NY; Art Inst Chicago; Victoria & Albert Mus, London; Nat Portrait Gallery, Nat Mus Am Art & Smithsonian Inst, Washington, DC; and many others. *Exhib:* One-man shows, Mus Mod Art, NY, 75 & 84, Galleria Civica D'Arte Moderna, Torino, 75 & Metrop Mus Art, NY, 77; Irving Penn: Master Images, Nat Mus Am Art & Nat Portrait Gallery, Washington, DC, 90, Irving Penn: Platinum Prints, Nat Gallery Art, Washington, DC, 2005; numerous others nat & internationally. *Awards:* Hasselblad Award, 85; Prix Nadar, 91. *Bibliog:* John Szarkowski (auth), Irving Penn, New York, 84. *Publ:* Auth, Moments Preserved, 60; Worlds in a Small Room, 74; Inventive Paris clothes, 1909-1939, 77; Flowers, 80; Issey Miyake, 88; Passage, 91. *Mailing Add:* c/o Irving Penn Studios 89 Fifth Ave New York NY 10003

PENNEY, CHARLES RAND
COLLECTOR, PATRON
b Buffalo, NY, July 26, 23. *Study:* Yale Univ, BA; Univ Va, LLB & JD; State Univ NY, Hon DFA, 95. *Collection Arranged:* Prints from the Charles Rand Penney Found, traveling NY & Tex, 64-75; Selections from the Charles R Penney Collection, Lakeview Gallery, NY, 70; Prints From the Charles Rand Penney Foundation, Niagara Co Community Col Mus, 71 & 77; Staffordshire Pottery Portrait Figures, Niagara Co Hist Soc, 72; 44 Charles Burchfield Drawings & two paintings, Charles Burchfield Ctr, Buffalo, 73; Decade, Graphics in the Sixties, 74; NY State Photographers, 74; Victorian Staffordshire Figurines, Carborundum Mus of Ceramics, Niagara Falls, 74 & Columbus Gallery of Fine Arts, Ohio, 76; Charles Burchfield: The Charles Rand Penney Collection, traveling throughout US, 78-81; The Graphic Art of Emil Ganso, Univ Iowa Mus Art, 79; The Charles Rand Penney Collection: Twentieth Century Art, traveling throughout US, 83-88; The Charles Rand Penney Collection of Western New York Art, Burchfield Art Ctr, 92-93; The Charles Rand Penney Collection of Works by Charles E Burchfield, Burchfield-Penney Art Ctr, Buffalo State Col, 94; The Charles Rand Penney Collection of Works by Roycroft Artists, Burchfield-Penney Art Ctr, Buffalo State Col, 94; The Charles Rand Penney Craft Art Collection, Burchfield-Penney Art Ctr, Buffalo State Col, 94; Selections from the Charles Rand Penney Collection of Prints of Niagara Falls, Mediatheque Municipale Jean Levy, Lille, France, 2002; Selections from the Charles Rand Penney Collection of Prints of Niagara Falls, Centre Culturel Mousckonnois Mouscron, Belgium, 2003. *Awards:* Distinguished Service to Culture Award, State Univ NY Col Potsdam, 83; President's Distinguished Serv Award, Buffalo State Col, 91. *Mem:* Am Ceramic Circle; hon life mem Rochester Art Club; hon trustee Buffalo Soc Artist; and many others. *Collection:* International contemporary art; works of Charles E Burchfield and Emil Ganso; Western New York artists; Spanish-American Santos and Retablos; Victorian Staffordshire pottery portrait figures; American antique historic glass and textiles; American antique pressed glass; international primitive art; US World's Fairs & Expositions; Niagara Falls Print Collection; Tiffany Collection; Mr Planter's Peanut Collection; American Carnival Chalk Figurines; African Art Collection; New Guinea Art Collection; Western New York Art Collection; Haitian Art Collection; Eskimo Art Collection. *Mailing Add:* c/o Burchfield-Penney Art Ctr Buffalo State Col 1300 Elmwood Ave Buffalo NY 14222

PENNEY, JACQUELINE
PAINTER, INSTRUCTOR
b Roslyn, NY, Mar 26, 30. *Study:* Phoenix Sch Design, New York, 48; Black Mountain Col, 49; Inst Design, Chicago, 50, with Tom Hill, Carl Molno, Charles Reid, Frank Webb, Robert E Wood & Christopher Schink. *Work:* Port Authority, World Trade Ctr, NY; Stony Brook Sch, NY; Eastern Long Island Hosp, Greenport, NY; Unitarian Universalist Church, Oak Park, Ill; Jane Voorhees Zimmerli Art Mus, Rutgers State Univ, NJ. *Comn:* Cutchogue Pub Libr, Cutchogue, NY. *Exhib:* White Containers, Guild Hall Mus, East Hampton, NY, 86; What Comes After Winter, Audubon Artists Juried Exhib, 86; Nat Asn Women Artists Traveling Show, 88, 89 & 96; Monhegan Backyard, San Diego WC So Int, 89; Dancing in the Light, Salmagundi Club, NY, 92. *Teaching:* Art workshops acrylic & watercolor, 77-. *Awards:* ER Langer-Seligson Mem Award, Nat Asn Women Artists, 89; First Prize Best Landscape, Artist's Mag; Landscape Award, Mid-Atlantic Regional Watercolor Exhib, 90; William Meyerowitz Mem Prize, Nat Asn Women Artists, 86. *Bibliog:* Paul Demery (auth), An artist dreams in Cutchogue, Long Island Traveler-Watchman, 3/17/83; Marion Wolberg Weiss (auth), Downtown Cutchogue (cover), Honoring the Artist of East End, 10/9/92; 1998 National Competition, Artist's Mag, 12/98; Linda S. Price (Auth), Get the most out of painting abroad, Watercolor Mag, 99; M Stephen Doherty, Special report: 16 artists that paint together in Colorado, spring, 2000. *Mem:* Artist Equity New York; Nat Asn Women Artists; Salmagundi Club, New York, 92; Nat Asn Am Penwomen, 92. *Media:* Acrylic, Watercolor. *Publ:* Auth, Painting Watercolor Greeting Cards, North Light Books; A painting in progress--from far to near, Palette Talk Mag, 92; Still lifes that wont stay still, Am Hist Mag, 12/92; Discover the Joy of Painting with Acrylics, North Light Books, 2001; co-auth, The Artful Journal, A Spiritual Quest, 2002. *Dealer:* Penney Art Gallery & Studio 270 North St Cutchogue, NY 11935. *Mailing Add:* 270 North St PO Box 959 Cutchogue NY 11935

PENNINGTON, CLAUDIA
MUSEUM DIRECTOR
Pos: Dir, Key West Mus Art & Hist, Fla, 2000-. *Mailing Add:* Key West Mus Art & Hist 281 Front St Key West FL 33040

PENNINGTON, ESTILL CURTIS
HISTORIAN, CURATOR
b Paris, Ky, Oct 3, 50. *Study:* Univ Ky, BA, 72; Univ Ga; George Washington Univ. *Collection Arranged:* A New Quarter: Contemporary New Orleans Artists, 83; Birney Imes III: An exhib of photographs, 84; Storytime: Art as Episode, 85; William Edward West (1788-1857): Kentucky Painter (auth, catalog), 85; Reveries & Mississippi

Memories, 86; A Southern Collection, Morris Mus Art, 92, Will Henry Stevens, An Eye Transformed, A Hand Transforming, 93, Gracious Plenty, American Still Life Art in Southern Collections, 95, Echoes and Late Shadows, The Larger World of Southern Impressionism, 96, Frontier Sublime: Alaskan Art from the Juneau Empire Collection, 97. *Pos:* Guest cur & asst registrar, Nat Portrait Gallery, 77-78; art historian, Archives Am Art, 78-83; mus dir, Lauren Rogers Mus Art, Laurel, Miss, 83-87; cur, Ogden Collection, New Orleans, 87-88 & Morris Mus Art, 89-. *Awards:* Fel Royal Soc Arts. *Mem:* Miss Inst Arts & Letts (pres, 85-); Am Asn Mus; Victorian Soc Am. *Res:* American painting and portraiture. *Publ:* Auth, Joseph Cornell: Dimestore Connoisseur, 83 & Painting Lord Byron: An Account of William Edward West, 84, Archives Am Art J; The Climate of Taste in the Old South, Southern Quart, 85; collabr, The South on Paper: Line, Color & Light, Robert Hicklin, Inc, 85. *Mailing Add:* c/o Morris Mus Art One 10th St Augusta GA 30901-1134

PENNINGTON, JULIANA
DESIGNER, GRAPHIC ARTIST
b Catskill, NY, Jan 13, 50. *Study:* Foothill Col, AA(fine arts), 71; Humboldt State Univ, BA(fine arts, printmaking), 74; Calif Col Arts & Crafts, 86-87; paper and book intensive with Nance O'Banion, 97, San Francisco Ctr for Book, 2000-05. *Work:* Randall Mus & City San Francisco, Calif. *Comn:* Beyond Recycling, Norcal Waste Systems Inc, San Francisco, Calif, 95; cast paper sculpture, San Francisco Recycling Prog, Calif, 95. *Exhib:* Floculators Past, Present & Couchers, Randall Mus, San Francisco, Calif, 91; Little Art, Palo Alto Cult Ctr, Calif, 94; Reduce, Reuse, Recycle, San Francisco Int Airport, Calif, 95; Recycling: Preserving Natural Resources and Building a Sustainable Society (traveling exhib), San Francisco War Mem Bldg & One Market Plaza, San Francisco, Calif, 95-97; Friends of Dard Hunter Paper Conf, Sonoma, Calif, 98, Chicago, Ill, 99. *Pos:* Guest cur, Sanitary Fill Co Artist-in-Residence prog, San Francisco, Calif, 94-97; San Francisco Int Airport Comn, Calif, 95; Earth Options 90, Fort Mason Ctr, San Francisco, Calif, 90; Graphic Designer, de Young Mus/Fine Arts Mus San Francisco, 97-99, sr graphic designer, 2000-. *Teaching:* Instr papermaking, Randall Mus, San Francisco, Calif, 93-2001; guest lectr, graphic design, Acad Art, San Francisco, Calif, 95; instr, papermaking & printmaking, Kala Inst, Berkeley, Calif, 96-98; guest lectr, Univ Calif, Berkeley Coll Environ Design, 2000; artist book studio, Legion of Honor Mus, 2001; instru, art, papermaking, Waldorf High Sch, San Francisco, Calif, 2004-05; guest lectr papermaking, Acad Art Univ, 2004-06. *Awards:* Design Award, Am Planning Asn, Planning & Law Div, Logo Design Competition, 88; Honor Award, Communications, Am Soc Landscape Archits Ann Awards, 90; Nat Communs Merit Award, Am Soc Landscape Architects, Ann Awards, 97; Am Planning Asn Nat Pub Edn Award, 98. *Bibliog:* Communications, Landscape Archit Mag, 11/90 & 11/97; Robert Reed (auth), Recycling: Pictures & story, Recycle Today, 10/96; Marcia McNally (auth), Activist of the month, Sustainable Activist/Urban Ecology, 11/96. *Mem:* Am Inst Graphic Arts (environ comt, 94-); YLEM-Artists Using Sci & Tech; Friends Dard Hunter Papermaking Mus. *Media:* Papermaking, Printmaking; Installations. *Publ:* Auth, About Handmade Paper, Randall Mus, 94; Illusr, Palo Alto Comprehensive Plan, 1996-2010, City of Palo Alto, 96; designer, Blueprint for a Sustainable Bay Area, Urban Ecology, 96; designer exhib pub, Fine Arts Mus San Francisco, 97-. *Mailing Add:* 546 Shotwell St San Francisco CA 94110

PENNINGTON, SALLY
PAINTER
b Seattle, Wash, 53. *Study:* Mills Col, MFA(painting), 83. *Exhib:* Pro Arts Ann, Oakland, 85; Introduction Show, Triangle Gallery, San Francisco, 86; Connected by Nature, Pro Arts, Oakland, 86; Gallery Artists, Triangle Gallery, 86; Six East Bay Artists, Mills Col Art Gallery, Oakland, Calif, 89. *Teaching:* Instr, Diablo Valley Col, Calif, 83-87; Edmonds Community Col, Wash, currently. *Awards:* Catherine Morgan Trefethew Fel in Art, 82; Visual Artists Fel Grant, Nat Endowment Arts, 87. *Dealer:* Triangle Gallery 95 Minna St San Francisco CA 94105. *Mailing Add:* 23216 SE 31st St Issaquah WA 98029

PENNY, DONALD CHARLES
CRAFTSMAN, SCULPTOR
b Atlanta, Ga, Oct 5, 35. *Study:* Ga Tech, 1957-58; Ga State Univ, with Joe Perrin & Joe Almyda, BBA, 1961; Fla State Univ, with Karl Zerbe & Ralph Hurst, MS, 1963; Penland Sch, studies with Cynthia Bringle, 1966. *Work:* Metrop Mus Art, Miami; Ahmadu Bello Univ, Zaria, Nigeria; Macon Mus Arts & Sci, Ga; Valdosta State Univ, Ga; Renwick Gallery, Washington. *Comn:* Ga Coun Arts & Humanities, Valdosta, 81-82; Emory Univ, Atlanta, Ga, 81-82; and others. *Exhib:* Mint Mus Art, Charlotte, NC, 67, 69 & 70; Smithsonian Inst, Washington, 70; solo exhibs, Metrop Mus & Art Ctr, Miami, Fla, 70, Brenau Col, Gainesville, Ga, 89, Fla Landscape, Loundes/Valdosta (Ga) Arts Coun, 97; Greenville Co Mus, SC, 74; Furman Univ-R J Reynolds, Winston-Salem, NC, 77; Mus Arts & Sci, Macon, Ga, 82 & 89; Fla Sch Art, 89; Broward Community Col, 92; Lowndes/Valdosta Arts Coun, 2000; Mus Contemp Art, Atlanta, 2003; BascomLouiseGallery, Asheville, NC, 2003. *Teaching:* Instr, Palm Beach Jr Col, West Palm Beach, Fla, 61-63; prof art, Valdosta State Univ, Ga, 63-91; sr lectr, Ahmadu Bello Univ, Zaria, Nigeria, 72-73; prof emer art, Valdosta State Univ, Ga, 92. *Awards:* Best Show, Columbus Mus Arts & Crafts, Ga, 69; First Prize, St Augustine Festival, Fla, 70; Purchase Award, High Mus Art, Atlanta, Ga, 71; Purchase Award, Macon Mus Arts & Sci; Award Sculpture, Gala 2000, Gainesville, Ga. *Bibliog:* Barclay F Gordon (auth), Record houses: 1978, Archit Record Mag, 5/78; The connection, Atlanta Impressions Mag, summer 81; Alexandra Mettler (auth), Emory's Cannon Chapel: Master touches, Atlanta Mag, 12/81; American Craft, June/July, 2002; Valdosta Daily Times, June 9, 2002. *Mem:* Am Crafts Coun (trustee emer); Ga Designer Craftsman (vpres, 68); Nat Coun Educ Ceramic Arts; Lowndes/Valdosta Arts Comn; Southern Art League. *Media:* Clay. *Publ:* Auth, Nigerian Crafts, Nat Coun Educ Communication Arts. *Dealer:* Signature Shop Atlanta GA; Classic Art & Frame Valdosta GA; Blue Spiral 1 Asheville NC; Summit One Gallery Highlands NC. *Mailing Add:* Little River Studio 8601 Morven Rd Hahira GA 31632

PENTAK, STEPHEN
PAINTER, EDUCATOR
b Denver, Colo, Aug 24, 51. *Study:* Union Col, NY, BA, 73; Tyler Sch Art, MFA, 78. *Work:* Schenectady Mus, NY; Free Libr Philadelphia; Columbus Mus Art; Wexner Ctr, Columbus. *Comn:* State Auto Insurance, Columbus; Thomson Electronics, Columbus. *Exhib:* Selected Works, Sutton Place, London, 82 & Gallerie D'Arte Mod Ca'Pesaro, Venice, 83; solo exhib, Jan Cicero Gallery, Chicago, 83 & Noel Butcher Gallery, Philadelphia, 83, Univ Akron, 87, J Rosenthal, Chicago, Wexner Ctr Arts, Columbus, 92, Toni Birckhead, Cincinnati, Linda Schwartz, Lexington, Ky, 97, Bonfoey, Cleveland, Ohio, 98 & Marie Park, Dallas, Tex, 98; Landscape Anthology, Grace Borgenicht Gallery, NY, 88; Ohio Selections IX, Cleveland Ctr Contemp Arts, 90; Rivers Revisited, Linda Schwartz Gallery, Cincinnati, 99; Common Ground, The Artist House, Jerusalem, Israel, 2000. *Collection Arranged:* Four Landscape Painters, Concept Art, Pittsburgh, 97; Back to Reality, Riffe Gallery, Columbus, 98. *Teaching:* Vis asst prof, Art Inst Chicago, 81-82; prof, Ohio State Univ, Columbus, currently. *Awards:* Ohio Arts Coun Individual Artists Fel, 85, 89 & 97. *Bibliog:* Lorraine Padden (auth), Columbus Art, 1/92; K Rouda (auth), Article, Columbus Monthly, 9/94; Sally Vallongo (auth), rev, ARTnews, 3/95. *Media:* Oil on Panel & Paper. *Publ:* Auth, Gregory Amenoff's new pictures, 81 & Daryl Hughto, 81, Arts Mag; coauth, Design Basics (with David Lauer), Harcourt Brace, 94. *Dealer:* Jan Cicero Chicago; Concept Art Pittsburgh. *Mailing Add:* 211 Greenglade Ave Worthington OH 43085-2264

PENTELOVITCH, ROBERT ALAN
PAINTER
b Minneapolis, Minn, Oct 13, 55. *Study:* Minneapolis Col Art & Design, BFA, 78; San Francisco Art Inst, MFA, 80. *Work:* Walker Art Ctr & Regis Corp, Minneapolis, Minn; Chicago Inst Arts; Martin Marietta Corp, NY; Maslon, Kaplan, Borman & Brand, Minneapolis; Robin Farkas, NY; Gen Electric Group, NY. *Exhib:* solo exhibs, Trumbull Art Guild, Warren, Ohio, 85 & Arras Gallery, NY, 86; Zumbach Gallery, NY, 88 & 89; Greenleaf Gallery, Nags Head, NC, 92-94; Animal Imagery, Juried, Madison, NJ, 92; Alaska Mus Hist & Art, 93; Nabisco Gallery, NJ, 2002; Cooper Classics Collection, NY, 2003; and others. *Awards:* First Place, Minneapolis Col Art & Design, 77; Award of Excellence, Concours Auto Art, Oakland Univ, Troy, Mich, 85; Fel, John Simon Guggenheim Mem Found, 91. *Mem:* Artists Equity Asn. *Media:* Acrylic. *Publ:* Contribr, Edsel Owners News, 79 & 80, & Automotive Showcase, 1/82. *Dealer:* Cooper Classic Collections 137 Perry St New York NY. *Mailing Add:* 340 W 55th St Apt 2D New York NY 10019

PENTZ, DONALD ROBERT
PAINTER, PRINTMAKER
b Bridgewater, NS, Sept 18, 40. *Study:* Mt Allison Univ, Sackville, NB, BFA, 66; Univ Regina, Sask, MFA, 79; Banff Sch Fine Art, Alta, 79. *Work:* Art Gallery NS, NS Art Bank, Halifax; Can Coun Art Bank, Ottawa; Imperial Oil, Calgary, Alta; Osaka Found Culture, Japan. *Comn:* Selected Birds, Parks Can, Newfoundland, 82. *Exhib:* Young Artists of the Prairies, Walter Phillips Gallery, Banff, Alta, 79; Force Field Series, Art Gallery NS, Halifax, 79; RCA Centennial Exhib, CNE Bldg, Toronto, 80; Emerging Canadian Artists, Muttart Gallery, Calgary, Alta, 81; Atlantic Artists, Shell Can, Calgary, Alta, 81; Studio 21, Halifax, 91; Kejimkujik Nat Park, NS, 99; Southern Vt Arts Ctr, Manchester, Vt, 2000; Trinity Galleries, NB, 2001. *Teaching:* Instr art, privately, 70-2002, Univ Regina, Sask, 77-79 & Mt St Vincent Univ, Halifax, NS, 80. *Awards:* Prof Artists Award, 75 & NS Talent Trust, 78, NS Govt; Can Coun Grant, 80; NS Arts Grant, 2002. *Bibliog:* Janet Smith (producer), D Pentz--Wildlife Artist, CBC-TV, 83; Arts Atlantic, 88; # 37 Arts Atlantic, 90; # 42 Arts Atlantic, 92; NS Visual Arts News, 2000. *Mem:* Visual Arts NS; Royal Can Acad; Can Soc Paiters in Watercolour. *Media:* Acrylic, Oil, Watercolor. *Specialty:* Trinity Gallery,. NB: Realism; Fog Forest Gallery, NB: Realism; Studio 21, NS: Abstract. *Dealer:* Studio 21 5435 Spring Garden Rd Halifax NS Can B3J 1G1; Trinity Galleries 128 German St St John NB Can E2L 2E7; Fog Forest Gallery 14 Bridge St Sackville NB Can E4L 3N5; Peer Gallery 167 Lincoln St Lunenburg NS Can. *Mailing Add:* RR1 Pleasantville Lunenburg NS B0R 1G0 Canada

PEPICH, BRUCE WALTER W
MUSEUM DIRECTOR, CURATOR
b Elmhurst, Ill, June 5, 52. *Study:* Northern Ill Univ, De Kalb, BA(art hist), 74. *Collection Arranged:* Lee Weiss: 25 Years in Wisconsin, 87 & Wis Craft Masters, 88; For the Birds: Artists Examine Aviary Abodes, 90; Artists and the American Yard: Lawn Gnomes, Pink Flamingoes and Bathtub Grottos, 91; Craft: The Discerning Eye, 91; Walter Samuel Hamady: Handmade Books, Collages and Sculptures, 91; Watercolor Wisconsin: Celebrating 25 Years, 91; Just Plane Screwy: Metaphysical and Metaphorical Tools by Artists, 92; Pets: Artists and an American Obsession, 93, From Our Vault to the Studio: American Crafts Artists and the Collection, 93, JoAnna Poehlmann: Books, Sculptures and Works on Paper, 1964-1994, 94, The Aesthetics of Athletics: Artists View Games, Sports and Exercise, 94, The Object Redux: Re-Used, Re-Newed and Re-Invested, 94, Wustum Mus Fine Arts, Racine, Wis. *Pos:* Cur, Univ Art Collection, Northern Ill Univ, 71-74; writer & contribr, Art Gallery Int Mag, 88-90. *Awards:* Endowment Arts Avan Program, Overview Panel, 6/92. *Mem:* Am Craft Coun; Am Asn Mus; Contemp Glass Ctr Am, Millville, NJ (bd trustees, 94-); Textile Art Ctr, Chicago, Ill (adv bd, 94-); Friends Fiber Int (prof adv comt, 93-).

Publ: Auth, Chicago New Art Forms Brings Spotlight to Craft, The Crafts Report, 12/90; Walter Hamady, with essays by Buzz Spector & Tom Olson, Wustum Mus, 3/91; The Art of Lee Weiss: Poetry in the Natural Landscape, Wis Acad Review, Fall, 94. *Mailing Add:* Charles A Wustum Mus Fine Arts 2519 Northwestern Ave Racine WI 53402

PEPPARD, BLAYLOCK A
PAINTER
b Burlington, Vt, Dec 28, 52. *Study:* St Lawrence Univ, Canton, NY, BA(art honors), 75; Maryland Inst Col Art, Hoffberger Sch Painting, study with Grace Hardigan, Sal Scarpitta & Robert Moskowicz, MFA, 79. *Work:* Lewis & Clarke Mus, Portland, Ore; St Lawrence Univ, Canton, NY; Hagstromer Col, Stockholm, Sweden; Best Products, Ashland, Va; Berger Col, NY. *Exhib:* Pace Gallery, Philadelphia, 80; Art Fair, Stockholm Mus, Sweden, 81; solo shows, Concord Gallery, NY, 82 & 83; Everson Biennial, Everson Mus, Syracuse, NY, 84; Art Quest, Sharadin Mus, Kutztown Univ, Pa, 86; Proj Studio Installation, PS1, Long Island City, NY, 86; St Lawrence Univ, 98. *Pos:* Tech Etching, Parker Etching Studio, New York, 83-84; installation technician, Queens Mus, Flushing, NY, 83-85; Exhibs coordr, Jewish Mus, New York, 85-86. *Teaching:* Painting instr, New York Univ, 82-83; vis lectr, St Lawrence Univ, Canton, NY, 83. *Awards:* Painting Fel, Nat Endowment Arts, 90. *Bibliog:* Sylvia Falcon (auth), Blaylock Pepperd, Arts Mag, 83; Katherine Howe (auth), Blaylock Pepperd, Images & Issues Mag, 83; Art Quest '86, Film/Artquest/Slabey, 86. *Mem:* Col Art Asn; Orgn Independent Artists. *Media:* Oil, Beeswax. *Mailing Add:* 231 W 29th St New York NY 10001

PEPPARD, JACQUELINE JEAN
PAINTER, INSTRUCTOR
b Calif, Feb, 12, 54. *Study:* Univ Colo, studied fine art, 76-78; Colo Inst Art, AA, 81; studied with Frank Web, 82. *Work:* Telluride Coun Arts & Humanities Gallery, Bank Telluride & Mountain Village Metro Dist Offices, Telluride, Colo. *Comn:* Posters, Telluride Jazz Festival, Telluride, Colo, 87 & 88; poster, San Miguel River Coalition, Telluride, Colo, 94. *Exhib:* Watercolor West 20th Ann, Riverside Art Mus, Riverside, Calif, 88; 89th Ann Watercolor Exhib, Nat Arts Club, NY, 88; Watercolor West 21st Ann, San Bernardino Co Mus, Redlands, Calif, 89; Western Fedn Watercolor Soc 15th Ann, El Cajon Arts Ctr, El Cajon, Calif, 90; Colo Watercolor Soc State Exhib, Denver Hist Mus, 94. *Teaching:* Teacher watercolor landscape, AHA Sch Art, Telluride, Colo, 94-. *Awards:* Brush & Palette Club First Place Watercolor Landscapes, 39th Ann Nat Exhib, 86; Grant, Telluride Coun Arts & Humanities, 89; Second Place, NMex Watercolor Soc Nat, 90. *Bibliog:* Dinah B Witchel (auth), Colors of the Southwest, Snow Country Mag, 1/90; Art Goodtimes (auth), For art's sake, Telluride Mag, winter 90; M Stephen Doherty (auth), 5 ways to strengthen your landscapes, Watercolor 91/Am Artist Mag, spring 91. *Mem:* Signature mem Watercolor West; signature mem Nat Watercolor Soc. *Media:* Transparent Watercolor on Paper. *Publ:* Auth, True tones/Jacqueline Peppard colors the world her way, Southwest Art Mag, 8/94; contribr, Splash III/105 of America's Best Contemporary Watercolorists; auth, A Place of a Different Color, Watercolor Magic Mag, winter 98. *Dealer:* Antonia Clark Toh-Atin Gallery 145 W 9th St Durango CO 81301

PEPPER, BEVERLY
SCULPTOR, PAINTER
b Brooklyn, NY, Dec 20, 22. *Study:* Pratt Inst; Art Students League; Studied with Fernand Leger & Andre L'hote. *Hon Degrees:* Pratt Inst, D (fine arts), 82; Md Inst, D (fine arts), 83. *Work:* Albright-Knox Art Gallery, Buffalo, NY; Mass Inst Technol, Boston; Fogg Art Mus, Cambridge, Mass; Walker Art Ctr, Minneapolis; Metrop Mus Art, NY; Whitney Mus Am Art, NY. *Comn:* Jerusalem Ritual sculptures, Jerusalem Found, Israel, 94; Todi columns, Venice, Italy, 95; Sentinels of Justice columns, Kansas City Fed Bldg, Mo, 97; Sacramento Stele sculptures, Calif Environ Protection Agency, Sacramento, 2000; Split Ritual, Nat Arboretum Friendship Garden, Washington, 1992; Panel Screen, Societe des Amis du National d'Art Moderne, Centre Georges Pompadou, 1992; Palingenesis, Credit Suisse, Zurich, Switzerland, 1992-94; Split Ritual II, Grounds for Sculpture, Hamilton, NJ, 96; Manhattan Sentinels, Federal Plaza, NY, 93-95; New Central Libr Project, Minneapolis,. *Exhib:* San Francisco Mus Mod Art, 76; Seattle Mus Contemp Art, 77; Earthworks & Land Reclamation, Seattle Mus, 79; Nat Collection Arts, Smithsonian Inst, Washington, DC, 80; Laumeier Int Sculpture Park, St Louis, 82; one-woman shows, Charles Cowles Gallery, NY, 90, 94, 97 & 98, Metrop Mus Art, NY, 91, Contemp Sculpture Center, Japan, 91; Cleopatra's Wedge, Battery Park, Pub Art Fund, NY, 93; Ternana Altar II, White House Exhib II, Washington, DC, 95; Teatro Celle in Context, Pistoia, Italy, 98; Retrospective, Albright-Knox Art Gallery, Buffalo, NY, 1970, Brooklyn Mus, NY, 1987, Ctr for Fine Arts, Miami, Fla, 1987, Forte Belvedere, Firenza, Italy, 1998, Palais Royal, Paris, France, 99, Marlborough Gallery, NY, 99, 2001, 03, Casal Solleric, Majorca, Spain, 2004. *Pos:* Artist-in-residence, Southeastern Ctr Contemp Arts, 81, Am Acad, Rome, 86 & Sante Fe Inst Fine Arts, 91, 93 & 94. *Awards:* Nat Endowment Arts Grant, 75 & 79; Hon Award, Nat Women's Caucus, Queens Mus Art, 94; Alexander Calder Prize, 99; Allied Arts and Craftsmanship Award, Am Inst Architects, 99; Preparatory Vision award, Xavier Col, 1999; Legends award in Sculpture, Pratt Institute, 2003. *Bibliog:* Vittorio Armentano (auth), B P Making Sculpture (film), G Ungaretti, narrator, 70; Amphisculpture (film), Barbara Rose & Beverly Pepper, narrators, 77; Rosalind Krauss (auth), Beverly Pepper-Sculpture in Place, Abbeville Press, 86; Suzaan Boettger (auth), Endless columns: the quest for infinite extension, Sculpture, 1-2/94; William Zimmer (auth), Sculptures and abstract expressionist prints in close harmony, NY Times, 4/3/94; Robert Hobbs (auth), Beverly Pepper: In the Querenia, Sculpture, Nov-Dec, 1994; Abby Remer (auth), Pioneering Spirits, The Lives and Times of Remarkable Women Artists in Western History, Davis Publs, 97; Barbara Rose (auth), Beverly Pepper: Three Site-Specific Sculptures, Spacemaker Press, 98; Tim Engle (auth), Sky high, Kansas City Star, 9/20/98; Anne Barclaw Morgan (auth), Memory, Monuments, Mystery and Iron: An Interview with Beverly Pepper, Sculpture, 4/98; Robert Hobbs (auth), Beverly Pepper at the Fattoria di Celle, Gori Collection, Societa Editrice Umberto Allemandi & Co, Italy, 98; Carlo Bertelli (auth), Beverly Pepper at Forte Belvedere, Trent Anni Di Scultura, Electa, Milano, 98; Maria Lluisa Borras (auth), Beverly Pepper: Una Poetica de L'Espai, Ajuntament de Palma, Casal Solleric, Spain, 2004. *Media:* Cast Iron, Earthwork, Stone, Bronze. *Specialty:* Sculptue. *Publ:* Art Fundamentals: Theory and Practice, McGraw Hill Higher Education, New York, 2002; Launching the Imagination: A Comprehensive Guide to Basic Design, McGraw Hill Higher Education, New York, 2002; Sculpture in Place, Western Wash Univ, Bellingham, 2002. *Dealer:* Marlborough Gallery 40 W 57th St New York NY 10011. *Mailing Add:* Marborough Gallery 40 W 57th St New York NY 10011

PERA, ISABELLA
SCULPTOR
b Trivero, Italy, Sept 24, 45. *Study:* State Univ NY Cortland, BA, 73; Univ Ill Urbana-Champaign, MFA, 77. *Work:* Sheldon Swope Art Mus, Terre Haute, Ind; Del Mar Col, John Seaman Collection, Corpus Christi, Tex; Kirkland Fine Arts Ctr, Millikin Univ, Decatur, Ill; Almidones Mejicanos Bldg, Guadalajara, Mex; Italian Cult Ctr, Chicago. *Exhib:* One-woman shows, Gilman Galleries, Chicago, 77, Freeport Art Mus, Ill, 79, Sheldon Swope Art Mus, Terre Haute, 80 & 88, Ital Cult Ctr, Chicago, 80 & Burpee Art Mus, Rockford, Ill, 81; 30th & 31st Ann Mid-States Art Exhib, Evansville Mus Art & Sci, Ind, 77-78; Art Expo, NY, 84 & 85; and others. *Collection Arranged:* 7th Ann Mid-States Traveling Art Show, Evansville Mus Art & Sci, 77-78. *Awards:* Art Casting of Colo Award, Foothills Art Ctr, 79; First Prize Sculpture, La Junta Fine Arts League, 79; First Prize Sculpture, Italian Cult Ctr, Chicago, 81; and others. *Bibliog:* Janelle Hirchert (auth), Artistry in bronze wins recognition, News Gazette, 76; Harold Haydon (auth), Art, Sun Times, Chicago, 77; Nina Rubel (auth), Relief in bronze, Heartland Beat, Kerning Arts Press, 81. *Mem:* Int Sculpture Ctr. *Media:* Bronze; Epoxy

PERCY, ANN BUCHANAN
CURATOR, HISTORIAN
b Lynchburg, Va, Nov 13, 40. *Study:* Sweet Briar Col, BA, 62; Pa State Univ, MA, 65; Courtauld Inst Art, Univ London, PhD, 74. *Collection Arranged:* Giovanni Benedetto Castiglione: Master Draughtsman of the Italian Baroque (auth, catalog), Philadelphia Mus Art, 71; A Scholar Collects: Selections from the Anthony Morris Clark Bequest (co-ed, catalog), Philadelphia Mus Art, 80; New Art on Paper 1 and 2 (coauth, catalog), Philadelphia Mus Art, 88, 96; Francesco Clemente: Three Worlds (coauth, catalog), Philadelphia Mus Art, 90; Art in Rome in the Eighteenth Century (coauth, catalog), Philadelphia Mus Art, 2000, Mus Fine Art Houston, 2000. *Pos:* Art hist ed, Pa State Univ Press, 69-72; asst cur drawings, Philadelphia Mus Art, 72-74, assoc cur drawings, 74-84, acting cur drawings, 81-84, cur, 84-. *Awards:* Fulbright-Hays Scholar, 64-65; Chester Dale Fel, 68-69; Vis Scholar, J Paul Getty Mus, 87. *Mem:* Print Coun Am. *Res:* Seventeenth and eighteenth century Italian drawings and paintings; contemporary drawings. *Publ:* Auth, Castiglione's chronology: Some documentary notes, Burlington Mag, 67; coauth, Philadelphia: Three Centuries of American Art, Philadelphia Mus Art, 76; Bernardo Cavallino of Naples, 1616-1656; catalogs, Cleveland Mus Art, Kimbell Art Mus, Ft Worth & Museo Pignatelli Cortes, Naples, 84-85; Ital Master Drawings, Philadelphia Mus Art, Pa, 2004. *Mailing Add:* Philadelphia Mus Art PO Box 7646 Philadelphia PA 19101

PEREGRIN, MAGDA ELIZABETH
PAINTER, INSTRUCTOR
b Budapest, Hungary, Jan 2, 23. *Study:* John Huntington Polytech Sch, cert, 44; Pasadena City Col, cert, 52; Rex Brandt workshop, Oriental Brush Painting with Ning Yeh. *Work:* Smithsonian Inst, Washington; Arcadia Meth Hosp, Arcadia, Calif; City of Hope, Duarte, Calif; Home Saving & Loan; Hillcrest Congregational Church, Whittier, Calif. *Comn:* Painting, Unical, Los Angeles, Calif, 75. *Exhib:* Edward Dean Mus Invitational, Cherry Valley, Calif, 79; Brand Libr Art Gallery, Glendale, Calif, 80, 81 & 83; Nat Watercolor Soc Ann, Calif, 81 & 93; Watercolor West Ann, Riverside, Calif, 84, 86, 87, 88, 90, 92, 93 & 94; Pasadena Soc Artists Ann, San Bernadino Co Mus, Calif, 84-88; Invitational, Mus Hist & Art, Ontario, Calif, 85; Yosemite Renaissance Nat Exhib, Fresno, Calif, 86 & 95; San Diego Int, San Diego Watercolor Soc, 86, 87 & 88; Pasadena Arts Alliance, 89; Downey Mus Art, 90; Brea Cult Ctr, 90; Calif Watercolor West, 90-94. *Pos:* Staff artist, Am Greetings, Cleveland, Ohio, 44-50. *Teaching:* Instr watercolor, Foothill Creative Arts Group, Sierra Madre, Calif, 82- & Yosemite Art & Activity Ctr, Calif, 82-. *Awards:* Windsor & Newton Award, 81 & Challis Gallery Award, 82, Watercolor West Ann; Purchase Awards, Hillcrest Invitational, 89, 90, 91, 92, 93, 94 & 95; Best Landscape Watercolor Ann Award, Pasadena Presby Church, 96. *Mem:* Watercolor West (bd mem, 77-79); Pasadena Soc Artists; Mid-Valley Arts League Inc (bd mem, 75-76 & 78); Creative Arts Group. *Media:* Transparent Watercolor. *Mailing Add:* 8517 Ravendale Rd San Gabriel CA 91775

PEREHUDOFF, WILLIAM W
PAINTER
b Saskatoon, Sask, Apr 21, 1918. *Study:* Colorado Springs Fine Arts Ctr; Ozenfant Sch Art, New York; Univ Sask, Emma Lake, workshops with Cherry, Noland & Greenberg; Carnegie Inst of Technol, Pittsburgh, PA. *Hon Degrees:* Univ Regina, LLD, 2003. *Work:* Glenbow Mus, Calgary, Alta; Mendel Art Gallery, Saskatoon; Edmonton Art Gallery; London Art Gallery, Ont; Nat Gallery Can, Ottawa, Ont; Portland Art Mus, Portland, OR; The Art Gallery of Nova Scotia. *Comn:* Mural, Toronto Dominion Bank, Regina, 75. *Exhib:* Solo exhibs, Mendel Art Gallery, Saskatoon, Sask, 65, Edmonton Art Gallery, Alta, 72-73, Glenbow Alta Inst (with catalog), Noah Galdowsky Gallery, NY, 74, 76; Calgary, 77-78, Meredith Long

Gallery, NY, 78, 80; Theo Waddington Gallery, London, Eng, 79, Waddington Galleries, NY, 82, Eva Cohon Gallery Ltd, Chicago, Ill, 88, Waddington Gorce Inc, Montreal, Que, 90, Mirium Shiell Fine Art Ltd, Toronto, Ont, 90; Mirium Shiell Fine Art, Toronto, 90, 93, 2000; Douglas Udell Gallery, Vancouver, BC, 98; Art Placement, Saskatoon, 98, 99, 2003; Winchester Galleries Victoria, 98, 2004; Douglas Udell Gallery, Edmonton, Alberta, 99, 2001; Mendel Art Gallery, Saskatoon 2002; Modern Painting in Canada (with catalog), Edmonton Art Gallery, 78; Seven Prairie Painters (with catalog), Art Gallery Ont, 78-79; Aspects of Canadian Painting in the Seventies (with catalog), Glenbow Mus, Calgary, Alta, 80; The Heritage of Jack Bush, A Tribute, The Robert McLaughlin Gallery, Oshawa, Ont, 81; The Flatside of the Landscape, The Emma Lake Workshop, Mendel Art Gallery, Sask, 89; A Critic's Collection, Palm Springs, Calif, 2004, Atrium Gallery, Ontario Col of Art & Design Toronto Ontario, Triangle Workshop Artists; Palm Springs Desert Mus Clement Greenberg, Three Generations Art Gallery, London Eng, 2005; and others. *Teaching:* Instr, Emma Lake Art Workshop, Emma Lake, Sask, 88. *Awards:* Order of Canada; Saskatchewan Order of Merit; Saskatoon Centennial Medal; Nat Award Painting, Univ Alta. *Bibliog:* Clement Greenberg (auth), Painting and Sculpture in Canada, Can Art, 63; Karen Wilkin (auth), William Perehudoff, Art Int, 77; Joan Murray (auth), The Best Contemporary Canadian Art, Hurtig Publ, Edmonton, 87; Kellag Alan (auth) Perehndoff Refines Redefines His No 71, 99; Gorgeous Abstracts, Edmenton Journal, 2001; The Hudson Review, 55th Anniversary Review, Winter 2004; David Evison (auth) column for Piri Halasz; From the Mayor's Doorstep (internet newletter) London England, 2005, (http://pir.home.mindspring.com/pmaro5.html). *Mem:* Royal Can Acad Art. *Media:* Acrylic on Canvas. *Dealer:* Douglas Udell Galleries Vancouver, BC and Edmonton, Alberta; Winchester Galleries, Victoria, BC; New Zones Gallery, Calgary, Alberta; Art Placement, Saskatoon, Sask; Mirium Shiell Fine Art Ltd. Toronto, Ontario; Waddington/Gorce, Montreal, Quebec. *Mailing Add:* 1131 Second St E Saskatoon SK S7H 1R4 Canada

PERELMAN, JEFFREY E
COLLECTOR
Study: Univ Ill, BA (with hon); Ill Inst Tech, Chicago-Kent Col Law, JD. *Pos:* former owner & mgr, Commodities Brokerage Firm; Sterling Real Estate Partners, Chicago, 96-. *Awards:* Nominated Top 200 Art Collectors, ARTnews Mag, 2006. *Mailing Add:* Sterling Real Estate Ptnre 1033 Skokie Blvd Ste 600 Northbrook IL 60062

PERELMAN, RONALD OWEN
COLLECTOR
b Greensboro, NC, 43. *Study:* Univ Pa, BA, 64; Wharton Sch Fin, MBA, 66. *Pos:* With, Belmont Industries Inc, 66-78; chmn, chief exec off, MacAndrews & Forbes Group Inc (subsidiary), New York City, 78-; chmn, chief exec off, dir, MacAndrews & Forbes Holdings Inc, Wilmington, Del, 83-; chmn, chief exec off, dir, Revlon Group Inc (subsidiary MacAndrews & Forbes Group Inc), 85-, Revlon Inc (subsidiary), New York City, 85-; chmn, Nat Health Laboratories Inc, La Jolla, Calif, 85-, Andrews Group Inc, La Jolla, 85-; pres bd of trustees, Solomon R Guggenheim Mus, 95-. *Awards:* Achievements; being named one of World's Richest People by Forbes in 99, 2000-2004; Named one of Top 200 Collectors, ARTnews Mag, 2004. *Collection:* Contemporary art. *Mailing Add:* Revlon Group Inc 625 Madison Ave 8th Fl New York NY 10022-1894

PERESS, GILLES
PHOTOGRAPHER
b Neuilly-sur-Seine, France, Dec 29, 46. *Study:* Inst d'Etudes Politiques, dipl, 68; Univ Vincennes, dipl, 71. *Work:* Art Inst Chicago; Mus Fine Arts, Houston; Minneapolis Inst Art; Mus Mod Art & Metrop Mus Art, NY; Arts Coun-Great Britian, Bibliotheque Nationale, Paris; First Bank, Minn. *Comn:* Double Diary of the Twin Cities, First Banks Minnesota, Minneapolis, 86. *Exhib:* Photo Politic, PS 1/Inst Art & Urban Resources, NY, 80; Paris: Magnum, Palais du Luxembourg, Paris & traveling, 81; Photographie Français d'Aujourd'hui, Mus d'Art Mod, Paris, & traveling, 84; Telex: Iran, PS 1/Inst Art & Urban Resources, NY, 84; Magnum: Concert, Mus d'Art, Fribourg, Switz, 85; The Indelible Image, Corcoran Gallery, Washington, DC & traveling, 85; On the Line: New Color Photojournalism, Walker Art Inst, Minneapolis & traveling, 86; Power in the Blood: The North of Ireland, Art Inst of Chicago, 92; one-man show, Palais de Tokyo, Paris, 93; Sex and Crime, The Silence, silver print installation: Sprengel Mus, Hannover, Ger, 96; Bosnia: Avant/Apres Guerre, digital print installation: Parc de la Villette, Paris, France, 98; and many others. *Pos:* Exec, Magnum Photos, Inc, currently. *Teaching:* Lectr photog, Int Ctr Photog, NY, 80-86, RI Sch Design, 82, Harvard Univ, 86-87. *Awards:* Nat Endowment Arts Grants, 79 & 84; Art Director's Club Award, New York Times, 97; Northampton Film Festival Award, Eye Witness Photo & Journalistic Impact, 98. *Bibliog:* Charles Hanson (auth), Iran: Another view, Afterimage, fall 82; Michel Maingois (auth), L'Iran de Peress, Photo Mag, Paris, 5/8/84; Pete Hamill (auth), Prey for the dead, Am Photog, 8/84. *Mem:* Am Soc Mag Photogrs (vpres, 84-85, pres, 86-). *Publ:* Telex: Iran, Aperture/Contrejour, 84; contribr, Identities, Exposition Palais du Tokyo, Paris (exhib catalog), Editions du Chene, 85; Men's Lives, Random House, 86; auth, An Eye for an Eye: Northern Ireland 1970-1986, Aperture, 87; Power in the Blood: The North of Ireland, Jonathan Cape, Eng, Parkett, Zurich, 93. *Mailing Add:* 141 West 24 St New York NY 10011

PEREZ, VINCENT
PAINTER, ILLUSTRATOR
b Jersey City, NJ, July 17, 38. *Study:* Pratt Inst, BFA; Univ Am, Mex; Calif Col Arts & Crafts, MFA. *Work:* Mus Art, Calif Palace Legion Hon, San Francisco; Oakland Art Mus, Calif; Playboy Enterprises, Chicago; Time Inc, NY; and many others. *Comn:* Mural, Arleigh Gallery, San Francisco, 69; portrait of State Supreme Court Judge Peters, comn by Clerks of Supreme Court for Univ Calif, Berkeley Law Sch, 74; woodcuts, Civic Arts Asn, Walnut Creek, Calif, 74. *Exhib:* One-man shows, Calif Col Arts & Crafts, 77 & Hoover Gallery, 80; 12 Artists, Calif Col Arts & Crafts, 78; Human Form, Walnut Creek Col, 78; Palo Alto Cult Ctr, 80; Ctr Visual Arts, 86. *Teaching:* Prof drawing & anat for artists, Calif Col Arts & Crafts, 66-. *Awards:* Union Independent Col Art Res Grant, 70; Best of Show, Tech Writers Convention, Los Angeles, 72; Gold Medal, Acad Italy, 80; Gertrude B Murphy Award, 84. *Bibliog:* Fred Martin (auth), San Francisco letter, Art Int, 66; Cecille McCann (auth), Vincent Perez, FMb Fine Arts, 69; Palmer French (auth), San Francisco artists, Artforum, 69. *Mem:* Bohemian Club; San Francisco Soc Illusrs; Union Independent Col Art. *Media:* Mixed. *Publ:* Illusr cover, Time Mag, 69; illusr, Art & Tools, 72; Archives of Institutional Change Humanizing Technology, 73; Psychol Today, 73; Playboy, 74. *Mailing Add:* Fine Arts Calif Col Arts & Crafts 5212 Broadway Oakland CA 94618-3941

PEREZNIETO, FERNANDO
PAINTER, SCULPTOR
b Mex, Aug 12, 38. *Study:* Univ Nat Autonoma Mex, Architect, 62; studied etching, Villa Schifandia, Florence, Italy, 77. *Work:* Mus de la Cudad de Mex, Mus Nac de la Estampa, Fomento Cult Banamex, Mexico City; Inst de Cult de Tabasco, Villahermosa, Tab; Bellas Artes, San Miguel, Mex. *Comn:* Quijote's Sculpture, Black Marbel, Mus Del Quijote Guanajuato, Mex; I Offer You My Heart Sculpture, White Marbel, City of Villahermosa, Tabasco, Mex. *Exhib:* 650 Aniversary of the City, Mexico City Mus, 75; Memories & Inventions, Univ Calif, Los Angeles, 80; L'Amour Pur La Musique, Municipal Mus, Castres, France, 81; Oniric Memories, Canning House, London, 87; Musica y Acompanamiento, Mus Nac de la Estampa, Mexico City, 94. *Pos:* archit. *Awards:* Premo Naz Pitura, Comune di Lampedusa, Italy, 84; Premio Ocho Columnas de Oro, Mex, 96; Premio Juchiman de Plata, Tabasco, Mex, 96. *Bibliog:* Gloria Cosi (auth), Pereznieto - Cento maghi unacitta, Eco D'Arte Moderna, 3-4/84; Thoughts on the work of FP, Castello Mediceo, Italy, 89; Alain Rener (auth), Pereznieto, L'art en mediterrnee, Montecarlo Cote D'Azur, 11/91. *Media:* All Media. *Publ:* Auth, Images of the Consciousness, Ed Unam, 80; Story of a Spell, Il Candelaio - Frenze, 82; Divertimento Erotico, Formal, 87; The Magic World of Fernando Pereznieto, Fund Tabasco, 94; Pereznieto - Sculpture, Ed Themis, 94. *Dealer:* Galerie D'Art Fernando Pereznieto 17 Ave Auber, Nice, 06000, France; Galeria Estela Shapiro Victor Hugo 72 Mex 11590. *Mailing Add:* Colina 47 Lomas De Bezares DF 11910 Mexico

PERGOLA, LINNEA
PAINTER, PRINTMAKER
b Los Angeles, Calif, Sept 23, 53. *Study:* Univ Northridge, Los Angeles, BA, 76. *Exhib:* Ambassador Gallery, NY; Mus Flying, Los Angeles; Fine Art Mus, Long Island, NY; Martin Lawrence Galleries, Los Angeles, Chicago, & NY; Roberts Gallery, Scottsdale, Ariz. *Publ:* Illusr, I create a world-it's mine to enter, and share, SunStorm Fine Art, 95. *Mailing Add:* c/o Pierside Gallery 300 Pacific Coast Hwy Suite 108 Huntington Beach CA 92648

PERHACS, LES
SCULPTOR, INDUSTRIAL DESIGNER
b Studio City, Calif, Oct 5, 40. *Study:* Chouinard Art Inst, 58; Pratt Art Inst, studied with David Smith, Salvador Dali & Willem Dekooning, 59-60; Art Ctr Sch Design, Los Angeles, Calif, 58; Sch Archit & Design, Univ Southern Calif, 61-62; Wildlife Studies, US Dept Interior, 67-79. *Work:* Frye Art Mus, Seattle, Wash; Whatcom Mus, Bellingham, Wash; State Capitol Mus, Olympia, Wash. *Comn:* People's Nat Bank, Lynden, Wash, 79; First City Nat Bank, Houston, Tex, 80; US Bank, Seattle, Wash, 83; Paragon Ranch Ltd, Denver, Colo, 90; San Diego Intl Airport, Calif, 98; and others. *Exhib:* Group show, Royal Ont Mus, Can, 75; Sculpture by Les Perhacs, McNay Art Inst/Mus, San Antonio, Tex, 78; Sculpture of Les Perhacs, State Capitol Mus, Olympia, Wash, 79; Wildlife Sculptures, Frye Art Mus, Seattle, Wash, 80; Artists of Am, State Hist Mus, Denver, Colo, 81-86, 90, 95, 96 & 2000; 30th Ann Group Show, Total Arts Gallery, Taos, NMex, 99. *Teaching:* Guest lectr indust design, Univ Calif, Los Angeles, 68. *Awards:* Nat Alcoa Indust Design Award, Alcoa Aluminum, 62. *Bibliog:* Mary Balcomb (auth), Stylized interpretations, Southwest Art, 3/80; Mary Balcomb (auth), Beyond accurate representation, Am Artist, 4/91; Judy Hughes (auth), Using art as a language, Wildlife Art News, 11/92. *Mem:* Nat Sculpture Soc. *Media:* Stone, Bronze, Steel. *Publ:* Contribr, Les Perhacs, Sculptor, Putnam Macdaniel/Mary Balcomb, 78; auth, An artist's perspective, Wildlife Art News, 11/92. *Dealer:* Perhacs Studio Fallbrook Calif; Total Arts Gallery Taos NM. *Mailing Add:* 2540 Wilt Rd Fallbrook CA 92028

PERKINS, A ALAN
CERAMIST, ENAMELIST
b Toronto, Ont, Nov 30, 15. *Study:* Danforth Tech Sch, Toronto, dipl; Ont Col Art, Toronto, scholar; Brookfield Craft Ctr, Conn, with Margaret Seeler & Francis Felton. *Work:* Ont Inst of Studies, Toronto; Ont Craft Coun Permanent Collection, Toronto, Confedn Centre Gallery & Mus, Charlottetown, PEI, Can; Chalmers Collectors Col Mus of Civilization, Ottawa, Can. *Comn:* Mural, Cochran Murray Co, Toronto, 69; modular assemblage, Cadillac Develop Corp, Toronto, 72, Crown Life Insurance Head Off, Toronto, & George Brown Col, Toronto, Can, 90; and others. *Exhib:* First World Craft Exhib, Ont Sci Centre, Don Mills, 74; Ont Craft Coun Traveling Exhib, 77-78; Biennale Int, Limoges, France, 88; Kunstverein Coborg, W Ger: 3rd Salon; Int Del Esmalte, Madrid, Spain. *Pos:* Tread bd dir, Ont Craft Found, Toronto, 68-69. *Teaching:* Instr enameling & jewelry arts, George Brown Col, Toronto, 68-; instr glazes on metal, Toronto Bd Educ, 68-87. *Awards:* Adelaide Merriot Award of Excellence, Can Nat Exhib, 70; Award of Excellence, MAKE Exhib, Ont Can Guild of Crafts, 71; Best in Show, Graphics, Aviva Art Show, 81; and others. *Bibliog:* Una Abrahamson (auth), Crafts Canada, The Useful Arts, Clarke Irwin & Co Ltd, Toronto, 74; David Piper (ed), Canadian Interiors, Maclean Hunter Publ, 74; J Hartley Newman

(auth), Wire Art, Crown Publ, New York, 75; Glass on metal, Enamelist Soc Int, Vol 5, No 2, 4/86. *Mem:* Soc Can Artists (chmn exhib comt, 76-77); Ont Soc Artists; Ont Crafts Coun (secy-treas bd dir, 68-70); Metal Arts Guild, Ont; assoc mem, Soc NAm Goldsmiths. *Media:* Multimedia. *Dealer:* Harbinger Gallery Waterloo ON Can; Gallery House Sol Georgetown ON Can

PERKINS, LOIS BOUTHILLIER
PAINTER, EDUCATOR
b Asbestos, Que, June 23, 37; US citizen. *Study:* Fla Atlantic Univ, BFA, 81, independent study, Beijing PR of China, 88, London, Paris, Rome, 89. *Work:* Judge James R Knott Ctr Hist Preserv, Delray, Fla; Pompano Beach Pub Libr, Fla; Broward Co Court House, Ft Lauderdale, Fla; Chende Teachers Col, People's Repub China; Private Collections, Mr Sam Sneed & Dr & Mrs M Weinbaum. *Comn:* Decorate a floor, Mr & Mrs Frank, Pompano, Fla. *Exhib:* Sch Exhib, Boston Mus Fine Art, Mass, 60-61; Broward Co Libr, Pompano Beach, Fla, 80-94 & 96-98; 36th All-Fla Juried Exhib, Boca Raton Art Mus, 87; Soc Four Arts, Palm Beach, Fla, 88 & 91; Curzon Gallery, Boca Raton Hotel & Club, Fla, 89. *Pos:* Mem, Community Appearance Comt, Pompano Beach, Fla, 80-81 & 89, 2000 Plus comt, Pompano, Fla, 95. *Teaching:* Instr, pottery & painting, Broward Co Sch System, Fla, 75-89; instr, painting, Broward Co Community Col, 88, 2000-01; youth prog, Fla Atlantic Univ, 92; weekly art prog, Deerfield, Fla, 94-, City Libr, Lighthouse Point, Fla, 2000-; painting Boca Raton (Fla) Resort and Club, 98-99. *Bibliog:* Dorothy Anne Flor (auth), feature article, Ft Lauderdale News & Sun Sentinel, 4/17/83; Pat Curry (auth), feature article, Ft Lauderdale News & Sun Sentinal, 3/4/90; Tamara Kerrill (auth), feature article, Ft Lauderdale News & Sun Sentinal, 6/19/92. *Mem:* Fla Arts Ed; Fla Prof Artists Inc. *Media:* All Media; Bronze Metalic Powders. *Publ:* Columnist monthly column, Paint Drops, Observer, Deerfield Publ Inc, Fla, 96

PERKINSON, ROY L
CONSERVATOR, HISTORIAN
Study: Atelier Chapman Kelly, Dallas, Tex, 60-61; MIT, Cambridge, Mass, BA, 63, post grad studies, 64-65; Sch Mus Fine Arts, Boston, 64-69; Boston Univ, MA(art hist), 67; apprentice to FW Dolloff, Conservator Prints & Drawings, Mus Fine Arts, Boston, 67-70. *Hon Degrees:* Lorenzo Award, Prof Picture Framers' Asn, 1979; Nat Endowment for the Arts, 1994; Sheldon and Caroline Keck Award, 1999. *Pos:* Asst Conservator prints & drawings, Mus Fine Arts, Boston, 67-71, assoc conservator, 71-73, conservator, 76-; conservator prints & drawings, Fine Arts Mus San Francisco, 73-76; designer, Western Regional Paper Conserv Lab, Fine Arts Mus San Francisco, 73; vis comt, Int Mus Photog, George Eastman House, Rochester, NY, 79-82; acad rev comt mem, Winterthur Grad Prog in Conserv & Early Am Studies, 86-94; conserv assessment comt, Mus Fine Arts, Boston, 90-91, ethics code comt, 94-95, conserv comt, 94-, head paper conserv, 98-. *Teaching:* Various lectures & workshops, 74-99; guest lectr, J Paul Getty Mus, Malibu, Calif, 4/94 & Nat Gallery Am Art, Washington, 10/95. *Awards:* Lorenzo Award, Prof Picture Framers' Asn, 79; Res grant for paper hist, Dir Mus Fine Arts, Boston, 93; Prof Develop Award, Nat Endowment Arts, 94. *Mem:* Fel, Am Inst Conserv; Fel, Int Inst Conserv; Nat Conserv Adv Coun; Nat Inst Conserv; Print Coun Am. *Publ:* Auth, Conserving works of art on paper, Mus News, Am Asn Mus, Washington, 77; coauth, Questions concerning the design of paper pulp for repairing art on paper, In: Preservation of Paper and Textiles of Historic and Artistic Value, Am Chemical Soc, Washington, 77; contribr, Mary Cassatt: The Color Prints,Abrams, New York, 89; auth, Notes on media and papers, In: Awash in Color: Homer, Sargent and the Great American Watercolor, Mus Fine Arts, Boston, Bulfinch Press, Little, Brown & Co, Boston, 93; coauth, Printmaking terminology, In: Emil Nolde: The Painter's Prints, Mus Fine Arts, Boston, 95; coauth, Les papiers bleus: identification de colorants, 96. *Mailing Add:* 365 Weston Rd Wellesley MA 02181

PERLE, VIRGINIA
PAINTER
b East Orange, NJ, 42. *Study:* Montclair State Col, NJ, 63; Ocean Co Col, NJ; student of Lucille Geiser. *Work:* 65 Print editions of NYC; Ocean Co Cult and Heritage Soc; Toms River Seaport Soc; lobby, McGuire Air Force Base, NJ; and others. *Exhib:* Art in the Park, Central Park, NY; Thompson Park Art Ctr, Monmouth, NJ; Congressional Off Bldg, Rotunda, Wash, DC; Central PA Festival of Arts, 79-96; solo exhib, Rotunda, State Dept Off, Trenton, NJ, 99; and others. *Awards:* Scholarship grant, Art Ctr of Oranges; First place, Point Pleasant Festival Arts and Crafts, 2001. *Mem:* Ocean Co Artist Guild (pres, formerly). *Media:* Watercolor. *Specialty:* Landscapes, still lifes, cityscapes and shore scenes. *Mailing Add:* 1427 Holmes Ave Toms River NJ 08753

PERLESS, ROBERT
SCULPTOR
b New York, NY, Apr 23, 38. *Study:* Univ Miami, Coral Gables, Fla. *Work:* Aldrich Mus Contemp Art, Ridgefield, Conn; Okla Art Ctr, Oklahoma City; Phoenix Art Mus, Ariz; Univ Northern Iowa, Cedar Falls; Whitney Mus Am Art, NY; others; Bard Col, Annandale on Hudson, NY; Bucknell Univ, Lewisburgh, PA; Miami Univ, Oxford, Ohio. *Comn:* Xerox Int Hq, McLean, Va, 93; 555 Madison Ave, NY, 94; Univ Conn, Storrs, 95; Bristol-Myers Squibb, New Brunswick, 96; Rusk Inst, NY, 98; others. *Exhib:* Recent Acquisitions, Whitney Mus Art, NY, 70; Recent Sculpture, Taft Mus, Cincinnati, Ohio, 80; group shows, Aldrich Mus Contemp Art, Ridgefield, Conn, 87, 94, 97, 98 & Stamford Mus Art, Conn, 88; Conn Biennial, Art New Eng (with catalog), Bruce Mus, Greenwich, Conn, 89; Andre Emmerich Top Gallant Farm, Pawling, NY, 91, 92, 93, 94, 95 & 96; others; City of Corpus Christi, Tex, 2002; USVC, Heber City, UT, 2004; Salt Lake Community Col, Salt Lake City, UT, 2000; Syracuse Hancock Int Airport, Syracuse, NY, 99. *Bibliog:* Structural drama for a New Canaan poolhouse, Archit Dig, 8/89; Art in public high places, Palm Desert Sun, 8/91; Somewhere over the rainbow, Hartford Courant, 8/16/95; others; Greenwich Time, Artist's Engergy Reflected in Work, 97; From Greenwich with Light, Fairfield Co Times, 97; New York Times, What 72 Artists Figured Out About Boxes 1 by 1 by 1, 2000; Art at Transit Sites, Sculpture Magazine, 2000; Corpus Christi Caller Times, Onion's Belt Shows City's Coastal History, 2001; Stamford Advocate & Greenwich Times, Towering Controversy, Stamford Advocate & Greenwich Times, 2002. *Mem:* ISC, Sculptor's Guild. *Media:* Aluminum, Stainless Steel; Prisms. *Mailing Add:* 37 Langhorne Ln Greenwich CT 06831-2611

PERLIN, BERNARD
PAINTER, ILLUSTRATOR
b Richmond, Va, Nov 21, 18. *Study:* Nat Acad Design, with Leon Kroll, 36-37; Art Students League, with Isabel Bishop, William Palmer & Harry Sternberg, 36-37; also in Poland. *Work:* Tate Gallery, London; Nat Collection Fine Art, Smithsonian Inst; Mus Mod Art & Whitney Mus Am Art, NY; Va Mus Fine Arts; and others. *Comn:* US Post Off Dept, 40. *Exhib:* Brussels World's Fair, 58; Detroit Inst Art, 60; Pa Acad Fine Arts, 60; retrospective, Univ Bridgeport, 69; and many other group & one-man shows. *Teaching:* Instr, Wooster Community Art Ctr, Danbury, Conn, 67-69. *Awards:* Fulbright Fel, 50; Guggenheim Fels, 54-55 & 59; Nat Inst Arts & Lett Award, 64; and others. *Bibliog:* Lloyd Goodrich & John I H Baur (auths), American Art of Our Century, Whitney Mus Am Art, 61; Daniel M Mendelowitz (auth), A History of American Art, Holt, 61; Selden Rodman (auth), Conversations with Artists, Capricorn Press, 61; and others. *Mem:* Nat Acad (assoc 1957-94, academician 1994-). *Publ:* Illusr, Life & Fortune Mags. *Mailing Add:* 56 Shadow Lake Rd Ridgefield CT 06877-1017

PERLIN, RUTH RUDOLPH
EDUCATOR, ART HISTORIAN
b Washington, DC. *Study:* Wellesley Col, BA, 57; Metrop Mus Art, Inst Fine Arts, 61-62; New York Univ Inst Fine Arts, MA, 61-63. *Pos:* officer bd, Mus Educ Roundtable, 78-81; contrib ed, Sch Arts Mag, 78-82; proj dir, laserdisc, 83 & producer, digital image base/laserdisc, Am Art, Nat Gallery Art, Wash, 93; dir, Educ Tech, The Phillips Collection, 2001; spl asst to dir, Interpretation and Technological Initiatives, The Phillips Collection, Wash, 2001. *Teaching:* Head docent training art hist, Baltimore Mus Art, 65-69, lectr, 70-72; instr art hist, Towson State Col, Md, 67-69. *Awards:* Cine Golden Eagle, 83-86 & 88-90; Mus Educator of Yr, Mus Div, Nat Art Educ Asn Eastern Region, 93. *Mem:* Am Asn Mus (vchair, 96-98, chair media and tech standing prof com, 98-2000, bd media and tech standing prof com, 2000-, coun of SPCS, 98-2000); Nat Art Educ Asn, Mus Educ Div (eastern region dir, 95-97); Non Print Mats (comn, 96-2003). *Res:* Collections, exhibitions of The Phillips Collection; 19th & 20th century painting; 19th & 20th century American art. *Specialty:* 19th & 20th century European and American Art. *Publ:* coauth, A video disc resource for interdisciplinary learning, Art Educ, Vol 48, No 3, 17-24, 5/95; Worlds of meaning, Art Educ, Vol 51, No 5, 25-28 & 45-48, 9/98; prodr, dir European Art from the Nat Gallery of Art (digital imagebase/laserdisc & videocassette), 2000; prodr, dir, writer Jacob Lawrence: Over the Line (interactive web pgm), 2001, prodr Jacob Lawrence CD-ROM, The Phillips Collection, 2002; prodr, Am Art at Phillips Collection (interactive web program), 2005. *Mailing Add:* c/o The Phillips Collection 1600 21st St NW Washington DC 20009-1090

PERLIS, DONALD M
PAINTER
b New York City, Jul 29, 41. *Study:* Art Students League, 61; Sch Visual Arts, NY City, 65; Skowhegan Sch, 65. *Work:* exhib in group shows Whitney Mus, NY City. *Exhib:* one-man show Sindin Gallery, New York City, 94, 95; Walter Wickiser Gallery, New York City, 96-97; Claudia Carr Gallery, New York City, 99; Graham Gallery, 71, 75, Sindin Galleries, 93, 95, Charas-Elbohio, 93; solo shows, Denise Bibro Gallery, 2001-2005. *Mem:* Nat Acad. *Publ:* Doc film on artist produced by Time Capsule Films, 1993; auth, (monogr) Allegories of Love, 1995. *Dealer:* Denise Bibro Fine Art 329 W 20th St New York NY 10011. *Mailing Add:* 105 E 9th St New York NY 10003-5401

PERLMAN, BENNARD BLOCH
PAINTER, WRITER
b Baltimore, Md, June 19, 28. *Study:* Carnegie-Mellon Univ, BFA, 49; Univ Pittsburgh, MA, 50. *Work:* Peale Mus & Baltimore Mus Art, Baltimore, Md; Univ Ariz, Tucson; Univ Md, College Park; Fed Reserve Bank, Balt; Am Airlines, Dallas. *Comn:* Mural, 66 & History of Gardenville (oil), 80, City Baltimore. *Exhib:* Baltimore Mus Art; Corcoran Gallery Art, Washington, DC; Carnegie Mus, Pittsburgh; Pa Acad Fine Arts, Philadelphia; 76 one-man shows. *Pos:* Art critic, The Daily Record, Baltimore, 84-92, Maryland Maturity, 92-93, South Fla Times, 99-2004; contribr, The Balt Sun, 48-, The New York Times, 87-. *Teaching:* Prof & chmn dept art, Community Col Baltimore, 54-86; vis lectr, Oxford Univ, Eng, 75 & Dartmouth Col, 81. *Awards:* Freeland Art Award, Md Artists Exhib, Baltimore Mus Art; First Prize & Mus Purchase, Peale Mus Ann; First prize & Purchase, Easton Md Acad of the Arts. *Bibliog:* Md Pub Television, 2005. *Mem:* Artists Equity Asn (nat vpres, 69-71 & 77-79); Baltimore Mus Art Artists Comt (chmn, 59-61 & 69-70); Greater Baltimore Arts Coun (pres, 64-66); Col Art Asn. *Media:* Oils, Ink. *Interests:* Late 19th- Early 20th Cen Am Art. *Publ:* Auth, Arthur B Davies: Drawings and Watercolors (exhib catalog), Baltimore Mus Art, 87; Robert Henri: His Life and Art, Dover, 91; ed, Revolutionaries of Realism: The Letters of John Sloan and Robert Henri, Princeton Univ Press, 97; The Lives, Loves and Art of Arthur B Davies, State Univ NY Press, 98; ed, American Artists, Authors and Collectors: The Walter Pach Letters 1906-1958, State Univ NY Press, 2002. *Mailing Add:* 2944 Wood Valley Dr Baltimore MD 21208

PERLMAN, CARA
SCULPTOR
b New York, NY. *Study:* RI Sch Design, Providence, BFA, 73. *Exhib:* TV Newsroom, Am Fine Arts, NY, 90; Summer Group Exhib, Fawbush Gallery, NY, 90; Drawing, Fawbush Gallery, NY, 90; Richard Anderson Gallery, NY, 92 & 93; Signs of Life (with catalog), Univ Galleries, Ill State Univ, Normal, 92; Wadsworth Anthenium,

Hartford, Conn, 93; 1920, Exit Art, NY, 93; Peephole Installation, Postmasters Gallery, NY, 97; Barbara Gross Gallery, 98; Portraits, Trans Hudson Gallery, NY, 99; plus many others. *Pos:* Set designer, Frankfurt Ballet, Ger, 83-91. *Awards:* NY Found Grant Sculpture, 89; Guggenheim Found Grant Sculpture, 97; Pollock/Krasner Found Grant, 99. *Bibliog:* Sara Schmerler (auth), Projects at Roosevel Is, Time Out NY, 8/21-28/96; Carlo McCormick (auth), Cara Perlman at Deitch projects, ArtNet, 9/97; Roberta Smith (auth), Cara Perlman, NY Times, 9/26/97. *Media:* Plastics. *Publ:* Auth, Fingerpaint Portraits, 83; Slingerland, Ballet Frankfurt, Ger, 91. *Mailing Add:* 40 Lispenard St New York NY 10013

PERLMAN, HIRSCH
PAINTER
b Feb 7, 60. *Study:* Yale Univ, BA, 82. *Exhib:* Solo exhibs, Cable, NY, 87, Galerie Claire Burrus, Paris, France, 88, 91 & 93, Shodhalle, Zurich, Switz, 90, Galerie Hufkens, Brussels, Belg, 90, Monika Sputh Galerie, Koln, Ger, 91, 94 & 97, Interim Art, London, Eng, 91, Feature, NY, 92 & Donald Young Gallery, Seattle, Wash, 93, Blum & Poe, Santa Monica, Calif, 2001, Donald Young Gallery, Chicago, Ill, 2002; Whitney Mus Am Art, NY, 89; After and Before, Renaissance Soc, Chicago, 94; Radical Scavenger(s): the Conceptual Vernacular in Am Art (catalog), Mus Contemp Art, Chicago, 94; When Attitudes Become Form: Selections From a Contemp NJ Collection, Montclair Mus, NJ, 94; Notational Photog, Metro Pictures & Petzel Borgmann Gallery, NY, 94; Temporary Translation(s), Deichtorhallen, Hamburg, Ger, 94; Passions Privees, ARC, Paris, France, 95; Art in Chicago 1945-1995 (with catalog), Mus Contemp Art, Chicago, 96; Fake Ecstasy With Me, Mus Contemp Art, Chicago, 97; Next, Blum & Poe, Santa Monica, Calif, 97; Hello Mr Soul, Gallery 400, Univ Ill Circle, Chicago, 99; No Harm in Looking, Mus of Contemp Art, Chicago, Ill, 2001, (Tele)visions, Kunstyhalle, Vienna, Switz, 2001; Whitney Biennial, Whitney Mus Am Art, NY, 2002; Extreme Existence, Pratt Manhattan Gallery, NY, 2002; LA on My Mind, Mus Contemporary Art, LA, 2002; Zones, Art Gallery Hamilton, Ontario, Canada, 2003; Outlook: Int Art Exhibition, Athens, Greece, 2003; 100 Artists See God (traveling); Premiere, A Gavlak Projects Production, NY, 2003. *Teaching:* Assoc prof scupture, UCLA, currently. *Awards:* Nat Endowment Arts, 89 & 91; Louis Comfort Tiffany Found Grant, 91. *Bibliog:* Fred Camper (auth), Minute art, Chicago Reader, 3/25/94; Laurie Palmer (auth), Repeat after me, Frieze, 7/94; Regina Hackett (auth), review, Seattle Post-Intelligencer, 11/25/94. *Publ:* Contribr, Artists Writings: Twice-Told Tales, Art J, fall 89; auth, Contingency, Iron & Solidarity, Artforum, 12/89; coauth (with Jeanne Dunning), Introduction to the Relationship Between Art & Pervision, DU, 6/91; coauth (with Jeanne Dunning), Getting to Know the Law or Make Things Mean What I Want Them to Mean or A Collection of Quotes I Like, Dirty Data (catalog), Ludwig Mus, Aachen, Ger; auth, Exhibit Z 1 (Judicial), Framework, vol 5, issued 2 & 3, 92. *Dealer:* Donald Young Gallery 933 W Washington Blvd Chicago IL 60607. *Mailing Add:* UCLA Dept Art 1100 Kinross Ave Ste 245 Los Angeles CA 90095

PERLMAN, JOEL LEONARD
SCULPTOR, INSTRUCTOR
b New York, NY, 43. *Study:* Cornell Univ, BFA, 65; Cent Sch of Art & Design, London; Univ Calif, Berkeley, MA, 68. *Work:* Whitney Mus Am Art; Los Angeles Co Mus; Johnson Mus, Cornell Univ; Metrop Mus Art, NY; Hirshhorn Mus & Sculpture Garden. *Comn:* Night Traveler (outdoor sculpture), Storm King Art Ctr, 77; Tenneco World Hq, Greenwich, Conn, 96; Kane Sports Ctr, Cornell Univ, 96; ABN Amro Plaza, Chicago, Ill, 2004; Hebrew Home at Riverdale, NY, 2005. *Exhib:* Whitney Mus Am Art Biennial, 73; Contemp Reflections, Aldrich Mus Contemp Art, 73; Roy Boyd Gallery, Chicago & Los Angeles, 78, 80, 81, 83, 86, 88 & 96; Eve Mannes, Atlanta, 93; Retrospective (with catalog), Glen Horowitz Gallery, East Hampton, 96; Century Asn, NY, 96; Roy Boyd, Chicago, Ill, 96; Kouros Gallery, NY, 2000, 2002 & 2004; Roy Boyd, Chicago, 2003 & 2005. *Teaching:* Instr sculpture, Sch Visual Arts, 73-. *Awards:* Nat Endowment Arts Grant, 79; Reynolds Aluminum Award, 87; Special Prize, Fujisankei Biennale, Japan, 95; Fel Guggenheim Found, 1974. *Bibliog:* Barbara Pollack (catalog), 2000; Jason Andrew (catalog), 2000; Peter Barton (interview), 2000; Jonathan Goodman, review Art in Am, 2002; Philip F. Palmedo (monograph), Joel Perlman, A Sculptor's Journey, Abbeville Press, 2006. *Mem:* Sculptors Guild; Century Asn New York. *Media:* Welded Steel, Cast Bronze. *Interests:* motorcycles, sports, dogs. *Publ:* Joel Perlman, New Sculpture 97-2000; Douglas Maxwell, article Sculpture Mag, 2002. *Dealer:* Kouros Gallery NYC; Roy Boyd Gallery Chicago. *Mailing Add:* 250 W Broadway New York NY 10013-2431

PERLMUTTER, LINDA M
PAINTER, INSTRUCTOR
b New York, NY, Mar 1, 43. *Study:* Hunter Col, BA, 63, MA, 67; China Inst, Calligraphy, NY, 69; Art Student's League, with Mario Cooper, 71-81. *Work:* Gabelli Funds Inc, Rye, NY; Powell Duffryn Inc, Bayonne, NJ; Yonkers Bd Educ, NY; Blue Cross Blue Shield Md, Baltimore; Ernst & Young, Stamford, Conn. *Comn:* Marriott Corp, comn by Baird Eaton, Tarrytown, NY, 85. *Exhib:* Filth, Hudson River Mus, Yonkers, NY, 71; Beaux Arts, State Univ NY, Purchase, 78; Nat Asn Women Arts Traveling Exhib, Sarah Lawrence Col, Bronxville, NY, 85, Jesse Besser Mus, Alpena, Mich, 86, Schenectady Mus, NY, 86 & Adelphi Univ Mus, Garden City, NJ, 87; River Gallery, Irvington, NY, 90, 92, 94, 97 & 2000. *Pos:* Art supervisor, New York City Bd Educ, 68-69; art dir, N Tarrytown Art in the Park, 86-90; pres, Odyssey Art Ctrs, 95-present. *Teaching:* Fine arts, New York City Bd Educ, 66-69; instr, Creative Use Art Media, State Univ NY, 69 & Odyssey Art Ctrs, 75-present. *Awards:* Best in Show, Ossining Women's Club, 78; Nat Asn Women Artists Traveling Exhib, 85; Ada Cecere Mem Award, Nat Asn Women Artists Ann, 89. *Bibliog:* Harriett Edelson (auth), Genius Culled from Natural Phenomena, Gannett, 77; Helene Brooks (auth), A singular woman, McCall's Mag, 79; Phyllis Riffel (auth), Organization and Creativity Makes Artists' Life Productive, 83; Valerie Bohigian (auth), Lady-Bucks, Dodd Mead & Co, 87. *Mem:* Nat Asn Women Artists (bd mem, 82-95); Katonah Mus Artist's Asn. *Media:* Watercolor, Acrylic. *Specialty:* Watercolors, Oils, Pastels. *Interests:* Travel, Boating, Gardening. *Publ:* H George Caspari Inc as notecards, 78-present, Posters. *Dealer:* River Gallery Main St Irvington NY 10533. *Mailing Add:* 470 Bellwood Ave Sleepy Hollow NY 10591

PERLMUTTER, MERLE
PRINTMAKER
b London, Eng, Apr 16, 36; US citizen. *Study:* Art Students League, with Ethel Katz; Pratt Inst, Brooklyn, NY; Ruth Leaf Graphic Workshop, Douglaston, NY. *Work:* Portland Mus Art, Wash; Musee de Petit Format, Couvin, Belgium; New York City Pub Libr, 42nd St Branch Print Collection; Housatonic Mus Art, Bridge Port, Conn; Newark Pub Libr, NJ. *Exhib:* Eleven one-person shows, Soc Am Graphic Artists, Taiwan, China, 84, Silvermine Gallery, Conn, 85, Ariz State Univ, Phoenix, 85, Katonah Gallery, NY, 86, Hudson River Mus, 88 & QCC Gallery, Queens Community Col, New York City; Boston Printmakers Nat Competition, Mass, 74, 76, 79, 80 & 83; Pratt Int Miniature Graphics Exhib, 75, 77, 81, 83, 85 & 87; Premio Int Biella Por L'Incisione, Italy, 76 & 80; Miami Int Biennial, Metrop Mus & Art Ctr, Fla, 77 & 80; Martha Jackson Gallery, NY, 79; NY State Mus, Albany, 81; Third & Fourth Int Biennial, 87-89; Taipei Fine Arts Mus, Taiwan, China; Tucson Mus Art, Ariz; Biennial graphic Art, Mus Mod Art, Ljublyana, Yugoslovia; Mus Mod Art, Wakayama, Japan, 88; Rufino Tamayo Mus, Chapultepec, Mex; Noyes Mus, NJ, 90. *Teaching:* Instr etching & printmaking, Ruth Leaf Graphic workshop, Douglaston, NY, 76-; guest printmaker prints & techniques, Grey Art Gallery & Study Ctr, NY Univ, 76. *Awards:* Two Gold Medals & Silver Medal, Audubon Artist Nat Competition, NY, 75, 77, 80, 84 & 88; Creative Artist Pub Serv Prog Fel, 76; Soc Am Graphic Artists Award, 78, 80, 90, 91 & 97; and many others. *Bibliog:* Ruth Leaf (auth), Intaglio Printmaking Techniques, Watson-Guptill, 77; Jacquline Brody (auth), Prints Published, Print Collectors News Lett, 9-10/78; Phyllis Braff (auth), articles, New York Times, 11/4/84 & 9/15/85; Carol Wax Abrams (auth), The Mezzotint, 90. *Mem:* Boston Printmakers, Mass; Audubon Artists; Soc Am Graphic Artists. *Media:* Intaglio, Etching. *Mailing Add:* 20 Cherry Ave New Rochelle NY 10801-5304

PERLOFF, MARJORIE G
CRITIC, HISTORIAN
b Vienna, Austria, Sept 28, 31; US citizen. *Study:* Barnard Col, AB, 53; Catholic Univ, MA, 56, PhD, 65. *Teaching:* Prof English, comparative literature & art literature, Univ Southern Calif, 77-86, Stanford Univ, 86-; Sadie D Padek chair humanities, 91-. *Res:* Modern and postmodern poetry and painting; artists books; intermedia. *Publ:* Auth, The Dance of the Intellect, Cambridge Univ Press, 85; The Futurist Moment, Univ Chicago Press, 86; Poetic License, Studies in Modernist & Postmodernist Lyric, Northwestern, 90; Radical Artifice, 92; Wittgenden's Ladder, 96; and others. *Mailing Add:* 1467 Amalfi Dr Pacific Palisades CA 90272

PERLOW, KATHARINA RICH
DEALER, GALLERY DIRECTOR
b Vienna, Austria; US citizen. *Study:* Hunter Col (art hist), 75-77. *Pos:* Dir, Jack Gallery, New York, formerly; partner, A M Sachs Art Gallery, 83-85; pres & dir, Katharina Rich Perlow Gallery, New York, 85-. *Bibliog:* Cover, Profile of a Galerist, 11/1991; Talk Show, Lynn Graham's Transetters, 9/29, 10/6/2001; Juor: Temple Univ, Alumni Exhib, Philadelphia, Pa; Juror: Schoharie Art Ctr, Coblcshill, NY. *Mem:* Mus Mod Art, NY; Metrop Mus Art, NY; Whitney Mus Am Art; Guggenheim Mus Art; Norman Rockwell Mus; Berkshire Mus; Soc Illusr. *Media:* Painting, Sculpture photography. *Specialty:* Contemporary art, 20th century, Jon Schueler, John Ferren, Stephen Dietemann, Gertrude Greene, Brian Yoshimi Isobe, Stephen Pace, Ian Hornak, Michael Harnett, Scott Kahn, Joe Naujokas, Steven Katz, Lani Irwin, Balcomb Greene, Abigail Varela, Tom Ferrara, Sally Michel, Jacob Kainen, Richard Segalman, David Ahlsted, Larry Rivers, Michele Harvey, William Clutz, Gail Boyajian, Diane Brawarsky, Robert Goodnough & Monica Rich Kosann. *Interests:* Art, music and sports. *Collection:* Ecclectic private collection of our gallery, artists and others. *Mailing Add:* Katharina Rich Perlow Gallery The Fuller Bldg 41 E 57th St 13th Fl New York NY 10022

PERLS, KLAUS G
DEALER
b Berlin, Ger, Jan 15, 12; US citizen. *Study:* Univ Basel, Switz, PhD, 33. *Pos:* Partner, Perls Galleries, 37-; trustee, Metrop Mus, New York, 92. *Mem:* Art Dealers Asn Am. *Specialty:* Modern masters. *Publ:* Auth, Complete works of Jean Fouquet, 40; Maurice de Vlaminck, 41. *Mailing Add:* 4 N Lake Rd Armonk NY 10504

PERREAULT, JOHN
CRITIC, CURATOR
b New York, NY, Aug 26, 37. *Exhib:* Pattern Painting, PS1, NY, 77; Usable Art, Queens Mus, NY, 81; Streamline Design, Queens Mus, NY, 84; Am Craft Mus, NY, 92 & 93; Urban Glass, NY, 94. *Pos:* Art critic, Village Voice, New York, 66-74 & 87-; sr art critic, Soho News, New York, 75-82; cur, Everson Mus, 83-84; dir visual arts, Snug Harbor Cult Ctr, Staten Island, NY, 85-88; sr cur, Am Craft Mus, 90-. *Teaching:* Vis prof, Univ Calif, San Diego, 76; prof art criticism, Univ Ariz, Tucson, 79 & State Univ NY, Binghamton, 81. *Awards:* Art Criticism Fels, Nat Endowment Arts, 73 & 79. *Bibliog:* Alex Gildzen (ed), John Perreault issue, Serif, Kent State Univ Libr, Ohio, Vol XI, fall 74. *Mem:* Am Sect Int Asn Art Critics (pres, 78-81); Col Art Asn; Am Asn Mus; Nat Coun Educ Ceramic Arts; Nat Writers Union. *Res:* Contemporary art, American ceramic art and design and crafts. *Publ:* Auth, articles in Artforum, Art Am, Arts, Artscanada, Art Int; Auth, Drawings & Watercolors of Philip Pearlstein, Abrams, 88; Philip Pearlstein; Drawing & Watercolors, Abrams; and many others. *Mailing Add:* 54 E Seventh St New York NY 10003

PERRET, DONNA C
ART DEALER, CONSULTANT
b Jackson, Miss, June 23, 49. *Study:* Miss State Col Women, BS, 72. *Pos:* Dir, Galerie Simonne Stern, New Orleans; bd mem, Contemp Arts Ctr, 88-93; vpres policy & planning, Arts Coun New Orleans, 96. *Awards:* Times Picayune Woman to Watch 90; YWCA Roll Model, 93. *Mem:* Contemp Arts Ctr; Warehouse District Art Asn, New Orleans; New Orleans Mus Art-Friends of Cont Art; Arts Coun New Orleans; Art Table. *Specialty:* Contemporary fine art

PERRIN, ALAIN-DOMINIQUE
COLLECTOR
b Nantes, France, Oct 10, 42. *Study:* Degree in business, Ecole des Cadres, 69. *Pos:* Sales rep, Cartier, Paris, 69-70; gen mgr Les Must de Cartier, 71-76, chief executive officer, 76-81; chmn, Chief Exec Officer Cartier Inte, Cartier SA, 81-88; chief executive officer, Piaget/Baume & Mercier/Aldebert, 88-; Chief Exec Officer Richemont Group, 2001-; Lectr, Ecole des Hautes Etudes Commls, Paris, 86; wine producer Chateau La Grezette, Cahors, 84. *Awards:* Recipient World Star trophy, 85, Phoenix award, 87, Trophée de l'Entreprise, 88, Officer, Order of the Legion of Honour, 2002; named one of top 200 collectors, ARTnews Magazine, 2004. *Bibliog:* (auth): Les Seigneurs du Cahors, 88. *Collection:* Contemporary art, especially minimalism; photography. *Mailing Add:* Cartier Internat 51 Rue François 1 er Paris 75008 75008 France

PERRONE, JEFF
CERAMIST
b Atwater, Calif, 53. *Exhib:* Univ Art Gallery, Calif State Univ and travelled, 83; White Columns, NY, 84; Bernice Steinbaum Gallery, NY, 86; What's New?, Am Ceramics Since 1980: The Alfred and Mary Shands Collection, J B Speed Mus, Louisville, Ky, 87; Charles Cowles Gallery, NY, 87; plus others. *Teaching:* Instr, Sch Visual Arts, NY, 77-83, Univ Tex, San Antonio, 84 & Brown Univ, Providence, RI, 86. *Awards:* Nat Endowment Arts, 78. *Bibliog:* J Kozloff (auth), Like a dense curry with coconut milk, Am Ceramics, 5/4/87. *Mailing Add:* c/o Gallery Camino Real Gallery Ctr 608 Banyan Tr Boca Raton FL 33431

PERRONI, CAROL
COLLAGE ARTIST, PAINTER
b Boston, Mass, July 28, 52. *Study:* Boston Mus Sch, Mass, 70-71; Bennington Col, BA, 76; Skowhegan Sch Painting & Sculpture, 78; Hunter Col, NY, MFA, 83. *Work:* RI Hosp, Providence. *Exhib:* Solo exhibs, Boston City Hall, 78, Hunter Col Gallery, Ny, 83 AS220, Hera Gallery, Wakefield, RI, 95 & 98, Providence RI, 96 & Community Col RI, Lincoln Campus Gallery, 96; Gallery X, Fed Reserve Bank Boston Gallery, 96; Fall Painting Show, Sarah Doyle Gallery, Brown Univ, Providence, RI, 96; Ann Holiday Art Bazaar, Art Adv/Boston, Quincy, Mass, 96; Illusions of the Millennium, Renaissance Gallery, Fall River, Mass, 98. *Pos:* Studio asst for Isaac Wilkin, Bennington, Vt, 73-74, Mel Bochner, New York, 79 & Lee Krasner, E Hampton, 80; libr asst, Simmons Col Libr, 77-78; bookkeeper, Int House, New York, 79-80; res asst, Art News Mag, New York, 81; tech asst, Avery Archit & Fine Arts Libr, New York, 81-83; intern, Greenspace Gallery, New York, 82-83; librarian/researcher, Kennedy Galleries Inc, New York, 84-86; prog specialist/art teacher, Swinging Sixties Sr Citizen Ctr, Brooklyn, NY, 86-87; Arts in Educ Prog, RI, 93-96. *Awards:* Grant, Flintridge Found, 93. *Bibliog:* Bill Van Siclen (auth), Taking a fresh approach to ancient themes, Providence J, Providence, RI, 8/96; Alicia Craig Faxon (auth), Gallery Night/Providence, Art New Eng, Brighton, Mass, 12/96-1/97; Juliet Pennington (auth), Artist strives for a three-dimensional look, Sun Chronicle, Attleboro, Mass, 6/97. *Mem:* Hera Educ Found (bd dir, 94). *Media:* Oil, Acrylic; Collage. *Publ:* Auth of biographies of 35 Am Artists, Aspects of America: The Land & the People 1810-1930 (with catalog), Kennedy Galleries, New York, 5/85. *Dealer:* Art Advisory Boston 1245 Hancock St Suite 26 Quincy MA 02169. *Mailing Add:* 154 Lancaster St Providence RI 02906

PERROTTI, BARBARA
PAINTER, INSTRUCTOR
b Akron, Ohio. *Study:* Paier Sch Art, New Haven, Conn; Madison Sch Art, Robert Brackman, Conn; Burt Silverman, Cinnaminson, NJ; with Greg Kreutz, Maitland, Fla; Lois Griffiel, Willow Wisp Farm Studio, Fairview, NC. *Work:* Ormond Memorial Art Mus, Ormond Beach, FL; Doan Col, Rall Gallery, Crete, Nebr; Mus Arts & Sci, Daytona Beach, Fla; Ponce Inlet Town Hall, Fla; St. Joe Corp, Port St Joe, Fla. *Comn:* Kent Cottage (mural), Stuart Treatment Ctr, Daytona Beach, Fla, 86; mural, Family Study Ctr, Ormond Beach, Fla, 87; oil painting, Walt Disney-Epcot, 92; portrait of Chapman S Root, Mus Arts & Sci, Daytona Beach, Fla, 93; Portrait-Cold War Soldier Nat Inf Mus, Fort Benning, GA. *Exhib:* Of the Figure II, Ctr Arts, Vero Beach, Fla, 90; one-woman show, Poetry in Pose, Casements Cult Ctr, Ormond, Fla, 90, Inspirations, Cult Art Ctr, Valdosta, Ga, 94; Two Women/Two Painters, Ormond Art Mus, Ormond Fla, 93; One Women Show, Romancing the Landscape, Ctr for the Arts, Val Dosta, GA; Small Works Show, Mill Gallery, Taos, NMex, 2005; Group Invitational, Fla on my mind, Sm Trust, 2004, Matheson Mus, A Painted History of Alachua county, 2006; Epcot Int Garden Festival, 2004-2006. *Pos:* Guest Cur, Casements Cult Ctr; E Coast Plain Air-Shows, 2004-2007. *Teaching:* Instr oil portrait workshops, New Smyrna Beach, Fla, 94, Cult Art Ctr, Valdosta, Ga, 94 & Casements Cult Ctr, Ormond, Fla, 94; Instr oil painting, Art League, DAytona Beach, 79-2007; John C Campbell Folk Sch, Inst Oil & Pastel, Brasstown, NC, 2004-2007; Inst Child Plein Air-Ctr for the Arts, New Smylna Beach, FL, 2004. *Awards:* Epcot Int Garden Festival Plein Air Event, 3rd Place Award, 2004; Art League Daytone, Fiquratively speaking, 2005; Inte Plein Air Paintings, Signature status, 2006. *Bibliog:* Patricia Sporer, Up Close & Natural, Orlando Sentinal, 2002; Cindy Crawford, Artists Paint, Photo; Jim Tiller, New Journal, 2004. *Mem:* Am Impressionist Soc; Plein Air, Fla; Int Plein Air Painters; Sig mem, Fla Ambassador; Nat Mus women Arts, vol. Co. Chapter; Group of eight (co-founder). *Media:* Oil, Acrylic & Pastel. *Specialty:* Fine Art & Framing. *Dealer:* Metrop Art & Framing, 46 E Granada Blvd, Ormond Bch, FL; Soho Muriael Atlanta, Ga; St Augustine Gallery 75 King St St Augustine Fla. *Mailing Add:* 1411 N Beach St Ormond Beach FL 32174-3401

PERRY, CHARLES OWEN
SCULPTOR
b Helena, Mont, Oct 18, 29. *Study:* Yale Univ, MA(archit). *Work:* Art Inst Chicago; Univ Ind Mus Art, Bloomignton; San Francisco Mus Art, Calif; Mus Mod Art, NY; Hood Mus, Dartmouth, NH; Smithsonian Inst, Washington, DC. *Comn:* Hyatt Regency Hotel, San Francisco, Calif, 73; Gen Elec Hq, Conn, 74; Ministry of Defense, Riyadh, Saudi Arabia, 75; Nat Air & Space Mus, Washington, DC, 76; Zeimu Univ, Tokyo, Japan, 98; Barnett Plaza, Tampa, Fla, 86; Shell Oil, Melbourne, Australia; One-man shows include Hansen Gallery, San Francisco, 64, Waddell Gallery, New York City, 67, 70, Dartmouth Col, 1973, Arts Club, Chicago, 73, Auguste st-Gaudens Mus, NH; exhibited in group shows at Whitney Mus, 64, 66, Spoleto Festival, 67, Venice Biennale, 70, Quadrienalle di Arte de Roma, 77, Katonah Gallery, NY; represented in permanent collections at Mus Modern Art, New York City, Art Inst Chicago, San Francisco Mus Art, Univ Ind Mus Art, Dartmouth Col, Univ Mich, Nat Air and Space Mus, IBM, Charlotte, NC, Hyatt Regency, San Francisco, Fed Reserve Bank, Minneapolis, Barnett Plaza, Tampa, Lincoln Ctr, Dallas, Shell Oil Bldg, Melbourne, Australia, GE Hdqrs, Fairfield, Conn, Bushnell Park, Hartford, Conn, Crystal City, Arlington, Va, Zeimu Univ, Tokyo, Kokubu Civic Ctr, Japan; patentee in furniture design field. *Exhib:* Fed Reserve Bank, Minneapolis, Minn, 73; Whitney Mus Am Art, NY, 64 & 66; Venice Bienale, 70; Quadriennale di Roma, Italy, 77; one-man shows, Alpha Gallery, 70, Hopkins Art Ctr, Dartmouth, 72 & Arts Club of Chicago, 72; Cummer Gallery, Mus Art, Jacksonville, Fla 82; and others; St Gaudens Mus, Agustus, NH, 2000. *Collection Arranged:* Arts Club of Chgo, 72; Hood Mus, Dartmouth Col, 72; Cummer Gallery Mus Art, Jacksonville, Fla, 82; St Gandens Mus, Agustus, NH, 2000. *Pos:* Lectr, State Univ, NY, Albany, 92, 94 & 96, Smithsonian Inst, Washington, DC, 96, Univ Calif, 8/98 & Univ De Los Paises Vazcos, San Sebastian, Spain, 98. *Teaching:* Am Acad in Rome, 69 & Dartmouth Col, 73. *Awards:* Prix de Rome in Archit, 64-66; Am Inst Steel Design Award, 68 & 70; Nat Acad Design, New York, 87. *Mem:* Nat Acad, NY; Century Asn, NY. *Media:* Metal

PERRY, DONALD DEAN
PAINTER, EDUCATOR
b Hutchinson, Kans, Sept 29, 39. *Study:* Pittsburg State Univ, BFA, 62; Kans State Univ, MS, 67; Univ Wis-Madison, MFA, 67. *Work:* IBM Corp, United Telecommun Systems Inc, AT&T Corp, Kansas City, Mo; Software AG NAm, Chicago. *Comn:* Wildlife Panorama, Marshfield Libr, Wis, 70; sculpture installation, Security Benefit Building, Topeka, Kans. *Exhib:* Nat Print Exhib, State Univ NY, Potsdam, 67; Miami Graphics Biennial Int, Metrop Mus, Fla, 74; Nat Print & Drawing Exhib, Univ NDak, Minot, 76; Ann Printmaking West, Logan, Utah, 78; Ann Nat Drawing & Small Sculpture Show, Ball State Univ, Ind, 80; Telec III Int Exhib, Art Res Ctr, Kansas, City, Mo, 85; Abstract Paper (three-person exhib), Batz-Lawrence Gallery, Kansas City, 86; Hypergraphics Int VIII Exhib, Bannister Gallery, RI Col, Providence, 87; Dakotas 100 Int Works on Paper Exhib, Dickinson State Univ, NDak & Univ SDak, Vermillion, 88; Ann Faculty Art Exhib, Norman R Eppink Art Gallery, Emporia State Univ, Kans, 93-98; Kansas Abstract Artists Exhib, Cafe Gallery, Wichita Art Mus, Kans, 94; Constructions, Dykes Libr Art Gallery, Univ Kans Med Sch, 95; Prismacolor and Acrylic Works on paper, Emporia Arts Coun, Kans, 97; 29th Ann Smoky Hill Art Exhib, Hays Arts Ctr, Kans, 98; and many others; US Printmakers, Franco-Am Inst, Rennes, France, 2000; 12th Ann Nat Art Competition, Univ Art Gallery, Truman State Univ, Kirksville, Mo, 2000; Forty-Fifth Ann Nat Print Exhib, Hunterdon Mus Art, Clifton, NJ, 2001; Fourteenth Parkside Nat Small Print Exhbit, Communications Arts Gallery, Univ Wis-Parkside, Kenosha, 2001; Dirty Dozen Plus One, City Arts Gallery, Wichita, 2002; Print Jumble, Art and Design Gallery, Univ Kan, 2002; Sixteenth Parkside Nat Small Print Exhib, Communication Arts Gallery, Univ Wis-Parkside, Kenosha, 2003. *Pos:* Mem bd dir, Community Arts Inc, Emporia, 73-74; dir, Univ Art Galleries, Emporia State Univ, 79-2001, chair art dept, 77-84, 92-2000. *Teaching:* Instr drawing & printmaking, Univ Wis, Marshfield, 67-72; prof art, Emporia State Univ, Kans, 72-, chmn art dept, 77- 84, 99-2000. *Awards:* Purchase Award, Miami Graphics Biennial, 74; Art Enhancer award, Kan Art Edu Asn, 92. *Mem:* Emporia Arts Coun, Kans. *Media:* Screenprint; Acrylic. *Mailing Add:* 1636 Dover Rd Emporia KS 66801

PERRY, EDWARD (TED) SAMUEL
ADMINISTRATOR
b New Orleans, La, 37. *Study:* Baylor Univ, BA, 61; Univ Iowa, MA, 66, PhD, 68. *Pos:* Dir film dept, Mus Mod Arts, NY, 75-78; chair, Salzburg Seminar on Film, 94. *Teaching:* Prof cinema & chmn dept, Univ Iowa, Univ Tex & NY Univ, 69-75; Luce vis prof cinema, Harvard Univ, spring 75; chmn, Arts Div, Middlebury Col, 78-97; Am Film Inst Ctr for Advanced Film Study, 81-87; Fletcher prof arts, dir arts, Middlebury Col, 97-. *Mem:* Soc Cinema Studies; Speech Commun Asn (mem res bd, 74-). *Publ:* You Are What You Look At, No 76 Film Cult, 92; How Can One Sell the Air? The Book Publ Co, 93; Il mestiere di vivere, il mestiere di vivere, Arion, spring & fall 92 & 93; A Secret Place, With A View in American Identities, ed by Robert Pack & Jay Parini, Univ Press of New England Press, 94; Antonioni: Poet of Images, by William Arrowsmith, Oxford Univ Press, 94; My Reel Story, Univ Press of New England, 2000; Buky Schwartz: The Seeing I, Acad, Chicago, 2004; ed, The Impulse to Preserve, NY, Other Press, 2006; Masterpieces of Modernist Cinema, Ind Univ Press, 2006. *Mailing Add:* 49 South St Middlebury VT 05753

PERRY, FRANK
SCULPTOR
b Vancouver, BC, Jan 15, 23. *Study:* Univ BC, BA, 49; Cent Sch Arts & Crafts, London, Eng; Regent Poly, Chelsea Sch Art, London. *Work:* Granite carving, Vancouver Art Gallery, BC, 98; Vancouver Art Gallery; Univ BC Sch Archit; Art Gallery Greater Victoria, BC; Univ Victoria; London Art Gallery, Ont. *Comn:* Bronze fountain, Crescent Apts, West Vancouver, 61; cor-ten welded, Fed Govt Bldg, Victoria, 66; bronze cast, Playhouse Theatre, Vancouver, 67 & BC Govt for Prov Bldgs, 73. *Exhib:* Montreal Mus Fine Arts, 58; Winnipeg Show, 58; BC Centennial Outdoor Show, 58; BC Centennial Outdoor Sculpture Show, 67; Burnaby Art Gallery, 77. *Pos:* Pres, Northwest Inst Sculpture, 59-60. *Awards:* First Prizes, Montreal Mus Fine Arts, Winnipeg Show & BC Centennial Outdoor Show, 68; Grand Prize, BC Centennial Outdoor Sculpture Show, 67; Rothman Award, 67. *Mem:* Sculptor's Soc Can; Sculptor's Soc BC; Royal Can Acad Art. *Media:* Bronze, Welded Steel. *Mailing Add:* 137 W 17th St No 402 North Vancouver BC V7M 1V5 Canada

PERRY, GREGORY J
MUSEUM DIRECTOR
Study: Univ Ill, Urbana-Champaign, BA, 82; DePaul Univ, JD, 90; Sch of Art Inst Chicago, MA in modern art hist, theory and criticism, 2003. *Pos:* Assoc Robert W Smith & Assocs, Ill, Hillside, and Fein and Seeskin; assoc dir devel, spec projects Art Inst Chicago; assoc dir, Jane Voorhees Zimmerli Art Mus, Rutgers Univ, NJ, 2000-02, acting dir, 2002, dir, 2003-. *Mailing Add:* Rutgers Univ Jane Voorhees Zimmerli Mus 71 Hamilton St New Brunswick NJ 08901

PERRY, KATHRYN POWERS
COLLAGE ARTIST, PAINTER
b Chico, Calif, Mar 13, 1948. *Study:* Stanford Univ, 68; Concordia Col, BA, 70: Art Students League, Studies with Will Barnet, Knox Martin, Gregory d'Alessio & Robert B Hale, 71-74; Emily Ferrier-Spear Scholar, 73-74; Sch Visual Arts, 78-79. *Comn:* various private comns, 1990-1994; various small works, 2002-2006. *Exhib:* Solo exhib, Aames Gallery, NY, 76, Berg Art Ctr, Moorhead, Minn, 77; Ore Independent Artists, Arte Fiera, Bologna, Italy, 78; Marietta Nat, Ohio, 79; Ligoa Duncan Gallery, NY, 79; and other group exhibs. *Pos:* Art dir, Metrop Opera Guild, New York, 83-89. *Awards:* ECHO Leader Award for Educational Brochure Design, 86. *Bibliog:* Review of four Concordia College artists, Fargo Forum, 5/70; Rob Edelman (auth), Three Brooklyn artists probe their role in society, Courier-Life, 7/74; New York Challenges Artists, Concordia, winter 78; Asketch in time, Skagit Valley Herald, 5-2006. *Mem:* Life mem Art Students' League; charter mem Nat Mus Women Arts. *Media:* Pastel, watercolor, mixed media, acrylic. *Mailing Add:* PO Box 373 Lopez WA 98261

PERRY, LINCOLN FREDERICK
PAINTER, SCULPTOR
b New York, NY, May 28, 1949. *Study:* Columbia Univ, BA, 71; Queens Col, MFA, 75. *Work:* Bayly Mus, Charlottesville. *Comn:* Work & Leisure (murals), John Hancock, Inc, Boston, 84; triptych, Solomon Brothers, NY, 86; MetLife (murals) St Louis, Mo, 88; Mural for 1700 Pennsylvania Ave, Washington, 90. *Exhib:* Tatistcheff Gallery, NY, 80, 82, 84, 86, 88 & 90; Contemp Realism, NY Coun Arts Mus, NY, 82; Bodies and Souls, Artists Choice Mus, NY, 83; New Talent-NY, Sioux City Art Mus, 84. *Teaching:* Asst prof painting & drawing, Univ NH, Durham, 75-80, Univ Ark Fayetteville, 83-84 & Univ Va, 85. *Awards:* Nat Endowment Arts Grant, 84. *Bibliog:* James Cooper (auth), rev, News World, 81 & 82; Eunice Agar (auth), Lincoln Perry, Am Artist, 84; Liebemann Butler (auth), intro to catalog, Sioux City Art, 84. *Media:* Oil, Terra Cotta

PERRY, REGENIA ALFREDA
HISTORIAN
b Virgilina, Va, Mar 30, 41. *Study:* Va State Col, BS, 61; Case Western Reserve Univ, MA(Va Mus Fine Arts Out of State Fel), 62; Univ Pa, 63-64, PhD(art hist), 66; Yale Univ, 70-71. *Pos:* Spec res asst, Cleveland Mus Art, 64-65; vis scholar, Piedmont Univ Ctr, Winston-Salem, 71-72. *Teaching:* Asst prof art hist, Howard Univ, 65-66; asst prof art hist, Ind State Univ, Terre Haute, 66-67; prof art hist, Va Commonwealth Univ, 67-90, emer prof, 90-. *Awards:* Danforth Found Post-Doctoral Fel, 70-71. *Mem:* Col Art Asn Am; Am Asn Mus; Soc Archit Historians; Am Asn Univ Prof. *Publ:* Auth, James Van Derzee--Photographer, 73; Free Within Ourselves: African American Artists in the Collection of the National Museum of American Art, 92; Harriet Powers's Bible Quilts, Rizzoli, NY, 94. *Mailing Add:* 3404 Moss Side Ave Richmond VA 23222-1826

PERSHAN, MARION
PAINTER - WATERCOLOR, OIL, LECTURER
b New York, NY. *Study:* Hunter Col, with William Starkweather, BA, 38; Pratt Inst, 40, Nat Acad Fine Arts, with Louis Bouche, 53; Art Students League, with Edwin Dickinson & Frank Mason, 54; watercolor with Edgar Whitney. *Work:* Dow Chemical Corp, Midland, Mich; Cardiology Assoc, Westport, Conn, 2000. *Comn:* watercolor, comn by Dr Ralph Kirmaer, 92; watercolor, comn by Dr Robert Moskowitz, 93; watercolor, comn by Dr Lawrence Kaplan, 98; watercolor, comn by Joseph Jensen, 98; Capital M, NY; and others. *Exhib:* Catherine Lorillard Wolfe Arts Club, Nat Arts Club, NY, 76-83 & 90; Salmagundi Club, NY, 81; 157th Ann, 82 & 159th Ann, 84, Nat Acad Design, NY; Knickerbocker Artists, 85-87; Madison Sq Garden, NY, 86; Lincoln Ctr, NY, 87; Nature Ctr Westport, Conn, 90-95; Art Expo, Fla, 97-2005. *Collection Arranged:* Brooklyn Comes to the Met, Metrop Mus of Art, 76 & 77; Long Island Univ, 88; Brooklyn Mus, 90. *Pos:* Art dir, Camp Roselake, Honesdale, Pa, 54-55; art dir, Camp Racquette Lake, NY, 57; juror, Nat Shows Catherine Lorillerd Wolfe Art Ctr, NY 85-89. *Teaching:* Instr & coordr art, New York City Pub Sch, 60-77. *Awards:* Gold Medal of Honor, Catherine Lorillard Wolfe Club, Inc, 79 & Silver Medallion, 82; Best in Show, Nat Arts Club, 82; Second Prize Watercolor, Knickerbocker Artists, 82 & Gold Medal, 85; Cynthia Goodgal Mem Award, 83; Top Award Watercolor, Hudson Valley Art Asn, 87. *Bibliog:* Walter Cruickshank (auth), Art Rev, Flatbush Life, 5/8/71; Les Krantz (auth), Am Artists. *Mem:* Catherine Lorillard Wolfe Art Club Inc; Knickerbocker Artists; Hudson Valley Art Asn; Asn Am Watercolor Soc. *Media:* Watercolor and Oils. *Specialty:* Contemporary realism. *Interests:* Visual art enjoyment. *Collection:* Consists of large 28x36 and medium watercolor paintings. *Publ:* Auth, Language Arts in the Art Curriculum, Fac News Asn, 4/72; illusr cover design, Career Opportunities Exposition, Am Educ Asn, 10/73. *Dealer:* Grand Central Art Galleries New York NY. *Mailing Add:* 209-25 18th Ave Bayside New York NY 11360

PERSKY, ROBERT S
WRITER, PUBLISHER
b Jersey City, NY, Jan 5, 30. *Study:* NY Univ, 49; Harvard Law Sch, JD, 52. *Pos:* Ed, The Photograph Collector, 80-96; publ, The Consultant Press Ltd. *Mem:* Am Photog Hist Soc. *Publ:* Auth, The Artist's Guide to Getting & Having a Successful Exhibition, Consul Press; ed & publ, The Photographic Art Market, Vol III-XIII; Guide to Tax Benefits: For Collectors, Dealers & Investors, third ed, Consultant Press, 91. *Mailing Add:* c/o The Photograph Collector 163 Amsterdam Ave New York NY 10023

PERUO, MARSHA
PAINTER, PRINTMAKER
b Brooklyn, N Y. *Study:* Queens Col, BA, 71; Pratt Inst, MFA, 80. *Exhib:* Miniature Painters, Sculptors & Gravers Soc Washington 58th Ann Int Exhib, DC, 91; Am Soc Contemp Artists Ann Exhib, Broome St Gallery, NY, 92; Am Soc Contemp Artists 75th Anniversary Exhib, Broome Street Gallery, NY, 93; Am Soc Contemp Artists Exhib Paintings, Graphics, Sculptures, Lever House, NY, 94; Miniature Art Soc Fla 21st Ann Int Show, Belleview-Mido Resort Hotel, Clearwater, Fla, 96; Nat Collage Soc 13th Ann Exhib, Stocker Ctr Gallery, Lorain Co Comm Col, Elyria, Ohio, 97. *Awards:* Dorothy Fiegen Mem Award for Graphics, 62nd Ann, Am Soc Contemp Artists, 80. *Mem:* Am Soc Contemp Artists (awards chmn, 80-81, corresp secy, 81-83, dir, 83-85, 1st vpres, 85-87); NY Artists Equity Asn. *Media:* Mixed Media. *Mailing Add:* 55 W 14th St New York NY 10011

PERZYNSKI, BOGDAN P
VIDEO ARTIST
b Poznan, Poland. *Study:* Acad Fine Arts, Poland, MFA. *Work:* Muzeum Narodowe, W Poznaniu; De Saisset Mus, Santa Clara, Calif; Mus Fine Arts, Houston, Tex; Univ Art Mus, Univ Calif, Santa Barbara; Bibliot Publiczna, Zielona Gora. *Exhib:* Positions, Mexie Arte Mus, Austin, Tex, 84; Faculty Show, Univ Art Mus, Santa Barbara, Calif, 85; Cafedegli Artisti, De Saisset Mus, Sanat Clara, Calif, 87; Ann Fac Shows, Jack Blanton Mus Art, Austin, Tex, 87-2000; Piwna RO/26, Muzeum Akademii Sztuk Pigknychi, Warsaw, Poland, 94; One-man shows, Arlington Mus Art, 96, Univ Art Gallery, Dallas Visual Art Ctr, 97 & Jade S Blanton Mus Art, 98. *Teaching:* asst prof, Acad Fine Arts, Pozhau, Poland, 80-83; lectr, Univ Calif Santa Barbara, 84-87; assoc prof, Univ Tex, Austin, 87-. *Mem:* Col Art Asn. *Mailing Add:* 4305 Shaolwood Ave Austin TX 78756

PESNER, CAROLE MANISHIN
ART DEALER
b Boston, Mass, Aug 5, 37. *Study:* Ecole du Louvre, Inst d'Art et d'Archit, Paris, 58; Smith Col, Northampton, Mass, BA, 59. *Pos:* Pres, Kraushaar Galleries, New York, currently. *Mem:* Art Dealers Asn Am Inc; Int Fine Print Dealers Asn. *Specialty:* 20th century and contemporary American art. *Publ:* Auth & coauth, Kraushaar Gallery Publ & Catalogs. *Mailing Add:* Kraushaar Galleries 724 Fifth Ave New York NY 10019

PETER, FRIEDRICH GUNTHER
PAINTER, CALLIGRAPHER, GRAPHIC DESIGNER
b Dresden, Ger, Feb 23, 33. *Study:* Hochschule fuer Bildende Kuenste, WBerlin, Ger, 50-56; Meisterschueler Dipl in lettering & graphic design, 56-57. *Comn:* Murals, 90 ft for World Coun Churches 6th Assembly, 83, City of Vancouver Street Banners, 95; postage stamp designs, Can Post, Govt Can, for Can Nat Anthem, 80, Can Constitution, 82, Terry Fox, 82, Multiculturalism, 90; 100 dollar gold coin, 82 & 20 dollar silver Olympics coin, 88, One dollar special issue coin, 93, Royal Can Mint; four 50-cent proof coins, Can Sports Series, 98; illus, cover designs & calligraphy for publs, Oncken & Kreuzverlag Publ, Ger; and others. *Exhib:* solo shows, Following Higher Orders, Gulf War Drawings at Gallery Alpha and Lookout Gallery, UBC, Vancouver, BC, 91; The Art of the Coin, Royal Canadian Mint, Roy Thompson Hall, Toronto, Ont, 92; one-man shows Lookout Gallery, Regent Col, Univ BC, 89, 92, 99, 2001, 2006 & Ferry Bldg Gallery, West Vancouver, BC, 94; Landscapes and Scriptures, Ferry Bldg Gallery, West Vancouver, BC, 96; Invitational traveling exhib calligraphy, Christians Visual Arts, 97. *Collection Arranged:* 26 Letters (traveling exhib), Fine Arts Gallery, Univ BC, Vancouver. *Pos:* Educator, regional rep & found Mem, Graphic Designers, Can, 58; Postage Stamp Design Sub-Comt, Postage Stamp Adv Comt, Can Post, Fed Govt Can, 82-85. *Teaching:* Instr graphic design, Vancouver Sch Art, BC, 59-78, chmn dept, 76; instr graphic design, Emily Carr Col Art & Design, Vancouver, BC, 76-94, Emily Carr Inst Art & Design, 94-98. *Awards:* Nat Competition, Royal Can Mint, 81, 82, 88 & 92; First Prize in Latin Category; winner typeface design competitions, Vivaldi Internat Typeface Corp, NY, 61, Magnificat, Letraset Internat, London, Sanbika, Morisawa Corp, Osaka, Japan, 87, Shinko, 90, Peter Roman, 93. *Bibliog:* Television interview, Coin & medal designers, Sunday Arts Entertainment, Can Broadcasting Corp, 90; Canada at the Millenium, Heirloom Press, 2000; Natl Archives, Canada; 26 Extraordinary Canadians, CFMT Intl, Rogers TV

Studio C, 2002; Canada at the Millennium, Can Heirloom Series, 2000. *Mem:* Royal Can Acad; Graphic Designers Can (fell). *Media:* painting, calligraphy, lettering, drawing, graphic design. *Specialty:* Painting, acrylic, watercolors, misc media. *Interests:* Hiking, Backpacking, Travel; Coin designs for a number of intl typeface design competetions. *Publ:* Auth & ed, Idea Mag, No 110, Yoshinobu Kawasaki, 72; Novum education Vancouver School of Art, Novum/Gebrauchsgraphik Mag, 3/75; illusr, Der Turm, Ulrich Schaffer (auth), Oncken, Ger, 79; Wenn Mauern fallen, U Schaffer (auth), Kreuz Verlag (publ), Ger, 90; Talking with Friedrich Peter (illus interview) Graphic Design Journs, Graphic Designers of Can, 2001. *Dealer:* Bel Art Gallery Inc 2171 Deep Cove Rd North Vancouver BC Canada V7G1S8. *Mailing Add:* 193 E St James Rd North Vancouver BC V7N 1L1 Canada

PETERS, ANDREA JEAN
PAINTER
b Boston, Mass, Dec 27, 47. *Study:* Vesper George Sch Art, Boston, 65-66; Mass Col Art, Boston, 66-68; Roger Curtis, Gloucester, 78-83. *Work:* Warner & Stackpole, Boston; MBNA Am; Axelrod Enterprises, Tex; Voltaix Corp, NJ; Russell Reynolds Associates, Boston, MA; AUSAM Intl; Farnsworth Art Mus, Rockland, Maine. *Exhib:* 17th Nat Works on Paper, Harnett Hall Gallery, Minot State, NDak; Bates Col Mus Art, Lewiston, Maine, 98; Notations of Color: oil sketching in Maine; 8th Int Exhib, Am Intercontinental Univ, Atlanta, 98; USArtists, Pa Acad Fine Arts, Pa, 2000. *Awards:* Daniel B Hoye Mem Award, 86 Hoyt Nat, 86; Pearl Paint Award, 15th Ann Pastel Soc Am, 87; J Giffuni Scher Award, 16th Ann Pastel Soc Am, 88; & others. *Bibliog:* Miles Unger (auth), Art Review, Boston Sunday Globe, 9/90; Charlotte Floyd (auth), Artist Portrait, The Minuteman Chronicle, 9/90; Philip Isaacson (auth), Art Review, Maine Sunday Telegram, 6/97 & 7/2004; Carl Little (auth), The Art of Maine in Winter, Downeast Books, 2002. *Mem:* Am Artists Prof League, NY; Pastel Soc Am, NY (master pastelist); North Shore Arts Asn, Mass; Copley Soc Boston, Mass (copley artist); Maine Coast Artists. *Media:* Oil, Pastel. *Dealer:* Gleason Fine Art Boothbay Harbor ME

PETERS, DIANE (PECK)
PAINTER, MURALIST
b Corpus Christi, Tex, May 14, 40. *Study:* Univ Okla Art Workshop, with Milford Zornes, 75; Class with Chen Chi, 76, Master Class in Watercolor, with Edward Betts, 78 & 84; La Tech Univ, with Douglas Walton, 78. *Work:* Corpus Christi Mus, Tex; McAllen State Bank, McAllen, Tex; Incarnate Word Convents, Corpus Christi, Tex, Lyon, France, Nairobi, Kenya, E Africa, Mex, Cleveland, Ohio, Victoria, San Antonio & Houston, Tex; mural, Incarnate Word Sisters, 75th Jubilee, Kenya Africa; Mura, Incarnate Word Sisters, 25th Jubilee, Kenya, E Africa. *Comn:* Seascape mural, Dr & Mrs William Roof; Lake wildlife mural, John Peters Mem, 86; In The Beginning Was The Word (Incarnate Word Missions in Africa) 96 & And The Word Was Made Flesh (mural), Order Incarnate Word, Corpus Christi, Tex, 95; The Baptism of Jeanne Chezard De Matel, France, 97; Series of the Tribe of Kenya, 97; Ascension, Bishop Peter Kairo, Kenya; mural, Tribal Peace Below Mt Kenya, Incarnate Word Sisters Regional House, Nairobi, Kenya, 2006. *Exhib:* 39th Watercolor Soc Ala Ann Nat Competition, Birmingham Mus Art, Ala; Allied Artists Am 65th Ann Exhib, Nat Acad Galleries, NY; Salmagundi Club 2nd & 3rd Ann Non-mem Exhib, Salmagundi Galleries, NY; Southwestern Watercolor Soc Ann Membership Exhib, Dallas; Tex Watercolor Soc Exhib, 84; traveling exhib, mural Venerable Jeanne Chezard De Matel, Incarnate Word Convent, Tex, France, Kenya, 96, Incarnate Word Int Reunion, Ohio, 96; Africa A Printed Diary, Art Ctr Corpus Christi, 2005. *Awards:* Purchase Award, Tex Watercolor Soc, 84; Best of Show Award, Art Community Ctr Exhib, 89 & 98; First Place Watercolor, Art Ctr Corpus Christi, 98. *Bibliog:* Lee Dodds (auth), Tonkaland a winner, Corpus Christi Times, 6/79; Spotlight Ed (auth), Local artist has show in New York, Corpus Christi Times, 12/79; Local Artist Honored, Corpus Christi Caller Times, 5/90. *Mem:* Corpus Christ Art Ctr. *Media:* Watercolor, Acrylic; Aqua Media. *Interests:* Sailing, opera. *Publ:* Illusr, cover, Star to Star, 1/72; cover, Giving (catalog), 85; cover, The Cooking Habit, 87; paintings featured, The Artist Mag, 5/88; paintings featured, The New Spirit of Watercolor, North Light Books, 4/89. *Dealer:* Diane Peters Art Studio. *Mailing Add:* 6653 Downing # 16 Corpus Christi TX 78414

PETERS, JIM (JAMES) STEPHEN
PAINTER, SCULPTOR
b Syracuse, NY, Aug 3, 45. *Study:* US Naval Acad, Annapolis, Md, BS, 67; Mass Inst Technol, Cambridge, Atomic Energy Comn fel, 67-69, MS, 69; Md Inst, Col Art, MFA, 77. *Work:* Flint Inst Art, Mich; Cent Cult Art Contemp, Mex City; Provincetown Art Asn & Mus, Mass; Ctr Fine Arts, Vero Beach, Fla; William Benton Mus, Univ Conn, Storrs. *Exhib:* Exxon Invitational, Solomon R Guggenheim Mus, 85; Fables and Fantasies, Duke Univ Mus Art, Durham, NC, 89; Am Art Today, Fla Int Univ, Miami, 89; The Art Show, 7th Regiment Armory, NY, 89; I, Myself and Me, Midtown Payson Gallery, NY, 92; Solo exhib, Age of Drawing: An Int Scene CDS Gallery, NY, 98, Collection of Provincetown Art Asn & Mus, Nat Art Club, NY, 2000, Redo China, Ethan Cohen Fine Arts, NY, 03, Cape Mus Art, Dennis, Mass, 04. *Pos:* Chmn, visual comt, Fine Arts Work Ctr, 85-89, 94- & fel, 82-84, Provincetown, Mass. *Teaching:* Artist-in-res, Hartwick Col, Oneonta, NY, 90-94. *Awards:* Fel & cash painting grant, Mass Artist Found, 85 & 88; Adolph & Esther Gottlieb Individual Artists Grant, 99; Mass Artist Grant, 2002. *Bibliog:* Lisa Denison (auth), New Horizons in American Art (exhib catalog), Solomon R Guggenheim Mus Found, 85; Vasari Diary (auth), Obsessed with women, Art News, 5/91; Ann Wilson Lloyd (auth), Jim Peters, Art Am, 10/91; Grace Giveck (auth), Art in Review, NY Times, 10/15/99; Cate McQuaid (auth), Shedding Light on the Tensions of Initamcy, Boston Globe, 8/30/02. *Media:* Oil, Mixed on Canvas; Wood Constructions & Wax. *Dealer:* CDS Gallery 76 E 79th St New York NY 10021. *Mailing Add:* PO Box 1171 Truro MA 02666-1171

PETERS, JOHN D
PAINTER
b Dover, NH, Jan 23, 48. *Study:* Univ NH, BA, 71. *Hon Degrees:* fellow in the arts, Univ NH. *Work:* Dolan Art Ctr Gallery, Locust Valley, NY; Univ NH Collection, Durham, NH; Ferry St Inns Collection, Detroit; Danish Consulate, Detroit. *Comn:* Triptych Spring, Summer, Fall, Motor City Ventures, Detroit, 91. *Exhib:* Solo-exhib, Peters Circus, Dolan Ctr for the Arts, 2001; Solo-exhib, Eve Poppers, Ambleside Galleries, Grosse Point, MI, 02; Flowers, Fruit & Wheatfields, The Cascades, Telluride, CO, 02; group exhib, Amsterdam-Whitney Gallery, Chelsea, NY, 2004; Scarab Club group exhibs, 2005-06. *Collection Arranged:* Charfoos & Christensen PC; Inns on Ferry St. *Pos:* Assoc prof, Wayne State Univ, 1978-. *Teaching:* Instr, Univ Toledo, Ohio, 72-73. *Awards:* 1st Place, NH Dept of Forrestry, 67; Global Competition, Amsterdam-Whitney Gallery, Chelsea, NY, 2003. *Mem:* Oil Painters of Am; Allied Artists Am. *Media:* Oil on canvas. *Res:* Painting techniques in the 1600s and 1700s. *Specialty:* Contemp Am Art (paintings, sculpture & photog). *Interests:* Archeology, world hist & antiquities. *Collection:* Heland (Va), Mandt (NY), Gross (Fla), Christensen, French, Charfoos, Trojanowski, Harbut, Baas (Mich), Mandt (Calif). *Publ:* The Hand Painted Photographs of Charles Henry Sawyer, Treasure Press, 02; Classic Hand Painted Photographs Are Fine Art, Antiques & Auction News, 02. *Dealer:* Juris Galleries, 5510 Woodward Ave, Detroit, MI 48202. *Mailing Add:* 5510 Woodward Ave Detroit MI 48202

PETERS, LARRY DEAN
DIRECTOR, PAINTER
b Manhattan, Kans, July 15, 38. *Study:* Washburn Univ, BFA, 62; Southern Ill Univ, with Nicholas Vergette, MFA, 65. *Work:* Afghanistan Embassy, Kabul; Singapore Embassy: art in eth Embassy Prog, Temp Loans, Union Pacific Corp; Mulvane Art Mus, Washburn Univ; Wichita Ctr for the Arts. *Exhib:* 16th Mid-Am Exhib, William Rockhill Nelson Gallery, Kansas City, Mo, 66; North Coast Col Soc Ann Exhib, Ohio, 86; Highland Community Col, 96; Wichita Ctr Arts, Kans, 98; Pittsburgh State Univ, 2000; McPherson Col, 2001; Strecker-Nelson Gallery, Manhattan, Kans, 2002. *Collection Arranged:* Hard Mud: 30 Contemporary Works of Ceramics from the Permanent Collection of the Topeka & Shawnee Coun Pub Libr, Nat Ceramic Educ Conf, Kansas City, Mo, 89; Timock-Babu-Ferguson-Leedy-Pinnell, Kansas City Art Inst Ceramic Fac, 93; Topeka Competition 20, 96; Topeka Competition 22, Mulvane Art Mus, Washburn Univ, Topeka, 2001; Mid-West Contemp Clays, Cedar Rapids Mus Art, Iowa; Hard Mud II: 90 Contemp Works in Clay from the Permanent Collections of the Topeka & Shawnee Co Pub Libr. *Pos:* Readers adv, Dept Fine Arts, Topeka & Shawnee Coun Pub Libr, 65-73, gallery dir, Gallery Fine Arts, 73-. *Teaching:* Instr pottery, Washburn Univ Topeka, Kans, 69-70. *Awards:* Kansas Governor's Arts Award for Arts Advocacy, 90. *Mem:* Am Asn Mus; Mountain Plain Mus Asn (bd mem, 98-); Kans Mus Asn (bd mem, 79-); Kans Artist Craftsmen Asn (secy, 69-71, pres, 71-73); Mulvane Art Ctr (pres, 89-90); Local Arrangements Chair, Mountain Plains Mus Assoc, 2002. *Media:* Mixed Media. *Collection:* Ceramics and Regional Painting and Prints. *Dealer:* Collective Gallery Topeka Kans. *Mailing Add:* Alice C Sabatini Gallery 1515 W Tenth Topeka KS 66604

PETERSEN, FRANKLIN G
PAINTER
b Staten Island, NY, July 19, 40. *Study:* Art Students League, 69-73. *Comn:* Portraits, Admiral A B Durek, US Navy, Washington, DC, former Gov Malcom Wilson, NY, former Atty Gen Louis J Lefkowitz, NY, Fed Judge Irving R Kaufman & Very Rev James Fewhagen, pres, General Theological Seminary NY for Allin Collection, Fordham Law Sch, NY. *Exhib:* Salmagundi Club, NY, 72-78; Nat Arts Club, NY, 73-76; Staten Island Mus Ann, 74-75; Allied Artists, Nat Acad, NY, 74-75; Pentagon Exhib, Washington, DC, 75; Nacal Artists Exhib, US Navy War Mus, Washington, DC, 75; NY Press Club, 78; and others. *Awards:* Greenshields Found Grant, 73; Stacey Mem Grant, 74; Pouch Award, Staten Island Mus, 75. *Mem:* Life mem Art Students League (secy, 72). *Media:* Oil. *Dealer:* Portraits Inc 985 Park Ave New York NY 10028; Portraits Brokers 36 B Church St Birmingham AL 35213. *Mailing Add:* 8178 Deerbrook Cir Sarasota FL 34238-4375

PETERSEN, ROLAND CONRAD
PAINTER, PRINTMAKER
b Endelave, Denmark, Mar 31, 26; US citizen. *Study:* Univ Calif, Berkeley, AB, 49 & MA, 50; San Francisco Art Inst, 51; Calif Col Arts & Crafts, summer 54; Atelier 17, Paris, with Stanley W Hayter, 50, 63 & 70; Islington Studio, London, 77; The Print Workshop, London, 80. *Work:* Mus Mod Art & Whitney Mus Am Art, NY; Philadelphia Mus Art, Pa; Nat Collection Fine Arts, Washington, DC; Univ Reading, Eng; San Francisco Mus Mod Art; Hirshhorn Mus & Sculpture Garden, Washington, DC; M.H. de Young Mem Mus, San Francisco, Calif; Oakland Mus, Calif; Mus Contemp Art, San Diego, Calif; Va Museum Fine Art, Richmond, Va; Santa Barbara Art Mus, Calif. *Comn:* Dams of the West (portfolio of 25 color prints), US Dept Interior, Bur Reclamation, Washington, DC, 70. *Exhib:* Carnegie Inst Int, Pittsburgh, 64; 25th Ann Exhib Contemp Art, Art Inst Chicago, 65; one-man shows, Staempfli Gallery, NY, 63, 65 & 67, Phoenix Art Mus, Ariz, 72, Santa Barbara Mus, Calif, 73 & Rorick Gallery, San Francisco, 81-85; Vanderwoude/Tananbaum Gallery, NY, 87-89; Harcourts Gallery, San Francisco, 89-91; John Natsoulas Gallery, Davis, Calif, 98-2000; Hackett-Freedman Gallery, San Francisco, Calif, 2002-2004. *Pos:* Mem educ process, Col Lett & Sci, Univ Calif, Davis, 65, mem exec comt, 65-66. *Teaching:* Instr painting, Wash State Univ, 52-56; prof painting & printmaking, Univ Calif, Davis, 56-91; instr printmaking, Univ Calif, Berkeley, 65. *Awards:* Guggenheim Fel, 63; appointee, Inst Creative Arts, Univ Calif, 67 & 70; Fulbright Travel Award, 70. *Bibliog:* Andree Marchal-Workman (auth), article, Artweek, 81; Kenneth Baker (auth), article, San Francisco Chronical, 89; Bruce Nixon (auth), Art of Calif, 91; Paul Karlstrom (auth), Book Forward, Hackett Freedman Gallery, 2002; Douglas, Bullis

(auth), 100 Artists of the West Coast, Schiffer Publ, Atglen, Pa, 2003; Catalog Forward, Bruce Guenther, Hackett-Freedman Gallery, 2004. *Mem:* Intercontinental Biog Asn; Calif Soc Etchers; San Francisco Mus of Modern Art, Oakland Art Mus San Jose Art Mus, Crocker Art Mus. *Media:* Acrylic, Oil. *Res:* Intaglio Printing. *Specialty:* Modern & Contemporary. *Interests:* Nature. *Publ:* catalogs, Harcourts Gallery, 89, 91 & 93; catalog, Maxwell Gallery, 95; Hackett-Freedman Gallery, 2002-2004. *Dealer:* Hackett Freedman Gallery, San Francisco. *Mailing Add:* 1148 Crespi Dr Pacifica CA 94044

PETERSON, DOROTHY (HAWKINS)
PAINTER, EDUCATOR
b Albuquerque, NMex, Mar 14, 32. *Study:* Univ NMex, Albuquerque, BSEd, 53; Dallas Mus Sch, studied painting with Otis Dozier, 63-64; Univ Tex, Permian Basin, Odessa, MA, 79. *Work:* First Nat Bank Chicago Collection, Ill; Eastern NMex Univ, Roswell; Immaculata Hosp, Westlock, Alta, Can; Mus Southwest, Midland; Odessa Col, Tex. *Comn:* Library Windows, Jal, NMex Jr High Sch; murals, Tarahumara Sch, Creel, Chi, Mex; catalog cover, ENM Univ, Roswell, 94-96. *Exhib:* Solo exhibs, Carlsbad Mus, NMex, 85, Mus Southwest, Midland, Tex, 85 & Thompson Gallery, Univ NMex, Albuquerque, 86; Eastern NMex Univ, Portales, 88; Centennial Gallery, Univ NMex, 89; Art Inst Permian Basin, Odessa, Tex, 94. *Pos:* Comnr, NMex Arts Comn, Santa Fe, 83-96; artist rep, NMex Arts & Crafts Fair, Albuquerque, 84-86. *Teaching:* Instr painting, Midland Col, Tex, 71-75, Roswell Mus, 81-83; prof art hist, Eastern NMex Univ, Roswell, 89-2000; painting instr, NMex Military Inst, Roswell, 92, 94. *Awards:* Tricentennial Award, Masterworks, 2004; Third Place Award, Tex Watercolor Soc, 2005; First Place Award, Watercolors Masterworks, 2005. *Bibliog:* NMex Mag, 5/89& 2/2006. *Mem:* NMex Watercolor Soc; Nat Watercolor Soc, Signature Mem, 2001; Tex Watercolor Soc, Signature Mem, 2006. *Media:* Oil, Watercolor. *Specialty:* Landscape, Figure. *Publ:* Savoring the Southwest, RSG Pub, 83 & 98; Artists of NMex, Mtn Pub, 89 & 93. *Dealer:* Benson Fine Arts Box 10 San Patricio NM. *Mailing Add:* PO Box 915 Roswell NM 88202

PETERSON, GWEN ENTZ
PRINTMAKER, GRAPHIC ARTIST
b Newton, Kans, Mar 8, 38. *Study:* Northern Colo Univ, BFA, 59; Goshen Col, Florence, Italy, 77; Univ NMex, 77-79. *Work:* Golden Collection, Eastern NMex Univ; AT&T; Albuquerque Nat Bank; Miller Libr, McPherson Col; Jonson Collection. *Comn:* Frame Work, Wright Edge Advert Agency. *Exhib:* Solo exhibs, Jonson Gallery, Univ NMex, 75, 77, 79 & 81, McPherson Col, Kans, 2003; retrospective, Thompson Gallery, Univ NMex, 84; Johnson's Gallery, Madrid, NM, 2001. *Pos:* Independent artist, currently. *Teaching:* Instr pub sch, Colby, Kans, 59-61, Denver, Colo, 61-62 & Lake Bluff, Ill, 65-66. *Awards:* Prof Competition Award, NMex State Fair, 78, 80, 82 & 83; Poster Award, NMex Arts & Crafts Fair, 82; Purchase Award, Art in Pub Places, Fairbanks, Alaska, 86; Banner Design Award, Nat Presbyn Mariners, 97. *Bibliog:* Jean Blackmon (auth), Gwen Peterson, Southwest Profile, 9-10/84. *Media:* Serigraphy. *Interests:* Hiking. *Mailing Add:* 3717 General Patch NE Albuquerque NM 87111

PETERSON, HAROLD PATRICK
LIBRARIAN
b Chicago, Ill, Aug 27, 35. *Study:* Harvard Col, AB; Univ Wis, MA. *Pos:* Ed-in-chief, Minneapolis Inst Arts, 72-82, art head librn, 72-. *Mem:* Art Libr Soc NAm; Col Art Asn; Midwest Art Hist Asn. *Interests:* Decorative arts, history of printing, illustration of books. *Publ:* Ed, Victorian High Renaissance, 78, New Treasures at the Inst, 78, Millet's Gleaners, 78 & Treasures of Hermitage Mus of Leningrad, 79, Minneapolis Inst Arts; Chinese Jades: Archaic & Modern, Tuttle, 77; Five Hundred Years of Sporting Books, Manuscripts, Prints & Drawings. *Mailing Add:* Minneapolis Inst Arts 2400 Third Ave S Minneapolis MN 55404

PETERSON, KRISTIN
SCULPTOR, ASSEMBLAGE ARTIST
b Urbana, Ill, May 17, 54. *Study:* Kansas City Art Inst, Mo, BA 78; Univ Calif, Davis, MFA, 82. *Exhib:* One-woman shows, Performance Project, Diablo Valley Community Col Art Gallery, Pleasant Hill, Calif, 81 & 92, Master of Fine Arts Exhibit, Mem Union Art Gallery, Univ Calif, Davis, 82, Joseph Chowning Gallery, San Francisco, Calif, 87, 89 & 93; Functional Fantasy, Transamerica Pyramid Lobby, San Francisco, 90; Holiday Exhib, Joseph Chowning Gallery, San Francisco, Calif, 91; Couturier Gallery, Los Angeles, Calif, 92; Sun Gallery, Hayward, Calif, 92; Images of Us, Bedford Gallery, Regional Ctr Arts, Walnut Creek, Calif, 92. *Teaching:* Teaching asst, Univ Calif, Davis, 80-82; vis artist, Vacaville State Prison, Calif, 87 & 89, Humboldt State Univ, Arcata, Calif, 90; vis artist lectr, Calif State Univ, Chico, 89, Dominican Col, San Rafael, Calif, 90, San Francisco Art Inst, Calif, 91, Diablo Valley Community Col, Pleasant Hill, Calif, 92 & Calif Col Arts & Crafts, 92. *Awards:* Humanities Grant, Univ Calif, Davis, 81; First Prize & Hon Mention, Calif State Fair, Cal Expo, Sacramento, 85; Nat Endowment Arts Grant, 86. *Bibliog:* Terri Cohn (auth), Everyday Form and Function, ArtWeek, 10/90; Edie Meidav (auth), Our Tangled Hearts, ArtWeek, 2/92; Mary Hull Webster (auth), A Conversation with Kristin Peterson, ArtWeek, 2/92. *Media:* Mixed Media. *Publ:* Contribr, Voyeurism strong in Beth Foley paintings, Chico Enterprise/Record, 4/89; Story lines, Chico New & Rev, 4/89; Everday form and function, ArtWeek, 10/99; Our tangled hearts, ArtWeek, 2/90; A conversation with Kristin Peterson, ArtWeek, 2/92. *Dealer:* 1717 17th St San Francisco CA 94103

PETERSON, LARRY D
PAINTER, EDUCATOR
b Holdrege, Nebr, Jan 1, 35. *Study:* Kearney State Col, BA, 58; Northern Colo Univ, MA, 62; Univ Kans, EdD, 75. *Work:* Univ Minn; US Nat Bank, Omaha; Univ Nebr, Kearney; Nebr Art Collection; 540 works in pvt collections; Sheldon Art Gallery, Lincoln, Nebr. *Comn:* Acrylic & oil paintings, First Methodist Church, Kearney; watercolor paintings, Kearney state Bank, 80. *Exhib:* Col St Mary, Omaha, 80; Landworthy Watercolor Exhib, Seward, 85-91; Six-State Competitive, McCook Col, 88-91; Nebr Art Mus, 89; Nebr Art Educators Exhib, Nebr Wesleyan Univ, Lincoln, 90-94; Fred Wells, Twelve-State Exhib, Nebr Wesleyan Univ, Lincoln, 91 & 93. *Pos:* Dir, Mus Nebr Art & Kearney Artists Guild. *Teaching:* Instr art, North Platte Pub Schs, 58-65; North Platte Col, 66-67; prof art, Univ Nebr, Kearney, 67-2000; grad asst, Univ Kans, Lawrence, 70-71. *Awards:* Gold Medal Award, Calvatone, Italy, 86-88; Pratt-Heins Award, Kearney State Col, 87; Gov Ben Nelson's Award & One of Am Best, Art In Park, Kearney, 94; 30 Years Serv Award, Asn Nebr Art Club, Lincoln, 94; Art & Entertainment Person of Yr, Kearney Daily Hub, 2002. *Bibliog:* Nancy Kalis (auth), article, Art Rev, 68; Reva Remy (auth), one-man rev in Rev Mod Art, Paris, 68 & 72; Tom Norwood (auth), Contemporary Nebraska Art and Artists, Univ Nebr, 78; Nebraska Art Asn, Sheldon Art Gallery, Lincoln, 88. *Mem:* Nat Art Educ Asn (nat comt, 83-84); Nebr Art Teachers Asn (past pres); Asn Nebr Art Clubs (past pres); Kappa Pi (past pres, Beta Beta Chap). *Media:* Watercolor, Acrylic. *Publ:* Coauth, John Lundgren, His Geese Were Made For Hunting, Decoy Mag, Natl Publ, 9/92; John Lundgren, Decoy Maker, Mag, Nebraskland State Publ, 11/93; Cy Blacks Counterfeit Canadas, article, 11/95; contrib ed, Paper decoys, Nebraskaland State Publ, 10/96; Decoy Mag, article, 5/96. *Dealer:* Mus Nebr Art 2401 Central Ave Kearney NE 68847. *Mailing Add:* Studio 44 4 Seminole Ln Kearney NE 68847

PETERSON, ROBYN G
CURATOR
b San Francisco, Calif, Jan 17, 58. *Study:* UCLA, BA, 79; Univ Wis - Madison, MA, 82, PhD, 87. *Collection Arranged:* Brilliance In Glass; Lost Wax Glass Sculpture of Frederick, 93; Finding New Worlds; American Frontier Photography (with catalog), Rockwell Mus, 93, Edward Borein (with catalog), 97 & Warp & Weft; Navajo Weaving (with catalog), 97; Fabric of Life; Photographs of John Smart, 94; Transforming Trash; Bay Area Fiber Art auth, catalog), Turtle Bay Mus, 2000; Richard Wilson: Paintings from the Nineties, Turtle Bay Mus., 2000; Putting the Pieces Together: Contemporary Quilts by Californians, 2000; Ansel Adams: Masterworks, 2002; Inspired Obsessions: Redding Collectors, 2002; The Earth is Singing: The Art of Frank LaPena, 2003. *Pos:* cur collections, Rockwell Mus, Corning, NY, 88-99; dir collections & res, Turtle Bay Mus, Redding Calif, 99-. *Mem:* AAM; CAA; AHAA; GAS. *Interests:* 19th & 20th Century American Art; Ecological Art. *Mailing Add:* Turtle Bay Mus PO Box 992360 Redding CA 96099

PETHEO, BELA FRANCIS
PAINTER, PRINTMAKER
b Budapest, Hungary, May 14, 34; US citizen. *Study:* Univ Budapest, MA, 56; Acad Fine Arts, Vienna, with A P Guetersloh, 57-59; Univ Vienna, 58-69; Univ Chicago, MFA, 63. *Work:* Hungarian State Mus Fine Arts, Budapest; Kunstmus, Bern, Switz; Boston Public Libr; Tweed Mus, Duluth, Minn; Plains Art Mus, Fargo, NDak; Minn Mus Art, St Paul; and others. *Comn:* Kindliche Untugenden (mural), Asn Austrian Boyscouts, Vienna, 58; The History of Handwriting (exhib panel), comn by Noble & Noble Publ for Hall of Educ, NY World's Fair, 64; Summer Day at The Gallery, Holiday Inn, St Cloud MN, 2004; and others. *Exhib:* Hamline Univ, 66; Coffman Gallery, Univ Minn, 69; Moorhead State Univ, 69; Biennale Wis Printmakers, 71; Duluth: A Painterly Essay, Tweed Mus Art, Minn, 75; B P Themes: 1953-1983, CSB Gallery, St Joseph, Minn, 83; and others. *Teaching:* Instr art, Univ Northern Iowa, 64-66; assoc prof art & artist-in-residence, St John's Univ, 66-80, prof, 80-97, prof emer, 97-. *Awards:* Purchase Award, Pillsbury Invitational, 81; Burlington-Northern Fac Excellence Award, 92, Camargo Found Fel, Cassis, France, fall 94; and others. *Bibliog:* J Gray Sweeney (auth), Bela Petheo: Painter of the Center in an Age of Extremes (monogr), St John's Univ Publ, 85; Arts Salutes Bela Petheo, Arts, Minneapolis, 12/87; Bela Petheo, Works Between 1985-2000, A Retrospective (catalog), 2001. *Mem:* Rotary Internat (hon). *Media:* Oil, Acrylics; Lithography. *Res:* German Expressionism, litho techniques. *Interests:* Art history, psychology of art. *Publ:* The college art gallery, Art J, summer 71; Lithography: an introduction, traveling exhib, 78; Kokoschka Remembered, Arts(Minneapolis), 12/87; Mission and Commissions: Oskar Kokoschka in Minnesota, 1949-1957 (monogr), SJU Press, 91; The Dimensions of Agreement: Arnheim & the Painter, J Aesthetic Educ, winter 93; plus others. *Dealer:* Groveland Gallery 25 Groveland Terrace Minneapolis MN 55403; Probst Gallery 46 E Superior St Chicago IL 60611. *Mailing Add:* 400 NE Riverside Dr Saint Cloud MN 56304

PETHICK, JERRY THOMAS BERN
SCULPTOR, ASSEMBLAGE ARTIST
b London, Ont, Sept 22, 35. *Study:* Chelsea Polytechnic London, Gt Brit, Dipl Art, 60; Royal Col Art, London, Gt Brit, ARCA(sculpture), 64. *Work:* Art Gallery Ont, Toronto; Seattle Arts Comn; Vancouver Art Gallery; Biblioteque Nat, Paris. *Comn:* Vowe Land Piece, Mr & Mrs H Peake, Sussex, 68; padded wall (junkie), Methadone Centre, San Francisco, 72; turret installation, Mr & Mrs D DeVost, Hornby Island, BC, 84; outdoor installation, Toronto Sculpture Garden, 92. *Exhib:* Trales Discovery, Vancouver Art Gallery, 84; Can Biennial, Nat Gallery Can, Ottawa, 89; Material Space, S Alta Art Gallery, Lethbridge, 91; one-man show, Ctr Int D'Art Contemairaine, Montreal, 92, The Power Plant, Toronto, 92; Notion of Nothing, Stadt Gaerie, Saarbruchen, Ger, 94. *Pos:* Pres, Young Common Wealth Artists (UK), 59-61; co-founder & instr, Sch Holography, San Francisco, 70-73. *Teaching:* Instr sculpture, San Francisco Art Inst, 69-70 & Emily Carr Inst Art & Design, 85-86. *Awards:* Grant, 84-90 & Media Arts Grant, Can Coun, 92. *Bibliog:* Billy Little (auth), Voluminous luminositiey, Capilano Review, 89; Barbara Fischer (auth), The Sequin Veil, Texts Winter 9, 92; Mathew Kangas (auth), Material Space (exhib catalog), Lethbridge, 92. *Mem:* Art Gallery Ont, Toronto; Chelsea Arts Club, London; Western Front, Vancouver; Can Indian Artcrafts, Montreal. *Media:* Mixed, Photo. *Publ:* Contribr,

Holography Book, Avon, 80; auth, Lae Dot, Press Gang, 86; contribr, Virtual Sem on the Bioapparatus, Banff Centre, 91; Research & Reverie, Presentation House, 94. *Dealer:* Catriona Jeffries Gallery 3149 Granville St Vancouver BC V6H 3K1 Canada. *Mailing Add:* 1210 Savoie Rd Hornby Island BC V0R 1Z0 Canada

PETITTO, BARBARA BUSCHELL
PAINTER, CURATOR
b Jersey City, NJ. *Study:* NJ Ctr Visual Arts, studies with Robert Anderson & Phil Sherrod, cert, 85; Art Students League, NY, studies with Pousette-Dart, 90; Montclair Art Mus, with Miriam Bearman, 93. *Work:* Interior Sensations, Marinac, NY; Palisades Amusement Park Hist Soc; Cliffside Park Libr, NJ. *Comn:* Numerous pvt comns. *Exhib:* Int Juried Show, Palmer Gallery, NJ Ctr Visual Arts, 85, 92 & 98; solo exhibs, Co Col Morris Learning Resource Ctr Gallery, Randolph, NJ, 86, NJ Ctr Visual Arts, Mem Gallery, World Trade Ctr, Corner Gallery, 89 & 90, Allied Corp, Florham Park, NJ, 89, Dominion Country Club, San Antonio, Tex, 89 & Wippanong Libr, Whippany, NJ, 89; NJ Prints, Montclair Art Mus, NJ, 91; Art NJ, Ben Shahn Gallery, William Paterson Col, 92 & 94; Nat Soc Painters in Casein & Acrylic, Salmagundi Club, NY, 96; Nat Asn Women Artists, 96, 98, 99 & 2000; Ward-Nasse Gallery, Soho, NY, 96-98; Johnson & Johnson World Hq, New Brunswick, NJ, 98; Morris Co Libr, 2003. *Pos:* Artist-in-residence, St Elizabeth Acad, Convent, NJ, 88-90; cur, Ward-Nasse Gallery, Color, Divine Madness, 96. *Teaching:* Art teacher acrylics, Morris Co Art Asn, 86; art fac, Acad St Elizabeth, Convent, NJ, 92-94. *Awards:* Rudolph Voekler Mem Award, Art Ctr NJ, 82; Award of Excellence, Middlesex Co Mus, 91; Award of Excellence, Manhattan Arts Int Cover Art, 94-98; Mary K Karasick Memorial Award, NAWA Atetier 14, 2000; Papermill Award, Nabisco Brands, Inc. *Bibliog:* June W Hayes (auth), A villa in the hills, San Antonio Homes & Gardens, 87; Martin Parsons (auth), Barbara Petittos painterly knockout punch, Artspeak, 89; Elizabeth Wilford (auth), A gifted colorist artist of the 90s, Manhattan Arts, 94; articles in Art In America, Art News, Art Forum, New York Times, & Business and Art Jour.; and many others. *Mem:* Nat Asn Women Artists Inc; Nat Soc Painters Casein & Acrylics; Artists Equity; NJ Ctr Visual Arts; Catherine Lorillard Wolfe Art Club, NY. *Media:* Acrylic, Impasto. *Publ:* Feature article, Alumnae St Elizabeth, winter 89; The figure as muse, Trenton Times, Artworks, 90; Manhattan Arts Mag, 94. *Dealer:* Nexus Gallery 345 E 12th St New York NY; Ward-Nasse Gallery 178 Prince St New York NY

PETLIN, IRVING
PAINTER
b Chicago, Ill, Dec 17, 34. *Study:* Art Inst of Chicago, BFA, 52-56; Yale Univ, MFA, with Josef Albers, 59. *Work:* Art Inst Chicago; Jewish Mus, NY; Mus Mod Art, NY & Whitney Mus Am Art, NY; Metrop Mus, NY; Hirshhorn Mus, Wash; Ark Art Ctr, Little Rock; Centre Georges Pompidou, Paris; Des Moines Art Ctr, Iowa; First Nat Bank of Chicago; Hood Mus of Art, Dartmouth Col, Hanover, NH; Mus Contemp Art, Chicago, Ill; Los Angeles Co Mus, Calif; San Fransisco Mus of Contemp Art, San Francisco, Calif; de Young Mus of San Francisco, Calif; Pa Acad of Art, Philadelphia, PA. *Exhib:* Art Inst of Chicago, 53, 56 & 72; Mus d'Art Mod, Paris, 61-66; Chicago Imagist Art, Mus Contemp Art, Chicago, 72; Whitney Mus Am Art, NY, 73; Retrospective, Palais des Beaux-Arts, Brussels, Belg, 65; Neuberger Mus, State Univ NY Col, Purchase, 78; Arts Club Chicago, 78; Wiessewald, Kent Fine Art, NY, 86; 25 yr Retrospective Pastels, Kent Fine Art, NY, 88; The World of Bruno Schulze, Krugier, Geneva, 92 & 97; Jan Krugier Gallery, NY, 98; Contini Gallery, Venice, Italy, 98; solo exhibs, Irving Petlin Memoire du voyage, voyage de la memoire, Galerie Thessa Herald, Paris, 99, Basel 2000, Krugier-Ditesheim Art Contemporain, Switz, 2000 & Irving Petlin, Galleria Tega, Milano, Italy, 2001; and others; group exhibs, Light into Darkness, Kent Gallery, NY, 96, Leon Golub, RB Kitaj, Irving Petlin, Kent Gallery, NY, 97 & Chicago Loop: Imagist Art 1949-1979, Whitney Mus of Am Art, Stanford, CT, 2000; Jan Krugier Gallery, The Wolrd of Paul Celan, Geneva, 2003; Galerie Jan Krugier, Basel Int, 2001-2004. *Teaching:* Vis artist, Univ Calif, Los Angeles, 63-66; artist-in-residence, Dartmouth Col, fall 83; vis prof, Cooper Union, New York, 77-89 & Pa Acad Grad Prog, 90-96. *Awards:* Ryerson Fel, 56; Copley Found Grant, 61; Guggenheim Found Fel, 71. *Bibliog:* Michel Butor (auth), Spiral, 65; RB Kitaj (auth), Irving Petlin: Rubbings, 78; Edward Fry (auth), Irving Petlin: Kent, 87. *Mem:* Century Club, NY; Nat Acad. *Media:* Oil on Canvas; Pastel on Paper. *Publ:* Coauth (with M Palmer), A Song for Sarah; Auth, Irving Petlin: 25 Yrs of Pastels, Paul Cummings, 88; Arte Americana e arte europea a NY ed oltre: 41 east 57th St, Terzocchio, 3/89; Coauth (with Michael Brenson), Irving Petlin, New York Times, 1/6/89; coauth (with Wroblewska and Zielinski), Irving Petlin: Bruno Schulz's World, Varsovie: Galeria Kordegarda (catalogue), 93; Paul Cummings (auth), Irving Petlin the Patels, NY, 88; (auth), The world of Edmond Jabes. *Dealer:* Kent Fine Art 67 Prince New York NY 10012; Krugier-Ditesheim 29-31 Grand-Rue Geneve 1204

PETRACCA, ANTONIO
PAINTER, PHOTOGRAPHER
b Rochester, NY, June 6, 45. *Study:* Rochester Inst Tech Sch Art, BFA, 67, MFA, 69. *Work:* Mem Art Gallery, Rochester, NY; George Eastman House, Int Mus Photog, Rochester; Albright-Knox Mus, Buffalo, NY; NY Hist Soc; Mus of City of NY. *Comn:* Subway mural, Metrop Transit Authority Arts for Transit, NY, 92; Putt Modernism, Hole No 6, Artists Space, NY, 93; Patrons Print (award), Mem Art Gallery, Rochester, NY, 78. *Exhib:* Altered Landscape, Albany Inst Hist & Art, NY, 90; NY State Art Exhib, Herbert Johnson Mus, Cornell Univ, NY, 91; Isn't It Romantic?, Art Initiatives, NY, 94; Mem Gallery Selections, Albright-Knox Mus, Buffalo, NY, 96 & 97; 4 Artists From NY, Galerie Bhak, Seoul, Korea, 97; Psychological Realism, Castle Gallery, Col New Rochelle, NY, 98; Elbow Room, Kim Foster Gallery, Turner, NY, 2000; solo exhibs, Kim Foster Galleru, NY, 95-97, 97, 99, 2000, 2002, Galerie Bhak, Seoul Korea, 99, Oxford Gallery, Rochester, NY, 95, 99 & 2003, SUNY, Oswego, NY, 99; Inst of Hist & Art, NY, 2002; Flowers East, London, Eng, 2002; Fanelli Show, OK Harris Gallery, New York City, NY, 98; US Embassy, Caracas, Venezuela, 2004-2005. *Collection Arranged:* Performance Art, New Music, Nyack Center for Arts, Nyack, NY, 88. *Pos:* Dir & chief cur, Pyramid Art Ctr, Rochester, NY, 77-87; dir performing arts, Monroe Community Col, Rochester, NY, 88-89. *Teaching:* Adj instr painting, Rochester Inst Tech, NY, 82-83; Instr painting, Allofus Art Workshop, Rochester, NY, 71-77. *Awards:* Art Matters Inc Grant, 92; Best of Show, Casa Italiana, Nazereth Col, 92. *Bibliog:* Putt Modernism (TV doc), CBS Sunday Morning, 11/14/93; William Zimmer (auth), Definitive Decade Show, NY Times, 10/30/94; Margaret Mooreman (auth), Review of Exhibition, Art News, 10/97; Ken Johnson (auth), Review of Exhibition, NY Times, 9/13/02; Melissa Kuntz (auth), Review of Exhibition, Art in America Mag. *Media:* Oil on wood constructions. *Dealer:* Kim Foster Gallery 529 W 20th St New York NY 10011; Oxford Gallery 267 Oxford St Rochester NY 14607. *Mailing Add:* 552 Broadway 4th Fl New York NY 10012

PETRIE, FERDINAND RALPH
PAINTER, ILLUSTRATOR
b Hackensack, NJ, Sept 17, 25. *Study:* Parsons Sch Design, New York, cert advert, 49; Art Students League, with Frank Reilly; Famous Artists Course Illus, cert, 59. *Work:* Nat Collection Fine Art, Smithsonian Inst, Washington; Indianapolis Mus Art; JF Kennedy Libr, Boston; US Navy Combat Art Gallery, Washington; US Coast Guard, Washington. *Comn:* Salvation Army Nat Hq, NY; US Commemorative Stamp, 80. *Exhib:* Am Artists Prof League Grand Nat, NY, 71-79; Am Watercolor Soc Travel Exhib, 73, 75-78. *Pos:* Illusr, J Gans Assoc Studio, NY, 50-69, Salvation Army, 75-86. *Teaching:* pvt instr watercolor, 72-78; instr, DuCret Sch Art, 75-77, Ridgewood Art Inst, 80-85. *Awards:* Salmagundi Club Awards, 70-83; US Navy Gold Medal for Watercolor, 74; Gold Medal, Hudson Valley Art Asn, 76 & Rockport Art Asn, 71-96. *Mem:* NJ Watercolor Soc; Artists Fel; Rockport Art Asn. *Media:* Watercolor, Oil. *Publ:* Illusr, Reader's Digest covers, 77 & 79; auth, Drawing Landscapes in Pencil, Watson-Guptill, 79, The Color Book, 81, The Alkyd Book, 82 & Watercolorists Guide Series, 83-85. *Mailing Add:* 51 Vreeland Ave Rutherford NJ 07070-2227

PETRIE, SYLVIA SPENCER
PRINTMAKER, PAINTER
b Wooster, Ohio, June 15, 31. *Study:* Col Wooster, BA; State Univ Iowa, with Mauricio Lasansky & Eugene Ludens; Univ RI. *Work:* Art Ctr Mus, Wooster Col; Hasbro Children's Hosp, Providence, RI; Providence Public Libr; Boston Pub Libr; Newport Art Mus, RI. *Exhib:* Soc Am Graphic Artists 63rd Nat Print Exhib, NY; solo exhib, Vet Mem Auditorium, Providence, RI, 94-95; By Virtue of Excellence, Bell Gallery, Brown Univ, Providence, RI, 95; Hunterdon 40th Nat Juried Print Exhib, Clinton, NJ, 96; Springfield Art Mus, Mo, 90; Albrecht-Kemper Mus Art, St Joseph, MO, 2000. *Pos:* Vis artist, Title III Prog, Coventry Elem Schs, RI, 75-77. *Awards:* Netta Strain Scott Prize Art, Wooster Col, 53; First Prize & Purchase Award, Fantle's, 56; First Prize, South Co Art Asn Open Juried Art Ann, 93 & 94; and many others; Awards, open juried exhibs, Providence Art Club, 90, 91, 97. *Bibliog:* Elizabeth Findley (auth), Petrie prints and pastels depend on point of view, Eve Bulletin, Providence, 10/15/77; Edward Sozanski (auth), Print forms offer intriguing tones, Providence Sunday J, 10/15/78; Arline Fleming (auth), Variety of Interest Reflected in Work of Peace Dale Artist, Providence Jr Bull, 3/4/87. *Mem:* Print Consortium, Kansas City, Mo; Nineteen on Paper, Providence, RI; South Co Art Asn. *Media:* Intaglio, Collagraph; Oil, Pastel, Monotype. *Publ:* Illusr, From under the Hill of Night, Vanderbilt Univ, 69; The Idol, 73 & Time Songs, 79, Biscuit City Press. *Dealer:* David Charles Gallery 263 S Main St Providence RI 02903. *Mailing Add:* 200 Dendron Rd Peace Dale RI 02879

PETRO, JOE, III
PRINTMAKER, PAINTER
b Lexington, Ky, May 3, 56. *Study:* Univ Tenn, 74-79. *Work:* Jimmy Carter Pres Libr, Atlanta, Ga; Am Acad Arts & Lett, NY; Ind Art Ctr, Indianapolis; Univ Ky Art Mus, Lexington. *Comn:* Sculpture TV, State Ky, Lexington, 92; silkscreened ed & poster, David Suzuki Found, Vancouver, Can, 93; silkscreen ed in collab with Ralph Steadman, 94; silkscreen ed & poster, Greenpeace, Canada, 94, 96 & 99; silkscreen ed in collab with Jonathen Winters, 97-99; silkscreen ed in collab with Ken Kesey, 97-99; Poster in collab with Barnum Mus, Bridgeport, Conn, 98-99. *Exhib:* Liberty Gallery, Louiseville, Ky, 89; Artists Attic, Lexington, Ky, 98. *Awards:* Cert Merit, Graphic Arts Awards Competition, Heidelberg, USA, 91, 92, 93, 94, 96 & 97. *Bibliog:* Craig Latscha (auth), Joe Petro III: A Printmaker of Many Interests, Screenprinting, 80, 107-111, 12/90; Terry Pope Freas (auth), Absolute Statehead, Young Am Artists gain Nat recognition, Sunstorm, Vol 18, pp 28-31, 93. *Media:* Silkscreen. *Dealer:* John Cavaliero Fine Arts 229 E 42nd St New York NY 10017. *Mailing Add:* PO Box 2166 Lexington KY 40588-2166

PETRO, JOSEPH (VICTOR), JR
PAINTER, ILLUSTRATOR
b Lexington, Ky, Nov 4, 32. *Study:* Transylvania Col, with Victor Hammer; grad sch, Cincinnati Med Sch, art as appl to med. *Work:* Hermitage Mus, Leningrad, USSR. *Comn:* Series of paintings of all Triple Crown winners for Oaklawn Park, 73-77; mural, Hardin Mem Hospital, 82; commemorative mural, St Johns Hosp, Anderson, Ind, 90; life size series of portraits of judges, Fayette Courthouse & US Fed Bldg, Lexington, Ky, 90; designer of 1992 Ky bicentennial postage stamp for the US Postal Serv, Washington, DC, 92; and many others. *Pos:* Publ, series ltd number collector prints, 54-79; consult, Spindletop Res, Inc, Lexington, 65-68; head, Dept Appl Art, Loyola Univ of Chicago, Rome Ctr, Italy, 69-77; cult adv, US Info Serv, Am Embassy, Rome, Italy, 73-77; designer, Franklin Mint, Franklin Ctr, Pa, 80-. *Teaching:* Vis prof art, John Cabot Int Col, Rome, Italy, 75-76; prof art, Transylvania Univ, Lexington, Ky, 78- & artist-in-residence, 82-; consult, adv, Dept Army, Nat Endowment Arts, Washington, DC, 86-. *Awards:* Morrison Medallion, Transylvania Univ, 83. *Mem:* Soc

Illusr; Southeastern Ctr Contemp Art; Artists Equity, Washington, DC; Nat Soc Arts & Letts, Washington, DC. *Media:* Acrylic, Oil. *Publ:* Illusr, var publ including Thoroughbred Rec, Nat Geog, Holiday, Better Homes & Gardens & others. *Mailing Add:* 357 Henry Clay Blvd Lexington KY 40502

PETRULIS, ALAN JOSEPH
PRINTMAKER, PHOTOGRAPHER
b Queens, NY, June 20, 54. *Study:* Queens Col, BA, 1977; Md Inst Col Art, MFA, 1979. *Work:* Brooklyn Mus, Brooklyn, NY; Mus City NY, NY; NY Transit Mus, NY. *Exhib:* The Highland Set, Mus Hudson Highlands, Cornwall, NY, 1989; Hudson Valley Photography, Hudson River Mus, Yonkers, NY, 1995; New York by New Yorkers, Mus City of NY, NY, 2002; Transit Views, NY Transit Mus, NY, 2003; Impressions of NY, NY Hist Soc, NY, 2004; Tide Lines, Noble Maritime Collection, Stanten Island, NY, 2006. *Pos:* Dir, First Street Gallery, NY, 1983-1989. *Awards:* Cannon Prize, 159th Exhib, Nat Acad Design, 1984; Ralph Fabri Prize, 161st Exhib, Nat Acad Design, 1986; Adriana Brina Award, Pastel Soc Ann, Pastel Soc Am, 1986. *Bibliog:* Madaline Rogers (auth), Only in New York /Local Color, Daily News Mag, 1985; Jerry Morgan, His Brush Captures the Outer Boroughs, News Day, 1985. *Mem:* Soc Am Graphic Artists; NY Etchers Soc. *Media:* Etching. *Publ:* Contribr, Art & the Law (bk), West Publ, 1996; contribr, Impressions of New York (bk), Princeton Archit Press, 2005. *Mailing Add:* 164-11 Underhill Ave Flushing NY 11365

PETTERSON, MARGO
PAINTER
b Los Angeles, Calif, Jan 12, 44. *Study:* San Bernardino Valley Col, AA, 81. *Work:* CM Russell Mus, Great Falls, Mont; Holy Cross Hosp, Cleveland, Ohio; High Desert Cult Art Inst, Victorville, Calif. *Comn:* Collections of Wayne & Ann Miller, Myron Achenbach & Mr & Mrs Wm Tamietti. *Exhib:* Gold Medal Exhib, Calif Art Club, 95-97; Calgary Stampede, Can, 96-2005; Am Art in Miniature, Gilcrease Mus, Tulsa, OK, 1998-2006; Draft Horse Classic, Grass Valley, Calif, 2000-2006; Am Acad Equine Art, Lexington, KY, 2002 & 2004. *Awards:* 2nd Place, Calif State Fair, 2002; Best of Show, Snake River Showcase, Snake River Art Guild, 1995; Best of Show, Draft Horse Classic, 2004; Best of Show, Western States Horse Expo, 2006. *Mem:* Calif Art Club; Oil Painters of America; Women Artists of the West. *Media:* Oil, Pastel. *Interests:* The human figure; Equine paintings in the Western style. *Publ:* Sarah H Crampton, Romantic Sesibliity of Margo Petterson, Equine Visions Mag, 2002; Elizabeth Stevens, Romancing the Old West, Big, Bear Life & Grizzly, 2000. *Dealer:* Ken McDonald, 6834 Granola Las Vegas Nev 89103. *Mailing Add:* 165 Pinon Place Coleville CA 96107-9400

PETTIBON, RAYMOND
VIDEO ARTIST
b Tucson, Ariz, June 16, 1957. *Study:* Univ Calif, Los Angeles, BA, 77. *Exhib:* Heart, Mind, Body & Soul, Whitney Mus Am Art, NY, 97-98 & Hindsight: 56 Recent Acquisitions, 98-99; Double Trouble: The Patchett Collection, Mus Contemp Art, San Diego, 98; Sea Change, Parrish Art Mus, Southampton, NY, 98; LA Current: Looking at the Light: 3 Generations of Los Angeles Artists, Armand Hammer Mus Art & Cult Ctr, Univ Calif, Los Angeles, 99; Life Lessons: How Art Can Change Your Life, The Judy and Stuart Spence Collection, Laguna Art Mus, 99; It's Only Rock and Roll Currents in Contemp Art, Austin Mus Art, 99; one man show, The Drawing Ctr, New York City, 99, Philadelphia Mus of Art, 99, Mus of Contemp Art, Los Angeles, 99, Galerie Meyer Kainer, Vienna, 99, Sadie Coles HQ, London, 2000, David Zwirner Gallery, New York City, 2000, Hauser +Wirth, Zurich, Switzerland, 2000, Regen Projects, Los Angeles, 2000, Contemp Fine Arts, Berlin, 2000, MAK, Vienna, 2000 & 2001, David Zwirner Gallery, 2000, Mus of Art, Calif, 2000, The Whitechapel, London, 2000 & Plots Laid Thick, MACBA, Barcelona, Spain, 2002; LA-ex, Mus Villa Stuck & Marstall, Munich, Ger, 2000; Am Art, Galerie Fudolfinum, Munich, 2001; Das Gute Leben, Galerie Gebr, Lehmann, Dresden, Ger, 2001; Sammlung Hauser und Wirth Part 2-Alternating Current, Sammlung Hauser & Wirth, 2001; Location Drawing, Lawing Gallery, Houston, 2001; Drawing Exhib, Lawing Gallery, Houston, 2001; group exhibs, Ten Yrs, Galerie Hauser & Wirth, Zurich, Switz, 2002, Colorblind: Works in Black and White, Ikon Ltd/Kay Richards Contemp Art, Santa Monica, Calif, 2002, 2004, Permanent Collection Galleries, Post-1945 Art, Dallas Mus of Art, Dallas, Tex, 2002. *Awards:* Recipient Awards Painting, Sculpture, Printmaking, Photog, & Craft Media, Louis Comfort Tiffany Found, 1991, Wolfgang-Hahn-Prize, Ludwig Mus, Cologne, Ger, 2001, Busksbaum Award, Whitney Mus Am Art, 2004. *Mailing Add:* David Zwirner Gallery 525 W 19th St Chester MA 01011-2808

PETTIBONE, JOHN WOLCOTT
CURATOR, ADMINISTRATOR
b Springfield, Ohio, Jan 30, 42. *Study:* Wittenberg Univ, 62-63; Cleveland Inst Art, 63-65, Ford grant, 64. *Work:* Am Red Cross, Washington, DC; Town of Rockport, Mass. *Exhib:* Rockport Art Asn, 71-83; Am Fortnight Exhibition, Hong Kong, 73. *Pos:* Dir marketing, Hammond Castle Mus, Gloucester, Mass, 83-85, cur, 85-90, exec dir/cur, 90-; instr drawing, Rockport Pub Schs, 73-78, Endicott Col, 85; registrar, Higgins Armory Mus, Worcester, Mass, 78-83. *Teaching:* Instr drawing, Lakewood Pub Schs, Ohio, 59, Springfieid Art Asn, Ohio, 61-63, Rockport Pub Schs, 73-78 & Endicott Col, 85-86. *Mem:* Rockport Art Asn; Arms & Armour Soc, London; Japanese Sword Soc USA. *Media:* Conte Crayon, Silverpoint. *Dealer:* Rockport Art Asn 12 Main St Rockport MA 01966. *Mailing Add:* 509 Washington St Gloucester MA 01930-1749

PETTIBONE, RICHARD H
PAINTER, SCULPTOR
b Los Angeles, Calif, Jan 5, 38. *Study:* Pasadena City Col, AA, 59; Otis Art Inst, MFA, 62. *Work:* Israel Mus, Jerusalem; De Mennil Found, Houston; Rose Art Mus, Brandeis Univ; Art Mus, Princeton Univ, NJ; Mus Mod Art, NY; San Francisco Mus Calif; Los Angeles Co Mus; and many others. *Exhib:* Small Objects, 77, Art About Art, 78, Whitney Mus, NY; Art Against AIDS, Nature Morte, NY, 87; Aspects De L'Art Du XXe Siecle L'oeuvre re produite, Abbay Ste Andre Ctr Contemp Art (catalog), France, 91; Art Apropriates Art (catalog), Calif State, Fullerton, 91; Quotations, Aldrich Mus Contemp Art, 92; Curt Marcus Gallery, 93, 96, 99, 2001; Arts Club of Chicago, Ill, 2001. *Awards:* Nat Endowment Arts Grant, Sculpture, 88; Pollack Krasner Found, award, 93. *Bibliog:* Richard Pettibone at Curt Marcus. Art News, 92; Duncan, Michael (auth.) Richar Pettibone at Curt Marcus, Art in America, 97; Humphrey, David, Richard Pettibone at Michael Kohn, Art Issues, 90. *Media:* Oil on Canvas, Silkscreen on Canvas; Wood. *Dealer:* Curt Marcus 578 Broadway New York NY 10012. *Mailing Add:* Star Rte Charlotteville NY 12036

PEVEN, MICHAEL DAVID
PHOTOGRAPHER, EDUCATOR
b Chicago, Ill, Apr 12, 49. *Study:* Univ Ill, Chicago, AB, 71; Sch Art Inst Chicago, MFA, 77. *Work:* Ctr Creative Photog, Tucson; Humanities Res Ctr, Austin; Mus Contemp Art, Chicago; Mus Mod Art, NY; Nat Gallery Art, Ottawa, Ont, Can. *Exhib:* Alternative Image II, Kohler Art Ctr, Sheboygan, 84; Offset: Survey of Artists Books (with catalog), Hera Found, Wakefield, RI, 84; one-man shows, Art Arts Ctr, Little Rock, 85, Amarillo Mus Art, 94, Daum Mus Contemp Art, Sedalia, No, 2003, Art Ctr of Ozark, 2004, Univ Mus, Southern Ill Univ, Carbondale, Ill, 2005; Photog Book Art in the United States, 91, travel, 94; Camera Obscura, Obscura Camera, Rymer Gallery Saic, Chicago, Ill, 94; Exploring Sight: Young Photographers of the 70's, Amon Carter Mus, Ft. Worth, Tex, 2006; and others. *Teaching:* Prof art, Univ Ark, Fayetteville, 77-. *Awards:* Artists Fel, 82 & Photographers Fel, 83, Mid-Am Art Alliance; Photographers Fel, Ark Art Coun, 86 & 90; Master Teaching Award, Fulbright Col, 92. *Bibliog:* T Brown & E Partnow (auths), McMillian Biographical Encyclopedia of Photographic Artists and Innovators, 83. *Mem:* Soc for Photog Educ. *Media:* Photography, Book Arts. *Publ:* Auth, Snatches--or Man Made Wonders, Verb: Print, 79; Prophesy Panorama, 82, The Marriage of Heaven & Hell, Part 1, 86 Global Family, 90, Primitive Press; Cradle of Civilization, Primitive Press, 93; Slugs and Roses, Primitive Press, 2001; auth, Drive by Shootings, Primitive Press, 2004; Open.Heart Surgery, Primitive Press, 2006. *Dealer:* Vamp & Tramp Booksellers LLC 1951 Hoover Ct Ste 105 Birmingham Ala 35226; Printed Matter 195 10th Ave New York NY 10011; Art Metropole 788 King St West Toronto Ontario Can M5V 1N6. *Mailing Add:* 514 N Mission Blvd Fayetteville AR 72701-3519

PEYSER, JONATHAN
SCULPTOR
b Boston, Mass, 61. *Study:* Univ Rochester, BA (eng) 1983; Art Students League, NYC; self taught. *Work:* Pvt collections, Paris, NY, Barcelona & Spain. *Exhib:* The Arsenal Gallery, New York City; Concept Ethnic, Paris, France, 2001; solo exhib, Duggal Underground Gallery, SoHo, New York City, Escabelle Antiques Gallery, New York City, Tehen Boutique, SoHo, New York City, 2000; Tribeca Open Artist Studio Tour, New York City, 2001; group exhib, The Wreath, Millennial Interpretation, The Arsenal Gallery, New York City, 96 & 99; Audubon Artists Inc 60th Aniv Show, Salmagundi Club, NY, 2002; Rythms & Restraints, Steven Amedee Gallery, NY, 2003; Leather Sculptures of Johathan Peyser, Donghia Furniture Textiles, NY, 2004; Live Drawings, Gallery 51, Montclair, NJ, 2005; Sotheby's Ann Coalition for the Homeless Exhib & auction, NY, 2006. *Pos:* cur, New York City Dept Parks & Recreation, 89-94; asst pub art coordr, 89-91; coordr, Arsenal Gallery, 89-91, dir, 91-94. *Teaching:* Sculpture, art reviewer/writer, 2002; sculpture instr, Monmouth Univ, NJ, 7/2003. *Awards:* Artist-in-Residence Award; Found Corbero. *Bibliog:* Bob Creps (auth), Jonathan Peyser Biographical Encyclopedia of Am Painters, Sculptors & Engravers with th US, Colonial to 2002, Dealer's Choice Books, Vol 1, pg 1081; Donghia Furniture/Textiles, Leather Sculptures, Johathan Peyser, Town & Country, NY, 5/2005; Donghia Furniture/Textiles, Leather Sculptures, Jonathan Peyser, Interior Design, NY, 6/2005. *Mem:* Int Sculpture Ctr; Modern Art Foundry. *Media:* Steel, bronze, stone, silver & leather. *Specialty:* Formalist abstract sculpture. *Publ:* auth & illusr, John Duff at Baumgartner Gallery, Sculpture (pp 61-62), Wash, DC, 3/2002; auth, IK-Joan King at the United Nations, Sculpture (pp 87-89), Wash, DC, 9/2002; auth & illusr, Declaring, Defining and Dividing Space: A Conversation with Richard Serra, Sculpture (pp 28-35), Wash, DC, 10/2002. *Mailing Add:* 200 Columbia Heights # 8 Brooklyn NY 11201

PEYTON, ELIZABETH JOY
WRITER, PAINTER
b Danbury, Conn, Dec 20, 65. *Study:* Sch Visual Arts, NY City, BA, 87. *Work:* Mus Modern Art, 1998, Examining Pictures, Mus Contemp Art, Chicago, 1999, Whitney Biennial, Whitney Mus Am Art, 2004. *Exhib:* exhibs incl Art of Four Decades 1958-1998, San Francisco, Remix: Contemp art & pop, Tate Liverpool, 2002, Cher peintre- Peintures figuratives despuis l'ultime Picabia, Centre Pompidou, Paris, 2002, Inaugural Exhib, Regen Project, Los Angeles, 2003, New Paintings, 2003, EDITION SPECIALE, Galerier Suzanner Tarasieve, Paris, 2003, Aldrich Contemp Art Mus, Ridgefield, Conn, 2006. *Awards:* Larry Aldrich Found Award, 2006. *Publ:* Auth: Live Forever, 1997, Craig, 1998. *Mailing Add:* c/o Reagan Projects 629 N Almont Dr Los Angeles CA 90069

PEZZUTTI, SANTO C
PAINTER
b Fontanafredda, Italy. *Study:* Art Students League, NY; Newark Sch Fine and Industrial Arts; student of John Grabach. *Work:* Private Collections, Mont; South Africa; Argentina. *Exhib:* Nat Acad of Design, NY; Monmouth Mus; Newark Mus; solo exhib, Phoenix Gallery, NY, Carrimore Gallery, NY, Monmouth Univ, NJ, Emory Univ, Atlanta, Ga. *Pos:* Exec Art Dir, Dancer Fitzgerald Advert Agency, Madison Ave, NY. *Teaching:* instr, Summit Art Ctr, NJ; instr, Guild Creative Art; workshops instr, Ocean Co Art League; instr, Bloomfield Art League. *Awards:* 1st Prizes: Monmouth

Mus, Guild Creative Art, Monmouth At Counc. *Mem:* NY Watercolor Soc; Art Dir Club, NY. *Media:* Oil, Watercolor & Acrylic. *Interests:* People and Marine subjects. *Publ:* Illusr, The Best in Watercolor, NY Illusr Club. *Dealer:* Anchor & Palette Gallery. *Mailing Add:* 50 Conover Ln Red Bank NJ 07701

PFAFF, JUDY
SCULPTOR, EDUCATOR
b London, Eng, 1946. *Study:* Washington Univ, St Louis, BFA, 71; Yale Univ, MFA, 73. *Work:* Whitney Mus & Mus Mod Art, NY; Albright Knox Mus, Buffalo, NY; Brooklyn Mus, NY; High Mus, Atlanta. *Comn:* Special installation, Wacoal Ctr, Tokyo, Japan, 85 & Spokane, Wash; site specific comn, GTE, Irving, Tex, 91; Pa Convention Ctr, Philadelphia, 94. *Exhib:* Whitney Biennial, Dragon Group, Whitney Mus Am Art, Columbus, Ohio, 75; Rorschach, Ringling Mus, Sarasota, Fla, 81; Solo exhib, Rock-Paper-Scissors, Albright Knox Mus, Buffalo, NY, 82; Int Survey of Recent Painting & Sculpture, Mus of Modern Art, NY, 84; An Am Renaissance, Painting & Sculpture since 1940, Mus of Art, Ft Lauderdale, Fla, 85; Recent Aquisitions, Whitney Mus, NY, 86; Landscape as Metaphor, Denver Art Mus & Columbus Mus Art 94 & 95; Am Acad Arts & Letters Invitational Exhib NY, 94; Recent Drawings, Andre Emmerich Gallery, NY, 94; Rose Art Mus, Brandeis Univ, Waltham, Mass, 95; and others. *Pos:* Co-chair, Undergrad Dept Art, Bard Col. *Teaching:* Instr sculpture, Yale Univ & Skowhegan Sch of Painting, formerly; prof Visual Arts, Columbia Univ, 92-94; prof Visual Arts, Bard Col, 95-. *Awards:* Creative Artists Pub Serv, 76; Nat Endowment for the Arts Fel, 79 & 86; Guggenheim Fel, 83; Bessie Award, 84; MacArthur Fel, 2004. *Bibliog:* Wade Saunders (auth), Talking Objects, interviews with 10 younger sculptors, Art in Am, 10/85; John Russel (auth), Bright young talents: 6 artists with a future, New York Times, 5/16/86; Jerry Salz (auth), What's an artist's artist?, Art & Auction, 93. *Media:* All. *Mailing Add:* Bard Coll PO Box 5000 Annandale On Hudson NY 12504-5000

PFAFFMAN, WILLIAM SCOTT
SCULPTOR, DRAFTSMAN
b Albany, Ga, July 10, 54. *Study:* Auburn Univ, BFA, 76; Hunter Col, City Univ, NY, MA, 78. *Work:* John F Kennedy High Sch, Bronx, New York City; Dept of Parks, Brooklyn, NY; Lookout Sculpture Park, Pa. *Comn:* Artpark Proj Comn, Natural Heritage Trust, Lewiston, NY, 84; Sculpture Chicago, Burnham Park Planning Bd, Chicago, Ill, 85; sculpture, NY State Coun Arts, Bronx, NY, 87; Brooklyn Bears Greenthumb Project, NY Dept Gen Serv, 88; Mus in the Schs 1.S.49, Brooklyn, NY, 99. *Exhib:* Am Pantheon, City Univ NY Grad Ctr, 82 & Art on the Beach, Battery Park City, NY, 82; Spec Proj Exhib, Proj Studios One, Queens, NY, 83. *Pos:* Artist-in-residence, Athena Found; dir, Scott Pfaffman Gallery, NY; co-founder, Kentler International Drawing Space, KIDS. *Teaching:* Drawing instr, PS6, New York City, 2004. *Awards:* Annual Award, Am Acad Arts & Lett, 85; Artist Fel, Pollack-Krasner Found, 86. *Bibliog:* Martignioni (auth), Socrates Sculpture Park, Athena Found, 86; Allen Rokach (auth), article, Sculpture Mag, Int Sculpture (tr, 87). *Mem:* Brooklyn Waterfront Artists Coalition (vpres); Found Community of Artists; Am Coun Arts. *Media:* Sculpture. *Publ:* Auth, Five years of outdoor sculpture, Brooklyn Waterfront Artists Coalition, 87. *Dealer:* Scott Pfaffman Gallery 35 E 1st St New York NY 10003. *Mailing Add:* 360 Van Brunt St Brooklyn NY 11231

PFAHL, JOHN
PHOTOGRAPHER
b New York, NY, Feb 17, 39. *Study:* Syracuse Univ, BFA, 61, MA, 68. *Hon Degrees:* Niagara Univ Hon Dr Fine Art, 90. *Work:* George Eastman House, Rochester, NY; Albright-Knox Art Gallery, Buffalo, NY; Art Inst Chicago; San Francisco Mus Mod Art; Los Angeles Co Art Mus. *Exhib:* The Social Scene Mus of Contemp Art, La, 2000; Photog? A Facet of Modernism, San Francisco Mus Mod Art, 86; Playing Off Time, Aldrich Mus, Ct, 99; Perpetual Mirage, Whitney Mus of Art, New York City, 96; one-man shows, Albright-Knox Art Gallery, Buffalo, NY, 90, Chicago Art Inst, 91, High Mus, Atlanta, Ga, 92 & Los Angeles Co Mus Art, 93; Crossing the Frontier, San Francisco Mus of Modern Art, Calif, 96; The Real West, Denver Art Mus, Colo, 96; Nina Freudenheim, Inc, NY, 2000; Piles, Janet Borden, Inc, NY, 2002. *Teaching:* Prof photog, Rochester Inst Technol, NY, 68-82. *Awards:* Nat Endowment Arts Photog Fel, 77 & 90; NY State Creative Artists Prog Serv Photog Grant, 79. *Bibliog:* Peter Bunnell (auth), Altered Landscapes, Friends Photog, 81; Estelle Jussim & Anthony Bannon (coauths), Arcadia Revisited, Castellani Art Mus, 88; Estelle Jussim (auth), A Distanced Land, Albright-Knox Art Gallery, 90. *Publ:* Contribr, Photography from 1839 to Today, George Eastman House, 99, Am Am. Century of Photography, Abrams, 99, The Altered Landscape, Nev Mus of Art, 99, Landscape 2000, Univ of Wyo Art Mus, 2000, The Social Sci Mus of Contemporary Art, 2000; On the Art of Fixing a Shadow, Bullfinch Press, 89; Aperture No 120: Beyond Wilderness, Aperture Found, 90; auth, Tainted Prospects, Castellani Mus, 91. *Dealer:* Janet Borden Inc 560 Broadway New York NY 10012. *Mailing Add:* c/o Janet Borden 560 Broadway New York NY 10012

PFEIFER, MARCUSE
ART DEALER, GALLERY DIRECTOR
b Little Rock, Ark, Nov 4, 36. *Study:* Sarah Lawrence Col, AB, 58. *Collection Arranged:* Gravure, 74; American Indian Photographs from the 19th & Early 20th Century, 74; Cyanotype, 75; The Male Nude (auth, catalog), Marcuse Pfeifer Gallery, 78; The Dividing Line, Screens by Nine Photograhers & Thirteen New Americans, Arles, France, 86; Photos of Heinrich Harrer from early 40's Tibet, Am Mus Nat Hist, 91-92. *Pos:* Asst to dir, New Sch Art Ctr, New York, 66-70; dir photog art, Robert Schoelkopf Gallery, New York, 70-76; gallery owner, Marcuse Pfeifer Gallery, New York, 76-91. *Awards:* American Photographers Award, 83; Invited Colloquium Speaker, Sorborne, 88 & Harvard, 90. *Bibliog:* Article in Am Photogr, 5th Anniversary Issue, 83. *Mem:* Asn Int Photography Art Dealers (pres, 80-82); Art Table. *Specialty:* Photography. *Publ:* Auth, Thank Heaven for Little Girls-Lewis Carroll, Bk Forum, 79; coauth, On Collecting Photographs, Asn Int Photog Art Dealers

PFEIFFER, PAUL
ARTIST
b Honolulu, 66. *Exhib:* A Place Called Lovely, Green Naftali Gallery, NY, 99; KW Inst Contemp Art, Berlin, 2000; Whiteny Mus Am Art, 2001; Venice Biennial, 2001; Mus Contemp Art, Chicago, 2002-2003; James Cohan Gallery, NY, 2003; Mori Art Mus, Tokyo, 2004; Inst Contemp Arts London, 2004; Inst Contemp Arts, Boston, 2005; San Diego Mus Art, 2005; Kunsthaus Zürich, 2006; representing Galerie Carlier, Germany, Gió Marconi Gallery, Milan, Galleria Maze, Turin, Thomas Dance Gallery, London, The Project, LA, Adam Baumgold Gallery, NY. *Mailing Add:* 108 E 4th St Apt 21 New York NY 10003

PHARIS, MARK
CERAMIST
b Minneapolis, Minn, 47. *Study:* Univ Minn, BFA, 71 with Warren Mackenzie and Curt Hoard. *Work:* Victoria & Albert Mus, London, Eng; Univ Colo; Univ Wis, River Falls; State Col Ceramics, NY; also pvt collections of Robert Pfannebecker, Joan Mannheimer, Daniel & Caroline Anderson, Dr & Mrs Edward Okun, Betty & George Woodman and many others. *Exhib:* Solo exhib, Hadler Rodriguez, NY, Pro Art, St Louis, 87, 89 & 92, Garth Clark Gallery, NY, 87, 89 & 94; Rhode Island Sch Design, Providence, RI; Marion Art Ctr, Lancaster, Pa; Minneapolis Art Inst, Minn; Victoria & Albert Mus, London, Eng; Univ Minn, St Paul. *Teaching:* Assoc prof, Art Dept, Univ Minn, currently. *Awards:* Fel, Nat Endowment Arts, 86; Two Nat Endowment Grants for Individual Craftsmen; Minn State Art Coun Grant. *Media:* Clay. *Mailing Add:* c/o Univ Minn Art Dept 216 21st Ave S 208 Art Bldg Minneapolis MN 55455

PHELAN, ANDREW L
EDUCATOR, WRITER
b Bryn Mawr, Pa, May 8, 43. *Study:* Pratt Inst, BS, 65, MFA, 69; NY Univ, PhD, 86. *Exhib:* Solo show, Snug Harbor Cult Ctr, Staten Island, NY, 80. *Collection Arranged:* RB Sprague, Fred Jones Jr Mus of Art, New York, 10/01 to 12/01; Fritz Scholder, Recent Works, Fred Jones Jr Mus of Art, New York, 5/02 to 9/02; Jim Waid, Recent Works, Fred Jones Jr Mus of Art, New York, 10/02 to 12/02; Elias Rivera, The Other Side of the Street, Oklahoma City Mus of Art, 10/3 to 1/04; John Fincher, Boughs Branches and Limbs, Oklahoma City Mus of Art, 10/04 to 11/04; National Cowboy & Western Heritage Mus, 10/2005-11/2005, Nelson Shanks, In the Clanic Tradition, 2/2006-3/2006, Fred Jones Jr Mus of Art, Norman, Okla. *Pos:* Consult & adv, Yugen Kashia Gregg Int, Tokyo, Japan, 90-92. *Teaching:* Dean acad affairs, assoc dean to dean art & design, chair art educ, Pratt Inst, Brooklyn, NY, 72-90; dir & prof, Sch Art, Univ Okla, 92-. *Mem:* Nat Asn Sch Art & Design; Col Art Asn. *Res:* Technology and the arts; history of innovation in the artists education or training. *Publ:* Auth, The Bauhaus & studio art education, Art Educ, 81; The impact of technology & post modern art, Art Educ, 84; The Albers Project - A model for multi-media courseware, Tech Horizons Ed, 88; 50 years at the Sch for Am Craftsmen, Ceramics Monthly, 2/95; Rowantrees Pottery, Ceramics Monthly, 2/98; Western Waver in Oklahoma, Ceramics Monthly, 11/04. *Mailing Add:* 1811 Quail Creek Dr Norman OK 73026-0944

PHELAN, ELLEN DENISE
PAINTER
b Detroit, Mich, Nov 3, 43. *Study:* Wayne State Univ, BFA, 69, MFA, 71. *Work:* Detroit Inst Arts; Mus Mod Art, NY; Whitney Mus Am Art; Walker Art Ctr; Brooklyn Mus; High Mus of Art; Metrop Mus Art, NY; Fogg Mus, Harvard Univ; McNay Art Mus; Baltimore Mus; Mass Inst Technol; Allen Mem Art Mus, Oberlin Col; Hood Mus Art, Dartmouth Col. *Exhib:* New Art for the New Year, Mus Mod Art, NY, 78; Drawings, Albright-Knox Art Gallery, Buffalo, NY, 79; Am Abstraction Now, Inst Contemp Art, Va Mus, Richmond, 82; Out of Square, Cranbrook Acad Art, Bloomingfield Hills, Mich, 84; The New Romantic Landscape, Whitney Mus Am Art, Stamford, Conn, 87; Recent Drawings, Whitney Mus Am Art, NY, 88; Contemp Environment, Mus Mod Art, 89; The 80's in Review: Selections from the Permanent Collection, Whitney Mus Am Art, Fairfield Co, Conn, 89; Drawings of the Eighties from the Collection of the Mus Mod Art, NY, 89; solo exhibs, Asher/Faure, Los Angeles, 89, 92 & 94, Baltimore Mus Art, 89, Susanne Hilberry Gallery, Birmingham, Mich, 90, Barbara Toll Fine Arts, NY, 84-94, Member's Gallery, Albright-Knox Art Gallery, Buffalo, NY, 91 & Univ Art Gallery, Univ Mass, Amherst, 92, traveling, 93, Patricia Faure Gallery, Santa Monica, Calif, 94 & 99, Donna Beam Gallery of Art, Univ Nev, Las Vegas, 98; Cincinnati Art Mus, 94; Am Acad of Arts and Letters, 95; Open Ends (1960-2000): Innocence and Experience, 2000; and many others. *Teaching:* Instr painting, Calif Inst Arts, 78-79 & 83; instr painting & drawing, Sch Visual Arts, 81-83; instr, Bard Col, 81-94, Calif Inst Arts, 83; prof studio art, Harvard Univ, 95-, dir Carpenter Ctr for the Visual Arts, 96-, chair dept visual and environmental studies, 99-. *Awards:* Nat Endowment Arts Grant, 78-79; Arts Achievement Award, Wayne State Univ, 88; Academy Award, Am Acad Arts & Lett, 94; NY Times Fel, Am Acad in Rome, 99. *Bibliog:* Francine Hunter McGivern (auth), Excerpts from an interview with Ellen Phelan, NY Arts, 12/99; Barry Schwabsky (auth), Ellen Phelan-Senior & Shopmaker Gallery, ArtForum, 5/2000; Lill Wei (auth), Art in America, July, 2002; and others. *Media:* Oil, Gouache. *Dealer:* Ameringer Yohe Fine Art, 20 W 57th St, New York, NY. *Mailing Add:* 130 E 67th St New York NY 10021

PHILBIN, ANN
MUSEUM DIRECTOR
b Boston, Mass, Mar 21, 52. *Study:* Univ NH, BA in Art Hist, BFA in Painting, 1976; NYU, MA in mus studies/arts admin, 1982. *Pos:* res, Frick Art Reference Libr, New York City, 1977-79; asst to dir, prog coordr, Artists Space, 1979-80; asst cur coordr, The New Mus, 1980-81; cur, Ian Woodner Family Collection, 1981-83; asst dir, Grace Borgenicht Gallery, 1983-85; dir, Curt Marcus Gallery, 1985-88; account dir, Art

Against AIDS Livet Reichard Inc, 1988-90; dir, The Drawing Ctr, 1990-1999, UCLA Hammer Mus Los Angeles, 1999-. *Awards:* Recipient Best Monographic Mus Show Nationally Award for exhib Lee Bontecou: A Retrospective, Inter Asn Art Critics/USA, 2004. *Mailing Add:* Univ of Calif UCLA Hammer Museum 10899 Wilshire Blvd Los Angeles CA 90024

PHILLIPS, ALICE JANE
PAINTER
b New York, NY, Aug 30, 47. *Study:* NY Univ, with Chuck Close & John Opper, BS, 70, MA, 72. *Work:* Aldrich Mus Contemp Art, Conn; Mus City New York, Brooklyn Mus, Chase Manhattan Bank, Shearson Lehman Hutton, NY. *Exhib:* Works on Paper--Women Artists, Brooklyn Mus, 75; Contemp Reflections, Aldrich Mus, Conn, 77; Fifteen New Talents, Aldrich Mus, Conn, 79; Paperworks 80, Hudson River Mus, Yonkers, NY, 80; Solo exhib, David Findlay Galleries, NY, 82, van Straaten Gallery, Chicago, 83, Dubins Gallery, Los Angeles, 83, 84, 86 & 88 & Gallery 500, Elkins Park, Pa, 88, 91 & 95; Printed By Women, Port of Hist Mus, Philadelphia, Pa, 83; Art of the 1970s & 1980s, Aldrich Mus, Conn, 85; Am Art: Am Women, Stamford Mus, Conn, 85; Natural Image, Stamford Mus, Conn, 89; Salute to Women, Nat Mus Women Arts, Washington, 91; group exhib, State Univ NY, Stonybrook, 94; Alice Phillips & Raymond Tomasso, Gallery 500, Philadelphia, 95; Pulse Points, Harvard Univ, Cambridge, Mass, 96; Generations, AIR Gallery, NY, 97; The Square Show, Ceres Gallery, NY, 01; Art Strokes, Broome St Gallery, NY, 02; group exhib, Pace Univ Gallery, NY, 03. *Teaching:* Adj asst prof art & drawing, NY Univ, 81-82. *Bibliog:* Mary Vaughn (auth), article in Arts Mag, 1/82; Grace Glueck (auth), article in NY Times, 1/27/84; Mila Andre (auth), article in NY Daily News, 8/5/94. *Mem:* Women in Arts Found (exec coordr, 78-80, secy, 80-82); Women's Caucus Art (exec bd, 94-2000). *Media:* Acrylic, Pastel. *Dealer:* Gallery 500 Church & Old York Rds Elkins Park PA 19117. *Mailing Add:* 32 Greene St New York NY 10013

PHILLIPS, ARTHUR BYRON
PAINTER, SCULPTOR
b Dec, 1, 30. *Study:* Pa Acad Fine Arts, Univ Pa, BFA, 1956, MFA, 1958; Sorbonne, Audit, 57; Universita Internationale Dell Arte-Firenze, doctorate, 60. *Work:* Mus Fine Arts, Boston, Mass; Brandywine River Mus, Chadds Ford, Pa; Guild Hall, East Hampton, NY; Everhart Mus & Marywood Col, Scranton, Pa; Elvejem Mus Art & Sordoni Gallery Wilkes Col, Wilkes Barre, Pa; Audubon Artists, Nat Acad, NY; Everhart Mus & Guild Hall Mus, East Hampton. *Comn:* portrait, comn by Marlene Dietrich, Paris, France, 80; portrait, comn by Amanda K Berls, NY, 83; portrait, comn by Ruth H Yerion, NY, 83; portrait, comn by Greta Keller, Vienna, Austria, 85; portrait, comn by Olga Mack, NY, 99. *Exhib:* Meticulous Realism, Univ Md, College Park, 66; Three Centuries of the Am Nude, NY Cult Ctr, 75; A Tribute to Am Painting, Coe-Kerr, NY, 76; Berls - Yerion Collection, Brandywine Mus, 81; Portraits: Guild Hall, East Hampton, NY, 83 & Winterscape, 89; Long Island Painters, World Mus, East Hampton, NY, 93. *Awards:* Cresson European Travel Award, Pa Acad Fine Arts, 54; Parrish Art Mus Gold, Southampton, NY, 73; Best in Show, Guild Hall, East Hampton, NY, 75; 3 Centuries of the Am Nude by Cutural Friedrich der Grosse award, Frankfort, Am Ger; Beauharhis, Paris, 97. *Bibliog:* Ami Wallack (auth), Portraits Real & Imagined, Newsday, 80; David Shirley (auth), The New Realism, New York Times, 81; Marhorni Sharp Young (auth), Winterscape, New York Times, 83. *Mem:* Frick Mus & Libr; SP Morgan Libr; Pollack-Krasner Study Ctr (adv bd, 2000); Everhart Mus (adv, 68-); Children's Mus; Metrop Mus; Parrish Mus; Brandywine River Mus & Conservancy. *Media:* Egg Tempera, Watercolor; Clay, Metal. *Publ:* auth, The Great American Nude, Praeger, 74; auth, Winterscape, Hampton Press, 82; contribr, Artist and Their Cats, Mid March Art Press, 90; contribr, First Light - Arthur Byron Phillips, Roselyn Tiecher, 96; Portraits Real and Imagined, The Artistic Impact of the WPA, 1985. *Dealer:* 443 West 21st St New York NY 10021. *Mailing Add:* c/o Mr Phillips 28 Tyrone Dr East Hampton NY 11937

PHILLIPS, BERTRAND D
PAINTER, PHOTOGRAPHER
b Chicago, Ill, Nov 19, 38. *Study:* Art Inst Chicago, with Paul Wieghardt & Leroy Neiman, BFA; Northwestern Univ, MFA. *Work:* Governors State Univ, Park Forest South, Ill; David & Alfred Smart Gallery, Univ Chicago, Ill; Du Sable Mus African Am Hist, Chicago; Art Inst Chicago; Erie Art Ctr, Pa; and others. *Exhib:* Art Inst Chicago, 78-80; Ill State Mus, 78 & 80; Nat Mus Haitian Art, 79-80; Cult Ctr Guyana, 79-80; NAME Gallery, Chicago, 81; Mid-Am Biennial Nat Exhib, Owensboro Mus Fine Arts, Ky, 82; and many others. *Teaching:* Instr drawing & painting, Elmhurst Col, 70-72; asst prof drawing & painting, Northwestern Univ, 72-79; vis artist, Sch Art Inst Chicago, 81-. *Awards:* George D Brown Foreign Traveling Fel, Art Inst Chicago, 61; Governor's Purchase Award, State Ill. *Bibliog:* Elton Fax (auth), Black Artists of the New Generation, Dodd Mead & Co, 77; and others. *Media:* Oils, Acrylic. *Mailing Add:* 6617 S Perry Ave Chicago IL 60621-3806

PHILLIPS, BONNIE
DEALER, PAINTER
b Salt Lake City, Utah, July 8, 42. *Study:* Univ Utah, BA. *Work:* Salt Lake Art Ctr, Utah; Utah Mus Fine Arts, Salt Lake City; Braithwaite Gallery, Southern Utah State Col, Cedar City. *Exhib:* Intermountain Biennial, Salt Lake Art Ctr, 66-77; Utah State Ann Exhib, 81-84; Women Artists of Utah, Springville Mus Art, 84; Nat Mus, Taipei, Taiwan, 85; two-person show, Collett Art Gallery, Weber State Col, Ogden, Utah, 86. *Pos:* Co-owner, Phillips Gallery, Salt Lake City, currently. *Awards:* Purchase Prize, Utah 81; Award of Merit, Utah '84; Best of Show, Utah Watercolor Soc, 86. *Mem:* Utah Watercolor Soc. *Media:* Watercolor, Gouache

PHILLIPS, DICK (RICHARD) CORTEZ
PAINTER, INSTRUCTOR
b Ft Worth, Tex, May 6, 33. *Study:* Texas A & M Univ, BBA, 55; with Milford Zornes, 73; also with Robert E Wood, 74, 77-88. *Work:* City of Himeji, Japan; Old Jail Art Ctr, Albany, Tex; Desert Cabaleeros Mus, Wickenburg, Ariz; City Scottsdale, Ariz; Chandler Ctr Arts, Ariz; Fine Arts Center, Breckenridge, Tex. *Comn:* Int Paper Corp, Memphis, Tenn; Phoenix Mutual Life Insurance Co, Hartford, Conn; paintings, Lewis & Roca, Phoenix, 87; W L Gore & Assoc, Phoenix, 91. *Exhib:* Watercolor Exhib, US State Dept, toured Taiwan, 75; Rocky Mountain Nat, Golden, Colo, 78; Am Watercolor Soc Ann, Nat Acad Design, NY, 78 & 86; Watercolor Biennial, Ctr Arts, Scottsdale, Ariz, 78 & 80; Nat Watercolor Exhib, 85 & 92-95, 2001; painting selected for exhib, US Amb to UN, Geneva, Switz, 2001; and others. *Teaching:* Pvt lessons, Phoenix, Ariz, 72-; instr, Sch Int Training, Univ Okla, 77 & 78; Scottsdale Artists Sch, 2001-. *Awards:* Merit Awards, Western Fedn Watercolor Anns, 75, 79, 80, 83 & 94; Best of Show, Southwest Watercolor Soc, 77; First Place, Watercolor West, 1982, 2000 & Am Watercolor Soc Traveling Exhib, 1986; Challenge Award, Challenge of Champions Exhib, Houston, 2003. *Bibliog:* Barbara Pearlman (auth), Making changes, Ariz Arts & Lifestyle, 81; Betsy Dillard Stroud (auth), Abstract art: what is it?, Int Artist, 98; Betsy Dillard Steaud (auth), The Window to your Creativity, Watercolor Magic, 2004. *Mem:* Scottsdale Artists League; Ariz Watercolor Soc (bd dir, 73-77); Nat Watercolor Soc; Watercolor West. *Media:* Acrylic, Oil, Watercolor. *Publ:* Illusr, Si! Si! Mrs Crusoe, Franklin Publ, 70; Vitality Mag (cover), 90; Freshen Your Paintings with New Ideas, North Light Books; The Best of Watercolor 2, Quarry Bks, 97; Faces of Arizone, Art Renaissance Found, 99; Painting from the Inside Out, by Betsy Dillard Stroud, Northlight Books; Betwy Dillard Stroud (auth), The Artist's Muse, Northlight Books. *Dealer:* Raku Gallery 250 Hull Ave Hwy 89A Jerome AZ 86331; Duly-Jones Gallery, 7100 Main St, Scottdale, AZ, 85251; Hellea Art Images, 11015 Elm St, Omaha, NE, 68144; Tamarack Gallery, 4262 Gulf Shore Blvd. North Naples, FL, 34103; Courtyard Gallery, 813 E Buffalo, New Buffalo, MI, 49117. *Mailing Add:* 7829 E Hubbell Scottsdale AZ 85257

PHILLIPS, DUTCH (JAMES) O, JR
GALLERY DIRECTOR, DEALER
b Ft Worth, Tex, Mar 29, 44. *Study:* Univ Tex, Austin, BA, 67. *Pos:* Dir, Ft Worth Gallery, formerly; dir, Dutch Phillips & Co, 94-. *Specialty:* Contemporary painting and sculpture; Pre-Columbian and African art. *Mailing Add:* Dutch Phillips & Co 4109 El Campo Ave Ft Worth TX 76107

PHILLIPS, ELLEN T
SCULPTOR, ASSEMBLAGE ARTIST
Study: San Diego State Univ, MFA, 85. *Work:* Downey Mus Art, Calif; Alexandria Mus Art, La; Nat Handicraft Mus India, New Delhi; Hoyt Inst Fine Arts, New Castle, Pa, and over 75 pvt collections; solo exhib, Chadron State Coll, 99. *Comn:* Ceramic tile & bronze participation wall, Children's Hosp, San Diego, (collab), 93; polychrome wood relief, Malabar Libr, Los Angeles Cult Affairs Dept, (collab), 93-96; hist benches in photoetched granite & concrete, decorative fencing, pillars, Dairy Mart Rd & Bridge Proj, City of San Diego, 95-2000; 17 abstract metal bird forms, Washington St, City San Diego, Mission Hills Asn (collab), 95-2000. *Exhib:* Solo exhibs, Athenaeum Music & Arts Libr, La Jolla, Calif, 91, Miracosta Col, Oceanside, Calif, 91, Southwestern Col, Chula Vista, Calif, 92, Univ Pacific Art Gallery, Stockton, Calif, 92, Minot State Univ, NDak, 94, McHenry Co Col Gallery, 95 & Hyde Gallery, Grossmont Col; Girllila Art Invitational, Simay Space, San Diego, 2002; Little by Little, Mus Photographic Arts, San Diego, 2002; 4th Ann Nat, Kaufman Gallery, Shippensburg Univ, Pa, 2003; An Open Book, Gallery West, Cuyahoga Community Col. Cleveland, 2004; Low Altitude/High Altitude, Gallery Contemp Art, Univ Colo, Colorado Springs, 2004; Artists Architects: Modeling Our World, Southwestern Col Art Gallery, Chula Vista, Calif, 2005; and others. *Pos:* Show comt, Calif Fibers, 85-; bd mem, COVA, 87-91, Allied Craftsmen, 87-92 & SDMA Artist Guild, 88-92; design team, Indian School Road/Canal Bank Proj, City of Phoenix, Ariz, 91-92. *Teaching:* Instr 2- & 3-D design crafts, San Diego State Univ, 82-89; instr 3-D design crafts, Mesa Col, San Diego, 88-93; instr 3-D design, Grossmont Col, 95. *Awards:* Best Concrete Bridge Award, Am Concrete Inst, 2000, Am Pub Works Asn, 2000; Potnam Award, League of Calif Cities, 2001. *Bibliog:* D Gage (auth), Ellen Phillips: Going Public, Fiber Arts, 1-2/93; Discovery Award-Gold Winners, Art in Calif, 1/93; The Children's Wall, Sculpture Mag, 9-10/93. *Mem:* Calif Fibers; Allied Craftsmen; SDMA Artist Guild. *Media:* All Media. *Publ:* Auth, Line up, Carolyn Price Dyer, 2-3/88; ISTL/WAC Newslett, San Diego State Univ, spring 89. *Mailing Add:* 9463 Mesa Vista La Mesa CA 91941

PHILLIPS, GIFFORD
COLLECTOR, WRITER
b Washington, DC, June 30, 18. *Study:* Stanford Univ, 36-38; Yale Univ, BA, 42. *Mem:* Trustee Mus Mod Art, NY; trustee Phillips Collection, Washington, DC; trustee Rothko Found, NY; trustee Pasadena Art Mus (pres, 73-74, secy-treas, 75-76); Mus Mod Art Int Coun (bd dir); Los Angeles Co Mus Art Contemp Art Coun. *Collection:* Contemporary American painting and sculpture. *Publ:* Auth, Arts in a Democratic Society, 66; auth, articles, Art News, Artforum & Art Am. *Mailing Add:* 3881 Old Santa Fe Tr Santa Fe NM 87505

PHILLIPS, HARRIET E
ILLUSTRATOR, BOOKMAKER, COLLAGIST, PAINTER
b New York, NY. *Study:* Hunter Col, BA, 51, Art Students League, NY, studied under Frank J Reilly, Col Physicians & Surgeons, Columbia Univ, NY, with Alfred Feinberg, courses & workshops at Ctr Bk Arts, NY, Womens Studio Workshop, Rosendale, NY & Fashion Inst Technol, NY. *Exhib:* Okla Mus Natural Hist, Norman, 93; Oshkosh Pub Mus, Wis, 93; Houston Mus Natural Sci, 93; RW Norton Art Gallery, Shreveport,

La, 93; Art & the Animal, Bennington Ctr Arts, Vt, 94; Nat Tour, Soc Animal Artists, 94-95, Disney's Animal Kingdom Park Ann Show, 98; Soc Animal Artists Ann Show, Witte Mus, San Antonio, 96; Nat Asn Women Artists Regional Invitational, Unison Arts & Learning Ctr, 98; Nat Asn Women Artists Show, Hutchinson Gallery, CW Post Col, 98; solo show, Unitarian Church, Rock Tavern, NY; group shows, Hiram Blauvelt Mus, Oradell, NJ, John Wehle Gallery of Sporting Art, Mumford, NY, Garrison Art Ctr of Sarasota, Sarasota, Fla, Banana Factory, Bethlehem, PA, Woodstock Artist Asn, Woodstock, NY, Haworth Libr Gallery, Haworth, NJ, Nat Asn Women Artists, NY; Bennington Art Center, Bennington, Vt. *Pos:* Med Art Service, 59-; Owner, Med Art Serv, 59-95; Owner, the HEP Press, 94-. *Teaching:* Instr med illus, Col Physicians & Surgeons, Columbia Univ, 66-68; instr air brush, BOCES, Orange City, NY, 90-. *Awards:* Paper Grant, 86 & 91; Puffin Grant, Puffin Found, 94; Stelly Sterling Mem Award, Nat Asn Women Artists, 95. *Mem:* Life mem Art Students League; Nat Asn Women Artists (rec secy, exhib comt); Soc Animal Artists (rec secy, exec bd, 90-); Women Studio Workshop, Rosendale, NY; and others; Woodstock Artist Asn Mus, Woodstock, NY. *Media:* Bookmaking, Collage, Acrylic. *Publ:* illusr & coauth, Understanding the Human Form, Avery Publ Group, 81; illusr, Adrenal Disorders, Thieme Med Publ, 89; ed & illusr, Black Dirt, pvt publ, 91; auth & illusr, ABC Mammals, Internet publ, 2005; auth & illusr, Animals in Black & White, Internet publ, 2005; Donald Richard Miller, Catalogue 2003, The Hep Press

PHILLIPS, JAMES M
MUSEUM DIRECTOR, COLLECTOR
b Philadelphia, Pa, July 18, 46. *Study:* Glassboro State Col, BA, 75. *Work:* Antietam Nat Mus, Sharpsburg, Md; and others. *Comn:* Sculpture-medallion, Spec Forces Regiment, 91. *Exhib:* Washington Co Mus Fine Arts, 86. *Pos:* Dir, Antietam Nat Mus, 68-; Bladesmiths Soc, 86-; bd dir, Am Mus Comt, 92. *Teaching:* Lectr, Univ Wyo, 83; Armed Forces Inst Pathology, 88; OP Gator, 88. *Awards:* Best of Show Award, Connie Kalitta Service Inc, 85. *Mem:* Co of Military Historians; Am Bladesmiths' Soc; Asn Former Intelligence Officers; Spec Forces Asn. *Res:* Clandestine weapons and equipment, subminiature cameras-photo devices, US elite Forces. *Collection:* Artifacts of soldiers who fought in the Civil War through the Viet Nam Wars; uniforms, weapons, photographs, paintings, documents and writings of participants; espionage and intelligence literature and related material. *Publ:* Auth, Stand in the Door, 88; coauth, Bowie Knives, 92; contribr, The Microcol, 92; Subminature Photography, 92; OSS Weapons, 94; and others. *Mailing Add:* PO Box 168 Williamstown NJ 08094

PHILLIPS, LAUGHLIN
MUSEUM CHAIRMAN, DIRECTOR
b Washington, DC, Oct 20, 24. *Study:* Yale Univ, 42-43; Univ Chicago, MA(philos), 49. *Pos:* Chairman & dir, Phillips Collection, Washington, DC, 72-02, dir, 72-92, chairman emeritus, currently. *Awards:* Officier, Arts et Lettres, France. *Mem:* AAMD, 79-92; Cosmos Club, Washington, DC. *Mailing Add:* 26 Parsonage Ln Washington CT 06793

PHILLIPS, MICHAEL
PAINTER, SCULPTOR
b New York, NY, Feb 22, 37. *Study:* Inst Fine Arts, NY, with HW Janson & Robert Goldwater, MA, 62. *Work:* Inst Contemp Art, Boston; Sonesta Hotels; Rose Art Mus, Brandeis Univ, Mass; Bowdoin Col Art Mus, New Brunswick, Maine. *Comn:* Mural, Inst Contemp Art, Boston, 70; sculpture, City of Boston, 70; painting, Sonesta Hotel, Amsterdam, Holland, 83. *Exhib:* One-man shows, Inst Contemp Art, Boston, 70, Frank Marino Gallery, NY, 82, Univ Va, Charlottesville, Va, 96; 12 Americans, Moma, Buenos Aires, Argentina, 87-88; Recent Guggenheim Paintings, IPA, Boston, Mass, 90, 92; Abstraction Per Se, Pratt Inst, NY, 92; Artists Space Anniversary Exhib, NY, 94; Voices, IPA, Boston, Mass, 94; The Power of Abstraction, 8th Floor Gallery, NY, 97; and others; SC Centennial, SC State Mus, 2000. *Teaching:* Vis artist painting, Univ SC, Columbia, 81; prof painting, Col Charleston, SC, 84-; vis artist, Am Acad Rome, 87 & 94; vis artist, Cardiff Col Art, Wales, United Kingdom, 88-89. *Awards:* Nat Endowment Arts Grant Painting, 80-81; (Caps) NY Fel in painting, 80; Painting Grant, SC Arts Comm, 85-86; Guggenheim fel, 89-90. *Bibliog:* Mary Sherman (auth), Three galleries invite closer look, Boston Globe, 5/30/90; Cate McQuaid (auth), Light shows, Southend News, Boston, Mass, 5/10/90; Nancy Stapen (auth), Michael Phillips, Boston Globe, 1/27/94. *Mem:* Col Art Asn. *Media:* All. *Publ:* Auth, New Options in Painterly Abstration, OIA, New York, 79; Painting Self Evident: Evolutions in Abstraction, Gibbes Mus, Charleston, SC, 92; Phoebe Helman Mem Exhib (catalog), 95; Reconsidering Modernism, Line, 2004. *Dealer:* Joan Sonnabend/Obelisk Gallery Boston MA 02108. *Mailing Add:* Charleston College Art Dept Charleston SC 29424

PHILLIPS, RICHARD
PAINTER
Study: Mass Col Art, BFA(painting), 84; Yale Univ Sch Art, MFA(painting), 86. *Work:* Albright-Knox Art Gallery, Buffalo; Chase Bank, Zurich; Mod Art Mus, Ft Worth; Whitney Mus Am Art, New York; Memphis Mus, Tenn. *Exhib:* One-person exhibs, Laurie Rubin Gallery, NY, 90, Elizabeth Koury, NY, 92, White Columns, NY, 94, Knoxville Paintings, Edward Thorpe Gallery, NY, 95, New Paintings, Turner & Runyon Gallery, Dallas, 97 & Shoshana Wayne Gallery, Santa Monica, 97; Signs of Support: Furniture Forms in Contemp Art, John Michael Kohler Art Ctr, Sheboygan, Mich, 90; 20th Anniversary Benefit Show, White Columns, NY, 90; Not on Canvas, Asher Faure Gallery, Los Angeles, 91; Tattoo, Andrea Rosen Gallery, NY, 92; 5 Painters, Edward Thorp Gallery, NY, 93; David's Friends, Bernard Toale Gallery, Boston, 94; Transfixed, Gavin Brown Enterprises, NY, 96; Painting Into Photog-Photog Into Painting, Mus Contemp Art, North Miami, 96; Whitney Mus Am Art Biennial, NY, 97; Prophecy of Pop, Contemp Arts Ctr, New Orleans, 97. *Awards:* Ellen Battel Stockel Fel, Yale/Norfolk, 83; Pace Gallery Award, Mass Col Art, 84 & Lawrence Kupferman Award, 84; J Richardson Dilworth Materials Grant, Yale Univ Sch Art, 86. *Bibliog:* Jack Bankowsky (auth), Exhibition Preview Winter/Spring '97, Artforum, 1/97; Whitney Biennial Buzz (front pg), Art Am, 2/97; Roberta Smith (auth), A new surge of growth, just as death cut it off, NY Times, 2/14/97

PHILLIPS, ROBERT J
FILMMAKER, PHOTOGRAPHER
b Montclair, NJ, Feb 28, 46. *Study:* Jersey City State Col, BA(art educ), 68: New York Univ Grad Sch Arts, MFA(phogog, film & TV), 72; Found for Mind Res, Pomona NY, creative actualization with Dr Jean Houston, Res & Teaching Assoc, 75-I Fairleigh Dickinson Univ, EdD, 88. *Exhib:* Faculty Show, Caldwell Coll, 86 & 90. *Pos:* Designer of high sch film educ prog, identified as exemplary model curriculum site by Am Film Inst, DC, 68-70; coordr, Film Festival, 19th Congress Int Soc for Educ Through Art, 69; asst proj dir, NJ State Coun on Arts, Inner City Arts Proj, Hoboken, NJ, 70; proj dir, Summer Arts Workshop for Mentally Handicapped, Title VI grant, East Orange, NJ, 71; chmn, Comt for Creative Actualization, New Ways of Being Inst Conf, Minneapolis, Dallas, Los Angeles & NJ, 78-79. *Teaching:* Instr art, Photog & film, Woodbridge Sr High Sch, NJ; educator-at-large, master classes & teacher-in-service training in creative actualization, camera arts & fine arts, schs, communities & cols throughout the east, 72-; adj instr, creative actualization & camera arts, Caldwell Col, NJ, 72-; art dir/designer, creative dir & dir mktg communications, WLMW & Assocs, Bozell Inc, FDS/Merrill Lynch. *Awards:* Bronze Phoenix Award for outstanding creative achievement in filmmaking, Atlanta Int Film Festival, Ga, 74; Award for Outstanding Achievement in film direction, in graphic design, Int Creativity Ann, Art Direction Mag, 74; Cert Excellence, filmmaking, NJ Art Dir's Club, 75; plus others. *Media:* Video Tape, Multi Media. *Publ:* Filmmaker & photog, Qualify (film), Net Channel 13, New York, 71; Choice Not Chance (film), 74 & Daydreams and Indecision, 79, NJ State Dept Educ; Asbury Park--A Renaissance, Asbury Park Dept Community Affairs, 79; Art and Multi-Sensory Learning (filmstrip), Educ Frontiers Assocs, 80-90. *Mailing Add:* 6 Linda Lane Edison NJ 08820

PHILLIPS, SANDRA
CURATOR, HISTORIAN
Study: Bard Col, AB(John Bard Fel, Regents Scholar), 67; Bryn Mawr Col, MA(Woodrow Wilson Fel), 69; City Univ New York, PhD(art hist), 85. *Exhib:* exhib curated, Picture Magazines before LIFE, Woodstock, NY, 82, Allen Memorial Art Gallery, Oberlin Col, 90, Mus Photog Arts (catalogue), San Diego, 1991, Detroit Inst Arts, 92, Int Ctr Photog, NY, 95, Yale Univ Art Gallery, 96, Mus Photog Arts, San Diego, Jan-March, 2001, Reagan Louie, Sex in Asia, SFMOMA, Aug, 2003-Jan, 2004, and many others. *Collection Arranged:* Wright Morris: Origin of a Species (auth, catalog), San Francisco Mus Mod Art, 92; Dorothea Lange (auth, catalog), San Francisco Mus Mod Art, 94; William Klein New York 1954-1955 (auth, catalog), San Francisco Mus Mod Art, 95; Crossing the Frontier: Photographs of the Developing West, 1849 to the Present (auth, catalog), 96; Commonplace Mysteries: Photos by Peter Hujar, Andrea Modica, and Bill Owens, 96; Police Pictures: The Photograph as Evidence (auth, catalog), San Francisco Mus Mod Art, 97; Photography After Modernism: Extensions into Contemporary Art, San Francisco Mus Mod Art, 98. *Pos:* Cur & art dept assoc, Bard Col, 68-77; photog historian, Catskill Ctr Photog, 80-85; cur, Vassar Col Art Gallery, Poughkeepsie, NY, 86-87; cur photog, San Francisco Mus Mod Art, 87; sr cur photog, San Francisco Mus Mod Art, 99; Delivered lectures on Dorothea Lange, Contemp Am Photography, Catholic Univ, Milan, March, 2001-May, 2002. *Teaching:* Lectr art hist, Bard Col Independent Study Prog, 71-77; part-time lectr, State Univ NY, 77-86; guest lectr art hist, Mills Col, 80; instr hist photog, Parsons Sch Design, New Sch Soc Res, 81-86; part-time lectr, contemp art, San Francisco State Univ, 89, contemp photog, San Francisco Art Inst, 93. *Awards:* Travel Grant, Am Hungarian Found, 82; Travel Grant, National Endowment Arts, 89; Resident, Am Acad Rome, Jan-March, 2000; Several Exhib Grants, 1991-2000. *Mem:* Col Art Asn; Hudson River Heritage. *Publ:* Meditations on the document (essay), In: Public Information: Desire, Disaster, Document, Distributed Art Publ, 94; Bill Dane Dentro Y Fuera (essay), In: Colleccion Granada Disputacio de Fondo de Granada, Publicaciones de la Diputacion Provincial de Granada, 95; John Gutman (essay), In: Pacific Dreams: Currents of Surrealism and Fantasy in California Art, 1934-1957, Univ Calif Los Angeles Armand Hammer Mus Art & Cult Ctr, 95; Archive, DoubleTake, fall 96; Abelardo Morell and Tom Roma, 2nd Tokyo Int Photo-Biennale, 97; Introduction, Thomas Roma, Sicilian Passage, Powerhouse Books, NY, 2003; and many others

PHILLIPS, TONY
PAINTER, DRAFTSMAN
b Miami Beach, Fla, Sept 16, 37. *Study:* Trinity Col, Hartford, BA(cum laude), 60; Sch Art, Yale Univ, BFA, 62, MFA, 63. *Work:* Art Inst Chicago; Mus Contemp Art, Chicago. *Exhib:* Art Inst Chicago, 73, 85, 87 & 89-90; Indianapolis Mus Art, 82; one-man shows, Marianne Deson Gallery, Chicago, 82 & 86, Hyde Park Art Ctr, Chicago, 93 & Lyons-Wier Gallery, Chicago, 93 & 95; Mus Contemp Art, 83; Reveries, Ford Ctr Fine Arts, Knox Col, Galesburg, Ill, 96; Dogs! Mus of Contemp Art, Chicago (and traveling), 83; Lyonswier Gallery, 2000; Printworks, Chicago, 00; Judith Raphael & Tony Phillips, Gallery of Ind Univ NW Gary, 2003; Gescheilde Gallery, Chicago, 2003, (solo show); The 179th Ann Invitational, Nat Acad Mus, NY, 2004. *Pos:* Prof Emer, Sch of Art Inst of Chicago. *Teaching:* Instr painting & design, Palo Alto Art Ctr, Calif, 65 & Sch Visual Arts, NY, 65-68; artist-in-residence, Univ Pa, Philadelphia, 68-69; prof & chmn dept painting & drawing, Art Inst Chicago, 98-2001; vis artist & lectr, var univs & art schs, 71-96. *Awards:* Ann Arbor (super 8) 76; Pringes for films at Toronto Film Festival in 76 (super 8); Fel, Nat Endowment for the Arts, 78 & 85; Jacob & Bessie Levy Prize, 85; Fel, Ill Arts Coun, 84, 88 & 90. *Bibliog:* Robert Berlind (auth), rev, Art in Am, 7/86; Jasmes Yood (auth), essay,

Spirited Visions, Univ Ill Press, 91; Alan Artner (auth), rev, Chicago Tribune, 4/2/93; also reviews 5/2/85 & 1/24/2003. *Mem:* Col Art Asn. *Media:* Oil, Pastel, Film. *Res:* Psychological Narrative. *Specialty:* Contemp Art. *Interests:* Ormithology. *Collection:* Art Inst of Chicago; Mus of Contemp Art. *Publ:* Auth, Joseph Beuys at the Art Institute, Quart Mag Art Inst Chicago, spring 74; Leon Golub: Portraits of political power, New Art Examiner, 1/78; Essay on Drawing, Whitewalls, spring 86. *Dealer:* Gescheidle Gallery, 118 N. Peoria St. Chicago, IL, 60607. *Mailing Add:* 807 W 16th St Chicago IL 60608

PHILLIS, MARILYN HUGHEY
PAINTER, INSTRUCTOR
b Kent, Ohio, Feb 1, 27. *Study:* Ohio State Univ, BS, 49; Toledo Mus Art Sch Design, 61; studied with Fred Leach, Jeanne Dobie, Edward Betts & Glenn Bradshaw. *Work:* Springfield Mus Art, Springfield, Ohio; EF McDonald Co, Gem Savings, Dayton; Rolls Royce Ltd, Palmyra, NY; Neumann Indust, Cleveland; Dean Witter Reynolds Inc, Jackson, Miss; Holiday Inns, Memphis, Tenn; On Line Computer Libr Ctr, Dublin, Ohio; Ohio Univ-Lancaster; Ohio Univ-Eastern; Heritage Hall Mus, Talladega, AL; Monroe Community Col, MI. *Comn:* Harpischord decorative design, comn by Rosalyn Schneider, 84; abstr painting, Dr & Mrs Eugene Schmiedl, 88. *Exhib:* Am Watercolor Soc, Nat Acad Gallery, NY & traveling, 74, 76, 78, 79, 82, 89, 91, 95, 96, 97 & 2002; Nat Watercolor Soc, Laguna Beach Mus & Palm Springs Mus, Calif, 74, 80, 83, 89, 96 & 01; Watermedia Exhib, Springfield Art Mus, Ohio, 81 & 83; Ohio Northern Univ, 84; Davis & Elkins Univ, Elkins, WVa, 86; Zanesville Art Ctr, Ohio, 87; Watercolor Exhib, Nat Taiwan Art Educ Inst, Taipei, 94; Cheekwood Mus, Botanical Ctr, Nashville, Tenn, 95; New York City Lincoln Ctr, 04; Straphmore Hall, MD, 2004; Idaho Falls Art Ctr, North Ariz Univ. *Pos:* Illusr, Western Reserve Mag, 74-78, co-ord, 93, 95, 97, 99 & 2002; seminar, Stretching Boundaries for Creative People Int. *Teaching:* Instr art, Edison State Community Col, 76; instr watercolor, Springfield Art Ctr, Ohio, 76-84; guest lectr and instructor painting throughout US; juror nat painting and all media exhibs. *Awards:* Inductee Hall of Fame Fine Arts Category, Kent, Ohio, 2000; Inductee Hall of Fame Cult Arts Category, Wheeling WV, 2000; Named Master Artist Mixed Media, Am Arts Mag, 1996; William Church Osborne Award Am Watercolor Soc, 1998; Ohio Watercolor Soc Gold Medal, 1993; 1st award Watercolor West, 1990; 2d award Southern Watercolor Soc, 2001; Ohio Watercolor Soc, North Coast Award, 2004. *Bibliog:* Mike Ward (auth), The New Spirit of Watercolor, North Light, 89; Nita Leland (auth), The Creative Artist, North Light, 90; Gerald Brommer (auth), Understanding Transparent Watercolor, Davis Publ, 93; Vicki Lord (auth), Painting Acrylics, North Light, 96; Mary Todd Beam (auth), Celebrating Your Creative Self, F&W Publ, 2001. *Mem:* Am Watercolor Soc (bd dir, 91-93 & newsletter ed); Allied Artists Am; Watercolor West; Ohio Watercolor Soc (rec secy, 79-82, vpres, 82-89 & pres, 90-96); Soc Layerists Multimedia (vpres, 88-93); Nat Watercolor Soc (chair jury selection 2001). *Media:* Watermedia, Collage. *Res:* Architectural res historic homes, Piqua, OH; exploring art as bridge between art and science. *Publ:* Illusr, Historic Piqua: An Architectural Survey, Piqua Br, Am Asn Univ Women, 76; auth, Painting from the imagination, Artists Mag, 1/85; Watermedia techniques for releasing the creative spirit, Watson Guptill Pub, 92; Painting from the inner spirit, Watercolor Magic, 6/96; Learning from the Art Masters, Am Art Publ, 6/96; auth, Alchemy of a Creative Idea in: Bridging Time and Space, Maskowitz Publ, 98, Quiet your inner critic, Artist Mag, 4/2003 & Art and Healing, Watercolor Mag, spring 2003; The Artist Mag, Art Clinicd, June/04; Watercolor Magic Mag, Studio Staples, April/05. *Dealer:* Win Dodrill 4853 Nugent Dr Columbus OH. *Mailing Add:* 72 Stamm Cir Wheeling WV 26003

PHILLPOT, CLIVE JAMES
WRITER, LIBRARIAN
b Thornton Heath, Eng, June 26, 38. *Study:* Polytech of N London, ALA, 67; Univ London, Dipl HA(with distinction), 74; Fel Lib Asn UK, 90. *Collection Arranged:* The Art Press (auth, catalog), Victoria & Albert Mus, London, 76 & Art Gallery of Ontario, Toronto, 79; Fluxus: Selections from the Silverman Collection (auth, catalog), Mus Mod Art, NY, 88; Artist/Author: Contemporary Artists' Books (auth, catalog), US Tour; Live in Your Head (auth, catalog), Whitechapel Art Gallery, 1998-1999, London & Museu do Chiado, Lisbon, 2000 & 01; Outside of a Dog (auth, catalog), Baltic, Gateshead, 2003-04. *Pos:* Librn, Chelsea Sch Art, London, 70-77; dir libr, Mus Mod Art, New York, 77-94; freelance writer & art libr consult. *Mem:* Art Libr Soc NAm (pres, 89-90); Int Asn Art Critics. *Res:* Word & Image; marginal art, Ray Johnson. *Interests:* Contemporary art. *Publ:* Britain at the Venice Biennale 1895-1995, British Coun, 95; More Works by Ray Johnson, Moore Col, 91; Artist/Author: Contemporary Artist's Bks, AFA, 98; Ed Ruscha Editions 1959-99, Walker Art Ctr, 99; Michael Porter: Gwavas Lake, Tate, 2001. *Mailing Add:* 3 Pevensey Ave London N11 2RB United Kingdom

PHOENIX, KAOLA ALLEN
COLLAGE ARTIST, PAINTER
b Cincinnati, Ohio, June 16, 52. *Study:* Univ NC, Chapel Hill, BA(art), 74. *Work:* R J Reynolds, Winston-Salem, NC; NCNB, Charlotte, NC; Duke Med Ctr, Durham, NC; Chapel Hill Children's Clinic, Chapel Hill, NC. *Exhib:* Forty-eighth Southeastern Competition for Drawing, Photog & Printmaking, Southeastern Ctr Contemp Art, 80; Charlotte Juried Exhib, Spirit Sq Galleries, NC, 81; Ensemble: Collage & Assemblage, Green Hill Art Ctr, Greensboro, NC, 82; Southeastern Graphics, Mint Mus Art, 82; Collage: Southeast, Southeastern Ctr Contemp Art & traveling with Southern Arts Fedn, 82-83; Xerox Show, Southeastern Ctr Contemp Art, 84; Women Printmakers of the Southeast, McKissick Mus, Columbia, SC, 84; The Artist's Self, Southeastern Ctr Contemp Art & traveling with Southern Arts Fedn, 85-86. *Awards:* Juror's Merit Award, Charlotte Exhib, 81; Best in Show Purchase Award, Southeastern Graphics Invitational, NC Nat Bank, 82; Grant, funded by Nat Endowment Asn & Feminist Am Art Inst, Visual Artists' Exchange in collaboration, 83. *Bibliog:* Allen, Irwin, Holsenbeck & Foster (producers), Birth Days: A Collaborative Room Installation (videotape), 82. *Media:* Miscellaneous. *Mailing Add:* 103 Longwood Dr Chapel Hill NC 27514-9502

PIANO, RENZO
ARCHITECT
b Genoa, Italy, Sept 14, 37. *Study:* Milan Polytech Sch Archit, 64; Stuttgart Univ, Ger, Hon Dr, 90; Univ Delft, Neth, Hon Dr, 91. *Exhib:* Int Bauhausstellung, Berlin, Ger, 85; Mass Inst Technol, Boston, 85; Univ New S Wales, Sydney, Australia, 86; Palladio's Basilica, Vicenza, Italy, 86; Vancouver Mus, Can, 86; 9H Gallery, London, Eng, 87; Menil Mus, Houston, Tex, 87; Sorbonne Chapel, Paris, France, 87; Vieille Charite, Marseille, France, 88; Expo 2000, Moscow, Russia, 88; Royal Inst Brit Architects, London, Eng, 89; Toko Mus, Tokyo, Osaka, Nagoya & Sapporo, Japan, 90; Archit League, NY, 92; Menil Collection, Houston, Tex, 93; Aedes Gallery, Berlin, Ger, 93; MOPT Gallery, Madrid, Spain, 93; Carnegie Mus Art, Pittsburgh, Pa, 94; Art Inst Chicago, 94; GA Gallery, Tokyo, Japan, 94; Neth Archit Inst, Rotterdam, 95; Light Construct, Mus Mod Art, NY, 96; Potsdamer Platz Exhib, Genova, Italy, 96; Ital Design, Triennale, Milano, Italy, 96; VI Int Exhib Archit Biennale, Venezia, Italy, 96; Out of the Blue, Kunst-und Ausstellungshalle, Bonn, Ger, 97, Villa Pignatelli, Napoli, Italy, 97 & MA Gallery, Tokyo, Japan, 98; Renzo Piano Workshop, Beyeler Fondation, Riehen, Basel, Switz, 97; Roma Auditorium, La Serra, Rome, Italy, 97; and many others. *Awards:* Hon Fel, Am Acad Arts & Lett, 94; Telecom Prize, Napoli, Italy, 96; Diploma Europe Award Steel Structures, Lingotto, Torino, Italy, 97; Pritzker Architecture Prize, 98. *Mailing Add:* Renzo Piano Workshop 36 Rue des Archives Paris 75004 France

PIASECKI, JANE B
ADMINISTRATOR
b Brooklyn, NY, Jan 21, 53. *Study:* Brooklyn Mus Art Sch, 72-75; City Univ New York-Col Staten Island, AS(liberal arts), 78, BS(econ, 82; City Univ New York-Baruch Col, MBA, 85. *Pos:* Accounting asst, Brooklyn Botanic Gardens, 73-76; asst mgr finance & personnel, Brooklyn Mus, 76-80; bus & personnel mgr, NY Hall Sci, 80-85; assoc dir, Newport Harbor Art Mus, 85-93; assoc dir, Inst of Am Indian Arts Mus, 93-95; vpres, finance and Chief Financial Officer, Nat Hist Mus, Calif, 96-. *Teaching:* Calif State Univ, Fullerton, 99. *Mem:* Art Pub Places (comt, 88-92); Int Coun Mus (mgt comt, 92-92); Am Asn Mus, Mus Mgt Comt, (chmn, 2000-04); Calif Asn Mus (treas, 92-93). *Publ:* Int Coun of Mus Newsletter, 2002. *Mailing Add:* c/o Nat Hist Mus Los Angeles Co 900 Exposition Blvd Los Angeles CA 90007

PIATEK, FRANCIS JOHN
PAINTER, EDUCATOR
b Chicago, Ill, Dec 9, 44. *Study:* Sch Art Inst Chicago, BFA & MFA. *Work:* Art Inst Chicago; Ill State Mus; First Nat Bank Chicago; Kemper Insurance Bong Warren Corp; John D & Catherine T MacArthur Found. *Comn:* Mural, Main State Bank Chicago, 72. *Exhib:* Whitney Mus Am Art Ann Exhib Contemp Am Painting, 68; one-man shows, Hyde Park Art Ctr, 69, Phyllis Kind Gallery, 72, NAME Gallery, Chicago, 75 & Roy Boyd Gallery, 84-87; Chicago Art Inst; Surfaces, 2 Decades of painting in Chicago Terra Mus Am Art, 87; Art in Chicago 1945-1995, Mus Contemp Art. *Teaching:* Instr painting, Art Inst Chicago; instr painting, Wash Univ, St Louis. *Awards:* Art Inst Traveling Fel, Francis Ryerson, 67; Pauline Potter Palmer Award, 68 & John G Curtis Prize, 69, Chicago & Vicinity Shows; Nat Endowment Arts, Visual Arts Fel, 85. *Bibliog:* Franz Schulze (auth), Frantastic Images: Chicago Art since 1945, Follett Publ Co, 72; Franz Schulze (auth), Artists the Critics Are Watching Art News, 5/81; Mary Mathews Gedo (auth), Abstraction As Metaphor: The Evacative Imagery of William Conger, Miyoko Ito, Richard Loving & Frank Piatek, Arts Mag, 10/82. *Media:* Painting, Multi Media. *Mailing Add:* 3925 N Troy St Chicago IL 60618-3407

PICCIANO, LANA PATRICIA PICCIANO
OIL PAINTER, GLICEE'S
b Evanston, Ill. *Study:* Bloomfield Col, BA, 69; Art Students League, with Vaclav Vytlacil, scholar, 70-72 & with Theodoras Stamos, scholar, 71-72; Provincetown Workshop, with Leo Manso & Victor Candell, 74. *Work:* Int Monetary Fund, Washington; Bell Laboratories, Holmdel & Parsippany, NJ; Integrated Resources, Inc, NY; Wertheim Schroder & Co, Equitable Ctr, NY; Morrison & Foerester, NY. *Comn:* Painting, Bell Laboratories, Holmdel, NJ, 80; painting, Lutz and Carr, NY, 87; painting, Jad Corp of Am Col Point, NY, 89; painting, comn by Mr & Mrs Martin Gottlieb, Boca Raton, Fla, 89. *Exhib:* Shirley Scott Gallery, Southampton, NY, 87-91; Contemp Artists, Islip Art Mus, East Islip, NY, 88; 100 Yrs/100 Works, Women Artists Today Salute Their Centennial, Islip Art Mus, East Islip, NY, 89, Fine Arts Mus of South Mobile, Ala, 89 & Chattanooga Regional Hist Mus, Tenn, 89; The New Romanticism, 8th Plaiedes Gallery, NY, 90; Works Gallery, NY, 1991-2006. *Teaching:* Painting, Alliance for the Arts, Fort Myers, Fla, 2003-2004. *Awards:* Ford Found Grant for Study; Christian Bucheit scholar; Art Students League scholar. *Bibliog:* First Place in Oils, Framingham Ann Competition, 74; Best in DC Slide Registry & Best of DC Artists, D Christensen, 82. *Mem:* Artists Equity NJ (pub relations dir, 79-81); Nat Asn Women Artists (financial relations dir, 86-88); Artist Equity NY. *Media:* Oil on Canvas. *Specialty:* Works Gallery 2350 Madison Ave NYC. *Interests:* Kriya meditation, yoga, tennis. *Publ:* Auth, An Illustrated Survey of Leading Contemporaries, Am Artists, 90; New York Art Review, Les Krantz, 90. *Mailing Add:* 14271 Reflection Lakes Dr Fort Myers FL 33907

PICCILLO, JOSEPH
PAINTER
b Buffalo, NY, Jan 9, 41. *Study:* State Univ NY Col Buffalo, MFA, 64, fel, 68, 69 & 72. *Work:* Mus Mod Art, NY; Brooklyn Mus; Art Inst Chicago; Butler Inst Am Art, Youngstown, Ohio; Minn Mus Art, Minneapolis; Metrop Mus, NY. *Exhib:* Smithsonian Inst Traveling Drawing Exhib, 71; Monique Knowlton Gallery, 80, 81 & 83; Betsy Rosenfield Gallery, 80, 83; one-man shows, Monique Knowlton, NY, 84 & 96, Betsy Rosenfield, Chicago, 80, 85, 86, 88, 91 & 94, Elliot Smith Gallery, St Louis, Mo, 86 & 88, 94, Barbara Fendrick Gallery, NY, 88, Brendan Walter Gallery, Los Angeles, Calif, 90 & 92, Perimeter, Chicago, 97, 99, 2002, & 06, Chase Gallery, Boston, 99, 2000, 03, Robert Kidd Gallery, Birmingham, 99 & 2002, R Duane Reed Gallery, St Louis, 2003, Gallery Camino Real, Boca Raon, Fla, 2003; Chase Gallery, Mass, 2000. *Pos:* Consult, NY State Coun Arts, 75-77. *Teaching:* Prof art, State Univ NY Col Buffalo, 67-. *Awards:* Childe Hassam Purchase Award, Am Acad Arts & Lett, 68; Nat Endowment for Arts fel, 79. *Bibliog:* Diane Cochrane (auth), J Piccillo's game structures, Am Artist, 12/73. *Publ:* Illusr (covers), Poverty in America, 5/17/68 & Black vs Jew-A tragic confrontation, 1/31/69, Time Mag; contribr (cover), Art Gallery Int, 90. *Mailing Add:* 812 Elmwood Ave Buffalo NY 14222

PICCIRILLO, ALEXANDER C
PAINTER, INSTRUCTOR
b Brooklyn, NY, Jun 27, 52. *Study:* Brooklyn Mus Art Sch - 1968-70; Special studies with Burton Silverman - 1972-75; Sch of Visual Arts, BFA, 1974. *Comn:* mem pastel, Bd Educ, Nutley, NJ, 1989. *Exhib:* Ann Exhib, The Nat Acad of Design, New York, 1975; Ann Exhib, Pastel Soc Am, New York, 1985-; Art Achievement Awards, Artist's Soc Int, San Francisco, 1986; Int Juried Show, Bergen Mus, Bergen Co, NJ, 1991-92; Int Juried Show, New England Fine Arts Inst, Boston, 1993; Int Juried Show, Patterson Mus, NJ, 1994; Master Pastelist Exhib, Hammond Mus, N Salem, NY, 1995; Int Juried Show, NJ Ctr Visual Arts, Summit, 1996. *Teaching:* Instr genre painting & drawing, Yard Sch Art Montclair Art Mus, NJ, 1983-; instr representational painting & drawing, NJ Ctr Visual Arts, Summit, 2001-06; instr painting & drawing all media, Livingston Art Asn, NJ, 2001-. *Awards:* Columbus Citizens, 1987 & Beatrice Camer, 1988, Ann Exhib, Pastel Soc of Am; Best in Show, Am Artist Prof League, NJ, 1989. *Bibliog:* John Zeaman (auth), Every lawn a king every man isolated, Bergen Record, 5/91; Patricia C. Turner (auth), Art in the ring, NJ Star Ledger, 7/92; William Zimmer, How a curator turns into a judge, NY Times, 4/96. *Mem:* Elected mem Pastel Soc Am, 1985; Yard School of Art Bd Trustees (faculty liaison) 1985-1994; elected master pastelist, Pastel Soc Am, 1987; elected mem Degas Pastel Soc, 1988; elected mem Art Ctr of NJ, 1989. *Media:* All Media. *Publ:* Contribr, The Art of Pastel Portraiture, Watson-Guptill, 1996; contribr, The Best of Oil Painting, Quarry, 1996; contribr, Portrait Inspirations, Rockport, 1997; contribr, The Best of Pastel I & II, Quarry, 1998 & 2000; contribr, The Best of Sketching & Drawing, Quarry, 1999. *Dealer:* Gallery 214 214 Glenridge Ave Montclair NJ 07042. *Mailing Add:* 26 Vine St Nutley NJ 07110-2636

PICCOLO, RICHARD
PAINTER
b Hartford, Conn, Sept 17, 43. *Study:* Pratt Inst, 66; Art Students League, 67; Brooklyn Col, MFA, 68. *Work:* Crown Am Corp, Johnstown, Pa; Grosvenor Int, Sacramento, Calif; also pvt collections of Lillian Cole, Sherman Oaks, Calif, Mr & Mrs Robert Emery, San Francisco, Graham Gund, Boston, Robert Gutterman, San Francisco, Dr & Mrs Joseph Jennings, San Francisco and others. *Comn:* Mural, Crown Am Corp, Johnstown, Pa, 89; mural, Lobby Park Plaza Tower, Grosvenor Int, Sacramento, 91-94; Aer, Ignis, Terra, Aqua (mural), US Bank Plaza, Sacramento, Calif, 91-94. *Exhib:* Solo exhibs, Robert Schoelkopf Gallery, NY, 75, 79, 83 & 89, Suffolk Community Col, Long Island, 76, Am Acad, Rome, Italy, 77, Galleria Temple, Rome, Italy, 79, Galleria il Gabbiano, Rome, Italy, 85 & Contemp Realist Gallery, San Francisco, 89 & 95; The Ital Tradition in Contemp Am Landscape Painting (with catalog), Gibbes Mus Art, Charleston, SC with Spoleto Exhib, 90; Figure, Contemp Realist Gallery, Calif, 90; Paintings from Contemp Realist Gallery, NY Acad Art, 91-92; New Am Figure Painting, Contemp Realist Gallery, San Francisco, 92; Drawings by Am Artists, Contemp Realist Gallery, San Francisco, 93; Homage to the First 100 Yrs of Cinema, Il Gabbiano Gallery, Rome, Italy, 96; Still Lifes, Contemp Realist Gallery, San Francisco, Calif, 96; Re-presenting Representation III (with catalog), Arnot Art Mus, Elmira, NY, 97; 10th Ann Exhib, Hackett-Freedman Gallery, San Francisco, 97; Artists Who Look Back: Spirituality in Contemp Art (with catalog), Museo Italo Americano, San Francisco, Calif, 98. *Teaching:* Instr, Pratt Inst, New York, 66-68, Pratt Inst, Tyler Sch Art, Rome, Italy, 69-95 & Univ Notre Dame, Rome Prog, 84-95; dir, Pratt Inst, Rome Prog, 80-95. *Awards:* EA Abbey mem Scholar, 73-75; Nat Endowment Arts Grant, 89. *Bibliog:* Alfred Kay (auth), Grand Canvas, Sacramento Bee, 4/92; Thomas Bolt (auth), New American Figure Painting, Contemp Realist Gallery, San Francisco, 92; Richard Piccolo (exhib catalog), Contemporary Realist Gallery, San Francisco, 95; Elizabeth Helman Minchilli (auth), Homage to the First 100 Years of Cinema, Artnews, 96; and others. *Mailing Add:* c/o Contemporary Realist Gallery 250 Sutter St 4th Fl San Francisco CA 94108

PICKETT, JANET TAYLOR
ARTIST
b Ann Arbor, MI Aug 13, 48. *Study:* Univ Mich, Sch of Art, BFA, 1970; Univ Mich, Rackham Sch Grad, MFA, 1972; Textile Design, Fashion Inst Technol, 1979; Graphic Art, Parsons Sch of Design, NY, 1980; Studied with Sam Gilliam, Vermont Studio Sch,. *Work:* Studion Mus of Harlem; Newark Public Libr; Univ Mich Sch of Social Work; Schomburg Center NYC; Found Valpariso, Mojacar, Spain. *Comn:* Hands on Healing (mural), Univ of Medicine & Dentistry, 1986-98; eight works of art commissioned by The Washington State Art Commission for Our Art-Our Selves: Art as Autobiography, 1990; banners depicting joy in movement (canvas), UMDNJ Sch of Osteopathic Medicine, Stanhope, NJ; 10 48x60 canvas flags, Johnson & Johnson, Research Facility, Princeton, NJ; outdoor mosaic project, New Community Corp of Newark; outdoor sculpture & mosaic project, Rutgers Univ, Camden Campus. *Exhib:* Art As Autobiography, Bellevue Art Mus, Bellevue, Washington, 1990; Book of Embraces, Jersey City Mus, Jersey City, NJ, 1996; More than One Way Home, Montclair Art Mus, Montclair, NJ, 1997; Religion in the 21st Century, Newark Mus of Art, 2003; Icons, Symbols & Alters, Noyes Mus, Oceanville, NJ, 2004. *Teaching:* Prof art, Essex Co Col, Newark, NJ, 1973-2004; adj prof, Bloomfield Col, Bloomfield, NJ,. *Awards:* Glass Blowing Fel, Pilchuck Sch, 1998; Found Valpariso, Mojacar, Almeria, Spain, 2001; MidAtlantic Arts Found, Commissioned Garden Sculpture, Rutgers Univ, Camden, 2002. *Bibliog:* Phil Lane & John Givens (coauths), Working Title (documentary), 2006. *Mem:* Montclair Art Mus (bd of trustees, 2006); Studio Montclair. *Media:* Mixed Media, Works on Paper. *Publ:* Gumbo YaYa, African American Women Artists; More Than One Way Home, exhib catalog, Monclair Mus, 1997. *Dealer:* Tarin Fuller Fine Arts, Newark NJ. *Mailing Add:* 50 Pine St # 205 Montclair NJ 07042

PICKETT, KERI L
PHOTOGRAPHER
b Charleston, SC, June 4, 59. *Study:* Moorhead State Univ, BA, 82. *Work:* Winona State Univ, Minn; Houston Mus Fine Arts; Minneapolis Inst Art; Rourke Art Gallery, Moorhead, Minn; Museet for Fotokunst, Odense, Denmark; pvt collection of Michael Stipe, Bill Hunt, Peter Hay Halpert. *Comn:* Horizon Organic; American Express; Abbott Northwestern Hospital. *Exhib:* Five Jerome Artists, Minn Col Art & Design Gallery, Minneapolis, 91; Celebrate Freedom, Los Angeles Photo Ctr, 92; solo shows, Love in the 90's Jon Oulman Gallery, Minneapolis, 94, Int Photog Hall of Fame and Mus, Oklahoma City, 97, Photo Passage, Toronto, 97, NAFOTO, Int Photog Festival, Sao Paulo, 97, Opolousas (La) Mus Art, 98, New Orleans Mus Art, 98, SE Mus Photog, Daytona Beach, Fla, 98 & Chilean Inst Cult, Santiago, 2000, Tibetan Portraits from the Kingdom of Lo and India, Minneapolis Photographer's Gallery, 95 & Int Photog Hall of Fame and Mus, 95, Faeries, Tweed Mus, Duluth, Minn, 98, Nash Gallery, Univ Minn, Minneapolis, 98, McKnight Found Photog Fel Exhib, 98 & Plains Art Mus, Fargo, ND, 99; Southeast Mus Photog, 97; Exhib Minn 2000 Documentary Project, Minn Hist Soc, St Paul, 2000; Fotofest: Discoveries fo the Meeting place, Erie Ironworks, Houston, 96; 8″X10″: Contemp Am Photog, Godwin-Ternbach Mus, Queens Col/CUNY, Flushing, NY, 96; Delirium, Ricco Maresco Gallery, NY, 97. *Pos:* Free-lance photogr, currently; free-lance writer; speaker, Nat Asn Med Dirs Conv, 97, 5th Annual Heartland Long-Term Care Symposium, Kansas City, 98, AAUW Assembly, 2000. *Teaching:* Ms Found Nat Girls Initiative Photog Proj, 91; Youth Photog Prog, Film in the Cities, St Paul, Minn, 91; collabr audio visual, Earth Survival Sch, 92; MCAD lectr, 93-96. *Awards:* McKnight Found Fel, Film in the Cities, 92 & 97; Bush Found Artists Fel, 92; Book Award for Love in the 90s, Am Photog, 96; & others; McKnight Foundation Photoghraphy Fellowship; Jerome Foundation Grant to Apeture on behalf of FAERIES; Lambda Literary Award, Best Fine Art Book, 2000. *Bibliog:* Cover story, Village Voice, 1/3/95; article, Dallas Morning News, 11/25/95; article, Los Angeles Times Sun, 1/21/96; Open shutters, City Pages, 6/7/2000; article, Editorial Photographers, Lightstackers. *Mem:* Panelist, Minn State Arts Bd Photog. *Publ:* Articles in Life Mag, People Mag, Stern Mag, Am Photo Mag, Photo Dist News Mag, Das Magazin, Der Spiegel, Sports Illustrated, Geo, Time Mag, and others; auth, Love in the 90s, Warner Books; BB & Jo, The Story of a Lifelong Love, a Granddaughter's Portrait; FAERIES: Visions, Voices & Pretty Dresses, Aperture Publ, 2000; Minnesota in Our Time: A Photographic Portrait, 12 Photographers Document the Turn of the Century, Minn Hist Soc Press, 2000; contribr, The Mission Inside the Church of Jesus Christ of Latter-Day Saints, 95; Hugs and Kisses, Abbeville Press, 98; Our Grandmother's Loving Portraits by 74 Granddaughters, 98; At Grandmother's Table: Women write about Food, Life the Enduring Bond between Grandmothers and Granddaughters, Fairview Press, 2000; Saving Body & Sout, The Mission of Mary Jo Copeland, Shaw, 2004. *Mailing Add:* 413 E Hennepin Ave Minneapolis MN 55414-1005

PICKFORD, ROLLIN, JR
PAINTER
b Fresno, Calif. *Study:* Calif State Univ; Stanford Univ, BA; also with Alexander Nepote, Ralph DuCasse, James Weeks & Joseph Mugnaini. *Work:* Springfield Art Mus, Mo; State of Calif Collection, Sacramento; Ford Motor Co, Dearborn, Mich; City of Santa Paula, Calif; Monterey Peninsula Mus Art; and others. *Comn:* UNICEF Card (UN painting), comn by United Nations, NY. *Exhib:* Watercolor USA, Springfield, MO, 62, 65, 66 & 97; Mainstreams Marietta, Ohio, 68; Austrian-Am Exchange Exhib, Linz, Salzburg & Vienna, Austria, 72; Taiwan-Am Exchange Exhib, 73; Royal Watercolor Soc, London-WCoast Watercolor Soc Exchange Exhib, 75-76; Fresno Art Mus Residency, 89; and others. *Teaching:* Instr art, Fresno State Col, 48-62. *Awards:* Best of Show, All-California Exhib, 60; First Prize & Purchase Award, Watercolor USA, 62; First Prize & Purchase Award, Calif State Fair, 63. *Mem:* West Coast Watercolor Soc; Watercolor USA Honor Soc; Carmel Art Asn; Monterey Mus Art; Santa Cruz Art Mus. *Media:* Multimedia. *Publ:* Illusr, stories by William Saroyan, Lincoln-Mercury Times & Ford Times, 50s; auth, A philosophical approach to watercolor, 69 & The California style, 85, Am Artist; California Light: The watercolors of Rollin Pickford, 98. *Mailing Add:* 930 E Sierra Madre Fresno CA 93704

PICOT, PIERRE
PAINTER
b Tours, France, Jan 11, 48. *Study:* Calif State Univ, Northridge, 66-69; Univ Calif, BFA, 70; Calif Inst Art, MFA(design), 73. *Work:* Los Angeles Co Mus Art, Calif; Security Pac Bank, Los Angeles, Calif; Patrick J Lannan Found, Los Angeles, Calif; Yale Sch Art Mus, New Haven, Conn; City of Rennes Munic Collection, France.

Exhib: One-man shows, Jan Baum Gallery, Los Angeles, Calif, 81, 82 & 85, Richard L Nelson Gallery, Univ Calif, Davis, 83, Guggenheim Gallery, Chapman Univ, Orange, Calif, 92, La Criée Munic Gallery, Rennes, France, 94, Inst Franco-Am, Rennes, France, 96 & New Image Art, Los Angeles, Calif, 98; Directions '83, Hirshhorn Mus, Washington, DC, 83; Sunshine & Shadow, Recent Painting in Southern Calif, Univ Southern Calif, Fisher Gallery, 85; Miracles & Mysteries, Calif State Univ, Dominguez Hills, 86; Downey Mus Art, Calif, 89; Variations, Cal Arts Painting, R Bachofner Gallery, Santa Monica, Calif, 90; Domestic Setting, Susan Landau Gallery, Los Angeles, Calif, 93; Galerie du Placard, St Briac, France, 96; Sala Exposiciones Exoma, Cuenca, Spain, 97; Enghien-les-Bains, France, 2000; Works on Paper, Armory Center for the Arts, Pasadena, Calif, 2006. *Pos:* Puplisher/designer, Art in Los Angeles Mag, 87-91; contrib critic, Artweek Mag, 88-90, Visions Mag, Los Angeles, 91-94, New Art Examiner, 91-94; contrib ed, Artweek, 87-91, New Art Examiner, 91-92, Visions, 91-93 & Prism, 95; Vis lectr, Otis Art Inst Grad Sch, Los Angeles, Calif. *Teaching:* vis artist, Claremont Grad Sch, Calif, 81 & 83; vis artist, lectr, Calif State Univ, Fullerton, 82; Instr fine arts, Art Ctr, Pasadena, Calif, 83-; vis lectr, Univ Southern Calif, Los Angeles, 83-85 & Otis/Parsons, Los Angeles, Calif, 86-87. *Awards:* Art Fel, Nat Endowment Arts, 87; Award of Excellence, Art Dirs Club Houston; Silver Award of Excellence, Univ & Col Designers Asn, 88. *Bibliog:* William Wilson (auth), LA Times, 80; Suzanne Muchnic (auth), LA Times, 12/11/81; Louis Fox (auth), Artweek, 12/81; Susan Larsen (auth), Artforum, 3/83; Betty Brown (auth), Arts Mag, 2/83; Christopher French (auth), Artweek, 12/3/83; Kristine MacKenna (auth), LA Times, 7/5/85; Joan Hugo (auth), LA Weekly, 7/25/85. *Publ:* Auth, The Archipelago of time: Charles Garabedian, Los Angeles Louver Gallery, Venice, Calif, 96; Sexy, Sensual Abstraction in California, 1950s-1990s, Armory Center Arts, Pasadena, Calif, 96. *Mailing Add:* 3516 Crestmont Ave Los Angeles CA 90026

PIEHL, WALTER JASON, JR
PAINTER, EDUCATOR
b Marion, NDak, Aug 1, 42. *Study:* Concordia Col, BA, 64; Univ NDak, MA, 66; Univ Minn, 69. *Work:* Pillsbury Co, St Paul, Minn; Fed Reserve Bank Minneapolis; NDak Governor's Collection, Bismarck; Plains Art Mus, Moorhead, NDak. *Comn:* Mosaic mural, Devils Lake Sioux Tribe, NDak, 71; Univ NDak Mobile Art Gallery Graphic, Art Gallery Asn, NDak statewide tour, 79. *Exhib:* 19th Ann Drawing, Ball State Mus, Muncie, Ind, 73; Ann Images, Anoka Ramsey Col Gallery, Minn, 73; Midwestern Graphics, Tulsa City Libr Mus, Okla, 74; 15th Ann Nat Graphics, Okla Art Ctr, Oklahoma City, 74; one-man shows, Dynamics of Rodeo & Landscape, Univ Art Galleries, Grand Forks, NDak, 75 & 81 & Rodeo Imagery, Plains Art Mus, Moorhead, Minn, 66, 69, 70 & 76. *Collection Arranged:* Great Plains Traveling Exhib, 70-71; Northwest Biennial Invitation (auth, catalog), 71; Artrain (traveled), 75; Dakota Made, Mobile Gallery, 79; Nat Watercolor Invitation (auth, catalog), 79-80. *Teaching:* Instr art, Valley City State Col, NDak, 67-68; from asst prof to assoc prof art, Minot State Col, NDak, 69-. *Awards:* Purchase Awards, Nat Graphics, Univ NDak, 72 & Northwestern Bak Corp, 74 & Drawing USA, Minn Mus Art, 73. *Bibliog:* Nancy Edmonds Hanson (auth), Contemporary artists of the west, NDak Horizons, 75; article, Art Voices South, 81. *Mem:* NDak Art Gallery Asn (vpres, 79-80); NDak Coun on Arts. *Media:* Mixed. *Dealer:* Wildine Gallery 903 Rio Grande Blvd NW Albuquerque NMex 87104. *Mailing Add:* 11000 86th St SE Minot ND 58701-2457

PIENE, CHLOE
DRAFTSMAN, VIDEO ARTIST
Study: Columbia Univ, New York City, BA, 93; Goldsmiths College, United Kingdom, MFA, 97. *Work:* Mus Mod Art, NY; Whitney Mus Am Art, NY; Walker Art Ctr, Minneapolis; San Francisco Mus Mod Art, San Francisco; FNAC, France; FRAC, France; Sammlung Hoffman, Berlin; Ctr Nat D'Art et de Cult George Pompidou, Paris. *Exhib:* Me & More, Kunst Mus, Luzerne, 2003, Whitney Biennial, Whitney Mus Am Art, NY, 2004, Spirit, Galerie Nathalie Obadia, Paris, 2004, Videorome II, Bates College Mus Art, 2004, Boys Will Be Boys?, Mus Contemp Art, Denver, 2005. *Mailing Add:* c/o Klemens Gasser & Tanja Grunert 524 W 19th St New York NY 10011

PIENE, OTTO
SCULPTOR, PAINTER
b Laasphe, Westphalia, Ger, Apr 18, 28. *Study:* Blocherer Art Sch & Acad of Fine Arts, Munich, 48-50; Dusseldorf Art Acad, WGer, 50-53; Univ Cologne, WGer, 53-57. *Hon Degrees:* Univ Md, hon DFA. *Work:* Albright-Knox Art Gallery, Buffalo, NY; Mus Mod Art, NY; Carnegie Inst Int Mus Art, Pittsburgh, Pa; Nat Gallery of Can, Ottawa, Ont; Stedelijk Mus, Amsterdam, Holland; Nat Gallery, Berlin; and others. *Comn:* Olympic Rainbow, Munich, 72; Light sculptures, Hawaii Capitol, Honolulu; Galaxy, Cambridge, Mass. *Exhib:* Sixteen Ger Artists, Corcoran Gallery of Art, Washington, DC, 62; one-man shows, Mus Am Ostwall, Dortmund, 67, Trumbull Col, Yale Univ, New Haven, Conn, 69, Centro de Arte y Communicacion, Buenos Aires, Art, 72 & Kolnischer Kunstverein, Cologne, 73; Documenta 4 Group Zero, 64; Earth, Air, Fire, Water: Elements of Art, Mus Fine Arts, Boston, Mass, 71; Hayden Gallery, Mass Inst Technol, Cambridge, Mass, 75; Documenta 6, Ctr Advan Visual Studies, Mass Inst Technol, 77; Fitchburg Art Mus, Mass, 77; Stadtisches Kunstmuseum, Dusseldorf, Ger, 96; and many others. *Pos:* Dir, Ctr Adv Visual Studies, Mass Inst Technol, Cambridge, 74-94, dir emer, 94-. *Teaching:* Prof environmental art, Sch Archit & Planning, Mass Inst Technol, 72-94, prof emer, 94-. *Awards:* Prize, Int Biennial Prints, Tokyo Mus Mod Art, 72; Kepes Prize, Mass Inst Technol, 92; Prize, Paper Biennale, Dueren, Ger, 94; Sculpture prize, Am Acad Arts, 96. *Bibliog:* Heiner Stachelhaus & Jurgen Claus (auth), Otto Piene, Essen, Ger, 83; Manfred Schneckenburger, et al (auth), Otto Piene und das cavs, Karlsruhe, Germany, 88; Stephan von Wiese (auth), Otto Piene, Dusseldorf, Ger, 96; and many others. *Mem:* Deutscher Kunstlerbund; European Acad Art & Sci. *Media:* Multimedia. *Publ:* Auth, Rainbows, 71, More Sky, 73; co-auth Zero, 1958-61, Dusseldorf, Germany, Cambridge, Mass, 73; coauth & co-ed, Sky Art (conference catalogs), Cambridge, Mass, 81, 82 & 83; co-auth, co-ed Lightsorot, New York, NY, 87; and others. *Mailing Add:* 383 Old Ayer Rd Groton MA 01450

PIEPENBURG, ROBERT
SCULPTOR
b Detroit, Mich, Oct 28, 41. *Study:* Eastern Mich Univ, BS, 64, MA, 65, MFA, 73. *Work:* Detroit Inst Arts; Smithsonian Inst. *Comn:* Mural, Liberty State Bank, Clinton, Mich, 81; sculpture, Fed Mogul World Hq, Southfield, Mich, 82; fountain, Sheraton Hotel, Novi, Mich, 82; wall relief, Delta Airlines Terminal, Orlando, Fla, 90; wall sculpture, Hurley Hosp, Flint, Mich, 94. *Exhib:* Solo exhib, Robert Kidd Gallery, Birmingham, Mich, 80; Wichita Art Mus, Kans, 81; Ceramic League of Miami, 88; Univ Mich, Ann Arbor, 90; Concordia Col, Ann Arbor, 96; Mott Community Col, Flint, Mich, 96; Eastern Mich Univ, 98. *Teaching:* Instr ceramics, Oakland Community Col, Ill, 69-, Vancouver Sch Art, 76, Tyler Sch Art, 77 & Eastern Mich Univ, 84. *Awards:* Nat Endowment Arts Fel, 80; Mich Coun Arts Creative Artist Grant, 81, 86 & 90. *Bibliog:* Tim Andrews (auth), Raku: A Review of Contemporary Work Black/Chilton, 94; J Fairbanks & A Fina (auths), The Best of Pottery, Rockport, 96; Susan Peterson (auth), The Craft and Art of Clay Prentice Hall, 98. *Mem:* Nat Coun Educ Ceramic Arts. *Media:* Ceramics, Welded Steel. *Publ:* Auth, Raku Pottery, Pebble Press, 98; Auth, The Spirit of Clay, Pebble Press, 98; Treasures of the Creative Spirit, 98

PIERCE, ANN TRUCKSESS
PAINTER, EDUCATOR
b Boulder, Colo, Aug 28, 31. *Study:* Univ Colo, Boulder, BFA, 53, MFA, 55; Yale Univ summer sch, fel, 53; study with Bernard Chaet, Gabor Peterdi, Jimmy Ernst, N Marsicano; workshops with Harold Gretzner, Robert E Wood, Morris Shubin, Jade Fon, George Post, Tom Hill, Tom Nicholas, Millard Sheets, Glenn Bradshaw, Jane Burnham, William B Lawrence & George Gibson. *Work:* Tri-Counties Bank, Mangrove; Pillsbury Branches, Chico, Calif; Yale Univ, New Haven, Conn; Forum Gallery, NY; Calif State Univ, Chico; Univ Colo, Boulder. *Comn:* Oil painting, Colo State Univ, Fort Collins. *Exhib:* Rocky Mt Nat Watermedia Exhib, Foothills Art Ctr, Golden, Colo, 74, 77-79, 81-83, 85, 88 & 89; San Diego Watercolor Soc Nat, Cent Fed Tower Plaza Gallery, 76-78 & 80-84; Scottsdale Watercolor Biennial, Scottsdale Ctr for Arts, Ariz, 78 & 80; Ann Exhib Watercolor Soc Ala, Birmingham Mus Art, 78 & 79; Watercolor West, Riverside Art Ctr, Calif, 79, 81-83, 87 & 88; Nat Watercolor Soc, Desert Mus, Palm Springs, Calif, 79-81 & traveling exhib, 79, 80, 82 & 88; Watercolor USA, 80 & 88; Watercolor Now, Springfield Art Mus, 87, 89 & 90; Aqueous '87, Owensboro Mus Fine Art, Ky, 87; New Visions Cult & Agr, Marshfield Clurie, Wis, 96; Watercolor West 29th Ann, Riverside Art Mus, Calif, 97; Nat Watercolor Okla, Kirkpatrick Gallery, Okla City, 98. *Teaching:* Grad asst drawing & watercolor, Univ Colo, Boulder, 53-54, instr, summers, 59 & 62; prof drawing & watercolor, Calif State Univ, Chico, 64-95, chmn art dept, 80-83, numberous workshops, Calif & Nev, 90-2001. *Awards:* Springfield Art Mus Award, Watercolor USA, 80; Purchase Awards, Joyce Media, Nat Watercolor Soc, 80 & Hutchings, Watercolor West, 81; First & Second Prize, Calif State Fair, 82; Award of Excellence & Purchase Award, Lodi Ann, 83. *Bibliog:* Watercolor 89, Am Artist Mag Publ, 89; Greg Albert (auth), Splash, North Light Bks, 91; The Best of Watercolor, Rockport Publ, 95. *Mem:* Nat Watercolor Soc; West Coast Watercolor Soc; Watercolor West; Rocky Mountain Nat Watermedia Soc; Nat Asn Women Artists; Watercolor USA. *Media:* Watercolor. *Dealer:* Vagabond Rose 236 Main Chico CA 95928. *Mailing Add:* 819 Shepard Ln Chico CA 95926-2941

PIERCE, CHARLES ELIOT, JR
ADMINISTRATOR, DIRECTOR
b Springfield, Mass, Dec 25, 41. *Study:* Harvard Col, BA, 64; Harvard Univ, PhD, 70. *Pos:* Dir, Pierpont Morgan Libr, NY. *Mailing Add:* Pierpont Morgan Library 29 E 36th St New York NY 10016

PIERCE, CONSTANCE LAUNDON
PRINTMAKER, PAINTER
b Cleveland, Ohio, May 24, 46. *Study:* Cleveland Inst Art, BFA, 73; Col Art, Md Inst, Baltimore, MFA(Hoffberger fel), 75. *Work:* Nat Mus Women in Arts, Georgetown Univ Spec Collections, Ctr Art & Relig Collection, Cath Univ Am Fine Arts Collection, Nat Gallery Art Rare Books & Sketchbooks Collection, Nat Inst Health Fine Arts Collection, Washington; Massillon Mus Art, Ohio. *Exhib:* One-woman shows, Dadian Gallery, Washington, 92, Washington Print Gallery, Washington, 93, Nat Mus Women in Arts, Washington, 94, Riverside Gallery, NY, 94 & Newman Gallery, Capitol Hill, Washington, 95; Yale Univ Divinity Library (CT), 98; Regina Quick Arts Ctr. (NY), 2003; Henry Luce III Ctr for Arts & Religion (DC), 2005; Paper Chase, Miss Mus Art, Jackson, 95; Monotypes Nat Invitational, Indiana Univ, Pa, 96; SKETCHBOOKS, Eudora Welty Libr Gallery, Jackson, Miss, 97; 11th Miniature Print Int (traveling), 97-98; Greenwich Arts Ctr (CT), 2000; Macy Gallery of Columbia Univ (NY), 2000; Georgetown Univ Fairchild Gallery (DC), 2000; Henry Luce III Ctr for the Arts (DC), 2001; Foundry Gallery (DC) 2004; Easton Academy of the Arts (MD) 2004; Glenview Mansion Gallery (MD), 2005;. *Collection Arranged:* Nat Mus Women in the Arts (DC); Smithsonian Archives of Am Art, (DC); Nat Gallery Art Rare Book Library (DC); Yale Center British Art Sketchbook Archives (CT); Yale Art of Book Collection (CT); Georgetown Univ. Special Col. (DC); Henry Luce III Center for Arts (DC); National Inst of Health Art Col. (DC); Massillon Art Mus (OH), Int'l Marion Research Inst. (OH); Southern Graphics Council Archives (MS). *Pos:* Artist-in-residence, Ctr for Art & Relig, Washington, DC, 90-92; guest cur, Dadian Gallery, Washington, DC, 91-92; fac, Smithsonian Inst Art Studio, 91-97; vis

artist-in-residence, Millsaps Col, Jackson, Miss, 94-97; Penland Sch Summer Prog, NC, 95. *Teaching:* Fac monotype & painting, Lafayette Col, Easton, Pa, 78-81; monotype & sketchbook, Smithsonian Inst Art Studio, 91-. *Awards:* Helen Green Perry Award, Europen Travel, Cleveland Inst, Ohio; Summer Res Fel, Lafayette Col, Res Comt, 78; Artist-in-Residency Fel, Magi Endowment Comt, Cath Univ, Washington, 90; Catholic University of Am: Magi Endowment Grant (DC), 93--94; Martine-Keenan Grants (NY) 2003, 2005; Journey Project Grants from Lilly Endowment, Inc, St. Bonaventure Univ (NY), 2003-05;. *Bibliog:* JW Mahoney (auth), Catalog Essay, Exhib Catalog, 92; Douglas Utter (auth), New monotypes, New Art Examiner, 93; Richard Freis (auth), The Discipline of Images: The Art of Constance Pierce, IMAGE J, 96. *Mem:* Col Art Asn; Women's Caucus for Art, DC Chap; Md Printmakers Asn; Washington Cult Alliance; Christians in Visual Arts; MD Printmakers Assoc; Southern Graphic Council (MD);. *Media:* Painting, Monotype, Works on Paper, Sketchbooks, Imaging Journals. *Mailing Add:* PO Box 144 Olean NY 14760

PIERCE, DANNY P
SCULPTOR, PAINTER
b Woodlake, Calif. *Study:* Schouinard Inst Art, Los Angeles; Am Art Sch, New York; Brooklyn Mus Art Sch; Univ Alaska. *Work:* Mus Mod Art, NY; Nat Libr, Paris; Nat Mus Sweden, Stockholm; Huntington Libr, San Marino, Calif. *Comn:* Eskimo scene panels, 62, abstract design in concrete for cafeteria bldg, 63, Univ Alaska; Logging (diorama), White River Hist Soc Mus; 3 murals, Kent, Wash. *Exhib:* Traveling Exhib Prints, Europe, Eurasia, 59-62; Northwest Printmakers Int, Seattle Art Mus, 68; Washington Art, Worlds Fair, Osaka, Japan, 70; Edge of the Sea, Bradley Gallery, Milwaukee, 73, 75, 77, 79 & 81; one-man show, Small Bronzes, 74 & Oostduinkerke, Belgium, 80. *Pos:* Artist-in-residence, Univ Alaska, 59-63. *Teaching:* Assoc prof art, Univ Wis, Milwaukee, formerly, emer prof, formerly, retired full prof & prof emer, 84. *Awards:* Green Memorial Award for Best Oil, Conn Acad Art, 49; Purchase Award, Libr Cong, 52, 53 & 58; Northwest Printmakers International Award, Seattle Art Mus, 68. *Media:* All. *Publ:* Auth & illusr, Cattle Drive, 76, 77, Shepherdess of Monument Valley, 79, Man, Horse, Sea, 80, Sea Wreck, 81 & Birds, 81; Golden Seas, Horse Logging; Sugaring Fever, 89; Irish Vignettes, 92. *Dealer:* Jube Gallery 243 First Ave Kent WA. *Mailing Add:* 330 Summit Ave N Kent WA 98031-4714

PIERCE, DIANE JEAN
PAINTER, ILLUSTRATOR
b Evanston, Ill, Apr 9, 52. *Study:* Univ Utah, 70-76. *Work:* Springville Mus Fine Arts, Utah; Nat Girl Scout Coun Am, Utah; Prof Figure Skaters Hq, Sun Valley, Idaho. *Comn:* Portraits, comn by James Montgomery, Salt Lake City, 91-92; portrait, comn by Sen Blaze Warton, Salt Lake City, 94-95; portrait, comn by John & Jane McCoy. *Exhib:* Springville Nat Salon, Springville Mus Fine Arts, Utah, 85; Univ Utah, Springville Mus Fine Arts, Utah, 87; Nat Asn Women Artists, NY, 87; Park City Open, Kimbal Art Ctr, 89, 90 & 93; 100 Yrs 100 Women traveling exhib, Nat Ash Women, NY, 89-91; Out of the Land, Springville Mus Fine Arts, Utah, 92. *Pos:* Artist & cur, Devereaux Mansion, 84-87; artist, New Dimensions Gallery, 94-. *Awards:* Artists Fel Inc, NY, 93; Merit Award, Springville Mus, 95; and others. *Bibliog:* Charlotte Romney Howe (auth), Artists who to kids, minor masterpiece, Parent Express, 9/88; Richard Christensen (auth), Business booms at art galleries, Desert News, 12/9/90; Vern Swanson (auth), Utah Artists, 91. *Mem:* Nat Asn Women Artists, NY; Salt Lake Art Ctr, Utah. *Media:* Oil, Pastel. *Publ:* Auth, Women Artists of Utah, Springville Mus Fine Art, 84; Utah Women Artists, Utah Div Am Asn Univ Women, 89; Out of the Land: Utah Women, Springville Mus, 92. *Dealer:* 1323 S 6th East. *Mailing Add:* 160 W 200 St Redmond UT 84652

PIERCE, PATRICIA JOBE
ART DEALER, HISTORIAN
b Seattle, Wash, May 18, 43. *Study:* Univ Conn, 64; Boston Univ Sch Fine & Appl Arts, BFA, 65, Harvard Univ, 89-90. *Comn:* Camden Hist Soc, 1967, 71; El Paso Art Mus, Tex, 1972; William Penn Mem Art Mus, Pa, 1976; Schenectady Mus, NY, 1982; Art video, comn by Finlay Holiday Film Corp, 90; Republican Conv Art, Houston, 92. *Exhib:* Design Ctr, Boston, 92; Bridgewater State Col, Anderson Gallery, Mass, 92; Daniel Reni, Boston, 92; Gallery, Nantucket, 92-96. *Pos:* Pres, Pierce Galleries, Inc, Hingham, Mass, 68-; owner, Pierce Galleries Publ Co, 80-; exclusive agent, Kahlil Gibran, & Samuel Rose, Rep of the art estate of W S Barrett (1854-1927); Chauncy F Ryder, N A Marguerite S Pearson, J W S Cox & Louise Woodroofe; prof mgr, World Champion Tae Kwon Do Martial Artists, 82-; prof art appraiser, Appraisers Asn Am, NY, 74-. *Teaching:* Tae Kwon Do. *Awards:* Golden Poet Award, Calif, 88, 89 & 90; Citation for Patriotism & Coverage, Pres Bush's Task Force, 89; Presidential Comn, Washington, DC, 92; and others. *Mem:* Patron Brockton Art Ctr; Nat Writer's Club; Nat Writer's Union; Int Platform Asn; Presidential Task Force, 92-94 & 96; Appraisers Asn Am. *Res:* The life & work of Edward Henry Potthast, JAM Whistler, Elvis Presley, bluesman B B King & Stevie Ray Vaughn & Aerosmith; Cape Ann painters; surrealism; The Ten Am Painters. *Specialty:* Am paintings from Hudson River Sch through 1940 Modernism. *Collection:* Nineteenth century American & French impressionists, William S Barrett, Jane Peterson, E C Tarbell, J W S Cox, J J Enneking & Walter Granville Smith, realism, Pino de Angelico, sculpture by Kahlil Gibran; Claude Monet, Childo Hassan, F.C. Frieske, Richard Miller, Maurice Prendergast. *Publ:* The Watercolored World of J W S Cox, 81; The Prophetic Odessey of Richard Earl Thompson, Am Impressionist, 82; Edward Henry Potthast: More than One Man, 90; The Master's Touch, 90; The Ultimate Elvis, Simon & Schuster, 94; Edmund C Tarbell and the Boston School, 1980; The Ten American Painters, Rumford Press, 1980; Love, Fine Art Pub, NY, 2000; Art Collecting and Investing, 2003; and others. *Mailing Add:* c/o Pierce Galleries Inc 721 Main St Rte 228 Hingham MA 02043

PIERSON, JACK
ARTIST
b Plymouth, Mass, 60. *Study:* Mass Col Art, BFA, Boston. *Work:* Whitney Mus Am Art, NY, 1994, 1995, 2004; Mus Contemp Art, Chicago, 1995; Defining the Nineties, Mus Contemp Art, Miami, 1996. *Exhib:* One-man shows incl, Simon Watson, NY, 1990, Pat Hearn Gallery, NY, 1991, Richerd Kuhlenschmidt Gallery, Los Angeles, 1991, 1992, Tom Cugliani Gallery, NY, 1992, White Columns, NY, 1992, Jack Hanley Gallery, San Francisco, 1993, Regen Projects, Los Angeles, 1994, Edward Hopper & Jack Pierson: Am Dreaming, Luhring Augustine Gallery, NY, 1994, 1996, Fine Arts Work Ctr, Provincetown, Mass, 1994, Tex, Gallery, Houston, 1995, Parco Gallery, Tokyo, 1995, White Cube, London, 1996, Galerie Philippe Rizzo, Paris, 1996, Taka Ishii Gallery, Tokyo, 1995, Pay Me In Coke, 1998, An Artificial Night, Ginza Art Space, Tokyo, 1998; exhib in group shows at The Moderns, Feature, NY, 1995, Defining the Nineties, Mus Contemp Art, Miami, 1996. *Mailing Add:* c/o Cheim & Read Gallery 547 W 25th St New York NY 10001

PIET, JOHN FRANCES
SCULPTOR, INSTRUCTOR
b Detroit, Mich, Feb 23, 46. *Study:* Detroit Soc Arts & Crafts, BFA, 73; Wayne State Univ, MFA, 75. *Comn:* Detroit Bank & Trust, Mich, 72; Pingree City Park, Detroit, Mich, 73; Grand Circus Park, Mich Coun Arts, 75; sculpture, KMart Courtyard, KMart Int, Troy, Mich, 79; Oakland Univ, Rochester, Mich, 81. *Exhib:* Tradition & Invention, Kresge Art Gallery, Mich State Univ, East Lansing, Mich, 77; Kick Out the Jams, Detroit Inst Arts, 80 & Mus Contemp Art, Chicago, 81; Detroit Artists, Cranbrook Acad Art, West Bloomfield, Mich, 80; Meadowbrook Invitational, Oakland Univ, Rochester, Mich, 81; and others. *Awards:* Nat Endowment Arts Grant, Oakland Univ Festival, 81. *Bibliog:* Robert Pincus-Witten (auth), Islands in the blight, Arts Mag, 1/78; Mary S Smyka (auth), Dreams in steel, Detroit Monthly Mag, 80; Dennis A Nawrocki (auth), Art in Detroit public places, Wayne State Press, 80. *Media:* Steel. *Dealer:* Cantor-Lemberg Gallery 538 N Woodward Ave Birmingham MI 48010. *Mailing Add:* 25501 Edgemont Dr Southfield MI 48034-2201

PIJANOWSKI, EUGENE M
EDUCATOR, CRAFTSMAN
b Detroit, Mich, Oct 5, 38. *Study:* Wayne State Univ, BFA, 65, MA, 67; Cranbrook Acad Art, Bloomfield Hills, Mich, MFA, 69; Tokyo Univ Art, 69-71. *Work:* The Art Gallery of Western Australia, Perth; Nat Mus Mod Art, Kyoto; Nat Mus Art; Smithsonian Inst, Washington, DC; Detroit Inst Art; Am Crafts Mus, NY. *Exhib:* Contemp Metalcraft, Seoul, Korea, 88; Fourth Int Non Arts Forays Exposition, Navy Pier, Chicago, 88, 89, & 90; Crafts Today-USA traveling exhib (15 countries), 89-93; Sculptural Concerns: Contemp Am Metalworking, Contemp Arts Ctr, Cincinnati & Ft Wayne Mus, 93-94; Int Jewelry Biennele, Kunsthal, Rotterdam, 93; Sculptural Concerns, 93-96. *Pos:* Assoc dean & prof, Sch Art, Univ Mich, Ann Arbor, currently. *Teaching:* Instr metalwork, jewelry & crafts design, San Diego State Univ, Calif, 72-73; lectr Japanese metalworking, over 88 workshops throughout the US, Europe, Japan and Australia; assoc prof metalwork, jewelry & three-dimensional design, Purdue Univ, West Lafayette, 73-81; prof, Sch Art, Univ Mich, Ann Arbor, 81-. *Awards:* Fulbright Fel, Vienna Inst Appl Arts, Austria, 85; Herbert Hofman Prize Schmuck gene, 87; Best of Show, The Wichita Nat, 87. *Bibliog:* Mokume-Gane (film), Oberon Films, 81; Sculptural Concerns (video-one of 5 artists interviewed), 93. *Mem:* Distinguished mem, Soc NAm Goldsmiths. *Media:* Non-ferrous Metals. *Publ:* Contribr to 30 books on metalwork, 73-94; coauth, 15 articles on Lamination of nonferrous metals by diffusion: Adaptations of the traditional Japanese technique of Mokume-Gane, Goldsmiths J, 77; Mokume-Gane, Craft Horizons, 78; Chong Hap design: Korea, Goldschneide Zeitung, 81; Refractory metals, Jewel, Japan, 82; Update II: Mokume-Gane, Metalsmith, 83. *Mailing Add:* Univ Mich Sch Art Ann Arbor MI 48109

PIJOAN, IRENE MARIA ELIZABETH
PAINTER, INSTRUCTOR
b Laursanne, Switzerland, Nov 12, 53; US citizen. *Study:* Univ Calif, Davis, MFA, 80. *Hon Degrees:* Artist grant, NEA, 1982 & Art Matters, 1996; Artist in Residence, Calif State Univ, 1998. *Work:* Guggensheim Mus, NY; Oakland Mus, Calif; Univ Art Mus, Univ Calif, Berkeley; Roswell Mus & Art, NMex; painting, Sant Clara Pub Libr, Calif, 2001. *Comn:* theatrical set, Lines Ballet Co, San Francisco, 98; metal works, Harborview Res Ctr, Seattle, 99-2000; painting, Highland Hosp, Oakland, Calif, 2000-01. *Exhib:* One-woman show, Roswell Mus & Art Ctr, 82, DeSaisset Mus, 84; New Horizons in Am Art, Guggensheim Mus, 85; 42nd Bicennial of Am, Corcoran Gallery, 91; From the Studio, Oakland Mus, 92; Rena Brawlen Gallery, San Francisco, 98; Art at the Millenium, Univ Mus, Berkeley, 98; one-woman retrospective, Dean Lesher Ctr for the Arts, Bedford Col, Walnut Creek, Calif, 2001. *Teaching:* assoc prof, San Francisco Art Inst, 83-. *Awards:* Nat Endowment for the Arts Grant, 82; Art Matters Grant, 96; Artist in Residence Calif State Univ, 98. *Bibliog:* New Horizons at Guggensheim, NY Times, 85; Local painter's canvases really add up, San Francisco, 90; Abstract and personal, Washington Post, 91; Artweek focus: Irene Pijoan, Artweek, 91. *Media:* Paper, Aluminum, Paint. *Dealer:* Rena Bransten Gallery 77 Geary St San Francisco Ca 94108. *Mailing Add:* San Francisco Art Inst 800 Chestnut St San Francisco CA 94133

PIKE, JOYCE LEE
PAINTER, WRITER
b San Fernando, Calif, July 25, 29. *Study:* Sergei Bongart Sch Art, 55-57; Los Angeles Valley Col, 58-62; Art League Los Angeles, 60-63. *Work:* Fort Hays State Univ, Kans; Brandes Art Inst, Northridge, Calif; Scottsdale Artists Sch, Ariz; Arnot Art Mus, Elmira, NY; Beijing Mus, China. *Comn:* Pico Adobe San Fernando Hist Soc, Calif, 72; Ralph Liebman, Los Angeles, Calif, 82; A J Diani Corp, Santa Maria, Calif, 83;

USAF, 92. *Exhib:* One person shows, Brand Libr, Glendale Calif, 73, Eng Gallery, Beverly Hills, Calif, 84 & Americana Gallery Carmel by the Sea, Calif, 85; Artists of Am, 90-94; Am Artists Prof League, 90; Arnot Mus, 92. *Pos:* Vpres, San Fernando Valley Art Club, Calif, 68-72; dir, Pikes School Workshops, Pacific Grove, Calif, 72-88; consult, Art Video Prod, 83-88. *Teaching:* Instr Fine Arts, Art League Los Angeles, Calif 57-88, Art Students League, Northridge, Calif, 78-88 & Scottsdale Artists Sch, Ariz, 87-2003; instr editing, Los Angeles Valley Col, Calif 61-78. *Awards:* Spec Merit Award, Artists of the Southwest, Southern Calif Arts Coun, 70 & Oil Painters Am, 2001-03; Best of Show, Catalina Festival of Arts, Calif, 72; Best of Show, Pasadena Festival of Arts, Calif, 81; Am Artists Prof League Award for Floral. *Mem:* Emer mem Woman Artists Am West; Am Inst Fine Arts; Calif Coun Arts; San Gabriel Fine Arts Inc; Calif Art Club; fel Am Artist Prof League NY; master signature mem Oil Painters Am. *Media:* Oils. *Res:* Reference art material. *Publ:* Auth & illusr, Painting Floral Still Lifes, Northlight Publ Co, 83; auth, Oil Painting, A Direct Approach, 88-90 & Painting Flowers with Joyce Pike, 92, Writers Digest. *Mailing Add:* 2536 Bay Vista Ln Los Osos CA 93402

PILDES, SARA
PAINTER, COLLAGE ARTIST
b New York, NY. *Study:* Pratt Inst; Col City of NY, with Doris Cross; Brooklyn Mus with Harold Baumbach. *Work:* Doane Col Mus, Crete, Nebr. *Exhib:* Stuhr Mus, Grand Island, Nebr; Governor's Mansion, Lincoln, Nebr; Raymond Duncan Gallery, Paris, France; Galerie Int, NY; Loeb Ctr, NY Univ; and others. *Pos:* treas, Metrop Painters & Sculptors, 82-. *Mem:* Nat Asn Women Artists; Artists Equity; Metrop Painters & Sculptors; Burr Artists. *Media:* Acrylic. *Mailing Add:* Logan Square E Two Franklin Town Blvd Philadelphia PA 19103

PILE, JAMES
PAINTER
b Pueblo, Colo, Nov 7, 43. *Study:* Univ Nebr, BFA, 65, MFA(Woods Fel), 71. *Hon Degrees:* Univ de Sonora, Hermosillo, Mexico, hon diploma, 72. *Work:* Sioux City Art Ctr, Iowa; Krasdale Foods Inc, Bronx, NY; Kalicow Corp, NY; Phoenix Art Mus, Phoenix, Ariz; Univ de Guadalajara, Guadalajara, Jal, Mexico. *Exhib:* Solo exhib, PM & Stein Gallery, 82, Bernice Steinbaum Gallery, 84, 86 & 89, NY & Udinotti Gallery, Scottsdale, Ariz, 2001, 2003; Time Out-Sports & Leisure in Am, Tampa Mus, Fla, 83; Cowboys & Indians-Common Ground, Boca Raton Mus & Lock Haven Art Ctr, Orlando, Fla, 85; The City Observed-Point of View, Bronx Mus Arts, NY, 86; Annual Hassam & Speicher Purchase Exhib, Am Acad Arts & Lett, NY, 87 & 88; West Art & the Law, St Paul, Minn, 88, 89 & 93; Univ de Guadalajara, Guadalajara Jal, Mexico, 2000 Solo Exhib. *Teaching:* Prof painting & drawing, Ariz State Univ, Tempe, 71-06, prof emer, 2006. *Awards:* Visual Artists Fel, Nat Endowment Arts, 87. *Bibliog:* Peter Schwepker (auth), Summer's scattered rewards, Artspeak, Vol III, No 25, 6/24/82; Donald Locke (auth), Jim Pile: New Icons for the southwest, Artspace, spring 82; Renee Phillips (auth), James Pile at Bernice Steinbaum, Manhattan Arts & Entertainment, 84. *Media:* Painting, Collage. *Dealer:* Udinotti Gallery Scottsdale AZ. *Mailing Add:* 9465 E Irwin Ave Mesa AZ 85209

PILGRIM, DIANNE HAUSERMAN
MUSEUM DIRECTOR, HISTORIAN
b Cleveland, Ohio, July 8, 41. *Study:* Pa State Univ, Univ Park, BA (art hist), 63; New York Univ, Inst Fine Arts, MA, 65; City Univ New York Grad Ctr, 71. *Collection Arranged:* American Impressionist and Realist Paintings and Drawings from the Collection of Mr & Mrs Raymond J Horowitz (auth, catalog), Metrop Mus Art, NY, 73; American Renaissance 1876-1917 (auth, catalog), traveling, Brooklyn Mus, Nat Collection Fine Arts, DC, Fine Arts Mus San Francisco, Denver Art Mus, 79-80; Renovation of 21 Period Rooms at the Brooklyn Mus, 80-84; The Machine in America 1918-1941 (auth, catalog), Brooklyn Mus, Mus Art Carnegie Inst, Pittsburgh, Los Angeles Co Art Mus & High Mus, Atlanta. *Pos:* Asst to dir, Pyramid Galleries, Ltd, DC, 69-71; researcher, Metrop Mus Art, New York, spring, 71 & res consult, 72-73; asst to dir, Finch Col Mus Art, New York, summer, 71; chmn, Decorative Arts, Brooklyn Mus, 73-88; dir, Cooper-Hewitt Mus, 88-. *Teaching:* Adj asst prof museological problems: the period rooms, Columbia Univ Sch Archit & Planning, 76-78. *Awards:* Chester Dale Fel, Metrop Mus Art, 66-68; Alumni Achievement Award, Pa State Univ, 90. *Mem:* Decorative Arts Soc; Soc Archit Hist; Friends of Clermont; Victorian Soc in Am. *Res:* American 19th and 20th century decorative arts and paintings. *Publ:* Auth, Alexander Roux, his plain and artistic furniture, 2/68 & Reopening of the period rooms at the Brooklyn Museum, 10/84, Antiques; Inherited from the past: the American period room, 5/78 & The revival of pastels in nineteenth century America: the Society of Painters in Pastel, l0/78, Am Art J; Eighteenth century American interiors, Apollo, 4/82; The American Renaissance 1876-1914, 79 & The Machine Age in America 1918-1941, 85, Brooklyn Mus, NY. *Mailing Add:* 295 Central Park W No 17 New York NY 10024-3008

PILLSBURY, EDMUND P
MUSEUM DIRECTOR
b San Francisco, Calif, Apr 28, 43. *Study:* Yale Univ, BA(hist art), 65; Univ London, Courtauld Inst Art, MA, 67, PhD, 73; Univ NTex, Hon Dr Fine Arts, 96. *Hon Degrees:* Univ N Tex, Hon Dr. *Pos:* Cur Europ art, Yale Univ Art Gallery, 72-76, asst dir, 75-76 & bd govs, 90-; former dir, Yale Ctr Brit Art, Yale Univ, chmn adv comt, 76-80; Chief Exec Officer, formerly, Paul Mellon Ctr Studies Brit Art, London, bd govs & adv coun, 76-80; founding chmn, Villa I Tatti Coun, 79-84; dir, Kimbell Art Mus, 80-98; vpres, Kimbell Art Found, 80-; mem, Presidential Task Force Arts & Humanities, Washington, 81; trustee, Ft Worth Symphony Orchestra, 81-82, Ft Worth Country Day Sch, 82-94, Am Fed Arts, NY, 82-83, Ft Worth Opera Asn, 84-86, St Paul's Sch, Concord, NH, 85-96, Burlington Mag Found, 87-96, Asn Art Mus Dirs, 89-90 & Chinati Found, Marfa, Tex, 98-; vis comt, Sherman Fairchild Paintings Conserv Ctr, Metrop Mus Art, NY, 82-; art adv panel, IRS, US govt, 82-84 & Fed Coun Arts & Humanities, Indemnity Prog, 84-87 (chmn, 85-87); bd dir, Master Drawings Asn, NY, 87-; bd advs, Art Dept, Univ NTex, Denton, 90-; juror, Asn Soutien & Diffusion d'Art, Paris, 94-; chmn int adv bd, State Hermitage Mus, St Petersburg, Russ, 97-; co-chmn, Am Friends Hermitage, 99-; Chief Exec Officer, Peters Fine Art Gallery, Dallas, 99-; consult, Bellagio Gallery Fine Arts, Las Vegas. *Teaching:* Lectr art hist, Yale Univ, 72-76, adj prof, 76-80; adj prof art & art hist, Tex Christian Univ, Ft Worth, 85-. *Awards:* Chevalier l'Ordre Arts & Letts, Ambassador of French Repub to US, 85; Premio Cult Città di Bassano del Grappa, Italy, 92; Chief of Mission, UNESCO Campaign to Save Hermitage Mus, St Petersburg, Russ, 93; and others. *Mem:* Master Drawings Asn, NY (bd dir, 87-); Am Acad Arts & Sci. *Publ:* Contribr, The Cabinet Paintings of Jacopo Zucchi: Their Meaning and Function; Monuments et Mémoires: Foundation Eugéne Piot, LXIII, 80; auth, The rebirth of Venus: Titian and Picasso, Art News, 4/83; Chuck Close and the art of anti-portraiture, Perspectives, Vol 3, No 11, Contemp Art Mus, Houston, Tex, 85; Paul Mellon as Collector and Patron of British Art, Selected Acquisitions 1976-1980, In Honor of Paul Mellon, Collector and Benefactor: Essays, John Wilmerding (ed), Wash Nat Gallery Art, 86; foreword, In Pursuit of Quality, The Kimbell Art Museum, An Illustrated History of the Art and Architecture, 87

PINARDI, ENRICO VITTORIO
SCULPTOR, PAINTER
b Cambridge, Mass, Feb 11, 34. *Study:* Apprentice with Pelligrini & Cascieri, five yrs; Boston Archit Ctr; Sch Mus Fine Arts, Boston; Mass Col Art, BS(educ); RI Sch Design, MFA. *Work:* Worcester Art Mus, De Cordova Mus, Lincoln & Boston Inst Contemp Art, Mass; Chase Manhattan Bank, NY; Marmonac, San Ambogio Yalp, Verona, Italy; Rose Art Mus, Brandeis Univ, Waltham, Mass; Boston Pub Libr, Mass. *Exhib:* New Eng Art Part IV Sculpture, 64 & Surrealism, 70, De Cordova Mus; painting, sculpture, Pucker Gallery, Boston, Mass, 80, 88, 97, 2002; sculpture, Vorpal Gallery, NY, NY, 91; printing, Tufts Univ, 2004. *Teaching:* Instr sculpture, Worcester Art Mus Sch, 63-67; prof, RI Col, formerly, emer prof, currently. *Media:* Wood. *Dealer:* Pucker Gallery 171 Newbury Boston MA 02116. *Mailing Add:* 87 Child St Hyde Park MA 02136-1732

PINAULT, FRANÇOIS-HENRI
COLLECTOR
b Rennes, France, May 28, 1962. *Study:* Grad, Ecole des Hautes Etudes Commerciales (HEC), 85. *Pos:* Internal sales to mgr procurement Pinault-Printemps-Redoute SA (now known as PPR SA), 87-89, gen mgr, France Bois Industries, 89-90, chmn, Chief Exec Officer Pinault Dist, 91-97, chmn, Chief Exec Officer, CFAO (Compagnie Française de l'Afrique Occidentale), 93-97, chmn, Chief Exec Officer Fnac Group, 97-2001, asst gen mgr, 2000, co-mgr, Financière Pinault, 2001-03, chmn Artémis Paris, 2003-, bd dir, Gucci Group, 99-, mem, supervisory bd, 2001-; chmn, mgt bd, PPR SA, Paris, 2005-, Chief Exec Officer, 2005-, Bd dir, Financière Pinault Pinault-Printemps-Redoute SA (now known as PPR SA), bd dir, Finaref, bd dir, Fnac SA, bd dir, Rexel, bd dir, Soft Computing, bd dir, TV Breizh; mem, managing bd, Château Latour; chmn, supervisory bd, PPR Interactive; permanent rep Artémis on supervisory bd Conforma Holding, Guilbert; permanent rep Finacière Pinault on bd dir, Bouygues. *Awards:* Named one of Top 200 Collectors, ARTnews Mag, 2004. *Collection:* Contemporary art. *Mailing Add:* PPR SA 10 Ave Hoche Paris France

PINCKNEY, STANLEY
PAINTER, TAPESTRY ARTIST
b Boston, Mass, Sept 30, 40. *Study:* Famous Artist Sch, Westport, Conn, 57-61; Mus Sch Fine Arts, Boston, Mass, 67. *Work:* Nat Ctr African-Am Art, Roxbury, Mass; Mus Dynamique, Dakar, Senegal, W Africa; Palace de l'Pres, Dakar. *Comn:* Tapestry, Mus Sch Fine Arts, Boston, 75. *Exhib:* A Century of the Mus Sch, Boston Mus Fine Arts, 77; African-Am Master Artists-in-Residency Prog Exhib, Dodge Libr Gallery, Northwestern Univ, 78 & Univ Lowell, 79; Recent Tapestries, Mus Sch Fine Arts Gallery & Boston Mus Fine Arts, 78; Resist-Dyed Tapestries, Stanley McCormick Gallery, Boston Archit Ctr, 79; Traveling Scholarship Exhib, Mus Fine Arts, Boston, 81; Object of the Month, Mus Fine Arts, Boston, 84; Art in Craft Media, Newton Arts Ctr, Newtonville, Mass, 88; and others. *Collection Arranged:* Twelve Black Artists, Rose Art Mus, Brandeis Univ, 69; Osubamba (auth, catalog), Boston Ctr for the Arts, 76 & Cyclorama Gallery, Boston, 76; A Century of the Museum School (auth, catalog), Boston Mus Fine Arts, 77. *Teaching:* Instr African & traditional arts, Mus Sch Fine Art, Boston, 72-. *Awards:* 19th Albert H Whitin Fel, Boston Mus Fine Arts, 69; Ford Found Fac Enrichment-Artist Grant, Mus Sch Fine Art, 78; Blance E Colman Fel, 78; Mellon Found, Fac Enrichment Grant, Mus Sch Fine Arts, 87; and others. *Media:* Watercolor. *Publ:* Beyond Tradition (exhib catalogue), New England Fiber Collective, 83; auth, article, Am Crafts Mag, 86. *Mailing Add:* Dept African Arts 230 Fenway Boston MA 02115

PINCUS, DAVID N
COLLECTOR
b Philadelphia, Pa. *Pos:* Trustee, Philadelphia Mus Art, 74-, Fairmount Park Art Asn, 76- & Pa Acad Fine Arts, 79-. *Collection:* Contemporary sculpture; New York school of abstract expressionists; major contemporary European artists. *Mailing Add:* 1319 Remington Rd Wynnewood PA 19096-2331

PINCUS, LAURIE JANE
PAINTER, SCULPTOR
b New York, NY, Dec 14, 51. *Study:* Bard Col, with Murray Reich, Matt Phillips; Sarah Lawrence Col, with Richard Povsette-Darte, BA, 75; Pacifica Grad Inst, MA, 94. *Work:* Los Angeles Co Mus Art; Univ Calif Los Angeles; LA Foret Mus, Tokyo; Norton Family Collection; Los Angeles Woman's Clinic. *Comn:* Tom & Betty

(sculpture), Takashimaya Dept Store, Osaka, Japan, 85-90; spec art proj, Fuji Television, Tokyo, Japan, 90, Hollywood Roosevelt Hotel, Hollywood, Calif. *Exhib:* Calif Contemp Artists, Laguna Art Mus, Calif, 87; Guest Artist, Orange Co Ctr Continuing Art, Santa Ana, Calif, 89; 10 Yr Survey Show, LaBand Art Gallery, Loyola Marymount Univ, Los Angeles, 89; Am Pop Cult Today III, LA Foret Mus, Tokyo, Japan, 89; External Fantasies, Internal Realities, Security Pac Corp, Gallery at Plaza, Los Angeles, 91; Three From LA, Pima Community Col, Tucson, Ariz, 90; The Dream - A Performance, Cas de Maria church, Santa Barbara, Calif, 92; Am Studio at World Design Center, Gifu, Japan, 2000; Group Shows, NTT Japan, Calendar Projects by World-Famous Artists, 97, Obsessions, UCSB Women's Ctr Gallery, Santa Barbara, Calif, 97, Laguna Art Mus, Calif, 97, Angels Over Gifu, World Design Gallery, Japan, 2002; and others. *Pos:* artist-in-residence, World Design Ctr, Gifu, Japan, 2000. *Teaching:* West Side Arts Ctr, Junior Arts Ctr & Los Angeles Children's Mus; Santa Barbara's Children's Creative Projects, Carpinteria Sch Dist, Calif. *Bibliog:* Marva Marrow (auth), Inside The LA Artist, Penegrine Smith Books, 88; Betty Brown (auth), Exposures: Women & Their Art, New Sage Press, 89; Kei Nagashima (auth), America Pop Culture Today, Vol 3, Seibundo Shinkosha, 90. *Mem:* Westside Arts Ctr, Santa Monica (bd dir, currently); Friends Jr Arts Ctr, Los Angeles (bd dir & Joanna Cotsen fel comt); Artists Equity; Calif Arts Standards Comt; Soc Writers & Illus of Childrens Books. *Media:* Mixed Media, Paper, Acrylic; Wood. *Dealer:* USSO Toyko Japan; Takum Studio Gifucity Japan. *Mailing Add:* 629 Miramonte Dr Santa Barbara CA 93109

PINCUS-WITTEN, ROBERT A
EDUCATOR, WRITER
b New York, NY, Apr 5, 35. *Study:* Cooper Union, Emil Schweinburg Grant, 56; Univ Chicago, MA(dept fel), 60, PhD(dept fel), 68; Univ Paris, Sorbonne, exchange fel, 63-64. *Pos:* Assoc ed, Arts Mag, 63-90; ed, Artforum Mag, 66-76; dir, Gagosian Gallery, New York, 90-96, dir exhib, C & M Arts, NY, 96-. *Teaching:* Emer prof art hist, Queens Col & Grad Ctr, City Univ New York. *Mem:* Col Art Asn (life mem). *Res:* Symbolism; the history of contemporary art and photography. *Specialty:* Abstract expressionism; 20th Century Masters. *Publ:* Auth, Occult Symbolism in France, Josephin Peladan and the Salons de la Rose-Croix, Garland Press, 76; Post-Minimalism, Art of the Decade, 77 & Entries (Maximalism), Art at the Turn of the Decade, 83, Out of London Press; Eye To Eye, Twenty Years of Art Criticism, UMI Res Press, 84; and others. *Dealer:* Twentieth Century and Modern Masters. *Mailing Add:* L & M Art 45 E 78th St New York NY 10021

PINDELL, HOWARDENA DOREEN
PAINTER, EDUCATOR
b Philadelphia, Pa, Apr 14, 43. *Study:* Boston Univ Sch Fine & Applied Arts, BFA, 65; Cumminton Sch Arts, 63; Sch Art & Archit, Yale Univ, MFA, 67 Mass Col Art, Hon Dr, 97. *Hon Degrees:* Hon Dr Mass Col Art, Hon Dr, 97, Parsons Sch of Design and New School Univ, 99. *Work:* Mus Contemp Art, Chicago; Fogg Art Mus, Harvard Univ; Whitney Mus Am Art, Mus Mod Art, Metrop Mus Art, NY; Philadelphia Mus Art; Chase Manhattan Bank, NY & Tokyo; High Mus, Atlanta; Toledo Art Mus; NY Pub Libr; Detroit Inst of the Arts. *Comn:* Comn by IBM, 85; comn by GSA, 87; Metrop Mus Art, 91; Lehman Col, Bronx, NY, 93; Phoenix Int Airport, 96. *Exhib:* Mus Mod Art, NY, 71, 76, 85, 89 & 96; Fogg Art Mus, Harvard Univ, 73; Mus Mod Art, Paris, 75; Inst Contemp Art, Boston, 77; Oakland Mus, 77, 81 & 92; Stadtische Kunsthalle Dusseldorf, Ger, 77; Los Angeles Co Mus Art, 78; New Orleans Mus Art, 78 & 89; Wadsworth Atheneum, 78 & 89; Nat Gallery Art, Washington, 78 & 92; Kunstmus Bern, Switz, 79; Metrop Mus Art, NY, 79 & 82; Everson Mus Art, 81; Va Mus Fine Arts, 87; Mus Fine Arts, Houston, 87; Baltimore Mus Art, 87; Philadelphia Mus Art, 88, 90, 93 & 94; Denver Art Mus, 89; Brooklyn Mus, 89 (2 exhibs), 90; Albright-Knox Art Gallery, 92 & 93; Mus Fine Arts, Boston, 92; Inst Contemp Art, Boston, 93; High Mus Art, 93; retrospective (traveling), 94; solo exhibs, George N'Namdi Gallery, Birmingham, Mich, 95, Arting Gallery, Cologne, Ger, 95, Bethel Col Art Gallery, St Paul, Minn, 96, Charter Oak Cult Ctr, Hartford, Conn, 96, N'Namdi Gallery, Chicago, 96, Kane Col, NJ, 97 & Suffolk Community Col, NY, 97; Bearing Witness: African Am Women Artists, traveling to Minn Mus Am Art & Edwin A Ulrich Mus Art, among others, 96; At the Foreground of Paths, Skoto Gallery, NY, 96; Religion: Through Brown Eyes, Minority Arts Coun, Philadelphia, 96; A Slave Ship Speaks: The Wreck of the Henrietta Marie, Spirit Sq Ctr Arts & Educ, Charlotte, NC, 96, The Thurlow Tibbs Collection, Corcoran Mus Art, 96; Witness to our Time: Hocardena Pindell, Heckscher Mus, Huntington, NY, 99. *Collection Arranged:* The War Show, Ann McCoy, 83; Michael Singer: Ritual Series, Retellings, 87; Poetic Liscence, 90; Liliana Porter, Staller Fine Arts Ctr, Art Gallery, State Univ NY, Stony Brook, 98; Staller Fine Arts Ctr, Art Gallery, State Univ NY, Stony Brook. *Pos:* Exhib asst, Mus Mod Art, New York, 67-69, cur asst, 69-71 & asst cur, prints & illus books, 71-77, assoc cur, 77-79. *Teaching:* Assoc prof, State Univ NY, Stony Brook, 79-84, prof, 84-; vis artist fac, Skowhegan Sch Painting & Sculpture, Maine, summer 80 & Vt Studio Sch, Johnson, summer 85; vis prof art, Yale Univ, New Haven, Conn, 95-99. *Awards:* Nat Endowment Arts (painting), 72-73 & 83-84; Guggenheim Fel Painting, 87-88; Col Art Asn Artist Award for Distinguished Body of Work, 90; Artist Award Studio Mus in Harlem, 94; Joan Mitchell Painting Award, 94; Artist Award for Disting Svc to the Profession, Women's Art Caucus, 98. *Bibliog:* Nancy Heller (auth), Women Artists, An Illustrated History, Ableville Press, New York, 91; Clarence White (auth), Howardena Pindell, Art Papers, 7-8/91; Charles Hagen (auth), Who's on first?, NY Times, 8/2/91. *Mem:* Col Art Asn; Int Art Critics Asn. *Media:* Acrylic on Canvas. *Publ:* Auth, California Prints, Arts Mag, New York, 5/72; Ed Ruscha: Words, Print Collectors Newslett, 1/73; Robert Rauschenberg: Link, Mus Mod Art, 10/75; Alan Shields: Tales of Brave Ulysses, 1/75 & Artists' Periodicals: Alternative Space, 9/77, Print Collector's Newslett; Convenant of Silence: Defacto Censorship, 10/90 & 11/90; New Art Examiner, 3rd text, 9/90; The Heart of the Matter: The Writings and Art of Howardena Pindell, Midmarch Arts Press, New York, 97. *Mailing Add:* State Univ NY Dept Art Stony Brook NY 11794-5400

PINKEL, SHEILA MAE
PHOTOGRAPHER, COMPUTER GRAPHICS
b Newport News, Va, Aug 21, 41. *Study:* Univ Calif, Berkeley, BA, 63, MFA, 77; Univ Calif, Los Angeles, with Robert Heinecken. *Work:* Walker Art Ctr, Minn; Moca, Los Angeles Co Mus, Calif; Ctr Creative Photog, Tucson; Mus Mod Art & Int Mus Photog, George Eastman House, NY; Seattle Mus Art; San Francisco Mus Mod Art; Calif Mus Photography. *Comn:* Cyanotype mural, Park La Brea Towers, Los Angeles, Calif, 76; Metrorail Station, Los Angeles, 93. *Exhib:* Light from Illumination to Pure Radiance, San Francisco Mus Mod Art, 85; Art in Environment, San Francisco Mus Arts & Crafts, 93; solo exhibs, Prague, Czech, 93; Reinventing Documentary, Purdue Univ, 94; Reinventing Emblems, Yale Univ, 95; Contemp Photog; The California Focus, Univ Calif, Los Angeles & Armond Hammer Mus Art, 95; Platt Gallery, Univ Judaism, Los Angeles, 96; San Francisco Camera Work Gallery, 97, Calif Mus Photog, 98, Supacorn Univ, Thailand, 2000. *Collection Arranged:* Multicultural Focus (auth, catalog), Cross Cultural Photog Exhib. *Teaching:* Instr photog, Univ Calif Exten, Los Angeles, 76-83, Otis Parsons Art Inst, 81-83, Sch Art Inst Chicago, 83 & Calif Inst Arts, 84-86; assoc prof, Pomona Col, 86; Friends Photo Workshops, 87 & 88; Visual Studies Workshops, 93. *Awards:* Sloan Found Grant, 87-88 & 90; Artist of the Year, City Santa Monica, 88; Visual Studies Book Publ Awar,d 93; Hammer Award, Ctr for The Study Political Graphics, 95. *Bibliog:* Sylvia Moore (auth), Yesterday and Tomorrow: Collection Women Artists, Midmarch Press, NY, 89; Paul Von Bauer (auth), Other Voices, Other Visions, 95; Bethann Kevus (auth), Naked To The Bone, 97. *Mem:* Los Angeles Ctr Photog Studies (vpres, 78-83); Soc Photog Educ (nat bd mem, 86-90); Col Art Asn. *Media:* Black & White, Xerography. *Publ:* coauth, Kou Changs Story, 93; Guest ed, Art & Social Issues, vol 5, Leonardo, 93. *Mailing Add:* 210 N Ave 66 Los Angeles CA 90042-2927

PINKNEY, JERRY
ILLUSTRATOR
b Philadelphia, Pa, Dec 22, 39. *Study:* Philadelphia Mus Col Art, 58-60. *Work:* Mus Am Illus, NY; H C Taylor Art Gallery, NC A & T State Univ; Miami-Dade Pub Libr; Afro-Am Hist & Cult Mus, Philadelphia; Air & Space Mus, Washington, DC. *Comn:* 10 US Postal Stamps, US Postal Serv, Washington, DC, 77-86; limited edition poster, Negro Ensemble, NY, 82; limited edition books, Franklin Libr, NY; NASA Art Team (painting), NASA, 82; Cover & interior illus, Nat Geog Mag, Washington, DC, 84. *Exhib:* Through Am Eyes; Moscow Int Bk Fair, USSR, 89; Biennale Illustrations, Bratislave, Chechoslovakia, 89; Soc Illustrators, 86-90; solo exhibs, Schomburg Ctr for Res, NY, 90. *Pos:* Mem, comts at US Postal Serv, Washington, DC, 82-. *Teaching:* Vis critic illus, RI Sch Design, 69-70, adj prof, 70-71; assoc prof illus, Pratt Inst, Brooklyn, NY, 86-; Distinguished vis prof, Univ Del, Newark, 86-87, assoc prof, 88-92. *Awards:* Randolph Caldecott Medal of Hon (bk), Mirandy and Brother Wind, 89; Coretta Scott King Award (bk), Mirandy and Brother Wind, 89; Award, Libr of Congress Books for Children (bk), More Tales of Uncle Remus, 89; award, The Year's Best Illustrated Book for Children, New York Times, 89; award, The Year's Twelve Outstanding Works for Children, Time Mag, 89; First Place, New York Bk Show; Randolph Caldecott Medal of Hon (bk), The Talking Eggs. *Bibliog:* Donald Stermer (auth), Jerry Pinkney, Communication Art Mag, 5-6/75; Nick Meglin (auth), The strength of weakness, Am Artist Mag, 1/82; Jerry Pinkney, Idea Mag, Japan, 82. *Mem:* Soc Illusrs. *Media:* Watercolor. *Publ:* Illusr, The Tales of Uncle Remus, 88; More Tales of Uncle Remus, 89; Home Place, Macmillan, 90; Further Tales of Uncle Remus, 90; Pretend You're Cat, 90. *Mailing Add:* 41 Furnace Dock Rd Croton On Hudson NY 10520-1406

PINSKER, ESSIE
SCULPTOR
b New York. *Study:* Brooklyn Col, BA; Art Students League, New York Univ NY (with Vincent Glinsky); Mus Mod Art; New Sch Soc Res (with Leo Manso); Cambridge Univ, Eng; Oxford Univ, Eng. *Comn:* marble sculpture, Marriott Hotels, USA, Minneapolis, Minn, 88; Bronze Sculpture RD SCINTO/Enterprise Corp, 88; bronze sculpture, Granard Comm Ltd, 89; painted steel sculpture, Tauck Tours, Westport, Conn, 90; steel sculpture, Queensboro Steel, Wilmington, NC, aluminum sculpture, City of Brea, Calif; bronze sculplture, KOCE PBS-TV, Orange Co, Calif, 2000; bronze sculpture, Ctr for Universal Truth, San Juan Capistrano, Calif; bronze sculpture, Anne Frank in the World, Calif; many others. *Exhib:* solo exhibs, Lifetime Retrospective (with catalog), Las Vegas Art Mus, Nev, 97, Vorpal Gallery, NY, Bodley Gallery, NY, Ross Watkins Gallery, Palm Desert, Calif, Left Bank Gallery, Dove Canyon, Calif; group exhibs, Lever Bros, NY, 81; Arco Int Art Fair, Madrid, Spain, 88; Galleri Atrium, Stockholm, Sweden; Sandra Higgins Fine Arts, London, Eng; Gallerie Ilse Lommel, Leverkusen, Ger; Feingarten Galleries, Los Angeles, Calif; many others. *Collection Arranged:* Permanent Mus Collections: Portland Art Mus Portland, OR; Nat Portrait Gallery, Smithsonian Inst; City of Peace, Rondine, Italy; Everson Mus, Syracuse, NY; Las Vegas Art Mus; Aldrich Mus Contemp Art, Ridgefield, Conn; War Mem, Yehud, Israel; Okla Art Ctr; Minn Mus Art; Mus Arts & Scis, Daytona Beach, Fla; Mus Mod Art, Warsaw, Poland; Orange Co Mus Art, Newport Beach, Calif; UCLA Med Ctr; Ctr for the Arts, Vero Beach, Fla; Vassar Mus, Poughkeepsie, NY; Fordham Univ at Lincoln Ctr; Rutgers Camden Collection of Art, NJ; Pace Univ, NY; Hinkhouse Collection, Eureka Col, Ill; NECCA Mus, Brooklyn, Conn; New Sch for Social Rsch, NYC. *Awards:* Sculpture Award, Knickerbocker Artists 24th Ann Exhib, 74; Sculpture Award, Metrop Life Ann Exhib; Lumiere Award, Ctr for Universal Truth, San Juan Capistrano, Calif; Anne Frank to Steven Spielberg for the film Schindler's List, Humanitarian Award. *Bibliog:* Benjamin Epstein (auth), Sculptor Fashions a Return to Form, Los Angeles Times, 98; Sean Simon (auth), Essie Pinsker, A Major Sculpture Retrospective, Artspeak, 97; Laurie Mendenhall (auth, brochure), Essie Pinsker: A Profile, Las Vegas Art Mus, 97; David

Mann (auth, brochure), Essie Pinsker, Stones & Steel, Bodley Gallery, NYC, 81; Vorpal, David Shapiro Art Critic, The Art of Essie Pinsker; Las Vegas Art Mus James Mann curator, Essis Pinsker and Sculptor Today. *Mem:* Artists Equity, New York. *Media:* Stone, Metal. *Mailing Add:* 23123 Ventura Blvd Ste 211 Woodland Hills CA 91364-0706

PINTO, JODY
PUB ARTIST
b New York, NY, Apr 8, 42. *Study:* Pa Acad Fine Arts; Philadelphia Col Art, BFA, 73. *Work:* Philadelphia Mus Art & Pa Acad Fine Arts, Philadelphia; Nat Gallery Art, Washington, DC; Whitney Mus Am Art, NY; NY Pub Libr, New York City; Guggenheim Mus, NY. *Comn:* Fingerspan Bridge, Fairmont Park, Philadelphia, Pa, 87; Papago Park/City Boundary and South Ave Streetscape/Park/Patrick Park Plaza, Phoenix, Ariz, 92; Metro-Link (light rail system), St Louis, Mo, 93; San Antonio Convention Ctr, 95; Rio Salado Park & Open Space Master Plan, Tempe, Ariz, 99; Pasadena City Col Sculpture Garden, Pasadena Col, 02; Light Islands, Tokamachi City, Japan, 2000; Kakaako Waterfront Park Master Plan, Hawaii Community Devel Authority, 2000; Vallejo Downtown/Waterfront Master Plan, City of Vallejo Redevelopment Agy, 2000; Beach Improvement Group Project, Santa Monica, Calif, 2000; Riverside Park, New York City, 01. *Exhib:* Hal Bromm Gallery, 78-87; 1979 Biennial, Whitney Mus Am Art, NY, 79 & 81; Venice Biennial 1980, Italy; Tel-Hai 80 Conference, Israel; Inst Contemp Art, Philadelphia, 84; and many other solo and group exhibs. *Teaching:* Pa Acad Fine Arts, 78-; RI Sch Design, 80-83. *Awards:* NY Found Arts Grant, 93; Joan Mitchell Found Grant, 94; Fedn Design Achievement Award, 95; Design Excellence Award, AIA, 96; Design for Transp Award, NEA, 96; Nat ASA Honor Award, 92, 02; and others. *Bibliog:* Lucy Lippard (auth), Overlay, Pantheon Bks, 83; Penny Bach & Pamela Houk (auth), Art for the Public: New Collaborations, Dayton Art Inst, Ohio, 88; Patricia Phillips (auth), The Once & Future Park, Prine Arch Press, 93; Sculpting With The Environment, Van Nostrand Reinhold, 94; and others. *Media:* Natural & Industrial Materials. *Publ:* Auth, Excavations and Constructions: Notes for the Body/Land, Marian Locks Gallery, 79. *Mailing Add:* 124 Chambers St New York NY 10007

PINZARRONE, PAUL
PAINTER
b Mich. *Study:* Univ Ill, BFA(painting), 73. *Work:* Butler Inst Am Art, Youngstown, Ohio; Ill State Mus, Springfield; Kemper Insurance, St Xavier Col & Union League, Chicago. *Exhib:* New Horizons in Art, Chicago, 75, 76 & 80; 28th Ill Exhib, Springfield, 75; 39th & 40th Midyear Exhibs, Butler Inst, 75 & 76; Mainstreams 75-, Marietta Int, Ohio, 75; one-man shows, Joy Horwich Gallery, Chicago, Ill, 76, 77, 80 & 83, Rockford Arts Coun, 88, Rockford Arts Coun, 89 & Univ Wis, 90, Kortman Gallery, Rockford, Ill, 2005. *Teaching:* Instr art, Rock Valley Col, Rockford, Ill, 75-76 & 78, Rockford Col, 76; guest lectr, Univ Miami, 77, Gloria Luria Gallery, Miami, 77, Regent Art Asn, 78, St Xavier Col, Chicago, 80 & Highland Col, 81. *Awards:* First Prize, New Orleans Int, 75; First Prize, Ill State Fair Prof, 75; First Prize, Art Inst Juried, Chicago, 84. *Bibliog:* Article, New Art Examiner, Chicago, 12/80; Carrie Rebora & Laura Cottingham (auths), article in The Chicago Art Review, 81. *Media:* Airbrush, Digital Media. *Mailing Add:* 1617 24th St Rockford IL 61108

PIONK, RICHARD C
PAINTER
b Moose Lake, Minn, Apr 26, 38. *Study:* Studies with Daniel E Greene, 76-77; David A Leffel & Sidney E Dickinson, 77-78; Art Students League, New York, cert, 83. *Work:* Pastel Soc Gallery & Salmagundi Club, NY; Kidder Peabody, NY; Am Home Prod, NY. *Comn:* Completed over 35 portrait commissions in the past 10 years. *Exhib:* The Still Life, Hermitage Found Mus, Norfolk, Va, 85; Connoisseur Gallery, NY, 87-94; Gregory Gallery, Conn, 91-94; Hammond Mus, Salem, NY, 95; Francesca Anderson Fine Art, Lexington, Mass, 94; Butler Inst, Ohio, 2000, 2003; Suzhou, China, 2003; Taiwan, 1994. *Collection Arranged:* cur Constable exhib, Salmagundi Club, NY, 2000; cur travel exhib Salmagundi Club Collection, 1996. *Pos:* Exhib chmn & 1st vpres, Pastel Soc Am, NY, 78-; instr pastel-still life & portrait painting, Pastel Soc Am Studio, Nat Arts Club, NY, 82-; control bd, Allied Artists Am, NY, 88, treas, 84-86; bd dir, Artists Fel, NY, 84-; instr pastel-portraiture, Summit Art Ctr, NJ, 84-85; control bd, Art Students League, NY, 84-88. *Teaching:* Art Students League & Pastel Soc Sch, NY. *Awards:* Henry Gasser Mem Found, 85; Newington Award, Hudson Valley Art Asn, 86 & 94; Stevenson Portrait Award, Nat Arts Club, 92 & 94; over 100 awards for oils & pastels from all art organizations. *Bibliog:* Rachel Wolf (ed), Basic Still Life Techniques, Northlight, 94; David P Richards (auth), Finding Your Personal Artistic Style, Northlight, 95; Hazel Harrison (auth), Painting Shapes and Edges, Northlight, 96. *Mem:* Allied Artists; Pastel Soc Am; Audubon Artists; Nat Arts Club; Salmagundi Club (pres, 94-); and others. *Media:* Pastel, Oil. *Dealer:* Portnoy Gallery Carmel CA; Windward Gallery NY; Geary Gallery, New York; Mufalli Gallery, Naples, Fla. *Mailing Add:* 1349 Lexington Ave Apt 8B New York NY 10128

PIOTROWSKI, KIMBERLY E
PAINTER
b Buffalo, NY, Aug 27, 65. *Study:* State Univ NY, Buffalo, 83-84; Art Inst Chicago, BFA, 87. *Exhib:* Abstract: Chicago 1993, Klein Art Works, Ill, 93; Chicago Abstract Painters, Evanston Arts Ctr, 95; Wanderlust, Arts Coun Chicago, 95; Milk and Muscle, Design Arts Coun, Santa Barbara, Calif, 95; Take a Holiday, Prarie State Col, Chicago, 96; The Leaf, the Blossom or the Bolt?, Hyde Park Arts Ctr, Chicago, 97; Collaborations, Printworks, Chicago, 98; Traces, Ukranian Nat Mus & Libr, Chicago, 98; Sextabos, Hyde Park Art Ctr, Chicago, Ill, 99; one-woman show, Fassbender Gallery, Chicago, Ill, 2000-. *Pos:* Dir, Dart Gallery, Chicago, 91-93; gallery mgr, Adams Fine Arts, Chicago, 93-95; exec dir, McLean Co Arts Ctr, Bloomington, Ill, 97-98. *Awards:* Visual Arts Grant, Elizabeth Found Arts, New York, 98. *Mem:* Nat Mus Women Arts, Washington, DC; Chicago Artists Coalition; Art Inst Chicago. *Media:* Oil, Acrylic. *Dealer:* Fassbender Gallery 309 W Superior St Chicago IL 60610; Stefan Stux Gallery, 529 W 20th St 9th Fl, NYC, 10011

PIPER, ADRIAN MARGARET SMITH
CONCEPTUAL ARTIST, WRITER
b New York, Sept 20, 48. *Study:* Sch Visual Arts, AA (fine art), 69; City Col New York, BA(philos), 74; Harvard Univ, Cambridge, Mass, MA(philos), 77 & PhD(philos), 81. *Hon Degrees:* Calif Inst Arts, Valencia, 1992; Mass Col Art, DA. *Work:* Art Inst Chicago; Baltimore Mus Art; Brooklyn Mus; Metrop Mus Art; High Mus Art, Atlanta; Denver Art Mus; Kunstverein München; Mus Mod Art, NY; Mus Contemp Art, Chicago; Whitney Mus Am Art; and others. *Exhib:* 557,087, Seattle Art Mus (traveling), 69; Information, Mus Mod Art, NY, 70; Paris Biennale, Mus Art Mod, Paris, 71 & 77; one-woman shows, Wadsworth Atheneum, 80 & Whitney Mus Am Art, 90; Commitment to Print, Mus Mod Art, NY, 88; Signs, Art Gallery Ont, Toronto, 88; L'Art Conceptuel: Une Perspective, Mus Art Mod, Paris, 90; The Art of Advocacy, Aldrich Mus Contemp Art, Ridgefield, Conn; Visions/Revisions, Denver Art Mus, 91; What it's Like, What it is, No 3, Dislocations, Mus Mod Art, NY, 91; Open Mind: The LeWitt Collection, Wadsworth Atheneum, Hartford, 91; The Theater of Black Refusal: Black Art & Mainstream Criticism, Univ Calif Fine Arts Gallery, Irvine, 93; L'Hiver de l'Amour, Mus Art Mod, Paris, 94; Thirty Years, Aldridge Mus Contemp Art, Ridgefield, Conn, 94; Mappings, Mus Mod Art, NY, 94; Black Male: Representations of Masculinity in Contemp Am Art, Whitney Mus Am Art, 95, Options 2: Selections from the Modern & Contemp Permanent Collection, Denver Art Mus, 95; It's Not a Picture, Galleria Emi Fontana, Milan, 95; Cornered, Paula Cooper Gallery, NY, 95; Art with Conscience, Newark Art Mus, NJ, 96; Now Here, La Mus Mod Art, Humlebaek, Denmark, 96; Reconsidering the Object of Art: 1965-1975, Mus Contemp Art, Los Angeles, 96; Thinking Print: Books to Billboards 1980-95, Mus Mod Art, NY, 96; Hidden in Plain Sight: Illusion in Art from Jasper Johns to Virtual Reality, Los Angeles Co Mus Art, 97; Devant l'histoire, Centre Georges Pompidou, Paris, 97; retrospective, Lamoca, 2000, New Mus, NY, 2000-2001; The Color Wheel Series, Paula Cooper Gallery, 2000; solo shows, New Mus, 2000-2001, Thomas Erben Gallery, 2000-2001 & Lamoca,; Adrian Piper: A Retrospective, 99-2001: Adrian Piper Seit 1965, General Found, 2002-2003; Adrian Piper Over the Edge, Emi Fontana Gallery, Milan, 2002. *Teaching:* Prof Philos, Wellesley Col, Mass, Harvard Univ, Stanford Univ, Univ Mich, Georgetown & Univ Calif, San Diego. *Awards:* Visual Artists' Fel, Nat Endowment Arts, 79 & 82, Artists Forums Grant, 87; Gugenheim Meml Found Fel, 89; Skowhegan Medal, 95. *Bibliog:* David Joselit (auth), Object lessons, Art in Am 84, 2/96; Gary Kornblau (auth), 1965-75: Reconsidering the object of art, Art Issues, 2/96; Museum of Contemporary Art at the temporary contemporary, The Print Collector's Newsletter, 2/96. *Media:* Installation, Video; Photo Text. *Publ:* Auth, Decide Who You Are, Reframings: New American Feminist Photographers, Temple Univ Press, Philadelphia, 95; Mortal Remains, Intermedia Arts, Minn, 96; Withdrawal clarified, Art in Am 84, 3/96; Dickinson's charm, NY Review Bks XLIII, 10/3/96; Out of Order, Out of Sight, MIT Press, 96. *Dealer:* Paula Cooper Gallery 534 W 21st St New York NY 10011; Robert Del Principe. *Mailing Add:* Adrian Piper Research Archive Postfach 54 02 04 Berlin 02135 D-10042 Germany

PIPKIN, MARY MARGARET
ARTIST
b San Angelo, Tex, Mar 17, 51. *Study:* Univ Tex, BA, MA; student, Brooklyn Mus Art Sch, 73-74. *Work:* One-woman shows incl Zigler Mus, Jennings, La, 2002, Mus Southwest, Midland, Tex, 2003, San Angelo Mus Fine Art, Tex, 2004, Sci Mus WVa, Roanoke, 2004, Mus Arts & Sci, Daytona Beach, Fla, 2004, Elliot Mus, Stuart, Fla, 2005. *Exhib:* One-woman shows, Addison/Ripley Gallery, Wash, Jennings, La, 2002, Louisburg Col, NC, 2003, Art Station, Stone Mountain, Ga, 2003, Anderson Art Ctr, Ind, 2003, US Botanic Garden, Wash, 2003, Olbrich Botanical Gardens, Madison, Wis, 2004, Dunedin Fine Arts Ctr, Fla, 2005, Bob Rauschenberg Gallery, Edison Col, Fort Meyers, Fla, 2005

PIRKL, JAMES JOSEPH
EDUCATOR, DESIGNER, PAINTER
b Nyack, NY, Dec 27, 30. *Study:* Pratt Inst, cert adv design, 51 & BID, 58; Wayne State Univ; Syracuse Univ, 81. *Hon Degrees:* Univ Monterrey, Hon diploma, Mexico, 81. *Exhib:* Syracuse Univ Fac Show, 65-91; The Future Is In Our Hands, Domus Acad, Tokyo, 96. *Pos:* Jr designer, General Motors Design staff, 58-59, designer, 59-60, sr designer, 61-64 & asst chief designer, 64-65; principal, James Joseph Pirkl/Transgenerational Design, NMex, 93-; adv, Universal Kitchen proj, RI Sch Design, 97-98; exec dir, Transgenerational Design Matters, Albuquerque, NMex, 2005-. *Teaching:* Instr, Ctr for Creative Studies, Detroit, Mich, 63-65; asst prof indust design, dept of design, Syracuse Univ, 65-68, assoc prof, 69-73, prof, 74-92, prof in charge, Indust Design Prog, 79-85, chmn, dept of design, 85-92, emer prof, 93-. *Awards:* Fel, Indust Designers Soc Am, 85; Sr Res Fel, ALL Univ Gerontology Ctr, Syracuse Univ, 90; Gold Indust Design Excellence Award, Indust Designers Soc Am & Bus Week Mag, 94; Educ award, Indust Designers Soc Am, 2001. *Bibliog:* Designing for the Elderly, Int Coun Soc Indust Design (interview), Nordmore LOKALTV, Kristionsund, Norway, 10/89; Talk of the Nation (invited guest), Nat Pub Radio, 98; This Bold House (article), AARP The Magazine, 9-10/2003. *Mem:* Indust Designers Soc Am (chmn cent NY chap, 77-79, vpres, mid-east region, 80-82, dir, 86-88, life); Human Factors Soc (life); Nat Asn of Sch of Art & Design; Author's Guild. *Media:* Oil, Pen and Ink, Computer Graphics. *Res:* Transgenerational Design: Making products & environments compatable with those physical & sensory impairments associated with human aging, which limit independence, & accomodate the widest range of ages & abilities. *Interests:* Promoting the concept of

transgenerational design through education, writing & consulting. *Publ:* Coauth, Guidelines and Strategies for Designing Transgenerational Products, Copley, 88; many articles in mag, 88-97; Transgenerational Design: Products for an Aging Population, John Wiley & Sons, 94. *Mailing Add:* 2007 Quail Run Drive NE Albuquerque NM 87122

PISANI, JOSEPH
MURALIST, PAINTER
b New Rochelle, NY, Oct l, 38. *Study:* San Francisco Art Inst; Calif Col Arts & Crafts, with George Post, Richard Diebenkorn, Nathan Oliveira & Ralph Borge, BFA. *Work:* Dept of Defense & Hq Dept of Army, The Pentagon, Arlington, Va; The White House, Washington, DC; US Army Collection; US Air Force Collection; Royal Embassy of Saudi Arabia; pvt collection of Prince Bandar Al Saud; plus others. *Comn:* Mondavi Tomb, Caesar Mondavi Family, St Helina, Calif, 62; General Marshall Mem Corridor, comn by Secy of the Army, Pentagon, 75; Army Bicentennial Murals, comn by Secy of Defense, 75-76; Gen Pershing mural, comn by Gen Yerks, Ft Myer, Va, 77-78; Gen MacArthur Mem, 81, Anzus Mem Corridor, 82, Military Womens Corridor, 83, Eisenhower Corridor, 85, Military Intelligence Corridor, 86 & Gen Mark Clark Display, 86, comn by Secy of Defense Weinberger, Pentagon, 90, Portrait Comm King Fahd, Saudi Arabia. *Exhib:* Army Wide Art Exhib, Pentagon, 63, 65; Corcoran Washington Area Show, 69; Artist Equity Group Shows, Washington, DC, 72 & 73; Va Beach Art Shows, 73 & 75. *Pos:* Chief graphic arts, Chief of Staff (Personnel), Pentagon, 67-73; graphic designer, Dept of Defense, 73-75; art dir, US Army Hq, 75-88; dir, Art Gallery 101-Ltd. *Awards:* Outstanding Achievement in Art, Bank of Am, 61; Scholar to Study Fine Arts, Scholastic Mag, 62; First Prize for Painting, Art League Va, 70; and many other awards. *Bibliog:* Article, Art Voices/South, 5-6/78. *Mem:* Portrait Soc Am. *Media:* Mixed; Watercolor. *Interests:* photography, painting. *Publ:* Illusr, Yorktown 1781-1981 Poster, 81; 1980 & 1981 Army Weapon Systems Covers; The Many Faces of Christ, Washington Post. *Dealer:* Art Gallery 101 10640 Main St Fairfax VA 22030. *Mailing Add:* 2658 Quincy Adams Dr Herndon VA 22071

PISANO, RONALD GEORGE
HISTORIAN, CONSULTANT
b New York, NY, Dec 19, 48. *Study:* Adelphi Univ, Garden City, NY, BA; Univ Del. *Collection Arranged:* An American Place (auth, catalog), 81, The Long Island Landscape, 1865-1914: The Halycon Years (auth, catalog), 81 & The Long Island Landscape, 1914-1946: The Transitional Years (auth, catalog), 82, Parrish Art Mus, Southampton, NY; American Paintings from the Parrish Museum, (auth, catalog), Coe-Kerr Gallery, New York, 82; A Leading Spirit in American Art: William Merritt Chase, 1849-1916, Henry Art Gallery & Metrop Mus Art (auth, book), 83-84; Heckscher Mus, 87; The Art Students League Traveling Exhib: Selections from the Permanent Collection (auth, catalog), Nassau Co Mus of Fine Arts, 88; Centenial Celebration Nat Asn Women Artists (auth cat); Henry & Edith Mitchill Prellwitz & the Peconic Art Colony, Mus at Stony Brook, 96. *Pos:* Dir exhib, Baruch Col, New York, 74-76; consult cur of Am art, Heckscher Mus, Huntington, NY, 75-77; guest cur, Mus of Stony Brook, NY, 77, 78, 85 & 90; assoc cur, Parrish Art Mus, Southampton, NY, 77-79, dir, 79-81, pvt art consult, 81-. *Awards:* A Conger Goodyear Award, Adelphi Univ, 71; Stebbins Family Res Grant, Heckscher Mus, 72-73; Distinguished Art Historian Award, Grand Cent Art Gallery, 79. *Mem:* Col Art Asn. *Res:* Late 19th and early 20th century American art; William Merritt Chase; artists of Long Island. *Publ:* Auth, William Merritt Chase, Watson Guptill, 79; Long Island Landscape Painting, 1820-1920, Little Brown, 85; Idle Hours: Americans at Leisure, 1865-1914, Little Brown, 89; Long Island Landscape Painting in the 20th Century, Little Brown, 90; Summer Afternoons: Landscape Painting: Landscape Paintings of William Merritt Chase, Little, Brown & Co, 93; auth, The Tile Club and the Aesthetic Movement in America (1877-1887), Abrams, 99. *Mailing Add:* 375 Riverside Dr New York NY 10025

PISKOTI, JAMES
PRINTMAKER, PAINTER
b Logan, WVa, July 5, 44. *Study:* Univ Mich, Ann Arbor, BS(design), 67; Yale Univ, MFA, 69. *Work:* Detroit Inst Arts; Bradley Univ; City of Stockton, Calif; Minot State Col; Calif State Univ, Stanislaus. *Exhib:* Rutgers Nat 96 Works on Paper, Rutgers Univ Campus, Camden, NJ, 96; Pacific Prints - 8th Biennial Print Competition & Exhib, Pac Art League, Palo Alto, 96; Stockton Nat Print & Drawing Exhib, Haggin Mus, 96; 70th Crocker-Kingsley Juried Exhib, Crocker Mus, Sacramento, 96, 72nd Exhib, 2000; Int Print Triennial 97 Cracow, Poland & other countries, 97. *Teaching:* Lab asst Intaglio Printmaking Studio, Univ Mich, 65-67; teaching asst printmaking, Yale Univ, 68-69; vis lectr printmaking, Southern Conn State Col, spring 69; prof fine art, Calif State Univ Stanislaus, Turlick, 69-. *Awards:* Award of Excellence, Calif State Fair, 1987, Sacramento, 87; Cash Merit Award, Univ Mus, Miss, 1/90-3/90; Pac Art League Serigraphy Award & Timothy Duran Purchase Award, Pac Art League, Palo Alto, Calif, 5/90-6/90. *Bibliog:* Peter Fierz (auth), Young American Painter, Der Kunst, 69; Gabor Peterdi (auth), Four prints, Eye-Mag of Yale Arts Asn, 69; Whos Who Am, 86-. *Mem:* Calif Soc Printmakers; Los Angeles Printmaking Soc. *Media:* Acrylics; Color Intaglio. *Dealer:* John Natsoulas Gallery Davis CA. *Mailing Add:* 11 River Garden Ct Sacramento CA 95831

PITCHER, JOHN CHARLES
PAINTER
b Kalamazoo, Mich, Aug 6, 49. *Study:* Self taught. *Work:* Anchorage Mus Hist & Art, Alaska; Nat Wildlife Fedn, Washington, DC; Univ Alaska Mus; Leigh Yawkey Woodson Art Mus, Wausau, Wis; Juneau Empire, Alaska. *Exhib:* British Mus Nat Hist, London, 82; Alaska's Artists in Washington, DC, Capitol Rotunda Rm, 83; Alaska State Mus, 84-85; Beijing Natural Hist Mus, China, 86; Original Art Showcase, Can, 89-94; Southeastern Wildlife Expo, Charleston, SC, 94. *Teaching:* Leads workshops & gives slide/lectures on drawing & painting wildlife. *Awards:* First Place, Nat Exhib Wildlife Art, Anchorage Audubon Soc, 83; one of the featured artists, First Ann Pac Rim Wildlife Art Show, 88, 91-92; Keynote speaker, workshop presenter Alaska Loon Festival, Anchorage, 90. *Bibliog:* Elaine Rhode (auth), John Pitcher: In perspective with nature, Alaska J, autumn 79; Sandy Preston (auth), John Pitcher, perfect squares, Midwest Art (Now US Art), 88; Patricia Black Bailey (auth), John C Pitcher, Southwest Art, 3/92. *Mem:* Soc Animal Artists Inc. *Media:* Watercolor; Oil, Acrylic. *Publ:* Illusr, A Guide to the Birds of Alaska, Alaska NW Publ Co, 80; contribr-illusr, bird sect rev, World Bk Encycl, 81; illusr, Field Guide Birds of NAm, Nat Geographic Soc, 83; Birds of the Seward Peninsula, Alaska, brina Kessel, Univ Alaska Press, 89. *Mailing Add:* RR 1 Box 138 Dorset VT 05251

PITTMAN, LARI
PAINTER
b Los Angeles, Calif, 52. *Study:* Univ Calif, Los Angeles, 70-73; Calif Inst Arts, Valencia, BFA, 74, MFA, 76. *Work:* Carnegie Inst Art, Pittsburgh, Pa; Corcoran Mus Art, Washington, DC; Eli Broad Family Found, Los Angeles Co Mus Art, Mus of Contemp Art, Los Angeles, Calif; Phoenix Mus Art, Ariz; San Francisco Mus Mod Art, Calif; Whitney Mus Am Art, NY; Mus of Contemp Art, Monterrey, Mex; Newport Harbor Art Mus, Newport Beach, Calif; Weatherspoon Art Gallery, Univ of NC. *Exhib:* Biennial Exhib, Whitney Mus Am Art, NY, 87, 93 & 95; solo exhibs, Jablonka Gallery, Cologne, Ger, 93, Paintings & Works on Paper 1989-1993, Mandeville Gallery, Univ Calif, San Diego, 93 Rosamund Felson Gallery, Los Angeles, Calif, 93, Tex Gallery, Houston, 94, Jay Gorney Mod Art, NY, 94, Studio Guenzani, Milan, Italy, 95, Los Angeles Co Mus Art, 96, Greengrassi, London, Eng, 96, Centre d'Art Contemporain, Geneva, Switz, 99, ICA, London, Eng, 99, Spacex Gallery, Exeter, Eng, 98, Regen Projects, Los Angeles, 98, 2001, Barbara Gladstone Gallery, NY, 99, 2002, Studio Guenzani, Milan, Italy, 2000; 42nd Biennial Exhib Contemp Am Painting & Animal Farm, 94, James Corcoran Gallery, Santa Monica, Calif; Love in the Ruins, Long Beach Mus Art, Calif, 94; The Arabesque, PPOW Gallery, NY, 94; In Retrospect: Paintings of the 80's, Rosamund Felsen Gallery, Los Angeles, Calif, 94; 1995 Whitney Biennial Exhib (with catalog), Whitney Mus Am Art, NY, 95 & Czech Mus Mod Art, Czech Repub, 95; 1997 Whitney Biennial Exhib, Whitney Mus Am Art, NY, 97; Elusive Paradise: Los Angeles Art from the Permanent Collection, Mus Contemp Art, Los Angeles, 97-99; LA Current: Looking at the Light: 3 Generations of Los Angeles Artists, Univ Calif Los Angeles, Armond Hammer Mus Art & Cult Ctr, 98; and many others; The Rowan Collection: Passion and Patronage, Mills Col Art Mus, Oakland, Calif, 99; Armand Hammer Mus, Los Angeles, 99; Secret Victorians: Contemp Artists and a 19th Century Vision, Bighton Mus, 99; Examining Pictures, Whitechapel Art Gallery, London, 99, Mus Contemp Art, Chicago, 99; The Am Century: Art and Cult, 1900-2000, Whitney Mus Am Art, 99; Departures: 11 Artists at the Getty, The J Paul Getty Mus, Los Angeles, 2000; Secret Victorians, The Fabric Workshop and Mus, Philadelphia, Pa, 2001. *Pos:* Bd dir, Santa Monica Mus Art, 93. *Teaching:* Prof fine arts, Univ Calif, Los Angeles, 93-. *Awards:* Art Matters Grant, 86; Fel, Nat Endowment Arts, 87, 89 & 93; Fel, Calif Arts Coun, 90; Flindridge Found Awards for Visual Artists, 99; Skowhegan Medal for Painting, 2002. *Bibliog:* Christopher Knight (auth), A Suggestion of Cultural Edginess, Los Angeles Times, 3/10/94; Stuart Servetar (auth), True Lies, False Falseness & Defensive Vulnerability, New York Press, 10/19/94; Amelia Jones (auth), Lari Pittman's Queer Feminism, Art & Text, Sydney, Australia, 12/94; and many others; Donald Britton (auth), cover, Art Issues, 5/90. *Mem:* Los Angeles Contemp Exhibs (bd dir, 86-91). *Mailing Add:* c/o Barbara Gladstone Gallery 515 W 24th St New York NY 10011

PITTORE , CARLO
PAINTER, MURALIST
b Long Island, NY, May 14, 43. *Study:* Tufts Col, BA, 66; Acad di Belle Arti, Rome, 71-73; Brooklyn Mus Art Sch, 78. *Hon Degrees:* Maine Col Art, BFA Hon, 2000. *Work:* Mus Mod Art Libr, NY; Sackner Archive, Miami, Fla; J Paul Getty Inst Art Hist & Humanities, Los Angeles, Calif; Sohm Arch; Sonia Henie Mus, Carlo Pittore Archive Int Mail Art, Oslo. *Comn:* Mural, Fedn of Handicapped, NY; portraits, K Bradford, D Stover & W Dana. *Exhib:* No Se No, NY, 85; NAME Gallery, Chicago, 86; Portland Mus Biennial, 2003; Fitzpatrick Gallery, Portland, Maine, 94, 96, 99; Avcocisco Gallery, Portland, 2001. *Collection Arranged:* Bern Porter Retrospective, Franklin Furnace & travelling, 79. *Pos:* Ed, Me Mag, 80-86; Cult Coun Fdn CETA Artists Proj, NY. *Teaching:* Instr, Acad Carlo Pittore, Bowdoinham, Maine; Univ Maine, Augusta. *Awards:* Max Beckmann Scholar, 77 & 78; Maine Col of Art Award, 83. *Bibliog:* Articles, Art News, 12/81 & New Art Examiner 4/85. *Mem:* Union Maine Visual Artists (pres). *Media:* Oil, Pencil. *Publ:* Ed, Colleagues, 80 & illusr, The Adventures of Carlo Pittore, 80, Pittore Euforico; illusr, Boxers, 82 & The Man With an Egg, 83, Bern Porter; Keith Haring Journals, Viking Penguin NY, 96

PITTS, RICHARD G
PAINTER, PRINTMAKER
b Ft Monmouth, NJ, Oct 15, 40. *Study:* Newark Sch Fine Arts, 61; Pratt Inst, BFA, 68; New York Studio Sch, Paris, 72. *Work:* Anot Mus Art, Elmira, NY; General Electric Co, NY; Port Authority of New York; Continental Insurance Co, New Brunswick, NJ; Univ Va Mus, Charlottesville, Va; Univ SC; Askville Art Mus; Coos Art Mus; Reading Public Mus. *Comn:* Mural, Chelsea Health & Fitness, 91-92. *Exhib:* Solo exhib, David Findlay Jr, 83 & 85, Randolf Manchon, Ashland, Va, 84, Rutherin Gallery, Columbus, Ohio, 85, Deutche Bank Gallery NY, 93 & Caesarea Gallery, Boca Raton, Fla, 94; Contemp Images, Mendik Gallery, NY, 86; First Street Gallery Invitational, 86; Shirley Goodman Resource Ctr, FIT Galleries, 87; Cedar Art Ctr, Corning, NY, 92; Mus at FIT, NY, 99; and others. *Pos:* Chmn, Artist Bd, Artist Choice Mus, currently. *Teaching:* Assoc prof painting, Kansas City Art Inst, 70-73; prof fine arts, Fashion Inst Technol, 73-. *Bibliog:* Judd Tully (auth), Richard Pitts One Man Show, Arts Mag,

2/85; Jacqueline Hall (auth), Landscapes, Columbus Dispatch, 5/85; Animal Life at One Penn Plaza, Art World, 11/87; David Matlock (auth), Nature and Art, Art World, 4/88; Abigail Wender (auth), Paintings by Richard Pitts, Diversion Mag, 8/88. *Media:* Oil on Canvas. *Dealer:* David Findlay Jr Inc 41 E 57 St New York NY 10022; Carola Van der Houten 390 West End New York NY 10024. *Mailing Add:* 233 W 18th St New York NY 10011-4500

PITTS, SHARON
PAINTER
b Chicago, IL, Dec 4, 47. *Study:* Univ Ill, BA, 1970; The Barnes Found, 1976-1978; Mass Col of Art, studied under Patricia Tobacco Forrester, 2001. *Work:* Widener Univ Mus of Art, Chester, Pa; Colgate Palmolive Corp, NYC; Pfizer Inc, Morris Plains, NJ; Sankyo Pharma Inc, Parsippany, NJ; Senior Care & Activities Center, Montclair, NJ. *Comn:* CBS Inc, NY, 1983. *Exhib:* Flora, Univ City Arts League, Philadelphia, Pa, 1980; Montclair Art Colony, Past & Present, Montclair Art Mus, Montclair, NJ, 1997; Allied Artists Mems Exhib, Butler Inst Am Art, Youngstown, Ohio, 2001; Connections, Kunstlerbund, Graz, Austria, 2004; Butler 69th Midyear, Butler Inst Am Art, Youngstown, Ohio; Allied Artists Am 93rd Ann Exhib, Nat Arts Club, NYC, 2006; Visions in Watercolor, Dupre Gallery, Montclair, NJ, 2006. *Pos:* Pres, PS Art Tours, Montclair, NJ, 2005-; Watercolor workshops, Les Pradailles, France & Gold Coast Watercolor Soc, Fort Lauderdale, Fla, 2006. *Teaching:* Instr, watercolor, Adult Sch of Montclair, NJ, 1995-2005; Instr, Montclair Art Mus, 1999-. *Awards:* 1st Prize Watercolor, The Art Show, Town of Montclair, 1988; 1st Prize Watercolor, Art in the Park, Montclair Co-Op Sch, 1990; Best in Show, 5th Ann Juried Show, Louisa Melrose Gallery, 2004. *Bibliog:* Sheryl Weinstein (auth), Watercolorist Showcases Blooming Creations, Star Ledger, 1997; William Zimmer (auth), Three Rare Invitations to Inner Sanctum, NY Times, 1997; Teri Murphy (auth), Louisa Melrose Gallery Presents Art Blooms, Nouveau, 2005. *Mem:* Women Artists of Montclair (publicity), 1992-2003; Studio Montclair Inc (publicity), 1995-2005; Artists Fel (exhib chair), 1997-; Allied Artists of Am (dir watercolor), 97-. *Media:* Watercolor, Acrylics, oils. *Dealer:* Essex Fine Arts Gallery Diane Israel 13 S Fullerton Montclair NJ 07042. *Mailing Add:* 184 Christopher St Montclair NJ 07042

PITTS, TERENCE RANDOLPH
DIRECTOR, CURATOR
b St Louis, Mo, Feb 5, 50. *Study:* Univ Ill, Champagne-Urbana, BA (lit), 72, MA (libr sci), 74; Univ Ariz, MA (art history), 87. *Collection Arranged:* Contemporary Photography in Mexico, 78; Edward Weston: Color Photography, 86; One Hundred Years of Photography in the American West, 87; Photography in the American Grain, 88; 4 Spanish Photographers, 88; Reframing America (auth, catalog), 96; Crafting Light: The Photographs of Laura Volkerding, 98; Media Amnesia: Robert Heinecken 1966-2000, Cloister St Trophime, Les Rencontres Internationales de la Photographie, Aries, France, 2000. *Pos:* Cur, Ctr for Creative Photog, Tucson, Ariz, 78-89, dir, 89-2000; exec dir, Cedar Rapids Mus Art, Iowa, 2000-. *Awards:* Mus Fel, Nat Endowment for Arts; US-Spanish Joint Com for Cult and Educ Coop Grant, 85; Univ of Ariz Research Sabbatical, Spring 92. *Mem:* Am Asn of Mus. *Publ:* Auth, 100 Years of Photography in the American West, Phoenix Art Mus, 87; auth, Edward Weston: Color Photography, Ctr for Creative Photog, 86; auth, Photography in the American Grain, Ctr for Creative Photog, 88; Auth, Public places/private spaces: American photography 1960-70, decade by decade, Little Brown, 89; auth, 4 Spanish Photographers, Ctr for Creative Photog, 88; auth, Reframing America: Points of Entry, Ctr for Creative Photog and Univ of NM, 95; Edward Weston, Cologne: Taschen, 99. *Mailing Add:* Cedar Rapids Mus of Art 410 Third Ave SE Cedar Rapids IA 52401

PITYNSKI, ANDRZEJ P
SCULPTOR
b Ulanow, Poland, Mar 15, 47; US citizen. *Study:* Acad Fine Arts in Cracow, Poland, MFA(sculpture), 74; Art Students League, New York, 75. *Work:* Portrait bust M Curie (bronze on granite, 7'), Bayonne, NJ; Sculpture Partisans (aluminum, 3'), Polish Am Mus, Port Washington, NY. *Comn:* Ignacy Paderewski, 12' Cracow, Poland 73; Avenger (bronze on granite, 36'), Polish-Am Veterans US, Doylestown, PA, 87; Katyn-1940 (bronze on granite, 38'), Katyn Mem Fund, Comt Jersey City, 91; Pope John Paul II (bronze on granite, 12'), Polish Am Cong, NY, 91; Blue Army Monument (bronze on granite, 48), Polish Am Veterans, Warsaw, 98. *Exhib:* Allied Artists Am, Nat Art Club, NY, 94; Nat Sculpture Soc, Am Tower, NY, 95; retrospective, Polish Army Mus, Warsaw, Poland, 95 & 96; Contemp Artist's Guild, Broom Street Gallery, Soho, NY, 96; Audubon Artists, Fed Hall, NY, 96; and others. *Pos:* Asst to sculptor Alexander Ettl, Sculpture House, NY 75-79; supv modeling, enlarging, resins & moldmakings, Johnson Atelier Tech Inst Sculpture, Mercerville, NJ 79-. *Teaching:* Instr Sculpture, Rider Univ, Lawerenceville, NJ, 92. *Awards:* Silver Medal Honor, 72nd Ann Exhib, Allied Artists Am, NY, 85; Allied Artist's Am Mem & Asn Award, 81st Ann Exhib, NY, 94; Gold Medal Honor, 54th Ann Exhib, Audubon Artist's Soc, NY, 96, Silver Medal, 55th Ann Exhib, 97 & 56th Ann Exhib, 98. *Bibliog:* Donald M Reynolds (auth), Masters of American Sculpture, Abbeville Press, 94; Mirek Kin (producer), Avenger (20 min film), Polish, TV, 95; Irena Grzesiuk-Olszewska (auth), Polish Monuments from 1945-1995, Warsaw, Poland, 95. *Mem:* Contemp Artists Guild, NY; Audubon Artists, NY; Allied Artists Am, NY; fel mem Nat Sculpture Soc, NY; Am Medallic Sculpture Asn, NY. *Media:* Meral Cast-Bronze, Aluminum. *Mailing Add:* 90 Dupont St Brooklyn NY 11222

PIWINSKI, CARL B
ARTIST
b Lexington, Ky, Mar 25, 58. *Study:* Univ Ky, BA (art studio), 1992. *Work:* Smithsonian, Wash DC, Md. *Exhib:* Carl Piwinski and Jim Shambho Drawing and Sculpture, Lexington Arts and Cult Coun, Lexington, Ky, 1993. *Interests:* New media illustration, video, performance, environ, artist book, functional/nonfunctional art neon craft, art furniture in installation. *Publ:* Contempory Folkart: A Collectors Guide, Abbeville, 1999. *Mailing Add:* 3272 Saxon Dr Lexington KY 40503-3429

PIZZAT, JOSEPH
EDUCATOR, COLLAGE ARTIST
Study: Kalamazoo Col, Mich, BA, 49, MA, 50; Columbia Univ Teachers Col, New York, EdD, 55; vis scholar, Pa State Univ, 59 Pratt Inst, New York, 61. *Comn:* Stations of the Cross, Mercyhurst Col, Erie, Pa, 94. *Exhib:* One-man shows, Tapings 1975, Ivy Sch Prof Art, Pittsburgh, PA, 76, Spirituality & Religionty in Am, Albuquerque, 1997, Words-Image-Faith, Srehcen Gallery, Erie, Pa, 1997, Visions Gallery, Alrich, NY, 1998, Totally Digital, Invitational, Colo, 1999, Gicrube!, Johnson-Homrick House Mus, Ohio, 2002; Nat Christian Fine arts Exhib, San Juan Col, Farmington, NMex, 97, 98 & 99; Mary & The Arts (traveling exhib) Mariological Soc Am, Ohio, 98-99; Works of Faith, Portland, Oreg, 99, 2000, 2001, 2002; Appalachian Corridors Exhib, Charleston WVa, 2003. *Collection Arranged:* Pizzat Art Loan Collection, Northwest Renna Region, 1995-. *Teaching:* Prof art & chmn art prog, SW Minn State Col, Marshall, 67-71; prof art, Mercyhurst Col, Erie, Pa, 71-, chmn, creative arts div, 71-78, prof emeritus, 99-. *Awards:* Outstanding Educator Am Award, Southwest Minneapolis, 70 & Mercyhurst Coll, 75; Outstanding Art Educator Award, Pa Art Educ Asn, 81. *Mem:* US Prof Tennis Asn; Pa Art Educ Asn; Nat Art Educ Asn; Northwest Renna Artists Asn. *Media:* Pressure Sensitive, Self-Adhesives. *Res:* Pressure sensitive art, a visual-tactile art system using self-adhesive & pressure sensitive materials as primary art media. *Interests:* playing professional tennis; teaching. *Publ:* I'm a right brained person, why me God?, Nat Art Educ Asn Art Educ J, 79; The Book, A Learning Experience, 86 what!, 6/90, Kites: An art flight of fantasy, 10/91, Presenting Pres/sent Art, 10/92, Arts & Activities; What's Up? Art's Up-that's what!, 6/90, Kites: An art flight of fantasy, 10/91, Presenting Pres/sent Art, 10/92, Art & Activities; The Spiritual Dimensions in Child Development, The Pa Art Educ, fall 98; An Open Letter to Pope John Paul, Ministry & Literacy, 11/2000. *Mailing Add:* 2046 Charleston Ave Erie PA 16509-1765

PIZZUTI, RONALD A
COLLECTOR
Study: Kent State Univ, BS, 62. *Pos:* Chmn, Chief Exec Officer, Pizzuti Cos, Columbus, Ohio, 76-; fac comn, Ohio Arts & Sports, currently; bd trustees, Kenyon Col, currently; bd dir, Kent State Found, currently; chair bd trustees, Kent State Univ. *Awards:* recipient Shining Stars of Seminole Co, Lifetime Achievement award, 2002; Named one of Top 200 Collectors, ARTnews mag, 2003-06. *Mem:* Columbus C of C (exec comt, currently). *Collection:* Modern & contemporary art

PLACE, BRADLEY EUGENE
EDUCATOR, GRAPHIC ARTIST
b Rule, Tex, Nov 4, 20. *Study:* Tex A&M Univ, 38-40; NTex Univ, with Carlos Merida & Ivan Johnson, BS, 42. *Pos:* Mem visual arts adv panel, Okla Arts & Humanities Coun, 72-; mem selection comt, Art for Pub Places, Tulsa, 75-. *Teaching:* From asst prof to prof lettering & typography, Univ Tulsa, 47-86, chmn dept art, 64-86, emer prof art, 86. *Awards:* Brad Trust Scholar, 73. *Bibliog:* Jenk Jones, Jr (auth), Honor roll for May, Tulsa Tribune, 71; Connie Cronley (auth), Profile of a teacher of artists, Tulsa, 6/14/73; Myrna Smart (auth), Dilemma of penal reform, Arts & Humanities Coun Tulsa & KTEW-TV, 5/74. *Mem:* Tulsa Advert Fedn; Tulsa Art Dir Club (exec bd, 70-75, 77 & 81-, pres, 74-75); Tulsa Arts & Humanities (mem bd, Chmn Mayor's Arts Comn, 77). *Mailing Add:* 2156 S Fulton Pl Tulsa OK 74114 2250

PLAGENS, PETER
PAINTER, CRITIC
b Dayton, Ohio, Mar 1, 41. *Study:* Univ Southern Calif, BFA, 62; Syracuse Univ, MFA, 64. *Work:* Baltimore Mus Art; Albright-Knox Gallery, Buffalo, NY; Hirshhorn Mus, Washington, DC; Santa Fe Mus Art, NMex; Tawaraya, Kyoto; Denver Art Mus, Colo. *Exhib:* 24 Young Los Angeles Artists, Los Angeles Co Mus Art, 71; Continuing Abstraction, Whitney Mus Downtown, NY, 74; Los Angeles Selections from the Art Lending Service, Mus Mod Art, NY, 76; 40th Ann Mid-Yr Show, Butler Inst Am Art, 76; Painting & Sculpture in Calif: The Modern Era, Nat Collection Fine Arts, Smithsonian Inst, Washington, DC, 77; Works on Paper, Inst Contemp Art, Va Mus Fine Arts, Richmond, 80; solo exhibs, Univ Art Mus, Calif State Univ, Long Beach, 85, Jan Cicero Gallery, Chicago, Ill, 85 & 98, Nancy Hoffman Gallery, NY, 87, 90, 92, 96 & 97, Jan Baum Gallery, Los Angeles, 88, Akron Art Mus, Ohio, 96, Jan Cicero Gallery, Chicago, 98, Nancy Hoffman Gallery, NYC, 99, 01, Las Vegas Art Mus, 00-01; Primarily Paint, Mus Contemp Art San Diego, La Jolla, Calif, 97; Nancy Hoffman: A Perspective on Art, Flanders Contemp Art, Minneapolis, Minn, 97; 25 Yrs, Nancy Hoffman Gallery, NY, 98; small scale LARGE SCALE, Nancy Hoffman Gallery, NY, 98; From Diptychs to Polyptychs, Nancy Hoffman Gallery, NY, 98; plus many others. *Pos:* Designer, Barth & Dreyfuss Inc, Los Angeles, 64-65; cur, Long Beach Mus Art, Calif, 65-66; ed comt, J Los Angeles Inst Contemp Art, 74-75; contrib ed, Artforum, 66-76; chmn bd dir, Los Angeles Inst Contemp Art, 77-79; art critic, Newsweek Mag, 89-. *Teaching:* Instr, Univ Tex, Austin, 66-69; assoc prof art, Calif State Univ, Northridge, 69-78, Univ Southern Calif, 78-80; chmn, dept art, Univ NC at Chapel Hill, 80-83, prof, 80-84; prof, Hofstra Univ, Hempstead, NY, 85-. *Awards:* John Simon Guggenheim Fel in Painting, 72-73; Nat Endowment Arts, Grant in Art Criticism, 73-74, Fel in Painting, 77-78; Sr Fel, Nat Arts Journalism Prog, Columbia Univ, 98. *Bibliog:* Holland Cotter (auth), Peter Plagens at Nancy Hoffman, Art in Am, 9/90; MA Greenstain (auth), Whitewash, Artweek, 2/6/92; Herne Pardee (auth), Peter Plagens, Artnews, Summer 92. *Publ:* Auth, Ecology of evil, 12/72, Peter and the pressure cooker, 6/74 & None dare call it BoHo, 9/75, Artforum; Sunshine Muse: Contemporary Art on the West Coast, Praeger Publ, 74; Moonlight Blues: An Artist's Art Criticism, UMI Research Press, 86. *Dealer:* Jan Cicero Gallery Chicago IL. *Mailing Add:* c/o Nancy Hoffman Gallery 429 W Broadway New York NY 10012

PLANKEY, ELLEN J
PAINTER
b Pittsfield, Mass. *Study:* Wm Schultz Schl of Art, Lenox, Mass - 1962-86; Eliot McMurrough Sch of Art study under Chas Reid, Robert E Wood, Haywood Veaf, Indialantic, Fla, 1964-66. *Hon Degrees:* Pastel Soc of Am, Master Pastellist. *Work:* Mint Mus Art, Charlotte, NC; Vero Beach Mus Art, Fla; City of Indialantic, Fla; Alabama Power Co, Birmingham; Peoples National Bank, Naples, Fla. *Exhib:* one man retrospective, Mint Mus Art, Charlotte, NC, 1978; one-man show, Fla Southern Col, Lakeland, 1979 & Brevard Art Ctr & Mus,. Melbourne, Fla, 1983; Rocky Mountain Nat, Foot Hills Art Ctr, Golden, Colo, 1994; Fla Watercolor Soc, Fla Art Mus, Sarasota, 1995. *Teaching:* instr art, Studio, Melbourne, Fla, 1968-80; instr art, workshops in Fla, 1980-1986. *Awards:* First Prize, Rocky Mountain Nat, Intermedia Exhib, 1994; Best of Show, Pastel Soc of Am, 1976; Best of Show, Fla Watercolor Soc, 1995. *Bibliog:* J. Phyllis Hattan (auth), Plankey: The Search for the Light, Arts & Expressions, July & Aug 1984; Carole Surface (auth), Artist Brushes Love & Light, Orlando Sentinel, 7/1987; Bebe Raugel (auth), Artist Winning Watercolor of 1995, Artists Mag, 9/1995. *Mem:* Pastel Soc of Am, Nat Arts Club, New York City, 1963-; Arts Students Guild of Brevard (pres 1983); life charter mem Fla Watercolor Soc (pres 1983). *Media:* Acrylic, Oil, Pastel, Watercolor. *Mailing Add:* 2255 Abalone Ave Indialantic FL 32903

PLASTER, ALICE MARIE
PAINTER, INSTRUCTOR
b Hickory, NC. *Study:* Md Inst, Col Art, BFA, 77. *Work:* George Wash House Mus, Bladensburg, Md; Nat Automotive Hist Collection Art, Detroit. *Comn:* Mural, Md Nat Capital Park & Planning Comn, Riverdale, 79. *Exhib:* Urban Landscapes, 3rd Ann Juried Visual Arts Exhib, Strathmore, Hall Arts Ctr, Rockville, Md, 88; Mansion Art Gallery, Rockville, 91; Ballasai Gallery, Laurel, Md, 91; Venable Neslage Galleries, Washington, 91; George Meany Ctr Labor Studies Gallery, Silver Spring, 94; National Automotive History Collection Campaign 100 Exhibit, Detroit, Mich, 96; Discovery Galleries, Ltd, Bethesda, Md, 96-; Open Exhib, Nat Mus Women Arts, Bell Atlantic Gallery, Ernst Community Cult Ctr, Northern Va Community Col, 97-99, 2002-2004; Art Expo, NY, 98. *Pos:* Graphic artist, Prince George's Co Mem Libr System, Hyattsville, Md, 80-. *Teaching:* Instr painting, Md Nat Capital Park & Planning Comn Montpelier Cult Arts Ctr, 86-. *Awards:* Cash Award, Nat Soc Arts & Letters, 73; 1st Prize Award, Oil, Open Exhib, Juror J Carter Brown, Dir Emer, Nat Gallery Art, Annadale, VA, 93. *Bibliog:* The Prince Georgian, (Publ Cover Artist), Wash Post, 6/17/88; Concours d'Elegance, British Car Day (video), Visual Edge Productions, Potomac, 92; Automobile Artist-Jaguars Across America (video), British Cars Across America Series, No 4, Brit Car Films, London, Eng, 98. *Mem:* Arts Council Fairfax Co, VA; Walters Art Mus, Baltimore, MD. *Media:* Oil, Pencil. *Publ:* The Prince Georgian (cover), Wash Post, 6/17/88; illusr, Writer's Choice, Ligature, Inc, 93; Old Cars Weekly (cover), Krause Publs Inc, Vol 23, No 2, 1/13/94 & Vol 23, No 5, 4/21/94. *Mailing Add:* Reflective Images P O Box 680 Bowie MD 20718

PLATTNER, PHYLLIS
PAINTER
b New York, NY, Apr 25, 40. *Study:* Bennington Col, BA, 60; Brooklyn Mus Sch, 59; Claremont Grad Sch, Calif, MFA, 62. *Work:* St Louis Art Mus; Springfield Art Mus, Mo; The Kemper Group, Chicago; Xerox Corp, Stamford, Conn. *Comn:* Three-panel watercolor, Coinco, St Louis, 84; five-panel curved watercolor, IBM Bus Machines, Rochester, Minn, 85. *Exhib:* New Acquisitions, St Louis Art Mus, 83; Solo exhibs, BZ Wagman Gallery, St Louis, 85 & 86, Fendrick Gallery, Washington, 86 & 89, Esther Saks Gallery, Chicago, Ill, 87 Locus, St Louis, Mo, 89, Steven Scott Gallery, Baltimore, Md, 89 Brody's Gallery, Washington, 91-92 & Elliot Smith Gallery, St Louis, Mo, 92; Contemp Works on Paper, Frumkin & Struve Gallery, Chicago, 85; Watercolor USA: The Monumental Image, Springfield Art Mus, 86; and other one-man exhibs. *Teaching:* Vis assoc prof painting, Washington Univ, St Louis, 81-85 & 91-93, vis assoc prof watercolor, 85-87; instr, Md Inst Col Art, Baltimore, Md, 87-. *Awards:* Mayor's Award for the Arts, St Louis, 84; Mid-Atlantic States Nat Endowment Arts, 88. *Bibliog:* Robert Duffy (auth), It's a jungle in there, St Louis Post Dispatch, 84; Betsy Goldman (auth), Phyllis Plattner, Am Artist Mag, 85. *Media:* Oil, Watercolor; Oil Pastels. *Dealer:* R Duane Reed Gallery 1 N Taylor St Louis MO 63141; Elliot Smith Gallery 4727 McPherson Ave St Louis MO 63108. *Mailing Add:* 6204 Redwing Rd Bethesda MD 20817

PLATZKER, DAVID
BOOK DEALER, CURATOR
b Palo Alto, Calif, Sept 22, 65. *Study:* St Lawrence Univ, BA, 87; student, St Lawrence Univ, London, 86-87. *Collection Arranged:* Claes Oldenburg/John Baldessari, Brush Art Gallery, Canton, NY, 92; Claes Oldenburg: Multiples 1964-1990, various cities, 92-97; Claes Oldenburg: Books and Ephemera, 1960-1994, Glen Horowitz Bookseller, East Hampton, NY, 94, Printed Matter, Inc, NY, 94; Claes Oldenburg: The Geometric Mouse, Susan Inglett Gallery, NY, 94-95; Donald Judd: Drawings, Susan Inglett Gallery, NY, 96; Books by Edward Ruscha, Printed Matter, Inc, NY, 96; Claes Oldenburg: Printed Stuff (with Richard H Axsom), Madison (Wis) Art Ctr, 97, Columbus (Ohio) Mus Art, 98, Detroit (Mich) Inst Art, 98; Some More Books by Dieter Roth, Printed Matter, NY, 97; The Information Age: Baldessari, Barry, Huebler, Weiner, 1969-1971, Susan Inglett Gallery, NY, 98; Hard Pressed: 600 Years of Prints and Process (with Elizabeth Wyckoff), AXA Gallery, NY, 2001. *Pos:* Vpres, exec bd dir, Printed Matter Inc, 92-98, dir exhib, 94-97, dir, 98-2004; Cur, Claes Oldenburg and Cossje van Bruggen, 89-98; Independent cur, 98-; host, Recorded Matter, WPS1 Art Radio, 2003-; proj dir, Art Spaces Archives Proj, 2004-. *Awards:* Wittenborn Mem Bk Award, ARLS, 97; Mus Publ Award, Am Asn Mus, 98. *Res:* Pop art; conceptual art; artists' publications. *Specialty:* Artists' books & editions. *Interests:* Conceptual arts, minimal arts, pop art. *Publ:* Contribr, John Baldessari, Rizzoli, 89; Claes Oldenburg: An Anthology, Guggenheim Mus, New York, 95; co-auth, Printed Stuff: Prints by Claes Oldenburg, Hudson Hills Press, 97; co-auth, Hard Pressed: 600 Years of Prints and Process, Hudson Hills Press, 2000. *Dealer:* Specific Object 100 Wooster St New York NY 10012. *Mailing Add:* 100 Wooster St New York NY 10012

PLEAR, SCOTT
PAINTER
b Vancouver, BC, Mar 26, 52. *Study:* Univ BC, BFA, 76; Univ Sask, with Emma Lake, 77, 80, 84, 85 & 88; Triangle Artists Workshop, Pine Plains, NY, 82. *Work:* Edmonton Art Gallery, Alta; The Art Bank; Burnaby Art Gallery, BC; Art Gallery Greater Victoria, BC; Surrey Art Gallery, BC. *Exhib:* The Current Generation, Edmonton Art Gallery, 83; solo exhibs, Scott Plear: Recent Paintings, Edmonton Art Gallery, Alta, Grand Forks Art Gallery, BC, Burnaby Art Gallery, 87, BC House, London, Eng, 95, Vanderleelie Gallery, Edmonton, Alberta, 97 & Swift Current, Nat Exhib Centre, Saskatchewan, 98; North of the Border, Whatcom Mus Hist & Art, Bellingham, Wash, 90; My Own Space, Edmonton Art Gallery, Alta, 93; Driven to Abstraction, Surrey Art Gallery, BC, 93; Ten Painting Yrs (with catalog), Grand Forks Art Gallery, BC, 94; Harlech Biennale, Wales, 96; Cuillin Bantock/David Lemon/Scott Plear, Grand Forks Art Gallery, Grand Forks, BC, 99; Spiritus Forma, Grand Forks Art Gallery, Grand Forks, BC, 2001; Jerusalem, Jewish Community Centre, Vancouver, BC, 2002; Harbingers, HSBC Bank Atrium, Vancouver, BC, 2003; Full Fathom, Petley Jones Gallery, Vancouver, BC, 2003; With Flying Colours, Fran Willis Gallery, Victoria, BC, 2005; Banners & Standards, Petley Jones Gallery, Vancouver, BC, 2005; Agnes Burgera Gallery, Edmonton, Alberta, 2006. *Pos:* Guest artist, Mbile Int Artists' Workshop, Zambia, 93; with Saskatchewan Invit Artist's Workshop, Emma Lake, Saskatchewan, 2000. *Teaching:* Instr, Univ BC, 78-79; asst prof, Univ Alta, 83; fac mem, 1986-, Langara Col, dept chmn, 92-94, div chmn, 94-2001. *Bibliog:* Roger H Boulet (auth), Scott Plear, Recent Paintings, The Edmonton Art Gallery, 87; Robert Amos (auth), Victoria Times Colonist, 92; Gilbert Bouchard (auth), Edmonton J, 2006. *Mem:* Royal Canadian Acad of Arts. *Media:* Acrylic. *Publ:* Mythos, 2003; Harbingers, 2003; Full Fathom, 2004; With Flying Colours, 2005; Banners & Standards, 2005. *Dealer:* Virginia Christopher Fine Arts 816 11th Ave SW Calgary Alberta Can; Petley Jones Gallery 2235 Granville St Vancouver BC; Agnes Bugera Gallery 12310 Jasper Ave Edmondon AB Canada. *Mailing Add:* 106-237 E 4th Ave Vancouver BC V5T 4R4 Canada

PLETCHER, GERRY
PAINTER, PRINTMAKER
Study: Edinboro State Univ, BS; Pa State Univ, MA(fine arts); also with Montenegro, Carol Summers, Harold Altman, Nelson Sandgren & Shobaken; Vanderbilt Univ, Nashville, PhD. *Work:* Evansville Mus Arts & Sci, Ind; Fisk Univ, Tenn; Jacksonville State Univ, Ala; Tenn Arts Comn; Tenn Botanical Gardens; First Am Bank, Nashville; and others. *Exhib:* Cent South Art Exhib, Nashville; Nat Acad Design 145th Ann, NY; Wonderworks Four, Nat Print Show, Nashville; Springfield Nat Exhib, Ill; Brooks Mem Gallery, Memphis; Gallery Contemp Art, NC; and others. *Teaching:* Prof art, Tenn State Univ, currently. *Awards:* Graphics Purchase Award, 22nd Ann Mid-States Art Exhib, Evansville Mus Arts & Sci; seven Purchase Prizes, Tenn Arts Comn; Purchase Award, 13th Ann Tenn All-State; Purchase Award, Jacksonville Nat, Ala; and others. *Bibliog:* Artists USA, 72-73; Am Printmakers, 74; Who's Who Am Art, 83-92. *Media:* Acrylic, Oil; Etchings, Woodcuts. *Mailing Add:* 605 Brook Hollow Rd Nashville TN 37205-3119

PLETKA, PAUL
PAINTER, PRINTMAKER
b San Diego, Calif, 1946. *Study:* Ariz State Univ, Tempe; Colo State Univ, Ft Collins. *Work:* San Antonio Mus Art, Tex; Milwaukee Fine Arts Ctr, Wis; St Louis Art Mus, Mo; Minneapolis Inst Art, Minn; Phoenix Art Mus, Ariz; and others. *Comn:* Ghost Dancer (lithograph), Phoenix Art Mus, Ariz, 77; Those Living at the Sunrise (lithograph), Heard Mus, Phoenix, Ariz, 79; Papageno (poster), St Louis Opera Theater, Mo, 80. *Exhib:* Four Corners Biennial, Phoenix Art Mus, Ariz, 77; one-man show, El Paso Mus Art, Tex, 78; A Sense of Space, Univ NMex Art Mus, 79; Eiteljorg Collection, Indianapolis Mus Art, 79; Here and Now, Albuquerque Art Mus, NMex, 80. *Awards:* Certificate of Excellence, Chicago, 76; Nat Watercolor Soc Award, Watercolor USA, 77. *Bibliog:* Edna Gundersen (auth), Pletka bares Indian souls on canvas, El Paso Times, 5/13/78; Ed Montini (auth), Unmasking a dedicated artist, The Ariz Republic, 3/22/81; Edna Gundersori (auth), Pletka, Northland Press, 83. *Media:* Acrylic, Watercolor. *Mailing Add:* PO Box 34095 Santa Fe NM 87594-4095

PLETSCHER, JOSEPHINE MARIE
LIBRARIAN, PRINTMAKER
b Muscatine, Iowa. *Study:* Immaculate Heart Col, BA, 62, MA, 64; Univ Calif, Los Angeles, Santa Monica Col, Calif. *Comn:* Feel Free (poster), Wilson Libr Bulletin, Bronx, NY, 69. *Exhib:* Iowa Artists 4th Ann Exhib, Des Moines Art Ctr, 52 & 11th Ann Iowa Artists Exhib, 59; Calif State Fair, Sacramento, 62; Hillcrest Festival Fine Arts, Whittier Calif, 96; Gallery at City of Calabasa, Calif, 97; McKenzie Gallery, Los Angeles, Calif, 68; City of Pasadena, Fgn Cities Affiliation Travel Exhib, Japan, Ger, 72-73. *Collection Arranged:* Mexican Festival--Arts and Crafts, Pasadena Pub Libr, 72. *Pos:* Fine arts coordr, Pasadena Pub Libr, Pasadena, 64-82; reference librn, Rio Hondo Col Libr, Whittier, Calif, 83- & Santa Monica Comm Col, Libr, Calif, 95-06. *Awards:* Watercolor Hon Award, Des Moines Art Ctr, 59 & State Calif, 62; Recognition Award, Pasadena Pub Libr, 68. *Bibliog:* Larry Palmer (auth), Local art and artists, Pasadena Star News, 7/13/69; Jack Birkinshaw (auth), Joy of children painting is captured on librarian's film, Los Angeles Times, 9/4/69; Arthur Plotnik (auth), This is a library feel free, Wilson Libr Bulletin, 11/69. *Mem:* Art Libr Soc NAm; Hollywood Art Coun; Los Angeles Co Mus Art; Friends of Corita Art Ctr; and

others. *Media:* Serigraphy. *Interests:* Architecture, graphics, printmaking and rare art objects. *Collection:* Corita Kent original prints with archives. *Publ:* Illusr, Immaculate Heart College--Announcement of Courses, Immaculate Heart Col, 63-64; illusr & contribr, Painting from the heart, Business: Pasadena CofC, 5/69; Illusr, Learning By Heart, Bantan, 92; illusr and contribr, Primary Colors (film), 1991; contribr, Clifford Coffin, Stewart, Tabor & Chang, 1997; illusr & contribr, Life Stories of Artist Corita Kent, Loste, 2000. *Mailing Add:* 1231 S Bundy Dr No 3 Los Angeles CA 90025

PLEVIN, GLORIA JOY
PAINTER, PRINTMAKER
b Pittsburgh, Pa, July 25, 34. *Study:* Ohio Univ, AA, 54; Cooper Sch Art, 74; Cleveland Inst Art, 75-85. *Work:* Cleveland Mus Art; Butler Inst Am Art, Youngstown, Ohio; Jewish Community Ctr, Cleveland, Ohio; Univ Hosps of Cleveland, Ohio; Temple Emanuel, Cleveland, Ohio; BF Goodrich Corp Hdqtrs, Charlotte, NC; Cleveland Clinic; plus others. *Comn:* Rabbi Alan Green Portrait, Temple Emanuel, University Heights, Ohio, 78; bridal canopy, Temple Emanuel, University Heights, Ohio, 84; Amish Fields (monoprint tryptich), University Hosp, Cleveland, 93; Univ Print Club, Etching Edit, 2000. *Exhib:* Chautauqua Nat, Chautauqua Art Asn Galleries, NY, 73-75; Mid-Year Show, Butler Inst Am Art, Youngstown, Ohio, 74; Access Ann, Adams Mem Gallery, Dunkirk, NY, 87; Am Drawing Biennial, Muscarelle Mus Art, Williamsburg, Va, 88; Interiors, Mansfield Art Ctr, Ohio, 90; Chautauqua Vistas, solo, Butler Inst Am Art, Salem, Ohio, 93; Print Collection of J Marlin Casker, Prendergast Gallery, Jamestown, NY, 98; Artists Archives, 2002; Dead Horse Gallery, 2001; Many Faces of Cleveland, Cleveland Artists Foundation, 2002; Ohio Print Biennial, 1999-2001; Kelly Randall Gallery, 2002; Parallel Lives, Gloria Plevin & Bonnie Dolin, Ursuline Col Women's Invitational, 2004. *Pos:* Owner & dir, Gloria Plevin Gallery, Chautauqua, NY, 85-2002. *Awards:* Helen Logan Award, Chautauqua Nat, 73; Purchase Award, 85, Best Show, 89, Jewish Community Ctr Ann; Gov's Award, Ohio Arts Coun, 99. *Bibliog:* Dick Wooten (auth), The Cleveland connection, Salem News, 10/7/93; Helen Cullinan (auth), Plevin Displays a New Love, Cleveland Plain Dealer, 95; Lois Wiley (auth), Art on common ground, Erie Times, 8/16/96; Oral History Interview, Artists Archives, 2002; Fresh Ink (interview), Zygote Press, spring/summer 2002. *Mem:* New Orgn Visual Arts (pres, 82-84); Womens Mus Arts; Cleveland Artists Found; Cleveland Print Club; Artists Archives of Western Reserve. *Media:* Acrylics; Pastels, Monopaints. *Publ:* Portfolio 83 (Paula L Grooms, dir/coordr), New Orgn Visual Arts, 93; The Art of Gloria Plevin (monogr), Ohio Artists Now, 98; Herb Ascherman (auth), The Artists Project, 2002. *Dealer:* The Verne Collection 2207 Murray Hill Rd Cleveland OH 44106. *Mailing Add:* 13901 Shaker Blvd Suite 1A Cleveland OH 44120

PLOCHMANN, CAROLYN GASSAN
PAINTER, GRAPHIC ARTIST
b Toledo, Ohio, May 4, 26. *Study:* Toledo Mus Art Sch Design, 43-47; Univ Toledo, BA, 47; State Univ Iowa, MFA, 49, with Alfeo Faggi, 50; Southern Ill Univ, 51-52. *Work:* Evansville Mus Arts & Sci, Ind; Knoxville Mus Art, Tenn; Butler Inst Am Art, Youngstown, Ohio; Univ Chicago Librs Collection; West Collection, St Paul, Minn. *Comn:* mural, North Side Old Nat Bank, Evansville, Ind. *Exhib:* Evansville Mus Arts & Sci, 62, 68 & 79; one-man shows, Witte Mus, San Antonio, Tex, 68, Toledo Mus Art, 65 & Kennedy Galleries, NY, 73, 81, 83, 87, 89, 92, 94, 95 & 98; 164th Prints & Drawings Ann, Pa Acad Fine Arts, Philadelphia, 69; Knoxville Mus Art, Tenn, 91; Purch Exhib, 45th & 48th Ann Am Acad Arts & Letts, 93; Kutztown Univ, 96. *Teaching:* Supervisor art, Southern Illinois Univ Training Sch, 49-50. *Awards:* George W Stevens Fel, Toledo Mus Art, 47-49; Tupperware Art Fund First Award, 53; Emily Lowe Found Competition Award, 58; First Award, Art and the Law, West Collection, 85. *Bibliog:* Selden Rodman (auth), Geniuses and other Eccentrics, Green Tree Press, San Francisco, 97; Michael Kammen (auth), The Creative and Enigmatic Imagery of Carolyn Gassan Plochmann, Kennedy Catalogue, 98; Matthew F Daub (auth), A Charmed Vision: The Art of Carolyn Plochmann, Evansville Ind Mus Arts & Sci, 90; and others. *Media:* Oil, Acrylic; Graphics. *Publ:* Auth, University Portrait: Nine Paintings by Carolyn Gassan Plochmann, Southern Ill Univ Press, 59; auth, Introductory Statement, Kennedy Galleries One-man show (catalog), 92; and others. *Dealer:* Kennedy Galleries 730 Fifth Ave New York NY 10019. *Mailing Add:* 5729 S US Hwy 51 Carbondale IL 62901-8298

PLOSSU, BERNARD
PHOTOGRAPHER
b Dalat, SVietnam, Feb 26, 45. *Work:* Bibliotheque Nat, Paris; Amon Carter Mus, Ft Worth, Tex; George Eastman House, Rochester, NY; Ctr Creative Photography, Tucson, Ariz; Niepce Mus, Chalon, France; Mus Fine Arts, Santa Fe, NMex; Albuquerque Mus, NMex. *Exhib:* Plossu by Atelier Fresson, Eaton-Shoen Gallery, San Francisco, 82; solo exhib, Etherton Gallery, Tucson, Ariz, 82; The Spirit of Traveling, Arles Photo Fest, Arles, France, 82; In Place, Albuquerque Mus, NMex, 82; two-person show, Hoshour Gallery, Albuquerque, NMex, 83; The Mexican Voyage, Eaton-Schoen Gallery, San Francisco, 84. *Teaching:* Photography workshops, Okla Summer Arts Inst, 83. *Bibliog:* Gilles Mora (auth), La rupture creatrice du Voyage Mexicain, Cahiers Photo, 81; L Sherman & S Parks (auths), I photograph the weather, Artlines, 81; M Foley (auth), Bernard Plossu, Artspace, 81; Gilles Mora (auth), Bernard Plossu, Camera, 86. *Publ:* Photogr, Surbanalism, Chene, France, 72; Go West, Chene, France, 72; Le Voyage Mexicain, Contrejour, France, 79; Egypte, Photoeil, France, 79; New Mexico Revisited, Univ NMex Press, 83. *Mailing Add:* c/o Galerie Michele Chinette 24 Rue Beabourg Paris 75003 France

PLOTEK, LEOPOLD
PAINTER
b Moscow, USSR. *Study:* McGill Univ, Montreal; Sir George Williams Univ, Montreal, BFA, 70; study with Roy Kioyooka & Yves Gaucher; Slade Sch Art, London, Eng, study with William Townsend, 70-71. *Work:* Montreal Mus Fine Arts; Mus d'Art Contemporain; Concordia Univ; Can Coun Artbank; Alcan Aluminum; others. *Exhib:* 49th Parallel, NY, 89; Univ Que, Montreal, 92; Cenacle, 7 Montreal Painters, 93; Hidden Values, McMichael Can Collection, Kleinburg, 94; Artcité: quand Montréal devient Musée, Mus Contemp Art, Montreal, 2001; Leonard & Bina Ellen Gallery, Montreal, 2002; Solo exhibs, Vehicule Art, Montreal, 72 & 74, Weissman Gallery, Concordia, Que, 75, Galerie Optica, Montreal, 76, Galerie Yajima, Montreal, 79, 81 & 83, Olga Korper Gallery, Toronto, 84, 86, 88, 90, 93, 95, 97, 2002, Concordia Art Gallery, Concordia Univ, Montreal, 90 & Saidye Bronfman Ctr, Montreal, 92, Galerie Eric Devlin, Montreal, 2002. *Awards:* Alfred Pinsky Medal in Fine Arts; Four Can Coun Arts Coun; two travel grants to Italy. *Mailing Add:* c/o Olga Korper Gallery 17 Morrow Ave Toronto ON M6R 2H9 Canada

PLOTKIN, LINDA
PAINTER, PRINTMAKER
b Milwaukee, Wis, Dec 21, 38. *Study:* Univ Wis, Milwaukee, BA, 61; Pratt Inst, Brooklyn, NY, MFA, 62. *Work:* Metrop Mus Art & Mus Mod Art, NY; Bibliotheque Nationale, Paris, France; Libr Cong, Washington, DC; Brooklyn Mus, NY. *Exhib:* 30 Yrs of Am Printmaking, Brooklyn Mus, NY, 76; 10th Ann Tokyo Int Print Biennial, Tokyo, Japan, 77; 30 Am Printmakers, Ohio State Univ, Columbus, 81; Int Print Exhib, Taipei Mus, Taiwan, 84; Va Mus Print Invitational, Va Mus Art, Richmond, 86. *Teaching:* Asst prof art, Pa State Univ, State Col Pa, 62-77; artist in residence, St Mary's Col, Notre Dame, Ind, 85; State Univ NY, Purchase, 86-. *Awards:* MacDowell Fel, 76, 78 & 79; Ossabaw Island Fel, 78; Camargo Found Fel, 81. *Bibliog:* Judd Tully (auth), Linda Plotkin, Arts Mag, 5/19/84; James Watrous (auth), A Century of American Printmaking, 84. *Mem:* Soc Am Graphic Artists (bd mem, 83-); Int Graphic Artists Found; Artists Equity. *Publ:* Contribr, In Praise of Women Artists (calendar), Bo-Tree Prods, 85. *Dealer:* G W Einstein Inc 591 Broadway New York NY. *Mailing Add:* 55 Perry St No 3A New York NY 10014-3218

PLOTNICK, HARVEY BARRY
COLLECTOR
b Detroit, Mich, Aug 5, 41. *Study:* Univ Chicago, BA, 63. *Pos:* Ed, Contemp Books, Inc, Chicago, 64-66, pres pub, 66-94; Chief Exec Officer, Molecular Electronics Corp, Chicago, 2000-01, Paradigm Holdings, Inc, Chicago, 94-. *Awards:* Names one of Top 200 Collectors, ARTnews Mag, 2005-06. *Mem:* Trustee Univ Chicago, (trustee, 94-); Argonne Nat Laboratory, (bd gov, 2001); Chicago Acad Scis (bd dir, currently). *Collection:* Old Master prints, Islamic Ceramics & rare books. *Mailing Add:* Paradigm Holdings Inc 2 Prudential Plaza Ste 3150 Chicago IL 60601-6790

PLOTT, PAULA PLOTT AMOS
PAINTER, SCULPTOR
b Wichita, Kans, Sept 22, 46. *Study:* Wichita State Univ, BFA (cum laude), 68; Univ Ore, MFA (summa cum laude), 70. *Work:* Wichita Art Mus, Kans. *Comn:* Carved reception desk & 12 paintings, J P Weigand & Sons Real Estate, Wichita, 76-77; Day in the Life of an Aztec (paintings), Taco Tico, Inc, 78-84; Symphony Calendar, Wichita Symphony, 79-80; panel designs, Trinity Methodist Church, Hutchinson, Kans, 80-81; Herbal Calendar, 87 & Wildflowers Calendar, 88, 89, 90 & 91 Wildlife Fedn; Lipton Herbal Tea Calendar, 89 & 90, Commemorative Cup, 90, Lipton Tea Co; Wichita Art Mus Commemorative Christmas Ornament, 89. *Exhib:* One-woman shows, Mus Fine Art, Los Gatos, 75, Wichita Gallery Fine Art, 78, Wichita Art Asn, 82 & Birger Sandzen Gallery Art, 83; Kansas Watercolor Tri State Show, 81, Seasons Greetings Invitational, 81, Facets in Wood, 84, Woods Worthy Christmas, 85, Wichita Art Mus; Plott Toy Shop, 86, 87, 88, 89 & 90. *Collection Arranged:* Historic Cowtown, Religion in 1863, 82-83. *Pos:* Designer & graphic coordr, US Govt, Stuttgart, WGer, 71-73; tech adv, Chabot Galleries, 75-76; lectr religious symbolism, Methodist Church, 79-82; League artist pub relations, Jr League Wichita, 84-86; artist, Propellor Mag, currently. *Teaching:* Guest lectr Western art, Kurisini Inst Int, Dar Es Salaam, Tanzania, 67; teaching asst painting, Univ Ore, Eugene, 69-70. *Awards:* First Place & Grand Prize, Religion Art Festival, Congregational Church, 82. *Bibliog:* E O'Hara (auth), A woman for all seasons: Religious symbolism, The Wichitan City Mag, 82; Wonder of wood, Colonial Homes, 12/88. *Mem:* Wichita Artists Guild; Kans Watercolor Soc; Nat League Am Pen Women (treas, 85-86). *Media:* Watercolor; Woodcarving, Relief. *Publ:* Illusr, Diagnostic & therapeutic implications of schizophenic Art, J Arts & Psychotherapy, 84; Country Wildlife, Hammond Publ, 85; auth, Seasons of Inspiration, 86 & Paula Plott's Herbal, 87, Hammond Publ; Wild Flowers, 89, 90 & 91. *Dealer:* Wichita Gallery Fine Arts 4th Financial Ctr Wichita KS 67201. *Mailing Add:* 350 S Fountain St Wichita KS 67218

PLOUS, PHYLLIS
CURATOR
b Green Bay, Wis. *Study:* Univ Wis, with Oskar von Hagen & James Watrous, BA, 47; Univ Col London; Univ Calif, Santa Barbara. *Collection Arranged:* Ralph A Blakelock retrospective & tour (coauth, catalog); Charles Demuth retrospective & tour (coauth, catalog); 19 Sculptors of the 40's; Sculptors in the 50's, catalog & tour; Sculptural Perspectives in the 70's catalog; Richard Diebenkorn, Intaglio Prints 1961-1978, catalog; Dark/Light: Extensions of Photography, catalog and tour; New York, Report on a Phenomenon, catalog; Terry Winters, Painting & Drawings, catalog & tour; Abstract Options, (coauth, catalog), tour; Knowledge (coauth, catalog), tour; Carroll Dunham (catalog), Paintings & Drawings, 96. *Pos:* Asst to dir, Santa Barbara Mus Art, 54-56; asst to dir, Univ Art Mus, Univ Calif, Santa Barbara, 63-72, cur, 72-92. *Awards:* Nat Endowment Arts Fel, Mus Professionals, 80. *Mem:* Am Asn Art Mus; Col Art Asn Am; Southern Calif Art Writers Asn; Int Coun Mus. *Mailing Add:* 33219 SE 15th St Washougal WA 98671-6814

PLOWDEN, DAVID
PHOTOGRAPHER, WRITER
b Boston, Mass, Oct 9, 1932. *Study:* Yale Univ, BA, 55; pvt study with Minor White, Nathan Lyons, 59-60. *Work:* George Eastman House, Rochester; Albright-Knox Gallery, Buffalo; Mus Contemp Photog, Chicago; The Baly Mus, Univ Va, Charlotteville; Albin O Kuhn Libr, Univ Md. *Comn:* Design resources photog study,

Dept Transportation, Washington, 66; Bridges of NAm, photog study, Smithsonian Inst, Washington, 69-72; Railroad men, photog study, Smithsonian Inst, Washington, 76; Chicago industry, photog study, Chicago Hist Soc, 80-85; State Hist Soc Iowa, 87; Iowa Humanities Bd & Nat Endowment Humanities, 87-88. *Exhib:* Photog in the Fine Arts V, Metrop Mus Art, NY, 67; solo exhibs, Smithsonian Inst, 71, 75, 76 & 89, Chicago Hist Soc, 85, Kunst Mus, Luzern, Switz, 87, Iowa State Mus, 88, Mid-Am Arts Alliance, Exhibs USA, 90-93, Kathleen Ewing Gallery, Washington, 94 & Univ Miami, 96; The River, Walker Art Ctr, Minneapolis, Minn, 76-77; Industrial Sites, Whitney Mus, NY, 79; Chicago: The Architectural City, Art Inst Chicago, 83; An Open Land: Photographs of the Midwest 1852-1982, Art Inst Chicago, 83 & traveling, 83-86; Road & Roadside, Ill State Univ, 87 & Art Inst Chicago, 87; Trains, Boats & Planes, Witkin Gallery, NY, 88; The Photographer & the Railroad, Univ Louisville, 89; Three Decades of Midwest Photog, Davenport Mus Art, Iowa, 92; Plain Pictures: Images of the Am Prairie, Univ Iowa Mus Art, 96 & traveling, 97; When Aaron met Harry: Chicago Photog 1948-1971, Mus Contemp Photog, Chicago, 96 & 98; Beinecke Rare Book and Manuscript Libr, Yale Univ, 97; Baly Mus, Univ Va, Charlottesville, 97; Albright-Knox Gallery, Buffalo, 97-98; Albin O Kuhn Libr & Gallery, Baltimore, 98; Tatar/Alexander Gallery, Toronto, 99; Passages: A Forty Yr Retrospective, Laurence Miller Gallery, NY, 00; Chicago Cult Ctr, 03; Peter Fetterman Gallery, Santa Monica, Calif, 00. *Pos:* Photogr & writer, 62-. *Teaching:* Assoc prof design, Inst Design, Ill Inst Technol, Chicago, 78-84; lectr, Univ Iowa, Iowa City, 85-88; vis prof, Grand Valley State Univ, Allendale, Mich, 88-89 & 91-; artist-in-residence, Univ Baltimore, Inst for Publ Design, 90-91. *Awards:* Guggenheim Found Fel, 68; Wilson Hicks Award, Univ Miami, 77; Seymour & Knox Found, 87; Hon Imagemaker, Soc Photog Educ, Mideast Region, 02. *Bibliog:* David McCullough (auth), Brave Companions, 92. *Mem:* Am Soc Media Photogr. *Publ:* Auth, An American Chronology, Viking, 82; A Time of Trains, Norton, 87; A Sense of Place, Norton, 88; End of an Era: The Last of the Great Lakes Steamboats, Norton, 92; Small Town America, Abrams, 94; Imprints the Photographs of David Plowden, Bulfinch, 97; Bridges: The Spans of North America, Norton, 02; David Plowden: The American Barn, Norton, 03; auth, A Handful of Dust: Photographs of Disappearing America, Norton, 2006. *Dealer:* Lawrence Miller Gallery 20 West 57th Street New York NY; Catherine Edelman Gallery 300 W Superior St Chicago Ill 60610. *Mailing Add:* 609 Cherry St Winnetka IL 60093

PLUMB, JAMES DOUGLAS
PAINTER, EDUCATOR
b New Haven, Conn, Dec 20, 41. *Study:* Univ Va; Philadelphia Col Art, BFA. *Work:* Acad Arts, Easton, Md. *Exhib:* Ann Md Show, Acad Arts, Easton, Md, 74, 78, 79 & 81; Art Asn Newport Ann Show, RI, 75; Conn Acad Arts Ann Show, Wadsworth Atheneum, 75; Five From the Eastern Shore, 76 & Md Biennial, 78, Baltimore Mus Art. *Collection Arranged:* Collection of the Academy of the Arts, 175 Works (auth, catalog), 79; College Show (auth, catalog), Contemporary Maryland Photographers (auth, catalog), 79; Eight Artists' Invitational Shows (auth, catalog), 79; Contemporary Works on Paper, 80. *Pos:* Cur, Acad Arts, Easton, Md, formerly. *Teaching:* Instr painting & drawing, Acad Arts, Easton, MD, 71-76; lectr art hist, State Extension Home Economics & Improvement, Univ Md, 73-76, assoc prof, Cheaspeake Col, 90-. *Awards:* Acad Arts Ann Show Awards, 74, 78 & 80; Best in Show, Easton Lions' Club Show, 75. *Media:* Oil on Canvas, Pencil on Paper. *Dealer:* David Adamson Gallery 406 7th St NW Washington DC 20004. *Mailing Add:* PO Box 1088 Easton MD 21601

PLUMMER, CARLTON B
PAINTER, INSTRUCTOR
b Brunswick, Maine. *Study:* Vesper George Sch Art, dipl, 48-51; Mass Col Art, BS, 55-58; Boston Univ, MFA, 61-64. *Work:* Mus Military Art, Washington, DC; First Nat Bank Boston, Mass; Mus Fine Arts, Springfield, Mass; Aetna Insurance Co, Hartford, Conn; Miniature Artists Am, Clearwater, Fla. *Comn:* Faces of America, Old Forge, NY. *Pos:* Free-lance illusr, own pvt studio, Summerville, Mass, 53-58; art coodr, Chelmsford Sch System, Mass, 58-64; instr watercolor, own pvt workshop studio, Boothbay, Maine, 78-; vpres, New Eng Watercolor Soc, 79-82, pres, 82-84. *Teaching:* Prof art, drawing & painting, Univ Mass, 64-86, prof emeritus; watercolor workshops in Boothbay, Maine, throughout US & Abroad, 78; nat and int workshops, 75-. *Awards:* Wash Sch Award, Am Watercolor Soc Ann, 79; Gold Medal Hon, Am Artists Prof League, 83; Gold Medal Hon, Allied Artists Am, 96; Gold Medal Hon, Salmagundi Club, 98. *Bibliog:* Nita Leland (auth), Exploring Watercolor, North Light Publ, 85; Watercolor Demo (film), Chelmsford Cable TV, 86. *Mem:* Am Watercolor Soc; Allied Artists Am; Guild Boston Artists; Rocky Mountain Nat Watermedia Soc; New Eng Watercolor Soc; San Diego Watercolor Soc. *Media:* Watercolor, Oil. *Publ:* Auth, Using diagonal compositions in watercolor, 82 & Capturing the essence of a scene, 84, Am Artist; Exploring Watercolor, Northlight Publ, 85; Best of Watercolor III, Northlight Publ, 93; The Transparent Watercolor Wheel, Watson/Guptil Publ, 94; Best of Watercolor I, Northlight Publ, 94. *Dealer:* Guild of Boston Artists Newbury St Boston MA; Wisc Bay Gallery Wiscasset ME. *Mailing Add:* c/o Birdsnest Gallery 12 Mount Desert St Bar Harbor ME 04609

POCHMANN, VIRGINIA
PAINTER, DRAFTSMAN
b Starkville, Miss, Mar 13, 38. *Study:* Univ Wis, Madison, BS, 59; Am Acad Art, Chicago, Ill, 66-68; De Burgos Sch Art, Washington, DC, 68-70. *Work:* City of Sunnyvale Permanent Collection. *Exhib:* Am Watercolor Soc Ann, NY, 82; Rocky Mountain Nat Watermedia Exhib, Golden, Colo, 82, 84 & 86; Watercolor USA, Springfield Art Mus, Mo, 83; 15th Ann Watercolor West, Harrison Mus Art, Logan, Utah, 83; Watercolor West Ann, Riverside, Calif, 83, 85 & 86; West Coast Watercolor Soc, Monterey Peninsula Mus Art, Calif, 84; San Diego Watercolor Soc Int Exhib, Calif, 84; one-person shows, Fireside Gallery, Carmel, Calif, 84 & 85; 65th Ann, Nat Watercolor Soc, Brea, Calif, 85; Bernard Galleries, Walnut Creek, Calif, 88; Foliage and Flowers, Sunnyvale, Calif, 88. *Pos:* Retired. *Awards:* Purchase Award, La Watercolor Soc Exhib, Pontchartrain Clinic, 85; Cash Award, WTex Watercolor Soc Nat Exhib, Mus Tex Tech, 85; First Award, Northern Calif Watercolor Competition, Pacific Art League, Palo Alto, 85. *Mem:* Nat Watercolor Soc; Artists Equity; WCoast Watercolor Soc (treas, 84-85). *Media:* Watercolor, Pen, Ink. *Publ:* Contribr, Gerald Brommer, Watercolor & Collage Workshop, Watson-Guptill, 86; Contemp Women Artists, (calender), Pomegranate Publ Co, Petaluma, Calif, 89; Contribr, Exploring Painting, Davis Publ Co, 87; contribr Understanding Transparent Watercolor, Brommer, Davis Pub Co, 93; contribr Splash 2, Watercolor Breakthroughs, North Light, 93; and others. *Mailing Add:* 235 Oak Rd Alamo CA 94507

PODUSKA, T F
LECTURER, PAINTER
b Cedar Falls, Iowa, Dec 6, 25. *Study:* Univ Northern Iowa, BA(art educ). *Work:* Denver Art Mus, Contemp Collection; Atlantic Richfield Corp; Amoco; Int Bus Machines; Exeter; and others. *Exhib:* Colo Womens Col, 79; Aspen Inst, 79; Univ Wyo, 80; Watercolor USA, Springfield, Mo, 80; Carson-Sapiro Gallery, Denver, 82; and others. *Pos:* Lectr, consult & proj asst, Colo Coun Arts & Humanities, 73. *Teaching:* Bus skills workshops, 75. *Awards:* Colo Governor's Award for Arts & Humanities, 77; Merit Award, Nat Acad of Design, 77. *Mem:* Alliance Contemp Art; Asian Art Asn. *Media:* Water Media, Paper. *Publ:* Coauth, Insuring the artist's work, Am Artist Bus Lett, suppl, 74; Business Practices for Artists, Artists Equity Asn, 75. *Dealer:* Melinda Percell Fine Art Denver CO. *Mailing Add:* 10233 W Powers Ave Littleton CO 80127-1814

POEHLMANN, JOANNA
ILLUSTRATOR, PRINTMAKER
b Milwaukee, Wis, Sept 5, 32. *Study:* Layton Sch Art, four-year dipl, 54; Kansas City Art Inst, 55; Marquette Univ, 58; Univ Wis, Milwaukee, 65 & 85. *Work:* Milwaukee Art Mus; Victoria & Albert Mus, London; Ruth & Marvin Sackner Archive Concrete & Visual Poetry, Miami Beach, Fla; Int Print Biennial, Embragel, Cabo Frio, Brazil; New York Pub Libr, NY; Mus Kunsthandwerk, Frankfurt, Ger; Istvan Kiraly Muzeum-Szekasfechevar, Budapest, Hungary; and others. *Comn:* Animal note cards, Recycled Paper Co, Chicago, 81-83; Ed of Hand Colored Lithograph, Quad/Graphics Inc, Pewaukee, Wis, 87 & 93; Poster Design, Charles Allis Art Mus, Milwaukee, 88; 50th Anniversary card design, Wustum Mus Art, Racine, Wis, 91; Artist Book Retirement Gift, Midwest Express Airlines, Milwaukee, Wis. *Exhib:* Retrospective, Drawings, Collages, Mindscapes, Milwaukee Art Mus, 66; Wisconsin Directions I & II, Milwaukee Art Mus, 75 & 78; Works on Paper, Art Inst Chicago, 78; Prints, Multiples, Art Inst Chicago, 81 & Nat Mus Am Art, 82; 10 Yr Retrospective 1964-1994, Wustum Mus Fine Arts, Racine, Wis, Charles Allis Art Mus, Milwaukee, Wis, 91; Verbal Text/Non-Verbal Context: Handmade Books, Milwaukee Art Mus, 92; Cross Section World Financial Ctr, NY, 92; Artists Books in the USA, Galerie Druck & Buch, Tübingen, Ger; Retrospective, Wis Acad Art, Sci & Lett, 92; Book Arts in the USA, Ctr Bk Arts, NY, 90 (Touring Africa through 92); and others. *Teaching:* Assoc lectr, Univ Wis, Milwaukee. *Awards:* Purchase Awards, 20th Bradley Nat Print & Drawings Exhib, Bradley Univ, Peoria, Ill, 85, 22nd Nat Works on Paper Biennial, Univ of Del, Newark, 86, 10th Print Nat, Univ Dallas, Irving, Tex, 88 & Univ NDak Print & Drawing Ann, Grand Forks, 88; Milwaukee Co Individual Art Fel, 93; Arts/Midwest Regional Visual Artist Fel, Nat Endowment Arts, 94-95. *Bibliog:* Laura Murphy (auth), Art in Wisconsin, 4/87; Printworld Directory/87-88, 91-92; article, Am Crafts Mag, 4-5/96. *Mem:* Printforum Milwaukee Art Mus; Ctr Bk Arts, NY; Columbia Col, Chicago Ctr Book Paper Arts. *Media:* Hand Color Stone Lithography; Artists Books. *Publ:* Illusr, The chimp who went fishing, Int Wildlife Mag, 78; auth & illusr, The Day Before Christmas, Western Publ Co, 79; illusr, A Nutrition Monograph for Taking Off Pounds Sensibly, Tops Club, 80; auth & illusr, So have a Canary, self publ, 87; Love Letters, Food for Thought & Cancelling Out, Abbeville Press, Inc, 91. *Dealer:* Patti Gilford Fine Arts 444 N Wells St Chicago IL 60610; Tony Zwicker 15 Gramercy Park New York NY 10003. *Mailing Add:* 1231 N Prospect Ave Milwaukee WI 53211-3013

POGANY, MIKLOS
PAINTER, PRINTMAKER
b Budapest, Hungary, Feb 4, 45. *Study:* St Procopins Col, BA, 65; Univ Chicago, MA, 65, PhD, 72. *Work:* Metrop Mus Art, NY; Philadelphia Mus Art, Pa; Phillips Collection, Washington, DC; Victoria & Albert Mus, London, Eng; Nat Mus Am Art, Washington. *Exhib:* The Am Artist as Printmaker, Brooklyn Mus, NY, 83; Contemp Am monotypes, Chrysler Mus, Norfolk, Va, 85; 1987 Invitational, New Britain Mus Am Art, Conn, 87; Contemp Art Exhib, Spencer Mus, Lawrence, Kans, 87. *Awards:* SECA Award Painting, San Francisco Mus Mod Art, 77; Grant for Printmaking, Conn Comn Arts, 80; Louis Comfort Tiffany Found Award, 81. *Dealer:* Victoria Munroe Gallery 415 W Broadway New York NY 10012

POHLMAN, LYNETTE
MUSEUM DIRECTOR, CURATOR
Study: IA State Univ, BA, 1972, MA in applied art, 1976. *Exhib:* Cur Emperors, Shoguns and Kings, 1981, Fiber to Glass, 1987, Land of Fragile Giants: Landscapes, Environs and Peoples of the Loess Hills, 1994-96, The Golden Age of Glass: 1875-1939, 1999. *Pos:* Dir, chief cur, Univ. Mus at IA State Univ. *Teaching:* Adj prof art & design IA State Univ; organizer Art in State Bldgs Progressive. *Awards:* Recipient Christian Petersen Design Award, 2004. *Mem:* Asn Col and Univ Mus and Galleries (found mem). *Mailing Add:* Iowa State Univ Brunnier Art Mus Iowa State Ctr Schman Continuing Edn Bldg Ames IA 50011

POKORNY, JAN HIRD
ARCHITECT, EDUCATOR
b Brno, Czechoslovakia, May 25, 1914. *Study:* Tech Univ, Engr-Archit, Prague, 37; Columbia Univ, MS(archit), 41. *Work:* princ works incl: Taylor Mem Libr and Reeves Student Union Bldg at Centenary Col for Women, Hackettstown, NJ, Lewisohn Hall at Columbia Univ, (with Damaz and Weigel) Student Union Bldg, Admin Bldg, Libr and Fine Arts Bldg at NY State Univ, Stony Brook, (with David Todd Assts) master plan Libr, Auditorium and renovated Music Bldg, Speech and Theatre Bldg, Lehman Col-City Univ NY; housing at Grasslands Westchester Med Ctr housing for Urban Devel Corp, in Middletown, Elmira and Wayne Co, NY, Corp offs for Samuel H Kress Found, Ambassador's Off US Mission to UN, Off John and Marry R Markle Found; restoration of: Schermerhorn Row Block, S St, Seaport, New York City, Monsignor McGolrick Park Shelter, Brooklyn, Sloppy Louie's Restaurant, S St, Seaport, New York City, Shellens Gallery of Brooklyn Hist, Brooklyn Hist Soc, Firemen's Mem, New York City, Church of Incarnation, New York City, Morris-Jumel Mansion, New York City, Century Club Facade, New York City. *Pos:* Gen practice archit, Prague, 38-39; designer Winn-Roensch & Brezner, Detroit, 42, Leo Bauer, Detroit, 42-44, Skidmore, Owings & Merrill, New York City, 44-45; Chief Exec Officer, Jan Hird Pokorny (architect), 45-71, 77-; dir, evening prog in archit, 57-73, partner Pokorny & Pertz, 71-77, archit mem Art Comn City NY, 73-77. *Teaching:* Assoc prof, Columbia Sch Archit, 58-74; prof, archit Grad Sch Archit, Planning & Preserv, 74-82, prof emer, 82-. *Awards:* Recipient Ethnic New Yorker award by Mayor of NY, 85, Lifetime Preservation award Columbia Alumni, 90, Felber Gold medal Czech Tech Univ, 91, James William Kideney award, Am Inst of Archits, 92, award for Morris-Jumel restoration NY City Landmarks Comn, 93, "Quintessential Architect" Am Inst of Archits NY State Fels award, 2000. *Mem:* Fel Am Inst of Archits (awards of merit 55, 61,74, NY state asn award 75, Bard award 85, Arthur Ross award); Nat Acad; Clubs: Century Asn. *Publ:* Contributor articles to prof jour. *Mailing Add:* JanHird Pokorny Associates Floor 12 A 39 West 37th St New York NY 10018

POLAN, ANNETTE
PAINTER, DRAFTSMAN
b Huntington, WVa, Dec 8, 44. *Study:* Hollins Col, Va, BA(art hist), 63-67; Ecole du Louvre, Paris, 64-65; Tyler Sch Art, Philadelphia; Corcoran Sch Art, Washington. *Work:* Huntington Mus, Huntington, WVa; WVa Coun Arts & Humanities, Charleston, WVa; Nat Drug Abuse Coun, Washington; Columbia Hosp Women, Washington; Hill & Knowlton, Washington; and many others pub & pvt. *Comn:* Portraits: Am Pharmaceutical Asn, Washington, 90; Hon Sandra Day OConnor, US Supreme Ct; Bergen Brunswig Corp, Orange, Calif, 90; Coun For Relations, NY, 95; Gov Gaston Caperton, Charleston, WVa, 96. *Exhib:* Am Genius, Corcoran Gallery, Washington, 76 & Hemicycle, 92; one-person exhibs, Foundry Gallery, 76 & 83, Wallace Wentworth Gallery, Washington, 85, Marywood Mus Art, Marywood Col, Scranton, Pa, 89, Montrose Gallery, Fredricksburg, Va, 90, Agardhs Gallery, Bastad, Sweden, 92, Gustaf Nord, Stockholm, Sweden, 92; Ann Art Auction, Washington Proj for the Arts, Wash, 91-98; Figure, Ctr Street Gallery, Manassas, Va, 92; The Woman's Show, Cur for Hon Eleanor Holmes Norton, Washington, 92; Stockholm Art Fair, Sweden, 93; Portraits, Georgetown Univ, Washington, DC, 93; Susan Conway Gallery, Washington, DC, 95; Cult Ctr, Charleston, WVa, 96; Gallery Samtah, Seoul, Korea, 96; Sunrise Mus, Charleston, WVa, 98; Md Art Place, Baltimore, 98; Huntington Mus of Art, Huntington, WVa, 2000; and many others. *Pos:* Artist-in-residence, Art Therapy Italia, Vignale, Italy, 86; vis artist, Landscape Painting Prog, La Napoule, France, 87; dir Corcoran Summer Prog, La Napoule, 88; pres, Fac Asn, Corcoran Sch Art, Washington, DC, 88-89, chmn painting dept, 91-92; guest lectr Contemp Am Portraiture, China, & Japan, 89, Nat Trust Sydney, 96 & Seoul, Korea, 97; artist-in-residence, La Napoule, France, 90; juror, many orgns & galleries, 90-93; presenter, Mod Artists' Mat & Their Conservation Implications, Smithsonian Inst, Washington, DC, 91. *Teaching:* Asst prof fine art, Corcoran Sch Art, Washington, DC, 74-. *Awards:* DC Comn Arts & Humanities Grants in Aid, 85 & 93; Distinguished Alumnae Award, Baldwin Sch, Bryn Mawr, Pa, 98; Award Batuz Found, Soc Imaginaire Pgm, Altzella, Ger, 99. *Mem:* Corcoran Fac Asn (pres, 88-89); Washington Proj for the Arts, Washington (bd dir, 94-). *Media:* Painting, Drawing. *Publ:* Illusr, Say What I Am Called, Selected Riddles from the Exeter Book, Sibyl-Child Press, 88; illusr, Relearning the Dark, Washington Writers Publ House, Washington; cover designer, Doers of the Word, Oxford Univ Press, 95. *Dealer:* Susan Conway Gallery Washington DC 20007. *Mailing Add:* 4719 30th St NW Washington DC 20008

POLCARI, STEPHEN
HISTORIAN, ADMINISTRATOR
b Boston, Mass, Jan 22, 45. *Study:* Columbia Col, BA, 67; Columbia Univ, MA, 71; Univ Calif, Santa Barbara, PhD, 80. *Pos:* Cur, DeCordova Mus, Lincoln, Mass, 76; dir, Archives Am Art, NY. *Teaching:* Asst prof mod art, Univ Ill, Urbana, 79-83; State Univ NY, Stony Brook, 83-90. *Awards:* Rubinstein Mus Fel, Whitney Mus Art, 77; Nat Endowment Humanities, 82; Inst Advan Study, Princeton, 82; Nat Mus Am Art, 91. *Mem:* Col Art Asn; Alumni of Inst Advanced Studies. *Res:* Intellectual, cultural & political history and the development of modern art, especially abstract expressionism, modern and American Art, the Depression and War, 1930-1950s. *Publ:* Martha Graham & Abstract Expressionism, Smithsonian Studies in Am Art, 90; Orozco & Pollock: Epic Transfigurations, Am Art, 92; Barnett Newman, The Broker Obelisk, Art J, 94. *Mailing Add:* Dir NY Archives Am Art 1285 Sixth Ave New York NY 10019

POLEDNA, MATHIAS
VIDEO ARTIST
b Vienna, Austria, 65. *Study:* Student Univ Applied Arts; Student, Univ Vienna, Austria. *Exhib:* Principal works include: Produktion Pop (with Martin Beck & Jon Savage), 1996; Fondazione, Generali Found,Vienna, Austria, 1998; Actualite, 2001; Sufferers' Version, 2004; Zones of Disturbance, Graz, Austria, 1997; Grazer Kunstverein, 2001; Richard Telles Fine Art, Los Angeles, 2002, 2005; Mus Mod Art Found, Austria, 2003; MUMOK, Vienna, Austria, 2003; Galerie Meyer Kainer, 2004; Witte de With Center Contemp Art, Neth, 2006; group shows: 3 Berlin Biennale, Martin-Gropius-Bau, Berlin, 2004; 20/20 Vision, Stedelijk Mus Post CS, Amsterdam, Neth, 2004; Liverpool Biennial, Tate Liverpool, Eng, 2004; Occupying Space/Wasting Time, Haus, London, 2005; Whitney Biennial: Day for Night, Whitney Mus Am Art, 2006. *Mailing Add:* c/o Richard Telles Fine Art 7380 Beverly Blvd Los Angeles CA 90036

POLESKIE, STEPHEN FRANCIS
ARTIST, PRINTMAKER
b Pringle, Pa, June 3, 38. *Study:* Wilkes Col, BA, 59; New Sch Social Res, 61. *Work:* Whitney Mus Art, Metrop Mus Art, Mus Mod Art, NY; Victoria & Albert Mus; Tate Gallery, London. *Comn:* Aerial Theatre, Toledo, Ohio, 84 & Richmond, Va, 85; Int Video Festival, Locarno, Switz, 85; Zone Art Ctr, Springfield, Mass, 88; Aerial Theatre, Southampton Performance Festival, Eng, 89. *Exhib:* Word & Image-Posters and Typography (1879-1967), Mus Mod Art, NY, 68; Recent Acquisitions: Prints and Drawings, Metrop Mus Art, 69; Oversize Prints, Whitney Mus Am Art, 71; one-man exhibs, Palace of Cult & Sci, Warsaw, Poland & Gallery of Mod Art, Gdansk, 79; Stadt Mus, Kassel, WGer, 86; Lee Art Gallery, Clemson Univ, SC, 90; Nine Colums Gallery, Brescia, Italy, 91; Glenn Curtis Mus, Hammodsport, NY, 93; Caproni Mus, Trento, Italy, 95; and others. *Pos:* Founder & dir, Chiron Press, New York, 63-68. *Teaching:* Instr, Sch Visual Arts, New York, 66-68; assoc prof silk-screen & contemp art issues, Cornell Univ, 68-81, prof, 81-200, prof emer, 2000-; vis prof, Univ Calif, Berkeley, 76. *Awards:* Carnegie Found, 67; New York State Coun Arts, 73; Best Found, 85. *Bibliog:* Peter Frank (auth), Flights of Fancy, catalog essay, Richmond, Va, 85; Enrico Crispolti (auth), catalog essay, Rome, 87; Alison Lurie (auth), catalog essay, Eng, 89. *Media:* Aerial Theatre Performance, Screen Printing. *Publ:* Auth, Dell'arte e del Volo, Dars Milano, 84; Art and Flight: Historical Origins to Contemporary Works, Leonardo, 85; Reasons for Aerial Theatre, Art Criticism, 86. *Mailing Add:* OnagerEditions PO Box 849 Ithaca NY 14851-0849

POLING, CLARK V
HISTORIAN
Study: Yale Univ, BA, 62; Columbia Univ, MA, 66, PhD, 73. *Collection Arranged:* Bauhaus Color, 76, Contemporary Art in Atlanta Collections, 76 & Contemporary Art in Southern California, 80, High Mus Art; Kandinsky: Russian and Bauhaus Years, 1915-1933, Guggenheim Mus, 83; Henry Hornbostel-Michael Graves, Emory Univ Mus, 85. *Teaching:* Asst prof mod art, Emory Univ, 73-79, assoc prof, 79-88, prof, 88-, dir, 88-86, chmn Mus Art & Archeol, 87-. *Awards:* Kress Found Fel, 64-65; Deutscher Akad Austauschdienst Grant, 77 & 81; Nat Endowment Humanities Stipend, 78; Woolford B Baker Serv Award, Emory Univ and the Michael C Carlos Mus, 01. *Mem:* Col Art Asn; Twentieth Century Art Soc (bd dir, 88-). *Res:* Early 20th century European art and theory, especially surrealism: contemporary American art. *Publ:* Auth, Geometric abstraction: A new generation, Inst Contemp Art, Boston, 81; Kandinsky's Teaching at the Bauhaus, Rizzoli, NY, 87; The City and Modernity: Art in Berlin in the First World War and Its Aftermath, Art in Berlin 1815-1989, High Mus Art, Atlanta, 89. *Mailing Add:* c/o Art Hist Dept Carlos Hall Emory Univ Atlanta GA 30322

POLLACK, REGINALD MURRAY
PAINTER, SCULPTOR
b Middle Village, NY, July 29, 24. *Study:* Apprentice to Moses Soyer, 41; study with Wallace Harrison, 46-47; Acad Grande Chaumiere, Paris, 48-52. *Work:* Whitney Mus Am Art & Mus Mod Art, NY; Tel Aviv Mus, Jerusalem Mus & Haifa Mus, Israel; Nat Mus Am Art & Hirshhorn Mus & Sculpture Garden, Washington, DC; Brooklyn Mus; Rockefeller Inst. *Comn:* Peace (greeting card), Jewish Mus, NY, 61; painting for Great Thoughts of Western Man series, Container Corp Am, 64; cover for State of NY Dir, Bell Tel Co, 68-69; Chinese animal destiny calendar, Colgate-Palmolive Co, 72; Jacob's Dream (103' painting), Washington Cathedral, 74; Touche Ross New Perspective Awards, 79. *Exhib:* 63 one-man shows, 12 at Peridot Gallery, NY, 49-69, Felix Landau Gallery, Los Angeles, Washington Project for Arts: Retrospective, 77 & Jack Rasmussen Gallery, Washington, DC, 78-82; Whitney Mus Am Art, 53, 55, 56, 58 & 62; The Tartt Gallery, Washington, DC, 86; Denise Cade Gallery, NY, 86; Arctic Images Gallery, Colo, 87; The Gallery, Leesburg, Va, 92. *Pos:* Mem bd trustees, Washington Proj for the Arts, DC, 75-80; dir, The Gallery, Leesburg, Va, 92-94. *Teaching:* Vis critic art, Yale Univ, 62-63; instr art, Cooper Union, 63-64; staff mem, Human Rels Training Ctr, Univ Calif, Los Angeles, Lake Arrowhead, 66; pvt art classes, 67-69; instr, Quaker Half-Way House, Los Angeles, 68; vis artist, Mat Res Lab, Pa State Univ, 77 & 78. *Awards:* Prix Othon Friesz-V, Paris, 56; Prix des Peintres Etrangers - Laureate, Paris, 58; Ingram-Merrill Found Grants in painting, 64 & 70-71. *Media:* Oil; Bronze, Wood. *Interests:* painting, sculpting. *Publ:* Auth & illusr, The Magician and the Child, Atheneum, 71; illusr, Ctr for Dem Insts Mag, 3/72; auth, To artists with love & Brancusi's sculpture versus his home, Art News; illusr, Sounds Freedomring, Martin, Holt-Rinehart & Winston; Ted Knight (auth), Oedipus, 73; O is for Overkill, Viking, Pollack; The Enjoyment of Music, Machlis, Norton. *Mailing Add:* 2283 E Smokewood Ave Palm Springs CA 92264

POLLARD, HERSCHEL NEWTON
PAINTER, INSTRUCTOR
b Chadbourn, NC, Apr 6, 38. *Study:* Vanderbilt Univ, BA, 1960, PhD, 1972. *Work:* National Gallery, London, Eng. *Exhib:* One-man show, The Parthenon, Nashville, Tenn, 1972 & Nat Trust Larson Gallery, Naples, Fla, 2000 & Goff Gallery at Visual Arts Ctr, Punta Gorda, Fla, 2003; Glimpses of the Sea, Mus of Everglades, Naples, Fla, 1998; The Easter Exhib, Cape Coral Arts Studio, Fla, 1999; People, Places, Things, Impac Univ, Punta Gorda, Fla, 2004; The Entombment, Ave Maria Univ,

Naples, Fla, 2004-05; one man retrospective, Arts & Humanities Gallery, Port Charlotte, Fla, 2005. *Pos:* proj coord, Television, Radio & Film Comm, 1962-64; bd chmn, Von Leibig Ctr for the Arts, Naples, Fla, 2003-04; bd chmn, Visual Arts Ctr, Punta Gorda, Fla, 2005-. *Teaching:* instr, Pollard Studio, Chattanooga, Tenn, 1986-; instr painting, Cape Coral Arts Studio, Fla, 1999-2004; instr drawing & painting, Art League of Bonita Springs, Fla, 1996-99; instr painting & sculpture, Von Leibig Ctr for Arts, Naples, Fla, 1999-2003 & Visual Arts Ctr, Punta Gorda, Fla, 2001-. *Awards:* First Judges Award, Visual Arts Ctr Fifth Nat Art Exhib, 2004; Bowles Award for Portraiture, Faces & Figures, Bill & Susanne Bowles, 2005; First Place, Nat Aviation Art Exhib, 2006. *Bibliog:* M. Gomez (auth), The 2005 H Pollard Retrospective, CESA Press, 2005. *Mem:* Von Leibig Ctr for the Arts (pres 2002-03); Art Council of SW Fla (rep 2002-03); Visual Arts Ctr (pres 2005-06); Peace River Nat Arts Festival (plan bd chmn 2006); Nat Aviation Art Exhib (chmn 2006). *Media:* Acrylic, Oil. *Res:* Italian baroque art; ancient Greek, Chinese & Roman coin-making techniques. *Publ:* auth, The Art of Frances Morton Pollard, 2000, The Madman of Arles, 2003, Plllard's Brief Handbook for Painters, 2004 & Pollard's Infinite Palette, 2006, CESA Press; ed, A Life Remembered, CESA Press, 2004. *Dealer:* L M Gomez 1001 Montlake Rd Soddy-Daisy TN 37379. *Mailing Add:* 27121 Solomon Dr Punta Gorda FL 33983

POLLARD, JANN LAWRENCE
FINE ARTIST, INSTRUCTOR
b Mt Pleasant, Iowa, Apr 11, 42. *Study:* Univ Colo, BFA, 1963; Col San Mateo, studied technical arts, San Mateo, Calif. *Comn:* Karen Brown Guides; Princess Cruise, 2005. *Exhib:* One-woman shows, The Gallery, Burlingame, Calif, 1991, 93, 95-96, 98-99, 2001-2002, & 2004-2005, The Cottage Gallery, Carmel, Calif, 1991, 93, 95 & 98; Images of Filoli, Filoli Gardens, 98; juried shows, Calif Watercolor Asn, 98, Nat Watercolor Soc, 99; California Watercolorists Invitational, 99; Watercolor USA, 2001; numerous others. *Teaching:* instr, watercolor workshops, France, Italy, England, Mexico, Calif, 95-; instr, Calif Watercolor Asn, 2001; instr, watercolor workshops, Filoi Nat Trust Garden, 96-. *Awards:* 3rd Prize, 30 & 1 Artists Ann, San Mateo, Calif, 1996; Patron Purchase award, Watercolor USA, 2001; Outstanding Achievement award, Calif Watercolor Asn, 2002. *Bibliog:* Jan Wright Bressler (auth), Almost Famous Recipes, Gentry Mag, 2002; Theodora Philcox (auth), Landscapes in Watercolor, AVA Publ, SA, Switzerland, 2002; Margot Schulzke (auth), A Painter's Guide to Design & Composition, North Light Books, 2005. *Mem:* Calif Watercolor Asn (signature mem, ann show dir, 1997-98, fundraising dir, 1997-98, newsletter editor, 1999 & 2000 & newsletter dir, 2000 & 2001); Nat Watercolor Soc (signature mem); Soc Western Artists (signature mem); ASID (profl mem). *Media:* All Media. *Publ:* Cover artist, Karen Brown Travel Books, 91; auth, The Artist & Computer can be Friends, Int Artist mag, Issue 5, 99; coauth, Creative Computer Tools for Artists, Watson-Guptill Publs, 2001. *Dealer:* The Gallery, Burlingame, CA; New Masters Gallery, Carmel, CA. *Mailing Add:* 105 La Mesa Dr Burlingame CA 94010

POLLARO, PAUL
PAINTER
b Brooklyn, NY. *Study:* Flatiron Sch Art, NY; Art Students League, Pratt Graphic Ctr. *Work:* Mus NMex, Santa Fe; Jan Perry Mayer Collection; Chrysler Mus; Orlando Mus Art, Fla; Notre Dame Univ Mus Art, South Bend, Ind. *Exhib:* Ann, Pa Acad Fine Arts, Philadelphia, 64; Nat Inst Arts & Lett, 69 & 72; Artists of the 20th Century, Mus Mod Art, NY, 70; Artists at Work, Finch Col Mus, 71; Babcock Gallery, NY, 73; Louis Newman Gallery, Beverly Hills, Calif; L K Meisel Gallery, NY; one man exhib, Chrysler Mus, 91; Janus Gallery, Santa Fe, NMex, 92. *Pos:* Assoc dir, The MacDowell Colony, 73-77. *Teaching:* Instr painting, New Sch Social Res, 64-69; asst prof painting, Wagner Col, 69-72; vis artist, Notre Dame Univ, summers 65 & 67. *Awards:* Second Prize, Jersey City Mus, 62; MacDowell Colony Fels, 66, 68 & 71; Tiffany Found Grant, 67. *Media:* Acrylic, Oil. *Publ:* Articles in: Art in America, Art News, Arts, NY Times, Art Space, Art New Eng, Art Int. *Mailing Add:* Norway Hill Hancock NH 03449

POLLEI, DANE F
MUSEUM DIRECTOR, CURATOR
b Fond du Lac, Wis. *Study:* Beloit Col, BA. *Collection Arranged:* Wayang Puppets: Art of Indonesia, Logan Mus Anthropology, 84; German Expressionism, Wright Mus Art, 85; Beloit and Vicinity, Wright Mus Art, 86; Franklin Boggs and V O Schaffer: Art and Architecture, Freeport Art Mus, Ill, 88; Scenes of Madagascar: Ethnographic Portraits 1890-1930, Freeport Art Mus, Ill, 88; The Art of Persuasion: Posters from the World Wars, Kenosha Hist Mus, 90; The Art of the Wheel: Nash Advertising; It Came from Hollywood: B-Movies of the 50's & 60's; The Photographs of Louis Thiers (auth catalog), 97. *Pos:* Asst cur, Logan Mus Anthropology, 83-85; asst to dir, Wright Mus Art, 85-86; dir, Freeport Art Mus, Ill, 87-89; exec dir, Kenosha Hist Mus, 89-. *Teaching:* Instr, mus studies, Univ Wis, Oshkosh, 87; instr, Am Indian art, Highland Community Col, 88-89, instr anthropology, 88-89. *Mem:* Am Asn Mus; Wis Art Educ Asn. *Publ:* Ed, Westword Traveller, Wis Heritage Tourism Newspaper; auth, Focus on Louis Thiers: A Photographers View of Kenosha, 98

POLLIEN, ROBERT L
PAINTER, PRINTMAKER
b Bridgeport, Conn, Nov 21, 60. *Study:* Trinity Col, BA, 81; Univ Pa, MFA, 84; Studied in Skowhegan, 84. *Work:* Farnsworth Mus, Rockland, Maine. *Exhib:* Skowhegan at Fifty: The Maine Legacy, Maine Coast Artists Gallery, Rockport, Maine, 96. *Teaching:* instr drawing and design, Univ Southern Maine, 86-92. *Awards:* Grant, Ludwig Vogelstein Found, 91-92; Individual fel, Maine Arts Comn, 2000. *Media:* Oil. *Mailing Add:* PO Box 658 Mount Desert ME 04660

POLLITT, JEROME JORDAN
HISTORIAN, EDUCATOR
b Fair Lawn, NJ, Nov 26, 34. *Study:* Yale Univ, New Haven, Conn, BA, 57; Columbia Univ, New York, PhD, 63. *Pos:* Ed-in-chief, Am J Archeol, 74-78. *Teaching:* Prof classic art & archeol, Yale Univ, 62-. *Publ:* Auth, The Art of Greece: Sources and Documents, 64 & The Art of Rome: Sources and Documents, 65, Prentice-Hall & Cambridge Univ Press, 83 & 90; Art and Experience in Classical Greece, Cambridge Univ Press, 72; The Ancient View of Greek Art, Yale Univ Press, 75; Art in the Hellenistic Age, Cambridge Univ Press, 86 & Personal Styles in Greek Sculpture, 96. *Mailing Add:* Dept History of Art PO Box 208072 New Haven CT 06520

POLLOCK, BRUCE
PAINTER, SCULPTOR
b Painesville, Ohio, July 7, 51. *Study:* Carnegie-Mellon Univ, 70; Cleveland Inst Art, BFA, 76; Tyler Sch Art, MFA, 78. *Work:* Philadelphia Mus Art; Prudential Insurance Co. *Comn:* 12th Walnut brick-walk, Redevelop Authority Philadelphia. *Exhib:* Solo exhibs, Alan Stone Gallery, NY, 82, Karen Lennox Gallery, Chicago, Ill, 82, Laurence Miller Gallery, NY, 84, Jeffrey Fuller, Philadelphia, 84, Cavin-Morris Gallery, NY, 86, Janet Fleisher Gallery, Philadelphia, 87-95, Pa Acad Fine Art, Philadelphia, 90-92; Pertaining to Philadelphia, Philadelphia Mus Art, 83; Contemp Philadelphia Artists, Philadelphia Mus Art, 90; On the Moon, Univ Sci Ctr, Philadelphia, 92; Ritual and Response Abstract, Hicks Art Ctr, Newton, Pa, 93; Prison Sentences: The Prison Site/The Prison as Subject, Moore Col Art, Philadelphia, 94; Artists of Northern Liberties, Paley Design Ctr, Philadelphia, 95; Biennial 1996, Del Art Mus, Wilmington, 96. *Teaching:* Drexel Univ, Philadelphia. *Awards:* Fel, Macdowell Colony, Peterborough, NH, 87; Distinguished Artist Award, Contemp Philadelphia Artists, Philadelphia Mus Art, 90; Pollock-Krasner Found Grant, 91. *Bibliog:* Reviews in Artforum, 10/79, Art in America, 10/82, New Art Examiner, 10/82, 3/83, 3/88 & 5/92; Edward J Soznaski (auth), Philadelphia Inquirer, 3/19/94; Mark Gallini (auth), Seven Arts Mag, 10/95. *Media:* Acrylic, Oil. *Publ:* Illusr, Metapsychology Mag, Vol I No II, autumn, 85

POLONSKY, ARTHUR
PAINTER, EDUCATOR
b Lynn, Mass, June 6, 25. *Study:* Boston Mus Sch, with Karl Zerbe, dipl (with highest honors), 48; Europ Traveling Fel, 48-50. *Work:* Fogg Mus, Harvard Univ, Cambridge; Mus Fine Arts, Boston; Addison Gallery Am Art, Andover; Walker Art Ctr; Stedelijk Mus, Amsterdam, Holland. *Comn:* Stone with the Angel (portfolio of ten original lithographs), Impressions Workshop, Inc, Boston, 69. *Exhib:* Art Today-50, Metrop Mus Art, NY, 50; one-man show, Boston, NY & Washington, 51-98; Starr Gallery, Boston, 87; Fitchburg Art Mus, Mass, 90; Boston Pub Libr, 90, 93, 96 & 99; Palais Universitaire, Strasbourg, France, 95; Boston Expressionism, Paul Creative Arts Ctr, Univ NH, 2000; Decordova Mus, Lincoln, Mass, 03; Kantar Fine Arts, Newton, Mass, 02. *Pos:* Founding mem & dir, Artists' Equity Asn, 48-67. *Teaching:* Instr painting, Boston Mus Sch, 50-60; asst prof painting, drawing & design, Brandeis Univ, 54-65; assoc prof painting, drawing & design, Boston Univ, Coll of Fine Arts, 65-90, prof emer, 90. *Awards:* Tiffany Found Grant for Painting, 51-52; First Prize, Boston Arts Festival, 54; Purchase Award, Drawings '74, Wheaton Nat Exhib, Wheaton Col, 74; Named Copley Master Copley Soc Boston, 86. *Bibliog:* reviews of exhibs in Art News, Arts Mag, NY Times, Time Mag, New Yorker Mag & others, 48-99; Archives Am Art, Smithsonian Inst, 72; Nathan Goldstein (auth), The Art of Responsive Drawing, Prentice Hall, 73, 77 & 84; Nathan Goldstein (auth), Figure Drawing, Prentice-Hall, 76; Judith Bookbinder (auth), Boston Expressionism, Univ Press New Eng, 2005; and others. *Media:* All. *Publ:* Illusr, Sexual Decisions, Little, Brown & Co, 80; Poetry in Motion, Sundance Publ, 87; Léo Bronstein (auth), Kabbalah And Art, Brandeis Univ Press, 78; Richard Jones (auth), The Dream Poet, Schenkmann Books, 81; Sadie, Remember, Sundance Publ, 92; and others. *Dealer:* Kantar Fine Arts Newton MA 02458; Francesca Anderson Fine Art Lexington MA. *Mailing Add:* 364 Cabot St Newtonville MA 02460

POLSHEK, JAMES
ARCHITECT
b Akron, Ohio, Feb 11, 30. *Study:* Case Western Reserve Univ, BS, 51; Yale Univ, MArch, 55. *Hon Degrees:* Pratt Inst, Hon DFA, 95; New Sch Univ, Hon DFA, 99; NJ Inst Technol, LHD, 2002. *Comn:* designer, Brooklyn Mus, entry pavillion & plaza, Brooklyn, NY; co-designer, Am Mus Nat Hist, Rose Center for Earth & Space, NY; designer, The Santa Fe Opera, NMex; designer, Scandanavia House: The Nordic Center in Am, NY; designer, William J Clinton Presidential Ctr, Little Rock, Ark, 2004. *Pos:* I M, Pei & Assocs, New York City, 55-56; Ulrich Frazen & Assoc, New York City, 57-60; Westermann & Miller & Assocs, 60-61; pvt Practice Archit, 62-80; special adv for planning & design to the Pres, Columbia Univ, 72-87; founder, Polshek Partnership Architects, 80-. *Teaching:* Columbia Univ, Grad Sch Archit, Planning & Preservation, dean, 72-87, prof archit, 72-2002, prof emeritus archit, 98-. *Awards:* Fulbright Fel, 56-57. *Mem:* Am Acad Arts & Sciences (fel); Archit, Designers & Planners for Social Responsibility (founder, mem bd adv); Nat Acad (fel); Cathedral of St. John the Divine (regent); NY Sch Design (adv bd); Temple Hoyne Buell Center, Study of Am Archit, Columbia Univ (founder, former mem bd dir); Regional Plan Asn (bd mem); Lycée Français de NY (adv comt); Am Inst Archit (col of fel). *Mailing Add:* Polshek Partnership Architects LLP 320 W 13th St New York NY 10014

POLSKY, CYNTHIA HAZEN
ADMINISTRATOR, COLLECTOR
b New York, NY, Feb 16, 39. *Study:* Art Students League; New Sch Social Res; Marymount Manhattan Col, BA; Fordham Univ, MBA. *Work:* Corcoran Gallery Am Art, Washington, DC; Israel Mus, Jerusalem; Ulrich Mus of Art, Wichita, Kans; Fogg Art Mus, Cambridge, Mass; USIA Collection, London, Eng; and others; Johnson Mus

at Cornell Univ, Ithaca, NY; NY Acad Scis and Rockefeller Univ, NY. *Exhib:* One-person shows, Benson Gallery, Bridgehampton, Long Island, NY, 68, Comara Gallery, Los Angeles, 69, Artisan Gallery, Houston, Tex, 70, Palm Springs Desert Mus, 72-73 & Crispo Gallery, NY, 73 & 74; Ulrich Mus of Art, Wichita, Kans, 77. *Pos:* Trustee, Metrop Mus Art, chmn comt membership & visiting comt for 20th cent art, mem exec comn, aquisitions comt, adv comt Asian Art, educ comn, currently; hon trustee, Storm King Art Ctr, Mountainville, NY, chmn, acquisitions comt, mem exec comt, nominating comn; hon life trustee, Friends Asian Arts, Asia Soc, NY; chmn, Patrons Pierpont Morgan Libr, NY; trustee, Am Acad in Rome, co-chair, comn for Sch of Fine Arts, mem executive comn, nominating comn; adv comn, Cult Affairs NY. *Bibliog:* Judith Denham (auth), article, in: Art Week, 73; Alfred Frankenstein (auth), article, in: San Francisco Chronicle, 73. *Mem:* Comm on Indo-US Ed, Asia Soc; Collectors' Comt, Nat Gallery Art, Washington, DC; Collections Comt, Harvard Univ Art Mus; New York City Comn to the UN. *Publ:* Auth, Indian Paintings from the Polsky Collection, The Art Mus, Princeton Univ, 82; Cynthia Polsky, Paintings 1973-1974, 90. *Mailing Add:* 667 Madison Ave 15th Fl New York NY 10021

POLZER, JOSEPH
HISTORIAN
b Vienna, Austria, May 7, 29; US citizen. *Study:* Univ Iowa, BA(art), 50, MA(art hist), 52; Inst Fine Arts, NY Univ, PhD(art hist), 63. *Teaching:* Instr, Univ Kans, 57-58; lectr, Univ Buffalo, 58-62; from asst prof to prof, Univ Louisville, 62-73; prof art, Queen's Univ, Kingston, formerly, Univ Calgary, Alberta, Can, currently. *Res:* Late Rome, Middle Ages, Renaissance. *Publ:* Auth, articles in Late Antique Medieval & Renaissance Art. *Mailing Add:* Dept Art Univ Calgary 2500 University Dr NW Calgary AB T2N 1N4 Canada

POMEROY, FREDERICK GEORGE
PAINTER, RESTORER
b Oakland, Calif, Aug 30, 24. *Study:* Calif Col Arts & Crafts, Oakland, AB(scholar), 53; Ecole de Beaux Arts, Fontainebleau, France, with Lucien Fontanarosa, cert, 51; La Grande Chaumiere, Paris, France, cert, 51; Centre Universitaire de la Mediterrane, Nice, France, cert, 65. *Comn:* Murals commissioned privately in Pebble Beach, Calif, 58 & Carmel Valley, Calif, 58; Restorations, Beeches Gallery, Carmel, Calif, 86-. *Exhib:* James Phelan Competition, San Francisco Mus Art, 50; Recent Paintings, Marjory Evans Gallery, Carmel, Calif, 86; Local Color, Sangre de Cristo Arts Ctr, Pueblo, Colo, 89; Celebration of Plein Air Painters, Pacific Grove Art Ctr, Calif, 91; Open Studio Tour, Monterey Peninsula Artists, 93; Monterey Peninsula Mus Art, 96; Invitational Exhib, Pac Grove Art Ctr, 97; Homage to Mother Earth, Environ Res Ctr, Santa Cruz, Calif, 97-98; Local Color, Alvarado Gallery, Monterey, Calif, 99; Art in the Park, Carmel Valley, Calif, 2005. *Teaching:* Instr art, Robert Luis Stevenson Sch & local schs, Pebble Beach, Calif, 54. *Awards:* French Govt Cult Relations Prize, 51; Kiwanis of Pacific Grove First Prize in Watercolor, 5th Ann Competition, 69; First Prize, Pacific Grove Mus 13th Ann Competition, 77. *Bibliog:* Lyman Pitman (auth), Natures detail, Chieftain, Pueblo, Colo, 3/12/89. *Mem:* Monterey Peninsula Watercolor Soc. *Media:* Oil, Watercolor. *Specialty:* Int painting, figure, landscape, still-life. *Publ:* Illusr, Trees of the San Francisco Bay Area, Univ Calif Press, 59; The Poetry Shell, Mag of Verse, fall 77 & spring 78. *Dealer:* Collectors Gallery Mission St bet 5th & 6th Carmel CA 93921. *Mailing Add:* 88 Boronda Rd Carmel Valley CA 93924

POMEROY, LYNDON FAYNE
SCULPTOR
b Sidney, Mont, Mar 9, 25. *Study:* Mont State Univ, BS, 52, MAA, 60. *Work:* Yellowstone Art Ctr, Billings, Mont; Mont State Hist Mus, Helena. *Comn:* Loggers, Savings & Loan, Green Bay, Wis, 80; Ditch Builder, Hist Centennial Co, Worland, Wyo, 89. *Exhib:* Nat Religious Art Exhib, Detroit, Mich, 64. *Teaching:* Asst prof, Northern Mont Col, 53-58; Eastern Mont Col, 58-61. *Awards:* Mont State Gov's Arts Award Visual Arts, 91. *Mem:* Growth Thru Art for Disabled Adults (bd dir, 90); Stillwater Soc. *Media:* Steel. *Mailing Add:* 5000 Rimrock Rd Billings MT 59106-1313

POMEROY, MARY BARNAS (MRS F G POMEROY)
PAINTER, ILLUSTRATOR
b Frankfurt am/Main, Ger, Mar 3, 21; US citizen. *Study:* Studied with Carl Barnas, Quito Eduador, 38-46; Pa Acad Fine Arts, with Daniel Garber, Roy Nuse, Franklin Watkins & Henry Pitz, 46-48. *Work:* Univ Calif Dept of Botany, Berkeley; Hunt Inst Botanical Doc, Carnegie-Mellon Univ, Pittsburgh, Pa. *Comn:* Geological Illustrations, comn by Dr Sauer, Univ Cent, Quito, Ecuador, 40; Fruits & Vegetables (paintings), comn by Mrs Foote, Carmel Valley, Calif, 74; Flowering Trees of America (Plate design), Franklin Mint Corp, Pa, 79; Restorations, Beeches Gallery, Carmel, 87-; Wildflowers of the Asilomar Dunes (poster), Asilomar Operating Corp & Dept Parks, Pacific Grove, Calif, 89-90. *Exhib:* Solo exhib, Wildflowers of Ecuador, Universidad Cent, Quito, Ecuador, 40, Ecuadorian Wildflowers & Fungi, Acad Nat Sci, Philadelphia, Pa, 46 & Acad Sci, Golden Gate Park, San Francisco, Calif, 48 & Jungle Flowers, Mus of Mo Botanical Gardens Traveling Show, Mo, 74; Int Exhib of Botanical Art & Illus, Hunt Inst, Pittsburgh, Pa, 64, 72 & 77; Exhib Contemp Botanical Artists & Illusr, Cleveland Mus Art, Ohio, 66; California Land & Seascapes, Portraits, Florals, Marjorie Evans Gallery, Carmel, Calif, 81-86; Natural Color, Sangre de Cristo Art & Conf Ctr, Pueblo, Colo, 89; Celebration of Plein Air Painters, Pacific Grove Art Ctr, Calif, 91; Open Studio Tour, Monterey Peninsula Artists, 93; Homage to Mother Earth, Environ Resource Center, Santa Cruz, Calif, 97-98. *Collection Arranged:* Hunt Inst for Documentation (Botanical Art from Equador & Calif). *Pos:* Illusr, Fossil Foraminifera & Shells, Int Petroleum Co, Guayaquil, Ecuador, 43-44; botanical illusr, Univ Calif Berkeley for H Mason & others, 47-53; free-lance painter & illusr, 53-. *Teaching:* Pvt lessons in watercolor & botanical illust,Berkeley, Caif, 50; pvt workshops in outdoor landscape in watercolor, Carmel, Calif, 66, 67 & 69. *Awards:* Pa Acad Fine Arts, First Prize in Anatomy & Animal Drawing, Students Work Acad Gallery, Philadelphia, 47; Mus Nat Hist Best Monterey Co Subject, 14th Ann Watercolor Competition, 78 & Best Small Painting, 18th Ann Watercolor Competition, 82, Pacific Grove. *Bibliog:* Pat Griffith (auth), Carmel Valley's nature artist M B Pomeroy, Carmel Valley Outlook, 10/12/72; art ed, A calendar full of birthday flowers, Carmel Pinecone, 10/27/83; Lyman Pittman (auth), Nature's details, colors, inspire California couple, Pueblo Chieftain, 3/12/89. *Mem:* Monterey Peninsula Watercolor Soc. *Media:* Watercolor, Pen & Ink. *Publ:* Illusr, Las Plantas, Publicaciones de las Univ Cent, Quito, Ecuador, 39; A Flora of the Marshes of California & Native Trees of the San Francisco Bay Region, Univ Calif Berkeley Press, 59; Saloya, 67 & Eduador's edible jewels, 69, America's Mag, Pan-Am Union Publ; Birthday Flowers, Landmark Calendars, 84. *Dealer:* Beeches Gallery PO Box 4092 Carmel CA 93921; The Artisan's hand Gallery 19 E Carmel Valley Rd Carmel Valley CA 93924. *Mailing Add:* 88 Boronda Rd Carmel Valley CA 93924

PONCE DE LEON, MICHAEL
PRINTMAKER, PAINTER
b Miami, Fla, July 4, 22. *Study:* Univ Mex, BA; Art Students League; Nat Acad Design; Brooklyn Mus Art Sch; also in Europe. *Work:* Mus Mod Art & Metrop Mus Art, NY; Nat Gallery Art & Smithsonian Inst, Washington, DC; Brooklyn Mus; collection of prints added to NY Pub Libr Collection, 02; and others. *Comn:* Many print editions, 60-; ten prints, US State Dept, 66; glass sculpture, Steuben Glass, 71; 100 prints, Pioneer Moss, Inc, annually, 68-83. *Exhib:* Mus Arte Mod, Paris; Victoria & Albert Mus, London; Venice Bienale, 70; Mus Mod Art & Metrop Mus, NY; Smithsonian Inst, Washington, DC; and others. *Pos:* Int Cult Exchange, US State Dept, teaching, lect & travel, Yugoslavia, 65, India & Pakistan, 67-68, Spain, 71 & SAmerica. *Teaching:* Instr printmaking, Hunter Col, 59-66; prof, New York Univ, 77 & Pratt Inst, 78; instr printmaking, Art Students League, 78-, Berkeley Univ, Calif, Univ Calif, Los Angeles, and others. *Awards:* More than 65 medals & awards, incl Tiffany Found Grants, 54 & 55; Fulbright Grants, 56 & 57; Guggenheim Found Grant, 67. *Bibliog:* G Peterdi (auth), Printmaking, Macmillan, 72; F Eichenberg (auth), The Art of the Print, Abrams, 77; D Saff (auth), Printmaking History and Process, Holt, Rinehart & Winston, 78. *Mem:* Soc Am Graphic Artists (treas, 68); Asn Am Univ Prof. *Media:* All Graphic Media. *Publ:* Contribr, Experiments in three dimensions, Art Am, 68; auth, The collage intaglio, 72; The collage-intaglios of Michael Ponce de Leon, Am Artist, 8/74; History of an Art, Skira (in 4 languages), 81; History of International Art, Academia Italia (in 4 languages), 81. *Dealer:* Jane Haslem Gallery 2121 P St NW Washington DC 20036; AAA Gallery 663 Fifth Ave New York NY

POND, CLAYTON
PAINTER, PRINTMAKER
b Long Island, NY, June 10, 41. *Study:* Carnegie Inst Technol, BFA, 64; Pratt Inst, MFA, 66. *Work:* Smithsonian Nat Air & Space Mus, Nat Gallery Art & Nat Collection Fine Arts, Washington; Mus Mod Art, NY; Boston Mus Fine Arts; Philadelphia Mus Art; Art Inst Chicago; Los Angeles Co Mus; and many others. *Comn:* Large painted construction, 1985-86 Fly-by of Halley's Comet, Nat Air & Space Mus, Washington; Kentucky Derby Dandies, Petro III Editions, painting, ltd ed serigraph, prints & poster, Gov John Y & Phyllis George Brown, Ky, 81; 3-D painting on plexiglass-acquiring constellation Orion, NASA (Nat Aeronautic & Space Admin), 81; large painted sculpture & study painting, Printing Press, Motter Printing Press Co, York, Pa, 88; large painted sculpture & study painting, The Intimidator, Anderson Gallery, Buffalo, NY, 91. *Exhib:* One-man shows, Assoc Am Artists Gallery, NY, 66, Martha Jackson Gallery, NY, 68, 72, 73, 75 & 77, Jack Gallery, NY, 79 & 84, Hammer Galleries, NY, 80 & 91, Linden Gallery, NY, 81, Dwight Frederic Boyden Gallery, St Mary's Col, Md, 83 & 92, Schenectady Mus Art, NY, 86, Elvejhem Mus, Madison, Wis, 86 & DeGraaf Fine Arts, Chicago, 87, 89, 91 & 93, Hammer Galleries, New York City, 91, St Mary's Coll Md, 92, DeGraaf-Forsyth Galleries, Saugatuck, Mich, 93, W Palm Beach, Fla, 99.; Whitney Mus Am Art Ann, NY, 67; New Am Prints Traveling Exhib, US Info Agency, 8 countries, 73; 23rd Libr Cong Exhib, Nat Collection Fine Arts, Smithsonian Inst, 73; Vision of Flight, 1988-1992, Int traveling exhib 13 mus NASA art collection; Deitrich Gallery, NY, 95 & 96; Modern Masters Gallery, NY, 96; De Graaf Fine Arts, Chicago, 2001. *Teaching:* Instr photog & printmaking, C W Post Col, Long Island Univ, 66-68; adj instr serigraphy, Sch Visual Arts, New York, 68-70; guest lectr, Univ Wis-Madison, spring 72; vis prof, St John's Univ, Queens, NY, 90-91. *Awards:* State Dept Grant, Smithsonian Inst Int Art Prog & Abby Gray Found, 67; Purchase Award, Boston Printmakers 20th Ann Exhib, Boston Mus, 68; Nat Endowment Arts Grant, 73. *Bibliog:* Una Johnson (auth), American Prints and Printmakers, Doubleday & Co Inc, Garden City, NY, 80; Dorothy A Spencer (auth), The Colorful World of Clayton Pond, cover & feature article, Am Artist Mag, Billboard Publ Inc, New York, 3/81; Stella Pandell Russell (auth), Art in the World, Holt Rinehart & Winston, New York, 84. *Mem:* Albany Print Club. *Media:* Acrylic Paintings, Reliefs; Serigraphy. *Publ:* Articles in Artist's Proof, Pratt Graphic Art Ctr, New York, Vol VI, 66 & Vol VIII, 68. *Dealer:* Anderson Gallery 1 Martha Jackson Pl Buffalo NY 14214. *Mailing Add:* 835 Dockbridge Way Alpharetta GA 30004

PONDICK, RONA
SCULPTOR, ENVIRONMENTAL ARTIST
b Apr 18, 52. *Study:* Queens Col, BA, 74; Sch Art, Yale Univ, MFA, 77. *Work:* Whitney Mus Am Art; Los Angeles Co Mus; Mus Contemp Art, Los Angeles; Brooklyn Mus; Israel Mus, Jerusalem. *Exhib:* Solo shows, Inst Contemp Art, Boston, 89, Israel Mus, 92, Cincinnati Art Mus, 95, Brooklyn Mus, 96-98; Whitney Bienniel, Whitney Mus Art, 91; Corporal Politics, MIT List Visual Arts Ctr, Cambridge, Mass, 92; Vber-Leben, Bonner Kunstuerein, Bonn, Ger, 93; Configura 2, Erfurt, Ger, 95. *Awards:* Mid-Atlantic Arts Grant, 91; Guggenheim fel, 92; Rockefeller Found Fel, 96.

Bibliog: Terry R Myers (auth), Presenting pleasures: Urgent sculpture of Rona Pondick, Arts Mag, 90; Jerry Saltz (auth), The Living Dead Life of the Body, Balcon, 91; Mark Wilson (auth), Het liminale lichaam: De Deelden van Rona Pondick, Metropolis, 94. *Mailing Add:* 32 Cooper Sq New York NY 10003

PONSOT, CLAUDE F
EDUCATOR, PAINTER
b Rabat, Morocco, May 29, 27; US citizen. *Study:* Atelier Perrier/Jaudon, 47-50; Atelier Andre L'hote, 48-50; Atelier Fernand Leger, 49-50. *Work:* Associated Metals & Minerals Corp, NY; pvt collections, Monique Ponsot, Barbara Baranowska, NY; pvt collection Mr & Mrs M Kesdekian, Tex; Boltax Gallery, Shelter Island, NY. *Comn:* Graphics, LaGuardia Community Col, NY, 79-80 & St John's Univ, 81; South Oaks Hospital, Amityville, 81; and others. *Exhib:* One-man show, Galerie Maitre Albert, Paris, 76; Cabinet des Estampes, Biblioteque Nat, Paris, 78; Brand X, Glendale, Calif, 80; In the Best Tradition, Heckscher Mus, Huntington, 81; Firehouse Gallery, Nassau Community Col, NY, 82 & 83; and others. *Collection Arranged:* Philippe Tailleur, Nimes, France. *Teaching:* Prof art, St John's Univ, New York, formerly. *Awards:* Pat Lambert Award, Shreveport Art Guild; Purchase Award, Images-Shapes 76, Plattsburgh; Patron Purchase Award, Watercolor USA, Springfield Mus, 77. *Bibliog:* Jean Parris (auth), articles, Newsday, 79-81; biog, WCUSAHS newsletter, 97. *Mem:* Watercolor USA Hon Soc. *Media:* Oil, Watercolor. *Res:* Lascaux, The Painters of Yesterday. *Specialty:* Boltax Gallery, One man show 1002. *Interests:* Romanesque art France; caves arts. *Dealer:* Kimberly Greer Gallery Northport Village NY 11768. *Mailing Add:* 8047 235th St Queens Village NY 11427

PONTYNEN, ARTHUR
EDUCATOR, ADMINISTRATOR
b Brooklyn, NY, Mar 23, 50. *Study:* Univ Iowa, Iowa City, PhD, 83. *Teaching:* Asst prof art hist, Stephen F Austin State Univ, 85-89, Univ Wis, Oshkosh, 89-95, assoc prof, 95-, dept chair, 97-2003, full prof, 2006. *Awards:* Fel, Smithsonian Inst, Washington, DC, 79-80; Salvatori Fel, Heritage Found, Washington, DC, 91-93. *Mem:* Col Art Asn. *Res:* Art theory and philosophy. *Publ:* Auth, A Winter landscape: Reflections on the theory & practice of art history, Art Bull, 86; A cosmopolitan critique of multiculturalism & Oedipus wrecks: PC & liberalism, Measure, 92-93; Beauty vs aesthetics, chapter in Moral Education: An Interdisciplinary Approach, 94; Taoism & Confucianism, Dictionary of Art, 96; Ready Reference: Censorship, Nat Endowment Arts; Art, Science and Postmodern Society, Am Outlook, 11-12/2000; Beauty and the Enlightened Beast, Am Outlook, 2001; The Aesthetics of Race vs The Beauty of Humanity, Am Outlook, 2002; For the Love of Beauty: Art, History, and the Moral Foundation of Aesthetic Judgement (Transaction Pub, 2005). *Mailing Add:* Univ Wis Oshkosh WI 54901

POOLE, LESLIE DONALD
PAINTER, PRINTMAKER
b Halifax, NS, May 3, 42. *Study:* Prince of Wales Col, Charlottetown, PEI, 60; Univ Alta, Edmonton, BFA, 67; Yale Univ, MFA, 70. *Work:* Can Coun Art Bank, Ottawa; Beaverbrook Art Gallery, Fredericton, NB; Confederation Ctr Art Gallery, Charlottetown, PEI; Hyatt Hotel, Chicago, Ill; Vancouver Art Gallery, BC. *Comn:* Portrait lieutenant gov, Prov Alta, 73; mural, Minto Suite Hotel, Ottowa, Ont, 89; Trimark Mutual Funds, Toronto, Ont, 94. *Exhib:* Solo exhib, Confederation Ctr Art Gallery, Charlottetown, PEI, 73, Edmonton Art Gallery, 74, Encounters with the Goddess, Surrey AG, BC, 91, Kamloops Art Gallery, BC, 92-94 & SFU Art Gallery, Vancouver, 95, Shadow/Light: new paintings, Heffel Gallery, 98, Aspen paintings, Scott Gallery, 99, Leslie Pooe's Diary, Gallery at Coperley House, Burnaby, BC, 2000; Memento Mori, Teck Gallery, Simon Fraser Univ at Harbor Ctr, Vancouver, 96; Shadow Paintings, Canadian Art Galleries, Calgary, Alta, 97; Landscpes with Cows paintings, Bauxi Gallery, Toronto, 99; After Bonnard, Winchester Galleries, 2000; Simon Fraser Univ, Vancouver, 04; Scott Gallery Edmonton, 05. *Teaching:* Lectr design, Univ Alta, Edmonton, 71-72; instr painting, Banff Sch Fine Arts, 73; lectr drawing, Vancouver Community Col, 75-87. *Awards:* Can Coun Arts Grants, 72, 74, 75 & 80. *Bibliog:* Glenn Howarth (auth), An ecumenical intent, Vanguard Mag, Vancouver, 78; David Watmough (auth), Not exactly limpid Pooles, Interface, Alta, 81; Capilano Rev, No 34, 85. *Media:* Acrylic; Lithography. *Dealer:* Gary Maier New Westminster BC Can. *Mailing Add:* 526 Fourth St New Westminster BC V3L 2V6 Canada

POOLE, NANCY GEDDES
GALLERY DIRECTOR
b London, Ont, May 10, 30. *Study:* MacDonald Col, McGill Univ, dipl, 49; Univ Western Ont, BA, 55; Univ Western Ont, LLD, 90. *Hon Degrees:* Univ Western Ont, LLD, 90; ORDGR of Canada, 2004. *Collection Arranged:* SW18-London, Rothman Gallery, Stratford, Can, 69; Canadian Printmakers, 70 & Jack Chambers, 79, Canada House Gallery; British Printmakers, Ont galleries tour, 71; Victorian Artists, London Regional Art Gallery, 86. *Pos:* Dir & owner, Nancy Poole's Studio, 69-78; chmn governing coun, Ont Col Art, 73-74; gov, Univ Western Ont, 74-95; interim dir, London Regional Art Gallery, 81, exec dir, London Regional Art & Hist Mus, 85-95. *Awards:* Mayor's New Year's Honours List, 84; Women of Distinction Award, 84; Award of Merit, Univ Western Ont, 85. *Mem:* Hardy Geddes House (bd dir); London Health Asn (bd dir); London Social Planning Coun (vchmn). *Specialty:* Living Canadian aritsts with emphasis on London painters. *Publ:* Auth, Jack Chambers, pvt publ, 78; The Art of London: 1830-1980, Blackpool Press, 84. *Mailing Add:* 420 Fashawe Park Rd London ON N5X 2S9 Canada

POON, HUNG WAH MICHAEL
PAINTER
b Canton, China, Oct 30, 42. *Study:* Sir Robert Black Col, Hong Kong; Hwa Kui Col; Hong Kong Acad Fine Arts. *Work:* Int Young Men's Club, Osaka, Japan; Hong Kong Acad Fine Arts. *Exhib:* Hong Kong Acad Alumnus Club Fine Arts; Hong Kong Art's Festival; Hist Mus Southern Fla, 98-99; traveling exhib, Tallahassee, Orlando & Tampa, Fla, 98-99. *Teaching:* Vpres, Int Studio Chinese Art, 76--88; teacher, Hong Kong Govt Middle Sch. *Mem:* Chinese Art Asn, Hong Kong; Kwong Ngar Calligraphy Soc, Hong Kong. *Media:* All media. *Mailing Add:* 15221 SW 89th Ave Miami FL 33157

POON, YI-CHONG SARINA CHOW
PAINTER, CALLIGRAPHER
b Canton, China; Jan 26, 44. *Study:* Sir Robert Black Col of Educ, Hong Kong; Hwa Kui Col; Studio of Chinese Art. *Work:* Univ Toronto, Canada; Mus Miami, Fla; Int Y's Men's Club, Osaka, Japan; Sir Robert Black Col Educ. *Exhib:* Asia Mod Art Exhib, Art Gallery Tokyo, Japan; Mus Hist, Taiwan; Art Mus of Korea; Hong Kong Art's Festival; The Burger King World Hq, Miami, Fla. *Teaching:* Pres, Int Studio Chinese Art, 67-88; prof, dept extramural studies, Chinese Univ, Hong Kong, 79-80; principal, Kei Yam Sch, 70-85; Kei Ho Sch, 85-88. *Mem:* Chinese Art Asn, Hong Kong; Kwong Ngar Calligraphy Soc; Asia Artist Asn. *Mailing Add:* 15221 SW 89th Ave Miami FL 33157

POONS, LARRY
PAINTER
b Tokyo, Japan, Oct 1, 37. *Study:* Boston Mus Fine Arts Sch, 59. *Work:* Mus Mod Art, Metrop Mus Art, Solomon R Guggenheim Mus, Whitney Mus Am Art, NY; Albright-Knox Art Gallery; Stedelijk Mus, Holland; Woodward Found, Washington, DC; Mus Fine Arts, Boston, MA; Philadelphia Mus Art, PA; Tate Gallery, London, Eng. *Exhib:* Art Inst Chicago, 66; Corcoran Gallery Art, 67; Whitney Mus Am Art Ann, 68 & 72 & Whitney Biennial, 73; Albright-Knox Art Gallery, Buffalo, NY, 68 & 70; retrospective, Boston Mus Fine Arts, 80; Mus Fine Arts, Boston, Mass, 82; Fort Worth Art Mus, Tex, 85; Galleria Chisel, Milan, Italy, 86; Hokin Gallery, Bay Harbor, Fla, 87; Meadow Brook Art Gallery, Rochester, MI, 88; Daniel Newburg Gallery, NY, 89-90; solo exhibs, Helander Gallery, Palm Beach, Fla, 90, Salander-O'Reilly Galleries, NY, 90, 92, 94, 95 & 96, Beverly Hills, 91, Berlin, Ger, 92, Gallery Afinsa, Madrid, Spain, 91, Meredith Long & Co, Houston, 91, Univ Miami, 93, Frederick Spratt Gallery, San Jose, Calif, 94 & 96 & Ruth Bachofner Gallery, Santa Monica, 95; The Brushstrokes and its Guises, NY Studio Sch, 94; Seven Painters, Nicholas Alexander Gallery, NY, 95; Addison Gallery of Am Art: 65 Yrs, Addison Gallery, 96; Color Field, the Classic Years: 1960-75, Andre Emmerich, 96. *Teaching:* Vis fac, NY Studio Sch, 67, Bennington Col & Art Students League, 97-. *Awards:* Francis J Greenburger Found Award, 88. *Bibliog:* Roberta Smith (auth), Art Review, NY Times, 8/9/96; Karen Wilkin (auth), Partisan Review, Vol LXIII, No 3, 96; Karen Wilkin (auth), Partisan Review, No 4, 96; David Ebony (auth), Art in Am, 1/97; Karen Wilkin (auth), Art in America, 5/2006. *Media:* Painting acrylic on canvas. *Publ:* Auth, The Structure of Color, 71. *Dealer:* Salander O'Reilly Gallery 20 E 79th St New York NY 10021; Jacobson Howard 22 E 72nd St New York, NY 10021. *Mailing Add:* 831 Broadway New York NY 10003

POOR, ANNE
PAINTER
b New York, NY, Jan 2, 18. *Study:* Bennington Col; Art Students League, with Alexander Brook, William Zorach & Yasuo Kuniyoshi; Acad Julian, Paris, painting with Jean Lurcat & Abraham Rattner. *Work:* Whitney Mus Am Art; Brooklyn Mus; Art Inst Chicago; Wichita Mus; Des Moines Art Ctr; plus others. *Comn:* Murals, Pub Works Admin, Depew, NY & Gleason, Tenn, 37; murals, Skowhegan Sch Painting & Sculpture, 54, South Solon Free Meeting House, Maine, 57. *Exhib:* Artists for Victory, Metrop Mus Art, 42; Am Brit Art Ctr, NY, 44, 45 & 48; Maynard Walker Gallery, NY, 50; seven shows, Graham Gallery, NY, 57-79; Dinten Fass Gallery, NY, 92; plus others. *Teaching:* Mem fac painting & dir, Skowhegan Sch Painting & Sculpture, 47-61, gov & trustee, 63-. *Awards:* Edwin Austin Abbey Mem Fel for Mural Painting, 48 & First Prize for Landscape Painting, 70, Nat Acad Design; Nat Inst Arts & Lett Grant in Art, 57. *Bibliog:* Alan Gussow (auth), A sense of place, Friends of Earth, Sat Rev Press, 72. *Mem:* Artists Equity Asn; Nat Acad; Am Acad Arts & Letters. *Media:* Oil, Watercolor. *Publ:* Illusr, Greece, Viking Press, 64. *Dealer:* William O Reilly New York NY. *Mailing Add:* 1150 5th Ave New York NY 10128-0724

POOR, ROBERT JOHN
HISTORIAN
b Rockport, Ill, July 10, 31. *Study:* Boston Univ, BA, 53 & MA, 57; Univ Chicago, with Ludwig Bachhofer, PhD(art hist), 61. *Collection Arranged:* Art of India (exhib catalog), 69 & Far Eastern Art in Minnesota Collections (exhib catalog), 70, Univ Minn Gallery; Hanga, The Modern Japanese Print (exhib catalog), Minn Mus Art, St Paul, 72. *Pos:* Consult Asian art, Minneapolis Inst Art, formerly; cur Asian art, Minn Mus Art, St Paul, formerly. *Teaching:* Asst prof Asian art, Dartmouth Col, 61-65; from assoc prof Asian art to prof art hist, Univ Minn, Minneapolis, 65-. *Res:* Chinese bronzes. *Publ:* Auth, Notes on the Sung archaeological catalogs, 65 & auth, Some remarkable examples of I-Hsing ware, 66-67, Arch of Chinese Art Soc Am; auth, Ancient Chinese Bronzes, Inter-Cult Arts Press, 68; auth, Evolution of a secular vesseltype, 68 & On the Mo-tzu-Yu, 70, Oriental Art. *Mailing Add:* Dept Art Hist Univ Minn 338 Management & Economics 271 19th Ave S Minneapolis MN 55455

POPE, MARY ANN IRWIN
PAINTER
b Louisville, Ky, Mar 8, 32. *Study:* Art Ctr, Louisville; Univ Louisville; Cooper Union. *Work:* Mint Mus, Charlotte, NC; Huntsville Mus of Art; Fine Arts Mus S, Mobile, Ala; Zerox; McGraw Hill. *Comn:* Boy Scouts Am; Kaiser, Atlanta, Ga. *Exhib:* Watercolor USA, 1982, 83, 87, 88, 89, 2003 & 04; Birmingham Biennial, 83 & 85;

Art Quest, 85; Nat Biennial Invitational, Watercolor USA, 89; Voices Rising, Nat Mus of Wome in the Arts, 2000; Adirondacks Nat Exhib Am Watercolors, 2002; Butler Inst Am Art, 2005; Nat Watercolor Soc, 2006; plus others. *Awards:* Gallery Award, Grand Nat Exhib, Miss Mus Art, 98; Merit Award, Exhib South, 95 & 98; Watercolor USA, 89, Greg C. Thielen Award, 2004; & others. *Bibliog:* Patricia Seligman (auth), Painting Skies; Ruth Appelhof (auth) Voices Rising (catalog), 2000; Splash 7, Northlight Pub, 2002; Splash 8, Northlight Pub, 2004; Master Painters of the World, US Showcase, Int Artist; and others. *Mem:* Kentucky Watercolor Soc; Ala Watercolor Soc; Nat Honor Soc-Watercolor USA. *Media:* Oil, Watercolor. *Dealer:* Corporate Art Source Montgomery AL. *Mailing Add:* 1705 Greenwyche Rd SE Huntsville AL 35801

POPINSKY, ARNOLD DAVE
SCULPTOR, CERAMIST
b Bronx, NY, Aug 21, 30. *Study:* Albright Art Sch, State Univ NY, Buffalo, BS; Univ Wis-Madison, MS; Alfred Univ. *Comn:* Metal sculpture, Wright Art Ctr, Beloit, Wis, 64; 3 cast iron plaques, 64 & aluminum sculpture, 68, Beloit Col, Wis. *Exhib:* Colt & Popinsky, Wright Art Ctr, Beloit, Wis, 67; one-man shows, Lang Art Ctr, Claremont, Calif, 69, Univ WFla, Pensacola, 73 & Fishey Whale Gallery, Milwaukee, Wis, 75; Wis Designer-Craftsman, Milwaukee Art Ctr, 73. *Pos:* Artist-in-residence, Inst Artes Plasticas, Univ Guadalajara, Mex, 64-65 & Univ WFla, Pensacola, 72-73; gallery owner, Arnold Popinsky Gallery & Arboretum Market, Austin, Tex; owner, Clarksville Pottery & Am Crafts Gallery, Austin, Tex, 76-; Clarksville Pottery Studio Inc, 91; mem bd dir, Austin Contemp Visual Arts Asn, 78. *Teaching:* Prof sculpture & ceramics, Beloit Col, Wis, 57-76. *Mem:* Col Art Asn; Am Craft Coun; Austin Contemp Visual Arts Asn; Rock Prairie Arts Coun. *Media:* Clay, Metal. *Mailing Add:* 5101 Crestway Dr Austin TX 78731-5405

POPLAWSKA, ANNA
EDUCATOR, CRITIC
Teaching: teacher, in field. *Mem:* Chicago Art Critics Asn. *Publ:* Contribr to monthly art columns in the following publs: Footlights Playbill, Yoga Chicago, Wednesday Jour of Oak Park; freelancer Chicago Artist's News. *Mailing Add:* 1017 S Harlem Forest Park Forest Park IL 60130

POPOVAC, GWYNN
PAINTER, SCULPTOR
b Wilmington, Del, Dec 1, 48. *Study:* Univ Calif, Los Angeles, Eng lit, honors, 66-71. *Work:* Detroit Med Hosp. *Comn:* Mask for Kabuki play, The Dream of Kitamura, Sierra Repertory Thea tre, 92. *Exhib:* Behind the Disguise, Olive Hyde, Fremont City Gallery, Calif, 89; The Art of the Mask, Hearst Gallery, Moraga, Calif, 91; Habitat masks & hexapods, Wellspring Gallery, Santa Monica, 94; Chicago Sch Fine Arts. *Bibliog:* Liz Winter (auth), Behind the disguise, Monitor, Fremont, Calif, 10/25/89; Gary Linehan (auth), Working in the bugs, Union Democrat, Sonora, Calif, 4/3/92; Ann Batchelder (ed & auth), Swatches, Fiberarts, 94. *Media:* Mixed Media, Oil, Fibers. *Publ:* Auth, Ripe plums, Ms Mag, 7/84; Wet Paint, Houghton Mifflin & Ballantine, 86; illusr, Wet Paint (dust jacket for hardback ed), Houghton Mifflin & Ballantine, 86; auth & artist, Conversations with Bugs (Writing J & calendar), Pomegranate, 93; Limited Editions-Insect Series, Apple Jack, 96. *Dealer:* Vault Gallery 42 S Washington Sonora CA 95370; Anderson Gallery 7 N Saginaw Pontiac MI 48342. *Mailing Add:* 17270 Robin Ridge Sonora CA 95370

PORGES, MARIA FRANZISKA
SCULPTOR, PRINTMAKER
b Oakland, Calif, 54. *Study:* Yale Univ, BA, 75; Univ Chicago, Ill, MFA; studied with Bob Peters. *Work:* Mus of Modern Art, San Francisco, Calif; Scottsdale Mus of Art, Ariz; di Rosa Found; Phillip Morris Collection; Oakland Mus of Calif; Berkely Art Mus. *Comn:* 6 pieces, CalPERS HQ, 2006. *Exhib:* Albuquerque Mus Art, NMex, 2000; Palo Alto Art Ctr, Calif; Pratt Inst, Brooklyn, NY; Midway Gallery, Chicago, Ill; John Berggruen Gallery, San Francisco; Solo exhib, James Harris Gallery, Seattle, Wash, 2001, David Beitzel Gallery, New York City, Mus of Modern Art, San Francisco, Calif, Sheppard Art Gallery, Univ Nev, Reno. *Teaching:* instr, Stanford Univ, currently; instr, Univ Calif, Berkeley; adj prof, Calif Col Arts, San Francisco, currently. *Awards:* SECA Award, Mus Modern Art, San Francisco, Calif; Individual Artists Grant, Calif Arts Coun, 90; John McCarron Criticism Grant, San Francisco Artspace, Calif. *Mem:* AICA; Col Art Asn. *Media:* Wax, Bronze & Paper. *Dealer:* John Berggruen Gallery San Francisco. *Mailing Add:* 5174 Trask St Oakland CA 94601

PORTA, SIENA GILLANN
SCULPTOR
b New York, NY, Nov 5, 51. *Study:* Art Students League, 69-70; Brooklyn Col, NY, BS(studio arts), 77; Pa State Univ, MFA (sculpture) 79. *Work:* Fulbright Comn, Reykjavik, Iceland; Hafnarborg Mus, Iceland; Robert L Yaeger Health Ctr, Pomona, NY; Jacob Riis Nat Park, Ft Tilden, NY; Binsons Veor Trust, Cornwall, England. *Comn:* Co Rockland, NY; St Philip Church, Norwalk, Conn. *Exhib:* Solo exhibs, Dominican Col, Blauvelt, NY, 80 & Mari Galleries, Ltd, Mamaroneck, NY, 85, 14 Sculptors Gallery, 85, 87 & 90, Mid Hudson Arts & Sci Ctr, Poughkeepsie, NY, 92-93, Noho Gallery, NY, 03 & 05; A B Condon Gallery, NY, 82-83; 14 Sculptors Gallery, 82-83; Blue Hill Cult Ctr, Pearl River, NY, 95; NJ City Univ, 98; Nassau Community Col, NY, 98; Group exhibs, Notre Dame Univ, 90, Lehigh Univ, 92, Adelphi Univ, 2000, St Thomas Aquinas Coll, 2000; Hafnarborg Mus, Iceland, 02-03; Snaeflsnes Reg Mus, 02-03; Ramapo Coll, Krejkeit & Pascal Gallery, 01; McLevy Green, Bridgeport, Conn, 05; Sculpture at Lockwood Mathews Mansion Mus, Norwalk Conn, 2006. *Pos:* Scenic artist, Metrop Opera, New York, 87-92 & numerous broadway shows, 92-; vpres, 14 Sculptors Gallery, 87-89, pres, 89-91; cult comt co-chair, Partners Americas, Rockland Co, NY, 92-97. *Teaching:* Adj prof, Bergen Community Col, Paramus, NJ, 84-85, St Thomas Aquinas Coll, Sparkill, NY, 2000-, Ramapo Coll, Mahwah, NJ, 2001-. *Awards:* Artist-in-Residence, Brisons Veor, Cape Cornwall, England, 03; NY State Coun Arts Grant, 86; USIA Granttee, Partners of the Americas, 92; NYFA, decentralization grantee, 1986 & 2002. *Bibliog:* Aspects of the Arts, Siena Porta, Sculptor (video), TKR Channel 30, 91; Broadcast, TKR Channel 30, 91; Vivien Raynor (auth), NY Times, 7/16/95; Oscar Corall (auth), Newsday, 4/2000. *Mem:* Col Art Asn; Art/Science Collab, Staten Island, NY. *Media:* Sprayed Metals, Plastics. *Publ:* Illusr, Southern Ocean Atlas, Columbia Univ Press, 82; auth, Spray metal (article), Maquette Mag, Int Sculpture Soc, Washington, 94; Gallery & Studio (review), 9/03. *Dealer:* Noho Gllaery, 530 W 25th St NY. *Mailing Add:* PO Box 46 Palisades NY 10964

PORTER, ALBERT WRIGHT
EDUCATOR, PAINTER
b Brooklyn, NY, Nov 25, 23. *Study:* Ecole Des Beaux-Arts, Paris; Chouinard Art Inst; Univ of Calif, Los Angeles, BA; Calif State Univ, Los Angeles, MA; Otis Art Inst. *Work:* Los Angeles City Art Comn; Utah State Univ; Las Vegas Art Mus. *Exhib:* Nat Watercolor Soc, Laguna Beach, Calif, 69; Southern Calif Expo, Del Mar, 72; Watercolor West, Riverside Art Mus, Calif, 74; Nat Watercolor Soc, Northridge, Calif, 77; Nat Watercolor Soc, Palm Springs, 83; Nat Watercolor Soc, Whittier, Calif, 86; San Diego Watercolor Soc, 94; many one-man shows & group shows, Village Square Gal, Montrose, Calif, 1955-2005. *Pos:* Art supervisor, Los Angeles City Schs, 58-71. *Teaching:* Prof art, Calif State Univ, Fullerton, 71-89, prof emer, 89-. *Awards:* Cash Award, Nat Watercolor Soc, Del Mar Col, 72. *Bibliog:* Gerald Brommer (auth), Understanding Transparent Watercolor & Joseph Mugnaini (auth), Expressive Drawing, Davis Publs. *Mem:* Nat Watercolor Soc (1st vpres, 77); Watercolor Wes. *Media:* Watercolor, Drawing Media. *Publ:* Auth, Shape and Form: Design Elements, 74, Pattern: A Design Principle, 75, The Art of Sketching, 77, Exploring Visual Design, 78 & Expressive Watercolor Techniques, 82, Davis Publ; auth, Exploring Visual Design, 3d ed, 2000. *Dealer:* Village Sq Gallery 2418 Honolulu Ave Ste C Montrose CA 91205. *Mailing Add:* 8554 Day St Sunland CA 91040

PORTER, JEANNE CHENAULT
EDUCATOR, HISTORIAN
b New York, NY, Mar 18, 44. *Study:* Barnard Col, Columbia Univ, BA, 65; Univ Mich, Ann Arbor, MA, 66 & PhD(Ford Found Graduate Fel & Fulbright Grant), 71; Univ Florence, Rome & Ghent (Belgian Govt Grant). *Collection Arranged:* Bradley Tomlin: A Retrospective View, traveling exhib (auth, catalog), Hofstra Univ, 75-76; Bradley W Tomlin, City Univ NY. *Teaching:* Assoc prof, Finch Col, New York, 72-74 & Pa State Univ, 74-. *Awards:* Fulbright Grant to Rome, 68-69; Belgian Govt Grant, 68. *Mem:* Col Art Asn Am. *Res:* Abstract Expressionism (American), and Spanish, French and Italian Baroque Painting. *Publ:* Auth, Bradley Walker Tomlin: Early paintings & intimations, Archives Am Art J, 74; Bradley Walker Tomlin: A painter's painter, Arts Mag, 75; Painting and Sculpture in the Samuel Gallu Collection (catalog), 80 & Works on Paper: Henry Varnum Poor (catalog), 83, Pa State Press; Tomlin (catalog), Munson-Williams-Proctor Inst, Utica, NY, 89; contribr, Munson-Williams-Proctor Inst (catalog), Baroque Publ. *Mailing Add:* 525 W Park Ave State College PA 16803-3432

PORTER, KATHERINE PAVLIS
PAINTER, EDUCATOR
b Cedar Rapids, Iowa, 41. *Study:* Boston Univ, 62; Colo Col, BA, 63; Colby Col, LHD, 82; Bowdoin Col, LHD, 92. *Work:* Metrop Mus Art, Mus Mod Art, Whitney Mus Am Art, Guggenheim Mus, New Mus Contemp Art, NY. *Exhib:* Collaboration, Inst Contemp Art, Boston, 69; Annual, Whitney Mus Am Art, NY, 69; Katherine Porter: Works on Paper, Fine Arts Mus San Francisco, 80; Recent Acquisitions, Mus Mod Art, NY, 83; I am an Am Drawings, Cape Split Pace Gallery, Addison, Maine, 84; Contemp Drawings from the Last Three Decades, Mus Mod Art, NY, 85; 1988 Invitational, New Britain Mus Am Art, 88; On the Edge, Portland Mus, Maine, 93; and many others. *Collection Arranged:* Painting Self-Evident, Picolo Spoleto Festival, 92. *Teaching:* Instr, Stanford Univ, Columbia Univ & Sch Visual Arts, Tyler. *Bibliog:* Peter Frank (auth), Rev, Art News, 2/76; Stacey Moss (auth), Rev, Art in Am, 6/76; William Zimmer (auth), Airing out the grid, SoHo News, 8/78; and others. *Dealer:* Les Yeux de Monde 841 Wolf Trap Rd Charlottesville VA 22911; Salander O'Reily 79th St New York NY. *Mailing Add:* Rue St Paul Ouest No 24 Montreal PQ H2Y 1Y8 Canada

PORTER, LILIANA
PAINTER, PRINTMAKER, VIDEO ARTIST
b Buenos Aires, Arg, Oct 6, 41; US citizen. *Study:* Nat Sch Fine Arts, Buenos Aires; printmaking, Iberoamerican Univ & La Ciudadela, Mexico City. *Work:* Mus Mod Art & Metrop Mus Art, NY; Mus Fine Arts, Philadelphia; Mus de Bellas Artes, Buenos Aires, Arg, Caracas, Venezuela & Santiago, Chile; La Bibliot Nat, Paris; Hunter Mus Art, Chattanooga, Tenn; Bronx Mus, NY; plus many others. *Comn:* Alice; The Way Out, 4 Mosaic Murals, MTA Subway Line 1-9, 50th station, New York City; Untitled with Rabbit, Mural, three dimensional installations, Lavaugh Robert Moore Day Care Center, Brooklyn; The Traveler, glass mosaic mural, Domenech Train Station, San Juan, Puerto Rico, 2003. *Exhib:* Solo-exhibs, Mus Mod Art, NY, 73, Weatherspoon Art Gallery, Univ NC, Greensboro, 91, Inst de Cult, San Juan, PR, 91, Bronx Mus Arts, NY, 92, Archer M Huntington Art Gallery, Univ Tex, Austin, 93, Steinbaum Krauss Gallery, NY, 93 & Gallery Contemp Art, Sacred Heart Univ, Fairfield, Conn, 94; A Retrospective of Graphic Art 1968-1993, Reading Pub Mus, Pa, 93; Reclaiming Hist, El Mus del Barrio, NY, 93; El desdoblamiento, el simulacro y el reflejo, Inst de Cooperacion Iberoamericana, Buenos Aires, Argentina, 94; Toys/Art/Us, Castle Gallery, Col New Rochelle, NY, 94; Art & the New Novel, Arnot Art Mus, Elmira, NY, 94; Latin Am Women Artists 1915-1995 (traveling), Milwaukee Art Mus, 95;

Poetry in Paradox, Univ Art Gallery, NMex State Univ; Monique Knowlton, 96; and others. *Pos:* Co-dir, Studio Porter-Wiener, 79-. *Teaching:* Instr etching, NY Graphic Workshop, 65-68; adj lectr graphics, State Univ NY, Purchase, 87; instr, printmaking workshop, NY, 88; prof, Art Dept, Queens Col, NY, 91-. *Awards:* Travel Grant, Nat Endowment Arts Int, 94; Regional Fel, Nat Endowment Arts Mid Atlantic, 94; NY Found Arts Grant, 96; and others. *Bibliog:* James Collins (auth), articles in Artforum, 73 & Arts Mag, 5/77. *Media:* Video. *Publ:* Contribr, Wrinkle, 68, Nail, 73 & String, 73, New York Graphic Workshop; For You (16 mm film), 99; Drum Solo (19 minute video), 2000. *Dealer:* Hosfelt Gallery, San Francisco, Calif; Annina Nossei Gallery, New York City; Sicardi Gallery, Houston, Tex; Ruth Benzacar Gallery, Buenos Aires, Argentina. *Mailing Add:* 720 Greenwich St 10G New York NY 10014

PORTER, RICHARD JAMES
GALLERY DIRECTOR
b Bellefonte, Pa, Jan 2, 50. *Study:* Pa State Univ, BA, 71, MA, 73, PhD, 83. *Collection Arranged:* Sidney Goodman: Paintings, Drawings & Graphics 1959-1979 (coauth, catalog), Mus Art, Pa State Univ, Queens Mus, Columbus Mus Art & Del Art Mus, 80-81; Henry Varnum Poor (coauth, catalog), Mus Art, Pa State Univ, Burchfield Ctr, Everson Mus & Nat Acad Design, 83-84. *Pos:* Registrar & cur Am art, Mus Art, Pa State Univ, Pa 78-85; dir, Joe & Emily Lowe Art Gallery, 85-86; chmn, Grad prog in Mus Studies, Syracuse Univ, 85-86; sales assoc, Villager Realty, 86-87 & Assoc Realty, 87-90; assoc broker, Assoc Realty, 90-92; broker/partner ReMax Ctr Realty, 92; dir, Wally Findlay Galleries, 2006. *Teaching:* Instr art hist, Middle Tenn State Univ, 73-76; adj assoc prof art hist, Juniata Col, 84. *Mem:* Am Asn Mus; Mid Atlantic Asn of Mus; Col Art Asn. *Res:* American and European art, 17th century to present, particularly American & French 18th-20th centuries. *Specialty:* 19th & 20th Century French paintings, Contemporary American & European art. *Publ:* Auth, A newly discovered painting by Ammi Phillips, Conn Hist Soc Bull, 79; Introduction, selected works from the collection of Samuel Gallu, Pa State Univ, 80; Jerome Witkin, A Decade of Work (exhib catalog), 82; Henry Varnum Poor, 1887-1970 (exhib catalog), 83; The oil paintings of Henry Varnum Poor, Arts Mag, 85. *Mailing Add:* 308 E 79th St Apt 9J New York NY 10021

PORTER, SHIRLEY
PAINTER
b Tallahassee, Fla. *Study:* Fla State Univ, BS(educ), 62; Univ SFla, MA(educ), 69. *Work:* Tweed Mus, Duluth, Minn; Montgomery Co Dept Parks, Rockville, Md; Utah State Univ. *Exhib:* Am Watercolor Soc, Nat Acad Gallery, NY, 75-77 & 79; Allied Artists, Nat Acad Gallery, 75-77; Nat Acad Design, Nat Acad Gallery, 77-81; Rocky Mountain Nat Watermedia, Foothills Art Ctr, Golden, Colo, 78, 80 & 81; Watercolor USA, Springfield Art Mus, Mo, 79. *Awards:* David Soloway Mem Award, 77 & Gold Medal, 78, Allied Artists; Silver Medal, 80 & Gold Medal, 81, Baltimore Watercolor Soc. *Mem:* Am Watercolor Soc; Allied Artists Am; Audubon Artists; Nat Watercolor Soc; Midwest Watercolor Soc; and others. *Media:* Watercolor. *Mailing Add:* 14315 Woodcrest Dr Rockville MD 20853-2334

PORTMAN, BRIAN
PRINTMAKER
b Woonsocket, RI, 1960. *Study:* RI Sch Design, BFA, 83; Artist-in-Residence Core Prog, Glassell Sch Art; Mus Fine Arts, Houston, Tex, 83-85. *Work:* Centro Cult del Arte Contemporaneo, Mexico City, Mex; Mus Fine Art, Houston, Tex; Dallas Mus Art, Tex; Univ Tex Austin Art Galleries; Walker Art Ctr, Minneapolis, Minn; Old Jail Arts Ctr, Albany, Tex; Compaq, Houston, Tex. *Exhib:* Solo exhibs, List Art Ctr, Brown Univ, Providence, RI, 83, Hiram Butler Gallery, Houston, Tex, 88, 90 & 92, Barry Whistler Gallery, Dallas, Tex, 93 & Robert McClain & Co, 94 & 96, The Glassell Sch of Art, Mus of Fine Arts, Houston, Tex 2000, Barbara Davis Gallery, Houston, Tex, 2001; Small Wonders, Barry Whistler Gallery, Dallas, 93; The Big Picture, Barry Whistler Gallery, Dallas, 94; The Tex Collection: Tex Mod & Post-Mod, Mus Fine Arts, Houston, 96; Brian Portman & Alfred DeCredico, Robert McClain & Co, Houston, 96; The Texas Collection of the Mus of Fine Arts, Houston: Texas Modern and Post-Modern, Mus Fine Arts, Houston, 96; Cerling Etching Studio, The First Five Yrs 1990-95 (with catalog), Transco Tower Gallery, Houston, Tex, 96; Little Treasures, Robert McClain & Co, 97; Abstraction: Painting Sculpture, Robert McClain & Co, 98; group exhib, Barbara Davis Gallery, Houston, Tex, 2000. *Awards:* Europ Honors Prog, Rhode Island Sch Design, Providence; Anne Giles Kinbrough Grant, Dallas Mus Art, 88; Visual Arts Fel, Nat Endowment Arts, 89-90. *Bibliog:* Lisa Broadwater (auth), Whistler focuses on the big picture, Dallas Morning News, 1/7/94; Shermakaye Bass (auth), A really big show at Barry Whistler Gallery, Dallas Morning News, 1/10/94; Janet Kutner (auth), DMA acquires 2 new works, Dallas Morning News, 3/25/94

PORTMAN, JOHN C, JR
ARCHITECT
b Walhalla, SC, Dec 4, 24. *Study:* Us Naval Acad, Midshipman, 44; Ga Inst Tech, BS in Archit, 50; Ga Inst Tech, DFA, 93; Emory Univ, DFA, 93; Atlanta Col Art, DFA, 93. *Work:* Prin works incl: The Regent Hotel, Marina Sq, both Singapore, Embarcadero Ctr, The Pan Pacific-San Francisco, San Francisco Fashion Ctr, Hyatt Regency O'Hare Hotel, Chicago, Peachtree Ctr, Atlanta; George W Woodruff Physical Educ Ctr, R Howard Dobbs Student Ctr, both Emory Univ, Atlanta, Atlanta Merchandise Mart, Atlanta Apparel Mart, Atlanta Decorative Arts Ctr, Atlanta Gift Mart, Inforum, One Peachtree Ctr, Kennedy Community Ctr and Middle Sch, Hyatt Regency Hotel, Westin Peachtree Plaza Hotel, Atlanta Marriott Marquis, Northpark Town Ctr, Riverwood, Greenbriar Shopping Ctr, Olympic Village Housing, all Atlanta, Blue Cross-Blue Shield Bldg, Chattanooga, Ft Worth Nat Bank Bldg and Garage, Brussels Int Trade Mart, Dana Fine Arts Bldg at Agnes Scott Col, Decatur, Ga, Renaissance Ctr, Detroit, Bonaventure Hotel, Los Angeles, NY Marriott Marquis, Rockefeller Ctr renovation, New York City, Shanghai Centre, Dream Lake Villas, Hangzhou Qiantang River City, Shandong Bldg, Guomai Bldg, BAODA Bldg, Senfuli Building, S Renzhill Complex, Peoples Republic of China, Capital Sq, Kuala Lumpur, Malaysia. *Pos:* Individual practice, 53-56; partner, Edwards and Portman (Archit), 56-68; princ, John Portman and Assocs, 68-; chmn, Chief Exec Officer, The Portman Cos., Atlanta, 71-; bd dir, Nations Bank; pres Cent Atlanta Progress, 70-72; bd dir, Aaron Rents, Inc, 2006-. *Awards:* named Outstanding Young Man of Yr, Ga Junior CofC, 1959; Silver medal for innovative design Ga chap Am Inst of Archit, 81; Atlanta Downtown Partnership's Resurgens award, Design of Peachtree Plaza. *Mem:* Fel Am Inst of Archits; Nat Coun Archit Registration Bd; Am Inst Interior Designers; Soc Int Bus Fel; World Trade Club (founding); Nat Acad. *Publ:* Co-auth: The Archit as Developer, 1990. *Mailing Add:* Portman Holdings LLC Ste 4600 303 Peachtree St NE Atlanta GA 30308

PORTNOW, MARJORIE ANNE
PAINTER
b New York, NY, Sept 30, 1942. *Study:* Western Reserve Univ, with Dr Sherman E Lee, BA(art hist), 64; Skowhegan Sch Painting, with Lenart Anderson, A Leslie & A Katz, 65; Brooklyn Col, with P Pearlstein & G Laderman, MFA(painting), 72. *Hon Degrees:* Nat Acad (National Acadamicicum From Member national Acad of Design). *Work:* Metrop Mus Art, Chase Manhattan Bank, New York, NY; Albany Inst Art, NY; Gibbs Mus, SC; Middlebury Col Mus; Sheldon Art Mus, Lincoln, Nebr; and others. *Exhib:* Am Acad & Inst Arts & Lett, NY, 80, 90, 92, 94 & 96; Recent Developments in Am Landscape, Whitney Mus, Stamford, Conn; Graham Gund Collection, Mus Fine Arts Boston, 82; The Ital Tradition on Contemp Landscape Painting, Gibbs Mus, Charleston, SC; The Landscape in 20th Century Am Art: Selections from the Metrop Mus Art, 91; Rediscovering the Landscape of the Americas, Gerald Peters Gallery, Santa Fe; A Century, Painters and Sculptors at MacDowell Colony, Currier Gallery; Green Woods and Crystal Waters: The Am Landscape Tradition Since 1950, Philbrook Mus Art, 99; Peter Rose Gallery, New York City, 2003; Hollins Univ 2000; Oxbow Gallery, 2005. *Pos:* Fac, NY Studio Sch, 94-95 & Pa Acad Fine Arts, 95-2003; Western Conn State Univ, Fac, 2003-2006; Fine Arts Work Ctr, Provincetown, MA,. *Teaching:* Fac, Vt Studio Sch, 87-2000, Univ Pa (Grad Sch), 88-91, Pa Acad Art, 88-91 & 94-2000, Skowhegan Sch, 89, Univ Calif, Santa Cruz, 92-93, & NY Studio Sch, 95. *Awards:* Bunting Fel, Radcliff, 70-72; Louis Comfort Tiffany Found Grant, 72 & 78; Nat Endowment Arts Grant, 80 & 94; NY Found Arts Award, 86; Hassam Purchase Prize, Am Acad & Inst Arts & Lett, 90 & 94-95. *Bibliog:* R Milazzo (auth), Realism After 7PM-Realist Painting After E Hopper, 90; A Gussow (auth), The Artist as Native, Babcock, 93 & Rediscovering the Landscape of the Americas, 96; R S Torr & T Wolf (auths), Community of Creativity: A Century of MacDowell Artists, 96; The American Landscape Tradion Since, 1950; Greenwoods and Crystal Waters, John Author. *Mem:* NY Artists Equity Asn; Nat Acad. *Media:* Oil. *Specialty:* Contemporary oil Paintings. *Dealer:* Contemp Realist Gallery San Francisco CA; Fischbach Gallery 29 W 57th St New York NY 10019; Grigr Clark Gallery, Burlington, UT; Julie Heller Gallery, Provincetown, MA. *Mailing Add:* 67 Vestry St New York NY 10013

PORTNOY, THEODORA PREISS
DEALER
b New York, NY. *Study:* Manhattanville Col; Sarah Lawrence Col, BA. *Pos:* dir, Theo Portnoy Gallery, formerly, bd mem, currently; bd dir, Cornell Art Mus; chmn acquisitions, Rollin's Col. *Specialty:* Sculpture with emphasis on work that has evolved from craft media, clay, glass, wood and forged steel. *Mailing Add:* 10518 Wood Chase Cir Orlando FL 32836

POSEN, STEPHEN
PAINTER
b St Louis, Mo, Sept 27, 39. *Study:* Washington Univ, St Louis, Mo, BFA, 62; Yale Univ, New Haven, Conn, MFA, 64. *Work:* Va Mus Fine Arts, Richmond; Chase Manhattan Bank; Pa Acad Fine Arts, Philadelphia; Solomon R Guggenheim Mus, NY; JB Speed Art Mus, Louisville, Ky. *Exhib:* The Inflated Image, Mus Mod Art, NY, 69; solo exhibs, OK Harris Gallery, NY, 69, 71 & 74, Robert Miller Gallery, NY, 78 & Jason McCoy, NY, 86 & 89; Highlights of the 1970-71 Art Season, Aldrich Mus, Ridgefield, Conn, 71; Whitney Mus Painting Ann, Whitney Mus Am Art, NY, 72; 71st Am Exhib & New Realism, Art Inst Chicago, Ill, 74; Eight Contemp Am Realists, 77 & Contemp Am Realism Since 1960 (catalog), traveling, Pa Acad Fine Arts, Philadelphia; Reality of Illusion, Denver Art Mus, Colo, traveling, 79; Twenty Artists: Yale Sch of Art, 1950-70 (catalog), Yale Univ Art Gallery, New Haven, Conn, 81; Texas, Real, Really Real & Super Real: Directions in Contemp Am Realism (catalog), San Antonio Mus Art, Tex, traveling, 81; The Image of Am Painting & Sculpture 1950-1980, Akron Art Mus, Ohio, 81; Am Super Realism from the Morton G Neumann Family Collection, Terra Mus Am Art, Evanston, Ill, 83; Am Realism: Twentieth Century Drawings & Watercolors (catalog), San Francisco Mus Mod Art, Calif, traveling, 85; More Than Meets the Eye: The Art of Trompe l'oeil Columbus Mus Art, Ohio, traveling, 86; Two Generations of Creativity, 80 Washington Sq E, NY, 89; Yale Collects Yale, Yale Univ Art Gallery, New Haven, Conn, 93. *Awards:* Fulbright Grant, 64-66; Creative Artists Pub Serv Grant, 72; Guggenheim Fel, 87. *Bibliog:* A Mackie (auth), Dialectic in modernism: The paintings of Stephen Posen, Art Int, 1/80; John Arthur (auth), Realism/Photorealism, Philbrook Art Ctr, 80; John L Ward (auth), American Realism: 1945-1980, UMI Res Press, 89. *Mailing Add:* 115 Spring St New York NY 10012

POSKAS, PETER EDWARD
PAINTER
b Waterbury, Conn, Oct 29, 39. *Study:* Univ Conn, 57-60; Paier Sch Art, 60-62; Univ Hartford, BS, 62-65. *Work:* Mint Mus, Charlotte, NC; Gen Foods Corp, White Plains, NY; FMC Corp, Chicago; Raht-West Mus, Wis; Frye Mus, Wash. *Comn:* Landscape, Metropolitan Life, NY, 89. *Exhib:* Solo exhibs, Mazur Mus, Monroe, La, 72,

Mattatuck Mus, Waterbury, Conn, 74 & Hunter Mus Art, Chattanooga, Tenn, 84; Hassam Speicher, Am Acad & Inst Arts & Lett, NY, 77; Butler Inst, Youngstown, Ohio, 77; Artists of Am, Colo Heritage Ctr, Denver, 82-83; The Conn View, P P William Benton Mus Art, Storrs, Conn, 84; The Recognizable Image, Bruce Mus, Greenwich, Conn, 85; Acts of Season, Southern Alleghenies Mus Art, Loretto, Pa, 86; Brigham-Young Mus, Provo, Utah, 97. *Bibliog:* John Arthur (auth), Peter Poskas, Arts Mag, 83; Theodore Wolf (auth), Mondrian would have liked it, Christian Sci Monitor, 84; Michael Brenson (auth), Peter Poskas, NY Times, 84. *Media:* Oil. *Publ:* Coauth, Peter Poskas, Watson-Guptill, 87 & 92. *Dealer:* Spanierman Gallery 45 E 58th St New York NY. *Mailing Add:* Nettleton Hollow Rd Washington CT 06793

POSNER, HELAINE J
GALLERY DIRECTOR, CURATOR
b New York, NY, Nov 17, 53. *Study:* Georgetown Univ, BA(art hist), 75; George Washington Univ, MA, 78. *Collection Arranged:* Jasper Johns Prints: Three Themes (coauth, catalog), Whitney Mus Am Art, 78; Selection from the Chase Manhattan Bank Art Collection (auth, catalog), 81, Martin Puryear Sculpture (coauth, catalog), 83 & Anish Kapoor, 86, University Gallery, Univ Mass, Amherst. *Pos:* Cur asst to dir, Chase Manhattan Bank Art Prog, New York, 78-81; chief cur, Nat Mus of Women in the Arts, Washington, DC, 88-90; cur, MIT, List Visual Arts Ctr, Cambridge, formerly; cur, Int Ctr of Photography, currently. *Teaching:* Asst prof, dept art, Univ Mass, Amherst, 81-88, cur collections & educ, University Gallery, 81-84, dir, 84-88. *Mem:* Am Asn Mus; New Eng Mus Asn. *Res:* Modern and contemporary art. *Specialty:* Development of permanent collection of 20th century works on paper. *Mailing Add:* 135 Green St Apt 4N New York NY 10012

POSNER, JUDITH L
DEALER, PUBLISHER
b Milwaukee, Wis, Sept 22, 41. *Study:* Univ Wis, BFA. *Work:* Broward Co Libr - AGAM; Milw Exhbn/Conv Ctr-Arena Mecca. *Pos:* Dir & pres, Posner Fine Art, currently. *Teaching:* Instr, Comprehensive Employment & Training Act, Milwaukee, formerly. *Awards:* Hands That Svc, Mt Sinai Hosp, Milwaukee. *Bibliog:* Curtis Casewitt (auth), Making a Living in the Fine Arts, Macmillan. *Mem:* Indust Found Am Soc Interior Designers; Prof Tempo, Milwaukee Art Dealers Asn (past pres); Int Soc Appraisers; Picture Framers Asn; Woman in Hospitality NEWH Orgn. *Specialty:* Nineteenth and twentieth century American and European painting, sculpture and graphics and tribal art. *Interests:* Golf, Travel. *Publ:* Publisher of posters & prints. *Mailing Add:* 13234 G Fiji Way Marina Del Rey CA 90292

POST, ANNE B
SCULPTOR, GRAPHIC ARTIST
b St Louis, Mo. *Study:* Bennington Col, BA(fine arts); study with Simon Moselsio, Stephen Hirsch & Edwin Park; study in Europe. *Work:* Israel Mus, Jerusalem; Maison Francaise; Cooper Union Mus Gallery; Norfolk Mus; Va Bennington Visual Arts Mus; and others. *Exhib:* St Louis Mus Art; Univ NJ Mus; benefit exhib, Acad Medicine, NY; Bennington Mus Art; Bennington Col Visual Arts Mus; AIR Gallery, NY; and others. *Teaching:* Drawing & sculpture, Army Hosps, WVa, Tex, Mo & Settlement House, St Louis, 42-46. *Bibliog:* Gunter Klotz (auth), Zcichnunsen und skulpturen der Anne Post, Klotz-Makowckie, 65. *Mem:* Artists Equity; Metrop Mus; Native Am Found. *Media:* Wood, Stone; Watercolor, Guache. *Mailing Add:* 29 Washington Sq W New York NY 10011

POSTIGLIONE, COREY M
PAINTER, EDUCATOR, CRITIC
b Chicago, Ill, July 25, 42. *Study:* Univ Ill, Circle Campus, BA; also with Martin Hurtig & Roland Ginzel; Sch Art Inst Chicago, MA(20th century Art Hist). *Exhib:* One-man shows, Evanston Art Ctr, Ill, 72, Mayer Kaplan JCC, Skokie, Ill, 73, Jan Cicero Gallery, Chicago, 76, 78, 83, 85, 95 & 97, Columbia Col Gallery, Chicago, 81 & 97-98 & Passages, Oakton Community Col, 98; New Works on Paper, Jan Cicero Gallery, Chicago, 91; Labyrinth Series, Jan Cicero Gallery, Chicago, 93; Exquisite Corpse, Transmission Gallery, Glasgow, Scotland, 94; Lakeside Views, Evanston Art Ctr, 94; Blink (installation work) Northern Ill Univ Gallery, Chicago, 2000; and others; Brad Cooper Gallery, Tampa, Fla, 2003. *Collection Arranged:* Art in Chicago, 96, 98, 2000 & 2002. *Pos:* Contribr ed, New Art Examiner, New Art Asn, 75-76; asst dir, Jan Cicero Gallery, Chicago, 77-84; contrib ed Dialogue, 89-2002, ArtForum, 2003. *Teaching:* Instr painting, Evanston Art Ctr, Ill, 71-79, Ill Inst Technol, 75-83, Columbia Col, Chicago, 79-89, Art Inst Chicago, 81-83 & Univ Ill, Chicago, summer 83; Art Inst Chicago, 81-; Instr art history and criticism, Columbia Col, Chicago, 90-, tenured prof, 96-, 2D design studio, 99-. *Awards:* 3rd Prize, Italian American Exhib; Merit Award Evanston and Vicinity Exhib, Ill. *Bibliog:* James Yood (auth), Chicago draws, New Art Examiner, 12/86; Michael Rooks (auth), article, New Art Examiner, 3/98; Esther Hammer (auth), article, Tampa Tribune, 11/2/2002. *Mem:* Chicago Art Critics Asn; Am Abstract Artists, NY. *Media:* Multimedia. *Publ:* Contribr, Dictionary of American Biography, Macmillian, 94. *Dealer:* Kathie Shaw Chicago IL; Brad Cooper Tampa FL. *Mailing Add:* Columbia Coll Dept Art & Design 623 S Wabash Rm 1004 Chicago IL 60625

POTANIN, VLADIMIR
PATRON
b Moscow, Jan 3,1961. *Pos:* With USSR Minister For Trade, 1983-90; found, pres, Interros For Trade Asn, 1990-92, pres, chmn, 98-; vpres, joint stock comml bank MFK Bank, 1992-93; founder, pres, UNEXIM Bank (United Export/Import Bank), 1993-96, 97-98; first dep prime minister Russia, 1996-97. *Mem:* Russian Fedn Govt Coun on Entrepreneurship, Asn Russian Banks Coun; chmn, Nat Coun Corp Governance; founder, Vladimir Potanin Charitable Fund; trustee, Solomon R Guggenheim Found, 2002-; chmn bd dir Hermitage-Guggenheim Fund, 2002-; chmn bd trustees, State Hermitage, 2003-. *Mailing Add:* Interros Co 9 Bolshaya Yakimanka St Moscow 119180 Russia

POTOTSCHNIK, JOHN MICHAEL
PAINTER, INSTRUCTOR
b St Ives, Cornwall, Eng, Nov 14, 45; US citizen. *Study:* Wichita State Univ, BFA, 68; Art Ctr Col Design, 69-71; Lyme Acad Fine Arts, 93. *Work:* Blue Cross Blue Shield, SC; City of McKinney (Collin Co Courthouse), Tex; City of Carrollton (City Hall), Tex; Kansas City Southern Railroad, Mo; City of Schlumberger, Tex. *Exhib:* Am Art in Miniature, Thomas Gilcrease Mus, Tulsa, Okla, 93-94, 99-2001, 2004 & 2006; Miniatures, Albuquerque Mus, NMex, 93-2002; Oil Painters of Am Nat Show, 94, 96-97, 99 & 2001-2003; Great Am Artists Exhib, Cincinnati, OH, 99-2005; Salon Int, San Antonio, Tex, 2004-2006. *Pos:* Newsletter ed, Artists & Craftsman Assoc, 83-85, first vpres, 85-86, pres, 86-88. *Teaching:* Assoc prof art, Collin Co Community Col, 94-; pvt lessons, 89-98. *Awards:* George Washington Honor Medal, Freedom's Found Valley Forge, 84, 86, 92 & 95; John Steven Jones Fel, Bosque Co Conservatory of Fine Arts, Roland & Joyce Jones, 92; Oil Painters of Am, 2001; 1st Place, Landscape, Art Renewal Center, 1st Int Salon, 2004. *Bibliog:* Peter Anderson (auth), Introductions, Southwest Art Mag, 87; Paul Soderberg (auth), Masters and Mentors, Plein Air Magazine, 2005. *Mem:* Outdoor Painters Soc (sig mem); Oil Painters Am (sig mem). *Media:* Oil. *Publ:* Contribr, Am Artist, BFI Communs, 90; The Artist's Mag, 8/94, 5/95, 12/95, 4/96, 6/96; 200 Great Painting Ideas for Artists, North Light Books, 98; Internat Artist, Oct/Nov 2000; Expressing the Visual Language of the Landscape, Int Artist Publ, 2002. *Dealer:* American Legacy Gallery 5911 Main St Kansas City MO; G Stanton Gallery 3412 Rosedale Dallas TX; Greenhouse Gallery of Fine Art 6496 N New Braunfels San Antonio Tex; New Masters Gallery Dolores between Ocean & 7th Carmel Calif; Rutledge Street Gallery 508 Rutledge St Camden SC. *Mailing Add:* 6944 Taylor Ln Wylie TX 75098

POTTER, (GEORGE) KENNETH
PAINTER, PRINTMAKER
b Bakersfield, Calif, Feb 26, 26. *Study:* Acad Art, San Francisco, 47 & 48; Acad Frochot, Paris, with Metzinger, 50-52; Inst Statale Belli Arte, Florence, Italy, summer 51; study in Sicily, 53; San Francisco State Univ, BA, 74, teaching credential San Francisco State Univ, 1976. *Work:* Admiral's Conference Room, USS Enterprise; Univ San Francisco Collection; City of San Francisco Art Comn; San Diego Mus Fine Art. *Comn:* Dome (stained glass & resin), Soc Calif Pioneers, Hale Mem Gallery, Civic Ctr, San Francisco, 74; triptych (stained glass & resin windows), Univ Calif, San Francisco, Moffitt Hosp, San Francisco, 76; hist mural (ink & acrylic on canvas), Corte Madera Recreation Ctr, Calif, 99; Le Marin, cement & styrofoam sculpture, W Robert Griswold Jr, Tiburon, Calif, 2002; watercolors & prints, Embassy Suites Hotel, Sacramento. *Pos:* Art dir, McCann-Erickson Inc Advert, Rio de Janeiro, 54-55, Johnson & Lewis Advert, San Francisco, 57 & Michelson Advert, Palo Alto, 59-60; artist demonstr, Grumbacher Inc, New York, 78-79. *Teaching:* Instr watercolor, Civic Art Ctr, Walnut Creek, Calif, 68-70, Acad Art, San Francisco, 70, San Francisco State Univ, 74 & 75 & Richmond Art Ctr, Calif, 78-79. *Awards:* First Award Watercolor, Alameda Co Fair Statewide Competition, 74, 79 & 85; Best of Show, Calif Arts League Sixth Ann Nat Open, 88 & 98; First Place, 7th Nat Open, Calif Arts League, 99; Best of Show Award, Calif, 99, Wash, 2002. *Bibliog:* Christian Sci Monitor cover spread, 2/1949; California Style Watercolor Artists 1925-1955, Gordon McClelland Hillcrest Press, 1987; California Watercolors 1850-1970, Hillcrest Press, 2003. *Mem:* West Coast Watercolor Soc (pres, 68-70); life mem, Marin Soc Artists; AWS (signature mem); Watercolor Artists Sacramento; Northern Calif Arts Asn. *Media:* Watercolor, Miscellaneous Media. *Publ:* Toward Diversity California Post War Watercolors, Gordon McClelland (auth), Antiques & Fine Art 1-2/91, California Watercolors 1850-1970, Hillcrest Press, 2003; Review of California The Urban Tempo, Charlotte Berney (auth), Antiques & Fine Art, 3-4/91; Switzerland In Watercolor-Watercolors By Kenneth Potter, 2003. *Dealer:* Michael Johnson Fine Art PO Box Fall Brook CA 92088; Calif Art Gallery 305 N Coast Hwy Ste A Laguna Beach CA 92651. *Mailing Add:* 4824 Skyway Dr Fair Oaks CA 95628

POTTER, TED
PAINTER, ADMINISTRATOR
b Springhill, Kans, Dec 6, 33. *Study:* Northwestern Univ; Univ Kans; Baker Univ, BFA; Univ Calif, Berkeley; Calif Col Arts & Crafts, MFA. *Work:* Calif Col Arts & Crafts, Oakland; Univ Kans Art Gallery, Lawrence; Wake Forest Univ, Winston-Salem; Vanderbilt Univ, Nashville; Glaxo Inc, RTP, NC; and many pvt collections. *Exhib:* Solo exhibs, State Univ, Salem Col, Winston-Salem, Barbara Fiedler Gallery, Washington, DC, Morehead Galleries, Greensboro, NC & Marita Gilliam Gallery, Raleigh, NC, 89; New Orleans Acad Fine Art, 84. *Pos:* Dir art, Glide Found, 65-67; dir, Southeastern Ctr Contemp Art, Winston-Salem, 68-; dir, Awards Visual Arts, Nat Artist Fel Prog, Atlanta Ctr Arts, New Smyrna Beach, Fla. *Mem:* NC State Arts Soc (adv coun, 69-72); NC State Arts Coun. *Dealer:* Estelle Dodge Associates New York, NY; Barbara Fiedler Galleries Washington DC. *Mailing Add:* c/o Southeastern Ctr Contemporary Art 750 Marguerite Dr Winston Salem NC 27106-5861

POTTS, TIMOTHY
MUSEUM DIRECTOR
Pos: dir media and telecommunications group, corporate finance department Lehman Brothers, NYC and London; Head Nat Gallery of Victoria, Australia; dir, Kimbell Art Mus, Ft Worth, Tex, 1998-. *Teaching:* prof Univ Melbourne; adjunct prof, La Trobe Univ, Melbourne. *Publ:* Author: (monograph) Mesopotamia and the East: An Archaeological & Historical Study of Foreign Relations 3400-2000 BC, 1995; editor: Kimbell Art Museum: Handbook of the Collection, 2003; co-editor: Culture Through Objects: Ancient Near Eastern Studies in Honour of P. R. S. Moorey, 2003. *Mailing Add:* Kimbell Art Museum 3333 Camp Bowie Blvd Fort Worth TX 76107

POULET, ANNE LITLE
MUSEUM DIRECTOR
b Washington, Pa, Mar 20, 1942. *Study:* Sweet Briar Col, BA(cum laude), 1964; NY Univ Inst Fine Arts, NYU, MA, 1970. *Exhib:* Corot to braque, Mus of Fine Arts, Boston, 79; Clodion Terracottas in North Am Collections, The Frick Collection, 84; Clodion, Musee du Louvre, 92; Jean-Antoine Houdon: Sculptor of the Enlightenment, Nat Gallery of Art, Wash, DC, 03. *Pos:* Cur, Dept European Decorative Arts and Sculpture Mus Fine Arts, Boston, cur emer, 99—; dir, The Frick Collection, New York City, 2003—. *Awards:* Recipient Ford Found Grant, 70; Iris Found Award, 2000; Kress Fel, Nat Gallery Art; Chevalier de l'Ordre des artes et des lettres. *Mem:* French Heritage Soc (co-founder, vchmn bd, 82-2003); Am Acad Arts & Sciences. *Publ:* Co-auth: (catalogue) Clodion (1738-1814), Jean-Antoine Houdon (1741-1828): Sculptor of the Enlightenment; (co auth) Nudity and Chstity: Houdons Statue of Diana in the Light of Newly Discovered Documents, Sculptures Journax X, Sept 03; Auth: (exh catalogue) Jean-Antoine Houdon: Sculptor of the Enlightenment, National gallery of Art. *Mailing Add:* The Frick Collection 1 E 70th St New York NY 10021-4967

POULIN, ROLAND
SCULPTOR
b Apr 17, 40. *Study:* Ecole des Beaux-Arts de Montreal, 64-69, Atelier Mario Merola, 69-70, Univ Laral, PhD, 80. *Work:* Mus d'Art Contemporain, Montreal, PQ; Mus du Quebec; Nat Gallery, Ottawa, Ont; Mus des Beaux-Arts de Montreal; Art Gallery Ont, Toronto. *Exhib:* Solo exhibs, Mus D'Art Contemporain, Montreal, Can, 71 & 83, Agnes Etherington Art Ctr, Kingston, Can, 84, Olga Korper Gallery, Toronto, Can, 88, 90, 91, 93 & 96, Mus Folkwang Essen, 92, Galerie Rochefort, Montreal, Que, 92, Nat Gallery Can, Ottawa, Ont, 94 & Art Gallery North York, Ont, 95; Quebec '88--A Selection, Art Gallery Toronto Art Rental, 88; Historical Rouse: Art in Montreal, Power Plant, Toronto, 88; 49th Parallel, NY, 89; Cologne Art Fair, Ger. *Pos:* Instr sculpture, Univ du Que a Montreal, 71-72; instr composition, Col du Vieux-Montreal, 72-74, Col Brebeuf, 75-76; instr sculpture, Univ Laval, Quebec, 73-81, Concordia Univ, Montreal, 82-83, Univ Ottawa, 87-. *Awards:* Ozias Leduc Prize (Visual Arts), Emile Nelligan Found, 92. *Bibliog:* Gilles Daignault (auth), La nouvelle sculpture de Roland Poulin, Le Devoir, Montreal, 5/17/86; Norman Theriault (auth), L'oeuvre d'art prend le pas sur l'histoire, Forces, No 84, Montreal, winter 89; Chantal Pontbriand (auth), Roland Poulin, No 53, Parachute, Montreal, 89. *Mailing Add:* c/o Olga Korper 17 Morrow Ave Toronto ON M6R 2H9 Canada

POULOS, BASILIOS NICHOLAS
PAINTER, EDUCATOR
b Columbia, SC, Dec 15, 41. *Study:* Atlanta Sch Art, BFA, 65; Tulane Univ, MFA, 68; Univ SC. *Work:* Mus Fine Arts, Houston; Chase Manhattan Bank, NY; Voores Mus, Athens; Tulane Univ, New Orleans, La; New Orleans Mus Art; and others. *Exhib:* One-man exhibs, High Mus Art, Atlanta, 65, LaGrange Col, Ga, 84, McIntosh/Drysdale Gallery, Houston, 85, Harris Gallery, Houston, 86, Caroline Lee Gallery, Houston, 87, Meredith Long Gallery, Houston, 92 & Galveston Arts Ctr, Tex, 94; Contemp Reflections, Aldrich Mus Contemp Art, 74; 35th Biennial, Corcoran Gallery Art, Washington, 77; Fresh Paint: The Houston Sch, Mus Fine Arts, Houston, 85; Petit Format, Kouros Gallery, NY, 87; Large Scale/Small Scale, Sewall Art Gallery, Houston, 89; A Sense of Place, Transco Gallery, Houston, 93; Foreign Influences, Mus ETex, Lufkin, 93; New Gallery, Houston, Tex, 96, 98, 01; Selini Gallery, Athens, Greece, 98; Theophilos Gallery, Athens, 01. *Teaching:* Prof studio art, Rice Univ, Houston, 85-. *Awards:* Fine Arts Found Grant, Atlanta, Ga, 65; French Govt Grant, 65-66; Guggenheim Found Fel, 73-74. *Bibliog:* Mimi Crossley (auth), Poulos at Watson De Nagy, Art in Am, 77. *Media:* Acrylic on Canvas, Wood. *Res:* Figuration/Structure

POUNIAN, ALBERT KACHOUNI
PAINTER, CURATOR
b Chicago, Ill, Mar 7, 24. *Study:* Art Inst Chicago, BFA, 48, MFA, 49. *Work:* Borg-Warner Corp, Chicago; Ill Bell Tel, Chicago; Harper Col, Palatine, Ill; Barat Col, Lake Forest, Ill. *Exhib:* Chicago & Vicinity, Art Inst Chicago; Ringling Mus, Sarasota, Fla; Northwest Territory, Springfield, Ill; Violence in Contemp Am Art, Mus Contemp Art, Chicago, 68. *Pos:* Consult & contribr, Am Educ Encycl; coordr, Nat Upward Bound Exhib, Off Econ Opportunity, 66 & consult, 67-68; corp art cur, Continental Ill Nat Bank & Trust Co, Chicago, 79-89; founding chmn, Asn Corp Art Curators, Chicago, 80; consult, Nixon Assoc, Chicago, 89-. *Teaching:* Instr, painting & drawing, Art Inst Chicago, 48-56; lectr art hist, Lake Forest Col, 50-65; prof painting & drawing, Barat Col Lake Forest, 49-79 & chmn art dept, 70-74; Fulbright-Hays exchange prof, Sch Fine Arts, Ulster Col, Northern Ireland Polytechnic, Belfast, Northern Ireland. *Mem:* Am Asn Univ Prof. *Media:* Acrylic, Pen & Ink. *Publ:* Auth, articles, Am Educ Encycl. *Mailing Add:* 970 Ivy Ln Deerfield IL 60015-2231

POUPENEY, MOLLIE
CERAMIST, WRITER
b Oregon, 26. *Study:* Univ Calif, BA, 69. *Work:* Oakland Mus, Calif; Saks Fifth Ave Am Craft Collection, San Francisco, Calif; US State Dept. *Exhib:* Solo exhibs, Valley Arts Gallery, Walnut Creek, Calif, 68, 70, Scott Gallery, Orinda, Calif, 78, Antonio Prieto Gallery, Mills Col, Oakland, 81 & Oakland Mus, Calif, 82; Calif Artists, Oakland Mus, Calif, 81; Invitational 1984, Craftsman's Gallery, Scarsdale, NY, 84; Five Western Artists, Artisans Am Fine Crafts, Tex, 86; Los Angeles Int Art Show, Barclay Simpson Fine Arts, Calif, 87; Jewel Savadelis Collection, Triton Mus, Santa Clara, Calif, 88; Renwick Gallery, Smithsonian, Wash, DC, 88. *Pos:* Ed cartoonist, Out to Lunch (comic strip), The Sun, Orinda-Walnut Creek, Calif, 62-72. *Teaching:* Chico Art, 62-74 & Ceramics, 73-76, Orinda, Calif. *Awards:* Purchase Award, San Francisco Art Comn, 76 & Exhib Award, 77. *Mem:* Asn Calif Ceramic Artists; Cali Contemp Craft Asn. *Media:* Clay, Paint. *Publ:* Auth, articles, Oregon Revisited, Ceramics Monthly, 97; Daddy for Sale, 98. *Dealer:* The Gallery 329 Primrose Rd Burlingame CA 94010; Barclay Simpson Fine Arts Gallery Lafayette LA. *Mailing Add:* 21 Francisca Dr Moraga CA 94556

POUSETTE-DART, JOANNA
PAINTER
b New York, NY, 1947. *Study:* Bennington Col, BA, 68. *Work:* Mus Mod Art, Solomon R Guggenheim Mus, Citibank, Fox Glynn & Melamed, Lehman Brothers, McCrory Corp, Wells Rich & Greene, Brooklyn Mus, NY; Indianapolis Mus, Ind; Portland Art Mus, Ore; Coopers & Lybrand, Houston, Tex; Security Pacific Nat Bank, Calif. *Comn:* Doumani House (mosaics & architect), comn by Robert Graham, Los Angeles. *Exhib:* Solo exhibs, Susan Caldwell Gallery, NY, 76, 78, 79 & 83, Janus Gallery, Los Angeles, Calif, 81 & Schmidt-Dean Gallery, Philadelphia, Pa, 88, Tenri Gallery, NY, 95; Painting and Sculpture Today 1980, Indianapolis Mus Art, Ind, 80; Collectors Gallery XVI, Marion Koogler McNay Art Inst, San Antonio, Tex, 82; Recent Acquisition: Paintings & Sculpture, 83 & Contrasts of Form: Geometric Painting 1960-1980, 85-86, Mod Mus Art, NY; Drawings, Gallery 201, traveling, 86; Abstractions Self-Evident, Piccalo Spaleto, Charleston, SC, 91. *Teaching:* Instr, Ramapo Col, NJ, 72-76 & Hunter Col, 86-; Instr, Yale Univ, Norfolk, Conn, 97. *Awards:* John Simon Guggenheim Mem Fel, 81; Nat Endowment Arts Grants, 89-90. *Bibliog:* Lenore Malen (auth), New York Reviews, ARTnews, 10/88; Vered Leib (auth), Joanna Pousette-Davis: Exploring the Possibilities of Dialogue, Arts, 4/88. *Mailing Add:* 433 Broome St New York NY 10013

POWELL, DAN T
PHOTOGRAPHER
b Richland, Wash, July 12, 50. *Study:* Cent Wash Univ, with Jim Sahlstrand, BA, 73, MA(art), 77; Univ Ill, with Art Sinsabaugh & Luther Smith, MFA(art), 80. *Work:* Hallmark Collection, Kansas City, Mo; Calif Inst Arts; Art Inst Chicago, Ill; Midwest Mus Am Art, Elkhart, Ind; Ill State Univ, Normal; Polaroid Corp; Mus Fine Art, Houston; Portland Art Mus. *Exhib:* Summer Light, Light Gallery, NY, 82; Group exhib, Fifth Vienna Int Biennial, Austria, 82, Chicago Art Inst, 88, San Francisco Mus Mod Art, 88; four-person exhib, San Francisco Camerawork, 83; Susan Spiritus Gallery, Los Angeles, 83; Evolving Abstraction in Photog, Anita Shapolsky Gallery, New York City, 89; Royal Col Art, London, 93; Am Made, The New Still Life, Isetan Mus Art, Tokyo, Japan; Comdeso/Cawler Gallery, New York City, 94; Elizabeth Leach Gallery, Portland, 95. *Teaching:* Asst prof, Univ Northern Iowa, 80-; assoc prof, Univ Ore, Eugene, 87-. *Awards:* Second Award, Contemp Photoworks, Univ NMex, 80; Best of Show, Midwest Photo 80, Midwest Mus Am Art, 80; Best of Prints & Drawings, Iowa Artists, Des Moines Art Ctr, 82. *Bibliog:* Joan Murray (auth), rev of New Photographics, 79 & Diane Neumaier (auth), Visual & Verbal Language, 80, Artweek; Barbara Westerfield (auth), Constructed Realities, Art News, 86. *Media:* Photography. *Dealer:* Olson/Larsen Gallery De sMoines IA

POWELL, EARL ALEXANDER, III
DIRECTOR, HISTORIAN
b Spartanburg, SC, Oct 24, 43. *Study:* Williams Col, BA, 66; Harvard Univ, MA, 70, PhD, 74. *Hon Degrees:* Otis Parsons Inst, DFA, 87; Williams Col, DFA, 93. *Pos:* Cur Michener Collection, Univ Tex, Austin, 74-76; mus cur & asst to asst dir, Nat Gallery Art, Wash, 76-78, exec cur, 79-80, dir, 92; dir, Los Angeles Co Mus Art, 80-92. *Teaching:* Teaching fel fine arts, Harvard Univ, 70-74; asst prof Am art, Univ Tex, Austin, 74-76. *Awards:* King Olav Medal, Norway; Officier dans l'Ordre des Arts & Lett Award, France; Grand Off Order Infante D Henrique Med, Govt Portugal, 95; Williams Coll Bicentennial Medal, 95; Mexican Cult Inst Award, 96; Commendatore dell 'Ordine al Merito della Republica Italiana, Govt Italy, 98; Chevalier of Legion Honor Award, French Govt, 2000. *Mem:* Am Fedn Arts (trustee); Ga O'Keefe Found (trustee); Nat Trust Historic Preservation (trustee); White House Historical Asn (trustee); Asn Art Mus Dirs; Comt for Preservation of White House; Fed Coun on Arts and Humanities; Nat Coun Arts; Pres's Comt on Arts and Humanities; US Comn Fine Arts (chm); Morris & Gwendolyn Cafritz Found (trustee); John F. Kennedy Ctr Performing Arts (trustee); Am Acad Arts & Sciences; Am Philosophical Soc. *Res:* English influences in the art of Thomas Cole. *Publ:* Coauth, American Art at Harvard (catalog), 73; auth, Catalogue Raisonne of the Michener Collection, 78; Thomas Cole, Monograph, Abrams, NY, 1990; plus article & catalogue essay on Am art; and others. *Mailing Add:* Nat Gallery Art 2000B S Club Dr Hyattsville MD 20785

POWELL, GORDON
SCULPTOR
b Decatur, Ill, May 4, 47. *Study:* Sch Art Inst, Chicago, BFA, 75; Univ Ill, MFA, 80. *Work:* Cresap, McCormick and Paget, Chicago; Levy Organization, Chicago; Prudential Insurance; Saks Fifth Ave, Portland, Ore; State Ill Collection, Springfield; Millikin Univ. *Comn:* Wine Label Imagery Series, Benziger Family Wines. *Exhib:* New Horizons in Art, Cult Ctr, Chicago, 84; 81st Exhib Artists of Chicago & Vicinity, Art Inst Chicago, 85; Fetish Show-Obsessive Expressions, Rockford Art Mus, 86; Extended Boundaries, Cult Ctr, Chicago, 86; Columnar, Hudson River Mus, Yonkers, 88; Body Fragments, Shea and Beker Gallery, NY, 89; The Chicago Show, Chicago Cult Ctr, Ill, 90; Summer 1990, Rosa Esman Gallery, NY, 90; one-person exhibs, Roy Boyd Galleries, Chicago, 82, 83, 85, 86 & 89, Santa Monica, Calif, 87 & Vaughan & Vaughan, Minneapolis, Minn, 90, Univ N Iowa, Cedar Falls, Roy Boyd Gallery, Chicago, 91, Chicago Cult Ctr, 96, William Rainey Harper Coll, Palatine, Ill, 2000, Perimeter Gallery, Chicago, 2001; Rockford (Ill) Art Mus, 92, Ukrainian Inst Modern Art, Chicago, 97; Perimeter Gallery, Chicago, 98, Elgin (Ill) Coll, 2001. *Teaching:* Instr, Rockford Col, 90; adj asst prof Sch of Art, Art Inst Chicago, 96. *Awards:* Artist-in-Residence, ArtPark, Lewiston, NY, 85, Yaddo, Saratoga Springs, NY, 93; Fel

Nat Endowment Arts, 86; Prix de Rome, Am Acad Rome, 87-88; Vis artist Am Acad, Rome, 94; Visual Artists fel, Ill, Arts Coun, 97, Enrichment grant, Sch of Art Inst Chicago, 98, 2000. *Bibliog:* Emerging Sculptor Show, The New York Times, 12/11/87; reviews, Chicago Tribune, 7/16/82, 89, 91, 93, Los Angeles Times, 11/17/87, Evanston Rev., 95. *Media:* Wood. *Dealer:* Gordon Powell Studio 1117 W Lake St Chicago IL 60607. *Mailing Add:* 319 N Thatcher River Forest IL 60305

POWELL, JOSEPHINE
PHOTOGRAPHER
b 1919. *Study:* Cornell Univ, BA; Columbia Univ (Sch of Social Work), MA. *Work:* has photographed cultures all over the world including the Middle East, the Indian sub-continent adn Africa. *Exhib:* Represented in permanent collections of Ctr for Anatolian Ethnography and Textile Studies, Instanbul, Frine Arts Library, Harvard Univ. *Pos:* Asst, Int Refugee Orgn, United Nations, 1946-52; freelance photographer, 1952-; co-founder (with Harald and Renata Böhmer), DOBAG Project. *Awards:* George Hewitt Myers Award for Lifetime Achievement, The Textile Mus, 2006

POWELSON, ROSEMARY A
PAINTER, PRINTMAKER
b La Junta, Colo. *Study:* Univ Nebr, Lincoln, BFA, 71; Mich State Univ, East Lansing, MFA, 74. *Work:* Art Inst Chicago; Cranbrook Acad Art, Bloomfield Hills, Mich; Hackley Art Mus, Muskegon, Mich; Kalamazoo Inst Art, Mich; Sioux City Art Ctr, Iowa; Lower Columbia Col, Longview, Wash. *Comn:* Mich bicentennial portfolio prints in collotype, Nat Endowment Arts, Alma, Mich, 76; Prints 83 (portfolio), Lower Columbia Col Found, Longview, Wash, 83. *Exhib:* One-woman show, Alma Col, Mich, 78; Kans 5th Nat Small Paintings & Drawings, Art Gallery, Ft Hayes State Univ, 81; Wash Women Art, Art Gallery, Eastern Wash Univ, Cheney, 81; Print Exhib, Fort Steilacoom Community Col, Tacoma, Wash, 83; Print Exhib, Ore State Univ, Corvallis, Ore, 84; Invitational Group Show, Clatsop Community Col, Astoria, Ore, 85. *Pos:* Humanities consult, Wash Humanities Project, Olympia, 81-. *Teaching:* Instr painting & drawing, Alma Col, Mich, 75-78; instr design & drawing, Ft Steilacoom Community Col, Tacoma, Wash, 78-79; instr art hist & design, Lower Columbia Col, Longview, Wash, 79-. *Awards:* Purchase Award, 33rd Ann Fall Show, 71; Merit Award, Saginaw Ann Area Art Exhib, 77. *Media:* All Media. *Publ:* Producer, Women in Art (film), Wash State Humanities Project, Olympia, 81. *Mailing Add:* Art Dept PO Box 3010 Lower Columbia Col Longview WA 98632

POWERS, DONALD T
PAINTER
b Madison, Tenn, May 20, 50. *Study:* Tenn Technol Univ, 69-70; David Lipscomb Col, 70-72. *Work:* Smithsonian Inst Nat Portrait Gallery, Washington, DC; Emory Univ, Atlanta; Ga Mus Art, Univ Ga, Athens; Am Acad & Inst Arts & Lett, New York, NY; Mus Mod Art, Haifa, Israel. *Comn:* Portrait of Jimmy Carter, Friends of the President, Washington, DC, 85; portrait of His Holiness the Dalai Lama, 90. *Exhib:* Jimmy Carter in Plains, Hunter Mus Art, Chattanooga, Tenn, 86; Art and the Law, Minn Mus Art, St Paul, Minn & Moscarelle Mus, Col William & Mary, Williamsburg, Va, 87; The Eternal Landscape, Southeastern Ctr for Contemp Art, Winston-Salem, NC, 91; 17th Art & the Law Exhib, Kennedy Galleries, NY & Loyola Law Sch, Los Angeles; The Artist as Native, Babcock Galleries, NY, Middlebury Col Mus Art, Albany Inst Hist & Art, Owensboro Mus Art, Westmoreland Mus Art & Md Inst & Col Art; Coast to Coast: The Contemp Landscape in Fla (with catalog), Daytona Mus Arts & Sci, Gulf Coast Art Mus, Bel Aire, Lowe Mus, Miami & Pensacola Mus Art, 98-; Am Embassy, Rome, 2001-04. *Pos:* Art Dir, TN State Mus, Nashville, 73-76. *Teaching:* Priv teaching to Pres Jimmy Carter. *Awards:* Lyndhurst Prize, Lyndhurst Found, 84-86; Purchase Award, West Publ Co, 87. *Media:* Egg Tempera, Oil. *Specialty:* Realism. *Publ:* Auth, The Artist As Native, Pomegranate Books, 93; Illustrator The Silver Donkey, Candlewick Press, Cambridge, 2005. *Dealer:* Stonehenge Gallery, Montgormery, AL. *Mailing Add:* 217 Edgewood Dr PO Box 3295 Thomasville GA 31799

POWERS, JOHN & KIMIKO
COLLECTOR
Mr Powers b Mt Vernon, NY, Aug 5, 16; Mrs Powers b Tokyo, Japan, Aug 26, 36. *Study:* Mr Powers, Princeton Univ, BA, 38; Harvard Law Sch, LLB, 41; studied with John McRosenfield, 68-98; Colo State Univ, LLD, 90; Mrs Powers, Int Christian Univ, Tokyo, grad, 58. *Collection Arranged:* Traditions of Japanese Art, Harvard, Seattle, Princeton, 70; Extraordinary Persons: Japanese Artists (1560-1860), 88; Edo Period Art, Harvard Univ, 98. *Teaching:* Adj prof, Aspen Inst Humanistic Studies, Colo State Univ. *Bibliog:* John M Rosenfield & Shujiro Shimada (auths), Traditions of Japanese Art: selections from the Kimiko & John Powers Collection, Fogg Art Mus, Harvard Univ, 70. *Collection:* Antique Japanese painting, sculpture, ceramics, bronze from pre-history to 1868; contemporary art 1958-1998. *Mailing Add:* 13114 Hwy 82 Carbondale CO 81623

POWERS, LINDA S
Study: Davenport Univ, Undergrad degree in Sales and Marketing. *Pos:* With Amway Corp, Digital Equipment Corp, IBM Corp; marketing dir, private country club; founder, pres Arts & Crafts Asn Am, 1999—. *Mailing Add:* Arts and Crafts Assn Am 4888 Cannon Woods Ct Belmont MI 49306

POWERS, W ALEX
PAINTER
b St Charles, Va, Apr 25, 40. *Study:* Emory & Henry Col, Emory, Va, BA, 62; Eliot McMurrough Sch Art, Indialantic, Fla, 67-69; Art Students League, Woodstock, NY, 69. *Work:* SC State Art Collection, Columbia; Trammel Crowe Co, Charlotte, NC; Waccamaw Art & Crafts Guild, Myrtle Beach, SC; Coca Cola, Charlotte, NC. *Exhib:* Am Watercolor Soc, NY, 76, 88, 90 & 92; Nat Watercolor Soc, Los Angeles, 84-86 & 94; San Diego Watercolor Soc Int Exhib, 85-86 & 91-92 & 94; Rocky Mountain Nat, Golden, Colo, 90; Watercolor USA, Springfield, Mo, 91. *Teaching:* Self-employed teacher, watercolor workshops throughout US, Canada & Abroad, 72-. *Awards:* Best-of-Show, Okla Patrons Gala Watercolor Exhib, 86; Best-of-Show, Ky Watercolor Soc, 93 & 94; 2nd Award, Watercolor Soc Ala Nat Exhib, 93 & 94. *Bibliog:* Everything You Always Wanted to Know About Watercolor, Watson-Guptill, 92; Splash 2, Northlight Publ, 93; Exploring Transparent Watercolor, Davis Publ, 93. *Mem:* Nat Watercolor Soc; Southern Watercolor Soc; Waccamaw Arts & Crafts Guild, SC (pres, 76, vpres, 86); SC Watercolor Soc. *Media:* Watercolor, Drawing. *Publ:* Am Artist Mag, 2/85; Artist's Mag, 2/85; auth, Painting People in Watercolor, Watson-Guptill Publ, 89. *Mailing Add:* 401-72nd Ave N Apt 1 Myrtle Beach SC 29572-3814

POWLEY, DONALD
PAINTER
b St Louis, Mo, 1955. *Study:* Washington Univ, St Louis, Mo, BFA, 79. *Work:* Chase Manhattan Bank, NY. *Exhib:* Solo exhibs, Cash/Newhouse, NY, 86 & 87, Julian Pretto, NY, 88 & 89, White Columns, NY, 90 & Rubenstein/Diacono, NY, 93; Strategies for the Next Painting (with catalog), Wolff Gallery, NY, 91; Cotextures & Constructures (with catalog), Rubenstein/Diacomo Gallery, NY, 92; The Mechanical Drip, Greenberg Gallery, St Louis, Mo, 92; The Return of the Cadavre Exquis, Drawing Ctr, NY, 93; Numbers, Letters & Markings, Hirschl & Adler Modern, NY, 94; and others. *Awards:* Visual Arts Fel, Painting, Nat Endowment Arts, 87. *Bibliog:* Carin Kuoni (auth), Interview, J Contemp Art, Vol 4, No 1, 91; Mario Diacono (auth, essay), Donald Powley (exhib catalog), 93; Ingrid Schaffner (auth, essay), Cursive, Parkett, No 42, 94. *Mailing Add:* RD 1 Box 308 Stamford NY 12167

POZZATTI, RUDY O
PRINTMAKER, PAINTER
b Telluride, Colo, Jan 14, 25. *Study:* Univ Colo, BFA & MFA; Hon LHD, Univ Colo, 73; also with Wendell H Black, Max Beckman & Ben Shahn. *Work:* Mus Mod Art, NY; Libr Cong, Washington, DC; Art Inst Chicago, Ill; Sheldon Mem Art Mus, Lincoln, Nebr; Cleveland Mus Art, Ohio; Univ Art Mus, Bloomington, 2002, Evansville Mus Art, 2002; rep in permanent collections, Mus Modern Art, New York City, Libr. Congress, Wash, Art Inst Chicago, Cleveland Mus Art. *Comn:* Spec Print Eds, Cleveland Print Club, Cleveland Mus Art, 54; Int Graphic Arts Soc, NY, 58-61 & 63; Conrad Hilton Hotel, NY, 61; Clairol, Inc, comn for NY World's Fair, 63; Ferdinand Roten Galleries, Baltimore, Md, 67 & 68; Rochester Print Soc, NY, 98; Int Print Symposium, Cortona, Italy; Corcoran Mus, Washington DC, 2001; and others. *Exhib:* Young Americans, Whitney Mus Am Arts, NY, 61; Stampe di Due Mondi: Prints of Two Worlds, Tyler Sch Art, Rome, Italy, 67; 20 Yr Retrospective, Sheldon Mem Art Gallery, Univ Nebr, 69; Artists Abroad, Inst Int Educ, Am Fedn Arts, NY, 69; Int Cult Conf, Budapest, Hungary, 85; Rudy Pozzatti, Four Decades of Printmaking (82 works with catalog), Mitchell Mus, Mt Vernon, Ill, Traveling Show, 92-93; one man retrospective, Ind Univ Art Mus, 2001. *Pos:* US State Dept Cult Exchange Proj, USSR, 61, Yugoslavia, 65 & Brazil, 74; artist-in-residence, Roswell Mus & Art Ctr, 79. *Teaching:* Asst prof printmaking & painting, Univ Nebr, 50-56; prof printmaking, Ind Univ, 56-72, distinguished prof, 72-91. *Awards:* Guggenheim Fel, 63-64; George Norlin Silver Medal, Asn Alumni of Univ Colo, 72; Rockefeller Grant, Belaggio, Italy, 95. *Bibliog:* Norman Geske (auth), Rudy Pozzatti; American Printmaker, Univ Kans, 71; Richard Taylor (auth), Pozzatti (film), Artists in America, NETV, 71; Nancy Carroll (auth), A visit with Rudy Pozzatti, North Shore Art League, 72. *Mem:* Soc Am Graphic Artists; Am Color Print Soc; Col Art Asn, NY; Nat Acad (assoc, 81, acad, 91). *Media:* All Media. *Dealer:* The Gallery 109 E Sixth St Bloomington IN 47401; Soraya Planning & Design 233 Wacker Dr Suite 845 Chicago IL 60608. *Mailing Add:* 117 S Meadowbrook Ave Bloomington IN 47408

POZZI, LUCIO
PAINTER, PRINTMAKER
b Milano, Italy, Nov 29, 35; US citizen. *Study:* Sculpture with Michael Noble. *Work:* Mus Modern Art, NY; Mus Contemp Art, Chicago; Detroit Art Inst; Fogg Mus, Cambridge, Mass; Museo Pecci, Prato, Italy. *Exhib:* John Weber Gallery, NY, 93, 96, 2000; Carlo Grossetti, Milan, 96; ESSO Gallery, NY, 99; Hindsight/Foresight, Bayly Mus, Charlottesville, Va, 2000; Ben Shahn Gallery, Paterson Univ, NJ, 2002; Kalamazoo Inst Arts, Mich, 2002; Anderson Gallery, Drake Univ, Des Moines, 2002; Grossetti Arte, Milan, 2003; retospectives, Kunsthalle, Bielefeld, Ger, 82, Badischer Kunstverein, Karlsruhe, Ger, 83, Mus New Art, 2001, Kalamazoo Inst Art, Mich, 2002. *Pos:* Art writer & critic various art publications. *Teaching:* Asst prof art & art hist, Cooper Union, 69-75; vis prof art, Princeton Univ, 75; instr art, Sch Visual Arts, 78-; sr critic, Yale Univ grad sculpture prog, 90. *Awards:* Nat Endowment Arts Fel, 83. *Bibliog:* David Shapiro (auth), An interview with Lucio Pozzi, NY Art J, 11/79; J Van Der Marck (auth), Reconnecting (exib catalog), Detroit Art Inst, 87; Tiffany Bell (auth), Lucio Pozzi Peccolo, Haley, 91. *Mem:* Am Abstract Artists. *Media:* Acrylic, Oil; All Media. *Publ:* Auth, Five Stories, 75 & 78; 475 years, 80-; A User's Manual to Approch the Art of Lucio Pozzi, 2000. *Mailing Add:* 101 A Mercer St New York NY 10012

PRACKO, BERNARD F, II
PAINTER, SCULPTOR
b Ada, Okla, Jan 17, 45. *Study:* NMex Military Inst, AA, 65; Univ Colo, BA, 70; Ariz State Univ Sch Fine Art, 92. *Work:* Sun Cities Art Mus, Ariz; Ariz State Univ Sch Art, Tempe; Univ Colo Govs Collection, Boulder. *Comn:* Man in the Cosmos, SCI, Scottsdale, Ariz, 91; Jack Healy (untitled 92/20p), Amnesty Int, Washington, DC, 92. *Exhib:* For Amnesty Int, Sena Gallery Invitational, Santa Fe, NMex, 91; Sacred Spaces, Long Island, 91; Roaring Fork Ann, Aspen Art Mus, Colo, 92; Art Plates-A

Gala, Nelson Fine Art Mus, Tempe, Ariz, 92; Egyptian Echoes, Sun Cities Art Mus, Ariz, 93. *Bibliog:* Lynn Pyne (auth), Sounds move artist, Phoenix Gazette, 7/92; Ann Bonnano (dir), Pracko - His Art (film), Video Media Productions, 7/92. *Media:* Acrylic on Canvas; Metal, Stone. *Publ:* Contribr, Amnesty Int Calendar, 90. *Dealer:* FayBer Assoc 4333 Civic Ctr Plaza No 110 Scottsdale AZ 85251

PRACZUKOWSKI, EDWARD LEON
PAINTER, EDUCATOR
b Norwich, Conn, May 25, 30. *Study:* Norwich Art Sch, fine arts dipl, 50; Sch Mus Boston, cert with hons in painting, 56, Clarrisa Bartlett travel fel & grad cert, 59; Tufts Univ, BS(art educ), 58; Cranbrook Acad, MFA, 65. *Work:* Slater Mem Mus, Norwich, Conn, 81; City of Seattle, Wash. *Exhib:* Drawing USA, St Paul Art Ctr, Minn, 66 & 69; Nat Polymer Exhib, EMich Univ, 67 & 68; 11th Ann Nat Drawing Exhib, Oklahoma Art Ctr, 69; one-man shows, Greenwood Gallery, Seattle, Wash, 81 & 83, Foster White Gallery, 86 & Pima Community Col, Tucson, Ariz, 89; Living With the Volcano, The Artists of Mt St Helens, Mus Art, Wash State Univ, 83; Int Artist Exchange Exhib, Seattle Chap Artists Equity, 90, 92 & 93. *Teaching:* Assoc prof drawing & painting, Univ Wash, 65-. *Awards:* First Prize Painting, Int Arts Festival, Detroit, 65; MacDowell Colony Grants, 66 & 69; Wash Water Power Award, Spokane Ann, 81. *Mem:* Edward MacDowell Colony, NY; Allied Artists, Seattle, Wash; Artists Equity, Seattle Chap (pres, 91-92). *Media:* Oil, Acrylic

PRADO-ARAI, NAMIKO
VISUAL ARTIST
b Mexico City, Mex. *Study:* Escuela Nacional de Artes Plasticas, UNAM, Mex, Maestría, 92; Univ Paris VIII, Maîtrise, 96; Ecole des Hautes Etudes en Sciences Sociales, Paris, DEA, 98; Escuela Diseno INBA, Mex, Diplomado Compugafia, 00. *Work:* Bibliotheque Nationale de France-Estampes, Paris; Fondation Culturelle du Mexique, Paris; Aeroports de Paris; Colegio de España, Paris; Maison du Mexique-Cite Int Universitaire, Paris; Ambassade de France, Mex. *Comn:* mural Museo de Ciencias-Universum, UNAM, Mex City, 00-01. *Exhib:* Encuentro Nacional Arte Joven, Mus Carrillo Gil, Mexico City, 92; Arte Joven en San Carlos, Mus de la Ciudad de Mex, Mexico City, 92; Cinco en la Grafica, Mus Universitario del Chopo, Mexico City, 93; Salon D'Art Contemporian, Mairie de Montrouge, France, 96; Biennale de Jeune Peinture, Mus D'Art Contemporian, Nice, France, 96; Novembre a Vitry, Galerie Guy Moquet, France, 97; Prize Johny Walker, Museo de Arte Moderno, Mexico City, 98; Casa de Francia, Mex City, 2000 & 2001; Catalogo de Ilustradores, Centro Nacional de las Artes Mex City, 2000; Cuerpo en Movimiento, Mus Universum, 2003; Niche Gallery, Tokyo, Japan, 2003, 2006; Trajections, Espace Beaurepaire, Paris, 2002; Nippon Int Contemp Art Festival, Tokyo, 2003; Casa Lamm, Mexico, 2004; La Source, Villarceaux Chateau, 2005. *Awards:* Intern, Peggy Guggenheim Found, 92; Spadem Prize, Paris, 93. *Bibliog:* Aline Brandauer (auth), Travail Recent, Paris-Mexico, France, 93; Christine Frerot (auth), La Realite de L Abscence, Mex Embassy, France, 94; Elia Espinosa (auth), Lo Infinito Cotidiano, Revista UNAM, Mex, 96; Santiago Espinosa del los Monteros (auth), Energia, 2001. *Mem:* Soc des Auteurs Arts Graphiques & Plastiques; Asn Artistas Plasticos Mex; Asn Int d'Arts Plastiques, UNESCO, Fed Mexicana de Univ. *Media:* Oil pastel, paper, mixed media. *Specialty:* Painting, drawing, etching, illustration, jewelery creations. *Dealer:* Niche Gallery 3-12 Ginza 3 Chome Tokyo Japan; Cerro del Jabali 9 Pedregal de San Francisco CP 04320 Mexico. *Mailing Add:* 18 Rue du Plan de l'autre Bailly France 78870

PRAKAPAS, DOROTHY
DIRECTOR
b New York, NY, May 13, 28. *Study:* Hunter Col, New York, BA(art), 49; Fashion Inst Technol, BS(drafting & design), 51; Parson's Sch Design, with Hananiah Harari, 52; Sch Visual Arts, Advert Design, 54. *Pos:* Animator, Lee Blair Film Graphics, 52-54; stylist, Playtex, 55-62; fashion design, Mercantile, 62-76; dir, Prakapas Gallery, 76-93; retired. *Mem:* Art Dealer's Asn Am; Asn Int Photog Art Dealers. *Specialty:* Twentieth century modernism with special emphasis on photography. *Mailing Add:* One Northgate 6B Bronxville NY 10708

PRAKAPAS, EUGENE JOSEPH
ART DEALER, EDITOR
b Lowell, Mass, July 29, 32. *Study:* Yale Univ, BA, 53; Oxford Univ, Eng, with Balliol, MA, 59. *Pos:* Co-dir, Carus Gallery, 73-75; vis cur, San Francisco Mus Mod Art, 86; dir, Prakapas Gallery, New York, currently. *Mem:* Art Dealers Asn Am; Asn Int Photog Art Dealers. *Specialty:* Twentieth century modernism, with special emphasis on photography. *Publ:* Auth, Bauhaus Photography, Mass Inst Technol Press, 85. *Mailing Add:* c/o Prakapas Gallery One Northgate Apt 6B Bronxville NY 10708

PRALL, BARBARA JONES
PAINTER; INSTRUCTOR
b Cedar Rapids, Iowa, July 4, 32. *Study:* Kirkwood Community Col, AA, 1973; Upper Iowa Univ, BA in Art Educ (magna cum laude), 1975; Iowa Univ, 1978-85; studies with Burt Silverman, John Howard Sanden, Daniel Green & Bob Gerbracht among others. *Comn:* Lake Louise (mural), comn by Erwin Besler, Dyersville, Iowa; Last Supper (mural), Open Bible Ch, Des Moines; Dyersville, USA (mural), Dyersville Nat Bank; mural, Harvs Auto Body, Iowa City. *Exhib:* Kalispell Mt Boyd Tower West Lobby, Univ Iowa Hosp; Marion Hist Soc, Racine, Wis, Cannon Falls, Minn, Owatonna, Minn & Edina, Minn, others; Operation Wildlife Art Show, Kansas City, Kans. *Pos:* owner, artist, Barb's Art Barn, Delhi, Iowa, Pinicon Acres Fine Art's Farm,Central City, Iowa & Barb's Fine Art Gallery & Studio, Marion, Iowa. *Teaching:* art teacher, grades 1-8, Central City Commnity Schs, Iowa; art instr, Barb's Art Barn, Delhi, Iowa, Pinicon Acres Fine Arts Farm, Central City, Iowa & Barb's Fine Art Gallery & Studio, Marion, Iowa. *Awards:* Best of Show landscape, Operation Wildlife; Artist of Yr, Upper Iowa Univ; winner calendar choice, Farmer's State Bank. *Mem:* Am Soc Portrait Artists; NY Portrait Soc. *Media:* Oil, Acrylic, Watercolor, Pastel. *Mailing Add:* c/o Barb's Fine Art 788 6th St Marion IA 52302

PRAMUK, EDWARD RICHARD
PAINTER
b Akron, Ohio, Feb 14, 36. *Study:* Kent State Univ, BFA, MA; Queens Col, grad study; Akron Art Inst; also with John Ferren, James Brooks & Louis Finkelstein. *Work:* New Orleans Mus Art; Cornell Univ; Pan Am Life Corp; Banc Texas, Houston. *Comn:* Paintings, James Talcott Inc, NY, 74. *Exhib:* Pelham-Von Stoffler Gallery, Houston, Tex, 78; Edinboro State Univ, Edinboro, NY, 78; one-man shows, Contemp Art Ctr, New Orleans, 80, First St Gallery, NY, 83 & 85 & Entergy Ctr, New Orleans, 97; Landscape, Cityscape, Seascape, Contemp Art Ctr, New Orleans, 86; Louisiana Landscape, Downtown Gallery, New Orleans, 90; Sylvia Schmidt Gallery, New Orleans, 91, 93, 94, 96 & 98; and others. *Teaching:* Prof art, La State Univ, 64-. *Awards:* Award, La Prof Artists, Baton Rouge, 71; Purchase Award, 7th Nat Drawing & Sculpture Show, 73; Purchase Award, New Orleans Mus Art, 74. *Media:* Acrylic. *Publ:* Contribr, two colorplates, How to Make an Oil Painting, Watson-Guptill, 90; Nine colorplates, Georgia Rev, Winter 98. *Mailing Add:* La State Univ Dept Fine Arts Baton Rouge LA 70808

PRANGE, SALLY BOWEN
CERAMIST, SCULPTOR
b Valparaiso, Ind, Aug 11, 27. *Study:* Univ Mich, Ann Arbor, BA. *Work:* Victoria & Albert Mus, London, Eng; William Hayes Ackland Mem Art Ctr, Univ NC, Chapel Hill; NC Mus Art, Raleigh; Smithsonian Inst, Washington; Mus Art, Pa State Univ, University Park; Mus Int Ceramics, Faenza, Italy; J Patrick Lannan Found Cont Art, Palm Beach, Fla; Everson Mus Art, Syracuse, NY; Hickory Mus Art, Hickory, NC; NC State Univ, Raleigh; Southern Prog Corp, Birmingham, Ala, 90. *Comn:* Booke & Co, Winston-Salem, NC; Wachovia Bank, Winston-Salem, NC; Glaxo-Welcome, Res Triangle Park, NC; SAS Inst Res, Triangle Park, NC. *Exhib:* Am Ceramic & Sculpture Show, Butler Inst Am Art, Youngstown, Ohio, 67-68 & 71; Kyoto Crafts Ctr, Japan, 86; Tyndall Galleries, Durham, NC, 92 & 95; Durham Art Guild, NC, 93; Lee Hansley Gallery, Raleigh, NC, 92, 95 & 96; Greenville Art Mus, NC, 95; Green Hill Ctr NC Art, Greensboro, 97; Fayetteville Mus Art, NC, 97; Am Embassy, Tokyo, Japan; A Different Turn, NC Pottery Mus, Pinehurst, NC; Ceramics Viewpoint 98, Grossmont Col, El Cajon, Calif; Monarch Nat Competition, Kennedy, Douglas Ctr; Durham Art Coun, NC, 2000; Gallery C Raleigh, NC, 2000. *Pos:* Juror & vis lectr. *Teaching:* Instr ceramic pottery, Univ NC, Chapel Hill, 65-66; instr, Arrowmont, Gatlinburg, Tenn, 79 & 80, Penland Sch Crafts, NC, 81, NC State Univ Crafts Ctr, Raleigh, 82, Univ Calif, San Diego Craft Ctr, 82 & Greenwich House Pottery, New York, 83; guest lectr, Brit Craftsmen Potters Asn, London, 80, Int Mus Ceramics, Faenza, Italy, 80, Octagon Ctr, Ames, Iowa, 84, Kansas City Inst, Mo, 85 & Greenhill Ctr NC Arts, 85. *Bibliog:* Lloyd Herman (auth), American Porcelain: New Expressions in an Ancient Art, 80; Peter Lane (auth), Studio Potter, 81, Studio Ceramics, 85 & Studio Porcelain, 86; Katherine Pearson (auth), Am Crafts, 83. *Mem:* Tri-State Sculptors Guild; Am Crafts Coun; World Crafts Coun; Piedmont Crafts Guild, Winston-Salem; Nat Coun Educ Ceramic Art. *Media:* Clay. *Publ:* Ceramic Form: Shape & Decoration, 88; Hist of Am Ceramics, Elaine Levin, 89; The Best of Pottery, Rockport Publ, 89; The Craft & Art of Clay, Susan Peterson, 89. *Dealer:* ART Gallery New Bern NC; Gallery C Raleigh NC; Tyndall Galleries Durham Nc; Penland Gallery NC; WDO Gallery CharlotteNC. *Mailing Add:* 6421 Heartwood Dr Chapel Hill NC 27514

PRATT, ELIZABETH HAYES
PAINTER, INSTRUCTOR
b Dayton, Ohio, 27. *Study:* Dayton Art Inst, 45; Col William & Mary, BA (art), 49; Workshops with Eliot O'Hara Na, Charles Demotropolis & James Twitty, 56-60; Studied with Murray Wentworth & Joan Rothermel, 78-85. *Work:* Cape Mus Fine Arts, Dennis, Mass; Int Monetary Fund, Washington DC; US Cath Conf, Washington DC; Superior Ct DC; Citibank, NY; Cahoon Mus, Cotuit, Mass. *Comn:* King of Morocco (portrait), comn by king's cousin, 59; watercolor landscape, Nat Asn Manufacturers, Washington DC, 74; paintings, Inst Irish Studies Stonehill Col, North Easton, Mass, 82; illus, June Fletcher, What Should I Do?, Snow Libr, Orleans, Mass, 96; painting, Orleans CofC, Mass, 97; painting, Harvard Law Sch Libr, 83. *Exhib:* One-man show, Art Complex Mus, Duxbury, Mass, 79; Face of Am (nat portrait show), Art Ctr Galleries, Old Forge, NY, 94; Audubon Artists Ann Nat, 94, 95, 96, 97, 98, 99, 2000; Ga Watercolor Soc Nat, Chattahoochee Valley Art Mus, La Grange, Ga, 95; Rocky Mountain Nat, Foothills Art Ctr, Golden, Colo, 96; Masters of Watercolor, New Bedford Art Mus, 2006. *Pos:* bd dir, Washington Watercolor Soc, 71-77; dir, Spectrum Gallery, Georgetown, Va, 72-73. *Teaching:* instr watercolor, Creative Arts Ctr, 79-86, 98-2002, Castle Hill Ctr for Arts, 82-2001, Cape Mus Fine Arts, 90-92; lectr art, Cape Mus Fine Arts, 96. *Awards:* Rocky Mountain Nat Golden Artist Award, New Berlin, NY, 86; Dean L Rubin Award, Audubon Artists, 99. *Bibliog:* James Hanson (auth), Artists in Residence, Boston Mag, 86; Cindy Nickerson (auth), Watercolorist Loves Spontaneity, Cape Cod Times, 89; Carol K Dumas (auth), Going for the Gold, Cape Codder Arts Sect, 93. *Mem:* Audubon Artists (juried mem); Copley Soc (juried mem); New Eng Watercolor Soc (juried mem); Provincetown Art Asn; Creative Arts Ctr Chatham. *Media:* Watercolor. *Specialty:* Oils, watercolors, pastels, original works of fine art. *Publ:* auth, Experiments with Watercolor, Artists Mag, 89; contribr, C LeClair, The Art of Watercolor, Watson Guptall, 94, The Best of Watercolor, Vol I & 3, 95, 99, Best of Watercolors-Painting Composition, 97 & Watercolor Expressions, Rockport Publ, 2000. *Dealer:* Addison/Holmes Box 2756 43 Rt 28 Orleans MA 02642; The Capley Soc of Boston 158 Newbury St Boston 02116. *Mailing Add:* PO Box 238 - 180 Mill Rd Eastham MA 02642

PRAVDA, MURIEL
INSTRUCTOR, RESTORER
b Brooklyn, NY, 25. *Study:* Brooklyn Col Journalism, AA, 47; Traphagan Sch Fashion (cert), 47; S Fla Art Inst, (cert), 75-92, Bruno Luchese Seminars, 80-91, (cert); Atterbury Sch Sculpture, (cert). *Work:* N Miami Mus, Fla; Int Boat Show, Miami Beach; Hollywood Art Guild, Fla; Community Art Alliance, Hollywood, Fla. *Comn:* John Kennedy, pvt comn, Dallas, Tex, 89. *Exhib:* One-woman show, S Fla Art Inst, Miami, 87; Sculpture Show, Gallery Turnberry, NMiami Beach, 89; Faculty Show, Discovery Ctr, Ft Lauderdale, 89; Miniature Show, Del Bello Gallery, Toronto, Can, 90; Leonard Art Gallery, Ft Lauderdale, 90; and others. *Pos:* Restorer paintings, Lang Gallery, Jamaica Estates, NY, 70-80, asst sales, 70-80. *Teaching:* Instr clay sculpture, S Fla Art Inst, 80-, lectr sculpture workshop, 82-84. *Awards:* Second Place Sculpture, Fresh Meadows, Merchants, 78; First Place Sculpture, 81 & Merit Award Sculpture, 82, Miami Art League; Silver Poet, Writer's Lullaby, 90 & Gold Poet, Song of the World, 91, World of Poetry. *Bibliog:* M L Pesora (auth), Art show sizzles, Hollywood Sun, 91; Cindy Stauger (auth), News item, Sun Sentinal, 89; Florence Gould (auth), Inside Art (Hallandale) Sculpture, Hallandale Press, 87. *Mem:* Community Art Alliance; charter mem Nat Mus Women Arts; assoc mem Nat Sculpture Soc; Int Sculpture Soc. *Media:* Clay. *Publ:* Sculptures, Friends and Neighbors Column, 88, Hallandale Press; Poem, The Survivors, Miami Herald, 9/92. *Mailing Add:* 8308 NW 80th St Tamarac FL 33321-1628

PREBLE, MICHAEL ANDREW
ADMINISTRATOR, PHOTOGRAPHER
b July 27, 47; US citizen. *Study:* Cornell Univ, BA, 69; Calif State Univ, Mass, 77. *Exhib:* Photowork, 90, Univ Miami, 90; 40th Ann Juried Exhib, Boca Raton Mus Art, 91; Architectural Photo Competition, AIA Gallery, Miami, 91; 23rd Ann Prints, Drawing & Photos, Ark Arts Ctr, 95; 8th Ann ArtWave, Ohr Arts & Cult Ctr, Biloxi, 95. *Pos:* Chief cur, Bass Mus Art, Miami, 87-89; ed & vpres publ, Int Voyager Media, 89-94; assoc dir/educ, Ark Arts Ctr, 96- & dir, Mus Sch, currently. *Publ:* Ed & contribr, William Baziotes, Paintings & Works on Paper 1952-1961, Blum Helman Gallery, 88; auth, Colonial architecture in the Caribbean, IVM, 90; Artist's Colonies-Bob Edelson, Bacardi Gallery, 91; The reel tropics: Filmmaking in the Caribbean, IVM, 91; Vacation St Maarten/St Martin, St Maarten Tourism Asn, 96

PREEDE, NYDIA
PAINTER, ILLUSTRATOR
b Manhattan, NY, Nov 7, 26. *Study:* Art Students League, Fine & Applied Arts Diploma, 45; Pratt Inst, 45-46; Columbia Univ, 49; Sch Visual Arts, 57; Monmouth Col, BA, 62, MA, 73. *Work:* Yergeau Mus Int D'Art, Que; Coast Guard Art Prog 4 Works, Washington DC; Plucking Strings, Monmouth Co Libr System; Collage, Award sale, Fells Point Gallery; Oceanport, car repair inspection station, 3 works tech; Plane Firsta, pvt, seascapes. *Exhib:* Nat Asn Women Artists Traveling Exhib, 91-92; Small Works, Concordia Col, 92; Contemp Artists, Gelabert Studios, 93; Points of View, Agora Gallery, 93; Europa Bombal Palace, Lisbon, Port, 94; You, Me & Them, Women in the Arts, Cork Gallery, Lincoln Ctr Performing Arts, NY, 96; Earth-Water, Agora Gallery, 97; solo exhibs New Yorker Show, Barcelona, 90, Gallery 402, NY, 99; WIA Peekskill Flat Iron Gallery, 99; Ceres Hallelujah Invitational, 99; Coast Guard Art Program, Wash DC, 2000; and others. *Pos:* prof adv bd, Am Biographical Inst, 2003; bd dirs, Am Artists Prof League, 2004-. *Awards:* Charles Horman Mem Prize, 88; 1st Place, Alternate, Nat Forest Stamp Prog (tour USA), 91-92; Nat Arts Club Award, 96; and others. *Mem:* Nat Asn Women Artists (juror, 90-92); Women in Art; Nat Endowment Arts; NJ Educ Asn; Col Art Asn; Nat Arts Club Asn; Coast Guard Art Program; fel, Am Artists Prof Leauge; Am Asn Univ Women; Nat Soc Painters; Nat League Am Penwomen; NJ Watercolor Soc; Miniature Painters Sculptures & Gravers; Nat Collage Soc. *Media:* Acrylic, All Media. *Dealer:* Pen & Brush 116 E 10th St New York NY. *Mailing Add:* 249 B Eaton Crest Dr Eatontown NJ 07724

PREISS, ALEXANDRU PETRE
DESIGNER, ILLUSR
b Bucharest, Romania, Oct 4, 52. *Study:* N Grigorescu Fine Arts Inst, Bucharest, BA & dipl, 76 cert, 77; Purdue Univ, MA, 81. *Work:* Greater Lafayette Mus Art, Ind. *Comn:* Homage: The Soldier (environmental sculpture), Greater Lafayette Mus Art, Ind, 82. *Exhib:* Smithsonian Inst Traveling Exhib, 82; Summer Invitational Show, Pleiades Gallery, NY, 83; one-man show, Second Street Gallery, Charlottesville, Va, 84; 11th Biennial Graphic Design, Brno, Czech, 84; Great Ann Int Exhib, Ctr Int D'Art Contemporain, Paris, France, 86; and others. *Pos:* Owner, Kennedy & Preiss Design, Honolulu, HI, 86-. *Teaching:* Asst prof graphic design, Purdue Univ, W Lafayette, Ind, 81-86 & Univ Hawaii at Manoa, Honolulu, 86-88. *Awards:* Silver Medal, 11th Biennial Graphic Design, Brno, Czech, 84; Pele Award of Excellence in Illus, AAF Hawaii, 89; Award of Excellence, IABC, Hawaii, 89. *Bibliog:* Marion Garmel (auth), Purdue designer creates superb homage, Indianapolis News, 82. *Media:* Mixed, Photo-collage. *Interests:* Dog Agility. *Publ:* Contribr, American Illustration 2, Am Illus Inc, New York, 83; illusr, Heart to Heart: A Discussion of Sexual Assault, Honolulu, 91; No Way Out, Honolulu Mag, 9/93; The Stress of Paradise, Honolulu Mag, 4/94. *Mailing Add:* 2118 Kuhio Ave No 701 Honolulu HI 96815

PREKOP, MARTIN DENNIS
PAINTER, SCULPTOR
b Toledo, Ohio, July 2, 40. *Study:* Cleveland Inst Art; Cranbrook Acad Art, MFA; RI Sch Design, MFA; Slade Sch Art, London, Eng. *Work:* Univ Ill, Edwardsville. *Exhib:* Roof Works, Mus Contemp Art, 72; Art Inst Chicago, 74 & 75; one-man shows, Photographs, Yale Univ, 75, Name Gallery, Chicago, 75; Jan Cicero Gallery, Chicago, 79 & 84; LYC Gallery, Cumbria, Eng, 81. *Pos:* Dean, Art Inst Chicago, 88. *Teaching:* Prof & grad prog chmn painting, sculpture & photog, Art Inst Chicago, 66-, chmn Freshman Found, 70-73, chmn grad div, 73-77, chmn painting dept, 78- & chmn undergrad div, 82-93; dean, Col Fine Arts, Carnegie-Mellon Univ, Pittsburgh, 93-. *Awards:* Fulbright Fel, US State Dept, 65; Artists grant, Ill Arts Coun, 85; Fel, Nat Endowment Arts, 87. *Bibliog:* Jan Vendermark (auth), Roof Works Rev, Artforum, 72. *Media:* All. *Mailing Add:* Col Fine Arts Carnegie-Mellon Univ 5000 Forbes Ave Pittsburgh PA 15213

PRENT, MARK
ENVIRONMENTAL ARTIST, SCULPTOR
b Montreal, Que, Dec 23, 47. *Study:* Sir George Williams Univ, Montreal, 66-70, BFA, 70, study with John Ivor Smith. *Work:* Art Gallery of Ont, Toronto; Art Bank of Can; Mus Du Quebec; Mus D'Art Contemporain; Nat Gallery Can; Mus D'Art Joiette, Quebec; Reflex Modern Art Mus, Amsterdam, Holland; Mus Des Beaux Arts De Sherbrooke, Quebec. *Comn:* Le Festin Chez la Comtesse Fritouille, staged by Suzanne Lantagne, Espace Libre, Montreal, 87. *Exhib:* Eighth Biennale de Paris, Nat Mus Mod Art, France, 73; one-man shows, Akademie der Kunste (auth, catalog), Berlin, Ger, 75-76, Kunsthalle Nuremberg, Ger, 76, Stedelijk Mus (auth, catalog), Amsterdam, The Neth, 78, Mus d'Art Contemporain (auth, catalog), Montreal, 79 & Galerie Esperanza, Montreal, 86; Maison Cult Rennes, France, 80-81; one-man show, Power Plant (catalog), Toronto, Ont, 87, Chaffee Gallery, Rutland, Vt, Galerie Esperanza, Montreal, Que, 88, Isaacs Gallery, Toronto, 90, Galerie De La Tour, Basel, Switz, 93 & Centre Exhib Circa, Montreal, Que, 93, Espace D Rene Harrison, Montreal, 2000, Galerie Bernard, Montreal, 2001; performances, Le Festin Chez La Comtesse Fritouille, Espace Libre, Montreal, Can, 87; Tetsuro Fukuhara and BODHI SATTVA with Mark Prent and Sue Real, traveling show, 91; Winds from the future, Tokyo, Japan, 92; Pupae, Montreal, Can, 96. *Awards:* Guggenheim Mem Found Fel, 77; Can Coun Sr Arts Award, 78-81, 85-88, 91 & 96; Art Matters Inc, 87, 88 & 94; Can Coun Proj Cost Grant, Japan-Can Fund, 90, 92 & 93. *Bibliog:* Hartmut Kraft (auth), Antiasthetica 1978, Helmut Braun Kg, Koln, WGer, 78; Brian McNeil (dir film documentary), Mark Prent: Overmood, 80; Martial Ethier (dir film documentary), Prent's Universe, 97. *Mem:* Can Artists Representatives; Royal Can Acad; Int Sculpture Asn. *Media:* Polyester Resin, Fiberglass. *Mailing Add:* 35 Bank St Saint Albans VT 05478

PRENTICE, DAVID RAMAGE
PAINTER, PRINTMAKER
b Hartford, Conn, Dec 22, 43. *Study:* Hartford Art Sch. *Work:* Wadsworth Atheneum, Hartford; Yale Univ, New Haven, Conn; Mus Mod Art, NY; Corcoran Gallery Art, Nat Gallery, Washington, DC; Aldrich Mus, Ridgefield, Conn. *Exhib:* One-man shows, Livingstone-Learmonth Gallery, 75, NY & Genesis Gallery, NY, 78; Other Ideas, Detroit Inst Fine Arts, Mich, 69; Prospect, Dusseldorf, Ger, 69; Whitney Mus Am Art Ann, NY, 70; From Los Angeles & other places, Silverman Gallery, Los Angeles, 78. *Teaching:* Guest instr painting, Hartford Art Sch, Univ Hartford, fall 70. *Media:* Acrylic. *Mailing Add:* 654 Broadway New York NY 10012-2327

PRESCOTT, KENNETH WADE
MUSEUM DIRECTOR, ADMINISTRATOR
b Jackson, Mich, Aug 9, 20. *Study:* Western Mich Univ, BS; Univ Del, EdM; Univ Mich, MA & PhD. *Collection Arranged:* Ben Shahn Retrospective Exhib, Nat Mus Mod Art, Tokyo & other Japanese mus (with catalog), 70 & 91; Jack Levine Retrospective Exhib, Jewish Mus, New York, 79-80; Burgoyne Diller Exhibs, Meredith Long & Andre Emmerich & Harcourts Gallery, 79-92; Complete Grafic Work of Ben Shohn, KWP. *Pos:* Dir, Kansas City Mus, Mo, 54-58 & NJ State Mus, 63-71; managing dir, Acad Nat Sci, Philadelphia, 58-63; prog officer, Div Arts & Humanities, Ford Found, New York, 71-74. *Teaching:* Adj prof changing perspectives in the humanities, Grad Sch, Temple Univ, 60-70; prof art & chmn art dept, Univ Tex, Austin, 74-84, emer prof, currently. *Mem:* Tex Asn Schs Art; Am Color Print Soc (hon vpres, 68-71); Col Art Asn Am; Nat Coun Art Adminr (chmn, 79-80); Am Fedn Arts. *Res:* Preparation for exhibitions and Catalogue Raisonne on contemp American artists (Shahn, Levine, Diller, Browne, Hunt, de Creeft, Lorrie Goulet, James Chapen, Hunt Slonem & others). *Collection:* Works of contemporary American artists. *Publ:* Auth, Ben Shahn: A Retrospective (catalog), 76-77; Jack Levine: A Retrospective (catalog), 78; Burgoyne Diller 1938-1962, Paintings, Drawings and Collages (catalog), 79; The Prints and Poster of Ben Shahn, 82; The Prints and Posters of Jack Levine, 83. *Mailing Add:* 1 Towers Park Lane Suite 2302 San Antonio TX 78209

PRESSER, ELENA
ASSEMBLAGE ARTIST
b Buenos Aires, Nov 3, 40; US citizen. *Study:* Dade Community, AA, 75. *Work:* Fla Capitol, Dept Nat Resources & Art Pub Places, Fla; Ala Power Co, Birmingham, Ala; IBM, Gaithersburg, Md. *Comn:* Anna Magdalena Bach Notebook, Ruth & Marvin Sackner Arch, Miami Beach, Fla, 85; Italian Concerto-J S Bach, comn by Dr & Mrs Roley Kohen, Miami Beach, Fla, 87. *Exhib:* Solo exhibs, Elena Presser: Bach's Goldberg Variations, Frances Wolfson Art Gallery, Miami, Fla, 85, Meadows Mus & Gallery, Dallas, Tex, 87, Mus Contemp Hispanic Art, NY, 87 & Elena Presser: Transpositions, Moore Col Art, Philadelphia, Pa, 88; group shows, Calligraffitti, Leila Taghinia Micani Gallery, NY, 84, Collage: The State of the Art, Bergen Mus, Paramus, NJ, 85, Southern Abstraction, City Gallery Contemp Art, Raleigh, NC, 87 & Expresiones Hispanas, Ctr Fine Arts, Miami, Fla, 89. *Awards:* Purchase Award, House of Repr, 79; Purchase Award, Fla Dept State, 81; Artist-in-Residence Fel, D Jerassi Gounf, 85. *Bibliog:* John & Joan Digby (auth), The Collage Handbook, Thames & Hudson Inc, 85; Marvin Sackner (auth), Ruth & Marvin Sackner Arch Concrete & Visual Poetry, Ruth & Marvin Sackner, 86. *Mem:* Women's Caucus For Art, Miami Chap, (bd dir 83-85); Lowe Art Mus, 78-88; Ctr Fine Arts, 88; Bass Mus, 84-88; Soc Layerists Multi-Media, 87-88. *Media:* Wall Relief Assemblage. *Mailing Add:* 7020 SW 100th St Miami FL 33156

PRESSLY, NANCY LEE
CURATOR, ADMINISTRATOR
b Suffern, NY, Feb 11, 41. *Study:* Goucher Col, BA, 62; Columbia Univ, with T Reff, L Hawes & O Brendel, MA, 69; Inst Fine Arts, with W Rubin, R Rosenblum & G Schiff, 69-71. *Collection Arranged:* The Pursuit of Happiness: A View of Life in Georgian England (auth, catalog), 77 & The Fuseli: Circle in Rome: Early Romantic Art of 1770s (auth, catalog), 79, Yale Ctr Brit Art; A Birthday Celebration: Recent Gifts and Acquisitions, 1981 (auth, catalog), 82, Salome: La belle dame sans merci (auth, catalog), 83 & Revealed Religion: Benjamin West's Commissions for Windsor Castle and Fonthill Abbey (auth, catalog), 83, San Antonio Mus Art. *Pos:* Cataloger Am art, Metrop Mus Art, New York, 69-71; assoc res & asst cur, Yale Ctr Brit Art, 71-79; chief cur, San Antonio Mus Art, 81-84; asst dir, Mus Prog, Nat Endowment Arts, Washington, DC, 84-92; pres, Nancy L Pressly & Assocs, 92-. *Awards:* Paul Mellon Vis Sr Fel, CASVA, Nat Gallery Art, fall 92. *Bibliog:* Hilton Kramer (auth), Henry Fuseli: A leader in Romanticism, Sunday New York Times, 9/16/79; John Ashbery (auth), Dark satanic mills, New York Mag, 10/6/79; Gert Schiff (auth), article, Arts Mag, 12/79. *Mem:* Col Art Asn; Am Asn Mus; Soc 18th Century Studies. *Publ:* Auth, Whistler in America: An album of early drawings, Metrop Mus J, 72; James Jefferys and the master of the giants, Burlington Mag, 4/77; Guy Head and his echo flying from Narcissus: A British artist in Rome in the 1790s, Bull Detroit Inst Arts, 82; Museum Design: Planning & Building for Art (intro & proj dir), Oxford Univ Press, 93. *Mailing Add:* 6135 31st St NW Washington DC 20015-1515

PRESSLY, WILLIAM LAURENS
HISTORIAN, EDUCATOR
b Chattanooga, Tenn, Apr 1, 44. *Study:* Princeton Univ, BA, 66; Inst Fine Arts, New York Univ, PhD, 73. *Teaching:* Asst & assoc prof 18th-19th century European art, Yale Univ, 73-82; sr lectr, Univ Tex, Austin, 82-83; assoc prof, Duke Univ, 85-87; assoc prof, Univ Md, 87-93, prof, 93-. *Awards:* Morse Fel, Yale Univ, 75-76; Guggenheim Mem Fel, 83-84; Inst Advan Study, Princeton, 94-95. *Mem:* Fel Royal Soc Arts, London; The Am Soc for Eighteenth Century Studies; Col Art Asn; Walpole Soc, London; Phi Beta Kappa Soc. *Publ:* Auth, The praying mantis in surrealist art, Art Bull, 12/73; The Life and Art of James Barry, Yale Univ Press, 81; James Barry: The Artist as Hero, Tate Gallery, London, 83; A Catalogue of Paintings in the Folger Shakespeare Libr, Yale Univ Press, 93; The French Revolution as Blasphemy: Johan Zoffany's Paintings of the Massacre at Paris, August 10, 1792, Univ Calif Press, 99. *Mailing Add:* 6135 31st St NW Washington DC 20015

PRESTON, ANN L
SCULPTOR
b Seattle, Wash, 42. *Study:* Swarthmore Col, Pa, 59-61; Sch Mus Fine Arts, Boston, 62-66; Tufts Univ, Boston, BFA, 68; Calif Inst Arts, Valencia, MFA, 80. *Work:* Chase Manhattan Bank, NA, NY; Carnation Corp, Los Angeles; Phoenix Art Mus, Ariz; Anaheim Marina, San Francisco, Calif. *Comn:* Los Angeles Cent Publ Libr; Los Angeles Transportation Comn, Willow Sta; San Francisco Courthouse, Family Court; San Francisco Int Airport. *Exhib:* Solo exhibs, Atlantic Richfield Co, Ctr Visual Arts, Los Angeles, Calif, 81, Pence Gallery, Santa Monica, Calif, 86-91, Barbara Toll Fine Arts, NY, 87, 88, 91 & 94, Los Angeles Contemp Exhibs, 88, Guggenheim Gallery, Chapman Univ, Orange, Calif, 92 & Rosamund Felsen Gallery, Los Angeles & Santa Monica, Calif, 93, 95; Selections from the Carnation Co Collection, Armory Ctr Arts, Pasadena, Calif, 90; In Her Image, Barbara Toll Fine Arts, NY, 90; The Lick of the Eye, Shoshana Wayne Gallery, Santa Monica, Calif, 91; From Studio to Station: Pub Art on the Metro Blueline, FHP Hippodrome Gallery, Long Beach, Calif, 92; Recent Work, Rosamund Felsen Gallery, Los Angeles, Calif, 93; The Figure as Fiction: The Figure in Visual Art and Lit, Contemp Arts Ctr, Cincinnati, 93; Gallery Artists, Barbara Toll Fine Arts, NY, 93; DAMNED, Life, Death & Surface, John Thomas Gallery, Santa Monica, 94; Hooked on a Feeling, Kohn Turner Gallery, Los Angeles, 94; Wax, Nohra Haime Gallery, NY, 95; The Anamorph, Anaheim, Calif, 95; From LA With Love, Galerie Praz-Delavallade, Paris, 95; Chimera, Angels Gate Cult Ctr, San Pedro, Calif, 97; Plastered, Shoshana Wayne Gallery, Santa Monica, Calif, 97. *Awards:* Nat Endowment Arts Fel, 88. *Bibliog:* Benjamin Weissman (auth), rev, Artforum, 10/93; Michael Duncan (auth), LA rising, Art Am, 12/94; Peter Frank (auth), Art pick of the week, LA Weekly, 6/15/95; numerous newspapers, mags, art publs. *Dealer:* Rosamund Felsen Gallery Bergamot Sta B-4 2525 Michigan Ave Santa Monica CA 90404. *Mailing Add:* 24618 Golf View Dr Valencia CA 91355

PRESTON, GEORGE NELSON
HISTORIAN, EDUCATOR
b Dec 14, 38; US citizen. *Study:* City Col New York, BA, 62; Columbia Univ, MA, 68, PhD, 73. *Collection Arranged:* African Art: Rare and Familiar Forms (auth, catalog), State Univ New York Art Gallery, Potsdam, 76; The Innovative African Artist (auth, catalog), Ithaca Col Mus Art; Permanent Installation, African Hall, Brooklyn Mus, 68-78; Ancient Terracottas of Ghana and Mali (with catalog), 81-82. *Pos:* Spec consult, Brooklyn Mus, 68. *Teaching:* Asst prof art, Rutgers Univ, Livingston Col, 70-72; asst prof art, City Col, City Univ New York, 72-80, assoc prof, 81-, prof art hist, 95-. *Awards:* Fels, Ford Found, 68-70 & 72 & Kress Found, 69; Res Award, Res Found City Univ New York, 81-82. *Mem:* Columbia Univ Seminar Primitive & Pre-Columbian Art; Washington Hq Asn, NY (bd dir, 79-); Int Asn Art Critics. *Res:* Conceptual and culture historical aspects of African art; contemporary American artists whose styles are outside the definition of the most popular isms. *Publ:* Auth, Dynamic/Static, African Art as Philosophy, Interbook, New York, 74; Jay Milder: Painter of discovery, resolution and rediscovery, 11/76 & Against the grain: The paintings of Ann Tabachnik, 2/79, Arts Mag; Reading the Art of Benin, Images of Power: Royal Court Art of Benin, New York Univ, 81. *Mailing Add:* c/o Art Dept City Col City Univ NY Convent Ave & 138th New York NY 10031

PRESTON, MALCOLM H
CRITIC, PAINTER
b West New York, NJ, May 25, 20. *Study:* Univ Wis, BA; Columbia Univ, MA & PhD. *Work:* Hofstra Univ Collection; Portland Mus; Queens Mus, NY; Islip Art Mus; Cape Cod Mus Fine Arts; and others. *Exhib:* Mourlot Galerie; ACA Gallery; Eggleston Gallery; SAC Gallery; AAA Gallery; and others. *Pos:* Dir, Inst Arts, Hofstra Univ, 60-64; art critic, Newsday, 68-85 & Boston Herald Traveler, 70-72. *Teaching:* Asst instr fine arts, New Sch Social Res, 40-41; instr, Adelphi Univ, 47-48; prof, Hofstra Univ, 49-74. *Awards:* Joe & Emily Lowe Found Educ Res Grant, 50; Ford Found Grant, 56 & 57; Shell Oil Res Grant, 64. *Mem:* Nat Soc Lit & Arts; CAA. *Media:* Oil, Serigraphs. *Res:* Florality of Am Art; use of computer data to identify artists style. *Publ:* Contribr, Christian Sci Monitor, Arts Mag, Boston Globe & other mag & newspapers; writer, producer & principal performer, Arts Around Us & American Art Today (Ford Found-sponsored nat educ television series), 55-56. *Dealer:* Heller Gallery Provincetown, MA. *Mailing Add:* Box 182 Truro MA 02666

PREUSS, ROGER
PAINTER, WRITER
b Waterville, Minn, Jan 29, 22. *Study:* Minneapolis Col Art & Design, BFA. *Work:* Nat Wildlife Gallery, Smithsonian Hall Philately, Washington, DC; Minn Mus Am Art; Blauvelt Art Mus, Oradell, NJ; Weisman Art Mus, Univ Art Mus, Univ Minn, Minneapolis; CM Russell Mus, Great Falls, Mont; and others; Voyageyrs Nat Park Interpretive Ctr, International Falls, Minn; Roger Preuss Wildlife Art Coll, Ctr for Western Studies, Sioux Falls, SD; Luxton Mus, Banff, Alberta; plus others. *Comn:* 150 paintings of wildlife, Thos D Murphy Co, Red Oak, Iowa, 54; Commemorative Centennial Pheasant Stamp Design, 81; Gold Waterfowl Medallion, Franklin Mint, 83; Gold Wildlife Medallion, Wildlife Mint, 88; 40th Commemorative Fed Duck Etching, 89. *Exhib:* Solo exhibs, Kerr's Gallery, Beverly Hills, Calif, 47, Albert Lea Art Ctr, Minn, 63, Gallery Western Art, Helena, Mont, 64, Merrill's Gallery Fine Art, Taos, NMex, 80, Faribault Art Ctr, Minn, 81, travelling exhib, Weyerhaeuser Mus, Little Falls, Minn, 95; Joslyn Art Mus, 48; retrospective, LeSueur Co Hist Mus, Elysian, Minn, 76; Blauvelt Art Mus, Oradell, NJ, 90; Rochester Art Ctr, 91; Metaphorical Fish (traveling show), 92; Minn Hist Soc Hill House, 92; Bemidji Art Ctr, 93; Waseca Art Ctr, Minn, 96; Elysian State Bank, Minn, 96; LeSueur Co Court House, Minn, 97; Stark Mus, Orange, Tex, 75; plus others. *Pos:* Vpres & chmn emer Fine-Arts Bd, Wildlife Artists of the World; critic, Wildlife Art News. *Teaching:* Sem lectr wildlife painting, Minneapolis Col Art; speaker's bur, Minneapolis Inst Arts. *Awards:* Nat Endowment Humanitites Grant, 95; Partners for Wildlife Award US Interior Dept, 93; Achievement Award Visual Arts, N Oaks Club, 93; Fed Roger Preuss Waterfowl Prodn Area (first one named for an artist) US Fish & Wildlife Svc, LeSueur Co, Minn, 97; Pub Serv Award Dept Interior, 96; plus others. *Bibliog:* Judy Cathey (auth), LeCenter dedicates Preuss art, New Prague Times, 6/18/96; Roger Preuss receives nation's highest civilian award, Wildlife Art Mag, 97; Preuss honored by Interior's Prestigious Public Service Award, Minn Waterfowler Mag & Duck's Unlimited Leader, 97. *Mem:* Emer Soc Animal Artists; Fel Int Inst Arts; Minn Artists Asn (dir & vpres, 53-56); found charter mem Wildlife Artists World; Nat Wildlife Fedn; emer mem Am Artis Prof League. *Media:* Oil, Watercolor. *Publ:* Auth & illusr, The official wildlife of America calendar, 53-; American game birds, 64; illusr, Twilight over the wilderness, 71; contribr & illusr, Nat Wildlife, Country Gentleman, Contemp Western Artists, Wildlife Art News, Art West, Art Impressions (Can), Today's Art & many other nat periodicals & ltd ed prints by Wildlife Am; auth, Is wildlife art recognized fine art?, 86; Wildlife Art Can be Fine Art too, 88; plus others. *Dealer:* Wildlife of Am Box 580004-WA Minneapolis MN 55458. *Mailing Add:* c/o Wildlife of Am Box 580004-WA Minneapolis MN 55458

PREWITT, MERLE R(AINEY)
PAINTER
b Fayetteville, NC, Mar 15, 28. *Study:* Duke Univ, 50; Fayetteville Tech Community Col with Tom Moore, Lyn Padrick, Petra Gerber & Kerstin Weldon. *Work:* Fayetteville Diagnostic Ctr, Cape Fear Studios & Jr League Fayetteville, NC; Cooperative Savings & Loan, Wilmington, NC; MacPherson Presbyterian Church, Fayetteville, NC; First Presby Church, Fayetteville, NC; New S Bank; pvt collections. *Comn:* 3 dogs - Singleton, Crab-Arts & Crab Dog. *Exhib:* Pembroke Art Mus, Pembroke Univ, NC, 93; solo show, Cape Fear Studios, Fayetteville, NC, 93 & 95; Miniature Painters, Sculptures & Graphics Soc Washington DC, Art Club Washington, 94; Colored Pencil Soc Am, Oswego, Wash, 94; Moore Co Competition, Campbell House, Southern Pines, NC, 94; 1998 Winter Olympics, Nagano Japan, 98; Marilyn Wilson Gallery; Seaside, Nags Head, NC, 93; El Dorado Gallery, Colorado Springs; and others; Moore Co Competition, 97, 02; Olympics Show, Nagano Japan, 1997-2005. *Pos:* Bd dir, Fayetteville Art Guild, 88-93; Cape Fear Studios, 91-. *Awards:* Cooperative Savings & Loan Purchase Award, Artquest of Wilmington, 91; Emerging Artist Grant, NC/Cumberland Co/Fayetteville Art Coun, 93; Best local artist, Fayetteville, Nebr, 2004; Campbell House, NYC, 2004; Artist of Year, Fayetteville Cumberland Cty Art Council, 2006. *Mem:* Fayetteville Art Guild; Miniature Painters, Sculptors & Grafters of Washington, DC; Moore Co Art Coun; Fayetteville/Cumberland Co Art Coun; Fayetteville Art League; Colored Pencil Soc Am; NC Watercolor; Miniature Art Soc Fla; Fayetteville Mus Art Colored Pencil Soc Am; Am Watercolor Soc. *Media:* Watercolor, Colored Pencil, Pen, Pastel, Oil & Paste. *Specialty:* Floral, still life, animals, birds; minatures. *Collection:* Co-op Savings Loan, Wilmington, NC; first Pres. *Dealer:* Cape Fear Studios 148-1 Maxwell St Fayetteville NC 28305-5205. *Mailing Add:* 416 Devane St Fayetteville NC 28305-5205

PREY, BARBARA ERNST
PAINTER
b Manhasset, NY, Apr 17, 57. *Study:* Williams Col, Williamstown, Mass, BA(honors in art), 79; Univ Wurzberg, Ger, (Fulbright scholar, 80; Harvard Univ, MDiv, 86. *Work:* Williams Col Mus Art, Williamstown, Mass; GE Capital Gallery, Stamford, Conn; Henry Luce Found, NY; Farnsworth Art Mus, Rockland, Maine; pvt collection

of Pres & Mrs George Bush; and others; Pres and Mrs George Bush, The White House; Office of the First Lady of NY. *Comn:* Paintings, Prince Castell, Ger, 80; President's House, Williams Col, Williamstown, Mass, 86; Site of New Art Complex, Shadyside Acad, Pittsburgh, Pa, 93; US Embassy, Paris, France; Bloomberg Bus News Holiday Card, 95 & 97; NASA Art Collection; The White House Christmas Card, 03; NASA: The Internat Space Station; Commission X-43, Shuttle relaunch, 2005; US Arts in Embassies Program, Oslo, 03. *Exhib:* Brooklyn Mus, NY, 75; Farnsworth Mus Art Benefit Auction Exhib, Rockland, Maine, 94; Westmoreland Mus Art; Recent Acquistions, Farnsworth Art Mus, 97; Guild Hall Mus, East Hampton, NY, 97; Express Yourself, Portland Mus Art, Maine, 97; Young Collectors Choice, Hecksher Mus, Huntington, NY, 99; Art in Miniature, Gilcrease Mus, 2000; Lightscapes, Jensen Fine Arts Mus, 2001; and others. *Collection Arranged:* Pres and Mrs. George Bush; The White House; The farnsworth Art Mus; Williams College. *Pos:* Mod Painting Dept, Sotheby's Auction House, NY, 81-82; illusr, The New Yorker, 81-; Gourmet Mag, 82-; travel sect, New York Times, 87-88; poetry columnist, Good Housekeeping, 87-92. *Teaching:* Vis lectr western christian art, Taiwan Col & Sem, 86-87; Artist in Residence, Westminister Sch, Simsbury, Conn, 97. *Awards:* Henry Luce Found Grant, 86; Jean Thoburn Award, Pittsburgh Watercolor Soc, 94; Best Show, Westmoreland Mus Art, 96; NY Senate Women of Distinction Award, 2004. *Bibliog:* Art Market, Int Art Newspaper, 1/99; Critic's Choice, NY Daily News, 1/99; Inspirations, Maine PBS, 2001; many others. *Mem:* Nat Mus Women in Arts. *Media:* Watercolor. *Publ:* Profiles, The Observer-Reporter, 1/93; illusr, Williams Col Bicentennial Calendar, 92-93; Watercolor Wins Award, Pittsburgh Watercolor Soc, 94; cover, Am Artist Mag Watercolor, 94 & Dan's Papers, The Hamptons, 99, 2000; Barbara Ernst Prey: The Trace in the Mind-An artists Response to 9/11, 02; Works on Water, 2005. *Dealer:* Jensen Fine Arts. *Mailing Add:* 22 Pearl St Oyster Bay NY 11771

PREZIOSI, DONALD A
HISTORIAN, CRITIC
b New York, NY, Jan 12, 41. *Study:* Fairfield Col, BA, 62; Harvard Univ, MA, 63, PhD, 68. *Teaching:* Asst prof art hist, Yale Univ, 67-73 & Mass Inst Technol, 73-77; assoc prof, State Univ NY, Binghamton, 78-86; prof, Univ Calif Los Angeles, 86-. *Awards:* Fels, Nat Endowment Humanities, 73-74, Ctr Advan Study Visual Arts, Nat Gallery, 81-82 & Ctr Advan Study, Stanford Univ, 83-84; Am Coun Learned Soc, 89-90. *Mem:* Col Art Asn Am; Archaeol Inst Am; Semiotic Soc Am (vpres, 83-84, pres, 84-85). *Res:* Ancient art and architecture; contemporary theory and criticism. *Publ:* Auth, The Semiotics of the Built Environment, Ind Univ Press, 79; Architecture, Language and Meaning, 79 & Minoan Architectural Design, 83, Mouton; Constructing the origins of art, Art J, 83; Rethinking Art Hist, Yale Univ Press, 89

PRICE, ANNE KIRKENDALL
CRITIC
b Birch Tree, Mo, June 14, 22. *Study:* Univ Mo, Columbia, BJ; Univ Ga, Athens, art seminars; Southern Regional Educ Bd workshop for art critics. *Pos:* Art critic, Morning Advocate, Baton Rouge, La, 60-. *Awards:* Humanities Coun Award for Serv to the Arts, Greater Baton Rouge Arts, 86; Award, Women Achievement, Arts & Humanities, 94; Governor's Award for Lifetime Achievement in the Arts, 98. *Mem:* Capitol Corresp (pres, 68); Baton Rouge Arts Coun; Baton Rouge Little Theater (bd mem). *Mailing Add:* c/o Morning Advocate 525 Lafayette Baton Rouge LA 70802

PRICE, ARTHUR D
DESIGNER, PHOTOGRAPHER
b Edmonton, Alta. *Work:* Can Mus Civilization, Ottawa, Ont; Nat Gallery Can, Ottawa, Ont; Windsor Art Gallery, Ont; Ottawa Gallery, Ont. *Exhib:* Art Price Show, Montreal Mus Fine Arts. *Awards:* New York Award Metal Sculpture, Am Design Coun. *Media:* Sculpture & photography, design. *Publ:* Auth, A Cross Section of Work, Le Droit; Happiness Is Where You Find It, Le Droit

PRICE, BARBARA GILLETTE
ADMINISTRATOR, PAINTER
b Philadelphia, Pa, June 26, 38. *Study:* Univ Ala, BFA, 66, MA, 68. *Work:* Univ Ala, Tuscaloosa; Dept Health, Educ & Welfare N Portal Bldg, Washington, DC; Ferris State Col, Mich. *Exhib:* One-woman shows, Foundry Gallery, Washington, DC, 76, Spiritscapes, Cranbrook Acad Art Mus, Bloomfield Hills, Mich, 80, Landscapes of the Mind, Ferris State, Big Rapids, Mich, 81, Md Inst, Col of Art, Baltimore, 82, Schweyer Galdo Galleries, Birmingham, Mich, 82, Notre Dame Col, Baltimore, 85, Columbia Asn Ctr for Arts, Md, 89; Faculty Show, Md Inst Col of Art, 83 & 85-92; Artscape, Baltimore, 86; Art in the Bell Tower, Baltimore, 88; Intimate Works, Morris Mechanic Theatre Gallery, 89; one-person show, Le Ninfee, Loyola Col, Baltimore, Md, 91; group exhib, Members Only Premiere, Artshowcase, Baltimore, Md, 90, Reverberations: 4 Voices, Barbara Price, Nancy K Roeder, Jann Rosen-Queralt and Jo Smail, Roper Gallery, Frostburg State Univ, 91, Media-Mix, Artshowcase, Baltimore, Md, 91; Finding Beauty in the Ordinary, John Dorsey, Baltimore Sun, 91. *Pos:* Dean, Cranbrook Acad Art, 78-82; vpres, Acad Affairs, Maryland Inst, Col Art, 82-93; pres, Moore Col Art & Design, 94-. *Teaching:* Asst prof art, Corcoran Sch Art, DC, 70-78, dir summer prog, 75-78. *Bibliog:* Marsha Miro (auth), Celebration of legacy, Detroit Free Press, 2/21/82; Jeanne Heifeitz (auth), Price landscapes explore territory of Psyche, Jewish Times, 83; Mike Guliano (auth), Barbara Price at the Columbia Art Center, Columbia Flyer, 89. *Mem:* Nat Coun Art Adminr; Col Art Asn; NASAD; Am Asn of Higher Educ. *Media:* Oil, Acrylics. *Publ:* Ed, Sculpture at Cranbrook (catalog), Cranbrook Acad Art Mus, 79; Spiritscapes (catalog), Ferris State Col, 81. *Mailing Add:* 11141 69th Terr Miami FL 33173-2103

PRICE, BURDON See Price, Helen Burdon

PRICE, DIANE MILLER
ASSEMBLAGE ARTIST, COLLAGE ARTIST
b Paterson, NJ, Sept 13, 43. *Study:* RI Sch Design, 61-63; Parsons Sch Design, New York, 63-64; Monclair State Univ, NJ, papermaking as art form with Anne Chapman, BA, 84. *Work:* Reader's Digest, Pleasantville, NY; Educ Testing Serv, Princeton, NJ; Blue Cross/Blue Shield, Wilmington, Del; Crane Mus Papermaking, Dalton, Mass. *Exhib:* NJ State Mus, Trenton, 86; Paper: By Hand, Lib Gallery, Printmaking Coun NJ, North Branch, 94; Paper Works & Habitats, Pierro Gallery, South Orange, NJ, 95; NJ Arts Ann, Noyes Mus, Oceanville, 98; solo show, Interchurch Ctr Galleries, New York City, 2000; In the Spotlight, Nat Asn Women Artists. Gallery, New York City, 2004. *Awards:* Fel Grant, NJ State Coun, 86-87; Eve Helman Award, 102nd Ann Mems Show, Nat Asn Women Artists, 90; Medal of honor & Elizabeth S Blake Meml Award; Best Mixed Media Award, Gaelen Gallery, Whippany, NJ, 2004. *Mem:* Nat Asn Women Artists (asst awards chair, 86-98); Printmaking Coun NJ; Visual Arts Ctr NJ. *Media:* Handmade Paper; Assemblage, Collage. *Publ:* The Art of the Miniature, Jane Freeman, Watson-Guptill Pubs, 02. *Dealer:* Rabbet Gallery 120 Georges Rd New Brunswick NJ 08901. *Mailing Add:* 61 Winged Foot Dr Livingston NJ 07039-8228

PRICE, HELEN BURDON
PAINTER, PRINTMAKER
b St Louis, Mo, Sept 23, 26. *Study:* La State Univ, Baton Rouge, BS, 46; Johns Hopkins Univ, Baltimore, Md, BS & RN, 49; studied with Gerry Samuels, Budd Hopkins, DeLaMonica, John Heliker, Ken Nishi. *Work:* Dames & Moore, Blue Hill Ctr, NJ; Women's Ctr, Hackensack, NJ; Morgan Lewis & Bockius, New York City; Berlex Lab Inc, Montville, NJ; and others. *Exhib:* Thirty-two solo exhibs in NY & NJ; many 2 to 4 person & group exhibs; several traveling painting & printmaking exhibs in US, India & Italy. *Pos:* Dir & cur, Vineyard Theatre Gallery & Gallery 108, NY, 77-87; critquer, Teen Festival, NJ, 95-2001. *Awards:* Found Award, Nat Asn Women Artists Ann Exhib, Zuita & Joseph Akston, 87; Exhib Award, Ringwood Manor Exhib, W Wing Gallery, 88; Blake Mem Award, Nat Asn Women Artists Ann Exhib, Elizabeth Stanton Blake, 91; NAWA Medal of Honor, 95, Doris Kreindler Meml Award, 98, Gladys B Blum Meml Award, 99. *Mem:* Nat Asn Women Artists Inc (vpres, 89-92, pres, 93-)95; Salute to Women in Arts; Painting Affil Art Ctr Northern NJ; Artists Equity NY. *Media:* Acrylic, Collage. *Publ:* Contribr (auth P Knapp), Strictly business, Artist's Mag, 1/93. *Dealer:* Broadfoot and Broadfoot Boonton, NJ. *Mailing Add:* 151 Tweed Blvd Grandview NY 10960

PRICE, JOAN WEBSTER
ENVIRONMENTAL ARTIST, SCULPTOR
b Camden, NJ, Jan 8, 31. *Study:* Tyler Sch Art, Temple Univ, BFA, 54; Columbia Univ, MA, 58, EdD, 71. *Work:* Brooklyn Mus; Bronx Mus Arts; Mus Mod Art; Brit Mus, London; NJ State Mus; Solomon R Guggenheim Mus, NY. *Exhib:* Quietude Garden Gallery, 94-98; Noyes Mus Art, NJ, 94; The Art of Science the Science of Art, 60th Anniversary Exhib Am Abstract Artists, Westbeth Gallery, NY, 96; Pioneers of Abstract Art, Am Abstract Artists, 1936-1996 (with catalog), Stanley Mishkin Gallery, Baruch Col, 96; The Glove Project, Visual Art Center, Summit, NJ, 96; Post Modern Techno Art ASCI, eight floor/project space, NY, 96; Am Abstract Artists 60th Anniversary (with catalog), James Howe Fine Arts Gallery, Kean Col, 96; Rauma Art Mus (with catalog), 97. *Collection Arranged:* University Artists-Teachers (auth, catalog), Bronx Mus Art, 76; Women Artists 78, City Univ New York Grad Ctr, 78; Works on Paper Am Abstract Artists, Betty Parsons Gallery, 79; Ageless Perceptions I & II: Forms of Figuration I, Forms of Abstraction II, SoHo 20, New York, 88 & 89. *Pos:* Vpres & bd gov, Inst Study Art in Educ, 76-78; co-vpres, Higher Educ, NYCATA, 83-84. *Teaching:* Asst prof painting & design, Suffolk Community Col, NY, 65-67; lectr art educ, Queens Col, NY, 67-68; prof environ art, newform-intermedia, City Col NY, 68-94, grad dir, 94, prof emer. *Awards:* Fel, Va Ctr Creative Arts, 84; Art Educator Award, Art Works, 85. *Bibliog:* William Zimmer (auth), American Abstract Artists look back at 50 year history, NY Times, 3/30/86; Virginia Watson-Jones (auth), Contemporary American Women Sculptors, Oryx Press, 86; Les Krantz (auth), illus survey of the city's mus, galleries & leading artists, The New York Art Review, 88; and others. *Mem:* Am Abstract Artists; Art & Sci Collab Inc; Artists Using Sci & Technol; Int Sculpture Ctr; Univ Coun Art Educ. *Media:* All. *Publ:* Auth, A Response for an Environmental Response Center, NY State Arts & Humanities, 71; VTR: The Observed and the Observer, NY State Publ, 75; Light Boxes, NY State Art Teachers, 75; coauth, Sun altar, Landscape Archit, 11/80

PRICE, JOE (ALLEN)
SERIGRAPHER, INSTRUCTOR
b Ferriday, La, 35. *Study:* Northwestern Univ, Evanston, Ill, BS, 57; Art Ctr Col Design, Los Angeles, with Glenn Vilppu, 67-68; Stanford Univ, Calif, MA, 70. *Work:* Philadelphia Mus Art, Pa; Nat Mus Am Art, Washington; Libr Congress, Washington; Achenbach Found Graphic Art, Legion Honor, San Francisco; San Francisco Mus Mod Art; Mus Int Contemp Graphic Art, Fredrikstad, Norway. *Comn:* Print, Int Graphic Arts Found, Darien, Conn. *Exhib:* One-man shows, Tahir Gallery, New Orleans, 82, New Talent in Printmaking, Asn Am Artists, NY & Philadelphia, 84, Triton Mus Art, Santa Clara, 86, Ankrum Gallery, Los Angeles, Calif, 86, Huntsville Mus Art, Ala, 87, Gallery 30, San Mateo, Calif, 88, 91 & 97, Arches Paper Printed on Paper, Talens Headquarters, South Hadley, Mass, 98, Robert Wright Community Gallery, Col of Lake Co, Grayslake, Ill, 2003, Carnegie Visual Arts Ctr, Decatur, Ala, 2005; Sixth Int Exhib Botanical Art, Hunt Inst, Carnegie-Mellon Univ, Pa, 88; Fourth Int Biennial Print Exhib '89, Taipei Fine Arts Mus, Taiwan, Rep of China; Directions in Bay Area Printmaking: Three Decades, Palo Alto Cult Ctr, 92-93; Alabama Impact: Contemp Artists with Alabama Ties, Fine Arts Mus of the South & Huntsville Mus Art, 95; Agart World Print Festival, Ljubljana, Slovenia, 98; Am Botanical Prints of

Two Centuries, Hunt Inst, Carnegie-Mellon Univ, Pa, 2003. *Pos:* Chmn art dept, Col San Mateo, Calif. *Teaching:* Prof studio drawing & chair art dept, Col San Mateo, Calif, 70-94. *Awards:* Louis Lozowick Mem Award, Audubon Artists 36th Ann, 78; Lessing J Rosenwald Prize, Philadelphia Print Club Int, 79; Ture Bengtz Mem Purchase Award, 39th NAm Print Exhib, New York, 86; Creative Achievment Award, Calif State Legislature, 89; Audubon Artists Silver Medal Honor in Graphics, 91. *Bibliog:* Duane Wakeham (auth), Joe Price: Serigraphs in light and tone, Am Artist, 10/77; Tom Cervenak (auth), Bay area printmakers, Visual Dialog, spring 78; Prints Charming, Pol, Sydney, Australia, 1/80; Mary Ann & Mace Wenniger (coauths), Secrets of Buying Art, 10/90. *Mem:* Calif Soc Printmakers; Boston Printmakers; Am Color Print Soc; Audubon Artists; Print Club, Philadelphia. *Media:* Serigraphy, Watercolor. *Dealer:* M Lee Stone Fine Prints Inc 2101 Forest Ave Ste 130 San Jose CA 95128. *Mailing Add:* 6221 Cartwright Ave North Hollywood CA 91606

PRICE, JOE D & ETSUKO
COLLECTOR
Pos: Founder, shin'enkan found, for Japanese art, Corona del Mar, Calif; bd dir, Friends of Kebyar, 83. *Awards:* Names one of Top 200 Collectors, ARTnews Mag, 2004. *Collection:* Edo-period Japanese art. *Mailing Add:* PO Box 1111 Bartlesville OK 74005

PRICE, KENNETH
PRINTMAKER, SCULPTOR
b Los Angeles, Calif, 1935. *Study:* Chounard Art Inst; Los Angeles Co Art Inst; Univ Southern Calif, BFA, 56; State Univ NY at Alfred, MFA, 59. *Work:* Los Angeles Co Mus Art; Albright-Knox Art Gallery; Dallas Art Mus; Mus Modern Art, Whitney Mus Am Art, NY; Philadelphia Mus Art; San Francisco Mus Modern Art; Seattle Art Mus; Art Inst Chicago; St Louis Art Mus; Victoria & Albert Mus. *Exhib:* Recent Acquisitions, Whitney Mus Am Art, 67; one-man exhibs, James Corcoran Gallery, Los Angeles, 76, 82, 87, 91 & 92, Los Angeles Co Mus Art, 78, George Lavrov Gallery, Paris, 89, Rena Bransten Gallery, San Francisco, 89, Sena West Gallery, Santa Fe, 90, Charles Cowles Gallery, NY, 92 & LA Louver, 94, 96 & 97; Tamarind: Homage to Lithography, Mus Mod Art, NY, 69; 7th Ann Nat Print Exhib, Brooklyn Mus, NY, 70; Nine Print Portfolios, Mus Mod Art, NY, 70; Contemp Am Sculpture, Whitney Mus Am Art, 70; Gemini: Technics and Creativity (with catalog), Mus Mod Art, NY, 71; Contemp Am Art: Los Angeles, Ft Worth Art Ctr Mus, Tex, 72; Clay (with catalog), Whitney Mus Am Art, 74; Sculpture: Am Directions, 1945-1975, Smithsonian Inst, 75; 30 Yrs of Am Printmaking, Brooklyn Mus, 76; Painting and Sculpture in Calif: The Modern Era (with catalog), San Francisco Mus Mod Art, 76; 200 Yrs of Am Sculpture (with catalog), Whitney Mus Am Art, 76; Directions (with catalog), Hirshhorn Mus & Sculpture Garden, Washington, DC, 79; Contemp Sculpture, Mus Mod Art, NY, 79; Biennial Exhib (with catalog), Whitney Mus Am Art, 79 & 81; Los Angeles Prints, 1883-1980 (with catalog), Los Angeles Co Mus Art, 80; Ceramic Sculpture: Six Artists (with catalog), Whitney Mus Am Art & San Francisco Mus Mod Art, 81; Art in Los Angeles, 17 Artists in the Sixties (with catalog), Los Angeles Co Mus Art, 81; 100 Years of Calif Sculpture, Oakland Mus, Calif, 82; An Int Survey of Recent Painting and Sculpture (with catalog), Mus Mod Art, NY, 84; LA Hot and Cool: Pioneers, Mass Inst Technol, 88; The Cowles Art Show, Cowles Gallery, NY, 89; Calif Finish Fetish, Univ Southern Calif, Los Angeles, 91; Selections from Permanent Collection, Mus Contemp Art, Los Angeles, 91; Shigariki Mus Ceramic Art, Tokyo, 91; Contemp Crafts and the Saxe Collection, Toledo Mus Art & St Louis Art Mus, 93; New Sculpture, LA Louver, Venice, Calif, 94; A Calif Collection, Hunsaker/Schlesinger, Santa Monica, Calif, 95; and many others. *Awards:* Tamarind Fel, 68-69; Artists Award, Am Acad Arts & Letters, 98. *Bibliog:* Thomas Hess (auth), Art, New York Mag, 12/74; Judith Tannenbaum (auth), Kenneth Price--Willard, Arts Mag, 2/75; Kenneth Price at Willard, Art in Am, 5-6/75. *Dealer:* La Louver 45 N Venice Blvd California Venice CA 90291. *Mailing Add:* c/o LA Louver 45 N Venice Blvd Venice CA 90291

PRICE, LESLIE KENNETH
PAINTER, EDUCATOR
b New York, NY. *Study:* Sch Visual Arts, NY, 63-64; Pratt Inst, with James Gahagan, Ernest Briggs, G Laderman, BFA, 69; Mills Col, Oakland, Calif, MFA, 71. *Work:* Oakland Mus, Calif; Johnson Publ Co, Chicago. *Exhib:* Blacks USA, NY Cult Ctr, 73; New Directions in Afro-Am Art, Cornell Univ, Ithaca, NY, 74; Berkeley Art Ctr, Calif, 76; San Jose Mus, Calif, 76; Studio Mus in Harlem, NY, 77. *Teaching:* From assoc prof painting to prof art, Humboldt State Univ, Arcata, Calif, 72-. *Awards:* Painting Award, Pratt Inst, 68; Award of Merit, Calif Palace Legion Honor, 73; Honorarium, Cornell Univ, 74. *Bibliog:* Alfred Frankenstein (auth), article, San Francisco Chronicle, 11/77. *Mem:* Nat Conf of Artists. *Media:* Acrylic, Graphite. *Publ:* Contribr, Black Artists on Art, Vol II, Contemporary Crafts, 72; Existence Black, Southern Ill Univ, 72; contribr, Directions in Afro-American Art, Cornell Univ, 74. *Mailing Add:* Humboldt State Univ Dept Art Arcata CA 95521

PRICE, MARLA
MUSEUM DIRECTOR, CURATOR
Study: PhD in Art Hist. *Pos:* Assoc cur, of 20th-century art Nat Gallery Art, Washington, DC; chief cur, Modern Art Mus Ft Worth, Tex, 1986-91, dir, 1991-. *Mailing Add:* Modern Art Mus Ft Worth 3200 Darnell St Fort Worth TX 76107-2872

PRICE , MARY SUE
MUSEUM DIRECTOR
Study: Allegheny Col, BA in Eng, 73; Caldwell Col, DHC (hon). *Pos:* With textbook pub co, New York City; superv pub relations Newark Mus, 75, deputy dir, 90-93, dir, 93-. *Mem:* Asn Art Mus Dir, Am Asn Mus, NJ Asn Mus (bd dir, currently). *Mailing Add:* Newark Mus 49 Washington St Newark NJ 07102

PRICE, MICHAEL BENJAMIN
SCULPTOR, EDUCATOR
b Chicago, Ill, Oct 21, 40. *Study:* Univ Ill, Urbana-Champaign, with Frank Gallo, AB, 63, MA, 64; Tulane Univ, MFA(sculpture). *Work:* Berman Mus, Ursinus Col, Collegeville, Pa; Carleton Col Permanent Collection, Northfield, Minn; Art Gallery Mus, Mobile, Ala; Hamline Univ, Permanent Collection, St Paul, Minn; Governor's Mansion, St Paul, Minn; and others. *Comn:* Albright Col, Reading, Pa; Moravian Col, Bethlehem, Pa; St Charles Borromeo, Kettering, Ohio; Cincinnati Bicentinnial Riverwalk, Covington, Ky; Church of the Incarnation, Centerville, Ohio; and others. *Exhib:* One-man shows, Vincent Price Gallery, Chicago, 69, Krasner Gallery, NY, 73-74, 76-77 & 80, Imprimatur, St Paul, Minn, 84, Waterloo Munic Art Gallery, Iowa, Mussavi Art Ctr, NY, 87 & Berman Mus, Collegeville, Pa, 88; C G Rein Gallery, Scottsdale, Ariz, 79; Imprimatur Gallery, St Paul, Minn, 84; Int Juried Art Competition, NY, 85; Mussavi Art Ctr, NY, 85; and others. *Teaching:* Instr sculpture, Univ Ala, Huntsville, 66; prof sculpture, drawing & art hist, Hamline Univ, 70-, chmn art dept, 80-. *Awards:* Top Honor Award, Excellence on the Waterfront, Cincinnati Bicentennial, 89; Agnes Hulburd Award in the Humanities, 93; Richard P Bailey Journalism Award, Hamline Univ, 98. *Mem:* Col Art Asn Am. *Media:* Cast Bronze. *Mailing Add:* 1954 Laurel Ave Saint Paul MN 55104

PRICE, MORGAN SAMUEL
PAINTER, INSTRUCTOR
b Cleveland, Ohio, Feb 9, 47. *Study:* Ringling Sch Art, Cert, 68, with Loran Wilford, 66-68 & Carl Cogar, 76. *Work:* Goddard Art Ctr, Ardmore, Okla; Libr Cong, Washington, DC; Kirchman Corp Gallery, Orlando, Fla. *Comn:* Oil painting, St Mary's Catholic Church, Annapolis, Md, 68, Walker Oil, 73, painting, comn by Mr & Mrs Norman Yodi, 78, 79, 80 & 81, Gant Oil Co, 78, Woodruff Oil Co, 80, Ardmore, Okla, Law Offices of Tanya Plant 78, Law Offices of Mort Rosenblum 75-80, Orlando, Fla. *Exhib:* Salmagundi Club, NY, 88, 90-91; 78th Ann Exhib, Allied Artists Am, NY, 89 & 91 & 92; Brevard Cult Alliance, Savannahs, Merritt Island, Fla, 90; Quintuple Galerie, Argenteuil, France, 91; one-woman show, State of Fla, Capitol Bldg, Tallahassee, 91, McDonald Douglas Corp, Kennedy Space Ctr, 91 & Brevard Mus Art, Melbourne, Fla, 92, Marie Ferrer Gallery, 92; The Cloisters, Sea Island, Ga, 91; Arts of the Park (Top 100), Nat Park Acad, Jackson Hole, Wyo, 92; Pastel Soc Am, NY, 92. *Pos:* artist, Hallmark Cards, Kansas City, Mo; vpres, Knickerbocker Artists, New York, 91-92. *Teaching:* Instr oil painting, Goddard Art Ctr & Mus (oil, watercolor & pastel), Ardmore, Okla, 72-; workshops, oil, painting, watercolor & pastel, Throughout US & Europe, 72-. *Awards:* Joseph Hartley Award, Ann Open Show, Salmagundi Club, 90; Leon Stacks Mem, 78th Ann Exhib, Allied Artists, 91; Salmagundi Club, New York, New York, Antonio Cirino Award for a Pastel 1991; New Mems Show Oil Award Copley Soc Boston, Mass, 91; and many others. *Bibliog:* Dorothy Michaels (auth), Knowing How to Determine Value and Intensity, Am Artists, 6/91. *Mem:* Fel, Am Artists Prof League; Salmagundi Club; Copley Soc Boston; Pastel Soc Am; Knickerbocker Artists, NY (vpres, 91-92); Allied Artists Assoc, NY; Audobon Artists Asso, NY; Oil Painters of Am; Asn Pour La Promotion Du Patrimoine Artistique Francais. *Media:* Oil, Watercolor. *Publ:* Oil Painting with a Basic Palette. *Mailing Add:* PO Box 150247 Altamonte Springs FL 32715-0247

PRICE, RITA F
PAINTER, PRINTMAKER
b Bronx, NY. *Study:* Art Inst Chicago, BFA, 82; Univ Ill, Chicago, 83. *Work:* Carter Presidential Libr & Policy Ctr Mus, Atlanta, Ga; Int Mineral & Chemical Corp, Northbrook, Ill; Schiff, Hardin & Waite, Chicago, Ill; Ctr Prof Advan, E Brunswick, NJ; Renaissance No Shore Hotel, Northbrook, IL. *Comn:* A Place Where a Dreamer Goes, comn by Mr & Mrs Marshall Field, Chicago, 88; Cheries Garden, comn by Cherie Melchiorre, Chicago. *Exhib:* Curs Choice Collectibles, Prints & Drawings, Art Inst Chicago, 86; Ill Regional Print Show, Dittmar Gallery, Northwestern Univ, Evanston, Ill, 87 & 98; Ann Exhib, Am Jewish Arts Club, Spertus Mus, Chicago, 87, 88, & 89; 100 Yrs/100 Artists Traveling Exhib, 89; Nat V Print Exhib, Haggin Mus, Stockton, Calif, 90; Traveling Print Exhib, India, 90-91 & Nat Asn Women Artists, NY, 98-99; Women in the Visual Arts, Boca Raton, Fla; Boca Mus Artists Guild, Boca Raton, Fla; NAWA Fla, Judges Recognition, 2004-2005. *Pos:* Asst dir admis, Art Inst Chicago, 83-85, asst dir, non-degree progs, 85-88 & dir alumni affairs, 88-93. *Teaching:* Instr experimental printmaking N Shore Art League, Winnetka, Ill, 84-; instr printmaking, Sch Art Inst, Chicago, 88-94; instr printmaking, Ox-Bow, Saugatuck, Mich, 88 & Evanston Art Ctr, Ill, 95. *Awards:* Award of Excellence, N Shore Art League, Ann Exhib, 82, Am Jewish Arts Club, 86, 87, 88, 90, 91, 92, 93, 97 & 98, Munic Art League, Chicago, 89 & Old Orchard Art Festival, 91; Women in the Visual Arts, Boca Raton, Fla. *Bibliog:* Les Krantz (auth), The Chicago Art Rev, Am Reference Inc, 89; Louise Dunn Yochim (auth), Harvest of Freedom, Am Reference Inc, 89; Ivy Sundell (auth), The Chicago Art Scene, Woods Publ, 98. *Mem:* Nat Asn Women Artists; N Shore Art League (bd dir, vpres & pres, 73-); Chicago Soc Artists; Chicago Arts Coalition; Evanston Art Ctr (bd trustees, 92-); Nat Alumni Asn of Sch of Art Inst/Chicago (pres); plus others. *Media:* Acrylic, Oil; All Media. *Dealer:* Deer Path Art Gallery Lake Forest IL. *Mailing Add:* 8204 Casa Del Lago Apt 240 Boca Raton FL 33433-2185

PRICE, SARA J
PAINTER, PHOTOGRAPHER
Study: Pratt Inst, BFA, 76; New Sch Soc Res, 77-80; study with Burt Silverman, William Katavolos & Don Stacy. *Exhib:* Nat Exhib, Heckscher Mus, Huntington, NY, 85 & 86; Talent, Allan Stone Gallery, NY, 86 & 88-91; Giannetta Gallery, Philadelphia, Pa, 89; Nat Asn Women Artists, traveling exhib, Washington Cty Mus Fine Arts, Hagerstown, Md, 88, Greenville Mus Art, NC, 89, Butler Inst Am Art, Youngstown, Ohio, 89, Jesse Besser Mus, Alpena, Mich, 90 & Sansker Kendra Mus, Ahmedebad, India, 89-90; Mus Southwest, Midland, Tex, 91; Richmond Art Mus, Ind,

92. *Pos:* Freelance photogr, Tomlin Art Co, 77-92. *Awards:* Silver Medal/Printmaking, Int Art Competition, 84; Award of Excellence, Huntington Township Art League, 85; Purchase Award, Hoyt Inst Fine Arts, 86. *Mem:* Nat Asn Women Artists (exec bd 90-); NY Artists Equity Asn; Asn Flatbush Artists. *Media:* Oil on Paper, Watercolor. *Mailing Add:* 59 Sullivan St New York NY 10012-4306

PRIEST, TERRI KHOURY STRUCKUS
PAINTER
b Worcester, Mass, Jan 20, 28. *Study:* Worcester Art Mus Sch, Mass, 47-48; Quinsigamond Community Col, Worcester, 72 & 73; Univ Mass, Amherst, BFA(painting), 75, MFA(painting), 77. *Work:* Worcester Art Mus, Mass; Aldrich Mus Contemp Art, Ridgefield, Conn; DeCordova Mus, Lincoln, Mass; Bundy Art Ctr, Waitsfield, Vt; Springfield Art Mus, Springfield, Mass. *Comn:* Three color serigraph, Worcester Art Mus, 77; ltd ed print, Holy Cross Col, Worcester, 81; Bishop Ireton Hish Sch, Alexandria, Va, 2004; and others. *Exhib:* New Eng Women, DeCordova Mus, Lincoln, 75; Painting Invitational, Brockton Art Ctr, Mass, 75; one-person shows, Drawings, Worcester Art Mus, Mass, 76 & Wash World Gallery, Wash, DC, 81; Paperworks, Hudson River Mus, NY, 80; Survey Show, Cantor Art Gallery, Holly Cross Col, Worcester, Mass, 2005. *Pos:* Instr, Hampshire Col, Amherst, Mass, 75; vis cur, Col Art Gallery Prog, Worcester Art Mus, 79. *Teaching:* Assoc prof intermediate painting, visual design & color, Col Holy Cross, Worcester, formerly; retired. *Awards:* Kinnicutt Travel Award, Worcester Art Mus, 74; Charles & Roseanna Batchelor Summer Fel, Holy Cross Col, Worcester, 81; Res & Publ Award, Holy Cross Col, 82, 84 & 86. *Bibliog:* Nina Kaiden & Bartlett Hayes (auth), Artist and Advocate, Renaissance, 67; Roger T. Dunn (auth), Terri Priest Interactions: Paintings & Works on Paper (monogr & catalog), Col Holy Cross, Worcester, Mass. *Mem:* Boston Visual Artists Union; Col Art Asn; Worcester Art Mus. *Media:* Oil; Pastel. *Mailing Add:* 5 Pratt St Worcester MA 01609

PRIETO, MONIQUE N
PAINTER
b Los Angeles, Calif, 62. *Study:* UCLA, BFA, 87; Calif Inst Arts, BFA, 92, MFA, 94. *Exhib:* Wight Gallery, Univ Calif, Los Angeles, 87; Corazon Mexicana, Bacilla Hernandez Gallery, Long Beach, Calif, 89; Happy Show, Lockheed Gallery, Valencia, Calif, 94; Temporary, Thesis Show, Mus Contemp Art, Los Angeles, Calif, 94; solo exhibs, ACME, Santa Monica, Calif, 94, 95, 96, 97, 99, 00, 01, Bravin Post Lee, NY, 96, Anderson Gallery, Va Commonwealth Univ, Richmond, 97, Pat Hearn Gallery, NY, 97, 98, 99, Robert Prime, London, Eng, 98, Corvi-Mora, London, 00, 02, Cheim & Read, NY, 02, Il Capricorno, Venice, Italy, 03; The Speed of Painting, Pat Hearn Gallery, NY, 96; Chalk, Factory Place Gallery, Los Angeles, 96; LA Current: New View, Univ Calif Los Angeles/Armand Hammer Sales & Rental Gallery, Los Angeles, 97; group exhibs, Pat Hearn Gallery, NY, 01, Tate Liverpool, 01, Palm Beach Inst Contemp Art, Lake Worth, Fla, 01, Kerling Gallery, Dublin, 01, Mus Contemp Art, Denver, 01, Cirrus Gallery, Los Angeles, 02, Portland Art Mus, Ore, 02, ACME, Los Angeles, 02, 03, Royal Acad, London, 02, Kresge Art Mus, East Lansing, Mich, 02, Kunstmus Wolfsburg, Ger, 03, Marella Arte Contemporanea, Milan, Italy, 03. *Collection Arranged:* Mus Contemp Art, San Diego; Mus Contemp Art, Los Angeles; Los Angeles Co Mus Art; Whitney Mus Am Art, New York City; Orange Co Mus Art, Newport Beach, Calif; Kresge Art Mus, Mich State Univ, East Lansing. *Awards:* Louis Comfort Tiffany Found Biennial Competition, 97, Grant, 98. *Bibliog:* David Pagel (auth), Adding a splash of fun to abstraction, Los Angeles Times, 12/5/97; Peter Frank (auth), article, LA Weekly, 12/12/97; Dave Hickey (auth), Top ten X 12, Artforum, 12/97; Martin Coomer (auth), Monique Prieto, Time Out, London, 10-11/2000; David Pagel (auth), A Breakthrough in Dark, Abstract Dramas, LA Times, F36, 12/21/2001; Blake Gopnik (auth), LA Consequential, Washington Post, 1, G6-7, 2002. *Dealer:* Acme, 6150 Wilshire Blvd, 1&2, LA 90048. *Mailing Add:* 1942 N Alvarado St Los Angeles CA 90039

PRIMM, SYLVIA MARIE
ARTIST
b Atlanta, Ga, Apr 13, 51. *Study:* Univ Fla, BFA; Fla State U, MFA. *Work:* Nat Cattleman's Asn Polit Action Com, Washington. *Comn:* painted ceramic plate, R & M Montgomery Art Ctr, West Palm Beach, Fla, 1995; carousel horses, comn by Mrs D Epson, Lake Park, Fla, 1997; painted night stand, comn by Mrs D Miller, Indiantown, Fla, 1998; contemporary impressionism, comn by Mr & Mrs K Mosely, Jupiter, Fla, 2000; portrait, comn by Mrs M Gallo, Palm Beach Gardens, Fla, 2002; W Rogers Primm, Palm Beach Gardens, Fla; Arch & Fine Arts Libr, Univ Fla. *Exhib:* Benefit Tea Party, Ann Norton Sculpture Gardens & Mus, West Palm Beach, Fla, 1995; Marden Gallery Exhib (Easter Egg), Norton Mus Art, West Palm Beach, Fla, 2001. *Pos:* dir, ArtBizs.net. *Teaching:* instr drawing, adult education, Jupiter Community Sch, 93-94; instr drawing & painting R&M Montgomery Art Ctr, West Palm Beach, Fla, 93-97; instr drawing, Lighthouse Gallery Sch, 95. *Awards:* Unity Mural certificate. *Mem:* Martin Co Art Asn; Hobe Sound Fine Art League; Women Art; Palm City Art Asn. *Publ:* Illustrator, Botany Lab Manaul, Univ Fla, 86

PRINA, STEPHEN JAMES
ARTIST, EDUCATOR
b Galesburg, Ill, Nov 3, 54. *Study:* Carl Sandburg Col, Galesburg, Ill, AA, 74; Northern Ill Univ, Dekalb, Ill, BFA, 77; Calif Inst Art, Valencia, Calif, MFA, 80. *Work:* Mus Contemp Art, Los Angeles, Calif; Mus Mod Art New York City; Whitney Mus Am Art; Garr+233 Art Musee D'Art; Contempopain De Nimes, France. *Comn:* Los Angeles Munic Libr, 93; Galerie Gisela Capitain, 99; Margo Leavin Gallery, 99, Friedrich Petzel Gallery, New York City, 98, 99 & 2001, Musee D'Art Moderne Et Contemporain (MAMCO), Geneva, Switzerland, 98; Frankfurter Kunstuerein, Ger, 2000, Hamburger Gahnhof, Berlin, Ger, 2000, Art Pace, San Antonio, Tex, 2000. *Exhib:* Striking Distance, Mus Contemp Art, Los Angeles, Calif, 88; BiNational: Am Art of the Late 80's, Inst Contemp Art, Boston, Mass, 89-90; solo exhibs, Galerie Gisela Capitain, Koln, 90, 93 & 96 Luhring Augustine Gallery, NY, 90, 92, 93 & 96, Galerie Fricke, Dusseldorf, Ger, 91, Galerie Peter Pakesch, Wien, 91, Galerie Max Hetzler, Koln, 91, Margo Leavin Gallery, Los Angeles, 93 & 96 & DAAD Galleries, Berlin, 96; Allegories of Modernism: Contemp Drawing, Mus Mod Art, NY, 92; After & Before, Renaissance Soc, Univ Chicago, 94; Die Orte der Kunst, Sprengel Mus, 94; Exposure, Luhring Augustine, NY, 96; a/drift, Bard Ctr Curatorial Studies, NY, 96; Pittsburgh Ctr for the Arts, 98, Charim Klocker, Vienna, Austria, 98, Crossings Kunsthalle, Vienna, 98, INIT-Kunst-Halle, Berlin, 99, Mus Contemp Art, Sydney, Australia, 2001. *Teaching:* Instr, Art Ctr Col Design, 80-; Calif Inst Arts, 87. *Awards:* Individual Artist Fel, Nat Endowment Arts, 88; Englehard Found Award, Englehard Found, Boston, 88; Ind Artsist Fel, NEA, 90. *Bibliog:* Kristine McKenna (auth), Getting his chaos in order, Los Angeles Times/Calendar, 1/21/96; Susan Kandel (auth), Memories of Prina's past benefit present installation, Los Angeles Times, 1/25/96; Dennis Cooper (auth), Real life rock Dennis Cooper's top ten, ARTFORUM, summer 96; and others. *Publ:* Coauth (with Christopher Williams), A Conversation with Shelia Mc Laughlin & Lynne Tillman, LAICA Journal, 85; auth, The Twenty-Six Inch Experience, TV Guides, 85; coauth (with Christopher Williams), By These Walls (exhib catalog), Cal Arts: Skeptical Beliefs, 88; It was the best he could do at the moment, Mus Boymans-van Beuningen, 92; Johanna Fahmels Monolog, Johanna Faehmels Monologue, Walther Konig, 94. *Dealer:* Galerie Gisela Capitain Koln Germany; Margo Leavin Gallery Los Angeles CA; Friedrich Petzel Gallery New York NY. *Mailing Add:* 4411 Los Feliz Blvd Apt 1102 Los Angeles CA 90027-2143

PRINCE, ARNOLD
SCULPTOR, EDUCATOR
b Basseterre, St Kitts, West Indies, Apr 17, 25. *Study:* Brit Coun with John Harrison, Jose DeCreeft, William Zorach & John Hovvannes; Art Students League. *Work:* First Vest Pocket Park, NY; Art Students League. *Comn:* Concrete sculpture, City North Adams, Mass, 68; gate post sculpture, Spruces Residential Park, 72; concrete sculpture, comn by Robert Potrin, Stamford, Vt, 73. *Exhib:* St Marks on the Bowery, 64; Sculptors Guild Exhib, Mus RI Sch Design, 69-75; Slide Show Collection of Afro-Am Artists, Univ Ala, 71; Boston Pub Libr, 73; group show RI Sch Design, 75. *Teaching:* Dir sculpture educ, Fed Govt Poverty Proj Harlem, HARYOU, 64-67; adj prof sculpture, North Adams State Col, 70-72; asst prof fine arts & sculpture, RI Sch Design, 72-82. *Bibliog:* Article in Village Voice, 12/65; article in NAdams Transcript, 66-71. *Mem:* Sculptors Guild NY. *Media:* Wood, Stone. *Publ:* Auth, Carving Wood and Stone, Prentice Hall, 80. *Dealer:* Sculptors Guild Inc 75 Rockefeller Plaza New York NY 10020. *Mailing Add:* c/o Sculptor's Guild Inc 110 Greene St New York NY 10012

PRINCE, RICHARD
PHOTOGRAPHER
b Panama Canal Zone, Aug 6,49. *Work:* Whitney Mus Am Art & Mus Mod Art, NY; Haus due Kunst, Munich, Ger; San Francisco Mus Art, Calif; IVAM Centre del Carne, Valencia, Spain. *Exhib:* Inst Contemp Art, London, Eng, 83; Centre Nationalidad Art Contemporian, Grenoble, France, 88; Spirinal Am, IVAM Centre del Carne, Valencia, Spain, 89; Whitney Mus Am Art, NY, 92; Whitney Biennial, Whitney Mus Am Art, NY, 97; one-man shows, White Cube, London, Eng, 97, Mus Haus Lange, Krefeld, Ger, 97, Barbara Gladstone Gallery, NY, 98, 2000, Sabine Knust, Munich, Ger, 99, Sadie Coles HQ, London, Eng, 99, 2001, Jabklonka Galerie, Köln, Ger, 2000, Partobject Gallery, Weaver Carboro, NC, 2000, MAK Ctr for Art and Archit, Los Angeles, 2000, Micheline Szwajcer, Antwerp, 2001, Skarstedt Fine Art, NY, 2001, Mus für Gegenwartskunst, Basel, Switz, 2001, Neue Galerie im Höhmann-haus, Augsburg, 2001, Kunsthalle Zurich, Switz, 2001, Barbara Gladstone Gallery, NY, 2002, Patrick Painter, Inc, Santa Monica, Calif, 2002; Marianne Boesky Gallery, NY, 98; Cleveland Mus of Art, Ohio, 98; Mus of Am Art, Pa Acad Fine Arts, 98; Whitney Mus Am Art, NY, 99; Mus Contemp Art, Chicago, 99; Whitechapel Art Gallery, London, 99; Barbara Gladstone Gallery, NY, 99; Galleria Franco Noero, Turin, Italy, 2001; Royal Acad of Arts, London, Eng, 2001; Mus of Contemp Art, Miami, Fla, 2001; Jablonka Gallery, Cologne, Ger, 2001; Mus of Mod Art, NY, 2001; Aldrich Mus Contemp Art, Ridgefield, Conn, 2001; Cheim & Reid Gallery, NY, 2001; Short Stories, Henry Art Gallery, Seattle, Wash, 2002; Pub Affairs, Kunsthaus, Zurich, 2002; Chic Clicks: Creativity and Commerce in Contemp Fashion Photog, the Inst of Contemp Art, Boston, Mass, 2002. *Pos:* Odd jobs Time Life, New York City, 1973-1985; ed cover photog Mademoiselle Mag, 1985; full-time artist, 1985-; Mem "Picture" Generation of artists 1970s, New York City. *Awards:* Recipient Nat Endowment award, 1985. *Bibliog:* David Humphrey (auth), New York Fax, Art Issues, No 54, 3-4/98; Richard Price Party, Dazed and Confused, London, 3/98; Richard Prince & Glen O'Brien (auths), Are we having fun yet, Blind Spot, 11/98. *Mem:* Mem The Off, NY (pres 1979-80). *Media:* Mixed Media. *Mailing Add:* c/o Barbara Gladstone Gallery 515 W 24th St New York NY 10011

PRINCE, RICHARD EDMUND
SCULPTOR, EDUCATOR
b Comox, BC, Apr 6, 49. *Study:* Univ BC, BA(art hist), 71 & study, 72-73; Emma Lake Artists Workshop, Sask, with Ron Kitaj, 70. *Work:* Nat Gallery Can, Ottawa; Vancouver Art Gallery, BC; Govt of BC, Victoria Art Collection; Can Coun Art Bank, Ottawa, Can; Glenbow Mus, Calgary, Can; and others. *Comn:* Can Pavillion, Expo 86, Vancouver, Can; Concord Pac Developments Ltd, City of Vancouver, 96; CK Choi Inst Asian Research, 97. *Exhib:* One-man shows, Issacs Gallery, Toronto, 78 & 82 & Figure Structures, Burnaby Art Gallery, BC, 79, Hamilton Art Gallery, Ont, 84; Canadian Cult Ctr, Rome, Italy, 87; 49th Parallel Gallery, NY, 89; A New Decade: Vancouver, Alta Col Art Gallery, Calgary, 79; Vancouver Heritage, Vancouver Art Gallery, 83; Reflecting Paradise, World Expo 93, Seoul, South Korea, 93; Strangers in the Arctic, Rundertaarn Mus, Copenhagen, Denmark & Mus Contemp Art, Helsinki,

Finland, 96; MacLaren Art Ctr, Barrie, Can, 2000; and others. *Teaching:* Instr sculpture, Vancouver Community Col, BC, 74-75; instr fine arts & sculpture, Univ BC, 75-; vis lectr sculpture, Univ of BC, 77-78, asst prof sculpture, 78-83, assoc prof, 83-2003, prof 2003-. *Awards:* Art Vancouver for 74 Award, City of Vancouver, 74; Can Coun Arts Grant, Govt Can, 75; Can Coun Arts Grant, 77-78. *Bibliog:* Joan Lowndes (auth), Richard Prince: bringing the outdoors in, Artscanada, Toronto, 10-11/78; Arthur Perry (auth), Richard Prince: figure structures, Vanguard Vancouver, BC, 11/79; Joel Kaplan (auth), Richard Prince, Parachute, Montreal, Que, summer 85; Stephen Godfrey (auth), Focus on Richard Prince, Can Art, fall 88; JP Borum (auth), Richard E Prince, Artforum, New York, 1/90; Ian Thom (auth), Art BC, Douglas & MacIntyre, Vancouver, BC, 2000; Anne Newlands (auth) Candian Art Fire Fly Books, Buffalo, NY, 2000; Arthur Williams (auth), Beginning Sculpture, Davis Publ Inc, Worcester, MA, 2004; Arthur Williams (auth), The Sculptor Reference, Davis Publ Inc, Worcester MA, 2004. *Mem:* Life mem Royal Can Acad; Univ Art Asn Can. *Media:* Multimedia. *Dealer:* Equinox Gallery 2321 Granville St Vancouver BC Can V6H 3G3. *Mailing Add:* Univ BC Dept Art Hist & Vis Art 6333 Memorial Rd Vancouver BC V6T I2Z Canada

PRINTZ, BONNIE ALLEN
PAINTER, PHOTOGRAPHER
b Luray, Va. *Study:* Va Commonwealth Univ, Richmond, BFA, 68; Hunter Col, New York, MA, 70. *Work:* Baltimore Mus Art, Baltimore Life & Ballard Spahr Andrews & Ingersoll, Baltimore, Md; Corcoran Gallery Art & Bechtel Corp, Washington, DC; Towson Univ, Baltimore, Md. *Exhib:* one-person exhib show, Baltimore Mus Art, 79; Corcoran Gallery Art, Washington, DC, 79, 82 & 88; William Penn Mem Mus, Harrisburg, Pa, 79-80 & 82; Va Mus Fine Arts, Richmond, 80 & 83; Baltimore Mus Art, 80, 83 & 86; McIntosh/Drysdale Gallery, Washington, DC, 87; Galerie Des Saints Peres, Paris, France, 92; Exposition D'Art Contemporain, Paris, France, 93; Fraser Gallery, Georgetown, Washington, DC, 97, 98 & 99; Bendann Art Gallery, Baltimore, Md, 99; Md Art Place, Baltimore, 99; Fish out of Water, Baltimore Pub Art Exhib, 2001; Art Works, Pub Television, MPT, MD; Party Animals, Arts Commn, Washington, DC, 2002. *Pos:* Tech asst spec collections, Mus Mod Art, New York, 68-70. *Teaching:* Instr fine arts, Md Inst, Col Art, Baltimore, 72-73, 76 & 79-89. *Awards:* Alliance Independent Col Art Grant, 85; Yaddo Fel, 88 & 89; Fel Painting, Md State Arts Coun, Baltimore, 98. *Bibliog:* Allan Ripp (auth), Polaroid photos allow artists to develop their talents, News Am, Baltimore, 12/31/78. *Media:* Oil. *Publ:* Illusr, Frank Young's Visual Studies: A Foundation Course for the Visual Arts, Minneapolis Col Art & Design, 85; New American Paintings, Whitney Mus Am Art, New York, Open Studios Press, Mass, 94. *Dealer:* Barbara Feeser Art Assocs Baltimore MD; Susan Perrin Art Consult Baltimore MD. *Mailing Add:* 1104 Regester Ave Baltimore MD 21239

PRIOLA, J JOHN
PHOTOGRAPHER, INSTRUCTOR
b Dec 30, 60. *Study:* Met State Col, Denver, BFA (with honors), 84; San Francisco Art Inst, MFA, 87. *Work:* Met Mus Art, NY; Mus Mod Art, NY; Art Inst Chicago; Philadelphia Mus Art; Los Angeles Co Mus Art. *Comn:* five black & white photographs, Banana Republic, Los Angeles, 96. *Exhib:* In a Different Light, Univ Art Mus, Berkeley, Calif, 95; Prospect '96, Schirn Kunsthalle, Frankfurt, Ger, 96; Crossing the Line, Art Inst Chicago, 2000; Now! Modern Photographs from Permanent Collection, Met Mus Art, NY, 2000; Beyond Boundaries, Santa Barbara Contemp Arts Forum, Calif State Univ Long Beach, 2000-01. *Teaching:* adj prof photog, San Francisco Art Inst, 98-99; adj prof photog, Calif Col Arts & Crafts, 99-2000. *Awards:* Individual Photog Fel, Found Fels Collection, Princeton Univ, Aaron Siskind Found, 98. *Mem:* San Francisco Mus Mod Art; Ansel Adams Ctr: Friends of Photog; San Francisco Camerawork. *Publ:* auth, Once Removed: Portraits by J John Priola, Arena Edits, 98. *Dealer:* Fraenkel Gallery. *Mailing Add:* Calif Coll Arts & Crafts 5212 Broadway at College Ave Oakland CA 94618

PRIP, JANET
CRAFTSMAN, SCULPTOR
b Hornell, NY, June 17, 50. *Study:* Moore Col Art, 68-70; RI Sch Design, BFA, 74. *Work:* RI Sch of Design Mus, Providence; Boston Mus Fine Arts; Am Craft Mus, NY. *Exhib:* Feature Show, Joanne Rapp Gallery, Scottsdale, Ariz, 93; Am Craft Mus, NY, 93; New Acquisitions Show, Craft Today USA, 93; Peter Joseph Gallery, NY, 94; Contemp Art RI, RI Sch Design Mus Art, Providence, 94; and others. *Awards:* Fel, Nat Endowment Arts, 86; Merit Award, Guild Am Craft Awards, 87. *Bibliog:* Jamie Bennet (auth), American Holloware: Changing Criteria, Metalsmith, summer 84; Sarah Bodine (auth), Janet Prip, Metalsmith, fall 88. *Media:* Bronze, Pewter. *Mailing Add:* 38 Rosemary Ln Jamestown RI 02835

PRITZKER, JOHN A.
COLLECTOR
Study: Menlo Col, grad; Univ Denver Col Hotel and Restaurant Management, grad. *Pos:* various positions to divisional vpres Calif, Hyatt; pres, Hyatt Ventures Inc; founder, pres, Red Sail Sports Inc, 88-; exec vpres bus develop, Key3Media Events Inc, 2000; bd dirs, Zoomedia Inc; trustee, San Francisco Mus Modern Art; dir, Pritzker Found, Pritzker Cousins Found, Children Now; bd dirs, Univ Calif San Francisco Found. *Awards:* Named one of Forbes 400 Richest Americans; Named one of Top 200 Collectors, ARTnews mag, 2005-06. *Mailing Add:* Red Sail Sports 1 Ferry Bldg Suite 255 San Francisco CA 94111

PRITZKER, THOMAS JAY
PATRON
b Chicago, Ill, Jun 6, 50. *Study:* Claremont Men's Col, BA, 71; Univ Chicago, MBA, JD, 76. *Pos:* Assoc, Katten, Muchin, Zavis, Pearl & Galler, Chicago, 76-77; exec vpres, Hyatt Corp, 77-80, pres, 80-2002, chmn, Chief Exec Officer, 99-, Hyatt Int Corp, 99-; partner, Pritzker & Pritzker, Chicago, 80-; Bd trustees, vchmn, Art Inst Chicago, 88-; bd trustees, Univ Chicago, currently. *Mem:* Am Bar Asn; Ill Bar Asn; Chicago Bar Asn. *Mailing Add:* Hyatt Corp 200 W Madison St 38th Fl Chicago IL 60606

PRITZLAFF, (MR & MRS) JOHN, JR
COLLECTORS
Mr Pritzlaff, b Milwaukee, Wis, May 10, 25; Mrs Pritzlaff, b St Louis, Mo. *Study:* Mr Pritzlaff, Princeton Univ, BA, 49; Mrs Pritzlaff, Briarcliff Col. *Pos:* Mr Pritzlaff, US Ambassador to Malta, 69-72; Ariz State Sen, formerly; mem bd dir, Heard Mus, Phoenix, Ariz, 76-77; Mrs Pritzlaff, pres, bd dir, Phoenix Art Mus. *Mailing Add:* 7352 E McLellan Blvd Scottsdale AZ 85250-4523

PROCHOWNIK, WALTER A
EDUCATOR, PAINTER
b Buffalo, NY, Dec 12, 23. *Study:* Art Inst Buffalo; Art Students League. *Work:* Albright-Knox Art Gallery, Burchfield Ctr, State Univ NY, Buffalo; Norfolk Mus Arts & Sci, Va; Minn Mus Arts, St Paul; Houston Mus Art; Ball State Univ Art Gallery, Muncie, Ind. *Comn:* You the People (mural), Co of Erie, Rath Off Bldg, Buffalo, 74; mural, Blue Cross Bldg, Buffalo, NY, 88. *Exhib:* One-man shows, Member's Gallery, Albright-Knox Art Gallery, Buffalo, 64, Col of Wooster, Ohio, 66, Chautauqua Art Asn Gallery, NY, 68 & Burchfield Ctr, Buffalo, 75 & 89; Smithsonian travel tour, 68-69; Barbara Schuller Gallery, 93; Rochester Inst Technol, 95; State Univ NY, 95. *Teaching:* Prof, State Univ NY, Buffalo, 63-95. *Awards:* First Oil Award, Chautauqua Art Asn, 58; Purchase Prize, Drawings USA, 63 & 66; Perkin-Elmer Corp Award, Silvermine Guild, 69. *Mem:* Patteran Artists. *Media:* Oil, Multimedia. *Dealer:* Barbara Schuller Gallery 345 Franklin St Buffalo NY 14202. *Mailing Add:* 734 Richmond Ave Buffalo NY 14222-1159

PROHASKA, ELENA ANASTASIA
CONSULTANT, CURATOR
b Southampton, NY, Sept 3, 46. *Study:* NY Univ, Washington Sq Col, BA, 70; Univ Va, Charlottesville, with William Seitz & Frederick Hartt, MA, 72; New Sch; NY Univ, 97. *Work:* Investment Counrs, NY. *Collection Arranged:* Monthly exhibs, (auth, catalogs), Upstairs Gallery, East Hampton, NY, 72-74; Twelve Americans: Masters of Collage, Crispo Gallery, New York, 77; Artists of the Springs, East Hampton, NY, 81; East Hampton Hist Soc Invitational, 86; Consult & Appraiser, Artists of the Hamptons, Guernsey's Auctioneers, 92. *Pos:* Owner, Elena Prohaska Fine Arts; cur, Art Collection, EM Warburg, Pincus, New York & London, 84-; co-cur photographs & paintings, East Hampton Marine Mus, 95-96; mem, Univ Va Coun Arts, currently; adv coun, Bayly Mus Art, Univ Va, Charlottesville; sculpture adv, archit & design firms, currently; co-dir, co-owner, Prohaska Vetter Fine Arts, Ltd, New York, 99-. *Teaching:* Docent & art lectr, Guggenheim Mus, New York, 74-76; instr art, Town Sch, New York, 74-77. *Mem:* Appraisers Asn Am, NY; Nat Arts Club (photography com), NY; USPAP (cert). *Specialty:* Contemporary paintings, sculpture and photographs; also specialize in advising private and corporate clients on art acquisitions; appraisals provided for insurance, gift and replacement purposes

PROMUTICO, JEAN
PAINTER
b Baltimore, Md, Nov 23, 36. *Study:* Md Inst Col Art, with Lila Katzen & Jon Schueler, BFA(painting & drawing), 66; Univ NMex, Albuquerque, with John Kacere, MA(painting & art hist), 68. *Work:* Fine Arts Mus NMex, Santa Fe; Univ Art Mus, Univ NMex, Albuquerque; Roswell Mus & Art Ctr, NMex; Lynn Mahew Gallery, Ohio Wesleyan Univ, Delaware; Roanoke Mus Fine Arts, Va. *Exhib:* Mus Fine Arts NMex, Santa Fe, 1973, 1975, 1989; Roswell Mus Art Ctr, NY, 1974, 79, 90; First Western States Biennial traveling exhib, 1979; San Francisco Mus Modern Art, 1981; Bruce Mus, Greenwich, Conn, 1985; NJ Ctr Visual Arts, Summit, 88; The Painter's Light, PMWG, Stamford, Conn, 89; Port Washington Pub Libr, Port Washington, NY, 93; Artafare Auction, Md Inst Col Art, Baltimore, 95; La Mama La Galleria, NY, 95; Fay & Friends, Md Inst, Baltimore, 97; Tai Gallery, 2000, 02, 04, 06, The Actors Inst, NY, 2000-2002; Anderson Mus Calif. *Awards:* Nat Endowment Arts Grant, 74; Artist-in-Residence Grant, Roswell Mus & Art Ctr, 78-79 & 90-91; Nat Studio Program Grant, PSI Mus, New York, 81. *Bibliog:* William Peterson (auth), Jean Promutico, Artspace, spring 79; Gerrit Henry (auth), NY Review, Art News, 9/81; article, William Peterson (auth), Santa Fe, Artspace, fall 83. *Media:* Acrylic, Miscellaneous Media, Oil. *Dealer:* Tai Gallery 159 W 25th St NYC 10001. *Mailing Add:* 463 West St D-351 New York NY 10014-2032

PRONIN , ANATOLY
PHOTOGRAPHER
b Leningrad, USSR, Oct 28, 39; US citizen. *Study:* State Univ Leningrad, Russia, (journalism), 62-65. *Work:* Brooklyn (NY) Mus; Metrop Mus Art, NY; Libr Congress, DC; Bibliot Nat, Paris; Staatliche Mus Berlin, Ger. *Exhib:* 33 Photo Salon, Photographic Asn Calcutta, India, 89; 128 Int Exhib Pictorial Photog, Edinburgh (Scotland) Photo Soc, 90; 43 South African Int Salon, Johannesburg, 90; Ghetto - Traces of Memory, NY Pub Libr, 90; Old Vocies, New Faces, Nat Jewish Mus, Washington DC, 92; USE, Contacts/Proofs, Jersey City (NJ) Mus, 90, 93; Natural History, Katlin Ewing Gallery, Washington DC, 93; Children of Leningrad, MBM Gallery, NY, 96; Fellow Exhib 99, Hunterdaon Mus Art, Clinton, NJ, 99, CHUBB Atrum Gallery, NJ, 2000; Propagandist and Romantic: Contemp Russian Photog,

Priebe Art Gallery, Univ Wis, Oshkosh, 2002; New York City Photog in Black and White, Michael Ingbar Gallery, NY, 2003. *Awards:* Silver Medal, Int Photo Exhib, Berlin, Ger, 71; First place, USSR Photog Exhib, Moscow, 78-79; Cert of Excellence, Art Dir Club NJ, 88; NJ State Coun Arts Fel, 90, 99. *Publ:* contribr, Encyl Brittanica, 86, 92; contribr, Graphis Photo 89, Graphis mag, Switzerland, 89; contribr, Power of Art, Harcourt Brace, 95; contribr, Facing the Music, Simon & Schuster, 96; contribr, Encarta, Microsoft, 97, 2006. *Mailing Add:* 315 Eastern St Apt D-1613 New Haven CT 06513

PROPERSI, AUGUST J
ADMINISTRATOR, PAINTER
b Bronx, NY, Apr 3, 26. *Study:* Sch Art Studies, with Isaac Soyer & Sol Wilson, 46-47; Sch Visual Arts, with Jack Sheridan, Ben Dale & Francis Criss, grad, 50; Conference Conservation of Paintings, Brooklyn, Mus, 62. *Work:* Veterans Administration Hospital, Montrose, NY. *Exhib:* Artists USA, Bohman Gallery, Stockholm, Sweden, 68; 50 State Competition, Duncan Galleries, Paris, France, 68; Am Artists, Propersi Gallery D'Arte, Scarsdale, NY, 68 & 80; Propersi Galleries, Greenwich, Conn, 77-84; Conn Inst of Art Galeries, 95-01. *Collection Arranged:* American Artist (auth catalog), 68; American's 1930 (auth catalog) Depression Artists, 75. *Pos:* founder and dir, Propersi Galleria D'Art, Scarsdale, NY, 68-70; founder & pres, Propersi Galleries & Sch Art Inc, 70-84; founding pres & chmn, Conn Inst Art, 94-; chmn Conn Inst Art, 95-01. *Teaching:* Dir & instr life drawing, The Little Studio, Pelham, NY, 59-68; dir & instr fine arts, Propersi Gallerie D'Arte, 68-70; chmn fine and commercial art, Propersi Sch Art, Inc, 70-84. *Awards:* Prix d'Paris, 50 States Competition, Raymond Duncan Galleries, 68; Skills 2000 Regonition Award, Col Career Asn; Cert Achievement, Team Leader Workshop, Nat Asn Trade & Tech Schs, 86. *Bibliog:* Les Krantz (ed & publ), American Artist-an illustrated survey of contemporary Americans, 85; Who's Who in the East, Marquis, 20th ed, 86; Les Krantz (auth), American References Inc, NY Art Rev, 88. *Mem:* Artist Guild (bd dirs, 53); Am Veterans Soc Artists (bd dir, 68); Alpha Beta Kappa Hon Soc, 85. *Media:* Pastels, Oils. *Specialty:* Listed American painters and European painters--19th & 20th centuries. *Mailing Add:* 225 Magnolia Ave Mt Vernon NY 10552-3732

PROSS, LESTER FRED
PAINTER
b Bristol, Conn, Aug 14, 24. *Study:* Oberlin Col, BA, 45, MA, 46; Ohio Univ, with Ben Shahn, summer 52; Skowhegan Sch Painting & Sculpture, summer 53; with Simon, Zorach, Levine, Hebald & Bocour; Univ Colo Kyoto Sem, Japan, 75-76; study painting with Kono Shuson. *Exhib:* More than Land or Sky: Art from Appalachia, Nat Mus Am Art, Smithsonian Inst, Washington, 81-82, Traveling Exhib, 82-84; Headley-Whitney Mus, Lexington, Ky, 83, 89, Kentucky to Ecuador, 89-90; one-person shows, Ky Guild Gallery, 88, Prestonsburg Col, 90; retrospective, Doris Ulmann Galleries, Berea Col, 90; group show, Yeiser Art Ctr, Paducah, 92; Morgan Gallery, Transylvania Univ Lexington, 93; Paramount Gallery - Ashland, KY, 93; Kentucky Guild, Lexington, 94; and others. *Pos:* Bd dir, Doris Ulmann Found, 60-84; chmn adv bd, Appalachian Mus, Berea Col, 69-84. *Teaching:* Prof art, Berea Col, 46-91, chmn dept, 50-84; Fulbright lectr painting & art hist, Univ Panjab, Pakistan, 57-58; vis assoc prof art educ & hist, Union Col, summer 61; vis prof art, Am Univ Cairo, 67-68; Bryant Drake guest prof art, Kobe Col, Japan, 84-85. *Awards:* Haskell Traveling Fel, Oberlin Col, 57-58; Fulbright Lectureship, Pakistan, 57-58; Merit Award, UK Appalachian Ctr, 87. *Mem:* PKP, Berea Arts Council; fel Ky Guild Artists & Craftsmen (pres, 61-63). *Media:* Oil, Watercolor. *Publ:* Auth, Five Expressionists, Allen Mem Art Mus, Oberlin, Ohio, 46; Celebration, Berea Col, Ky, 78; illusr, The Passion, Mountain Life & Work, Berea, 51. *Dealer:* The Gallery, 114 Main St, Berea, KY 40403. *Mailing Add:* 104 Peachbloom Cir Berea KY 40403

PROVAN, DAVID
SCULPTOR
b Los Angeles, Calif, Oct 3, 48. *Study:* Yale Univ, BA, 79; Royal Col Art, MA, 81. *Work:* Univ Calif, San Diego; Ise Art Found, Tokyo; Brooklyn Union Gas Co, NY; Metrop Transportation Authority, NY; Yale Univ Art Gallery. *Comn:* Mural, Santa Barbara City Col, 77. *Exhib:* Freedom of Speech, Univ Calif, Berkeley, 90; Invitational 1990, Grace Borgenicht Gallery, NY, 90; Lyric Thought, Lyric Form, Parkland Col Art Gallery, Champaign, Ill, 92; Influenced by Architecture, Fitchburg Art Mus, Mass, 94; Cultured Pearl, Seoul Metrop Mus Art, Korea, 96. *Bibliog:* Edith Newhall (auth), Installation, New York Mag, 12/4/95; Walter Robinson (auth), Subway spinners, Art in Am, 1/96; Natasha Duré, Underground movement, Metropolis Mag, 5/96. *Mem:* Int Sculpture Ctr; Am Crafts Asn. *Media:* Welded Steel, Aluminum. *Mailing Add:* 10 Strong Pl Apt 1 Brooklyn NY 11231-3720

PROVDER, CARL
PAINTER, INSTRUCTOR
b Brooklyn, NY, Feb 7, 33. *Study:* Pratt Inst, BFA; Columbia Univ, MA, prof dipl; Inst Allende, MFA; Educ Alliance Art Sch; Art Students League; NY Univ; Acad Belli Arti, Perugia; with Samuel Adler. *Exhib:* Contemp Artists of Brooklyn, Brooklyn Mus, 72; Painters & Sculptors Soc, Jersey City Mus, NJ, 72; La Jolla Mus, 74 & 75; San Diego Mus, 75 & 79; Laguna Beach Mus, Calif, 77; and others. *Pos:* Mem, San Diego Mus Art & La Jolla Mus Contemp Art. *Teaching:* Instr fine arts, Bd Educ, New York, 64-73 & San Diego Community Col, 74-83; pvt instr, 75-; instr, Mira Costa Col, 76-77 & Mendocino Art Ctr, 80-81. *Awards:* First Prize-Mixed Media, Southern Calif Expo, Del Mar, 77 & Third Prize Mixed Media, 79; Purchase Award, Small Image Art Show, San Diego, 78-80; First Prize Painting, San Diego Art Inst Ann, 80 & Hon Mention, 81; Second Prize Painting, 82; Third Prize Painting, 83. *Bibliog:* Denise Draper (auth), An exhibit that passes the test, Coast Dispatch, 1/21/78; Richard Reilly (auth), Artist's work is from within, 1/22/78 & Joan Levine (auth), Art on a cul-de-sac, 10/19/78, San Diego Union. *Mem:* Artists Equity Asn (vpres, 76-79); San Diego Artists Guild; Soc Layerists in Multi-Media. *Media:* Oil, Mixed Media. *Publ:* Auth, A colorists approach to abstract painting, Today's Art, Vol 26, No 11, 78. *Mailing Add:* 1416 Elva Terr Encinitas CA 92024

PROVISOR, JANIS
ARCHITECT
b Brooklyn, NY, 46. *Study:* Univ Mich, Sch archit & Design, 66; Univ Cincinnati, Col Design, Art & Archit, 68; San Francisco Art Inst, BFA, 69, MFA, 71. *Work:* Albright-Knox Art Mus, Buffalo, NY; The Annex, Tucson, Ariz; Ludwig Mus, Aachen, Ger; Univ Art Mus, Berkeley, Calif; Oakland Art Mus, Calif; and others. *Comn:* Times Square Project, Proskauer Rose Goetz & Mendelsohn, NY, 91. *Exhib:* One-person exhibs, Gloria Luria Gallery, Miami, Fla, 90, Lisa Sette Gallery, Scottsdale, Ariz, 90, Dorothy Goldeen Gallery, Santa Monica, Calif, 90, Eugene Binder Gallery, Cologne, Ger, 91, San Francisco Art Inst, Calif, 91, Barbara Toll, NY, 92, Timothy Brown Fine Art, Aspen, Colo, 92, Plum Blossoms Gallery, Art Asia Hong Kong, 93 & Dorothy Goldeen Gallery, Santa Monica, Calif, 93; Contemp Prints, Gallery 44, 90, 20th Anniversary Visiting Artist Prog, Univ Art Gallery, Colo Univ, Boulder, 92; Post Earthquake Prints, Crown Point Press, San Francisco, Calif, 90; The Common Wealth Exhibition, Roanoke Mus Fine Art, Va, 90; Woodcuts, Crown Point Press, 90, The Tree, Elysium Art Gallery, 91, Sheh Zand Proj, NY, 92; Works on Paper, Timothy Brown Fine Arts, Aspen, Colo, 91; Presswork: The Art of Women Printmakers, Nat Mus Women in the Arts, Washington, DC, 91; Vital Forces, Hecksher Mus, Huntington, NY, 91; Miniatures, Lisa Sette Gallery, Scottsdale, Ariz, 92; Big Ideas, Tucson Mus Art, Ariz, 92; Abstract Paintings, Dorothy Goldeen Gallery, Santa Monica, Calif, 92. *Teaching:* Vis artist, Anderson Ranch Arts Ctr, Snowmass, Colo, 90 & 92, State Univ NY, Purchase, 92. *Awards:* Ford Found Grant, Univ Tex, 78; Nat Endowment Arts, Individual Artist's Fel, 80, 85 & 91; Colo Coun Arts & Humanities Fel, 88. *Bibliog:* B A M (auth), Anish Kapoor, Janis Provisor, Crown Point Press, Art News, 4/92; Allan Schwartzman (auth), Landscapes of the Mind, Aspen Mag, midsummer 92; Jane Wilson (auth), Artist Comes 'Home' with New Work, Aspen Times, 8/8/92. *Mailing Add:* c/o Crown Point Press Gallery 20 Hawthorne St San Francisco CA 94105

PROWN, JULES DAVID
ART HISTORIAN
b Freehold, NJ, Mar 14, 30. *Study:* Lafayette Col, AB, 51; Harvard Univ, AM(fine arts), 53; Univ Del, AM(early Am cult), 56; Harvard Univ, PhD(fine arts), 61. *Hon Degrees:* Yale Univ, Hon AM, 71; Lafayette Col, Hon DFA, 79. *Collection Arranged:* John Singleton Copley Exhib (auth, catalog), 65-66 & American Art from Alumni Collections, 68, Yale Univ Art Gallery; travelling exhib, 65-66 & American Art from Alumni Collections, 68, Yale Univ Art Gallery. *Pos:* Asst to dir, William Hayes Fogg Art Mus, Harvard Univ, 59-61; cur, Garvan & Related Collections of Am Art, Yale Univ, New Haven, 63-68; dir, Yale Ctr Brit Art, New Haven, 68-76; assoc dir, Nat Humanities Inst, New Haven, 77. *Teaching:* Fel art hist, Harvard Univ, Cambridge, Mass, 56-57; from instr to prof, Yale Univ, 61-86, Paul Mellon prof hist of art, 86-99, Paul Mellon prof emeritus, 99-. *Awards:* Guggenheim Fel, 64-65; Blanche Elizabeth MacLeish Billings Award, Yale Univ, 66; Robert C Smith Award, Soc Arch Historians, 83; George Washington Kidd Award, Lafayette Col, 86; Iris Found Award for Outstanding Contbns to the Decorative Arts, Bard Grad Ctr for Studies in the Decorative Arts, 01; Lawrence A Fleischman Award for Scholarly Excellence in Field of Am Art Hist, 01; William Clyde DeVale Award for scholarship and teaching, Phi Beta Kappa, Yale Univ, 2005. *Mem:* Am Soc 18th Century Studies (exec bd mem, 73-76); Col Art Asn (bd dir, 75-79); Benjamin Franklin Fel Royal Soc Arts; Am Antiquarian Soc (mem coun, 77-94). *Res:* American and English art; John Singleton Copley; Benjamin West; Winslow Homer; material culture. *Publ:* Thomas Eakins' Baby at Play, Studies in the History of Art, Nat Gallery Art, Washington, Vol 18, 121-7, 85; Benjamin West's Family Picture: A Nativity in Hammersmith, in John Wilmerding, ed, Essays in Honor of Paul Mellon, Washington, 269-81, 86; Charles Willson Peale in London, Charles Willson Peale: New Perspectives, A 250th Anniversary Celebration, Univ Pittsburgh Press, 91; Expedition against the Ohio Indians under Colonel Bouquet: Two Early Drawings by Benjamin West, in Guilland Sutherland, ed, British Art 1740-1820: Essays in Honor of Robert R Wark, Huntington Library, 92; The Truth of Material Culture: History or Fiction, in Steven Lubor and W David Kingery, eds, History from Things: Essays on Material Culture, Smithsonian Inst Press, 93; John Singleton Copley, 2 vols, 66; American Painting from Its Beginnings to the Armory Show, 69; The Architecture of the Yale Center for British Art, 77; Art as Evidence: Writings on Art and Material Culture, 02. *Mailing Add:* Dept Art Hist Box 208272 Yale Univ New Haven CT 06520

PRUITT, LYNN
SCULPTOR, ASSEMBLAGE ARTIST
b Washington, DC, May 24, 37. *Work:* Marlboro Hall, Prince George Com Col, Largo, Md. *Comn:* Sculptured canvas wall relief, Naval Acad, Annapolis, Md, 76. *Exhib:* Corcoran Gallery Art, Washington, DC, 65 & 72; one-person shows, Md Artists Today, East Coast Univ Tour, Baltimore Mus, 75 & 76, Nat Audubon Soc, Chevy Chase, Md, 77 & Nourse Gallery, Washington, DC, 80; Am Chairs, Form, Function & Fantasy, John Michael Kohler Arts Ctr, Sheboygan, Wis, 78; Washington Proj for the Arts, DC, 80; and others. *Pos:* Juror, Prince George's Community Col, 72-75, Nat Inst Health, 73-75, Md Col Art, 76 & Scholastic Art Awards, Washington, DC, Md & Va, 77-78; dir & consult, Holden Gallery, Inc, Kensington, Md, 76-. *Teaching:* Instr basic art, Jewish Community Ctr, Rockville, Md, 74-. *Awards:* First in Painting, 68, 69 & 70, Best in Show, 68, 69 & 70 & First in Sculpture, 70, 71, 73 & 74, Nat Inst Health, Bethesda, Md. *Mem:* Washington Womens Arts Ctr; Am Crafts Coun. *Media:* Plaster. *Dealer:* Nourse Gallery Washington DC 20013. *Mailing Add:* 12806 Poplar St Silver Spring MD 20904

PRUITT, ROBERT A
ARTIST
b Houston, Tex, 75. *Study:* S Tex Univ, BFA; Univ Austin Tex, MFA. *Exhib:* This do in Remembrance of Me, 2005; group shows at Splat Boom Pow!: The Influence of Cartoons in Contemp Art, Contemp Art Mus; Come Forward: Emerging Art in Tex, Dallas Mus Art; Whitney Biennial: Day for Night, Whitney Mus Am Art, 2006; I Call My Brother Sun Because He Shines Like One, Clementine Gallery, NYC. *Pos:* Mem Otabenga Jones & Assoc, Houston, 2002; arts coord, Project Row Houses. *Awards:* Recipient Artadia Award, 2004. *Mailing Add:* Project Row Houses 2500 Holman PO Box 1011 Houston TX 77251-1011

PRUNEDA, MAX
SCULPTOR
b Laredo, Tex, 48. *Study:* Univ Tex, Austin, BFA, 73. *Exhib:* One-person shows, Brigitte Schluger Gallery, Denver, Colo, 89 & 91, Gallery Elena, Taos, NMex, 89, 90 & 91, Quintana Gallery, Portland, Ore, 89, 90, 91 & 92, Ralph Greene Gallery, Albuquerque, NMex, 92-, Bentley Gallery, Scottsdale, Ariz, 94-, Okun Gallery, Santa Fe, NMex, 94- & Art of the People, Portland, Ore, 98; Gallery Elena, Taos, NMex, 92; Gudalajara Int Book Fair, Mex, 94; Klein Horowitz Gallery, Santa Fe, 95 & 96; Gallery 10, Carefree, Ariz, 97; Crossing Cultures, Lewallen Contemp Gallery, Santa Fe, 98; Pedestals and Stretchers, Lewallen Contemp Gallery, Santa Fe, 98; and others. *Awards:* Nat Endowment Arts Fel, 88; Cult Arts Coun Houston Grant, 89. *Bibliog:* Mag of Arts, 1/94; Wesley Pulkka (auth), Renacimiento, NU-CITY, 11/93; Raquel Tibol & Maria Elena Alvarez (auth), Critic digs deep into New Mexican art, Albuquerque J, 12/11/94. *Dealer:* Art of the People Portland OR. *Mailing Add:* 2226 C Los Padillas Rd SW Albuquerque NM 87105-7168

PRYSTAUK, ELISSA
PAINTER
Study: Rutgers Univ, BFA; Newark Sch Fine and Indust Art; Sch Visual Arts, NY; Urbino Univ, Italy. *Exhib:* Am Artist Prof League; 74th Grand Nat Show, Salmagundi Club; John Stobart Gallery, Martha's Vineyard; Cropsey Mus, Hudson Valley; Salmagundi Club, Catharine Lorillard Wolfe Art Club, Pastel Soc Am, Pen & Brush. *Awards:* Edward Tadeliss Mem Award, Community Arts Asn Nat Show. *Bibliog:* aritcles, The Best of Oil Painting, Savvy Living Mag & Morris Mag. *Mem:* Salmagundi Club, NY; signature mem, Pastel Soc Am (PSA). *Media:* Pastels and Oils. *Interests:* Traveling the local countryside as well as abroad. *Mailing Add:* 20 Knox Hill Rd Morristown NJ 07960-3502

PUCKER, BERNARD H
ART DEALER
b Kansas City, Mo, Oct 19, 37. *Study:* Columbia Univ, BA, 59; Hebrew Univ, Jerusalem, 60; Brandeis Univ, MA, 66. *Pos:* Dir, Pucker Gallery, Boston, currently. *Mem:* St Botolph Club. *Specialty:* Contemporary artists; Chagall graphics; Israeli artist Bak, Sharir; New England artists such as Ali and Jim Schantz; fantastic realist artists like Shigeru Matsuzaki; Southern African works; bronzes by David Aronson, Igor Galanin, porcelains by Brother Thomas, Tetsuzo Shinzaka Hamzar, W Tsuchiya, K Masuzaki; photogs Baking, Marin Mutter

PUCKETT, RICHARD EDWARD
PAINTER
b Klamath Falls, Ore, Sept 9, 32. *Study:* Southern Ore of Educ; Lakeforest Col; Univ of San Fran, BA. *Teaching:* Instr, Ft Sheriden Arts & Crafts, 1957-68; instr, Camp Irwin, Calif, 1958-60; instr, Ft Ord Arts & crafts Cntr, Calif, 1960-86. *Awards:* First place sculpture, Monterey Fair, 1979; third place sculpture, Monterey Fair, 1979; first place Army, Dept of Army Shown at Smithsonian Mus, 1978-85. *Mem:* Salimas Valley Art Assoc, (pres, 2000-2003); Monteren Mus of Art; Int Soc of Acrylic Painters. *Media:* Acrylic, Oil. *Interests:* Art, history, antiques & gardening. *Collection:* Over 800 paintings, graphics, art objects & antiques. *Dealer:* Sasoontsi Gallery 40 Central Ave Salinas Calif 93901. *Mailing Add:* 210 San Miguel Ave Salinas CA 93901-3021

PUETT, GARNETT G
SCULPTOR
b Hahira, Ga, 59. *Study:* Uni Wash, Seattle, BA, 81. *Work:* Brooklyn Mus, NY; Edward R Broida Trust Collection, Calif; First Nat Bank Chicago Collection; Hirshhorn Mus & Sculpture Garden, Washington, DC; Laumier Sculpture Park, St Louis, Mo. *Exhib:* Solo exhibs, Univ Wash, Seattle, Wash, 81 & 83, Laumier Sculpture Park, St Louis, Mo, 87, Glenn/Dask Gallery, Los Angeles, Calif, 89, Pittsburgh Ctr Arts, 90 & Southwest Ctr Contemp Arts, Winston-Salem, NC, 93; Galerie Georges Verney, Carron, Villeurbanne, France, 89; Lead and Wax, Stephen Wirtz Gallery, San Francisco, Calif, 90; Curt Marcus Gallery, NY, 91; Transformers: A Moving Experience, Auckland Art Gallery, NZ, 96; and others. *Awards:* Nat Endowment Arts, 88. *Bibliog:* Ingrid Schaffner (auth), Flash Art Int, 1-2/89; Eric Gibson (auth), Decade in review, Sculpture, 5-6/89; The Sciences, 3-4/92; and others

PUGH, GRACE HUNTLEY
PAINTER, ART HISTORIAN
b Schenectady, NY, Sept 25, 12. *Study:* Wellesley Col, 30-32; Barnard Col, BA(fine arts), 34; Nat Acad Design, with Leon Kroll, Charles Hinton & Ivan Olinsky, 34-36; with Samantha Littlefield Huntley, 34-38; Parsons Sch Design, summer 37; Art Students League, with Reginald Marsh, summer 38. *Work:* Barnard Col; 100 Friends of Pittsburgh Art & Montefiore Hosp, Pittsburgh; Mamaroneck Free Libr, NY; Westchester Co Art in Pub Places, White Plains, NY. *Comn:* Harbor mural, St Thomas Episcopal Church, Mamaroneck, 63-66; paintings, Mamaroneck Harbor, Dime Savings Bank, Mamaroneck, 75, Mill Stream, Harrison, NY, 76 & Scarsdale Summer, Scarsdale, NY, 77. *Exhib:* Artist Equity Exhib, Whitney Mus Am Art, NY, 51 & Riverside Mus, NY, 53; NY State Painters, NY State Bldg-World's Fair, Flushing, 65 & Butler Art Inst, Pa; one-woman shows, Sails, Wildcliff Mus, New Rochelle, NY, 75 & Rockport Art Asn, Mass, 76 & 80; Franklin & Marshall Col, 74, Pa; Gloucester Sawyer Libr, 78, Mass; 13 Artist Exhib, Rockport Art Asn, Mass, 93; 36th Nat Open Juried Exhib, Mamaroneck Artists Guild, 94; and others. *Pos:* Chmn art, Mamaroneck Free Libr, 50-87; artist-in-residence & adv fine arts, Village of Mamaroneck, 77-; first chmn, Mamaroneck Hist Preserv Adv Comt, archit art, 82. *Teaching:* Artist-in-residence & head dept art, Briarcliff Jr Col, Briarcliff Manor, NY, 36-40; art instr, Westchester Co Workshop, White Plains, 61-63. *Awards:* Grace Huntley Pugh Day, Village Mamaroneck, with commendation from Pres Bush, 10/17/82 & 6/14/91; Cert, Federated Conservationists Westchester Co, NY, 91; 50 Year Cert Appreciation, Rockport Art Asn, 94. *Bibliog:* Jim Kinter (auth), Show mirrors artist's strong moods, Intel J Newspaper, 74; Herb Rosoff (auth), The pro's nest meet with Grace Huntley Pugh, Palette Talk Mag, 77. *Mem:* Am Watercolor Soc; Rockport Art Asn; Mamaroneck Artists Guild (pres, 53-55, 61-63, dir, 53-80); Artists Equity. *Media:* Oil, Watercolor. *Publ:* auth, Buoy 16, Mamaroneck Harbor, Village of Mamaroneck; illusr, Sound Seasonings (cookbook), Jr League Westchester, NY, 90; 10 Year Recognition as Creator/producer/host of Down Memory Lane (film), Mamaroneck Hist Soc, 94; illusr, Rebuilding the Pigeon Cove Breakwater, Town Rockport Ann Report, Mass, 94; auth, The Last 100 Years, Village of Mamaroneck Centennial Book-Celebration, 95; and others. *Mailing Add:* 823 Stuart Ave Mamaroneck NY 10543

PUJOL, ELLIOTT
EDUCATOR, MEDALIST
b Memphis, Tenn, June 4, 43. *Study:* Southern Ill Univ, BS(theatre), 68, with Brent Kington, MFA(art), 71; Penland Sch, with Arline Fisch, 70. *Work:* Minn Mus Art, St Paul; Sheldon Mem Art Gallery, Lincoln, Nebr; Topeka Public Libr; Wichita Art Mus; Louisiana Sch Visually Impaired; Samuel Dorsky Mus of Art, New Paltz, NY. *Comn:* Pendulum (sculpture), Kansas State Univ Col Eng, 83. *Exhib:* Brookfield Craft Ctr, Conn, 80; Basketry: Tradition in New Form, Traveling Exhib, Inst Contemp Art, Boston, Mass, Cooper-Hewitt Mus, NY & Greenville Co Mus Art, NC, 83; Super Bowls - Gallery Eight, La Jolla, Calif, 88; Am Craft at the Armory, NY, 88; Univ of Ore Mus of Art Traveling Metals Exhib, 88-89; Fiber/Metal Invitational USA 1992, Craft Alliance Gallery, St Louis; Kansas Chooses Kansas II, Mulvane Art Mus, Topeka; Steel City: Contemp Am in Metal, Sangre de Crist Arts Ctr, Pueblo Co; and others. *Collection Arranged:* First Blacksmith Conference, Carbondale, Ill, 70; Third National Student Metal International (auth, catalog), Tyler Sch Art, 72; Summer Vail Metal Symposium, Colo, 74; American Metal Work (auth, catalog), Sheldon Mem Art Gallery, 76; First National Ring Show, Athens, Ga & Manhattan, Kans, 77; Kansas Artist Craftsmen Assoc Exhib & Conference, Manhattan Arts Ctr, KS, 05. *Pos:* Guest artist, Penland Sch, NC, 71, 73, 76, 79, 89, 92, 96 & 03, Arrowmont Sch, Gatlinburg, Tenn, 73, 79, 86 & 92 Brookfield Craft Sch, Conn, 73, 76 & 79, Summer Vail, Colo, 74-84 & 47th Ann Conf Mid Am Col Art Asn, St Louis. *Teaching:* Instr jewelry & silversmithing, Tyler Sch Art, Philadelphia, 71-73; prof metalsmithing, Kans State Univ, Manhattan, 73-; studies abroad, Univ Ga, Cortona, Italy, 93. *Awards:* First Place, Mus Contemp Crafts, Copper Develop Asn, 71; 50 Outstanding Craftsmen, Penland Sch, Nat Endowment for Arts, 71; Purchase Award, Renwick Gallery, DC, 74; Master Metalsmith, Nat Ornamental Metal Mus, Memphis, Tenn, 2005. *Bibliog:* Philip Morton (auth), Contemporary Jewelry, Holt, Rinehart, Winston, 70; Oppi Untracht (auth), Jewelry Concepts and Techniques, Doubleday, 71; plus var newspaper articles. *Mem:* Am Crafts Coun; Artist Blacksmith Asn NAm; Kans Artist Craftsmen Asn (pres, 96-98); Soc NAm Goldsmiths. *Media:* All. *Res:* Argentium Sterling Silver. *Dealer:* J Cotter Gallery Vail CO 81657. *Mailing Add:* 2002 Rockhill Cir Manhattan KS 66502

PUJOL, ERNESTO
PAINTER
b Havana, Cuba, 57. *Study:* Universidad de Puerto Rico, Rio Piedras, BA(visual arts), 79. *Work:* Bronx Coun Arts, Longwood, NY; Int Univ, Miami; Mus Art, Ft Lauderdale, Fla; Asociacion de Artistas Plasticos de Cuba, Havana; El Museo del Barrio, NY. *Exhib:* Solo exhibs, Experimento en Tematica Religiosa, Taller D'Jevarez, San Juan, PR, 84, New Work, Cavin-Morris, NY, 93, Installations, Int Arts Relations, NY, 94, Taxonomies, Galeria Ramis Barquet, Monterrey, Mex, 95, The Children of Peter Pan, Casa de las Americas, Havana, Cuba, 95, Collapses, Frederic Snitzer Gallery, Miami, Fla, 95 & Winter, Iturralde Gallery, Los Angeles, 96; One Hundred Hearts, Nat Arts Club, NY, 90; 11th Ann Exhib, Bronx Mus Arts, NY, 91; Material Revisions, Brattleboro Art Mus, Vt, 92; Paper Visions V, Housatonic Mus Art, Bridgeport, Conn, 94; Inquisitive Art, Reed Col Art Gallery, Portland, Ore, 94; Iconography of Exile, Seton Hill Col, Pa, 95; Other Choices Other Voices, Islip Art Mus, Long Island, NY, 95, & Recent Acquisitions, 96; Reaffirming Spirituality, El Museo del Barrio, NY, 95; Boat Images from South Fla Collections, Miami-Dade Pub Libr, 95; The House Project, Mus Contemp Art, Los Angeles, 95; Cuba Siglo XX - Modernidad y Sincretismo, Centro Atlantico de Arte Moderno, Las Palmas, 96; and others. *Awards:* Cintas Found Fel, Arts Int, Inst Int Educ, NY, 91; Visual Arts Fel, Pollock-Krasner Found, NY, 93; Reg Painting Fel, Mid Atlantic Arts Found/Nat Endowment Arts, Baltimore, Md, 94. *Bibliog:* Yolanda Woods (auth), Ernesto Pujol - Signos de la Memoria, Revista Casa, Havana, Cuba, 95; Ruth Behar (auth), Bridges to Cuba, Puentes a Cuba, Univ Mich Press, 95; Victoria Looseleaf (auth), Home is where the heart is, Los Angeles Downtown News, 11/27/95. *Mailing Add:* 210 Dean St Brooklyn NY 11217-2298

PULITZER , EMILY RAUH
COLLECTOR, CONSULTANT
b Cincinnati, Ohio, July 23, 33. *Study:* Bryn Mawr Col, AB, 55; Ecole du Louvre, Paris, student, 56; Harvard Univ, MA, 63. *Hon Degrees:* Univ Mo, LHD, 89; Aquinas Inst, St Louis, DFA, 2002; St Louis Univ, DFA, 2003; Washington Univ, St Louis, HHD, 2005. *Pos:* Mem staff, Cincinnati Art Mus, 56-57; asst cur drawings Fogg Art

Mus, Harvard, 57-64, asst to dir, 62-63; cur, City Art Mus, St Louis, 64-73; mem painting and sculpture comt, Mus Modern Art, 75-; chmn visual arts comt, Mo Arts Coun, 76-81; bd dir, Mark Rothko Found, 76-88, Grand Ctr, 93-95, 99-, St. Louis Symphony Orchestra, 94-; co-chmn, fel Fogg Art Mus, 78-; memr bd, Inst Mus Serv's, 79-84; bd dir, Forum, St Louis, 80-, pres, 90-94; comnr, St Louis Art Mus, 81-88, vchmn, 88; chmn, collections comt Harvard Univ Arts Mus, 92-; bd dir, Pulitzer Inc, currently. *Awards:* Recipient St Louis award for contrib to arts community, 2003; Named one of Top 200 Collectors, ARTnews Mag, 2003-06. *Mem:* Am Fedn Arts (dir, 76-89); St Louis Mercantile Libr Asn (bd dir, 87-93); Mo Women's Forum. *Collection:* Abstract expressionism, cubism & post impressionism art

PUNIA, CONSTANCE EDITH
PAINTER
b Brooklyn, NY. *Study:* Brooklyn Mus Art Sch; oil with Edwin Dickinson & Yonia Fain; oil and sumi-e with Murray Hantman. *Exhib:* Les Surindependants, Paris, 75; Grand Prix Humanitaire de France, Paris, 75; Des Artistes Francais, Grand Palais, Paris, France, 76 & 77; Sun Yat Sen Ctr of Asian Studies at St John's Univ, Jamaica, NY, 76; Nat A Arts Club, New York, NY, 77; Meridien House Int, Washington, DC, 86. *Awards:* Silver Medal & Laureate of Honor, Grand Prix Humanitaire de France, 75; Bronze Medal, Akad Raymond Duncan, 75; Order of Merit Medal, Acad of Sci & Human Rels, Dominican Repub; Palme D'Or. *Mem:* Nat League Am Pen Women; Sumi-E Soc Am. *Media:* Oil, Sumi-e. *Mailing Add:* 519 Magnolia Ave Brielle NJ 08730

PUNIELLO, FRANCOISE SARA
LIBRARIAN
b Boston, Mass, June 3, 47. *Study:* RI Col, BA, 69; Rutgers State Univ NJ, MLS, 70, MA(art hist), 77. *Pos:* Assoc dir pub service, Douglass Lib, 85-88; dir, Mabel Smith Douglass Libr, 88-97; assoc dir, New Brunswick Campus Librs, Rutgers Univ, 97-2003; acting dir, New Brunswick Campus Libr, 2003. *Mem:* Am Libr Asn (art section). *Res:* Women artists and how to research their lives and works. *Interests:* Women artists. *Publ:* Auth, Elsie Driggs in Past and Promise: Lives of New Jersey Women, Scarecrow, 90; Women Painters born after 1900 in Women Artists in the United States, GK Hall, 90; coauth, Abstract Expressionist Women Painters: An Annotated Bibliography, Scarecrow Press, Lantham, Md, 96. *Mailing Add:* 302 Harrison Ave Highland Park NJ 08904

PURA, WILLIAM PAUL
PRINTMAKER, PAINTER
b Winnipeg, Man, Dec 19, 48. *Study:* Sch Art, Univ Man, BFA, 70; Ind Univ, Bloomington, MFA, 73. *Work:* Art Bank, Can Coun, Ottawa, Ont; Miller Brewing Co, Milwaukee, Wis; Prudential Life Insurance Co, Minneapolis; Gallery III, Univ Man, Winnipeg; Wilfred Laurier Univ, Kitchener, Ont. *Exhib:* Solo exhibs, Gallery III, Univ Man, Winnipeg, 80, Ukrainian Inst Mod Art, Chicago, 84 & Winnipeg Art Gallery, 85; Virginia Beach Art Ctr, Va, 79; Charlotte Printmakers, NC, 79; Contemp Can Printmaking, Australia, 85-86. *Teaching:* Prof, Sch Art, Univ Man, 73-. *Awards:* Print & Drawing Coun Can, Opus Frames Ltd, Vancouver, 80; Art Ventures Grant, Man Arts Coun, 85; Explorations Grant, Can Coun, 86. *Mem:* Man Printmakers Asn; Can Artists Representation. *Media:* Lithography; Acrylic, Oil. *Publ:* Auth, A quiet in the land, Arts Manitoba, spring 85; George Flynn interview, Border Crossings, winter, 88. *Dealer:* Can Art Galleries 110 8th Ave SW Calgary AB T2P 1B3; The New Van Straaten Gallery 742 N Wells St Chicago IL 60610. *Mailing Add:* Univ Man Dept Art Winnipeg MB R3T 2N2 Canada

PURCELL, ANN
PAINTER
b Arlington, Va, Nov 18, 41. *Study:* Corcoran Sch Art, DC; George Washington Univ, BA (fine arts), 73; NY Univ, MA (lib studies), 95. *Work:* Corcoran Gallery Art, Washington; Phillips Collection, Washington; Albright-Knox Mus, Buffalo, NY; Nat Gallery Art, Washington; Milwaukee Art Mus; and others. *Exhib:* 19th Area Exhib, Corcoran Gallery Art, Washington, 74; one-woman show, 5 Washington Artists, 76 & Corcoran Fac Exhib, 76; Group Show, Selected, Southern Alleghenies Mus Art, Loretto, Pa, 78; 5 Artists, Mus Fine Arts, St Petersburg, Fla, 78; Selected Works from Tibor de Nagy, Mint Mus, Charlotte, NC, 79; plus many others. *Collection Arranged:* Nat Gallery Art; Phillips Collection; Nat Mus Women in the Arts; and others. *Teaching:* Instr painting & drawing, Smithsonian Inst, Washington, 74-78, Corcoran Sch Art, 74-79, Parsons Sch Art & Design, 83-. *Bibliog:* Jane Livingston (auth), Five Washington Artists, Garamond Press, 76; article, Arts, 11/83. *Mem:* New York Artists Equity Asn; Col Art Asn. *Media:* Acrylic. *Dealer:* Tibor de Nagy Gallery 29 W 57th St New York NY 10019; Osuna Gallery 2121 P St NW Washington DC 20037. *Mailing Add:* 155 Henry St 8F Brooklyn NY 11201-2563

PURDUM, REBECCA
PAINTER
b Idaho Falls, Idaho, June 16, 59. *Study:* St Martins Sch Art, London, Eng 80; Skowhegan Sch Painting & Sculpture, Maine, 81; Syracuse Univ, NY, BFA, 81. *Work:* Munson Williams-Proctor Inst, Utica, NY; List Visual Arts Ctr, Mass Inst Technol, Cambridge, Mass; Mus Mod Art, Ft Worth, Tex; Herbert F Johnson Mus Art, Cornell Univ, Ithaca, NY. *Exhib:* 10 plus 10: Contemp Soviet & Am Painters, Mod Art Mus Ft Worth, traveling exhib, San Francisco Mus Art, Albright-Knox Gallery, Corcoran Gallery, Moscow, Tbilisi & Leningrad, 89-90; Jack Tilton Gallery, NY, 89, 91, 93, 95, 98 & 2000; List Visual Arts Ctr, Mass Inst Technol, 90; Whitney Biennial, NY, 91; Repicturing Abstraction, Va Mus Fine Arts, Anderson Gallery, Marsh Gallery & 1708 Gallery, Richmond; The Poetic Object: Paintings of Rebecca Purdum, Marywood Univ, Scranton, Pa, 97; After the Fall, Snug Harbor Ctr, Staten Island, NY, 97; After Nature, Herter Arts Gallery, Univ Mass, Amherst; one-man show, Lebanon Valley Col Mus Art, Annville, Pa; No Greater Love: Abstraction, Tilton/Kustera Gallery, NY, 02; Regional Selections 30, Hood Mus, Dartmouth Mus, Hanover, NH, 03; Tilton Gallery, 2005. *Awards:* Eugene M McDermitt Award, Mass Inst Technol; Louis Comfort Tiffany Found Award; Joan Mitchell Found Grant, 2005. *Bibliog:* Mary Haus (auth), Rebecca Purdum, Artnews; Wendy Beckett (auth), The Mystical Now Art and The Sacred, Universe Press; Rebecca Purdum, New Yorker, 4/2000, 10/2001. *Media:* Oil. *Dealer:* Jack Tilton Gallery 8 East 76th St, NY. *Mailing Add:* PO Box 20 Ripton VT 05766

PURDY, DONALD R
PAINTER
b Conn, Apr 10, 24. *Study:* Univ Conn, BA; Boston Univ, MA. *Work:* New Britain Mus; Colby Col; Chase Manhattan Bank Collection; Univ Kans; Chrysler Mus; Butler Inst, Ohio. *Exhib:* USA Int Show; Silvermine Guild Artists; Audubon Artists; Allied Artists Am; Hudson Valley Exhib, 85. *Awards:* Gold Medal, Allied Artists Am; First Prize, Silvermine Guild Artists; Jane Peterson Award, Audubon Artists; Hudson Valley Award. *Bibliog:* F Whitaker (auth), article, Am Artist. *Mem:* Am Fedn Arts; Allied Artists Am; Silvermine Guild Artists. *Media:* Oil. *Collection:* American and Barbizon; Impressionist. *Dealer:* Hammer Gallery E 57th St New York NY 10022; Flemington Art Gallery Main St Flemington NJ 08822; Greenwich Gallery 6 West Putnam Ave Greenwich CT 06830. *Mailing Add:* 70 Poverty Hollow Rd Newtown CT 06470-1872

PURDY, HENRY CARL
PAINTER, EDUCATOR
b Wolfville, NS, Nov 6, 37. *Study:* NS Col Art, Halifax, assoc, 58. *Work:* Confederation Ctr Arts, Island Art Collection, Charlottetown, PEI; Dofasco Steel, Hamilton, Ont; NB Mus, St John; Art Ctr Gallery, Univ NB, Fredericton; PEI Mutual Fire Insurance. *Comn:* carved wooden mural, Can Coast Guard Col, Sydney, NS, 81; carved sculpture, St Assissi Church, 90; stained glass window, Trinity United & Southport Church, 90-91; Royal Can Mounted Police Hq, PEI; Queen Elizabeth Hosp, PEI. *Exhib:* Ars Sacra Int, St Mary's Art Gallery, Halifax, 79; Maritime Art Asn, Eptek Exhib Ctr, Summerside, PEI, 79; Royal Can Acad Arts Ann, Toronto Exhib Ctr, 80; Between Two Islands, Visby Art Gallery, Sweden, 81; solo exhib, St John City Hall Gallery, NB, 83; and over 100 other exhibs through 97; Designed gold coin, Royal Canadian Mint, 99. *Collection Arranged:* Island Visual Artists, 82 & 83. *Pos:* Mem, Can Coun, 84-90; bd mem, Confedn Ctr Arts, 84-91; task force mem, Higher Educ Arts, Can, 92-93. *Teaching:* Instr commercial design, Holland Col, 69-77; dir art & crafts, Sch Visual Arts, 77-92; private instr painting & drawing, 92-. *Awards:* Centennial Awards, Gold Medal Sculpture, 63 & Gold Arts Medal, 73, Prov PEI; Outstanding Craftsperson, PEI, 92; FRA Arsenault Sr Arts Award, PEI, 96; 125 commemorative medals, Govt Can. *Bibliog:* Pat Murphy (auth), Look out, Here comes Henry Purdy, Axiom Mag, 3/76; Rich Smith (dir), Henry Purdy--Artist (video), Confederation Ctr Arts, 78; various newspaper articles. *Mem:* Royal Can Acad Art (elected 78, vpres Atlantic region, 78-84); Can Soc Educ Through Art; PEI Crafts Coun (pres, 96-97); Royal Soc Arts; PEI Coun Arts (chmn bd, 78-83). *Media:* Acrylic, Welded Steel. *Interests:* photography, teacing, nature. *Publ:* Auth, Me Too, Holland Press, 74; illusr, Icons of Poverty & Riches, 81 & Francis, 83, A Arsenault; contribr, Sand Patterns--A Commemorative Issue, Sand Patterns Group, 83; illusr, PEI Sketchbook, 81; auth, Epigrammatically Yours Adrien, 91. *Mailing Add:* 6 St Peters Rd Charlottetown PE C1A 5N2 Canada

PURI, ANTONIO
PAINTER
b Chandigarh, India. *Study:* Academy of Art, San Francisco, Calif, 1986; Coe Co, IA, BA, 1989; Univ of IA, Col of Law, JD, 1995. *Exhib:* Foot in the Door, Minneapolis Inst of Art, Minneapolis, Mnn, 2000; Four Visions, Bergen Mus of Art, Paramus, NJ, 2004; Outside the Mandala, Philadelphia Art Alliance, Philadelphia, Pa, 2005; Path of Technology & Cosmology, Noyes Mus of Art, Oceanville, NJ, 2006; Micro to Macro, W Chester Univ, W Chester, Pa, 2006. *Collection Arranged:* Noyes Mus, NJ; Bergen Mus of Art & Sci, NJ; Planet Art Mus, S Africa; Post & Schell, Philadelphia, Pa; Ritz Theatre, NJ. *Media:* Acrylic, Oil, All Media. *Dealer:* Heineman Myers Comtemp Art Bethesda MD; Robert Roman Gallery, Scottsdale, AZ. *Mailing Add:* 1001 White Horse Pike Haddon Township NJ 08107

PURNELL, ROBIN BARKER
PAINTER
b Norwood, Mass, Jul 5, 51. *Study:* Mass Col Art, BFA, 71; Samos Sch Art, studied with Aristotle Solunias, 73-74; Mukina Inst Art, Ste Petersburg, Russia, studied with Alexander Kondractieu, 99-2000. *Hon Degrees:* Mass Col Art, Honors, 75. *Work:* Rappahannock Pub Libr, Wash, Va. *Comn:* Mary Mochary, Nat Mus of Women in Arts; Linda Dietel, Wife of former headmaster of Emma Ward Sch; Jon Purnell, Am Ambassador to Uzbekistan; Ambassador & Mrs Julius Walker, Ambassador to West Africa; many more. *Exhib:* Portrait Exhib, Soviet Cult Found, St Petersburg, Russia, 91; Painters St Petersburg, Hermitage Mus, Russia, 91; One Woman Show, Dostoyevsky Mus, St Petersburg, Russia, 92, Catherine's Palace, Catherine's Palace, Pushkin, Russia, 92, Walker Arts Ctr, Woodberry Forrest, Orange, Va, 97; Russian Artists, Anna Gallery, Brussels Belgium, 92; Journey's, Kasteey Mus, Almaty, Kazakstan, 99; Summer Exhib, Royal Acad Art, London, 2002; group exhib, Mass Col Art, 72-74, Middle St Gallery, Wash, Va, 86-98, 90 & 93, Ariadna Gallery, St Petersburg, Russia, 92, Kasteev Mus, Almaty, Kazakhstan, 99, Royal Acad Arts, London, Eng, 2002,. *Pos:* Display dir, Lodge at Harvard Sq, Boston, Mass, 75-78. *Teaching:* instr, life drawing, anatomy, Middle St Gallery Wash, Va, 86-87, instr, origami workshop, 86; instr, pastel poortraiture, Artists Studio Wash Va, 87-88. *Bibliog:* B Martinenko (auth), Robin B Purnell, Evening Leningrad News, 5/91; Dr Vacheslau Mukin (auth), Robin B Purnell, Universal Commodity Exchange, 9/92;

Janet Wilson (auth), From Russia with Love, Wash Post, 6/19/93. *Mem:* Middle St Gallery Wash, Va (bd dir, 86-87); Ki Theatre, Wash, Va (bd dir, 86-87); RAAC, Rappahannocr Asn for Arts in Community (bd dir, 87-88); Artists Group, Wash, Va (founder, 2001-05). *Media:* All Media, Lecturer. *Dealer:* Robin B Purnell PO Box 416 Washington Va 22747. *Mailing Add:* PO Box 416 Washington VA 22747

PURTLE, CAROL JEAN
HISTORIAN, EDUCATOR
b St Louis, Mo, Feb 20, 39. *Study:* Maryville Univ, St Louis, BA(magna cum laude), 60; Manhattanville Col, MA, 66; Washington Univ, St Louis, PhD, 76. *Teaching:* Instr art hist, Washington Univ, St Louis, 70-76; assoc prof art & coordr art hist, Univ Memphis, 77-93, prof art, 94-; instr art hist, Benjamin Rawlins, 2005-. *Awards:* Advan Res Fel, Belgian-Am Educ Found, 74-75; Nat Endowment Humanities Summer Fel, 82 & 88; Coolidge Fel, 85; NEH Travel Grant, 89; Kress Found Grant, 97; Royal Flemish Acad Science & Arts, Belgium, 2003; Visiting Foreign Res Scholar, Ghent Univ, 2005. *Mem:* Historians Netherlandish Art (nat pres, 83-85); Col Art Asn Am; Southeastern Col Art Conf; Midwest Art Hist Soc; Centre europ d etudes bourguignonnes. *Res:* Painting of Jan van Eyck; 15th century devotional images; relationship between word and image in church-related art. *Publ:* Auth, The iconography of Campin's madonnas in interiors: a search for common ground, Robert Campin, New Directions in Scholarship, London, 96; Le Sacerdoce de la vierge et l'enigme d'un parti iconographique exceptionnel, Revue du Louvre, 12/96; ed, Rogier van der Weyden: St Luke Drawing the Virgin, Selected Essays in Context, Brepols, 97; auth, Rogier's St Luke and the Crossroads of Scholarship, 97; Narrative time and metaphoric tradition in the development of Jan Van Eyck's Washington Annunication, Art Bulletin, 3/99; Assessing the Evolution of Van Eyck's Ieonography through technical study of the Washington Annunciation II, Investigating Jan Van Eyck, London, 2000; H. Verougstraeto Leuven (ed), Jan Van Eyck's Madonna in a Church: Re-viewing Stylistic Assumptions in Jeronic Bosch et son Entourage, 2003; The Context & Jan Van Eyck's Approach to the Thyssen Diptych in Prayers and Portraits: Unfolding the Netherlandish Diptych: Essays in Context, New Haven, 2006. *Mailing Add:* 8519 Hunters Horn Germantown TN 38138-6290

PURYEAR, MARTIN
SCULPTOR
b Chicago, Ill, May 23, 41. *Study:* Cath Univ Am, Washington, BA(art), 63; studied wood craftsmanship with African carpenters, Sierra Leone, 64-66; Swed Royal Acad Art, Stockholm, guest student, 66-88; Yale Univ Sch Art & Archit, MFA(sculpture), 71. *Hon Degrees:* Yale Univ, hon degree, 94. *Work:* Mus Mod Art & Whitney Mus Am Art, NY; Art Inst Chicago; Walker Art Ctr, Minneapolis, Minn; Los Angeles Co Mus; Addison Gallery Am Art, Andover, Mass; Getty Center, Los Angeles; and others. *Comn:* Ampersand, Minneapolis Sculpture Garden, Walker Art Ctr, 88; GRIOT New York (set design), collab with Garth Fagan Dance Co, Garth Fagan & Wynton Marsalis, Brooklyn Acad Music, 91; Steven Oliver Art Ctr, San Francisco, 94; Battery Part Authority, NY, 95; Univ Wash Pub Art Comn, Seattle, 96; set design, Garth Fagan Dance Co. *Exhib:* Galerie Remmert und Barth, Duesseldorf, 98; McKee Gallery, NY, 2000, 2002-2003, 2005; Berkeley Art Mus and Pacific Film Arch, Calif, 2001; Addison Gallery Am Art, Andover, Mass, 2002; Donald Young Gallery, Chicago, 2002-2003, 2005; Corcoran Gallery Art, Wash, DC, 2003; Mus Fine Arts, Boston, 2003; Irish Mus Mod Art, Dublin, 2004; St Louis Art Mus, 2005; Mus Contemp Art, Cleveland, 2006; representing Barbara Krakow Gallery, Boston, Donald Young Gallery, Chicago, McKee Gallery, NY, Greg Kucera Gallery, Seattle. *Pos:* Vis artist, Skowhegan Sch Painting & Sculpture, Maine, 80 & Am Acad Rome, 86. *Teaching:* Secondary sch instr Eng, French, biology & art, Sierra Leone, W Africa, 64-66; asst instr, Yale Univ, New Haven, Conn, 69-71; asst prof art, Fisk Univ, Nashville, 71-73 & Univ Md, College Park, 74-78; prof art, Univ Ill, Chicago, 78-88. *Awards:* Grand Prize for best artist, Sao Paulo Bienal, Brazil, 90; Skowhegan Medal for Sculpture, Skowhegan Sch Painting & Sculpture, New York, 90; Col Art Asn Award, 93. *Media:* All Media. *Mailing Add:* c/o Donald Young Gallery Ltd 933 W Washington Blvd Chicago IL 60607

PUTTERMAN, FLORENCE GRACE
PAINTER, EDUCATOR
b Brooklyn, NY, Apr 14, 27. *Study:* New York Univ, BS; Bucknell Univ; Pa State Univ, MFA, 73. *Work:* Metrop Mus Art, Everson Mus, Brooklyn Mus, NY; Art Inst Chicago; Nat Mus Women Arts, Washington; Philadelphia Mus, Pa; NJ State Mus, Trenton; and others. *Comn:* Harris Saving Bank, Harrisburg, Pa, 80; Geisinger Med Ctr, Women's Hosp, Sunbury Community Hosp, Sunbury, Pa. *Exhib:* Abstraction: Monotype, Univ Mus, Indiana, Pa; Philadelphia Watercolor Soc Ann, Woodmere Mus, 92; Fla Artists Statewide Exhib, Ringling Mus, Sarasota, Fla, 94; Erie Art Mus Ann, 95; Haggin Mus Ann, Stockton, Calif, 95; Saginaw Art Mus, Saginaw, Mich, 2000; Lancaster Mus, Lancaster, PA, 2001; Albany Art Mus, Albany, GA, 2002; Ten Yr Retrospective, Lore Degenstein Gallery, Susquehanna Univ, Selinsgrove, Pa, 2003; Walton Art Ctr, Fayetteville, Ark, 2004; Projects Gallery, Phila, 2006; Susquehanna Art Mus, Harrisburg, Pa, Gallery 10, Washington, DC, Ormond Beach Mus, Ormond Beach, Fla, 2006. *Pos:* Founder & pres, Arts Unlimited, Selinsgrove, Pa, 65-78; cur, Milton Shoe Co Print Collection, Pa, 70-; bd dir, Art Gallery, Bucknell Univ, Lewisburg, Pa. *Teaching:* Artist in residence, Fed Title III Prog, 67-68 & 69-70; instr, Lycoming Col, Williamsport, Pa, 73-75; instr, Susquehanna Univ, 84-; instr, Monotype Workshop, Bennington Col, Vt, 89. *Awards:* Nat Endowment Arts, 79-80; Distinguished Alumni Award, Sch Arts & Archit, Pa State Univ; Nat Medal Honor, Nat Asn Women Artists. *Bibliog:* New American Monotypes, 79-80; articles, Am Artist, 7/79 & 2/81; The Nation, Art News, 1/83; New Art Examiner, 90; Art News. Nov, 2002; Art News, summer 2006. *Mem:* Boston Printmakers; Nat Asn Women Artists; Soc Am Graphic Artists (vpres); Nat Colorprint Soc; Florida Printmakers. *Media:* Oil, Acrylic. *Publ:* Southwest Art, 6/88; Twenty Year Survey, Palmer Museum, Pa State Univ Publ, 90; Encountering the Narrative In Florence Puttermans Work, Susquehanna Univ Publ, 93; Cryptic Tidings, 97, Metaphoric Fables, 99, Art at the 4 Corners, 2000; Allusive Metaphors, 2002. *Dealer:* Allyn Gallup, 556 Pineapple Ave, Sarasota, FL, 34236; Walter Wickiser, 568 Broadway, NY, 10012. *Mailing Add:* 3 Fairway Dr Selinsgrove PA 17870

PUTTERMAN, SUSAN LYNN
CURATOR, ADMINISTRATOR
b Zurich, Switzerland; US citizen. *Study:* Bennington Col; Barnard Col, BA, 75; Hunter Col, MA(art hist). *Collection Arranged:* Inside/Outside/On the Wall: Sculpture Invitational, 2003; Portaits, Myths & Stories: Three Photographers, 2004; Barbara Schwartz: Shaped Paintings (1998-2004), 2004; Are you Ready for Social Security?, 2005. *Pos:* Dir, Gallery Ilene Kartz, New York, 90-92; cur, Hebrew Home for the Aged, Riverdale, 94-. *Bibliog:* William Zimmer (auth), An artist with a sharp eye for the seams, NY Times, 5/21/95; Francine Silverman (auth), Two exhibits focus on parent/child relationship, Riverdale Rev, 11/23/97; Vivien Raynor (auth), From the famous to the nameless, NY Times, 6/14/98; Jonathon Goodman (auth), Inside/Outside/On the Wall, Hebrew Home for the Aged, Sculpture Magazine, 6/04; Pre-Teen Turf, The Riverdale Review, 3/11/04; Alex Friedman (auth), Getting Better with Age, the Riverdale Press, 2/3/05. *Mem:* Nat Asn Corp Art Mgrs; Am Asn Mus; Arts & Bus Coun; Mayo Smith Soc; IAPAA, ArtTable, Am Asn Mus; Arts & Business Council. *Specialty:* Contemporary Art. *Collection:* 20th C Art, including works by Christian Boltanski, Frederic Brenner, Christo, Amy Cutler, Joan Mitchell, Joel Perlman, Pablo Picasso, Andy Warhol, William Wegman. *Publ:* Auth, Art in the nursing home, Nursing Homes Mag, 6/97. *Mailing Add:* The Hebrew Home for the Aged at Riverdale 5901 Palisade Ave Riverdale NY 10471

PYLE, MELISSA BRONWEN
PAINTER, SCULPTOR
b Neptune, NJ, May 7, 63. *Study:* Moore col Art and Design, BFA, 85. *Comn:* mural, Mrs Wilhamena Hardee, Alicante, Spain, 95; botanical oil painting, Dr Jason Connor, Villanova, Pa, 95; botanical oil painting, Ms Jeanette Petti, Oceanport, NJ, 2000; landscape oil painting, Mr & Mrs Joel Lizotte, Red Bank, NJ, 2000; landscape oil painting, Mr & Mrs Keith Olson, Naples, Fla, 2000. *Exhib:* Color Now, Main Line Ctr for the Arts, Bryn Mawr, Pa, 96; From Paper to Cloth, Moore col Art and Design, Philadelphia, Pa, 96; solo exhib, Thistledown Gallery, Spring Lake, NJ, 98 & Elzeard Gallery, Baltimore, Md, 2000; Monmouth Co Arts Coun juried exhib, Monmouth Mus, Lincroft, NJ, 99; 13th Ann juried exhib, Art Alliance, Red Bank, NJ, 99; An Affair of the Art, Walt Disney Imagineering, Los Angeles, Calif, 2000-2001; mem exhib, Woodmere Art Mus, Chestnut Hill, Pa, 2001; group exhib, Jersey Shore Ctr for the Arts, Ocean Grove, NJ, 2004 & Frederick Art Gallery, Allenhurst, NJ, 2006; Audubon Artists Juried Nat exhib, Salmagundi, New York City, 2006. *Pos:* Master Designer & Mgr, Smudges Inc, Chestnut Hil, Pa, 87-92; Sole Proprieter, M Bronwen Pyle Hand Painteds, Philadelphia, Pa, 91-95. *Teaching:* Facilitator, The Artist's Way, Abington Art Ctr, Jenkintown, Pa, 97; Adj Prof, Color Theory, Moore col Art and Design, Philadelphia, Pa, 97-2003. *Awards:* MCAC Award, Monmouth Co Arts Coun, Monmouth Mus, Lincroft, NJ, 99; Wall Found for Educ Excellence, Wall High Sch, Wall, NJ, 2000. *Mem:* The Guild Creative Art, Shrewsbury, NJ (assoc mem); The Artists Group, Philadelphia, Pa (co-creater/facilitator, 95); Artsbridge, Lambertville, NJ (assoc mem); Audubon Artists Nat Art Soc, NY. *Media:* Acrylic, Oil; Mixed Media. *Publ:* auth, Wall township artist gives new life to conventional form, The Herald of Wall Township, 98; auth, Melissa Bronwen Pyle, The Times at the Jersey Shore, 98; auth, On display, Asbury Park Press, 99; auth, Living the material world, MCAC 21st ann show, Asbury Park Press, 2000. *Dealer:* Frederick Art Gallery 401 Spier Ave Allenhurst NJ 07711; Web of the Quill Gallery 5 bay Rd Brooklin Maine 04616. *Mailing Add:* PO Box 382 Spring Lake NJ 07762

PYZOW, SUSAN VICTORIA
PAINTER, PRINTMAKER
b Bronx, NY, Oct 27, 55. *Study:* Cooper Union, BFA, 76; Buffalo Univ, 78. *Exhib:* Art & Law Exhib, Minn Mus Art, St Paul, 80; Committed to Print, Mus Mod Art, NY, 88; Committed to Print, Spencer Art Mus, Kansas City, Kans, 90; Art at the Armory: Occupied Territory, Mus Contemp Art, Chicago, Ill, 92; Am Artists Prof League Nat Competition, Salmagundi Club, NY, 92; 57th Midyear Exhib, Butler Inst Am Art, Youngstown, Ohio, 93; 58th Midyear Exhib, Butler Inst Am Art, Youngstown, Ohio, 94; Pastel Soc of Am Nat Competition, Nat Arts Club, NY, 94; Contemporary Printmakers, Seton Hall, NJ, 2004; Paul Marcus & Susan Pyzon, Two Contemporary Printmakers, The Old Paint Shop, NY, 2006. *Teaching:* Instr intaglio & drawing, Buffalo Univ, NY, 77-78; drawing & watercolor, Parsons Sch Design, New York, 84-. *Awards:* Purchase prize, Fed Res Bank of NY, 2000; First place acrylic, Joyce Dutka Arts Found, 2002; Nat League of Am, Pa Women Grant in Art, 2004. *Mem:* Nat Asn Women Artists. *Media:* Oil, Acrylic, Printmaking. *Mailing Add:* 505 E 14th St New York NY 10009

Q

QUACKENBUSH, ROBERT
PRINTMAKER, PAINTER, ILLUSTRATOR-CHILDRENS BOOKS, CONSULTANT
b Hollywood, Calif, July 23, 29. *Study:* Art Ctr Col Design, Pasadena, Calif, BA, 56; Pratt Graphic Art Ctr, with John Ross & Clare Romano, 61. *Work:* Whitney Mus, NY; Smithsonian Inst, Washington, DC; Mazza Collection Gallery, Findlay Col, Ohio; Lena Y de Grummond Collection, Univ Southern Miss; Kerlen Collection, St Paul, Minn; Mrs George Roy Hill, Mrs Norton Simon, Beulah Campbell Col, NC, de

Grummond Collection, Univ So Miss. *Comn:* Paintings, US Dept Interior, 68 & US Air Force Mus, 69, Washington, DC. *Exhib:* Audubon Artists Ann, Nat Acad Art Galleries, 60; Continental American Print Show, Whitney Mus, 62; Nat Acad Arts Ann, 66; Soc Illustrators Ann, Soc Illustrators Gallery, 68, 70 & 84; New Acquistions, Mus Am Illus, 84, NY. *Pos:* Artist, writer, art therapist, lectr. *Teaching:* Instr painting & bk illus, Sch Visual Arts, 68-73; instr painting & illus, Robert Quackenbush Studio-Gallery, 68-; guest lectr, worldwide tours to universities, schs & libraries, 68-. *Awards:* Citation, 50 Best Books Exhib, Am Inst Graphic Arts, 62; Edgar Allen Poe Spec Award for Best Juvenile Mystery, Mystery Writers Am, 82; Citations (2), Best Children's Books of 1992, Soc Illustrs, 92; Gradiva Award for best children's book of 1998; Holland Soc Gold Medal for distinction in art and literature, 2000. *Bibliog:* The art of Robert Quackenbush, Am Artist Mag, 65; Morton Schindel (dir), Signature Collection, Weston Woods Studio, 76; Something about the author, Gale Research Inc, Vol 7, 89; Something about the author, Gale Research Inc, Vol 133, 02. *Mem:* Auth Guild; Holland Soc, NY; Mystery Writers of Am. *Media:* All Media. *Res:* Understanding the Symbolic Communications of Children through their Art, Intl Univ for Grad Studies. *Interests:* Psychoanalytic Research. *Publ:* Illusr, The Pilot (by James Fenimore Cooper), 68 & The Life of Washington (by Rev Mason L Weems), 74, Ltd Ed Club; The Scarlet Letter (by Nathaniel Hawthorne), Reader's Digest Bks, 84; auth & illusr, Robert Quackenbush's Treasury of Humor, Doubleday, 90; Batababy, Random House, 97; Daughter of Liberty, Disney Hyperion, 99; Miss Mallard Mysteries, animated film series, Cinar in co-prodn with Shanghai Animation Film Studio, 2000. *Dealer:* Robert Quackenbush Studios 223 E 78th St New York NY 10021. *Mailing Add:* 460 E 79th St New York NY 10021

QUAM, CAROLE C
PAINTER
b Grass Valley, Calif, Mar 22, 44. *Study:* Univ Idaho, 62-65; Univ Alaska, Anchorage, BFA, 91. *Work:* Univ Alaska Mus, Fairbanks. *Exhib:* Solo shows, Univ Alaska, Anchorage Campus Ctr Gallery, 91, Rogue Community Col, Grants Pass, Ore, 93, Civic Ctr Gallery, Fairbanks, Alaska, 94, Alaska Pac Univ, 95, 99, Clatsop Community Col, Astoria, 96, La State Univ, Shreveport, 96; Northern Nat, Nicolet Col Gallery, Rhinelander, Wis, 93; XXV All Alaska Juried, Anchorage Mus, Alaska, 94 & 96; group show, Sinclair Community Col, Dayton, Ohio, 94, Artists Gold Rush, Collector Art Gallery, Washington, 95, Fairbanks Arts Asn, 96, Alaska State Mus, 96; Mary Mary, Woman Made Gallery, Chicago, 96; Solo shows, Erb Mem Union Gallery, Univ Ore, Eugene, 97, The Barn Gallery, Middle Tenn State Univ, Mur Freesboro, 97, Nordic Heritage Mus, Seattle, Wash, 97 & Univ Gallery, Univ Mass, Lowell, Mass, 98; group shows, Narratives, Woman Made Gallery, Chicago, 97 & Figuresque, The Art Ctr, Mt Clemens, Mich, 98. *Awards:* Anchorage Mus Best Fibre, Earth, Fire & Fibre, 87; Career Opportunity Grant, Alaska Arts Coun, 94; Residency Ragdale Found, 99. *Bibliog:* Dimetra Makris (auth), First Prize Quilts, Simon & Schuster, 84; Heather Robertson (auth), In the gallery, Fairbanks Arts, 94; Tom Nicholas (auth), The Best of Oil Painting, 96. *Mem:* Mensa. *Media:* Oil. *Publ:* Contribr, Hayden's Ferry Review, Ariz State Univ, 94

QUAYTMAN, HARVEY
PAINTER
b Far Rockaway, NY, Apr 20, 37. *Study:* Syracuse Univ; Tufts Univ; Boston Mus Fine Arts Sch, BFA & grad degree. *Work:* Tate Gallery, London; Whitney Mus Am Art & Mus Mod Art, NY; Israel Mus, Jerusalem; Carnegie Inst of Technol, Pittsburgh, Pa, and others. *Exhib:* Solo exhibs, David McKee Gallery, NY, 75, 77, 78, 80, 82, 84, 86, 87, 88, 90, 93, 96, 98 & 2000, Galerie Nordenhake, Malmo, Sweden, 82, 86, 87, 90, 93 & 96, Nielsen Gallery, Boston, Mass, 76, 78, 80, 83, 86, 89, 93, 95 & 2000, Gilbert Brownstone Gallery, Paris, 90; Henie-Onstaad Art Center, Oslo, Norway, 96; Corcoran Biennale, Corcoran Gallery Art, Washington, DC, 87; Generations of Geometry, Whitney Mus Am Art, Equitable Ctr, NY, 87; Mus Mod Art, NY, 87-88; Germans Van Eck Gallery, NY, 89; 1989 Ljubljana Bienale 18, Int Centre Craphic Art, Yugoslavia, 89; 50 Yrs Collecting: Art at IBM, IBM Gallery Sci & Art, NY, 89; Abstraction in the Eighties, Rose Art Mus, Brandeis Univ, Waltham, Mass, 90; Tel Aviv Mus Art, Israel, 92; 48th Ann Am Acad Purchase Exhib, Am Acad Arts & Lett, NY, 97; Queens Artists: Highlights of the 20th Century, Queens Mus Art, NY, 97; The Edward R Broide Collection, Orlando Mus Art, Fla, 98; Then and Now: Nielson Gallery 35th Ann Exhib, Nielsen Gallery, Boston, Mass, 99; and others. *Teaching:* instr, Boston Mus Fine Arts Sch, Middlebury Col, Essex Col Art, Colchester, Eng & Sch Visual Arts, NY, formerly; instr, Cooper Union, Parsons Sch Design, NY; vis lectr, Harvard Univ, 82 & 83; adj asst prof, Hunter Col, 83. *Awards:* Guggenheim Fel, 79 & 85; Artist Fel, Nat Endowment Arts, 83; Am Acad Arts & Letters Award, 97. *Bibliog:* Peter Clothier (auth), Harvey Quaytman, Artnews, 5/88; Charles Hagan (auth), Harvey Quaytman, Artforum, 12/88; Ellen Handy (auth), Harvey Quaytman, Arts, 1/89. *Media:* Miscellaneous Media. *Mailing Add:* McKee Gallery 745 5th Ave New York NY 10151

QUENTEL, HOLT
PAINTER
b Milwaukee, Wis, 1961. *Study:* Lawrence Univ, 79-83; Sch Art Inst Chicago, 84-85; Princeton Univ, 86-87. *Work:* Milwaukee Art Mus. *Exhib:* One-woman shows, Stux Gallery, Boston, 87, Stux Gallery, NY, 87, 88 & 90, Wriston Mus, Lawrence Univ, 89, State of Ill Gallery, Chicago, 89; All Quiet on the Western Front, Espace Dieu, Paris, 90; Bayly Mus, Va, 90; Mayor Rowan Gallery, London, 90; Stuttering, Stux Gallery, NY, 90; Outside Am: Going into the 90's, Fay Gold Gallery, Atlanta, 91; The Fetish of Knowledge, Real Art Ways, Hartford, 91; Invitational, Tony Shafrazi Gallery, NY, 91; Theoretically Yours, 92; and many others. *Awards:* Elizabeth Richarson Award, 83; Smith Merit Scholar, Sch Art Inst Chicago, 84-86; Nat Endowment Arts, 89. *Bibliog:* Michael Archer (auth), I Don't Like Eggs: Janet Green, British Collector, On Art & The Art World, Artscribe, summer, 90; Phyllis Freeman (auth), New York: Harry N Abrams Inc, New Art, 90; Gretchen Faust (auth), Holt Quentel, Arts, 1/91; and others. *Mailing Add:* 114 Bridgemann Rd London N11 BH United Kingdom

QUICK, EDWARD RAYMOND
MUSEUM DIRECTOR
b Los Angeles, Calif, Mar 22, 43. *Study:* Univ Calif, Santa Barbara, with Dr Herbert Cole, BA, 72, MA, 77. *Collection Arranged:* Art Inc, 79; George Sugarman, 81; Views of a Vanishing Frontier, 84; Johann Berthelsen, 88; Swope Art Mus Collections, 87. *Pos:* Asst cur, Santa Barbara Mus Art, Calif, 77-78; registrar, Montgomery Mus Fine Arts, Ala, 78-80; dept head, Joslyn Art Mus, Omaha, Nebr, 80-85; dir, Sheldon Swope Art Mus, Terre Haute, Ind, 86-95, Berman Mus, Anniston, Ala, 95-. *Teaching:* Mus Mgt, Ind State Univ, Terre Haute, 89-. *Mem:* Am Asn Mus (map surveyor, 85-); Inst Coun Mus; Arts Illiana (bd pres, 86, secy, 88); Asn Ind Mus (bd, 88-); Midwest Mus Conf. *Publ:* Contribr, Regional styles of drawing in Italy: 1600-1700, Univ Calif, Santa Barbara, 77; Registrars on Record: essays on museum collections management, Am Asn Mus, 88; ed, Johann Berthelsen: An American master painter, Swope Art Mus, 88. *Mailing Add:* 5363 Brenda Ave San Jose CA 95124

QUIDLEY, PETER TAYLOR
PAINTER
b Boston, Mass, Dec 20, 45. *Comn:* Paintings, Westinghouse, Ft Lauderdale, Fla, 68; portraits of 4 kings, Kingdom of Saudi Arabia, Raytheon Corp, Saudi Arabia, 79; Death of Socrates (copy), Anheuser-Busch, St Louis, 93. *Exhib:* One-man shows, Gallery Juarez, Palm Beach, Fla, 73 & Luminous Interiors, Copley Soc, Boston, Mass, 96; Int Art Expos, Jeddah Dome, Saudi Arabia, 78-79; Evolution of an Artist, Cahoon Mus Am Art, Cotuit, Mass, 94; Federal Reserve Group Show, 94; Portrait Group Show, Copley Soc Boston, 94; Places for the Muse, Cape Mus Fine Art, 98. *Awards:* Robb Saggandorf Mem Award, Copley Member Show, Yankee Mag, 92; First Prize Painting, Winter Member Show, Copley Soc Boston, 93; Evelyn Strand Dibner Award, Cape Cod Art Asn Show, 93. *Bibliog:* Tim Wood (auth), Introducing Peter Quidley, A Plus, 12/93; Anna Crebo (auth), Artist Peter Quidley, Cape Cod Life Mag, 4/94; Debbie Forman (auth), Master of romance paints with purpose, Cape Cod Times, 7/22/94. *Mem:* Copley Soc Boston; Am Soc Marine Artists; Am Soc Portrait Artists; US Coast Guard Artists. *Media:* Oil. *Dealer:* Quidley & Company 26 Main St Nantucket Mass 02554. *Mailing Add:* PO Box 129 South Chatham MA 02659

QUIGLEY, ROBERT WELLINGTON
ARCHITECT
b Calif, 45. *Study:* Univ Utah, Bachelor, 69. *Comn:* Prin works include San Diego New Main Libr (Honor award, Am Inst of Archit San Diego, 98), Sherman Heights Community Ctr (Citation, Am Inst of Archit San Diego, 90, Orchid, San Diego Chap Am Inst of Archit, 92, Merit award, Am Inst of Archit San Diego, 96), Baltic Inn, San Diego (Honor award, Am Inst of Archit San Diego, 87, Panda award, City of San Diego, 88), 202 Island Inn (One of "Ten Best Designs of 1992," Time Mag., 93, Nat Am Inst of Archit Honor award, 93, Merit award, Am Inst of Archit San Diego, 93, Honor award with Distinction, Am Inst of Archit Calif Coun, 94), Solana Beach Transit Station (Orchid, San Diego Chap, Am Inst of Archit, 96, Honor award, Am Inst of Archit Calif Coun, 98), Escondido Transit Station (Citation, Am Inst of Archit San Diego, 90, Orchid, Am Inst of Archit San Diego, 91, Beautification award, City of Escondido, 90); San Diego Children's Mus, Calif, Student Academic Services Facility, Univ Calif San Diego, San Diego Historic Harbor Front, West Valley Branch Libr (Divine Detail, Am Inst of Archit San Diego, 2003, Merit award, Am Inst of Archit Santa Clara, 2004), Leslie Shao-ming Sun Field Station, Stanford Univ (Merit award, Am Inst of Archit San Diego, 2003, Honor award, Am Inst of Archit Santa Clara, 2004, COTE Top Ten Green Buildings, Nat Am Inst of Archit, 2005), Opportunity Ctr for the Midpeninsula (Advocacy Planning award, Northern Sect Am Planning Asn, 2003), Shaw Lopez Park, Casa Feliz, and several others. *Exhib:* solo exhibitions, Retrospective, Southern Calif Inst of Archit, Santa Monica, 82, Exhibit of Recent Work, UCLA, 84, Recent Work, Portland State Univ, 91, exhibitions include Visual Communication Towards Architecture, Installation Gallery, San Diego, 82, Don Clos Pegase Competition, San Francisco Mus Contemporary Art, 85, The Emerging Generation in the USA, Global Architecture Gallery, Tokyo, Japan, 87, Five Choose Five, Nat Am Inst of Archit Conf, St. Louis, 89, Fabrications, San Francisco Mus Modern Art, 98, Books, Bytes and Mortar, Mus Contemporary Art, San Diego, 2001, Modern Trains and Splendid Stations, Art Inst Chicago, 2002, and several others. *Pos:* Archit Peace Corps, Chile; prin, Quigley Archits, San Diego, Palo Alto, 74-. *Teaching:* Adj prof, archit Univ Calif, San Diego; vis design prof, Harvard Univ Grad School Design, 91, Univ Tex, Austin, 94, Univ Calif, Berkeley, 97 & 98; spkr. in field; invited juror and advisor. *Awards:* Named Headliner of Yr in Archit, San Diego Press Club, 95; named one of 100 Foremost Architects of the World, AD 100, Archit Digest, 91, 88 San Diegans to Watch in '88', San Diego Mag, 88, The San Diego 50 People to Watch in 1997; recipient Presidential Commendation for Exemplary Community. Serv, 88, Firm award, Am Inst of Archit Calif Coun, 95, The Irving Gill award, Am Inst of Archit San Diego, 97, Maybeck award, Am Inst of Archit Calif Coun, 2005, several mag. and community program awards, several awards for design excellence from the Nat Am Inst of Archit, Am Inst of Archit Santa Clara, Am Inst of Archit San Diego, and Am Inst of Archit Calif Coun; fellow Inst for Urban Design, 96. *Mem:* Fel, Am Inst of Archit; Nat Acad of Design. *Publ:* co-auth: Bldgs & Projects, 1996. *Mailing Add:* Quigley Architects 434 W Cedar St San Diego CA 92101

QUIGLEY, ROBIN L
JEWELER, METALSMITH
b New York, NY, 47. *Study:* Tyler Sch Art, Elkins Park, Pa, BFA, 74; RI Sch Design, Providence, MFA, 76. *Exhib:* Craft Today USA, Musee Des Arts Decoratifs, Paris, France, 89; Function--Non-Function, Rezac Gallery, Chicago, Ill, 89; New Bronze Age, Soc Art Crafts, Pittsburgh, Pa, 91; Neoteric Jewelry, Snug Harbor Cult Ctr, Staten Island, NY, 91; Am Jewellery & Metalwork, Art Gallery Western Australia, Perth, 92; and others. *Teaching:* Prof, Philadelphia Col Art, 76-78; asst prof, RI Sch Design, 81-. *Awards:* Craftsman Fel, Nat Endowment Arts, 79 & 86. *Media:* Precious Metals, Bronze. *Mailing Add:* RI Sch Design-Jewelry Dept 2 College St Providence RI 02903

QUILLER, STEPHEN FREDERICK
PAINTER, PRINTMAKER
b Osmond, Nebr, Aug 15, 46. *Study:* Colo State Univ, BA, 68. *Work:* City Medford Art Collection, Ore; Colo Coun Arts; Colo Springs Fine Arts Ctr; Luther Bean Mus & Adams State Col, Alamosa, Colo; Berman Mus Art, Collegeville, Pa. *Comn:* Gov's Export Award (painting), Colo Coun Arts, Denver, 79; City of Creede (mural), Colo Coun Arts. *Exhib:* One-man show, Foothills Art Ctr, Golden, Colo, 73; Am Watercolor Soc, 73, 76, 94, 95, 96, 97, 98, 99, 01-05 & Nat Soc Painters Casein & Acrylic, 74 & 76-78, Nat Acad Design, NY; Rocky Mountain Nat, Foothills Art Ctr, Golden, Colo, 74-75, 77-79 & 81; Watercolor USA, Springfield Art Mus, Mo, 77; Am & Ital Printmakers, Sangre de Cristo Art Ctr, Pueblo, Colo, 80; and others. *Collection Arranged:* Charles & Nancy Wallisk Collection, Bean ARt Mus, Adams State Coll, Alamosa, Colo. *Teaching:* Instr art, SW Watercolor Soc, Dallas, spring 76; instr art, NMex Watercolor Soc, Albuquerque, spring 79; guest artist-in-res intaglio, Adams State Col, Alamosa, Colo, fall 81; instr painting & printmaking, Adams State Col, 81-89. *Awards:* Gov's Award, Colo Coun Arts, 79; Greathouse AWard & Medal, Am Watercolor Soc, 97; Louis Kaep Award, 1999, Am Watercolor Soc, 99; Philadelphia Watercolor Soc Award, Nat Watercolor Soc, 2004; Winsor & Newton Award, Am Watercolor Soc, 2005. *Bibliog:* Web Allison (auth), Steve Quiller: Creede's artist-in-residence, Colo Country Life, San Luis Valley, 11/72; GA Minshew (auth), Spotlight on the artist, Scene, SW Watercolor Soc, 4/75; Susan Meyer (auth), 40 Watercolorists And How They Work, Watson-Guptill, 78. *Mem:* Nat Soc Painters Casein & Acrylic; Watercolor West; Artists Equity Asn; Watercolor Asn Ala; Am Watercolor Soc. *Media:* Watercolor, Acrylic; Casein, Intaglio. *Publ:* Auth, Water Media: Watercolor & Gouache (video), Water Media: Acrylic & Casein (video), Color Concepts (video) & Color for the Painter (video), Chrysal Productions; Water Media Techniques, Watson-Guptill, 83, Water Media: Processes and Possibilities, 86, Color Choices, 89, Acrylic Painting Techniques, 94, Painter's Guide to Color, 2000; auth, Mastering Color and The Plein Air Experience (video), 04; auth, Watercolor Workshop (video), 04. *Dealer:* Mission Gallery, Taos, NMex; Quiller Gallery, Creede, Colo. *Mailing Add:* PO Box 160 Creede CO 81130

QUINLAN, ROBERT CONRAD
PATRON
Study: Yale Univ, 1954. *Pos:* Partner, Quinlan & Field Real Estate, New York City, currently; chmn, Columbus Ave Bus Improvement Dist, currently. *Mem:* Whitney Mus Am Art, New York City, (bd trustees, currently); NY Landmarks Conservancy, (bd dir, currently); Friends of Upper East Side Hist Dist; Preserv League of NY State; Hist House Trust. *Mailing Add:* Quinlan & Field 101 W 70th St 2N New York NY 10023

QUINN, BRIAN GRANT
SCULPTOR, PAINTER
b Wahoo, Nebr, Oct 21, 50. *Study:* Nebr Wesleyan Univ, BAE; Ariz State Univ, MFA. *Work:* Weber State Col, Odgen, Utah; Ariz State Univ, Tempe; Tucson Art Mus, Ariz; Yuma Art Ctr, Ariz; Shemer Art Ctr, Phoenix, Ariz; Phoenix Childrens Hosp; Catholic Diocese Wichita. *Comn:* sculpture, Median Inst, Pittsburgh, Pa, 83; sculpture, Northern Ariz Univ, 83; sculpture, Nebr Wesleyen Univ, 87; sculpture, Lincoln Nebr Pub Sch, 87; sculpture, Glendale Community Col, 90; relief sculpture/painting, Phoenix Children's Hosp, Ariz. *Exhib:* Ariz Biennial, Tucson Art Mus, 80-84; 1st & 2nd Northern Ariz Univ Sculpture Invitational, 80 & 81; 13th-18th Midwestern Invitationals, O'Rourke Gallery, Moorhead, Minn, 81-86; 17th Ann Nat Drawing & Small Sculpture Show, Del Mar Col, Tex, 83; Redefining the Lathe-Turned Object, Ariz State Univ, 93; solo exhib, Shemer Art Ctr, Phoenix, Ariz, 2001; and others. *Pos:* Preparator, Phoenix Art Mus, 75; artist-in-residence, Nat Endowment Art, 75-76; dir bd, Japanese Sword Soc US, 94-2004; Pres, Japanese Sword Soc US, 2004-. *Teaching:* Vis instr sculpture, Glendale Community Col, 76-90; lectr sculpture, Ariz State Univ, Tempe, 80 & 81; prof sculpture & jewelry, Glendale Community Col, 90-94, cur art collection, 90-94. *Awards:* Fred Wells Purchase Award, Small Sculpture and Drawing Exhib, Nebr Wesleyan Univ, 76; Jurors Award, First & Third Ariz Wood-in-Art Exhib, 77-79, Ariz State Univ; Jurors Award, Galeria Mesa, 85; Fulbright Mem Fund Scholar, Japan, 2001; The Sch the Art Inst Chicago's Teacher Inst in Contemp Art Scholar, 2005. *Bibliog:* Barbara Cortright (auth), Brian Quinn at Northern Arizona Univ and the University of New Mexico, Artspace, spring 84; Jessica Benton Evans (auth), Brian Quinn an interview, The Ashes, 4/94; Jennifer Franklin (auth), The shape of things/gardens of stone, life, Scottsdale Progress, 4/7/94. *Mem:* Southern Asn of Sculptors; Japanese Sword Soc of the US; Cent Ariz Mus Asn; Orders & Medals Soc Am; Am Soc Military Insignia Collectors. *Media:* Mixed Media. *Interests:* Art; Militaria & Antique Arms Collector. *Dealer:* Faust Gallery 7103 E Main St Scottsdale AZ 85251; Ann Jacob Gallery Phipps Plaza 3500 Peachtree Rd NE Atlanta GA 30326. *Mailing Add:* 6132 E Lincoln Dr Paradise Valley AZ 85253-4256

QUINN, THOMAS PATRICK, JR
PAINTER
b Honolulu, Hawaii, June 5, 1938. *Study:* Col of Marin, Kentfield, Calif, 56-58, Art Ctr Col Design, Pasedena, Calif, BA, 58-63. *Work:* Leigh Yawkey Woodson Art Mus, Wasau, Wis; Nat Wildlife Art Mus (permanent collection), Jackson, Wyo. *Comn:* Painting, Monterey Bay Aquarium, Calif, 84. *Exhib:* Nat Exhib Alaskan Wildlife, Alaskan Mus Art, Anchorage, 82; The Nature of the Best, Southern Alleghenies Mus Art, Loretto, Pa, 86; solo exhib, Frederic Remington Art Mus, Ogdensburg, NY, 88; NY Mus Natural Hist; Alexander Koenig Mus, Bonn, Ger; Nat Acad Western Art, Nat Cowboy Hall Fame, Oklahoma City, 93; Nat Wildlife Art Mus, Jackson, Wyo; Gilcrease Mus, Tulsa, Okla, 92; 25 Artists Nature Exhib, Zeist, The Neth, 92. *Awards:* Gold Medal, Nat Acad Western Art, Okla City, 93; Master Wildlife Artist Award, Leigh Yawkey Woodson Art Mus, Wasaw, Wis, 98. *Bibliog:* Thomas Fox (auth), The elusive quality of a wild thing, Southwest Art, 83; Tom Davis (auth), Influencing the eye, Wildlife Art News, 87; M Stephen Doherty (auth), Thomas Quinn, Am Artist, 88. *Mem:* Trumpeter Swan Soc. *Media:* Mixed Media. *Publ:* Auth, First Person, Sports Illus, 83; The Working Retrievers, E P Dutton, 83; contribr, Wildlife Painting Techniques of Modern Masters, Watson Guptill, 85; Wildfowl Art, Ward Found, 86; Auth, R Riviere, Thomas Quinn on Art: Illustration and Inspiration, Art Today, 87; Wind, Wad & Waterverf (Dutch), 91. *Dealer:* Gerald Peters Gallery 1011 Paseo de Peralta Santa Fe NM 87501. *Mailing Add:* PO Box 225 Point Reyes Station CA 94956-0225

QUINN, WILLIAM
PAINTER
b St Louis, Mo, Sept 5, 29. *Study:* Washington Univ, BFA, study with Paul Burlin & Carl Holty; Univ Ill, MFA, 57. *Work:* Butler Inst Am Art, Youngstown, Ohio; Brooks Mem Art Gallery, Memphis, Tenn; Nelson-Atkins Gallery, Kansas City, Mo; St Louis Art Mus; Weatherspoon Art Gallery, Univ NC; High Mus, Atlanta, Ga; Tampa Mus, Fla; Mus of the Arts, Ft Lauderdale, Fla; Mulvane Art Ctr, Washburn Univ, Topeka, Kans; Drury Col, Springfield, Mo; Univ Mo, Columbia; Webster Univ, St Louis,. *Comn:* Oil painting, Sea Watch (48x60), Four Seasons Hotel, Fayence, France, 2006. *Exhib:* Twenty-six one-man shows US, Europe & Mexico. *Teaching:* Formerly Prof painting & drawing, Washington Univ,. *Awards:* Miliken Travel Scholar, Washington Univ, 58; Fulbright Alternative, 1962; Cité Des Arts Fel, Paris, France, 82; Painting Fel, Nat Endowment Art, 86; and over 36 other awards in regional museums & galleries. *Bibliog:* Numerous newspaper & magazine articles & photos. *Media:* Oil, Gouache; Acrylic. *Dealer:* Manna Kunsthuis Bruges Belgium. *Mailing Add:* 17 Ave du General Leclerc Vence 06140 France

QUINONES KEBER, ELOISE
HISTORIAN, EDUCATOR
b Los Angeles, Calif. *Study:* Columbia Univ, PhD, 84. *Pos:* mem, Seminar Arts Africa, Oceania & Americas, Columbia Univ. *Teaching:* Prof art hist, Baruch Col, City Univ New York, 86- & Grad Ctr, 91-. *Awards:* Getty Publ Award, 92-93; Fel, Am Coun Learned Soc, 87-88 & 93-94, Nat Endowment Humanities, 93-94; John Simon Guggenheim Found Fel, 98-99. *Mem:* Col Art Asn; Asn Latin Am Art; Am Soc Ethnohistory. *Res:* Aztec art and culture; early colonial Mexican art; manuscripts and early ethnohistorical texts. *Publ:* Coauth, Art of Aztec Mexico: Treasures of Tenochtitlan, Nat Gallery Art, 83; co-ed, The Work of Bernardino de Sahagun, Univ Tex Press, 88; Mixteca-Puebla: Discoveries and research in Mesoamerican art and archaeology, 94 & ed, Chipping Away on Earth: Studies in Prehispanic and colonial Mexico, 94, Labyrinthos Press; auth, Codex Telleriano-Remensis: Ritual Divination and History in a Pictorial Aztec Manuscript, Univ Tex Press, 95; ed, Precious Greenstone, Precious Quetzal Feather: Mesoamerican Essays in Honor of Doris Heyden, Laybrinthos Press, 2000; ed, Representing Aztec Ritual: Performance, Image & Text in the Work of Sahagún, Univ Colo Press, 2002. *Mailing Add:* Dept Art History CUNY Graduate Ctr 365 5th Ave New York NY 10016

QUIRARTE, JACINTO
HISTORIAN, ADMINISTRATOR
b Jerome, Ariz, Aug 17, 31. *Study:* San Francisco State Col, BA, 54, MA, 58; Nat Univ Mex, PhD, 64. *Pos:* Dir cult affairs, Ctr Venezolano Am, Caracas, 64-66; bd mem & vpres, San Antonio Arts Coun, 73-77; mem visual arts & humanities panel, Tex Comn on the Arts & Humanities, 76-80. *Teaching:* Art instr, Colegio Americano, Mexico City, 59-61; asst to Alberto Ruz Lhuillier, Seminario de Cultura Maya, Nat Univ Mex, 61-62; dir cult affairs, Centro Venezolano Americano, Caracas, 64-66; vis prof hist contemp art Latin Am & pre-Columbian art, Yale Univ, New Haven, Conn, 67; prof hist pre-Columbian, Colonial & contemp art of Mex & Guatemala, Univ Tex, Austin, 67-72; vis prof hist pre-Colombia art of Mesoamerica & Colonial art of Latin Am, Univ NMex, 71; dean, Col Fine & Applied Arts, Univ Tex, San Antonio, 72-78; dir & prof art hist, Res Ctr Visual Arts, 77-98. *Mem:* Mid-Am Col Art Asn; Soc for Am Archaeol; Int Cong of Americanists; Int Cong of the Hist of Art; Int Cong of Ethnology & Anthrop. *Publ:* Auth, El estilo artistico de Izapa, Cuadernos de Historia del Arte, No 3, Instituto de Investigaciones Esteticas, Univ Nac Autonoma de Mexico, 73; auth, Izapan style art--a study of its form and meaning, Studies in Pre-Columbian Art & Archaeology, No 10, Dumbarton Oaks, Washington, DC, 73; auth, Mexican American Artists, 73 & Maya Vase, (in prep), Univ Tex Press, Austin, Art and Architecture of the Texas Missions, Univ Tex Press, Austin, 2002. *Mailing Add:* Dept Visual Arts Univ Tex 6900 North Loop 1604 W San Antonio TX 78249-0642

QUIRK, THOMAS CHARLES, JR
PAINTER, SCULPTOR
b Pittsburgh, Pa, Dec 31, 22. *Study:* Edinboro Univ PA, BS, 48; Univ Pittsburgh, MEd, 64. *Comn:* St Mary's Church, Kutztown, Pa; Holy Spirit Lutheran Church, Emmaus, Pa. *Exhib:* Pa Acad Fine Arts Ann, Philadelphia, 69; Drawing & Small Sculpture Ann, Ball State Univ, 71; Nat Acad Design Ann, NY, 74; Philadelphia Watercolor Club Ann, 74 & 79; Philadelphia Watercolor Club, 76; Ann Nat Soc of Painters in Casein & Acrylic, NY, 76 & 79; Mary in Art, Milwaukee, Wis, Dayton, Ohio & Washington, DC, 98-99; and others. *Collection Arranged:* Butler Inst Am Art, Youngstown, OH; Chatham College, Pittsburgh, PA; Pittsburgh Public Schools, Pittsburgh, PA; Millersville Univ, PA; Rutgers Univ, NJ. *Pos:* Artist-in-residence, Everhart Mus, Scranton, Pa, 72-. *Teaching:* Emer prof art, Kutztown Univ, Pa, 66-89. *Awards:* Dawson Mem Prize, Philadelphia Watercolor Club, 74; Crest Award, Philadelphia Watercolor Club, 97; Religious Art Award in Visual Arts-Sculpture, AIA, St Mary's Church, Kutztown, Pa, 99. *Mem:* Nat Sculpture Soc; Philadelphia Watercolor Club. *Media:* Multimedia, Stone, Wood, Clay. *Publ:* Auth, Reptiles and Amphibians, Dover Publs; Fishes of the Western Atlantic, Dover Publs; Illusr, Ghost Garden, Hela Feil (auth), Atheneum Press. *Mailing Add:* 310 E Main St Kutztown PA 19530

QUIROZ, ALFRED JAMES
PAINTER, EDUCATOR
b Tucson, Ariz, May 9, 44. *Study:* San Francisco Art Inst, BFA, 71; RI Sch Design, MAT, 74; Univ Ariz, MFA, 84. *Work:* Mus Fine Arts NMex, Santa Fe; Tucson Mus Arts; Scottsdale Mus Contemp Art; NY Pub Libr Print Collection, Manhatten. *Comn:* Housing projs, City of Tucson, Ariz, 86; Novus Ordo (mural), San Francisco Ctr Arts, 93. *Exhib:* Evidence, San Antonio Mus Art, 86; Counter Colonialismo, Heard Mus, Phoenix, 92; Year of the White Bear, Mex Fine Arts Mus, Chicago, 92 & Walker Art Ctr, Minneapolis, 92; Chicago Codices, Mex Mus, San Francisco, 92; La Frontera, Mus Contemp Art, San Diego, 93; In Out of the Cold, Ctr Arts, Yerba Buena Gardens, San Francisco, 93; Works: On Paper, Galeria Mesta Bratislavy, Slovkia, 94. *Pos:* Resident artist (mural), Ariz Comn Arts, Phoenix, 85-89. *Teaching:* Prof painting & drawing, Univ Ariz, Tucson, 89-. *Awards:* Best of Show, Ariz Biennial, Tucson Mus Art, 86; Ariz Arts Award Fel, Tucson Comn Found, 88; Visual Arts Fel, Ariz Comn Arts, 89-95. *Mem:* Col Art Asn; Nat Artists Arts Orgn; Asn Latin Am Art. *Media:* Oil, Wood panel. *Dealer:* Davis-Dominquez Gallery Tucson AZ. *Mailing Add:* 2726 E Winchester Vista Tucson AZ 85713

QUISGARD, LIZ WHITNEY
PAINTER, SCULPTOR
b Philadelphia, Pa, Oct 23, 1929. *Study:* Md Inst Col Art, dipl, 49, BFA(summa cum laude), 66; studied with Morris Louis, 57-60; Rinehart Sch Sculpture, MFA, 66. *Work:* Univ Baltimore; Johns Hopkins Univ; Libyan Mission UN, Englewood, NJ, Can Imperial Bank Com, NY, Great Northern Nekoosa Corp, Norwalk, Conn, Quality Inns, Newark, NJ, Datalogy Corp, Valhalla, NY, Rosenberg Diamond Corp, NY, Ctr Club, Baltimore, Md; Fordham Univ, NY; Miss Mus, Jackson; Am Airlines, Dallas, Tex; Coca Colo Co of Brazil, Sao Paulo, Brazil; plus others. *Comn:* Mural painting, Urban Wall, Atlanta, Ga, 90; floor painting, Vets Stadium, Philadelphia, 92; mural painting, Royal Caribbean Cruise Line, Oslo, Norway, 96; mural painting, Sinai Hosp, Baltimore, 96; mural painting, Meridian Co, Indianapolis, 96. *Exhib:* Corcoran Biennial Am Painting, 63; Univ Colo Show, 63; Am Painting & Sculpture Ann, Pa Acad Fine Arts, 64; Art Inst Chicago Ann, 65; solo exhibs, Henri Gallery, Washington, DC, 87, Savannah Col Art & Design, Savannah, Ga, 87, Three Financial Plaza, Chicago, 88, Franz Bader Gallery, Washington, DC, 89, Fairleigh Dickinson Univ, Hackensack, NJ, 90, Herr-Chambliss Gallery, Hot Springs, Ark, 90 Retrospective Gallery, La Jolla, Calif, 90; Broadway Windows, NY, 92; Asheville Mus, NC, 95; Richmond Mus, Ind, 96; Austin Mus, Tex, 97. *Pos:* Theatre designer, Goucher Col, Theatre Hopkins & Ctr Stage, Baltimore, 66-; art critic, Baltimore Sun, 69 & 70; area reviewer, Craft Horizons Mag, 69-75. *Teaching:* Instr painting & design, Baltimore Hebrew Congregation, 62-; instr painting & color theory, Md Inst, Baltimore, 65-80; lectr design, Goucher Col, 66-69; lectr art hist, Univ Md, Catonsville, 69-70; instr painting, Baltimore Jewish Community Ctr, 62-80. *Awards:* Rinehart Fel, Md Inst, 64-66; Best in Show, Loyola Col, 66; Florsheim Art Fund Grant, 91; and others. *Bibliog:* B Rose (auth), article, Art Int, 11/62; articles, Arts Mag, 11/62 & Art News, 11/62, Baltimore Sun, 4/78 & 10/88, Artspeak, 11/84 & 9/85, Manhatten Arts, 3/84, New Art Examiner, 3/89, NY Times, 2/90 & 7/92. *Media:* Oil, Watercolor; All media. *Publ:* Auth, Baltimore's top twelve, Baltimore Mag, 5/69; auth & illusr, An artist's travel log, Baltimore News Am, 71; illusr, Shore Writers' Sampler, Friendly Harbor Press, 87. *Mailing Add:* 113 Elizabeth St New York NY 10013

R

RAAB, GAIL B
COLLAGE ARTIST, PAINTER
b New York, NY, Jan 15, 34. *Study:* Univ Colo with Louis Shanker, 53; Univ Mex, 54; Tyler Sch Fine Arts, BFA with honors, 55; Queens Col. *Work:* Philadelphia Mus; Seventeen Mag, NY; Scherling-Plough Corp, NJ; CBS Recordings, NY. *Comn:* Paintings, Columbia Broadcasting, NY, 86; wall assemblage, Schering-Plough Corp, NJ, 88; wall collages, Haines, Lundberg Waehler, NY, 89; Miniature Mus, Amsterdam, 96. *Exhib:* Solo-exhibs, Viridian Gallery, NY, 80, 82, Whitney-Clark Gallery, Lenox, Mass, 88 & Bachelier, Cardonsky, Kent, Conn, 90 & 96, Pepper Gallery, Boston, Mass, 99, OK Harris Gallery, New York City, 2000; Paper Works, Berkshire, Pittsfield, Mass, 88 & 89 & Nassau Co, NY, 88 & 89; Nat Asn Women Artists Juried Show, Nat Acad Design, NY, 88 & 89; Marabella Gallery, Bks & Co, NY, 90; OK Harris, NY, 1995, 1997, I Love NY Benefit, 2001, Collage & Assemblage, 2002; OK Harris Gallery, NY, 97, 2004; UTE Stebich Gallery, Lennox, Mass, 98; Ensembles, Pepper Gallery, Boston, 2003; Hidell Brooks Gallery, Charlotte, NC, 2004; SKH Gallery, Great Barrington, Mass, 2005. *Pos:* Art Reach dir, Whitney Mus, NY, 89-90. *Awards:* Medal of Honor, 80 & C Winston Mem Prize, 88, Nat Asn Women Artists; Martha Reed Mem Award. *Bibliog:* Jeanne Paris (auth), The artists inspiration, Newsday, 6/2/78; Jerry Tallmer (rev), New York Post, 6/3/78; Margaret Pomfret (rev), Arts Mag, 1/80. *Mem:* Nat Asn Women Artists (exec bd); Long Island Craftsman Guild. *Media:* Mixed Media, Acrylic, Collage, Paper. *Interests:* Collecting found objects to incorporate in collages of hist meaning. *Dealer:* OK Harris Gallery, 383 W Broadway, New York, 10012; Pepper Gallery,38 Newbury St, Boston, 02116. *Mailing Add:* 300 E 74th St No 25G New York NY 10021

RAASH, KATHLEEN FORECKI
PAINTER
b Milwaukee, Wis, Sept 12, 50. *Study:* Univ Wis, Eau Claire, BS, 72; Univ Wis, Milwaukee, MFA, 78. *Work:* Univ Wis, Eau Claire & Madison; Fine Arts Gallery, Univ Wis, Milwaukee; Miller Brewing Co, Milwaukee, Wis; Fed Reserve Bank, Minneapolis, Minn; Rhinelander Med Ctr, Wis; Univ Hosp, Madison, Wis. *Exhib:* Artists Chicago & Vicinity, Art Inst Chicago, 80; solo exhibs, Duluth Art Inst, Minn, 84, Wis Acad, Madison, 96 & Wis Union Theater, Univ Wis, Madison, 2000, Mount Senario Col, Ladysmith, Wis, 2001; two person shows, W Bend Art Mus, Wis, 95 & Ctr Visual Arts, Wausau, Wis, 98, State Reginal Ctr, Eau Claire, Wis, 2002, Nicolet Col, Rhinelander, Wis, 2005; group exhibs, View from Four Corners, Minnetonka Ctr, Wayzata, Minn, 96, Gallery 110 North, Plymouth, Wis, 2001, Bloomington Art Ctr, Bloomington, Minn, 2001; The Art Garden, Paine Art Ctr, Oshkosh, Wis, 98; Woodward Gallery, NY, 2000; Watrous Gallery, Madison, Wis, 2004. *Teaching:* summer art instr, Univ Wis, Milw, 1978; Instr, Treehaven Tomahawk, Univ Wis, Stevens Point, 98. *Awards:* Purchase Award, United Bank & Trust of Madison, 78, Wis Arts Bd, 2001, Hon Mention, Paine Art Ctr, Wis, 2002. *Media:* Oil. *Publ:* auth, Pamela Powers, Creative State, Eau Claire Leader, 2/2002; Kit Basquin (auth), Second anniversary show, New Art Examiner, 3/80; Dean Jenson (auth), Forecki Show, Milwaukee Sentinel, 1/16/81; Joy Marquardt (auth), Rippling Waters, Wausau Daily Herald, 4/23/98. *Dealer:* Peltz Gallery 119 E Knapp St Milwaukee WI 53202; Woodwalk Gallery 8496 Hwy 42, Fish Creek, Wis, 54212; Riveredge Galleries 432 E Main St Mishicot WI 54228; Premier Gallery 141 S 7th St Minneapolis MN 55402; Moondeer Gallery 10362 Main St Boulder Junction WI. *Mailing Add:* W 1630 Bear Trail Rd Gleason WI 54435

RABB, JEANNETTE See Solomon, (Mrs) Sidney L

RABB, MADELINE M
CONSULTANT
b Jan 27, 45. *Study:* Univ Md, College Park, 61-63; Md Inst Col Art, Baltimore, BFA(painting), 66; Ill Inst Technol, Inst Design, MS(visual design), 75. *Exhib:* In Our Own Image: Works by Woman, Capital East Graphics, Washington, DC, 80; The Chicago Exchange Group, Chicago State Univ Gallery, 81; The Young Collector's Sale, Renaissance Soc Invitational, Univ Chicago, 82; Jazzonia Gallery, Detroit, Mich, 83; Members Show, Arts Club Chicago, 84-85; Exhibs of Artists Mems, Arts Club, Chicago, 84-2001. *Pos:* Asst dir art & production, Tuesday Publs, Chicago, 66-68; vpres-bus manager, Myra Everett Designs Inc, Chicago, 77-78; account exec, Corporate Concierge, Chicago, 78-79; owner, Madeline Murphy Rabb Studio, Chicago, 79-83; exec dir, Chicago Office Fine Arts, 83-90; pres, Murphy Rabb Inc, Chicago, 91-. *Awards:* Numerous Awards for work and service to publ. *Bibliog:* Big City Cultural Bosses (article), Ebony Mag, 88. *Mem:* Arts Club Chicago; Nat Conf Artists; Chicago Artists Coalition; Art Table Inc; Ill Arts Alliance; Women's Bd, Md Inst Coll of Art. *Media:* Fine Arts. *Publ:* Auth, Removing Cultural Viaducts: Initiatives for Traditionally Underserved Audiences, Connections Quarterly, 86; Chicago: An Artistic Renaissance Under Way, Am Visions Mag, 87. *Mailing Add:* c/o Murphy Rabb Inc 400 S Green St Unit G Chicago IL 60607-3533

RABBIT, RUNNING See Red Star, Kevin (Running Rabbit)

RABINOVICH, RAQUEL
PAINTER, SCULPTOR
b Buenos Aires, Arg, Mar 30, 29, Am citizen. *Study:* Univ Cordoba, Arg; Univ Edinburgh; Atelier Andre LHote, Paris. *Work:* Ark Art Ctr, Little Rock; Miami Art Mus; Reading (Pa) Pub Mus; World Bank Fine Art Collection, Washington, DC; NJ State Mus, Trenton. *Comn:* Emergences (site specific sculpture installations on Hudson River shores), ongoing; sculpture mem, Threshold, Marbletown, NY. *Exhib:* Eric Stark Gallery, NY, 91-92; Presence/Absence, Trans Hudson Gallery, NJ, 95; Lehigh Univ Art Galleries, Pa, 96; Trans Hudson Gallery, NY, 2000; Collaborative Concepts, NY, 2003; Hudson River Mus, NY, 2003; Weatherspoon Art Mus, NC, 2004; Yellow Bird Gallery, NY, 2005; Lesley Heller Gallery, NY, 2006. *Teaching:* Lectr, Whitney Mus, 83-86 & Marymount Manhattan Col, 84-90, NY. *Awards:* Fel, Nat Endowment Arts, 91 & US/France Paris residency award, 92; NY State Coun Arts Grant, 95; grant, Pollock-Krasner Found, 2001. *Bibliog:* Michael Kimmelman (auth), Art Rev, NY Times, 90; Fatima Bercht (auth), catalog essay, 90; Patrick Smith (auth), article, catalog essay, 92; Nicole Krauss (auth), Art in Am, 1999; William Zimmer (auth), Art Review, NY, 2004. *Mem:* Am Abstract Artists. *Media:* Oil; Stone, Rivers & Mud. *Publ:* Auth, The Dark is the Source of Light, Contemporary Artists Collection, Sta Hill Arts. *Mailing Add:* 141 Lamoree Rhinebeck NY 12572

RABINOVICH, RHEA SANDERS See Sanders, Rhea Sanders Rabinovich

RABINOVITCH, WILLIAM AVRUM
PAINTER, FILMMAKER
b New London, Conn, Sept 16, 36. *Study:* Worcester Polytech Inst, BSME, 58; Boston Mus Sch Fine Arts; San Francisco Art Inst, MFA, 73; Whitney Mus, independent study prog, 73. *Work:* Mus Mod Art, Wendy's, NY; Fairmont Hotel, San Francisco; Mercedes Benz Show Room, San Rafael, Calif. *Comn:* Mural, Fairmont Hotel, 77-2005; US Post Off, Canal St, NY, 87-2005; Pablo Picasso (video doc), comn by Marc Ham, Metrop Mus Art, 94. *Exhib:* One-man exhibs, Pac Grove Art Ctr, 91, Wendy's, NY, 95-2005, Soho Arts Festival, Artist's Studio Tour, 96-, Ross Power Gallery, Miami, Fla, 98-2001; Cineprobe Series, Mus Mod Art, NY, 2001; plus many others. *Pos:* Dir, Whitney Counterweight, 77, 79 & 81; dir & producer, Art Seen (cable show), NY, 93-99; bd dir, Artist Talk on Art Symp Series, NY, 93-2005; proj dir, DVD Arts Proj, 2001; producer cable TV, Manhattan Neighborhood Network, NY, 93-2003; dir, producer, creator, Pollock Squared, feature film, 99-2005. *Awards:* Nat Endowment Arts Grant, 77; Video Prod Grant, Time/Warner-Manhattan Neighborhood Network, 94 & 2000; Leonhardt Found, 99. *Bibliog:* New York Arts Mag, 2003; Fine Arts Guide to Marketing and Self-Promotion, 2003; Don Wigal (auth), Jackson Pollock: Veiling the Image, 2005. *Media:* Multi. *Res:* DVD 15 Year Video Archive of Visual Arts in NY. *Publ:* Cover artist, Jacob Boehme & Gregory of Nyssa: The Life of Moses, Paulist Press, 78; dir, Full Length Feature Movie on Jackson Pollack, 2001. *Dealer:* Ross Power Gallery 3701 NE 2nd Ave & 37th St Miami FL 33137. *Mailing Add:* PO Box 403 Canal St Station New York NY 10013

RABINOWITCH, DAVID
SCULPTOR
b Toronto, Ont, Mar 6, 43. *Study:* Univ W Ont, BA. *Work:* Mus Mod Art, NY; Boston Mus Fine Arts; Mus Contemp Art, Los Angeles; Nat Gallery Can, Ottawa; Art Gallery, Ont, Toronto, Can; Mus Fine Arts, Montreal, Can; Bibliot Nat Centre Pompidou, Paris; Fogg Art Mus, Harvard; Nat Gallery, Berlin; Mus Ludwig, Cologne and others. *Comn:* Clocktower and PS1, NY, 76; Forum Metall, City of Linz, Austria, 77; Documenta VI-Viii, Kassel, Ger, 77, 82 & 87; Situation Kunst, Ruhr Univ, Bochum, Ger, 86-90; Muzeum Historii Miasta, Lodz, Poland, 90; Cathedral Notre Dame de Boarg, Digue, Reigional Systems Cult Affairs, France, 93; Tapestry, Le Dorat Collegiate Church, France, 99; Carved Systems in Involution (sculpture, with Steven Oliver), Oliver Ranch, Geyserville, Calif, 2001. *Exhib:* One-man shows, Richard Bellamy/Oil & Steel, NY, 78-92, Mus van Hedendaagse Kunst, Gent, Belg, 78, Mus Haus Lange, Krefeld, Ger, 78, Galerie Mailhot, Montreal, 79, Haus Ester, Krefeld, Ger, 87, Kunsthalle Tubingen, Ger, 87, Kunsthalle Bielefeld, Ger, 88, Kunstmuseum Düsseldorf, Ger, 88, Flynn, NY, 89-92, Galerie Nächst St Stephan, Vienna, 90, Renos Xippas, Paris, 91 & Kunsthalle Baden-Baden, 92, Kunstmuseum Winterthur, Switz, 93, 2004, Galerie Nationale du Jeu de Paume, Paris, 93, Peter Blum, NY, 93-2003, Glypotothek, Munich, 94 & Akira Ikeda Gallery, NY, 94, Zacheta Gallery of Contemp Art, Starmach Gallery, 99; Art Gallery Ont, Toronto, 68-; Nat Gallery Can, Ottawa, 68-; Mus Mod Art, Paris, 72, 77, 82 & 91; Mus Mod Art, NY, 77 & 79; Kaiser-Wilhelm Mus, Krefeld, Ger, 92; Mus des 20 Jahrhunderts, Vienna, 93; Kuntshaus, Zurich, 94; Städtische, Chemnitz, Ger, 95; Sammlangen Fogg Mus, Harvard Univ, 96; Lokhalle, Gottingen, 2001; Mus Art Contemporain of Montreal, 2003; Nat Gallery Can, 2004. *Teaching:* Instr, Yale, 74-75 & Kunstakademie Dusseldorf, 84-. *Awards:* Guggenheim Fel, 75; Can Coun Lynch Staunton Award, 77; Nat Endowment Arts, 86. *Bibliog:* Kenneth Baker (auth) Art in America, 74, 75; Donald Kuspit (auth), Artforum, 92; Catarina Neiman (auth), David Rabinowitch: Tyndale Contructions, 90; Whitney Davis, Pacing the World, 1996. *Media:* All. *Publ:* Auth, article, Artforum, 91; article, Parkett, 91; article, Blast, 91; interview, Das Kunstwerk, 91; article, Drawings of a Beech Tree, Düsseldorf, 92; article, Kunst und Kirche, 93. *Mailing Add:* 639 Second St Greenport NY 11944

RABINOWITCH, ROYDEN LESLIE
SCULPTOR
b Toronto, Ont, Mar 6, 43. *Study:* Self taught. *Work:* Guggenheim Mus, NY; Kunsthaus Zurich, Switz; Stedelijk Mus, Amsterdam, Neth; Watari Mus Contemp Art, Tokyo, Japan; Kunstmuseum, Düsseldorf, Ger. *Comn:* Rotation and Translation of the Top, comn by Sarabhai family, The Retreat Ahmedabad, India, 83; Eloges de Fontenelle, Toronto Conv Ctr, Can, 84; Tomb of Dr Josef Hoet, Ghent, Belg, 87; Judgement on the Keplerian Revolution, Furkapasshohe, Swiss Alps, 87. *Exhib:* SMAK, Ghent, 99; Limerick City Mus, Ireland, 2000; Galerie Foksal, Warsaw, 2001; Irish Mus Mod Art, Dublin, 2003; Musée des Beaux-Arts, La Chaux-de-Fonds, Switz, 2004; Beijing Biennale, China, 2005; Marta Herford, Ger, 2005. *Pos:* Life mem, Clare Hall, Cambridge Univ, Gt Brit, 86-. *Teaching:* Adj prof hist art, Leiden Univ, Neth, 94; Maxwell Cummings Disting lectr, McGill Univ, Montreal, 2002. *Awards:* Lynch Staunton Award of Distinction, Can Coun, 85; Officer of the Order of Can, 2002; Queen Elizabeth Golden Jubilee Medal, 2003. *Bibliog:* Adolf Krischanitz (auth), Royden Rabinowitch, Wiener Secession, Vienna, 91; R H Fuchs (auth), Royden Rabinowitch, Sculpture 1962/1992, Haags Gemeentemuseum, The Hague, 92; Robert Kwak (auth), Royden Rabinowitch's Judgment on the Copernican Revolution: The Virtual Documentary, DXNet, Toronto, 2002. *Media:* Mixed. *Publ:* Auth, Development of the Early Sculpture Leading to the Most Recent Sculpture, Orchard Press, 83; auth, Mankind Breaking Through the Clouds of Heaven Recognizing New Spheres, Determining the Ethics of Stan Laurel & Oliver Hardy, Technical Univ, Berling, Ger, 2006. *Dealer:* Ian Mccallum. *Mailing Add:* Jan Verspeyenstraat 15 B-9000 Ghent Belgium

RABKIN, LEO
SCULPTOR, PAINTER
b Cincinnati, Ohio, July 21, 1919. *Study:* Univ Cincinnati; NY Univ. *Work:* Mus Mod Art, Whitney Mus Am Art, Guggenheim Mus, NY; Smithsonian Inst; Bass Mus, Fla; Brooklyn Mus, NY; NC Mus, Raleigh; Newburger Mus, Purchase, NY; Cincinnati Ar Mus, Ohio; Baruch Gallery, SUNY, NY; Tel-Aviv. *Exhib:* Seven Painting & Sculpture Biennials, Whitney Mus Am Art, 59-69 & Drawings & Watercolor, 74 & 75; A Plastic Presence, San Francisco Mus Art, Milwaukee Art Ctr & Jewish Mus, 70; Storm King Art Ctr, Mountainville, NY, 70; one-man shows, La Jolla Mus Contemp Art, 81 & Marilyn Pearl Gallery, NY, 81, 83, 84, 86, 89 & 90, Drew Univ, NJ & Herbert Lust Gallery, NY, 96; Art Concrete, Nuremberg, WGer, 83; Persistence of Abstraction, Wichita, Kans, 92; Va Lust Gallery, NY, 96; Lust Gallery, NY, 99; Boxes Exhib, Roslyn Libr, NY, 2000; and others. *Pos:* Mem bd dir, Fine Arts Fedn, NY, 70-, hon vpres, 89-. *Awards:* Ford Found Award for Watercolor, 61; First Prize for Watercolor, Silvermine Guild Artists, 61; Richard Florsheim Art Fund, 98. *Bibliog:* Clarence Bunch (auth), Acrylic for Sculpture & Design, Van Nostrand Reinhold, NY, 72; Robert Bishop (auth), American Folk Sculpture, EP Dutton & Co Inc, NY, 79; Robert Bishop (auth), Treasure of American Folk Art, Harry N Abrams Inc, NY, 79. *Mem:* Am Abstr Artists (pres, 64-78); US Comn Int Asn Art (secy, 68-70); Fine Arts Fedn (bd dir), NY. *Media:* Shadow Box Constructions, Works on Paper, Digital Print, Shadows. *Collection:* Dorothea & Leo Rabkin: outsiders art; 20th Century American Art (outsider), Shaker Artifacts & Furniture; Glyptic (Sumerian); Primitive American Folk Art, AAA Journals, 2000, 03. *Publ:* Ed, American Abstract Artists, 1936-1966. *Dealer:* Lust Gallery 61 Sullivan New York NY 10012. *Mailing Add:* 218 W 20th St New York NY 10011

RABY , JULIAN
GALLERY DIRECTOR
b London, Eng, 50. *Study:* Univ, Oxford, PhD in Oriental Studies, 81. *Pos:* Lectr, in Islamic Art & Archit Univ, Oxford, Eng, 79-2002; chmn of curs, Oriental Inst, 91-93, 95-2000; chmn of bd, fac of Oriental Studies, 93-95; Found, former co-owner Azimuth Eds publ. *Teaching:* dir, Freer Gallery of Art and Arthur M Sackler Gallery, Smithsonian Instit, Wash, 2002-. *Mem:* Fel, Soc of Antiquaries; Coun of Britis Inst of Archaeology and Hist, Amman, Jordan. *Publ:* Series found and editor Oxford Studies in Islamic Art; auth: Venice, Durer, and the Oriental Mode, 1982, IZNIK: The Pottery of Ottoman Turkey, 1989, Turkish Bookbinding in the 15th Century, The found of a Court Style, 1993, Qajar Portraits, 1999. *Mailing Add:* Freer Gallery of Art Smithsonian Instn MCR707 PO Box 37012 Washington DC 20013-7012

RACHOFSKY, HOWARD
COLLECTOR, PATRON
Pos: bd dirs, Dallas Symphony Asn, Dallas Mus Art, NY City Dia Ctr Arts, E Dallas Community Sch, Tate Lecture Series, Southern Methodist Univ; adv dir, Booker T Washington Magnet High Sch for Performing and Visual Arts, Dallas Theater Ctr, Dallas Archit Found, Univ Tex Sch Archit; founder, bd dirs, Dallas Ctr for Performing Arts Found, chair site design comt; mem adv bd, Wharton Club, Dallas/Ft Worth, Dalls Bus Comt for the Arts; founder, Howard Earl Rachofsky Found; mem investment comt, St Phillips Acad. *Awards:* Named one of Top 200 Collectors, ARTnews mag, 2003-06. *Mailing Add:* Dallas Ctr for Performing Arts 2106 Boll St Dallas TX 75204

RACITI, CHERIE
PAINTER
b Chicago, Ill, June 17, 42. *Study:* Univ Ill, Urbana, 60-61; Memphis Col Arts, Tenn, 63-65; San Francisco State Univ, BA, 68; Mills Col, Oakland, MFA, 79. *Work:* San Francisco Mus of Mod Art, Calif; Mills Col, Oakland; San Francisco Redevelopment Agency. *Exhib:* Whitney Mus Am Art Biennial, NY, 75; Los Angeles Inst Contemp Art, Calif, 76 & 78; one-woman shows, Adaline Kent Award Exhib, San Francisco Art Inst, 77, Fuller-Goldeen Gallery, San Francisco, 79, Marianne Deson, Chicago, 80, Long Beach Mus, Calif, 82 & Mills Col Art Mus, 98; Angles Gallery & Fresno Mus, 87; Reese Bullen Gallery, Humboldt State Univ, Arcadia, Calif, 90; Terrain, San Francisco, Calif, 92; In/Out of the Cold, Inagural Exhib, Ctr Arts, San Francisco, 93; two person show, Santa Monica Col, 98; 25/25 Southern Exposuer 25th Ann Exhib, 99; Art Coun Awards, Jernigan Wicker Fine Arts, 2000; Conceptual Color, Santa Cruz Mus, 03; New Geometries, Thatcher Gallery, Univ San Francisco, 2004. *Teaching:* prof art, San Francisco State Univ, 89-; prof, Calif State Univ, Hayward, 74; prof, San Francisco Art Inst, 78; prof, San Francisco State Univ, Col Creative Arts, 77-. *Awards:* Trefethen Fel, Mills Col, 79; Eureka Fel, Fleishhacker Found, 88; Djerassi Resident Artist Prog, 94; Brit Travel Grant, 95; Tyrone Guthrie Ctr, Ireland, 95; Millay Colony Arts, Austerlitz, NY, 99; Juror's Award, The Art Coun, Inc, San Francisco, 2000; Va Ctr Creative Arts, 2005. *Bibliog:* Thomas Albright (auth), Art in the San Francisco Bay Area, 1945-1980, Univ Calif Press, 85; Marlena Donohue (auth), LA Times, 1987; Moira Roth (ed), Connecting Conversations: Interviews with 28 Bay Area Woman Artists, Eucalyptus Press, 88; Judy Moran (ed), New Langton Arts, The First Fifteen Years, New Langton Arts, San Francisco, 90; Keith Lachowicz & Mark Johnson (auths, catalog) Mills College Museum 15 Year Survey, 98; Alicia Miller (auth), Art Week, 1999; Jeff Kelley (auth), Art Week, 1999; DeWitt Cheng (auth), Art Week, 10/2004; Colin Berry (auth), Art Week, 11/2004. *Mem:* San Francisco Art Inst Artist Comt (mem, 74-85); New Langton Arts (bd mem, 88-92). *Media:* Acrylic, Mixed Media. *Mailing Add:* 365 San Jose Ave San Francisco CA 94110

RACKUS, GEORGE (KEISTUS)
PAINTER, PRINTMAKER
b Lithuania, May 29, 27; Can citizen. *Study:* Wayne Univ, 48-50; Ont Col Art, 50-52; with Andre L'Hote, 52-55; Ecole des Beaux Arts, Paris, 52-55. *Work:* Victoria & Albert Mus, London; New York Cent Libr; Nat Gallery Can; NB Mus, St John; Contemp Mus, Sao Paulo, Brazil; Lithuanian Art Mus, Vilnius; R McLaughlin Gallery, Can; Art Gallery Ont, Can; and others. *Comn:* Murals (anodized aluminum), Howoco, Brussels, 69, Alcan Aluminum Ltd, Toronto, 70, Shell Can, Oakville, Ont, 70, Univ Western Ont, London, 71 & Dental Arts Bldg, Dunnville, Ont, 75. *Exhib:* Solo exhib, Galerie Foyer des Artists, Paris, 54-59, Anodized Aluminum Works, Commonwealth Inst, London, 70 & Anodized Aluminum Works & Prints, NB Mus, St John, 73; Agnes LeFort Galerie, Montreal, 60; Picture Loan Soc - Gallery, Toronto, 60, 63, 65, 66, 69 & 71; Gallery Moos, Toronto, 62; Fifth Ann Exhib Can Art, Montreal Mus, 62; Can Nat Art Gallery Tour for Australia, Nat Art Gallery, Victoria, 67, Nat Gallery, S Australia, Adelaide, 67 & Art Gallery New SWales, Sydney, 68; Vilnius Contemp Mus, Lithuania, 79, 87 & 88; Brand Libr Art Gallery, Glendale, Calif, 81; Grimsby Art Gallery, Can, 86; Peel Region Art Gallery, Brampton, Can, 87; Goethe Inst, Toronto, 87; traveling exhibs, Lithuania Mus Tour, 88 & art exhib, Dum Polonii, Warsaw & Paltusky, Poland, 89-90. *Pos:* Admin & Cur, Glenhyrst Arts Coun, Brantford, Can, 62-63; admin, Colour & Form Soc, Can, 85-89, admin, 89-. *Teaching:* Instr art, Dundas Valley Art Sch, Ont, 65-66, McMaster Univ, Hamilton, Ont, 68-69 & Brock Univ, St Catharines, Ont, 77-78. *Awards:* Print of Yr, Soc Can Painter-Etchers & Engravers, 71; Graphic Award, Baltic Roots, Baltic Studies Asn, 78; First Prize Anodized Aluminum Work, Colour & Form Exhib, 81. *Bibliog:* Robert Ayre (auth), article, Montreal Star, 62; Robert Percival (cur), doc, New Brunswick Mus; Paul Duval (auth), doc, 88. *Mem:* Ont Soc Artists Can (pres, 86-88); Colour & Form Soc Can (pres, 74-76 & 79-84); Print Consortium, USA. *Media:* Anodized Aluminum, Lithography. *Publ:* Auth, British sculpture at Montreal Museum, Wkly, 61; A painter speaks up, Globe & Mail, 62; Anodized aluminum as an art media, 71 & Exploring new media, Vol II, 71, Arts Mag, Can. *Mailing Add:* 1998 Lakeshore Rd W Mississauga ON L5J 1J8 Canada

RADAN, GEORGE TIVADAR
ADMINISTRATOR, HISTORIAN
b Budapest, Hungary, Dec 31, 23; US citizen. *Study:* Univ Budapest, MA, 46 PhD, 48, with Peter Pazmany; Ecole de Louvre, Paris AEM, 67. *Work:* Nat Maritime Mus, Haifa, Israel. *Collection Arranged:* Ships through the Ages (with catalog), Nat Maritime Mus, 55. *Pos:* Dir archeol, Ky State Univ & Wayne State Univ, 70-76; dir archeol excavations, Siena, 84. *Teaching:* Prof art hist, Villanova Univ, Pa, 60-, chmn dept art, 63-; prof art hist, Am Col in Paris, 66-67. *Awards:* Am Coun Learned Soc Scholarship to Hungary Acad Sci, 73 & 75; Outstanding Fac Publ Award, 85. *Mem:* Col Art Asn; Asn Ancient Historians; Italian Art Soc. *Media:* Archaeologist. *Res:* Art historian dealing with ancient art and archeology. *Interests:* Naval Decoration. *Publ:* Auth, An Introduction to Ancient Art and Architecture, 67, Del Villanova Press; Coauth, The Archeology of Roman Pannonia, Univ Ky Press, 80; The Sons of Serulon, Jewish Maritime Hist, 80; The Villanova University Art Collection: A Guide, Villanova Press, 86; Lecceto, Silvania Editoriale, 91; Augustine in Iconography, Lang, 98; and others. *Mailing Add:* Dept History Villanova Univ Villanova PA 19085

RADECKI, MARTIN JOHN
ADMINISTRATOR, CONSERVATOR
b South Bend, Ind, Jan 4, 48. *Study:* Ind Univ, AB, 70; Intermuseum Conserv Lab (internship), 74-75. *Exhib:* Forgery: The Steele/Forsyth Controversy, 89. *Collection Arranged:* Conservation of Indiana Governors Portraits, Indianapolis Mus Art, 78. *Pos:* Apprentice conservator, Indianapolis Mus Art, 71-73, asst conservator, 73-74, actg chief conservator, 75-; conserv intern, Intermuseums Conserv Lab, 74-75, chief conservator, 75-. *Mem:* fel Am Inst Conserv Historic & Artistic Works; Int Inst Conserv Historic & Artistic Works. *Res:* Treatment of blanched paintings; methods of forgery detection, specifically on late 14th-early 20th century American paintings. *Mailing Add:* 9029 Chestnut Ct Indianapolis IN 46260-1055

RADES, WILLIAM L
PAINTER, SCULPTOR
b Milwaukee, Wis, Aug 13, 43. *Study:* Univ Wis, Milwaukee, BFA, 65, MFA, 68; San Francisco Art Inst, with Ron Nagle & Jack Jefferson, 66. *Work:* Santa Barbara Mus Art, Calif; Am Telephone & Telegraph, NY; Minneapolis Inst Art, Minn; Georgia Pacific Corp, Portland, Ore; Eastern Wash Univ, Cheney. *Comn:* Drawing on paper, Wash State Arts Comn & Evergreen State Col, Olympia, 79; painting on paper, Wash State Arts Comn, Olympia, 80; painted wood relief, Wash State Arts Comn, Spokane, 82. *Exhib:* Oregon Artists Under 35, Portland Art Mus, 74 & 77; Drawing USA, Minn Mus Art, 77; Washington Painting, Tacoma Art Mus, 77, 79 & 81; 21st Nat Chautauqua Exhib Am Art, NY, 78; Illusionism: Handmade, Henry Art Gallery, Univ Wash, Seattle, 81; Northwest Perspectives, traveling exhib in US, 82-84. *Teaching:* Instr drawing, Univ Wis, Milwaukee, 65-68; asst instr ceramics, San Francisco Art Inst, 66; vis asst prof drawing, Ore State Univ, 72-74. *Awards:* Purchase Awards, Pensacola Nat Drawing Competition, Visual Arts Gallery, 76, Drawing USA, Minn Mus Art, 77 & Fourth LaGrange Nat Competition, CVAA Gallery, 78. *Bibliog:* Bill Rades paintings, Artweek, 74; Mus interview, KTRS Pub TV, 82; Harvey West (auth), The Washington Year, Univ Wash Press, 82. *Mem:* Col Art Asn. *Mailing Add:* 12709 Lake City Blvd SW Tacoma WA 98498-4211

RADOCZY, ALBERT
PAINTER
b Stamford, Conn, Oct 24, 1914. *Study:* Parsons Sch Design; Cooper Union, grad. *Work:* Brooklyn Mus, NY; Ball State Teachers Col, Ind; Lyman Allyn Mus, Conn; Sloan-Kettering Mem. *Comn:* Tapestry murals, Allegheny Col, Meadville, Pa, 66. *Exhib:* NJ State Mus Ann, Trenton, 61; Whitney Mus Am Art Ann, NY, 62; Brooklyn Mus Nat Print Exhib, NY, 62; Mus Mod Art Lending Collection, 65; Bergen Community Mus, 73; The Figure in Drawing, Univ of Bridgeport, 77. *Teaching:* Lectr drawing, Cooper Union, 50-55; prof design, City Col New York, 55-. *Awards:* Purchase Award, Ball State Teachers Col, 59. *Media:* Oil. *Dealer:* Romantiquities Art Gallery 759 Greenwich St New York NY 10014. *Mailing Add:* 61 Cedar St Cresskill NJ 07626

RADOVICH, DONALD
PAINTER, EDUCATOR
b Nazareth, Pa, Jan 3, 32. *Study:* Univ NMex, BFA, 56, with Randall Davey & Kenneth Adams, MA, 60; also in San Miquel Allende, Mex, 70. *Work:* Univ NMex Mus, Albuquerque; State Capitol, Santa Fe, NMex; Nat Wildlife Fedn, Washington, DC. *Exhib:* Wave Hill Mus, Bronx, NY, 82; Ark Wildlife Fedn Traveling Exhib, 85; Colo Ctr Arts, Grand Junction, 86; one-man exhib, Nat Wildlife Fedn, Washington, 88, Am Birding Asn Exhib, Park City, Utah, 96-, Wilson Club Conv, Manhattan, Kans, 97. *Teaching:* Prof painting, Western State Col, Gunnison, Colo, 64-88, emer prof, 88-; instr, Nat Wildlife Fedn, Washington, DC & Estes Park, Colo, 78-85; Keynote Address, Guild of Natural Science Illustrators 1992, Rocky Mountain Biological Laboratory, 90-92. *Awards:* Gold Medal, Nat Exhib, Tubac, Ariz, 65; Purchase Award, Nat Exhib, Cedar City, Utah, 68. *Bibliog:* J W Campbell (auth), Donald Radovich: Artist, naturalist, teacher, Southwestern Art, Vol IV, No 4, 74. *Mem:* Kappa Pi (sponsor, 65-). *Media:* Oil, Watercolor. *Publ:* Colorado Birds, Denver Mus Nat Hist, 92; Atlas-Birds Monteray Co, Calif, 93; Birdfinding in Colorado, Am Birding Asn, Holt, 97; Guide to Birds of West Indies, Princeton Press, 98; State of Ind, Wildlife Calendar, 99-2000

RADY, ELSA
CERAMIST, SCULPTOR
b New York, NY, July 29, 43. *Study:* Chouinard Art Sch, 62-66. *Work:* Smithsonian Inst, Renwick Gallery, Washington, DC; Boston Mus Fine Arts; Victoria & Albert Mus Art, London, England; Brooklyn Mus, NY; Los Angeles Co Mus Art; Metrop Mus Art; NYNEX Corp, White Plains, NY; Chase Manhattan Bank, NY; General Motors, NY; Am Med Int Inc, Beverly Hills, Calif; Denver Art Mus; and many others. *Comn:* Sculptures, Jules Stein Eye Inst, Univ Calif, Los Angeles, 66 & Disneyland, 67. *Exhib:* Craftsmen USA '66, Los Angeles Co Mus Art, 66; Am Porcelain, Renwick Gallery, Smithsonian Inst, Washington, DC, 80; Pacific Connections, Los Angeles Co Mus Art, 85; solo exhibs: Garth Clark Gallery, NY, 85, Jan Turner Gallery, Los Angeles, 87 & 88, Holly Solomon Gallery, NY, 87 & Lily (catalogue), 90, Ochi Gallery, Suny Valley, Idaho, 90 & Still Life (catalogue), Isetan Fine Arts Inc, Tokyo, Japan, 91; Am Potters Today, Victoria & Albert Mus, London, Eng, 86; World War II Holdings, Metrop Mus Art, NY, 89; Selections from the Joyce & Jay Cooper Collection of Contemp Ceramics, Nelson Fine Arts Ctr, Ariz State Univ Art Mus, 89-90; Building a Permanent Collection: A Perspective on the 1980s, Am Craft Mus, NY, 90; 28th Ann Ceramic Exhib (catalogue), Everson Mus Art, Syracuse, NY, 90; Southeast Bank Collects, A Corporation Views Contemp Art, Harn Mus Art, Univ Fla, West Palm Beach. *Awards:* Nat Endowment Fel, 81; Calif State Arts Comn Grant, 83. *Bibliog:* William Wilson (auth), California ceramics: shape of things to come, Los Angeles Times, 8/9/84; Mac McCloud (auth), Elsa Rady: porcelain vessels, Am Ceramics, Vol III, No 4, 85; Gerrit Henry (auth), Elsa Rady, Art News, Vol 85, No 2, 86; and others. *Media:* Ceramics; Porcelain. *Publ:* Ornaments aand Surfaces on Cermics, Kunst & Handwerk, 77; Studio Porcelain, Chilton Book Co, 80; Porcelain: Tradtions and New Visions, Watson-Guptill, 81; Ceramics of the 20th Century, Rizzoli, 82; American Crafts: A Source Book for the Home, Stewart, Tabori, Chang, 83

RAFFAEL, JOSEPH
PAINTER, PRINTMAKER
b Brooklyn, NY, Feb 22, 33. *Study:* Cooper Union, 53-54, Yale Sch Fine Arts, BFA, 56, studied with Josef Albers. *Work:* Metrop Mus Art, Whitney Mus Am Art, NY; San Francisco Mus Mod Art; Libr Cong, Hirshhorn Mus & Smithsonian Inst, Washington; Oakland Mus, Calif; Mint Mus, Charlotte, NC; and many others. *Exhib:* The Modern Era: Bay Area Update, San Francisco Mus Mod Art, 77; Eight Contemp Am Realists, Pa Acad Fine Arts, Philadelphia, 77; Drawings of the 70's, Soc Contemp Art, Art Inst Chicago, 77; one-man exhibs, San Francisco Mus Mod Art, 78-79, Butler Inst Am Art, 91, Hunter Mus Art, Chattanooga, Tenn, 92, Naples Philharmonic Ctr, Fla, 92, Louis Newman Galleries, Los Angeles, 92, Nancy Hoffman Gallery, NY, 92, 94, 96, 97 & 98 & Images Gallery, Toledo, Ohio, 95, The Canton Mus Art, Ohio, 98-99, Nancy Hoffman Gallery, NYC, 99, 01, 02; Art at Work: Recent Art from Corporate Collections, Whitney Mus Am Art, 78; New Am Monotypes, Smithsonian Inst, 79; The Decade in Review-Selections from the 1970's, Whitney Mus Am Art, 79; New Dimensions in Drawing, Aldrich Mus Contemp Art, 81; Contemp Am Realism since 1960 (traveling), Pa Acad Fine Arts, 81-83; A Private Vision: Contemp Art from the Graham Gund Collection, Mus Fine Arts, Boston, 82; Purchases of the Hirshhorn Mus, 1974-1983, Hirshhorn Mus & Sculpture Garden, 83; The Am Artist as Printmaker: Twenty-Third Nat Print Mus Exhib, Brooklyn Mus, NY, 83; Albright-Knox Art Gallery, 83; Reflections of Nature: Flowers in Am Art, Whitney Mus Am Art, 84; 50th Ann Midyear Show, Butler Inst Am Art, 86; Modern Am Realism, Sara Roby Found Collection, Nat Mus Am Art, Smithsonian Inst, 87; Close Focus: Prints, Drawings and Photographs, Smithsonian Inst, 87; California A to Z and Return, Butler Inst Am Art, 90; The Flower in Am Art, Butler Inst Am Art, 91; Nat Midyear Exhib, Butler Inst Am Art, 92; First Sightings, Denver Art Mus, 93; 57th Ann Midyear Exhib, Butler Inst Am Art, 93; Collector's Show, Ark Arts Ctr, Little Rock, 95-96; Small Scale, Nancy Hoffman Gallery, NY, 96; Painting '96, Kutztown Univ, Pa, 96; In Bloom, NJ Ctr Visual Arts, Summit, 96; Health & Happiness in Twentieth-Century Avant-Garde Art, Binghamton Univ Art Mus, NY, 96; Canton Mus Art, Ohio, 98-99; group exhibs, Nancy Hoffman Gallery, 01, 02, Taipei Gallery, New York City, 01, Ark Art Ctr, Little Rock, 01, 02, Yale Univ Sch Art, New Haven, Conn, 01, Art Foundry Gallery, Sacramento, 02, Selby Gallery, Ringling Sch of Art and Design, Sarasota, Fla, 02, TIAA/CREF, New York City, 02. *Collection Arranged:* Art Inst Chicago; Butler Inst Am Art, Youngstown, Ohio; Denver Art Mus; Fort Worth Art Mus, Tex; Smithsonian Inst; Joslyn Art Mus, Omaha, Nebr; Libr Congress, Washington, DC; Los Angeles Co Mus Art; Metrop Mus Art; Mint Mus, Charlotte, NC; Oakland Mus, Calif; Philadelphia Mus Art; San Francisco Mus Modern Art; Va Mus of Fine Arts, Richmond; Walker Art Ctr, Minneapolis; Whitney Mus Am Art, NY. *Teaching:* Instr art, Univ Calif, Davis, 66, Sch Visual Arts, New York, 67-69; assoc prof art, Univ Calif, Berkeley, 69; prof art, Calif State Univ, Sacramento, 69-74. *Awards:* Fulbright Fel to Florence & Rome, 58-59; LC Tiffany Found Fel, 60; First Prize & Purchase Award, Oakland Mus, Calif, 75. *Bibliog:* Gloria Smith (auth), The Eyes Have It: Joseph Raffael (film), NBC-TV, 72; Wm S Wilson (auth), The paintings of Jos Raffael, Studio Int, 5/74; Jerome Tarshis (auth), Nature upclose, Horizon, 9/78. *Media:* Oil, Watercolor; Lithography. *Mailing Add:* c/o Nancy Hoffman Gallery 429 W Broadway New York NY 10012

RAFFAEL, JUDITH K See North, Judy K Rafael

RAFFERTY, ANDREW
PAINTER, PRINTMAKER
Study: Boston Univ, BFA, 84; Yale Univ, MFA, 88. *Work:* Rhode Island Sch Design, Providence. *Exhib:* Mary Washington Col, Fredericksburg, Md, 87; Srathmore Hall Art Ctr, Rockville, Md, 88; Gallery Ohio, Nagoya, Japan, 92; Trenton State Col, NJ, 93; solo exhib, Hackett-Freedman Gallery, San Francisco, 94. *Teaching:* Lectr lithography, Yale Univ Sch Art, New Haven, Conn, 89-91; asst dir/instr etching, Yale Summer Sch Art, Norfolk, 88-93; fac printmaker, RI Sch Design, Providence, 91-93. *Bibliog:* Portraying the world as he finds it: The narrative paintings of Andrew Rafferty, American Artist, 95; Realism, Artnews, 96. *Mailing Add:* c/o Hackett-Freedman Gallery 250 Sutter St 4th Fl San Francisco CA 94108

RAFFERTY, JOANNE MILLER
PAINTER, COLLAGE ARTIST
b Morristown, NJ, May 31, 48. *Study:* Daemen Col, NY, with James Kuo & Jay Jodway, BS(art educ), 70; State Univ NY, Buffalo, 75, Art Educ, permanent cert. *Work:* Albright Knox Art Gallery, Buffalo, NY; Master Charge Int, NY; Bankers Trust, NY; Equitable Life Insurance, Atlanta, Ga; Dun & Bradstreet, NY; USBS Corp Headquarters, Hartford, Conn; General Motors; Exxon Corp; IBM; American Express; AT&T; Marriott Hotels; Nabisco Corp; Merril Lynch; Compuserve, NY. *Comn:* lobby, Int Bus Machines, comn by Armand Avakian, architect, Harrison, NY, 89; main lobby, Clark State Performing Arts Ctr, Springfield, Ohio, comn by Art Exchange, Columbus, Ohio, 93; main lobby, CompuServe, 5th Ave, NY, 95; main lobby, Crestar Bank, Richmond, Va, 92; main lobby, Warner Lambert Corp Hq, comn by Cloninger Fine Art, NJ, 97; main lobby, Chubb Insurance, Philadelphia, Pa, 03; int hq, Pub Svc Electric and Gas, Newark, NJ, 02. *Exhib:* solo exhibs, Broden Gallery, Madison, Wis, 91-99, 2006 & Chasen Galleries, Sarasota, Fla, 93-99, 2006, Rima Fine Art, Scottsdale, Ariz, 2001, 2005; Nat jurored Exhib Painting & Sculpture, Mus Great Plains, 84b; People's Choice Exhib, Long Beach Island Fdn Arts & Sci, Loveladies, NJ, 90; AmeriFlora, 92; Huntington Nat Bank, Columbus, Ohio, 92; Starfish Found Invitational Exhib, 93; Nat Asn Women Artists, W Broadway, NY, 94; NJ Favorite Artists Exhib, Nabisco Corp Hq, Hanover, NJ, 98; Nat Asn Women Artists Millennium Collection Exhib, Comn on the Status of Women, UN lobby, New York City, 02; NJ Ctr for Vis Arts - A Decade of Papermaking, 03; Gallerie des Artes, Sarasota, Fla, 03; Chasen Galleries, Richmond, Va, 03; Blank Canvas Benefit: For Art's Sake, Vision Arts Center NJ, 2006. *Teaching:* Instr art, Middleport Central Schs, NY, 70-71; Amherst Central Schs, NY, 71-76; Educ Dept, Montclair Mus, 94. *Awards:* NJ Watercolor Soc Award, 89; Winsor & Newton Award of Achievement, NJ Watercolor Soc Found 45th Anniversary Show, 92; Phillips Award, 50th Ann Open Exhib, Monmouth Mus, 92. *Bibliog:* J Taylor Basker (auth), Art at the Reece Galleries, Art Speak, 4/87; Susan Fields (auth), Publishers refine lines and grow, Art Business News, 4/89; Robert Merritt (auth), Rafferty paintings, Richmond Times Dispatch, 5/92; F B Glucksman (auth), Turn your passion into your profession, Income Opportunities, 1/94; Kevin Lynch (auth), Abstract art is in again, The Capital Times, 5/2000; Cindy Potters (auth), Home is Where the Art Is, Newark Star Ledger, 9/2005; Helena Miehle (auth), Joanne Rafferty: Beyond the Horizon, Fine Art Mag, 3/2006. *Mem:* Nat Asn Women Artists; NJ Watercolor Soc; New York Artists Equity. *Media:* Acrylic, Watercolor. *Dealer:* Excel Fine Art 313 Columbus Ave NY NY 10023; Rime Fine Art 7077 E Main St, Scottsdale, AZ; Uphouse Fine Art Publ, Scottsdale, AZ. *Mailing Add:* 14 Mackenzie Ln N Denville NJ 07834

RAFSKY, JESSICA C
COLLECTOR
b New York NY, Sept 18, 24. *Study:* George Washington Univ; NY Univ. *Mem:* Whitney Mus; sustaining mem Mus Mod Art; assoc Metrop Mus Art; assoc Am Fedn Arts. *Collection:* Contemporary art. *Mailing Add:* 200 E 62nd St New York NY 10021-8209

RAGGIO, OLGA
HISTORIAN, CURATOR
b Feb 5, 1926. *Study:* Liceo EO Visconti, Rome, BA(with hon), 44; Lycee Chateaubriand, Rome, Baccalaureat I, 45; Vatican Libr, dipl, 47; Sch Art Hist & Archaeol & Sch Mod Lang, Univ Rome, PhD(cum laude), 49; Inst Fine Arts, 51-53. *Exhib:* Patterns of Collecting: Selected Acquisitions 1965-1975 (coauth & ed, catalog), 75, Highlights from the Untermeyer Collection, 77-78, The Splendor of Dresden, 78-79, Treasures from the Kremlin, 79, & The Vatican Collections: The Papacy and Art, 83. *Collection Arranged:* Cent Europ Decorative Arts, 89, Europ Sculpture Ct Galleries, 90-96 & Metro Mus Art, New York. *Pos:* Cur asst, Dept Europ Sculpture & Decorative Arts, 52-54, asst cur, 54-63, assoc res cur, 63-68, cur, 68-71, chmn dept, 1971-2001, Disting rsch cur, 2001-, Metrop Mus Art, NY. *Teaching:* Adj asst prof fine arts, Inst Fine Arts, NY Univ, 64-67, adj assoc prof fine arts, 67-68, adj prof fine arts, 1968-2000. *Awards:* Metrop Mus Trustee Fel, 69; Am Coun Learned Socs Grant-in-aid, 76-77; Res Fel, Am Acad, Rome, '83; Andrew W Mellon Found Grant, 90-94; Salimberri Prize, San Severino, Italy, 2001. *Mem:* Col Art Asn Am; Am Mus Asn; Int Coun Mus Orgn; Renaissance Soc of Am. *Res:* Italian & French sculpture, Renaissance & Baroque. *Publ:* Auth, The Velez Blanco Patio, Metrop Mus Art Bulletin, Vol XXIII, pages 141-176, 64-65; Vignola, Fra Damiano et Gerolamo Siciolante à la Chapelle de la Battie d'Urfé, La Revue de l'Art, 29-52, 72; coauth, Die Bronzen der Furstlichen Sammlungen Liechtenstein, (17 entries) Frankfurt, Liebghaus, 86; New Galleries for French and Italian Sculpture at the Metropolitan Museum of Art, Gazette des Beaux Arts, Vol VI, 231-252, 12/91; The Cubbio Studiolo and its Conservation, New York, 1999, vol 1 of 2. *Mailing Add:* 64 E 94th St No 7C New York NY 10128-0773

RAGINSKY, NINA
PAINTER, PHOTOGRAPHER
b Montreal, Que. *Study:* Rutgers Univ, BA, 62. *Work:* Nat Film Bd Can; Edmonton Art Gallery; George Eastman House; Nat Gallery Can. *Exhib:* Int Photo Show, Nat Gallery Can, 68; Vision and Expression, George Eastman House, Rochester, NY, 69; solo exhibs, San Francisco Mus Art, 75 & Art Gallery Ont, 79; Between Friends, Field Mus, Chicago, 76; Nancy Hoffman Gallery, New York City. *Teaching:* Instr photog, Emily Carr Col Art, Vancouver, 72-81; workshops, Univ Ottawa, Univ Victoria & Banff Sch Fine Arts. *Awards:* Can Coun Grant, 76; Officer, Order of Can, 85. *Bibliog:* Geoffrey James (auth), An inquiry into the aesthetics of photography, Arts Can, 12/74. *Mem:* Royal Can Acad Art. *Media:* Oils. *Collection:* Sol Lewitt Collection, National Gallery of Canada, George Eastman house, univ of Victoria, Canadian Mus of Contemporary Art photography, Ottawa. *Publ:* Vision & Expression, Horizon Press, 69; An Inquiry into the Aesthetics of Photography, Arts Can, 75; Banff Purchase, Wiley, 79; Aperture 88, Aperture, 82; Between Friends; Nat Film Board Image Series, 1, 2, 3, 5, 6. *Mailing Add:* 272 Beddis Rd Salt Spring Island BC V8K 2J1 Canada

RAGLAND, BOB
PAINTER, INSTRUCTOR
b Cleveland, Ohio, Dec 11, 38. *Study:* Rocky Mountain Sch Art, Denver, Colo; study with Phil Steele. *Work:* Denver Pub Libr; Karamu House, Cleveland; Irving St Ctr, Cult Arts Prog, Denver; Created Mayor's Awards, Denver, Colo, 92. *Comn:* Logo, Metro State Col Black Student Union, 74; art print, Big Sisters Colo, 75; Mayor's Arts Awards, Denver, Colo, 93; Governor's Recycling Awards, Denver, Colo, 94. *Exhib:* 16th Ann Drawing Exhib, Dallas Mus Fine Art Traveling Exhib, 67; one-man show, Cleveland State Univ, 68, Denver Nat Bank, Colo, 80-81, Century Bank Cherry Creek, Denver, Colo, 80-81; Group Exhib, Boston, Mass Tubman Gallery, 81; Anniversary Art Exhib, Channel Six PBS, 91-93; Colo Pub Educ & Business Coalition Art Exhib, 93-96; Savageau Gallery, 96. *Collection Arranged:* Kaiser Permanente Colo; Denver Pub Libr, Colo; Colo State Univ; Channel 4 TV-Denver, Colo; Denver Pub Schs, Colo. *Pos:* Chmn, Arts & Humanities Comt, 68-69; lectr, Afro-American art of the 60's & 70's; founding fac mem, Auraria Campus, Community Col, Denver, 70-72; visual arts coordr, City Spirit Proj, 78; Free Counseling, Art Career Coach, Denver Colo. *Teaching:* Instr painting & drawing, Denver Pub Libr, 69-71 & Eastside Action Ctr, Denver, 69-71; artist-in-residence, Model Cities Cult Arts Ctr Workshop, 71-73; artist/teacher, KRMA-TV; instr, Gove Community Sch, 79-; instr, Metrop State Col, Denver, Colo; instr, Arapahoe Community Col, Littleton, Colo; vis artist, Cole Sch Arts, 93-95 & Urban Peak Ctr Homeless Youth, 96-97; artist-in-residence, Denver Pub Sch, 96-97 Denver Post, 1/81; artist-in-residence, Career Educ Ctr, 96-, Art Career Coach, 80-; Bob Ragland Talks About Art and Artists, Mary Motian-Meadows, Denver, Urban Spectrum, 11/2002. *Awards:* Recognition Award, KCNC-TV & Denver Ctr Performing Arts, 86, Foot Hills Art Ctr, Golden, Colo, 2001. *Bibliog:* Diane Wengler (auth), Bob Ragland- He's learned to survive by using his wits and considerable talent, Gazette-Telegraph, Colo Springs, 4/81; Alexandra King (auth), article, Street Talk Mag, Denver, 10/81; Bonnie McCune (auth), What to do until rich & famous, This Week in Denver, 11/22/82; Carson Reed (auth), Denver artist is more method than madness, Up the Creek Newspaper, 1/25/85; James J Lewis (auth), Making the Art is only Half of the Job, Sol Day News Arts & Entertainment, 98; Outlaw Artist's Work Reflects Neighborhood, Denver Post, 3/28/2005. *Mem:* Colo Black Umbrella. *Media:* All Media; Metal, Welded. *Res:* Oral history project with Colorado artists over the age of fifty. *Interests:* collecting art books. *Collection:* Traditional renderings of the figure and landscape in all mediums. *Publ:* publ, Colorado Gallery Guide, 78-; contribr, Black Umbrella/Black Artists Denver; Dick Kreck, Artist will throw in a sculpture at this half off sale, Denver Post, 9/28/98 & 3/28/2005; GoGo Mag, Bob Ragland, Non Starving Artist, 10/2002; Art Talk Mag, Ariz, 12/98. *Dealer:* Bob Ragland Studio 1723 E 25 Ave Denver Co 80205. *Mailing Add:* 1723 E 25th Ave Denver CO 80205

RAGLAND, JACK WHITNEY
PAINTER, PRINTMAKER
b El Monte, Calif, Feb 25, 38. *Study:* Ariz State Univ, BA & MA, with Dr Harry Wood, Arthur Jacobson & Ben Goo; Univ Calif, Los Angeles, with Dr Lester Longman, Sam Amato & William Brice; Akad Angewandte Kunst; Akad Bildenden Kunste; Graphische Bundes-Lehrund Versuchsanstalt, Vienna; with Bill Bowne, San Diego, Calif, Ted Goerschner, Fallbrook, Calif, Tim Clark, David Leffel, Sherry McGraw, John Cosby, Pasadena, Calif. *Work:* Albertina Mus, Vienna, Austria; Phoenix Art Mus, Ariz; Bibliotheque Nat, Paris; Kuns Mus, Basel, Switz; Los Angeles Co Mus, Calif; Vintage Car Poster Designs, Fallbrook, 2003-05. *Comn:* Portrait, Henry Nollen, Equitable Life Insurance, 73; stained glass windows, Methodist Church, Perry, Iowa, 74; painting, Mary Kay Ryan, 2006; mural paintings, Alan & Jean Silberman, 2006; signature painting, Beucler Signature Homes & Malabar Rancho (hqs), Fallbrook, Calif, 2006. *Exhib:* Exhib Nat Recognized Artists, Seattle, 63 & Ft Lauderdale, Fla, 64, 65; Iowa Ann Exhib, Des Moines, 70 & 72; Artists Fedn Traveling Exhib, Eight Midwest States, 75; Southern Calif Exhib, Del Mar, Calif, 81, 83-96; Designer Show Case, Pasadena, 95 & San Diego, 95-98; Desert Plein Air Master Show, 2000, 2001. *Pos:* Owner, Jack Ragland Atelier, 1976-2006. *Teaching:* Grad asst drawing & painting, Univ Calif, Los Angeles, 61-64; instr drawing & painting, Ariz State Univ, summer 63; art dept head & assoc prof art hist, drawing, printmaking & painting, Simpson Col, 64-76; Private workshops, 84-2006. *Awards:* Grand Purchase Prize, Ariz Ann, Phoenix Art Mus, 61; Painting Selected for Prize Winning Paintings, Book II, Allied Publ, 62; First Prize, Prints & Graphics, Iowa State Fair, 74; First Prize, Acrylic Painting, Southern Calif Exhib, Del Mar, 84; Best of Show, 1st & 3rd Prize, 2 Hon Mentions, Calif State Fair, Sacramento, 2005; First & 3rd Prize, Hon Mention, Calif State Fair, Sacramento, 2006. *Bibliog:* Am Artist Mag, 10/94; Decor and Style, 95-2006; San Diego Life Styles, 95-98. *Mem:* Calif Art Club; Fallbrook Art Assoc. *Media:* Acrylic, Oils; Serigraphy. *Specialty:* romantic impressionist & abstract paintings, representational works. *Interests:* singing, dancing, traveling the world. *Dealer:* Desert Art Source Palm Desert CA; French Gallery & Jacque Company Fallbrook CA; Eagle Gallery La Jolla CA. *Mailing Add:* 5555 8th St Fallsbrook CA 92028-9602

RAGUIN, VIRGINIA C
HISTORIAN, CONSULTANT
b New York, NY, Feb 24, 41. *Study:* Marymount Col, Tarrytown, NY, BA(magna cum laude), 63; Univ Toulouse, France, cert, 64; Yale Univ, with Summer McK Crosby, PhD, 74. *Collection Arranged:* Col Gallery Prog, Worcester Art Mus, 75-84; Northern Renaissance Stained Glass (with catalog), Cantor Gallery, Holy Cross, 87; Glory in Glass (with catalog) Am Bible Soc, New York, 98. *Pos:* Dir, Census Stained Glass Windows Am, 82-; hist res consult, Stained Glass Mag, 83-; consult, Mem Hall Restoration, Harvard Univ, 85-; stained glass res, Boston, Charleston & Birmingham dioceses (currently). *Teaching:* Prof art hist, Col Holy Cross, 74-. *Awards:* Fulbright Scholar, 64; Woodrow Wilson Fel, 64; Nat Endowment Humanities Educ Proj Grant, 77-80; Nat Endowment Humanities Technology Grant, 98. *Mem:* Int Ctr Medieval Art; Col Art Asn; Soc Archit Historians; Société Francaise d'Archéologie. *Res:*

Medieval Renaissance and Modern stained glass; Medieval iconography. *Publ:* Auth, Isaiah master of the Sainte-Chapelle in Burgundy, Art Bull, 77; Stained Glass in Thirteenth-Century Burgundy, Princeton, 82; Worcester's Tradition of Stained glass, Worcester Art Mus J, 83; coauth, Stained Glass Before 1700 in American Collections, Nat Gallery, 85-88; auth, Revivals Revivalists and Architectural Stained Glass, Soc Archit Historians J, 90; co-ed, Artistic Integration in Gothic Buildings, Toronto, 95. *Mailing Add:* 280 Boston Ave Medford MA 02155

RAGUSA, ISA
HISTORIAN
b Rome, Italy, Dec 30, 26; US citizen. *Study:* New York Univ, BA(magna cum laude), 47, Inst Fine Arts, MA, 51, PhD, 66. *Pos:* Reader & acting dir, Index Christian Art, formerly; res art hist, Princeton Univ, formerly. *Teaching:* Vis scholar, Inst Fine Arts, NY Univ, 83-84; vis prof, Univ Cattolica del Sacro Cuore, Milan, 92-93. *Mem:* Medieval Acad Am; Col Art Asn; Renaissance Soc; Int Ctr Medieval Art. *Publ:* Coauth (with RB Green), Meditations on the Life of Christ, Princeton Univ Press, 61 & 77; auth, Porta patet vitae Sponsus vocat Intro venite and the Inscriptions of the lost Portal of the Cathedral of Esztergom, Zeitschrift fur Kunstgeschichte, 43, 77; Il manoscritto ambrosiano L 58 Sup: L'infanzia de Cristo e le fonti apocrife, Arte Lombarda, 83, 87; The iconography of the Abgar Cycle in Paris, Ms lat 2688 and its Relationship to Byzantine Cycles, Miniature, 2, 89; Mandylion-Sudarium: the 'Translation' of a Byzantine Relic to Rome, Arte Medievale, V, 91. *Mailing Add:* 30 W 12th St New York NY 10011-8635

RAHJA, VIRGINIA HELGA
PAINTER, ADMINISTRATOR
b Aurora, Minn, Apr 21, 21. *Study:* Hamline Univ, BA, 44; Sch Assoc Arts, DFA, 66. *Exhib:* Walker Art Ctr; Minn State Fair, Minn Art Inst; Hamline Galleries; Col of Visual Arts, Univ Minn; plus many other exhibs & ann. *Pos:* Asst supt fine arts, Minn State Fair, 44-48. *Teaching:* Assoc prof painting, Hamline Univ, 43-48 & dir, Hamline Galleries, 45-48; prof painting, Co of Visual Arts, St Paul, 48-65, dean, 48-73, dir and pres, 75-86. *Mem:* Col Art Asn Am; Am Asn Univ Women. *Media:* Oil. *Mailing Add:* 550 Summit Ave Saint Paul MN 55102

RAHR, STEWART & CAROL
b Feb 19, 1948. *Collection Arranged:* Impressionist & modern art. *Awards:* Named one of top 200 collectors, ARTnews Magazine, 2004. *Mailing Add:* Kinray Inc 152-35 10th Ave Whitestone NY 11357-1233

RAIMONDI, JOHN
SCULPTOR
b Boston, Mass, May 29, 48. *Study:* Mass Col Art, BFA, 73. *Work:* Nat Mus Am Art, Smithsonian Inst, Washington, DC; Milwaukee Art Mus, Wis; Mus Fine Arts, Boston; Newark Mus, NJ; Okla Mus Art, Oklahoma City. *Comn:* Lupus, Cabot, Cabot & Forbes, Lotus Corp, Cambridge, Mass, 85; Aquila, Lincoln Prop Co, Miami, Fla, 86; Dance of the Cranes, Omaha Airport Auth, Nebr, 88; Artorius, Stanhope PLC Stockley Park Ltd, London, Eng, 89; Athleta, Univ Nebr, Kearney, 90. *Exhib:* C Grimaldis Gallery, Baltimore, 90; Helander Gallery, Palm Beach, Fla, 91; Stars in Fla, Mus Art, Ft Lauderdale, 92; Romantic Abstraction: A 20-Year Survey of Works by John Raimondi, traveling exhib (catalog), Stuart & Vero Beach, Fla, 92; The Hyde Collection, Glens Falls, NY, 92; and others. *Teaching:* Artist-in-residence, Portland Regional Vocational Tech Ctr, Maine, 75, San Angelo Independent Sch Dist, Tex, 79 & Univ Nebr, Kearney, 89. *Awards:* MacDowell Colony Fel, 82. *Bibliog:* John Raimondi: Artist-in Residence, Nat Endowment Arts, Guggenheim Productions, Washington, DC, 75; Harry Rand (auth), cover story, Arts Mag, 4/83; Dance of the Cranes, Pub Broadcasting System Documentary (film), 89. *Mem:* Mass Coun Arts & Humanities. *Media:* Bronze, Steel. *Mailing Add:* c/o Dolly Fiderman Fine Arts 100 University Ave SE Golden Valley MN 55414

RAINER, YVONNE
FILMMAKER, EDUCATOR
b San Francisco, Calif, Nov 24, 34. *Hon Degrees:* Mass Col of Art, Hon Dr Fine Arts, 88; RI School of School of Design, Hon Dr Fine Arts, 88; Art Inst Chicago, Hon Dr Fine Arts, 93; CA Inst of Arts, Hon Dr Fine Arts, 93. *Work:* Mus Mod Art, NY; Pac Film Arch, Berkeley, Calif; British Film Inst, London, Eng; Munich Film Mus, Ger; Australian Film Inst, Canberra, Australia. *Exhib:* retrospective, Whitney Mus, NY, 86; Carnegie Mus Art, Pittsburgh, 91; Vienna Film Casino, Vienna, 94; Am Ctr, Paris, 95; San Francisco MOMA, 97; Walter Reade Theater, 97; Ctr for Media Cult/NYU, NY, 99. *Teaching:* instr, Art Inst Chicago, 98, Columbia Univ, 99 & Whitney Mus, NY, 74-. *Awards:* Guggenheim, 69 & 98; NEA, 72, 74, 85, 88, 90 & 95; MacArthur, 90-95. *Bibliog:* Teresa deLauretis, Technologies of Gender, Indian Univ Press, 87; Peggy Phelan (auth), Unmarked: The Politics of a Performance, Routledge, 93; Shelly Green (auth), The Films of YR, Scarecrow Press, 94. *Mailing Add:* 72 Franklin St New York NY 10013

RAINS, BAXTER
SCULPTOR, CONSULTANT
b Emory University, Ga, July 2, 38. *Study:* Atlanta Col Art; Ga State Univ, Atlanta, BVA(visual arts), 68; Univ de Guanajuato, Inst Allende, Mex, MFA, 74. *Work:* Radford Univ Sculpture Garden, Va; Ga State Univ Mus, Atlanta; Univ de Guanajuato, Inst Allende, San Miguel de Allende, GTO, Mex; Municipality of Toronto, Can; Brevard Mus Art & Sci, Melbourne, Fla. *Comn:* Sculptures, St Francis Gardens, Albuquerque, NMex, 78; sculpture, comn by King Sims, Atlanta, Ga, 79; sculpture, comn by Parkway Co, Dorsey, Md, 88; sculptures, comn by Count Roger de la Burde, Powhatan, Va, 89 & 90; sculpture, comn by Hilda Knothe, Cocoa Beach, Fla, 93. *Exhib:* High Mus Art, Atlanta, Ga, 69; Mint Mus Art, Charlotte, NC, 70; Esculturas de Baxter Rains, Galeria Roma, San Miquel de Allende, Mex, 73-74; Inaugural Exhib, Galeria de Los Jovenes, Mexico City, Mex, 74; Art to Touch, Colo Fed Savings, Denver, 77; Shidoni Ann Outdoor Sculpture Show, Tesuqui, NMex, 77-78; Baxter Rains: Sculptures, Gallery Danielli, Toronto, Ont, 79; Briggs & Rains: Wood Works, Wash World, 79; Faculty exhib, Ctr for the Arts, Vero Beach, Fla, 2000, 10, 02; Brevard Mus Art & Sci, Melbourne, Fla, 2003; Vero Beach Mus Art, Fla, 2003; Indian River Sculpture Gallery, Vero Beach, Fla, 2004. *Collection Arranged:* Art to Touch (auth, catalog), Colo Fed, Denver, 77; Special Museum of Touch (auth, catalog), Arts Festival Atlanta, 81-82; Judy Chicago's: The Dinner Party, Sculptural Arts Mus, 82; The Great Garden Sculpture Show (auth, catalog), Atlanta Botanical Garden, 82; German & American Handcrafted Furniture, Regency-Hyatt House, Atlanta, 83; Allan Welch Outdoor Installation sculpture, Veira, Fla, 2004. *Pos:* Dir, Evening Sch, Atlanta Col Art, Ga, 69-71; found & exec dir, Sculptural Arts Mus, Atlanta, Ga, 80-82 & Vector Arts Endowment, Indian Harbour Beach, Fla, 97-; vpres, Hope Dragon Found, Indian Harbour Beach, Fla, 96-97; bd dir, Arts Festival of Atlanta, Ga, 82-85; bd dir, Ga Woodworkers Guild, Atlanta, 1982-84. *Teaching:* Instr drawing, Atlanta Col Art, Ga, 69-71; prof art, Westminster Sch, Atlanta, 69-71; dir evening sch, Atlanta Col Art, Ga, 70-71; maestro art hist, Univ de Guanajuato, Inst Allende, Mex, 72-75; adj prof drawing and sculpture, Ctr for the Arts, Vero Beach, Fla and Indian River Community Col, Fort Pierce, Fla, 2000-. *Awards:* First Award in Sculpture, Fine Arts League Nat Award Exhib, La Junta, Colo, 77; First Award in Sculpture, Telfair Acad of Arts and Sci, Savannah, Ga, 71. *Bibliog:* Articles in Maquette Mag, Int Sclupture Ctr, Washington, DC, 11/94, Annual Guide to Artists, Art in Am, 95-96, Florida Today, 92 & 96; Pam Harbaugh (auth), The Quite Sculpture of Baxter Rains, Fla Today Newspaper, 92. *Mem:* Vector Arts Endowment (bd governors). *Media:* Mixed Media with Wood. *Publ:* Guest columnist, Florida Today Newspaper, Melbourne, 7/94; co-publ & contribr, Studio Link Newsletter, Port Canaveral, Fla, 94; auth, To Be Artists, 3/94 & Desultorious to Dedication, 6/94, Studio Link Newsletter; Show People Beauty and It Restores Hope, Fla Today Newspaper, 7/30/94; Studio Link, A Newsletter, Studio Barbara Osmundsen & Baxter Rains, 94. *Dealer:* Carol Minton 250 Ocean View Lane, Indiatlantic, FL 32908. *Mailing Add:* 135 Tomahawk Dr Apt B1 Melbourne FL 32937

RAISELIS, RICHARD
PAINTER, EDUCATOR
b Bridgeport, Conn, July 15, 51. *Study:* Skowhegan Sch painting & sculpture, 72; Yale Univ, BA, 73; Tyler Sch Art of Temple Univ, MFA, 76. *Work:* Chemical Bank, NY; Exxon Corp; Fidelity Investments; Mich Bell, Detroit; Univ Iowa Mus Art; Boston Univ Photonics Ctr; Wellington Mgmt Co, Boston; Boise Mus of Art, Idaho; Butler Inst of Am Art; Wright State Univ, Dayton, Ohio, 2003. *Comn:* Boston Univ, Photonics Ctr, 98. *Exhib:* Am Realism: 20th drawings & watercolors, San Francisco Mus Mod Art, 85; Am Acad of Arts and Letters, NY, 90, 2001; Robert Schoelkopf Gallery, NY, 91; Elevated Outlook: Urban Landscapes, Cedar Rapids Mus Art, Iowa, 95; Gerold Wunderlich & Co: The Urban Landscape, NY, 95; Nat Acad of Design, 171st Ann, NY, 96, 175th Ann, 2000; solo exhib, Gallery NAGA, Boston, Mass, 96, 99, 2002, 2006; Landscapes, Wright State Univ, 2003; Realism Now, Vose Contemp, Boston, 2003; Ocean View, Monserrat Col Art, Beverly, Mass, 2004; Different Views, Washington Art Asn, Washington Depot, Conn, 2006; 181st Ann, Nat Acad Mus, NY, 2006; The First Ten Years, Simmons Col, Boston, 2006. *Collection Arranged:* Pittura Figurativa Americana, Temple Univ, Rome, Italy, 88. *Teaching:* Asst prof art, Univ Mich Sch Art, 83-89, Temple Univ, Rome, Italy, 86-88; asst prof art, Boston Univ Sch Visual Arts, 89-96, assoc prof, 96-. *Awards:* Louis Comfort Tiffany Found Grant, 99; Purchase Prize, Am Acad of Arts and Letters, NY, 2001; Phil Desind Painting Prize, Butler Inst Am Art, Youngstown, Ohio, 2004; Artists Resource Trust Grant, Berkshire Taconic Community Found, 2005. *Bibliog:* Judith Reynolds (auth), Out in the Open, Rochester City Newspaper, 6/89; Miles Unger (auth), Art New Eng, 4-5/96; Holland Cotter (auth), article, NY Times, 7/26/96; Andrew Forge, Ten Figurative Painters in New England: An Artist's Choice, 2000. *Media:* Oil. *Publ:* Auth, Don Shields, Detroit Focus Quarterly, Vol 3, No 3, 9/84. *Dealer:* Gallery NAGA 67 Newbury St Boston MA 02116. *Mailing Add:* 21 Arapahoe Rd Newton MA 02465-2202

RAKOCY, WILLIAM (JOSEPH)
MURALIST, MUSEOLOGIST
b Youngstown, Ohio, Apr 14, 24. *Study:* Butler Inst Am Art, with Clyde Singer, 39-41; Am Acad Art, 44; Kansas City Art Inst, with Ross Braught, Ed Lanning & Bruce Mitchell, MFA, 51. *Work:* US Naval Training Sta, Great Lakes, Ill; YMCA, Youngstown; Butler Inst Am Art; El Paso Mus Art, Tex. *Comn:* Mural, Woodrow Wilson High Sch, Youngstown, 46; four murals (with Robert Sonoga & Chet Kwiecinski), McSorleys Colonial Rest, Pittsburgh, Pa, 55; three murals, YMCA, Youngstown; three murals, Mesa Inn, El Paso, Tex, 75; fourteen dioramas, Cavalry Mus & Wilderness Park Mus, El Paso, Tex, 78. *Exhib:* Butler Inst Am Art Ann, 55; one-man show, Juarez, Mex, 79 & 81, El Paso Mus Art, 86 & Quintas Gameros Mus, Chic City, Mex. *Pos:* Founder, Bill Rakocy-Fine Arts, El Paso, Tex; cur educ, El Paso Mus Art, 71-73; cur var mus, El Paso, Tex, 73-85; installation cur, Wilderness Park Mus, 77. *Teaching:* Instr painting & drawing; prof painting & drawing, Col Artesia, 67-71; vis prof, Sull Ross State Univ, 89-. *Awards:* Art Travel Grant to Study in Italy, Ital Businessmen, Kansas City, Mo, 53; Area Award in Watercolor, Butler Inst Am Art, 56-60. *Mem:* Kansas City Area Artists Asn; El Paso Art Asn; founder Rio Bravo Watercolorists; Western Asn Art Schs & Univ Mus; El Paso Hist Soc; Am Soc Appaisers. *Media:* Oil, Watercolor. *Interests:* Promote art auctions to assist artists via sales and scholarships; publisher of art and history books; founder and manager of Raks Art and History Museum, Ruidoso, New Mexico. *Publ:* Auth, A Western Portfolio, 65; Art Reporter, 72; Sketches & Observations, 72; Images, Paso del Norte, 79 & Villa Raids 80, Col NMex; Mogollon Diary No 2. *Mailing Add:* 4210 Emory Way El Paso TX 79922

RAKOVAN, LAWRENCE FRANCIS
PRINTMAKER, PAINTER
b Eleria, Ohio, Oct 26, 39. *Study:* Detroit Soc Arts & Crafts; Wayne State Univ, BS; RI Sch Design, MA. *Work:* Brooklyn Mus, NY; Colby Col; Calif Col Arts & Crafts, Oakland; Bowdoin Col Mus Art; Univ Maine, Orono; Bates Col, Lewiston, ME. *Comn:* 14 Stations of the Cross & exterior monumental cross with stoneware reliefs of The Four Evangelists, St Charles Borromeo Church, Brunswick, Maine, 75. *Exhib:* Two-man show, St Peter's Ctr, NY, 73; Maine 75, Bowdoin Col, 75; Sculpture in Wood, Maine Festival of Arts, Bowdoin Col, 77; one-man shows, Treat Gallery, Bates Col, 76, Univ Southern Maine, 84 & Merrill Art Gallery, Nichols Col, Dudley, Mass, 85; juried competitions, Mamaroneck Artist Guild, Nat Exhib, 85, Chautauqua Nat Exhib Am Art, Chautauqua Inst, NY, 85, Fine Arts Inst, San Bernardino Co Mus, Redlands, Calif, 85, 13th Int Dogwood Arts Fest, Atlanta, Ga, 86, Springfield Art League 67th Nat, Mus Art, Mass, 86, & Arts Asn Harrisburg, Pa, 86; Sketch Book of Tibet, Univ Southern Maine Environ Studies Ctr, 98-99; Ctr Maine Contemp Art, Rockport, 2006. *Collection Arranged:* Maine to Tibet, Me Art Gallery, 99. *Pos:* Dir, Chocolate Church Art Gallery Ctr Arts, Bath, Maine, 84- 91. *Teaching:* Assoc prof painting & printmaking, Univ Southern Maine, 67-2006; vis prof art, Univ Maine, Augusta, 79-80. *Awards:* State of Maine Res Grant, 73. *Mem:* Copley Soc, Boston, Mass; Skowhegan Sch Painting & Sculpture. *Media:* Oil, Stone Lithography. *Interests:* Paintings and Textiles of Ctrl Asia; History of the ancient silk road. *Dealer:* Barridoff Gallery Portland ME. *Mailing Add:* Upper Maine St Brunswick ME 04011

RALEIGH, HENRY PATRICK
PAINTER, WRITER
b New York, NY, Feb 5, 31. *Study:* Pratt Inst, BS, 56 & MS, 59; New York Univ, PhD, 63. *Exhib:* The New Response, 86; Mus Hudson Highlands, 87; Rice Gallery, Albany, NY, 87; Woodstock Sch Art, 88; Park W Gallery, Kingston, NY, 94; and others. *Teaching:* Chmn art dept, Pratt Inst Art Sch, 61-68; prof painting, art criticism & aesthet, State Univ NY, New Paltz, 68-, chmn studio art & art hist, 68-74 & co-dean fac fine & performing art, 71-73. *Awards:* Travel Grant, 7th Int Am Coun Learned Soc, Cong, Rumania, 72; Prize Winner, 4th Nat Painting Exhib, Woodstock, NY. *Media:* Oils. *Res:* Application of value study to examinations of contemporary art and art criticism. *Publ:* Auth, Art and the public, 79 & The Ambiguous Art (film), 82, J Aesthetic Educ; Post Modernism in the Visual Arts, Hofstra Univ, 86; auth, Art Times (film); The Liberal Education of the Artist & Ortegay Gasset, Sch Visual Arts, NY, 87; Myth of the Artist, Sch Visual Arts, NY, 90. *Mailing Add:* 16 Deerpath Dr New Paltz NY 12561-2811

RALES, MITCHELL P
COLLECTOR
b 56. *Study:* DePauw Univ, bachelor's degree; Miami Univ, Ohio, grad, 78. *Pos:* Partner Equity Group Holdings, Washington, 79-; pres Danaher Corp, 84-, bd dirs, chmn exec comt, 90-; founder, dir, Colfax Corp, 95-; chmn, Capital Campaign for Hosp Sick Children; treas, trustee, chmn, Capital Campaign of Norwood Sch; mem adv coun, Miami Univ, Ohio; bd trustees, Hirshhorn Mus and Sculpture Garden; mem trustees coun, Nat Gallery Art. *Awards:* Named one of Top 200 Collectors, ARTnews mag, 2003-06. *Collection:* Modern and Contemporary Art. *Mailing Add:* Danaher Corp 2099 Pennsylvania Ave Northwest 12th Fl Washington DC 20006-6800

RALES, STEVEN M
COLLECTOR
b Pittsburgh, Pa, Mar 31, 51. *Pos:* ptnr Equity Group Holdings, 79-; chmn bd, chief exec officer, Danaher Corp, Washington, DC, 84-2001, chmn, 2001-. *Awards:* Named one of Top 200 collectors, ARTnews mag, 2003-06. *Mailing Add:* Danaher Corp 2099 Pennsylvania Ave NW 12th Fl Washington DC 20006

RAMANAUSKAS, DALIA IRENA
PAINTER, DRAFTSMAN
b Kaunas, Lithuania, Jan 10, 36; US citizen. *Study:* Southern Conn Col, BS(art educ). *Work:* Prudential Insurance Co; Smithsonian Inst, Washington, DC; Va Mus, Richmond; Chase Manhattan Bank; Calif Palace, Legion Hon; New Britain Mus Am Art; Mineeapolis Inst Art; Univ Mass Art Gallery; Dade Community Col, Miami, Fla. *Comn:* Spec drawing, Fidelity Investments, Boston, Mass, 95; Harvard Bus Sch; Parthenon Investments, Boston. *Exhib:* Am Drawing 1927-1977, Minn Mus Art, St Paul; solo shows, O K Harris Gallery, NY, 77-79, Capricorn Gallery, Washington, DC, 77, 82, 85, 90, 93 & 96, Stockholm Int Art Expo, 81 & Payson Weisberg, NY, 84; Chicago Expo, 82; Mainstream America, Butler Inst, Ohio, 87; 41st Ann Art Northeast USA, Silvermine, Conn, 90; Earth Art, Tokyo, Japan, 90; Irving Galleries, Palm Beach, Fla, 91-92; and others. *Awards:* Am Drawing 20th Ann Purchase Award, Norfolk Mus Arts & Sci, 63; Purchase Award American Drawing, Minn Mus Art, St Paul. *Bibliog:* Rev, Artforum, 4/74; M L D'Otrange Mastai (auth), Illusionism in Art, Abaris, 76; Watercolor, fall 92; Paris Review, 76; Watercolors, American Artist Publ, 92. *Media:* Acrylic, Watercolor. *Dealer:* Capricorn Gallery Washington DC; ALVA New London CT. *Mailing Add:* PO Box 264 Main St Ivoryton CT 06442

RAMIREZ, JOEL TITO
PAINTER, CALLIGRAPHER
b Albuquerque, NMex, June 3, 23. *Study:* Univ NMex, with Randall Davey, Kenneth M Adams & Ralph Douglass; also with Enrique Montenegro & Raymond Jonson. *Work:* Mus NMex, Santa Fe; Univ Albuquerque; NMex State Univ; Univ NMex. *Comn:* Arrival (mural), Rio Rancho Hawk Missile Armory, Volunteer Calvary From Pa (mural), Modern Age (mural); Santa Fe Trail (mural), Fort Union, Springer, NMex; portrait, La Casa Senior Ctr, Clovis, NMex; Moon Glow (painting), Clayton Patrol Yard; San Ysibro (painting), Eunice Community Ctr, NMex, Toward Windmill (painting); 100 Years (poster), Friends of the Libr; and many others. *Exhib:* War with Japan, 47; Fiesta Show, Mus NMex, 62; Art Intimates, Galerie de Paris, NY, 65; Museo Ibariano Arte De Norte America, Madrid, Spain, 85-86; 300 Centennial Poster Celebration, Albuquerque, NMex; and others. *Pos:* First vpres, NMex Art League, 58-59; assoc ed & art dir, El Clarin; art dir, Quijotes De America. *Teaching:* Teacher oil painting, Ramirez Art Studio, 65-73. *Awards:* Anitiqua, Fine Arts Mus, Santa Fe, James T Forrest, 62; Los Trampas, Fiesta Show, Bernique Longley, 63; Nat Contest Columbus & the New World First Prize, Art Studio League, Denver, 91 & 92; and others. *Bibliog:* Jacinto Quirate (auth), Southwest Artists, Exxon Oil Co, 73 & Mexican-American Artists, Univ Tex, Austin, 74; Frank Duane (auth), Pilgrims to the West, KLRN-TV, San Antonio, Tex, 73. *Mem:* Int Soc Artists. *Media:* All Media, Oil. *Interests:* reading, history & contemporary events. *Publ:* Contribr, After Cortez, 73; illusr, Juan Diego and the Virgin of Guadalupe, 75; St Bernadette of Lourdes, 75; Across America, McDougal, Littell & Co, 86; text books for 8th grade literature 87-88 & art work studies, 88-89; Insignia, for 98th Bombardment Gr, Freedom Force, 90. *Mailing Add:* 10305 Santa Paula NE Albuquerque NM 87111

RAMIREZ, MARI CARMEN
CURATOR
Study: Univ Puerto Rico, Rio Piedras, BA(magna cum laude), 75; Univ Chicago, MA(art hist), 76, PhD(art hist), 89; Mus Management Inst, W Asn Art Mus, Univ Calif, Berkeley, 79. *Work:* co-cur, (with Hector Olea) (exhib) Inverted Utopias: Avant-Garde Art in Latin Am, 2004, co-cur, (with Beverly Adams) Encounters/Displacements: Alfredo Jaar, Luis Camnitzer, Cildo Meireles, cur, David Alfaro Siqueiros, Cantos Paralelos: Visual Parody in Contemp Argentinean Art, Global Conceptualism: Points of Origin (Latin Am section). *Collection Arranged:* Puerto Rican Painting: Between Past and Present, Squibb Gallery, Princeton, NJ, 87; De Oller a los Cuarenta: La Pintura en Puerto Rico de 1900 a 1948, Univ Puerto Rico Mus, Rio Piedras, 87-88; Abstraccion-Figuracion/Figurative-Abstract (reinstallation), Permanent Collection Latin Am Art, Archer M Huntington Gallery, Univ Tex, Austin, 89; Liliana Porter: Retrospectiva de Obra Grafica, 1964-1990, Exposicion Homenaje, IX Bienal de San Juan del Grabado Latinoamericano y del Caribe, 91; Domingo Garcia: Icons of our History, Univ Puerto Rico Mus, Rio Piedras, 91; The School of the South: El Taller Torres-Garcia and Its Legacy, Archer M Huntington Art Gallery, Univ Tex, Austin, Centro de Arte Reina Sofia, Madrid, Spain, Mus de Arte de Monterrey, Mex, Mus Tamayo, Mex City & Bronx Mus Arts, NY, 91; Liliana Porter: Fragments of the Journey, 1968-1991 (with catalog), Bronx Mus Arts, NY, 91; Encounters/Displacements: Alfredo Jaar, Luis Camnitzer, Cildo Meireles, Archer M Huntington Art Gallery, Univ Tex, Austin, 92; Universalis (with catalog), XXIII Sao Paulo Bienal, 96; Re-Aligning Vision: Alternative Currents in South American Drawing (with catalog), El Mus del Barrio, NY, 97, Ark Art Ctr, Little Rock, 97, Archer M Huntington Art Gallery, 98, Mus de Bellas Artes, Caracas, 98, MARCO, Monterrey, 98-99 & Miami Art Mus, 99; David Alfaro Siqueiros (with catalog), XXIV Bienal de Sao Paulo, Nucleo Historico, 98; Cantos Paralelos: Visual Parody in Contemporary Argentinean Art (with catalog), Jack S Blanton Mus Art, Austin, 99 & Phoenix Art Mus, Ariz, 99; Global Conceptualism: Points of Origin (with catalog), Queens Mus Art, NY, 99. *Pos:* Asst dir, Ponce Mus Art, 77-79; cur, Epstein Photog Arch, Dept Art, Univ Chicago, 81-82; dir, Mus Anthropology, Hist & Art, Univ Puerto Rico, Rio Piedras, 85-88; cur Latin Am Art, Jack S Blanton Mus Art & adj lectr Art Dept, Univ Tex, Austin, 89-2000; Worthman Cur, Latin Am Art Mus Fine Arts, Houston, 2001-; dir, Inter Ctr for the Arts of the Am, 2001-. *Teaching:* Instr Hist W Painting Survey, Docent Prog, Ponce Mus Art, 78-79; Mod Art Europe & Latin Am, Dept Fine Arts, Univ Puerto Rico, Rio Piedras, 88; Mex Avant-Garde, Art Hist & Inst Latin Am Studies, Dept Art, Univ Tex, Austin, 90 & 95; Multiculturalism & Visual Arts, Art Hist & Inst Latin Am Studies, Dept Art, Univ Tex, Austin, Spring 93; Globalization & Art Am, Ctr Curatorial Studies, Bard Col, Fall 98. *Awards:* Mellon Summer Res Grant, Inst Latin Am studies, Univ Tex, Austin, 91; Peter Norton Family Found Award Curatorial Excellence, 97; Getty Curatorial Residence Fel, Ctr Curatorial Studies, Bard Col, 98-99. *Mem:* Am Soc (visual arts bd, 97-); Col Art Asn (bd dir, 90-94); Latin Am Studies Asn. *Publ:* Auth, Blue-Print Circuits: Conceptual Art and Politics in Latin America, Latin Am Art Twentieth Century, Mus Mod Art, New York, 93; Con-Sensualismo Caribeno: Las Casas de Antonio Martorell, Art Nexus, 1-3/94; co-ed, Beyond Identity: Globalization and Latin American Art, Univ Minn Press, in press; Ed & contribr, Latin American Art in the Collection of the Archer M Huntington Art Gallery, Univ Tex Press, in press; plus many others; Editor: (books) El Taller Torres-Garcia: The Sch of the South and Its Legacy, 1992; Collecting Latin America Art for the 21st Century, 2002; Questioning the Line: Gego in Context, 2003; co-auth (with Hector Olea): Inverted Utopias: Avant-Garde Art in Latin Am, 2004. *Mailing Add:* Mus Fine Arts PO Box 6826 Houston TX 77265-6826

RAMOS, JULIANNE
ADMINISTRATOR, CONSULTANT
b New York, NY. *Study:* Dominican Col, BA, 75; Columbia Univ, MFA, 91. *Pos:* Exec dir, Rockland Ctr Arts, 84-. *Teaching:* Adj prof, Marketing the Arts, New York Univ, spring 93. *Awards:* JP Getty Trust Fel, Getty Leadership Inst. *Mem:* Am Fedn Art (dirs forum). *Dealer:* Rockland Ctr Arts New York NY. *Mailing Add:* 5 Old Farm Ct West Nyack NY 10994

RAMOS, (MEL) MELVIN JOHN
PAINTER, EDUCATOR
b Sacramento, Calif, July 24, 35. *Study:* Sacramento Jr Col, with Wayne Thiebaud, 54; San Jose State Col, 55; Sacramento State Col, BA, 57 & MA, 58. *Work:* Mus Mod Art, NY; Neue Galerie, Aachen, Ger; Oakland Art Mus & San Francisco Art Mus, Calif; Guggenheim Mus; Indianapolis Mus; Nat Gallery, Washington, DC; and others. *Comn:* Paintings, Time Inc, NY, 68 & Syracuse Univ, NY, 70. *Exhib:* Pop Art USA, Oakland Mus & Six More, Los Angeles Co Mus, Calif, 63; Human Concern, Personal Torment, Whitney Mus Am Art, NY, 69; Pop Art Revisited, Hayward Gallery, London,

69; Looking West, Joslyn Art Mus, Omaha, Nebr, 70; Am Pop Art, Whitney Mus Am Art, 74; Krannert Mus, Univ Ill, Champaign, 74; Cornell Univ, Ithaca, NY, 74; Retrospective, Mus Havs Lange, Krefeld, WGer, 75; solo exhib, Schaufenstergalerie, Frankfurt, Ger, 91, Louis K Meisel Gallery, NY, 91, ARTAX, Düsseldorf, Ger, 92 & Galerie B Haasner, Wiesbaden, Ger, 92; Hand-Painted Pop: Am Art in Transition, 1955-62 (catalog), Mus Contemp Art, Los Angeles, 92; and others. *Teaching:* Assoc prof painting, Calif State Univ, Hayward, 66-92, prof art, 80-, prof emer. *Awards:* Nat Endowment Artist Fel, 86; US-France Exchange Fel, 86. *Bibliog:* Liz Claridge (auth), Mel Ramos, Mathews Miller Dunbar, London, 75; Mel Ramos--Watercolors, Lancaster-Miller, 79; Claudia Betti & Teel Sale (auths), Drawing: A Contemporary Approach, Chicago, 245,246, 92. *Mem:* Visual Artists & Galleries Asn Inc. *Media:* Oil, Watercolor. *Publ:* Contribr, History of Modern Art, 69, Erotic Art 2, 70, Art Now/New Age, 71, The High Art of Cooking, 72 & Art as Image & Idea, 72. *Dealer:* Louis K Meisel Gallery 141 Prince St New York NY 10012. *Mailing Add:* 5941 Ocean View Dr Oakland CA 94618

RAMOS, THEODORE
PAINTER, MURALIST
b Oporto, Portugal, Oct 30, 28; British citizen. *Study:* Royal Acad Schs, London, Eng, RAS Dipl, 54. *Work:* Nat Portrait Gallery, London; Guildhall Chamber, Windsor, Berks, Eng; Royal Acad Arts, London; Government House, Perth, W Australia. *Comn:* H M Queen Elizabeth the Queen Mother, Irish Guards, 78 & 94; The Transfiguration, Distillers Company, London, 79; H R H the Duke of Edinburgh Grenddier Guards, 89; H M Queen Elizabeth II, Grenadier Guards, 91; J Ortiz-Patiño, the Duke of Devonshire, the Grand Duke of Luxembourg, Pres of Valderrama Golf Club, 96. *Exhib:* Bicentenary Exhib, Royal Acad Arts, London, 68; 20th Century Portraits, Nat Portrait Gallery, London, 80 & 89. *Teaching:* Vis lectr fine art, Brighton Col Art, Eng, 59-65; Harrow Sch Art, Eng, 64-67; Royal Acad Arts, London, 60-84. *Awards:* Silver Medal, Royal Acad Schs, 54. *Mem:* Painter Stainers; Founders Co; E India Club. *Media:* Oil. *Publ:* Illusr, Chinese Art, Pelican & Thames & Hudson, 55; Monumental Brasses, Penguin Books, 57. *Dealer:* Portraits Inc 985 Park Ave New York NY 10028; Harley Art Brokers 13 Overstrand Mansions Prince of Wales Dr London SW11 4HA. *Mailing Add:* Studio 3 Chelsea Farm House Milmans St London SW10 OBY England United Kingdom

RAMSAUER, JOSEPH FRANCIS
PAINTER
b Chicago, Ill, Aug 12, 43. *Study:* Southern Ill Univ, Carbondale, BA, 67, MFA, 69; also with David Slivka. *Work:* Univ Galleries, Southern Ill Univ; Louisville Arts Club; AMOCO Corp of Chicago; Abbott Labs, Abbott Park, Ill; Augustana Col. *Comn:* Saukenuk Indian Mem, Ill State Bicentennial Comn, Black Hawk Col, Ill, 76. *Exhib:* Mid-Am Two, City Art Mus of St Louis, 69; Mid-Miss Valley Ann, Davenport Mus Art, Iowa, 70, 74-77, 80 & 81; 19th Mid South Biennial, Brooks Mem Art Gallery, Memphis, 75; Washington & Jefferson Nat, Washington & Jefferson Col, Washington, Pa, 76; Am Painters in Paris, Paris Convention Ctr, France, 76; Ann Seven State Competition, Univ Wis, Platteville, 77; 41st Nat Ann Midyear Show, Butler Inst of Am Art, Youngstown, Ohio, 77 & 93; 69th Ann Jury Exhib, Birmingham Mus of Art, Ala, 77; Tex Fine Arts Asn Traveling Exhib, 78. *Collection Arranged:* Spectrum Invitational, Davenport Mus Art, Iowa, 72; Black Hawk Col & Ill Cent Col Art Fac Exhib, 74; 31st Ill Invitational, Ill State Mus, 79; Two Midwest Artists, Sangamon State Univ, Springfield, Ill, 81. *Teaching:* Prof art, Black Hawk Col, 69-87, chmn art dept, 71-83. *Awards:* Best of Show, Ann Seven State Competition, Univ Wis, 77; First Place in Acrylic Division & The Judges Award, Pilot Club of Golden Sands Int Fine Arts Exhib, 77; First Place in Painting, Boston Mills Art Festival, Peninsula, Ohio, 84 & 87. *Mem:* Deaf Artists of Am Inc. *Media:* Acrylic on Canvas

RAMSEY, DOROTHY J
PAINTER, WRITER
b Northampton, Mass, May 1, 35. *Study:* Northampton Commercial Col, 54; Smith Col, 75-76; pvt study with Helen Van Wyk, Roger Curtis & Michael Stoffa. *Work:* New England Telephone. *Exhib:* Burr Artists Ann Exhibs, NY, 82-85; Salmagundi Club Ann Exhibs, NY, 82-87 & 90-; North Shore Arts Asn, Gloucester, Mass, 82-; Rockport Art Asn, Mass, 84-. *Pos:* Dir & instr oil painting, Ramsey Art Studio, 77-80; owner & operator, Michael Stoffa Gallery, Rockport, Mass, 80-. *Teaching:* Ramsey Art Studio, Northampton, MA,77-80. *Mem:* Rockport Art Asn; North Shore Arts Asn, Gloucester, Mass (secy, 80-84, mem bd, 80-90); Salmagundi Club, NY; Artist Fel, NY. *Media:* Oil. *Specialty:* Paintings & Prints, Traditional. *Publ:* Best Poems of 2000, "Wintry Day", In: Poetry's Elite. *Dealer:* Michael Stoffa Gallery

RANALLI, DANIEL
ARTIST, EDUCATOR
b New Haven, Conn, Oct 17, 1946. *Study:* Clark Univ, Worcester, Mass, BA, 68; Boston Univ, MA, 71. *Work:* Boston Mus Fine Arts; San Francisco Mus Mod Art; Mus Mod Art, NY; Baltimore Mus Fine Arts; Rose Art Mus, Brandeis Univ, Waltham, Mass; and others. *Comn:* New Works, Mass Council Arts, Photographic Resource Ctr, 81. *Exhib:* One-man shows, Mass Inst of Technol Photog Gallery, 77, Foto Gallery, NY, 78, Carl Siembab Gallery, Boston, 78, 79 & 82, Brent Sikemma Gallery, Boston, 1983, Vision Gallery, Boston, Alfred Univ, NY, 94,& DNA Gallery, Provincetown, 95, 96, 97, 99, 2001, 2002; group shows, Inst Contemp Art, Boston, 81, Boston Mus Fine Arts, 81, 2001, San Francisco Mus Mod Art, Baltimore Mus Fine Arts, 81, 89, Rose Art Mus, Mass, 92, DeCordova Mus, Mass, 87, 2000, Provincetown Art Mus, 1999, Duxbury Art Mus, 1999, Fitchburg Art Mus, 1991, Harvard Fogg Art Mus, 1989, St Petersburg Mus Fine Arts, 1987, Fuller Art Mus, 1983, Franklin Institute Mus, 1983, Provincetown Art Mus, 1982, Southern Alleghenies Mus Art, 1981, Addison Gallery Am Art, 1980, RH Fleming Mus, Univ Vt, 1980, Worcester Art Mus, 1978; and many more. *Collection Arranged:* Elements of Landscape, Boston Univ Art Gallery, 83 & Earthworks, 89. *Pos:* Prog dir, The Artists Found, 75-79; exec dir, Truro Ctr Arts, 79-81; actg dir, Boston Univ Art Gallery, 82-83; dir, Arts Admin Prog, Lesley Col Grad Sch, Cambridge, Mass, 84-92, Boston Univ, 92-, founding dir, grad program arts admin. *Teaching:* Prof, Lesley Col Grad Sch, Cambridge, 84-92; assoc prof art hist dept, Boston Univ, currently. *Awards:* Individual Artist Fel, Nat Endowment Arts, 81; Mass Arts Lottery Grant, 83; Earthwatch Artists Fel, 93. *Bibliog:* article, Camera Arts, 5/83; C Temin (auth), Mingling scientific detachment & personal passion, Boston Globe, 12/7/89; numerous others. *Mem:* Mass Alliance Art Educ (bd trustees, 76-79); Photog Resource Ctr, Boston; Boston Visual Artists Union (vpres, 77); Am Asn Mus; Coll Art Asn. *Publ:* Auth, Forum (monthly column), Art New Eng, 82; coauth, Darkroom Dynamics, Curtin & London, 78; contrib ed, Provincetown Arts, Mass; Daniel Ranalli: Projects & Photographs, 94. *Dealer:* Artstrand Gallery Provincetown MA. *Mailing Add:* 75 Richdale Ave Cambridge MA 02140

RAND, ARCHIE
PAINTER, MURALIST
b New York, NY, Aug 13, 49. *Study:* City Col New York, 65-66; Art Students League NY, 67-68; Pratt Inst, Brooklyn, BFA, 70. *Work:* Montclair Art Mus; Bibliotheque Nationale, Paris; San Francisco Mus Mod Art; Jewish Mus, NY; Casa Italiana, Columbia Univ. *Comn:* 12 stained glass windows, Anshe Emet Synagogue, Chicago, 80; three stained glass windows, Temple Sholom, Chicago, 83; exterior murals, Michlalah Col, Jerusalem, 83; murals, Fresco, Hebrew Home Greator Wash, 87, Chapters, Freyer Found, NY, 88; Castellani Art Mus (with Robert Creeley), Buffalo, 98. *Exhib:* Solo exhibs, Columbia Univ, 95, Univ Wis, 97, Aljira Ctr Contemp Art, NJ, 98, Jewish Mus Md, 98 & Interchurch Ctr, NY, 98; Columbia Univ, 92; Centre l'Echange de Perrache, France, 93; Worcester Mus, Mass, 94; Feigensen-Preston Gallery, Detroit, Mich, 91 & 92; Schmidt-Dean Gallery, Philadelphia, 91, 92 & 95; Baum Gartner Gallery, Washington, 91 & 95; John Post Lee Gallery, NY, 92; Philadelphia Mus Art, 92; and others. *Pos:* Designer, Rambusch Stained Glass Studios, 83, Edward Fields Tapestries Inc 83-84 & Xicon Animation Inc, 87; US rep, UNICEF Art Coun, 85-; acting dir, Hoffberger Grad Sch Painting, Md Inst, 89-90; co-chair, Studio Arts Prog, Col Art Asn, 92-94, chair, 94-; acq comt, George Mus, NY, 92-. *Teaching:* Vis prof, State Univ Ill, Normal, 84, Va Commonwealth Univ, 85, Columbia Univ, RI Sch Design, State Univ NY, Albany, Brooklyn Col, 90 & Univ Syracuse, 91; grad fac, Bard Col, 86-91 & Sch Visual Arts, 88-91 & 93-; assoc dir grad prog, Md Inst Col Art, 89-; prof art, Columbia Univ, 92-; artist-in-residence, Hoffberger Grad Sch Painting & Mt Royal Grad Sch Art, Md Inst, Col Art, 92-93; dir painting & drawing, Columbia Univ, NY, 97-. *Awards:* Engelhard Award, 85; awards, Visual Arts, 87; NY Found Arts Fel, 90; The Sienna Award, Ital Acad Advanced Studies in Am, 95; Lifetime Achievement Award for contrib to Visual Arts. *Bibliog:* Barry Schwabsky (auth), Archie Rand connections, Art Mag, 6/84; John Yau (auth), Archie Rand, Art Forum, 86; Barry Schwabsky (auth), What is painting about--a conversation with Archie Rand, ARTS Mag, 4/87. *Mem:* Nat Soc Mural Painters (bd mem); Int Soc Film Animators; IFRAA Am Inst Architects. *Media:* Acrylic on Canvas; Stained Glass, Fresco. *Publ:* Auth, The victory of the futile, ARTS Mag, 11/88; Trevor Winkfield's good show, Arts, 9/89; illusr, Two or Three Things, Collectif Generation, 90; coauth (with Malcolm Morley), Sensation without memory, Tema Celeste, No 32-3, autumn 91. *Mailing Add:* 326 55th St Brooklyn NY 11220

RAND, HARRY
HISTORIAN, EDUCATOR
b New York, NY, Jan 10, 47. *Study:* City Col New York, BA, 69; Harvard Univ, AM, 71, PhD, 74. *Pos:* Contrib ed, Arts Mag, New York, 75-92; cur 20th century painting & sculpture, Nat Mus Am Art, Washington, 79-93, Sr cur, 93-; hon ed, Leonardo, Berkeley, 83-; consult, Nat Acad Sci, 84, Consanti Found, 89-, World Bank, 94-95; sr cur cult history, Smithsonian Inst, Wash. *Teaching:* Asst prof mod art & methodology, State Univ NY, Buffalo, 74-76. *Awards:* Rockefeller Found Develop Grant, 83; Smithsonian Inst Res Opportunities Grant, 85, 87, 90 & 91; Scholarly Studies Grant, Smithsonian Inst, 87-95; Getty Found Curatorial Fel, 2003. *Bibliog:* Hilton Kramer (auth), The pictures in the paintings, 6/21/81 & A true museum of record, 2/14/82, NY Times; Washington Times, Black Angel: The Life of Arshille Gorky, by Eric Gibson, April 30, 2000, pg B 7-8; Christian Science Monitor, A Building With Wavy Floors and Rooftop Tress, May 10, 2000, Shira J. Boss, p 14; New York Times, July 12 2000, Life Story of an Artist Who Embraced Mystery, by Roberta Smith, p B 8; German Life, June/July 2000, Jochen Seidel by Ferdinand Protzman, pg 16-19; New Times (Phoenix, AZ) October 21, 2002, Exile Adrift by Deborah Sussman Susser; Washington Post, December 5, 2002, Preserving A Tradition and Views of a Capital, by Judith Havemann; New York Observer December 8, 2003, Gorky's Oeuvre: Despite Hommages, Works Were Diary by Hilton Kramer, p1; 20; David M. Knight Playing God with the World, Endeavor (UK) vol 28, #3, September 2004, p 90-91; Beth Py-Lieberman, George Washington Sat Here, From the Attic, Smithsonian Mag, February, 2005, p 48. *Mem:* Explorers Club, NY. *Res:* History of modern art; problems of methodology and implications. *Publ:* Auth, Manet's Contemplation at the Gare St Lazare, UCal Press, 87; Paul Manship, Smithsonian Press, 89; Hundertwasser, Taschen, 91; Gorky, UCBC Press, 91; Julian Stanczak, State Univ NY, 92; auth, Color: Suite in Four Parts, DOV Press, 93; auth, The Clouds, DOV Press, 96; contbr, The Dictionary of Art, MacMillan Ltd; coauth, From Idea to Matter, Anderson Gallery Publ, 2005; auth numerous exhibition catalogs including Vincent Pepi, Art Gallery, NY State Univ at Stony Brook, 96, Merrill Mahaffey: Cue from Manet, Palm Springs Desert Mus, 00, From Idea to Matter: 9 Sculptors, Anderson Gallery, Va Commonwealth Univ, 00, William Scharf: History Painter, essay in Phillips Collection, Washington, 00. *Mailing Add:* 5511 Greystone St Chevy Chase MD 20815-5556

RANDALL, LILIAN M C
CURATOR
b Berlin, Ger, Feb 1, 31. *Study:* Mt Holyoke Col, BA, 50; Radcliffe Col, MA, 51, PhD, 55; Hon degree, Towson State Univ, 93. *Work:* Walters Art Gallery, Baltimore, Md. *Collection Arranged:* Armenian Manuscripts, Walters Art Gallery, Baltimore, Md, 74; Printed Books before 1500, Walters Art Gallery, 77; Splendor in Books, Grolier Club, New York, 77-78; An American Art Agent in Paris, George A Lucas (1857-1909), Walters Art Gallery, 78-79; Illuminated Manuscripts: Masterpieces in Miniature, Highlights from the Collection of the Walters Art Gallery, 84-85. *Pos:* Asst dir, Md Arts Coun, 72-73; cur manuscripts & rare books, Walters Art Gallery, 74-95. *Teaching:* Vis lectr medieval illumination, Johns Hopkins Univ, 64-68. *Awards:* Phi Betta Kappa, Sesquicentennial Award, Mount Holyoke Col, 87. *Mem:* Grolier Club; Int Ctr Medieval Art (bd dir, 78-82, 95-98); Baltimore Bibliophiles (pres, 81-83). *Res:* Medieval and Renaissance European illumination. *Publ:* auth, The Diary of George A Lucas: An American Art Agent in Paris, (2 vols), Princeton Univ Press, 79; auth, A Nineteenth-Century Medieval Prayerbook Woven in Lyon, In: Art the Ape of Nature: Studies in Honor of HW Janson, Harry N Abrams, 81; auth & ed, Medieval and Renaissance Manuscripts in the Walters Art Gallery: France, 875-1420, 89 & 1420-1540, 92, & Belgium 1250-1530, 97, Johns Hopkins Univ Press. *Mailing Add:* 301 Kendall Rd Baltimore MD 21210-2562

RANDLETT, MARY WILLIS
PHOTOGRAPHER
b Seattle, Wash, May 5, 24. *Study:* Whitman Col, BA, 47; photog with Hans Jorgensen, Seattle, 48. *Work:* Dept Photog & Prints, Metrop Mus Art, NY; Arch Am Art, Nat Collection Fine Arts, Nat Portrait Gallery, Washington, DC; Manuscripts Div & Spec Collections, Univ Wash Collections, Seattle, Wash State Capitol Mus, Olympia, Wash; Western Wash State Univ, Bellingham. *Comn:* Wash State Artists (photog), Wash State Libr, Olympia, 68; doc ser (photogs), Noguchi Skyviewing sculpture, Western Wash Univ, Bellingham, 70, Tony Angell's of raven, Pacific NW Bell, Seattle, 78, Artists, Everett, 80, 4 artists for Kingdome, King Co Arts Comn, Seattle, 78-80, Wash. *Exhib:* One-woman shows, Northwest Portfolio: The Photog of Mary Randlett, Off of the Gov, Olympia, Wash, 91, Stonington Gallery, Seattle, Wash, 92 & Grad Sch Design, Dept Landscape Archit, Harvard Univ, 96, Inside Back Cover: Lit Portraits of Mary Randlett,Tacoma Pub Libr, Tacoma, Wash, 97, The Light and The Landscape,Hendersons House, Tumwater, 98, Portraits of Writers, Nortwest Bookfest, Pier 48, Seattle, 98, In Love With Light, Mus Northwest Art, 99 & Liquid Light, Port Angeles Fine Arts Ctr, 2000, Mary Randlett and The Creative Neighborhood Safeco Plaza, Seattle, 2002, Mary Randlett Portraits on the Arts Community, Wright Exhib Square, Seattle, 2002-2003, Northwest Masters Selection, City of Seattle's One Percent For Art City Space, 2004, Walla Walla Community Col, Wash, 2004, Wash State Libr, Olympia, 2005, Ecology Building, Lacey, Wash, 2005, Skinner Bldg, Univ Wash, Seattle, 2005-2006; Group shows, Blue Prints: 100 Yrs of Seattle Architecture, Mus Hist & Indust, Seattle, Wash, 94; River History, Skagit Valley Hist Mus, Wash, 95; Seattle Comes to Christ Church, Christ Church, NZ, 96; Guy Anderson: In Celebration, Mus NW Art, Wash, 96; Northwest Landscape: Clayton James, Mary Randlett, Paul Havas, Lucia Douglas Gallery, Wash, 96; Present & Future: Architecture in Cities, XIX Congress of the Int Union of Architects Barcelona, Spain, 96; Guy Anderson Northwest Master, Seattle Art Mus, 96; Philip McCracken Bronzes, Valley Mus Northwest Art, La Conner, Wash, 93 & Jacob Lawrence, 97; Jacob Lawrence, Instrument of Change: James Schoppert 1947-1992, Anchorage Mus Hist & Art, Anchorage, Alaska, 97 & Burke Mus Nat Hist & Cult, Seattle, Wash, 98; A Century of Photographs of the Western Landscape: The Paving of Paradise, Seattle Art Mus, Seattle, Wash, 98; 18th Ann Northwest Inter Art Comp, Whatcom Arco Exhib Gallery, Bellingham, Wash, 98; George Tsutakawa, Seattle Art Mus, 98; A Tribute to Del McBride, Henderson House Mus, Tumwater, Wash, 98 & Wash State Capital Mus, Olympia, 99; From Tractors to Tornadoes: Photographers of the Rural Landscape, Whatcom Mus, Bellingham, Wash, 99; 14th Ann Works from the Heart, Cheney Cowles Mus, Spokane, Wash, 99; Rock, Paper, Scissors, Henderson House Mus, Tumwater, 99; The View from Here: 100 Artists Mark the Centennial of Mount Rainier Nat Park, Mus Northwest Art, Laconner, Wash, 2000; Instrument of Change: James Schoppert Retrospective, Mus Am Indian, New York City, 99; Olympia Through Artists Eyes, Wash State Capitol Mus, 2000; Morris Graves: Journey Mus of Northwest Art La Conner, Wash, 2000; Leo Kenny: Celebrating the Mysteries, A Retrospective, Mus of Northwest Art, 2000; The Governors Heritage Award 1989-2000, Olympic, Wash, 2001; Over the Line: The Art and Life of Jacob Lawrence, The Phillips Collection, Washington, DC, 2002; Roderick Haig-Brown Exhib, Cambell River Mus, BC, 2002; Iridescent Light Artists and Portraits, Rainier Club, Seattle, 2002; Jacob Lawerence Seattle Art Mus, Seattle WA, 2003; New Acquisition for the Collection Tacoma Art Mus, Tacoma, 2003; John Cole Whatcom Mus, Bellingham, WA, 2003; Philip McCracken: 600 Moons, MONA, La Conner, Wash, 2004; Mary Randlett: Nature Photographs, Lucia Douglas Gallery, Bellingham, Wash, 2005; Sequoia Miller-Transplants: Pottery, Place & the Pacific Northwest, Univ Portland, Ore, 2006. *Awards:* Gov Award, Wash, 83; Individual Artists Award, King Co Arts Comn, Seattle, 89; GAP Award, Artists Trust, 89 & 92; Allied Arts Grants, 98; Matrix Table, Woman of Achievement, Seattle, Wash, 99; Allied Arts Found Grant, 2000; Nancy Blankenship Pryor Award Recipient, 2001; Artists Trust Lifetime Achievement Award, 2001; Honary Mem of Seattle Chap of Am Inst of Architects, 2002; Hist Makers Award-Mus of Hist and Industry, Seattle, 2003; Alumnus of Merit Award Whitman Col, 2003. *Bibliog:* Robert Atwan & Valeri Vinokurov (auths), Openings: Original Essays by Contemporary Soviet and American Writers, Univ Wash Press, Seattle, Wash, 90; Arthur Kruckeberg (auth), The Natural History of Puget Sound Country, Univ Wash Press, Seattle, Wash, 91; Jim Rupp (auth), Mary Randlett (photogr), Art in Seattle's Public Places, Univ Wash Press, Seattle, 92; Marilyn Symmes (ed), Fountains: Splash and Spectable, Water and Design from the Renaissance to Present, Rizzoli Int, 98; Mark Tobey (auth), Museo Nat Centro de Arte Reina, Sofia, Spain, 98. *Mem:* Am Soc Mag Photogr; AIA Seattle (hon mem), 2002. *Publ:* Auth, To Know a River, Roderick Haig-Brown, Lyons Burford, New York, 96; The Confederate Raider in the North Pacific: The Saga of the SCC Shenandoah, 1864-65, Wash State Univ Press, 96; Sine Die: A guide to the Washington State Legislative Process, 1977 edition, Edward D See Berger, Univ Wash Press, 96; Seeing with Music: The Lives of Three Blind African Musicians, Simon Ottenberg, Univ Wash Press, 96; The Eighth Lively Art, Wesley Wehr, Univ Wash Press, Seattle, 2000; The Eighth Lively Art, Wesley Wehr, Univ Wash Press, Seattle, 2000; Seattle Waterways, J Scott Rohrer, Pudget Sound Maritime Hist Soc, Seattle, 2001; Geology & Plant Life, Arthur Kruckeberg, Univ Wash Press, Seattle, 2001; John Hoover, Art & Life, Julie Decker, Univ Wash Press, Seattle, 2002; John Cole, Deloris Tarzan Ament, Whatcom Mus, Bellingham, 2003; 600 Moons: 50 Years of Philip McCracken's Art, Deloris Tarzan Ament, Univ Wash Press, Seattle, 2004; The Quick, Katrina Roberts, Univ Wash Press, Seattle, 2005; Sketchbook: The 30s & the Northwest School, William Cumming, Univ Wash Press, Seattle, 2006. *Dealer:* Martin Zambito 721 East Pike Seattle WA 98122-3719. *Mailing Add:* PO Box 11238 Olympia WA 98508-1238

RANDOLPH, LYNN MOORE
PAINTER
b New York, NY, Dec 19, 38. *Study:* Univ Tex, Austin, BFA, 61. *Work:* The Mary Ingraham Bunting Inst, Radcliffe/Harvard; The Menil Collection, Houston; Ariz State Univ Mus; Nat Mus Women in Arts; San Antonio Mus Fine Arts; and others. *Exhib:* solo exhibs, Contemp Arts Mus, Houston, 78, Graham Gallery, 84, 86 & 91, The Texas Landscape 1900-1986, Mus Fine Arts, Houston, 86, Bunting Inst, Radcliffe Col, 90, Everyday Miracles: Retablos, Ex Votos and Contemp Texas Artists, Contemp Art Mus, Houston, Tex, 90 & Virgins in Vertigo and Juicy Women, Lynn Goode Gallery, 95, Joan Wich Gallery, 2003 & 06; The Vulnerable Body, Artscan Gallery, 2000; Waco Art Center, Tex, 2001; D Berman Gallery, Austin, Tex, 2002; Spirits on the Coast, Joan Wich Gallery, 2003; Democracy in Am, Ariz State Univ Mus, Tempe, Ariz, 2004; Cover Art, The Nation, Sept 13, 2004. *Awards:* Residency at Yaddo, June 87; Fel, The Bunting Inst, Radcliffe Col, 89-90. *Bibliog:* Articles in Houston Press, 93-97; Donna Harawa (auth), Modest Witness, Second Millennium, 96; Deborah J Haynes (auth), The Vocation of the Artist, Cambridge Univ Press, 97. *Mem:* Nat Women's Caucus Art (regional vpres, 82-86); Houston Women's Caucus Art (pres, 79-80); Lawndale Art Ctr (artist bd, 92-95). *Media:* Oil. *Publ:* Auth, Beyond political and economic equality, Women Artists' News, 83; A Return to Alien Roots: Painting Outside Mainstream Western Culture, Radcliff Papers, 90. *Dealer:* Joan Wich Gallery, Houston, TX. *Mailing Add:* 1803 Banks Houston TX 77098

RANKAITIS, SUSAN
PAINTER, PHOTOGRAPHER
b Cambridge, Mass, Sept 10, 49. *Study:* Univ Ill, Champaign, BFA(painting), 71; Univ Southern Calif, Los Angeles, MFA(painting & photog), 77. *Work:* Ctr Creative Photog, Tucson, Ariz; San Francisco Mus Mod Art, Calif; Los Angeles Co Mus Art, Calif; Nat Mus Am Art; Art Inst, Chicago. *Exhib:* Solo exhibs, Los Angeles Co Mus Art, 83, Meyers/Bloom, Santa Monica, Calif, 89 & 90, Schneider Mus, 90, Ctr Creative Photog, 91, Ruth Bloom Gallery, Santa Monica, 92, Robert Mann Gallery, NY, 94 & 97, Mus Contemp Photog, Chicago, 94, Mus of Photog Arts, 2000 & Europos Parkas, Vilnius, Lithuania, 2005; group exhib, San Francisco Mus Mod Art, 87 & 89, Santa Fe Art Mus, 87, Axiom Ctr Arts, Eng, 87-88, Los Angeles Co Mus Art, 88 & 2000, Nat Mus Am Art, 89, Tokyo Metrop Mus Photog, 96; NC Mus Art, 2004; and others. *Pos:* Selector, Bingham Educ Trust, 97-2002. *Teaching:* Fletcher Jones chair in art (prof), Scripps Col. *Awards:* Avery Fel to China, 2001; Artist Scholar in Residence, Borchard Found, 2004; Award in Visual Arts, Flintridge Found, 2004. *Bibliog:* Andy Grundberg & Kathleen Gauss (auths), Photography and Arts Interactions Since 1946, Abeville Press; Susan Kandel (auth), Susan Rankaitis, Meyers/Bloom Gallery, 90; Denise Miller Clark (auth), Susan Rankaitis, Abstracting Technology, Science & Nature, 94, Mus Contemp Photog, Chicago; Diana Gaston (auth), Susan Rankaitis: Drawn From Science, 2000; Lyle Rexer (auth), The Antiquarian Avant-Garde, 2002; Paschal & Dougherty (auths), Detying Gravity: Contemporary Art & Flight. *Mem:* Col Art Asn. *Media:* Miscellaneous Media. *Dealer:* Robert Mann Gallery 210 Eleventh Ave New York NY 10001. *Mailing Add:* 3117 Lansbury Claremont CA 91711

RANKIN, DON
PAINTER, INSTRUCTOR
b Dec 9, 42. *Study:* Famous Artists' Sch; also with Bill Yeager; Samford Univ, BA(fine art & psychol); Union Inst, Cincinnati, PhD Visual Art. *Comn:* Birmingham Centennial Commemorative Coins, Arlington Shrine, 70, Univ Ala Med Complex, 71 & Birmingham-Jefferson Civic Ctr, 71; prints, First Nat Bank, Tuscaloosa, 74-76; painting, Country Club Birmingham, 79; Watercolor & print, comn by Air War Col, class of 90, Maxwell AFB, Montgomery, Ala; and others. *Exhib:* The Am Barn & Its Translation in Watercolor, Chautauqua Art Asn Exhib Am Art, NY, 79; 3rd Ann Exhib Southern Watercolor Soc, NTex State Univ Galleries, Denton, 79; Southern Connections - a Nat Invitational, Blount Collection, Montgomery, Ala, 86; Invitational Exhib, Southern Watercolor Painters, Takarazuka, Japan, 90; 16th Ann Juried Exhib, Southern Watercolor Soc, Strathmone Hall, Baltimore, 93-; Ala Artists Traveling Exhib, Wiregrass Mus Art, Dothan, Ala; 17th Ann Juried Exhib, Southern Watercolor Soc, The Parthenon, Nashville, Tenn, 94; PhD exhib, Samford Univ, 98. *Teaching:* National & international watercolor workshops for various art associations; instr, Samford Univ, asst prof. *Bibliog:* Featured artist, watercolor page, Am Artist, 3/80; Elizabeth Leonard (auth), Painting the Landscape, Watson-Guptill; Watercolor 89, Am Artist; reviews, NY Art Rev, 89, Am Artist (video), 6/90 & Artist's Mag (video), 7/90. *Mem:* Ala Watercolor Soc; charter mem La Watercolor Soc; Southern Watercolor Soc; Indian Arts & Crafts Asn. *Media:* Watercolor, Egg Tempera, Oil. *Res:* Papermaking among N Am Indians. *Publ:* Auth, Mastering Glazing Techniques in Watercolor,

Watson-Guptill, 86; Painting from Sketches, Photographs and Imagination, Watson-Guptill, 87; Fifty Most Asked Questions About Watercolor Glazing Techniques, Watson-Guptill, 91; All You Ever Wanted to Know about Watercolor, Watson/Guptill, 7/93. *Dealer:* EC May & Co. *Mailing Add:* 3412 Wellford Cir Birmingham AL 35226

RANSOM, BRIAN
CERAMIST
Study: Univ Puget Sound, Tacoma, Wash, 72-73; RI Sch Design, Providence, 73-74; NY State Col Ceramics at Alfred Univ, New York, BFA(art), 76-78; Universidad de San Marcos (res in Pre-Columbian musical instruments), Lima, Peru, 78-79; Univ Tulsa Okla, MA(ceramics, anthropologh), 83-84; Claremont Grad Sch, Calif, MFA(sculpture), 84-85. *Work:* Everson Mus Ceramics, Syracuse, NY; NY State Col Ceramics Mus, Alfred, NY; also pvt collections of Edward Judd, Lynn Bonyhadi-Scheicher, Pat & Darrel Maveety and others. *Exhib:* Solo exhibs, Couturier Gallery, Los Angeles, 89, 90, 94 & 99, Art Space, Winnipeg, Man, Can 91, Conejo Ballery Art Mus, Thousand Oaks, Calif, 91, El Camino Col, Torrance, Calif, 94, Mendicino Art Ctr, Fla, 95, Elliot Gallery, St Petersburg, Fla, 98 & Univ Fla, Gainesville, 98; Faith Nightingale Gallery, San Diego, 90; Hollywood Bowl Mus, Hollywood, Calif, 92; Riverside Community Col Gallery, Calif, 92; Present Art II, Couturier Gallery, 93; Wabash Col, Torrence, Calif, 94; Mus Nebr Art, Kearny, 96; Tustin Renaissance Gallery, Calif, 96; Penland Sch Gallery, NC, 97; Newport Harbor Art Mus, Calif, 98; Diane Nelson Fine Art, Laguna, Calif, 98; Couturier Gallery, 99; and many other performances. *Pos:* Artist-in-residence, Calif Arts Coun, 92. *Teaching:* Numerous lectrs & workshops, Music & Sculpture, 79-90; Art teacher, Univ Calif-Los Angeles extension, Chino Inst Men, Calif, 88-89; ceramics & glaze calculation instr, Chaffey Col, Calif, 90; ceramics teacher, Scripps Col, Claremont, Calif, 91, First St Gallery, Claremont, Calif, 92-95; asst prof art, Eckerd Col, St Petersburg, Fla, 95-. *Awards:* Res Fel, Univ Tulsa, Okla, 85; Visual Artist Fel Sculpture, Nat Endowment Arts, 86; Artist in Res Fel, Calif Arts Coun, 92. *Bibliog:* Ray Hughey (auth), The sound vision of artist musician Brian Ransom, News Chronicle, Thousand Oaks, Calif, 9/13/91; Joseph Woodward (auth), Sound sculptor, The Los Angeles Times Arts & Entertainment, 10/24/91; Anne Klarner (auth), Best bet, The Los Angeles, 11/5/92. *Publ:* Auth, The Enigma of the Peruvian Whistling Water Vessel, Univ Mo, Columbus, Ohio, 85; contribr (with patrick O'Hearn), music sound track for film "The Destroyer" released by MGM, 87; auth, Sounding Clay, Ceramics Monthly, vol 36, no 8, p 30-34, 88; Sounding Clay (music), Hubba Hubba Studio, Hubbard, Ore, 90; The Enigma of Whistling Water Jars in Pre-Columbian Ceramics, Experimental Musical Instruments, Vol 14, No 1, 98. *Mailing Add:* c/o Couturier Gallery 166 N La Brea Ave Los Angeles CA 90036

RANSOM, HENRY CLEVELAND, JR
PAINTER
b Chattanooga, Tenn, Aug 19, 42. *Study:* Univ Ga, BFA, 64, MFA, 72. *Work:* Montgomery Mus Fine Art, Ala; Mint Mus Art, Charlotte, NC; Hunter Mus Art, Chattanooga, Tenn; Columbus Mus Art, Ohio. *Exhib:* one-man shows, Mint Mus Art, 76, Hunter Mus Art, Chattanooga, 76, Montgomery Mus Fine Art, 76 & Far Gallery, NY, 78; Southern Realism, Miss Mus Art, Jackson, 79; New Am Still Life, Westmoreland Co Mus Art, Greenburg, Pa, 79; Henry W Ranger Exhib, Nat Acad Design, NY, 80; 46th Ann Nat Midyear Show, Butler Inst Am Art, Youngstown, Ohio, 82; 45th Ann Exhib, Soc Four Arts, Palm Beach, Fla, 83. *Awards:* Atwater Kent Award, 39th Ann Exhib, Soc Four Arts, Palm Beach Fla, 77; Purchase Award, Mint Mus Art Biennial, 77; Julius Hallgarten Prize, 155th Ann Exhib, Nat Acad Design, New York, 80. *Media:* Oil, Pencil. *Publ:* Contribr, Ga Rev, Univ Ga Press, 76

RAPOPORT, SONYA
CONCEPTUAL ARTIST
b Boston, Mass. *Study:* Mass Col Art; New York Univ, BA; Univ Calif, Berkeley, MA. *Work:* Stedelijk Mus, Amsterdam, Holland; Grey Art Gallery, New York Univ; Indianapolis Mus Art, Ind; Oakland Art Mus, Calif; Crocker Art Mus, Sacramento, Calif; NY Mus Mod Art. *Comn:* Abstract painting (acrylic/canvas), Hall of Justice, Hayward, Calif, 76. *Exhib:* One-person shows, Calif Palace Legion Honor & Crocker Art Mus, 64 & 74, Peabody Mus, Harvard Univ, Cambridge, Mass, 76 & Kuopio Mus, Finland, 92; Art Scene, San Francisco Mus Mod Art & Baltimore Mus Art, 65 & 73; Book Arts III, Nat Mus Women, Washington, 90; Books as Metaphor for Art: Beyond Words, vol 1 & 2, Crafts & Folk Art Mus & Calif Craft Mus, San Francisco, 90; 4th Int Symp Electronic Art, FISEA, Minneapolis, Minn, 93; NY Digital Salon, 95-96; Col Art Asn, Montreal, Can, 2001; Bienial, Buenos Aires, 2002; SETI Workshop, Paris, 2003. *Pos:* Reviewer, Leonardo Mag. *Teaching:* San Francisco Art Inst, 74; New Sch Social Res, New York, 81; Sarah Lawrence Col, Bronxville, NY, 84; Univ Calif, Berkeley, 88; Ohio State Univ, 92. *Awards:* Vera Adams Davis Mem Award, 63 & Rhea Keller Mem Prizes, 65, San Francisco Mus Art; Individual Juror's Award, Richmond Art Ctr Ann, Calif, 66; Eyes & Ears Found Grant, 82; Calif Art Coun Grant for Telecommun, 88. *Bibliog:* Stephen Moore (auth), Sonya Rapoport--An Aesthetic Response, Union Gallery, San Jose State Univ, 78 Rapoport, Ctr Visual Arts, 79; Edgar Buonagurio (auth), Interaction art & science, Truman Gallery review, Arts Mag, 4/79; Patricia Zimmerman (auth), Metaphysical or Virtual Reality, Soma Mag, Vol 18, spring 92; and others in LAICA J, 82 High Performance, 83, 88 & Heresies, 86; Judy Malloy (ed) Artswire, 99, 2000. *Mem:* Womens Caucus Art; Pacific Ctr Book Arts; Ylem; Kala Inst. *Media:* Scanning, Copy Images; Computer interactive. *Specialty:* Gender, Genetic Engring, Religion. *Interests:* Digital Art Theory, Gender Theory, Installation Art. *Publ:* Auth, About Me, 79, Surface, 80, Chelate, 80 & The Remainder, 80, The Animated Soul-Gateway To Your Ka, pvt publ; Transgenic Bagel, 1998; Redeeming the Gene, 2001. *Mailing Add:* 6 Hillcrest Ct Berkeley CA 94705

RAPP, M YVONNE
ART DEALER, LECTURER
b Lancaster, Pa, July 27, 35. *Study:* Thomas More Col, BA(arts admin), 78. *Pos:* Gallery guide, Cincinnati Art Mus, Eden Park, Ohio, 70-78; docent, J B Speed Art Mus, Louisville, Ky, 79-81; own-dir, Yvonne Rapp Gallery, 82-. *Teaching:* Instr contemp art, Bellarmine Col, 92-. *Specialty:* Contemporary painting, drawings and sculpture. *Mailing Add:* c/o Yvonne Rapp Gallery 2117 Frankfort Ave Louisville KY 40206

RASCOE, STEPHEN THOMAS
PAINTER, EDUCATOR
b Uvalde, Tex, May 8, 24. *Study:* Univ Tex, Austin; Art Inst Chicago, BFA & MFA. *Work:* Dallas Mus Fine Arts; Southern Methodist Univ, Dallas; Ford Motor Co, Dearborn, Mich; Blanton Mus Art, Univ Tex at Austin; Tex A&M Univ Gallery; Houston Mus of Fine Arts; Art Mus South Tex, Corpus Christi; Arlington Mus Art, Tex; Memory Tech, Plano, Tex. *Comn:* Rancho Seco Land & Cattle Co, Corpus Christi, Tex, 67; Tex Instruments Corp, Dallas, 67; Arlington Bank & Trust Co, Tex, 69; First Nat Bank, 69 & Lakewood Bank, 71, Dallas. *Exhib:* Longview Ann, Tex, 57-86; Artists West of the Mississippi, Denver, 67; San Antonio Hemisphere, Tex, 68; Tex Ann Painting and Sculpture Exhib, 56, 57, 58, 59, 60; Mary Nye Contemp Art Gallery, Dallas; Arlington Mus of Art, Arlington, Tex, One Man Show, June 88; Galerie Kornye West, Ft Worth, Tex, One Man Show and 80th Birthday Celebration, May 8, 2004. *Teaching:* Assoc prof art, Univ Tex, Arlington, 64-92. *Awards:* Houston Mus Fine Arts Purchase Award, Tex Show, 56; First Prize, Tex Painting & Sculpture Show, Dallas Mus, 57; DD Feldman Award, 58 & Purchase Award, 59. *Bibliog:* Texas Painting and Sculpture: 20th Century, 71; Pecos to Rio Grande, Tex A&M Press, 83; Dallas Home Design Mag. A Voyage of Discovery by Steve Carter, Sept. 2003. *Mem:* Dallas Art Asn; Ft Worth Art Asn; STex Art League (pres, 60-61); Arlington Art Asn (pres, 67-68). *Media:* Oil. *Dealer:* Galerie Kornye West 1601 Clover Ln Fort Worth TX 76107, telephone 817-763-5227. *Mailing Add:* 2002 Westview Terr Arlington TX 76013

RASCON, ARMANDO
CONCEPTUAL ARTIST, CURATOR
b Calexico, Calif, Dec 9, 56. *Study:* Col Creative Studies, Univ Calif, Santa Barbara, Calif, BA, 79. *Work:* Franklin Furnace, NY; Steel, Clarence & Buckley, San Francisco, Calif; US-Mex Border Fence, Bi Nat Mural Proj, 95. *Exhib:* The AIDS Time line, Univ Art Mus, Berkeley, 89; Tattoo Collection, Jennifer Flay Galerie, Paris, France, 92; Existential Monochrome, Southern Exposure, San Francisco, Randolph St Gallery, Chicago, 92; Mis/Taken Identities, Univ Art Mus, Santa Barbara, 92; Occupied Aztlan, Art Inst San Francisco, 94; Xicano Anesthetic, Intar, NY, 94; Video Collection, Mus Mod Art, NY, 95; Blue Star Arts Space, San Antonio, Tex, 98; and others. *Pos:* Art dealer, conceptual artist, cur, educator, painter, photogr & video. *Teaching:* Univ Calif, Davis, 88; Calif Col Arts & Crafts, Oakland, Calif, 91. *Awards:* Fel, Nat Endowment Arts, 87; Calif Arts Coun, 98; US-Mex Fund Cult Grant, 98. *Bibliog:* Suzaan Boettger (auth), The impolite figure, Art forum, 10/83; Judith Christensen (auth), Business as usual, Artweek, 12/12/87; Lydia Natthews (auth), Armando Rasan at Souhern Exposure, Visions, spring 92. *Publ:* Ed, The Multicultural Reading Room at Randolph Street Gallery, Artpapers. *Mailing Add:* c/o Terrain Gallery 165 Jessie St 2nd Flr San Francisco CA 94105

RASKIND, PHILIS
SCULPTOR, INSTRUCTOR
b New York, NY. *Study:* Art Students League; Nat Acad Sch Fine Arts, cert, 73. *Work:* Elizabeth T Greenshields Mem Found, Montreal, Can. *Comn:* Peace Medal US & N Vietnam, pvt comn, NY, 73; theatre masks for New York City Opera, Conn Opera Co, 73-75; bust: Pompidou, Waxworks, Can, 74; miniature series, Quantum Arts, NY, 78-79; life-size figure for WAM Satta, 82; portrait bust, Sculpture Group, New Am Libr, 84. *Exhib:* Catharine Lorillard Wolfe Art Club, Nat Arts Club, NY, 72-79; Nat Sculpture Soc, NY, 72-80; Pen & Brush Club, NY, 75, 76, 78 & 79; Nat Acad Fine Arts Exhib, Nat Acad Fine Arts, 76-78; Salmagundi Club, NY, 79. *Pos:* Ed newsletter, Catharine Lorillard Wolfe Art Club, 75-78. *Teaching:* Instr sculpture, Manhattan Community for Psychotherapy, 73-75; instr sculpture, Am Telegraph & Telephone Adult Educ Prog, New York, 73-74; instr, Fashion Inst Technol, New York, 85-87. *Awards:* Gold Medal, Pen & Brush Club, 78; Bronze Medal, Catharine Lorillard Wolfe Art Club, 77; Kalos Kagathos Found Award, Nat Sculpture Soc, 82; and others. *Mem:* Catharine Lorillard Wolfe Art Club (sculpture chmn, 75-78); Nat Art League; Vis Artists & Galeri Galleries Asn; Int Soc Artists; Artists Equity Asn. *Media:* Clay; Wood. *Dealer:* Belanthi Gallery 142 Court St Brooklyn NY. *Mailing Add:* 330 Third Ave No 15G New York NY 10010-3705

RASMUSSEN, ANTON JESSE
PAINTER, ADMINISTRATOR
b Salt Lake City, Utah, Nov 12, 42. *Study:* Univ Utah, BFA, 67, MFA, 74. *Work:* Utah Mus Fine Arts, Eccles Health Sci Libr, Univ Utah, Salt Lake City; Davis Co Libr, Farmington, Utah. *Comn:* Oil paintig, Bountiful, 76 & three panels, Clearfield, 77, Davis Co Libr, Utah; oil painting, four panels (4 ft x 5 ft), Salt Lake Int Airport, Utah. *Exhib:* Utah Painting 75, Utah Mus Fine Arts, Salt Lake City, 75; one-man exhibs, Davis Co Libr, S Davis Br, Bountiful, Utah, 76, N Davis Br, Clearfield, Utah, 76 & Eccles Health Sci Libr, Univ Utah, Salt Lake City, 76; Two Utah Artists, Boise State Univ, Idaho, 77. *Pos:* Dir, Bountiful Art Ctr, Univ Utah Exten, Bountiful, 74-84; asst dir, Prog for Higher Educ, Davis Co/Univ Utah, Bountiful, 75-84. *Teaching:* Adj asst prof art, Univ Utah, Salt Lake City, 74-84. *Bibliog:* Claudia Sisemore (producer, color film), Anton J Rasmussen--painter of abstractions from nature, pvt publ, 77. *Media:* Oil. *Mailing Add:* 1321 Penn St Salt Lake City UT 84105

RASMUSSEN, ROBERT (REDD EKKS) NORMAN
SCULPTOR, CERAMIST
b Oslo, Norway, Feb 11, 37. *Study:* San Francisco Art Inst, BFA, 59; Calif Col Arts & Crafts, MFA, 70. *Work:* San Francisco Mus Mod Art, San Francisco; Los Angeles Co Mus Art, Los Angeles; Mills Col Art Gallery, Oakland. *Exhib:* Mix, San Francisco Mus Art, 73; Ceramic Sculpture, San Francisco Art Inst, 74; Newport Harbor Art Mus, Newport Beach, Calif, 81; New Mus, NY, 81; Artists Space, NY, 82; Joseph Chowning Gallery, San Francisco, 83 & 86; Ten Yrs Later, Calif State Univ Fullerton, Calif, 87; New Langton Arts, San Francisco, 87; and others. *Teaching:* Instr ceramics, San Francisco Art Inst, 71-; instr ceramics, Univ Wis-Madison, summer, 75. *Awards:* Nat Endowment Arts, 81. *Mailing Add:* PO Box 210462 San Francisco CA 94121-0462

RASTO See Hlavina, Rastislav

RATCLIFF, CARTER
CRITIC, WRITER
b Seattle, Wash, Aug 20, 41. *Study:* Univ Chicago, BA, 63. *Pos:* Assoc ed, Art News, 69-72; adv ed, Art Int, 70-75; contrib ed, Art in Am, 76-, Saturday Rev, 80-82; ed adv comt, Sculpture, 92-. *Teaching:* Workshop dir, Poetry Proj, St Mark's Church, New York, 69-70; vis prof, Hunter Col, New York, 85-86 & 96-98; lect at numerous insts & univs. *Awards:* Poets Found Grant, 69; Nat Endowment Arts Fels, 72 & 78; Guggenheim Mem Found Fel, 76; Mather Award, 87. *Res:* Post-war American art. *Publ:* Auth, Andy Warhol: Inflation artist, Artforum, 3/85; Gilbert & George: The Singing Sculptures, McCall, 93; Ellsworth Kelly: Curves, Guggenheim Mus, 96; The Fate of a Gesture: Jackson Pollock and Postwar American Art, Ferrar, Straus & Giroux, 96; Out of the Box: The Reinvention of Art 1965-75, Allworth, 2000

RATH, ALAN T
SCULPTOR
b Cincinnati, Ohio, 59. *Study:* Mass Inst Technol, BSEE, 82. *Work:* Denver Art Mus, Colo; Oakland Mus, Calif; San Diego Mus Contemp Art, La Jolla, Calif; Walker Art Center, Minn; Orange Co Mus Art, Newport Beach, Calif; and others. *Exhib:* Solo exhibs, ctr Advanced Visual Art, MIT, 84 & 94, Walker Art Ctr (traveling), 91, Haines Gallery, San Francisco, 95, 96 & 98, Contemp Arts Mus, Houston (with catalog), 95, Nelson Gallery, Univ Calif, Davis (with catalog), 96 & Aspen Art Mus, Colo, 96; Site Santa Fe, NMex, 98; Dorfman Projects, NY, 98; Yerba Buena Ctr for Arts, San Francisco, 98; Mus Contemp Art, Scottsdale, Ariz, 99; Mus Art, Austin, Tex, 99; Track 16 Gallery, Santa Monica, Calif, 2002. *Awards:* Nat Endowment Arts Fel, 88; John Simon Guggenheim Mem Found Fel, New York, 94. *Bibliog:* Peter Boswell (auth), Alan Rath (brochure), Walker Art Ctr, Minneapolis, Minn, 91; Alan Rath (catalog), Gallery 210, Univ Mo, St Louis, 92; Ken Baker (auth), Alan Rath: digital world, Artnews, 5/92. *Dealer:* Carl Solway Gallery 424 Findlay St Cincinnati OH 45214; Haines Gallery 49 Geary St Fl 5 San Francisco CA 94108. *Mailing Add:* 830 E 15th St Oakland CA 94606

RATHBONE, ELIZA EURETTA
CURATOR
b St Louis, Mo, Sept 3, 48. *Study:* Smith Col, 67-68; New York, with Horst W Janson, William Rubin, Gert Schiff & Robert Rosenblum, BA, 72; Courtauld Inst, Univ London, with John Golding, MA, 74. *Collection Arranged:* Modigliani: An Anniversary Exhibition, 83; Mark Tobey: City Paintings (auth, catalog), 84; Susan Rothenberg (auth, catalog), 85; Duncan Phillips: A Centennial Exhib, 86; Bill Jensen (auth, catalog), 87; Nicolas de Stael in America (coauth, catalog), 90; Brancus: Photographs and Sculpture, 94; Impressionists on the Seine: A Celebration of Renoir's Luncheon of the Boating Party, (coauth, catalog), 96; Jake Berthot: Drawing into Painting, 96; Impressionists in Winter: Effects de Neige (coauth, catalog), 98; Honore Daumier, 2000; The Eye of Duncan Phillips, 2000 (co-auth); Impressionist Still Life (co-auth catalog), 01. *Pos:* Asst cur 20th century art, Nat Gallery Art, Washington, DC, 77-85; from assoc cur to chief cur, Phillips Collection, Washington, DC, 85-. *Awards:* Chevalier in the Order of Arts and Letters, French Govt, 02. *Publ:* Coauth, Art at Mid-century: The Subjects of the Artist, Nat Gallery of Art, 78 & The Morton Neumann Family Collection, 80; auth, Art Beyond Isms: Masterworks from El Greco to Picasso in the Phillips Collection, 02; Nicholas de Stael in Am, 1990; Impressionists on the Scene, 1996; Impressionists in Winter, 1998; Discovering Neilton Avery. *Mailing Add:* c/o The Phillips Collection 1600 21st St NW Washington DC 20009

RATHBONE, PETER B
APPRAISER, COLLECTOR
Study: Boston Univ, BA. *Pos:* Dir, Am paintings, drawings and sculpture dept, Sotheby's, NYC, 76-. *Mailing Add:* Sotheby's 1334 York Ave New York NY 10021

RATHBUN, WILLIAM JAY
CURATOR
b Sioux City, Iowa, June 19, 31. *Study:* Univ Wash, BA, 54, MA(art hist), 66. *Collection Arranged:* Song of the Brush: Japanese Paintings from Sanso Collection (auth, catalog), 79, Treasures of Asian Art from the Idemitsu Collection (auth, catalog), 81, Yo no Bi: The Beauty of Japanese Folk Art (auth, catalog), 83 & 50 Years: A Legacy of Asian Art, 83, Seattle Art Mus. *Pos:* Asst cur, Seattle Art Mus, 73-76, assoc cur Asian painting, 76-78, cur Japanese art, 78-. *Teaching:* Asst art hist, Univ Wash, Seattle, 66-67; asst prof, Portland State Univ, 70-71. *Awards:* Governor's Writers' Award, 84. *Mem:* Oriental Ceramic Soc, London; Japan Soc. *Publ:* Coauth, Asiatic Art in the Seattle Art Museum, Seattle Art Mus, 73; contribr, A Myriad of Autumn Leaves, New Orleans Mus Art, 83; Asian Art Collection (catalog), Seattle Art Mus (in prep). *Mailing Add:* Seattle Art Mus 1400 E Prospect St Seattle WA 98112

RATHLE, HENRI (AMIN)
PAINTER
b Cairo, Egypt, Nov 4, 11; US citizen. *Study:* Self-taught; Royal Palace, with El Hawawini, 29-30; also studied with Henry Gasser, 70; Fac de Medecine de Paris, MD, 38. *Work:* Phoenix Fire Mus & Mus of City, Mobile, Ala. *Comn:* President Nixon, Washington, DC, 69; Oakley and Southern Belle, Emperor Clocks, WGer, 73; President Charles deGaulle, comn by J F Bezou, New Orleans, La. *Exhib:* One-man shows, Percy Whiting Art Ctr, Fairhope, Ala, 68, Biloxi Municipal Art Gallery, Miss, 68, Jackson Co Col, Gautier, Miss, 68 & Fine Arts Mus South, Mobile, Ala, 72. *Awards:* Purchase Award, Bellingrath Gardens, Mobile, Ala, 70; Purchase Award, Fine Arts Mus South, Mobile, Ala. *Bibliog:* John Fay (auth), Masculinity found in art, Mobile Register, 3/67; J F Bezou (auth), Exposition a Biloxi, France-Amerique, 2/68; German & Swedish Monographs, 78. *Mem:* Mobile Art Asn; Easte. *Media:* Acrylic, Watercolor, Oil. *Mailing Add:* 756 Sullivan Ave Mobile AL 36606

RAUF, BARBARA CLAIRE
INSTRUCTOR, PAINTER
b Covington, Ky, Mar 13, 44. *Study:* Thomas More Col, AB, 68; Univ Cincinnati, BFA, 74; Univ Pa, MFA, 77. *Work:* Atkins & Pearce Manfacturing, Co, Cincinnati, Ohio; Saint Clair Med Ctr, Morehead, Ky; Admin Bldg, Sci Wing & Chancellors Room, Thomas More Col, Crestview Hills, Ky. *Comn:* Amy (portrait), comn by Mr & Mrs George Deitmaring, Ft Mitchell, Ky, 80; Asa (portrait), Atkins & Pearce Co, Cincinnati, 81; pres series & chancellor series (portraits), Thomas More Col, 84-86 & 96; Pat (portrait), comn by Dr & Mrs Forrest Calico, Ft Mitchell, Ky, 85. *Exhib:* Inst Contemp Art, Philadelphia, 75, 76 & 77; solo exhibs, Carnegie Art Ctr, Covington, Ky, 92, Clermont Art Gallery, Eatavia, Ohio, 93, The Gallery, Covington, Ky, 93 & Dayton Visual Art Ctr, 95; Southern Ohio Mus, 96; Univ Cincinnati Gallery, 97; Cathedral Gallery, 98, 2002, 03 & 04; Annex Gallery, 2005. *Pos:* Dir, Thomas More Gallery, Thomas More Col, 78-. *Teaching:* Asst prof art & dept chair, Thomas More Col, 77-83, assoc prof, 83-97, prof, 98. *Awards:* Advan Inst Development Grants, US Govt; Ky Found Women, 90; Outstanding Teacher of the Year, 2001. *Bibliog:* B Wheatley (auth), Carnegie Center today, Kenton Co Recorder, 84; Mary McCarty (auth), Portrait painter, Cincinnati Mag, 85. *Mem:* Contemp Art Ctr, Cincinnati; Col Art Asn; Carnegie Art Ctr. *Media:* Oil, Pencil. *Mailing Add:* 840 Tater Knob Rd Peebles OH 45660

RAUSCHENBERG, ROBERT
PAINTER, PHOTOGRAPHER
b Port Arthur, Tex, Oct 22, 25. *Study:* Kansas City Art Inst & Sch Design, 46-47; Acad Julian, Paris, 47; Black Mt Col, with Josef Albers, 48-49; Art Students League, with Vaclav Vytlacil & Morris Kantor, 49-50. *Hon Degrees:* Grinnell Col, LHD, 67; Univ Southern Fla, LHD, 76. *Work:* Albright-Knox Art Gallery; Whitney Mus Am Art; Wadsworth Atheneum; Tate Gallery, London; Mus Mod Art, NY; Neue Galerie, Aachen, Ger; Moderna Museet, Stockholm, Sweden; Hirshhorn Mus, Washington, DC; and many others. *Exhib:* Solo exhibs, Galerie Mathilde, Amsterdam, 79, Espace Nicois d' Art et de Cult, Nice France, 86, Museo Nacional, Havana, Cuba, 88, Galerie Alfred Kren, Cologne, Ger, 88-89, Central House Cult, Tretyakov Gallery, Moscow, Russia, 89, Nat Art Gallery, Kuala Lumpur, Malaysia, 90, The Silk Screen Paintings 1962-1964, 90-91, Whitney Mus Am Art, NY, 90 & 2000, ROCI, Nat Gallery Art, Wash, DC, The Early 1950's, Guggenheim Mus, 92, Hiroshima City Mus Contemp Art, Japan, 93, Mandarin Oriental Fine Arts, Hong Kong, 94, Nat Mus of Art, Osaka, Japan, 94, Buckminster Fuller Inst, Santa Barbara, Calif (traveling), 95-96, UN Main Lobby, NY, 96; Retrospective, Nat Collection Fine Arts, Washington, DC, Mus Mod Art, NY, San Francisco Mus Mod Art, Albright-Knox Gallery, Buffalo, NY & Art Inst Chicago, 77-78, Solomon R Guggenheim Mus & Guggenheim SoHo, NY (traveling), 97-98; Guggenheim Mus, NY, 85 & 88; Sogetsu Art Mus, Japan, 88; Mus Mod Art, NY, 88; Whitney Mus Am Art, Stamford, Conn, 88 & 89; Galerie Kaj Forsblom, Helsinki, Finland, 88; Corcoran Gallery Art, Washington, DC, 89 & 90; Heland Wetterling Gallery, Stockholm, Sweden, 90; Milwaukee Art Mus, Wis, 90; Art Gallery Ont, Can, 90; Makuhari Messe, Japan, 90; LA Louvre, Venice, Calif, 90. *Pos:* neurosychiatric tech, Calif Naval Hosps; founder Overseas Culture Interchange traveling exhib, 85-. *Awards:* Grand Prix D'Honneur, 13th Int Exhib Graphic Art, Ljubljana, Yu; Gold Medal, Oslo, Norway; Officier, Ordre des Arts et Lettres, Ministry Culture & Commun, France; Grand Prize, Venice Biennale, 64; Praemium Imperiale, Japan Art Assoc, 98; 1st Prize Int Exhib Prints Gallery Modern Art, Ljubljana, Yugoslavia, 63, Corcoran Biennal Contemp Am Painters, 65; Painting and Sculpture Medal, Skowhegan Sch, 82; Grammy Award, 84. *Bibliog:* Rauschenberg: Modern Masters '89, Viikonvaihde, Helsinki, Finland, 6/3/89; Nava Semel (auth), Robert Rauschenberg, Studio Art Mag (in Hebrew), Israel, 12/89; Henry Kamm (auth), Rauschenberg Show Heralds Union of the Arts in Berlin, New York Times, 3/10/90; Daniel Waterman (auth), Rauschenberg's Bandages, ArtNews, 5/90. *Mem:* Nat Acad Design (assoc, 82, acad, 85); Am Acad and Inst Arts and Letters. *Mailing Add:* c/o Pace Wildenstein 32 E 57th St New York NY 10022-2513

RAVENAL, JOHN B
CURATOR
Study: Wesleyan Univ, BA(art hist), 82; Columbia Univ, MA(art hist), 87, MPil(art hist), 90. *Work:* Cur (exhibs) robert lazzarini, Va Mus Fine Arts, 2003—04 (Award for Best Exhib of Digital Art, Asn Independent Art Critics/USA, 2005). *Pos:* Res, in contemp art, Wadsworth Atheneum, Hartford, Conn, 82—85; asst cur, 20th-century art Philadelphia Mus Art, 91—97; assoc cur, 20th-century art, 97—98; cur of art, after 1900 Va Mus Fine Arts, Richmond, 98—. *Mailing Add:* Va Mus Fine Arts 200 N Blvd Richmond VA 23220-4007

RAVETT, ABRAHAM
FILMMAKER, PHOTOGRAPHER
b Poland, Aug 2, 47; US citizen. *Study:* Brooklyn Col, BA, 68; Mass Col Art, BFA(film-photog), 75; Syracuse Univ, MFA(filmmaking), 78. *Exhib:* Cineprobe, Mus Mod Art, NY, 86; New Eng Film Festival, Boston, Mass, 86 & 90; Image Forum, Tokyo, 87; Anthology Film Archives, NY, 89; Collective for Living Cinema, NY, 90; Mus Mod Art, NY, 91; Edison Black Maria, 91. *Pos:* Artist-in-residence, The Artist Found, Boston, 79. *Teaching:* Assoc prof film-photog, Hampshire Col, Amherst, Mass, 79-. *Awards:* Andrew Mellon Found Grant, 81, 87, & 90; Artist Found Fel, Boston, 83; Nat Endowment Arts Grant, 85, 87 & 92; Japan-US Friendship Comn Grants, 83, 85, 87 & 90; Mass Productions, 88-89. *Mailing Add:* 193 Nonotuck St Florence MA 01062-1907

RAVIV, ILANA
PAINTER, PRINTMAKER
b Tel Aviv, Israel, Nov 29, 45; US & Israeli citizen. *Study:* League NY, with Robert Delamonica, Knox Martin & Bruce Dorfman, 80-84. *Work:* Holocaust Mem Mus, Washington, DC. *Comn:* mural, City of NY, 87. *Exhib:* one-woman shows, Nat Arts Club, New York City, 2000, Castra Gallery, Haifa, Israel, 01, Wilfrid Israel Art Mus, 01-02, Painters and Sculptors Asn, Tel-Aviv, 02, BoxHeart Gallery, Pittsburgh, 04. *Mem:* NY Artist Equity Asn; Painters & Sculptors Asn, Israel; Nat Asn Acrylic Painters. *Media:* Acrylic, All media; Serigraphy, Silkscreen. *Mailing Add:* 400 Central Park W Apt 18T New York NY 10025

RAY, CHARLES
SCULPTOR
b Chicago, Ill, 53. *Study:* Univ Iowa, Iowa City, BFA(cum laude), 75; Mason Gross Sch Art, Rutgers, MFA, 79. *Work:* Whitney Mus Am Art, NY; Newport Harbor Art Mus. *Exhib:* one-man shows, 64 Market St, Venice, Calif, 83, Mercer Union, Toronto, 85, Feature, Chicago, 87, NY, 89, 90, 91 & 92, Burnett Miller, Los Angeles, 88, The Mattress Factory, Pittsburgh, 89, Galerie Claire Burrus, Paris, 90, Feature, NY, 90, 92 & 93, Donald Young Gallery, Seattle, Wash, 92, Galerie Metropol, Vienna, Austria, 93, Rooseum-Ctr for Contemp Art, Malmo, Sweden, 94, Kunsthalle Bern, Switz, 94, Kunsthalle Zurich, Switz, 94, Studio Guenzani, Milan, 96, Regen Proj, Los Angeles, 97, Whitney Mus of Am Art, 98, Mus of Contemp Art, Los Angeles, 98, Mus of Contemp Art, Chicago, 98; Recent Drawings, Whitney Mus Am Art, NY, 90; Helter Skelter: LA Art in the 1990's (with catalog), Mus Contemp Art, Calif, 92; Whitney Biennial, Whitney Mus Am Art, NY, 97; The Am Century: Art and Cult 1900-2000, Whitney Mus of Am Art, New York City, 99; Regarding Beauty: A View of the Late Twentieth Century, Smithsonian Inst Hirshhorn Mus, 99; Let's Entertain, Walker Art Ctr, 2000; Barbara Gladstone Gallery, New York City, 2000; Made in Calif: Art, Image and Identity 1900-2000, Los Angeles Co Mus of Art, 2000; Au-dela du Spectacle, Centre Pompidou, Paris, 2001; Open Ends: Art Since 1960, Mus of Modern Art, New York City, 2001; Pollock to Today: Highlights from the Permanent Collection, Whitney Mus, 2002; A Room of Their Own, Mus of Contemp Art, Los Angeles, 2001. *Awards:* NJ Coun on the Arts Grant, 80; Nat Endowment Arts, 85 & 88; Larry Aldrich Found Award, 97. *Bibliog:* Christopher Knight (auth), An Art of Darkness at MOCA, Los Angeles Times, F1, F4-F5 (reproduction), 1/28/92; Susan Kandel (auth), LA in Review, Arts, 98-99, 4/92; Hunter Drohojowska (auth), LA Raw, Artnews, 78-81, 4/92. *Mailing Add:* c/o Regen Projects 629 N Almont Dr Los Angeles CA 90069

RAY, CHRISTOPHER T
SCULPTOR, CRAFTSMAN
b Albany, NY, May 7, 37. *Study:* Pa Acad Fine Arts, 60. *Work:* Mus Am Jewish Hist & Port of Hist Mus, Philadelphia; Pa State Mus, Harrisburg. *Comn:* Sculptured gates, Penn's Landing Sq, Philadelphia, 73; pub sculpture, Scheie Eye Inst, Philadelphia, 75, First Pa Bank, Philadelphia, 76 & Great Valley Corp Ctr, Malvern, Pa, 79; sculptured gate/bas-relief, Chestnut St Park, Philadelphia, 79. *Exhib:* Figure & Fantasy, 75 & Animal Art, 81, Smithsonian Inst, Washington, DC; Am Craft Show, Philadelphia Mus Art, 77; Sculpture Outdoors, Temple Univ, Ambler, Pa, 79; Mod Wrought Ironwork & Sculpture Int Exhib, Lindau, Ger, 81; Ornamentalism, Hudson River Mus, Yonkers, NY, 83; and others. *Pos:* Pres/founder, GENUS Collab, Philadelphia, 77-. *Bibliog:* Donna Z Meilach (auth), Decorative & Sculptural Ironwork, Crown Publ; R Jensen & P Conway (coauth), Ornamentalism, Potter, Inc; B Brolin & J Richards (coauth), Architectural Ornament, Van Nostrand Rheinhold Co, 82. *Mem:* Artists' Equity Asn (vpres, 76-78); fel Pa Acad Fine Arts; Artists-Blacksmiths Asn NAm; Am Crafts Coun. *Media:* Forged Iron, Carved Wood

RAY, DEBORAH See Kogan, Deborah

RAY, TIMOTHY L
PAINTER, EDUCATOR
b Indian Head, Sask, Sept 26, 40. *Study:* Univ Man, BFA; Univ Ark, MFA. *Work:* Winnipeg Art Gallery, St John's Col, Man; Sioux City Art Ctr, Iowa; Moorhead State Univ Found, Minn; Royal Bank Can, Monteal, Que. *Comn:* Kinetic sculpture, City of Winnipeg, 77. *Exhib:* Four Artists, Minneapolis Inst Arts, 80; Invitational Exhib, Univ SDak, Vermillion, 86; Studio Visits, NDak Mus Art, Grand Forks, 86; NDak Centennial Art Exhib, traveling, 88. *Teaching:* Prof art, Moorhead State Univ, 70-96; retired. *Awards:* First Prize, Red River Ann, 66; Royal Trust Award, Manisphere, 72 & Outstanding Am, 74. *Bibliog:* William Hegeman (auth), Four artists, Minneapolis Star-Tribune, 80; Robert Enright (auth), Departures and arrivals, Arts Manitoba, 83; R McIlroy (auth), Ray's art, Winnipeg Free Press, 84. *Media:* Acrylic. *Publ:* Auth, One Hundred Years of Art, Moorhead State Univ, 87; The Importance of Being Low Tech, Border Crossings, 92; Imponderable joys, work of Austin Cooper, Art Gallery SWMB, 94. *Mailing Add:* 1006 4th Ave N Moorhead MN 56560

RAYBURN, BOYD (DALE)
PAINTER, PRINTMAKER
b Carriere, Miss, May 12, 42. *Study:* Univ Southern Miss, BS, 64; Univ Miss, MFA, 70. *Work:* DeCordova Mus, Lincoln, Mass; High Mus, Atlanta; Mint Mus, Charlotte, NC; Southeastern Ctr Contemp Art, Winston-Salem, NC; Yale Univ Art Gallery. *Exhib:* 20th Southeastern Exhib, High Mus, Atlanta, 65; Piedmont Painting & Sculpture, Mint Mus, Charlotte, NC, 71; Audubon Artist Ann, Nat Acad Gallery, NY, 73; two-person show, Mint Mus, Charlotte, NC, 74 & Miss Mus Art, Jackson, 77; Hunterdon Print Exhib, Hunterdon Art Ctr, Clinton, NJ, 78. *Pos:* Bd dir, Nat Asn Independent Artist. *Teaching:* Instr art, Univ Miss, 69-70; instr printmaking, Ga Southwestern Col, 72-73; asst prof, La State Univ, Shreveport, 80-82. *Awards:* Purchase Award, DeCordova Mus, 77 & Southeastern Ctr Contemp Art, 78; Rembrandt Graphic Award, Boston Printmakers Exhib, 90; 1st Place Printmaking, Coconut Grove Arts Festival, 2002. *Mem:* Boston Printmakers; Southeastern Printmakers Asn; Nat Asn Independent Artists. *Media:* Monotype. *Dealer:* Lagerquist Gallery 3235 Paces Ferry Place NW Atlanta GA 30305. *Mailing Add:* 1538 Jones Rd Roswell GA 30075-2726

RAYDON, ALEXANDER R
DEALER, COLLECTOR
Study: Tech Univ Munich, grad. *Pos:* Dir, Raydon Gallery. *Mem:* Int Coun Mus. *Res:* American art of the nineteenth and early twentieth centuries. *Specialty:* Paintings, sculpture, prints and drawings from the Renaissance to the present, with emphasis on the nineteenth and early twentieth centuries. *Interests:* fine art from Renaissance to present. *Publ:* Ed, Americans Abroad, 72; Charles Burchfield--Master Doodler, 72; American Scene--American Artists Abroad, 75-77; Masters in European Portraiture, 76; Am Watercolor Painting, 80

RAYEN, JAMES WILSON
PAINTER, EDUCATOR
b Youngstown, Ohio, Apr 9, 35. *Study:* Yale Univ, BA, BFA & MFA; with Josef Albers, Sewell Sillman & Rico Lebrun. *Work:* Addison Gallery Am Art, Andover, Mass; Yale Univ, New Haven, Conn; Wellesley Col, Mass; First Nat Bank, Boston; Mint Mus, NC; Harvard Univ, Cambridge, Mass. *Comn:* Marriott Hotel Corp; Hyatt Hotel Corp. *Exhib:* One-man shows, Durlacher Brothers Gallery, NY, 66 & Eleanor Rigelhaupt Gallery, Boston, 68; 10 Yr Retrospective, Brockton Art Ctr, Mass, 73; Recent & Revised, Wellesley Col Mus, 78; Chapel Gallery, Boston, 84; Rice Pollack Gallery, Provincetown, Mass, 95. *Pos:* Bd dir, N Bennet St Sch, Boston; bd dir & vpres, Boston Acad Music. *Teaching:* Prof, Wellesley Col, 61-, Elizabeth Christy Kopf chair in studio art, 83. *Awards:* Ital Govt Grant in Painting, 59-60; Ford Found Grant in the Humanities, 69-70; Wellesley Col Fac Grant, summer 75, spring 84, 85, 91, 92 & 93; Mass Coun Arts Grant Printmaking, 88. *Bibliog:* Robert Taylor (auth), Boston Globe, 73; Christine Temon (auth), Boston Globe, 83, 90. *Media:* Acrylic, Watercolor; Monotype, Oil. *Dealer:* Gallery 79 Boston Mass. *Mailing Add:* Wellesley Col Art Dept Jewett Arts Ctr Wellesley MA 02481

RAYMOND, LILO
PHOTOGRAPHER
b Frankfurt, Ger, June 23, 22; US citizen. *Study:* Photog Sem, with David Vestal, 61-63. *Work:* Sheldon Mus Art Gallery, Mus Mod Art & Metrop Mus, NY; High Mus, Atlanta; New Orleans Mus Art. *Exhib:* Still Life in Photog, Helios Gallery, NY, 76; Contrasts Gallery, London, Eng, 80; Woodman Gallery, Morristown, NJ, 81; Photo West, Carmel, 82; Baker Gallery, Kans, 82; and many one woman shows. *Teaching:* Mem sem photog, Sch Visual Arts, New York, 78-, Maine Photog Workshop, Rockport, summer 79 & Int Ctr Photog, New York, winter 79. *Awards:* Creative Artists Pub Serv Prog Grant, 78. *Bibliog:* Sir Cecil Beaton (auth), The Magic Image, Little Brown & Co, 75; Alicia Wille (auth), Lilo Raymond, gravure portfolio, Popular Photog, 77; Richard Blodgett (auth), A Collectors Guide, Ballatine Bks, 79. *Publ:* Photogr, Classic County Inns of America, Knapp Press & Holt, Rinehart & Winston, 78. *Dealer:* Marcuse Pfeifer 825 Madison Ave New York NY 10021. *Mailing Add:* Cutler Hill Rd Eddyville NY 12401

RAYNER, GORDON
PAINTER
b Toronto, Ont, 1935. *Work:* Philadelphia Mus Art; Mus Mod Art, NY; Can Coun, Ottawa, Ont; Hirshhorn Collection, Nat Gallery Can, Ottawa. *Comn:* Wall mural, Bank of Montreal, Toronto, 70; building facade & canopy, Ontario Hydro/Ont Place, Toronto, 71; outdoor wall mural, Benson & Hedges Tobacco Co, Toronto, 71; Tempo (ceramic tile mural), Toronto Transit Comn, 77. *Exhib:* Sixth Biennale of Can Painting, Nat Gallery Can, Ottawa, 65; Mus Mod Art, NY, 67; Coughtry/Rayner/Markle, Nat Gallery Can (traveling), Ottawa, 68; Toronto Painting 1953-1965, Nat Gallery Can, 72; Artists Jazz Band, Mus d'Art Contemporian, Montreal, 74-75; Survey Can Painting, Art Gallery Ont, Toronto, 75; Artists Jazz Band, Beaubourg Centre, Can, Paris, France, 78; Paradise, The Isaacs Gallery, 79. *Teaching:* Painting, Three Schs Art, Toronto, 68-77; teacher painting & founder, For Art's Sake Inc, Toronto, 77-80. *Awards:* First Prize, Graphics 12th Winnipeg Art Show, 70; Can Coun Sr Arts grant, 73 & 75. *Bibliog:* Barrie Hale (auth), Gordon Rayner: The first decade, 2/70 & Theodore Heinrich (auth), Edging up to paradise, 5/6/79, Artscanada. *Media:* Acrylic, Collage. *Mailing Add:* 1493 Dupont St Toronto ON M6P 3S2 Canada

RÉ, PAUL BARTLETT
GRAPHIC ARTIST, SCULPTOR
b Albuquerque, NMex, Apr 18, 50. *Study:* Calif Inst Technol, BS, 72, with honors. *Work:* Univ Calif Art Mus, Berkeley; Oakland Mus, Calif; Fine Arts Mus NMex, Santa Fe; J B Speed Mus Art, Louisville, Ky; Wichita Art Mus, Kans; Paul Ré Collection and Sculpture Garden, Univ NMex, Albuquerque. *Comn:* Series of 6 large

drawings, comn by Jim Freeman, Kyoto, Japan, 76; series of 7 large drawings, comn by Fredrick Shair, Altadena, Calif, 81; Touchable Art for the Blind and Sighted (hand made bk), Perkins Sch Blind, Watertown, Mass, 83, Can Nat Inst Blind, Edmonton, Can, 83 & Deutsche Blindenstudienanstalt, Marburg, Ger, 86. *Exhib:* Paul Ré: Drawings and Paintings, Jonson Gallery, Univ NMex Art Mus, Albuquerque, 78, New Works by Paul Ré, Jonson Gallery - Univ NMex Art Mus, 2001; Graphic Design, XIII Biennale, Monrovia Gallery, Brno, Czech, 88; Touchable Art: An Exhibit for the Blind and Sighted by Paul Ré, J B Speed Mus Art, Louisville, Ky, 85; Wichita Art Mus, Kans, 86; Albuquerque Mus Art, NMex, 86; Aitken Bicentennial Exhib Centre, St John, NB, Can, 89; Colorado Springs Pioneers' Mus, Colo, 90; Santa Barbara Mus Art, Calif, 91; Paul Ré: Shaping Serenity, Karpeles Mus, Newburgh, NY, 2002. *Pos:* Dir, Paul Ré Collection and Archives, 96-; adv bd, Mus Am Folk Art, 86-94. *Awards:* Helene Wurlitzer Found Residency Grant, Taos, NMex, 82 & 84; Publ Award for Touchable Art (book chpt) Spirit of Enterprise: The 1990 Rolex Awards, Geneva, Switzerland, 90; Legion of Hon (one of five worldwide for promoting peace through art), United Cult Convention, 2005; Paul Bartlett Ré Peace Prize. *Bibliog:* Dennis Wepman (auth), Ré, Paul B, Contemp Graphic Artists, 88; Beryl Dakers & Mark Shaffer (auths), Touchable Art by Paul Ré (TV doc), SCETV, 90; Interview by Dennis Wepman, The Dance of the Pencil, J Print World, 94. *Mem:* Int Soc Art Sci & Technol; Int Soc Interdisciplinary Study of Symmetry. *Media:* Drawings, Thermoformed Reliefs, Réograms (hybrid hand-digital prints). *Publ:* Auth, My Drawings and Paintings, Leonardo XIII-2, 80, My Drawings and Paintings: An Extension, Leonardo XIV-2, 81 & On the Progression of My Figurative Drawings, 82, Leonardo XV-2; Touchable Art: A Book for the Blind and Sighted, 83 & The Dance of the Pencil: Serene Art by Paul Ré, 93, Paul Ré Archives. *Dealer:* The Paul Ré Archives. *Mailing Add:* 10533 Sierra Bonita Ave NE Albuquerque NM 87111

READ, DAVE (DAVID) DOLLOFF
PHOTOGRAPHER, EDUCATOR
b Belfast, Maine, July 14, 38. *Study:* Ohio Univ, BFA, 63, MFA, 65. *Work:* Mus Mod Art, NY; Libr Cong, Washington, DC; Mus Fine Arts, St Petersburg, Fla; Univ Mich, East Lansing; Univ Louisville, Ky. *Exhib:* Photog Fine Arts, Metrop Mus Art, NY, 67; Photog Art Form, Ringling Mus, Sarasota, 77; Dave Read Photog, Mich State Univ, 77 & Light Factory, Charlotte, NC, 78; Dave Read: 1st Mid-west Photogs, Sheldon Art Gallery, Lincoln, Nebr, 80; Photographs by Dave Read, Friends Photog, Carmel, Calif, 83. *Collection Arranged:* Flash (photog by Mertin, Hume, Cohen & Bishop, auth, catalog), Miami Dade Community Col, 76. *Teaching:* Instr photog, Univ NMex, Albuquerque, 65-66; assoc prof photog, Miami-Dade Community Col, Fla, 69-77; prof photog, Univ Nebr, Lincoln, 78-. *Awards:* Artist's Fel, Mid-Am Arts Alliance & Nat Endowment Arts, 83. *Mem:* Soc Photog Educ; Friends of Photog. *Media:* Silver Prints. *Publ:* Contribr, Afterimage, Visual Studies Workshop, 81; Electronic Flash Photography, Van Nostrand Reinhold, 80; contribr, Exposure, 79. *Mailing Add:* 626 SE 35th Ter Cape Coral FL 33904-4941

READMAN, SYLVIE
PHOTOGRAPHER
b Quebec City, Que, Aug 10, 58. *Study:* St-Foy Col, DEC, 80; Laval Univ, Que, BA, 81; Concordia Univ, Montreal, MA(photog), 89. *Work:* Can Contemp Mus Photog, Ont; Contemp Art Mus Montreal, Que; Mus Que; Winnipeg Art Gallery, Man; Bibliotheque Nat De Paris, France. *Exhib:* Group exhibs, Can Mus Contemp Photog, 91 & 92, Nickle Art Gallery, 93 & Frac De L'ile De France, Paris, 96; Les Decennies De La Métamorphose, Musee Du Que, 92; solo exhibs, Contemp Art Montreal, 93 & Edmonton Art Gallery, 96. *Bibliog:* Daniel Leger C Simon (auth), Sylvie Readman, Gallery S Lallouz, 92; Paulette Gagnon (auth), Sylvie Readman, Contemp Art Mus Montreal, 93; Lucy R Lippard (auth), The Lure of the Local, spring 97. *Dealer:* Samuel Lallouz 4295 St Laurent Montreal PQ H2W 1Z4 Canada. *Mailing Add:* 1747 boul Boucherville Rd Saint Bruno PQ J3V 4H2 Canada

REAGAN, ROURK C
PAINTER, PHOTOGRAPHER
b Baltimore, Md, Jan 5, 1970. *Study:* Scuola Lorenzo de Medici, Florence, Italy, BFA prog, 90; Art Inst Chicago, BFA, 91; Claremont Grad Univ, MFA, 2000. *Exhib:* Love, Power & Magic, Atelier 751, Taos, NMex, 94; Lachsa Retrospective, Downey Mus Art, Calif, 96; Am Signature, Fine Art Living, Melbourne, Australia, 97; Agora Gallery, NY, 97; La Casa de la Cultura Mex, San Jose, Calif, 97; D C Gallery, Claremont, Calif, 98; 1st Int Biennial Contemp Art, Trevi Flash Art Mus, Italy, 98. *Teaching:* instr, Los Angeles Co High Sch for Arts; instr, San Antonio Col; instr, The Buckley Sch. *Media:* Oil, Mixed Media. *Dealer:* Gunther Nachtrab Atelien 751 Box 22 Taos NM 87109. *Mailing Add:* 1760 Garfield Pl Los Angeles CA 90028-5904

REBAUDENGO, PATRIZIA SANDRETTO RE
COLLECTOR
b Turin, Italy. *Pos:* Founder, chairwoman Fondazione Sandretto Re Rebaudengo, Turin, Italy, 95-, Centro per l'Arte Contemporanea, Turin, Italy, 2002-. *Awards:* Named one of Top 200 Collectors, ARTnews Mag, 2003-06; recipient Montblanc Arts Patronage award, 2003. *Mem:* Inter Council, Tate Gallery, London, Inter Council and Friends of Contemp Drawing, Mus Modern Art, New York City. *Collection:* Contemporary art. *Mailing Add:* Fondazione Sandretto Re Rebaudengo Via Modane 16 Turin i 10141 Italy

REBBECK, LESTER JAMES, JR
GALLERY DIRECTOR, PAINTER
b Chicago, Ill, June 25, 29. *Study:* Art Inst Chicago & Univ Chicago, hist with K Blackshear, BAEd, MAEd, 59; also painting with Wieghardt, drawing with Isoble McKinnon. *Comn:* Paintings & prints, comn by William Fischer, 69. *Exhib:* Mus Sci & Industry, Chicago, 83; Ill State Mus, Springfield, 83; Peace Mus, Chicago, 83; Fort Wayne Mus Art, Indiana Ex, 89-90; Ninth Biennial Nat Small Print Exhib, Sixty Sq Inches, Purdue Univ Galleries, 94; and others. *Pos:* Gallery dir, Countryside Art Gallery, Arlington Heights, Ill, 63-68; gallery dir, Chicago Soc Artists Gallery, 67-68. *Teaching:* Asst prof art appreciation & painting, Harper Col, 67-71. *Awards:* GI Show Medal Award, Art Inst Chicago, 53; First Place Oils, McHenry Art Fair, 60, Best of Show, 62. *Bibliog:* Nicolo Pan Epinto & Calogero Panepinto (coauths), Tendenze E Testimonianze Del Arte Contemporanea, Accademia Italia, 83; Lis Krantz (auth), American Artists, Facts on File Publs, New York/Oxford, Eng, 85; Les Krantz (ed), The New York Art Review, Am References Inc, 88. *Mem:* Col Art Asn Am. *Media:* Oil on Canvas; Wood Sculpture. *Dealer:* Nahan Galleries 381 W Broadway New York NY 10012. *Mailing Add:* 2041 Vermont St Rolling Meadows IL 60008

REBER, MICK
SCULPTOR, PAINTER
b St George, Utah, June 6, 42. *Study:* Brigham Young Univ, BFA & MFA; independent studies in San Francisco, Chicago, Montreal, New York & Paris. *Work:* Springville Art Mus; Brigham Young Univ, Utah; Southern Utah State Col. *Comn:* Hilton Hotel Corp, Nev; paintings, 20th Century Fox, 73; Don Rey Advert, Nev. *Exhib:* Mainstreams Exhib, Marietta Col, Ohio, 74; Western State Art Found Traveling Exhib, San Francisco Mus of Mod Art, Denver Art Mus & Seattle Art Mus, 78; one-man shows, Gallery Sloan, Scottsdale, Ariz, 90, Byrne-Getz Gallery, Aspen, Colo, 90 & Presden Gallery, Santa Fe, NMex, 90; and others. *Teaching:* Prof advan painting & sculpture, Ft Lewis Col, Durango, Colo. *Awards:* Painting Award, Springville Nat, Springville Mus of Art, Utah, 70; First Cash Award, Four Corners Biennial, Phoenix Art Mus, 73. *Bibliog:* H Lester Cooke (auth), A Biennial of Painting & Sculpture (catalog); Arthur Williams (auth), Sculpture (cover story), Santa Fean Mag. *Media:* All Media

REBHUN, PEARL G
PAINTER, PRINTMAKER
b New York, NY, Feb 20, 24. *Study:* Studied with Isaac Soyer, Leo Manso, Shirley Gorelik, Jerry Okomoto & Jerry Samuels. *Work:* Nassau Mus Fine Art, Roslyn, NY; Trinity Col, Hartford; Public Serv Gas & Elec Utility, NJ; Martha Lincoln Gallery, Vero Beach, Fla; Isis Gallery, Port Washington, NY; Ft Lauderdale Mus, Juried Exhib: Hortt. *Comn:* Oppenheim, Appel Dixon & Co, NY, 78; Brookhaven Bursing Corp, Nassua Co, 79; Fleischmanns Distilling Corp, New Hyde Park, 80; Forest Elec Corp, NY, 87. *Exhib:* Palazzo Vecchio, Florence, Italy, 83; Mencul Ctr Arts, Cairo, Egypt, 83; Parrish Mus Art, Southampton, NY, 83; Hecksher Mus Art Ann, Huntington, NY, 85; Ft Lauderdale Mus Art, 90-91; and others. *Awards:* Grumbacher Award for Outstanding Contrib to the Arts, 76; Elizabeth Erlanger Award of Merit, Nat Asn Women Artists, 79; Chase Manhattan Bank Purchase Award, Nassau Mus Fine Art, 85; First prize, Boca Raton Mus Art, Artists Guild, 2001. *Mem:* Nat Asn Women, New York (bd mem 80-91); Old Sch Square Cult Arts Ctr, Delray, Fla, 91-92; Boca Raton Mus Art, 92. *Publ:* NY Times, Newsday. *Mailing Add:* 3541 NW 61st Cir Boca Raton FL 33496

RECANATI, DINA
SCULPTOR
b Cairo, Egypt. *Study:* Art Students League, with Jose de Creft, 59-62. *Work:* Israel Mus, Jerusalem; Tel Aviv Mus; Ben Gurion Airport, Tel Aviv; Tel Aviv Univ, Israel; Jewish Mus, NY; Herrzliah Mus, Continental Grain Collection, NY. *Comn:* Gate (bronze), Ministry of Transportation, Israel, 74; Gates (spec bronze ed), Am-Israel Cult Found, NY, 76; Israel Chancellery, Washington, DC, 80; President's Garden Collection, Jerusalem; Weizmann Inst Sci, Rehovot, Israel. *Exhib:* July M Gallery, Tel-Aviv, 81-84; Jewish Mus Sculpture Garden, NY, 81-84; Mus Contemp Art (with catalog), Ramat Gan, Israel, 89; Barbican Art Gallery, London, Eng, 90; Installation Ben Gurion Airport, 92; and others. *Bibliog:* Amnon Barzel (auth), Pillars and Parchments, 86; Prof M Omer (auth), Transformation from Within, Cimaise, 87 & Signs of Survival in the Culture of Decay, 89; Gil Goldfine (auth), Through the Trees, Jerusalem Post, 89; and others. *Media:* Bronze, Wood. *Publ:* Contribr, The Artist's Notebook, Gordon Galleries, Israel, 75. *Dealer:* Julie M Gallery Tel Aviv Israel. *Mailing Add:* 136 Grand St Apt 6E New York NY 10013

RECTOR, MARGE (LEE)
PAINTER, SCULPTOR
b Norman, Okla, Aug 4, 29. *Study:* Tex Tech Univ, BA(com art), 50; studied at Dallas Mus Fine Arts (painting & life drawing), 65-66, Chapman Kelley (critique & life drawing), 65-66 Col Marin (ceramic & sculpture), 75-78. *Exhib:* Tex Painting & Sculpture Exhib, Dallas Mus Fine Arts, 66 & 71; Butler Inst Am Art, Youngstown, Ohio, 66 & 70; 8th Ann Eight State Exhib Painting & Sculpture, Okla Art Ctr, 66; Color Talk & Personal Motives, Agora Gallery, NY, 93 & 94; Expanding Consciousness, Abney Galleries, NY, 94; Critics Choice, Montserrat Gallery, NY, 94. *Collection Arranged:* Public; McDermott-Smyzer Collection, Dallas TX; Private: Donald W Seldin-Dallas TX, Ellen Hansen, Columbus, NC; Christine & Bill Berry-Tiburon, CA. *Pos:* Artist, Bozell & Jacobs, 50-52; free lance com artist, Dallas, Tex, 52-65; fine arts gallery affil, Atelier Chapman Kelly, 66-73. *Awards:* Humble Oil & Refining Co Award, 66; Best in Show Circuit Award, Tex Fine Arts Asn, 67; Minnie Belle Heep Award, Tex Fine Arts Asn, 68. *Bibliog:* Timothy Rose & Marge Rector, Ways to Shape Space, Artweek, 76; Marge Rector's Abstracts Start 6 week Show at Library, Marin Scope, 2/77. *Mem:* Marin Arts Coun. *Media:* Acrylic. *Interests:* Gardening, Reading. *Publ:* Contribr, California Art Review, Am References, 89; Encyclopedia of Living Artists 8, Art Network, 94; Color Talk Agora, Manhattan Arts Int, 1-2/94. *Mailing Add:* 25 San Carlos Sausalito CA 94965

REDD, RICHARD JAMES
PRINTMAKER, EDUCATOR
b Toledo, Ohio, Oct 22, 31. *Study:* Toledo Mus Sch; Univ Toledo, BEd, 53; Univ Iowa, MFA, 58, study with Eugene Ludins & Mauricio Lasansky. *Work:* Allentown Art Mus, Pa; Lehigh Univ, Bethlehem, Pa; Philip & Muriel Berman Collection, Allentown; Kutztown Univ, Pa; East Stroudsburh Univ, Pa; Joan Milla Moran

Collection; Allentown Symphony Orchestra Collection; Community Music School, Allentown. *Exhib:* One-man shows, Allentown Art Mus, 61, Kemerer Mus, Bethlehem, Pa, 80 & Zhejiang Art Acad, Hangzhou, China, 89 & 92; Mushroom Magic, Reading Mus, 82; Breaking with Tradition, Int Quilt Exhib, 83; 30 yr Print Retrospective, Lehigh Univ, 88; Jiangsu Art Gallery, Nanjing, China 92; Banana Factory, Bethlehem, Pa, 99; Hill Sch, Pottstown, Pa, 2000; Raab Gallery, Phila, Pa, 2002; 21 Years of Collagraph Prints Retrospective, Banana Factory, Bethlehem, PA, Aug-Sept 2005; Swann Gallery, Jenkintown, Pa, 2006. *Teaching:* Prof, Lehigh Univ, 58-95, prof emeritus, 96-; chmn dept fine art, 70-76; cur, Masks: Other Faces, Kemerer Mus, 88; lectr in China, 89 & 92. *Awards:* Recognition Award, Bethlehem Fine Arts Commision, 94; Prize, 9th Nat Print Show, Moravian Col, 94 & Woodmere Art Mus, Philadelphia, 96; Print Prize, Phillips Mill, New Hope, Pa, 01; Am Color Print Soc Print Prize, Philadelphia, 06. *Mem:* Lehigh Art Alliance (bd dir, 72-75, 86-96, pres, 76-77); Printmaking Coun NJ (bd dir, 93-96); Kemerer Mus, Bethlehem (bd dir, 78-88); Am Color Print Soc (Phila chap). *Media:* Intaglio, Collagraph. *Dealer:* JMS Gallery, Philadelphia, Pa; Premier Gallery, New Hope, Pa; Swan Gallery, Jenkintown, Pa. *Mailing Add:* 1749 Stonesthrow Rd Bethlehem PA 18015-8935

REDDINGTON, CHARLES LEONARD
PAINTER, EDUCATOR
b Chicago, Ill, Mar 22, 29. *Study:* Art Inst Chicago, with Paul Wieghardt, dipl, 54, BFA, 58; Southern Ill Univ, MFA, 70. *Work:* Commonwealth Govt Collection, Canberra, Australia; Art Gallery NSW, Sydney; Nat Gallery Victoria, Melbourne; Western Australian Art Gallery, Perth; Southern Ill Univ, Carbondale. *Comn:* Harold Mertz Pub Collection, NY, 63; Four Color Lithographs, Nat Gallery Victoria, Melbourne, 64. *Exhib:* Australian Painting Today, 64; Young Contemporaries of Australia, Japan, 65; Travel Exhib of Art, Ind, 71; one-man show, Swope Art Gallery, Terre Haute, Ind, 73; G Bablo, Acad D'Arts, Rivera dei Fiori, Bordighera, Italy; and many others. *Pos:* Dir educ abroad, Ind State Univ, Terre Haute, 75-93. *Teaching:* Lectr drawing & painting, NSW Univ, Sydney, 63-66; prof painting, Ind State Univ, Terre Haute, 70-93. *Awards:* Willis Painting Award, H O Willis Corp, Inc, Sydney, 65; Louis Comfort Tiffany Grant, 70; Works on Paper Prize, Indianapolis Mus, 72; and many others. *Bibliog:* Robert Hughes (auth), Art in Australia, Pelican Books, 70; James Gleeson (auth), Modern Painters, Landsdowne Press, 71; Alan McCulloch (auth), Encyclopedia of Australian Art, Hutchinson & Co. *Mem:* Col Art Conf; Art Inst Chicago Alumnae; Int Inst Conserv Historic & Artistic Works; Ind Arts Comn. *Media:* Acrylic, Oil. *Mailing Add:* 735 W Division Chicago IL 60610-1005

REDDIX, ROSCOE CHESTER
PAINTER, EDUCATOR
b New Orleans, La, Nov 15, 33. *Study:* Southern Univ, BA; Univ New Orleans; Ind Univ, Bloomington, MS(art educ); Univ Southern Miss; also with Dr Eddie Jordan; Vanderbuilt Univ, Nashville, Tenn, PhD. *Comn:* Pastic painting, Southern Univ New Orleans; painting, Superdome, New Orleans, La. *Exhib:* Expo 72, La Artist Exhib, Ill State Univ; NJ State Mus; Black Artist, Ind Univ; one-man shows, Ala State Univ, Southern Univ New Orleans & DeWitt Hist Soc, Ithaca, NY. *Pos:* Bd dir, New Orleans Mus Art. *Teaching:* Instr art, Shreveport, La & New Orleans, La; from asst prof to assoc prof art, Southern Univ New Orleans, 74-, asst to chancellor, 92-. *Bibliog:* Samella S Lewis & Ruth Waddy (auth), Black artist on art, Contemp Crafts. *Mem:* Nat Conf Artist (state dir, 73); Col Art Asn; Creative Artists Alliance New Orleans. *Media:* Oil. *Publ:* Contribr, Black Artist on Art, Vol 2, 71. *Mailing Add:* 1330 Cambronne St New Orleans LA 70118-2002

REDDY, KRISHNA N
PRINTMAKER, SCULPTOR
b Chittoor, Andhra State, India, July 15, 25. *Study:* Int Univ Santiniketan, India, dipl (fine arts), 47; Univ London Slade Sch Fine Arts, cert (fine arts), 52; Acad Grande Chaumiere, Paris, with Zadkine, cert (fine arts), 55; Atelier 17, Int Ctr Gravure, Paris, 55; Academie DiBelle Arti DiBrera, Milan, with Marino Marini, cert (fine arts), 57. *Work:* marble sculpture, Carrara, Ital, 76; bronze sculpture, Demonstrators, Collectors Guild, NY, 77; Mus Mod Art, NY & Paris; Libr Cong, Nat Galleries, Smithsonian Inst, Washington, DC; Metrop Mus Art, NY; British Mus, London; Albertina Mus, Vienna; Chicago Art Inst. *Comn:* Monumental sculpture in marble, Int Sculpture Symposium, St Margarethan, Austria, 62 & Montreal, 64. *Exhib:* One-man shows, Madison Art Ctr, 73, Assoc Am Artists, NY, 74, Univ Calif Gallery, Santa Cruz, 75 & Galerie Vivant, Tokyo, 78; Retrospectives, Bronx Mus Arts, NY, 81; Lalitkala Akademi, New Delhi, 84; Museo del Palacio de Bellas Artes, 88. *Pos:* Dir art dept, Col Fine Arts, Kalakshetra, Madras, 47-49. *Teaching:* Prof & co-dir printmaking, Atelier 17, Int Ctr Graphics, Paris, 57-76; prof & dir graphics, printmaking prog, Dept Art & Art Educ, NY Univ, 77-. *Awards:* Padma Shree, Pres India, 72; Printmaker Emer Award, Southern Graphics Council, 2000; Prof Emer of Art and Art Educ, Pres NY Univ, 2001. *Bibliog:* S W Hayter (auth), About Prints, 64 & New Ways of Gravure, 66, Oxford Univ Press, London; Gabor Peterdi (auth), Printmaking, Macmillan Co, New York, 71; Una Johnson (auth), American Prints and Printmakers, NY, 80; The Great Clown, Gallerie Borjeson, Malmo, Sweden, 85; Peggy Roalf (auth), Looking at Paintings: Circus, 93. *Mem:* Soc Am Graphic Artists. *Media:* Engraving, Etching; Stone. *Publ:* Auth, Intaglio Simultaneous Color Printmaking, State Univ New York Press, Albany, 88; New Ways of Color Printmaking: Significance of Materials and Processes, Aianta Press & Vadehra Art Gallery, New Delhi, 97. *Dealer:* Sylvan Cole Gallery 101 W 57th St New York NY 10019. *Mailing Add:* 80 Wooster St New York NY 10012

REDGRAVE, FELICITY
PAINTER, PRINTMAKER
b UK, 1920; Can citizen. *Study:* Sheridan Col, Oakville, Ont, dipl(hon, graphic design), 70; Univ Guelph, Ont, BA(hon; fine arts), 73; Univ Toronto, BEd(art), 75. *Work:* Can Art Bank, Ottawa; Esso Resources Ltd, Calgary, Alta; Lavalin Inc, Montreal; Teleglobe, Montreal; Telesat, Ottawa. *Exhib:* Solo exhib, Images of Nova Scotia & Newfoundland, Harbour Front, Toronto, 77, Art Gallery of Nova Scotia, 78, Confederation Ctr, Charlottetown, PEI, 80, Night-Spaces, St Mary's Univ, Halifax, NS, 84 & Moncton Univ, 86; Night Radio, Galerie Sans Nom, Moncton, 87; McPherson Libr, Univ Victoria, 92; Videographe, Montréal, Que, 94. *Pos:* Contrib ed, Art mag, 78-82; art crtic, Discussion Concordia Univ, Montreal, 80; contrib writer, Arts Atlantic, 81. *Teaching:* Vis artist, Univ Toronto, York Univ, 77 & Univ Waterloo, 79 & 81; lectr, Owens Art Gallery, Mt Allison Univ, NS, 85. *Awards:* Can Coun B Grant, 83-84; Intermedia Group & video Grants, 87-88; Exploration Grant, 89. *Bibliog:* Susan Gibson (auth), article, Vangard Mag Review, 85; Univ Guelph Alumni Mag, 94. *Mem:* Visual Arts NS; Can Artists Representation; NS Printmakers Asn; Community Arts Coun, Victoria, BC. *Media:* Acrylic, Graphite. *Publ:* Auth, Tom Forrestal, Arts Atlantic, 79; Marlene Creates and Pat Martin Bates at Mt St Vincent's Art Gallery, 85; Brian Porter at Dalhousie Art Gallery, 85; John Neville, Art Gallery NS, 88. *Dealer:* Winchester Galleries 1545 Fort St Victoria BC V8S 1Z7. *Mailing Add:* 1545 Fort St Victoria BC V8S 1Z7 Canada

REDING, BARBARA ENDICOTT
ARTIST
b New York, NY, Jan 31, 39. *Study:* b Brigham Young Univ, BA, 60; grad work, Univ Calif. *Work:* Art Mus of Santa Cruz; Tate Mus, London; Bank of Am; Plantronics Corp; Landmark Properties. *Comn:* Double Tree Hotel, Monterey, Calif. *Exhib:* NAPA Exhibit, Santa Fe, NM, 2002. *Collection Arranged:* Westminster exhib, London, Tate Mus, London, Colton Hall Cult Arts exhib, Monterey, Calif, Napa Signature exhibs, Monterey, Calif, New Orleans, La. *Pos:* Plein Air Instr, Santa Cruz Art League, 94-96; Plein Air Instr, Ireland, 96-2002. *Teaching:* studio private and group instructions. *Awards:* Best of Show, Capitala Plein Air Competition, 02; Best of Show, Santa Cruz, 99. *Bibliog:* Monterey Co Herald, 00; Santa Cruz Sentinel, 70-89. *Mem:* Nat Acrylic Painters Asn (signature mem); Cent Coast Painters; Carmel Colorist; Carmel Art Found; Santa Cruz Art League. *Media:* Oils. *Specialty:* Calif Plein Air Works, Calif Impressionists. *Mailing Add:* PO Box 755 Capitola CA 95010

REDINGER, WALTER FRED
SCULPTOR, MURALIST
b Wallacetown, Ont, Jan 6, 40. *Study:* Beal-Spec Art, London, Ont; Meinsinger Sch Art, Detroit; Ont Col Art, Toronto. *Work:* Nat Art Gallery, Ottawa; Stratford Art Gallery; St Thomas Art Gallery; Univ Western Ont; Univ Sask. *Comn:* Nat Parks Comn, Ottawa, 78; Por & Assocs, 79; Oakville Art Gallery, Ont; Garlick Gardens, 83; Dr R Redinger, Louisville, Ky. *Exhib:* Montreal Mus Fine Arts, Que, 64; Survey 68, Montreal Mus Fine Arts, 68; group show, Montreal Mus Fine Arts, 68; Ont Centennial Exhib, Toronto, Art Gallery Ont, 68; The Hart of London, Nat Gallery Can, 68; Can Artists, Art Gallery Ont, 68; Plastic Presence, Milwaukee Art Ctr, 69; Plastics, San Francisco Mus Art, 69; Sensory Perceptions, Art Gallery Ont, 70; 3 D's into the 70's, Art Gallery Ont, 70; St Thomas Art Gallery, Ont, 73; London Regional Art Gallery, 77; Opening Celebrations, London Regional Art Gallery, 80; group show, Ctr Contemp Art St Thomas, 92; Three Elgin Co Artists, St Thomas Art Gallery, 92; Hart of London, London Regional Art Gallery, 93; one-man show, Beyond Survival, London Regional Art Gallery & Christopher Cutts Gallery, Toronto, 94; group show, Mitchel Algus Gallery, NY, 95; Michael Gibson Gallery, London, Ontario, Small & Mighty, small works by maj artists, 2003; St Thomas Pub Art Ctr, Organic Works on Paper, 2004; Mitchell Algus Art Gallery, NY, God Seekers, 2005. *Pos:* Resident artist, Univ Western Ont. *Awards:* Sculpture Prize, Montreal Mus Fine Art, 68; Can Coun Jr Awards, 68-71, Sr Awards, 73, 74, 78-80 & 87; Victor Lynch-Staunton Award, 77; Pollack-Krasner Award, 2004-2005. *Bibliog:* Peter Crass, 75 & 76; Phil Ross & Walter Redinger, Landscape Vision & Dreams, 82; Beyond Survival, Int Film Festival, Halifax, NS, 96; Redinger at work-Documentary, 2005. *Mem:* Royal Can Acad Arts. *Media:* Fiberglass, Steel. *Dealer:* Mitch Algus, 511 West 25th St New York, NY, 212-242-6242. *Mailing Add:* 25761 Silver Clay Hene R #3 West Lorne ON NOL2PO Canada

REDMOND, CATHERINE
PAINTER
b Jamestown, NY, June 3, 43. *Study:* Cornell Univ, Ithaca, NY, 61-62; Harpur Col, State Univ NY, Binghamton, AB, 66; Art Students League, New York, 69-74. *Work:* Butler Inst Am Art; Art Students League NY; Luther Col, Decorah, Iowa; Progressive Insurance Corp & Cleveland Clinic Found Collections, Cleveland, Ohio; Reading Mus, Reading, Pa. *Comn:* View from Euclid, Cleveland Clinic Found, Ohio, 85; Winter Westside, Cardinal Fed Savings Bank, Cleveland, Ohio, 86; View from Downtown, Transohio Bank, Cleveland, 87; 17 Views of NY, Dreyfus Corp, 92. *Exhib:* Biennial One, Contemp Art Ctr, Cincinnati, 86; The City as Subject, Butler Inst Am Art, 88; Urbanology, Mary Grove Col Gallery, Detroit, 89; The Artist as Native, Babcock Galleries, NY, 93-94; Rediscovering the Landscape of the Americas, Gerald Peters Gallery, Santa Fe, NMex, 96-97; NY Collection, Albright-Knox Art Gallery, NY, 98; NY Night and Day, David Findlay Jr Contemp Art, NY, 01; Kindred Spirits, David Findlay, Jr Contemp Art, 02; Points of View, David Findlay Jr Contemp Art, NY, 02; Value and Presence, List Gallery, Swarthmore Col, Pa, 03; Twelve: Catherine Redmond, David Findlay Jr Contemp Art 2003, Thru the Ether, Dean's Gallery, Pratt Inst. *Teaching:* Asst prof painting, Cleveland Inst Art, 85-90; instr, Art Students League, NY, 90-; vis asst prof, Sch of Art and Design, Pratt Inst, NY, 1999; Aju Associate Prof Sch of art and Design, Pratt Inst 2005-. *Bibliog:* Erica-Lynn Gamino (auth), Creations at Goodheart, Southampton Press, 4/29/98; John Driscoll (auth), The Artist & American Landscape, First Glance Bks Inc, 98; Phyllis Braff (auth), 3 artists & a solid view of individual directions, NY Times, 4/19/98; Christopher Willard, "Creating Contrasts with Conte Crayons," American Artist, 2/99; Cynthia Dantzic (auth), 100 New York Painters, Schiffer Publ Co, fall 2006. *Mem:* Art Students League NY (bd control, 72-74); Artists Fel. *Media:* Oil. *Mailing Add:* 156 Chambers St New York NY 10007

REDMOND, ROSEMARY
PAINTER
b Anchorage, Alaska, Mar 16, 52. *Study:* Univ Alaska, BFA, 82; Pratt Inst, grant & fel, MFA, 85. *Work:* Anchorage Mus Hist & Art, Alaska; Alaska State Coun Arts; Mat-Su Coll; Palmer, Alaska; Univ Alaska, Fairbanks Mus. *Exhib:* Nat, Current Visions, Germanow Gallery, Rochester, NY, 86; Nat, New Am Talent, traveling, Tex Fine Arts Assoc, Austin, 89; solo exhibs, Visual Arts Ctr Alaska, Anchorage, 91, Kendall Gallery, New York, NY, 91, Anchorage Mus Hist & Art, Alaska, 95, Alaska Pac Univ, 98, Bunnell Gallery, Homer, Alaska, 2000, Decker Morris Gallery, Anchorage, Alaska, 2000, Alaska Pacific Univ, 2004, Bitoz, Anchorage, Alaska, 2004 & Bunnell Gallery, Homer, Alaska, 2006; Garr Gottstien Gallery, 98; group show, Alaska Pacific Univ, 2004. *Teaching:* adj prof art, Matanuska Susitna Campuses, Univ Alaska, Anchorage. *Awards:* Fel, Yaddo Corp, 89; Grants, Artists Space, New York, 90 & 91; Alaska State Coun Arts, 2000; Website Award, Northwestern States Art coun, 99. *Bibliog:* Julie Decker (auth), Icebreakers-Alaska's Most Innovative Artists, textbook, Alaska Sate Coun on Arts and Alaska Humanities Forum, 99; John Branson (auth), Bristol Bay, From Hinterlands to Tidewater, textbook, Nat Park Svc; Painting the Railroad, Anchorage Daily News, 08/11/2006. *Media:* Acrylic, Oil; Miscellaneous Media. *Interests:* abstraction, symbology. *Publ:* Auth, An Eskimo in Touch with Two Cultures, Alaska Mag, 11/79. *Dealer:* Nemo Art Gallery 200 W 34th Anchorage AK 99501. *Mailing Add:* 440 E 15th Terr Anchorage AK 99501

RED STAR, KEVIN (RUNNING RABBIT)
PAINTER, PRINTMAKER
b Lodge Grass, Mont, Oct 9, 43. *Study:* Inst Am Indian Art, Santa Fe, NMex, 62-65; San Francisco Art Inst, 65-67; Mont State Univ, 68-69; Eastern Mont Col, Billings, BA, 72. *Work:* Northern Plains Mus, Browning, Mont; Inst Am Indian Art Mus, Santa Fe, NMex; Denver Art Mus, Colo; Shenyang Nat Art Mus, Liaoning, China; Rocky Mountain Coll, Billing, Mont; and others. *Comn:* Mural, Crow Tribal Office, Crow Agency, Mont. *Exhib:* Wheelwright Contemp Indian Artist Show, Wheelwright Ceremonial Art Mus, Santa Fe, 78; 100 yrs of Native Am Painting, Okla Mus Art, 78; Indian Images '80, Natural Hist Mus, Denver; Peking Exhibit of Am Western Art, China, 81; Lublin Collection, NY, 86 & Greenwich, Conn, 87; Segal Gallery, New York City, 87; El Taller Gallery, 88; Mus of the Rockies, Bozeman, Mont, 95; Kevin Red Star Gallery, Red Lodge, Mont, 97, 2000, 2001, 2002; Ramscale Gallery, New York City, 97; Autry Mus of Western Heritage, Los Angeles, 97, 98-2003; Red Lodge North Gallery, Billings, 98, 99; Ventana Fine Art Gallery, Santa Fe, 98, 99, 2000, 2001 & 2003; Denver Art Mus, 98; Wilde Meyer Gallery, Scottsdale, Arix, 2000; Sutton West Gallery, Missoula, Mont, 2000, 2002 & 2003; Frame Hut & Gallery, Billings, 2000; Martin-Harris Gallery, JacksoHhole, Wyom, 2000; Big Horn Gallery, Cody, Wyom, 2000n; Mus Nebr Art, Kearney, 2000, 2002; Buffalo Bill Hist Ctr, Cody, 2000; Coeur d'Alene Tribal Art Show & Auction, 2001, 2002; Sorrel Sky Gallery, Durango, Colo, 2002; Lloyd Kiva New Gallery, Santa Fe, 2002; Eiteljorg Mus, Indianapolis, 2002 & 2003; Buffalo Bill Hist Ctr, Cody, 2002; Indian Artist's of Am Show, Scottsdale, 2003; Yellowstone Art Mus, Billings, 2003; one-person shows, Northcutt Steele Gallery, Billings, 89, El Taller Gallery, Santa Fe, 90, Ventana Fine Art Gallery, Santa Fe, 98, 2001, 2002, Healing Environ Gallery, Billings Deaconess Hosp, 98, Kevin Red Star Gallery, 98, 99, CM Russell Mus, 99, Carbon Co Arts Guild & Depot Gallery, Red Lodge, Mont, 2000, Holter Mus, Helena, 2000, Martin-Harris Gallery, 2001, Rich Haines Gallery, Hackson Hole, 2002 & Mt San Antonio Col Gallery, 2002; two-person show, Sutton West Gallery, 2001. *Collection Arranged:* 77 West Coast Experience (auth, catalog), Tokyo, Japan; American Indian Art Exhibition, Espace Pierre Cardin, Paris, 79; The Real People, Havana, Cuba, 79; Santa Fe Festival of the Arts, 78-81; American Indian Art in the 80's, Native Am Ctr Living Arts Mus (auth, catalog), Niagara Falls, NY, 81. *Teaching:* Instr art, Lodge Grass, Mont, 73-74, Inst Am Indian Art, Santa Fe, 75-76. *Awards:* Governor's Trophy, Scottsdale Nat Indian Art Exhib, 65; First Place, Cent Wash State Col Art Exhib, Ellensburg, Wash, 74. *Bibliog:* Scott E Dial (auth), Visual portrayals of Kevin Red Star, Southwest Art, 2/76; Penny Cox (auth), Red Star: Modern mystic and on the move, Santa Fe Profile Mag, 12/79; Jamake Highwater, The Sweet Grass Lives On, Harper & Row, 79-80. *Mem:* Harvard Project. *Media:* Acrylic, Oil; Lithography, Etchings. *Mailing Add:* PO Box 269 Roberts MT 59070

REECE, MAYNARD
PAINTER, ILLUSTRATOR
b Arnolds Park, Iowa, Apr 26, 20. *Work:* Cent Nat Bank, Des Moines, Iowa; Norwest Bank, Des Moines; Leigh Yawkey Woodson Art Mus, Wausau, Wis. *Comn:* Designs for postage stamps, Govt of Bermuda, 65; First Iowa Duck Stamp, State Conserv Comn, 72; Marshlander Mallards, Ducks Unlimited Inc, 73; Canada Geese & Mallards, Winnebego Indust; Canada Geese, Remington Arms, Bridgeport, Conn, 76; Am Artist Collection, 85. *Exhib:* Various mus throughout the US & Can. *Awards:* Five Time Winner, Fed Duck Stamp Competition; Ark Duck Stamp Award, 82; Tex Duck Stamp Award, 83; Master Artist, Leigh Yaukey Woodson Art Mus, Wausau, Wis. *Bibliog:* John Diffely (auth), Maynard Reece: Wildlife artist, Am Artist, 78; Chuck Wechsler (auth), I've been there with Maynard Reece, Wildlife Art News, 84; M Stephen Doherty (auth), Am Artist, 85; Mark E Stegmaier (auth), Maynard Reece: Celebrator of the marsh, Midwest Art, 85. *Mem:* Grand Cent Art Galleries New York; hon trustee Ducks Unlimited Inc; Soc Animal Artists; Nat Audubon Soc; Outdoor Writers Asn Am (past bd mem). *Media:* Oil, Watercolor; Stone Lithography. *Publ:* Illusr, Life, Outdoor Life, Sports Afield & others; auth & illusr, Fish & Fishing, Meredith, 63; illusr, Waterfowl in Iowa & Iowa Fish & Fishing, Iowa Conserv Comn; auth & illusr, Waterfowl Art of Maynard Reece, Abrams, 85; Upland Bird Art of Maynard Reece, Abrams, 97. *Dealer:* Mill Pond Press Inc 310 Center Court Venice FL 34292. *Mailing Add:* 5315 Robertson Dr Des Moines IA 50312

REED, CLEOTA
HISTORIAN, LECTURER
b Chicago, Ill. *Study:* Syracuse Univ, BFA, 75, MA, 76. *Awards:* Am Philos Soc Grant, 76 & 98; Nat Endowment Humanities Fel, 80 & 91; Merit Award, NY Regional Coun Hist Agencies, 85. *Mem:* Am Ceramic Circle, Tile Heritage Found. *Res:* American & English ceramic tiles; arts and crafts movement; John Gough Nichols and the Gothic revival. *Publ:* Auth, Irene Sargent: A Comprehensive Bibliography, Syracuse Univ: Courier, 81; William Ittner & H Mercer: Art & Architecture, Erie Co Hist Soc, 82; ed, Henry Keck Stained Glass Studio 1913-1974, Syracuse Univ Press, 85; auth, Henry Chapman Mercer and the Moravian Tile Works, Univ Pa Press, 87; Syracuse China, Syracuse Univ Press, 97; The Tiles of Erie, Erie Mus Art, 99. *Mailing Add:* 329 Westcott St Syracuse NY 13210

REED, DAVID
PAINTER
b San Diego, Calif, Jan 20, 46. *Study:* Reed Col, BA; New York Studio Sch; Skowhegan Sch Painting & Sculpture. *Work:* Metrop Mus Art, NY; Mus Contemp Art, San Diego; Mus Nat d'Art Mod, Centre George Pompidou, Paris; Wexner Ctr Arts, Columbus, Ohio; Mus Moderner Kunst, Frankfurt & Main, Germ; Mus Moderner Kunst, Stiftung, Ludwig, Vienna, Austria; Albright Knox Art Gallery, Buffalo, NY; Hirshhorn Mus, Washington, D.C.; Kunstmuseum St. Gallen, St. Gallen, Switz; Kaiser Wilheim Mus, Krefeld, Ger. *Exhib:* Asher/Faure Gallery, Los Angeles, 88, 97 & 2002; one-man shows, Max Protetch Gallery, 89, 91, 92 & 95, 98, 99, 2002 & 2004, Galerie Rolf Ricke, Cologne, Ger, 91, 93, 97, 2000 & 2003; Leave Yourself Behind. Paintings & Special Projects 1967-2005, Ulrich Mus of Art, Witchita, Kans, Roswell Mus & Art Ctr, NMex & Luckman Gallery, Los Angeles. *Teaching:* vis artist, Calif Inst Arts, Valencia, 94. *Awards:* Rockefeller Found Grant, 66; Fel, Guggenheim Found, 88; Nat Endowment Arts, 91; Skowhegan Medal for Painting. *Bibliog:* David Reed (interview), ART Press, William Bartman Found, 90; Arthur Danto & Hanne Loreck (auths), David Reed (exhib catalog), Kolnischer Kunstverein, 95; Elizabeth Armstrong, Dave Hickey & Mieke Bal (auths), David Reed Paintings: Motion Pictures (exhib catalog); and others; David Reed: You Look Good in Blue (ex cat) Kunstmuseum St. Gallen, Switz, 2001; Painting Pictures (ex cat) Kunstmuseum Wolfsburg, Ger, 2003; High Times, Hard Times: New York Painting 1967-1975 (ex cat), 2006. *Media:* Oil & Alkyd on Canvas. *Publ:* auth, Memories of Rome, New Observations, #68, 6/89; Reflected light; In siena with Beccafumi, Arts Mag, pgs 52-53, 3/91; Two Bedrooms in San Francisco (essay, exhib catalog), San Francisco Art Inst, 92; Step into Liquid, in: Richard Allen Morris Retrospective, 58-2004 (exib cat 2004). *Dealer:* Max Protetch Gallery 511 W 22nd St New York NY 10011. *Mailing Add:* 506 Greenwich St New York NY 10013

REED, DENNIS JAMES
CURATOR, DESIGNER
b Culver City, Calif, Oct 30, 46. *Study:* Calif State Univ, Fullerton, BA, 69, MA, 71; MMI, Univ Calif, Berkeley, 83. *Collection Arranged:* Japanese Photography in Los Angeles, 1920-1945 (auth, catalog), 82 & The Furniture of Gustav Stickley, 83, Art Gallery, Los Angeles Valley Col; Japanese Photography in America 1920-1940 (auth, catalog), Japanese-Am Cult Ctr, 86; Travel Exhib 88-89: Oakland Mus, Rahr-West Art Mus; Whitney Mus Am Art, Corcoran Gallery Art; Southern Calif Pictorialism: Its Mad Aspects, The Huntington; and other exhibs. *Pos:* Dir, Conejo Valley Art Mus, 78-80 & Art Gallery, Los Angeles Valley Col, 80-91. *Teaching:* Prof art, Los Angeles Valley Col, 80-91, dean fine, performing and media arts, 91-. *Awards:* Award of Excellence, Am Fed of the Arts; Award, Parallels and Contrasts, Am Inst Graphic Arts, 89. *Res:* Pictorial photography. *Publ:* Auth, Japanese Photograph in Am 1920-1940, 86; Richard Pettibone, Forty Years of California Assemblage, Wight Art Gallery, Univ Calif-Los Angeles, 89; Pictorialism in California: Photographs, 1900-1940, J Paul Getty Mus & Huntington Libr, 94. *Mailing Add:* c/o Los Angeles Valley Col Dean of Arts 5800 Fulton Ave Valley Glen CA 91404

REED, JESSE FLOYD
PAINTER, PRINTMAKER
b Belington, WVa, July 25, 20. *Study:* Grand Cent Sch Art, 39-42; Art Students League, 45-47; Davis & Elkins Col, BA; WVa Univ, MA. *Work:* Huntington Mus, WVa; Rosenberg Libr, Galveston, Tex; Avampato Discovery Museum, WVa; George Wash Univ, Wash, DC. *Exhib:* Print Show, Brooklyn Mus, 49; Libr Cong, 55; Print Club Albany Ann; Boston Printmakers Ann. *Teaching:* Prof emer art & hist, Davis & Elkins Col, 49-97. *Awards:* Purchase Award, Print Club Albany, 74; Merit Award & Purchase Award, Charleston Art Gallery, WVa, 75; Merit Award, Cult Ctr, WVa, 79. *Mem:* Salmagundi Club; life mem, Boston Printmakers; found mem, WVa Watercolor Soc; life mem, Print Club Albany. *Media:* Watercolor; Aquatint Etching. *Dealer:* Artists at Work 329 Davis Ave Elkins WV. *Mailing Add:* 4 Lincoln Ave Elkins WV 26241-3669

REED, PAUL ALLEN
PAINTER
b Washington, DC, Mar 28, 19. *Study:* San Diego State Col, Calif; Corcoran Sch Art, Washington, DC. *Work:* In over 50 pub collections, including: San Francisco Mus Art; Hirshhorn Mus, Washington, DC; Corcoran Gallery Art & Nat Mus Am Art, Washington, DC; Detroit Inst Art; Walker Art Ctr, Minneapolis; Phillips Collection, Washington, DC. *Exhib:* 25th Ann Soc Am Art, Art Inst Chicago, 65; Washington Color Painters, Washington, DC, Tex, Calif, Mass & Minn, 65-66; 250 Yrs Am Art, Corcoran Gallery Art, 66; Jackson Pollock to the Present, Steinberg Gallery, Washington Univ, St Louis, 69; Inaugural Exhib, Wadsworth Atheneum, Hartford, Conn, 69; Washington 20 Yrs, Baltimore Mus Art, 70; one-man shows, Phoenix Art Mus, 77, Watkins Gallery, Am Univ, The Arts Club, Washington, DC, 1997, Montgomery Col, Takoma Park Md, 2001, Marymont Univ, Arlington, Va, 2002. *Pos:*

Graphics Dir, US Peace Corps, 1962-1971. *Teaching:* Instr painting, Art League Northern Va, 71-74; asst prof & coordr first yr core prog, Corcoran Sch Art, 71-80. *Bibliog:* Barbara Rose (auth), The primacy of color, 5/64 & Legrace Benson (auth), Washington Scene, 69, Art Int; Walter Hopps (auth), The Vincent Melzac Collection, Corcoran Gallery Art, 71; Claudine Humblet (auth), The New American Abstraction, 1950-1970. *Media:* Acrylic, Gouache. *Mailing Add:* 3541 N Utah St Arlington VA 22207

REED, ROBERT JAMES, JR
PAINTER, EDUCATOR
b 38. *Study:* Morgan State Col, Baltimore, BS, 58; Yale Univ, BFA, 60, MFA, 63; Minneapolis Col Art and Design, DFA (hon), 2001. *Work:* Group exhibs, Albright-Knox Art Gallery, Hirshhorn Mus and Sculpture Garden, Minneapolis Inst Arts, Walker Art Ctr, Whitney Mus Am Art, Yale Univ Art Gallery, solo exhibs, Bayly Mus, Va, Washburn Gallery, NY, Whitney Mus Am Art, Represented in permanent collections, Bayly Mus, Va, Hirshhorn Mus and Sculpture Garden, Walker Art Ctr, Whitney Mus Am Art, Yale Univ Art Gallery. *Exhib:* Group exhibs, Albright-Knox Art Gallery, Hirshhorn Mus and Sculpture Garden, Minneapolis Inst Arts, Walker Art Ctr, Whitney Mus Am Art, Yale Univ Art Gallery solo exhib, Bayly Mus, Va, Washburn Gallery, NY, Whitney Mus Am Art, Represented in permanent collections, Bayly Mus, Va, Hirshhorn Mus and Sculpture Garden, Walker Art Ctr Whitney Mus Am Art, Yale Univ Art Gallery. *Pos:* Dir art div, Yale Summer Sch Music and Art, 1970-75. *Teaching:* Mem fac, Skidmore Col, Minneapolis Col Art and Design, head Found Studies Div, 1964; mem painting fac, Yale Univ, New Haven, 1969-; mem fac, summer prog Pont-Aven Sch Contemp Art, France, 2005. *Awards:* grantee Nat Endowment for the Arts, 1980; Recipient Distinguished Teaching of Art Award, Col Art Asn, 2004; Yaddo Fel. *Mailing Add:* Yale Univ Sch Art Holcombe T Green Jr Hall 1156 Chapel St New Haven CT 06520

REED, WALT ARNOLD
HISTORIAN, DEALER
b Big Spring, Tex, July 21, 17. *Study:* Pratt Inst; NY-Phoenix Sch Design; also with Franklin Booth. *Comn:* Designer US postage stamp series, 50 state flags, US Postal Serv, 76. *Pos:* Art dir, CARE, New York, 52-55; ed, North Light Publ, Westport, 72-78; proprietor, Illus House, 75-. *Teaching:* Art instr, Famous Artists Sch, Westport, Conn, 57-66, asst to dir, 66-72. *Awards:* Wrangler Award for Best Western Art Book, Cowboy Hall Fame & Western Heritage Ctr, 72. *Mem:* Appraisers Asn Am Inc; New York Soc Illusr; Sanford Low Mem Collection Am Illus, New Brit Mus Am Art, Conn. *Res:* American illustrations, 1860-2000. *Specialty:* American and Some European Illustration Art work, 1860-2005. *Publ:* Auth, Harold Von Schmidt Draws and Paints the Old West, 72 & John Clymer, 76, Northland; The magic pen of Joseph Clement Coll, North Light, 78; The Illustrator in America 1880-1980, Madison Sq Press, 84; The Art of Tom Lovell, Greenwich Workshop, 93; ed, Visions of Adventure, Watson Guptill, 2000; Auth, The Illustrator in America 1860-2000, rev. ed., 2001. *Dealer:* Illustration House Inc 110 West 25th St NY NY 10001. *Mailing Add:* Seven Belaire Dr Westport CT 06880

REEDY, MITSUNO ISHII
PAINTER
b Osaka, Japan, Jan 18, 41; US citizen. *Study:* Laguna Gloria Art Mus Sch, 76; Elizabeth Ney Mus Sch, 77-79; Scottsdale Art Sch, 92; Studied with Daniel Greene & Albert Handell. *Work:* Oklahoma Heritage Mus, Oklahoma City, Okla; Greenwood Cult Ctr, Tulsa, Okla; Univ Oklahoma, Norman, Okla; US District Court House, Oklahoma City, Okla; Purdue Univ, West Lafayette, I. *Exhib:* Pastel Soc Am Ann; Catherine Lorillard Wolfe Art Club Ann; Contemp Pastel Soc of Japan Ann; solo exhib, Firehouse Art Ctr, Norman, Okla & Kirkpatrick Ctr, Oklahoma City, Okla; Governors Gallery, Oklahoma City. *Bibliog:* Article in Focus, Santa Fe, 6-7/95; article in Nichols Hills News, Oklahoma City, 2/02; Art Treasures of Okla Capitol, 2003. *Mem:* Pastel Soc Am; Portrait Soc Am; Pastel Soc Japan. *Media:* Pastel; Oil. *Publ:* The Best of Oil Painting, Rockport Publ, Mass, 96; The Best of Pastel, 96, Portrait Inspirations, 97, Floral Inspirations, 97, The Best of Pastel II, 99, Rockport Publ. *Dealer:* The Howell Gallery 6432 N Western Oklahoma City OK; Stroke of Genius www.portraitartist.com. *Mailing Add:* 1701 Denison Norman OK 73069

REEDY, SUSAN
PAINTER
b Buffalo, NY, June 1, 56. *Study:* State Univ NY, Buffalo, MFA(painting), 81. *Work:* Mem Art Gallery, Univ Rochester, NY; Roswell Park Cancer Ins, Buffalo, NY; Castellani Art Mus, Niagara Falls; Mobil Oil Corp, NY; Rich Products Corp, Buffalo, NY; Standard Fed Bank, Troy, Mich; Automobile Association of Am, Amherst, NY; Hospice Foundation of Buffalo, NY. *Exhib:* Works on Canvas & Paper, Goldman-Greenfield Galler, Amherst, NY, 85; Works on Canvas, OK Harris Gallery, NY, 88; Ann Midyear Exhib, Butler Inst Am Art, Youngtown, Ohio, 90 & 92; Recent Works on Canvas & Paper, Castellani Art Mus, Niagara Falls, 93; Ann Rochester Finger Lakes, Mem Art Gallery, NY, 95 & 96; Nat Varied Exhib, Gallery 84, NY, 96 & 97; Silent Soliloquy, Amherst Mus, NY, 97; Selected Works II, Albright-Knox Gallery, Buffalo, NY, 97; Marymount Mahattan Col Art Gallery, NY, 2002; From NY to Western NY Collectiors Gallery, Albright-Knox Art Gallery, Buffalo, NY. *Awards:* Manufacturers & Traders Trust Co Award, Albright-Knox, 80; Directors Choice Award, 54th Rochester-Finger Lakes Exhib, Meml Art Gallery, Rochester, NY, 95; Dorothy Cripps Salo Meml Award for Outstanding Non-Representational Painting, 55th Rochester Finger Lakes Exhib, Meml Art Gallery, Rochester, NY, 96. *Bibliog:* Richard Huntington (auth) Show full of surprises reflects penney's sensibilities, The Buffalo News, 7/15/97, Measured skill, 9/95; Lynn Nicholas (auth) Reedy's mixed media, The Niagara Gazette, 2/93. *Mem:* Roswell Park Alliance Art Com. *Media:* Acrylic on Canvas, Collage. *Interests:* Figure skating. *Mailing Add:* PO Box 733 Buffalo NY 14051

REEL, DAVID MARK
MUSEUM DIRECTOR, CURATOR
b Pa, Nov 21, 69. *Study:* Dickinson Col, Carlisle, PA, BA, 92; NY Univ, NY, MA, 94. *Collection Arranged:* Ordered Chaos: Surrealist Art from the Coll, Dickinson College, Carlilsle, PA, 91-92; Papers opf Joseph Huston, Pennsylvania State Capitol Preservation Committee, Harrisburg, PA, 91; Leon Golb: Worldwide, Dickinson College, Carlisle, PA, Chicago Cultural Ctr, Chicago, IL, 93; The Words of War: Documents of WWII, from Forbes Magazine Coll, Forbes Gallery, NY, 94-95; Faberge in America, Metropolitan Mus Art, New York, NY, HM DeYoung Memorial Mus, San Fransisco, Mus Fine Art, Richmond, VA, New Orleans Mus Fine Art, LA, Cleveland Mus Art, OH, 96-97; The Great American Place: Saratoga Springs, Forbes Gallery, New York, NY, 97; Carl Faberge: Goldsmith to the Tsar, Natl Mus, Stockholm, Sweeden, 97; Highlights from the Forbes Magazine Collection, Forbes Gallery, NY, 97; Art of the Panama Canal, West Point Mus, United States Military Academy, NY, 99; The Panama Canal and the Art of Contruction, Williams College, MA, 99-2000; Come Join us Brothers: African-American in the US Army, West Point Mus, United States Military Academy, NY, 2001-2003; Timeless Treasures: 200 yrs of West Point Memories, West Point Mus, United States Military Academy, NY, 2001-2002; Tabletops and Tradition: The Officers Mess and Cadet Mess at West Point, West Point Mus, United States Military Academy, NY, 2002-2003; Gallantry.Above and Beyond the Call of Duty.Civil War Medals of Honor, West Point Mus, United States Military Academy, NY, 2003-2004; The Wes Point Mus: A mus for the Army, West Point Mus, United States Military Academy, New York, NY. *Pos:* cur, Forbes Magazine Coll, New York, NY, 93-98; Chief cur art, West Point Mus, United States Military Academy, West Point, New York, 98-2006, dir, 2005-. *Teaching:* Instr arts, United States Military Academy, West Point, NY, 98-. *Mem:* Am Asn Mus; Army Mus Asn, USA; Nat Trust for Historic Preservation; NY Univ Arts Alumni Adv Council, VPres 2002-03. *Res:* Artwork depicting Am Amy actions, Military portraiture and battle scenes. *Publ:* Auth, Western Passages, West Point, Points West, Denver Art Mus, 2002. *Mailing Add:* West Point Mus US Mil Acad West Point NY 10996

REEP, EDWARD ARNOLD
PAINTER, WRITER
b Brooklyn, NY, 18. *Study:* Art Ctr Col Design, cert, 41; also with E J Bisttram, Stanley Reckless, Willard Nash & Barse Miller. *Hon Degrees:* East Carolina Univ, MA, 56. *Work:* Los Angeles Co Mus, Calif; 66 works, US War Dept, Pentagon; Grunwald Graphic Arts Collection, Univ Calif, Los Angeles; Lytton Collection, Los Angeles; State of Calif Collection, Sacramento; Nat Mus Am Art, Smithsonian Inst, Washington, DC. *Comn:* Three panels of early conquests in Calif, SAm & US (with Gordon Mellor), USA Private's Club, Ft Ord, Calif, 41; Painter's Impression of International Airports (10 pages in full color), Life Mag, 6/56; Impressions of the Berlin Wall, Ger, US Govt, 71. *Exhib:* Whitney Mus Am Art Ann, NY, 46-48; Los Angeles Co Mus Ann, 46-60; Corcoran Gallery Art Biennial, Washington, DC, 49; Nat Acad Design, NY; Nat Gallery Art, Washington, DC. *Pos:* Coord art chmn, Los Angeles City Art Festival Exhibs, 51; official war artist & corresp, World War II. *Teaching:* Instr painting & drawing, Art Ctr Col Design, Los Angeles, 46-50; instr painting & drawing & chmn, Dept Painting, Chouinard Art Inst, Los Angeles, 50-69; prof painting, artist in residence, E Carolina Univ, 70-85, prof emer, currently. *Awards:* First Prize in Oil Painting, Los Angeles All City Ann, 63; Nat Endowment Arts Grant, 75; Lifetime Achievement Gold Medal, Watercolor USA, 99, Nat Watercolor Soc, 2002; and others. *Bibliog:* Schaad (auth), Realm of Contemporary Still-life, 62 & Mugnaini (auth), Drawing, a Search for Form, 65, Van Nostrand Reinhold; James Jones (auth), World War II, Grosset & Dunlap, 75; Robert Henkes (auth), Themes in American Painting, 95. *Mem:* life Nat Watercolor Soc (pres, 57-58); Watercolor USA Soc. *Media:* Oil, Watercolor. *Publ:* Auth, The Content of Watercolor, Van Nostrand Reinhold, 83; A Combat Artist in World War II, Univ Press, Ky, 87; They Drew Fire, TV, Book, 2000. *Dealer:* Gordon McClelland. *Mailing Add:* 9021 Crowninshield Dr Bakersfield CA 93311

REESE, MARCIA MITCHELL
SCULPTOR
b Cleveland, Ohio. *Study:* Case Western Reserve Univ, BA, 51. *Work:* Hofstra Mus, Hofstra Univ, Godwin-Ternbach Mus, Queens Col, NY, Filderman Gallery, Hempstead, NY; MONY Financial Services World Headquarters, NY; many nat & int collections. *Exhib:* Solo shows, CAPA Rotational Art Exhib, 80, Bloomingdale's, Model Room #3, NY, 81, Chemical Bank, North Shore Towers, 82, Port Washington Libr Gallery, 82, Bryant Libr Gallery, 86, Gallery Lincoln Ctr, 86, Plandome Gallery, 91, Shelter Rock Gallery, 95; Elaine Benson Gallery, Bridgehampton, NY, 83; Nat Asn Women Artists, NY, 84-2004; Guild Hall Mus, East Hampton, NY, 87-90; Shelter Rock Gallery, 95; Heckscher Mus Art, 96; A Jaim Marunouchi Gallery, New York City, 99-02. *Awards:* Cleo Hartwig Mem Award, Nat Asn Woman Artists, 89; Dr Max Ellenberg Award, Nat Asn Women Artists, 91; Nassau Co Mus Art, 92; Artists Network of Great Neck, 90, 93, 95, 96; Nat Asn Women Artists, 2003; and others. *Bibliog:* interview, On Long Island, WLIW-TV, 91; Stone Stories (video), 97; Artscene on Long Island (video), Cablevision Channel 44 & 25, 9/97. *Mem:* Nat Asn Women Artists (exec bd, 94- & chmn sculpture jury 94-96, chmn jury awards, 96-98); Sculptors Inc (pres); Stone Sculpture Soc NY; Artists Network Great Neck (archivist, 88-90 scholarships, 90-); Archeol Inst Am, LI Soc (vpres, grants chair). *Media:* Stone. *Publ:* Hofstra Univ, Catalog of Art in Their Museum Collection, 89; Capturing the Esssence of Their Vision & Form (catalog), Hofstra Univ, 94; Art Calendar Monograph, ps 92-93, 98. *Mailing Add:* 246 Oriole Ct Manhasset NY 11030

REESE, THOMAS FORD
HISTORIAN, ADMINISTRATOR
b New Orleans, La, Oct 9, 43. *Study:* Fac Filosofia y Letras, Univ de Madrid, 63-64; Tulane Univ, BA, 65; Yale Univ, MA, 69, PhD, 73. *Collection Arranged:* Buenos Aires 1910: Memorias del Porvenir, Mercado del Abasto, Buenos Aires, May-June 99. *Pos:* exec dir, Stone Ctr Latin Am Studies, Tulane Univ, New Orleans, La. *Awards:*

John Simon Guggenheim Mem Found Fel, 76-77; Academico correspondiente, Real Acad de Bellas Artes de San Fernando, Madrid, 77; Samuel H Kress Sr Fel, Ctr Advan Study in Visual Arts, Nat Gallery Art, Washington, 83. *Mem:* Col Art Asn Am; Soc Archit Historians; Am Soc Hispanic Art Hist Studies; Asn Latin Am Art; Asn Res Insts in Art Hist. *Res:* History of the arts of Spain and Portugal; Latin American Colonial Art; European architecture since 1400. *Publ:* Auth, The Architecture of Ventura Rodriguez, Garland Publ Inc, 76; intro to Libro de diferentes pensamientos unos imbentados y otros delineados por Diego de Villanueva, Real Academia de Bellas Artes de San Fernando, 80; ed, Studies in Ancient American and European Art--The Collected Essays of George Kubler, Yale Univ Press, 85, Buenos Aires: Centro de estudios avenzados de la Universidad de Buenos Aires, 99; introd to La configuracion del tiempo--Observaciones sobre la historia de las cosas, Editorial Nerea, Madrid, Spain, 88; coauth, Boehm, Gehry, Hollein and Stirling in Los Angeles--The Competition Entries for the Walt Disney Concert Hall, Zodiac 2, Milan, Italy, 9/89. *Mailing Add:* 5825 Pitt St New Orleans LA 70115

REESE, WILLIAM FOSTER
PAINTER
b Pierre, SDak, July 10, 38. *Study:* Wash State Univ; Orange Coast Col; Los Angeles Trade Tech Sch; Art Ctr Sch Design, Los Angeles. *Work:* Frye Art Mus, Seattle, Wash. *Comn:* Painting, Walter Lommell Hosp, Woodburn, Ore, 72; paintings, St Francis Hotel, San Francisco, 72. *Exhib:* Rocky Mountain Nat, Golden, Colo, 75, 76 & 77; Am Watercolor Soc Show, 76; Pastel Soc Show, 76-77; NAWA Show, Cowboy Hall of Fame, Oklahoma City, 77; one-man show, Frye Art Mus, 77; and others. *Awards:* Leon Augustine Hermitte Award, Puget Sound Exhib, Frye Mus, 75 & 77; House of Heydenryk Award, Nat Arts Club, 77; Best Show, Mus Great Plains, 78. *Bibliog:* Mary N Balcomb (auth), William F Reese: Form follows function, Am Artist Mag, 12/78; Laurel Andrews (auth), The visual poetry of William F Reese, Art West Mag, fall 79; Mary N Balcomb (auth), The art of painting, Southwest Art Mag, 10/82. *Mem:* Puget Sound Group Northwest Painters (secy, 70-71, treas, 71-72); Nat Acad Western Art; Whiskey Painters Am; Pastel Soc Am; Soc Animal Artists. *Media:* Oil, Watercolor. *Mailing Add:* c/o Wichita Gallery Fine Art 100 N Broadway Ste 230 Wichita KS 67202-2212

REESER, ROBERT D
EDUCATOR, ADMINISTRATOR
b Orangeville, Ill, Mar 4, 31. *Study:* Northern Ill Univ, BS, 53; Univ Denver, MA(art), 59; Ohio State Univ, PhD(art educ), 74. *Work:* Burpee Art Gallery, Rockford, Ill. *Pos:* Assoc dean, Sch Arts & Letters, Calif State Univ, Los Angeles, 87-94; retired. *Teaching:* Prof art, Calif State Univ, Los Angeles, 71-94. *Mem:* Calif Art Educ Asn (pres, 76-78); Nat Art Educ Asn; Artists Equity Asn; Int Soc Educ Art. *Res:* Teaching of secondary school art; aesthetics, art criticism and art history. *Mailing Add:* 1308 Emerald Dr Santa Maria CA 93454-3242

REEVES, DANIEL MCDONOUGH
VIDEO ARTIST, INSTALLATION ARTIST
b Washington, DC, Aug 1, 48. *Study:* Ithaca Col, BS, 76. *Work:* Mus Mod Art; Pac Film Archives. *Exhib:* High Mus Contemp Art, Atlanta, Ga; Mus Mod Art & Whitney Mus Am Art, NY; Tate Gallery, UK; Pearce Inst, Glasgow, Scotland; Long Beach Mus Art, Calif; Nat Video Festival/Am Film Inst, Los Angeles, Calif; and others. *Pos:* Exec dir, Shakti Productions, Greenwich Village, NY & Tarbert, Scotland, UK. *Awards:* Fel & Grant Nat Endowment Arts, 80-94; NY State Coun on the Arts Prodn Grants, 80-94; Fel, John S Guggenheim Found, 83-84; NY Found Arts Fel, 87; Scottish Arts Council Grants, 90-92. *Mem:* Media Alliance; Asn Independent Video & Filmmakers. *Media:* Video, Film. *Publ:* Single channel video tapes, Smothering Dreams, Nat Video Festival Blue Ribbon Winner, 82; Mosaic for the Kali Yuga, 85; Sabda, Nat Video Festival Blue Ribbon Winner, 85; Ganapati/A Spirit in the Bush, 86; Sombra a Sombra, 88; video installations, The Well of Patience, 89, Eingang/The Way In, 90 & 93, Jizo Garden, 92, Obsessive Becoming, 95 & Forty Nine Bodhisattvas, 97. *Mailing Add:* 12 Glasgow St Scotland G129PR United Kingdom

REEVES, ESTHER MAY
PAINTER
b Riverside, Calif, Oct 12, 37. *Study:* Calif State Univ-Fullerton, MA, 86, MFA, 88; studied with H Ralph Love. *Work:* United First Methodist Church, Riverside, Calif; Truth Consciousness-Poona Ashram, India. *Comn:* Angel of Light (mural), Truth Consciousness, Boulder, Colo, 81; Fallopian Tissue & Dermal Pore, Riverside City Col-Life Sci Dept, Calif, 83 & 84; Landscape with Ducks, comn by Jones, Riverside, Calif, 83; portrait, comn by Headman, Orange, Calif, 88; portrait, comn by Bavaresco, Sacramento, Calif, 92. *Exhib:* Solo shows, Progressive Creativity, Inland Empire Gallery, 83 & Arising from Scripture, Riverside Art Mus, Calif, 92; Images 87, Bowers Mus, Santa Ana, Calif, 87; Grace Street Artists, Corona Gallery Ltd, Calif, 87; In Praise of Maleness, Piret's Gallery, Costa Mesa, 87; Celebration, Grand Hotel, Anaheim, 87; The Art of Love, Riverside Art Mus, 90; Wildlife Art, San Bernardino Art Mus, Calif, 90; Invitational, Capitol Bldg, Sacramento, Calif, 2000. *Pos:* Illusr & secy, Riverside Unified Sch Dist, 60-61; instr, Calif State Univ-Fullerton, 88-89. *Teaching:* Instr beginning drawing, Calif State Univ, 88-89. *Awards:* Best of Show, Grumacher Award, M Grumbacher Inc, 89; Best of Show, Ann Exhib, Clarks, 90; Best of Show, Riverside Art Mus, 99. *Bibliog:* Melody Rogers (host), Two on the Town (CBS-TV), Joel Tator, 87; Joey Bavaresco (host), The World of Joey Bavaresco (TV), Ron Gallup, 92. *Media:* Oil on Canvas. *Specialty:* Decorative Art, Western Art Landscapes. *Interests:* Gardening. *Dealer:* Art Angles Gallery 940 W Chapman Ave Orange CA 92868; Blue Jay Gallery 27248 St Hwy 189 Blue Jay CA 92317. *Mailing Add:* 5415 Via San Jacinto Riverside CA 92506-3650

REEVES, JAMES FRANKLIN
HISTORIAN, COLLECTOR
b Huntsville, Ala, July 4, 46. *Study:* Univ Ala, Huntsville, BA(art hist), 72; Vanderbilt Univ, Nashville, Tenn, MA(art hist), 75. *Collection Arranged:* Gilbert Gaul, (with catalog), Tenn Fine Arts Ctr, Nashville & Huntsville Mus Art, 75. *Pos:* Asst, P L Hay House Mus, Macon, Ga, 66-67; asst to dir, 73-75, cur Huntsville Mus Art, 75-77. *Mem:* Col Art Asn Am; Southeastern Col Art Conf; Kappa Pi (pres local chap, 71-72). *Res:* Gilbert Gaul, 1855-1919; Huntsville architecture, 1820-1975. *Collection:* 19th and 20th century American paintings; 18th and 19th century American decorative arts; 19th century European paintings; Oriental porcelains and sculpture. *Mailing Add:* 2005 Kildare St Huntsville AL 35811

REEVES, JOHN ALEXANDER
PHOTOGRAPHER
b Burlington, Ont, Can, Apr 24, 38. *Study:* Sir George Williams Art Sch, Montreal, 56-57; Ont Col Art, Toronto, 57-61, AOCA. *Work:* Nat Film Bd Can, Ottawa; Archives Canada; Dept Indian & Northern Affairs, Ottawa; Can Mus Contemp Photog, Ottawa; Nat Libr Can, Ottawa. *Exhib:* One-man shows, 30 Portraits of Women, Deja Vue Gallery, Toronto, 77, The Magic Word, Nat Archives Can, 81, Inuit Art World, Can Ctr Photog, Toronto, 82, Corkin Gallery, Toronto, 83, Can Cult Ctr, Rome, 91, About Face (traveling exhib), Cambridge, Simcoe & Brantford Art Galleries, Ont, 92 & Exile's Exiles, Bystriansky Gallery, Toronto, 92; Academic Images, Can Ctr Photog, 82; Creative Canadians (traveling exhib), Dept External Affairs, Ottawa, 82; Authors, Harbourfront Gallery, Toronto, 83; and others. *Pos:* Critic, host, Toronto Rev, Can Broadcasting Corp, Radio, 68- 71. *Teaching:* Instr photog, Ontario Col Art. *Awards:* Am Inst Graphic Arts Award, 63 & 68; Award of Merit, Art Dir Club, Toronto, 71, 72, 76 & 77; Int Asn Printing House Craftsmen, 77. *Bibliog:* Charles Oberdorf (auth), articles, 11/72 & 6/77 & Gunter Ott (auth), Sand on the beach, 87, Camera Can Mag; Gary Michael Dault (auth), article, Toronto Star, 6/77; Gary Michael Dault (auth), Inuit Art World Catalogue, 82. *Mem:* Royal Can Acad Art; Can Asn Photogs & Illusrs Communs. *Publ:* Auth, John Fillion--Thoughts About My Sculpture, Martlet Press, 68; God's Big Acre--Life in 401 Country, Methuen, Can, 86; About Face, 90 & Exile's Exile, 92, Exile Eds, Toronto; Jazz Lives, McClelland & Stewart, Toronto, 92; Incontro, Conere Italy & Canada Meet Exile Eds, Toronto, 96. *Dealer:* Feheley Fine Arts 14 Hazelton Ave Toronto ON M5R 2E2 Canada. *Mailing Add:* 33 St Paul St Toronto ON M5A 3H2 Canada

REFF, THEODORE
HISTORIAN
b New York, NY, Aug 18, 30. *Study:* Columbia Col, BA, 52; Harvard Univ, MA, 53, PhD, 58. *Collection Arranged:* Cezanne Watercolors (ed, catalog), M Knoedler & Co, New York, 63; Degas in the Metropolitan, Metrop Mus, New York, 77; Cezanne: the Late Work, Mus Mod Art, New York, 77; Manet and Modern Paris, Nat Gallery, Washington, DC, 82-83. *Teaching:* Prof art hist & mod art, Columbia Univ, 57-; vis prof, Univ Mich, Princeton Univ, John Hopkins Univ & NY Univ; Slade prof, Cambridge Univ; plus others. *Awards:* Chevalier, Ordre des Palmes Academiques, 87. *Mem:* Col Art Asn Am (dir, 77-81); Int Found Art Res (dir, 80-); Swann Found Caricature (dir, 82-89); Psychoanalytic Perspectives Art (dir, 84-90); Soc Paul Cezanne (pres, 98-). *Res:* 19th and 20th century art; relations between art and literature. *Publ:* Auth, Manet: Olympia, Penguin, 76; ed, Modern Art in Paris, 1850-1900, Garland, 81; auth, Manet and Modern Paris, Univ Chicago Press, 83; co-auth, Two Cezanne Sketchbooks, Philadelphia Mus Art, 90; Jean-Louis Forain: The Impressionist Years, Memphis, 95. *Mailing Add:* 435 RSD Apt 92 New York NY 10025

REGAN, BETSEY
PAINTER
b Long Branch, NJ, Feb 22, 54. *Study:* Monmouth Univ, BA, 82; Temple Univ, MS, 89. *Work:* Pfizer Collection, NY; Common Health Collection, Parsippany, NJ; Quantum Group, Parsippany, NJ. *Comn:* portrait, comn by Julie Corbisiero, Toms River, NJ 98 & 2000; portrait, comn by Annie Santulli, Rumson, NJ, 99; paperworks, comn by Maryann Sciarappa, Ocean NJ, 2000. *Exhib:* MCAC Show, Monmouth Mus, Middletown, NJ, 94-2001; New Jersey Arts Ann, NJ State Mus, Trenton, 94 & 99; Juried National, Aljira, Newark, NJ, 95 & 96; Watchung Arts Ctr Invitational, Watchung, NJ, 96; Noyes State Mus, Oceanville, NJ, 99. *Awards:* Best of Show, City W/O Walls Gallery, 94, 95 & 97; Best of Show, Art Alliance, 99. *Bibliog:* Barry Schwabsky (auth), Familiar Made Different, NY Times, 9/21/97 & New Jersey Arts Annual, 8/1/99; Pat Summers (auth), New Jersey Arts Ann, The Trentonian, 8/11/99. *Mem:* Art Alliance, Red Bank, NJ (cur, 90-2000). *Media:* Oil; Plaster. *Mailing Add:* 96 Swimming River Rd Lincroft NJ 07738

REGAT, JEAN-JACQUES ALBERT
SCULPTOR, MURALIST
b Paris, France, Sept 12, 45. *Study:* Univ Alaska, BA; Soc Beaux Arts, France. *Work:* Sheik Zayed Ben Sultan Al-Nahyan, Pres of United Arab Emirates, Abu Dabi; Fairbanks North Star Borough Pub Libr, Alaska; Soroptimist Int of Anchorage; RCA Alascom, Anchorage; Kobuk Valley Jade Co, Alyeska. *Comn:* The Man Who Became Caribou (bas relief wood), Noatak Artic Sch Dist, 81; Miners of the Yukon (tryptic bas relief wood), Yukon Off Supplies Co, 82; Delta Pastoral (bas relief wood), Delta Greely Sch Dist, 82; The Resolution (bronze & bas relief wood), Carr-Gottstein Ltd; St Joseph & St Francis, St Anthony Cath Church Anchorage, 83. *Exhib:* One-man show, Artique Ltd, Anchorage, 72-77; Heritage Northwest Gallery, Juneau, 73-74; House of Wood, Fairbanks, 74-80; Erdon Gallery, Houston, Tex; Rendezvous Gallery, Anchorage. *Bibliog:* Judy Shuler (auth), Jacques & Mary Regat, Alaska J autumn 77;

Nancy Cain Schmitt (auth), Ancient legend of Sedna is captured in bronze, Anchorage Times, 5/20/79; Mary Sawyer-Albert (auth), Stories carved in wood and stone, Jacques and Mary Regat, Southwest Art, 8/79; plus others. *Media:* Stone, Wood. *Dealer:* House of Wood 529 Fourth Fairbanks AK 99701. *Mailing Add:* 518 Pearl Dr Anchorage AK 99518-1833

REGAT, MARY E
SCULPTOR, MURALIST
b Duluth, Minn, Nov 12, 43. *Study:* Univ Alaska. *Work:* Anchorage Fine Arts Mus, Alaska; Soroptimist Int of Anchorage; Kobuk Valley Jade Co, Alyeska, Alaska; Fairbanks North Star Borough Pub Libr; RCA-Alascom, Anchorage. *Comn:* Trail of 98 (bas relief wood), Pioneers Asn Alaska, 79; Creek Woman (bas relief wood & bronze), Kokanok, Peninsula Sch Dist, 80; Huskies (bronze), Kotzebue Artic Sch Dist, 82; Dance of the Oomialik (sculpture), Gottstein Inc, 82; High, Wild and Free (sculpture), Greyling, Iditarod Sch Dist, 83. *Exhib:* One-woman show, Artique Ltd, Anchorage, 72-77; House of Wood, Fairbanks, 74-80; Erdon Gallery, Houston, Tex; Boreal Traditions Gallery, Anchorage; plus others. *Awards:* Sculpture Award, Design I, 71; Purchase Award, Anchorage Fine Arts Mus, 71. *Bibliog:* Judy Schuler (auth), Jacques and Mary Regat, Alaska J, autumn, 77; Nancy Cain Schmitt (auth), Ancient legend of Sedna is captured in bronze, Anchorage Times, 5/20/79; Mary Sawyer-Albert (auth), Stories carved in wood and stone, Jacques and Mary Regat, Southwest Art, 8/79; plus others. *Mem:* Artist Guild; Anchorage Fine Arts Mus Asn. *Media:* Wood, Bronze. *Dealer:* Boreal Traditions 939 W 5th Ave Suite J Anchorage AK 99501; New Horizons 519 1st Ave Fairbanks AK 99701. *Mailing Add:* 518 Pearl Dr Anchorage AK 99518-1833

REGER, LAWRENCE L
ADMINISTRATOR
b Lincoln Nebr, June 23, 39. *Study:* Univ Nebr; Vanderbilt Univ, JD, 64. *Pos:* Dir prog develop & coord, Nat Endowment Arts, DC, 71-78; dir, Am Asn Mus, DC, 78-86; pres, Heritage Preserv, 86

REGINATO, PETER
SCULPTOR
b Dallas, Tex, Aug 19, 45. *Study:* San Francisco Art Inst, 63-66. *Work:* Metrop Mus Art, Chase Manhattan Bank, NY; Houston Mus of Fine Arts; Mint Mus Art, Charlotte, NC; Brown Univ, RI; Boston Mus Fine Arts, Mass; Corcoran Gallery Art, Washington, DC; Storm King Art Ctr, Mountainville, NY; Univ Fla, Gainesville; Richard Brown Baker Collection, Yale Univ, New Haven, Conn. *Comn:* High Plains Drifter (large sculpture), Allen Ctr, Houston, Tex; Outdoor Sculpture Exhib, Rutgers State Univ, Camden, NJ, 78; sculpture, Glick Orgn, Promenade Bldg, NY; City of Hope Sculpture Garden, Duarte, Calif; Outdoor sculpture Woodland Corp, Houston, Tex. *Exhib:* Peter Reginato/Jane Manus: Two Visions of Abstract Construction, Mus Art, Ft Lauderdale, Fla, 91; Adelson- William Bendleston Galleries, NY, 92; Donna Kline, Jewish Mus, Boca Raton, Fla, 94; Palm Springs Mus, Fla, 94; Small Wonders, Adelson Gallery, NY, 96; Welded! Sculputre of the Twentieth Century, neuberger Mus of Art, NY, 99; Paint on Metal, Tucson Mus of Art, 2005; Merry Peace, Sideshow Gallery, Williamsburg, NY; New Additions Outdoors, Grounds for Sculpture. *Teaching:* Adj lectr sculpture, Hunter Col, 71-73. *Awards:* John Simon Guggenheim Mem Found Fel, 76; Purchase Award, Hirshhorn Mus, Washington, DC, 79; Clayworks Residency, Nat Endowment Arts, 84. *Bibliog:* Jean Lawlor Cohen (auth), Sculpture thrives in Washington law firms, Washington Lawyer, Vols 2 & 3, 1-2/88; Margo Guralnick (auth), Timely Obsessions, House & Gordon, 9/89; Carter Ratcliff (auth), Reginato's improvisations, Art in Am, No 12, 12/89; Ken Johnson (auth), Teting the durability of welding, New York Times; Karen Wilkin (auth), Drawing in space, Ars Longa; plus others. *Media:* Painted Welded Steel, Clay. *Mailing Add:* 60 Greene St New York NY 10012

REHM, CELESTE L
PAINTER, EDUCATOR
b Bayshore, NY, Apr 19, 48. *Study:* Pratt Inst, NY, MFA, 73. *Work:* SDak State Univ; Portsmouth Arts Ctr, Va; Chautauqua Art Asn, NY; Chattahoochee Valley Art Asn, Ga; Boulder Community Hosp, Colo. *Exhib:* Solo shows, Loveland Mus & Gallery, Colo, 91, Tenn Tech Univ, Cookeville, 92, Ganymede Gallery, NY, 92, Artsquad Contemp Fine Art, Easton, Pa, 93 & Univ La, Shreveport, 94; The Camera's Eye, Mus NW Colo, Craig, 95; Americas 2000: All Media Competition, NW Art Ctr, Minot, NDak, 95; Magnum Opus VIII, Sacramento Fine Arts Inc, Carmichael, Calif, 95; Women & Surrealism, Woman Made Gallery, Chicago, 95. *Teaching:* Assoc prof fine arts, Univ Colo, Boulder, 73-, var art-related courses. *Awards:* First Place for Graphics, Eleanor Bliss Ctr Arts; Univ La honorarium & travel expenses; Award Merit & Gift Cert Award, Sacramento Fine Arts Ctr. *Bibliog:* Gregory Battcock (auth), Super Realism, EP Dutton, 74; Gerald F Brommer (auth), Drawing: Ideas & Techniques, Davis, 88. *Mem:* Nat Asn Women Artists. *Media:* Oils, Pen & Ink. *Publ:* Auth, Art Careers & The Business of Art, Higher Educ Sub Comt State Career Educ Adv Coun Colo, 81

REIBACK, EARL M
SCULPTOR, KINETIC ARTIST
b Brooklyn, NY, June 30, 48. *Study:* Lehigh Univ, Pa, BA(lit) & BS(eng physics); Mass Inst Technol, MS(nuclear eng). *Work:* Whitney Mus Am Art & Mus Mod Art, NY; Philadelphia Mus Art; Milwaukee Art Ctr; New Orleans Mus Art; and 34 other mus; David Bemant Light Collection, Whitney Brevard Col. *Comn:* 70' Lumia light sculpture, Las Vegas Hilton, Nev, 68; Coty Awards (mural of light), Metrop Mus Art, 70; Lumia light sculpture, comn by Hugh Heffner, 71. *Exhib:* solo exhibs, Metrop Mus Art, NY, 67, Moos Gallery, Montreal, Can, 70, Waddell Gallery, NY, 72 & 73, Colibri Gallery, San Juan, PR, 74, Estes Robles Gallery, Los Angeles, Calif, 75 & 82, Electric Gallery, Toronto, Can, 71, 76 & 84 & OK Harris Gallery, NY, 95; Brooklyn Mus, NY, 68 & 69; Milwaukee Art Ctr, Wis, 69; Metrop Mus Art, NY, 69; Philadelphia Mus Art; Albright-Knox Art Gallery, Buffalo, NY; Long Beach Mus Contemp Art, Calif; Aldrich Mus Contemp Art, Ridgefield, Conn; Mus d'Art Contemporain, Montreal, Que; US Cult Ctr, Tel Aviv, Israel; Fine Arts Gallery, Ankara, Turkey; Mus Mod Art, NY; Baltimore Mus Art, Md; Walker Art Ctr, Minneapolis, Minn; Hayden Gallery, Cambridge, Mass; Whitney Mus Art, 94; Cite des arts et des nouvelles technologies, Montreal, Can, 96; Long Beach Mus Art, Calif, 97; Age of Technology, San Jose Mus Art, 98; and others. *Collection Arranged:* New Am Films & Videos at Whitney Mus Am Art, 1994; Cité des Arts et des novvelles tech de Montréal, 1996. *Teaching:* Instr, NY Univ Sch Continuing Educ, currently; lectr, Met Mus Art, NY Univ, Columbia Univ, City Col NY, Univ Denver, Mass Inst Tech, many others. *Mem:* Art & Sci Collaborations Inc; Whitney Mus Art (permanent artist mem). *Media:* Electronics, Light. *Interests:* Human develop. *Publ:* Auth, articles, Fortune Mag, 1968, House & Garden, 1/69 & Electronics Age, spring 70, Encyclopedia Britanica Yearbook of Science & the Future, 1971. *Mailing Add:* 20 E Ninth St New York NY 10003

REICH, OLIVE B
PAINTER
b Brooklyn, NY, Mar 1, 35. *Study:* Mt Holyoke Col, South Hadley, Mass, BA, 56; Art Students League, 66-67; Craft Students League; Parsons Sch Design. *Work:* Brooklyn Botanic Garden/Nature Conser, NY; Health & Hospital Corp, NY; Mount Holyoke Col Mus of Art; Brooklyn Botanic Garden Health & Hosp Corp, NY; Cantor Fitzgerald, NY. *Comn:* Series of drawings, comn by Union Chapel Grove, Shelter Island, NY, 76-86; Centennial Celebration (painting), comn by Fox River Paper Co, Appleton, Wis, 84; Series of homes on Shelter Island, NY, 2000-04. *Exhib:* solo exhibs, Present Day Club, Princeton, NJ, 78 & Brooklyn Botanic Garden, NY, 86, Mayer, Brown & Platt Law Firm, NY, 96, Nat Arts Club, NY, 2001, Cook Pony Farm Gallery, Sag Harbor, NY, 2002, Nat Arts Club, NY, 2001, 2005, Clayton Libertore Gallery, Bridgewhampton, NY, 2002; Monmouth Mus, Lincroft, NJ, 90; Adelphi Univ, NY, 90; CW Post Univ, Brookville, NY, 92; Brooklyn Borough Hall, 96; Art Ctr, Sarasota, Fla, 2000; Walter Greer Gallery, Hilton Head, SC, 2000. *Pos:* Instr watercolor, YWCA, 74-77, own studio, 78-, Brooklyn, NY & Aquarelle Studio, Shelter Island, NY, 83-88. *Awards:* Catharine Lorillard Wolfe Art Club Award, 99; Halpern Mem Award, Nat Asn Women Artists, 99; Four Awards, Nat Asn Women Artists, 99-2004; 1st Place, East End Ats Coun, 2005. *Bibliog:* Barbara Dunne (auth), Reich exhibts watercolor, Shelter Island Reporter, 84; Dawn Goris (auth), From Art of the Bay Ridge/Profile Olive Reich, Here's Brooklyn Mag, 89; Kim Covell (auth), Olive Reich, An artist in search of happy homes for her work, Shelter Island Reporter, 2000; An Island Sheltered - Olive Reich, Sally Flynn, Dans Papers, 2001; Featured Artist, N Fork Section, Dan's Papers, 2005. *Mem:* Artists Alliance of East Hampton; Audubon Artists; Artists Equity; Contemp Artist Guild (corresp secy, 80-); Catharine Lorillard Wolfe Art Club (exec bd, 85-88); exhibiting mem, Nat Arts Club. *Media:* Watercolor. *Interests:* Theatre, ballet, decorating, traveling and gardens; Environ preserv. *Publ:* Illusr, God's Summer Cottage, Shelter Island Hist Soc, 80; Chronicle of Shelter Island churches, MIT Graphics, 83; Shelter Island Yacht Club-A History, Mad Printers, 86; Cover, Art Calendar, 92; contribr, Manhattan Arts Int Mag, 96. *Dealer:* Annyx Gallery Sag Harbor NY; Island Home Gallery Shelter Island Heights NY. *Mailing Add:* 7518 Third Ave Brooklyn NY 11209

REICHEK, ELAINE
CONCEPTUAL ARTIST
b New York, NY, Apr 30, 43. *Study:* Brooklyn Col, BA, 63; Yale Univ Sch Art & Archit, BFA, 64. *Work:* Norton Gallery Art, West Palm Beach, Fla; Portland Art Mus, Ore; Arthur Anderson & Assoc; AT&T; New Sch Social Res. *Exhib:* Out of the House, Whitney Mus Am Art, 78; NY Collection, Albright-Knox Art Gallery, 78; Site Seeing Travel & Tourism in Contemp Art, Whitney Mus Am Art, 91; solo exhibs, Jewish Mus, NY, 94, Stichting de Appel, Amsterdam, 94, Ctr Res Contemp Art, Univ Tex, Arlington, 94, Michael Klein Gallery, NY, 95, Univ Arts, Philadelphia, Van Every Smith Gallery, Davidson Col, NC, 96 & Mus Mod Art, NY, 99; Labor of Love, New Mus, NY, 96; A Bare Wall, Michael Kelin Gallery, NY, 96; Model Home, PS1, The Clocktower, NY, 96; Embeded Metaphor (traveling), 96; Making Pictures: Women and Photog, 1975-Now, Nicole Klagsbrun, NY, 96; Art on the Edge of Fashion, Ariz State Univ Art Mus, Tempe, 97; Ethno Antics, Nordiska Museet, Stockholm, 98; Loose Threads, Serpentine Gallery, London, 98; Dimensions of Native Am: the Contact Zone, Mus Fine Arts, Fla State Univ, Tallahassee & Appleton Mus Art, Ocala, Fla, 98; Palais Des Beaux Arts, Brussels, 2000; "When This You See," MoMA Project Room and Nicole Klagsbrun Gallery, 1999; "MADAM I'M ADAM," Shoshana Wayne Gallery, Los Angeles, 2003; "Online Project," Gardner Museum, Boston, 2003. *Teaching:* Guest lectr, Bryn Mawr, Pa, 89, Kent State Univ, Ohio, 89, Hobart-William Smith Col, Geneva, NY, 89, Everson Mus, Syracuse, NY, 90, Syracuse Univ, NY, 90, Art of the Middle Ages. Recent Work by Mid Career Feminists, Women's Caucus Art, NY, 90, Ethnicity/Ethnography: The Uses and Misuses of Traditional Aesthetics by Contemp Artists, Col Art Asn, NY, 90. *Awards:* Creative Artists Pub Serv Grant, NY State Coun Arts, 83; New York Found Grant, 88; Louis Comfort Tiffany Found Award, 94. *Bibliog:* Arnd Schneider (auth), Uneasy Relationships, Contemporary Artists & Anthropology, J Mat Cult, 7/96; Robin Rice (auth), Now Who's Laughing, Philadelphia City Paper, 10/96; Jeanne Nugent (auth), Museum Focus, Philadelphia Weekly, 9/18/96; Fall Preview, Seven Arts, Philadelphia, 9/96. *Mem:* Women's Caucus Art. *Publ:* Auth, Liberals at War (article, book review), Artforum, 1/90, 23-24. *Dealer:* Nicole Klagsburn 526 W 26th St New York NY 10001; AIR Gallery 63 Crosby St New York NY 10013. *Mailing Add:* 140 Riverside Dr New York NY 10024

REICHEL, MYRA
TAPESTRY ARTIST, WEAVER

b Philadelphia, Pa, June 19, 51. *Study:* Philadelphia Col Art, 69-71, apprenticed with Nora Johnson, 81-82, study workshops with Mary Lane, 88-89; Bryn Mawr Col, BA, 95. *Work:* Hercules Corp, Wilmington, Del; Fox Co, Chesterbrook, Pa; Educ Testing Serv, Princeton, NJ; Wolf Block Schorr Solis, Cohen, Philadelphia, Pa; Dupont Corp, Wilmington, Del. *Comn:* Colo Mountains (tapestry), comn by Dr Richard Small, Reading, Pa, 80; Spring Dreams (tapestry), comn by George & Toni Wiswessler, Reading, Pa, 81; Miroian Dream (tapestry), comn by Helene & Walter Sencer, NY, 85; Night tales (tapestry), comn by Arthur Gershkoff, Merion, Pa, 88; Star Flower (tapestry), comn by Jean Bradley, Philadelphia, Pa, 88; Daybreak, Lee MacIlhenney, 89. *Exhib:* One-person show, Hudson River Mus, Yonkers, NY, 85, Del Ctr Contemp Arts, Wilmington, 85, Henry Chauncy Conf Ctr, Educ Testing Serv, Princeton, NJ, 87; Biennial Art/Craft Exhib, Del Art Mus, Wilmington, 89; Philadelphia Guild of Handweavers, Swedish Mus, Pa, 92; Bryn Mawr Col, 93; Abington Art Ctr, 94; Liberty Place, Philadelphia, Pa, 98; Am Express Fin Svcs, Plymouth Meeting, PA, 2000; Art of the State, Susquehanna Art Mus, Harrisburg, Pa, 2002; Sedwick Art Center, Alma Gallery, Phildelphia, 2003. *Pos:* Asst dir Mcpl Planning, Borough of Norristown. *Teaching:* Philadelphia Guild of Handweavers, 84-92; Community Arts Ctr, Wallingford, Pa, 91; artist-in-residence, Pa Coun Arts, 93-95; Powell Elem Sch; Gillespie Middle Sch. *Mem:* Philadelphia Guild of Hand Weavers. *Publ:* Contribr, Handmade Charter Issue, FiberArts, 81. *Mailing Add:* 121 E Sixth St Media PA 19063

REICHERT, DONALD KARL
PAINTER, PHOTOGRAPHER

b Libau, Man, Jan 11, 32. *Study:* Univ Man Sch Art, with Robert A Nelson & George Swinton, BFA, 56; Inst Allende, Mex, with James Pinto; Emma Lake Artist's Workshops, with Jules Olitzki, Stepan Wolpe, Lawrence Alloway, John Cage & Frank Stella. *Work:* Nat Gallery Can; Art Gallery Ont; Winnipeg Art Gallery; Can Coun Art Bank; Montreal Mus Fine Arts. *Exhib:* Winnipeg Show Nat Biennial; Montreal Spring Show Nat; Nat Gallery Biennial; solo-exhibs, Winnipeg Art Gallery, 60, 69, 75, 83 & 92; Visua '67, Nat Exhib. *Pos:* Founding pres, Winnipeg Artists Co-op Inc, Site Gallery, 95. *Teaching:* Artist-in-residence, Univ NB, 61-62; prof painting, Univ Man Sch Art, 64-88, emer prof, 90. *Awards:* Can Coun Sr Nat Awards, 67 & 74; Visual Arts Grant, Manitoba Arts Coun, 89. *Bibliog:* Don Reichert, Artist in the Landscape, CBC Film, 82; Robert Enright (auth), Balancing the instrument of art, Arts Manitoba Mag, 83; Don Reichert, A Life in Work (monogr), Winnipeg Art Gallery, 95. *Mem:* Royal Can Acad Arts. *Media:* Acrylic, Watercolor. *Mailing Add:* 228 Glenwood Crescent Winnipeg MB R2L 1J9 Canada

REICHERT, MARILYN F
MUSEUM DIRECTOR

b Cincinnati, Ohio. *Study:* Bryn Mawr Col, BA, 58; Xavier Univ, MEd, 78. *Exhib:* William Zorach Paintings & Sculpture, 94; Jerusalem Album: Vintage Photographs 1860-1905, 96; Henry Mosler Rediscovered: Drawings & Paintings, 96; Artisans in Silver: Judaica Today, 97; Kenneth Treister: A Sculpture of Love and Anguish, 98; June Wayne: The Dorothy Series, 99. *Mem:* Am Asn Mus; Asn Col & Univ Mus; Ohio Mus Asn. *Mailing Add:* Hebrew Union Col-Jewish Inst Religion Skirball Mus 3101 Clifton Ave Cincinnati OH 45220

REID, CHARLES CLARK
WRITER, PAINTER

b Cambridge, NY, Aug 12, 37. *Study:* S Kent Sch; Univ of Vt, 57; Art Students League, study with Frank Reiley, 59. *Work:* Yellowstone Art Ctr, Billings, Mont; Brigham Young Univ, Salt Lake City, Utah; Smith Col Mus, South Hampton, Mass. *Comn:* US Postage Stamp to Commemorate Family Planning, US Postal Dept. *Exhib:* Nat Acad of Design, Am Watercolor Soc & Am Inst of Arts & Letters, NY; Far Gallery, NY; Munson Gallery, Mass & NMex; exhibs incl Govt House, Madeira, Portugal, 1961; Roko Gallery, New York City, 1973-74; Gallery Fair, Mendocino, Calif, 1991-92; Stremmel Gallery, 2005. *Pos:* Assoc, Nat Acad, New York City, 1980-83, academician, 1983-. *Awards:* Salmagundi Award, Allied Artists, 75; Silver Medal, Soc Illustrs, 83; Adolph & Clara O'Brig Prize, Nat Acad, 87 & 92. *Mem:* Mem Nat Acad of Design (assoc, 75, acad, 83, 1st Altman prize, 2nd Altman prize, Julius Hulgarten award, Clark prize, Salmagundi award 1975, Ranger fund, Emil Dines award, Obrig prize), Nat Watercolor Soc, Century Assoc. *Media:* Watercolor; Oil. *Publ:* Auth & illusr, Figure Painting in Watercolor, 72, Portrait Painting in Watercolor, 73, Flower Painting in Oil, 76 & Flower Painting in Watercolor, 79, Watson-Guptil; Painting What You Want To See, 83; Pulling Your Paintings Together, 85; Painting by Design, 88; Painting Flowers in Watercolor with Charles Reid, 2001. *Dealer:* Munson Gallery Chatham MA. *Mailing Add:* Munson Gallery 800 Main St Chatham MA 02633-2735

REID, FREDERICK W
PATRON

Study: Univ Calif, Berkeley, BA, 73. *Pos:* Va positions, Pan Am World Airways, Am Airlines, 76-87; commercial managing dir, Am Airlines, London, 87-91; sr vpres, Lufthansa, 91-97; exec vpres, chief marketing off, Delta Airlines Inc, Atlanta, 98-2004; Chief Exec Officer, Virgin Am, Inc, New York City, 2004-; bd trustees, Solomon R Guggenheim Found, currently; bd dir, High Mus Art, Atlanta; adv bd, Taub Inst for Res on Alzheimer's Disease & the Aging Brain. *Mailing Add:* Virgin Electronic 65 Bleeker St Fl 6 New York NY 10012

REID, KATHARINE LEE
MUSEUM DIRECTOR, CURATOR

Study: Harvard Univ, MFA, 1966; Instiut d'Art et Archaelogie, Sorbonne, Paris; BA magna cum laude, Vassar Coll. *Pos:* Cur Toledo Mus Art, Ohio, David and Alfred Smart Mus, Univ Chicago, Ackland Art Mus, Univ NC, Chapel Hill; asst dir Art Inst Chicago, 1982-86, deputy dir, 1986-91; dir Va Mus Fine Arts, 1991-2000, Cleveland Mus Art, 2000-; Chair vis comt Frances Lehman Loeb Art Ctr, Vassar Col. *Mem:* Am Fedn of Arts, Am Asn Mus, Am Asn Mus Dir (pres 2000-01, mem bd trustees, formerly). *Mailing Add:* Cleve Mus Art 11150 East Blvd Cleveland OH 44106

REID, LAURIE FRANCES
PAINTER

b Minneapolis, Minn, 64. *Study:* Univ Strasbourg, dipl, 84; Reed Col, BA, 86; Calif Col Arts & Crafts, MFA, 96. *Work:* San Francisco Mus Mod Art, Fine Arts Mus San Francisco Achenbach Found, San Francisco; San Jose Mus Art, Calif; Philadelphia Mus Art, Pa; Nora Eccles Harrison Mus Art, Utah State Univ, Logan. *Exhib:* New Am Talent, Austin Mus Art, Tex, 96; Selections 1996 Fall, The Drawing Ctr, NY, 96; Master Works on Paper, De Young Mem Mus, San Francisco, Calif, 98; In Over Our Heads, San Jose Mus Art, Calif, 98; Images and Ideas, Berkeley Art Mus, Calif, 98; 1999 Biennial Exhib, Orange Co Mus Art, Newport Beach, Calif, 99; Seca Award Show, San Francisco Mus Mod Art, Calif, 99; Whitney Biennial, Whitney Mus Am Art, NY, 2000; Vivid, Stephen Wirtz Gallery, San Francisco, Calif, 2001, The Kiang Gallery, Ga, 2002, James Harris Gallery, Seattle, Wash, 2001, 2003; In the Making: Contemp Drawings from a Pvt Collection, Univ Gallery, Fine Arts Ctr, Univ Mass Amherst, 2003. *Awards:* Cadogan fel, San Francisco Found, 95; Seca Award, Seca Award Show, San Francisco Mus Modern Art, 99. *Bibliog:* The Eds (auth), The Max factor, Art Forum, 3/2000; Katy Siegel (auth), Biennial 2000, Art Forum, 5/2000; Thomas Hoving (auth), My eye, Artnet.com, 4/12/2000. *Media:* Watercolor. *Dealer:* Stephen Wirtz Gallery 49 Geary St San Francisco CA 94108. *Mailing Add:* 1410 Josephine St Berkeley CA 94703

REID, LESLIE
PAINTER, PHOTOGRAPHER

b Ottawa, Ont, Feb 8, 47. *Study:* Queen's Univ, Kingston, Ont; Byam Shaw Sch Art, London, Eng; Chelsea Sch Art, London, Eng; Slade Sch Art, London, Eng. *Work:* Nat Gallery Can, Ottawa; Can Coun Art Bank, Ottawa; Agnes Etherington Art Ctr; Montreal Mus Fine Arts; Mus d'Art Contemporain, Montreal; and others. *Exhib:* Nat Gallery Can, Ottawa, 75, 78 & 84; solo shows, Biennalede de Paris, 77, Mira Godard Gallery, Toronto, 78, 81 & 84, Can Cult Ctr, Paris, 80, Can House Gallery, London, 80 & Galerie Jolliet, Montreal, 82; Ottawa Art Gallery, 90; Mary Porter Sesnon Gallery, Santa Cruz, 91; Galerie l'autre Equivoque, Ottawa, 93, 96 & 98; Robert Mclaughlin Gallery, Oshawa, 94; Agnes Etherington Art Ctr, Kingston, 96; Carleton Univ Art Gallery, Ottawa, 96; and others. *Teaching:* Prof painting & drawing, Univ Ottawa, Ont, 72-, chmn art dept, 80-81, 85-86 & 87-88, co-chair, 96-98. *Awards:* Ed Award, First Can Biennial Prints & Drawings, Can Coun, 74, 75, 76, 77, 79, 83 & 89; Ont Arts Coun Grant, 78, 83, 84, 90 & 95; Arts Abroad Grant, 91; and others. *Bibliog:* Rolando Castellon (auth), Leslie Reid, Meridian Gallery, San Francisco, 91; Sandra Dyck (auth), Surfacing - Leslie Reid, Carleton Univ Art Gallery, 96; Jan Allen (auth), Fertile Ground, Agnes Etherington Art Ctr, 96; and others. *Mem:* Royal Can Acad; Can Artist Representation; Univ Art Asn Can. *Media:* Oil, Cibachrome. *Dealer:* Galerie L'Autre Equivoque 333 Cumberland St Ottawa K1N 7J3 Canada; Gallery One 121 Scollard St Toronto M5R 1G4 Canada. *Mailing Add:* Univ Ottawa Dept Visual Arts Ottawa ON K1N 6N5 Canada

REID, SHEILA
ASSEMBLAGE ARTIST, WRITER

b Minneapolis, Minn. *Study:* Monteith Experimental Col, Wayne State Univ; Ctr Creative Studies Art Col; Ecole Nationale Superieure des Beaux-Arts, Paris. *Work:* Solomon Guggenheim Mus, NY; Musee d'Art Moderne, Saint-Etienne, France; Davis Mus, Wellesley, Boston; Mus Arts & Sci, Daytona Beach, Fla; Supreme Court of the US, Chambers RB Ginsburg; Utah Mus of Fine Arts, Salt Lake City; Fyns Kunst Mus, Denmark; Harrison Mus Art, Logan, UT; Univ Jacksonville Mus, Fla; McAllen Int Mus, Tex; Midwest Mus Am Art, Ind. *Exhib:* Musee de Luxembourg, Paris, 84; Maier Mus, Lynchburg, Va, 86; Mus Univ Miss, 86; Nexus Found Today's Art, Philadelphia, 87; New Am Art, Inst Contemp Art, London, 88; Thoughts Without Words, Art Gallery Greater Victoria, Can, 90 & Gulbenkian Mus, Lisbon, Port, 91; FYNS Kunst Mus Odense, Denmark, 91; Musee d'Art Contemporain, Chamaliéres, France, 91; Uncensored, Harrison Mus Art, Logan, Utah, 94; Imperceptible Icons, Midwest Mus Am Art, Elkart, Ind, 96. *Pos:* Artist. *Media:* Installation. *Publ:* Auth, Art Without Rejection, Rush Ed, 94; ed, Irony & Rude Questions, A Journal, Rush Ed, 96; A Place in the Future, 1/2 hour Film. *Mailing Add:* c/o Rush Editions BP 13 Vence 06141 Cedex France

REID JENKINS, DEBRA L
PAINTER, ILLUSTRATOR

b Grand Rapids, MI, Mar 24, 55. *Study:* Kendall Sch of Design Grand Rapids, 1973-75; Aquinas Col, 1978-90. *Work:* Muskegon Mus Art, Mich; Butterworth Hosp Helen Devos Women & Childrens Centre, Grand Rapids, Mich; Spectrum Fred & Lena Meijer Heart Centre, Grand Rapids, Mich; Am South Bank, Birmingham, Ala; Grand Valley State Univ, Grand Rapids, Mich. *Exhib:* Regional, Muskegon Mus Art, Mich, 1993; one-woman show, Frederick Meijer Botanical Gardens, Grand Rapid, Mich, 1997. *Awards:* Emerging Artist, Am Artist Mag, 1995. *Bibliog:* Emerging Artist, Am Artist Mag, 1995. *Mem:* sig mem, Pastel Soc Am; Soc Gilders. *Media:* Oil. *Interests:* Tai chi feldenkrais, philosophy, kayaking. *Publ:* illus, I Wanted to Know all About God, Eerdmans, 1993; illus, I See the Moon, Eerdmans, 1997; illus, My

Freedom Trip, Boyds Mills Press, 1998; illus, Here is Christmas, Waterbrook Press, 2000; illus, Glory, Eerdmans, 2001. *Dealer:* Arthur Frederick Button Gallery 161 Blue Star Hwy Douglas, MI 49406-0400; Keith Miller Hawthorn Gallery 2017 3rd Ave N Birmingham AL 35203. *Mailing Add:* 1323 Alden Nash Ave NE Lowell MI 49331

REIF, (F) DAVID
SCULPTOR, EDUCATOR, PAINTER
b Cincinnati, Ohio, Dec 14, 41. *Study:* Univ Cincinnati, 60-63; Sch Art Inst Chicago, BFA, 68; Yale Univ, with J Tworkov, J Rosati, R Serra, R Morris & A Held, B Rose, et al, MFA, 70. *Work:* Weatherspoon Art Gallery, Univ NC, Greensboro; Univ Wyo Art Mus, Laramie; Asheville Art Mus, NC; Wichita Art Mus, Kans; Renwick Gallery, Smithsonian Inst, Washington. *Exhib:* group shows: Joslyn Art Mus, Omaha, Nebr, 78 & 79, Springville Art Mus, Utah, 79, Miss Mus Art Traveling Show, 81-, Flatworks, Washington Project Arts, Washington, 83-84, Univ Northern Ariz Art Mus, La Sculpture Tour (with catalog), (La Coun Arts), Wyo Biennials, (touring West, US), The Human Figure, Woy Ctr Arts, Jackson Hole, 2006, Navigation/Negotiation, Gene Siskel Film Ctr Gallery, Art Inst Chicago, 2006; one-man shows, Slusser Gallery, Univ Mich, Ann Arbor, 80, Dorsky Gallery, NY, 80, One West Ctr Contemp Art, Ft Collins, Colo, 91, Univ Wyo Art Mus, 93, Western Wyo Community Col, Rock Springs, 99, Casper Col Goldstein Gallery, Casper, Wyo, 2003. *Pos:* Juror, Uccross Artists Residency Prog, Wyo; vis artist, Univ Mich, Univ Wis, Madison, Univ Houston, Northern Ariz, Univ Colo State Univ & Centenary Col; mem adv bd, Wyo Arts Coun & chair, 93-96; selection comm, Wyo Arts Coun, Percent for Art Construction Proj, 97; owner, Reif Artworks & Design Consulting; landscape & art design consulting, wyo. *Teaching:* Assoc prof, Univ Wyo, Laramie, 70-80, prof, 81-2003, distinguished prof emeritus, 2004-; assoc prof, Univ Mich, Ann Arbor, 80-81. *Awards:* Best Sculpture Award, Joslyn Art Mus, Omaha, 78; Emerging Artist Grant, Nat Endowment Arts, 79-80; Teaching Excellence Grant, Univ Wyo, 98. *Bibliog:* George P Tomko (auth), Regionalism, Seven Views, Joslyn Art Mus, 7-8/79; Martha Keller (auth), Art, a catalyst to thought and dialog, Ann Arbor News, Mich, 8/16/81. *Mem:* Col Art Asn; Int Sculpture Ctr, Washington. *Media:* Mixed Media. *Publ:* Auth, Contemporary art on the Wyoming frontier: 1978, Wyo News Mag, 8/78. *Mailing Add:* 3340 Aspen Lane Laramie WY 82070

REILLY, BERNARD FRANCIS
HISTORIAN, CURATOR
b Philadelphia, Pa, June 7, 50. *Study:* Villanova Univ, BA, 72; Bryn Mawr Col, with Arthur Marks, MA(hist art), 74. *Exhib:* Caricature Since 1870, Libr Cong, Washington, DC, 79. *Collection Arranged:* American Political Prints (cataloged), Libr Cong, 78; Applied Graphic Art, Libr Cong; Photographs from 1845 to 1876 (cataloged), Libr Co Philadelphia. *Pos:* Cur prints & drawing, Libr Co Philadelphia, 74-77; cur popular & applied graphic art, Prints & Photographs Div, Libr Cong, 78-87, head cur, Prints & Photog Div, Libr Congress, formerly; dir res & access, Chicago Hist Soc, 97-. *Teaching:* Am political art, Humanities Prog, Georgetown Univ, 81-92. *Mem:* Am Asn Mus. *Res:* History of 19th century painting, graphic art and photography, particularly landscape; history of political art from Renaissance to current times with emphasis on theory of expression. *Publ:* Auth, Drawings of Nature and Circumstance, Caricature since 1870, contribr, Posada's Mexico, Libr Cong, 79; auth, American Political Prints in the Library of Congress, GK Hall, 89. *Mailing Add:* Chicago Hist Soc Clark St at North Ave Chicago IL 60614-6099

REILLY, JACK
PAINTER, VIDEO ARTIST
b Pittsburgh, Pa, Nov 4, 50. *Study:* Fla State Univ, BFA, 76, MFA, 77. *Work:* Oakland Mus Art, Calif; Matthews Ctr Mus, Ariz State Univ, Tempe; Arco Ctr Visual Arts, Am Airlines, Los Angeles, Calif; Fresno Metrop Mus, Calif; Co of San Diego Pub Art Fredric Weisman Found, Los Angeles; Retrospective, Channel Islands Art Ctr, Camarillo, Calif, 2002; Magnum Opus, Ventura Co Govt Center, Ventura, Calif, 2003; Electronics Alive, Univ Tampa, Fla, 2003. *Comn:* Pub Art Comn, Co San Diego; Painting Am Airlines. *Exhib:* Reality of Illusion, Denver Art Mus, Colo, Oakland Mus Art, Calif & Toledo Art Mus, Ohio; Am Painters in Paris, Ctr Int, Paris, France, 75; New Floridians, Jacksonville Art Mus, 77; Eyes and Ears, Calif Mus Sci, Los Angeles, 78; one-man show, Matthews Ctr Mus, Ariz State Univ, Tempe, 80; Laguna Beach Mus Art, Calif; Downtown Los Angeles, Palm Springs Mus, Calif. *Pos:* chair, art dept, Calif State Univ, Channel Islands, prof, 2001-; bd dir, Ventura Co Arts Coun, Calif. *Teaching:* Adj instr painting, Fla State Univ, 78; vis prof painting, Ariz Western Col, Yuma, 80-81; instr, Otis-Parsons Art Inst, Los Angeles, 85-86; prof, Calif State Univ, Northridge, 87-2001. *Awards:* Best Show, Alexandria Mus Art, 94; Best Experimental Film, Univ Cincinatti Film Festival, 94; Best Captioned Video Poem, Nat Poetry Asn, 96; Best 3D Art, Carnegie Mus, Oxnard, Calif, 2001; Jury Award for Best Screenplay, Silver Spocket Film Competition, Fla, 2002. *Bibliog:* Linda Jacobson (auth), article, Arts Mag, 12/81; Edward Lucie-Smith (auth), article, Am Art Now, 85; Morrow Marva (auth), Inside the Los Angeles, Artist, 88; Shauna Snow (author), Article, The Fugue A Public Art Commission, Los Angeles Times, 10/90; Josef Woodard (auth), A Wild Ride Through Art History, Los Angeles Times, 9/2002. *Mem:* Col Art Asn Am; Los Angeles Contemp Exhibs. *Media:* Acrylic, Oil; Digital Media. *Res.* Investigation into the relationships between digital media and traditional painting techniques. *Publ:* Auth, Shelia Ruth, A Discourse on Flowers Rev, 1/85 & Ed Paschike, Exhib Rev, Artweek, 12/90. *Dealer:* Image Mod Gallery 2674 Main St Ventura Calif 93003. *Mailing Add:* PO Box 7017 Santa Monica CA 90406

REILLY, JOHN JOSEPH
PAINTER, INSTRUCTOR
b Brooklyn, NY, June 9, 42. *Study:* Newark Sch Fine Art studied with James McGinley, 1988; studied with Burt Silverman (2 yrs), Everett Raymond Kinstler (10 yrs). *Work:* Joy Malin Fine Art, NYC; Lambertville Gallery Fine Art, NJ; Highlands Art, Chester, NJ; Richland Fine Art, Nashville, Tenn; McPhee Fine Art, Stone Harbor, NJ. *Comn:* Portrait, comn by Judge Macstein, Long Island, 1999; mural (30'x40'), Dal Archit, Bayonne, NJ, 2000; Kearny Bank, Kearny, NJ, 2003; Ste John on the Mountain, comn by Mary E Bittrich, 2006; Vanderneer House, comn by Mary E Bittrich, 2006. *Collection Arranged:* Salmagundi Club, NY, 1990-2002; Nabisco Gallery, Hanover, NJ, 1997; Children's Specialized Hosp, Mountainside, NJ, 2001; Johnson & Johnson, 2002; Clarence Dillon Libr, Bedminster, NJ, 2006. *Pos:* Dir, Elliot J Axelrod, NYC, 1965-1990; Somerset Art Asn, Somerset, NJ, 2001-2004; Ridgewood Art Asn, 2003-2005. *Teaching:* Sch Visual Arts, NYC, 1980. *Mem:* Artist Fel; Somerset Art Asn; Summit Art Asn. *Media:* Oil. *Publ:* TV (short segment on Channel 9), John Rouland, 2002; ed, NJ section NY Times, 2004; ed (article), Bernardsville News, 2005; ed (article), Weekender Local News, 2006. *Mailing Add:* 211 Pickle Rd Califon NJ 07830

REILLY, NANCY
PAINTER
b Bryn Mawr, Pa, Mar 29, 27. *Study:* Portraiture with Samuel E Brown, Westport, Conn & Mimi Jennewein, NY. *Comn:* Numerous portraits & landscapes, pvt collections. *Exhib:* Nat Arts Club, NY, 1971-2005; Wadsworth Atheneum, Conn Acad Fine Arts, Hartford, 81; Am Artists Prof League, Salmagundi Club, NY, 1985-2004; Salmagundi Club, NY, 89; Acad Artists, 90-96; Butler Inst of Am Art, Youngstown, Ohio, 2001; New Britain Mus Am Art, Conn, 2001; incl in invitational traveling exhib with Allied Artists of Am to 8 mus throughout US, 2003-. *Pos:* volunteer artist Norwalk Hosp Rehabilitation Unit, 84-95. *Teaching:* demonstr lectr portrait painting Bridgeport Art League, Conn, Milford Art League, Conn, Pen & Brush Club, New Haven, Conn, Conn Classic Arts Asn, Allied Artists Am, Kent Art Asn, Conn, SCAN, Newtown, Conn. *Awards:* Bruce Stevenson Award, Nat Arts Club, 78, 88 & 91; Claude Parsons Mem Award, Nat Arts Club, NY, 2003; First prize, 106th Annual Exhib Artist Mem Exhib, 2005. *Mem:* Allied Artists Am Inc (hon, bd dir, 91-98); Nat Arts Club; Pastel Soc Am; fel Am Artists Prof League; Hudson Valley Art Asn; Artists Fel NY. *Media:* Oil, Pastel. *Collection:* Slide collection; Smithsonian Institute, Washington, D.C.; University of Connecticut, Farmington. *Mailing Add:* Nine Marilane Rd Westport CT 06880

REILLY, RICHARD
DIRECTOR, HISTORIAN
b New York, NY, Mar 13, 26. *Pos:* Consult, James S Copley Libr & Art Collection, La Jolla; fine arts adv, James S Copley Found. *Publ:* Auth, A Promise Kept, 83. *Mailing Add:* PO Box 1530 La Jolla CA 92037

REIMANN, ARLINE LYNN
PRINTMAKER, PAINTER
b St Louis, Mo, Nov 25, 37. *Study:* Rutgers Univ, BA, 74; Montclair State Univ, NJ, MA, 80. *Work:* Newark Pub Libr Fine Print Collection, NJ; Montclair State Univ, Upper Montclair, NJ; Jane Voorhees Zimmerli Art Mus, New Brunswick, NJ; Bailey Matthew Mus, Sanibel, Fla; Black Hills Inst, SD. *Exhib:* Jane Voorhees Zimmerli Art Mus, 98 & 99; Prince St Gallery, Soc Am Graphic Artists, NY, 99; Worldwide Feminist Expo, Baltimore, Md, 2000; Nat Asn of Women Artists United Nations, 02; Soc Am Graphic Artists, Old Print Shop, New York City, 04; Ringling Mus Sch Art, Sarasota, Fla, 2006; Venezuelan Consulate, New York City, 2006; Goggleworks, Reading, Pa, 2006; and others. *Awards:* Best Show, Lincoln Ctr, 81; Hon Mention, Nat Juried Exhib Small Works, Montclair State Univ, NJ, 95; Aida Whedon Mem Award, Nat Asn Women Artists, NY, 96. *Mem:* Nat Asn Women Artists (chmn travel printmaking exhib, 84-86 & 87-89 & printmaking jury 87-89 & 95-97); Audubon Artists (recording secy, 91-97); Soc Am Graphic Artists; Phi Beta Kappa. *Media:* Intaglio-Etching, Monotype. *Mailing Add:* 546 Hillrise Pl Walnut Creek CA 94598

REIMANN, WILLIAM P
SCULPTOR, EDUCATOR
b Minneapolis, Minn, Nov 29, 35. *Study:* Yale Univ, BA, 57, BFA, 59, MFA, 61; with Josef Albers, Rico Lebrun, Robert M Engman, James Rosati, Gilbert Franklin, Seymour Lipton, Gabor Peterdi, Neil Welliver & Bernard Chaet. *Work:* Mus Mod Art, Whitney Mus Am Art & Rockefeller Univ, NY; Boston Mus Fine Arts; Nat Gallery Art, Washington; City of Holyoke, Mass. *Comn:* Relief-mural, First Church of Christ, Boston, Mass, 81; suspended sculpture, Shell Oil Corp, Houston, Tex, 81 & Southwestern Bell Telephone Co, 86; Designated Artist, Radnor Twp, Pa, Blue Route Enhancement Proj, 89-96; Sandblasted Relief, Boston Red Sox Baseball Club, Fenway Park, Mass, 90; water feature, Mass Turnpike Authority, 96; relief sculpture, Mass Port Authority, 96. *Exhib:* Structured Sculpture, Galerie Chalette, NY, 61-68; Sculpture Ann, 64-65 & Young Americans, 65, Whitney Mus Am Art; Int Exhib Contemp Painting & Sculpture, Carnegie Inst, Pittsburgh, 67-68. *Teaching:* Asst prof art, Old Dom Col, 61-64; lectr visual & environ studies, Harvard Univ, 64-, Carpenter Ctr Visual Arts, spring 71, sr preceptor visual & environ studies, 75-, head tutor dept visual studies, 86-. *Media:* Plexiglas, Stone. *Mailing Add:* One Gerry's Landing Cambridge MA 02138-5511

REIMERS, GLADYS ESTHER
SCULPTOR, INSTRUCTOR
b Yonkers, NY. *Study:* Art Students League, New York, 60; Sculpture Ctr, New York, 65-69; Studied metal sculpture with Herb Kallems, 66. *Work:* Newark Mus, NJ; AAUW Traveling Collection; Rockwell Int, Pittsburgh, Pa; British Pelroleum, London. *Comn:* Caring (marble sculpture), Union Co / Westlake Special Sch, NJ, 86. *Exhib:* one-women shows, Morris Pine Gallery, Fair Lawn, NJ, 79, Caldwell Col Gallery, NJ, 80 & Palmer Mus, Springfield, NJ, 2001; Cork Gallery, Lincoln Ctr, NY, 87; Audubon Artists Ann Exhib, Salmagundi Club, NY, 98; Biennial Exhib, Trenton State Mus, NJ & Newark Mus, NJ. *Teaching:* instr sculpture workshop, Town of Westfield, NJ, 82-94 & Somerset Art Asn, Bedminster, NJ, 90-. *Awards:* Hirsch

Award, Audubon Artists Nat Show, 96, Cleo Harting Award, 98; Women of Achievement Award for Union Co, NJ State Legislature, 99. *Mem:* Audubon Artists; New York Soc Women Artists; NJ Ctr for Visual Arts; Somerset Art Asn. *Media:* Stone, Wood. *Dealer:* Braunsdorf Gallery Westfield NJ. *Mailing Add:* 837 Fairacres Ave Westfield NJ 07090

REINERTSON, LISA
SCULPTOR
b Washington, DC, May 15, 55. *Study:* Univ Calif, Davis, BA, 82, MFA, 84; Skowhegan Sch Painting & Sculpture, Scholar, 83. *Work:* Martin Luther King (bronze bust), Calif State Univ, Chico; ceramic, Davis Art Ctr, Calif. *Comn:* Martin Luther King Jr (terra cotta portrait), King Law Sch, Univ Calif, Davis, 87; portrait, George Washington HS, San Francisco, Calif, 89; Martin Luther King Jr (full size bronze), City of Kalamazoo, Mich, 89. *Exhib:* Fifty-ninth Ann Crocker-Kingsley Exhib, Crocker Art Mus, Sacramento, Calif, 84; City of Savona, Italy; Introductions, Dorothy Weiss Gallery, San Francisco, 89; Reynolds Gallery, Univ Pac, Stockton, Calif, 90; Figures in Ceramics, La State Univ, Baton Rouge, 90. *Teaching:* Vis artist & instr ceramics, La State Univ, Baton Rouge, 84; lectr ceramics & drawing, Calif State Univ-Stanislaus, 86-87; asst prof ceramics, Calif State Univ, Chico, 87-. *Awards:* Grand Central Gallery Educational Asn Award, New York, 85; Research Award, Calif State Univ, Chico, 89. *Bibliog:* Saunthy Singh (auth), Lively ceramic sculpture, Artweek, 10/86; Craig Thomas (auth), Kalamazoo Gazette, 89; Elaine Levin (auth), Contemporary Ceramics: The Artists of TB9 (exhib catalog), 89. *Mem:* Col Art Asn. *Media:* Clay. *Mailing Add:* John Natsoulas Gallery 140 F St Davis CA 95616

REININGHAUS (SMITH), RUTH
PAINTER
b New York, NY, Oct 4, 22. *Study:* Studied with Bob Maione & Rudy Colao, 57-62, Nat Acad Design, with Morton Roberts, 62; Frank Reilly Sch Art, with Frank Reilly, 63; Art Student's League, with Robert Philip & Robert Beverly Hale, 68; New York Univ. *Work:* Murtugh D Guinness. *Comn:* numerous private collections. *Exhib:* Allied Artists Am Ann, Nat Acad Design, NY, 72 & 87; Hammer Gallery, NY, 1974; Salmagundi Club Ann, NY, 74-; Far Gallery, NY, 1975; Catherine Lorillard Wolfe Art Club Ann, NY, 78-; Knickerbocker Artists, 85-; solo exhib, Petrucci Gallery, 88; Pastel Soc Am Ann, 88-; Heidi Neuhoff Gallery Inc, NY, 90; John Lane Gallery, Rheinbeck, NY; Regianni Gallery, NY. *Pos:* Draftsmen, Engineering Aide, Allied Control Co, 41-45, 52-60; Freelance tech illusr, 60's; Management Info, Bell Helicopter, Iran, 77-79; Sr CHartist, Economics, Bankers Trust, 80-85. *Teaching:* Instr oil painting, Bankers Trust, New York, 71-99 & Kittredge Club for Women, 72-77. *Awards:* J Giffuni Purchase Award, Pastel Soc Am Ann, 1988; Medal Honor, Salmagundi Club, 1989; Silver Medal Award for Excellence in Pastel, Art Spirit Found, 2006; over 50 award in juried ann shows. *Bibliog:* Lucien Mandose (auth), 58th Ann Allied Artists Am Exhib, La Rev Mod, Paris, 72; Raymond Steiner (auth), Profile, Art Times, 8/89; Jennifer McGhee Siler (alumnae ed), New York artist pursues international following, Adelphean, summer 91; 200 Great Painting Ideas for Artists, in Carole Katchen; The Best of Pastel 2, by Pastel Soc Am; Pastel Artist Intl, Jan/Feb, 2001. *Mem:* Salmagundi Club (dir at large, 74-77, chmn admiss, 81-83, pres, 83-87 & cur, 89-2004); Fel Am Artist's Professional League; Catherine Lorillard Wolfe Club (bd dir, 87-); Hudson Valley Art Asn; Pastel Asn Am (bd dir, 87-89); Pen & Brush Club, 80-90; NACAL (Navy Art Cooperation & Liaison) 70-80; COGAP (Coast Guard Art Program) 80-90; Am Artist Professional League, 1971-; Music Box Soc; Salmagundi Club; and others. *Media:* Oils, Pastels. *Dealer:* Salmagundi Club New York NY. *Mailing Add:* 222 E 93rd St Apt 26A New York NY 10128-3758

REINKER, NANCY CLAYTON COOKE
PAINTER, SCULPTOR
b Owensboro, Ky, July 6, 36. *Study:* Kent State Univ; Cleveland Inst Art; Silvermine Sch Art; Critique with Robert Reed, Sculpture with Stanley Bleifeld; ConnGraphicarts Ctr with Robert Reedat, etching with Vijay Kumar. *Work:* New Haven Paint & Clay Club, New Haven, Conn; Housatonic Community Col, Bridgeport, Conn. *Exhib:* solo exhib, Silvermine Hayes Gallery, New Canaan, Conn, 92 & Farrell I Gallery, Art Place, Southport, Conn, 93, 95 & 98; Conn Art, Stamford Mus, Conn, 92; Faber Birren Color Show, Stamford Mus, Conn, 93; Art Place, Southport, Conn, 93, 95, 98 & 2000; Farrell I Gallery, 98; United Nations Regeneration Exhib, New York City, 99; Norwalk Community Col, 99 & 2000; Artspace, Hartford, Conn, 99; Gallery Irohani, Sakii City, Japan, 2000; 100th Ann Exhib, New Haven Paint and Clay Club, 2000; Katonah Mus Art, 2001; Art of Northeast, 2001, 2002; Erector Square Gallery, New Haven, Conn. *Pos:* vpres, Art Place Gallery, 91-92; pres, Inst for Visual Artists, 92, 93; Chmn, Western Comn Arts, 93-94; bd mem, Silvermine Guild of Artists, 94-99. *Awards:* Painting Award, Conn Women Artists, 91; Merit Award, New Haven Paint & Clay, 93; R Chitwood Prize, Greenwich Art Soc, Randolph Chitwood, 94. *Bibliog:* Ann R Langdon (auth), Art New Eng, June-July, 94; Wm Zimmer (auth), NY Times, 12/17/95 & 1/20/91; Kate Jennings (auth), Westport News, 11/17/96. *Mem:* Nat Asn Women Artists; Inst Visual Arts (pres, 92-93); Conn Women Artists; Art Place (vpres, 91-92, pres, 94); Women's Caucus Art; and others; Silvermine Guild Artists. *Media:* Mixed Media on Wood, Canvas & Vellum. *Dealer:* Silvermine Guild of Artists 1037 Silvermine Rd New Canaan CT 06840; Art Place 400 Center St Southport CT 06490. *Mailing Add:* 87 Valley Forge Rd Weston CT 06883

REINKRAUT, ELLEN SUSAN
PAINTER
b East Orange, NJ Jul 3, 49. *Study:* Univ of Cincinnati, BFA, 1971; Arts Students League, NY City, Studied with Bruce Dorfman/Norman Lewis, 1975-79. *Work:* Muhlenberg Col, Pa; McCarter and English, Law Off, NJ; McBride Corp, NJ; Maxwell Us Headquarters, NJ; JMS Advisory, Mass. *Exhib:* Paterson Mus, Paterson, NJ, 1992; Morris Mus, Morristown, NJ, 2002-04; Phillips Mus of Art, Lancaster, Pa, 2003; Bergen Mus, Paramus, NJ, 2004; Monmouth Mus, Monmouth, NJ, 2004. *Teaching:* art instru, dir, Dunellen Pub Sch, 1975-91; art instr, Art Ctr of Northern NJ, 2003-04. *Awards:* Art Asn Award, Maurice Pine Gallery, 1993; Int Exhib, 93 S Art Gallery, NY, 1998; fifth annual art exhib, NAWA, 2004. *Mem:* Nat Asn of Women Artists; The Soc of Layerist in Multi Media; Studio Montclair; Salute to Women in the Arts. *Media:* Oil. *Mailing Add:* 706 Clove Ln Franklin Lakes NJ 07417

REIQUAM, PETER
SCULPTOR
Study: Univ Tex, El Paso, 77-79; Univ Wash, BFA, 82; Yale Univ, MFA, 84. *Work:* Maeany Hall Performing Arts, Seattle, Wash; Froula Park, Seattle, Wash; Kent Parks Dept, Wash; Tri-Met Airport, Portland, Oreg; Kent Animal Control Shelter, Wash; LA Co Metro, Los Angeles. Calif. *Comn:* Pedaling Man (mechanical sculpture), REI-Redmond Town Ctr, Wash, 98; mechanical sculpture, MTV's The Real World - Seattle, 98; sculpture, MTV's The Real World - Hawaii, 99; mechanical sign, Tacoma Screw Products, Wash, 2000; sculpture pieces, Real Networks Corp, 2000. *Exhib:* one-man shows, Nine-One-One, Seattle, Wash, 85, Raw Space/ARC Gallery, Chicago, Ill, 86, Cornish Col Arts, Seattle, 87 & VOX Gallery, Portland, Ore, 91; Table Lamp & Chair, Portland, Ore, 92; Suburbia, Marylhunst Art Gym, Ore, 93; Art in Architecture, Washington Trade & Conv Ctr, 94; Focus on Fire, Bellevue Conv Ctr, Wash, 94; Lead Gallery, 96, 97 & 99; Port Angeles Fine Arts Center, Wash, 98 & 2000; McAllen Int Mus, Tex, 99. *Pos:* sculpture fabrication, New Art Projects Co, Seattle, Wash. *Teaching:* Sculpture instr, Pratt Fine Arts Ctr, Seattle, Wash, 84-98, head dept & head facility technician, 85-96; sculpture instr, Cornish Col Arts, 88; sculpture instr, Univ of Wash, 2002, 2003. *Awards:* Visual Artists Fel, Nat Endowment Arts, 86; Merit Award, Art Quest, 87; Grant, King Co Arts Comn, 91. *Bibliog:* Nice doggie, Seattle Times, 5/91; Arts/industry program enters 20th year, Kohler People, winter 94; Cast-iron collaboration, Am West Airlines Mag, 5/94; Twisting traditions, Seattle Mag, 11/95; Putting their mettle to the metal, Seattle Times, 2/98. *Media:* Metal, stones & concrete. *Collection:* Kohler Co, Kohler Wis; Trimet, Portland, Ore; Univ of Wash Pub Art collection, Seattle; City of Seattle, Wash; LA Co Metro, Los Angeles, Calif. *Mailing Add:* 6107 S Hazel Seattle WA 98178

REIS, MARIO
PAINTER
b Weingarten, Ger, 1953. *Study:* Dusseldorf Art Acad, 73-78; study with Prof Gunther Vecker, 78-79. *Work:* Ministerium fur Wissenschaft und Kunst des Landes; Baden-Wurttemberg; Stadische Galerie Ludenscheid; Mus der Stadt Gelsenkirchen; Ulmer Mus. *Exhib:* One-man shows, Unge Kunstneres Samfund, Oslo, Norway, 86, Galerie Vayhinger, Radolfzell, 86, Fenderesky Art Gallery, Belfast, Ireland, 86, Galerie Dorothea van der Koelen (with catalog), Mainz, 86, Galerie Monochrom, Aachen, 87, Gallery Carla Fuehr, Munchen, 88, Salon des Modernes Mus, Belgrad, Yugoslavia, 88; Stadisches Bodenses-Mus (with catalog), Freidrichshafen, 86; Nur Rost---? (with catalog), Skulpturenmuseum Glaskastn, Marl, 86; Kunstmuseum Karlsruhe, 88; Kunstmuseum Dusseldorf, 88. *Media:* Watercolor. *Mailing Add:* Philip Bareiss Gallery 15 Route 150 PO Box 2739 Taos NM 87571

REISS, ROLAND
SCULPTOR, PAINTER
b Chicago Ill, May 15, 29. *Study:* Univ Calif, Los Angeles, BA, 55, MA, 57; also at Am Acad Art, Chicago. *Work:* Los Angeles Co Mus Art; Laguna Art Mus, Laguna Beach, Calif; Oakland Mus, Calif; Hallmark Inc; Newport Harbor Art Mus, Newport Beach, Calif. *Exhib:* Biennial, Whitney Mus Am Art, NY, 75; one-person exhib, Los Angeles Co Mus Art, 77; Documenta 7, Kassel, Ger, 82; 20 Am Artists, Mus Mod Art, San Franciso, 82; Currents, Inst Contemp Art, Boston, 83; Boxes, Mus Tamayo, Mexico, 85; Avant Garde in the 80s, Los Angeles Co Mus Art, 87; Contemp Calif, Taipei Fine Arts Mus, Taiwan, 87; Ace Contemp Exhibs, 87, 88 & 89; solo exhib, Ace Contemp Exhibs, Los Angeles, 88; Montgomery Art Gallery, Claremont, Calif, 90; Barnsdall Munic Art Gallery, Los Angeles, 91; Univ Ariz Mus Art, Tucson, 92; Neuberger Mus Art, State Univ NY, Purchase, 92; Palm Springs Desert Mus, 92. *Teaching:* Asst prof art, Univ Calif, Los Angeles, 57; from asst to assoc prof, Univ Colo, Boulder, 57-61; chmn & prof, Claremont Grad Univ, 71-. *Awards:* Visual Arts Fel, Nat Endowment Arts, 71, 77, 80 & 87. *Publ:* Auth, Roland Reiss, A Seventeen Year Survey, Fels Contemp Art. *Mailing Add:* Dept Art Claremont Grad Univ 251 E Tenth St Claremont CA 91711

REITZENSTEIN, REINHARD
SCULPTOR, ENVIRONMENTAL ARTIST
b Uelzen, Ger, May 27, 49; Can citizen. *Study:* Ont Col Art. *Work:* Art Gallery of Ont; Can Coun Art Bank; Nat Gallery Can; Mem Univ Art Gallery; Government of Ont. *Comn:* Wall relief, Govt of Ont, Can, 85; outdoor sculpture, Mem Univ Art Gallery, St John's Newfoundland, 85; Pergola (sculpture), Western Univ, 93; Arch (sculpture), McDonald Stein Art Gallery, Ont, 94. *Exhib:* Nat Gallery Can, 74 & 77; Landscape Canada Traveling Exhib, Art Gallery Ont & Edmonton, 76; one-man shows, Carmen Lamanna Gallery, Toronto, 75-90, Olga Korpa Gallery, Toronto, Ont, 93, Can; Royal Botanical Gardens, Sculpture Symposium, 83; Lutz Teutluzf Gallery, Brock Univ, 99; Royal Botanical Gardens, Burlington, Ont, 2000. *Pos:* dir sculpture, State Univ NY, Buffalo, 2000-. *Teaching:* Instr, Univ Guelph, 80-98, Brock Univ, 90-94, Univ Waterloo, 83, Toronto Sch Art, 98-2000, Sheridan Col, 2000. *Awards:* Can Coun Proj Cost Grants, 74 & 76-84 & Art Grants, 78-88. *Bibliog:* Carol Corbel (auth), article, Globe & Mail, Toronto, 3/86; Kate Tayler (auth), Can Art, 90; John K Grandf (auth), Sculpture Mag, 94, 99 & 2000, Vies Des Arts, 2000, Le Sabord, 2000, Espace, 2000. *Media:* Mixed Media, All Media. *Publ:* Auth, Natural Areas Divisions Charter, 75; According (record album), 80; Reinhard Reitzenstein, C Dewdney Art Gallery of Hamilton, 89; World Tree, Ted Fraser Confed Centre Arts, PEI, 93. *Dealer:* Olga Korper Gallery 17 Morrow Ave Toronto Can. *Mailing Add:* 146 Ridge Rd W Grimsby ON L3M 4E7 Canada

REKER, LES
PAINTER, EDUCATOR
b Indianapolis, Ind, Aug 7, 51. *Study:* Ind Univ, Bloomington, BFA, 73; Queens Col, MFA, 75; study with Robert Birmelin & Gabriel Laderman. *Work:* Reading Mus, Reading, Pa. *Comn:* Landscape paintings, Hawk Mountain Sanctuary, Kempton, Pa, 82 & Republic Bank, Dallas, 84. *Exhib:* In Praise of Space, Westminster Col, New Wilmington, Pa, Gross-McCleaf Gallery, Philadelphia, Pa & Parsons Sch Design, NY, 77-78; Christmas Invitational, Allentown Art Mus, Allentown, Pa, 77 & 78; Co-op Invitational, Philadelphia Art Mus, 81; Queens Alumnus, Godwin-Ternbach Mus, Flushing, NY, 82; Sherry French Gallery, NY, 83-86; Art of Our Time, Temple Emanuel, Woodcliff-Lake, NY, 84; Emerging Realists: Sherry French Gallery, NY, 84; Emerging Realists: East Meets South, Col Mainland, Texas City, Tex, 86. *Collection Arranged:* Contemporary Narrative Figure Painting (auth, catalog), 85 & Landscapes of the Hudson River Sch (auth, catalog), 86, Payne Gallery, Moravian Col; Artificial Light: Paintings by William Haney (auth, catalog), 85; Robert Arneson (auth catalog), 87; Clarence Carter. *Pos:* Dir & cur, Payne Gallery, Moravian Col, Bethlehem, Pa, 84-; asst prof art, Moravian Col, Bethlehem, Pa, 84. *Teaching:* Instr art hist, Leigh Co Community Col, Schnecksville, Pa, 78-83; asst prof drawing, Kutztown Univ, Kutztown, Pa, 83-84; asst prof studio & art hist, Moravian Col, 84-. *Bibliog:* Hedy O'Beil (auth), reviews, Arts Mag, 6/78 & 1/84; Freddie Kaplin (auth), Landscape painting in America, Am Artist, 2/84. *Mem:* Asn Col & Univ Gallery & Mus; Am Asn Mus. *Media:* Oil on canvas. *Dealer:* Sherry French Gallery 41 W 57th St New York NY 10019. *Mailing Add:* 1200 Main St Bethlehem PA 18018

RELKIN, MICHELE WESTON
PAINTER, INSTR
b Calif, Jan 17, 46. *Study:* Santa Monica Col, Lucille Brown Green Studio, AA, 66. *Work:* Clinton Libr, Ark; Whitehouse, Presidential Col, Washington, DC; Galleria Ortiz, San Antonio, Tex; Johnson Corp Gallery Coll, Los Angeles, Calif; Ronald Raegan Pres Libr and Mus, Semi Valley, Calif. *Comn:* CD Cover Art, George Gamez, Los Angeles, Calif, 2004; Socks in Blue Room, Los Angeles Mus Art, Los Angeles, Calif; Children Art & Music Festival, Dorothy Chandler Pavillion, Los Angeles, Calif. *Exhib:* From Washington to Clinton, Ronald Reagan Mus, Semi Valley, Calif, 93; Black Tie & Blue Jeans, Congo Valley Art Mus, Thousand Oaks, Calif, 92; Internet Mail Art, Pasadena Armory Ctr, Pasadena, Calif, 92; Parade of Animals, Lancaster Mus Art, Lancaster, Calif, 94; Los Angeles Co Mus, Los Angeles, Calif, 97; Atkinson Gallery, Santa Barbabra Col, Santa Barbara, Calif, 97; Permanent Collection, Clinton Pres Libr, Ark, 2004. *Collection Arranged:* Cur, Gallery 9, 98. *Teaching:* Artist in Residence, Walnut Canyon Elem, 97-2004; Vis Artist, Pub & Pvt Sectors, Santa Fe, NMex. *Awards:* Woman of the Yr, Santa Monica Col, Calif, 65; Printmaking Award, Moorpark Col, Santa Monica, CA, 91; Honorable Mention, Thousand Oaks Juried Exhib, Katherine Lill, 99. *Bibliog:* Dialogue with Georgia O'Keefe, Studio Zine Magazine, 2001; Patty Jean Levine (auth), Presidential Pets, Thousand Oaks Star, 2004. *Mem:* NAWA, 95-; Book Artists Group, 2005. *Media:* Mixed Media, Acrylic, Found Objects. *Dealer:* Galleria Ortiz, San Antonio, TX. *Mailing Add:* 6 Dandelion Cir San Antonio TX 87506

REMBERT, VIRGINIA PITTS
EDUCATOR, ART HISTORIAN
b Birmingham, Ala, Nov 15, 21. *Study:* Univ Montevallo, BA, 42; Columbia Univ, MA, 44, univ traveling fel, 67, Am Asn Univ Women fel, 67, PhD, 70; Univ Wis, MA, 59. *Work:* NC State Mus, Raleigh; Univ Ala Birmingham; Univ Ala Tuscaloosa; Univ Montevallo; Birmingham Mus of Art. *Exhib:* Ala State Exhib, Birmingham, 43; NC State Exhib, Raleigh, 48 & 49; Ala Watercolor Soc, Birmingham, 62 & 86; Univ Faculty Exhibs, 81-90; Cabiness Gallery, Birmingham, 98; Donahue-Sosinski Gallery, NY, 95; Ramapo Collection, 98. *Pos:* Pres, Birmingham Art Asn, 70-71 & Ala Watercolor Soc, 62-63; chmn, comt to study baccalaureate degree, Univ Ark, Little Rock, 85-86. *Teaching:* Instr art, Beloit Col, 53-55; asst prof art hist, Mass Col Art, 56-60; from asst prof to prof art & chmn dept, Birmingham Southern Col, 60-73; prof art & chmn dept, Univ Ala, Birmingham, 74-75, Univ Ala, Tuscaloosa, 81-90 & prof emer, 90, head, fine arts area, Col Educ, 84-86; Donaghey Distinguished prof art & art hist, Univ Ark, Little Rock, 75-81; lectr, Fine Arts Club, Vanderbilt Univ, 79, Birmingham Mus Art, 82-88, Montgomery Mus Art, 83; Columbia Mus Art, 88. *Awards:* Pres Award, Univ Montevallo, 81; Cert Merit, Southeastern Col Art Asn; Distinguished Career Award, Soc Fine Arts, Univ Ala, 93. *Bibliog:* Bosch, Parkstone Press, 2004; Mondrian in the USA, Parkstone, 2002; Chapter in Dorothy Gillespie, Radford Univ, 98; Journal Articles: 11 from 76-84; Reviews: 31 from 68-2005; Popular Press: 11 from 56-83. *Mem:* Col Art Asn; Southeastern Col Art Asn (bd dir, 74-76, 88-91, pres, 77-78, chmn ann meeting, 78 & 86). *Media:* Drawing, Photography. *Res:* Mondrian's life, work and influence in America; Bolotowsky, Von Wiegand, Baber & Gillespie; modernism & post-modernism in art and architecture. *Interests:* Photog, painting, drawing, traveling. *Collection:* The N Carolina Mus of Art; The Univ of Alabama at Birmingham; The Univ of Alabama, Tuscalousa; The Altamont School. *Publ:* Column, Birmingham News, 66-73; contribr, Mass Col Art Alumni Bulletin, 58 & Southeastern Col Art Asn Rev, 68-78; Arts Mag, 76-83; Woman's Art Journal, 82-2004 (18 reviews one article). *Mailing Add:* 1831 28th Ave S Apt 420 Birmingham AL 35209-2613

REMINGTON, DEBORAH WILLIAMS
PAINTER
b Haddonfield, NJ, Jun 25, 35. *Study:* San Francisco Art Inst, BFA, 55; studies in Asia, 57-59. *Work:* Whitney Mus Am Art, NY; Mus Boymans von Beuningen, Rotterdam, Holland; Centre d'Art et de Cult George Pompidou, Paris; Nat Mus Am Art; Art Inst Chicago. *Comn:* Cleveland Print Club, 90. *Exhib:* One-person shows, Bykert Gallery, NY, 67, 69, 72 & 74, Galerie Darthea Speyer, Paris, 68, 71, 73 & 92, Hamilton Gallery, NY, 77, Jack Shainman Gallery, NY, 87, Shoshana Wayne Gallery, Los Angeles, Calif, 88, Mitchell Algus Gallery, New York City; 71st Am Exhib, Art Inst Chicago, 74; Painting Endures, Inst Contemp Art, Boston, 75; 20 Yr Retrospective (with catalog), Newport Harbor Art Mus, Calif, 83; 20 Yr Retrospective, Oakland Mus Art, Calif, 84; The Stamp of Impulse, Worcester Art Mus, Mass, 2001-04; Nora Eccles Harrison Mus of Art, Logan, Utah, In the Spirit of the Times, (exhib catalog) 2003-04. *Teaching:* Cooper Union, New York, 73-96; New York Univ, 94-99; Nat Acad Design, NYC, 2003. *Awards:* Guggenheim Fel, 84; Pollock-Krasner Found grant, 99; B Altman Prize for Painting, 178 Annual Exhib, Nat Acad, NY, 2003. *Bibliog:* R C Kenedy (auth), Deborah Remington, Art Int, summer 74; Donald B Kuspit (auth), Deborah Remington: Autonomy and absences in the visual koan, Art Int, summer, 79. *Mem:* Nat Acad Design, NY (acad, 99); Benjamin Altman prize for painting 178th Ann, Exhib 2003. *Media:* Oil, Drawing. *Specialty:* Fine Art. *Dealer:* Galerie Darthea Speyer 6 Rue Jacques Callot Paris 75006. *Mailing Add:* Nat Acad Design 5 E 89th St New York NY 10128

REMSEN, JOHN
PAINTER, CONSULTANT
b Glen Cove, NY, Apr 21, 39. *Study:* Pratt Inst, BFA; NY Univ, MA(art educ). *Exhib:* Postcards From Our Friends, A.I.R. Gallery, NYC, 2003; Alpan Gallery, Huntington, NY, 2003 & 2005 & 2006; Abstraction at 40, Gallery North, Setauket, NY, 2005; Of Nature and the Hand (curator & exhib), Port Jefferson Village Ctr, NY, 2006; Re/Opening, Alpan Gallery, Huntington, NY, 2002; One-man show, Canios Bookshop, Sag Harbor, NY, 1992, New Works on Paper, Nesé Alpan Gal, Roslyn, NY, 1992, horse show paintings, Prism Gallery, Port Jefferson, NY, 1999, Abstract Landscapes, West Beth Gal, NYC, 2001 & paintings from 1980-2001, Gallery Rood, Eastport, NY, 2001. *Pos:* Mgr & dir contemp art gal, NYC, Calif & Long Island, NY; independent cur & reviewer of fine arts for various publ; critic, Sunstorm & Times Beacon newspapers, NYC. *Teaching:* Instr, high schools, Long Island, NY. *Media:* Acrylic, Wood Construction. *Specialty:* Contemporary painting, assemblage, sculpture & environments. *Dealer:* Alpan Gallery. *Mailing Add:* PO Box 2803 East Setauket NY 11733-0860

REMSING, JOSEPH GARY
PAINTER, SCULPTOR
b Spokane, Wash, Sept 18, 46. *Study:* San Jose State Univ, BA & MA. *Work:* De Saisset Mus, Univ Santa Clara; Oakland Mus. *Comn:* Maj sculptural comn, State of Calif, 78. *Exhib:* One man exhibs, Willima Sawyer Gallery, San Francisco, 71, 73, & 74; Int Sculpture Competition, State of NJ, traveling, 79-80; Djurovich Gallery, Sacramento, Calif, 85; Palo Alto Cult Ctr, 85; Chuck Levitan Gallery, NY, 86; Lighting Collaberative, NY, 87; Modesto Col Calif, 89 & 94; and others. *Teaching:* Instr, Modesto Jr Col, 71-. *Awards:* Award, Maryville Col, Tenn, 70; Award, Calif Arts Comn, 70. *Bibliog:* Articles in San Francisco Chronicle, 9/8/69 & 5/7/71, Artforum, 11/69 & Art Wk, 5/71, 4/72 & 6/74; and others. *Mailing Add:* Modesto Jr College Art 124 435 College Ave Modesto CA 95350

RENDELL, JOHNATHON
APPRAISER
Mailing Add: Christie's 20 Rockefeller Plz New York NY 10020

RENDL, M(ILDRED) MARCUS
PAINTER, WRITER
b New York, NY, May 30, 28. *Study:* NY Univ, BS, 48, MBA, 50; Radcliffe-Harvard, PhD, 54. *Hon Degrees:* Dean Brown Cronkite Fel, Radcliffe Col, 50-51; Anne Radcliffe Fel, SubSahara Africa, 58-59. *Comn:* Cover for ann meeting, Allied Social Sci Asn, 94. *Exhib:* Art of the Northeast, Silvermine Guild Ctr Arts, New Canaan, 86; Phoenix Gallery, NY, 89; Lever House Gallery, NY, 90; Cork Gallery, NY, 90; Greater Hartford Archit Conservancy, Conn, 91; Barnum Festival Art Exhib, Discovery Mus, Bridgeport, Conn, 95 & 96; Ward Nasse, 99, 2000-; fine art Liliana Gallery, Lenox, Mass, 2001-2003; Nat Asn Women Artists, 115 yr Anniversary Show, World Trade Ctr, NY, 2004; Pen & Brush Non-Member Show, NY, 2004; Nat Asn Women Artists, New York City, 2005; Catherine Lorilland Wolfe Art Asoc, 2006. *Pos:* Art econ consult. *Awards:* Faber Birren Color Award; Metrop New York City Award. *Mem:* Women's Caucus Arts, Miami, San Antonio; Artists Equity Asn; Southwest Soc Economists; Western Economics Asn; Women Arts Found, NY; Nat Asn Women Artists New York City; Allied Artists of Am Inc, Asn Artist; Catherine Lorilland Wolfe Art Asoc, New York City. *Media:* Oil, Acrylic; Ink. *Res:* Economics of art; complex art appraisals and pricing art; art as investment or money substitute; art as consumer durable good and valuation. *Interests:* Organizer Rendl Fund for Slavic Art at Mus of Mod Art, NY, Harvard Univ Art Mus, Busch Reisinger Mus, 99-, Cambridge, Mass, and The Rendl Fund for Conservation of Slavic Artifacts at Peabody Mus Archeology and Ethnology, Cambridge, Mass, Rendl Fund, Harvard Mus Natural History, 2000. *Collection:* Rendl Fund for Czec Art; Metrop Mus, New York City, 2006. *Publ:* Auth, Economics of the fine arts: Fad, fashion and value, Eastern Community Col Asn, 84; Pricing contemporary art & Economic issues in the arts, Women Arts Found, 86-90; When Is a Price of Fine Art, The Price ?, Am Soc Bus & Behav Sci, 96 & Price Distortion (Fine Art) Caused by Source of Purchase, 96. *Dealer:* Art Commun Int On-Line Gallery 210 W Rittenhouse Sq Philadelphia PA; Liliana Fine Arts Gallery Lenox MA; Ward-Nasse Gallery, New York, NY; Chelsea Ward-Nasse Gallery, New York, NY. *Mailing Add:* Art Complex PO Box 814 New Canaan CT 06840

RENEE, LISABETH
SCULPTOR, ASSEMBLAGE ARTIST
b Brooklyn, NY, July 28, 52. *Study:* Univ Puget Sound, Tacoma, Wash, 72-73; State Univ NY, Buffalo, BA, 77; Art Students League, New York, studied drawing with Marshall Glasier & Anthony Palumbo, sculpture with Jose Decreeft & Sidney Simon, painting with Knox Martin & Theodoros Stamos, 78-80; New Sch Social Res, New

York, with Dorothy Gillespie & Alice Baber, 79; Long Island Univ, MFA, 82; Rollins Col, Winter Park, Fla, teaching cert, 84; Univ Cent Fla, Orlando, EdD, 96. *Comn:* Mural (8ft X 11ft), State Univ NY, Buffalo, 76; Peaches on the Roof (mural), comn by Dr Michael Reeves, Montgomery, Ala, 84; Jet (floor installation), McCoy Elementary Sch, Orlando, Fla, 85. *Exhib:* Solo exhibs, The Painted Box, Ctr Arts, Vero Beach, Fla, 86 & Harris, Atlantic Ctr Arts, New Smyrna Beach, Fla, 92; Creatures of Creativity Invitational Exhib, Seminole Community Col, Sanford, Fla, 93; Underwraps Invitational Exhib, Harris House, Atlanta Ctr Arts, New Smyrna Beach, Fla, 93, 94 & 95; Nat Art Educ Asn Exhib, Baltimore, Md, 94; Traditions, Translations & Transformations Invitational, Orlando, Fla, 96; and others. *Pos:* Dir, Southern Artists' Registry, Winter Park, Fla, 84-87; juror, Riverfront Fine Arts Festival, Seminole Community Col, 90 & Ponce Inlet Art Festival, 92; dir, W Campus Art Gallery, Valencia Community Col, Orlando, 96-. *Teaching:* Instr studio art, Long Island Univ, Greenvale, NY, 80-82, Orange Co Pub Schs, Fla, 83-86 & Seminole Co Pub Schs, Fla, 86-94; adj fac drawing, Rollins Col, Winter Park, Fla, 83; adj fac art educ, Univ Cent Fla, 94-95, vis instr & coordr art educ, 95-96; adj fac humanities, Valencia Community Col, 95-96, prof humanities & fine arts, 96-. *Awards:* Ace Scholar, 92 & 96; Kimball Grant, Fla Dept Educ, 95; Invision Grant, Fla Div Blind Servs, 95. *Bibliog:* Art Rev, Tampa Art Today, Channel 8, Tampa, Fla, 10/85; Teacher excels in art fields, Wings, spring 88; Jim Murphy (auth), Contemporary art lost and found, Orlando Sentinel, 11/6/92. *Mem:* Women's Caucus Art; Col Art Asn; Int Sculpture Ctr; Nat Art Educ Asn; Fla Art Educ Asn, (central Fla regional rep). *Media:* Mixed. *Publ:* Ed, Children and the Arts: A Sourcebook of Arts Experiences for School Age Childcare Programs, 90 & Children of the Arts: A Sourcebook of Arts Experiences for Pre-Kindergarten Programs, 90, Fla Dept Educ, Tallahassee; Cooperarive Art, The ARTISTeacher, 91; auth, the Phenomenological significance of aesthetic communion, Univ Cent Fla, Orlando, 96. *Mailing Add:* 20 Cobblestone Way Casselberry FL 32707-5410

RENEE, PAULA
TAPESTRY ARTIST, PAINTER
b Hackensack, NJ. *Study:* Rockland Community Col, Suffern, NY, 70-71; Ramapo State Col, Mahwah, NJ, 73; Fairleigh Dickenson Univ, Teaneck, NJ, 73-77; Art Ctr Northern NJ, Tenafly, 77-80; Thomas A Edison Col, Princeton, NJ, 78; OCCC Sch Art, Demarest, NJ, 78-80; State Univ NY, Empire Col, AS, 90; studied with John McQueen, Albertje Koopman & Hugh Mesibov. *Work:* Nat Inst Design, Ahmedabad, India; The Wood Sch, NY; Sealy Mattress; AT&T; also pvt collection of Mary Tyler Moore; and many others; AT&T Internat Marketing, NY; Bramwell Capital Management, NY; Travelers Insurance, Hartford, Conn; Warner Lamber, Morris Plains, NJ; The Wood School, NY; Worthington Hotel, Ft Worth, Tex; many others. *Comn:* Tapestry, Sheraton Hotel, Chicago, Ill, 88; handwoven Moroccan bldgs, Stouffers' Resort, Indian Wells, Calif, 89; Our Lady of Peace Mausoleum at St Nicholas Cemetery, Lodi, NJ, 91; tapestry (with Sidney Simon), W Point Jewish Chapel, US Army Military Acad; GE Capital, Stamford, Conn; Tobu Hotel, Kinshicho, Japan, Presidential Suite and 17 lobbies; Ramada Inn, Albuquerque, NMex; Biomatrix, Ridgefield, NJ; A T Clayton, Greenwich, Conn; Tetko Corp, Briarcliff Manor, NY; University Club, Durham, NC; Town Club, Corpus Christi, Tex; collection of Mary Tyler Moore; Nat Inst of Design, Ahmedabad, India; Olin Corp, Stamford, Conn; others. *Exhib:* Hudson River Mus Westchester, Yonkers, NY; New London Art Soc Gallery, Conn; L'Atelier Gallery, Piermont, NY; Images Gallery, Briarcliff Manor, NY; Bergen Mus Arts & Sci, Paramus, NJ; Silo Gallery, New Milford, Conn; Reece Galleries, NY; Rawls Mus Art, Courtland, VA, 2000-01; al Arts, Farmville, VA, 2000-01; Picture This Gallery, Westport, Conn, 2000-01; ENMU-R, Roswell, NM, 2002; Amm Crafts Gallery, Cleveland, Ohio, 2002; Wooster Art Ctr, Danbury, Conn, 98; New Canaan Soc for Arts, Nw Canaan, Conn, Ann Photog Show 2006 & Spectrum, ann juried art show, 2006, Rockwell Gallery, Wilton Conn, Solo Exhib 2006, Merging Elements; others. *Pos:* Artist-in-residence, Bergen Community Col, Paramus, NJ, Studio/Gallery-Hackensack, NJ, 78-79. *Teaching:* OCC Sch Art, Demarest, NJ, 85. *Awards:* 9th Place, Int Art Competition, Harrison, NY, 85; David Blick Award, SCAN, 2000; 1st Place, Richter Art Ctr, Danbury, Conn, 2001, 02, 04, 2nd Place 03; 2nd Place, Art Soc Old Greenwich, 2004; New Canaan Soc for Arts, 2nd Place 2006; numerous others. *Bibliog:* June Avignon (auth), Colorful masks can't disguise her whimsical art, North Jersey Suburbanite, 2/1/84; Edith Sobel (auth), Artist fabricates symbolic tapestry, Fed News, 8/85. *Mem:* Soc Creative Arts Newtown Conn; Ridgefield Guild Artists; Candlewood Camera Club; Westport Arts Ctr; Wilton Arts Coun. *Media:* Gouache, Oil; Loom-woven Fiber, tapestry, dimensional paper, photographyconstructions. *Publ:* Illusr, Photo Cover, Shuttle Spindle & Dyepot Mag (Handweavers Guild of Am), 81, 86; auth, Shuttle, Spindle & Dyepot (mag, cover), Handweavers Guild Am, Bloomfield, Conn, 86; photograph and article, Fiberarts, Asheville, NC, 11/86 & 12/86, 9-10, 98; Creative thought, Religious Sci Int, Spokane, Wash, 5/90; mag cover, Sci of Mind Mag, Church Relig Sci, Los Angeles, Calif, 7/90, 4/91 & 10/92; Westport Mag, 10/02; Savvy Living mag, 11-12, 2000; Connecticut Mag, 6/00; auth, Pages of Revelations, Artbuilders Inc Collection Metropolitan Mus Art and Newark Libr. *Dealer:* Fenn Gallery Woodbury Conn; PS Gallery Litchfield Conn; Barn Gallery New Fairfield CT; Bethel Art Junction Bethel CT; Fiberworks Nyack NY; Picture This Westport CT; Hartford Framing East Hartford CT; Walker Kornbluth Gallery Fairlawn NJ; Jewel Spiegel Gallery Englewood NJ; Galleria D'Arte Ridgefield Conn; Brookfield Craft Ctr Brookfield Conn. *Mailing Add:* Birchwood 27 Crow's Nest Ln - 16D Danbury CT 06810

RENFRO, CHARLES
ARCHITECT, EDUCATOR
Comn: works incl, Blur Bldg (Progressive Archit Design award), media pavillion for Swiss EXPO 2002, designed viewing platform for Ground Zero, NY City, Brasserie Restaurant, NY (James Beard Found award for Best New Restaurant Design), Slither, Gifu, Japan, The American Lawn: Surface of Everyday Life, Canadian Centre for Archit, Montreal, 98, (permanent collections) Travelogues, Int Arrivals Terminal 4, JFK Airport, NY, (installation); The Desiring Eye: Reviewing the Slow House, Gallery MA, Tokyo, 92, Master/Slave, Fondation Cartier, Paris, InterClone Hotel, Ataturk Airport for Istanbul Biennial, 97. *Pos:* Collabr, Diller & Scofidio, 97—, partner, now Diller Scofidio & Renfro, currently. *Teaching:* adj asst prof, archit Columbia Univ Sch Archit, currently. *Publ:* dance collaborations, with the Lyon Ballet Opera of France and Charlerol/Danses of Belgium (touring exhib) EJM1: Man Walking at Ordinary Speed and EJM2: Inertia, 98, (web project) Refresh, Dia Art Found, (video installation) Pageant, Johannesburg Biennial & Rotterdam Film Festival, 97, (permanent installation) X,Y, Kobe, Japan, 97, (multi-media work for stage in collaboration with Builders Association) Jet Lag, 98 (Obie award for Creative Achievement), (pub. art commission, permanent video marques) Jump Cuts, United Artists Cineplex, San Jose, Calif, (collaborative dance work with Charlerol/Danses) Moving Target, (collaborative theater work with Dumb Type and Hotel Pro Forma) Business Class, Copenhagen Cultural Capital, (interactive video installation) Indigestion, Barbican Art Gallery, London, Walter Phillips Gallery, Banff, Canada, Biennial Nagoya, Japan, 97, (electronic project) Subtopia, Interstate Commerce Commission Gallery, Tokyo, 97. *Mailing Add:* Diller Scofidio & Renfro 36 Cooper Sq New York NY 10003

RENK, MERRY
GOLDSMITH, PAINTER
b Trenton, NJ, July 8, 21. *Study:* Sch Indust Arts, Trenton, NJ; Inst Design, Chicago. *Work:* Boston Mus Art; San Francisco Art Comn & Calif Craft Mus, San Francisco; Am Craft Mus, NY; Oakland Mus Art, Calif; Smithsonian Inst; Renwick Gallery; Private Collections. *Comn:* Wedding crown, comn by Johnson Wax, Objects, USA; copper sculpture, Contra Costa Jr Col Dist, Martinez, Calif; iron sculpture, Walnut Creek Pub Libr, Calif. *Exhib:* Messengers of Modernism, traveling through Quebec, US, Europe; one-woman shows, De Young Mem Mus, San Francisco, 71 & Mus Hist & Technol, Smithsonian Inst, 71-72; retrospective, Calif Craft Mus, San Francisco, 81; Le Trou Gallery, San Francisco, Watercolors, 86, 88 & 90; Depot Gallery, Mill Valley, Calif, 94. *Pos:* Self employed Goldsmith, until 83; Watercolor printer, 83-2005. *Teaching:* Instr enamel for jewelry, Haystack Mt Sch Crafts, Deer Isle, Maine; instr design, Univ Calif, Berkeley. *Awards:* Craftsman Grant, Nat Endowment Arts, 74; San Francisco Comn Awards Hon, 86-; Fel, Am Craft Coun, 94. *Bibliog:* Toni Greenbaum (auth), Messengers of Modernism; A Fried (auth), article, San Francisco Examiner, 3/71; Joan Watkins (auth), article, AM Crafts Mag, 4/81; and others; Opullen and Organic The Jewelry of Merry Renk, JP Watkins, April / May 81, American Craft Mag; Women Designers in the USA-1900-2000-Toni Greenbaum; Modernish Jewelry, 1930-1960, Marbeth Schon-2004. *Mem:* Metal Arts Guild Life (pres, 53); distinguished mem Soc NAm Goldsmiths. *Media:* Watercolor. *Specialty:* Contemp Art Crafts. *Interests:* painting, memories of peak or special life copying them for inclusion in binders events for my grandchildren. *Publ:* Auth, Design Autobiography, Goldsmith J, Summer, 80. *Dealer:* Mobilia 358 Huron Ave Cambridge MA 02138. *Mailing Add:* 17 Saturn St San Francisco CA 94114-1420

RENNER, ERIC
PAINTER, PHOTOGRAPHER
b Philadelphia, Pa, Nov 6, 41. *Study:* Univ Cincinnati, BS, 1964; Cranbrook Acad Art, MFA, 1968. *Work:* Mus Mod Art, NY; Nat Gallery Can, Ottawa; Mus Mod Art, Mexico City; Mus Art Sao Paulo, Brazil; Inst Contemp Art, Chicago; Graham Nash Collection; Bibliothèque Nationale, Paris. *Comn:* Photographs, State Ohio, State Off Tower, 74. *Exhib:* Nat Gallery Can, 71, 73 & 75; solo exhib, Mus Mod Art, Mexico City, 1971 & Mus Sao Paulo, Brazil, 1978, numerous others, incl Solo Photo, NY, San Francisco Art Inst, RI Sch Design, Mus Modern Art, Mexico City, Museu de Arte de Sao Paulo, Brazil, Nat Sch Photog, Buenos Aires, Univ NMex, Hollins Col, State Univ NY at Alfred; The Great West, Univ Colo, Denver, 79; The Extended Frame, Visual Studies Workshop, Rochester, NY, 80; Handmade Cameras, Tyler Sch Art, Temple Univ, 82; The Panoramic Image, Univ Southampton, Eng, 82; The Pinhole Image, Va Mus, Richmond, 83; Through a Pinhole Darkly, Fine Arts Mus Long Island, Ctr Contemp Arts Santa Fe, Museo de Arte Contemporaneo Sevilla, Spain, 1988; Centre Photographique d'Ile de France, Paris, Photog Mus Charleroi, Belgium, Saidye Bronfman Center, Montreal, 1989; Optical Alchemy, Rencontyres Int de la Photog d'Arles, France, 1996; The World Through a Pinhole, Michael Fowler Center, Wellington, New Zealand, 1997; Magiae Naturalis, Lonsdale Gallery, Toronto, Images from the Collection Nat Gallery Can, Ottawa, 1999; Sténopé Photog 1985-2000, Mediatheque Jean Levy, Lille, France, 2000; Pin:Whole, Univ Essex, Eng, 2001; Why Pinhole?, Visual Studies Workshop, Rochester, 2001; Dis/Content, Col Santa Fe, 2001. *Pos:* founder, dir, Pinhole Resource, 1984-. *Teaching:* Asst prof design, State Univ NY, Alfred, 1968-71; adj prof photog, Visual Studies Workshop, 1975; teacher, Espanola (NMex) Pub Schs, 1976; adult ed painting tchr, Col Santa Fe, 1976-1978; adj prof art appreciation, Western NMex Univ, 1979; instr photog, Tyler Sch Art, Philadelphia, summer session, 1985-1988; vis prof photog, Hollins Col, Roanoke, Va, 1991; vis artist-in-residence with Nancy Spancer, Hollins Univ, Va, Spring semester, 2002; tchr various workshops and lectrs, various cities, 1975-. *Awards:* Nat Endowment Arts Fel, 1976, 1979; Aaron Siskind Found grant, 1990; Am-Scandinavian Found Grant, 1987; J Paul Getty Trust grant, 1986. *Mem:* Soc Photog Educ. *Publ:* Auth, The Horsefetter, 77, Visual Studies Workshop; Pinhole Photography - Redicovery of a Historic Technique, Focal Press, 95, 2d edit, 99, 3d edit, 2004; Pinhole Jour, 1985-. *Dealer:* Jeffrey Fuller Fine Art 2108 Spruce St Philadelphia PA. *Mailing Add:* Star Rte 15 Box 1355 Hanover NM 88041

RENOUF, EDDA
PAINTER, PRINTMAKER
b Mexico City, Mex, June 17, 43; US citizen. *Study:* Academie Julian, Paris, 63-64; Sch Art, Columbia Univ, MFA, New York, NY, 71; Academie der Bildende Kunste, Munich, 69-70; Columbia Univ, Paris, France, painting fel, 71-72. *Work:* Art Inst Chicago, Ill; Nat Gallery Art, Washington, DC; Metrop Mus Art, Mus Mod Art &

Whitney Mus Am Art, NY; Australian Nat Gallery, Canberra, Australia; Centre Georges Pompidou & Bibliotheque Nationale, Paris; British Mus, London; Collection Lambert, Avignon, France; Corcoran Gallery, Washington, DC; Kunstmuseum, Winterthur, Switz; Mus Contemp Art, Los Angeles; Philadelphia Mus Art, Philadelphia, Pa. *Exhib:* Mus Mod Art, NY, 73, 77, 90 & 98; Whitney Mus Am Art, NY, 78, 79, 85; solo exhibs, Galerie Yvon Lambert, Paris, 1972, 1974. 1975, 1978, 1980, 1984, 1993, Frangoise Lambert Gallery, Milan, 1973, 1975, 1976, 1979, 1983, Daniel Weinberg Galley, San Francisco, 1977, 1979, Blum Helman Gallery, NYC, 1978, 1979, 1982, 1985, 1987, 1989, Elisabeth Kaufman, Basel, Switz, 94 & 96, Galerie Sollertis, Toulouse, France, 94, 96 & 98, Staatliche Kunsthalle Karlruhe, Ger, 97 & Hubert Winter, Vienna, 98, Joseph Helman Gallery, NYC, 2002, Nat Mus Women in the Arts, Washington, DC, 2004, Galerie Arnaud Lefebvre, Paris, 2006; group exhibs, Stedelijk Museum, Amsterdam, Fundamental Painting, 1975, Musée d Art Moderne, Paris, 1975, MoMA, NYC, Extraordinary Women, 1977, Metrop Mus Art, NY, 82 & 87; Lines of Vision: Drawings by Contemp Women (traveling exhib), Hillwood Art Gallery, Long Island Univ Brookville, NY, 89; Contemp Drawing-NY, Univ Calif, Santa Barbara, 78; Biennial Exhib, Whitney Mus of Am Art, 79; Drawing Acquisitions 1981-1985, Whitney Mus Am Art, 85; 20th Century Art, Metrop Mus of Art, NY 87; From Bonnard to Baselitz-Ten Yrs of the Collection 1978-88, Bibliot Nat de Paris, 92; From Minimal to Conceptual Art: Works From the Dorothy & Herbert Vogel Collection, Nat Gallery Art, Washington, DC, 94 & 98; Prints, Galerie Gisele Linder, Basel, Switz, 96 & 2004; Heureux le Visionnare, Centre National de l 'Estampe et de l'Art Imprime, Chatou, France, 97; From Minimal to Conceptual Art: Works from the Dorothy & Herbert Vogel Collection, Tel Aviv Mus Art, 98; La Collection Yvon Lambert, Yokoham Mus Art, Japan, 98; Prints & Drawings, Recent Acquisitions, Corcoran Gallery, Washington, DC, 2000; Paper Assets, Collecting Prints & Drawings, British Mus, 96-2001; La Cult Pour Vivre, De Georges Braque Aurelie Nemours, Centre Georges Pompidou, Paris, 2002; Mattisse to Freud: A Critic's Choice-The Bequest of Alexander Walker, The British Mus, London, 2004; Matisse to Freud, Hayward Gallery, London, 2006. *Teaching:* Vis prof, Ecole Nat Superieure de Beaux Arts, Paris, 95-96. *Awards:* Printmaking Grant, Nat Endowment Arts, 76; Pollock-Krasner Found Inc Grant, 90. *Bibliog:* C Beret, Interview with Edda Renouf, Art Press 1/73; Rolf-Gunter Dienst (auth), Sprache, Sichtbar-Die Marein Edda Renouf in Karlsruhe, Frankfurter Allegmeine Zeitung, 5/97; Thomas Clark (auth), From Dawn to Dusk to Midnight, Contemporary Art, London, 93; and many others; Maiten Bouisset (auth), Edda Renouf, Art Press 216, 9/96. *Media:* Acrylic, Oil; Pastel Chalk, Oil Pastels. *Publ:* Lines, Edizione Flash Art, Milan, 74; Lines and Non-Lines, Lapp Princess Press & Printed Matter Inc, New York, 77; Echoes, Graeme Murray Gallery, Edinburgh, Scotland, 79; Lines of Vision-Drawings by Contemporary Women, Hudson Hills Press, NY, 89; auth, 24 Signes, Editions Galerie Arnaud Lefebvre, 2006. *Dealer:* Arnaud Lefebvre Gallery 30 rue Mazarine 75006 Paris France; Galerie Sollertis 12 rue des Régaus Toulowe 31000 France; New Arts Gallery 513 Maple St Litchfield CT 06759; Kornelia Tamm Fine Arts 1012 Marques Pl #203B Santa Fe NM 87505. *Mailing Add:* 37 Rue Volta Paris 75003 France

RENSCH, ROSLYN
HISTORIAN, COLLECTOR
b Detroit, Mich. *Study:* Northwestern Univ, BM & MM; Univ Ill, MA(art hist); Univ Wis Madison, PhD(art hist), 64. *Pos:* Bd dir, Sheldon Swope Art Gallery, Terre Haute, Ind, 77-82, World Harp Congress, 83-89; harpist spec events, The Cloister, Sea Island, Ga, currently. *Teaching:* Lectr art hist & humanities & chmn div humanities, Nat Col Educ, 62-65; prof art hist & humanities, Ind State Univ, 65-88; lectr art hist & humanities, Elder hostel progs, Ga Southwestern Col & Mercer Univ, Golden Isles, Ga; adj fac Univ N Fla, Jacksonville, 2002-. *Mem:* Col Art Asn Am; Midwest Art Hist Soc; Int Ctr Medieval Art; life mem Art Inst Chicago. *Res:* Pre-Romanesque stone carving in the British Isles; representations of the harp in art monuments; American landscape painting; 18th-20th century harps. *Collection:* Harps (antiques & modern); art representations featuring the harp. *Publ:* Auth, Harp, its History, Technique & Repertoire, Praeger, 69 & Duckworth, 69; Development of the medieval harp: A re-examination of the evidence of the Utrecht Psalter and its progeny, Gesta, Vol 11, No 2; Harp carvings on the Irish crosses, Am Harp J, winter 74; Landscape painting in America to c 1900, Ind State Univ, 75; Harps & Harpists, Duckworth, 89 & Ind Univ Press, 89; Three centuries of harpmaking, Victor Saln Found, 2002. *Mailing Add:* 315 Forest Oaks Saint Simons Island GA 31522-2490

REPLINGER, DOT (DOROTHY THIELE)
WEAVER, DESIGNER
b Chicago, Ill, Jan 30, 24. *Study:* Sch Art Inst Chicago, BA(educ), study with Carolyn Howlett & Else Regensteiner. *Work:* Amerinvesco, Chicago; Caterpillar Int, Peoria, Ill; Haskins & Sells, Stand Oil Bldg, Chicago; State of Ill Bldg, Chicago; Waterfront Place, Seattle, Wash. *Comn:* Ark curtain, Sinai Temple, Champaign, Ill, 76; wall piece, Friends of Champaign Pub Libr, Ill, 78; Citizens Bank, Ind. *Exhib:* Craft Multiples, Renwick Gallery, Smithsonian Inst, Washington, DC, 75; Marietta Crafts Nat, Ohio, 75 & 77; Clay & Fiber--15 Viewpoints, Wustum Mus Fine Arts, Racine, Wis, 78. *Awards:* Craftsmen's Fel, Nat Endowment Arts, 76-77; Creativity Award, Miss River Craft Show, Brooks Mem Art Gallery, Memphis, Tenn, 76; Purchase Award, Mid-States Craft Exhib, Evansville, Ind, 77. *Mem:* Am Crafts Coun (state rep, 70-76); Handweavers Guild Am; Midwest Weavers Cong. *Media:* Fiber. *Mailing Add:* 403 Yankee Ridge Ln Urbana IL 61802

RESEK, KATE FRANCES
PAINTER
b Cleveland, Ohio. *Study:* Univ Wis, Madison, BS(fine arts); Columbia Univ, MFA, 69. *Work:* Aldrich Mus of Contemp Art, Ridgefield, Conn; Neuberger Mus, Purchase, NY; Housatonic Mus, Bridgeport, Conn; Columbia Univ. *Exhib:* One-man shows, Soho 20, NY, 74 & 76, Noyes, Van Cline & Davenport, NY, 77 & Bertha Urdang Gallery, NY, 77; Contemp Reflections 1974-1975, Aldrich Mus of Contemp Art, 75; 40th Ann Show, Butler Inst of am Art, Youngstown, Ohio, Ohio; New Acquisitions, Neuberger Mus, 76; New Acquisitions, Aldrich Mus of Contemp Art, 78; Penthouse Show, Mus Mod Art, 80-81; Adam Gimbel Gallery, NY, 81; and others. *Teaching:* Instr drawing/painting, State Univ NY, Purchase, 75-76, Fairleigh Dickinson Univ, Teaneck, NJ, 78-82, Brooklyn Mus, 83. *Awards:* Silver Hill Award/Painting, & Inez Leon Greenberg Award/Drawing, Silvermine 22nd New Eng Exhib; Yaddo Fel, 78 & 82; NJ State Coun Arts Grant, 83. *Bibliog:* Ellen Lubell (auth), Kate Resek, Arts Mag, 12/76; Holland Cotter (auth), article in NY Arts J, 9/77; Carrie Rickey (auth), Village Voice, 10/82. *Mem:* Women's Caucus of Art; Women in the Arts; Col Art Asn. *Media:* Pastel on Canvas. *Dealer:* Adam Gimbel Gallery 17 E 49th St New York NY. *Mailing Add:* 354 Bowery New York NY 10012-1113

RESIKA, PAUL
PAINTER
b New York, NY, Aug 15, 28. *Study:* With S Wilson, 40-44 & Hans Hofmann, 45-47, New York; also in Venice & Rome, 50-54. *Work:* Sheldon Mem Gallery, Univ Nebr-Lincoln; Univ Wyo, Laramie, Wyo; Whitney Mus, NYC; Hood Mus Dartmouth Hanover, NH; Mills Col, Oakland, Calif; Metropolitan Mus Art, NY. *Exhib:* Peridot Gallery, NY, 64-71; Washburn Gallery, NY, 73; Graham Gallery, NY, 77-84; Century Asn, NY, 82; solo exhibs, Artist's Choice Mus, NY, 85, Crane Kalman Gallery, London with Robert De Niro, 86, Kornbluth Gallery, Fairlawn, NJ, 86, Meredith Long Gallery, Houston, 86, 97, Long Point Gallery, Provincetown, 88, Mead Art Mus, Amherst Col, Mass, 91, Salander, O'Reilly Galleries, NY, 93, 94, 96, 99, 01, Gerald Peters Gallery, Santa Fe, 96, Lizan Tops Gallery, East Hampton, NY, 97, 98, Berta Walker Gallery, Provincetown, Mass, 00, 02, Alpha Gallery, Boston, 98, 02; Hackett-Freedman Gallery, San Francisco, Calif, 97; Air-Light-Color, Provincetown Art Asn & Mus, Mass, 8/97 & Berta Walker Gallery, 98; Lori Bookstein Gallery, NY, 98; Lizan-Tups Gallery, East Hampton, NY, 98; Group Exhibs: Ctr Figurative Paintings, New York City, 00, 01; NY Studio Sch, 02; Contemp Am Art in Embassies Program, Embassy of US of Am, Vienna, 02; and others. *Collection Arranged:* Am Acad Arts and Letters; Ark Art Ctr; Chase Manhattan Bank; Darmouth Col; Indianapolis Mus Art; Metrop Mus Art; Nat Acad Design, NYC; Nat Mus Am Art; Weatherspoon Art Gallery, NC; Mus Mod Art, NY. *Pos:* Artist in residence, Dartmouth Col, 72; chmn masters prog, Parsons Sch Design, NY, 78-90. *Teaching:* Adj prof painting & drawing, Cooper Union, 66-78; instr painting, Art Students' League, 68-69; instr, Skowhegan Sch Painting, 73 & 76; instr, Grad Sch, Univ Pa, 74 & 79. *Awards:* Fel, Guggenheim Mem Found, 84; Purchase Awards, Hassam Fund & Speicher Fund, Am Acad & Inst Arts & Letts, 86, 88 & 91; Benjamin Altman Landscape Prize, Nat Acad Design, 91, Adolph and Clara Obrig Prize, 96, Benjamin Altman Landscape Prize, 97; and others. *Bibliog:* Arturo Vivante (auth), Figures on the Beach, High Head Press, 92; W S DiPiero & Karen Wilkin (auths), Paul Resika Paintings, Salander-O'Reilly Galleries, New York, 93; David Bonetti (auth), Gallery Watch, San Francisco Examiner, 3/24/2000; and many others; Hilton Kramer (auth) NY Observer, NY Times; Vivian Raynor (auth), NY Times. *Mem:* Nat Acad Design (assoc, 76, acad, 78); Century Asn, NY; Am Acad Arts & Lett. *Publ:* Figures on the Beach, 92; Provincetown Pier Paintings, 95; John Russell (auth), NY Times. *Dealer:* Salander-O'Reilly Gallery 20 E 79th St New York NY. *Mailing Add:* 114 E 84th St New York NY 10028

RESNICK, DON
PAINTER
b New York, NY, May 19, 28. *Study:* Hobart Col, BA, 49; Int Acad of Fine Art, Salzburg, Austria, Cert, 57; studied with Oskar Kokoschka, 56-57, Raphael Soyer, Seymour Lipton, 58-59. *Work:* Hood Mus Art, Dartmouth Col, Hanover, NH; JB Speed Mus, Louisville, Ky; Portland Mus Art, Maine; Sheldon Mem Art Gallery, Univ Nebr, Lincoln; Nat Mus Am Art, Washington, DC; Bowdoin Coll Mus Art; Colby Col Mus Art; Williams Col Mus Art; Univ Mich Mus Art; Rose Art Mus, Brandeis Univ; Bates Col Mus Art; Farnsworth Art Mus, Rockland, Maine; others. *Exhib:* Long Island Artists, Nassau Co Mus Fine Art, Roslyn, NY, 89; Figurative Abstraction, Andrea Marquis Fine Arts, Boston, 89; Five over Five, Hobart Col, 94; Long Island Landscape, Firehouse Art Gallery, Nassau Community Col, 96; The Poetry of His Painting (with catalog), Odon Wagner Gallery, Toronto, 96; In Good Company, Heckscher Mus Art, Huntington, NY, 97; Poets and Artists: Collaborations, CW Post Hutchins Gallery, 98; Landscpaes, Wright Gallery, NY, 98; Overview, Hobart Col, Geneva, NY, 99; Odon Wagner Gallery, Toronto, 2000 & 2005; Earth, Sea and Sky (with catalog), Odon Wagner Gallery, 2002; Century Asn Ann, FAN Gallery, Philadelphia; Flanders Gallery, The Minn River Gallery, Damariscotta, Maine; Mint Mus Art, Charlotte, NC, 2003; Kresge Mus Art, Lansing, Mich, 2003; US Embassy, NATO, Brussels, Belgium, 2003; The Round Top Ctr for the Arts, Damariscotta, ME, 2005; Hammer Galleries, Contemp Artists, 2005; The Long Island Mus of Art, The Little Continent of Long Island-Paintings from the Permanent Collection, 2005; Union Col, Mandeville Gallery, 2005; The Century Asn, NY, 2006; Hammer Galleries, NY, 2006; River Gallery, Damariscotta, ME, 2006. *Awards:* First Prize, Long Island Artists, 58; Nominated, Am Acad & Inst of Arts & Lett, 82, 86; Millay Colony Found Arts, 89; Medal of Excellence, Hobart Col, 99. *Bibliog:* Joanna Silver (auth), Artist illuminates Africa, Boston Herald, 2/6/94; Terry Sullivan (auth), From eye to heart to hand, Am Artist, 8/96; Louis Simpson (auth), Donald Resnick Drawings, Grenfell Press, New York, 2000. *Mem:* Artist's Equity; Artists Fel; Century Asn. *Media:* Oil, Watercolor, Etching. *Publ:* illusr, The King My Father's Wreck & There You Are, Louis Simpson (auth), Story Line Press; contribr, The Best of Drawing and Sketching, Rockport Publ; Donald Resnick-Drawings, (by Louis Simpson), Grenfell Press, NY; Francois Villons-The Legacy and The Testament, (transl Louis Simpson), cover design & drawing; The Eye of God, a Life of Oscar Kokoschka, (by Susan Keegan). *Dealer:*

Hammer Galleries, 33 W 57th St., New York, NY 10019; Andrea Marquit Fine Arts 38 Newbury St Boston MA 02116; Odon Wagner Gallery, 196 Davenport Rd Toronto Ont M5R1J2; The River Gallery, Damariscotta, ME; Gakkery North, Setauket, NY. *Mailing Add:* 15 Revere St Rockville Centre NY 11570

RESNICK, MARCIA
PHOTOGRAPHER, CONCEPTUAL ARTIST
b New York, NY, Nov 21, 50. *Study:* NY Univ, 67-69; Cooper Union, BFA, 72; Calif Inst Arts, MFA, 73; Hunter Col, Tchng Cert, 92. *Work:* Metrop Mus Art & Mus Mod Art, NY; Tampa Mus Art, Fla; George Eastman House, Rochester, NY; Mus Fine Arts, Houston; San Francisco Mus; Santa Barbara Mus, Calif; Univ S Calif, Los Angeles. *Exhib:* Photog Unlimited, Fogg Mus, Harvard Univ, 74; Women of Photog, San Francisco Mus & Traveling Show, 75; Punk Art, Washington Proj Arts, 78; Book Art, Art Inst Chicago, 78; Kunst als Photographie 1879-1979, Tiroler Landesmuseum Ferdinandeum, Innsbruck, Austria, 79; Galerie Ricke, Cologne, 81; John Belushi, Univ Dallas, Tex, 87; Gallery Mod Objects, Los Angeles, Calif, 87; Suzan Cooper Gallery, NY, 87, 88 & 93; New Photographs, Old Friends, Oregon Sch Arts & Crafts, Portland, Ore, 89; Photog Collection of Robert Olden, Arles, France, 90; Open Mind: The Sol Lewitt Collection, Wadsworth Athenaeum, Hartford Ct, 91; Beat Art, Washington Sq, NY Univ, 94; The Cool & the Crazy, Earl McGrath Gallery, NY, 96; Half a Dozen Roses, Venice, Calif, 96 & 97; Gershwin Hotel, NY, 98, 99; Luhring-Augustine Gallery, NY, 99; Revelations-Familiar Faces, Greely Square Gallery, NY, 2000; NY City, New Wave Levis Internet Show, 2001; Punk Anthology, 2002; Bande á Part, Galerie du Jour Ágnes B, trav, 2006; plus many others. *Teaching:* Instr photog, Queens Col, Cooper Union, Int Ctr of Photog, Staten Island Col, City Univ NY & La Guardia Community Col, NY, 73-88; Instr photog, Pratt Manhattan, Manhattanville Col. *Awards:* Nat Endowment Arts Photography Grants, 75 & 78; Creative Artists Pub Serv Prog Grant, 77. *Bibliog:* Pop up people, Time-Life Yearbk, 74; Layered eye, Camera 35 Mag, 7/74; Peter Frank (auth), Picture books, Soho Weekly News, 7/17/75; Twelve hot photographers, Rolling Stone Mag, 5/77; Ben Lifson (auth), Growing pains..., Village Voice, 5/1/78; Alex Sweetman (auth), Exposure Mag, 78; Alan Sondheim (auth), Art Papers, 5/6/87; Ken Windkur (auth), Contemporary Photographers, St James Press, 88; Claude Solnicky (auth), Mirror Images, NY Mirror, 2/8/95. *Mem:* Soc Photog Educ. *Publ:* Auth, Landscape; See; & Tahitian Eve, 75; Re-visions; & Landscape-Loftscape, 78; Auth, Landscape, See & Tahitian Eve, 75; Auth Re-visions, Landscape-Loftscape, 78. *Dealer:* Galerie du Jour Agnes B 44 Rue Quincampoix Paris France 75004. *Mailing Add:* 2 Grove St 1F New York NY 10013

RESTIVO, CHARLES L
ADMINISTRATOR
Study: Rutgers Univ, BS, MBA; Steven Inst Tech, MS. *Pos:* pres, DeVry Inst Tech, Dallas; exec vpres & dir, Wade Col; pres, Ill Inst Art-Chgo, 2002-. *Mailing Add:* Ill Inst Art Off of Pres 350 N Orleans St Ste 136 Chicago IL 60654-1593

RETTEGI, STEVEN
PAINTER
b Marosvasarhely, Transylvania, Jan 11, 32; US citizen. *Study:* Private tutoring from Tonie Fricke, 41, Oskar Kokoschka, 52 & Ben Shawn, 54; Minn Sch Art, 53. *Work:* Capitol Building, St Paul, Minn; Duluth Mus Art, Minn; Univ Minn, Minneapolis. *Comn:* Painting, Here's Chicago Assoc; painting, Kon Tiki Country Club, Minneapolis, Minn. *Exhib:* Biannual Exhib, Minn Inst Art, Minneapolis, 63; Operation Democracy, Grenville Baker Club, Locust Valley, NY, 67; Am Artists Prof League, Lever Bldg, NY, 74 & 76; Hudson Valley Art Asn, Cult Ctr, White Plains, NY, 82, 88 & 94; Ann Exhib, Salmagundi Club, NY, 85. *Teaching:* Instr portraits, Minnetonka Ctr Art, Minn, 59-62; instr basic drawing, Minneapolis Sch Art, Minn, 62-63; instr composition, St Paul Sch Art, Minn, 62-63. *Awards:* Best Painting in Show, Am Artists Prof League, 74; Philip Isenburg Award, Salmagundi Club, 85; Isabel Steinschneider Mem Award, Hudson Valley Art Asn, 90 & 94. *Bibliog:* Steven Somody (auth), Life story & illustrations, Hungarian World Review, 76; Charles Movalli (auth), A conversation with Steven Rettegi, Am Artist, 83; Bela Petheo (auth), Kokoschka in Minn, St Johns Univ, 91. *Dealer:* Vern Carver Galleries LaSalle Ave Minneapolis MN. *Mailing Add:* 10 Fairview Ave Bayville NY 11709

REUMAN, SCOTT CAMPBELL
SCULPTOR, WRITER
b Long Branch, NJ, Aug 5, 49. *Study:* Brown Univ & Rhode Island Sch Design, AB & SCB, 72. *Work:* Pub Art Comn, State of Colo, Denver; Ark Mus Art, Little Rock. *Comn:* World Cup Ski Race, Vail Asn, Vail, Colo, 89; Entry Doors & Wall Art, Copper Mountain Resort, Copper Mountain, Colo, 90; Race Event Art, John Denver Ski Classic, Heavenly Valley, Calif, 91; Advertising Art, Absolut Vodka, Denver, Colo, 93; Grand Entry Doors Sculpture, Ed Trumble, Leanin' Tree Mus, Boulder, Colo, 2002. *Awards:* Purchase Award, Toys Designed by Artists, Arkansas Mus Art, 2003. *Media:* Stone, Wood, Metal, Synthetics. *Interests:* kayaking, backpacking, environmental activism. *Publ:* Auth, Health Consequences of the Population Explosion, World Bank Science, 98; auth, Recreation vs Preservation, can they Co-exist?, Boulder Chautauqua, 99. *Mailing Add:* 7425 Magnolia Rd Nederland CO 80466

REUTER, LAUREL J
MUSEUM DIRECTOR, WRITER
b Devils Lake, NDak, Oct 17, 43. *Study:* Univ NDak, MA, 74; interned at Minneapolis Inst Arts. *Collection Arranged:* Frontiers in Fiber (auth, catalog), US Info Agency tour to Asia, 88-90; Light & Shadow: Japanese Artists in Space, 94; Ignacio Iturria (auth, catalog), 96; Will Maclean (auth, catalog), 98. *Pos:* Founder & dir, NDak Mus Art, 70-; vis specialist, Nat Mus Jakarta, 90; vis critic, Univ Hawaii, 92 & Univ Ore, 95; served on numerous panels & as juror for founds & art groups; site vis, mus progs, 92, 94 & 97. *Teaching:* Lectured and conducted workshops at 13 nat mus in Pac Rim countries & China. *Awards:* Mus Internship Fel, Minneapolis Inst Arts, 72; Nat Endowment Arts Mus Prof Fel, 73, 90. *Bibliog:* Articles in New York Times, 11/23/97, Art News, 11/98 & Notable N Dakotans, 98. *Mem:* Am Asn Mus. *Res:* Shields of the American Indian; Contemporary Japanese art; Contemporary art in general. *Publ:* Auth, George Papageorge (catalog), 95; Autobiography (catalog), 96; auth & co-ed, Under the Whelming Tide: The 1997 Flood of the Red River of the North, 97; coauth (with Mildred Constantine), Whole Cloth, Monacelli Press, NY, 97; Will Maclean: From Scotland (catalog), 98. *Mailing Add:* 321 Princeton Grand Forks ND 58202

REVINGTON BURDICK, BETTY
COLLECTOR
Collection: Modern American painting and sculpture exhibited at major museums throughout the United States. *Mailing Add:* 3000 Woodkirk Dr Columbia MO 65203

REVITZKY, DENNIS L
PRINTMAKER, PAINTER
b Titusville, Pa, Apr 28, 47. *Study:* Gannon & Mercyhurst Cols, BA (Art Educ), 1969; Suny Brockport, NY, Grad studies (Fine Arts), 1971-1976. *Work:* Patron Print, Mem Art Gallery, Rochester, NY; Western Ill Univ, Macomb, Ill; Print Archives, Corcoran Gallery of Art, Wash DC; State Univ NY, Brockport, NY; Prudential Securities Inc, Rochester, NY. *Comn:* Edition of Serigraphs (Patron Print), Mem Art Gallery, 1984; Edition of 40 Linocuts, Print Soc of Nelson Atkins Mus of Art, Kans City, Mo, 1990. *Exhib:* Finger Lakes Exhib, Mem Art Gallery, Rochester, NY, 1980-81; Recent Prints & Drawings (solo), Gallery 34, Finger Lakes Community Col, Canandaigua, NY, 1991, 96; Everson Biennial, Everson Mus of Art, Syracuse, NY, 1994; 171st Ann Exhib, Nat Academy of Design, NY, 1996; Nat Print & Drawing Exhib, Bradley Univ, Peorial, Ill, 1998; 2000 Pacific States Biennial Nat Exhib, Univ of HI, Hilo, HI, 2000; 18th Los Angeles Printmaking Soc, Nat Print Exhib, Armory Ctr for the Arts, Pasadena, Calif, 2005; Reflections on the Nature of Things (solo), Ohringer Gallery, R.I.T., Henrietta, NY, 2005. *Teaching:* Instr Visual Arts, Livonia Central School Dist, Livonia, NY, 1970-2002. *Awards:* Roy M. Mason Mem Award (Nat Exhib), Batavia Soc of Artists, 1988; Jurors Award (Juried Spring Show), Erie Art Mus, 1993; Merit Award (Images 2002 Robeson Gallery, Penn State U), Central Pa Festival of Arts, 2002. *Bibliog:* Sherry Chayat (auth), Landscape Show Graces Gallery's New Home, Syracuse Herald Am, 1994; Elizabeth Forbes (auth), Etch A Sketch, Rochester Democrat & Chronicle, 1995; Los Angeles Printmaking Soc 18th Nat Exhib Catalog, Kitty Maryatt, Two Hands Press, CA, 2005. *Mem:* Soc of Am Graphic Artists (1991-); Los Angeles Printmaking Soc (1996-2005); Rochester Contemp (2002-); Boston Printmakers (2005-). *Media:* Serigraphy, Silkscreen, Woodcut, Linocut, Oil & Mixed media on canvas. *Dealer:* Gallery C 3532 Wade Ave Raleigh NC 27607. *Mailing Add:* 131 Monroe St Honeoye Falls NY 14472

REVRI, ANIL
PAINTER, GRAPHIC ARTIST
b New Delhi, India, Jan 8, 56. *Study:* Sir J J Sch Art, BFA(interior design), 76; Corcoran Sch Art, BFA(graphic design), 95. *Work:* Tempra Mus, Malta; DC Commn Arts & Humanities. *Exhib:* Senior Show, Corcoran Mus Art, Washington, DC, 95; Veiled Doorways '96 (coauth, catalog), Am Inst Architects, Washington, DC, 97; Baltimore Print Fair, Baltimore Mus Art, 98; Art Mus Am, Washington, DC, 98; Pyramid Atlantic: A Study in Collaboration, Fed Reserve Bd, Washington, DC, 98; 21st Ann Art on Paper, Md Fedn Art Gallery Circle, Annapolis, 98; Ctr Visual Arts, Int Show, Summit, NJ, 98; Malta Biennale, 99; solo exhib, Cult Crossings, The Milennium World Peace Summit, NY, 2000; F Donald Kenny Mus, St Bonaventure Univ, NY, 2001; Lichtenstein and Beyond; Recent Acquisitions of Modern Prints, Corcoran Gallery of Art, 2001; India; Contemp Art from Northeastern Pvt Collections, Jane Voorhees Zimmerli Mus, Rutgers Univ, NJ, 2002; In Search of Self (Solo) Corcaaoan Gallery of Art 2004. *Collection Arranged:* Ministry Energy, Oberoi Hotels, New Delhi; Air India, Great Eastern Shipping Co & Tata Sons, Ltd, Bombay; The Corcoran Gallery of Art; Library of Congress. *Awards:* Fel, Washington DC Comn Arts & Humanities, Nat Endowment Arts, 98. *Bibliog:* Suneet Chopra (auth), Art equity: opt for Indian images, Financial Express, India 12/22/96; Cornelia Ravenal (auth), Coming in from the cold, Interiors & Lifestyles, India Biannual, 97; Mahoney, J.W. Anil Revri's Inner Order, Washington Review, 2001-2002; Prakash, Uma, Keeping Faith, Asian Art News, March/April, 2001; Shaw-Eagle, Joanna, Print Masters at Corcoran, The Washington Times, 12/08/2001; O'Sullivan, Michael, Anil Revri's Doors of Perception at Corcoran, Washington Post, Weekend, 6/25/2004; McLaughlin, Caitlin, Painter of All Times, Asian Art News, Nov/Dec 2004; Amy, Michael, Anil Revri at the Corcoran, Art in America, Jan, 2005. *Mem:* Am Inst Graphic Arts; Art Dirs Club Metrop Washington DC; Allied Artists Am. *Media:* Oil on Canvas, Mixed media on Handmade paper. *Publ:* Illusr, Femina, 76-77 & Youth Times, 77, Times India; Highlights, Washington Art Assocs, fall 96. *Dealer:* Sundaram Tagore Gallery, NY. *Mailing Add:* 3201 Wisconsin Ave NW No 802 Washington DC 20016

REXROTH, NANCY LOUISE
PHOTOGRAPHER
b Washington, DC, June 27, 46. *Study:* Marietta Col, Ohio, 64-65; Am Univ, BFA, 65-69; Ohio Univ, MFA(photog), 69-71. *Work:* Mus Mod Art, NY; Smithsonian Inst & Libr Cong, Washington, DC; Biblioteque Nat, Paris, France; Ctr Creative Photog, Tucson, Ariz; Houston Mus Fine Arts; Minneapolis Art Mus; Corcoran Gallery Art, Washington DC; Univ Mass, Amherst; Santa Barbara Mus Art, Calif; Univ Ariz; Pecordova Mus Art, Mass. *Exhib:* One-person shows, Corcoran Gallery Art, Washington, DC, 73, Light Gallery, 75, 77 & 80, Grapestake Gallery, San Francisco, 78, Ctr Creative Photog, Tucson, 82, Silver Image Gallery, Columbus, Ohio, 78,

Jefferson Place Gallery, Washington DC, 74, Antioch Col, Noyes Gallery, Yellow Springs, 75, Weinstein Gallery, Minneapolis, 2000 & Steven Wirtz Gallery, San Francisco, 2000; Baltimore Mus Art, Md, 73; Smithsonian Inst, Washington, DC, 73; Halstead 381 Gallery, Birmingham, Mich, 77; Int Ctr Photog, NY, 78; Nat Mus Am Art, Washington, DC, 84. *Teaching:* Instr beginning-advan photog, Antioch Col, Yellow Springs, Ohio, 77-79 & Wright State Univ, 79-82. *Awards:* Nat Endoment for the Arts Award, 72; Ohio Arts Coun Grant, 81; Wright State Grant, 80. *Bibliog:* Janis Crystal Lipzin (dir), Trepanations (film). *Mem:* Soc Photog Educ; Am Asn Univ Women. *Media:* Photography. *Publ:* Auth, IOWA, 76 & The Platintotype 1977, 76, Violet Press; contribr, The Diana and the Nikon, Godine, 79; contribr, The Platinum Print, Graphic Arts Res Ctr-RIT, 80; and others. *Dealer:* Elclusive Light 135 E 74th St New York NY 10021

REYNARD, CAROLYN COLE
PAINTER, INSTRUCTOR
b Wichita, Kans, Aug 6, 34. *Study:* Wichita State Univ, BFA; Ohio Univ, MFA. *Work:* Wichita State Univ; State Univ NY Col Oswego. *Exhib:* Santa Barbara Art Mus, Calif, 60; Artists of Santa Barbara, Faulkner Gallery, Santa Barbara, 60-62; Artists of Central NY, Munson-Williams-Proctor Inst Mus Art, Utica, NY, 64-65 & 67; Barrett House Gallery, 70-; Mid-Hudson Armory Show, 90-91. *Teaching:* Instr art, Ohio Univ, 58-59; asst prof art, State Univ NY, Col Oswego, 63-69; instr art, Wappingers Cent Sch Dist, NY, 69-97, adminr/coordr fine arts dept, 78-79. *Awards:* Artists in Residence, WCSD, 2003-2006. *Mem:* Dutchess Co Art Asn. *Media:* Acrylic. *Publ:* Auth, I can't draw, 71 & Getting it all together, 74, Sch Arts. *Mailing Add:* 110 College Ave Poughkeepsie NY 12603

REYNOLDS, JAMES ELWOOD
PAINTER
b Taft, Calif, Nov 9, 26. *Study:* Kann Inst Art, Beverly Hills, Calif; Sch Allied Arts, Glendale, Calif. *Work:* Phoenix Art Mus, Ariz; Cowboy Hall Fame, Oklahoma City; Mus Southwest, Midland, Tex. *Comn:* Design gold & silver medals Cowboy Artists Am 8th Ann Exhib & future competitions, Cowboy Artists Am & Franklin Mint, 73; painting used by Marlboro for spec Christmas advert, Philip Morris Co, 85; plus many others paintings. *Exhib:* Cowboy Hall Fame, Oklahoma City, 69-73; Ann Cowboy Artists Am Show, Phoenix Art Mus, 73-75; Texas Art Gallery; Settlers West Gallery; O'Briens Gallery; Main Trail Gallery. *Teaching:* Instr, Scottsdale Artist's Sch, 83 & 84. *Awards:* Gold Medal First Prize, Cowboy Hall Fame, 71 & 78; Most Outstanding Western Painter, 74-75; Artist of the Yr, Tucson Festival of Arts, Ariz, 77; plus others. *Mem:* Cowboy Artists Am (secy, 72-73, vpres, 74-75, pres, 75-76); Western Art Asn, Phoenix; Ariz Artists in Action. *Media:* Oil. *Publ:* Contribr, Cowboy in Art, 68; West & Walter Bisom, Univ Ariz, 71; American cowboy in life & legend, Nat Geographic, 72; Renaissance of Western Art, Franklin Mint, 74; Western Painting Today, Watson-Guptill, 75. *Mailing Add:* 9185 E Los Gatos Dr Scottsdale AZ 85255

REYNOLDS, JOCK
CURATOR, EDUCATOR, GALLERY DIRECTOR
Study: Univ Ca, Santa Cruz, BA, 69; Univ Ca, Davis, MFA, 72. *Work:* Rep in permanent collections Smithsonian Nat Mus of Am Art, Corcoran Gallery of Art, Walker Art Ctr, Minneapolis Inst of Arts, Univ Wash Henry Art Gallery. *Pos:* dir, Wash Project of the Arts, Wash, 83-89. *Teaching:* assoc prof, dir, grad prog, Ctr for Experimental and Interdisciplinary Art San Francisco State Univ, 73-83; Henry J Heinz II dir, Yale Univ Art Gallery, New Haven, 98-; adj prof, Yale Univ, 1998. *Awards:* Recipient Fulbright Fel

REYNOLDS, JOHN (JOCK) M
DIRECTOR, WRITER
Study: Harvard Univ, AB, 66, MAT, 67. *Work:* Center Gallery, Bucknell Univ, Lewisburg, Pa; Freedman Gallery, Albright Col, Reading, Pa; Anderson Gallery, Va Commonwealth Univ, Richmond; Washington Project for Arts, Washington, DC. *Collection Arranged:* The First Texas Triennial, 88, Works From a Decade (with catalog), 88, The Border/La Frontera, 89, Everyday Miracles, 90 & Happy Families (with catalog), 90, Contemp Arts Mus, Houston, Tex. *Pos:* Dir, Yale Univ Art Gallery, 98-. *Teaching:* Asst prof art hist, Bucknell Univ, Lewisburg, Pa, 74-77, Albright Col, Reading, Pa, 77-81 & Va Commonwealth Univ, 81-86. *Res:* Contemporary art with sepecial interest in social and political content. *Publ:* Auth & ed, Sue Coe: Police State, 87 & Hunt Slonem: Baroque Beatitudes, 87, Va Commonwealth Univ; Belchite/South Bronx, Univ Mass, 88; Bill Viola: Works From a Decade, 88 & Ida Applebrong: Happy Families, 90, Contemp Art Mus, Houston. *Mailing Add:* c/o Yale Univ Art Gallery PO Box 208271 New Haven CT 06520-8271

REYNOLDS, PATRICIA ELLEN
PAINTER
b Portchester, NY, Apr 6, 34. *Study:* State Univ NY; studied with Mario Cooper, 79, Barbara Necchis, 81 & Jeanne Dobie, 82, Marilyn H Phyllis, 98, Cheng Khee-Chee, 2000. *Work:* Temple Univ; State Vt, Montpelier; IBM Corp, Burlington, Vt; Gen Electric Corp, Schenectady, NY; Int Trade & Commerce, Montreal, Que & Waitsfield, Vt; Shelburne Mus, Vt; plus others; North County Cult Ctr. *Comn:* Acrylic collage mural, Pizzagalli Construction Corp, Burlington, Vt, 79. *Exhib:* Solo exhib, US Nat Tour Univs, 82-84; Mid-West Watercolor Soc, Davenport Art Gallery, Iowa, 83, 89 & 92; Allied Artists Exhib, 87 & 91; State Univ NY Art Mus, 96; Hyde Collection; Cayuga Mus; Remington Mus; Headley-Whitney Mus, 90-91; and many others; 25 Yr Retrospective State Univ NY, 96. *Pos:* Treas, Adirondack Art Asn, 62-65, dir gallery, 66-77; consult, Coun Arts (Essex & Clinton Co). *Teaching:* instr workshops State Univ New York, Clinton Community Col. *Awards:* Award, Am Watercolor Soc, 82 & 87; Award, Midwest Watercolor Soc, 92; Award, State Univ New York Multi-Focus, 92; and others. *Bibliog:* Watercolor Mag, 96; Topia Mag, 97; Art in US Embassies (catalog), 98; Best of Watercolor series Am Artist Watercolor mag. *Mem:* Watercolor Soc, Cent NY, Asn Am & Nat; assoc Allied Artists Am; Omicron Delta Kappa; Transport Watercolor Soc Am (signature mem). *Media:* All Media. *Interests:* Cultivation of orchids indoors for painting subjects impression landscapes in watercolor and oil. *Publ:* Watercolor, Am Artist Mag; Several Best of Watercolor series; 25 tips by the best of MWS, Midwest Watercolor Soc. *Mailing Add:* East Side Studio #828 Point Rd Willsboro NY 12996

REYNOLDS, ROBERT
PAINTER, EDUCATOR
b San Luis Obispo, Calif, Mar 7, 36. *Study:* Art Ctr Col Design, Los Angeles, Calif, BPA; Calif Polytech State Univ, San Luis Obispo, MA; also with Lorser Fettelson, Harry Carmean, Robert Clark, Arne Nybak & Joe Henninger. *Work:* San Luis Obispo Co, Calif; Mus Nat Hist, Morro Bay, Calif; Mus Nat Hist, Santa Barbara, Calif; Calif Polytechnic Univ, San Luis Obispo; over 1200 pvt collections. *Comn:* ltd ed print, Natural Hist Asn Central Coast, Calif, 82; painting & prints, Mozart Festival, San Luis Obispo, Calif, 88; paintings & serigraphs, San Luis Obispo Co Symphony, 88; post card stamp design, US Postal Serv, 88; Ser of Paintings, Bear Valley Lodge, Bear Valley, 96. *Exhib:* solo exhibs, retrospective, Art Ctr, San Luis Obispo, 75, Allan Hancock Col, Santa Maria, 80, Clark Galleries, Bakersfield, 88, Hutchins Gallery, Cambria, 88 & 90, Calif Polytechnic Univ Union Galeria: 89 & 93 Vision Art Gallery, Morro Bay, Calif, 91 & 94, Johnson Art Gallery, San Luis Obispo, Calif, 98, 99, 2000; traveling exhib, Ford Motor Co, Dearborn, Mich, 77-78; Cunningham Art Mus Watercolor Exhib, Bakersfield, Calif, 78; solo exhibs, Harbinger Gallery, Arnold, Calif, 98, 2000 & 2002, Johnson Art Gallery, San Luis Obispo, Calif, 98, 99, 2000-2002 & 2005, Elverhoj Mus Hist & Art, 2004; Featured Artist/Poster, Bear Valley Music Festival, Bear Valley, Calif; Biennale Internazionale Dell'Arte Contemporanea, Florence, Ital, 2003. *Pos:* Pres, Art Asn, San Luis Obispo, Calif, 68-69; mem design & review bd, City of San Luis Obispo, 68-73; mem bd of trustees, San Luis Obispo Art Ctr, 69-78; founding mem, Cent Coast Watercolor Soc, Calif, 77-, pres, 80-81. *Teaching:* Prof art, drawing & painting, Dept Art, Calif Polytech State Univ, 64-, actg dept head, 82-83, chmn, dept art & design, 84-86; art instr drawing & painting, Evening Div, Cuesta Community Col, 72-76, Robert Reynolds Watercolor Workshop, 74-. *Awards:* Bronze Award Winner, Nat Painting Competition, Artist's Mag (Landscape Div), 96; Distinguished Teaching Award, Calif Polytech Univ, 88-89; Calif Poly President's Art Award, Calif Poly Univ, San Luis Obispo, Calif, 93; Gold Award Winner, Calif Discovery Awards Art Competition, 94; Purchase Prize, Ironstone Vineyard's Nat Art Competition, 2000; Selected The Central Coast Wine Classic Commemorative Artist, 99, 2000; Central Coast Wine Classic Commorative Artist, 99, 2000 & 2002. *Bibliog:* Stephen L Smith (auth), The Art of Robert Reynolds, Cent Coast Art Guide, 93; Splash 3, North Light Bks, 94; April Karys (auth), Learning from nature's art, Focus/Telegram-Tribune Newpaper, 3/94; James Hayes (auth), feature article, Robert Reynolds, Central Coast Magazine, CA, 2004; The Art of Robert Reynolds: Quiet Journey, Calif Poly Tech Univ, San Luis Obispo, 2006. *Mem:* San Luis Obispo Art Ctr; San Luis Obispo Arts Coun. *Media:* Multimedia. *Publ:* Watercolor Page, Am Artist, 3/88; Artist's Mag, 90; coauth, Design Secrets, Watercolor Magic Mag, 93; illusr, Painting Nature's Peaceful Places, North Light Bks, 93; How to be a rock star, Artist's Mag, 94; Painting the Figure, Watercolor Mag (Am Artist), 96; Redicovering Reynolds, New Times, 6/1/2000, 98; Painting the Wild Fields, Telegram Tribune Focus, 6/98, San Luis Obispo, 98; cover artist, Splash 9: Best of Watercolor, North Light Books, 2006

REYNOLDS, VALRAE
CURATOR
b San Francisco, Calif, Dec 18, 44. *Study:* Univ Calif, Davis, BA, 66; New York Univ, MA, 68, cert mus training, 69. *Collection Arranged:* Chinese Art from the Newark Museum, China Inst, 80; Tibet, A Lost World (auth, catalog), 81-82 & Japan, The Enduring Heritage, 83, Newark Mus; 16 permanent galleries of Asian Art, Newark Mus, 89; Cooking for the Gods: The Art of Home Ritual in Bengal, 95-96; From the Sacred Realm, Treasures of Tibetan Art (auth, catalog), Newark Mus, 99; Tibet: Mountains and Valleys, Castles and Tents, Paine Webber Art Gallery, New York, 2001; Williams Coll Mus of Art, 2003. *Pos:* Ford Fel arms & armor dept, Metrop Mus Art, New York, fall 68; Ford Fel Islamic ceramics, Asian Art Mus, San Francisco, spring 69; asst cur Oriental collection, Newark Mus, 69-70, cur Oriental collection, 70-. *Teaching:* Instr Tibetan art & civilization, Columbia Univ, 96. *Awards:* Nat Endowment Humanities Grant Film Production, 72-74; Nat Endowment Arts Grant Publ, 82-83, 85-86 & 99; J Paul Getty Grant Publ, 86, 88-91; Nat Endowment Arts Spec Artistic Initiative Grant galleries & progs, 88; Asian Cult Coun grants, travel, 89; Nat Endowment Humanities galleries & progs, 90-91; nat Endowment Arts Grant Exhib, 98-99; Freeman Found Grant progs, 02-03. *Mem:* Comt SAsian Art; Asia Soc; Japan Soc; Tibet Soc. *Res:* Arts of Tibet, India and Himalayas. *Publ:* Auth, Tibet, A Lost World, Ind Univ Press, 79; Chinese Art from the Newark Museum, China Inst, 80; The Newark Museum Tibetan Collection, Vol I, 83 & Vol III, 86; Japan, the enduring heritage, Newark Mus Quart, 83; A Tibetan Buddhist Altar, Newark Mus, 91. *Mailing Add:* Newark Mus 49 Washington St Newark NJ 07101

REYNOLDS, WADE
PAINTER
b Jasper, NY, 29. *Study:* Self-taught. *Work:* Santa Barbara Mus Art, Calif; Cleveland Mus Art, Ohio; Miami Inst Fine Art, Fla; Times-Mirror Corp, Los Angeles; Palm Springs Desert Mus, CA. *Comn:* Official Portrait Gov Deukmejian, State of Calif, 89. *Exhib:* Solo Exhib, Realism, Calif Palace Legion Honor, 67-68 & California Visions, Santa Barbara Mus, Calif, 77; Prints, Miami Inst Art, 79; Retrospective, Pioneer Mus, Stockton, Calif, 82; Selections from Ellen & Jerome Westheimer Collection, Okla Art Ctr, 88; Johnson & Johnson Gallery, San Francisco, Calif, 2003; Arnot Mus, 2004. *Teaching:* Acad Art Col, San Francisco, 96-98; Art Inst Southern Calif, Laguna,

97-2003. *Awards:* Best Show, Madonna Festival, San Luis Obispo, Calif, 77 & Miami Print Biennial, 79. *Bibliog:* Frankenstein (auth), New realists, San Francisco Chronicle, 67; Stowens (auth), Intense realism, Am Artist, 1/81; Pincus (auth), Los Angeles Times, 6/25/82. *Media:* Oil, Acrylic. *Publ:* Auth, Painting Faces and Figures, Carole Katchen/Watson-Guptil, 86

REZAC, RICHARD
CONCEPTUAL ARTIST, SCULPTOR
b Lincoln, Nebr, Feb 17, 52. *Study:* Pacific Northwest Col Art, Portland, Ore, BFA, 74; Md Inst, Col Art, Baltimore, MFA, 82. *Work:* Art Inst Chicago. *Exhib:* Solo exhibs, Susanne Hilberry Gallery, Birmingham, Mich, 87, 89 & 93, Feature, NY, 92, 93 & 95, Cedar Rapids Mus Art, Iowa, 93, Feigen Inc, 94 & 96, Marc Foxx, Santa Monica, 95 & Rena Bransten Gallery, San Francisco, 96; Abstract: Chicago 1996, Klein Gallery, Chicago, 96; Drawing in Chicago Now, Columbia Col Art Gallery, 96; Art in Chicago: 1945-1995 (with catalog), Mus Contemp Art, Chicago, 96; AbFab, Feature, NY, 96. *Pos:* Gallery dir, Pac Northwest Col Art, Portland, Ore, 77-80. *Teaching:* Instr painting & design, Mt Hood Community Col, Creshaw, Ore, 79-80 & Portland State Univ, Ore, 82-83; instr drawing & design, Pac Northwest Col Art, Portland, 82-84; instr drawing & three-dimensional design, Sch Art Inst Chicago, Ill, 85-; vis artist, Univ Chicago, 86, 88 & 90, adj fac, 91; adj assoc prof, Sch Art Inst Chicago, 91-. *Awards:* Visual Artist Fel Grants, Nat Endowment Arts, 76 & 86 & Ore Arts Comn, 83; Prof Grants, Art Matters Inc, New York, 87 & Chicago Artists Abroad, Ill, 88; fel grant, John Simon Guggenheim Mem Found, 89; Louis Tiffany Fel, 93. *Bibliog:* Alan Artner (auth), Rezac's pieces: his sensuous sculpture makes an appeal to touch, Chicago Tribune, 96; Judith Russi Kirshner (auth), Rev, Artforum, 1/97; Michelle Grabner (auth), Rev, Sculpture, 1/97. *Mailing Add:* c/o Mark Foxx Gallery 6150 Wilshire Blvd Los Angeles CA 90048

RHODES, CURTIS A
PAINTER, PRINTMAKER
b Butler, Mo, Nov 5, 39. *Study:* Univ Kans, BFA, 62; Ohio Univ, MFA, 66. *Work:* Univ Kans Spencer Mus Art, Lawrence; Flint Inst Arts, Mich; Grand Rapids Art Mus, Mich; Kalamazoo Art Ctr, Mich; Trisolini Gallery, Ohio Univ. *Comn:* Multi-color lithograph, Oxbox Sch Art, Sagituck, Mich, 73; multi-color photo-etching, Detroit Print Workshop, Mich, 76; five multicolor lithographs, comn by Terry Allen, 81; four multicolor lithographs, comn by new art examiner of artist Ed Paschke, 85; three color lithograph, comn by Dan Leary, 93-94; one-person show, Kalamazo Inst Arts, 98. *Exhib:* Butler Ann, Butler Inst Art, Youngstown, Ohio, 60; And Another, Western Mich Univ, Kalamazoo, 66; Nat Painting & Sculpture Invitational, Flint Inst Art, Mich, 66-67 & 70; Paper as Medium, Smithsonian Invitational & Traveling Exhib, Washington, 79-81; Another View, Nat Invitational Contemp Prints, Fosdick-Nelson Gallery, Alfred Univ, NY, 90. *Collection Arranged:* 3rd Nat Drawing-Prints (auth, catalog), Juried Drawing-Prints, 68; Multiples USA (auth, catalog), Nat Juried Invitational Exhib of Prints, 70; Markings, Major Int Exhib of Prints, 75; Strike/Restrike-The Revitalized Print (with catalog), traveling exhib, 83-86. *Pos:* Visual arts adv, Mich Coun Arts, 75-78. *Teaching:* Prof, Western Mich Univ, Kalamazoo, 66-. *Awards:* Nat Endowment Arts Fel, 74-75; Ford Found Awards, 77-82; Mich Coun Arts Fel, 84-85 & 90-91. *Bibliog:* Kathy Clark (auth), Twinrocker: Collaboration in Custom Papermaking, Fine Print, 77 & Pigments and Dyes in Hand Papermaking, Tamarind Tech Papers, 78. *Media:* Color Lithography, Paint. *Publ:* Mayan Legends/Replies, Limited Ed, Twinrocker Paper Mill, 81. *Dealer:* Thomas Holowitz Gallery Detroit MI. *Mailing Add:* Western Mich Univ Dept Art Kalamazoo MI 49008

RHODES, DAVID
EDUCATOR
Study: Wesleyan Col, BA (philos); Columbia Univ (attended). *Pos:* Pres Sch Visual Arts, New York City, 78-. *Mem:* Comn Higher Educ Middle States Asn Col & Sch, (appointment 2003-04), Regants Adv Council Inst Accreditation, Comn Higher Educ, Asn Proprietary Col (bd trustees 89-, chmn fed affairs comt 89-). *Mailing Add:* Sch Visual Arts Office of the Dean 209 E 23d St New York NY 10010

RHODES, JAMES MELVIN
GLASS BLOWER, SCULPTOR
b Gorman, Tex, Dec 1, 38. *Study:* Univ Wis, Mechanical eng; Univ Hawaii, BA. *Work:* State Found on Cult & the Arts, Hawaii. *Comn:* Glass mural, Steven B Dixon, 83. *Exhib:* Honolulu Acad Arts, Hawaii, 72; two-man shows, The Foundry, Honolulu, Hawaii, 72 & 74, Metes & Bounds, Sausalito, Calif, 74, Hand & Eye, Honolulu, 74, Downtown Gallery, Honolulu, Hawaii, 77 & Sculptore, Hawaii, 80; VAC Hawaii, 87. *Pos:* Chmn, Easter Art Festival, Hawaii, 76; vpres, Big Island Artists Guild, Hawaii, 76. *Teaching:* Instr arts & crafts, Schofield Arts & Crafts, Wahiawa, Hawaii, 70-74; instr off hand glass blowing, The Foundry, Honolulu, Hawaii, 70-74. *Awards:* Am Fac Award, Hawaii Craftsmen Show, 73; Campus Ctr Bd Award, Univ Hawaii Show, Univ Hawaii, 74. *Mem:* Hawaii Concert Soc; E Hawaii Cult Coun. *Media:* Blown glass

RHYNE, CHARLES SYLVANUS
HISTORIAN
b Philadelphia, Pa, Mar 29, 32. *Study:* Wittenberg Col, AB, 54; Univ Chicago, MA, 56, advan study, 56-60; Fulbright fels, Courtauld Inst, Univ London, 62-64. *Work:* Mr & Mrs Paul Mellon; Yale Ctr British Art. *Collection Arranged:* Lee Kelly: Outdoor Pub Sculpture in the Northwest, 10/76, Miriam Schapiro: Anatomy of a Kimono, 4/78 & Francise Grossen: Fiber as Sculpture, 8/78, Reed Col Art Gallery, Expanding the Circle: the Art of Guud San Glans, Robert Davidson, 8/98; and others. *Pos:* Chief reader, Advan Placement Prog, Art Hist of Art Educ Testing Serv, Princeton, NJ, 70-75; bd dir, Portland Ctr for the Visual Arts, 73-80; dir art gallery, Reed Col, 74-80; mem long-range planning comt, Portland Art Mus, 75-77. *Teaching:* Instr art hist & humanities, Reed Col, 60-62, from asst prof to assoc prof art hist, 62-68, prof, 68-; vis teacher art hist, Mus Art Sch, Portland, 74-75; prof emer, 97-. *Awards:* Sr Fel, Ctr Advan Study Visual Arts, Nat Gallery Art; Younger Humanities Fel, Nat Endowment Humanities, 72-73; Resident fel, Yale Ctr for Brit Art, 78; and others. *Mem:* Col Art Asn; sr fel Ctr Adv Study Visual Arts; Soc Archit Historians; Soc of Indust Archaeol; res fel Yale Ctr British Art; Am Inst for Conservation; Int Inst for Conservation. *Res:* History and interpretation of landscape painting: John Constable; images as evidence & digital images; philosophy and practice of conservation (preparing intro text). *Publ:* Auth, Constable Drawings and Watercolors in the Collections of Mr & Mrs Paul Mellon at the Yale Ctr for Brit Art, Part I, Authentic Works, Part II, reattributed works, Master Drawings, Vol XIX, No 2, 4/81, Archit of the Getty Ctr, 97, 2000, Constable's First Two Six-Foot Landscapes, Studies in the History of Art, Nat Gallery Art, Washington, DC, Vol XXIV, 90; John Constable: Toward a Complete Chronology, 90; Computer Images for Research, Teaching and Publication in Art History and Related Disciplines, Comn on Preserv & Access, 96; Expanding the Circle: The Art of Guud San Glans, Robert Davidson, Cooley Mem Art Gallery, Portland, Ore, 98; Changing Approaches to the Conservation of the Totem Poles, Int Inst for Conserv, 2000. *Mailing Add:* Reed Col 3203 SE Woodstock Blvd Portland OR 97202-4336

RICCIO, LOUIS NICHOLAS
PAINTER, CURATOR
b Jersey City, NJ, Oct 19, 31. *Study:* Art Instructions Inc, 1947-1950; Instr with John Grabach, 1955-1957; Newark Sch of Fine Art & Industrial Art, Carmella DeFronzo Art Sch, 1965-1968. *Work:* Noyes Mus, Oceanville, NJ; When Pigs Fly Gallery, Asbury Park, NJ; Ocean Co Col Gallery, Toms River, NJ; Bordentown Gallery-Laurelton Art GAllery, Bordentown, NJ; Audubon Artist-Salmagundi Club, NY; NJ State Show Gallery, Flemington, NJ. *Comn:* Billboard, O'Mealia Outdoor Adv Co, Jersey City, NJ, 1950-1970; House murals, Jersey City, NJ, 1950-2006; portrait, EXPO 67, Montreal, Can, 67; Outside wall murals, Jersey City, NJ, 1970-1987. *Exhib:* 15 Ann statewide Exhib, Jersey City Mus, NJ, 1967; NJ State 1st Place Pen-Ink, Manalapan Munic Libr, Manalapan, NJ, 1993; Audubon Artists Art Soc, Salmagundi Art Club, NY, 2005-2006; NJ State Juried Exhib, Ocean Co Guild, Island Heights, NJ, 2006. *Collection Arranged:* Ocean Co Col NJ Anns, Seniors Exhib, 1998-2006; NJ Open State Juried, Am Artists Pro League, 2006. *Pos:* Billboard pictorial artist, O'Mealia Outdoor Adv Co, Jersey City, NJ, 1950-1973; sign painter, Lou Riccio Sign Co, 1973-2000. *Teaching:* Instr sign painting, Newark Sch of Fine & Indust Art, NJ, 1984-1986; instr art (oil pen-ink drawing), Manasquan High Sch, Leisure Knoll, NJ 1987-2006; instr, Ocean Co Col, NJ, 2000-2006. *Awards:* John Grabach Award, Am Artist Prof League, 1997-2004; Beatrice Jackson Award, Salmagundi Club, Audubon Artists Inc, NY, 2005; Best in Show, Am Artist Prof League, 2006; Pen & Ink Award, Sr Citizens Show, Flemington, NJ; Watercolor Award, Ocean Co Artist Guild, Island Heights, NJ, 2006. *Bibliog:* Susan Weiner (auth), Show Recognizes Talent of Artist, Senior Scoop, 2000; Carolyn Van Houten (auth), seniority/Art, Ocean Co Observer, 2006; Lynne Salisbury (auth), Festival of Art 2006, Community News, 2006. *Mem:* Am Artist Prof League, NJ; Ocean Co Artist Guild, NJ; Manasquan River Group, NJ; Laurelton Art Soc, NJ; Audubon Artists Inc, NYC. *Media:* Oil, Watercolor, Pen & Ink. *Publ:* Auth, Portraits and Still Life in Oils, Manasquan River Group Artists, 2002; contrib, illusr, Coffee House, Carpenter Gothic Press, 2005. *Dealer:* When Pigs Fly Gallery 568 Cookman Ave Asbury Pk NJ 07712. *Mailing Add:* 1501 Jackson St Point Pleasant Beach NJ 08742

RICE, ANTHONY HOPKINS
HISTORIAN, ARTIST
b Angeles Pampanga, Philippine Islands, July 21, 48. *Study:* Va Commonwealth Univ, Richmond, BFA, 70; Univ NC, Chapel Hill, MFA, 72. *Work:* NY Pub Libr; Nat Mus Am Art, Smithsonian Inst, Washington; Victoria & Albert Mus, London, Eng; Nat Mus Am Art, Washington, DC. *Comn:* Indoor environmental sculpture, Sarasota Sq Mall, Sarasota, Fla, 89. *Exhib:* New Sculpture, Washington, Baltimore, Richmond, Corcoran Gallery, Washington, DC, 70; Translucent and Transparent Art, St Petersburg Mus Art, Fla, 71; Renwick Gallery, Smithsonian Inst, Washington, 81; Brooklyn Mus Art, NY, 88; Nat Sculpture '89, Libr Congress, Washington, 89; Gallery Camina Real, Boca Raton, Fla, 90; one-man shows, Mary Ryan Gallery, NY, 89, Kathy Albers Gallery, Memphis, Tenn, 90, 92, 93 & 96, McIntosh Gallery, Atlanta, Ga, 92, 94 & 95 & Miramar Gallery, Sarasota, Fla, 92, 93, 94, 95 & 96. *Teaching:* Coordr art hist prog, Ringling Sch Art & Design, Sarasota, Fla, 85-, fac mem, 85-; actg dean liberal art, 95-96. *Awards:* Visual Arts Fel Award in Painting, Nat Endowment Arts. *Bibliog:* Greg Thielew (auth), article, Art Voices, 3/81. *Mem:* Col Art Asn; Am Asn Univ Prof. *Media:* Modern Art. *Dealer:* Mary Ryan Gallery New York NY. *Mailing Add:* 2319 Roselawn Cir Sarasota FL 34231

RICE, EDWARD
PAINTER
b Augusta, Ga, Feb 24, 53. *Study:* Freeman Schoolcraft, 72-80. *Work:* Gibbes Mus Art, Charleston, SC; Morris Mus Art, Augusta, GA; NationsBank, Charlotte, NC; State SC, Columbia; Springs Industries, NY. *Exhib:* Mint Mus Biennial, Charlotte, NC, 88; SC Arts Commission Fel Retrospective, SC State Mus, Columbia, 90; solo exhib, Tree Paintings, Heath Gallery, Atlanta, 90; SC Expressions, Columbia Mus Art, 92; The Artist as Native, Babcock Galleries, NY, 93; Lure of the Lowcountry, Gibbes Mus Art, Charleston, SC, 94; Vividly Told, Morris Mus Art, Augusta, Ga, 94; and others. *Awards:* Merit Award, Mint Mus Biennial, Charlotte, NC, 88; SC Arts Commission Visual Arts Fel, 88; Nat Endowment for Arts Regional Fel, Southern Arts Fedn, 88. *Bibliog:* Jeffrey Day (auth), Resurrecting the mundane, The State, 3/1/92; Estill Pennington (auth), A Southern Collection, Augusta, 92; Allan Gussow (auth), The Artist as Native: Reinventing Regionalism, San Francisco, 93. *Dealer:* Hodges Taylor Gallery 227 N Tryon St Charlotte NC 28202. *Mailing Add:* 502 Lucerne Ave North Augusta SC 29841

RICE, NANCY NEWMAN See Newman-Rice, Nancy

RICE, NORMAN LEWIS
PAINTER, EDUCATOR
b Aurora, Ill, July 22, 1905. *Study:* Univ Ill, BA, 26; Art Inst Chicago, 26-30. *Pos:* From asst dean to dean, Art Inst Chicago, 30-43; dir, Sch Art, Syracuse Univ, 46-54; dean, Col Fine Arts, Carnegie-Mellon Univ, 54-72, emer dean, 72-. *Teaching:* Instr drawing & design, Art Inst Chicago, 28-43; prof painting, Syracuse Univ, 46-54; prof painting & hist art, Carnegie-Mellon Univ, 54-73; dean, prof emeritus, Col Fine Arts, 73. *Mem:* Fel Nat Asn Schs Art & Design; fel Am Coun Arts in Educ; plus others. *Media:* Paint, Print. *Mailing Add:* 201 E End Ave No 1 Pittsburgh PA 15221-2760

RICE, SHELLEY ENID
CRITIC, HISTORIAN
b Bronx, NY, Aug 20, 50. *Study:* Smith Col, 68-69; State Univ NY, Stony Brook, BA(summa cum laude), 72; Inst Fine Arts, New York Univ, MA, 75; Princeton Univ. *Work:* Parisian Views, 1997; Inverted Oddyseys, 1999. *Exhib:* Deconstruction/Reconstruction, New Mus, NY,1980; The Eye of the Beholder, ICP, 1997; Inverted Oddyseys, Grey Art Gallery, 1999-2000. *Collection Arranged:* Avon Collection of Contemporary Women's Photography, 97. *Pos:* Photog critic, Village Voice, 76-77; columnist, SoHo Weekly News, 78-79; freelance cur & critic, 78-; staff writer, Artforum Mag, 80-82; cur Deconstruction/Reconstruction, The New Mus, 1980. *Teaching:* Assoc Arts Prof, NYU; Grad Faculty, School of Visual Arts, New York, NY. *Awards:* Fulbright Sr Res Grant, France, 88-89 & Fulbright Sr Scholar Teaching Grant, Turkey, 98-99; PEN/Jerard Award for Non-Fiction Essay, 89; Guggenheim Found Fel, 92-93. *Mem:* Nat Writers Union; Col Art Asn; Am Sect Int Asn Art Critics; PEN/Am; Art Table. *Res:* Historical and contemporary photography; contemporary multi-media art. *Publ:* Fields of Vision (exhib catalog), Landmarks, Bard Col, 84; Lartigue: Le Choix du Borheur, Paris, Minister of Culture, France, 92; Parisian Views, MIT Press, 97; Inverted Odysseys, MIT Press, 99; The Book of 101 Books, A Roth (D.A.P.), 2001. *Mailing Add:* 721 Broadway 8th Fl New York NY 10003

RICH, DAVID
PAINTER, EDUCATOR
b Chicago, Ill, Sept 21, 52. *Study:* Philadelphia Col Art, 70-72; Kansas City Art Inst, BFA, 74; Univ Ore, MFA, 76. *Work:* IDS Corp Collection, Piper Jaffray Collection, Northwestern Nat Life Collection & Abbott-Northwestern Collection, Minneapolis, Minn; 3 M Collection, St Paul, Minn. *Comn:* Three murals, City of St Paul, 84; two paintings, Marquette Bank, Minneapolis, 85; four paintings, McCormick Place, Chicago, Ill, 98. *Exhib:* One-man shows, Univ Minn, Nash Gallery, 83, Franz Bader Gallery, Washington, DC, 86, Minn Inst Arts, 87, Satori Fine Art, Chicago, 97, Dolly Fiterman Fine Art, Minneapolis, 85, 92 & 98, First St Gallery, NY, 91, 93, 98, 95 & 2000, Gallery Co, Minneapolis, 2005; group show, 2D on 3D, Minn Inst Arts, 89, Grimaldis Gallery, Baltimore, MD, 2004; Am Still Life, Minn Mus Art, St Paul, 92; ann exhib, Nat Acad Mus, NY, 96; group show, Minn Inst Arts, Minn Mus Art; Frye Mus, Seattle, 2002. *Teaching:* Instr painting & drawing, Minn Mus Art, 77-87; fac, Minn Col Art & Design, 85-, fac sabbatical grant, 2001. *Awards:* Proj Assistance Grant, Minn State Arts Bd, 84, 90, 2005 & Career Opportunity Grant, 90; Puffin Found Artist Fel, NJ, 96, 99, 2004; Minn Col Art & Faculty Grants, 2001, 2003, 2005. *Bibliog:* Nancy Roth (auth), Meetings & Archetypes, Minneapolis Inst Arts, 87; David Nye Brown (auth), David Rich (exhib essay), Dolly Fiterman Fine Arts, 98; Norman Lundin (auth), A Decade of Contemporary American Figure Drawing, 2002. *Mem:* Col Art Asn; Traffic Zone Ctr Visual Art, Minneapolis, Minn. *Media:* Oil. *Publ:* Contribr, Exploring Painting, Davis Publs, 88; Tikkun, Inst Labor & Mental Health, 89; Journal of the American Planning Association, Hunter Col, NY, 90. *Mailing Add:* 436 Smith Ave N Saint Paul MN 55102

RICH, GARRY LORENCE
PAINTER
b Newton Co, Mo, Nov 11, 43. *Study:* Kansas City Art Inst, BFA; New York Univ, MA. *Work:* Whitney Mus Am Art, NY; Aldrich Mus Contemp Art, Ridgefield, Conn; Phoenix Art Mus, Ariz; Nelson Gallery Art, Kansas City, Mo; Miami Art Ctr, Fla. *Exhib:* Whitney Mus Am Art Ann, 71; Highlights of the Season, Aldrich Mus Contemp Art, Ridgefield, 71; one-man shows, Max Hutchinson Gallery, NY, 71-72, 74, 77, 79, 81, 83 & 85, Henri Gallery, Washington, DC, 72 & Gallery A, Sydney, Australia, 72. *Teaching:* Asst prof painting, New York Univ, 65-71, Hofstra Univ, 71-72 & Bard Col, 72. *Awards:* Max Beckman fel, Brooklyn Mus, 66; Nat Coun Arts Award, 67; Nat Endowment Art, 74. *Bibliog:* Domingo (auth), Color abstractionism, 12/70 & Bowling (auth), Color & recent painting, 72, Arts Mag; Ratcliff (auth), Young New York painters, Art News, 70. *Mailing Add:* 167 Crosby St New York NY 10012-2709

RICHARD, JACK
PAINTER, RESTORER
b Akron, Ohio, Mar 7, 22. *Study:* Chicago Prof Sch Art, scholar; Univ Ohio, Athens; Kent Univ; Akron Univ; also with R Brackman, A Bohrod, Y Kunioshi, B Shahn, J Carroll & many others. *Work:* Canton Art Inst, Ohio; Umbaugh Pole Bldg Collection, Ravenna, Ohio; Woodrum Ins Collection, Stow, Ohio; Good Year Tire Co; Firestone Country Club; and many others. *Comn:* President & Mrs Eisenhower, Tupperware Int, Orlando, Fla; murals, Central Christian Church Kettering, Dayton; Valley Savings & Loan, Cuyahoga Falls; mural, First United Church of Christ, Akron; portraits, comn by Bing & Cathrine Crosby, Byron Nelson, Juan Rodrigues, President Gerald Ford, Bob Hope, Dinah Shore, Arnold Palmer, Nancy Lopez, President George Bush & Raymond Firestone. *Exhib:* Retrospective, Ambassador Col, Pasadena, 70; City Ctr Gallery, NY; Fifty Am Artists, Gallerie Int & Salmagundi Club, NY; Butler Inst Am Art Nat, Youngstown, Ohio. *Pos:* Illusr, Stevens-Gross Studios, Chicago. *Teaching:* Instr painting & design & dir, Cuyahoga Valley Art Ctr, Cuyahoga Falls, 53-63; instr, Woman's City Club, Akron, Ohio, 60-; instr painting & design & dir, Almond Tea Galleries, Cuyahoga Falls, 63-; instr, Madison Sch Art, Conn, 81. *Awards:* Purchase Award & Second Award Painting, Canton Art Inst; Best in Show Award, Akron Art Inst, 48; Huntington Hartford Fel, 58; Best in Show Award, ASA, 2001 & 02. *Bibliog:* Six Rotos, Beacon J, Knight Newspapers; M M (auth), Jack Richard Al Lavoro, Il Pungold Verde, Italy, 74. *Mem:* Artists, Ohio; Ohio Arts & Crafts Guild; Tri-Co Art Soc, Ohio; Akron Soc Artists; Cuyahoga Valley Art Ctr. *Media:* Acrylic, Oil. *Interests:* Assisting in training of young artists and rehabilitation use of arts. *Collection:* R Brackman, L Grell, R Skemp, G Eluegren, D Cornwell, Ball, Japanese Prints, A Loomis & 60 others. *Publ:* Illusr, Staley J, Ind, 43-45; The Helm Mag; Ohio Edison Ann Report, 60; Ohio Story, TV prog, Ohio Bell Tel. *Dealer:* Asahi Press. *Mailing Add:* c/o Almond Tea Galleries 2250 Front St Cuyahoga Falls OH 44221

RICHARD, PAUL
CRITIC
b Chicago, Ill, Nov, 22, 39. *Study:* Harvard Col, BA, 61; Univ Pa Grad Sch Fine Arts. *Pos:* Art critic, Washington Post, DC, 67-. *Mailing Add:* 1707 Columbia Rd NW Apt 519 Washington DC 20009

RICHARD, SALOMON E
PATRON
Study: Yale Univ, BA, 64; Columbia Univ, MBA, 67. *Pos:* Pres & managing dir, Spears Beznak Salomon & Farrell, 82-2000; pres, Mecox Ventures, New York City, 2000-; Sr adv, to David Rockefeller, currently; chmn adv bd, Blackstone Alternative Asset Mgt, currently; vchmn, Mus Modern Art, New York City, currently. *Mem:* Coun on Foreign Relations (dir & mem investment comt, currently); Rockefeller Univ (trustee & chmn investment comt, currently); NY Pub Libr, Alfred P Sloan Found (trustee, currently). *Mailing Add:* Mecox Ventures 610 5th Ave New York NY 10020

RICHARDS, BILL
PAINTER
b Grantsville, WVa, July 15, 36. *Study:* Ohio Univ, with Dwight Mutchler, BFA; Ind Univ, with Leon Golub & James McGarrell, MFA; Skowhegan Sch Painting & Sculpture. *Work:* Philadelphia Mus Art; Brooklyn Mus & Guggenheim Mus, NY; NJ State Mus Art, Trenton; Westinghouse Corp, Pittsburgh; and others. *Comn:* Diptych painting & performance, The Travelers Corp, TV Commercial, 86. *Exhib:* Friends Collect 20th Century, Philadelphia Mus Art, 67; Pa Acad Fine Arts Ann, 68; Whitney Mus Am Art Biennial, 75; solo exhibs, Marian Locks Gallery, Philadelphia, 75, Olympia Galleries Ltd, Philadelphia, 76, La Bertesca Gallery, Dusseldorf, 77, Ohio Univ, Athens, 79 & Ricco/Maresca Gallery, NY, 96; 19 Artists--Emergent Americans, Exxon Nat Exhib, Guggenheim Mus, 81; Westinghouse Collection, Loch Haven Art Ctr, Orlando, Fla, 83; NY Painting Today, Three Rivers Arts Festival, Pittsburgh, 83; Pa Acad Fine Arts, 85; Traveling Exhib, US & Canada, Independent Curators, Inc, 85-87; Painting, Beyond the Death of Painting, Kuznetsky Most Exhib Hall, Moscow, USSR, 89. *Pos:* Originator & dir Harlem Horizon Art Studio, Harlem Hosp Ctr, New York, 88-. *Teaching:* Assoc prof, Moore Col Art, 67-81, prof, 81-82. *Bibliog:* Victoria Donohoe (auth), rev in Philadelphia Inquirer, 5/75; Ann Jarmusch (auth), article, Art News 1/77; Peter Frank (auth), article, Art Am, 3/77. *Media:* Acrylic. *Mailing Add:* TRA Art Group 1700 Stutz Dr No 98 Troy MI 48084

RICHARDS, BILL (WILLIAM) A
DRAFTSMAN
b Brooklyn, NY, Sept 19, 44. *Study:* Pratt Inst, BFA, 66; Univ Iowa, MA, 68; Univ NMex, MFA, 70. *Work:* Chase Manhattan Bank, NY; Ill Bell Tel, Chicago; Asheville Art Mus, NC; Nat Mus Art, Washington, DC. *Exhib:* On Paper, Va Mus Fine Arts, 80; The Am Landscape: Recent Developments, Whitney Mus Am Art Fairfield Co Br, Stamford, Conn, 81; Contemp Am Realism Since 1960, Pa Acad Fine Arts, Va Mus Fine Arts, Oakland Mus Art & mus in Europe, 81-83; Nature Transformed, Anderson Gallery, Va Commonwealth Univ, 82; solo exhibs, Hite Art Inst, Univ Louisville, 83 & Moravian Col, Bethleham, Pa, 85; Am Realism, Twentieth Century Drawings and Watercolors, San Francisco Mus Mod Art, 85; Tomasulo Gallery, Union Col, Cranford, NJ, 86; Divergent Styles: Contemp Am Drawing, Univ Gal, Univ Fla, Gainsville, 90. *Teaching:* Asst adj prof drawing, State Univ NY, Purchase, 77-78; instr, Sch Visual Arts, 77-79 & Parsons Sch Design, 85-90. *Awards:* Creative Artists Pub Serv Grant, 75-76; Nat Endowment Arts Fel, 77-78. *Bibliog:* Vivian Raynor (auth), Art: A tranquil show of American landscape, New York Times, 5/15/82; Ronny Cohen (auth), Drawing the meticulous realist way, Drawing, 3-4/82; Antony Nicoli: (auth), Bill Richards, Arts, summer 85. *Mailing Add:* c/o Nancy Hoffman Gallery 429 W Broadway New York NY 10012

RICHARDS, BRUCE MICHAEL
PAINTER, PRINTMAKER
b Dayton, Ohio, Jan 28, 48. *Study:* Univ Calif, Irvine, BA, 70, MFA, 73. *Work:* Los Angeles Co Mus Art; San Francisco Mus Mod Art; Grunwald Ctr Graphic Arts, Los Angeles; La Jolla Mus Contemp Art, Calif; New Port Harbor Art Mus, Calif. *Comn:* Print, Graphic Arts Coun, Los Angeles Co Mus Art, 92. *Exhib:* Southern California Styles of the 60's & 70's, La Jolla Mus Art, 78; one-man show, Laguna Beach Mus, Calif, 81 & 86, Los Angeles Munic Art Gallery, 84; 20th Century Watercolors Yesterday & Today, Long Beach Mus Art, Calif, 88; Individual Realities in the California Art Scene, Se Zon Mus Art, Tokoyo, Japan, 91; End of the Century, Los Angeles Co Mus, 97. *Awards:* Painting Fel, Nat Endowment Arts, 76; 8th Nat Exhib 1st Award, Los Angeles Print Soc, 84; City of Los Angeles Individual Artist Grant, Los Angeles Munic Art Gallery, 97-98. *Bibliog:* Michael Smith (auth), Bruce Richards

- A Selection of Paintings and Watercolors, Baxter Art Gallery, 79; Donald Carrol (auth), Bruce Richards: Recent Images (exhib catalog), Los Angeles Munic Art Gallery, 84; Joan Hugo (auth), Bruce Richards (exhib catalog), Laguna Beach Mus, 86. *Media:* Oil, Watercolor. *Mailing Add:* c/o Hamilton Press Gallery 1317 Abbott Kinney Blvd Venice CA 90291

RICHARDS, DAVID PATRICK
PAINTER, WRITER
b Abington, Pa, Sept 14, 50. *Study:* Kutztown Univ, BS, 73; Lehigh Univ, 78-80; Studied with Michael Kessler, 93. *Work:* Muhlenberg Col, Allentown, Pa; Salisbury Univ, Md. *Exhib:* Allentown Arts Mus Biennial, Pa, 84; Nat Watercolor Soc, Muckenthaler Cult Ctr, Los Angeles, 84; Am Watercolor Soc, Salmagundi Club, NY, 84, 87, 91; Pa Watercolor Soc, Port Hist Mus, Philadelphia, 87; Allied Artists Am, Nat Arts Club, NY, 99. *Pos:* freelance auth, 84-. *Teaching:* spec educ art instr, Vitalistic Therapeutic Ctr, Allentown, Pa, 74-80; gen art workshop facilitator, 80-95; vis artist, Northern Lehigh Sch Dist, Pa, 90-92. *Awards:* Shalin Award, AWS, 84; Muckenthaler Award, Nat Watercolor Soc, 88; Law Award, Allied Artists Am, 99; Gold brush, Audubon artists, 2005. *Bibliog:* Greg Albert (auth), Splash: America's Best Watercolors, North Light Books, 91; Daniel J Lombardo (auth), Arts and Humanities, Libr Jour, 9/1/95; Rachel Wolf (auth), A Variety of Personal Textures, Painting Textures in Watercolor, F & W Publ, 98; Betsy Dillard Stroud (auth), The Artist's Muse, North Light Book, 2006. *Mem:* American Watercolor Soc; Nat Watercolor Soc (Regional rep); Nat Soc Painters Casien & Acrylic (board dirs & publicity chmn 98-2005); Allied Artists Am; Audubon Artists. *Media:* Acrylic, Oil, Watercolor. *Publ:* auth, David P Richards, Am Artist Mag, 84, The Peacefulness of Pointillism, Watercolor Magic, 93, How to Discover Your Personal Painting Style, N Light Books, 95, Becoming a Message Maker, Artists Mag, 96; contribr, Basic Nature Painting, N Light Books, 98; Moving on to move ahead, Watercolor magic, 2006. *Mailing Add:* 1006 Caravan Way Salisbury MD 21804

RICHARDS, EUGENE
PHOTOGRAPHER, LECTURER
b Dorchester, Mass, Apr 25, 44. *Study:* Northeastern Univ, Boston, BA(Eng), 67; Mass Inst Technol, grad level study with Minor White. *Work:* Mus Mod Art, NY; Mus Fine Arts, Boston; Addison Gallery Am Art, Andover, Mass; J B Speed Art Mus, Louisville, Ky; Everson Mus, Syracuse, NY. *Comn:* Art in Public Places, Mass Artists Found, Boston, 78. *Exhib:* We the People, Smithsonian Inst, DC, 75; Photogs, J B Speed Art Mus, Louisville, Ky, 76; Recent Acquisitions, Mus Fine Arts, Boston, 76 & Fourteen New Eng Photogrs, 78; Recent Acquisition Show, Addison Gallery Am Art, Andover, Mass, 77; one-man show, Photogs, Folkwang Mus, Essen, WGer, 79; Mass Art Found Winners, Worcester Art Mus, Mass, 80. *Pos:* Artist-in-residence, Maine Photo Workshop, Rockport, 77-78 & Int Ctr Photog, New York, 78-79; nominee mem, Magnum Photos, New York, 78-. *Teaching:* Instr photog, Art Inst Boston, 74-76 & Union Col, Schenectady, NY, 77. *Awards:* Nat Endowment for Arts grant, photog, 74 & 83; Mass Artists Found, 78 & fel, 79; Guggenheim fel, photog, 80. *Bibliog:* Lou Stettner (auth), A look at forgotten books, Camera 35, 3/78; Vickie Goldberg (auth), Half dirty realities, Am Photogr, 78; Julia Scully (auth), Dorchester days, Mod Photog, 6/79. *Mem:* Photog Resource Ctr. *Publ:* Auth, Few Comforts or Surprises: The Arkansas Delta, Mass Inst Technol, 73; Contribr- Photographer's Choice, Addison House, 76; contribr, Family of Children, 77 & contribr, Family of Women, 78, Ridge Press; auth, Dorchester Days, Many Voices Press, Wollaston, Mass, 78. *Mailing Add:* c/o Many Voices 472 13th St Brooklyn NY 11215-5207

RICHARDS, GLENORA
PAINTER
b New London, Ohio, Feb 18, 09. *Study:* Cleveland Sch Art, with Rolf Stohl. *Work:* Philadelphia Mus Art; Nat Collection Fine Arts, Smithsonian Inst; US Post Off; 2 miniatures, Worcester Art Mus, Mass, 94; 4 miniatures, Yale Mus Am Art, 95. *Comn:* Mr & Mrs Lamont DuPont Coply, 80. *Exhib:* Philadelphia Watercolor Soc Show, 47; Nat Asn Women Artists, Nat Acad, NY, 53-74; Royal Soc Miniature Painters Exhib, London, 58, 95; Smithsonian Mus Traveling Show, 66; Westminster Gallery, London; and others. *Awards:* Best Show, Fla Miniature Int Show, 88; First in Portraiture, Miniature Painters Sculptors & Gravers Soc Washington, 91, 00; First Portraiture, Miniature Art Soc Fla, 92. *Bibliog:* Frederick Whitaker (auth), The art of painting portraits in miniature, Am Artist Mag, 58. *Mem:* Miniature Painters, Sculptors & Gravers Washington; Whiskey Painters Am; Soc Miniature Painters, NJ & Fla. *Media:* Watercolor on Ivory. *Publ:* Auth, Good things come in small packages, North Light, 72; auth, The magic of miniatures, Dynamic Maturity, 76; auth, North Light Collection II, 79. *Mailing Add:* 87 Oak St New Canaan CT 06840

RICHARDS, JEANNE HERRON
PRINTMAKER, PAINTER
b Aurora, Ill. *Study:* Univ Iowa, with Mauricio Lasansky, BFA, 52, MFA, 54; Atelier 17, Fulbright grant, 54-55, with Stanley William Hayter. *Work:* Lessing J Rosenwald Collection, Nat Gallery Art; Prints & Photographs, Libr Cong, Washington, DC; Nat Mus Am Art, Washington, DC; Sheldon Mem Art Galleries, Univ Nebr-Lincoln; British Mus, London, Eng. *Exhib:* NW Printmakers, Seattle Art Mus, 53 & 61; Bay Printmakers, Oakland Mus Art, Calif, 56-59; Boston Printmakers, Boston Mus Fine Arts, 56-57, 59 & 61; Prints From Brooklyn Mus Nat, Am Fedn Arts US Tour, 56; Intaglio Prints USA, US Info Agency Tour S Am, 59; Nat Print & Drawing, Dulin Gallery of Art, Knoxville, Tenn, 68; one-man show, Univ Ill, Champaign, 69; Sheldon Mem Art Galleries, Univ Nebr, Lincoln, 70; 19th Area Exhib, Corcoran Gallery Art, Washington, DC, 74; plus others. *Teaching:* Asst instr drawing, Univ Iowa, 55-56; asst prof prints & drawing, Univ Nebr-Lincoln, 57-63. *Awards:* Purchase Award, Corcoran Gallery Art, 57; Purchase Award, Print Club Albany 13th Nat, 69; SW Printmakers Purchase Prize to Philadelphia Mus of Art in hon of Carl Zigrosser, 76. *Bibliog:* Archives of American Art, Smithsonian, 83. *Media:* Etching

RICHARDS, ROSALYN A
DIRECTOR
b Palo Alto, Calif, Sept 21, 47. *Study:* RI Sch Design, BFA, 69; Yale Univ Sch Art, MFA, 75. *Work:* Chicago Art Inst; Yale Univ Art Gallery; Minneapolis Inst Art; Hood Mus, Dartmouth Col; Grunwald Ctr for Graphic Arts, UCLA. *Exhib:* 6th Ann Mid Yr Exhib, Butler Inst Am Art, Youngstown, Ohio, 00; two-person exhib, Munson Williams Proctor Inst, Sch Art, Utica, NY, 01; Global Matrix Int Print Exhib, Purdue Univ Galleries, W Lafayette, Ind, 02, Wright State Univ, Dayton, Ohio, 02; Three Artists, Dowd Fine Arts Gallery, SUNY, Cortland, NY, 03; Solo Show, Howard Co Ctr for the Arts, Ellicott City, Md, 02. *Teaching:* Asst prof art, Dartmouth Col, Hanover, NH, 76-82; prof art, Bucknell Univ, Lewisburg, Pa, 82-. *Awards:* Purchase Award, Delta Small Prints Exhib, Ark State Univ, 00; Purchase Award, Mid Atlantic New Painting, Mary Washington Col, 97; Ragdale Found Fel, Lake Forest, Ill, 03. *Mem:* Womens Studio Workshop; CAA; SAGA; Print Ctr. *Media:* Prints, Drawings. *Publ:* Diane Lesko, Rosalyn Richards Catalogue, Center Gallery, Bucknell Univ, 90. *Dealer:* Sande Webster, 2081 Locust St, Philadelphia, PA, 19103. *Mailing Add:* 1195 Smoketown Rd Lewisburg PA 17837

RICHARDS, SABRA
PRINTMAKER, PAINTER
b Utica, NY. *Study:* Syracuse Univ BFA(cum laude), 58; Bennington Col & Parsons Sch Design, 83-86. *Work:* Mus Arts & Sci, Daytona Beach, Fla; Mem Art Gallery, Univ Rochester, NY; Syracuse Univ Fine Arts Collection, NY; NY State Fine Arts Collection, Albany; City of Ann Arbor Fine Arts Collection, Mich. *Comn:* Six Works, IBM, Atlanta, Ga, 84; 4 ft x 5 1/2 ft piece, Humana Hosp, Louisville, Ky, 85; 12 pieces, Temple Univ, Philadelphia, 86; 2 pieces, IBM lobby installation, San Francisco, 87; 4 ft X 9 ft piece, Ann Arbor Pub Libr. *Exhib:* Hunterdon Nat Print Show, traveling exhib, 79-83; Nat Asn Painters Acrylic, traveling exhib, 80-82; solo exhibs, Visions of the Sea, Krasl Mus Art, St Joseph, Mich, 85 & State Univ NY, Rockefeller Ctr Art, Fredonia, NY, 86; Six Artists, Rochester Inst Technol, NY, 87; Collages, Neville Sargent Gallery, Chicago, 88; Hand Made Paper, Rubiner Gallery, Detroit, 88. *Teaching:* Instr, painting, St John Fisher Col, Rochester, NY, 78-82; Artist-in-residence, Artpark, Lewiston, NY, 81. *Awards:* Miller Mem Award, Nat Asn Women Artists; 1st Prize painting, Syracuse Univ, 73; 1st Prize graphics, World Orchid Show, Am Orchid Soc, 84. *Bibliog:* Karen Wenger (auth), Not just hand painted, Screen Printing, 85; Sebby Jacobson (auth), Sabra Richards, Rochester Times-Union, 86; Jan Serasky (auth), Sabra Richards, Artist Mag, spring 89. *Mem:* Nat Asn Women Artists; Arena Group (treas, 88, vpres, 90), Rochester, NY; Ohio Designer Craftsmen. *Media:* Collage; Handmade Paper. *Mailing Add:* 1747 W Bloomfield Rd Honeoye Falls NY 14472-9215

RICHARDS, TALLY
DEALER, WRITER
b Clarkston, Ga. *Pos:* Dir, Tally Richards Gallery, Taos, 69-91, Tally Richards Gallery, Palm Desert, 83-85 & 95-. *Mem:* Taos Art Asn; Soc Muse Southwest. *Specialty:* Contemporary art by Southwest artists. *Publ:* Auth, Scholder, Darthmouth: Renewed commitments, Southwest Art Mag, 74; Lary Bell, 75; Indian in Paris, Am Indian Art Mag, 77; Tally 13, collected stories, 80; Three AM, Puerto Del Sol, 82; The Paintings of DH Lawrence, Visions of NM Mag, 88. *Mailing Add:* 203 Ledoux St Taos NM 87571-5943

RICHARDSON, FRANK, JR
MURALIST
b Baltimore, Md, Jan 14, 50. *Study:* Community Col Baltimore, AA; Md Inst Col Art, BFA; Towson State Col; Riverside Art Ctr with Jacob Laurence, Romare Bearden. *Work:* ILE-IFE Mus Afro-American Cult, Philadelphia; ThirdWorld Mus, 111 & Assoc, Baltimore; Merabash Mus, Inc, Willingboro, NJ; Old Slave Mart Mus, Charleston, SC; Nat Ctr Afro-American Artists, Inc, Dorchester, Mass. *Comn:* Mural for film Amazing Grace, 74; mural, Enoch Pratt Free Libr, Baltimore, 74; Black Art (murals), FAN: Baltimore Arts Tower, 74; Amen America, (murals with Berkeley S Thompson), Asn Black Arts/East, Nat Endowment Arts, 75. *Exhib:* First and Second Wide-Regional, Black Art Show, Baltimore; Black Mural Painter, Inst Art Ctr, Lima, Peru, 75; Mural Painter, Univ Pretoria, Repub South Africa, 75. *Collection Arranged:* An Evening With the Links, 74; Awards Extravaganza 74. *Teaching:* Dir graphics, Sinai Druid Camp, Baltimore, 71-72; dir, Mus Prep Sch, 72-; instr printing, Career Opportunities Inc, Baltimore, 71-. *Awards:* Best Black Art Work in Show, Black Cult Endowment, 69; Children's Hour Prog, Md Art Coun, 74; Third World Prep Sch, Nat Endowment Arts, 75. *Bibliog:* Averil Jordan-Kadis (auth), Colorful mural, Baltimore Sun, 67; Priscilla Coger (auth), Mr Richardson's beautiful wall, Baltimore Afro-American, 72; James Kelmartin (auth), Museum unit to expand, News American, 75. *Mem:* Asn Black Arts/East. *Media:* Paint. *Mailing Add:* 3016 Baker St Baltimore MD 21216

RICHARDSON, JEAN
PAINTER, SCULPTOR
b Hollis, Okla, Feb 10, 40. *Study:* Wesleyan Col, Macon, Ga, BFA, 62; Arts Student League, New York, 78. *Work:* Arthur Anderson Cos, St Charles, Ill; State Collection of Okla, Oklahoma City; Fed Reserve Bank of Kansas City; US State Dept, Copenhagen, Denmark; Col Law, Univ Okla. *Comn:* Murals, State Capitol Okla, Okla House of Reps, Oklahoma City, 76; mural, Co Courthouse, Okla Co, Oklahoma City, 92; murals, Sarkey Law Ctr, Oklahoma City Univ, Okla, 94. *Exhib:* West 80 Exhib, Minn Mus Art, Minneapolis, 80; Okla Artist Showcase, Goddard Mus Arts, Ardmore, 81; Arts Place Exhib, Okla Art Mus, Oklahoma City, 91; Am Art in Miniature Ann, Thomas Gilcrease Mus, Tulsa, Okla, 93 & 94; Oklahoma Illustrations, Mabee Gerrer Mus, Shawnee, Okla, 94. *Pos:* Judge design & illus, Okla Book Awards, 95-. *Bibliog:* Joan Carpenter (auth), Plains Myths & Other Tales, John Szoke Graphics, 88 &

Turning Toward Home: The Art of Jean Richardson, 98; Sandy Clarke (auth), Jean Richardson, A certain mystique, Equine Images, summer 90. *Mem:* Nat Women Arts; Okla Visual Artists Coalition. *Media:* Acrylic; Miscellaneous Media. *Publ:* Santa Fean Mag, 84 & 87; Southwest Profile Mag, 85; Art Gallery Mag, 85; Western Art Digest, 86. *Dealer:* John Szoke Edits 591 Broadway 3rd Flr New York NY 10012. *Mailing Add:* 12700 N Council Rd Oklahoma City OK 73142

RICHARDSON, JOHN ADKINS
HISTORIAN, EDUCATOR
b Gillette, Wyo, Oct 24, 29. *Study:* Eastern Wash State Univ, BA, 51; Columbia Univ, New York, MA, 52, EdD, 58. *Teaching:* Asst prof art hist, State Univ NY, 57-58; asst prof art hist, Fresno State Col, Calif, 58-59; prof art hist, Southern Ill Univ, Edwardsville, 59-96, prof emer art hist, 96-. *Mem:* Col Art Asn; Am Soc Aesthetics. *Res:* Art as intellectual-cultural history in late nineteenth and earlier twentieth centuries. *Collection:* Southern Ill Univ, Edwardsville. *Publ:* Auth, Art: The Way It Is, Abrams/Prentice-Hall, 74, rev ed, 80, 86 & 92; The Complete Book of Cartooning, Prentice-Hall, 76; Design: Systems, Elements, Applications, Prentice-Hall, 83; contribr, Cultural Literacy & Arts Education, Univ Ill Press, 91; auth, From Pure Visibility to Virtual Reality in an Age of Estrangement, Praeger, 98; Along a Far Horizon, Bookman, 2005. *Mailing Add:* 11 W Broadway Bangor ME 04401

RICHARDSON, SAM
SCULPTOR, EDUCATOR
b Oakland, Calif, July 19, 34. *Study:* Calif Col Arts & Crafts, BA, 56 & MFA, 60. *Work:* Dallas Mus Fine Art, Tex; Denver Art Mus; M H De Young Mem Mus, San Francisco; Milwaukee Art Ctr; Nat Mus Am Art, Smithsonian Inst, Washington, DC. *Exhib:* Plastic as Plastic, 63 & Creative Casting, 73, Mus Contemp Crafts, NY; New Media, New Methods, Mus Mod Art, NY, 69; Whitney Mus Am Art, 68-69; Stanford Univ, Calif, 72; Vassar Col, 72; Rutgers Univ, 75; Vpres US Home, Artists Pac Coast States, 80; and others. *Teaching:* Instr art, Oakland City Col, 60-61; art dir, Mus Contemp Crafts, New York, 61-63; asst prof art, San Jose State Univ, 63-66, assoc prof art, 67-72, prof art, 72-. *Dealer:* Martha Jackson Gallery 521 W 57th St New York NY 10019; Hansen Fuller Goldeen Gallery 228 Grant Ave San Fransisco CA. *Mailing Add:* Sch Art & Design San Jose State Univ One Washington Sq San Jose CA 95192-0089

RICHARDSON, TREVOR J
GALLERY DIRECTOR, CURATOR
b Nov 7, 50; United Kingdom citizen. *Study:* Univ Mass, Amherst, MFA, 82. *Collection Arranged:* Fantasies, Fables & Fabrications: Photoworks from the 1980's, Herter Gallery, Univ Mass, Amherst, 89; Meg Webster: Sculpture Projects (auth, catalog), Weatherspoon Art Gallery, Univ NC, Greensboro, 89, Ida Applebroog: Selected Paintings: 1982-90 (auth, catalog), 93 & Pink Lady (auth, catalog), 94. *Pos:* Cur exhib, Weatherspoon Art Gallery, Univ NC, Greensboro, 90-95; cur galleries, Manchester Col, St Paul, Minn, 95-97; dir, Herter Gallery, Univ Mass, Amherst, 97-. *Teaching:* Asst prof, Univ Mass, Amherst, 97-. *Awards:* Spec Proj Award, Southeast Mus Asn, 92. *Mem:* Am Asn Mus; Col Art Asn; Mass Soc Prof. *Res:* Contemporary American and European art. *Publ:* Auth, Contemporary American College. 1960-85, Univ Mass, Amherst, 86; Fractions of the Self: The Portrait in Contemporary Photography, Univ NC, Greensboro, 93. *Mailing Add:* Univ Mass 125A Herter Hall Amherst MA 01003

RICHARDSON, W C
PAINTER, EDUCATOR
b San Diego, Calif, May 15, 53. *Study:* Univ NC, Chapel Hill, BFA (studio art, with hons), 75; Wash Univ, St Louis, MFA, 77. *Work:* Hirshhorn Mus & Sculpture Garden, Washington; Ackland Art Ctr, Chapel Hill, NC; Corcoran Gallery of Art, Washington. *Comn:* Reston Town Ctr, Va, 90; Nat Airport Terminal, 94-95. *Exhib:* Md Biennial, Baltimore Mus Art, 80, 83; one-person shows, Osuna Gallery, Washington, 82, 85 & 87, Baumgartner Galleries Inc, Washington, 89, 91, 93, 95 & 98, Univ NC, Chapel Hill, 94 & Baumgartner Gallery, NY, 2000, Fusebox, Washington 02, 03 & 05, Kiang Gallery, Atlanta, 04; Wash Show, Corcoran Gallery Art, Washington, DC, 85; two-person show, Va Mus Fine Arts, Richmond, 86; Washington/Moscow Art Exchange, Tretyakoff State Mus, Russia, 90; Abstract Icons, Roanoke Mus Fine Arts, Va, 92; WPA at the Hemicycle, Corcoran Gallery Art, Washington, DC, 92; The Far Light, Fine Arts Gallery, Millersville Univ, Pa, 94; Art Sites 96, WPA/Corcoran Cent Armature Annex, 96; Fine Arts Ctr, Provincetown, Mass, 96; Remote Sensing, Cheryl Numark Gallery, Washington, DC, 97; Chance and Necessity, Md Art Place, Baltimore, 97; Kiang Gallery, Atlanta, 2000; Broadway Gallery, NY, 05. *Teaching:* Assoc prof painting & drawing, Univ Md, College Park, 78-. *Awards:* First Prize, Md Biennial, Baltimore Mus Art, 83; Artist's Fel, Md State Arts Coun, 81, 87, 98 & 02; First Prize, McLean Proj Arts, Va. *Bibliog:* Ferdinand Protzman (auth), City Focus, Art News, 11/97; JoAnna Shaw-Eagle (auth), WC Richardson, Wash Times, 3/22/98; Ferdinand Protzman (auth), WC Richardson, Wash Post, 4/2/98; Ingrid Perez (auth), WC Richardson, ArtNews, 11/2000; Jonathan Gilmore (auth) WC Richardson, Art in America 5/01; Glen Dixon (auth), Swing Shift, Wash City Paper, 6/03. *Mem:* Wash Proj Arts; Md Art Place; Sch 33 Art Ctr, Baltimore; CAA. *Media:* Oil, Alkyd. *Res:* Contemporary Art. *Specialty:* Contemporary Art. *Interests:* Contemporary Art Theory, mathmatics, physics, music, non-western art. *Collection:* Hirshorn Museum & Sculpture Garden; Corcovan Gallery of Art; Federal Reserve Bank of Richmond; Federal Reserve Bank of Baltimore. *Publ:* Substance and Doubt (catalog essay), Recent Paintings, Proj Space, WPA/Corcoran, Washington, DC, 98; Enter Decatur Blue (catalog essay), DB Sides, The Wardhouse, Wash, 02. *Dealer:* Fusebox 1412 14th St NW Washington DC 2005; Kiang Gallery 1545 Peachtree St NE Atlanta GA. *Mailing Add:* 4309 Sheridan St University Park MD 20782

RICHARDSON, WC
PAINTER
Work: Hirshhorn Twenty-five: Celebrating Modern & Contemp Art, Hirshhorn Mus & Scuplture Garden, 1999; North Terminal, Ronald Reagan Nat Airport. *Exhib:* One-man shows, Loyola Univ, Baltimore, 2004, Fusebox Gallery, Washington DC, 2002, 2003, Baumgartner Gallery, New York City, 2000; Exhib incl, WC Richardson: New Paintings, Klang Gallery, Atlanta, 2004. *Awards:* Individual Artist Award, Maryland State Arts Coun, 2002; Visual Arts Fel, Md State Arts Coun, 81, 87, 98, 2002. *Mailing Add:* Univ of Md 1211 Art/Sociology Bldg College Park MD 20742-1311

RICHENBURG, ROBERT BARTLETT
PAINTER, SCULPTOR
b Boston, Mass, July 14, 17. *Study:* George Washington Univ; Boston Univ; Corcoran Sch Art; Art Students League, With Reginald Marsh & George Grosz, Ozenfant Sch Art; Hans Hofmann Sch Fine Art, NY & Provincetown. *Work:* Mus Modern Art, NY; Whitney Mus Am Art, NY; Philadelphia Mus Art, Philadelphia, PA; Hisrshhorn Mus, Washington, DC; Pasadena Mus Fine Art, Pasadena, Calif. *Exhib:* One-person exhibs, Chrysler Art Mus, Provincetown, Mass, 58, RI Sch Design, Providence, 60, Santa Barbara Mus, Calif, 61, Upstairs Gallery, Ithaca, 76 & 81, Benton Gallery, Southampton, NY, 86-88, Guild Hall Mus, East Hampton, NY, 92, Rose Art Mus, Brandeis Univ, Waltham, Mass, 93, Staller Ctr Arts, SUNY, Stonybrook, NY, 94, Pollock-Krasner House, East Hampton, NY, 94, and many others; group exhibs, Solomon R Guggenheim Mus, 61, Whitney Mus Am Art, 61, 63 & 68, NY; Inter Selection Contemp Painting & Sculpture, Dayton Art Inst, Ohio, 62; Biennial Am Painting, Cocoran Mus Art, Washington, DC, 63; James A Michener Collection, Allentown Art Mus, Pa, 63; Larry Aldrich Mus, Ridgefield, Conn, 64; Emerging Decade, Seattle Art Mus, 65; Hilles Collection of Paintings & Sculpture, Mus Fine Arts, Boston, 66; Kunstverein Wolfsburg, Galerie Für Mod Für Kunst, Golar, Ger, 83; Guild Hall Mus, East Hampton, NY, 83-84, 86 & 2003; Parrish Art Mus, Southampton, NY, 99-2001; Heckscher Mus Art, Recent Additions to Permanent Collection, Huntington, NY, 2002; Rockford Art Mus, Ill, 2004; Westport Arts Ctr, Conn, 2005; Ark Arts Ctr, Little Rock, 2005. *Teaching:* Lectr, Pratt Inst, Cooper Union, 51-64, New York Univ, 60 61, Cornell Univ, 64-67, Hunter Col, 67-70 & Ithaca Col, NY, 70-83. *Bibliog:* Dorothy Seckler (auth), Artists In America: Victims of the cultural boom? 12/63 & Fifty-six painters and sculptors, 8/64, Art in Am; Donald Judd (auth), articles in Arts, 4/62 & 4/63; Dore Ashton (auth), Art USA 1962, 3/62, 2/65, Studio Mag; James A Michener (auth), James A Michener on Richenburg, 11/62, Art Voices; Rose CS Slivka (auth), Robert Richenburg at MB Modern, Art in America, 11/2001; Robert Long (auth), Robert Richenburg: Six Decades of Making Art, a profile, East Hampton Star, 12/5/2002; and many others. *Mem:* Artists Alliance, East Hampton; life mem Art Students League. *Dealer:* David Findlay Jr Fine Art NYC and Thomas McCormick Chicago IL. *Mailing Add:* 1006 Springs Fireplace Rd East Hampton NY 11937

RICHMOND, REBEKAH
PRINTMAKER, PAINTER
b Ashland, Ky. *Study:* Ringling Sch Art; Univ Ky, Lexington; Art Inst Pittsburgh. *Work:* Coos Art Mus, Coos Bay, Ore; Mus Prints & Printmaking, NY; Nat Arts Club, NY. *Comn:* Presentation Print, Print Club Albany, 76-77. *Exhib:* Ann Artists Salon, Okla Mus Fine Art, 75 & 77; solo exhib, Albany Inst Hist & Art, 77; April Salon, Springville Mus Art, Utah, 77, 78, 80 & 82; Colorprint USA, Tex Tech Univ, 80; Audubon Artists Ann, Nat Arts Club, NY, 81; 3rd Brit Int Miniature Exhib, 97; Irish Int Print Exhib, 98. *Awards:* Gold Medal Hon, Acad Artists Asn, Mass, 78 & 79; Anna Hyatt Huntington Bronze Medal, Catharine Lorillard Wolfe Art Club, 79; Hugh D Botts Award, Salmagundi Club, 92. *Mem:* Salmagundi Club; Hudson Valley Art Asn; Soc Am Graphic Artists; Am Artists Prof League; Acad Artists Asn. *Media:* Etching, Oils. *Dealer:* Kerwin Galleries 1107 California Dr Burlingame CA 94010. *Mailing Add:* PO Box 468 Ashland KY 41105-0468

RICHTER, GERHARD
PAINTER
b Dresden, Ger, Feb 9, 32. *Study:* Kunstakademie, Dresden, Ger, 51-56, Dusseldorf, 61-63. *Exhib:* Mobelhaus Berges, Dusseldorf, 1963, Galerie Heiner Friedrich, Munich, 1964, 67, 70, 72, Galerie Rene Block, 1965, 69, 74, White Wide Space Gallery, Antwerp, 1967, Galerie Ricke, Kassel, 1968, Galleria del Naviglio, 1969, Palais des Beaux-Arts, Brussels, 1970, Galerie Konrad Fischer, Dusseldorf, 1970, 72, 75, 83, Mus Folkwang, Essen, 1970, 80, Kunstverein, Dusseldorf, 1971, Galerie Thomas Borgmann, Cologne, 1971, 84, Galerie Rudolph Zwirner, Cologne, 1972, Galerie Seriaal, Amsterdam, 1973, Onnasch Gallery, NY, 1973, Galleria La Bertesca, Milan, 1973, Galerie Rolf Preisig, Basle, 1975, Nova Scotia Col Art, Halifax, 1978, Whitechapel Art Gallery, London, 1979; Ger Art in the 20th Century, Royal Acad Arts, London & Staatsgalerie, Stuttgart, Ger, 85; Mus Nat d'Art Mod, Ctr Georges Pompidou, Paris, France, 87; Singular Objects, Nat Mus Mod Art, Tokyo & Kyoto, Japan, 95; solo exhibs, Wako Works Art, Tokyo, Japan, 97, La Biennale di Venezia 47th, Venice, 97, Anthony d'Offay, London, Eng, 98, Sprengel Mus, Hannover, 98, Kaiser Wilhelm Mus, Krefeld, 98, Stadtische Galerie im Lenbachhaus, Munchen, 98 & Astrup Fearnley Museet, Oslo, 99, Kaiser Wilhelm Mus Krefeld, Ger, 00, Wako Works of Art, Tokyo, 01, 02, Marian Goodman Gallery, NYC, 01, Deutsche Guggenheim, Berlin, 02, Mus Modern Art, 02, City Gallery, Wellington, New Zealand, 02; Antwerpen Open, Belgium, 2000-01, Fundación La Caixa, Madrid, 2000-01; Sun Valley Ctr for the Arts, Ketchum, Idaho, 02, Marian Goodman Gallery, New York City, 02, Kaiser Wilhelm Mus Krefeld, Ger, 02, Dia Ctr for the Arts, New York City, 02-03; exhib in group shows at Whitechapel Art Gallery, London, Stedelijk Mus, Amsterdam, Kunsthalle, Royal Acad London, Los Angeles Co Mus Art; represented in permanent collections Kunstmuseum, Dusseldorf, Neue Gallery, Mus

Folkwang, Nationalgalerie, Berlin, Kunstmuseum, Basle, Guggenheim Mus, NY; auth: Bericht uber eine Demonstr, 1963, Gerhard Richter: Atlas von de fot, 1972, Gerhard Richter: Atlas der Fotos, Collgen und Skizzen, 1976. *Teaching:* Guest prof, HfBK, Hamburg, 67 & Col Art, Halifax, 78; prof, Kunstakademie, Dusseldorf, 71. *Awards:* Junger Western Art Prize, Recklinghausen, 67; Arnold Bode Prize, Kassel, 81; Oskar Kokoschka Prize, Vienna, 85; Praemium Imperiale Award, Japan Art Asn, 97; Wexner Prize, Wexner Ctr for the Arts, 98. *Bibliog:* Peter Schjedahl (auth), Images count, Village Voice, 5/23/95; Roberta Smith (auth), A German master takes an epic journey, NY Times, 6/4/95; Benjamin H D Buchloh (auth), Divided memory and post-traditional identity: Gerhard Richter's work of mourning, October, winter 96. *Mem:* Am Acad Arts and Sci (hon foreign). *Mailing Add:* c/o Marian Goodman Gallery 24 West 57th St New York NY 10019

RICHTER, HANK
PAINTER, SCULPTOR

b Cleveland, Ohio, Oct 10, 28. *Study:* Philadelphia Mus Sch of Art. *Work:* DeGrazia-Gonzales Cult Ctr & Mus, Casa Grande, Ariz; Valley Nat Bank Collection, Phoenix; First Nat Bank Collection, Tucson, Ariz; Read Mullan's Gallery Western Art, Ariz State Univ; Principia Col, Elsah, Ill; Wells Fargo Bank, Tucson, Ariz. *Comn:* Ted DeGrazia portrait (ltd edition pewter bas-relief plate) & Tracks Across America (series of six ltd edition pewter bas-relief sculptures), comn by Richard Smith, Century Reproductions, Inc, Wilmington, Mass, 77; three 50 year commemorative belt buckle sculptures, Western Savings & Loan, Phoenix. *Exhib:* San Dimas Am Indian & Cowboy Artists Soc Show, Calif, 77-93; First Fed Savings & Loan Traveling Exhib; Western Gallery, 1st Interstate Bank, Tucson, Ariz; Gene Autry Mus Western Heritage, 95-96; Mountain Oyster Club Ann; and others. *Pos:* owner, Hank Richter Studio. *Teaching:* Student instr anat, Philadelphia Mus Sch Art, 49-50; instr creative design, Kachina Sch Art, Phoenix, 54-56; sculpture instr & drawing instr, Principia Col, Elsah, Ill; instr pvt classes, currently. *Awards:* Gold Medal, Atlanta Film Festival, 69; Golden Eagle, CINE/USA, 69; Silver Medal, W/C Sandimas Art Festival, Calif, 2001. *Bibliog:* The West & Walter Bimson, Univ Ariz Press, 72; Pat Broder (auth), Bronzes of the American West, Abrams, 75; Lil Rhodes (auth), A man and his art, Southwest Art, 78. *Mem:* Am Indian & Cowboy Artists Soc (past pres); Art Group 12, Payson, Ariz; Artists of Renown; Peoria Fine Art Assoc, Ariz; Oil Painters of America. *Media:* Oil, Watercolor; Bronze, Graphite. *Res:* Artist Mourgue from 1960. *Specialty:* Oils, Watercolors of ranch life giclees LTD. Ed prints. *Interests:* Reading-illustrations (book). *Dealer:* ARR West Galleries Main St Scottsdale AZ; Espritdecor 5533 N 7th St Phoenix AZ 85014; Dow Gallery, Ft worth, Tex; Centenica Gallery, Ft Collings, Colo; Galleria Tubac, Tubac, Ariz. *Mailing Add:* 1221 W Carol Ann Way Phoenix AZ 85023-4497

RIDDLE, JOHN THOMAS, JR
SCULPTOR, PAINTER

b Los Angeles, Calif, Mar 18, 33. *Study:* Los Angeles City Col, AA, 60; Los Angeles State Col, BA, 66; Calif State Univ, MA, 73. *Work:* High Mus Art, Atlanta, Ga; Golden State Mutual Life Inst Co, Calif State Univ, Los Angeles; Oakland Mus, Calif; Albany Mus Art, Ga. *Comn:* Murals, Bank of Am (2 br), Los Angeles, 70; The Operation (welded steel), Los Angeles Co Mental Health Clinic, 72; relig murals, Shrine of Black Madonna, Atlanta, 74; Expelled Because of Their Color (bronze), State of Ga, Atlanta, 77; Spirit Bench 1, City of Atlanta, 78; Painted, Welded, Sculpture Walls, Mid-Town Marta Sta, Atlanta, Ga. *Exhib:* Black Artists, Oakland Mus, Calif, 73; Calif Artists, Calif State Univ, Sacramento, 74; Artists in Ga, High Mus Art, Atlanta, 75-80; Calif Artists, the Black Experience, State Capitol, Sacramento, Calif, 76; Black Artists S, Huntsville Mus Art, Ala, 78; 8th Ann Art Festival, Martinique, WI, Port de France, 79; Calif African-Am Mus, Los Angeles, 89; William Grant Still Gallery, Los Angeles, Calif, 92. *Pos:* Dir, Neighborhood Arts Ctr, Inc, Atlanta, 75-81. *Teaching:* Instr ceramics & sculpture, Pub Schs, Los Angeles & Beverly Hills, Calif, 66-73; asst prof painting, Spelman Col, Atlanta, 79-80; asst dir, Atlanta Civic Ctr, 84-92. *Awards:* Emmy Award, TV Acad Arts & Sci, 71; Ga Gov Award Visual Art, 81. *Bibliog:* Lewis Productions, Three artists, Lewis, Riddle, Pajaud, 68; Larry Stuart (auth), Renaissance in black, KNBC, 10/71; Lewis & Waddy (coauth), Black Artists on Art, 2 vols, Contemp Crafts, 72. *Mem:* Black Artists Atlanta; Ga Coun for Arts; Gov Artist-in-Schs; Atlanta Urban Design Comn, 90-91. *Publ:* Contribr, Prints by American Negro Artists, Cult Exchange Ctr, 67; Black Artists on Art, 2 vols, Contemp Crafts, 71; Art: African American, Harcourt-Brace, 78. *Dealer:* Camille Love 3230 Kingsdale Dr SW Atlanta GA 30311. *Mailing Add:* 3034 Rebecca Dr SW Atlanta GA 30311-1920

RIDER BERRY, TARAH J
PHOTOGRAPHER, INSTRUCTOR

b New York, NY, 1963. *Study:* Ariz State Univ, BA(art hist). *Work:* Scottsdale Mus Contemp Art & Scottsdale Cult Coun; Phoenix Arts Comn & PMH Found, Phoenix. *Comn:* Picture This (photographic portfolio), Phoenix Arts Comn, 95 & 98; Documentary, Scottsdale Cult Coun, 96; Animal Rites, Ariz Comn Arts, 97. *Exhib:* I Can Fly: Photographs by Tarah Rider Berry (with catalog), Scottsdale Ctr Arts, 96; Annual Collectors Exhibition, Houston Ctr Photog, 96; Souls, AP Tell Gallery, Phoenix, 97; Tucson Biennial, Tuscon Mus Art, 97; My Life: Photographs of Children Living in Phoenix, Ariz Comm Arts Traveling Exhib, 97-98; Another Arizona, Nelson Art Mus, Ariz State Univ, Tempe, 98; Building for the Millennium, Scottsdale Mus Contemp Art, 98. *Teaching:* Instr photog, Pub Art Projs City of Phoenix, 95 & 98. *Awards:* Visual Arts Grant, Ariz Comm Arts, 96 & Artist Proj Grant, 97; Flow Fund Grant, Rockefeller Found, 98. *Bibliog:* Gia Cobb (auth), By the people, for the people, Ariz Repub, 9/14/97; Richard Nilsen (auth), The jury is in, Arizona State University exhibit, Ariz Repub, 3/29/98. *Mailing Add:* 6212 S 8th Pl Phoenix AZ 85040

RIDLON, JAMES A
SCULPTOR, ASSEMBLAGE ARTIST

b Nyack, NY, July 11, 34. *Study:* Syracuse Univ, BA, 57, MFA, 65; San Francisco State Col, 58-59. *Work:* Munson-Williams-Proctor Inst, Utica, NY; Julliard Sch, NY; Rochester Mem Gallery, NY; Everson Mus, Syracuse, NY; Smithsonian Inst, Washington; and others. *Comn:* Assemblage, ABC, NY, 58; Outland Trophy, Football Writers Asn Am, 88; Disneyland, 89; HSE, 90. *Exhib:* New Paintings, Everson Mus Art, 74; one-man retrospective, Logan Alexander Ctr Creative Arts, Concord Col, 75; Lubin House Gallery, NY, 77; Herbert F Johnson Mus, Cornell Univ, Ithaca, NY, 77; Canton Art Inst, Canton, Ohio, 89; and others. *Pos:* Chmn, CORE Dept, Syracuse Univ, 82-. *Teaching:* Prof sculpture & studio arts, Syracuse Univ, 68-74, prof sculpture & synaesthetic educ, 74-81, prof, Sch Art Design, 82-. *Awards:* Purchase Prize, 32nd Ann Exhib, Munson-Williams-Proctor Inst, 68; First Prize in Sculpture, 10th Ann Westchester Art Soc Exhib, 70; First Prize Sculpture, NY State Fair, 92; and others. *Publ:* Contribr, Synaesthetic Education, Syracuse Univ, 71; auth, Synaesthetic education as a basis for symbolic expression, Humanities J, 5/73; co-producer & dir, Icons and Eclecticism (film), Syracuse Univ, 81; producer & dir, Artist-Athlete (film), Syracuse Univ, 82; co-producer & dir, The Wonder of Friction (film), Syracuse Univ, 83. *Dealer:* Oxford Gallery 267 Oxford Rochester NY 14607. *Mailing Add:* 4468 E Lake Rd Cazenovia NY 13035

RIEBER, RUTH B
PRINTMAKER, PAINTER

b New York, NY, Mar 9, 24. *Study:* New York Univ, BS, 45; Art Students League, 47; Columbia Univ, MFA, 48. *Work:* Westinghouse Electric, Pittsburgh, Pa; Pub Serv Electric & Gas Co, Newark, NJ; State NJ Dept Treasury, Trenton; Newark Teachers Union, NJ; Jane Voorhees Zimmerli Art Mus, Rutgers, NJ; and others. *Exhib:* NJ Invitational Graphics, Morris Mus Art & Sci, 80; Nat Asn Women Artists Centennial Celebration (juried, travel), India, 89; solo exhibs, Insights, Saint Peters Church Gallery, NY, 87, Relief Print, Johnson and Johnson World Hq, New Brunswick, NJ, 90 & Works on Paper, Int Church Ctr, NY, 91; Hudson River Open 91, Hudson River Mus, Yonkers, NY, 91; SUNNY Westchester Community Col, NY, 96. *Teaching:* Teacher art, Bd Educ, NY, 46-49; art therapist, Teaneck Sch System Spec Educ, NJ, 68-74; printmaker specialist, Project Impact Arts in Educ Found, NJ, 85-92. *Awards:* Medal of Honor, Catherine Lorillard Wolfe Art Club, 83, 84, 86, 94, 95 & 97; Graphics Award, Nat Asn Women Artists, Janet Turner, 84; Purchase Award, Nat Print 86 Exhib, Trenton State Col, 86 & 96; and others. *Bibliog:* Dori Halasz (auth), A Show in Trenton Survey's States Art, NY Sunday; Eileen Watkins (auth), Shedding Artistic Light on Women's Issues, The Star Ledger, 3/5/88; Vivian Raynor(auth), Well Known Artists Join the Crowd at NY Art Gallery Auction, NY Times, 6/21/92. *Mem:* Nat Asn Women Artists; Print Coun NJ; Painting Affiliates, NJ; Audubon Artists; Catherine Lorillard Wolfe Art Club; NY Soc Women Artists. *Publ:* Collaborative Artist Book Project, Int Printed ed, ed VIII, 96, ed IV, 97 & 98. *Mailing Add:* 407 Warwick Ave Teaneck NJ 07666

RIEGLE, ROBERT MACK
ART DEALER, COLLECTOR

b Sedan, Kans, Nov 11, 24. *Study:* Tex A&M Univ, College Station, 43; Univ Kans, Lawrence, BS(archit), 50. *Pos:* Dir, Wichita Gallery Fine Art, currently. *Specialty:* Original fine paintings and sculpture; realism, impressionism and expressionism. *Collection:* Contemporary realists and impressionists of the southwest; oils, watercolors and pastels; bronze sculpture. *Mailing Add:* Wichita Gallery Fine Art Bank of America Ctr 100 N Broadway Ste 210 Wichita KS 67202

RIES, MARTIN
PAINTER, PRINTMAKER

b Washington, DC, Dec 26, 26. *Study:* Corcoran Gallery Art, 40-44; Am Univ, with William Calfee, Jack Tworkov & Leo Steppat, BA, 50; Hunter Col, MA, 68, with Leo Steinberg, William Rubin, Ad Reinhardt & E C Goossen. *Work:* Pace Univ Mus; Riverside Mus Collection, Rose Art Mus, Brandeis Univ; Corcoran Mus, Washington,; NY Pub Libr Print Collection; Netherlands Consulate; Housatonic Mus, Bridgeport, Conn; Rose Art Mus, Brandeis Univ; Manhattan Psychiat Ctr, Ward's Island, NY; William Calfee Found, Md; Rabobank of the Nederlands, Chicago; Watkins Gallery, Am Univ. *Exhib:* Corcoran Gallery Art, 52; Mus Mod Art, 56; Paul Gallery, Tokyo, Japan, 68; Verfeil, France, 73; Stamford Mus, Conn, 87; Inst Contemp Art, London, 88; Raja Idris Gallery, Melbourne, Australia, 89; Homages, Images, Jaxtapositions, 2/20 Gallery, NY, 96; others; Watkins Gallery, Washington, DC, 2000; solo show, Karpeles Mus, Newburgh, NY, 2002. *Pos:* Asst dir pub rels, Nat Cong Comt, 51; asst dir, Hudson River Mus, Yonkers, NY, 57-67; adv, Westchester Cult Ctr, 65-67; contrib ed, Arts Mag; art ed, Greenwich Village News; bd dir, Artists Representing Environ Art; juror Inst Int Educ, J William Fulbright Art Scholarships, UN. *Teaching:* Instr medieval art hist, Marymount Col, 59; instr mod art hist, Hunter Col, 63-67; prof hist art, color theory, printmaking, drawing & painting, Long Island Univ, 68-94. *Awards:* Honorable Mention, 52nd Nat Soc Arts & Lett Award, Corcoran Gallery Art; Critics Choice, Whyte Gallery, 57; Yaddo Fel; Research-Time Award, Long Island Univ. *Bibliog:* Masters & Houston, Psychedelic Art, Grove Press, NY, 68; C Dantzic (auth), Design Dimensions, Prentice-Hall, NJ. *Mem:* Asn Int des Critiques d'Art, Am Sect; Artists Equity Asn; Am Soc Contemp Artists. *Media:* Acrylic, Silk Screen Printing. *Res:* Braque's Atelier and the Symbolic Bird; Abstract-Perspectivism of John Hultberg; Andre Masson: Surrealism and its Discontents; Willem de Kooning's Asheville. *Publ:* Endowments for Great Society, Art Voices Mag, 65 & New Art: Anthology, Dutton, 66; Picasso and the Myth of the Minotaur, Art J, winter 72-73, portion reprinted in: Picasso in Perspective, Prentice Hall, 75; Environmental Art: Working with Elements, video produced by AREA; Braque's ateliers and the symbolic bird, J Aesthetic Educ, summer 95; US ed, Irony & Rude Questions, Nat Writers Union; Art research & visuals for TV documentary, The Feuding Tombs of

Christopher Columbus, Newman Assocs, Washington, 92; The Ecstasy of Discontent, Art e Dossier, Florence, Italy, 4/2002; Andre Masson: Surrealism and His Discontents, Art Jour, 2002; numerous reviews, introductions to catalogs, gallery/artists news releases. *Dealer:* Aaron Berman 660 E 19 St Brooklyn NY 11230; Glass Gallery 315 Central Park West New York NY 10025. *Mailing Add:* 36 Livingston Rd Scarsdale NY 10583

RIESS, LORE
PAINTER, PRINTMAKER
b Berlin, Ger; US citizen. *Study:* Art Acad, Contempora (Bauhaus Sch), Berlin; Sumi Drawing & Calligraphy, Tokyo; Art Students League. *Work:* Corcoran Gallery Art, Washington, DC; Tel Aviv Mus & Israel Mus, Jerusalem; US Embassy, Japan & Korea; pvt collections in US, Japan, Belg, Eng & Israel; AT&T; and others. *Comn:* Ed of etchings, Mickelson Gallery, Washington, DC, 71. *Exhib:* One-man shows, Old Jaffa Gallery, Israel, 70, 73, 75 & 79, Nora Art Gallery, Jerusalem, 71, 74 & 82, Jeanne Frank Gallery, NY, 78 & Park Village West, London, 79 & 80; Linden Galleries, NY, 81, Artist Studio, NY, 82, 85 & 90, Park West Gallery, London, Eng, 83, Lillian Heidenberg Gallery, NY, 84, Zack Schuster Gallery, Boca Raton, Fla, 85, 86 & 89. *Awards:* William McNulty Merit Award, Art Students League, 64; M J Kaplan Prize, Nat Asn Women Artists, 69; Gallery of Graphic Art Award, Int Miniature Print Exhib, 71. *Bibliog:* T Ichinose (auth), Colorful abstract oils by Lore Riess, Mainichi Daily News, 65; articles in Jerusalem Post, 7/70 & 3/71. *Media:* Acrylic, Pastel. *Dealer:* Margaret Lipworth, FL; Adler Arts Int Washington DC. *Mailing Add:* One Lincoln Plaza Apt 23B New York NY 10023

RIFKA, JUDY
PAINTER
b New York, NY, Sept 25, 45. *Study:* NY Studio Sch, Cert, 67; Suny Empire Westbury, BA, 94; Adelphi Univ, MA, 95. *Work:* Boston Mus Fine Arts; NY Pub Libr; Eli Broad Family Found, Los Angeles; The Mint Mus, Charlotte, NC; Kemper Mus Contemp Art, Kans City, Mo. *Comn:* Bistro 110, Levy Corp & Doug Roth, Chicago; Bistro 100, Nations Bank Bldg, Levy Corp & Nations Bank, Charlotte, NC; Union Square Cafe, Daniel Meyer, NY, 86 & 04; Madison Square Garden, MSG Corp, NY, 89; Ericcson Stadium, Charlotte, NC, 96. *Exhib:* Biennial, Whitney Mus, NY, 75, 83; Documenta 7, Kassel, Ger, 82; Back to USA, Kunst Mus, Luzerne, 84; Borrowed Embellishments, Kansas City Art Inst, Kansas City, 87; Making Their Mark, Cincinatti, Denver, New Orleans Mus & Pa Acad, 89; The Future Now, Bass Mus, Miami, 89; Beyond the Pale, Irish Mus Modern Art, Dublin, 94; Grey Art Gallery, NY Univ, 2006; Berkeley Art Mus, 2006; Andy Warhol Mus, 2006. *Teaching:* asst prof, Hofstra Univ, 95-96. *Bibliog:* Joseph Masheck (auth), Modernities, Pa Univ Press, 93; Ann-Sargent Wooster (auth), Judy Rifka, Arts Mag, 91; Vincent Carducci (auth), Judy Rifka at Alley Culture, Art in Am, 98; Brooklyn Rail, Political Cartoons, 2004. *Mem:* Whitney Mus; Friend New Mus. *Media:* Oil. *Collection:* Metrop Mus Art, NY; NY Pub Libr. *Publ:* Auth/illusr, Judy Rifka's Polaroid Album of Premierem, Kunst Forum, 85; illusr, Opera of the Worms, Solo Press, 85; Making Thier Mark, Cincinatti Art Mus, 89; illusr, A Still Small Voice, Delacorte, 2000. *Dealer:* C Hendricks Alley Culture PO Box 441261 Detroit Michigan 48244. *Mailing Add:* 53 Market St Apt 4B New York NY 10002

RIFKIN, NED
CURATOR, MUSEUM DIRECTOR
b Florence, Ala, Nov 10, 49. *Study:* Syracuse Univ, AB, 1972; Univ Mich, MA, 1973, PhD, 1976-77. *Collection Arranged:* Stay Tuned, New Mus, New York, 81; Leon Golub, New Mus, New York, 84; Paradise Lost/Paradise Regained, New Mus Am Pavilion, Bienale di Venezia, 84; Spectrum (New Series), Corcoran Gallery Art, Washington, DC, 84-86; Signs, The New Mus, New York, 85; Works (New Series), Hirshhorn Mus, Washington, DC, 86-91; 40th Corcoran Biennial (painting), Corcoran Gallery Art, Washington, DC, 87; Robert Muskowitz (with catalog), Hirshhorn Mus & Sculpture Garden, Washington, DC, 89. *Pos:* Cur/asst dir, New Mus Contemp Art, 81-84; cur contemp art, Corcoran Gallery Art, 84-86; chief cur, Hirshhorn Mus & Sculpture Garden, 86-91, dir, 2002-05; junior dir, High Mus Art, Atlanta, 1991-1999; dir, Menil Collection and Found; Houston, 2000-02; Smithsonian Int Art Mus Div, 2004-; under section, for art Smithsonian Inst, 2004-. *Teaching:* Asst prof art hist, Univ Tex, Arlington, 77-80. *Awards:* Curators Award, Art Matters Inc, 91. *Mem:* Asn Art Mus Dirs. *Publ:* Auth, Antonioni's Visual Language, UMI Res Press, 81; Sean Scally: 20 years, 1976-1995, (in press), Thames & Hudson. *Mailing Add:* Smithsonian Inst Bldg 1000 Jefferson SW MRC 041 Washington DC 20560

RIGBY, IDA KATHERINE
CRITIC, HISTORIAN
b Los Angeles, Calif, May 10, 44. *Study:* Stanford Univ, BA, MA; Ecole des Beaux Arts, Tours, France; Univ Calif, Berkeley, MA, PhD(art hist), 74. *Teaching:* Asst prof mod art hist, Univ Montana, Missoula, spring 72; instr, Newcomb Col, Tulane Univ, New Orleans, 72-74; asst prof, Univ Victoria, BC, 74-76; prof mod & contemp art, San Diego State Univ, 76-. *Awards:* Kress Found Grant; Grant, Deutscher Akademischer Austauschdienst, Bonn. *Mem:* Col Art Asn; Art Historians of Southern Calif. *Res:* German Expressionism; German Expressionist artists and politics; politics of opposition and official collaboration in Germany during the 1930's; art criticism. *Publ:* Auth, Karl Hofer, Garland Publ, 76; The Expressionist Artist and Revolution, 1918-1922 & Entartte Kunst, 1933-1938, In: German Expressionist Art: The Robert Gore Rifkind Collection, Univ Calif, Los Angeles Press, 77; Franz Marc's wartime letters from the front, 1880-1916, Univ Calif Berkeley, 79; Wichner Collection, Long Beach Mus Art, 81; An Alle Kunstler War Revolution Weimar: German Expressionist Prints, Drawings, Posters and Periodicals for the Robert Gore Rifkind Foundation, San Diego State Univ Press, 83. *Mailing Add:* Sch Art Design & Art Hist San Diego State Univ San Diego CA 92182

RIGG, MARGARET R
ASSEMBLAGE ARTIST, CALLIGRAPHER
b Pittsburgh, Pa, Dec 14, 29. *Study:* Carnegie-Mellon Univ, 45-50; Fla State Univ, BA, 51; Scarrett Col; Presby Sch, MA, 55; George Peabody Col; Chicago Art Inst, 63; painting with Edmund Lewandowski & Florence Kawa; design & theory with Mathias Goeritz; Chinese calligraphy with Tsutomu Yoshida, Kim Kee-Sung, Kim Hahn & Tennyson Chang; Am calligraphy with Corita Kent & Jan Steward; Brit calligraphy with George L Thompson. *Work:* Tenn Collection, Smithsonian Inst; Yamada Gallery, Kyoto, Japan; Turku Univ Mus, Finland; NH Mus, Manchester; Korea Fulbright House, Seoul. *Comn:* Stained glass windows, Mexico City Nat Cathedral, 61; stained glass window, communion table, lectum & celtic cross, Univ NC, Chapel Hill, 62; calligraphy mural, Experiment House, Vere, Jamaica; calligraphy, CBS-TV News, 69 & 71; calligraphy letterhead & gates to campus, Eckerd Col, 72. *Exhib:* Solo shows, calligraphy, Hannover, Ger, 84, calligraphy & paintings, Montreat, NC, 85, calligraphy, Buenos Aires, Argentiana & Salvador, Bahia, Brasil, 86 & calligraphy, Cult Olympics, Seoul, Korea, 87; calligraphy, Tokyo, Japan, 88, Galeria Pequena, St Petersburg, Fla, 90; Gararia Pequena, St Petersburg, Fla, 91; Aura group, Philadelphia, Pa, 92; St Petersburg visual artists, Univ SFla, 92; and others. *Pos:* Art dir, Bd Publ, Fla State Univ, 51-53; owner & publ, Possum Press; art ed, Motive Mag, Nashville, Tenn, 54-65. *Teaching:* Artist-in-residence, Fla Presby Col, 65-67; prof visual art, Eckerd Col, 67-; dir, Elliot Teaching Gallery, Eckerd Col, 81-88. *Awards:* Stone Lectr, Princeton Seminary, Princeton, NJ, 71; Fulbright-Hays Sr Res Grant in Chinese Calligraphy, Korea, 72. *Bibliog:* Contribr, Amenu Alphabet Workbook, 89; The Cherry Tree Alphabet, 94; A SHAHN Alphabet Workbook, 95; The Cherry Tree Alphabet, 98. *Mem:* Int Soc Women Calligraphers; Soc Italic Handwriting; Nashville Artist Guild (pres, 63-64); Fla Artist Group, Inc; St Petersburg Soc Scribes (founder & 1st pres, 78-); Soc Arts, Religion & Contemp Cult (ARC), NY. *Media:* Acrylic, Mixed Media; Pen & Ink, Markers, Calligraphy. *Publ:* Pro-Nica, logo & art, Religious Soc Friends (Quakers) (relief to Nicaragua), 89; front cover logo design, Human Quest Mag, 90. *Dealer:* Carol Ridge St Petersburg Fla. *Mailing Add:* 6909 Dr MLK Jr St #380 Saint Petersburg FL 33705-7380

RIGGIO, LEONARD
BOOK DEALER, COLLECTOR
b 41. *Study:* NY Univ, student. *Hon Degrees:* Baruch Col of City Univ NY, Hon Dr; Bentley Col, Hon Dr. *Pos:* Merchandise mgr, NY Univ Bookstore, NY City, 62-65; pres, Chief Exec Officer, bd dirs, Barnes & Noble Bookstores, Inc, 65-86; founder, Chief Exec Officer, pres, treas, Barnes & Noble Inc, NY City, 1986-2002, chmn bd, 86-; chmn bd, principle beneficial owner, Software Etc Stores Inc, Minneapolis, MBS Textbook Exchange Inc, Columbia, Mo; chmn bd, Dia Art Found, 1998-2006, bd mem, 2006-; bd dirs, Childrens Defense Fund, Black Childrens Community Crusade, Brooklyn Tech Found, Italian Am Found. *Awards:* Recipient Ellis Island Medal of Honor, Frederick Douglas Medallion, Americanism award, Anti-Defamation League, 2002; Named one of Top 200 Collectors, ARTnews mag, 2003-06; Named to Acad of Distinguished Entrepreneurs, Babson Col, Retailing Hall of Fame, Tex Agr & Mechanical Univ, 2005. *Collection:* Contemporary Art. *Mailing Add:* Barnes & Noble Inc 122 5th Ave 4th Fl New York NY 10011-5605

RIGGS, GERRY
MUSEUM DIRECTOR, EDUCATOR
b Frankfurt, Ger, Dec 12, 1950; US citizen. *Study:* Univ Okla, BFA(art), 79, Masters Liberal Studies, 87. *Collection Arranged:* The Fahrenheit Group, 94; NeoGeo, 95; AAA plus, 95; On Colorado, 5 Photographers, 96; Co-cur, Boardman Robinson's Circle, 96. *Pos:* Dir & cur, C B Goddard Ctr Visual & Performing Arts, Ardmore, Okla, 87-90; cur fine art, Colorado Springs Fine Arts Ctr, 90-91; dir, Gallery Contemp Art, Univ Colo, Colorado Springs, 91. *Teaching:* Asst prof mus studies, Univ Colo, Colorado Springs, 91-. *Mem:* Am Asn Mus; Colo-Wyo Mus Asn; Asn Col & Univ Mus & Galleries; Mountain Plains Mus Asn. *Publ:* Contribr, Facets of Modern Art, Heritage Media Graphics, 87; auth, The Rug Route: From Istanbul to Bokara, Colorado Springs Fine Arts Ctr, 90. *Mailing Add:* 318 Locust Dr Colorado Springs CO 80907-4348

RIGLEY, FREDERICK WILDERMUTH
PAINTER, INSTRUCTOR
b Owosso, Mich, July 1, 14. *Study:* Art Students League NY; Ringling Sch Art & Hilton Leech Studio Sch, Sarasota, 32-36; studied with Adrian Pillars, Enrique Elferez, Emile Agruppe, John F Carlson, George Bridgman & others. *Work:* Ind Univ, Bloomington; Univ Del, Newark; N Shore Arts Asn, Glouster, Mass; Gen Motors Corp, Anderson, Ind; Eaton Nat Bank & Trust Co, Ohio. *Comn:* Paintings, Gen Motors Corp, Anderson, Ind; paintings, Outdoor Ind Mag, Indianapolis. *Exhib:* Cedar Key Art Festival, Fla, 85; Hoosier Salon, Indianapolis, 98; Ind Heritage Arts, Nashville, 98. *Teaching:* Instr, Indianapolis Art League, 51-76; artist-in-residence painting, Univ Del, 64. *Awards:* Selection Purchase Prize, Hoosier Salon, Kappa Kappa Kappa. *Mem:* Brown Co Art Guild (pres, 75); Hoosier Salon; Ind Artists Club (former pres); N Shore Arts Asn (former pres); Eastern Shore Art Asn. *Media:* Oil, Acrylic. *Dealer:* Artists Colony Inn & Art Gallery 105 S Van Buren St Nashville IN 47448. *Mailing Add:* PO Box 427 Nashville IN 47448

RILEY, BARBRA BAYNE
PHOTOGRAPHER, EDUCATOR
b Brooklyn, NY, Dec 20, 49. *Study:* Sch Visual Arts, New York, cert(fine arts), 70; Calif State Univ, Sacramento, BA, 72, MA, 74. *Work:* Dallas Mus Art; Mus Fine Art, Houston; Laguna Beach Mus Art, Chase Manhattan Bank, NY; Atlantic Richfield Co. *Comn:* Photographers Portray the Family, Women & Their Work, Nat Endowment Arts, Austin, Tex, 81; 24 photographs, Corpus Christi Nat Bank, 81; Texas Commerce Bank, Corpus Christi. *Exhib:* Solo exhib, Art Mus STex, Corpus Christi, 79; Contemp

Photog as Phantasy, Santa Barbara Mus Art, Calif, 82; Texas Landscape 1900-1986, Mus Fine Arts, Houston, 86; Houston Ctr for Photog, 86; Texas Women, Nat Mus Women in Arts, Washington, DC, 88; 150 Yrs of Photog, Laguna Gloria Art Mus, Austin, Tex, 89. *Collection Arranged:* Return to Beyond the Valley of Photography, Weil Gallery, Corpus Christi State Univ, 81; Touched by Man--Landscape Photographs from Around the World, Weil Gallery, Corpus Christi State Univ, 90. *Teaching:* From asst prof to prof photog & design, Corpus Christi State Univ, Tex, 82-. *Bibliog:* Ellen Wallenstein (auth), Ties that bind, Artweek, 12/81; Suzanne Winkler (auth), Where's the family, Tex Monthly, 1/82. *Mem:* Tex Photog Soc; Houston Ctr for Photog; Art Mus S Tex (bd trustees). *Media:* Silver Prints, Non-Silver Processes. *Dealer:* Carrington/Gallagher 7979 Broadway San Antonio, TX 78209. *Mailing Add:* c/o Wilhelmi-Holland Gallery 300 S Chaparral Corpus Christi TX 78401

RILEY, BRIDGET LOUISE
PAINTER
b London, Apr 24, 31. *Study:* Goldsmith's Sch Art, London, 49-52; Royal Col Art, 52-55; Ulster Univ, 86. *Hon Degrees:* Manchester Univ, Dlit(hon), 76. *Pos:* With, J Walter Thomspon, London, 58-59; trustee, Nat Gallery London, 81-88. *Teaching:* Part time teacher, Hornsey Col Art, London, 60-61. *Awards:* AOCA critics prize John Moores Exhib, Liverpool, 63; travel bursary, 64; Int Prize, Painting XXXIV Venice Biennale, 68; Ohara Mus Prize, Tokyo Print Biennale, 72; Decorated comdr; Order Brit Empire; Recipient Peter Stuyvesant Found. *Publ:* auth, Paintings from the 60's & 70's, London, Serpentine Gallery, 99; auth, Selected Paintings 1961-1999 (Dusseldorf: Kunstverein fur die Rheinlande und Westfalen; Ostfildern: Cantz Publishers, 99); auth, Works 1961-1998 (Kendal, Cumbria: Abbot Hall Art Gallery & Mus, 98); auth, Dialogues on Art (London: Zwemmer, 95). *Mailing Add:* Pace Wildenstein Galleries 32 E 57th St 2nd fl New York NY 10022

RILEY, SARAH A
PAINTER, EDUCATOR
b Richmond, Va, July 1, 47. *Study:* Tyler Sch Art, Rome; Va Commonwealth Univ, BFA; Univ Mo, Columbia, 77, MFA, 82. *Work:* Chesapeake & Pacific Telephone Co; Springfield Art Mus, Mo; Vivian & Gordon Gilkey Ctr Graphic Arts, Portland, Ore. *Comn:* Painting, Univ Mo Hosp & Clinics, 83. *Exhib:* Va Mus Fine Arts Next Juried Show, 83; Watercolor USA, Springfield Art Mus, Mo, 83 & 88; 2nd Nat Small Print & Drawing Exhib, Cobleskill, NY, 84; one-woman shows, Wichita State Univ, 85 & Leedy-Voulkes Gallery, Kansas City, Mo, 90; Mid-Four Ann Juried Exhib, Nelson Atkins Mus, Kansas City, 87; Fourth Clemson Nat Print & Drawing Exhib, SC, 89; Greater Midwest Int, Warrensburg, Md, 96. *Pos:* Dir, Davis Art Gallery, Stephen's Col, Columbia, Mo, 83-94. *Teaching:* Prof drawing & painting, Stephens Col, 82-94, actg head art dept, 85-86, prog dir art area, 86-94; prof & chairperson, SE Mo State, 94-. *Awards:* First Patroness Award, Mid-Four Ann Juried Exhib, Nelson-Atkins Mus, Kansas City, 87; Purchase Award, Springfield Mus Art, 88; 1st Place Award, 47th Spiva Ann Competition, Spiva Art Ctr, Joplin, Mo, 97; and others. *Bibliog:* Donald Hoffman (auth), article, Kansas City Star, 6/20/82; article, New York Art Rev, 88. *Mem:* Col Art Asn; Watercolor USA Hon Soc; assoc mem, Kans Watercolor Soc. *Media:* Drawing, Paint. *Publ:* Charlottesville First Folio, 71. *Dealer:* Reynolds-Minor Gallery 1514 W Main St Richmond VA 23220; Sherry Leedy Contemp Art 1919 Wyandotte Kansas City MO 64111. *Mailing Add:* 34 N Fountain St Cape Girardeau MO 63701-7302

RILEY, TERENCE
CURATOR, ARCHITECT
Study: Univ Notre Dame, BA (archit), 1978; Columba Univ, MA (archit and urban planning). *Collection Arranged:* Cur, Paul Nelson: Filter of Reason, Arthur Ross Archit Galleries, Columbia Univ, 1989; cur, Light Construction; cur, The Un-Private House; cur, Mies in America, 2001; cur, On-Site: New Architecture in Spain, 2006. *Pos:* Partner (with John Keenen) archit practice; dir, Arthur Ross Archit Galleries, Columbia Univ, until 1991; cur dept archit and design, Mus Modern Art, NY, 1991, chief cur, 1992-2002, staff liaison to architect selection comt, Philip Johnson chief cur archit and design, 2002-06; dir, Miami Art Mus, Fla, 2006-; trustee, Fundació Mies van der Rohe, Barcelona, Spain, currently; mem adv bd, Parsons Grad Sch Design, currently. *Teaching:* Prof, Harvard Univ, Columbia Univ. *Mem:* Am Inst Architects. *Publ:* Contributes articles to professional journals. *Mailing Add:* Miami Art Museum 101 West Flager St Miami FL 33130

RINDER, LAWRENCE R
CURATOR, WRITER
b New York, NY. *Study:* Sch Visual Arts, NY, 82; Reed Col, Ore, BA (art), 83; Hunter Col, NY, MA (art), 90. *Collection Arranged:* Searchlight, UAC Inst (auth, catalog), 99; Capp St Project: Jim Hodges, CCAC Inst, 2000; 2000 Biennial, Whitney Mus Am Art, NY, 2000; Bitstreams, Whitney Mus Am Art, 2001. *Pos:* Cur, 20th century art and contemporary projects and cur MATRIX program, Berkeley Art Mus, 1988-98; founding dir, Wattis Inst, Calif Col Arts, San Francisco; Anne and Joel Ehrenkranz cur contemporary art, Whitney Mus Am Art, NY, 2000-04, adj cur, 2004-. *Teaching:* Adj prof art history and archaeology, Columbia Univ; dean grad studies, Calif Col Arts, San Francisco, 2004-. *Mailing Add:* Calif College of Arts 1111 Eighth St San Francisco CA 94107-2247

RINDFLEISCH, JAN
DIRECTOR, CURATOR
Study: Purdue Univ, BS, 62, San Jose State Univ, MFA, 79; Mus Mgt Inst, J Paul Getty Trust, 89. *Collection Arranged:* Art Collectors in and Around Silicon Valley, 4/85; Art of the Refugee Experience, 3/88; Drawing from Experience: Artists over Fifty, 2/90. *Pos:* Dir, Euphrat Gallery, De Anza Col, Cupertino, Calif, 79-. *Teaching:* Instr studio art/art hist, De Anza Col, Cuperinto, Calif, 79-85. *Awards:* Asian Heritage Coun Arts Award, 88; Woman Achievement, Santa Clara Co, 89. *Bibliog:* Cordell Koland (auth), Euphrat Gallery fights cultural deprivation in the valley, Bus J, 3/25/85; Theresa Hong Bailar (auth), Focus on Jan Rindfleisch, Silhouette Mag, 4/89; Eric Reyes (auth), A Room of One's Art, Metro, 4/90. *Mem:* Am Asn Mus; Calif Confederation Arts; Western Mus Conf; Comt Arts Policy, Santa Clara Co (comt mem, 85-); Arts Coun Santa Clara Co (bd mem, 88-). *Publ:* Auth, Art, Religion, Spirituality, Euphrat Gallery, 82; Art Collectors in and Around Silicon Valley, Euphrat Gallery, 85; Content: Contemporary Issues, Euphrat Gallery, 86; Art of the Refugee Experience, Euphrat Gallery, 88. *Mailing Add:* Euphrat Mus Art De Anza Col 21250 Stevens Creek Blvd Cupertino CA 95014

RINEHART, MICHAEL
EDITOR
b Miami, Fla, Dec 27, 34. *Study:* Harvard Univ, BA, 56; Courtauld Inst, Univ London, 57-59. *Pos:* Ed-in-chief, BHA Bibliography of the History of Art. *Mem:* Col Art Asn; ARLIS/NA. *Publ:* Ed, B Berenson, Italian Pictures of the Renaissance, Florentine School, London, 63; auth, A Drawing by Vasari for the Studiolo of Francesco I, Burlington Mag, 64; auth, Practical Support on an International Basis for the Bibliography of Art History, CNRS, Paris, 69; auth, A Document for the Studiolo of Francesco I in Art the Ape of Nature, Abrams, 81; auth, Art databases and art bibliographies: A survey, Art Librs J, 82; and others. *Mailing Add:* 415 Central Park W New York NY 10025-4856

RINGGOLD, FAITH
PAINTER, SCULPTOR
b New York, NY, Oct 8, 30. *Study:* City Col New York, BS, 1955, MA, 1959, DFA, 1989; DFA, 1991; Moore Col Art, DFA, 1986; Wooster Col Art, DFA, 1987; Brockport State Univ, DFA, 1992; Calif Col Arts & Crafts, DFA, 1993; DFA MA Col of Art, 1991; DFA RI Sch of Design 1994; DFA Parsons Sch of Design 1996; DFA Russell Sage Col 1996; DEd Wheelock Col 1997; DHL Molloy Col 1997; DHL Bank St. Col of Edu 1999; DFA Marymount Manhattan Col 1999; DHL Mary Grove Col 2000; DHL St. Joseph Col 2004; DFA Bloomfield Col 2005. *Hon Degrees:* Hon Dr, William Paterson Univ & Sch of Chicago Art Inst, 2001. *Work:* Chase Manhattan Bank, NY; Studio Mus, Harlem, NY; High Mus Art, Atlanta, Ga; Philip Morris Collection, NY; Newark Mus, NJ; Metrop Mus Art, Solomon R Guggenheim Mus, NY; Boston Mus Fine Art. *Comn:* Williams Col, Williamstown, Mass, 1988; High Mus Art, Atlanta, Ga, 1988; Committed to Print, Mus Mod Art, NY, 1988; Tradition & Conflict: Images of a Turbulent Decade, 1963-1973, Studio Ms Harlem, NY; Oprah Winfrey, Harpo Prod, 1990-91. *Exhib:* Mem for Martin Luther King, Mus Mod Art, NY, 1968; Women Choose Women, NY Cult Ctr, 1973; retrospectives, Rutgers Univ Art Gallery, 1973, Studio Mus Harlem, NY, 84 & Fine Arts Mus of Long Island, traveling, 1990-93; Jubilee, Boston Mus, 1975; Second World Black & African Festival Arts & Cult, Lagos, Nigeria, 1977; Whitney Biennial, 1985; one-person shows, Wooster Col, Columbus, Ohio, 1985, Bernice Steinbaum Gallery, NY, 1986, Baltimore Mus, Md, 1987, Deland Mus Art, Fla, 1987 & Bernice Steinbaum Gallery, NY, 1988; The Decade Show, Studio Mus Harlem, 1990; Hudson River Mus Westchester, Yonkers, NY, 1996; San Diego Children's Mus, 1997; Adams Art Gallery, Dunkirk, NY, 1998; Jane Voorhees Zimmerli Art Mus, Rugers Univ, NJ, 1999; Faith Ringgold: Coming to Jones Rpad and Other Stories, ACA Galleries, 2001. *Pos:* Founder, Coast to Coast: A Women of Color Nat Artists' book proj, 1988; independent cur, Detroit Focus Gallery, 1989, African Am Mus Fine Art, 1990 & SoHo 20 Gallery, New York, 1990. *Teaching:* Prof art, Univ Calif, San Diego, 1984-; Prof Emeritus U of CA (1984-2002). *Awards:* National Endownment for the arts 1978: sculpture, 1989 painting; Solomon Guggenbieem fd. fellowship 1987 (painting); La Napoule Found Award, 1990; Coretta Scott King Award, 1992; Caldecott Honor, 1992; Visionary Woman award, Moore Coll. Art & Design, 2005. *Bibliog:* Leslie Sills (auth), Inspirations: Stories about Women Artists, Albert Whitman & Co, Ill, 1988; Arlene Raven, Cassandra L Langer & Joanna Frueh (co-eds), Feminist Art Criticism: An Anthology, 1988; Faith Ringgold, A 25 Yr Survey, Fine Arts Mus Long Island, 1990. *Mem:* Women's Caucus Art; Col Art Asn. *Media:* painting and mixed. *Specialty:* contemporary art (AM). *Interests:* art, children, philanthrapy. *Publ:* Contribr, Confirmation: An Anthology of African American Women Writers, William Morrow, 1983; auth, Tar Beach, Crown Publ, 1991; Dinner at Aunt Connie's House, 1993 Hyperion; Bonjour Lonnie, 1996 Hyperion; My Dream of Martin Luther King 1995 Crown Publ; Talking to Faith Ringgold 1995, Crown Publ.; Invisible Princess 1999. Crown Publ.; Aunt Harriet's Underground Railroad in the Sky, Crown Publ, 1993; If a Bus Could Talk: The Story of Rosa Parks, 1999 auth Simon Schuster; Counting to Tar Beach 1999, Crown Publ.; Cassie's Colorful Day 1999, Crown Publ.; Cassie's Word Quilt, Crown Publ. 2000; O Holy Night, 2004 Harper Collins Publ.; Three Witches 2005 Harper Collins Publ. *Dealer:* ACA Gallery 529 West 20th St., New York, NY 10022. *Mailing Add:* PO Box 429 Englewood NJ 07631

RINGIER, MICHAEL
COLLECTOR
b Switzerland. *Pos:* With Grüner & Jahr, H Bauer; mgt team Ringier Group, Zurich, Switzerland, 84-85, chmn dir, 85-90, pres board dir, 90-97, Chief Exec Officer, 91-2003; pres board dir Ringier Holding AG, 2003. *Awards:* Named one of Top 200 Collectors, ARTnews Magazine, 2004. *Mem:* Bilderberg Group. *Collection:* Contemporary art. *Mailing Add:* Ringier AG Pressehaus 1 Dufourstrasse 23 Zurich CH-8008 Swaziland

RINGNESS, CHARLES OBERT
EDUCATOR, PRINTMAKER
Study: St Cloud State Univ, BS, 68; Univ NMex, 70; Tamarind Lithography Workshop, Los Angeles, Master Printer(Ford Fel Grant), 70; Univ Cincinnati, MFA, 83. *Work:* Mus Mod Art, NY; Los Angeles Co Mus Art, Calif; Amon Carter Mus Western Art, Ft Worth, Tex; Canada Coun Art Bank, Ottawa; Pasadena Art Mus, Calif;

Art Gallery, Ont, Toronto. *Exhib:* One-man shows, Univ Cincinnati, Art Gallery, 73, Gallery Moos, Toronto, 79, 81, 83 & 85, Phillis Needlman Gallery, Chicago, 83, Condesso Lawler Gallery, NY, 83 & 84, Art Gallery, Ont, Toronto, 84, Helandenr Rubinstein Gallery, Palm Beach 85 & Malton Art Gallery, Cincinnati, 86 & 90, Lydon Fine Art, Chicago, 90, Peter M David Gallery, Minneapolis, 90; Canadian Biennial, Winnipeg Art Gallery, Man, 81; Condesso/Lawler Gallery, NY, 83 & 84; Van Straaten Gallery, Chicago, 85. *Teaching:* Asst prof, Univ SFla, 70-76, graphicstudio mgr, 71-76; assoc prof, Univ Sask, 76-85, prof, 85-. *Awards:* Ford Fel Grant, 68-70; Prizes for prints & drawing, Art Gallery Brant Inc, Brantford, Ont, 80 & 81; Kathleen Fenwick Award, Edmonton Art Gallery, 80; Sask Sr Arts Bd Grant, 82-83. *Bibliog:* Marshall Webb (auth), article, Arts West, 12/79; Carol Phillips (auth), article, Artscanada, 4/80; Charlie Crane (auth), Anti-multiple printmaker, Artmagazine, 6/80; articles in Palm Beach Daily News, Cincinnati Post & NY Times. *Mem:* Col Arts Asn, NY; Print & Drawing Coun Can; Canada Artists Representation. *Media:* Mixed. *Dealer:* Gallery Moos 136 Yorkville Ave Toronto ON Canada M5R 1C2; Lydon Fine Arts Chicago Ill. *Mailing Add:* Univ Sask Dept Art & Art History 3 Campus Dr Saskatoon SK S7N 5A4 Canada

RIPPE, DAN (CHRISTIAN)
PAINTER, INSTRUCTOR
b Giradote, Columbia, May 26, 34. *Study:* North Texas Univ, 53-57; Famous Artist Sch, 60-63; Studied with Paul Strisik. *Work:* US Army Med Training Ctr, San Antonio; Stockholm Univ Sch Med, Sweden,; Univ Tex Law Sch, Austin; E/Sys Ross Perot, Dallas. *Comn:* murals, US Army Med Training Ctr, San Antonio, 59; mountain & Aspen scenes, comn by Dr Christian D Rippe IV, Denver, 2000. *Exhib:* Coppini Acad Show, Panhandle Plains Hist Mus, Canyon, Tex, 68-74; Nat Acad Design, NY, 76; D'Art Mus & Gallery, Dallas, 79; Am Watercolor Ann, Nat Acad Design, NY, 76; Salmagundi Club, NY, 80, 97; Law Sch Mus, Univ Tex, Austin, 81; Land & Light Show, Mary Bryan Mem Gallery, Jeffersonville, Vt, 98 & 2001; Audubon Artists, Inc, Nat Acad Design, NY, 76. *Pos:* artist, engineer, Heath & Co, Dallas, 62-78; art dir, engineer, Tandy Electronics, Arlington, Tex, 85-96. *Teaching:* instr oil painting, Artisan Shop, Ruidoso, NMex, 74-75; instr oil techniques, Carrizo Lodge, NMex, 76-78; instr oil & aquamedia, Williamson Gallery, Dallas, 78-80. *Awards:* Outstanding Mural Award, Med Training Ctr, US Army, 59; Best of Show, Tex Fine Arts Asn, 75; Tara Fredrix Canvas Award, Audubon Artists 55th Ann, 97. *Bibliog:* Living - New Approach, Dallas Times Herald, 77; From Field to Studio (film), Metrop Libr System, Okla City, 83; Profile, Dan Rippe, Hensley Gallery Southwest, 98. *Mem:* Whiskey Painters Am; Audubon Artists, Inc; Salmagundi Club. *Media:* Oil, Watercolor. *Publ:* illusr, Drawing for the Student, N Tex Univ Press, 56-. *Dealer:* Hensley Gallery Southwest 311 N Pueblo Rd Taos NM 87571. *Mailing Add:* 717 West Cheryl Ave Hurst TX 76053

RIPPEL, M (MORRIS) CONRAD
PAINTER
b Albuquerque, NMex, Jan 23, 30. *Study:* Univ NMex, BS(Archit Eng), 58. *Work:* NMex Dept Development, Santa Fe; West Texas Mus, Lubbock; Denver Art Mus, Colo; Valley National Bank, Phoenix. *Exhib:* Retrospective, Haley Libr, Tex, 79; Nat Acad Western Art, Nat Cowboy Hall Fame, Okla, 75-81; Artists of Am Exhib, Colo Heritage Ctr, Denver, 81; Western Heritage, Houston, Tex, 81. *Pos:* Design architect, Chambers & Campbell Architects, 64-67. *Awards:* Prix de West, Nat Cowboy Hall Fame, 79; Gold Medal Watercolor, Nat Cowboy Hall Fame, 78 & 79. *Bibliog:* Susan E Meyer (auth), The watercolor page, Am Artist, 72; Mary Carroll Nelson (auth), A serious realist, Southwest Art, 80; Jean Jordan (auth), From blueprints to egg tempera, NMex Mag, 81. *Mem:* Nat Acad Western Art. *Media:* Egg Tempera; Drybrush Watercolor. *Dealer:* Settler's West Galleries 6420 North Campbell Ave Tucson AZ 85718. *Mailing Add:* 1317 NE Florida St Albuquerque NM 87110-6803

RIPPEY, CLAYTON
PAINTER, MURALIST
b La Grande, Ore, Apr 24, 23. *Study:* Northwestern Univ; Stanford Univ, with Daniel Mendelowitz, Ray Faulkner & Anton Refrigier, BA & MA; San Jose State Col, with George Post; Inst Allende, Mex, with James Pinto & Fred Samuelson. *Work:* Pepsi Cola, Bakersfield, Calif; Dance Mag Hq, NY; Wakayama Castle, Japan; Missions of Calif, Mexicali, Bakersfield, Calif; World of Legends, Los Altos, Calif. *Comn:* 2 murals (12' x 48'), Valley Plaza, Calif; Calif mural (12' x 46'), Tenneco Corp; mural (4' x 10') & mural (9' x 25'), Bakersfield, Calif; set of doors, Leo Lambile, Orras, Wash. *Exhib:* Lucian Labaudt Gallery, San Francisco, 55; Bakersfield Mus Art, Calif, 58, 61 & 66; Circulo de Belles Artes, Palma, Spain, 60; Haggen Mus, Stockton, Calif, 64; Galerie Yves Jaubert, Paris, France, 73; and over 85 solo-shows. *Pos:* Chmn art dept, Bakersfield Col, 69-72. *Teaching:* Prof art, Bakersfield Col, 49-67 & 69-80; prof art, Maui Comm Col, 68-69. *Awards:* Top 100 Arts for Parks, 90; Artist of the Year, 97, Sponsor Artist, 98, Wash. *Bibliog:* Contemporary Personalities, Parma, Italy, 81; murals by Mueller; Elan Mag, 90. *Media:* Acrylics, Watercolor; Mosaics. *Dealer:* Ryan Gallery 4270 N Highway 101 Lincoln City OR 97367; Scott Milo Gallery 420 Commercial Avenue Anacortes WA 98221. *Mailing Add:* 226 Keller St Petaluma CA 94952

RIPPON, RUTH MARGARET
SCULPTOR, CERAMIST
b Sacramento, Calif, Jan 12, 27. *Study:* Calif Col Arts & Crafts, with Antonio Prieto, BA, 47, MFA, 51; San Francisco Sch Fine Arts, with Joan J Pearson, scholar. *Work:* Crocker Art Mus, Sacramento; Vice President's House, Washington; Bemidji State Univ; Calif Expos & Fair, Sacramento; Mem Gallery Rochester; and many pvt collections. *Comn:* Life-size sculpture group, Mother w/children, Pavilions, A Robert Powel Development, Sacramento, 89; Freeport Sq, Sacto Sculpture Lifesize, 91; The Children's Hour, life-size sculpture group, Sierra Health Found, Garden Hwy, Calif; 3 discs (large wall), comn by Mr & Mrs Michael Heller, Gold River, Calif, 97; Leaping Koi (pond Sculpture), comn by Mr & Mrs Paul Fong, Sacramento, Calif, 98; Walting, UC Med Ctr, Sacto, CA; Life Size Bronze Woman Reading Carca, 2004. *Exhib:* One-woman shows, Artists Contemp Gallery, Sacramento, 79, 82 & 86, Univ Pac, Stockton, Calif, 76, Univ Rochester, NY, 76, Michael Himovitz Gallery, Sacramento, 90 & John Natsoulas Gallery, Davis, Calif, 95; 20-Yr Retrospective, Crocker Art Mus, Sacramento, 71; Oakland Mus, 74; Crocker Kingsley Retrospective, Sacramento, 75; Drawing Show, Sacramento City Col, 78; Col Holy Names, 82; Retrospective Calif State Univ, 87; Exhib Ceramic Conf, John Natsoulas Gallery, Davis, Calif, 91, 92, 93 & 94; Bronze UCD Med Ctr, Sacramento, Calif, 2000; 50 Year Retrospective, Fresno Art Mus, 02-03; and others. *Teaching:* Crafts dir, Presidio of San Francisco, 54-56; prof ceramics, Calif State Univ, Sacramento, 56-87 (Prof Emer, 87-). *Awards:* Many Purchase Awards, Calif State Fair & Expos, Sacramento, 48-66; Presidents Wives Series, San Francisco Potters Asn, DeYoung Mus, 69-70, Excellence in craftsmanship, AIA for Lollies, Powell Pavilion, 87; designated Woman Artist of the Year, Coun of 100, Fresno; designated as a Calif Living Treasure, Creative Arts League of Sacramento, 02. *Bibliog:* Oppi Untracht (auth), Ruth Rippon, Sgraffito Through Glaze, 57 & Fred Ball (auth), Ruth Rippon Retrospective, 71, Ceramics Monthly Mag; Ruth Holland (auth), Rippon Retrospective, Creative Arts League 71 Catalog, 71; Calif State Univ Retrospective catalog, 87; brochure, Fresno Art Mus, 03. *Mem:* Creative Arts League Sacramento; Asn Calif Clay Artists; Crocker Art Mus Asn. *Media:* Stoneware Clay, Watercolor, Pencil. *Dealer:* Solomon Dubnick Gallery Sacramento CA. *Mailing Add:* 98 Sandburg Dr Sacramento CA 95819

RIPPON, THOMAS MICHEAL
SCULPTOR, COLLECTOR
b Sacramento, Calif, Apr 1, 54. *Study:* Apprenticeship with Robert Arneson, Calif, 70-74; Sch Art Inst Chicago, MFA(Nelson Raymond Fel), 79. *Work:* San Francisco Mus Mod Art, Calif; Renwick Gallery, Smithsonian Inst, Washington; Contemp Art Mus, Honolulu, Hawaii; Erie Art Mus, Pa; Crocker Art Mus, Sacramento, Calif. *Comn:* Univ Mont, 96. *Exhib:* The Great Am Foot, Am Craft Mus, NY, 78; Clay Routes, San Francisco Mus Mod Art, Calif, 79; Wedgewood's Contemporaries, Philadelphia Mus Mod Art, Pa, 80; The Clay Figure, Am Craft Mus, NY, 81; Am Porcelain, Renwick Gallery, Smithsonian Inst, Washington, 81; Painting & Sculpture Today, Indianapolis Mus Art, Ind, 82; First Int Crafts Triennial, Art Gallery Western Australia, Perth, 89; New Masters Exhib (2 person), Huntington Mus Art, WVa, 91. *Pos:* Chmn, Dept Art, Univ Mont, 89-. *Teaching:* Asst prof fine art, Univ Nev, Reno, 87-89; vis prof fine art, Univ Calif, Davis, 89; assoc prof fine art, Univ Montana, Missoula, 89-. *Awards:* Artist Fel, Nat Endowment Arts, 74, 81. *Bibliog:* Vicki Halper (auth), Clay Revisions, Seattle Art Mus, 87; Ingrid Evans (auth), Cheerful Agglomerations, Artweek, 88; Nancy Bless (auth), Tom Rippon-A Poet's Game, John Michael Kohler Art Ctr Exhib Catalog, 93. *Mem:* Nat Coun Arts Adminrs; Col Art Asn. *Media:* Porcelain, Ceramic. *Collection:* Contemporary American Folk Art-naive-untrained contemporary painting, drawing & sculpture. *Dealer:* John Natsoulas Gallery 140 F St Davis CA 95616; John Elder Gallery 529 W 20th St New York NY 10011. *Mailing Add:* Univ Mont Dept Art Missoula MT 59812

RIPPS, RODNEY
PAINTER
b New York, NY. *Study:* York Col, BA, 72; Hunter Col, MA, 72 73. *Work:* Isreal Mus, Jerusalem; Rothchild Bank, Zurich, Switz; Brooklyn Mus; New Orleans Mus; LaJolla Mus; and others. *Exhib:* Critics Choice, Munson-Williams-Proctor Inst, Utica, NY, 77; one-man shows, Nancy Lurie Gallery, Chicago, 77, Brooke Alexander Gallery, NY, 77 & 78 & Galerie Daniel Templon, Paris, 78, Univ Art Mus, Calif State Univ, Long Beach, 84, Carl Solway, Cincinnati, Ohio, 86, Berkshire Mus, Pittsfied, Mass, 88 & Kim Foster Gallery, NY, 97-98; Holly Solomon Gallery, NY, 80-81; Univ Kentucky Art Mus, Lexington, 82; Joslyn Art Mus, Omaha, Nebr, 82; Univ Tex, Austin, 83; Jacksonville Art Mus, Fla, 83; Ronald Felman Gallery, NY, 84; Jewish Mus, NY, 86; Berkshire Mus, Pittsfield, Mass, 90; Marisa Del Re Gallery, NY, 91. *Pos:* Vis artist, Art Inst Chicago, 77, Ill State Univ, Bloomington, 78, Marisa Del Re, New York, 85 & Princeton Univ. *Teaching:* Instr painting, Brooklyn Mus Art Sch, 74-76. *Awards:* Nat Endowment Arts, 79 & 90. *Bibliog:* John Russell (auth), Painting 1985, The New York Times, 2/1/85; Anthony Bannon (auth), Anything goes, Buffalo News, 1/18/85; Stephen Westfall (auth), Ripps romantic theatre, Art in Am, 1/86. *Mem:* Abstract Artist Asn. *Mailing Add:* 535 Dean St # 901 Brooklyn NY 11217-2184

RIPSTEIN, JACQUELINE
PAINTER, WRITER
b Mex City, Mex. *Study:* Self taught. *Work:* Posada Hermandad, Toledo, Spain; Mus/Biblioteca Galeria Dos Puertas, Mex City, Mex; Biblioteca Cuernauaca, Mex. *Exhib:* St Carmen Mus, Mex City, Mex, 90; Jewish Community Ctr, Mus Community Ctr, Houston, 92; Centro Arte Cult, Posada Hermandad, Toledo, Spain, 94; Plastique Found Napoleon, Art Plastique Found, Paris, 95; Grand Prix Acquitaire & Grand Prix Paris Art, Mus Art Mod, Unet, France, 95; Kolel Art Show, Synagogue Caracas, Venezuela, 96. *Pos:* Staff artist, City Aventura, 96. *Teaching:* Instr children's art, South Beach Alternative Sch, 95 & Aspira of Fla United Way Educ Prog, 95; Dancing hands art, Moca Mus, 96. *Awards:* Dipl Honneur Encourgemont Pub, Oevre Francaise d'entraide Sociale, 95. *Bibliog:* Alberto Peldez (auth), Art Inquisitions Events Spanish TV; Joaquin Bravo, Hola Mag, 94; Cover Art Expressions, Henk Abbink, 96. *Media:* Oil, Poetry. *Publ:* Auth, Voices Esteticas II, Govt Mex, Ignacio Flores Autura, 79. *Dealer:* William Levine 761 Palmer Ave Holmdel NJ 07733; Wilm Fine Arts 168 Mercer St 2nd Floor Soho NY. *Mailing Add:* 2800 Williams Island Blvd No 804 Miami FL 33160-4935

RISBECK, PHILIP EDWARD
GRAPHIC ARTIST, EDUCATOR
b Kansas City, Mo, July 25, 39. *Study:* Univ Kans, BFA, 62, MFA, 65. *Work:* Sheldon Gallery Art, Lincoln, Nebr; Union Soviet Artists Collections, Moscow; Libr Cong; Wilanov Poster Mus, Warsaw; Moravian Mus, Brno, Czechoslovakia. *Exhib:* Int Poster Biennale, Zacheta Mus, Warsaw, 66, 68, 70, 72, 74, 76, 78, 84, 86, 88, 90, 92, 94, 2000 & 02; Graphic Design Biennale, Moravian Mus, Brno, Czechoslovakia, 66, 70, 74, 78, 82, 84, 86, 88, 90, 92, 94, 98, 2000 & 02; Posters USA, Mead Libr Ideas, NY, 75; Am Poster, 45-75, Smithsonian Inst, 76; Jurors Exhib, Cordegarda Gallery, Warsaw, 80; one-man exhibs, Gallery Union Soviet Artists, Moscow, 83, traveling exhib, 83-84 & Porto Museo de Los Soares, Portugal, 84, M'ARS Gallery, Moscow, Russia, 04; and many others. *Pos:* Co-dir, Colo Int Poster Exhib, 79-. *Teaching:* Prof art, Colo State Univ, 65-, dept chmn, 93-03. *Awards:* Durrell Award Res, Colo State Univ, 82; Outstanding Prof, Col Arts, Humanities & Soc Sci, Colo State Univ, 83; Honorable Diploma, Un Coun for Publ Awards for Outstanding Contrib to Graphic Design, 04. *Bibliog:* Richard Coyne (auth), Colorado State University Poster Exhibition, Commun Arts Mag, 79; Silas Rhodes (auth), Colorado State University Art Program in Graphics, Graphis, Zurich, 82; Oleg Savostiuk (auth), Philip Risbeck-An artist of the USA, Art Mag, Moscow, 84; Lanny Sommese (auth), Showroom: Phil Risbeck Novum, Gebrachs Graphik, 2000; Lanny Sommese (auth), Colo State Univ Graphic Design, Novum Gebrachsgraphik, 2004. *Mem:* Art Dirs Club Denver (pres, 81-82, mem bd, 81-); Univ & Col Designers Asn; Int Typography Alliance; Int Cong Graphic Design. *Publ:* Auth, Eighth International Poster Biennale in Warsaw, Graphis Press, Zurich, 80; Third, Fourth & Fifth Colorado International Poster Exhibition, Graphis, 84, 86 & 88. *Mailing Add:* 1113 Parkwood Dr Fort Collins CO 80525-1928

RISE, JOHN ERNEST
PAINTER
b Albuquerque, NMex, Nov 30, 54. *Study:* Tamarind Litho Workshops, with Garo Antresian, 74-75; Ariz State Univ, with Jim Pile, BFA, 76; Univ NMex, with John Wenger, MA(grad asst), 77. *Work:* Mus Albuquerque; Roswell Mus & Arts Ctr, NMex; Prudential Life Insurance Co, Los Angeles; Ariz State Univ, Tempe; Am Oil Co, Denver; and others. *Exhib:* One-man shows, William Sawyer Gallery, San Francisco, 79 & traveling show in Mex, 81-82; Here and Now, Mus Albuquerque, 80; Joslyn Art Mus, Omaha, 80; New Mexico Artists, Sarah Blaffer Mus, Univ Houston, 81; and others. *Pos:* Pres & gen mgr, Best Moulding Frames, 80-. *Awards:* Alumni Asn Award, Ariz State Univ, 76; Jurors Award, 8 West Biennial, Grand Junction, Colo, 80. *Bibliog:* Thomas Albright (auth), Decadence, motion, San Francisco Chronicle, 80; William Peterson (auth), New Mexico art, Portfolio Mag, 81; William Peterson (auth), New Mexico art, Art Am, 81. *Mem:* Nat Art Materials Trade Asn. *Media:* Oil, Chalk Pastel. *Dealer:* William Sawyer Gallery 3045 Clay St San Francisco CA. *Mailing Add:* 3816 Manchester Dr NW Albuquerque NM 87107-3020

RISELING, ROBERT LOWELL
EDUCATOR, PAINTER
b Sioux City, Iowa, June 5, 41. *Study:* Univ Northern Iowa, BA, 63, MA, 66; State Univ Iowa, 64; Univ Wis-Madison, MFA, 72. *Work:* Memphis Brooks Mus Art, Memphis Col Art, Tenn; Tenn State Mus, Nashville; Hamline Univ, St Paul, Rochester Art Ctr, St Cloud Univ, Anoka-Ramsey St Jr Col, Wilmar & City of St Cloud, Minn; Univ Northern Iowa, Cedar Falls; and many others. *Exhib:* One-man shows, Maka Gallery, Rock Island, Ill, 65 & 71, Univ Northern Iowa, Cedar Falls, 66, Rochester Art Ctr, Minn, 67, Hamline Univ, Minn, 67, 71 & 73, St Cloud State Univ, Minn, 68, 70 & 72, Edythe Bush Theatre, St Paul, Minn, 71 & Univ Wis, Madison, 72; Memphis Col Art, Tenn, 75 & 82, Commerce Sq Gallery, Tenn, 77, Theatre Memphis, Tenn, 78, Galveston Arts Ctr, Tex, 80, Clark Turner Gallery, Tenn, 82, Alice Bingham Gallery, Tenn, 83 & Albers Gallery, Tenn, 86; Jewish Community Ctr, Memphis, Tenn, 87 & Crown Plaza Hotel Gallery, Memphis, Tenn, 88; group shows, Luther Col Fine Arts Festival Exhib, 65 & 67, Luther Col Watercolor, Prints and Drawing, 65-66, 3rd Ann, Waterloo, Iowa, 66, Charles E MacNider Mus Painting and Drawing Exhib, Mason City, Iowa, 66, Minn State Fair, 66, Luther Col Drawing, Water, Print Show, 69 & Minn Printmakers, 70; Midwest Drawing Invitational, N Hennepin State Jr Col, 71, 8th Ann, Waterloo, Iowa, 71, 40th Ann Arrowhead, Tweed Gallery, Duluth, Minn, 73, 17th Ann Delta, Ark Arts Ctr, Little Rock, 74, Tenn Bicentennial, Nashville, 76, 11th Ann Prints and Drawings, Ark Art Ctr, Little Rock, 78 & Memphis in May Exhib, 81; Art in the Eighties, Tenn State Mus, Nashville, 81, Tenn State Mus, Nashville, 84, Memphis Ctr Contemp Art, Tenn, 89 & Flora, Goldsmiths Botanic Gardens, Memphis, Tenn, 90. *Teaching:* Instr art, Monticello, Iowa, 63-65; grad asst, Dept Art, Univ Northern Iowa, 65-66; asst dir & resident artist, 66-67, dir art, Rochester Art Ctr, 67; instr dept art, St Cloud State Univ, 67-71; teaching asst, Dept Art, Univ Wis, 71-72; asst prof, Dept Art, St Cloud State Univ, 72-74; asst prof, Memphis Col Arts, Tenn, 74-78, assoc prof, 78-, prof, 90-; vis artist, Lake Placid Sch Arts, NY, 81, Univ Northern Iowa, Cedar Falls, 83, Alfred Univ, NY, 83, Pac Northwest Col Art, Portland, Ore, 86 & fac, Gov Sch Arts Murfreesboro, Tenn, 89 & 90. *Awards:* First Award Painting, 8th Ann, Waterloo, 71; Second Award Painting, 40th Ann Arrowhead, Tweed Gallery, Duluth, Minn, 73; Purchase Award, Tenn Bicentennial, 76. *Media:* Acrylic, Collage. *Mailing Add:* 1273 N Pkwy Memphis TN 38104

RISHEL, JOSEPH JOHN, JR
CURATOR
b Clifton Springs, NY, May 15, 40. *Study:* Hobart Col, BA, 62; Univ Chicago, MA, 65. *Exhib:* Art in France Under the Second Empire, Philadelphia, 78-79, Detroit, 78-79, Paris, 78-79; Masters of 17th-Century Dutch Landscape Painting, Rijksmus Amsterdam & Mus Fine Arts, Boston, 87-88. *Collection Arranged:* Painting in Italy in the 18th Century: Rococo to Romanticism (co-ed, catalog), Chicago, Minneaolis & Toledo, 70-71; Art in France Under the Second Empire (auth, catalog), Philadelphia, Detroit, Paris, 78-79; Sir Edwin Landseer (auth, exhib catalog); Cezanne in Philadelphia Collections (auth, exhib catalog); British Painting in the Philadelphia Museum of Art from the Seventeenth through the Nineteenth Century; Claude Monet: Philadelphia, 87; Henry P McIlhenny Collection, 87-88; Masters of 17th-Century Dutch Landscape Painting, 87-88; Masterpieces of Impressionism and Post-Impressionism: The Annenberg Collection, 89. *Pos:* Cur, European painting before 1900 & John G Johnson Collection, Philadelphia Mus Art, 71-; cur, Rodin Mus, Philadelphia. *Teaching:* Instr art hist, Wooster Col, Ohio; lectr spec exhibs, Art Inst Chicago. *Mem:* Mus Loan Network; William Penn Found; Am Fedn Arts; Fel Am Acad Arts & Scis; Chevalier dans l'Ordre des Arts et des Lettres. *Publ:* The Hague School: some forgotten pictures in the collection, Philadelphia Mus of Art Bull, 15-27, 7-9/71; auth, Landseer: Queen Victoria's favorite painter copied in America, 19th Century Mag, Vol 7, autumn 81; A Lyonnais flower piece by Antoine Berjon (1754-1843), Philadelphia Mus Art Bull, Vol 78, No 336, 16-24, fall 82; contribr, Great French Paintings from the Barnes Found, (catalog), New York, Knopf, 93; co-editor Mus Studies, jour of Art Inst of Chicago; Degas and the Dance, exhib catalogue, Detroit Inst Arts, 02, Philadelphia Mus Art, 03. *Mailing Add:* 2322 Delancey St Philadelphia PA 19103

RISLEY, JOHN HOLLISTER
SCULPTOR
b Brookline, Mass, Sept 20, 19. *Study:* Amherst Col, BA(cum laude); RI Sch Design, BFA; Cranbrook Acad Art, MFA. *Work:* Wesleyan Univ; Fred Olsen Found, Conn; Hartford Jewish Community Ctr, Conn; Rose Art Gallery, Brandeis Univ. *Comn:* Wood & metal relief, IBM Hq, NY, 65; wrought iron relief, Cleveland Garden Ctr, Ohio, 66; copper relief, Nat Bank, Quarryville, Pa, 71; wood & metal sculptures, Brookside Elementary Sch, Waterville, Maine, 70; bronze sculpture, Univ Maine, Portland, 70. *Teaching:* Prof sculpture, Wesleyan Univ, 54-, chmn dept art, 68-93. *Awards:* Drakenfield Prize, 18th Ceramic Ann, 54; New Haven Arts Festival Sculpture Prize, 66; First Prize, Int Festival Humor and Satire, Bulgaria. *Publ:* Auth, The King is Moved, Princeton Univ Press, 10/94. *Mailing Add:* Wesleyan Univ Dept Art Middletown CT 06457

RISS, MURRAY
PHOTOGRAPHER, EDUCATOR
b Poland, Feb 6, 40; US citizen. *Study:* City Univ New York, BA; Cooper Union Sch Art; RI Sch Design, with Harry Callahan, MFA. *Work:* Mus Mod Art, NY; Bibliot Nat, Paris; Art Inst Chicago; Nat Gallery Art, Can; New Orleans Mus Fine Arts. *Comn:* Photograph Reelfoot Lake, State of Tenn, 72. *Exhib:* Mus Mod Art, NY, 70-71; one-man shows, Minneapolis Mus Fine Art, 71, Visual Studies Workshop (traveling show), NY, 76-78, Projects Inc, Cambridge, 79 & Southern Artist (worldwide traveling exhib), US Info Agency, 76; Fantastic Photog USA, six maj mus in Europe, 78; Photographer's Gallery, London, Eng, 79; Rhodes Col, Memphis, 80; Big Shot, Univ Ala, 83; Askew Nixon Gallery, 94-. *Pos:* Vis sr lectr, Univ Haifa, Israel, 75-76; cur, Emerging Southern Photographers, Memphis Col Art, 92. *Teaching:* Prof photog, Memphis Col Art, 68-86, head dept photog, 68-86. *Awards:* Nat Endowment Arts Grant, 79. *Bibliog:* William Parker (auth), Introduction to my portfolio, Ctr Photog Studies, 75. *Publ:* Illusr, Sleep Book, Harper & Row, 74; Good Abode: Architectural History of Shelby County, Towery Press, 83; The Guide to Mud Island, MM Publ, 87; Elmwood 2002, Elmwood Publ, 2003. *Dealer:* Visual Studies Gallery Rochester NY. *Mailing Add:* 1306 Harbert Ave Memphis TN 38104

RITCHEY, RIK
PAINTER, SCULPTOR
b Mountainhome AFB, Idaho, Mar 3, 53. *Study:* Wash State Univ, BA(fine art), 78; Mills Col, MFA(painting), 83. *Work:* Art Beam, Seoul, Korea; San Jose Mus Art, Calif; City of Pusan, Korea; Calif State Univ, Bakersfield. *Comn:* The Four Seasons after SFB Morse (bronze), Symp 94 Open Air, Pusan, Korea, 94. *Exhib:* One-man shows, Pascal de Sarthe Gallery, San Francisco, 89, IPOMAL Gallery, Landgraaf, The Neth, 90, New Sculpture, William Sawyer Gallery, San Francisco, 91, Tissue, In Khan Gallery, NY, 94, Fong Gallery, San Jose, Calif, 97 & New Paintings and Works on Paper, Klein Art Works, Chicago, Ill, 98; Oakland Artists '90, Oakland Mus, Calif, 90; Monoprints, Riverside Mus Art, Calif, 91; Material Abstraction (with catalogue), Seomi Gallery, Seoul, Korea, 92; Codified Desires (with catalog), traveling, 96 & 97; Blue, In Khan Gallery, NY, 97; Contemp Abstraction, Klein Art Works, Chicago, Ill, 98. *Pos:* Chairperson, Educ Subcomt ISC 1994 Biennial, Int Sculpture Ctr, Washington, DC, 93-94. *Teaching:* Instr studio art/theory, Univ Calif, Berkeley, 92- & Acad Art Col, San Francisco, 92-95; instr sculpture, Sierra Nev Col, Incline Village, Nev, 98. *Awards:* Inventer '89: La Cite du Bicentenaire Concours, La Villette Grand Halle, Paris, 87; Ann Flanagan Fel, Fel Exhib, KALA, 89-91; Artist Fel in Visual Arts, Calif Arts Coun, 90. *Bibliog:* Peter Selz (auth), Rik Ritchey, Art News, 5/89; Kenneth Baker (auth), Vigor and diversity in Oklahoma, San Francisco Chronicle, 14, 5/18/90; Roger Anderson (auth), Oaklandish art, Eastbay Express, 30-31, 6/22/90. *Mem:* Int Sculpture Ctr, Washington, DC. *Media:* All Media. *Publ:* Contribr, Small Arena for Heroics, Eye Mag, San Francisco, 85. *Dealer:* Dong Jo Chang In Khan Gallery 415 W Broadway New York NY 10012. *Mailing Add:* 667 11th St Oakland CA 94607

RITCHIE, CHARLES MORTON, JR
PAINTER, PRINTMAKER
b Pineville, Ky, Nov 21, 54. *Study:* Univ Ga, Athens, BFA, 77; Carnegie Mellon Univ, MFA(grad fel), 80. *Work:* Nat Gallery Art, Washington, DC; NY Pub Libr; Boston Pub Libr, Mass; Butler Inst Am Art, Youngstown, Ohio; Va Mus Fine Arts, Richmond; Fogg Art Mus, Harvard Univ Art Mus, Cambridge, Mass; Balt Mus Art, Md; Boise Art Mus, Idaho; Chrysler Mus, Norfolk, Va; Corcoran Gallery Art, Washington; Phila Mus Art, Pa. *Exhib:* Solo exhibs, The Interior Landscape, Marsh Art Gallery, Univ Richmond & Va Mus Fine Arts, 93-95, Works on Paper 1983-96, Butler Inst Am Art,

Youngstown, Ohio, 96, recent work, Numark Gallery, Washington, DC, 98, drawings & prints, Mary Baldwin Col, Staunton, Va, 98 &Spheris Gallery, NY, 2000; 171st Ann Exhib, Nat Acad Design, NY, 96; Prints Washington 1997, Corcoran Gallery Art, Washington, DC, 97; 61st Ann Mid-Year Exhib, Butler Inst Am Art, Youngstown, Ohio, 97; 40th Chautauqua Nat Exhib Am Art, NY, 97; group exhibs, Butler Inst Am Art, 99 & 2000, Washington Art Club, DC, 2001, Pepper Gallery, Boston, 2002, Swarthmore Col, Pa, 2003 & others. *Pos:* Staff artist, Univ Ga, 76-77; art dir, TFC Inc, Atlanta, Ga, 77-78; staff asst, Nat Gallery Art, Washington, DC, 81-85, res asst, 85-88 & asst cur dept mod prints & drawings, 88-. *Teaching:* Instr drawing, Carnegie Mellon Univ, Pittsburgh, Pa, 78. *Awards:* Individual Artist Fel, Arts Coun Montgomery Co, Md, 96; Individual Artist Award, Md State Arts Coun, 98; The MacDowell Colony Fel, 99; Individual Artist Award, Md State Arts Coun, 2000. *Bibliog:* Richard Waller (auth), Charles Ritchie: The Interior Landscape, Marsh Art Gallery, Univ Richmond, 94; Gabriella Fanning (auth), Working Proof: Charles Ritchie, On Paper, Vol 1, No 1, 29, 9-10/96; Jacqueline Brody (auth), Prints and Photographs Published: Charles Ritchie, Print Collector's Newsletter, Vol XXVII, No 1, 29, 3-4/96; Steven Zevitas (auth), New American Painting 33, Open Studios Press, Wellesley, Mass, 2000; Joanna Shaw-Eagle (auth), Print Masters at Corcoran, The Washington Times, 8/2001. *Mem:* Washington Print Club, DC; Print Coun Am. *Media:* Watercolor, Conte Crayon; Intaglio Printmaking, Lithography. *Publ:* Coauth, The 1980's: Prints from the Collection of Joshua P Smith, 89, Art for the Nation: Gifts in Honor of the 50th Anniversary of the National Gallery of Art, 91 & The Robert and Jane Meyerhoff Collection 1945-95, 95, Nat Gallery Art; auth, Gemini GEL: Recent Prints and Sculpture, Nat Gallery Art, 94; auth, Max Webers Modern Vision, 2000; and many others. *Dealer:* Center Street Studio 369 Congress St Boston MA 02210. *Mailing Add:* 3107 Lee St Silver Spring MD 20910-1052

RITCHIE, MATTHEW
PAINTER
b London, 64. *Study:* Boston Univ, BFA, 82; Camberwell Sch Art, BFA, 83-86. *Exhib:* Andrea Rosen Gallery, NY, 1999-2000, 2002, 2005; Mass Mus Contemp Art, North Adams, 2000; Lehmann Maupin Gallery, NY, 2000; San Francisco Mus Mod Art, 2001; Sammlung Goetz, Munich, 2001; Sydney Biennial, 2002; Inst Contemp Art, Philadelphia, 2002; Palais de Tokyo, 2003; Deste Found, Ctr Contemp Art, Athens, 2004; Whitney Mus Am Art, NY, 2005; St Louis Art Mus, 2006; represented by Atle Gerhardsen, Berlin, Parkett Editions, Zurich, Andrea Rosen Gallery, NY, Two Palms, NY. *Media:* miscellaneous. *Mailing Add:* Andrea Rosen Gallery 525 W 24th St New York NY 10001

RITCHIE, WILLIAM (BILL) H, JR
PRINTMAKER, VIDEO ARTIST
b Yakima, Wash, Dec 24, 41. *Study:* Cent Wash State Col, BA, 64; San Jose State Col, MA, 66; studied with Rolf Nesch, Norway, 69, intern Nat Ctr for Experiments in Television, 74; Studied Worldwide, 83. *Work:* Philadelphia Mus Art, Pa; US Info Agency, Japan; Seattle Art Mus, Wash; Tacoma Art Mus, Wash; Segovia Biennial, Spain. *Comn:* Print, Henry Gallery Asn, Seattle, Wash, 70; sculpture, City of Seattle, Wash, 77; prints, CDROM Publisher's Club, Seattle, Wash; Videotape, King Co Arts Comn, 80. *Exhib:* Nat Print Exhib, Libr of Cong, Washington, 71; Brit Int Print Biennale, Bradford Galleries, Eng, 72; NWest Film & Video Exhib, Portland Art Mus, Ore, 73 & 74; Am Printmaking, Brooklyn Mus Art, NY, 76; Boston Printmakers 29th Nat, DeCordova Mus, Lincoln, Mass, 77; Portopia, Kobe, Japan, 81; Perspectives: 100 Yr Washington Art, Tacoma Art Mus, 89; Northwest Vision, Seattle Art Mus, Wash, 90. *Collection Arranged:* Ritchie's Video Archives Northwest Regional Multimedia Arts. *Pos:* Art prof, Univ Wash, Seattle, 66-85; corp exec artist, Ritchie's, Inc, 90-96. *Teaching:* Prof art, Univ Wash, Seattle, 66-85; vis prof media arts, Evergreen State, Wash, 87, Univ Ore, 89 & Highline Community Col, 94; instr, Myartpatron.com, 2000-. *Awards:* Research Grants, Printmaking, Video & Computer Art, 70-76; First Prize, First NWest Film & Video Festival, Portland Art Mus, Ore, 73; Nat Endowment Arts Fel, 74. *Bibliog:* Korot & Schneider (coauths), Video Art, Harcourt, Brace, Jovanovitch, 76; F Eichenberg (auth), The Art of the Print, Harry N Abrams, 76; V Ancona (auth), Bill Ritchie: Video in the Northwest, Videography Mag, Vol 12, No 6; Lois Allan (auth), Contemporary Printmaking in NW, 97. *Mem:* Washington Software Asn (foundine mem digital media alliance 96-97). *Media:* All print media; Video and Computer Graphics. *Specialty:* diplayes tech assisted arts, research & dev. *Publ:* Auth, Behind Time in the Electronic Age, Ritchie's Video, 82; Print 'N Video News, Ritchie's Video, 85-87; Art of Selling Art, Ritchie's Perfect Press, 89; Reinventing Art Studios: Between Tradition and Technology, 93. *Dealer:* Emeralda Works Artist's Gallery 5th & Aloha PO Box 9627 Seattle WA 98109. *Mailing Add:* 500 Aloha-105 Seattle WA 98109-3901

RITTER, RENEE GAYLINN
PAINTER
b Bronx, NY. *Study:* Queens Col, NY, BA; Long Island Univ, Greenvale, NY, MFA. *Work:* Islip Art Mus, NY; Muscarelle Mus Art, Williamsburg, Va; Famli Mus, Hempstead, NY; Danville Mus Art, VA; Jane Voorhees Zimmerli Art Mus, Rutgers, NJ. *Exhib:* Sivermine Guild for Arts, New Canaan, Conn, 81, 83, 86, 92 & 94; Heckscher Mus Art, Huntington, NY, 90, 92, 94 & 96; Del Mus Art, Wilmington, 92; Art on Paper, Md Fedn Art, Md, 94, 95 & 96; Eleftherias Park Art Ctr, Athens, Greece, 96; Rathbone Gallery, Sage Col, Albany, NY, 96. *Pos:* Lectr, Nassau Co Mus Art, 79-91; exec bd, Nat Drawing Asn, 91-98. *Teaching:* Adj prof, art, CW Post Ctr, Long Island Univ, NY, 82-. *Awards:* Award of Excellence, Long Beach Mus, 87 & 88; Donn Steward Graphic Award, Heckscher Mus, 90; Purchase Prize, Muscarelle Mus Art, Williamsburg, Va, 96. *Bibliog:* Numerous articles including, NY Times, Newsday, Artspeak & Artists Mag, Christian Sci Monitor. *Mem:* Nat Asn Women Arts. *Media:* Paint, Collage. *Dealer:* Reece Gallery 24 W 57 St New York NY; Nese Alpan Gallery Huntington NY. *Mailing Add:* 62 Birchwood Park Dr Jericho NY 11753

RITTS, EDWIN EARL, JR
ADMINISTRATOR, MUSEUM DIRECTOR
b Pittsburgh, Pa, Nov 11, 48. *Study:* Wilmington Col, AB, 70; Univ Cincinnati, grad prog, 71; Univ NC, cert arts mgt, 85. *Collection Arranged:* Andrew Wyeth in Southern Collections, 76; Richard Hunt, Mountain Flight, 77; Pvt collection of Arthur & Holly Magill, 81; New Modern Painting, Harsh Images on Canvas, 84; America's Impressionists, 86. *Pos:* Pres, SC Artist's Guild, 74-75; treas, SC Mus Asn, 74-76; chmn art sect, NC Mus Conf, 89-91. *Teaching:* Lectr art markets, SC Gov Sch, 82; adj prof mus studies, Univ NC, 84-86. *Mem:* Am Asn Mus; NC Mus Conf. *Mailing Add:* c/o Historic Greenville Foundation 540 Buncombe St Greenville SC 29601-1906

RITZ, LORNA J
PAINTER, SCULPTOR
Study: Worcester Art Mus, 63-65; Boston Mus Fine Arts, 65; Art Students League, 66; Skowhegan Sch Painting & Sculpture, Scholar, 68; Pratt Inst, BFA, 69; Cranbrook Acad Art, Bloomfield Hills, Mich, MFA(painting & sculpture), 71. *Work:* Bank of Boston, Int Bank New Eng & High Voltage Eng, Shrafts Ctr, Boston; Mt Holyoke Col Art Mus; Hale & Dorr Lawfirm, Boston & NY; Veridex; Johnson & Johnson. *Exhib:* Solo exhibs, Nat Arts Mus, Teguciagalpa, Honduras, 83, Boston Visual Artists Union, 85, Augusta Savage Gallery, New Africa House, Univ Mass, Amherst, 87, Nicole C Gallery, Boston, 90, NACUL Archit Ctr, Amherst, Mass, 90 & Harriet Tubman House, Boston, 91; Art in Embassies Program, Washington, DC, paintings located in Guatemala City, Brazzaville, the Congo, Banjul, The Gambia, Valetta, Malta and Praia & Cape Verde; Lopoukhine Gallery, Boston, 88; Nat Asn Women Artists, Jacob Javits Ctr, NY, 89; Grossman Gallery, Sch Mus Fine Arts, Boston, 89; Lacoste Exhib, Mona Bismarck Found, Paris, 91; Portland Mus Art, Maine, 99; The Painting Center, 2003; Oxbow Gallery, Northampton, MA, 2004. *Teaching:* Asst prof painting, Univ Minn, 76-77; vis asst prof, Brown Univ, RI, 78 & Dartmouth Col, NH, 78-79; lectr, univs & insts throughout US and world; New York Studio School, New York, NY. *Awards:* US Info Agency Grant Awards, Vt, Partners of Americas, to paint, exhibit, lectr & teach at Univ Honduras, 83, Mass Partners of Americas, to teach, lectr & exhib at Inst de Belles Arted, Medelin, Columbia, 90; Esther & Adolph Gottlieb Found Emergency Grant Award, 88; Pollock Krasner Found Grant Award, 90, 99, 2004. *Media:* oil on linen. *Mailing Add:* 1245 S East St Amherst MA 01002

RITZER, GAIL L
COLLAGE ARTIST, CERAMIST
b Indianapolis, Ind, Jan 9, 54. *Study:* Univ Mo-Columbia, BS(art educ), 74; E Carolina Univ, MFA(ceramics/painting), 82. *Work:* Greenville Mus Art, NC; NC Mus Crafts; Psychology Clinic, Va Commonwealth Univ; Mendenhall Galleries, E Carolina Univ; Community Coun Arts, Kinston, NC. *Comn:* Ceramic sculpture, Bloomingdale's, NY, 85; ceramic mural, Southern Women's Show, Raleigh, NC, 86; ceramic sculpture, NC Solar Asn, Raleigh, 86; ceramic sculpture, Sch Textiles, NC State Univ, 90; tile mural, NC Arts Coun/Elmhurst Sch, Greenville, 96. *Exhib:* NC Artists Exhib (with catalog), NC Mus Art, 80; NC Sculpture Exhib (with catalog), Northern Telecom Corp, Research Triangle, 84; Fantastic Fibers (with catalog), Yeiser Art Ctr, Paducah, Ky, 96; Form & Freedom (with catalog), Int Quilt Festival, Houston, 96; one-women show, E Carolina Univ, Greenville, NC, 96; Expressions of Freedom (with catalog), Int Quilt Study Ctr, Lincoln, Nebr, 98; NC 20th Century Masters, Lee Hansley Gallery, Raleigh, NC, 2000; Reformations (with catalog), The Courthouse Galleries, Norfolk, Va, 2000; Remembrance: Women, Bloomsburg Univ, Pa, 2000; Women Artists: Works from the Greenville Mus Art Collection (with catalog), NC, 2001; NC Art Quilts (with catalog), Green Hill Ctr for NC Art, 2001; Story Quilts (with catalog), Univ Mo, St Louis, 2001; Story Quilts, Greenville Mus of Art, Greenville, NC, 2002; Art Quilts, East Carolina Univ, 2004; Women of the GMA, E Carolina Univ, 2005; Imago Dei (with catalog), E Carolina Univ, 2006; Juried Nat Art Exhib, Chadron State Col, Nebr, 2006; Small Works Invitational Salon Exhib (with catalog), New Arts Program, Kutztown, Pa, 2006. *Teaching:* instr classes in mixed media, Greenville Mus of Art, 90-. *Awards:* Visual Artists Proj Grant, NC Arts Coun, 96, Emerging Artist Grant, 96, Regional Artist Proj Grant, 97 & 2001; Regional Artist Proj Grant, 2005. *Bibliog:* Lynn Lewis Young (auth), The Quintessential Quilt, Quilts Inc, 96; Gail L Ritzer (auth), Mommy, sew me a Story, Art/Quilt Mag, Lynn Lewis Young Publ, 97. *Media:* Mixed Media. *Publ:* auth, Expressions of Freedom: Quilts Celebrating Human Rights, Quilters Newsletter Mag, 3/99; auth, Fiberarts Design Book 7, Susan Mowery (ed), Kieffer Lark Books, 2004; auth, Quilting Arts Magazine, John P. Bolton Publ, summer 2005, No 18. *Dealer:* Lee Hansley Gallery, 225 Glenwood Ave, Raleigh, NC, 27603. *Mailing Add:* 1318 Red Banks Rd Greenville NC 27858

RIVERA, ELIAS J
PAINTER
b Bronx, NY, April 18, 1937. *Study:* Art Students League, 55-61, with Frank Mason; pvt study with Steve Raffo, 61-64. *Work:* Ga Mus Fine Arts, Athens; Adelphi Univ, Long Island, NY; Vassar Mus, Poughkeepsie, NY. *Comn:* Mural, Banco de Ponce, Rockefeller Plaza, NY, 73; four paintings and one bronze plaque, pvt comn by Fortunoff family, NY, 80. *Exhib:* Community Gallery, Brooklyn Mus, NY, 69; Nat Acad Design, NY, 71, 73, 74, 77 & 78; Crimes of Passion, Chrysler Mus, Norfolk, Va, 81; Santa Fe Festival Arts, NMex, 83 & 84; Ctr Contemp Arts, Santa Fe, 85; Miniature Show (91, 92), Albuquerque Art Mus, NMex, 93; Cacciola Gallery, NY, 93; The Americas: A Latin Connection, Nev Inst Contemp Art, 93; one-man exhib, Visions of Solola, Riva Yares Gallery, Santa Fe, NMeax & Scottsdale, Ariz, 95; Riva Yares Gallery, Santa Fe, NMex, 95 & 97. *Awards:* Best Painter, De Puerte Rico Inst, 72; Purchase Prize, Ann Show, Am Acad & Inst Arts & Lett, 78; Creative Artists Pub Serv Award, 81. *Media:* Oil. *Mailing Add:* c/o Georgetown Gallery Art 3235 P St NW Washington DC 20007

RIVERA, FRANK
PAINTER
b Cleveland, Ohio, Aug 28, 39. *Study:* Yale Univ Grad Sch Fine Arts, with Alex Katz & Jack Tworkov, BFA, 62; Univ Pa, with Pi Dorazio, Savelli, Helen Frankenthaler & Ludwig Sander, MFA, 67. *Exhib:* Ann Am Painting & Sculpture, Pa Acad Fine Arts, 68; NJ State Mus Painting & Sculpture Ann, 72; Univ Rochester Gallery Art, 72; Susan Caldwell Gallery, NY, 74; 1975 Biennial Exhib Am Art, Whitney Mus Am Art, 75; Ellarslie Mus, Trenton, NJ, 84; Abington Art Ctr, Pa, 87; Considine Gallery, Princeton, NJ, 89; Mariboe Gallery, Swig Art Ctr, Hightstown, NJ, 95 & 97; City Without Walls, Urban Gallery; New Art & Artists, Newark, NJ, 99. *Pos:* Staff Art Critic & Rev, Town Topics Publ, Princeton, NJ, 99. *Teaching:* Prof painting & design, Mercer Col, Trenton, NJ, 67- Trenton Times, 3/23/75. *Awards:* Nat Endowment Humanities Grant for Study & Travel in France, 72-73. *Bibliog:* Wendy Heisler (auth), Windsor-Hights-Herald, Princeton, NJ, 95; Richard Shea (auth), Time Off Mag, Princeton, NJ, 97; Dan Bischoff (auth), Newark Star Ledger, 99. *Media:* Oil on Canvas. *Publ:* critic/art reviewer US1, Princeton, NJ. *Mailing Add:* 110 Broad St Hightstown NJ 08520

RIVERA, GEORGE
MUSEUM DIRECTOR, PAINTER
b Japan, Nov 5, 55; US citizen. *Study:* San Jose State Univ, BA, 79, MA, 82. *Exhib:* San Jose Mus Art, 88; de Saisset Mus, 93; Los Gatos Mus Art Hist, 99; Washington Sq Gallery, 2001; D P Fong Galleries, 2001, 02, 03; Euphrat Mus Art, Cupertino, Calif, 2003-2004; Los Gatos Mus Art, Los Gatos, Calif, 2005. *Pos:* cur, Triton Mus Art, Santa Clara, Calif, 86-94, asst dir & chief cur, 94-97, exec dir, 97-. *Teaching:* Assoc fac art, Mission Col, Santa Clara, Calif, 86-; instr, Exten Prog, Univ Calif, Berkeley, 96- & Pac Art League, Palo Alto, 98-; instr, DeAnza College, Cupertino, CA. *Awards:* Asian Heritage Award, 92; Critics Choice Award, 96; Jean Bock Spirit of Art Award, 2000. *Media:* Oil, Charcoal, Acrylic, Watercolor, Mixed Media. *Dealer:* dp Fong Gallery San Jose Calif; Michael Himovitz Gallery Sacramento Calif; Washington Square Gallery San Francisco CA; Togonon Gallery, San Francisco Gallery, San Francisco, CA. *Mailing Add:* Triton Museum of Art 1505 Warburton Ave Santa Clara CA 95050

RIVO, SHIRLEY WINTHROPE
PAINTER
b Toronto, Ont; US citizen. *Study:* Kean Univ, BA, & teaching certification, 77, MA, 80; studied with Carl Burger, Vito Giacalone, James Howe, Wanda Gromodska, Joseph Loeber, Nicholas Reale, Michael Metzger. *Work:* Winter in the Park, Schering-Plough, Corp Hq, Madison, NJ; painting, Johnson & Johnson, World Hq, New Brunswick, NJ, 94; Nat Baseball Hall Fame & Mus, Cooperstown, NY; Statue of Liberty Nat Monument, Liberty Island, NY, 99; Yankee Stadium, Bronx, NY, 98; Cooperstown, NY, 1998; Brooklyn Botanic Garden, NY; Morris Mus, Morristown, NJ; Nabisco Corp Hqs, Hanover, NJ; The New York Botanical Garden, Bronx, NY 2005; Summit Free Pub Libr, Summit, NJ, 2006. *Comn:* Revelation For Centennial of Brooklyn Bridge, 1983, Morris Mus, Morristown, NJ. *Exhib:* One-woman exhibs, Chemical Bank, NY, 77, St Barnabas Med Ctr, Livingston, NJ, 78, NJ Ctr Visual Arts, Summit, NJ, 79 & 85, Ciba-Geigy Corp, Summit, NJ, 79, Exxon Corp, Linden, NJ, 84, Chubb Corp World Hq, Warren, NJ, 85, Johnson & Johnson, World Hq, New Brunswick, NJ, 94, Schering Plough, Kenilworth, NJ, 94; Images, Members Gallery, NJ Ctr Visual Arts, AT&T, Prudential, Chubb, 88, 90 & 91; Arts Counc of Morris Area at Schering Plough, Madison, NJ, 92; Award of Merit, Paper Mill Playhouse, Millburn Short Hills Arts, 95; Salmagundi Club, NY, Nat Soc Painters, 96, 97, 98 & 2000; Union Co Arts Exhib, NJ Ctr Visual Arts, 96; paintings, NJ Sen Robert C Torricelli Senate Off, Washington, DC, 97-98; Seton Hall Univ, 98; Paper Mill Play House, Renee Foosaner Gallery, 98; 2-person exhib, Schering-Plough, Madison, NJ, 2000; Two- Person Exhibition, Overlook Hospital, Summit, NJ, 2003; One Woman Exhibition, Johnson & Johnson Health Care, Piscataway, NJ, 2004, Photographs, Visual Arts Center NJ at Summit Free Pub Libr, 2006. *Pos:* Window display designer, Display Craft & Belg Stores, 44-53; theatrical design & decor, Actors Co, Toronto, Ont, 51-53; needlepoint design, Creative Yarn Kits Inc, New York, 65-72. *Teaching:* Substitute teacher art, various high schs NJ, 77-90. *Awards:* Award of Excellence, Mill Playhouse, NJ, 90, 91 & 95; Award of Merit, Atrium Gallery, Morristown, NJ, 97; Award of Excellence in Photograph, Atrium Gallery, 99; The Outstanding Achievement in Amateur Photography Award for 2004 from The Int Soc of Photographers, Owing Mills, MD; Merit Award for photography, Renee Foosaner Gallery, Papermill Playhouse, NJ, 2003. *Bibliog:* Andrea Kannape (auth), New York Times, 11/1/98; Kristie Hanley (auth), The Star-Ledger, 10/22/98; Mitchel Seidel (auth), The Star-Ledger, 10/23/99, 3/8/2006; Liz Keill (auth), Summit Herald, 2/18/2006. *Mem:* NJ Ctr Visual Arts (prog chmn, 1979-1984); Millburn-Short Hills Art Ctr (bd trustees, 1986-2006); NJ Ctr Visual Arts (chmn of classes, 1990-1998); Nat Mus Women in Arts; Nat Soc Painters in Acrylic & Casien. *Media:* Oil, Acrylic, Photog. *Interests:* Writing, film, science. *Mailing Add:* 32 Summit Rd New Providence NJ 07974

RIZZI, JAMES
PAINTER, PRINTMAKER
b Brooklyn, NY, Oct 5, 50. *Study:* Miami Dade Jr Col, AA, 72; Univ Fla, BFA, 74. *Work:* Brooklyn Mus, NY; Isetan Sagamihara, Kanagawa, Japan; Seibu Parco, Chiba, Tokyo, Japan; Int Olympic Mus, Lausanne, Switz, 96. *Comn:* 45-meter outdoor mural, Eric's Bar & Grill, NY, 75; painting, Werzalit AG, Ger; ltd ed collector's China vase, candlestick holders, canister, plate, expresso cup, decorative box & pitcher, Rosenthal China, 94-95; exterior of Boeing 757 in celebration of their 40th anniversary, 96; paintings, Int Olympic Mus, Lausanne, Switz; Painted Smart Car, Spiral Garden, Tokyo; Origina Art, Siemens Corp, 01; Exterior of train, City of Heilbronn, Ger, 02. *Exhib:* 30 Yrs of Am Printmaking, Brooklyn Mus, NY, 76; one-man shows, Fine Art Mus, Hempstead, Long Island, Tsukuba City Mus, Japan, 92, Kunst Mus Limburg, Ger, 96, Univ Fla, Gainesville, 96, Int Olympic Mus, Lausanne, Switz, 96 & Ctr Arts, Vero Beach, Fla, 97. *Awards:* Guest of Hon, United Hospital Fund, 92; Guest of Hon, Am Anorexia/Bulimia Asn, 93; Citation, Atlanta Olympic Comt, 96; Sport Artist of Yr, US Sports Acad, Ala; Invited Artist World Economic Forum, Davos, 98. *Bibliog:* Gerrit Henry (intro auth), James Rizzi 3-D, Constructions, 88 & Glenn O'Brien (auth), Rizzi, 92, John Szoke Graphics; Juan Antonio Samaranch (intro auth) & George Plimpton (auth), James Rizzi-Dreams of Sport, Olympic Mus & Study Ctr, 96. *Media:* Acrylic, Oil; Miscellaneous Media. *Publ:* Auth, 3-D Constructions, John Szoke Graphics Inc, New York, 88; Rizzi, John Szoke Graphics Inc, New York, 92; feature article with cover, Dan's Papers, 8/96; The New York Paintings, Prestel-Verlag, Ger, 96; Christmas Cooking in NY, Mary Hahn verlag, Muenchen, Germany, 97; American Cookies & More, Sudwest Verlag, Germany, 00. *Mailing Add:* c/o John Szoke Editions 591 Broadway 3rd fl New York NY 10012-3232

RIZZIE, DAN
COLLAGE ARTIST, PAINTER
b Poughkeepsie, NY, May 23, 51. *Study:* Hendrix Col, Conway, Ark, BA, 73; Southern Methodist Univ, Dallas, Tex, MFA, 75. *Work:* Dallas Mus Fine Arts & Univ Gallery, Southern Methodist Univ, Tex; Witte Mus, San Antonio, Tex; Brooklyn Mus, NY; Mus Mod Art, NY Pub Libr, Metrop Mus Art, NY; Univ Tex, Austin. *Comn:* Akard Mall banners, City of Dallas, Tex, 79; Signa Life Insurance, Dallas, 94. *Exhib:* one-man shows, Lizan Tops Gallery, East Hampton, NY, 97, 99, Allene Lapides Gallery, Santa Fe, 97, 98, 99, Dan Rizzie: Works on Paper, Dueringer Gallery, Jackson, Miss, 98, Liz Mayer Fine Art, New York City, 97, West End Fine Arts Gallery, West Palm Beach, Fla, 97; Black and, Flatbed Gallery, Austin, Tex, 99; Flatbed Press Impressions, Amarillo Mus Art, Tes, 99; Mutiple Impressions, ACA Gallery, Austin, 99; Flatbed at Ten, Flatbed Press, Austin, 99; 3 Americans, Wilson Stephens Fine Art, London, 99; Flatbed Selections, Flatbed Gallery, Autstin, 2000. *Teaching:* Instr lithography & drawing, Southern Methodist Univ, Dallas, 74-75; instr drawing, Richland Col, Dallas, 75-76; instr painting & drawing, Eastfield Col, Dallas, 76-80. *Awards:* Best of Shows, Tex Painting & Sculpture, 76, Shreveport Ann, 77 & Tarrant Co Ann, 78. *Bibliog:* Festival, The East Hampton Star, 20, 10/28/99; Marion Walberg Weiss (auth), Honoring the Artist: Dan Rizzie, Dan's Papers, 10/15/99. *Media:* Drawing, Collage. *Publ:* Betsy Craz (auth), A Cinema Toast, In Style, 304, 6/99,. *Dealer:* Allene La Pedes Gallery 217 Johnson St Santa Fe NM. *Mailing Add:* PO Box 1672 Sag Harbor NY 11963

RIZZOLO, LOUIS (LOU) B M
ENVIRONMENTAL ARTIST, PAINTER
b Ferndale, Mich, Oct 8, 1933. *Study:* Western Mich Univ, with Harry Hefner, BS(art), 56; Univ Iowa, with Frank Wachowiak & Maurico Lasansky, Ky, MA(art), 60, post grad studies, Univ Ga, with Lamar Dodd, 69-70. *Work:* Mich Artist Permanent Collection, Battle Creek Mus Art; Western Mich Univ Collection, Kalamazoo; Kalamazoo Inst Art, Mich; Chicago Inst Arts, Oxbow Prog; Univ Iowa. *Comn:* Mind Energy (multi-media performance), Mich Found Art, Detroit, 85; Mind Events (multi-media performance), Upjohn Co, Kalamazoo, Mich, 86; Skye Gondola (interactive light art work), Dow Corning/Midland Ctr Art, 86-87. *Exhib:* Construction to Performance, Minn Mus Am Art, St Paul, Minn, 86; North Skye, Mich Technol Univ, Handcock, Mich, 88; Oxbow Light, Chicago Inst Arts, Oxbow Prog, Saugatuck, Mich, 88 & 89; Calgary Skye, Mt Royal Conserv Int Workshop, 90; Swiss Skye, Nat Conserv, Lake Geneva, Lausanne, Switz, 91; Lyon Skye, Lyon Conserv Nat de Region, Lyon, France, 94; Scottish Royal Acad Int Workshop, 95; Konserthus Norway Int Workshop, 97; Palais des Festivals, Int Workshop, Biarritz, France, 98; Bjergsted Install, Stavanger Norway, 2002; Fear/Fun, Multimedia Performance WMU, 2002; Starr Earthwork, Albion, 2002. *Pos:* Dir & artist, Rizzolo & Assoc, ILWC (Art/Tech Collaborative), Glenn, Mich, 1979-2003. *Teaching:* Prof art painting, drawing & multi-media, Western Mich Univ, 1964-2003, Int Workshops, Md, 1989-2003; watercolor painting instr, Kalamazoo Inst Arts, 1968-81. *Awards:* W K Kellogg Found Expert-in-Residence, Kellogg Skye Environ Art, 92; Mich Millennium Proj State Grant, Mich Coun Arts & Cult Affairs, 96-97 & Nat Endowment Arts Regrant, 98; Fetzer Inst, 1999, 2000; Richard Florsheim Art Fund, 2002; Starr Commonwealth, 2000-2002; artist residency, W R Kellogg Found World Pece Art Initiatives. *Bibliog:* Review, New Art Examiner, Chicago, Ill, 11/84; Fetes d'ete, Int Workshops, Lyon, France, 7/94; Rizzolo Ganther (dir), Michigan Millennium (film), Ganther Films, Chicago, 11/96; Art for Peace, Reclaiming Children & Youth, Sculpture Nat Jour Beijing, 2003. *Mem:* Mich Watercolor Soc; Int Soc Arts & Technol; World Forum on a Coustic Ecology. *Media:* Environmental Light Art; Watercolor. *Publ:* Contribr, Int Skye Art Catalog, 1st & 2nd ed, MIT Press, 83 & 91; Emphasis Art, Int Textbook, 89; The Fourth Coast, Penguin Books, 95; Best of Watercolor, 95, Creative Inspriations, 96, Rockport Publ. *Mailing Add:* PO Box 62 Glenn MI 49416

ROATZ See Myers, Dorothy Roatz

ROBB, CHARLES
PAINTER
b Toronto, Ont, June 28, 38. *Study:* Ont Col Art, AOCA, 59, with Jock MacDonald, John Alfson & Carl Schaefer. *Work:* Can Coun Art Bank, Ottawa; Citicorp Ltd, Toronto; Kitchener/Waterloo Art Gallery, Ont; Esso, Calgary, Alta; Art Gallery London, Ont, Can; and others. *Exhib:* One-man shows, Pollock Gallery, Toronto, 77-82 & Gallery One, Toronto, 82-90; three-man show, Agnes Etherington Art Centre, Queens Univ, Kingston, Ont, 77; Art for Bus Sake, Art Gallery Ont, Toronto, 75; Lefebvre Galleries, Edmonton, Alta, 81; Kitchener/Waterloo Art Gallery, Ont, 81; and others. *Bibliog:* D Adlow (auth), Stripes by Robb, Christian Sci Monitor, 64; Kay Woods (auth), Charles Robb, Arts Canada, 77 & 81; Seeing it Our Way, Portrait of Charles Robb (film), Canadian Broadcasting Corp. *Media:* Acrylic. *Mailing Add:* 121 Nymark Ave No 104 Willowdale ON M2J 2H3 Canada

ROBB, DAVID METHENY, JR
HISTORIAN, MUSEUM DIRECTOR
b Minneapolis, Minn, Apr 12, 37. *Study:* Princeton Univ, BA, 59; Yale Univ, MA, 67; Attingham Summer Sch, 78; Mus Mgt Inst, Univ Calif, Berkeley, 83. *Collection Arranged:* The Book of Hours of Charlotte of Savoy, 73; Star Spangled History, 75-77; Louis I Kahn: Sketches for the Kimbell Art Museum (auth, catalog), 78; Elisabeth Louise Vigee Le Brun, 82; Vivid Colors: Three Pastel Artists, 93; co-cur, Early Alabama: Our Land and Lifeways, 98. *Pos:* Res asst, Nat Gallery Art, DC, 63; cur, Collection of Mr & Mrs Paul Mellon, 63-65; curatorial fel, Walker Art Ctr, Minneapolis, 67-69; cur, Kimbell Art Mus, Ft Worth, Tex, 69-74, chief cur, 74-83 & acting dir, 79-80; dir, Telfair Acad Arts & Sci, Savannah, 84-85 & Huntsville Mus Art, Ala, 85-95; dir emer, Huntsville Mus Art, 95-. *Awards:* Ford Found Cur Training Fel, 68-69. *Mem:* Col Art Asn; Am Asn of Mus; Soc Archit Historians. *Res:* American and European portrait painting; architectural and landscape photography; southern landscape painting; 19th century southern photography. *Publ:* Ed, Kimbell Art Mus Catalogue, 72; Louis Kahn: Sketches for the Kimbell Art Mus, 78; Kimbell Art Mus Handbook, 81. *Mailing Add:* 506 Lanier Rd Huntsville AL 35801

ROBB, LAURA ANN
PAINTER, INSTRUCTOR
b Winfield, Kansas, Apr 5, 55. *Study:* Art Students Acad, 70-71; studied with Michael Aviano, 72-73, with Richard Schmid, 74. *Exhib:* Miniatures 2000, Albuquerque Mus Art, NMex, 2000; Am Art in Miniature, Gilcrease Mus, Tulsa, Okla; Salon D'Arts, Denver, Colo, 2002-2006; guest artist, Western Rendezvous Art, Helena, Mont, 2006. *Teaching:* instr oil painting, Scottsdale Artists Sch, Ariz, 93-99, Valdes Art Sch, Santa Fe, 94-2001, Fechin Art Inst, Taos, NMex, 2000-2001. *Awards:* Grumbacher Gold Medal, Catherine Lorillard Art Club, 86; John F and Anna Lee Stacey Scholar award, 91; Liquitex Award, Oil Painters of Am juried exhib, 96. *Media:* Oil, Watercolor. *Publ:* contribr, The Subject is Merely A Vehicle, Art of the West, 90; Laura Robb, Southwest Art, 92; Emerging Realist Painters, Art-Talk, 96; Contemporary American Oil Painting, Jilin Publ House, 99; A Personal Sense of Beauty, Southwest Art, 4/2001; In the Studio, Southwest Art, 1/2002; An All-Consuming Passion, Arts of the West, 5/2003-6/2003; A Sharp Eye, The Artist's Magazine, 9/2003; The Cultural Times, 9/2006. *Dealer:* Claggett / Rey Gallery 100 East Meadow Dr Vail CO 81657

ROBB, PEGGY HIGHT
PAINTER, INSTRUCTOR
b Gallup, NMex, Sept 14, 24. *Study:* Univ NMex, BFA & MA, with Raymond Jonson & Kenneth Adams; Art Students League, New York, 64. *Work:* Univ NMex, Albuquerque; Guangzhuo Art Inst, China, 84. *Comn:* Stained glass window & portraits, Christian Ctr, Albuquerque, 75; McDonnell-Douglass Aircraft, St Louis, Mo, 79. *Exhib:* Southwestern Fiesta, NMex Art Mus, Santa Fe, 66; Sun Carnival Art Exhib, El Paso, Tex, 71; Centre Int D'Art Contemporian, Paris, 83; Inst Art, Guangzhuo, China, 84; NMex State Fair, 86; Biennial exhib, Ariz, Colo, NMex, Tex & Utah, 87; Expressions of Faith, Scottsdale, Ariz, 87; Christians in the Visual Arts, Washington, 87; Graham Ctr Mus, Wheaton, Ill, 87 & 89; Sacred Arts 200, Civic Ctr Mus, Philadelphia, 89. *Pos:* Juror, Statewide Exhib, 81, 87, 89, 91; bd dir, Col Fine Arts, Univ NMex, 89-. *Teaching:* Univ NMex, Continuing Educ. *Awards:* First Prize, NMex State Fair, 59 & 63; Exhib Awards, St John's Episcopal Cathedral, Albuquerque, 78 & 79; Jurors Award, Nat Christian Fine Arts Exhib, Farmington, NMex, 96. *Bibliog:* Conceptions Southwest, Southwest Art Mag, Univ NMex, 85. *Mem:* Albuquerque Asn United Artists; Christians in the Visual Arts; Albuquerque Arts Alliance. *Media:* Acrylic, Oil. *Mailing Add:* 7200 Rio Grande Blvd NW Albuquerque NM 87107

ROBBIN, TONY
PAINTER, SCULPTOR
b Washington, DC, Nov 24, 43. *Study:* Columbia Univ, BA, 65; Yale Univ, MFA, 68. *Work:* Whitney Mus Am Art, NY; Neuberger Mus, Purchase, NY; Loch Haven Art Ctr, Orlando; Crysler Mus, Norfolk, Va; Del State Mus, Wilmington. *Comn:* Prudential Insurance, Newark, NJ, 82; Southeast Bank, Miami, Fla, 83; United Bank, Houston, 83. *Exhib:* Le Wouvean Mus, Lyon, France, 80; McNay Art Inst, San Antonio, 83; Loch Haven Art Ctr, Orlando, 83; Concepts in Construct, Neuberger Mus, Purchase, NY, 84; Computers & Art, IBM Gallery, NY, 88; Kaos, Chicago Acad Sci, 89; solo exhibs, Am Assoc, Advancement Science, Washington, DC, 92 & Boston Meeting, 93, Fordham Univ, NY, 92 & Williams Gallery, Princeton, 92; Structure of Symmetry, Hungarian Nat Gallery, Budapest, 89; Bronx Mus Arts, 91; The William Collection, Princeton, 92; Contemp Develop Design Science, 95; Building for the Future, Istanbul Mus, 96; Am Asn Advan Sci, Fordham Univ, Univ Sci, Philadelphia, Univ Fla, Greenville, 2006. *Awards:* Artist Fel, Nat Endowment Arts, 75; Nat Science Found Grant, 89. *Bibliog:* Linda Henderson (auth), Princeton Univ Press, 83; David Curtis (auth), To the Nth Dimension, Innovations/PBS, 87; Cynthia Goodman (auth), Distal Visions, Henry Abrams, 87. *Media:* Acrylic, Sculpture. *Publ:* Chuangtze, Main Currents, 75; Painting & Physics--4 Dimensions, Leonardo, 84; Quasi crystals for Architecture, Leonardo, 89; Auth, Fourfield: Computers, Art & the 4th Dimension, 92; auth, Engineering a New Architecture, 96; auth chpt, Beyond the Cube, by J Francis Gabriel, 97; auth numerous articles. *Mailing Add:* 423 Broome St New York NY 10013

ROBBINS, DAVID A
CONCEPTUAL ARTIST, WRITER
b Whitefish Bay, Wis, Apr 17, 57. *Study:* b Brown Univ, Providence, RI, BA, 79. *Work:* Mus Boymans von Beunigen, Rotterdam, Holland; Univ Chicago. *Exhib:* Presi Per Incantemento, Padiglione d'Arte Contemporanea, Milan, Italy, 88; The Photog of Invention, Nat Mus Am Art, Smithsonian, Washington, DC, 89; Image World, Whitney Mus Am Art, NY, 89; D&S Austellung, Kunstverein, Hamburg, Ger, 89; Das Offentliche Bild, Forum Staatpark, Graz, Austria, 91; numerous solo exhibs. *Bibliog:* Doris Von Dratein (auth), David Robbins, Kunstforum, 88; Joshua Decter (auth), Psychosafari, Artscribe, 91; Olivier Zahm (auth) The Wanderer, Texte Zur Kunst, 91. *Media:* Photographs, Sculpture. *Publ:* Auth, The Camera Believes Everything, Eds Schwarz, Stutgart, 88; Foundation Papers from the Archives of the Institute for Advanced Comedic Behavior, NY, 92; auth of more than 30 essays & articles

ROBBINS, EUGENIA S
WRITER, EDITOR
b New York, NY, Apr 22, 35. *Study:* Smith Col, BA. *Pos:* ed, Art & Auction, 80; news ed, Art Express, 81-; secy, Iriquois Co, formerly & Ctr Can Archit Adv Bd, formerly; dir, Friends of the Vt State House; chmn, Langeview House Restoration, 82-84. *Teaching:* Instr, Union Col, Schenectady, NY. *Media:* Print. *Res:* Persian art and architecture; modern art and architecture; Art books; history of photography; historical preservation on prints and drawings; early photography, American art. *Collection:* 19th and 20th century paintings, drawings, and prints. *Publ:* Auth & coauth, articles in Studio Int, Art in Am, Art and Auction & NY Post; auth, Art, Collier's Yr Bk; auth, regular column in Art J & rev in Art in Am & Art J; Toulouse Lautrec; and others. *Mailing Add:* 28 Walker Rd Braintree VT 05060

ROBBINS, HULDA D
PAINTER, PRINTMAKER
b Atlanta, Ga, Oct 19, 10. *Study:* Pa Mus Sch Indust Art, Philadelphia; Prussian Acad, Berlin, with Ludwig Bartning; Barnes Found, Merion, Pa. *Work:* Metrop Mus Art, NY; Victoria & Albert Mus, London, Eng; Bibliot Nat, Paris; Art Mus Ont; Smithsonian Inst, Washington. *Exhib:* Portrait of Am, NY & Tour, 45-46; Current Am Prints, Carnegie Inst, Pittsburgh, 48; Nat Print Ann, Brooklyn Mus & Tour, 48-49; Nat Exhib Prints, Libr Cong, Washington, 56; US Info Agency Print Exhib Europ Tour, 72-. *Teaching:* Instr basic & advan serigraphy, Nat Serigraph Soc Sch, 54-60; instr creative painting, Atlantic Co Jewish Community Ctr, Margate, NJ, 60-67. *Awards:* Purchase Award, Prints For Children, Mus Mod Art, 41; Paintings by Printmakers Award, 47 & Babette S Kornblith Purchase Prize, 49, Nat Serigraph Soc. *Mem:* Print Club; Am Color Print Soc. *Media:* Oil. *Dealer:* The Picture Store Boston MA; William P Carl Fine Prints Boston. *Mailing Add:* 16 S Buffalo Ave Atlantic City NJ 08406

ROBBINS, JACK C
PAINTER, SCULPTOR
b Dallas, Tex. *Study:* Univ NTex, study with Robert Wade, BFA, 77; Univ Tex, San Antonio, MFA, 94. *Work:* Mus Mod Art, Ft Worth, Tex; ARTPACE Found Contemp Art, San Antonio, Tex; City Pub Art Coll, Dallas; Barrett Coll Tex Art, Dallas. *Comn:* City billboard, Patrick Media Co, Arlington, Tex, 87; pedestrian tunnelway, City of Dallas, 96. *Exhib:* Social Distortions, Los Angeles Contemp Exhibs, 86; Tornadoes Twister of Fate, Vanderbilt Univ, 90; Prints from Permanent Collection, Ft Worth Mus Mod Art, 90; 40 Texas Printmakers, Laguna Gloria Mus, Austin, Tex, 92, Return of Cadavre Exquis, The Drawing Ctr, NY, 93. *Bibliog:* Janet Kutner (auth), Dallas Morning News, 9/90; Joel W Barna (auth), Tex Architect, 2/94; Dan Goddard (auth), San Antonio Expos News, 6/95. *Media:* Installation. *Dealer:* Parchman-Stremmel Presa St San Antonio TX

ROBBINS, JOAN NASH
PAINTER, COLLAGE ARTIST
b Kalamazoo, Mich, Nov 24, 41. *Study:* Western Mich Univ, BA, 63; Oakland Univ, MA, 69. *Comn:* Jungle Story (series of 4 collages), St Louis Fed Savings & Loan, 84; Growth (series of 4 collages), Gen Am Life, St Louis, 85; Rivers Run (diptych collage), AT&T, St Louis, 85; Dance (diptych collage), AT&T, St Louis, 86. *Exhib:* An Art Affair, Westport, St Louis, 82 & 84-86; San Diego Int, 85; Watercolor Missouri, William Woods Col, Fulton, Mo, 85; 10th Okla Ann, Norman Gallery, Lawton, Okla, 85; 10th Nat Ann, Southern Watercolor Soc, Okla Art Ctr, Oklahoma City, Okla, 86. *Teaching:* Pvt instr, collage & watermedia, in studio & in workshops. *Awards:* Moerschel Award, St Charles 17th Ann Show, 82; Merit Award, An Art Affair, Show, St Louis, 83; Norman Gallom Award, Watercolor, Okla 10th Ann, 85. *Mem:* Southern Watercolor Soc; Midwest Watercolor Soc; St Louis Art Guild; North Coast Collage Soc. *Media:* Watercolor, Collage. *Mailing Add:* 204 N Gilmore St Charleston MO 63834

ROBBINS, MICHAEL JED
PAINTER, PRINTMAKER
b New York, NY, June 15, 1949. *Study:* High Sch Music & Art, New York, dipl, 66; Cooper Union, New York, BFA, 70; Syracuse Univ, MFA (teaching fel), 71. *Work:* Mus City NY; Brooklyn Mus; Mus Liege, Belg; Smithsonian Inst Nat Gallery Art, Washington, DC; Rutgers Univ, NJ; Univ NC, Greensboro; Mus of Boverie Park, Brussels, Belgium. *Comn:* Posters, Molissa Fenley Dance Co, NY, 80; on site oil on panel mural, ESPA Dept Store, 84; banners & posters, 84-85, Ito Yokado Corp, Tokyo; outdoor banners, St Marks Church, NY, 87. *Exhib:* Drawings, Czech Mus Mod Art, 76; Recent Drawings by Younger Artists, Whitney Mus, 78; Art in the 70's-Richard Brown Baker Collection, Rochester Univ Mus, 79; The Block Print, Whitney Mus, 82; NY in Print, Mus City NY, 82; Paintings, Prints, Trustees Collection, Albright-Knox Mus, 86; Am Expressionists, Montclair Mus, NJ, 87; Prints, Rutgers Univ, 88; traveling exhib, Robi Collection, Smithsonian Inst Nat Gallery Art, 98. *Pos:* Fine Artist, currently; Minister, currently. *Teaching:* Asst instr art & drawing, Syracuse Univ, 70-71; sub-instr painting, Cooper Union, 76 & 80-85. *Awards:* CAPS Grant, NY, 78; NEA Grant, 85. *Media:* Oil Painting; Linocuts. *Specialty:* Prints, drawings, works of the 1920s, 30s & 40s. *Interests:* Art, ministry, lecturing. *Collection:* Museum of the City, New York; The Brooklyn Museum, New York City; The collection of Richard Brown Baker, New York City; The Metropolitan Museum of Art, New York City; The Smithsonian Inst Nat Gallery of Art, New York City. *Dealer:* Ellen Sragow 67-73 Spring St New York NY. *Mailing Add:* 136 E 208 Norwood NY 10467

ROBBINS, PATRICIA
PAINTER
b Brooklyn, NY, Oct 27, 51. *Study:* American Univ, Washington, DC, BA, 73; Johns Hopkins Univ, Baltomore, MD, MLA, 77. *Work:* Morgan Stanley Regional Headquarters, San Luis Obispo, Calif. *Comn:* Painting, Botanical Garden, Calif, 2005; painted Violin Mozart Int Music Festival, 2006. *Exhib:* Asian Style, McConnell Gallery, San Luis Obispo, Calif, In the Tin Gallery, San Luis Obispo, Calif, Roofs, Doors, Windows, San Luis Obispo Art Center, 2004; New Art, Fogg Mus Contemp Art, Boston, Mass, Asian Style 2005, Excellent Experiences Gallery, San Luis Obispo, Calif, Miniatures, Monterey Mus Art, Biennial Exhib, Monterey Mus Art, Monterey, Calif, Small Works Exhib, Bakersfield Mus Art, Bakersfield, Calif, 2005; Biennial Exhib, Monterey Mus Art, Miniatures, Monterey Mus Art, Monterey, Calif, Configurations, San Luis Obispo Art Center, San Luis Obispo, Calif, Sacred Women, Art Harvest, Sacramento, Calif, Nat Asn Women Artists Small Works Exhib, Karpeles Libr Mus, 54th Haggin Juried Exhib, Haggin Mus, Stockton, Calif, Nat Asn Women Artists 117th Ann Exhib, Reading, Pa, 2006; Solo exhibs, City of Paso Robles, Paso Robles, Calif, Postcards, Excellent Experiences Gallery, San Luis Obispo, Calif, Postcards 2, Excellent Experiences Gallery, Santa Cruz, Calif, 2006. *Awards:* Elizabeth Horman Mem Award, 2005; Hon Mention 2nd City Coun Gallery Exhib. *Mem:* Nat Asn Women Artists (juried mem); Nat Asn Independent Artists; San Luis Obispo Oil, Pastel & Acrylic Group; Women Painters West (juried); Women Caucus Art; Int Asn Acrylic Painters; Col Art Asns. *Media:* Acrylic, oil. *Mailing Add:* 7170 Cerro Robles San Luis Obispo CA 93401

ROBBINS, TRINA
CARTOONIST, ILLUSTRATOR
b Brooklyn, NY, Aug 17, 38. *Exhib:* Corcoran Gallery, Washington, DC, 69; Global Space Invasions, San Francisco Mus Mod Art, 78; Pork Roasts, Univ BC Fine Arts Gallery, Vancouver, 81. *Awards:* Inkpot Award, San Diego Comic Art, 77. *Bibliog:* Ronald Levitt Lanyi (auth), Trina, Queen of underground comics, Univ Calif, Davis, 78; Sharon R Gunton (ed), Contemporary Literary Criticism, Vol 21, Gale Res, 82. *Publ:* Ed & contribr, It ain't me, Babe, 70 & contribr, Wimmen's Comix No 1-6, 72-76, Last Gasp; Wet Satin No 1 & 2, Krupp/Last Gasp, 76 & 78; auth & illusr, Flashback Fashions, Price, Stern, Sloan, 83; coauth, Women and the Comics, Eclipse Enterprises, 85; and others. *Mailing Add:* 1982 15th St San Francisco CA 94102

ROBBINS, WARREN M
MUSEUM DIRECTOR, EDUCATOR
b Worcester, Mass, Sept 4, 23. *Study:* Univ NH, BA, 45; Univ Mich, MA, 49; Del State Univ, LHD, 2001. *Hon Degrees:* Lebanon Valley Col, Pa, Hon DL, 75; Int Col, Los Angeles, LHD, 79; Univ NH, LHD, 79; Frostburg State Univ, LHD, 96. *Collection Arranged:* The Sculptor's Eye, Chaim Gross Collection, 76; The Traditional Art of the Nigerian People: The Ratner Collection, 77; Art of Zaire: The Bronson Collection, 78; Traditional Sculpture from Upper Volta, 79; The Useful Arts of Kenya, 79; African Puppetry, 80; Selections from the Permanent Collections, 80-81; Traditional Costumery and Jewelry in Africa, 81; Traditional Costumes and Jewelry of Egypt, 81; Forms and Influences of African Art, Washington Proj Arts, 85; African Art, Frostburg State Univ, 93; Mondrian & African Art, Nat Acad Sci, 92; Ben Shahn on Human Rights, Am Univ & US Dept Health & Human Serv, 92-95; African Art & Textiles, Dept Health & Human Serv, 93; African Textiles, Frostburg State Univ, 94; African Textiles, Univ Mich, 96; The Language of African Art (traveling), Frostburg State Univ & Del State Univ, 96-97; Ben Shahn on Human Rights, Del State Univ & Univ Mich, 96-97; and others; 5000 Objects of African Art. *Pos:* Founder & dir, Robbins Ctr Cross Cult Commun, 63-; founding dir, Mus African Art, 64-82; founding dir emer & sr scholar, Nat Mus African Art, Smithsonian Inst, 82-; bd mem, Duke Ellington Sch Arts. *Teaching:* Lectr African art, Mus African Art, Washington, DC, 64-. *Awards:* Phelps-Stokes Aggrey Medal, 93; Univ Mich Regents Alumni Outstanding Achievement Award, 94; Robbins Ctr Grad Studies Dedication Award, Univ Mich Sch Art & Design, 96. *Bibliog:* Steve Rosoff (auth), The collector, Mich Alumnus, 1/92; Josephine Gregory (auth), Making connections work, UNH Alumni Companion, 92; Roulhac Toledano (auth), A collector and his collections find two houses better than one, Roll Call, 7/93; and others. *Mem:* Cosmos Club; DC Comn Arts & Humanities; Am Asn Mus; Libr Congress Arts Comn, Univ Mich Nat Adv Bd. *Res:* Influence of African Culture on Modern Art. *Collection:* Traditional African Art and Textiles. *Publ:* Auth, African Art in American Collections, Vol I, Praeger, 66; African Art in American Collections, Vol II, Smithsonian, 89; Making the galleries sing, Mus News, 9-10/94; Art, science & education in a democratic society, Lib Educ, fall 96; The malling of a museum: African art goes elite, while the audience just goes away, Wash Post, 9/29/96. *Mailing Add:* 530 Sixth St SE Washington DC 20003

ROBERSON, SAMUEL ARNDT
ARCHITECTURAL HISTORIAN, EDUCATOR
b Honolulu, Hawaii, May 5, 39. *Study:* Williams Col, BA, 61, MA, 63; Salzburg-Klessheim Sch, cert, 65; Yale Univ, PhD, 74. *Collection Arranged:* American Paintings from a Private Long Meadow Collection, Amherst Col, 71; Five College Modern Architecture, Amherst Col, 72; Early Chicago Architecture, Herron Sch Art, 80. *Pos:* Consult, Eye of Thomas Jefferson Bicentennial Exhib, Nat Gallery Art, Washington, DC, 74-76; acad coordr, Nat Endowment Humanities Learning Mus Prog, Indianapolis Mus Art, 76-80; dir, Historic Indianapolis Inc, 80-; comnr, Ind Film Comn, 83-; adj assoc prof Am studies, Sch Liberal Arts, Ind Univ, 84-. *Teaching:* Instr art hist, Williams Col, 61-63, Yale Univ, 64-66, Princeton Univ, 66-68 & Amherst Col, 69-72; asst prof, Herron Sch Art, 72-76, chmn art hist, 72-80, assoc prof, 76-; vis assoc prof, Ind Univ, Bloomington, 76. *Mem:* Soc Archit Historians; Col Art Asn; and others. *Res:* Eighteenth and nineteenth century American architecture and landscape gardening. *Publ:* Auth, The Technical Creation of the Greek Slave, 65 & coauth, The Greek Slave, 65, Newark Mus; contribr, Praeger Encyclopedia of Art, Praeger Publ, 71; auth, Indiana Historic Sites and Structures Reports, 80-; Historic American Buildings Survey in Indiana Catalog, 83. *Mailing Add:* Herron Sch of Art 1701 N Pennsylvania Indianapolis IN 46202

ROBERSON, SANG
CRAFTSMAN
b Greenville, Miss, Feb 7, 38. *Study:* Sophie Newcomb Col, Tulane Univ; Daytona Beach Community Col; Arrowmont, Gatlinburg, Tenn; Penland Sch, NC; Univ Miss, BA. *Work:* Mus Arts & Sci, Daytona Beach, Fla; Off Chief Exec Officer, Walt Disney World, Fla; Orlando City Collection, Fla; DeLand Mus Art, Fla; also pvt collections of Dan Rather, CBS News, Steffi Graf, Ger, Jane Fonda & others. *Exhib:* Solo exhibs, Decorative Touch, Greenville, Miss, 89, Gallery 500, Elkins Park, Pa, 93, Albers Gallery, Memphis, Tenn, 93, Hibbard-McGrath Gallery, Breckenridge, Colo, 94 & 96, Sampson Galleries, Stetson Univ, DeLand, Fla, 95 & Ormond Mem Art Mus, Ormond Beach, Fla, 96; Pa Acad Art, Philadelphia, 92; Philadelphia Mus Art, 92 & 94; Florida's NEA & SAF Recipients Exhib, Fla Craftsmen Gallery, St Petersburg, Fla, 97; SOFA-MIAMI, Gingrass Gallery, Milwaukee, Wis, 97; Smithsonian Craft Show, Washington, 97 & 2000; Beyond Function, Columbus Mus Art, Ga, 97; Sophia Wanamaker Gallery, San Jose, Costa Rica, 2001; Fla Craftsmen Gallery, St Petersburg, Fla, 2001; Wyndy Moorhead Fine Arts, New Orleans, La, 2001; Gayle Wilson Gallery, Southampton, NY, 2001. *Awards:* Nat Endowment Arts Visual Artist Fel, 94; Award Excellence Southeastern Crafts Regional Exhib, Tampa Mus Art, Fla, 95; First Place Ceramics, Am Craft Expo, Evanston, Ill, 96; Award Excellence, Am Craft Coun Atlanta, 2000. *Bibliog:* Southern Homes Mag, 7/90; Ceramics Monthly, 5/92; The Year of American Craft Desk Diary, Harry N Abrams Publ, New York, 93. *Mem:* Am Craft Asn (bd dir, 93); Piedmond Craftsmen; Arts Coun Volusia Co; Am Craft Coun; Fla Craftsmen (secy exec bd, 88-89); Fla Dept Cult Affairs (visual arts fel panel). *Media:* Terra Cotta, Terra Sigillata. *Dealer:* Blue Spiral Ashville NC; Albers Fine Art Gallery Memphis TN. *Mailing Add:* 19 Orchard Lane Ormond Beach FL 32176

ROBERSON, WILLIAM
TAPESTRY ARTIST, COLLAGE ARTIST
b Ripley, Miss, Feb 15, 39. *Study:* Memphis State Univ; Memphis Col Art, BFA; Ind Univ. *Work:* Ark Art Ctr, Little Rock; Tenn Craft Collection, Craft Mus, Nashville; 1st Nat Bank, Orlando, Fla; Falls Creek State Park, Tenn; and others. *Comn:* Tapestries, comn by Lausanne Sch, Memphis, 70, Jewish Community Ctr, Memphis, 71, Holiday Inns of Am, Aberdeen, Tex, 73, Opryland Hotel, Nashville & First Tenn Bank, Memphis. *Exhib:* Young Americans, Mus Contemp Crafts, NY, 69; Piedmont Craft Exhib, Sneed Mus, Charlotte, NC; Miss Arts Festival, Jackson; Southeastern Craftmen Show, San Antonio, Tex. *Pos:* Assoc dean. *Teaching:* Assoc prof fiber design, Memphis Col Art, 69-. *Mailing Add:* 694 N Trezevant St Memphis TN 38112

ROBERT, JEAN See Ipoustéguy, Jean Robert

ROBERTS, CLYDE HARRY
PAINTER, INSTRUCTOR
b Sandusky, Ohio, June 12, 23. *Study:* Cleveland Inst Art, dipl, 46; Columbia Univ, MA, 49; also with John Pike, Robert Brackman, Edgar Whitney & William Schultz. *Work:* Washington Co Mus Fine Arts, Hagerstown, Md; Ford Times Gallery, Dearborn, Mich; State House, Annapolis, Md; Merchants & Farmers Bank; Washington Co Hosp Ctr. *Comn:* Murals, Rocco's Restaurant, 87, Washington Co Tourism Ctr, 89; hist painting, Renfrew Mus, Waynesboro, Pa, 91. *Exhib:* Many exhibs, Baltimore Watercolor Open, Cumberland Valley Exhib, Cleveland Mus May Show, Valley Art Asn Gallery; one-man show, Pa State Univ, 79. *Pos:* pres Valley Art Asn, 90-91, 99-2002. *Teaching:* Instr painting, Hagerstown Cmty Col, 57-; supvr art, Washington Co Bd Educ, 68-81; retired; instr watercolor, Mont Alto Campus, Pa State Univ; instr art teacher educ, Shepherd Col, WVa, 89; pvt studio painting, 92. *Awards:* First Prize, Cumberland Valley Artists, 88, 89, 90, 93, 94, 96, 98, 2000 & 2006; Artists Members Award, Baltimore Watercolor Club, 71, 74, 98, 99, 2000; First Award, Pa Watercolor Soc, 81; First Prize, Baltimore Watercolor Soc, 2005; and others. *Bibliog:* G Horn (auth), article, Art Today, 68; feature article, Painting--Materials and Techniques, Timmons, 79; article, US News & World Report, 82; Palette Talk, 94. *Mem:* Nat Art Educ Asn; fel Royal Soc Art, Lifetime mem; Pa Watercolor Soc; Valley Art Asn; Art Alliance; signature mem, Pa Watercolor Soc; life mem, Baltimore Watercolor Soc. *Media:* Watercolor. *Specialty:* Benjamin Art Gallery, Hagerstown. *Interests:* Photography. *Collection:* Washington County Museum of Fine Art. *Publ:* Illusr, Ford Times Mag, 58; contribr, Sch Arts, 68; Artists News Unlimited, 71; Nat Geog Sch Ed, 73; auth, article, Palette Talk, 80. *Dealer:* Little Gallery Montalto PA 21722; Mansion House Art Ctr Hagerstown MD 21740; Benjamin Art Ctr Hagerstown. *Mailing Add:* 219 N Colonial Dr Hagerstown MD 21740

ROBERTS, DONALD
EDUCATOR, PRINTMAKER
b Wolfeboro, NH, Nov 24, 23. *Study:* Vesper George Sch of Art, Boston, cert; RI Sch of Design, Providence, BFA; Ohio Univ, Athens, MFA. *Work:* Cleveland Mus of Art; Tate Gallery, London; Rosenwald Collection, Los Angeles; Seattle Mus, Wash; Libr of Cong, Washington, DC. *Exhib:* Dayton Art Inst, Ohio, 60, 65 & 74; 1st-3rd Lithography Ann, Tallahassee, Fla, 64-67; The Print Club, Philadelphia, 68; Contemp Am Prints, Krannert Mus, Champaign-Urbana, Ill, 70; Huntington Galleries, WVa, 71; and others. *Teaching:* Prof printmaking, drawing & painting, Ohio Univ, Athens, 53-. *Awards:* Tamarind Lithography Grant, 62; Purchase Award, 9th Ann Paint of the Yr, Mead Corp, 63; Pennypacker Award, 4th Ann Soc Am Graphic Artists, 65. *Bibliog:* William Sargent (auth), American Printmakers, Ashland Oil Corp, 76. *Mailing Add:* 6555 Frum Rd Athens OH 45701

ROBERTS, HELENE EMYLOU
HISTORIAN, EDITOR
b Seattle, Wash, Mar 23, 31. *Study:* Univ Wash, BA, 53, MA, 57, ML, 61. *Pos:* Art librn, Dartmouth Col, Hanover, NH, 63-66 & slide librn, 68-70, cur visual collections, Harvard Univ, 70-94; adv ed, Victorian Periodical Newslett, 75-; ed, Visual Resources, currently. *Awards:* Librn Res Fel, Harvard Univ Libr, 80-81; Distinguished Serv Award, Visual Resources Asn, 91. *Mem:* Historians Brit Art; Col Art Asn; Res Soc for Victorian Periodicals (treas, 70-75); Am Soc Picture Professionals; Visual Resources Asn. *Res:* Dante Gabriel Rossetti; Victorian Art; Eighteenth and nineteenth century art periodicals; images of women in art; Associationalism & gothic revival. *Publ:* Auth, The sentiment of reality, Thackeray's art critism, In: Studies in the Novel, Vol 13, 81; Exhibition and review: the periodical press and the Victorian art exhibition system, In: Victorian Periodical Press, Leicester Univ Press, 82; ed, Art History through the Cameras Lens; auth, Cardinal Wiseman, the Vatican & the Pre-Raphaelites, In: Pre-Raphaelite Art in Its European Context, Assoc Univ Presses, 95; ed, Encyclopedia of Comporative Iconograpy, Fitzroy Dearborn, 98; auth, The Persistence of My Thological, Religious and Literary Narratives in Works of Art In: Images and Belief, Princeton Univ Press, 1999. *Mailing Add:* 80 Lyme Rd No 331 Hanover NH 03755

ROBERTS, HOLLY L
PAINTER, PHOTOGRAPHER
b Boulder, Colo, Dec 22, 51. *Study:* Univ NMex, BA, 73; Ariz State Univ, MFA, 81. *Work:* San Francisco Mus Art; Ctr Creative Photog, Tucson, Ariz; Mus Photog Art, San Diego, Calif; Los Angeles Mus Contemp Art; Art Inst Chicago; and others. *Exhib:* Crosscurrents: Recent Additions to the Collection, San Francisco Mus Art, 86; Photog & Art: Interactions Since 1946, Los Angeles Co Mus Art, 87; solo exhibs, Friends Photog, San Francisco, 89, Lowe Art Gallery, Syracuse Univ, NY, 90, La Photographie en Miettes, Musee Nat d'Art Moderne, Centre Georges Pompidou, Paris, 92, Presentation House, North Vancouver, BC, Can, 92, Mesa Col Art Gallery, San Diego, 93, Saddlebrook Col Art Gallery, Mission Viejo, Calif, 93, Linda Durham Gallery, Santa Fe, NMex, 93, Ctr Photog Art, Carmel, Calif, 93, Roger Williams Univ, Bristol, RI, 94 & Robert Koch Gallery, San Francisco, 94; Am Art Today: Surface Tension, Art Mus, Fla Int Univ, Miami, 92; New Acquisitions/New Work/New Directions, Los Angeles Co Art Mus, 92; Diverse Directions, Tex Christian Univ, Fort Worth, 93; Beyond Boundaries, Light Factory, Charlotte, NC, 93; 4x4: Late Modern; Photog Between the Edges, Mus Fine Arts, Santa Fe, NMex, 94. *Awards:* Fel Photog, Nat Endowment Arts, 86 & 88; Ferguson Grant, Friends of Photog, Carmel, Calif, 86. *Bibliog:* Northwest by Southwest; Painted Fictions, Palm Springs Desert Mus, Calif, 90; David Featherstone (auth), Holly Roberts, Friends of Photography, 90; Gerald Lang & Lee Marks (auth), The Horse: Photographic Images, 1839 to the Present, Harry N Abrams, 91. *Mailing Add:* 251 Alamos Corrales NM 87048

ROBERTS, LUCILLE (MALKIA) D
PAINTER, EDUCATOR
b Washington, DC. *Study:* Howard Univ; Univ Mich, AM; New York Univ; Acad Grande Chaumiere, Paris; Univ Ghana; also with Jose Gutierriez, Mexico City, Mex. *Work:* Atlanta Univ; WVa State Col; Jefferson Community Col, Water Town, NY. *Exhib:* One-man shows, Porter Gallery, Howard Univ, 71 & Col Mus, Hampton Inst, 72; Nat Exhib Black Artists, Smith-Mason Gallery, Washington, DC, 71; Black Artists Exhib, Afro-Am Cult Ctr, Cleveland State Univ, 72. *Teaching:* Asst prof art, DC Teachers Col, Washington, DC, 65-78, assoc prof, 78-; vis assoc prof African & Afro-Am art, State Univ NY Col Oswego, 70-71; retired. *Awards:* First Prize, Mem Show, 65 & Evening Star Award, 66, Soc Washington Artists; James A Porter Award, Cleveland State Univ, 72. *Bibliog:* Lewis & Wadday (auths), Black Artists on Art, 69; J Edwin Atkinson (auth), Black Dimensions in Contemporary Art, Carnation Co, 70. *Mem:* Nat Conf Artists; Black Acad Arts & Lett; Soc Washington Artists; DC Art Asn. *Media:* Oil, Acrylic

ROBERTS, MARK DENNIS
PHOTOGRAPHER, CURATOR
b Los Angeles, Calif, Mar 10, 43. *Study:* Stanford Univ, Palo Alto, Calif, MA, 62; studied photog with Ansel Adams, 56-57, Imogen Cunningham, 63-64 and Pierre Cordier, 82. *Work:* Minn Mus Art, St Paul; Minn Inst Arts, Minneapolis; Mus Mod Art, NY; Huntington Hartford, Los Angeles; Ecole Nationale de la Photographia, Arles, France; Vatican Mus, Italy; Mus D'Arte Moderna, Milan; Paul Getty Mus, Malibu, Calif. *Exhib:* Lincoln Ctr Gallery, NY, 77; Provincetown Art Mus, Mass, 85; Am Acad, Paris, France, 90; Ecole Nat De La Photographis, Arles, France, 95; one-person, Am Acad Rome, Italy; Miami Nat Expo, 2000; Miami Mayors Exhib, 02; Art Basel, Miami, 02. *Collection Arranged:* Vera Stravinsky Gouaches and Watercolor, 85; Photographs by Igor and Vera Stravinsky, 87-88; Kirlian Imagery, 92; Alternative Image, 96; Contemp Nudes, 96. *Pos:* Dir, J Hunt Gallery, 72-80 & Imprimator, Ltd, 80, Minneapolis; Dir, Roberts & Assocs, Palm Beach, Fla. *Bibliog:* Tom Adair, Wyld Rice, KTCA-PBS, 77; John Barnier, Images, KUOM Radio, 81; Tom Adair (auth), Belle Russe, Renaissance House, Ltd, 86. *Publ:* Illusr, Hennepin Government Center, Archit Forum, 80; Mark Roberts, Photogrs Forum, 80; Adam without Eve, Christopher Street, 84 & Artnews, 85; Ideas and images, Photo Design, 86; 200 Photographic Innovators; Salon Album of Vera Stravinsky, Princeton Univ Press. *Dealer:* Roberts and Assocs Palm Beach FL. *Mailing Add:* Roberts & Assocs 277 Royal Poinciana Way Palm Beach FL 33480

ROBERTS, RUSSELL L
PAINTER
b Sept 9, 53. *Study:* Vassar Col, BA (eng lit); Sch Mus Fine Arts, dipl; Boston Univ, MFA (painting). *Exhib:* Tsai Performance Art Ctr, Boston Univ, 95; MFA Thesis Exhib, Boston Univ Art Gallery, 95; Traveling Scholars Exhib, Mus Fine Arts, Boston; Outside the Box, Horn Gallery, Babson Col, Mass; Spirit of Landscape, V, Nielsen Gallery, Boston, 2000; Boston Drawing Project, Bernard Toale Gallery, Boston, 2001; one-man show, Danforth Mus, Framingham, Mass, 2001, Sherman Gallery, Boston Univ, 2001, Farrell-Pollock Gallery, Brooklyn, NY, 2001 & Hanes Art Ctr, Univ NC, Chapel Hill, 2003; Intersection: Couples in Mixed Media, DNA Gallery, Provincetown, Mass, 2002; Merry II, Sideshow Gallery, Brooklyn, NY, 2002. *Pos:* Artist-in-residence, Univ NC, 2003. *Teaching:* Asst prof painting, Mass Col Art, 2000-01; vis asst prof, Pratt Inst, 2001-2002 & 2002. *Awards:* Charles Cumming Mem Travel Grant, Sch Mus Fine Arts, Boston, 96; Guggenheim Fel Painting, 97-98; Artist Books Finalist Grant, Mass Cult Coun, 2002. *Mailing Add:* 15 Gramercy Park S #11A New York NY 10003-1705

ROBERTS, STEVEN K
SCULPTOR, PRINTMAKER
b San Diego, Calif, Dec 2, 54. *Study:* Washington & Lee Univ, Va, BA, 76; also with Ju Ming, Taiwan, 76. *Work:* Nat Mus Am Art & Fed Deposit Insurance Corp, Washington, DC; Nat Mus Hist, Taipei, Taiwan; Gen Motors, Detroit; Am Tel & Tel, Rosalyn, Va. *Comn:* Poster, comn by City Councilman John Wilson, Washington, DC, 80; stained glass window, Rivertown Gen, Occuquan, Va, 80; painting, Am Systs Corp, Annandale, Va, 82; sculptural portrait, pvt comn by Melvin Watson & family, Lynchburg, Va, 84; wall murals, pvt comn by Anita & Burton Reiner, Bethesda, Md, 86. *Exhib:* 36 Hours, Mus Temporary Art, Washington, DC, 78; Sculpture Conference, Lansburg Bldg, Washington, DC, 80; 57th Ann Int, Print Club, Philadelphia, 81; Am Printmakers in Moscow, US Embassy, Moscow, USSR, 84; North Miami Mus & Art Center, N Miami, Fla, 84; Kathleen Ewing Gallery, Washington, DC, 85. *Bibliog:* Paul Waley (auth), US sculptor deeply influenced, The China News, 9/19/76; Ellen Edwards (auth), Art-Show & Tell, 4/26/80 & Jo Ann Lewis (auth), Art in boxes: surprises inside, 3/12/83, Washington Post. *Mem:* Washington Proj Arts, DC; Print Club, Philadelphia. *Media:* Wood, Steel; Serigraphy. *Dealer:* Kraskin Gallery 9812 Falls Rd Potomac MD 20854. *Mailing Add:* 1731 Harvard St NW Washington DC 20009

ROBERTS, WILLIAM EDWARD
PAINTER, EDUCATOR
b Cleveland, Ohio, July 1, 41. *Study:* Kent State Univ, BFA, 68, MA, 71; Cornell Univ, lithography with Arnold Singer, 73. *Work:* Everson Mus Art, Syracuse, NY; Kent State Univ, Ohio; IBM Corp, Albany, NY; NY Racing Asn, Elmont; Seagrams Inc, NY. *Exhib:* One-man show, Everson Mus Art, 74; 55 Mercer, NY, 81; Saratoga Performing Art Ctr, NY, 82; Hartell Gallery, Cornell Univ, 82; Dayspring Gallery, Saratoga Springs, NY, 82-86; Handwerker Gallery, Ithaca Col, 83; Schweinforth Art Ctr, Auburn, NY, 85; Shearson Lehman Am Express, Ithaca, NY, 86; Herbert Johnson Mus, Cornell Univ, 91; Tyler Art Gallery, SUNY Oswego, NY, 91. *Pos:* Instr, Cayuga Correctional Facility, 90-. *Teaching:* Assoc prof painting, Wells Col, Aurora, NY, 71-86, prof, 86-; instr painting, Auburn Prison, NY, 75-77. *Awards:* Purchase Awards, State Univ NY, Potsdam, 73 & Erie Pa Ann, Marine Midland Bank, 73; Purchase Award, Erie, Pa Ann, Marine Midland Bank, 73; First Place in Painting, Skaneateles Art Assoc, NY, 90. *Bibliog:* Millie Wolff (auth), Artist's racing series has King's excitement, Palm Beach Daily News, 3/14/79; Charlene Johnson (auth), Saratoga on a grand scale, Horsemen's J, 8/83; Lee Scott (auth), Aurora artist paints life on the fast track, Ithaca J, 2/20/84; Message to the Future, Binghamton, NY, 91; and others. *Mem:* Col Art Asn; Am Asn Univ Prof. *Media:* Oil,. *Mailing Add:* Wells Rd Aurora NY 13026

ROBERTSON, CHARLES J
ADMINISTRATOR
b Houston, Tex, Sept 12, 34. *Study:* Univ Va, BA, 56; Harvard Univ, MA, 58; Courtauld Inst, Univ London, 60; George Wash Univ, JD, 64. *Pos:* Assoc dir, NC Mus Art, 75-77; asst dir mus resources, 77-86; dep dir, Smithsonian Am Art Mus, 86-2001; asst to dir, 2002-. *Mem:* Octagon House Mus (adv comt, 89-97, chmn, 93-96); Victorian Soc Am (bd dir, 90-, vpres, 94-2000); Am Asn Mus (treas, 81-83); Am Archit Found (regent, 93-96); Hist Preservation Review Bd Washington DC; Cosmos Club Hist Pres Found (trustee, 93-, tres 99-). *Mailing Add:* Nat Mus Am Art Smithsonian Inst Washington DC 20560

ROBERTSON, DAVID ALAN
MUSEUM DIRECTOR, EDUCATOR
b Jefferson City, Mo, Oct 10, 50. *Study:* Univ Mo, Ba, 73, MA, 76; Kress fel, London, 76, Vienna, 80; Penfield Scholar, Studies in Vienna, Austria, 81-82; Univ Pa, PhD, 83; Fulbright, Munich, 89. *Collection Arranged:* Context & Collab in Contemp Art, Dickinson, 86; On Loan from the Metrop Mus, Dickinson, 87; Leon Golub: World Wide (auth, catalog), Dickinson/Chicago Cult Ctr, 93; Sacrificial Images of Christ (1350-1750) (auth, catalog), Loyola D'Arcy Gallery, 94. *Pos:* Curatorial asst, Yale Ctr Brit Art, New Haven, Conn, 77-78; staff supervisor Rosenbach Mus and Libr, 80-82; dir, Dickinson Col, Carlisle, 1982-2002; founding dir, Trout Art Gallery, Dickinson Col, 82-91; mem selection comt, Fulbright Comn, Bonn, Ger, 89; Fulbright professorship, Univ Munich, 89-90; grant reviewer, Inst Mus Serv's, Wash, 89-91; dir, Martin D'Arcy Gallery, Loyola Univ, Chicago, 92-95 & Univ Ore Mus Art, 96-2000; dir, Mary and Leigh Block Mus Art Northwestern Univ, Evanston, Ill, 2002-, lectr Art Hist Dept, 2003-; assoc dir, Smart Mus, Univ Chicago, 2000-2002; dir, Block Mus, Northwestern Univ, 2002-. *Teaching:* Teaching asst art hist, Univ Pa, Philadelphia, 78-81; assoc prof, Dickinson Col, Carlisle, Pa, 82-91. *Awards:* Kress fel Kress Found, London, 1976, Vienna, 1980, Penfield fel Univ Pa, Vienna, Austria, 1981-82. *Mem:* Ill Medieval Asn (pres, 94); Am Asn Mus; Historians Netherlandish Art; Asn Col and Univ Mus and Galleries (bd mem, 2006-). *Res:* Late-medieval German art; contemporary American art. *Specialty:* Prints & drawings. *Publ:* Coauth, Toshiko Takaezu: ceramics, textiles, bronzes, Dickinson Col, 83; auth, Michelangelo's St

Proculus reconstructed, Art Bull, 83; coauth, The art & science of Eadweard Muybridge, Dickinson Col, 85; co-ed, Essays in Medieval Studies, 94-96; auth, Bridging the Pacific through Art, UNESCO Mus Intl, 2000. *Mailing Add:* Mary and Leigh Block Mus Art Northwestern Univ 40 Arts Circle Dr Evanston IL 60208

ROBERTSON, E BRUCE
HISTORIAN, CURATOR
b Dunedin, New Zealand, May 14, 55. *Study:* Swarthmore Col, BA(hons), 76; Yale Univ, MA, 78, MPhil, 80, PhD, 87. *Collection Arranged:* The Art of Paul Sandby (auth, catalog), Yale Brit Art Ctr, 85; Dutch Landscape Prints, Allen Art Mus, 86. *Pos:* Assoc cur Am paintings, Cleveland Mus Art, 87-91; chief cur, Ctr for Am Art. *Teaching:* Instr, Univ Del, Newark, 82 & Oberlin Col, Ohio, 83-87; asst prof, Case Western Reserve Univ, Ohio, 87-90; assoc prof, Univ Calif, Santa Barbara, 94-98, prof, 98-. *Mem:* Col Art Asn; Am Studies Asn. *Res:* British and American painting to 1945. *Publ:* Coauth, Views and visions, Corcoran Gallery Art, 86; auth, Reckoning with Winslow Homer: His Late Paintings and Their Influence, 90; Marsden Hartley, 95; Am Realist Prints, 95; auth & coauth, Perils of the Sea & Yankee Modernism (essays), Picturing Old New England: Image and Memory, Nat Mus Am Art, 99; Ruth Harriet Louise and Hollywood Glamour Photography, 2002; Sargent and Haly, 2003. *Mailing Add:* c/o Art Hist Dept Univ Calif Santa Barbara CA 93106

ROBERTSON, JOAN ELIZABETH MITCHELL
GRAPHIC ARTIST
b Washington, DC, June 11, 42. *Study:* Bucknell Univ, Lewisburg, Pa, BA(art), 64; Univ Iowa, MA(printmaking), 67, studied with Mauricio Lasansky. *Work:* Kemper Group, Long Grove, Ill; Chemical Bank, NY; First Nat Bank, Chicago; Southland Corp, Dallas, Tex; Ill State Mus, Springfield; Blount Inc, Montgomery, Ala. *Exhib:* Works on Paper by Artists of Chicago and Vicinity, Art Inst Chicago, 78; one-person shows, Donnelly Libr Gallery, Lake Forest Col, Ill, 79 & Loyola Univ, Chicago, 81 & Saginaw Art Mus, 98; Nat Prints & Drawing Competition, DeKalb, Ill, 81; Ill State Fair, Prof Art Exhib, 89; Flora 88 & 90, Chicago Botanic Garden, 88, 90 & 96; Karga Art Ctr, St Joseph, Mich, 97; Jan-Cicero, Chicago, 98. *Collection Arranged:* Kemper Nat Insurance Companies art collection, purchase, brochure preparation & monthly exhibs, 73-; Couples I and Couples II, Suburban Fine Arts Ctr, Highland Park, Ill, 83 & 84; A Celebration of Women (catalog), David Adler Cult Ctr, Libertyville, Ill, 92. *Pos:* Art cur, Kemper Nat Insurance Companies, Long Grove, Ill, 73-; gallery coordr, Lake Forest Col, Ill, 81-84. *Awards:* Award Merit, Flora, 88; Chicago Botanic Garden, 88; President's Purchase Award, Elgin Community Col, Ill, Works on Paper, 90; and others. *Bibliog:* Lydia Murman (auth), Joan E Robertson, New Art Examiner, 6/81; Sandy Riemer (auth), Color puts life into her pencil drawings, Sunday Herald, 4/81; Garrett Holg (auth), An exhibition for art and nature lovers at Botanic Garden, Waukegan News-Sun, 2/11/88; and others. *Mem:* Asn Corp Art Curators, Chicago; Nat Asn Corp Art Mgt, NY; David Adler Cult Ctr, Libertyville, Ill (bd dir, 90-93). *Media:* Colored Pencil. *Mailing Add:* c/o James S Kemper Found Long Grove IL 60049

ROBERTSON, LORNA DOOLING
PAINTER
b New York, NY, Aug 29, 29. *Study:* Purdue Univ, BS, 51; Cornell Med Ctr, MS, 52. *Hon Degrees:* Hans Hofman Sch, NY, 60-64; Art Students League, NY. *Work:* Curwen & Chilford Mus, Cambridge, England; Tate Mus Print Collection, London, England. *Exhib:* Solo exhib, Willow Gallery, NY, 92 & Gallery Herouet, Place de Voges, Paris, France, 94; Exhib Hall & Mus, Palais des Congres, Marseille, France, 94; Osaka Int Art Festival, Osaka, Japan, 94; 12th Int Biennial of Humor and Satire in Art, Gabrovo, Bulgaria, 95; Ann Juried Exhib, Hui-No eau, Maui, Hawaii, 2000. *Awards:* Gold Medal, Palais DeCongres, Mme Grimaldi, 94; First Prize, First Internat Female Artist Exhib, 94; Bronze Medal, L'Bradem Francouse Soc, 95. *Mem:* Vt Studio Ctr. *Media:* Oil, All Media. *Publ:* illusr, Social Problems, Allyn & Bacon, 2000. *Mailing Add:* 13656 Lake Jane Rd Orlando FL 32832

ROBERTSON, NANCY ELIZABETH See Dillow, Nancy Elizabeth Robertson

ROBERTSON, RUTH
ART DEALER, PAINTER
b Philadelphia, Pa, Dec 22, 49. *Study:* Va Commonwealth Univ, BFA, 73. *Work:* James F Lewis Mus, Baltimore; CID Collection, Sao Paolo, Brazil; Santos Cult Inst, Sao Paolo; Mus of Contemp Art, Washington, DC. *Exhib:* Between the Light & Dark, Nat Theater, Havana, Cuba, 2002; Recent Works, Mus of Contemp Art, Wash, DC, 97; Sations of the Cross, DC AA Ctr, Wash, DC, 99. *Pos:* Photography Cur, Mus of Contemp, DC, 98-2000; Gallery Dir, Dist West Fine Art, Leesburg, VA, 2000; dir, E-Moca.com, 95-, mem bd 2003-; owner, dir, Ruth Robertson Fine Art, 2004-. *Teaching:* Art Instr, Bishop O'Connell HS, 91-98; instr, VA Commonwealth Univ, Graduate Sch Fine Art, 2004-. *Awards:* Presidential Citation, Univ Richmond, 94; Nominated for Whitney Biennial, Whitney Mus of Am Art, 98, 2000. *Mem:* NVCC adv comt fine arts, 2001-; Am Soc Landscape Painters. *Media:* Painting, Photography, Mixed Media. *Specialty:* Contemporary Fine Art. *Publ:* DC Arts, At MOCA DC, 99; Arts/Corcoran Dir, 2002; Washington Review, The Cabinet of Good & Evil, 98. *Dealer:* District West Fine Art 3 1/2 S King St Leesburg Va 20175. *Mailing Add:* 602 Third St Herndon VA 20170

ROBINS, JOYCE
SCULPTOR, LANDSCAPE ARCHITECT
b Greenville, SC, Aug 23, 44. *Study:* Cooper Union, BFA, 66; Yale Summer Sch, 66; City Col NY, BSLA, 95. *Exhib:* Solo shows, Nobe Gallery, NY, 79, 55 Mercer St Gallery, NY, 80-81, 83-84, 86-88, 90-91, 93-94 & 96, Vassar Col Art Gallery, Poughkeepsie, NY, 92; Function, Gallery 128, NY, 95; Domestic Policies, Art Gallery State Univ NY, 95; Insites II: Lower East Side Artists Re-think Neighborhood Streets, Abrons Art Ctr, Henry St Settlement, NY, 96; Vis Fac, Col Ctr Gallery, Vassar Col, Poughkeepsie, NY, 96. *Pos:* Bd mem, 55 Mercer St Gallery, New York, 90-96, Springside Landscape Restoration, Poughkeepsie, NY, 95-2001. *Teaching:* Instr sculpture, Vassar Col, Poughkeepsie, NY, 96-2001. *Awards:* NY State Creative Artists Pub Serv Grant for Sculpture, 82. *Bibliog:* David Carrier (auth), Joyce Robins, Art in Am, 3/87; Yanick Rice Lamb (auth), Flag deconstruction, NY Times, 1/94; Holland Cotter (auth), NY Times, 9/97 & 10/97. *Media:* Bronze, Ceramic. *Dealer:* Pierogi 2000 177 N 9th St Brooklyn NY 11211. *Mailing Add:* 70 Hester St New York NY 10002

ROBINSON, AMINAH BRENDA LYNN
SCULPTURE, PAINTER
b Columbus, Ohio, 1940. *Study:* Columbus Art Sch (now Columbus Col Art and Design), BA, cum laude, 1960. *Work:* Poindexter Village Quilt, 1966-84; (sculpture) Gift of Love, 1974; Journal, 1980; To Be a Drum (Jazz), 1996-98. *Comn:* Murals, Columbus Metrop Library. *Exhib:* Columbus Mus Art; Akron Art Mus; Oakland Mus; Baltimore Mus Art; Studio Mus, Harlem; San Francisco Craft and Folk Mus; Retrospective, Brooklyn Mus Art, 2006; Summer Favorites, Hammond Harkins Gallery, 2006. *Teaching:* Tchr art, Columbus Dept Recreation and Parks, since 1972. *Awards:* Int Studios Fellow; Bob Blackburn Print Shop Fellow, NY; Governor's Award for Visual Arts, 1984; Individual Artist Fellowship, Ohio Arts Council, 1980 and 1987, 1991-92; John D and Catherine T MacArthur Found Fellow, 2004. *Bibliog:* Carol Miller Genshaft, Leslie King-Hammond, Ramona Austin and Annegreth Nil (authors) Symphonic Poem: The Art of Aminah Brenda Lynn Robinson, 2003. *Mailing Add:* c/o Hammon Harkins Galleries Ltd 2264 East Main St Columbus OH 43209

ROBINSON, AVIVA
PAINTER
b May 24, 33. *Study:* Univ Mich, 1951; Wayne State Univ, BS, 1951-55. *Work:* Detroit Inst Arts, Mich; Univ Mich, dearborn. *Exhib:* Rubiner Gallery, 1984; Cantor & Lemberg Gallery, 1986; Kidd Gallery, 1988, 90; Edge Gallery, 1994; Nat Paper Invitational, Univ of Mich Sch of Art, 1996; Uzelac Gallery, 1998. *Teaching:* teacher, art, Oak Park High Sch, 1954-55. *Awards:* Johns Manville award, Rocky Mountain Nat Watercolor, 1976; Mich Watercolor soc, award, 1976, 79, 80 & 82; Womens Industry Painting award, 1988. *Mem:* Detroit Inst Arts (bd of dir, 1995-); Mus of Arts & Design (bd, 1996-2005). *Media:* Watercolor. *Publ:* Corinne Abatt (auth), Variations on the Theme, The Birmington Eccentric (11/1984); Aviva Robinson at Cantor & Lemberg Gallery, The Detroit News (9/1986); Corinne Abatt (auth), Crating Dimensional Relationships, The Birmington Eccentric (9/1986). *Mailing Add:* 1589 Kirkway Bloomfield Hills MI 48302

ROBINSON, CHARLOTTE
PAINTER, PRINTMAKER
b San Antonio, Tex, Nov, 24. *Study:* Art Students League, 48; New York Univ, 49; Corcoran Art Sch, 51-53. *Work:* Mus Espanol de Arts Contemporaneo, Madrid; Philip Morris Inc, New York; McNay Art Mus, San Antonio, Tex; Nat Mus Women Arts, Washington, DC; The White House, Washington, DC; Musea al De Arte Contemporanes, Lisbon, Portugal New School for Social Research, NY. *Exhib:* Mint Mus, Charlotte, NC, 77; solo exhibs, McNay Art Mus, San Antonio, Tex, 86, Lowenstein Libr Gallery, Fordham Univ, NY, 90, San Antonio Art Inst, Tex, 91 & Masur Mus Art, Monroe, La, 93, Savannah Col Art & Design, 97 & Duke Univ Law Sch, Durham, NC, 98; Twentieth Yr Invitational Show, Rutgers Univ, New Brunswick, NJ, 92; Emerson Art Ctr, McLean, Va, 93 & 96; Northern Va Community Col, Fairfax, 99; Tiknor Hall, Harvard Yard, Cambridge, Mass, 96; solo shows, Lee Hausley Gallery, Raleigh, NC, 2002: Emerson Gallery, McLain Art Ctr, VA, 2003; Southwest Ctr for Art & Crafts-San Antonio, Tex, 2004; The Am Ctr for Physics, 2005, College Park, MD. *Pos:* Trustee, Bronx Mus, NY, 76-77; vis artist, Southwest Craft Ctr, San Antonio, Tex, 85 & 86. *Teaching:* Painting Instr, Torpedo Factory, Alexadria, Va, 67-75; Instr drawing, Smithsonian Assoc Prog, Washington, DC, 76-; instr art world sem, Washington Women's Art Ctr, Washington, DC, 76-80. *Awards:* Scholar, Student Exhib, Corcoran Art Sch, Washington, 51; Grants, Nat Endowment Arts, 77, 78 & 81; Fel, Va Ctr Creative Arts, 90. *Bibliog:* Women in the Arts, Charlotte Robinson, The Washington Post, 79; The Artist & The Quilt, Time Mag, 83; A New Kind of Art, NY Times Mag, 82; Joan Arbeiter (auth), Talks with Women Artists, Scarecrow Press, 96; Dan Goddard (auth), Nature in painting, San Antonio Express, 97; Mary Shuter (auth), Underwater art Savannah Morning News, 97. *Mem:* Nat Women's Caucus Art (bd dir, 82-84); Col Art Asn. *Media:* Oil; Lithography. *Res:* Research agricultural water withdrawel that protects Va waterways & downstream residents. Part of ongoing (since 96) project for my "Waterwaste" series of paintings. *Specialty:* American Contemp Art, with Emphasis on Modernisums. *Interests:* Environment (clean water), Swimming. *Publ:* Ed, The Artist & The Quilt, Knopf, 10/83. *Dealer:* Lee Hansley Gallery 225 Glenwood Ave Raleigh NC 27603. *Mailing Add:* 6324 Crosswoods Dr Falls Church VA 22044

ROBINSON, CHRIS (CHRISTOPHER) THOMAS
CONCEPTUAL ARTIST, EDUCATOR
b Huntington, NY, Mar 18, 51. *Study:* Fla State Univ, BFA, 73; Univ Mass, MFA, 75. *Work:* Arch Am Art, Washington, DC; Univ South; SC State Art Collection, Columbia; Southern Graphics Coun; Univ Miss. *Comn:* Installations, Ninth Nat-Int Sculpture Conf, New Orleans, 76, Nat Sculpture Conf, Jonesboro, Ark, 77, Arcosanti Festival Art in the Environment, Cordes Junction, Ariz, 78, Col Art Asn, New Orleans, 80 & Eastern Ill Univ, 81; The Laser (installation), SC State Mus, Columbia, 89; Viscom, Southern Bell Regional Hq, Charlotte, NC, 91; 25th Annual Governors Carolighting, State Capitol, Columbia, SC, 92; First Night, Releigh Bicentennial, NC,

92. *Exhib:* Artists Biennial, New Orleans Mus Art, 77; solo exhib, Atlanta Art Workers Coalition Gallery, 80 Solo exhibs, Univ NC, Col at Charleston, 87, Art in Transit, Arts Festival Atlanta, 89; Fact, Fiction and Fantasy: Recent Narrative Art in the Southeast, Traveling Exhib, Ewing Art Gallery, Univ Tenn, Knoxville, 87; Traces, Proposals, Plans & Documentations, Trahern Gallery, Austin Peay State Univ, Clarksville, Tenn, 93; Centennial Exhib, SC State Mus, Columbia, 94; Art in Transit, Arts Festival Atlanta, Ga, 94; Emblems, Yale Univ Art Gallery, 95; plus many others; Clemson Nat Print & Drawing Exhib, Clemson Univ, 98; Ormond Meml Art Mus, 99; Views From the Edge of the Century, Florence Mus of Art, 2000. *Collection Arranged:* Nat Sculpture Exhib, 76, 78 & 79. *Pos:* Dir, Northern Projects, Operation Raleigh, Chile; bd trustees, Lexington Co Sch Dist Five; leader, US Expeditions (sci, serv, adventure), Operation Raleigh, Alaska, Colo & NC, 88; dir grad studies, Univ SC, 90; pres, SC Sch Bd Asn, Columbia, 98. *Teaching:* Assoc visual arts, Univ Mass, Amherst, 73-75; from instr to assoc prof, Univ SC, Columbia, 75-; guest artist, Univ Ala, Huntsville, 77, Univ South, Greensboro Col, Brevard Col & Univ Cent Ark. *Awards:* Merit Award, 18th Ann Juried Show, Anderson Co Arts Ctr, 93; Merit Award, What is Drawing Now, Weber State Univ, 2000; Distinguished Serv Award, Nat Sch Bds Asn, 98. *Bibliog:* Elizabeth George (auth), Laser artist beams brush towards space shuttle, Greenville Piedmont, 3/10/78; Ron Jones (auth), Techno-aesthetics in South Carolina, Art Papers, 3-4/81; Linda Shrives (auth), Outline of a dream, Columbia Record, 4/13/84; Michael Farley (auth), USC art instructor lives life full of adventure, The Charlotte Observer, 7/7/85; Beverly E Simmons (auth), University professor leads five month research mission, The State, 1/16/86. *Mem:* Col Art Asn; Southern Asn Sculptors (bd mem, 75-80); Southeastern Col Art Conf. *Media:* Computers, Light. *Res:* Experiential investigation of exploratory processes in science and technology as an impetus to the expansion of the visual arts process. *Publ:* Auth, Astronautics as an impetus to visual art, In: Proceedings of the 33rd International Astronautical Federation Congress, 82; Cultural dichotomy: An artist's role in scientific and space exploration, Art Papers, 5-6/85; Sky Art and Power chap Sky Art Book Ctr for Adv Visual Studies, Mass Inst Technol, in press; Art & Technol, Koger Ctr Prog, 89; The Visual Artist's Role in Scientific & Space Exploration, 41st Int Art Found Congress, Dresden, Ger; What Happens When the Lights Go Out, SECAC, Norfolk, VA; Idea vs Object Revisiting Conceptual Art Through the Digital Looking Glass, SECAC?MACCA; Laser Light Scanning, Mixed Messages Conf, Univ North Carolina, Charlotte. *Mailing Add:* 201 Steeple Crst N Irmo SC 29063

ROBINSON, CLEO
DIRECTOR
Study: Denver Univ, degree in Dance Educ Psychology, DFA (hon), 91. *Pos:* Founder, exec, artistic dir, choreographer Cleo Parker Robinson Dance, Denver. *Teaching:* Mem dance, expansion arts and inter-arts panels Nat Educ Asn; bd dir, Denver Ctr Performing Arts; teacher in workshops. *Awards:* Recipient Thelma Hill Ctr for the Performing Arts award, 86; named one of Colo 100, 92, Colo Gov's award for Excellence in the Arts; named to Blacks in Colo Hall of Fame, 94. *Mem:* Int Asn Blacks in Dance (2nd vpres). *Publ:* Co-creator (documentary) African-Americans at Festae, Run Sister Run, (film) Black Women in the Arts, (music video) Borderline. *Mailing Add:* Cleo Parker Robinson Dance 119 Parker Ave Denver CO 80205

ROBINSON, DUNCAN (DAVID)
DIRECTOR, HISTORIAN
b Kidsgrove Staffs, Eng, June 27, 43. *Study:* Clare Col, Cambridge, Eng, BA, 65, MA, 69; Yale Univ, Mellon Fel, 65-67, MA, 67. *Collection Arranged:* Stanley Spencer (auth, catalog), 75 & William Nicholson, 80, Arts Coun Gt Brit; British Watercolors, Brisbane, Australia, 82; and several exhibs of British Contemp Art. *Pos:* Asst keeper paintings & drawings, Fitzwilliam Mus, Cambridge, Eng, 70-76, keeper, 76-81; dir, Yale Ctr Brit Art, 81-95 & Fitzwilliam Mus, Cambridge, Eng, 95-2007; master, Magdalene Col, Cambridge, Eng, 2002-. *Teaching:* Lectr art hist, Univ Cambridge, Eng, 70-81; adj prof hist Art, Yale Univ, 81-95; fel, Clare Col, Cambridge. *Awards:* Fel Royal Soc of Arts, United Kingdom; Fel Soc of Antiquaries, United Kingdom. *Mem:* Blake Trust (UK); Walpole Soc (UK). *Res:* History of British Art concentrating on later 18th and 19th century contemporary art. *Specialty:* World-wide fine & decorative arts. *Publ:* Auth, Companion Volume to the Kelmscott Chaucer, Basilisk Press, 75; Stanley Spencer, Phaidon, 79 (rev 90); coauth, Morris & Company in Cambridge, Cambridge Univ Press, 80; auth, Town Country, Shore and Sea: British Drawings and Watercolors from Van Dyck to Nash, Cambridge, 82. *Mailing Add:* Fitzwilliam Mus Trumpington St Cambridge CB2 1RB United Kingdom

ROBINSON, FRANKLIN W
MUSEUM DIRECTOR, HISTORIAN
b Providence, RI, May 21, 39. *Study:* Harvard Univ, BA, 61, MA, 63, PhD, 70. *Pos:* Dir, Williams Col Mus Art, 76-79, Mus Art, RI Sch Design, 79-92 & Herbert F Johnson Mus Art, Cornell Univ, 92-. *Teaching:* Asst prof art hist, Dartmouth Col, 69-75; assoc prof & dir grad prog art hist, Williams Col, 75-79. *Awards:* Fulbright Fel, 61-62. *Mem:* Am Asn Mus Dir. *Res:* Baroque art; prints and drawings. *Publ:* Auth, 100 Master Drawings from New England Private Collections, 72; Gabriel Metsu, 75; Dutch Life in the Golden Century, 75; Seventeenth Century Dutch Drawings from American Collections, 77; Dutch and Flemish Paintings from the Ringling Museum, 80; Fresh Woods and Pastures New, 99. *Mailing Add:* Herbert F Johnsons Mus Art Cornell Univ Ithaca NY 14853

ROBINSON, JAY
PAINTER
b Detroit, Mich, Aug 1, 15. *Study:* Yale Col, BA; Cranbrook Acad Art, MFA. *Work:* Cranbrook Mus, Bloomfield Hills, Mich; Detroit Inst Art; Houston Mus Fine Arts; J B Speed Mus, Louisville, Ky; Philbrook Art Ctr, Tulsa. *Exhib:* Audubon Artists, NY; Carnegie Inst Int, Pittsburgh; Corcoran Gallery Art Biennial, Washington, DC; Nat Acad Design, NY; Pa Acad Fine Arts, Philadelphia. *Teaching:* Private lessons. *Awards:* Louis Comfort Tiffany Found Fel, 49; seven Childe Hassam Fund Purchase Awards, Am Acad Arts & Lett. *Media:* Miscellaneous, Acrylic & Mixed. *Collection:* Jason Schoen. *Mailing Add:* 305 E Landing Williamsburg VA 23185-8254

ROBINSON, LIBBY
PAINTER, SCULPTOR
b New York, NY. *Study:* Art Students League(drawing), 49-51; studied painting with John Von Wicht, New York, 49-51. *Exhib:* Bronx Mus, 90; The Kendall Gallery, NY, 91; Noho Gallery, NY, 91; Noho Invitational, 92; Contemp Artists for Global Peace, Casa Arg en Israel, 93; and others. *Awards:* Susan Hirschfeld, Asn Cur, The Solomon Guggenheim Mus, NY, 89. *Bibliog:* Leslie Plummer (auth), article, New York Arts J, 9/79; Renee Phillips (auth), article, News World, East Side Weekly, 12/80; reviews, Artpseak, 9/1/83, 1/15/85, 7/1/86 & 11/16/86. *Mem:* NY Artists Equity; Women in Arts, NY; Women's Caucus Arts. *Publ:* Auth, catalogue, Discoveries V, 89. *Dealer:* Noho Gallery 168 Mercer St New York NY 10012

ROBINSON, LILIEN FILIPOVITCH
HISTORIAN, EDUCATOR
b Ljubljana, Yugoslavia, Feb 7, 40; US citizen. *Study:* George Washington Univ, BA, 62, MA, 65; Johns Hopkins Univ, PhD, 78. *Pos:* Chmn dept art, George Washington Univ, 76-2000. *Teaching:* Lectr art introd & surveys of Western art, George Washington Univ, 64-65, asst prof 19th century art & surveys of Western art, 65-76, assoc prof 19th century Europ art, 76-79 & prof 19th century Europ art, 80. *Awards:* Outstanding Teacher Award, Columbian Col, George Washington Univ, 88; Trachtenberg Serv Award; The George Washington Award. *Bibliog:* Boris Weintraub (auth), The professor's enthusiasm is contagious, Washington Star, 10/27/79. *Mem:* Col Art Asn; Am Asn Advancement Slavic Studies; N Am Soc Serbian Studies. *Res:* 19th-century French painting and academic painting; Serbian 19th-century secular art. *Publ:* Auth, Clarice Smith, Wildenstein Galleries, 86; Barye & the Nineteenth Century Sculptural Tradition, Barye and Patronage in Antoine-Louis Barye, Corcoran Gallery Art, Washington, DC, 88; Anna Elizabeth Klumpke: Duty and the Dedicated Spirit, Ariz State Univ, 93; Arthur Hall Smith: Repeat Works on Paper, LRC Gallery, Charles County Community Col, 93; Nineteenth-Century Serbian Painting: A Confluence of Nationalism & Secularism, Serbian Studies, Vol 16, 2/2003; introduction, Clarice Smith: Patterns in People, Places and Things, Richard Green Galleries, London, 2002; Clay Variance, The Lyons Agy, Alexandria, Va, 1995. *Mailing Add:* Dept Art George Washington Univ 801 22nd St NW Washington DC 20052

ROBINSON, MARGOT STEIGMAN
PAINTER, SCULPTOR
b New York, NY. *Study:* Art Students League, with Harry Sternberg, 47; Robert Blackburn's Creative Workshop, 49-55; painting with John Von Wicht, 53-55; Gerard Koch Studio, Paris, 68; Donald Mavros Studio, New York, 71-72. *Work:* Am Express Co, New York; Data Processing Co, Boston & Chicago; Continental Grain Co, Columbus, Ohio; Bronze mem, Jervis Pub Libr, Rome, NY. *Comn:* Bronze memorial, Jervis Pub Libr, Rome, NY. *Exhib:* Whitney Mus Am Art, NY; Womens Caucus Art Painters Puzzle Project, Port Authority, NY, 90; solo exhib, Tom Kendall Gallery, NY, 90 & Noho Gallery, NY, 92; Cincinnati Art Mus, Ohio; Brooklyn Mus, NY; Cie Mod et Contemporaine, Paris, France, 91; Contemp Artists for Global Peace, Casa Argentina en Israel Tierra Santa, 93; Forgiveness/or Not, Ceres Gallery, NY, 96; Hallelujah, Ceres Gallery, NY, 2002. *Pos:* Dir, Creative Graphic Workshop, New York, 52-54; registr, Nat Acad Sch of Fine Arts, New York, 55-57; vpres, Noho Gallery, New York, 76-77, secy, 77-78. *Bibliog:* Sean Simon (auth), Artspeak, 11/89; Claude Le Suer (auth), Artspeak, 1/90; Bruno Palmer Poroner (auth), article, Artspeak, 6/92; Edgar Buonagurio (auth), Arts Mag, 4/1978; James T McCartin (auth), essay, 1982; Ellen Lee Klein (auth), 1985. *Mem:* New York Artists Equity; Women in the Arts; Womens Caucus Art, New York & Nat. *Media:* Acrylic, Oil; Miscellaneous Media. *Publ:* Contribr, Modern Sculpture, calendar, Cedco Publ Co, San Rafael, Calif, 90. *Dealer:* Aldona M Gobuzas. *Mailing Add:* 141 Joralemon St Brooklyn NY 11201

ROBINSON, MARY ANN
PAINTER, EDUCATOR
b McPherson, Kans, Sept 24, 23. *Study:* Kans State Univ, BS, 45; McCormick Theological Sem, MA, 55; Wichita State Univ, MA, 72; studied under Maude Ellsworth, Jan Lundgren, Robert Kisskaden, Robert Wood & James Pike. *Work:* Galaxy Series. *Exhib:* Am Contemp Arts & Crafts, Fla, 73; Birger Sandzen Mem Gallery, 80-92; Kans Watercolor Soc Mem Exhib, Lawrence, Kans, 88; Wichita Art Mus Watercolor Exhib, 89; Ellsworth Art Gallery, Kans, 91; Pratt Art Gallery, Pratt, Kans, 92; Friendship Gallery, McPherson Col, 96; The Gallery, McPherson Col, 95-2000. *Collection Arranged:* Nat Art Exhibition, 1989-1998. *Pos:* Supvr art pub sch, McPherson, Kans, 47-49; dir, Friendship Hall Gallery, McPherson Col, Kans, 63-86; co-sponsor & dir, Aesthetics Nat Art Exhib, 89-98. *Teaching:* Assoc prof art educ & art hist & chmn dept art, McPherson Col, Kans, 63-86, emer prof, 86-. *Mem:* Kans Watercolor Soc (bd mem, 77-79); McPherson Mus & Art Found (bd mem, 86-90); Opera House Preserv Co (bd mem, 86-90); McPherson Arts Coun; charter mem Nat Mus Women in the Arts; Aesthetics Ltd (bd mem, 89-98); Rayner Soc. *Media:* Watercolor, Acrylic. *Publ:* Illustrated Survey of Leading Contemporaries, 90. *Mailing Add:* 601 S Walnut McPherson KS 67460

ROBINSON, SALLY W
PRINTMAKER, WEAVER
b Detroit, Mich, Nov 2, 24. *Study:* Bennington Col, BA; Wayne State Univ, MA & MFA; Cranbrook Acad Art; also with Hans Hofmann, Paul Feeley, Karl Knaths & Leon Kroll. *Work:* Chase Manhattan Bank, New York; Detroit Inst Arts; K-Mart Hq; and pvt collections. *Exhib:* Toledo Mus, Winston Traveling Show; Zella 9 Gallery,

London, Eng; Troy Art Gallery, 78; Detroit Inst Arts, 78; Cliche-Verre, nat exhib, Detroit Inst Arts & Houston; and others. *Pos:* Mem, Gov Comn for Art in State Bldgs, Mich, 78-79; bd mem, Mus Art, Univ Mich, currently; vis fel, Williams Col Mus Art, currently. *Teaching:* Instr silk screen, Wayne State Univ, 73-74. *Awards:* Second Prize, Bloomfield Art Asn, 72; Second Prize, Soc Women Painters, 74 & First Prize, 75. *Mem:* Friends Mod Art; Founders Soc; Detroit Artists Market; Soc Women Painters; Bloomfield Art Asn; Fel Williams Col Mus Art; Guggenheim Mus; Cooper Hewitt Mus; Whitney Mus Mod Art; and others. *Specialty:* Printmaking. *Interests:* Botany and Art. *Publ:* Contribr, Mich Art J, 76; auth, Cliche-Verre: Hand Drawn, Light Printed, 80. *Dealer:* Klein-Vogel Gallery 4520 N Woodward Royal Oak MI 48053; Rina Gallery E 74th St & Madison New York NY 10021. *Mailing Add:* 639 Eagle Watch Ln Osprey FL 34229

ROBINSON, THOMAS V
DEALER, COLLECTOR

b Ft Worth, Tex, Feb 9, 38. *Study:* Tex Christian Univ, 56-57; Carlsbad-Oceanside Col, 57-58; Tex Wesleyan Col, 59-60; Univ Houston, 88-89. *Exhib:* Inst Allerde, San Miguel de Allerde, Mex, 81; Edinburgh Int Festival, 83-86; Am Festival, Glasgow, Scotland, 85; Casa de la Cultura, Quito, Ecuador, 87; Mus Mod, Cuenca, Ecuador, 87; Mus Munic de Guayaquil, Ecuador, 94. *Collection Arranged:* Ben Shahn 1930-1969, 70; Auther G Dove 1920-1940, 71; Am Landscape, 73; Western Am Art 1860-1940 (auth, catalog), 74; Networking, Int Exchange Prog, 82-86 & 87-95. *Pos:* Dir, Robinson Galleries, 69-, pres, 77-90; dir, Ben Shahn Foundation, New York, 71-75; bd mem, Houston Art Dealers Asn, 81-83 & 94-97, pres 95-96; chmn, art travel studies & bd mem, Instituo de Arte Grace, Ecuador, 88; publ, Pasaporte Á USA; chmn, Kuumba House Found, 93-94; rep, Paul Suttman Sculpture Estate, currently. *Awards:* Consulor Corps Comt, 89; Inst Hispanic Cult, 90; Leadership Award, Ecuadorian-Am Chamber Commerce, 90. *Bibliog:* Thomas V Robinson, SW Art Mag, 71; Donna Tennant (auth), Gallery-Inst Exchange, Houston Chronicle, 81; Internation exchange, Artscene, Houston, 83; International networking, Houston Chronicle, 84; El Commercial, Quito, Ecuador, 87 & 94. *Mem:* Cultural Arts Comt Houston Chamber Com; Tex Arts Alliance; Cultural Arts Coun Houston; Houston Art Dealers Asn (treas, 80-81, dir, 83-97, pres 95-96). *Specialty:* Twentieth century figurative expressionists and outsider artists of the Americas; Contemporary painting, sculpture, performance, video and all media objects. *Publ:* Coauth, Kachinas-Paone, Encino Press, 76; International Fine Art Collector, 90; auth, PasaporteÁ Houston, 94-95; A Traves de los Ojos de Texas, 95. *Mailing Add:* Robinson Galleries Inc 2307 W Alabama St Houston TX 77089

ROBISON, ANDREW
MUSEUM CURATOR, WRITER

b Memphis, Tenn, May 23, 40. *Study:* Princeton Univ, AB & PhD; Oxford Univ, MA; Fulbright Res Scholar, India. *Collection Arranged:* Giovanni Battista Piranesi & Picasso Prints, 70, Princeton Univ; diverse print & drawing exhib, Nat Gallery of Art, 74-; 18th century Venetian Illus Bks, Grolier Club, 81; Prints From an Alumni Collection, Princeton Univ Art Mus, 82; Uncommon Piranesis, Grolier Club, 88; The Glory of Venice, Royal Acad, London, 94-95; Ernst Ludwig Kuichner, Nat gallery of Art and Royal Acad, Lodon, 03. *Pos:* Cur & head dept prints & drawings, Nat Gallery Art, 74-, sr cur, 83-91, Mellon sr cur 91-; pres, Print Coun Am, 75-81; mem ed adv bd, Master Drawings, 81-; pres, Int Adv Comn Keepers Pub Collections Graphic Art, 84-88; bd dir, Drawing Soc, 84-. *Teaching:* Instr & asst prof, Univ Ill, 70-74. *Awards:* Ateneo Veneto, 90. *Bibliog:* Der Zusammendenker, Weltkunst, 10/04. *Mem:* Grolier Club, NY; Master Drawings Asn (int ed adv bd, 81-); Drawing Soc (bd dir, 84-); Print Coun Am (pres, 75-81). *Res:* Eighteenth century Italian graphic art; early German prints and drawings; German expressionism. *Collection:* Prints and 18th century Italian drawings and illustrated books. *Publ:* Paper in Paris, 77; German Expressionist Prints from the Collection of Ruth & Jacob Kainen, 85; Piranesi: Early Architectural Fantasies: A Catalogue Raisonne of the Etchings, 86; Durer to Diebenkorn, 92; The Glory of Venice: Art in the Eighteenth Century; Building a Collection, 97; A Century of Drawings, 01; and others. *Mailing Add:* Graphic Arts Div Nat Gallery Art Washington DC 20565

ROBLES-GALIANO, ESTELA
PAINTER

b Mayaguez, PR, Mar 28, 43. *Study:* U PR, Mayaguez, BA, 1963; Art Ctr Francisco Oller, Aguadilla, PR, studies with Antonio Loro, 1973-78. *Work:* Clínica San Francisco, Guadalajara, Mexico; U PR, Aguadilla; Autoridad Comunicaciones, San Juan, PR; Aguadilla Art Mus. *Comn:* cover and interior for telephone directory (12 paintings), Autoridad Comunicaciones, Caguas, PR, 92-93; cover telephone directory (25 paintings), PR Telephone Co, San Juan, 92-93; cover, The Tourist's Tlephone Directory Quickguide, ITT Intermedia, Inc, Hato Rey, PR, 92-93; cover for Maldita Sea la Justicia (auth Jorge Chear Cacho), 97; Literature in Painting (10 paintings), Hewlett-Packard Caribe, Aguadilla, PR, 2000. *Exhib:* 10th Ann NDak Nat Exhibit, Minot, NDak Art Gallery, 87; Int Art Competition, Pfeiffer Gallery, NY, 88 & Agora Gallery, NY, 93; 48th Ann Anniversary Nat Art Competition, Lake Worth, Fla Art League, 89; Watercolor Asn PR Ann Exhib, Graphic Art Mus, San Juan, 90; Int Showcase Traditional Marine Art, Gloucester Fine Arts, Mass, 91; Las Americas en Encuentro Musical, Las Americas Mus, San Juan, 93; 22nd Ann Pa Watercolor Soc, So Alleghenies Mus, Ligonier Valley, Pa, 2001. *Pos:* juror, lectr watercolor, Ramey Sch, CABA, Aguadilla & Univ PR, Mayagüez, 99-2000. *Teaching:* prof humanities I & II, Cath Univ PR, Aguadilla, 64-71; art instr drawing & painting, Colegio San Carlos, Aguadilla, 78-80 & Univ PR, Aguadilla, 82-84; workshop instr, Centro Arte Borinké, Aguadilla, 94-96; lectr, Univ PR, Centro Mujer y Salud, San Juan, 96. *Awards:* Cert of Excellence, Internat Art Competition, I a C, NY, 88; Langnickel award, 48th Annaul Nat Art Competition, Lake Worth Art League, 89; Disting Woman, Senate of PR, 95 & 98; homage, Exch Club, 92, Union Am Women, 92 & Women Civic Club, 98. *Bibliog:* Reinaldo Silvestri (auth), Esteal Robes y su mundo pictórico, Visión de Puerto Rico, 5/89; subject of video Down to Sea, North Am Marine Art Soc, 91; Randi Hoffman (auth), Mysticism at Agora Gallery, 94. *Mem:* Watercolor Asn PR (publicity chmn 1997, 98 & 99); Nat Exhib Day PR Painter (founder, pres. assessor, 1998-99, 2000-03); Aguadilla Art Mus (assessor 1980-2003); Am Soc Portrait Artists; Nat Mus Women in the Arts; PR Watercolorists Asn. *Media:* Watercolor. *Dealer:* West Gallery - Alicia Martinez McKindley 24 W Mayagüez PR 00680. *Mailing Add:* McKindley 24 Mayaguez PR 00680

ROBLETO, DARIO
ARTIST

Study: Univ Tex, San Antonio, 91-93; Univ Tex, El Paso, 93-96; Yale Summer Sch Music & Art, 96; Univ Tex, San Antonio, BFA, 96-97. *Teaching:* Vis lectr, Corcoran Col Art & Design, Wash, 2001; instr, Univ New Orleans, 2001; instr, Calif Inst Arts, Valencia, 2002; instr, Calif Col Arts & Crafts, San Francisco, 2002; instr, Loyola Marymount, Los Angeles, 2002. *Mailing Add:* c/o Acme 6150 Wilshire Blvd #1 Los Angeles CA 90048

ROCAMORA, JAUME
PAINTER

b Tortosa, Spain, July 6, 46. *Study:* Taller Sch Art, Tortosa, Spain, 56; studied with Joan Llimona, Cercle Artistic Sant Lluc, Barcelona, 69. *Work:* Mus Popular Contemp Art, Villafamés, Spain; Zabaleta Mus, Quesada; Munic Mus Fine Arts, Cholet, France; Mus Leopod-Huesch, Dûren, Alemania; Mus Dibujos, Larres, Spain. *Comn:* Mural collage, Casa Diocesana d'Espiritualitat, Tortosa, Spain, 86; mural collage, Hotel Berenguer IV, Tortosa, Spain, 86; Serigrafia, Ministry of Trabajo, Madrid, 89 & 90. *Exhib:* Elements Primaris, Mus Popular Contemp Art, Villafamés, 84; Ocuvres 1983-1988, Mus Munic Fine Arts, Cholet, 89. *Bibliog:* J Corredor Matheos (auth), El Arte Mental de Jaume Rocamora, catalog, 85; Josep Miquel Garcia (auth), La percepció implica pensament, catalog, 86; Arnau Puig (auth), Intención ensimismada, catalog, 91. *Mem:* Noesis Found, Calaceite, Spain (vpres, currently). *Media:* Collage. *Publ:* Illusr, Textos Bàsic de Edicions de Filosofia, Santa Coloma de Gramenet, 91; Xle, Festival de Música Felip Pedrell, Tortosa, 91; Ediciones del Ministerio de Trabajo, Madrid, 91; L'Organització Territorial en Vegueries, Tortosa, 91. *Mailing Add:* Argentina 13 Tortosa Spain 43500

ROCCO, RON (RONALD) ANTHONY
SCULPTOR, VIDEO ARTIST

b Ft Hood, Tex, Nov 21, 53. *Study:* Fordham Univ, BS, 71; State Univ NY, Col, Purchase, BFA (state regents scholar) 76; Ctr Advan Visual Study/Mass Inst Technol, with Herr Otto Piene, 83. *Work:* Raw Data for the I V, Showing Room, NY, 79; Laser Sculpture/Dance, Herbert F Johnson Mus, Ithaca, NY, 81; Zaroffs Tale, Solomon R Guggenheim Mus, NY, 83; Buddah Meets Einstein at the Great Wall, Asia Soc, NY, 85; Grammage Theatre, Temple, Ariz, 86. *Comn:* Altair, 77 & Meketra, 78, Festival Ithaca, NY; The Horizon is Nothing More Than the Limit of Our Sight, Brooklyn Mus, NY, 90. *Exhib:* Artist & the Computer, Bronx Mus Art, NY, 85; solo exhibs, Special Projects, PS1, Inst Art & Urban Resources, NY, 87, The Waterline Project, Found Art Garden, Amsterdam, The Neth, 89 & The Berlin Project (auth, catalog), Kunstlerhaus Bethanien & Amerika Haus, Berlin, Ger, 91; Technological Muse, Katonah Mus Art, 90; Working in Brooklyn-Installations, Brooklyn Mus Art, NY, 90. *Collection Arranged:* American Video Selections/The Video Image Invitational, Found Georgio Ronchi, Capri, Italy, 85. *Pos:* Resident video artist, Experimental TV Ctr, Owego, NY, formerly; int artist-in-residence, Kunst & Complex, Rotterdam, Neth, 92. *Teaching:* Guest lectr, Cornell Univ, Watermargin Ser, Ithaca, NY, 77, Columbia Univ, Sch Arit Hist, NY, 82, Harvard, Sch Archit, Cambridge, Mass, 88; guest fac, Banff Ctr Arts, Banff, Can, formerly. *Awards:* NY State Coun Arts Award, In Light of Sound, 85; NY Found Arts Award, The Waterline Project, 89; Neth/Am Found Award, The Waterline Project, Dutch Consulate Gen, 89. *Bibliog:* Jennifer Dunning (auth), Dance--laser sculpture, New York Times, 5/26/81; Jenya Gould (auth), Brooklyn artists-open studios, Greenline Press, 5/90; Jeanne Greenberg (auth), Working in Brooklyn-Installations, Brooklyn Mus, 8/3/90. *Mem:* Conf on Commun Technol & Traditional Cult (conf partic 83). *Media:* Metal, Video. *Interests:* digital media, physics biol scis. *Publ:* Auth, Private Parts, Kunst & Complex, Rotterdam, Neth. *Dealer:* Peirogi 200 Gallery 177 N 9th St Brooklyn NY 11211; Galene Volcker &Friends Orawenburger Str 2 10178 Berlin Germany

ROCHE, (EAMONN) KEVIN
ARCHITECT

b Dublin, Ireland, Jun 14, 22. *Study:* Nat Univ Ireland, BArch, 45; Ill Inst Tech, Postgrad, 48. *Hon Degrees:* Wesleyan Univ, DFA (hon), 81; Nat Univ Ireland, DSc (hon), 77; Yale Univ, DFA (hon), 95. *Comn:* Prin works incl Ford Found Hdqs, 67, Oakland (Calif) Mus, 68, Metrop Mus Art, NY, Creative Arts Ctr, Wesleyan Univ, Middletown, Conn, 71, Fine Arts Ctr, Univ Mass, 71, Union Carbide Corp World Hdqs, Conn, General Foods Corp Hdqs, Rye, NY, 77, 78, Conoco Inc Hdqs, Houston, 79, Central Park Zoo, NY, 80, DeWitt Wallace Mus Fine Arts, Williamsburg, Va, 80, Bouygues World Hdqs, Paris, 83 JP Morgan and Co Hdqs, NY, 83, UNICEF Hdqs, NY, 84, Leo Burnett Co Hdqs, Chicago, 85, Corning (NY) Inc Hdqs, 86, Merck & Co Hdqs, NJ, 87, Dai Ichi Hdqs./Norinchukin Bank Hdqrs, Tokyo, 89, Nations Bank Hdqs, Atlanta, 89, Pontiac Marina Pvt Ltd; Singapore, 90, Metrop, Madrid, 90, Borland Inter Headquarters, Scotts Valley, Calif, 90, Tanjong & Binariang/Ampang Tower, Kuala Lumpur, Malaysia, 93, Mus Jewish Heritage Holocaust Mem, NY, 93, Tata Cummins Private Ltd, Jamshedpur, India, 94, Vis Ctr, Columbus, Ind, 94, Cummins Engine Co APEX Manufacturing Facility, 94, Lucent Techs. Hdqs, Murray Hill, NJ, 96, Wuxi Newage Cummins Wuxi, China, 96, Total Systems Serv Corp. Headquarters, Columbus, Ga, 97, student housing and student union NY Univ, NY 2003, central athletic facility Mass Inst of Tech, Cambridge, 2000, Lucent Tech. Research and Development Facilities, various locations incl The Neth and Ger, 2001,

Shiodome Block B Devel, Tokyo, 2003, Santander Central Hispano, Madrid, 2001-, Securities & Exchange Comn Hdqrs, Wash, 2001-, Bouygues SA Holding Co Hdqrs, Paris, 2002-, Nat Conf Ctr, Dublin, 2002-. *Pos:* With Eero Saarinen & Assocs Bloomfield Hills, Mich, 50-61; partner, Kevin Roche John Dinkeloo & Assoc, Hamden, 66-. *Awards:* Recipient Creative Arts award Brandeis Univ, 67; AS Bard award City Club NY, 68, 77, 79; Albert S Bard award, 90. *Mem:* Fel Am Inst of Archits; Am Asn for Advancement of Sci; Nat Acad (assoc, 67, acad, 73); Am Acad of Arts and Letters (pres, 94-97); Munic Art Soc, NY. *Mailing Add:* Kevin Roche John Dinkeloo & Assoc 20 Davis St PO Box 6127 New Haven CT 06517-3501

ROCHÉ, ROBERT (RICHARD)
PAINTER
Study: Apprenticeship, studio of Sebastian Cruset, 31-32; Nat Acad Design, New York, 33-36; Art Students League, 36-40; Columbia Univ, 1941. *Work:* NY Racing Asn, Aqueduct, Long Island & Belmont, Elmwood; Nat Mus Racing, Saratoga, NY; Wilmington Race Track, Del; USAF, Offutt, Nebr; numerous pvt collections. *Comn:* Saratoga Race Track Series, NY Racing Asn, Long Island, 60, painting of Man O War, 61 & Belmont Race Track Series, 63; plus private commissions. *Exhib:* One-man shows, Frank K M Rehn Galleries, NY, 49 & 52 & Am Watercolor Soc, NY; Silvermine Guild Artists, Norwalk, Conn, 51-54; Salmagundi Club, NY, 54 & 55; Retrospective, USAF Acad, Colo, 88; Retrospective of NYRA Racing Yrs, Paintings & Drawings, Nat Mus Racing, Saratoga Springs, NY, 2000-2001; many others. *Pos:* Cur, Mus Fine Arts, Richmond, Va, 47-48; radio art prog, NH 68-70; writer, Nat Antiques Rev, Portland, Maine, 69-71; owner, RRR Assoc & RR Prints. *Teaching:* Instr painting & drawing, own pvt art sch, 42-64. *Bibliog:* Payton Boswell & G Leonard Gold (auth). *Mem:* Am Watercolor Soc; Royal Soc Arts. *Media:* All Media. *Res:* Art and the Mentally Sick, Northhampton, MA. *Interests:* Art, Music, Literature, rare books, farming, raising animals, sports, etc. *Publ:* Illusr, Birds and Beasts of Mark Twain, Univ Okla Press, 66; and prints of own work; Paintings in Various Publications. *Mailing Add:* Windswept Farm PO Box 467 York ME 03909

ROCHE-RABELL, ARNALDO
PAINTER
b Santurce, PR, 55. *Study:* Sch Archit PR, 74-78; Art Inst Chicago, BFA(James Nelson Raymond Fel), 82, MFA, 84. *Work:* Art Inst Chicago; Hirshhorn Mus & Sculpture Garden, Washington, DC; Metrop Mus Art & Mus del Barrio, NY. *Exhib:* Recent Acquisitions, Hirshhorn Mus & Sculpture Garden, Washington, DC & Museo del Barrio, NY, 91; Myth and Magic: Am Art of the 1980's, Museo de Arte Contemporaneo, Monterrey, Mex, 91; Cruciformed: Images of the Cross Since 1980, Cleveland Ctr Contemp Art, Ohio, 91-92; Awards in the Visual Arts 10, Southeastern Ctr Contemp Art, Hirshhorn Mus & Sculpture Garden, Washington, DC, Albuquerque Mus Art, Hist & Sci, NMex & Toledo Mus Art, Ohio, 91-92; 40th Anniversary Exhib: Selections from the Richard Brown Baker Collection, Frumkin/Adams Gallery, NY, 92; Latin Am Artists of the Twentieth Century, Mus Mod Art, NY, Estacion Plaza de Armas, Seville, Centre Georges Pompidou, Paris, Mus Ludwig, Cologne, 92-93; Selections from the Collection, Hirshhorn Mus & Sculpture Garden, Washington, DC, 94; Caribbean Visions: Contemp Painting and Sculpture, Art Serv Int, 95; The Reconstructed Figure: The Human Image in Contemp Art, Katonah Mus Art, NY, 95; Azaceta, Bedia, Roche, George Adams Gallery, NY, 95 & Going Places, 96; Art in Chicago: 1945-1995, Mus Contemp Art, Ill, 96-97; Caballos: Political Animals, Azaceta, Bedia, Benedit, Elso, Roche, George Adams Gallery, NY, 97; FIA 1997, Caracas, 97; Annual Collectors Show, Ark Arts Ctr, Little Rock, 98; Latin-Am Group Show (Azaceta, Bedia, Roche, Palazyan), George Adams Gallery, NY, 98; and many others. *Awards:* Medallion of Lincoln Award, presented by Mr James Thompson, Gov Ill, 81; 2nd Ann Biennial Painting Prize, Cuenas, Ecuador, 89. *Bibliog:* Enrique Garcia Gutierrez (auth), Arnaldo Roche-Rabell: Los Premeros Diez Anos (exhib catalog), Museo de Arte Contemp, 92; and many others. *Mailing Add:* c/o George Adams Gallery 41 W 57th St 7th Fl New York NY 10019

ROCHETTE, ANNE MONIQUE
SCULPTOR
b Oullins, France, Jan 5, 57. *Study:* Ecole Nationale Des Beaux Arts, Paris, dipl fine arts, 79; New York Univ, MA, 82. *Work:* Fond Nat D'Art Contemporain, France; Collections de la Ville de Paris, France. *Exhib:* Ateliers 81-82, Mus Mod Art, Paris, 82; one-person exhibs, Pains & Pleasures, Julian Pretto/Berland/Hall Gallery, NY, 90, Ecole Nat Superieure des Beaux Arts, Paris, 94, Maison d'Art Contemporain Chaillioux, Fresnes, 95, Un Pas de coté, Galerie Jaqueline Moussion, Paris, 95 & Le Quai, Mus des Beaux-Arts, Mulhouse Statengalerie, La Haye, Pays-Bas; Galerie Attia Bousbaa, Paris, 96; Inter/References, De l'Inde à l'Autre, Ecole des Beaux-Arts, Rouen, 96; Galerie J Rabouan/Moussion, FIAC, Paris, 96; Dessein de Dessins, Galerie des Ateliers, Galerie A Vivas, Paris, 96. *Teaching:* Asst prof, Tyler Sch Art, 86-87; vis prof, Parsons Sch Design, 87-88 & sr sculpture critic, 93; asst prof, NY Studio Sch, 87-90; asst prof, RI Sch Design, 87-90; resident critic, Vt Studio Ctr, 91; prof, Ecole Nat Superieure des Beaux-Arts, Paris, 93-. *Awards:* Nat Endowment Arts Fel, 90; New York Found Arts Fel, 91; Leonard de Vinci Award, France, 93. *Bibliog:* Philippe Dagen, Le Monde, 5/95 & 9/95; Sophie Thuot, Galeries Mag, 7/95; Michel Nuridsany, Le Figaro, 9/95. *Media:* Sculpture. *Publ:* Auth, Ariane Lopez-Huici, Art in Am, 93; Savage Mercies (Annette Messager), Art in Am, 94; Revitalizing the Louvre, Art in Am, 94; Erik Dietman, Art in Am, 94; Figures of Estrangement (Thomas Schutte), Art in Am, 95. *Mailing Add:* 315 Berry St No 7N Brooklyn NY 11211

ROCKBURNE, DOROTHEA
PAINTER, SCULPTOR
b Montreal, Que; US citizen. *Study:* Black Mountain Col, Ecole Des Beaux Arts, Montreal; Montreal Mus Sch, Can. *Hon Degrees:* Hon Degrees, Col for Creative Studies, Hon Doctor of Fine Arts, 2002. *Work:* Mus Mod Art, Whitney Mus Am Art & Metrop Mus Art, NY; Philadelphia Mus Art; Corcoran Gallery, Washington; Guggenheim Mus, NY; J Paul Getty Trust, Calif; Nat Mus of Women in Art; Philadelphia Mus of Art; Auckland City Art Mus; Brooklyn Mus of Art; Nat Galleries, Washington, DC; Houston Mus of Fine Arts; and many other collections. *Comn:* Mural, Sony Corp, NY, 93; mural, Ganek Residence, 93; mural, Hilton Hotel, San Jose, Calif, 93; mural, Portland Maine Courthouse, 94; mural, Univ Mich, Ann Arbor, 97. *Exhib:* One-woman show, Margo Leavin Gallery, Los Angeles, Calif, 82, Galleriet, Lund, Sweden, 83, Xavier Fourcade, NY, 86, Arts Club, Chicago, Ill, 87, Andre Emmerich Gallery, 88, 89, 90, 91, 92 & 94, Guild Hall Mus, 95 & Portland Mus Art, 96, Lawrence Rubin, Greenberg, Van Doren Fine Art, NY, 2000; Viewpoints: Postwar Painting & Sculpture, Guggenheim Mus, NY, 89; Geometric Abstraction, C Grimaldis Gallery, Baltimore Md, 95; Jason McCoy Gallery, NY, 95; More than Minimal: Feminism & Abstraction in the 70's, Rose Art Mus, 96; Bare Bones, TZ Art & Co, NY, 96; group exhibs: Marcus Ritter, NY, The Selby Gallery, Fla, The Nat Acad of Design, NY, The Armory Show, 2002; Reina Sophia Mus, Spain, 2003; Mus Fine Arts, MA, 2003; Cleveland Mus Art, OH, 2003 & 06; Guggenheim Mus, NY, 2004; LA MOCA, CA, 2004; Addison Gal Am Art, MA, 2004; Bruce Mus, Conn, 2004; Boca Raton Mus Art, FL, 2005; Betty Cunningham Gal, NY, 2005; Spanierman Gal, NY, 2005; Black Mountain Col, NC, 2005; Greenberg Van Doren Gal, NY, 2006; Nat Acad Design, NY, 2006; MOMA, NY, 2006. *Pos:* Mem, Artists' Advisory bd, New Mus, NY; bd mem & trustee, Independent Curators Inc & Art in General, NY; adv bd, Art Omni, NY. *Awards:* Guggenheim Fel, 72-73; Painting Award, Art Inst Chicago, 72; Nat Endowment Arts Fel, 74-75; Brandeis Univ Creative Arts Award, 85; Col for Creative Studies, Hon Doctor of Fine Arts Degree, 2002; Francis J Greenburger Award, Art Omi Int, 2003. *Bibliog:* Robert Storr (auth), Painterly Operations, Art Am, 2/86 & Rockburne's Wager (exhib catalog), Andre Emmerich Gallery, 88; Michael Brenson (auth), A new-world painter views the masterpieces of old-world innovators, 4/29/88 & Egyptian art is alive & well in the West, 12/31/89, NY Times; Lilly Wei (auth), Dorothea Rockburne, Stargazer, Art in Am, 10/94; John Yau (auth), Light and Dark (exhib catalog), Andre Emmerich Gallery, 89; Carter Ratcliff, Out of the Box: The Reinvention of Art, 1965-75, NY, 2000. *Mem:* Nat Arts Club; Art in Gen Century Club; Nat Acad. *Media:* Various Media. *Res:* Astronomy, Physics, Mathematics, Philosophy. *Specialty:* Estab and Emerging Contemp Artists. *Dealer:* Artemis Greenberg Van Doren Fine Art, NY. *Mailing Add:* 140 Grand St # 2WF New York NY 10013

ROCKEFELLER, DAVID
COLLECTOR
b New York, NY, June 12, 1915. *Study:* Harvard Univ, BS, 36; Univ Chicago, PhD, 40; LLD, Columbia Univ, 54, Bowdoin Col, 58, Jewish Theol Sem, 58, Williams Col, 66, Wagner Col, 67, Harvard Univ, 69, Pace Col, 70, St John's Univ, 71, Univ Liberia, 79. *Hon Degrees:* Numerous hon degrees from US & foreign univ, 54-87. *Pos:* hon chmn, Int House, 40-, dir, 40-63; trustee, Rockefeller Univ, 40-95, Carnegie Endowment Int Peace, Hist Hudson Valley, 81—; Asst regional dir, Office Defense, Health & Welfare Serv's, 41-42; asst mgr for dept, Chase Nat Bank, New York City, 46-47; asst cashier, 47-48, 2d vpres, 48-49, vpres, 49-51, sr vpres, 51-55; pres, Morningside Heights, Inc, 47-57, chmn, 57-65; bd overseers, Harvard Col, 54-60, 62-68; exec vpres, Chase Manhattan Bank (Chase Nat Bank merged with Bank of Manhattan), 55-57; vchmn bd, Chase Manhattan Bank, 57-61, pres, chmn exec comt, 61-69, chmn, 69-81, Chief Exec Officer, 69-80; exec comt, chmn, Downtown Lower Manhattan Asn, 58-75; chmn Int Exec Serv Corps, 64-68; Active Urban Develop Corp, NY State Bus Adv Coun, 68-72; US Adv Comt on Reform on Int Monetary System, 73-77, US exec comt, Dartmouth Conf Bd Inst Int Econs, Am Friends of LSE, US Hon Fel LSE, Bus Comt for Arts; co-founder, Trilateral Comn, 73-91, N Am chmn 81-92, hon chmn, 92; chmn, Rockefeller Brothers Fund, 81-87, vchmn, 68-80; chmn Chase Int Adv Comt, 81-99, Rockefeller Group, Inc, 81-95, NY Clearing House, 71-78, Ctr for Int-Am Relations, 66-70, Overseas Develop Coun, US-USSR Trade & Econ Coun Inc; chmn Am Soc, 81-92, hon chmn, 92-, New York City Partnership, 79-88, Captain Army of the US, 42-45, N African Theatre of Operations, ETO; chmn, Rockfeller Ctr Properties Trust, Inc, 96-; trustee & chmn bd trustees, Mus Mod Art, NY, emer chmn, currently; trustee, chmn emer, Mus Modern Art, New York City; life trustee, Univ Chicago; hon trustee, Rockefeller Family Fund. *Awards:* World Brotherhood Award, Jewish Theological Sem, 53; Recipient Merit Award NY chap Am Inst of Archits, 65; Gold medal, Nat Inst Social Scis, 67; Medal of Honor for City Planning New York City, Am Inst Architects, 68; C Walter Nichols award NY Univ, 70; Regional Planning Asn Award, 71; Charles Evans Hughes Award Nat Conf of Christians & Jews, 74; Hadrian Award, World Monuments Fund, 94; US Presidental Medal of Freedom, 98; Named one of Top 200 Collectors, ARTnews Mag, 2004; Decorated Legion of Honor France, Order of Arts & Letters; Order of the Liberator San Martin, Argentina, Order of Valor, Rep of Cameroun, Order of Boyaca, Colombia, Order of Christopher Columbus, Domincan Republica, Nat Order of Merit, Ecuador, Knight Comdr.'s Cross of the Order of Merit, Ger, Order of the Republic, Guinea, Gwengha Medal of the Rep of Korea,Order of the Aztec Eagle, Mex, Order of the Throne, Morocco, Hilal-i'Quaid-e-Azam, Pakistan, Order of Vasco Nunez de Balboa, Panama, Order of Manuel Amador Guerrero, Panama, Nat Order Merit/Grand Cross, Paraguay, Order of Merit, Italy, Order of Southern Cross, Brazil, Order of the White Elephant & Order of Crown, Thailand, Order of the Cedars, Lebanon, Order of the Sun, Peru, Nicholas Copernicus award, Porland; Order of Prince Henry the Navigator, Portugal, National Order of the Lion, Rep of Senegal, Order of Francisco de Miranda, Venezuela, Order of the Humane African Redemption, Liberia, Order of the Crown, Belgium, Nat Order of Ivory Coast, Grand Cordon Order of Sacred Treasure, Japan, Order Bernardo O'Higgins, Chile. *Mem:* Coun Foreign Relations (dir, 49-51, vpres, 51-70, chmn, 70-85), Japan Soc, Int House, Bilderberg Conf, Harvard Club, Univ Club, Century Club, The Links, The Knickerbocker. *Interests:* collecting 19th-century American art, impressionism and modern art, porcelain; sailing. *Collection:* Paintings, modern art. *Publ:* Auth, Unused Resources and Economic Waste, 40; auth, Creative Management in Banking, 64. *Mailing Add:* 30 Rockefeller Plaza Rm 5600 New York NY 10112

ROCKEFELLER, JOHN (JAY) D, IV
COLLECTOR
b New York, NY, June 18, 37. *Study:* Int Christian Univ, Tokyo, 57-60; Harvard Univ, BA, 61. *Hon Degrees:* Eleven from US Col & Univ. *Awards:* 200 Leaders in Am, Time Mag, 75; Named one of Top 200 Collectors, ARTnews Mag, 2004, 2005, 2006. *Mem:* Charleston Rotary; Nat Gov Asn (chmn, formerly). *Collection:* 19th Century Am Art & Am Impressionism. *Publ:* Auth, The Japanese Student, New York Times Mag, & Life 6/60. *Mailing Add:* 531 Hart Senate Off Bldg Washington DC 20510

ROCKEFELLER, SHARON PERCY
COLLECTOR
b Oakland, Calif, Dec 10, 44. *Study:* Stanford Univ, BA(cum laude), 66. *Hon Degrees:* DPS, Alderson-Broaddus Col, WVa, 77; LLD, Univ Charleston, WVa, 77 & Beloit Col, Wis, 78; LHD, W Liberty State Col, WVa, 80, Hamilton Col, NY, 82 & Wheeling Col, WVa, 84. *Awards:* Named Washingtonian of Year, Washingtonian Mag, 94; Nat Endowment for the Humanities, 94; Distinguished Broadcaster Award, 94; named one of Top 200 Collectors, ARTnews Mag, 2004, 2005, 2006; recipient Charles Frankel Prize; Woman of Vision Award; Women in Film & Video Award; CINE Lifetime Achievement Award. *Mem:* Stanford-in-Washigngton Coun (chmn, formerly); Fel, Am Acad Arts & Sci's; Smithsonian Am Art Comn (bd mem, currently). *Collection:* 19th century American Art & American Impressionism

ROCKLIN, RAYMOND
SCULPTOR, EDUCATOR
b Moodus, Conn, Aug 18, 22. *Study:* Educ Alliance, New York, with Abbo Ostrovsky; Cooper Union Art Sch, with Milton Hebald & John Havannes, BFA(Skowhegan Scholar). *Work:* Whitney Mus Am Art, NY; Provincetown Mus Art, Mass; Temple Israel, St Louis; Skowhegan Sch Painting & Sculpture; Birds, Stainless Steel, Manocherian, NY; plus others. *Comn:* Wall brass, comn by Mrs Beskind, NY, 62; wall brass, comn by Mrs Nina Waller, Baltimore, 63; four religious sculptures, White Plains Hosp, NY, 79; brass horse (16'x9'), Mr Stahmer, Yorktown Heights, NY, 88. *Exhib:* One man shows, Tanager Gallery, 56, Am Univ, 56, Oakland Art Mus, 59, Santa Barbara Mus Art, 59, Univ Calif, Berkeley, 59, Pomona Col, 60, Ball State Univ, 64, Briarcliff Col, 73, Mardin Gallery, 87; Stable Gallery, Bertha Schaeffer Gallery, AAA Gallery, Galleria Tiberna in Rome; plus others. *Teaching:* Guest artist, Am Univ, 56 & Ball State Teachers Col, summer 64; asst prof art, Univ Calif, Berkeley, 59-60; prof art, Borough Manhattan Community Col, City Univ New York, currently. *Awards:* Fulbright Grant, Italy, 52-53; Yaddo Found Fel, 56; First Prize for Sculpture, Pocantico Women's Club Award, New York, 75; plus others. *Bibliog:* M Seuphor (auth), Raymond Rocklin, The Sculpture of this Century, 61; F Hazan (auth), article, Dictionary Mod Sculpture; and others. *Mem:* Sculptors Guild; Am Abstract Artists; Fedn Mod Painters & Sculptors. *Media:* Mixed. *Dealer:* Sculptors Guild 110 Greene St New York NY 10012

RODA, RHODA LILLIAN SABLOW
PAINTER, TAPESTRY ARTIST
b Port Chester, NY, 1926. *Study:* Univ Wis; Rochester Inst Technol; Art Students League; also with Frank Vincent DuMont & Frank Reilly. *Comn:* Cranbrook 50th Anniversary (needlepoint rug), Cranbrook Acad, Bloomfield Hills, Mich, 73; needlepoint designs of main altar area & furniture, Christ Episcopal Church, Detroit, Mich, 75 & main altar rug, 82; needlepoint designs altar seats & kneelers, St James Church, Birmingham, Mich, 83; needlepoint design, Church of the Holy Sepulcher, Jerusalem, 94. *Exhib:* Allied Artists Am, Nat Acad, NY, 69; Ahda Artzt Gallery, NY, 70; Needle Arts Gallery, Birmingham, Mich, 71, 74 & 76; Lever House, NY, 77. *Pos:* chmn, organizer juried craft show, Purchase Col Performing Arts Center, Purchase, NY, 98, 99, 2000. *Bibliog:* Lesley Umans (auth), Encaustic painting, Reporter Dispatch, AP, 7/70 & Creative stitchery, Women's Wear Daily, 8/71; Lillian Braun (auth), 3-D needlepoint, int, Detroit Free Press, 10/74. *Media:* Oil, Acrylic. *Mailing Add:* Rural Dr Scarsdale NY 10583

RODAN, DON
PHOTOGRAPHER, PAINTER
b Cincinnati, Ohio, June 30, 50. *Study:* Cooper Union Art Sch, BFA, 74. *Work:* Int Mus Photog, George Eastman House, NY; Australian Nat Gallery, Canberra; Williams Col Art Mus, Mass; The Polaroid Collection, Cambridge, Mass; San Francisco Mus Mod Art, Calif; Kunstmuseum, Basel, Switz; Walker Arts Ctr, Minneapolis, Minn; Nat Gallery, Washington, DC; Mus Fine Arts, Houston. *Exhib:* One-man shows, The Greek Myths, Int Mus Photog, George Eastman House, 77 & Castelli Gallery, NY, 79, Immortal Stories: Recent Color Drawings, Leo Castelli Gallery, NY, 86; One of a Kind Color, Houston Mus Fine Arts & Corcoran Gallery, 79-80; Exploration of a Medium, Rheinisches Landes Mus & Frakfurter Kunst Verein, Ger, 80 & 81; Fabricated to be Photographed, San Francisco Mus Mod Art & Albright-Knox Gallery, 80; New Voices 2, Allen Mem Art Mus, Ohio, 81; La Photographie en Amerique, Galerie Texbraun, Paris, 82; Arranged Images, Boise Gallery Art, Idaho, 83; Three Dimensional Photographs, Herman Wunsche, Bonn, WGer, 83; The Family of Man, PS 1, Long Island City, NY, 84; Extending the Perimeters of Twentieth-Century Photog, San Francisco Mus Mod Art, 85; Fabrications: Staged, Altered and Appropriated Photographs, Int Ctr of Photog, NY 87 & Carpenter Art Ctr, Harvard Univ, Cambridge, Mass, 88. *Awards:* Nat Endowment Arts Fel, 84-85. *Bibliog:* Richard Whelan (auth), New York Reviews: Don Rodan, Art News, 5/79; Sally Eauclaire (auth), The New Color, Abbeville Press, 81; Carter Ratcliff (auth), Tableau photography from Mayall to Rodan, Picture Mag #18, fall 81; Andy Grundberg (auth), Exploring the improbable, New York Times, 7/11/82; Ronny H Cohen (auth), Image scavengers, photography, an exhibition, Print Collector's Newletter, 5-6/83; John Russell (auth), Don Rodan, Immortal Stories: Recent Color Drawings, NY Times 3/14/86; Anne Hoy (auth), Fabrications: Staged, Altered and Appropriated Photographs, Abbeville Press, NY 87. *Media:* Color Pencil on Linen, Cibachrome Color

RODE, MEREDITH EAGON
PRINTMAKER, EDUCATOR
b Delaware, Ohio, Mar 27, 38. *Study:* Corcoran Sch Art, 55-58; George Washington Univ, BA, 58; Art Students League, New York, (scholar), study with George Grosz & Harry Sternberg, 59; Univ Md, MFA, 74; Union Inst, PhD, 94. *Work:* Southern Graphics Print Collection, Univ Miss, Oxford; Univ Md Col Permanent Collection; Dundalk Col; Univ Dist Columbia Permanent Collection; Nat Mus Women in Arts. *Exhib:* Baltimore Mus Art, Md, 77; Utah Mus Fine Arts, Salt Lake City, 77; Contemp Printmaking in Maryland, (juried) Baltimore, MD, 83; Dundalk Col Gallery Invitational, self-portraits, 91; US Dept State Art in the Embassies Prog, Nassau, Bahamas, Kinshasa, Zaire, Vienna, Austria, Port-Au-Prince, Haiti, Brazzaville, the Congo & Geneva, Switz; Mus Modern, in New Delhi, India, Beijing, China, 2002. *Pos:* Actg chmn, Federal City Col, Washington, DC, 71-72. *Teaching:* Instr studio art, Corcoran Sch Art, 62-68; assoc prof studio art, Univ DC, 68-78, prof, 78-. *Awards:* Fac Res Grant, Univ DC, 85-86, 86-87; Fel, Ctr Applied Res, 88-89; Sussman Award, Union Inst, 94; Nat Educ Asn Award, 2000. *Bibliog:* UDC Special Art Collection catalog, 84. *Mem:* Women's Caucus Art (nat vpres, 75-76); Founds Art Theory & Educ; Arts Coun African Studies Asn; Col Art Asn; and others. *Media:* Multimedia. *Res:* Visual Culture (global). *Publ:* Auth, articles, Art J, Col Art Asn, 75; illusr, Earth Day, 90, Quicksilver Comm, Inc; auth, Thought on Action, The NEA Higher Educ J, 2000; auth, Fate in Review, Foundations in Art, Theory and Education, 2000. *Mailing Add:* Univ DC 4200 Connecticut Ave NW Washington DC 20008

RODEIRO, JOSE MANUEL
PAINTER, MURALIST
b Tampa, Fla, Feb 5, 49. *Study:* Univ Tampa, Fla, BA, 71; Pratt Inst, Brooklyn, MFA, 73; Ohio Univ, Athens, Ohio, PhD, 76. *Work:* Washington Co Mus, Hagerstown, Md; Oscar Cintas Found, NY; City of Tampa, Fla; Oscar Cintas Found Collection, Fla Int Univ Mus, Miami, Fla. *Comn:* Arrival of De Soto in Florida (mural), Convention Center, Tampa, Fla, 80; Tampa the Craddle of Cuban Independence (mural), Fla, 90; The Ransoming of Frederick (mural), Walkersville, Md, 92. *Exhib:* Four Allegheny Artists, Md Art Place, Baltimore, 83; one-person shows, Nicholas Roerch Mus, NY, 85 & Washington Co Mus, Md, 88; Inaugural Exhib, Casal de Sarria, Barcelona, Spain, 86; Grace Harkin Gallery, NY, 88; Rosenberg Gallery, Baltimore, Md, 90; Lucia Gallery, NY, 90; Washington Co Mus, Md, 97; Face-to-Face, Washington Co Mus, Hagerstown, Md, 2001; Visual Imagery of Latinas/os Exhib, Mason Gross Sch Art Gallery, Rutgers, State Univ NJ, 2001; Corazones Unidos, Newark Mus, 2002; Kenkelaba Gallery, New York City, 2002; Transcultural NJ, Perth Amboy Gallery, Perth Amboy, NJ. *Pos:* Professor of Art, New Jersey City Univ, Jersey City, NJ, 2003-. *Teaching:* Vis prof, Pratt Inst, Brooklyn, 75-77; adj prof art, Univ SFla, Tampa, 77-79; asst prof, Frostburg State Univ, Md, 79-84, assoc prof, 84-93; artist-in-residence, Md State Arts Coun, 92; assoc prof, Art Dept, NJ City Univ, 93-. *Awards:* Oscar B Cintas Fel in painting, 82; Best of Show, Washington Co Mus, 85; Vis Artist Fel in painting, Nat Endowment for the Arts, 86-87; Best of Show, Lucia Gallery, 88; Lectr Res Fulbright Grant, Nicaragua, 94-95. *Bibliog:* Nico Suarez (auth), Amnesis Art, Lascaux Pub, 88; Murals article, St Petersburg Sun Times, 11/11/90; Presencia Revista, La Paz, Bolivia, 9/12/93; The Hispanic Outlook in Higher Education, Paramus, NJ, 1/2002; Transcultural New Jersey Vol II, 2005; Neo-Latino, Perth Amboy Galleries Publ, Perth Amboy, NJ, 2004-2005; Visual Imagery of Latinoas/os in New Jersey, Rutgers Univ, 2002. *Mem:* Art South Inc; Md Fedn Art; Md State Arts Coun Visual Arts Panel; Friends of Art NJ; Ctr for Latino Arts & Culture; Council on Hispanic Affairs; Neo-Latin Group, Newark, NJ. *Media:* Oil, Acrylic. *Res:* Grolier's Encyclopedia Latina (Aesteics, Cuban-Americans). *Interests:* Poetry. *Publ:* Art of the 60's & 70's, Wash Co Mus Fine Arts, Hagerstown, 90; Contemporary Nicaraguan Art, Frostburg State Univ Press, 91; Ron Felbers Searchers (cover), Omni Mag, St Martins Press, NY, 11/94; and others; cover design, illusr, Amnesia Tango, Cedar Hill Pub, 98; cover design, Infinite Days, BOP Press, 2003. *Dealer:* Clayton Galleries Tampa FL; Lucia Gallery New York NY; Alan Britt, Baltimore, MD. *Mailing Add:* New Jersey City Univ 2039 Kennedy Blvd Jersey City NJ 07305-2152

RODRIGUEZ, GENO (EUGENE)
PHOTOGRAPHER, MUSEUM DIRECTOR
b New York, NY, June 2, 40. *Study:* Hammersmith Col Art, London, NDD, 66; Int Peoples Col, Elsinore, Denmark. *Work:* Metrop Mus Art; Everson Mus Art; Int Ctr for Photog, NY; Am Mus Natural Hist, NY; Mus Contemp Art, Caracas, Venezuela. *Exhib:* One & two-person exhibs, Wadsworth Atheneum, Hartford, Conn, 76, Aternative Ctr for Int Arts, NY, Studio Arte 2001, Castressata, Italy & Centro Arte Galeter, Brescia, Italy, 77, Mus Contemp Art, Caracus, Venezuela & II Diaframma Gallery, Milan, Italy, 79, Cayman Gallery, NY & Real Art Ways Gallery, Hartford, Conn, 80, Jayne H Baum Gallery, NY, 86, CEPA Gallery, Buffalo, NY, 87 & Sheldon Memorial Art Gallery, Univ Nebr, Lincoln, 89; Graham Mod, NY, 87; San Diego Mus Art, Calif, 87; Photog on the Edge (catalog), The Patrick & Beatrice Haggerty Mus Art, Marquette Univ, Milwaukee, Wis, 88; The Photog of Invention: Am Photogrs of the Eighties (catalog), Nat Mus Am Art, Smithsonian Inst, Washington, DC, 89; Fantasies, Fables and Fabrications: Photoworks from the 80's traveling exhib, Univ Mass, Amherst, Herter Art Gallery, also traveling: Delaware Art Mus, Wilmington; Lamont Gallery, Phillips Exeter Acad, Andover, Mass; Univ Mo, Gallery Art, Kansas City; Mus Contemp Art, Ostende, Belgium; Mus Contemp Photog, Antwerp, Belg & Mus Contemp Art, Florence, Italy, 89; and others. *Collection Arranged:* Dia Dos Los Muertos III: Homelessness, 90; Peter Dean: A Retrospective, 90; Keith Morrison: Recent Paintings, 90; Syncretism: Art of the 21st Century, 91; Artists of Conscience: 16 Years of Social & Political Commentary, 92; Made in America: Art of the Great Lakes States, 86. *Pos:* Pres, founder, Inst Contemp Hispanic Art, 72-74, Enfoco: Latin Am Photog Collaborative, 73-74, Alternative Mus, 75-. *Teaching:* Instr photog, Rutgers Univ, 77-78; instr photo critique, Sch Visual Arts, New York, 77-. *Awards:* Distinguished Am Vis to Africa, Phelps Stokes Fund, 77; Artist Nat Endowment Arts

fel, 79; Ludwig Vogelstein Found Fel, 81. *Mem:* Am Asn Mus (cur comt, exec mem, 85-86). *Media:* Photo-assemblage. *Publ:* The Islands: Worlds of the Puerto Ricans, Harper & Row, 74; auth, Mira Mira Mira Puerto Rican New Yorkers, Forum Press, 75. *Mailing Add:* 32 W 82nd St Apt 9A New York NY 10024

RODRIGUEZ, ROCIO A
PAINTER
b Caibarien, Las Villas, Cuba, 52. *Study:* Univ Ga, BFA, MFA. *Work:* High Mus Art, Atlanta, Ga; Hyatt Hotel Int, Paris, France; Kidder Peabody & Co, Atlanta, Ga; 3M Co, St Paul, Minn; Mus Art, Ft Lauderdale, Fla. *Comn:* Hartsfield Int Airport, Atlanta, Ga; Culpepper, McAuliffe & Meaders, Atlanta, Ga; Hyatt Hotel Corp, Atlanta, Ga; Troutman and Sanders, Atlanta, Ga. *Exhib:* Summer Selections, Carl Solway Gallery, Cincinnati, Ohio, 86; State of the Arts of Georgia Exhib, Contemp Art Ctr, New Orleans, La, 88; Latin Am Artists of the Southeast Coastal Region, Contemp Art Ctr, New Orleans, La, 88; Spotlight on Georgia Artists, Trinity Sch, Atlanta, Ga, 88; Southern Expressions: A Sense of Self, High Mus Art, Atlanta, Ga, 88; Gathering for a Figurative Myth, Univ Ala, Tuscaloosa, 89; Birmingham Biennial V, Birmingham Art Mus, Ala, 89; one-woman shows, McIntosh Gallery, Atlanta, Ga, 89, Sandler Hudson Gallery, Atlanta, Ga, 91, 93 & 95, Studio Exhib, Atlanta, Ga, 92, Brenau Col, Gaineseville, Ga, 95, Nexus Contemp Art Ctr, Atlanta, Ga, 96, Fay Gold Gallery, Atlanta, Ga, 98, 99 & 2000, Hamphill Fine Arts, Washington, DC, 99 & Cheekwood Mus Art, Nashville, Tenn, 2000; High Mus Art, Atlanta, Ga, 90; Vital Signs, Nexus Contemp Arts Ctr, Atlanta, Ga, 91; Angry Love, Arts Festival, Atlanta, Ga, 92; Galerie Simonne Stern, New Orleans, La, 92; Montgomery Biennial, Montgomery Mus Fine Arts, Ala, 94; Michael Solway Gallery, Cincinnati, Ohio, 96; 9 Women in Georgia, Nat Mus Women Arts, Washington, DC, 96; Defying the Southern Sterotype, Sandler Hudson Gallery, Atlanta, Ga, 96; Big, Ga Mus Art, Athens, 97; r Emote, Hyde Park Ctr, Chicago, Ill, 97; Joy of the Journey: Visual Accounts of Ten Women Artists in Georgia, Spelman Mus, Spelman Col, Atlanta, Ga, 97; Breaking Barriers, Mus Art, Fort Lauderdale, Fla, 97; New Orleans Triennial, New Orleans Mus, La, 98. *Awards:* Ford Found Fel, 1978; Oscar B Cintas Fel, 1980; Atlanta Ga Mayor's Fel Arts, 1990; Southern Artists Fedn/Nat Endowment Arts Regional Fel, 90 & 96; Southern Regional Vis Artists Award, Am Acad Rome, 97. *Bibliog:* Catherine Fox (auth), Georgia sampler, Atlanta Jour & Constitution, 2/19/95; Catherine Fox (auth), Smudged effects reveal Rodriquez's state of mind, Atlanta Jour & Constitution, 6/9/95; Kathy Maschke (auth), Rocio Rodriguez at Sandler Hudson Gallery, Art Papers, 10-11/95; Glen Harper, Rodriguez, Lindsay take personal, cultural journeys, Atlanta Jour & Constitution, 2/9/96; Jill Jordan Sieder, Breaking through, ten Atlantans on the brink of making it big in 1997, Atlanta Mag; Ferdinand Protzman, Arts, Washington Post, 3/18/99; Michael Plante, Art Am, 3/99. *Mailing Add:* 902 Barnett St Atlanta GA 30306

RODRIQUEZ, ERNESTO ANGELO
PAINTER, DESIGNER
b New York, NY, 47. *Study:* Parsons Sch Design, 65-68; New Sch Social Res/Parsons, BFA, 79. *Work:* Hudson River Mus, Yonkers, NY. *Comn:* Linen fabric design, comn by Miss Iris Roberts, NY, 89; linen designs, comn by D Calahan, NY, 89; floral fabric designs, comn by H Rodriquez, NY, 90, 2002; football fabric, comn by S Brathwait, NY, 90; marine fabric design, comn by S Willard, NY, 90-91; grand piano, comn by P Candide, NY, 2002; Portrait and Egyptian Temples, comn by James Patton, NY, 2004. *Exhib:* Hudson River Mus, Yonkers, NY, 81; Hispanic Experience, Long Beach Mus Art, NY, 82; St Francis Assisi, NY, 84; Int Art Gallery, Bogota, Colombia, 86; Art Communication Int, Philadelphia, 96; Pa Hotel, NY, 89; Madison Square Garden, NY, 89; Durban Art Gallery, South Africa, 99; Hilltop, Inc, NY, 2002-03; Jano R Co, NY, 2002-03. *Teaching:* Coordr, Camp Oakhurst, NJ, 82-86; instr crafts, Jewish Guild for Blind, 86-87; instr art, St Francis Assisi, NY, 84-89 & 91-93. *Awards:* Max Beckman Fel, 1968. *Bibliog:* Mantle Fielding's Dictionary of American Painters, Sculptors and Engravers, 2001; Biographical Encyclopedia of American Painters, Sculptors and Engravers of the US, Colonial to 2002. *Mem:* Philadelphia Mus Art; Boston Mus Fine Art. *Media:* Oil, Acrylic, color pencils, conte crayon. *Res:* making discoveries in balance, form and color applicaitons in Leonardo da Vinci; Abstract's semi-abstracts; Hieronymus Bosch, Paul Klee study artist's usage of light, color & composition. *Specialty:* Landscapes; Still Life; Group scenes; Portraits. *Interests:* Res in Portraiture, Studying Landscape Photog. *Collection:* Dr. Livette Johnson, NYC; James Patton, NYC. *Publ:* Intergalactic Poetry Messenger, 94; New Art International, 2006. *Dealer:* Ernesto Rodriguez. *Mailing Add:* 55 Overlook Terr 4H New York NY 10033

ROEDIGER, JANICE ANNE
ARTIST
b Trenton, NJ. *Study:* Graduate Certificate Penna Academy of the Fine Arts. *Work:* Abington Pub Libr; Abington Meml Hosp; Rohm and Haas, Philadelphia; Boro of Harvey Cedars, Harvey Cedars, NJ; Glen Meade Trust, Philadelphia. *Exhib:* Pa Acad Fine Arts, fellowship exhibs; Nat Drawing, Coll NJ, 98; Woodmere Mus, Philidelphia, Pa. *Collection Arranged:* Curator Faculty Exhibs, Long Beach Island Found, 99-2003. *Teaching:* Docent, Pa Acad of the Fine Arts, 92-2003; instr, Long Beach Island Found Arts, Loveladies, NJ, 94-2001; Docent Mus instr Long Beach Island Foundation of the Arts, 2005. *Awards:* Woodmere Endowment Meml Award, Woodmere Mus, Philadelphia, 99; Presidents Award, Chellenbam Ctr for the Arts, 01. *Mem:* Pa Acad Fine Arts; Philadelphia Art Alliance; Philadelphia Mus of Art; Woodmere Mus. *Media:* Painting-Oil/Acrylic-Drawing. *Specialty:* Fine Art. *Interests:* Teaching, Traveling, Theater, Classical Music. *Publ:* Linda Stein, Defying Expectations, Art Matters, 94; Eileen Eskin Renounded Artist in our Midst, Graystone Gazette, 02. *Dealer:* The Philadelphia Mus Art Box 7646 Philadelphia PA 19101-7646; Lambertville Gallery Fine Art 20 N Union St Lambertville NJ 08530. *Mailing Add:* 1250 Greenwood Ave Apt 211 Jenkintown PA 19046

ROESCH, ROBERT ARTHUR
SCULPTOR, DESIGNER
b Buffalo, NY, June 25, 46. *Study:* State Univ NY; Pratt Inst, study with David Lee Brown. *Work:* Fidelity Bank, Philadelphia; Marine Midland Bank, NY; State Univ NY, Farmingdale. *Comn:* Sculpture, Cynmark Group, Suffern, NY, 84; sculpture, Boca Raton Redevelopment, Fla, 85. *Exhib:* New Directions in Sculpture, Heckscher Mus, NY, 77; Wistariahurst Mus, Holyoke, Mass, 77; Art Alliance, Philadelphia, 80; Bennison Bldg, Long Island, NY, 81; Beaver Col, Pa, 83. *Teaching:* Adj prof, 3-D design, Southampton Col, NY, 75-84, Parsons Sch Design, New York, 84-85 & Acad Fine Arts, Philadelphia, 86-. *Bibliog:* Jessica Darraby (auth), article, in: Designer's West, 86. *Media:* Steel and Similar Metals. *Dealer:* David Segal Gallery 568 Broadway New York NY 10012; Nerlino Gallery 96 Green St New York NY. *Mailing Add:* 1201 S Fifth St Philadelphia PA 19147

ROGALSKI, WALTER
PRINTMAKER, LECTURER
b Glen Cove, NY, Apr 10, 23. *Study:* Brooklyn Mus Sch, with Xavier Gonzalez, Arthur Osver, C Seide & Gabor Peterdi, 47-51. *Work:* Mus Mod Art; Brooklyn Mus; Cleveland Mus Art; Fogg Mus Art; Seattle Art Mus; plus many others. *Exhib:* Six shows, Brooklyn Mus, 51-68; Soc Am Graphic Artists, 66 & 69; Cincinnati Mus Asn, 68; Am Fedn Arts Traveling Exhib, 69; Nat Print Exhib, Potsdam, NY, 69; plus many others. *Teaching:* Prof graphic art, Grad Sch Art & Design, Pratt Inst, currently. *Awards:* Prizes, De Cordova & Dana Mus, 61 & Yale Gallery Fine Arts, 61; Purchase Prize, Asn Am Artists, 66; plus others. *Mem:* Soc Am Graphic Artists. *Mailing Add:* 15 Cross St Locust Valley NY 11560

ROGERS, ART
PHOTOGRAPHER
b Wilson, NC, Sept 13, 48. *Work:* Joseph Seagrams & Sons Calif Photog Collections, NY; Arch Univ Ariz, Tucson; San Francisco Mus Mod Art, Calif; Ctr Creative Photog/Archive, Tucson, Ariz; Int Ctr for Photography, NY; The Archive, Tucson, Ariz. *Exhib:* SECA, San Francisco Mus Mod Art, Calif, 82; Photographs, CEPA Gallery, Buffalo, NY, 83; 10,000 Eyes, ASMP, Int Ctr Photog, NY, 91; Time and Motion, Int Ctr Photog, NY, 93; Family Values, PHOTOS Gallery, San Francisco, 93; Portraits for Families, Old Bank Bldg Gallery, Point Reyes, Calif, 95; Yesterday and Today, Bolinas Mus, Calif, 99. *Teaching:* San Francisco Art Inst, 68-73, Indian Valley Col (Col Marin), Ignacio, Calif, 76-79 & Point Reyes Nat Seashore Field Sem, 78-80. *Awards:* Guggenheim Fel; Fel, Nat Endowment for the Arts; Fel, Marin Arts Coun; SECA/San Francisco Mus of Modern Art Award. *Mem:* Am Soc Mag Photogs; Marin Arts Coun. *Dealer:* Photos 403 Francisco St San Francisco CA 94133. *Mailing Add:* 6 Cypress Rd PO Box 777 Point Reyes Station CA 94956-0777

ROGERS, BARBARA
PAINTER, EDUCATOR
b Newcomerstown, Ohio, Apr 28, 37. *Study:* Ohio State Univ, BSc; Univ Calif, Berkeley, MA. *Work:* San Francisco Mus Mod Art; Oakland Art Mus, Calif; Univ Calif, Berkeley; Prudential Ins Co, Calif; San Jose Mus Art. *Exhib:* One-person exhibs, San Francisco Mus Mod Art, 73, Michael Berger Gallery, Pittsburgh, Pa, 78 & 81, Fuller Goldeen Gallery, San Francisco, Univ Pac Gallery, Stockholm, Calif, 87, Frauen Mus, Erfurt, Ger, 92, Ga State Univ, 93, Selby Mus Bot & Arts, Sarasota, Fla, 94 & Univ Ariz Mus Art, 94; 71st Am Exhib, Art Inst Chicago, 74; two-person exhib, Embracing Change, San Jose State Univ, Calif, 89; Bridges: Artists Responses to Disaster, Berkeley Art Ctr, Calif, 90; Recent Paintings, Sandy Carson Gallery, Denver, Colo, 97; Earthly Pleasures: the Garden as Source, Jewish Community Ctr, Tucson, Ariz, 97; The Permanet Collection 1997: Recent Acquisitions, San Jose Mus Aart, Calif, 97; Recent Paintings: Her Garden, Objects and Sites Remembered, Temple Gallery, Tucson, 98; Retrospective: Works on Papers, Ohio State Univ, Columbus, 98; Pleasures of the Palettess Auction, The Phoenician, Scottsdale, Ariz; Another Arizona: A State Wide Juried Exhib, Nelson Fine Arts Ctr, Ariz State Univ, Tempe, 98; Human Nature, Allrich Gallery, San Francisco, Calif, 92; Personal Eden, One West Art Ctr Inc, Ft Collins, Colo, 96; Ponds: The Garden Mirror'd, Frederick Spratt Gallery, San Jose, Calif, 95. *Pos:* Mem, exhib comt, San Francisco Art Inst, 75, bd trustees, 80; artist consult, Adv Coun, Grumbacher Inc, Cranbury, NJ, 94. *Teaching:* Vis lectr drawing & painting, Univ Calif, Berkeley, 72-73; vis artist painting & drawing, San Francisco Art Inst, 74-76, 83-85, prof, 83-, chmn painting, 86-88; vis artist painting & grad sem, Univ Wash, Seattle, 75; instr painting & drawing, San Jose State Univ, 78-82; prof painting, Univ Ariz, Tucson, 90-98, grad coordr, Dept Art, 91-92, dir, Grad prog, 92-93. *Awards:* Int Travel Grant, Univ Ariz, 91; Prof Develop Grant, Com on Arts, Ariz, 91; Fine Arts Summer Res Incentive Grant, Univ Ariz, Tucson, 92-93. *Bibliog:* Thomas Albright (auth), Art in the San Francisco Bay Area, 1945-1980, Univ Calif Press, 85; Angelika Storm-Rushe (auth), Reverence for the Water, General-Anzeiger, 1/92; New American Paintings, Open Studios Press, Wellesley, Mass, 97; plus many reviews in magazines & newspapers. *Mem:* Col Art Asn; Women's Caucus for Art. *Media:* Oil, Mixed Media. *Mailing Add:* 6161 N Camino Padre Isidoro Tucson AZ 85718

ROGERS, BRYAN LEIGH
SCULPTOR, EDUCATOR
b Amarillo, Tex, Jan 7, 41. *Study:* Yale Univ, New Haven, Conn, BE, 63; Univ Calif, Berkeley, MS, 66, MA, with Jim Melchert, Peter Voalkos, Mark DiSuvero, Arnaldo Pomodoro, Eduardo Paolozzi & Robert Morris, 69, PhD, 71; Akademie der bildenden Künste, Munich, Germany, 74-75. *Work:* San Francisco Mus Mod Art, Calif. *Comn:* Mannesmann Demag Corp, Pittsburgh, Pa, 93. *Exhib:* Umbrella Show, San Francisco Mus Mod Art, Calif, 74 & Laguna Beach Mus Art, Calif, 74; San Francisco/Science Fiction, Clocktower Gallery, NY, 85; Mechanical Contraptions, Objects Gallery, Chicago, 92; ARTEC 93, Nagoya, Japan, 93; On the Nature of the Machine, Chicago

Cult Ctr, 93; Pittsburgh Biennial, Pittsburgh Ctr Arts, 94; and others; Allegheny Col Gallery, Headville, Pa, 97; Aichi Art Gallery, Nagoya, Japan, 97. *Pos:* ed, Leonardo Journal, San Francisco, Calif, 82-85; dir, Studio for Creative Inquiry, Carnegie Mellon Univ, 89-2000. *Teaching:* Lectr art, Univ Calif, Berkeley, 72-73; prof art, San Francisco State Univ, 75-88; prof art & dept head, Carnegie Mellon Univ, 88-2000; prof art & dean, School Art & Design, Univ Michigan, An Arbor, 99-. *Awards:* Artist's Fel, Nat Endowment Arts, 81 & 82; Res Fel, Mass Inst Technol, 81; fel, Deutscher Akademischer Austauschdienst, Ger, 74-75. *Bibliog:* Gerhard Lischka (auth), Das Poetische ABC, Benteli Verlag, Bern, 85; Jim Jenkins/Dave Quick (coauth), Motion Motion Kinetic Arts, Gibbs-Smith, 89. *Media:* Electromechanical Installations. *Publ:* The Umbrella Series, Leonardo, Pergamon, 76, Timepieces, 81 & Odyssetron, 84; Apples and Bouillabaisse, Art/Cognition, 92. *Mailing Add:* Univ Mich Sch Art and Design 2055 Art & Arch Bldg Ann Arbor MI 48109

ROGERS, EARL LESLIE
PAINTER, EDUCATOR
b Oakland, Calif, July 8, 18. *Study:* Los Angeles Valley Col, 49-52, AA, Pierce Col, 58, Northridge State Univ, 58-59, Univ Calif in Los Angeles, 67, Sergei Bongart Sch Art, 67-68, MA equivalency, Merced Col, 96. *Work:* Bear Valley Mus, Calif; Mariposa Co Historical Mus, Calif; Seattle Pub Libr Capitol Hill Branch, Seattle, WA; John C Fremont Hosp Mariposa, Calif; Merced Col Merced, Califo. *Comn:* John C Fremont portrait, Soroptimists Int, Mariposa, Calif, 69; memorial painting, John C Freemont Hosp staff, 72; Early Mariposa (mural), Mariposa Mus & Hist Ctr, Inc, 79; portrait of Yosemite Indian leader, Mariposa Arts Coun, 84; memorial portrait painting, Friends of Mariposa Co Libr, 86. *Exhib:* Yosemite Art Pl, Yosemite Nat Park, Calif, 71; Society of Western Artists, Fashion Fair, Fresno, Calif, 77; 31st Ann Soc Western Artists, Hall of Flowers, Golden Gate Park, San Francisco, Calif, 78; Cong Washington Art Show, Cannon Bldg Rotunda, Washington, 82; solo exhib, US Post Off, Mariposa, Calif, 86, Bear Valley Hist Bon-Ton, Calif, 99. *Pos:* Pres, West Valley Artist Asn, San Fernando Valley, 67-68; art dir, Yosemite Nat Park, Calif, 73; mem, 15th Cong Dist Arts Comt, 80-82. *Teaching:* Teacher art, Mariposa Co High Sch, 69-70; instr oil & watercolor painting, Earl Rogers Studio Workshops, 69-96, 70-2003; instr art, Merced Col, 69-2006. *Awards:* Soc Western Artists Neva Rall Mem Award, San Francisco Hall of Flowers, 78; Cong Cert Special Recognition, Washington Cong Art Show, 82. *Bibliog:* Janis McCrae (auth), Mariposa's gold rush mural, Merced Sun Star, 80; Doris Jamgotchian (auth), Earl Rogers exhibit, Mariposa Gazette, 86; Leslie Bonner (auth), portrait workshop, The Catalyst-Merced Col, 94. *Mem:* Soc Western Artists; Pastel Soc West Coast; Mariposa Arts Coun, Inc; Oil Painters Am, Sierra Artists. *Media:* Oil, Acrylic. *Specialty:* Contemp Traditional Paintings, all media & subject matter. *Interests:* Piano, Books. *Publ:* Illusr, Model Cities Program-City of Los Angeles, Off of the Mayor, 67; City of Los Angeles-Engineering Procedure, Los Angeles City Coun, 67; From the Kitchen of Ruth Robeson, Robeson Realty, 71; Mariposa History Center Tour Guide, Mariposa Mus & Hist Ctr Inc, 72; The Catalyst, Merced Col, 90; illusr, Yosemite (1958-1961): Exploits of a Former Employee, 2005. *Dealer:* Arbor Gallery 645 W Main St Merced CA 95340. *Mailing Add:* 5323 Hwy 49 N Mariposa CA 95338

ROGERS, JOHN H
SCULPTOR, CONSULTANT
b Walton, Ky, Dec 20, 21. *Study:* Eastern Ky Univ; Tyler Sch Art, Temple Univ, BFA & MFA. *Work:* Ala Archives, Montgomery; Marine Corps Art Collection, Marine Corps Mus, Washington, DC; Auburn Univ, Ala; Dept Defense, Pentagon, Washington, DC; NDak Mill & NDak Mus Art, Grand Forks, 81 & 92. *Comn:* Bust of Gen H M Smith USMC, Ala Archives, Montgomery, 69; mem plaque of Lt Gen J A Chaisson, USMC, 75; baptistry, St Paul's Episcopal Church, Grand Forks, NDak, 83; Peace Garden Award Medallion, Univ NDak, 85; bust of Gen C B Cates USMC, Tenn State Mem Mus, Nashville & Marine Corps Univ, Quarntico, Va. *Exhib:* Artists in Vietnam, Smithsonian Traveling Exhib Serv, 68-70; Atlanta Col Art Fac Exhib, High Mus Art, Ga, 72; Inaugural Exhib, USMC Hist Ctr, Wash, DC, 77; solo show, Art Gallery, Univ NDak, 81; John Rogers, Elder & Younger, Art Gallery, Univ NDak, 92; Sculptures in the Garden, NC Botanical Garden, Chapel Hill, 93-2001; Bronze Sculpture, Keep Morisi, dedicated to NCO's, 2003. *Pos:* Acad dean, Minneapolis Col Art & Design, 64-68; asst head, Marine Corps Combat Art Prog, Washington, DC, 68-69, head, 69-70; dean, Atlanta Col Art, Ga, 70-73; dean col fine arts, Univ NDak, 73-80; sculptor in residence, Syracuse Univ, 80-81; pres, Docents NC Mus Art, 97-98. *Teaching:* Sr sem humanities, Atlanta Col Art, 70-71; prof fine arts & sr symp, Univ NDak, 73-80, prof visual arts, 81-85; adj prof basic design, Syracuse Univ, 80-81, emer prof visual arts, 85-; vis lect sculpture, Earlham Coll, 89; docent, NC Mus Art, Raleigh, 91-2002. *Mem:* Fel & life mem Nat Asn Schs Art & Design; Am Crafts Coun; Int Sculpture Ctr; Tri-State Sculptors Guild. *Media:* Wood; Miscellaneous. *Res:* Arts & Aging. *Publ:* Coauth, Aging & creativity, In: Lifelong Learning and the Visual Arts, Nat Art Educ Asn, 80. *Mailing Add:* 5522 Hideaway Dr Chapel Hill NC 27516

ROGERS, JOSEPH SHEPPERD See Nevia, Joseph Shepperd Rogers

ROGERS, MALCOLM AUSTIN
MUSEUM DIRECTOR
b Scarborough, Yorkshire, England, Oct 3, 48. *Study:* Oxford Univ, BA, MA, 76, DPhil, 76. *Pos:* asst keeper, Nat Portrait Gallery, London, 74-83, deputy dir, 83-85, dep keeper, 85-94; Ann & Graham Gund dir, Mus of Fine Art, Boston, Mass, 94-; mem Harvard overseers comt Visit the Art Mus; trustee Found for the Arts, Nagoya, Japan. *Awards:* comdr Order Brit Empire, 04. *Mem:* Fel Soc Antiquities; Am Asn Mus; Am Asn Mus Dirs; Beefsteak Club; Liveryman Girdlers Co; Alogonquin Club (hon); Commercial Club of Boston; Wednesday Evening Club; Thursday Evening Club. *Publ:* Blue Guide Museums and Galleries of London, 83; contribr, The Companion Guide To London, Blue Guide, 92; contribr, William Dobson 1611-46: The Royalists at War, 83-84; contribr, Camera Portraits, 89-90; auth, Dictionary of British Portraiture, 4 Vols, 79-81. *Mailing Add:* Mus Fine Arts 465 Huntington Ave Boston MA 02115-5597

ROGERS, MILLARD FOSTER, JR
MUSEUM DIRECTOR, HISTORIAN
b Texarkana, Tex, Aug 27, 32. *Study:* Mich State Univ, BA(honors), 54; Univ Mich, MA, 58; Victoria & Albert Mus, London, 59, with John Pope-Hennessy, Xavier Univ, Cincinnati, LHD, 87. *Collection Arranged:* New Eng Glass Co, 1818-1880, Toledo Mus Art, 63; Indian Miniature Painting, 71 & Canadian Landscapes, Univ Wis, 73; Treasure From the Tower of London, 82-83; Masterworks from Munich, Cincinnati Art Mus, 88-89. *Pos:* Asst to dir, Toledo Mus Art, Ohio, 59-63, cur Am art, 64-67; dir, Elvehjem Art Ctr, Univ Wis, Madison, 67-74; dir, Cincinnati Art Mus, 74-94, emer dir, 94-. *Teaching:* Prof art hist dept, Univ Wis, Madison, 67-74; vis prof, Principia Col, 84; adj prof, Univ Cincinnati, 86-90. *Awards:* Gosline Fel, Toledo Mus Art, 58-59; Samuel B Sachs Prize, 83. *Mem:* Asn Art Mus Dirs; Am Asn Mus; Mariemont Preservation Found (pres 84-90 & 94-). *Res:* Junius Brutus Stearns, 1815-1885; Mary M Emery, Collector and Philanthropist, 1844-1927. *Publ:* Spanish paintings in the Cincinnati Art Museum, 78; Auth, Favorite paintings from the Cincinnati Art Museum, Abbeville Press, 80; Sketches & Bozzetti by American Sculptors, 1800-1950, Cincinnati Art Mus, 87; Rich in Good Works: Mary M Emory of Cincinnati, Univ Akron Press, 2000; John Nolen and Mariemont: Building a New Town in Ohio, Johns Hopkins Univ Press, 2001

ROGERS, MURIEL I
PAINTER
Study: Georgian Court Col, graduate. *Exhib:* NJ Watercolor Soc Ann Open Juried Show, 97, 99, 2001 & 05; Garden State Watercolor Soc Open Juried Show, 98-2003, 04 & 06; Guild of Creative Art Juried State Show, 2000-05; Am Artist Prof League, NJ, 2000-02; New Am Gallery Juried Nat Watercolor Show, 2003. *Collection Arranged:* Georgian Court Col; Monmouth Co Park System; Am Reinsurance Corp; Kirkland & Ellis; KFR Consult & Adminr, Inc; Nationwide Insurance. *Teaching:* Instr, watercolor painting, pvt sessions, currently. *Awards:* NJ Watercolor Soc Peoples' Choice Award, 97; Am Artists Prof League, NJ, 99; Guild of Creative Art State Show Award, 2000 & 03; First Place Watercolor Award, Anchor & Patelle Gallery, NJ, 2006. *Bibliog:* Articles in Am Artist; articles Watercolor, winter 97; aritcles, To the Shore Once More, Vol I & II; cover artist, Jersey Shore Home & Garden, 2000 & 04; articles, Jersey Shore Mag, 98-2006. *Mem:* NJ Watercolor Soc; Garden State Watercolor Soc; Am Artist Prof League; Guild of Creative Art; Manasquan River Group Artists. *Media:* Oil & Watercolor. *Dealer:* Anchor Palette Gallery Bay Head; Matawan Art Gallery Aberdeen; New America Internet Gallery. *Mailing Add:* 33 Beaver Dam Rd Colts Neck NJ 07722

ROGERS, OTTO DONALD
PAINTER, EDUCATOR
b Kerrobert, Sask, Nov 19, 35. *Study:* Sask Teacher's Col, cert, 53; Univ Wis, BSc(art educ), 58, MA(fine art), 59. *Work:* Nat Gallery Can, Ottawa; Montreal Mus Fine Arts; Nat Mus Iceland, Reykjavik; Fredericton Art Gallery, NB; Windsor Art Gallery, Ont. *Comn:* Sculpture in steel (with George Kerr, architect), Prince Albert Regional Libr, 65. *Exhib:* Biennial, Nat Gallery Can, 66, Royal Can Acad Art Exhib, 70; Directors Choice Exhib, sponsored by Can Coun, Confedn Art Gallery & Mus, Charlottetown, PEI, 68; Art in Saskatchewan, Waddington Fine Arts Gallery, Montreal, 69; Art Bank Can Exhib, Mendel Gallery, Saskatoon, 72. *Teaching:* Prof painting, Univ Sask, 59-, head dept art, 73-88. *Awards:* Sr Award for Study in Europe, 67-68. *Bibliog:* R Harper (auth), History of Canadian Painting, 66; W Townshend (auth), Canadian art today, Studio Int, 70; C McConnell (auth), Otto Rogers, Arts Can, 71. *Mem:* Royal Can Acad Art. *Media:* Acrylic

ROGERS, P J
PRINTMAKER, COLLAGE
b Rochester, NY. *Study:* Wells Col, BA; Univ Buffalo; Acad Fine Arts, Vienna; Art Students League; also with Victor Hammer, Lazlo Szabo & Robert Brackman. *Work:* Akron Children's Hosp; Ohio Arts Coun, 98; Cleveland Art Mus; Art Complex Mus, Duxbury, Mass; Hahn, Loeser and Parks, Law Off, Cleveland, Ohio. *Comn:* Portrait of founder, Novatny Electric Co, Akron, 67; poster for opening of new theater, Akron Weathervane Theater, 70; portrait of Dr DJ Guzzetta, pres, Univ Akron, 75; Ohio Arts Coun, 94; Children's Hospital, 94. *Exhib:* Maison des Arts et de la Cult, Quebec, 98; Olin Art Col, Kenyon Col, 2000; PJ Rogers Retrospective, Harris-Stanton Gallery, Akron, Ohio, 2001; SAGA 69th Nat Juried Exhib, The Art Students League of NY, 2002; All Ohio Landscape Juried Rosewood Gallery, Kettering, Ohio, 2002; Wooster Mus Art, NY, 2003; Susan Teller Gallery, NY, 2004; one-person show; Harris Stanton Gallery, Akron, Ohio, 2005, 808 Gallery Boston Univ, Boston, Mass, 2005; Hollar Soc Gallery, Prague, 2006. *Pos:* Art preparator, Buffalo Mus Sci, 52-55. *Teaching:* Instr painting, Buffalo Mus Sci, 55; instr arts & crafts, Univ Akron Spec Progs, 58. *Awards:* Purchase Award, Print Club, Philadelphia, 90-91; Prof Develop Assistance Award, Ohio Arts Coun, 93; Purchase Award, Col NJ, 97. *Bibliog:* Stevens (auth), Aux Etats-Unis, expositions diverses, PJ Rogers, La Rev Mod. *Mem:* Boston Printmakers; Soc Am Graphic Artists, NY. *Media:* Aquatint-etching, Mixed Media & Digital Inkjets Prints. *Publ:* Contribr, The Gamut, (six aquatints), Cleveland State Univ, Ohio, 80 & 90; American Artists, Krantz Co Publ, 85 & 92. *Dealer:* Harris Stanton Gallery 2301 W Market St Akron Ohio 44313. *Mailing Add:* 954 Hereford Dr Akron OH 44303

ROGERS, PETER WILFRID
PAINTER, WRITER
b London, Eng, Aug 24, 33. *Study:* St Martins Sch Art, London, Eng. *Work:* Bristol Art Gallery, Eng; Roswell Mus, NMex; Macnider Mus, Mason City, Iowa; Mus Southwest, Midland, Tex; Fine Arts Mus, Santa Fe, NMex. *Comn:* Mural, Tex State Archives & Libr, Austin, 64; 48 paintings & drawings of Alaska, Atlantic Richfield Co, Los Angeles, 70-71; mural, Tex Tech Mus, 74; mural, Anaconda Co, Denver; mural, Arcomex, Mexico City. *Exhib:* One-man shows, Fairmount Gallery, Dallas, 69, Artium Orbis, Santa Fe, 71-72, Grace Cathedral, San Francisco, 73 & Janus Gallery, Santa Fe, 75; Heard Mus, Phoenix, Ariz, 75; plus others. *Bibliog:* Mary Carroll Nelson (auth), Peter Rogers: Journeyman Artist, American Artist, 76; Mary Carroll Nelson (auth), Profiles: Peter Rogers, Art Voice South, 3/80; Isabelle Howe (auth), The Murals at Texas Tech. *Media:* Oil, Acrylic. *Res:* Edward de Vere and the Sonnets of Willm Shakespeare. *Publ:* Auth & illusr, A Painter's Quest, Bear & Co. *Mailing Add:* PO Box 214 San Patricio NM 88348

ROGERS, RICHARD L
EDUCATOR, ADMINISTRATOR
b New York, NY, Sept 17, 49. *Study:* Yale Col, BA, 71; Yale Divinity Sch, MAR, 73; Univ Chicago, 77-80; Bankstreet Col Educ, MSed, 89. *Pos:* Vpres & secy, New Sch Soc Res, 82-94; pres, Col for Ctr Creative Studies, 94-. *Teaching:* Foote Sch, New Haven, Conn, 74-77; instr liberal arts, Parsons Sch Design, New York, 87-94. *Mailing Add:* 201 East Kirby Detroit MI 48202

ROGERS, SARAH
CURATOR
b Buffalo, NY, Aug 8, 56. *Study:* Wells Col, Aurora, NY, BA, 78; Northwestern Univ, Evanston, Ill, MA, 80. *Collection Arranged:* Doug & Mike Starn, Contemp Arts, Cincinnati, 85-90; Trilogy Inaugral Exhibs, Wexner Ctr, 89-90; Lorna Simpson: Interior/Exterior-Full/Empty, Wexner Ctr, 97; The Body and the Object: Ann Hamilton, Wexner Ctr & tour, 96-98; Evidence: Photography & Site, Wexner Ctr & tour, 97-98; Body Mecanique: Artistic Explorations of Digital Realms, Wexner Ctr, 98. *Pos:* Intern, Nat Endowment Arts, Walker Art Ctr, Minneapolis, 80-81; asst dir, New Gallery Contemp Art, Cleveland, 81-82; cur, Contemp Arts Ctr, Cincinnati, 82-; dir exhibs, Wexner Ctr Arts, Columbus, currently. *Teaching:* adj prof, Dept Art, Ohio State Univ, currently. *Awards:* Abby Grey Fel, Nat Endowment Arts, 80. *Mem:* Col Art Asn. *Publ:* Segments I-III (catalogs), Contemp Arts Ctr, 84-85; Nam Jine Paik, Video Flag X (catalog), Contemp Arts Ctr, 85; interview, Doug & Mike Starn, Abrams, 90. *Mailing Add:* c/o Wexner Ctr Arts Ohio State Univ N High St at 15th Ave Columbus OH 43210-1393

ROGOVIN, MARK
MURALIST, MUSEUM DIRECTOR
b Buffalo, NY, July 31, 46. *Study:* Mexico, with Elizabeth Catlett Mora & David Alfaro Siqueiros, 64-68; RI Sch Design, Providence, BFA, 68; Art Inst Chicago, MFA, 70. *Comn:* Outdoor mural (18ft x 89ft), side of Am Nat Bank, comn by Rockford Evening Cosmopolitan Club, Ill, 75; indoor mural, Col of Dupage, Glen Ellyn, Ill, 75; Outdoor mural, comn by several neighborhood orgn on Chicago's West Side, 76. *Exhib:* Murals for the People, Mus of Contemp Art, Chicago, 71; Street Art--Pub Murals in the USA (Bicentennial traveling exhib), Amerika-Haus, W Berlin, 76; Mural Art USA (traveling exhib); porcelain enamel mural, Percent for Art Comn, Chicago. *Pos:* Dir & co-founder, Pub Art Wkshp, 72-81 & Peace Mus, 81-86. *Teaching:* Sch prog artist, Urban Gateways, Chicago, 73-81; artist-in-residence murals, Col DuPage, Glen Ellyn, Ill, spring 75, Univ Nebr, Omaha, 77, Univ Ill, Champaign, 78. *Mem:* Chicago Artists Coalition. *Publ:* Auth, Mural Manual, Beacon Press. *Mailing Add:* 930 Dunlop Ave Forest Park IL 60130

ROGOVIN, MILTON
PHOTOGRAPHER
b New York, NY, Dec 30, 1909. *Study:* Columbia Univ, BS, 31; State Univ NY, Buffalo, MA, 72; Univ Buffalo, Hon Dr, 94, Buffalo State Col, Hon Dr, 94 & D'Youville Col, Hon Dr, 94. *Hon Degrees:* Univ Buffalo, Hon Dr, 94, Buffalo State Col, Hon Dr, 94 & D'Youville Col, Hon Dr, 94. *Work:* Metrop Mus Art & Mus Mod Art, NY; Libr Cong, Washington; Bibliot Nat, Paris; Albright-Knox Art Gallery; San Francisco Mus Art. *Comn:* Eight porcelain enamel panel portraits, Niagara Frontier Transit Authority, Buffalo, NY, 83. *Exhib:* One-man exhibs, Albright-Knox Art Gallery, 75 & 85, Brooklyn Mus, 85, Nat Mus Am Hist, Smithsonian Inst, 92, Art Inst Chicago, 93, Rochester Inst Technol, 94, Int Labor Orgn, Geneva, Switz, 95 & NY State Mus, 96; Fotografiska Mus, Stockholm, Sweden, 78; Dartmouth Col, NH, 86; Nationalities Cult Palace, Beijing, 87; Burchfield-Penny Art Ctr, Buffalo, 94; Mex Fine Arts Mus, Chicago, 94; Int Labor Orgn, Geneva, Switz, 95; Mus Berliner Arbeiterleben, Berlin, 95. *Awards:* W Eugene Smith Mem Fund Award, 83; Arts & Sci Distinguished Achievements Award, State Univ New York, 89; Gov's Art Award NY State, 2000. *Bibliog:* James N Wood (auth), Lower West Side, Albright-Knox Gallery Art, 75; Ann Rogovin (auth), Learning by Doing, Westinghouse Learning Corp, 79 & Let Me Do It, Harper & Row, 79; Jack Foran (auth), The workhouse views, Afterimage, Rochester, NY, 4/83; Fred Licht (auth), Photography class acts, Art in Am, New York, 2/84; and many others. *Publ:* Auth, The Forgotten Ones, Univ Wash Press, 88; Portraits in Steel, Cornell Univ Press, 91; Triptych Buffalo's Lower West Side Revisited, WW Horton & Co, 94. *Mailing Add:* c/o The Rogovin Collection 930 Dunlop Forest Park IL 60130

ROHM, ROBERT
SCULPTOR
b Cincinnati, Ohio, Feb 6, 34. *Study:* Pratt Inst, BID, 56; Cranbrook Acad Art, Bloomfield Hills, Mich, MFA, 60. *Work:* Mus Mod Art, Metrop Mus Art, Whitney Mus Am Art, NY; Kunsthalle, Zurich, Switz; Mus Fine Art, Boston; Metrop Mus Art, NY; The Rose Art Mus, Brandeis Univ, Waltham, Mass; Newport Art Mus, Newport, RI; Tucson Mus Art, Ariz; Munson-Williams Proctor Mus Art, Utica, NY; Flint Inst of Arts, Mich; Butler Inst Am Art, Youngstown, Ohio; Harn Mus, Univ Fla, Gainsville; Amarillo Mus Art, Tex. *Exhib:* Solo exhibs, O K Harris Works of Art, NY, 70-2002 & 05, Worcester Art Mus, Mass, 78, Nielsen Gallery, Boston, Mass, 85, 86, 92, 93, 02, Cumberland Gallery, Nashville, Tenn, 86 & 93, New Work: Sculpture & Drawing, Fine Arts Ctr, Univ RI, Kingston, 88 & 94, Lenore Gray Gallery, Providence, RI, 90, 90, 93 & 95, Salve Regina Univ, Newport, RI, 93, 2003 & Bannister Gallery, RI Col, Providence, 98, wheaton Col, Norton, Mass, 02; Totem: Sculpture by Ellen Driscoll, Christopher Hewat, Robert Rohm, Ursula von Rydingsvard, Addison Gallery Am Art, Phillips Acad, Andover, Mass, 89; 10 Yrs of Boston Art, Nielsen Gallery, Boston, Mass, 91; Drawing, Lenore Gray Gallery, Providence, RI, 91; Whats Next, Soma Gallery, San Diego, 93; Concept in Form: Artistd Sketchbooks & Maquettes, Palo Alto Cult Ctr, Calif, 95; and others. *Teaching:* Instr sculpture, Columbus Col Art & Design, 56-59; instr sculpture, Pratt Inst, 60-65; prof sculpture, Univ RI, 65-95, emer prof, 95-. *Awards:* Guggenheim Found Fel, 64; Fel, RI Coun Arts, 73, 82 & 93; Nat Endowment Arts Award, 74 & 86. *Bibliog:* Kenneth Baker (auth), review, Art Am, 5/84; Ronald J Onorato (auth), Robert Rohm, Arts Mag, 1/85; Robert C Morgan (auth), Review, Arts Mag, Summer, 89; J Bowyer Bell (auth), Review Robert Rohm, Review Mag, 11/99. *Media:* Welded Metal with other materials. *Specialty:* Contemp Art. *Publ:* Robert Rohm: Selected Works 1975-1985, Nielsen Gallery, Boston, Mass, 85; Robert Rohm, Nielsen Gallery, Boston, Mass, 2001. *Dealer:* OK Harris Works of Art 383 W Broadway New York NY 10012; Nielsen Gallery 179 Newbury St Boston MA 02116. *Mailing Add:* PO Box 1679 Charlestown RI 02813

ROHRBACHER, PATRICIA
PAINTER, INSTRUCTOR
b Marblehead, Mass, Dec 4, 40. *Study:* Studied with David Leffel, BS (92-94), DL (85-93). *Hon Degrees:* Studied with Harvey Dinnerstein and Burton Silverman, HD (91-99). *Comn:* Still life paintings, Silonex Inc, Montreal, 95; Floral landscape, Frances Kalil, Montreal, 96; Floral landscape, Pamela Foss, Bronxville, NY, 98; Floral painting, Paintings Direct.com, NY, 99; numerous portraits. *Exhib:* Soc Illusr, Mus of Am Illus, NY; Art Club Mem Exhib, Broome St, NY, spring 99; Exhib Akron Soc Artists, Emily Davis Gallery, Akron Univ, fall 2000; Oil Painters of Am, Dunton Gallery, Arlington Hgts, Ill, 2000; Hilligoss Galleries, Chicago; Nicholas Taos Fine Art Gallery, Taos, NMex; Mather Gallery; Woman Art Exhib, Case Western Reserve Univ, Cleveland, Ohio; Cincinnati Art Club, 2002. *Teaching:* Private lessons at art studio since 96. *Awards:* scholar, Pastel Soc Am, 89; merit scholar, Art Student League, 90; award, Catherine Lorillard Wolfe, 95; Margaret Dole Portrait Award, 99; Award of Excellence, Oil Painters of Am, 2000. *Bibliog:* Review Pastel Soc 89 Exhib, Park E Publ, 10/89; J Sanders Eaton (auth), Reviw of CLWAC 99 Members, Gallery Studios, 5-6/99. *Mem:* Art Students League NY, 85-99; Akron Society Artists; PSA; Am Artists Prof League; Audubon Artists; Knickerbocker Artists; Oil Painters of Am; Catherine Lorillard Wolfe Art club. *Media:* Oil, Pastel. *Publ:* Illus, Annual of American Illustration, Madison Square Press, 88, 90, 91, 93 & 94. *Dealer:* Lawrence Churski Gallery Ghent Rd Ghent OH 44333; Art and Frame Gallery 85 Pondfield Rd Bronxville NY 10708. *Mailing Add:* 971 Gavington Pl Akron OH 44313-8002

ROJEK, CHRISTINE
SCULPTOR
b Chicago, Ill, Jan 15, 49. *Study:* Univ Ill, Champaign-Urbana, BFA, 71; Am Sch Fountainebleau, France, 71. *Work:* Col DuPage, Northeastern Ill Univ, Robert Mayor, Kenneth Schroeder, AIA, LI Aronson, Lawrence Edwards, Walter Netch & Robert Winslow, Chicago, Ill. *Comn:* Sculpture, James Nagle, AIA, Chicago, 88; Capitol Develop Bd State Ill, Percentage for Art Prog, Art & Archit Com Northeastern Ill Univ Physical Ed Bldg, 88-90; Univ Akron, Ohio, 91; Kinetic mall sculpture, Woodlands, Tex, 94; Roberto Clemente HS Plaza, Chicago, Ill; Chicago Children's Mus, Navy Pier, 95; 2 inter-active/kinetic environments, Stratford Square, Bloomingdale, Ill, 99; hanging painted metal sculpture, Stonebriar Ctr, Frisco, Tex, 2000; kinetic fountain play area, Park Place, Tucson, Ariz, 2001. *Exhib:* Vicinity Show, Art Inst Chicago, Ill, 73; solo exhibs, Artemisia Gallery, Chicago, Ill, 78, Gilman Gallery, Chicago, Ill, 79, Col DuPage Performing Arts Ctr Gallery, Glen Ellyn, Ill, 87 & Sonic, Pneumatic, Eccentric Sculpture, Zolla/Lieberman Gallery, Chicago, Ill, 87; Sculpture Chicago (with catalog), Ill, 87; Zolla/Lieberman Gallery, Chicago, Ill, 89, 91, 96 & 97; The Renaissance Soc, Chicago, Ill, 91; 10th Anniversary Exhib, William E Gahlberg Art Gallery, Col DuPage, 96; Int Sculptor Exhib, Pier Walk, Navy Pier, 97 & 98; Kinetic Art in Folk Tradition: A Sense of Whimsy, Tarble Art Ctr, 98; and others; Maquettes Exhibit for large sculptures, Columbia Col, 99; large scale pub sculptures exhib, Rome, Italy, 2000. *Pos:* pub sculptor, Columbia Col, Chicago, 93-. *Awards:* Proj Completion Grant, 80, 81 & 82 & Fel Grants, 83, 84, 86, 87 & 89, Ill Arts Coun; Visual Artists Fel Grant, Nat Endowment Arts, 86. *Media:* Aluminum, Steel. *Mailing Add:* 711 S Dearborn No 502 Chicago IL 60605

ROKEACH, BARRIE
PHOTOGRAPHER, WRITER
b Huntington Beach, Calif, Mar 11, 50. *Study:* Univ Calif, Berkeley, BA, 70, MA, 74. *Work:* Oakland Mus Nat Hist; Bank of Am, San Francisco; Hewlett Packard, Consolidated Freightway, Palo Alto; Citicorp, NY. *Exhib:* Images From Above, Ryder Gallery, Chicago, 83; An Intimate Look, Neikrug Gallery, NY, 84; Aerial Photog, Art Ctr, Waco, Tex, 86; Aerial Photog, Tweed Mus, Duluth, Minn, 87; Oakland Mus, Calif, 90; Calif Mus Sci & Indust, Los Angeles, 91; and others. *Teaching:* Instr, Univ Calif Berkeley, 77-78 & 84. *Awards:* Calif Design Award, Art Dirs, 92. *Bibliog:* Paul Raedeke (auth), article, Photo Metro, 83; Lucas Blok (auth), Portfolio, Vantage Point, 84; Brenda Kahn (auth), Aerial photography, Zoom, 86. *Mem:* Am Soc Media Photogrs (exec bd & ed, 68-). *Publ:* Contribr, 24 Hours in the Life of Los Angeles, Van der Marck, 84; Ireland: A Week in the Life of a Nation, Century Hutchinson, 86; Thailand: Seven Days in the Kingdom, Times Ed, 87; Auth-illusr, Timescapes: California Aerial Images, Westcliffe, 89; Auth-illusr, Kodak Guide to Aerial Photography, Silver Pixel, 96. *Mailing Add:* 499 Vermont Ave Berkeley CA 94709

ROLLAND , PETER GEORGE
ARCHITECT
b Frankfurt, Ger, Jul 2, 30. *Study:* Del Valley Col, BSc, 52; Harvard Univ, MLA, 55. *Work:* Principal landscape archit, New Parliament House, Canberra, Australia, 1980, State Univ of NY, Col at Purchase, 1964-75. *Pos:* Chief site planner, Perkins & Will Archits, White Plains, NY, 55-60; project landscape archit, Lawrence Halprin & Assoc, San Francisco, 60-63; prin, Peter G Rolland & Assoc, Rye, NY, 63-89; partner, Rolland/Towers UC, New Haven, 1981-. *Teaching:* Andrew Mellon vis prof Yale Univ Sch Forestry, 1979; fac Sch Archit, Yale Univ, 1973-; vis prof Harvard Grad. Sch Design, 1990. *Awards:* Design award Am Inst of Archits, 75, 78, 85, 90, 92, 94; Recipient Arthur Brown award Del Valley Col, 78; Rome Prize fel Am Accad in Rome, Pierson Col fel Yale Univ, 82-92. *Mem:* Fel Am Soc Landscape Archits; Nat Acad of Design (assoc, 91, acad, 94); Australian Inst Landscape Archits. *Mailing Add:* Rolland/Towers Site Planners & Landscape 85 Willow St New Haven CT 06511-2668

ROLLER, MARION BENDER
SCULPTOR, PAINTER
b Boston, Mass. *Study:* Vesper George Sch Art, dipl; Art Students League, with John Hovannes; Greenwich House, with Lu Duble; Queens Col, BA; also watercolors with Edgar Whitney. *Work:* Am Numismatic Soc; Nat Acad Design; Am Numismatic Asn, Colorado Springs, Colo; Smithsonian, Washington. *Comn:* Head of child, Nassau Ctr Emotionally Disturbed Children, Woodbury, NY, 68; Relief portrait of Ethel Traphagen & commemorative medal, Traphagen Sch, 82-83; portrait of Margaret Sussman, Pen & Brush, 83-84; Women & Youth (7' bronze sculpture), St Mary's Family Servs, Syosset, NY, 88; 3 Dancing Figures - in memory of Rosemary Harris (poet), 94; and many pvt comns of portraits, figures & animals. *Exhib:* sculpture, Can Mus, Ottawa, 92; The Fall of the Berlin Wall, FIDEM, Budapest, 93; 5 medals, Franklin Mint (traveling exhib), 94; Newark Mus, 95-96; Nat Sculpture Soc Ann, 96-97, 2000 & 01; Masterworks of Am Sculpture 1893-1999, Fleischer Mus, Scottsdale, Ariz, 99-2000; many others; Inst of Am Art, 2001, Nat Acad Ann, 2001. *Teaching:* Instr art, Fashion Inst Technol, 67-72; Traphagen Sch, 73-91, Sculpture Ctr, 77-; Sculptor in residence, 1999-2000. *Awards:* Audubon Artists Award, 94; Multiple Awards, Pen & Brush, 96, 97, & 2000; Chaim Gross Found Award, Audubon Artists, 96 & 97, Gold Medal Honor, 98; medal Int Exhib of Medallic Art Mus Beelden ann Vee, 98; award for Medallic Sculpture Pen & Brush, 99; medal of Ethel Traphagen Medallic Art Co, 2001. *Bibliog:* Gustav Kramer (auth), Profile, Hudson Register Star, 65 & 10/3/75; Ed Reiter (auth), reviews in NY Times, 5/8/83; Helen Barett (ed), article in Pen & Brush Bull, 86; Featured in Film, The Making of a Bronze Monument. *Mem:* Nat Acad Design; Pen & Brush (co-chmn, 67, chmn, 82-, vpres 92-94); Fel Nat Sculpture Soc (rec secy, 82-85, sec, 86-89, 91-93 & 94-); Audubon Artists (treas, currently, pres, 94-); Am Medallic Sculpture Asn; Margaret Sussman award 2000, Charlotte Dunwiddie award for medallic art 2000, Allied Artists Am (pres, formerly, Silver medal honor, Sybil and Bob Porton award, Helen Gapen Oehler Mem award, 91), Am Medallic Sculpture Asn, Fine Arts Fedn. *Media:* Mixed. *Publ:* Auth, The challenge of space, Nat Sculpture Soc Rev, spring 82; several art book reviews, Nat Sculp Rev, summer 81, 82, 84, 86, 87, 88, 89. *Mailing Add:* 30 W 60th St No 8A New York NY 10023

ROLLER, RUSSELL KENNETH
EDUCATOR, PRINTMAKER
b Chicago, Ill, Oct 6, 38. *Study:* Ill Wesleyan Univ, BFA, 63; Southern Ill Univ, MFA, 65. *Work:* Univ Wisconsin, Eau Claire; Emporia State Col, Kans; Northern State Col, Aberdeen, SDak. *Exhib:* Int Miniature Print Exhib, Pratt Graphics, NY, 79; 34th Ann Exhib Chicago & Vicinity Artists, Art Inst Chicago, 85. *Teaching:* Asst prof printmaking, Emporia State Col, Kans, 65-70; assoc prof printmaking, Northeastern Ill Univ, 70-76, prof & chmn art dept, 76-. *Media:* Intaglio, Acrylic

ROLLINS, TIM
PAINTER, INSTRUCTOR
b Pittsfield, Maine, 1955. *Study:* Sch Visual Arts, BFA, 78; New York Univ, MA, 80. *Work:* Philadelphia Mus Art; Mus Mod Art, NY; Mint Mus, Charlotte, NC. *Exhib:* All shows collaborations with KOS; Bi National: Am Art of the Late 80's, Mus Fine Arts, Boston & Kunsthalle, Dusseldorf, 88; Amerika, Dia Art Found, NY, 89-90; Wadsworth Atheneum, Harford, Conn, 90; The Temptation of St Antony, Mus fur Gegenwartskunst, Basel, 90; Amerika, Mus of Contemp Art, Los Angeles, Calif, 90. *Teaching:* Artist & teacher, Learning to Read through the Arts Prog, Bd Educ, New York, 80-82 & Div Spec Educ, New York, 82-; founder, Kids of Survival (KOS) & Art & Knowledge Workshop Inc, 82. *Awards:* Artists-in-Educ Grant, 83 & 84, Expansion Arts Grant, 85 & 86 & Visual Artists Fel, 86, Nat Endowment Arts; Artists-in-Educ Award, 86 & Spec Art Servs Grant, 88, NY State Coun Arts; Joseph Benys Prize, 89. *Bibliog:* Berman (auth), Parkett #20, 89; Amerika, Dia Art Found; Arthur Danto (auth), Tim Rollins & KOS, The Nation, 1/22/90. *Mailing Add:* c/o Dia Ctr Arts 548 W 22nd St New York NY 10011

ROLLMAN, CHARLOTTE
PAINTER
b Harrisburg, Ill, Oct 15, 47. *Study:* Murray State Univ, Ky, BFA, 69; Univ Ill, Champaign, MFA, 71. *Work:* Capitol State Bank, Continental Banking Co, St Louis, Mo; McDonald's Corp, Heart Hanks Radio, Phoenix, Ariz; State of Ill Bldg, Harris Bank, Chicago; Nev State Univ, Reno; Evansville Mus Art & Sciences, Ind; and others. *Comn:* John Gardener Tennis Resort, Sedona, Ariz; Jan Cicero Gallery, Chicago; Locus Gallery, St Louis, Mo; Suzanne Brown, Scottsdale, Ariz. *Exhib:* One person exhibs, Roy Boyd Gallery, Chicago, 84, Suzanne Brown Gallery, 85, Locus Gallery, 88, Univ Wis Ctr/Rock Co, Janesville, 91, Cornucopia, Dorothea Thiel Gallery, S Suburban Col, S Holland, Ill, 91, River of Life, Perry Rotunda Theatre Gallery, Aurora Univ, 93, Riverscapes, Campbell House, Kane Co Forest Preserve Cult Ctr, 93, Midstates Contemp Gallery, Evansville, Ind, 93, River of Life, Kishwaukee Col, 93, Source, Strategy, Reflection, Northern Ill Univ, Art Mus, 94, Flood Plain, AES Gallery, Chicago, Ill, 94 & Eastern Infulence, New Harmony Contemp Gallery Art, Ind, 94; Utopia: Envisioning a Dream, The Forum Gallery at Jamestown Community Col, NY, 92; 16th Harper Nat Print & Drawing Exhib, Harper Col, Palatine, Ill, 92; Owensboro Nat Bank & the Arts: Part IV, Owensboro Mus Fine Arts, Ky, 92; Art on Paper 92, Md Fedn Art, MFA Gallery on the Circle, Annapolis. *Pos:* Colorist & textile designer, Gallery Studio, NY, 76-77; supvr silk painting & textile designer, Nicole Ltd, Chicago & Rio Rancho, NMex, 80-84; textile design & stylist, Thybony Wallcovering, Chicago, Ill, 84-88. *Teaching:* Instr drawing & design, Ball State Univ, 71-75; asst prof art, Northern Ill Univ, 86-92, assoc prof art, 93-. *Bibliog:* Judd Tulley (auth), Icons in Art (review), Am Artist Pub, spring 94. *Media:* Watercolor, Drawing. *Publ:* Illusr, New American Dictionary of Music, Penguin Bks, NY, 91; New International Dictionary of Music, Penguin Bks, NY, 92 & 93. *Mailing Add:* 184 McLaren Dr S #4-C Sycamore IL 60178

ROLLY, RONALD JOSEPH
DEALER
b Waterbury, Conn, Dec 31, 1937. *Pos:* Dir, Rolly-Michaux Galleries, Boston, 1969-. *Specialty:* 20th century Europ masters and contemporaries; paintings, sculpture and graphics; French Impressionists and Post-Impressionists. *Mailing Add:* c/o Rolly-Michaux Galleries LTD 290 Dartmouth St Boston MA 02116

ROLOFF, JOHN (SCOTT)
SCULPTOR, ENVIRONMENTAL ARTIST
b Portland, Ore, Sept 20, 47. *Study:* Univ Calif, Davis, BA; Calif State Univ, Humboldt, MA. *Work:* Nat Mus Am Art, Wash; San Francisco Mus Mod Art, Calif; Oakland Mus, Calif; Newport Harbor Mus, Newport Beach, Calif; Art Mus, Univ Calif, Berkeley; and others. *Comn:* Deep Gradient/Suspect Terrain (Seasons of the Sea Adrift), Yerba Buena Gardens, San Francisco, Calif, environmental sculpture, San Francisco Redevelopment Agency, 93; Fragment: The Hidden Sea (Island of Refuge), envionmental sculpture, Stanford Univ, Stanford, Calif, 93; The Middle of the World, mult-media sculpture, Staten Island Ferries, NY (with W Klotz), 2000-05; Site Index, environmental sculpture, Sch of Archit and Landscape Archit, UM, Minneapolis, Minn (with R Krinke), 2000-2006; Untitled environmental sculpture I-5 Open Space Project, Pro Parks Levy, Seattle, Wash, 2003-05. *Exhib:* Whitney Biennial, Whitney Mus of Am Art, NY, 75; OK Art Contemp Art Ctr, Ohio, 75; Second Newport Biennial; The Bay Area, Newport Harbor Mus, Newport, Beach, Calif, 86; Vanishing Ship (Greenhouse for Lake Lahontan), Matrix Exhib, Univ Art Mus, UC Berkeley, Berkeley Calif, 87; The Boat Show, Smithsonian Inst, Washington, DC, 89; Facing Eden; 100 Yrs of Landscape Art in the Bay Area, MH De Young Memorial Mus, San Francisco, Calif, 95, 98; The Rising Sea, Mus of Contemp Art, Lake Worth, Fla, 98; Morphology of Change, Lance Fung Gallery, NY, 99; John Roloff; Displacement, John Michael Kohler Art Ctr, Sheboygan, WI, 2000; Original Depositional Environment, Gallery Paule Anglim, San Francisco, Calfi, 2001; Holocene Passage, Archivio Emily Harvey, NEXT, Venice Architectural Biennale, Venice Italy, 2002; The Snow Show, Kemi Finland, 2004; Technological Sublime, Univ of Colo, Boulder, Colo, 2005. *Teaching:* Prof, Sculpture Dept, Univ Ky, 74-78 & Univ Southern Calif, 87-88; Prof, Chmn of Sculpture Dept, Co-Coord, Ctr for Art and Sci, San Francisco Art Inst, 88-present. *Awards:* Visual Arts Award, Nat Endowment Arts, 77, 80 & 86; Guggenheim Fel, 83; Visual Arts Award, Calif Arts Coun, 90. *Bibliog:* John Roloff, Univ Art Mus, Artforum, Nov 87, pg 144; Becker, Lisa Tamaris, John Roloff; Displacements, solo exhib catalog, J.M Kohler Arts Center, Sheboygan, WI 2000; Morgan, Robert, John Roloff's Rising Sea, catalog essay, Mus of Contemp Art, Lake Worth, FL, 98. *Publ:* Auth, Kiln projects, Artery Mag, 2-3/83; Untitled Essay, Ten Years Later, Exhib, catalog, CSU, Fullerton, CA, 87; 51 Million BTU's, docmentation catalog, 90; Organic Logic, New Observations Mag, #127, NY, co-editor, with Mark Barlett, Fall/Winter, 2000; Devonian Shale; Aquifer I, limited first edition of 4 books, Fractal Terror Press, Oakland, CA, 2001. *Dealer:* Gallery Paule Anglim 14 Geary St San Francisco CA 94108; Lance Fung Gallery 537 Broadway New York NY 10012. *Mailing Add:* 2020 Livingston St Oakland CA 94606

ROMAN, SHIRLEY
PRINTMAKER, PAINTER
b New York, NY. *Study:* Am Artists Sch; Brooklyn Mus Sch; Queens Col; also with Gregorio Prestopino, Raphael Soyer, Ruth Leaf & Agnes Mills. *Work:* De Cordova Mus, Lincoln, Mass; Readers Digest, Pleasantville, NY; Slater Mus, Norwalk, Conn; Butler Mus Am Art; Libr Cong, Washington, DC; Fed Reserve Bank, Richmond, Va. *Exhib:* Philadelphia Print Club, 69-74; Soc Am Graphic Artists; Pratt Graphics Miniature Show; Boston Printmakers Asn, 73; Audubon Artists, Taipei, Taiwan, 80; Nat Asn Women Artists, 80-99; Madison Art Guild, 1997-2003. *Awards:* Purchase Prize, Boston Printmakers 25th Ann, 73; Medals of Hon, Nat Asn Women Artists, 76, 79, 82 & 86; and others. *Bibliog:* Ruth Leaf (auth), Intaglio Printmaking Techiques. *Mem:* Madison Art Guild; Nat Asn Women Artists; Soc Am Graphic Artists; Nat Art League. *Media:* Etching; Watercolor. *Mailing Add:* 5019 Sheboygan Ave Apt 203 Madison WI 53705

ROMANO, CLARE
PAINTER, PRINTMAKER
b Palisade, NJ, 22. *Study:* Cooper Union Sch Art, 1939-43, BFA; Ecole Beaux-Arts, Fontainebleau, France. *Work:* Mus Mod Art, Whitney Mus Am Art & Metrop Mus Art, NY; Libr of Cong & Nat Collection Fine Arts, Washington, DC; British Mus, London; Ftizwilliam Mus, Cambridge, England; Brooklyn Mus; Smithsonian Inst; Philadelphia Mus; Mus Modern Art, Cairo, Egypt; White House. *Comn:* Tapestry, Mfrs Hanover Bank, NY, 69; mural, Northern Valley Savings & Loan, Englewood, NJ, 79; Texas Tech, Portfolio, 1998; Casanatense, Rome, Italy, Portfolio, 1997; Nat Acad Design,

Portfolio, 1997. *Exhib:* 2nd Triennial Int Exhib Woodcuts, Ugo Carpi Mus, Italy, 72; Am Prints, US Info Agency, Australian Nat Mus, Canberra, 72; Hane Haslem Gallery, Washington, DC, 81, 88 & 93; Queensland Col Art, Brisbane, Australia, 82; AAA Gallery, NY, 82; NJ State Mus, Trenton, 85; Benton Gallery, Southampton, NY, 91; Steinbaum-Krauss Gallery, New York City, 97; Mus Modern Art, Cairo, Egypt, 98; Denise Bibno Gallery, New York City, 99; Rutgers Univ, 2002; Nat Acad Design, 2000, 2002; Houghton Col, 2000. *Pos:* Asst to Herbert Bayer, 43-46. *Teaching:* instr printmaking, New Sch Social Res, 60-73; adj assoc prof printmaking, Pratt Graphic Arts Ctr, 63-87; prof printmaking, Pratt Inst, 64-94, emeritus; vis artist, Brisbane Col Art, Australia, 82; vis artist Baltimore Col Art, Pa; Pratt in Venice, Italy, drawing & printmaking, 88-. *Awards:* MacDowell Fel, 74, 76, 78, 82 & 87; Distinguished Teacher Award, Pratt Inst, 79; NJ State Counc Arts Grant, 80; Lifetime Achievement Award, Soc Am Graphic Artists, 2002; Fulbright Grant, Inst Statale Arte, Florence, Italy, 58-59; Clinedinst Art Achievment Award, Artist Fel, New York, 1991. *Bibliog:* Jules Heller (auth), Printmaking Today, Holt, Rinehart & Winston, 72; Fritz Eichenberg (auth), The Art of the Print, Abrams, 77; Eldon Cunninham (auth), Printmaking, A Primary Form of Expression, Univ Press Colo, 92. *Mem:* Soc Am Graphic Artists (pres, 70-72); Nat Acad Design (assoc, 70, acad, 79, vpres, 87-). *Media:* Painting, Acrylic & Oil, Printmaking, Collagraph, Woodcut & Etching, Art of the Book. *Publ:* Co-illusr, Leaves of Grass, 64; auth, Artist's Proof, 64 & 66; American Encyclopedia, 71; coauth, The Complete Printmaker, 72 & 89 & The Complete Collagraph, 80, Free Press. *Dealer:* Susan Teller Gallery 568 Broadway New York NY 10012; Jane Haslem Gallery 406 Seventh St NW Washington DC 20004. *Mailing Add:* PO Box 1122 New York NY 10159-1122

ROMANO, SALVATORE MICHAEL
SCULPTOR, KINETIC ARTIST
b Cliffside Park, NJ, Sept 12, 25. *Study:* Art Students League, with Jon Corbino; Acad Grande Chaumiere, Paris, with Edouard Georges & Earl Kerkam. *Work:* Brooklyn Bridge Cent (by Creative Time NY), 83; The Children's Mus of Manhattan, NY, 97; Chase Manhattan Bank, NY; Nassau Co Mus Fine Art, NY; Mass Mus Fine Art, Amherst; Moma. *Exhib:* Bali Miller Gallery, NY, 88; Water Installation, Sculpture Ctr, (with catalog), NY, 90; solo show, Andrea Zarre, NY, 94; Robert Parde Gallery, 2000; Pratt Inst Campus, 2001; Galleria Bate Leur, Rome, Italy; Rutgers State Univ NJ Art Libr, New Brunswick, 2003; Samuel Dorsky Mus Art, New Paltz, NY, 2004; Delaware Valley Arts Alliance, Harrisbrug, N.Y., 2005. *Teaching:* Adj instr sculpture, Cooper Union Sch Arts & Archit, 68-70; lectr painting & sculpture, Lehman Col, 69-71, prof, 72- & Rutgers State Univ, New Brunswick, 2004-06; lectr kinetic sculpture, US Info Serv, Brazil, 72 & Rutgers Univ, 79; prof emer, Herbert H Lehman Col, CUNY, Bronx, NY. *Awards:* Nat Endowment Arts, 79-80; Fac Res Award, City Univ NY, Lehman Col, 80-81; McDowell Coloy Fel, 80 & 81; NY Found Arts Award, 85-86, 89-90; Delaware Valley Art Alliance Award, 2002. *Bibliog:* Michael Brenson (auth), Time, 9/7/90; Elena Hartney (auth), Art in Am, 11/90; Bruce Altshuler (auth), The Avant Garde in Exhibit, 94; Robert Morgan (auth), Int Sculpture Mag, 5/2001. *Mem:* Artist Equity; Int Sculpture Ctr. *Media:* Plastics, Wood; Metal, Water, Coopper, Brass. *Specialty:* Painting, sculpture, performances. *Publ:* Auth, article, Lehman Col Art News Lett, 71. *Dealer:* Robert Pardo 121 E 31st St New York NY 10016. *Mailing Add:* 83 Wooster St New York NY 10012

ROMANS, VAN ANTHONY
SCULPTOR, DESIGNER
b Baltimore, Md, Jan 13, 44. *Study:* Univ Calif, Fullerton, BA(art design), studied with Dextra Frankel; Univ Southern Calif, studied 3-D arts & mus design with Lee Chesney, MFA. *Work:* Claremont Grad Sch Gallery, Calif; Univ Southern Calif, Los Angeles; Calif State Univ, Fullerton; Orange Coast Col, Costa Mesa, Calif. *Comn:* Westcliff Shopping Ctr (designed), comn by Richard Marowitz, 76; Courtyard Shopping Ctr (designed), comn by Jerry Stout, 77. *Exhib:* One-man shows, Oakland Mus Art, Calif, 71 & Univ Southern Calif, Los Angeles, 72; Six Promising Young Sculptors, Claremont Cols, Calif, 73; Environments/Spaces, Orange Coast Col, 75; Spaces, Pac Design Ctr, Calif, 76; and others. *Collection Arranged:* Thonet & Thereafter, show of chair hist incl Bauhaus (auth, catalog), Japanese Sword Show, collection from collectors & from Los Angeles Co Art Mus, Western Indian Show--Dan Namingha & Persian Rug Show (designed exhib), 57 rugs from cols & collections, Orange Coast Col Art Gallery. *Pos:* Dir display prog, Orange Coast Col, Costa Mesa, Calif, 73-, dir galleries interior design, 75-; mem, Orange Co Art Alliance, Calif, 77; lectr, Newport Harbor Art Mus, Newport Beach, Calif. *Teaching:* Prof design & exhib design/visual promotion, Orange Coast Col, Costa Mesa, Calif, 73-, prof design & visual promotion, currently; asst prof design, Univ Southern Calif, Los Angeles, 73-82. *Awards:* Most Outstanding Educator, Orange Coast Col, 75. *Bibliog:* Wilson (auth), Sculpture, 74. *Mem:* Am Soc Interior Designers. *Media:* Metal. *Mailing Add:* Dept Art PO Box 5005 Orange Coast Col 2701 Fairview Rd Costa Mesa CA 92628-5005

ROMBERG, OSVALDO
ARCHITECT
b Buenos Aires, Arg, 1938. *Study:* Colegio Nac de Buenos Aires, 50-55; Univ de Buenos Aires, Facultad de Architectrua, 56-62. *Work:* The Haifa Mus, Israel; The Israel Mus, Jerusalem; Jewish Mus, NY; Kunst Mus, Bonn; Leopold-Hoesch Mus, Duren; Libr congress, Washington, DC; Ludwig Mus, Cologne; Muhka Mus Contemp Art, Antwerp; Mueso do Bellas Artes, Buenos Aires; Mus Modern Art, NY; Mus Moderner Kunst, Vienna; Philadelphia Mus, Pa; Tel Aviv Mus, Israel; Wilheml Hack Mus, Ludwigshafen, Duisburg. *Exhib:* Building Footprints (with catalog), Israel Mus, Jerusalem, 91; Romberg: Art about Art, Artifact Gallery, Tel Aviv, 91; New Works, Galerie Heike Curtze, Vienna, 93 & Galerie Shuppenhauer, Cologne, 91 & 93; La Vie en Valise, The Artists as a Curator (with catalog), Fundacion San Telmo, Buenos Aires, Arg, 93; On Scale (with catalog), Sprengel Mus, Hanover, 93; Building Footprint III (with catalog), Mus Moderner Kunst, Vienna, 93; Re-Citing, Books and Short Stories, Gimel Gallery, Jerusalem, 94; Recent Works, Ingrid Dacic Gallery, Tubingen, 94; New Books and Short Stories, Galerie Hohenthal und Bergen, Cologne, 95; The Return of Martin Steel, Artists Space, NY, 95; 2000/2000 Even Traveling Exhib (with catalog), 96; Bypass, Kunstmuseum Bonn, Ger, 97; Stefan Stux Gallery, NY, 97; plus many others; solo exhibs, fundacion Xavier Corbero, Barcelona, 96, Junstmuseum, Bonn, 97, 99, Univ of Arts, Philadelphia, Pa, 2000, Domgrabungsmuseum, Salzburg, Austria, 2000. *Teaching:* Instr, Pa Acad Fine Arts, currently. *Mailing Add:* 561 Broadway 48 New York NY 10012

ROMERO, MEGAN H
PAINTER, DEALER
b Chicago, Ill, Sept 22, 42. *Study:* Ind Univ, BA, 65; Univ Chicago, with Max Kuhn; Univ NMex, with Charles Mattox, MA, 69. *Work:* Univ NMex Fine Arts Mus, Albuquerque; Mus NMex, Santa Fe. *Exhib:* Intrinsic Art, Friends Contemp Art, 71, Denver; Fall Invitational, Roswell Mus & Art Ctr, NMex, 72; one-man show, Lerner Heller Gallery, NY, 72; Fine Arts Mus NMex, Biennial, 73; Seven Artists, Francis McCray Gallery, Western NMex Univ; and others. *Pos:* Owner, Hill's Gallery, Santa Fe, currently. *Awards:* Southwest Biennial, Mus NMex, 72. *Bibliog:* Donna Meilach (auth), Leather Book, 71; article, Art in Am, 8/72; article, Southwest Art Gallery Mag, 12/72. *Mem:* Mus NMex Found. *Specialty:* Contemporary New Mexico fine arts and crafts. *Publ:* Auth, Aiming at the creative environment, SW Art Gallery Mag, 11/71 & 1/73; contribr, Craft Horizons, 12/71. *Mailing Add:* 1469 Canyon Rd Santa Fe NM 87501

ROMERO, RACHAEL L
PAINTER, PRINTMAKER
b Adelaide, S Australia, July 14, 53. *Study:* S Australian Art Inst, 70-72; San Francisco State Univ, 75-78; Antioch Univ, MA, 92. *Work:* Mus Mod Art & Whitney Mus, NY (artists bks); Cooper Hewitt Mus, NY; Lahti Mus, Finland; Libr Cong, Washington; Santa Fe Mus. *Comn:* Mural, US Post Off, NY; mural, Subway, NY. *Exhib:* Committed to Print, Mus Mod Art, NY & 89, Newport Art Mus, 89; Homeless: The Street and other Venues, DIA Art Found, NY, 89; The Decade Show (with Group Mat), Studio Mus, Harlem, NY, 90; A Different War: Vietnam in Art, DeCordova Mus, Lincoln, Mass, 90, Akron Art Mus, 90 & Whatcom Mus, Bellingham, Wash, 90. *Teaching:* Artist/educ art & printmaking, various non-profits, 87-90; artist/educ art educ, Pratt Inst, Brooklyn, 89-90, art hist, Bosphorus Univ, 92-93. *Awards:* Award Merit, Hispanic Festival Arts, Mus Sci & Ind, Chicago, 82; Fel, Residency, MacDowell Colony, 89; Fel, Yaddo, Saratoga, NY, 91-92. *Bibliog:* Deborah Wye (auth), Committed to Print, Mus Mod Art, 88; Peter Plagens (auth), A painful war's haunted art, Newsweek, 9/11/89. *Mem:* Col Art Asn. *Media:* All Media

ROMEU, JOOST A
CONCEPTUAL ARTIST, DESIGNER
b Bremerhaven, Ger, Jan 16, 48; US citizen. *Study:* Drexel Univ, BS. *Work:* Kansas City Art Inst; MTL Gallery, Belg. *Exhib:* Deurle, Belg, 73; Projekt '74, Koln, Ger; Diskussies Omtrent Joost A Romeu, Univ Antwerp, Belg, 75; Idea Warehouse, NY, 75. *Bibliog:* Foote (auth), The apotheosis of the crummy space, Artforum; J L Mackie (auth), The Directon of Causation; Merleau Ponty (auth), Primacy of Perception. *Publ:* Art after philosophy, 73; auth & illusr, ONCE1, ONCE2. *Mailing Add:* PO BOX 1322 Gualala CA 95445-1322

ROMNEY, HERVIN A R
ARCHITECT
b Havana, Cuba, 41; US citizen. *Study:* Cooper Union, 62-65; L'Ecole Speciale d'Architecture, Paris, 70; Catholic Univ, Washington, DC, BArchit, 73; Yale Univ Sch Archit, Master's, 75. *Comn:* Il Gattopardo, Ambassador J A Correa, Quito, Equador, 76; Babylon (condominium), Pac Developers, Miami, 77; Atlantis (condominium), Stonecrest Development, Miami, 79; Palace (condominium), Helmsley-Spear, Miami, 79, Helmsley Ctr, 81. *Exhib:* Inst Archit & Urban Studies, Rome, 79; Cooper Hewitt, NY, 79; Yale Art Gallery, New Haven, Conn, 80; Inst Fine Arts, Chicago, 80; Mus Contemp Arts, La Jolla, 81; Contemp Arts Mus, Houston, 82. *Pos:* Designer, Harrison & Abramovitz, New York, 61-65; proj designer, Andrault-Parat, architects, Paris, 69-70; architect & environmental designer, South Am, 75-76; principal & founder, Arquitectonica Int Corp, Miami, 76-; founder & pres, Hervin Romney Architect Inc, Miami, 85-. *Awards:* Cintas Fel, UN Inst Int Educ, 74-75; Design Citations, Progressive Archit, 78 & 80; Fla Am Inst Archit, 82; First Prize, Dade Co Prototype Sch Competition, Miami, 85; Miami Design Preservation League, 90; Fla AIA Design Award, 89. *Bibliog:* Color-architecture, Life Mag, 4/81; articles, Newsweek 11/8/82 & House & Garden, 6/83. *Publ:* Ed, Perspecta 15, Yale Archit Papers, 75. *Mailing Add:* 2940 S Le Jeune Rd Miami FL 33134-6604

RONAY, MATTHEW
SCULPTOR
b Louisville, 76. *Study:* Md Inst Col Art, Grad, 98; Yale Univ, MFA, 2000. *Work:* Whitney Biennial, Whitney Mus Am Art, NY, 2004. *Exhib:* One-man shows incl Gallery Luhmann, Nils Staerk, Copenhagen, 2002, Galerie Grimm/Rosenfeld, Munich, 2003, Vedanta Gallery, Chicago, 2003; exhib in group shows at Richard Telles Gallery, Los Angeles, 99, Andrew Kreps Gallery, New York City, 2000, Exit Art, 2001, Marc Foxx, Los Angeles, 2001, 2002, Dorsky Gallery, Long Island, NY, 2002, Wattis Inst for Contemp Arts, San Francisco, 2002, Logan Gallery, 2002, Gallery Luhmann, Nils Staerk, Copenhagen, 2002, Inst Contemp Art, Boston, 2002, Gallery 2 Andrea Rosen, New York City, 2002, The Stars Are So Big, The Earth Is So Small.Say As You Are, Esther Schipper, Berlin, 2004. *Awards:* Recipient award for set design, NY Int Fringe Festival, 2001; Named Invited Exhib, 2004 Biennial Exhib, Whitney Mus Am Art, NY, 2004

ROOD, KAY
PAINTER, PRINTMAKER
b Omaha, Nebr, May 19, 45. *Study:* Univ Iowa, BA, 68, with Maurico Lasansky, Stuart Edie & James Lechay; Ecole des Beaux Arts, 68. *Work:* Seattle Art Mus; City of Seattle, One Percent For Art, Portable Works Collection; Washington State, One Percent For Art, Art in Public Places; King Co Arts Commission Portable Purchase Collection; Portland, Art Mus. *Exhib:* Washington Women Artists, Eastern Wash State Univ, Cheney, 81; Ten Monotype Artists, 82 & Contemp Seattle Art, 83, Bellevue Art Mus, Wash; Northwest Print Council in China, Cent Fine Arts Acad, Beijing, China, 86; Northwest Now, 86 & Kay Rood: Recent Monotypes, 87, Tacoma Art Mus, Wash; Sixth Ann Northwest Int Art Competition, 86 & Kay Rood, 92, Whatcom Mus, Bellingham, Wash; First Impressions: Northwest Monotypes, Seattle Art Mus, 89. *Pos:* Artist-in-residence, Centrum Found, 84 & 88, Marrowstone Press, Pt Townsend, 86. *Awards:* Juror's Award Painting & Drawing, Sixth Ann Northwest Int Art Competition, 86. *Bibliog:* Matthew Kangas (auth), Kay Rood: The gesture and the void, West Art, 10/22/82; Lynn Smallwood (auth), Studies in monotype, The Seattle Weekly, 10/17/84; Ron Glowen (auth), The fascination of process, Artweek, 5/24/86. *Mem:* Northwest Print Coun, Portland, Ore (bd dir, 84-92). *Media:* Miscellaneous Media; Monotype. *Publ:* Contribr, Perspectives in New Music, Six Images, vol 28, no 2, 90; Five Pears or Peaches (cover art), short stories by Reginald Gibbons, Broken Moon Press, Seattle, 91; Modernism & Beyond: Women Artists of the Pacific Northwest, ed, Laura Brunsman, Midmarch Arts Press, New York, 93. *Mailing Add:* 922 E Denny Way Seattle WA 98122

ROOKE, FAY LORRAINE
ENAMELIST, INSTRUCTOR
b Chatham, Ont, Dec 22, 34. *Study:* Ont Col Art, Toronto, AOCA, 56; internat specialized enamel techniques. *Work:* Royal Can Acad Arts, 86; Claridge Investments, Montreal, Quebec, 89; Can Craft Collection, Mus Civilization. *Comn:* Enamel celebratory object, Claridge Invest, Que; enamel object, Glenn Gould Prize, Toronto, Ont, 90; enamel triptych, Capex 78; enamel Cross & objects/containers, Loretto Abbey Chapel, Toronto; champleve chandalier panels, St Elaias Byzantine Rite Catholic Chruch, Homestead, Pa. *Exhib:* Solo-exhibs, Koffler Gallery, North York, Ont, 86, Can Clay & Glass Gallery, Waterloo, Ont, 93 & Harbinger Gallery, Waterloo, Ont, 95; Peninsula Fine Arts Gallery, Hampton, Va, 95; mus Contemp Art, Caracas, Venezuela, 96; Burlington Art Ctr, Ont, 97; int invitational exhibs, South Korea, Tokyo, France, US. *Pos:* Vpres & exec bd mem, South Hills Arts League, Mt Lebanon, Pa, 70-72; found bd dir, Renaissance Ctr Arts, Pittsburgh, Pa, 71-72; dir, Enamelist Soc, Newport, KY, 89-95; adj panel, Pereny Flat Bed Enamel Furnace, Cleveland, Ohio, 93-, Can Clay & Glass Gallery, Waterloo, Ont, 94-; juror, Designer Crafts 94, Hamilton Regional Arts Coun Ont Enamelist Soc IV Biennial, Cleveland, Ohio, 93-, The Color of Fire: Mississauga, ON, 2002; conf. chair & exhibs coord, Crossing Boundaries, Enam Soc, Waterloo, 99. *Teaching:* Prog coordr enamel, Ont Col Art & Design,Toronto, 79-95; guest enamel instr, NS Col Art & Design, Halifax, 94; instr enamel, Brock Univ, St Catherines, Ont, 87, 88 & 92, St Lawrence Col, 84-2006; Int Workshops, Caracas, Venezuela 96, Sydney & Brisbane, Australia, 98, 2003, San Diego, Calif, 2000, 01, Newark, NJ, 2005. *Awards:* Thompson Enamels Award & Alice Wilick Robyns Mem Award, 85; Grand Prize Winner, 9th Cloisonne Jewelry Contest, Tokyo, Japan. *Bibliog:* Current Exploration in Glass & Enamel, Koffler Gallery, North York, Ont, 86; film, Faces in small places: Fay Rooke, CKUR Barrie, Ont-TV Series, 84 & CBC Nat Television, Sunday Arts, 90, 91 & 92; Enamelist Supremo, Craftarts #50, Australia. *Mem:* Royal Can Acad Arts (coun mem, 86-88 & exec bd mem, 86-); Metal Arts Guild; Ont Col Art Alumni Asn (mem-at-large, 84-85); Enamelist Soc (trustee, 89-95, conf chair, 99); Ont Crafts Coun. *Media:* Enamelled Forms, Enamel Jewelry. *Res:* Larger fine art objects in multiple enamel techniques, specializing in plique-à-jour. *Publ:* Ornament and Object, Barros, 97; The Art of Enamling, 2004; A Fine Line, Crawford Dundurn Press, 98; The Art of Fine Enameling, 2002; Craft Arts: International # 50, 2000; The Color of Fire, 2002. *Mailing Add:* 842 Forest Glen Ave Burlington ON L7T 2L2 Canada

ROOSEN, MIA WESTERLUND
SCULPTOR
b New York, NY, 42. *Study:* Art Students League; New York Univ. *Work:* Metrop Mus Art, Guggenheim Mus, Storm King Art Ctr, NY; Albany Mus Art, Ga; Art Gallery Ont, Toronto. *Exhib:* Forum 76, Montreal Mus Fine Arts, 76; one-woman shows, Storm King Art Ctr, 80-94, New Mus Contemp Art (with catalog), NY, 80, Leo Castelli Gallery, NY, 76, 79, 82, 86, Shoshana Wayne Gallery, Calif, 89, 95, 99, Joseloff Gallery, Harry Jack Gray Ctr, Univ Hartford, Conn, 89, Lennon Weinberg Inc, 91, 93, 96, 98, 01; Nat Gallery Can, Ottawa, 80; In Three Dimensions: Women Sculptors of the 90s; Indoor Exhibs; Part II: Beyond Gender, Snug Harbor Cult Ctr, 95; The Material Imagination, Solomon R Guggenheim Mus, 96; Appraising Abstraction, Art Initiatives, NY, 96; Borders, Crossings, Passages: Outdoor Sculpture Exhib, Skidmore Col, Saratoga Springs, NY, 96; The Uneasy Surface: Points of Turbulence in Contemp Art, Fine Arts Ctr Galleries, Univ RI, Kingston, 96; Hanging by a Thread, Hudson River Mus, Yonkers, NY, 97; Montclair Art Mus, NJ, 99-00; Herter Art Gallery, Univ Mass, Amherst, 01; Five Myles, Brooklyn, NY, 02; and others. *Collection Arranged:* Albany Mus Art, Ga; Albright-Knox Art Gallery, Buffalo, NY; Art Gallery Ont, Toronto; Metrop Mus Art; Nat Gallery Can; Guggenheim Mus; Univ Calif, Berkeley; Yale Art Gallery, New Haven, Conn. *Awards:* Can Coun Art Grant, 74; Nat Endowment Arts, 88-89; John Simon Guggenheim Mem Found Fel, 93; Fulbright Fel, 96. *Bibliog:* Lilly Wei (auth), Mia Westerlund Roosen at Storm King Art Center, Art Am, 12/94; A studio visit with Mia Westerlund Roosen, Paris Rev, spring 95; Nancy Princenthal (auth), Mia Westerlund Roosen at Lennon, Weinberg, Art Am, 7/96; Ann Landi (auth), Mia Westerlund Roosen, Lennon, Weinberg, ARTnews, 2/02; Holland Cotter (auth), Archit for One, NY Times, 5/3/02

ROOSEVELT, MICHAEL ARMENTROUT
PRINTMAKER, WRITER
b Philadelphia, PA. *Study:* Carnegie-Mellon Univ, BFA, 70; Tyler Sch Art, MFA, 86; Atelier 17, Paris - SW Hayter (Private Stuy), 67-85; NY Acad Fine Arts, Grad Sch of Figure Study, 95. *Work:* Woodmere Mus Art, Philadelphia, PA; Sherman Hines Mus, Liverpool, NS CND; Lessing Rosenwald Coll, Abington, PA. *Exhib:* solo shows, The Print Club, Philadelphia, PA, 70, NS Col of Art & Design, Halifax, NS, 71, Galerie Harriet Woolley, Paris, FR, 86, The Print Club, Philadelphia, PA, 86, Sherman Hines Mus, Liverpool, NS CND, 97, Woodmere Art Mus, Philadelphia, PA, 98; group show, RI Col, Providence, RI, 89; 62nd Int of the Print Club, Philadelphia, PA, 86; PA Painters & Printmakers, PA State Univ, Univ Park, PA, 88. *Mem:* The Print Ctr (formerly Print Club), Philadelphia, PA, (bd mem, 84-86); Vis Arts Nova Scotia; Nova Scotia Printmakers Asn; Vt Crafts Council; The Authors Guild; Soc Canadian Artists. *Media:* Printmaking. *Publ:* Auth, Universal Multiplication of Intelligence, Institutes Press, 80; illusr, Enouhg, Inigo, Enough, Institute Press, 84; auth, Joseph Hecht, Dolan/Maxwell, 85; auth, Stanley William Hayter (1901-1988), www.contrepoint.com, 2004. *Mailing Add:* PO Box 179 Greensboro Bend VT 05842-0179

ROOTS, GARRISON
SCULPTOR, EDUCATOR
b Abilene, Tex, June 25, 52. *Study:* Mass Col Art, with George Greenmayer, Harris Barron & Jana Longacre, BFA(with hon), 79; Wash Univ, with Howard Jones & James Sterritt, MFA, 81. *Work:* Denver Art Mus, Colo; City of Dallas; Laumeier Sculpture Park, St Louis; City of Miami, City of Memphis. *Comn:* Aspen Art Mus, Colo, 89; City of Denver, New Denver Airport Proj, 90; City of Dallas, 1993 Dallas Conv Ctr Expansion Proj, 91-93; Miami Int Airport 96-; Memphis/Shelby Co Airport, 99. *Exhib:* solo exhibs, Contemp Arts Ctr, New Orleans, 84, Alternative Mus, NY, 86, Cincinnati Artist Group, 89, Inst Design & Experimental Art, Sacramento, Calif, 92, SW China Normal Univ, Chongqing, Beibei, 93, Art Galleries, Univ Colo, Boulder, 93 & Laumeier Sculpture Mus, St Louis, 96; ARTPARK, Lewiston, NY, 86; Aspen Art Mus, Colo, 89; Contemp Art Ctr Santa Fe, N Mex, 90; SPACES S, Cleveland, Ohio, 91; FUSE, Boulder, Colo, 95; Lawndale Art Ctr, Houston, Tex, 95; Buffalo Bayou Artpark, Houston, Tex, 95; Larumeier Sculpture Mus, St Louis, 96; Bemis Ctr Contemp Art, Omaha, Nebr, 99. *Pos:* Med artist/photogr, Mass Eye & Ear Infirmary, Boston, 76-79; asst to dir, Laumeier Sculpture Mus, St Louis, 79-81; artist/consult, Denver Art Ctr, Denver Comn on Cult Affairs, Colo, 86-87. *Teaching:* Teaching/tech asst, Wash Univ, St Louis, 79-80; instr, Swain Sch Design, New Bedford, Mass, 81-82; asst prof, Univ Colo, 82-88, assoc prof & dir sculpture, 88-97, assoc chmn grad studies, 96-98, prof, 98-. *Awards:* Fel Award for Sculpture, Nat Endowment Arts, 81 & 84; Travel Grants Mex, China, Ecuador & Chile, Univ Colo, 92-98; Fel Award, Westaf/ Nat Endowment Arts, 95. *Bibliog:* Beth Chic (auth), Dialouge, 91; Steven Litt (auth), The Plain Dealer, 91; Randall Davis (auth), Artweek, 92; and many others. *Mem:* Nat Endowment Arts; Colo Coun Arts & Humanities; Col Art Asn; FUSE, Boulder, Colo. *Dealer:* Robischon Gallery 1122 E 17 Ave Denver CO; William Campbell Gallery Ft Worth TX. *Mailing Add:* 803 Tenacity Dr Longmont CO 80504-7333

ROPHAR
PAINTER
b Los Angeles, Calif, Dec 19, 35. *Study:* Self taught. *Work:* Bolshoi Theatre, Moscow, Russia; Am Cancer Prevention Ctr, Los Angeles, Calif; Bank Yokohama, Japan. *Comn:* Dancer/Portraits, comn by Ruth St Denis, Los Angeles, Calif, 59; Study of Anna Pavlova, comn by James A Doolittle, Los Angeles, Calif, 72; Total Design Concepts, comn by Liberace, Los Angeles, Calif, 73; 17th Century Fantasy (portrait), comn by Dr Richard Ellenbogen, Los Angeles, 83; White Tigers, comn by Jim Simon, Scottsdale, Ariz, 92. *Exhib:* One-man shows, 21 Turtle Creek Club, Dallas, 71, residence of Baroness von Boehm, Berlin, Ger, 73, Marina City Club, Marina Del Rey, Calif, 76 Regional Conf ASID, Los Angeles, Calif, 81, Pomeroy Gallery Fine Arts, Carmel, Calif, 89 & Ctr Arts Galleries, Hawaii, Honolulu, 90-91. *Awards:* Rotary Club Award, Art Contest, Rotary Club Int, 51-57; Hon Mem, Regional Conf ASID, Los Angeles Chap, 81. *Media:* Acrylic, All Media. *Mailing Add:* 4242 Beethoven St Los Angeles CA 90066

ROPP, ANN L
PAINTER, GALLERY DIRECTOR
b LaCrosse, Wis, Nov 14, 46. *Study:* Univ Ill, BFA, 71; Columbia Univ, MFA, 89. *Work:* Evansville Mus Art, Ind; NY Pub Libr, NY. *Pos:* Gallery dir, East Tenn State Univ, Johnson City, Tenn, 89-. *Teaching:* Instr printmaking, East Tenn State Univ, 92-. *Awards:* Fel, Nat Endowment Arts, 94. *Media:* Oil, Watercolor. *Mailing Add:* Slocumb Galleries Dept Art East Tenn State Univ Johnson City TN 37614-0708

ROREX, ROBERT ALBRIGHT
EDUCATOR, HISTORIAN
b Alexandria, La, Sept 9, 35. *Study:* Hendrix Col, BA, 57; Univ Ark, MFA, 60; Princeton Univ, MA, 69, PhD, 75. *Teaching:* Asst prof, Hendrix Col, 60-61; actg asst prof, Univ Kans, Lawrence, 68-70; instr, Univ Iowa, Iowa City, 70-75, asst prof art hist, 75-79, assoc prof, 79-. *Mem:* Col Art Asn; Mid-Am Col Art Asn; Midwest Art Hist Soc. *Res:* Chinese art & archeology; Japanese art & archeology; Sung, Ming & Liao painting. *Publ:* Coauth, Eighteen Songs of a Nomad Flute: The Story of Lady Wen-Chi, Metrop Mus Art, 74; auth, Setting out at dawn on an autumn river: A painting by Wang Hui, Artibus Asiae, 79; auth, Eighteen songs of a nomad flute, 8/81 & Chunghi Choo: Works in metal and silk, 10/82, Orientations; auth, Some observations on Harold Osborne's The Aesthetics of Chinese Pictorial Art, J Theory & Criticism Visual Arts, 82. *Mailing Add:* 610 Beldon Ave Iowa City IA 52246

RORICK, WILLIAM CALVIN
PAINTER, INSTRUCTOR
b Elyria, Ohio, June 23, 41. *Study:* Studied drawing, painting, & sculpture at NY Academy of Art, Art Students League, Nat Academy of Design, Sch of Visual Arts, Lyme Academy of Art. *Comn:* many comn portraits in corporate, institutional, public & pvt collections. *Exhib:* Portraits Only Int Juried Competition, Wash, DC Soc Portrait Artists, Wash, DC, 1998; Juried Exhib, NY Society of Portrait Artists, Salmagundi Club, NY, 2002; Faces of Newtown, Booth Libr, Newtown, Conn, 2005; Drawings Only Exhib, Portrait Soc of Atlanta, Ga, 2005; 55th Ann Nat Exhib of Contemp Realism in Art, Acad Artists Asn, First Church Gallery, Springfield, Mass, 2005. *Teaching:* Instr (cert leader), Portrait Club of Greater Southbury, Conn. *Awards:* Randolph Chitwood Award, Greenwich Art Soc, 1996; 1st Place Award in Pastel, Graphics, Mixed Media, Conn Classic Arts, 2001; Meritorious Serv, NY Soc of Portrait Artists, 2002; Vernon W Hill Mem Award, Conn Pastel Soc, 2003; Honorable Mention, Conn Soc of Portrait Artists, 2004; Acad Artists Award, Pastels Acad Artists Asn, 2005. *Bibliog:* Who's Who in the East, 1995-1996; Who's Who in Am, 1997-; Who's Who in the World, 2004-; Who's Who in Educ, 2005-. *Mem:* Conn Classic Arts (Publicity Chair), 1996-1999); Soc of Creative Artists of Newtown (Bd Dir, Corresp Secy/Mem), 1999-2002; NY Soc of Portrait Artists (Leadership Team), 2002; Acad Artists Asn (Elected Artist), 2004; Audubon Artist; Arts & Crafts Asn of Meriden. *Media:* Pastel, Oil. *Res:* Locator Index to the Portraits of Thomas Sully, 1783-1872. *Dealer:* Gallery at Kent Conn. *Mailing Add:* 63 Beacon Hill Dr Southbury CT 06488-1914

RORSCHACH, KIMERLY
MUSEUM DIRECTOR
Study: Brandeis Univ, BA; Yale Univ, PhD in art hist. *Pos:* Cur, Philadelphia Mus Art, Rosenbach Mus & Libr, Philadelphia; Dana Feitler dir, Smart Mus Art, Univ Chicago, 1994-2004; dir, Nasher Mus Art, Duke Univ, Durham, NC, 2004-. *Mem:* Asn Art Mus Dir. *Mailing Add:* Nasher Mus Art PO Box 90732 Durham NC 27708

ROSAND, DAVID
HISTORIAN, CRITIC
b Brooklyn, NY, Sept 6, 38. *Study:* Columbia Col, AB, 59; Columbia Univ, MA, 62, PhD, 65. *Collection Arranged:* Titian and the Venetian Woodcut (auth, catalog), Nat Gallery Art, Washington, DC, 76; The Pastoral Landscape (coauth, catalog), Nat Gallery Art, Washington, DC, Philipps Col, Washington, DC, 88; Robert Motherwell On Paper: Gesture, Variation, Continuity (coauth, catalogue), Wallach Art Gallery, Columbia Univ, New York, 97. *Teaching:* Dept Art History & Archaeology, Columbia Univ, New York, 64-. *Awards:* Fulbright Fel, 71-72; Nat Endowment Humanities Fel, 71-72, 85-86, 91-92; Guggenheim Fel, 74-75. *Res:* Venetian painting; Renaissance tradition; graphic arts; criticism of drawing; Abstract Expressionism. *Publ:* Auth, Titian, Abrams, 78; Painting in Cinquecento Venice: Titian, Veronese, Tintoretto, Yale Univ Press, 1982, rev ed Cambridge Univ Press, 1997; The Meaning of the Mark: Leonardo and Titian, Spencer Mus Art, Univ Kansas, 88; coauth, Places of Delight: The Pastoral Landscape, Clarkson N Potter, 88; Myths of Venice: The Figuration of a State, Univ North Carolina Press, 2001; coauth, Robert Motherwell on Paper: Drawings, Prints, Collages, Abrams, 1997; Drawing Acts: Studies in Graphic Expression and Representation, Cambridge Univ Press, 2002. *Mailing Add:* Dept Art Hist & Archeol Columbia Univ New York NY 10027

ROSAS, MEL
PAINTER, EDUCATOR
b Des Moines, Iowa, June 1, 50. *Study:* Drake Univ, with Jules Kirschembalm, BFA, 71; Tyler Sch Art, with John Moore & Steven Greene, MFA, 74. *Exhib:* Corcoran Gallery Art, 74; Eastern Mich Univ, Ypsilanti, 78, Cantor/Lemberg Gallery, Birmingham, Mich, 81 & 84 & Community Arts Gallery, Wayne State Univ, Detroit, 88; Cranbrook Art Mus, 79 & 80; Brooklyn Mus, 81; Butler Inst Am Art, 87; Portals, Maxwell Davidson Gallery, NY, 95; Maxwell Davidson Gallery, 2000, 2001; The Art Show, ADAA, NY, 2001; Art Palm Beach, Fla, 2001; Water and Other Stories, Maxwell Davidson Gallery, NY, 2003; Everyday Mysteries: Paintings by Mel Rosas, The Muskegon Mus, Muskegon, Mich, 2005; After the Rain, Maxwell Davidson Gallery, NY, 2005. *Teaching:* Instr, Univ Calgary, Alberta, 75-76; prof, Wayne State Univ, Detroit, 76-. *Awards:* Fac Res Grants, Wayne State Univ, Detroit, 87 & 90; Creative Artists Grant, Mich Coun Arts, Detroit, 87; Nat Endowment Arts Grant, 93; Creative Artist Grant, Artserve of Mich, 99-2000; The Elizabeth Found for the Arts Grant, NY. *Bibliog:* Harry N Abrams (publ), Tools as Art, Thr Hechinger Collection; Nathan Goldstein (auth), The Art Responsive Drawing, Prentice Hall. *Media:* Oil, Drawing. *Dealer:* Maxwell Davidson Gallery

ROSE, HERMAN
PAINTER, PRINTMAKER
b Brooklyn, NY, Nov 6, 09. *Study:* Nat Acad Design, 27-29. *Work:* Whitney Mus Am Art, Mus Mod Art, NY; Univ Tex; Univ Nebr; Smithsonian Inst Print Collection; and others. *Exhib:* Mus Mod Art, 48 & 52; 15 Americans, Whitney Mus Am Art, 48-58 & 72; Pa Acad Fine Arts, 52; one-man shows, ACA Gallery, 52 & 55-56, Forum Gallery, NY, 62 & Zabriskie Gallery, 67, 69, 72 & 74. *Teaching:* Instr, New Sch Social Res, 54-55 & 63-; instr, Hofstra Col, 59-60; artist in residence, Univ Va, 66; vis prof, Univ NMex, 70-71. *Mem:* Nat Acad (assoc, 74, acad, 76). *Mailing Add:* 463 West St No H821 New York NY 10014

ROSE, LEATRICE
PAINTER, INSTRUCTOR
b New York, NY, Jun 22, 24. *Study:* Cooper Union, 45; Art Students League, 46; Hans Hofmann Sch, 47. *Exhib:* Artists Ann, Whitney Mus Am Art, 50; one-woman shows, Zabriske Gallery, 65, Landmark Gallery, 74, Tibor de Nagy Gallery, 75, 78 & 81 & Armstrong Gallery, 85, Cyrus Gallery, 89; Women Choose Women, NY Cult Ctr, 73; Nat Acad Design Ann, 74-76; Whitney Mus Am Art, Downtown, 78; Hans Hofmann as Teacher: Drawings by his Students, Metrop Mus Art, 79; Contemp Naturalism, Nassau Co Mus Fine Arts, 80; Contemp Still Life, One Penn Plaza, NY, 85; Am Academy of Arts & Letters, 91,92; Nat Acad of Design Ann 92-2003; Cherry Stone Gallery, Wellfleet, MA, 2004. *Teaching:* Instr painting, State Univ NY, Stony Brook, 74-75, Sch Visual Art, New York 77, Art Students League, currently. *Awards:* Nat Endowment Arts Grant, 77; Gottlieb Found Award, 80; Esther and Adolph Gottlieb Found Grant, 88; Am Acad Arts and Letts Painting Award, 92; Nat Acad Design Painting Award, 92; Carlson Award Best Still Life, Nat Acad Design, 99. *Bibliog:* John Ashbery (auth), Dash, Dodd & Rose, 3/74 & Lawrence Campbell (auth), article, 10/85, Art in Am; April Kingsley (auth), The Lugano review, Art Int, 3/20/74; Lawrence Alloway (auth), Art, The Nation, 10/25/75; Barbara Guest (auth), article, Arts, summer 85; Woman's Art Journal 94-95. *Mem:* Nat Acad of Design (assoc, 92, acad, 94). *Media:* Oil on canvas. *Collection:* Lisa Felgy-Chemical Bank, Metropolitan Mus. *Mailing Add:* 463 West St Apt A924 New York NY 10014

ROSE, PEGGY JANE
PAINTER, INSTRUCTOR
b Plainfield, NJ Oct 4, 47. *Study:* Univ Tex, BA with with high honors, Austin, Tex, 1971; Acad of Art Col, BFA with distinction, 1980; Private studios: Peter Blos, 1982-1984; Daniel Greene, 1983; Burton Silverman, Hudson River Valley Studio, NYC, spring & summer 1998; Teachers as Scholars, Princeton U, 2006. *Work:* Mercer Co Cult & Heritage Comn Collection, Trenton, NJ. *Exhib:* Pastels USA, Pastel Soc W Coast, Roseville Art Center, Sacramento, Calif, 1996-1999; Pastels Only Ann Exhits, Nat Arts Club, NY, 1998-2005; Catherine Lorillard Wolfe Art Club, Nat Art Club, NY, 2000, 2002, 2004; Allied Artists Am Ann, Nat Arts Club, NY, 2002-2003; Audubon Artists Inc Ann Exhib, Salmagundi Club, NY, 2002-2003; 21st & 22nd Ellerslie Open Exhibts, City of Trenton Mus, Trenton, NJ, 2003-2004. *Teaching:* Fac, Figure, Portrait, color drawing & Painting, Acad Art Col, (Univ) San Francisco, Calif, 1983-1997; Fac, Illus drawing & painting, Calif Col Arts & Crafts, Oakland, Calif, 1985-1986; Fac, gen art, Montgomery Twp, Sch Dist, Skillman, NJ, 2005-. *Awards:* Best of Show, Pastels in Light, Pastel Soc W Coast, 1996; Gold Medal of Honor, Catherine Lorillard Wolfe Art Club 106th Exhib, 2002; Gold Medal of Honor, Allied Artists of Am 89th Exhib, 2002. *Bibliog:* Nancy Cushing (auth), Rose Paintings are Pure Pleasure, Mill Valley Record, 1987; Ian Seldon (auth), Three Cheers, Diablo Arts Mag, 1992; Int Showcase Prize Winners, Int Artist Mag, 2003. *Mem:* Pastel Soc W Coast (signature mem), 1999-; Allied Artist Am (signature mem), 2002-; Pastel Soc Am (master pastellist), 2004-; Catherine Lorillard Wolfe Art Club (full mem), 2005-. *Media:* Pastel, Oil. *Publ:* Auth, Whistler's Pastels in Venice, Their Innovations & Their Impact on Pastel in Am, Pastel Soc Am, 2003; Auth, A Celebration of Pastel, Ann Exhib, Pastelagram Mag, winter 2004. *Mailing Add:* 12 Perry Dr Princeton Junction NJ 08550-2803

ROSE, PETER HENRY
DEALER
b New York, NY, Feb 25, 35. *Study:* Hamilton Col, BA; Univ Pa, MA; Columbia Univ; Ecole Superieure, Univ Paris. *Pos:* Co owner, Peter Rose Gallery, currently. *Mem:* Arts & Bus Coun New York. *Specialty:* Nineteenth and twentieth century contemporary American art; major French impressionist paintings. *Mailing Add:* c/o Peter Rose Gallery 200 E 58th St No 20C New York NY 10022

ROSE, ROBIN CARLISE
PAINTER, SCULPTOR
b Ocala, Fla, Sept 3, 1946. *Study:* Fla State Univ, BFA, 68, MFA, 70. *Work:* Corcoran Gallery, Phillips Collection & Nat Mus Am Art, Washington, DC; Jacksonville Mus Fine Art, Fla; Hirshhorn Mus & Sculpture Garden, Washington, DC. *Comn:* IBM, Gaithersburg, Md; Signet Bank, Washington, DC; Shea Beker Gallery, NY; Grand Hyatt, Washington, DC. *Exhib:* M-13 Gallery, NY; WPA, Washington, DC; Corcoran Gallery Art, Washington, DC; White Columns, NY. *Bibliog:* Stephen Westfall (auth), rev, Art in Am, 5/86. *Media:* Encausitic, Silverpoint. *Dealer:* Fendrick Gallery 3059 M St NW Washington DC 20007. *Mailing Add:* 2900 Fessenden St NW Washington DC 20008

ROSE, ROSLYN
COLLAGE ARTIST, PHOTOGRAPHER
b Irvington, NJ, May 28, 29. *Study:* Rutgers Univ; Pratt Graphic Ctr; Skidmore Col, BS. *Work:* NJ State Mus, Trenton; Newark Mus, NJ; Citibank of NY, Moscow, Russia; Newark Pub Libr, NJ; Zimmerli Mus, Rutgers Univ, New Brunswick, NJ; McAllen Int Mus, Tex; Noyes Mus, Oceanville, NJ; Readers Digest Collection, Pleasantville, NY; Voorhees-Zimmerli MusNew Brunswick, NJ; Stevens Inst, Hoboken, NJ; and others. *Comn:* Etchings, NY Graphic Soc, Ltd, Greenwich, Conn, 70-80 & John Szoke Gallery, NY, 81-85; UNICEF Card, 79-80; etched metal wall-relief, Pub Serv Elec & Gas Co, Newark, NJ, 80. *Exhib:* Liberated Printmakers (traveling), NJ Coun Arts, 1972; solo exhibs, Robins Hutchins Gallery, 78, George Frederick Gallery, Rochester, 1981, Arnot Art Mus, elmira, 1982, Nathans Gallery, West Paterson, 1984,1986, 1989, 1997, 1999, Gallery 3, Hoboken, NJ, Pen & Brush Club, NYC, 1998, New Century Artist Inc, NYC, 2003, Symposia, Hoboken, NJ, 2005, Hoboken Hist Mus, Hoboken, NJ, 2006,; Black-White & Color, Printmaking Coun, NJ, 1982; Western CO Art Center, Grand Junction, CO, Catherine Lorillard Wolfe Art Club, NY, Penn & Brush Club, 2000; Faces, Period Gallery, Omaha, Nebr, Bristol Art Mus, Bristol, RI, 2001; Mountain Art Show, Bernardsville, NJ, Cambridge Art Asn, Cambridge, Mass, 2002; Case Western Reserve Univ, Cleveland, Ohio, Nat Asn Women Artists, NY, Seton Hall Univ, South Orange, NJ, 2003; Lee Co Alliance of the Arts, Fort Myers, Fla, Studio Seto, Boston, Mass, 2004; Somerville Art Mus, Somerville, Mass, AIR Gallery, NY, Stevens Inst Technol, 2005; DeVos Mus, Northern Mich Univ, Marquette, Mich, Ceres Gallery, NY, GoggleWorks Center for the Arts, Reading, Pa, 2006. *Pos:* Bd dir,

Printmaking Coun NJ, 80-85; jury ch printmaking, Nat Asn Women Artists, 86-88, jury chair works on canvas, 93-96, vpres, 97-2000; co-founder, Hob'Art cooperative gallery, Hoboken, NJ, corresponding secy, 2002-2006. *Teaching:* Instr printmaking, Newark Mus, 72-82. *Awards:* Georgi Memorial Graphic Prize, 77, Innovative Painting Prize, 90, Nat Asn Women Artists; Mixed Media Award, Salmagundi Club, 95; Mixed Media Award, Pen & Brush Club, 96, 97 & 98; Innovative Award, Western Colo Art Ctr, Grand Junction, 2000; Directors Award, Period Gallery, Omaha, Neb, 2001; ISEA Award, 2003; Nat Asn Women Artists Computer Art Award, 2003; Lee Co Alliance, 2004; Best in Show Award, Mountain Art Show, 2004; Computer Art Award, Intl Soc of Experimental Artists. *Bibliog:* J H Newman & L S Newman (auths), Plastics for the Craftsman, Crown, 72; Thelma R Newman (auth), Innovative Printmaking, Crown, 77; Manhattan Arts Mag, 1/98. *Mem:* Nat Asn Women Artists (printmaking jury ch, 86-88 & 2000-03, vpres, 97-99); Printmaking Coun NJ (bd dir, 80-85); Assoc Artists NJ (exec bd, 86); Artist Equity Asn, Inc; Pen and Brush Club, NY (chair open exhib 1998-2001); Hob'Art cooperative gallery. *Media:* Assemblage Digital Montage & Transfer Photography. *Publ:* Auth, Outline of Printmaking, NJ Coun Arts, 72. *Dealer:* Ceres Gallery 547 W 27th St New York NY 10001. *Mailing Add:* 321 Newark St Hoboken NJ 07030

ROSE, SAMUEL
PAINTER, MURALIST
b Cleveland, Ohio, Sept 17, 41. *Study:* Cape Cod Sch Art, Provincetown, with Henry Henche; Cooper Sch & Kent State Univ; Boston Atelier, with R H Ives Gammell; also with Basil Kalashnifoff, Cleveland. *Work:* Maryhill Mus Art & St Ignatius Church, Washington, DC; Nat Fire Protection Asn; Brockton Mus; Pierce Galleries Inc, Hingham, Mass. *Comn:* Many, incl Maharaj Ji, Mrs F Lee Bailey, Patricia Barlow & Patricia Pierce. *Exhib:* Nat Arts Club, NY, 69; Copley Art Soc & Concord Art Asn, 71; Jordan Marsh, Boston, 72-73; one-man shows, Concord Art Asn, 75, Pierce Galleries, Inc, 79, 80, 88 & 90, Hammer Galleries, NY, 85; and others. *Teaching:* Pvt art classes. *Awards:* First Prize, Concord Art Asn, 63, 67 & 69; Greenshields Grant, Montreal, 63-70; Nat Fire Protection Asn; Julias Hallgarten Prize, NAD, 68. *Mem:* Copley Soc; Salmagundi Club; Guild Boston Artists; Concord Art Asn; Am Artists Prof League. *Media:* Oil. *Publ:* Edmund C Tarbell and the Boston School, 80; Samuel Rose, Surrealist, 76. *Dealer:* Pierce Galleries Inc Hingham MA 02043. *Mailing Add:* c/o Pierce Galleries Inc 721 Main St Hingham MA 02043-3326

ROSE, THOMAS ALBERT
SCULPTOR
b Washington, DC, Oct 15, 42. *Study:* Univ Wis, Madison, 60-62; Univ Ill, Urbana, BFA, 65; Univ Calif, Berkeley, MA, 67, study grant to Univ Lund, 67-68. *Work:* Univ NMex Mus, Albuquerque; Libr Cong, Washington; Minneapolis Inst Art; Walker Art Ctr, Minneapolis; Brooklyn Mus, NY; plus others. *Comn:* Park St Loft One, Springfield, Mass; chapel, St Lukes Episcopal Church, Minneapolis; set design, Fool for Love, Cricket Theater, Minneapolis; set design, Circus, Theater de Jeune Lune, Minneapolis; Minn Zoological Gardens. *Exhib:* Walker Art Ctr, Minneapolis, 74; Small Objects, Whitney Mus Am Art, NY; Scale & Environment, Walker Art Ctr; outdoor sculpture exhib, Wave Hill, NY, 81; Sheldon Mus Art, Univ Nebr, Lincoln; Thomson Gallery, Minneapolis, 91; Minneapolis Inst Art, 92; Frederick R Weismann Mus, Minneapolis, 94; Nat Mus Art, Tirana, Albania, 94; Tweed Mus Art, Univ Minn, 95; Steinbaum/Krauss Gallery, NY, 96 & 97; Socrates Sculpture Park, NY, 96; Bernice Steinbaum Gallery, Miami, Fla, 2001, 2003; Exercises, The Drawings of Merce Cunningham, Nash Gallery, Univ Minn, 2005; Luxun Acad Art, Shenyang, China, 2006. *Teaching:* Instr sculpture, Univ Calif, Berkeley, 68-69; instr sculpture & graphics, NMex State Univ, 69-72; instr sculpture, Univ Minn, Minneapolis, 72-81, assoc prof, 81-83, prof, 83-; prof art, Univ Minn. *Awards:* Jerome Found Fel, 93-94; Dayton Hudson Travel Grant, Italy, 94; McKnight found fel, 95; Rockfeller Found, Bellagio, Italy, 1993; McKnight Fel/photog, 2002. *Bibliog:* John Ligon (prod), Encounters with Minnesota Artists (film); Eleanor Heartney (auth), Tom Rose: Access to Hidden Worlds (article); Ann Klefstad (auth), Five McKnight Artists; Mark Cohen (auth), Provisional Locations, Review Mag, 3/1999. *Media:* Mixed Media. *Publ:* Auth, Winter Book, Minn Ctr Book Arts, 95. *Dealer:* Bernice Steinbaum Gallery 3550 N Miami Ave, Miami FL. *Mailing Add:* 91 Nicolet St Minneapolis MN 55401

ROSEMAN, STANLEY
PAINTER, DRAFTSMAN
b Brookline, Mass, Sept 4, 45. *Study:* Cooper Union Col Art & Archit, BFA, 67; Pratt Inst, MFA, 72. *Work:* Nat Gallery Art, Washington, DC; Albertina, Vienna; Israel Mus, Jersusalem; Bibliothèque Nat France, Paris; Staatsliche Graphische Sammlung, Munich; Prentenkabinet Kunsthistoiche Inst der Rijksuniversiteit Te Leiden. *Exhib:* One-man shows, Performing Arts in Am (auth catalog), Mus Performing Arts, Lincoln Ctr, NY, 77, Saami People of Lappland, Peabody Mus, Yale Univ, 77, Thomas Mann Archiv, Zurich, 81, Zeichnungen aus Klöstern, Albertina (1st Am artist), Vienna, 83 & Dessins sur la Danse à l'Opéra de Paris (auth catalog), Bibliothèque Nat France, 96; Ashmolean Mus, Oxford, 80; Bibliot Royale, Brussels, 80; Nat Gallery Art, Washington, DC, 82; Mus des Beaux-Arts, Bordeaux, 85; Nat Gallery Ireland, Dublin, 86; Theatre Mus, Victoria & Albert Mus, London, 87; Mus Ingres, Montauban, 87. *Awards:* Artistic Achievement Among the Saami People of Lappland, The Explorers Club, New York, 77. *Bibliog:* David Shirey (auth), Paintings by Stanley Roseman glow with a shiny dignity, NY Times, 8/21/77; Stanley Roseman, Drawing the Monastic Life (film), Thames TV, Eng, 79; John Groser (auth), How an artist captured the pure face of sanctity, The Times-London, 4/8/80. *Media:* Oil; Chalk, Pencil. *Publ:* Illusr, Faces Behind the Monastery Wall--The Monastic Life in Europe, Deventer, 92. *Dealer:* Ronald Davis Postfach 2607 6002 Lucerne Switzerland; Ronald Davis BP 219 F-75765 Paris Cedex 16 France

ROSEMAN, SUSAN CAROL
PRINTMAKER, PAINTER
b Philadelphia, Pa, June 20, 50. *Study:* Art Inst Pittsburgh, 67; Pa Acad Fine Arts, cert, 68-73. *Work:* Allentown Art Mus, Pa; Springfield Free Pub Libr. *Exhib:* Japan Int Artists Soc, Prefectural Mus, Nara, China, 81-82; Nat Print Exhib, Trenton State Col, NJ, 86; James A Michener Art Mus Bucks Binnial I, Doylestown, Pa, 92; 10th Biennial Nat Printshow, Payne Gallery, Moravian Col, Bethlehem, Pa, 96; Donald B Palmer Mus, Springfield, NJ, 96; The Learning Studio, Longhorn, Pa, 99; PC NJ Newark Mus, NJ, 99. *Pos:* exhib committee, fel, Pa Acad Fine Arts, 91-; Pres, Riverbank Arts Inc, Stockton, NJ, 94-. *Awards:* Fel, Pa Acad Fine Arts, Ft History Mus, 88; 2nd Place, Graphics Art Show at the Dog Show, 95; Purchase Prize Award, 98th Ann Juried Exhib Fel, PASA, Westchester Univ, 95 & 10th Biennial Nat Print Show, Payne Gallery, Bethlaham, Pa, 97. *Mem:* Printmaking Coun NJ; Pa Acad Fine Arts; Woodmere Art Mus. *Media:* All. *Publ:* Auth, rev, Art Matters, 12/84, 10/89. *Mailing Add:* 6588 Groveland Rd Pipersville PA 18947

ROSEN, ABY
COLLECTOR
Comn: Helped develop properties at 390 Park Ave, NY City, 400 Park Ave, NY City, 516 fifth Ave, NY City, 275 Madison Ave, NYC, 636 Madison Ave, NY City, and many other commercial and residential properties. *Pos:* Cofounder RFR Holding LLC, NY City; works with Ian Schrafer. *Awards:* Named one of Top 200 Collectors, ARTnews mag, 2006; recipient Man of Yr Award, Spring Ahead Gala, Jeffrey Modell Found, 2000

ROSEN, ANNABETH
CERAMIST, SCULPTOR
b Brooklyn, NY, Jan 15, 57. *Study:* NY State Col Ceramics-Alfred Univ, BFA, 78; Cranbrook Acad Art, Bloomfield Hills, Mich, MFA, 81. *Work:* Alfred Univ Ceramics Mus; Muchael O'Conner, Horsham, Eng; Robert Pfannebecker, Lancaster, Pa; Dorothy Weiss Gallery, San Francisco, Calif; Mel & Hope Barkan, pvt collection, Boston, Mass. *Exhib:* Dorothy Weiss Gallery, San Francisco, 95, 96 & 97; solo-exhib, Revolution, Ferndale, Mich, 95; New (York) Visions Watershed Benefit, David Beitzel Gallery, NY, 96; New Eng Ceramic Artists (catalog), Boston Atheneum, 96; one-woman shows, The Alternative Work Site, Omaha, Nebr, 86; Jane Harsook Gallery, New York City, 89; Challenge Exhib #3, Samuel S Fleisher Meml, Phila, 90; Revolution, Ferndale, Mich, 95; Nelson Gallery, Univ Calif Davis, 97; Dorothy Weiss Gallery, San Francisco, 99; John Michael Kohler Art Ctr Mus, Sheboygen, Wis, 2000; Magic and Ritial: Hannukkiahs Through Contemp Eyes, Steinbaum Drauss Gallery, NY, 99; Ceramic Nat 2000, Everson Mus, Syracuse, NY, 2000; Defining Moments In Contemp Ceramics, Los Angeles Co Mus, Calif, 2000; The Snake in the Garden, Aberystwyth Arts Ctr, Wales, 2001. *Teaching:* Instr, Ohio State Univ, Columbus, 87, Tyler Sch Art, Temple Univ, Philadelphia, Pa, 89-92, RI Sch Design, Providence, 90 & 91, Sch Art Inst Chicago, Ill, 91, Univ Arts, Philadelphia, 91-93 & Bennington Col, Vt, 93-97; prof, Univ Calif, Davis Arneson, 97-. *Awards:* Nat Endowment Arts Craftsman Fel, 79 & 86; Pen Coun Arts Craftsman Fel, 92; Pew Fel, 93. *Bibliog:* Jim Melcert (auth), rev, Am Ceramics; Peter Schjeldahl & Allison Britton (authors), The American Way (exhib, catalog); Peter Schjeldahl (auth), reprinted essay, Am Ceramics, Vol 11/2, spring 94. *Mem:* Cal Art Asn; Nat Coun Educ Ceramic Arts; Tile Heritage Found. *Publ:* Auth, Out of the Melting Pot, NY Times, 11/17/88; Mysterious Works, Courier Times, 11/22/90; On Galleries, Philadelphia Inquirer, 11/29/90; Views on Use: Function in American Ceramics, Ceramic Rev, 7-8/93; Visual Art, Visible Thinking, The Int, 94. *Mailing Add:* Univ Calif Davis Art Bldg 1 Sheilds Ave Davis CA 95616

ROSEN, CAROL M
SCULPTOR, COLLAGE ARTIST
b New York, NY. *Study:* Hunter Col, BA, 54, MA, 62; Pratt Graphics Ctr, New York. *Work:* Smithsonian Inst, Washington, DC; Rutgers Univ, Newark, NJ; Scanoil Corp, NY; AT&T, NJ; Newark Mus, NJ; NJ State Mus; Bristol-Myers Squibb; Noyes Mus; Tel Aviv Univ; Jewish Nat & Univ Libr, Jerusalem; and others. *Exhib:* Paperworks, Alberta Col Art, Can, 83; Constructed Image, Constructed Object, Alternative Mus, NY, 84; Grounds for Sculpture, Hamilton, NJ, 96; Gary Snyder Fine Art, New York City, 2002; Museo de Arte y Diseno Comtemporanio, San Jose, Costa Rica, 2002; solo shows, NJ State Mus, Trenton, 86, Oberlin Col, 2003, William Paterson Univ, 2004, Dana Libr, Rutgers Univ, 2006; Nat Mus of Women Arts, Wash, 2004; Group Exhibs, Wellesley Col, 2005, Col of NJ, 2006. *Collection Arranged:* co-curator, Paper: Surface and Image, Printmaking Coun NJ, 81; Sculptors Proposals for Large Scale Works, 14 Sculptors Gallery, 88; Form & Space: A Dialogue, Hunterdon Mus Art, 98. *Teaching:* Teacher art, Pub Sch, Bronx, NY, 54-59; printmaking, painting, papermaking, art hist, Pub Sch, West Orange, NJ, 59-85; retired. *Awards:* Purchase Award, NJ Mus, 69; Fel NJ State Coun, 80 & 83. *Bibliog:* Vivien Raynor (auth), Collages from assorted everyday items, New York Times, 80; Pat Malarcher (auth), An artist's radical shift, New York Times, 86; Barry Schwabsky (auth), Visual Voyages, New York Times, 96. *Mem:* Printmaking Coun NJ (bd dir, 88-90); Aljira, Hunterdon Mus of Art. *Media:* Mixed Media & Digital Prints. *Interests:* Reading, gardening. *Publ:* Auth, Donald Judd at Marfa, Arts Mag, 88; 10,000 Things I know about her: Judy Pfaff's Recent Work, Arts Mag, 89; Sites and installations, Arts Mag, 90; Christian Boltanski: Traces of the Dead, Sculpture, 6/99; What Are You Looking At? the Sculpture of Tony Oursler, Sculpture, 5/2000. *Mailing Add:* Ten Beavers Rd Califon NJ 07830

ROSEN, DIANE
PAINTER, MURALIST
b New York, NY. *Study:* French Govt Fel Painting, Independent Study, 81; Art Students League, with Robert Beverly Hale & Daniel Greene, 78-80; Nat Acad Design, with Harvey Dinnerstein, 79; Goucher Col, BA cum laude, 70. *Work:* Pastel Soc Am, National Arts Club, NY. *Comn:* Mural (oil, 7 x 10 ft), comn by Victoria

Hunter-Gohl, NY, 92; mural (acrylic 6 X 16 ft), Robert Vissichio, NY, 93; mural (acrylic 8 X 17 ft), Bruce Selfon, Washington, DC, 94; mural (acrylic 5 x 13 ft), comn by Pamela Swedelson, Woodbury, NY, 96; mural (oil, 60 x 54 ft) comn by Constance Slaughter, London, Eng, 95; mural (acrylic 8 x 6 ft), comn by M E Bernal, San Antonio, Tex, 97; and others. *Exhib:* 19th Ann Pastel Soc Am, Nat Arts Club, NY, 91; True Love & Other Stories, Gallery Stendhal, NY, 91; Ann Combined Media Exhib, Salmagundi Club, NY, 92; Pastels USA, 6th Ann Pastel Soc West Coast Int Open Exhib, Sacramento Fine Arts Mus, Carmichael, Calif, 92; Hammond Mus Invitational, N Salem, NY, 95, Bard Coll, Annandale-on-Hudson, NY, 79; solo show, Two Visions Gallery, Washingtonville, NY, 94, Walter Wickiser Gallery, NY, 95, 04, S E Feinman Gallery, NY, 96, Wyckoff Gallery, NJ, 95-, Mark Gruber Gallery, New Paltz, NY, 95-02; Gayle Clark Fedigan Gallery, Cornwall Univ, 2002-; Catharine Lorillard Wolfe Art Club Ann Nat Arts Club, NY, 2002, 2006; Butler Inst Am Art Nat Show, Youngstown, Ohio, 2002, 2004-2005; Pastel Soc Am Curator Series Show, 2002-2003; Pastel Soc Am Ann, NY, 03, 04; Allied Artists Am Ann, NY, 03; Women's History Month Invitational Show, Howland Cult Ctr, Beacon, NY, 05; Hopper House Art Ctr Ann, Nyack, NY, 2006. *Pos:* Creative dir, vpres, Wilcox & Assoc, NY, 84-88; creative dir/owner, Diane Rosen Communs, NY, 88-90; Sole proprietor, Diane Rosen Studio, 91-. *Teaching:* Teacher art, Parsons Sch Design, NY; teacher, Birch Wathen Sch, NY; teacher, Pastel Soc Am Sch, NY. *Awards:* President's Award, 6th Ann Pastel Soc West Coast Int Open, 92; A & A Giffuni Purchase Award, Pastel Soc Am, 95; Salmagundi Club Award, Catharine Lorillard Wolfe Art Club 106th Ann Exhib, 2002; elected Master Panelist, Pastel Soc Am, 03; Joseph V Giffuni Mem Award, Pastel Soc Am, 03; Dianne Bernhard Gold Medal award for Pastel, Allied Artists Am, 03; Dianne B Bernhard Prize for Pastel, Butler Inst Am Art, 2006. *Bibliog:* Elizabeth Exler (auth), The classical in the contemporary art of Diane Rosen, Manhattan Arts, 92; Kathy Swanwick (auth), Giving form to humanity, The Times Herald-Record, 94; EC Lipton (auth), New Voices, Artspeak, 94; Barbara Fischman (auth), Seeing the World Afresh, Pastel Soc Am Mag, 96; Kristina Feliciano (ed), Best of Pastel 2, Rockport Pub, 98; Keith Crandell (auth), Remembering Adam In Noho, The Villager, 2000; J. Sanders Eaton (auth), Pastels Only Celebrates a Major Medium, Gallery Studio Mag, 04; Loraine Crouch (auth), Diane Rosen, Pastel Journal, 2005; Maureen Bloomsield & James Markle (ed), Pure Color - The Best of Pastel, North Light Books Publ, 2006. *Mem:* Pastel Soc Am; Salmagundi Club, NY; Allied Artists Am; Am Artists Prof League; Hudson Valley Pastel Soc; Arts Coun Orange Co. *Media:* Oil, Pastel. *Publ:* Auth & ed, Pastelagram, Newsletter Pastel Soc Am, 91, 92; auth, Interpreting Classical Form with Abstract Underpainting, Am Artist Mag, 03; auth, Create Evocative Figures, Pastelagram, Newsletter, Pastel Soc Am, 04. *Dealer:* Walter Wickiser Gallery, NY. *Mailing Add:* 26 Sixth Ave Nyack NY 10960

ROSEN, HY (HYMAN) JOSEPH
CARTOONIST, SCULPTOR
b Albany, NY, Feb 10, 23. *Study:* Art Inst Chicago; Art Students League; State Univ NY, Albany; Stanford Univ, Fel. *Comn:* Seal of City of Albany (over life size bronze sculpture) Tricentennial Park, Albany, NY 86; Christopher Columbus bust (1 1/2 life size), Troy, NY, 92; Gray Rider (7' bronze statue), NY State Trooper Acad, Albany; 11' Statue 2 Bronze Bas Relief, NY State Women's Veterans Mem. *Pos:* Ed cartoonist, Albany Times-Union, 45 yrs; ed cartoonist, Hearst Newspapers & Heritage Found, Washington; freelance art work, various clients, 89-. *Teaching:* Instr cartooning, State Univ NY, Albany, formerly; instr, Russell Sage Evening Division Col, currently. *Awards:* Top Award, Nat Conf Christians & Jews, 62; Am Legion Fourth Estate Awards, 62nd Nat Conv, 80; Ink Bottle Award, Asn Am Cartoonists, 90. *Mem:* Asn Am Ed Cartoonists (pres, 72). *Media:* Ink. *Publ:* Auth, As Hy Rosen Saw It, 70; Do They Tell You What to Draw?, 80; co-auth, Peter Slocum, From Rocky to Pataki, Syracuse Univ Press, 98

ROSEN, KAY
PAINTER
Study: Newcomb Col Tulane Univ, BA; Northwestern Univ, MA. *Exhib:* Whitney Biennial, Whitney Mus Am Art, 91; solo exhibs, Feature, NY, 93, Mus Contemp Art, Chicago, 94, Shoshana Wayne Gallery, Santa Monica, Calif, 94, Indianapolis Mus Art, Forefront Gallery, Ind, 94, Victoria Miro Gallery, London, Eng, 94, Galeria Massimo de Carlo, Milan, Italy, 94 & Galerie Erika & Otto Friedrich, Berne, Switz, 95; Awards in Visual Arts 10 (with catalog), Hirshhorn Mus, Washington, DC, Albuquerque Mus, NMex & Toledo Mus Art, Ohio, 91; Synesthesia: Sound & Vision in Contemp Art, San Antonio, Tex, 94; The Use of Pleasure, Terrain, San Francisco, Calif, 94; Murder, Bergamot Station, Los Angeles; Five Words or Less, Mus Mod Art, Melbourne, Australia; and many others. *Pos:* Adv mem, Visual Arts Panel, Ind Arts Comn, 86, Arts Midwest Focus Groups, 88; cur, Sch Art Inst Chicago, 88; panelist, Interdisciplinary Inspiration, Midwest Col Art Asn Conf, Cincinnati, Ohio, 89, Mass Artists Fel Prog Painting Panel, 90; grad critique panelist, Sch Art Inst Chicago, 89; rev panelist, Arts Midwest New Partnership Grants Visual Artists, 90; speaker & panelist, Mountain Cake Symp, Va, 90; Respondent, Stillstand switches, Shedhalle, Zurich & Mus fur Gestaltung, 91; grad fac adv, Sch Art Inst Chicago, 92; guest speaker, Michael M Williamson Mem Lect, Is Poetry a Visual Art, Ind State Univ, Terre Haute, 93. *Teaching:* Vis artist, Sch Art Inst Chicago, 88, Univ Chicago, 90; lectr, Inter-Arts at Columbia Series, Columbia Col, 89, Womens History Month, Ind Univ Northwest, Gary, 92 & Arts & Letters, Language as Image in Art, 92. *Awards:* Nat Endowment Arts Visual Arts Grants, 87 & 89; Awards, Visual Arts (AVA) 10 Fel, 90. *Bibliog:* Kathryn Hixson (auth), review, Flash Art, 1-2/94; Terry Myers (auth), Bloc: Kay Rosen, BlocNotes, 1/94; Terry Myers (auth), Painting camp, Flash Art, 11-12/94. *Mem:* Visual Arts Panel, Ind Arts Comn; Arts Midwest Focus Groups. *Publ:* Spunky International (ed), Billy Miller, New York, 92; The Progressive Corporation Annual Report (91), The Progressive Corp, Mayfield Heights; Promotional Copy, Robin Kahn, New York, 93; L'Endroit Ideal (Ideal Place) Un Livre Eric Troncy (book), Nice, France, 93; Bcoming Apart, Du, Zurich, Switz. *Mailing Add:* 6925 Indian Boundary Gary IN 46403

ROSENBAUM, ALLEN
MUSEUM DIRECTOR
b New York, NY, 37. *Study:* Queens Col, City New York, BA, 58; Inst Fine Arts, New York Univ, MA, 62. *Pos:* Lectr, Educ Dept, Metrop Mus Art, 64-69, sr lectr, 71-72; asst dir, Shickman Gallery; asst dir, Art Mus, Princeton Univ, 74-, dir, 80-98; vis committee, Meadows Mus, SMU, Dallas; vis committee dept of the art, Africa, Oceania and the Americas, Metropolitan Mus Art; Board Godwin Ternbach Mus, Queens College, City of New York; consultant, Henry & Rose Pearlman Foundation, New York, NY. *Teaching:* Instr, Sch Gen Studies, Queens Col, City Univ New York, 61; instr, Sch Fine Arts, Univ Calif, Irvine, 72; lectr, Nat Gallery of London, 2000 & Metrop Mus Art, NY, 2001. *Awards:* Fulbright Fel Hist Art, Rome, 62-63. *Mem:* Asn Art Mus Dirs. *Publ:* Auth, Titian and Giotto in Padua, Marsyas, Studies Hist Art, Vol 8, 66-67; Old Master Paintings from the Collection of Baron Thyssen Bornemisza, Int Exhibs Found, Washington, 79; The museum program vis-a-vis the art department & other disciplines, In: Museum in Academe II, Vassar Col Art Gallery, 4/8/88; Peter Jay Sharp, In: The Peter Jay Sharp Collection (exhib catalog), Sotheby's, New York, 94. *Mailing Add:* 205 E 78th St Apt 10C New York NY 10021

ROSENBAUM, EVELYN ELLER See Eller, Evelyn Eller Rosenbaum

ROSENBAUM, JOAN H
MUSEUM DIRECTOR
b Hartford, Conn. *Study:* Hartford Col Women, AA; Boston Univ, BA; Hunter Col(art hist); Jewish Theological Seminary Am, Dr, 93. *Hon Degrees:* Jewish Theological Scm Am, D Hebrw Letters, 93. *Pos:* Cur asst, Mus Modern Art, NY, 66-72; dept head, Mus Prog, NY State Coun Arts, 73-79; trustee, Artist Space, NY, 82-; consult, Michael Washburn & Assocs, 79-80, Am Asn Mus, Mus Assessment Prog, 79-; dir, Jewish Mus, NY, 81-. *Awards:* European travel grantee, Int Coun Mus, 72; Achievement Award, E Manhattan Chamber Com, 89; Distinguished Alumni Award, Boston, Mass, 94; Diploma, Chevalier Order Arts & Letters, 99. *Mem:* Asn Art Mus Dirs; Coun Am Jewish Mus; Am Asn Mus; ICOM; Art Table. *Res:* History of Jewish museums in America and Europe. *Publ:* Introd, Treasures of the Jewish Museum (catalog), Universal, 26; numerous catalog introductions. *Mailing Add:* c/o The Jewish Mus 1109 Fifth Ave New York NY 10128

ROSENBERG, ALEX JACOB
CURATOR, CONSULTANT, APPRAISER
b New York, NY, May 25, 19. *Study:* Philadelphia Mus Art; Albright Col, Philadelphia Univ, BS, 48; Instituto De Arte Superior, ScD (art), 2003. *Hon Degrees:* HLD, Hofstra Univ, 1989. *Collection Arranged:* An American Portrait 1776-1976 Traveling Exhib (original print & multiple sculpture portfolio; ed, catalog), 76-77; Marc Tobey Retrospective, 77 & 81; James Coignard Traveling Exhib, 82-83; Henry Moore (Mother & Child, co-cur & assoc ed, catalog), Mus Traveling Exhib, 87-88; co-cur, The Prints of Romare Bearden, co-ed catalog, Mus Traveling Exhib, 92-96; Henry Moore Traveling retrospective, Havana, Cuba & 4 other Latin American Venues, 97-99; Alex & Carole Rosenberg Coll, Freedman Gallery, Albright Coll, Reading, PA. *Pos:* Publ & ed-in-chief, Transworld Art Corp, NY, 69-88; dir & bd mem, Artist's Rights Today Inc, 76-86; dir, Alex Rosenberg Gallery, NY, 77-88; assoc dir, Snug Harbor Cult Ctr, 83-88; dir, Ardmore Affiliates Ltd, 85-; trustee, Mus Borough Brooklyn, 86-88; Abbott Group, 87-89; Neikrug-Rosenberg Assoc Inc, 89-90; adv comt mem, Hofstra Mus, 89-93; trustee, Philadelphia Col Textiles & Sci, 91-95; dir, Tel Aviv Mus Art, 2001; adj asst prof, NY Univ, 95-2000; chair, Salvador Dali Research Center, NYC, 2006. *Teaching:* Lectr, New Sch Social Res, Parsons Div, 79-88; Appraising Modern Art, NY Univ, 92-95, Adjunct Asst Prof & Business of Appraising, 93-; Vis Prof, Advan Inst Arts, Havana, Cuba, 93-. *Awards:* Alex Rosenberg Gallery-Hofstra Univ, 95; Repub Cuba-Order of Cult, 95; Graham J Littlewood Award, Philadelphia Col Textiles & Sci, 96; Honorary fel Tel Aviv Mus Art, 2002; Bronze Circle mem, Alex & Carole Rosenberg Studio, Albright Col; Service Diploma, Nat Mus Fine Art, Havana, Cuba; Lifetime Achievement Award, Nat Arts Club, 2004. *Mem:* Asn Artist Run Galleries (bd dir, 79-83); Fine Arts Publ Asn (vpres & dir, formerly); Fine Arts Publ Asn (pres, 84-86); sr mem Am Soc Appraisers (bd examiners, 87-); Cert Mem, Appraisers Asn Am (vpres, 92-94, pres, 94-96); Nat Arts Club, 1990-. *Specialty:* Modern art. *Publ:* Ed, The 12 Tribes of Isreal--Dali, 73, The Prophets--R Rubin, 73, Homage to Tobey, 74, Our Unfinished Revolution--Calder, 76 & An American Portrait 1776-1976, 76, Transworld Art; The Art, Science and Business of Appraising, 2000; and others. *Mailing Add:* Alex Rosenberg Fine Art and Appraisers 3 E 69th St New York NY 10021

ROSENBERG, BERNARD
PUBLISHER, BOOK DEALER
b New York, NY, Aug 2, 38. *Study:* City Col of New York, cert advert. *Pos:* Owner, Olana Gallery. *Res:* American art; decorative art; libr bldg consult. *Publ:* Auth, Olana's Guide to American Artists, A Contribution Toward a Bibliography, Olana Gallery, 2/78, supplement, vol 2, 80. *Mailing Add:* 2 Carillon Rd Brewster NY 10509

ROSENBERG, CAROLE HALSBAND
ART DEALER, ADMINISTRATOR
b New York, NY, Nov 16, 36. *Study:* Hunter Col, Brooklyn Col, BA; Yeshiva Univ; New York Univ. *Exhib:* Women Beyond Borders, Havana, Cuba. *Collection Arranged:* An American Portrait 1776-1976; Mark Tobey Retrospective (ed, catalogue), 77 & Yaacov Agam (ed, catalogue), 77; Belkys Ayon, Mass Col Art. *Pos:* vp, Alex Rosenberg Fine Art. *Awards:* Spec Prize for Publ, Seventh Int Triennial of Colored Graphic Prints, Grenchen, Switz, 76; Lotus Medal of Merit. *Bibliog:* Metaphor/Commentaires: Artists from Cuba, forward. *Mem:* Nat Arts Club; Women's City Club; Lotos Club (art comt, mem found); Art Table; Am Friends Ludwig Found Cuba (pres). *Specialty:* contemporary, modern, Cuban art. *Collection:* contemporary, modern, Cuban art. *Mailing Add:* 3 E 69th St New York NY 10021

ROSENBERG, CHARLES MICHAEL
HISTORIAN, EDUCATOR
b Chicago, Ill, Aug 3, 45. *Study:* Swarthmore Col, Pa, BA, 67; Univ Mich, Ann Arbor, MA, 69, PhD, 74. *Teaching:* Asst prof renaissance art, State Univ NY, Brockport, 74-80; Prof renaissance art, Univ Notre Dame, 80-. *Awards:* Fel, Harvard Ctr, 85-86; Rome Prize, NEH, 2000-01. *Mem:* Renaissance Soc Am; Centro di Studi Europa delle Corti; Italian Art Soc. *Res:* Renaissance patronage; portraiture. *Publ:* Auth, Courtly decorations and the decorum of interior space, 82, Raphael and the Florentine Istoria, 86 & Borsian imagery in the heavenly zone in the Sala dei Mesi, 89; Fifteenth Century North Italian Painting & Drawing: Bibliography, GK Hall, 86; Four Este Monuments and Urban Development in Renaissance Ferrara, Cambridge Univ Press, 97. *Mailing Add:* 410 Manitou Pl South Bend IN 46616

ROSENBERG, HERB
SCULPTOR, DESIGNER
b New York, NY, Feb 4, 42. *Study:* Ecole Des Beaux Arts, Paris, 63; State Univ NY, Binghamton, BA, 64; Pratt Inst, MFA, 67; Hertfordshire Col Art & Design, Eng, PhD, 92. *Work:* Zimmerli Mus, New Brunswick, NJ; Robeson Archives, NY; Inst Expressive Arts, Goteborg, Sweden; Seybold Sculputre Garden, Malibu, Calif. *Comn:* Landscape fountain, Mosbacher Inc, Paris, France, 85; plynth neon, Mobil Oil Corp, NY, 88; Holocaust Memorial, Hollis Hills Temple, NY, 89; interior lobby, JCS Designs, NY, 90; 40' Millenium Sculpture (stainless), NJ City Univ, 98. *Exhib:* Retrospective, Jersey City State Col; Light & Illusion, State Mus, Trenton, NJ, 85, Sculpture Soc, Sydney, Australia, 90, Acad Fine Arts, Beijing, China, 90 & Gallerie des Acts UNESCO, Paris, 91; Salone d'Automne, Paris, 85; New Sweden Invitational, Fine Arts Palace, Stockholm, 88; Art Int Invitational, World Expo '88, Brisbane, Australia; MAC 2000, Paris, 92; and others. *Pos:* Cur, Fine Arts Collection, Jersey City State Col, 85-; exec dir, Heights Artist Asn, 88; juror, Hong Kong Mus Biennial, 92-94; bd dir, Centre Bres d'Or Hurley Found, currently. *Teaching:* Lectr design, Drexel Inst Design, 69-71; instr photog, Baruch Col, NY, 75-78; prof sculpture, NJ State Univ, 71-. *Awards:* Design research, Jersey City Col, 86-89; Grant, Canada Coun, 88; Award, Essex Cty Arts Coun, 88. *Bibliog:* Walter Zabinski (auth), Imogene Coca by Herb Rosenberg, Newsweek, 84; Eric Bersh (auth), Light and Illusion, Video Press Packs, 86; CBC Mainstreet, 92. *Mem:* Int Sculpture Ctr; Am Art Therapy Asn; Australian Sculpture Soc; Centre Bras d'Or Cult Ctr. *Media:* Stainless Steel, Bronze; Wood, Glass. *Res:* perceptions in Russian/Hertfudshire church. *Interests:* Environ installations. *Collection:* Barbara Eliren & PJ Sey Bald. *Publ:* Auth, Drawing within a drawing, Am Art Therapy Asn, 80. *Dealer:* 14 Sculptors Gallery New York NY; Viridian Gallery 24 W 57th St New York NY 10019. *Mailing Add:* 408 Ogden Ave Jersey City NJ 07307

ROSENBERG, JANE
ILLUSTRATOR, PAINTER
b New York, NY, Dec 7, 49. *Study:* Beaver Col, with Jack Davis, BFA, 71; New York Univ, with Sol Lewitt, MFA, 73. *Work:* Amerada Hess, NY. *Comn:* Scenes of the Operas (notecard ser), Metrop Opera Guild, NY, 86. *Exhib:* Review, Preview, Judith Christian Gallery, NY, 81; Invitational Show, 55 Mercer Gallery, NY, 82; The Original Art: Celebrating the Fine Art of Children's Book Illustration, Master Eagle Gallery, NY, 85-86; The Art of the Fairy Tale, Every Picture Tells A Story Gallery, Los Angeles, 91; Jane Rosenberg-Theatreworks, Summerlin Libr & Performing Arts Ctr, Las Vegas, 95. *Bibliog:* Tessa Rose Chester (auth), Children's Literature, London Times, 4/11/86; San Francisco Chronicle, Bk Rev, 12/3/89; Deirdre Donahue (auth), Tune in to classical music, USA Today, 12/5/94. *Mem:* Soc of Children's Books Writers and Illustrators. *Media:* Childrens Books; Watercolor, Gouache. *Specialty:* Children's book illustration. *Publ:* Auth & illusr, Dance Me a Story: Twelve Tales from the Classic Ballets, Thames & Hudson, 85; Sing Me a Story: The Metropolitan Opera's Book of Opera Stories for Children, 89; Play Me a Story: A Child's Introduction to Classical Music Through Stories and Poems, Alfred A Knopf, Inc, 94. *Dealer:* Every Picture Tells A Story: A Gallery of Original Art from Children's Books 1318 Montana Ave Santa Monica CA 90403. *Mailing Add:* 2925 Nichols Canyon Rd Los Angeles CA 90046

ROSENBERG, MARILYN R
PAINTER, PRINTMAKER
b Philadelphia, Pa. *Study:* Empire State Col, State Univ NY, BA(studio art), 78; New York Univ, MA, 93. *Work:* Ohio State Univ Libr; King St Stephen Mus, Hungary; Tate Gallery Libr, England; Chelsea Sch of Art Libr, England; Canberra Sch Art Libr, Australia; Harvard Univ, Yale Univ, Ind Univ, Brown Univ, Georgetown Univ, Getty Rsch inst for History of Art and Humanities, Calif; London Col Printing; NY Pub Libr; Oberlin Col Libr, Ohio; Mus Fine Arts, Boston. *Exhib:* Color-Copier Aesthetic in Artist Books, Libr Mus Mod Art, NY, 94-95; Spring Garden, Mus Arts Nebr, Kearney, 95; Reinventing the Emblem (with catalog), Yale Univ Art Gallery Sculpture Hall, New Haven, Conn, 95; Paper, Art & the Book, Ctr Bk Arts, NY, 96; Women Artists Series 25th Ann Exhib, Douglas Libr & Mason Gross Sch Arts Galleries, Rutgers Univ, New Brunswick, NJ, 96; Women of the Book (traveling), 97-2003; Writing to Be Seen, NY Ctr for Book Arts, 2002-03; solo exhib, McHenry Co Col, Crystale Lake, Ill, 97, John Jay Col Gallery, NY, 99, Westchester Community Col Gallery, Valhalla, NY, 2002; MN Ctr for Book Acts; An Am Avant Garde, Ohio State Univ Libr, Columbus, 2002; Changing Pages (with catalog), Collins Gallery, Univ Strathclyde, Glasgow, Scotland, 98-; Printed and Bound, Peck Arts Ctr Gallery, Central Wyoming Col, Reneiton, Wyo, 2003; The Book Unbound Redux, Durango Arts Ctr, Colo, 2004; New Editions., O'Hanlon Ctr Arts, Mill Valley, Calif, 2005; The Artist and the Book, Pelham Art Ctr, NY, 2006; and others. *Teaching:* Fac, Pratt Inst, Manhattan, (Graphic Ctr), New York, 85-86; visiting artist lectr various art insts and orgns, 85-; pvt teaching, 80-99. *Awards:* Meyer Katz Meml Award for Innovative Graphics, Harrison Coun for the Arts, 82; grant, The Writer's Ctr Offset Works, 83; grant, Internat Graphic Arts Found, 86. *Bibliog:* Jason Thompson (auth), Making Journal by Hand, Rockprot Pub, 2000; Bob Grumman and Craig Hill (coauth), Writing to Be Seen, Runaway Spoon Press & Score Pub, 2001; Ori L Saltes (auth), Fixing the World, Univ Press of New England/ Brondius Univ Press, 2003. *Mem:* Ctr for Book Arts, NYC. *Media:* Artists Books, Visual Poetry. *Publ:* Contribr (with David Cole), A Point of View, Visual Poetry: The 90's, Kaliningrad-Koenigsberg, Russia, 98; 7 Poets, 7 Poems: A Portfolio of Visual Poems, Hermetic Press, 94; auth & illusr, Xerolage No 25, Rumble-Strips, Xexoxial Eds, 94; contribr, Visuelle Poesie aus den USA Experimentelle Texte, Siegen Univ, Gesamthochschule, 95, Bibliophilos, vol IV, no 3, winter 2000, Movable Stationery "Interfolds", vol 7, no 2, May 99; Martha Hellion (ed), Artists' Books. Vol 1 pf 2. pg 184 & 201, 2003; contribr, Coner Feature, pg 2, Interfolds, Spring 2003. *Dealer:* Printed Matter 77 Wooster St New York NY 10012; Vamp and Tromp Booksellers LLC South Hall Bldg 1951 Hooper Ct Suite 105 Birmingham AL 35226-3606. *Mailing Add:* 67 Lakeview Ave W Cortland Manor NY 10567

ROSENBERG, TERRY
PAINTER, SCULPTOR
b Hartford, Conn, 54. *Study:* Miami-Dade Community Col, AA, 74; Univ Miami, Coral Gables, BFA, 76; NY State Col Ceramics, Alfred Univ, MFA, 78. *Work:* Albright-Knox Art Gallery, Buffalo; Walker Art Ctr, Minneapolis; Smart Gallery, Univ Chicago; Brooklyn Mus, NY; Nelson Atkins Mus, Kansas City; and others. *Exhib:* The UFO Show, Queens Mus, Flushing, NY, 82; Raw Edge: Ceramics of the 1980's, Everson Mus, Syracuse, NY, 83; Modern Masks, Whitney Mus Am Art, NY, 84; A Passionate Vision: Contemp Ceramics, DeCordova Mus, Lincoln, Mass, 84; Between Sci & Fiction, Sao Paulo Bienal, Brazil, 85; The Eloquent Object, Traveling Exhib, Philbrook Art Ctr, Tulsa, Mus Fine Arts, Boston & Oakland Mus, Calif, 86-; one-man show, Drawings Inside the Dance (auth, catalog), Sheldon Mem Art Gallery, Lincoln, Nebr, 95; Coral Springs Mus of Art, Coral Springs, Fla, 2002, Univ of Wyoming Art Mus, 2004, Laramie, WY; Berman Art Mus, Collegeville, PA. *Collection Arranged:* Fine Arts Mus of San Francisco, CA; Virginia Mus of Fine Arts, Richmond Addison Gallery of American Art, Andover, MA; Berkeley Art Mus, CA; Arkasas Arts Center, Little Rock. *Awards:* Award, Bemis Found, Omaha, 87; Award, NY Found Arts, 89; Nebr Arts Coun, 96. *Bibliog:* Nicholas Moufarrege (auth), Terry Rosenberg, Arts Mag, 9/82; Alan Artner (auth), Chicago Tribune, 11/26/82; Grace Glueck (auth), Terry Rosenberg, NY Times, 11/9/84; Kendall, Richard, NY Arts; Anderso, Jack, NY Times, 2001. *Media:* Mixed. *Publ:* Projections, Leonardo Mag, 96; Generatrix, Uno Editions, Univ Nebr, Omaha, 96; Inside the Dance 95 Sheldon Mem Art Gallery, Lincoln, Nebr; Hypersurface Architecture II, Ad, 99; Giguring Motion: Terry Posenberg, Smart Art Press, 2002. *Mailing Add:* 96 Grand St Apt 3F New York NY 10013-2660

ROSENBLATT, ADOLPH
PAINTER, SCULPTOR
b New Haven, Conn, 33. *Study:* Sch Design, Yale Univ, BFA, 56, with Albers, Brooks & Marca-Relli, Peterdi, Chait. *Work:* NY Times; Libr Cong, Washington; Ft Wayne Mus Art, Ind; Carlisle Mus Art, Pa; Milwaukee Art Mus, Wis. *Exhib:* One-man shows, Toledo Mus Art, Ohio, 78, Minneapolis Inst Art, 82 & Tibor de Nagy Gallery, NY, 82; Cooperstown Hall of Fame, NY, 83; Haggerty Mus Art, Marquette Univ, 96; Charles Allis Art Mus, Milwaukee, 1999 & 04; Piano Gallery, Milwaukee, 2000-01; Betty Brinn Mus, Milwaukee, 2000-; Chapman Hall, Univ Wis-Milwaukee, 2000-. *Teaching:* From assoc prof to prof, Univ Wis-Milwaukee, 66-99; prof emeritus, Univ Wis-Milwaukee, 1999-. *Awards:* Wis Arts Bd, 85-86; Res Award, Univ Wis-Milwaukee, 86; Midwest Arts Grant, 95-96. *Bibliog:* Robert Berlind (auth), Adolph Rosenblatt, Art in Am, 9-10/78; Milwaukee Journal; Milwaukee Sentinel. *Mem:* Milwaukee Artists Resource Network; Allis Art Mus; Milwaukee Art Mus; Walkers Point Ctr for Art. *Media:* Polychrome, Clay. *Publ:* Auth, Book of Lithographs, Peter Deitsch Gallery, New York, 71; producer, dir & ed, Underpass (film), 74 & Daydream Diner (film), 75. *Dealer:* www.rosenblattgallery.com. *Mailing Add:* 4211 N Maryland Ave Milwaukee WI 53211

ROSENBLATT, JAY HOWARD
FILMMAKER, VIDEO ARTIST
b Brooklyn, NY, Feb 25, 55. *Study:* State Univ NY, Buffalo, BA, 76; Univ Ore, MS, 81; San Francisco Univ, MA, 88. *Work:* Chicago Art Inst; Australian Nat Libr, Australia; Screenings Sundance Film Festival, Park City, Utah, 91, 95, 98, 99, 2000, 2001, Film Forum, NY, 97 & 2000, Carolina Film & Video Festival, 98, 99 & 2000, Los Angeles Ind Film Festival, 2000, Fla Film Festival, 2000, Phila Festival World Cinema, 98, 99 & 2000, Athens Internat Film & Video Festival, 98, 99 & 2000, Atlanta Film & Video Festival, 2000, Palm Springs Short Flm Festival, 98, 2000, Chicago Underground Film Festival, 98, 2000, Mill Valley Film Festival, 98, 99, 2000, Denver Internat Film Festival, 98, 99 & 2000, Outfest Film Festival, Los Angeles, 94 & 2000, Cinematexas, Austin, 98, 99 & 2000, UCLA/IDA Salon, 2000; internat screenings Tampere Interat Shorts Film Festival, Finland, 2000, It's All True Documentary Film Festival, Brazil, 2000, European Media Art Festival, Osnabruck, Ger, 95, 98 & 2000, Images Film Festival, 2000, Vila do Conde Internat Short Film Festival, 91, 95, 98 & 2000, Norwegian Short Film Festival, 2000, Odense Film Festival, Denmark, 98 & 2000, Voper Film Festival, Switzerland, 95, 98, Uppsala Internat Short Film Festival, 2000. *Exhib:* Retrospectives, Denver Int Film Festival, Colo, 95, Impakt Film Festival, The Neth, 96, San Francisco Cinematheque, Calif, 97, British Short Film Festival, 98, Sao Paulo Int Short Film Festival, Mus Image & Sound, 98, Brussels Film Mus, Belg, 98; One person shows European Tour of Paris, Brussels & 5 cities in The Neth, 98, Sao Paulo Int Short Film Festival, Brazil, 98, Brit Short Film Festival, London, 98, Northwest Film Ctr, Portland Art Mus, 98, Mus Modern Art, NY, 99, Film Forum, NY, 2000. *Pos:* Bd mem, Ann Arbor Film Festival, 98-. *Teaching:* Instr film, San Francisco State Univ, 89; vis artist, San Francisco Art Inst, 93; instr, Univ Calif, Santa Cruz, 92; asst prof, Col San Mateo, 92-; instr grad

documentary filmmaking, Stanford Univ, Palo Alto, 99-2000; instr beginning film and video, Calif Coll Arts & Crafts, Oakland; guest filmmaker, Sch Art Inst Chgo, 96, Stanford Univ, 95, 98; San Francisco Art Inst, 2003-06. *Awards:* Guggenheim Fel, John S Guggenheim, 98; Distinguished Doc Award, Int Doc Asn, 98; Rockefeller Fel, 99; First Prize, Viper Festival, Switzerland, 95; Best Experimental Film, Melbourne Internat Film Festival, Australia, 95, Sinking Creek Film Festival, 95, Humboldt Film & Video Festival, 98; Best Documentary, Tampere Internat Film Festival, Finland, 95, Aspen Shortsfest, 98; Grand Prize, Hamburg Internat Short Film Festival, Ger, 95; Honorable Mention, Visions du Reel Documentary Film Festival, Switzerland, 96; Best Documentary, Vila do Conde Internat Short Film Festival, Portugal, 98; Best of the Best, Charlotte Film Festival, 95; First Place Film, Athens Internat Film & Video Festival, 95; Best of Festival, Humboldt Film & Video Festival, 96; Best Short Film, Hamptons Internat Film Festival, 98; Grand Jury Price, Fla Film Festival, 98; Jury Award, Sundance Film Festival, 98; Disting Documentary Award, Internat Documentary Asn, 98; Best Editing, Ann Arbor Film Festival, 99 & 2000; Best Experimental Film, Humboldt Internat Film Festival, 2000; First Prize, Big Muddy Film Festival, 2000; Grand Prize, USA Film Festival, 2000; Artforum Best of 2000 List; Best Short Short, Aspen Shortsfest, 2001. *Bibliog:* Buried Memories: The Films of Jay Rosenblatt, cover story Releast Print, 98; The Films of Jay Rosenblatt, Christian Sci Monitor, 2000; Twenty Four Frames to the Brain, Shout, 2000; Boyx II Men, Jewish Week, 2000; Never a dull moment in Rosenblatt's shorts, NY Post, 2000; Primal Therapist, Village Voice, 2000; Lost & Found: The Philosophical Appropriations of Jay Rosenblatt, Filmmaker, 2000; The Films of Jay Rosenblatt, Time Out NY, 2000; Trivialities of Despots, Told Without A Smile, NY Times, 2000; Lost & Found: Filmmaker Jay Rosenblatt, LA Weekly, 2000; Times When Less Is More Profound, NY Times Arts & Leisure, 2000; The 10-Minute Masterpiece, cover story SF Weekly, 2000; Jay Rosenblatt's Excavations of the Psyche, cover story The Independent, 2000. *Mem:* AIVF; Internat Documentary Asn; Acad Motion Picture Arts and Sci. *Media:* Film. *Publ:* Contribr, Blood Test (film), 85, Paris X 2 (film), 88, Short of Breath (film), 90, The Smell of Burning Ants (film), 94 & Human Remains (film), 98; co-dir (with Jennifer Frame) A Pregnant Moment, 99, (with Dina Ciraulo) Drop, 99, (with Caveh Zahedi) Worm, 2001; Restricted, 99, King of the Jews, 2000, Nine Lives (The Eternal Moment of Now), 2001, Prayer, 2002, Friend Good, 2003, I Used To Be a Filmmaker, 2003, I Like It A Lot, 2004, Phantom Limb, 2005, I'm Charlie Chaplin, 2005, Afraid So, 2006, I Just Wanted To Be Somebody, 2006; appearances on Sundance Channel, 2000, NY & Co with Leonard LOpate, WNYC Radio, 2000, Peter Bochan Show, WBAI Radio, 2000, Independent View, KQED TV, 2000. *Mailing Add:* 4159 20th St San Francisco CA 94114-2824

ROSENBLATT, SUZANNE MARIS
PAINTER, WRITER
b Hackensack, NJ, 37. *Study:* Cent Sch Arts & Crafts, London, 57-58; Oberlin Col, Ohio, BA, 59; Cooper Union, 60; Art Students League, 61-63. *Work:* City Ctr, Libr Performing Art, Guggenheim Mus, Mus Mod Art, Artists Books Collections, NY. *Comn:* Courtroom drawings, WISN-TV, Milwaukee, 73-77 & Milwaukee's Pub TV, 74. *Exhib:* One-woman shows, Oshkosh Pub Mus, Wis, 72, New York City Ctr Gallery, 76 & others; Ft Wayne Mus Art, Ind, 76; Performing Arts Ctr, Milwaukee, 76-87; Long Island Univ, Brooklyn, NY, 80; Gallery Wis Art, 92; Piano Gallery, Milwaukee, 2000-01; Charles Allis Art Mus, Milwaukee, Wis, 2004. *Teaching:* Artreach, 1989-98. *Awards:* Hon Mention, Media Am, Seattle, Wash, 75; Artreach Teaching Grants, Junior League, 89 & 94, Milwaukee Found, 90, Bader Found, 93 & Poets & Writers, 94; Taparts Grant, 94. *Bibliog:* Donald Key (auth), Show of painted people shadowed by circus, Milwaukee J, 71; Edith Brin (auth), Milwaukee J, 91; Harvey Taylor (auth), Shepherd Express, 91. *Mem:* Milwaukee Artists Resource Network; Wis Painters & Sculptors; Milwaukee Earth Poets; Grass Roots. *Media:* Acrylic, Ink. *Interests:* Tai chi; environmental causes; dance; gardening. *Publ:* Producer, dir & ed, Animated film paintings & drawings of dancers, 76; auth, Memorandance, Marcel Dekker, 78; Changes in the Lake, 82; Some Poems, 87; Shorelines, Gallery of Wis Art, 91; illus in On the Waterbed They Sank To Their Own Levels, Carnegie Mellon, 2000. *Dealer:* www.rosenblattgallery.com. *Mailing Add:* 4211 N Maryland Ave Milwaukee WI 53211

ROSENBLUM, ELIZABETH
PAINTER
b Manhattan, NY, 54. *Study:* Barnard Col Columbia Univ, New York, 72-77; Tufts Univ, Medford, Mass, BFA, 80; Boston Mus Fine Arts, dipl, 81, Fifth Yr Cert, 82. *Work:* DeCordova Mus & Sculpture Park & Rose Art Mus, Brandeis Univ, Lincoln, Mass; Fed Reserve Bank Boston, Mass; Fuller Mus Art, Brockton, Mass; Gen Electric, Conn. *Exhib:* Solo shows, Lillian Immig Gallery, Emmanuel Col, Boston, Mass, 90, Akin Gallery, Boston, Mass, 90, Bunting Inst Radcliffe Col, 92 & Gallery NAGA, Boston, Mass, 92 & 93; Gallery NAGA, Boston, Mass, 92 & 94; 249 A Street, The 10th Anniversary, Fed Reserve Bank of Boston Gallery, 93; Rooms with Views: Body, Nature, Cult, Politics, Newton Arts Ctr, Newtonville, Mass, 94; Sex Blind, Gallery 28, Boston, Mass, 94; Rose Art Mus, Brandeis Univ, Waltham, Mass, 2000; Gallery NAGA Boston, Mass, 2002; group exhib, Columbia Univ, NY, 96. *Awards:* Visual Artists Fel, Nat Endowment Arts & Humanities, 87; Fel Painting, Mass Coun Arts & Humanities, 89; Fel, Bunting Inst, Radcliffe Col, 91-92. *Bibliog:* Miles Unger (auth), Art New Eng, 12/92-1/93; Francine Koslow Miller (auth), Elizabeth Rosenblum: Gallery NAGA, Art Forum, 1/93; Eve Ensler & Stacey Schrader (eds), Childhood sexual abuse, Central Park, spring 93; and others. *Dealer:* Gallery NAGA Fine Art Inc 67 Newbury St Boston MA 02116. *Mailing Add:* 3 Sheridan Sq Apt 3L New York NY 10014

ROSENBLUM, ROBERT
HISTORIAN
b New York, NY, July 24, 27. *Study:* Queens Col, BA, Yale Univ, MA; New York Univ, PhD. *Hon Degrees:* Queens Col, PhD, 92, Oxford Univ, MA, 73. *Teaching:* Instr hist art, Univ Mich, 55-56; assoc prof hist art, Princeton Univ, 56-66; prof hist art, New York Univ, 67-. *Awards:* Frank Jewett Mather Award Art Criticism, Col Art Asn Am, 81; Fel Am Acad Arts & Sci; Chevalier de la Légion d'Honneur, 2002. *Res:* Modern art, 1760 to the present. *Publ:* The Dog in Art from Rococo to Post-Modernism, 88; The Romantic Child from Runge to Sendak, 88; Paintings in the Musee d'Orsay, 89; The Jeff Koons Handbook, 92; Andy Warhol Portraits, 93; auth, Introducing Gilbert & George, 2004. *Mailing Add:* NYU Dept Fine Arts 100 Washington Sq E 303 Main Bldg New York NY 10003

ROSENFELD, RICHARD JOEL
DEALER
b Philadelphia, Pa, May 31, 40. *Study:* Pratt Inst, New York, MFA, 64; Univ Pa, Philadelphia & Pa Acad Fine Art (coordinated prog), BFA, 62. *Pos:* Mgr, Artists Galleries, Cheltenham, Pa, 67-72; co-dir, Longman Gallery, Pa, 72-75; dir-owner, Rosenfeld Gallery, Philadelphia, Pa, 76-. *Teaching:* Instr painting & art hist, Perkiomen Sch, Pennsburg, Pa, 63-65. *Bibliog:* Susan Perloff (auth), article, Pa Gazette, 6/77. *Mem:* Fel Pa Acad Fine Arts. *Specialty:* Contemporary art, all media including crafts. *Mailing Add:* Rosenfeld Gallery 113 Arch St Philadelphia PA 19106

ROSENFELD, SAMUEL L
ART DEALER, APPRAISER
b New York, NY, July 27, 31. *Study:* Univ Pa, BS, 51; Harvard Univ, MBA, 53. *Pos:* Owner, Rosenfeld Fine Art, New York, currently. *Mem:* Appraisers Asn Am (bd dir, cert). *Specialty:* American art in the realist & modernist tradition in all media, mainly from 1910 to World War II emphasizing the WPA period, the Eight & Ash Can school. *Collection:* Modern American realists, especially WPA period; Trench art; Rogers groups; Doulton Lambeth stoneware pottery; cast iron boot jacks. *Mailing Add:* Rosenfeld Fine Art 303 E 57th St # 41G New York NY 10022-2947

ROSENFELD, SARENA
PAINTER
b Elmira, NY, Oct 17, 40. *Study:* Otis Art Inst, currently; Idylwild Sch Music & Art, currently. *Work:* Tishman Corp, Los Angeles, Calif; Ruhr Univ Bochum, Ger; South Africa Asn Arts South Transual, Johannesburg, S Africa; Univeritatlinikum Benjamin Franklin, Berlin, Ger; Gallery 444, San Francisco, Calif. *Awards:* Tapestrey in Talent, San Jose Arts Coun, 89; Best of Show, Glendale Reg Arts Coun, 95; Sweepstakes Award, Santa Monica Arts Coun, 98. *Bibliog:* Michael Colbruno (auth), Fauvism Live at Robert Dana Gallery, San Francisco Sentinel, 91; Chris Culwell (auth), Wild about Sarena, San Francisco Sentinel, 92; Patrick Lagreca (auth), On the Wall & Off the Wall, Marina Union, 98. *Mem:* Nat Mus Women in the Arts, Wash, DC. *Media:* Oils on canvas. *Interests:* volunteer, Los Angeles Zoo. *Dealer:* Gallery 444 444 Post St San Francisco CA 94102; CODA Gallery Palm Desert Calif. *Mailing Add:* 6570 Kelvin Ave Canoga Park CA 91306

ROSENFELD, SHARON
PAINTER
b New York, NY, Apr 8, 54. *Study:* Pratt Inst, BFA, 77; NY Univ, MA, 83. *Work:* Mus Nat Arts Found, NY. *Exhib:* Solo exhibs, 80 Washington Sq E Gallery, NY, 83, Mead Data Cent, Pan Am, NY, 90, Mighael Ingbar, NY, 91, Righetti Knie Fine Arts Trading, Muri-Bern, Switz, 92, Century Galleries, Henley on Thames, Eng, 92 & Gallery Galimberti, Vaduz, Liechtenstien, 92; State of the Art, Boston, 93; Art Addiction (with catalog), Stockholm, Sweden, 93; Le Livre d'or des Collectionneurs et Amatueurs d'Art, Paris, 93; Jadite Gallery, NY, 96; Martha's Vineyard, Old Sculpting Gallery, 96; Mayer, Brown & Platt, NY, 97; Sylvia White Gallery, NY, 98; and others. *Awards:* Ford Found Studio Art Award, 77; Artist in Residence Grant, Millay Colony Arts, 85. *Media:* Acrylic on Linen, Watercolor. *Publ:* Reviews, Arts Mag, 4/84; Contribr, Profile, Manhattan Arts, 6/89; Le Livre d'or des Collectioneuers et Amateurs d'Art, Paris, 93. *Dealer:* Sylvia White Gallery 560 Broadway New York NY 10012. *Mailing Add:* 16 E 96th St Apt 4B New York NY 10128

ROSENFIELD, ANDREW M
PATRON
b Chicago, Ill, Sept 20, 51. *Study:* Kenyon Col, BA(hon), 73; Harvard Univ, MA, 78; Univ Chicago, JD(cum laude), 78. *Pos:* Pres, founder, Lexecon Inc, Chicago, 77; founder, chmn, UNext, 2000-; managing partner, Gleacher & Co LLC; bd trustees, Univ Chicago, 96-; vchmn bd trustees, Art Inst Chicago. *Teaching:* adj prof, Northwestern Univ Law Sch, 85-86; lectr, in law Univ Chicago, 86-; lectr numerous law & bus seminars, currently. *Mem:* Order of Coif Clubs; Chicago, Standard (bd dir, 85-); Bar: Ill, 78. *Mailing Add:* Univ Chicago Law Sch 1111 E 60th St Chicago IL 60637

ROSENFIELD, JOHN M
EDUCATOR, CURATOR
b Dallas, Tex, Oct 9, 24. *Study:* Univ Calif, Berkeley, BA, 45; Univ Iowa, Iowa City, MFA, 49; Harvard Univ, PhD, 59. *Collection Arranged:* Japanese Art of Heian Period (auth, catalog), Asia House, New York, 67; Traditions of Japanese Art (auth, catalog), Fogg Mus, Harvard, 70; Courtly Tradition in Japanese Art & Literature (coauth, catalog), Fogg Mus, Harvard, 73; Journey of the Three Jewels (coauth, catalog), Asia House, New York, 79; Masters of Japanese Calligraphy (coauth, catalog), Japan Soc, New York, 84. *Pos:* Cur Asian art, Fogg Art Mus, Cambridge, Mass, 76-91; actg dir, Harvard Univ Art Mus, 82-85. *Teaching:* Asst prof oriental art, Univ Calif, Los Angeles, 57-60; prof E Asian art, Harvard Univ, Cambridge, Mass, 65-91, emer prof,

91-. *Awards:* Order of the Rising Son, Japan, 88; Distinguished Teaching Award, Col Art Asn, 94. *Publ:* Auth, Dynastic Arts of the Kushans, Univ Calif, 67; ed, Song of the Brush: Japanese Paintings from the Sanso Collecion, Seattle Art Mus, 79; coauth, The Japanese Courtier: Painting, Calligraphy and Poetry from the Fogg Art Mus, The Philip Hofer Collection, Santa Barbara Mus Art, 80; Masters of Japanese Calligraphy 8th-19th Century, Japan Soc, NY, 84. *Mailing Add:* Harvard Univ Dept Fine Arts Cambridge MA 02138

ROSENQUIST, MARC H
SCULPTOR
b Amityville, NY, May 5, 55. *Study:* Syracuse Univ, BFA, 79. *Work:* Newark Pub Libr, NJ; Zimmerli Mus Art, New Brunswick, NJ; NJ State Mus, Trenton; Newark Mus, NJ. *Exhib:* Newark Mus, NJ, 61; NJ Mus, Trenton, 85; Philadelphia Mus Art, Pa, 90. *Awards:* Louise Cramer Found Award, Artnew, Philadelphia Mus Art, 90; Nat Endowment Arts, 90; NJ State Coun Arts, 90. *Bibliog:* Paula Marincola (auth), Contemporary Philadelphia Artists, Philadelphia Mus Art Catalog, 4/90; Anne Levin (auth), Two Trenton residents, Gain Nat Arts Award, Trenton Times, 11/6/90; Vivien Raynor (auth), Creations by Fellowship Winners, NY Times, 7/28/91. *Media:* All. *Dealer:* Larry Becker 43 N Second St Philadelphia PA 19106. *Mailing Add:* 103 Locktown-Flemington Rd Flemington NJ 08822

ROSENSAFT, JEAN BLOCH
CURATOR, MUSEUM DIRECTOR
b New York, NY, Jan 6, 54. *Study:* Barnard Col, BA, 73; New York Univ Inst Fine Arts, 73-77. *Collection Arranged:* The Eichmann Trial, Chagall and the Bible, Justice in Jerusalem Revisited, Jewish Mus, 86, 87; David Newman, Ran Oron, Rage/Resolution, Rebirth After the Holocaust: The Bergen-Belsen Displaced Persons Camp, 45-50, Hebrew Union Col, Jewish Inst Relig, 95, 96, 97, 2000. *Pos:* Spec asst publs, Mus Mod Art, New York, 83-84; dir pub progs, Jewish Mus, New York, 84-86, asst dir educ, 86-89; exhib dir, Hebrew Union Col-Jewish Inst Relig, 94; mus dir, Hebrew Union Col, Jewish Inst Relig Mus, 2000. *Teaching:* Gallery lectr modern art, Mus Mod Art, New York, 77-80, Nat Endowment Arts lectr(collections), 79-80, spec asst independent sch prog, 80-83. *Bibliog:* Chagall & the Bible, 1987; Maty Grunberg: Selected Works, 1966-2006; Vision of Sigmund R Balka, 2006. *Mem:* Chmn, UJA Womens Task Force Arts Comt, 95; Coun Jewish Am Mus (officer, 96-2001). *Specialty:* Contemp art. *Publ:* Auth, Giorgio De Chirico, Mus Mod Art, 82; Chagall and the Bible, Universe Books, 87; ed, The Collectors Room: Selections from the Steinhardt Collection, 93, David Newman - Breaking the Tablets, 95 & Ran Oron - Planes, 96, Hebrew Union Col-Jewish Inst Relig; 30 Pieces/30 Years, Sculpture by Ann Sperry, 2003; auth, Archie Rand: The 19 Paintings, 2004. *Mailing Add:* Hebrew Union College Jewish Inst Religion 1 W 4th St New York NY 10012

ROSENTHAL, DEBORAH MALY
PAINTER, EDUCATOR
b New York, NY, Jan 16, 50. *Study:* Smith Col, with Leonard Baskin, 66-68; Barnard Col, BA, 71; Pratt Inst, with George MacNeil, MFA, 74; Queens Col, with Ilya Bolotowsky, 74. *Comn:* Stained Glass Windows, Ansche Chesed Congregation, NY. *Exhib:* Solo exhibs incl Bowery Gallery, NY, 86, 87, 91, 93, 96, 99, Eve's Vocabulary, Hebrew Union Col, NY, 99, others. *Pos:* Critic, Arts, Artforum & New York Arts J, 75-; artist & cur, Cult Coun Fedn, 78-80. *Teaching:* Guest lectr, Queens Col, Univ NH & Parsons Col, 77-; lectr, Sch Visual Arts, New York, 80-82; fac mem, New Sch Social Res, 81-; prof of art, Rider U, Lawrenceville, NJ; guest lectr Sch of the Art Inst of Chicago, Am Univ. *Awards:* Critic's Award, Nat Endowment Arts, 79-80. *Mem:* Col Art Asn; Int Asn Art Critics. *Media:* Oil. *Publ:* Auth, Metaphor in Painting, 78, auth, The lesson of the master: Paul Klee, 78, auth, Interview with Andre Masson, 80 & coauth, Zone painting, 81, Arts Mag; auth, Ilya Bolotowsky, Harry N Abrams, 82. *Dealer:* Bowery Gallery New York NY. *Mailing Add:* 250 W 85th St No 5D New York NY 10024

ROSENTHAL, DONALD A
HISTORIAN, CRITIC
b Jersey City, NJ, Oct 7, 42. *Study:* Yale Univ, BA(magna cum laude); Princeton Univ; Hunter Col, MA; Columbia Univ, MPhil, PhD. *Collection Arranged:* Charlotte Dorrance Wright Collection, Philadelphia Mus Art, 78, George Eastman Collection, Mem Art Gallery, Rochester, 79; Monet in London, High Mus Art, Atlanta, 88; Thomas Cornell: Paintings, Bowdoin Col Mus Art, 90; Latin American Colonial Art from the Mabee-Gerrer Museum, Chapel Art Ctr, 94; Carl Barnas 1879-1953; Crossing Continents, Chapel Art Ctr, 2000. *Pos:* Res asst, Metrop Mus Art, New York, 74-77; asst cur Europ painting, Philadelphia Mus Art, 77-79; cur collections, Mem Art Gallery, Rochester, NY, 79-85; chief cur & cur europ art, High Mus Art, Atlanta, 86-89; assoc dir, Bowdoin Col Mus Art, 89-91; dir, Chapel Art Ctr, St Anselm Col, Manchester, NH, 91-2001; critic, Art New England, Boston, 2001-. *Mem:* Col Art Asn; Int Coun Mus. *Res:* European art of the 18th & 19th centuries; history of photography. *Publ:* Géricault's Expenses for The Raft of the Medusa, Art Bull, 80; Orientalism: The Near East in French Painting, 1800-1880, 82 & La Grande Manière: Historical and Religious Painting in France, 1700-1800, 87, Rochester. *Mailing Add:* 2050 Massachusetts Ave #306 Cambridge MA 02140

ROSENTHAL, EARL EDGAR
EDUCATOR, HISTORIAN
b Milwaukee, Wis, 21. *Study:* Univ Wis, Milwaukee, BA, 43; New York Univ, PhD, 53. *Hon Degrees:* Univ Granada, Spain, PhD (hon), 94. *Pos:* Asst dir, Milwaukee Art Inst & Layton Art Gallery, 52-53. *Teaching:* Prof hist art, Univ Chicago, 54-91, emer prof, 91-. *Awards:* Order of Merit, King of Spain, 6/89; Cultural History Prize, Junta De Andaluca, 95. *Mem:* Col Art Asn Am; Soc Archit Historians (dir, 57-58 & 59-60); Am Soc Hispanic Art Hist Studies; Hispanic Soc Am; corresp mem Acad San Fernando, Madrid; Honor the Acad Artes de Bellas de Granada, 99; Santa Barbara Sculpture Guild, 98-. *Media:* Clay, Pastel. *Res:* Renaissance archit and sculpture in Italy and Spain. *Interests:* Sculpture in Clay, Portraits and human figures, painting in pastel and water color. *Publ:* Auth, The Cathedral of Granada, 61 & The Palace of Charles V in Granada, 85 & 88, Princeton Univ Press; Michelangelo's Moses, Art Bulletin, XLVI, 64; Die Reichskrone, In: Jahrbuch der Kunsthistorischen Sammlungen in Wien, 71; Invention of columnar device of Charles V, J Warburg Inst, 73; transl of El Palacio de Carlos V en Granada, Alianza, Madrid, 88, Arquitectura Imperial, Granada, 88, La Catedral De Granada, Granada, 90 & The Uniqueness of the Renaissance in Spain, Gazette Des Beaux-Arts, 12/93; De Egas Al Siloe, La Sante Catedral, Granada, 2005. *Mailing Add:* 203 Hitchcock Way Apt 214 Santa Barbara CA 93105-4078

ROSENTHAL, HOWARD
SCULPTOR
b Mar 4, 48. *Study:* RI Sch Design, Providence, BFA, 69; Pratt Inst, Brooklyn, NY, MFA, 80. *Comn:* Outdoor sculpture, Crosby Gardens, Toledo, Ohio, 89-90; outdoor sculpture, Snug Harbor Cult Ctr, Staten Island, NY, 91. *Exhib:* Solo shows, 22 Wooster Gallery, NY, 86, Intersection Arts, San Francisco, Calif, 86, White Gallery, Tokyo, Japan, 89 & Ihara Ludens Gallery, NY, 90; Pratt Inst, Brooklyn, NY, 91; Cleveland State Univ, Ohio, 91; Int Contemp Art Fair, Yokohama, Japan, 92. *Teaching:* Lects & presentations, var col, mus & univ, 84-91; asst prof art, Conn Col, New London, 84-87 & 88-89; vis instr New Forms, Grad Sch Art & Design, Pratt Inst, Brooklyn, NY, 91-92; vis instr sculpture, Barnard Col, Columbia Univ, New York, 92. *Awards:* Grant, Corp Pub Broadcasting, 85; Nat Endowment Arts Fel, 90. *Bibliog:* Amy Sparks (auth), Unreal vistas, Cleveland Ed, 4/25/91; Gretchen Faust (auth), New York in review, Arts Mag, 11/91; Jennifer Dunning (auth), A collaboration in individuality, NY Times, 1/3/92. *Mailing Add:* 65 Spring St Apt 9 New York NY 10012

ROSENTHAL, JOHN W
PHOTOGRAPHER, PUBLISHER
b Munich, Ger, Mar 25, 28; US citizen. *Study:* Univ of Chicago, BA(liberal arts). *Pos:* Commercial photogr, Koopman-Neumer, Chicago, Ill, 55-65; owner-dir, Rosenthal Art Slides, Chicago, 60-95. *Teaching:* Helped photograph the collections & taught photogrs at the Art Inst of Chicago & Mus of Contemp Art, 70-77. *Bibliog:* Norine Cashman, Slide Buyer's Guide, Libr Unlimited, 90. *Media:* Slides. *Specialty:* Extensive collection 36,000 of high quality slides pertaining to art and art history. *Publ:* Auth, Rosenthal Art Slides, The 90's Catalog, Part I: Painting and Sculpture, Part II: Architecture & Decorative Arts

ROSENTHAL, MARK L
CURATOR, HISTORIAN
b Philadelphia, Pa, Aug 9, 45. *Study:* Temple Univ, AB, 63; Univ Iowa, MA, 71, PhD, 79. *Collection Arranged:* Andre, Buren, Irwin, Nordman: Space as Support (auth, catalog), 79; Franz Marc (auth, catalog), 79; Neil Jenney (auth, catalog), 81; Juan Gris (auth, catalog), 83-84; Jonathan Borofsky (auth, catalog), 84-85; Anselm Kiefer (auth, catalog), 87-88; Joseph Johns (auth, catalog), 88-89. *Pos:* Assoc cur, Wadsworth Atheneum, Hartford, Conn, 74-76; cur collections, Univ Art Mus, Berkeley, Calif, 76-83; cur 20th century art, Philadelphia Mus Art, Pa, 83-, Nat Gallery Art, Washington, DC & Solomon R Guggenheim Mus, NY, 97-; cur, 20th century art, Nat Gallery Art, Washington, DC; cur, 20th century art, Solomon R Guggenheim Mus, NY, currently. *Mem:* Col Art Asn. *Res:* Various topics in twentieth century art. *Publ:* Auth, Paul Klee, Phillips Collection, 81; The prototypical triangle of Paul Klee, 82 & Picasso's night fishing at Antibes, 83, Art Bulletin; auth, Picasso's night fishing at Antibes, Art Bulletin, 83. *Mailing Add:* c/o Solomon R Guggenheim Mus 1071 5th Ave New York NY 10128

ROSENTHAL, RACHEL
PERFORMANCE ARTIST
b Paris, France, Nov 9, 26; US citizen. *Study:* New Sch Soc Res, New York; Sorbonne, Paris; also with Hans Hoffmann, Karl Knaths, William S Hayter, John Mason, Merce Cunningham & Erwin Piscator. *Hon Degrees:* Art Inst Chicago, hon dr. *Work:* Los Angeles Pub Libr, Calif. *Comn:* KabbaLAmobile, Mus Contemp Art & Mark Taper Forum, Los Angeles, 84; Los Angeles Festivals, 87 & 90; filename: FUTURFAX, Whitney Mus, 92; Zone, UCLA Ctr Performing Arts, 94. *Exhib:* Soldier of Fortune, Art Inst Chicago, 81; KabbaLAmobile, Mus Contemp Art, Los Angeles, 84; Was Black, John Anson Ford Theatre, Los Angeles, 86; Rachels Brain, Los Angeles Festival & throughout US & Europe, 87-89; Pangaean Dreams, 90; Amazonia, 90-91; Timepiece, Calif State Univ, Los Angeles, 96; UR-BOOR, Los Angeles Theatre Ctr, 2000; and others. *Collection Arranged:* Jon & Lillian Lovelace, Bob Rauseneuberg, LA Pub Libr. *Pos:* Dir, Instant Theatre, Los Angeles, 74-76; founding mem bd dir, Womanspace, Los Angeles, 72-74, co-chmn, 73-74; founding mem, Double X, Los Angeles, 74-76; dir, Espace DBD, Los Angeles, 80-83; exec dir, The Rachel Rosenthal Co, Los Angeles, Calif, 89-. *Teaching:* Performance, Claremont Grad Sch, Calif, 79, Otis/Parsons Inst Design, Los Angeles, 80-81, Espace DBD, Los Angeles, 81-96 & Univ Calif, Irvine, 82; vis artist, Univ Colo, Boulder, 83 & Calif State Univ, Long Beach, 81-83, New York Univ & Univ Calif, Los Angeles; workshop residency, Galerie 101, Ottawa, 89; performance lect, San Francisco Art Inst, 90; Art Gaia Art, Univ Calif, Santa Barbara, 91; performance, CSU Summer Arts, Humbolt State Univ, Calif, 91-94; Chaos, Movement Res Inc, New York, 92 & 94; Who Needs Artists, Carnegie Mellon Univ, Pittsburgh, Pa, 92; Omega Inst, NY, 95 & 96; Calif State Univ, Los Angeles, 96-99. *Awards:* OBIE Award, Village Voice, 89; Solo Performance Fel, Nat Endowment Arts, 90, 93 & 94; J Paul Getty Trust Fund for Visual Arts, 95-; Living Cult Treasure Fel, City of Los Angeles Cult Affairs Dept, 2000; Merrit Award, Asn Performing Arts Presenters, 2001. *Bibliog:* Jan Breslauer

(auth), Inside the Rosenthal zone, Los Angeles Times, 2/6/94; 50 ways to be a feminist, MS Mag, 7/94; Rachel Rosenthal (mongr), John Hopkins Univ Press, 97. *Mem:* Int Asn Art Critics; New Mus Contemp Art (adv bd); Mus Contemp Art; Santa Monica Mus Art. *Media:* Theatre; Artist books; Painting. *Interests:* Animal rights. *Publ:* Filename: Futurfax (audio cassette), New Am Radio, 91; Animal human hybrid images in the Western World, American writing, A Mag, 94-95; Tatti Wattles, A Love Story, Smart Art Press, 96; Pangaean Dreams, Word Plays 6, John Hopkins Univ Press, 96; Rachel's Brain and Other Storms, Continum Press, UK, 2001. *Mailing Add:* 2847 S Robertson Blvd Los Angeles CA 90034

ROSENTHAL, SEYMOUR
PAINTER, LITHOGRAPHER
b Bronx, 21. *Study:* Self taught. *Work:* Metrop Mus Art, City NY Mus, NY; IBEW Arch; Technion Bldg, Haifa, Israel; Santa Barbara Mus Art, Calif; Harry S Truman Libr, Independence, Mo; NY Pub Libr; Forty-two (42) original Lithos in NY Metro Mus Art; Yale Univ, New Haven, Conn; Pres Richard Nixon Libr; Smithsonian Nat Musof Am Art, Wash; Theodore Herzel Inst, 515 Park Ave, NY City, 64. *Comn:* Drawings of children, NY Bd Educ, 57; painting of Moses, borough pres off, Queens, NY, 62; Pfizer Pharmaceutical; Pfizer, Parke Davis. *Exhib:* one-man shows, Community Church, 35th St & Park Ave, New York City, 67, Suffolk Mus, 68, ACA Gallery, NY, 69, Daruma Gallery, Cedarhurst, NY, 91 & Educ & Cul Fund Elect Indus, Flushing, NY, 92; Art Dealers Choice Exhib, 67; Indianapolis Mus Art, 72; Creative Journey into an Artist's Mind, Am Jewish Congress House, NY, 90; Mus of the Suffolk; Jewish Community Ctr, Comack, NY, 2000 & 05; Temple Beth Shalom, 2000. *Awards:* Saint Gaudens Medal for Fine Draughtsmanship; Citation of Honor from the Benjamin Rosenthal Chap of Am Jewish Congress, 92. *Bibliog:* Edwin Newman (commentator), Today Show, NBC TV, 70; Life & Works of Seymour Rosenthal, ABC TV, 10/82; Live at Five, NBC TV, 4/1/88; Chauney Howell (commentator), TV Cable New York One, 10/19-10/23/94; Views, ABC TV channel 7, 10/22/94. *Mem:* Artists Equity Asn; Comt Arts & Lit in Jewish Life; Jewish Fedn Philanthropies; United Jewish Appeal. *Media:* Watercolor, Oil; OriginalLithographs. *Collection:* Paul Robeson, Edward G Robinson, Huntington Hartford, Prime Minister of Isreal Golda Meir, Isaac Stern, Leonard Bernstein, Harry Van Arsdale Jr, Pete Seeger, Nathan Cummings. *Publ:* Illusr, Parke Davis Med J, & Scope, 56; contribr, Commonwheel, Vol 90, No 15; The World of Seymour Rosenthal, 76; illustr, Jewish calendars, various supermarkets, US, 94-98, 99, 2000. *Dealer:* SKM Inc 6431 Inkster Rd Ste 118 Bloomfield Hills MI 48301-1311; ACA Gallery 529 W 20th St New York NY 10011

ROSENTHAL, STEPHEN
PAINTER
b Richmond, Va, May 28, 35. *Study:* Art Students League, with Edwin Dickinson; Tyler Sch Fine Arts, Philadelphia, with Boris Blai, BFA, 60. *Work:* Arts Club Chicago; Yale Univ Art Gallery, New Haven, Conn; Art Fund, NY; Metrop Mus of Art, NY. *Exhib:* Am Acad Arts & Lett, NY, 63; Amon Carter Mus, Ft Worth, Tex, 64; Int Watercolor Biennial, Brooklyn Mus, NY, 65; Herron Inst, Indianapolis, Ind, 67; Pa Acad Fine Arts Biennial Exhib, Philadelphia, 67; John Gibson Gallery, New York, NY, 87; Steven Rosenberg Gallery, New York, NY, 87; one-man shows, Eric Stark Gallery, NY, 91 & Gallerie Wasserman, Munich, Ger, 92. *Pos:* Bk reviewer, Arts Mag, New York, 71-72. *Teaching:* Instr design, Cooper Union, New York, 66-67; lectr painting, Univ NC, Greensboro, 71-72; vis instr, Parsons Sch of Design, 86-. *Awards:* Mason Lord Prize, Baltimore Mus Art, 67. *Bibliog:* Raymond Charmet (auth), Un jeune Americain, Arts Mag, 66; Leach Levy (auth), The drawn line in painting, Parker St 470, 71. *Media:* Tempera. *Mailing Add:* 39 Bond St New York NY 10012

ROSENTHAL, TONY (BERNARD)
SCULPTOR
b Highland Park, Ill, Aug 9, 1914. *Study:* Univ Mich, BFA, 36; Cranbrook Acad Art; Hofstra Univ, Hon, doctorate, 1989. *Work:* Guggenheim Mus, Mus Mod Art, Whitney Mus Am Art, NY; Israel Mus, Jerusalem; Albright-Knox Art Gallery, Buffalo. *Comn:* Cube, Alamo, NY, 66; large cube, Univ Mich, Ann Arbor, 68; bronze disk, Rondo, NY Pub Libr, 69; Indiana totem, Ind Univ Art Mus, Bloomington, Ind, 71; Police Plaza Sculpture, NY, 74. *Exhib:* Nine Whitney Mus Am Art Ann, 53-72; Recent Sculpture USA, Mus Mod Art, 59; one-man shows, Catherine Viviano, NY, 50-60, Kootz Gallery, NY, 60-66; Knoedler & Co, NY, 66-77; Denise Rene, Paris, 88; Maxwell Davidson, NY, 89. *Awards:* Outstanding Achievement Award, Univ Mich, 67; First Prize, Iron & Steel Inst, 75; Sculpture Award, Am Inst Arts & Letts, 89. *Bibliog:* Gibson Danes (auth), Bernard Rosenthal, Art Int, 68; Sam Hunter (auth), Rosenthal: Sculptures, 68; Edward Albee (auth), Reacting to Rosenthal, Decade, 79. *Mem:* Nat Acad of Design (assoc, 92, acad, 94). *Dealer:* Andre Emmerich Sculpture Farm Pawling NY

ROSENZWEIG, DAPHNE LANGE
HISTORIAN, MUSEUM CONSULTANT
b Evanston, Ill, July 7, 41. *Study:* Mt Holyoke Col, AB; Columbia Univ, MA & PhD; Univ Wis; Corcoran Sch Art; Fulbright Fel, Nat Palace Mus, Taiwan. *Collection Arranged:* Art of the Orient: Eighth Century to the Present, Univ NMex, 72; Fine Arts Group Collection of Later Chinese Painting (with catalog), 94; Yangtze River Collection of Later Chinese Jade (with catalog), 95; Power and Pride in Later Korean Painting, 96. *Pos:* Owner, Rosenzweig Assoc (personal property appraisals); Bd mem, vis collections committee, Mus Japanese Art. *Teaching:* Lectr Oriental art, Univ NMex, Albuquerque, 69-73; asst prof Oriental art, Oberlin Col, 73-77; asst prof, Univ SFla, 78-94; from inst to prof Art hist, Ringling School Art Design, 92-. *Awards:* Fulbright Fel, Repub China, 67-69; Columbia Univ Grant, 69; Mary E Wooley Fel, 70. *Mem:* Soc Study Chinese Relig; Int Chinese Snuff Bottle Soc; Asn Asian Studies; Am Oriental Soc (Fel); China Inst; Fla Token Kai; Col Art Asn. *Res:* Painting the Wing Dynasty of China, with emphasis on court painting and modern Chinese jades; Japanese prints, Korean painting. *Collection:* Chinese paintings, Oriental ceramics; modern Japanese prints. *Publ:* Reassessment of Painters and Paintings at the Early Ch'ing Court, Artists and Patrons: Some Social and Economic Aspects of Chinese Painting, Univ Wash Press, 89; auth, A Chinese Chronology & Appraisal of Chinese Jade, Jade, Anness Publ & Nostrand-Reinhold, 92; coauth, Collection of the Museum of Fine Arts, St Petersburg, Fla, 93; auth, The Paintings of Cheng Haw-chien, Taipei, 94; Appraisal of Japanese Prints (3rd edition). *Mailing Add:* Ringling School of Art & Design 2700 N Tamiami Tr Sarasota FL 34234

ROSENZWEIG, PHYLLIS D
CURATOR
b Brooklyn, NY, Dec 27, 43. *Study:* Hunter Col, City Univ New York, BA, 64; Inst Fine Arts, New York, MA, 95. *Collection Arranged:* The Thomas Eakins Collection (auth, catalog), Hirshhorn Mus & Sculpture Garden, Smithsonian Inst, Washington, 77, Arshile Gorky: The Hirshhorn Museum & Sculpture Garden Collection, 79; The Fifties: Aspects of Painting in New York, 80; Larry Rivers, The Hirshhorn Mus and Sculpture Garden Collection, 81; Directions 83 & 86; Content: A Contemporary Focus, 84; Sol Lewitt Works, 87; Directions: Sherrie Levine, 88; Krzysztof Wodiczko Works, 88; Daniel Buren Works, 89; Directions, Susana Solano, 89; Lawrence Weiner Works, 90; Thomas Struth: Museum Photographs, 92; Joseph Kosuth Works, 92; Glenn Ligon: To Disembark, 93; Cindy Sherman: Film Stills, 95; Byron Kim: Grey-Green, 96; Kiki Smith:Night, 97; Directions: Dana Hoey, 2001; Directions Marina Abramovic-The Hero, 2002; Directions: Gabriel Oruzco-Photographs, 2004. *Pos:* Curatorial asst, Hirshhorn Mus & Sculpture Garden, 71-76, assoc cur, 76-00; curator, works on paper, 2000-. *Mem:* Col Art Asn. *Res:* contemp and modern prints, drawings, and photos. *Mailing Add:* Hirshhorn Mus & Sculpture Garden Smithsonian Inst MRC 350 PO Box 37012 Washington DC 20013-7012

ROSER, CE (CECILIA)
PAINTER, VIDEO ARTIST
b Philadelphia, Pa. *Study:* Berlin Fine Arts Acad, 52-53. *Work:* Guggenheim Mus, NY; Mus Mod Art, NY; Brooklyn Mus, NY; Nat Mus Art, Washington, DC; The Brit Mus, London, Great Britain; Newark Mus Art, NJ; Bibilotheque Nat, Paris, France; and others. *Exhib:* Int Watercolor Biennial, Brooklyn Mus, 63; Women Choose Women, NY Cult Ctr, 73; Works on Paper/Women Artists, Brooklyn Mus, 75; Art & Poetry, Tweed Mus Art, Duluth, Minn, 77; New Acquisitions, Guggenheim Mus, 82; Am Abstr Artists, Bronx Mus, 86; New Spaces/New Faces, East Hampton Guild Hall Mus, 87; Int traveling show Tikanoja, Rovaniemi & Josensuu Art Mus, Finland, 88; plus many others. *Pos:* Producer & pres, Artists Video Arch, New York, 77-. *Bibliog:* Rosemary Daniell (auth), Elegant explosions East and West mingle in Roser act, Atlanta Constitution, Ga, 7/5/67; Lane Dunlop (auth), article, 9/77 & Joan Marter (auth), article, 2/80, Arts Mag; plus others. *Mem:* Founder Women in the Arts (first exec-coordr, 74-76, bd mem at large, 76-78); Women's Caucus for Art; Am Abstr Artists. *Media:* Oil, Watercolor; Collage. *Dealer:* Ingber Gallery 415 West Broadway New York NY 10012. *Mailing Add:* 355 Riverside Dr New York NY 10025

ROSKILL, MARK WENTWORTH
HISTORIAN, CRITIC
b London, Eng, Nov 10, 33. *Study:* Trinity Col, Cambridge, BA, 56, MA, 61; Harvard Univ, MA, 57; Courtauld Inst, Univ London, 57; Princeton Univ, MFA & PhD, 61. *Teaching:* Instr & asst, Princeton Univ, 59-61; from instr to asst prof, Harvard Univ, 61-68; assoc prof, Univ Mass, Amherst, 68-72, prof, 72-. *Awards:* Am Coun Learned Socs Fel, 65-66 & 74-75. *Mem:* Col Art Asn Am. *Res:* Nineteenth & twentieth century art; criticism; history of photography; methodology of art history. *Publ:* Contribr, Atlantic Brief Lives, 71; auth, What is Art History, 76 & 89; The Interpretation of Cubism, 85; Interpretation of Pictures, 89; Klee, Kandinsky and the Thought of their Time: A Critical Perspective, 92; The Languages of Landscape, 96. *Mailing Add:* Univ of Mass Dept of Art Amherst MA 01003

ROSLER, MARTHA (ROSE)
ARTIST, WRITER
b Brooklyn, NY, July 29, 43. *Study:* Brooklyn Mus Art Sch; Brooklyn Col, BA; Univ Calif, San Diego, MFA. *Work:* Canada Coun, Ottawa; Arts Coun Great Britain, London; Whitney Mus Am Art; Inst Valencia Arte, Moderna, Spain; Neue Galerie, Graz, Austria. *Exhib:* Information, Disaster, Document, San Francisco Mus Mod Art (inaugural exhib); one-person shows, Long Beach Mus Art, Calif, 77, Whitney Mus Am Art, NY, 77, Installation Gallery, San Diego, 86, Dia Art Found, 89, Palais des Beaus Arts, Brussels, 94, Contemp Arts Ctr, Cincinnati, 94, CEPA Gallery, Buffalo, 99; Whitney Mus Am Art Biennial, 79, 83, 87 & 89; Video of the Seventies--The Greatest Hits, Inst Contemp Art, Boston & traveling, 83; New Am Video Art: A Historical Survey, Whitney Mus Am Art, NY, 84; Difference: On Representation & Sexuality, 84 & The Art of Memory, the Loss of History, 85, New Mus of Contemp Art, NY; The Arts for Television, Stedelijk Mus, Amsterdam & Mus Contemp Art, Los Angeles, traveling, 87-88; The First Generation: Women & Video 1970-1975, ICI traveling, 93-95; War Works, Victoria & Albert Mus, London, 94-95; retrospectives, London, Vienna & Geneva, currently. *Teaching:* Instr, San Diego State Univ, 75-76 & Univ Calif San Diego, 75-78; instr photog, Orange Coast Col, Costa Mesa, 77-79; instr film, photog & media, Univ Calif, Irvine, 78-79; vis prof art, Simon Fraser Univ, Vancouver, 80, NY Univ & Cooper Union; asst prof, Rutgers Univ, 80-85, assoc prof, 85-90, prof, 90-, dir grad studies, 92-95; studio instr, Whitney Independent Study Prog; vis assoc prof, Univ Calif, San Diego, 86; vis lectr, Univ Capetown, 90; prof, visual arts, Rutger Univ, NJ. *Awards:* Line Artist's Book Grant, 83; NY Found Arts Fel, 85; Women Photogr's Catalogue Grant, NY Found Arts, 96. *Bibliog:* Craig Owens (auth), The Discourse of Others: Feminism & Postmodernism, The Anti-aesthetic, 83; Brian Wallace (auth), Living Room, Art in Am, 92; Laura

Cottingham (auth), Crossing Borders, Frieze, 11/93. *Mem:* Assoc Independent Video & Film; Col Art Asn; Media Alliance. *Media:* Images & Texts. *Res:* Relationships between representations and power in daily life and in the public sphere. *Publ:* Auth, Service: A triology on colonization, New-Found Career, 78; Martha Rosler: Three Works, NS Col Art & Design Press, 81; Lookers, buyers, dealers, and makers: Thoughts on audience, Art After Modernism, New York, 85; Shedding the Utopian Moment (video), Block, 86; Born to be Sold: Martha Rosler Reads the Strange Case of Baby M (video), 88. *Dealer:* CEPA Gallery 617 Main St Suite 201 Market Arcade Complex Buffalo NY 14203-1400. *Mailing Add:* 143 McGuinness Blvd Brooklyn NY 11222

ROSS, CHARLES
ENVIRONMENTAL ARTIST, SCULPTOR
b Philadelphia, Pa, Dec 17, 37. *Study:* Univ Calif, AB, 60, MA, 62. *Work:* Whitney Mus Am Art; French Ministry of Culture; Indianapolis Mus Art; Walker Art Ctr, Minneapolis; Los Angeles Co Mus Art, Calif; Lannan Found, Mus NMex; Frederick A Weisman Mus, Minneapolis, Minn; French Min of Culture; plus numerous others; Nat Mus Am Indian, Smithsonian Instution, others. *Comn:* Dwan Light Sanctuary, United World Col, Montezuma, NMex; Cook Inst, Grand Rapids, Mich; Plaza of the Americas, Dallas; Solar Spectrum, Harvard Bus Sch Chapel; Year of Solar Burns, Chateau D'Oiron, France; Saitama Univ, Japan; US Fed Courthouse, Tampa, Fla; Meiji Univ, Tokyo; Nat Mus Am Indians. *Exhib:* Renwick Gallery, Smithsonian, Washington, DC; Stadtizches Mus, W Ger; Centre Georges Pompidou, Paris, 77; Albright Knox, Buffalo; Hirshhorn Mus, Washington, DC; Mus Contemp Art, Chicago; Yale Univ Art Gallery; Stadtisches Mus, WGer; Mus Fine Arts, Boston; solo shows, Richard Humphrey Gallery, NY, 95 & Mus d'Arte y Diseno Contemporaneo, San Jose, Costa Rica, 1996; NTT Intercomm Ctr, Tokyo, 97; Lyon Biennal, Lyon, France, 2000. *Teaching:* Assoc prof, Cornell Univ, 64; instr, Univ Calif, 65, Sch Visual Arts, New York, 67, 70 & 71 & Herbert Lehman Col, 68; adj prof, Col Santa Fe, NMex, 94-2000. *Awards:* Am Inst Graphic Arts Award, 1976; Boston Soc Architects, 92; Interfaith Forum Relig Art & Archit, 92; NCAA Award Distinction, 97; Washington Bldg Cong Award, Spectrum 8, Nat Mus Am Indian (NMAI), 2005. *Bibliog:* Giles Tiberghein (auth), Land Art, C Eds, Carre, Paris, 93, Princeton Archit Press, 95; Baile Oaks (auth), Sculpting with the Environment, Int Thomson Publ Inc, London, pages 46-55, 95; Jan Adlmann, Contemporary New Mexico Artists: Sketches & Schemas, Craftsman House, Australia, 96; Patrick Werkner (auth), Star Axis, Diadelos, 6/15/93; Harold Linton (auth), Color in Architecture, McGraw-Hill, 99; Anne-Marie Charbonneaux and Norbert Hillaire (eds), Architectures de Luriere, Marvel, 2000. *Publ:* Auth, Sunlight Convergence-Solar Burn, Univ Utah Press, 76; Charles Ross: The Cosmos, Architecture, 5/84; Sculpting the Environment-A Natural Dialogue, Van Nostrand & Rienhold, 94. *Dealer:* Loic Malle 167 Blvd Haussmann Paris France 75008. *Mailing Add:* 383 W Broadway New York NY 10012

ROSS, CONRAD H
PAINTER, PRINTMAKER
b Chicago, Ill, Apr 26, 31. *Study:* Univ Ill, BFA, 53; Univ Chicago, 54; Univ Iowa, MFA, 59; Masereel Ctr Graphic Arts, Kasterlee, Belgium, 87, 92 & 95. *Work:* Libr Cong, Washington; Springfield Art Mus, Mo; Norfolk Mus Arts & Sci, Va; Dallas Mus Fine Arts, Tex; Macon Mus Arts & Sci, Ga. *Exhib:* one-man show, Augusta Col, Ga, 79, Univ Ctr Gallery, Huntsville, Ala, 96, Malone Univ, Troy, Ala, 98 & Jacksonville State Univ, Ala, 99; Southeastern Graphics Invitational, 81; Art Dept Gallery, Jacksonville State Univ, Ala, 85; Exhib US-UK Print Connection, An Int Exchange, Los Angeles Printmakers Soc & Printmakers Coun of Great Brit, 88-89; Artsplosure, Raleigh, NC, 89; Artist Selects, Comer Art Mus, Sylacauga, Ala, 89; Through the Yrs, Drawing, Painting, Prints, Chattahoochee Valley Art Mus, LaGrange, Ga, 2003. *Pos:* Bd dir, Southeastern Col Art Conf, 79-82; publ, Wycross Press, 89-. *Teaching:* Instr drawing, design, lettering & art appreciation, La Polytech Inst, 61-63; asst prof drawing & printmaking, Auburn Univ, 63-81, assoc prof, 81-83, prof, 83-97, emer prof art, 97-; vis lectr drawing & printmaking, Kans Univ, 68; instr, Arrowmont Sch Arts & Crafts, Gatlinburg, Tenn, 83; artist-in-residence, Univ Ga Summer Abroad Prog, Cortona, Italy, 84. *Awards:* Louis Comfort Tiffany Found Grant printmaking, 60; Auburn Univ Res Grant-in-Aid, 65-68, 70 & 73; Purchase Award, LaGrange Nat II, Prints and Drawings, Ga, 75; Tech Asst Grant, Ala State Arts Coun, 97; 35th Ann Montgomery Art Guild Mus Exhib Award, Montgomery Mus Fine Arts, 2003; Best of Show, Tenn Valley Art Asn Exhib South, 2005. *Bibliog:* Stevens Seaberg (auth), The Daemons Face: An Artists Discovery of the Metaphors of Child Abuse, Vol 28, Leonardo; Noble Press, Vol XXII No 4, The Print Collectors Newsletter, 9-10/91; The China Collés, Vol 22 issue No 1, Auburn Circle, winter 96; Jason Nix (auth), Fine Print, Opelika, Auburn News, 9/04; Wycross Press, The Jour of the Mid Am Print Coun, Vol 11, 1, Spring/Summer, 2005; Wellbeing., Jour of the Print World, page 15, Spring, 2005. *Mem:* Ala Art League (pres, 78-80); Southeastern Graphics Coun (vpres, 78-80); Col Art Asn Am. *Media:* Oil, Intaglio. *Publ:* Contribr, Artists' proof the annual of prints and printmaking, 70; The monoprint and the monotype: a case of semantics, Art Voices/South, 78/79; Approaches to Drawing: Activity in the Southeast, SECAC Rev, 81. *Mailing Add:* 447 Wrights Mill Rd Auburn AL 36830-5914

ROSS, DAVID ANTHONY
MUSEUM DIRECTOR
b New York, NY, Apr 26, 49. *Study:* Syracuse Univ, BS, 71. *Collection Arranged:* Traveling exhib, Circuit: A Video Invitational (survey of video art, 68-72), 72-74; Southland Video Anthology (survey of video art in Southern Calif, 68-75, with catalog), Long Beach Mus Art, 75 & 77; Richard Avedon: Retrospective, Univ Art Mus, Berkeley, 80; Inst Contemp Art, Boston, 82-84 & 86; The BiNational: American and German Art of the Late 80's, Inst Contemp Art, Boston & Kunsthalle, Dusseldorf, 89-98; Between Spring and Summer: Soviet Conceptual Art in the Era of Late Communism (traveling exhib), Inst Contemp Art, Boston, Tacoma Art Mus, Wash & Des Moines Arts Ctr, Iowa, 90; William Wegman, Kunstmuseum Lucerne & Whitney Mus Am Art, 91-92; Multiple Identity (traveling exhib), Whitney Mus Am Art, NY, Nat Gallery, Athens, Greece, Contemp Art Mus, Barcelona, Spain, Kunst Mus, Bonn, Ger & Costello de Rivoli, Turin, 96-97; Bill Viola: a 25 Year Survey (traveling), Whitney Mus Am Art, New York, 98-99; Diebenkorn, San Francisco Mus Modern Art, Calif, 98-99. *Pos:* Asst dir, Everson Mus Art, Syracuse, 71-72, cur video arts, 71-74; deputy dir TV & film, Long Beach Mus Art, 74-77; chief cur, Univ Art Mus, Univ Calif, Berkeley, 77-81; dir, Sam Rayburn House, Bonham, Tex, fomerly, Boston Inst Contep Art, 82-91, Whitney Mus Am Art, NY, 91-98 & San Francisco Mus Mod Art, 98-. *Teaching:* Lectr video performance, San Francisco Art Inst, 70-82; lectr video art, Grad Sch, Univ Calif, San Diego, 74-82; lectr, Calif Col Arts and Crafts, 82, Harvard Univ, 83-91 & Sch Art, Columbia Univ, NY, 97-98. *Awards:* John D Rockefeller III Found Res Study Grant, 74. *Mem:* Am Asn Mus; Advocates for Arts; Am Asn Mus Dirs; Trustee, Tiffany Found, NY. *Res:* Relationship between development of new art and context that supports art in American society and development of new support structures. *Publ:* Coauth, Douglas Davis: Videotapes, Manifestos, Drawings and Objects, 72; Frank Gillette: Video Process & Metaprocess, 73; Nam June Paik: Video & Videology, 74; Peter Campus: Video Works, 74; auth, Southland Video Anthology, 75 & 76-77. *Mailing Add:* San Francisco Mus Modern Art 151 Third St San Francisco CA 94103-3159

ROSS, DOUGLAS ALLAN
SCULPTOR, INSTRUCTOR
b Los Angeles, Calif, Jan 23, 37. *Study:* Carleton Col, BA, 59; Minneapolis Col Art & Design, 59-61; Univ Minn, MFA, 65. *Work:* Northrup Gallery, Univ Minn, Minneapolis; Ill State Univ, Normal; Sheldon Art Gallery, Lincoln, Nebr; Prudential-Bache Securities, NY; McDonalds Corp, Chicago, Ill. *Exhib:* Okla State Univ, Stillwater, 88; 20th Ann Joslyn Biennial, Joslyn Art Mus, Omaha, Nebr, 88; Central Time Zone Sculpture Exhib, Nebr Weslyan Univ, Lincoln, 89; 6th Ann Exhib, Kansas City Artists Coalition, Mo, 89; 60th Ann Exhib, Art Asn Harrisburg, Pa, 89; 12th Ann Art Exhib, Milford Fine Arts Coun, Conn, 89; Chicago Int New Art Forms, Navy Pier, Chicago, 89; Sculpture Now, Spokane Ctr Gallery, Wash, 89; solo exhibs, Drury Col, Springfield, Mo, 90, Eastern Mont Col, Billings, 90, MC Gallery, Minneapolis, Minn, 90 & Ralston Fine Arts, Johnson City, Tenn, 91. *Collection Arranged:* First Great Plains sculpture Exhib, Sheldon Mem Art Gallery, Lincoln, Nebr, 75; Drawings by Sculptors, SW Mo State Univ, 75 & Syracuse Univ, NY, 76; Second Ann Great Plains Sculpture Exhib, Sheldon Mem Art Gallery, 76; Nebr Alumni, Nebr Mus Fine Arts, 76. *Teaching:* From asst prof to assoc prof sculpture/drawing, Univ Nebr, Lincoln, 66-79, prof, formerly; lectr grade II sculpture, Manchester Polytech, Eng, 69-70. *Awards:* Juror's Award, NJ Ctr Arts, 90; First Prize, Greater Midwest Int III, Warrensburg, Mo, 90; Purchase Award, One-man Show, Muhlenberg Col, 76. *Mem:* Mid-Am Col Art Asn (prog dir & exhib dir, 75-76). *Media:* Mixed. *Dealer:* MC Gallery Minneapolis MN. *Mailing Add:* Univ Neb 207 Woods Art Bldg Lincoln NE 68588-0144

ROSS, JAIME
GRAPHIC ARTIST, PAINTER
b New Haven, Conn, Aug 14, 46. *Study:* Princeton Univ; Univ Colo, BA, 69, MFA, 71, studied with Roland Reiss and George Woodman. *Work:* Oslo Fine Arts Mus, Norway; Alvord Mus Fine Art, Portugal; Univ Colo, Boulder; Los Angeles Inst Contemp Art. *Comn:* Billboard, ABC Records, Los Angeles, 76; mural, Fiat, Milan, 78; distributional sculpture, Alvord Inst, Oporto, Portugal, 84; mural, Santa Fe Pub Schs, 85 & NMex Arts Comn, Ojo Caliente, NMex, 86. *Exhib:* Wit and Whimsey, Cambridge Mus Fine Arts, Eng, 77; Small Wonders, Univ BC, Vancouver, 81; Contemp Cartoons, Lisbon Fine Arts Mus, Portugal, 84; Western States Biennial, Fine Arts Mus NMex, Santa Fe, 82; Color, Oslo Fine Arts Mus, Norway, 83. *Pos:* Artist-in-residence, NMex Arts Comn, 85-86; painter, designer & illusr for various ad agencies, animation studios & mags, Los Angeles, 76-78. *Teaching:* Instr painting & drawing, Univ Ill, 71-72; instr painting, Univ Colo, 75. *Media:* All. *Dealer:* Ed Thomas Fine Art Taos NM; El Zocalo Santa Fe NM. *Mailing Add:* Catchwater Farm PO Box 44 Carson NM 87517

ROSS, JAMES MATTHEW AKIBA
ASSEMBLAGE ARTIST, PHOTOGRAPHER
b Ann Arbor, Mich, Sept 8, 31. *Study:* Univ Mich, AB, 51; Cranbrook Acad Art, MFA(painting), 60; Rockham Sch Grad Studies, Ann Arbor; Acad Belle Arti, Rome. *Work:* Butler Inst Am Art; Cranbrook Mus Art; Wustum Mus, Racine, Wis; Madison Art Ctr, Wis; Detroit Inst Art. *Exhib:* Detroit Inst Art & Pa Acad Fine Arts, 59-60; Walker Art Ctr, 59-60; Wis Painters & Sculptors Ann, Milwaukee Art Ctr, 63-65; 100 Yrs of Navajo Weaving, Univ Wis-Platteville, 91; Uncommon Thread, West Bend Mus Art, Wis, 94; In a Modern Vernacular Navajo Textile, Chicago Cult Ctr, 95; and others. *Teaching:* Asst prof art, Univ Wis-Platteville, 62-80, assoc prof fine arts, 80-90. *Awards:* Fulbright Grant Painting to Italy, 60 & 61; Prizes, Wis Painters & Sculptors, 63 & Mich Fine Arts Exhib, 64; Individual Artist Fel, Wis Arts Bd, 92-93. *Bibliog:* Surface Appearances: The Painted Photograph, Kohler Art Ctr (pending). *Mem:* Col Art Asn Am; Wis Painters & Sculptors Soc; Am Asn Univ Prof. *Mailing Add:* 310 High St Mineral Point WI 53565-1219

ROSS, JANICE KOENIG
PAINTER
b Harrisburg, Pa, 26. *Study:* Pa State Univ, BA, 47; Univ Ill, MFA, 54; Fulbright-Hays seminar, Pakistan, summer 86. *Work:* Mr & Mrs Harper; Beauregard Family; Family Portrait; Conversation, Sarah & Emily, Birthday, & many others. *Comn:* portraits Auburn Univ Col Vet Med. *Exhib:* Solo exhibs, Ga Inst Technol Student Ctr Gallery, 80 & Chattahoochee Valley Art Asn Gallery, 83; The Human Figure, Arts Festival of Atlanta, 89; Hearthstones I, Space One Eleven, Birmingham, Ala, 91; Patchwork of

Many Lives, Huntsville Mus Art, 92; Montgomery Mus Fine Arts, 93; Red Clay Survey, Huntsville Mus Art, 98; Albany Arts Gallery, Calif, 2000; (with Conrad Ross), Through the Yrs, Chattahoochee Valley Art Mus, LaGrange, Ga, 03. *Pos:* Artist-in-residence, Art Studios Abroad Prog, Univ Ga, 84; founder, Studio 218, Auburn, Al, 1980. *Teaching:* Prof art, Tuskegee Univ, Ala, 68-91. *Awards:* Nat Endowment Humanities Fel, 81-82; Fulbright-Hays Fel, Pakistan, 86; Residency, Hambidge Ctr, Rabun Gap, Ga, 97, 2000. *Bibliog:* Susan Hood (auth), Through the years, Auburn Univ, Montgomery, 2003; John M. Williams (auth), Art papers, 1/89 & 2/89. *Mem:* Col Art Asn; Women's Caucus Art (nat adv bd, 88-91); Southeastern Women's Caucus Art (mem secy-treas, 78-80); and others. *Media:* Oil, Pastel. *Specialty:* Alabama Artists. *Collection:* Alabama Power Co, Auburn Univ, Montgomery Al; Craig & Goulden Architects, Greenville, SC; Intertape Systems, Inc., Winston-Salem, NC; & many private collections. *Publ:* Co-Auth, MFA Survey, Col Art Asn, fall 78; Eight from Auburn, Art Voices South, 1-2/80; Agnes Bradley Taugner profile, Artcraft, 2-3/80. *Dealer:* Rattling Gourd Gallery 6214 Stage Rd PO Box 69 Loachapoka AL 36865. *Mailing Add:* 447 Wrights's Mill Rd Auburn AL 36830

ROSS, JOAN M
PAINTER, INSTRUCTOR

b Brooklyn, NY, Apr 23, 31. *Study:* St Joseph's Col, Brooklyn, NY, BA, 53; St Elizabeth's Col, Convent Station, NJ(continuing educ), 80-84; studied with Betty Lou Schlemm, Robert Laessig & Robert Wade, art Workshops 84-85. *Work:* Lakeland State Bank, Sparta, NJ, 91; Sussex Co Libr, Vernon, NJ, 93; Permanent Collection, US Coast Guard; Operation Smile HQ, Va, 96; Intrawest-Mountain Creek, Vernon, NJ, 2000. *Comn:* Watercolor-landscapes, J Kane, Hygrade Corp, Philadelphia, Pa, 80; watercolor-landscapes, comn by Dr & Mrs William R Magee, Norfolk, Va, 94-96; watercolor-landscapes, comn by Senator & Mrs Robert E Littell, Franklin, NJ, 91 & 95; Dr & Mrs Joseph D'Onofrio, Sparta, NJ, 93, 95 & 97; Mr & Mrs Samuel Lewin Highland Lakes NJ, 02-04; Mr & Mrs Steve Oroho, 2006. *Exhib:* NE Watercolor Soc, Hall Fame Mus, Goshen, NY, 76-98; Salmagundi Club Ann, NY, 85-05; Am Artists Prof League, Grand Nat, Salmagundi, NY, 86-02; NJ Watercolor Soc, Monmouth Mus, 95-04; Hudson Valley Art Asn, Hastings on Hudson, 91-04; NJ Watercolor Soc, Monmouth Mus, 91 04; Morris Mus, 01-02. *Pos:* Treas, vpres & chmn adv bd, Sussex Co Arts Coun, 77-98; pres, Vernon Township Cult Soc, 80-82; pres, Northeast Watercolor Soc, 86-94; vpres, NJ Watercolor Soc, 99-2000, pres, 04-06. *Teaching:* Chmn & vprincipal dept art & sci, Immaculate Conception Regional Sch, 68-90; instr art & watercolor workshops, demonstr art groups, NY, NJ & Pa, 90-06; Official US Coast Guard Artist, 90-06. *Awards:* John Pike Mem Award, Northeast Watercolor Soc, 91 & 92; Ogden Pleissner Mem Award, Salmagundi Club Ann, 96-04; Helen G Ohler Mem Award, 97 & Claude Parson Mem Award, 99, Am Artists Prof League; Award of Excellence, RI Watercolor Soc, 2000; Award of Excellence, Northeast Watercolor Soc, 2002; Award of Excellence, NJ Water Color Soc, 2004; Presidents Award, Am Artist Prof League, 2005; David H. Wright Award & Best of Show, Skylands Juried Exhib, 2005; Essex Watercolor Club Award of Merit, 2006. *Bibliog:* Mark Fitzgibbon (auth), Immortalizing Vernon, Vernon News, 3/86; Jim Cordes Beacon (auth), Recording a vanishing scene, NJ Herald, 8/86; Maura Rossi (auth), Beauty around her, The Beacon, Paterson, NJ, 86; Beth Ambrose Vernon Artist, NJ Herald, 02, 04 & 06; and others. *Mem:* Am Artist Prof League; Salmagundi Club; Essex Watercolor Club; Hudson Valley Art Asn; Northeast Watercolor Soc (vpres, 83-86 & 93-94, pres, 86-88); NJ Watercolor Soc (pres); NJ Am Artists Prof League; Ecology Committee, Highland Lakes, NJ (chm). *Media:* Watercolor, Oil. *Dealer:* Port of Call Warwick NY; Artery Gallery Milford PA; Cardinal Art Gallery Vernon NJ. *Mailing Add:* 1181 Lakeside Dr E Highland Lakes NJ 07422

ROSS, JOAN STUART
PAINTER, PRINTMAKER

b Boston, Mass, Sept 21, 42. *Study:* Conn Col, with R Lukosius & W McCloy BA, 64; Yale Univ, with J Albers, G Peterdi & Sillman, 65; Univ Iowa, with M Lasansky & E Ludins, MA, 67, MFA, 68. *Work:* Seattle City Light Collection; Oregon Arts Found, Salem; Seattle Art Mus; Sea First Bank; King Co Harborview Hosp. *Comn:* Environ sculpture, Seattle Arts Comn & Nat Endowment Arts, Seattle, 76; five woodcut prints, King Co Arts Comn, 78-79; 7 mixed-media panels, King Co Archit Div, 80; painting, Seafirst Bank, Seattle, 86; King Co Justice Ctr, 97. *Exhib:* Original Ed, traveling exhib, Oregon Arts Found, 78; 31st Spokane Ann Exhib, Cheney-Cowles Mem Mus, 79; Rutgers Nat Drawing, Rutgers Univ Mus, 79; New Ideas IV, Seattle Art Mus, 81; Northwest Now, Tacoma Art Mus, 86; Focus: Seattle, San Jose Art Mus, 86; NW Monotypes, Seattle Art Mus, 89; Betty Bowen Mem Exhib, Seattle Art Mus; Familie-Portrait Exhib, Norway, Nordic Heritage Mus, Vesterheim Mus, 1999-2000; Univ Puget Sound, Tacoma Wash, 2005. *Pos:* Mem, Seattle Arts Comn, 81-85; chair, Art in Pub Places Comn, 83-85; Bumbershoot Festival Comn, 85-91. *Teaching:* Instr printmaking & drawing, Seattle Pac Univ 68-88; instr printmaking, Factory Visual Art, 74-76; instr drawing, Green River Community Col, 78; instr drawing, Univ Wash, 88-91; instr drawing, Edmonds Community Col, 92-96; instr art, monotype & painting, N Seattle Community Col, 96-. *Awards:* Gaiser Award, Cheney-Cowles Mem Mus, 79; Betty Bowen Award, Seattle Art Mus, 81; Rome Fel, Northwest Inst Archit & Urban Studies in Italy, 93. *Bibliog:* L. Allan, Contemp Printmaking in NW, 97; M. Kangas, Family Portrait Seattle Times, 2000; Doc, Artists Express, SCC-TV. *Mem:* Northwest Print Coun (charter mem); Seattle Bk Arts Guild; founding mem Seattle Print Arts. *Media:* Acrylic, Mixed Media, Encaustic, Oil. *Interests:* Published poet, member, Village Idioms, Seattle. *Publ:* Backbone: Seven Northwest Poets, 77 & Talk and Contact, 78, Seal Press; Fifty Northwest Artists, Chronicle Books, 83; two covers, Copper Canyon Press, 86-89; Bumbershoot Arts Festival, poster, 92; NW Originals, Matrimedia Press, 1992; Contemporary Printmaking in the Northwest, 96. *Dealer:* Seattle Art Museum Rental & Sales Gallery; Patricia Cameron Gallery Seattle. *Mailing Add:* 4102 Second Ave NW Seattle WA 98107

ROSS, JOHN T
PRINTMAKER, EDUCATOR

b New York, NY, Sept 25, 21. *Study:* Cooper Union Art Sch, with Morris Kantor & Will Barnet, BFA; New Sch Social Res, with Antonio Frasconi & Louis Schanker; Columbia Univ, 53. *Work:* Libr Cong, Hirshhorn Mus & Nat Collection Fine Arts, Washington; Metrop Mus Art, & Whitney Mus, NY; Brit Libr, Victoria & Albert Mus, London; NY Pub Libr; Smithsonian Inst. *Comn:* Ed prints, Hilton Hotel, 63, Asn Am Artists, 64, 66 & 72, Philadelphia Print Club, 67, NY State Coun Arts, 67 & Int Poetry Forum, 68. *Exhib:* Second Int Color Print Exhib, Grenchen, Switz, 61; Int Biennale Gravure, Cracow, Poland, 68; Prize-winning Am Prints, Pratt Graphic Art Ctr, NY, 68; Nat Acad Fine Arts, Amsterdam, The Neth, 68; Biennial Print Exhib, Calif State Col, Long Beach, 69; and others. *Pos:* Coun, Ctr Book Arts, currently; pres, US Comt-Int Asn Art, 67-69; chmn, dept art Manhattanville Col, Purchase, NY, 1964-86. *Teaching:* Instr printmaking, New Sch Social Res, 57- & Pratt Graphics Ctr, 63-; prof art, emer, Manhattanville Col, 64-; demonstr & lectr, US Info Agency Exhib, Romania & Yugoslavia, 64-66. *Awards:* Louis Comfort Tiffany Found Grant Printmaking, 54; citation for prof achievement, Cooper Union Art Sch, 66; B W Clinedinst Award Artists Fel, 91; McDowell Colony Fel, 1978, 82, 87. *Bibliog:* Articles, Am Artist, 52-81, Artists Proof, 64 & Art in Am, 65; auth, F Geierhaas, The Creative Act, Int Print Soc, 84. *Mem:* Soc Am Graphic Artists (pres, 61-65, exec coun, 65-); Nat Acad Design (assoc, 70, acad, 83); Ctr Book Arts, NY; Philadelphia Print Club; Grolier Club, NY. *Media:* Prints, Artists Books. *Publ:* coauth, The Complete Printmaker, 72 & 90 & The Complete Collagraph, 80, Free Press, NY; dir, High Tide Press, New York, NY, 1991-; Illusr, many bks; Artists Books, High Tide Press. *Dealer:* Susan Teller Gallery 568 Broadway New York NY. *Mailing Add:* PO Box 1122 New York NY 10159-1122

ROSS, RHODA HONORE
PAINTER, INSTRUCTOR

b Boston, Mass, Dec 24, 41. *Study:* Carnegie-Mellon Univ; RI Sch Design, BFA; Yale Univ, with Jack Tworkov, Al Held, Lester Johnson & Bernard Chaet, MFA; Skowhegan Sch Painting & Sculpture, Fashion Inst Technol, AAS. *Work:* Mus City NY; The White House, Washington; Julliard Sch, Chemical Bank, & Can Imperial Bank of Commerce, NY. *Comn:* Paintings, Russian Tea Room, NY; paintings, Smith Barney, Harris, Upham & Co, NY; Waldorf Astoria Hotel, NY; paintings, First Deposit Corp, San Francisco, Calif; portrait, retiring pres, Lehman Col, NY; and others. *Exhib:* Watercolor USA, Springfield Art Mus, Mo; The Subway Show, Lehman Col Art Gallery, NY; Art in the Garden, Cape Mus Fine Arts, Dennis, Mass; Nat Asn Women, Pace Univ Art Gallery, NY; Artists traveling exhib, Nicolasen Art Mus, Wyo, Lewiston Art Ctr, Mont, Jesse Besser Mus, Mich & S Roper Gallery, Md; Am Univ, Washington; NY Studio Sch, NY. *Pos:* Treas, RI Sch Design Alumni Exec Comt, formerly; juror, Nat Asn Women Artists, formerly. *Teaching:* Instr New York Univ, presently. *Awards:* First Prize, Mademoiselle Mag; Susan B Whedon Prize, Yale Univ; Grumbacher Gold Medal. *Mem:* Nat Asn Women Artists; Womens Caucus Art; Graphic Artists Guild; Nat Asn Women Artists. *Media:* Oil, Watercolor. *Publ:* Am Artist; UNICEF; Am Psychologist Mag. *Dealer:* The North End Gallery Boston MA; Wally Findlay Galleries NY Palm Beach Fla Chicago IL. *Mailing Add:* 473 West End Ave New York NY 10024

ROSS, STEPHEN M
PATRON

Study: Univ Mich, BS, 62; Wayne State Univ, JD; NYU, LLM(taxation). *Pos:* Dr Insignia Fin Group, Inc; Dir, Juvenile Diabetes Found; founder, dir, Charter Munic Mortgage Acceptance Co; founder, chmn, Chief Exec Officer, The Related Cos LP, New York City; bd trustees, Solomon R Guggenheim Mus; trustee, Jackie Robinson Found; Jewish Asn for Serv for Aged. *Mem:* Real Estate Bd NY (dir, currently). *Mailing Add:* The Related Cos LP 60 Columbus Cir New York NY 10023

ROSS, SUEELLEN
PAINTER, PRINTMAKER

b Oakland, Calif, July 12, 41. *Study:* Univ Calif, Berkeley, BA, 65, MA, 69, Sch Visual Arts, New York, NY, 78-79. *Work:* Leigh Yawkey Woodson Art Mus. *Comn:* bittern in reeds, Safeco Insurance Co, Seattle, Wash, 86. *Exhib:* Survival to Sport, Whatcom Mus Hist & Art, Bellingham, Wash, 86; Birds in Art, Leigh Yawkey Woodson Art Mus, Wausau, Wis, 87, 89, 91-95, 97, 99, 00-04; Arts for Parks, 91 & 92; Naturally Drawn, Leigh Yawkey Woodson Art Mus, Wausau, Wis, 92, Wildlife: The Artists View, 93 & 96; Wildlife Art Sale, Christie's, South Kensington Ltd, London, Eng, 96; and others. *Teaching:* Instr fine arts, Frye Art Mus & Daniel Smith Inc, 97, 99; instr fine arts, Dillman's, 2000, 01, 05, 06. *Awards:* Region I Winner, poster, Arts for Parks, 91. *Bibliog:* Bart Rulon (auth), Painting Birds Step by Step, N Light Bks, 96; Rachel Wolf (ed), The Best of Wildlife Painting, N Light Bks, 97; plus others; Bart Rulon (auth), Artist's Photo Reference: Songbirds, North Light Books, Cincinnati, 2004. *Mem:* Signature mem NW Watercolor Soc; Colored Pencil Soc Am. *Media:* Hand Colored Etchings; Mixed Media. *Publ:* Auth, Paint Radiant Realism with Mixed Media, N Light Bks, 99; Jamie Gildow, Colored Pencil Explorations, N Light Books, 02; auth, Living Color, The Artist's Magazine, Jan, 2001. *Dealer:* Howard/Mandville Gallery 120 Park Ln Kirkland, WA 98033. *Mailing Add:* 1909 SW Myrtle Seattle WA 98106

ROSS, WILBUR LOUIS, JR
COLLECTOR

b Weehawken, NJ, Nov 28, 37. *Study:* Yale Univ, AB, 59; MBA with distinction, Harvard Univ, 61. *Pos:* Assoc, Wood, Struthers and Winthrop, New York City, 63-64; pres, Faulkner, Dawkins & Sullivan Securities Corp, 64-76; sr managing dir, Rothschild, Inc, 76-2000; Chief Exec Officer, News Comms, Inc, 96-98; chmn, chief investment off, Rothschild Recovery Fund, 97-2000; chmn, Chief Exec Officer W L

Ross & Co LLC, 2000-; bd dir, Biocraft Labs Inc, Rutherford, NJ, FurVault Inc, New York City, Investors Insurance Co, Lawrence Harbor, NJ, Revere Copper and Brass Co, Stamford, Syms Corp, Secaucus, NJ, Am Bankruptcy Inst, Wash, Allis Chalmers Corp, Milwaukee, KTI Inc, RH Cement Co, Seoul, Korea, Tong Yang Life Insurance Co, Seoul, Kansai Sawayaka Bank, Osaka, Fresca Credit Card Co, Osaka; fin adv equity holders comt Texaco Co, AH Robins Co, Pub Serv NH; hon economic ambassador from Korea to APEC Investment, Montana, 99; chmn Asia Recovery Fund LP, WL Recovery Fund LP, Asia Co, Investment Partners L.P; chmn, Clarent Hosp Corp, Int Steel Group, Inc, Cleveland, 2002-, Ohizumi Manufacturing Co, Japan, 2003- Burlington Industries, 2003-, Marquis Who's Who LLC, 2003-; dir, Nikko Electrical Co, Japan; treas, NY State Dem Comt, 80-83, Am Fedn Arts, 93-, The New Mus, 93-; vchmn, Brooklyn Mus, 81-; chmn, univ coun comt, on art Yale Univ, 83-88; chmn, Nat Acad Design, New York City, 85-, Am Art Forum, Smithsonian Inst, 87-; trustee, vchmn, Nat Mus Am Art, Wash, 86-91, chmn, 91-; trustee, Mus Am Fin Hist; trustee, Sarah Lawrence Col, 86-, chmn art gallery, 84-; pres, Parrish Art Mus, 91-95; chmn, NY Hist Soc, 93-94; bd dir, Smithsonian Inst Nat Bd, 94-, chmn bd, 95; nat chmn, Smithsonian Bicentennial Celebration, 96; trustee Gustave Hyde Ctr Nat Mus Am Indian, 2001-, Nat Mus Am Fin Hist; bd dir, Turnaround Mgt Asn, 2001-; chmn, Absolute Recovery Hedge Fund, Ltd, Hamilton, Bermuda, Taiyo Fund, 2003-, Japan Real Estate Recovery Fund, 2003-, With US Army, 61-63. *Mem:* Fel, Jonathan Edward Col Yale Univ, Metrop Mus Art; mem Fin Analysts Fedn (chartered), Century Asn, The Bus Round Table, Southampton Bath & Tennis Club (chmn bd dir), Harvard Bus Sch Club NY (bd dir), Beach Club, Club Colette, Palm Beach Fla

ROSSEN, SUSAN F
HISTORIAN, EDITOR
Study: Smith Col, AB(art hist), 63; Univ of Mich, Wayne State Univ, MA(art hist), 71. *Pos:* Asst cur educ, Detroit Inst Arts, 64-68, assoc cur Europ art, 71-72, sr ed & coordr of publ, Detroit Inst Arts, 72-81; exec dir publs, Art Inst Chicago, 81-. *Teaching:* Lectr 19th century art, Univ Detroit, 71. *Awards:* Am Art Mus Asn; Art Mus Asn, Chicago Book Clinic; ARLIS. *Mem:* Int Asn Mus Pubs; Col Art Asn. *Res:* Nineteenth and twentieth century art and women artists, women as patrons of the arts; 20th century illustrated books. *Publ:* The Photography of Gustave Le Gray; Ed, Henri Matisse Paper Cut-Outs, 77; The Golden Age of Naples: Art and Civilization Under the Bourbons 1734-1805, 81; auth, Primer for seeing: The Gallery of Art interpretation of Katharine Kuhs crusade for modernism in Chicago, Art Inst Chicago Mus Studios, Vol 16, No 1, 90; ed, Ivan Albright, 96. *Mailing Add:* Art Inst Chicago 111 S Michigan Ave Chicago IL 60603-6110

ROSSMAN, MICHAEL
DRAFTSMAN, PAINTER
b Chambersburg, Pa, Apr 4, 41. *Study:* Pratt Inst, Brooklyn, BID, 63 & MFA(sculpture). *Work:* Philadelphia Mus Art; Woodmere Mus, Philadelphia, Pa. *Exhib:* Artists Choose Artists, Inst Contemp Art & More Gallery, Philadelphia, 91; More Gallery, 95, 2000; From Durer to Doag, Philadelphia Mus Art, 2006. *Teaching:* Prof, Univ Arts, Philadelphia, 66-; lectr, Barnes Found, Lower Merion, Pa, 2003-. *Awards:* Nat Endowment Art Fel, 91; Bietzel Award for Teaching, 98. *Media:* Graphite Paper. *Specialty:* Contemporary American Art. *Dealer:* Charles More Gallery Philadelphia PA 19103. *Mailing Add:* 819 N 21st St Philadelphia PA 19130

ROSSMAN, RUTH SCHARFF
PAINTER, INSTRUCTOR
b Brooklyn, NY. *Study:* Cleveland Inst Art; Case-Western Reserve Univ, BS; Kahn Inst Art; Univ Calif, Los Angeles; also with Sueo Serisawa & Rico Lebrun. *Work:* Pa Acad Fine Arts; Univ Redlands; Nat Watercolor Soc; Brandeis Inst; Ahmanson Collection, Calif; plus others. *Exhib:* Recent Paintings USA: Figure, Mus Mod Art, NY, 61; Crescent Gallery, New Orleans, 77, 78; Rocky Mountain Nat, Colo, 77 & 81; Denver Art Mus; Venice Art Walk, Venice, Calif, 92-98, 99; Platt Art Gallery, Univ Judaism, Los Angeles, 94; A Retrospective, 98; and others. *Teaching:* Teacher art, Pub Sch Syst, Canton, Ohio; teacher art, Canton Art Inst; instr, Arts & Crafts Ctr, Los Angeles. *Awards:* Purchase Award, Pa Acad Fine Arts, 65; All-City Ann Purchase Awards, Los Angeles, 65 & 69; Rocky Mountain Nat, 77; plus others. *Bibliog:* William Wilson & Henry Seldis (auths), articles, Los Angeles Times, 63 & 6/66; States Item, Times-Picayune World Art, New Orleans, 12/77; Robert Perine (auth), The California Romantics - Harbingers of Watercolorism, Artra Publ Inc, 86. *Mem:* Nat Watercolor Soc (secy, 73-74, 1st vpres, 74-75, pres, 75-76). *Media:* Acrylic, Oil. *Mailing Add:* 1843 El Camino De La Luz Santa Barbara CA 93109-1924

ROSTER, FRED HOWARD
SCULPTOR, EDUCATOR
b Palo Alto, Calif, June 27, 44. *Study:* Gavilan Col, AA; San Jose State Col, BA & MA; Univ Hawaii, MFA & with Herbert H Sanders. *Work:* Honolulu Acad Art, Hawaii; State Found Cult & Arts, Honolulu; Contemp Arts Ctr Hawaii; Hawaii Loa Col, Kailua; St Francis Hosp, Honolulu. *Comn:* Sand cast mural, Ft Derussy, 75; bronze bust of former Gov John Burns, State Found Cult & The Arts; Kekuanaoa bronze portrait, 79; bronze & stainless steel mural, Physical Educ Facility, Univ Hawaii, Manoa, 82; bronze, stone & stainless steel sculpture, Honolulu Int Airport, 83. *Exhib:* Artists of Hawaii Ann, Honolulu Acad Art, 75-76, 79 & 81; Hawaii Craftsmen's Ann, Honolulu, 69-72 & 75-80; one-man shows, Contemp Arts Ctr Hawaii, 72, Gima's Art Gallery, Honolulu, 75 & 78 & Corpus Christi Univ, Tex, 80. *Teaching:* Instr ceramics, San Jose State Col, 68-69; asst prof sculpture, Univ Hawaii, 69-78, assoc prof, 78-. *Awards:* Elizabeth Moses Award, San Francisco Potter's Asn, 68; Sculptural Grant Award, Windward Artists Guild, 71; Hawaii Craftsman Award, 74. *Mem:* Honolulu Acad Art. *Media:* Mixed. *Mailing Add:* 1841 Halekoa Rd Honolulu HI 96821

ROTENBERG, JUDI
PAINTER, ART DEALER
b Boston, Mass. *Study:* Boston Univ, BFA; studied privately in Paris, Mex & Israel. *Exhib:* Le Salon 80, Soc des Artistes Francais, Paris, 80; DeCordova Museum; Holyoke Mus Show; Societarian de Societe des Beaux Art. *Pos:* Dir, Judi Rotenberg Gallery, Boston & Square Circle Gallery, Rockport, Mass. *Teaching:* Spain Univ, Madrid, 98; Young President's Orgn, 98. *Mem:* Rockport Art Asn. *Media:* Acrylic, Watercolor. *Specialty:* 20th century American art. *Mailing Add:* Judi Rotenberg Gallery 130 Newberry St Boston MA 02116

ROTH, FRANK
PAINTER
b Boston, Mass, Feb 22, 36. *Study:* Cooper Union, 54; Hofmann Sch, 55. *Work:* Albright-Knox Art Gallery, Buffalo, NY; Whitney Mus Am Art, Metrop Mus Art, Mus Mod Art, NY; Santa Barbara Mus Art, Calif; Baltimore Mus Art; Walker Art Ctr, Minneapolis; Tate Gallery, London, Eng; David Rockefeller Collection, NY; and others. *Exhib:* one person exhibs, Martha Jackson Gallery, NY, 67, 68, 70 & 71, Gimpel & Weitzenhoffer, NY, 74, O K Harris Works Art, NY, 75, Louis K Meisel Gallery, NY, 81, 82, 84 & 85, Martha White Gallery, Louisville, Ky, 81, Sindin Gallery, NY, 91 & 93; Va Mus Fine Arts, Richmond, 70; Indianapolis Mus Art, Ind, 70; Louise Himmelfarb Gallery, Bridgehampton, NY 77 & 78; David Anderson Gallery, Buffalo, NY, 91, 93 & 99; Bologna Lawdi Gallery, East Hampton, NY, 92, 93; Sindin Gallery, NY, 94, 97, 99; Hermitage Arts, Amsterdam, The Neth, 96; Radford Univ Mus, Va, 99; many others. *Pos:* panelist, Col Art Asn, New York, 78. *Teaching:* Instr painting, State Univ Iowa, summer 64; instr painting & drawing, Sch Visual Arts, NY, 63--; Ford Found artist-in-residence, Univ RI, 66; artist-in-residence, Univ Wis, Madison, 70; instr, Univ Calif, Berkeley, 68 & Univ Calif, Irvine, 71; vis lectr, Bellville Area Col, Ill, 76, Maryland Inst Art, Baltimore, Md, 77; vis critic, Md Inst Art, Baltimore, 78-88. *Awards:* Prix de Rome, Chaloner Prize Found Award, 61; Guggenheim Fel, 64; Minister Foreign Affairs Award, Int Exhib Young Artists, Tokyo, Japan, 67; Nat Endowment for Arts, 77. *Bibliog:* Phyllis Braff (auth), The Emotional Intensity of Devotion, NY Times, 1/3/93; Jacquely Campbell (auth), Precise in Speech and Painting, spec to J Bull, 96; James Michner (auth), Art Voices Who's Who in American Art, NY Times Mag, 4/7/96. *Media:* Arcylic. *Mailing Add:* 120 Accabonac Rd East Hampton NY 11937

ROTH, JACK (RODNEY)
PAINTER
b Brockway, Pa, Mar 13, 27. *Study:* Calif Sch Fine Arts, with Mark Rothko & Clifford Still, 49-50; State Univ Iowa, with James Lechay, MFA, 51-53; Duke Univ, PhD, 62. *Work:* Mus Mod Art, NY. *Awards:* Guggenheim Fel, 79-80. *Media:* Acrylic, Watercolor. *Mailing Add:* 32 Clinton Ave Montclair NJ 07042

ROTH, LELAND M(ARTIN)
HISTORIAN, WRITER
b Harbor Beach, Mich, Mar 22, 43. *Study:* Univ Ill, Urbana, BA(archit), 66; Yale, MA, 71, PhD, 73. *Teaching:* Instr, Univ Ill, Urbana, 66-67 & Ohio State Univ, Columbus, 71-73; asst prof, Northwestern Univ, 73-78; assoc prof, Univ Ore, Eugene, 78-90, prof, 90-, Marion Dean Ross prof archit hist, 92-. *Awards:* Founders Award, Soc Archit Historians, 79; Nat Endowment Humanities Fel, 82-83; Kamphoefner Fel, 85. *Mem:* Col Art Asn; Soc Archit Historians (dir, 77-80); Nat Trust Hist Preserv; Vernacular Archit Forum. *Res:* American architecture, 1850-1950; history of urban America; history of American art, 1850-1930; Native American Architecture. *Publ:* Ed, Monograph of the Work of McKim, Mead & White, B Blom, 73; auth, The Architecture of McKim, Mead & White, 1870-1920: A Building List, Garland Publ, 78; A Concise History of American Architecture, 79, ed, America Builds: Source Documents in American Architecture, 83, auth, McKim, Mead & White, Architects, 83 & Understanding Architecture, 93, Harper Collins; American Architecture; A History 2001, Westview Press; Understanding Architecture, Westview Press, 2nd ed, 2006. *Mailing Add:* Art Hist Dept Univ Ore Eugene OR 97403-5229

ROTH, MARIAN
PHOTOGRAPHER
b Brooklyn, NY, Apr 28, 44. *Study:* Brooklyn Col, BA, 64; Univ Iowa, MA, 66; Univ Iowa, PhD, 68. *Exhib:* 2nd Ann Int Pinhole Exhib, Wnesdale Gallery, Toronto, 00; 3rd Int Pinhole Exhib, Toronto, 01; 2001 Ann, Decordova Mus, Lincoln, Ma, 01; Pinhole Pictures, June Bateman Gallery, NY, 02. *Teaching:* Fac Pinhole, Fine Art Work Center, 99-; Ast Prof Photog, Cazenovia Col, NY, 80-92. *Awards:* Photog Award, Ma Cult Coun, 98; Guggenheim, 00. *Mem:* Provincetown Art Asn and Mus; Provincetown Cultural Coun. *Publ:* Eric Renner (auth), Pinhole Photog, Focal Press, 99; Sara London (auth), Marian Roth, Art New England, 00; Rosalind Smith (auth), The Pinhole Thing, Photog Fourm, 01. *Mailing Add:* 2 Allerton St Provincetown MA 02657

ROTH, MICHAEL S
ADMINISTRATOR, EDUCATOR
Study: Wesleyan Univ, BA; Princeton Univ, MA; Princeton Univ, Phd in hist. *Comn:* Archit, Film, Photog & Urban Landscape, 2001, Disturbing Remains: Memory, Hist, & Crisis in Twentieth Century, 2001. *Exhib:* cur, (exhib) Sigmund Freud: Conflict & Cult, Libr. Congress, 1998. *Pos:* Assoc dir, Getty Res Inst, chrmn, Res & Educ Dept; pres, Calif Col Arts, San Francisco, 2000-. *Teaching:* HB Alexander Prof, Humanities & Cult Studies Claremont Grad Sch. *Publ:* Auth: Freud: Conflict & Culture, 1998; auth: Looking for L.A. *Mailing Add:* Calif Col of the Arts Off of the Pres 1111 Eighth St San Francisco CA 94107

ROTH, MOIRA
EDUCATOR, HISTORIAN
b London, Eng, July 24, 33. *Study:* New York Univ, BA, 59; Univ Calif, Berkeley, MA, 66, PhD, 74. *Hon Degrees:* San Francisco Art Inst, Hon Dr, 94. *Teaching:* Acting asst prof art hist, Univ Calif, Irvine, 70-72; lectr art hist, Univ Calif, Santa Cruz, 73-74; from asst to assoc prof, Univ Calif, San Diego, 74-86, chmn, Visual Arts Dept, 82-83; prof art hist & Trefethan endowed chair, Mills Col, 86-. *Awards:* Lifetime Achievement Award, Women's Caucus Art, 98; Frank Jewlett Mather Lifetime Achievement Award in art criticism, 2000. *Mem:* Col Art Asn (bd dir, 92-96). *Res:* Performance art, Marcel Duchamp, American Multicultural & women's contemporary art. *Publ:* Ed & contribr, The Dual Citizenship: Art of Carlos Villa, Visions, fall 89; auth, A Trojan Horse (essay), Faith Ringgold: A Twenty Year Retrospective (catalog), 90; contribr, Shigeko Kubota: Video Sculpture (catalog), 91; The Power of Feminist Art: The American Movement of the 1970s, History and Impact, 94; ed, We Flew Over the Bridge: Memoirs of Faith Ringgold, 95. *Mailing Add:* Dept Art Mills Col Oakland CA 94613

ROTH, RICHARD
PAINTER, EDUCATOR
b Brooklyn, NY, June 22, 46. *Study:* Cooper Union, BFA, 69; Tyler Sch Art, Temple Univ, MFA, 77. *Work:* Akron Art Inst, Ohio; Chase Manhattan Bank Collection, NY; NY Univ Art Collection; First Nat City Bank Collection, NY; Wexner Ctr for the Arts, Columbus. *Comn:* Sculpture, Tipton Assocs, 87; Ohio State Univ Hosp, 89; Bowling Green State Univ, 97. *Exhib:* 1969 Ann Exhib of Contemp Am Painting, Whitney Mus Am Art, NY, 69-70; Group shows, Contemp Arts Ctr, Cincinnati, 88, Dart Gallery, Chicago, 88, Penine Hart Gallery, NY, 90, Bess Cutler Gallery, NY, 90 & Mus Mod Art, Saitama, Japan, 94; One-person shows, Toni Birckhead Gallery, Cincinnati, 90, Feigen Inc, Chicago, 91; Calif Mus Photog, Univ Calif Riverside, 98; Shillam & Smith 3, London, UK, 98. *Teaching:* Asst prof & dir, Prog Fundamentals & Spec Classes, Art Inst Chicago, 77-81; prof, Dept Art, Ohio State Univ, 81-99; prof, chair painting & printmaking dept, Va Commonwealth Univ. *Awards:* Nat Endowment Arts, Visual Artists Fel, Painting, 91; Ohio Arts Coun Individual Artists Fel, 91. *Publ:* Beauty Is Nowhere: Ethical Issues in Art and Design, G & B Arts Int, with Susan King Roth; also Color Basics, with Stephen Pentak, Thompson-Wadsoworth. *Mailing Add:* Painting & Printmaking Dept Va Commonwealth Univ 1000 W Broad St Richmond VA 23284

ROTH, STEVEN
PATRON
Study: Dartmouth Col, AB, 62, MBA, 63. *Pos:* With Kenilworth Assoc, NJ, 75-79; co-founder, managing gen partner, Interstate Properties, 79-; Chief Exec Officer, chmn bd, Vornado Realty Trust, New York City, 89-; Chief Exec Officer, Alexander's Inc, currently. *Mem:* Intrepid Mus Found, New York City; New York Univ Sch Med Found; Whitney Mus Am Art, New York City, (trustee, currently); Jewish Theological Seminary Am (bd dir, currently); Amos Tuck Sch, Dartmouth Col, (bd dir, 81-87). *Mailing Add:* Vornado Realty Trust 888 Seventh Ave New York NY 10019

ROTHAFEL, SYDELL
PAINTER
b Brooklyn, NY, June 11, 31. *Study:* Goucher Col, Towson, Md, 53; Brooklyn Col, NY, studied with Anderson, D'Arcangelo, BA (fine arts), 80; post grad studies, 81-82; New Sch, studied with Anthony Toney & Henry Pearson. *Work:* Queensboro Pub Libr, NY; World Women Online, Ariz State Univ. *Exhib:* Brooklyn Mus, 77; Creativity, Bentley Gallery, Lawrence, NY, 90; New Yorkers In Barcelona, Banco-Hispano-Americano Cartoon Gallery, Barcelona, Spain; Visions & Diversity, Staten Island Mus, NY, 92; Perceptions of Beauty, Ariel Gallery, 92; Int Bienniale, Tonniens, France, 93; Beams of Light, Salon du vieux Columbiers, Paris, 93; A Woman's Place, Prince Street Gallery, 95. *Pos:* Exhib chmn, Sumi-e Soc Am, 77-78; pres, Japan-Am Sumi-e Club, 83-86; artist-in-residence, Hilai Int, Ma'alot, Israel, 93. *Teaching:* Instr art, Freeport Arts Coun, 81-82, adult ed, Brookside Jr HS, 82-83, Alley Pond Environ Ctr, 87-88, Ryan Ctr Gateway Nat Park. *Awards:* Presidents Award, Japan House Gallery, Sumi-e Soc Am, 76; Hon First Prize, Cork Gallery, Japan Am Sumi-e Soc, 83; Soho NY Int Prize Winner, Agora Gallery, 92. *Bibliog:* Ariel Gallery (auth), Perceptions of Beauty, Manhattan Arts, 91; Jeanne Russel (auth), The beauty that winter was, Newsday, 3/96. *Mem:* NY Artists Equity Asn; Womens Caucus Art; Burr Artists. *Media:* Acrylic. *Dealer:* Lenox Artisans Gallery Lenox MA; Bradford Collection. *Mailing Add:* 326 Beach 142nd St Neponsit NY 11694

ROTHENBERG, BARBARA
PAINTER, EDUCATOR
b New York, NY, June 21, 33. *Study:* Univ Mich, 52-54; Bennington Col, with Paul Feeley, BA(cum laude), 56; Columbia Univ Teachers Col, MA, 56; NY Univ, with Esteben Vicente & Samuel Adler, 56-58. *Work:* Housatonic Mus Art, Bridgeport, Conn; Readers Digest Corp, Pleasantville, NY; CDC Financial, Farmington, Conn; Smithsonian Inst; United Nations, NY; Pitney-Bowes, GE. *Comn:* Tapestry, Sofia Assocs, NY, 85; Jacob's Ladder (20' mural), Temple Israel, Westport, Conn, 94. *Exhib:* Northeast Ann, Silvermine Guild Arts Ctr, 76, 79, 80, 82-83, 93-94, 97 & 98; Collage, Silvermine Guild Arts Ctr, 79; New Dimensions in Drawing, Aldrich Mus, 81; solo exhibs, Ingber Gallery, NY, 88, Conn Gallery, Marlborough, 88, Newspace Gallery, Manchester Community Col, Conn, 91, Conn Comn Arts, Hartford, 94, Mort Rosenfeld Gallery, Westport Art Ctr, Conn, 96, Discovery Mus, Bridgeport, Conn, 97 & Silvermine Guild Arts Ctr, 98, UN Invitation, 99, Gallery of Contemp Art, Sacred Heart Univ, 2000; Out of Longing and Out of Song, Silvermine Guild Arts Ctr, 2005; The Big Hike, Silvermine Guild Arts Ctr, 90; Modern Times, Katonah Mus, NY, 92; Investing in Dreams, William Benton Mus Art, Storrs, Conn, 95; Silvermine Invitational, Kohn, Pederson, Fox, NY, 95; India: Reflections of a Country, Krasdale Gallery, NY, 95; Archeology of the Spirit, Gallery Brocken, Koganei, Japan, 96; Paessagio Gallery, Hartford, Conn, 98; West Wind Gallery, Up from Earth, 2004; Hebrew Union Inst Mus, The Art of Aging, 2003-2004; solo show, Out of Longing & Out of Song, Silvermine Guild Art Center, 2005; Song of the Earth, Van Brunt Gallery, 2006. *Collection Arranged:* Word/Image, Westport Art Ctr, 2003. *Pos:* Moderator-organizer, Inst Visual Artists, Silvermine Guild Arts Ctr, 85, 2000; lectr, Friends Music, 85, Fairfield Univ, 87 & 89 Westport Arts Ctr, 87 & 89 & Westport Continuing Educ, 87; moderator & panelist, Inst Visual Artists, Silvermine Guild Arts Ctr & Conn Gallery, Marlborough, 89; lectr & vis artist, Silvermine Guild Arts Ctr, 89, Westport Arts Ctr, 91-92, 93 & 95, New Brit Mus Art, 91-93, Fairfield Univ, 91-93, Harvard Club India, 91-93, Univ Hyderabad, India, 91-93, Discovery Mus, Bridgeport, Conn, 92, Great Neck Libr, 92, Delhi Col Art, 92, India Int Ctr, 92, Friends Music, 93, Port Wash Libr, 93, Hewlett-Woodmere Libr, 95, Inst Asian Studies, NY, 95, Long Beach Island Found Arts & Sci, Loveladies, NJ, 96 & Weir Farm Historic Site, 98. *Teaching:* Instr art, City Col NY, 58-60 & Silvermine Sch Arts, 80-83 & 96-2006; adj assoc prof art, Housatonic Community Col, 70-82, Sch Visual Arts, NY, 80-82, Sacred Heart Univ, 80-88 & Fairfield Univ, Conn, 86-98; adj prof fine arts, Fairfield Univ, 88-98; guest lectr & critic, RI Sch Design, 92; instr, Silvermine Guild Sch Arts, 94-2005 & Victor D'Amico Inst Art, Amagansett, Long Island, 96, 97, 98, 2000 & 2001. *Awards:* Indo-Am Fulbright Grant, 92-93; Best Show for Painting on paper, Discovery Mus, Conn, 96; Artist-in-Res, Weir Farm, 98; Artist-in-Res, Virginia Ctr for the Creative Arts, 2000. *Bibliog:* Vivian Raynor (auth), review, NY Times, 1/96; Sachidananda Mohanty (auth), In search of Ragamala, SPAN Mag, 1/96; Art New Eng, 97; LP Streitfeld Review, The Advocate, 2003; Nancy Hull-Duncan (auth), Out of Longing & Out of Song (catalog), 2005. *Mem:* Col Art Asn; Womens Caucus Arts; Westport-Weston Arts Coun; Silvermine Guild Ctr Arts (mem bd, 78-80); Fulbright Asn. *Media:* Oil, Pastel; Collage. *Interests:* Music, Poetry, Travel, Dance. *Publ:* Auth, On painterly painting, Women Artists News, 81; Connecticut women artists, Conn Mag, 81. *Dealer:* Silvermine Guild New Canaan CT; Westport Art Ctr. *Mailing Add:* 303 Bayberry Ln Westport CT 06880

ROTHENBERG, SUSAN
PAINTER, PRINTMAKER
b Buffalo, NY, Jan 20, 45. *Study:* Cornell Univ, BFA, 66; George Wash Univ, 67; Corcoran Mus Sch. *Work:* Mus Mod Art, Whitney Mus Am Art, NY; Albright-Knox Art Gallery, Buffalo, NY; Walker Art Ctr, Minneapolis, Minn; Mus Fine Arts, Houston; Fogg Art Mus, Harvard Univ, Cambridge, Mass. *Exhib:* New Acquisitions, Extraordinary Women & Am Drawn & Matched (with catalog), 77, Prints from Blocks, Gauguin to Now (with catalog), 83, An Int Survey of Recent Painting & Sculpture (with catalog), 84 & Allegories of Modernism: Contemp Drawing (with catalog), 92, Thinking Print: Books to Billboards, 1980-95 (with catalog), 95, Mus Mod Art, NY; solo exhibs, Recent Work (with catalog), Walker Art Ctr, Minneapolis, Minn, 78, Los Angeles Co Mus Art, Calif, traveling, 83-85, Paintings & Drawings 1974-1192 (with catalog), Albright-Knox Art Gallery, Buffalo, NY, traveling, 92-94, Focus Series, Va Mus Fine Arts, Richmond, 95, Mus Art Contemp Monterrey, Mex, 96, Drawings & Prints (catalog) Herbert F Johnson Mus Art, Cornell Univ, Ithaca, NY, 98-99 & Paintings from the 90's (catalog) Mus Fine Arts, Boston, 2000; New Image Painting (with catalog), 78-79, 1979 Biennial Exhib (with catalog), 79, A Decade in Review: Selections from the 1970's, 79, Focus on the Figure: Twenty Years (with catalog), 82, Block Prints, 82, 1983 Biennial Exhib (with catalog), 83, Minimalism to Expressionism: Painting & Sculpture Since 1965 from the Permanent Collection, 83, Visions of Childhood: A Contemp Iconography, 84, 1985 Biennial Exhib (with catalog), 85, Four Printmakers, 85, Three Printmakers, 86 & Evolutions in Expression, 94, Whitney Mus Am Art; Am Paintings of the 1970's, Albright-Knox Gallery, NY, traveling, 78-80; A New Bestiary: Animal Imagery in Contemp Art, Va Mus Fine Arts, 81; 74th & 75th Am Exhib (with catalog), Art Inst Chicago, Ill, 82 & 86; New Figuration in Am (with catalog), 83, 1988-The World of Art Today (with catalog), 88, & 25 Americans: Paintings in the 90s, 95, Milwaukee Art Mus, Wis; 47th Ann Mid-Yr Exhib (with catalog), 83 & 50th Nat Mid-Yr Exhib, 86, Butler Inst Am Art, Youngstown, Ohio; Images & Impressions: Painters Who Print (with catalog), Walker Art Ctr, Minneapolis, Minn, 84; States of War: New European & Am Paintings (catalog) & Virginia & Bagley Wright Collection, 99, Seattle Art Mus, 85; Boston Collects: Contemp Painting & Sculpture, Boston Mus Fine Arts, Mass, 86-87; The Int Art Show for the End of World Hunger, Minn Mus Art, St Paul, traveling, 87-91; Timely & Timeless (with catalog), Aldrich Mus Contemp Art, Conn, 93-94; A NY Time: Selected Drawings of the Eighties, Bruce Mus, Greenwich, Conn, 95; 7 Artists, Cleveland Mus Art, 95; XXV Years, John Berggruen Gallery, San Francisco, 95; Diary of the Human Hand, Galerie Centre Arts Saidye Bronfman, 95; Powerful Expressions: Recent Am Drawings (with catalog), Nat Acad Design, 96; Thinking Print: Books to Billboards 1980-95 (catalog), Mus Mod Art, NY, 96; Hirshhorn Collects: Recent Acquisitions 1992-96 (catalog), Hirshhorn Mus & Sculpture Garden, Washington, 97; Eye of Modernism, Georgia O'Keeffe Mus, Santa Fe, NMex, 2001; Sperone Westwater, NY, 2001, 02. *Collection Arranged:* A Guide to the Collection of the Museum Fine Arts, Houston, Tex; The Image in American Photography & Sculpture 1950-1980 (auth, catalog), Akron Art Mus. *Awards:* Creative Artists Pub Serv Prog Grant, NY State Coun Arts, 76-77; Guggenheim Fel Painting, 80; Award Painting, Am Acad Arts & Letts, 83. *Bibliog:* Anne Midgette (auth), Words Worth a Thousand Pictures, Wall St J, 9/22/99; Jason Edward Kaufman (auth), The Gallery: Chaos and Crowds, Wall St J, 1/5/2000; Elisa Turner (auth), Mythic Proportions, Artnews, 5/2001. *Mem:* Nat Acad. *Media:* Acrylic and Flashe or Oil on Canvas or Paper, Aquatint; Lithography. *Publ:* Contribr, New Image Painting, Whitney Mus, 78; American Paintings: The Eighties, Barbara Rose/Vista Press, 79. *Mailing Add:* c/o Sperone Westwater 415 W 13th St #2 New York NY 10014-1104

ROTHOLZ, RINA
PRINTMAKER
b Israel; US citizen. *Study:* Pratt Graphic Arts Ctr, New York; Brooklyn Mus Art Sch, NY. *Work:* Boston Mus Fine Arts; Rose Art Mus, Brandeis Univ; Mus Mod Art, NY; Israel Mus, Jerusalem; Albright-Knox Art Gallery, Buffalo, NY; and others. *Comn:* Ed of 50 prints, 69 & ed of 200 prints, Commentary Libr Collection of Art Treasure; Blue Disc (greeting card design), UNICEF, 72; 36 ingots (reprod by Franklin Mint), Judaic Heritage Soc, 73-78. *Exhib:* One-man shows, Pucker/Safrai Gallery, Boston, 72, 74, 77 & 81 & Port Washington Libr, NY, 75; Boston Printmakers Ann & Traveling Shows, 67-79; Queens Mus, NY, 74; Potsdam Print Exhib, State Univ NY Col, Purchase, 76; and others. *Teaching:* Lectr & demonstr, Bd Coop Educ Serv, Scholars in Residence Prog, Nassau Co, NY. *Awards:* First Prize for Graphics, Port Washington Ann, 70; Purchase Prize, Nassau Community Graphic Exhib, 72 & 73; Prize in Graphics, Nat Asn Women Artists, 72 & 74. *Mem:* Boston Printmakers; Graphic Arts Coun NY; Nat Asn Women Artists; Prof Artists Guild. *Res:* Discovered process of Tuilegraphy, which is the carving of vinyl asbestos tiles while they are still warm, then printing the tiles as intaglio plates to achieve a variety of textures, shapes, and high reliefs. *Publ:* Auth, Tuilegraphy, Artist's Proof, Vol 7. *Mailing Add:* 42 Shepherd Ln Roslyn Heights NY 11577

ROTHSCHILD, BARBARA R SIMON
PAINTER
b Chicago, Ill. *Study:* Art Inst Chicago; Am Acad Art, Chicago; Col New Rochelle, BA(art ed), 74, MA(art ed), 78. *Work:* Greenburgh Pub Libr, Elmsford, NY; Larchmont Libr, NY; Free reading room, Rye, NY. *Exhib:* Artists Guild, Norton Gallery, W Palm Beach, Fla, 91-93; Palm Beach Watercolor Soc, Cornell Mus, Delray Beach, Fla, 93; Bay Ann Tri-State, Visual Arts Ctr, Panama City, Fla, 95; Tallahassee Watercolor, Le Moyne Art Found, 95 & 96; Best of the Gallery, Mus New Arts, Ft Lauderdale, 96; Boca Raton Mus Art, Fla, 98, 2000; Mus Fine Arts, St Petersburg, Fla; Hudson River Mus, Yonkers, NY; Coral Springs Fla Mus, 98. *Pos:* Instr contemp painting, Boca Mus Art, Fla, 88-96. *Teaching:* Prof drawing, Mercy Col, Dobbs Ferry, NY, 85-87. *Awards:* Second Prize, Gold Coast Watercolor Soc, 92 & 95; Merit Award, Arizona Aqueous, 93; Second Prize and Special Award, Palm Beach Watercolor Soc,; Several awards, Prof Artsits Guild, Fla, 98-. *Bibliog:* J Pat & Cindy Breedlove (dirs), Artists of Florida III, Mountain Productions, 94; Linda Selichia (auth), Barbara Rothschild, XS Mag/Sun Sentinal, 2/6/96. *Mem:* Exhibiting mem, Florida Watercolor Soc; signature mem, Gold Coast Watercolor Soc; Women in the Visual Arts; Palm Beach Watercolor Soc; Boca Mus Artsists Guild. *Media:* Water Media, Acrylic. *Dealer:* Conservant, Boca Raton, Fla; Lupine Gallery, Monhegan, Maine

ROTHSCHILD, JOHN D
DEALER
b Chicago, Ill, June 22, 40. *Study:* Mass Inst Technol, BS, 62; Columbia Univ, MBA, 64. *Pos:* Owner, Rothschild Fine Arts Inc, currently. *Specialty:* European and American paintings, drawings and sculptures by the masters, from French impressionists up through the present. *Publ:* Contribr, I Love New York Guide, Macmillan, Danger: Poets at Play; A Story for the Eleventh Hour, E M Donahue. *Mailing Add:* 5346 E Sapphire Ln Paradise Valley AZ 85253-2531

ROTHWELL, JUNKO ONO
PASTEL
Study: Okayama Univ, Japan. *Work:* George Wash Univ Hosp; Southern Co; Continental Telephone; Northwest Mem Hosp Chicago; Prime Bank, Nations Bank. *Exhib:* Nat Exhib: Am Artists Prof League Nat Exhib, Pastel Soc Am, NY, Patel Soc Japan, Tokyo. *Awards:* Am Artists Prof League Dianne B Bernhard Award in Pastel. *Bibliog:* Best of Pastel, Rockport Publishers, 96; Best of Flower Painting 2, North Light Books, 99; articles: Unforgettable Landscapes, Different Approaches to Light and Texture, Pastel J, 5/200-6/200; article: A Lesson from the East, The Artist's Mag, 6/2004; Caroling Purtell (auth), Junko Ono Rothwell, The Pastel J, 8/2004. *Mem:* Pastel Soc Am; Atlanta Artists Club (mem excellence); Southeastern Pastel Soc; Fel, Am Artist Prof League, NY; Pastel Soc, Japan. *Media:* . *Dealer:* Lagerquist Gallery; Vista Gallery Atlanta Ga; Anderson fine Art Gallery; St Simons Island; Georgia and Spruce Creek Gallery Va. *Mailing Add:* 3625 Woodstream Circle Atlanta GA 30319

ROTTERDAM, PAUL ZWIETNIG-ROTTERDAM
PAINTER
b Austria, Feb 12, 39; US citizen. *Study:* Acad & Univ Vienna. *Work:* Graphische Sammlung Albertina, Vienna, Austria; Metrop Mus, Mus Mod Art & Guggenheim Mus, NY; Mus Nat d'Art Moderne, Paris; and others. *Exhib:* 8th Biennial, Tokyo, 65; Whitney Biennial Am Art, 75; Acquisitions, Guggenheim Mus, 75; Susan Caldwell Gallery, NY, 75; Mus de l'Abbaye St Croix, Les Sables d'Olonne, France, 76; Mus de Nice, France, 77; Birmingham Mus Art, Ala, 77; Ark Arts Ctr, 95; and others. *Teaching:* Lectr painting, Harvard Univ, 68-88 & Cooper Union Sch Art, 74-75. *Bibliog:* Alvin Martin (auth), Paul Rotterdam: The 14 Stations of the Cross, Univ Tex, 80; Carter Ratcliff (auth), Paul Rotterdam: Selected Paintings, Storrer, 82; Townsend Wolfe (auth), Paul Z Rotterdam, A Drawing Retrospective, The Ark Arts Ctr, Littlerock, 95; Carl Aigner, Paul Rotterdam Work list 53-2004; Prestel Publ., London, NY. *Dealer:* Denise Cade 1024 Madison Ave New York NY 10021; Adams Middleton Gallery 3000 Maple Ave Dallas TX 75201. *Mailing Add:* PO Box 952 North Blenheim NY 12131-0952

ROUKES, NICHOLAS M
SCULPTOR, WRITER
b San Jose, Calif, Nov 22, 25. *Study:* San Jose State Col, Calif; Fresno State Col, BA, 49; Stanford Univ, MA, 51. *Work:* Can Coun Art Bank, Ottawa. *Comn:* Kinetic Light, Provincial Judges Court; column, Calgary, Alta, 74. *Teaching:* Prof art educ, design & sculpture, Univ Calgary, Alta, 66-88, prof emer art, 88-. *Media:* Mixed Media. *Res:* New media for art creativity. *Publ:* Auth, Art Synectics, 81; Acrylics Bold and New, 82; Design Synectics, 88; Sculpture in Paper, 92; Humor in Art, Davis Publ, 97

ROUSSEAU, IRENE VICTORIA
SCULPTOR, WRITER
Study: Hunter Col, with Tony Smith, AB; Claremont Grad Sch, MFA; NY Univ, PhD. *Work:* Metrop Mus Art, Mus Mod Art & Guggenheim Mus Art, NY; Smithsonian Inst, Washington; Philadelphia Mus Art; Brit Mus, London. *Comn:* Mosaic mural, Holocaust Mem, The Brotherhood Synagogue, NY, 86; series of metal wall relief sculptures, Capital Sports Inc, Stamford, Conn, 89-90; mural wall relief, Beacon Hill Club, Summit, NJ, 92; mosaic mural, Overlook Hosp Found, Summit, NJ, 93; mosaic murals, Concert Hall, La Roche, Switzerland, 95 & 96. *Exhib:* one-person exhib, Gallery Saint Agnes, Denmark, 86 & Bridges '97, Univ Calif, Berkeley, 97, Weston Gallery, Sch Artchit, NJ Inst Tech, Newark, 2003; Drawing Exhib, Philadelphia Mus Art, Pa; Weatherspoon Art Gallery, Univ NC, Greensboro, 83; Moody Art Gallery, Univ Ala, 83; 50th Anniversary 1936-1986 Am Abstract Artists, Bronx Mus Arts, 86; Int Art Competition, Gallery 54, NY, 89-90; Noyes Mus, NJ, 94; Columbia Mus, SC, 95; 1st Int Art Bienniale, Malta, 95; Mosaic: Ancient Medium/Modern Expressionism, Int AIEMA Conf, Lausanne, Switz, 97; Ecole Francaise de Rome, Italy, 2001; Polytech Inst, Freiburg, Ger, 2002; NJ Inst Tech Sch Architecture, 2003; Univ Granada, Spain, 2003; NJ Inst Tech, Weston Art Gallery, 2004; Yellow Bird Gallery, Newburg, NY, 2005; Science & Art, Int Interdisiplinary Conf, Athens, Greece, 2005; Renaissance Banff, Banff Art Ctr, Alberta, Can, 2005; trav exhib, Soc Math, France & The Min Culture, 2005. *Collection Arranged:* Language of Abstraction & Works on Paper, 79 American Abstract Artists, Betty Parsons Gallery, 79; American Abstract Artists: The Early Years, mus traveling show, 80 & 81; Abstraction in Action, City Gallery, New York, 82. *Pos:* Invited speaker, Noyes Mus, NJ, 94 & Mus African Art, NY, 94, Univ Sydney, Australia, 96, Int Soc Arts, Mathematics & Architecture, Freiburg, Germany, 2002, Mathematical Commections in Art, Music & Sci/Int Soc Arts, Mathematics & Architecture, Granada, Spain, 2003, NJ Inst Tech, 2004; invited artist, Harold Berg Endowment, Art Dept, Colo Col, Colo Springs, 2002. *Teaching:* prof, William Paterson Col, Wayne, NJ, formerly. *Awards:* ER Squibb and Sons Sculpture Award; Presentation Design Award, Am Inst Architects, 95; Installations Winner, Biennale for US, Malta, 97. *Bibliog:* Roskilde Avis (auth), Drom, fantasi realiteter og Illusioner, 6/28/86; Synagogue to Unveil Mosaic Mural, Town and Village, NY, 5/1/86; Arthur Williams (auth), Sculpture: Technique-Form-Content, Davis Publ, Inc, Worcester, Mass, 88; Ed McCormack (auth), World Class Winners at Art Gallery 54, Artspeak, NY, 1/1/90; Jennifer Lawson (auth), Holocaust mural, The Jewish Week, Inc, New York, 5/9/86. *Mem:* Col Art Asn; ISC; Fine Arts Fedn; Am Inst Architects (chair archit dialogue comt, 94-95); AIEMA. *Media:* Stone, Glass. *Res:* Mosaics: ancient medium/modern expression, a series of lectures based on research of ancient mosaics, how these were used to structure space in architecture, and how these methods have evolved in the contemporary use of mosaics as a medium. *Interests:* interdisciplinary creative art using concepts of science and mathematics. *Publ:* Contrib, Perle Fine Arts, 6/82; Hiroshi Murata, Arts, 1/83; Nassos Daphnis: An Artist in the Art World, Arts, 5/83; Offset Technology as a fine arts medium, Arts, 3/84; auth, Spectral Light as Sculptured Space, BRIDGES, 2001; auth, Geometric Mosaic Tiling on Hyperblic Sculptures, Univ Granada, Spain, 2003; auth, Mosaics as a Concept for Mathematics & Science, AIEMA Publ, Int Conf Antique & Medieval Mosaics, Rome, Ital, 2004; auth, Language of Abstraction, Pan Hellenic Soc, Athens, Greece, 2005; auth, Mosaic Art from Pebbles to Pixels, Renaissance Banff, BRIDGES, 2005. *Mailing Add:* 41 Sunset Dr Summit NJ 07901

ROUSSEAU-VERMETTE, MARIETTE
TAPESTRY ARTIST, EDUCATOR
Can citizen. *Study:* Ecole des Beaux Arts, dipl, 48; Oakland Col Arts & Crafts, Calif, 48-49. *Work:* Nat Gallery, Ottawa; Mus Contemp Art, Montreal; Winnipeg Art Gallery, Man; Quebec Mus, Quebec City; Metrop Mus Art, NY; Am Craft Mus, NY; and others. *Comn:* Kennedy Ctr theater curtain, comn by Can Govt, Washington, DC, 70; tapestry mural, Exxon Corp, Rockefeller Ctr, NY, 71; tapestry mural, Royal Bank Hq, Toronto, 77; Concert Hall ceiling, Toronto, 77-83; theatre curtain, Can Embassy, Washington, DC, 88-89. *Exhib:* Mus des Beaux Arts, Montreal, 61; 1st Biennale Tapestry, Mus Cantonal des Beaux Arts, Lausanne, Switz, 62, 65, 67, 71 & 77; Triennale, Milan Mus, 68; Contemp Tapestries, Mus Mod Art, NY, 68; Retrospective, Quebec City Mus, 72; Fiber Works, Mus Mod Art, Kyoto & Tokyo, Japan, 77-78; New Tapestry, Mus d'Art Contemp, Montreal, 77-78; The Art Fabric-Mainstream, traveling USA, 81-84. *Collection Arranged:* Metiers d'Art 2 & 3, Paris, Brussels, London & traveling; Mikrokosma, Europ & Can cities, 82-85. *Teaching:* Prof art, archit, Banff Sch Fine Arts, 77-80, head fiber arts dept, 80-85. *Awards:* 1st Prize, Concours Artistiques de la Province, Govt Que, 57; 2nd Prize, Can Handicraft Guild, Montreal, 61; Cert Hon, Can Conf Arts, 74; Order of Can, 76-. *Bibliog:* André Kuenzi (auth), La Nouvelle Tapisserie, Bibliot des Arts, Paris, 81; Vincent Tovell, interview, Hand & Eye-Fiber, Can Broadcasting Corp, 84; Pasia Schonberg, interview, Life: In a Flash of Lightning, TV Ont, 84-85. *Mem:* Can Soc Decorative Art & Design (vpres, 86); Soc Que de la Tapisserie Contemp (vpres, 81, pres, 86); Royal Can Acad Arts (elected mem, 73). *Media:* Fiber Art. *Res:* addition of fiber optics to traditional tapestries. *Specialty:* Pauli Art/Brown Grotta, Fiber Art. *Interests:* Nature. *Dealer:* Alice Pauli 9 rue de Port-Franc Lausanne 1003 Switzerland; Brown Grotta Gallery 276 Ridgefield Rd Wilton CT 06897. *Mailing Add:* 373 Rue Morin Ste Adele PQ J8B 2P8 Canada

ROUSSEL, CLAUDE PATRICE
SCULPTOR, EDUCATOR
b Edmundston, NB, July 6, 30. *Study:* Ecole Beaux-Arts, Montreal, PQ, 50-56; Can Coun Sr Traveling Fel, Europe, 61. *Work:* Smithsonian Inst, Washington; NB Mus, St John; Can Coun Art Bank; Portland Mus, Maine; New Brunswick Art Bank; New Brunswick Mus, Beaverbrook Art Gallery. *Comn:* Exterior sculpture & interior mural, Univ Moncton Nursing Pavilion, 71; Sailing Olympics, Kingston, Ont, 76; Int Sculpture Garden, Seoul Olympics, 88; Moncton 100 Monument, 90; Clement Cormier Monument, Univ Moncton, 90; and others; Exterior mural, Caisse Populaire

Moncton, 99. *Exhib:* Survey 69, Montreal Mus Fine Arts, 69; Owens Art Gallery, 75 & 79; Ctr d'Art du Montreal, Royal, 82; Beaverbrook Art Gallery, 84-88; Univ Moncton Art Gallery, 84; retrospective, Univ Moncton Art Gallery, 93; Claude Roussel Virtual Gallery; Topomania, New Brusnwick Mus, 2000; Festival Int Des Artvisuels, Caraquet, NB, 2003; Crea-Passion Univ Monicton Art Gallery, 2004. *Collection Arranged:* 41 public comns. *Pos:* Asst cur, Beaverbrook Art Gallery, Fredericton, 59-61. *Teaching:* Instr art, Edmundston Pub Schs, 56-59 & Univ Moncton, 63-91 (ret); prof emer, Univ Moncton, 98; prof emer, Royal Canadian Acad, 2000. *Awards:* Order of Can, 84; McCain Exhib, Beaverbrook Art Gallery, Fredericton, NB, 89; Current Award, Can Soc Educ Art, Ont, 96; Order of NB, 2002; Diplome De Medaille Dargent, Art-Sciences-Letters, France, 2004; Lifetime Award (Lt Gov), 2005. *Bibliog:* articles, Arts Atlantic, fall 77 & spring 83; Claude Roussel, Sculpteur, Sculptor, Edition D'Acadie, 87; Calude Roussel, Retrospective (video), 95; Bravo TV, Shaping Art, 2005. *Mem:* Asn Des Artistes Acadiens. *Media:* Wood, Enamel, Mixed Media. *Interests:* Documenting Biog Documents. *Collection:* Smithsonian; Seoul Olympic Sculpture Garden; New Brunswick Mus; Confederation Art Gallery; Beaverbook Art Gallery; 15 other insts. *Publ:* Coauth, The Visual Arts, In: The Acadians of the Maritimes, 82. *Mailing Add:* 50 allee des Arts Cap-Pele NB E4N 1R2 Canada

ROUTON, DAVID F
PAINTER, DRAFTSMAN
b Jackson, Tenn, Dec 6, 31. *Study:* Mexico City Col, BFA, 59; Univ Iowa, MFA, 63. *Work:* Sheldon Mem Art Gallery, Lincoln, Nebr; Univ Nebr, Lincoln; Univ Minn Art Mus, Minneapolis; Sioux City Art Ctr, Iowa; Col Notre Dame Md, Baltimore; Deane Col, Crete Nebr; Mus Nebr Art, Kearney, Nebr; and others. *Comn:* Portrait Carl T. Curtis, US Nat Park Serv, NPS Regional Bldg, Omaha, Nebr. *Exhib:* 24th Bradley Nat, Bradley Univ, Peoria, Ill, 93; 10th Art in the Woods Exhib, City Overland Park, Kans, 93; Galerie Tempo, Roeselane, Belgium, 93-94; Galerie Magenring, Hagen, Ger, 94; 28th Ann Nat Drawing & Small Sculpture Show, Del Mar Col, Corpus Christi, Tex, 94. *Teaching:* Instr, Mich State Univ, E Lansing, 63-64; Asst prof drawing & painting, State Univ NY, Plattsburg, 64-66 & Univ Minn, Minneapolis, 66-72; prof drawing & painting, Univ Nebr, Lincoln, 76-97, emeritus, 97-. *Awards:* Canson/Mi-Teintes Award Pastel, 29th Ann Chautauqua Nat, Chautauqua Inst, NY, 86; Jurors Merit Award, La Grange Nat XV, 90; Merit Award, Anderson Winter Show, Anderson Fine Arts Ctr, 93. *Mem:* Col Art Asn. *Media:* Oil; Drawing. *Publ:* Illusr, Ten Years in Nevada, 85, All is But a Beginning, 86, Martha Maxwell, Rocky Mountain Naturalist, 86, Emily: The Diary of a Hard Worked Woman, 87, Life in Alaska, 88, Univ Nebr Press; Sod House Days, Univ Press, Kans, 83. *Mailing Add:* 120 Woods Hall Lincoln NE 68588-0114

ROUX, BARBARA AGNES
ENVIRONMENTAL ARTIST, SCULPTOR
b Huntington, NY, Feb 28, 46. *Study:* State Univ NY, Col Old Westbury, BA, 79; Hunter Col, City Univ NY, MFA, 85. *Work:* Islip Art Mus, East Islip, NY; Heckscher Mus, Huntington, NY; Brooklyn Mus, Brooklyn, NY; Metropolitan Mus Art, NY; Cincinnati Mus, Cincinnati, Ohio; Libr, Whitney Mus, NY; Nat Mus of Women in eth Arts, Libr Collection. *Exhib:* Outdoor Sculpture Now, Islip Art Mus, East Islip, NY, 89; Collaborations: Word and Image, Pages Turned, Miami Univ Art Mus, Oxford, Ohio, 91; Featured Artists of the Permanent Collection, Islip Art Mus, 93; Eighteen Suffolk Artists, Univ Art Gallery, State Univ NY at Stony Brook, 95; What on Earth?, Wave Hill, Bronx, NY, 97; Country Pleasures, Heckscher Mus, Huntington, NY, 98; Elements 2000, Saug Harbor Cult Ctr, Newhouse Ctr Contemp Art, Staten Island, NY, 2000; Utopia/Dystopia, Byrdclffe Arts Colony, Woodstock, NY, 2000; Invisible Forest, Walter Wickiser Gallery, NY, 2003, Within the Land, Islip Art Mus, NY, 2003; Artists, Neighbors, Friends, Heckscher Mus, NY, 2003; Hidden Forrest Exhibit, AIR Gallery, NY, 2005. *Awards:* Alumni Award of Excellence, Communications & Creative Arts, Col Old Westbury, State Univ NY, 4/98; Artist Residency, Andy Warhol Preserve, The Nature Conservancy, 2005. *Bibliog:* Judy Collischan Van Wagner (auth), Barbara Roux, Arts Mag, 5/90; Helen A Harrison (auth), Pitting Man Against Nature Roux review, New York Times, 8/90; Interview with Barbara Roux, Artscene on Long Island, CableTV, 2/2000; Vivien Raynor (auth), A Show That Tweaks Ecological Concers, NY Times, 9/97; Phyllis Braff (auth), The Intellectual Translated into the Visual, NY Times, 1/99; Amy Storts (auth), Barbara Roux, NY Arts Mag, 2/02; Islip Art Mus, Within the Land, 2003; David Everitt (auth), The Woods and Wetlands Are Her Inspiration, NY Times, 11/03. *Mem:* Artists in Residence, New York. *Media:* Installation Art, Sculptural Environments. *Publ:* Coauth, The Opaque Glass, Water Mark Press, 84; Soc of Plants, Barbara Roux, 2001; Barbara Roux, Huntington, NY. *Mailing Add:* 20 Lloyd Pt Dr Huntington NY 11743

ROVNER, MICHAL
VIDEO ARTIST, PHOTOGRAPHER
b Tel Aviv, Israel, Nov 7, 57. *Study:* Tel Aviv Univ, Israel, BA(cinema/televison & philos), 81; Bezalel Acad Art, Jerusalem, hon BFA, 85. *Work:* Mus Mod Art, Metrop Mus, Whitney Mus American Art, Guggenheim Mus, NY; Art Inst Chicago & Mus of Contemp Art Chicago; Los Angeles Co Mus; Mus Fine Arts Houston; Corcoran Gallery Art, Washington, DC; Israel Mus; MACRO: Museo d'arte contemporanea, Rome; Musée de l'Elysée, Lausanne; Tel Aviv Mus, Israel. *Comn:* Installation Tel/Hill (mural), Colonnade House, Tel Aviv, 95; Installation Co-Existence (several murals overhanging Syrian-African break); Construct Process-Artist's Mus, Mitzpe-Ramon, Israel, 95. *Exhib:* Over 40 solo exhibs in video and film incl: Sky Line, Tel Aviv Mus Art, 88, Tel Aviv Mus Art, (exhib catalog) 90; Collection & Grant Winners, Am Israeli Cult Fund, Tel Aviv Mus Art, 90; Recent Acquisitions, Tel Aviv Mus Art, 91; Maison Cult Mercier, Montreal, 91; Grant Winners, Am Israeli Cult Fund, Haifa Mus Mod Art, Israel, 91; Tel Aviv Mus Art, 93; First Image: Eight Photogrs for the 90s, Laura Carpenter Fine Arts, Santa Fe, NMex, 93; In-Camera, Santa Fe Mus Art, NMex, 93; Art Inst Chicago 93 (exhib catalog), & Israel Mus, (exhib catalog) Jerusalem, 94; Contemp Women Photogrs, Mus Fine Arts Houston, 94; New Photog, Mus Mod Art, NY, 94; Moholy-Nagy and Present Company, Art Inst Chicago, 95; Beyond the Looking Glass: Contemp Women Photographers, David Adamson Gallery, Washington, 95; Desert, John Hansard Gallery, Univ Southampton, Eng, 96; Michal Rovner: The Space Between, Whitney Mus of Am Art, 2002; Against Order? Against Disorder?, Israeli Pavilion at the 50th Int Art Exhib, Venice Biennale, 2003; Michal Rovner: in stone, PaceWildenstein Gallery, 2004. *Pos:* Co-dir, Camera Obscura Sch Art, Tel Aviv, 78-; script writer & dir asst, Robert Frank, 90-91. *Teaching:* Instr photog criticism, Camera Obscura Sch Art, Tel Aviv, 85-88. *Awards:* Am Israeli Cult Fund Grant, 87, 89, 90-91; Jerar Levi Prize for contributions to progress of photog, Israel Mus, Jerusalem, 85; Polaroid Award, 88. *Bibliog:* Walter Keller (auth), Ani-Mal, Selection of the Artist's Work, Parkett, Zurich, 90; Jennifer L Riddel (auth), Reviews: Michal Rovner at Rhona Hoffman Gallery, New Art Examiner, 11/95; Simon Morrissey (auth), Reviews: Michal Rovner at Montage Gallery and Stephen Friedman Gallery, London, creative camera, 12-1/95-96. *Media:* Video. *Publ:* Contribr, Meetings, 86; coauth (with Robert Frank), One Hour-C'est Vrai (script), 90; auth, Decoy (exhib catalog), S Bitter-Larkin Gallery, 91. *Dealer:* Rhona Hoffman Gallery. *Mailing Add:* Pace Wildenstein Gallery 32 E 57th St 2nd Fl New York NY 10022

ROW, DAVID
PAINTER
b Portland, Maine, Aug 31, 49. *Study:* Yale Univ, BA(cum laude), 72, Yale Sch Art, with Al Held, MFA, 74. *Work:* Carnegie Mus Art, Pittsburgh, Pa; Brooklyn Mus Art, NY; Cleveland Mus Art; Hood Mus Art, Dartmouth Col; Wash Nat Airport; and others. *Comn:* Triptych, Richard Lewis Assocs, NY, 87; mural, Washington Nat Airport, 94. *Exhib:* Solo exhibs, John Good Gallery, NY, 87, 89, 91 & 93, Richard Feigen Gallery, Chicago, Ill, 91, Fujii Gallery, Tokyo, Japan, 91, Pamela Auchincloss Gallery, NY, 94, Locks Gallery, Philadelphia, Pa, 95 & Andre Emmerich, NY, 95 & 96; Armand Hammer Mus Art, Univ Calif Los Angeles, 95; Galerie Thomas von Lintel, Munich, 95 & 97; Turner, Byrne & Runyon, Dallas, 96 & 98; Contemp Arts Forum, Santa Barbara, 96; Mus Beaux Arts, La Chaux de Fonds, 96; Brandstelter & Wyss, Zurich, 98. *Teaching:* Instr drawing & photo, Rutgers Univ, NJ, 77-78; instr drawing & color, Sch Visual Arts, NY, 77-91; vis critic, Tyler Sch Art, 81, Bates Col, 87, Pratt, 88, NY Studio Sch, 90, Syracuse Univ, 93 & Kent State, 94; asst prof, Pratt Inst, Brooklyn, NY, 86-87; vis prof advan painting, Cooper Union Arts & Sci, NY, 94-95, Sch Visual Arts, graduate program, NY, 96-99; vis lectr & painting critic, Mt Royal Sch Art, Md Inst, 96 & Princeton Univ, NJ, 98. *Awards:* Scholar of the House in Painting, Yale Univ, 71-72; Yale-Norfolk Scholar, Norfolk Summer Sch Art & Music, 71; Grant in Painting, Nat Endowment Arts, 87. *Bibliog:* Roberta Smith (auth), Palettes full of ideas about what painting should be, NY Times, 11/1/96; John Zinsser (auth), Continuous Model: The Paintings of David Row, Edition Lintel, Munich, Ger; Alfred MacAdam (auth), Studio: David Row, Art News, 6/97; and others. *Mem:* Am Abstract Artists. *Media:* Oil, Fresco. *Dealer:* Andre Emmerich Gallery 41 E 57th St New York NY 10022; Galerie Thomas Von Lintel 10 Residenzstrasse Munich Germany. *Mailing Add:* 476 Broadway New York NY 10013

ROWAN, DENNIS MICHAEL
PRINTMAKER, EDUCATOR
b Milwaukee, Wis, Jan 6, 38. *Study:* Univ Wis, BS, 62; Univ Ill, MFA, 64. *Work:* Art Inst Chicago; Boston Mus Fine Arts; Seattle Art Mus, Wash; Okla Art Ctr, Oklahoma City; Honolulu Acad Arts, Hawaii. *Exhib:* Boston Mus Fine Arts, 61, 64-65, 68-69 & 70; Walker Art Ctr, Minneapolis, 62; Chicago Art Inst, 62 & 66; Pa Acad Fine Arts, 63; Seattle Art Mus, Wash, 63-65, 67, 70 & 71; Okla Art Ctr, 68, 70 & 72; Miami Art Ctr, 73; Brooklyn Mus, NY, 73; Calif Palace Legion Honor, San Francisco, 73; Vienna Graphics Biennale, Austria, 73; US Nat Mus, Washington, DC, 74; Kansas City Art Inst, 75; 3rd Biennale Int de l'Image, Epinal, France, 75; and many others. *Teaching:* Prof art, Univ Ill, Urbana-Champaign, 64-, assoc ctr advan study, 71-, prof sch art & design, currently. *Awards:* Purchase Award, 2nd Biennale Int Gravure, Cracow, Poland, 68; Yorkshire Arts Asn Purchase Prize, Brit Int Print Biennale, 70; Juror's Prize, Graphikbiennale Wien, Europahaus, Vienna, Austria, 72. *Media:* Intaglio. *Publ:* Contribr, Prize-winning graphics, Vol 3, 65 & Vol 4, 66; contribr, John Ross & Clare Romano's Complete Printmaker, Free Press, New York & Collier-Macmillan Ltd, Toronto, 72; contribr, Walter Chamberlin's Etching & Engraving, Thames & Hudson, London, 72 & Viking Press, New York, 73. *Mailing Add:* 101 S Scarbrorough Sidney IL 61877

ROWAN, FRANCES PHYSIOC
PAINTER, WOODCUTTER
b Ossining, NY, Dec 17, 1908. *Study:* Randolph-Macon Woman's Col, 29-30; Cooper Union, BFA, 36; also graphics with Harry Sternberg & woodcuts with Carol Summers, 65-73. *Work:* Randolph-Macon Woman's Col, Lynchburg, Va; Freeport High Sch, NY; Cotton Inc. *Exhib:* Brooklyn Mus 11th Nat Print Show, 58; Audubon Artists, 58 & 59; Am Fedn Arts Traveling Show, 58-59; Knickerbocker Artists, 61; Silvermine Guild Artists 6th & 14th Nat Print Show, 66 & 80; one-man show, Sarasota Art Asn, 81. *Teaching:* Instr drawing & painting, Country Art Gallery, Westbury, NY, 55-66; instr drawing & painting, Five Towns Music & Art Found, 70-72; instr drawing, still life & figure, Longboat Key Art Ctr, 77-. *Awards:* First Prizes, Hofstra Univ, 57 & Sarasota Art Asn, 79 & 82; Flax Award, Knickerbocker Artists, 61; and others. *Mem:* Prof Artists Guild; Silvermine Guild Artists; Longboat Key Ctr for the Arts. *Media:* Graphics; Oils. *Mailing Add:* 601 Broadway Longboat Key FL 34228

ROWAN, HERMAN
PAINTER, EDUCATOR
b New York, NY, July 20, 23. *Study:* Cooper Union; San Francisco State Col; Kans State Col, BS; State Univ Iowa, MA & MFA. *Work:* Walker Art Ctr, Minneapolis; Brooklyn Mus, NY; Univ Notre Dame, South Bend, Ind; Columbus Mus, Ohio; San Diego Gallery Fine Arts, Calif; Tweed Mus, Duluth, Minn. *Exhib:* Grand Central

Moderns, NY, 60, 63 & 65; San Francisco Mus Nat Ann, 63; Southwest Ann, Houston Mus, 63; Walker Art Ctr Exhib, 65; Box-Top Art, Tour NZ Galleries, 71-72; Mitzi Landau Gallery, Los Angeles, 82; Tweed Mus Art, Duluth, Minn, 86; retrospective, Katherine Nash Gallery, Univ Minn, 93. *Teaching:* Prof painting, Univ Minn, Minneapolis, 63-93, emer prof, 93-. *Awards:* Lyman Award, Albright Gallery, 59; Purchase Prize, San Diego Gallery Fine Arts, 63. *Media:* Oil. *Collection:* Brooklyn Mus, Tweed Mus, Duluth. *Mailing Add:* Regis Center for Arts E208 405 21st Ave S Minneapolis MN 55455

ROWAN, (C) PATRICK
PAINTER, SCULPTOR
b Milwaukee, Wis, Jan 7, 37. *Study:* Univ Wis-Madison, BSArch, 62; Univ Wis-Milwaukee, BFA(painting), 68, MS(painting), 70; Univ Fla, Gainesville, MFA(sculpture), 71. *Work:* Kearney State Col, Nebr; Univ Wis-Milwaukee; Joslyn Art Mus, Omaha, Nebr; Sheldon Art Gallery; Springfield Art Mus, Mo; and others. *Comn:* Sculpture installations, St John's Univ Art Ctr, Minn, 98. *Exhib:* One-man exhibs, 34 paintings & sculptures, Wis, Fla, Nebr, SDak, Pa, Iowa, Ark, Mo, Colo & Minn, 70-98; Invited Exhibs, Gallery Tempo, Roselaire, Belgium, Gallery Epikur, Wuppertal, Ger & Belgium Ministry, Brussels, 90-98; Reflections of Faith (nat sculpture), Concordia Col, Ann Arbor, Mich, 96; Contemp Works of Faith (sculpture), Columbus Mus, Ohio, 97; Impressions, Blanden Art Mus, Fort Dodge, Iowa, 2000; Religious Sculpture 2000, Cath Univ Am, Washington, DC, 2000; Works of Faith 2000, Portland, Oreg, 2000; over 80 others. *Teaching:* Instr, Univ Wis-Milwaukee, 69-70; prof sculpture, painting & drawing, Univ Nebr, Lincoln, 71-99, prof studio art, 71-. *Awards:* Grant, Univ Nebr, Lincoln, 95, 96, 97, 98, 99, 2000. *Bibliog:* Jon Nelson (auth), Artists work, Lincoln J, 91; V A Christensen (auth), Catalogúe sculpture-Rowan, Spiva Art Ctr, Joplin, Mo, 93; Kyle Macmillan (auth), Review, Omaha World Herald, 96-98. *Mem:* Asn Int Artists; Irish Am Cult Inst; Int Sculpture Ctr; Sculpture's Soc Ireland; Christians in Visual Arts. *Media:* Acrylic, Oil; Wood Fabrication & Carving. *Publ:* Contribr, Poetry Across the Universe Anthology, Nat Libr Poetry, 96; Meditations, Cader Publ Ltd, 97; Reflections, Poets Int Soc, 97

ROWAND, JOSEPH DONN
GALLERY DIRECTOR, ART DEALER
b Champaign-Urbana, Ill, July 11, 42. *Study:* Southern Ill Univ, BFA, 64; Ont Sch Art; Parsons Sch Design, New York. *Collection Arranged:* Vic Huggins, 78, 81, 85, 89 & 93, Dorothy Gillespie, 81, 84, 88 & 92 Maud Gatewood, 83, 87, 89, 91 & 93, Mary Lou Higgins, 84, 87 & 91, Edith London, 82, 84, 86, 89 & 91; Raymond Chorneau, 85, 88 & 91, Andrew Braitman, 92, Will Dexter, 90, Claytopia, 90 & Thomas Sayre, 92; Group Fiber Show 87, Somerhill Gallery, Chapel Hill, NC. *Pos:* Panel mem, How to Buy & Enjoy Contemp Art, City Gallery Contemp Art, Raleigh, NC, 88; adv bd, City Mag, 91 & NC Home Mag, 92; Town Chapel Hill Pub Art Endowment Coun, 91 & 92; owner & dir, Somerhill Gallery, currently; plus numerous juror & adminr positions for arts orgns. *Teaching:* Guest lectr, Sandhills Community Col, Carthage, NC, 85, Arts on the River Festival, Savannah Arts Asn, Ga, 88, Duke Univ Continuing Educ Fac, 89 & 90 & Wake Visual Arts Asn, Raleigh, NC, 92; NC Cent Univ Fine Art of Collecting Symp, 87. *Bibliog:* Kay McClain (auth), Chapel Hill Newspaper, 89; Jo Schwarts (auth), Art Bus News, 90; Katheleen Christianson & Fred Park (auths), article, Bus Properties, 91; and others. *Mem:* NC Mus Art Found; Duke Univ, Mus Art (bd dir, 92-95); Art Advocates NC; Akland Mus Assocs; Southeastern Ctr Contemp Art; and others. *Specialty:* Contemp American Artists of Southeastern US

ROWE, CHARLES ALFRED
PAINTER, ILLUSTRATOR
b Great Falls, Mont, Feb 7, 34. *Study:* Mont State Univ, 52-53; Southern Methodist Univ, 56-57; Univ Chicago, 59-60; Art Inst Chicago, BFA, 60; Tyler Sch Art, Temple Univ, Philadelphia, MFA, 68; also with John Rogers Cox, Boris Margo, Max David Brill, Leroy Neiman & James Paulus. *Work:* Victoria & Albert Mus, London; Noel Goldblatt Collection, Chicago; Michael Landon Productions, Hollywood; Banco De Granda, Spain; Star Shower Found, Graveson-en-Provence, France; NASA Space Mus, Cape Canaveral, Fla; and numerous others. *Comn:* Designed a coord arts coun symbol & related printed materials for Mont Arts Coun, Missoula, 73; designed numerous fabrics for major accounts for Galleon Fabrics, Inc, NY, 74-; USAF Pentagon, Washington, DC, 89, 91 & 92; NASA Mus, Cape Kennedy, Fla, 89. *Exhib:* Dallas Mus Fine Art, 57; Art Inst Chicago, 59; Los Angeles Co Mus, Calif, 65; one-man exhibs, Newark Gallery, Del, 67-69, Mickelson Gallery, Washington, DC, 70 & 74, C M Russell Mus, Great Falls, 72-74, 76, 78, 80, 82-87, 89, Pleiades Gallery, NY, 77 & 81, Sala de Exposiciones, Almunecar, Spain, 88, West Chester Univ, Pa, 92 & Soc Illusrs, NY, 93 & 2004; Mid-Year Show, Butler Inst Am Art, Youngstown, Ohio, 69; 37th Mid-Year Show, Butler Inst Am Art, Youngstown, Ohio, 73; Ball State Nat Drawing & Small Sculpture Show, Ball State Univ, Muncie, Ind, 74; C M Russell Mus Invitational, Great Falls, Mont, 86-91; Nat Drawing Exhib: Exhibits USA, Kansas City, Mo, 89-91; USAF Exhib, Soc Illusrs, NY, 89 & 91; Our Own Show, Soc Illusrs, NY, 90-2006; Atrium Gallery, NY, 95; Hauptman & Greenwood Collections, NY, 94; Kevin Costner, Hollywood, Calif, 95; plus over 200 others exhibs. *Collection Arranged:* Univ Del, Mont. State Collection, Mont. State Univ Del State Collection, Great Falls Pub Schs, Michael Landon Prodns, Calif, Jerry Pinkney, Croton-on-Hudon, NY, Kau Collection, Charlotte, NC, Meredith Corp, Des Moines, Collection Knissel, Austria, Archives Victoria and Albert Mus, London, artists USAF Nat. Collection, Washington, Jacqueline Pierson, Nice, France, Banco De Granada, Granada, Spain, artists USAF Nat Collection, Washington; NASA Space Mus, Hauptman and Greenwood Collections, NYC, Bush Collection, Swampscott, MA, Star Shower Foundation, Graveson, Provence, France, Vera Haas, Dallas, Baker, Honolulu; fabric designer Galleon Fabrics, Inc, NYC, Jones of NY, Saks Fifth Ave, Kevin Kilner, Jordan Baker, Hollywood, Calif, 1987, Steele Big Fork, Mt, Kevin Kostner Collection, 1997, designer graphics Mont. State Arts Coun, Del. state duck stamp, 1981. *Pos:* Graphic designer & consult, Chicago, Ill, 57-60; graphic package designer, Am Can Co, Bellwood, Ill, 60-62; graphic designer, Abrams-Bannister Engraving, Inc, Greenville, SC, 62-64; life drawing prog, Greenville Mus Art, 62-64; artist-in-residence, Nat Endowment Arts & Humanities, 72-73; design consult, Galleon Fabrics, Inc, First Run Fabrics, Inc & TAGS, 74-83. *Teaching:* Prof drawing, painting, illustrator & graphic design, Univ Del, 64-; exchange prof, Univ Ariz, 83-84; Prof Emer, 97. *Awards:* Nat Endowment Arts & Humanities Grant, 72-73; Unidel Grant, 89; President's Grant, 1/90; and many others. *Bibliog:* Three present rewarding results of sabbatical leaves, Univ Del, News Update, 88; Sara Albert (auth), Potpourri, Cecil Co Arts Coun, 89; Article in Grand Rapids Press, 12/4/89. *Mem:* Soc Illusrs, NY. *Media:* Oil, Acryllic; Watercolor. *Publ:* Illusr, State duck stamps, New York Art Review, Harshman & Houk; Artists in the Schools-Communities, 72-88, Mont Arts Coun, 88; Duck Stamps and Prints, the Complete Federal and State Ed, Hugh Lauter Levin Assoc, Inc, 88, reved, 91; The New York Art Review, Am References, Inc, 88; artist, Huang Trial, WNSTV Channel 2 & WPVI Channel 6, 89. *Dealer:* Hardcastle Gallery Newark DE; Artistic Gallery Bear DE. *Mailing Add:* Chapel Hill 133 Aronimink Dr Newark DE 19711

ROWE, MICHAEL DUANE
PAINTER
b Lykens, Pa, Nov 5, 47. *Study:* Art Inst Pittsburgh, Pa, 71-72. *Work:* Southern Allegheny Mus Art, Loretto, Pa. *Exhib:* Dia de los Muertos, Alternative Mus, NY, 90, 94 & 95; 56th National Mid Yr, Butler Inst Am Art, Youngstown, Ohio, 90 & 92; Images, Pa State Univ, 92 & 93; Pa Council of the Arts, Pa State Mus, Harrisburg, 86 & 87; Works on Paper, Del Cen Conte Art, Wilmington, 93; Magic Realism, Southern Allegheny Mus, Loretto, Pa, 96, 97 & 99; Whitaker Arts/Scis, Harrisburg, Pa, 2000. *Awards:* Grant, Art Matters, 88; First Prize, Delaplaine Gallery, 89; Fel, Pa Coun Arts, 93. *Bibliog:* Michael Tomor (auth), Magic Realism, Art Review, 99. *Media:* Oil. *Specialty:* printing, sculpture. *Dealer:* Mangel Gallery 1714 Rittenhouse Sq Philadelphia PA 19103. *Mailing Add:* 814 Meadow Ln Camp Hill PA 17011-1545

ROWE, REGINALD M
PAINTER, SCULPTOR
b New York, NY, Dec 8, 20. *Study:* Princeton Univ, BA, 44; Art Students League, with Louis Bosa, 46-47; Inst Allende, Univ Guanajuato, 58-59, MFA, 59. *Work:* McNay Mus, San Antonio; Arts Coun San Antonio; Univ Tex Health & Sci Ctr; San Antonio Mus Art; St Thomas Univ, Houston, Tex. *Comn:* Mural & outdoor sculpture, Hemisfair 1968, San Antonio, Tex, 68. *Exhib:* One-man shows, Welluns Gallery, NY, NY, 52, 53 & 56, Bianchini Gallery, NY, NY, 60, Ruth White Gallery, NY, 64 & 70, Marion Koogler McNay Mus, San Antonio, Tex, 77, Wallace Wentworth Gallery, Wash, DC, 85, Locus Gallery, San Antonio, 87, Read Stremmel Gallery, San Antonio, 87, Milagros Contemp Gallery, San Antonio, 93 & 95; Retrospective, Marion Koogler McNay Mus, San Antonio, 96; Evanston Art Ctr, Ill, 98; Joan Grona Gallery, San Antonio, Tex, 99 & 2001; Semmes Gallery, Univ Incarnate Word, San Antonio, Tex, 2000; Southwest Sch Art & Crafts, San Antonio, Tex, 2003; Baylor Univ, Waco, Tex, 2005. *Pos:* Chmn exhibs, Witte Mus, 65-67. *Teaching:* Instr painting & design, San Antonio Art Inst, 64-84; vis artist, Univ NFla, 75, Southwest Craft Ctr, 84-87 & San Antonio Art Inst, 87-. *Awards:* San Miguel Allende, 60. *Bibliog:* Ernest Hemingway (auth), catalog statement for first New York show, 52; reviews in Arts, Art News, Artweek, Pictures on Exhib, Times, Tribune & Art Int, 52-70; rev, San Antonio Express, SA Light, 65-97. *Mailing Add:* 219 W Gramercy San Antonio TX 78212

ROWLAND, ADELE
PHOTOGRAPHER
b Ft Rodman, Mass, Dec 4, 15. *Study:* Carnegie Mellon Univ, 34-35; Univ Southern Calif, BS, 38, MS, 42; Univ Calif, Berkeley, PhD, 49. *Work:* Bibliotheque Nationale, Paris, France; Grunwald Ctr Graphic Arts, Univ Calif, Los Angeles; San Francisco Mus Mod Art, Calif; Libr Cong, Washington, DC; Nanjing Mus Art, China. *Comn:* Greek photomontage, Occidental Life, Los Angeles, Calif, 77; wall mural (7 ft), Kapalua Bay Hotel, Maui, Hawaii, 78; seven wall murals, Torrey Pines Bank, La Jolla, Calif, 85; two wine-country murals, comn by pvt home, Napa, Calif, 89; three Wis photomontages, Hitachi Data Systems, Palo Alto, Calif, 93. *Exhib:* Light Images, Chrysler Mus Art, Norfolk, Va, 78; Haiku Photog Prints, San Jose Mus Art, Calif, 79; Adele's Recent Counterpoint Images, Hearst Gallery, St Mary's Col, Moraga, Calif, 89; Counterpoint Images of Am Dr Adele, Nanjing Mus Art, China, 92; Les Artistes Francais, Le Salon 93, Grand Palais, Paris, France, 93; 138th Ann Int Print Exhib, Royal Photog Soc Gt Brit, Octagon House, Bath, Eng, 94; Panorama de l'Art Vivant '97, Salon d'Automne, Espace Eiffel Branly, Paris, France, 97; Int Dominican Artists, Piazza della Minerva, 42, Rome, 00; Imaginary Imagery, Oakland Munic Water Gallery, Calif, 01; Salon d'Automne, Espace Auteuil, Paris, 01; Int Artists, La Galerie Int, Palo Alto, Calif, 01; Am Artists, France-Ameriques, Paris, 02; Int Artists, Alliance Francaise, San Francisco, 03. *Teaching:* Assoc prof Eng, Calif State Univ, Fresno, 40-50; assoc prof humanities, hist art & photog, Dominican Col, San Rafael, Calif, 51-75 & resident artist, 75-. *Awards:* Award of Distinction, Royal Photog Soc Gt Brit, 94; Most Talented Artist Silver Medal, 7th Int Exhib, Peder Russu, Stockholm, Sweden, 97; Fra Angelico Award for Excellence in Art, Lifetime Achievement Award, Dominican Inst Arts, 98; US Dominican Artist Rep, Convocation of Leading Internat Dominican Artists, Rome, 00. *Bibliog:* Gary Peterson (auth), Marvelous transformation, San Rafael News Pointer, 3/2/94; Unsigned, Spirit and Tradition in American Art, Art Pictorial, Tokyo, Vol 10, 96; B Winegarner (auth), Dominican artist honored with art award, News Pointer, 9/22/98. *Mem:* Alliance Women Artists; Royal Photog Soc Gt Brit. *Interests:* the photomontage aspect of photography. *Mailing Add:* Artist-in-Residence Dominican Univ Calif 50 Acacia Ave San Rafael CA 94901

ROWLAND, ANNE
PHOTOGRAPHER
b Washington, DC. *Study:* Am Univ, 79; Sch Mus Fine Arts, Boston, BFA, 82; Calif Inst Arts, 87-89. *Work:* Bank of Boston; Spencer Mus, Kans; Houston Mus Fine Art, Tex. *Exhib:* Solo exhibs, Hera Coop Gallery, Wakefield, RI, 83, Sch Art, Univ Denver, Colo, 84, Burlington Co Col, Pembrerton, NJ, 84, Zoe Gallery, Boston, 86, 87 & 91, Tartt Gallery, Washington, DC, 90, Greg Kucera Gallery, Seattle, 90-91 & Jayne Baum Gallery, NY, 93; Twelve on 20 x 24, Mus Fine Arts Sch, Boston, 84; Boston Now: Photog, Inst Contemp Art, Boston, 85; 50th Anniversary Celebration, Inst Contemp Art, Boston, 86; The Photog of Invention: Am Pictures of the 1980's, Nat Mus Am Art, Smithsonian, Washington, DC, 89, travelled to Walker Art Ctr, Minneapolis, 89; This is My Body, Greg Kucera Gallery, Seattle, 94; Sum of the Parts, Univ Hawaii Art Gallery, Honolulu, 94; Contemp Collections of the Los Angeles Ctr for Photog Studies, Gallery at 777, Los Angeles, 94; About Face, Real Art Ways, Hartford, Conn, 94; and others. *Awards:* Fel, Nat Endowment Arts, 86; Photog Fel, Mass Coun Arts & Humanities, Artists' Found, 85. *Bibliog:* Miyoshi Barosh (auth), Photo essay, Now Times, Los Angeles, 92; Michael Duncan (auth), Hollywood, Hollywood, Art Issues, Los Angeles, No 26, 1-2/93; Vince Aletti (auth), Voice Choice, Village Voice, NY, 3/9/93. *Dealer:* Tartt Gallery 2017 Q St NW Washington DC 20009. *Mailing Add:* c/o Jayne H Baum Gallery 26 Grove St 4C New York NY 10014

ROYAL, RICHARD P
CRAFTSMAN
Study: Inst de Cultural, Guadalajara, Mex, 73; Cent Wash Univ, 70-74; Pilchuck Glass Sch, Stanwood, Wash, 78-84. *Work:* Washington Trust Bank, Spokane; Wash State Arts Comn, Olympia; Seattle Children's Theater; IBM Collection, NY; High Mus Art, Atlanta; Mint Mus of Art, Charlotte; and others. *Comn:* Wash Governor's Award, Wash State Arts Comn. *Exhib:* One-man shows, Foster/White Gallery, 86, 87, 89, 91, 93, 94, 96 & 98 Lyons/Matrix Gallery, Austin, Tex, 92, Margo Jacobson Gallery, Portland, Ore, 93, 97 & 99, Friesen Fine Art, Sun Valley, Idaho, 93, 94 & 99, Vespermann Gallery, Atlanta, Ga, 94, Grand Central Gallery, Tampa, Fla, 95 & 98, Elaine Horwitch Gallery, Scottsdale, Ariz, 95, Marx Saunders Gallery, Chicago, 2000 & Riley Hawk, Cleveland, 2000; C Corcoran Gallery, Muskegon, Mo, 88, 89 & 90; Masterworks: Pacific NW Arts and Crafts Now, Bellevue Art Mus, Wash, 91; Clearly Art: Pilchuck's Glass Legacy, Whatcom Mus Hist & Art, Bellingham, Wash, 92; Nine Decades: Northern California Craft Movement, 1907-Present, Calif Col Arts & Crafts, Oakland, Calif, 93; Collective Brilliance: Contemp Glass, Albany Mus Art, Ga, 94; Northwest Glass: Park I, NW Mus Art, La Conner, Wash, 95-96; Heir Apparent: Translating the Secrets of Venetian Glass, Bellevue Art Mus, Wash, 97; Progressions in Glass, Contemp Art Ctr of Virginia Beach, 97; Founder's Circle Collection, Mint Mus of Arts and Crafts, Charlotte, NC, 2000. *Pos:* Designer/production artist, Glass Eye Studio, Seattle, Wash, 82-84; prof artist, currently. *Teaching:* Gaffer, Dale Chihuly Studio, Seattle, Wash, 78- & Benjamin Moore Studio, Seattle, Wash, 85-; instr, Pilchuck Glass Sch, Stanwood, Wash, 81- & gaffer, 83-90; instr, Haystack Mountain Sch Crafts, Deer Isle, Maine, 89; instr, New Orleans Sch Glassworks, La, 93; workshop instr, Ohio State Univ, 99. *Awards:* Nat Endowment Arts Fel Award, 88; Wash Gov Award, Wash State Arts Comn, 89. *Bibliog:* Southwest Art Mag, 2/94; Matthew Kangas (auth), rev, Glass Mag, fall 94; Glass & Art Mag, fall 94 & 95; Am Craft Mag, Apr/May 95; and others. *Mailing Add:* William Traver Gallery 110 Union St # 200 Seattle WA 98101

ROYBAL, JAMES RICHARD
PASTEL, PAINTER
b Santa Fe, NM, Aug 23, 52. *Study:* Highlands Univ, Las Vegas, NMex, 1971-1972; NMex State Univ, 1973-1975; Albert Handel-Pastel Hall of Fame, 1994-1995. *Comn:* Life size Geronimo, Mr. James Garrow, Santa Fe, NMex, 2003. *Exhib:* NMex State Fair Prof Fine Arts, Albuquerque State Fair Grounds, Albuquerque, NMex, 1971; NMex State Fair Prof Fine Arts, NMex State Fair, Albuquerque, NMex, 1978-1981, 1986, 1988; Santa Fe Festival of the Arts, Convention Center, Santa Fe, NMex, 1979-1980; Taos Arts Asn, Vistas, Stables Art Center, Taos, NMex, 1986; NMex State Fair, Permanent Collection, Gov's Gallery, Santa Fe, NMex, 1987; Miniatures, Albuquerque Mus of Art, Albuquerque, NMex, 1991-1994. *Teaching:* Instr, Pastel Painting, Valdes Art Workshops, Santa Fe, NMex, 2005-2006. *Awards:* First Place & Purchase Award, NMex Fair Prof Fine Arts Show, Fair, 1978; Best of Show, NMex State Fair Prof Fine Arts Show, Fair, 1986, 1988; Southwest Art Magazine Award, 2003. *Bibliog:* Daniel Gibson (auth), Artist of the Year, Santa Fean Mag, 1978; Peggy & Harold Samuels (auths), Contemporary Western Artist, Southwest Art Mag, 1982; Joy Waldren Murphy (auth), Best Part is Art, Santa Fean Mag, 1987. *Mem:* NMex Pastel Soc; Nat Sculpture Soc. *Media:* Painter, All Media, Sculptor, Bronze, Metal cast w/stone. *Specialty:* Representational Art - Western. *Interests:* Oil painting proficiency. *Publ:* Auth, Sculptor James Roybal (cover), 1979; auth, Exploring all Possibilities, Santa Fean Mag, 1994. *Dealer:* Alexandra Stevens Gallery of Fine Arts 820 Canyon Rd Santa Fe NM 87501; Grimshaw Fine Art 132 Kit Carson Rd Taos NM 87571. *Mailing Add:* 25 Lone Pine Spur Santa Fe NM 87505

ROYCE-SILK, SUZANNE
CONSULTANT, CURATOR
b Oakland, Calif, Dec 26, 35. *Study:* Univ Calif, Berkeley, BA(hist art), 83. *Collection Arranged:* Parker Edwards, George Scott Miller, Louis Siegriest, Bolinas Mus, Calif, 92; Gordon Onslow Ford (auth, catalog), Bolinas Mus, Calif, 93; Richard & Martha Shaw, Robert Hudson, Cornelia Schulz-The Stinson Years (auth, catalog), Bolinas Mus, Calif, 93; Calif Contemporary: Three Coastal Collections, Bolinas Mus, Calif, 98; Gordon Onslow Ford Mirando en lo profundo, Seeing in Depth, Fundacion Eugenio Granell, Santiago de Compostela, Spain, 98; Fletcher Benton, Solid Geometry, Sheldon Mem Art Gallery, Univ Nebr, Lincoln, 99. *Pos:* Spec projs coordr, Phillips Collection, Washington, DC, 83-84, corp progs mgr, 84-86; art communs consult, Suzanne Royce & Assocs, San Francisco, 87-. *Mem:* Am Asn Mus; Nat Asn Corp Art Mgt; Coun Univ Art Mus, Berkeley; Col Art Asn. *Publ:* Auth, The Years at White Gate Ranch (exhib catalog), Bolinas Mus, Calif, 95. *Mailing Add:* 1408 Kearny St San Francisco CA 94133

ROYER, MONA LEE
PAINTER
b Washington, DC, June 5, 44. *Study:* Dayton Art Inst, 53; Famous Artists Sch, 66; Wright State Univ, BFA(hons), 78; Georgetown Univ, 85; Alliance Francaise, Paris, 85; Casa Italiana, Washington, 95; Riverbend Art School, Ohio, Roberson Studio, Hawaii, Tepping Studio, Ohio. *Work:* Joan Rivers, NY; The Embassy of Europ Economic Community, Washington; Xerox Corp & Ohio Vision Serv, Columbus, Ohio; Nat Portrait Gallery, Washington; Pat Summerall, Dallas, Tx; Nieman Marcus, Washington, DC; KY Fried Chicken, Lousiville, KY; I Magnin, MD; Burke & Herbert Bank, VA; Kettering Foundation, Ohio; Nolan Miller, Hollywood. *Comn:* Andy Williams, Branson, Mo; Visitors Service Staff, Nat Gallery Art, Washington; DM Graves Jr, Asn Old Crows; Hist Soc Bermuda; Joan Rivers, NY; Judith Lieberer Handbags; Painted Violin for Arlington, Symphony, VA; National Gallery Orchestra, Washington, DC; Gold Cup Title & Escrow, VA; Rolls Royce, USA, 2006; Nat Symphony Orchestra, 2006. *Exhib:* Galerie Julian, 92-; One-man shows, Nat Gallery Art, Washington, You'll Love It Gallery, Palm Beach, 94 & 95, Fashion Accessories Expo, NY, 94, Gramercy Park Gallery, NY, 94 & 95, Saks Fifth Ave, Washington, 94, 95 & 96, Christina's, Martha's Vineyard, 94 & 95 & Russell Senate Rotunda, Washington, 97; Broadway Gallery, Fairfax, Va, 98; Toledo Mus Art, Ohio; Columbus Mus Fine Art, Ohio; Iranian Embassy; Brit Embassy; Capitol Hill; Phillips (mus) Mansion; Marin Price Gallery, Chevy Chase, Md, 2000; Foliograph Gallery, DC, 2001-2005; Art & Frame by Valentin, 2002-2003; Mt Vernon Plantation, Va, 2003; Riverbend Designs, WVa, 2005; Watercolors of Colombus Gallery, 9 Yrs; Sisco Systems Beastie Bizaar, 2004-2006; Nat Symphony Show House, 2006; and others. *Pos:* prof painter (artist), Sales Art/Dayton, selling through galleries and out of his own studio, 67-68; dealer & consult, 69-; exhib aide & art info specialist, Nat Gallery Art, Washington, DC; licensed tour guide, (Art Specialists Tours); sketch artist, Nat Gallery of Art Concert Series, Washington, DC, 2000-2006. *Teaching:* Independent Art Marketing, 94-. *Awards:* Second in Painting, Nat Arboretum, Washington, 89; One Artist Hon, Toledo Mus Art, 95. *Bibliog:* Jacqueline Hall (auth), Enjoying paintings, Columbus Dispatch, 78 & 79; Kay Blue (auth), article, Wright State Alumni News, 91; Kristen Hartke (auth), Hill Rag, Art Critic, Washington, 91; Alexandria Gazette, 2000, plus others. *Mem:* Guild Prof (Art) Tour Guides; Nat Trust Hist Preserv; Nat Capitol Hist Soc; Blair House. *Media:* Oil, Watercolor. *Publ:* Delta Queen Cover, CFA program, Cincinnati, 68; Eight art covers, Hill Rag, Washington, 85-91; art covers, Foxhall Gazette, Fagon Publ, Washington, 90-91; auth, Journal of electronic warefare, 92; cover art, Wright State News, 92; self-pub Pastel Cats, 92, 2000; Self Published Society Works called My Mother's Friends. *Dealer:* Foliograph Gallery Washington DC; Dinunzio Designs Warrenton Va; Marin Price Gallery Washington DC (Chevy Chase); Toledo Mus of Art. *Mailing Add:* PO Box 34 Mount Vernon VA 22121

ROZIER, ROBERT L
PAINTER
Study: St Mary's Seminary Col, Perryville, Mo, BA, 72; Mich State Univ, East Lansing, MFA, 81. *Exhib:* Columbia Art League Ann Exhib, Columbia, Mo, 77; Knollwood Gallery, Western Mich Univ, Kalamazoo, 80; All Area 1985 Exhib, Saginaw Art Mus, Mich, 86; Nat Juried Exhib, Arlington Art Asn, Arlington Mus Art, Tex, 87; Four Views of the Figure, Pontiac Art Ctr, 88; solo exhibs, Flora Kirsch Beck Gallery, Alma Col, 83, Colby-Sawyer Col, New London, NH, 84, Creative Arts Gallery, Mt Pleasant, Mich, 87, Saginaw Valley State Univ, 88. *Teaching:* Instr painting, drawing, watercolor, Art Reach Mid-Mich, Mt Pleasant, 81-82; instr illus, Lansing Community Col, 82; asst prof, Alma Col, Mich, 83-. *Media:* Watercolor. *Dealer:* Cade Gallery, Royal Oak, MI. *Mailing Add:* 416 Yale Ave Alma MI 48801

ROZMAN, JOSEPH JOHN
PAINTER, EDUCATOR
b Milwaukee, Wis, Dec 26, 44. *Study:* Univ Wis, Milwaukee, BFA(with honors), 67, MFA, 69. *Work:* Southwest Tex State Col; Carroll Col; Waukesha, Wis; Racine Art Mus, Wis; Georgetown Univ, Washington, DC; Milwaukee Art Mus; and others. *Comn:* Complete ed of etchings for membership drive, Milwaukee Art Ctr, 69; Award Emblem Design, Lakefront Festival of Arts, Milwaukee Art Ctr, 73 & 77; PBS Great TV Auction (poster), WMVS TV, 78. *Exhib:* 19th, 20th & 21st Boston Printmakers Nat, Boston Mus Fine Arts, 67-69; Nat Print & Drawing Exhib, Okla Art Ctr, Oklahoma City, 67-68 & 72; Int NW Printmakers Exhib, Seattle Art Mus & Portland Art Ctr, 68 & 69; Printmaking: Wisconsin Editions, Milwaukee Art Mus, 72; one-man show, Milwaukee Art Mus, 73 & Joy Horwich Gallery, Chicago, 80 & 83; Artists/Toys Exhib, Milwaukee Art Mus, 77 & 79; Works on Paper, Art Inst Chicago, 78; Wisconsin Directions Two: Here & Now, Milwaukee Art Mus, 78; Watercolor USA, Springfield Art Mus, 81; Prints & Multiples, Art Inst Chicago, 81; Wis Masters Exhib, Wis Acad Arts & Scis, 86; The Aesthetic Excursion: Artists Look at Travel & Transportation, Wustum Mus Fine Arts, Racine, 89; Fourth Int Biennial Print Exhib, Taipei Fine Arts US, Taiwan, Rep of China, 90; Watercolor Wisconsin: Celebrating 25 Years, Charles A Wustum Mus Art, Racine, 91; and others. *Teaching:* Instr design & printmaking, Univ Wis-Milwaukee, 67-69 & 72-73; instr printmaking, Milwaukee Art Mus, 68-76; instr printmaking & painting, Carthage Col, 69-72; vis lectr art, univ Wis-Parkside, 70-71; instr printmaking & design, Layton Sch Art & Design, 73-74; prof printmaking, painting & photography, Mt Mary Col, Wis, 75-; artist-in-residence, Univ Wis-Platteville, 83; dir, fine art prog, Mount Mary Col, Milwaukee, Wis, 02-. *Awards:* Logan Award, Art Inst Chicago, 66, Curtis Award, 81; Edgewood Col Award,

Madison Nat Watercolor Exhib, 88; Janey & Carl Moebius Award for Excellence, Alumni Art Show 15, Univ Wis-Milwaukee Art Mus, 89; William Bushel Purchase Award, Watercolor Wis, 92. *Bibliog:* Dean Jensen (auth), Art in a cold climate, Wisc Acad Rev, 3/83; James Auer (auth), Rozman combines patience craft & vision, Milwaukee J, 91; Elizabeth McGowan (auth), Wet & wild, J Times, 6/13/96. *Mem:* Milwaukee Art Mus; Racine Art Mus. *Media:* Watercolor; Miscellaneous Media. *Mailing Add:* 5125 Darby Pl Racine WI 53402

RUB, TIMOTHY F
MUSEUM DIRECTOR
Study: Middlebury Col, BA in Art Hist, 1974; NYU, MA in Art Hist, 1979; Yale Univ, MBA, 1987; Harvard Univ, Postgrad, 1998. *Mailing Add:* Cincinnati Art Mus 953 Eden Park Dr Cincinnati OH 45202

RUBELL, DONALD
COLLECTOR
Pos: Gynecologist and hotel executive; retired. *Awards:* Named one of Top 200 Collectors, ARTnews Magazine, 2004, 2005, 2006. *Collection:* Contemporary art. *Mailing Add:* The Rubell Art Collection 95 Northwest 29th St Miami FL 33127

RUBELLO, DAVID JEROME
PAINTER, PHOTOGRAPHER
b Detroit, Mich, Sept 3, 35. *Study:* La Accademia Di Belli Arti, Rome, with Franco Gentilini, BFA, 61; Det Kongelige Akademi, Copenhagen, with Richard Mortensen, 63-66; Univ Mich, Ann Arbor, with Guy Palazzola, MFA, 72. *Work:* Philip Morris Collection, Washington; Tate Gallery, London; Victoria & Albert Mus, London; Brit Libr; Mus Mod Art, NY; Stanford Univ; Rijksmuseum, The Hague; Book Mus, The Hague; and others. *Comn:* Mural-painting, New Detroit, Inc, Mich, 72; mural-painting, Residential Col, Ann Arbor, Mich, 73. *Exhib:* One-man show, Slusser Art Gallery, Univ Mich, 78, Shippensburg State Univ, 84; Reform Function, Detroit Arts Mkt, 93; Ann Celebrate Mich Artists, P Cart Ctr, Rochester, 94, 95 & 96; Photo Nat 2, Ella Sharp Mus, Mich, 95; Patrimonio Invitational, Wayne State Univ Gallery, Detroit, 96; New Life Forms, Maniscalco Gallery, Grosse Point, Mich, 2000; Null Dimension, Fulda, Ger, 88; Systemica Constructive Art, Madrid, 89; Archive 90s, Amsterdam, London; Konkrete Minitures Invitational, Amsterdam, 81; Planet Art Gallery, Capetown, S Africa, 99; Detroit Focus, 2000. *Pos:* Artist coordr, Italian-Am Archives, Warren, Mich, 87, dir, 88. *Teaching:* Lectr, Univ Mich, Ann Arbor, 73-74; asst prof art, Pa State Univ, University Park, 74-80; assoc prof art, Towson State Univ, Md, 80-81 & Univ Mich, Ann Arbor, 87-90; lectr, Ctr Creative Studies, Detroit, Mich, 97-99. *Awards:* Fel, Va Ctr Creative Arts, 81; Mich Coun Arts Grant, 87; Mich Coun Arts Grant, 87-88. *Bibliog:* Blank page, B-4 Publ, London 90; Structurist, No 37-38, 97-98 & No 41-42, 2001-02; New Life Forms, Black & White Fine Art Photog, 6/2001. *Mem:* Mich Photog Hist Soc. *Media:* Acrylic, Wood. *Publ:* Auth, Reflection and form; Auth, My Sicilian Garden, Poetry & Photographs, 2004; Contrib articles to prof journals including: The Structurist, 99-2002; Featured prof artist profile B&W Fine Art Photog Mag, June, 2001. *Dealer:* Arnold Klein Gallery Royal Oak MI. *Mailing Add:* 22062 27 Mile Rd Ray MI 48096

RUBEN, ALBERT
PAINTER
b New Orleans, La, Dec 4, 18. *Study:* Univ Calif, Los Angeles, BA(hon; art), 41; Art Students League, with Robert Brackman & F V Dumond, 44-46. *Work:* Elizabeth Greenshields Found, Montreal. *Exhib:* Solo exhib, Regina Gallery, NY, 55, Studio Gallery Workshop, NY, 59 & Doll & Richards, Boston, 61; Butler Mus Am Art, 60; Nat Acad Ann Exhib, NY, 72; Allied Artists Am Ann Exhib, NY, 75-78. *Teaching:* Instr painting, Pels Sch Art, NY, 65-66 & Montserrat Sch Art, Mass, 73-74. *Awards:* Gold Medals, Am Veterans Art Soc, 57 & Rockport Art Asn, 68 & 80. *Mem:* Allied Artists Am; Rockport Art Asn; North Shore Art Asn; life mem Art Students League NY. *Media:* Oils. *Mailing Add:* 2A Old Harbor Rd Rockport MA 01966

RUBIN, DAVID S
CURATOR, WRITER
b Los Angeles, Calif, June 18, 49. *Study:* Univ Calif, Los Angeles, AB, 72; Harvard Univ, MA(art hist), 74; Mus Mgt Inst, 89. *Exhib:* Drawing Conclusions I & II, NY Arts Gallery, 2003; Cursive, Teari Cultural Inst, 2005; Draw, Scissors, Paper, Domestic Setting, 2006. *Collection Arranged:* Black and White are Colors (auth, catalog), Galleries Claremont Cols, 79, & Contemporary Triptychs (auth, catalog), 82; Jay DeFeo (auth, catalog), San Francisco Art Inst, 84, Wally Hedrick (auth, catalog), 85 & Concerning the Spiritual (auth, catalog), 85; William Baziotes (auth, catalog), Freedman Gallery, 87, Computer Assisted (auth, catalog) 87 & Edward Albee Collection, 88; Painting from the San Francisco Bay Area (auth, catalog), Paine Art Ctr, 88; Cynthia Carlson (auth, catalog), 89; Contemp Hispanic Shrines (auth, catalog), Freedman Gallery, 90; Art About AIDS, 89, Donald Lipski (auth, catalog) 90, Freedman Gallery; Cruciformed (auth, catalog), Cleveland Ctr Contemp Art, 91; Petah Coyne (auth, catalog), Cleveland Ctr Contemp Art, 92; Ellen Brooks (auth, catalog), Cleveland Ctr Contemp Art, 93; Old Glory: The American Flag in Contemporary Art (auth, catalog), Cleveland Ctr Contemp Art, 94; It's Only Rock & Roll: Rock & Roll Currents in Contemporary Art (auth, catalog), Exhib Mgt Inc, 95; Elusive Nature (auth, catalog), Cuenca Biennial, 96; Phoenix Triennial (auth, catalog), 98; Photographs Now (auth, catalog), 2000; Chelsea Rising (auth, caralog), 2001; Al Held (auth, catalog), 2002; Douglas Bourgeois (auth, catalog), 2003; Birdspace: A Post Audubon Artists Aviary, (auth, catalog) 2004; Tomer Ganihar: Raving in the Desert (auth, catalog), 2005; The Culture of Queer: A Tribute to JB Harter (auth, catalog), 2005. *Pos:* Asst dir, Galleries Claremont Cols, 77-; contrib ed, Arts Mag, NY, 79-81; cur, Los Angeles Visual Arts, 82; dir, Santa Monica Col Art Gallery, 82-83; dir exhibs, San Francisco Art Inst, 83-85; adj cur, San Francisco Mus Mod Art, 83-85; guest cur, Paine Art Ctr, Oshkosh, Wis, 86-88; dir, Freedman Gallery, Albright Col, Reading, Pa, 86-90; assoc dir & chief cur, Cleveland Ctr Contemp Art, 90-94; cur 20th century art, Phoenix Art Mus, 94-99; US Comnr, 1996 Cuenca Biennial of Painting, 96; cur visual arts, Contemp Arts Ctr, New Orleans, 2000-06; cur, contemp art, San Antonio Mus Art, 2006-. *Teaching:* Lectr art hist, Sch Visual Arts, NY, 76-77; asst prof art hist, Scripps Col, Claremont, Calif, 77-82. *Awards:* Nat Endowment Arts Mus Fel, Fogg Art Mus, 75-76; summer fel, Guggenheim Mus, 76; Visual Arts Achievement Award, N Ohio LIVE Mag, 92 & 94. *Mem:* Col Art Asn; Int Asn Art Critics; Am Asn Mus; Assoc Art Mus Cur. *Res:* Contemporary art, twentieth century art, automatism, abstract expressionism, Californian art. *Publ:* Jean St Pierre, Re-Dact, 84; Fritz Scholder: Flirting with Posessions, 97; American Dreamer: The Art of Philip C Curtis, 99; auth, Reminders of Invisible Light-The Art of Beth Ames Swartz, 2002; auth, Baby-Boom Daydreams: The Art of Douglas Bourgeois, 2003; auth, Celebrating Freedom: The Art of Willie Birch, 2006. *Dealer:* Ogden Mus Southern Art. *Mailing Add:* 427 Quentin Dr San Antonio TX 78201

RUBIN, DONALD VINCENT
SCULPTOR
b New York, NY, July 10, 37. *Comn:* US Army War Col, Carlisle Barracks, Pa; Am Polled Hereford Asn; Del River & Bay Auth. *Exhib:* Soc Animal Artists Exhib Conv, NY, 79; one-man shows, Brass Door Galleries, Houston, 77, Hunter Gallery, San Francisco, 77, Indian Paint Brush, Vail, Colo, 77-94 & Huntsville Mus Art, Ala, 78; Nat Sculpture Soc 47th Ann Exhib, NY, 80; and many others. *Pos:* Bd Dirs, Huntsville Mus Art, 81-89. *Awards:* Richman Award for Sculptures, Salmagundi Club, 75, 76, 77, 80 & 89; DeBellis Award, 79; Elliot Liskin Sculpture Award, 81, 87 & 94; and others. *Bibliog:* Ralph Perril (auth), Donald Rubin (Huntsville Alabama), Art Voices South Mag, 7-10/78; Cover Photo Polled Hereford World, 10/88; Francis Robb (auth), Don Rubin American Realistic Sculptor (monogr), Art Press, 11/88. *Mem:* Am Artists Prof League; Soc Animal Artists; Artists Fel; Salmagundi Club. *Media:* Bronze. *Specialty:* Western Art. *Interests:* Portrait Relief Sculpture. *Collection:* Army War Coll; Delaware River and Bay Authority; Huntsville Mus of Art. *Dealer:* J N Bartfield Art Galleries 30 W 57th St New York NY 10019; Indian Paint Brush 183 Gore Creek Dr Vail CO 81657. *Mailing Add:* 712 Forrest Heights Dr SE Huntsville AL 35802

RUBIN, IDA ELY
CONSULTANT, WRITER
b New York, NY. *Study:* Wells Col, Aurora, NY, BA(with high honors), 44; NY Univ Inst Fine Arts, 44-49; Belg-Am Educ Fel, Brussels, 51. *Collection Arranged:* The Guennol Collection (ed, catalog), Metrop Mus Art, NY, 69; Collection of Mr and Mrs John D Rockefeller, III, NY; Collection of Mr and Mrs David Rockefeller, NY; and others. *Pos:* Exec dir, 20th Int Cong Art Hist, Columbia Univ & NY Univ, 59-61; dir develop, Inst Fine Arts, NY Univ, 62-64; spec consult, Art Gallery, Ctr Inter-Am Rels, NY, 66-69; adv, Coun of Doc Int, Film & Video Found, Washington, DC, 98. *Teaching:* Art of Latin Am, Manhattanville Col, Purchase, NY, 70-71. *Awards:* Award for Contributions to the Arts, Mass Inst Technol, 89. *Mem:* Univ Andes Found; Am Found; Coun Arts Mass Inst Technol; and others. *Res:* Cross-cultural influences of Latin American and European art. *Publ:* Ed, Acts of the 20th International Congress of Art History, 4 vols, Princeton Univ, 63; The Drawings of Morris Graves, NY Graphic Soc, 75; auth, Text on Eduardo Ramirez Villamizar, In: Panorama Artistico Colombiano, Lithografia Arco, Bogota, 77; and others

RUBIN, IRWIN
PAINTER, DESIGNER
b Brooklyn, NY, July 26, 30. *Study:* Brooklyn Mus Sch Art; Cooper Union Art Sch; Yale Univ, BFA & MFA. *Exhib:* Fla State Univ, 60; Baltimore Mus Art, 60; Bertha Schaefer Gallery, NY, 60-63; Stable Gallery, NY, 64; Byron Gallery, 65; and others. *Pos:* Art dir, McGraw-Hill Bk Co, New York, 58-63; art dir, Harcourt Brace Jovanovich, Inc, New York, 71-92. *Teaching:* Instr drawing & color design, Univ Tex, 55; asst prof, Fla State Univ, 56-58; instr, Pratt Inst, Brooklyn, 64-68; prof art, Cooper Union Art Sch, 67-. *Publ:* Auth, Permanency in collage, Arts Mag, 57. *Mailing Add:* 680 Croton Lake Rd Mt Kisco NY 10549

RUBIN, LAWRENCE
ART DEALER, COLLECTOR
b New York, NY, Feb 22, 33. *Study:* Brown Univ, BA, 55; Univ Paris. *Pos:* Pres, M Knoedler, New York, formerly; art adv panel, IRS; principal, Galleria Lawrence Rubin, Milan Italy, formerly; principal partner, Lawrence Rubin Greenberg Van Doren Fine Art, New York, 99-. *Mem:* Art Dealers Asn (vpres). *Specialty:* Twentieth century contemporary paintings sculpture and drawings; artists Adolph and Esther Gottlieb Found, Inc, Michael David, Richard Diebenkorn, Estate of Herbert Ferber, Glenn Goldberg, Nancy Graves, Howard Hodgkin, Robert Motherwell, Robert Rauschenberg, Estate of David Smith, Frank Stella, Donald Sultan, John Walker. *Collection:* Contemporary painting and sculpture. *Mailing Add:* Greenberg Van Doren Gallery 730 5th Ave New York NY 10019

RUBIN, SANDRA MENDELSOHN
PAINTER
b Santa Monica, Calif, Nov 7, 47. *Study:* Univ Calif, Los Angeles, BA, 76, MFA, 79. *Work:* Los Angeles Co Mus Art; Santa Barbara Mus Art; Univ Calif, Los Angeles; Boise Art Mus, Idaho. *Exhib:* Exhib of Contemp Los Angeles Artists, Nagoya City Mus, Nagoya, Japan, 82; A Heritage Renewed, Univ Art Mus, Santa Barbara, 83; solo exhib, Los Angeles Co Mus Art, Calif, 85, Claude Bernard Gallery, NY, Pieces from Life, LA Louver, Venice, Calif, 92; Am Realism: Twentieth-Century Drawings & Watercolors, San Francisco Art Mus, 86; The Janss Collection, Boise Art Mus, Idaho, 88; Calif Cityscapes, San Diego Mus Art, 91; Cityscapes, Community Arts Inc & Los Angeles Stories, Jack Rutberg Fine Arts, Los Angeles, Calif, 93. *Awards:* Young

Talent Purchase Award, Los Angeles Co Mus Art, 80; Nat Endowment Arts Artist's Fel Grant, 81 & 91. *Bibliog:* David Hale (auth), Capturing the Californias, Fresno Bee, 10/4/92; Andy Brummer (auth), The face of the place-the city of Los Angeles gets itself painted, Visions, winter 92; Pat Leddy (auth), Dreamtown, Los Angeles stories at Jack Rutberg Fine Arts, Artweek, 3/93. *Media:* Oil on Canvas. *Dealer:* LA Louver Gallery 55 N Venice Blvd Venice CA 90291. *Mailing Add:* PO Box 627 Boonville CA 95415

RUBINFIEN, LEO H
PHOTOGRAPHER, FILMMAKER
b Chicago, Ill, Aug 16, 53. *Study:* Reed Col; Calif Inst Arts, BFA, 74; Yale Univ Sch Art, MFA, 76. *Comn:* Grandola Alentejo Province, Portugal, 2000-01; Citigroup, 2005-06. *Exhib:* Solo exhibs, Metrop Mus Art, NY, Philiadelphia Col Art, Robert Mann Gallery, NY, Seattle Art Mus, Seibu Art Forum, Tokyo & Cleveland Mus Art, Fraenkor Gallery & Castelli Graphics; The New Color, Int Ctr Photog, NY, 81; New Am Color Photog, Inst Contemp Arts, London, 81; Color & Colored, San Francisco Mus Mod Art, Calif, 81; Color as Form, George Eastman House, Rochester, NY & Corcoran Gallery, Washington, DC, 81; Recent Acquisitions, Mus Mod Art, NY, 84; New Directors, New Films, Mus Mod Art, NY, 89; group shows, Met Mus Art, NY, Robert Mann Gallery. *Collection Arranged:* Cleveland Mus Art; San Francisco Mus Mod Art, Calif; Metrop Mus Art & Mus Mod Art, NY; Corcoran Gallery Art; Seattle Art Mus. *Teaching:* Instr photog, Swarthmore Col, 77 & Sch Visual Arts, NY, 78-87; assoc prof art, Fordham Univ, 81-87; vis lectr, Cooper Union, 82; instr, Reed Col, 2001; instr, NY Univ, 2001-; Sch Visual Arts, 2000-04. *Awards:* Guggenheim Found Fel, 82-83; Asian Cult Coun Fel, 84; fel, Int Ctr Advanced Studies, NY Univ, 98; Japan Found, 2002. *Bibliog:* Pete Karmel (auth), The anxious moment, Soho News, 11/4/81; Prudence Carlson (auth), article, Art in Am, 3/82; Ian Buruma (auth), New York Review of Books, 10/92; and others. *Media:* Photography. *Publ:* Auth, Love-Hate Relations, Artforum, 78 & The Man in the Crowd, In: Photography in Print, 81, Touchstone Press; 10 Photographs in Camera Mainichi, 5/84; dir & co-writer, The Money Juggler (56 min film), 88; dir & coauth, My Bed in the Leaves (film), 90; auth (bks), A Map of the East, David R Godine Inc, Boston, 92; auth, The Poetry of Plain Seeing, 12/2000, Perfect Uncertainty, 3/02, The Mask Behind the Face, 6-7/04, Where Diane Arbus Went, 10/05, Art in America; auth (bk), Shomei Tomatsu: Skin of the Nation, Yale Univ Press & San Francisco MOMA, 2004; and many others. *Dealer:* Robert Mann Gallery 210 11th Ave New York NY 10001. *Mailing Add:* 145 Nassau St New York NY 10038

RUBINSTEIN, CHARLOTTE STREIFER
WRITER, CURATOR
b New York, NY, Dec 14, 21. *Study:* Brooklyn Col, BA, 41; Teachers Col, Columbia Univ, MA, 46; Otis Art Inst, Los Angeles, MFA, 69. *Collection Arranged:* Women USA Nat Exhib (with catalog), Nat Endowment Arts, 73; Women Sculptors of the Nineties, 96. *Teaching:* Instr art hist, appreciation & design, Fullerton Col, 71-74. *Awards:* Best Humanities Bk of 1982, Asn Am Publ, 82; Individual Res Grant, Am Asn Univ Women, 84-85; Nat Award, Womens Caucus Art, 94. *Mem:* Col Art Asn; Women's Caucus Art; Art Lib Soc NAm. *Res:* All aspects of history of American women artists. *Publ:* Auth, The early career of Frances Flora Bond Palmer (1812-1876), Am Art J, fall 85; The first American women artists, Women's Art J, spring-summer 82; American Women Artists: From Early Indian Times to the Present, G K Hall/Avon Bks, 82; American Women Sculptors: A History of Women Working in Three Dimensions, G K Hall, 90; Fanny Palmer: The Work Horse of Currier & Ives, 97. *Mailing Add:* 3420 Lady Hill Rd San Diego CA 92130-1806

RUBINSTEIN, RAPHAEL
CRITIC
b Lawrence, Kans, July 22, 55. *Study:* Bennington Col, BA, 79. *Pos:* Managing ed, Flash Art, 89-90; Assoc ed, Art in Am, 94-96, sr ed, 97-. *Awards:* John McCarron Award. *Publ:* Auth, Europa resurgent: nouveau realisme, 88, Outstations of the post modern, 89 & A hemisphere decentered: Mexican art comes north, 91, Arts Mag; Sight unseen: Derrida at the Louvre, 91 & The painting undone: supports/surfaces, 91, Art Am. *Mailing Add:* Art in America 575 Broadway New York NY 10012

RUBINSTEIN, SUSAN R See SuZen, Susan R Rubinstein

RUBY, LAURA
SCULPTOR, PRINTMAKER
b Los Angeles, Calif, Dec 7, 45. *Study:* Univ Southern Calif, BA (English), 67; San Francisco State Col, MA (English), 69; Univ Hawaii, MFA(art), 78. *Work:* Honolulu Acad Arts, Hawaii State Fedn Cult & Arts, Honolulu; Erie Mus, Pa; Soc Am Graphic Artists, NY; McNeese State Univ, La, Univ of Dallas, TX. *Comn:* Richard Street YWCA (screenprint), Hawaii YWCA, 86; Film Crew at Diamond Head (screenprint), Honolulu Printmakers, 88; Stage Set--Mise en Scene (site specific mixed media sculpture), Hawaii St Fedn Cult & Arts, Honolulu, 91; Site of Passage-Chinatown (site-specific mixed media sculpture), City & Co of Honolulu, 94; Elvis & Marilyn (site-specific installation), Honolulu Acad Arts, Hawaii. *Exhib:* Honolulu Acad Arts, 87, 95, 2005; 12th Nat Los Angeles Printmaking Soc, Marymount Univ Gallery, Los Angeles, 93; Univ Iowa Mem Union, 95; Georgia Southern Univ Art Gallery, 96; Mus Nebr Art, 97; Tex Wesleyan Univ East Rm Gallery, 2001; Morningside Col Eppley Art Gallery, Iowa, 2002; Denison Univ Art Gallery, Ohio, 2003; Walking on Water, SUNY Brockport Tower Fine Arts Gallery, NY, 2005; and others. *Pos:* Ed, Fate in Review, 93-2001. *Teaching:* Instr, Univ Hawaii, Honolulu, 77-; instr, Chaminade Univ, Honolulu, 80-81. *Awards:* Award in Sculpture, Artquest 86, Los Angeles; Lace Artist Proj Grant New Forms Regional Initiative, Los Angeles, 91-92; Purchase Awards & Catalogue Cover Art Award, 65th Soc Am Graphic Artists Nat Print Exhib, New York, 93. *Bibliog:* Marcia Morse (auth), A Tribute to Diamond Head, Honolulu Star Bull, Hawaii, 3/16/86; Joan Rose (auth), Installation Sculptures Invite Viewer Participation, Honolulu Star Bull, 4/5/92; Reuel Denney (auth), Laura Ruby's Nancy Drew Series, Honolulu Acad Arts Catalogue, 4/95. *Mem:* Col Art Asn; Found Art Theory & Edn Asn Art Editors; Jean Charlot Found; Honolulu Printmakers, Am Print Alliance,. *Media:* All; Screenprinting. *Res:* Land & Power in Hawaii, Moiliili, (a Hawaii Community). *Publ:* Drawing on a Sleuth: The Case of the Nancy Drew Series, Rediscovering Nancy Drew (ed by Carolyn Stewart & Nancy Tillman Romalov), Univ Iowa Press, 95; Diamond Head Contemporary Impressions, Am Print Alliance, Vol 6, No 2, fall 98; Cultural Determination of Visual Perception: The Unavoidable Condition that could Liberate, FATE in Rev, vol 23, 2001; editor, Moili'ili-The Life of a Community, 2005. *Dealer:* Ramsay Mus 1128 Smith St Honolulu HI 96817. *Mailing Add:* 509 University Ave 902 Honolulu HI 96826

RUDA, EDWIN
PAINTER
b New York, NY, May 15, 22. *Study:* Columbia Univ, MA, 49; Sch Painting & Sculpture, Mexico City, 49-51; Univ Ill, MFA, 56. *Work:* State of NY Collection, Albany Mall; Indianapolis Mus Art, Ind; Dallas Mus Art, Tex; Nat Gallery of Australia, Canberra; Mass Inst Technol, Cambridge; Corcoran Gallery, Washington; Port Authority of NY. *Exhib:* Smithsonian Traveling Exhib, Latin Am, 66; Systemic Painting, Guggenheim Mus, 66 & Whitney Mus Am Art Painting Ann, 69, NY; Paintings on Paper, Aldrich Mus Contemp Art, Ridgefield, Conn; 73 Biennial, Whitney Mus Am Art, NY; Contemp Am Painting & Sculpture, Krannert Art Mus, Univ Ill, Urbana, 74; 10th Anniversary Exhib 1964-1974, Aldrich Mus Contemp Art, 74; Baltimore Mus, 75, Drawing Show, 76; Benefit Exhib for Udine, Italy, NY Univ, 76; June Kelly Gallery, New York, NY, 87-95; Condeso Lawler Gallery, New York, NY, 87-88; one-person exhib, Paula Cooper Gallery, NY, 69, 71, 73 & 75, Gallery A, Sydney, Australia, 73, June Kelly Gallery, NY, 88, 92 & 95 & Condeso/Lawler Gallery, NY, 88; and others. *Pos:* Co-founder, Park Pl Gallery Art Res. *Teaching:* Instr painting, Univ Tex, Austin, 56-59 & 78, Sch Visual Arts, NY, 67-71, Pratt Inst, Syracuse Univ & Ohio State Univ, 78 & Tyler Sch Art, Philadelphia, 79. *Awards:* Creative Artists Pub Serv Fel, 78-79. *Bibliog:* Carter Ratcliff (auth), Striped for action, Artnews, 2/72; Dore Ashton (auth), New York commentary, Studio Int, 2/70; Peter Schjeldahl (auth), In and out of step in Soho, New York Times, 10/73; and many others. *Publ:* Auth, Park Place 1963-67: some informal notes in retrospect, Art Mag, 67. *Dealer:* June Kelly Gallery 591 Broadway New York NY 10012. *Mailing Add:* 44 Walker St New York NY 10013

RUDENSTINE, ANGELICA ZANDER
HISTORIAN, CURATOR
b Ger. *Study:* Oxford Univ, Eng, BA, 59, MA, 60; Smith Col, MA, 61. *Collection Arranged:* Art of the Russian Avant-Garde: The George Costakis Collection Traveling Exhib (auth, catalog), 82-84; Kazimir Malevich, 90-91; Piet Mondrian, 94-96. *Pos:* Cur, Mus Fine Arts, Boston, 60-68 & Guggenheim Mus, NY, 69-82; freelance cur, 82-; prog off, mus & conserv, Andrew W Mellon Found, 93-. *Teaching:* Adj prof 19th & 20th century art hist, Inst Fine Arts, NY Univ, 85-86. *Awards:* Guggenheim Fel, 83; Alfred H Barr Award, 87; Mitchell Prize, 88. *Mem:* Col Art Asn Am; Am Acad, Rome (trustee & chmn, fine arts comt, 80-92); Int Coun Mus. *Res:* 20th century European and American art. *Publ:* Auth, Guggenheim Mus Collection: Paintings 1880-1945, 76; Russian Avant Garde Art: The George Costakis Collection, 81; Peggy Guggenheim Collection, Venice, Abrams, 85; Modern Painting-Drawing-Sculpture Collected by Emily & Joseph Pulitzer, Jr, Harvard Univ Press, 88; Piet Mondrian 1872-1944, Mondadori, 94. *Mailing Add:* Andrew Mellon Found 140 E 62nd St New York NY 10021

RUDINSKY, ALEXANDER (JOHN)
PAINTER
b Corvallis, Ore, Feb 4, 57. *Study:* Ore State Univ, 75-76; Univ Mass, 76-77; Syracuse Univ, BFA(studio arts), 79; Univ Calif, Irvine, MFA(studio arts, Regents fel), 89. *Work:* Portland Art Mus, Ore; Univ Calif, Irvine; Hewlett Packard, Corvallis, Ore; Hufstedler, Miller, Kaus & Beardsley, Newport Beach, Calif; Williamette Valley Co, Eugene, Ore. *Comn:* Mural, Crescent Valley High Sch, Corvallis, Ore, 75; mural, Benton Co Courthouse, Corvallis, Ore, 76; stage set for Journey, Univ Mass, Amherst, 77; neighborhood photomural, Mt Scott/Arleta Community Ctr, Portland, Ore, 82; mural, Show Biz Expo, Los Angeles, Calif, 92. *Exhib:* Fine Arts Inst 28th Ann, San Bernardino Co Art Mus, Redlands, Calif, 93; 58th Nat Exhib, Cooperstown Art Asn, NY, 93; Nat Small Oil Painting Exhib, Wichita Ctr Arts, Kans, 94; Neighborhoods of the '90's: 53rd Ann Nat, Braithwaite Fine Arts Gallery, Southern Utah Univ, Cedar City, 94; City Art Invitational, Millard Sheets Gallery, Los Angeles Co Fair, Pomona, Calif, 94. *Pos:* Installation consult, Alexander Rudinsky Studios, Portland, Ore, 85-87; gallery preparator, Elizabeth Leach Gallery, Portland, Ore, 86; self-employed fine artist, 85-94. *Teaching:* Instr drawing & bus art, Pac Northwest Col Art, Portland, Ore, 86-87; instr film & video, Marylhurst Col, Ore, 86-87; teaching asst contemp art, Univ Calif, Irvine, 87-89. *Awards:* Multi-Arts Grant, Metrop Comn, Portland, Ore, 82; Fine Arts Res Grant, Univ Calif, Irvine, 89. *Bibliog:* Cathy Curtis (auth), The preoccupation behind creation, LA Times, Orange Co Ed, 5/8/88; Randy Gragg (auth), Gallery's mixed bag of new works, Oregonian, 2/17/90; Nancy Kapitanoff (auth), Sharing life's crosses, LA Times, San Fernando Ed, 7/2/93. *Mem:* Seeing It Through Exhibitions. *Media:* Oil on Canvas, Ceramics. *Publ:* Illusr, Seven Slovak Stories, Gregorian Univ Press, Rome, 80; Jozef Mak, Slavica Pub, Columbus, 85. *Dealer:* Lynn Shue The Village Galleries 120 Dickenson Ave Lahaina Maui HI 96761

RUDMAN, JOAN (COMBS)
PAINTER, INSTRUCTOR
b Owensburg, Ind, Oct 7, 27. *Study:* Mich State Univ, BA(art educ), MA(art); Art Student's League, Woodstock, NY, with Arnold Blanch, Walter Plate & Richard Segalman also with Edgar A Whitney, Walter DuBois Richards, Diana Kan & Charles Reid. *Work:* Combe Inc, Kresgie Mus. *Exhib:* Wadsworth Atheneum; Acad Fine Arts

& Watercolor Soc, New Brit Mus Am Art; Nat Arts Club Open Watercolor Show, 69 & 78; Am Watercolor Soc, 74, 77 & 84; Mus Fine Arts, Springfield, Mass, 77; Salmagundi Club, 78; Nat Acad Design, NY, 86; and others. *Pos:* Asst Ed, Newsletter (Am Watercolor Soc). *Teaching:* Instr, King Sch, Stamford, Conn, Round Hill Community House, Greenwich, Conn & Continuing Educ Classes, Stamford, currently; artist-in-residence, Southern Vermont Art Ctr, Manchester, currently; artist-in-residence, Manchester, Vt, 6/2000. *Awards:* Best in Show & Russell Purchase Award, Old Greenwich Art Soc, 91; Winsor-Newton Plaque & Award, Hudson Art Asn, 91; Hon Mention in Graphics, Catherine Lorillard Wolfe Art Club, 91; first in watercolor, Founder's Show Art Soc, Old Greenwich, 99; Mrs John Newinton 1st Award (pencil), HVAA 69th Annuak, 2000; and others. *Mem:* Am Watercolor Soc, 84- (bd dir, 87-); Am Artists Prof League; Hudson Valley Art Asn (bd dir, 71-, vpres, 99, pres, 2000); hon mem, Columbia Univ Alumni Club; Nat Press Club, Washington; Mich State Univ Alumni Club; and others. *Media:* Watercolor. *Publ:* Artist in Special Tribute, HVAA Catalog Ann, Newspaper Press Releases, Gannett Chain, 72-. *Mailing Add:* 274 Quarry Rd Stamford CT 06903

RUDQUIST, JERRY JACOB
PAINTER, EDUCATOR
b Fargo, NDak, June 13, 34. *Study:* Minneapolis Col Art & Design, BFA, 56; Cranbrook Acad Art, MFA, 58. *Work:* Univ Minn Gallery, Minneapolis; St Cloud State Col, Minn; Anoka Ramsey State Jr Col, Minn. *Comn:* San Disc (8' X 8' painting), Whitney Fine Arts Ctr, Minneapolis Community & Tech Col, 95. *Exhib:* Walker Art Ctr, Minneapolis, 58, 60, 62, 65 & 77; Minn Portfolio (traveling exhib, Middle East & Europe), St Paul Gallery, 60; Denver Art Mus, Colo, 63; Joslyn Mus Art, Omaha, Nebr, 64, 68 & 70; Birmingham Mus Art, Ala, 66; Art in the Embassies Prog, US State Dept, 68-71; one-man exhibs, Walker Art Ctr, Minneapolis, 63 & Minneapolis Inst Arts, 64, 71 & 75; Drei Amerikaner aus dem Mittleren Western, Mannheimer Symposion der Kunste, WGer, 72; Colo 1st Nat Print & Drawing Competition, 74; We Too/Come From, 39th Midwestern Invitational, Rourke Art Gallery Mus, Moorhead, Minn, 98; John, Fine Arts Exhibit, Minn State Fair, 98, Petunia, 97; Art on the Plains, Plains Art Mus, Fargo, NDak, 99. *Teaching:* Prof art, Macalester Col, 58-; vis lectr & critic art, Boston Univ, summer 69. *Awards:* Spec Donor & Purchase Award, Walker Art Ctr, 62; Purchase Award, Minneapolis Inst Arts, 65; Purchase Award, World Print Competition, San Francisco, 73. *Bibliog:* Dan Paris (auth), Rudquist (film), produced by Minneapolis Inst Arts, Macalester Col & Minn State Arts Coun, 71; Samuel Sachs II (auth), Jerry Rudquist: Recent works, Minneapolis Inst Arts, 71. *Media:* Oil. *Mailing Add:* c/o Art Dept MacAlester Col 1600 Grand Ave Saint Paul MN 55105

RUDY, HELEN
PAINTER, INSTRUCTOR
b New York, NY Aug 2, 25. *Study:* Hunter Col, BA; Ridgewood Art Inst; Art Sch Northern NJ. *Comn:* Pvt Collections. *Exhib:* Ann Exhibs, Hudson Valley Art Asn; Grand Nat, Am Artists Prof League; Ann Juried Exhib, Allied Artists Am; Ann Juried Exhib, Audubon Artists; Butler Mus, Youngstown, OH; Valley Hospital, Ridgewood, NJ; Cork Gallery, Lincoln Ctr, NY. *Pos:* Coast Guard Artist; juror, West Essex Art Asn & Kent Art Asn, Conn. *Teaching:* instr, painting, currently; teaching asst, Ridgewood Art Inst, currently; monitor, Art Sch Nothern, NJ, currently. *Awards:* Awards for Juried Shows; Am Artists Prof League, Kent Art Asn, Hudson Valley Art Asn, Suburban Art League, Allied Artists Am; Silver Medal Honor, Ann Exhib, Audubon Artists, 2004. *Mem:* Allied Artists Am (bd dir, currently); Am Artists Prof League (bd dir, currently); Catharine Lorillard Wolfe Art Club; Hudson Valley Art Asn (bd dir); Kent Art Asn. *Media:* Acrylic, Oil & Pastels. *Dealer:* Westwood Art Gallery Westwood NJ. *Mailing Add:* 856 Hillcrest Rd Ridgewood NJ 07450

RUEHLICKE, CORNELIA IRIS
PAINTER
b Berlin, Ger. *Study:* Acad Fine Arts, Stuttgart, Ger, MFA, 79; studied painting with Kurt Sonderborg; studied sculpture with Alfred Hrdlicka. *Work:* Hampton Arts Comn, Va; Somerset Co Col, NJ; Haag & Haag Gmbh, Leonberg, Ger; Duszinsky Gmbh, Hoefingen, Ger; Art Space, Nishinomiya, Japan. *Comn:* Artists of Worldwide Attention, ARS Nova. *Exhib:* Palm Springs Desert Mus, Calif; San Diego Art Inst; Nat Exhib of Women's Work on Paper, Women's Found Genesee Valley, Rochester, NY; Time Capsule, Paula Cooper Gallery, NY; HUB Galleries, Pa State Univ; O'Keefe Ctr for Arts, Toronto, Can; Monmouth Col Art Gallery, NY; Consulate Gen of Ger Cult Ctr, NY; Goethe Inst, Toronto, Can; Gasteig Cult Ctr, Munich; San Francisco Mus Mod Art; Allentown Art Mus, Pa; Guggenheim Mus; San Bernardino Co Mus, Calif; Berkshire Mus, Mass; Mus Mod Art, Bordeaux, France; Newport Art Mus, RI; Atlantic Ctr for the Arts, Fla; NJ Ctr Vis Arts, Morristown, NJ. *Awards:* Hub Galleries Cent Pa Fest Arts Merit Award, Pa State Univ, 93; Hampton Arts Comn Mayor's Purchase Award Charles H Taylor Arts Ctr, 93; Marc Printmaking Award, Peninsula Fine Arts Ctr, 94; Elizabeth Found for the Arts Studio Ctr, 00, 02; Cons Gen of Ger Grant, 99. *Mem:* Brooklyn Waterfront Artists Coalition; Elizabeth Found for the Arts. *Media:* Oil, Acrylic, Watercolor. *Publ:* Auth, Promotional Copy, M Somerby, New York, 93; Diversions, Hampton Arts Comn, 94; Time Capsule, Creative Times & SOS Int, 95; Crossings, Vol III, Brooklyn Waterfront Artists Coalition, 96; disc covers, Louisville First Editions, for music by Morton Gould, Walter Piston, and Roy Harris. *Mailing Add:* 35 W 16th St No 4 New York NY 10011

RUEPPEL, MERRILL C
MUSEUM DIRECTOR
b Haddonfield, NJ, May 7, 25. *Study:* Beloit Col, BA, 49; Univ Wis-Madison, MA, 52, PhD, 55. *Pos:* Dir, Dallas Mus Fine Arts, Tex, 64-73, Mus Fine Arts, Boston, Mass, 73-75 & Contemp Mus, Honolulu, Hawaii, 91-95. *Teaching:* Assoc prof art hist, Washington Univ, St Louis, Mo, 63. *Publ:* Auth, Sculpture, Twentieth Century (exhib catalog), 64; Dubuffet (exhib catalog), 66; Mark Tobey Retrospective (exhib catalog), 68; Masterpieces of Japanese Art (exhib catalog), 69; James Brooks (exhib catalog), 72. *Mailing Add:* 766 Chestnut St Needham MA 02192-2740

RUFE, LAURIE J
MUSEUM DIRECTOR
b Pa. *Study:* Va Commonwealth Univ, BA in Art Hist. *Pos:* Intern, Richmond Fine Arts Mus, Hist. House Mus; with Mercer Mus, Doylestown, Pa; oral hist proj, Wyo; with Douglas Co Coun for the Arts and Humanities, Colorado Springs; dir, Custer Co Art Ctr, Montana; deputy dir, Roswell (NMex) Mus and Art Ctr, Roswell, 1987-98; dir, Tucson Mus Art, 1998-. *Mailing Add:* Tucson Mus Art 140 N Main Ave Tucson AZ 85701

RUFFING, ANNE ELIZABETH
PAINTER
b Brooklyn, NY. *Study:* Cornell Univ, BS; Drexel Inst Technol; also studied with John Pike. *Work:* Metrop Mus Art, NY; Brooklyn Mus, NY; Nat Gallery Art, Washington, DC; Whitney Mus Am Art, NY; Libr of Nat Collection of Fine Arts, Smithsonian Inst, Washington, DC; and many others. *Comn:* Four Wildlife Drawings, Johnston Hist Mus, North Brunswick, NJ, 76; four hist landmark lithographs, NY State Senate, comn by City of Kingston, NY, 76; porcelain series, Danbury Mint, Norwalk, Conn, 81-82; porcelain series, Oxmoor House, Birmingham, Ala, 83-85; ltd ed print, Nat Wildlife Fedn, Washington, DC, 88. *Exhib:* Rocky Mountain Nat Watermedia Exhib, Golden, Colo, 76; 25th Ann Exhib Painting & Sculpture, Berkshire Mus, 76; one-woman shows, Art in Industry, IBM Corp, NY, 66 & A E Ruffing Exhib, Hall of Fame, Goshen, NY, 71; 4th Ann Exhib, Midwest Watercolor Soc, Manitowoc, Wis, 80; and others. *Awards:* Int Women's Year Award, Int Women's Festival, D Gillespie, 76; Spec Merit Award, Midwest Watercolor Soc, 80. *Bibliog:* Bruce Henry Davis (auth), Introducing the art of A E R, 1/77, Memories of Childhood, 2/77 & Glimpses of yesterday, 7/77, Collector's News, Am Masters Found. *Media:* Watercolor, Ink. *Publ:* Illusr, Ideals Old Fashioned Issue (title page plus two others), Ideals, 75

RUFFNER, GINNY MARTIN
SCULPTOR, GLASSBLOWER
b Atlanta, Ga, June 21, 52. *Study:* Univ Ga, BFA(drawing, painting, cum laude), 74, MFA, 75. *Work:* High Mus, Atlanta, Ga; Corning Mus Glass, NY, Cooper-Hewitt Mus, NY; Toledo Mus Art, Ohio; Mus des Arts Decoratif, Lausanne, Switz; Metrop Mus Art, NY. *Comn:* Sculpture & mural, S Park Community Ctr, Seattle, 89; sculpture, Security Pacific Bldg, Seattle, 90; sculpture, Absolut Vodka, 90; playground, William T Machan Sch, Phoenix, Ariz, 93. *Exhib:* Mus Louvre, Paris, 89; Am Craft Mus, NY, 90; Detroit Inst Arts, Mich, 91; Espace Duchamp-Villon, Rouen, France, 91; Renwick Gallery, Smithsonian Inst, Washington, 92; Museo Correr, Venice, Italy, 96; Metrop Mus Art, NY, 96; and others. *Pos:* Dir, Glass Art Soc, 88-91, pres, 90-91; ed adv, Glass Mag, New York, 89-94; trustee, Pilchuck Glass Sch, Stanwood, Wash, 91-, vpres, 94-; comnr, Seattle Arts Comn, 91; dir, New York Experimental Glass Workshop, 92-94; contemp art coun prog comt, Seattle Art Mus, currently. *Teaching:* Adj instr watercolor & art appreciation, DeKalb Col, Clarkston, Ga, 77; vis scholar glassblowing, Penland Sch Crafts, NC, 79; lectr, Nat Sculpture Conf, Cincinnati, 87; lectr, Bellevue Mus, Wash, 88; instr, Pilchuck Glass Sch, 84-89 & Univ d'été, Sars-Poteries, France, 90; conf coordr, Glass Art Soc, Seattle, 90; exhib cur, Tacoma Art Mus, Wash, 91. *Awards:* Visual Artist Fel, Nat Endowment Arts, 86; Outstanding Contrib Award, UrbanGlass, New York, 95; Woman of the Year, Palm Springs Desert Mus, Calif, 96. *Bibliog:* Matthew Kangas (auth), Unraveling Ruffner, Glass Mag, spring 91; Bonnie Miller (auth), Why Not?: The Art of Ginny Ruffner, Tacoma Art Mus, in asn with Univ Wash Press, Seattle & London, 95; Ellen Pall (auth), Starting from scratch, NY Times Mag, 9/25/95. *Mem:* Glass Art Soc; Am Craft Coun; Am Sci Glassblowers Soc. *Media:* Glass, Metal. *Publ:* Auth, Speaking of glass/women sculptors, Am Craft Mag, 10/88; co-ed, Glass: Material in the Service of Meaning, Tacoma Art Mus, in asn with Univ Wash Press, Seattle & London, 91; and others. *Mailing Add:* 5000 20th Ave NW Seattle WA 98107

RUFFO, JOSEPH MARTIN
PRINTMAKER, ADMINISTRATOR
b Norwich, Conn, Dec 6, 41. *Study:* Pratt Inst; Cranbrook Acad Art. *Work:* Ark Art Ctr, Little Rock; Mus Mod Art, Salvador, Brazil; Memphis Col Art, Tenn; Miss Art Asn, Jackson; Sheldon Mem Art Gallery, Lincoln, Nebr; and others. *Comn:* American Tool Co; Cliffs Notes Inc. *Exhib:* Third Biennial Rutgers Nat Drawing Exhib, State Univ NJ, Camden Col Arts & Sci, 79; Potsdam Prints, 16th Nat, 82; 11th Nat Prints & Drawing Exhib, Minot State Col, 82; La Grange Nat, 82; 23rd Nat Print Exhib, Hunterdon Art Ctr, Clinton, NJ, 79; Images Aluminum, Tamarind Prints Traveling Exhib, Macalester Col, 79-80; solo exhib, Sheldon Mem Art Gallery, Lincoln, Nebr, 87. *Pos:* Head dept art, Univ Northern Iowa, Cedar Falls. *Teaching:* Instr art, Memphis Acad Arts, 64-68; instr art, Fla Mem Col, 69-77; asst prof art & chmn dept, Barry Col, 69-74, chmn div fine arts, 74-77; prof art, Univ Northern Iowa, 77-84; chmn dept art and art hist, Univ Nebr, 84. *Awards:* Fulbright Grant, Brazil, 63; Best in Show, 12th Ann Mid South Exhib, 67; Purchase Prize, 10th Dixie Ann Prints & Drawings, 68. *Mem:* Nat Coun Art Adminrs; Nat Asn Schs Art & Design; Col Art Asn; Am Arbitration Asn. *Media:* All Media. *Mailing Add:* Dept Art & Art Hist Univ Nebr Lincoln 14th & R St Lincoln NE 68588

RUFO, CAESAR ROCCO
MEDALIST, SCULPTOR
b Philadelphia, PA, Aug 15, 29. *Study:* Temple Univ, with Raphael Sabatini, Philadelphia; Studied at Pa Academy Fine Arts; Studied at Philadelphia Col Art. *Work:* La Scala Mus, Milan, Italy; Metrop Opera House Mus, New York; Franklin Mint Mus, Franklin Center, PA; Smithsonian Inst, Washington, DC; Belskie Mus Art & Science, Closter, NJ. *Comn:* bronze bust, comn by Dr. John Esposito, PA, 1971; plaque, Nat Liberty Corp, Springfield, PA; monument, Virginia Military Inst, Lexington, VA, 1983; life size statue, Villanova Univ, PA, 1985; bronze relief wall plaques, comn by Dr PM Lincoln Jr, Boston, MA, 1986. *Exhib:* Metrop Centennial Medal, 21st World Expos, New York, 1987. *Pos:* Sr medallic sculptor, Franklin Mint, PA, 1965-1978; chief sculptor, Roger Williams Mint, Attleboro, MA, 1978-1983; vpres art dept, Highland Mint, Melbourne, FL, 1991-. *Teaching:* Instr sculpting tech, Delaware County, PA, 1960-1965. *Mailing Add:* 504 Eaton Way West Chester PA 19380

RUGGIERO, LAURENCE J
MUSEUM DIRECTOR
b Paterson, NJ, Mar 25, 48. *Study:* Univ Pa, BA, 69, MA, 73, PhD, 75; Boston Univ, MBA, 79. *Pos:* Consult projs, J Paul Getty Mus Found, Los Angeles & Boston Mus Fine Arts; asst to pres, Metrop Mus Art, New York, 78-81; exec dir, Oakland Mus Asn, Calif, 81-85; dir, John & Mable Ringling Mus Art, Sarasota, 85-92; assoc dir, Charles Hosmer Morse Mus Am Art, Winter Park, Fla, 92-, dir, 95. *Teaching:* Asst prof hist art, Univ Ill, Chicago Circle, 73-77. *Awards:* Kress Found Fel, 1972. *Mem:* Col Art Asn; Am Asn Mus. *Mailing Add:* c/o Charles Hosmer Morse Mus Am Art 445 Park Ave N Winter Park FL 32789

RUGGLES, JOANNE BEAULE
PAINTER, EDUCATOR
b New York, NY, May 19, 46. *Study:* Akron State Univ; Ohio State Univ, with Sidney Chafetz, BFA(painting) & MFA(painting, printmaking & photography). *Work:* Ohio State Univ, Columbus; Calif Polytech State Univ, San Luis Obispo; Calif State Library, Sacramento; Wesleyan Col, Macon, Ga. *Exhib:* 6th, 7th, 8th & 9th Int Exhib Original Drawings, Mus Mod Art, Rijeka, Yugoslavia, 78, 80, 82 & 84; Eigth Premio Biella Per L' Incisione, Italy, 80; Second Int Exhib of Prints and Drawings, Mus Arts & Sci, Wesleyan Col, 83-84; Cabo Fio I & II Int Print Biennal, Brazil, 83 & 85; Intergraphic '84, Exhibit Ctr, Berlin, 84; Int Print Exhib: 1983 Repub of China, Taipei City Mus Fine Arts, Taiwan, 83-84; Prints USA, Nat Mus, Singapore & Nat Gallery, Bangkok; Art Ctr, 84, Silpakorn Univ, Bangkok, 97; Royal Soc Artists Gallery, Birmingham, Eng, 97; Prints USA Museo Carvillo Gil, Mexico DF, 87; Westminster Gallery, London, 99; Black Sheep Gallery, Hawarden, Wales, 99; US Embassy, Luanda, Angola, 99-2003; Durham Art Gallery, 2000; AIM for Arts Int Open, 2000, Performance Works Gallery, Vancouver, BC, Canada, 2000; US Embassy, Freetown, Sierra Leone, 2005-08. *Pos:* Cur, Exhibs Univ Art Gallery, Cal Poly, 89-98; reviewer, Applications for Dorland Mountain Arts Colony, 89-2004; panelist to review art in pub places applicants, San Luis Obispo Co, 92; mem, San Luis Obispo Co Arts Coun Adv Bd, 2000-02. *Teaching:* Lectr drawing & painting, Ohio State Univ, 70-71, Allan Hancock Col, 71-76 & Cuesta Col, 77-79; lectr drawing & printmaking, Calif Polytech State Univ, 73-80, assoc prof, 83-88, prof, Dept Art & Design, 88-2004; emeritus prof, 2004. *Awards:* Jurors Award, Cabo Frio Int, Brazil, 83; Purchase Award, Minot State Univ, 96; Selected Artist of 1997, US State Dept Art Embassies Prog, 97; John McKee Meml award, 45th Internat, San Diego Art Inst, 01; Donald Pierce Meml award, Am Soc Contemp Artists 84th Ann, 02; Cal Poly award, Outstanding Res, Creative Activity & Prof Develop, 04; Individual Artists Grant, James Irvine Found Art Inspires Grant Prog in Conjunction with Slo Community Found, 2005. *Bibliog:* Glen Starkey (auth), The arts: Earth Angels, New Times, 7/18-25/96; Monica Fiscalini (auth), Searching for celestial & other heavenly bodies, San Luis Obispo Co Telegram Tribune, 8/16-27/96; Teresa Mariani (auth), What is it with you artists, always drawing nudes, San Luis Obispo Co Telegram Tribune, 8/16-27/96. *Mem:* Nat Asn Women Artists; Calif Soc Printmakers; Am Soc Contemp Artists; Nat Oil & Acrylic Painters Soc; Nat Acrylic Painters Asn. *Media:* Mixed Media; Acrylics, Oil Pastels. *Publ:* Co-auth, Darkroom Graphics: Creative Photographic Techniques for Photographers and Artists, Amphoto, 75; contribr, Encyclopedia of Photography, Amphoto/Eastman Kodak, 78. *Mailing Add:* Box 46 San Luis Obispo CA 93406

RUGOLO, LAWRENCE
PRINTMAKER, EDUCATOR
b Milwaukee, Wis, Oct 2, 31. *Study:* Univ Wis, Milwaukee, BA(art & art educ), 54; Univ Iowa, MFA, 59. *Work:* IBM, St Louis, Mo; Hunterdon Art Ctr, Clinton, NJ; State Univ NY Col, Potsdam; Ark Arts Ctr, Little Rock; Arts Coun Collection, Tulsa, Okla; plus others. *Comn:* Mural, First Nat Bank, Columbia, Mo, 79. *Exhib:* One-man shows, Albrecht Art Mus, 75, NE Mo State Univ, 81 & Lindenwood Col, St Louis, Mo, 88; La Grange Nat XVII, Nat Exhib Painting, Drawing & Prints, CVAA, Ga, 92; Valdosta Works on Paper IV, Valdosta State Col, 92; 24th Bradley Nat Print & Draw Exhib, Bradley Univ, Peoria, Ill, 93; 38th Nat Print Exhib, Hunterdon Art Ctr, Clinton, NJ, 94; NPVAG Nat Exhib, Scottsbluff, Nebr, 94. *Teaching:* Prof screenprinting & design, Univ Mo, Columbia, 74-95, chmn art dept, 73-96. *Awards:* Purchase Awards, 28th Nat Print Exhib, Hunterdon Art Ctr, Clinton, NJ, 84 & 19th Ann Anderson Winter Show, Ind, 89; Best of Show, No Platte Valley Artist's Guild Nat Juried Art Show, Scottsbluff, Nebr, 90. *Mem:* Print Consortium, St Joseph, Mo; Col Art League. *Media:* Screenprinting. *Mailing Add:* Univ Mo Dept Art Columbia MO 65211

RUHE, BARNABY SIEGER
PAINTER, CRITIC
b New York, NY, Aug 10, 46. *Study:* US Naval Acad, BS, 68; Md Inst, Col Art, with Ed Dugmore, Sal Scarpitta & Babe Shapiro, MFA(painting), 75; NY Univ, PhD, 89. *Work:* Lincoln & Great Neck Schs; Muhlenberg Col, Lincoln & Great Neck; Sidney Lewis Mus; Patterson Mus; Conejo Valley Art Mus. *Comn:* Marathons, City Allentown, 80; Conejo Valley Art Mus, 90. *Exhib:* Pleiades, NY, 76, 77 & 79; 5 solo-shows, Barbara Braathen Gallery, NY, 85-88; Conejo Valley Art Mus, 90. *Collection Arranged:* WC4 Box 83 10,000, New York Mail Concept Exhib. *Pos:* Dir, cur & producer, Whitney Counterweight, NY, 77, 79, 81 & 83; Sr art ed, Art World, 80-90; artist & lectr, Mus Mod Art, NY, 90-91. *Teaching:* Instr, Art hist, US Naval Acad, 72-75; instr Shamanistic painting workshops, Muhlenberg Col & Great Neck Ctr, 81-. *Awards:* Nat Endowment Arts Dirs Grant, 77; Prize, Allentown Art Mus, 79; Comn Visual Arts Grant, NY, 83, 86. *Bibliog:* Vic Miles (interviewer), Ruhe marathon painting, CBS TV, New York, 1/79 & NBC TV, 2/80; Myra Goldfarb (auth), Zen in Ruhe Painting, Call Chronicle, 5/79; Brad Swift, Bill Paige & Nina Barbier (dirs), Movies on Ruhe. *Mem:* Valley Arts Coun (founding mem, 76-); Artists Talk on Art, NY (bd dir, 89-91). *Media:* Oil, House Paint. *Publ:* Auth, Art of Making Boomerangs, American Woodworking, Rodale Press, 91. *Dealer:* Helen Turner 185 E 85th New York NY 10028. *Mailing Add:* 4926 Mountain Dr Emmaus PA 18049

RUMFORD, RONALD FRANK
PRINTMAKER, PAINTER
b Ft Meade, Md, May 28, 62. *Study:* Univ Arts, Philadelphia, BFA, 84. *Work:* NY Pub Libr, NY; Camden Co Cult & Heritage Soc, Haddonfield Twp, NJ; Ballinglen Arts Found, Bally Castle, Rep Ireland; Philadelphia Mus Art; Print and Picture Collection, Free Libr of Philadelphia, Pa. *Comn:* Lunamoth, Univ Print Club, Cleveland, Ohio, 96. *Exhib:* Images of N Mayo Fel Exhib, Philadelphia Art Alliance, Pa, 94; solo exhibs, The Print Ctr, 95 & Univ Arts, 95; One Over One, Rubicon, Dublin, Ireland, 97; New Prints: Bridgewater Lustberg, Blumenfeld Gallery; Challenge Exhib: Fleisher Art Mem, Philadelphia, Pa; New Prins, Locus Gallery, St Louis, Mo, 2000; The Print Ctr, 2002; Sch House Ctr, Provincetown, Ma, 2002; Abington Art Ctr, Jenkintown, Pa, 2003. *Pos:* Assoc dir, Dolan/Maxwell Inc, Philadelphia, 88-91, dir, 91-. *Awards:* Alexander Award, Cheltenham Art Ctr, 89; Purchase Prize, Camden Co, NJ, 89; Miriam McCall Award, 90. *Bibliog:* Edward Sozanski (auth), Museums and Galleries, Philadelphia Inquirer, 6/16/95, 10/22/2000, 6/16/2002. *Mem:* Printcenter, Philadelphia; Int Fine Print Dealers Asn; Green St Artists Cooperative (found pres, 90-92); Sketch Club (Philadelphia chap). *Media:* Print Making. *Publ:* Working Proof: Art on Paper, 00. *Dealer:* Blumenfeld Fine Art Brooklyn NY. *Mailing Add:* 5225 Greene St Philadelphia PA 19144

RUPP, SHERON ADELINE
PHOTOGRAPHER, EDUCATOR
b Mansfield, Ohio, Jan 14, 43. *Study:* Denison Univ, BA, 65; Univ Mass, MFA, 82. *Work:* Mus Mod Art, NY; Fogg Art Mus, Harvard Univ; Columbus Mus Art, Ohio; Smithsonian Mus, Washington, DC; J Paul Getty Mus, Los Angeles, Calif; Mus Fine Arts, Boston; and others. *Exhib:* Recent Acquisitions, Mus Mod Art, NY, 87; Rose Art Mus, Waltham, Mass, 88; Portland Sch Art, Maine, 89; Pleasures & Terrors of Domestic Comfort, Mus Mod Art, NY, 91; The Magic of Play, Dir Guild of Am, Los Angeles, Calif, 94; Columbus Mus Art, Ohio, 98; Cleveland Mus of Art, Ohio, 00; Smithsonian Inst, Game Face, DC, 01. *Teaching:* Instr photog, Northfield Mt Hermon Sch, 82-83 & Holyoke Community Col, 86-88; vis asst prof, Hampshire Col, 85-87; vis lectr, Amherst Col, Mass, 94. *Awards:* Photog Fel, Mass Artists Found, 84 & 87; Visual Arts Fel, Nat Endowment Arts, 86 & 94; John Simon Guggenheim Mem Award, 90. *Bibliog:* For Kids' Sake - Photographs of Today's Youth, PRC-Boston, 85, Cross Currents, Cross Country, PRC Boston & San Francisco camera work, 88; Northampton Postcards, Smith Col Art Mus, Northampton, Mass, 90; Peter Galassi (auth), Pleasures & Terrors of Domestic Comfort, Mus Mod Art, New York, 91. *Mem:* Photog Resource Ctr. *Media:* Photography. *Collection:* Berman Collection; Hallmark Collection & Photography, KC, Mont. *Publ:* Auth, Sheron Rupp Color Photographs, Helicon Nine, J Women's Arts & Lett, 86. *Mailing Add:* 364-C Hatfield St Northampton MA 01060

RUPPERSBERG, ALLEN
CONCEPTUAL ARTIST
b Cleveland, Ohio, Jan 5, 44. *Study:* Chouinard Art Inst, BFA, 67. *Work:* Guggenheim Mus Art, Mus Mod Art, Whitney Mus Am Art, NY; Los Angeles Co Mus, Calif; Addison Gallery Am Art, Andover, Mass; Milwaukee Art Mus, Wis; Los Angeles Co Mus Art, Mus Contemp Art, Los Angeles, Calif. *Exhib:* 557,087, Seattle Art Mus, Wash, 69; Ann Exhib: Contemp Am Sculpture, Whitney Mus Am Art, NY, 70; 24 Young Los Angeles Artists, Los Angeles Co Mus Art, Calif, 71; Pier 18, Mus Mod Art, NY, 71; Biennial Exhib, Whitney Mus Am Art, NY, 75; Calif Painting & Sculpture, The Modern Era, Smithsonian Inst, Washington, DC, 76; Theodoran Awards: Nine Artists, Solomon R Guggenheim Mus, NY, 77; Am Narrative Story Art, Contemp Arts Mus, Houston, 77; Book Works, Mus Mod Art, NY, 77; Ft Worth Art Mus, Tex, 77; Am Exhib, Art Inst Chicago, Ill, 80; LA Hot & Cool, Mass Inst Technol, Cambridge, 87; Boys and Girls, Men and Women, Addison Gallery Am Art, Andover, Mass, 90; Word as Image (with catalog), Milwaukee Art Mus, Wis, 90; Biennial 1991 (with catalog), Whitney Mus Am Art, NY, 91; one-man shows, frac Limousin, France, 92, Jay Gorney Mod Art, NY, 93 & 94, Linda Cathcart Gallery, Los Angeles, 93, Raum fur Aktueller Kunst, Vienna, Austria, 94, Galerie de Expeditie, Amsterdam, The Neth, 94, Galerie Gabrielle Maubrie, Paris, France, 94, Studio Guenzani, Milan, Italy, 94 & Pontikus, Frankfurt, Ger, 98; The Elusive Object, Recent Sculpture from the Permanent Collection of the Whitney Mus Am Art (with catalog), Whitney Mus Am Art, 93; For 35 Yrs: Brooke Alexander Editions, Mus Mod Art, NY, 94; L'Hiver de lAmour (with catalog), Mus Mod Art, Paris, 94; Ideas and Objects: Selected Drawings and Sculptures from the Permanent Collection, Whitney Mus Mod Art, NY, 94; Drawn in the 70's, Brooke Alexander Gallery, NY, 94; In the Field: Landscape in Recent Photog, Margo Leavin Gallery, Los Angeles, 94; Five Longish Wood Sculptures, Feature, NY, 94; Cocido y Crudo (with catalog), Mus Nac, Ctr de Arte Reina Sophia, Madrid, Spain, 94; Musee d'art Modenne et contemporian, Geneve, Switz, 98; Fonds Fegional d'Art Contemporain, Marseille, France, 98; and others. *Awards:* Grant, Nat

Endowment Arts, 76 & 82; Theodoran Award, Guggenheim Mus, 77; Guggenheim Fel, 97. *Bibliog:* Judd Tully (auth), Galeries de New York, Beaux Arts, Paris, 6/94; Raphael Rubenstein (auth), Gorney review, art in Am, 11/94; Alain-Henri Francois (auth), Maubrie review, Voir, Switz, 11/94. *Publ:* Auth, The Secret of Life and Death, Black Sparrow Press, 85; Art Paper, 4-9/88, Art Paper, 9/88, Artist's Page; Our House is very Beautiful at Night, Alti Novri (Utrecht), Vol 2, No 1, 92; Western/Allen Ruppersberg: A Different Kind of Never-Never Land (exhib publ), De Appel, Amsterdam, 92. *Mailing Add:* 532 La Guardia Pl # 656 New York NY 10012

RUPPRECHT, ELIZABETH
INSTRUCTOR, PAINTER
b Paris, France, Mar 28, 32; US citizen. *Study:* Sch of Art Inst Chicago, BFA, 54, MFA, 65. *Comn:* portraits, Wyler Children's Hosp, Chicago, Ill, 80. *Pos:* dir, Oxbow Sch Art, Saugatuck, Mich, 58-63, bd dir, 57-, pres, 66, secy, 67-89. *Teaching:* prof drawing, painting & color, Sch of Art Inst Chicago, Ill, 60-. *Awards:* John Quincy Adams Foreign Traveling Fel, 55. *Media:* Acrylic, Oil. *Mailing Add:* 5421 N Laporte Chicago IL 60630

RUSAK, HALINA R
LIBRARIAN, PAINTER
b Navahradak, Belarus; US citizen. *Study:* Douglass Col, New Brunswick, NJ, BA, 54; Rutgers Univ, New Brunswick, MLS, 56, MA, 76. *Work:* Nat Art Mus, Belarus; Douglass Col, NJ; Zimmerli Art Mus, New Brunswick, NJ; Jane Voorhees Zimmerli Art Mus, New Brunswick, NJ. *Exhib:* One-woman shows, NJ State Mus, Trenton, 77, Georgian Court Col, Lakewood, NJ, 77, SOHO 20, NY, 79, 84 & 87, 89 & 94, Byelorussion Inst Arts & Sci, NY, 82, Franklin Libr, Somerset, NJ, 82, Ortho Pharmaceutical Corp Art Gallery, Raritan, NJ, 86, Johnson & Johnson Int Hq Gallery, New Brunswick, NJ, 87, Symbols of Resiliency, SoHo 20, NY, 94 & Miracles & Disasters, 97; Women Artists, Paul Robeson Gallery, Newark, NJ, 79-80 & Nabisco World Hq, East Hanover, NJ, 80; Women Artists Series, Walters Hall Gallery, New Brunswick, 81 & Douglass Col Libr, 84; Women's Spheres, Middlesex Co Mus, Piscataway, NJ, 83-84; Slavic Art Exhib, NY, 88; Double Blind, SoHo 20, NY, 96; Belarus: 10 Yrs After Chemoby, Capital Children's Mus, Washington, DC, 96 & Johnson & Johnson World Hq, New Brunswick, NJ, 97; Graphic Work, Hunterdon Art Mus, 96; Transmission, NY-Amsterdam, De Zaaijer, The Neth, 98; Mem Exhib 1999, Hunterdon Mus of Art, Clinton, NY, 99. *Pos:* Art bibliographer & slide librn, Douglass Col, New Brunswick, 56-83; art librn & head, Rutgers Univ, New Brunswick, 83-; consult ed, Art Reference Services Quarterly, 91-. *Teaching:* Bibliog instr, art, Rutgers Univ, New Brunswick, NJ, 83. *Awards:* Preservation Grant for Elephant Folio, State of NJ; Res Coun Grant for Publ, Am Abstract Women Painters; Res Coun Grant for Publ, Art & Archit Polacak Principality. *Bibliog:* Women Artists Series Representative Works, 1971-84, Douglass Col, 84; Women Artists Series: 25 Years 1971-1996; My Land Minsk, Rutgers Univ, 96. *Mem:* Art Libr Soc NAm (vchmn, 84-85 & pres, 85-86, NJ chap); Women's Caucus Art; Col Art Asn. *Media:* Acrylic. *Res:* Women's art history; Belarusan arts history; architectural history and preservation; abstract expressionist woman artists. *Publ:* Auth, New and adequate space for the art library, ARLIS/NJ Newsletter, spring, 90; Ann Ryan, In: Past and Promise: lives of New Jersey Women, Scarecrow Press, 90; co-auth, American Women Painters Born After 1900, In: Women Artists in US, GK Hall, 90; The Art Library: A New Landmark, J Rutgers Univ Libr, 92; Coauth, Abstract Expressionist Women Painters, Scarecrow Press, 96. *Dealer:* SOHO 20 Gallery 469 Broome St New York NY 10013. *Mailing Add:* Art Libr Voorhees Hall-Rutgers Univ CAC-71 Hamilton St New Brunswick NJ 08903

RUSCHA, EDWARD JOSEPH
PAINTER, FILMMAKER
b Omaha, Nebr, Dec 16, 37. *Study:* Chouinard Art Inst, Los Angeles, Calif, 1960. *Work:* Mus Mod Art & Whitney Mus Am Art, NY; Los Angeles Co Mus Art; Joseph Hirshhorn Collection, Washington, DC; San Francisco Mus Mod Art; restrospective of works on paper J Paul Getty Mus Los Angeles, 1998; retrospective of career Hirshhorn Mus, 2000; Sculpture Garden, Washington, DC, 2000; Mus Contemp Art, Chicago, Miami Art Mus, Modern Art Mus, Ft Worth, Tex; also others. *Comn:* Mural, Metro Dade Co Art in Pub Places, 85; mural, Denver Pub Libr, 94-95; painting, JP Getty Ctr Auditorium, Los Angeles, 97. *Exhib:* Mus Contemp Art, Los Angeles, 81; One-man exhib tour, San Francisco Mus Mod Art, 82-83; Whitney Mus Am Art, Los Angeles Co Mus Art; Contemp Arts Mus, Houston; Vancouver Art Gallery; ICA, Nagoya, Japan, 88; Whitney Biennial, Whitney Mus Am Art, NY, 97; and others; exhib, Gagosian Gallery, Beverly Hills, 1999, Metro Plots, NY, 1999. *Pos:* US Rep, Venice Biennale, 2005. *Teaching:* Lectr painting, Univ Calif, Los Angeles, 69-70. *Awards:* Nat Coun Arts Grant, 67; Nat Endowment Arts Grant, 69 & 78; Tamarind Lithography Workshop Fel, 69; Guggenheim Found Fel, 71; Skowhegan Sch Painting & Sculpture Award in Graphics, 74. *Bibliog:* Geoffrey Haydon (dir), Edward Ruscha (film), British Broadcasting Corp, 79; Dave Hickey (auth), Available Light, Hudson Hills Press, 82; Peter Plagens (auth), Ed Ruscha, Seriously, Hudson Hills Press, 82; plus many others. *Mem:* Fel: Am Acad Arts & Sci; Am Acad Arts and Letters (mem dept art). *Publ:* Auth, Twenty Six Gasoline Stations, 63, Various Small Fires, 64, Every Building on the Sunset Strip, 66, Real Estate Opportunities, 70, A Few Palm Trees, 71, Heavy Industry Publs; Guacamole Airlines, Abrams, 80; and others. *Dealer:* Gagosian Gallery 456 North Camden Beverly Hills CA 90210; Anthony d'Offay Gallery 9 Dering St London W1R 9AA England. *Mailing Add:* 90 Gagosian Gallery 980 Madison Ave New York NY 10021-1848

RUSH, ANDREW
PRINTMAKER, SCULPTOR
b Mich, Sept 24, 31. *Study:* Univ Ill, BFA(hons), 53; Univ Iowa, MFA, 58; Fulbright fel, Florence, Italy, 58-59. *Work:* Uffizi Mus, Florence, Italy; Libr Cong, Washington; Dallas Mus Art; Seattle Art Mus. *Comn:* Law Prints (portfolio of three offset lithographs), Lawyers Publ Co, 68 & 74; ed etchings, Tucson Art Ctr, 71; large scale tile mural, Univ Ariz Health Sci Libr, 95. *Exhib:* US Info Serv Traveling Exhib to Europe & Latin Am, 60-65; Graphic Art USA, Am prints to Soviet Union, 63; Brooklyn Mus Biennial, 64; 50 Am Printmakers, Am Pavilion, NY World's Fair, 64-65; Intag 71, 30 Printmakers, San Fernando State Univ, 71; Tucson Gateway Project, 02. *Pos:* Founding mem, Rancho Linda Vista Community Arts, 69; guest cur, Tucson Mus Art, 88. *Teaching:* Assoc prof art, Univ Ariz, 59-69; vis artist-in-residence, Ohio State Univ, 70. *Awards:* Seattle Mus Int Printmakers Award, 63; Purchase Award, Brooklyn Mus Biennial, 64. *Bibliog:* Article, Southwest Art Gallery Mag, 3/72. *Media:* All. *Publ:* Prog cover artist, Tucson Symphony & Ariz Theatre & Opera Co, 78-83; illusr, The Rule of Two, Oracle Press, 84; A Voice Crying in the Wilderness, St Martins Press, 90; Ask Marilyn, St Martins Press, 92. *Mailing Add:* Rancho Linda Vista Star Rte 2360 Oracle AZ 85623

RUSH, DEBORAH
PAINTER, SCULPTOR
b Buffalo, NY, Oct 29, 52. *Work:* Arabian Horse Trust-Permanent Collection, Westminster, Colo. *Comn:* Mural, Town Historical, Elma Hist Soc, NY, 76; mural, Pioneer/Indian History, Canaseraga Cent Sch, NY, 86; mural, Town Historical, Elma Town Hall, 8/2003. *Exhib:* Allentown Art Festival, Buffalo, NY, 73; Crabbet Symposium, Denver, Colo, 84; Egyptian Event, Lexington, Ky, 84, 90, 91, 94-2006; US Nat Arabian Show, Louisville, Ky, 88, 92 & 94-98; World Cup, Tampa, Fla, 89; Mus European Art, April Group Juried Exhib (nude studies), Clarence, NY, 2004; Int Arabian Horse Show, HRH Royal Jordan Stables, Amman, 10/05; one-man show, Fountain Arts Ctr, Belmont, NY, 9/06. *Teaching:* Creative sculpting ceramic-clay, Iroquois Cent Sch, 72-; drawings & sketching, Adult Educ Prog, Elma, NY, 75-; private tutor, 1987-2005; premier one-day art seminar, Mashav Hn'yoger, Israel, 2005; instr, drawing, sketch, pastel painting, clay culture curriculum, Wellsville Creative Arts Ctr, NY, 2006. *Bibliog:* D Hamrick (auth), Rush's Passion--, Arabian Horse Express, 9/86; S Leadley (auth), The Easel, Arabian Visions, 2/92; Arabian Horse World, Pyramid Report, 2/05 & 4/06; Arabian Horse, Profile of the Artist, Times, 4/06. *Mem:* Lifetime honorary mem, Arabian Horse Assoc of NY, 2002; Allegany Artisan's Art Soc. *Media:* Porcelain; Pastel, Pencil. *Dealer:* The House of Horses 14459-1 W Grove Rd Forreston IL 61030. *Mailing Add:* 5071 State Rte 244 Belmont NY 14813

RUSH, JEAN C
EDUCATOR, PAINTER
b Bloomington, Ill, Nov 21, 33. *Study:* Ill Wesleyan Univ, BFA, 55; Univ Iowa, MFA, 58; Univ Ariz, PhD, 74. *Work:* Libr Congress, Washington, DC; Dallas Mus Fine Arts, Tex. *Exhib:* 13th Nat Exhib Prints, Libr Congress, Washington, DC, 55; 11th Exhib Southwest Prints & Drawings, Dallas Mus Fine Arts, Tex, 61; Ariz Women's Caucus for Art Statewide Show, 79. *Pos:* Coordr art educ prog, Univ Ariz, 78-80 & 81-88; co-ed, Studies in art education, Nat Art Educ Asn, 81-83, sr ed, 83-85; dir, Ariz Inst Elementary Art Educ, 86-87. *Teaching:* Lectr art educ, Univ Ariz, 71-75, asst prof art educ, 75-80, assoc prof, 80-89, prof, 89, emer prof, 89-; prof & admin chmn art dept, Ill State Univ, 89-91, prof, 91-96, emer prof, 96-. *Awards:* First Prize, Ariz State Fair, 60; Purchase Prize, Dallas Mus Fine Arts, 61; June King McFee Award, Nat Artists Equity Asn, 85. *Mem:* Col Art Asn; Int Soc Educ through Art; Nat Art Educ Asn. *Media:* Oil, Pencil. *Res:* Visual perception, art learning discipline-based art lesson, Studies in Art Educ, 87. *Publ:* Coauth, Teaching Children Art, Prentise Hall, 97. *Mailing Add:* RR 2 PO Box 59 Heyworth IL 61745

RUSH, JON N
SCULPTOR, EDUCATOR
b Atlanta, Ga, Sept 24, 35. *Study:* Art Inst Chicago, 53-55; Cranbrook Acad Art, with Tex Schiwetz, 55-59, BFA & MFA. *Work:* Columbus Mus Art, Ohio; Univ Mich, Ann Arbor. *Comn:* Sculpture, Southwestern Mich Col, Dowagiac, 84; sculpture, Domino World Hq, Ann Arbor, 89; sculpture, ISR, Univ Mich, 89; sculpture, Wallenberg Mem, Univ Mich, Ann Arbor, 95. *Exhib:* Hong Kong Int Competition, China, 62; Bundy Art Gallery, Waitsfield, Vt, 63; Fifteen Mich Sculptors, City of Lansing, 76; Meadowbrook Outdoor Sculpture, Rochester, Mich, 81; Mich Outdoor Sculpture II, S Field, 89; Mich Sculpture, Midland Ctr Arts, 02. *Teaching:* Prof sculpture, Univ Mich, 62-. *Awards:* Sculpture Award, All Mich Artists, Flint Inst Art, 72; Sculpture Prize, Mich Outdoor Sculpture II, S Field, 89; 1st Place, Art in Pub Places, Mich Coun Arts, 90. *Media:* Metal, Stone. *Mailing Add:* 7930 Fifth St Dexter MI 48130

RUSH, KENT THOMAS
PHOTOGRAPHER, PRINTMAKER
b Hayward, Calif, Jan 16, 1948. *Study:* Calif Col Arts & Crafts, BFA, 70; Univ NMex, Albuquerque, MA, 75; Univ Tex, Austin, MFA, 79. *Work:* Oakland Mus, Calif; McNay Mus, San Antonio; Albuquerque Mus, NMex; Inst De Obra Grafica De Oaxaca, Oaxaca, Mex; Humanities Res Ctr, Univ Tex, Austin; Ctr Fine Print Research, Col West of England, Bristol, UK; Auchenbach Found Graphic Arts, San Francisco, Calif. *Exhib:* One-man shows, Univ Art Mus, Univ NMex, Albuquerque, 90, Inst Cult Peruano Norte Americano, Lima, Peru, 90, Dowd Fine Arts Ctr, State Univ NY, Cortland, 92, Martin Mus Art, Baylor Univ, Waco, Tex, 94, Art Pace, San Antonio, Tex, Legion Arts/CSPS, Cedar Rapids, Iowa, 2002; Blue Star Art Space, San Antonio, Tex, 93; Ctr for Photog, Woodstock, NY, 93; Santa Fe Mus Fine Arts NMex, 93; San Antonio Mus Art, Tex, 94; Diverse Works, Houston, Tex, 94; SE Mus Photog, Daytona Beach, Fla; Retrospective, McNay Art Mus, 98; Amarillo Mus Art, Tex, 2003; Art Gallery, Ctr Fine & Performing Arts, Texas A&M Int Univ, Laredo, Tex, 2006. *Teaching:* Instr, San Antonio Art Inst, 76-79; lectr, Calif Col Arts & Crafts, Oakland, 80-81, San Francisco Art Inst, 82; prof, Univ Tex, San Antonio, 82-06; instr, Santa Reparata Grafic Arts Ctr, Florence, Italy, 84 & 97, Taller Delas Artes Plasticas Rufino Tamayo, Oaxala, Mex, 88 & Universidad Catolica, Lima, Peru, 90. *Awards:* Sr Fulbright Fel, Taller Rufino Tamayo, Oaxaca, Mex, 88; MidAm Arts Alliance & Nat Endowment Arts Fel in Photog, 90-91; Partners of the Americas Grant, Univ Catolica,

Lima, Peru, 90. *Bibliog:* Diane Armitage (auth), Kent Rush, Recent Photographs, THE Mag, Santa Fe, NMex, 12/93; Lyle Williams (auth), Kent Rush: A retrospective, San Antonio: Marian Koogler McNay Art Mus, 1998; Anjali Gupta (auth), Foundabstraction, San Antonion Current Mag, 6/14/2000. *Mem:* Southern Graphics Coun; Soc Photog Educ. *Publ:* Auth, Collotype: An Extension of Lithography, Tamarind Papers, 87. *Dealer:* Parchman-Stremmel Galleries San Antonio Tex; Hare & Hound Press San Antonio Tex. *Mailing Add:* Dept Art & Art History Univ Tex San Antonio One UTSA Circle San Antonio TX 78249-0642

RUSH, MICHAEL JAMES
MUSEUM DIRECTOR, WRITER
b Orange, NJ, Apr 30, 49. *Study:* St Louis Univ, BA, 1971, MA, 72; Harvard Univ, PhD, 80. *Work:* Centre Georges Pompidou, Paris; Kunsthalle, Zurich; Whitney Mus, NY. *Exhib:* Brooklyn, 2001; Video Jam, 2001; Sue Williams, 2002; Sculpture Now, 2002. *Pos:* founding dir, New Haven Artists' Theater, 85-2000; dir, Palm Beach Inst of Contemp Art, 2000-. *Teaching:* Harvard Univ, 79-80, Boston Col, 80, Yale Univ, 87-90, Duke Univ, 90. *Awards:* Found for Contemp Performing Arts, 92; Nat Endowment for the Arts, 93; New Eng Found for the Arts, 94. *Bibliog:* A Klein (auth), NY Times, 86-95. *Mem:* Am Asn Mus; Int Asn of Art Critics; Dramatists' Guild; Asn Independent Video and Filmmakers. *Media:* Video. *Publ:* auth, New Media in Late 20th Century Art, Thames and Hudson, 99; auth, Video Art, Thames Hudson, 2003; featured writer in NY Times, Art in Am, Newsweek.com. *Mailing Add:* Palm Beach Inst Contemp Art 601 Lake Ave Lake Worth FL 33460

RUSHWORTH, MICHELE D
PAINTER, INSTRUCTOR
b Toronto, Ont, Can, Oct 16, 58, US Citizen. *Study:* Queen's Univ, BFA, 76-78; Ont col Art and Design, with William Whitaker, Tony Ryder, Juliette Aristides & Calvin Goodman, 78-80. *Comn:* Official Portrait of Washington Governor Gary Locke, State Wash, Olympia, Wash, 2005; Portrait of Pacific NW Ballet Directors, Pacific NW Ballet, Seattle, Wash, 2005; Official Portrait of Nevada Gov Kenny Guinn, State Nev, Carson City, Nev, 2006; Portrait of Law Dean, Campbell Univ, Buies Creek, NC, 2006; mural with 30 portraits, Peel Co Bd Educ, Toronto, Can. *Exhib:* Salmagundi Club Allied Artists Am Nat Arts Club Am Watercolor Soc juried exhib, New York, NY, 85-88; Rutgers Univ Regional Int show, NJ, 85-88; Pa Watercolor invitational show, Pa. *Bibliog:* CBS News (television), Portrait of a Hero, CBS News The Early Show, 9/3/2002; Sherry Grinderland (auth), Portrait colorful tribute to former state leader, Seattle Times, 1/4/2006; Cy Ryan (auth), Seattle artist picked to paint Guinn, Las Vegas Sun, 8/23/2006. *Mem:* Portrait Soc Am. *Media:* Oil on Canvas. *Dealer:* Portrait Brokers of Am 36-B Church St Birmingham Ala 35213. *Mailing Add:* 22930 SE 27th Ct Sammamish WA 98075

RUSSELL, JEFF See Jeff

RUSSELL, ROBERT PRICE
PAINTER, EDUCATOR
b Rochelle, Ill, June 23, 39. *Study:* Kansas City Art Inst, Mo, BFA, 61; Southern Ill Univ, Carbondale, MFA, 63. *Work:* El Paso Mus Art, Tex; Idaho State Univ, Pocatello; Roswell Mus & Art Ctr, NMex; Springfield Art Mus, Mo. *Comn:* Painting/Drawing, Westin-Crown Ctr Hotel, Kansas City, Mo, 87. *Exhib:* One-person shows, Jan Weiner Gallery, Kansas City, Mo, 87, 89 & 92, Kauffman Galleries, Houston, 89 & 91 & Jack Meier Gallery, Houston, 94, Jazz Connection, Jack Gallery, 98. *Pos:* Artist-in-residence, Area arts prog, Wis, 66-67, Hanover Col, Ind, 73, Roswell Mus & Art Ctr, NMex, 74-75 & Idaho State Univ, Pocatello, 79 & 82. *Teaching:* Instr art, Univ Wis-Stevens Point, 63-66; prof, Pittsburg State Univ, Kans, 67-. *Awards:* Tech Assistantship Grant in Lithography, Kans Arts Comn & Nat Endowment Arts, 85. *Bibliog:* Greg Field (auth), Readable references rescue abstract art, Forum, 9/87. *Media:* Acrylic, Monotype. *Dealer:* Jack Meier Gallery 2310 Bissonnet Houston TX 77005

RUSSELL, ROBERT S
SCULPTOR
b Fitchburg, Mass, Nov 10, 19. *Study:* Univ of NH, Keene, BA, 1966; Columbia Univ, MA, 1969; Columbia Univ, EdD, 1976. *Work:* Perm Collections: Fitchburg Art Mus, Fitchburg, MA, Mills Col, Oakland, Calif; City Univ NJ, Three Bronze Sculptors, Jersey City, NJ; Wavehill Ctr, Eagle Garden Sculptor, Riverdale, NY City. *Exhib:* One man show incl: Dow Gallery, TC Columbia New York City, 1967; World Craft Conf, Lima, Peru, 1968; Hudson Co Paints & Sculpture Show, Jersey City, NJ, 1970; group show incl: Juried New York City Loeb Ctr, Univ Counc for the Arts, New York City, 1984. *Pos:* cur, Mus Am Indian Art, formerly. *Teaching:* student asst, Columbia Univ, 1965-66; instr, CUNJ, Jersey City, NJ, 1966-89; prof emerites, NJCU; retired. *Mem:* Univ Coun for the Arts (treas, formerly). *Mailing Add:* 44 College Dr Jersey City NJ 07305

RUSSIN, ROBERT I
SCULPTOR, EDUCATOR
b New York, NY, Aug 26, 1914. *Study:* City Univ New York, BA, 33 & MS, 35; Beaux Arts Inst Design, 35-36. *Work:* Evanston Post Off, Ill; Conshohocken Post Office, Pa; Bicentennial Monument, Cheyenne Visitors' Ctr, Wyoming Crystal, State Off Bldg, Cheyenne, Wyo; Chthonodynamis, Granite monument, Dept Energy Bldg, Washington, 92; monument (acrylic, steel & bronze), Herschler State Office Building, Cheyenne; monument (marble head), Juan Pablo Duarte, Santo Domingo; portrait, Charles Bluhdorn; busts, Lincoln, Milward Simpson, James Forest & Pres J Balaguer of Dom Rep; Man and Energy (monument), Casper CofC, Wyo; and many other monuments and sculptures. *Comn:* Spirit of Life (bronze & marble), City Hope Nat Med Ctr, Duarte, Calif; Fountainhead (steel), City Hall, Casper, Wyo; marble carving, Univ Wyo; Prometheus (bronze), Casper Pub Libr, Wyo; Helios Dallas (bronze & marble), Lincoln Ctr, Dallas; Joie de Vie, bronze fountain sculpture, Pomona Col, Claremont, Calif; Pan-American Family (marble), Dominican Repub; Einstein, Gershwin, IB Singer medals for Magnes Mus, Berkeley, Calif; Freedom Fighter Monument (bronze) & monumental Holocaust figure, Tucson Jewish Community Ctr, Ariz; L'Charm (Bronze & Granitic), Nat'l Jewish Medical & Research Center, Denver, CO. *Exhib:* Pa Acad Fine Arts Sculpture Biennial, Philadelphia, 66; one-man shows, Tucson Fine Arts Ctr, 66, Colo Springs Fine Arts Ctr, 67, Palm Springs Desert Mus, Chas G Bowers Mem Mus, Judah L Magnes Mem Mus, Berkeley, Calif, 70, Galleria d'Arte Mod, Santo Domingo, 76-77, Riggins Art Gallery, Scottsdale, Ariz, 89 & Univ Wyo Art Mus, 91, Tubac Ctr of Arts, Ariz, 95, Old Town Gallery, Park City, Utah, 98, Maxwell Gallery, San Francisco, 98; and many others. *Teaching:* Instr sculpture, Cooper Union Art Inst, 44-47; prof sculpture, Univ Wyo, 47-86, univ artist, 79-86, prof emer, 87-. *Awards:* Lincoln Sesquicentennial Medal, US Cong, 59; Alfred GB Steel Award, Pa Acad Fine Arts, 61; Charles GB Steele Sculpture Award, Pa Acad Fine Arts, 66; Einstein & Gershwin medals, Magnes Mem Mus, Berkeley, Nat Mus Art, Santo Domingo, Dom Rep, 75; Order of Duarte, Sanchez & Mella, by Pres Joachim Balaguer, Dominican Repub, 77; Former Faculty Distingsuished Award, Univ Wyo, 2000. *Bibliog:* RT Northen (auth), Russin's metal magic, Empire Mag, 2/56; Tom Francis (auth), Robert Russin, Wyoming sculptor, Am Artist, 1/60; F K Frame (auth), Russin's Lincoln, Empire Mag, 2/26. *Mem:* AAUP; Int Sculpture Soc; Sculptors Guild; Nat Sculpture Soc; Col Art Int Inst Arts & Letters. *Media:* Miscellaneous Media. *Publ:* Contribr, A new sculptural medium, Col Art J, 56, The Lincoln monument on the Lincoln highway, Lincoln Herald, 61 & A university bronze foundry, 63, Am Artist

RUSSO, ALEXANDER PETER
PAINTER, EDUCATOR
b Atlantic City, NJ, June 11, 22. *Study:* Pratt Inst, 40-42; Swarthmore Col, 47; Bard Col, summer 47; Columbia Univ, BFA(Breevort-Eickenmeyer Fel), 52; Acad Fine Arts, Rome, Fulbright Grant, 52-54; Univ Buffalo, 55. *Work:* Albright-Knox Gallery, Buffalo, NY; Nat Collection Fine Arts, Washington, DC; Fed Ins Deposit Corp, Washington, DC; Acad Arts & Lett, NY; Delgado Mus of Art, New Orleans, La. *Comn:* Encaustic mural, Telesio Interlandi, Capo San Andrea, Sicily, 53; var design comns, Doubleday Publ Co, Dutton Publ, Birge Co & Cohn Hall Marx, 56-60; acrylic painting series, US Navy Dept, 64; acrylic mural, Dr Martin Cherkasky, NY, 70; Vet Mem sculpture, Frederick, Md, 75. *Exhib:* Carnegie Nat, Pittsburgh, 46; Int Exhib, Bordighera, Italy, 53 & 54; Four Am Artists Exhib, Biblioteca, Rome, 54; Albright-Knox Gallery Regional, Buffalo, NY, 56; Corcoran Biennials, Washington, DC; and many one-man shows. *Pos:* Combat artist, US Navy Dept, Washington, DC, 42-46; actg art dir, Sewell, Thompson, Caire Advert, New Orleans, 48-49; freelance artist & designer, var agencies & orgns, New York, 58-60; guest lectr art, Roanoke & Hollins Cols, Univ Southern Ill, Miss Art Asn, and others; art consult, Univ Publications of Am, Frederick, Md, 80-; guest art critic, Southampton Press, summer 88 & 91. *Teaching:* Assoc prof painting & drawing, Corcoran Sch Art, 61-70, chmn fac & painting dept, 66-69; prof art & chmn dept, Hood Col, 71-85, prof art, 86-90, prof emer, 90; vis prof art, Inst Allende, San Miguele de Allende, Mex, 92 & 93. *Awards:* Guggenheim Fel, Painting, 47-48, 49-50; Fulbright Grant (painting), Rome, 52-54; Grantee, India, US-Indo Subsomm, on Ed & Culture, 84. *Bibliog:* Carl Fortes (auth), Tape on aesthetics and teaching methods of Alexander Russo, Boston Univ, 68; Anne M Jonas (auth), Focus on: Alexander Russo, The Art Scene, 70/71. *Mem:* Col Art Asn; Arts Club Washington (chmn exhibs, 70-71); Artists Equity; Soc Washington Artists; Edward McDowell Colony; Md State Arts Coun. *Media:* Acrylic, Oil. *Publ:* Illusr, To All Hands, an Amphibious Adventure, 44 & Many a Watchful Night, 45, McGraw; auth, Profiles on Women Artists, Univ Publ Am, 83; The Challenge of Drawing, Prentice-Hall, 86; Vigmettes, poems by Alexander Russo, Morris Publ, 96. *Mailing Add:* PO Box 1377 Wainscott NY 11975

RUSSO, SALLY FULTON HALEY See Haley, Sally

RUSSOTTO, PAUL
PAINTER, EDUCATOR
b New York, NY, May 28, 44. *Study:* Art Students League, 62-63. *Work:* Metrop Mus Art, NY; Heckscher Mus Fine Art, Huntington, NY; Tokai Bank Ltd, Chicago; Gen Electric Corp; Ciba-Geigy Corp, Ardsley, NY; Brooklyn Mus; NY Pub Libr; Rochfort-en-Terre FDN, Brittany, France; Asheville Art Mus; Accademia D'Arte Dino Scalabrino, Montelatiniterme, Italy. *Comn:* Work for Permanent Installation for Mus of Peace, Comune Di Murlo (si) Italy, 2004. *Exhib:* NY/Beijing, Beijing Art Inst, Shanghai Mus, 87; Invitational, Am Acad Arts & Letters, NY, 93 & 97; Recent Acquisitions, Heckscher Mus Fine Art, Huntington, NY, 2000; Omaggio A Marino Marini, Acad Scalabrino, Montecatini Terme, Italy, 2000-2001; Angeli, Rome, Florence, Montecatini Terme, Venice, Romania, 2001-02; numerous others. *Teaching:* instr painting & drawing, Parsons Sch Design, NY, 78-80, NY Studio Sch of Drawing, Painting & Sculpture, NY, 80-82 & Vt Studio Ctr, Johnson, Vt, 85-2001. *Awards:* Rouchefort-en-Terre Found Award, 95; Purchase Award, Am Acad Arts & Letters, 97; Edwin Palmer Mem Prize, Nat Acad Design, 2000; Henry Ward Ranger Purchase award, 2001. *Bibliog:* Eleanor Heartney (auth), Paul Russotto at Ingber, Art In America, 12/86; Gerard Haggerty (auth), Crux of Change, Cover Mag, 1/94; Vincent Katz, Paul Russotto, Art in America, 5/94; Valentine Tatransky (auth), Men & their Bodies, Cover Mag, 80-81; Peter Bellamy (auth), The Artist Project: Portraits of the Real Art World / New York 1981-1990, In Pub, NY, 91; Alan Jones (auth) Drawing the Line, Paul Russotto Drawing Disegni, 2002; Alan Jones, 8 Artisti Da New York, Accademia Darte Dino Scalabrino, Montecatini terme, Italy. *Mem:* Nat Acad Design (assoc, 93, acad, 94); cert. of merit 1996; Palmer Mem prize 2000; Henry Ward Ranger award 2001. *Media:* Oil. *Publ:* Boundary 2: A Journal of Postmodern Literature & Culture, SUNY Binghamton, 85-86. *Dealer:* Seraphin Gallery Philadelphia Pa. *Mailing Add:* PO Box 385 Canal St Sta New York NY 10013-0385

RUST, DAVID E
CURATOR, COLLECTOR
b Bloomington, Ill. *Study:* Harvard Col, BA; NY Univ Inst Fine Arts, MA, 63. *Collection Arranged:* English Drawings & Watercolors, 62; Old Master Drawings from Chatsworth, 69; Nathan Cummings Collection, 70; Francois Boucher: 100 Drawings (asst auth, catalog), 73; French Paintings from the Alisa Mellon Bruce Collection (auth, catalog), 78; Manet and Modern Paris, 82-83. *Pos:* Cur Fr, Brit & Spanish Paintings, Nat Gallery Art, Washington, DC, 61-83; adv panel, Art Pub Places, Dade Co, Fla; dir, Tissot Exhib, 84-85. *Collection:* Paintings and drawings, mostly European sixteenth-nineteenth century; American nineteenth century and some contemporary. *Publ:* Auth, Twentieth Century Paintings & Sculpture of the French School in the Chester Dale Collection, 65; Eighteenth & Nineteenth Century Paintings & Sculpture of the French School in the Chester Dale Collection, 65; The drawings of Vincenzo Tamagni da San Gimignano, Report & Studies Hist Art, 68; Small French Paintings from the Bequest of Alisa Mellon Bruce, 78. *Mailing Add:* 2812 P St NW Washington DC 20007

RUST, EDWIN C
SCULPTOR, ADMINISTRATOR
b Hammonton, Calif, Dec 5, 1910. *Study:* Cornell Univ; Yale Univ, BFA; also with Archipenko & Milles; Southwestern at Memphis, Hon DFA, Memphis Col Art, Hon DFA. *Work:* US Ct House, Washington; Univ Tenn Ctr Health Serv; Univ Miss, Oxford; Univ Tenn, Knoxville; Memphis Acad Arts, Tenn; Ouchita Baptist Univ, Arkadelphia, Ark; Memphis Brooks Mus Art. *Exhib:* Whitney Mus Am Art, NY, 40; Carnegie Inst Int, Pittsburgh, 40; Philadelphia Mus Art, 40 & 49; Mus Mod Art, NY, 42; Brooks Mem Mus, 50 & 52. *Pos:* Dir, Memphis Acad Arts, 49-75, emer dir, 75-. *Teaching:* Assoc prof sculpture, Col William & Mary, 36-43, head, Dept Fine Arts, 39-43. *Mem:* Nat Sculpture Soc. *Mailing Add:* 3725 Waynoka Ave Memphis TN 38111-6113

RUTA, PETER PAUL
PAINTER
b Dresden, Ger, Feb 7, 18; US citizen. *Study:* Art Students League, 38-42 & 45-46; Acad Fine Arts Venice, 47-49, degree; Acad Venice, 48. *Work:* Uffizi Gallery, Florence, Italy; Univ Southern Ill; State NMex; Mus City NY. *Exhib:* One-man shows, Larcada Gallery, NY, 76, Sunne Savage Gallery, Boston, 80, Sch House Gallery, Truro, Mass, 83, Acad Gallery, New Orleans, 83, 89, 92 & 95, 01 & Munson Gallery, Santa Fe, NMex, 85-88, 93, 97, St Johns Col, Santa Fe, NMex, 97, Bamring Gallery, NY, 2003, Mus of City NY, 2004,. *Collection Arranged:* ND Mus of Art, 02. *Pos:* Ed, Arts Mag, 68-71 & Int Art Exhibs, 69. *Awards:* Fel, Pollock-Krasner Found, 88 & 95, 02; Fel, Va Ctr Creative Arts, 89; Fel, Roche Fort En Terre, France, 1994, 2000, 04, 06. *Mem:* Art Students League New York. *Media:* Oil. *Mailing Add:* Studio B 647 463 West St New York NY 10014

RUTHLING, FORD
PAINTER, SCULPTOR
b Santa Fe, NMex, Apr 23, 33. *Study:* With Randall Davey; largely self taught. *Work:* Mus NMex; Wichita Falls Fine Art Mus; Univ Utah Collection; and others. *Comn:* US Pueblo Pottery Postage Stamp (4 thirteen cent stamps), 77; and others. *Exhib:* Nelson Atkins Mus; Mus NMex; Oklahoma City Mus Fine Art; Dallas Mus Fine Art; Wichita Falls Mus Fine Art; Roswell Art Mus, 79; and others. *Pos:* Cur Exhibs, Mus Int Folk Art, 1965-68. *Teaching:* at NMex State Pennitentiary, 1973-. *Awards:* 2006 Governor's Art Award; 4 Top Awards at competition for Int Incarcerated Prisoners. *Media:* Oil, Graphics; Metal, Wood, Mono Prints. *Collection:* Folk Art, Latin Religous Santos, Retablos, Reliquaries & Paintings; African Antique Art; Indian Jewelery; Pottery; Textiles. *Publ:* Various. *Mailing Add:* 313 E Berger St Santa Fe NM 87501

RUTHVEN, JOHN ALDRICH
PAINTER, LECTURER
b Cincinnati, Ohio, Nov 12, 24. *Study:* Univ Cincinnati Art Acad; Ctr Acad Com Art; Miami Univ, Ohio, DHL; St Francis Col, Loretto, Pa, DHL. *Work:* Hermitage Mus, Leningrad, Russia; Neil Armstrong Space Mus, Wapakoneta, Ohio; Ruthven Conf Ctr, Middletown, Ohio; White House, Washington; Cincinnati Natural Hist Mus. *Comn:* Cardinals for Gov Conf, State Ohio, Columbus, 68 & Eagle to the Moon, 69; Colonial Williamsburg Ser, Va, 70-75; Cardinal, USSR, 70; Miami Indian, Miami Univ, 74; Bankers' Life & Casualty. *Exhib:* Ducks Unlimited, Hilton Head, SC, 72; Ohio State Fair, Columbus, 74; White House Reception, 76; Leigh-Yawkey-Woodson Mus, Wausau, Wisc, 76 & 77; Wildlife Festival, Easton, Md, 77; Artists Am, Denver; Soc Animal Artists; Bennington Ctr Arts, NJ, 96; Cannon House, Washington, 96. *Pos:* Mem bd dir, Cincinnati Nature Ctr, 69; trustee, Cincinnati Natural Hist Mus, 75; trustee, Ducks Unlimited, Ohio Nature Cons Bd, currently. *Awards:* Sachs Fine Art Award, Cincinnati Art Acad, 69; Ducks Unlimited, 1st Art of Yr, 82; 1st Ohio Animal Stamp, 88; Pacific Flyaway Artist, Ducks Unlimited, 1989; recipient Irma Lazarus Award for sustained arts excellence, Ohio Govs Awards for the Arts, 2001; Nat Medal of Arts, 2004. *Bibliog:* Jerry Bowles (auth), John Ruthven, Acquire Mag, 73; Cincinnati Art, Town & Country, 75; Art of Life, film-doc, WCET-TV, 96. *Mem:* Soc Animal Artists NY; Audubon Soc; Nature Conservancy; Grouse Soc; Wild Turkey Fedn. *Media:* Opaque Watercolor. *Publ:* Coauth, Topflight, 69; auth, Carolina Paraquet, Audubon Mag, 72; auth, In the Audubon Tradition, Hennegan, 94; Wings of Encouragement, Helen Steiner Rice Found, 95; Ohio Wildlife Guidebook, Ohio Div Wild, 96. *Mailing Add:* Wildlife Internationale Inc 202 E Grant Ave Georgetown OH 45121

RUTLAND, LILLI IDA
PAINTER, ILLUSTRATOR
b Dothan, Ala, Jan 3, 18. *Study:* Univ Ala, 50-52; study with Claude Peacock, 50-52. *Work:* Governors Mansion, Montgomery, Ala; Houston Mem Libr & Rose Hill Elem Sch, Dothan, Ala. *Comn:* Yearbook cover, Young Jr High Sch, Dothan, Ala, 33. *Exhib:* King Alfred Daffodils, Panama City Art Mus, Fla, 60; First Snow and Wild Flowers, Montgomery Mus Fine Arts, Ala, Daytona Mus Arts & Sci, Daytona Beach, Fla, Mobile Art Gallery, Ala & Birmingham Mus Art, Ala, 76; Daybreak, 84 & Southern Magnolias, 84, City Nat Bank Gallery, Dothan, Ala; solo exhib, Southeast Ala Med Ctr Gallery, Dothan, Ala, 85. *Pos:* Illusr, Training Aids, Ft Rucker, Ala, 67-75. *Awards:* First in Watercolor, Houston Co Fair, City of Dothan, 60; First in Watercolor, Dothan Wirgrass Art League, 73; Best of Show in Watercolor, Dothan Bank & Trust Co, 73. *Mem:* Dothan Wirgrass Art League (secy, 62); Portrait Club, Washington, Conn. *Media:* Watercolor. *Mailing Add:* 106 Charleston Ln Dothan AL 36301-4234

RUTSTEIN, REBECCA
PAINTER
b Philadelphia, Pa, Jun 25, 71. *Study:* Wash Univ, St Louis, studied Art Hist & Studio Art, 89-90; Cornell Univ, BFA, 93; Univ Pa, MFA, 97. *Work:* Philadelphia Mus Art Mus Restaurant, 2004. *Exhib:* Solo exhib incl, Painting and Drawings, Tjaden Gallery, Ithaca, NY, 93, Painting and Collages, Morgan Print Gallery, Univ Pa, Philadelphia, 96, Small Works/Sacred Spaces, 97, Recent Works, Lockjaw Gallery, Philadelphia, 99, Paintings, Drawings & Illuminations, 2000, Erasure, Tribes Gallery, New York City, 2000, Second Skin, In Rare From Gallery, Lambertville, NJ, 2000, Shifting Images, Bridgette Mayer Gallery, Philadelphia, 2002, Love & Subduction, 2004, Underworld, Fleisher Art Mem, Philadelphia, 2002, Breaking Boundaries, Canopy Adventures, List Gallery, Swarthmore Col, Pa, 2004, Ebb and Flow, Bridgette Mayer Gallery, 2005; group shows incl Dear Fleisher, Fleisher Art Meml, Phila, 2004; Tierney Communications, Pa, 2004, 05, 06; Art of the State, The State Mus Pa, 2005; Sum of All Parts, Bridgette Mayer Gallery, 2006. *Teaching:* Artist-in-residence Vt Studio Ctr, Johnson, 97, Banff Centre for the Arts, Can, 2003, Can, 2004; visiting artist and lectr, Swarthmore Col, 2004, Bucks County Community Col, 2005, Main Line Unitarian Church, Pa, 2005; guest critic, Univ Arts, Phila, 2006. *Awards:* Named Degree Marshall (Valedictorian), Fine Arts Dept, Cornell Univ, 93; Overseers Scholar Fel, Univ Pa, 95-96; recipient Piero Dorazio Color Award, Grad Sch Fine Arts, Univ Pa, 96; Charles Addams Mem Prize, 97; Natvar Bhavsar Prize for group exhib East/West Visions In Between, Arthur Ross Gallery, Philadelphia, 97; Pew Fel in the Arts, 2004; Bridgette Mayer Gallery Travel Grant, 2005; Pa Council Arts Grant, 2006. *Mailing Add:* c/o Bridgetta Mayer Gallery 709 Walnut St Philadelphia PA 19106

RUTTINGER, JACQUELYN
PAINTER, GALLERY DIRECTOR
b Great Falls, Mont, July 21, 40. *Study:* Univ Wash, Seattle, 58-60; Art Inst Chicago, BFA(hon), 63; Northern Ill Univ, MA, 76, MFA, 77; Gov's State Univ, 81-83, Post-grad work in Printmaking. *Work:* Ill State Mus, Springfield; State Ill Percent Art, Northern Ill Univ, DeKalb & Eastern Ill Univ, Charleston; Millikin Univ, Decatur, Ill; Sheldon Swope Art Mus, Terre Haute, Ind; Western Mich Univ, Kalamazoo, & Downtown Grad Ctr, Grand Rapids, Mich; Am Council on Education, Washington, DC. *Comn:* 2 paintings, Appl Technol Bldg, Grand Rapids Community Col, Mich, 92. *Exhib:* One-person show, Kalamazoo Inst Arts, Mich, Saginaw Art Mus, Mich & Jesse Besser Mus Alpena, Mich; State of Mich Commerce Dept & State Suptd of Schs Offs, State Off Bldgs, Lansing, Mich, 96; Four from Kalamazoo Krasl Art Ctr, St Joseph, Mich, 99; Farnham Galleries, Simpson Col, Indianolo, Iowa; Recent juried, Behind the Walls, Nat juried show, Univ Wisc-Green Bay, 2000; Shared Journey, Greate Lafayette Mus of Art, Indianina, 2001; 75th Muskegon Mus Art Regional, MI, 2004; Jackson Area Show, Ella Sharp Mus, Jackson, MI, 2005, Best of Show Award. *Pos:* Dir exhib & vis artist progs, art dept, Western Mich Univ, Kalamazoo, 86-. *Teaching:* chmn art dept, St Mary-of-the-Woods Col, 83-85. *Awards:* Ill Art Coun, Grant, 81-82; Creative Artists Grant, Arts Found Mich & Mich Coun Arts & Cult Affairs, 96-97; Best of Show, Jackson Area Show, Ella Sharp Mus, Mich, 96. *Mem:* Arts Coun Greater Kalamazoo; Mich Mus Assoc; ArtServ Mich. *Media:* Acrylic Airbrush Paintings, Prismacolor Drawings. *Specialty:* Contemporary Art. *Publ:* 33rd Annual Drawing & Small Sculpture Show (exhib catalog), Ball State Univ Art Gallery, 87; Recent Trends in Painting: The 11th Michigan Biennial (exhib catalog), Kresge Art Mus, Mich State Univ, 89; Haworth Col Bus Fine Art Collection (catalog), Western Mich Univ, 91; Hidden Treasures, Int Libr Photog, Owings Mills, Md, 2000. *Mailing Add:* 1110 Dwillard Dr Kalamazoo MI 49048-2259

RUTZKY, IVY SKY
SCULPTOR, PAINTER
b New York, NY, Nov 19, 48. *Study:* Penland Sch, NC, 69; Univ NMex, BFA, 73. *Work:* Glacial, Macomb Community Col, Warren, Mich; New Mus, NY; Detroit Inst Ats, Detroit, MI. *Comn:* Sculpture, Simone Forti for dance performance, Austria & NY. *Exhib:* Iandor Gallery, Newark, NJ, 2001 & 2003; Cass Cafe, Detroit, MI, 2001; Equus, Mehu Gallery, New York, NY 2002, 2003 & 2005; Germaine Keller Gallery, Garrison, NY, 2002; Ana Valentine Gallery, Livingston, MT, 2004. *Awards:* Nat Endowment Arts Grant, 85 & 89. *Bibliog:* Dennis Nawrocki & Tom Holleman (auth), Art in Detroit Public Places, Wayne State Univ Press, 80; Ruth & Louis Redstone (auth), Public Art/New Directions, McGraw-Hill, 81; Discovering Fossil Fishes (auth), 96; Discovery.com Website. *Media:* Pastel. *Publ:* Keith Johnson (auth), Threshold, Art Express, 5-6/81, Discovering Fossil Fishes, 96, numerous illustrations for children's sci books for Scholastic Inc., Newbridge Educational, others. *Dealer:* PF Galleries 213 E 14 Mile Rd Clawson MI 48017; Mehu Gallery 21 W 100th St New York NY 10025. *Mailing Add:* 317 W 21st St 4D New York NY 10011

RUYLE, LYDIA MILLER
PRINTMAKER, EDUCATOR
b Denver, Colo, Aug 4, 35. *Study:* Univ Colo, Boulder, BA (magna cum laude), 57; Univ Northern Colo, MFA, 72; Syracuse Univ, int study, Renaissance Art, Italy; Romanesque Art, France, Spain, 85; Santa Reparata Graphic Arts Ctr Workshops, Florence, Italy, 1988-2000; Sch Art Inst Chicago, study in Indonesia, 93; Phi Beta Kappa. *Work:* Nat Mus Women Arts, Washington; Citicorp, Denver; McDougal-Littell Publs, Evanston, Ill; Lincoln Ctr, Ft Collins, Colo; Union Colony Civic Ctr, Sr Ctr, Greeley, Colo. *Comn:* print ed of lithographs, Am Hist Soc Gers from Russia, Lincoln, Nebr, 80; print eds for United Way, Weld Co, Colo, 80-91; environ sculpture, Artspicnic Festival, Greeley, Colo, 85; graduation banners, Univ Northern Colo, 96; cast paper sculptures, Children's Hosp, Denver, 92. *Exhib:* Nat Asn Women Artists Ann Exhibs, NY, 82-92; Exchange Exhib, Traveling Printmaking, Bombay, India, 89-90, throughout US, 92-93; one-woman show, The Goddess in the Desert, Palm Springs, Calif, 98, Language of the Goddess & Crop Circle, Loveland, Colo, 98, Re-Imaging Revival: The Divine Feminine, Minneapolis, Minn, 98, Nat United Methodist Churches Conf, Orlando, Fla, 98, The Language of the Goddess Conf, Calif Inst Integral Studies, San Francisco, 98, circles of Light/Techno Cosmic Mass with Mathew Fox, Glen Miller Ballroom, Univ Colo, 98 & The Greenest Branch: Conf for 900th Birthday of Hildegard of Bingen, Burlington, Vt, 98; Univ Tex Health Scis Ctr, San Antonio, Tex, 92; Quattro Amici, Santa Reparata Graphic Arts Ctr, Florence, Italy, 92; Goddesses in the Himalayas, Fatan Mus, Nepal, 2000; Goddess in Eastern Europe, Hady Gallery, Brno, Czech Repub, 2001; Dialy Ctr Visual Arts, Boulder, Colo, 2003; Boise State Univ, ID, 2003; Univ Missouri, Columbia, MO,2003; New Col, San Francisco, Calif, 2003; Serbian Academy of Arts & Sci, Novi Siad, Serbia, 2004; UCLA's Fowler Mus, Los Angeles, Calif, 2004; Women's AIDS conf Kenya, 2004; UC Boulder, Colo 2005; Marin Servs Women Gala, 2006; Sekmet Festival, Indian Springs, Nev, 2006; Healing Retreat, Machu Picchu, Peru, 2006; Mysteries of Ancient Greece, 2006; Goddess Conversations, Paris, France, 2006; and many others. *Pos:* Gov appointed bd mem, Colo Coun Arts Humanities, 77-82; comnr, Colo Comn Higher Educ, 83-85; Presenter/owner, Goddess Tours, Ya-Ya Journeys, 93-. *Teaching:* Creative Arts Ctr, Greeley, Colo, 68-78; adj fac, Printmaking, art hist & art appreciation, Univ Northern Colo, 80-; workshop presenter, univs serv clubs, prof asns throughout US & abroad, 85-; Vis artist, Col of the Desert, Palm Springs, Cal, 94-95; Univ of CO, Boulder, 2005. *Awards:* Juror's Award, Manhattan Nat Print, 84; Printmaking, 86, Works on Paper, 91, Nat Asn Women Artists Ann; Honored Alumni Award, Univ N Colo, 96; Arts Alive! Award, City of Greeley, Colo, 2005. *Bibliog:* Judy Chicago (auth), The Birth Project, Doubleday & Co, 85; Linda Anderson (auth), Greeley's Goddesses, Spectrum UNC, 90; Mary Carroll Nelson (auth), Affirming Wholeness, Southwest Art/CBH Publ, 6/92. *Mem:* Nat Asn Women Artists, NY; Los Angeles Printmaking Soc; Women's Caucus Art, Philadelphia; Soc Multi-Media Layerists, Albuquerque, NMex; Colo Art Educs Asn. *Res:* Research and use inherited images of divine feminine in collagraph print & icon banners; Black Madonnas as icon images of healing. *Specialty:* Artist Cooperative. *Interests:* travel. *Publ:* Contribr, Layering, Soc Layerist in Multimedia, Albuquerque, 91 & 98; illusr, The Great Goddess, An Introduction to Her Many Names, Shef, Boulder, 92; auth & illusr, The Goddess Has A Thousand Faces, Inner Eye Press, Tucson, Ariz, 92; auth, Goddess Icons, Spirit Banners of the Divine Feminine, Woven Word Press, 2002; illusr, Dark Mother, African Origins and Godmothers, Lucia Chiavola Birnbaum, iUniverse, 2002; (auth) Turkey Goddess Icons Spirit Banners of the Divine Feminine, Hitit Publ, Istanbul, 2005; (cover & illusr) Prayers and Seven Contemplations of the Sacred Mother, Mary E Kingsley, 2004; auth & illustr, Lydia Ruyle: Fifty Years of Herstory in Art, 1955-2005 (exhib catalog), 2005; cover, Making Place, Making Self, Ashgate Press, Eng, 2005. *Dealer:* Madison & Main Gallery. *Mailing Add:* 2101 24th St Greeley CO 80631

RUZ, THELMA
SCULPTOR
b Mexico, June 4, 49. *Study:* Haddox Acad, 66; study with Enrique Jolly, Moyado, Palma Cajiga. *Work:* Grupo Arte Contemporaneo, Mexico. *Comn:* Bronze sculpture, Patrimono de la Nacion. *Exhib:* Galena Ultra, Galena Alexandra, Galena Nona, Mex; 8 solo exhibs in Mex & Los Angeles. *Media:* Bronze. *Mailing Add:* Privada de Ahuehuetes Sur No #18 Bosques de las Lomas Mexico 17000 Mexico

RYAN, DAVID MICHAEL
CURATOR
b Lincoln, Nebr, July 10, 39. *Study:* Univ Nebr, BFA & BA, 62; Univ Nebr Law Sch, 62-63; Univ Denver, MA, 65. *Collection Arranged:* Sixth Minn Biennial, 68; Documents as Art, 69; Barry Le Va: Piece One and Two, 69; Richard Avedon, 70; Art Deco, 71; American Indian Art: Form and Tradition, Minneapolis Inst Arts, 72; Aycock, Holste, Singer, 80; Josef Hoffmann: Design Classics, 82; Twentieth Century Drawings, 83; Pop Art Print (auth, catalog) 84; Focus Series, Ft Worth Art Mus, 79-85; Modernism at Norwest (auth, catalog), 88-89; Modernist Ceramics: 1880-1940 (auth, catalog), 90-91; Modernist Lighting: 1900-1940 (with catalog), 91-92; Women in Modernist Design, 1900-1945 (auth, catalog), 92-93; The American Moderne: 1920-1940 (auth, catalog), 93-94; Art Nouveau in Europe (auth, catalog), 94-95; Vienna Moderne: 1895-1930 (auth, catalog), 95-96; Modernist Metalwork: 1900-1940 (auth, catalog), 96-97; Scandinavian Moderne 1900-1960 (auth, catalog), 97-98; Fin de Siecle, 1899 & 1999 (auth, catalog); The Art of Design: 1880-1940 Masterworks from the Norwest Collection, Kimbell Art Mus, Ft Worth, Tex, 98; Milestones of Modernism: Modernisty Design, Norwest Collection, 99; Innovation & Grace: Modernist Glasswork, 1890-1940 (auth, catalog), 99-2000; Reflections of A New Era, Modernist Metalwork, 1880-1940, 99-2000; Japonisme: A Synthesis in Modernity, 1880-1920 (auth, catalog), Norwest Ctr, Minneapolis, 2000-01; Letter Perfect: The Art of Modernist Typography, 1896-1953 (auth, catalog), Minneapolis Inst Arts, 2001-. *Pos:* Mus intern, Denver Art Mus, 64-65; cur asst, Walker Art Ctr, 65-68; cur exhibs, Minneapolis Inst Arts, 68-72, adj cur design, 99-; asst dir, Am Fedn Arts, New York, 73-74; asst dir mus prog, Nat Endowment Arts, 74-79; dir, Ft Worth Art Mus, 79-85, Des Moines Art Ctr, 86, arts prog, Norwest Corp, Minneapolis, 87-99; cur design, Minneapolis Inst Arts, 2003-. *Publ:* Auth, Guide to the Painting and Sculpture Collection, Ft Worth Art Mus, 83; Md Invitational, 88; Baltimore Mus Art, 88; coauth, Modernism: Modernist Design, 1880-1940, 98; Letter Perfect; The Art of Modernist Typography, 1896-1953, Pomegranate, San Francisco, 2001. *Mailing Add:* 2001 W 86th St Minneapolis MN 55431

RYAN, ELIZABETH
PAINTER
b New York, NY. *Study:* With Ed Whitney, Ivan Olinsky & Bruce Stevenson. *Work:* Va State Col, Richmond; Frye Mus, Seattle. *Exhib:* Am Watercolor Soc Traveling Exhib, 82-83; Nat Acad Design; Salmagundi Club; and others. *Awards:* Edna P Stauffer Award, 93; Bee Paper Co Award, 93; F Ballard Williams Fund Award, 93. *Mem:* Am Watercolor Soc (treas, 70-73); Allied Artists Am; Audubon Artists (treas, 84-94); Salmagundi Club. *Media:* Watercolor. *Mailing Add:* 910 Boylston St No 319 Chestnut Hill MA 02167

RYAN, JOYCE ETHEL
ILLUSTRATOR, PAINTER
b Atlanta, Ga, Aug 29, 49. *Study:* Univ Ga, BFA, 1972. *Work:* Ronald Reagan Presdl Lib, Simi Valley, Calif. *Comn:* Longhorn Dolphin, Dances with Dolphin, Corpus Christi, Tex. *Exhib:* Group shows include Maryland Ctr Arts, Annapolis, 83; Am Group Exhib of Gak Ahm & Students, Sejong Cult Ctr, Seoul, Korea, 85; Tubac Ctr Arts, Ariz, 87. *Bibliog:* Judith Rees (auth), book rev, Arts & Humanities, Lib Jour, 4/1/91; Amy Myers-Payne & Cathy Johnson (auths), From the artist's book shelf, Artist's Mag, 5/93; Judith Yankielunlind (auth), book rev, Arts & Humanities, Lib Jour, 4/94. *Mem:* San Antonio Watercolor Group; Art Ctr Corpus Christi. *Media:* Watercolor. *Publ:* Illustrator, Seoul Sketches, Hollym Corp, 85; auth, illustrator, Travelling with Your Sketchbook, North Light, summer, 88; auth, illustrator, Traveling with Your Sketchbook, Butterfly Books, 90, Calligraphy: Elegant and Easy, Butterfly Books, 94 & Drawing at Home, Butterfly Books, 96; Tex Watercolor Soc: Fifty Years of Excellence, 99. *Dealer:* Sable V Fine Art Gallery 2211 The Strand Ste 105 Galveston TX 77550. *Mailing Add:* c/o Sable V Fine Art Gallery 2211 Strand Galveston TX 77550

RYAN, RICHARD E
PAINTER, PRINTMAKER
b London, Eng, Feb 14, 50, US citizen. *Study:* Stanford Univ, BA, 72; Yale Univ Sch Art, MFA, 79. *Work:* Middlebury Col Gallery, Utah; Calif Mus Legion Hon, San Francisco, Calif. *Comn:* 4 paintings for tearoom, Hotel Seneyan, Jakarta, Indonesia, 97; painting for dining room, Peninsula Hotel, NY, 98; 4 paintings, MGM Grand, Casino & Hotel, Las Vegas, Nev; 2 mural sized paintings for hq lobby, Carr Am Corp, Washington, DC, 99. *Exhib:* The Classic Tradition, Aldrich Mus, Ridgefield, Conn, 85; Tradition & Innovation 1500-1989, Calif Palace Legion Hon, San Francisco, 89; Contemp Realist Gallery, 93-95. *Pos:* self-employed painter. *Teaching:* Asst prof, Ind Univ, Bloomington, 79-81; Vassar Col, 81-85; assoc prof, Yale Univ Art, 85-94; sr critic, post-bac painting prog, Brandeis Univ, Mass. *Awards:* Nat Endowment Arts Fel Grant, 93; Ingram Merrill Found Grant, 95; John Simon Guggenheim Mem Found Fel, 2000. *Bibliog:* Charles Jencks (auth), Post Modernism: the New Classicism in Art and Architecture, Rizzoli, NY, 87

RYBCZYNSKI, WITOLD MARIAN
ARCHITECT, EDUCATOR
b Edinburgh, Scotland, Mar 1, 43. *Study:* Loyola Col, Montreal, 60; McGill Univ, BArch, 66, MArch, 72, DSc, 2002. *Pos:* res assoc, McGill Univ, 72-75, asst prof, archit, 75-80, assoc prof, 80-86, prof, 86-93; Consult UN, Manila, 76, Int Devel. Res Ctr, Ottawa, 77, Banco de Mex, 79-80; sr fel, Design Futures Inst, 2003. *Teaching:* Pvt practice, archit, Montreal, 70-82; Meyerson prof, of Urbanism Univ Pa, 94-. *Awards:* Progressive Architect Design award, 91; Jurzykowski Found award, 93; Athaneum Lit prize, 97 & 2001. *Mem:* Fel, Am Inst Archit; US Commission Fine Art. *Publ:* Auth: Paper Heroes: A Review of Appropriate Technol, 1980, Taming the Tiger: The Struggle to Control Technology, 1983, Home: A Short History of an Idea, 1986, The Most Beautiful House in the World, 1989, Waiting in the Weekend, 1991, Looking Around: A Journey Through Archit, 1992, A Place for Art, 1993, City Life: Urban Expectation in a New World, 1995, A Clearing in the Distance, 1999 (J. Anthony Lukas Book Prize, Christopher award), One Good Turn, 2000, The Look of Archit, 2001, The Perfect House, 2002; contrib ed: Saturday Night, 1990—2001; contributing auth Booknotes: Stories from Am Hist, mem adv. board Encyclopedia Americana; founding editor: Wharton Real Estate Rev, 1996-

RYCHLAK, BONNIE L
SCULPTOR, CURATOR
b Culver City, Calif, July 7, 51. *Study:* Univ Calif, Los Angeles, BA, 73; Univ Mass, Amherst, MFA, 76. *Work:* Harvard Univ. *Comn:* Wall sculpture, NY, 94. *Exhib:* Rastovsky Gallery, NY, 88; Solo shows, Rastovsky Gallery, NY, 89, Shoshana Wayne Gallery, Santa Monica, Calif, 91, Sculpture Ctr 2d Gallery, NY, 93, Gallery Three Zero, NY, 94; Shoshana Wayne Gallery, Santa Monica, 89; Stux Gallery, NY, 90; Penine Hart Gallery, 90; Emily Sorkin Gallery, NY, 90; Sue Spain Fine Art, Los Angeles, Calif, 90; Hallwalls Pleasure, Buffalo, NY, 91; Int House, NY, 92; 55 Ferris St, NY, 92; T'zart - Test Wall, NY, 93; Adam Baumgold Gallery, NY, 94; Otis Fine Arts, NY, 96; Silverstein Gallery, NY, 98; R&F Gallery, Kingston, NY, 99; Momenta Benefit Exhib, NY, 2000. *Collection Arranged:* Isamu Noguchi-Rosanjın Kitaojı (auth, catalog), Sezon Mus Art, Tokyo, Japan, 96; Noguchi and The Figure (auth, catalog), Mus Arte Contemporaneo Monterrey and Mus Rufino Tamayo, 99. *Pos:* Asst, Isamu Noguchi, 80-88; dir collections & cur, Isamu Noguchi Found, 80-.

Awards: NEA, 76-77; Bellagio Residency, Rockefeller Found, 85; Prix de Rome Am Acad Rome, 90. *Bibliog:* Arlene Raven (auth), Well healed, The Village Voice, 2/94. *Mem:* Col Art Asn; Asn Am Mus; Int Cong Art Historians; Orgn Independent Artists. *Media:* Found objects. *Mailing Add:* 248 Lafayette St New York NY 10012

RYDEN, KENNETH GLENN
SCULPTOR
b Chicago, Ill, May 16, 45. *Study:* Univ Wis, Superior, BFA; Univ Kans, Lawrence, MFA; study with Bernard Frazer, Eldon Tefft & Victor Timmerman. *Work:* Grover Hermann Fine Arts Ctr, Marietta, Ohio; Swope Art Gallery, Terre Haute, Ind; Southern Ill Univ Art Collection, Edwardsville; Wabash Col Art Collection, Crawfordsville, Ind; Kans State Univ; and others. *Comn:* Delyte Morris Mem, Southern Ill Univ at Edwardsville, 76 & John Rendleman Mem, 76; Greenville City Sq, 80; 10 Yr Mem, Southern Ill Univ, Sch Med, Springfield. *Exhib:* Mainstreams 73, Grover M Hermann Fine Arts Ctr, Marietta, Ohio, 73; one-man exhibs, Univ Wis-Superior, Ark State Univ, Jonesboro, Univ Notre Dame, Kans State Univ, Manhattan & Roberts Wesleyan Col, Rochester; Houghton Col, NY, 80; and many others. *Teaching:* Instr sculpture, Univ Mo, Columbia, 70-73; asst prof sculpture, Southern Ill Univ, Edwardsville, 73-78; assoc prof & chmn art dept, Greenville Col, Ill, 78-; assoc prof, Anderson Col, Ind, 83-. *Awards:* Purchase Award, Mainstreams 73, Grover M Hermann Fine Arts Ctr, 73; Top Purchase Award, 33rd Ann Wabash Valley Sheldon Swope Art Gallery, 77; First in Sculpture, Int Platform Asn Artists Exhib, 82. *Mem:* Nat Col Art Asn; Southern Sculptors Asn; Nat Sculpture Ctr; Int Platform Asn; Washington Arts Club, Washington, DC. *Media:* Multimedia, Metals. *Dealer:* Prairie House Gallery 3013 Lindburgh Blvd Springfield IL. *Mailing Add:* Dept Art Anderson Univ 1100 E 5th St Anderson IN 46012

RYERSON, MITCH
CRAFTSMAN
b May 16, 55. *Study:* Washington Co Vocational Tech Inst, Lubec, Maine, 73-74; Boston Univ, BAA (furniture design), 82. *Work:* Cambridge Pub Libr, Mass; Mus Fine Arts, Boston; ARC Int, NY; Workbench Corp, NY; and many others. *Exhib:* New Furniture, Victoria & Albert Mus, London, Eng, 84; New Art Forms Expo, Franklin Parrasch Gallery, Washington, DC, 89; Furniture: Contemp Expressions, Lyman Allyn Art Mus, New London, Conn, 89; Contemp Furniture: 13 Major Figures, Gallery NAGA, Boston, Mass, 89; New Am Furniture (traveling), Mus Fine Arts, Boston, 89; Art That Works, Mint Mus Art, Charlotte, NC, 90; Art For Everday, Snyderman Gallery, Philadelphia, PA, 90; Surfaces/Group Furniture Exhib, Clark Gallery, Lincoln, Mass, 90; Conservation by Design, RI Sch Design, 93; Clocks, Clark Gallery, Lincoln, Mass, 94; Art Furniture Invitational, Helander Gallery, Palm Beach, Fla, 94; The Chair: Deconstructed/Reconstructed, Sybaris Gallery, Royal Oak, Mich, 95; Mirrors by Studio Furnituremakers, Gallery NAGA, Boston, 96; Mitch Ryerson, Forms & Furniture, Cambridge Arts Coun, Mass, 96; Seats of Meaning, Tufts Univ Gallery, 96; Studio Report, Clark Gallery, Lincoln, Mass, 96; Trashformations, Whatcom Mus, Bellingham, Wash, 97; Mitch Ryerson, New Furniture, Sybaris Gallery, Royal Oak, Mich, 97; Living Room, Dining Room, Gallery, Clark Gallery, Lincoln, Mass, 97; Entry, Clark Gallery, Lincoln, Mass, 2000; Sculpture for the Outdoors III, Clark Gallery, Lincoln, Mass, 2000; Salon Show, Clark Gallery, Lincoln, Mass, 2001. *Teaching:* Instr, Penland Sch Crafts, NC, 87 & 97, Swain Sch Design, New Bedford, Mass, 88 & Haystack Mountain Sch, 97. *Awards:* Nat Endowment Arts Fel, 88; Cambridge (Mass) Arts Coun Fel, 88 & Proj Grant, 97; Travel Award, Philadelphia Furniture Show, 96. *Bibliog:* Eric Gibson (auth), Artist crafts imaginative replies to old furniture, Washington Post, 4/24/90; John Updike (auth), Art & Antiques, 2/90; Patricia Conway (auth), Art For Everyday, Clarkson Potter, New York, 90. *Dealer:* Clark Gallery PO Box 339 Lincoln Station MA 01773. *Mailing Add:* 12 Upton St Cambridge MA 02139

RYMAN, ROBERT
PAINTER
b Nashville, Tenn, May 30, 30. *Study:* Tenn Polytech Inst, 48-49; George Peabody Col, 49-50. *Work:* Mus Mod Art, Solomon R Guggenheim Mus & Whitney Mus Am Art, NY; Ctr Pompidou, Paris; Carnegie Inst, Pittsburgh; Kunsthaus, Zurich; Albright-Knox Art Gallery; and many others; Whitney Mus Am Art, 99-2000. *Comn:* The Charter Series: A Meditative Room, Gerald S Elliott; Art Inst Chicago. *Exhib:* Solo exhibs, The Charter Series: A Meditative Room for the Collection of Gerald S Elliott, Art Inst Chicago & San Francisco Mus Art, 87-88, New Paintings, Pace Gallery, NY, 90 & 92-94, Renn Espace d'Art Contemporain, Paris, Hallen fûr neve Kunst, Schaffhausen, Switz, 91-93, Galerie Konrad Fischer, Dûsseldorf, 92, Victoria Miro Gallery, London, 93, Musée d'art Contemporaine, Bordeaux, 93-94 & Galerie Marc Blondeau, Paris, 94, Betsy Senior Gallery, NY (traveling), 94-96, Studio 7 L, Paris, 99, Haus der Kunst, Munich, Ger (traveling), 2000-01; The Brushstroke and Its Guises, NY Studio Sch Drawing, Painting & Sculpture, 94; Painting, Rhona Hoffman Gallery, Chicago, 94; The Tradition of the New: Postwar Masterpieces from the Guggenheim Collection, Solomon R Guggenheim Mus, NY, 94; White Works, Pace Wildenstein, NY, 94; On A Clear Day, Staatliche Kunsthalle Baden, Baden, 94; Dream of the Absolute, Galerie Beyeler, Basel, 94; James Cohan Gallery, 2001-02; Richard Gray Gallery, New York City, 2001-02; and many other one-man & group exhibs. *Pos:* Mem, Art Comn NY, 82-. *Awards:* Medal, Skowhegan Sch Painting, 85; Praemium Imperiale award for painting, Japan Art Asn, 2005. *Bibliog:* Saul Ostrow (auth), Reviews: Robert Ryman, Flash Art, 5/94; Steven Vincent (auth), Dream of the absolute at Beyeler, Art & Auction, 6/94; Deidre Stein (auth), John Cage chance collection, Artnews, 9/94; and many others. *Mem:* Am Acad Arts & Lett; Comnr, New York City Art Commission; Art Comn, NY (bd dir, 91-)

S

SAAR, BETYE
ASSEMBLAGE ARTIST, COLLAGE ARTIST
b Los Angeles, Calif, July 30, 26. *Study:* Univ Calif, Los Angeles, BA; Univ Southern Calif; Long Beach State Col; San Fernando Valley State Col. *Work:* Univ Mass, Amherst; Wellington Evest Collection, Boston; Golden State Mutual Life Ins Collection, Los Angeles; Los Angeles Co Mus Art; Univ Calif Mus, Berkeley. *Comn:* Mural, Los Angeles, 83; mural, Newark Sta, NJ, 84; Metrorail Sta, Miami, Fla, 86. *Exhib:* Sculpture Ann, 70 & Contemp Black Artists in Am, 71, Whitney Mus Am Art, NY; Black Artist Exhib, Los Angeles Co Mus Art, 72; one-woman exhibs, Whitney Mus Am Art, 75, Jan Baum/Iris Silverman Gallery, Los Angeles, 77, 79 & 81, Univ Art Gallery, Univ NDak, 79 & Mandeville Art Gallery, Univ Calif, San Diego, 79, Personal Icons, Univ Art Mus, Univ NMex, 99, Betye Saar: As Time Goes By 1591-1591, IconsSavannah Coll of Art & Design, Ga, 2000; Painting/Sculpture in Calif: Mod Era, San Francisco Mus Mod Art, 76 & Smithsonian Inst, Washington, DC, 77; Monique Knowlton Gallery, NY, 76 & 81; San Francisco Mus Mod Art, 77; Studio Mus Harlem, NY, 80; Connections, Mass Inst Tech, Cambridge, 87; African Am Art: 20th Century Masterworks, VII, Michael Rosenfeld Gallery, NY, 2000. *Teaching:* Vis artist, Calif State Univ, Hayward, fall 71; prof art, Calif State Univ, Northridge, 73-75 & Otis Art Inst, 76-84; instr, Univ Alaska, summer 79 & Univ Calif, Los Angeles, 84-. *Awards:* Purchase Award, Calif State Col, Los Angeles, 72; Nat Endowment Arts Award, 74 & 84; The Visual Arts Award, The Flintridge Found, Pasadena, Calif, 97-98; Nat Artist Award, Anderson Ranch Art Ctr, Colo, 99. *Bibliog:* Spirit Catcher: The Art of Betye Saar, The Originals: Women in Art series, WNET-PBS, NY; Houston Conwill (auth), Interview with Betye Saar, Black Art, 79; Eleanor Munro (auth), Originals: American Women Artists, Simon & Schuster, 79; Lynn Miller & Sally Swenson (auths), Lives & Works: Talks with Women Artists, Scarecrow Press, NJ, 81; Clothier (auth), Betye Saar (catalog), Mus Contemp Art, Los Angeles, 84. *Media:* Multi. *Publ:* Auth, Handbook, 67. *Dealer:* Monique Knowlton New York NY. *Mailing Add:* c/o Michael Rosenfeld Gallery 24 W 57th St New York NY 10019

SAARI, PETER H
PAINTER, SCULPTOR
b New York, NY, Feb 15, 51. *Study:* Sch Visual Arts, 69-70; C W Post Col, BFA, 74; Tyler Sch Art, Rome, Italy, study with Stephen Greene, 72-73; Yale Sch Art, study with William Bailey & Al Held, MFA(fel), 76. *Work:* Hirshhorn Mus, Washington, DC. *Comn:* John O Shoosan (Co), Baliston, Va; Bruce Kouner (residence), Millbrook, NY. *Exhib:* Solo exhibs, Helander Gallery, Palm Beach, Fla, 87, OK Haris Works of Art, NY, 87 & 93, Robert Schoelkopf Gallery, NY, 88, Tortue Gallery, Santa Monica, Calif, 89, Fendrick Gallery, Washington, DC, 90 & OK Harris Works Art, NY, 93, 98, 2001, Disjecta Membra, Broadway Windows, NY, 2001; New York-NY, Helander Gallery, Palm Beach, Fla, 86-87; Mainstream Am: The Collection of Phil Desind & 51st Ann Nat Mid-Year Exhib, Butler Inst Am Art, Youngstown, Ohio; Classical Myth and Imagery in Contemp Art, The Queens Mus, Flushing, NY, 88; Art After Art (with catalog), Nat Co Mus Art, Roslyn Harbor, NY, 94 & 95. *Collection Arranged:* Hirshhorn Mus & Sculpture Garden, Smithsonian Inst, Washington, DC; Israel Mus, Jerusalem. *Teaching:* Asst instr advan painting, Yale Sch Art, New Haven, Conn, 75-76; guest lectr, St Lawrence Univ, 78. *Bibliog:* Ninon Gaulthier (auth), Impressions de New York, Finance, France, 4/87; A Question of Space: Architectural Inquiries (catalog), The Rye Arts Ctr, NY, 87; Richard Martin and Harold Koda (coauthor), The Historical Mode: Fashion and Art in the 1980's, Rizzoli, New York, 80. *Dealer:* OK Harris 383 W Broadway New York NY 10012. *Mailing Add:* 69 Whitney Short Hills NJ 07078

SAATCHI, CHARLES
COLLECTOR
b Jun 9, 43. *Study:* Christ's Col, Finchley, student. *Pos:* Assoc dir, Collett Dickenson Pearce, 66-68; dir, Cramer Saatchi, 68-70; co-founder, dir, Saatchi & Saatchi, plc, London, 70-93, pres, 93-95; partner, M & C Saatchi Agency, 95—; founder, Saatchi Gallery, London, 2003. *Awards:* Named one of Top 200 Collectors, ARTnews Mag, 2004. *Collection:* Contemporary Art, especially British. *Mailing Add:* 36 Golden Sq London United Kingdom W1R 4EC

SABELIS, HUIBERT
PRINTMAKER, PAINTER
b Wageningen-Gelderland, Neth, Feb 28, 42; Can citizen. *Study:* Tech Sch Art, Neth, with Bloothoofd, 57-60; Art Instr Schs Inc, Minneapolis, 64; lino printmaking with Senggih, 73; serigraphy with Rol Lampitoc, 81-86. *Work:* Royal Ont Mus, Toronto; Philippine Nat Mus, Manila; UNESCO Japan, Tokyo; Nat Libr, Paris, France; HRH Prince Bernard of Neth; Vatican Collection; Librijeciy Art Gallery, Neth; and many others. *Exhib:* One-man shows, Woodstock Pub Art Gallery, Can, 80, Laurier Gallery, Waterloo, Can, 81 & Galerij 3, The Neth, 81, US, Phillipines, Australia, Japan, Israel & Colombia; Saxe Gallery, Toronto, Can, 81. *Awards:* Haiez Award IV, Mostra Mondiale di pittura Cresentino, 79. *Bibliog:* Articles, Arts mag, Arts Queensland, Toronto Calendar Mag. *Media:* Acrylic, Watercolor; Serigraphy

SABLOW, RHODA LILLIAN See Roda, Rhoda Lillian Sablow

SABO, BETTY JEAN
PAINTER, SCULPTOR
b Kansas City, Mo, Sept 15, 1928. *Study:* Univ NMex; with Randall Davey, Carl von Hassler, Charles Reynolds & Al Merrill. *Work:* Albuquerque Mus; Mus Sasebo, Japan; Pub Serv Co, NMex; United NMex Bank; Wells Fargo Bank. *Comn:* Christmas Greeting, Phelps-Dodge Collection, 81; 36 Collographs, St Joseph Rehabilitation

Hosp, 90; 5 bronze figures (sculpture), Sun Health Care, 94; 2 bronze figures (sculpture) & group 24 bronze figures (sculpture), City of Albuquerque, NMex; 7 bronze figures (scuplture), Univ NMex; Bronze Figure, Mt Union Col Alliance, Ohio; Bronze Figure, Juan Diego High School, Draper, UT. *Exhib:* Albuquerque I, Albuquerque Mus, 68; Catharine Lorillard Wolfe Exhib, Nat Acad, NY, 71 & Nat Arts Club, NY, 72-73; Allied Artists, 78-80; Am Acad Art, NY, 80; Margaret Jamison Presents, NMex, 84-86; NMex Tapestries, 84-85; Magnifico, Gov Exhib, Albuquerque; Arte Grande Outdoor Sculpture, Albuquerque, 91; Magnifico 90-94, Albuquerque; Sedona Sculpture Walk, Ariz, 91-94; NM Community Found, 91-92. *Collection Arranged:* Miniatures, Albuquerque Mus, 91-2002. *Pos:* Chmn, Albuquerque Arts Bd, 88-90; guest cur, Miniatures, 91-94, Albuquerque Mus; chmn, Bernalillo Co Arts Bd, 93-94. *Bibliog:* Flo Wilks (auth), The colorful way of the land, SW Art, 12/77; Women on the Arts, Southwest Art, 4/81; M C Nelson (auth), New Mexico is warm when its Cold, Art Lines, Winter 86-87; S H McGarry (auth), Schooled in the Art of Collecting, Southwest Art, 1/87; J A Baldinger (auth), Colorful Artists Run the Spectrum, NMex Mag, 6/91; Fabulous Fountains, Southwest Art, 8/92. *Mem:* Catharine Lorillard Wolfe Art Club; NMex Art League; Am Artists Prof League. *Media:* Oil; Metal Cast. *Mailing Add:* 705 Parkland Cir SE Albuquerque NM 87108-3318

SACCOCCIO, JACQUELINE
ARTIST
b Providence, RI, 1963. *Study:* RI Sch Design, BFA in painting, 1985; Sch of the Art Inst of Chicago, MFA in painting, 1988; L'Universita per Stranieri, Perugia, Italy, 1990. *Exhib:* Solo exhibs incl, Lauren Wittels Gallery, New York City, 1997; White Columns, New York City, 2001; Galerie Michael Neff, Frankfurt, Ger, 2003. *Teaching:* Adj fac, RI Sch Design. *Awards:* Edward L Ryerson Traveling Fel, 1988; Fulbright-Hays Found Grant/Miguel Vinciguerra Award, 1990-91; John Simon Guggenheim Mem Found Fel, 2000; Harold M English/Jacob H Lazarus-Met. Mus Art Rome Prize Fel; Am Acad in Rome, 2004-05. *Mem:* Col Art Asn

SACHS, KATHERINE STEIN
HISTORIAN, COLLECTOR
Study: Univ Pa, graduate, 69. *Pos:* Res coordr, Philadelphia Mus Art, curently; chmn bd, overseers Inst Contemp Art, Univ Pa, 98-. *Awards:* Named one of Top 200 Collectors, ARTNews Mag, 2004, 2005, 2006. *Mem:* Contemp collector's comt Harvard Univ Art Mus; Tate Int (coun mem, currently); gov Ferkauf Grad Sch Psychology, Yeshiva Univ (chmn bd, currently); Pa Women, (mem trustee coun, 2000-). *Collection:* Contemporary Art. *Mailing Add:* Philadelphia Mus of Art Benjamin Franklin Pkwy Philadelphia PA 19130

SACHS, KEITH L
COLLECTOR
Study: Univ Pa, 1967; Harvard Law Sch, 1970. *Hon Degrees:* Hebrew Univ, Jerusalem, PhD(hon), 2003. *Pos:* Chmn, Saxco Int Inc, Horsham, Pa, currently. *Awards:* Named one of Top 200 Collectors, ARTnews Mag, 2004. *Mem:* Philadelphia Mus Art (trustee, currently); Am Friends of Hebrew Univ (chmn bd, currently). *Collection:* Contemporary Art. *Mailing Add:* Saxco Int Suite 225 200 Gibraltar Rd Horsham PA 19044

SACHS, SAMUEL, II
MUSEUM DIRECTOR, HISTORIAN
b New York, NY, Nov 30, 35. *Study:* Harvard Univ, AB(cum laude); NY Univ Inst Fine Arts, AM. *Collection Arranged:* The Past Rediscovered, XIX Century French Painting 1800-1900, 69; Fakes and Forgeries (with catalog), 73; Grant Wood, 83. *Pos:* Asst prints & drawings, Minneapolis Inst Arts, 58-60, chief cur, 64-73, dir, 73-85; asst dir, Univ Mich Mus Art, 62-64; dir, Detroit Inst Arts, 85-97; dir, Frick Collection & Frick Art Ref Libr, 97-. *Teaching:* Lectr art hist, Univ Mich, Ann Arbor, 62-63. *Mem:* Am Fedn Arts; Col Art Asn Am. *Res:* Fakes and forgeries; American 19th and 20th century painting. *Publ:* Auth, Reconstructing the whirlwind of 26th St, Art News, 2/63; Drawings and watercolors of Thomas Moran, In: Thomas Moran (catalog), Univ Calif, Riverside, 63; American Paintings at the Minneapolis Institute of Arts, 71; Art forges ahead, Auction Mag, 1/72; Favorite Paintings from the Minneapolis Institute of Arts, Abbeyville Press, 81. *Mailing Add:* Frick Collection 1 E 70th St New York NY 10021

SACKLER, MORTIMER DA
PATROL
Study: Harvard Univ, BA, MD; NYU, MBA. *Pos:* Founder, chmn, co-Chief Exec Officer, Purdue Pharma LP; bd mem, eMagin Corp; bd trustees, Solomon R Guggenheim Mus. *Mailing Add:* 15 E 62nd St New York NY 10021

SACKS, BEVERLY
ART DEALER, CONSULTANT
Study: Beverly: Brooklyn Col, BA. *Exhib:* African-Am Artists; Woman at Her Easel; The Fine Line; Wonderous Imagery; All the Isms. *Pos:* Beverly: Consult, Phillips & Son & Neale, Am Illusr; owners, Sacks Fine Art; permanent collection, Comt Soc Illusr Mus Am Illus. *Bibliog:* Antique & Arts Weekly, 10/17/80; Maine Antique Digest, 11/80; Buying American painting, Boston Sunday Globe, 11/23/80. *Mem:* Appraisers Asn Am; Soc Illusr (trustee). *Specialty:* American paintings; 19th and early 20th century American illustrations and paintings; American works on paper; African American, modernist, WPA, regional, abstract; women artists. *Collection:* African American, abstract and surrealists. *Publ:* Rube Goldberg, Early Works, 81; African-American artists of the Harlem Renaissance period and later, 91. *Mailing Add:* Beverly Sacks Fine Art 229 E 60th St Ste 3 New York NY 10022-1444

SACKS, STEVE G See Sax, (Steve G Sacks)

SADAO, SHOJI
ARCHITECT, ADMINISTRATOR
b Jan 2, 27. *Study:* Cornell Univ, BArch, 54. *Work:* Mus Mod Art, NY. *Pos:* exec dir, Isamu Noguchi Found Inc, Long Island City, NY, 90-03. *Teaching:* assoc prof architecture & design, SUNY, Buffalo, 76-78

SADE, SHULI
SCULPTOR, PHOTOGRAPHER
b Jerusalem, Israel, Oct 20, 52; Am & Israeli citizen. *Study:* Bezalel Acad Art & Design, BFA, 76; postgrad Sch Visual Arts, New York, 87-89. *Exhib:* Socrates Sculptor, Indust Temple, Long Island, NY, 93; Design Sculptor Park, Boyd Park, New Brunswick, NJ, 93; Imprint, AIR Gallery, NY, 94; Industrial, Cerstosa, Venice, Italy, 94; solo photog, Columbia Univ, Sch Archit, Hoffman Gallery, Portland, Ore, Vision Gallery, San Francisco & Schneider Gallery, Chicago, 96; Lemberger Mus Photog, Israel, 00; photogs, Mead Mus Amherst, 03; and others. *Pos:* Cur, USIS, Jerusalem, Am Embassy, 76-82; art dir, Parade, AZYF, 90-92. *Teaching:* Instr three dimensional design, Parsons Sch Design, 90-91; instr archit design, Univ Pa, Bezalel Acad, Israel. *Awards:* Painters Fel, Nat Endowment Arts, 91-92; Art Grant, Aid, New York, 1994-2000. *Bibliog:* Various interviews & reviews including, Art TV, 6/92 & Art Talk, 8/92. *Mem:* Soc Indust Archeol-Nat. *Media:* Oil; Industrial Materials. *Specialty:* photography. *Dealer:* Talli's Fine Arts Israel; Vission Gallery NY. *Mailing Add:* 55 W 14th St Apt 16F New York NY 10011

SADEK, GEORGE
EDUCATOR, DESIGNER
b Czech, Oct 12, 28; US citizen. *Study:* Hunter Col; City Univ New York, BA; Ind Univ, MFA. *Work:* Mus Mod Art, NY; Libr Cong; Morgan Libr; Bienecke Libr, Yale Univ. *Exhib:* Type Dir Club NY, 69; Am Inst Graphic Arts, 70; Typomondus, Frankfurt, Ger, 71; Mus Mod Art, Japan, 84; Corcoran Gallery Art, Washington, 95; M F Gallery, Prague, 94; Cooper Hewitt, NY, 96. *Pos:* Pres, Col Arts Asn, 76-78. *Teaching:* From instr to asst prof graphic design, Ind Univ, 60-66; prof graphic design, Cooper Union, 66-93, chmn dept art, 66-68, dean, Sch Art, 68-93, Ringling Sch Art, Sarasota, Fla, 93-. *Awards:* Medal, Masaryk Acad Arts, Prague, 93; Brno Int Bienalle Award, 96. *Bibliog:* Articles, Am Inst Graphic Arts J, 68 & Print, 70. *Mem:* Am Inst Graphic Arts (bd mem, 69-72); Col Art Asn (vpres, 74-76, pres, 76-78). *Media:* Typography. *Mailing Add:* 97 Sunset Dr Sarasota FL 34236-5571

SADIK, MARVIN SHERWOOD
DEALER
b Springfield, Mass, June 27, 32. *Study:* Harvard Univ, AB, 54, AM, 61. *Hon Degrees:* Bowdoin Col, DFA, 78. *Pos:* Curatorial asst, Worcester Art Mus, Mass, 55-57; cur & dir, Bowdoin Col Mus Art, 61-67; dir, Univ Conn Mus Art, 67-69; dir, Nat Portrait Gallery, Smithsonian Inst, 69-81. *Teaching:* Instr fine arts, Harvard Col, 58-60. *Awards:* Knight of Dannebrog, Denmark; Smithsonian Gold Medal For Exceptional Service, 81. *Mem:* Colonial Soc Mass; Am Antiquarian Soc; fel Morgan Libr; Century Asn; Grolier Club. *Publ:* Auth, Leonard Baskin, 71; auth, Christian Gullager, Portrait Painter to Federal America, 76; auth, Wedgewood Portraits and the American Revolution, 76; co-auth, American Portrait Drawings, 80; auth, Portraits of George Bellows, 81; auth, Colonial and Fed Portraits at Bowdin Col, 66; auth, The Drawings of Hyman Bloom, 68; auth, The Paintings of Charles Hawthorne, 68; auth, Edith Halpert and the Downtown Gallery, 68; auth, The Life Portraits of John Quincy Adams, 70. *Mailing Add:* PO Box 6360 Scarborough ME 04070

SADLE, AMY ANN BRANDON
PRINTMAKER, PUBLISHER
b Council Bluffs, Iowa, Aug 3, 40. *Study:* State Univ Iowa, 58-61; Ed Whitney Watercolor, 73; Univ RI, 65-. *Work:* Statute of Liberty Mus, NY; Des Moines Art Ctr, Des Moines, Iowa; Univ Nebr Ed TV & Agr Dept; Mc Cook Col, Nebr. *Comn:* St Theresa Church, Sta of the Cross, Mitchell, Nebr, 80; stained glass window, Cath Church, Torrington, Wyo, 80; portrait, Indian Comn, Lincoln, Nebr, 83. *Exhib:* East Meets West, Jacob Javitz Ctr, NY, 89; Nat Tour of Impact. *Collection Arranged:* Impact the Art of Nebraska Women, 88-90; Unitarian Gallery, Kansas City, Mo, 94; McCook Col, McCook, Nebr, 94; Needles & Thread, 95-98. *Pos:* Art gallery dir, W Nebr Art Ctr, 74-76; corp dir, Impact, Nebr, 87-94. *Teaching:* Instr, Painting, W Nebr Community Col, Scottsbluff, Nebr, 72-81; workshop instr, Midwest 72-00; residence artist, Nebr Arts Coun, 2000-. *Awards:* Nebr Arts Award, ANAC, 88; Top Award, Ottawa Nat, Sylvania, Ohio, 95; Amsterdam Art Competition Award, 98; First Place, San Diego Nat Print. *Bibliog:* Krantz, Calif Art Review. *Mem:* Fla Print Club; Asn Nebr Art Clubs, (pres comts 75-96). *Media:* Woodcut, Watercolor. *Res:* Encaustic Book; monoprint book. *Interests:* Travel; research. *Publ:* Auth, ed & illusr, Home of Wooden Men and Iron Ships, private publ, 79; ed, Her Barnyard Brush, Country People, 81; auth, Doing My Thing in Tune, Pallet Talk Mag, 88; ed, Impact, art of Nebr women, private publ, 89, Hunter Hall, 2001 & 2004. *Dealer:* Artist's Cooperative 405 S 11th Omaha NE; Ward & Ward Kansas City Mo. *Mailing Add:* Box H Syracuse NY 68446

SADOW, HARVEY S, JR
CERAMIST, SCULPTOR
b New York, NY, June 29, 46. *Study:* Knox Col, Ill, BA, 68; Sch Art & Art Hist, Univ Iowa, MA(ceramics), 70, MFA(ceramics, sculpture), 71. *Work:* Yingge Mus Art, Taipei, Taiwan; Mus Fine Arts, Boston; High Mus Art, Atlanta; Mus Ceramic Art, Alfred, NY; Everson Mus Fine Art, Syracuse, NY; and others. *Comn:* Mixed media wall installation, Decatur Mem Hosp, Ill, 73; mixed media sculpture, World Bank, Washington, 85; mixed media sculpture, MNC Financial Ctr, Columbia, Md, 87;

ceramic wall installation, Williams & Connolly, Washington, 93; ceramic vessel, White House, 93. *Exhib:* 20 Year Retrospective Exhib (traveling), William Benton Mus Art, Tampa Art Mus, Racine Art Mus & Decorative Arts Mus, Little Rock, Ark, 88; Int Raku Invitational Biseul Art Ctr, Gyungbuk, S Korea, 2001; Int Contemp Ceramic Art, Shijingyi Art Mus, Foshan, China, 2002; Generations: Impending Lineage, Art & Industry Gallery, San Diego, Calif, 2003; 21st Century Ceramics, columbus Col of Art & Design, Columbus, Ohio, 2003; Taiwan Biennial, Yingge Mus of Art, Taipei, Taiwan, 2004. *Teaching:* Millikin Univ, Decatur, Ill, 71-73, Univ Wis, Whitewater, 73-77 & Canberra Art Inst, Australia, 88 & 91; numerous lect & workshops, incl: Smithsonian Inst, Washington, Sydney Col Art, Sydney, NSW, Australia, Am Ceramics Soc, Los Angeles, Corcoran Sch Art, Washington, Col William & Mary, Williamsburg, Va & Purdue Univ, West Lafayette, Ind; hd ceramics & sculpture dept, Armory Art Ctr, West Palm Beach, Fla, 98-2004; chmn ceramics dept, Armory Art Ctr Art, West Palm Beach, Fla. *Awards:* Juror's Award, Md Biennial, Baltimore Mus Art, 80; Lennox Award for Excellence in Ceramics, Lennox China Co, 84; Fla Artists Fel, State of Fla, 91; Presidential Citation, 94. *Bibliog:* Hildegard Cummings (auth), Harvey Sadow: Toward a vessel aesthetic, Univ Conn, 88; Robert Ellison (auth), Harvey Sadow, Am Ceramics, 7/89; Linda Marx (auth), Sadow lands, Ocean Drive Mag, 10/94; Gerry Williams, Harvey Sadow, Studio Potter Mag, 12/98; The Revelance of Handmade Pottery in the Twenty First Centrury, by Harvey Sadow, Ceramics Monthly, 2004; Contemp Ceramics in Am Pub Art & Architecture, by Harvey Sadow, Design & Use of World Bldg Cermacics, pub Artrend Studios, Guangzhou, china, 2002; My Secret Life as a Shino Addict & Carbon Trapper, by Harvey Sadow, Studio Potter Mag, 2002. *Mem:* Nat Coun Educ Ceramic Arts; Am Crafts Coun; Fla Craftsmen; Int Sculpture Ctr; Col Art Asn. *Media:* Ceramics; Mixed Media. *Collection:* Biseul Art Center, Gyungbuk, S Korea; Boca Raton Mus of Art, Boca Raton, Fla; Canberra Art Inst, Canberra, Australia; Decorative Arts Mus, Little Rock, AR; Everson Mus of Art, Syracuse, NY. *Mailing Add:* c/o Sadow Art Studios 9540 Quail Trail Jupiter FL 33478

SADOWSKI, CAROL (LOUISE) JOHNSON
PAINTER
b Chicago, Ill, 1929. *Study:* Art Inst Chicago Scholar, 42-43; Wright Jr Col, AAS, 49. *Work:* Mus Fla Hist, Tallahassee; Elliot Mus, Stuart, Fla; Hollywood Art & Cult Ctr, Fla; Ernest Hemingway Home & Mus, Key West, Fla; Hemingway Mus, San Francisco; Presidential Palace, Havana, Cuba; The Vatican. *Comn:* Paintings, San Augustin Antiqua Found, St Augustine, Fla, 85; Atlantic Bank, Fort Lauderdale; Bonnet House Fla Trust, Ft Lauderdale. *Exhib:* Solo exhibs, Scenes of Fla, Mus Fla Hist, Tallahassee, 84, Hemingway's Haunts, Elliot Mus, Stuart, Hemingway's Home & Mus, Key West, Hist Mus S Fla, Miami, 86, Marjorie Kinnan Rawlings-Cross Creek, Thomas Ctr Arts, Gainesville, Fla, 85 & Mus Fla Hist, Tallahassee 85 & 87; Marjorie Kinnan Rawlins-Cross Creek, Mus Fla Hist, Tallahassee, 85. *Teaching:* Art teacher, adult ed, Malverne High Sch, 68-69. *Awards:* Appreciation Award, City of Hollywood, Fla; Hemingway Medal, Ernest Hemingway Mus, San Francisco de Paula, Cuba. *Bibliog:* Paul Heidelberg (auth), Canvassing Hemingway's life, Ft Lauderdale Sun Sentinal, 5/15/88; Hooked On Hemingway's Haunts, Stuart McIver (auth), Gold Coast Mag; Hemingway's Key West, Stuart McIver (auth), Pineapple Press, Inc. *Mem:* Mus Art Fort Lauderdale, Fla; Fla Hist Assocs; charter mem Women in the Arts Nat Mus, Washington, DC; Chopin Found US. *Media:* Oil, Watercolor. *Specialty:* Fine Art of Am & Europ Artist. *Interests:* Swimming, bike riding. *Collection:* Actors; Burt Reynolds, Jamses Caan, Nadji Jameel Emir of Bahrain, David Usher Pres.; Greenwich Workshop & Harcourt Sylvester, Philanthropist of Palm Beach. *Dealer:* Gingerbread Sq Gallery Key West FL; De Bruyne Fine Art Gallery Naples FL; Patricia Cloutier Gallery Jequesta FL. *Mailing Add:* Sheridan By The Beach 1480 Sheridan St Apt B-17 Hollywood FL 33020

SAFER, JOHN
DESIGNER, ENVIRON ARTIST
b Washington, DC, Sept 6, 22. *Study:* George Washington Univ, AB, 1946; Law Sch, Havard Univ, LLB, 1949. *Hon Degrees:* Lees-McRae Col, LLD, 1994; Daniel Webster Col, Dlitt, 2003. *Work:* Baltimore Mus Art, Md; Corcoran Gallery Art, Washington; Nat Air and Space Mus, (Smithsonian Inst), Washington; Philadelphia Mus Art, Pa; San Francisco Mus Art; and others. *Comn:* Search, 20 ft bronze, Harvard Bus Sch, 84; Web of Space, Nat Air & Space Mus Trophy, 84; Timepiece, (World's largest clock, Guinness Bk of Records), Int Sq Bldg, Washington, 85; Challenge: Christa McAuliffe Mem, Bowie New Town Ctr, Bowie, Md, 88; Ascent, 75 ft steel, NASM, 2003. *Exhib:* One-man shows, US Embassy, London, 72 & 89, Nat Air & Space Mus (Smithsonian Inst), Washington, 84, Norton Gallery Art, Palm Beach, Fla, 85, & Espace Pierre Cardin, Paris, 89; Int Monetary Fund, Wash, 01; Frederik Meijer Sculpture gardens, Grand Rapids, MI, 01; Daniel Webster Col, Nashua, NH, 02; Dayton Art Institute, Dayton, Ohio, 03. *Collection Arranged:* Pathway II, American Hospital of Paris, France; Pathway, Dayton Art Institute, Nashua, NH; The Dancer & the Dance, Friends of Art in Embassies. *Bibliog:* Charles Mann (auth), article, An Artistic Bent, Pursuits Mag, 88 (cover); CJ Houtchens, (auth), article, Dossier Mag, The Art of John Safer, 89; Walter Boyne (auth), David Finn (photo), book, Art in Flight, 92. *Mem:* Cosmos Club, Washington, DC. *Media:* Metal, Lucite. *Mailing Add:* 183 Chain Bridge Rd McLean VA 22101

SAFF, DONALD JAY
PAINTER, EDUCATOR
b New York, NY, Dec 12, 37. *Study:* Queens Col, City Univ NY, BA, 59; Columbia Univ, MA, 60; Pratt Inst, MFA, 62; Teachers Col, Columbia Univ, EdD, 64; Univ So Fla, DFA 1999; Fulbright Grant (Italy), 64-65; Inst Statale Di Belle Artis Urbino, Italy, 65. *Work:* Metrop Mus Art, Mus Mod Art, Brooklyn Mus, & Nelson Rockefeller Collection, NY; William Hayes Fogg Art Mus, Harvard Univ & Mus Fine Arts, Boston, Mass; Philadelphia Mus Art; Nat Gallery Art, Libr Cong, Washington; Butler Inst Am Art, Ohio; and many others. *Comn:* Int Graphic Arts Soc, 67, 68 & 71. *Exhib:* Smithsonian Inst, 61; Fanesi Gallery, Ancona, Italy, 64; solo exhibs, Galleria Academia, Rome, 65, La Colomba Gallery, Bologna, Italy, 66, Byron Gallery NY, 68, Toronto Art Gallery, 70, Galleria D'Arte Moderna, Udine, Italy, 81 & Gemini, GEL, Los Angeles, 85; Canadian Int Print Exhib, Vancouver, 67; Loch Haven Art Ctr, Orlando, 70; Edison Community Col, Ft Myers, Fla, 80; Huntsville Mus Art, Ala, 81; Libr Congress, 84; retrospective, Tampa Mus Art, 89 & Va Beach Ctr Arts, 91; and many others. *Pos:* Co-dir, Pyramid Arts Ltd, Tampa, Fla, formerly; dir graphic studio, Univ SFla, 68-76 & 85-90 & dean, Col Fine Arts, 71-82; dir & cur, Rauschenberg Overseas Cult Interchange, 84-91; consult, Art J, formerly; dir, Saff Tech Arts, Inc, 90- & Knoedler & Co, New York, 94-95. *Teaching:* Instr printmaking & design, Teachers Col, Columbia Univ, summers 65 & 66; assoc prof printmaking & design, Univ SFla, Tampa, 65-67, chmn visual arts dept, 67-71, distinguished prof, 82, distinguished prof emer, 96 & emer dean, 89. *Awards:* Individual Artist Grant, Fla Endowment Arts, 80; Pennell Comt, Libr Cong, 79-86; Univ Serv Medallion, Univ S Fla, 93. *Bibliog:* article, Print Collector's Newslett, 7-8/72, 5/79, 1/81; Graphic studio: Contemporary Art from the Collaborative Workshop at the University of South Florida, Nat Gallery Art, Washington, 91; Interview: Donald Saff, Sculpture Mag, 11/94. *Mem:* Nat Coun of Art Adminrs (mem bd dir, 73-75); Int Coun Fine Arts Deans; Col Art Asn; mem & founder, Nat Coun of Art Adminrs, (bd dir, 73-75). *Publ:* Coauth, Fables, 79 & Constellations, 80, Getler/Pall Gallery, NY; Jim Dine: Youth and the Maiden, Waddington Graphics, 89; Rauschenberg Overseas Culture Interchange (catalog), Nat Gallery Art, 91; Conservation of matter: Robert Rauschenberg's art of acceptance, Aperture Mag, 91. *Mailing Add:* PO Box 408 Royal Oak MD 21662

SAFTEL, ANDREW P
PAINTER, SCULPTOR
b New Bedford, Mass, June 13, 59. *Study:* San Francisco Art Inst, BFA, 81. *Work:* Knoxville Mus Art, Tenn; Tenn State Mus, Nashville; Nashville Int Airport; Metro Atlanta Chamber of Commerce; Asheville Art Mus. *Comn:* Paintings, Southcentral Bell, Nashville, 94; Painting & Sculpture, Hartsfield Int Airport, Atlanta, 96; sculpture, St Andrews Sewanee Sch, Tenn, 2000; sculpture, Episcopal Sch, Portland, Oreg, 2002; sculpture, Knoxville Conventin Ctr, Tenn, 2002. *Exhib:* One-man show, Confluence, Knoxville Mus Art, 95; Serenade the Procession, Tenn State Mus, Nashville, 96; Spirit Sq Ctr Arts, Charlotte, NC, 96; Cheekwood Mus Art, 99. *Teaching:* printmaking, Penland Sch Crafts, 2001, Haystack Mt Sch Crafts, 2002, Arrowmort Sch Arts & Crafts, 2002. *Awards:* Fel, Tenn Arts Comn. *Bibliog:* Catherine Fox (auth), The Southern Artist, Southern Accents, 5/91; Suzanne Stryk (auth), Confluence: Objects by Andrew Saftel, Art Papers, 7/95; Bilen Mesfin (auth), Emerging Artist: Andrew Saftel, Art & Antiques, 12/2002. *Dealer:* Lowe Gallery 75 Bennett St Atlanta GA 30309; Cumberland Gallery Hillsboro Cir Nashville TN 37215. *Mailing Add:* Rte 1 Box 214 Pikeville TN 37367

SAGANIC, LIVIO MICHELE
SCULPTOR
b Vidovici, Yugoslavia, Aug 19, 1950, US citizen. *Study:* Pratt Inst, BFA, 74; Yale Univ, MFA, 76. *Work:* Albright-Knox Art Gallery, Buffalo, NY; Montclair Mus, NJ; Newark Mus, NJ; Chase Manhattan Bank, NY; Exxon Corp, NY. *Comn:* Student Recreational Ctr, Jersey City State Col, 93-94; State House Complex, Trenton, NJ, 94-95; Rowan Col NJ, Glassboro, 94-95; Vet Mem Home, Menlo Park, NJ, 96-98; NJ Transit Light Rail System, Hudson Co, NJ, 97-99. *Exhib:* solo exhibs, NJ State Mus, Trenton, 82, Univ NC, Chapel Hill, 86, Hal Bromm Gallery, NY, 88, Montclair Mus, NJ, 88, Morris Mus, Morristown, NJ, 93 & Kouros Gallery, NY; Landscape into Sculpture, Barbara Krakow Gallery, Boston, 83; Sacred Spaces, Everson Mus, Syracuse, NY, 87; 19th Biennial, Middleheimein Mus, Antwerp, Belg, 87; NJ sculptors, NJ Ctr Visual Arts Summit, 96. *Teaching:* Prof fine arts, Drew Univ, Madison, NJ, 76-. *Awards:* Louis Comfort Tiffany Found Award for Sculpture, 79; Sculpture Fel Award, Nat Endowment Arts, 80; Sculpture Fel Award, New York Found Arts, 87. *Bibliog:* April Kingsley (auth), Obsession is with permanence, Arts Mag, 11/85; Stephen Westfall (auth), review, Art in Am, 9/88; William Zimmer, (auth), Glass Sculptures That Look Like Paintings, NY Times, 4/17/96. *Media:* Stone, Water

SAHAGIAN, ARTHUR H
PAINTER, INSTRUCTOR
b Cleveland, Ohio, Oct 16, 24. *Study:* Western Reserve Univ, & Cleveland Inst Art, 47; Northeastern Ill Univ, MA, 72. *Work:* John Fitzgerald Kennedy Libr, Boston, Mass; Eisenhower Nat Site Mus, Gettysburg, Pa; Miss Mus Art, Jackson, Miss; Nat Civil Rights Mus, Memphis, Tenn; DuSable Mus, Chicago, Ill. *Comn:* oil portrait, Nancy Reagan, Say No Found, Ventura, Calif, 87; oil portrait, Chicago Transit Authority, Chicago, Ill, 88; oil portrait, Gerald Ford, Pres, Calif, 89. *Exhib:* Watts in Calie, DuSable Mus, Chicago, Ill, 80; Presidential Showing, Herbert Hoover Mus, Iowa, 88; permenant collection, Lindon Baines Johnson Mus, Houston, Tex, 89; permenant collection, Miss Mus Art, Jackson, Miss, 95; 6 Squares, Clown Hall Fame Mus, Delavan, Wis, 98; Lillies Won't Do, Mus Human Rights, Memphis, Tenn, 2006; and many others. *Pos:* Art Supv, Garfield Heights bd educ, Cleveland, Ohio, 47-50; Dir, Nat Arts Found, Chicago, Ill, 94-98; Owner, Arthurian Gallery, Skokie, Ill, 98-2002. *Teaching:* Art Teacher, Chicago bd educ, Chicago, Ill, 67-90, Smith Ctr, Skokie, Ill, 85-98 & Highland Park, Ill, 2000-2001. *Awards:* 1st Place, Renata Gallery, 87; Special Recognition, Skokie Art Show, 90-93; 1st Place, Prism Art Gallery, Evanston Ill, 93. *Bibliog:* Nation Medal of Arts, Arts Nomination, Armenian Mirror, 98; Myrna Petlicki, Artists Surveys, Pioneer Press, 2001; Unveiled in Skokie, Lerner Papers, Alen Kaleta 2004. *Mem:* Nat Art Found (bd mem, 85); programs, Skokie Artists Guild, 88 & Armenian Artist Asn, 98; Skokie Fine Arts Comt (bd mem, 92-96). *Media:* Oil Painting. *Publ:* auth, Authurian Approach, Arthurian Gallery, 82; auth, Sahagians Armenia, St Vartans, 2000; auth, Reflections on the Century, Nat Arts Found, 2001; auth, Reflections on America, Nat Arts Found, 2004. *Dealer:* Harry Hagen NAF Gallery 4448 Oakton Ave Skokie Ill 60076. *Mailing Add:* 8725 Karlov Skokie IL 60076

SAHLMAN, SONDRA LIPTON See Lipton, Sondra

SAHLSTRAND, JAMES MICHAEL
PHOTOGRAPHER
b Minneapolis, Minn, May 4, 36. *Study:* Univ Minn, BA, MFA. *Work:* New Photographics Exhib, Central Wash Univ, 1972-88. *Comn:* Photographs SE Wash, Walla Walla Community Col, 76-77 & photographs E Wash, Eastern Wash Univ & Turnbull Game Reserve Res Sta, 77, Wash State Arts Comn. *Exhib:* Young Photographers Traveling Exhib, 68-70; Be-ing without Clothes, Mass Inst Technol, 70; Photo-Media, Mus Contemp Crafts, NY, 71; San Francisco Mus Art, 72; Synthetic Color, Univ Southern Ill, 74. *Pos:* Pres, Roslyn Arts, 72-. *Teaching:* Assoc prof photog, Cent Wash Univ, Ellensburg, 65-. *Mem:* Soc Photog Educ. *Media:* Color, Multiple Image. *Mailing Add:* 12060 Hwy 10 Ellensburg WA 98926

SAHLSTRAND, MARGARET AHRENS
PRINTMAKER, CRAFTSMAN
b St Louis, Mo, Oct 1, 39. *Study:* Lindenwood, Col, St Charles, Mo, 61; Univ of Iowa, Iowa City, printmaking, MFA, 64; also in Japan, 81-83. *Work:* Kobe Mus Fine Arts, Hygo Prefecture Mus Collection, Japan; Okla Art Ctr, Oklahoma City; Wash State Printmakers Collection, Evergreen State Col, Olympia; Nat Collection Art, Washington, DC. *Comn:* Cast paper murals, W Valley Sr High Sch, Yakima, Wash, 80 & Western Paper Co, Kent, Wash, 81. *Exhib:* Solo exhibs, Cast Paperworks, Slocumb Gallery, E Tenn State Univ, Johnson City, 77; 1st Editions Graphics Competition, Ore Arts Comn, Salem, 76; World Print Competition, San Francisco Mus Art, 77; Paper as Medium, SITES, Smithsonian Inst, Washington, DC, 78-; Cast Paper, Pratt Graphics Ctr, NY, 78; Works in Handmade Paper, Jerusalem Theater, Israel, 83; Paper Innovations, Mingei Int Mus, La Jolla, Calif, 85; Arts of the Book, The Akuin Soc, Vancouver, BC, 86. *Pos:* Proprietor, Icosa Studio & Papermill, Ellensburg, currently. *Teaching:* Retired. *Awards:* Cannon Prize, Printmaking, Nat Acad Design, New York, 66; Purchase Award, Statewide Services, Univ Ore, Eugene, 75; Fac Res Grant, Cent Wash Univ, 78; First prize, Paper Fair III Exhib, Vancouver, BC, 85. *Mem:* Northwest Book Arts Guild; Northwest Designer Craftsmen. *Publ:* Auth, Paper clothing, Fiberarts, Vol II, No 2, 84 & Hyakomantoh, No 61, Tokyo, 85; Japanese paper textiles, Paper Innovations, Mingei Int Mus, 85. *Mailing Add:* 12060 Hwy 10 Ellensburg WA 98926

SAID, WAFIC RIDA
COLLECTOR
b Damascus, Syria, 39. *Pos:* Banker UBS, Geneva, 62; founder TAG System Construction, Saudi Arabia, 69, SIFCORP Holdings, 81, Sagitta Asset Mgt, London & Dublin, 95; Founder, Karim Rida Said Found, Eng, 82, chmn, Said Holdings Ltd. *Awards:* Named to Ordre Cherifien, Morocco; recipient Sheldon medal, Oxford Univ, 2003; named one of Top 200 Collectors, ARTNews Mag, 2004. *Mem:* Court Benefactors Oxford Univ; trustee Said Bus Sch Found; gov Royal Shakespeare Co, London. *Specialty:* Old Masters, British Sporting Art & Impressionism. *Mailing Add:* c/o Karim Rida Said Foundation 4 Bloomsbury Place London United Kingdom WC1A 2QA

ST CLAIR MILLER, FRANCES
PRINTMAKER, PAINTER
b Croydon, Eng, Feb 15, 47. *Study:* Slade Sch Art; Univ Col, London. *Work:* Adelphi Univ, Long Island, NY; Citibank, AT&T, IBM, NY. *Comn:* Portfolio of Prints, Shell Oil, UK, 80; Edition of Prints, P&O; Eng, 94. *Exhib:* Solo exhibs, Graffiti Gallery, London, 78 & 79 & Hereford City Art Gallery, 92; Tolly Cobbold Eastern Arts, Fitzwilliam Cambridge, 83; Slade Ladies, Mall Galleries, London, 90. *Pos:* Master printer, Studio Prints, formerly & Octopus Press, currently. *Teaching:* Art of printmaking, Sir John Cass Col, Eng, currently. *Mem:* Printmakers Coun; Chelsea Arts Club. *Media:* Etching

ST DENIS, PAUL ANDRE
PAINTER, INSTRUCTOR
b Chicago, Ill, Nov 16, 38. *Study:* Cleveland Inst Art, BFA; Kent State Univ, MA; additional study with Julian Stanczak. *Work:* Tweed Mus, Duluth, Minn; Massillon Mus, Ohio; Utah State Univ, Logan; Columbia Mus Art, SC. *Comn:* Cleveland Pub Libr. *Exhib:* Butler Inst Am Art, Youngstown, Ohio, 68 & 70; Canton Art Inst, Ohio, 73; Aqueous Open, Pittsburgh Watercolor Soc, 74 & 75; Watercolor West, Utah State Univ, 76-79; Nat Watercolor Soc, Laguna Beach Mus Art, Calif, 76-88 & 92; Adirondacks Nat Exhib Am Watercolors, 91; and others. *Pos:* Chmn art dept, Interlochen Ctr Arts, Mich, summers, 69-81; chmn found, Cleveland Inst Art, 94-. *Teaching:* Prof painting, Kent State Univ, Ohio, 68-70, Cooper Sch of Art, Cleveland, 70-80 & Cleveland Inst of Art, 73-. *Awards:* First Prize Gold Medal, Ohio Watercolor Soc, 89, 90 & 94; William Kowalsky Award, Adirondacks Nat Exhib Watercolors, 91; First Prize, Nat Watercolor Soc, 92. *Bibliog:* The Artist Mag, 9/90, 9/93 & 7/94; Splash, 90 & Splash II, 91, North Light/FW Publ. *Mem:* Am Watercolor Soc; Nat Watercolor Soc; Ohio Watercolor Soc. *Media:* Acrylic, Watercolor. *Dealer:* Belstone Gallery Traverse City MI; Vigland Gallery Benzonia MI. *Mailing Add:* 28007 Sites Rd Bay Village OH 44140

ST FLORIAN, FRIEDRICH GARTLER
EDUCATOR, ARCHITECT
b Graz, Austria, Dec 21, 32; US citizen. *Study:* Tech Univ Graz, dipl(archit), 58; Ecole Nat Superiure d'Archit, Brussels, Belg, 55-56; Atelier, with Victor Bourgeois; Columbia Univ, March, 62. *Work:* Mus Mod Art, NY; Mass Inst Technol, Cambridge; Mus Art, Providence; Pompidou Centre, Paris. *Exhib:* One-man shows, Mod Museet, Stockholm, 69, Hayden Gallery, Mass Inst Technol, 73, Mus Art, Univ Tex, 76, Drawing Ctr, NY, 79 & Walker Art Ctr, Minneapolis, 80; Archit Studies & Proj, Mus Mod Art, NY, 75; RI Sch Design Mus Art, 77; Centre Georges Pompidon, 94; Visionary Architecture in Austria, Biennale Di Venezia, 96; From Bauhaus to Pop, Mus Mod Art, NY, 96. *Teaching:* From asst to prof archit design, RI Sch Design, 63-, chmn archit div, 77-78, dean archit, 78-88. *Awards:* Fulbright Fel, 61-62; Fel, Ctr for Advan Visual Studies Fel, Mass Inst Technol, 71-77; Nat Endowment Arts Awards, 73-74 & 76-77; Fel, Am Acad in Rome, 85-; Finalist, Nat World War II Mem, Am Battle Monuments Comn, 96. *Mem:* Am Inst Architects. *Publ:* Auth, On my imaginary architecture, Leonardo, 77. *Mailing Add:* Rhode Island Sch Design 112 Union St Providence RI 02903-1753

ST GEORGE, WILLIAM (M)
PAINTER, INSTRUCTOR
b Canton, Mass, Jan 13, 39. *Study:* Sch Mus Fine Arts, Boston, Mass, 69-. *Work:* Scudder, Stevens & Clark Mutual Funds, Int Place, Wertheim Schroder & Co Inc, Colonial Mgt, Exec Off Gillette, Boston, Mass, The Alexander Law Firm, San Jose, Calif, Can Imperial Bank of Commerce, Ackerley Communications, Seattle, Wash, Kuhns Brothers Investment Banking, Greenwich, Conn, Societ?mmobilier Trans, Qu?c; also pvt collections of John Davidson, Undersecy Finance, Nuevo Leon, Mex, Gulston & Storrs, Attys Law, Law Off Hale & Dorr, Law Off Atwood & Cherney; Boston Globe Newspaper. *Comn:* corp bldg, New World Power Corp, Lime Rock, Conn, 95; Boston paintings, Boston Globe, Mass, 95; Boston Col & Middlebury Col, Alexander Law Firm, San Jose, Calif, 96; Baupost Financial Group, Cambridge, Mass, 98; Citizen's Bank, Boston, Mass, 98, Bank of Canton, Canton, Mass, 99. *Exhib:* One-man shows, J Todd Galleries, Wellesley & Lexington, Mass, 91, Lime Rock Galleries, Lakeville, Conn, 91, E L Wilde Gallery, Avon, Conn, 92, Michael Thompson Galleries, San Francisco, Calif, 93, Open Studios, Boston, Mass, 94 & 96, S Rotunda Art Gallery, Hynes Auditorium, Boston, Mass, 96; Boston Painters, Judi Rotenberg Gallery, Boston, Mass, 95; Fall Exhib, Copley Soc, Boston, Mass, 95; Corp Prog, De Cordova Mus, Waltham, Mass, 96; Kennedy Galleries, Provincetown, Mass & Key West, Fla, 96; St George Gallery, Boston, 2001-; Boulevard Gallery, Newport, RI, 2003; Linden Galleries, Rowley, Mass, 2005; Willoughby Galleries, Martha's Vineyard, Mass,; Boston Art, Boston, Mass, 2005. *Pos:* Guest demonstr oil painting, various New Eng art groups, 91-; producer & host, Impressions (weekly art show), Cablevision Television Group; artist instructor, gallery owner, St George Gallery, Boston, Mass. *Teaching:* Instr oil painting, Blackburn Hall, Walpole, Mass, 98, Steinert Hall, Boston, 98, 2001, St. George Gallery, Boston, Mass, on going. *Awards:* Am Artist Ser Feature Artist, PAK 2000, 92; Two Collection Best Show, Channel Two Auction, WGBH Boston, 94; Artist of the year, Monco charity horse show, Monico, Calif, 2005. *Bibliog:* Showcase: A celebration of the arts, Newbury Street Guide salutes William St George, Newbury St Guide, Boston, Mass, 3/3/94; Art of all styles, Boston Herald, 11/17/95; Alexander Berman (dir), The Painter (film), 95; Equine Vision Mag, The Horse in Landscape, Fall 2004. *Mem:* Copley Soc Boston; Mus Fine Arts Advan Painting Group, Boston, Mass; Cambridge Art Asn. *Media:* Oil. *Specialty:* Boston Cityscapes, Equestrian, Swimmers, Stilllife, Landscapes, Portraits. *Interests:* Location for DNC Reception July 2004; Woman's Caucus Group/Maryland and Delware Delegates Reception; NABB Reception and wine tasting, charity event. *Publ:* Auth, Expressions (newsletter), St George Gallery, Boston, Mass; contribr, The Two Collection Catalog (cover), WGBH, Boston, Mass, 94; auth, Final touches: Painting en plein air, Pleiades, 3-4/95; contribr, Boston Bar J (cover), 11-12/95, 96, 97. *Mailing Add:* c/o St George Gallery 245 Newbury St Boston MA 02116

ST JOHN, ADAM
CRAFTSMAN
b Tampa, Fla, Feb 24, 52. *Study:* Self-taught. *Work:* Mus Fine Arts, Houston, Tex; San Antonio Mus Asn Collection, Texas. *Comn:* Future Perfect One table, Houston, Tex, 86; Paradise: The Chair, West Palm Beach, Fla, 86; Remember the Alamo, Amarillo, Tex, 87; Pueblo Santa Fe chair, Santa Fe, NMex, 89; Texas Virgin Bed, Houston, 90. *Exhib:* The Chair Fair, Int Design Ctr, NY, 86; Materials: Hard & Soft, Denton Arts Coun, Tex, 87; Furniture of the 80's, Hokin-Kaufman Gallery, Chicago, IL, 88; one-man show, Parkerson Gallery, Houston, Tex, 86; two-person show, O'Kane Gallery, Houston, Tex, 90. *Pos:* Int exec dir, Am Soc Furniture Artists, 91-. *Teaching:* Painted illusions, Trompe l'Oeil, Art League Houston, 88-; continuing educ Faux finishes, Univ Houston, 90-; art for detained youth, Harris Co Juvenile Detention Ctr, 90-. *Awards:* Honor Award, 1986 Furniture Design, Texas Homes Mag, 86; Meadows Found Award, 87; Outstanding Artist Award, IAC New York '88, 88. *Bibliog:* 397 Chairs, Archit League NY, Abrams, NY, 88. *Mem:* Art League Houston (bd dir, 88-90); Am Craft Coun; Am Soc Interior Designers; Am Soc Furniture Artists (found & Pres, 89-). *Media:* Mixed. *Publ:* Article, Los Angeles Mag, 86, ID, 87, Ambienture, 87, Ultra, 88. *Mailing Add:* PO Box 35339 Houston TX 77235-5339

ST JOHN, TERRY N
PAINTER, CURATOR
b Sacramento, Calif, Dec 24, 34. *Study:* Univ Calif, Berkeley, AB; San Francisco Art Inst, spec study with James Weeks; Calif Col Arts & Crafts, Oakland, MFA. *Work:* Mills Col, San Francisco; Oakland Mus. *Exhib:* James D Phelan Award Show, Calif Palace Legion Honor, 65; one-man show, Crown Col, Univ Calif, Santa Cruz, 75 & Contemp Realist Hackett-Freedman Gallery, San Francisco, 94; Contemp Realist Hackett-Freedman Gallery, San Francisco, 90; Gallery North, Setauket, NY, 90; Art Los Angeles Expos, Realist Hackett-Freedman Gallery, 92; Chicago Int Art Expos, Realist Hackett-Freedman Gallery, 93; New Bay Area Painting, Contemp Realist Hackett-Freedman Gallery, 94; Hackett Freedman Gallery, San Francisco, 01-03. *Collection Arranged:* Dilexi Years Revisited, (co-curator, auth, catalog), 83. *Pos:* Assoc cur, Oakland Mus, 69-90; head art dept, Col Notre Dame, Belmont, Calif, 90-97. *Teaching:* Outdoor Painters Proj, Univ Calif, Santa Cruz, 79-88; Col Notre Dame, Belmont, 90-2000. *Bibliog:* Thomas Albright (auth), Art in the San Francisco

Bay Area, Univ Calif Press, 85. *Media:* Oil. *Publ:* Auth, Society of Six (catalog), Oakland Mus, 72; Louis Siegriest: A painter's topography, Currant Mag, 75; Impressionism: The California View, Oakland Mus, 81. *Dealer:* Hackett-Freedman Gallery San Francisco. *Mailing Add:* 5340 Locksley Ave Oakland CA 94618

ST. LIFER, JANE
CONSULTANT, ART DEALER
b New York, NY, Apr 19, 56. *Study:* Syracuse Univ, BFA, 1978; The New Sch Soc Res, 1979; Arizona State Univ, 1980; NJ City Univ, MA (educ), 1996; George Washington Univ, (cert), 2002. *Collection Arranged:* Will Barnett A Poster Retrospective, Digital Sand Box Gallery, 2002-2003; Will Barnet A Poster Retrospective, Cape Cod Mus Art, 2005-2006. *Pos:* Dir graphics & publ, Hammer Galleries, New York, NY, 1981-1986; sales mgr, Gallery Urban, Nagoya, Japan & New York, NY, 1986-1988; asst dir, Grand Central Art Galleries, New York, NY, 1993-1994; pres, St. Lifer Fine Art Inc, New York, NY, 1988-; cur & dir, Digital Sandbox Gallery, 1999-. *Mem:* Am Soc Appraisers; Auctioneers Asn Inc, NY (vpres); Dog Fanciers Club Inc, NY (secy); Int Found Art Res, NY; Nat Arts Club, NY; Nat Mus Women in the Arts, DC. *Media:* Appraiser of 19th & 20th century paints, prints & sculpture. *Res:* Appraiser of 19th & 20th century paintings, prints & sculpture. *Mailing Add:* 140 Riverside Blvd #323 New York City NY 10069

ST MAUR, KIRK
SCULPTOR, PAINTER
b July 7, 1949. *Study:* Quincy Col; Univ Minn; Carleton Col, BA, 72; Academia di Belle Arti, Florence, Italy, 72-75, studied anat with Harkevitch; asst to R Puccinelli, Univ Int de Belle Arte, 73 & 74; Villa Schifanoia, Florence, MA, studied with E Manfrini; Simi Studio, Florence, 74-78. *Work:* State of Ill Mus; Lindbergh Mus, St Louis; H M Seymour Libr, City of Le Bourget, France; Pere Marquette State Park (monument); St Louis Univ. *Comn:* Heroic bronze of St Michael, Church of Buriano, Italy, 79; Quest (bronze monument), Ore State Univ, 83; The Sentinel (monument), City of Richmond, Calif, 84; Indian monument, City of Duluth, 92; Marathon, St Louis Univ, 94. *Exhib:* Quincy Art Ctr, 74 & 85; Am Artists Prof League, 82, 86, 87,92, 93 & 96; Knickerbocker Artists, 1983-1989; John Pence Gallery, 84; Acad Artists Asn, 1986-1989, 1991; Int Art Expo, Los Angeles, 88; and others. *Teaching:* Prof sculpture, Gonzaga Univ, 78-79. *Awards:* Knickerbocker Artists Award, 84; Acad Artist Asn Award, 86; Medal of Honor, City of LeBourget, France, 88; Best of Show, Billy Graham Mus, 95. *Bibliog:* Mario Bucci (auth), Kirk McReynolds, Sansoni Editrice, Florence, Italy, 77; articles in Rome Daily Am, San Francisco Examiner, 79 & 83, Oakland Tribune, 84 & St Louis Post Dispatch, 93 & 96. *Mem:* Fel Am Artists Prof League; Hudson Valley Art Asn. *Media:* Bronze, Oils. *Publ:* Am Arts Quart, spring 92; Christianity and the Arts, spring 96. *Mailing Add:* PO Box 158 Payson IL 62360-0158

ST TAMARA, KOLBA TAMARA STAHANOVICH
PAINTER, PRINTMAKER
b Navahradak, Repub Belarus; US Citizen. *Study:* Western Col, Oxford, Ohio, BA; Columbia Univ, MFA, with John Heliker; Art Students League, with Seong Moy. *Work:* Nat Mastacki Mus, Minsk, Repub Belarus; Hrodzienski Historyka-Archealahichny Mus, Hrodno, Repub Belarus; Mus Belaruskaha Knihadrukavannia, Polatsak, Repub Belarus; Ablasny Krayaznauchy Mus, Vitsiebsk, Repub Belarus; Navahradski Hist-Krayaznauchy Mus, Navahradak, Repub Belarus; Soros Found, Minsk, Belarus; Columbia Univ, NY; NY Pub Libr, NY; Zimmerli Art Mus, Rutgers Univ, New Brunswick, NJ; plus others; Belarusan Embassy to the UN, New York City; Belarusan Consulate, New York City; Mus F Skaryna, Homiel, Belarus. *Comn:* Four Icons, Belarusan Church, Cleveland, Ohio; woodcut portrait of Dr Francisak Skaryna, comn by Dr V Kipel, NY Pub Libr, 68. *Exhib:* Vitsiebski Ablasny Krayaznauchy Mus, Vitsiebsk, Repub Belarus, 97; solo exhibs, Nat Art Mus, Repub Belarus, 94, Hrodzienski Dziarzauny, Hist-Archeol Mus, Repub Belarus, 96, Vitsiebski Ablasny Krayaznauchy Mus, Vitsiebsk, Belarus, 97, Lidzea Nat Gallery, Lida, Belarus, 96, Mus Belaruskaha Knlhadrukavannia, Polatsak, 97; Clwac, New York City, 94; Western Col, Oxford, Ohio, 96; The Capital Children's Mus Washington, DC, 96; Hunterdon Art Ctr Clinton, NJ, 96; Zimmerli Art Mus, New Brunswick, NJ, 96; Johnson & Johnson World Headquarters, New Brunswick, NJ, 97; Everhart Gallery, Basking Ridge, NJ, 97; CLWAC, New York City, 98, 99, 2001 & 2003; Guild of Creative Art, Shrewsbury, NJ, 2000; Art Alliance, Red Bank, NJ, 2001; Salmagundi Club, New York City, 2001-2003; Custer Co Art Ctr Miles City, MT, 2001; National Drawing, Erwing, NJ, 2002. *Awards:* Gold Medal, CIWAC, Nat Acad Design, NY, 71; 1st Place, FACET, Taos, NMex, 85; Cert of Excellence, Nat Small Painting Exhib, Albuquerque, NMex, 87; Samuelballin Mem Award, Salmagundi Club, 2001; Honorable Mention, Custer Co Art Ctr, Miles City, MT, 2001. *Bibliog:* Tatsiana Antonava (auth), St Tamara: Her Cosmos Began in Navahrudak, Zviazda, 10/6/94; S Y Kryshtapovich (auth), Stahanovich Tamara, Belarus-Belarusan Encyclopedia, 95; Valyantsia Tryhubovich (auth), St Tamara: My-America, My-Belarus, Mastatstva, 4/98. *Mem:* Guild Creative Art, NJ; Catherine Lorillard Wolfe Art Club, NY; Print Club, NY; Belarusan Inst Arts & Sci, NJ; Art Alliance, NJ; Salmagundi Club, New York City; The Nat Mus of Women in the Arts, Washington, DC. *Media:* Oil, Graphics. *Interests:* Nature, Photography; ethnic folk art; AM Indian Art;. *Collection:* Hudson River Painter; Icons. *Publ:* Auth & illusr, Save that Racoon & Chickaree, a Red Squirrel, Harcourt, Brace, Jovanovich; illusr, Biography of a Polar Bear, G P Putnam's Sons, 72; Animal Games, Holiday House, 76. *Mailing Add:* 211 Hockhockson Rd Tinton Falls NJ 07724

SAITO, SEIJI
SCULPTOR
b Utsunomiya, Japan, 1933. *Study:* Tokyo Univ Art, BFA(sculpture), clay modeling with Tsuruzo Ishii & MFA(stone carving), with Kametaro Akashi; Brooklyn Mus Art Sch, Scholar, 8 yrs; granite carving with Odillo Begg; Ottavino Granite Corp, NY. *Work:* Methodist Hosp, Brooklyn, NY; Isaac Delgado Mus Art, New Orleans; Non-Ferros Int Corp & Kowa Realty, NY; The Toyo Trust & Banking Co, Ltd, NY; Wichita Mus; Tochigi Mus, Japan; Taiyo Kobe Bank, NY; Utsukushigahara Open Air Mus, Japan; Salisbury State Univ, Md; Daiwa Security & Trust Co, NJ; Utsunamiya High Sch, Tochigi, Japan. *Comn:* Buddha (stone sculpture), Gyokusendo, Okinawa, Japan, 81. *Exhib:* One-man shows, Samanthe' Gallery, NY, 68 & 70, New Sch, NY, 78, Warner Commun Bldg, 79, Tokyo Gallery, Tokyo, Japan, 79 & Gallery Seiho, Tokyo, 90; Azuma Gallery, NY, 75; Mid-Hudson Art & Sci Ctr, Poughkeepsie, NY 80; FIDEM Int Exhib, Florence, Italy, 83; Nat Sculpture Soc Ann Show, 70, 89 & 93, 100th Ann Show, Seravessa, Italy, 94; and others. *Teaching:* Instr sculpture, Brooklyn Mus Art, summer 74, 76, 84, 85; Art Student League New York, 98-. *Awards:* Cert Merit, Ann Exhib of Nat Acad Design, New York, 73; Many Awards, Nat Sculpture Soc Ann Exhibs, New York, 76-96, 2004; Merit Prize, Hakone Open-Air Mus, Japan, 80. *Mem:* Nat Sculpture Soc. *Media:* Stone, Bronze, Wood. *Specialty:* Gallery Seiho (specializing in sculpture), Tokyo, Japan. *Publ:* Art Text book, article, Expressions, McMillan, New York & Sculpture Rev. *Mailing Add:* 925 Union St Apt 1G Brooklyn NY 11215

SAITO, YOSHITOMO
SCULPTOR
b Tokyo. *Study:* Jiyugakuen Col, Tokyo, BS-E, 80; Calif Col Arts & Crafts, Oakland, MFA, 87. *Exhib:* Solo exhibs, Fuller Gross Gallery San Francisco, 88; Shidoni Contemp Gallery, Tesque, NMex & Mincher/Wilcox Gallery, San Francisco, 90, Haines Gallery, San Francisco, 91, 93 & 95, Zwillingswerke AG, Solingen, Ger, 92, Univ Art Gallery, Sonoma State Univ (with catalog), Rohnert Park, Calif, 95 Haines Gallery, San Francisco, Calif, 97, 99, 01, Marshall Univ Art Gallery, Huntington, WV, 03. *Teaching:* Lect, Sonoma State Univ, 89, Univ Calif, Berkeley, Southern Ill Univ, Carbondale, 90, Calif State Univ, Hayward, 90-96; Artist-in-Residence, Southern Ill Univ, Carbondale, 90. *Awards:* Gold Award, Art Calif Mag Discovery Award, 92; Reg Fel, Western States Art Fedn/Nat Endowment Arts, 93; Fel Grant, Nat Endowment Arts, 94. *Bibliog:* Jamie Brunson (auth), San Francisco/Pleasanton Fax, Art Issues, 11-12/97; Topics - Sculptor Yoshitomo Saito, Mon Mag, 12/97; John Rapko (auth), article in Art Week, 11/95. *Media:* Bronze. *Mailing Add:* c/o Haines Gallery 49 Geary St 5th fl San Francisco CA 94108

SAKAOKA, YASUE
SCULPTOR
b Himaji-City, Hyogo-Prefecture, Japan, Nov 12, 33; Nat US. *Study:* Reed Col, BA, 59; Portland Mus Art Sch, cert; Univ Ore, MFA, 63; Rinehart Inst Sculpture, 63-65; CUNY, Brooklyn, 72-73; Ohio Univ, 77-79. *Work:* Portland Mus Art, Ore; Arnot Mus, Elmira, NY; Zanesville Art Ctr, Ohio; Schumacher Gallery, Capital Univ, Columbus. *Comn:* Concrete Panels, Jasper Park, Ore, 63; a play sculpture, Columbus Acad, Ohio, 80-81 & Godman Guild, 83; a tapestry, Epiphany Lutheran Church, Pickerington, Ohio, 84-85; Four Seasons, Worthington Arts Coun, 93; Goodwill Rehabilitation Ctr, Columbus, Ohio, 93-94; St Helen's Church, Dayton, Ohio, 1999-2000; Worthington Comm Ctr, 2004. *Exhib:* Paper Exhibs, 81 & Best of 1986, 86, Columbus Cult Arts Ctr, Ohio; Pub Sculpture in Columbus, Ohio State Univ Art Gallery, 84; Ohio Selection Dayton Art Inst, 89; Pebbles Cast on the Water (with catalog), Worthington Arts Coun, Ohio, 93; Reflections of Japan in Ohio Visual Arts (with catalog), Ohio State Univ, 94; and others. *Collection Arranged:* Many exhibs at St Paul's Col in Va including Robert Dilworth's work, 66-77; View of Columbus (with catalog), Artreach Gallery, Columbus, Ohio, 82; A Photographic Exhib: Sculpture on the Grass (with catalog), 83; Franklin Co Sculptors (a catalogue), Columbus, Ohio, 83; Stivers Sculpture Invitational, Ohio, 96 & 99; Installation, Nat City Bank Center, IMPEL Design with Miami Valley Arts Cooperative, Dayton, Ohio, 2001. *Pos:* vis artist, Stivers Sch for the Arts, Dayton, Ohio, 89-. *Teaching:* Asst prof art, St Paul's Col, Va, 67-77; asst prof sculpture & art hist, Mansfield State Univ, Pa, 77-78; lectr, Ohio State Univ Continuing Educ, 80-; resource fac, Capital Univ Without Walls, Colo, Ohio, 81-86; vis prof studio art & humanities, Ohio Dominican Col, 95. *Awards:* Pollock-Krasner Found Award, 87-88; Apprenticeship Award, Ohio Arts Coun, 89-92, 97 & 2001-2002; Best, Outdoor Sculpture Competition, Olde Towne East, Columbus, Ohio, 94. *Bibliog:* Fred Kalister (auth), Yasue Sakaoka in Dialogue, Ohio Found Arts, 82; Charles Dietz (auth), Yasue Sakaoka (exhib catalog), Zanesville, Art Ctr, Ohio, 85; John Seto (auth), Sakura in Buckeye, Lima Art Asn, 90-91. *Mem:* Col Art Asn; Int Sculpture Ctr; Dayton Visual Arts Ctr. *Media:* All. *Res:* Japanese Folk Art; Italian Scupltors. *Interests:* Visual Arts. *Publ:* Auth, article, Sculpture Quart, Vol II, No 1, 74; Fragments: A review of a Whitney exhibtion in sculpture, Southern Asn Sculptors, summer 76; many catalogs & videos. *Dealer:* Mary Baskett Cincinnati OH; Muse Gallery, Columbus, Ohio. *Mailing Add:* PO Box 09428 Columbus OH 43209-0428

SAKOGUCHI, BEN
PAINTER
b San Bernardino, Calif, 38. *Study:* San Bernardino Valley Col, 56-58; Univ Calif, Los Angeles, BA, 60, MFA, 64; Calif State Univ, Los Angeles, 82-83. *Work:* Brooklyn Mus, NY; Chicago Art Inst; Mus Mod Art, NY; Nat Mus Am Art, Smithsonian Inst, Washington; Philadelphia Mus Art, Pa; Hirshhorn Mus, Smithsonian Inst, Washington. *Comn:* Etching, Container Corp Am, 65. *Exhib:* Solo exhibs: Los Angeles City Col, 03, and many others pre-2000; Shifting Perceptions: Contemp Los Angeles Visions, Pacific Asia Mus, Pasadena, Calif, 2000; Made in Calif: Art, Image and Identity, 1900-2000, Los Angeles Co Mus of Art, 2000; 46th Biennial Exhib: Media/Metaphor, Corcoran Gallery of Art, Washington, 2000; Represent, Kellogg Gallery, Calif State Polytechnic Univ, Pomona, 2001; 3rd Int Biennial Exhib of Contemp Art, Florence, Italy, 2001; Smile, Oceanside Mus of Art, Calif, 2002; The Story is in the Telling, Armory Ctr for the Arts, Pasadena, Calif, 2002; In Their Own League, Saddleback Coll Art Gallery, Mission Vielo, Calif, 2003; Issho/Together, Meridian Gallery, San Francisco, 2004; and many others pre-2000. *Teaching:* Prof art, Pasadena City Col, Calif, 64-97. *Awards:* Nat Endowment Arts Fel, 80 & 95; Pasadena Arts Comn Fel,

91; J Paul Getty Trust Fund Visual Arts Fel, Calif Community Found, 97; Lila Wallace-Reader's Digest Fund Artists at Giverny Fel, 97; Calif Arts Concil Fel, 03; and others. *Bibliog:* Lucy Lippard (auth), A Different War (exhib catalog), Whatcom Mus Hist Art, 90, Walter Gabrielson (auth), Ben Sakoguchi, Addictions (exhib catalog), Santa Barbara Contemp Arts Forum, 91; Andrew Perchuck (auth), Ben Sakoguchi's America, Artists of Conscience II (exhib catalog), Alternative Mus, 92; Michael Duncan (auth), Ben Sakoguchi at Luckman Fine Arts Gallery, California State University, Art in America, Nov 99, p 150. *Publ:* Special issue on nuclear disarmament, Village Voice, 6/15/82; 10: Artist as Catalyst (portfolio), ed/100, Alternative Mus, 92. *Mailing Add:* 1183 Avoca Ave Pasadena CA 91105

SAKSON, ROBERT (G)
PAINTER
b Trenton, NJ, Feb 13, 38. *Study:* Trenton Jr Col, AA, 58. *Work:* Hunterdon Co Libr, Felmington, NJ; AT&T Longlines, Bedminster, NJ; US Coast Guard, Mich; Ellarslie, Trenton City Mus, NJ; Princeton Univ Art Mus, NJ. *Comn:* Paintings for Calendar, Best Foods Corp, Ridgwood, NJ, 86; paintings of Phillipsburg, NJ, Carteret Savings Bank, 86, 87 & 88; location paintings, Avon Corp, NY, 89 & 90; series paintings, Waterloo Village, Horizon Bank, Morristown, NJ, 88, 89 & 90; painting of Palmer Square, Collins Develop Corp, Princeton, NJ, 90; Best Portfolio- 9 paintings of Philadelphia for The Chubb Insurance Group Corp offices, Philadelphia, PA. *Exhib:* Am Watercolor Soc Ann Exhibs, NY, 68-95; Allied Artists Am, Nat Arts Club, NY, 83, 86 & 87; Audubon Artists Ann, Nat Arts Club, NY, 88; Knickerbocker Artists Ann, Salmagundi Club, NY, 89; In Our Circle, James Michener Art Mus, Doylestown, Pa, 91; Historic NJ: A Contemp View, Bristol Myers-Squibb Gallery, Princeton, 91; and others. *Pos:* Watercolorist. *Teaching:* Instr master classes watercolor, Somerset Art Asn, Far Hills, NJ, 70-; instr watercolor, Morris Co Art Asn, Morristown, NJ, 89-, Perkins Ctr Arts, Moorestown, NJ, Long Beach Island Gallery Watercolor Workshops. *Awards:* Silver Medal of Honor, NJ Watercolor Soc, 76, 83 & 92; Gold Medal, Allied Artists Am, 83; Elizabeth Callan Mem Medal & Dolphin Fel, Am Watercolor Soc, 93; and others. *Mem:* Am Watercolor Soc; Allied Artists Am (juror, currently); Audubon Artists Am (juror, currently); Knickerbocker Artists (juror, currently); Pastel Soc Am (juror, currently); NJ Watercolor Soc & Garden State Watercolor Soc; Phila Watercolor Soc. *Media:* Watercolor, Pastel. *Publ:* Contribr, Painting Light & Shadow, Painting Texture, Best of Watercolor 1 and 2, Rockport Publ; Painting with the White of Your Paper, Splash 2 and 4, North Light Bks; Painters of the River towns, River Arts Press, 2002. *Dealer:* Coryell Gallery Lambertville NJ. *Mailing Add:* Ten Stacey Ave Trenton NJ 08618-3421

SAKUYAMA, SHUNJI
PRINTMAKER, PAINTER
b Harbin, Manchuria, July 29, 1940, Japan citizen. *Study:* Tokyo Gakugei Univ, BA, 65; Brooklyn Col, MFA, 72; Pratt Graphics Ctr. *Work:* Brooklyn Mus; Berkshire Mus, Pittsfield, Mass; City Mus, NY; New Sch Art Ctr, NY; NY Hist Soc; 21 Century Pear Mus, tottori, Japan. *Exhib:* One-man shows, Paintings, 72 & Prints, 94, Berkshire Mus, Takano Gallery, Tokyo & Chinoh Gallery, NY; 21st Nat Print Exhib, 78; NY Album, Brooklyn Mus, 79; NY Collects, City Mus, NY, 81; Gene Baro Collects, Brooklyn Mus, 83. *Teaching:* Instr Japanese brush work, Long Island Univ, Brooklyn Ctr, 77-78. *Awards:* Painting Awards, New Eng Art Exhib, New Canaan, Conn, 72 & Berkshire Art Asn Exhib, 75. *Media:* Lithography; Acrylic, Oil. *Publ:* Auth, Cynthia Pantzic, Design Dimensions, Prentice Hall. *Dealer:* Chino Art Gallery 575 5th Ave New York NY 10017. *Mailing Add:* 915 President St Brooklyn NY 11215

SAL, JACK
PHOTOGRAPHER, PAINTER
b Waterbury, Conn, Mar 28, 54. *Study:* Philadelphia Col Art, BFA, 76; Art Inst Chicago, MFA, 78. *Work:* Detroit Inst Arts, Mich; Ctr for Creative Photog, Tucson, Ariz; Mus Mod Art, NY; Int Mus Photog, Rochester, NY; Yale Univ Art Gallery, New Haven, Conn; Mus Ludwig, Köln, Ger; and others. *Comn:* Earth Work, Off Cult Affairs, New Haven, Conn, 79; Grant, Conn Comn for Arts, 80; Fresco mural, Univ Bridgeport, 84; Fresco mural, Padua, Italy, 86; Am Cult Heritage Abroad and City of Kielce, Poland, 2005. *Exhib:* Prints in the Cliche-Verre, Houston Mus Fine Art, 80; One-man shows, Northlight Gallery, Tempe, Ariz, 80 & Recent Camera Works, Photog Workshop, New Canaan, Conn, 80, Mus Ludwig, Köln, Ger, 95; Light Gallery, NY, 81; Int Ctr Photog, NY, 81; Ferns Gallery, Hull, Eng, 82; Mus Mod Art, NY, 83; Hudson Ctr, 85; Gallery Multigraphic, Venice, 01; Salt Ctr, Denmark, 02; and others. *Pos:* Cur, Light Gallery, 85-. *Teaching:* Assoc prof, Int Ctr Photog-NY Univ, Rutgers Univ, 85; chmn photog dept, Moore Col Art & Design. *Awards:* Mellon Fel, 82; Vis Artist Am Acad in Rome, 86-87. *Bibliog:* S D Peters (auth), Interview/Jack Sal, Int Mus Photog, 79; Roger Baldwin (auth), Jack Sal/camera images, Views, 80; Glassman/Symmes, Prints in the Cliche-Verre, Detroit Inst Arts, 80; Wire/works (auth) Salon Verlag, 2000; M & M (editors), Primary drawings, 2001. *Media:* Pigment, Light-Sensitive Paper. *Publ:* Auth, Cliche-verre: cameraless images, Portfolio Mag, 79; contribr, Prints in the Cliche-Verre, Detroit Inst Arts, 80; contribr, Connecticut Photographers, Art Resources of Conn, 80; contribr, Photographers Hand, Int Mus Photog/George Eastman House, 80; auth, Mark/Making, Combinations Press, 81. *Dealer:* Brigitte Schenk Gallery Köln Ger. *Mailing Add:* 431 E Sixth St New York NY 10009

SALADINO, TONY
PAINTER, PRINTMAKER
b New Orleans, La, June 5, 43. *Study:* La State Univ, BS, 64; self-taught as artist. *Work:* Nat Mus Fine Arts, Hanoi, N Vietnam; Mus Int Art, Bahia, Brazil; Tex State Univ; Wichita Falls Mus & Art Ctr, Tex; Mus Art & Archaeol, Univ Mo. *Comn:* Mem Hosp, San Antonio, Tex; Circle Theatre, Fort Worth, Tex. *Exhib:* Central Texas Biennial, The Art Center, Waco, Tex, 89 & 92; Nat Works on Paper, Univ Miss, 90; Small Impressions 1990, The Printmaking Coun of NJ, Somerville; Pac States Nat Print Exhib, Univ Hawaii, Hilo, 90; Am Realism Competition, Parkersburg Art Center, WVa, 90; The Print Club of Albany, NY, 92; 5th Ann Nat Art Exhib, Cooperstown Art Asn, NY, 92; New Traditions: Contemp Mezzotints, Bradley Univ, Peoria, Ill, 94; and others. *Teaching:* Instr, 1-wk workshop, Imagination Celebration, Ft Worth Sch District, 90; monotype workshop, Oxbow Summer Sch Art, Saugatuck; instr painting, Mod Art Mus, Ft Worth, Tex, 92-. *Awards:* Purchase Award, Am Realism Competition, Parkersburg Art Ctr, Va, 90; Purchase Award, Univ Wis, Parkside, 90; Delta Nat Small Prints Exhib Purchase Award, Ark State Univ, 97; Bank Am Award, Presentation is the Art of City, Ft Worth, Tex, 2004. *Bibliog:* Article, NY Times, 12/17/89; article, the Art Calendar, 2/92; David Band (auth), Enrich Your Paintings with Texture, North Light Bks, 94; others. *Mem:* Int Mezzotint Soc. *Media:* All Media. *Interests:* Argentine Tango, Span Study. *Collection:* Michael and Susan Dell Foundation, Austin, Texas; Fort Worth Public Library Foundation, Fort Worth, Texas; Winstead Seachrest & Minick, PC, Austin, Texas. *Publ:* The Artist's Mag, 89; The Art Calendar, 92; La Semana, Fort Worth, 6/2000; Austin American Statesman, Austin, Tex, 12/2004; Crosswinds Weekly, Albuquerque, 7/2004. *Dealer:* Milan Gallery Ft Worth TX; B Deemer Gallery Louisville KY; Running Ridge Gallery 640 Canyon Rd Santa Fe NMex; Waterstreet Gallery 546 Butler St Saugatuck Mich; Lagerquist Gallery 3235 Paces Ferry Pl NW Atlanta Ga; Gallery at Snoal Creek 1500 W 34th St Austin Tex. *Mailing Add:* 756 Norwood Hurst TX 76053

SALEMME, LUCIA AUTORINO
PAINTER, WRITER
b New York, NY, Sept 23, 19. *Study:* Privately with Gustavo Cenci, 30-35 & Baroness Hilla Von Rebay, 41; Art Student League, 38. *Work:* Whitney Mus Am Art; Nat Gallery Art, Washington; Elsa Picone, Rome, Italy; Metrop Mus Art, NY; Mus Art, Bates Col, Lewiston, Maine; Mr Lindsey Gruson, NY Times Washington Bureau, Washington; Ross Contantine Gallery, NY. *Comn:* Mosaic mural, Mayer & Whittlesey, NY, 58; portraits, 59-72; art restoration, Manhattan House murals, 77 & Art Students League collection, 78. *Exhib:* One-woman exhibs, NY Univ Lubin Ctr, 62, Dorsky Gallery, NY, 65 & 86, Grand Central Moderns Gallery, NY, 65, William Zierler Gallery, NY, 72 & 74, Fair Lawn Libr, NJ, 76, Cape Split Place Gallery, Maine, 77; Pen & Brush Gallery, NY, 88-2000; Susan Teller Gallery, NY, 89; Assoc Am Artists, 90; Mus Art, Bates Col, Lewiston, Maine, 96; Southeast Mo Mus Art, 1998. *Pos:* Chair, Brush Div, Pen & Brush Inc, 94-. *Teaching:* Instr, People's Art Ctr, Mus Mod Art, 57-61; adj prof painting & drawing, NY Univ, 59-70, assoc prof, 75; instr painting & drawing, Art Students League, 70-91. *Awards:* Pen & Brush Graphics Awards, 84-94; Grumbacher Watercolor Award, 85; Oil Awards, 89, 90, 91, 92, 93 & 94. *Mem:* Artists' Equity; Pen & Brush Inc, NY; Nat Soc Mural Painters. *Media:* Oil, Watercolor. *Publ:* Auth, Color Exercises for the Painter, 70 & Compositional Exercises for the Painter, 73, Watson-Guptill; The Complete Book of Painting Techniques, Macmillan, 82. *Dealer:* Assoc Am Artists Gallery 20 W 57th St New York NY; Susan Teller Gallery 568 Broadway New York NY 10019. *Mailing Add:* 463 West Street 641B New York NY 10014

SALGIAN, MITZURA
ARTIST
b Bucharest, Romania; US citizen. *Study:* Nicolae Grigorescu Art Inst, Bucharest, MA, 1976. *Exhib:* solo exhibs, Escada Quatro Gallery, 1995, Arte Varia Gallery, 1996, Portals Gallery, 1999-2004; group exhibs, Saginaw Art Mus, 98, Midwest Mus Am Art, 98-99; 92nd Exhib, Conn Accad Fine Arts, 2003; Danville Mus of Fine Arts & Hist, Danville, Va, 2004; The Butler Inst Am Art, 2004; Bergstrom-Mahler Mus, 2004; Huntsville Mus Art, 2004; Mus Texas Tech Univ, 2005; Catharine Lorillard Wolfe Art Club 109th Ann Open Juried Exhib, Nat Arts Club, NY, 2005. *Collection Arranged:* Marquis Luc de Clapiers; Angelo Loggia, Rome; Onik Sahakian, Lisbon & NY, many others; Mimi Adler, NY; Gilbert Kahn, Newport, RI. *Awards:* John Young Hunter Award, Allied artists of Am, 1990; Honourable Mention Midyear Show Award, Butler Inst of Am Art, 2004; Tamsin L Holzer Memorial Award, Catharine Lorillard Wolfe Art Club, 2005; Mervin Honig Memorial Award, Allied Artists Am. *Mem:* Allied Artists of Am; Flushing Coun Culture & Arts. *Media:* Oil, Egg Tempura, Pastel, Watercolor. *Mailing Add:* 60-11 Broadway Apt 1F Woodside NY 11377

SALINAS, BARUJ
PAINTER, PRINTMAKER
b Havana, Cuba, July 6, 35; US citizen. *Study:* Kent State Univ, BArch. *Work:* Mus de Arte Mod, Mexico City, Mex; San Antonio Mus Art; Mus Arte Siglo XX, Alicante, Spain; McNay Mus Art, San Antonio; Museo Maria Zambrano, Velez-Malaga, Spain; Museo Nacional D'Art de Catalunya, Barcelona, Spain. *Comn:* Murals, Sephardi Sch, Mex DF; paintings, Edificio la Victoria, Mex DF, 79; paintings, Europ Am Bank, Miami, Fla, 82; Stained Glass Windows (3) and a Mural, Inst Cult Mexico-Israel, Mexico City, 93. *Exhib:* One-man shows, Harmon Gallery, Fla, 75 & 83, EditArt, Geneva, Switz, 75, 77, 79, 83, 85, 88 & 91, 94, 96, 2000, 02 & 04, Mus Carrillo Gil, Mex, 81, 94, 96, 2000, & Galeria Joan Prats, NY, 82; Mus de Arte Mod, Mexico City, Mex, 88; Shuyu Art Gallery, Tokyo, Japan, 94; Musee Des Tapisseries, Aix-en-Provence, 98; retrospective, Espace Vallon, Editart, Geneva, 2000, Galeria Trazo, Mex, 2002; New Works, Central Conn State Univ, S Chen Art Ctr, Hartford, Conn, 2002; Pintar de Palabras, Centro Cult Espanol, C Gables, Fla, 2003; Claros Del Bosque, Frances Wolfson Gallery, Miami, Fla, 2004; Layers, Univ Buffalo Art Center, Buffalo, NY, 2006. *Teaching:* Instr seminars graphic work, Winchester Sch Art & Sch Visual Arts, Barcelona, Spain, 92-94; Instr seminar paintings, Sch Visual Arts NY, summer 93; Prof painting, MDCC Interam Campus, Miami, Fla, prof art, 2005-2006; Instr, Miami Dade Col, 99-2006. *Awards:* Cintas Fel, Inst Int Educ, 69 & 70; First Prize, VI Bienal, Degrabado Latinoamericano de San Juan, PR, 83. *Bibliog:* Wifredo Fernandez (auth), Baruj Salinas su mundo pictorico, Ed Punto Cardinal, 71; Gloria Moure, Carlos Franqui, Wifredo Fernandez & Jose A Valente (auths), Baruj Salinas,

Ediciones Poligrafa, Espana, 79; Octavio Armand, Carlos Monsivais, Michel Butor, Jose A Valente, (auths), Baruj Salinas, Mus Arte Mod, Mexico City, 88; Carlos M Luis (auth), Pintar De Palabras, Centro Cult Espanol, Miami, Fla, 03. *Media:* Acrylic, Miscellaneous Media. *Interests:* Reading; Classical Music; Travel. *Publ:* Resumen AIP, 71; Narradores Cubanos de Hoy, 75; Revista Escandalar, NY, 81; co-illusr, Tres Lecciones de Tinieblas, with J A Valente, Ediciones la Gaya Ciencia, Barcelona, 82; Trois Enfants Dans La Fournaise, Michel Butor, 88. *Dealer:* Galerie Editart Route de Ore-Bots 20 1215 Geneva Switzerland. *Mailing Add:* 2740 SW 92nd Ave Miami FL 33165

SALINGER, ADRIENNE
PHOTOGRAPHER, EDUCATOR
b Los Angeles, Calif. *Study:* Sch Art Inst Chicago, with Joyce Neimons, MFA(photog), 86. *Work:* Los Angeles Co Mus Art; Mus Fine Arts, Houston; Nat Gallery Can, Ottawa; Bibliotheque Nationale, Paris; Int Polaroid Coll, Cambridge, Mass. *Exhib:* The Photog of Invention, Nat Mus Am Art, Washington, 89; Pleasures & Terrors of Domestic Comfort, Mus Mod Art, NY, 91; Recent Acquisitions, Mus Fine Arts, Houston, 91; Observing Traditions: Contemp Photog, Nat Gallery Can, 93; solo exhib, San Jose Mus Art, Calif, 95; Sala El Tunel, Inst Chileno Norteamericano, Santiago, Chile, 96; In My Room, Scottsdale Ctr Arts, Ariz, 96; Alt Youth Media, New Mus, NY, 96. *Teaching:* Assoc prof photog, Syracuse Univ, 88-. *Awards:* James D Phelan Award in Photog, 87; MacDowell Colony, fel, 96. *Bibliog:* Dennis Cooper (auth), Teenage fan club, SPIN, 6/95; Dulcie Leimbach, A room of their own, NY Times, 10/15/95; Bobbie Ann Mason (auth), Overdue books, Doubletake, winter 96. *Mem:* Col Art Asn; Soc Photog Educ. *Media:* Photography. *Publ:* Auth, In My Room: Teenagers in Their Bedrooms, Chronicle Books, 95. *Dealer:* Stephen Wirtz Gally 49 Geary St San Francisco CA 94109

SALLE, DAVID
PAINTER
b Norman, Okla, Sept 28, 52. *Study:* Calif Inst Arts, Valencia, BFA, 73 & MFA, 75. *Work:* Boymans Mus, Rotterdam, Holland; Basel Kunst Mus, Switz; Mus Contemp Art & Los Angeles Co Mus Art, Calif; Whitney Mus Am Art, Mus Mod Art & Metrop Mus Art, NY; Art Inst Chicago; Nat Gallery, Washington and many others. *Exhib:* Le portrait dans l'art contemporain, Musee D'Art Moderne et D'Art Contemporian, Nice, 92; Solo shows, Fantomas Series, Daniel Templon Gallery, Paris, 92, Am Social Dance, Galerie Bruno Bischofberger, Zurich, 92, Galeria Soledad Lorenzo, Madrid, 92, New Paintings & Drawings, Jason Rubell Gallery, Palm Beach, 93, New Works, Newport Harbor Art Mus, Calif, 93, Mary Boone Gallery, NY, 94, Gagosian Gallery, NY, 94, 2001, Guild Hall Mus, East Hampton, NY, 94, Galerie Bruno Bischofberger, Zurich, 95, Itochu Gallery, Tokyo, 98, Museo d' Arte Contemporanes, Torino, Italy, 99, and many others.; NY on Paper Galerie Thaddeus Ropac, Paris, 93; Portraits de Femmes, Galerie Beaubourg, Venice, 94; Galerie Bernd Kluser, Munich, 96; Saatchi Gallery, London, 98; Contemp Art Ctr, Long Island, 2000 and many others. *Awards:* Creative Artists Pub Serv Prog Grant, 79. *Bibliog:* Grace Glueck (auth), Artists who scavenge from the media, New York Times, 1/9/83; Roberta Smith (auth), Appropriation uber allies, Village Voice, 1/11/83; Michael Brenson (auth), New York vs Paris: Views of an art reporter, NY Times, 1/16/83; Eleanor Heartney (auth), David Salle at Mary Boone, ArtNews, 88; Robert Storr (auth), Salle's gender machine, Art Am, 88; Laura Cottingham (auth), David Salle, Flash Art, 88; Interview with Frederic Tuten, Art in America, 97; Exhibition Young Americans, The London Times, 98; Peter Plagens (auth.) Amsterdam Artforum, 99; James Reginato (auth.) W, 2001. *Mailing Add:* C/o Gagosian Gallery 980 Madison Ave New York NY 10012

SALLICK, LUCY ELLEN
PAINTER, INSTRUCTOR
b Boston, Mass, Sep 21, 37. *Study:* Univ Mich, 55-58; New York Univ, BA, 59, painting, 60-62; Art Students League, 64-65; Corcoran Sch Art, 66-68. *Work:* Bruce Mus, Greenwich, Conn; Rahr West Mus, Manitowoc, Wis; Housatonic Mus Art, Bridgeport, Conn; Univ Mich Art Mus, Ann Arbor; Town of Westport, Conn. *Comn:* Painting, Brunswick Savings Inst, Maine, 75. *Exhib:* Contemp Reflections, Aldrich Mus, Ridgefield, Conn, 75; solo exhibs, Rutgers Univ, New Brunswick, NJ, 77, Canton Art Inst, Ohio, 80 & Bowdoin Col Mus Art, Brunswick, Maine, 87; Childe Hassam Purchase Exhib, Am Acad & Inst Arts & Lett, 76-83; Contemp Naturalism, Nassau Co Mus Fine Arts, NY, 80; Conn Painters, Wadsworth Atheneum, 83; Contemp Landscape Painting, Wesleyan Univ, Conn, 83; Contemp Am Still Life, One Penn Plaza, NY, 85. *Teaching:* Instr painting, Silvermine Guild Sch Arts, 77- & Lyme Acad Fine Arts, 85-. *Awards:* Eloise Egan Mem Award, New Eng Ann Silvermine Guild, 75 & Guild Award, 79. *Bibliog:* Lawrence Alloway (auth), Lucy Sallick, Fairleigh Dickinson Univ, 75; John Russell (auth), article, New York Times, 9/23/77; Gerrit Henry (auth), article, Art in Am, 2/83. *Mem:* Women's Caucus Art; Silvermine Guild; Soho 20. *Media:* Oil, Watercolor. *Dealer:* G W Einstein Co Inc 591 Broadway New York NY 10012. *Mailing Add:* 77 Long Lots Rd Westport CT 06880

SALLOUM, JAYCE P
CONCEPTUAL ARTIST, VIDEO ARTIST
b Kelowna, BC, Apr 30, 58. *Study:* San Francisco Art Inst, BFA, 80; Univ Calif, San Diego, MFA, 88; studied with Whitney Independent Studio Prog, 88-89. *Work:* Bibliotheque Nationale, Paris, France; Can Mus Contemp Photog, Ottawa, Ont; Int Polaroid Collection, Offenbach, Ger; Long Beach Mus Art, Calif; Artbank, Can Coun, Ottawa, Ont. *Comn:* Open Channels, Long Beach Mus Art, Calif, 88. *Exhib:* The Call: Personal insights on the Middle East & N Africa, Long Beach Mus Art, Calif, 92; Beyond Glory: Re-presenting Terrorism, Md Inst Col Art, Baltimore, 92; Bonoff Souvenier, Can Mus Contemp Photog, Ottawa, Ont, 92; Demontage: Appropriation, Recycling, Valencia Inst Modern Art & Museo Nat Ctr Art, Spain, 93; one-man show, Artists Space, NY, 94. *Awards:* Can Coun Grants, 81-93; NYSCA Grant, NYSCA, 89; NYFA Fel, NYFA, 94. *Bibliog:* Richard Rhodes (auth), Alternate Photography, YYZ Toronto, 83; Amiel Alcaly (auth), Culture without a country, Afterimage, 5/90; Tony Reveaux (auth), Mugadimal Li-Nihayat Jidal, Artweek, 3/7/91. *Mem:* Col Art Asn; Asn Independent Video Film; Media Alliance. *Media:* Installation, Video. *Publ:* Auth, New Canadian Photography, Can Ctr, Photog, 82; Ausstellungsraum, Shin-Shin Gallery, 91; Canada(s), Semiotext(E), 94; coauth, Documents, 94; auth, Felix, Felix/Standby, 94-95

SALMINEN, JOHN THEODORE
PAINTER, INSTRUCTOR
b Minneapolis, Minn, Jan 18, 45. *Study:* Univ Minn, Duluth, BS (art educ) 1968, MEd (art educ) 1974; Univ Minn with Cheng Khee Chee -1982-84. *Work:* Nat Watercolor Soc, San Pedro, Calif; Univ Minn, Tweed Mus, Duluth; Springfield Art Mus, Mo; 1st Bank Fine Arts Collection, National. *Comn:* Paintings, Duluth Visitors & Conv, Minn, 1983; paintings, Seaway Port Auth, Duluth, Minn, 1996; mag covers, Seaway Port Auth, Duluth, Minn, 1998-; purchased paintings, St Mary's Duluth Clinic, Minn, 2005. *Exhib:* Tweed Mus of Art, Duluth, Minn, 1988; Allied Artistss Am, New York City, 1995, 96, 98, 99; Am Watercolor Soc, Salmagund Club, New York City, 1995-2001, 2003, 05, 06; Audubon Artists, New York City, 1997, 2002-03; Neville Mus, Green Bay, Wis, 1998; Nat Acad 173rd Annual Exhib, New York City, 1998; Nat Arts Club Open Exhib, New York City, 1998. *Pos:* Nominations chmn, TWSA, 2000-05; dir, Am Watercolor Soc, 2002-04. *Teaching:* Instr art, I.S.D., Duluth, Minn, 1969-2001; instr, Col St Scholasticia, Duluth, Minn, 1984; instr, Fullbright Exchange, Edinburgh, Scot, 1984-85; instr, watercolor, 2001-. *Awards:* Grant recipient, Marie Walsh Sharpe Found, Colorado Springs, Colo, 1995; First Place Experimental, Artists Mag Art Comp, 2000; Silver Star, Nat Watercolor Soc, 2005; Gold Medal, Am Watercolor Soc, 2006. *Bibliog:* Michael J. Burlinham (auth), An Urban Realist Takes on the Big Apple, Am Artist Watercolor, 1999; Loraine Crouch (auth), Staying in the Flow, Watercolor Magic Yearbook, 2004. *Mem:* Dolphin fellow Am Watercolor Soc (dir, 2002-2004); signature mem Nat Watercolor Soc; master status Transparent Watercolor Soc of Am (nom chair, 2000-2005); Sylvian Groose Pennsylvania Watercolor Soc; signature mem Watercolor West. *Media:* Watercolor. *Publ:* Auth Bright Lights, Dark City, Watercolor Magic/FandW, 1999; East Meets West (interview of Cheng Khee Chee), Watercolor Magic/Fiw pub, 2000; Auth Expressing the Language of the Landscape, Int Artist Pub Inc, 2002; On the Street, Artists Mag, F&W Pub, 2004; Crough, Mesch & Moorman (auth), View from the Top, Watercolor Magic Fiw Pub, 2005; Every Picture Tells a Story, Int Artist Pub Inc, 2006. *Dealer:* Amican Legacy Gallery Jack Olsen 5911 Main St Kansas City MO 64113. *Mailing Add:* 6021 Arnold Rd Duluth MN 55803

SALMON, RAYMOND MERLE
CARTOONIST, EDUCATOR
b Akron, Colo, Sept 6, 31. *Study:* Mesa Col; Univ Denver; Chicago Acad Fine Arts; Univ Colo; Calif Col Arts & Crafts; San Francisco State Univ; Colorado Springs Fine Arts Ctr; Univ Northern Colo, BA & MA(fine arts). *Work:* Libr Commun & Graphic Arts, Ohio State Univ. *Exhib:* Univ Denver Art Mus, 55; Colorado Springs Fine Arts Ctr, 61; Tacoma Art Mus, Wash, 64; State Univ Mo, 65; Master Cartoonists Exhib, Parke-Bernet, NY, 71. *Pos:* Free lance graphic artist, Salmon Studios, Calif, 60-; cartoonist; creator cartoon panel, The Little Man. *Teaching:* Art educ, John F Kennedy Univ, 66-74; art educ, commercial dept, Solano Community Col, 71-; Chapman Col, 88. *Mem:* Nat Cartoonists Soc, NY; Soc Prof Journalists. *Media:* Pen and Ink, Watercolor. *Publ:* Cartoons in Saturday Review, FM and the Fine Arts Mag, Writer's Digest, Life Mag & Newspapers. *Mailing Add:* 717 Alabama St Vallejo CA 94590

SALOMON, JOHANNA
PAINTER, INSTRUCTOR
b Passaic, NJ, Jan 29, 44. *Study:* Art Ctr NJ, with Denise Collins, Florence Hurewitz, Leonard Agronsky, Gerald Samuels, Philip Pearlstein and Charles Reid, 86-96; Art Students League, with Knox Martin & Christine Jordan, 90-91. *Comn:* mural, Holley House for Children, Hackensack, NJ, 87. *Exhib:* Catherine Lorrilard Exhibit, Nat Arts Club, NY, 90, 92; Gallery 108, Vineyard Theater, NY, 90; Three Worlds of Realism, Williams Ctr Arts, Rutherford, NJ, 91; Festival Exhibit, Bergen Mus Arts & Sci, Paramus, NJ, 91; Figuratively Speaking, Art Ctr NJ, New Milford, 91; Paterson Mus, NJ, 92; Cork Gallery, Avery Fisher Hall, NY, 94; Belskie Mus Art and Sci, 2002. *Teaching:* instr watercolor, acrylic, oil, Emerson Bd Educ, NJ, 92-2001, Art Ctr Northern NJ, 99-, Bergen Community Coll, Paramus, NJ, 2000-; instr watercolor, Ridgewood Bd Educ, NJ, 93-. *Awards:* WInsor & Newton Painting Award, Hackensack Art Club, 85; Grumbacher Award, Hackensack Art Club, 89; Best in Show, Westwood Chamber Com, NJ, 89. *Bibliog:* Will Grant (auth), About NY in the Galleries, Artspeak, 5/1/90; Alexandra Shaw (auth), Salute to Women in the Arts, Mahattan Arts Int, 9-10/94. *Mem:* Art Ctr NJ Watercolor Affiliates (pres, 90-95, educ com, 90-94); Salute to Women in the Arts; Art Ctr NJ Painting Affliates; Communtiy Arts Asn; Ridgewood Arts Coun. *Media:* Watercolor, Acrylic. *Dealer:* Michael Fitzsimmons Westwood Gallery 10 Westwood Ave Westwood NJ 07675. *Mailing Add:* 29 Powell Rd Emerson NJ 07630-1446

SALOMON, LAWRENCE
SCULPTOR, EDUCATOR
b Chicago, Ill, July 18, 40. *Study:* Art Inst Chicago; Univ Ill, BFA; Univ Chicago. *Exhib:* Chicago Biennial, 68 & Critic Choice, 69, Art Inst Chicago; Lyman Wright Art Ctr, Beloit, Wis, 70; The Five: Pub Works, Univ Chicago, 71; Art for Pub Places, Dept Housing & Urban Develop Nat Competition, 73; Cool Abstraction, Richard Gray Gallery, Chicago, 76; Romantic Structures: Abstract Art in Chicago Traveling Exhib, Univs Mo & Kans, 78; and others. *Teaching:* Assoc prof fine art, Univ Ill, Chicago Circle, 65-. *Awards:* Art in Pub Places Award, Nat Competition, Dept Housing &

Urban Develop, 73. *Bibliog:* Amy Goldin (auth), Greasy kid stuff, Art Gallery Mag, 73; articles, Art in Am, 77; C L Morrison (auth), Chicago dialectics, Art News, 2/78. *Mem:* The Five; Participating Artists Chicago (secy, 68-70); Art Pub Places (bd dir, 78-). *Media:* Metal. *Dealer:* Jan Cicero Gallery 433 N Clark Chicago IL. *Mailing Add:* 2116 N Bissell Chicago IL 60614

SALT, JOHN
PAINTER
b Birmingham, Eng, 1937. *Study:* Slade Sch Fine Arts, London, 60; Birmingham Col Art, Eng, 68; Md Inst Col Art, Baltimore, MFA, 69. *Exhib:* Die Metamorphose des Dinges, Palais des Beaux-Arts, Brussels, 71; Relativerend Realisme, Stedelijk van Abbemuseum, Eindhoven, The Neth, 72; Sharp-Forcus Realism, Sidney Janis Gallery, NY, 72; Verkehrskultur, Westfalische Kunstverein, Munster, WGer, 72; solo exhibs, Louis Meisel Gallery, NY, 94, White Chevy Red Trailer: John Salt Paintings, Prints and other Works from 1953-1997, Wolfhampton Mus & Art Galleries, Silk Top Hat Gallery, Ludlow, Eng, 97; Paperwork, Louis W Meisel Gallery, NY, 96; Our Century: Selections (with catalog), Housatonic Mus Art, Bridgeport, Conn, 97; Photorealists (with catalog), Savannah Col Art & Design, Ga, 97. *Teaching:* Instr, various cols of art, Eng, 60-67 & Md Col Art, Baltimore, 67-68. *Bibliog:* Helen Harris (auth), Town an Country, Art and Antiques: The New Realists, 242, 244, 246-247, 10/78; The New Republic (cover), 3/15/80; Gerrit Henry (auth), John Salt, O K Harris, 121, 7/91. *Media:* Oil. *Mailing Add:* c/o O K Harris Works of Art 383 W Broadway New York NY 10012

SALTER, RICHARD MACKINTIRE
PAINTER
b Iowa City, Iowa, May 7, 40. *Study:* Northern Ariz Univ, BA, 64; Univ Guanajuato, Inst Allende, Mex, MFA, 68. *Work:* Arthur Adams Western Collection, Beloit, Wis; US Dept Interior, Washington, DC; Miller Brewing Co, Milwaukee, Wis; Univ Wis, Green Bay; Northern Ariz Univ. *Comn:* Com Design, US Borax Co, Boron, Calif, 65-66; Photography, Orput & Orput, Architects, Rockford, Ill, 71. *Exhib:* Mitchell Mus, Mt Vernon, Ill, 81; Smithsonian Inst, 82; Kennedy Ctr, 82; one-person show, Alverno Col, Milwaukee, 82; Appleton Gallery Fine Arts, Wis, 83; and many other group and one-man exhibs. *Teaching:* Instr painting, Stanislaus State Col, 68; instr creative photog, Univ Wis-Green Bay, 73. *Awards:* First Prizes, Red Cloud Indian Art Show, Pine Ridge, SDak & Heard Indian Art Show, Phoenix. *Bibliog:* Platt Cline (auth), NAU Show, Ariz Daily Sun, 73; Barbara Manger (auth), Salter Exhib, Mid-West Art Mag, 74 & 77. *Mem:* Rockford Art Asn; Wis Painters & Sculptors Asn; Col Art Asn Am. *Media:* Acrylic, Mixed. *Dealer:* Segal Gallery New York NY; Cudahy Gallery Milwaukee Art Ctr Milwaukee WI. *Mailing Add:* 414 Forest Rd Mt Dora FL 32757

SALTZ, JERRY
CRITIC, CURATOR
b Chicago, Ill, Feb 19, 51. *Study:* Art Inst Chicago, BFA, 73; Fashion Inst Tech, Grad Studies, 89 & 90. *Collection Arranged:* Recent Tendencies in Black & White, Sydney Janis Gallery, 73; A Drawing Show, Cabel Gallery, New York, 87; and over 75 shows at NAME Gallery, Chicago, 73-78. *Pos:* Founder & dir, NAME Gallery, 73-78; contrib, ed Arts Mag, 87-; contrib ed, Balcon Mag, 89; contribr, Flash Art. *Awards:* Nat Endowment Arts Grant, 80. *Publ:* Coauth, Sketchbook with Voices, Alfred Van der Marck, 86; auth, Beyond Boundaries: New York's New Art, Alfred Van der Marck, 87; numerous exhibition catalog essays. *Mailing Add:* 40 E Ninth St Apt 3-D New York NY 10003

SALTZMAN, MARVIN
PAINTER
b Chicago, Ill, 1931. *Study:* Art Inst Chicago, 54-56; Univ Southern Calif, BFA, 58, MFA, 59. *Work:* Nat Mus Am Art, Washington; Univ Calif, Berkeley Art Mus; Ackland Art Mus, Chapel Hill, NC; NC Mus Art; Nat Acad Sci, Washington, DC. *Exhib:* Los Angeles Artists & Vicinity Ann, Los Angeles Co Mus, 57-59; solo, Nat Acad Sci, Washington, 87; Durham Arts Coun, NC, 91; Peninsula Fine Arts Ctr, Newport News, Va, 92; Greenville Mus Art, NC, 93; Waterworks Ctr, Salisbury, NC, 93; Ackland Art Mus, NC, 97; French Embassy, Washington, DC, 99-2007; and many others. *Teaching:* prof painting, Univ NC, Chapel Hill, 67-97, studio chmn, 67-74 & 86-88, chmn fine arts div, 76-79, emer prof, 97-. *Awards:* Pogue Fel, 78-79; Sam Ragan Award, St Andrews Col; NC award, Fine Arts, 98. *Media:* Oil, Graphite. *Publ:* Places: Graphite Drawings, 98; Serigraphs & Poems, Chapel Hill Gravel, 72. *Dealer:* info@rcgallery.com (Raleigh Contemp Gallery); Minta@mintabell.com (Minta Bell Design); www.broadhurstgallery.com (Broadcast Gallery); www.gierek.com (Joseph Gierek Fine Art). *Mailing Add:* 717 Emory Dr Chapel Hill NC 27517-3011

SALVEST, JOHN
SCULPTOR, EDUCATOR
b Kearny, NJ, Feb 13, 55. *Study:* Duke Univ, BA, 77; Univ Iowa, MA (English), 79, MFA, 83. *Work:* NJ State Mus, Trenton; Bristol-Myers Squibb Collection, Princeton, NJ; DePauw Univ Permanent Art Collection, Greencastle, Ind; Zimmerli Mus Rutgers Univ, New Brunswick, NJ; Univ Iowa Mus Art, Iowa City. *Comn:* sculpture, Salina Art Ctr, Kans, 98; sculpture, Ark State Univ, Jonesboro, 99; sculpture, Memphis Pub Libr, Tenn, 2001; sculpture, Cannon Ctr for the Performing Arts, Memphis, 2003; sculpture, Hartsfield Int Airport, Atlanta, 2004. *Exhib:* Brooks Biennial, Memphis Brooks Mus Art, Tenn, 92; Tijd Tekens (Marking Time), Gallery Quartair, The Hague, The Neth, 95; New AmTalent, Austin Mus Art, Tex, 96, 97; Triennial, New Orleans Mus Art, 98, Birdspace, Contemp Arts Ctr, New Orleans, 2004, What Business Are You In?, Atlanta Contemp Ctr, 2005; solo- show Inventory: Selections & Evaluations, City Gallery at Chastain, Atlanta, Ga, 96; Meditation 7.21, Forum for Contemp Art, St Louis, Mo, 97; Nothing Endures, New Mus Contemp Art, NY, 98; Time on His Hands, Phoenix Art Mus, Ariz, 99-2000; Texture, Ark Arts Ctr, Little Rock, 2002; New Glory, Cheekwood Mus Art, Nashville, Tenn, 2002; Fly, etc., Bernice Steinbaum Gallery, Miami, Fla, 2005; No Time for Sorrow, Morgan Lehman Gallery, NY, 2006. *Teaching:* prof art, sculpture, Ark State Univ, Jonesboro, 89-; vis artist sculpture, Univ Memphis, Tenn, 85-86. *Awards:* Ark Arts Coun fel, 92; Nat Endowment for the Arts fel, 93; Pollock-Krasner Found Grant, 98. *Bibliog:* Felicia Feaster (auth) Inventory: Selections & Evaluations, City Gallery at Chastain, 96; Debra Wilbur (auth) Studio View: John Salvest, New Art Examiner, 3/98; Kim Levin (auth) Time on His Hands, Phoenix Art Mus, 99. *Mem:* Coll Art Asn; Southeastern Coll Art Conf. *Media:* Mixed Media, Objects and Installations. *Publ:* coauth Composition Book, Salina Art Ctr, 95. *Dealer:* Rudolph Projects 1836 Richmond Ave Houston TX 77098. *Mailing Add:* 1224 W Matthews Jonesboro AR 72401

SAMARAS, LUCAS
SCULPTOR
b Kastoria, Greece, Sept 14, 36; US citizen. *Study:* Rutgers Univ, with Alan Kaprow, BA, 59; Columbia Univ, with Meyer Schapiro, 59-62. *Work:* Solomon R Guggenheim Mus, Metrop Mus Art, Whitney Mus Am Art, Mus Mod Art, NY; Albright-Knox Art Gallery, Buffalo, NY; Los Angeles Co Mus Art; Fogg Art Mus, Harvard Univ, Cambridge, Mass; Mus Contemp Art, Chicago; Hirshhorn Mus & Sculpture Garden, Smithsonian Inst, Washington; Aldrich Mus Contemp Art, Ridgefield, Conn; and others. *Exhib:* solo exhibs, Mus Mod Art, NY, 75 & 92, Inst Contemp Art, Boston, 76 & 83, Walker Art Ctr, 77, Pace Gallery, NY, 93, Pace Wildenstein, NY, 94 & 96, Gallery Seomi, South Korea, 95 & Galerie Xippas, Paris, 97 & 2000; Two Hundred Yrs of Am Sculpture, Whitney Mus Am Art, NY, 76; retrospective, Mus Contemp Art, Chicago, 71, Denver Art Mus (traveling), 82 & 88, Polaroid Int Collection, Cambridge, Mass (traveling), 83, Yokohama Mus of Art, Japan (traveling), 91-92; Forty Yrs of Sculpture, Solomon R Guggenheim Mus, NY, 85; 75th Am Exhib, Art Inst Chicago, 85-86; Enigmatic Objects; Sculpture from the Permanent Collection, Whitney Mus Am Art, NY, 88-89; Identity; Representations of the Self, Whitney Mus Downtown Fed Reserve Plaza, NY, 88-89; Vanishing Presence, Walker Art Ctr, Minneapolis, 89; Aldrich Mus Contemp Art, Ridgefield, Conn, 94; 47th Ann Am Acad Purchase Exhib, NY, 95; Deformations: Aspects of the Modern Grotesque, Mus Mod Art, NY, 96; Pastels by Ten Contemp Artists, DC Moore Gallery, NY, 96; Inside, Henry Art Gallery, Univ Wash, Seattle, 97; The Pop 60's: Transatlantic Crossing, Fundacao das Descobertas/Centro Cult de Belem, Portugal, 97; Pace Wildenstein, NY, 97-98; Off Limits: Rutgers Univ and the Avant-Garde, 1957-1963, Newark Mus, NJ, 99; Photofictions, PaceWildenstein Gallery, New York City, 2003; PhotoFlicks (iMovies) and PhotoFictions (A to Z), PaceWildenstein Gallery, New York City, 2005. *Teaching:* Instr, Brooklyn Col, 71-72. *Bibliog:* Goings on about town: art, The New Yorker, 3/15/93; Christina Mango (auth), The oral matrix, The Arts in Psychotherapy, 93; Carol Vogel (auth), Inside art, NY Times, 2/11/94. *Publ:* Auth, Autopolaroid, Art in Am, 11/70, Vol 58, 66-83; The art of portraiture in the words of four New York artists, NY Times, 10/31/76, 29; Clay and bronze, Artforum, 3/82, Vol 20, 57 63. *Mailing Add:* c/o Pace Wildenstein Gallery 32 E 57th St 2nd Fl New York NY 10022

SAMBURG, GRACE (BLANCHE)
PAINTER, LITHOGRAPHER
b New York, NY. *Study:* Art Students League, painting with Morris Kantor & Raphael Soyer; New Sch for Social Res, stage design & lighting; Contemp Art Gallery Graphic Workshop, with Michael Ponce de Leon; also with Philip Guston. *Work:* Slide Collection, Mus Fine Arts, Boston. *Exhib:* Silvermine Guild of Artists Ann, New Canaan, Conn, 59; Works on Paper, Brooklyn Mus, NY, 75; Chatham Col, Pittsburgh, Pa, 76; Randolph-Macon Women's Col, Lynchburg, Va, 77; solo exhibs, Kornbluth Gallery, Fairlawn, NJ, 83 & Péne DuBois Gallery, NY, 86; Green Mountain Gallery, NY, 73; John McEnroe Gallery, NY, 96; and others; Prince St Gallery Invitational, NY, 2001; Long Beach Island Found 3rd Ann Juried Competitional, 2002. *Bibliog:* Lawrence Campbell (auth), article, Art News, 9/73; Gordon Brown (auth), article, Arts Mag, 11/73; Lucy Lippard (auth), From the Center, Feminist Essays on Women's Art, Dutton, 76; Lucy Lippard (auth), Household images in art, Ms Mag, 9/73. *Mem:* Women in the Arts. *Media:* Oil on Canvas. *Publ:* Contribr, Arts Mag, & Art News, 67. *Dealer:* Kornbluth Gallery Fair Lawn NJ; Péne DuBois Gallery New York NY. *Mailing Add:* 63 Highwood Terrace Weehawken NJ 07087-6814

SAMIMI, MEHRDAD
ILLUSTRATOR, PAINTER
b Mashad, Aug 14, 39; US citizen. *Study:* Sch Archit, Univ Ariz, 64. *Work:* Calif State Capitol, Sacramento; Cosmopolitan Fine Arts, La Jolla, Calif; Lynn House, City Comn Art, Antioch, Calif. *Comn:* Governor's portrait, Sacramento, Calif, 92; portrait of Clarence Woodard of Orinda, Calif, comn by Woodard's children, 92; mayoral portrait, New Orleans Gallier Hall, 93; recreation of fire destroyed portrait, comn by Judith Woods, Oakland, Calif, 93; portrait, comn by Dr & Mrs Safavi, Dallas, Tex, 94. *Exhib:* Solo exhibs, Art Circle, Vancouver, BC, 86, Los Angeles, Calif, 87; group exhib, Kertesz Fine Art, San Francisco, Calif, 90; Oakland Art Asn, Kaiser Ctr, Oakland, Calif, 91, Pan Pacific, Oakland, Calif, 92; Inside/Outside, Lynn House, Antioch, Calif, 94. *Teaching:* Pvt lessons landscape, still lifes & portrait, 90-94. *Awards:* Art Calif Mag Discovery Award, Juried Traditional Realist, 93. *Bibliog:* Doc, Univ Ariz, 63; Portrait lost in Oakland fire reborn, San Francisco Chronicle, 93; Portrait lost in fire reborn, Assoc Press, 93. *Mem:* Calif Art Club; Smithsonian Nat Portrait Gallery. *Media:* Oil. *Dealer:* Cosmopolitan Fine Art 7932 Girard Ave La Jolla CA 92037. *Mailing Add:* 6 Sunrise Hall Rd Orinda CA 94563

SAMPLE, STEVEN BROWNING
PATRON
b St Louis, Mo, Nov 29, 40. *Study:* Univ Ill, BS, 62, MS, 63, PhD, 65. *Hon Degrees:* Numerous hon degrees from US cols & univs, 89-95. *Pos:* Timpanist St. Louis Philharmonic Orchestra, 55-58; Sr scientist, Melpar Inc, Falls Church, Va, 65-66; deputy dir, Ill Bd Higher Educ, Springfield, 71-74; exec vpres accad affairs, dean Grad

Col, prof electrical engineering, Univ Nebr, Lincoln, 74-82; trustee, Univ at Buffalo Found, 82-91, Studio Arena Theatre, Buffalo, 83-91, Western NY Pub Broadcasting Asn, 85-91; bd dir, Buffalo Philharmonic Orchestra, 82-91, Regenstrief Med Found, Indianapolis, 82-, Res Found State Univ NY, 87-91; chmn, Western NY Regional Econ Develop Coun, 84-91; mem bd dir, Dunlop Tire Corp, 87-91, Greater Buffalo CofC, 85-91, United Way Buffalo and Erie Co, 85-91; chmn, Gov's Conf on Sci & Eng Educ, Res & Devel, 89-91; trustee, LEARN, 1991-; pres, Univ Southern Calif, Los Angeles, 91-, prof, electrical engineering, 91-, Robert C Packard pres.'s chmn, 1995-; mem bd dir, 1st Interstate Bancorp, 91-96, Galaxy Inst Educ, 91-94, Niagara Mohawk Power Corp, 88-91; bd dir, Los Angeles chap World Affairs Coun, Hughes Galaxy Inst Educ, 91-94; mem bd, gov Los Angeles Annenberg Metrop Project (LAAMP), 94-2000; mem bd dir, Western Atlas, Inc, 94-97; mem, Calif Bus-Higher Educ Forum (CBHEF), 95-97; sr warden, Church of Our Savior, 96-98; vestry Church of Our Savior, 96-2001; mem bd trustees, J Paul Getty, currently; bd dir, Rebuild Los Angeles Comt, Coalition of 100 Club, Los Angeles; bd dir, Univ Southern Calif Keck Sch Medicine. *Teaching:* Assoc prof, electrical eng, Purdue Univ, Lafayette, Ind, 66-73; prof electrical & computer eng, State Univ NY, Buffalo, 82-91. *Mem:* Nat Asn State Univ & Land-Grant Col (educ telecommunications comt, 82-83, chmn coun pres, 85-86, educ & tech comt 86-87, exec comt, 87-89); Asn Am Univ (vchmn, 97-98, tenure comt 97-2001, chmn 98-99, assessing quality of univ educ & res comt 2000-, co-chmn task force on res accountability 2001-02, internationalization comt 2002-); Am Acad Arts & Sci, Asn Pacific Rim Univ (co-founder, chmn, 97-2002); Knight Comn on Intercollegiate Athletics. *Publ:* Auth, Contrarian's Guide to Leadership, 2001; contribr, articles to prof jour. *Mailing Add:* Univ So Calif Off of Pres Univ Park Admin 110 Los Angeles CA 90089-0012

SAMPSON, FRANK
PAINTER, PRINTMAKER
b Edmore, NDak, Mar 24, 28. *Study:* Concordia Col, BA, 50; Univ Iowa, MFA, 52; studied printmaking with Mauricio Lasansky, 56-59. *Work:* Libr Cong, DC; Walker Art Ctr, Minneapolis; Nelson-Atkins Mus, Kansas City; Sheldon Mem Art Ctr, Lincoln, Nebr; Joslyn Art Mus, Omaha, Nebr. *Exhib:* One-man shows, Walker Art Ctr, Minneapolis, 54, Sheldon Mem Art Ctr, Lincoln, Nebr, 64 & Denver Art Mus, 75; Mid-Am, Nelson-Atkins Mus, Kansas City, 65; 13th Am Drawing Biennial, Norfolk Mus Arts, Va, 69; 21st Nat Exhib Prints, Libr Cong, Washington DC, 69; Drawings from Nine States, Mus Fine Arts, Houston, Tex, 70; Regionalism: Seven Views, Joslyn Art Mus, Omaha, Nebr, 79; Hanga Ann, Tokyo Metrop Art Gallery, Japan; retrospective, Boulder Mus Contemp Art, Boulder, Colo, 97; Arvada Art Ctr, CO, 2003. *Teaching:* Prof painting, drawing & printmaking, Univ Colo, Boulder, 61-90, prof fine arts emer, 90-. *Awards:* Fulbright Grant (painting & printmaking), Brussels, Belg, 59-60; Ford Purchase, Walker Biennial, 64; Purchase Prize, Minn Mus Art, St Paul, 71. *Bibliog:* Michele de Ghelderode (auth), D'ou Viens Tu, Beau Nuage?, Le Cahier des Arts, Bruxelles, Belg, 4/61; Walter Simon (auth), The collector, Colo Quart, Univ Colo, summer 77; Merrill Mahaffey (auth), Contemporary western painting, the new western art, Southwestern Art, fall 77. *Media:* Oil, Acrylic. *Dealer:* Sandy Carson Gallery 760 Santa Fe Drive Denver CO 80204; Mary Belochi 227 Juniper CT Boulder CO 80304 EXHIBITREK. *Mailing Add:* 1912 Columbine Ave Boulder CO 80302

SAMSON, CARL JOSEPH
PAINTER, INSTRUCTOR
b Sandusky, Ohio, Jan 7, 61. *Study:* Study under Allan R Banks, 75-79 & 81-83, R H Ives Gammell, 79-80 & Richard (Atelier) Lack, 83-85. *Work:* Music Hall Grand Gallery, Cincinnati, Ohio; Ohio State Senate Chambers, Capitol Bldg, Columbus; Northminster Presby Church, Tucson, Ariz. *Comn:* Sen Stanley Aronoff (portrait), 93, Sen Theodore Gray (portrait), 94, State of Ohio, Columbus; Hershel Farmer (portrait), Cintas Corp, Cincinnati, Ohio, 93; James DeBlasis (portrait), Cincinnati Opera Inc, Ohio, 93; Patricia Corbett, Corbett Found, Cincinnati, Ohio, 95. *Exhib:* Solo show, Cincinnati Art Galleries, 95; PAPA Ann Catalina Show, Avalon, Calif, 95; ASCR Traveling Exhib, Boston, Minneapolis, Milwaukee, 96; The Legacy Lives, Lever House Gallery, NY, 96; Am-Rus Plein-Air Exhib, Kolomna, Russ, 96. *Teaching:* Instr drawing, Atelier Fine Arts, Sandusky, Ohio, 81-83; pvt instr, Cincinnati, Ohio, 86-; asst dir drawing & painting, Atelier Plein Air Studies, Safety Harbor, Fla, 94-. *Awards:* John Howard Sanden Award for Excellence in Portrait Painting, Nat Portrait Sem, Atlanta, 93; Artist's Mag Award, Cincinnati Art Club Viewpoint Exhib, 95; Portrait Inst Award for Distinguished Achievement in Portrait Painting, Nat Portrait Competition, New York, 96. *Bibliog:* Mary McCarty (auth), It's the real thing, Cincinnati Mag, 10/92; Owen Findsen (auth), Prized portraits-Cincinnatian Carl Samson paints his way to top prize in prestigious competition, Cincinnati Enquirer, 5/24/93; M Stephen Doherty (auth), Prize-winning portrait-painting techniques, Am Artist, 12/96. *Mem:* Am Soc Classical Realism; Am Artists Prof League; Cincinnati Art Club (vpres); Am Soc Portrait Artists. *Media:* Oil on Linen Canvas. *Publ:* Auth, A journey through Monet country, 6/91 & Cincinnati past & present, spring 92, Classical Realism Quart, Am Soc Classical Realism; Three steps to polished portraits, Artists Mag, 6/94; contribr, Realism in Revolution-The Art of the Boston School, Taylor Publ Co, 85. *Dealer:* Cincinnati Art Galleries 605 Main St Cincinnati OH 45202. *Mailing Add:* 2152 Alpine Pl Cincinnati OH 45206

SAMTEN, LOSANG
ARTIST
b Ribuce Chang, Tibet, 53. *Study:* Namgyal Monastery, Dharamsala, India, Ordained as Buddhist monk, 67, 85; Trinity Col, Hartford, Conn, DD (hon), 94; Maine Col Art, Portland, AtD (hon), 95. *Work:* Has created sand mandalas at, Am Mus Natural Hist, NY, 88, 96, 2001; Univ Pa Mus Archaeology and Anthropology, Philadelphia, 89; Natural Hist Mus, LA, 89, 99; Asian Mus Art, San Francisco, 91; Metrop Mus Art, NY City, 94; Philadelphia Mus Art, 96, 97, 2001; Temple Gallery, Philadelphia, 2003; Has created sand mandalas at, Am Mus Natural Hist, NY City, 88, 96, 2001, Univ Pa Mus Archaeology and Anthropology, Philadelphia, 89, Natural Hist Mus, Los Angeles, 89, 99, Asian Mus Art, San Francisco, 91, Metrop Mus Art, NY, 94, Philadelphia Mus Art, 96, 97, 2001, Temple Gallery, Philadelphia, 2003, Phillips Mus Franklin and Marshall Col, Lancaster, Pa, 2003, Helena Art Mus, Mont, Nev Art Mus, Reno; Helena Art Mus, Montana, Nevada Art Mus, Reno. *Pos:* Ritual dance master, Namgyal Monastery, Dharamsala, India; personal attendant to the Dalai Lama, 1985—1988; founder, spiritual dir, Tibetan Buddhist Ctr of Philadelphia, 89-; Cenrezig Himalayan Cultural Ctr, El Paso, Tex, 90—; Chenrezig Tibetan Buddhist Ctr, Middletown, Conn, 94—, Lake Tahoe Chenrezig Ctr, Nevada. *Awards:* Nat Heritage Fel; Nat Endowment for the Arts, 2002; Pew Fel in the Arts, 2004. *Publ:* Has created sand mandalas at, Am. Mus Natural History, New York, NY, 88, 96, 2001, Univ Pennsylvania Mus Archaeology and Anthropology, Philadelphia, 89, Natural History Mus, LA, 89, 99, Asian Mus Art, San Francisco, 91, Metropolitan Mus Art, New York, NY 94, Philadelphia Museum Art, 96, 97, 2001, Temple Gallery, Philadelphia, 2003, Phillips Mus Franklin and Marshall Col, Lancaster, Pennsylvania, 2003, Helena Art Mus, Montana, Nevada Art Mus, Reno; actor, religious advisor (films) Kundun, 97. *Mailing Add:* Tibetan Buddhist Ctr of Phila 134 Heather Rd Upper Darby PA 19082

SAMUELS, JOHN STOCKWELL, III
COLLECTOR, PATRON
b Galveston, Tex, Sept 15, 33. *Study:* Tex A&M Univ, BA, 54 & MS, 54; Harvard Univ, BL, 60. *Collection:* American, French, Italian & Pre-Columbian paintings and decorative arts. *Mailing Add:* 1702 Broadway Galveston TX 77550

SAMUELS (JOESAM), JOE
SCULPTOR
b Harlem, NY, 39. *Study:* Univ Mass, Amherst; self taught. *Work:* Cleveland Rapid Transit System, Ohio; Anchorage Mus Hist & Art; Univ of Central Fla, Orlando; 53 sculptures, Hide n Seek; Sadie, Wilmington/Imperial Metro Rail Station, Los Angeles, Calif. *Exhib:* Oakland Mus, Collectors Gallery, Calif; No Am Sculpture Exhib, Golden, Colo; Nat Black Arts Festival, Atlanta, Ga; Museo Nat de Belles Artes, Santiago, Chile; Solo exhib, Albertson-Peterson Gallery, Winter Park, Fla, Morgan/Monceaux Gallery, Seattle, Wash, Mus of African Art, Los Angeles, Calif, 2000, Richmond Art Ctr, Calif, 2001. *Awards:* Compton Found Fel; Nat Endowment for Arts, 85-86; Artist-in-Residence, Djerassi Found, 99. *Media:* Mixed. *Mailing Add:* PO Box 883894 San Francisco CA 94188

SAMUELSON, FRED BINDER
PAINTER, EDUCATOR
b Harvey, Ill, Nov 29, 25. *Study:* Sch Art Inst Chicago, BFA, 51 & MFA, 53; Univ Chicago, 46-53. *Work:* Denver Art Mus, Colo; Witte Mus, San Antonio, Tex; Ohio Univ, Athens; Tex Fine Arts Asn, Laguna Gloria Mus, Austin. *Comn:* Acrylic mural, Hemisfair 68, San Antonio. *Exhib:* 60th Ann Exhib Western Art, Denver Art Mus, 54; 20th Ann Tex Painting & Sculpture Exhib, Dallas Mus Fine Art, 58; Southwest Am Art Ann, Okla Art Ctr, 60; Segundo Festival Pictorico Acapulco, 64; 53rd Tex Fine Arts Asn Ann, 64. *Teaching:* Prof painting & drawing, Inst Allende, San Miguel de Allende, Mex, 55-63, head grad studies & painting, 65-; chmn fac, San Antonio Art Inst, 63-64. *Awards:* Purchase Award, Denver Art Mus, 54; Purchase Award, Tex Fine Arts Asn, Laguna Gloria Mus, Austin, 64; Purchase Award, Ohio Univ, Athens, 64. *Bibliog:* Leonard Brooks (auth), Oil Painting Traditional and New, 59 & Wash Drawings, 61, Van Nostrand Reinhold; interview, Time-Life, 65. *Media:* Acrylic. *Mailing Add:* 133 Valencia Rd Rockledge FL 32955

SANABRIA, ROBERT
SCULPTOR, WRITER
b El Paso, Tex, Aug 20, 31. *Study:* Univ Md, BA, 65, MFA, 79. *Work:* Wichita Art Mus, Kans; Tweed Mus Art, Duluth, Minn; Miss Mus Art, Jackson; Univ Md, College Park; US Ambassador Residence, Mexico City. *Comn:* bonze/copper abstract tree sculpture, comn by Dr Wm Rutherford, Wash, 91; bronze/copper abstract tree sculpture, comn by Beth Sholom Synagogue, Fredrick, Md, 94; bronze/copper fountain sculpture, Dr & Ms Ronald Hodges, Eugene, Ore, 96; abstract bronze/copper flame sculpture, comn by Kemp Mill Synagogue, Silver Spring, Md, 2000; Menorahs, Beth Sholom Synagogue, 2004; bronze/copper abstract tree sculpture, Ralph Terkowitz, McLean, Va, 2005; bronze/copper abstract tree sculpture, Shady Grove Adventist Hosp, Rockville, Md, 2006. *Exhib:* Md Col Art & Design, Silver Spring, 90; Fridholm Fine Arts Gallery, Asheville, NC, 91; Invitational Outdoor Sculpture Exhib, Montgomery Col, Rockville, Md, 92; Invitational, Washington Abstract Sculpture, The Am Univ, Washington, DC, 93; Art in Pub Places, Glenview Mansion, Rockville, Md, 96; Sculpture on the Grounds, Rockville Civic Ctr Park, Rockville, Md, 98; and others; Flora: Sculptures of Natural World, Botanic Garden, Washington, DC. *Pos:* Artist-in-residence, Fairfax Co Sch, Mobil Oil Co, 92. *Teaching:* Instr sculpture, Art League Workshops, Alexandria, Va, 75-78. *Bibliog:* CB Tomlins, (auth) Water Sculpture: USA, 86; Galleries, Washington Post, 90; Gale Woldron (auth), On a Grand Scale, Loudoun Mag, summer 2006. *Mem:* Loudoun Arts Coun, Leesburg, Va (vpres, 87-92); Washington Sculptor's Group, Washington, DC. *Media:* All Media, Metal-Welded. *Publ:* Auth, Fees for commissions, Sculptors' Int, Vol 1, No 6, 83; A World Apart, A World of Art, Vol 5, No 6, 11-12, 2000; Stewing in the Melting Pot, Capital Books, 2001; Stewing in the Melting Pot: The Memoir of a Real American. *Mailing Add:* 18163 Canby Rd Leesburg VA 20175

SANABRIA, SHERRY ZVARES
PAINTER
b Washington, DC, Oct 18, 37. *Study:* George Washington Univ, BA, 59; Am Univ, MFA, 74. *Work:* Phillips Collection, Columbia Hosp Women, Washington Convention Ctr, Washington Post, Student Loan Marketing Asn, George Washington Univ & Nat Asn Retired Persons, Washington, DC; Phillip Morris Co & Charles E Smith Co,

Richmond, Va; Frostburg State Col, Md; First Nat Bank Boston, Mass; US Holocaust Mem Mus, Washington; Am Univ, Washington, DC; Benchmark Capital, Menlo Park, Calif, McGraw-Hill Publishers, NYC, New Yor. *Comn:* Crystal City Park IV; Vice Pres US Residence Found, Washington, DC. *Exhib:* solo exhibs, Phillips Collection, Wash, 80, Baumgartner Galleries, Washington, 81, 83, 86 & 88, KPMG Peat Marwick, Washington, 89, David Adamson Gallery, Washington, DC, 89, 91, 93 & 95, Ellis Island Immigration Mus, NY, 91, Marymount Univ, Mclean, Va, 91, Dorothy McRae Gallery, Atlanta, Ga, 94, Washington Hebrew Congregation, 98, Eastern Loudown Libr Sys, Va, 2000, Am Inst Arch Hdqr Gallery, Washington, DC, 2002, Rentz Gallery, Richmond, Va, 2004, Washington Co Mus Fine Arts, Hagerstown, Md, 2005; group exhibs, Am Acad Arts & Letters, New York City, 83; 22nd Area Exhibit: Works on Paper, Corcoran Gallery, 80; Nat Works on Paper, Univ Richmond, Va, 92; 26th Univ Del Biennial, Del, 94; Art Sites 6, GRACE, Va, 94; B'nai B'rith Kluznick Mus, 96; Gallery Henoch, NY, 99; Md Art Place, 2000; Nat Gallery Bermuda, Hamilton, 2003. *Bibliog:* New American Paintings, 94, 2002 & 06; Madelyn Rosenberg (auth), Am Artist Mag, 3/2003; Ori Z Soltes (auth), Fixing the World, Univ Pres New England, 2003; Logan Ward (auth), Southern Accents, 10/2003 & Virginia Living, fall 2005; Joe Shannon (auth), Art in America, 4/2003. *Mem:* Wash Women's Caucus; Loudoun Arts Coun. *Media:* Acrylic. *Mailing Add:* 18163 Canby Rd Leesburg VA 20175

SANBORN, JIM (JAMES)
SCULPTOR
b Nov 14, 45. *Study:* Art & Archeol Prog, Oxford Univ, United Kingdom, 67; Randolph-Macon Col, Ashland, Va, 68; Pratt Inst, MFA(sculpture), 71. *Work:* US Fed Courthouse, Little Rock, Ark; Biology Dept, MIT, Cambridge; Nat Oceanic & Atmospheric Admin, Silver Spring, Md; Cent Intelligence Agency, Langly, Va; Nat Endowment Arts, Washington. *Comn:* granite water wave generator, Nat Oceanic & Atmospheric Admin; bronze, petrified wood, Cent Intelligence Agency. *Exhib:* Va Mus Fine Arts, 73, 77, 83 & 88; solo shows, Va Mus Fine Arts, 74 & 78, Nancy Drysdale Gallery, Washington, 92 & 94, Corcoran Gallery Art, Washington, 92, Orlando Mus Fine Arts, Fla, 93 & Grimaldis Gallery, Baltimore, 96; Baltimore Mus Art, 76 & 78; Corcoran Gallery Art, 74, 78 & 85; AVA 7, Carnegie-Mellon Art Gallery & Los Angeles Co Mus Art, 88; Grimaldis Gallery, Baltimore, 91; Dialogue with Nature, Phillips Collection, Washington, 92; Metaphysical Metaphores, High Mus Art, 94; Va Mus Fel Recipients, Peninsula Fine Arts Ctr, Newport News, Va, 95; Pub Art Biennial, Neuberger Mus, Purchase, NY, 97. *Awards:* Grant, Art Matters Inc, 90; Va Mus Fine Arts, Fel, 91; Pollack Krasner, 92. *Bibliog:* Colin Hughes (auth), Secret messages of the CIA, London Independent, 1/17/90; Joshua Remo (auth), CIA cryptic on artwork, Boston Globe, 7/4/90; Jack Rosenberger (auth), The CIA's top secret sculpture, Art Am, 3/91; and others. *Dealer:* Laurence Miller Gallery 138 Spring St New York NY. *Mailing Add:* 903 Girard St NE Washington DC 20017

SANCHEZ, BEATRICE RIVAS
ADMINISTRATOR, PRINTMAKER
b San Antonio, Tex, June 17, 41. *Study:* Del Art Ctr, 65-69; Montgomery Col, 70-71; Univ Mass, MFA, 75. *Work:* McNay Mus, Trinity Univ, Tex; Univ Tex Health Sci Ctr; Fla State House Rep; St Johns Col, Fla. *Comn:* Two Hundred Years of Graphics (poster), STex Print Soc, San Antonio, 76. *Exhib:* Color Print USA, Tex Tech Univ, 75; Women Artists of San Antonio, Univ Tex, 76; Womens Nat Exhib, Galarie Triangle, Washington, DC, 80; Montgomery Co Regional Juried Exhib, Greater Reston Arts Ctr Ann Juried Exhib, Md, 81; Southern Graphic Couns 190th Ann Conf Exhib, Kansas City, Mo, 91. *Pos:* Mem bd trustees, Native Am & Alaskan Indian Cult Inst, Santa Fe, NMex; mem, Comm on Accredidation, Nat Asn of Schs of Art & Design; mem, Capital Campaign Honorary Comt, Col Art Asn; pres, Kansas City Art Inst, 87-; gov, Am Royal Asn; adv Bd Mem, Conelo Studios, Chicago. *Teaching:* Artist-in-residence printmaking & drawing, Trinity Univ, Tex, 76; coordr fine arts prog, Fla Sch Art, Palatka, 76-78; acad & assoc dean, Md Col Art & Design, 78-82; dean, Cranbrook Acad Art, 82-. *Awards:* Second Prize, Eighth Ann Parkville Art Exhib, Md, 68; Third Place, Dept Commerce Exhib, Washington, DC, 69; First Prize, Creative Painting, Md Sch Art, 69. *Mem:* Nat Coun Art Admin. *Publ:* Contribr, Spectrum Fine Arts, 74 & 75 & Chomo-Uri Mag, summer 75

SANCHEZ, JOHN
PAINTER, PHOTOGRAPHER
Exhib: solo exhib, Emblems of a Prior Order, UCLA, Los Angeles, Calif, 2004; Resident Artists' Exhib, Cooper Union, New York City, 2004; Portraits, Cooper Brook Gallery, 2004; An American Album, J Paul Getty Mus, Los Angeles, Calif, 2004; Amory Ctr for the Arts, Los Angeles, Calif; Berkeley Art Ctr, Berkeley, Calif; Contemporary Arts Forum Gallery, Santa Barbara, Calif. *Awards:* Artist's Residency, Cooper Union for the Advan of Sci & Art, New York City, 2004. *Media:* Painting, Photography, Filmmaking. *Mailing Add:* PO Box 50434 Santa Barbara CA 93108

SANCHEZ, THORVALD
PAINTER
b Havana, Cuba, June 11, 33; US citizen. *Work:* Milwaukee Art Ctr, Wis. *Exhib:* Pintura Cubana, Caracas, Venezuela, 72; 15th Ann Hortt Competition, Ft Lauderdale, Fla, 73; 35th Ann Exhib, Soc Four Arts, Palm Beach, Fla, 73; East Coast Painters, Longboat Key Art Ct0, Sarasota, Fla, 74; Fla Artists, Norton Mus, West Palm Beach, 75. *Awards:* Best of Show Award, Fla Gulf Coast 9th Show, High Mus Art, Atlanta, Ga, 74. *Bibliog:* Georgia Dupuis (auth), Transition theme of Sanchez work, Palm Beach Post, 74. *Mem:* Fla Artist Group. *Media:* Acrylic, Collage. *Dealer:* Center Gallery 327 Acadia Rd West Palm Beach FL 33401. *Mailing Add:* 1029 N Palmway Lake Worth FL 33460-2313

SAN CHIRICO, JOANIE
ARTIST
Comn: Public Art Library Project, Atrium, Ocean County Library Headquarters, Toms River NJ; Wallhanging,World Trade Center Memorial, NY. *Exhib:* Uncommon Threads/Uncommon Women, Cleopatra Steps Out Gallery, Asbury Park, NJ, 2000; Fiber Revolution, Brodsky Gallery, Chauncey Conference Ctr, Princeton, NJ, 2003; Beyond the Stitch, Ocean Co Artists' Guild, Island Heights, NJ, 2004; Common Thread, Phoenix Gallery, NY, 2005; Beyond the Stitch II, Ocean Co Artists' Guild, Island Height, NJ, 2006. *Collection Arranged:* E-Conversation Keeps a Group Connected, Surface Design Asn Newsletter, summer 2004; Creating Opportunities in Art Galleries, The Professional Quilter, winter 2005; Spotlight on Education: The Quilt/Surface Design Symposium, Suface Design Asn J, spring 2005. *Bibliog:* Footnotes, Jersey Footlights, NY Times, 2003; Feature Story, Weekend, Ocean Co Observer, 2004; New Zealand Quilter, 2005. *Media:* Independent Curator. *Publ:* Surface Design Asn Newsletter, Summer, 2004; The Prof Quilter, Winter, 2005; Surface Design Asn Journal, Spring, 2005. *Mailing Add:* 1064 Lake Placid Dr Toms River NJ 08753

SANDEL, RANDYE NOREEN
PAINTER, PRINTMAKER
b Los Angeles, Calif, June 2, 42. *Study:* Univ Calif, Los Angeles, BA(Latin), 63, MFA(painting & printmaking), 69, studied with William Brice, Richard Diebenkorn & Arman. *Work:* River Forest State Bank, Ill; Security Pacific Nat Bank, Century City, Sunnyvale, Whittier & Sacramento, Calif. *Comn:* Four pastel drawings, Devon Indust Exec Offices, Northridge, Calif, 85. *Exhib:* Current Directions in Southern Calif Art, Los Angeles Inst Contemp Art, 78; Art from Los Angeles, San Francisco Mus Mod Art, Ft Mason, Calif, 86; solo exhib, Univ Gallery, Calif State Univ, Northridge, 88 & Riverside Mus, Calif, 89; Scrapes, Jose Drudis Gallery, Baida Mt St Marys Col, Brentwood, Calif, 89; Divergent Similarities, Occidental Col, 96; Dogs & Cats in Art, Danville Fine Arts Ctr, 96. *Teaching:* Assistantship drawing & painting, Univ Calif, Los Angeles, 67-69; art instr, Los Angeles Harbor Col, Wilmington, Calif, 69-86 & Los Angeles Valley Col, Van Nuys, Calif, 70-89. *Awards:* Pick of the Week, Los Angeles Weekly, 85. *Bibliog:* Merle Schipper (auth), Randye Sandel, Images & Issues, 10/83; Appreciating Art (documentary), Financial News Network, Cable TV, 10/90; Ray Zone (auth), Randye Sandel, Art Scene, 4/96. *Media:* Oil Painting, Oil Pastel Drawing. *Publ:* Contrib, Moon in Capricorn, Dreamworks, 82, Dream Landscapes, Dreamworks, 83, Southwest Dream Landscapes, Dreamworks, 86, Human Sci Press Inc; Art Scene, D'Art, 98. *Dealer:* Sherry Frumkin Gallery 2525 Michigan Ave Unit I Bergamont Sta Santa Monica CA 90404

SANDELMAN, JONATHAN (JON) E
PATRON
Study: Adelphia Univ, BA; Cardozo Sch Law, JD. *Pos:* Deputy head global equities, managing dir, equity derivatives Salomon Brothers, formerly; head equity fin, prod NationsBank (now Bank Am Securities), New York City, 98-2002; head equities, Bank Am Securities LLC, 2002-04, pres, 2004-, head debt & equities, 2004-. *Mem:* Whitney Mus Am Art (trustee, currently). *Mailing Add:* Bank of Am Securities LLC 9 W 57th St New York NY 10019

SANDEN, JOHN HOWARD
PAINTER, INSTRUCTOR
b Austin, Tex, Aug 6, 35. *Study:* Minneapolis Sch Art, BFA, 56; Art Students League, New York; Houghton Col, DFA, 94. *Work:* US Capitol & NASA Hq, Washington, DC; Fifth Ave Presby Church & New York Univ, NY; Royal Palace, Oyo, Nigeria. *Pos:* Pres & found, Portrait Inst, New York, 74-; chmn & found, Nat Portrait Sem, 79-. *Teaching:* Instr, Art Students League, 71-. *Awards:* John Singer Sargent Medal, Am Soc Portrait Artists, 94. *Bibliog:* Doreen Mangan (auth), Portrait of a portraitist, Am Artist Mag, 3/75; Joe Singer (auth), Painting Men's Portraits, Watson-Guptill, 76 & 77; Eunice Agar (auth), John Howard Sanden, Am Artist Mag, 11/83. *Mem:* Leading Am Portrait Painters (coun mem). *Media:* Oil. *Publ:* Auth, Painting The Head in Oil, 76 & Successful Portrait Painting, 81, Watson-Guptill. *Dealer:* Portraits Inc 985 Park Ave New York NY 10028; Portraits South 4008 Barrett Dr Raleigh NC 27609. *Mailing Add:* 100 Cains Hill Rd Ridgefield CT 06877

SANDER, SHERRY SALARI
SCULPTOR
b McCloud, CA, July 16, 41. *Work:* Denver Zoo, Denver, Colo; Nat Mus of Wildlife Art, Jackson, Wyo; City of Bend, Bend, Ore; Okla City Zoo, Oklahoma City, Okla; Benson Park Sculpture Garden, Loveland, Colo; Leanin' Tree Mus Western Art, Boulder, Colo; Buffalo Bill Mus, Cody, Wyo; Genesee Country Mus, Mumford, NY; Gerald Ford Amphitheater, Vail, Colo; High Desert Mus, Bend, Ore; Leigh Yawkey Woodson Art Mus, Wausau, Wis; Big Sky Resort, Huntley Lodge, Big Sky, Mont; Kentucky Dept Fish & Wildlife Resources, Frankfort, Ky; Int Mus Contemp Masters Fine Art, San Antonio, Tex. *Comn:* Grizzly Monumental, Big Sky of Montana, Big Sky, Mont, 1990; Whitetail Deer Monumental, Private Party, Aspen, Colo, 1995. *Exhib:* Birds in Art, Leich Yawkey Woodson Art Mus, Wausaw, Wis, 1990, 1992, 1994-1996, 1998-1999; Rendezvous '95, Thomas Gilcrease Mus, Tulsa, Okla, 1995; 100 Years of NSS of USA in Italy, Palazzo Mediceo, Seravezza, Italy, 1998; Masterworks of Am Sculpture, Fleischer Mus, Scottsdale, Ariz, 1999; Wildlife Art for a New Century II, Nat Mus of Wildlife Art, Jackson, Wyo, 2005. *Pos:* Juror, CM Russell Auction, 1980; Juror, Society of Animal Artists, NY, 1993. *Teaching:* Instr, Scottsdale Artists Sch, Scottsdale, Ariz, 1989. *Awards:* Gold Medal, Nat Acad of Western Art (NAWA), 1983; Best of Show, CM Russell Auction, CM Russell Mus, 1988; Purchase Award, Patron's Choice, Int Masters, Int Mus of Contemp Masters, 2002. *Bibliog:* Greenhouse Gallery (auth), Leading Ladies Part I, Am Art Collector,

2006; Joan Brown (auth) Sculptor Creates a Wildlife Haven, Wildlife Art, 2006; Vickie Stavig (auth), Magical Medium, Art of the West, 2006. *Mem:* Allied Artists of Am; Nat Acad of Western Art (NAWA); Nat Sculpture Soc; Soc of Animal Artists. *Media:* Metal, Cast (Bronze). *Mailing Add:* PO Box 5448 Kalispell MT 59903-5448

SANDERS, JOOP A
PAINTER
b Amsterdam, Holland, Oct 6, 1921; US citizen. *Study:* Art Students League, with George Grosz; also with De Kooning. *Work:* Stedelijke Mus, Amsterdam; Munic Mus, The Hague; Belzalel Mus, Jerusalem; Dillard Univ. *Exhib:* Ninth St Show, 51; Stable Shows, 52-55; one-man retrospective, Stedelijke Mus, 60; Carnegie Inst, 60; Options, Mus Contemp Art, Chicago, 68; one-man show, Alfred Kren Gallery, NY, 86; Gallery Biderman, Munich, Ger, 92. *Teaching:* Vis lectr, Carnegie Inst Technol, spring 65; prof painting, State Univ NY Col, New Paltz, 66-; vis lectr, Univ Calif, Berkeley, spring 68. *Awards:* Longview Found Fel, 60-61; Carnegie Inst Technol Res Found Awards, 71-72. *Media:* Oil, Acrylic. *Mailing Add:* 157 Lake Dr Lake Peekskill NY 10537

SANDERS, RHEA SANDERS RABINOVICH
PAINTER, WRITER
b Charleston, SC, Nov 6, 23. *Study:* With Maurice Sterne, 40-44; Pratt Graphics, NY, 83; Cooper Union Sch Continuing Educ, New York, 92. *Work:* High Mus, Atlanta, Ga; Univ SC, Columbia; British Mus Libr, London; Rare Bks Collection, New York Pub Libr; Gibbes Art Mus, Charleston, SC; and others. *Exhib:* NY Tech Col, Brooklyn, 93; First Street Gallery, NY, 94; Ctr for Book Arts, NY, 94; Members Gallery, Albright-Knox Mus, Buffalo, NY, 94; Made by Hand, NGO Forum on Women, Beijing, 95; Juried Arts Competition, Jacques Marchais Mus Tibetan Art, Staten Island, NY, 95; New Work, First St Gallery, NY, 96; and others; NY Pub Libr, 1997; Saho 20 Gallery, New York City, 2000; Prince St Gallery, New York City, 2000; Biennial 2001, Flushing Town Hall, 2001; Queens Community Col, New York City, 2002; Snug Harbor Cult Ctr, NY, 2002; LaGuardia Community Col, Queens, NY, 2002; Berliner Kunsthalle, Berlin, Ger, 2002; NY Pub Libr, NY, 2002; Prince Street Gallery, NY, 2004. *Awards:* Artist Space Grant, 80, 83; Orgn Independant Artists Grant, 80; Visual Artists Fel Grant, Nat Endowment Arts, 85; Resident Fel, Karolyi Found, Vence, France, 89; Resident Fel, Mishkenot Sha'ananim, Jerusalem, Israel, 93. *Media:* Miscellaneous Media. *Publ:* Auth & illusr, The Fire Gardens of Maylandia, Tradd St Press, 80; Lecture on Egg Tempera (film), Paragon Cable, New York, 90; Rhea Sanders Talks About Her Solo Show (film), Paragon Cable, New York, 94; auth & illusr, At Ravemel 1927, 83. *Dealer:* Prince Street Gallery 530 W 25th St 4th Flr New York NY 10001. *Mailing Add:* 617 W End Ave New York NY 10024-1607

SANDERSON, CHARLES HOWARD
PAINTER, EDUCATOR
b Hamilton, Kans, Mar 6, 25. *Study:* Kans State Univ; Emporia State Univ, Kans; Wichita State Univ, BS(art educ); Ft Hays State Univ, Kans, MS(art educ). *Work:* Wichita Art Mus, Kans; Springfield Art Mus, Mo; Hockaday Ctr for the Arts, Kalispell, Mont; Birger Sandzen Mem Gallery, Lindsborg, Kans; Wichita Ctr Arts; and others. *Comn:* Faceted stained glass windows, Ascension Lutheran Church, Wichita, kans, 80; five piece mural, Central State Bank, Junction City, Kans, 86. *Exhib:* One-man show, Wichita Art Mus, Kans, 65-80; Sanderson-Booty Exhib, Galerie Monti-Carlo, Charleroi, Belg, 72; Am Painters in Paris, France, 76; Watermedia Nat, Kalispell, Mont, 85; Rocky Mountain Nat, Golden, Colo, 86; and others. *Collection Arranged:* Group Two--Invitational Kans Exhib, Century II Concert Hall Foyer, Wichita, 72-75; Kans Watercolor Soc Five-State. *Teaching:* Instr art, Kans Pub Schs, 51-85; instr painting, Wichita Art Asn, Kans, 58-71; instr teaching methods, Friends Univ, Wichita, 68-74; lectr & instr, Kans Art Educators Workshop, Wichita, 72-75; instr watercolor, Wichita State Univ Continuing Educ, 75-81, asst prof art, 85-. *Awards:* Kans Watercolor Soc Tri-State Exhib Award, 70-73, 75-76 & 80-81; Kans Watercolor Soc Spec Juror's Award, Wausau Wis Festival of Art, 88; Kans Gov's Art Award, 88. *Bibliog:* Watercolor, Acrylic, Sculpture & Demonstration (four educ videotapes), Wichita Bd of Educ, 77; Eileen O'Hara (auth), The painter and the business manager, Wichitan Mag, 5/81; feature article, Wichita Eagle Beacon, 4/85; Best of Kansas Art & Craft, Kansas Dept of Commerce, 88. *Mem:* Founder Kans Watercolor Soc (pres, 71-72, 79-86 & 89); Wichita Artists Guild; Whiskey Painters Am; Kans Cult Trust, Scholastic Art Awards Comt. *Media:* Watercolor, Acrylic. *Mailing Add:* 902 Waddington Ave Wichita KS 67212-4158

SANDERSON, WARREN
ART HISTORIAN, LECTURER, ARCHIT
b Boston, Mass, Feb 9, 31. *Study:* Boston Univ, MA, 56; NY Univ Inst Fine Arts, PhD, 65. *Pos:* Pres Emer, Can Nat Comt of Int Comt of Hist of Art (Paris); pres asn Villard de Honnecourt for the Interdisciplinary Study of (Medieval) Sci, Tech & Art (Avista, 1992-2000; pres asn for Art Hist, 2001-2002. *Teaching:* Prof hist art & archit, Univ Ill, Chicago, 66-70; prof art hist & criticism, Concordia Univ, Montreal, 76-2006; vis prof art hist, Univ Trier, Ger, 77, 78 & 83; vis prof archit hist, Univ Cologne, Ger, 89; vis scholar, Harvard Fine Arts, 90. *Awards:* Fulbright Fel, 66, 82, 83; Deutsche Forschungsgemeinschaft, 77, 78 & 83; Can Coun Award, 80, 86-89, 96-99; Thyssen Found Award. *Bibliog:* Jeffrey Horrell (auth), article, Art Doc, 10/82; Diane Kay (auth), article, Art Int, 1/3/83; Elaine Cohen (auth), Sharing the joy & discovery of fine works of art, Suburban, 9/28/83; Nigel Hiscock (auth) The Wise Master Builder: Platonic Geometry in Cathedrals, Ashgate Publ (in Speculum), 2002-2004. *Mem:* Soc Archit Historians; Int Comt Hist Art (pres emer, Can Sect); Univ Arts Asn Can; Asn Art Hist (pres 99-01); Col Art Asn Am; Asn Villard d'Honnecourt for Interdisciplinary Study of Medieval Sci, Technology & Art (pres 92-2000). *Res:* Western art and architecture; Carolingian & Ottonian; art and architecture since 1950. *Interests:* Politics, Edn, Scis, Art, Music. *Publ:* Coauth, Hommage--Joseph Beuys 1986, Vie Des Arts, 87; auth, Considerations on the Ottonian Monastic Church of Saint Maximin at Trier, Baukunst Des Mittelalters in Europa Hans Erich Kubach Zum Ft Geburtstag, 89; Art Et Hyperactivite Un perspective Tres Visuelle, Prisme (Psychiatrie, Recherche et Intervention en Sante Mentale de L'enfant), Montreal 93; Early Christian Buildings, 300-600, Astrion Publ, 94; auth, Carolingian, Ottonian & Romanesque Buildings, 760-1130, Astrion Publ, in prep; auth, The Plan of St Gall Reconsidered, in Speculum, A Journal of Medieval Studies (Cambr.MA) 60/3, p615-632, 85; auth, Medieval rchitecture and Liturgy 750-1400, in Macmillan Dictionary of Art, Lodon, 96; auth, Carolingian Aachen., in Avista Forum Journal, 13/1, p1-14 / 8 illus, 01; auth Geometry on a Carolingian Wall, chapter 1 in Ad Quadratum: Practical Application of Geometry in Medieval Architecture, Ashgate Publ, London, 02; auth, The Practical Application of Geometry in Medieval Architecture, Nancy Wu (ed), Ashgate Publ, London, 2002; auth, Monastic Architecture and tech Gorze Reforms Reconsidered, chapter 4 in The White Mantle of Churches.Around the Millenium, Ashgate Publ, UK, 03. *Mailing Add:* 107 Covington Lane Shelburne VT 05482

SANDGROUND, MARK BERNARD, SR
COLLECTOR, PAINTER
b Boston, Mass, June 6, 32. *Study:* Univ Mich, BA, 52; Univ Va, LLB, 55, JD, 71 & PhD, Johnson & Wales Univ, 2000. *Work:* The First Chartered Collection, Cracked Eggshells from Pacifica, Delmura Art Inst, 2004. *Exhib:* Hard on the Cutting Room floor, demonstration of film gastronomics, 92. *Pos:* chmn, The Orient House, Istanbul, Turkey, 2000. *Teaching:* Prof humanities & cooking, Free Col, Belgravia, Lower Sch, 65-66; lectr, Johnson & Wales Univ, RI. *Awards:* Star of Mex 1992; Order of the Grand Papal Soc for Peace & Friendship, Columbia, 92; Order of the Grand Enchalata, Mex, 93. *Bibliog:* D Kane (auth), Killer Kane and the White Princess, McGraw, 72; The Gypsie princess (film), Anon, 72. *Mem:* Friends of Corcoran Gallery Art (bd dir, 67-, pres, 68-70); Osuna Gallery Inc, Washington, DC & Miami, Fla. *Res:* Graphic works of Jose Louis Cuevas. *Specialty:* Masterpieces from Eastern Shore, Oil on Crab Shells; Unique Collection of paintings and recipies. *Collection:* Cuevas, Rico Lebrun & Anne Truitt. *Publ:* Auth, Collected letters from unknown artists, 1846-1871, private publ, 52; Erotica from the Falls Church Collection, 72; Specialties at The Sign of The Whale, 92. *Mailing Add:* Suite 600 8000 Towers Crescent Dr Vienna VA 22180

SANDLER, BARBARA
PAINTER
b New York, NY, Sept 14, 43. *Study:* Art Students League, George Bridgeman scholar, 63, also with Edwin Dickenson & Robert Beverly Hale. *Work:* Mus Mod Art, NY; Chicago Art Inst; Joseph Hirshhorn Mus, Washington, DC; Chase Manhattan Bank; Manufacturers Hanover Trust; Hearst Corp; Royal Saudi Arabian Naval Base; Dance Collection Lincoln Ctr. *Comn:* Poster & lithograph for Bicentennial, Spec Proj Group, Chicago, 75; posters, Circle in the Square Theatre, NY, 77-78; covers for Harpers & Sat Rev Mag; var record covers for Columbia & Verve Records; poster PBS Mobil Oil Mystery Series. *Exhib:* one-person shows, Segal Gallery, NY, 81 & 83-85, Mary Martin Gallery, Aspen, Colo, 83, Trabia-Macafee Gallery, 89, The Ctr Show, 89, Art in Embassies-US State Dept, 89 & Dance Collection Lincoln Ctr, 91; Micro '83 Int Exhib, Stockholm, Sweden, 83; Zeus Trabia Gallery, 86; group exhib, Art in General, 93; group exhib, Lennon Weinbers, 94. *Awards:* Elizabeth T Greenshields Mem Found Grant, 74. *Bibliog:* Articles, Archit Digest, 2/76, Print Mag, 79, Graphis Mag, 80, Arts Mag, 5/83, 5/84, 4/86 & 5/89, Downtown Mag, 12/86, Village Voice, 89, NY Native, 89 & Dance Mag, 1/89. *Media:* Oil, Graphite. *Publ:* Illusr, The Long View, Knopf, 74; Indian Oratorio, Ballantine Bks, 75; contribr, Super Realism, Dutton, 75. *Mailing Add:* 221 W 20th St New York NY 10011

SANDLER, IRVING HARRY
CRITIC, HISTORIAN
b New York, NY, July 22, 1925. *Study:* Temple Univ, BA, 48; Univ Pa, MA, 50; NY Univ, PhD, 76. *Pos:* Art critic, Art News, 56-62 & NY Post, 60-65; contrib ed, Art Am, 72. *Teaching:* Instr art hist, NY Univ, 60-71; prof, State Univ NY Col Purchase, 71-. *Awards:* Tona Shepherd Fund Grant Travel in Ger & Austria; Guggenheim Found Fel, 65; Nat Endowment Humanities Fel, 80. *Bibliog:* Jay Jacobs (auth), Of myths and men, Art Am, 3-4/70; Rosalind Constable (auth), The myth of the myth-makers, Washington Post Bk World, 11/29/70; Gesture makers and colourfieldsmen, Times Lit Suppl, 6/8/71. *Mem:* Int Asn Art Critics (pres, Am Section, 70-75); Col Art Asn Am (bd dir, 86); Artists Space (co-founder, 73). *Res:* American art since 1930. *Publ:* Auth, The New York School: Painters and Sculptors of the Fifties, Harper & Row, 78; Alex Katz, Abrams, 79; Al Held, Hudson Hills, 84; American Art of the 1960s, 88; Mark di Suvero, 96. *Mailing Add:* SUNY Purchase Col Humanities Div 735 Anderson Hill Rd Purchase NY 10577-1400

SANDLIN, DAVID THOMAS
PAINTER, PRINTMAKER
b Belfast, N Ireland, Nov 9, 1956. *Study:* Univ Ala, Birmingham, BA, 79. *Work:* Gallery X, Kansas City; Chase Manhattan Bank, NY. *Exhib:* Birmingham Art Asn Show, Birmingham Mus, 79 & 80; Excerpts from East Village, Va Beach Arts Ctr, 84; Innocence and Experience, Greenville Co Mus, 85; New Work from NY, Barbara Farber Gallery, Amsterdam, The Neth, 85; Painting and Sculpture 1986, Indianapolis Mus, 86; Prints, Pub and Pvt 1986, Brooklyn Mus, 86; Focus NY, Moos Art Gallery, Miami, 86; Investigations, McIntosh-Drysdale Gallery, Washington, DC, 86; solo exhibs, Kwok Gallery, NY, 83, Gracie Mansion Gallery, NY, 84-86 & Brunswick Gallery, Missoula, Mont, 85. *Pos:* Founding mem, Print Co-op, NY, 80-81. *Teaching:* Mgr, printmaking shop, Sch Visual Arts, 82-, teacher lithography, 85-. *Awards:* Jurors Award, Birmingham Art Asn, Birmingham Mus, 79. *Bibliog:* M Brenson (auth), rev, New York Times, 85; M Cone (auth), Prints about prints, Print Collectors Newslett, 85; D Rubey (auth), Sarcastic quotations, Arts Monthly, 85. *Media:* All. *Mailing Add:* 58 E First St New York NY 10003

SANDMAN, ALAN
SCULPTOR, PUBLISHER
b New York, NY, Nov 1, 47. *Study:* Self taught. *Work:* Community Gallery Art, Santa Fe Community Col, Gainesville, Fla. *Comn:* Fountain sculpture, C Beville Landscape Designer, 78; Univ Lutheran Church, 78. *Exhib:* Solo exhibs, Santa Fe Community Col, 75, Springdale Park, Atlanta, 79 & DeKalb Community Col, Clarkson, Ga, 86; Great Garden Sculpture Show (with catalog), Atlanta Botanical Garden, Sculptural Arts Mus, 82; Sculpture Tour (with catalog), Univ Tenn, Knoxville, 85 & 86; Sculpture Tour (with catalog), Walters State Community Col, Morristown, Tenn, 86-87; Sculpture to Touch, Martin Luther King Libr for the Blind (with printed & braille catalogs), Washington, 87. *Pos:* Bd mem, Atlanta Artworks Coalition, 79-82, pres, 80-82; visual arts chmn, Decatur Arts Fest, 87; System operator/publisher, ARTLINK7, 88-91; Co-founder, Decatur Arts Alliance, 87. *Awards:* Exhib Grant, Atlanta Bur Cult Affairs, 79. *Bibliog:* Larry Smith (auth), Sculptor Uses Live Models, Gainesville Sun, 10/12/75; Grant Carrington (auth), Shapes in Stone, Vol 2, No 21, New Look, 10/15/75; Metro Scenes, Atlanta Constitution, 10/18/84. *Media:* Cast, Stone. *Publ:* Artlink (auth), Leonardo Jour. of Internat Soc Arts, 91; Illustration HO-1, The Sculptor's Bible, Quarto, Inc, 2005. *Dealer:* Art Int 394 Fourth St Atlanta GA 30308. *Mailing Add:* PO Box 5595 Atlanta GA 31107

SANDMAN, JO
PHOTOGRAPHER, ENVIRONMENTAL ARTIST
b Boston, Mass, Mar 22, 31. *Study:* Brandeis Univ, AB, 52; with Hans Hofmann, Provincetown and NY, 52-53; Hunter Col, with Robert Motherwell, 53; Univ Calif, Berkeley, MA(art), 54; Radcliffe Col, MAT, 56. *Work:* Addison Gallery Am Art; Dallas Mus Fine Arts; NY Univ; Mass Inst Technol; Portland Mus of Fine Art, Oregon Rose Mus, OR; Brandeis Univ, MA; Seattle Mus Art, Seattle, WA. *Comn:* Video piece for TV, Nat Endowment Arts, Rockefeller Found & Mass Coun Arts, Boston, 75; Removal Drawing, Bicentennial Painting Comn, Boston 200, 75. *Exhib:* Flush with the Walls, Mus Fine Arts, Boston, 71; Drawings from Two NY Galleries, Va Mus Fine Arts, (traveling), 73-75; solo exhibs, Addison Gallery Am Art, Phillips Acad, Andover, Mass, 74, Stux Gallery, Boston, 81 & 83, O K Harris Works of Art, NY, 73, 75, 82 & 94, 2001, Grey Art Gallery, NY Univ, NY, 78, Group Gallery, Provincetown, Mass, 83, 84 & 85, DeCordova Mus, (installation) Lincoln, Mass, 86 & Mobius, Boston, Mass, 88 & Thomas Segal Gallery, 89; On the Wall (installation), Inst Contemp Art, Boston, 76; Prospectus: Art in the Seventies, Aldrich Mus Contemp Art, Ridgefield, Conn, 79; Addison Gallery Am Art, Andover, Mass, 81; Boston Now: Abstract Painting, 81 & Boston Now: Works on Paper, Inst Contemp Art, Boston, 88; Andrea Marquit Gallery, Boston, 94 & 95; and many others; Gallery Kayafas, Boston 2003; New Eng Sch of Art & Design, Boston 2002; Mercer Gallery, NY. *Teaching:* Vis artist, lectr & critic painting, various art sch & col, 56-. *Awards:* Sculpture Fel, Mass Coun on Arts & Humanities, 84; Citation for Excellence, Boston Soc Architects, 90; 2nd place, Best Mid-career Show, IAAC, Boston, MA. *Bibliog:* Cate McQuaid, Two Artists Explore Their X-Ray Vision, Boston Globe, July 2003; D Lynne Plummer (auth), Fragility Caught on Film, South End News, July 2003; Robert C Morgan (auth), Jo Sandman: The Elusive Image, Provincetown Arts, 2001. *Media:* Miscellaneous. *Specialty:* photography. *Dealer:* Gallery Kayafas 450 Harrison Ave Boston MA 02118. *Mailing Add:* 1 Fitchburg St Studio C-507 Somerville MA 02143

SANDOL, MAYNARD
PAINTER
b Newark, NJ, 1930. *Study:* Newark State Col, 52; also with Robert Motherwell. *Work:* Newark Mus Art; Wadsworth Atheneum, Hartford, Conn; Princeton Univ, NJ; Finch Col Mus, NY; Joseph Hirshhorn Collection, Washington, DC; also pvt collections. *Comn:* Dr John Murray, CLinton, NJ; Salvitore & Sandra Tobia, Toms River, NJ. *Exhib:* Corcoran Gallery of Art, Washington, DC; Mus Mod Art, NY; NJ Pavilion, NY World's Fair; NJ State Mus, Trenton; NJ Masters, 1980; and others. *Teaching:* instr, US Army, 53-55; tchr, art, Newark Pub Schs, NJ, 55-56, East Paterson, NJ, 65-67; instr art hist, Farleigh Dickinson Univ, Madison, 65-67, Co Col Morris, NJ, 81, 82; tchr art & humanities, Hackettstown High Sch, NJ, 64-98. *Bibliog:* William H Gerdts, Jr (auth), Paintings and Sculpture in New Jersey, Van Nostrand, 64. *Media:* Oil, Acrylic. *Dealer:* Stanley Gallery Livingston NJ. *Mailing Add:* 2073 N Barrington Dr Fayetteville AR 72701-3061

SANDOVAL, ARTURO ALONZO
EDUCATOR, WEAVER
b Española, NMex, Feb 1, 42. *Study:* Univ Portland, Oreg, 59; Calif State Univ, Los Angeles, with Virginia Hoffman & Michael Schrier, BA, 64, MA, 69; Cranbrook Acad Art, with Richard Devore, Robert Kidd & Gerhardt Knodel, MFA, 71. *Work:* Mus Mod Art, Design & Archit, NY; Smithsonian Inst Art, Renwick Gallery, DC; Rocky Mt Quilt Mus, Golden, Colo; Mus of Art and Design, NY; Nat Hispanic Cult Ctr, Albuquerque, NMex; Cityscape No 6, JB Speed Art Mus, Louisville, Ky, 2000; others. *Comn:* fiber art quilt, Citizens Fidelity Bank & Trust, Louisville, Ky, 90; fiber art quilt, Fed Reserve Bank, Cincinnati, Ohio, 91; fiber art, UFCW of the AFL/CIO, Washington, 92; The Atlanta Clock (with Aaron Alvic Schroeder), Atlanta Hartsfield Airport, 99; Sparkle, Horsemania, Lexington Arts and Cult Coun, Lexington, Ky, 2000; GSA, AIA, 6th District Courthouse, London, Ky. *Exhib:* Pacesetters and Prototypes, Detroit Inst Art, 73; Textiles: Past & Prologue, Greenville Co Mus Art, SC, 76; 8th Int Biennial Tapestry, Mus Cantonal des Beaux Arts, Lausanne, Suisse, 77; New Acquisitions: Design Collection, Mus Modern Art, NY, 79; Art Fabric: Mainstream, Mus Mod Art, San Francisco, Calif, 81; one-man show, J B Speed Art Mus, Louisville, Ky, 81, Indianapolis Art Ctr, Ind, 2000, Commonwealth Int Conv Ctr, Louisville, Ky, 2000, Wingspan Gallery, Lexington, Ky, 2000, Cult Arts Gallery, Indianapolis, Ind, 2002, Cult Arts Gallery, Indianapolis, Ind, 2002, Southwest Art and Craft Ctr, San Antonio, Tex, 2003 & Cerlan Gallery, Lexington, Ky, 2003; 8 State Crafts, J B Speed Art Mus, Louisville, Ky, 84, New Works/New Artists IV, 89; one-man retrospective, Network Gallery, Cranbrook Acad Art Alumni Art Space, Pontiac, Mich, 98, Art Mus, Univ Ky, Lexington, 98, Columbus State Univ, Ga, 99, Campbell Hall Gallery, Western Ore Univ, Monmouth, 99, Reed Gallery, Univ Cincinnati, Ohio, 2000, St Louis Community Col, Mo, 2001 & La Col, Pineville, 2003; 3rd Ann Renaissance Regional, Visual Arts Gallery, Renaissance Ctr, Dickson, Tenn, 2001; Ahora, Visual Arts Galleries, Albuquerque, NMex, 2002; Homage to 911, Cerlan Gallery, Lexington, Ky, 2002; Breaking from Tradition: Quilt Explorations, Mus Am Quilter's Soc, Paducah, Ky, 2003; others. *Pos:* freelance designer & illusr, Western Lighting Corp, Los Angeles, 64; supervisor, Carding Mill, Edison Inst, Dearborn, Mich, 71; cur, Bernhart Gallery, Univ Ky, Lexington, 79, Student Ctr, Lexington, 84, State Capitol, Frankfort, Ky, 84; co-cur, Chanlder Medica Ctr, Lexington, Ky, 91; bd dir, Lexington Arts and Cultural Ctr, Ky, 2002. *Teaching:* teaching asst, Calif State Univ, Los Angeles, 68 & 69, instr, 70; instr, Sch Art and Design, Southern Ill Univ, Carbondale, 71, asst prof, head weaving/textiles prog, Col Commun and Fine Arts, Ewardsville, Ill, 71-74; from asst prof to assoc prof, Col Arts and Scis, Univ Ky, Lexington, 74-86, head fiber prog, 76-present, prof, 86-, acting dir undergrad studies, 88. *Awards:* Craftsman's Fel, Nat Endowment Arts, 73, Visual Arts Fel, 92; Al Smith Fel, Ky Arts Coun, 87; NEA Artist Residency, Pyramid Atlantic, 96; Al Smith Profl Svc Award, Ky Arts Coun, Frankfort, Ky, 97; Rude Osolnik Award, Ky Craft Mktg Program, and the Ky Art and Craft Found, Frankfort, 97; First place, Reverse Raffle, Lexington Art League, Ky, 99; Ky Gov Artist Award, 2003. *Bibliog:* Art Jester (auth), Faith and values: crown jewel, Lexington Herald-Leader, 02/14/2001; Christine Zoller (auth) Local talk, southeast, Surface Design Newsletter, Vol 14, No 2, 2001, Vol 15, No 2, 2002; Charles Talley (auth), Sandoval's Double Terrorist - deja vu all over again?, Friends Fiber Art Int, 4/2002. *Mem:* Am Craft Coun; Surface Design Asn; Ky Guild Artists and Craftsmen; Fiber Guild Lexington; Ky Mus Art & Craft (cur, 85); Louisville Visual Arts Asn. *Media:* Non-Woven Materials, Mylar. *Res:* Active investigation in using recycled industrial linear tapes, films and cables in the creation of mixed media art works. *Specialty:* Fine arts and craft work. *Collection:* textiles from around the world. *Publ:* Coauth, The creative process, Fiberarts, 48-50, 11-12/1983; auth, The Artist as Revelator, Fiberarts/Lark Press, 1/2 90; coauth, Quilt National: The Best Contemporary Quilts, Lark Books, 2001. *Dealer:* Linda Schwartz Gallery PO Box 120188 Covington KY 41012-0188; Cerlan Gallery 522 W Short St Lexington KY 40508. *Mailing Add:* 509 Quail Run Lexington KY 40517-2009

SANDROW, HOPE
PHOTOGRAPHER
b Philadelphia, Pa, Dec 31, 51. *Study:* Philadelphia Col Art, 72-75. *Work:* Metrop Mus Art; Baltimore Mus Art; Houston Mus Fine Arts; Minn Mus Art; Henry Art Gallery, Mus Mod Art. *Comn:* Dakis Joannou, Athens, Greece, 87; Artforum Maga, 90; Vera List, 92; Artist in the Community, Southeastern Ctr Contemp Art, 94; Material Matters, Creative Time, NY, 95. *Exhib:* Solo exhibs, Philadelphia Col Art, 84, Haggery Mus, Milwaukee, Wis, 86, Gracie Mansion Gallery (with catalog), NY, 86, 88, 89 & Southeastern Ctr Contemp Art (with catalog), 95, Whitney Mus (with catalog), Philip Morris, 98; Painting & Sculpture Today-Biennial, Indianapolis Mus, 86; Directions-Biennial (with catalog), Hirshhorn Mus, Washington, 86; The New Shape of Content, Whitney Mus Art (with catalog), 87; Photo on the Edge, Haggerty Mus, Milwaukee, 88; Am Photos of the 80s (with catalog), Nat Mus Am Art, Washington, 89, Sequence (con) Sequence, Blum Art Inst, Bard Col, 89; Fantasies, Fables & Fabrications, Herter Art Gallery, Univ Mass, 89-91; Grey Art Gallery, NY Univ, 91; Dia De Los Muertos, Alternative Mus, 91; Tradition & the Unpredictable, Houston Mus Art, 94. *Pos:* Founder & pres, Artist & Homeless Collaborative. *Awards:* Art Matters Award, 91; Manhattan Borough Pres Citation for Excellence in Arts, 91; Mayor Dinkins Superstar Award, 92; Govs Award Skowhegan Sch of Painting & Sculpture, 94; Nat Endowment Arts, Artists Fel, 90 & 94. *Bibliog:* Nina Felshin (ed), The Spirt of Art as Activism, Bay Press; Reading in Comtemporary Poetry, Dia Found, 88; Julia Ballerini (auth), Sequence con Sequence, Aperture, 89. *Mem:* Women's Action Coalition. *Media:* Photography, Mixed Media. *Publ:* Art Forum, 80 90 & 91; Art in Am, 84, 90, 93 & 94; Village Voice, 87, 89, 90, 93, 95, 97 & 98; Boston Review, 89; Flash Art, 10/91; Vogue, 91; and others. *Mailing Add:* 5 E 16th St New York NY 10003

SANDUSKY, BILLY RAY
PAINTER, PRINTMAKER
b Bowling Green, Ky, Oct 23, 45. *Study:* John Herron Sch Art, Ind Univ, BFA, 68, Tulane Univ, New Orleans, La, MFA, 70; Academia di Belle Arte, Florence, Italy, 75. *Work:* Midwest Mus Am Art, Elkhart, Ind; Evansville Mus Arts & Sci, Ind; South Bend Regional Mus Art, Ind; Santa Raparta Graphic Art Ctr, Florence; Tulane Univ, New Orleans; Wilfrid Laurier Univ, Waterloo, Ont, Can. *Exhib:* One-person shows, Palazzo Strozzi, Florence, 76, S Bend Art Ctr, 82 & 90 & Purdue Univ, Lafayette, Ind, 86; Ind Artists Show, Indianapolis Mus Art, 83; Realism Today, Mus Arts & Sci, Evansville, 85-86; La Grange National XI, Lamar Dodd Art Ctr, Ga, 86; Art USA, Grand Junction, Colo, 89; South Bend Regional Mus Art, 96; Colfax Cult Ctr, South Bend, 96. *Teaching:* Assoc prof painting, chmn dept art, St Mary's Col, Notre Dame, Ind, 80-. *Awards:* Saint Mary's Col Fac Teaching Grants, 90 & 94; Lilly Open Fel, Lilly Found, 92; 1st place Fine Arts, 4th Airbrush Excellence Nat Competition, Airbrush Action Mag; and others. *Mem:* Col Art Asn; Mid-Am Col Arts Asn (exec bd); Mid-Am Print Coun (exec bd). *Media:* Acrylic, Oil; Lithography, Etching. *Mailing Add:* St Mary's Col Art Dept Notre Dame IN 46556

SANDWEISS, MARTHA ANN
MUSEUM DIRECTOR
b St Louis, Mo, Mar 29, 54. *Study:* Harvard Univ, BA, 75; Nat Endowment for Humanities Fel, Nat Portrait Gallery, Washington, 75-76; Yale Univ, MA, 77, Fel, Ctr Am Art & Mat Cult, 77-79, PhD, 85. *Collection Arranged:* A Knot of Dreamers: The Brook Farm Community, Nat Portrait Gallery, 76; Pictures from an Expedition: Early

Views of the American West (auth, catalog), Yale Univ Art Gallery, 78; Carlotta Corpron: Designer with Light (auth, catalog), 80; Masterworks of American Photography (auth, bk), 82; Carleton E Watkins: Photographer of the American West (introd, bk), Amon Carter Mus; 83; Carl Mydans, Amon Carter Mus, 85; Richard Avedon: In the American West, 85; Laura Gilpin: An Enduring Grace (auth, bk), Amon Carter Mus, 86; Eliot Porter (introd, bk), Amon Carter Mus. *Pos:* Cur photographs, Amon Carter Mus, Ft Worth, Tex, 79-86, adj cur photographs, 87-89; dir, Mead Art Mus, Amherst Col, 89. *Teaching:* Assoc prof Am studies, Amherst Col, currently. *Awards:* George Wittenborn Award, 87; Nat Endowment Humanities Fel for Independent Scholars, 88; Am Coun Learned Soc Fel, 96. *Publ:* Ed, Historic Texas: A Photograhic Portrait, Tex Monthly, 86; Contemporary Texas: A Photographic Portrait 86; coauth, Eyewitness to War: Prints and Daguerreotypes of the Mexican War, 1846-1848, Smithsonian Press, 89; ed & coauth, Photography in Nineteenth-Century America, Abrams, 91; co-ed, Oxford History of the American West, 94. *Mailing Add:* Amherst Col Mead Art Mus Amherst MA 01002

SANGIAMO, ALBERT
EDUCATOR, PAINTER
b Brooklyn, NY. *Study:* Brooklyn Col, AB; Yale Univ, BFA & MFA. *Work:* Baltimore Mus, Md. *Exhib:* Smithsonian Traveling Exhib Am Drawing, 65; one-man shows, Baltimore Mus, 69, Towson State Col, 71, Decker Art Gallery, Md, 75 & Md Arts Coun Traveling Show, 75. *Teaching:* Instr painting & drawing, Md Inst Col Art, 61-, chmn found dept, 61-73, chmn dept fine arts, 73-. *Awards:* Grand Prize, Baltimore Mus, 59; Purchase Prizes, St Paul Arts Ctr, 64. *Media:* Synthetic Charcoal, Acrylic. *Mailing Add:* 1715 Bolton St Baltimore MD 21217

SANGUINETTI, EUGENE F
ADMINISTRATOR, LECTURER
b Yuma, Ariz, May 12, 17. *Study:* Univ Santa Clara, BA, 39; Univ Ariz, 60-62. *Collection Arranged:* Selected Drawings from the Collection of Edward Jacobson, 70; Drawings by Living Americans, Objects from Buddhist Cultures & Etching Renaissance in France: 1850-1880, 71 (with catalog); Drawings by New York Artists (with catalog), Prehistoric Utah Petroglyphs & Pictographs & Ron Resch and the Computer, 72; Abraham Walkowitz Retrospective (with catalog), 74; plus other retrospectives & one-man exhibs. *Pos:* Dir, Tucson Mus & Art Ctr, Ariz, 64-67; dir, Utah Mus Fine Arts, Univ Utah, Salt Lake City, 67-; judge art shows, Colo, Utah & Idaho, 68-72, Bellevue & Seattle, Wash, 75. *Teaching:* Lectr art hist, Univ Ariz, 62-64; adj prof art, Univ Utah, 67-. *Mem:* Asn Am Mus; Western Asn Art Mus; Col Art Asn Am; Asn Archit Historians; Am Fedn Arts. *Res:* American art of the first half of the 20th century. *Specialty:* Paintings, tapestries and furniture from American and European periods; Oriental material; Egyptian and Cyprist antiquities; French and English objects and decoration. *Publ:* Contribr, Alexander H Wyant Retrospective, 68; contribr, John Marin Drawings Retrospective, 69; contribr, Alex Katz Retrospective, 71; contribr, Social Concern and the Worker: French Prints from 1830-1910, 73

SANIN, FANNY
PAINTER
b Bogota, Colombia, Nov 30, 38. *Study:* Univ Ill, 63; Univ Los Andes, Bogota, MFA, 60. *Work:* Nat Mus Women in the Arts, Washington, DC; New Orleans Mus Art; Mus of Art of the Americas, Washington, DC; Interamerican Development Bank, Washington, DC; Greater Lafayette Mus Art, W Lafayette, Ind. *Comn:* set for Walt Whitman's A Clear Midnight, Am Soc, NY. *Exhib:* Mus Fine Arts, Caracas, 67; Edinburgh Festival, Scotland, 67; Mus Modern Art, Mexico City, 79; Jersey City Mus 86; Mus Modern Art, Retrospective, Bogota, 87; Latin-Am Women Artists 1915-1995, Milwaukee Art Mus, 95; Colors: Contrasts & Cultures, Discovery Mus, Bridgeport, Conn, 97; Color and Symmetry-Retrospective, Luis Angel Arango Cult Ctr, Bogota, 2000; Mus of Abstract Art Manuel Felquerez, Zacatecas, Mex, 2001. *Awards:* Medellin Award, Colteger Internat Biennial, 70; Canadian Club Award, US Art Tour, NY, Canadian Club, 85; Colombia External Excellence Award, Miami, 2006. *Bibliog:* Margaret Barlow, Women Artists, Hugh Lauter Levin Asocs, 99; Robert Henkes, Latin Am Women Artists of the US, McFarland, 99; Nancy G Heller, Why a Painting is like a Pizza, Princeton Univ Press, 02. *Mem:* Nat Arts Club, NY. *Media:* Acrylic. *Dealer:* Andrea Marquit 71 Pinckney St Boston MA 02114; Latin Collector 37 W 57th St New York NY 10019; Alonso Garces Galeria, Cra 5 No 26 92, Bogota, Colombia. *Mailing Add:* 345 E 86th St Apt 17C New York NY 10028

SANSONE, JOSEPH F
CRAFTSMAN
b Mt Vernon, NY, Oct 20, 22. *Exhib:* Milton Glazer, Univ Minn, Minneapolis, 88; Frank Stella, Los Angeles; Richard Haas, San Francisco. *Pos:* Pres, Archit Wallcovering Inc, 60-; Painting & Decorating Contractors Am, 70-71. *Teaching:* Instr mural installation, various trade unions (CETA sponsored), 60-. *Awards:* First Prize, Painting & Decorating Contractors Am, 87, 88 & 89, Second Prize, 88. *Mem:* Painting & Decorating Contractors Am. *Publ:* Coauth, PWC Mag, Finan Publ, 70-90; coauth, American painter-decorator, Voss Publ, 70-90; coauth, Journal of Property Mgt, NAR, Chicago, 90. *Mailing Add:* 10846 N 34th Pl Phoenix AZ 85028

SAN SOUCIE, PATRICIA MOLM
PAINTER, INSTRUCTOR
b Minneapolis, Minn, Nov 4, 31. *Study:* Univ Wis, graphics with Warrington Colescott, John Wilde & Alfred Sessler, painting with Dean Meeker & Santos Zingale, BS(applied art), 53; NJ Ctr Vis Arts, NJ, painting. *Work:* Springfield Art Mus, Mo; Chattahoochee Art Mus, Ga; Butler, 85; and others. *Comn:* Casio Int Off, NJ & NY. *Exhib:* Am Watercolor Soc, 72-76; solo exhib, Acad Arts, Easton, Md, 83; Butler Inst Am Art, 86; Watercolor USA Hon Soc, 89-97. *Collection Arranged:* Invitational exhib at Parkland Col Art Gallery, Champaign, IL, State of the Art Exhib, Feb-Mar, 99, curated by Glenn Bradshaw,; Butler Inst of Am Art Midyear, 85; Touring exhibs in Chateau de Tours, France and Taiwan Art Mus, China; Cultural Exchange, Zheljiang Art Mus, Hangzhow, China, 94; Jane Voorhees Zimmerli Art Mus, New Brunswick, NJ,permanent collection, two watercolors, 94; Artists Collab Books Editions IV, V, VI in collections, Newark Mus and Mus of Modern Art Libr s, Artists Libr of the Victoria and Albert Mus, London, Nat Gallery of Art Libr, Washington; Chattahoochee Valley Art Mus, LaGrange, GA, 96; Southwestern WC Milan, Itlay Invitational Exchange, 2001; 40 Watercolorists Selected to show in irvine, IA & Milan Italy; Myrtle Beach, SC. *Pos:* Jury selection chmn, St Louis Artists Guild, 68-71; gallery exhib comt, Summit Art Ctr, NJ, 73-79; pres, NJ Watercolor Soc, 88-90; bd, Watercolor USA Honor Soc, 94-2003. *Teaching:* Instr, Princeton Art Asn, NJ, 75-76; fac mem, Summit Art Ctr, NJ, 83- & ARTWORKS, Trenton, NJ, 92-; instr numerous workshops, Kanuga, NC, Acapulco, Mex, Canada; Oregon College of Arts & Craft, Sitka Ctr of the Arts, Otis, OR. *Awards:* Walser Greathouse Award & Gold Medal, Am Watercolor Soc, 91; Arches Special Papers, Third Award, Ajomari Inc, 91; Ariz Aqueous Award for Excellence, Tubac Ctr Arts, 91, 98. *Bibliog:* Color section, Master Class in Watercolor, Edward Betts, 75; Watermedia Techniques for Releasing the Creative Spirit, Marilyn Hughey Phillis, 92; color inclusion, Splash I and II, Rachel Wolf, 93; How to Discover Your Personal Painting Style, David P Richards, 95; Abstracts, 96; Exploring Color II, Nita Leland, 98; How to Use and Control Color. *Mem:* Nat Watercolor Soc; Signature mem Am Watercolor Soc; Watercolor USA Honor Soc; AWS; Dolphin Fel; Northwest Watercolor Soc; NJW Watercolor Soc; Rocky Mountain Watercolor Soc; Watercolor Soc Oregon. *Media:* Watercolor, Gouache. *Interests:* Landscapes; Whimsies. *Publ:* Auth, article, Artists Mag, 1/91; auth, article, Watercolor, Fall, 97; auth, article, Watercolor Magic, Fall, 99; Beth Patterson (auth), Artists Mag, 2003. *Dealer:* Lawrence Gallery Rt 18 Sheridan OR; Howden Arts Gallery West Linn OR; The Attic Gallery Portland OR. *Mailing Add:* 11777 SE Timber Valley Dr Clackamas OR 97086-8388

SANT, VICTORIA P
MUSEUM DIRECTOR
Study: Stanford Univ, BA. *Pos:* Docent, Nat Gallery Art, Wash, DC, 83-85, chmn trustees coun, 2001—2002; pres, The Phillips Collection, 2003—; Co-founder, pres, Summit Found, Summit Fund of Wash, currently. *Mailing Add:* Summit Found Ste 525 2100 Pennsylvania Ave NW Washington DC 20037

SANTIAGO, RICHARD E
SCULPTOR, EDUCATOR
b Mar 29, 48. *Study:* Univ S Fla, Tampa, BA(art educ), 74, MA(art educ) 77; Univ Utah, Salt Lake City, MFA(sculpture), 84; studied with Stephen Antonakos, Sculptor, NY. *Work:* Tampa Mus Art & Berkeley Prep Sch, Tampa, Fla; First Fla Bank, Clearwater, Fla; Univ Utah, Mus Fine Arts, Univ Utah, Art Dept & Salt Lake City Art Ctr, Salt Lake City; Nora Eckles Harrison Mus Fine Art, Logan, Utah; also pvt collections of Stephen Antonakos, Peter Frank & James Whitecotton. *Exhib:* ASA Gallery, Albuquerque, NMex, 83; solo exhibs, Gittins Gallery, Salt Lake City, Utah, 83 & 84, Univ Utah, Mus Fine Arts, Salt Lake City, 83 & 84, Univ S Garage Gallery, Sarasota, Fla, 86, Fla Ctr Contemp Art, Tampa, 88, Michael Murphy Gallery, Tampa, Fla, 89, Fla Towers Bldg, Tampa, 90, Tampa Mus Art, Fla, 90 & C Company, Chicago, Ill, 91; Utah Arts Coun, Salt Lake City, 84; Bellair Art Ctr, Bellair, Fla, 87; Ridge Art Asn, Winter Haven, Fla, 87; The Arts Ctr, St Petersburg, Fla, 87, 88 & 92; Fla Ctr Contemp Art, Tampa, 87 & 88; PSA Architects Inc, St Petersburg, Fla, 89; N Miami Ctr Contemp Art, Fla, 91; PJC Gallery, Pensacola, Fla, 92. *Teaching:* Instr art, Hillsborough Co Pub Schs, Fla, 75-; instr design & sculpture, Univ Utah, Salt Lake City, 80-82 & 91. *Awards:* Emerging Artists Grant, Arts Coun Tampa/Hillsborough, Tampa, Fla, 89; Master Assoc, Atlantic Ctr Arts, New Smyrna Beach, Fla, 89; Individual Artist Fel, Fla Arts Coun, Div Cult Affairs, Tallahassee, Fla, 90. *Media:* Neon, Site Specific Installation. *Mailing Add:* 7107 N 18th St Tampa FL 33610-1257

SANTIAGO-IBARRA, BEATRICE MAYTE
EDITOR, CRITIC
b Santurce, PR, Feb 17, 49. *Study:* Univ PR, Rio Piedras, BA(comparative lit), 75; Centro de Estudios Avanzados, MA(lit & arts), 98. *Work:* Museo Casa del Rey, Dorado, PR; Arsenal de la Marina, Instituto de Puerto Rican Cultura & Museo las Americas, San Juan, PR, Museo Casa Alonso, Vega Baja, PR; Feria de Arte Contemporanio, Madrid, Spain. *Comn:* Cultural Doradina, Municipo de Dorado, PR, 85-86; Organizadora Brenal de San Juan, Instituto de Puerto Rican Cultura, PR, 86-98; Monumentos Turismo, Compania de Turismo, San Juan, PR, 88. *Pos:* Pub relations art, Univ Sacred Heart, 80-84; dir cult affairs, Casa del Rey, Dorado City Hall, 85-86; gen coordr, San Juan Print Biennial Latin Am & Caribbean Countries, Instituto Puerto Rican Cultura, 86-98; critic, 80-. *Teaching:* Prof, Acad Santa Teresito, 77-80; prof art & pub relations, Univ Sacred Heart, PR, 80-84. *Awards:* First Prize of Literature, Book of Poems, La Habana, Cuba, 74. *Bibliog:* Several articles in El Mundo Newspaper, 77-82. *Mem:* Am Asn Mus; Asn Art Critics. *Res:* Financial aspects supporting biennials. *Publ:* Auth, Siembra Para No Decir Adios (poetry), Taller Quinque, 71; En el Silencio de las Desgarradurcas (poetry) & El Asesinato de Casandra Ramirez (fiction), 86, Coqui-Zahori-Editorial. *Mailing Add:* Inst Puerto Rican Culture Apartado 9024184 San Juan PR 00949

SANTINI, DEBRAH A
PAINTER, PRINTMAKER
Study: Univ Mass, BFA(painting), 83, MFA(printmaking), 94; Pratt Inst, 83-84; Univ Hartford, MA Ed(printmaking), 88. *Work:* Gardiner Art Gallery, Okla State Univ, Stillwater; Agawam Pub Libr, Mass; Smith Col Rare Bk Room, Neilson Libr, Northampton, Mass; Dept Art, Ga Col, Milledgeville; and many others. *Exhib:* Solo exhibs, Univ Hartford, Conn, 87, Western New Eng Col, Springfield, Mass, 89, Springfield Cent Gallery, Mass, 88, Fitchburg Mus Fine Arts, Mass, 93 & Pioneer

Valley Reading Coun, Am Int Col, Springfield, Mass, 93; Third & Fourth Int Biennial Print Exhib, Taipei Mus Arts, Taiwan, Peoples Repub China, 88 & 90; Parkside Nat Small Print Exhib, Univ Wis, Kenosha, 91; Picture This: Children's Book Illustrators, Holyoke Children's Mus, Mass, 91; Cimarron Nat Award Winners Invitational Exhib, Okla State Univ, Stillwater, 92; Pressed and Pulled IV: The 4th Georgia Collage Printmaking Invitational Exhib, Milledgeville, 95; Art Alumni Exhib, Arno Maris Gallery, Westfield, Mass, 95; Image and Text, Steven F Austin Univ, Nacogdoches, Tex, 97; Southern Fedn Arts/Nat Endowment Arts Visual Arts Fel Exhib, Southeast Ctr Contemp Art, Winston-Salem, NC, 97; Teaching Art: Regional Fac Invitational, Columbus Mus, Ga, 98; Pressed & Pulled VII: 7th Ann Printmaking Invitational, Milledgeville, Ga, 98; Minn Nat Print Biennial, Univ Minn, Minneapolis, 98; Animal Stories, Woman Made Gallery, Chicago, Ill, 98; Printmaking Today, Visual Arts Alliance Nashville Am Pop Cult Gallery, Tenn, 98; and others. *Teaching:* Instr art, Granby Mem High Sch, Conn, 89-90 & Suffield High Sch, Conn, 90-91; adj prof, Univ Hartford, Conn, 91-92; Univ Mass, Amherst, 91-93; assoc prof, State Univ W Ga, Carrollton, 94-. *Awards:* Nat Endowment Arts/Southern Artists Fedn Grant, 96; Hon Men, Printmaking Today, Visual Arts Alliance Nashville, Tenn, 98; many purchase awards, 91-96. *Res:* Memories of Cappocietta Rossa. *Publ:* Illustr, The Bably Who Would Not Come Down, 89, Santa's Secret Helper, 90 & Tululips, 92, rev 96, Picture Bk Studio, Saxonville, Mass; Time to fly, US Kids Mag, Middleton, Conn, 91; When a friend dies, 91 & The strange disappearance of Mr Stone's lunch, 92, Cricket Mag, Peru, Ill; Cinderella, Boyds Mills Press, Honesdale, Pa, 94; The Last Dance, 95, Wishing, 97 & When Young Melissa Sweeps, 99, Peachtree Publ. *Mailing Add:* Univ West Georgia 1601 Maple St Carrollton GA 30118

SANTLOFER, JONATHAN
PAINTER
b New York, NY, Apr 26, 46. *Study:* Boston Univ, BFA, 67; Pratt Inst, MFA, studied with George McNeil, 69. *Exhib:* Solo exhibs, Inst Contemp Art, Tokyo, Japan, 78, 85 & 96, Ruth Bachofner Gallery, Los Angeles, Calif, 91, Galleria Peccolo, Italy, 92, James Graham & Sons, NY, 94, 98 & 01, Jim Kempner Fine Arts, NY, 98; Photographism (in painting), Pratt Manhattan Gallery, NY, 96; Portraits, James Graham & Sons, NY, 96; And I Quote, Pavel Zoubok at Mary Delahoyd Gallery, NY, 98; Pattern, James Graham & Sons, NY, 99; Portraits, Jim Kempner Fine Art, NY, 99; Waxing Poetic: Encaustic Art in Am, Montclair Art Mus, NJ, 99 & 2000; and others. *Teaching:* Instr art hist/studio, Jersey City State Col, NJ, 74-79; instr contemp art, The New Sch, New York, 76- Columbia Univ, 87-90; resident artist, Am Acad Rome, 89-90. *Awards:* Skowhegan Scholar, Summer Painting Grant, Skowhegan Sch of Painting & Sculpture, Maine, 67; Nat Endowment Arts Fel in Painting 81 & 89; Yaddo Fel, 95-99. *Bibliog:* Eleanor Moretta (auth), Photographism (exhib catalog), Pratt Galleries, NY, 96; Jonathan Goodman (auth), Jonathan Santlofer at James Graham & Sons & Jim Kempner Fine Art, Art in America, 4/99; Ken Johnson (auth), Jonathan Santlofer, The New York Times, 4/01. *Media:* Multimedia. *Dealer:* Graham Modern Gallery 1014 Madison Ave New York NY 10021; Jim Kempner Fine Arts 501 West 23 St New York NY 10011. *Mailing Add:* 151 W 28th St New York NY 10001

SANTORE, JOSEPH W
PAINTER
b Philadelphia, Pa, Dec 15, 45. *Study:* Philadelphia Col Art, BFA, 69; Univ Ariz, 70-71; Yale Univ, MFA, 73. *Exhib:* Solo exhibs, Yale Univ, 73, Edward Thorp Gallery, 82, 84, 87, 90 & 93, NY Studio Sch, 95, Philadelphia Art Alliance, Pa, 97 & Phoenix Art Mus, 2000; Whitney Biennial, Whitney Mus Am Art, 91; Leo Castelli Gallery, NY, 93; Skowhegan 93, Colby Col Mus Art, 93; Waterworks, Edward Thorp Gallery, NY, 94; Summer Group, Edward Thorp Gallery, NY, 94; 70th Ann Exhib of the Nat Acad Design, NY, 95; A Gift of Vision: The William and Susan Small Collection, Tucson Mus Art, Ariz, 95; Painting Faculty Exhib, NY Studio Sch, 96; Am Still Life, Aspen Art Mus, Colo, 96; The Figure Revisited, Gallery at Hasting-on-Hudson, NY, 97; Gallery Group Exhib, Edward Thorp Gallery, NY, 97 & 98; Contemp Selections from the Nat Acad at Silvermine, Silvermine Guild Galleries, New Canaan, Conn, 98; Drawing Plus One, NY Studio Sch, NY, 98; 174th Ann Exhib, Nat Acad Design, NY, 99; Kinds of Drawing: NY, NC, Western Carolina Univ, Cullowhee, NC, 99; The Figure: Another Side of Modernism, Newhouse Ctr Contemp Art, Snug Harbor, NY, 2000; and many others. *Teaching:* Fac, NY Studio Sch, New York City. *Awards:* John Simon Guggenheim Mem Fund Fel Grant, 88-89; Am Acad & Inst Arts & Letters Award, 89; Nat Endowment Arts Fel, 93-94. *Bibliog:* Haines Sprunt Tate (auth), At home with the paradoxical, the ambiguous and the random, Maine Times, 9/10/93; Eileen Watkins (auth), Review, Star-Ledger, 7/4/93; Alisa Tager (auth), Patrick Dunfey, Joseph Santore, Artnews, 9/93; Edward J Sozanksi (auth), Traditional fare rendered unconventionally, The Philadelphia Inquirer, 6/27/97; Karen Sandstrom (auth), Exhibit captures a place in memory, The Plain dealer, 4/30/98; Dorothy Shinn, Show disproves adage "Those who can't.", The Beacon Jour, 4/12/98. *Mem:* Am Acad & Inst Arts & Lett; Nat Acad (assoc, 93, acad, 94-)

SANTOS, ADELE NAUDE
ARCHITECT, URBAN DESIGNER
Study: Archit Asn, London, dipl, 61; Univ Pa, MArch & MP; Harvard, MArch in UD. *Pos:* Professorships grad prog at Harvard, Rice Univ & Univ Pa, chmn dept archit, 81-87; founding dean, Sch Archit, Univ Calif, San Diego, formerly; Univ Calif, Berkeley, 94-. *Awards:* Int design competitions. *Publ:* Published work in journals world-wide. *Mailing Add:* c/o Adele Santos & Assoc 33 Zoe St San Francisco CA 94107

SAPHIRE, LAWRENCE M
WRITER, ART DEALER
b Brooklyn, NY, Jan 12, 31. *Study:* Yale Univ, BA, 52, writing with Robert Penn Warren; Yale Sch Fine Arts, 51-53; Univ Paris I at Sorbonne, two dipl. *Pos:* Dir, Blue Moon Gallery, NY; ed, Blue Moon Press, Yorktown Heights, NY. *Res:* Modern prints, particularly Leger, Andre Masson. *Specialty:* Modern European painting, sculpture, graphics, original print publications in books and albums. *Publ:* Auth & ed, Sea Bird Saga (including Wallace Putnam lithographs), Blue Moon Gallery, 66; Poems (including Andre Masson etchings), Ed de la Lune Bleue, 74; Andre Masson/Second Surrealist Period, 75, The Genius of Andre Masson (catalogs), 76, Fernand Leger/Complete Graphic Work, 78, Blue Moon Press; Andre Masson/The Illustrated Books, 94, Patrick Crater Publ; Andre Masson, Complete Graphic Work, Blue Moon Press, 90. *Mailing Add:* 808 Broadway New York NY 10003

SAPIEN, DARRYL RUDOLPH
PAINTER
b Los Angeles, Calif, Mar 12, 50. *Study:* Fullerton Col, AA, 71; San Francisco Art Inst, BFA, 72, MFA 76. *Work:* Art Mus, Univ Calif, Berkeley; Oakland Mus, Calif; San Francisco Mus Mod Art; Solomon R Guggenheim Mus, NY. *Comn:* This is Not A Test, Soc Encouragement Contemp Art, San Francisco, 76; "Pixellagem," Commissioned Set Design for San Francisco Ballet, 83; Lobby Installation, Nat Automobile & Casualty Co, Pasadena, Calif, 93. *Exhib:* Within the Nucleus (performance), San Francisco Mus Mod Art, 76; Painting & Sculpture in Calif: The Mod Era, Nat Collection Fine Art, Washington, DC, 76; Space, Time, Sound, a Decade in the Bay Area, San Francisco Mus Mod Art, 79; Hero (performance), Newport Harbor Art Mus, Calif, 80; 19 Artists--Emergent Americans, Solomon R Guggenheim Mus, NY, 81; Am Roulette, Solomon R Guggenheim Mus, NY, 81; Artspace Painting Grant Award, San Francisco Artspace, 88; Digital Visions: Computers and Art, Everson Mus Art, Syracuse Univ, NY, 88; The Written Word, Richmond Art Ctr, Richmond, Calif, 90; San Francisco Art Comn Gallery, 91; Recent Work, San Francisco City Col, 96; Facing Eden 100 Yrs of Landscape Art in the Bay Area, MH de Young Mus, San Francisco, 95; Recent Work, Opts Art Gallery, San Francisco, 94; Eyecharts, Wienstien Gallery, San Francisco, 98. *Pos:* Sr computer graphics artists, Amdahl Coop, 84-86. *Teaching:* Lectr, San Francisco State Univ, San Francisco Inst. *Awards:* Nat Endowment Arts Awards, 73, 79 & 92; Louise Riskin Award, Video Pavillion, San Francisco Art Festivel, 75; Artspace Painting Grant, 88. *Bibliog:* Charles Csuki (auth), Music & Dance J a Paint Machine, Computer Graphics & Applications, 8/85; Christine Tamblyn (auth), Darryl Sapien at Art Space, Artnews, 11/88; Ken Baker (auth), Darryl Sapien at Opts Art, San Francisco Chronicle, 11/30/94. *Media:* Paintings; Multi-Media Installations. *Publ:* Auth, Splitting the axis & Video art and the ultimate cliche, La Mamelle, 76; contribr, Other Sources (catalog), San Francisco Art Inst, 76; Oggi in California, Data, 77; auth, Crime in the streets, High Performance, summer 79; What is performance art?, Intersection Newslett, 81. *Dealer:* Mendoza Gallery Latin American Art. *Mailing Add:* 4333 Balboa St San Francisco CA 94121

SAPP, WILLIAM ROTHWELL
SCULPTOR, EDUCATOR
b Cape Girardeau, Mo, July 4, 43. *Study:* Univ Mo, Columbia, MA, 67; Wash Univ, MFA, 78; Southeast Mo State Univ. *Work:* Univ Ark & State Capitol, Little Rock; Comptroller of the US Currency, Oklahoma City; N Ark Med Ctr, Harrison, AK; Harlin Mus, West Plains, MO. *Comn:* J P Harlin Portrait Sculpture, comn by Harlin family, 73; Ark Gov Bailey, 88; St Redhead, Casa de la Cultura, Santa Cruz, Bolivia, 88; Ark Gov Faubus, 89; Claude Parrish Onc Hosp, 90. *Exhib:* Ark Arts Coun Fel, Winners, pub Serv Gallery, Little Rock, Ark, 85; Mid Am Arts Asn/NEA Winners Exhib, Salina Arts Ctr, Kans, 86; Casa dela Cultura/Taller de Artes Visuales, Santa Cruz, Bolivia, 88; Dogs, Memphis Ctr Contemp Arts, 89; SAF/NEA Winners, New Orleans Cont Arts Ctr, 94; Mus Univ, Medellin, Colombia, 95; Casa de la Cultura, Santa Cruz, Bolivia, 96; Biblioteca Luis Angel Arango, Bogota, Colombia, 96; Instituto Iberoamericano, Santa Cruz, Bolivia, 98; Centro Colombia Americano, Medellin, Colombia, 98. *Teaching:* Asst Prof, Adams State Col, Alamosa, Co, 67-73; assoc prof, Univ Ark, Little Rock, 78-89; assoc prof, sculpture, Univ Ga, Athens, 89-95. *Awards:* MAAA/NEA Fel, 85; AAC Vis Arts Fel, 86; SAF/NEA Fel, 93; Sculpture Award, Fla Nat, Tallahassee, Fla, 94. *Mem:* Int Sculpture Ctr; Mid-Am Col Art Asn. *Media:* All Media, Handformed Paper. *Mailing Add:* Lamar Dodd Sch Art Dept Art Univ Georgia Athens GA 30602

SARANTOS, BETTIE J
PAINTER, PRINTMAKER
b Aug 15, 34. *Study:* Workshops with Dong Kingman, Betty Lou Schlem, Charles Movali, Frank Webb, Charles Reid, Gerald Brommer & others, 79-; Zhejiang Acad Arts, Hangzhou, China, cert, 86. *Work:* Nat Croquet Gallery, Newport, RI; RI Hosp Corp Collection, Providence; Arts & Crafts Inst, Weifang, China; Smithsonian Inst-White House Easter Egg Collection, Washington, DC. *Exhib:* Taipei Exhib of Am Brush Painters, Taipei, Repub of China, 84; one-woman show, Univ Conn, Storrs, 85; Zhejiang Acad Arts, Hangzhou, China, 86; Newport Art Mus, RI, 95, 97 & 98-2003; Art Complex Mus, Duxbury, Mass, 2003. *Pos:* Dir, Roger King Gallery Art, Newport, RI, 85-95. *Teaching:* Oriental brush painting, Swinburne Sch, Newport, RI, 74-94 & RI Sch Design Continuing Educ. *Awards:* First, Channel 36, Providence, RI, 84; First & Best of Show, War Col Mus, 95; Florence Brevoort Kane, Providence Art Club, 98. *Bibliog:* Barons (auth), Who's Who in Interior Design, int ed, 91; Spencer Berger (auth), Bettie J Sarantos-Not just the lady artist of the croquet world, RI First Online Mag, 98; studio tour & interview, Cox Cable Television, 98. *Mem:* Copley Soc, Boston; SUMI-E Soc Am Inc; Am Artists Chinese Brush Painting; Nat Mus Woman Artists, Washington, DC; Providence Art Club; Art League of RI. *Media:* All Media. *Dealer:* Roger King Fine Art 21 Bowens Wharf Newport RI 02840; Jesica Hagen Fine Art 51 Bellevue Ave Newport RI 02840. *Mailing Add:* Studio One 1 Hope St Newport RI 02840

SARET, ALAN DANIEL
SCULPTOR, PAINTER
b New York, NY, Dec 25, 44. *Study:* Cornell Univ, BArch, with Peter Kahn & Alan Atwell; Hunter Col, with Robert Morris. *Work:* Mus Mod Art, Whitney Mus Am Art, NY; Detroit Inst Art; Art Gallery Ont; Ft Worth Art Mus, Tex; Dallas Art Mus & Art Mus STex; Allen Art Mus, Oberlin Col. *Comn:* Ghosthouse, Artpark, Niagara, NY, 75; Home and Away (environ mosaic), Greater Pittsburgh Int Airport, 92. *Exhib:* Whitney Ann, 69 & Whitney Biennial, 77, Whitney Mus Am Art, NY; Recent Acquisitions, Mus Mod Art, NY, 75-76; one-man shows, Charles Cowles Gallery, NY 80 & 82, Rudolph Zwirner Gallery, Cologne, Ger, 81, Nigel Greenwood Gallery, London, 82, Daniel Weinberg Gallery, Los Angeles, 83 & 89, Albright-Knox Gallery, Buffalo, NY, 83 Alan Saret: Recent Sculpture & Drawings, Margo Leavin Gallery, Los Angeles, 86 & Lorence Monk Gallery, NY, 89; Recent Developments in Sculpture, Whitney Mus Am Art, 81; Images of the Unknown, PS 1, Long Island City, NY, 86; Natural Form and Forces, MIP Bank Boston, Mass, 86; Eccentric Abstraction, Blum Helman Gallery, NY, 86; Retrospective exhib, Inst Art Urban Resources, PS 1, Long Island City, NY, 90; Web of Pythagoras, 99. *Pos:* Founder & dir, ALAEL, 74-77. *Teaching:* Vis artist sculpture, Univ Calif, Irvine, 78. *Awards:* Guggenheim Fel, 69; Nat Endowment Arts Fel, 75; CAPS Grant, 76. *Bibliog:* Suzanne Muchnic (auth), A show that is wired for brightness, Los Angeles Times, 6/9/86; Cynthia Goodman (auth), Digital Visions, Everson Mus Art, 87; Michael Brenson, rev, NY Times, 5/29/87; Robert Morgan (auth), Eccentric abstraction and postminimalism, Flash Art, 1/2/89; Michael Kimmelman (auth), Exploring the connections in a multi-faceted Career, NY Times, 1/26/90. *Media:* Multimedia. *Publ:* Auth, The Ghosthouse, ALAEL, 76; coauth (with Klaus Kertess), Matter Into Aether, Newport Harbor Art Mus, Newport Beach, Calif, 82. *Mailing Add:* 65 S 11th St Brooklyn NY 11211

SARETZKY, GARY DANIEL
PHOTOGRAPHER, HISTORIAN
b Newton, Mass, 46. *Study:* Univ Wis, BA, 68, MA, 69; Thomas Edison Col, studied with Peter Bunnell, William Barksdale, Duane Michals, Frederick Sommer, Eva Rubinstein & Charles Harbutt. *Work:* Hist Soc of Princeton, NJ. *Exhib:* 2nd Biennial NJ Artists Exhib, NJ State Mus, 79; Images: The Art of Photog, Monmouth Mus, 81; Living in Am, Noyes Mus, 88; Stated as Fact, NJ State Mus, 90; TAWA in the USSR, Soviet Artists Gallery, Moscow, 90. *Collection Arranged:* Educ Testing Service Archives, Princeton, NJ; Hopewell Mus, NJ; Herman Witkin Papers; Louis H Draper Papers; George Eastman House; Mercer Co Cult & Heritage Comn Collection, Trenton, NJ; Margaret Bourke-White: In Paint, Rutgers Univ, 2006. *Pos:* Archivist, Monmouth Co, 94; self-employed photographer, photo conservator & consult, presently. *Teaching:* Assoc prof photog, Mercer Co Community Col, 77- & Trenton State Col, 85-93. *Awards:* Purchase Award, Mercer Co Photography, 78, 80, 82 & 83; First Prize, Princeton Art Asn, 79; Best in Show, Mercer Co Photography, 80. *Mem:* Am Inst Conserv Photo Materials Group; History Photog Group; Trenton Artists Workshop Asn (pub relations dir, 85-87); Soc Photog Educ; Princeton Preservation Group (pres, 2004-). *Media:* Silver Gelatin. *Res:* History of photog. *Publ:* Auth, The effects of electrostatic copying on modern photographs, 86 & Recent photographic conservation and preservation literature, 87, Picturescope; Photographic conservation, Conservation Admin News, 88; North American business archives, Business History Bull, 90-91; Elias Goldensky: Wizard of Photography, Pa History, 97; Margaret Bourke-White: Eyes on Russia, Photo Review, 99, She Worked Her Head Off: Edwin and Louise Rosskam & the Golden Age of Documentary Photography Books, 2000; Nineteenth Century NJ Photographies, NJ Hist, 04; Margaret Bourke-White: In Print (auth, catalog), Rutgers Univ, 2006. *Mailing Add:* 700 Trumbull Ave Lawrenceville NJ 08648

SARGENT, J MCNEIL
PRINTMAKER, PAINTER
b Wilkesboro, NC. *Study:* Univ Calif, San Diego BA; Pratt Graphics Ctr, New York; Art Students League; La Reparata Graphic, Florence, Italy; Sch Prof Art, New York; Atelier 17, Paris; NY Univ. *Work:* Nat Biblioteque, Paris; Libr Cong, Washington, DC; NZ Embassy, Washington, DC; Imperial Savings & Loan, Westwood, Calif; Pratt Graphics Ctr, NY; Smithsonian Inst, Washington, DC; Internationale Grafiek, Maastricht, Neth; and many others. *Comn:* Wall paintings, Glendale Fed Bank, San Diego, 75; five color intaglio ed, Orr's Graphic Ctr, San Diego, 76-77; wall paintings, Calif First Bank, San Diego, 77, comn by Sen Edward Brooks & Barry Goldberg, Washington, DC, Jose Manual Salazar, Spanish Ambassador, Washington, DC & Robert Goulet, Las Vegas. *Exhib:* Calif-Hawaii Biennial, San Diego, 76; Palace Fine Arts, Mexico City, 76; 50 Calif Printmakers Nat Tour, 76 & 77; Soc Am Graphic Artists, NY, 77; Yokohoma Citizens Mus, Japan, 79; one person shows, Riverside Mus, Calif, Tarbox Gallery, San Diego, Foxhall Gallery, Washington, DC, Queens Gallery, Lake Havasu, Ariz, Knowles Art Ctr, La Jolla, Calif, Las Vegas Art Mus, Nev & many others. *Pos:* Prof illusr, publ & advert agencies, NY & Washington, DC, 50-68; vchmn docent, Fine Arts Gallery Mus, San Diego, 74-75. *Teaching:* Instr design & drawing, Luther Rice Col, Franconia, Va, 70-71; instr advan oil, San Diego Community Col, 71-78; instr, Mira Costa Col, 79-. *Awards:* San Diego Top Woman Artist, 80; Purchase Awards, Southern Calif Expo, 81 & Pratt Graphics Ctr, 82; Awards, SW Ann Regional, Washington, DC, 68-70; and others. *Mem:* Artists Equity Asn San Diego (founder, 72, pres, 73 & 74); Calif Art Comn; Printmaker's Atelier (dir, 82-83); and others. *Media:* Intaglio, Oil. *Publ:* Contribr, M Petersen (auth), On view, Jean Braley, Applause, 11/80. *Dealer:* Rancho Santa Fe Art Gallery Rancho Santa Fe Calif

SARGENT, MARGARET HOLLAND
PAINTER
b Hollywood, Calif, 27. *Study:* Univ Calif, Los Angeles, 45-47; Tokyo, Japan, 56; with Herbert Abrams, NY, 59-61 & Marcos Blahove, Fairfax, Va, 69; Art Students League, with John Sanden, 74. *Work:* British Piano Mus, Middlesex, Eng; US Military Acad Mus; US Air Force Acad; USA Pentagon; US Naval Acad; US Naval War Col; Hawaii State Found; Navy Combat Artists; Nat Portrait Gallery, US; and others. *Comn:* Portrait, President Gerald Ford, Time, Inc; Judge Wm Matthew Byrne, Jr, US District Ct; Secretary of State and Mrs Alexander M Haig; playwright Tennessee Williams; Jules S Stein; Prince Turki Saud; Governor George Ariyoshi, Hawaii; Army Chief of Staff, General John A Wickham; Lew R Wasserman; Dorothy Stimson, Bullitt; Kent Kresa, CEO, Northrop Grumman, 2003; portrait, Mary Maxwell Gates & William Gates Sr; Jonathan Varat, Dean, UCLA School of Law, 2004. *Exhib:* One-man shows, Turkish Am Asn, Ankara, 63, Frye Art Mus, 71 & 84, Woodside Gallery, Seattle, 72 & Excelsior Club, NY, 74-75; group shows, Salmagundi, NY; plus many others. *Pos:* Owner-dir, Sargent Portraits, Los Angeles, currently. *Teaching:* Lectr,Metrop Mus Art, 2001; instr video, Camelot Productions, currently. *Awards:* H M Salmagundi Award; Naval Award Outstanding Achievement in Oil Painting, 77; First Prize Prof Oils, AFL-CIO's 10th Ann, Los Angeles, 79; and others. *Bibliog:* numerous articles in Town & Country, Forbes, Time, Inc, Am Artist, Southwest Art, Money, Palm Springs Life, Baltimore Sun & many others, 76-2000. *Mem:* Salmagundi Club; Am Portrait Soc; Coun Leading Am Portrait Painters (founder); Am Soc Portrait Artists; West Coast Soc Portrait Artists (judge); Portrait Soc of Am. *Media:* Oil. *Specialty:* Oil Portraits. *Mailing Add:* 2750 Glendower Ave Los Angeles CA 90027

SARGENT, RICHARD
PAINTER, PHOTOGRAPHER
b St Louis, Mo, 1932. *Study:* Univ Southern Calif, BFA, 54 & MFA, 56. *Comn:* Mural, Audio Workshop, NY; painting, Int Sci & Technol Mag, 63. *Exhib:* One-man shows, NY Times, 58, Nonagon Gallery, NY, 61 & Heads, Berkeley Art Ctr, 68; Santa Rosa Jr Col, 80; Ammo Gallery, Brooklyn, NY, 85; The Breakfast Group 20th Anniversary Show, Landes Gallery, Berkeley, Calif, 94, Bedford Gallery, Walnut Creek, Calif, 97; Berkeley City Club, 98; Drawings, Madame's Gallery, 99; Print, June Steingart Gallery, 2003. *Collection Arranged:* David Anderson Sculpture, 72; Berkeley City Limits, 73; Water Works, 75; Fiber Space, 75; Joseph Rees, Neon-Argon, 75; Three Allegorical Painters: Jimenez, Pratchenko, Ross, 77; Barbara Spring, Wood Sculpture, 77; The Outdoor Studio: Carlin, Holdsworth, St. John, 77; Robert Loberg, Paintings, 1977; Berkeley Before 1950: Historical Photographs, 86-93. *Pos:* Cur, Long Beach Mus Art, 64-65, Berkeley Art Ctr, 69-78 & Berkeley Hist Soc, 85. *Awards:* Fel, Edward MacDowell Colony, 59 & 63; Hon Mention, 50 paintings, Civic Arts Gallery, Walnut Creek, Calif, 69. *Mem:* Artists Breakfast Group. *Media:* Oil; Archival Inkjet Printing. *Publ:* Illusr, New York Times, 59, Western J Surgery, Obstet & Gyn, 59, Africa Today, 61 & 62; Poems Read in the Spirit of Peace & Gladness, 66; San Francisco Earthquake, 68; photos, The Studio Potter, 84, Fine Woodworking, 86, 87, 88, Am Crafts, 88, Woodwork, 90, 92, 93 & 94 & Macrobiotic Times, 90; 20th Century Glass: a New Definition, 93; Ceramics Monthly, 2004, 2005, 2006. *Mailing Add:* 2316 McGee Ave Berkeley CA 94703

SARKISIAN, PAUL
PAINTER
b Chicago, Ill, Aug 18, 28. *Study:* Art Inst Chicago 45-48; Otis Art Inst, Los Angeles 53-54; Mexico City Col, 55-56. *Work:* Metrop Mus Art, Solomon R Guggenheim Mus, NY; Corcoran Gallery Art, Washington; Santa Barbara Mus, Calif; Chicago Art Inst; Milwaukee Art Ctr, Wis; Sheldon Mem Art Gallery, Lincoln, Nebr; Ron Judish Gallery, Denver, Colo. *Exhib:* Late Fifities at the Ferus, Los Angeles Co Mus Art, Calif, 68; one-man exhibs, Corcoran Galllery Art, 69, Mus Contemp Art, Chicago, 72, Nancy Hoffman Gallery, NY, 78, 80 & 82, Arts Club Chicago, 79, traveling exhib, Wright State Univ, 80, Arco Ctr Visual Arts, Los Angeles, Calif, 81, Frederick Gallery, Washington, 81, Aspen Ctr Visual Arts, Southwest Artist Series, Colo, 82 & Tomasulu Gallery, Cranfield, NJ, 94; Whitney Ann, Whitney Mus Am Art, NY, 69; Documenta, Ger, 72; San Francisoc Mus, Calif, 76; Visions Distinguished Alumni 1945 to Present, Chicago Art Inst, Ill, 76; Prospectus: The Seventies, Aldrich Mus, Ridgefield, Conn, 79; First Western States Biennial Exhib, Western Collection Fine Arts, San Francisco Mus Mod Art, Seattle Art Mus, Univ Hawaii, Newport Harbor Art Mus, 79-80; NY Gallery Showcase, Okla Art Ctr, 81; 46th Ann Nat Midyear Show, Butler Art Inst Am Art, 81; Alcove Show, Santa Fe Art Mus, 89; Pacific Enterprise Collection (catalog), Libr Towers, Los Angeles, Calif, 90; The Allure of Illusionism: Trompe L' Oeil-In Contemp Am Painting, Nora Eccles Harrison Mus Art, Utah State Univ, Logan, 92; Trompe L' Oeil-Illusionism: Curators' Forum (catalog), Hans & Walter Bechtler Gallery, Charlotte, NC, 93; Postmark, Santa Fe, NMex, 2000; and others. *Teaching:* Vis prof painting, Pasadena Art Mus, Calif, Univ Southern Calif, Los Angeles, 69, Los Angeles Art Ctr, 69, Univ Calif, Berkeley, 70, Univ Ore, Eugene, 71 & Univ SFla, Tampa, 72. *Media:* Air Brush. *Mailing Add:* 258 Tano Rd Santa Fe NM 87501

SARNOFF, ARTHUR SARON
PAINTER, ILLUSTRATOR
b Brooklyn, NY, Dec 30, 12. *Study:* Indust Sch Art; Grand Cent Sch Art; also with Harvey Dunne; Kansas Univ, Hon Dr. *Work:* Bass Mus; Springfield Mus; Parrish Mus; Hartford Mus; Nat Art Mus Sport, NY. *Comn:* Fine art prints, Arthur Kaplan Co, Donald Art Co & Cataldi Fine Art Prints; portraits Pres Kennedy, Bob Hope and others. *Exhib:* Int Art Galleries; Continental Art Galleries; Sports in Action, Grand Cent Art Galleries; Nat Acad Art; De Ligny Gallery; Zantman Gallery; Findley Gallery. *Teaching:* Instr Boca Raton Mus Art, 85-95. *Awards:* Outdoor advert award, Art Dirs Club; Art League Nassau Award; Allied Artists Award; Allied Artists Awards, 90 & 91. *Mem:* Soc Illusrs; Allied Artists Am; Prof Art Guild. *Media:* Oil, Acrylic. *Publ:* Illusr, Saturday Evening Post, Colliers, Good Housekeeping, Cosmopolitan, Red Book, McCalls, Women's Home Companion, Ladies Home J and others

SAROFIM, FAYEZ S
COLLECTOR
b Nov, 19, 28. *Study:* Univ Calif, Berkeley, BS (food technology), 49; Harvard, MBA, 51. *Pos:* Founder, chmn, pres, Fayez Sarofim & Co, 58—; bd mgr Mem Sloan-Kettering Cancer Ctr, currently; council mem Rockefeller Univ; bd dirs Alley Theatre, Houston Ballet Found, Mus Fine Arts, Houston, Tex Heart Inst. *Awards:* Named one of Top 200 Collectors, ARTnews, 2004, 2005, 2006. *Mem:* Houston Symphony Soc (vice chair bd dirs, formerly). *Collection:* Coptic sculpture; old masters, 19th century art, American impressionism, modern & contemporary art. *Mailing Add:* Fayez Sarofim & Co Ste 2907 Two Houston Ctr Houston TX 77010

SAROFIM, LOUISA STUDE
COLLECTOR
Pos: Chair Houston Grand Opera Studio; pres bd trustees The Menil Collection, currently; trustee adv Rice Univ; hon chair The Drawing Ctr, NY. *Awards:* Named one of top 200 collectors, ARTnews mag, 2006. *Bibliog:* Coauth (with Matthew Drutt and Anna Gaskell), Anna Gaskell: Half Life, 2003. *Mailing Add:* The Menil Collection 1511 Branard Houston TX 77006

SARSONY, ROBERT
PAINTER, PRINTMAKER
b Easton, Pa, Jan 1, 38. *Work:* Butler Inst Am Art, Youngstown, Ohio; NJ State Mus, Trenton; Joslyn Art Mus, Omaha, Nebr; Nat Mus Am Art, Smithsonian Inst, Washington; Univ Kans Mus Art, Lawrence; and others. *Exhib:* Allied Artist Show, NY, 63-65; one-man shows, Capricorn Galleries, Bethesda, Md, 67-78; Christopher Gallery, NY, 78-80; Meinhard Galleries, Houston, Tex, 82-83; Harris Gallery, Dallas, Tex, 85-87; and others. *Bibliog:* John S Le Maire (auth), Robert Sarsony, NJ Bus Mag, 69; Philip Desind (auth), article, Southwest Art, 4/80; Dennis Wepman (auth), article, Sunstorm Arts Mag, fall 91. *Media:* Oil, Watercolor; Serigraph, Lithography. *Publ:* Contribr, Sunstorm Arts Mag, 10/91; US Art, 8/97. *Dealer:* DeBruyne Fine Art Naples FL; Robert Sarsony Portfolio Cary NC; The Little Gallery Moneta VA; Discovery Galleries Bethesda Md

SASAKI, TOSHIO
SCULPTOR, ENVIRONMENTAL ARTIST
b Kyoto, Japan, Nov 24, 46. *Study:* Aichi Prefectual Univ Fine Art, BFA, 72; Brooklyn Mus Art Sch, 74. *Work:* Manhattan Psychiatric Ctr Sculpture Garden, Ward's Island, NY; NY Aquarium, Brooklyn, NY; Staten Island Psychiatric Ctr, NY; Cent Park Dept Park & Recreation, NY; Aquarium Wildlife Conserv, Brooklyn, NY. *Comn:* Wall sculpture, comn by New York City; The First Symphony of The Sea (332 ft sculptural wall), comn by New York's Percent for Art Prog, Dept Cult Affairs, NY Aquarium, 86-92; Moving Earth, Cent Park, Dept Park & Recreation, NY, 89. *Exhib:* Japanese Artist in Brooklyn, Brooklyn Mus, 75; solo exhibs, Studio Show, Brooklyn, NY, 78, 112 Workshop Inc, NY, 78, PS 1 Inst Urban Resource, Long Island City, NY, 80 & Storefront Art & Architecture, NY, 82; Metaphysical Vistas, Cleveland State Univ, Ohio, 91; Humanity & Money, Zeku Art Gallery, Paris, France, 92; Diversity Int Traveling Exhib, Brandywine Workshop, 93; A Celebration of Asian/Pacific Am Art, Tweed Gallery, NY, 94; Friends, 55 Mercer Gallery, NY, 94. *Awards:* Visual Artist Fel, Nat Endowment Arts, 86; Award of Merit, Concrete Industry Bd Inc, NY, 92; Award of Excellence in Design, Art Comn City New York, 92. *Bibliog:* 1992 in Review: Public Art (pictorial rev), Art Am Ann, 93; Esther Iverem (auth), Artist in the Boroughs-Coney Island's Sea Wall Brings Art to Boardwalk, NY Newsday, 6/29/93; Lucie Young (auth), Currents, NY Times, 7/29/93. *Mem:* Int Sculpture Ctr. *Publ:* Crossed Culture, ed by Rotunda Gallery, Brooklyn, NY; Noah's Art, ed by Dept Park & Recreation, NY; Project & Proposal, ed by Dept Cult Affairs, NY; Project DMZ, ed by Kyong Park, Storefront for Art & Archit, NY, 88; Public Art in Chinatown, ed by Robert Lee, Asian Am Arts Ctr, NY, 88

SASSONE, MARCO
PAINTER, PRINTMAKER
b Florence, Italy, July 27, 42. *Study:* Ist Galileo Galilei, Florence; Acad Fine Arts, with Silvio Loffredo, Florence. *Work:* Los Angeles Co Mus Art; Nat Art Gallery, Wellington, NZ; Galleria d'Arte Int, Florence; Hunt-Wesson; Laguna Art Mus, Calif. *Comn:* Mural, Palio D'asti, San Francisco. *Exhib:* One-man shows, Wally Findlay Galleries, Beverly Hills & NY, 77-79, Wally Findlay Galleries, Beverly Hills, Calif, 82, Bernheim-Jeune, Paris, France, 88, Diane Nelson Gallery, Laguna Beach, Calif, 87, Buschlen-Mowatt Gallery, Vancouver, Can, 90, Ital Cul Inst, San Francisco, Calif, 89 & 91 & Pasquale Iannetti Galleries, San Francisco, 93; group show, Nat Acad Design, NY, 77; Laguna Art Mus, Laguna Beach, Calif, 79; Munic Art Gallery, Los Angeles, 88; group show, Basel Art Fair, Ger, 90; group show, Chicago Int Art Expo, 90; Los Angeles Contemp Exhib, 92; Mus Italo Americano, San Francisco, 94. *Pos:* Lectr-guest artist, Bowers Mus, Santa Ana, Calif, 70, San Bernardino Mus Art, Calif, 78, Laguna Beach Mus Art, 78, Orange Coast Col, Costa Mesa, Calif, 78, Laguna Beach Arts Comn, Calif, 78-81 & Kern Co Art Educ Asn, Bakersfield, Calif, 79. *Awards:* Gold Medal, Ital Acad Arts, Lit & Sci, 78; Off Knight, Ital Repub, 82; Day named in honor, Mayor Frank Jordan, San Francisco, 3/30/94. *Bibliog:* Donelson F Hoopes (auth), monogr, 79, Arti Grafiche Il Torchio, Florence, Italy; John Wilson (producer), Sassone (film), Fine Arts Films Inc, 76; Peter Clothier (auth), Home on the Street (catalog), 94. *Media:* Oil; Watercolors. *Publ:* Critic, William Wilson, Los Angeles Times, 11/14/75; Sassone Serigraphs, Arti Grafiche, Florence, Italy, 9/84; Janet Dominik (auth), Sassone (catalog), Bernheim Jeune, Paris, France, 88; Peter Clothier (auth), Sassone (catalog), Ital Cult Inst, San Francisco, Calif, 91; Kenneth Baker (critic), San Francisco Chronicle, Apr 17, 94; and others. *Dealer:* Pasquale Iannetti Art Gallery 522 Sutter St San Francisco CA 94102

SATIN, CLAIRE JEANINE
SCULPTOR, ILLUSTRATOR
b Brooklyn, NY, Jan 9, 42. *Study:* Pratt Inst, with Calvin Albert, MFA, 68; Sarah Lawrence Col, with Theodore Roszak, BA, 56. *Work:* Victoria & Albert Mus, London; Getty Ctr Hist Art & Humanities, Los Angeles; Mus Mod Art, NY; Mus Art, Ft Lauderdale, Fla; King Stephen Mus, Szekesfeherdr, Hungary; and others; Rare Books Collection, Library of Congress. *Comn:* Chapman Chronicles, State of Alaska, Fairbanks, 92; Alphawalk 2 (250 ft walkways, auth, catalog), Hillsborough Co, Tampa, Fla 97; Alphastory: Series of 6 Installations (auth catalog), Broward Co, Pembroke Pines, Fla, 98. *Exhib:* Int Biennial Paper Art, Leopold-Hoesch Mus, Duren, Ger, 86 & 90; Artists Bks USA, Am Ctrs, New Delhi, India, 87 & Buchandlung Hugo Frick, Tubingen, Ger, 91-; Bookworks (auth, catalog), Nat Mus Women Arts, Washington, Dc, 93; Sculpture, Bookworks & Related Objects, Art & Cult Ctr, Hollywood, Fla, 93; Visual Arts Fel Exhib (auth catalog), SE Ctr Contemp Art, Winston-Salem, NC, 97; S Fla Cult Consortium Award, Miami Art Mus, Fla, 97-98; El Arte de Los Libros Artista (auth catalog), Instituto de Artes Graficas, 98; State Fla Individual Artist Fel Statewide Exhib (auth catalog), 98-99; and many others; Harper Collins Pubs Gallery, NY, 97. *Pos:* bd mem, Broward Co Cult Affairs Coun, Ft Lauderdale, Fla, 75-83, hon chair, 81-; dir, Broward Community Col Gallery, Ft Lauderdale, Fla, 75-76; bd mem, Art Pub Pl, Broward Co, Fla, 79-83. *Teaching:* Instr art educ, Brooklyn Mus, Dept Educ, 58-59 & fine arts, Broward Community Col, Ft Lauderdale, Fla, 71-83; workshops & lect. *Awards:* Tiffany Found Grant Sculpture, 68; Fla State Individual Artist Fel, Statewide Exhib, 78, 97 & 98; Cult Consortium Fel, Miami Art Mus, State Fla Consortium, 97-98; Memorial Fndtn Jewish Culture, 2001. *Mem:* Int Sculpture Ctr, Washington, DC; Center Bk Arts, NY; Am Craft Coun; Fonteneda Soc (bd mem, 97-); Guild Bookworkers, Chicago; and others. *Media:* Book Arts, Sculpture, Public Art, Mixed Media. *Dealer:* New York, NY Rep: Gabriela Herrera; Art Vitale, Miami; Lame Duck Books, Brookline, MA; Priscilla Juvezis, Cambridge, MA. *Mailing Add:* Artworks/Artspace 101 SW 1st St Dania FL 33004

SATO, MASAAKI
PAINTER
b Kofu, Japan, Feb 28, 41. *Study:* Kofu Saito Fine Arts Inst, Japan; Heatherley Sch Fine Arts, London, Eng; Brooklyn Mus Art Sch, NY; Pratt Inst. *Work:* Aldrich Mus Contemp Art, Ridgefield, Conn; Mus Honolulu Acad Art; Minn Mus Art, Minneapolis; ETenn State Univ; Mus Mod Art, La Tertulia, Cali, Columbia; and others. *Comn:* Big Apple (sculpture), Eye Messe Yamanashi, Yamanashi Prefectural, Japan, 95. *Exhib:* One-man shows, Brooklyn Mus Little Gallery, 73, Soho Ctr Visual Artists, NY, 76 & Edward Williams Col, NJ, 77; Yamanashi Prefectural Mus (auth, catalog), Japan, 90; OK Harris Works of Art, NY, 92, 95 & 96; and many others. *Awards:* 9th Nat Print & Drawing Exhib, Minot, NDak; Rockford Int Print Exhib, Ill, 79; 40th N Am Print Exhib, Brockton Art Mus, Mass, 88. *Bibliog:* Richard Walker (auth), Gallery reviews, Art Rev, 8/31/68; Arthur Bloomfield (auth), An artist of many styles, San Francisco Examiner, 9/24/73; Malcolm Preston (auth), Westbeth connection, Newsday, 7/31/75; John Canaday (auth), It's spring in Connecticut and new talent blooms, 5/9/76; Michael Brenson (auth), Off the beaten paths at city treasure houses, 1/13/84 & Michael Brenson (auth), Weekend reviews, 6/21/85, New York Times. *Mem:* Contemp Artists Orgn; Am Soc Contemp Artists. *Media:* Acrylic, Oil. *Publ:* Auth, The Frederick R Weisman Foundation Collection of Art, Tsurumoto Room Co Ltd, Japan, 86; Japanese Anti-Art: Now and Then, Nat Mus Art Osaka, Japan, 91; ARTODAY, Phaidon Press Ltd, London, 95. *Dealer:* OK Harris 383 W Broadway New York NY 10012. *Mailing Add:* 55 Bethune St New York NY 10014

SATO, NORIE
ENVIRONMENTAL ARTIST, SCULPTOR
b Sendai, Japan, July 19, 49. *Study:* Univ Mich, BFA, 71; Univ Wash, MFA, 74. *Work:* Brooklyn Mus; Philadelphia Mus Art; Seattle Art Mus; Guggenheim Mus. *Comn:* Westside Light Rail, Portland, Ore, 92-98; Miami Int Airport, 96-06; Sound Transit, Seattle, 98-; Univ Wash/Cascadia Community Col, Bothell, 2000; Seattle Justice Ctr, 2000-02; and others. *Exhib:* Thirty Yrs Am Printmaking, 76 & Eight West Coast Printmakers, Brooklyn Mus, 78; 5th Int Brit Print Biennale, Bradford, Eng, 76; Northwest '77, Seattle Art Mus, 77; Proj Video XXIV, Mus Mod Art, NY, 79; Lande, Ritchie & Sato, Vancouver Art Gallery, BC, 79; Videoviewpoints, Mus Mod Art, NY, 80; 19 Artists-Emergent Americans, Guggenheim Mus, 81; solo shows, Linda Farris Gallery, 81, 82, 83, 86, 87, 90, 93 & 95 & Elizabeth Leach Gallery, 89, 91, 94 & 97; Seattle Art Mus, 84; Reed Col, 87; 15th Ave Studio II, Henry Art Gallery, Seattle, 87; Home Show, Santa Barbara Contemp Arts Forum, 88; Contemp Voices: Washington Sculptors, Bellevue Art Mus, 93; Alcott Gallery, Univ NC, Chapel Hill, 2000. *Teaching:* Cornish Col, Seattle, 84-87; Western Wash Univ, Bellingham, fall 89; Univ Mich, Ann Arbor, 98. *Awards:* Wash State Arts Com, 90; Artist Trust Fel, 94; George Tsutakawa Award for Advancement of Pub Art, 97. *Mem:* COCA, Seattle, (bd mem); Reflex, Seattle, (bd mem); WESTAF, Santa Fe, (bd mem); Col Art Asn (bd mem); Pub Art Network Coun; On The Boadrs (bd mem, secy). *Media:* Electronic, Mixed. *Mailing Add:* 619 Western Ave PO Box 14 Seattle WA 98104

SATORSKY, CYRIL
PAINTER, PRINTMAKER
b London, Eng. *Study:* Leeds Col Art, nat dipl design; Royal Col Art, Royal scholar, traveling scholar, res scholar, ARCA & first class hon degree. *Work:* Cincinnati Art Mus; Wooster Col; Essex Community Col. *Exhib:* Philadelphia Print Club Ann; Rental Gallery, Baltimore Mus, 70; Sixth Dulin Nat Print Show, Knoxville, Tenn, 70; one-man show, Gallery Four, Alexandria, Va, 74 & Grimaldo Gallery, Baltimore, 78. *Pos:* Adv to univ publ, Univ Tex, Austin, 62-65. *Teaching:* Prof illus & printmaking, Md Inst Col Art, 65-. *Interests:* music, arts of India & Japan. *Publ:* Auth & illusr, A pride of Rabbis, Aquarius, 70; illusr, Frenchman & the Seven Deadly Sins, Scribners, 71; illusr, Sir Gawain & the Green Knight, Limited Ed Club, 72; Illusr, Country J. *Dealer:* Gallery K 2032 P St NW Washington DC 20036. *Mailing Add:* ARCA 4488 Circle Rd Core des Neiges Montreal PQ H3W-1Y7 Canada

SATTLER, JILL
PHOTOGRAPHER, PAINTER
b New York, NY, Jan 3, 47. *Study:* Chouinard Art Inst, Los Angeles, 68 (with scholarship & honors), Univ Calif, Santa Barbara; pvt study as well as manuscript painting with student of Royal Scribe to Queen of Eng. *Work:* Pvt collections of Cher (worn during acceptance of Acad Award for Moonstruck), Diane English (writer, exec producer of Murphy Brown & featured in ELLE Mag); photog portraits of Beatrice Wood (100th birthday), Chantal of Good Morning Am & Sandy Duncan. *Comn:* Many public & pvt comns. *Exhib:* CL Clark Galleries, Bakersfield, Calif, 91; Painting & Photog Exhib, Karpeles Manuscript Mus, 93-94; Photog Exhib, Carnegie Art Mus, Ventura, Calif, 94; Art Mus Santa Cruz Co; Ron Breeden Gallery, Orange Co, 95; Contemp Arts Forum Santa Barbara; De La Guerra Gallery & Frameworks, Santa Barbara, Calif, 97; Photog portrait, Beatrice Wood's 105th Birthday (with catalog), Milagros Nest Gallery, Ojai, Calif, 98; Photog portrait with Beatrice Wood's Vessels and Figures, Ojai Valley Mus, Calif, 98. *Pos:* Own, Jill Sattler Embellishments & Jill Sattler Photog. *Teaching:* Instr photog hand tinting, Carnegie Art Mus, Santa Barbara City Col, Santa Barbara Photog & Learning Tree Univ, Thousand Oaks. *Bibliog:* Chouinard: An Art Vision Betrayed, Astra Publ Inc, 86; A Survey of the States Museums, Galleries and Artists, Calif Art Rev, 90 & A Survey of Leading American Contemporaries, 90, Am References Publ Co. *Publ:* Jewelry photos only in Elle Mag, Ladies Home J Memories Mag (front cover), Artspace Mag Scene, Los Angeles Times, Vanity Fair Mag. *Mailing Add:* PO Box 50041 Santa Barbara CA 93150

SATUREN, BEN
PAINTER, EDUCATOR
b Somerset, Pa, Dec 10, 48. *Study:* Iowa State Univ, BS, 70; Calif Col Art & Crafts, 84; Santa Rosa Jr Col, 2000-05, Col NAUI, 99-2000; Adobe Photoshop cert., 2004. *Work:* Chinese Med Acad Sci, Beijing, China & Shanghai Second Med Univ; Leigh Yawkey Woodson Art Mus, Wausau, Wis; Bell Mus Natural Hist, Minneapolis, Minn. *Comn:* Silkscreen seriagraph, comn by Dr William Bigler, San Francisco State Univ, Calif, 85; World Wildlife Fund/SAO Tome Cachets & Stamps, Comn by Intercontinental Philatelics, Inc, Southampton, NJ, 92; Marine Wildlife Poster, Nature Discovery Press, 90; A Tribute to Tidepools (mural), Petaluma Wildlife & Natural Sci Mus, Calif, 93; Sea Turtles of the World, Nature Discovery Press, 95. *Exhib:* Wildlife in Crisis, Cent Park Wildlife Conserv Ctr, NY, 93 & 94; Art and the Animal, Bennington Ctr Arts, Vermont, 94 & 96; Houston Mus Natural Sci, 95; Scripps Inst Steven Birch Aquarium & Mus, La Jolla, Calif, 95; Detroit Zoological Gardens, 96; Romberg Tiburon Ctr (SFSU), 2000-2001; and others. *Teaching:* Instr 3D moderling & animation, Col of Marin, 2000, Santa Rosa Jr Col, 2001, 02; instr, Acad Art Univ, San Francisco, Calif, 2004; instr animal illus, Sonoma State Univ, 2005, 06. *Awards:* Cash Award Winner, Artist's Liaison, 88; Third Place, Seascape, and Merit Awards, Wildlife Art Show, Los Angeles Audubon, 87; Artist of the Year, Proj Reefkeeper, Miami, Fla, 94. *Bibliog:* Colleen Francis (auth), Diving for Art, Calif Diving News, 88; Colleen Francis (auth), Below the Surface, Artist's Mag, 4/89; Colleen Francis (auth), Artist Vignette: Ben Saturen, Wildlife Art News, 3-4/90. *Mem:* Soc Animal Artists; Artists Guild San Francisco; San Francisco Soc Fine Arts. *Media:* Oil; Silkscreen Serigraphy. *Publ:* Bay Area Naturalist, Marjorie Ruegg, 82; 1987 Artists' Profile, Wildlife Art News, 87, 89, 90; Profile of Wildlife Artists, Southwest Art, 88; Tropical sea creatures for all to see, The Press Democrat, 94; Undersea Artistry, Petaluma Argus-Courier, 95. *Dealer:* Saturen Studio 10A 7th St Petaluma CA 94952. *Mailing Add:* 10 7th St Apt A Petaluma CA 94953-4038

SATZ, JANET
PAINTER, EDUCATOR
b Chicago, Ill, Apr 20, 1933. *Study:* Pratt Inst, BFA, 74; NY Univ, MA, 77, Doctor of Arts Fel, 77-79. *Work:* Smithsonian Inst; Southern New Eng Tel, Fairfield, Conn; Housatonic Col Mus Art, Bridgeport, Conn; Town Westport Collection Art, Conn; Spencer Mus of Art, Univ of Kans, Lawrence, Kans; Fairfield Univ, Conn; Marlboro Col, Marlboro, VT; Sprint Collection of Art, Kansas City MO; Albert A Greenberg Collection, Chicago, Ill; and others. *Exhib:* Chicago & Vicinity Ann, Art Inst Chicago, 69; New Reflections, Aldrich Mus Contemp Art, Ridgefield, Conn, 77; Women's Art, Grad Ctr, City Univ NY, 78; solo exhibs, Carlson Gallery, Bridgeport Univ, Conn, 79, Henry Chauncey Conf Ctr, ETS, Princeton, NJ, 81, Stamford Mus, ART/EX Gallery, Conn, 87, Joy Horwich Gallery, Chicago, Ill, 94 & Norman R Eppink Art Gallery, Emporia State Univ, Kans, 94, Morgan Gallery, Kansas City, 2001; Int Delle Arti Palasso Grassi, Venice, Italy, 79; White House Easter Egg Collection, Mus Art, Sci & Indust, Bridgeport, Conn, 85; 40th Art of Northeast USA, Silvermine Guild Ctr Arts, New Canaan, Conn, 89; Central Mo State Univ, Warrensburg, 91; Kans Ten, Mulvane Art Mus, Washburn Univ, Topeka, 91; 12th Benefit Art Auction, Mus Contemp Art, Chicago, 96; White Gallery, Butler Comm Col, El Dorado, Kans, 97; Shaffer Gallery, Barton Comm Col, Great Bend, Kans, 97; Manhattan Ctr Arts, Kans, 98; Suburban Fine Arts Ctr, Highland Park, IL, 97; Wichita Art Mus, Wichita Kans, 1998; Stockdale Gallery, William Jewel Collape, 2002; Strecher-Nelson Gallery, Manhattan, Kans, 2004; Fields Gallery, Lawrence, Kans, 2006. *Pos:* Dir educ, Whitney Mus Am Art Branch, Fairfield Co, Stamford, Conn, 81-89, educ consult, 89-90; Kans Arts Comn appointment, major grants panelist, prof develop panelist, 90-93. *Teaching:* Lectr & dir mus docent training, Whitney Mus Am Art, Stamford, Conn, 81-90. *Awards:* Prof Develop/Kans Artist Fel, Nat Endowment Arts & Kans Arts Comn, 94; Exhib Award, Muchnic Gallery, Atchinson, Kans, 97; Collborate Lithography Project grant, Kans Arts Commission, 1991; Barbara Rensner Cash Award, Wichta Mus, Kans, 98. *Bibliog:* J Burnham (auth), monograph, Arts Mag, 2/73; Jacqueline Moss (auth), Stamford Museum celebrates, The Advocate, 4/13/82; Vivien Raynor (auth), Contemporary Solo Shows in Hartford and Marlborough, NY Times, 1/24/88. *Media:* acylic, mixed media, college. *Interests:* Contemporary Art. *Publ:* A Community of Artists: A Chronicle of Painters, Sculptors and Cartoonists of Westport-Weston, 1900-1985. *Dealer:* Dennis Morgan Gallery, 2011 Tracey Ave. KS City, MO 64108. *Mailing Add:* 3713 Quail Creek Ct Lawrence KS 66047

SAUDEK, MARTHA FOLSOM
PAINTER
b Palo Alto, Calif, Nov 27, 23. *Study:* Pomona Col, BA, 47. *Comn:* Oil painting, Palos Verdes Neighborhood Church, Calif, 93; oil paintings, Kaiser Permanente Hosp, Riverside, Calif, 94 & Lancaster, Calif, 95. *Exhib:* Oil Painters Am, Chicago & Long Grove, Ill, 92-93 & San Antonio, Tex, 96; Int Artists Invitational, Dr Sun Yatsen Mem Hall, Taipei, Taiwan, 92-95; Women Artists & the West, Tucson Mus Art, 94-95; Salmagundi Club, NY, 93-94; Arts for the Parks, Jackson, Wyo, 94, 95 & 96. *Pos:* Pres, Women Artists West, 92. *Teaching:* Instr oil landscape painting, Calif Art Inst, Westlake Village, 92-94. *Awards:* Eleanor Libby Best Landscape Award, Scottsdale Artists Sch, 92; Grumbacher Gold Medal, 94. *Bibliog:* Shirley Behrens (auth), Going for it, Art of the West, 1/94; Carol Katchen (auth), Painting with Passion, North Light Books, 94; Patricia Seligman (auth), How to paint trees flowers & foliage, BT Batsford Ltd, 94. *Mem:* Assoc mem Oil Painters Am; Calif Art Club; assoc mem Allied Artists Am; Women Artists of the West (treas, 88, 2nd vpres, 89, pres, 90); assoc mem Am Artists Prof League. *Media:* Oil. *Dealer:* Morseburg Galleries 9089 Santa Monica Blvd Los Angeles CA 90069

SAUER, JANE GOTTLIEB
SCULPTOR, CURATOR
b St Louis, Mo, Sept 16, 37. *Study:* Washinton Univ, St Louis, Mo, BFA, 59; studied with Leslie Laskey, 76-78. *Work:* Wash Univ Steinberg Mus, St Louis Art Mus, Mo; Erie Art Mus, Pa; Nordenfjeldske Kunstinndustrimuseum, Tronndheim, Norway; Wadsworth Atheneum, Hartford, Conn; Mus Suwa, Japan; and others. *Exhib:* Denver Art Mus, traveling to JB Speed Art Mus, 86; Mus Cantonal Beaux-Arts, Lausanne, Switz, 92; St Louis Art Mus, 93 (two exhibs), 94 & 95 (two exhibs); Newport Harbor Art Mus, 93; Fiber: Five Decades from the Collection, Am Craft Mus, NY, 95; Breaking the Barriers: Recent Am Craft (traveling), Portland Art Mus, Madison Art Ctr, Wis, Albany Art Mus, Ga & Am Craft Mus, NY, 95; Thread, Baribican Ctr, London, Eng, 98; Mint Mus Craft & Design, Inaugural Gift, 2000; Ark Art Mu Fiber Forms, 2000; Univ Nebr, 2001; R Duane Reed Gallery, St Louis, 2001; Mus Fine Arts, Santa Fe, 2003. *Collection Arranged:* Baskets & Beyond, St Louis, 98; Under The Japanese Influence, St Louis, 99; Inventions & Construction, St Petersburg, Fla, 2000; The Art of Basketry, Santa Fe, 2003. *Pos:* Studio artist, lectr & workshop leader, 76-; lectr, various univs & orgns, US, 77-; vis artist/lectr numerous schs & mus, 77-94; consult, Harris Stowe Col, St Louis, Mo, 80-84. *Teaching:* Art teacher, Jefferson Barrocks Sch Dist, St Louis, Mo, 59-63; artist-in-residence, New City Sch, St Louis, Mo, 76-78. *Awards:* Visual Artists Grant, Nat Endowment Arts, 84 & 90; 15th Biennale Int de la Tapisserie Lausanne, Mus Cantonal Des Beaux-Arts, Switz, 92; Distinguished Alumni Award, Wash Univ, St Louis, Mo. *Bibliog:* Rita Reif (auth), Weavers aren't the whole story in fiber art, NY Times, 4/23/95; Jane Sauer (auth), Janet Kaplos, Catalogue for Making A Difference: Fiber Sculpture, 2000; Bruce Pepich (auth), Impassioned Form (catalogue), Univ Nebr, 2001. *Mem:* Am Craft Coun (bd trustees, 92- & chmn, 97-2000); St Louis Artist Coalition (bd trustees, 84-86); Forum Contemp Art, St Louis, Mo (bd dir, 90-); Nat Coun Sch Art, Wash Univ, 95-; Int Women's Forum; Mus Found NMex (bd dir, 2002-03). *Media:* Structured Fiber. *Dealer:* R Duane Reed Gallery 7513 Forsyth, St Louis, MO 63105; Thirteen Moon Gallery Santa Fe NM 87501. *Mailing Add:* 1379 Cerro Gordo Santa Fe NM 87501

SAUL, ANDREW M
COLLECTOR
b NY City, 46. *Study:* Wharton Sch Fin, Univ Pa, BS, 68. *Pos:* Exec vpres, Brooks Fashion Stores, 68-80, pres, 80-85, BR Investors, 85-86; gen partner, Saul Partners, 86-; dir, Caché Inc, 86-, chmn, 93—2000; chair Federal Retirement Thrift Investment Bd; commissioner Metrop Transportation Authority, NY, 96-; mem exec comt Mt Sinai Medical Ctr, chair audit comt; trustee Federation Jewish Philanthropies, United Jewish Appeal, Sarah Neuman Nursing Home; trustee and chair council Metrop Mus Art. *Awards:* Named one of Top 200 Collectors, ARTnews Mag, 2004, 2005, 2006. *Collection:* Chinese Bronzes, Modern & Contemporary Art, especially Postwar Americans. *Mailing Add:* Caché Inc 1440 Broadway New York NY 10018

SAUL, PETER
PAINTER
b San Francisco, Calif, Aug 16, 34. *Study:* Stanford Univ; Calif Sch Fine Arts, San Francisco, 50-52; Wash Univ, with Fred Conway, BFA, 56. *Work:* Art Inst Chicago; Whitney Mus Am Art, Metrop Mus Art, Mus Mod Art, NY; San Francisco Mus Mod Art; Carnegie Inst, Pittsburgh; Los Angeles Co Mus Art; Carnegie Inst, Pittsburg; Madison Art Mus, Wis; and many others. *Exhib:* One-man exhibs, Frumkin/Adams Gallery, NY, 89, 90, 92, 93, 95, Galerie Bonnier, Geneva, Switz, 90, 95, Krannert Art Mus, Univ Ill, Champaign, 90-91, Art Mus, Washington Univ, St Louis, 90-91, Galerie Du Ctr, Paris, (with catalog) 91, 97 & 2000, Herbert Palmer Gallery, Los Angeles, 94, George Adams Gallery, NY, 96, 98 & 99 & Nolan Eckman Gallery, 98 & (with catalog) 2000, Galerie Charlotte Moser, Switz, 2002, Nolan-Eckman Gallery, NY, 2002; The Soc of Contemp Am Art, Art Inst Chicago, 62-65; 67th Ann Am Exhib (with catalog), Art Inst Chicago, 64; Social Comment in Am, Mus Mod Art, NY, 68; Paris Biennale Int (with catalog), Mus Mod Art, Paris, 68; Human Concern/Personal Torment (with catalog), Whitney Mus Am Art, NY, 69-70; 70th Am Exhib (with catalog), Art Inst Chicago, 72; 72nd Am Exhib, Art Inst Chicago, 76; Art About Art (with catalog), Whitney Mus Am Art, NY, 78; The Figurative Tradition and the Whitney Mus (with catalog), Whitney Mus Am Art, NY, 80; Made in the USA: Art from the '50s and '60s (with catalog), Va Mus Fine Arts, Richmond, 87; Committed to Print, Mus Mod Art, NY, 88; Calif A to Z and Return (with catalog), Butler Inst, Youngstown, Ohio, 90; Hand-Painted Pop: Am Art in Transition, 1955-1962 (with catalog), Whitney Mus Am Art, NY, 92-93; Quotations (with catalog), Aldrich Mus Contemp Art, Ridgefield, Conn, 92; Masters of Satire (with catalog), William King Regional Arts Ctr, Abingdon, Va, 94; Old Glory: The Am Flag in Contemp Art (with

catalog), Cleveland Ctr Contemp Art, Ohio, 94; Grotesque, Mus Mod Art, NY, 95; Auction 98, Denver Art Mus, Colo, 97; Pop Surrealism (with catalog), Aldrich Mus Contemp Art, Ridgefield, Conn, 98; Made in Calif: Art, Image and Identity 1900-2000 (with catalog), Los Angeles Co Mus Art, 2000-01; George Adams Gallery, 2002, 03; Contemp Arts Mus, Houston, Tex, traveling to Inst of Contemp Art, Boston,Mass, 2003; Los Angeles Co Mus of Art, Calif, 2000-01; Snug Harbor Cult Ctr, Staten Island, NY, 2000-01. *Awards:* New Talent Award, Art in Am Mag, 62; William & Norma Copley Found Grant, 62; Nat Endowment Arts Grant, 80. *Dealer:* George Adams Gallery 41 W 57th St New York NY 10019

SAULSON, HAROLD
PAINTER
b New York, NY, Dec 10, 53. *Study:* Bard Col, BFA, 76. *Exhib:* Ann Plumb Gallery, NY. *Awards:* Nat Endowment Arts Grant, 87. *Mailing Add:* 73 Leonard St New York NY 10013

SAUNDERS, EDITH DARIEL CHASE
PAINTER, INSTRUCTOR
b Waterville, Maine, Mar 19, 22. *Study:* Univ NC, Greensboro, with Robert Partin, Boris Margo, Gilbert Carpenter & Madam Sun To-Ze Hsu; John Brady Sch Art, Blowing Rock, NC; studied with Maria D'Annuzio in Florence, Italy & Leroy Neiman, Philip Moose, Blowing Rock, NC. *Work:* Wachovia Bank; Reynolds Tobacco; Southport Libr, NC; Hunt Mfg Co Collection; Westminster Presbyterian Church, Knoxville, Tenn. *Exhib:* Island Gallery, Manteo, NC; Contemp Graphic Artists (traveling exhib); Weatherspoon Art Gallery, Greensboro; Regional Gallery, Boone, NC; Assoc Artists of NC; Mint Mus Art, Charlotte, NC; Art Gallery Originals, Winston-Salem, NC, 94; and others. *Collection Arranged:* Arts Coun Gallery, Winston-Salem, 57, 62, 64, 65, 77 & 81; Southeastern Art Festival, Winston-Salem; Arts & Sci Mus, Statesville, NC; Herman Art Gallery, Statesville, NC; Contemp Graphic Artists (nat traveling exhib); Regional Gallery, Boone, NC; Hickory Mus of Art, NC; Greenville Art Gallery, NC; Caldwell Arts Coun, Lenoir, NC. *Pos:* Art chmn-coordr, Winston-Salem Women's Club, 60-61; columnist, Edy and Art (weekly), The Suburbanite, 74-76 & 77-78. *Teaching:* Inst privately in home, painting. *Awards:* Purchase Prizes, Northwest Art Exhib, Lowe's Collection, Lowe's Co, 62 & Southport Art Festival, City of Southport, NC, 63; Hunt Mfg Purchase Award, Watercolor Soc of NC, 75. *Mem:* Assoc Artists Winston-Salem; Watercolor Soc NC. *Media:* Acrylic, Watercolor. *Publ:* Artists of Florida vol II, Mountain Productions Tex, Inc; Artists of North Carolina vol I, Mountain Productions Tex, Inc. *Dealer:* Lewis Interiors 2809 Gates Head Dr Winston-Salem NC 27106. *Mailing Add:* 2250 Hilltop Dr Winston-Salem NC 27106

SAUNDERS, J BOYD
PRINTMAKER, EDUCATOR
b Memphis, Tenn, June 12, 37. *Study:* Memphis State Univ, BS; Univ Miss, MFA; Bottega Arte Grafica, Florence, Italy. *Work:* Denison Univ; SC State Collection, Mus Art, Columbia; Bottega Arte Grafica; Cent Art Acad, Beijing, China. *Comn:* Mixed media altar panel, Guess Chapel, Univ Church, Oxford, Miss, 62; mem portrait comn, Tipoff Club, Columbia, SC, 69; oil mural, Univ House, Univ SC, 72. *Exhib:* Soc Washington Printmakers 24th Nat, Smithsonian Inst, 62; First Int Printmaker's Exhib, Gallerie Bottega & Arte Grafica, Florence, 67; 34th Graphic Arts & Drawing Nat, Wichita, Kans, 69; Fifth Dulin Print & Drawing Competition Nat, Knoxville, Tenn, 70; 15th NDak Print & Drawing Ann, Grand Forks, 72. *Pos:* Staff artist, Dan Kilgo & Assocs, Tuscaloosa, Ala, 59-60; designer & illusr, Chaparral Press, Kyle, Tex, 63-65. *Teaching:* Instr art, Univ Miss, 61-62; instr art, Southwest Tex State Col, 62-65; prof art, Univ SC, 65-. *Awards:* Third Prize, Sixth Ann Mid-South Exhib Paintings, Prints & Drawings, Memphis, Tenn, 61; Grand Prize, Guild Columbia Artists, 71; Purchase Prize, 15th NDak Ann Print & Drawing Competition, 72. *Bibliog:* Jack Morris (auth), Boyd Saunders, printmaker, Contemp Artists SC, 69; Beryl Dakers (producer), Boyd Saunders (video tape), WSCE-TV, 79; Gita Maritzer Smith (auth), The Storyteller's Art of Boyd Saunders, WLC Press, 84. *Mem:* Print Coun Am; Guild SC Artists; Columbia Art Asn; Southeastern Graphics Coun; Am Asn Univ Prof. *Publ:* Illusr, Bosque Territory: A History of an Agrarian Community, 64; illusr, Lyndon Baines Johnson: The Formative Years, 65; auth, A summer's printmaking in Florence, Art Educ J, 68. *Dealer:* Trans Designs Inc 1000 Transart Pkwy Woodstock GA 30188. *Mailing Add:* 533 Mallard Dr Chapin SC 29036

SAUNDERS, RAYMOND JENNINGS
PAINTER, EDUCATOR
b Pittsburgh, Pa, Oct 28, 34. *Study:* Pa Acad Fine Arts, nat scholastic scholar, 53-57; Univ Pa, nat scholastic scholar, 54-57; Carnegie Inst Technol, BFA, 60; Calif Col Arts & Crafts, MFA, 61. *Work:* Pa Acad Fine Arts, ARA Serv, Philadelphia; Mus Mod Art, & Whitney Mus Am Art, NY; San Francisco Mus Mod Art; Crocker Art Mus, Sacramento, Calif; Oakland Mus, Calif; and others; Hunsaker/Schlesinger Fine Art, 2001; Centre Jerome Cuzin, France, 2002; Schneider Mus Art, Southern Ore Univ, 2004; rep in permanent collections, Mus Modern Art, New York City, Whitney Mus Am Art, New York City, Philadelphia Mus Art, Chrysler Mus, Va. *Comn:* Los Angeles Bicentennial Anniversary Poster Comn, 80; US Olympic poster, 84; exhib poster, Hunsaker/Schlesinger Gallery, Los Angeles, 87. *Exhib:* Mus Mod Art, NY, 68, 70, 72-73 & 74; Philadelphia Art Mus, Pa, 68, 72-73, 74 & 78; Thirty Contemp Black Artists, San Francisco Mus Art, Calif, 69; Metrop Mus, NY, 70; Card Design, Mus Mod Art, NY, 70; Whitney Mus Am Art, NY, 70 & 74; Recent Aquisitions, Mus Mod Art, NY, 71; Contemp Black Artists in Am, Whitney Mus Am Art, NY, 71; Pa Acad Fine Arts, Philadelphia, 72-73, 74 & 79; San Francisco Mus Mod Art, Calif, 72-73 & 74; Biennale, Whitney Mus Am Art, NY, 72-73; Corcoran Gallery Art, Washington, 74; Tweed Mus Art, Duluth, Minn, 74; Va Mus Fine Arts, Richmond, 74; Graffitti, San Francisco Mus Mod Art, Calif, 78; Paper on Paper, San Francisco Mus Mod Art, Calif, 79; Masterpieces from the Permanent Collection, San Francisco Mus Mod Art, Calif, 80; Resource/Reservoir: Collage and Assemblage, San Francisco Mus Mod Art, 82; Second Western State Exhib/The 38th Corcoran Biennial Exhib of Am Painting, Corcoran Gallery Art, Washington, 83, Brooklyn Mus, NY, 84, Long Beach Mus, Calif, 84 & San Francisco Mus Mod Art, Calif, 84; Resource/Reservoir: CCAC 75 Years, San Francisco Mus Mod Art, Calif, 83; The Human Condition: SFMMA Biennial III, San Francisco Mus Mod Art, Calif, 84; Made in USA Traveling Exhib, Univ Art Mus, Berkeley, Calif, Nelson-Atkins Mus Art, Kans, Mo & Va Mus Fine Art, Richmond, 87; Raymond Sauders: New Work, Oakland Mus, Calif, 94; Recent Acquisitions, Metrop Mus Art, NY, 95; Seven African-Am Artists, Encino Art Gallery, Sacramento, 96; It's Only Rock and Roll Traveling Exhib, Contemp Arts Ctr, Cincinnati & Addison Gallery Am, Phillips Acad, Andover, Mass, 96; Seeing Jazz, Smithsonian Inst, Washington, DC, 97-99; solo exhibs, Raymond Saunders: Distinguished Fac Exhib, Calif Col Arts & Crafts, Oakland, Calif, 97; Strength & Diversity: A Celebration of African-Am Artists, Carpenter Ctr for the Visual Arts, Harvard Univ, Mass, 2000; Hunsaker Schlesinger Fine Art, Santa Monica, Calif, 97 & Hunter Col, City NY Fine Arts Bldg Gallery, NY, 98; New Works, Stephen Wirtz Gallery, San Francisco, 99, 2001; Cooley Gallery, Reed Col, Portland, Ore, 2000, Art with Elders, MH DeYoung Mus, San Francisco, 2000. *Pos:* Nat consult urban affairs, Vol Teaching Serv, NY, 68; art consult, Dept Black Studies, Univ Calif, Berkeley, 69. *Teaching:* Prof painting, Calif State Univ, Hayward, 68-88; Ais critic, RI Sch Design, 68, vis artist, 72; vis artist, Yale Univ, 72; prof, Calif Col Arts & Crafts, Oakland; prof, painting, drawing Calif Col Arts and Crafts, Oakland, 1988-. *Awards:* Nat Inst Arts & Letts Award, 63; Guggenheim Award, 76; Nat Endowment Arts Award, 77 & 84; Visual Arts, Southeastern Ctr Contemp Art, 89. *Bibliog:* Kenneth Baker (auth), Raymond Saunders' signs of the times, San Francisco Chronicle, 7/10/94; Victoria Dalkey (auth), Exhibits give two views, Sacramento Bee, 2/18/96; Donald Miller (auth), Colorful, Cool and Colorblind: The Life and Art of Raymond Saunders, Pittsburgh Post Gazette, 4/11/96. *Mem:* Fel Am Acad Rome; Nat Acad (assoc, 92, acad, 94-). *Media:* All. *Publ:* Auth, Black is a color, pvt publ, 68; Raymond Saunders, Stephen Wirtz Gallery, San Francisco, Intro by Toni Morrison, fall 93; Raymond Saunders: Recent Work, Oakland Mus, 94. *Dealer:* Stephen Wirtz Gallery San Francisco CA. *Mailing Add:* Painting & Drawing Dept Calif Col Arts & Crafts 5212 Broadway Oakland CA 94618-1426

SAUNDERS, RICHARD HENRY
MUSEUM DIRECTOR, HISTORIAN
b Rochester, NY, Aug 13, 49. *Study:* Bowdoin Col, BA, 70; Univ Del (Winterthur Prog), MA, 73; Yale Univ, MA, 76, PhD, 79. *Collection Arranged:* Daniel Wadsworth: Patron of Arts, Wadsworth Atheneum, 81; Celebrating Vermont: Myths and Realities, Middlebury Col. *Pos:* Cur, Am paintings, Wadsworth Atheneum, Hartford, Conn, 78-81; dir, Christian A Johnson Mem Gallery, Middlebury Col, Vt, 85-91; Middlebury Col Mus Art, 92-. *Teaching:* Lectr, art hist, Yale Univ, 77-88; asst prof art hist, Univ Tex, Austin, 81-85; asst prof art, Middlebury Coll, Vt, 85-95, assoc prof, 95-. *Awards:* Samuel H Kress Found Fel, Courtalld Inst, London, 76-77; Andrew Wyeth Fel, Yale Univ, 75-76. *Mem:* Col Art Asn; Nat Trust Hist Preserv; Yale Club, NY. *Publ:* Coauth, American Colonial Portraits: 1700-1776, Smithsonian Inst, Ore, 87; auth, Collecting the West: The CR Smith Collection of Western American Art, Univ Tex Press, 88; auth, John Smibert: Colonial Americas First Portrait Painter, Yale Univ Press, 95. *Mailing Add:* Middlebury College Museum of Art Middlebury VT 05753

SAUNDERS, WADE
SCULPTOR, CRITIC
b Berkeley, Calif, Sept 13, 49. *Study:* Wesleyan Univ, Conn, BA, 71; Univ Calif, San Diego, MFA, 74. *Work:* Corcoran Gallery Art; Baltimore Mus Art; Mus Contemp Art, Chicago; Philadelphia Mus Art; Metrop Mus Art. *Exhib:* Solo exhibs, Newspace Gallery, Los Angeles, 77, 79, 81, 83 & 85, Charles Cowles Gallery, NY, 81 & 82, C Grimaldis Gallery, Baltimore, 83, 84, 88 & 93, Lawrence Oliver, Philadelphia, 84 & 86 & Diane Brown Gallery, 84, 85, 86, 88 & 90. *Teaching:* Asst prof, Tyler Sch Art, 78-82 & Pa State Univ, 82-84; assoc prof, RI Sch Design, 84-90. *Awards:* Nat Endowment Arts, 88; John Simon Guggenheim Fel, 89; Fulbright Res Sch, 93. *Bibliog:* David Tannous (auth), article, Art in Am, 10/80; Reagan Upshaw (auth), article, Art in Am, 6/82; Phyllis Derfner (auth), Art in Am, 11/85; Michael Brenson (auth), article, NY Times, 4/17/88; Nancy Princenthal (auth), Art in Am, 11/88. *Publ:* Auth, Touch and eye "50's" sculpture, 82, Talking objects, 85, Making art, making artists, 93, Figures of estrangement, 95 & Ends and means, 96, Art Am. *Mailing Add:* 315 Berry St Brooklyn NY 11211-5112

SAUTER, GAIL E
PAINTER
b San Antonio, Tex, July 16, 49. *Study:* Univ Okla, BFA, 70; Va Ctr Creative Arts, fel, 91-92. *Work:* Painting, Solomon Brothers, NY; painting, Chubb Life Am, Concord, NH; painting, Browning Ferris Industs, Boston; painting, Northern Telecommunications, Manchester, NH; painting, Arthur Anderson & Co, Concord, NH. *Exhib:* Nat Ann Exhib, Pastel Soc Am, New York, 83-90; Statewide Asn Exhib, Currier Mus, Manchester, NH, 83-92; Invitational Nat, Salmagundi Club, New York, 86-87; The Subject is Water, Newport Art Mus, RI, 87; Nat Color Show, Faber Birren Exhib, Stamford, Conn, 88 & 92; and others; Europastel, Russian Fedn, St Petersburg, Russia; UNESCO "Pastellisti Contemporanei", Cuneo, Italy; Art du Pastel, Normandy, France. *Awards:* Isenberg, Giffuni, Armstrong, Pastel Soc Am Nat, 83, 86 & 88; Grumbacher Gold Medal, Pastel Soc Can, 85; McCarthy, Salmagundi Club, 86. *Mem:* Pastel Soc Am (master status); Copley Soc (full artist status); NH Art Asn; League NH Craftsmen; Womens Caucus, Boston Chap. *Media:* Oil, Pastel. *Publ:* Illusr, Sudden Harbor, Orchises Press, 91; Auth, The Best of Pastels, Rockport Press. *Mailing Add:* 9 Government St Kittery ME 03904

SAVAGE, JERRY
PAINTER
b Chicago, Ill, Sept 2, 1936. *Study:* Art Inst Chicago, BFA, 59; Univ Southern Calif, MFA, 62. *Work:* Kemper Collection, Longrove, Ill; Krannert Art Mus, Urbana, Ill; pvt collection, George Irwin, Quincy, Ill. *Exhib:* Solo exhibs, Allen Frumkin Gallery, 69, Zaks Gallery, 78, 81, 86 & 88, Chicago, Ball State Univ, Muncie, Ind, 87 & Gallery K, Washington, DC; Human Concern-Personal Torment, Whitney Mus Am Art, NY, 69; Extraordinary Realities, Whitney Mus Am Art, NY, 69; Illinois Artist '76 Traveling Exhib, Ill, 76; Contemp Currents in Am Art, Fung Ping Shun Mus, Hong Kong, 82; Illinois Artists, Nat Gallery Art, Kuala Lumpur, Malaysia, 83; Am Art, Bejing, China, 87; Kunstwerke Aus Papier, Hamburg, Ger, 87; Hamburg Media Serv, Hamburg, Ger, 88. *Teaching:* Prof painting, Univ Ill, Champaign, 62-. *Awards:* Drawing Award, Los Angeles Co Mus, 61; Guggenheim Fel, 64-65; Ctr Advanced Study Assoc, Univ Ill, 74-75; Ford Found Grant, 75-76. *Bibliog:* Franz Schultz (auth), rev, Chicago Sun Times, 69; Dennis Adrian (auth), profile, Art Now-USA, 5/86; Daniel Reich (auth), rev, New Art Examiner, summer 86. *Media:* All Media. *Dealer:* Zaks Gallery 620 N Michigan Ave Chicago IL. *Mailing Add:* 203 S David Sidney IL 61877

SAVAGE, NAOMI
PHOTOGRAPHER
b NJ, June 25, 27. *Study:* Bennington Col; and with Man Ray. *Work:* Mus Mod Art, NY; Fogg Mus, Boston; NJ State Mus; Univ Kans, Ill & Princeton. *Comn:* 8 x 50 ft wall of photo engravings, LBJ Presidential Libr, Austin, Tex, 72; 60 tennis photographs, Youth Tennis Found, Princeton, NJ, 73-74. *Exhib:* Always the Young Stranger, Mus Mod Art, NY, 53; Photog as Printmaking, Mus Mod Art, 68; Two Generations of Photographs-Man Ray & Naomi Savage, NJ State Mus, 68; Light & Lens-Methods of Photog, Hudson River Mus, Yonkers, NY, 73; Women of Photog, San Francisco Mus Art, 75; Photog Disclosures, Squibb Gallery, Princeton, NJ, 82; one-man exhibs, Photographs, Noyes Mus, Oceanville, NJ, 83. *Awards:* Photography, Cassandra Found, 70; Nat Endowment Arts Grant, 71. *Bibliog:* Julia Scully (auth), Everchanging faces of Naomi Savage, NJ State Mus, 68; Contemporary Photographers, St Martins Press, NY, 82; N Rosenblum (auth), A World History of Photography, Abbeville Press, NY, 84. *Media:* Miscellaneous Media. *Dealer:* Snyder Fine Art 20 W 57th St New York NY 10019. *Mailing Add:* 41 Drakes Corner Rd Princeton NJ 08540

SAVAGE, ROGER
PAINTER, PRINTMAKER
b Windsor, Ont, Sept 25, 41. *Study:* Mt Allison Univ, Sackville, NB, Can, BFA, 63; study with Alex Colville, Lawren Harris, Jr & E B Pulford. *Work:* Confederation Ctr Art Gallery & Mus, PE; Art Gallery NS, Halifax, NS; Can Coun Art Bank, Ottawa, Ont; Glenbow Mus, Calgary, Alta; Can Found, Ottawa, Ont. *Comn:* Can $100 Gold Commemorative Coins, Royal Can Mint, Ottawa, 78 & 81; watercolors, Bowater Mersey Paper Co, 81; Serigraphs, Halifax Sheraton Hotel, 85; drawings, Liverpool Int Theatre Festival, 92, 94, 96, 98, 2000 & 02; portrait, Queens Gen Hosp Found, Liverpool, 97. *Exhib:* Aquarelles, Centre de Congres, Montreux, 90; Arctic in Palmengarten, Palmengarten, Frankfurt, 91; Gotlands Konst Mus, Visby, 92; NS Printmakers, Art Gallery, Mt St Vincent Univ, Halifax, 94; North of the Border, Wiregrass Mus, Dothan, Ala, 95; Malschule Gallery, Weimar, Ger, 99; Russignol Cult Ctr, Liverpool, 2003. *Pos:* Vis artist, Art Gallery, Corner Brook, Nfld, 77, Summerside, PEI, 78, Univ Moncton, 79, Arctic Awareness Prog, 91 & Camp Otto Fiord, 92; Printworkshop BBK, Berlin, 88-92; juror, Far & Wide exhib, Art Gallery NS, Halifax, 96; vis artist, Weimar, Ger, 99. *Teaching:* Instr, Annapolis Royal Community Arts Coun, NS, 86 & var ann self-conducted painting workshops 2004, & Bermuda, 98, Tatamagouche Ctr, 99, Weimar, Ger, 99 & 2000. *Awards:* Can Coun Grants, 70 & 80; Brucebo Found Scholar, 80; Award, Province NS, 80; NS Skills Dev for Prof Artist, 89; Int Cult Relations, foreign affairs dept, Ottawa, 99. *Bibliog:* Pat Laurette (auth), Roger Savage: A Survey, Art Gallery NS, 79; Elizabeth Jones (auth), Roger Savage: An intractable essence, Arts Atlantic, 3/81; Marilyn Vance (auth), Roger Savage: Artist, Visual Arts News, Vol 7, No 4, 85; Janice Carbert (auth), Canadian Ency, 2000; John Murchie (auth), New Acquisitions, Roger Savage, Art Gallery, 1999. *Mem:* Can Artists Representation; Visual Arts NS; Royal Can Acad Arts; Print Consortium; CARFAC Copyright Collective. *Media:* Watercolor; Serigraphy. *Dealer:* Savage Gallery 611 Mersey Point Rd Liverpool NS B0T 1K0. *Mailing Add:* 611 Mersey Point Rd RR 1 Liverpool NS B0T 1K0 Canada

SAVAS, JO-ANN
PAINTER, INSTRUCTOR
b Opelika, Ala, Jan 30, 34. *Study:* Auburn Univ, BS(art educ; Alpha Delta Pi Scholar). *Exhib:* NY World's Fair; Chateau de la Napole, Cannes, France; Southern Contemporaries Collection of Sears-Roebuck; Int Women's Show; Nat Women's Watercolor Exhib; and others. *Pos:* Tech illusr, Army Ballistic Missile Agency, Redstone Arsenal, Ala, 57-58; brochure designer, Huntsville Symphony Orchestra, 72-; dir art dept, Madison Acad, Huntsville, Ala, 74-77; chmn dept art, Stone Middle Sch. *Teaching:* Pvt art instr, Huntsville. *Mem:* Huntsville Art League & Mus Asn; Huntsville Art Educ Asn; Nat Asn Women Artists. *Media:* Multimedia. *Mailing Add:* 3506 May Dr SE Huntsville AL 35801

SAVENOR, BETTY CARMELL
PAINTER, PRINTMAKER
b Boston, Mass, Sept 2, 27. *Study:* Jackson von Ladau Sch Fashion; Mass Col Art; Brandeis Col, with Mitchel Siporin; Mass Col of Art, BFA. *Hon Degrees:* Mass Col of Art. *Work:* Liberty Mutual Insurance Co; Bank Boston; First Capital Bank Concord, NH; New Eng Life Insurance Co; TECO Energy Corp, Fla; and others. *Comn:* Needlepoint design, Temple Sinai, Springfield, Mass, 88. *Exhib:* RI Watercolor Soc Nat Exch, Tokyo, Japan, 87-88; Nat Asn Women Artists USA Centennial (traveling), NY, 88-89; Nat Asn Women Artist 100 Works (traveling), India, 89-90; Ga Watercolor Soc traveling exhib, 96; one-woman shows, Cataumet Arts Ctr, Mass, 96, Market Barn Gallery, Mass, 98 & Mazur Art Gallery, Mass, 98; Nat Asn wome Artists, US Traveling Painting Exhib, 98-99. *Pos:* Instr Demonstrations. *Teaching:* Instr in home studio, cruises, juror. *Awards:* First Prize Graphics, All New Eng Exhib, Cape Cod Art Asn, 93, 94 & 95, 98, 99, 2000, First Place Mixed Media, 02; Best In State, Nat League Am Pen Women, 95 & 38th Nat Biennial Award Excellence, 98; Juror's Choice, Falmouth Artists' Guild, Open Exhib, 96; Bronze Medal, Catherine L Wolfe Art Club, NY, 2000; Belle Kramer Meml Award, Nat Asn Women Artists, 02. *Bibliog:* Mary Ann Wenninger (auth), Collograph Printing, Watson Guptil, 80; Best of Watercolor Painting Textures & Best of Watercolor II, Rockport Publ, 98, 99. *Mem:* Nat Asn Am Penwomen; New Eng Watercolor Soc (past dir); Monotype Guild New Eng; Womens Contemp Artists; Northwest Watercolor Soc/Wash; Nat Asn Women Artists/NY; FLAG Fla; ISEA (Int Soc of Exp); NWWS (Northeast Wat Soc); SWS (Southern Water Soc). *Media:* Watercolor; Graphics; Mixed Media. *Specialty:* Contemporary Fine Arts. *Interests:* Sculpting; Tennis, Swimming, Decorating Jewelry designs. *Collection:* Fairfield Med Asn, Calif; Bank Boston; Sheraton Corp; Meadows Country Club, Fl. *Publ:* Colcograph Painting/ Watson-Guyotil: Painting Textures; Collected Best of Watercolors; The Best of Watercolor 2; The Best of Watercolor 3; Rockport Publishers. *Dealer:* Art Three Manchester NH; Gallery 333 MA Diane Levine Fine Arts MA. *Mailing Add:* 4305 Highland Oaks Cir Sarasota FL 34235-5173

SAVILLE, KEN
SCULPTOR, CRAFTSMAN
b Hanging Rock, WVa, Jan 9, 49. *Study:* Austin Peay State Univ, BS, 71. *Work:* Albuquerque Mus; Mus NMex, Santa Fe; Libr Cong; New Mus, NY; Univ Idaho. *Comn:* Sculpture, City Albuquerque, one percent for the Arts Prog, 86. *Exhib:* Drawings USA, Minn Mus Art, 77; Artwords and Bookworks, Los Angeles Inst Contemp Art, 78; New Epiphanies, Gallery Contemp Art, Univ Colo, 82; Arteder, Muestra Int Arte Grafico, Bilboa, Spain, 82; Arts New Mexico, Gallery Contemp Art Latin Am, Washington, DC, 84; Mus NMex, 91; Roswell Mus, 91. *Pos:* NMex Arts Div Grants Awards Juror, 84. *Teaching:* Artist in residence, NMex Arts Div, 78-83 & 88-97, Tex Comm Arts, 90 & Mus Int Folk Art, Santa Fe, 96-97; instr, Independent artwork, 78-. *Awards:* Jurors Award, Southwest Fine Arts Biennial, 76; Award Merit, Craftworks V, 83. *Bibliog:* Michael Reed (auth), article, Artspace, summer 83; Sandy Ballatore (auth), New Mexico Sculptors, El Palacio, spring/summer 90; Mary Carroll Nelson (auth), Ken Saville salvages joy from sorrow, NMex Mag, 5/93. *Media:* Polychromed Wood; Colored Pencil. *Dealer:* Obsidian Gallery St Philips Plaza No 90 4340 N Campbell Ave Tucson AZ 85718; Maripesa Gallery 3500 Central SE Suitek Albuquerque NMex 87106. *Mailing Add:* Box 4662 Albuquerque NM 87196

SAVINAR, TAD
VIDEO ARTIST
b Portland, Ore, 1950. *Study:* Colo Col, BA(studio arts), 73. *Work:* Portland Art Mus, Ore; Mus Mod Art & Chase Manhattan Bank, NY; Nat Archives, Smithsonian Inst, Washington, DC; Univ Calif Art Mus, Santa Barbara. *Comn:* State Lands Bldg, Boise Cascade, Ore, 90; US Customs Off, Nat Endowments Arts, 90; Mentor Graphics Hdq, Ore, 90; Harborview Hosp, Seattle, Wash, 91-96; Westside Light Rail, Design Team, Portland, Ore, 92-97. *Exhib:* Solo exhibs, Los Angeles Inst Contemp Art, 83, Ctr Contemp Art, Seattle, Wash & Reed Col, Portland, Ore, 84, New Mus Contemp Art, NY, 85, Elizabeth Leach Gallery, Portland, Ore, 88, 89, 91 & 92, Fabric Workshop, Philadelphia, 92, Savage Fine Art (with catalog), Portland, 94 & Art Gym, Marlhurst Univ (with catalog), Portland, 99; Portland Art Mus, Ore, 91, 93, 95, 98 & 99; Elizabeth Leach Gallery, Portland, Ore, 93; Art Gym, Marylhurst Col, Portland, Ore, 94; Savage Fine Art, Portland, Ore, 93; Meyerson Nowinski, Seattle, 96, 97 & 98; and others. *Collection Arranged:* Mus Mod Art; Nat Archives, Smithsonian Inst; Portland Art Mus, Oreg; Univ Calif Art Mus, Santa Barbara; Norton Mus Art, West Palm Beach, Fla; Fabric Workshop Mus, Philadelphia. *Teaching:* Instr, Marylhurst Col, Ore, 79-86. *Awards:* Grant, Metrop Arts Comn, 84, 86, 87 & 91; Nat Endowment Arts grant, 84, sculp fel, 84, painting fel, 95; Gov Arts Award, Ore, 98. *Publ:* Auth, The 4 Mickies, Artists Repertory Theatre, 88; Brushfires, Portland Civic Theater. *Dealer:* Savage Fine Art 1419 SW Park Portland OR 97201. *Mailing Add:* PO Box 10798 Portland OR 97296

SAVITT, SAM
PAINTER, ILLUSTRATOR
b Wilkes-Barre, Pa. *Study:* Pratt Inst; Art Students League; drawing with Paul Brown, painting with Howard Trafton & John Vickery & sculpture with Seymour Lipton. *Work:* St Lawrence Univ, Canton, NY; Grumbacher Collection, NY; and pvt collections including William Randolph Hearst, Jr, Raymond Firestone, August Busch, Dr Jere Lord, Jr, George C Haas, Howard H Newman & Meriwether Hudson. *Comn:* Posters, Nat Horse Show, NY, 80, 89 & Lipizzaner Stallions, 82; polo poster, BMW, 86; Ky Derby, 91; portrait racehorse "Forego" for Ky Mus of the Horse. *Exhib:* Int Sports Core, Oak Brook, Ill, 75; one-man shows, Piccolo Mondo, Palm Beach, Fla, 74, Gallery at Noroton, Darien, Conn, 81 & Northridge Gallery, Ridgefield, Conn; Am Acad Equine Artists, Morven Park, Leesburg, Va, 81; Soc Animal Artists, Acad Natural Sci, Philadelphia, 81; Bancroft Libr, Berkeley, Calif, 86; and others. *Pos:* Official artist, US Equestrian Team, 60-. *Teaching:* Guest lectr horses in art, 55-; yearly workshop, drawing & painting, Scottsdale Artists' Sch, Scottsdale, Ariz, Joseph Art Sch, Ore; dean Am Acad Equine Art, Lexington, Ky; Fechin Inst, San Cristobal, NMex. *Awards:* Jr Bk Award, Boys Clubs Am, 58; Lit Guild Award, 73; 73 Distinguished Achievement Awards, City Wilkes-Barre, Pa; Equine Artist of Distinction Award & Lifetime Achievement Award, NAm Horseman's Asn, 98. *Bibliog:* Felice Buckvar (auth), Animals fascinate artist, NY Times, 11/11/84; Nancy T Marr (auth), Savitt is a true aficionado, Chronicle of the House, 2/86; Equus Mag,

11/87 & 6/94; Thoroughbred Times, 8/20/94. *Mem:* Soc Animal Artists; Soc Illusr; Graphic Artists Guild; Authors Guild; Am Acad Equine Art (dir, painting). *Media:* Mixed. *Publ:* Auth & illusr, Vicki and the Brown Mare, 76, Dingle Ridge Fox and Other Stories, 78 & One Horse, One Hundred Miles, One Day, 81, Dodd Mead Co; auth & illusr, Draw Horses with Sam Savitt, Viking Press, 81; auth, A Horse to Remember, Viking Press, 84. *Dealer:* Gallery One, Mentor, OH; Black Horse Press Box 302 North Salem NY 10560. *Mailing Add:* PO Box 302 North Salem NY 10560

SAVOY, CHYRL LENORE
SCULPTOR, EDUCATOR
b New Orleans, La, May 23, 44. *Study:* La State Univ, BA(art); Acad Fine Arts, Florence, with Gallo & Berti; diploma di Profitto, Universita degli Studi di Firenze, Florence; Wayne State Univ, MFA(sculpture); TH Harris Vocation Tech Sch, diploma (welding), 72. *Work:* Alexandria Mus Art, La; Couvent St Dominique de la Gloire de Dieu, Maison Mere des Dominicaines, Flavigny, France; Our Lady Star of the Sea, Cameron, La; Sixtus Vezie, Cath Mission, Willowvale, Transkie, SAfrica; Savoy Med Ctr, Mamou, La; Frank R Savoy Cancer Ctr. *Comn:* New Orleans Mus of Art, St John the Baptist (sculpture design), Our Lady Star of the Sea, Cameron, La, 73; portrait, comn by FC Barksdale Assocs, Savoy Med Ctr, Mamou, La; Digittactus (sculpture), comn by Alexandria Mus Art, 91. *Exhib:* Detroit Inst Arts, 71; Ark Art Ctr, 71; New Orleans Mus Art, 72; Mint Mus Art, 73; Am Painters in Paris, Palais de Congres, Paris, 75; Galeria de Artes Plasticas, Monterrey, Mex, 87; Wang Cult Art Ctr, Columbia, Mex, 87; New Orleans Contemp Art Ctr, 89; Alexandria Mus Art, 90 & 93; Escuela de Humanidades, Univ de las Americas, Pueblo, Mex, 96; Circumscriber-Drawing the Line, Northeastern State Univ, Tahleguah, Okla, 2001; one-person exhib, Univ de las Americas, Puebla, Mex, 2003. *Pos:* Art comm chmn & bd mem, RS Barnwell Garden & Art Ctr, Shreveport, La, 76-77; juror, numerous local, regional and state art exhibs. *Teaching:* Asst prof fine arts, La State Univ, Shreveport, 73-77; Assoc prof sculpture & drawing, Univ La, Lafayette, 78-. *Awards:* Artist Exhib Award, New Orleans Mus Art, 71; Samuel Wiener Sculpture Award, 73; Instrnl Improvement Grants, Dept Fine Arts, Univ Southwestern, 86 & 87; Octava Premio Naz Danza Mex 1987 Finalist, Palacio Bella Artes, Mexico City, 87; Beacon Club Teacher of the Year Award, Univ, of LA, Lafayette, 2000; Borst Grant; Interdisciplinary Foundry and Mold Making Studio Development Spring, 2004. *Bibliog:* Virginia Watson-Jones (auth), Contemporary American Women Sculptors, Oryx Press, 86; Arthur Williams (auth), Sculpture: Technique-Form-Content, Davis Publ Inc, 89; Making Their Mark-Women Artists Move Into the Mainstream, Abbeville Press, 89; Beginning Sculpture by Arthur Williams, Davis Studio Series, Davis Pub, 2004; The Sculptural Reference, by Arthur Williams, Sculpture Books, Sculpture Books Pub, 2004; Who's Who Among America's Teachers, 2003-2004. *Mem:* Artist's Alliance. *Media:* Wood, Mixed Media. *Interests:* Music, Intramedia Collaborations. *Collection:* New Orleans Mus of Art, Alexandria Mus of Art, Alexandria LA. *Mailing Add:* PO Box 573 Youngsville LA 70592

SAWADA, IKUNE
PAINTER
b Japan, Aug 30, 36. *Study:* Kyoto Art Univ, BFA. *Work:* Seattle Art Mus; Art Gallery Gtr Victoria, BC; Brooklyn Col; Art Univ Kyoto. *Comn:* Mural, Puget Sound Mutual Savings Bank, Seattle, 75; King Co Bldg, Seattle, Wash, 76; Safeco Insurance Co, Seattle, 80. *Exhib:* Ann Exhib Northwest Artists, Seattle Art Mus, 71-75; Wash State Artmobile Exhib, 72; Ann Puget Sound Area Exhib, Charles & Emma Frye Art Mus, Seattle, 72 & 75; Nat Art Competition, Springfield Art Mus, Utah, 75; Asian Artist Exhib, Western Wash State Col Mus, 75. *Teaching:* Teacher art & art hist, Pub High Sch, Japan, 60-65. *Awards:* Lulu Fairbanks Award, Found Int Understanding Through Students, 70; Second Place Award, Fed Way Arts Festival, Washington, 72; Honorable Mention Award, Ann Exhib Northwest Artists, Seattle Art Mus, 74. *Bibliog:* Natsuhiko Tsutsumi (auth), People in Seattle, Katei-Zenka, 75. *Media:* Oil, Watercolor. *Mailing Add:* 637 Pleasant Walla Walla WA 99362

SAWAI, NOBORU
PRINTMAKER
b Takamatsu, Japan, Feb 18, 31; US citizen. *Study:* Augsburg Col, Minneapolis, BA, 66; Univ Minn, MFA, 69; Yoshida Hanga Acad, Tokyo, woodcut printmaking with Toshi Yoshida, 70. *Work:* Nat Gallery Can, Ottawa; Glenbow Mus, Calgary, Alta; Edmonton Art Gallery, Alta; Winnipeg Art Gallery, Man. *Comn:* Sculpture, Trinity Lutheran Congregation, Minneapolis, 67. *Exhib:* 38th Ann Exhib, Japan Printmakers Asn, Tokyo, 70; Can Nat Exhib, Toronto, 73; 1st Ann Nat Print Exhib, Los Angeles, 73; 2nd NH Int Graphics Ann, 74; 11th Int Biennial Graphic Art, Ljubljana, Yugoslavia, 75. *Teaching:* Instr printmaking, drawing & art hist, Berea Col, Ky, 70-71; asst prof printmaking, Univ Calgary, 71-94. *Awards:* Manisphere Award, Manisphere 10th Ann Show, 73; Purchase Award, London Mus, Ont, 74; Edition Award, Art Gallery Brant, Brantford, Ont, 75. *Bibliog:* Dennis Elliot (auth), 12th Annual Calgary Graphic Show, Arts Can Mag, 72; Ruth Weisberg (auth), Prints of wit and humor, W Coast Art Works, 5/4/74; Rino Boccaccini (auth), Noboru Sawai, Voce di Ferrara, 9/21/74. *Media:* Woodcuts, Etching. *Mailing Add:* 662 Alexander No 4 Vancouver BC V6A 1C9 Canada

SAWKA, JAN A
PAINTER, PRINTMAKER
b Zabrze, Poland, Dec 10, 46. *Study:* Polytech Inst, MA, 72 & Art Acad, MA, 72, Wroclaw, Poland. *Work:* Mus Mod Art, NY; Centre Georges Pompidou, Paris, France; Stedelijk Mus, Amsterdam, Holland; Libr Cong, Washington, DC; Nat Mus, Warsaw, Poland. *Comn:* Grateful Dead-Stadium Sets, 89 & 93. *Exhib:* Solo shows, Wilanow Mus, 76 & Poster Mus, Warsaw, Poland, 80; Musee d'Art Moderne, Paris, 78; Smithsonian Tour Show, 79-80; Toyoma Mus, Japan, 85; Musee D'Affiche, Paris, 86. *Pos:* Resident artist, Pratt Manhattan Ctr, 82-86. *Awards:* Oscar De La Peinture Award, 7th Int Painting Festival, Cagnos-sur-Mar, France, 75; Gold Medal, 7th Int Poster Biennale, Warsaw, Poland, 78; Silver Medal, 14th Int Graphic Art Biennale, Brno, Czechoslovakia; Artist Laureate, 7th Int Poster Exhib, Ft Collins, Colo. *Bibliog:* Syzmon Bojko (auth), Jan Sawka, Graphics Mag, Zurich, Switz, 81; James Beck (auth), The conversation, Arts Mag, 83. *Media:* Acrylic, Mixed Media. *Publ:* A Book of Fiction, Clarkson N Potter, New York, 86. *Mailing Add:* 54 Old State Rte 213 High Falls NY 12440-5103

SAWYER, HELEN See Farnsworth, Helen Sawyer

SAWYER, MARGO
SCULPTOR, ENVIRONMENTAL ARTIST
b Washington, DC, May 6, 58. *Study:* Brighton Polytechnic Fac Art, Gt Britain, 76-77; Chelsea Sch Art, London, Hon BA, 77-80; Skowhegan Sch Painting & Sculpture, 80; Yale Univ, MFA, 80-82. *Work:* Leon Hess; Prudential Insurance; Chemical Bank; Samuel P Harn Mus Art, Univ Fla; Progressive Corp. *Comn:* Birdhouse Proj, Hong Ning Apts, NY, 86. *Exhib:* Solo exhibs, Spec Proj, PS1, Long Island, NY, 89, Barbara Toll Fine Arts, NY, 89 & 91, Women & Their Work, Austin, Tex, 92 & 98, Projects, Diverworkds, Houston, Tex, 94, Sagacho Exhib Space, Tokyo, 96, Austin Mus Art, 98 & Galviston Art Ctr, 99; Skowhegan ten yr retrospective, Leo Castelli Gallery, NY, 86; Meyers-Bloom Gallery, Santa Monica, Calif, 89; Archer M Huntington Art Gallery, Austin, Tex, 90; Contemp Sculpture, Harn Mus Art, Univ Fla, 92; Drawing-Crossing the Line Diverse works, Houston, Tex, 94; plus many others. *Collection Arranged:* Austin Mus Art. *Teaching:* Assoc prof, Univ Tex, Austin, 88; assoc prof, Univ Tex, Austin. *Awards:* Nat Endowment Visual Arts, 86; Fel, Acad in Rome, 86-87 & Japan Found Visual Arts, 96; Grant, NY State Coun Arts, 87, Fulbright Sr Res to India, 82 & 83 & to Japan, 95-96. *Bibliog:* Patricia Phillips (auth), Margo Sawyer & Mark Walczak the bird house project, Artforum, 12/86; Michael Kimmelman (auth), Margo Sawyer,NY Times, Living Arts, 2/24/89; John Clarke (auth), Margo Saywer at diverseworks, Art in Am, 9/94. *Mailing Add:* Univ Tex Dept Art & Art Hist Art 3-338 Austin TX 78712

SAWYER, MARIA ARTEMIS PAPAGEORGE See Artemis, Maria Artemis Papageorge

SAX, (STEVE G SACKS)
PAINTER, CARTOONIST
b Brooklyn, NY, Jan 2, 60. *Study:* Sch Visual Arts, 82-84; Art Students League, 84-89. *Work:* Nat Baseball Hall Fame, Cooperstown, NY; Basketball Hall Fame, Springfield, Mass; Hockey Hall Fame, Toronto, Ont; Pelham Art Ctr, NY; Del Art Mus, Wilmington; and others. *Comn:* Ball Park, Queens, NY; Sargent Garcias, Queens, NY; 3 Sticks on a Fat Lady, NY; Popilini, NY; Alamo, Brooklyn, NY. *Exhib:* Teamwork, Krasdale Foods, Lehman Col Art Gallery, White Plains, NY; "Batter Up" the Art of Baseball, Pelham Art Ctr, NY; Nat Baseball Hall Fame, Cooperstown, NY, 89-94; The Artist and the Baseball Card, Syracuse Univ Lowe Gallery, NY, 92, Tex Christian Univ, Ft Worth, 94 & Brigham Young Univ, Provo, Utah, 94; Great Moment from the 50s, Basketball Hall Fame, Springfield, Mass, 93; Rock & Roll, Ambassador Gallery, NY, 97-98; solo exhib, Paintings & Sculpture, Butler Inst Am Art, Youngstown, Ohio, 98. *Bibliog:* Joe Gerson (auth), Cooperstown, Newsday, 8/93; Georgett Gouveia (auth), Baseball Art, Gannett, 94. *Media:* Acrylic, Oil. *Mailing Add:* PO Box 593 Forest Hills NY 11375

SAXE, ADRIAN A
CERAMIST
b Glendale, Calif, 1943. *Study:* Chouinard Art Sch, 65-69; Calif Inst Arts, BFA, 74. *Work:* Everson Mus Art, Syracuse, NY; Los Angeles Co Mus Art, Calif; Mus Art, Carneige Inst, Pittsburgh, Pa; Nelson-Atkins Mus Art, Kansas City, Mo; Renwick Gallery, Nat Collection Am Art, Smithsonian Inst, Washington, DC; Brooklyn Mus of Art, NY; The Metropolitan Mus of Art, NY; The White House, Washington, DC; and many more. *Comn:* Installation for 1st contemp art exhib at Getty Mus, Los Angeles Departures, 11 Artists at the Getty. *Exhib:* Solo exhibs, Frank Lloyd Gallery, NY, 85, 87, 88 & 90-97, Los Angeles, 85, The Am Hand, Washington, DC & Univ Mo Art Gallery Kansas City, 87 & 89, Saxe Retrospective 1970-92 Los Angeles Co Mus of Art traveled to Mus of Contemp Ceramic Art, Shigarski, Japan and the Newark Mus; Group exhibs, LA Post Cool, San Jose Mus of Art, Calif, 2002, Great Pots: Contemp Ceramics From Function to Fantasy, Newark Mus, NJ, 2003; Contemp Ceramics, Muscarelle Mus Art, Col William & Mary, Williamsburg, Va, 86; Craft Today: Poetry of the physical, Am Craft Mus, NY, 86; Am Potters Today, Victoria & Albert Mus, London, 86; New Clay, Univ Art Gallery, Calif State Univ, San Bernardino, Calif, 86; Am Ceramics Now, Everson Mus, 87; Chinese Influence on Am W Coast Contemp Art, 88; Kansas City Collects, Nelson Atkins Mus, Mo, 89; Am Clay Artists, Port Hist Mus, Philadelphia, 89, Vessels From Use to Symbol, Am Craft Mus, NY, 90; The Art Cup, Garth Clark Gallery, Los Angeles, 94; Current Trends in Ceramics: Vessels and Objects (with catalog), Aichi Perfectual Ceramic Mus, Japan, 94; The Splendor of Porcelain, Los Angeles Co Mus Art, Calif, 97; A Survey of Southern Calif Ceramics, Pasadena City Col, Calif, 98; The Hague, The Neth, 99; White House Collection of Am Crafts, Mus Art, Univ Mich, Ann Arbor, 2000; and many others. *Teaching:* Instr, Calif State Univ, Long Beach, 71-72; assoc prof art and head of ceramics, Univ Calif, Los Angeles, 73-. *Awards:* Fac Grant, Art Coun, Univ Calif, Los Angeles, 84; Artist Fel, Nat Endowment Arts, 86; US/France Exchange Fel, US Info Agency & Govt France, 87; NEA Grant, 92; Flintridge Found Visual Artists Award, 2001; Guggenheim Found Fel, 2002. *Bibliog:* Garth Clark (auth), Adrian Saxe: an interview, Am ceramics, Fall 82; Jan Axel & Karen McCready (auths), porcelain: Traditions and New Visions, Watson-Guptill, 81; Judith Bettleheim, Pacific Connections, Am Crafts, 4/86; Barbara Mayer (auth), Contemporary American Craft Art: A Collector's Guide, Peregrine Smith Books, 88; De Waal, Edmund (auth.) Design Sourcebook Ceramics, London, New Holland (pubs.), 2000. *Dealer:* Frank Lloyd Gallery 170 S La Brea Ave Los Angeles CA 90036. *Mailing Add:* Univ Calif Dept Art 1300 Dickson Art Ctr 405 Hilgard Ave Los Angeles CA 90095-1615

SAXE, HENRY, OC
SCULPTOR
b Montreal, Que, Sept 24, 37. *Study:* Ecole Des Beaux Arts, Montreal, 56-62. *Work:* Nat Gallery Can; Montreal Mus Fine Arts; Mus Art Contemporain, Montreal; Mus de Que; Queens Univ, Ont; and others. *Comn:* Govt Ocean Bldg, Calgary Alta. *Exhib:* Bienale de Paris, 68; Salon Int Pilot Galleries, Lausanne Switz, 70; Int Sculpture, Middleheim, Antwerp, 71; Bienale, Venice, 78; Retrospective, Mus d'Art, Contemporain Montreal, Que, 94; and many others. *Awards:* Grants, 67-69 & Sr Awards, 73, 77, 81, 84, 87 & 91, Can Coun Arts; Order Can, 88; Paul Emile Borduas Prize, 94. *Bibliog:* Jennifer Lynton (auth), Abstract Beauty in Sculpture, Queen's J, Kingston, 10/83; Elio Grazioll (auth), Aurora Borealis, Flash Art, No 124, Milan, 10/11/85. *Dealer:* Galerie Kozen. *Mailing Add:* PO Box 143 Tamworth ON K0K 3G0 Canada

SAYLES, EVA
PAINTER
b June 10, 28. *Study:* Brooklyn Col, BA, 49; Art Students League, with Will Barnet, Burban & Palumbo, 60-62 & 84-86; Sch Visual Arts; Pratt Inst. *Exhib:* Marcolio Ltd, NY, 69; Pen & Brush Club, NY, 70; solo exhibs, St Bartholemew's Church, NY, 70, Pen & Brush Club, 71 & mos Eno Art Gallery, Port Chester Coun Arts, 92; Knickerbocker Artists; Queens Mus, 83; Port Chester Coun for the Arts, NY, 92; Nat Asn Women Artists; Greenwich Art Soc. *Awards:* Oil Painting Award, Nat Asn Women Artists; Scholarships, Art Students League, 84 & 85. *Mem:* Nat Asn Women Artists (chairperson pub relations comt, 86-88). *Media:* Oil, Pencil. *Interests:* Art, music, science, philosophy, literature, poetry, dance & singing. *Publ:* Article in Greenwich Time Newspaper, 4/92; plus poems and articles published in The Am Bard, Greenwich Times and others. *Mailing Add:* PO Box 510 Port Chester NY 10573-0510

SAYLORS, JO AN
SCULPTOR, INSTRUCTOR
b Lewisberg, Tenn, Apr 23, 32. *Study:* Scottsdale Artists Sch, studied with Edward Fraughton, 86. *Work:* Will Rogers Mus, Claremore, Okla; Collection of Pres Suharto, Jakarta, Indonesia; Territorial Mus, Guthrie, Okla; Am Petroleum Mus, Ponca City, Okla; Childrens Hosp, Dallas. *Comn:* Stations of the Cross, Episcopal Church, Ponca City, 80; seal fountain, comn by Margo Kay Shorney, Oklahoma City, 82; life-sized bronze, Ponca City Libr, 88; Lady of Justice, Okla Found, 91; One & 1/4 life size Centennial Bronze, Centennial Found, 93; and others. *Exhib:* Am Royal Art Show, Am Royal Bldg, Kansas City, Mo, 81; Art Ann III & IV, Oklahoma City & Tulsa, 82-83; Nat Audubon Soc Invational, Tulsa, 83; N Am Sculpture Show, Golden, Colo, 84; Artists of Am Rotary Show, Denver, Colo; Am Rotary Show, Denver, Colo, 98; and others. *Teaching:* Instr, Scottsdale Artists Sch, Ariz & Loveland Acad Art, Colo. *Awards:* Gallery Owners Award, Art Ann III, Oklahoma City, 82; First Prize for Sculpture, Nat Audubon Soc, 83; Merit Award, Int Western Wildlife Show, Okla Gallery Owners Asn, 85. *Bibliog:* Article, Southwest Art, 4/89, Vail Mag, winter 90; cover, Santa Faen, 12/89. *Media:* Bronze. *Dealer:* Knox Galleries Denver Vail Beaver Creek CO & Naples FL; Alterman-Morris Galleries Dallas Houston TX Santa Fe NM & Hilton Head Island SC. *Mailing Add:* Knox Galleries 1512 Larimerst R 15 Denver CO 80202

SAYRE, ROGER L
SCULPTOR, PAINTER
b Sandusky, Ohio, Sept 19, 41. *Study:* Sch of Dayton Inst, BFA, 73; Univ Cin, MFA, 76, MA, 77. *Work:* Ind Univ Mus, Ohio; Dayton Art Inst, Ohio; Brooklyn Mus, NY; Wooster Col Mus, Ohio; Opposing Sculptural Forms, Contemp Art Ctr, Cinncinati, Ohio. *Comn:* sculpture, Ohio State Univ Hosp, Columbus, 73; prints, Sears Bldg, Chicago, Ill, 74; sculpture, UCF Cinncinati, Ohio, 76; sculpture, Citizen Fed Ctr, Dayton, Ohio, 91; sculpture, City of Dayton, Ohio, 92. *Exhib:* City of Chicago, Pub Sch, Ill; All Ohio Painting Sculpture, 69; Honor Exhib Ohio Arts Coun, 73; City of Toronto, Can, 75; Nat Gallery, Washington, DC, 94; Dayton Art Inst, Ohio, 2000; Steve Martin's Gallery, New Orleans. *Teaching:* asst prof 3-D design, Univ Dayton; asst prof drawing, Univ Cin; head program sculpture, Ind Univ East. *Awards:* Scholar, Ford Found, 67; Purchase awards, All Ohio Painting & Sculpture Exhib, 94 & All-Ohio Graphics Biennial; Atelier scholar Dayton Art Inst; Individual Artist fel Montgomery Co Arts & Cult Dist. *Mem:* Ohio Arts Coun; Dayton Art Inst; Cin Contemp Arts Ctr; Dayton Visual Arts Ctr; Montgomery Co Cooperative Arts Coun. *Media:* All Media. *Publ:* major works published in Le Revue Moderne, Exponent, Art in Am, Art Forum, Dialogue Mag, Dayton Mag, Am Contemp Artists, Viva Mag & The New Art Examiner. *Dealer:* TRA Art Gallery Troy Mich. *Mailing Add:* 215 McDaniel St Apt 809 Dayton OH 45405-4827

SAYWELL, EDWARD
CURATOR
Exhib: Cur (exhibs) Christopher Wilmarth: Drawing into Sculpture, 2003, The Privilege of Solitude: Alfred Jensen and Forest Bess, 2004 (Award for Best Show in a Commercial Gallery Nationally, Int Assoc Art Critics/USA, 2005). *Pos:* John S Newberry Res Asst, assoc cur; Charles S Cunningham Sr, Cur Assoc. *Teaching:* Lynn and Philip A Straus Intern Dept Drawing, Fogg Art Mus, Harvard Univ, Cambridge, Mass, 96-97. *Mailing Add:* Fogg Art Mus Harvard U 32 Quincy St Cambridge MA 02138

SAZEGAR, MORTEZA
PAINTER
b Teheran, Iran, Nov 11, 33; US citizen. *Study:* Univ Tex, El Paso, BA, 55, BS, 56; Baylor Univ Col Med, 56-57; Cornell Univ, 58-59. *Work:* Whitney Mus Am Art, NY; San Francisco Mus Art; Corcoran Gallery Art, Washington, DC; Prudential Ins Co, Newark, NJ; Tehran Mus Contemp Art. *Exhib:* One-man shows, Poindexter Gallery, NY, 64-77; Art Inst Chicago, 65; Whitney Mus Am Art Ann, 69-70; Cleveland Mus Art, 72; Corcoran Gallery Art, 73. *Bibliog:* Donald B Goodall (auth), Color Forum, Univ Tex Art Mus, 72; Gene Baro (auth), The Way of Color, Corcoran Gallery Art, 73; Lucy R Lippard (auth), Intricate Structural Repeated Image, Tyler Sch Art, Temple Univ, Philadelphia, Pa, 79. *Media:* Acrylic, Watercolor. *Mailing Add:* 1223 Homeville Rd Cochranville PA 19330

SCALA, JOSEPH A
SCULPTOR, PAINTER
b Queens, NY, Feb 20, 40. *Study:* C W Post Col, BS, 62; Cornell Univ, MFA(sculpture), 71. *Work:* Metrop Mus Art, NY; Herbert Johnson Mus, Ithaca, NY; Battelle Mem Inst, Acad Contemp Problems, Columbus, Ohio; Lehigh Univ, Penn. *Comn:* Laser sculpture, Andrew Dickson White Mus, Ithaca, NY, 70; Sound/Light Sculpture, Rochester Jr League, 70; Cybernetic Fountain, Cornell Univ Physics Dept, 72. *Exhib:* Some More Beginnings, Brooklyn Mus, 68; Mirrors, Motors, Motion, Albright-Knox Gallery, Buffalo, NY, 70; one-person shows, Everson Mus, Syracuse, NY, 72 & W Broadway Gallery, NY, 76; Can Comput Show Art Exhib, Toronto, Ont, 75; Computers & Art, IBM Gallery, New York, NY & traveling, 87-88. *Collection Arranged:* Current-New York (auth, catalog), Syracuse Univ Lowe Art Gallery, 80; Tibor de Nagy Collection, Syracuse Univ Lubin House Gallery, 80; A Contemporary Art Collection: Clement Greenberg, Syracuse Univ. *Pos:* Pres & founder, Collaborations in Art, Sci & Technol Inc, 69-79; dir, Lowe Art Gallery, Syracuse Univ, 78-85, dir, Lubin House Gallery, 79-82. *Teaching:* Instr multi-media, Cornell Univ, 70 & 71; assoc prof art & technol, Syracuse Univ, 71-85, chairperson museology prog, 78-85, prof computer graphics & museology, 85-86, prof computer graphics art, 85-92, emer prof, 92-. *Awards:* Winner Young Sculptors Competition, Sculptors Guild, New York, 69; New York State Coun Arts Grants, 70-85; Inst Mus Serv, Nat Endowment Arts, 85-86. *Bibliog:* Milford Kime (auth), Laser art, Laser Focus, 73; Arts Magazine, A Brief History of Siggraph Art Exhibition, 4/1982, page 13; Patric D. Prince, Brave New World; ACM Siggraph 89-Leonardo, 7/1989, page 3. *Media:* Ceramic, wood, acrylic, Mixed media, computer. *Publ:* Auth, Teaching Art Through Computer Graphics, Nat Computer Conf PRoceedings, ed Stanley Winkler, AFIPS Press, 1976, Vol 45, No 1, 185-189; auth, Current/New York:Recent Works in Relief, 1980. *Mailing Add:* 2381 Fairbanks Rd New Woodstock NY 13122

SCALERA, MICHELLE ANN
CONSERVATOR
b Montclair, NJ, May 7, 52. *Study:* Kean Univ, BA (art hist & fine arts), 1974; Universita Internazionale dell' Arte, Florence, Italy, MA, 1974-76; Conservation Studio apprentice to Prof Paolo Gori, Florence, Italy, 1976-80. *Hon Degrees:* Kean Univ, Phi Kappa Phi. *Pos:* chief conservator, Ringling Mus Art, Sarasota, Fla, 1985-. *Teaching:* Ringling Mus Art, 2001-06. *Awards:* ADDY Award, Techno-Vouet, 2004; Davis award, Fla Asn Mus, 2005. *Mem:* AAM-ICOM Am Asn Mus; AIC Am Inst Conserv; Florida Art Mus; Materials Research Soc; Int Inst Conservation. *Publ:* auth, JRS Micro-Raman Spectroscopic Study, Lapatsa, 2005; auth, JRS Micro Raman Study, Della Robbia (in prep); auth, Ca d'Zan The Restoration of Ringling Mansion (in prep); contribr auth, Encore, 2006. *Mailing Add:* 8019 Indigo Ridge Terr University Park FL 34201

SCALISE, NICHOLAS PETER
PAINTER
b Meriden, Conn, June 4, 32. *Study:* Horace C Wilcox Tech Sch, Meriden; Paier Sch Art, New Haven, Conn, 59. *Work:* Midstate Med Center, Meriden, Conn; City Hall, Meriden, Conn; Meriden Pub Libr. *Comn:* Our Lady of Mt Carmel Church, Meriden, 89; Miller Co, Meriden, 94. *Exhib:* Nat Art League, NY, 69; Butler Inst Am Art, Youngstown, Ohio, 69, 87-88 & 98; Wadsworth Atheneum, Hartford, Conn, 72; Silvermine Exhib, Conn, 77 & 81; New Eng in Winter Watercolor Exhib, De Cordova Mus, Lincoln, Mass, 77 & 78; Addison Gallery Am Art, Phillips Acad, Andover, Mass, 81; Holyoke Mus, Mass; New Brit Mus, Conn; Allied Artist of Am, NYC 79th Ann Exhib, 92; Nat Soc of Painters in Casein and Acrylic, New York City, The Elsie Ject-Key Memorial Award, 93; Academic Artists Assoc Springfield, MA 43rd Nat Exhib, 93 Academic Artists Award; Massey Fine Arts, Santa Teresa, NMex 92 Purchase Award and 93 First Place; Nat Exhib of Am Watercolors Arts Ctr Old Forge, NY Pulsifer Award and Selected Nat Travel Exhib, 96; Conn Pastel Soc Paul Mellon Art Ctr, Wlfd Conn, 97; Hudson Valley Art Assoc, NY 66th Ann Nat Exhib, President Mary LaGreca Award, 97; West Hartford Art League, Conn Open Juried Show, 97, One of Two First Place Awards. *Teaching:* Instr drawing & painting, Famous Artists Sch, Westport, Conn, 59-70. *Awards:* Meriden Hall Fame, 87; Second Prize Watercolor, Susquehanna Art Soc, Pa, 92; Cert Merit Watercolor, Nat Acad Design, New York, 92; and many others. *Bibliog:* Articles, North Light Mag, 7-8/77 & Am Artist Mus, 7/78, Am Artist Diary, 11/80; article & cover, Palette Talk, 80; American Artists of 86; Who's Who in American Art 88; Paler College of Art catalog 90-93; Rockport Publishers Best in Oil Painting, 96; Rockport Publishers Best in Watercolor 97; and others. *Mem:* Springfield Acad Artist; Meriden Arts & Crafts, Conn; Conn Acad Fine Arts, Hartford; Conn Watercolor Soc, Hartford; Knickerbocker Artists, NY. *Media:* Watercolor, All Media. *Publ:* Painting in Light and Shadow, Rockport Publ, 97, Portrait Inspirations, All Mediums, 97, The Best of Sketching and Drawing, 98 & 99 and other Best in Watercolor, Third ed, 99, included in seven Rockport Publ The "Best of Series". *Dealer:* Beaux Arts Gallery Woodbury CT. *Mailing Add:* 59 Susan Lane Meriden CT 06450-6848

SCALZO, JOYCE ANN
CERAMIST, CURATOR
b Utica, NY, Sept 29, 46. *Study:* Munson-Williams-Proctor Art Inst, with Vincent Clemente & John Von Bergen, 79-81. *Comn:* Wall sculptures, Breckenridge Resort Hotel, St Petersburg Beach, Fla; vessels & wall sculptures, Girard Jewelers Corp Off, St Petersburg, Fla & pres Weight Watchers, Palm Beach, Fla, 93. *Exhib:* Contemp

Relig Works, Schumacher Gallery, Capitol Univ, Columbus, Ohio; In Perspective/Out of Bounds, Fla Ctr Contemp Art, Ybor City, Fla, 87; Festival of States, Theodore Wolf, Juror Arts Ctr Asn, St Petersburg, Fla, 89; Arts in Embassies, Am Embassy, Madrid, Spain, 89-92; Crafts at the White House, White House, Washington, DC, 93; Water Lillies (exterior wall), comn by Ambassador & Mrs Mel Sembler, Treasure Island, Fla. *Collection Arranged:* Arts in Embassies (with catalog), Am Embassy, Madrid, Spain, 89; Rubadoux, Washington Irving Ctr, Madrid, 92; Return Engagement, Anderson-Marsh Galleries, 92. *Pos:* Dir, Gallery Mido, Clearwater, Fla, 94-; owner & dir, Scalzo Gallery, Bellair Bluffs, Fla. *Teaching:* Clay, Lee Co Pub Schs-Adult Educ, Fla, 81-83, St Petersburg Arts Ctr, Fla, formerly & Dunedin Arts Ctr, Fla, 93-. *Awards:* 2nd Place-Ceramics, Art at the Bluffs, 83-84; 2nd Place-Sculpture, Bay Pine Show, 84; First Place-Sculpture, Suntan Arts Ctr, 85. *Bibliog:* Angela Savko (auth), Arts critic, Ft Myers News Press; Charles Benbow (auth), Arts critic, St Petersburg Times, 84, 85 & 86; Mary Ann Marger (auth), Arts critic, St Petersburg Times, 88 & 89. *Mem:* Fla Craftsmen Inc (juried exhibitor, 93-); Womens Caucus Art; Clay Workers Guild Fla (pres, formerly); Arts Ctr Asn; Pinellas Arts Coun. *Media:* Porcelain. *Mailing Add:* c/o A Scalzo Gallery 8208 Forest Cir Seminole FL 34646

SCARBROUGH, CLEVE KNOX, JR
MUSEUM DIRECTOR, HISTORIAN
b Florence, Ala, July 17, 39. *Study:* Univ NAla, BS, 62; Univ Iowa, MA, 67. *Collection Arranged:* Pre-Columbian Art of the Americas, 70, Graphics by Four Modern Swiss Sculptors, circulated by Smithsonian Traveling Serv, 72- & Completed Charlotte Mus Hist, 76, Mint Mus Art, Charlotte, NC. *Pos:* Dir, Mint Mus Art, 69-76, Hunter Mus Art, Chattanooga, Tenn, 76-; mem visual arts adv panel, Tenn Arts Comn, 76, chmn comt, 77-81, rev comt, Art in Pub Places, 78. *Teaching:* Grad asst, Univ Iowa, 64-67; asst prof art hist, Univ Tenn, Knoxville, 67-69. *Mem:* NC Mus Coun (bd mem, 70-75); Southeastern Mus Assoc (bd mem & adv comt, 78-81 & 86-89); Chattanooga Cent City Coun (adv, 81-); Coun Am Asn Mus, 86-89; and others. *Publ:* Ed, North Carolinians Collect, 71; Graphics by Four Modern Swiss Sculptors, 72; British Painting from NC Mus Art, 73; Mountain Landscapes by Swiss Artists, 75. *Mailing Add:* Hunter Mus Art 10 Bluff View Chattanooga TN 37403

SCARPA, DOROTHEA
PAINTER, EDUCATOR
b Brooklyn, NY, July 24, 26. *Study:* Art Students League, 47-50; Mus Mod Art, painting, drawing & composition wood sculpture with Chaim Gross, 50. *Work:* East Stroudsburg Univ Collection. *Exhib:* One person show, East Stroudsburg Univ exhibs, 79-86, Dutot Mus, Del Water Gap, Pa, 80, Temple Gallery, Philadelphia, 87; Celebration of the Arts-Outdoors, Delaware Water Gap, Pa, 81-85; Lehigh Art Alliance Spring Shows, Muhlenburg Col, Allentown, 84; Spring & Winter Shows, Hunterdon Mus Art, Clinton, NJ, 88-98; Shawnee-on-Delaware, Worthington Ave Gallery, Pa, 93-; and many others. *Pos:* Bd mem, Community Art Asn, East Stroudsburg Univ, 80-84, pres, 85 & vpres, 86-. *Teaching:* Artist-in-residence, Dept Early Childhood & Elem Educ, E Stroudsburg Univ, 83-88, Pocono Mt, Elem Ctr, 87, Family of Artist Prog, Stroudsburg, Pa, 88, 91 & 93 & McKeel Child Care Ctr, E Stroundsburg Univ, 95; Special Arts Festival, E Stroudsburg Univ, 88-90; asst prog dir & Artist-in-Residence Penna Ctr of the Arts, Delaware, WaterGap, Pa, 91-92. *Awards:* Purchase Prize, 79 & Hon Mention, 82 & 84, Fall Show, East Stroudsburg Univ; First Prize Theme, Celebration of the Arts, Delaware Water Gap, 85. *Bibliog:* Karen Fisher (ed), Dorothea Scarpa, an artist after a challenge, Pocono Rec, Stroudsburg, Pa, 11/24/81. *Media:* Painting, Stone Carving. *Publ:* Illusr, Museums & Other Resources in Education (MORE), East Stroudsburg Univ, 11/83. *Mailing Add:* c/o McCullough 3410 Allandale Rd Tarpon Springs FL 34691-3303

SCARPITTA, SALVATORE
SCULPTOR, PAINTER
b New York, NY, 1919. *Study:* Study in Italy, 36-40, Royal Acad, Rome, Italy. *Work:* Stedelijk Mus, Amsterdam, Holland; Albright-Knox Art Gallery, Buffalo, Mus Mod Art, NY; Los Angeles Co Mus Art; Nat Mus, Milan Italy; Tel-Aviv Mus, Israel; Mus Mod Art, NY. *Exhib:* 28th Corcoran Biennial, Corcoran Gallery Art, Washington, DC, 63; 67th Ann Exhib: Painting & Sculpture, Art Inst Chicago, 64; one-man shows, Salvatore Scarpitta: Matrix (in cooperation with Leo Castelli), Univ Art Mus, Berkeley, Calif, 89, Sal Scarpitta (in cooperation with Leo Castelli), Scott Hanson Gallery, NY, 90, Sal Scarpitta: Race Car on Idaho Potato Track, Greenburg Wilson Gallery, NY, 90, Studio Guenzani, Milan, Italy, 90, Galleria d'Arte Niccoli, Parma, Italy, 90-91, Grand Salon Gallery, NY, 96 & Rhineheart Sch Sculpture, Baltimore, Md, 96; Buena Vista, John Gibson Gallery, NY, 89; All Quiet on the Western Front?, Espace Dieu, Paris, France, 90; Collins & Milatso Outdoor Sculpture Show, West Point, 94; Homage to Leo Castelli: His Gallery Artists, Contemp Arts Pavilion, Milan, Italy, 96; and others. *Teaching:* Artist-in-residence, Md Inst, Col Art, 66-. *Bibliog:* Harriet Janis & Rudi Blesh (auth), Collage, Personalities-Concepts-Techniques, Chilton, 62; Allen S Weller (auth), The Joys & Sorrows of Recent American Art, Univ Ill, 68; B H Friedman (auth), The ivory tower, Art News, 4/69. *Media:* All. *Mailing Add:* 2031 Oxford Rd New Oxford PA 17350

SCHAAD, DEE
EDUCATOR, CERAMIST
b Sutton, Nebr, Sept 6, 43. *Study:* Univ Nebr, Kearney, BA(art educ), 66, MS(art educ), 71; Univ Nebr, Lincoln Col Fine Arts, MFA, 73. *Work:* Univ Evansville, Ind; Mus Nebr Art, Kearney; Sheldon Swope Art Mus, Terre Haute, Ind. *Comn:* Risen Christ sculpture, St Vincent's Hosp, Indianapolis, Ind, 82; commemorative plaques, Pan Am Games, Indianapolis, Ind, 84. *Exhib:* Materials Hard & Soft, Ctr Visual Arts, Denton, Tex, 90; Int Ceramic Competition, San Angelo Mus Fine Art, Tex, 90; Clayfest VIII, Ctr Contemp Art, Indianapolis, Ind, 92; Natural Wonders, Culver Stockton Col, Canton, Mo, 94; Bald Headed Potters of Am, Grossmont Col, El Cajon, Calif, 95; Artists Who Teach, Concordia Col, St Paul, Minn, 95, Muskingum Col, New Corcord, Ohio, McMurray Univ, Abeline, Tex, 96; Plates & Platters, Studio Potters Network, Rochester, NY, 96, Ind Univ SE, New Albany, Ind, 96; Wall to Wall Ceramics, Univ Evansville, Ind, 97; Glazed Expressions, The Gallery at Studio B, Lancaster, Ohio, 98; Dinner Works, Louisville Visual Arts Assoc, Louisville, Ky, 99; Arthur Butcher Gallery, Concord Col, Athens, WVa, 2000; Hair Today Gone Tomorrow, Artists on Santa Fe, Denver, Colo, 2000; Clayfest 2001, Herron Gallery, Indianapolis, 2001; Contemp Hoosier Artists Sculpture Walk, Crown Hill Cemetary, Indianapolis, 2003; Shelddon Swope Mus, Terre Haute, Ind, 2004; Nat Coun on Educ for Ceramic Arts Invitational, Indianapolis, 2004; Ind Univ, Purdue Univ, Ft Wayne, 2004; Richmond Mus Art, Ind, 2004; Am Ceramic Soc Invitational, Ind Convention Ctr, Indianapolis, 2004; Pleasure of the Table Exhib, NCECA Nat Invitational Exhib, Indianapolis, Ind, 2004; Earth in Balance Regional Juried Competition, Rosewood Gallery, Kettering, OH, 2004; Ceramic Invitational Exhib, Armory Art Ctr, Palm Beach, Fla, 2005; Works on Walls Exhib, Texas Tech Univ, Lubbock, Tex, 2005; XXX Exhib, Santa Fe Clay, NMex, 2005; Ceramic Invitational Exhib, Thaddeus Gallery, LaPorte, Ind, 2005; Skin Deep Exhib, Francis Marion Univ, Florence, SC, 2006; Functionality, Dean Johnson Gallery, Indianapolis, Ind, 2006. *Teaching:* Prof, Univ Indianapolis, Ind, 75-, chair, Art Dept, 94-. *Awards:* Jurors Merit Award, Mat Hard & Soft Nat Craft Competition, 90; Dorothea Schlechte Merit Award, Mid-States Craft Exhib, 90; John Gormley Award, Clayfest VIII, Am Art Clay Co, 92; first place winner, Clayfest 2001, Herron Gallery, Indianapolis, Ind, 2001. *Mem:* Ind Artist Craftsmen (bd dir, 96-); Cent Ind Scholastic Awards (bd dir, 96-); Potters Guild Ind (pres, 90-91); Nat Coun Educ Ceramic Arts (bd dir, 2002-04, onsite liaison, 2002-04); Midwest Col Art Asn; ARTITUDE (bd mem, 2004-); Munce Fine Art Exec Comt. *Media:* Ceramics. *Publ:* Auth, A conversation with Carl Martz Potter, Arts Ind, 80; Light catcher - the work of Curt & Susan Benzelle, Dialogue Mag, 85. *Mailing Add:* Art Dept Univ Indianapolis 1400 E Hanna Ave Indianapolis IN 46227

SCHAB, MARGO POLLINS
ART DEALER
b Cincinnati, Ohio, Aug 4, 45. *Pos:* Pres, Margo Pollins Schab, NY. *Mem:* Pvt Art Dealers Asn. *Specialty:* Important prints, drawings, paintings and sculpture of the 19th and 20th century; Paintings, drawings & prints of the 19th and 20th Centuries. *Mailing Add:* 1000 Park Ave New York NY 10028

SCHABACKER, BETTY BARCHET
PAINTER
b Baltimore, Md, Aug 14, 25. *Study:* Conn Col Women; Marian Carey Art Asn, Newport, RI; Coronado Sch Art, Calif, with Monty Lewis; also with Gerd & Irene Koch, Ojai, Calif. *Work:* St John's Col, Santa Fe, NMex; Erie Art Mus, Pa; Western Union, NY; McGraw Edison, Columbia, Mo; Erie Zoo, Pa; and others. *Exhib:* 20 solo shows, Muses de Arte Moderne, Paris, France, Nat Acad Design; Butler Inst Am Art Ann, 64-77; St John's Col, Santa Fe, NMex, 90, 99; Soc Animal Artists (traveling), 91-92; Lightside Gallery, Santa Fe, NMex, 93; Sangre Cristo Arts Ctr, Pueblo, Colo; and others. *Pos:* Artist-in-residence, Lake Erie Col, 71. *Awards:* Nancy Hubbard Lance Award, Lake Erie Col, 71; First Toastmaster, Ann Fine Art Series, 73; Second Award, Nature Interpreted, Cincinnati Mus Natural Hist, 80; and others. *Bibliog:* Gerald Brommer (auth), Art of Collage, 77 & Collage Techniques, 94, Watson Guptil Publ. *Mem:* Nat Watercolor Soc; Collage Artists Am; Audubon Artists; Soc Animal Artists. *Media:* Watercolor, Mixed Media. *Mailing Add:* 1361 Fearrington Post Pittsboro NC 27312-5036

SCHACHTER, JUSTINE RANSON
GRAPHIC ARTIST, ILLUSTRATOR
b Brooklyn, NY, Dec 18, 27. *Study:* Tyler Sch Fine Arts, Temple Univ, scholar; Brooklyn Mus Art Sch, with John Bindrum, Milton Hebald & John Ferren; Art Students League, with Will Barnett. *Work:* Bellmore Pub Libr, NY; Island Trees Pub Libr, Levittown, NY; Wantagh High Sch, NY. *Comn:* Poster, NY State Parent-Teacher Asn, 70-73. *Exhib:* One-woman show, Ruth White Gallery, 61; Nat Asn Women Artists Traveling Graphics Show, US & Europe, 69-70; Am Soc Contemp Artists, NY, 49-95, 2000-06; and others. *Pos:* Dir graphic arts, Audio-Visual Educ TV, Mineola Pub Sch, 64-65; exec dir, Art Forms Creative Ctr, 71-73; owner, The Artist's Studio Gallery, 74-; designer & partner, Justine & Ruth Cards, 85-91; art dir, Long Island Pride Parade, 94-96, 97-02; ed/designer, Long Island Tidings Publ, 92-. *Teaching:* Artist in residence, Community Arts Prog, Wantagh High Sch, 72 & Syosset High Sch, 74. *Awards:* Awards for Mixed Media, Nassau Co Off Cult Develop, 70 & Am Soc Contemp Artists, 71 & 75; Lifetime Achievement Award Arts in Publ, Long Island Pride Parade, 2002; Dedidcation to Pflag Award, 15 yrs of Artisti Serv, 2002. *Bibliog:* Elyse Sommer (auth), Rock and Stone Craft, Crown, 72. *Mem:* Am Soc Contemp Artists (chmn admis, 68-71); Nat Asn Women Artists; Artists Equity Asn; Int Asn Arts. *Media:* Pen, Ink; Paper, Stone. *Publ:* Illusr, Long Island Free Press, 70-71; Make a Glad Sound, Consort Music, Inc, 74; You Can Play a Recorder, Music Minus One, illusr, Treasury of Stories, Waldman, 78; Long Island Pride Press, 94-; LI Pride Guide, 94-96, 2000. *Mailing Add:* 14 Trumpet Ln Levittown NY 11756

SCHACTMAN, BARRY ROBERT
PAINTER, EDUCATOR
b Newark, NJ, May 10, 30. *Study:* Univ of Miami; Art Students League; Rutgers Univ; Tyler Sch of Art of Temple Univ; Yale Univ Sch of Art, BFA, 58, MFA, 60, study with Josef Albers & Rico Lebrun. *Work:* Yale Univ Art Mus, New Haven, Conn; St Louis Univ, Mo; Mus of Israel, Jerusalem; Minn Mus Art, St Paul; Weatherspoon Art Gallery, Univ NC, Greensboro. *Comn:* Donald Finkel (portrait), Wash Univ, 98. *Exhib:* Drawing Soc National Traveling Exhib, Am Fedn Arts, 70-72; Drawing USA (nat traveling exhib), Minn Mus Art, St Paul, 71-73; Nat Invitational Drawing Exhib,

Mitchell Gallery, Southern Ill Univ, Carbondale, 75; Drawing Mo 1976, Bicentennial Invitational Exhib (traveling exhib), Albrecht Art Mus, St Joseph, Mo, 76; 30th Ann Hassam Purchase Fund Exhib, Am Acad & Inst Arts & Lett, NY, 78. *Pos:* Assoc dean, Sch Fine Arts, Washington Univ, St Louis, Mo, 77-79. *Teaching:* Instr drawing & design, Univ Tex, Austin, 59-61; prof drawing & painting, Washington Univ, St Louis, Mo, 61-92, emer prof, 92-. *Awards:* Purchase Prize, Drawing USA, Minn Mus Art, St Paul, 71; plus others. *Bibliog:* Gerald M Monroe (auth), Teaching drawing: The personal approach of Barry Schactman, Drawing Soc, 81 & Am Artist, 82; Bernard Chaet (auth), The Art of Drawing, Holt, Rinehart and Winston Inc, 83. *Media:* Pen and Ink, Charcoal; Oil. *Mailing Add:* 437 E Glendale Rd St Louis MO 63119

SCHAECHTER, JUDITH
STAINED GLASS ARTIST, PAINTER

b Gainesville, Fla, Feb 14, 61. *Study:* RI Sch Design, BFA(sculpture), 83. *Work:* Julie & Neil Courtney, Robert Ingersoll & John Wineman, Philadelphia, Pa; Corning Mus Glass, NY; Renwick Gallery, Nat Mus Am Art, Washington. *Exhib:* Art Around the Edges, Port Hist Mus, 89; Contemp Philadelphia Artists, Philadelphia Mus Art, Pa, 90; Renwick Gallery, Smithsonian Inst, 90; solo exhibs, La Luz De Jesus Gallery, Los Angeles, 92, Helander Gallery, 92 & 93, Snyderman Gallery, Philadelphia, 94, Inst Contemp Art, 95, John Michael Kohler Art Ctr, 95, Cincinnati Art Ctr, 96, Snyderman Gallery, Philadelphia, 97, 00, Pa Acad Fine Arts, Morris Gallery, 98, Agni Fine Arts, The Hague, The Neth, 99, Smalands Mus, Vaxjo, Sweden, 2000; Newport Art Mus, 93; Del Art Mus, 98; Tampa Mus Art, 99; Cornell Fine Arts Mus, Winter Park, Fla, 2000; DC Moore Gallery, New York City, 00; and others. *Teaching:* Artist-in-residence, glass prog, RI Sch Design, 85 & guest lectr, glass prog, 88; guest lectr glass prog, Tyler Sch Art, Temple Univ, 88, RI Sch Design, 88-90 & Glass Art Soc Conf, Kent State, Ohio, 88; guest lectr painting dept, Univ Arts, 89 & sculpture dept, Moore Col Art, 89; panelist, New Art Forms Expos, Chicago, Ill, 91. *Awards:* Fels in Visual Arts, Nat Endowment Arts, 86 & 88; Louis Comfort Tiffany Found Award, 89; Pa Coun Arts Fel Grant, 91; Joan Mitchell Award, NYC, 95; Leeway Found Award in Crafts, 99; Innovation and Techniques, Urban Glass, 00; and others. *Bibliog:* Shawn Waggoner (auth), The seduction of pain Judith Schaechter's stained glass world, Glass Art, 3-4/94; Jeanne Nugent (auth), Schaechter: wretched beauty, Glass, spring 94; Deni Kaurel (auth), Judith Schaechter: she cast pains in visions of beauty, Art Matters, 1/95; and others. *Mem:* Found Today's Art, Nexus, 83-. *Media:* Stained Glass. *Dealer:* Snyderman Gallery. *Mailing Add:* 1144 S 11th St Philadelphia PA 19147

SCHAEFER, GAIL
SCULPTOR

b NJ, June 11, 38. *Study:* Art Students League, with Kaz-Simon, 77-80, Scolar, 85-86; Ramapo Col, NJ, BA, 79; Nat Acad Design, Lucchesi scholar, 80-83. *Comn:* North Jersey Automobile MEM Plaque; BEC Manufacturing Corp; Trautwein Farms Inc. *Exhib:* Catherine Lorrilard Wolfe Nat Arts Club, NY, 78, 82 & 83; Allied Artists Am, Nat Acad Galleries, NY, 78, Am Acad & Inst Arts & Lett, 80 & Nat Arts Club, 81, 83, 87, 89, 90 & 91; Salmagundi Club, NY, 80; Nat Acad Design 157th Ann, NY, 82. *Teaching:* Instr studio classes, 77-; instr sculpture, Old Church Cult Ctr, Demarest, NJ. *Awards:* William Averbach-Levy Award, Nat Acad Design, 81; Medal Hon, Printers & Sculptors Soc NJ, 82; Anna Hyatt Huntington Award, Catherine Lorrilard Wolfe Art Club, 83. *Bibliog:* David Spengler (auth), Women of the arts, Record, 10/28/76; Diana Drew (auth), Sculptress has a way with children, Town News, 6/21/78; Terry Meyer (auth), Gail Schaefer's talent, Sunday Post, 7/16/78. *Mem:* Allied Artists Am; Painters & Sculptors Soc NJ; Catherine Lorrilard Wolfe Art Club; Nat Sculpture Soc. *Media:* Clay, Bronze. *Mailing Add:* 103 Commander Black Oradell NJ 07649

SCHAEFER, ROBERT ARNOLD, JR
PHOTOGRAPHER, LECTURER

b Cullman, Ala, Dec 1, 51. *Study:* Auburn Univ, BA, 75; Tech Univ Manchester, Eng, cert merit, 76; Techn Univ, Munich, dipl ingenieur, 78. *Work:* Biblio Nat, Paris; Stadt Mus, Munich, Ger; Philip Morris, Inc, NY; Huntsville Mus Art, Ala; Birmingham Mus Art, Ala; Mus Modern Art, NY. *Comn:* Wall mural, Interstate 280, City Birmingham, Ala, 71. *Exhib:* New Acquisitions, Birmingham Mus Art, Ala, 93; Am Zoo, 2 1/2 x 4 1/2 Galerie, Amersterdam, The Neth, 94; New Visions, Md Fedn Art, 94; Alabama Impact, Fine Arts Mus, Mobile, Ala, 95; Berlinier Ansichten, Aroma, Berlin, 95-96; New Works, Huntsville Mus Art, Ala, 96; Raab Gallery, Berlin, Ger, 97; Berlin Blau, Aroma Gallery, Berlin, 97-98; Robert A Schaefer Jr-25 Yrs of Photog, Huntsville Mus Art, Ala, 99-; Art on the Line Comes Inside, Philadelphia, Pa, 2000; plus others; The Silver Eye Ctr for Photog, Pittsburgh, PA, 2005. *Pos:* Dir pub relations, Soho Photo, 84-90. *Teaching:* Instr darkroom tech, Int Ctr Photog, NY, 82-84; Instr,Palladium printing, Soho Photo, NY, 87-91; Instr digital printing, Apple Computers, NY, 2001; NY Univ, currently; New Sch, NY, currently. *Awards:* SOS Award for New Works of Robert Schaefer in Orient, NY State Coun Arts, Long Island, 94. *Bibliog:* The Star Ledger, Newark, NJ, 2002; Photo Insider, Florham Park, NJ, 2000. *Mem:* NY Photogr. *Media:* Photography. *Res:* Alternative Photographic Developing Procesess Platinum, Paladium and Cyanotype. *Specialty:* Fine Art & Photography. *Interests:* Fine Art Films. *Publ:* Coauth, American pie, Foto Mag, 88; Bilder Leben (Art Life), Viktor Publ Co, Cologne, 94; Orient photographers 1885-1995, 95, Voyager, 96, Suffolk Times; Brennpunkt, Berlin, Ger, 97; Fotophile Photog Mag, NY, 97; Photography's Antiquarian Avant-garde, by Lyle Rexer, Abrams, 2002. *Dealer:* Charles Chamot Gallery, www.chamotgallery.com. *Mailing Add:* 44 E 21st St Apt 2R New York NY 10010-7220

SCHAEFER, RONALD H
PRINTMAKER, EDUCATOR

b Milwaukee, Wis, June 2, 39. *Study:* Univ Wis-Milwaukee, BS(art), 62; Univ Wis-Madison, MS(art), 63, MFA, 64. *Work:* Joslyn Mus, Omaha, Nebr; Tampa Pub Libr; First Nat Bank Minneapolis; and others. *Exhib:* Five Okla Printmakers Ann, 64-72; three Boston Printmakers Ann, 65-67; 12th & 19th Ball State Univ Drawing & Small Sculpture Ann, 66 & 73; Miami Biennial Print, 73; NH Int Ann, 73; and others. *Teaching:* Prof printmaking & chmn dept, Univ NDak, 65-. *Awards:* Twenty-five Printmakers Nat Invitational Purchase Award, Minot State Col, 71; Graphic Chem & Ink Co Award, First NH Print Int, 73; Purchase Award, Los Angeles, Print Exhib, 73. *Mem:* Print Club. *Media:* Etching, Intaglio. *Mailing Add:* 124 Central Ave New Rockford ND 58356

SCHAEFER, SCOTT JAY
CURATOR, HISTORIAN

b Chicago, Ill, Mar 30, 48. *Study:* Univ Ariz, BA, 70; Bryn Mawr Col, MA, PhD, 75. *Pos:* Asst cur paintings, Philadelphia Mus Art, 74; asst cur prints, Fogg Art Mus, Cambridge, Mass, 76-78; asst cur paintings, Mus Fine Arts, Boston, 78-80; cur Europ paintings and sculpture, Los Angeles Co Mus Art, 80-87; dir mus serv, Sotheby's, NY, 88-91, sr vpres, Old Master Paintings, 91. *Teaching:* Lectr, Philadelphia Col Art, 71-72; lectr, Harvard Univ, Cambridge, Mass, 76-79. *Mem:* Southern Calif Art Hist; Am Mus Asn. *Res:* Late 16th & 17th century Italian painting, 19th century French paintings. *Publ:* Auth, Drawings of the Studiolo of Francesco; a catalogue, Master Drawings, XX, 83; Drawings by Martin Freminet, Gazette Des Beaux-Arts, 1371, 83; Europe and beyond: Some paintings for the studiolo, Coun Europe, 3/84; A day in the country, Impression and the French Landscape, 84; Guido Reni, 88. *Mailing Add:* c/o Sotheby's 1334 York Ave New York NY 10021

SCHAEFFER, MARTHA J
ART DEALER

b Springfield, Mass, Jan 14, 48. *Study:* St Bonaventure Univ; Herbert Lehman Col, BA, 74. *Pos:* Owner, Schaeffer Fine Art, currently. *Specialty:* Impressionist, Modern and Contemporary Masters Works on Paper, Paintings and Sculpture. *Interests:* Art History, Film History, Theater History, 20th Century Fiction. *Mailing Add:* Riverdale Sta PO Box 1294 Riverdale NY 10471

SCHAEFFER, S(TANLEY) ALLYN
PAINTER, INSTRUCTOR, AURHOR

b Franklin, NJ, Nov 3, 35. *Study:* W Lester Stevens Studio, 50-60; Nat Acad Design, with Ivan Olinsky, 54-55; Art Students League (Schanackenberg Merit Scholarship), with Robert Brackman, 54-56, NY. *Work:* Shering Plough, Madison, NJ; Pastel Soc Am, NY; NJ Sports & Exposition Authority, East Rutherford, NJ; Monmouth Park, Oceanport, NJ; NJ Bell Telephone Co, Newark. *Comn:* Racing Paintings, Monmouth Park, Oceanport, NJ, 80-92; Revolutionary War Mural, (6x12), State Bank NJ, Springfield, 79; Mural School Life, (8x12), Long Branch Pub Sch, NJ, 83; Historic Drawing, Muhlenberg Hosp, Plainfield, NJ, 84; History of the Hambletonian, NJ Sports Authority, East Rutherford, 92. *Exhib:* Hudson Valley Art Asn Ann, White Plains Co Ctr, NY, 75-92; Pastel Soc Am Ann, Nat Arts Club, NY, 80-92; Hudson Valley group show, Hammond Mus, NY, 80; Pastel Soc Am Traveling Show, Eastern States, Fla & New Eng, 86; Salmagundi Ann; Thoroughbred Hall of Fame, Aiken, SC. *Pos:* Art ed, NJ Life Mag, Maplewood, 70-76 & NJ Music & Arts Mag, Chatham, 81. *Teaching:* Instr anatomy figure drawing, Du Sch Arts, Plainfield, NJ, 70-76; instr anatomy figure drawing, Spectrum Inst, Hillsboro, NJ, 75-80; instr painting, NJ Ctr Visual Arts, Summit, 82-. *Awards:* Mrs John Newington Award, Hudson Valley Art Asn, 95; Uschi Grueterica Award 23 Ann, Paste Soc of Am, 96; William O Zann Mem Award & Antonio Cirini Mem Award, Salmagundi Club, 2000. *Bibliog:* Wendon Blake (auth), Painting in Alkyd, Am Artists Mag, Billboard Publ, 80; George Maganan (auth), Interview S Allyn Schaeffer, Todays Art & Graphics, Sindicate Mag Inc, 81. *Mem:* Pastel Soc Am (bd mem, 91-); Hudson Valley Art; master pastelist, Pastel Soc Am; Salmagundi Club (New York City Art Comn), 41st Vice Pres; Served on the Board of all these Groups. *Media:* Oil, Pastel. *Publ:* Auth, The Oil Painter's Guide to Painting Trees, The Oil Painter's Guide to Painting Skies, 85, The Oil Painter's Guide to Painting Water, 86, Color Compositin & Light in the Landscape, 87 & Big Book of Painting Nature in Pastel, 93, Watson/Guptill; auth, Best of Pastel 2, Rockport Publ, 98. *Dealer:* The Sporting Gallery Inc 11 W Washington St Middleburg VA 22117; Sporting Scene Gallery Red Bank NJ; Swain Gallery Plainfield NJ, Contempory Am Painting. *Mailing Add:* 29 Woodland Ave Fanwood NJ 07023

SCHAFF, BARBARA WALLEY
ARTIST

b Plainfield, NJ, May 6, 41. *Study:* Syracuse Univ, BA, 1963; Pa Acad Fine Arts, cert degree, 1994; China Nat Acad Fine Art, Hangzhou, 1994. *Work:* Fuller Mem Art Mus, Brockton, Mass; Independence Found, Philadelphia, Pa; McGraw Hill Puiblishers, NY; NJ State Mus, Trenton, NJ; Pfizer Int, NY. *Comn:* NJ Natural Gas, Wall, NJ, 1983; Bell Communications Res, Red Bank, NJ, 1985; Barbara & Leon Goldstein, Mountain Lakes, NJ, 1985; Meldisco Corp, Mahway, NJ, 1987; Temple Univ Sch Law, Phila, 2004; Newark Mus, NJ, 2005. *Exhib:* NJ Designer Craftsmen, Newark Mus, NJ, 1973; NJ Artists Series, Reflections/Abstractions, NJ State Mus, Trenton, 1985; In Recognition of Excellence, Montclair Mus of Art, NJ, 1986; The Mus Restaurant, Philadelphia Mus of Art, Pa, 1999; Grounds for Sculpture, Toad Hall Gallery, Hamilton, NJ, 2003; 6th Biennal, AIR Gallery, NY, 2005. *Pos:* Fel Coun mem, Va Ctr for Creative Arts, Amherst, Va, 2005-; adv to the fac, BFA prog, Kean Col, Union, NJ, 1988-94; adv artists coun mem, Hunterdon Art Ctr, Clinton, NJ, 1988-89. *Teaching:* Long Beach Island for the Arts & Sci, summer 2005. *Awards:* Fel, NJ State Coun on the Arts, 1985; Blue Ribbon award, outstanding achievement, Long Branch Island Found for the Arts and Sciences, 1998-99; Fel, Pa Coun on Arts, 2004; Prize and Jurors award, Newark Mus, Perkins Ctr Art, 2005. *Bibliog:* Victoria Donohoe (auth), The Expressionist Gesture, Philadelphia Inquirer, 9/26/2004; Janet Purcell (auth), Allure of Orchids transforms potter to painter, The Times, Trenton, NJ, 8/1/2003; Eileen Watkins (auth), Former Potter turns her talent to porcelain tile paintings, The Sunday Star Ledger, 2/19/1989. *Mem:* Nat Arts Club, NYC. *Media:* Abstract - realism, expressionist. *Mailing Add:* 1520 Spruce St #906 Philadelphia PA 19102

SCHAFFER, DEBRA S
COLLAGE ARTIST, SCULPTOR
b New York, NY, Nov 22, 36. *Study:* Montclair State Col, BA, 58; Univ Md, with Kenneth Campbell, 79; Westchester County Cu, with Anthony Padovano, 82; Art Life Studio with Sebastiano Mineo; Pietra Santa Italy; Jane B Armstrong, VT. *Work:* Blue Heron Gallery, Wellfleet, Mass; Images Gallery, Briarcliff, NY; Tully Healthcare Ctr, Stamford Hosp, Conn; Temple B'nai Yisrael, Armonk, NY; North Castle Libr, Armonk, NY. *Comn:* owls & seals, comn by Dr & Mrs Bruce Brofman, Armonk, NY; harp seal, comn by Dr & Mrs David Schaffer, Philadelphia, Pa; Dr & Mrs George Ubogy, Greenwich, Conn; Mr & Mrs Paul Frankel, Armonk, NY; Dr & Mrs Steven Winter, Briarcliff, NY. *Exhib:* Allied Artists Am, NY, 89; two-person show, Westchester Cmty Col, NY, 90; Bergen Co Mus Arts & Sci, NY, 91; Art of NE USA Exhib, Silvermine, Conn, 94, 95, 96, 97, 99, 2000, 2002 & 2005; Katonah Mus, NY, 98; Hammond Mus, N Salem, 98 & 04; solo-show, Director's Choice, Silvermine Art Guild, 2003; Katonah Mus (Benny Andrews, juror), 2005; Westchester Biennial, Col New Rochelle, Castle Gallery, 2006. *Pos:* Pres, bd mem, juror, Mamaroneck Artists Guild, 77-88; juror, Nat Asn Women Artists. *Teaching:* instr sculpture, Heritage Hills, Somers, NY, 82-; Home Studio, 77-. *Awards:* First Prize Mixed Media, Ridgefield Guild Artists, Ann Juried Competition, 97, Robert Cottingham, 98; First prize Katonah Mus Artists Asn, 2000, Ellen Keiter, Hudson River Mus; First Prize mixed media, New Canaan Art Soc, 2002, and others; Mixed media award, Art of the Northeast Silvermine Cora Roseveas, MOMA, 97; First prize mixed media, Art of the Northeast Silvermine Alan Stone, 99. *Mem:* Nat Asn Women Artists; Silvermine Guild Arts Ctr; Katonah Mus Artists Asn. *Media:* Mixed Media Photo Collage, Wood, Stone. *Interests:* Bicycling, Knitting and travel. *Dealer:* Images Gallery Briarcliff Manor NY 10510; Haddad Lascano Gallery Great Barrington MA; Silvermine Guild of Art New Canaan CT. *Mailing Add:* Ten Windmill Pl Armonk NY 10504

SCHAFFER, RICHARD E(NOS)
PAINTER, PRINTMAKER
b Tucson, Ariz, Nov 25, 55. *Study:* Northern Ariz Univ, BFA, 79; Univ Ariz, MFA, 90. *Work:* Northern Ariz Univ Mus Art, Flagstaff, Ariz; Univ Ariz Collection, Bank One Art Collection, Tucson, Ariz; Univ Ariz Medical Ctr; Tucson Mus Art; St Elizabeth of Hungary Clinic. *Exhib:* Conversations in Color, Shemer Art Ctr & Mus, Phoenix, Ariz, 89; Ariz Alliances, Yuma Art Ctr, Yuma, Ariz, 92; Fragile Power, Newton Art Ctr, Cambridge, Mass, 93; Merged Realities, Cent Art Collectives & Slaundrau Sci Ctr, Tucson, Ariz, 96; Art Fac Exhib, Univ Ariz Mus Art, Tucson, Ariz, 96. *Pos:* Curatorial specialist, Univ Ariz Mus Art, 79-96, registrar, 96-; tech exhib consult, Etherton Stern Gallery, Tucson, Ariz, 90-92. *Teaching:* Adj prof, Dept Art, Univ Ariz, 96, 97; instr, Tucson Mus Art, 98-99. *Awards:* Cash Award, 11th Annual Two Flags Festival Arts Int, 82; 3rd Place Printmaking, Artquest Int Competition, 86. *Bibliog:* Michael Boyle (dir), The Rincon Proj, Ariz Illus, 89; Art in a bungalow, Southwest Profile, 9/89; Daniel Schacter (auth), Fragile Power: Exploration of Memory, Newton Art Ctr, 10/93. *Mem:* Prof Exhib Staffs Tucson (actg pres, 87-); Mus Asn Ariz; Mus Computer Network. *Media:* Installation, Printing

SCHAFFNER, J LURAY See Luray, J (Schaffner)

SCHAPIRO, MIRIAM
PAINTER, SCULPTOR
b Toronto, Ont, Nov 15, 23; US citizen. *Study:* Univ Iowa, BA, 45, MA, 46, MFA, 49; Col Wooster Ohio, Hon DFA, 83; Calif Col Arts & Crafts, Hon DFA, 89; Numerous hon degrees from US cols & univs 94-95. *Work:* Whitney Mus Am Art, Mus Mod Art, Metrop Mus Art, Brooklyn Mus Art, NY; Stanford Univ, Palo Alto, Calif; Hirshhorn Mus & Sculpture Garden, Nat Gallery Art, Washington; Mus Fine Arts, Boston, Mass; Hunter Mus Art, Tenn; and others. *Comn:* Scherzo, Orlando Airport, Fla, 80; Four Matriarchs (stained glass windows), Temple Shalom, Chicago, 84; Anna and David (sculpture), 1525 Wilson Blvd Bldg, Rosslyn, Va, 87; Eden (fan), Marriot Hotel, San Francisco, 89; Opening Night (painting), Pasquerilla Performing Arts Ctr, Johnstown, Pa, 91. *Exhib:* Solo exhibs, Twentieth Anniversary Celebration, ARC Gallery, Chicago, 93, Collaboration Series 1994: Mother Russia (with catalog), Steinbaum Krauss Gallery, NY 94, A Seamless Life, Sawhill Gallery, James Madison Univ, Harrisburg, Va, 96, A Woman's Way, Nat Mus Am Art, Smithsonian Inst, Washington, 97; Collaboration Series: Frida Kahlo and Me, Bernice Steinbaum Gallery, NY, 91; Graphic studio: Contemp Art from the Collaborative Workshop at the Univy of S Fla (with catalog), Nat Gallery Art, Washington, 91; Parallel Visions: Modern Artists and Outsider Art, Los Angeles Co Mus Art, Calif, 92; Women's Art, Women's Lives, Women's Issues, Tweed Gallery, NY, 93; The Label Show: Contemp Art & the Mus, Mus Fine Arts, Boston, Mass, 94; Division of Labor: Women's Work in Contemp Art (with catalog), Mus Contemp Art, Los Angeles, 95; Contemp Printmaking in Am: Collaborative Prints and Presses, Nat Mus Am Art, Washington, 96; Art Patterns, Austin Mus Art, Tex, 97; Hanging By a Thread (with catalog), Hudson River Mus Westchester, NY, 97; High Art/High Jinks in Contemp Art, Foster Gallery, Mus Fine Arts, Boston, 98; The Legacy, Brevard Mus Art & Sci, Fla, 98; Selections from SoHo: Steinbaum Krauss Gallery Artists, Ft Lewis Col Art Gallery, Colo, 98; and others; Flomenhaft Gallery, NY, 2006. *Pos:* Co-originator feminist art prog, Calif Inst Arts, 72-75; co-found, Feminist Art Inst, NY, 79; found mem, Feminist Art Inst, New York City; mem adv bd, Women's Caucus for Art; assoc mem Heresies Collective; lectr dept, art hist Univ Mich, 1987. *Awards:* Guggenheim Fel, Nat Endowment Arts, 76 & 87; Women's Caucus Art Award, 88; Rockefeller Found Grant, 93. *Bibliog:* Norma Broude & Mary Garrard (eds), The Power of Feminist Art: The American Movement of the 1970's, History and Impact, Harry N Abrams Inc, 94; Bill Meyers (auth), Genesis: A Living Conversation, Doubleday, 96; Downey, Giese & Metcalf (auths), United States History: In the Course of Human Events, West Publ Co, 97. *Mem:* Women's Caucus Art (nat adv bd, currently); Nat Acad (acad, 99-). *Media:* Acrylic, Oil. *Publ:* Coauth, Womanhouse (catalog), 72; Ed, Anonymous Was a Woman, 74 & Art: A Woman's Sensibility, 75, Feminist Art Prog, Cal Inst Arts; auth, Women and the Creative Process, Univ Man, 74; Rondo: An Artist's Book, Bedford Press, 90; Gardner, Art Through the Ages, 9th Ed, Harcourt Brace Jovanovich Inc, 90; Alphabet Book Mobile, Crazy Clothes Bookmobile, Kaleidoscope Bookmobile, Numbers Bookmobile, Pomegranate Artbooks, 93. *Mailing Add:* Steinbaum Krauss Gallery 3550 N Miami Ave Miami FL 33127-3112

SCHAR, STUART
ADMINISTRATOR, EDUCATOR
b Chicago, Ill, Aug 27, 41. *Study:* Univ Chicago, BFA, 63, MFA, 64, PhD(arts admin), 67. *Comn:* Painting for Frank Lloyd Wright house, Brookfield, Ill, 73; lithograph for Lyons Twp High Sch, City of LaGrange, Ill, 74; painting for Aurora Pub Libr, City of Aurora, Ill, 75. *Exhib:* Art Inst Chicago, 60-64, 70 & 74; Lexington Studios, Chicago, 64-65, 75-76; Printmaking 1969, Northern Ariz Univ, Flagstaff, 69; John Hancock Ctr, Chicago, 73; Columbus Gallery Fine Arts, Ohio, 76; Oberlin Col, Ohio, 77; Western Art League Asn, 77; and others. *Pos:* Res assoc higher educ, NCent Asn Cols & Sec Schs, 65, asst to exec secy, 66; admin asst to chmn art dept, Univ Ill, Chicago Circle, 66-69, actg chmn art dept, 69; artist-in-residence, Joliet Art League, Ill, 70-72; dir, Sch of Art, Kent State Univ, 75-83; co-dir, Blossom Kent Art, Music & Theatre summer progs, 75-83; dir, James A Michener Mus, Univ Galleries, Eells Outdoor Gallery & Jack Lord Purchase Collections, 75-83; coordr, Div Res & Serv, La State Univ, 84-86; dean, Hartford Art Sch, 86-; assoc vpres, Arts, 89-; actg dean, Hartt Sch Music, 89-90. *Teaching:* Asst prof rendering & drafting, Chicago Tech Col, 64, asst prof design & graphics, 65; asst prof art, Univ Ill, Chicago Circle, 66-70, assoc prof urban sci, 70-75; prof art, Kent State Univ, 75-83; Distinguished Prof, La State Univ, 83; prof art, Hartford Art Sch, 86-. *Awards:* Best of Show, Midway Studios, 72; Gen Motors Purchase Award, Art Inst, Chicago, 74; Best of Show, Western Art League Asn, 77; Lady Bing Fel Award, 86. *Mem:* Col Art Asn; Am Asn Univ Prof; Am Inst Planners. *Publ:* Coauth, Guide for the Evaluation of Institutions of Higher Education, NCent Asn Cols & Sec Schs, 66; auth, The education of an art student, Tallyrand, Vol 3, 70; coauth, A Self Study Report: The University of Illinois at Chicago Circle, Univ Ill, 71; Central Themes of Louisiana Architecture, Art & Humanities Coun, Baton Rouge, 84; Pathways to Art through Numbers, Apple Educ Found, 86; A Video Pilot: Significant Interiors Survey, Am Soc Interior Designers

SCHARF, KENNY
PAINTER
b Los Angeles, Calif, 58. *Study:* Sch Visual Arts, New York, BFA, 80. *Work:* Solomon R Guggenheim Mus; Stedelijk Mus, Amsterdam, Neth; Whitney Mus Am Art; Groninger Mus, Groningen, Neth; Museu Arte Mod Rio de Janeiro, Brazil; and others. *Comn:* Cosmic Cavern, VIP room for The Tunnel, NY, 95; porcelain design, Rosenthal China, Selb, Ger, 95; Absolut Scharf (billboard), Absolut Vodka, San Francisco, 95; signature watches for artist series, Swatch, NY & Switz, 95; textile design, Todd Oldham, NY, 95. *Exhib:* Whitney Mus Am Art, 83, 85, 88, 91 & 95; San Francisco Mus Mod Art, 84; Montreal Mus Contemp Art (with catalog), 84; Mus du Louvre, Paris, 92; New Figuration, Tucson Mus Art, Tex, 96; solo exhibs, Cotthem Gallery, Barcelona, Spain, 98, Kantor Gallery, Los Angeles, 98, McIntosh Gallery, Atlanta, 98, Galeria Ramis Barquet, Monterrey, Mex, 98, Galerie Hans Mayer, Dusseldorf, Ger, 99, Tony Shafrazi Gallery, NY, 2000 & Gagosian Gallery, Los Angeles, 2000; and others; Pop Surrealism, Aldrich Mus, Ridgefield, Conn, 98; Fashion at the Beach, Bass Mus, Miami, 98; Collaboration Transformation, Lithographs from the Hamilton Press, Univ of Okls, 98; Closet #16, Nexus Contemp Art Ctr, Atlanta, 98; Dreaming II, Contemp Am Art & Ancient Korea, Akira Ikeda Gallery, New York City, 99; On the Air, North Terminal Connector Gallery, San Francisci, 99; A Room with a View, Sixth @ Prince Fine Art, New York City, 99. *Pos:* Co-chair, Inter-Cambios Culturales El Salvador fund raiser (with Christy Turlington), New York, 96. *Bibliog:* and many others; Marion Wallberg (auth), Honoring the artist: Kenny Scharf, Dan's Papers, 1/21/2000; Mariuccia Casadio (auth), Kenny Schard, L'Uomo Vogue, 6/99; Camille Paglia (auth), Rock around the clock, Forbes ASAP, 11/30/98. *Media:* All. *Publ:* Auth, A Talk with Keith Haring, Flash Art, 1/85; designer, Total Cosmic Cavern (interactive Web environ), for TotalNY, New York, 96

SCHARF, WILLIAM
PAINTER
b Media, Pa, Feb 22, 27. *Study:* Samuel Fleisher Mem Art Sch, Philadelphia, Pa; Pa Acad Fine Arts, Philadelphia; The Barnes Found, Merion, Pa. *Work:* Neurosciences Inst, San Diego, Calif; Telfair Mus, Savannah, Ga; Frederick Weissman Mus, Malibu, Calif; Nat Acad Design Mus, NY City, 2003; Rose Art Mus, Brandeis Univ; Guggenheim Mus, NYC. *Exhib:* Am Acad & Inst Arts & Lett, NY, 91; Univ Mich Mus, 92; Phillips Collection, Wash, DC, 2000; Weissman Mus, Malibu, Calif, 01; PSI/Moma, NY, 02; Richard York Gallery, New York City, 02 & 04; Richard York Gallery, New York City, 05. *Teaching:* Instr painting, San Francisco Art Inst, 63, 66, 69, 74 & 89, Sch Visual Arts, NY, 65-69; lectr, Art Students League, 87-. *Awards:* Emmlen Cresson fel Pa Acad Fine Arts, 1948. *Mem:* Artists Equity Asn; Soc Illusrs; Nat Acad (acad, 02-). *Media:* All. *Dealer:* Meredith Ward NYC. *Mailing Add:* 75 Central Park W New York NY 10023

SCHEER, SHERIE (HOOD)
PHOTOGRAPHER, PAINTER
b Estherville, Iowa, Feb 15, 40. *Study:* Univ Iowa, 58-60; Univ Calif, Los Angeles, BA, 69, MA, 71. *Work:* Metrop Mus Art, NY; Fogg Art Mus, Harvard Univ; Israel Mus, Jerusalem; Minneapolis Inst Art, Minn; San Francisco Mus Mod Art. *Exhib:* Contemp Hand-Colored Photog, DeSaisset Mus, Santa Clara, Calif, 81; Summer Show V, Los Angeles Co Mus Art, 81; Five Photographers, Los Angeles Inst Contemp Art, 82; Artists' Tribute to Bertha Urdang, Israel Mus, Jerusalem, 82; Invitational: Bertha Urdang, London Regional Gallery, Ont, 83. *Teaching:* Instr photog, Univ Calif,

Los Angeles Exten, 82-84. *Bibliog:* Barbara Noah (auth), J Golden & S Scheer at the Womens Building, Art in Am, 3-4/78; Colin Westerbeck (auth), Reviews: New York, Artforum, 3/81; Anne Wagner (auth), Selections from An Interview with Sherie Scheer together with some suggestions for their use, J Womens Studies, winter 92. *Media:* Painted Photographs, Mixed Media. *Dealer:* Sherie Scheer Studio 31 Park Ave Venice CA 90291. *Mailing Add:* 31 Park Ave Venice CA 90291

SCHEIN, EUGENIE
EDUCATOR, GRAPHIC ARTIST
Study: Hunter Col, BA; Columbia Univ, MA; Art Students League, with De Muth & Bridgeman; studies in art & aesthetics at New York Univ & Univ NMex; Martha Graham Sch Dance. *Work:* Carvell Mus, La; Ga Mus Art, Athens; Lowe Art Mus, Coral Gables, Fla; Miami Mus Mod Art, Fla. *Exhib:* Int Watercolors, Brooklyn Mus; Soc Four Arts, Palm Beach; Lowe Mus, Univ Miami, Coral Gables, Fla; Hollywood Art & Cult Ctr, Fla; Butler Inst, Youngstown, Ohio; one-person shows, Midtown Gallery, Uptown Gallery & Salpeter Gallery, NY, Mexico City, Havana, PR, Barzasky Gallery, NY; Metamorphosis, Galleo, Miami Beach, 95; and others. *Teaching:* Instr, Hunter Col, 26-55 & Univ Miami, 56-60. *Mem:* Artists Equity Asn (vpres, 72-); Fla Artists Group; Nat Asn Women Artists. *Mailing Add:* 1070 Stillwater Dr Miami FL 33141

SCHEINER, MICHAEL L
CRAFTSMAN
b Philadelphia, Pa, June 22, 56. *Study:* Europ Hons Prog, Rome, 78-79; Ford Found Travel Grant, Murano, Italy, 80; RI Sch Design, BFA(sculpture/glass), 80; Ohio State Univ, MFA(sculpture/glass), 82. *Work:* Ark Art Ctr Decorative Arts Mus, Little Rock; Corning Mus Glass, NY; Mus Am Glass, Wheaton Village, Millville, NJ; permanent archit installation, RI Sch Design Mus Art, Providence; Nat Mus Am Art, Smithsonian Inst, Washington. *Exhib:* Solo exhibs, NY experimental Glass Workshop, NY, 90, Anne O'Brien Gallery, Washington, 90, William Traver Gallery, Seattle, 91, Woodmere Art Mus, Philadelphia, 91, Robert Lehman Gallery, NY, 93, Betsy Rosenfeld Gallery, 93, 95, Galeria Diners, Santa Fe de Bogota, Columbia, S Am, 97, Heller Gallery, New York City, 99; Clark Gallery, Lincoln, Mass, 96; Breaking the Mold: New Directions in Glass (with catalog), Huntsville Mus Art, Ala, 96; The Cutting Edge, Cape Mus Fine Arts, Dennis, Mass, 96; Infernal Inception, Boston Ctr Arts, 96; Hokkaldo Mus Mod Art, Sapporo, Japan, 97; The Glass Skin, Mus Fine Arts, Gifu, Japan, 98; Conning Mus Glass, NY, 98; The Glass Skin, Kunstsammlugen der Veste Colburg, Ger, 99, Kunstmus, Düsseldorf, Ger, 99; Margo Jacobsen Gallery, Portland, Oreg, 99; Transito, Mus Mod Art, Univ Nacional, Bogotá, Colombia, 00; Content, Clark Gallery, Lincoln, Mass, 01; Fuller Art Mus, Brockton, Mass, 01; Transparent Allusions, Newport Art Mus, RI, 02; Clearly Thinking, Phoenix Art Mus, 02. *Pos:* Set designer, Looking Glass Theater, Providence, RI, 78; technician, RI Sch Design, Providence, 82-83; acting dept head, glass dept, Univ Hawaii, Manoa, fall 96. *Teaching:* Artist-in-residence, Pilchuck Sch, Stanwood, Wash, 77, master glassblower-in-residence, 82 & instr, 90, 93, 01, 02; instr glass, RI Sch Design, Providence, 83-86, 88-96, 98-02, actg dept head, 96; summer instr, Haystack Mountain Sch Crafts, Deer Isle, Maine, 85, 87, 90 & 95; vis artist, Niijima Int Glass Arts Festival, Japan, 92; lectr, Univ de los Andes, Bogotá, Colombia, 00. *Awards:* Fel, New Eng Found Arts, 93; Nat Endowment Arts Fel, 94; Corning Mus Glass, Rakow Comn, 98; RI Sch Design, Faculty Devel Grant, 99; UrbanGlass Award for Innovative Use of Glass in Sculpture, 00; Fulbright Sr Scholar Fel, Grant for Rsch and Lecture, Host Instn, Univ Los Andes, Bogotá, Colombia, 00. *Bibliog:* New Glass Review 15, Corning Mus Glass, 94; Christine Temin (auth), Glass acts, Boston Globe, 96; Wash Post, 96. *Media:* Glass, Miscellaneous Media. *Dealer:* Larry Becker 43 N Second St Philadelphia PA 19106. *Mailing Add:* c/o Keer Design 10 Clinton St Central Falls RI 02863

SCHENCK, WILLIAM CLINTON
PAINTER, PRINTMAKER
b Aug 19, 47; US citizen. *Study:* Columbus Col Art & Design, 65-67; Kansas City Art Inst, BFA, 69. *Work:* Whitney Gallery of Western Art, Cody, Wyo; Brandeis Univ Mus, Boston, Mass; Smithsonian Inst, Washington, DC; Clymer Mus, Ellensburg, Wash; Brigham Young U, Provo, Utah; Tucson Mus Art, Tucson, Ariz; plus others. *Comn:* Paintings, Sky Harbor Int Airport, Phoenix, 79; paintings, IBM Corp, Tucson, Ariz, 81; Wells Fargo, Los Angeles, Calif, 83. *Exhib:* Wadsworth Atheneum, Hartford, Conn, 74; Rose Art Mus, Boston, 75; Grand Hornu Gallery, Belg, 76; Edwin Ulrich Mus, Wichita, Kans, 76; Navy Pier, Chicago, 81; 15-Year Retrospective, Scottsdale Ctr for the Arts, Ariz, 83; and others. *Bibliog:* Gregory Battcock (auth), Super-Realism: A Critical Anthology, E F Dutton, New York, 75; John Perrault (auth), Impressions of Arizona, Art Am, 81; Barbara Perlman (auth), Schenck's brand, Ariz Arts & Lifestyle, 81; Julie Sasse (auth) The Irony and the Ecstasy, The Paintings of Bill Schenck (catalog for Vanier Gallery Show), Nov, 99; Elizabeth Claire Flood (auth) Cowboys and Indians, 7/2000. *Media:* Oil; Serigraph. *Publ:* plus others. *Dealer:* Martin-Harris Gallery 268 Los Pinos Rd Santa Fe NM 87505. *Mailing Add:* 268 Los Pinos Rd Santa Fe NM 87505

SCHENK, JOSEPH BERNARD
DIRECTOR
b Glendale, Ariz, March 28, 53. *Study:* Huntingdon Col, Montgomery, Ala, BA, 75; Ball State Univ, Muncie, Ind, MA, 79; Univ Calif, Berkeley, Mus Mgt Inst, 86. *Collection Arranged:* Indiana Collects, 78; 20th Century Am Art, 79; Collections in Anderson, pvt collection survey, 79; Cochran Collection, 20th Century Graphics, 86; Art: On the Move, Nat Juried Invitational, 87; Mobile Collect, pvt collection survey, 92; FAMOS Collection Highlights 1991; Out of the Woods: Turned Wood by American Craftsmen, 92. *Pos:* Dir, Anderson Fine Arts Ctr, Ind, 76-79, Chattahoochee Valley Art Mus, 83-88, Fine Arts Mus South, Mobile, Ala, 88- & Mobile Mus Art, Ala, 99-. *Teaching:* Instr art appreciation, W Ga Col, Carrollton, 86-87. *Mem:* Am Asn Mus; elected treas, Southeastern Mus Conf, 98; Ga Citizens for Arts (treas, 87-88); Ala Mus Asn. *Res:* 19th and 20th century American art

SCHEPIS, ANTHONY JOSEPH
INSTRUCTOR, PAINTER
b Cleveland, Ohio, Mar 6, 27. *Study:* Cooper Sch Art, dipl; Cleveland Inst Art, cert; Kent State Univ, MA. *Work:* Canton Mus Art, Ohio; Massillon Mus Art, Ohio; Butler Inst Am Art, Youngstown, Ohio; Richmond Art Mus, Ind; Hoyt Art Inst Fine Arts, Pa. *Exhib:* Nat Mid-Year Show, Butler Inst Am Art, 55-74; Avanti Gallery, NY, 71; May Show, Cleveland Mus Art, 55-56, 66 & 73-89; Univ Mus, Ind Univ, Pa, 83; Cleveland/Toronto Exhib, Harbourfront Gallery, Toronto, 78; Univ Columbia Fine Arts Gallery, Mo, 80; Ft Wayne Mus Art, IN, 80; Albion Col, Mich, 85; Hoyt Art Inst, Pa, 96; Arnot Art Mus, NY, 96; Richmond Art Mus, IN, 2005; Cavalier Gallery, NY, 2005. *Teaching:* Prof drawing & painting, Cleveland Inst Art, Ohio, 79-96 & prof emeritus, 99-. *Awards:* Purchase Award, Butler Inst Am Art, 74; Painting Awards, Cleveland Mus Art, 78, 88, 89; Corning Award, Arnot Art Mus, NY, 96; and others. *Bibliog:* article, Cleveland Mag, 6/78; article, Ft Wayne Journals Gazette, 80; Cleveland Mus Art Bulletin, 5/88. *Mem:* Cleveland Artists Found. *Media:* Oil, Silkscreen. *Dealer:* Bonfoey Co Cleveland OH; Ctr of Earth Gallery Charlotte NC; Cavalier Gallery Greenwich Conn Nantucket MA. *Mailing Add:* 125 Osprey Heights Dr Winter Haven FL 33880

SCHER, JULIA
CONCEPTUAL ARTIST, VIDEO ARTIST
b Mar 9, 54. *Study:* Univ Calif Los Angeles, BA, 75; Univ Minn, MFA, 84. *Work:* Musee d'Art Moderne, Centre Geroges Pompidou, Paris; Musee Art Moderne, Geneve, Switz; Musee d'Art Contemporani de Barcelona, Spain; Neue Galerie am Landesmuseum Joanneu, Graz, Austria; Kôlnischer Kunstverein, Cologne, Ger. *Exhib:* 1989 Whitney Biennial, Whitney Mus Am Art, NY, 89; solo exhibs, Occupational Placement, Wexner Ctr Arts, Columbus, Ohio, 89-90, Don't Worry, Koln Kustverein, Cologne, Ger, 94, Forecast, Maurine & Robert Rothschild, Gallery, Bunting Inst, Radcliff Col, Cambridge, Mass, 97, The Komputer Kings, Schipper & Krome, Berlin, Ger, 98, Wonderland, Anderea Rosen Gallery, NY, 98, Predictive Engineering II, San Francisco Mus Mod Art, 99; The Raw & the cooked (cociday crudo), Reina Sofia, Madrid, Spain, 94; The End of the Avantgarde, Kunsthalle der Hypo-Kultur, Munich, Ger, 95; Push-ups, Factory-Athens Sch Fine Art, Greece, 96; The Art of Detection: Surveillance in Society, Mass Inst Tech Visual Art Ctr, Cambridge, 97; Performance Anxiety, Site Santa Fe, NMex, 98; Roomates, Mus Van Loon, Amsterdam, The Neth, 98. *Teaching:* Asst prof media & performing arts, Mass Col Art, 95-96; vis artist video, Mass Inst Technol, 95-96; Rennselaer Polytechnic Inst, Troy, NY, 97; Lectr Archit, Visual Arts, Mass Inst Tech, 97-2002. *Awards:* Bunting Fel, Harvard Univ, 96-97. *Mem:* Col Art Asn. *Media:* Mixed Media Installation; Audio, Web. *Dealer:* Andrea Rosen 525 W 24th St New York NY 10012. *Mailing Add:* 28 FOREST Somerville MA 02143

SCHERER, HERBERT GROVER
EDUCATOR
b Brooklyn, NY, May 16, 30. *Study:* Western Reserve Univ, BA(art), 53, MA(art hist), 60, MLS, 63. *Collection Arranged:* Marquee on Main Street: Jack Liebenberg's Movie Theaters, 1928-1941 (auth, catalog), Univ Minn Art Gallery, 82. *Pos:* Art librn, Syracuse Univ, 63-66 & Univ Minn, Minneapolis, 66-98; mem, Gorman Art Libr Endowment Adv Bd, 89-99; mem, Pub Art Rev Adv Comt, 94-98. *Teaching:* Instr art hist & methodology, Univ Minn, Minneapolis, 66-; lectr, 84-98. *Mem:* Art Libr NAm (charter mem & founder, 72) (Wittenborn Art Book Comt, 95). *Publ:* Auth, Program of the thirty-nine ceiling paintings of the Jesuit Church of St Ignatius in Antwerp, painted by P P Rubens in 1620, Am Philos Soc Yearbk, 68; auth, Minneapolis art deco extravaganza, Arts Mag, summer 71; dir, Streamlined Dreams (TV doc), KTCA, 80; auth, Marquee on Main Street: Jack Liebenberg's Movie & Theatres, J Decorative Arts, spring 86; Tickets to Fantasy, Hennepin Co Hist, fall 87; A tarnished Art Deco Gem, Minneapolis-St Paul, 3/88; Merging Subject Collections or Love's Labor Lost, The Architecture Library of the Future: Complexity and Contradiction, Ann Arbor Univ, Mich Press, 89, 105-111; Modernism at Norwest: An Interview with David Ryan, Journal of Decorative and Propaganda Arts, 14, Fall 89, 112-127. *Mailing Add:* 170 Wilson Library 309 19th Ave S Minneapolis MN 55455

SCHERPEREEL, RICHARD CHARLES
EDUCATOR, PAINTER
b Mishawaka, Ind, Dec 1, 31. *Study:* Univ Notre Dame, BFA & MFA; McMurry Col, MEd; George Peabody Col for Teachers, EdD. *Comn:* STex totems, Tex A&I Univ, Kingsville, 75. *Exhib:* Mid States Artist Exhib, 66-68; Found Exhib, Art Mus S Tex, 70-78; Del Mar Nat Drawing & Small Sculpture Exhib, 71; Tex Fine Arts Asn, 72-74. *Teaching:* Instr art, Irving Pub Schs, Tex, 59-60 & Elkhart, Ind, 60-63; prof & chmn dept art, Bloomsburg State Col, Pa, 64-68 & Tex A&M Univ, Kingsville, 68-. *Mem:* Nat Coun Art Adminr (bd dir, 72-78, secy-treas, 72-78); Art Mus STex (bd mem, 74-96, exhib policy bd, 96-); Tex Fine Arts Asn (bd dir, 71-74); S Tex Art League (pres, 72-73); Coastal Bend Art Educ Asn (pres, 73-74). *Mailing Add:* 1631 Santa Cecilia Dr Kingsville TX 78363

SCHEUER, RUTH
PAINTER, TAPESTRY ARTIST
b Wilson, NC, Aug 20, 52. *Study:* Univ NC, BFA(cum laude), 70; Les Manufactures Nationales Des Gobelins, Paris, France, invitational studies, 79-80; Univ Calif, San Francisco, MA(fine art), 81. *Work:* Am Embassy, Warsaw, Poland; Univ NC, Weatherspoon Gallery, Greensboro. *Comn:* Tapestry, IBM, White Plains, NY, 87;

tapestry, Nabisco-RJR, Altanta, Ga, 87; tapestry, Touche-Ross, Houston, Tex, 88; tapestry, Wilmington Trust Bank, Del, 89; tapestry, Bell Atlantic Hq, Philadelphia, Pa, 91. *Exhib:* Solo exhib, NJ State Mus, Trenton, 85, Weatherspoon Gallery, Univ NC, Greensboro, 91 & Va Ctr Arts, Richmond, 92; Int Textile Exhib, Kyoto Cult Mus, Japan, 87 & 92; The Narrative Voice (touring), Musée D'Aubusson, France, 89; Int Tapestry, Anchorage Mus, Alaska, 90 & Textile Mus; World Tapestry Today (touring), West Pac Gallery, Melbourne, Australia, 88. *Pos:* Founder & dir, Scheuer Tapestry Studio, 82-89; founder & pres, Ctr Tapestry Arts, NY, 89-92, InterArt Ctr, NY, 92-. *Awards:* Visual Arts Fel, Midatlantic/Nat Endowment Arts, 89; Fel Grant, NY Found Arts, 90. *Bibliog:* Manson Kennedy (dir), Narrative Voice (film), 89; Pamela Scheinman (auth), cover article, Urban Tapestry, Am Craft, 89; Beatrijs Sterk (auth), Stromungen Der Zeit Tap, Deutsches Textilforum, 90. *Mem:* Distant Lives/Shared Voices, Lodz, Poland (int steering comt, 92); Am Tapestry Alliance (vpres & bd dir, 82-89); San Francisco Tapestry Workshop (co-founder, 76-79). *Media:* Miscellaneous. *Mailing Add:* 41 Commerce St New York NY 10014

SCHIAVINA, LAURA M
PAINTER
b Springfield, Mass, Nov 27, 1917. *Study:* Traphagen Sch Fashion, NY, cert, 44-46; Art Students League, with Will Barnet, 73; studied with Paul Puzinas, Carl Molno & Don Stacy. *Work:* Metrop Club, NY; Queensboro Community Col Art Gallery, Bayside, NY; and other pvt collections. *Exhib:* Salmagundi Club, NY, 74-2005; Priva B Gross Int, Queensboro Community Col, Bayside, NY, 94 & 96; Art Ctr of Munic of Athens, Eleftherias Park, Greece, 96; Flushing Coun Cult & Arts Mems Exhib, 97, 99, 2000, 2002, 2004, 2005, 2006; Solo exhibs, 93 S Art Gallery, Nyack, NY, 98, Z Gallery, NY, 93, 94, College of Technology & Others (4 solos), Grace Gallery, 2005; Queens Mus of Art, 2001, 2002; Nat Asn of Women Artists, NY & other locations, 89-2005; and many other group exhibs. *Awards:* Irwin Z Lowe Mem Award, Nat Asn Women Artists Ann, 94; Kenneth W Fitch Award, Salmagundi Club, 96; Samuel T Shaw Mem Award, Salmagundi Club, 1998; Cash Award, Postcard Exhibit, Nat Collage Soc, 2000; Audrey Hope Shirk Mem Award, 2005; Dorothy L Irish Award, 2006; Nat Asn Women Artists. *Bibliog:* Rev, France-Amerique, Le Courrier des Estats Unis, 69; Dorothy Hall (auth), rev, Park East, New York, 69; article, Mixing pensions and painting, Marsh & McLennan News, 90; Artist in the 1990's, Manhattan Arts Mag, 9-10/92; Prof Cnythia Maris (auth) 100 New York Painters, 2006. *Mem:* Salmagundi Club; Women's Studio Ctr Inc; NY Artist's Equity; Nat Asn Women Artists; Audubon Artists. *Media:* Acrylic on Canvas & Paper, Watercolor & Collage Artists. *Mailing Add:* 35-25 78th St Jackson Heights NY 11372

SCHIEBOLD, HANS
PAINTER
b Freiberg, Ger, Feb 12, 38; US citizen. *Study:* Brigham Young Univ, Utah, BA, 68; Hartford Art Sch of Univ Hartford, Conn, MFA, 70. *Work:* Aldrich Mus Contemp Art, Conn; New Britain Mus Am Art, Conn; Brownsville Art Mus, Tex; Wichita Art Mus, Kans; Southern Conn State Col, New Haven; Lake Oswego Town Hall & Libr, Ore. *Comn:* Mural, Sedgewick Co Courthouse-Co Comnr, Kans, 81; 12 public murals, Kans Arts Commission & Wichita Arts Board, Kans, 80; 3 outdoor murals, Wesleyan Univ, Conn, 76. *Exhib:* Invitation Acad Exhib, Wadsworth Atheneum, Conn, 71-73; Contemp Reflections, Aldrich Mus, Conn, 74; one-man shows, Ctr Arts, Wesleyan Univ, Conn, 74, Razor Gallery, NY, 77, Mus Art, Okla, 80 & Wichita Art Mus, Kans, 81. *Teaching:* Asst prof painting & drawing, Wesleyan Univ, Conn, 70-78 & Wichita State Univ, Kans, 78-82. *Awards:* Best in Show, Greater Hartford Arts Festival, 72; First Prize, Conn Acad, 74 & Springfield Art League, Mass, 75. *Media:* Acrylic, Graphite. *Dealer:* Lawrence Gallery Portland OR; Lanning Gallery Sedona AZ; Vail Village Arts CO; Bronce Coast Gallery Cannon Beach OR; Rich Haines Gallery Park City UT; James Harold Gallery Tahoe City CA. *Mailing Add:* 13705 SW 118th Ct Portland OR 97223

SCHIEFERDECKER, IVAN E
PRINTMAKER, PAINTER
b Keokuk, Iowa, Apr 14, 35. *Study:* Univ Ill, BFA; Univ Iowa, MFA. *Work:* Colorado Springs Art Ctr; Ohio Univ; Dulin Art Gallery, Knoxville, Tenn; Springfield Art Mus, Mo; Montgomery Art Mus, Ala; and others. *Exhib:* Pa Acad Fine Arts Ann Prints & Drawings, 65; J B Speed Art Mus, Louisville, Ky, 77; Southeastern Juried Exhib, Fine Arts Mus South, Mobile, Ala, 87; Border To Border Nat Drawing Competition, Austin Peay Univ, Clarksville, Tenn, 87 & 89; Dwight Merrimon Davidson Print Exhib, Elon Col, NC, 91; Ky On Paper, Quito, Ecuador, 91; Swanson Cralle Gallery, Louisville, Ky, 90 & 93; and others. *Teaching:* Prof printmaking, Western Ky Univ, 64-81. *Mem:* Col Art Asn. *Mailing Add:* 1701 Dunlaney Way Bowling Green KY 42103

SCHIETINGER, JAMES FREDERICK
SCULPTOR, EDUCATOR
b Baltimore, Md, Sept 27, 46. *Study:* Fla Presby Col, 64-66; Fla Atlantic Univ, 67; Univ SFla, BA, 68, MFA, 71. *Work:* Univ SFla; Norton Gallery Art, West Palm Beach. *Exhib:* Twenty-fifth Ceramic Nat, Everson Mus, Syracuse, 69; New Photog, Cent Wash State Col, 71; Photo-Media Show, Mus Contemp Crafts, NY, 71; Light and Lens: Methods of Photog, Hudson River Mus, NY, 73; Images-Dimensional, Moveable, Transferable, Akron Art Inst, 73. *Teaching:* Instr art hist, Fla Atlantic Univ, 71; instr ceramics, Univ SFla, 71-72; instr art, Miami-Dade Community Col, Miami, 72-73; asst prof art, Univ Vt, Burlington, 77-78 & Millikin Univ, 78-. *Awards:* First Prize in Sculpture, Winter Park Art Show, 70; Technol & Artist-Craftsman Symposium Award, Octagon Art Ctr, 73; Best in Show, Los Olas Art Festival, Ft Lauderdale, 75. *Mem:* Am Crafts Coun. *Media:* Clay. *Mailing Add:* RR 1 Mount Auburn IL 62547-9732

SCHIFF, E JEAN
EDUCATOR
b Keokuk, Iowa, Oct 20, 29. *Study:* Chicago Art Inst, 49-52; Washburn Univ, 57-60; Univ Kans, 61-63; Col San Mateo, 63-64; Univ Denver, BFA, 66; Univ Colo, Boulder, MFA, 70; Art Students League, NY, 82, Michael Howard Studio, NY, 88-89; Ruth Franklin, Audio, NY, 89. *Work:* St Paul Fine Art Ctr, Minn; Wichita Art Asn; Bucknell Univ; Francis McCray Gallery, Western NMex Univ; Mulvane Art Ctr, Washburn Univ; and others. *Exhib:* Denver Art Mus, 67, 70, 71 & 74; Alumni Exhib, Univ Denver, 93; Kyle Belding Gallery, 93; Colo Watercolor Soc, 93; Colo State Fair, 94; Artists on Campus, Mizel Mus, 94; and others. *Teaching:* Instr drawing, Univ Colo, Denver, summer 70; instr drawing, Metrop State Col, 70-71, prof, 71-; vis prof drawing & video workshops, Loretta Heights Col, Denver, Colo, 74, Univ Colo, Colorado Springs, 75, Red Deer Col, Alta, Can, 76, Colo State Univ, Ft Collins, 77, 78 & 82, Univ Denver, 80, Washburn Univ, Topeka, Kans, 82, Sch Art Inst Chicago, 82, Inst de Arte Federico Brandt, Caracas, Venezuela, 89 & AIFS, Univ London, 94. *Awards:* Grad Fel, Univ Colo, Boulder, 70; Purchase Award, Stanislaus State Col, 72; Video Workshop fel, Chicago Art Inst, 82; and others. *Mem:* Alliance for Contemp Art; Denver Art Mus, Women's. *Mailing Add:* 1276 Corona St B-3 Denver CO 80218

SCHIFF, LONNY
PRINTMAKER, CONSERVATOR
b Columbus, Ohio, 1929. *Study:* Ohio State Univ, 48; Univ Ill, BA(hons), 53; Worcester Art Mus Sch, fine arts cert, 64; Impressions Workshop, etching study, 65; papermaking study, Rugg Road Handmade Papers, 84-87. *Work:* Fogg Art Mus; Brooklyn Mus; Rose Art Mus, Brandeis Univ, Waltham, Mass; NASA Space Art Mus, Kennedy Space Ctr, Cape Canaveral, Fla; Nat Mus Am Art, Washington; and others. *Comn:* Complete restoration of oils by Enneking, A C Goodwin, Largelliere, 80-84; wall graphics designer, Framingham Union Hosp, 82; Restoration Folk Paintings of Framingham Hist Soc, 86-89; First Street Cafe, East Cambridge, Mass, 88; NASA Space Ctr Mus, Cape Canaveral, Fla, 89-90. *Exhib:* Solo shows, Framingham State Col, Mass, 81, Bromfield Gallery, Boston, 81, Laughlin-Winkler Gallery, Boston, 82 & 85, Cambridge Multi Cult Art Ctr, Mass, 85, First Impressions Gallery, Toronto, Ont, Can, 90 & Randall Beck Gallery, 87, 89, 91, 92, 93, 94 & 95; Mus Mod Art, Gannett Corp, 87; Franz Bader Gallery, Washington, 88; Space Explorer's Asn Show, Riyadh, Saudi Arabia, 90; Reaching into Space, Ringling Sch Art, Sarasota, Fla 91; Print Show, Long Beach Island Found, Loveladies, NJ, 92; Exhib Women Artists of the NASA Art Prog, Nat Mus Women's Art, Washington, DC, 98. *Teaching:* Instr oil painting, Adult Classes, Worcester Art Mus, 63-67; instr art appreciation & techniques, Sudbury Art Asn, 68-69; instr printmaking workshop, Charles River Art Ctr, 68, lectr & demonstr of conservation Am folk art, 70-. *Awards:* Patron's Prize, Philadelphia Print Club, 86; Morse Graphics Prize, N Coast Collage Soc, Hiram, Ohio, 87; Top Prize, Berkshire Mus, Pitts Field, Mass, 82; plus others. *Bibliog:* At Home, Interview on Collaboration with Designer Fred Fiandaca, Boston Globe, 5/22/92. *Mem:* Int Inst Conservators Art, London; Philadelphia Print Club; Int Asn Astron Artists. *Media:* Collage, Prints. *Specialty:* Contemporary Print and Painting. *Publ:* New York Review of Art, 3rd ed, 88; cover illustr, Allyn & Bacon, Trade Div, Simmon & Schuster, Needham, Mass, 91-96; auth, NASA and the Exploration of Space, Stewart, Tabori & Chang, 98. *Dealer:* Kelly Barrett Gallery 129 Newbury St Boston MA 02116

SCHILDKNECHT, DOROTHY E
PAINTER
b Chicago, Ill, Sept 30, 43. *Study:* Am Acad Art. *Work:* St Patrick High Sch, Chicago; Lillian Berkley Collection, Calif, 2000. *Exhib:* Women Artists on the West, Calif, 90-91; Nat Asn Women Artists, NY, 91; Mountain Oyster Exhib, Tucson, Ariz, 93-94; Old West Mus Exhib, Cheyenne, Wyo, 94; Am Art Miniatures, Gilcrease Mus, Tulsa, Okla, 94; and others. *Teaching:* Oil painting, Mt Prospect Park Dist & Glenview Park Dist, 88-; adult educ, Oakton Community Col. *Awards:* Third Place, Nat Exhib NMex Small Picture, 91. *Mem:* Nat Asn Women Artists, NY; Palette & Chisel Acad Fine Art, Chicago; Women Artists of West. *Media:* Oil. *Publ:* Chicago Tribune, 8/92 & 7/96; Daily Herald, 1/94. *Dealer:* White Oak Gallery Edina MN; Cain Gallery Oak Park IL. *Mailing Add:* 1356 Whitcomb Des Plaines IL 60018

SCHIMANSKY, DONYA DOBRILA
LIBRARIAN, HISTORIAN
b Yugoslavia; US citizen. *Study:* Univ Belgrade, Yugoslavia, BA & MA(art hist); Univ Cologna, WGer, study with Prof Hans Kaufmann; Univ Hamburg, medieval art with Prof Wolfgang Schone; City Univ New York, MLS. *Pos:* Asst to chmn, The Cloisters, New York, 69-73; asst chief librn, Metrop Mus Art Libr, 73-76, mus librn, 76-. *Mem:* Int Ctr Medieval Art (secy, 69-74); Spec Libr Asn, New York (secy/treas, 78); Yugoslav Am Art Asn (bd dir, 79-); Art Libr Soc NAm. *Res:* Wall painting in Byzantine art; classification of art books. *Publ:* Auth, The study of medieval ecclesiastical costume, 71 & On stained glass, 72, Metrop Mus Art Bulletin; The Metropolitan Museum of Art Library Classification System: how it works, Art Libr Soc Newsletter, 76; Museum art libraries collection development policy in the United States, Art Librs J, 81. *Mailing Add:* 2025 Broadway No 14C New York NY 10023

SCHIRA, CYNTHIA
TAPESTRY ARTIST
b Pittsfield, Mass, June 1, 34. *Study:* RI Sch Design, BFA, 56; L'Ecole D'Art Decoratif, Aubusson, France, 56-57; Univ Kans, MFA, 67. *Hon Degrees:* RI Sch Design, hon DFA, 89. *Work:* Am Craft Mus, NY; Chicago Art Inst, Ill; Renwick Gallery, Nat Mus Am Art, Smithsonian, Washington; Metrop Mus Art, NY; Philadelphia Mus Art, Pa; Boston Muc of Fine Arts; De Young Mus, San Francisco; Mus Belleriven Zurich; Mus Art, RI Sch Design; Indianapolis Mus Art; Cooper-Hewitt Mus; Smithsonian, NY. *Comn:* Wall Hanging, Arrow Corp, 94;

Horsley Bridge Partners, San Francisco, 2005. *Exhib:* Solo exhibs: Mus Bellerive, Zurich, 79, Spencer Mus Art, Univ Kans, Lawrence, 87, Renwick Gallery, Nat Mus Am Art & Smithsonian, Washington, 87; Group exhibs: The Art Fabric: Mainstream, San Francisco Mus Mod Art, 81; Craft Today, Am Crafts Mus, 87; Int Textile Competition '89, Kyoto, Japan; Jacquard Proj, Mus Indust Kultur, Nuremberg, Ger, 91; First Textile Miniature Triennale, Gdynia, Poland, 93; 2010-Textiles & New Technology, Brit Craft Ctr, London, 94; Technology as Catalyst, Textile Mus, Wash, DC, 02; Miniature Textiles 2000, Mus of Art and Design, Helsinki, 2000. *Pos:* Chairperson bd trustees, Haystack Mountain Sch Crafts, Maine, 89-92; Honorary Trustee, Haystack School of Crafts, Deer Isle, ME, 2004-. *Teaching:* Prof textile design, Univ Kans, 76-99, prof emer, 99-. *Awards:* Fel Am Crafts Coun, 91; Gold Medal, Am Crafts Coun Col of Fel, 2000; Distinguished Educator Award; James Renwick Alliance, Smithsonian. *Bibliog:* Susan Axy (auth), A World of Costume & Design (exhib catalog), Mus Art, RI Sch Design, Providence, 89; Beatrijs Sterk (auth), High tech textilkunsk, Deutsches Textileforum Heft, 12/4/92; Joan Simon (auth), Cynthia Schira, portfolio collection, Telos Art Publ, 2003. *Mem:* Am Crafts Coun; Textile Soc Am. *Media:* Textiles. *Dealer:* Snyderman Works Gallery 303 Cherry St Phildelphia PA 19106. *Mailing Add:* Box 303 Westport NY 12993

SCHIRM, DAVID
PAINTER, EDUCATOR
b Pittsburgh, Pa, Mar 31, 45. *Study:* Carnegie Mus, BFA, 67; Ind Univ, MFA, 72. *Work:* Albright-Knox Art Gallery; Carnegie Mus Art; Nat Mus Art, Hanoi, Vietnam; Kaufman & Broad, Los Angeles; Burchfield Penny Art Ctr. *Exhib:* Directions, Hirshhorn Mus, Washington, 79; Painting & Sculpture Today, Indianapolis Mus Art, 80; Carnegie Int, Carnegie Mus, 82. *Pos:* Chair, Dept Visual Studies. *Teaching:* Lectr painting, Univ Calif Los Angeles, 77-81; asst prof, Univ Southern Calif, 82-83; prof, Univ Buffalo, 85-. *Awards:* NY Found for Arts, 91; Fulbright Fel, Fragile Petals, Fulbright Comn, 94-95; Fullbright Regional Res, India & Sri Lanka. *Bibliog:* Howard Fox (auth), Directions, Hirshhorn Mus, 79; Lucy Lippard (auth), A Different War, Vietnam in Art, 90; Susan Larsen (auth), David Schirm, Ind Univ, 94. *Mem:* Coun Int Exchange Schs. *Media:* Painting. *Mailing Add:* 3602 Rose Rd Batavia NY 14020

SCHJELDAHL, PETER
CRITIC, EDITOR
b Fargo, NDak, 42. *Study:* Carlton Col; New Sch, 60-65. *Pos:* Art critic, New York Sunday Times, 70-75, Village Voice, 81-82, Vanity Fair, 83-84 & 7 Days, currently; contrib ed, Art Am, currently. *Awards:* Frank Jewett Mather Award, Col Art Asn, 80. *Publ:* Auth: (poetry collections) White Country, 1968, An Adventure of the Thought Police, 1971, Dreams, 1973, Since 1964; New and Selected Poems, 1978, Sun, (books) Hydrogen Jukebox: Selected Writings of Peter Schjeldahl, 1978-1990, 1991, The Seven Days Art Columns, 1991, Columns and Catalogues, 1994; Auth, Cindy Sherman, Pantheon Books, 84; Eric Fischl, Art Am/Stewart, Tabori & Chang, 88; and articles in Artforum, Art News, Art Int, Art & Antiques, Camera Arts, Am Craft; co-founder poetry mag Mother; contributing editor Art in Am; contribr articles to art jours. incl Artforum, Art News, Art Inter, Art & Antiques, Camera Arts, Am Craft and others. *Mailing Add:* The New Yorker 4 Times Sq New York NY 10036-6592

SCHLAGETER, ROBERT WILLIAM
CONSULTANT, MUSEUM DIRECTOR
b Streator, Ill, May 10, 25. *Study:* Univ Ill, BA & MFA; Univ Heidelberg, cert; Univ Chicago; Harvard Univ. *Collection Arranged:* Fifty Years of American Art (1900-1950), 68; Winslow Homer's Florida (1886-1909), 77; George Inness, Florida & the South, 80; Martin Johnson Heade: St Augustine Years (with catalog), 81; Robert Henri & George Bellows (with catalog), 81. *Pos:* Dir, Mint Mus Art, Charlotte, NC, 58-66; assoc dir, Downtown Gallery, New York, 67; assoc dir, Ackland Art Ctr, Univ NC, Chapel Hill, 67-; dir, Cummer Gallery Art, Jacksonville, Fla, 76-92; fine Arts Consult, corp & pvt collections, currently. *Teaching:* Asst prof art hist, Univ Tenn, Knoxville, 52-58. *Publ:* Auth, Winslow Homer: Florida Years, 77; George Inness in Florida, 80; Martin Johnson Heade in Florida, 81. *Mailing Add:* 45 Katherine Blvd Apt 435 Palm Harbor FL 34684-3650

SCHLANGER, JEFF
SCULPTOR
b New York, NY, 37. *Study:* Swarthmore Col, BA; Cranbrook Acad Art, with Maija Grotell. *Work:* Sheldon Mem Art Gallery, Univ Nebr, Lincoln; Am Craft Mus, NY; Cranbrook Art Mus, Bloomfield Hills, Mich; Acad Art Mus, St Petersburg, Russ. *Comn:* Tile mural, Performing Arts Ctr, Eugene, Ore, 82. *Exhib:* Total Cup, Kanazawa City, Tokyo, Kyoto, Japan, 73; Contemp Crafts of the Americas: 75, Ft Collins, Colo, 75; The Object as Poet, Renwick Gallery, Smithsonian Inst, Washington & Mus of Contemp Crafts, NY, 77; one-man shows, State Col Ceramics, Alfred, NY, 78 & City Univ NY Grad Ctr Mall Gallery, 80; and others. *Teaching:* Instr ceramics, Hunter Col, 75 & Pratt Inst Grad Sch, 77; instr sculpture, State Univ NY, Purchase, 82; ceramics, Cranbrook Acad Art, 84. *Awards:* Tiffany Found Scholar, 67; Craftsmen's Fel Nat Endowment Arts, 73; Fel NY State Creative Artists Pub Serv, 81. *Mem:* Am Craft Coun; Int Sculpture Ctr. *Media:* Clay, Wood. *Publ:* Auth, Maija Grotell, Studio Potter Books, 96. *Mailing Add:* c/o Studio Spirale 556 Stratton Rd New Rochelle NY 10804-1108

SCHLEEH, HANS MARTIN
SCULPTOR
b Konigsfeld Schwarzwald, Ger, Oct9, 28; Can citizen. *Work:* Montreal Mus Fine Arts; Tel Aviv Mus, Israel; Art Gallery Winnipeg; Vancouver Art Gallery; Univ Sherbrooke, Can; Musée Contemporain. *Comn:* Limestone sculpture, Ciba Ltd, Montreal, 56; Swan (carrara marble), Pl Arts, Montreal, 65; copper sculptures, Arthur Maron Enterprises, Montreal, 67; limestone sculpture, Freiman Stores, Ottawa, 73. *Exhib:* Solo exhibs, Dominion Gallery, Montreal, 60-70, Que Sculptors Asn, Montreal, 65-70, Salon Jeune Sculpture, Paris, 66-67 & Expo 67, Montreal, 67; Exposition Int, Rodin Mus, Paris, 71; and others. *Bibliog:* Guy Robert (auth), L'Art au Quebec Depuis 1940, 40 & Ecole de Montreal, 64, La Presse. *Mem:* Royal Can Acad Arts. *Media:* Stone, Metal. *Mailing Add:* 2209 av Oxford Montreal PQ H4A 2X7 Canada

SCHLEINER, ANN-MARIE
GRAPHIC ARTIST
b Providence, 1970. *Study:* Univ Michoacan, Mex; Univ Kiel; Univ Calif, Santa Cruz; San Jose State Univ, MFA. *Work:* Madame Polly Game Patch, 1998; Epilepsy Virus Patch, 1999; Cracking the Maze, 1999; mutation.fem, 2000; Luckykiss xxx, 2000; Skool, 2001; Snow Blossom House, 2001; Anime Noir, 2002; Velvet Strike, 2002; Parangari Cutiri, 1999-; PS2 Diaries, 2004-; OUT: Operation Urban Terrain, 2004-. *Teaching:* Asst prof, interactive arts Technol, Univ British Columbia, Can, 99-2000; adj fac, of digital art Univ Calif, Irvine, 2001; asst prof, Univ Colo, Boulder, 2003-. *Mem:* fel, Akademie Schloss Solitude, 2003. *Mailing Add:* Univ Colo at Boulder Univ Art & Art Hist 318 UCB Boulder Boulder CO 80309

SCHLEMM, BETTY LOU
PAINTER, INSTRUCTOR
b Jersey City, NJ, Jan 13, 34. *Study:* Phoenix Sch Design, New York, scholar; Nat Acad Design, New York, scholar. *Work:* US Navy; 1st Nat Bank Boston; Andrew Mellon Collection; American Telephone & Telegraph; also in many other pvt & public collections. *Exhib:* Am Watercolor Soc; Butler Inst Am Art; Nat Acad Design; Allied Artists Am; Audubon Artists. *Pos:* Vpres, Boston Watercolor Soc; regional vpres, Am Watercolor Soc, 89-90 & dir, 90-92. *Awards:* Gold Medal, Rockport Art Asn, 81; Frederick B Robinson Award, Academic Artists, 81; Dolfin Fel, Am Watercolor Soc, 81 & Silver Medal, 64; and others. *Bibliog:* 100 Watercolor Techniques, Watson-Guptill, 69; Stephen Doherty (auth), Being An Artist, 92; Lewis Lehrman (auth), North Light, 92; and others. *Mem:* Am Watercolor Soc; Rockport Art Asn (pres, 95-97); Boston Watercolor Soc (vpres, 76-); and others. *Media:* Watercolor, oil. *Publ:* Auth, Watercolor page, Am Artist, 64 & 76; Painting with Light, Watson-Guptill, 78, 2nd ed, 79 & 3rd ed, 92; Learning from today's art masters, Am Artist Mag, 95; Watercolor Secrets for Painting, Light-North Light, 96. *Dealer:* Guild of Boston Artists 162 Newbury St Boston MA 02116; Rockport Art Asn 10 Main St Rockport MA 01966; State of the Art Gallery 1&2 Wanson St Gloucester MA 01930 & Pleasant St Gloucester MA 01930. *Mailing Add:* Caleb's Ln Rockport MA 01966

SCHLESINGER, CHRISTINA
PAINTER, MURALIST
b Washington, DC, Dec 19, 46. *Study:* Radcliffe Col, Harvard Univ, BA, 68; Zhejiang Acad Fine Arts, Hangzhou, China, 88; Mason Gross Sch Arts, Rutgers Univ, MFA, 95. *Comn:* The Peaceable: Kingdom, Kennedy Child Study Ctr, Bronx, NY, 91; The Big Splash, Greyhound Inc & City of Los Angeles, Percent for Art, Calif, 91; Fire Mural, DP Bean & Co, Jaffrey, NH, 92; East NY, Past, Present & Future, Sites Proj, Percent for Art, NY, 94; Chaqall Returns to Venice Beach, Cult Affairs Dept, City of Los Angeles, Venice, Calif, 96. *Exhib:* Mixed Use District, Clock Tower, NY, 90; Artists & Homeless Collaborative World Wall, Henry Street Settlement House, NY, 93; Other Choices, Other Voices, Islip Mus Art, NY, 95; Trees, Provincetown Art Asn, Mass, 95; Celebity Hood, Bronx Ctr Arts, NY, 96; Altered Egos, Hallwalls Contemp Art Ctr, Buffalo, NY, 97. *Pos:* Co-found, Social & Pub Art Resource Ctr, Venice, Calif, 76-. *Awards:* Grant, Pollock-Krasner Found Inc, 88; Grant, Adolph & Esther Gothlieb Found Inc, 89. *Bibliog:* Alan Barnett (auth), Community Murals: The People's Art, Art Alliance Press & Cornwall Bks, 94. *Media:* Oil; Acrylic. *Mailing Add:* 16 Deep Six Dr East Hampton NY 11937-1603

SCHLESINGER, JOHN
PHOTOGRAPHER
Study: Univ Minn, BA (philosophy & photography), 80, BS (art educ), 80. *Work:* Allen Mem Mus; Art Inst of Chicago; Bill Arning, NY; Bonni Benrubi, NY; Blue Mountain Center; and others. *Exhib:* Figures, Spaces and Structures, 1972-1983, Walker Art Ctr, Minneapolis, Minn, 85; Wider Perspectives, Mus Contemp Photog, Chicago, Ill, 85; Stills: From Cinema and Video into Photog, Seattle Mus, Wash, 86; Recent Acquisitions, Mus Mod Art, NY, 87; Poetic Injury: The Surrealist Legacy in Postmodern Photog, Alternative Mus, NY, 87; solo exhibs, Retrospective (with catalog) Writing Pictures, Julie Saul Gallery 96, Williamsburg Art NeXus, Brooklyn, Quotidan Gallery, San Francisco, 2001; group exhibs, The Artist as a Patron, The Alternative Mus, NY, Yard Sale, Downtown Arts Festival, NY Lab Sch, NY, 99, Our Town, Photo Gallery West, Philadelphia, Because Sex Sells, Nikolai Fine Arts, NY & Berlin Arts Fair, Ubu Gallery of NY, Berlin, FDR, 2000; and others. *Awards:* Fel, Nat Endowment Arts, 86; Louis Comfort Tiffany Award, 99; Aaron Siskind Fel, 2000; finalist, Rome Prize, 2001. *Bibliog:* Susan Zwinger (auth), Black is beautiful, Santa Fe Reporter, 11/29/85; Andy Grundberg (auth), Critics' choices, NY Times, 6/8/86; Leonard Boasberg (auth), The Philadelphia Inquirer, 1/31/2000. *Publ:* Award catalogue, Louis Comfort Tiffany Found, two photographs, 99-2000. *Mailing Add:* c/o Seraphin Gallery 1108 Pine St Philadelphia PA 19107

SCHLEY, REEVE, III
PAINTER
b NY City, NY, Mar 11, 36. *Study:* Yale Univ, BA, 59; Univ Pa, MFA, 62; studied with Josef Buchty, Munich, 55. *Work:* Exhib in group shows incl Spook Farm Gallery, Farm Hills, NJ, 1958, Hunterdon Co Art Ctr Ann, 1959, Pa Acad, 1966, NJ State Mus, Trenton, 1967, Tennessee Fine Arts Ctr, Nashville, 1973, Okl Art Ctr, Okl City, 1974, Butler Inst Am Art, Youngstown, Ohio, 1974, Drew Univ, 1975, Silvermine Guild Artists, 1975, Nat Acad of Design, 1977-78, Brooklyn Mus, 1984. *Exhib:* one-man

shows Vendo Nubes Gallery, Chestnut Hill, Pa, 67 & 71, Philadelphia Art Alliance, 69, Spook Farm Gallery, 70, Saratoga, Gallery, NY, 72-75, James Graham Gallery, NY, 73-2002, NJ State Mus, 78, Hull Gallery, Wash, 78, 80, Byck Gallery, Louisville, 79, Peale House Gallery, Pa Acad Fine Arts, 1980, Gallerie Arnoldi-Livie, Munich, 85, New Orleans Acad Fine Arts, 85, 96; represented in permanent collections NJ State Mus, Trenton, Nat Acad, Newark Mus, Brooklyn Mus, Yale Univ Art Gallery, Heublein Collection, Somerset Co Col, Tenneco Chems. *Teaching:* instr, watercolor Nat Acad, New York City, 81-. *Awards:* Best in Show award Hunterdon Co Art Ctr, 74; Laura M Gross Mem award Silvermine Guild Artists, 75; Recipient Ranger Fund purchase prize Nat Acad, 81 & 85, cert of merit, 78 & 95. *Mem:* Nat Acad (assoc, 80, acad, 94-). *Media:* Watercolor. *Mailing Add:* c/o James Grahm & Sons Inc 1014 Madison Ave at 78th St New York NY 10021

SCHLITTER, HELGA
PAINTER, SCULPTOR
b Mexico City, Mex; Can citizen. *Study:* Studied with Marcel Jean, 68-75. *Work:* Musee du Quebec; Ministry Multicultural Communities, Quebec Govt. *Comn:* Laure Gaudreault, Clermont, Québec, Andiwish:Lestortues, Interior floor mosaic, École L' Apprentisage, Québec, 99; Cirque, exterior wall installation, Ecole De Cirque De Québec, 2003; Un Drôle Ó Animal, exterior scuplture, École Primaire, 2003; Azi Mut Le Gardiev De L' École, exterior sculpture, École La Rose-Des-Vents, St Jean Chrysostome, Québec. *Exhib:* Pret d'oeuvres d'art, Musee du Que, 83, 85 & 86; Femmes-Forces Musee du Que, 87; Noel Reinvente, Musee du Civilisation, Que, 88; Quetzalpapalotl, le temple de l'oiseau-papillon, 84 & Recent Work, 86, La Chambre Blanche; Recent Work, Powerhouse, Montreal, 86; Des jaguar-des serpents-et des temples, Axe-Neo 7, Hull, Que, 86; BBK-Werkstattev, Freiburg, Ger, 92; De Quebec A Chicomoztoc Museo Carrillo Gil, Mex, D F, 94; Universidad La Salle, Mex, DF, 95; Galerie De L'Universite Laval, Que, 95; Centre D'Expositions De St-Jerome, Que, 97; Galerie Du Parc, Trois-Rivieres, Que, 98; Sculptures Et Mosaïques Galerie Trompe L'oeil, Cegep Ste-Foy, Qué, 2000; Jeux En Mosaique, Maison De La Cult, Notre-Dame-De-Grace, Montreal, Qué, 2001; Jardins De Cristal, Centre Diart De Baie-St-Paul, Qué, 2003. *Pos:* Mem exec coun, La Chambre Blanche, Quebec, 80-83, pres, 82-83; pres, Atelier le 88, Quebec, 80-88; mem exec coun, L'Oeil du Poisson, Quebec, 88. *Awards:* Quebec Cult Ministry Scholar, 88 & 94; Scholar of artistic exchange between Que & Mex, Ministry of External Affairs, 94; Scholar for Prof Studies in Barcelona, Ministry Art, Quebec, 98; Ministry of External Affairs of Can and Fonca (Fondo Nacinal Para La Cultura Mexico) Schlorship-Mexico/Can Exchange. *Bibliog:* Marie Delagrave (auth), Architec & paysages imaginaires, 1/28/84 & Helga Schlitter et le temple des papillons, 4/14/84, Le Soleil; Chantal Boulanger (auth), Atelier de l'artiste, Vanguard, 84; Dany Qunie (auth) Joies Exotiques, Le Soleil, Québec, 2/5/2000; Nathalie Côté (auth), La Menagerie De Verre, Voir, Québec, 2/10/2000. *Media:* Multimedia. *Mailing Add:* 169 St-Olivier Quebec PQ G1R 1G2 Canada

SCHLODER, JOHN E
DIRECTOR
Study: Duquesne Univ, BS, 1969; L'Ecole du Louvre, Paris, Diplôme d' Ancien Elève; L'Institut d' Archéologie Univ Paris-Sorbonne, 1973; Lurcy Fel, Columbia Univ, 1975; Traveling Fel, Univ Cambridge Eng, 1975-1976; Leverhulme Fel, 1977; Kellogg Project Fel, Smithsonian Inst, 1987; Columbia Univ, MPhil, 1980; L'Institut d' Art et d'Archéologie, Univ Paris-Sorbonne, PhD, 1988; J Paul Getty Trust, scholar, 1989; Japan Found vis schol, 1995. *Pos:* Chargé de Mission Musée du Louvre, Paris, 1979-1982; Asst cur, Cleveland Mus Art Edn Dept, 1982-1985, assoc cur, 1985-1986, adminr pub progs, 1986-1988, asst dir, edn & pub progs, 1988-1992; Dir Birmingham (Ala) Mus Arts, 1992-1996; Dir, Joslyn Mus Art, Omaha, 1997-2000; Dir, Mus Fine Arts, St. Petersburg, Fla, 2001. *Teaching:* Vis prof, Colégio Andrews, Rio de Janeiro, Brazil, 1980-1981; Vaculdade Candido Mendes, Rio de Janeiro, 1981-1982; Adj prof art hist, Case Western Reserve Univ, Cleveland, 1984-1992. *Awards:* French Govt Award of Achievement, 1975; Northern Ohio Live Mag, 1991. *Mem:* Am Asn Mus; Asn Art Mus (dirs); Int Lab Visitor Studies; Visitor Studies Asn; Ala Mus Asn; Birmingham Area Mus Asn; Soc de l'Historie de l'Art Francais; Rotary Club Birmingham. *Mailing Add:* Mus Fine Arts 255 Beach Dr NE Saint Petersburg FL 33701

SCHLOSBERG, CARL MARTIN
ART DEALER
b Los Angeles, Calif, Feb 5, 36. *Study:* Univ Calif, Los Angeles, BS, 58. *Pos:* Dir, Carl Schlosberg Fine Arts, 72-. *Mem:* Graphic Arts Coun, Los Angeles Co Mus; Univ Calif, Los Angeles Art Coun; Los Angeles Inst Contemp Art; Nat Soc Lit & Arts; Artists Equity Asn. *Specialty:* Contemporary paintings, graphics, tapestry, sculpture; publisher of Lee Waisler editions; twentieth century master prints; twentieth century American sculpture: Aldo Casanova, George Rickey, Oliver Andrews

SCHLOSS, ARLEEN P
PAINTER
b Brooklyn, NY, Dec 12, 43. *Study:* Parsons Sch Design, cert; New York Univ, BA; Art Students League. *Work:* Aldrich Mus Contemp Art, Ridgefield, Conn; Am Tel & Tel Longlines, NJ; Mus Mod Art Libr, NY; Lenbachhaus Mus, Munich, Ger. *Exhib:* Tenth Anniv Exhib, Aldrich Mus, Conn, 74; Contemp Reflections, 1971-74 Traveling Show, Am Fedn Arts, 75-77; Artists Books USA, Allen Mem Art Mus, Oberlin Col, 79; one-woman show, Diagrams, Rush Rhees Gallery, Rochester Univ, 75; Stadtische Galerie Im Buntentor, Bremen, Ger, 94. *Teaching:* Artist-in-residence art & music, NY Pub Schs, 67-75; guest lectr art, Rochester Univ, 75; guest prof, Hochschule fur Kunste, Bremen, Ger, 93. *Awards:* Video Fel, NY Found Arts, 92. *Bibliog:* Jill Dunbar (auth), Avant-Garde--The other end, The Villager, 12/8/77; Enrico Baj (auth), Panorama Mag, 6/86; Frances DeVuono (auth), New York Art Examiner, 89; Tobey Crockett (auth), High Performance Mag, 92. *Media:* Audio & Visual Materials. *Publ:* Contribr, Weaving: A Handbook of The Fibre Arts, Holt, Rinehart & Winston, 78. *Mailing Add:* 330 Broome St New York NY 10002

SCHMALTZ, ROY EDGAR
PAINTER, EDUCATOR
b Belfield, NDak. *Study:* Otis Art Inst, Los Angeles, 59-60; Univ Wash, Seattle, 57-59, 60-61; Akademie Der Bildenden Kunste, Munich, Ger, 65-66; San Francisco Art Inst, BFA, 63, MFA, 65. *Work:* Frye Art Mus, Seattle; San Francisco Art Inst & M H De Young Mem Art Mus, San Francisco; Mills Col, Oakland; Amerika-Haus, Munich, Ger; Univ Hawaii, Hilo; and others. *Exhib:* M H De Young Mem Art Mus, San Francisco, 69; San Francisco Mus Mod Art, 71; Oakland Art Mus, 79; Springfield Art Mus, Mo, 81; Butler Inst Am Art, Youngstown, Ohio, 81; Crocker Art Mus, Sacramento, 82; Appalachian State Univ, NC, 82; Univ Hawaii, Manoa, 83; and others. *Pos:* Artists bd, San Francisco Art Inst, 89-92. *Teaching:* Lectr, Col Notre Dame, Belmont, Calif, 68-70; lectr, M H De Young Art Mus, San Francisco, 69-70; prof, St Mary's Col, Moraga, Calif, 69-, chair, Dept Art. *Awards:* Fel, Fulbright, Munich, Ger, 65; Walnut Creek Civic Art Ctr Award, 82; San Francisco Art Comn Award, 85. *Bibliog:* Thomas Albright (auth), Art of the San Francisco Bay Area 1945-1980, Univ Calif Press, Berkeley; Bay Area Artists Calendar-1984, KQED TV; Les Krantz (auth), The Calif Art Review, Second ed, Am References, Chicago. *Media:* Oil, Watercolor. *Dealer:* Hackett-Freedman Gallery 250 Sutter St 4th Floor San Francisco CA 94108; Hearst Art Gallery Saint Mary's Col Moraga CA. *Mailing Add:* 1020 Whistler Dr Suisun City CA 94585

SCHMALZ, CARL (NELSON), JR
PAINTER, EDUCATOR
b Ann Arbor, Mich, Dec 26, 26. *Study:* Eliot O'Hara Watercolor Sch, summers 43 & 44; Harvard Univ, AB, 48, MA, 49, PhD, 58. *Hon Degrees:* Amherst Col, Hon MA, 69. *Work:* Walker Art Mus, Brunswick, Maine; Jones & Laughlin Steel Corp, Cleveland, Ohio; Diners Club Am; Blue Cross-Blue Shield; Hampshire Col; Kalamazoo Art Ctr; Naples Philharmonic Soc, Fla; Pelham Pub Libr, Mass. *Comn:* Amherst Savings Bank, Mass. *Exhib:* Am Watercolor Soc, 66, 68 & 70; Watercolor USA, Springfield, Mo, 70, 84 & 97; Wichita Centennial Nat Art Exhib, Kans, 70; Wall of Fame Bicentennial Exhib, Baltimore Watercolor Soc, 76 & 85; Boston Atheneum, 79; Govt House Gallery, Hamilton, Bermuda, 79 & Invitation, 86; plus others. *Pos:* Vpres & mem bd dir, Portland Mus Art, 57-62; art consult, O'Hara Picture Trust, 69-. *Teaching:* Asst prof art hist & assoc dir, Bowdoin Col, 53-62; prof art hist, Amherst Col, 62-94; dir pvt watercolor workshops, Kennebunkport, Maine, 70-89; private workshops nationally, currently. *Awards:* First Prize for Watercolor, Cambridge Art Asn Ann, 47; First Prize for Traditional Watercolor, Virginia Beach Boardwalk Show, 65; Southern Mo Trust Purchase Award, Watercolor USA, 70; Watercolor USA Honor Soc, 85; First prize, K'bunk River Club Ann, 85, Patron's Prize, 86; Arches Paper Award, Jim E Pinckley Purchase Award, Watercolor USA, 97. *Bibliog:* Wendon Blake (auth), The Artists Guide to Using Color, North Light Bks, Cincinnati, 92; Article in The Artist's Mag, Vol II, No I, 1/94; Splash 3: Ideas and Inspirations, North Light Bks, Cincinnati, 9/94. *Mem:* Col Art Asn. *Media:* Watercolor, Serigraph. *Publ:* Contribr, A staining and transparent palette, In: Watercolor Portraiture, Putnam, 49; auth, Watercolor Lessons from Eliot O'Hara, 74, Watercolor Your Way, 78 & Finding and Improving Your Painting Style, 86, Watson-Guptill; plus others. *Dealer:* Mast-Cove Gallery Kennebunkport ME; Windjammer Hamilton Bermuda. *Mailing Add:* 11 Cambridge Ct Kennebunk ME 04043-6980

SCHMANDT-BESSERAT, DENISE
HISTORIAN, ARCHAEOLOGIST
b Ay-Champagne, France. *Study:* Ecole du Louvre, Paris, 65. *Collection Arranged:* Permanent exhib, Near Eastern Collections (with catalog), Peabody Mus, Harvard Univ, 68; The Legacy of Sumer, the First Civilization (with catalog & children's catalog), 75 & Ancient Persia--The Art of an Empire, 78, Univ Tex Art Mus. *Pos:* Adv ed, Technology & Cult, 78-92; adv bd, Visible Language, 85-; ed bd, Written Commun, 93-95, Hedia Ecology, 2002- & Archaeol Odyssey, 2003-; curator, Legacy of the Middle East, exhib, Jeddah, Saudi Arabia. *Teaching:* Prof ancient Near East, Univ Tex, Austin, 72-; vis assoc prof, Dept Near Eastern Studies, Univ Calif, Berkeley, 87; guest scholar, Ger Archaeological Inst, Berlin, WGer, 87; guest scholar, Tsukuba Univ, Hiroshima Univ, Japan, 90. *Awards:* Nat Endowment Humanities, 79-80, 91 & 96; Ger Acad Exchange Serv Grant, 86; USIA Fel, Am Ctr Oriental Res, 95, 97, 2001; Named One of the 100 Authors of the 20th Century, Am Scientist, 99; Kayden Nat Univ Press Book Award, 92; Robert W Hamilton Author Award, 98; Walter J Ong Award Medi aEcology Asn, 2004; and others. *Mem:* Archaeol Inst Am (pres, Cent Tex Chap, 74-76, gov bd, 85-); Am Oriental Studies; fel Am Anthropological Asn; Am Sch Oriental Res; Ctr Int Ricerche Archeologiche Antropologiche e Storiche. *Res:* Symbolism in the Ancient Middle East. *Publ:* auth, The origins of writing, Written Commun, Vol 13, No 1, 86; Before Writing, 92, When Writing Came About, 96, Univ Tex Press; History of Counting, 2000; From Behind the Mask, Origini, Vol XXIV, 2002; Stone Age Death Masks, Archaeol Odyssey, Vol 6, No 2, 2003-; others. *Mailing Add:* 11 Hull Circle Austin TX 78746

SCHMID, RICHARD ALAN
PAINTER
b Chicago, Ill, Oct 5, 34. *Study:* Am Acad Art, Chicago, 52-55, with William Mosby. *Exhib:* Invitational Drawing Exhib, Otis Art Inst, Los Angeles, 66; 33rd Ann, Butler Inst Am Art, Youngstown, Ohio, 68; 23rd Ann Drawing Biennial, Norfolk Mus Arts & Sci, 69; 164th Ann, Pa Acad Fine Arts, Philadelphia, 69; Am Watercolor Soc Ann, Nat Acad Design Galleries, NY, 70-71; and many one-man shows throughout US, 58-72. *Awards:* Jane Peterson Prize, Allied Artists Am, 67; Gold Medal of Honor, Am

Watercolor Soc, 71, Gold Medal of Honor for Marianne, Am Artist, 72; and others. *Media:* Oil, Watercolor. *Publ:* Auth, Richard Schmid Paints the Figure, 73 & auth, Richard Schmid Paints Landscapes, 75, Watson-Guptill. *Dealer:* Talisman Gallery 115 SE 12th Bartlesville OK 74003. *Mailing Add:* c/o Tailsman Gallery 115 SE 12th Bartlesville OK 74003

SCHMIDT, CHARLES
PAINTER, CURATOR
b Pittsburgh, Pa, Mar 4, 39. *Study:* Carnegie-Mellon Univ, Pittsburgh, BFA (painting), 60; Cranbrook Acad Art, Bloomfield Hills, Mich, MFA(painting), 67. *Work:* Nat Air & Space Mus, Nat Gallery Art Rosenwald Collection, Washington; San Francisco Mus Art; Philadelphia Mus Art; Butler Mus, Youngstown, Ohio; Europ Space Agency, Paris, France. *Comn:* Painting, Nat Aeronautics & Space Admin, 80, 82, 83, 86 & 87; Mem mural of Challenger astronauts, US Senate for US Capitol, dedicated 87. *Exhib:* 164th Ann Exhib, Pa Acad Fine Arts, Philadelphia, 69; Nat Drawing Exhib, San Francisco Mus Art, 70; one-man shows, Lowe Art Mus, Syracuse Univ, NY, 73 & Rosenfeld Gallery, Philadelphia, 76, 80 & 83; Small Works, Newcastle upon Tyne Polytech Mus Art, Eng, 79; Artist and the Space Shuttle int tour, 82-87; The Art of Silverpoint, nat tour, 89; Myth & Psych, The More Gallery, Philadelphia, Pa, 98; Figure and Object, The More Gallery, Philadelphia, Pa, 2000; Museo Aeronautico, Rome, Italy; VA Air and Space Mus, Hampton, VA; US Capitol Bldg, Washington, DC; Syracuse Univ, Lowe Art Mus, Syracuse, NY; San Francisco Mus of Art, San Francisco, Calif; Philadelphia Mus Art, Philadelphia, PA; Nat Gallery of Art, Rosenwald Col, Washington, DC; Nat Air and Space Mus, Washington, DC; NASA, Washington, DC; Ark Art Ctr, Little Rock, Ark; European Space Agency, Paris, France. *Collection Arranged:* Silverpoint Etcetera: Contemporary American Metalpoint Drawings, traveling exhib, 10/92-10/93. *Pos:* Calligrapher, White House Social Staff, Washington, DC, 61-62. *Teaching:* Instr, Atlanta Col Art, Ga, 63-65; prof, Tyler Sch Art, Temple Univ, Philadelphia, 67-72, assoc prof, 72-81, prof, 81-; asst prof, Temple Abroad Tyler Sch Art Rome, Italy, 70-72. *Awards:* Dana Watercolor Medal, Pa Acad Fine Arts, 69; Purchase Award, Southern Ill Univ, Carbondale, 75; Purchase Award, West Collection, West Publ Co, St Paul, 84. *Bibliog:* Life on the new frontier, Look Mag, 1/2/62; The watercolor page, Am Artist Mag, 10/77; Mary Settegast (auth), Mona Lisa's Moustache, Phanes Press, 2001. *Media:* Oil. *Publ:* Illusr, Bioscience, by Platt & Reid, Reinhold Publ, 67. *Dealer:* Grey McGear Modern Inc Santa Monica CA. *Mailing Add:* 209 Ft Washington Ave Fort Washington PA 19034

SCHMIDT, EDWARD WILLIAM
PAINTER
b Ann Arbor, Mich, Apr 19, 1946. *Study:* Art Students League, 66-69; Skowhegan Sch Painting & Sculpture, 67; Ecole Beaux Arts, Paris, with R Chaplain-midi, 67-68; Pratt Inst, BFA, 71, Brooklyn Col, MFA, 74; Atelier 17, Paris with Stanley Hayter, 78. *Work:* Bayly Mus Art, Univ Va, Charlottesville; Am Acad Rome; Nat Acad of Design, NY; Ark Art Ctr, Little Rock; Elizabeth Greenshields Found, Montreal, Can. *Comn:* Mural, Alwyn Court, NY, 77; eight statues, Cincinnati Orchestra Pavilion, comn by M Graves, 85; four murals, Hotel Giorgio, Denver, 87; Quantum Corp, NY. *Exhib:* Salon Nat Beaux Arts, Grand Palais, Paris, 68; solo exhibs, Robert Schoelkopf Gallery, NY, 82, Stiebel Mod, NY, 92 & 94, NY Acad Art, NY, 92, Contemp Realist Gallery, San Francisco, 93, Hackett Freedman Gallery, San Francisco, 95 & More Gallery, Philadelphia, 97; Art & Archit & Landscape, San Francisco Mus Mod Art, 85; Centre Georges Pompidou, Paris, 88. *Teaching:* Assoc prof, New York Acad Art, 82-98; instr, Art Students League, 96-98. *Awards:* Nat Endowment Arts Grant, 85-86; Adolph & Ester Gottlieb Found Grant, 94-95; Arthur Ross Award in Painting, 98. *Bibliog:* Mark Helprin (auth), Arcadian lyricism of Edward Schmidt, Am Arts Quart, Spring 93; Edward Lucie-Smith (auth), Art Today, 95; Michael Graves (auth), Reading Edward Schmidt, Contemp Realist Gallery, 96. *Mem:* Soc Fel Am Acad in Rome; Nat Soc Mural Painters. *Media:* Oil. *Publ:* Ed cartoonist, Wall St J, 3/25/94, 7/25/94, 11/25/94 & 1/3/95. *Dealer:* Salander-O'Reilly Galleries 20 E 79th St New York NY; Hackett Freedman Gallery 250 Sutter St San Francisco CA 94108. *Mailing Add:* 6 Castle Rd Piermont NY 10968-1138

SCHMIDT, FREDERICK LEE
PAINTER
b Hays, Kans, Dec 11, 37. *Study:* Univ Northern Colo, BA; Univ Iowa, with Eugene Ludins & Stuart Edie, MFA; also with Joe Patrick & Howard Rogovin. *Work:* Joint Educ Consortium, Arkadelphia, Ark; Worthen Bank, Ark Arts Ctr, Historic Capitol Hotel, Ark State Capitol, Little Rock; Kimberly-Clark, Conway, Ark; Systematics-Little Rock, Ark; La Gas Co, Little Rock; St Vincents Hosp, Little Rock; KPMG Peat, Marwick, Cleveland, Ohio; Univ Ark Medical Center for the Aging, 2000. *Comn:* Stuck, Frier, Lane, Scott Archit, 82; Allison, Moses & Redden Archit, 86; J B Hunt Trucking Co & Cromwell Archit, 90. *Exhib:* Little Rock Arts & Design Fair, 77; 12th Ann Ark Artists Exhib, 78 & 79; 23rd & 24th Ann Delta Exhibs, Little Rock, Ark, 80 & 81; Arkansas Art on Exhibit, Arkadelphia, 82; one-man shows, Heights Gallery, 86 & Terretorial Restoration, Little Rock, Ark, 87; Terretorial Restoration, 89; Ark Art Ctr, Vineyard, Little Rock, 92; Pueblo State Bank, Salida, Colo, 2002. *Pos:* Artist/painter, 96-2005, ret; trainer, horse, currently. *Teaching:* Asst prof art, Northwestern Col, 68-70, Western Carolina Univ, 70-72 & Va Polytech Inst & State Univ, 72-76; instr, Ark State Univ & Ark Arts Ctr, 76-77, Univ Ark, Pine Bluff, 77-78, Ark Arts Ctr, 78-96. *Awards:* Purchase Awards, 12th Ann Ark Artists Exhib, 79 & 24th Ann Delta Exhib, 81; Governor's Award, Little Rock Arts & Design Fair, 80; Painting Invitational, Hendrix Col, Ark. *Media:* Acrylic, Oil. *Interests:* Horse trainer & instructor. *Mailing Add:* PO Box 344 Nathrop CO 81236

SCHMIDT, JULIUS
SCULPTOR
b Stamford, Conn, June 2, 23. *Study:* Okla Agr & Mech Col; Cranbrook Acad Art, BFA & MFA; with Ossip Zadkine, Paris, France, 53; Acad Belle Arti, Florence, Italy, 54. *Work:* Mus Mod Art, NY; Art Inst Chicago; Albright-Knox Art Gallery, Buffalo; Hirshhorn Mus; Whitney Mus Am Art, NY; 38 pub collections. *Exhib:* Sixteen Americans, Mus Mod Art, NY, 59; Hirshhorn Collection, Guggenheim Mus, NY, 62; Seventh Biennial, Sao Paulo, Brazil, 63; Sculpture in the Open Air, Battersea Park, London, Eng, 63; Biennial, Middleheim, Belg, 71; and 38 one-man shows. *Teaching:* Chmn dept sculpture, Kansas City Art Inst, 54-59; vis artist sculpture, RI Sch Design, 59-60 & Univ Calif, Berkeley, 61-62; chmn dept sculpture, Cranbrook Acad Art, 62-70; head dept sculpture, Univ Iowa, 70-93; retired. *Awards:* Guggenheim Fel, 64; Lifetime Achievement Award in Sculpture Education, Int Sculpture Ctr, 98. *Bibliog:* H Read (auth), Concise History of Modern Sculpture, Praeger, 64; Redstone (auth), Art in Architecture, McGraw, 68; Feldman (auth), Varieties of Visual Experience, Prentice-Hall; Empire State Plaza Art Collection & Plaza Memories, Rizzoli Int Publ. *Media:* Cast Bronze & Cast Iron. *Dealer:* Robert Kidd Gallery Birmingham MI; Karolyn Sherwood Gallery Des Moines IA. *Mailing Add:* 5 Highview Knoll NE Iowa City IA 52240

SCHMIDT, MARY MORRIS
LIBRARIAN
b Minneapolis, Minn, June 28, 26. *Study:* Univ Minn, BA, 47, MS(libr sci), 54 & MA(art hist), 55; Univ Paris, Fulbright fel, 56-57; New York Univ, 62-65. *Pos:* Art librn, Univ Minn, Minneapolis, 53-55; cataloger-reference librn, Metrop Mus Art, New York, 57-58; indexer, Art Index, H W Wilson Co, Bronx, 58-65, ed, 65-69; fine arts librn, Columbia Univ, New York, 69-77; librn, Marquand Libr, Princeton Univ, NJ, 77-89; spec projs librn, Princeton Univ, NJ, 89-91. *Mem:* Art Libr Soc NAm; Col Art Asn Am. *Res:* Rare 19th century art periodicals. *Interests:* Romantic book illustration; 19th century American art journals. *Publ:* Index to Nineteenth Century American Art Periodicals, Sound View Press, Madison, Conn, 99. *Mailing Add:* 29 Sergeant St Princeton NJ 08540

SCHMIDT, RANDALL BERNARD
SCULPTOR, EDUCATOR
b Ft Dodge, Iowa, Oct 2, 42. *Study:* Hamline Univ, BA; Univ NMex, MA. *Work:* Univ NMex Art Mus, Albuquerque; Univ Art Collections, Ariz State Univ, Tempe; Col Art Collection, Ariz Western Col, Yuma; Univ Art Collections, Pac Lutheran Univ, Tacoma, Wash; Yuma Fine Arts Asn. *Exhib:* Nat Crafts Exhib, Univ NMex Art Mus, 68; 25th Ceramics Nat, Everson Mus Art, Syracuse, NY, 68-70; Media 68 & Media 72, Civic Arts Gallery, Walnut Creek, Calif, 68-72; Southwest Crafts '70, Am Crafts Coun, Los Angeles, 70; Crafts 72, Richmond Art Ctr, Calif, 72. *Teaching:* Asst prof ceramics, Ariz State Univ, 68-75, assoc prof, 75-; guest artist, Pac Lutheran Univ, summer 71. *Awards:* Best of Show, 1st Ann Art Exhib, Phoenix Jewish Community Ctr, 68; Award, Media 68, Civic Arts Gallery, 68; Award, Four Corner Painting & Sculpture Biennial, Phoenix Art Mus, Ariz, 71; and others. *Mem:* Ariz Designer-Craftsmen; Nat Coun Educ Ceramic Arts. *Media:* Ceramics, Vinyl. *Res:* Exploration of expanded vinyl as a sculptural material. *Publ:* Contribr, Teaching Secondary School Art, W Brown Co, 71. *Mailing Add:* 6943 E Diamond St Scottsdale AZ 85257-3234

SCHMIDT, TERESA TEMPERO
PRINTMAKER, DRAFTSMAN
b Moscow, Idaho, July 16, 47. *Study:* Cent Wash Univ, BA, 69, MA 70; Wash State Univ, MFA, 72. *Work:* Fogg Art Mus, Harvard Univ, Cambridge, Mass; Springfield Art Mus, Springfield, Mo; Minot State Univ Art Dept, NDak; Norwich Sch Art & Design, Eng; Helen Spencer Mus Art, Lawrence, Kans. *Exhib:* Solo exhib, Manhatten Arts Ctr, Kans, 96, Norwich Sch Art & Design, Eng, 97, Leslie Powell Found Gallery, Lawton, Okla, 98, Union Gallery, Kans State Univ, 98, Emporia State Univ, Kans, 98 & Columbia Col, Mo, 98; 32nd Ann Nat Open, San Bernardino Co Mus Fine Arts Inst, Calif, 97; Small Works, Norwich Arts Coun Galery, Conn, 98; Georgetown Int Fine Arts Competition, Fraser Gallery, Washington, DC, 99; St Johns Univ, Jamaica, NY, 2000; 24th Jured Art Exhib, Dodge City Arts Coun, Kans, 2000; Drawing Connections, Beach Art Mus, 2000. *Teaching:* Teaching asst, Wash State Univ, Pullman, Wash, 70-72; instr, Kans State Univ Art Dept, 72-76, asst prof, 76-96; assoc prof, Kansas State Univ, 98-. *Awards:* Kans Arts Comn Matching Grant, Lawrence Lithography Workshop, 90; Fac Res Award, Kans State Univ, 85 & Fac Develop Award, 95; Artist's Residency Grant, Vt Studio Ctr, 97. *Publ:* Contribr, The Best of Printmaking, Rockport Publ, 97; The Sage National (catalog), Sage Col, Albany, NY, 97; 40th Chautauqua National Exhibition of American Art (exhibit catalog), Chautauqua Ctr Visual Arts, NY, 97. *Mailing Add:* 500 Oakdale Dr Manhattan KS 66502-3738

SCHMIT, RANDALL
PAINTER, COLLAGE ARTIST
b Newark, NJ. *Study:* Tex A&M Univ, Col Station, 73-75; Tex A&M Univ, Commerce Tex, BFA, 77 & MFA, apprentice to Ray Parker, 78-79. *Work:* Metrop Mus Art, New York, NY; New Orleans Mus Art & Ogden Mus Southern Art, New Orleans, La; Castellani Art Mus, Niagra, NY; Birmingham Mus Art, Birmingham, Ala. *Exhib:* Small Paintings, Betty Cunningham Gallery, New York, NY, 81; Romantic Science, One Penn Plaza Gallery, New York, NY, 87; New Acquisitions, New Orleans Mus Art, New Orleans, La, 87 & Apel Galeri, Istanbul, Turkey, 2000; Collage: New Applications, Lehman Col Art Gallery, New York, NY,91; The New York Collection, Albright-Knox Art Gallery, Buffalo, NY, 95; Seeing Jazz (catalog), Int Gallery, Smithsonian Inst, Washington DC; Hunter Mus Am Art, Chattanooga, Tenn; Huntington Mus Art, Huntington, WV; Mus of the SW, Midland, Tex; Bass Mus Art,

Miami Fla; Muson-Williams-Proctor Inst Mus Art, Utica, NY, 99; Winter Exhib, N Pointe Cult Ctr, Kinderhook, NY, 2005. *Teaching:* guest critic & adj fac, Studio Prog, SUNY at Empire State Col, New York, NY, 83; guest lectr, painting, Delgado Col & Univ New Orleans, New Orleans, La, 84, Parsons Sch Design, New York, NY, 95-96, SUNY at Purchase Schs Fine Art, 97 & US Consulate Gen, Instanbul, Turkey, 2000; guest lectr, Collaborative Master's Degree Prog, Bank St Col Educ/Parsons Sch Design, New York, NY, 94; guest critic & lectr, Md Inst Grad Sch Fine Arts, Baltimore, Md, 91, Skidmore Col, Saratoga Springs, NY & Bennington Col, Bennington, Vt, 92; guest critic & lectr, Studio Prog, SUNY at Empire State Col, New York, NY, 95. *Awards:* Ludwig Vogelstein Found Grant, Ludwig Vogelstein Found, 83; Invitational Travel Grant, Apel Galeri, US Consulate Gen, Instanbul, Turkey, 2000. *Bibliog:* Lowery Stokes Simms (auth), Randall Schmit (catalog), EM Donahue Gallery, NY, 90; Linda Yablonsky (auth), Randall Schmit, Artforum Vol XXXIII, No 3, 11/94; Tom Breidenbach (auth), Randall Schmit, The Country and Abroad, 12/2000. *Mem:* Mental Health Asn Comlumbia Greene Counties, Hudson, NY (bus adv coun, 2000-2006); Columbia Co CofC, Hudson, NY (mem comt, 2003-2006). *Media:* Painting, Collage. *Mailing Add:* PO Box 445 Hudson NY 12534-0445

SCHMITT, MARILYN LOW
HISTORIAN, ADMINISTRATOR
b Chicago, Ill, May 24, 39. *Study:* Lawrence Univ, Wis, BA, 60; Univ Calif, Berkeley, MA, 62; Seminar, Bibliotheque Royale, Brussels, 62; Yale Univ, PhD, 72. *Pos:* Trustee, Lawrence Univ, 95-98; 1st vpres, Abraham A Low Inst, 89-. *Teaching:* Vis lectureships, Univ of Nebr, 63, Univ of Colo, 75 & Southern Methodist Univ, 77; instr, Dickinson Col, Carlisle, Pa, 64-66; actg instr, Yale Univ, 69-70; asst prof art hist, Southern Conn State Univ, New Haven, 70-75; asst prof, Univ Miami, 75-78, assoc prof, 79-82; prog officer, J Paul Getty Trust, 83-84; prog mgr, Getty Art Hist Info Prog, 85, ret 99. *Awards:* Woodrow Wilson Fel, 60-61; Am Asn Univ Women Fel, 68-69; Individual Res Fel, Nat Endowment Humanities, 81-82; Earthwatch Research Expedition, 82. *Mem:* Col Art Asn Am; Int Ctr Medieval Art. *Res:* Romanesque sculpture in France; computerization of art-historical info; linking arts and humanities to new media. *Publ:* Auth, The carved gable of Beaulieu-les-Loches, Gesta, 75; Alice Neel, Arts Mag, 78; Random reliefs and primitive friezes: Re-used sources of Romanesque sculpture?, Viator, 80; Traveling carvers in the Romanesque: The case history of St Benoit-sur-Loire, Selles-sur-Cher, Meobecq, Art Bulletin, 81; coauth, Object, Image, Inquiry: The Art Historian at Work, 88; The Siren Song of Cybermedia, Mus News, 94

SCHMITZ, BARBARA
PAINTER, HISTORIAN
b Cincinnati, Ohio, 36. *Study:* Univ Chicago, AM, 60; Inst Fine Arts, New York Univ, MA & PhD, 81. *Awards:* Fulbright Grants for Research in India, 92-93 & 97-98; Indira Gandhi Nat Centre Arts, New Delhi, 95; Am Inst Indian Studies Grant, 98-99. *Res:* Islamic art history; painting and manuscript illustration of Persia, India, Turkey, and the Arab world. *Mailing Add:* 104 Churchill St PO Box 82 Bonnots Mill MO 65016

SCHMUTZHART, BERTHOLD JOSEF
SCULPTOR, EDUCATOR
b Salzburg, Austria, Aug 17, 28; US citizen. *Study:* Acad Appl Art, Vienna, Austria; masterclass for ceramics & sculpture. *Work:* Mr & Mrs Hirshhorn Collection; Fredericksburg Gallery Mod Art, Va. *Comn:* Christ (wood), St James Church, Washington, DC, 62, Christ (bronze), 64; bacchus fountain, Fredericksburg Gallery, 67; Christ (steel), St Clements Church, Inkster, Mich, 68, processional cross (bronze), 71; cross (guilded wood), Church of Reformation, Washington, DC, 74. *Exhib:* Washington Artists, Massilon Mus, Ohio, 69; Twenty Washington Artists, Nat Collection Fine Arts, Washington, DC, 70; Art Barn, US Dept Interior, Washington, DC, 71; Franz Bader Gallery, Washington, DC, 78-81; Nat Gallery Mod Art, New Delhi, India, 90; and others. *Pos:* chmn, Franz & Virginia Bader Fund. *Teaching:* Assoc prof sculpture & chmn sculpture dept, Corcoran Sch Art, Washington, DC, 63-81, prof, 81-94, prof emer, 94-. *Awards:* First Prizes, Wash Relig Arts Soc, 60 & Southern Sculpture, 66; First Prize Silver Medal, Audubon Soc, 71. *Bibliog:* Off Econ Opportunity (auth), A Face for the Future (film), Booker Assocs, Reston, Va, 65; Tools for Learning (film), Kingsbury Ctr, Washington, DC, 71. *Mem:* Am Asn Univ Prof; Guild Religious Archit; Artist's Equity Asn (pres, Washington, DC Chap, 73). *Media:* Multimedia. *Publ:* Auth, The Handmade Furniture Book, Prentice-Hall, 81. *Mailing Add:* 32 Layline Ln Fredericksburg VA 22406-4061

SCHNABEL, JULIAN
PAINTER
b New York, NY, 51. *Study:* Univ Houston, Tex, BFA, 73; Whitney Mus Independent Study Prog, New York, 73-74. *Work:* Tate Gallery, London; Centre Georges Pompidou, Paris; Whitney Mus Am Art, Mus Mod Art, Solomon R Guggenheim Mus & Metrop Mus Art, NY; Fogg Art Mus, Harvard Univ, Boston; Mus Contemp Art, Los Angeles; and many others. *Exhib:* Whitney Mus Am Art, 74, 81, 82, 83, 87 & 91; Inst Contemp Art, Boston, 82; Aldrich Mus Contemp Art, 82 & 94; Art Inst Chicago, 82 & 86; Contemp Arts Mus, Houston, 82 & 84; retrospectives, White Chapel Art Gallery (traveling), London, 86-88 & Mus Monterrey, Mex, 94; Manifeste, Centre Nat Art & Cult Georges Pompidou, Paris, 92; Am Art in the Twentieth Century: Painting & Sculpture 1913-1993, Royal Acad Arts, London, 93; The Portrait Now, Nat Portrait Gallery, London, 93-94; solo shows, Pace Wildenstein Gallery, NY, 96, 97, 98 & 99, Timothy Taylor Gallery, London, 97, Gallery Bruno Bischofberger, Zurich, 97-98, S London Gallery, Eng, 99, 1000 Eventi, Milan, Italy, 99, Galerie Thaddaeus Ropac, Salzburg, 99, Galerie Forsblom, Helsinki, 2000, Galleria Cardi & Co, Milan, 01; Summer Exhibition, Tony Shafrazi Gallery, NY, 96; Picasso: A Contemp Dialogue, Galerie Thaddaeus Ropac, Salzburg, 96; Biennale di Firenze: il tempo e la moda, Florence, 96; Pace Wildenstein Gallery, 96, 97, 98 & 99; Art/Fashion (with catalog), Guggenheim Mus SoHo, NY, 97; The Hirshhorn Collects: Recent Acquisitions 1992-1996, Hirshhorn Mus & Sculpture Garden, Smithsonian Inst, Washington, DC, 97; Anos 80/The Eighties (with catalog), Culturgest, Caixa Geral de Despositos, Lisbon, 98. *Bibliog:* Jerry Saltz (auth), A Year in the life: tropic of painting, Art in Am, 10/94; Mick Brown (auth), Something evil this way comes, Telegraph Mag, 10/1/94; Julian Schnabel retrospective, Flash Art News, 11/94; and others. *Publ:* Dir, producer, Basquiat (film), 96. *Mailing Add:* c/o PaceWildenstein 32 E 57th St New York NY 10022

SCHNACKENBERG, ROY
PAINTER, SCULPTOR
b Chicago, Ill, Jan 14, 34. *Study:* Miami Univ, Oxford, Ohio, BFA. *Work:* Whitney Mus Am Art, NY; Art Inst Chicago. *Exhib:* Whitney Recent Acquisitions Show, 67 & Whitney Ann, 67-69; New Am Realists, Goteberg, Sweden, 70; Beyond Illustration, The Art of Playboy World Tour, 71-; Recent Acquisitions Show, Art Inst Chicago, 71; Dept Interior Bicentennial Exhib, Corcoran Gallery, Washington, DC; and numerous one-man & int group shows. *Awards:* Copley Found Award, 67. *Mem:* Cliffdwellers; Arts Club Chicago. *Media:* Oil, Canvas; Mixed Media. *Mailing Add:* 180 E Pearson St Chicago IL 60611

SCHNEEMANN, CAROLEE
PAINTER, FILMMAKER
b Fox Chase, Pa, Oct 12, 39. *Study:* Bard Col, NY, BA; Univ Ill, Urbana, MFA; Columbia Univ Sch Painting & Sculpture, New York; New Sch Social Res, New York; Univ de Puebla, Mexico. *Work:* Mus Contemp Art, Chicago; Mus Mod Art, NY; Philadelphia Mus Art; Inst Contemp Art, London; San Francisco Mus Mod Art. *Exhib:* Palazzo Reale, Milan, 81; Max Hutchinson Gallery, NY, 82-83; Contemp Arts Ctr, Cincinnati, 90; Biennale Venezia, Italy, 90; San Francisco Mus Mod Art, 91; solo exhib, Kunstraum, Vienna, 95; Ctr Nat Art & Cult Georges Pompidou, Paris, 94-96; solo retrospective, New Mus Contemp Art, NY, 96; Frauen Mus, Bonn, Ger, 97; New Mus Contemp Art, NY, 97; Mus Contemp Art, Los Angeles, 98; Emily Harvey Gallery, NY, 2000; and others. *Pos:* Founder-dir, Kinetic Theatre, NY; vis artist, San Francisco Art Inst, Calif, 92. *Teaching:* Instr art, Art Inst Chicago, Ill, Univ Colo, Univ Ohio & Univ Calif, Los Angeles, Pratt Inst, NY. *Awards:* Individual Artist Grant, Gottlieb Found, 87; Guggenheim Fel, 93; Pollock-Krasner Grant, 96; Lifetime Achievement Award, Chicago Caucus for Women in the Arts, 2000; Distinguished Artist Award for Lifetime Achievement, Coll Art Asn, 01; Rockefeller Found Fel, 01. *Bibliog:* Linda M Montano (auth), Performance Artists Talking in the Eighties, Univ Calif Press, 83; Jitka Hanzlova (auth), Female, Deichtorhallen publ,; David Burrows (auth), Making a Scene, Univ of Central England; Art Monthly, Apr 2000. *Mem:* Women's Caucus Art; Col Art Assoc. *Publ:* Auth, Kenneth Anger's Scorpio Rising, Film Culture No 32, New York, 64; Love Paint Ritual Technicians of the Sacred, New York, 69; Banana Hands, Plays for Children to Direct, London, 70; More Than Meat Joy (complete performance works & selected writings), 78 & Carolee Schneemann: Early & Recent Work (monography of painting--constructions 1963-1983), 83, Documentext; Imaging Erotics: Carolee Schneemann's Body Politics, 97. *Dealer:* Elga Wimmer Gallery 560 Broadway New York NY 10012; Galerie Samuel Lallouz Montreal

SCHNEIDER, JANE HARRIS
SCULPTOR
b Trenton, NJ, Jan 2, 32. *Study:* Wellesley Col, Mass, BA; Barnard Col, New York; Columbia Univ, New York; Col New Rochelle, NY and Sch Indust Arts, Trenton, NJ; welding apprentice Bert Numme; studied woodworking with Lewis Korn. *Work:* Kutztown Univ, Pa; Ark Art Ctr, Little Rock; Munson-Williams-Proctor Inst, Utica, NY; NJ State Mus, Trenton; Univ Art Galleries, Univ of Wis, La Crosse; Davis Mus and Cult Ctr, Wellesley Col, Wellesley, Mass; Neuberger Mus, Purchase, NY; Fine Arts Mus of Long Island, Hempstead, NY; NY Hosp for Joint Diseases, NY; and several others. *Exhib:* solo exhibs, Steles in Steel, Fourteen Sculptors Gallery, 75, Sweet Deams & Nightmares, wood sculpture, June Kelly Gallery, NY, 2000 & 06, Myths as Muse, Atrium Gallery, St Louis, Mo, 2001, New Work, June Kelly Gallery, NY, 2003, 2006, and many others; The Year of the Woman-Reprise, Bronx Mus Arts, 76; Sculpture, Cath Univ Am, Washington, DC, 77; one-person show, New Eng Ctr Contemp Art, 78; Walking Trees, Found Gallery, NY, 81 & Little Ctr Gallery, Clark Univ, Worcester, Mass, 82; New Work in Wood, Philadelphia Art Alliance & Back to the Wall, 84; Wood Sculpture, Alternative Mus, NY, 85; Chimeras: Chisled and Sawn, Nassau Co Mus Fine Art, Roslyn, NY, 88; In the Making: Drawings by Sculptors, Sculpture Ctr Gallery & Sch, NY, 88; Nature of the Beast, Hudson River Mus Westchester, Yonkers, NY, 89; Means to Ends, Rockland Ctr Arts, W Nyack, NY, 90; Wild Women, Univ Wis, La Cross, 95; Immortals, Atrium Gallery, St Louis, Recycled Paper, 96; Generations, AIR Gallery, NY, 97; Love Affairs (with catalog), June Kelly Gallery, NY, 97, The Art Show, 98 & Sculpture on the Wall, 98; Soho 20 & Friends, Soho 20 Gallery, NY, 98; Quietude Garden Gallery Exhib, E Brunswick, NJ, 98; Out of the Woods, Delaware Valley Art Assoc, Narrowsburg, NY, 2002; The Art Show, Auspices ADAA, June Kelly Gallery at 7th Regiment Amory, NY, 1998-2003; and several others. *Collection Arranged:* Wood, US Courthouse, New York, 85 & Mixed Media-Mixed Mores, 86; The Significant Surface, Philadelphia Art Alliance, 90; Artists at Home, Bill Bace Gallery, 90; From Celestial to Earthly: Exploring the Environment Through Ourselves, Patterson Mus, NJ, 94-95. *Pos:* Found & dir, Larchmont, Little Art Sch, 63-78. *Teaching:* lectr at several col, univ and galleries, 76-98. *Awards:* Medal Honor Sculpture, Nat Asn Women Artists, 75; Int Women's Year Award, Int Women's Art Festival, 75-76; Target Presentations Found Community Artists, 80. *Bibliog:* Many articles in various magazines & newspapers, 75-98; Janet Koplos (auth), Jane Schneider at June Kelly, Art Am, 3/98; Nancy Grove (auth), Reviews: Jane Schneider at June Kelly, Art News, 3/98; Ken Johnson (auth), Jane

Schneider, Gallery Guide Soho, NY Times Weekend, 11/17/2000; Gallery Watch, Jane Schneider, Atrium Gallery, St Louis, Mo, Art & Antiques, 12/2001; and many others. *Mem:* NY Wellesley Artists; Women's Art Libr, London, 98; The Furniture Soc; Collaborative Concepts, Beacon, NY; Dia Found, NY; Wellesley Col Durant Soc, Mass. *Media:* Wood. *Specialty:* contemporary art. *Interests:* fabricating sculpture include, Aboriginal religious, Greek mythology, Egyptian hsitory, dream sequences, transgenics; Mutables. *Publ:* Auth, The Significant Surface, Curator's Talk, Philadelphia Art Alliance, 5-6/90; Creative Strategies: Breaking Through, Gallerie Artists News, Gallerie Publ, Vancouver, BC, Can, 10/91; Jane Schneider & The Dual Process of Her Art, Show & Tell, Vol 3, No 1, fall 96; and many others. *Dealer:* Atrium Gallery 4729 McPherson Ave St Louis MO 63108; June Kelly Gallery 591 Broadway New York NY. *Mailing Add:* 75 Grand St New York NY 10013

SCHNEIDER, JANET M
MUSEUM DIRECTOR, PAINTER
b New York, NY, June 6, 50. *Study:* Queens Col, City Univ New York, BA(fine arts, summa cum laude), 72; Boston Univ Tanglewood Inst, special study, fine arts, 71. *Exhib:* Solo Exhibs, Prince Street Gallery, 74, 76 & 81; Long Island Invitational, C W Post Art Gallery, 81; The First Eight Yrs, The Artists Choice Mus, 84. *Collection Arranged:* Sons and others: Women Artists See Men (auth, catalog), 75; Urban Aesthetics (auth, catalog), 76; Masters of the Brush: Chinese Painting and Calligraphy from the Sixteenth to the Nineteenth Century (auth, catalog), 77; Symcho Moszkowicz: Portrait of the Artist in Postwar Europe (auth, catalog), 78; Shipwrecked 1622: The Lost Treasure of Philip IV (auth, catalog), 81; Michelangelo: A Sculptor's World (auth, catalog), 83; Joseph Cornell, Revisited, (auth, catalog), 92; Blueprint for Change (coauth, catalog), Queensborough Pub Libr, 96. *Pos:* Cur, Queens Mus, 73-75, prog dir, 75-77 & exec dir, 77-89; exec dir, Cult Inst Group, 95-. *Teaching:* Instr mus cert prog, Hofstra Univ, 85-86. *Mem:* Gallery Asn NY State (bd dir, 79-81); Artists Choice Inc (bd trustees, 79-82); Cult Inst Group (chmn, 86-87); Mayor's Adv Comn Cult & Arts, NY. *Media:* Oil. *Dealer:* Prince St Gallery 121 Wooster New York NY 10012. *Mailing Add:* 35-39 159th St Flushing NY 11419

SCHNEIDER, JO ANNE
PAINTER
b Lima, Ohio, Dec 4, 19. *Study:* Sch Fine Arts, Syracuse Univ. *Work:* Butler Inst Am Art, Youngstown, Ohio; Syracuse Univ; Allentown Mus, Pa; St Lawrence Univ; Metrop Mus Art, NY; and others. *Exhib:* Corcoran Gallery Art, Washington, DC; Whitney Mus Am Art Ann, NY; 50 Yrs of Am Art, Am Fedn Art, 64; Childe Hassam Fund Exhib, Am Acad Arts & Lett, 71; plus one-man exhibs, 54-85. *Awards:* First Prize, Guild Hall, 67; Marion K Haldenstein Mem Prize, Nat Asn Women Artists, 70; Stanley Grumbacher Mem Award, Audubon Artists, 72. *Media:* Oil. *Mailing Add:* 35 E 75th St New York NY 10021

SCHNEIDER, JULIE SAECKER
PAINTER, DRAFTSMAN
b Seattle, Wash, Mar 7, 44. *Study:* Univ Wis, Madison, BS(art); Univ Wis, MFA(painting & drawing), 76. *Work:* Minn Mus Art, St Paul; Algur Meadows Mus, Shreveport, La; Rutgers Univ, Camden, NJ; State Univ NY Col, Potsdam; Indianapolis Mus Art. *Exhib:* Drawings USA Nat Exhibs (traveling show), Minn Mus Art, Saint Paul, 75 & 77; Am Drawings, Tidewater Art Coun & Portsmouth Community Art Ctr, Va, 76 & 78; Davidson Nat Print & Drawing Competition, Appalachian Nat Drawing Competition, Boone, 76, NC; Smithsonian Travel Exhibs, 76 & 78; Bradley Print & Drawing Competition, Bradley Univ, Peoria, Ill, 77, 79 & 85; Drawing Invitational, Goucher Col, Towson, Md, 85; Washington Community Artists, Jane Haslem Gallery, Washington, DC, 85; solo exhibs, Am Int Col, 80, Arlington Arts Ctr, Va, 85, Drawings, Fairweather-Hardin Gallery, 86, Jane Haslem Gallery, Washington, DC, 89 & 93, Tretyakov Gallery, Moscow USSR, 90-91, recent work, Arlington Arts Ctr, Va, 93, Legends Revisited, Peninsula Fine Arts Ctr, Newport News, Va, 96; Am realists (with catalog), San Francisco Mus Mod Art, Calif, 85-86; Realism/Idealism (with catalog), Jane Haslem Gallery, Washington, DC; Am Drawing, Boca Raton Mus Art; 12th Ann Int Drawing Invitational, Emporia, Kans; and others. *Pos:* Chair visual arts, Interlochen Ctr Arts. *Teaching:* Adj prof, Williams Col, 82-84; assoc prof, Northern Va Community Col, Alexandria; vis lectr, Va Mus Artists-in-residence series, Md Inst Col Art, Interlochen Ctr Arts, Towson State Univ; assoc prof & undergrad chair, Univ Pa, Philadelphia, 95-. *Awards:* Purchase Awards, Rutgers Nat Drawing 77, Drawings USA-77, Minn Mus of Art, St Paul, 77 & Bradley Print & Drawing, 79; Finalist, Mass Artist Found Grants, 80; Fel, Mid Atlantic Found, 88; Va Comn for the Arts Grant, 92; Arlington Comn for the Arts Grant, 94. *Bibliog:* American Realism, San Francisco Mus Mod Art & Abrams Press, 85; Pamela Kessler (auth), Galleries, Washington Post, 5/20/87; Brown & McLean (auth), Drawing from Life, Holt, Rinehart & Winston, 92 & 97; Nathan Goldstein (auth), Figure Drawing 4th ed, text bk, 93. *Mem:* Col Art Asn; FATE. *Media:* Graphite, mixed media. *Mailing Add:* c/o Jane Haslem Gallery 2025 Hillyer Pl NW Washington DC 20009

SCHNEIDER, KATY
PAINTER
Study: Yale Univ, BA; Ind Univ, MFA. *Pos:* Lecturer art Smith College, Northampton, Mass. *Awards:* Recipient Blanche Coleman Award, Purchase Prize, Am Acad of Arts and Letters; fel Guggenheim Mem Found, 2004; grantee Masss Cult Council Artists Grant, New England Found for Arts Regional Fel. *Mailing Add:* Smith Coll Dept Art Hillyer Hall Brown Fine Arts Ctr Northampton MA 01063

SCHNEIDER, KENNY
SCULPTOR, PAINTER
b Ellenville, NY, Jan 3, 39. *Study:* Univ Miami, BA in Art, 60; Summer Acad Bildende Kunst, Salzburg, Austria, 63; Adams State Col, MA in Art. *Work:* Palm Beach Internat Airport. *Comn:* Sculpture Art in Public Places, Seattle Arts Comn, 88; Sculpture, Community Redevelopment Agency, Los Angeles, 91-95; Sculpture, David W Bermant Found, Santa Barbara, Calif, 95; Sculpture, City of Miami Beach, Fla, 97; Sculpture, Buell Childrens Mus, Pueblo, Colo, 99; Homestead Park Proj, City of Collins, Colo; also pvt collections of Mel Brooks & Ann Bancroff, Gerald Robins, Michelle Isenberg, Barbara Marcus, Walter Annenburg Collection. *Exhib:* Solo Shows Galerie 99, Bay Harbor, Fla, 1st Ann Prize Competition, Provincetown Art Asn, 83, Ground Zero Gallery, Miami Beach, Fla, 88, Fiona Whitney Gallery, Los Angeles, 91; 4th Ann Small Works, Wash Sq E Galleries, NY Univ, 79; Mus Contemp Art, N Miami, Fla, 86; 29th Ann Hortz Mem Exhib, Mus of Art, Ft Lauderdale, Fla, 87; Humor in Art, Tempe (Ariz) Arts Ctr, 88; Nemiroff-Deutch Fine Art, Santa Monica, Calif, 91; Two-person exhib The Artists Gallery, Ojai, Calif, 95; Colorado Call, The Art Ctr Douglas Co, Castle Rock, Colo, 96; Awareness Alert Breast Cancer, WomenMade Gallery, Chicago, 98; 20th Ann Show Barbara Gillman Gallery, Miami Beach, Fla, 99; Co-Excellance 98 Traveling Exhib Alternative Arts Alliance, Denver, 98; Rocky Mt Biennial, Moca, Ft Collins, Colo. *Pos:* Presenter, Pueblo (Colo) Regional Arts Dialogue, Pueblo Community Col, 97; Panalist, Media Fel Awards, Colo Coun on the Arts; trustee & bd chmn, Spanish Peaks Regional Health Ctr; Pres, Huerfano Co Art Council, 98-2004. *Teaching:* Instr Art Hist, Art Appreciation, Drawing, Film Making, Trinidad State Jr Col, Walsenburg, Colo, 96, Multimedia Arts, Trinidad, 99-. *Awards:* Kolkoschka Prize Sommerakad for Bildende Kunst; Art in Cauly Sq Award; 8th Ann Small Works Nat Jurors Award, 24th Ann Small Painting Exhbn Jurors Award; NY Film Festival Silver Medal; Tampere Film Festival Award of Merit; Directors Award Colo Coun on Arts, 97; Visual Arts (3-D) Artist Fel, Colo Coun for the Arts & NEA, 99. *Bibliog:* S Derickson Moore (auth) World Class Art, Palm Beach Coun of Arts, Fla, 88; Helen Kohen (auth) Summer Dreams, Miami Herald, 88; Peter Frank (auth), Art Picks of the Week, LA Weekly, 91; James Rupp (auth) Art in Seattles Public Places: An Illustrated Guide, Univ Wash Press, 92; Pancho Doll (auth), Ojai Artist Kenny Schneider, LA Time, 95; Maja Beckstrom (auth) Pluggen In, Ventura Co Star, 95; Joseph Woodward (auth) This Artists Sense of Humor, LA Times, 95. *Mem:* Screen Actors Guild. *Media:* Sculpture, Painting, Video/Film. *Res:* Directed feature length dramatic film "Adonde Fue Juan Jose?", 2002. *Specialty:* Contemp Art. *Dealer:* Barbara Gillman 3814 NE Miami Ct Miami FL Tel 305-573-1920 800-688-7079. *Mailing Add:* PO Box 542 La Veta CO 81055

SCHNEIDER, LAURIE See Adams, Laurie Schneider

SCHNEIDER, LISA DAWN
DEALER, CRITIC
b Brookline, Mass, Nov 16, 54. *Study:* Boston Mus of Fine Arts Sch, Mass; DeCordova Mus; Syracuse Univ, Visual & Performing Arts Sch; Finch Col; Arts Sch League; Marymount Col, BA(fine arts). *Pos:* Asst dir, Galerie Denise/Rene, 76-77; art critic & art ed, Women's Week, 77-79; dir, Robert Freidus Gallery, NY, 78; assoc dir, Bertha Urdang Gallery, NY, 79-; exec dir, Cur Consul & Galleries, New York & Boston, 80-; cur, Fisher Brothers Collection, 82-; art correspondent, CNN, 99-. *Awards:* Third Annual Interiors Award, Ramco Co Art Collection. *Specialty:* Nineteenth & twentieth century Europe & American paintings, drawings, photography & sculpture. *Mailing Add:* 135 E 54th St New York NY 10022

SCHNEIDER, RICHARD DURBIN
CERAMIST, INSTRUCTOR
b Toledo, Ohio, April 5, 37. *Study:* Univ Toledo, BA, 63; Bowling Green State Univ, MA, 68. *Work:* Utah Mus Fine Arts, Salt Lake City; Cleveland Mus Art; Ohio Wesleyan Univ; Libbey-Owens, Ford Collection, Toledo. *Exhib:* Eighteenth Nat Las Vegas Art Exhib, Las Vegas Art Mus, 75; Materials & Techniques of 20th Century Artists, Cleveland Mus Art, 76; Lake Superior 4th Biennial Int Exhib, Tweed Mus Art, Duluth, Minn, 77; Beaux Art Designer, Columbus Mus Art, Ohio, 79; Eighth State Ann Craft Exhibition, JB Speed Art Mus, Louisville, Ky, 80; 28th Ann National Drawing & Sculpture, Ball State Univ, Muncie, Ind, 82; First Ann Am Ceramic Nat, Downey Mus Art, Calif, 83. *Collection Arranged:* Cleveland Clinic Found, Cleveland Mus Art. *Teaching:* Asst prof ceramics, Monroe Co Community Col, Mich, 69-71; assoc prof, Cleveland State Univ, Ohio, 71-. *Awards:* Special Award Sculpture, Cleveland Mus Art, 72; Purchase Award Ceramics, Butler Mus Am Art; Juror's Award for Drawing, Kansas 6th National Exhib, Ft Hays State Univ, 81. *Bibliog:* Lynette Rhodes (auth), Nine artisans, Craft Horizons, 74; Elizabeth McClelland (auth), Ceramic sculpture, Nat Orgn Visual Artists News, 80; Roger Welchans (auth), Dialogue, Ohio Arts J, 83. *Media:* Clay. *Specialty:* Painting & ceramics. *Publ:* Auth, Large thrown forms, 76 & Surface decoration on ceramic functional ware, 82, Ceramics Monthly. *Dealer:* River Gallery Old Detroit Rd Rocky River OH 44145. *Mailing Add:* 2610 Exeter Rd Cleveland Heights OH 44118

SCHNEIDER, ROSALIND L
VIDEO ARTIST, PAINTER
b New York, NY. *Study:* Sch Fine Arts, Syracuse Univ; State Univ NY, BA, 74. *Work:* US Info Agency, Washington, DC; Nynex Collection, NY; Dance Archives, Lincoln Ctr, NY; Donnell Film Libr, NY; Video Art Collection, Locarno, Switzerland; Metro Media Fibre Network; Libr Congress. *Exhib:* Yosemite Loop Extension, Mus of the Hudson Highlands, Cornwall, NY, 84; Ancient History, Bronx Mus, NY, 88; 10 Artists From NY, Kulturforum, Monchengladbach, Ger, 90; The Nature of the Beast, Hudson River Mus, Yonkers, NY, 90; Contemp Bestiary, Islip Art Mus, NY, 90; Women Avant Garde Filmmakers 1930-2000, Whitney Mus, NY, 2000; Chelsea Art Mus, NY, 2003; Monique Goldstrom Gallery, NY, 2003; Imaging the River, River Meditations, Hudson River Mus, NY, 04; Landscape Show, Van Brunt Gallery, Beacon, NY, 05; Wave Transformations, 911 Media Arts Ctr, Seattle, 05; River Fragmentations, Diva Art Fair, New York City, 05; Donnell Libr Media Ctr, 2005; Miami Beach Cinematheque, 2006; Art Miami (auth, catalog), 2006. *Pos:* exec dir, Film & Video Workshop, Inc. *Awards:* Directors Award, Biennial 2000, Westchester, 2000; Finalist, MTA Transit Commn for Dobbs Ferry Station, NY, 03; Film Presentation Grant, NY

Women Film & TV, 06. *Bibliog:* Jayanta Chatterjee & Hector Currie (eds), Women/Artists/Filmmakers, Univ Cincinnati Press, 76; Cynthia Nadelman (auth), Light & Lascaux, 92; Matt Freedman (auth), Wave Transformations, NY Hall Sci, 2000; William Zimmer (auth), Lights, Videos & Photos in a Biennial, 2000; Carlos Suarez de Jesus (auth), Riding the Earth's Curl, The New Times, 2006. *Mem:* Art Students League of NY. *Media:* Video & Film Installation. *Res:* internet site art in context. *Publ:* 10 Artists from New York, Kulturforum, Monchengiadbach, Ger, 90; Jules & Nancy Heller (eds) Encyclopedia of 20th Century Women Artists, Garland Publ, 92; Auth, Feminists Who Changed America 1963-1975, Univ Ill Press, 2006. *Dealer:* Diana Minotti Fine Art Inc; Van Brunt Gallery NY. *Mailing Add:* 40 Cottontail Lane Irvington NY 10533

SCHNEIDER, SHELLIE
COLLAGE ARTIST, PAINTER
b Brooklyn, NY, Oct 12, 32. *Study:* Cooper Union Art Sch, with Nick Marsicano & Leo Manso, 54; Hunter Col, with Tony Panzera, BA(cum laude, printmaking), 74; Queens Col, with Walter Kendra, MS(art educ), 77. *Work:* Voluntary Hosps Asn, Tampa, Fla; Chalgrin Co Ltd, Osaka, Japan; Am Stock Exchange, NY; Computer Assoc International, Islandia, NY. *Comn:* Triptych (collage), comn by Mr & Mrs Kurtz, Long Island, NY, 90; acrylic collage, comn by Dr & Mrs R Edwards, Long Island, NY, 92; acrylic collage (mural), comn by Mr & Mrs I Levy, Long Island, NY, 93; and others. *Exhib:* Nat Works on Paper '88, Firehouse Gallery, Nassau Community Col, Garden City, NY, 88; Traveling Nat Print Show, Nat Asn Women Artists, 89, 91, 96 & 99; Multi-Media Art Forum & Exhib, Hempstead House, Sands Point, NY, 91; one-person shows, From There to Here--In a Decade, Graphic Eye Gallery, Port Washington, NY, 91 & Manhasset Libr, Manhasset, NY, 94, Gallery North, Setauket, NY, 2000, Haddad Lascono Gallery, Great Barringten, Mass, 2004. *Pos:* Co-pres, Graphic Eye Coop Gallery, Port Washington, New York, 86, 87, 98 & 99; secy, Art Adv Coun, Port Washington Libr, NY, 93-98. *Teaching:* Art instr K-12 & adult educ, Port Washington, New York, 74-92; adj instr printmaking, C W Post Univ, New York, 80; adj asst prof art educ, Hofstra Univ, NY, 2001-2002. *Awards:* First Place, Sheffield Art League, 86; Award Excellence, Nassau Co Mus Fine Art, 86; Medal Honor, Nat Asn Women Artists, Leila Sawyer Mem, 88. *Bibliog:* Articles in Newsday, 10/84 & New York Times, 9/93 & 12/2002, 1/2005. *Mem:* Nat Asn Women Artists (jury selection, printmaking, 88); Sheffield Art League; Art Adv Coun, Port Washington Libr; Art League of Long Island. *Media:* Acrylic Paint, Mixed Media Collage. *Dealer:* Graphic Eye Coop Gallery New York; Lenox Fine Art Gallery MA. *Mailing Add:* 4 Miro Pl Port Washington NY 11050

SCHNEIDER, URSULA
PAINTER, SCULPTOR
b Zurich, Switz, 43. *Study:* Zurich Switz; Kunst Gewerbeschule, BFA, 63; San Francisco Art Inst, MFA, 68-72. *Work:* Univ Calif, Berkeley; US & Switz, Pvt Collections. *Exhib:* Solo shows include Braunstein Gallery, San Francisco, 86, 89, 92, 95, 98, 2001, 2003, Forum Febicus, Schaffhausen, Switzerland, 93, AIR Gallery II, NY, 96, 2002, 2005, Rockland Ctr Arts, 2006; group shows include Passages: A Survey of California Women Artists, 1945 to Present, Fresno Art Ctr and Mus, Calif, 87; Through the Land, Mary Delahoid Gallery, NY, 89; Hozschnitte, Forum Febicus, Schaffhausen, Switzerland, 89; Moku Hanga Traveling Exhib: Contemporary Japanese Woodcuts, N Am, 97; Matrix/Berkley: 20 Years, Berkley Art Mus, Univ Calif, 98; Sarah Lawrence Coll, Bronxville, NY, 99; Mixed Company: Women Choose Men, AIR Gallery, NY, 2004; Black and White, Edward Hopper House Art Ctr, Nyack, NY, 2005. *Teaching:* instr, painting, Sarah Lawrence Col, currently. *Awards:* New Talent Award, Oakland Mus, 74; Nat Endowment for Arts, 85. *Media:* Pastel, Acrylic & Oil. *Specialty:* Abstract, Panoramic Landscapes. *Mailing Add:* c/o Sarah Lawrence College Visual Art Dept 1 Mead Way Bronxville NY 10708-5999

SCHNEIDERMAN, RICHARD S
MUSEUM DIRECTOR
b NJ, June 27, 48. *Study:* Hartwick Col, BA, 70; Univ Cincinnati, MA, 73; State Univ NY Binghamton, PhD, 76. *Collection Arranged:* West Meets East, Impressionism in Nineteenth Century Prints, 78-80; J M W Turner Watercolors from the British Museum (auth introd, catalog), 82; Guardians of the Spire: The Gargoyle Image in Prints, 84; Drawings as Drawings: Works from the Ackland and the Weatherspoon, 87-88; Robes of Elegance: Japanese Kimono from the Sixteenth-Twentieth Centuries, 88; Nature into Art: English Landscape Watercolors from the British Museum, 91. *Pos:* Cur prints & drawings, Ga Mus Art, Univ Ga, Athens, 76-86, dir, 81-86; dir, NC Mus Art, Raleigh, 86-94. *Teaching:* Adj prof hist art, Tompkins-Cortland Community Col, Cortland, NY, winter 76; lectr mod art, State Univ NY Binghamton, summer 76; adj assoc prof, dept art, Univ Ga, 83-86. *Mem:* Am Asn Mus; Am Soc Aesthet; Col Art Asn; Asn Art Mus Dirs; Print Coun Am. *Res:* History of prints, primarily English and northern European. *Publ:* Contribr, A Catalogue Raisonne of the Prints of Sir Francis Seymour Haden, Robin Garton Fine Art Publ, 83; Masterpieces of European Printmaking: 15th-19th Centuries, Ga Mus Art, 84; A Catalogue Raisonne of the Prints of Charles Meryon (with Frank W Raysor II), Garton & Co, Scolar Press, 90. *Mailing Add:* 7161 Dickwoods Rd Afton VA 22920

SCHNEIER, DONNA FRANCES
DEALER
b St Louis, Mo, Mar 30, 38. *Study:* Brandeis Univ, BA; NY Univ, MFA; Inst Fine Art, NY Univ, PhD(art history). *Pos:* Pres, Gallery 6M, NY, 66-73 & Donna Schneier Fine Arts; consult contemp works art, Sothebys, 1990-1994. *Awards:* Visionary, Mus Art & Design, 2005. *Mem:* Am Craft Coun (bd trustees); Am Craft Mus (chairman & collections comt); First NY Bank For Business (bd advisors); Sch For Serv, Georgetown Univ (bd govs). *Specialty:* Post World War II Ceramics, Glass, Fiber, Metal & Wood. *Interests:* Contemp jewelry by artists. *Collection:* Zero Karat: contemp jewelry by artists. *Mailing Add:* 910 Fifth Ave New York NY 10021

SCHNITZER, ARLENE
PATRON
b Salem, Ore, Jan 10, 29. *Study:* Univ Wash, Seattle, 47-48; Portland Art Mus Sch, 59-61; studied with Michele Russo. *Pos:* Dir, Fountain Gallery of Art, Portland, Ore, 61-87; Exec vpres, Harsh Investment Corp, 50-; pres, Fountain Assoc, 86-; bd trustees, McCallum Theatre, Palm Desert, 2002-. *Awards:* Pioneer Award, Univ Ore, 85 & Distinguished Service Award, 91; Portland First Citizen Award, 95; Outstanding Philanthropist Award, 96. *Mem:* Nat Comt Performing Arts, Kennedy Ctr, 95-; Nat Coun Fine Arts Mus San Francisco, 95-. *Collection:* Primarily most noted artists of the Northwest; largest collection outside a museum of works by C S Price, including carvings. *Mailing Add:* 1121 SW Salmon St Portland OR 97205

SCHNITZER, KLAUS A
PHOTOGRAPHER
Study: State Univ NY, Albany, BA, 67; Ohio Univ, Athens, MFA, 71. *Work:* Mus Mod Art, NY; Witkin Gallery, NY; Brookdale Community Col, Lincroft, NJ. *Exhib:* Invitational, Bertha Urdang Gallery, NY, 77; one-man shows, Newark Mus, NJ, 77, Mem Fine Arts Ctr, Univ Colo, Boulder, 81 & Art Inst Chicago, Ill, 81; Hunterdon Art Ctr, Linton, NJ, 78; NY Univ East Galleries, 78; and many others. *Awards:* Nat Endowment Arts Photog Fel, 80; Montclair State Col Alumni Asn Grants, 78 & 80; Montclair State Col Research Grant & Release Time, 81-82. *Publ:* Ed & contribr, Sans Silver, Camera 25 Mag, 10-12/74; illusr, Ancient Glass at the Newark Mus, Newark Mus, 77; auth, New Jersey: Unexpected pleasures, United Jersey Banks & NJ Monthly, 80; auth, Capitol Story, New York State Publ, 82. *Mailing Add:* 551 Upper Mountain Ave Upper Montclair NJ 07043-1608

SCHNORRENBERG, JOHN MARTIN
HISTORIAN
b New York, NY, Dec 1, 31. *Study:* Univ NC, Chapel Hill, AB(Phi Beta Kappa), MA, 53; Princeton Univ, MFA, 57, PhD, 64. *Teaching:* Instr art hist, Columbia Univ, 58-59; from asst prof to prof art hist, Univ NC, Chapel Hill, 59-76; prof art, Univ Ala, Birmingham, 76-2002, chmn dept art & art hist, 76-90, prof Emer, 2002-. *Awards:* Tanner Award for Excellence in Teaching, Univ NC, Chapel Hill, 66; Nat Endowment for Humanities Jr Fel, 67-68; Southeastern Col Art Conference Award of Merit, 95. *Mem:* Col Art Asn; Medieval Acad Am; Soc Archit Historians; Southeastern Col Art Conf (ed, Review, 66-70, pres, 75-76 & 79-80). *Res:* Late gothic architecture, gothic survival, modern architecture. *Publ:* Ed & contribr, A Medieval Treasury From Southeastern Collections, Ackland Art Ctr, 71; Comedy in Western Art, Visual Arts Gallery, 78; Remembered Past, Discovered Future: The Alabama Architecture of Warren knight & Davis, 1906-1961, Birmington Mus Art, 99; Aspiration: Birmingham's Historic Houses of Worship, Birmingham Hist Soc, 2000

SCHNURR, ELINORE
PAINTER
b Sandusky, Ohio, 1932. *Study:* Cleveland Inst Art, BFA. *Exhib:* Recent Paintings USA/The Figure, Mus Mod Art, NY, 62; Butler Inst Am Art, Youngstown, Ohio, 62, 75, 81, 83, 84, 87, 98, 2001, 2002 & 2004; Cleveland Inst Art, Ohio, 83; Capricorn Galleries, Bethesda, Md, 84, 87 & 93; Nat Acad Design, NY, 86, 88, 90 & 93; Moran/Dervan, Fine Art, South Egremont, Mass, 93-98; Mus City NY, 94, 95 & 2000; DFN Gallery, NY, 97 & 98; EOS Gallery, Redlands, Calif, 2002 & 2004; Walter Wickiser gallery, NY, 2003. *Collection Arranged:* Cleveland Mus of Art; Mus of the City, NY; Mus of Fine Art, Fla; National Mus of Am Art, Wash, DC; Pfizer Inc, NY. *Awards:* CAPS Fel, NYSCA, 79; Thomas B Clarke Award, Nat Acad Design, New York, 86; Mid/Atlantic/Nat Endowment Arts, Fel, 94; Juror's Award, Armory Art Ctr, West Palm Beach, Fla, 2001; Golden Foundataion, 2001; Nat Midyear 2nd Place Award, Butler Inst Am Art, Youngstown, Ohio, 2002. *Bibliog:* New York, New York, Cleveland Inst Art Bull, fall 79; A Barnhill Portrait (film), 94; Painting the Town: Cityscapes of NY, 2000. *Media:* Oil, Watercolor. *Mailing Add:* 10-09 50th Ave Long Island City NY 11101

SCHOEN, (MR & MRS) ARTHUR BOYER
COLLECTORS
Mr Schoen, b Pittsburgh, Pa, Apr 17, 23; Mrs Schoen, b New York, NY, Sept 27, 15. *Study:* Mr Schoen, Princeton Univ, BA; Mrs Schoen, Columbia Univ; Grand Cent Sch Art, NY. *Pos:* Mr Schoen, bd adv, Ocean Learning Inst, West Palm Beach, Fla; dir & secy, Aqua Sol Inc; dir, Solar Micro Inc. *Mem:* Parrish Art Mus (Mrs Schoen, pres, 70-76, trustee); Meadow Club, Southampton. *Collection:* Paintings: 18th century English and American furniture; archaeological artifacts; Chinese porcelains; 10th & 12th century Persian pottery. *Mailing Add:* 1100 Park Ave New York NY 10128

SCHOENER, ALLON
DESIGNER, CONSULTANT
b Cleveland, Ohio, Jan 1, 26. *Study:* Yale Univ, BA, 46, MA, 49; Courtauld Inst Art, Univ London, 47-48. *Collection Arranged:* Lower East Side: Portal to American Life, Jewish Mus; Erie Canal: 1817-1967, NY State Coun Arts, 67; Harlem on My Mind, Metrop Mus Art, 69; Word From Jerusalem, Jewish Mus, 72; Life Aboard the Tall Ships for South Street, Seaport Mus, 76; The Family of Nations for the United Nations, Vienna, Austria, 79; Jewish Life in America, New York Pub Libr, 83; The Italian Americans--per terre assai lontane, Archivi Alinri, Florence, Italy, 89; Ellis Island, New York, 92. *Pos:* Asst dir, Jewish Mus, 66-67; visual arts prog dir, NY State Coun Arts, 67-72; consult traveling exhib, Smithsonian Inst, Washington, DC & Jewish Mus, NY; consult multiple exhib prog, Libr of Cong, Washington, DC. *Awards:* Nat Endowment Arts Proj Fel, 82. *Publ:* Ed, Portal to America, Holt, Rinehart & Winston, 67; Harlem on My Mind, Random House, 69, Dell, 79 & The New Press, 95; The American Jewish Album, Rizzoli Int Publ, 83; The Italian American, Macmillan, 87; illusr, History of the People, Norton, NY, 98. *Mailing Add:* PO Box 9 Hudson NY 12534

SCHOENHERR, JOHN (CARL)
PAINTER, ILLUSTRATOR
b New York, NY, July 5, 35. *Study:* Art Students League; Pratt Inst, BFA, study with Will Barnet & William A Smith. *Work:* Nat Park Serv, Washington; Kerlan Col, Univ Minn, Maples, Minn; Zimmerli Art Mus, Rutgers Univ, NJ; Genesee Co Mus, Mumford, NY; Hiram Blauvelt Art Mus, Oradell, NJ. *Exhib:* Artists of Am, Denver, Colo Hist Soc, 84, 85, 86, 87; Soc Illusr, NY, 64-68, 71 & 75; Contemp Am Illusr of Children's Bks, Rutgers Univ, NJ, 74; Royal Ont Mus, Toronto, Can, 75; Kent State Univ, 83; Hiram Blauvect Art Mus, 97. *Awards:* Soc Animal Artists Medal, 79 & 85; Silver Medal, Philadelphia Acad Natural Sci, 84; Caldecott Medal, 88; SAA Medal, 2003. *Bibliog:* Kingman, Foster & Lontoft (auths), Illustrators of Childrens Books 1957-1966, Horn Bk Inc, 68; Diana Klemin (auth), The Illustrated Book, Clarkson N Potter Publ, 70; C Hume (ed), From The Wild, Summerhill Press, 86. *Mem:* Soc Illusr; Soc Animal Artists. *Media:* Watercolor, Oil. *Publ:* Illusr, Rascal, EP Dutton, 63; auth & illusr, The Barn, Atlantic Mo Press, 68; illusr, Julie of the Wolves, Harper & Row, 72; Dune, Berkeley, 78; Owl Moon, Philomel, 87. *Dealer:* Spanierman Gallery New York NY. *Mailing Add:* 135 Upper Creek Rd Stockton NJ 08559

SCHOFIELD, ROBERTA
PAINTER
b Ronceverte, WVa, July 9, 45. *Study:* Univ S Fla, BA, 73, MFA, 79. *Work:* Federal Reserve Bank, Richmond, Va & Miami, Fla; Polk Mus Art, Lakeland, Fla; Jamestown Community Col, Olean, NY; Strathmore Hall Found, Rockville, Md; Gulf Coast Mus of Art, Largo, FL; and others. *Comn:* Painting, Jamestown Comm Col, 88. *Exhib:* Port Royal Plantation, Hilton Head Island, SC, 95; ISE Art Found, NY, 96; Waterworks Visual Arts Ctr, Salisbury, NC, 96; Cudahy's Gallery, Richmond, Va, 97; Valencia Community Col, Orlando, Fla, 98; Cudahy's Gallery, Richmond, Va, 93, 97, 99, 2002; Clayton Galleries, Tampa, Fla, 93, 99, 2005; 22nd Floor Capitol Gallery, Tallahassee, Fla, 2000; many others; Polk Mus, Lakeland, Fla, 2002; Greely Square Gallery, NY, 2001; Seton Hall Univ, Orange, NJ, 2002; Opus 39, St Augustine, Fla, 2003; Gulf Coast Mus Art, Key Largo, 2005; Boca Raton Mus Art, Fla, 2005; Pakhuis 6 Gallery, Rotterdam, Neth, 2006. *Pos:* Artistic dir, Fla Ctr Contemp Art, 87-88; exhib coordr, Tampa City Coun, 87-89 & 92-94; independent curator, 92-. *Teaching:* Instr, S Fla Jr Col, Avon Park Fla, 79-82, Univ Wis, Eau Claire, Wis, 83-84 & St Petersburg Jr Col, Clearwater, Fla, 89. *Awards:* Fla Arts Coun Fel, 87-88; Best in Show, Arts Ctr, St Petersburg, Fla, 2002; Best In Show, St Augustine Arts Ctr, Fla, 2004; and others. *Bibliog:* Adrienne Golub (auth), Art Papers, Atlanta, Ga, 10-11/93 & 9-10/98; Martha Mabey (auth), Schofield Unsettles, Pleases, Richmond Times-Dispatch, Va, 5/4/97; Roy Proctor (auth), Roberta Schofield's Vision of Interior Life on Display, Richmond-Times Dispatch, 10/31/99; and others. *Mem:* Women Caucus Art (chap secy, 87, treas, 88, publicity, 90); Nat Asn Women Artists; Fla Artists Group; Las Damas de Arte. *Media:* Oil, Color Pencil, Graphite, Photography. *Publ:* Auth-illusr, Gallerie Women's Art, Gallerie Pubs, 88; Cultural Affairs, Cultural Affairs Publ, 2002, 2003, 2005. *Dealer:* Clayton Galleries 4105 S MacDill Ave Tampa FL 33611. *Mailing Add:* PO Box 10561 Tampa FL 33679

SCHOLDER, LAURENCE
PRINTMAKER, EDUCATOR
b Brooklyn, NY, Nov 23, 42. *Study:* Carnegie Inst Technol, BFA; Univ Iowa, MA. *Work:* Ft Worth Art Ctr, Tex; Houston Mus Fine Arts; Brooklyn Mus, NY; Dallas Mus Fine Arts, Tex. *Exhib:* Am Graphic Workshops '68, Cincinnati Art Mus, 68; Multiples USA, Western Mich Univ, Kalamazoo, 70; Midwest Biennial, Joslyn Art Mus, Omaha, Nebr, 70 & 72; Seattle Print Int, Seattle Art Mus, 71; Libr of Cong 22nd Print Nat, Washington, DC, 71. *Teaching:* Asst prof printmaking, Southern Methodist Univ, 68-73, assoc prof, 73-81, prof, 81-. *Awards:* Purchase Awards, Young Printmakers, Herron Art Inst, 67 & Print & Drawing Nat, Okla Art Ctr, 68; Merit Award, Southwest Graphics, San Antonio, 72; Nat Endowment Arts Printmaker's Fel, 75. *Media:* Intaglio. *Dealer:* Gerald Peters Gallery 2913 Fairmount Dallas TX 75201. *Mailing Add:* 5239 Goodwin Ave Dallas TX 75206

SCHON, NANCY QUINT
SCULPTOR
b Boston, Mass, Sept 24, 28. *Work:* Children's Patio Newton Free Libr, Mass; Plotkin Mus, Phoenix, Ariz; M Maloney Properties, Boston, Mass; Beth Shalom, Needham, Mass; Sarah Pryor Living Mem, Wayland, Mass, 96. *Comn:* Nat Acad Sci, Washington, DC; Sweet Briar Col, Va; Jewish Home for the Elderly, Fairfield, Conn; Make Way for Ducklings, Boston Pub Garden, Mass & Novodevichy Park, Moscow, Russ, 91; Raccoons, Belle Meade, Nashville, Tenn, 94; and others. *Exhib:* One-person shows, Bristol Art Mus, RI, 78, Jerusalem Theatre Gallery, Israel, 79, Mass Inst Technol, Cambridge, Pierce Galleries, Hingham, Mass & Schönhaus Preview, Newton, Mass, 85; Concourse Art Gallery, Boston, 78; Richards Galleries, Hyannis, Mass, 80-81; Riji Gallery, NY, 81; Small Works, Rochester, NY, 84; Aetha Inst, Hartford, Conn, 84-85; Catherine Lorrilard Wolfe Ann, NY, 84-85; New Eng Sculptors' Asn Invitational, Boston, Mass, 85; Worcester Craft Mus, 86; Boston Mus, Mass, 86; Galleria de Tour, San Francisco; Rae Landers Gallery, East Brunswick, NJ; Raphael Galleries, La Jolla, Calif, Los Vegas, Nev; Wellesley Coll Mus, Mass; Univ of New Hampshire, Durham; Two Squares Gallery, Boulder, Colo; Springfield Mus of Fine Arts, Mass; George Walter Vincent Smith Art Mus, Springfield, Mass; and others. *Pos:* Gov's task force, Accessibility of the Arts (gov's comm), Boston, Mass, 72-74; Gov's Coun on Arts & Humanities, Boston, Mass, 72-75; founder, mem, Pub Media Found; adv bd Newton free Libr, Senior Citizens of Newton; bd dir, Newton Senior Ctr, Friends of Copley Sq. *Awards:* Good Samaritan Award, Easter Seal/Sculpture Competition, 73; Fel, Va Ctr Creative Arts, 85; Boston Preserv Award, Pub Art, 88; Joseph Henry Keenan Award, Mass Inst Technol, Cambridge; Browne Found Grant, 96; Wayland Cult Coun Grant, 96; Col Club Ann Career Award, 96; Woman of Distinction, Spar & Spindle Nat Girl Scouts Bachrach VIP Portrait Show, Newton Free Libr, 94; Historic Neighborhood Found Award; Cert of Recognition, Boston Mayor Raymond Flynn: for Art Award, Stamford Conn. *Media:* Bronze. *Mailing Add:* 291 Otis St Newton MA 02465-2531

SCHONZEIT, BENJAMIN
PAINTER
b Brooklyn, NY, May 9, 42. *Study:* Cooper Union, BFA, 64. *Work:* Brooklyn Mus Art; Denver Art Mus; Guggenheim Mus, NY; Metrop Mus Art, NY; Mus Contemp Art, Chicago; and many others. *Exhib:* Lowe Art Mus, Univ Miami, Fla, 72; Storm King Art Ctr, Mountainville, NY, 73; Art Inst Chicago, 74; Wadsworth Atheneum, Hartford, Conn, 74; Albright-Knox Art Gallery, Buffalo, NY, 75; Whitney Mus Downtown, NY, 75; Baltimore Mus Art, 75-76; Butler Inst Am Art, Youngstown, Ohio, 76; solo exhibs, Michael Berger Gallery, Pittsburgh, 79, Tomasulo Gallery, Union Col, Crawford, NJ, 79, Gibbes Art Gallery, Charleston, SC, 80, Nancy Hoffman Gallery, NY, 81 & DeGestlo Gallery, Cologne, Ger, 81, Del Art Mus, Wilmington, 84, Galerie 99, Bay Harbor Island, Fla, 88; Brooklyn Mus, 80; Guggenheim Mus, NY, 85; Am Icons, Fairleigh-Dickinson Univ, New Brunswick, NJ, 89; Charles Cowles Gallery, NY, 98; Baker Gallery, Boca Raton, Fla, 98-99; Gerald Peters Gallery, Santa Fe, NMex, 99. *Awards:* Butler Prize, Butler Inst Arts. *Bibliog:* Edward Lucie-Smith (auth), Superralism, Phaidon Press Ltd, 79; Louis K Meisel (auth), Photorealism, Abrams, Inc, New York, 80; Art Business News, 7/89. *Dealer:* Irving Galleries 332 Worth Ave Palm Beach FL 33480; Gerald Peters Gallery 1011 Paseo de Peralta Santa Fe NM 87501. *Mailing Add:* 107 Mercer St New York NY 10012

SCHOOLEY, ELMER WAYNE
PAINTER, EDUCATOR
b Lawrence, Kans, Feb 20, 16. *Study:* Univ Colo, BFA, 38; State Univ Iowa, MA, 41. *Work:* Mus Mod Art & Metrop Mus Art, NY; Hallmark Collection, Kansas City; Mus NMex, Santa Fe; Roswell Mus, NMex; Albuquerque Mus; Tucson Mus; Brooklyn Mus; Phoenix Art Mus; Libr of Congress. *Comn:* Fresco (with Gussie Du Jardin), Las Vegas, NMex Hosp, 50; also numerous pvt collections. *Exhib:* Houston Southwestern Exhib, 62; Kansas City Mid-Am Exhib, 64; Tucson Festival Art Exhib, 64; Eight State Exhib, Oklahoma City, 68; Biennial Southwestern Exhib, Santa Fe, 72; one-man shows, Tucson Mus Art Mus, Roswell Mus, NMex & Santa Fe Mus NMex, 92. *Pos:* Artist-in-residence, Roswell Mus, NMex, 77-78. *Teaching:* Asst prof, NMex Western Univ, 46-47; prof arts & crafts, NMex Highlands Univ, 47-77. *Awards:* Purchase Prize, Ford Found, 62; Honorable Mention, Kansas City Hallmark Purchase, 64; Prizes, Southwest Biennial, Santa Fe, 70, 72 & 74; NMex Governor's Award for Excellence in Visual Art, 86. *Bibliog:* Elmer Schooley, Munson Gallery Pub. *Media:* Oil. *Dealer:* Meyer Munson Gallery 225 Canyon Rd Santa Fe NM 87501. *Mailing Add:* Rte 1 1403 W Berrendo Roswell NM 88201

SCHORR, COLLIER
ARTIST
b NY City, 1963. *Study:* Sch Visual Arts, NY City, BFA. *Exhib:* International Ctr Photography Triennial, 2003; Whitney Biennial, Whitney Mus Am Art, NY City, 2002, 2006; Walker Art Ctr, Minnesota; Jewish Mus, NY City; Stedelijk Mus, Amsterdam; Consorcio Salamanca, Spain. *Mailing Add:* c/o 303 Gallery 525 W 22nd St New York NY 10011

SCHORR, PAUL C, III
PATRON
Pos: Pres, Chief Exec Officer, ComCor Holdings Inc, 88-; bd dir, Ameritas Life Insurance Corp, Schorr Family Co Inc, Nat Res Corp, Western Sizzlin Corp, Roanoke, Va, 94-; chmn, Western Sizzlin Corp (formerly Austin Steaks & Saloon), Roanoke, Va, 95-99, 2002-. *Awards:* Recipient Univ Nebr Builder Award, 84. *Mem:* Whitney Mus Am Art, New York City (trustee, currently). *Mailing Add:* ComCor Holdings Inc 6940 O St Lincoln Ste 336 Lincoln NE 68510

SCHOTTLAND, M
ILLUSTRATOR, PAINTER
b Brooklyn, NY, Nov 18, 35. *Study:* Pratt Inst, BFA, 57; New Sch, printmaking with Antonio Frasconi, painting with Gregorio Prestodino, 58-60. *Work:* Soc of Illustrators Permanent Collection, NY; US Army Military Hist, US Air Force Art Prog, Pentagon & Nat Parks Serv, DC. *Comn:* Postage stamp, US Postal Serv, DC, 76; painting, US Air Force, DC, 77; paintings for nat advert, Ingersoll Rand Corp, NJ, 78; painting for bk illus, Franklin Libr, NY/Philadelphia, 79; NASA, 83; and others. *Exhib:* Indust Arts Methods Ann Show, NY, 76; 200 Yrs Am Illus, NY Hist Soc, 77; Soc Publ Designers Ann Show, NY, 78-79; Soc Illustrators Ann Show, NY, 78 & 79 & 50 Yrs of Award Winners, 79; Art in Sci, Cincinnati Mus Art, 79; Smithsonian Inst, 83. *Pos:* Chmn Air Force Art Prog, US Air Force/Soc Illustrators, 76-79. *Teaching:* Guest lectr illus, Soc Illustrators, New York, 77, Sch Visual Arts, New York, 78, Fashion Inst Technol, New York, 79 & Philadelphia Col Art, 79. *Awards:* Hamilton King Award, Soc Illustrators Ann Show, 71; Best of Show, Indust Arts Methods Ann Show, 76; Awards of Distinctive Merit, Soc Publ Designers Ann Show, 77 & 79. *Mem:* Soc Illusrs; Comt to Save NY Libr Picture Collection (vpres, 78-80); Graphic Artists Guild, NY. *Media:* Tempera. *Mailing Add:* 2201 Massachusetts Ave NW Washington DC 20008

SCHRECK, MICHAEL H
PAINTER, SCULPTOR
b Austria; US citizen. *Work:* Ft Lauderdale Mus of Art; Heckscher Mus, NY; Metrop Mus, Miami; Mus Fine Arts, Lausanne, Switz; Tel Aviv Mus & Mus Mod Art, Haifa, Israel; Jacksonville Art Mus, Fla; Norton Gallery Arts; Currier Gallery Art, Manchester, NH; and others. *Comn:* Masada Monument, Hollywood, Fla. *Exhib:* Mus

Mod Art, Paris, 64; Palm Beach Gallery, Fla; Rauchbach Gallery, Bay Harbor, Fla, 82; Dyansen Gallery, NY; Patricia Judith Gallery, Boca Raton, Fla; Boca Raton Mus, Fla; and others. *Awards:* Grand Prix Int, Deauville, France; City of Hollywood Appreciation Award, Fla, 75; Academic Gold Medal, Accademia, Italia, 80; Diploma-Maestro Di Pittura, 82; Prix Int, Vichy, France. *Bibliog:* Alfred Werner (auth), Michael Schreck Sculpture, Univ Miami, 75; Richard A Madigan (auth), Michael Schreck Sculpture, Mus Palm Beach, 79. *Mem:* Life fel Royal Soc Arts, London; Am Fedn Arts; Artists Equity Asn; Accademia Italia, Italy. *Media:* Acrylic, Oil; Miscellaneous Media

SCHRECKENGOST, VIKTOR
DESIGNER, SCULPTOR
b Sebring, Ohio, June 26, 1906. *Study:* Cleveland Sch Art, 25-29; Kunstgewerbeschule, Vienna, Austria, 29-30. *Hon Degrees:* Cleve Inst Art, Hon Dr Fine Art, 1995; Case Western Reserve Univ, Hon Dr Humane Letters, 2002. *Work:* Cleveland Mus Art; Metrop Mus Art, Whitney Mus Am Art, NY; Memphis Mus Art; also in pvt collections; best known for Jazz Bowls he created beginning in the early 1930s. *Comn:* Designer K K Culver Air Trophy, Oberlin Mem Tablet; Early Settler, Lakewood HS, Ohio, 1954; sculpture for bird bldg, Cleveland Zoo, 1950, Pachyderm Bldg, 56; Cleveland Hopkins Airport, 56. *Exhib:* Major mus in US; also Century Progress, Chicago, 1933-34, Paris Int Expos, 1937, San Francisco & NY World's Fair, 1939-40. *Pos:* Head designer, Murray Ohio Mfg Co, Nashville; consult designer, Harris-Intertype Corp & divs; designer, Am Artists Group, Inc, NY; mem fine arts adv comt, Cleveland Planning Comn, from 1961. *Teaching:* Instr, Cleveland Sch Art,1930-72, head dept indust design, from 36, retired 1972, instr emeritus, 1972-. *Awards:* Spec & First Award, Cleveland Mus Art, 1955; Gold Medal Fine Arts, Am Inst Architect, 1958; Visual Arts Award, Women's City Club Cleveland, 1973; Governors Award for the Arts, State of Ohio, 2000. *Bibliog:* Henry Adams, CMA (auth), Viktor Schreckengost and 20th Century Design, 2000, rev 2004; Henry Adams (auth), Sunny Horton (ed), Viktor Schreckengost: American DaVinci, 2006. *Mem:* Fel Int Inst Arts & Lett; Cleveland Soc Artists; NY Archit League; Indust Designers Soc Am (past nat vpres & dir); Am Watercolor Soc; plus others. *Media:* Clay, Watercolor. *Mailing Add:* 2265 Stillman Rd Cleveland OH 44118

SCHREIBER, EILEEN SHER
PAINTER, PRINTMAKER
b Denver, Colo. *Study:* Univ Utah, 42-45; NY Univ Exten, 66-68; Montclair State Col, 75-79. *Work:* Citibank; AT&T Co; Johnson & Johnson; Georgia Pac; Champion Int Paper; Nabisco; Independence Bank, NY; plus others. *Comn:* NJ Beach Area, Broad Nat Bank, Newark, 70; Mitzubushi, Barclay Bank Eng. *Exhib:* NJ Mus, Trenton, 69 & 73; Am Watercolor Soc Nat, Nat Acad Galleries, NY; Audubon Artists, NY; Pallazzo Vecchio, Florence, Italy; Va State Mus, 75; Art Expo, NY, 86 & 87; Traveling show, Art Cult Ctr in Athena, Livingston Art Asn, 96. *Teaching:* former tchr art Jewish C Ctr, W Orange, NJ. *Awards:* Best Show Cash Award, Short Hills State Show, 76; Purchase Award, Tri-State Exhib, Somerset Co Col, 77; Best Show, Tri State Exhib, Somerset Col, 80; First Prize, Nat Asn Women Artist, 95. *Bibliog:* M Lenson (auth), article, Newark Eve News, 4/70; article, Newark Star Ledger, 6/74; Addison Parks (auth), article, Arts Mag, 12/79. *Mem:* Nat Asn Women Artists (chmn, 73-75); Artists Equity Asn, NY; Printmakers Coun; NJ Visual Arts. *Media:* Acrylic, Watercolor; Collage, Monoprints. *Specialty:* Southwest, contemporary. *Interests:* Photography, travel, music, art, golf. *Dealer:* South West Gallery, Baronegat Light, NJ; Many galleries in New York and Florida

SCHRERO, RUTH LIEBERMAN
SCULPTOR, PRINTMAKER
b New York, NY. *Study:* Columbia Univ, with Oronzio Maldarelli; Art Students League, with George Grosz; Tyler Sch Art, Temple Univ; Pratt Graphics Workshop & Manhattan Graphics Workshop; studies with Tony Kirk & Vijay Kumar. *Work:* Maywood Pub Libr, NJ; Harsen & Johns, Architects, Rochelle Park, NJ; Nabisco Brands Corp, Parsipanny, NJ; NY Univ Sch Law; Bergen Mus Art & Sci. *Comn:* Bronze portrait Hon Edward Weinfeld, comn by New York Univ Sch Law, 77. *Teaching:* Community Schools, Fairlawn & Glen Rock, NJ. *Awards:* Estelle Goodman Prize, Nat Painters & Sculptors Soc, 75; Exhib Am Drawings, Morris Mus, 84; Anna Hyatt Huntington Bronze Medal for Sculpture, 84, 89 & 98 & Gold Medal of Honor for Sculpture, Catharine Lorillard Wolfe Art Club, 97; Leila Gardin Sawyer Award for Etching, 99; plus others. *Bibliog:* NY Times, 79 & 84; Star Ledger, 80, 95 & 96. *Mem:* Artists Equity Asn NY; NY Soc Women Artists; Nat Asn Women Artists; Catharine Lorillard Wolfe Art Club; life mem Art Students League. *Media:* Clay, Miscellaneous Media; Etching, Mixed Media. *Dealer:* Wyckoff Gallery Wyckoff NJ. *Mailing Add:* 377 Rutland Ave Teaneck NJ 07666-2844

SCHREYER, CHARA
COLLECTOR
Pos: Chmn, Kadima Found, Mill Valley, Calif; trustee Mus Modern Art, San Francisco, Contemp Jewish Mus. *Awards:* Named one of Top 200 Collectors, ARTNews Mag, 2004, 2005, 2006. *Mem:* Mus Modern Art, San Francisco, Calif; Contemp Jewish Mus. *Collection:* Modern & Contemporary Art & Photography. *Mailing Add:* Kadima Found PMB 200 38 Miller Ave Mill Valley CA 94941

SCHROECK, R D
PAINTER, CONCEPTUAL ARTIST
b Buffalo, NY, June 28, 49. *Study:* Rosary Hill Col, BFA, 76. *Work:* Dartmoth Col Mus & galleries, Hanover, NH; Georgia State Univ, Atlanta; Cleveland Col Art & Design, Middlesbrough, Eng; Burchfield-Penney Art Ctr, Buffalo, NY; Cleveland Co Coun, Middlesbrough, Eng. *Exhib:* Western NY Exhib, Albright Knox Art Gallery, Buffalo, NY, 76, 80, 86, 94 & 96; 16th Biennal De Sao Paulo, 81; New Art of 1980-1990, Atelier Galeria, Dijon, France, 81; The Charles Rand Penney Collection of 20th Century Art, Rochester Art Gallery, NY, 83-84; Recent Acquisitions, Burchfield Penney Art Ctr, Buffalo, NY, 96. *Media:* Acrylic, Oil. *Mailing Add:* 14 Danforth St Buffalo NY 14227-1609

SCHROHENLOHER, SALLY A
PAINTER
b Cincinnati, Ohio, Feb 12, 57. *Study:* Univ Cincinnati, BFA, 79. *Work:* Borden Inc, Columbus, Ohio; Fidelity Investments, Atlanta, Ga; Cincinnati Bell Telephone, Ohio; Southern Ohio Mus, Portsmouth; EW Scripps Inc, La Jolla, Calif. *Exhib:* Faber Birren Color Show, Stamford Art Mus, Conn, 90; The Allen Collection, Miami Univ Art Mus, Oxford, Ohio, 94; Southern Ohio Mus, Portsmouth, 2000; South Bend Regional Mus Art, Ind, 2000; The Object Considered, Columbus Coll Art & Design, Ohio, 2000. *Awards:* Special Exhib Grant, Inst Mus Svcs, Nat Endowement for Arts, Wash, DC, 82; Individual Artist Grant, Summerfair Inc, Cincinnati, Ohio, 91; Ohio Arts Coun Award Fel, State of Ohio, Columbus, 2001. *Media:* Oil. *Dealer:* M Willis Fine Art 3235 Madison Rd Cincinnati Ohio 45209; Adam Whitney Gallery 8725 Shamrock Rd Omaha NE 68114; Anderson Fine Art Gallery 3309 Frederica Rd St Simons Island Ga 31522. *Mailing Add:* 5870 Blue Spruce Ln Cincinnati OH 45224-2856

SCHRUT, SHERRY
PAINTER, PRINTMAKER
b Detroit, Mich, Apr 27, 28. *Study:* Wayne State Univ, Detroit, BA(art), 50; Long Beach State Col, Calif & Univ Calif, Los Angeles. *Work:* Security Pac Nat Bank, Palm Desert, Calif; Cedars-Sinai Med Ctr, Thalians Bldg, Los Angeles; Int Cult Ctr for Youth, Jerusalem, Israel; Hebrew Union Col Skirball Mus, Los Angeles; Atlantic Richfield Co, Los Angeles; Wayne State Univ, Mich; IBM, Atlanta, Ga; Xerox Corp. *Comn:* Southern Calif Psychoanalytic Inst, Beverly Hills, 71 & 74; Sheraton Grande Hotel, Tokyo, Japan; MGM Grand Air, Lax Terminal Airport, Los Angeles; and others. *Exhib:* Los Angeles Inst Contemp Art, Century City, 75; Laguna Beach Mus Art, 76; Works on Paper, Newport Harbor Art Mus, Calif, 77; one-woman shows, Brand Libr & Art Ctr, Glendale, 72 & 79 & Galeria Del Sol, Santa Barbara, 76; Calif Mus Sci & Indust, 81; Hank Baum Gallery, San Francisco, 82; Eva Cohon Gallery, Chicago, Ill, 86. *Teaching:* Instr, Craft & Folk Art Mus, Los Angeles, 73-74. *Awards:* Second Prizes, Wayne State Univ, Detroit, 51 & Long Beach Mus Art, 53; First Prize, Westwood Ctr Arts, 68 & Riverside Mus Art, 80, Calif; Lucille Simon Purchase Award, Skirball Mus, Los Angeles. *Bibliog:* Barbara Probstein (auth), The fiery art, Home Mag, Los Angeles Times, 73 & Cloisonne enameling, Sch Arts Mag, Davis Publ, 1/75; W F Alexander (auth), Cloisonne Extraordinaire, California Contemporary Artists, In: Cloisonne & Related Arts, Wallace-Homestead Bk Co, 77; Designers West, Calif, 86. *Mem:* Southern Calif Designer-Crafts, Inc (treas, 75-78); Enamel Guild-West (mem bd, 77); Am Crafts Coun; World Crafts Coun. *Publ:* Contribr, Creative Stitchery, Crown Publ, 70; Porcelain Enamel, Historical, Contemporary, Industrial and Artistic, San Diego Univ Press, 76; Enameling for Secondary Schools, Lawrence Univ Press, RI, 76; Crafts 1976, Southern Calif Designer-Crafts, Inc, 76; The Center Mag, Ctr Democratic Insts, Santa Barbara, Calif, 78 & 79. *Dealer:* Ruth Bachofner Gallery Beverly Hills CA

SCHULE, DONALD KENNETH
SCULPTOR, INSTRUCTOR
b Madison, Minn, June 17, 38. *Study:* Univ Minn, sculpture with Richard Randall, Robert Mallory & James Wines, BFA, 64, MFA, 67. *Work:* Walker Art Ctr, Minneapolis; Sheldon Art Mus, Lincoln, Nebr; Univ Notre Dame, South Bend, Ind; Wichita Art Mus, Kans; Minn Mus Art, St Paul. *Exhib:* Walker Art Ctr, Minneapolis, 62 & 64; solo shows, Minneapolis Inst Arts, 70, Contemp Arts Mus, Houston, 75, Sheldon Art Mus, Lincoln, Nebr, 78 & Phyllis Kind Gallery, Chicago, 78; Allan Stone Gallery, NY, 73 & 77; Whitney Mus Am Art, NY, 77; Indianapolis Mus Art, 78; Nelson Mus, Kansas City, 83; Karen Lennox Gallery, Chicago, 83; Janet Fleisher Gallery, Philadelphia, 83; and others. *Teaching:* Assoc prof, Wichita State Univ, 67-78; lectr, Southwest Tex State Univ, San Marcos, 81-88 & Pa State Univ, 89-94. *Awards:* Purchase Prizes, Ford Found, 64 & Nat Endowment Arts, 70; 1st Prize, Wichita Art Asn, 72. *Bibliog:* Dona Z Meilach (auth), Woodworking: The New Wave, Crown Publ Inc, 81. *Media:* Wood, Stone. *Mailing Add:* 1721 Linden Hall Rd Boalsburg PA 16827

SCHULEIT, ANNA
ARTIST
b Mainz, Ger, 74. *Study:* RI Sch Design, BFA, 98; Dartmouth Col, MFA, 2005. *Exhib:* Solo shows include Nada Mason Gallery, Northfield, Mass, 2000, Northampton Ctr Arts, 2000; group shows include A Transatlantic Project, Muhle der schoenen Kunste, Ger, 95; Off the Wall, 16 S Main St Gallery, Providence, 98; Nat Prize Show, Cambridge Art Asn, Mus Fine Art, Boston, 98; Summer Show, Harvard Univ, 99; Kaelin Gallery, Boston, 2002; Pioneers of Public, Revolving Mus, Lowell, Mass, 2002; Inch x Inch, Arlington Ctr Arts, 2002; CHi of Ancestry, Gallery Luna, Salem, Mass, 2004; Medfield State Hospital Closing: Projections, Dept Mental Health, Westborough, Mass, 2004; The Matzo Files, NYC, 2004-2005; 1939 The Missing Year, New Art Ctr, Newton, Mass, 2005; Goliath, Brooklyn, 2006. *Pos:* Consultant Metrop Transit Authority, NY City, 2005. *Teaching:* Art instr Nightingale-Bamford Sch, 2005; guest lectr dept sociology Brown Univ, 99, 2002, 2005, Smith Col, 2000, River Valley Hospital, Middletown, Conn, 2000, Springfield Col, 2001, Brattleboro Mus and Art Ctr, 2001, The Delaney House, Holyoke, Mass, 2001, RI Sch Design, 2005; presenter Forum on Historical Records, Univ Mass Amherst, 2001, Nat Convention State Art Agencies, 2001, Sch Architecture McGill Univ, Montreal, 2003; vis artist Westborough State Hospital, Mass, 2001-2004; disting visitor Sch Art and Design, Univ Mich, 2006. *Awards:* Grad Alumni Award, Dartmouth Col, 2005, Thesis

Res Award, 2005; MacDowell Colony Fellow, 2002, 2005, Chubb Life Am Fellow, 2000-2001; Artist Grant, Elizabeth Greenshields Found, 96; Artist Grant, Northampton Arts Council, 2000; Artist Grant, Mass Found Humanities, 2000; MacArthur Fellow, John D and Catherine T MacArthur Found, 2006

SCHULLER, NANCY SHELBY
LIBRARIAN, HISTORIAN
b Austin, Tex, Aug 20, 42. *Study:* Univ Tex, Austin, BFA, 63, MA, 69. *Pos:* Prof librn dept art, Univ Tex, Austin, 67-77, cur visual arts, 77-. *Teaching:* Sr lectr, Univ Tex, Austin, 78-; lectr, Visual Resources Prof Workshops, 83-. *Awards:* Pres Award, Visual Resources Asn, 87; Distinguished Serv Award, Visual Resources Asn, 96. *Mem:* Art Libr Soc NAm (pres Tex chap, 80-83); Col Art Asn; Mid-Am Col Art Asn (chair, visual resources group, 77-79); Spec Libr Asn; Visual Resources Asn (vpres, 82, treas, 83-87). *Res:* Automated process for slide and photograph collections in the visual arts; subject indexing of slides and photographs of works of art; the image bank in visual arts. *Publ:* Auth, Slide collections, Tex Libr J, Vol 47, No 4; Strake College Book of Hours, Gothic & Renaissance Illuminated Manuscripts, Univ Tex, 71; compiler, Standard Abbreviations for Image Descriptions for Use in Fine Arts Visual Resources Collections, VRA Special Bull, No 2, 87; auth, Management for Visual Resources Collections, Librs Unlimited, 89; The Curator's Job Description: Development & Evaluation, Visual Resources, Vol 1, No 4, 90; Iconographic schemes & diagrams for descriptive cataloging of complex works of art, VRA Special Bull, 94. *Mailing Add:* Univ Tex 2709 Trail of the Madrones Austin TX 78746-2344

SCHULMAN, ARLENE
PHOTOGRAPHER, WRITER
b Bronx, NY, Aug 13, 61. *Study:* Art Students League, 92-94. *Work:* Mus City New York; NY Pub Libr; Nat Baseball Hall Fame, Cooperstown, NY; Int Boxing Hall Fame, Canastota, NY; Westinghouse Corp, Pittsburgh, Pa; plus pvt collections. *Exhib:* Solo exhib, Martin Luther King Jr Mem Lib, Washington, 86, Aurora, NY, NY 93 & Henry Street Settlement, NY, 95; Vassar Col, 96; and others. *Pos:* Freelance writer, 86-. *Teaching:* Instr, Ohio State Univ, Columbus, 96; instr, NY pub schs, 95-; instr, NY Pub Libr, 97-. *Awards:* Yaddo Fel, 94; Leonard I Shuger Award, Three Rivers Arts Festival, 94; A J Liebling Award for Outstanding Boxing Writing, Boxing Writers Asn Am, 96; and others. *Mem:* Prof Women Photographers Asn; Boxing Writers Asn Am; Newswomen's Club, NY; Asn Women Sports Media; Art Students League, NY. *Media:* Photography. *Interests:* Sculpture. *Publ:* Auth & illusr, The Prizefighters, Lyon & Burford, 94; auth, Muhammad Ali, Lerner, 96; auth & illusr, Carmine: The Story of a Boy Living with AIDS, 97; Robert F Kennedy: Promise for the Future, 98; TJ's Story: A Boy Who is Blind (bk), 98; 23rd Precinct: The Job, 01; On the Beat, 01. *Mailing Add:* Inwood Sta PO Box 460 New York NY 10034

SCHULSON, SUSAN
PAINTER, SILVERSMITH
b Racine, Wis, Nov 21, 41. *Study:* Lawrence Univ, BA, 63; Univ Ill, MFA(teaching asst), 78. *Work:* Mus Contemp Art, Chicago. *Exhib:* With Paper, About Paper, Albright-Knox Art Gallery, Buffalo, NY, 80; Navy Pier, Chicago, 81; Heresies, Grey Art Gallery, NY, 81; Swen Parson Gallery, 83; Ornaments as Sculpture, Sculpture Ctr, NY, 83; Critical Mixage, Galerie Lara Vincey, Paris, 85; and others. *Pos:* Ed, Le Corbusier Sketchbooks vols II-IV, Archit History Found, New York, 81-82; film producer & educator commercials & features in development, 83-94. *Teaching:* Instr printmaking, Evanston Art Ctr, Ill, 75-76, Univ Ill, 76-78, Searing Sch, New York, 80-81; guest lectr, Univ Chicago, 75-76, Sch Visual Arts, New York, 87 & 88. *Bibliog:* Joanna Frueh (auth), Susan Schulson at Zolla/Lieberman, Art Am, 79. *Mem:* Col Art Asn; Artist Equity; NY Acad Arts & Scis. *Media:* Miscellaneous Media. *Mailing Add:* 121 Wooster St New York NY 10012

SCHULTE, ARTHUR D
COLLECTORS
b New York, NY, 06. *Study:* Mr Schulte, Yale Univ; Mrs Schulte, Hunter Col, Columbia Univ, NY Univ. *Collection:* French, American, Italian and Greek paintings and sculpture. *Mailing Add:* 825 5th Ave New York NY 10021

SCHULTZ, CAROLINE REEL
PAINTER, LECTURER
b Evansville, Ind. *Study:* Art Ctr Col Design, Los Angeles, 58; Univ Ill-Urbana, 60-62; Wellfleet Sch, with W Kennedy, 60; Art Mart Sch, Martha's Vineyard; European Sch, Mallorca, Spain, 61; also with Nichola Ziroli & Billy M Jackson. *Work:* Mt Kenya Safari Club, EAfrica; Pavillon, Scottsdale, Ariz; New Masters, Carmel, Calif; Bruners Fine Art, Santa Rosa, Calif. *Comn:* Wildlife (screen), comn by John Batten, III, Twin Disc Corp, Racine, Wis, 75. *Exhib:* Game Coin, San Antonio, 75; Shikar Safari Club 75, San Diego Zoo, 75; Safari Int, Las Vegas, 76; Abercrombie & Fitch, San Francisco, 76; and other group and one-woman shows. *Pos:* US art dir, EAfrican Wild Life Soc, 75. *Teaching:* Lectr animal anat & Africa through the eyes of an artist, currently. *Awards:* Purchase Award, Comedians Classic, 72; Lenten Art Festival, San Diego, 72; Spec Award, Mt Kenya Safari Club, E African Wildlife Soc, 91; and others. *Mem:* San Diego Art Inst; La Jolla Art Asn; Desert Art Ctr, Palm Springs, Calif; Spanish Village Art Ctr. *Mailing Add:* 10405 Viacha Dr San Diego CA 92124

SCHULTZ, DOUGLAS GEORGE
DIRECTOR
b Oakland, Calif, Oct 3, 47. *Study:* Univ Calif, Berkeley, BA(art hist), 69, MA(art hist), 72; Inst Arts Admin, Harvard Univ, 71. *Collection Arranged:* Antoni Tapies: Thirty-Three Years of His Work, 77, In Western New York (coauth, catalog), 77, Piero Dorazio: A Retrospective, 79, Kenneth Nelson, 81, Chryssa: Urban Icons, 82, Robert Motherwell, 83, Beverly Pepper, 86, Albright-Knox Art Gallery. *Pos:* Curatorial intern, Albright-Knox Art Gallery, 72-73, asst cur, 73-75, assoc cur, 75-76, cur, 77-79, chief cur, 80-83, acting dir, 83, dir, 83-; mem professional adv comt, Arts Develop Servs, Buffalo, NY. *Teaching:* Adj prof art hist, State Univ NY, Buffalo, 75-79. *Mem:* NY State Coun Arts; Arts Develop Serv. *Mailing Add:* 1285 Elmwood Ave Buffalo NY 14222

SCHULTZ, JOHN BERNARD
EDUCATOR, HISTORIAN
b Pittsburgh, Pa, Nov 26, 48. *Study:* John Carroll Univ, BA, 70; Univ Pittsburgh, MA, 73, PhD, 82. *Pos:* Bd dir, Monogalia Arts Ctr, Morgantown, WVa, 82-84 & 94-; chmn, div art, WVa Univ, Morgantown, 89-94, assoc dean, Col Creative Arts, 94-. *Teaching:* Instr art hist, John Carroll Univ, Cleveland, Ohio, 74-75; from instr art hist to prof, WVa Univ, Morgantown, 77-90. *Awards:* Outstanding Teacher, 81, Innovation-Excellence Award, 85, Art Div, WVa Univ; Distinguished Prof Art, WVa Art Alumni Assoc, 88; Frick Fine Arts Distinguished Alumnus, Univ Pittsburgh, 93. *Mem:* Col Art Asn Am; Am Asn Hist Med. *Res:* Historical interrelationships between medicine and art. *Publ:* Auth, Art and Anatomy in Renaissance Italy, UMI Res Press, 85; A Fifteenth Century Papal Brief on Human Dissection, Medical Heritage, 86; coauth, Art Past/Art Present, Abrams, 90, 2nd ed, 94; Study Guide for Janson's History of Art, 4th ed, Prentice-Hall, 91, 5th ed, 95; With Gratitude to Eva Hubbard: A Celebration of Women Artists at WVa Univ (exhib catalog), 91. *Mailing Add:* WVa Univ Col Creative Arts PO Box 6111 Morgantown WV 26506-6111

SCHULTZ, MARILOU
WEAVER, INSTRUCTOR
b Safford, Ariz, Nov 6, 54. *Study:* Ariz State Univ, BA, 78, MA, 79. *Work:* Am Indian Sci & Eng Soc, Albuquerque, NM. *Comn:* Weaving, Intel Corp, Chandler, Ariz, 94; Germantown blanket, comn by a friend of Kevin Johnson, Phoenix, Ariz, 97; Ten Rugs in One Rug, comn by Mr & Mrs Craig Cummings, Paradise Valley, Ariz, 98; Ganado Red (on a loom), United Properties Inc, Sedona, Ariz, 98. *Exhib:* Ann Santa Fe Indian Market, SW Asn Indian Arts, NMex, 81-; Ann Navajo Show, Mus N Ariz, Flagstaff, 86-90; Ann Indian Fair & Market, Heard Mus, Phoenix, Ariz, 90-. *Pos:* Demonstr weaving, SW Mus, Mesa, Ariz, 97, Redhouse Inc, Scottsdale, Ariz, 98- & Heard Mus, Phoenix, Ariz, 98; Native Am adv bd, SW Mus, Mesa, Ariz. *Teaching:* Instr Navajo weavings, Omega Inst, Rhinebeck, NY, 98-2001 & Split Rock Arts Prog, Univ Minn, Minneapolis, Minn, 99-2005; Spinning Lofr, 2003-2005. *Awards:* Ariz Comn Arts Fel, 97; Best of Division Weavings, Heard Mus, Phoenix, Ariz, 97; Challenge Award, 96, 97, 2000. *Bibliog:* Fabric of Time (TV doc), KNXV-Channel 15, 12/97; CD Screen Saver, Santa Fe Indian Market, NMex, 98. *Mem:* SW Asn Indian Arts; Am Tapestry Alliance; ATALT; Heard Mus (Guild Member); and others. *Mailing Add:* 844 E Eighth Pl Mesa AZ 85203

SCHULTZ, SAUNDERS
SCULPTOR
b July 16, 27. *Study:* Wash Univ, St Louis, Mo, BFA, 50; Univ Ill, Urbana, MFA, 52; special study with Max Beckman, Paul Burlin & Fred Conway. *Work:* Morris Arboretum/Sculptural Park, Philadelphia; Broward Co--Art in Public Places Collection, Pompano Beach, Fla; Univ Ark Art Collection, Little Rock; Sculpture Fountain, Kansas City; St Louis Univ Hosp, Mo. *Comn:* Cosmos, is Prize-International Competition, Juffall Hq, Jedda, Saudi Arabia, 83; Light Rays, Maridian Hotel, Singapore, 83; Battle Bows-resulted from international Competition; Nurturing, Cath Cemeterics, St Louis, Mo, 89; Battle Bows, Tri-State Vet Mem, Dubuque, Iowa, 89; Flamma, One Pacific Place, Omaha, Nebr, 90-91. *Exhib:* Sculpture in Architectural Context, Fordham Univ, NY, 79; Centennial Alumni Exhib, Bixby Hall Gallery, Wash Univ, St Louis, Mo, 79; Sculpture Outdoors, Temple Univ, Philadelphia, Pa, 80; Int Sculpture Competition, Mercer Col, Trenton, NJ, 80; Interfaith Forum Exhibition on Religion, Art & Architecture, Washington, DC, 84; Sch Environ Design, Calif State Polytechnic, 88; Miss State Univ, 89; The Good Shephard & The Good Shephard Cross Archdiocese of City of Chicago & Catholic Cemeteries Chicago, Ill, 2005. *Teaching:* Guest lectr, numerous cols & univs incl Harvard Univ Sch Grad Sch Design, Columbia Univ Archit, Planning & Preserv, 77-. *Awards:* First Prize, Univ Wis, Green Bay, 75, Broward Co Housing Authority, 80, Washington, DC Hebrew Cong, 83, Nat Competition to create sculpture for Washington Hebrew Congregation, DC, 84, Tri-State Vets Mem, 87; Preservation by Design Award, Swain Sch Design, 89. *Bibliog:* George McCue (auth), Sculpture City: St Louis, Hudson Mills Press, 88; Lineatus, Hotel & Motel Mgt, Harcourt Brace & Jovanovich, cover photo, 88; plus others; Has delivered 11 Keynote addresses. *Media:* stainless, bronze, wood, marble, All. *Collection:* Umo Art Gallery, College of Fine Art, Univ of Neb, Omaha; US Embassey Fountain, Moscow, 83, Triyud, Temple Shaave Emerth, Crev Coeur, Mo. *Publ:* contribr, Nat Community Arts Program, US Dept Housing Urban Development, 73; auth, Washington Univ Mag, Washington Univ, St Louis, Mo, 79; auth, Religion and Theatre, Bethel Col, St Paul, Minn, 8/80; contribr, A Christian Response to the Holocaust, Stonehenge Books, 81; coauth, Art Guidelines, Salt River Project, Phoenix, 89. *Mailing Add:* 27 Covington Rd St Louis MO 63132

SCHULTZ, STEPHEN WARREN
PAINTER, EDUCATOR
b Chicago, Ill, Aug 28, 1946. *Study:* RI Sch Design, 65-67; San Francisco Art Inst, BFA, 71; Stanford Univ, MFA, 74. *Work:* Equitable Life Assurance Corp, NY; Univ Iowa Mus, Iowa City; Stanford Univ; Boise Mus, Idaho; Brunier Mus, Iowa State Univ; McNay Art Mus, San Antonio, Tex; Hallmark, St Louis, Mo. *Exhib:* Walker Art Ctr, 77; Awards in Visual Arts, Nat Mus Am Art, Washington, 82, Denver Art Mus, 83 & Des Moines Art Ctr, 83; Iowa Artists, Des Moines Art Ctr, 82; Sid Deutsch Gallery, NY, 84 & 86; Minneapolis Mus Art, 86; Artists Who Teach, Fed Res Gallery, Wasnington, 87-; Lowe Gallery, Atlanta, 93 & 95; Sinoway Gallery, Chicago, 96;

Chac Mool Gallery, Los Angeles, Calif, 98; Paris Gibsons Mus, Great Fall, Mont, 99; Victoria Boyce Gallery, Tucson & Scottsdale, Ariz, 2000; Frye Mus, Seattle, 2002; Salt Lake Art Ctr, 2003; Mus Art, Spokane, Wash, 2006. *Pos:* Rockefeller Found artist-in-residence, Bellagio Ctr, Lake Como, Italy, 84; artist-in-residence, George Rickey Workshop, East Chatham, NY & Camargo Found, Cassis, France, 85; Juror, Ill Art Coun Fels, 90; vis artist, Univ Tex, Arlington, 80, Belgrade Acad Fine Arts, Yugoslavia, 86-87 & Am Acad Rome, 98. *Teaching:* Prof, Univ Iowa, 75-94 & Univ Wash, Seattle, 2003. *Awards:* Tiffany Found Fel, 79; Awards in Visual Arts, Southeastern Ctr Contemp Arts, 81; Fulbright Fel, Int Exchange Scholars, 86; fels painting, Nat Endowment Arts, 90. *Bibliog:* RS Coburn (auth), Raising veil of emerging artist, Smithsonian Mag, 5/82; Southeastern Ctr Contemp Art, Awards in Visual Arts (film), PBS TV, 83; All art considered (interview), Nat Pub Radio, 5/19/82; Stephen Schultz, Selected Works, 88-94 (catolog); Johanna Hays, (essay), 95; Stephen Schultz, A Classic Vision, Paris Gibson Mus, 97. *Media:* painting and drawing. *Dealer:* Daniel Bessekche Gallery Paris. *Mailing Add:* 915 Poplar St Sandpoint ID 83864

SCHULZ, ANNE MARKHAM
HISTORIAN, EDUCATOR
b New York, NY. *Study:* Radcliffe Col, BA, 59; New York Univ, Inst Fine Arts, MA, 62, PhD, 68. *Pos:* Visiting scholar, Brown Univ. *Teaching:* Asst prof Renaissance art, Univ Ill, Chicago Circle, 67-68; vis lectr to vis prof & res assoc, Brown Univ, 68-. *Awards:* Basic Res Grant & Sr Fel, Nat Endowment Humanities, 82-86; Am Coun Learned Soc Sr Fel, 87-88; Fulbright Fel, Italy, 96-97; Associate, Vill I Tatti, Florence, Italy, 1983-4; Kress Fel, 1974-75, 1993-95, 2005-06. *Mem:* Col Art Asn; Renaissance Soc. *Res:* Venetian Renaissance sculpture; early Renaissance art. *Publ:* The sculpture of Giovanni & Bartolmeo Bon, Transactions Am Philos Soc, 78; Niccolo di Giovanni Fiorentino and Venetian Sculpture of the Early Renaissance, CAA Monographs Series 33, New York Univ Press, 78; Giambattista and Lorenzo Bregno: Venetian Sculpture in the High Rennaissance, Cambridge Univ Press, 91; Luciano Bellosi, Brunella Teodori & Giorgio Semmoloni (contrbs), Nanni di Bartolo e il portale della Basilica di San Nicola a Tolentino, Centro Di, Florence, Italy, 97; Giammaria Mosca called Padovano: a Renaissance Sculptor in Italy and Poland, (2 vols), Penn State Press, 98; The Sculpture of Bernardo Rossellino and his Workshop, Princeton Univ Press, 77; Antonio Rizzo, Sculptor and Architect, Princeton Univ Press, NJ, 1983; Manuela Moresi & Toto Bergamo Rossi (contrbs), The Badoer - Giustiniani Chapel in San Francesco della Vigna, Venice, Centro Di, Florence, Italy, 2003. *Mailing Add:* 192 Bowen St Providence RI 02906

SCHULZ, JUERGEN
EDUCATOR, HISTORIAN
b Kiel, Ger, Aug 18, 27; US citizen. *Study:* Univ Calif, Berkeley, BA, 50; Courtauld Inst Art, Univ London, PhD, 58. *Collection Arranged:* Master Drawings from California Collections (coauth, catalog), 1968; Caricature and Its Role in Graphic Satire (coauth, catalog), 1970; The Origins of the Italian Veduta (coauth, catalog), 1978. *Teaching:* From instr to prof hist art, Univ Calif, Berkeley, 58-68; assoc cur Renaissance art, Art Mus, 64-68; prof, Brown Univ, 68-, A V Rosenthal prof hist art, 90-94; SH Kress prof, Ctr for Advanced Study in the Visual Arts, Nat Gallery of Art, 2000-01. *Awards:* Grande Ufficiale, Stella Solidarieta Repub Italiana, 68. *Mem:* Col Art Asn Am; Soc Archit Historians; Centro Internaz Studi Architettura A Palladio Vincenza (mem comitato scienfifico). *Res:* History of Italian medieval architecture and urbanism; history of Italian 16th century art and architecture. *Mailing Add:* Prog Hist Art Brown Univ Box 1855 Providence RI 02906

SCHULZE, FRANZ
HISTORIAN, CRITIC
b Uniontown, Pa. *Study:* Northwestern Univ; Univ Chicago, B, 45; Art Inst Chicago, BFA, 49, MFA, 50, PhD, 45; Acad Fine Arts, Munich. *Work:* Art Inst Chicago, Ill; Mus Contemp Art, Chicago, Ill. *Exhib:* One man show Jan Cicero Gallery, Chicago, 98. *Pos:* Art critic, Chicago Daily News, 62-78; corresp ed, Art in Am, 65-; contrib ed, Art News, 75-; contrib ed, Inland Architect, 75-, Chicago Sun-Times, 78-85. *Teaching:* Instr, Purdue Univ, 50-52; prof, Lake Forest Col, 52-74, Hollender prof art, 75-91. *Awards:* Ford Found Critics Fel, 64; Harbison Award, Danforth Found, 71; Graham Found Advan Fine Arts Fel, 71 & 80; and others. *Mem:* Col Art Asn Am (bd dir, 81-82); Arch Am Art; Am Asn Univ Prof; Ragdale Found. *Media:* Painting; Drawing. *Res:* Art and architecture in the Midwest, especially Chicago. *Specialty:* Painting and drawing. *Publ:* Ed, Chicago's Famous Buildings, 1993; Philip Johnson: Life & Work, 1994; The Farnsworth House, 1997; others; auth, Mies van der Rohe: A Critical Biography, 1985; 30 Miles North, a History of Lake Forest College, Its Town and Its City of Chicago, 2000; coauth (with Kevin Harrington), Chicago's Famous Buildings, 5th edit, 2004. *Mailing Add:* Lake Forest Col Dept Art Lake Forest IL 60045

SCHULZE, PAUL
DESIGNER
b New York, NY, Feb 7, 34. *Study:* Parsons Sch Design, cert; NY Univ, BS(indust design), 60. *Work:* Corning Mus Glass; Nat Air & Space Mus, Washington, DC; NC State Univ; also numerous pvt collections. *Comn:* Crystal cross, Steuben Glass, St Clement's Episcopal Church, NY. *Exhib:* Studies in Crystal 1966, Steuben Glass, NY, 65; Islands in Crystal, Steuben Glass, NY, 66; New Glass, Corning Mus Glass, 79. *Pos:* Off interior design, Bus Equip Sales Co, New York, 60-61; designer, Steuben Glass, 61-69, asst dir design, 69-70, dir design, 70-87; prin, Paul Schulze Design, 87-. *Teaching:* Instr eng drawing & three dimensional design, Parsons Sch Design, 62-70. *Awards:* Student Competition Award, Am Soc Indust Designers, 59. *Bibliog:* Harry Abrams (auth), Contemporary Glass, Glass Animals, others. *Mem:* Guild for Organic Environment; Nat Alumni Coun Parsons Sch Design; NY State Craftsmen. *Media:* Glass, Mixed. *Publ:* Illusr, Organics, Steendrukkerij & Co, Holland, 61. *Mailing Add:* PO Box 134 New Suffolk NY 11956-0134

SCHULZKE, MARGOT SEYMOUR
PAINTER, WRITER
b San Francisco, Calif. *Study:* Brigham Young Univ, BA, 59, additional study with Albert Handell, Constance Flavell Pratt, William Schultz, Richard Yip & Frank Zuccarelli. *Work:* Sutter Auburn Faith Hosp, Calif; Blanning & Baker Inc, Sacramento; Auburn Diagnostic Soc & Surgery Ctr, Auburn, Calif. *Comn:* Shirley Canyon (pastel painting), Squaw Valley Auburn Diagnostic Ctr, Calif; 7 paintings, Sutter Auburn Faith Hosp, Auburn, Calif; Phipps Family At Home (group), comn by Dr & Mrs Mark Phipps, Auburn, Calif; Megan (portrait), comn by Mr & Mrs Steven Martini, Bellingham, Wash; portrait, Jason and Dallon Phipps, comn by Dr & Mrs Mark Phipps; Lee Remmel (portrait), comn by Richard Remmel. *Exhib:* Pastel Soc Am Nat Open Exhibs, Nat Arts Club, NY, 86-94; Pastel Soc West Coast Nat Open Exhibs, Ctr Galleries, Sacramento Fine Arts Ctr, Calif, 86-2003; 3rd Ann Orig Art Showcase, Prestige Gallery Ltd, Toronto, Can, 91; 69th Ann Spring Salon, Springville Mus, Utah, 93; Monmouth Mus, Lincroft, NJ, 94; NW Pastel Soc, Washington, 97; Ore Pastel Soc, Coos Bay Mus, 97; Audubon Artists of Am, Salmagundi Club, New York City, 2002; Triton Mus, Santa Clara, Calif, 2004; Degas Pastel Soc, 10th Biennial, New Orleans, 2004-05; Lauren Rogers Mus, Laurel, Miss, 2004-05; Haggin Mus, Stockton, Calif, 2006. *Pos:* Pres (founding), Pastel Soc West Coast, 85-88, & adv bd mem, 88-, pres, 95-97 & bd dir 85-; juror selection, Pastels USA, 2003, Sierra Pastel Soc Nat Open Exhib, 2002. *Teaching:* Lectr, creativity, oil painting, Educ Week Tours, Brigham Young Univ, Educ, 66-67; instr pastel & oil, Roseville Arts Ctr, 85-2005; instr pastel, Ultima Nat Art Symp, Yellowstone, 91; workshops, Mex, 98, 2001, 2002; High Sierra Workshop, 2003, 2006; prof emer, BYU, March, 2000. *Awards:* Distinguished Pastelist, Pastel Soc West Coast, 89; First Place, Sacramento Fine Arts Ctr, 3rd Nat Open, 90; Best of Pastel Award, Mother Lode Nat Open, 2000; and numerous others; awards in 14 Pastels USA Internat Exhibs; Distinguished Emer award, BYU; Pastel Laureate Award, PSWC Hall Fame, 2006. *Mem:* Am Artists Prof League, NY; Pastel Soc Am, NY; Pastel Soc West Coast, Sacramento (dist pastelist); Calif Art Club; Degas Pastel Soc; Am Soc Portrait Artists. *Media:* Pastel, Oil. *Res:* The arts. *Specialty:* Realist & impressionist galleries. *Interests:* Hispanic women & children; mountains, rivers & shore Sierras, Pacific Coast & SW; archit wealth of Europe,Near East & Mexico. *Publ:* featured artist, Pastel Interpretations by Madlyn Ann C Woolwich, Northlight, fall 93; featured artist, Best of Pastel, 96 & Landscape Inspirations, 97, Rockport Publ & Calif Season Mag, spring 99; Artspeak & The Westsider, New York City; cover artist & feature article, Guide to the Arts, summer 2002; over 3 doz articles, Pastel Journal, Artists Mag & Am Artists, 1992-2006; contribr, Pure Color: The Best of Pastel, Northlight, Cincinnati, 2006; auth, Guide to the Arts Mag, Grass Valley, Calif, 2001; contribr, Best of Pastel, Rockport Pubs, Mass, 1992; auth, A Painter's Guide to Design & Composition, North Light, Cincinnati, Ohio, 2006. *Dealer:* Sunset Oaks Gallery Auburn CA; Doiron Gallery Sacramento CA. *Mailing Add:* 1840 Little Creek Rd Auburn CA 95602

SCHUMACHER, JUDITH KLEIN
SCULPTOR
b Pittsburgh, Pa, 47. *Study:* Drew Univ, BA, 95; Mason Gross Sch Arts, Rutgers Univ, MFA; studied with John Goodyear, Robert Cooke & Lynne Allen. *Exhib:* Hunterdon Mus Art, NJ, 99; Greenwich St Studio Ctr, New York City; Gallery at Bristol-Myers Squibb, Princeton, NJ; Jane Voorhees Zimmerli Art Mus, Rutgers Univ, NJ, 2001. *Teaching:* instr, Visual arts, Middlesex Co Col, Edison, NJ, 97-2000; instr, ceramic sculpture, Rutgers Univ, 97-2000. *Media:* Ceramic. *Specialty:* Site Specific Installations. *Mailing Add:* 2155 Huntington Ct S Wexford PA 15090-7590

SCHURR, JERRY M
PAINTER, PRINTMAKER
b Philadelphia, Pa, May 4, 40. *Study:* Univ Pa, 58-59; Pa Acad Fine Arts, 58-60 & 65-69; Univ Hawaii, 59-60; Temple Univ, 61-63. *Work:* Philadelphia Mus Art, Pa; Del Art Mus, Wilmington; Portland Mus Art, Ore; Minneapolis Mus Art, Minn; US Dept State (Vienna Embassy), Vienna. *Exhib:* Ann Fel Show, Pa Acad Fine Arts, Philadelphia, 68, 69, 70, 74 & 86; Philadelphia Print Club, 74, 77, 78 & 86; The Philadelphia Civic Ctr Mus Exchange Exhib, Tel Aviv, Israel, 80; 65th Ann Multiple Impressions Traveling Show, Philadelphia Print Club, 80; Fel Show PAFA, Noyes Mus, NJ, 86; Nat Acad Art for the Parks, Smithsonian Inst, Washington, 87. *Teaching:* Instr serigraphy, Tyler Sch Art, Elkins Park, Pa, 77-78. *Awards:* Thouron Prize, Pa Acad Fine Arts, 66; Eugene Feldman Mem Prize, Philadelphia Print Club, Philadelphia Mus Art, 77; Nat Arts Club Purchase Prize, 79. *Bibliog:* Talking Posters, Art Bus News, 11/85; Victoria Donahoe (auth), The panorama of the west, Philadelphia Inquirer, 4/11/86; Roni Henning (auth), Silkscreen Painting, 10/94. *Mem:* Artist Equity; Philadelphia Print Club; Pa Acad Fine Arts (alumni). *Media:* Acrylic; Serigraphy, Silkscreen. *Dealer:* Summa Gallery 85th & Amsterdam New York NY; Ira Genstein 1121 Fox Chase Rd Jenkintown PA 19046

SCHUSELKA, ELFI
PAINTER, SCULPTOR
b Vienna, Austria, Feb 13, 40. *Study:* Art hist & theatre, Univ Vienna; Acad Arts, Vienna; photog, Graphic & Experimental Inst, Vienna; studied with Oskar Kokoschka, Sch of Vision, Salzburg, Austria; Art Students League, NY; Pratt Graphics Ctr, NY. *Work:* Albertina, Vienna, Austria; Amon Carter Mus Western Art, Ft Worth, Tex; Bibliot Nat, Paris, France; Nat Mus Hist, Taipei, Taiwan; Mus Mod Art, NY; Mus Contemp Art, Ibiza, Spain; Mus Int Contemp Graphic Art, Fredrikstad, Norway; Mus d'Art Contemporian, Skopje, Yugoslavia. *Exhib:* Brooklyn Mus Print Exhib, NY, 70 & 76; Exhib Graphic Art, Frechen, Ger, 76, 78, 83 & 90; solo exhibs, 55 Mercer Gallery, NY, 77, 79, 82 & 84, Condeso/Lawler, 80, 83, 85 & 87, Joan Hodgell Gallery, Sarasota, Fla, 85, Broadway Windows, NY Univ, 88 & Neue Galerie, Vienna, 88, Henry Chauncey Conf Ctr, Princeton, NJ, 90, Al Galerie, Stuttgart, 93, Glaskasten, Leonberg, Stuttgart, 96, Austrian Trade Comn, 2000; Musee de Petit Format, Couvin,

Belgium, 81, 83, 85, 87, 89, 91, 93, 98, 2000; Int Graphic Exhib, Taipei Fine Arts Mus, Taiwan, 83, 85, 89, 93, 99, 2000; Monumental Drawing, Brooklyn Mus, 86; Int Biennial Graphic Art Ljubljana, Tokyo, Japan, 88-89; Int Biennale Varna, Bulgaria, 89; Plaster in Contemp Art, Queens Mus, NY, 90; Int Triennial Graphic Art, Bitola, Macedonia, 94, 97, 2000; Austrian Trade Comn, New York City, 00; Glaskasten, Leonberg, Ger, 96; Group shows: Intern Biennale Bharat Bhavan, Roopankar, India, 02, 95, 91, 89, Musee du Petit Format, Couvin, Belgium, 02, 00, 98 93, 91. *Teaching:* Instr printmaking, Sch Visual Arts, New York, 70-73; instr art, Pratt/Phoenix Sch of Design, New York, 74 & Pratt Graphics Ctr, 78-80 & Baruch Col, City Univ New York, 89, 90, 91; vis artist Rutgers Univ, NJ, 76. *Awards:* Int Exhib Graphic Art Medal, Frechen, Ger, 78; Award, Ibizagraphic 82, Spain; NY Found Arts Grant, 86; Artist space, NYC, 88; Raciborz 2000, Poland, 00. *Bibliog:* Tiffany Bell (auth), article, Arts Mag, 1/78; Vivien Raynor (auth), NY Times, 8/6/78 & 12/26/82; Nancy Unger (auth), Gannett Newspaper, 1/21/83; Grace Glueck (auth), article, NY Times, 3/29/85; C Braunsteiner, Studio Interview for Seitenblicke, 99; Nora Novak, Cetatea Culturala, 01. *Dealer:* Al Galerie Edenhall Str 19 D-70597 Stuttgart Germany; Germany Glaskasten Leonberg Eltingerstr 11 Germany. *Mailing Add:* c/o Studio 13 133 Eldridge St New York NY 10002

SCHUSTER, CITA FLETCHER (SARAH E)
PAINTER, CONSULTANT
b El Paso, Tex, Sept 12, 29. *Study:* Vassar Col, AB, 50; Univ Tex, El Paso, with David Deming & Sally Bishop; Univ Calif, Los Angeles, Am Soc Appraisers sem fine arts; conserv & restoration with Nikoli Poloskov, 81; Cornucopia V, Am Soc Appraisers sem fine arts, London, 85. *Exhib:* One-man exhibs, Univ Tex, El Paso, 75 & 78; Int Woman's Art Slide Festival, 76; 19th Ann Sun Carnival Nat, El Paso Mus Art, Tex, 76-77; El Paso Designer Craftsmen Invitational, Univ Tex, El Paso, 78; Toys Designed by Artists, Ark Art Ctr, 79-80. *Pos:* Owner-dir, Two-Twenty-Two Gallery, El Paso, 63-72; fine art appraiser, 63-; chair art adv bd, El Paso Mus Art, 92-95; class I, curric adv & session leader, Leadership Art, El Paso; bd mem, Art Resources Dept, El Paso, Tex, 95-. *Teaching:* Session presenter, Leadership Art El Paso, 94; Ctr Lifelong Learning, Univ Tex El Paso, 96-98. *Bibliog:* Betty Chamberlain (auth), Professional page, Am Artist, 11/74; guest appearance, Spectrum - appraising fine arts, KCOS-TV, 86. *Mem:* Charter mem Visual Artists & Galleries Asn Inc; Appraisers Asn Am; founder Valuors Consortium, Houston; La Watercolor Soc; co-founder, Univ Tex El Paso, Friends Art, 87; sr mem Am Soc Appraisers (recertified, 98-03). *Media:* Watercolor, Acrylic. *Specialty:* Nineteenth and twentieth century painting, print and sculpture. *Publ:* Coauth, The Status Game, Avalon Hill, 82. *Mailing Add:* 5854 Mira Serena Dr El Paso TX 79912

SCHUSTERMAN, GERRIE MARVA
ART DEALER, GALLERY DIRECTOR
b Chicago, Ill, July 6, 28. *Study:* Univ Mich; Soc Arts & Crafts, Detroit; Univ Southern Calif, Irvine. *Pos:* Gallery dir, Art Angles Gallery, Orange, Calif, 71-. *Teaching:* Teacher & coordr, Rancho Santiago Community Col, 80-; Walker Elementary Sch, Santa Ana, Calif, 95. *Mem:* Prof Picture Framers Asn; Art Dealers Asn (bd mem). *Specialty:* Established regionalist artists. *Mailing Add:* Art Angles 940 W Chapman Ave Orange CA 92868

SCHUTTE, THOMAS FREDERICK
ADMINISTRATOR
b Rochester, NY, Dec 19, 35. *Study:* Valparaiso Univ, Ind, AB, 57; Ind Univ, Bloomington, MBA, 58; Univ Colo, Boulder, DBA, 63. *Pos:* Asst dean, Wharton Sch, Univ Pa, Philadelphia, 73-75; pres, Philadelphia Col Art, 75-83; dir, Union Independent Cols Art, 75; pres, RI Sch Design, 83-93; pres, Pratt Inst, Brooklyn, NY, 93-. *Interests:* American 18th and 19th century decorative arts. *Publ:* Auth, Is the antiques dealer aware of his economic position in the market place?, 1-5/63 & A salesmanship model for the antiques dealer, 4/64, Antiques Dealer; ed, An Uneasy Coalition: Design & Corporate America, Univ Pa, 75. *Mailing Add:* c/o Pratt Inst 200 Willougby Ave Brooklyn NY 11205

SCHWAB, CHARLES R
COLLECTOR
b Sacramento, Calif, 37. *Study:* Stanford Univ, 59, MBA, 61. *Pos:* mutual fund mgr, Marin Co, Calif, formerly; founder, chmn, Charles Schwab Corp, San Francisco, 71-, Chief Exec Officer, chmn, 71-2003, chmn, 2003-2004, Chief Exec Officer, chmn, 2004-; bd dir, The Gap, Inc, 86-2004, Seibel Systems, Inc; co-founder (with Helen Schwab) & chmn, Charles & Helen Schwab Found, 2001-; chmn, All Kinds of Minds Inst; bd trustees, Stanford Univ. *Awards:* Achievements inc, pioneer in discount brokerage bus, since 74; Named one of Top 200 Collectors, ARTnews Mag, 2004, 2005, 2006. *Collection:* Modern & contemporary art. *Publ:* Auth, How to be Your Own Stockbroker, 84, Guide to Financial Independence, 1998, You're Fifty - Now What?, 2001; coauth, (with Carrie Schwab Pomerantz): It Pays To Talk. *Mailing Add:* Charles Schwab & Co Inc 101 Montgomery St San Francisco CA 94104

SCHWAGER, MICHAEL R
EDUCATOR, CURATOR
b New York, NY, June 25, 53. *Study:* Calif Col Arts & Crafts, BFA, 75; John F Kennedy Univ, MA(mus studies), 82. *Collection Arranged:* One By Two: Artists in Collaboration, 92; Dangerous Pleasures: The Art of Judith Linhares (ed, catalog), 94; Private Visions: Artists' Sketchbooks, 95; The Urban Landscape: Recent Photographs, 95; Re-Presenting the Figure: The Body as Image & Object, 96. *Pos:* Exhib coordr, San Francisco Mus Mod Art, 84-88; cur, Richmond Art Ctr, Richmond, Calif, 88-90; dir, Univ Art Gallery, Sonoma State Univ, 91-. *Teaching:* Asst prof art hist, Sonoma State Univ, 94-; instr mus studies, Univ Calif, Berkeley, 96. *Mem:* Am Asn Mus. *Res:* Modern and contemporary art with an emphasis on Northern California art. *Publ:* Auth, Alvin Light: A Memorial Exhibition (brochure), San Francisco Mus Mod Art, 82; Viewpoints: 8 Installations (exhib catalog), Richmond Art Ctr, 91; Views from Afar: Contemporary German Art (exhib catalog), 93, Yoshitomo Saito: Bronze Sculpture 1986-1995 (exhib catalog), 95, Sonoma State Univ. *Mailing Add:* c/o Sonoma State Univ Univ Art Gallery 1801 E Cotati Ave Rohnert Park CA 94928

SCHWALB, SUSAN
PAINTER, INSTRUCTOR
b New York, NY, Feb 26, 44. *Study:* Carnegie-Mellon Univ, BFA, 65; Fel, Va Ctr Creative Arts, 73 & 92; MacDowell Colony, 74, 75 & 89; Yaddo, Saratoga Springs, NY, 81. *Work:* Brit Mus, London; Brooklyn Mus & Chase Manhattan Bank, NY; Ark Arts Ctr, Little Rock; Achenbach Found Graphic Arts, Fine Arts Mus San Francisco; Rose Art Mus, Waltham, Mass; Libr of Congress, Washington, DC; Israel Mus, Jerusalem; Nat Gallery of Art, Washington, DC; Mus of Fine Arts, Houston, Tex; Mus of Modern Art, NY; Fogg Art Mus, Cambridge, Mass; Mus of Fine Arts, Boston; and others. *Exhib:* Sacred Artifacts, Objects of Devotion, Alternative Mus, 82-83; one-woman shows, SOHO 20 Gallery, NY, 85 & 89, Brad Cooper Gallery, Tampa, Fla, 89, Yeshiva Univ Mus, 90, B'nai B'irth Klutznick Nat Jewish Mus, Wash, DC, 92-94, Andrea Marquit Fine Arts, Boston, 94, 96 & 99 & Am Cult Ctr, Jerusalem, Israel, 94, MY Art Prospects, 2001, Robert Steele Gallery, NY, 2003, 2005, 2006, Simon Gallery, Morristown, NJ, 2003 & 2006; Pino Molica Gallery (with catalog), 92-93; Cevini Haas, Scottdale, Ariz, 2002 & 2004; Solo Solomon Fine Arts, Seattle, 2005; Silverpoint Etcetra: Contemp Am Metalpoint Drawings, Art Arts Ctr, Little Rock, 92-93; Sanctuaries: Recovering the Holy in Contemp Art, Mus Contemp Relig Art, St Louis Univ, Mo, 93; Power, Pleasure, Pain: Contemp Women Artists and the Female Body, Fogg Art Mus, Harvard Univ, 94; Mus of Fine Arts, Houston, Tex, 2002; Danfoth Mus, 2004; and many more. *Pos:* Art dir, Aphra, Literary Mag, 74-75 & Women Artist News, 75-77. *Teaching:* Instr, Kean Col of NJ, 78-79, City Univ New York, 79-82 & Parsons Sch Art, 82; spec instr, Simmons Col, 88; vis assoc prof, Mass Col Art, Boston, 82-91; artist-in-residence, Tel Aviv Artists Studios, Mishkenot Sha'ananium, Jerusalem, Israel, 94. *Awards:* Comt for the Visual Arts Grant, New York, 77, 85 & 89; Int Commun Agency Travel Grant, 80. *Bibliog:* Cassandra Langer (auth), The Creation Series: 15 years of silverpoint, Women Artists News, fall 90; Helen A Harrison (auth), Contemporary metalpoint drawings, NY Times, 4/3/94; Alicia Faxon (auth), Doing nature in the 20th Century, Art New Eng, 6/94; Orisoltes Fixing the World Jewish American Painters in the 20th Cent., NE; Margaret Mathews Bernron, Light Touch, American Artist, Drawing, 2005. *Mem:* Coalition of Women's Art Orgn (exec comt, 77-78, vpres, 85-86); Col Art Asn; Women's Caucus Art (bd mem, 78-79, coord, Boston chap, 82-83). *Media:* Silverpoint Drawing, Acrylic. *Publ:* Illusr, Issue of Aphra, 73; contribr, Crafting with Plastics, Chilton Bk Co, 75; Women Artist News, Mid-March Assoc, 75-77; auth, Notes From Houston, Womanart, 78; contribr, Art New England, 95-. *Dealer:* Andrea Marquit Fine Arts Boston; Page Bond Gallery, Richmond, Va; Cervini Haas Gallery Scottsdale Ariz; Simon Gallery Morristown NJ; Brad Cooper Gallery Tampa Fla. *Mailing Add:* 10 Winsor Ave Watertown MA 02172

SCHWARCZ, JUNE THERESA
CRAFTSMAN, ENAMELIST
b Denver, Colo, June 10, 18. *Study:* Univ Colo, 36-38; Univ Chicago, 38-39; Pratt Inst, 39-41; Inst Design, Chicago, with Moholy Nagy. *Work:* Lannan Found, Palm Beach, Fla; Johnson Wax Collection; Kunstgewerbemuseums, Zurich, Switz; Nat Collection Fine Arts, Smithsonian Inst, Washington, DC; Mus Contemp Craft, NY; Met Mus Art, NY; Mus Fine Arts Boston; plus others. *Comn:* Enameled bowl with technique demonstration bowls, Mus Contemp Crafts, 58. *Exhib:* New Talent USA, Art in Am, 60; Objects USA, Johnson Wax Collection & Exhib, 69; one-man shows, Mus Bellerive (Kunstgewerbermuseum), Zurich, Switz, 71, Schmuckmuseum, Pforzheim, Ger, 72 & Mus Contemp Crafts, NY; two-man show, de Young Mus, San Francisco; Living Treasures of California, Crocker Mus, Sacramento, Calif, 85; Craft Today, Am Craft Mus NY, 86; Eloquent Object, Philbrook Mus Tulsa, Okla, 87; Retrospective, 40 yrs - 40 pieces, San Francisco Craft Mus, Calif, 98, Am Craft Mus, NY, 98 & Honolulu Acad Art, Hawaii, 99. *Awards:* Goldsmith 70, Minn Mus Art, 70; Fel, Am Craft Coun, 87; Gold Medal, Am Craft Coun, 96. *Bibliog:* Ventura (auth), June Schwarcz: Electroforming, Crafts Horizons, 11/65; Hammel (auth), June Schwarcz: Enamelist, Am Craft Mag, 10/81; Bennett (auth), article, Metalsmith, 83; Koplos (auth), June Schwarcz's Color Structures Metalsmith, 99; Forty Years/Forty Pieces, June Schwarcz, San Francisco Cart & Folk Art Mus (catalog), 98. *Mem:* Am Crafts Coun; No Calif Enamel Guild; The Enamelist Soc; Soc N Am Goldsmiths. *Media:* Enamel, Copper. *Interests:* Ethnic art. *Publ:* Contribr, Craftmen's World, 59 & Research in Crafts, 61, Am Crafts Coun; auth, The arts turn to plating, J Electroplaters Soc, 11/67

SCHWARM, HAROLD CHAMBERS
PAINTER, INSTRUCTOR
b Fairmont, WVa, May 5, 1925. *Study:* Univ Iowa, Iowa City, 45-48; Bradley Univ, Peoria, Ill, BFA, 51, MA, 52. *Work:* Kaiser Hosp, Milpitas, Calif; Univ Calif Cancer Ctr, Sacramento; Subway, Nuremburg, Ger; Galeria Aguntamiento, Naquera, Spain. *Comn:* Pier 66 (painting), Ft Lauderdale, Fla, 81; painting, Raley's Corp, Sacramento, Calif, 82; Kronick, Moskowitz, Tredmann & Girand (painting), Sacramento, Calif, 88; painting, McCuen & Steele, Rancho Condovg, Calif, 89; triptych, Hyatt Regency, Sacramento, 90. *Exhib:* Iowa Print Group, Philadelphia Mus Art, 47; Nat Print Ann, Brooklyn Mus, 48; Student show, Univ Iowa, Iowa City, 48; Painting, Butler Inst Am Art, 50; Bradley Prints, Art Inst Chicago, 54; Painting, Denver Art Mus, 63; Miniature show, Frye Art Mus, Seattle, 65; Claudia Chapline Gallery, Stinson Beach, Calif, 87-2005; Anagma Arte Contemp, Valencia, Spain; Galerie IM Gassla, Erlangen Ger, 95; Bay Model, Sausalito, Calif, 97; Bolinas Mus, Calif, 97; Civic Arts Plaza, Thousand Oaks, Calif, 99; Sf Art, Stasbourg, France, 2003; Strasbourg, France,

2003-04. *Pos:* Supervisor art serv, Southern Ill Univ, Carbondale, 55-59; designer, JB Talmadge Inc, Reseda, Calif, 72-74. *Teaching:* Instr sculpture & design, Bradley Univ, Peoria, Ill, 52-55; assoc prof graphic design, Calif State Univ, Northridge, 59-72. *Bibliog:* The Fine Art Index, 93, Internat'l Fine Art Refenence, Chicago; Art Fair Seattle, 93, Catalog; US Art Catalog, 95, Caskey, Lees; Who's Who in American Art, 2000. *Media:* Acrylic, Pastel, Watercolor. *Publ:* Contribr, California & the Western States, Roberts Publ Co, 63; illustr, many books for pvt & univ presses. *Dealer:* Claudia Chapline Gallery Stinson Beach CA. *Mailing Add:* c/o Claudia Chapline Gallery 3445 Shoreline Hwy PO Box 1117 Stinson Beach CA 94970

SCHWARTZ, ADRIENNE CLAIRE See Mim, Adrienne Claire Schwartz

SCHWARTZ, ALAN E
COLLECTOR
b Detroit, Mich, Dec 21, 25. *Study:* Univ Mich, BA, 47; Havard Law Sch, LLB, 50. *Hon Degrees:* Wayne State Univ, LLD, 83; Univ Detroit, LLD, 85. *Exhib:* Master Prints of Five Centuries, Detroit Inst Arts, Mich, 91; Univ Mich Mus Art; Univ Art Mus, Berkley; Art Gallery Ont; St Louis Art Mus. *Pos:* Assoc, Kelley, Drye & Warren, New York City, 50-52; dir, Detroit Symphony Orchestra; mem, Honigman, Miller, Schwartz & Cohn, Detroit, 52-; bd dir, Pulte Corp; bd dir, Detroit Renaissance, New Detroit, Jewish Welfare Fedn Detroit, Wayne State Univ Found; trustee, Community Found for Southeastern Mich, Interlochen Arts Acad; adv mem, Arts Comn, City of Detroit; mem investment comt, Kresge Found, Skillman Found Serv as ensign Supply Corps; vpres, bd dir, United Found. *Awards:* Recipient Mich Heritage Hall of Fame award, 84; George W Romney award for lifetime achievement in volunteerism, 94; Max M Fisher Community Serv award, 97; named one of Top 200 Collectors, ARTnews, 2004, 2005, 2006. *Mem:* Mich Bar Asn Clubs; Franklin Hills Co; Detroit, Econ. *Collection:* Old masters & modern prints. *Publ:* Ed, Harvard Law Rev, 50. *Mailing Add:* 4120 Echo Rd Bloomfield Hills MI 48302-1941

SCHWARTZ, AUBREY E
PRINTMAKER, SCULPTOR
b New York, NY, Jan 13, 28. *Study:* Art Students League; Brooklyn Mus Art Sch. *Work:* Nat Gallery Art, Washington, DC; Brooklyn Mus Art, Philadelphia Mus Art; Libr Cong, Washington, DC; Art Inst Chicago. *Comn:* Ed lithographs, Predatory Birds, Gehenna Press, 58, Midget & Dwarf, Tamarind Workshop, 60 & Bestiary, Kanthos Press, 61. *Exhib:* Young Am, Whitney Mus Am Art, 57; Print Coun Am Show, 57; one-man show, Grippi Gallery, NY, 58; Art USA, NY Coliseum, 59; Contemp Graphic Art, US State Dept, 59; retrospective, SUNY, Binghamton, NY, 97, McClaren Center, Barrie, Ont, Can, 2003; one-man show, Odon Wagner Gallery, Toronto, Can, 2003. *Teaching:* Prof art, State Univ NY, Binghamton, formerly; retired. *Awards:* Guggenheim Found Fel Creative Printmaking, 58-60; Tamarind Fel Creative Lithography, 60; First Prize Graphic Art, Boston Arts Festival, 60. *Dealer:* Odon Wagner Gallery 196 Davenport Rd Toronto ON M5R 1J2 Canada. *Mailing Add:* 104 Main St Afton NY 13730-3229

SCHWARTZ, BELLA
PAINTER, COLLAGE ARTIST
b New York, NY. *Study:* George Washington Univ, Washington, DC, BA, MA; Am Univ, Washington, DC. *Exhib:* Corcoran Gallery Art, Washington, DC, 56-57; Philadelphia Mus Art, 70; Washington Artists Equity, traveling, 72-73; Works on Paper Traveling Exhib, Kuumba Learning Ctr, 80. *Mem:* Washington Water Color Asn (pres, 72-74); Artists Equity Asn (pres, Washington area chap, 77-79); Women's Caucus Art. *Media:* Mixed. *Publ:* Ed, Paper: A Group Exhibition of Changing Uses and Concepts (exhib catalog), 12/79 & Clay: As Art and As Function, 11/81, Gallery 10 LTD, Washington, DC. *Dealer:* Studio Gallery 2108 R St NW Washington DC 20008

SCHWARTZ, BUKY
PAINTER
b Jerusalem, Israel, 32. *Study:* Avni Sch Art, Tel Aviv, Israel, 57-59, St Martin's Sch Art, London, Eng, 59-62. *Work:* Am Jewish Mus, Philadelphia; Rutgers Univ, New Brunswick, NJ; Jewish Mus, Bank Leumi Trust, Maritime Div Discount Banking, Ardin Co, Whitney Mus Am Art, NY; Israel Mus, Jerusalem; Tel Aviv Univ, Israel. *Exhib:* Solo exhibs, Eric Stark Gallery, NY, 89, Speces, Cleveland, Ohio, 89, Delta Gallery, Dusseldorf, Ger, 89, Spokane Ctr Gallery, Eastern Washington Univ, 90, Harn Mus, Gainesville, Fla, 96, Lutz Teutloff Gallery, Kohn, Ger, 92, Eric Stark Gallery, New York City, 89, Julie M Gallery, Tel Aviv, 99; Videosculpture Retrospective and Actual 1963-1989, Koln, Berlin, Zurich, 89; House 1990, Artists' Studios, Tel Aviv, Israel, 90; Frieze 1990, Paule Anglim Gallery, San Francisco, 90; Bookish Work, Reinpire Gallery, NY, 91; Video Sunflowers, Mucca Mus, Belg, 91; Video Sculpture, Middlebury Col, Vt, 92. *Awards:* Artpark, NYSCA Video Art Production Award, 83; Guggenheim Fel, USA, 87; Sculpture Grant, Nat Endowment Arts, 88; Guggenheim Grant for Publ, 90; Tel Aviv Found, Combining Art with Archit Prize, 1995; Pollock-Krasner Grant videosculpture, New York City, 92; Guggenheim Grant for Publ

SCHWARTZ, CARL E
PAINTER, PRINTMAKER
b Detroit, Mich, Sept 20, 35. *Study:* Art Inst Chicago, BFA; Univ Chicago, BFA. *Work:* Art Inst Chicago; Libr Cong & Smithsonian Inst, Washington, DC; Brit Mus; Brooklyn Mus Art; and many others. *Comn:* Northwestern Meml Hosp, Chicago, Ill; Lee Co Govt Bldg, Fla. *Exhib:* Am Painting Exhib, Smithsonian Inst, Washington, DC & traveling, 72; 18th Nat Print Exhib, Brooklyn Mus, 72-73; Calif Palace Legion of Honor, San Francisco, 73; Eight State Painting Exhib, J B Speed Mus Art, 75; one-man exhibs, Ill State Mus, 77, Ill Inst Technol, 77, Gallery 4, Alexandria, VA, 78, Art Inst Chicago, Jan Cicero Gallery, Chicago, 90; and many others. *Teaching:* Instr figure painting & drawing, NShore Art League, 58-85, Surburban Fine Arts Ctr, 60-85 & Deerpath Art League, Lake Forest, Ill & Edison Col, Ft Myers, Fla, Fla Gulf Coast Univ. *Awards:* Purchase Awards, J B Speed Mus Art, 73, Ill State Mus, 74 & Dickinson State Univ, 76; Artist Grumbacher Award, Logan Medal Art Inst Chicago, Ill, 88. *Bibliog:* Allan Davidson (auth), article, Art League News, 67; Thomas Carbol (auth), The Printmaker in Illinois, Ill Art Educ Asn, 72; Les Krantz (pub), American Artists, 85-90. *Mem:* NShore Art League; Fla Artist Group. *Media:* Acrylic; All

SCHWARTZ, DANIEL BENNETT
ILLUSTRATOR
b NY City, Feb 16, 1929. *Study:* Art Students League, 46; studied with Y Kuniyoshi; RI Sch Design, BFA, 49. *Exhib:* Solo shows include Davis Galleries, NY, 55, 56, 58, 60, Hirschl & Adler Galleries, NY, 63, Maxwell Galleries, San Francisco, 64, Badcock Galleries, NY, 67, FAR Galleries, NY, 70, Armstrong Galleries, NY, 85, 87, Hammer Galleries, NY, 94, Hudson River Gallery, Dobbs Ferry, NY, 2001; group shows at Albany Inst History and Art, Am Federation Arts, Bulter Inst Am Art, Library Congress, Nat Acad, Pa Acad Fine Art, Whitney Mus Am Art, Collection Nat Portrait Gallery, Munson-Williams-Proctor Inst, Bates Col, Brit Mus, Century Asn, as well as various others. *Teaching:* Instr private painting classes, 65-81, 90-95, Parsons Sch Design, 83. *Awards:* Louis C Tiffany Found Grant, 56, 60; 11 Gold Medals, Soc Illustrators, NY, 60-85; Purchase Prize, Am Acad Arts and Letters, 65, 84; Benjamin Altman Figure Prize, 92; named to Soc Illustrators Hall Fame, 2002. *Mem:* Nat Acad (acad, 97; Obrig Prize Painting, 90); Century Asn

SCHWARTZ, ELLIOTT S
PHOTOGRAPHER
Study: Univ Cincinnati, 71; Calif Inst Arts, BFA, 72; Yale Univ, MFA, 74. *Work:* Metrop Mus Art, NY; Int Ctr Photog, NY; Australian Nat Gallery, Canberra, Australia. *Exhib:* Photog as Fine Arts, Univ Fla, Gainesville, 74; Sequential Imagery in Photog, Broxton Gallery, Los Angeles, 76; Certain Landscapes, Castelli Photog, NY, 78; one-man shows, Galerie T Venster, Rotterdam, The Neth, 80, Sonnabend Gallery, NY, 81, Palazzo Dei Diamanti, Ferrara, Italy, 83, ICA, Boston, 85, Int Ctr Photog, NY, 87 & Jayne H Baum Gallery, NY, 90. *Awards:* Nat Endowment Arts Fel, 78 & 88. *Bibliog:* Stephen Westfall (auth), Art in America, 3/88. *Mailing Add:* 90 Fulton St New York NY 10038

SCHWARTZ, HENRY
PAINTER, INSTRUCTOR
b Winthrop, Mass, Oct 27, 27. *Study:* Sch Mus Fine Arts, Boston, dipl(traveling fel), 53; Akad Bildendekunst, Salzburg, Austria, with Oskar Kokoschka, dipl. *Work:* Mus Fine Arts, Boston; Wheaton Col, Mass; DeCordova Mus; Boston Pub Libr. *Exhib:* Five one-man shows, Boris Mirski Gallery, 56-68; Carnegie Inst Int, 61; Harvard Univ, 75; Boston Atheneum, 80; four one-man shows, Gallery Naga, 80-2004; Boston Expressionism, retrospective, De Cordova Mus, 86; 40 Year Retrospective, Fuller Mus, Brockton, Mass, 90; CoSo, Boston, A to Z, 3-4/2006. *Teaching:* Instr painting, Sch Mus Fine Arts, 56-90. *Awards:* Mus Sch Fel, 53; Ford Found Grant, 80. *Bibliog:* Christine Temin (auth), Boston Globe Profile, 90. *Media:* Oil, Acrylics; Assemblage. *Publ:* Illusr, filmstrip, United Churches of Christ, 61; illusr, Boston Mag, 64-65; Retrospective Catalog, Fuller Mus, Brockton, Mass, 90. *Dealer:* Gallery Naga 67 Newbury St Boston MA 02116. *Mailing Add:* Evan's Park 430 Centre St Apt 323 Newton MA 02458-2036

SCHWARTZ, LILLIAN (FELDMAN)
FILMMAKER
b Cincinnati, Ohio, July 13, 27. *Study:* Univ Cincinnati. *Hon Degrees:* Kean Col, NJ, LHD, 88. *Work:* Mus Mod Art, NY; Moderna Museet, Stockholm, Sweden; Stedlijk Mus Art, Amsterdam, Holland; Los Angeles Co Mus Art; Newark Mus Art, NJ. *Comn:* Painting/collage, Columbia Univ, NY, 67; murals, Int Bus Machines, Zurich, Switz, 72, sculpture, Miami, Fla, 77; New York Philharmonic, 76; mural, Am Telephone & Telegraph, Basking Ridge, NJ, 76; Hitachi, 88. *Exhib:* Mus Mod Art, NY, 68-69; Metrop Mus, NY, 72 & 73; Whitney Mus Am Art, NY, 73; 25th Int Film Festival, Cannes, France, 74; Hirshhorn Mus, Washington, DC, 75; Albright-Knox Art Gallery, Buffalo, NY, 76; Huntsville Mus, Ala, 78; Venice Biennial, 80; Grand Palais, Paris, 80; ELECTRA, La Musee d'Art Moderne de la Ville de Paris, France, 83; Lavillette, 88; IBM Gallery Sci & Art, 88; trav solo show, Retrospecitves of Film, 2006. *Collection Arranged:* Archive Coll, Ohio State Univ. *Pos:* Consult, Lucent Technologies Bell Labs Innovations, 2001. *Teaching:* Prof, Univ Md, 77-; adj prof, Kean Univ, Union, NJ, 81- & Rutgers Univ; grad fac, Sch Visual Arts, New York City, 90-92. *Awards:* Video Expos, Victor Co, Japan, 80; Artist of the Month, Hitachi, Japan, 88; Fel, World Acad Art & Sci; and others. *Bibliog:* Keating Productions, The Artist and the Computer (film), Am Telephone & Telegraph, 76; Jankel (auth), Creative Computer Graphics, Cambridge Press, 84; BBC special, Battle of the Wills, 94. *Mem:* Artists Equity Asn (NY & NJ); Artists League Cent NJ; Nat Acad Television Arts & Sci; Soc Motion Pictures & Television Engineers; Independent Cinema Artists & Producers; and others. *Media:* Computer, Video Books, DVD, DV. *Res:* artists & art analysis. *Publ:* Auth, The Computer Artist's Handbook (with Laurens R Schwartz), Norton Publ, 92; The Mask of Shakespeare, Pixel, 92; Electronic Restoration, Piero delle Francesca, Visual Computer, 92; Scientific American, 94; Leonardo: Appropriation Art, 96; co-auth, Leonardo da Vinci-The Hidden Mona Lisa, 2006. *Mailing Add:* 524 Ridge Rd Watchung NJ 07060

SCHWARTZ, MARVIN D
HISTORIAN
b New York, NY. *Study:* City Col New York, BS, 46; Inst Fine Arts, NY Univ, 47-51; Univ Del, MA, 54. *Collection Arranged:* 19th Century Am Tupperware Collection, Mus Modern Art. *Pos:* Jr cur, Detroit Inst Arts, 51-52; cur decorative arts & indust design lab, Brooklyn Mus, 54-68, ed publ, 59-60; adv dept design, Sears, Roebuck &

Co, 64-72; auth, weekly antiques column, New York Times, 66-72; lectr & consult, Metrop Mus Art, 68-; NY ed, Antique Monthly, 74-93. *Teaching:* Lectr, City Col NY, 48-51 & 56-64, State Univ NY, Purchase, 69-82 & NY Sch Interior Design, 94-. *Awards:* Stipend, Belg-Am Educ Found. *Mem:* Soc Archit Historians; Col Art Asn Am; fel HF DuPont Winterthur Mus; Nat Trust. *Res:* History of furniture. *Interests:* 19th century silver. *Publ:* Auth, Collectors Guide to American Clocks, 75; auth, Collectors Guide to American Silver, 75; plus many others; auth articles Grove Dict Art. *Mailing Add:* Educ Dept Metrop Mus of Art 5th Ave & 82nd St New York NY 10028

SCHWARTZ, RUTH
PAINTER, INSTRUCTOR
b Sept 24, 27. *Study:* NY Univ, with Leo Manso; Empire State Col, 84; Art in Am Sch, with Leo Manso, Great Neck, NY. *Work:* John T Mather Mem Hosp, Port Jefferson, NY; Atlantic Co Pub Libr, Atlantic City, NJ; Albright-Knox Art Gallery. *Exhib:* Long Island Artists, Nassau Co Mus Fine Arts, Roslyn Harbor, NY, 85; 43rd Western NY Exhib, Albright-Knox Gallery, Buffalo, NY, 90; Chautauqa Inst, NY; Burchfield Ctr, State Univ NY, Buffalo; State Col, Buffalo; Silvermine Guild of Artists, Inc, New Canaan, Conn; The Breakers, Palm Beach, Fla; Am Acad & Inst Arts & Letters, NYC; and others. *Teaching:* Instr, USDAN Ctr Performing & Creative Arts, Wheatley Heights, Long Island, NY, 81-88; Albright-Knox Art Gallery, Buffalo, NY, 89-; Art with Artists, Century Village, W Palm Beach, Fla. *Awards:* NAWA Award, 78, 80, 83, 85 & 88; Audobon Artists Citation of Merit, Am Acad & Inst Arts & Letters, 80; C Whinston Memorial Works on Canvas Award, Nat Asn Women Artists, 88. *Bibliog:* Park East (auth), article, Artspeak, 82; Malcolm Preston (auth), An invitational show, Newsday, 84. *Mem:* Nat Asn Women Artists (oil jury chmn, 80-81); Audobon Artists; Artist's Equity of NY; Buffalo Soc Artists (steering comt, 90). *Media:* All. *Interests:* Int Folk Dancing, Theater, Opera, Ballet, Piano. *Dealer:* Art Dialogue Gallery One Linwood Ave Buffalo NY 14209-2203; Albright-Knox Art Gallery, Buffalo, NY. *Mailing Add:* 1 Cambridge A West Palm Beach FL 33417-1301

SCHWARTZ, SING-SI
PHOTOGRAPHER
b New York, NY, Oct 20, 54. *Study:* New Sch for Social Res, advan photo printing with George Tice; psychol portraiture with Phillippe Halsman, 73; Rochester Inst Technol, AAS, 75, BS, 77; Artist in Res, Vermont Studio Ctr. *Comn:* Photograph, Burma Airline & posters, Burma Govt, 71; photograph, Vt Bi-Centennial Comn, 75; photographic mural, Wool Bur, Chicago Hq, 81; Eastern Spirit Western World, Transparencies in the film on artist, Diana Kan, 88. *Exhib:* One-man shows, Pen & Brush Club, NY, 77 & 85, Rochester Inst Tecnol, NY, 77, Dawson Gristmill Gallery, Vt, 77, Portchester Libr, NY, 78, Photographers Place, 86, Backer and Spielvogel, 86 & Nat Arts Club, NY, 88, Salmagundi Club, 2005. *Pos:* Mem staff, Villager Newspaper, New York, 68-74; photogr/correspondent, Cosmorama Pictorial, Hong Kong, 70-; photogr ed, New York Air, 83-85, & The New York Scene, 83-87. *Teaching:* Instr, Int Ctr Photog, New York, 81-88; adj prof, New York Univ, 83-84; Instr, New Brunswick Craft Sch, British Columbia, Can, 85. *Awards:* Elected as one of 100 outstanding Chinese abroad for accomplishments in photography, Chinese Govt, Taiwan, 71-77. *Bibliog:* Beautiful girls of Hong Kong seen through the eyes of photographer Sing-Si Schwartz, Ming-Pao Weekly, Hong Kong, 8/15/71; article, Interior Design, 10/81. *Mem:* Nat Arts Club; Am Soc Mag Photogr; assoc Allied Artists Am; Overseas Press Club. *Publ:* Photogr, Creating with Card Weaving, Crown Publ Inc, 73; photogr, The How and Why of Chinese Painting, Van Nostrand, 74; contribr, 40 American Watercolorists & How They Work, Watson-Guptill, 77; photogr, Joan Whitney Payson Gallery of Art, Westbrook Col, Maine, 77; photogr, A guide to flowers and flower painting, North Light, 80; Scientific Experiments for Kids, Harper & Row, 88; From the Desk of, Harcourt Brace Jovanovich, 89. *Mailing Add:* 15 Gramercy Park S Fl New York NY 10003

SCHWARTZ, THERESE
PAINTER, WRITER
b New York, NY, Dec 7, 28. *Study:* Corcoran Sch Art, Washington, DC; Am Univ; Brooklyn Mus Art Sch. *Work:* Corcoran Gallery Art, Smithsonian Inst & Howard Univ, Washington, DC; Nelson/Atkins Mus, Kansas City, Mo; Pepsico Collection, Purchase, NY; Ciba-Geigy Corp; Brooklyn Mus & New Sch Social Res, NY; Huntington Mus, San Francisco; plus many others. *Comn:* Mural, AEF Corp, Akron, Ohio, 96. *Exhib:* Humphrey Gallery, NY, 87-89 & 95; ARCO Int Art Fair, Madrid, Spain, 88; Humphrey Fine Art, NY, 89 & 92; Andrea Ross Gallery, Santa Monica, Calif, 90; B F Goodrich Co, Cleveland, 95; and others. *Pos:* Ed, NY Element, 68-72; contrib ed, Feminist Art J; mem bd dir, Princeton Arts J. *Awards:* Second Prize for Oils, Corcoran Gallery Art Regional Show, 52; New Talent USA Award, Art Am, 62; Women Artists Year Three, Mabel Smith Douglass Libr, Rutgers Univ, 73. *Bibliog:* Gerrit Henry (auth), Art in America, 6/92; Therese Schwartz, Artist as Witness, Homphrey, New York, 94; Anne M Carley (auth), Work of Therese Schwartz, WWW ARTS 4 ALL.com, 2000. *Mem:* Artists Equity. *Media:* All Media. *Publ:* Auth, Plastic Sculpture and Collage, Hearthside, 69; The politicalization of the avant-garde (ser), Art in Am, 11/71, 3/72, 3/73 & 1/74. *Dealer:* Richard Humphrey 2 West 45 St New York NY. *Mailing Add:* 161 W 75th St Apt 9A New York NY 10023

SCHWARZ, JUDITH
SCULPTOR, DRAFTSMAN
b Can, Nov 26, 44. *Study:* Univ BC, BA, 66; York Univ, MFA, 78. *Work:* Art Gallery Ont; Art Gallery Windsor; Hamilton Art Gallery; Nat Gallery Can; Oakville Galleries. *Comn:* Bronze sculpture, Skydome Corp, 90; Bronze & Steel sculpture, Waterpark Pl, 92. *Exhib:* Judith Schwarz, AGYU, York Univ, Toronto, 90; 9 x Toronto, Polytechnic Gallery, Newcastle-Upon-Tyne, Great Brit, 90; Legal Perspective, McMichael Can Art Collection, Kleinburg, Ont, 92; 64-94 Contemp Decades, ECIAD, Vancouver, Brit Columbia, 94; Fictive Space, Illingworth Kerr Gallery, Calgary, Alta, 94; Looking Back 111: 1986-1990, SAAG, Lethbridge, Alta, 95; Review 11, Mercer Union Gallery, Toronto, 96; Threshold, Power Plant, Toronto, Ont, 98. *Pos:* Mem bd, Mercer Union Gallery, 80-, Toronto Sculpture Garden, 84-88; pres, Mercer Union Gallery, 83-88; bd mem, Art Gallery York Univ, Toronto, 89-; bd mem, Art Gallery Ont, Toronto, 91-97. *Teaching:* Asst prof sculpture & drawing, York Univ, Toronto, Can, 78-, Assoc dir MFA Prog, 87-89, dir, MFA Prog, 94-97. *Awards:* Sr Grant Award, Ont Arts Coun, 93; Sr A Grant Award, Can Coun, 91, 92 & 96; Release Time Teaching Fel, York Univ, 96. *Bibliog:* Grant Arnold (auth), Disjunctions of Experience (exhib catalog), Art Gallery Windsor, 89; Annette Mangaard (dir), A Dialogue with Vision: The Art of Spring Hurlbut and Judith Schwarz (film), 90; Thomas McEvilley (auth), Fictive Space: The Collaboration of Judith Schwarz and Arlene Stamp (exhib catalog), Illingworth Kerr Gallery, 94. *Mem:* Adv mem Ont Arts Coun. *Dealer:* S L Simpson Gallery 515 Queen St W Toronto Ont M5V 2B4. *Mailing Add:* 26 Noble St Unit 7 Toronto ON M6K 2C9 Canada

SCHWEBEL, RENATA MANASSE
SCULPTOR
b Zwickau, Ger, Mar 6, 30; US citizen. *Study:* Antioch Col, BA, 53; Columbia Univ, MFA, 61; Art Students League, 68. *Work:* Am Airlines, Irvine, Calif; Jule Collins SMith Mus, Auburn, Ala; Comcraft Indust, Nairobi, Kenya; Southwest Bell, Houston; Heinrich Gruber House, Berlin, Ger; Colt Industs, NY; Columbia Univ, NY; Mus For Art, Sofia, Bulgaria. *Exhib:* Art of Northeast, Silvermine Guild, US Ann, 72, 76, 80, 95 & 98; Hudson River Mus Competitions, NY; Wadsworth Atheneum; New Britain Mus, Am Cult Ctrs, Egypt, Israel, Stamford Mus & Chesterwood Mus; one-woman show, Sculpture Ctr, NY; Katonah Gallery, Pelham Art Ctr, Berman/Daferner Gallery, NY; many others. *Pos:* Pres, Sculpture Guild, 80-83; trustee, Sculpture Ctr, NY, 80-86, cmn exhib comt, 84-86; bd dir, Fine Arts Fedn NY, 84 & Ams for Peace Now. *Awards:* Chaim Gross Found Award, 80; Medal of Honor, Nat Asn Women Artists, 81; Medal of Honor, Audubon Artists, 82. *Bibliog:* Padavano (auth), The Process of Sculpture, Doubleday, 81; Watson-Jones (auth), Contemporary American Women Sculptors, Oryx Press; Benton (auth), The Art of Welded Sculpture, Van Nostrand Reinhold. *Mem:* Sculptors Guild (pres, 80-83); Audubon Artists; Nat Asn Women Artists; NY Soc Women Artists; Silvermine Guild. *Media:* Welded Metal, Cast Metal and Wood. *Mailing Add:* 10 Dogwood Hills Pound Ridge NY 10570

SCHWEIG LANGSDORF, MARTYL
PAINTER, MURALIST
b St Louis, Mo, Mar 16, 17. *Study:* Washington Univ, AB; Colorado Springs Fine Arts Ctr, with Arnold Blanch & Boardman Robinson. *Work:* Whitney Mus Am Art, NY; Art Inst Chicago; Colorado Springs Fine Arts Ctr; Los Angeles Co Mus; St Louis Art Mus; Hirshhorn Mus & Sculpture Garden, Washington, DC; Brooklyn Mus; Miyagi Prefecture Mus Art, Japan; Calif Palace Legion Honor, San Francisco; Pa Acad Fine Arts; Ill State Mus; DuSable Mus, Chicago; Arnot Gallery, Elmira, NY; Greenville, SC Mus; Peace Mus, Chicago; Davenport Municipal Art Gallery, Iowa; Washington Univ, St Louis; Univ Ariz; Nat Mus Am Art, Washington, DC. *Comn:* Recorder of Deeds (mural), comn by Sect Fine Arts, Washington, 43; Darkness into Light (mural), Unitarian Church, Evanston, Ill, 62; 22 projections for Pierrot Lunaire, Fine Arts Quartet, Ill, 62; portraits, James Franck, Chandrasekar, Harry Kalven, Univ Chicago. *Exhib:* Am Drawing Biennial XXIV, Norfolk Mus Arts, 71; one-person shows, Art Inst Chicago, 76, Fairweather-Hardin Gallery, 77, 81, 83 & 88, Ill State Mus, 78, Lake Forest Col, 79 & Brooklyn Mus, 86; Oriental Inst Mus, Chicago, Ill, 87; Gibbes Mus, Charleston, SC, 88; Ill State Mus Art Gallery, Chicago, 90; Tokyo Expo, 90; Printworks Gallery, Chicago, 95, 97, 99, 2002, 04; and others. *Pos:* Art ed, Atomic Sci Bulletin, 45-72; exec comt, Artists Equity Asn Chicago, 58-69; bd dir, Arts Club & Oxbow; adv bd, Ragdale Found. *Teaching:* Instr painting, Univ Chicago, 65-70; artist-in-residence, Tamarind Inst, Univ NMex, 74. *Awards:* Logan Award & Medal, 50 & William Bartels Award, 57, Art Inst Chicago; Am Inst Archit Honor Award, 62. *Bibliog:* George McCue (auth), Martyl, St Louis Dispatch, 69; interview (film), WTTW Pub TV, 79; Michael Bonesteel, article, New Art Examiner, 83; History Channel, The Dooms Day Clock, 2003. *Mem:* Arts Club Chicago; Renaissance Soc (pres, 70-71); Oxbow Sch Art. *Media:* Acrylic; Ink. *Specialty:* Prints, Drawings & Paintings on paper. *Publ:* Contribr, Methods and Techniques of Gouache Painting, 46; auth, Cliches, old and new, St Louis Post-Dispatch, 67; New Art Examiner--Fred Sweet, 68; introduction to The Ste Genevieve Artists Colony & Summer sch Art, James G Rogers Jr, 98. *Dealer:* Printworks 311 W Superior Suite 105 Chicago IL 60610; Thea Burger Assoc PO Box 842 Barnard VT 05031. *Mailing Add:* 645 S Meacham Rd Schaumburg IL 60193

SCHWEISS, RUTH KELLER
SCULPTOR, DESIGNER
Study: Washington Univ, St Louis, fine arts cert; Cranbrook Art Acad, Bloomfield Hills, Mich, three yr int fel, sculpture with Carl Milles. *Work:* Many pvt collections. *Comn:* Blachette (bronze), Founder Monument, St Charles, Mo, 72; Children in the Rain, Ger Coun, Hamm, Ger, 73; Still Point (12 ft bronze fountain), Ritz-Carlton, Hotel, St Louis, Mo; bronze mem, Leif Sverdrup, St Louis, 79; Plaza Frontenac: In Paradise, St Louis, Mo, 87; Five eighteen ft Bronze Ballerinas, Adams Mark Hotel, Denver, Colo, 97; Elizabeth (17 ft sculpture), Clayton (Mo) Community Ctr. *Exhib:* Nat Acad Design, NY, 43; Detroit Art Mus Regional Show, Mich, 43; Pacific Show, Hawaiian Art Mus, Honolulu, 44; Int Art Show, Rotunda Gallery, London, 73; Ars Longa Gallery, Houston, 74. *Awards:* Mus Purchase Prize, Cranbrook Art Mus, 42; Ruth Renfrow Sculpture Prize, St Louis Art Mus, 45; Thalinger Sculpture Prize, St Louis Artists Guild, 50. *Bibliog:* Ruth Keller Schweiss, Gonterman Assoc, 65; The World of Ruth Keller Schweiss (film), Rick Noel, 74; picture story, St Louis Home/Garden, 79. *Mem:* Acad Prof Artists (exec dir, 68-83); Nat Soc Arts & Lett (corresp secy, 69-71, treas, 75-); Media Nine; St Louis Artists Guild (secy & mem bd, 65-67). *Media:* Bronze Castings of Limited Editions from Any Carved or Modeled Medium. *Mailing Add:* 4 Daniel Rd St Louis MO 63124

SCHWEITZER, JOHN ANDREW
COLLAGE ARTIST, CURATOR
b Simcoe, Ont, Can, Oct 6, 52. *Study:* Univ Western Ont, London, with Paterson Ewen & Michael Ondaatje, scholar, 73, Gold Medal Visual Arts, 73, BFA (hons, visual arts), 74; York Univ, Toronto, with Vera Frenkel & Sir Anthony Caro, MFA(painting), 78, Clement Greenberg, 79; Robert Motherwell, 89 & 91; Northrop Frye, 90. *Work:* York Univ, Toronto, Ont; Lynnwood Arts Ctr, Simcoe, Ont; Nat Capital Comn; La Citadelle, Quebec City; McIntosh Gallery, Univ Western Ont, London; Univ de Montreal, Que; Art Gallery Windsor, Ont; Mc Gill Univ, McCord Mus, Montreal, Que, Batcrest Ctr, Toronto, Ont; Bibliotheque Nat, Montreal; Musee de Joliette, Que; Univ Cape Brenton, Nova Scotia. *Comn:* Mus emblem, Ont Heritage Ctr, Delhi, Ont, 90; Mnemosyne (libr mural), Grand Erie Dist Bd Educ, Brantford, Ont, 91; The Equine Trilogy book design, comn by Dr JL Southin, McGill Univ, Montréal, Que, 94; Hosp Gén Montréal, Que, 96; Restaurant Toqué, Montréal, Que, 97; Astral Media, Montreal, Que, 99; comn by Charlie Trotter, Chicago, 2000; emblem, montreal Print Collectors Soc, 2001. *Exhib:* Homage to Duchamp, London Regional Art Gallery, Ont, 78; Accrochage Gallerie Suzanne Bollag, Zurich, 74; No Solution-A Suspense Thriller, Vancouver Art Gallery, BC, 78; Re:union, Art Gallery York Univ, Toronto, Ont, 80; Parallels; Girardoni: Schweitzer, Stephen Haller Fine Art, NY, 91; Sunt Lacrimae Rerum, Champigny, Montréal, Que, 92; Power Plant, Toronto, Ont, 97; The Pilgrimage, McGill Univ, Montreal, 97; Of Porphyry, Univ Western Ont, London, 99; The Erehwon Cycle, Centaur Theatre, Montreal, 99; The Arcadian Suite, Goethe-Institut, Toronto, Ont, 99; Galerie Christine Chassay, Montreal, Que, 2000; The Shapes of Time: 1991-2001, Visual Art Ctr, Montreal, Que, 2001. *Collection Arranged:* Mapplethorpe: 1978-1984, Galerie John A Schweitzer, 84; Bauhaus: Zweite Generation, Galerie John A Schweitzer, 85; Art Against AIDS (auth, catalog), Galerie John A Schweitzer, 86; Domus via Domus, Galerie John A Schweitzer, 88; Five Architectures (coauth, catalog), Galerie John A Schweitzer, 89; Duane Michals: Upside Down, Galerie John A Schweitzer, 89; Bolley Calzetta: Une Perspective de XV Ans (coauth, catalog), Galerie John A Schweitzer, 89. *Pos:* Vpres, Can Cult Progs, Montréal, Que, 80-84; trustee, La La La Human Steps Dance Co, Montréal, Que, 85-90; pres, Found John A Schweitzer, Montréal, Que, 94-; art comt, UNICEF, 95 ; acquistion comt, Univ de Montreal, Que, 2000-. *Teaching:* Asst prof painting, York Univ, Toronto, Ont, 76-78; Bishop's Univ, Lennoxville, Que, 83, McGill Univ, Montréal, Que, 85 & 95 & Banff Ctr, Alta, 87; Goethe Inst, Toronto, 2000. *Awards:* John G Rowe Fine Arts Scholar, Univ Western Ont, London, 73; Grant Hall Soc, Queen's Univ, Kingston, Ont, 96; Rector's Circle, Universite de Montreal, Que, 98; N C James Soc, Univ Western Ont, 99; President's Circle, Mus des Beaux-Arts de Montreal, 2000; Prix des Amisdm Mus d'Art Contemp, Montreal, Que, 2000. *Bibliog:* Howard Reitman (dir), Art Appreciation: City Beat (film), Can Broadcasting Corp, 94; Margaret Atwood (auth), Underbrush Man, 97; Ricardo L Castro (auth), The Pilgrimage, 98; James Miller (auth), Of Porphyry, 99; The Arcadian Suite, 99; John K Grande (auth) Border Crossings, 2000; Melanie Reinblatt (auth), ETC: MTL, 2000; Monique Brunet Weinmann (auth), Vie des Art, 2001; Ricardo L Castro (auth), The Shapes of Time: 1991-2001, 2001. *Mem:* Docomomo Int, Montréal, Que; Art & Design Coun Embassy Row, Montréal, Que (chmn, 92-); Montréal Print Collectors Soc. *Media:* Collage, Painting. *Collection:* 20th Century American & European painting, sculpture, photography, architectural and decorative arts; outsider and tribal art. *Publ:* Auth, Louis Comtois and the hagiographical icon, ELAAC, 90; Parallels; Girardoni: Schweitzer, Stephen Haller Fine Art, 91; Marcel Saint-Pierre, a theatrical prescience, ELAAC, 91; Anish Kapoor drawings at the Tate Gallery, London, ETC Montréal, 91; Peter Dickinson, ETC, Montréal, 96; XXV Reunion, Univ Western Ont Press, London, 99. *Dealer:* Galerie Christiane Chassay 358 rue Sherbrooke Est Montréal Québec Canada H2X 1E6. *Mailing Add:* 1545 Ave Docteur-Penfield Montreal PQ H3G 1C7 Canada

SCHWEIZER, PAUL DOUGLAS
ART HISTORIAN, MUSEUM DIRECTOR
b Brooklyn, NY, 46. *Study:* Marietta Col, Ohio, BA, 68; Univ Del, MA, 74, PhD, 79. *Collection Arranged:* Avant-Garde Painting & Sculpture in America: 1910-25 (collab effort, co-auth, catalog), Del Art Mus, spring 75; Edward Moran, Del Art Mus, 79; North Country Folk Art, 82, Cole's Course of Empire, 83 & The Voyage of Life: Paintings, Drawings, & Prints, 85, Munson-Williams-Proctor Inst, Utica, NY; 200 Yrs of Am Art, 86-87, The Art of Trenton Falls, 89, Munson-Williams-Proctor Inst, Utica, NY, 86-87; Alex Katz: A Drawing Retrospective, 91; Life Lines - Am Master Drawings, 1788-1962, Munson-Williams-Proctor Inst, Utica, NY, 94; Ferdinand Richardt's Drawings & Am: 1855-1859, 2007. *Pos:* Res consult, Choptank Collection, Middletown, Del, 76-77; cur collections, St Lawrence Univ, Canton, NY, 77-78, dir, Richard F Brush Art Gallery, 78-80; dir, Mus Art, Munson-Williams-Proctor Inst, Utica, NY, 80-; pres, bd of trustees, Williamstown Regional Art Conservation Lab, 87-91 & Gallery Asn NY State, 98-2000. *Teaching:* Instr art hist, Univ Del, Wilmington, 76; instr art hist, St Lawrence Univ, 77-78, asst prof fine arts, 78-80; adj fac Pratt at Munson-Williams-Procter Arts Inst, 2000-06. *Awards:* Unidel Fel, Univ Del, 72-76. *Mem:* Col Art Asn; Asn Art Mus Dirs. *Res:* John Constable and the Rainbow; American Painting and Sculpture of the 19th & 20th centuries; Historial American Drawings. *Publ:* Auth, John Constable, Rainbow Science and English Color Theory, Art Bulletin, 82; Literary source for Cole's Voyage of Life, 83 & Washington Irving's Friendship with William E West and the Impact of his History of New York on John Quider, spring 85, Am Art J; Who Was the Utica Artist, Clarion, 83; A note on the sources for W H Rinehart's Sleeping Children, MWPI Bulletin, 2/85; gen ed, Masterworks of Am Art at the Munson-Williams-Proctor Inst, Abrams, 88; William J Weaver & Polygraphy, Am Art J, 1999. *Mailing Add:* Munson-Williams-Proctor ArtsInst 310 Genesee St Utica NY 13502

SCHWENINGER, ANN ROZZELLE
ILLUSTRATOR
b Boulder, Colo, Aug 1, 51. *Study:* Univ Colo, 69-72; Calif Inst Arts, BFA, 73-75; also with Uri Shulevitz and Peter Hopkins, 75-. *Awards:* Notable Bk Award, Am Libr Asn, 82. *Media:* Watercolor, Pencil. *Publ:* Illusr, ABC Cat, Harper & Row, 83; illusr, Tales of Amanda Pig, Dial Press, 83; illusr, The Musicians of Bremen, 83 & illusr, Silent Night, 83, Western Publ; auth & illusr, Christmas Secrets, Viking Press, 84; and many others. *Mailing Add:* 2261 Rte 82 Ancram NY 12502

SCHWIEGER, C ROBERT
EDUCATOR, PRINTMAKER
b Scottsbluff, Nebr, Dec 5, 36. *Study:* Nebr Western Col, AA; Chadron State Col, BFA(educ); Univ Northern Colo, MA; Univ Denver, MFA. *Work:* Ohio State Univ; Miss Art Asn; Ga Inst Technol; Olivet Col, Mich; Oklahoma Art Ctr, Oklahoma City; and others. *Comn:* Gilded gold & mixed media on glass mural, Univ Northern Colo, 66. *Exhib:* Am Printmakers Invitational, Univ SDak; St Cloud State Univ; Univ Dallas; Prints of the 80's, Pratt Manhattan Gallery & Schafler Gallery, NY, 90; Nat Invitation Screenprint Traveling Exhib, Sch Mus Fine Arts, Boston, Mass; and others. *Teaching:* Assoc prof, Minot State Univ, 67-81, coordr art & prof, 81- 90, prof & chmn, dept art; prof & chmn, art dept, Mo Southern State Col, 90-91, prof art, 91-2000; adj prof art, Neb Wesleyan Univ, 2002-. *Awards:* Purchase Award, Univ Tex, Austin; Northwest Printmakers Int Jury Commendation, Seattle Art Mus, 71; 16th Nat Print & Drawing Exhib Jury Commendation, Okla Art Ctr, 74. *Bibliog:* The Complete Printmaker, Ross-Romano-Ross, rev ed, 89; Printmaking Techniques, Ayers Watson-Guptil Publ, 93; Waterbased Printing Inks Watercolor, Am Artist Publ, 93. *Mailing Add:* 7121 Shamrock Rd Lincoln NE 68506

SCOFIDIO, RICARDO & ELIZABETH DILLER
ARCHITECT, DESIGNER, EDUCATOR
Study: Diller: Cooper Union Sch Archit, BA (archit), 79. *Work:* Mus Mod Art, NY; San Francisco Mus Mod Art; Fond Nat d'Art Contemp; FRACs, France; Mus de la Mode, Paris. *Comn:* Cartier Found; Mus Mod Art, NY; New Mus, NY; Walker Art Ctr, Minneapolis; Palais des Beaux-Arts, Burssels. *Exhib:* Loophole, Mus Contemp Art, Chicago, 92; The Desiring Eye: Reviewing the Slow House (installation), Gallery MA, Tokyo, 92; Apparatus Drawing, Mus Mod Art, NY, 93; Case #00-17164, New Mus, NY, 93; Dysfunction, Ctr d'Art Contemporain de Castres, France, 93; Desiring Eye, I'dentity and Difference, Triennale, Milan, 94; Pelts, Thaddeus Ropac Gallery, Paris, France, 97; X, Y (permanent installation), Kobe, Japan, 97; Subtopia (electronic project), Int Ctr ICC Gallery, NTT, Tokyo, 97; Indigestion, Barbican Art Gallery, London, 97, Walter Phillips Gallery, Banff, Can, 97 & Biennial Nagoya, Japan, 97; Non-Place, San Francisco Mus Mod Art, 97; Interclone Hotel, Ataturk Airport, Istanbul Biennial, 97; Pageant (video installation), Johannesburg Biennial & Rotterdam Film Festival, 97; Slow House, At the End of the Century: One Hundred Years of Archit, Mus Contemp Art, Los Angeles, 98; Pub Faces/Pvt Places, Pusan Int Arts Festival, Korea, 98; Am Lawn; Surface of Everyday Life, Can Ctr Archit, Montreal, 98; His/Hers, Bathroom, Thomas Healy Gallery, NY, 98; Dress Code, Landesmuseum, Linz, Austria, 98; EJM1 Man Walking at Ordinary Speed, Dance Biennial Lyon, Ballet Opera, Lyon, 98. *Pos:* Scofido & Diller: Partner Diller & Scofidio (now Diller Scofidio & Renfro), New York City, 1979-. *Teaching:* Scofido: prof archit, The Cooper Union for Advancement of Sci & Art, currently; Diller: assoc prof archit design, Princeton Univ, NJ, 1990-, prof archit, currently. *Awards:* Chrysler Award Innovation in Design, 98-99; Fel, Graham Found Advancement Fine Arts, 98-99; Fel, NY Found Arts, 98-99; Brunner prize in Archit, Am Acad Arts & Letter, 2003. *Publ:* auths, Back to the Front: Tourisms of war/Visite aux armee: tourismes de guerre, FRAC Basse-Normandie, 94; Flesh: Architectural Probes, Princeton Archit Press, 95; Blur: The Making of Nothing, Abrams, 2002. *Mailing Add:* Diller Scofidio & Renfro 36 Cooper Sq New York NY 10003

SCOGIN, MACK
ARCHITECT, EDUCATOR
Study: Ga Inst Tech, Atlanta, BArch, 66. *Pos:* Sr design, archit Heery & Heery Archits & Engs, Inc, 67-81, vpres, coordr, 78-81, pres, COO, dir design, 81-84; principal, Scogin Elam & Bray Archits, Inc, Atlanta, 84-2000, Mack Scogin Merrill Elam Archits, Inc, Atlanta, 2000—. *Mem:* Nat Acad (assoc, 92, acad, 94-), Archit Soc, Atlanta (founding mem, mem bd sponsors 83—88); Am Inst of Archit's (nat comt on design, chmn steering comt 1987). *Mailing Add:* Mack Scogin Merrill Elam Archit Inc 111 JW Dobbs Ave Atlanta GA 30303

SCOTT, ARDEN
SCULPTOR
b Port Chester, NY, Oct 21, 38. *Comn:* Nassau Co Mus Fine Arts, NY, 77; pub sculpture, Riverhead, NY, 81; Atlanta Arts Festival, 83; Greenport Maritime Monument, 86. *Exhib:* Whitney Mus Biennial, 73; one-person shows, 112 Greene Gallery, NY, 74, AIR Gallery, NY, 97, AA Sites, NY, 2000, Oysterponds Mus, Orient, NY, 2004, Sculpture in the Garden, Greenpoint, NY, 2002; Aberdeen Arts Mus, Scotland, 83; Ways of Wood, Queens Col, NY, 84; Sculpture Ctr, NY, 84; Guild Hall Mus, EHampton, NY, 85; Live Steam Voices (performance), NY Harbor, 87 & Erie Canal, 88; Nat Print Exhib, Brooklyn Mus Art, 89; Cleveland Inst Art, Ohio,92; Printmaking Workshop Gallery, NY, 93; Sculpture Fest, Vt Arts Coun, Woodstock, 95; Outdoor Sculpture, SVt Art Ctr, Manchester, 96; Outdoor Sculpture Expo, Bristol, RI, 96; Parrish Art Mus, Southampton, NY, 98; Spirit of Place, Vt Arts Coun, Huntington, 98; Ahab's Wife, Newhouse Ctr Contemp Art, Staten Island, NY, 98; Sculpture in the Gardens, Erie Art Mus, Pa, 99; Van Deb Editions, Albright Knox, Buffalo, NY, 2002 & 2006; Long Island Maritime Mus, Sayville, NY, 2003; Northfork/Southfork, Parish AA Mus, Southampton, NY; Anthony A. Giordano Gallery, Dowling col, Oakdale, NY, 2006. *Teaching:* Prof sculpture, Bard Col, 75-, Parsons Sch Design, 78-85 &

Long Island Univ (semester prog), 91-95. *Awards:* NY State Coun Arts Award, 77; Guggenheim Fel, 81; Fel, NY State Found Arts, 88; Grant, Pollock-Krasner Found, 2001. *Bibliog:* Marcia Tucker (auth), Making it big, Ms Mag, 4/74; Brentano & Savitt, 112 Workshop/112 Greene, NY Univ Press, 81; Jack Somer (auth), A modern monument, Yachting Mag, 1/86; New York Times, 5/12/02, 8/4/02, 9/1/02, 5/15/04. *Media:* Miscellaneous. *Publ:* auth, (with Poppy Johnson), Sculpture and fiction, Bomb Mag, No 6, 83. *Dealer:* Richard Eagan Fine Art 72-74 Third St Hudson NY 12584; Kathryn Markel Fine Art 529 W 20th St 6W NY NY 10011; Van Deb Editions NY NY

SCOTT, B NIBBELINK (BARBARA GAE SCOTT)
PAINTER, SCULPTOR
b Columbia, Mo, July 23, 44. *Study:* With Daniel Greene, 82-83, Albert Handell, 84 & Herman Margulies, 85. *Work:* Wichita Art Asn & Fourth Financial Ctr, Wichita, Kans; Am Ambassador's Collection, London; Mr & Mrs Gerald Michaud pvt collection, Wichita, Kans. *Exhib:* Kans Pastel Soc First Nat, Wichita Art Asn Gallery, 86-87; Pastel Soc Am, Nat Arts Club, NY, 86-90; Third Salon des Pastellistes France, Centre Culturel de la Ville, Lille, France, 87; Am Aid Soc, Mall Gallerie's, London, 88; Fourth Salon des Pastellistes France, Centre Culturel de la Ville de Compiegne, France, 88; Cassatt Pastel Soc, Berkley Gallery, Scottsdale, Ariz, 89. *Pos:* Prog chmn, Community Art Guild, Wichita, Kans, 83-84, pres, 84-85. *Teaching:* Pvt lessons. *Awards:* Honorary Award, Kans Small Oil Painting Exhib, 82; Prix de International Honneur, Third Salon des Pastellistes de France, 87; First Place US, Fifth Salon des Pastellistes de France, 89. *Mem:* Kans Pastel Soc (founder, pres, 84-90); Pastel Soc Am; Salmagundi Club; Societe des Pastellistes de France (hon pres US, 87-90); Kans Acad Oil Painters. *Media:* Pastel, Oil; Clay. *Publ:* Auth, Discovering my potential with pastel, Am Artists, 7/87. *Mailing Add:* 301 N Crestway Wichita KS 67208

SCOTT, BILL EARL
PAINTER
b Cumberland, Md, May 6, 1935. *Study:* Self taught. *Work:* Barnett Bank, Tampa, Fla; Busch Gardens, Tampa, FL; Havatampa Inc,Tampa, FL; Leigh Yawkey Woodson Art Mus, Wausau, WI; Tampa Parks Dept, Tampa, FL. *Comn:* 300 hand colored prints, Arthur Andersen, Tampa, 93; painting, Art in State Bldg, Starke, Fla, 96; 6 pieces, Art in Public Places, City of Tampa, FL; 11 Brush and ink paintings, Tampa Parks Dept, Tampa, FL; 6 paintings, USAA, Tampa, FL. *Exhib:* Watercolor USA, Springfield Art Mus, Mo, 91; Southeastern W/C VI, Deland Mus Art, Fla, 91; Bird in Art Exhib, Leigh Yawkey Woodson Mus Art, Wis, 93; Fla Artists Group, Mus Art Sci, Daytona Beach, 94; Watercolor Soc of Ala, Gladsden Ctr, 95; 25th Ann Fla Watercolor Soc, St Petersburg, Mus Art, 96; Albemarle Gallery, London, 2006. *Mem:* Nat Watercolor Asn; Fla Watercolor Soc; Fla Artists Group; Prof Asn Visual Artists. *Media:* Watercolor, Acrylic. *Mailing Add:* 11865 34th St North Saint Petersburg FL 33716-1812

SCOTT, CAMPBELL
PRINTMAKER, SCULPTOR
b Milngavie, Scotland, Oct 5, 30; Can citizen. *Study:* Studied with S W Hayter, Paris; Glasgow Sch Art, Scotland. *Work:* British Mus, London; Bibliot Nat, Paris; Scottish Nat Gallery Mod Art; Montreal Mus Art Can; Victoria & Albert Mus; Art Gallery Ont Can; and others. *Comn:* Bronze sculpture, Pub Libr, Niagara Falls, Can; wood sculpture, Pub Libr, St Catharines, Can; Niagara on the Lake (mural), The Pumphouse Art Ctr; designed Addison Libr, St Mark's Church, Niagara-on-the-Lake, Can, 05. *Exhib:* FAAP Gravura, Sao Paulo, Brazil, 68; 1st British Int Print Biennale, Gt Brit, 69; Traveling Exhib, Nat Gallery Can, Ottawa, 69; 4th Am Biennial Engraving, Santiago, Chile, 70; Exhib Can Graphics, Can Embassy, Washington, DC, 71 & Pratt Inst, NY, 71; Niagara Pumphouse Visual Art Ctr, Can, 94, 99; designer, Addison Libr, Ont, Can, 2006. *Media:* Sculpture (bronze, aluminum), Graphics (woodcuts, etchings, engravings, computer laser prints), Jewelery (gold and silver), Architecture. *Publ:* Auth, article, City and Country Home, Maclean Hunter Publ, 9/85; article, House and Garden (Brit ed), Conde Publ, 11/87. *Mailing Add:* 89 Byron Niagara on the Lake ON L0S 1J0 Canada

SCOTT, CONCETTA CIOTTI
PAINTER, INSTRUCTOR
b Philadelphia, PA, Jan 17, 27. *Study:* Moore Col of Arts and Design, Assoc, 46-51. *Work:* Les Amis de la Grande Vigne Coll, Dinan, Brittany, France. *Exhib:* To Everything a Season, Charles Summer Sch Mus, Washington, DC, 90; Selections from Series, Barry Gallery, Marymount Univ, Arlington, VA, 94; Annual Juried Art Show, The Decoy Mus, Havre de Grace, MD, 95; 96th Int Jury Show, PWCS-Berman Gallery-Ursinus, Bryn Mawr, PA, 96; Int Miniature Show, MBGGS, Strathmore Hall, Bethesda, MD, 97-2004; Regional Juried Exhib, N Va Col Cult Ctr, Annandale, VA, 99; 101st Int Philadelphia Watercolor Soc, Gregg Ctr, Am Col, Bryn Mawr, PA, 2001; Multiples Exhib, Juried Wilson Hall, Moore Col Art, Philadelphia, PA, 2005; Vienna Mini Show, Va, 2005; Wash Watercolor Exhib, Strathmore Hall, Md, 2005; Juried Show, McLean Soc, 2005; 27th Juried Show, Va Watercolor Soc, 2006; 15th Juried Show, Central Va, 2006; Juried Show, Cumberland Art, Hagerstown, Md, 2006. *Pos:* Dir Art, Woodward & Lothrop Stores, Washington, DC, 59-63; Chmn, convention, Nat Women's League Am Pen Women, Washington, DC, 83-84; Chmn, programs & workshops, McLean Arts Club, McLean, VA, 2003-2005; vpres, McLean Art Soc, 2006-; Art Rep to Coun Arts Fairfax City. *Teaching:* teacher, Melrose Acad, Melrose Park, PA, 51-53; teacher, Montesorri Sch of McLean, McLean, VA, 75-95; instr, Design/Miniature Pkg, Art Asn Fairfax Cty, 95-2004. *Awards:* Winsor Newton & Plaque, Fourteenth Virginia Watercolor Show, Winsor Newton, 93; The Archers-D Smith Award, 101st Intl, PWCS, Philadelphia Watercolor Soc, Oct-Dec, 2001; Grant to paint, 1 month, at La Grande Vigne Dinan, France. *Bibliog:* Art News Editor, Fax News, C Scott, VA Tech, Fairfax Council of Arts Publ, 90; Rachel Woet (ed), Splash 6-Textures, North Light Books, Spring 2000; Tabitha Yeatts (auth), Framing the Still Life, Elan Magazine, D Reynolds Publ, Aug 2000 & 2005. *Mem:* Baltimore Watercolor Soc, Baltimore, MD; Philadelphia Watercolor Soc, Philadelphia, PA; Virginia Watercolor Soc, Roanoke, VA; Miniature Painters Scuptors, Gravers Soc, Wahington, DC; Nat league Am Pen Women, Washinton, DC; Potomac Valley Watercolor; Wash Watercolor Soc, Washington DC; Mclean Art Soc Art League, Alexandria, Va, Cider Paint Am Miniature Soc. *Media:* Pastels, Alkyds. *Res:* Miniature Art Hist: Middle E, India, W Europe. USA, 4th-20th century. *Interests:* painting; reading World News; music. *Collection:* MPR Asn, Alexandria, Va; Rosenberg Realtors MD; City of Dinan, France; Plv College Sweden, US. *Publ:* illusr, Move Over Mother Goose, Gryphon House, 87. *Mailing Add:* 1111 Dead Run Dr McLean VA 22101-2126

SCOTT, DAVID WINFIELD
PAINTER, CONSULTANT
b Fall River, Mass, July 10, 1916. *Study:* Art Students League; Harvard Col, AB; Claremont Grad Sch, MA & MFA; Univ Calif, Berkeley, PhD. *Pos:* From lectr art to prof, Scripps Col, 46-63; dir, Nat Collection Fine Arts, Washington, DC, 64-69; consult, Nat Gallery Art, Washington, DC, 69-84; mus consult, 84-; dir, Corcoran Gallery Art, Washington, DC, 90. *Media:* Acrylic. *Mailing Add:* 3016 Cortland Pl NW Washington DC 20008-3431

SCOTT, DEBORAH EMONT
CURATOR
b Passaic, NJ. *Study:* Livingston Col, Rutgers Univ, BA; Oberlin Col, MA. *Collection Arranged:* Veda Reed, 79; Alan Shields (auth, catalog), Memphis Brooks Mus Art, Memphis, Tenn, 83-84; David Saunders, 84; 50 Years of Collecting: The Friends of Art at the Nelson, 84; Highlights from Kansas City Art Institute Alumni, 85; Jonathan Borofsky (auth, catalog), 88; Judith Shea, 89; Gerhard Richter, 89; John Ahearn, 90; Kathy Muehlemann, 91; Nate Fors, 91; Julian Schnabel, 91; Shuttlecocks: the Making of a Sculpture (auth, brochure), 94; Joel Shapiro, 95; Lewis deSoto, 96. *Pos:* Asst cur, Allen Mem Art Mus, Oberlin, Ohio, 77-79; cur, Memphis Brooks Mus Art, Memphis, Tenn, 79-83; cur, 20th century art, Nelson-Atkins Mus Art, Kansas City, 83-, chief cur, 98-. *Bibliog:* Interview with Ursula Von Rydingsvard, Nelson Gallery Found & Yorkshire Sculpture Park, 97. *Mem:* Col Art Asn. *Res:* 20th century art. *Publ:* Auth, Winners, Nat Endowment for the Arts/Mid-America Arts Alliance, 3/87; The Nelson-Atkins Museum of Art Henry Moore Sculpture Garden, Nelson-Atkins Mus Art, 6/89; Joan Backes, Hafnarborg Inst Cult & Fine Art, Hafnarfjordur, Iceland, 8/91; Joel Shapiro: the Figure in Nature, In: Joel Shapiro: Outdoors, Walker Art Inst & Nelson-Atkins Mus Art, 6/95; A modern sculpture initiative recent acquisitions at the Nelson-Atkins Museum, Apollo Mag, 11/96; contrib Celebrating Moore: Works from the Henry Moore Foundation, 98, Modern Sculpture at the Nelson-Atkins Mus Art: An Anniversary Celebration, 99, (CD Rom) Masterworks for Learning: A College Collection Catalogue, Allen Memorial Art Mus, Oberlin Col, 98. *Mailing Add:* c/o Nelson-Atkins Mus Art 4525 Oak St Kansas City MO 64111

SCOTT, JOHN BELDON
HISTORIAN, EDUCATOR, WRITER
b Scottsburg, Ind, Aug 3, 46. *Study:* Ind Univ, BA, 68; Rutgers Univ, MA, 75, PhD, 82. *Pos:* Ed, Rutgers Art Rev, 78-79; Elizabeth M Stanley Prof of the Arts, 2004-, head art hist div, Sch Art and Art Hist; US Nat Comt, for the Hist of Art Int Congress of the Hist of Art, 2001-02. *Teaching:* Instr, Rutgers Univ, 77-79; lectr, Univ Pa, 81-82; assoc prof, Univ Iowa, 82-; vis mem Inst, Advanced Study, Princeton, NJ, 1991-92. *Awards:* Am Acad Rome Fel, 79-81; Delmas Found Fel, 82; Am Coun Learned Soc Fel, 84, 89; Am Philos Soc Grant, 84; Andrew W Mellon Fel, Univ Pa, 85; Nat Endowment of the Humanities Travel to Collections Grant, 1986; Gladys Krieble Delmas Found for Venetian Studies Grant, 1986; Nat Humanities Ctr Fel, 1993-94; Trinity Col Barbieri Grant in Italian Hist, Barbieri Endowment for Italian Culture, 1994; Marta Sutton Weeks Fel, Stanford Humanities Ctr, Stanford Univ, 1999-2000; Graham Found for Advanced Studies in the Visual Arts Research Grant, 1999; Am Philos Soc Sabbatical Fel, 2000. *Mem:* Col Art Asn (bd dir, 98); Soc Archit Historians (bd dir, 97-); Renaissance Soc Am; Midwest Art Hist Soc (bd dir, 1986-89); Col Art Asn (bd dir nominating comt, 1998); Soc Archit Historians (bd dir, 1997-2000). *Res:* Italian Renaissance and Baroque; northern Baroque. *Publ:* S Ivo Alla Sapienza and Borromini's symbolic language, J Soc Archit Historians, 82; Urban VIII, Bernini and the Contess Matilda, L'Age D'or Du Mecenat (1598-1661), Paris, 85; The Meaning of Perseus and Andromedia in the Farnese Gallery and on the Rubens House, J of the Warburg and Courtauld Inst, 88; Pietro da Cortona's Painted Ceilings of Palazzo Barberini, Princeton Univ Press, 90; Images of Nepotism: The Painted Ceilings of Palazzo Barberini, Princeton Univ Press, 90; and others; Auth: Images of Nepotism: The Painted Ceilings of Palazzo Barberini, 1991, Archit for the Shroud: Relic and Ritual in Turin, 2003 (Charles Rufus Morey Book Award, Col Art Asn, 2004), (articles have appeared in) Art Bulletin, Burlington Mag, Memoirs of Am. Acad Rome, Storia dell'Arte, J of the Warburg and Courtauld Inst, J of Soc Archit Historians. *Mailing Add:* Univ Iowa Sch Art & Art Hist Art Bldg 120 N Riverside Dr #100 Iowa City IA 52242-1706

SCOTT, JOHN FREDRIK
HISTORIAN, EDUCATOR
b Westfield, NJ, May 14, 36. *Study:* Princeton Univ, AB, 58; Johns Hopkins Univ, MAT, 62; Columbia Univ, PhD, 71. *Collection Arranged:* Before Cortes (coauth, catalog), Metrop Mus Art, 70; Ecuadorian Art (auth, catalog), Johnson Mus Art, 82; Taino Art from Dominican Republic (auth, catalog), Univ Fla Gallery, 85; Ancient Mesoamerica (auth, catalog), Univ Fla Gallery, 87; Lowe Art Mus (coauth, catalog), Univ Miami, 90; Human & Divine in Ancient Am Art, Harn Mus, 94; Harn Mus Art (auth), Art for the Next Life, Precolumbian Grave Objects, 2005-06. *Pos:* Res assoc, Metrop Mus Art, NY, 68-71; adj cur, Mus Fine Arts, Houston, 78-80. *Teaching:* Asst

prof primitive art, Cornell Univ, Ithaca, NY, 71-77; asst prof Rice Univ, Houston, 77-81; assoc prof Latin Am art, Univ Fla, Gainesville, 81-98 & prof 98-2006, prof emeritus, 2006-. *Awards:* Nat Endowment Humanities Grant, 74-75; Fel, US-Spanish Joint Comm, 88; Fulbright Fel, Colombia, 96. *Mem:* Col Art Asn; Archaeology Inst Am (vpres Houston soc, 80-81, pres Gainesville Soc, 83-87, sec 93-96, sec-treas 2000-04); Asn Latin Am Art (vpres Precolumbian, 83-86, pres, 87-88); Soc Am Archeology. *Res:* Pre-Columbian art, especially sculpture. *Interests:* Authentication of Pre-Columbian art. *Publ:* Latin America: Perspectives on a region, Art & Archit Latin Am Rep, 2nd ed, 98; Mexican Central and South American Art, Facts on File, NY, 96; Estilo Chorrera y su influencia en los Andes in Area Septentrional Andina, 98; Latin American Art: Ancient to Modern, Univ Press Fla, 99; Dressed to Kill, in Sport of Life and Death, 2001; Hombre-Pajaro En Andes Septentrionales, in Simbolismo y Ritual, 2004. *Mailing Add:* 3112 NW 57th Terrace Gainesville FL 32606

SCOTT, JOHN TARRELL
PRINTMAKER, SCULPTOR
b New Orleans, La, June 30, 40. *Study:* Xavier Univ La, BA, 62; Mich State Univ, sculpture fel, 64, MFA, 65; United Negro Col Fund Prog Fel, 83; Hand Hollow Fel, Studios of George Rickey, 83; United Negro Col Fund Distinguished Scholar, 86; Madonna Col, Livonia, Mich, LHD, 87; Tulane Univ, New Orleans, LHD, 97. *Hon Degrees:* Madonna Col, Livonia, Mich LHD, 87; Tulane Univ, LHD, 97. *Work:* Dallas Mus Art; Kresge Art Mus, Mich State Univ, East Lansing; Nat Mus Am Art, Smithsonian Inst, Washington; New Orleans Mus Art; also many pvt collections. *Comn:* Blues Migration (outside installation), Nat Mus Am Art, Smithsonian Inst, Washington, 89; Spiritgates, New Orleans Mus Art, 94; Man and his Development in Relationship to Water, Bd Comnrs, Port New Orleans, 95; Composition for a City Dance in Three Movements (3 part polychromed aluminum wall installation), Int Concourse, Atlanta Int Airport, 96; Ancestral Legacy, Xavier Univ, La, 98. *Exhib:* New Orleans Mus Art, 86 (two exhibs), 87, 90 & 93 (two exhibs); Hunter Mus Art, 91-92; solo exhibs, Southern Univ La, Baton Rouge, 92, Galerie Simonne Stern, New Orleans, 92, 93 & 95, McIntosh Gallery, Atlanta, 94, Nat Mus Am Art, Smithsonian Inst, Washington, 94-95 & Southeastern Univ, Hammond, La, 95; Seeing Jazz, Smithsonian Inst (traveling), Washington, 97-99; Arthur Roger Gallery, New Orleans, 99; Jazz: Visual Evidence, Univ Carolina, Chapel Hill, 2001; Powder Blue Circle Dance, Arthur Rogers Gallery, New Orleans, 2001. *Pos:* Asst printmaker under Charles Pollock, 64; mem, Mayor's Environ Design & Aesthetics Comn, 72, Comt Rev Grant Requests, Coun Arts Children, La State Univ System, 75, Selection Comt, Jazz & Heritage Crafts Festival, 77, Sculpture Selection Comt, Contemp Arts Ctr, New Orleans, 77, Community Adv Bd, New Orleans Ctr Creative Arts, 78, Mayor's Task Force on Arts Policy, New Orleans, 78, Mayor's Comt, Duncan Plaza Sculpture Garden, 79; set designer, New Orleans Sickle Cell Anemia Found Telethon, 74; co-host, Ninth Nat/Int Sculpture Conf, New Orleans, 76; bd mem, Contemp Arts Ctr, New Orleans, 77; Danforth Assoc, Danforth Found, 79; coun appointment, Canal Place Arts Coun, New Orleans, 83 & State Arts Coun (vchmn), 84; panel moderator, Benjamin Mays Acad Scholars Conf, 86; bd dir, New Orleans Cult Found Inc, 87 & Southern Arts Fedn (chmn vis arts plan comt, 88), 87; judge, Harambee Arts Festival, Tallahassee, 87, Nat Black Arts Festival, Atlanta, 88 & Slidell Cult Ctr, La, 93; guest speaker, NALAA Nat Conv, Washington, DC, 88; juror, Ann Arts Competition & Contemp Arts Ctr, New Orleans, 89 & Houston Arts Coun, 92; cur, Frank Hayden Mem Exhib, New Orleans Mus Art, 89; panelist, var mus & univs, 90-94. *Teaching:* Prof Fine arts, Xavier Univ of La, New Orleans, 65-, dept chair, 74-80; instr & workshop, New Orleans Pub Schs, La, 74-76; vis artist, Southern Meth Univ, Perkins Sch Theology, Dallas, 75, Univ Maine, Orono, 78, Benjamin Mays Acad, Ind, 84, Univ Pa, Ind, 84, Fla A&M Univ, Tallahassee, 85, Albany State Col, 85, Brandywine Workshop, 88 & 92, Washington Proj Arts, 88, Mich State Univ, 90, Univ Southern Ill, Evansville, 96, Ind Univ, Pa 98 & Univ Ga, 98; lectr & workshops, var mus & univs, 87-94; vis artist & lectr, Skidmore Col, Saratoga Springs, NY, 90; instr printmaking, Penland Sch Crafts, NC, 95 & 96; artist-in-residence, Pilchuck Glass Sch, Seattle, 96; vis artist & lectr, Univ of Penn, 98. *Awards:* Cert Special Cong Recognition for Serv to Community, Congressman William Jefferson, 95; Lifetime Achievement Arts Award, Arts Coun La, 95; Delgado Soc Award, New Orleans Mus Art, 96; Artie awrd, Delta Sigma Theta Sorority, Inc, 1996; Urban League Golden award, 1997; The Van Der Zee award, Brandywine Workshop, Philadelphia, 1997. *Bibliog:* Matthew Kangas (auth), Common ground, separate choices, Art Am, 3/92; article, New Orleans Tribune, 8/92; article, Times-Picayune, 6/16/92. *Mem:* New Orleans Arts Coun (bd dir, currently); Congo Square Arts Collective (asst dir, currently). *Media:* Mixed. *Publ:* Auth, Remembering a friend, Arts Quart, Vol XI, Issue I, 2-3/89; Quality: Who defines it & how, Connections Quart, Vol 8, No 5, 6/89. *Dealer:* Arthur Roger Gallery 432 Julia St New Orleans La 70130. *Mailing Add:* c/o Arthur Roger Gallery 432 Julia St New Orleans LA 70130

SCOTT, JOYCE T
PERFORMANCE ARTIST
b Baltimore, Md, Nov 15, 48. *Study:* Md Inst Col Art, BFA, 66-70; Instituto Allende, San Miguel de Allende, Guanajuato, Mex, MFA(crafts); Haystack Mountain Sch Crafts, weaving, beadworking, dyeing, 73 & 76. *Exhib:* One-person exhibs, Drew Univ Art Gallery, Madison, NJ, Brooklyn Col Art Gallery, NY & Esther Saks Fine Art Ltd, Chicago, Ill, 92; Diggs Gallery, Winston-Salem State Univ, NC, 92; Visual Arts Ctr, NC State Univ, Raleigh, 92; Eubie Blake Cult Ctr, Baltimore, Md, 92; and others. *Pos:* Guest cur, Walter's Art Gallery, Baltimore, Md, 88-89 & Artscape, Baltimore, Md, 89; lectr, var cols, mus & univs, 75-92; guest artist, Md Inst Col Art, Baltimore, Pratt Art Ctr, Seattle, Wash, Split Rock Art Prog, Duluth, Minn, The Shepardess, San Diego, Calif & Haystack Mountain Sch Crafts, Deer Isle, Maine, 92; artist-in-residence, Univ Del, Newark, 90, Contemp Arts Ctr, Cincinnati, Ohio, 92 & Pilchuck Glass Sch, Seattle, Wash, 92; bd trustees, Mus Contemp Arts, Baltimore, Md, currently; adv bd, Pub Art Fund, NY & Baltimore Film Forum, currently; hon bd, James Renwick Alliance, Smithsonian Inst, Washington, DC, currently. *Awards:* Nat Endowment Arts Fel, 88-89; Nat Printmaking Fel, Rutgers Ctr Innovative Printmaking, New Brunswick, NJ, 90; Art Matters Inc, NY, 92; Anonymous Was a Woman Foundation, 97. *Bibliog:* Stefany Tomalin (auth), Beads, David & Charles Publs, Devon, Eng; The Art of Politics, Contemporanea/Int Art Mag, Vol 1, No 4, 11-12/88; Arlene Raven (auth), Mojotech, Village Voice, 3/28/89. *Mem:* Fel ACC. *Publ:* contribr (with Lorraine Whittlesey), Try Me (CD), 2000

SCOTT, MICHAEL
PAINTER, PRINTMAKER
b Lawrence, Kans, 1952. *Study:* Kansas City Art Inst, BFA(Skowhegan Fel), 76; Univ Cincinnati, MFA, 78. *Work:* AT&T, Piscataway, NJ; Cincinnati Art Mus, Ohio; City of Covington, Ky; Ky Utilities, Carrollton, Ky; Manhattan Life Co, NY; and many others. *Comn:* Mural, Cincinnati Pub Libr, Ohio, 76; mural, comn by Bruce Shock, Cincinnati, 87. *Exhib:* Works on Paper, DeGraff Gallery, Holland, Mich, 88; solo exhib, DeGraff Gallery, Chicago, Ill, 88 & Sherry French Gallery, NY, 90, Joseph Chowning Gallery, San Francisco, Calif, 95, Cincinnati Art Gallery, 96, Cladbeck Gallery, Rockland Maine, 97, Linda Swartz Gallery, Lexington, Ky, 98 & Gerald Peters Gallery, Santa Fe, NMex, 99; Phoenix Installation, The Phoenix, Cincinnati, 89; Harmony & Discord, Va Mus Fine Arts, Richmond, 90; Waiting for Cadmium, Sherry French Gallery, NY, 90; The New Whitney Dissenters (traveling exhib), Sherry French Gallery, NY, Anchorage Mus Hist & Art, Alaska, Rockford Col Art Gallery, Ill & Fitchburg Art Mus, Mass, 92-93; Expedition: Everglades--River of Grass (traveling exhib), Sherry French Gallery, NY, Henry Morrison Flagler Mus, Palm Beach, Fla, Deland Mus Art, Fla, Ctr Arts, Vero Beach, Fla, Alexander Brest Gallery & Mus, Jacksonville, Fla, 94-96; 61st Ann Nat Competition, Butler Mus Art, 97; Expedition: Great Lakes-The Power of Water (traveling exhib), Sherry French Gallery, NY, Krasl Art Ctr, St Joseph, Mich, Flint Inst Art, Mich & Dennos Mus, Traverse City, Mich, 99. *Teaching:* Instr drawing, Art Acad Cincinnati, 80-. *Awards:* Bououn Award, 77. *Bibliog:* Jackie Barrett (auth), This event would make Cinderella proud, Cincinnati Enquirer, D-5, 3/29/89; Ivan Amoto (auth), Singing the Cadmium Blues (color reproduction), Sci News, 168-169, 9/15/90; James F Cooper (auth), American realists get back to nature (reproduction), NY City Tribune, 16, 10/11/90. *Media:* All Media

SCOTT, SAM
PAINTER
b Chicago, Ill, Apr 7, 40. *Study:* Univ Mich, BFA, 65; Md Inst Col Art, MFA, 69; also with Grace Hartigan, David Hare, Joseph Goto, Zubel Kachadoorian. *Work:* Mus NMex, Santa Fe; Roswell Mus Fine Art, NMex; AT&T Corp Bldg, NY; Univ Iowa Fine Arts Mus, Iowa City; Phoenix Fine Arts Mus, Ariz; Midlands Bank, Denver; Albuquerque Mus Contemp Art, NMex; and others. *Comn:* Mural painting, Westinghouse Elec Corp Bldg, Norman, Okla, 72; mural, Jelco Corp Bldg, Minneapolis, Minn, 72. *Exhib:* Keats Gallery, Santa Fe, 85; Conlon Grenfelly Gallery, San Diego, 86; Robischon Gallery, Denver, 87; Sena West Gallery, Santa Fe, 87; Tucson Fine Art Mus, Tucson, 87; 10 Take 10 (retrospective), Colorado Springs Fine Arts Mus, 77; Phoenix Art Mus, 79-80; Sacred Dimension, Robischon Gallery, Denver, 93; A Sacred Embrace, Mindy Oh Gallery, Chicago, Ill, 94; Recent Paintings, Univ Club Chicago/Mindy Oh Gallery, Chicago, 94, Select Art Gallery, Sedona, 95 & Robischon Gallery, Denver, 96, Sandra D'Emilio: A Curator's Vision, NMex Mus Fine Arts, Santa Fe, 95. *Pos:* Artist-in-residence, Sun Valley Ctr Arts & Humanities, Idaho, 75 & 76, Tucson Fine Art Mus Sch, Ariz, 87 & E Carolina Univ, Greenville, 88; panel coord mem, Tucson Vis Artists Consortium, 78-80. *Teaching:* Instr painting, Md Inst Col Art, 67-69; instr painting, St Johns Col, Santa Fe, 71; asst prof art, Univ Ariz, 78-83; vis assoc prof painting & drawing, Univ Tex, San Antonio, 90, Adams State Col, Alamosa, Colo, 92 & NMex Highlands Univ, Las Vegas, 92; vis prof painting, Tex A & M Univ, Corpus Christi, 96. *Awards:* Res & Mat Grant, Univ Ariz, Tucson, 80; Panel mem, Art in NMex, Int Contemp Art Fair, Los Angeles, 86; NMex Arts Comn Prize, 73. *Bibliog:* Linda Durham (auth), Artists of New Mexico, 88; Ernesto Mayans (auth), Men of the River, 88. *Media:* Oil on Canvas. *Publ:* Auth, Sam Scott, Southwest Profiles Mag, 87; 12 books and others. *Dealer:* Watson de Nagy Gallery 1106 Berthea Houston TX 77006; Sebastian Moore Gallery Denver CO; Artifold Gallery Santa Fe NMex. *Mailing Add:* 149 Mesa Verde St Santa Fe NM 87501

SCOTT, SANDY (SANDRA) LYNN
SCULPTOR
b Dubuque, Iowa, July 24, 43. *Study:* Kansas City Art Inst. *Work:* Wildlife World Mus, Monument, Colo; El Paso Zoo, Tex; Gilcrease Mus, Tulsa, Okla. *Comn:* Rodeo Events (etchings), Nat Cowboy Hall Fame, Oklahoma City, 78; Grand Slam, 79 & Bears of North America, 80, Nat Sporting Fraternity Ltd, NY; Kodiak Bears, WesTex Oil Co, El Paso, 80; Wood Ducks, Albuquerque, NMex, 81. *Exhib:* Am Artists Prof League, NY, 82 & 83; Catharine Lorillard Wolfe Art Club, NY, 82 & 83; Salmagundi Open Sculpture Exhib, NY, 83; NY Pen & Brush, 83; Ann Soc Am Impressionists Show, 84; more than fifty one-woman shows at galleries throughout the country. *Pos:* Background artist, Calvin Motion Pictures, Kansas City, Mo, 62-65. *Awards:* New York Pen & Brush Award, Ann Sculpture Exhib, 83; Medal Hon Sculpture, Catharine Lorillard Wolfe Art Club, 83; Barett-Colea Award & Salmagundi Club Cert Merit, Salmagundi Club Open Sculpture Exhib, 83; Sculpture Award, Pen & Brush, 83; Graphics Award, Am Artists Prof League, 84, Medal of Honor, sculpture, 85; Harriett W Frishmuth Mem Award, Catharine Lorillard Wolfe Art Club, 85. *Bibliog:* Sandy Scott: Etchings, Prints Mag, 7-8/81; Carrol Nelson (auth), Sandy Scott, In: Masters of Western Art, Watson-Guptill, 82; article, Artists of the Rockies, spring 83. *Mem:* Soc Animal Artists; Am Artists Prof League; New York Pen & Brush; Soc Am Impressionists. *Media:* Cast Bronze, Bronze. *Publ:* Illusr, The Ultimate Fishing Book, Houghton-Mifflin, 81. *Mailing Add:* c/o Knox Gallery 1512 Larimerst St R 15 Denver CO 80202-1514

SCOTT, SHIRLEY CLAY
ADMINISTRATOR
Study: Kent State Univ, PhD, 73. *Pos:* dean, Grad Col Western Mich Univ; dean, prof, Sch Art & Design Southern Ill Univ, 99-. *Mailing Add:* Art & Design So Illinois Univ Office of Dean Mailcode 4522 Carbondale IL 62901

SCRIBNER, CHARLES, III
HISTORIAN, LECTURER
b Washington, DC, May 24, 51. *Study:* Princeton Univ, AB, 73, MFA, 75, PhD, 77. *Pos:* Vpres, MacMillan Publ Co, 84-94; ed, Scribner, 94-; mem adv coun, dept art & archaelogy, Princeton, Univ, 83-91 & 99-, adv comt, Libr, 80-90 & 98-. *Teaching:* Instr Baroque art, Princeton Univ, 76-77, mem adv coun, Dept Art & Archaeol, 83-91. *Awards:* Thesis Prize, Princeton Univ, 73. *Mem:* Asn Princeton Univ Press. *Res:* Baroque art, especially religious art of Rubens, Bernini and Caravaggio--cultural world of the Counter-Reformation. *Publ:* Auth, Sacred architecture: Rubens' Eucharist tapestries, Art Bulletin, 75; Daniel Hopfer's Venus and Amor, Princeton Univ Art Mus Rec, 76; In Alia Effigie: Caravaggio's London Supper at Emmaus, Art Bulletin, 77; The Triumph of the Eucharist: Tapestries by Rubens, UMI Res Press, 82; Rubens and Bernini, Ringling Mus J, 83; Rubens: Baroque Artist, Renaissance Man, Abrams, 89; Gianlorenzo Bernini, Abrams, 91. *Mailing Add:* 155 E 72nd St # 5C New York NY 10021-4371

SCUCCHI, ROBIE (PETER), JR
EDUCATOR, PAINTER
b Lake Village, Ark, Apr 10, 44. *Study:* Ark State Univ, with Dan F Howard, BS(painting), 67; Southern Ill Univ, Edwardsville, painting with John Richardson, 70-71; Inst Allende, Univ Guanajuato, Mex, with James Pinto & Fred Samuelson, MFA(painting), 71. *Work:* Claypool-Young Art Gallery, Morehead State Univ, Ky; Matrix Art Gallery, Ind Univ, Bloomington; Grinstead Art Gallery, Cent Mo State Univ, Warrensburg; Jackson Hall Art Gallery, Ky State Univ, Frankfort; Gallery Fine Arts, Univ Ark, Little Rock. *Exhib:* Washington & Jefferson Col Gallery, Washington, Pa, 73 & 79; Birmingham Mus Art, Ala, 74; one-man shows, Jackson Hall Art Gallery, Ky State Univ, Frankfort, 81, Claypool-Young Art Gallery, Morehead State Univ, Ky, 81 & Matrix Art Gallery, Ind Univ, Bloomington, 82; Nat Arts Club, NY, 82-85, 87 & 88; Int Trade Mart Ctr, New Orleans, La, 82, 84 & 90; Ark Arts Ctr, Little Rock, 83, 84 & 88; Parthenon Art Mus, Nashville, Tenn, 83 & 86; W Nebr Art Ctr, Scottsbluff, 88, 90 & 92; Cottonlandia Mus, Greenwood, Miss, 92 & 95; Tenn Valley Art Mus, Tuscumbia, Ala, 96; and others. *Teaching:* Instr & head painting, drawing & design, NW High Sch, House Springs, Mo, 67-71; assoc prof art, Miss State Univ, Starkville, 71-96. *Awards:* Best Show Awards, St Charles Art Guild 4th Ann, Mo, 69 & Ark Bicentennial, 76; 2nd Place Purchase, Am Inst Architects, 72; Ann Art Exhib, Miss Artists, 92 & 95. *Mem:* Nat Soc Painters Casein & Acrylic; Col Art Asn Am; SE Col Arts Conf; Nat & Miss Art Educ Asn (state assemblyman, 78-79, state vpres, 78-80). *Media:* Charcoal, Acrylic. *Mailing Add:* 2402 Maple Dr Starkville MS 39759

SCULLY, VINCENT JOSEPH, JR
ARCHITECTURE, EDUCATOR, WRITER
b New Haven, Conn, 20. *Study:* Entered Yale Univ at age 16; Yale Univ, BA in English, 40; MA in art history, Yale Univ, MA in art hist, 47; Yale Univ, PhD in art hist, 49. *Teaching:* Mem fac, art hist Yale Univ, New Haven, 49-91, prof, art hist, 61-91; master Morse Col, 69-75; Sterling Prof, Emer of the Hist of Art, 91-; distinguished vis prof, Sch Archit Univ Miami, 92-. *Awards:* Named Jefferson Lectr, Nat Endowment of the Humanities, 95; inaugural Vincent Scully Prize, Nat Bldg Mus, Wash, DC, 99; Nat Medal of Arts, 2004. *Publ:* Auth: (books) The Shingle Style: Architectural Theory and Design from Richardson to the Origins of Wright, 55, Frank Lloyd Wright, 60, Modern Architecture: The Architecture of Democracy, 61, Louis I Kahn, 62, The Architectural Heritage of Newport, RI, 1640-1915, 67, American Architecture and Urbanism, 69, Pueblo Architecture of the Southwest, 71, The Shingle Style and The Stick Style: Architectural Theory and Design from Richardson to the Origins of Wright, 71, The Shingle Style Today: Or the Historian's Revenge, 74, Pueblo: Mountain, Village, Dance, 75, The Earth, the Temple, and the Gods: Greek Sacred Architecture, 79, Robert Stern, 81, Studies and Executed Buildings by Frank Lloyd Wright, 86, The Villas of Palladio, 86; auth: New World Visions of Household Gods and Sacred Places: American Art and the Metropolitan Museum, 1650-1914, 88, The Architecture of the American Summer: The Flowering of the Shingle Style, 89, The Architecture of Robert Venturi, 89, The Great Dinosaur Mural at Yale: The Age of Reptiles, 90, Architecture: The Natural and the Man-Made, 91, French Royal Gardens: The Design of Andre Le Notre, 92; book of essays: Modern Architecture and Other Essays, 2003; co-auth: (with C. Lynn, E. Vogt, P. Goldberger) Yale in New Haven: Architecture & Urbanism, 2004. *Mailing Add:* Yale Univ Dept Hist of Art 56 High St PO Box 208272 New Haven CT 06520

SCULTHORPE, PETER
PAINTER, PRINTMAKER
b Hamilton, Ontario, Can, 48. *Study:* PA Acad Fine Arts; studied with Art DeCost. *Work:* Butler Inst Am Art, Youngstown, Ohio; Bristol-Myers Squibb Gallery, NJ; Brandywine River Mus, Chadds Ford, Pa; Am Embassy, Copenhagen, Denmark. *Exhib:* Solo exhib, Frye Art Mus, Seattle Wash, Somerville Manning Gallery, Del, Judy Goffman Fine Arts Gallery, NY, Berman Mus Art Traveling Exhib, Pa, 99; Pa Acad Fine Arts, New Orleans Art Asn, La Audubon Artists Ann, NY, Somerville Manning Gallery, Greenville, Del, 2001. *Awards:* Award of Excellence, Am Artists Prof League, 84; Medal, Philadelphia Sketch Club, Pa, 86; Oil Painting Award, Nat Art League, 93. *Mem:* Watercolor USA, hon soc; Am Watercolor Soc; Nat Acad Design. *Media:* Oil & Watercolor. *Specialty:* Architectural Landscapes. *Mailing Add:* PO Box 410 Rockland DE 19732

SEABERG, LIBBY W
PAINTER, HISTORIAN
b New York, NY. *Study:* Queens Col, BA(cum laude), 57; Columbia Univ with Meyer Schapiro, MA, 64; Bryn Mawr Grad Sch; City Col Grad Painting Prog; New School with Jacob Lawrence. *Exhib:* Works on Paper/Women Artists, Brooklyn Mus, 75; Dimenseraction, Ammo's New Waterfront Mus, Brooklyn, 89; Physicality: An Exhib on Color Dimensionality in Painting, Hunter Col Art Galleries, NY, 91; Bubbles, Blisters and Pearls, Stern Sch, NY Univ, NY, 92; Private Papers: A Decade of Drawings, Queens Col Art Ctr, Flushing, NY, 95; Brushes with Sculpture, 55 Mercer Gallery, NY, 95; Clairvoyance, Dietz Gallery, NY, 2000; numerous group shows, NY & region, 2006-. *Collection Arranged:* curator/co-curator several exhbns. *Pos:* Libr, researcher, Whitney Mus Art, 68-76; asst cur contemp art & exhib coordr, Yeshiva Univ Mus, New York, 89-90. *Teaching:* lectr art hist & appreciation, Philadelphia Col Art, 64-65; lectr, Queens Col, Flushing, NY, 66; instr, Borough Manhattan Community Col, New York, 66-67. *Awards:* Vt Studio Colony (fel & artist in res), 89. *Bibliog:* Hilton Kramer (auth), A monumental muddle of American sculpture, New York Times, 3/28/76; Greg Gattuso (auth), Entertainment best bets, New York Newsday, 3/12/95; Joy Walker (auth), New York gallery walking, Next, No 36, spring, 96. *Mem:* Col Art Asn; Am Asn Mus; Artists Talk On Art; NY Artists Circle (bd mem). *Media:* Three Dimensional, Mixed Media. *Res:* Contemporary art merging painting & sculpture; American & 19th-20th-century art; the artist Janet Sobel. *Publ:* Contribr, Contemporary Black Artists in America (exhib catalog), 71 & Two Hundred Years of American Sculpture, 76, Whitney Mus Am Art; ed, Japanese Literati Painters: The Third Generation (exhib catalog), Brooklyn Mus, 77; ed, American Ceramics: 1876 to the Present, rev ed, Abbeville Press, 87; ed, NY, Judy Hoffman (review), Sculpture, Vol 22, 7-8/2003. *Mailing Add:* 667 Tenth St Brooklyn NY 11215

SEABERG, STEVE (STEVENS)
ASSEMBLAGE ARTIST, PERFORMANCE ARTIST
b Evanston, Ill, Sept 30, 30. *Study:* Northwestern Univ, BS, 52, MA, 61; Academie Grande Chaumiere, Paris, 56. *Work:* Art Bus Collection, State Ga, Atlanta; Albany Mus Art, Albany, Ga. *Comn:* Mural, comn by Ted Berrigan, NY, 66; mural, comn by Melvin Wildberger, Brooklyn, NY, 67; Lex et Domus (mural), The Law Office, Atlanta, 76; The Black Arts (mural), Nat Endowment Arts, Atlanta, 78; Hulsey Yard (murals), Seaboard Railway, Atlanta, Ga, 86. *Exhib:* Chicago and Vicinity, Art Inst Chicago, 60, Biennial Print & Drawing Exhib, 62; solo exhibs, Here Come de Judge-ment, Clocktower Gallery, NY, 79 & Ancestors, Malmo Konsthall, Sweden, 81; Artists in Georgia, High Mus Art, Atlanta, 80; Collage & Assemblage, Miss Mus Art, Jackson, 82; Leisure Am, Tampa Mus Art, Fla, 83; Birmingham Biennial, Birmingham Mus Art, Ala, 83; Centro Cult, Buenos Aires, 89; Children of Alcoholism, Little Beirut Art Space, Atlanta, 90; Children of Abuse, 800 East Art Space, Atlanta, 92. *Pos:* Artist & artist preparator, Field Mus Natural Hist, Chicago, 67-65; painter in residence, Neighborhood Art Ctr, Atlanta, 76-79; program dir, Arts Interface, Atlanta, 80-83, Atlanta Urban Design Comn, 85-; mgr, Nexus Theater, Atlanta, 88-90. *Teaching:* Vis lectr art hist, Northwestern Univ, 61-64; lectr & asst prof studio & art hist, Rutgers Univ, 67-70; instr humanities, Clark Col, Ga, 70-73. *Awards:* Nat Endowment Arts Visual Artist Fel, 78; Site Work Grants, Arts Festival Atlanta, 79-81; Third Prize, Birmingham Biennial, Birmingham Art Asn, 83. *Bibliog:* Oyvind Fahlstrom (dir, film), Sweden's TV, 68; Ann Livet (auth), Steve Seaberg's skeletons, Art Papers, 6/79; Tom Patterson (auth), Who is Steve Seaberg?, Brown's Guide to Ga, 8/82. *Publ:* Auth, Sunlight in Jungleland, private publ, 65; illusr, Om Baddrakter, Forfatterforlaget, 77; Song of Atlanta, Ali Baba, 81; The Iconography of Abuse, Seaberg, Atlanta, 94; The Demon's Face: An artisit's discovery of the metaphors of child abuse, Leonardo, Mass Inst Technol, 95; and others. *Mailing Add:* 683 Queen St SW Atlanta GA 30310-2611

SEABOURN, BERT DAIL
PAINTER, PRINTMAKER
b Iraan, Tex, 31. *Study:* Oklahoma City Univ, LHD, 97; Famous Artists Schs, Westport, Conn, cert(art); Univ Cent Okla; Okla Univ. *Hon Degrees:* Okla City Univ, LHD, 97. *Work:* Am Embassy, London; Smithsonian Mus Nat Hist, Washington; Pres Geral Ford Libr Collection, Mich; Vatican Mus Mod Religious Art, Italy; Nat Palace Mus, Taipei, Taiwan. *Comn:* Bronze sculpture, Southwestern Bell Tel, Okla City, 86; mural, Fox Television Channel 25, Okla City, 96; acrylic on linen, Episcopal Diocese Okla, 2000. *Exhib:* New Britain Mus Am Art, Conn, 79; Denver Mus Natural Hist, Colo, 80; Native Am Ctr Living Arts, Niagara Falls, NY, 81; Mus Natural Hist, Smithsonian Inst, Washington, DC, 83; Ming Chaun Col Taipei,Taiwan, 89; Mandarin Galleries, Singapore, 89; Moskow Univ, Ulyanovsk, Russia, 96. *Pos:* Artist & journalist, USN, 51-55; art dir & artist, Okla Gas & Elec Co, Oklahoma City, 55-77. *Teaching:* watercolor, acrylic & printmaking, City Arts Ctr, Okla City, 97-; adj tchr session classes, mixed media & surface texture, Univ Central Okla, 2002-04. *Awards:* First Prize (Watercolor), Okla Watercolor Asn, 74-75, 86, 96-97 & 2004; Gov Art Award, Okla, 81; Grand Award, Master Artists, Five Civilized Tribes Mus, 88, 97 & 2005; First Prize (Oil), Inter-Tribal Indian Ceremonial Art Show, Gallup, NMex, 89; Best of Show (watercolor), Okla Watercolor Asn, 91, 99-2000, 2002. *Bibliog:* Dick Frontain (auth), Cherokee artist Bert D Seabourn, Prairie Hawk, 79; Tricia Hurst (auth), Bert Seabourn common ties, Southwest Art, 81; Cecil Lee (auth), Bert Seabourn Paintings, Univ Sci & Arts, 2000. *Mem:* Okla Art Guild (pres, 70); Okla Watercolor Asn; Master Artists Five Civilized Tribes; Okla Visual Arts Coalition; Individual Artists of Okla. *Media:* Watercolor, Acrylic; Etching, Monotype. *Publ:* Auth & illusr, Indian Gallery, 72; Master Artists of the Five Civilized Tribes, 76; Vanishing Americans, 84; Seabourn Prints & Posters, 90; Illusr, The Father & Son Indian, Y Guide Manual. *Dealer:* Southwest Star Fine Art PO Box 37114 Kansas City MO 64138; 50 Penn Place Art Gallery 5000 N Pennsylvania Oklahoma City 73118. *Mailing Add:* 6105 Covington Ln Oklahoma City OK 73132

SEABOURN, CONNIE
PAINTER, PRINTMAKER
b Purcell, Okla, Sept 20, 1951. *Study:* Univ Okla, BFA, 81. *Work:* Gilcrease Mus, Tulsa; Talley Indust, Phoenix; Southwestern Bell Tel Co, Washington, DC; Heritage Ctr, Red Cloud Indian Sch, Pine Ridge, SDak; Tyson Foods Corp, Fayetteville, Ark. *Exhib:* Nat Printmaking & Drawing Show, Okla Art Ctr, 81; Night of the First Americans, John F Kennedy Ctr, Washington, DC, 82; Selected Works from Night of the First Americans, Smithsonian Mus, 82; Traditions & Transformations, Somerstown Gallery, Somers, NY, 83; Native Am Art--Three Artists, Twenty Six Horses, NY, 83; two-person exhib, New Trends Gallery, Santa Fe, 83; Eye of My Mind, San Diego Mus Man, 85; Southern Plains Indian Mus, Anadarko, Okla, 86; Kimball Art Ctr, Park City, Utah, 89. *Awards:* Powers Award, Red Cloud Art Show, 83. *Bibliog:* Jimmie Marshall (auth), The emerging of an artist, Art Gallery Mag, winter 80; Jimmie Marshall (auth), The best of both worlds: Connie Seabourn Ragan, Okla 81, 11/81; Dick Frontain (auth), The rising star of Connie Seabourn Ragan, Indian Trader, 10/82. *Mem:* Soc Layerists Multi Media. *Media:* Watercolor, Serigraphy. *Publ:* Auth, The Artist as Printmaker, 8/86. *Mailing Add:* PO Box 23795 Oklahoma City OK 73123

SEAMAN, DRAKE F
PAINTER
Study: Kachina Art Sch, with Jay Datus, 59-63; also murals with Ray Strong, 70. *Work:* Whitney Gallery of Western Art, Cody, Wyo; Phippen Mus Western Art, Prescott, Ariz. *Comn:* Landscape mural, Seventh Day Adventist Church, Santa Barbara, Calif; Prodigal Son (mural), St Joseph's Catholic Church, Williams, Ariz, 83. *Exhib:* Troys Cowboy Art Gallery, Scottsdale, 71-72; El Prado Gallery, Sedona, Ariz, 74-78; Am Painters in Paris, France, 75; McAdoo Gallery, Santa Fe, New Mexico, 92; plus others. *Teaching:* Instr landscape, Brooks Fine Arts Ctr, Santa Barbara, 69-70. *Bibliog:* Bob Austin (auth), Reflections on Oil, Austin Gallery, 70; article in SW Art, 4/76. *Media:* Oil, Sumi Ink. *Publ:* Auth (autobiog), Modern Veterinary Practice, 74; Animal Cavalcade, 74. *Mailing Add:* PO Box 23 Williams AZ 86046-0023

SEAMANS, BEVERLY BENSON
SCULPTOR
b Boston, Mass, Oct 31, 1928. *Study:* Mus Sch Fine Arts, Boston, 48-50; with George Demetrios & Peter Abate, 46-48. *Work:* Essex Inst & Peabody Mus, House of Seven Gables, Salem, Mass; Salem Hosp, Mass; Am Cathedral, Paris, France. *Comn:* Bronze, First Nat Bank Boston, Mass, 69; bronze, Salem Hospital, Mass, 76; bronze, Mass Inst Technol, 80; bronze, Camp Kieve, Nobleboro, Maine, 81; and other pvt collections. *Exhib:* Nat Sculpture Soc, NY, 73, 76-80; one-person shows, Essex Inst, Salem, 74, Mus Sci, Boston, 76, Pingree Sch, Hamilton, 75 & 77, Peabody Mus, Salem, 79-80, House of Seven Gables, Salem, Mass, 86, North Haven Gallery, Maine, 87 & Mem Art Gallery, Rochester, NY, 88, plus others; Abbot Pub Libr, Marblehead, Mass, 85; Trustees of Reservations, Beverly, MA, 2000; Marblehead HS, Marblehead, MA, 2001; Memorial Children's Sculpture, Prouts Necks, ME, 2003. *Awards:* First Prize, Marblehead Arts Asn, 76, 78 & 87; Silver Medal, Nat Sculpture Soc, 78. *Bibliog:* Sharron King (auth), Woman 75, Channel 4, Boston, 75. *Mem:* Fel Nat Sculpture Soc; New Eng Sculptors Asn; Copley Soc; Cambridge Arts; Marblehead Arts; Rockport Art Asn, Mass; Rebohoth Art League. *Media:* Bronze, Marble. *Mailing Add:* Ten Harbor View Marblehead MA 01945

SEARLE, WILLIAM ROSS
PAINTER
b Oak Bluffs, Mass, Sept 25, 36. *Study:* Mass Col Art, BFA, 1957—1961; RI Sch of Design, MFA, 1961—1963. *Work:* West Point Mus, NY; Rev Martin Luther King Jr Mus, Atlanta, Ga; New England Mus of Sports, Boston, Mass; Cape Cod Mus of Art, Dennis, Mass; Cahoon Mus of Am Art, Cotuit, Mass. *Comn:* 1797 and 1849 Salem Mass, Eastern Bank, Mass, 1985; 350th Anniversary Mural of Braintree Mass, 1990. *Exhib:* 1969 Invitational Exhib, Fitchburg Art Mus, Fitchburg, Mass, 1969; Art Galleries Invitational, China Trade Mus, Milton, Mass, 1979; Edge of the Sea, Cape Cod Mus of Art, Dennis, Mass, 2002; 2004 Invitational Exhib, Cape Cod Mus of Art, Dennis, Mass, 2004, 05, 06; Animal King Dom, Cahoon Mus of Am Art, Cotuit, Mass, 2005; World of Words, 2006. *Pos:* Chmn art dept, Lawrence Accad, Groton, Mass, 1963-70, dir, 1968-70; chmn, dir, art dept, St. Margarets-McTernan Sch, Waterbury, Conn, 1974-77; chmn, dir, art dept, Thayer Acad, Braintree, Mass, 1977-2000. *Media:* Watercolor, Acrylic & Oil. *Publ:* Leigh Harrington (auth), Art Imitates Life on Cape Cod, Where Mag, (spring/summer 2002); Judith Montminy (auth), Vogues Catch up Artists Vision, Boston Globe, (1/9/1994); Gerald R. Kelley (auth), The Arts of Summer, Grapevine, (7/12/1978); Saundra Tobins (auth), Inside Cape Cod Magazine, 8/2006. *Dealer:* J Miller Gallery Trinity Place Rte 28 Washpee Mass 02649; Kennedy Studios 66 Main St Vineyard Haven, MA 02568; Gardens Gallery Center of Fine Art 11611 Ellison Wilson Rd Palm Beach Gardens FL 33410. *Mailing Add:* 59 Shields Rd Mashpee MA 02649

SEARLES, CHARLES
PAINTER, SCULPTOR
b Philadelphia, Pa. *Study:* Pa Acad Fine Arts, four-year cert, 73. *Work:* First Pa Bank, Philadelphia; Harlem State Bldg, NY; Smithsonian Inst; Howard Univ; Philip Morris Corp; Arco Chemical Co; First Dist Self-Help Inc, Philadelphia, Pa, 90. *Comn:* Celebration (mural), Gen Serv Admin, Philadelphia, 76; Playtime (mural), City Philadelphia, 78. *Exhib:* Black Artist in Am, Whitney Mus Am Art, 71; Invisible Artist, Philadelphia Mus Art, 73; Jubilee, Boston Mus Fine Arts, 75; Afro-Am Abstract, PS1 Gallery, NY, 81; one-person shows, Landmark Gallery, NY, 81, Peale Gallery, Pa Acad Fine Arts, 82 & Sande Webster, Philadelphia, 83, 85, 87, 90 & 92; Black Art: Ancestral Legacy, Dallas Mus Art, Tex, High Mus, Atlanta, Ga. *Teaching:* Lectr drawing, Philadelphia Col Art, 73-. *Awards:* Cresson Award, Sr Show, Pa Acad Fine Arts, 71; Nat Endowment Fel Arts, 78; Creative Artists Pub Serv Fel, 80 & 81. *Media:* Acrylic; Painted Wood Sculpture. *Mailing Add:* 39 S Farragut St Philadelphia PA 19139

SEARS, STANTON GRAY
PAINTER, SCULPTOR
b Bethlehem, Pa, Oct 22, 50. *Study:* RI Sch Design, BFA, 73; Pa State Univ, MFA, 76. *Comn:* Sculptures, NH Art Asn, Manchester, 79 & 80; sculptures, Phillips Exeter Acad, NH, 81. *Exhib:* Stedman Art Gallery, Rutgers Univ, Camden, NJ, 79; Lee Hall Gallery, Northern Mich Univ, Marquette, 79; Allentown Art Mus, Pa, 79; De Cordova Mus, Lincoln, Mass, 79; Currier Gallery Art, Manchester, NH, 81; solo show, Plymouth State Col Art Gallery, Plymouth, NH, 81; Silvermine Guild Artists, New Canaan, Conn, 81; and others. *Teaching:* Instr, Pa State Univ, State Col, 75-78; instr, Univ NH, Durham, 80-81; instr, Manchester Inst Arts & Sci, NH, 81-83. *Awards:* Drawing Award, Educ Ctr Arts, New Haven, Conn, 78; Currier Award, NH Art Asn 34th Ann, Currier Gallery, 80; Award for Advanc Am Art, Arts Coun Holyoke, Mass, 81. *Bibliog:* David Elliot (auth), What are those stripes in the ravine, Univ NH Newspaper, 81; Laura Holland (auth), Sears' high overhead, Valley Advocate, 81; John Wharton (auth), David Fullam, Stanton Sears, Art New Eng, 81. *Mem:* Col Art Asn Am; NH Art Asn. *Media:* Graphite, Pastel; Welded Aluminum. *Dealer:* Boston Art Work 2345 Washington St Newton Lower Falls MA 02162. *Mailing Add:* McCalister-Art Dept-Dewitt Wallace Library 1600 Grand Ave Saint Paul MN 55105-1801

SEAWELL, THOMAS ROBERT
PRINTMAKER, PHOTOGRAPHER
b Baltimore, Md, Mar 17, 36. *Study:* Wash Univ, BFA, 58; Tex Christian Univ, MFA, 60. *Work:* Portland Mus Art; Libr Cong, Washington, DC; Mem Art Gallery of the Univ of Rochester, NY; Brooklyn Mus, NY; DeCordova Mus, Lincoln, Mass; Purdue Univ, West Lafayette, Ind, 83; JS Blanton Mus, Univ Tex, Austin; Dulin Gallery Art, Knoxville, Tenn; Pushkin Mus Art, Moscow; Del Mar Col, Corpus Christi, Tex; Brockton Art Ctr, Mass; US Info Agy; Univ ND; Alexandria Mus of Art; Ark Art Ctr; many others. *Comn:* Rochester Print Club; Geldermann Print Comn, 85-92; Merchants Nat Bank & Trust, 90; Print Club of Albany, 04. *Exhib:* 30 Yrs of Am Printmaking Including 20th Nat Print Exhib, Brooklyn Mus, 76; retrospective exhib, The Oswego Years, Tyler Art Gallery, State Univ NY, 91; Midwestern Univ, Wichita Falls, Tex, 93; Texas A&M Univ Commerce, 95; Columbia Col, SC, 96; Ceramic Vessel Making by Tex Artist, Richland Col, Dallas, 97, Irving Arts Ctr, Tex, 98, 13th San Angelo Nat Ceramic Competition, San Angelo Mus of Fine Art, Tex, 2000; and many others; Texas Prints, Univ Tex, Austin, 2001; Texas Mud, Ceramics by Texas Artists, Dallas Ctr Contemp Arts, 2002. *Teaching:* Prof drawing & printmaking, State Univ NY, Oswego, 63-91; retired; Vis artist, numerous sch art, 77-89, Print Symposium, Ox Bos, summer 85, Univ Dallas, 89, Henderson State Univ, 97 & ETenn State Univ, 97, Lousiana Col, 04. *Awards:* State Univ NY Res Found Printmaking Fels, 67, 70 & 74; over 60 prizes and awards, nat and regionals competitions. *Bibliog:* The Complete Collagraph, Romano & Ross, The Free Press, Macmillan, NY, 80; Eldon Cunningham (auth), Printmaking: A Primary Source of Expression; Richard Zakin (auth), Hand Formed Ceramics (Creating Form & Surface), Chilton Bk Co, 95. *Mem:* Boston Printmakers; Soc Am Graphic Artists; Philadelphia Watercolor Soc; Tex Sculpture Soc. *Media:* Printmaking, Ceramics, Photography. *Dealer:* Old Prints Shop New York NY. *Mailing Add:* 1513 Park Commerce TX 75428

SEAWRIGHT, JAMES L, JR
SCULPTOR, EDUCATOR
b Jackson, Miss, May 22, 1936. *Study:* Univ Miss, BA, 57; Art Students League, NY, 61-62. *Work:* Mus Mod Art, Whitney Mus Am Art & Solomon R Guggenheim Mus, NY; Larry Aldrich Mus, Ridgefield, Conn; Wadsworth Athenieum, Hartford, Conn. *Comn:* Electronic Environ, Seattle-Tacoma Int Airport, 73; outdoor sculpture, NJ State Mus, Trenton, 76; outdoor sculpture, Mobile Tech Ctr, Pennington, NJ; Sculpture Terminal C, Logan Int Airport, Boston. *Exhib:* Whitney Ann, Whitney Mus Am Art, 67; The Sixties, Mus Mod Art, 67; Focus on Light, NJ State Mus, Trenton, 68; Magic Theater, Nelson Gallery Performing Arts Found, Kansas City, Mo, 68; Cybernetic Serendipity, Inst Contemp Art, London, 69; Theodoron Awards Show, Solomon R Guggenheim Mus, NY, 69; Works for New Spaces, Walker Art Ctr, Minneapolis, 71; Art of the Space Age, Huntsville Mus Art, Ala, 78; Am Renaissance Mus of Art, Fort Lauderdale, Fla; one-man show, David Bermant Found, NY. *Pos:* Dir visual arts prog, Princeton Univ, 74-2003. *Teaching:* Teacher sculpture, Sch Visual Arts, New York, 67-69; lectr sculpture, Princeton Univ, NJ, 69-, prof visual arts, 92-. *Awards:* Nat Endowment Arts Comn, NJ State Mus, 76; Award of Merit, Miss Inst of Arts & Letters, 83; Acad Award in Art, Am Acad Arts & Letters, 97. *Bibliog:* Article, Life Mag, 4/67; Douglas Davis (auth), interview, Art Am, 1-2/68; Ralph T Coe (auth), The Magic Theater, Circle Press, 70. *Mem:* Am Abstract Artists. *Media:* Miscellaneous. *Publ:* Contribr, On the Future of Art, Viking, NY, 70. *Dealer:* OK Harris Works of Art 393 W Broadway NY NY 10012. *Mailing Add:* 421 Grahamtown Rd Middletown NY 10940

SEBASTIAN, JILL C
ENVIRONMENTAL ARTIST, SCULPTOR
b Libertyville, Ill, Mar 24, 1950. *Study:* Univ Wis-Milwaukee, MFA, 79. *Work:* Burpee Art Mus, Rockford, Ill; Haggerty Art Mus, Milwaukee Art Mus, Milwaukee, Wis. *Comn:* Toucan Du, New Orleans, La, 92; sculpture, Lake Terracce, Milwaukee, Wis, 98; Integrated Art, Midwest Express Conv Ctr, Milwaukee, Wis, 98. *Exhib:* Solo exhibs, Purdue Univ, W Lafayette, Ind, 83, Kit Basquin Gallery, Milwaukee, 83, Charles Wustum Mus, Racine, Wis, 84, Bertha Urdang Gallery, NY, 85, Loho Gallery,

Louisville, Ky, 86 & Wis Conv Ctr, Milwaukee, 96; Kohler Art Ctr, Sheboygan, Wis, 86; Walkers Point Ctr for Arts, 87; Dean Jensen Gallery, Milwaukee, 88 & 90; Michael Lord Gallery, Milwaukee, 91-92. *Pos:* Mem, Milwaukee Arts Bd, 91-93, pub art com, 97-2000; chair, Art Futures, 96-98. *Teaching:* Lectr film, design & drawing, Univ Wis-Milwaukee, 79-84; asst prof sculpture, Univ Denver, Color, 84-85; assoc prof, Milwaukee Inst Art & Design, 88-98. *Awards:* Grants, Wis Arts Bd, 81, 82 & 87, Milwaukee Artists Found, 82; Nat Endowment Arts Fel, 85; Sacajawea Award, 89; Milwaikee Artist of Yr, 97; named Artist of Yr, City of Milwaukee, 99. *Bibliog:* Christine Buth-Furness (auth), Jill Sebastian, New Art Examiner, 4/83; John Mominee (auth), Jill Sebastian, Wis Acad Rev, 3/85; Whitney Gould (auth), Midwest Express Ctr, Milwaukee J/Sentinel, 7/98. *Mem:* Col Art Asn; Riverwest Artist Asn. *Publ:* Auth & illusr, Cream City Rev, 81; Aviva Rahmani, rev, & Jim Brozak, rev, New Art Examiner, 84. *Dealer:* Michael H Lod Gallery 420 E Wisconsin Ave Milwaukee WI 53202

SEBEK, MIKLOS LASZLO
SCULPTOR, INSTRUCTOR

b Soskut, Hungary, Dec 6, 41; US citizen. *Study:* Budapest State Atelier of Fine Arts, 66; Budapest Tech Inst of Archit, 68; Montclair State Univ, BA (sculpture), 78. *Work:* bronze reliefs, Am Hungarian Mus, Passaic, NJ; steel sculpture, Clifton Arts Ctr, NJ; bronze sculpture, Rutgers Univ, NJ, Univ Gottingen, Ger & Bergen Co, NJ; bronze relief, Vatican City. *Comn:* bronze portrait of Mayor Chenoweth, Clifton Beautification Comm, NJ, 94 & Nutley, NJ, 97. *Exhib:* The State of the Arts in NJ, Morris Mus, NJ, 84, 1st Open Juried Art Exhib, Bergan Mus, Paramus, NJ, 84; Art Expo, Jacob Javits Ctr, NY, 87; For Arts Sake, Hunterdon Arts Ctr, Clinton, NJ, 89; Audubon, Nat Arts Club, NY, 80-96; Audubon, Salmagundi Club, NY, 81-2005; Interiorscapes, Monmouth Mus, NJ, 91; Artists from Hungary, Hungarian Embassy, Wash, 94. *Collection Arranged:* Sextet Marble, Morris Mus Arts & Sci, 2005. *Teaching:* instr, Bloomfield Art Ctr, NJ, 98; instr sculpture, Clifton Adult Sch, 94-2006. *Awards:* Best in Show Award, Art Ctr Caldwell, Col ND, 2002; Best of Show, Millburn Art Show, 2004; Best Sculpture, West Essex Art Show, 2005. *Bibliog:* NJ Coun on the Arts, Channel 50, 94; Tom Sullivan (auth) One City One Nation, Channel 19, 94; Steve Cooper (auth) Art in New Hampshire, WMUR-ABCTV, 2000. *Mem:* Audubon Artist (sr vpres, 99-2005, exhib chmn, 2003); Allied Artists Am (exhib chmn, 2006; S Vt Arts Center. *Media:* Bronze, Marble, Steel, Wood. *Publ:* Public Art, The Guild Archit Sculpture, 98. *Dealer:* Walker-Kornbluth Art Gallery Fairlawn NJ; Louisa Melrose Art Gallery Frenchtown NJ. *Mailing Add:* 112 Lafayette Ave Passaic NJ 07055

SEBELIUS, HELEN
PAINTER

b Assiniboia, Sask, 1953. *Study:* Univ Regina, Sask, 71-72; Alberta Col Art, Calgary, Dipl, 74-78; Banff Ctr, Alta, 80; Nova Scotia Col Art & Design, Halifax, MFA, 87. *Work:* Alberta Art Found; Can Coun Art Bank & Dept External Affairs, Ottawa; Grant MacEwan Col, Edmonton; Nickle Arts Mus, Calgary; Red Deer Col. *Exhib:* Solo exhibs, Gallery O, Toronto, Ont, 81, Olga Korper Gallery, Toronto, Ont, 83, 85, 88 & 91, Anna Leonowens Gallery, Halifax, NS, 87, New Gallery, Calgary, Alta, 87; Visions of Alberta, Muttart Art Gallery, Calgary, 88; Drawings/Motivations, Glenbow Mus, Calgary, Alta, 88; Four: Toyo Kawamura, New Gallery, Calgary, Alta, 88; OR Gallery, Vancouver, BC, 94. *Pos:* Guest speaker, Calif Col Arts & Crafts, Oakland, 81; asst dir, Snyder Hedlin Fine Art Consult, Calgary, Alta, 81-83; bd dir, Off Centre, Calgary, Alta, 84-85; adv bd, New Gallery, Calgary, Alta, 88-. *Teaching:* Instr textile & foundations, Alta Col Art Calgary, 81-85; vis artist & instr textiles, 87-88, instr drawing, 88-; instr foundations, Univ Calgary, Alta, 84, instr drawing 88-; instr papermaking, David Thompson Univ, Nelson, BC, 84, Red Deer Col, Alta, 85; teaching assitantships, Nova Scotia Col Art & Design, Halifax, 85-87, instr drawing, 87. *Awards:* Alta Cult Assts Award, 79; Project Grant, 82-83, Short Term Grant, 84, Travel Grant, 85, Can Coun; Project Grant, Alta Cult Project, 82-83. *Bibliog:* Nancy Tousley (auth), 5 plus 5, 9/27/85 & Drawings/Motivations, 10/5/88, Calgary Herald; Christiane Laforge (auth), Papiers Transformes 11, Le Quotidien, 5/16/87. *Media:* All media. *Mailing Add:* c/o Olga Korper Gallery 17 Morrow Ave Toronto ON M6R 2H9 Canada

SEBOROVSKI, CAROLE
PAINTER

b San Diego, Calif, 60. *Study:* Calif Col Arts & Crafts, BFA, 82; Hunter Col, MFA, 87. *Work:* Metrop Mus Art, Mus Mod Art, Whitney Mus Art, NY; Brooklyn Mus, NY; Baltimore Mus Art, Md; Cleveland Ctr Contemp Art, Ohio; Addison Gallery Am Art, Andover, Mass; Fogg Art Mus, Cambridge, Mass; Museo Cantonale d'Arte, Lugano, Switzerland; Tel Aviv Mus, Israel; Wadsworth Atheneum, Conn; Yale Univ Art Gallery. *Exhib:* Recent Acquisitons: Prints and Portfolios, Brooklyn Mus, NY, 86; Geometric Perspectives, Pfiser Inc, arranged by Mus Mod Art, NY, 91; one-person exhibs, Lorence-Monk Gallery, NY, 91, 92 & 93, Galerie Karsten Greve, Paris, 91, 92, & 94 Angles Gallery, Santa Monica, Calif, 91 & 92, Betsy Sr Contemp Prints, NY, 93, John Weber Gallery, NY & John Berggruen Gallery, San Francisco, 94 & 98, Cheryl Haines Gallery, San Francisco, 2000, Mitchell-Innes & Nash Gallery, NY, 2000, Miller Block Gallery, Boston, 2001; The Return of the Cadvre Exquis, traveling exhib, Corcoran Gallery Art, Washington, DC, 93; On Paper, Barbara Mathes Gallery, NY, 93; New Sculpture: Soft Surfaces, Transamerica Pyramid Lobby, San Francisco, 93; Contemp Abstract Am Prints, Addison Gallery, Andover, Mass, 93; Arthur M Sackler Mus, Harvard Univ Art Mus, Cambridge, Mass, 97; Sallonja, Palma de Mallorca, Baleares, Spain; Museo Cantopale d'arte, Lugano, Switz; Vassar Col, Poughkeepsie, NY; Gaga, NY, 98; Works on Paper, Mitchell-Innes and Nash, NY, 99; Into the New Century, Nohra Haime Gallery, NY, 99; Often, Margaret Thatcher Projects, NY, 99; Consonanze Museo Cantonale d'Arte, Lugano, Switz, 2000; Celebrating Modern Art: The Anderson Collection, San Francisco Mus Mod Art, Calif, 2000; End Papers: Drawings 1890-1900 and 1990-2000, Neuberger Mus Art, Purchase, NY, 2000; Minimalism, Jim Kempner Fine Arts, NY, 2001; others. *Awards:* Pollock-Krasner Found Grant, 86; Agnes Bourne Fel Visual Arts, 90; Nat Endowment Arts Grant, 91; Art Develop Comt Grant, 99. *Bibliog:* Susanne Henle (auth), Unbeschreiblich Weiblich, Frankfurter Allegmeine Zeitung, 7/4/92; John Good gallery review, The New Yorker, 8/92; Ann Wilson Lloyd (auth), Carole Seborovski at Karsten Greve, Art in Am, 12/92; Phyllis Braff (auth), Drawing is Another Kind of Language, The New York Times, 10/99; Mario Naves (auth), Currently Hanging, The New York Observer, 4/2000; Janet Koplos (auth), Carole Seborovski at Mitchell-Innes & Nash, Art in Am, 10/2000; others

SECKEL, CORNELIA
PUBLISHER, WRITER

b Queens, NY, Jun 28, 1946. *Study:* Queens Col, NY, BA, 68; Mich State Univ, East Lansing, MA, 73. *Awards:* Courage & Achievement Award, All Women in Bus, 85; Governors Citation, Governor Cuomo, NY, 94; Friend of Pastel award, Pastel Soc Am, 2001. *Mem:* Nat Arts Club; Artists Fel Inc; Catharine Lorillard Wolfe Art Club; Art Table Inc. *Res:* Cultural art. *Interests:* Travel; Gardening; Beach combing. *Publ:* columnist, Art Times. *Mailing Add:* c/o Art Times PO Box 730 Mt Marion NY 12456

SECKEL, PAUL BERNHARD
PAINTER, DESIGNER

b Osnabrueck, Ger, July 18, 18; US citizen. *Study:* London Cent Sch Arts & Crafts; Univ Buffalo, BFA; Yale Univ, MFA. *Exhib:* Recent Drawings, USA, Mus Mod Art, NY, 56; Drawings by Invitation, Flint Inst Art, 57; Exhib of Paintings Eligible for Purchase, Am Acad Arts & Lett, 63; Audubon Artists Ann; Art Commun Int: The Best Contemp Art, CD-ROM Ser, Juried Collection, 96. *Awards:* Emily Lowe Award, 63. *Mem:* New York Artists Equity Asn. *Media:* Acrylic, Oil. *Publ:* Auth, How to Make Original Color Lithographs--A Manual for Professional Artists, 70. *Mailing Add:* PO Box 268 Atlantic Beach NY 11509-0268

SEDERS, FRANCINE LAVINAL
DEALER

b Paris, France, Dec 12, 32; US citizen. *Study:* Univ Paris Law Sch, MLaws; Univ Wash, MLS. *Pos:* Mgr, Otto Seligman Gallery, Seattle, Wash, 65-66; pres & dir, Francine Seders Gallery Ltd, Seattle, 66-. *Mem:* North Seattle Community Col Found, 83-90 & 94-; Art Table, NY. *Specialty:* Contemporary paintings, sculpture and graphics. *Mailing Add:* 6701 Greenwood Ave N Seattle WA 98103

SEED, SUZANNE LIDDELL
PHOTOGRAPHER, WRITER

b Gary, Ind, Mar 8, 40. *Study:* Yale Univ Summer Sch Music Art, 61; Ind Univ, with Henry Holmes Smith, BA, 63; Art Inst Chicago, MFA, 82. *Work:* Chrysler Mus; Chase Manhattan Bank, NY; Exchange Nat Bank, Chicago. *Exhib:* Los Angeles Inst Contemp Art's Photog, Downey Mus Art, 80; Chicago Contemp Photog, Los Angeles Ctr Photog Studies, Calif, 81; Women/Image/Nature, Tyler Sch Art, Philadelphia, Pa & Rochester Inst Technol, NY, 81; and others. *Mem:* Soc Photogrs Communications; Soc Photogrs Educ; Writers' Guild. *Publ:* Auth & illusr, Saturday's Child, J Philip O'Hara, 73; contribr, Women See Men, McGraw Hill, 77; contribr, Women Photograph Men, Morrow, 77; auth & illusr, Fine Trades, Follett, 79. *Dealer:* Marjorie Neikrug 224 East 68th St New York NY 10021. *Mailing Add:* 175 E Delaware Chicago IL 60611

SEELBACH, ANNE ELIZABETH
PAINTER, INSTRUCTOR

b Detroit, Mich. *Study:* New York Univ, NYC, BA, 1967; Internationale Sommerakademie for Bildende Kunst, Salzburg, Austria, cert (painting), 1968; Hunter College (City Univ of NY), MFA, 1985. *Work:* The Newark Mus, Newark, NJ; Radcliffe Inst, Harvard Univ, Cambridge, Mass; Lyman Allyn Mus, New London, Conn; Frauen Mus, Bonn, Ger; Prudential Insurance Art Collection, Newark, NJ. *Exhib:* Newark Mus, Newark, NJ, 1984; Hudson River Mus, Yonkers, NY, 1984; Frauen Mus, Bonn, Ger, 1986-1988; Attleboro Mus, Attleboro, Mass, 1996; Smolyan Art Center, Smolyan, bulgaria, 2006. *Pos:* Curational asst, the costume inst, Metropolitan Mus of Art, NY, 1974-78; curator, Monhegan Mus, Monhegan Island Maine, 1992-95. *Teaching:* Instr, Univ RI, 1990; instr fundamentals, 3-D design, Parsons Sch of Design, 1994; instr watercolor, studio painting, Victor d'Amico Inst Art, Amaganset, NY, 1994-. *Awards:* Cash Prize, annual Juried exhib, Hudson River Mus, NY, 1984; MacDowell Colony Peterborough, NH, 1987; Triangle Artists Workshop, Pine Plans, NY, 1988; Honorary Prize, annual juried exhib, Monmouth Museum, NJ, 1989; Painting Fellowship, The Bunting Insti Gallery, Radcliffe College, 1990; Int Guest Artists, Bulgaria, 2006. *Bibliog:* Shirey L David (auth), Newark Whimsical Houses, NY Times (NJ sect, Pg 8), 12/1984; Hank Hoffman (auth), The Big Picture, New Haven Advocate, 4/2005. *Mem:* Artists Alliance E Hampton, East Hampton, NY. *Media:* All Media, Metal & Welded, Watercolor, Oil Paint. *Publ:* Auth, The Hunebedden Paintings, New Haven Advocate, 4/2005. *Dealer:* Kouros Gallery, 23 E 73rd St New York NY 10021. *Mailing Add:* PO Box 812 Amagansett NY 11930

SEEMAN, HELENE ZUCKER
WRITER, CURATOR

b New York, NY, Apr 20, 50. *Study:* Boston Univ, BA; Queens Col, NY, MLS. *Collection Arranged:* Photorealism Traveling Exhibition, NZ mus, 75-76; Audrey Flack, Univ Bridgeport, Conn, 75; Look Again, Taft Mus, Cincinnati, Ohio, 76; Rothmans of Pall Mall Traveling Exhibition, 77-78; New Realism, Jacksonville Mus, Fla, 77; Off the Beaten Path, Brainerd Gallery, State Univ NY Col, Potsdam, 77. *Pos:* Cur, Prudential Ins Co, NJ, 80- & 99-. *Teaching:* Lectr, New Sch, NY, 80 & 83, Avila Col, 81, Scripps Col, 82, Walker Art Ctr, 83, Fairleigh Dickinson Univ, NJ, 86, North

Gallery, Palm Beach, 90 & New York Univ, 92, 93 & 94. *Bibliog:* Randy Rosen (auth), Corporate collecting at a crossroads, Nat Arts Guide, 11-12/80; Connoisseur's corner, Wall St Transcript, 6/28/82; Keepers of corporate art, Fortune, 3/21/83; The corporate collector, Village Voice, 10/23/84. *Mem:* Asn Corporate Art Cur. *Interests:* Organization, research and published documentation of artists and special exhibitions. *Publ:* Coauth, SoHo, Neal Schuman, 79; The PhotoRealists, Abrams, 79; contribr, Alternative Careers for Librarians, Neal Schuman, 79

SEEREY-LESTER, JOHN VERNON
PAINTER
b Manchester, Eng, Dec 6, 45. *Study:* Salford Col Art, Lancashire, Eng, dipl art, 62. *Work:* Salford Art Gallery, Lancashire, Eng; Manchester Art Gallery, Eng; Leigh Yawkey Woodson Art Mus, Wausau, Wis. *Comn:* Drawing, Royal Lytham & St Ann's Golf Club, Cancer Soc fund raiser, British Open, 74; portrait of Lord Chalfont, Brit Indust Develop Corp, Eng, 75; painting of Giant Panda, World Wildlife Fund, 81. *Exhib:* Solo exhib, World Wildlife Fund, Ann Conf, Manchester, Eng, 82; Birds in Art, Leigh Yawkey Woodson Art Mus, Wausau, Wis, 83-94; World Wildlife Fund, Washington, DC, 84; Soc Wildlife Art for the Nation, Inaugural Exhibition, Guildhall Art Gallery, London, 85; Birds in Art, 87-94; Seerey-Lester Wildlife Art Seminars, Can, Fla, Guatamala, Eng & Alaska Masters, Watson-Guptill Publ, 85. *Teaching:* Seerey-Lester Wildlife Art Seminars, Can, Fla, Alaska, Mont, Calif, Colo, SC, Tikal & Eng. *Awards:* Artist Hall of Fame, US Art, 93; Award of Excellence, Soc Animal Artists; Master Artist, US Art, 98. *Bibliog:* Chuck Wechsler (auth), The arrival of John Seerey-Lester, Wildlife Art News, 85; Face to Face with Nature: The Art of John Seerey-Lester; other articles in US Art News, Southwest Art News & Prints & Wildlife Art. *Mem:* World Wildlife Fund; Soc Wildlife Art for the Nation (SWAN); Wilderness Soc; Audubon Soc. *Media:* Oil on Canvas, Acrylic on Panel

SEFARBI, HARRY
PAINTER
b Chester, Pa, 17. *Study:* Westchester State Teachers Col, Pa, 39; Pa Acad Fine Arts; Acad Grande Chaumiere, Paris; Barnes Found, Merion, Pa. *Exhib:* Pa Acad Fine Arts, 50; Penn State Univ; Philadelphia Art Alliance, Pa; Proctor Art Ctr, Bard Col, NY, 69; solo exhib, Galerie Huit, Paris, Green Hill, Lower Merion, Pa, 79, Woodmere Art Mus, Philadelphia, 91; Newman & Saunders Galleries, 2000 & 2004. *Teaching:* instr, Barnes Found. *Awards:* Philadelphia Regional Show, Pa, 65. *Media:* Oil on panel, acrylic, oil. *Specialty:* Figurative. *Mailing Add:* c/o Newman & Sannders Galleries 120 Bloomingdale Ave Wayne PA 19087

SEGAL, BARBARA JEANNE
SCULPTOR, INSTRUCTOR
b Bronxville, NY, Jan 27, 53. *Study:* Pratt Inst Technol, NY, 70-72, BFA, 96; L'Ecole Nationale Superieuve Des Beaux-Arts Paris, 72-74; Sch Visual Arts, 90-94. *Work:* Malcomb Forbes Collection, NY; Whitehouse Collection, City of Yonkers; Neuberger Mus of Art. *Comn:* sculpture park, Phillipse Manor Hall, The City of Yonkers, 2000-2001; Yonkers Sculpture Park on the Hudson, 2001-2003, Commissued by the City of Yonkers; Metropolitan Transportation Authority, 2005. *Exhib:* New Talent, Alan Stone Gallery, NY, 84-85; Art of Northeast Am, Silvermine Gallery, Conn, 86, 87 & 88; one-women shows, Gallery Henoch, 89, Westchester Gallery, 94, Over and Under, The Hudson River Mus, 98 & Women of Stone, Neuberger Mus Art, 2000; The Reality of Illusion, Contemp Grafts, Mus, Ore, 92; Musee Rodin, Hommagea Collamarini, Hokin Gallery, Fla, 93-94; Art as a Verb, Mus at Fashion Inst Tech, NY, 95; Virtual Bride, La Mama La Galleria, NY, 99. *Teaching:* Instr, private, formerly; instr stone carving, Sch Visual Arts, New York, 90-95; instr contemp sculpture, Westchester Art Workshop, 93-; instr, Nat Acad Design, 94; instr stone carving, Sch Visual Arts, 90-. *Awards:* Claudia & Maurice Stone Memorial Award, Silvermine Gallery, 88; Sculpture Award, Int Art Competition, 88; Hud Grant, 95; Mayoral Citation, 2000; Art Westchester Art, council, 2004; MTA/ Art for Transit. *Bibliog:* Patricia Malarcher (auth), 90's commentary in a classical medium (review), NY Times, 94; In Yonkers Hope is Chised in Stone, NY Times, 95, Roberta Hersenston (auth), NY Times, 98; Domenick Lombard, Art New England, 98; Beverly Russell (auth), Sculpture Mag, 98; Roberta Hershenson (auth), Works that Appear Soft but are Posed in Stone, NY Times, 2000; Carved in Stone, JournalNews, New York, 2000; Yonkers Waterfront Moves Ahead NY Times, Elsa Brenner, 3/2002; Sculpture Depicts City's River Links, Journal News, Caren Hatbfinger, 7/2003; Tograce Yonkers Station work that Mirrors the River, Roberta Hersherison, 2004. *Mem:* Art on Main Street, (chmn, 94); Yonkers Friends of the Arts, 2003-2005. *Media:* Stone, Metals. *Collection:* Small works & Public Art. *Publ:* Co-auth, Barbara Segal Sculptor, EGG, 90; New York Mode - Aus Marmor, Germany, 99. *Mailing Add:* 88 Alta Ave Yonkers NY 10705-1411

SEGAL, MARY
GRAPHIC ARTIST, PRINTMAKER
b Cincinnati, Ohio, Dec 25, 33. *Study:* Brown Univ, BA, 55; RI Sch Design; Akademie der Bildenden Kunste, Munich, Ger, 55-56; Laguna Col Art, with Paul Darrow, 65-69. *Work:* Sackner Arch of Concrete and Visual Poetry, Miami Beach; Ctr Arts, Vero Beach, Fla; Atlanta Women's Feminist Health Ctr; City Orlando; Larson Drawing Collection, Austin Peay State Univ, Clarksville, Tenn. *Exhib:* National Exhibit of Prints & Drawings, Bradley Univ, Peoria, 90-91; Autobiographical Subjects, Fla Ctr Contemp Art, Tampa, 91; one-person shows, Sarah Doyle Ctr, Brown Univ, Providence, 91, Wolfson Galleries, MDCC, Miami, 93, TULA Found, Atlanta, 94 & Atlantic Ctr Harris House, 94; Nat Mus Women, 96; South Fla Art Ctr, Miami; Dunedin Fine Arts Ctr, Fla, 97; Thomas Ctr Gallery, Gainexville, Fla, 97; Burns Rd Ctr Gallery, GardensArt, Palm Beach Gardens, 2001. *Pos:* Panelist nat conf, Women's Caucus Art, 95. *Teaching:* printmaking and mixed media, Ctr for The Arts, Vero Beach, Fla & Indian River Community Col, 90-2000. *Awards:* Hambidge Ctr Creative Arts Resident Fel, Rabun Gap, Ga, 91 & 94; Centrum Found Resident Fel Printmaking, Port Townsend, Wash, 92; SAF/Nat Endowment Arts Grant for Works on Paper, 92. *Bibliog:* Helen Kohen (auth), Text and images, Miami Herald, 93; Jo Ann Wein (auth), Mary Segal, SAF, 93; Philip E Bishop (auth), Some people call it eccentric, Orlando Sentinel, 94. *Mem:* Women's Caucus Art; Fla Printmakers Soc. *Media:* Collage, Mixed Media. *Dealer:* Mary Woerner PO Box 1647 Stuart FL 34995; Charles Kristen Gallery 3905 W 32nd Ave Denver CO 80212. *Mailing Add:* PO Box 861 Roseland FL 32957

SEGAL, TAMA & DAVID
DEALER, CURATOR
b Tama, b Brooklyn, NY, Feb 13, 49, b David, b Bronx, NY, Aug 31, 40. *Study:* Tama, Brooklyn Mus; Pratt Inst; New Sch; David, City Col, New Sch Social Res, BFA, 64. *Exhib:* Peter Max in Charlotte, 93; Thomas Kinkade, 1997-2005. *Pos:* Owners, Segal Fine Art, 77-. *Teaching:* Guest lectr contemp Native Am painting & sculpture, New Sch Soc Res. *Mem:* Munic Art Soc, NY; Santa Fe Festival Arts; Mus Am Indian; Mint Mus & Mint Mus Crafts. *Specialty:* contemporary Native American art. *Mailing Add:* 8047 Tifton Rd Charlotte NC 28226

SEGAL, THOMAS H
ART DEALER
b New York, NY, Feb 18, 40. *Study:* Univ Pa, BA, 61; Columbia Univ, MBA, 65. *Pos:* Pres, Thomas Segal Gallery, Boston, Mass, 76-96; trustee, Inst Contemp Art, 84-; vis comt, Dept Hist Art, Univ Pa, 91-97; trustee, Mass Col Art, 96-. *Mem:* Art Dealers Asn Am. *Specialty:* Impressionist, modern and contemporary art. *Publ:* Jasper Johns (catalog), Thomas Segal Gallery, 81; Helen Frankenthaler, Thomas Segal Gallery. *Mailing Add:* Thomas Segal Gallery 4 W University Pl Baltimore MD 21218

SEGALL-MARX, MADELEINE (MADDY MARX)
SCULPTOR, PAINTER
b New York, 52. *Study:* Univ Mich, BA; Art Students League, anat with Robert Beverly Hale, sculpture with Nat Kaz & Jose de Creeft, 77-80; studies at Foundries & Stoneyards of Pietrasanta, Italy. *Work:* Art Students League Permanent Collection, NY; Rothenberg Mem Mathematics Wall, Stuyvesant High Sch, NY, 99, Stuyvesant Centennial Wall, 2004. *Comn:* Stuyuesant High Sch, City NY, Rothenberg Mem & NY Street Tree Consortium, 90; The Childrens Ride (fiberglass pub sculpture), NY Dept Parks, 95; Collection of City of NY. *Exhib:* Sculptors League, Lever House, NY, 94; Audubon Nat Exhib, 94 & 95; Woodstock Artists Asn, 94; Soho Loft Pioneer Show, Puffin Found, NY, 96; Traveling Painting Exhib, Nat Asn Women Artists, 96-99; WaveCrest, Sculpture Park, Hyde Park, NY. *Pos:* Bd control, Art Students League, NY, 79-80; pres, Nat Asn Women Artists, 99-2002. *Teaching:* Instr sculpture, PS 41, NY, 93-96, Childrens Aid Soc, NY, 93-96 & Barrett House Sch Art, Poughkeepsie, NY, 94-. *Awards:* Medal Honor, Catherine Lorillard Wolfe Art Club, 91; Medal Honor & Amelia Peabody Award, Nat Asn Women Artists, 93, 97 & 2005; Excalibur Foundry Award, Pen & Brush, 94; Audubon Artists Award, Sculpture; Dutchess Co Exec Arts Award, 2006. *Bibliog:* William Zimmer (auth), Sculpture on 4 lush acres, NY Times, 9/6/92; Eileen Watkin (auth), East Brunswick gallery sculpture competition, Sunday Star Ledger, 9/13/92; Toby Axelrod (auth), A sculpture that won't offend anybody, New York Observer, 1/16/94; Stuart Leung (auth), Stuyvesant Legend Remembered with Memorial Wall, The Spectator, 12/99. *Mem:* Nat Asn Women Artists (1st vpres, 97-99, pres, 99-2002); Allied Artists Am; Audobon Artists; Catherine Lorillard Wolfe Art Club; Woodstock Artist Asn. *Media:* Miscellaneous Media. *Mailing Add:* 148 Greene St New York NY 10012

SEGGER, MARTIN JOSEPH
HISTORIAN, MUSEUM DIRECTOR
b Felixtowe, Eng, Nov 22, 46; Can citizen. *Study:* Univ Victoria, BA, 69, with Alan Gowans, dipl, 70; Warburg Inst, Univ London, with E H Gombrich, MPhil, 73. *Collection Arranged:* Arts of the Forgotten Pioneers (with catalog), Maltwood Mus, 71; Samuel Maclure-Architect, 74 & House Beautiful, An Exhibit of Decorative Arts 1860-1920 (with catalog), 75, BC Prov Mus; Colonial Painters of British Columbia, 79; The Victoria Portrait, 81; To Sir Yehudi Menuhin, 85; John Wright, Architect, 90. *Pos:* Dir, Maltwood Mus, Victoria, 71-, BC Heritage Trust, Provincial Heritage Adv Bd, Heritage Can & Int Coun Monuments & Sites Can; consult mus training, Egypt/UNESCO, 83; consult, Heritas Inc, 83; consult, Icom, Costa Rica, 89; chair, Int Comt Training of Mus Personnel, Int Coun Mus; vchair, BC Provincial Capital Comn; Pres, Soc of Architectural Hist, Pacific Northwest Branch; Pres, Commonwealth assn of Mus. *Teaching:* Lectr art hist & mus studies, Univ Victoria, BC, 71-. *Awards:* Lieut Gov Medal, BC Heritage, 89; Harley J McKee Award, Asn Preserv Technol; Award of Merit, Victoria Hallmark Soc; Queens Jubilee Medal; and others. *Mem:* Soc Archit Historians; Can Mus Asn (nat exec mem, 75-77); Soc Study Archit Can (vpres, currently); Royal Soc Arts Fel; and others; Commonwealth Asn Mus (pres). *Specialty:* fine & decorative arts. *Interests:* motor mechanics. *Publ:* Auth, Museum Operations Manual, 83; Samuel Maclure: An Architectural Biography, 86; The Development of the Gordon Head Campus, 88; Exploring Victoria's Architecture, 96; and others. *Mailing Add:* Maltwood Art Mus & Gallery Univ of Victoria PO Box 3025 St C Victoria BC V8W 3P2 Canada

SEGUIN, JEAN-PIERRE
PAINTER, PHOTOGRAPHER
b Montreal, Que, Feb 12, 51. *Study:* Cegep du Vieux-Montreal, DEC, 72; Univ de Que, Montreal, BA, 75, MA, 79. *Work:* Mus du Que; Conseil des Arts du Can, Ottawa; Univ du Que a Montreal; Steinberg; Mus d'Art Contemporain a Montreal. *Comn:* Stained-glass window, Govt du Que, Ville de la Baie, 86. *Exhib:* Gravure du Quebec, Mus d'Art Contemporain, Montreal, 74; Galerie Nat, Ottawa, Ont, 77; Jeune Contemporain 80, London Art Gallery, Ont, 80; ACTFART, Musée du

Saguenay-Lac-St-Jean, Chicoutimi, Oue, 85; Nommage à A Wharol, Galerie 13, Montreal, 87; Histoire De Collections, Mus d'Art Contemporain, Montreal, 88; Passages, Mus Du Saguenay, Que, 89; Le Blanc of MFS Nuits, éoifice Belgo, Montreal, 91; Two Cities/Latitudes Exchange, Lattitudes 53 Gallery, Edmonton, Alta, 95; Les Ateliers, S'Exposent, Montreal, 95; Autres Passages, CNE, Jonquiére, 95; Mobilier d'Artistes, Galerie Optica, 95. *Teaching:* Charge de cours activite de synthese, Univ Que, Montreal, 76-78 & prof painting & drawing, Univ Que, Chicoutimi, 79-717. *Awards:* Greenshield Fel, 75; ler Prix, Concours de Dessin & Biennale du Que, Govt du Que, 79; ler Prix Biennale Du, Que, 89. *Bibliog:* René Payant (auth), Dépeindre le photographique, Galerie Graff, 83; Giles Daigneault (auth), Jean-Pierre Seguin: Peindre ou feindre, Le Devoir, 83; Pierre Ouellet (auth), Le Savoir peint, Revue Protée, 85. *Media:* All. *Res:* Systems of representation & production of both photographic & pictorial portraiture. *Publ:* Coauth, Du neuf a cinq, Articule, 80; Entre le corps et la matiére, Intervention, 81; Ou, Langage Plus, 83; illusr, Langage et savoir, Protée, 85; Un Printemps Costaud, Vie Des Arts, 91. *Mailing Add:* Univ Quebec a Chicoutimi Art Dept Chicoutimi PQ G7H 2B1 Canada

SEHRING, ADOLF
PAINTER, SCULPTOR

b Urupino, Russia, June 8, 30; US citizen. *Study:* Berlin Acad Art, 46-49. *Work:* Bayly Mus; Chrysler Mus; Temple Univ; Am Embassy; St Mary's Inst; and others. *Exhib:* Youth Paints, Victoria & Albert Mus, London, Eng, 47; Qualite dela Vie, Grandpalais Salon, Paris, 75; Virginia Scene, Bayly Mus, Charlottesville, 78; Adolf Sehring, St Mary's Collection Mus, Mich, 78; Biannual Exhib, Va Mus Art, Richmond, 81; Chrysler Mus, 83. *Pos:* Lectr, varied civic groups, 72-81 & Lehigh Valley Art Groups, 75. *Awards:* First Prize of Gcr, Rias, Berlin, 46. *Bibliog:* Levin Houston (auth), Adolf Sehring and Realism, Kembel Publ, 77; S Bullard (auth), Sehring Paints, Daily Progress, 78; Rome Accepts Papal Portrait by Sehring, Assoc Press, 78; The Real World of A Sehring, English/Japanese; and numerous others. *Media:* All Media; Metal, Cast

SEIDE, PAUL A
SCULPTOR

b New York, NY, Feb 15, 49. *Study:* Egani Neon Glassblowing Sch, cert, 71; Univ Wis, BS(art), 74. *Work:* Nat Mus Mod Art, Kyoto, Japan; Corning Mus Glass, Corning, NY; Chrysler Mus Art, Norfolk, WVa; Mus des Arts Decoratifs, Lausanne, Switz; Lannan Found Mus, Palm Beach, Fla; and others. *Comn:* Swarovski World of Crystal, Wattens, Austria, 95. *Exhib:* One-man exhib, Heller Gallery, NY, 82, 84 & 88, Kurland Summers Gallery, Los Angeles, Calif, 84 & 86 & Habatat Galleries, Bay Harbour Islands, Fla, 85 & 87, Leo Kaplan Modern, NY, 98; Corning Mus Glass, NY, 78-79; Leigh Yawkey Woodson Art Mus, Wausau, Wis, 79, 81 & 88; Hokkaido Mus Mod Art, Sapporo, Japan, 82; Illumination: The Quality of Light, Pittsburgh Ctr for the Arts, Pa, 85; Luminosity, The Alternative Mus, NY, 86; The Saxe Collection, Mus Am Craft, NY, 87; Light and Transparency, Mus Bellerive, 88 & Illuminated Sculpture, Sanske Gallerie, 88, Zurich, Switz; Expressions en Verre II, Musee des Artes Decoratifs, Lausanne, Switz; Building a Permanent Collection, Mus Am Craft, NY, 90. *Pos:* Design dir & vpres, Milropa Studios, New York, 75-. *Teaching:* Instr, Milropa Studios, New York, 75-76 & New Sch Social Res, New York, 76-77. *Awards:* Res Grant, Union Molycorp, Los Angeles, 82. *Bibliog:* Judy Spurgin (auth), article, Art Craft Mag, 10-11/80; Sylvia Netzer (auth), Rays of Glass-Paul Seide, Neus Glas Mag, 3/88. *Mem:* Glass Art Soc. *Media:* Blown Glass, Neon. *Dealer:* Leo Kaplan Mod Art 41 E 57th St New York NY. *Mailing Add:* 29 W 17th St New York NY 10011

SEIDEN, ARTHUR
PAINTER, ILLUSTRATOR

b Brooklyn, NY. *Study:* Queens Col, BA(cum laude), 74; Art Students League, 8 yrs study with Will Barnet, S Dickinson, Charles Alston & Mario Cooper; New Sch, with Stuart Davis. *Work:* Kerlan Collection, Univ Minn; Philip Morris Corp & Kennedy Gallery, NY; Rutgers Univ, New Brunswick, NJ; Mazza Collection, New Britain Youth Mus; Univ Southern Miss; New Britain Mus Am Art. *Comn:* Hoffmann-LaRoche, Eli Lilly, Gen Motors, Hearst Pubs, others. *Exhib:* Am Watercolor Soc, Nat Acad Design, NY, 64, 67 & 68; one-man show, Lotos Club, NY, 74, 02; Lotos Club, 75; Am Watercolor Soc 123rd Ann Exhib, 90; Nat Acad 169th Ann Exhib, 94. *Collection Arranged:* Lotos Club, NY. *Pos:* guest instr, NY Univ. *Teaching:* Guest instr, New York City Community Col. *Awards:* Bk Awards, Am Inst Graphic Arts, 54, 57 & 61. *Mem:* Am Watercolor Soc; life mem Lotos Club; life mem Art Students League; Artist's Equity NY Inc; Soc Illusr; Artists Fel, Inc. *Media:* Transparent Watercolor, Gouache. *Specialty:* original illustrations. *Interests:* collecting autographs. *Publ:* Illusr, Train to Timbuctoo, Golden Bks, 51; Greek Gods and Heroes, 61, Big Treasure Book of Fairy Tales, 64 & Big Book of Kittens, 68, Grosset & Dunlap; Doc stops a war, Reader's Digest; Heroines of the American Revolution, 98. *Dealer:* Kendra Krienke Gallery. *Mailing Add:* 75 Lloyd Ln Lloyd Harbor NY 11743-9781

SEIDEN, KATIE
SCULPTOR, ASSEMBLAGE ARTIST

b New York, NY. *Study:* Sarah Lawrence Col, Bronxville, NY, BA, 58; New York Univ, New York, NY, MA, 60. *Work:* House of Humor & Satire, Gabrova, Bulgaria; Grand Manan Mus, New Brunswick, Can; Wash Co Mus Fine Arts, Hagerstown, Md; Helen S Keller Nat Ctr, Kingspoint, NY; Saint Mary Abbey, Mechanicsville, Md; Islip Art Mus, E Islip, Mid-Houston Arts & Sci Ctr, Poughkeepsie, NY. *Comn:* Sculpture (3 feet), comn by Mr & Mrs David Wood, Berkeley, Calig, 84; sculpture (7 feet), comn by Stephen Style, NY, 85. *Exhib:* Solo exhibs, Edward Williams Gallery, Hackensack, NJ, 84, Cent Hall Gallery, Soho, NY, 79, 82, 84, Five & Dime, East Village, NY, 87, Wash Co Mus Fine Arts, Hagerstown, Md, 88 & Sensory Evolution Gallery, NY, 87 & 88, San Francisco Int Airport, Calif, 88 & Myth & Reality, Gallery 10, Washington, DC, 90; Lines of Vision I: Drawings by Contemp Women Traveling Exhib, Islip Art Mus, E Islip, NY, 92, ARC Gallery, Chicago, 92; Lines of Vision II: Drawings by Contemp Women, US Info Agency Traveling Exhib, 89-90; Centennial Exhib Nat Asn Women Artists Traveling Exhib, 89- 90; The Expressionist Surface & Contemp Art in Plaster, Queens Mus, Flushing, NY, 90; Original Sin, Hillwood Art, Brookville, NY, 91. *Pos:* Arts ed & critic, Boulevard Mag, 87, 88 & 89; Exec ed & critic, Country Plaza Mag, 89, 90 & 91; arts ed & reviewer, The Gold Coast Gazette, Glen Cove, NY, 91-. *Awards:* Artists Grant, Artist Space, New York, 88-91; Puffin Found, 92; NY Found for the Arts & E End Arts Coun, 92. *Bibliog:* Michael Brenson (auth), Sculpture that springs from surrealism, The Sunday New York Times, 3/8/87; Karin Lipson (auth), Katie Seiden - The Outpost Artist, Newsday, 6/1/87; Diane Ketchum (auth), Katie Seiden - About Long Island, 12/4/88; Barbara Matilsky (auth), The Expressionist Surface: Contemporary Art in Plaster-Katie Seiden (exhib catalog), 90; Michael Brenson (auth), Plaster as a medium, not just an interim step, New York Times, 7/13/90. *Mem:* Nat Asn Women Artists; Hempstead Harbor Artists (bd mem, 84-85); Women's Caucus Arts. *Media:* Plaster, Miscellaneous Media. *Publ:* Auth, article, Central Hall Artists Newsletter, 76; Women Artists News, Midmarch Asn, 77; illusr, Sinister Wisdom, 84; feature art exhib (monthly), Boulevard Mag, 87, 88 & 89; illustr, Spiral Though, Front Cover, 89. *Dealer:* Country Art Gallery Locust Valley NY; Sensory Evolution Gallery 420 E 13th St East Village NY. *Mailing Add:* 52 Cromwell Pl Sea Cliff NY 11579

SEIDL, CLAIRE
PAINTER, PRINTMAKER

b Greenwich, Conn, May 17, 51. *Study:* London Polytech, Sir John Cass Col Art, 72; Syracuse Univ, Col Visual & Performing Arts, BFA(cum laude), 73; City Univ New York, Hunter Col, MFA, 82; Int Ctr Photog, 96-99. *Work:* Albright Col, Pa; Aldrich Mus, Conn; Citibank & Mobil Oil Corp, NY; Portland Mus Art, Maine; Pfizer Electric, NY; and others. *Comn:* two paintings, Miller, Anderson, Sherrard, MOMA Tower, NY, 88; four paintings,Reliance Insurance, NY, 89; painting/mural, Oxford Hills Comprehensive High Sch, S Paris, Maine, 97. *Exhib:* Solo exhibs, Hunter Gallery, NY, 82, John Davis Gallery, Akron, Ohio, 83 & 85, Stephen Rosenberg Gallery, NY, 86, 88, 90, 94, 96 & 99 Rosenberg + Kaufman Gallery, NY, 96, 99 & 2001, Claudia Carr Gallery, NY, 99, Icon Gallery, Brunswick, Maine, 2000 & A Ramona Space, NY, 2000; Works on Paper, Frick Gallery, Belfast, Maine, 92; Contemp Abstraction, O'Farrell Gallery, Brunswick, Maine, 92; The Tenth Summer, Stephen Rosenberg Gallery, NY, 93,; Paint and Paper, Rosenberg + Kaufman Fine Art, NY, 95, Painting, 97, Spatial Relations - Photographs, 99, Sun Signs, 2000 & Land Photographs, 2000; The Language of Art: Res Ipsa Loquitor Art Initiatives, NY, 95; Icon Gallery, Brunswick, Maine, 96 & 97; and others. *Teaching:* Vis artist, Ill State Univ, 84 & Syracuse Univ, NY, 85 & 86; lectr, Hunter Col, City Univ, NY, 85-90, asst prof, 90-95. *Awards:* Nancy Ashton Mem Fund Prize, 82; William Graf Fel, 82; Fel, Cummington Community of the Arts, 83. *Bibliog:* Marina Vaizey in Berlin: New work--New York, London Sunday Times, 10/30/83; Benjamin Forgey (auth), article, Washington Post, 7/20/85; Vivien Raynor (auth), New Currents in Watercolor, NY Times, 8/4/91; Sue Scott (auth) Art News, 9/96; Mario Naves (auth), New Art Examiner, 9/96; Lilly Wei (auth), Art In America, 1/97; Dominque Nahas (auth), Review, 1/99; Grace Glueck (auth), NY Times, 2/5/99. *Mem:* 22 Wooster (treas, 79-80). *Media:* Oils, Watercolor; Black & White Photog. *Dealer:* Rosenberg + Kaufman Fine Art 115 Wooster St New York NY 10012; Icon Contemp Art 19 Mason St Brunswick ME 04011; Claudia Carr Gallery 478 W Broadway New York NY 10012. *Mailing Add:* c/o Stephen Rosenberg & Kaufman Fine Art 115 Wooster St New York NY 10012

SEIDLER, DORIS
PAINTER, PRINTMAKER

b London, Eng. *Study:* Atelier 17, New York, with Stanley William Hayter. *Work:* Smithsonian Inst, Washington; Philadelphia Mus Art; Brooklyn Mus; Seattle Mus Art; Whitney Mus Am Art, NY; British Mus; and others; V&A Lonson, libr of Congress, Washington, DC; Pallant House, Chichester, England. *Exhib:* First & Second Hawaii Nat Print Exhib, Honolulu Acad Arts; Pa Acad Fine Arts, Philadelphia; Soc Am Graphic Artists; Jewish Mus, NY; Atelier 17, Brooklyn Mus, 78; Whitney Mus Am Art; Libr Cong, Washington; Nassau Co Mus Fine Art, NY; Pallant House, Chichester, Eng, 91; British Mus, 96; Alecto Exhib, Whitworth Gallery, Manchester, Eng, 2003; and others. *Awards:* MacDowell Artists Colony Fel, 66 & 75; Medal for Creative Graphics, Audubon Artists, 72; Awards, Soc Am Graphic Artists, 82, 83 & 85. *Bibliog:* Joly Patterson (auth), Chicago Soc Etchers, Farleigh Dickinson Univ Press, 2002; Tessa Sidey (auth), Editions Alecto Graphics, 1960-1981, 2003. *Media:* Acrylic; All Media. *Interests:* art, music, travel. *Publ:* Auth, articles in Artist Proof. *Dealer:* Anita Shapolsky Gallery 152 E 65th St New York NY 10012. *Mailing Add:* 14 Stoner Ave Great Neck NY 11021

SELF, DANA RAE
CURATOR, WRITER

b Fort Lauderdale, Fla, June 5, 59. *Study:* Stephens Col, BA, 81; Univ Kans, Lawrence, MA, 84. *Collection Arranged:* Subversive Domesticity, 95; Chihuly Over Venice: An American Premier, 96; Christian Boeltamski - So Far, 98; Alex Katz: Small Paintings, 2000; Robert Therrien, 2000; Ken Aptekar, 2001. *Pos:* asst cur, John Michael Kohler Arts Ctr, 93-94; cur, Ulrich Mus, Wichita State Univ, Kans, 94-96; cur, Kemper Mus Contemp Art, 96-. *Teaching:* adj instr art hist, Johnson Co Community Col, 91-93. *Mem:* Col Arts Asn; Am Asn Mus; PEO. *Res:* contemporary art. *Publ:* auth Subversive Dometicity, Wichita State Univ, 95; coauth Chihuly Over Venice, Portland Press, 96; auth Georgia O'Keefe: Intimate Landscapes, Univ Pub, 98; auth Shahzia Sikander, Kemper Mus, 98; coauth Alex Katz: Small Paintings, Kemper Mus, 2001. *Mailing Add:* Kemper Mus Contemp Art 4420 Warwick Blvd Kansas City MO 64111

SELIG, MANFRED
COLLECTORS, PATRONS
b Ger, Feb, 1909. *Exhib:* Henry Art Gallerie; Seattle Fry Mus. *Bibliog:* Michael Brenson (auth), New York Times, 12/16/88. *Collection:* Old and modern paintings; graphic art

SELIGER, CHARLES
PAINTER
b New York, NY, June 3, 26. *Work:* Metrop Mus Art, Mus Mod Art, Solomon R Guggenheim Mus & Whitney Mus Am Art, NY; Hirshhorn Mus, Washington, DC. *Exhib:* Intimate Abstractions, Jacksonville Art Mus, Jacksonville, Fla, 81; The Soloman R Guggenheim Mus, NY, 86; Nature into Art, Munson-Williams-Proctor Inst, Utica, NY, 87; Peggy Guggenheim's Other Legacy, The Soloman R Guggenheim Mus, NY, 87 & Collezione Peggy Guggenheim, Venice, Italy, 88; Visions of Inner Space, Univ Calif, Los Angeles, Wight Art Gallery, Los Angeles and Nat Gallery of Mod Art, New Delhi, India, 87-88; Abstract Expressionism: Other Dimensions, Jane Voorhees Zimmerli Art Mus, Rutgers Univ, NJ, and the Whitney Mus Am Art at Philip Morris, NY, 90; Art Of The Forties, Mus Mod Art, NY, 91; Kandinsky & the Am Avant Garde, 1912-1950, Dayton Art Inst, The Phillips Collection, Terra Mus Am Art, Amon Carter Mus, 92-93; one-man exhibs, Art of This Century Gallery, Williard Gallery, Andrew Crispo Gallery, Schlesinger Gallery, Michael Rosenfeld Gallery, NY & Galerie Lopes, Zurich, Switz. *Pos:* Distinguished vis prof, Robert H & Clarice Smith, George Washington Univ, 41-90; lectr, Katonah Art Mus, Katonah, NY, 4/90; panelist, Terra Mus Am Art, Chicago, 2/90; Whitney Mus Am Art, Philip Morris, New York, 11/90. *Bibliog:* Addison Parks (auth), Through the keyhole: some meaning and method to Charles Seliger, Arts Mag, 6/80; Mel P Lader & James Johnson Sweeney (coauths), Charles Seliger, Ways Of Nature (catalog), Andrew Crispo Gallery, NY; Gail Levin (auth), The Natural Magic of Charles Seliger (catalog), Michael Rosenfeld Gallery, NY. *Media:* Oil, Acrylic. *Dealer:* Michael Rosenfeld Gallery New York NY 212-247-0082. *Mailing Add:* 10 Lenox Ave Mt Vernon NY 10552-2408

SELIGMAN, THOMAS KNOWLES
DIRECTOR
b Santa Barbara, Calif, Jan 1, 44. *Study:* Stanford Univ, BA, 65; Acad of Art Col, San Francisco, BFA, 67; Sch of Visual Arts, New York, MFA, 68. *Collection Arranged:* Eskimo Art from the Toronto-Dominion Bank, 72, Man and Animals in Pre-Columbian Mesoamerica, 73, Australian Aboriginal Art from the Louis Allen Collection, 74, African & Ancient Mexican Art-The Loran Collection (coauth, catalog), 74-75, Fire, Earth & Water-Sculpture from the Land Collection of Mesoamerican Art (ed, catalog), Honolulu Acad of Arts & Seattle Art Mus, 75 & Masterpieces of Primitive Art from the Museum of Primitive Art in New York, 77, San Francisco Mus Fine Arts; Form & Freedom, Rice Inst Arts; The Art of Being Huichol, Field Mus, Chicago & Am Mus Natural Hist, New York; Treasures of Ancient Nigeria, co-organized with Detroit Inst Arts & Metrop Mus Art, 78-80; Bay Area Collects (coauth, catalog); Spirits, Gods and Kings; Forms and Forces: Dynamics of African Figurative Sculpture (coauth, catalogue), 88. *Pos:* Dir, Africana Mus, Liberia, Africa, 69-71; deputy dir educ & exhibs, Fine Arts Mus, San Francisco, 72-89; deputy dir operations and planning, Fine Arts Mus, San Francisco, 89-; dir, Cantor Arts Ctr, Stanford Univ, 91-. *Teaching:* Asst prof African art hist, Cuttington Col, Liberia, Africa, 69-71. *Awards:* Aid to Mus Prof Award, Nat Endowment Arts, 75 & 87; Award of Honor, Nat Inst Anthropology & History, Mex. *Mem:* Am Asn Mus; Friends of Ethnic Arts (dir, 74-); Am Fedn Arts (trustee & vpres); Cult Property Adv Comt to Pres of US, 88-92; Asn Art Mus Dirs. *Res:* African aesthetics; art in context in Liberia, Sierra Leone and Ivory Coast, Tuareg art of Niger and Algeria. *Publ:* Auth, African art at the MH de Young Memorial Museum, African Arts, Univ Calif, Los Angeles, Vol 7 (4); Educational use of an anthropology collection in an art museum, Curator, fall 74; An indigenous concept of fakes--authentic African art?, African Arts, Univ Calif, Los Angeles, Vol 9 (3); An Unexpected Bequest and an Ethical Dilemma featuring serpents and flowering trees, Fine Arts Mus of San Francisco, 88. *Mailing Add:* Cantor Arts Ctr Stanford CA 94305-5060

SELLA, ALVIN CONRAD
PAINTER, EDUCATOR
b West Hoboken, NJ, Aug 30, 19. *Study:* Yale Univ Sch Art; Art Students League, with Brackman & Bridgman; Columbia Univ, with Machau; Col Fine Arts, Syracuse Univ; Univ NMex; also in Mex. *Work:* Bristol Iron & Steel Co; Collectors of Am Art; Sullins Col. *Exhib:* Am Fedn Arts Traveling Exhib, 61-62; one-man exhibs, Centenary Col, Lauren Rogers Mus Art, Laurel, Miss, Munic Art Gallery, Jackson, Miss, Birmingham Mus Art, 69, Dick Jemison Gallery, Birmingham, 76, Moody Gallery Art, Univ Ala, Tuscaloosa, 95, Ala State Univ, Montgomery, 96, Stillman Col, Tuscaloosa, 98 & others; Birmingham Mus Art, 76; Watercolor Soc Ala, 76; Frank Fedele Fine Art, 84-86; Univ Ark, 85; and others. *Teaching:* Head, Dept Art, Sullins Col, 48-61; prof art, Univ Ala, 61-; vis prof, Spring Workshops, Miss Art Colony, 62-64 & Shreveport Art Colony, 64-68; artist-in-residence, Summer Sch Arts, Univ SC, 68. *Awards:* First Award, 54th Ann Miss Exhib; Third Prize, 7th Mobile Art Exhib, 72; 32nd Ann Watercolor Exhib First & Second Prize, Birmingham Mus Art, 72; others. *Mem:* Art Students League; Am Asn Univ Prof; Col Art Asn Am; fel Int Inst Arts & Lett. *Media:* All Media. *Dealer:* Galleria Atenea San Miguel de Allende Mexico, 95. *Mailing Add:* Univ Ala Dept Art Tuscaloosa AL 35486

SELLER, LINDA
ARTIST
b Brooklyn, NY, Sept 29, 54. *Study:* Hunter Col, 1972; Study with the Art Students League, 1973-82; Nat Acad of Design, 1985-88. *Work:* Trenton State Col, Trenton, NJ; Scott Mem Study Collection, Bryn Mawr, PA; Center for Book Arts, New York, NY. *Comn:* mural, comn by Lucinda C Collins, Brattleboro, Vt, 2005-06; mural, comn by HS Corwin, Boca Raton, FL, 2006. *Exhib:* HTAL Ann Juried Exhib, Heckscher Mus, Huntington, NY, 1990; Am Drawings Biennial, Muscarelle Mus Art, Williamsburg, VA, 1992; Selections from The Scott Mem Study Colllection, Bryn Mawr Col Center, Bryn Mawr, PA, 1993. *Awards:* Juror Award, Art Assoc of Harrisburg, 1991; First Place Juror Award, Muscarelle Mus Art, 1992; Janet Royce Award, Pastel Soc Am, 1994. *Mem:* Center for Book Arts; Guild of the Bookworker, New York, NY; Guild of the N Am Goldsmiths; Pastel Soc of Am; Craft Coun Am. *Media:* On Paper, Graphite, Ink, Pastel Watercolor. *Mailing Add:* 1665 Glenwood Rd Brooklyn NY 11230

SELLERS, JOHN LEWIS
EDUCATOR, DESIGNER
b Alexander City, Ala, Aug 28, 34. *Study:* Auburn Univ, BAA; Peabody Col, MA; also with Maltby Sykes for printmaking & Harry Lowe for painting. *Pos:* Art dir, Motive Mag, Nashville, Tenn, 65-67; assoc creative designer, McDonald & Saussy Agency, Inc, Nashville, 65-68; partner & creative dir, Les Hart Agency, Inc, Nashville, 68-70; art dir, Syracuse Scholar, 79-85, ed, 85-; co-dir, Drawing Nat, Everson Mus, 85-86. *Teaching:* Prof, Col Visual & Performing Arts, Syracuse Univ, 73-, chmn dept visual commun, 78-, chmn, Independent Study MFA progs, 73-. *Awards:* Magazine of the Year Award Runner Up, Mag Publ Asn, Mag Ed Asn & Columbia Univ Sch Journalism, 67; Best US Travel Brochure, Int Asn Travel Agents, 68; Merit Awards, NY Art Dir Club, 80, 82, 84 & 86. *Bibliog:* Don Barron (auth), Syracuse U: Preparation for the big world, Art Direction, 10/76; Jo Yanow (auth), John Sellers: The professional as educator, Graphics Today, Spring, 77; Paul Palange (auth), A teacher first, Syracuse Alumni Mag, Fall 77. *Mem:* Art Dirs Club NY; Am Inst Graphic Arts. *Res:* Creativity; Strategy. *Mailing Add:* Syracuse Univ Visual Commun Dept 102 Shaffer Syracuse NY 13244-1210

SELLERS, WILLIAM FREEMAN
SCULPTOR, PAINTER
b Bay City, Mich, June 1, 29. *Study:* Univ Mich, BArch, 54, MFA, 62. *Work:* Suspension, Six Cubes & Converging Cubes, Mem Art Gallery, Rochester, NY. *Comn:* Four Squares (painted steel), Student Asn, State Univ NY, Cortland, 69; reprogression, Sentry Group, Rochester, NY. *Exhib:* Sculpture & Prints Ann, Whitney Mus Am Art, NY, 66, Contemp Am Sculpture Ann, 68; Plus by Minus: Today's Half-Century, Albright-Knox Art Gallery, Buffalo, 68; Am Sculpture of the Sixties, Grand Rapids Art Mus, Mich, 69; Painting and Sculpture Today, Indianapolis Mus Art, 70; Installation, Carleton Col, 81; Contemp Sculpture, State Univ NY, 83; sculpture installation, Pyramid Arts Ctr, Rochester, NY, 87; working drawing & studies, Monroe Community Col, Rochester, NY, 87. *Teaching:* Instr design, Rochester Inst Technol, 62-65; asst prof sculpture, Univ Rochester, 66-70; asst prof art, Lehman Col, 70-, chmn dept art, 75-77; vis artist-teacher, Carleton Col, 81-; instr sculpture, Nazareth Col, 87. *Awards:* Jurors' Show Award, Mem Art Gallery, 66; Faculty Res Grant, Lehman Col, City Univ New York, 72-73. *Media:* Metal, Wood; Acrylic, Oil. *Dealer:* Oxford Gallery Rochester NY. *Mailing Add:* 192 Aberdeen St Rochester NY 14619

SELSER, CHRISTOPHER
DEALER, COLLECTOR
b Omaha, Nebr, Sept 15, 50. *Study:* Univ Ariz, BA, 77. *Collection Arranged:* 1000 Years Southwest Ceramic Art (auth, catalog), ACA Gallery, 81. *Pos:* Owner, Selser Gallery, Tucson; owner & dir, ACA Am Ind Arts, New York, formerly; Zaplin Lampert Gallery, Santa Fe, NMex. *Teaching:* Lect, New Sch, New York, 85. *Specialty:* American Indian Art. *Publ:* Auth, Navajo Weaving Tradition, E P Dutton, New York, 85

SELSOR, MARCIA LORRAINE
EDUCATOR, CERAMIST
b Philadelphia, Pa, Feb 1, 49. *Study:* Philadephia Univ Arts, BFA, 70; Southern Ill Univ, MFA, 74. *Work:* Northern Ariz Univ Galleries, Flagstaff; Yellowstone Art Ctr, Billings, Mont; Ill State Mus, Springfield; Mus Plastic Arts, Tumen, Russia; Mus Fine Art, Riga, Latvia; many others. *Comn:* Raku plaques, Deaconess Med Ctr, Billings, Mont, 89. *Exhib:* Western Ceramic Artists, N Ariz Univ Gallery, Flagstaff, 91; Dzintari Creative Arts, Ceramic Symp: Exhib Dzintari Creative Arts Ctr, Jurmala, Latvia, 91; solo exhibs, Marking the Millennium, Yellowstone Art Ctr, Billings, Mont, 91 & Recent Raku, Minot Art Gallery, NDak, 92; Year Am Craft, WWC, Rock Springs, 93; Fulbright Artists, Meridian Ctr, Washington, DC, 97; Wild Things, Peter's Valley, NJ, 98; Text and Texture, Broome St Gallery, NY, 98. *Pos:* Dir at large, Nat Coun Educ Ceramic Arts, 90; vis artist, Dzintari Creative Arts Ctr Soviet Artists Union, 91 & Uzbekisani Artists Union, 92; res artist, BANFF, 93; pres fac sen, Mont State Univ, Billings, 98-99; tech staff, Ceramics Monthly. *Teaching:* Prof ceramics, Mont State Univ, Billings, 75-92, prof art, 75-2000, prof emer; workshops Centro Agost, Spain, Sierra Nev Col, 98, Appalachian Ctr for Crafts, 2000. *Awards:* Sr Fulbright Scholar, US-Spain Joint Comt Educ & Cult Exchange, 85-86 & Uzbekistan, 94; Merit Award, 12th Ann NDak Nat Juried, Minot Art Gallery, 89; Member of Doboshu, Northern Ariz Univ, 91. *Bibliog:* Dr Louana Lackey (auth), Under a bigger sky, Montana's Marcia Selsor, Ceramics Monthly, 5/97; First Annual Clay Arters Exhibition, Ceramic Monthly, 98; Darryl Baird (auth), The Extruder Book, Am Ceramics Soc, 2000. *Mem:* Col Art Asn; Nat Coun Educ Ceramic Arts (dir-at-large, 90-91); Fulbright Asn; Am Anthropological Asn; Medieval Hispanists Soc. *Media:* Clay, Porcelain. *Publ:* Fulbright in Uzbekistan, Studio Potter, Vol 23, no 5, 95; Japanese Women Ceramists, Nat Coun Educ Ceramic Arts J, 43, 95-96; Once is Not Enough, An Historical Explanation of the Development of Multiple Firing Techniques, Nat Coun Educ Ceramic arts J, 97-98. *Dealer:* Toucan Gallery 2505 Montana Ave Billings MT 59101; Martin-Harris Gallery Jackson Hole WY. *Mailing Add:* 703 Burlington Billings MT 59101-0298

SELTZER, JOANNE LYNN
PAINTER, PRINTMAKER
b Philadelphia, Pa, June 21, 46. *Study:* Northwestern Univ, cert, 63; Univ Mich, BFA(painting & ceramics), 69; New Sch Social Res, 73; Pratt Inst, 74; Pratt Graphics Ctr, 74; NY Univ, MA(photog & art history) 79; Parsons Sch Design, 86-88 (perspective drawing). *Work:* Brooklyn Mus; Worcester Art Mus, Mass; Mus Contemp Art, Ghent, Belgium; Sunrise Mus, Charleston, WVa; Toledo Mus Art, Ohio; Indianapolis Mus Art, Ind; WVa Cult Ctr, Charleston. *Exhib:* Women Artists 1877-1977, Charlottenburg Palace, Berlin, 77; Travaux Sur Papier, Ctr Cult-Jacques Prevert, Paris, 81; Typich Frau, 81; Mapped Art, Charts, Roots, Regions traveling exhib, 81-83; Independent Cur Benefit, 85; 1978-79 Art-About the Strange Nature of Money, Stadtische Kunsthalle, Dusseldorf; and others. *Pos:* Inst, Nat Soc Col Dames State NY Art Archit & Decorative Arts Col Am, 86-88. *Teaching:* Guest lectr, Univ Iowa, 79, Univ Va, 79, Koninklijke Akad Bosch, Holland, 80 & 82, NY Univ, 81, Drew Univ, 81 & Conn Col, 82. *Bibliog:* Peter Frank (auth), article, Art News, 9/76; Lucy Lippard (auth), From the Center, EP Dutton, 77; Jos Knaepen (auth), article, Bulletin, Belg, 1/22/82; and others. *Media:* Oil; Silkscreen-Serigraphy. *Publ:* Contribr, Mus J, Amsterdam, 76, Kunstlerinnen Int, 77 & Flash Art, 77. *Mailing Add:* 210 Centre St New York NY 10013

SELTZER, PETER LAWRENCE
PAINTER
Study: Studied with Daniel Greene. *Work:* Butler Inst Am Art; New Britain Mus Am Art; Harvard Univ; paint & clay, New Haven, Conn. *Comn:* portrait, Harvard Univ, 2006. *Exhib:* Nat Acad Design, NY; Nat Arts Club, NY; Butler Inst Am Art, Ohio; New Britain us Am Art, Conn; Various solo and group exhib's. *Collection Arranged:* Corporate and pvt collections. *Awards:* Dianne B Bernhard Gold Medal, Pastel Soc Am, 2001 & 2002; Allied Artists Am Gold Medal Hon, Allied Artists Am, 2004; Best in Show, Int Exhib Pastels, Taiwan Ctr, NY. *Bibliog:* Pastel Journal, 2001; American Artist, 2004; Maureen Bloomfield (ed), Pastel Journal, 2006. *Mem:* Allied Artists Am; Pastel Soc Am. *Media:* Oils and Pastels. *Mailing Add:* 87 Main St N Woodbury CT 06798

SELTZER, PHYLLIS
PAINTER, PRINTMAKER
b Detroit, Mich, May 17, 28. *Study:* Univ Iowa, BFA & MFA; Lasansky's Workshop, sr study hist of technol, with M Kranzberg; Case Western Reserve Univ. *Work:* Brooklyn Art Mus; Cleveland Mus Art; Minn Mus Art, Minneapolis; Nat Gallery Art, Ottawa, Ont; Butler Mus, Youngstown, Ohio; Cleveland Clinic, Ohio; Citibank, NY; BP America, Cleveland, Ohio. *Comn:* Bicentennial print, Cleveland Area Arts Coun, 75; ed of 25, Exodus print, Cleveland Health Dept; elevators & etched mirrors, Stouffer's Inn on the Square, Cleveland, Ohio; Murals, Bistro des Artistes, Cleveland, Ohio. *Exhib:* May Show, Cleveland Mus Art, Ohio, 87 & 90 & Yr in Review, 90; Fla Printmakers Soc Ann, Tampa, 89; Art Expo, NY, 90; NY traveling, WGer, 90; NY Print Fair, 92; and others. *Pos:* Coordr fine arts, Cleveland Col, Case Western Reserve Univ, 66-70; interior designer, Dalton, Van Dijk, Johnson, Cleveland, 72-74; interior designer, 75-87. *Teaching:* Lectr art hist & printmaking, Lake Erie Col, Painesville, Ohio, 70-72; lectr art fund, Cleveland State Univ, 69-71. *Awards:* Purchase Award, Brooklyn Mus 19th Nat, 75; Tiffany Fel, Nat Congress Art & Design, 88; Artlink, 90. *Bibliog:* William Bierman (auth), Artist Improves on Technology, Akron Beacon J, 3/23/75; Helen Cullinan (auth), Venice is Source of Inspiration, Cleveland Plain Dealer, 8/7/88; Helen Cullinan (auth), A New Pespective on Spring Tradition, Cleveland Plain Dealer, 4/6/90. *Mem:* New Orgn Visual Arts (secy, 73, vpres, 74); Print Club Cleveland (pres, 83 & 84). *Media:* Oil; Heat Transfer Printing, Miscellaneous Media. *Publ:* Printworld, 83-87 & 90; Art Examiner, 90; An Illustrated Survey of Leading Contemporaries, Am Artists, 89 & 90; NY Gallery Guide, 90. *Dealer:* The Bonfoey Gallery Cleveland OH; John Szoke Gallery New York NY

SELVIG, FORREST HALL
HISTORIAN, WRITER
b Tacoma, Wash, Jan 3, 24. *Study:* Harvard Col, AB, 49; Univ Calif, Berkeley, 53-56. *Collection Arranged:* Selections From Richard Brown Baker Collection, 60; The Nabis, 61; Pavel Tchelitchew, 64; Jean Helion, 65; Charles Demuth (with catalog), 68; and others. *Pos:* Asst dir, Minneapolis Art Inst, Minn, 61-63; asst dir, Gallery Mod Art, New York, 63-65; dir, Akron Art Inst, 66-68; ed, New York Graphic Soc, Greenwich, Conn, 68-71. *Bibliog:* Ben Shahn Talks with Forrest Selvig, Arch Am Art J, Vol 17, 77. *Mem:* Am Asn Mus. *Res:* Late 19th century French painting, especially the Nabis and the Symbolists. *Publ:* auth, The Nabis and Their Circle, 62; American Collections, 63; ed, 19th Century Landscape Painting, 71; Mosaic Deterioration and Preservation, 80; ed & trans, Views of Florence in 120 Paintings by Fabio Borbottoni, Firenze Perduta, 82. *Mailing Add:* 244 Brattle St Cambridge MA 02138

SELVIN, NANCY
CERAMIST, SCULPTOR
b Los Angeles, Calif, 1943. *Study:* Univ Calif, Berkeley, BA, 69, with Voulkos & Ron Nagle, MA, 70. *Work:* Oakland Mus, Calif; Hokkoku Shimbun, Tokyo; Ariz State Univ Art Gallery, Tempe; Mint Mus, NC; Los Angeles Mus Mod Art; Nora Eccles Mus, Utah; Renwicke Gallery, Smithsonian Inst, Washington, DC. *Comn:* stone/text sidewalk inserts, In Berkeley 2000, City of Berkeley, Calif, 2000-01; Cafe Liliane, San Francisco, CA. *Exhib:* Mus Contemp Crafts, NY, 76; San Francisco Mus, 77; solo exhib, Calif Crafts Mus, Palo Alto, 82, Grossmont Col, Cajon, Calif, 90, Berkeley Civic Arts, Calif, 91, Richmond Art Ctr, Calif, 95, Works Gallery, Sonoma, Calif, 96, Charleston Heights Art Ctr, Las Vegas, Nev, 99 & Sybaris Gallery, Royal Oak, Mich, 99, Pence Gallery, Davis, Calif, 02, Tercera Gallery, Palo Alto, Calif, 03, Sybaris Gallery, Royal Oak, Mich, 04; Fac Exhib, San Francisco State Univ Art Gallery, 91; Artists Sketchbooks, Palo Alto Cult Ctr, Calif, 95; Kiddush Cup Invitational, Jewish Mus, San Francisco, 97; Teabowl Invitational, Lafayette Mus Art, Ind, 98; Celestial Seasonings, Boulder, Colo, 98; Ferrin Gallery, Northhampton, Mass, 98; Survey of Int Ceramics, Laguna Beach Art Mus, Calif, 98; Artesans Gallery, Mill Valley, Calif, 98; traveling, Color & Fire: Defining Moments in Studio Ceramics 1950-2000, 2000; Glimpse of the Invisible, Arvada Ctr for Arts, Colo, 2000; Selections from the Chasanoff Collection, Mint Mus, Charlotte NC, 2001; Scipps Col Collection, Claremont, Calif; Diverse Domain, Taipei, Taiwan, 2004. *Pos:* owner & founder, After School Arts, Cragmont Prospect Schs, 83-89; grants rev panelist, City of Oakland, 86-89 & 2000, pub art adv comt, 89-97, chair, 94-97; bd dir, ProArts, 87-94, pres, 89-91, chair nominations comt, 91-92, chair open studios comt, 90-91; dir, After Sch Art, 86- & San Francisco State Univ, 92; arts proj consult, Preserv Park, Oakland, 93 & Cult Arts Div, City of Oakland, 94; pub art adv comt, Alameda Co, 94-97; co-owner, Brushstrokes Studio, Berkeley, Calif, 95-98; art selection comt, Summit Hosp, Oakland, Calif, 96-; guest artist, Watershed Ctr Ceramic Arts, 98, bd trustees, 99-, pres bd trustees, 2000-04; CED coun bd, Univ Calif, 2005-. *Teaching:* Instr ceramics, Laney Col, Oakland, 73-86, program dir workshop series, 78-86; vis fac, State Univ NY, Albany, 70-72, Fashion Inst Design, San Francisco, 73, Univ Calif, Berkeley, 88, San Francisco State Univ, 92 & Pitzer Col, Claremont, Calif, 99; lectr, Calif Col Arts & Crafts, 99, Merritt Col, Oakland, Calif, 2000, Univ Utah, Salt Lake City, 2000, Casper Col, Wyo, 2000, Brookhaven Col, Dallas, 2000 & many others; vis fac, Univ California, Berkeley, CA, 2004. *Awards:* Craftsman Fel, 80 & Artist Fel, 88, Nat Endowment Arts; Skaggs Found Prog Develop Grant, 86; Business Arts Award, Oakland, 90; others; NEA Artist Fel, 80; Fel, California Arts Council, 2003. *Bibliog:* Up Front, Ceramics Monthly, 9/96; David M Brin, Nancy Selvin's Abstracted Forms, Ceramic Art & Perception, 98; Scott Dickensheets, Great Bowls of Fire, Las Vegas Weekly, 10/12/99; Susan Peterson (auth), The Craft of Art and Class, 99; Bai Ming (auth), Overseas Contemporary Ceramics, 2002. *Mem:* CED Alumni Coun; NCECA. *Media:* Mixed. *Publ:* Auth, Tepcoware, 8-9/82 & Bulmer brick and tile, 85, Am Craft Mag; auth, How I Got Here, Ceramics Monthly, 11/89; Decorating tile, Fine Homebuilding, 1/93; Fundamentally Clay: Cermaic Abstraction, 2006. *Dealer:* Pacini Lubel Gallery, Seattle, WA; Tercera Gallery, Palo Alto, CA; Snyderman Works Gallery, Philadelphia, PA. *Mailing Add:* 745 Page St Berkeley CA 94710

SELZ, PETER H
HISTORIAN, CURATOR
b Munich, Ger, Mar 27, 19. *Study:* Univ Chicago, fel, 46-54, MA & PhD; Univ Paris, Fulbright Award, 49-50. *Hon Degrees:* Calif Col Arts & Crafts, hon DFA, 67. *Collection Arranged:* Directions In Kinetic Sculpture (catalog), 65; Funk (catalog), 67; Richard Lindner, 69; Pol Bury, 70; Excellence, 70; Harold Paris (catalog), 72; Ferdinand Hodler (catalog), 72; The American Presidency in Political Cartoons (coauth, catalog), 76; German and Austrian Expressionism (catalog), 78; Two Decades of American Painting: 1920-1940 (catalog), Dusseldorf, Zurich & Brussels, 79; Max Beckmann: Self Portraits, 92; and many others. *Pos:* Head art educ prog, Inst Design, Ill Inst Technol, 53-55; chmn dept art & dir art gallery, Pomona Col, 55-58; chief cur painting & sculpture exhibs, Mus Mod Art, 58-65; dir, Univ Art Mus, Univ Calif, Berkeley, 65-73; ed, Art Am; mem consult comt, Art Quart; proj dir, Christo's Running Fence Project, Calif, 74-76. *Teaching:* Asst prof art hist, Inst Design, Univ Chicago, 53-54; chmn, Art Dept, Pomona Col, 55-58; prof art hist, Univ Calif, Berkeley, 65-88, prof emer, currently. *Awards:* Belg-Am Educ Found Fel, 53; Order of Merit, Fed Ger Repub, 63; Sr Fel, Nat Endowment Humanities, 72; Rockefeller Found Study Ctr, Bellagio, 94; and others. *Mem:* Col Art Asn Am (dir, 59-68). *Res:* 20th Century American and European Art. *Publ:* Art in Our Times, 81; Sam Francis, second ed, 82; Chillida, 86; Theories and Documents of Contemporary Art, 96; Max Beckmann, 96; Beyond the Mainstream, 97; Gottfried Helnwein, 97; Barbara Chase-Riboud, 99; Nathan Oliveira, 2002; Art of Engagement: Visual Politics in California and Beyond, 2006. *Mailing Add:* 861 Regal Rd Berkeley CA 94708

SELZNICK-DRUTZ, JUNE
PAINTER, EDUCATOR
b Toronto, Ont, Feb 14, 20. *Study:* Cent Tech Sch; Ont Col Art, grad(hons), 65. *Work:* McMaster Univ, Hamilton, Ont; Univ Waterloo, Ont; Royal Can Art Collection, Nat Gallery, Ottawa; Univ Guelph, Ont; London Trust Co, Ont; Citibank, Toronto; Hudson Bay Co, Toronto; and many others. *Comn:* Seeds of Spring Returning (serigraph ann print), Glenhyrst Art Asn, Brantford, Ont, 68-69. *Exhib:* One-man shows, Rebecca Sisler Gallery, Toronto, 78 & Prince Arthur Gallery, Toronto, 79; Ont Soc Artists, 80; Univ Ind, Elkhart, 80; Can Soc Painters Watercolor, 81; Second Int Watercolour Biennial, Mus Nac Aquarela, Coyoacan, Mex, 96; Cirle Art Gallery, Tohermoy, Ont, 2000; plus others. *Teaching:* Instr, Ont Col Art, Toronto, 67-86, Ont Dept Educ, summers 68-72, Ryerson Polytech Inst, Toronto, 72-73 & Toronto Art Sch, 66-75, retired. *Awards:* Honor award, Can Soc Painters Watercolor, 89; Honor Award & AJ Casson Medal, Soc Painters Watercolour, 93, Honour Award, 95, 97 & AJ Casson Award, 97. *Bibliog:* Robert Myers (auth), The youth cult maidens of June Drutz, Art Mag, Vol 6, No 22, 75. *Mem:* Royal Can Acad; Ont Soc Artists; Can Soc Painters Watercolor. *Media:* Tempera, Watercolor, Acrylic Tempera, Drawing. *Publ:* Article, Watercolor Magic, Cincinnati, Ohio, 99. *Dealer:* Circle Arts Gallery Tohermory Ont Canada. *Mailing Add:* 430 Annette St Toronto ON M6P 1R9 Canada

SEMAK, MICHAEL
PHOTOGRAPHER, EDUCATOR
b Welland, Ont, Jan 9, 34. *Study:* Ryerson Polytech Inst, Toronto, cert archit technol, 59. *Work:* Nat Gallery Can, Pub Arch, Ottawa; George Eastman House, Rochester, NY; Mus Mod Art, NY. *Comn:* Photographing Canada, Nat Film Bd, Ottawa, 64, 66, 67, 72 & 74; Photographing Tunisia, Nat Geog Soc, Washington, DC, 67; Photographing WVa, Time-Life Bks, NY, 68; Photographing Italy, Can Coun, Ottawa, 71; Photographing USSR, York Univ, Toronto, 75. *Exhib:* Ghana Image 4, Nat Film Bd, Ottawa, 69; Ghetto, New Sch Social Res, NY, 70; Mixed Subjects, Image Gallery,

NY, 71; Italy 1971, Il Diaframma Gallery, Milan, 73; Mixed Subjects, Deja Vue Gallery, Toronto, 75. *Pos:* Toronto chmn interarts, Canada-USSR Asn, 73-. *Teaching:* Lectr photog, Visual Arts Dept, Fac Fine Arts, York Univ, Toronto, 71-73, asst prof, 73-76, assoc prof, 77-. *Awards:* Gold Medal for Photog Excellence for Ghana Show, Nat Film Bd, 69; Award of Excellence in Photo-Jour, Pravda Newspaper, Moscow, 70 & 72; Excellence Int Fedn Photog Arts Dipl, Switz, 72. *Bibliog:* Don Long (auth), Tell a story, Can Photo Ann, 75. *Mem:* Royal Can Acad Art. *Publ:* Ed, Concerned photographer, Popular Photog, 70; Semak portfolio, Creative Camera, 70 & 73, Camera Can, 71 & Nuova Fotografia, 73; co-auth, Michael Semak monograph, Impressions Mag, 74; and others. *Mailing Add:* 1796 Spruce Hill Rd Pickering ON L1V 1S4 Canada

SEMCHISHEN, OREST M
PHOTOGRAPHER
b Mundare, Alta, Jan 9, 32. *Work:* Nat Film Bd, Can Coun Art Bank, Pub Archives, Ottawa; Edmonton Art Gallery, Alta; Nickle Art Mus, Calgary; Winnipeg Art Gallery, Can Ctr Archit, Montreal. *Comn:* Photog proj, Alta 75th Anniversary Comn, 80. *Exhib:* Byzantine Churches of Alta, Edmonton Art Gallery, 76, Confedn Art Gallery, Charlottetown, PEI, 77, Prov Mus, Edmonton, 81; Banff Purchase, Glenbow Mus, Calgary, 79; Points of View: Photos of Architecture, Vancouver Art Gallery, BC, 81 & Mus de Beaux Arts, Montreal, 81; Winnipeg Art Gallery, 96; Can Mus Contemp photog, Ottawa, 97. *Bibliog:* James Adams (auth), World through a radiologist's camera, Edmonton J, 81; Terry Fenton (auth), 4 Photographers, Update, Edmonton Art Gallery, 82. *Mem:* Friends Photog. *Publ:* Contribr, Byzantine Churches of Alberta, Edmonton Art Gallery, 76; The Banff Purchase, Banff Ctr, 79; Keepsake, Western Emerging Arts, 81

SEMEL, TERRY S
PATRON
b New York City, Feb 24, 43. *Study:* LI Univ, BS, 1964. *Pos:* Domestic sales mgr, CBS Cinema Ctr Films, Studio City, Calif, 1970-72; vpres, gen mgr, Walt Disney's Buena Vista, Burbank, Cali, 1972-75; pres, WB Distribrution Corp, Burbank, 1975-78; exec vpres, Chief Operating Officer, Warner Bros Inc, Burbank, 1979-80, pres, Chief Operating Officer 1980-94, chmn, co-Chief Exec Officer, 1994-99; chmn, Chief Exec Officer, Yahoo! Inc, 2001-; bd dir, Revlon, Polo Ralph Lauren Corp. *Mem:* Trustee, Solomon R Guggenheim Mus, Educ First, Cedars Sinai Med Ctr, Environ Media Asn. *Mailing Add:* Yahoo! Inc 701 First Ave Sunnyvale CA 94089

SEMMEL, JOAN
PAINTER
b New York, NY, 32. *Study:* Cooper Union, New York, dipl, 52; Art Students League, with Morris Kantor, 58-59; Pratt Inst, New York, BFA, 63, MFA, 72. *Work:* Chrysler Mus, Norfolk, Va; Brooklyn Mus, NY City; Parrish Mus of Art, Brooklyn, NY; Jocelyn Art Mus, Omaha, Nebr; Guild Hall Mus, East Hampton, NY. *Comn:* Portraits of: Chris Connell, Evelyn Wexler, Robin Oz, Frank Oz, Taylor Reznick, Eric Nord, Virginia Smith (pres, Vassar Col), V O'Leary, (pres, State Univ NY, Albany), Mary Hartman (dean, Douglass Col) & Delores Sloviter (judge) Philadelphia. *Exhib:* Solo exhibs, Greenville Co Mus Art, SC, 91, Skidmore Col, Saratoga Springs, NY, 92, State Univ NY, Oswego, 92, State Univ NY, Albany, 92, Bypass, NY, 93, Pratt Manhattan Ctr, NY, 93 & Brenda Taylor, NY, 96, Guild Hall Mus, Easthampton, NY, 98, Mitchell Algus Gallery, NY, 99 & 2003, Jersey City Mus, NJ, 2000; group exhibs: NJ Arts Ann, NJ State Mus, Trenton, 94, Sexual Politics, Armand Hammer, Mus, Berkeley, Calif, 96, The Figure, The Other side of Modernism, New House Ctr of Contemp Art, NY, 2000, Personal and Political, Guild Hall Mus, East Hampton, NY, 2003, Woman on Woman, The Whte Box, New York City, 2003, New York City DFN Gallery, 2004, Upstarts & Matriarchs Mizel Arts Ctr, Denver, Colo, 2005; Mathew Marks Gallery, NY, 99; Int Armory Show, NY, 2000. *Pos:* Prof Emer, Rutgers Univ, currently. *Teaching:* Md Inst Art, Baltimore, 73, Rutgers Univ, Livingston, NJ, 74-75, Brooklyn Mus Art Sch, 76-78 & Mason Gross Sch Arts, Rutgers Univ, New Brunswick, NJ, 78-2000, emer prof 2000-; Int Summer Acad of Fine Arts, Salzburg, Austria, 2000; Skowhegan Sch of Painting & Sculpture, 1991. *Awards:* Off Educ EPDA Fel, 70-72; Creative Artists Pub Serv Prog Award, NY State Coun on Arts, 75-76; Nat Endowment Arts Grant, 80 & 85; Richard Florikeim, Art Fund Grant, 96. *Bibliog:* Frances Borzello (auth) Seeing Ourselves, Women's Self-Portraits, Thams & Hudson, London, 98; Marie-Jo Bonnet (auth), Les Femmes Dans L'Art, Editions de la Martiniere Reproduction; Alan Tannenbaum (auth), New York in the 70's, Berlin, Ger; Erika Doss (auth), 20th Century Am Art, Oxford Hist of Arts Eries, Univ Press; Reckitt, (editor), Art and Feminism (Themes & Movements), Phaidon Press, London. *Mem:* Col Art Asn. *Media:* Oil. *Dealer:* Mitchell Algus 511 W 25th St New York NY 10011. *Mailing Add:* 109 Spring St New York NY 10012

SEMMES, BEVERLY
SCULPTOR
b Washington, DC. *Study:* Boston Mus Sch, Tufts Univ, BA(art hist), BFA(sculpture), 82; Skowhegan Sch Painting & Sculpture, Maine, 82; NY Studio Sch, New York, 83-84; Yale Sch Art, New Haven, Conn, fel, 85-87, Alice Kimball Eng Traveling Fel, 87, MFA(sculpture), 87. *Exhib:* Aldrich Mus Contemp Art, 93 & 96; Inst Contemp Art, Boston, 95; solo exhibs, Va Mus Fine Arts, 96, Galerie Bugdahn und Kaimer, Dusseldorf, 96, Irish Mus Mod Art, Dublin, 96, Whitney Mus Am Art at Philip Morris, 96, Michael Klein Gallery, NY, 96, Brooklyn Mus, 97 & Fabric Workshop, Philadelphia, 97; Bobyscape, Barbara Gross Galerie, Munich, 96; Functionally challenged, Ubu Gallery, NY, 96; L'art au Corps, le corps expose de Man Ray a nos jours, Mac Galeries contemp Mus Marseille, France, 96; Making Pictures: Women and Photog, 1975-Now, Nicole Klagsbrun, NY, 96; Art/Fashion, Guggenheim Mus SoHo, NY, 97; Masters of the Masters, Butler Inst Am Art, Youngstown, Ohio, 98; L'entrelacement et l'enveloppe, La Villa du Parc, Annemasse, France, 98; Fashion Happening, Gallery K, Washington, DC, 98. *Collection Arranged:* Whitney Mus Am Art, NY; Hishhorn Mus and Sculpture Garden, Washington, DC; Denver Art Mus, Colo; Irish Mus Modern Art, Mublin; Musee Dole, France; Microsoft Corp, Seattle, Wash; Progressive Corp,Cleveland, Ohio; The Refco Collection, Chicago, Ill. *Awards:* Artists Space Grant, 89; Mid-Atlantic Found Fel, Sculpture, 91; Nat Endowment Arts, Sculpture, 94. *Bibliog:* Elisa Turner (auth), Beverly Semmes, Norton Museum of Art, ARTnews, 10/96; Brian Fallon (auth), Exotic and compelling, Irish Times, 11/8/96; Cliona Harmey (auth), Twister, Beverly Semmes at IMMA, Sculptor's Soc Newslett, 11-12/96. *Dealer:* Leslie Tonkonow ARtwork & Projects 535 W 22d St New York NY 10011. *Mailing Add:* 29 15th St Apt B New York NY 10011-6864

SEMOWICH, CHARLES JOHN
HISTORIAN, PAINTER
b Binghamton, NY, 49. *Study:* State Univ NY, Binghamton, BA, 71; Cath Univ Am, MFA, 72; Int Col, PhD, 81; Woodstock Sch Art, NY, 89. *Work:* Roberson Ctr, State Univ NY, Binghamton, NY; Woodstock Sch Art, NY; Print Club Albany, NY; Newark Pub Libr, NJ. *Comn:* Murals, Rensselaer Riverfront Park, NY. *Exhib:* Schweinfurth Art Ctr, Auburn, NY, 92; spring exhib, Market Theatre Gallery, Albany, 94, RAMS, 95, State Univ NY, Binghamton, 96, Woodstock Sch Art, NY, 98 & Print Club Albany, 98; Northeast Prints, William Patterson Univ, 2000; one-person show, Print Club of Albany, 01; East of the Hudson, Fulton Street Gallery, Troy, NY, 99, Interpreting Landscape, 02; Mem, Fulton St Gallery, Troy, NY, 2005 & 06. *Collection Arranged:* Please Be Seated, Roberson Ctr, NY, 80; 16th Nat Print Show, Print Club Albany, NY, 89; D Lathrop Retrospective (with catalog), State Univ NY, Albany, 91; Nat Print Exhib, Print Club Albany & Schenectady Mus, 92, 98; 10 Exhib of Albany, Ctr Galleries. *Pos:* pres, Print Club Albany, 88-99, curator currently; mem, Mayor's Task Force Arts, Albany, 90-; artist-in-residence, Futton Street Gallery, Troy, NY, 01; juror, Albany Tulip Festival, 01-05; exec dir, Albany Ctr Galleries, Albany, NY, 2004-05. *Teaching:* Adj, Empire State Col, 78- & Chautauqua Inst, NY, summers 88-90; lectr, NY State Coun Humanities, 96. *Awards:* NY State Fair Awards Art, 72; Cogswell Award, Print Club Albany (disting mem), 99. *Bibliog:* Article, Capital District Bus Rev, 1/18/92. *Mem:* Print Club, Albany; Soc Am Graphic Artists (adv coun). *Media:* All Media. *Res:* American art, both fine and decorative; Joseph Antione Hekking; New York state furniture; American prints; African American Furniture. *Publ:* Auth, Historical ceramics-Englebert, Bulletin NY State Archeol Soc, 80; American Furniture Craftsmen Working Prior to 1920, Greenwood, 84; coauth, Dorothy Lathrop-A Centenary Celebration State Univ, NY, 92; auth, William Buttre, Furniture Hist, 93; articles in Dictionary of Art, 96. *Dealer:* LePetit Muse Pittsfield MA. *Mailing Add:* 242 Broadway St Rensselaer NY 12144

SEMPLE, JOHN PAULUS
PAINTER
b Easton, Pa, 30. *Study:* Hamilton Col, BA, 53; Mex City Col; Boston Univ, MFA; SKowhegan Sch Painting & Sculpture; studied with James Penney & Ivan Albright. *Work:* Univ Wis; Print Club Albany. *Exhib:* Pa Acad Fine Arts; San Diego Art Inst; Butler Inst Am Art, Youngstown, Ohio, 99; Boston Printmakers, 2001. *Awards:* Louis Comfort Tiffany Found Grant, 58; Grumbacher Gold Medal, Allied artists Am, 87; First prize, painting, Cape Cod Art Asn, 96. *Mem:* Boston Printmakers; Allied Artists Am; Audubon Artists; Print Club Albany. *Mailing Add:* PO Box 305 North Pomfret VT 05053

SENCIAL, GABRIEL JAIME
PRINTMAKER, PAINTER
b Medellin, Colombia, Jan 28, 47; US & Colombian citizen. *Study:* Medellin Fine Arts Inst, cert, 61-63; Univ Miami, with Eugene Massin, BA(art, art in our cchs scholar), 66-70; Santa Rosa Col, with Max Hein, certs, 82-91. *Work:* Lowe Art Mus, Coral Gables, Fla; Nat Inst Cult Inac, Panama; Univ Antioquia Mus, Mus de Antioquia, Medellin, Colombia; Sonoma Co Mus, Santa Rosa, Calif; Bristol Myers Squibb, The Netherlands; plus numerous other pvt and public collections. *Comn:* A View of Our Valley (350 sq ft), Alexander Sch Dist, Healdsburg, Calif, 88. *Exhib:* IV Medellin Biennial, Palace of Exhibs, Medellin, Colombia, 81; Panamenian Art Inst Collection, Palace of Exhibs, Panama City, 83; 35th Ann Mill Valley Art Festival, Calif, 90; 18th Open Studios, Somar Gallery, San Francisco, 91; Festival Latino, Sonoma Co Mus, Santa Rosa, Calif, 93-94; solo exhibs, Soundscape Gallery, Santa Rosa, Calif, 94, Quicksilver Gallery, Sebastopol, Calif, 89 & 3D Dynamic Gallery, Healdsburg, Calif, 98-99; 35th-38th Sonoma Ann Art Show, Calif, 96-98. *Pos:* Art dir, Artist Guild San Francisco, 91-94; cons in field, 72-80. *Teaching:* Teaching asst painting, Univ Miami, 67-68; teaching asst silkscreen, Santa Rosa Col, 88-92; artist-in-residence art, Healdsburg Sch Dist, 88-93. *Awards:* First Prize, 10th Nat Art Competition, Mus de Antioquia, 79; Discovery Awards, Art of Calif, 93. *Bibliog:* Jean Millewics (auth), The Art of G Sencial, US Info Agency, 80; Roger Kerraker (dir), Video disc on Colombia, Santa Rosa Col, 90; Julie & David Allen (dirs), Studio Views, KRCB-TV 22 PBS, 91; Art antiques and collectibles, Santa Rosa, Calif Press Democrat, 7/90; plus others. *Mem:* Artist Guild San Francisco; Cult Arts Coun Sonoma Co; Int Asn Artists (UNESCO), Paris; Artist Guild Santa Rosa; Valley of the Moon Art Asn. *Media:* All Media. *Interests:* Archaeology, nature, ethnic and primitive art, photography. *Publ:* Award Winner, Miami Herald, 6/6/66; Folk art to pop, El Tiempo, 3/20/80; article in Vision Time Mag, 8/25/80; Video disc on Gabriel Sencial, Press Democrat, 7/16/90; Spiritual Inspiration in Contemporary Art, 92. *Dealer:* Gallery One 209 Western Ave Petaluma CA 94952. *Mailing Add:* Artists Guild San Francisco 601 Van Ness Ave #E3-140 San Francisco CA 94102

SENDAK, MAURICE BERNARD
WRITER, ILLUSTRATOR
b Brooklyn, NY, June 10, 28. *Study:* Art Students League, 49-51. *Work:* Rosenbach Found, Philadelphia, Pa. *Exhib:* One-man show, Gallery Sch, Visual Arts, NY, 64; Ashmolean Mus, Oxford, Eng, 75; Morgan Libr, 88. *Pos:* Writer & illusr children's bks, 51-; Stage designer (costumes & sets), 80-. *Awards:* Caldecott Award for Where

the Wild Things Are, 63, In the Night Kitchen, 70 & Outside Over There, 81; Laura Ingalls Wilder Award, 83; Nat Medal Arts, presented by Pres Clinton, 97. *Publ:* Illusr, Dear Mili, 88; auth & illusr, We Are All in the Dumps with Jack and Guy, 93; illusr, The Miami Giant, 95; Panthesilea, 98; Swine Lake, 99. *Dealer:* Justin Schiller, New York. *Mailing Add:* 200 Chestnut Hill Rd Ridgefield CT 06877

SENDER, ADAM D
COLLECTOR
Pos: Gen partner, Exis Capital Mgt, New York City, 1998-. *Awards:* Named one of Top 200 Collectors, ARTnews Mag, 2004, 2005, 2006. *Collection:* Contemporary Art. *Mailing Add:* Exis Capital Mgt 875 Third Ave 29th fl New York NY 10022

SENIE, HARRIET F
HISTORIAN, CRITIC
b New York, NY, Sept 23, 43. *Study:* Brandeis Univ, BA, 64; Hunter Col, New York, MA, 71; Inst Fine Arts, New York, PhD (art hist), 81. *Collection Arranged:* Fabric into Art Traveling Exhib (auth, catalog), 80, William King Traveling Exhib (auth, catalog), 80, South Africa-South Bronx (auth, catalog), 81 & Landscape-Sculpture (auth, catalog), Amelie A Wallace Gallery, State Univ NY, Old Westbury; Sculpture for Public Spaces (auth, catalog), Marisa del Re Gallery, 86; George Rickey: Projects for Public Sculpture (auth, catalog), Neuberger Mus, 87; Memory as Metaphor, Pleiades Gallery, 96. *Pos:* Dir, Amelie A Wallace Gallery, State Univ NY, Old Westbury, 79-82; assoc dir, The Art Mus, Princeton Univ, 82-86; dir, Mus Studies Prog, City Col NY, 86-. *Teaching:* Adj prof art hist, Hunter Col, 74-78; asst prof, State Univ NY, Old Westbury, 79-82; prof, City Col NY, 86- & City Univ NY Grad Ctr, 97-; vis disting prof, Carnegie Mellon Univ, Pittsburgh, 2000. *Awards:* Eisner Scholars Award, City Col, 89; Nat Endowment Asn Mus studies grant, 87; PSC-City Univ UNY Res Grant, 88, 92, 95 & 96. *Mem:* Col Art Asn; Am Asn Mus; Soc Am Art Historians; Am Studies Asn; ArtTable. *Res:* Public art and contemporary culture. *Publ:* Contemporary Public Sculpture: Tradition, Transformation and Controversy, Oxford Univ Press, 92; co-ed & contribr, Critical Issues in Public Art: Content, Context and Controversy, Harper Collins, 92 & Smithsonian Inst Press, reissued 98; auth, Public art and the legal system, Pub Art Rev, fall/winter 94; contribr, Encyclopedia of New York City, Yale Univ Press, 95; Public Art in Brazil, Sculpture, 2/98 & Re-approaching Tony Smith, 11/98; contribr Complex Identities: Jewish Consciousness and Modern Art, Rutgers, 2000; auth article Harvard Design Mag, Fall/99; plus others. *Mailing Add:* 215 Sackett St Brooklyn NY 11231-3604

SENSEMANN, SUSAN
PAINTER, EDUCATOR
b Glen Cove, NY, Oct 6, 49. *Study:* Tyler Sch Art, Rome Italy, 70; Syracuse Univ, NY, BFA, 71; Tyler Sch Art, Philadelphia, MFA, 73. *Work:* Ill State Mus, Springfield; Southern Ill Univ Mus, Edwardsville; Lakeview Mus, Peoria, Ill; Univ Rochester, NY; Appalachian Col, Boone, NC. *Comn:* Five oil paintings, Ill Agricultural Asn, Bloomington, Ill, 79; two acrylic paintings, Hyatt Regency Hotel, Flint, Mich, 81; two watercolors, Western Hotels, Houston, Tex, 84; five paper pieces, Paper Press, Chicago, Ill, 84; two oils, IBM Tower, Atlanta, Ga, 88. *Exhib:* Ill Painters, Western Ill Univ, Macomb, 92; Open Surface: Nardi, Sensemann, Tinsley, State Ill Gallery, Chicago, 92; Roy Boyd Gallery, Chicago, Ill, 92; Artemesia, Chicago, Ill, 92; solo exhibs, Artemisia, Chicago, 93 & 94, Locus Gallery, St Louis, Mo, 94, SACI, Florence, Italy, 94, Roy Boyd Gallery, Chicago, Ill, 94 & Gallery Woong, Seoul, Korea, 95; Kunstler Haus Gallery, Ger, 98; Faeroernes Kunst Mus, Faroe Island, 98; Mus Arco, Madrid, Spain, 99; and others. *Teaching:* Assoc prof, Univ Ill, Urbana, 73-81, Chicago, 81-. *Awards:* Rice Award, Vicinity Show, Art Inst Chicago, 79; Capital Develop Bd, State Ill, 91; Mucia Travel Grant, Chicago/Seoul, Korea, 94. *Bibliog:* Alan Artner (auth), Sensemann puts the unseen of canvas, Chicago Tribune, 8/85; Kristen Schleifer (auth), Susan Sensemann Review, New Art Examiner, 6/92; Maud Lavin (auth), Susan Sensemann, Book Review: Cut With the Kitchen Knife, Design Issues, Mass Inst Technol Press, summer 94. *Media:* Works on Paper. *Publ:* Patty Carroll, James Yood, Spirited Visions, Univ Ill Press, 91. *Mailing Add:* Univ Ill Chicago Sch Art & Design 929 W Harrison 106 Jefferson Hall Chicago IL 60607-7038

SEPLOWIN, CHARLES JOSEPH
SCULPTOR
b New York, NY, July 19, 45. *Study:* Univ NH, BA(art); RI Sch Design, MFA(sculpture). *Work:* Municipal Fire House Ctr, NY; Titan Steel Corp, NY; Montclair State Col; Univ NH; Sherson-Hutton, NY. *Comn:* Gates, Caleia Fine Arts, Upper Montclair, NJ; One percent Prog for Art. *Exhib:* Aldrich Mus, 75; one-man show, Elizabeth Weiner Gallery, NY, 80; Sculpture Ctr, NY, 83; Cheltenham Art Ctr, Philadelphia, 83; Mus Mod Art Latin Am, Washington, DC, 83; Leslie Cecil Gallery, 86-; Recent Acquisitions, Art Mus Ams, Washington, DC, 92; and others. *Teaching:* Assoc prof, Montclair State Col, 74-. *Bibliog:* Articles in Craft Horizons, 8/74 & Arts Mag, 9/74. *Mailing Add:* 463 West St New York NY 10014

SEPPA, HEIKKI MARKUS
GOLDSMITH, EDUCATOR
b Sakkijarvi, Finland, Mar 8, 27; US citizen. *Study:* Georg Jensen Silversmiths, Copenhagen, 48-49; Cranbrook Acad Art, 60-61; Goldsmith Sch Helsinki, Cent Sch Indust Arts, Finland, Master Silversmith, 63. *Work:* Evansville Mus Sci & Art, Ind; Steinberg Gallery Art, Washington Univ, St Louis, Mo; Tex Tech Univ, Lubbock; Cranbrook Acad Art, Bloomfield Hills, Mich; St Louis City Art Mus. *Comn:* Over 200 pvt collections, St Louis area patrons, 65-78; The Search, W G Elliot Soc of Washington Univ, 69; Menorah Shaare Emeth Temple, St Louis, Mo, 80; Church St Michael & St George, St Louis, Mo, 90. *Exhib:* The Metalsmith, Phoenix Art Mus, Ariz, 77; 3-Exhib, Burnaby Art Gallery, BC, Can, 77; Goldsmiths Hall, London, Eng, 78; Schmuck Mus Pforzhaim, Ger, 79; solo shows, Ten Arrow, Cambridge, Mass, 82 & Wichita Arts Asn, 86. *Pos:* Head metal-arts studies, Art Ctr Sch, Louisville, Ky, 61-65. *Teaching:* Prof art metalsmithing, Sch Fine Arts, Washington Univ, St Louis, 65-92, emer prof, 92-; over 200 workshops in NAm & Europe. *Awards:* Craftsman Fel, Nat Endowment for the Arts, 75; dipl for lifetime work in profession, Precious Metal Indust League of Finland; Col of Fels, Am Crafts Coun, 87. *Bibliog:* Excellence, Am Craft Mag, 8/79; article, Form Mag, Seoul, Korea, 80; Washington Univ Mag, spring 81; and others. *Mem:* Founding mem Soc NAm Goldsmiths; Am Crafts Coun; Soc NAm Silversmiths. *Media:* Gold, Silver. *Publ:* Article on roll printing, Artisan/Craftsman, Can Craft Asn, 70; Auth, Form Emphasis for Metalsmiths, Kent State Univ Press, 78; Chapter on Reticulation, In: Metals Technic, Brynmorgan Press, 92; auth, Hopeasean Pajasta, 96, Coun of Edn, Finland

SERENYI, PETER
HISTORIAN, ADMINISTRATOR
b Budapest, Hungary, Jan 13, 31. *Study:* Dartmouth Col, AB, 57; Yale Univ, MA, 58; Washington Univ, PhD, 68. *Collection Arranged:* Contemporary Architecture in India, 76 & Le Corbusier in India, 80, Northeastern Univ Art Gallery & traveling; Hungarian Art: 1920-1970, Northeastern Univ Art Gallery, 81; Additions to Buildings: 1972-1982, 83 & Boston Architectural Competitions: 1960-1983, 84, Northeastern Univ Art Gallery & Boston Archit Ctr; Northeastern Univ Centennial Exhib, 97-98. *Teaching:* Chmn dept art & archit, Northeastern Univ, 81-96, prof emer, 96-. *Awards:* Graham Found Advan Studies Fine Arts Grant, 74-75; Fulbright Sr Res Grant, 74-75; Northeastern Univ Fac Develop Grant, 91; and others. *Mem:* Soc Archit Historians (vpres, New Eng chap, 77-78, pres, 78-79, dir, 79-82); Mass Comt Preserv Archit Records (dir, 79-81); Citizen Ambassador Prog Art Educ Deleg to People's Repub China, 91; Fulbright Asn, Eastern Mass Chap (pres, 98-). *Res:* Le Corbusier; modern architecture in India. *Publ:* Auth, Le Corbusier, Fourier and the Monastery of Ema, Art Bull, 67; ed, Le Corbusier in Perspective, Prentice-Hall, 75; auth, Mies' New National Gallery, Harvard Archit Rev, 80; Le Corbusier's Architecture in India, Le Corbusier Archive, 83; Sixty years of housing in Delhi, Techniques et Architecture, 85. *Mailing Add:* Dept Art & Archit Northeastern Univ 239 Ryder Ave Boston MA 02115

SERRA, RICHARD
SCULPTOR
b San Francisco, Calif, Nov 2, 39. *Study:* Univ Calif, Berkeley; Univ Calif, Santa Barbara, BA in English Lit, 61; Yale Univ, BFA & MFA, 64. *Hon Degrees:* Calif Col Arts & Crafts, PhD in Art (hon), 94. *Work:* Whitney Mus Am Art & Guggenheim Mus, NY; Stedelijk Mus, Amsterdam; Tate Gallery, London; Yale Univ Art Gallery, New Haven, Conn; and numerous pvt collections. *Comn:* London Stock Exchange, 87; sculpture, Rijksmuseum Kroller-Muller park, Otterlo, Neth, 88; Stacks, Yale Univ, New Haven, 90; Hall of Witness, US Holacaust Mem Mus, Wash; Mus Contemp Art, Barcelona,. *Exhib:* Solo exhibs incl: Galerie Francoise Lambert, Milan, 69, Portland Ctr for Visible Arts. 75, Mus Boymans-van Beuningen, Rotterdam, 80, Akira Ikeda Gallery, Tokyo, 87, Galerie Nordenhaken, Stockholm, 88, Gagosian Gallery, NY, 91, Ctr of Art Reina Sofia, Madrid, 92, Solomon R Guggenheim Mus, 93, Ctr for the Fine Arts, Miami, 94; Galerie M Bochum, Ger, 84; Stedilijik, The Neth, 88; IVAM Ctr, Valencia, Spain, 93; Jablonka Galerie, Cologne, Ger, 94; Mus Art Contemporaneo, Monterrey, Spain, 99; Whitney Mus Am Art, 2000; Whitney Biennial: Day for Night, Whitney Mus Am Art, 2006. *Awards:* Fulbright grant, 66, Guggenheim fel, 70, Skowhegan Sch Painting & Sculpture award, 75, named Fel, Bezalei Acad, Jerusalem, 83, Chevalier de lOrdre l' Arts et des Lettres, French Govt., 85, Officer, 91, recipient Wilhelm-Lehmbruck award for sculpture, Sculpture Ctr award for Distinction in Sculpture, 92, Praemium Imperiale, Japan Art Asn, 94; Gold Medal for Sculpture, Am Acad of Arts and Letters, 2001; Int Art award Cristóbal Gabarrón Found, 2005. *Bibliog:* Pincenthal, Nancy (auth.) The Print Collector's Newsletter, 91; Kimmelman, Michael (auth.), N.Y. Times, 99. *Mem:* Fel Acad Arts and Sci; Acad Universelles des Cultures. *Publ:* Richard Serra Writings & Interviews, Univ Chicago Press, 94; Richard Serra: Torqued Ellipses, Dia Center Arts, 97; Richard Serra Sculpture 1985-1998, Mus Contemp Art, Los Angeles, 98. *Dealer:* Gagosian Gallery 980 Madison Ave New York NY 10021. *Mailing Add:* 173 Duane St Fl 5 New York NY 10013-3334

SERRA, RUDY
SCULPTOR
b San Francisco, Calif, Apr 9, 48. *Study:* City Col San Francisco, AA; San Francisco State Col, BA; Univ Calif, Berkeley, MA & MFA. *Exhib:* San Francisco Art Inst, 73 & 76; 1975 Whitney Biennial, NY, 75; San Francisco Mus Mod Art, 77; Faculty Exhib, Univ Conn, 80-82; one-person shows, Univ Houston, 80, Baruch Col, 82 & Marianne Deson Gallery, 83; Oakland Mus, 82; Nassau Mus, NY, 85; Tomoko Liguori Gallery, NY, 88. *Teaching:* Vis asst prof sculpture, Calif State Univ, Chico, 75; asst prof, Am River Col, Sacramento, 76-77; vis asst prof sculpture, Univ Calif, Davis, fall 78; asst prof sculpture & drawing, Univ Conn, Storrs, 79-; State Univ NY, Purchase, 84, Sarah Lawrence Col, NY, 86-87, Bennington Col, Vt, 88. *Awards:* Nat Endowment Arts Grant, 76, 78 & 85. *Bibliog:* Roberta Smith (auth), Biennial review, Artforum, 5/75; Amy Goldin (auth), The New Whitney Biennial, Art Am, 5-6/75; Judith Dunham (auth), Introduction 75, Artweek, 7/75; Michael Brenson (auth), article, New York Times, 88. *Media:* Concrete, Hydracol. *Mailing Add:* 16 Greene St New York NY 10013

SESLAR, PATRICK GEORGE
WRITER, PAINTER
b Fort Wayne, Ind, Sept 20, 47. *Study:* Purdue Univ, BS (psychology), 69. *Exhib:* Coconut Grove Art Festival, Fla, 96; Cherry Creek Art Festival, Denver, 97; Masterworks in Miniature, Gallery One, Mentor, Ohio, 97-2000; Friends and Lovers, LeMoyne Art Found, Tallahassee, 2000. *Pos:* contribr editor, Artist's Mag, Cincinnati,

85-. *Awards:* Juror's Award, Cherry Creek Art Festival, Denver, Colo, 97; First placce painting, Maitland Arts Festival, 98. *Mem:* Nat Asn Independent Artists. *Media:* Oil. *Res:* Contemporary art technique and art marketing,. *Publ:* coauth, Painting Seascapes in Sharp Focus, 87, Painting Nature's Peaceful Places, 93, (auth) Wildlife Painting Step by Step, 95, Painting From Photographs, 99, The One-Hour Watercolorist, 2001, North Light Books. *Dealer:* Art Sales and Rental Gallery Philadelphia Mus Art 26th St & Benjamin Franklin Pkwy Philadelphia PA 19130. *Mailing Add:* 5580 La Jolla Blvd #334 La Jolla CA 92037

SETLOW, NEVA C (DELIHAS)
SCULPTOR, PAINTER
b New Haven, Conn, Dec, 40. *Study:* Empire State Col, BA. *Work:* Assoc Univs, Brookhaven Nat Lab, Upton, NY; Pittsfield City Bank, Mass; Islip Art Mus, NY. *Exhib:* Aldrich Mus, Ridgefield, Conn, 76; Guild Hall, East Hampton, 86-2002; Ward Nasse Gallery, NY, 92-97; Faber Biren Color Award Show, Stamford, Conn, 97, 01; The Altered Image, Islip Art Mus, Long Island, NY, 97, Eden Revisited, 2000; Exploring the Art of Space, Planetary Art Soc, Pasadena, Calif, 97; Firehouse Gallery, Garden City, NY, 97 & 2004; Salon des Femes, Southampton Cult Ctr, NY, 97; Tribute, Smithtown Arts Coun, 98; Pleiades Gallery 16th Juried Exhib, NY, 98; Broome St Gallery, Soho, NY, 99-2002; Huchins Gallery, Brookville, NY, 2000; Shelter Park Art Gallery, 2000 & 2006; Edison Gallery, Piqua, Ohio, 01; Huntington Arts Coun, Artrium, Melville, NY, 01; Grounds for Sculpture, Hamilton, NJ, 01; The Banana Factory, Bethlehem, PA, 02; East End Arts Coun, Riverhead, NY, 03; J Wayne Stark galleries, Texas A & M Univ, 04; Rosettastone Gallery, Juno, Fla, 04; East End Arts Council, The Skys the Limit, 05; Arts & Literature Laboratory, New Haven, Conn, 06; The Karpeles Libr Mus, Newburgh, NY, 06; Port of Call Gallery, Warwick, NY, 06. *Pos:* biology assoc, Brookhaven Nat Lab, Upton, NY, 76-96, guest app, 05. *Awards:* Silvermine Guild Artists 50th Ann Award, 72; Sculpture House Award, West Chester Art Soc, 73; Award of Excellence, Huntington Art League, 74; North Shore Art Guild Painting Award, 98, Sculpture Award, 98; Am Icon-Outer Space Sculpture Award, 01; Cleo Hartwig Award, Nat Asn Women Artists, 02; Nat ASN Woman Artist; Gretchen Richardson Memoral Award, 04; Am Soc of Contemporary Arts Award, 04; East End Arts Council, Hon Mention, 05. *Mem:* E End Arts Coun; Southampton Artists; Int Sculpture Ctr; Nat Asn Women Artists; Artist Equity of New York City; Am Soc Contemporary Artists, NY. *Media:* Plastic, Acrylic. *Specialty:* Contemporary Painting & Sculpture. *Interests:* Art and science, light art. *Publ:* Contribr, Art and Science: Similarities Disimilarities, Leonardo, Pergamon Press, Vol 27, No 3, 94. *Dealer:* Ward Nasse New York, NY. *Mailing Add:* Four Beachland Ave East Quogue NY 11942

SEVERSON, WILLIAM CONRAD
SCULPTOR
b Madison, Wis, Nov 22, 24. *Study:* Univ Wis, Madison, BS, AA, 47; Syracuse Univ, with Ivan Mestrovic, MFA(sculpture), 49; Susquahanna Univ, Hon PhD, 85. *Work:* Nat Cathedral Washington DC; Concordia Seminary, St Louis, Mo; St Louis Sculptors' Gallery, Mo; Cheltenham Art Asn, Philadelphia, Pa; Morris Arboretum, Philadelphia, Pa. *Comn:* Ciborium, Shrine Our Lady of Snows, Belleville, Ill, 64; Connectors, Blue Cross/Blue Shield, Chapel Hill, NC, 74; Solaris (bronze, solar), Tampa Electric Co, Fla, 80; Protein Cube, Ralston Purina, St Louis, Mo, 72; Primogenesis, Friends Mus Sci Nat Hist, St Louis, Mo, 81; Tri-State Vets Mem, Dubuque, Iowa, 89. *Exhib:* NY World's Fair, Mo Pavilion, NY, 65; Chillicothe, Mo State Council Arts, 65; Casa D'Artes, Taos, NMex, 70; Sculpture in Archit Concept, Fordham/Lincoln Ctr, NY, 76; 7th Ann, Shidonaa, Santa Fe, NMex, 81. *Pos:* Pres, St Louis Sculptors' Gallery, 64-68. *Awards:* First Place, Univ Wis, Green Bay, 77; Purchase Prize, Philip & Muriel Berman, 79. *Bibliog:* Thelma R Newman (auth), Plastics as Art Form, Chilton, 64; Theodore F Wolff (auth) Something for all to share, Christian Sci Monitor, 80; Louis G Redstone (auth), Public Art--New Directions, McGraw-Hill, 81. *Mem:* Int Sculpture Conf; Ecumenical Coun Drama & Art. *Media:* Steel, Bronze. *Mailing Add:* 21 Daniel Rd St Louis MO 63124-1809

SEVIGNY, MAURICE JOSEPH, II
EDUCATOR, ADMINISTRATOR
b Amesbury, Mass, July 24, 43. *Study:* Mass Col Art, BSEd, 65; Ohio State Univ, MA, 69, PhD, 77. *Teaching:* Asst prof art educ, Western Ky Univ, 69-76; teaching assoc, Ohio State Univ, 76-78; assoc prof art, chair, Div Art Educ, Bowling Green State Univ, Ohio, 78-81, dir, Sch Art, 77-85, prof, 81-; chmn dept art & Marguerite Fairchild centennial prof, Univ Tex, Austin, 86; dean Col of Fine Arts, Univ Ariz, 91. *Awards:* Award Excellence Dissertation Res, Rev Res Visual Arts Educ, 79; Ann Hollis Moore Award Disting Serv, Bowling Green State Univ Student Union, 82; Disting Alumnus, Ohio State Univ, 87; Educator of Yr Pacific Region High Edn Divsn NAEA, 96; Father of Yr, Tucson, Ariz, 98. *Mem:* Nat Coun Policy Studies Art Educ; Ohio Art Educ Asn (adv coun rep, 78, chmn Higher Educ, 79); Nat Art Educ Asn Higher Educ Div (chmn elect); Nat Coun Art Adminr; Nat Soc Schs Art & Design; Internat Coun of Fine Arts Deans. *Res:* Discipline based art education, studio learning and performance; assessment at the university level from the triangulated perspective of teacher, student, classroom ethnographer; lanquage and gender differences in non-verbal communication. *Publ:* Auth, Triangulation and descriptive research, Rev Res Visual Arts, 5/78; auth, Utilizing recorded materials for the clinical component of teacher training, In: Human Relations and the Clinical Component, Ohio Dept Educ, 80; auth, Triangulate inquiry: A methodology for the analysis of classroom interaction, In: Analysis of Discourse: Ethnographic Approaches, Ablex Publ, 81; Discipline Based Art Education and Teacher Education, J P Getty Ctr Educ, 86; contribr, Jour of Aesthetic Edn, Studies, and NAEA News. *Mailing Add:* 6463 E Paseo Otono Tucson AZ 85750

SEWELL, DARREL L
CURATOR, HISTORIAN
b Cushing, Okla, Dec 21, 39. *Study:* Univ Chicago, BA, 62, MA, 62. *Exhib:* Henry Ossawa Tanner, The Art Mus San Francisco, 91; Eastern State Penitentary, Philadelphia, Pa, 94; The Cadwalader Family: Art and Style in Early Philadelphia, Philadelphia Mus Art, 96; The Peale Family: Creation of an Am Legacy, 1770-1870, Philadelphia Mus Art, 96. *Collection Arranged:* Modern Jewelry, 64-86; Philadelphia: Three Centuries of American Art (auth, catalog), 76; Installation of American Collections, 77; American Presidential China, 77; The University of Pennsylvania: Collector and Patron of Art, 1779-1979, 79; Copley from Boston (auth, catalog), 80; Thomas Eakins: Artist of Philadelphia (auth, catalog), 81-82; One Hundred Years of Acquisitions, 83; Benjamin West in Pennsylvania Collections, 86; Diego Rivera, 86; The Helen Drutt Collection, 86-87; The Fairmount Waterworks, 88; Henry O Tanner (auth, catalog), 91. *Pos:* cur educ, Nat Collection Fine Arts, 70-73; cur, Am Art, Philadelphia Mus Art, 73-; chmn, Staff adv comt, Capitol Campaign, 86-89. *Teaching:* Instr art hist, Ohio State Univ, Columbus, 66-67 & Univ Ill, Chicago Circle, 68-70. *Publ:* Auth, What you see is what you get: An approach to the use of museums for education, Art Educ, 12/71; Auth, Henry O Tanner (with catalog), Philadelphia Mus Art, 91; Guide to the Thomas Eakins Research Collection with a Lifetime Exhibition Record and Bibliography, Philadelphia Mus Art, 96. *Mailing Add:* Philadelphia Mus Art PO Box 7646 Philadelphia PA 19101

SEWELL, JACK VINCENT
MUSEUM CURATOR
b Dearborn, Mo, June 11, 23. *Study:* St Joseph Jr Col, Mo, 41-43; City Col New York, 43-44; Univ Chicago, MFA, 50; Harvard Univ, 51-53. *Collection Arranged:* Complete reinstallation of Oriental Collections, Art Inst Chicago, 58; installation of Indian & SE Asian collections, Art Inst Chicago, 86. *Pos:* Mem staff, Oriental dept, Art Inst Chicago, 50-56, assoc cur Oriental art, 56-58, cur, 58-88, consult, 89-90, cur emer, 90-. *Mem:* Far Eastern Ceramic Group; Japan-Am Soc Chicago; The Cliff Dwellers; Arts Club Chicago. *Res:* Indian and Far Eastern art; arts of China; strength in delicacy--archaic Chinese bronzes and sculptures of Gandhara. *Publ:* Contribr, Archaeol & Chicago Art Inst Quart. *Mailing Add:* 618 S Prospect St Galena IL 61036

SEWELL, LEO
ASSEMBLAGE ARTIST, SCULPTOR
b Anapolis, Md, Sept 7, 45. *Study:* Univ Del, MA, 70. *Work:* Hartsfield Atlanta Airport, Ga; Express-Ways Children's Mus, Chicago; Ripley's Believe It or Not Mus, St Augustine, Fla; Philip & Muriel Berman Mus Art, Ursinus Col, Collegeville, Pa; Am Visiounary Art Mus, Baltimore, MD. *Comn:* NBC Corp Hq, Comn by Brandon Tartikoff, NY, 80; The Family, comn by Philip & Muriel Berman, Allentown, Pa, 83; Rocky, comn by Sylvester Stallone, Los Angeles, Calif, 85; Nolan Ryan, comn by Nike Corp, Portland, Wash, 92. *Exhib:* solo exhib, Children's Mus RI, Pawtucket, 89, Danville Mus Fine Art & Hist, Va, 90 & Livlan Mus Art, Tokyo, Japan, 92; Trash Menagerie, Express-Ways Children's Mus, Chicago, Ill, 90; Penis Art, University City Arts League, Philadelphia, 94; Recycle Reuse Recreate, USIA Traveling Exhib, 95; Fuller Craft Mus, Brockton, Mass; Lost & Found, Princeton, NJ; Art Works Gallery, Newark, Ohio. *Bibliog:* Cultural Connections, Temple Univ Press, 91; Hand and Home: The Homes of American Craftsmen, Little Brown Co, 94; Art with a Sense of Humor, Davis Publ, 96. *Mem:* Dumpster Divers Asn. *Media:* Found Objects. *Interests:* Found objects. *Publ:* Featured on many TV productions including You Asked For It, 81, Ripley's Believe It or Not, 82, Captain Noah, 85 & Earth Week Celebration on Mr Roger's Neighborhood, 90; auth, Artful Jesters, 10 Speed Press, 2003; auth, Found Object Art Schiffer, Publ LTD, 2001; auth, Humor in Art, Davis Publ, 97. *Dealer:* Connell Gallery 333 Buckhead Ave Atlanta GA 30305; Twist Gallery Portland OR; Works Gallery Philadelphia PA. *Mailing Add:* 3614 Pearl St Philadelphia PA 19104

SEWELL, RICHARD GEORGE
PRINTMAKER, PAINTER
b St Louis, Mo, Aug 22, 42; Can citizen. *Study:* Univ Nac Autonoma de Mexico, 65; Kansas City Art Inst, Mo, 66; Univ Mo, Kansas City, BA, 67. *Work:* Can Coun, Ottawa; The Gallery, Stratford, Ont; Nova Scotia Art Gallery, Halifax; Owens Art Gallery, Mt Allison, NB; Winnipeg Art Gallery, Man. *Exhib:* Beyond the Repeatable Image, Heywood, Tamasauskas, Sewell, Eng, Spain, Belg, Scotland, France, 84-85; New Work, May, Besant, Parker, Sewell, Alberta Col Art, Calgary, 88; Agnes Etherington Art Ctr, Kingston, Ont, 85; Univ Toronto, Erindale Campus, 90; solo exhib, Mem Univ St John's Newfoundland, 90. *Pos:* Co-founder & dir, Open Studio, Print Workshop, Toronto, Ont, 70-82; chmn, Print and Drawing Coun Canada, Toronto, Ont, Can, 89-91. *Teaching:* Univ Saskatchewan, Saskatoon, 81; Alberta Col Art, Calgary, 84-86; prof visual arts, Sheridan Col, Oakville, Ont, 86-; Ontario Col Art, Toronto, 88-. *Bibliog:* Linda Beattie (auth), Beyond the Repeatable Image, Heywood, Tamasauskas, & Sewell, Visual Arts, Ont, Toronto, 84; Louise Dompierre (auth), Paratactic Images Agnes Etherington Art Ctr, Kingston, Ont, 85; Deidre Hanna (auth), Chaos/Relief, NOW Mag, Toronto, Ont, 1/90. *Media:* All; Acrylic, Oil. *Publ:* Contribr, Open Studio-Ten Years (catalog), Open Studio, Toronto, Ont, 80; auth, StoneGrain Cycle, The Prints of Mark Critoph, The Gallery/Stratford, Ont, 84. *Mailing Add:* 49 Appleton Ave Toronto ON M6E 3A4 Canada

SEXAUER, DONALD RICHARD
INSTRUCTOR, PRINTMAKER
b Erie, Pa. *Study:* Col William & Mary; Edinboro State Col, BS; Kent State Univ, MA. *Work:* Butler Inst Am Art, Youngstown, Ohio; NY Pub Libr; Mint Mus Art, Charlotte, NC; Nat Mus Art, Smithsonian, Washington, DC; Libr of Cong, Washington, DC; and others. *Comn:* Print eds, Make Believe Print Club of Albany, Int Graphic Art Soc, 66, To Fly, To Fly, 66; Vietnam Fragments (folio), Off, Chief Mil Hist, Washington, DC, 71; Mecklenburg Bicentennial Comn (folio). *Exhib:* Soc Am

Graphic Artists, 64-; New Talent In Printmaking, NY, 66; 140th Ann, Nat Acad Design, 66; San Diego Print Exhib, 71; 16th Hunterdon Nat, Clinton, NJ, 72. *Teaching:* Prof printmaking, Sch Art, E Carolina Univ, 60-. *Awards:* Print Prize, Nat Acad Design 140th Ann, 66; Purchase Awards, Piedmont Print Ann, Mint Mus, 69-74; Purchase Awards, Bradley Print Show, Peoria, Ill, Soc Am Graphic Artists, 79 & 80 & Hunterdon Art Ctr, Clinton, NJ, 83 & 86. *Mem:* Soc Am Graphic Artists; Boston Printmakers; Audubon Artists. *Media:* Intaglio. *Publ:* Illusr, Red clay reader number 5, Southern Lit Rev, 68. *Mailing Add:* 109 Greenbriar Dr Greenville NC 27834

SEXTON, JANICE LOUISE
PAINTER, SCULPTOR
b Milwaukee, Wis, Oct 23, 1951. *Study:* Univ Mass, 1973-74; Univ Nev, Reno, 1984-85; Santa Rosa Community col, Santa Rosa, 1986. *Work:* Univ Mass-Dartmouth; State House Rotunda, Boston; Westport Townhall, Westport, Mass; Quadrangle, Springfield, Mass. *Comn:* Ocean Graphics (mural), Westport Mass, 2002; Town of Westport pub libr (mural), Westport, Mass, 1997; Chaney Instruments Nationwide Distribution (illus), Lake Geneva, Wis, 1998. *Exhib:* Waterfowl Stamp Competition (dept of fisheries and wildlife), Peabody Essex Mus, Salem, Mass, 1999-2003; Waterfowl Stamp Competition (dept of fisheries and wildlife), Mus of Sci at the Quadrangle, Springfield, Mass, 2002. *Collection Arranged:* Univ Mass-Dartmouth; State House Rotunda, Boston; Westport Townhall, Westport, Mass. *Teaching:* Art instr, Westbridge Water High School; Adult Edu, Bridgewater, Mass, 1984-1985; The Westeria Vine, Westport, Mass, 1991-1994; pvt art instr, oil painting, 95-99. *Awards:* Helen Ellis Trust Fund Grant, Town Hall-Westport, 1994-2001; Mass Arts Lottery Grant, 95; Prof Catagory Univ Mass, Dartmouth, Women's Ctr at U-Mass, 1997; Mass State Waterfowl (second pl), Peabody Mus, Mass Dept of Fisheries/Wildlife, 1999-2003; Mass State Waterfowl Stamp Design (second pl), 2006. *Bibliog:* Patricia O'Connor (auth), Times, 1993; Bill Hall (ed auth), Painting Wins Town Flag, The Chronicle, 1994. *Mem:* American Society of Marine Artists; Massachusetts State Arts Lottery Council, (treas, 1988-90); Westport Art Group; Int Soc Marine Artists (professional mem). *Media:* Acrylic, Oil, Watercolor & Clay. *Dealer:* Roshambo Art, Phoenix Ariz. *Mailing Add:* 191 Forge Rd Westport MA 02790

SEXTON, JOHN (WILLIAM)
PHOTOGRAPHER
b Maywood, Calif, May 22, 53. *Study:* Photog workshops with Ansel Adams, Wynn Bullock, Paul Caponigro & Brett Weston, 73-74. *Work:* Univ Ariz Ctr Creative Photog, Tucson; Polaroid Corp Collection, Clarence Kennedy Gallery, Cambridge, Mass; Newport Harbor Art Mus, Newport Beach, Calif; Monterey Peninsula Mus Art, Calif; China Photogrs Asn, Bening, Chica. *Exhib:* One-man exhib, Chapman Col, Orange, Calif, 76; Bell Gallery, Brown Univ, Providence, RI, 80; New Landscapes, Friends Photog Gallery, Carmel, Calif, 80; Message From The West Coast, Photo Gallery Int, Tokyo, 81; Focus Gallery, San Francisco, 81; and others. *Pos:* Co-dir & instr, Owens Valley Photog Workshops, Agoura, Calif, 76-; tech consult to Ansel Adams, Carmel, Calif, 79-82. *Teaching:* Instr, Cypress Col, Calif, 77-79; instr, Univ Calif, Santa Cruz, 80-81; instr, Ansel Adams Yosemite Workshops, 80-. *Awards:* Imogen Cunningham Award, Focus Gallery, San Francisco, 81. *Bibliog:* Ron Eggers (auth), Working with the masters, Rangefinder, 80. *Mem:* Friends Photog; Soc Photog Educ. *Publ:* Contribr, Photo-Image Mag, Lodestar Press, 76; Darkroom Photog Mag, Sheptow Publ, 79; The negative, New York Graphic Soc, 81; Zoom Mag, Joel Laroche-France, 81; coauth, Quiet Light, essays, 51 black & white reproductions, Bulfinch Press/Little, Brown & Co, 4/90, 2nd printing, 5/90. *Dealer:* Weston Gallery PO Box 655 Carmel CA 93921. *Mailing Add:* 291 Calle de los Agrinemsors Carmel Valley CA 93924-9725

SEYLE, ROBERT HARLEY
SCULPTOR, DESIGNER
b National City, Calif, Oct 9, 37. *Study:* La Sierra Col, Riverside, Calif; Otis Art Inst, Los Angeles, BFA, MFA. *Work:* Storm King Art Mus, Corning, NY; Palm Springs Desert Mus, Calif; Beneficial Ins Group, Los Angeles; Metro Media Studios, Hollywood, Calif. *Comn:* Nail sculpture 11, Henry J Ittleson, Jr, Palm Springs, 67; nail sculpture 89, Julian Brody, Des Moines, Iowa, 72; nail sculpture 110, Dr Alonzo Proctor, Lodi, Calif, 74; nail sculpture 125, Arthur Elrod Interiors, Palm Springs, 75; nail sculpture 154, Steve Chase, Palm Springs, Calif, 81. *Exhib:* One-man show, Palm Springs Desert Mus, 74; group show, Calif State Capitol Bldg, Sacramento, 75; Ankrum Gallery, Los Angeles, 78; Riverside Art Ctr, Calif, 78; San Bernardino Co Mus, 78; Calif Small Works Show, Santa Roca, Calif, 93 & 94; and others. *Teaching:* prof design & stained glass, Pac Union Col, Angwin, Calif, 91-. *Bibliog:* Ray Faulkner & Edwin Ziegfeld (auths), Art Today, Holt, Rinehart & Winston Inc; Bernard Morris (auth), California people, Eyewitness News, ABC-TV, 74; Noonday WVa, Channel 12, Clarksburg, WVa, 80

SEYLER, MONIQUE G
PAINTER
b Jersey City, NJ, Dec 3, 56. *Study:* Sorbonne, Paris, 76; Fu Jen Univ, Taiwan, ROC, 77-78; Seton Hall Univ, BA, 79; Art Students League, 83-85. *Work:* Zimmerli Mus, Rutgers Univ. *Exhib:* 2 woman exhib, Conscious Color, Lyrical Light, Westchester Community Col, 93; Emerging Artists, Elaine Benson Gallery, 95; Transition, Reggio Gallery, NY, 96; An Organic Palette, Manhattanville Col, 97; Recent Acquisitions, Zimmerli Mus, Rutgers Univ, 99; others; one-woman show Westchester Arts Coun, Valhalla, NY, 95, Nardin Galleries, Somers, NY, 97. *Collection Arranged:* Samuel C. Bernstein Co. *Pos:* Prog chair, Katonah Mus Artists Asn, 93-95; independent cur, Art & the Environ Exhib, Katonah Village Libr, 93, Waterworks, Paramount East Gallery, 94 & Multiples, Hastings Gallery, 95; founder/owner, Gallery Saint Martin, Inc. *Awards:* Painting Scholar, NJ Ctr Visual Arts; Miriam E Halpern Award for Works on Paper, Nat Asn Women Artists, 93; Hon Mention, Putnam Arts Coun, 93. *Bibliog:* Vivian Raynor (auth), More fantasies natural and cultural in arts council survey, NY Times, 11/19/95; Rose Slivka (auth), From the studio, E Hampton Star, 5/12/96; William Zimmer, Women's Work, Not all of it Ladylike, New York Times, 1/24/99. *Mem:* Nat Asn Women Artists. *Media:* Acrylic, Oil; Pastel. *Dealer:* Gallery Saint Martin Inc 7811 St Martins Ln Philadelphia PA 19118. *Mailing Add:* 7811 St Martin's Ln Philadelphia PA 19118

SEYMOUR, CLAUDIA
PAINTER
b St Paul, MN. *Study:* Duke Univ, BA, 1970; NY Univ, MA, 1979; Silvermine Art Sch, Conn, 1997-2000; Cape Cod Sch Art, 1999; Art Students League, NY, 2001-2003. *Exhib:* Catharine Lorillard Wolfe Art Club; Hudson Valley Art Asn; Int Asn Pastel Soc; Nat Exhib Pastel Soc, NMex, N Fla & W Coast; over 80 juried reg & nat exhib; Pastel Soc Am; Audubon Artists; Allied Artists Am; Am Artists Prof League. *Awards:* Numerous First Prize Awards and Best in Show Awards; Gold & Silver medals, Art Spirit Found. *Bibliog:* Michael Chesky Johnson (auth), Claudia Seymour, Pastel Journal, July-Aug 2003. *Mem:* Signature mem, Pastel Soc Am; Conn Pastel Soc; Painters Soc Cape Cod; Allied Artists Am; Am Artists Prof League. *Media:* Oils and Pastel. *Publ:* auth, Controlling the Light, Int Artist, June-July 2006. *Dealer:* Hoorn-Ashby Gallery 766 Madison Ave New York NY 10021. *Mailing Add:* 575 Silvermine Rd New Canaan CT 06840

SGOUROS, THOMAS
PAINTER
b Mass, 27. *Study:* RI Sch Design, BFA; RI Col, DFA (hon), 2001. *Exhib:* exhib in group shows at Parkland Art Gallery, 1999; One-man shows incl RI Watercolor Soc, 2004. *Pos:* Com illusr, New York City; prof, illustration RI Sch Design, Providence. *Awards:* Recipient Claiborne Pell award for excellence in arts, 2001. *Mem:* Nat Acad (assoc, 92, acad, 94-), Am Watercolor Soc, RI Watercolor Soc. *Mailing Add:* RI Sch of Design 2 College St Providence RI 02903

SHACK, RICHARD
COLLECTOR, PATRON
b New York, NY, May 15, 26. *Pos:* founder, chmn emer, Mus Contemp Art, Miami, Fla; chmn, Art Ctr S Fla, Miami Beach; print acquisitions comt, Whitney Mus; fine arts panel, Fed Reserve Bd. *Bibliog:* At Home With Art, Potter, 99; The World's Top 200 Collectors, Art News, summer 2000, 01 & 02. *Collection:* contemporary art. *Mailing Add:* 151 SE 15th Rd Miami FL 33129

SHADDLE, ALICE
SCULPTOR, COLLAGE ARTIST
b Hinsdale, Ill, Dec 21, 28. *Study:* Oberlin Col; Univ Chicago; Sch Art Inst Chicago, BFA & MFA. *Work:* Smithsonian Inst, Washington, DC; Muskegon Mus, Mich; State Ill Ctr Mus; Mus Contemp Art, Chicago. *Exhib:* Soft Edges, 54-55, Made With Paper, 67, Chicago Needs Famous Artists, 69 & Alternative Spaces, 84, Mus Contemp Art, Chicago; Soc for Contemp Art, 69, Exhib by Artist in Chicago & Vicinity, 75 & 85 & Prizewinners, 79, Art Inst, Chicago; Indianapolis Mus Art, Ind, 76; 26th Ill Invitational, Ill State Mus, Springfield, 76; Nat Drawing Show, Kohler Arts Ctr, Sheboygan, Wis, 76; Ill Traveling Sculpture Exhib II, 78-79. *Teaching:* Instr printmaking & drawing, Roosevelt Univ, Chicago, 65-67; children's painting teacher, Hyde Park Art Ctr, 55-98 & Triangle Art Ctr, 78-88, Chicago; Hyde Park Art Center, 1955-2006. *Awards:* Logan Medal, 75th Exhib by Artist of Chicago & Vicinity, Art Inst Chicago, 75; Ill Arts Coun Grant, 78; Nat Endowment Arts Grant, 79. *Bibliog:* Meilach & Ten Hoor (auth), Collage & Assemblage, Crown, 73; C L Morrison (auth, rev), Artforum, 76 & 78; Holly Day (auth), revs, Art in Am, 78 & 79. *Mem:* Artemisia Gallery & Fund (treas, 77-79); Hyde Park Art Ctr, Chicago; Art Inst Chicago (life mem). *Media:* Paper, Oil on Canvas, All Media. *Publ:* Contribr, Art: Choosing & Expressing, Benefic Press, 77, Leonardo, Vol II, Pergamon Press, 78, London, Eng; contribr, Perpetually Strange, Hyde Park Art Center, 2005. *Mailing Add:* 4858 S Kenwood Chicago IL 60615

SHADRACH, JEAN H
PAINTER, EDUCATOR
b La Junta, Colo. *Study:* Univ NMex; Constantine & Roman Chatov Studio, Atlanta, Ga; Alaska Methodist Univ, Sumie, with Diana Kan, Shozo Sato, Prof I-Hsing Ju, Ed Whitney, Gerald Brommer, Henry Wo, Katherine Liu & others. *Work:* Anchorage Fine Arts Mus & Aleyeska Pipeline Co, Anchorage; Frye Mus, Seattle; Standard Oil Co Calif; Price Waterhouse; Senator & Mrs Ted Stevens; British Petroleum Corp Hqs, Anchorage; and others. *Comn:* Anchorage Beautification, 70; Executive suites, ARCO & Aleyska Pipeline, 75; SOHIO painting, 80. *Exhib:* All Alaska Art Exhib, Anchorage, 68-72; Northwestern Watercolor Soc Ann, Seattle, 70; Design I, Anchorage, 71; Artists of Alaska, traveling, 71-75; Frye Mus, Seattle, 85; Sumie Soc Am, 87, 88, 91, 92, 93, 94, 97 & 98; Providence Hops, 90; Charter N Hosp, 98. *Pos:* Found, Artique, Ltd, Fine Art Gallery, Anchorage, 71-87. *Teaching:* Workshops, Foothills Art Ctr, Golden, Colo, 89-90; artist-lectr aboard Cunard Lines cruise ships, 89-92, 94-95 & 97; lectr-teacher, Univ Alaska, Cordova, Homer & Anchorage, 93-94, 97-98 & 99-2000; instr workshop, Sumie for cancer patients. *Awards:* Gov Award, Alaska, 70; Best Show, Alaska Watercolor, 88; Paul Schwartz Award, Sumie Soc Am, 93. *Bibliog:* Leo Krantz (auth), Contemporary Am Artists, 85 & 89; Article in Am Artist, 4/85 & Midwest Art, 9-10/87; Elizabeth Leonard (auth), Floral Painting, 86; Alaska People, 96. *Mem:* Alaska Artist Guild (pres, 70-71); Artists Equity Asn; Sumie Soc Am; Alaska Watercolor Soc. *Media:* Acryllic, Watercolor. *Specialty:* St Pierre Anchorage AK 99501. *Interests:* Teaching, Basics of Sumie and using magic & art in performance. *Collection:* B Donatello, F & V Prewitt. *Publ:* Auth, Okinawa Sketchbook, 62. *Dealer:* Scott Collection La Connor WA; Vickie Prewitt Anchorage AK; Birch Tree Gallery Soldotna Ark. *Mailing Add:* 3530 Fordham Dr Anchorage AK 99508

SHAFFER, FERN
PAINTER, LECTURER
b Chicago, Ill, Mar 29, 1944. *Study:* Univ Ill, BFA, 81, Columbia Univ, MA, 91; Studies in Univ Ill & Art Inst, Chicago, Ill. *Hon Degrees:* Honor Roll of Feminist Artist, Veteran Feminists of America. *Exhib:* Solo exhibs, Artemisia Gallery, Chicago, 81, 83, 85, 86 & 91, Centro Colombo Americano, Colombia, 95, Johnson State Col, Vt, 96, Mus Mod Art, Colombia, 96, Int Art Festival of Medellin 1997, Colombia, 97 & Olin Gallery, Roenoke Col, Va, 98; Peregrinajes Hacia Lo Sagrado, Mus Mod Art, Pereira, Colombia, 96; Art in Chicago 1945-95, Mus Contemp Art, Chicago, 96; Myths & Legends, Anchorage Mus Hist & Art, Alaska, 98; Spriritual Passports, Ill Art Gallery, Chicago, 98, Southern Ill Art Gallery, 98, Lockport, Ill, 99 & Ill State Mus, Springfield, 99; Then & Now, Northern Ill Art Mus Gallery, Chicago, 98; Lithuanian Mus, Vicnius, Lithuania, 99; Centro Colombo Americano, Medellin, Colombia, SAm, 2000; Galeria De Arte Fotografico, San Miguel de Allende, Mex, 2000; Turchin Ctr for Vis Arts, Appalachian State Univ, 2004; Portland Art Mus, 2005. *Pos:* Pres, Artemisia Gallery, 83-92. *Teaching:* Guest lectr, many incl Art Inst Chicago & Museo de Arte de Periera, Columbia, 84-98; instr, Humanities Inst, 89-90 & workshop, Art Inst Chicago, 97; lectr, Jewish Mus Lithuania, Vilnius, 99, Art Inst Chgo, 99 & 2000, Univ Antioquia, South America, 2003, Columbia College, 2004 & Nat Univ, Medillin, Colubmia, 2005. *Awards:* Nancy Grey Grant, 98; Copenhagen Grant, 98; Andrea Frank Found, 2000. *Bibliog:* Suzi Gablik (auth), Arts and the Earth, Orion, Autumn, 95; Boule Oakes (auth), Sculpture with the Environment, Van Nostrand Reinhold, 95; Juan Alberto Gaviria (auth), Desde el silencio, El Mundo Mag, 8/97. *Mem:* Womens Caucus Art (chmn, 90-91); Chicago Artists Coalition. *Media:* Acrylic. *Publ:* Auth, (catalog) Artemisia, 1983-88 & 93, Sacred Wild, Apexart, 2005. *Mailing Add:* 1310 N Spaulding Chicago IL 60651

SHAFFER, MARY
SCULPTOR
b Oct 3, 47. *Study:* Nat Endowment Arts Fel, 74; RI Sch Design, Nat Endowment Arts, 77; Wellesley Col, Huber Grant (study art in Czech), 79. *Work:* Grounds for Sculpture, Hamilton, NJ; Met Mus of Art, NY, NY; Toledo Mus Art, Toledo, Ohio; Stadt Mus, Fraunau, WGer; Columbus Mus of Art, Columbus, Ohio; NBC, Canadian CBS, Networks of Ger, France, Switz & France; Point of View, Shaffer Studios; The Judy Yougens Lecture Series, NBC coverage Canadian television; Mary Schaffer Lecture, Grounds for Sculpture, 99. *Comn:* Blumenthal Performing Arts Ctr, Charlotte, NC; Sara Lee Corp; Am Craft Mus, NY; Huntington Mus, Huntington, WVa; Providence Park Dept, Providence, RI. *Exhib:* Honolulu Acad Arts, Hawaii; Oakland Mus, Calif; Mus Fine Arts, Boston; Kestner Mus, Hanover, Ger; Kunstindusfriemuseet, Copenhagen, Denmark; Gemeentemus Arnhem, The Neth; Manchester City Art Galleries, Eng; Mus Kunsthandwerk, Frankfurt, Ger; Stedljk Mus, Amsterdam, The Neth; Nat Mus Fine Arts, Rio de Janeiro, Brazil, 91; Va Mus Art, 93; Ruffino Tamayo Mus, Mexico City; Halcone Open-Air Mus, Tokyo; Detroit Inst Art, Mich; Indianapolis Mus Art, Ind; Kunsthaus Am Mus, Koln, Ger; Corning Mus, NY; Am Craft Mus, NY; Tucson Mus Art, Ariz; Mus Mod Art, Koyto, Japan; Metrop Mus Art, NY, 96; Convergence IX; Int Sculpture Conf, RI Parks Dept, Providence, 96; New Look: Contemp Women Sculptors, Washington Sq, 96; 12 X 12, RI Sch Design, Providence, 96; People in Glass Houses, Robert Lehman Gallery, Brooklyn, NY, 96; solo exhibs, Sanske Gallery, 97, Habitat Galleries, Farmington Hills, Mich, 97, Marx Gallery, Chicago, 98, Heller Gallery, NY, 99, Mus Bellerive, Zurich, Switz, Mary Saunders Gallery, 2000, Chicago Art Fair, 2001; Hawk Gallery, Columbus, Ohio, 2003; Houston Ctr for Contemp Craft, Houston, Tex, 2004; group exhib, Breaking the Mold: Conceptual Glass, Arts Midland: Galleries and Sch of the Midland Ctr for the Arts, Midland, Tex, Cleveland, Ohio & Museo del Vidrio, Monterrey, Mex, 2001; group exhib, Sculpture in Glass, San Francisco Art Fair, Robert Berman Gallery, Los Angeles, Calif, Walton Arts Center, Fayetteville, Ark, 2002. *Teaching:* NY Univ; Wellesley Col; Univ RI, Kingston. *Awards:* Fel Individual Artists, DC Comn Arts & Humanities, 87 & Nat Endowment Arts, Washington, 94; Visionary Award, Am Craft Mus, NY, 95; Innovated use of Glass and Sculpture Award, Urban Glass, NY, 98. *Bibliog:* Bellerive Zurich GLAS, Band I 1945-1991, Zurich, 93; A Labor of Love: Distinction and Beyond, New Mus Contemp Art, New York, 96; Dan Klein & Attilia Dorigato (auths), International New Glass, Arenale Editrice, Italy, 96; Richard Wilfred Yelle (auth), Glass Art from Urban Glass, A Schiffer Art Book, 2000. *Media:* Glass, Metal. *Dealer:* Marx-Saunders Gallery Ltd 230 W Superior St Chicago IL 60610; The Gerald Peters Gallery Santa Fe NM. *Mailing Add:* PO Box 335 Marfa TX 79843

SHAFFER, RICHARD
PAINTER, PRINTMAKER
b Fresno, Calif, Mar 17, 47. *Study:* Univ Calif, Santa Cruz, BA (philos), 69; New Sch Social Res, New York, grad study philos; San Francisco Art Inst, BFA (painting), 73; Stanford Univ, Palo Alto, Calif, MFA (painting), 75. *Work:* Santa Barbara Mus Art, Calif; Roswell Mus & Art Ctr, NMex; La Jolla Mus Contemp Art, San Diego; Dallas Mus of Art, Tex; Nova Corp, Canada. *Exhib:* Roswell Mus 20th Anniversary Exhib, Roswell, NMex, 87; Am Acad & Inst Arts & Lett, NY, 86; La Jolla Mus Contemp Art, La Jolla Calif, 88; Nat Mus Am Art, Washington, DC, 82; John Berggruen Gallery, San Francisco, Calif, 88; and others. *Pos:* Artist-in-residence, Roswell Mus, 75-76, MacDowell Colony, Peterborough, NH, fall 77, Yaddo, Saratoga Springs, NY, spring 78, Ossabaw Found, Savannah, Ga, spring 79; vis artist, Univ Iowa, Iowa City, fall, 81; artist-in-residence, Bellagio Study & Conference Ctr, Lake Como, Italy, 83. *Teaching:* Instr printmaking, Univ Calif, Santa Cruz, summer 75; assoc prof painting & drawing, Univ Tex, Arlington, 78-83. *Awards:* Fulbright fel, Fulbright-Hays Exchange Act, 76-77; Nat Endowment Arts, painting, 81; Visual Arts Award for Painting, 82. *Bibliog:* Harry Rand (auth), Awards in the Visual Arts I, Southeastern Ctr Contemp Art, 82; Richard Shaffer (LA Lower, Susan Freudenheim) (coauth), article, Venice, Calif, 84; Annette Carlozzi (auth), 50 Texas Artists, Chronicle Books, San Francisco, Calif, 86. *Mem:* MacDowell Colony Fel. *Publ:* Auth, Andenken, L A Louver Publications Inc, 82. *Dealer:* La Louver 45 N Venice Blvd Venice CA 90291. *Mailing Add:* c/o L A Louver Inc 55 N Venice Blvd Venice CA 90291

SHAH, ELA
PAINTER, SCULPTOR
b Bombay, India, May 10, 48, US citizen. *Study:* SNDT Univ, Bombay, India, BA, 65; CN Col India, dipl(fine arts), 71; Montclair State Univ, MA, 80. *Work:* Permanent Mission of India to UN, NY; Univ Pa, Philadelphia; NJ State Mus, Trenton; Montclaire Art Mus, NJ; and others. *Comn:* Indoor mural, Temple at Leicefer, comn by Temple Comt, Leicester, UK, 85; outdoor mural, Riker Hill Art Park, comn by Ben Schaffer, Livingston, NJ, 88. *Exhib:* Five from India, Brookhaven Cult Ctr, NY, 90; Monmouth Mus, NJ, 90; one-person show, Oakside Bloomfield Cult Ctr, NY, 91; Sometimes My Eyes Blurr at Beaty, Asian Am Art Ctr, 92; Godess Festival of India, Am Mus Natural Hist, NY, 94; and others. *Pos:* Foreign chairperson, Nat Asn Women Artist; bd mem, Sculptor's Asn NJ, 80-94 & Indian Am Artists, 90-94. *Mem:* Sculptor's Asn NJ; Riker Hill Art Park Artist; Indian Am Artists; Miiniature Soc NJ. *Media:* All Media. *Mailing Add:* 550 Highland Ave Upper Montclair NJ 07043

SHAHEEN, GARY EDWARD
ADMINISTRATOR, COLLAGE ARTIST
b Binghamton, NY, Oct 21, 1952. *Study:* Royal Univ Malta, with Charles Eldred, 75; State Univ New York, Binghamton, with Angelo Ippolito & Aubrey Schwartz, BA(art), 75; Syracuse Univ Maxwell Sch, with Joseph Scala, 86. *Work:* Security Mutual Life Corp, Binghamton, NY. *Exhib:* State Univ NY-Binghamton Alumni Invitational, Univ Art Gallery, 83; Central Regional Exhib, Robinson Mem, Binghamton, NY, 86; Artists of Achievement, Lever House, NY, 88 & Stuhr Mus, Grand Island, Nebr, 90. *Pos:* Dir, Studio Sch & Art Gallery, Binghamton, NY, 80-87; bd mem, Broome Co Arts Coun, 85-87, Schnectady Co Arts Coun, 87-90; exhibs comt mem, Schenectady Mus, NY, 89-90. *Teaching:* Instr drawing, Robinson Mem, Binghamton, NY, 82-86; instr printmaking, Studio Sch/Art Gallery, Binghamton, NY, 84-86. *Awards:* Purchase Prize, Security Mutual Life, 82; Hon Mention, Visual Individualists, 89. *Mem:* Schenectady Co & Coun (bd dir, 87-90, visual arts comt, 90); Schenectady Mus & Planetarium (exhib comt, 89-90); A Place for Jazz Inc (bd mem, 90). *Mailing Add:* 1002 Bill Rd Schenectady NY 12303

SHAHLY, JEHAN
PAINTER
b Detroit, Mich, Dec 12, 28. *Study:* Mich State Univ, BA; Art Students League; New Sch Social Res; Hunter Col, MA. *Work:* San Francisco Mus Art; Univ Southern Ill; Univ Mass; Geigy Collection; Provincetown Art Asn Mus. *Exhib:* Grand Cent Mod Gallery, NY, 62 & 63; Six Painters, Kansas City Mus, 63; one-woman shows, Green Mountain Gallery, NY, 73, Ulster Co Community Col, 76 & Landmark Gallery, NY, 78; Caldbeck Gallery, Rockland, Maine, 86 & 88; Le Va-Tout, Waldoboro, Maine, 92; Coffey Gallery, Kingston, NY, 2001; Omega Inst, Rhinebeck, NY, 2002 & 03. *Pos:* Lectr, Guggenheim Mus, formerly; Gallery & mus tour guide, Great Neck Adult Prog, NY, formerly. *Awards:* Purchase Prizes, San Francisco Mus Art, 56 & Wichita Mus, Kans, 57; Creative Artists Pub Serv Grant, 76; Gottlieb Grant for Painting, 89. *Bibliog:* Lawrence Campbell (auth), article, Art News Mag, 11/73; April Kinsley (auth), article, Art Int, 1/74; Robbie Ehrlich (auth), article, Arts Mag, 12/78. *Media:* Oil. *Mailing Add:* 166 Moore Rd Germantown NY 12526

SHAHN, ABBY
PAINTER
b Long Branch, NJ, July 31, 40. *Study:* Skowhegan Sch Painting & Sculpture, 59-61; Calif Sch Fine Arts, San Francisco, 60; Art Students League, 60-61. *Work:* Hirshhorn Mus & Sculpture Garden, Washington, DC; Portland Mus, Maine; Colby Col, Waterville, Maine; Union Carbide; Walker Mus, Bowdoin Col, Brunswick, Maine. *Comn:* Door panels, Railroad Square Cinema, Waterville, Maine, 81; three paintings, Solon Elem Sch, Maine, 83; four paintings, Dept Disability, Old Max Bldg, Augusta, Maine, 85; mural, Univ Southern Miane, 90. *Exhib:* All Maine Biennial, Bowdoin Col, 79 & Portland Mus, 85; Ghost Dance, Univ Maine, Farmington, 83; Abstraction, Maine Coast Artists, Rockport, 85; Here and Now in Maine, Westbrook, 85; solo exhibs, Midtown, NY, 87-89. *Pos:* Mem, Maine Biennial Comt, Portland Mus Art, 81-83 & Visual Arts Panel, Maine State Comn, 79-83. *Teaching:* Instr mural proj, Skowhegan High Sch, 85 & Univ Southern Maine, 86; instr gifted class art, Madison High Sch, 86. *Bibliog:* Edgar Allen Beam (auth), 2 stars of the 3rd magnitude, Maine Times, 85; Susan Elizabeth Ryan (auth), Roy Slamm and Abby Shahn making art up country, Artists in Maine, summer 86; Ken Greenleaf (auth), One of the best artists, Maine Times. *Mem:* Union of Maine Visual Artists. *Media:* Egg Tempera. *Publ:* Illusr, Visions Mag, 70. *Dealer:* Midtown Payson Galleries 745 Fifth Ave New York NY 10151. *Mailing Add:* Rowell Mountain Rd Solon ME 04979

SHAHN, JONATHAN
SCULPTOR
Work: exhib in group shows at Vatican Mus, Rome, Art Mus, Princeton, NJ. *Comn:* prin works incl Martin Luther King Jr commission, NJ Transit, Jersey City, NJ, Franklin D Roosevelt Mem, Roosevelt, NJ. *Exhib:* One-man shows incl Mary Porter Sesnon Gallery, UC Santa Cruz, 1980, Hackett-Freedman Gallery, New York City, 2001; exhib in group shows at Nat Accad of Design, 1998, Cantor Fitzgerald Gallery, Harvard Col, 2001, O'Hara Gallery, New York City; Rep in permanent collections Nat Portrait Gallery, Wash. *Mem:* Fel: Nat Sculpture Soc; Nat Acad (assoc, 90, acad, 94-). *Mailing Add:* O'Hara Gallery Ste 1302 41 E 57th St New York NY 10022

SHAINMAN, JACK S
ART DEALER, GALLERY DIRECTOR
b Pittsfield, Mass, July 21, 57. *Study:* Am Univ, BA, 82. *Pos:* Owner, Jack Shainman Gallery, New York, NY. *Specialty:* Contemporary American, Canadian and European art of all media. *Publ:* Numerous reviews of the Jack Shainman Gallery in newspapers and mags. *Mailing Add:* Jack Shainman Gallery 513 W 20th St New York NY 10011

SHAKLEE, KIM
SCULPTOR
b Colo, 1956. *Study:* Colo State Univ, Forestry & Natural Resources. *Work:* Nat Acad Design, NY. *Exhib:* Am Art in Miniature, Thomas Gilcrease Mus, Tulsa, Okla, 2000-2002, 2004 & 2006; One artist Show, Marine Nat Bank, Naples, Fla, 2000; Plantation Wildlife Festival, Thomasville Cult Ctr, Ga, 2001; Wind River Valley Art Show, 52nd Ann Nat Exhib, Dubois, WY, 2001; Art of the Animal Kingdom VII, Bennington Ctr for Arts, VT, 2002; Mystic Int Maritime Exhib, Mystic Seaport Mus, Conn, 2002; Am Art in Miniature, Gilcrease Mus, Tulsa, Okla, 2002. *Collection Arranged:* Smithsonian Nat Zoological Park; Okla City Zoo; Benson Park Sculpture Garden, Loveland, Colo; Steamboat Springs Art Coun, Colo; Smithsonian Nat Zoological Park, Wash, DC; Maytag Park, Newton, IA. *Pos:* Northglenn Arts & Humanities Found, Northglenn, Colo, secy, 2004-2006 & bd dir, 2004-. *Awards:* Gold Medal of Hon, Allied Artists Am, NY, 2001; Gold Medal Award, Contemp Sculpture, Phippen Mus, Prescott, Ariz, 2002; Art of the West Publ Award & Best in Show 3-D, 5th Intl Comp, Women Artists of the West, Dubois, Wyo, 2003; Best of Show, Am Acad Women Artists, Tucson, Ariz, 2005. *Bibliog:* Cathy Abramson & Nancy Arbuthnot (auths), Wild Washington Animal Sculptures A to Z, Annapolis Publishing Co, 2005; Charles Raskob Robinson (auth), Notes from Brush Hill Studio, Am Soc of Marine Artists, 4/2002. *Mem:* Allied Artists Am; Catharine Lorillard Wolfe Art Club; Pen & Brush Inc; Am Artists Prof League (mem, Emer, currently); Am Acad Women Artists (signature mem); Women Artists of the West; Am Soc Marine Artists. *Media:* Metal. *Interests:* birding & photography. *Publ:* auth, Zoogoer, Editorial feature, Smithsonian Nat Zoo, 7-8/99; auth, Art of the West, Editorial feature, 11-12/99; auth, Wildlife Art, What Hot and What's What, 1-2/2003. *Dealer:* Mystic Maritime Museum & Gallery Mystic Conn; Lee Youngman Galleries Calistoga Calif; Howell Gallery Oklahoma City Okla; Gallery of the Rockies Colorado Springs, Colo. *Mailing Add:* 14599 Picadilly Rd Brighton CO 80601

SHALKOP, ROBERT LEROY
CONSULTANT
b Milford, Conn, July 30, 22. *Study:* Maryville Col, Tenn, 40-42; Univ Chicago, 46-50, MA, 49; Sorbonne, Univ Paris, 51-52. *Collection Arranged:* Arroyo Hondo, the Folk Art of a New Mexican Village (with catalog); Reflections of Spain: a Comparative View of Spanish Colonial Sculpture (with catalog), 68; Reflections of Spain II: Spanish Colonial Painting (with catalog), 69; 100 Years of Painting in the Pike's Peak Region (with catalog); Russian Orthodox Art in Alaska (with catalog), 73; Sydney Laurence, an Alaskan Impressionist (with catalog), 75; Eustace Ziegler (with catalog), 77; Contemporary Native Art of Alaska (with catalog), 79; Henry Wood Elliot (with catalog), 82. *Pos:* Dir, Rahr Civic Ctr, Manitowac, Wis, 53-56, Everhart Mus, Scranton, Pa, 56-62, Brooks Mem Art Gallery, Memphis, Tenn, 62-64; assoc dir, Colorado Springs Fine Arts Ctr & cur, Taylor Mus, 64-71; dir, Anchorage Mus Hist & Art, 72-87; Freelance Mus Consult, 88-92. *Mem:* Am Asn Mus. *Publ:* Auth, Wooden Saints, the Santos of New Mexico, 67; Sydney Laurence, His Life and Work, 82. *Mailing Add:* 309 W Marsh St Salisbury NC 99501

SHAMAN, SANFORD SIVITZ
MUSEUM DIRECTOR, CURATOR
b Pittsburgh, Pa, July 11, 46. *Study:* Ohio Univ, Athens, BFA, 68; State Univ NY Binghamton, 70-71; Villa Schifanoia Grad Sch Fine Arts, Florence, Italy, MFA, 74. *Collection Arranged:* Contemporary Chicago Painters (auth, catalog), Ohio State Univ, Fla State Univ, Univ SFla & Univ Northern Iowa Gallery Art, 77-78; De Kooning 1969-1978 (auth, catalog), Univ Northern Iowa Gallery Art, St Louis Art Mus, Contemp Arts Ctr, Cincinnati & Akron Art Inst, 78-79; Standards by Allan Kaprow (auth, catalog), Univ Northern Iowa Gallery Art; The Contemporary American Potter (ed & contribr, catalog), 80-82 & Noritake Art Deco Porcelains: Collection of Howard Kottler (auth, catalog), 82-84, Smithsonian Inst Traveling Exhibs; Philip Pearlstein: Painting to Watercolors (auth, catalog), Wash State Univ & Univ Northern Iowa, 83-84; Rodney Alan Greenblat's Reality & Imagination, Two Taste Treats in One (auth, catalog), Penn State Univ; Inst of Contemp Art, 86-87; Robert Yarber Paintings: 1980-88 (auth, catalog), Penn State Univ; Va Mus of Fine Arts; Mordecai Moreh, The Nocturnal Works (auth, catalog), Univ Haifa & Mishkan Le Omanut Mus Art Ein Harod, Israel; The Light of Yehoshua Grossbard, Univ Haifa, Omanut La'Am traveling exhib, Israel; Univ Haifa Oscar Ghez Collection: 18 Artists Who Perished in the Holocaust. *Pos:* Cur, Huntington Galleries, WVa, 74-75; asst cur, Mem Art Gallery, Rochester, NY, 75-77; dir, Gallery of Art, Univ Northern Iowa, Cedar Falls, 77-80; dir, Mus Art, Wash State Univ, Pullman, 80-84 & Palmer Mus Art, Pa State Univ, 80-89; evaluator, Am Asn Mus, Mus Assessment Prog, 85-88; dir fine arts exhib & collections, Univ Haifa, Israel, currently. *Teaching:* Vis lectr, WVa State Col, 75; adj fac, Univ Northern Iowa, 78 & mus studies, Univ Haifa, 89-. *Awards:* Villa Schifanoia Grad Sch Fine Arts Scholar, Florence, 72; Univ Northern Iowa Fac Res Award, 79-80; Nat Endowment Arts Fel, 83; B'nai B'rith Hillel Found Leadership Fel, Jewish Acad. *Bibliog:* Donald Miller (auth), A new art museum is his dream at Pennsylvania State, Pittsburgh Post Gazette, 2/24/87; Ethics and professionalism, Museum News, 12/88. *Mem:* Am Asn Mus; Pa Coun Arts, vchmn mus adv panel; Eastern Wash State Hist Soc (trustee, 82-84); Asn Col & Univ Mus & Galleries (vpres, 81-82, pres, 82-83); Forum of Art Mus, Israel. *Publ:* Coauth, Museum Programs: Public Escapism or Education for Public Responsibility?, 7/88; Education, Sunflowers and the New Vulgarity, Mus Media, Message, Routledge, London, 95; contribr, Chronicle of Higher Education, The Journal of Museum Education, The International Journal of Museum Management and Curatorship, Museologist, Art Mag, Christian Sci Monitor & Studio Israel; Interview with Belu-Simon Fainaru, J Contemp Art, Vol 7, 2, 95; Public Spaces-Private Art, Visitor Studies: Theory, Research and Practice, Vol 8, 1, 96. *Mailing Add:* Dir Fine Arts Exhib Univ of Haifa Mt Carmel Haifa 31905 Israel

SHAMBROOM, PAUL D
PHOTOGRAPHER
b Teaneck, NJ, Jan 26, 56. *Study:* Macalester Col, St Paul, Minn, 74-75; Minneapolis Col Art & Design, BFA, 75-78. *Work:* Whitney Mus Am Art & Mus Mod Art, NY; San Francisco Mus Mod Art; Los Angeles Co Mus Art; Walker Art Ctr, Minneapolis. *Exhib:* Recent Acquisitions in Photog, Mus Mod Art, NY, 93; Truths and Trials: Color Photog Since 1975, Minneapolis Inst Arts, 96; Crossing the Frontier: 1849 to the Present, San Francisco Mus Mod Art, 96; Hidden Places of Power, Walker Art Ctr, Minneapolis, 95; Biennial, Whitney Mus Am Art, NY, 97; Extra Ordinary: Am Place in Recent Photog, Madison Art Ctr, Wis, 2001; solo show, Mus Contemp Photog, Chicago, 2003. *Teaching:* Vis artist photog, Minneapolis Col Art & Design, 97-2000. *Awards:* Bush Found Fel, St Paul, 92 & 2002; Grant, Creative Capital Found, 2001; Guggenheim Fel, 2003. *Dealer:* Julie Saul Gallery 535 W 22nd St New York NY 10011. *Mailing Add:* 3754 Pleasant Ave #108 Minneapolis MN 55409-1277

SHANER, (GEORGE) DAVID
CERAMIST, CRAFTSMAN
b Pottstown, Pa, Nov 11, 34. *Study:* State Col, Kutztown, Penn, BS(art ed), 56; NY State Col Ceramics, Alfred Univ, MA(ceramic design), 59. *Work:* Royal Ont Mus, Toronto; Mus Contemp Crafts, NY; Everson Mus Art, Syracuse, NY; Nat Arts Collection, Smithsonian Inst, Washington, DC; Kansas City Art Inst, Mo. *Exhib:* Everson Mus Art, NY, 66 & 79; Craftsman USA, Mus Contemp Crafts, NY, 66; US Info Agency Exhib, Far East, Middle East, South Am & Africa, 74; Smithsonian Inst, Washington, DC, 79; Potters Dozen-NCECA, Univ Mich, Ann Arbor, 80; 8th Chunichi Int Exhib Ceramic Arts, Nagoya, Tokyo & Kanazawa, Japan, 80. *Pos:* Asst prof art, Univ Ill, Urbana, 59-63; res potter & dir, Archie Bray Found, Helena, Mont, 63-70; self-employed studio potter, Bigfork, Mont, 70-. *Awards:* Louis Comfort Tiffany Scholar Award, 63; Nat Endowment Arts craftsman fel, 73 & 78. *Bibliog:* Garth Clark (auth), A Century of American Ceramics: 1878-1978, 79; Peter Sabin (auth), David Shaner: Montana Conversation, Studio Potter Vol 8, No 1, Daniel Clark Found, 79; Harrington (auth), Northwest Ceramics, Univ Wash Press, 79. *Mem:* Archie Bray Found (trustee, 70-, chmn 76-); Mont Arts Coun (vchmn, 77-). *Mailing Add:* 7135 Mt Hwy 35 Bigfork MT 59911-6114

SHANK, J WILLIAM
CONSERVATOR
Study: Villa Schifanoia, Florence, Italy, Studied art hist and art conservation; NYU Inst Fine Arts, Grad studies; Harvard Univ, Advanced training in art conservation. *Work:* Cur (conserv based exhib) A Hidden Picasso, Guggenheim Mus, Bilbao, Spain, 2004. *Pos:* With Ctr for the Conserv of Fine Arts; mem staff, San Francisco Mus Modern Art, 85-2000, chief conservator, 91-2000; now with Conserv Resources Mgt; Found, Rescue Pub Murals (in cooperation with Heritage Preserv). *Awards:* Booth Family Rome Prize Fel for Historic Preserv and Conserv, Am Acad in Rome, 2004-05. *Mailing Add:* AM Acad Rome Via Angelo Massina 500153 Rome Italy

SHANKMAN, GARY CHARLES
PAINTER
b Washington, DC, Sept 30, 50. *Study:* Sch Fine & Applied Arts, Boston Univ, BFA, 68-73; Sch Arts & Sci, Am Univ, MFA, 73-75; Koninklijke Academie voor Schone Kunsten, Belg, 75-76; Skowhegan Sch, 78. *Work:* Mabee-Gerrer Mus Shawnee, Okla; Superior Ct Art Trust, Washington, DC; Nat Home Furnishings Asn, Chicago, Ill. *Comn:* Cover design ITT Int Fel Yearbook. *Exhib:* Solo exhibs, Still Life & Landscapes, Seta House, Antwerp, Belg, 76, H C Dickens, London, Eng, 82, Patterns of Light, Mickelson Gallery, Washington, 85, Reflections, 88 & Confections, 92, Painters Light, Shelnutt Gallery Rensselaer Polytechnic Inst, Troy, NY, 89 & Sunlight & White Lace, Mickelson Gallery, Washington, 96 & Broadway Gallery, 94, Yates Gallery, Siena Col, Loudonville, NY, 99, Canajohavic Libr & Art Gallery, Canajoharie, NY, 2001; Color-Expression, Perception & Meaning, Dietel Gallery, Troy, NY, 93; Landscape Show, Nisk Art Gallery, Wiskayuna, NY, 93; Quiet Elegance, Mickelson Gallery, Washington, 94; group exhib, Broadway Gallery, Albany, NY, 94 & Oak Room Artists Gallery, Schenectady, NY, 98, 2000, 03, Stillness, Parker Gallery, Washington, DC, 2002; Local Color Gallery, Lutham NY, 2003, Eastern State Regional; Arts and Eros, Parker Gallery, Washington DC, 2003; Group Shows; Train Station Gallery, West Stockbridge, MA, 2003; Winter Exhib; Firlefanz Gallery, Albany NY, 2004; Welcome Home; GCCA Mountaintop Gallery, Windham NY, 2004; regional exhib, Woodstock School of Art, New York, Vacancy, Washington Park Lake House, Albany, NY, 2005; small works show, Bennington Ctr for the Natural & Cult Arts, Vermont, 2006; 24th Annual Small Works Show, Schohurie Art Council, Cobleskill, NY, 2006. *Pos:* Artist in residence, City of Rockville, Md, 77; Artist-in-residence, State of Okla, 81. *Teaching:* Instr drawing & painting, Smithsonian Inst, Washington, 78- & Md Col Art & Design, 81-86; prof drawing & design, Sage Col Albany, NY, 86-. *Awards:* First Place, Nat Home Furnishing Asn, 85; First Place, Nat Landscape Competition, Tolley Galleries, Washington, 83; First Place, Joys of Summer, Lansingburgh Art Studio, NY, 96; Friendship Award, Colonie Artograph Inc, 2000; Merchandise Award, Colonie Nat, 2000; Awarded summer residencies at Artists' Enclave, I-Park, East Haddam, Conn, 2002, The Constance Saltonstall Found for the Arts, Ithaca, NY, 2001, The Brydclffe Artist Colony, Woodstock, NY, 97. *Bibliog:* John Greenya (auth), Painter's progress, Washington Post Mag, 80; Merrie Aiken (auth), An American artist paints English scene, 82 &

Lucia Anderson (auth), Time to do something for themselves, 84, Potomac News. *Mem:* Oakroom Artists. *Media:* Oil. *Specialty:* Traditional Painting, Prints, Drawings. *Collection:* Super Court Bldg, Washington, DC; Supr Court Art Trust, The Mabee-Gerror Mus, Shawnee, Okla; National Home Furnishings Asn, Chicago, Ill. *Dealer:* The Parker Gallery at Michelson's Framing 629 New York Ave NW Washington DC 20001. *Mailing Add:* 86 Lawnridge Ave Albany NY 12208

SHANNON, JOE
EDUCATOR, PAINTER
b Lares, Puerto Rico. *Work:* art shows, Art in Am; writer, (art related articles) Washington Times. *Exhib:* Studies Monuments & Variations, Haslem Gallery, 1983; Shoe Salesman, Corcoran Gallery, 1969. *Pos:* technician, Smithsonian Mus Nat Hist; cur, Hirshhorn Mus & Sculpture Garden. *Teaching:* prof, Corcoran Sch Art; instr, Md Inst Col Arts (MICA), Baltimore. *Mailing Add:* Maryland Institute College Art MICA 1300 Mount Royal Ave Baltimore MD 21217

SHANNON, R MICHAEL
PAINTER
b Lexington, Ky, Dec 29, 50. *Study:* studied with Henry Lawrence Faulker, 67-70, Ralph Wolfe Cowan, 74-75. *Work:* Fifth Third Nat Bank, Cincinnatti; First Security Nat Bank, Lexington, Ky; Am Savings & Loan, New York City; Stock Yard Bank, Louisville, Ky; Calumet Farm, Lexington, Ky. *Comn:* poster, Am Jazz festival, Lexington, Ky; paintings, Halleon Resort, Key West, Fla,; painting, comn by Mr & Mrs William DeVries, Louisville, Ky, Bank of Lexington, Ky, SCAPA, Lexington, Ky. *Exhib:* Henry Faulkner & Friends Spindletop, Lexington, Ky; World Equestrian, Ky Horse Park, Lexington; Nat Landscape Show, Martha White Gallery, Louisville, Ky; Our Fragile Environment, Martello Mus, Key West, Fla; Key West by Two, Living Arts & Sci Ctr, Lexington, Ky; one-man show, Heinsmith's, Lexington, Ky, Aristo's Gallery, Key West, Fla. *Media:* Acrylic, Oil. *Mailing Add:* 1935 Stanton Way Rm 233 Lexington KY 40511

SHANNONHOUSE, SANDRA
SCULPTOR
b Petaluma, Calif, May 19, 47. *Study:* Univ Calif, Davis, BS, 69, MFA(dramatic art), 73. *Work:* Utah Mus Fine Arts, Salt Lake City. *Comn:* Bronze sculpture, Benicia Pub Libr, Calif, 93; bronze & stone sculpture, City of Davis, Central Park, Calif, 95; bronze baptismal font, Davis Community Church, Calif, 98. *Exhib:* Solo exhibs, The Candy Store Gallery, 71, 74, 75 & 76, Quay Gallery, San Francisco, 75, 78 & 80, Memphis Acad Art, Tenn, 79, Pence Gallery, Davis, Calif, 80, Stephen Wirtz Gallery, Sacramento, Calif, 82, 84, 86, 90 & 91, City Gallery, Sacramento, 86, John Natsoulas Gallery, Davis, Calif, 92; Selections from the Joyce & Jay Cooper Collection of Contemp Artists, Ariz State Univ Art Mus, Nelson Fine Art Ctr, Tempe, 90; Hovikodden Int, Sonja Henie-Niels Onstad Mus, Olso, Norway, 90; Elizabeth Leach Gallery, Portland, Ore, 91; Contra Costa Collects, Bedford Gallery, Walnut Creek Art Ctr, Calif, 91; Sculptural Perspective for the Nineties, Muckenthaler Cult Ctr, Fullerton, Calif, 91; Bronze, Frumkin/Adams Gallery, NY, 91; Art Studio Alumni Exhib, Walter A Buehler Alumni & Visitors Ctr, Univ Calif, Davis, 92; From the Fire: Incendiary Spirits, Palo Alto Cult Ctr, Calif, 93; Sculpture from the Walla Walla Foundry, Greg Kucera Gallery, Seattle, 93; Pacific Rim Ceramic Sculpture, Honolulu Acad Arts, Hawaii, 93 & 94; Robert Arneson: Changing the Face of Am Ceramics, A Tribute, Kingsborough Community Col Art Gallery, Brooklyn, 94; Here and Now: Selections from the Rene and Veronica di Rosa Collection, Oakland Mus, Calif, 94; USA Within Limits, Documenta, Galleria de Arte & Ctr Book Arts, Sao Paulo, Brazil, 94; The Figure, John Natsoulas Gallery, Davis, Calif, 95; Concept in Form: Artists' Sketchbooks & Maquettes, Palo Alto Cult Ctr, Calif, 95-96; Cast Contemp Sculpture: Works from the Walla Walla Foundry, Sheehan Gallery, Whitman Col, Wash, 97; Ceramic Still Life: The Common Object, Oliver Art Ctr, Calif Col Arts & Crafts, Oakland, 97; L'Chaim: A Kiddush Cup, Jewish Mus, San Francisco, Calif, 97; Sculptural Perspectives for the New Millenium, LEF Found, St Helena, Calif, 98; A Feast fo the Eye, M H de Young Mem Mus, San Francisco, Calif, 98; Generations, B Sakala Garo Fine Art, Sacramento, 98; Kos Chaim--A Cup of Life, Margolis Gallery, Congregation Beth Israel, Houston, Tex, 99. *Teaching:* Lectr form in theatre, Univ Calif, Davis, 74; instr ceramics & drawings, Am River Col, Sacramento, Calif, 75-76; guest artist, Otis Art Inst, Los Angeles, Calif, 76-78; artist-in-residence ceramics, Oxbow Summer Sch Art, Saugatuck, Mich, 76-77. *Bibliog:* Suzanne Foley (auth), A Decade of Ceramic Art, San Francisco Mus Art, 72; Sandy Ballatore (auth), The California Clay Rush, Art in Am, 76; Mac McCloud (auth), Dealer's choice, Images & Issues, 9-10/83; Beth Coffelt (auth), Recent Bronzes, Stephen Wirtz Gallery. *Media:* Bronze, Clay. *Publ:* Illusr, Woman and Medicine (cover), Western J Med, 88; Modern Sculpture 1990 Calendar, Cedco Publ Co, San Rafael, Calif, 89; Cast Contemporary Sculpture, Walla Walla Foundry, Wash, 97. *Dealer:* Stephen Wirtz Gallery 345 Sutter St San Francisco CA 94108. *Mailing Add:* 430 1st St Benicia CA 94510

SHAP, SYLVIA
PAINTER
b Toledo, Ohio. *Study:* Otis Art Inst, 65; Univ Judaism, 68-71; Mentor Since Childhood. *Comn:* Portrait, comn by Audrey & Billy Wilder, Los Angeles, Calif, 82; portrait, comn by Henry Mancini, Los Angeles, 84; portrait, comn by Eileen & Peter Norton, Los Angeles, 87; portrait, comn by Victoria Principal, Beverly Hills, 92; portrait, comn by Anna & Rupert Murdoch, NY. *Exhib:* Contemp Southern Calif Art, Mus Fine Arts, Taipei, Taiwan & Los Angeles Municipal Gallery, 87; Hollywood: Portraits of Stars, Otis/Parsons, Los Angeles, 88; Some Members of My Family (solo exhib), Los Angeles Municipal Gallery, 88 & Art Mus S Tex, Corpus Christi, 89; Images of the Art World, Platt Gallery, Univ Judaism, Los Angeles, 97. *Collection Arranged:* Smithsonian Nat Portrait Gallery; Art Mus South Texas, Corpus Christi; Atlantic Richfield Co, Anchorage, Alaska; Los Angeles Co Mus Art; Los Angeles Music Ctr, Calif. *Pos:* Instr, Calif State, Fullerton, 83, Yeshiva Univ, Los Angeles, 86. *Teaching:* Gifted Children's Prog, Otis-Parsons, Los Angeles, 92; lectr, mus & univs; TV appearances. *Bibliog:* Articles in various mags, 89-92; Henry Stone (dir), Sylvia Shap, Portrait of the Artist (film), 92; Blair Bess (dir), Sylvia Shap, Portrait of the Artist in her own words (film), 92; Joan Quinn Profiles on Art, Cable Network TV, 94. *Media:* Oil, Miscellaneous Media. *Mailing Add:* 648 N Laurel Rd Los Angeles CA 90048

SHAPERO, ESTHER GELLER See Geller, Esther Geller Shapero

SHAPIRO, ADRIAN MICHAEL
LECTURER, WRITER
b Galveston, Tex, Apr 13, 50. *Study:* Univ Tex, Austin, BA(cum laude), 72, MA, 73; Ind Univ, Bloomington, PhD, 77. *Collection Arranged:* Slavko Kopac--Recent Work (coauth, catalog), 82; Claude Bellegarde--Homage to Color, 82. *Pos:* Contrib ed, Art Happenings mag, 80-86; Managing partner, FAME Gallery, Houston, 80-86; dir, Post Oak Fine Art Distribr, Houston, 81-88; secy, Texas Mod Art Found, 82-87. *Teaching:* Lectr, Univ Houston, 77-79; Our Lady of the Lake Univ, 87-, Texas Mod Art Found, 87-90. *Specialty:* Contemporary prints and art appreciation lectures. *Publ:* The origin of print collecting, Art Happenings Mag, 81; The search for original prints, Southwest Art Mag, 82; Corporate art collections, Art Happenings Mag, 83

SHAPIRO, BABE
PAINTER
b Irvington, NJ, May 4, 37. *Study:* NJ State Teachers Col, Newark, BS; Hunter Col, with Robert Motherwell, BS & MA, 58. *Hon Degrees:* Md Inst Col Art, Hon DFA, 2000. *Work:* Albright-Knox Art Gallery, Buffalo; Corcoran Gallery Art, Washington, DC; Scottish Nat Gallery of Mod Art, Edinburgh; Baltimore Mus Art, Md; Bayley Art Mus Univ Va; and many others. *Exhib:* NY's Worlds Fair, NY, 65; Cincinnati Mus Art, Ohio, 66; Indianapolis Mus Art, IN, 70; Baltimore Mus Art, Md, 70; Krannert Art Mus, Champagne-Urbana, IL, 80. *Pos:* Founder, dir emeritus, Mount Royal Grad Sch Art, Md Inst Col Art, Baltimore, 75-2000. *Teaching:* artist in res, Quincy Club, Quincy, Ill, 66; dir emer, Mount Royal Graduate School Art, MICA, Baltimore, MD, 2000. *Awards:* First Prize in Painting, Monmouth Col, NJ, 63; Purchase Prize Award, Bamberger's, 66; Ford Found Grant, 66. *Bibliog:* Hilton Kramer (auth), Art Once Cold, Now Romantic, The NY Times, Oct 69; Lincoln Johnson (auth), Paintings of Babe Shapiro, New Lugano Review, vol 8-9, 76; John Dorsey (auth), Retrospective reveals major change in Babe Shapiro's work, Baltimore Sun, 1, 4/3/90. *Mem:* Am Abstr Artists, NY. *Media:* Acrylic. *Mailing Add:* 31 Walker St New York NY 10013

SHAPIRO, DAVID
PAINTER, PRINTMAKER
b Brooklyn, NY, June 26, 44. *Study:* Skowhegan Sch Art, Maine, 65; Pratt Inst, BFA, 66; Ind Univ, Bloomington, MFA, 68. *Work:* Brooklyn Mus, Guggenheim Mus & Mus Mod Art, NY; San Francisco Mus Mod Art; Ft Lauderdale Mus Art, Fla. *Exhib:* Poindexter Gallery, NY, 71, 73, 74 & 77; Gloria Luria Gallery, Fla, 79, 81, 83, 85 & 88; Getler/Pall/Saper Gallery, NY, 81, 83 & 85; Jan Turner Gallery, Los Angeles, 87; Dolan/Maxwell Gallery, Philadelphia, 87 & 88; Fay Gold Gallery, Atlanta, 88. *Teaching:* Instr, Pratt Inst, 69-71; vis artist, Barnard Col, 72; guest artist, Kansas City Art Inst, 73; instr, Parsons Sch Design, 74-80. *Bibliog:* M L Thompson (auth), Cosmos and chaos, Arts Mag, 10/80; Jon R Friedman (auth), Elucidation in the art of David Shapiro, Arts Mag, 11/85. *Media:* Acrylic. *Dealer:* Dolan/Maxwell Gallery 154 Wooster St New York NY 10012. *Mailing Add:* 549 W 52nd St New York NY 10019-5012

SHAPIRO, DAVID JOEL
CRITIC, EDUCATOR
b Newark, NJ, Jan 2, 47. *Study:* Columbia Col, BA, 68; Clare Col Cambridge, Eng, BA, MA, 70- 74; Columbia Univ, PhD, 73. *Pos:* Ed Assoc, Art News, 69-70, Architectures Mag, 89-; ed bd, RES, Harvard. *Teaching:* Assoc prof, Wm Paterson, Wayne, NY, 80-; vis prof, architecture, Cooper Union, NY, 80-; asst prof, Columbia Univ, 73-79, Brooklyn Col, Princeton Univ. *Awards:* Zabel Prize, Nat Acad Inst Arts & Letters,77; Nat Endowment Humanities, for research in poetry & painting, 78; Nat Endowment Art, for poetry, 79. *Bibliog:* Stephen Paul Miller (auth), David Shapiro, Jasper Johns: An Analogy (Master's Thesis, City Col); Michael Simon, Padgett Shapiro Master's Thesis, Brown Univ. *Mem:* ed bd, RES Mag, Harvard/Peabody Mus; advisor, Poet's House. *Res:* Interdisciplinary modern Semiotics and aesthetics. *Publ:* Auth, John Ashbery's Poetry, Columbia Univ Press, 77; Jim Dine: Painting What One Is, Abrams, 80; Jasper Johns' Drawings, Abrams, 84; Mondrian Flowers, Abrams, 91; coauth, Artistic Collaboration in the 20th-Century Art, Smithsonian Inst Press, 84. *Mailing Add:* 3001 Henry Hudson Pkwy Bronx NY 10463-4717

SHAPIRO, JOEL ELIAS
SCULPTOR
b New York, NY, Sept 27, 41. *Study:* NY Univ, BA, 64, MA, 69. *Work:* Fogg Art Mus, Cambridge, Mass; Metrop Mus Art, Mus Mod Art, Whitney Mus Am Art & Brooklyn Mus, NY; Philadelphia Mus Art, Pa; Corcoran Gallery Art, Nat Gallery Art, Hirshhorn Mus & Sculpture Garden, Washington, DC; Art Gallery Ontario, Toronto; and many others. *Comn:* Sony Music Entertainment, NY, 94-95; Friedrichstadt Passagen, Berlin, Ger, 94-95; koln Sculpture Park, Cologne, Ger, 96-99; Embassy of the US, Ottawa, Can, 99. *Exhib:* Solo exhibs, Galerie Jamileh Weber, Zurich, 97, Addison Gallery Am Art, Andover, Mass, 98, Galerie Biedermann, Munich, 98, Haus der Kunst, Munich, 98, Pace Wildenstein, 98 & 99 & Am Acad Rome, 99, Mus Fine Arts, Boston, Mass, New Art Ctr, Salisbury, Eng, Yorkshire Sculpture Park, Wakefield, Eng, 99; New Dimensions in Drawing, Aldrich Mus Contemp Art, Conn, 81; Drawings from Georgia Collections, 19th & 20th Centuries, High Mus Art, Atlanta, 81; New

Acquisitions, Whitney Mus Am Art, NY, 81; retrospective of sculpture & drawing, Whitney Mus Am Art, NY & traveling, 82-84; IVAM Ctr Julio Gonzalez, Valencia, Spain & traveling, 90-91; Art at the End of the 20th Century: Selections from the Whitney Mus Am Art (traveling), 96-97; Twentieth Century Am Sculpture at the White House, Exhib V, Washington, 96-97; Masterworks of Modern Sculpture: The Nasher Collection (traveling), 96-97; Group show, Paula Cooper Gallery, NY, 96-97; and others; Joel Shapiro: Sculpture Traveling exhib, 2000-01; Timothy Taylor Gallery, London, 2000. *Awards:* Creative Arts Award, Brandeis Univ, 84; Skowhegan Medal for Sculpture, 86; Merit Medal for Sculpture, 90 & elected to Am Acad & Inst Arts & Letts, 98. *Bibliog:* Jeremy Gilbert-Rolfe (auth), Joel Shapiro: works in progress, 12/73 & Marc Field (auth), On Joel Shapiro's sculptures and drawings, summer 78, Artforum; Carter Ratcliff (auth), Joel Shapiro's drawings, Print Collector's Newlett, 3-4/78; Joel Shapiro: Sculpture and Drawing, Whitechapel Gallery, London, 80. *Mem:* Swedish Royal Acad Art. *Dealer:* Pace Wildenstein MacGill 32 E 57th St New York NY 10022

SHAPIRO, LOIS M
COLLAGE ARTIST, INSTRUCTOR
b Elizabeth, NJ, Nov 18, 32. *Study:* Fairleigh Dickinson Univ, BFA, 72; Kean Col, MA, 76; Montclair State Col, with Anne Chapman, 80-83. *Work:* Mus Mod Art, NY; Newark Mus, NJ; Noyes Mus, Oceanville, NJ; Montclair Mus, NJ; Library Congress, and others. *Exhib:* One-woman shows, Newark Mus, NJ, 84, Kent Place Gallery, Summit, NJ, 93, The Park Avenue Club, Florham Park, NJ, 96 & Icons/Iconography, Print Coun NJ, N Branch, 96; Contemp Papermakers, Print Coun NJ, North Branch, 93; Editions-The First Five Years, Newark Mus, NJ, 93; Papermade USA, Zimmerli Mus, New Brunswick, NJ, 93; Diversity in Paper, Univ of the Arts, Philadelphia, 94; Editions, Noyes Mus, Oceanville, NJ, 95; Spheres of Influence, NJ Ctr Visual Arts, Summit, 95, Celebrating Excellence, 96; Dimension Dementia, Print Coun, NJ, 95; Paper Made NJ, Gloucester Col, Sewell, NJ, 97. *Pos:* Dir Artmakers Gallery, Coop Gallery, Garwood, NJ, 73-79; bd dir, Watchung Art Ctr, NJ, 80-85; membership dir, Print Coun NJ, 85-90; co-ed, Editions, 89-; founder, Artshare, 92; creator & cur, The Glove Project, 96. *Teaching:* Instr handmade paper, Newark Mus, NJ, 87-, NJ Ctr Visual Arts, Summit, 88- & Printcouncil, NJ, 94-95; res artist, 96-97. *Awards:* NJ State Fel, NJ State Coun Arts, 86-87; Merit Award, Int Juried Show, 98. *Bibliog:* Rachael Mullin (auth), Artshare/Bringing Artists Together, Recorder Publ, 93; Barbara Goldstein (dir), Video Interview with Lois Shapiro, Monmouth Festival of Art, 94. *Mem:* NJ Designer Craftsmen; Printmaking Coun NJ; Guild of Papermakers; Friends Dard Hunter Papermakers. *Media:* Mixed Media. *Publ:* Ed, A Letter to a Friend, 90, coauth, In My Wildest Dreams, 91, Earth Mother/Mother Earth, 92, Voices and Visions, 93 & contribr, Icons, Editions, 94. *Mailing Add:* 11 Hyde Cir Watchung NJ 07060

SHAPIRO, MICHAEL EDWARD
ADMINISTRATOR, CURATOR
b New York, NY, Nov 15, 49. *Study:* Hamilton Col, BA, 72; Williams Col, MA(Kress Fel), 76; Harvard Univ, MA(Teaching Fel), 78, PhD, 80. *Collection Arranged:* Buffalo Bill Hist Ctr, Cody, Wyo, 88, Mus Fine Arts, Houston, Tex, 89 & Metrop Mus Art, New York, 89; Modern Art from the Pulitzer Collection: Fifty Years of Connoisseurship (auth, brochure), Fogg Art Mus, Harvard Col, 88 & St Louis Art Mus, 88; New Sculpture/Six Artists, 88 & Currents 41: Judy Pfaff, 90, St Louis Art Mus; George Caleb Bingham, St Louis Art Mus & Nat Gallery of Art, Washington, DC, 90; Rings Five Passions in World Art, 96; Impressionism Paintings Collected by European Museums, 98, 99. *Pos:* Guest cur, Nat Mus Am Art, 80-81; cur 19th & 20th Century art, St Louis Art Mus, 84-92, chief cur, 87-92, secr bd comnrs, 89-91; dir, Los Angeles Co Mus Art, 92-93; dir mus progs & chief cur, High Mus Art, Atlanta, Ga, 94-95, dep dir, chief cur, 96-99, dir, 2000-. *Teaching:* Asst prof, dept art, Duke Univ, Durham, NC, 80-84. *Publ:* auth Bronze Casting and American Sculpture, 84; Twentieth-Century American sculpture, Bull St Louis Art Mus, winter 86; contrib auth Frederic Remington The Masterworks, 88; Gerhard Richter: Paintings, Photographs and Prints in the Collection of the St Louis Art Mus, Bull St Louis Art Mus, summer 92; and others. *Mailing Add:* Director High Mus Art 1280 Peachtree St NE Atlanta GA 30309

SHAPIRO, ROBERT F & ANNA MARIE
COLLECTOR
b St Louis, Mo, Jan 19, 34. *Study:* St Louis Country Day Sch, graduate, 52; Yale Univ, BA, 56. *Pos:* Assoc, Lehman Brothers, New York City, 56-67, partner, 67-73, dir, sr managing dir, 70-73; bd, gov's Am Stock Exchange, 70-76; partner, Wertheim & Co, 74; exec vpres, Wertheim & Co, Inc, New York City, 74-75, pres, 75-86; co-chmn, Wertheim Schroder & Co, Inc, 86-87; bd dir, TJX Cos, Inc, Genaera Corp, The Burnham Fund, chmn, nominating comt, New York Stock Exchange, 80, mem, regulatory adv comt, 88—, surveillance comt, 89—; chmn, RFS & Assoc, Inc, New York City, 88-2004, New Street Capital Corp, 92-94; mem gov bd, Yale Univ Art Gallery, New Haven, 93-; vchmn, Klingenstein, Fields & Co, LP, New York City, 97-; trustee, Lenox Hill Hosp, Skowhegan, currently; trustee, Louis Comfort Tiffany Found, currently. *Awards:* Named one of Top 200 Collectors, ARTnews Mag, 2004. *Mem:* Securities Industry Asn (chmn, 85); Bond Club NY (pres, 87-88); Yale Club, Century Country Club & Knickerbocker Club. *Collection:* Contemporary art. *Mailing Add:* Klingenstein Fields & Co LLC 787 7th Ave New York NY 10019

SHARBAUGH, KATHRYN K
CERAMIST, DESIGNER
b Norwich, Conn. *Study:* Norwich Art Sch, 67; Kansas City Art Inst, BFA, 72; Cranbrook Acad Art, MFA, 74. *Work:* RI Sch Design, Providence, RI; Cooper-Hewitt, Smithsonian; Slater Mus, Norwich, Conn; Cranbrook Mus Art, Bloomfield Hills, Mich; Ark Art Ctr, Little Rock, Ark; Mokpo (S Korea) Mus Ceramics; Mus Het Kruithuis, s' Hertogenbosh, The Netherlands; pvt collections; Renwick Gallery, Smithsonian Am Art Mus, Washington; Besser Collection, Santa Fe, NMex; Pfannebecker Collection, Lancaster, Pa. *Comn:* Columbarium, Chapel of the Resurrection, St Paul's Episcopal Church, Flint, Mich, 94; commemorative plate series, Flint Cult Ctr Corp. *Exhib:* Mich Invitational, Flint Inst Arts, 90; Black & White, Kavesh Gallery, Ketchum, Idaho, 91; Teapots: Contemp Views, Pro-Art, St Louis, Mo, 92; Artistic Generations, Works Gallery, Philadelphia, Pa, 92; Teatime, Miller Gallery, Cincinnati, Ohio, 97; Plates Pewabic Pottery, Detroit, Mich, 97; The Art of Dinning, Ball State Univ, Muncie, Ind; Concours Int Ceramique, Mus Caronge (Switz). *Pos:* freelance pattern designer, Mikasa, Lauffer & Corning Glass Works; coord Capital Campaign, Flint Inst Arts, Mich, dir develop. *Teaching:* instr Flint Inst Arts. *Awards:* Nat Endowment Arts, 80-81 & 92-93; Fel, Mich Coun Arts, 85-94. *Bibliog:* Robert Bishop & Patricia Coblentz (auth), American Decorative Arts, Harry N Abrams, NY, 82; Duane Preble (auth), Artforms, Harper & Row, NY, 84 & The Best of Pottery, Quarry Books, 98; Ceramics: A Potter's Handbook, Nelson, Harcourt; Ceramics, Mastering the Craft, R Zakin, Krause; 500 Teapots, Lark Publ. *Mem:* Mayo Smith Soc; Rotary, Univ Mich Citizens Adv bd; Women's Forum. *Media:* high fired porcelain. *Publ:* Leslin Ferrin (auth), Teapots Transformed, Guild. *Mailing Add:* FIA 1120 E Kearsley Flint MI 48503

SHARLIN, JONATHAN
PHOTOGRAPHER, EDUCATOR
b Hackensack, NJ, Apr 20, 50. *Study:* Goddard Col, BA, 72; Visual Studies Workshop, SUNY, MFA, 78. *Work:* Fogg Art Mus Harvard Univ; Rose Art Mus Brandeis Univ; Mus Fine Arts, Houston; RI Sch Design Mus; Fidelity Investments & Polaroid Collection. *Exhib:* Representing Holocaust, Univ Southern Maine, Gorham, 96; Ancient Stones, Brown Univ List Art Center, Providence, RI, 97; Art Sentinels, RI Sch Design Mus, Providence, 99; Letters from the Middle East, St Mary's Coll, Notre Dame, Ind, 99, Artspace Gallery, Univ Va, Charlottsville, 99; Univ Mass, Lowell, Mass, 2001; Minn Ctr for Photog, 2002. *Teaching:* instr photog, RI Coll, 93-97, RI Sch Design, 1997-2003; instr photog, CC of RI, 84-05. *Media:* Photography. *Mailing Add:* 166 Lancaster St Providence RI 02906

SHARON, RUSSELL
PAINTER, SCULPTOR
b Minn, 48. *Study:* Univ Ams, Sch of Liberal Arts, Mexico City, Mex, 68-72; MIT, Student Art Asn, Cambridge, Mass, MA, 74-75. *Comn:* Outdoor sculptures, comn by Mr & Mrs Orton, Calif, 88. *Exhib:* Solo exhibs, Ctr for Fine Arts, Miami, Fla, 87, The Gallery, NY, 89, Barbara Greene Gallery, Miami, Fla, 90, Minneapolis Inst Art, Minn, 90. *Bibliog:* John Herzfeld (auth), article, Art News, 4/87; Helen H Kohen (auth), article, Miami Herald, 2/16/88; Leslie Judd Ahlander (auth), On Site Sculpting at Art Center, Miami News, 3/11/88. *Mailing Add:* 924 Lincoln Rd Apt 101 Miami FL 33139-2602

SHARP, ANNE CATHERINE
PAINTER, COLLAGE ARTIST
b Red Bank, NJ, Nov 1, 43. *Study:* Pratt Inst, Brooklyn, NY, BFA, 65, with Richard Lindner; Brooklyn Col, MFA, with Lee Bontecou & Jimmy Ernst, Laurence Campbell. *Work:* Albright-Knox Art Gallery, Buffalo, NY; St Vincent's Hosp, NY; NY Pub Libr; White House; Anchorage Mus Hist & Art, Alaska; Smithsonian, Nat Air & Space Mus, Washington, DC; US Geological Survey, Reston, Va. *Comn:* Libby Riddles - First Woman to Win the IDITAROD (poster), Libbys Blazing Stars, Alaska, 95. *Exhib:* Solo exhibs, NY Pub Libr, Epiphany Branch, 88, Books & Co, NY, 89, Kendall Gallery, NY, 90, Int Gallery Contemp Art, Anchorage, 93, US Geol Survey, Reston, Va, 94, Think Tank Gallery, NY, 94 & Stonington Gallery, Anchorage, 94, On Television Benefit, New York City, 98, 99, & 2000; Group Exhibs: Coos Art Mus, Ore, 90; Univ Alaska, Anchorage, 90, 91, 94 & 95; Rochester Mus & Sci Ctr, NY, 90-94; Nat Mus Women Arts, Washington, 91; Kikbuartsctr Gallery, Lawrenceville Sch, NJ, 1996; Blue Mountain Gallery, NY, 1998; AIR Gallery, NY, 2002-2006. *Pos:* family history project book, J Lindemann, 2004-2006. *Teaching:* Instr, NY Univ, 78, Sch Visual Arts, 78-89, Pratt Manhattan Ctr, 82-84, State Univ NY, Purchase, 83, Parsons Sch Design, NY, 84 90, Anchorage Mus Hist & Art, 90-95, Univ Alaska, Anchorage, 94-96 & Fashion Inst Technol, NY, 97-98. *Awards:* Teaching fel, Artist's Show, Brooklyn, NY, 72; Artist sponsor, Great Lakes Col Asn Apprenticeship Prog, 73-76; Artist-in-residence, Va Ctr Creative Art, 75, Artpark, 80; Pippin Award, OurTown, 84. *Bibliog:* NY Post, 12/7/91; Jerry Tallmer (auth), A Sharp View of the World; Mike Dunham (auth), Artists expanding the landscape, capturing the wild land, Anchorage Daily News, 11/14/93; Refreshing Collages, Anchorage Daily News, 11/6/94, Faculty Show, 9/12/95. *Mem:* Nat Mus Women Arts; Pratt Alumni Asn; Col Art Asn Am. *Media:* Oil, Acrylic; Collage. *Specialty:* Contemp art. *Publ:* Auth, Swimming in the mainstream with her, fall 86, Thoughtlines, fall 86, Univ Va Mag; Artists Vision of the Spirit, Anchorage Daily News, 7/31/94; The Art Scene - An Artists View, Anchorage Press, Alaska, 11/95-6/96; article, Anchorage Daily News, 4/6/97. *Dealer:* Decker Morris Gallery 621 W 6th Ave Anchorage AK 99501; Site 250 Contemporary Art 250 Cushman St Suite 2A Fairbanks AK 99701; ON Television, 388 Broadway, 2nd Fl, New York, NY 10013. *Mailing Add:* PO Box 1776 New York NY 10156-1776

SHARP, LEWIS INMAN
DIRECTOR
b New York, NY, Dec 22, 41. *Study:* Lewis & Clark, Col, Portland, Ore, BA, 65; Univ Del, MA, 68 & PhD, 80. *Pos:* Asst cur Am paintings & sculpture, Metrop Mus Art, New York, 72-75, assoc cur Am paintings & sculpture, 75-82, adminr, cur, 82-89; dir, Denver Art Mus, 89-. *Mem:* Asn Art Mus Dirs, 89-. *Publ:* Auth, John Quincy Adams Ward: History & contemporary influences, The Am Art J, Vol IV, 11/72; The Smith

Memorial, Sculptures of a City: Philadelphia's Treasures in Bronze & Stone, Walker Publ Co, 74; New York Public Sculpture by 19th Century American Artists, Metrop Mus Art, 74; contribr, The Architecture of Richard Morris Hunt, Univ Chicago Press, 86. *Mailing Add:* Denver Art Museum 100 W 14th Ave Pkwy Denver CO 80204-2749

SHARP, SUSAN S
PAINTER
b North Bergen, NJ, Jan 4, 42. *Study:* Syracuse Univ, 60-62; Univ Hartford, BS, 64. *Work:* Chase Manhattan Bank, Kidder/Peabody, NY; Town of Fairfield; General Elec, Conn; Huntington Bank, Columbus, Ohio; Trenwick Corp; Housatonnic Mus; Superior Courthouse State of Conn. *Exhib:* Conn Watercolor Soc, Wadsworth Atheneum, Hartford, 81; Winners Conn-Painters & Sculptors, Stamford Mus, 82; Art of Northeast, Silvermine Guild, 83, 85 & 89; Solo show, Water & Memory, Soho 20, NY, 92, Walter Wilkiser Gallery, NY, 99 & Housatonnic Mus, Bridgeport, Conn, 2001; Abstract Connections, Silvermine Guild, 92; Kohn Pederson Fox Gallery, NY; Looking East, Butters Gallery, Portland, Ore, 95; Surround, Reece Gallery, NY, 97; Housatonnic Mus Art, Conn Comn Gallery. *Teaching:* Painting, independent projs, Silvermine Guild. *Awards:* Fel, Conn Comn in the Arts in Painting, 2002. *Bibliog:* Roger Baldwin (auth), Art on the Town, Art New Eng, 85; Jude Schwendenwien (auth), A survey of Connecticut art, Art New Eng, 9/90; James Fox (auth), Gallery reviews, Art & Antiques, summer 92; William Zimmer (auth), rev, 1/24/99 & Vincent Lombardi (auth), rev, 3/26/99, NY Times Conn sect; Pat Rosoff (auth), Art New England, 2002. *Mem:* Silvermine Guild (bd 85-86, trustee); Inst Visual Artists (pres 90-91). *Media:* Acrylic, Oil. *Mailing Add:* 53 Wyldewood Rd Easton CT 06612-1528

SHARP, WILLOUGHBY
VIDEO ARTIST, CONSULTANT
b New York, NY, Jan 23, 36. *Study:* Brown Univ, BA; Univ Paris; Univ Lausanne; Columbia Univ, MA. *Work:* Guggenheim Mus & Mus Mod Art, NY; Boston Mus Fine Arts; Nat Gallery Art, Calif; plus others. *Exhib:* Information, Mus Mod Art, NY, 70; Earth, Air, Fire, Water: Elements of Art, Boston Mus Fine Art, 71; Circuit: A Video Invitational, Everson Mus Art, Syracuse, NY, Henry Gallery, Univ Wash, Cranbrook Acad, Bloomfield & Los Angeles Co Mus, plus others, 73-74; Kunst Bleibt Kunst: Project, 74, Cologne, Ger, 74. *Pos:* Dir, Kineticism Press, 68-; pres, Avalanche Video, 70-; vpres, Ctr New Art Activities, Inc, (Sharpcom), 74-; dir, Franklin Street Arts Ctr, NY, 76-82; dir, Worldpool, Toronto, 79; cur videos, Guggenheim Mus, NY, 79-80; owner, SharpGallery.com, NY; partner, ART-ENGINE, NY. *Teaching:* Prof humanities & sci, Sch Visual Art, 83-. *Awards:* Rockefeller Found Grant, 71; Kaplan Fund Grant, 71; Nat Endowment Arts Grant, 72 & 80; and others. *Bibliog:* Robert E Dallos (auth), Sculpture, NY Times, 8/30/67; Anthony Bannon (auth), Sharp puts himself into his art literally, Buffalo Eve News, 3/17/75; Douglas David (auth), Art, Newsweek, 7/21/75. *Dealer:* Willoughby Sharp Gallery 595 Main St 217 New York NY 10044

SHARPE, (NORMAN) BLAIR
PAINTER
b Montreal, Que, July 25, 54. *Study:* Kent Sch, WGer, A level, 72; Ottawa Sch Art, 73-74. *Work:* Can Coun Art Bank, Ottawa, Ont; Carleton Univ Art Gallery, Ottawa; City of Ottawa Collection; Ottawa Art Gallery; Regional Munic Ottawa-Carleton, Ont; Dept Fgn Affairs and Internat Trade, Can Embassy, Oslo, Norway. *Comn:* Painting, Mr & Mrs R McNally, Toronto, Ont, 88; mural, Jack Purcell Community Centre, comn by City of Ottawa, Art in Pub Pls Prog, 89; floor work, Smyth Transitway Station, Regional Municipality Ottawa-Carleton, Transart Prog, 90-91. *Exhib:* Regional Exhib, Agnes Etherington Art Ctr, Kingston, Ont, 81; Paint: The Expressive Touch, Gallery 111, Univ Manitoba, Winnipeg & Gairloch Gallery, Oakvill, 81, SAW Gallery, Ottawa, Ont & Cedar Ridge Gallery, Scarborough, Ont, 82; A Selection of Canadian Paintings, Art Gallery Harbourfront, Toronto, 81; Ottawa in The Hague, Artoteek The Hague, The Neth, 86; Studios: Work in Progress, Ottawa Art Gallery, 89; Blair Sharpe: 15 Yrs of Work, Ottawa Arts Gallery, Ottawa, 89 & Libr & Gallery, Cambridge, Ont, 90. *Teaching:* Instr, drawing & painting, Ottawa Sch Art, 74-79, instr, Painting, Drawing & Studio Seminar II, 88-. *Awards:* Post A Award, Brit Forces Educ, 73; Can Coun Arts Grant, 82; Region of Ottawa-Carleton "A" Grants, 93, 95, 99. *Bibliog:* David Burnett (auth), article, Artscanada, 5-6/77; Anna Babinska (auth), article, Artmag, Can, 2-3/80; Mayo Graham (auth), Blair Sharpe: 15 Years of Work (exhib catalog & monogr), Ottawa Arts Gallery, 90. *Mem:* Canadian Artists' Representation, Ont, (spokesperson, 83-86); Gallery 101 Artist's Ctr, Ottawa, Ont (bd mem, 90-95). *Media:* Acrylic, Watercolor. *Publ:* Auth, Juried exhibitions, In: Information for Artists, Canadian Artists Representation, Toronto, Ont, 88 & 90; Kenneth Lochhead: A Garden of Delights, Articles, Coun Arts Ottawa, 88; review, John Sadler, 9-10/89 & La premier recit: Carla Whiteside at Gallery 101, 1-2/90, articles, Coun Arts Ottawa; The Substance of Paint: An Interview with Richard Gorman (exhib catalog), Ottawa Art Gallery, 96. *Dealer:* Wallack Galleries 203 Bank St Ottawa ON Canada

SHARROW, SHEBA
PAINTER
b Brooklyn, NY, Apr 28, 26. *Study:* Art Inst Chicago, BFA, 48; Pa Acad Fine Art, 52; Tyler Sch Art, Temple Univ, MFA, 68. *Work:* Citibank, NY; Rite-Aid Corp; Armstrong World Indust; Steelcase Corp; Cigna Corp Am; and others. *Exhib:* solo shows, Hunterdon Art Ctr, Clinton, NJ, 94, Douglass Col, Rutgers Univ, 95, Gloucester Co Col, NJ, 95, Hopkins House Gallery, Camden Co, NJ, 95, APF Gallery, Philadelphia, 96, Jersey City Mus, 97 & Simon Gallery, Morristown, NJ, 2000; Gary Snyder Fine Art, New York City, 500 Works on Paper, 2002; Word/Image Westport Art Ctr, Westport, CT, 2003; Mind's Eye, White Birch Gallery, Media PA, 2004; Fellowship Show Rutgers Univ, Camden, NJ, 2004; Word/Image Westport Art Ctr, Westport, CT, 2004; Upcoming solo shows, Turchin Ctr for the Visual Arts, Boone, NC 2005; Wm Patterson Univ Wayne NJ, 2006; Pjenninger Gallery, Lancaster, PA, 2006. *Pos:* Assoc Prof of Art, Millersville Univ of PA. *Teaching:* Assoc prof, Millersville Univ, Pa, 68-; retired. *Awards:* Resident Fels, Va Ctr Creative Arts, 78, 79 & 81-96; Grant, Pollack-Krasner Found, 2000; Grant, Geraldine R Dodge Found, 2000; Pollock-Krasner Found Grant, 2000; NJ State Council on the Arts-Artist Grant. *Bibliog:* Star Ledger, Newark, NJ, Go Figure (Review), 2000; Philadelphia Inquirer, 5 Artists in Search of the Real, 2002; NY Times, (NJ) Review Bearing Witness, 2002; Art Matters, Philadelphia, PA, Deep in Sharrow Waters, 2002; Woman's Art Jour, Phildelphia, PA, Review of Catalogue, 2002; Autumn House Press, Pittsburg, PA, Not God After All, with/ Gerald Stern, 2004; WW Norton, New York City, Everything in Burning, G. Stern (cover), 2004. *Media:* painting. *Collection:* Jersey City Mus; Phillip Art Col, Franklin & Marshall College; Steelcase Corp; Armstrong World Industries; Cigna Corp of Am; Citibank of New York; Virginia Ctr for the Creative Arts; Millersville Univ; Rite Aid Corp; Jersey City Mus. *Publ:* Contribr, chap, Women's Studies and the Arts, Hacker Art Books, portfolio & cover, Poetry East No 30, DePaul Univ Press, 90; interview & work, Making Time for Making Art, Warner, Chicago Rev Press, 94; rev, Univ Tampa Press, 9/2000. *Dealer:* Snyderman Gallery Philadelphia PA; Simon Gallery Morristown NJ; White Birch Gallery, Media, PA. *Mailing Add:* 910 Abington Rd Cherry Hill NJ 08034-3902

SHASHATY, YOLANDA VICTORIA
PAINTER
b Chicago, Ind, Aug 13, 50. *Study:* Oberlin Col, BA, 72; Univ Wis-Madison, MA, 74. *Work:* Sunrise Mus, Charleston, WVa. *Exhib:* Directions 1986, Hirshhorn Mus, Washington, DC, 86; A View to Nature, Aldrich Mus Contemp Art, Ridgefield, Conn, 86. *Bibliog:* Michael Brenson (auth), New York Times, 86; Everett Potter (auth), Arts Mag, 88; Nancy Grimes (auth), Art News, 88. *Media:* Oil on Canvas. *Mailing Add:* 425 Riverside Dr Apt 8F New York NY 10025

SHATTER, SUSAN LOUISE
PAINTER
b New York, NY, Jan 17, 43. *Study:* Pratt Inst, BFA, 65; Skowhegan Sch Painting & Sculpture, summer 64-65; Boston Univ, MFA, 72. *Work:* Boston Mus Fine Arts; Univ Utah Mus, Salt Lake City; Art Inst Chicago; Philadelphia Mus Art; Dartmouth Col Art Mus; McMullen Mus of Art, Boston Col; Smithsonian Mus Am Art, Washington, DC; Nat Acad Mus, NY. *Comn:* Colo River in Utah (4ft x 8ft painting), America 1976, US Dept Interior, 75; Panorama of Manhattan Island (3 1/2ft x 12 1/2ft), Am Tel & Tel Co, NY, 77; seascape (5ft x 12ft), Bank New Eng, 88; Haleakala Crater (6 1/2 ft x 20 ft), J Campbell Estate, Maui, 94. *Exhib:* Boston Watercolor Today, Mus Fine Arts, Boston, 76; Am 1976 (traveling exhib), Corcoran Gallery Art, Washington, 77; NY Now, Phoenix Mus, Ariz, 79; Am Realism since 1960, Pa Acad, 81-83; Gund Collection, Mus Fine Arts, Boston, 82; Realist Watercolors, Fla Int Univ, 83; Am Realism: Twentieth-Century Drawings and Watercolors (traveling exhib), San Francisco Mus Mod Art, 85-86; A Contemp View of Nature, Aldrich Mus Contemp Art, Ridgefield, Conn, 86-87; solo exhibs, Heath Gallery, Atlanta, 87, Fischbach Gallery, NY, 88, 91, 92, 93, 96 & 97, Harcus Gallery, Boston, 90; The Subject is Water, Newport Art Mus, RI, 87; The World is Round: Contemp Panoramas, Hudson River Mus, Yonkers, NY, 87 89. *Pos:* Bd govt, Skowhegan Sch Photog, chmn 88-; instr, Sch Visual Arts, 83; Coun Nat Acad Art, NY, 98-99, pres, 2005. *Teaching:* Vis artist, Univ Pa, Philadelphia, 74-75 & 79, act chmn, 83-84; mem fac painting, Skowhegan Sch Painting, Maine, summers 77 & 79 & Benninton Col, 79; vis artist, Tyler Sch Art, 85, San Francisco Art Inst, 89, Brooklyn Col, NY, 91-95 & Univ Tex, 97; prof, Univ of NC, Greensboro, 2001-02. *Awards:* Nat Endowment Arts Grants, 80 & 87; NY State Found Arts Grant, 85; Grant, YADDO Corp, 95, 97, 2000 & 02; Ballinglen Artists Fel, Ireland, 1999; Brittany fellow Rochefort-en-Terre, 2002; Childe Hassam Purchase award, Am Acad Arts and Letters, 2003; Yaddo resident, Saratoga Springs, NY, 2001, 02; Pollock Krasner Found Grant. *Bibliog:* Sebby Wilson Jacobson (auth), THESE are landscapes?, Times-Union Rochester, 3/3/88; Do; Lori Hurwitz (auth), Contemporary Master: Susan Shatter, Am Artist, 12/90; Ann Wilson Lloyd (auth), rev of Fischbach Show, Art in Am, 10/93. *Mem:* Nat Acad (acad, 95-, W Paten Prize 2003, treas 1998-03, pres 2005-); The Century Club. *Media:* Watercolor, Oil. *Specialty:* Contemp Art. *Publ:* Illusr, Am Watercolors & Drawings (auth, John Arthur), Graphics Soc, NY, 80; Am Realism, Alvin Martin (auth), Abrams, NY, 85; Graphic Muse Prints by Contemp Am Women, Mt Holyoke Press, 87; Twentieth Century Watercolor, Christopher Finch (auth), Abbeville Press, NY, 88; American Figurative Art (auth, John Arthur), Miyasi Mus, Japan, 91. *Dealer:* Fischbach Gallery 29 W 57th St New York NY 10019; Harcus Gallery Seven Newbury St Boston MA 02116. *Mailing Add:* 26 W 20th St New York NY 10011

SHAW, DONALD EDWARD
SCULPTOR, PAINTER
b Boston, Mass, Aug 24, 34. *Study:* Boston Mus Sch Fine Arts. *Work:* Ark Arts Ctr, Little Rock; Atlantic Richfield Co, Los Angeles; Chase Manhattan Bank, NY; Mus Fine Arts, Houston, Tex; Smithsonian Inst, Washington, DC. *Comn:* Ark Arts Ctr, Little Rock, 88; Ark Col, Bateville, 92; Am Capitol, Houston; Bio-med Ctr, Univ Ark, Little Rock, 94. *Exhib:* Tex 30, Nave Mus, Victoria, Tex, 77; one-man show, Moody Gallery, Houston, Tex, 81 & 84; Mus Fine Arts, Houston, Tex, 89 & 94; Mid Am Mus, Hot Springs, Ark, 92. *Awards:* Travel Grant to Arg, Casa De'Arg, 77. *Bibliog:* Ann Holmes (auth), Fantastic artists, Southwest Art Gallery Mag, 2/72; N Laliberte & A Mogelon (auths), Art in Boxes, Van Nostrand, Reinhold Co, 74; Susie Kalil (auth, essay cat), Don Shaw, Ark Arts Ctr, Little Rock, 89. *Media:* Mixed. *Publ:* Contribr, Agencia Noticias Mex, 69 & cover illus, Southwest Art Gallery Mag, 72; Poverty Point, Sky Drawings Video, 91. *Dealer:* Hooks Epstein Houston TX. *Mailing Add:* 210 W Barraque Pine Bluff AR 71601

SHAW, ERNEST CARL
SCULPTOR
b New York, NY, Apr 17, 42. *Work:* Aldrich Mus Contemp Art, Ridgefield, Conn; Indianapolis Mus; Nelson Rockefeller; Wichita Art Mus, Kans; and others. *Comn:* Orlando Int Airport, Reading, Pa. *Exhib:* Storm King Art Ctr, Mountainville, NY, 77; Contemp Reflections, Aldrich Mus Contemp Art, 77; one-man shows, Storm King Art Ctr, 78, Hamilton Gallery Contemp Art, 78, Sculpture Now, NY, 78, Allentown Art Mus, 81, Wichita Art Mus, 81, Huntington Galleries, WVa, 81, Althea Viafora, NY, 86, Maxwell Davidson, NY, 88 & Williams Col Art Mus, Williamstown, Mass, 88; three-man show, Hamilton Gallery Contemp Art, 78; A M Sachs Gallery, 80; and other group and one-man shows. *Media:* Steel, Wood. *Mailing Add:* Two Wawarsing Rd New Paltz NY 12561

SHAW, ISABEL
SCULPTOR, GRAPHIC ARTIST
b New York, NY. *Study:* Bard Col, BFA, 52; Sch Visual Arts, Cooper Union. *Work:* numerous pvt collections in US, Eng, Hong Kong & Switz. *Exhib:* Solo exhibs, Anaya Gallery, Scarsdale, NY, 80, MAG Gallery, Larchmont, NY, 81 & 2000, Mari Gallery, Mamaroneck, NY, 81 & Gallery at Chappaqua Libr, NY, 95; Art Students League, NY, 90; Broome Street Gallery, NY, 91, 92 & 94; Pen & Brush Club, NY, 92; Westbeth Gallery, NY, 94; Kohn Pedersen Fox Gallery, NY, 96; and others. *Awards:* Merrit Award, New Rochelle Artists, NY, 74; First Place Sculpture, Beaux Arts Finale, Westchester Co, NY, 74; Sculpture Award, Mamaroneck Artists Guild, Lyla J Weiss Mem, 84. *Bibliog:* Review, NY Times, 1/22/95; interview, Scarsdale Inquirer, 10/27/2000. *Mem:* NY Soc Woman Artists; NY Artists Equity; Contemp Artists Guild NY; Hudson River Contemp Artists; Sculptors League, NY; Art Studio Club, NY. *Media:* Bronze, Wood. *Publ:* Contemp Women Artists (calendar), 88. *Dealer:* Roslyn Sailor Fine Arts Ltd Margate NJ & Philadelphia PA

SHAW, JIM
PAINTER
b Midland, Mich, Aug 8, 52. *Study:* Univ Mich, Ann Arbor, BFA, 74; Calif Inst Arts, MFA, 78. *Exhib:* Video and Dream, Mus Mod Art, NY, 90; Recent Drawings, Whitney Mus Am Art, NY, 90; Biennial Exhib, Whitney Mus Am Art, NY, 91; solo exhibs, Tex Gallery, Houston, 92, Massimo de Carlo, Milan, Italy, 92 & 96, Metro Pictures, NY, 92 & 93, Linda Cathcart Gallery, Santa Monica, Calif, 92 & 93, Rena Bransten Gallery, San Francisco, 94, Donna Beam Fine Art Gallery, Univ Nev, 95 & Cabinet Gallery, London, 96; Helter Skelter: LA Art in the 1990s, Mus Contemp Art, Los Angeles, 92; Songs of Innocence/Songs of Experience, Whitney Mus Am Art, Stamford, Conn, 92; Galleri Andreas Brändström, Stockholm, 95; Art on Pepr, Weatherspoon Art Gallery, Univ NC Greensboro, 95; Pay-Fi, Real Art Ways, Hartford, Conn, 96; It's Only Rock & Roll: Rock & Roll Currents in Contemp Art (with catalog), Bedford Gallery/Dean Lesher Regional Ctr Arts, Walnut Creek, Calif, 96; Exhibs incl What Exactly is a Dream and What Exactly is a Joke, Donna Beam Fine Art Gallery, 95, Galerie Praz-Delavallade, Paris, 97, 99, 2002, Frankfort Kunstverein, 98, From Head to Toe: Concepts of the Body in 20th Century Art, Los Angeles Co Mus Art, 98, Jim Shaw: Thrift Store Paintings, Inst Contemp Art, London, 2000, La Bienniale de Montreal 2000, 2000, The Artist's World, Calif Col Arts and Crafts, 2000, Biennale of Sydney, Mus Contemp Art, 2002, one-man shows incl The Goodman Image File and Study, Swiss Inst, 2002, O Kunsthaus Glarus, Ger, 2004. *Awards:* Nat Endowment Arts Grant, 87; Tiffany Found, 89; Fel Guggenheim Mem Found, 2004. *Bibliog:* David A Greene (auth), California Dreaming, The Village Voice, 96; Janet Preston (auth), New York Letter Bomb, Coagula Art J, No 24, 96; Ken Johnson (auth), California Dreamer, Art in Am, 12/96. *Publ:* Auth, Thrift Store Paintings, Heavy Industry Publ, 90; Dreams, Smart Art Press, Santa Monica, Calif, 95. *Dealer:* Linda Cathcart Gallery 924 Colorado Ave Santa Monica CA 90401; Metro Pictures 150 Greene St New York NY 10012. *Mailing Add:* Metro Pictures Gallery 519 West 24th St New York NY 10011

SHAW, JOHN PALMER
PAINTER, PRINTMAKER
b San Mateo Calif, Apr 23, 1948. *Study:* Art Students League; Pratt Inst; Md Inst Col Art, BFA, 72. *Work:* Mus Mod Art, NY; Brooklyn Mus, NY; Bank Am, San Francisco; NY Pub Libr. *Exhib:* Five Baltimore Artists, Baltimore Mus Art, 73; Ritz Show, Ritz, Washington, 83; Terminal Show, Brooklyn Terminal, 83; The Great East River Bridge Show, 83 & New Aquisitions, 86, Brooklyn Mus; New Talent, Leo Castelli Uptown, NY, 84; Stornaway Gallery, Montreal, 92; Artifice 96, Place Victoria Show, Montreal, 96; Galerie DuGazon-Couture, Montreal, 98; Dugazon Couture, Montreal, Can, 99 & 2000. *Teaching:* prof drawing, McGill Univ, 2006-. *Bibliog:* Beverly Mitchell (auth), Home again, Montreal Gazzette, 7/12/92; Lucinda Catchlove (auth), A painters painter John Shaw, Montreal Mirror, 11/10/92; Henry Lehmann (auth), Interiors, Exteriors, Montreal Gazzette, 10/3/98. *Media:* Encaustic, Oil. *Publ:* Ed, New Observations No 8, Lucio Pozzi, 83. *Dealer:* Christopher Baenninger. *Mailing Add:* 624 Rue Sainte-Madeleine Montreal PQ H3K 2L3 Canada

SHAW, JOSEPH WINTERBOTHAM
HISTORIAN, EDUCATOR
b Chicago, Ill, July 6, 35. *Study:* Brown Univ, BA, 57; Wesleyan Univ, MA, 59; Univ Pa, PhD, 70. *Hon Degrees:* Brown Univ, LHD, 87. *Teaching:* Asst prof, Univ Toronto, 70-73, assoc prof, 73-77, prof, 77-. *Awards:* Various res grants for Aegean Bronze Age archit and archaeology; Gold medal, Lifetime Achievement from the Archaelogical Inst Am, 2006. *Mem:* Can Mediterranean Inst; Am Sch Classical Studies; Archaeological Inst Am (pres, Toronto chap, 79-88, vpres); Soc Antiguaries; Royal Soc Can. *Res:* Bronze Age Aegean archaeology and art. *Publ:* Excavation at Kommos, Crete, Hesperia, 76-93; Coauth, Kenchreai, Vol 1, Brill, 78; auth, Consideration of the Site of Akrotiri as a Minoan Settlement, Thera & Aegean World, 78; Evidence for the Tripartite Shrine, Am J Archeol, 78; The Early Helladic II Corridor House, Am J Archeol, 87; Phoenician Shrine at Kommos, Am J Archeol, 89; coed & auth, Kommos An Excavation on the South Coast of Crete, I(1), I(2), II, III, IV, Princeton Univ Press, 90-; Kommos I, The Kommos Region and Houses of the Minoan Town, Part I, The Kommos Region, Ecology, and the Minoan Industries, Princeton, 95 & Part 2, 96; Kommos IV, The Greek Sanctuary, 2000. *Mailing Add:* Univ Toronto Fine Art/Grad Dept Hist Art Toronto ON M5S 13G3 Canada

SHAW, KAREN
PAINTER, CURATOR
b Bronx, NY, Oct 25, 47. *Study:* Hunter Col, City Univ New York, BFA, 65; grad work Hunter Col & C W Post, 70-71. *Work:* Herbert F Johnson Mus Art, Ithaca, NY; Israel Mus, Jerusalem; City Univ Grand Ctr, NY; Erasmus Haus, Basel, Switzerland; Mus Mod Art, NY. *Comn:* 11 large paintings, Mall, City Univ Grad Ctr, NY, 80; Installation: Effects of Acid Rain on the Great Lakes, LI Univ, Southampton Campus, 88; Installation, Het Apollohus, Eindhoven, Netherlands, 90; Pandora's Box, The Effects of Burning Fossel Fuels on the Environment, 90; Plato's Box in Pandora's Cave, Dowling Col, 91. *Exhib:* Book Works, Albright Knox Art Gallery, Buffalo, NY, 77; one-woman shows, Bertha Urdang Gallery, NY, 76 & 83, Dany Keller Galerie, Munich, WGer, 78 & 81, City Univ Grad Ctr, NY, 80 & 86, Corinne Hummel Galerie, Basel, Switz, 83, C Kermit Ewing Gallery Art & Archit, Univ Tenn, Knoxville, 86 & 91, Southampton Col, Long Island Univ, NY, 88 & Het Apollohuis, Eindhoven, The Neth, 90; Artists Books, Walker Art Ctr, Minneapolis, Minn, 81; Albright Knox Art Gallery, Buffalo, NY, 82; Dowling Col, Oakdale, NY; Women's Art Caucus, The Environment Show, Bronx, NY, 90; Anchorage Mus Hist & Art, Alaska, 90; Vital Signs, Artists Address the Environ, Henry St Settlement, NY, 90; and others. *Pos:* Cur, Islip Art Mus, 81-. *Teaching:* Asst prof art, Univ Tenn, 89-90; instr, Silvermine Art Sch, New Canaan, Conn, 89-; lectr Princeton Univ, 95, 99. *Awards:* Nat Endowment Arts, US Govt, 78-79; Found Karolyi, Vence, France, 88 & 89; New York Found Arts Grant, 92-93. *Bibliog:* Lenore Malen (auth), Karen Shaw: The reckoner, Arts Mag, 4/79; Helen Harrison (auth), New York Times, 9/22/91. *Media:* Acrylic, Oil. *Publ:* Contribr, A Big Jewish Book, Anchor Press Doubleday, 78; auth, Market Research, Univ Akron, Ohio, 78. *Dealer:* Tony Zwicker 15 Gramercy Park NY 10003; Art Resources Transfer New York NY 10011

SHAW, KENDALL (GEORGE)
PAINTER
b New Orleans, La, Mar 30, 24. *Study:* Ga Inst Technol, 44-46; Tulane Univ, BS, 49, MFA, 59; La State Univ, 50; New Sch Social Res, 50-52; Brooklyn Mus Art Sch, 53; also with Edward Corbett, Ralston Crawford, Stuart Davis, O Louis Guglielmi, George Rickey & Mark Rothko. *Work:* Mus Contemp Art, Nagaoka, Japan; NY Univ; Brooklyn Mus, NY; Everson Mus, Syracuse, NY; Neue Galerie Sammlung Ludwig, Aachen; Ogden Mus of Southern Art, New Orleans, La; Miss Mus of Art; Polk Mus of Art, Lakeland, Fla; Orlando Mus of Art, Fla; New Orleans Mus of Art, La. *Comn:* Chase Manhattan Bank. *Exhib:* One-man exhibs, Orleans Gallery, New Orleans, 60-61, 63, Tibor de Nagy Gallery, NY, 64, 65, 67 & 68, John Bernard Myers Gallery, NY, 72, Alessandra Gallery, NY, 77 & Lerner-Heller Gallery, 79, 81 & 82, Nature Morte Gallery, NY, 83, Bernice Steinbaum Gallery, NY, 91, Artists Space, NY, 92, Gallery S Orange, NJ, 98 & Univ Richmond, Va, 99, Tulane Univ, New Orleans, 2001; Contemp Painting, Mus Contemp Art, Nagaoka, Japan, 65; Modular Painting, Albright-Knox Art Gallery, 70; Sets for The First Reader by Gertrude Stein, Mus Mod Art & Metrop Mus Art, NY, 70-71; Pattern Painting, PS 1, NY, 77; Les Nouveaux Fauves, Die Neuen Wilden, Sammlung, Ludwig, 80; and others. *Collection Arranged:* Galerie Simone Stern, New Orleans, 68; Pattern & Decoration, Rive Univ, Houston, Tex, 77; Pattern & Decoration, Illinois Wesleyan Univ, Bloomington, 80. *Teaching:* Columbia Univ, NY, 61-66; Hunter Col, NY, 66-68; Parsons Sch Design, NY, 66-86; Lehman Col, NY, 68-70; Brooklyn Mus Art Sch, Brooklyn, NY, 70-76; retired. *Awards:* Disting Alumns, Tulane Col, 2001. *Bibliog:* Art Forum, 11/77; Articles, Arts Mag, 1/77 & Art News, 10/80, summer 82; Art & Artists, 8-9/86. *Mem:* Col Art Asn Am; NY Artists Equity Asn. *Media:* Acrylic, Collage. *Interests:* Peace on Earth. *Publ:* The Painter and the Photographer, Van Deren Coke, Univ of NMex, 72; Helicon Nine, 79; Richard Waller, Kendall Shaw, A Life's Journey in Art, Univ of Richmond, Va, 99; Tulane Univ, 2001; The Tulane Col Review, 2001, 02; CAC, New Orleans, 2003; and others. *Dealer:* Independent Artist. *Mailing Add:* 916 President St Brooklyn NY 11215-1604

SHAW, LOUISE E
DIRECTOR
b Quincy, Mass, Mar 16, 51. *Study:* Clark Univ, Worchester, Mass, BA, 73; Syracuse Univ, MFA, 81. *Exhib:* The World Unseen: When Science Meets Art. *Collection Arranged:* Obsession: Who What and Why People Collect, Traveling Exhbn, 97; Between Space and Time: Contemporary Norwegian Sculpture and Installation, 2000-01; Georgia Triennial, 01-02. *Pos:* Exec dir, Nexus Contemp Art Ctr, 83-98; freelance cur & consult, 80-; cur, CDC Mus, 2002-. *Awards:* Nat Endowment Arts Mus Fel, 88; ORISE Fel, 2002-2006. *Mem:* Cult Olympiad; Bus Coun Arts; Ga Asn Mus & Galleries; Art & Cult Comt, Atlanta; Ga Citizen for Arts; Atlanta Pub Art legacy Comt; and others. *Publ:* Vital signs, Nexus Contemp Art Ctr, 91; auth, Harry Callahan and His Students: A Study in Influence, Ga State Univ, 81; Between Space and Time: Contemporary Norwegian Sculpture and Installation, Norwegian Scultpure Asn, 2000; Georgia Triennial, 01. *Mailing Add:* 225 Melrose Ave Decatur GA 30030

SHAW, MARY TODD
SCULPTOR, PAINTER
b Gadsden, Ala. *Study:* Atlanta Col Art, cert, 41; Univ NC, Charlotte, BCA, 74; student, Ga Inst Technol, Am Univ Paris, Univ NC at Greensboro, Univ Salzburg, Austria. *Work:* Columbia Mus, SC; Mint Mus Art; Gibbs Gallery Art, Charleston, NC; Hickory Mus Art, NC. *Comn:* Monotypes, Art Coalition Charlotte, NC, 82. *Exhib:* Nat

Asn Women Artists Exhib, Nat Acad, NY & Royal Scottish Acad, Edinburgh; Piedmont Exhib, Mint Mus Art; State Dept Show, Mus Bella Artes, Buenos Aires; Hunter Mus Art Ann; Allied Artists Exhib, Nat Arts Club, NY; Exhib Va Artists, Va Mus Fine Arts; Southeastern, High Mus Art; Owings-Dewey Fine Art. *Teaching:* Instr drawing & painting, Mint Mus Art, 64-74; instr painting, Spirit Sq, 76- & Cent Piedmont Col, 79-80. *Awards:* Va Ctr Fel, Sweet Briar, Va, 84 & 85; Banff Ctr Fel, Alta, Canada; Best in Show, Springfest, Charlotte, NC, 86; over 90 others. *Bibliog:* Charlene Whisnant (auth), Red Clay Reader, Vol 1, 67, Vol 4, 68 & Vol 7, 70; Donaz Meilach & Evie Ten Hoor (auths), Collage & Assemblages, Crown Publ, 73; Virginia Watson Jones (auth), Contemporary American Woman Sculptors, Oryx Press, 86. *Mem:* Southern Graphics Asn; Tri-State Sculptors; Int Sculptors; Nat Asn Women Artists; NC Print & Drawing Soc. *Media:* Boxes. *Publ:* Auth, Tri State Sculptors Catalog, 85, 86, 87; Joseph Cornell (catalogue), Kawamura Mem Mus Art, Sakura City, Chiba, Japan, 93. *Dealer:* Ownings-Dewey Fine Art 76 East San Francisco St On The Plaza Santa Fe NMex. *Mailing Add:* 8919 Park Rd Apt 312 Charlotte NC 28210

SHAW, NANCY (RIVARD)
CURATOR, HISTORIAN

b Saginaw, Mich. *Study:* Oakland Univ, Mich, BA(studio art), 69; Wayne State Univ, Mich, MA(art hist), 73; Attingham Summer Inst, Eng, 77. *Collection Arranged:* The Art That is Life: The Arts & Crafts Movement in America 1875-1920; Thomas Hart Benton: An American Original, 89; American Paintings from the Manoogian Collection, 90; Gari Melchers: A Retrospective Exhibition, 90; Henry Ossawa Tanner, 91; American Paintings from the Monoogian Collection: A Private View (catalog), 93; The Art of Thomas Wilmer Dewing: Beauty Reconfigured, 96. *Pos:* Asst cur Am art, Detroit Inst Arts, 1972-1975, actg cur, 1975-1977, cur, 1977-1998, cur emer, 1998-. *Teaching:* Adj prof, Wayne State Univ, 1986-1998. *Bibliog:* Cotopaxi, Detroit Inst Arts Bull, 78. *Mem:* Decorative Art Chap, Soc Archit Hist. *Res:* Late Nineteenth and early twentieth century American painting and sculpture. *Interests:* Painting. *Publ:* auth introd to, American Paintings in the Detroit Institute of Arts: Works by Artists Born Before 1816, (1st of 3 vol on the collections), 91; auth & contribr, From the Hudson River School to Impressionism: American Paintings from the Manoogian Collection (exhib, catalog), 96; auth, Introduction to American Paintings in the Detroit Institute of Arts, Works by Artists Born between 1817 & 1847, 97; auth, Marriages, divorces and reconciliations: challenges in framing a museum collection, in The Gilded Age: The Art of the Frame, 2000; contribr, Calm in the Shadow of the Palmetto & Magnolia, 2003; contribr, American Paintings in the Detroit Institute of Arts, Works by Artists Born After 1847, 2005. *Mailing Add:* 9319 SE 137th St Rd Summerfield FL 34491

SHAW, PAUL JEFFERSON
CALLIGRAPHER, DESIGNER, HISTORIAN

b Ann Arbor, Mich, Sept 28, 54. *Study:* Reed Col, BA, 76; Columbia Univ, MA, 78, MPh, 80. *Comn:* Corp typeface, Origins, 91-92. *Exhib:* Brooklyn Art Mus, 83; Lettering Arts in the Zapftradition, Strathmore Hall, Bethesda, Md, 93; Alphabetics, Pratt Inst, Brooklyn, NY, 93; Calligrafia, Venice, Italy, 94; Paper, Art & the Book, Ctr Book Arts, NY, 96; solo exhibs, Asolo, Italy, 97 & St Paul, Minn, 98; group show, NY, 99. *Collection Arranged:* Calligraphy in the Graphic Arts, 81-89; Werner Schneider: Schriftkunst, 99; Words & Images, 83-87. *Pos:* Corresp, Calligraphy Rev, formerly; contribr, PRINT Magazine, NY. *Teaching:* Prof calligraphy, Sch Visual Arts, 79-85 & prof hist of graphic design, 2000-03, Long Island Univ, 81-89 & Parsons Sch Design, 85-, NYC Col of Tech, 2001, calligraphy, Univ Arts, 2006; prof lettering design, NY Inst Technol, 81-97. *Awards:* Fel, Biblio Soc Am, 2002; Am Acad in Rome, Italy, 2002; Alfred & Blanche Knopf Fel, Harry Ransom Humanities Ctr, Univ Tex, 2004. *Mem:* Soc Scribes Ltd (bd gov, 78-85); Type Director's Club; Am Ctr Design; Am Inst Graphic Artists; Asn Typografique Int; and others. *Media:* Ink, Gouache and Paper; Collage. *Res:* W A Dwiggins, Bartolomeo Sanvito, Andrea Bregno, George Salter. *Publ:* WA Dwiggins, Design Issues, 84; Letterforms, pvt publ, 87; Font Piracy: another view, Print, 94; Touchstones, 96; Blackletter: Type & National Identity (monograph), 98; Blackletter Type & National Identity: The Catalogue, 2000; A Chronology of Letterforms 1850-2000, vols I & II, 2000 & 01; Bartolomeo Sanvito, Parts I & II, Letter Arts Rev, 2003 & 2004. *Mailing Add:* 785 West End Ave New York NY 10025

SHAW, REESEY
PAINTER, SCULPTOR

b Jacksonville, Fla, Jan 11, 43. *Study:* Sch Fine & Appl Art, Boston Univ, 60-62; Md Inst Col Art, BFA, 64, MFA, 66. *Work:* Kaufman & Broad Collections, Los Angeles, Calif; AT&T, Los Angeles, Calif; Arco Corp Collection, Los Angeles, Calif. *Exhib:* La Jolla Mus Contemp Art, Calif, 74, 78 & 86; solo exhibs, San Diego Mus Art, 75 & Los Angeles Inst Contemp Art, 80, Calif; Personal Myth, Queens Mus, NY, 78; Private Icons, Bronx Mus, NY, 79; Painted Sculpture, Munic Art Gallery, Los Angeles, Calif, 82; Sunshine & Shadow, Univ Southern Calif, Los Angeles, 85; Retrospective, Selected Works 1980-1990 (auth, catalog), Mesa Col Art Gallery, San Diego. *Pos:* Cur, Felicita Found Arts, Calif, 87-89, artist dir, 89-91; dir galleries, Ctr for the Arts, Escondido, Calif, 91-93, vpres visual arts, 93-97; dir, Lux Art Inst, Rancho Santa Fe, Calif, 98-. *Teaching:* Asst prof art hist, Morgan State Univ, Baltimore, 66-69; lectr, Univ Calif, San Diego, 77-79; instr masters' classes, Claremont Col, Calif, 83. *Awards:* Art Guild Award, San Diego Mus Art, 75. *Bibliog:* John Russell (auth), When Art Imitates Anthropology, NY Times, 4/78; David Rubin (auth), Contemporary Tryptichs, Calif Technol-Pamona Col, 82; Ballatore (auth), The Psychological Tightrope, Images & Issues, 1/82. *Mem:* Am Asn Mus; Am Fed Arts; Calif Assembly Local Arts Agencies. *Media:* Encaustic Paint; Wood. *Publ:* Auth, Double Exposure, Images & Issues, 81; Inside: The Work of Saint Clair Cemin, Joel Otterson and Others, 96, coauth, Myths and Magical Fantasies, 96 & Tabletops Morandi's Still Lifes to Mapplethorpe's Flower Studies, 97, Calif Ctr Arts Mus, Escondido. *Mailing Add:* 7793 Senn Way La Jolla CA 92037

SHAW, RENATA VITZTHUM
ADMINISTRATOR

b Mantta, Finland, July 21, 26; US citizen. *Study:* Univ Chicago, MA(art hist), 49; Univ Helsinki, Finland, MPhilos(art hist), 51; Ecole de Louvre, Paris, dipl(museology), 52; Catholic Univ Am, MS(libr sci), 62. *Pos:* Reference librn art, Prints & Photog Div, Libr Congress, Washington, DC, 62-67, supervisory librn art, 67-71, bibliog specialist art, 71-81, asst chief prints & photog div, 82, actg chief prints & photog div, 83-84, asst chief prints & photog, 84-90. *Teaching:* Lectures in the Library of Congress on visual resources. *Mem:* Art Librn North Am; Spec Libr Asn; Am Libr Asn. *Res:* Art bibliography; collection development; visual librarianship; organization of visual collections; automation of library holdings, visual resources, production of videodisk of visual resources and retrieval of visual information. *Interests:* Development of a research collection in the field of art history. *Publ:* Auth, Handbook of Latin American Studies: Book Annotations, Univ Fla, 74; Quarterly Journal of the Library of Congress: Essays, Libr Cong, 75; Encyclopedia of Library & Information Science, Marcel Dekker, 77; Graphic Sampler: A Century of Photographs, 1846-1946, Libr Cong Collection, 80

SHAW, RICHARD BLAKE
SCULPTOR

b Hollywood, Calif, Sept 12, 41. *Study:* Orange Coast Col, 61-63; San Francisco Art Inst, BFA(Agnus Brandenstein Fel), 65; Alfred Univ, 65; Univ Calif, Davis, MA, 68. *Work:* Oakland Mus, Calif; San Francisco Mus; Nat Mus Art, Tokyo; Stedelijk Mus, Amsterdam, Holland; Whitney Mus Am Art, NY. *Exhib:* One-man shows, San Francisco Mus Art, 73, Braunstein/Quay Gallery, 69-94, A Survey, George Adams Gallery, NY, 98, Braunstein Quay Gallery, San Francisco, Calif, 98 & Tempe Arts Ctr, Ariz, 98; Whitney Mus Am Art, NY, 70 & 81; Int Ceramics, 1972, Victoria & Albert Mus, London, 72; The Chosen Object: Europ & Am Still Life, Joslyn Art Mus, Omaha, Nebr, 77; Newport Harbor Art Mus, Calif, 81; San Jose Mus Art, Calif, 81; Boise Gallery Art, Idaho, 81; Palm Springs Desert Mus, 87. *Teaching:* Lectr, Col Marin, Kentfiled, Calif, 77; lectr, Univ Calif Davis, 78; prof ceramics, Univ Calif, Berkeley, 87-. *Awards:* Nat Endowment Arts Grant, 70; Nat Endowment Arts Crafts Grant, 74; Fel, Am Crafts Coun, 98. *Bibliog:* Articles in Viking Press, 69 & Arts Can, summer 71; Catalog, Ceramic Sculpture, 78 & 81-83. *Mem:* Order Golden Brush; Int Soc Ceramists. *Media:* Ceramics, Mixed Media. *Mailing Add:* Univ Calif Berkeley Ceramics Dept Berkeley CA 94720-3750

SHAW-EAGLE, JOANNA
CRITIC

Pos: Art critic, Wash Times. *Publ:* Contribr articles to prof jour. *Mailing Add:* Wash Times 3600 New York Ave Washington DC 20002-1947

SHAWNA, MONTEPAULO
COLLECTOR

b Key Largo, Fla, Jun 1, 50. *Study:* Univ Miami, Fla, BA, 74; Fla State, MA, 84. *Pos:* Assoc cur, Disney Charactor Collector Gallery, Orlando, Fla, 90-95; Owner, Modern Collectibles, Miami, Fla, 96-. *Teaching:* Instr, collector workshops, Key Largo, Fla, 96-. *Awards:* Best of Show, Collector Exhib, Fla, 2001. *Interests:* Working with young artists and learning from their point of view. *Collection:* Disney and other cartoon charactor collections. *Mailing Add:* 52 Park Lane Rd New Milford CT 06776-2917

SHAY, ED
PAINTER

b Boston, Mass, Nov 12, 47. *Study:* Murray State Univ, Ky, BFA, 69; Univ Ill, Champaign, MFA, 71. *Work:* Minn Mus Art, St Paul; Univ NDak, Grand Forks; Dulin Gallery Art, Knoxville, Tenn; Bradley Univ, Peoria, Ill; Calif Col Arts & Crafts, San Francisco. *Comn:* Oil Planetarium, Ponderosa Collection, Dayton, Ohio, 74; wall graphic, Skate Away, Muncie, Ind, 77; billboard, Indianapolis Art League, Ind, 78. *Exhib:* 74th Chicago Artists & Vicinity Show, Chicago Art Inst, 73; World Print Competition, Calif Col Arts & Crafts, San Francisco, 73; Works On Twinrocker Handmade Paper, Ind Mus Art, Indianapolis, 75; Crimes of Passion, Univ Ky, Lexington, 77; Rutgers Nat Drawing 77, Camden Col Arts & Sci, NJ, 77; My Backyard: A Mid Career Retrospective of Paintings, Mt Vernon, Ill, 90 & State of Ill Art Gallery, Springfield, 91; Contemp Ill Watercolor Art Asn, 91; 8th Biennial Exhib, Tarble Arts Ctr, Charleston, Ill, 91; solo exhibs, Ctr Art Gallery, State of Ill, Chicago, 91, My Back Yard: A Mid-Career Retrospective of Painting, Ill Art Coun Traveling Exhib, 95; Cast in Carbondale, Evansville Mus Art, 93; Gallery Artists, Roy Boyd Gallery, Chicago, Ill, 94 & 95; Southern Ill Artists Open Competition, Mitchell Mus, Mt Vernon, Ill, 95; Twentieth Century Am Sculpture at the White House, Washington, DC, 96; Watercolor USA Honor Soc Biennial, Nat Invitational Exhib, Springfield Art Mus, Springfield, Mo, 97-98; Drawing/Watercolor: Illinois 12th Biennial Exhib, Tarble Art Ctr, E Ill Univ, Charleston, 98-99. *Collection Arranged:* Rollman-Shay, Not In New York Gallery, Cincinnati, Ohio, 74 & 76; Krannert Gallery, Univ Evansville, Ind, 74; Nancy Lurie Gallery, Chicago, Ill, 76; Roy Boyd Gallery, Chicago,. *Pos:* Vis artist, Studio Art Ctr Int, Florence Italy, 97, Burren Col Art, Ballyvaughn, Ireland, Ariz State Univ, Tempe, Ariz, 99. *Teaching:* Prof art & design, Southern Ill Univ, Carbondale, 86-. *Awards:* Purchase Awards, 55th Soc Am Graphic Artists Nat Print Exhib, New York, 77 & Drawings & Prints 77, Miami Univ, Oxford, Ohio, 77; Bronstein Purchase Award, Mid-States Exhib, Evansville Mus Art, Ind, 77; Special Asst Grant, Ill Art Coun, 88 & Exhib Grant, 91. *Bibliog:* Clinton Hillary Rodham & Tucker Marcia (auths), Twentieth Century American Sculpture at the White House, 96; Rob Erdle (auth), International Watercolor Biennial-East/West, Parkland Col Art Gallery, Champaign, Ill, 97; Gisele Alterberry (auth), Watercolor exhibit at Parkland joins east and west, The News-Gazette, F-4, 3/23/97. *Media:* Oil, Watercolor. *Mailing Add:* 1601 E Walnut Carbondale IL 62901

SHEA, JUDITH
SCULPTOR
b Philadelphia, Pa, Nov 13, 48. *Study:* Parsons Sch Design, AA, 69; Parsons/New Sch, BFA, 75. *Work:* Neuberger Mus, State Univ New York Col, Purchase; Hirschhorn Mus & Sculpture Garden, Washington, DC; Dallas Mus Fine Art; Walker Art Ctr, Minneapolis; La Jolla Mus Contemp Art, Calif; Minneapolis Sculpture Garden; Brooklyn Mus. *Comn:* Minn Sculpture Garden; Laumeier Sculpture Park, St Louis, Mo. *Exhib:* Biennial Exhib, Whitney Mus Am Art, NY, 81; Sculpture Now (with catalog), Va Mus Fine Arts, Richmond, 83; Directions 1983 (with catalog), Hirshhorn Mus & Sculpture Garden, Washington, DC, 83; one-person exhibs, Walker Art Ctr, 84, Hayden Gallery, 85, Acad Fine Arts, Philadelphia, Pa, 86, Nelson-Atkins Mus Art, Kansas City, Mo, 89, Whitney Mus Am Art at Phillip Morris, 92, St-Gaudens Nat Hist Site, Cornish, NH, 94 & Pub Art Fund Inc, Doris C Freedman Plaza, NY, 94; Contemp Cutouts (with catalog), Whitney Mus Am Art at Phillip Morris, 86; Structure to Resemblance: Work by Eight Am Sculptors (with catalog), Albright-Knox Art Gallery, 87; Enclosing the Void: 8 Contemp Sculptors (with catalog), Whitney Mus Am Art at Equitable Ctr, 88; Sculpture: Inside/Outside (with catalog), Walker Art Ctr, Minneapolis & Mus Fine Arts, Houston, 88; Making Their Mark: Women Artists Move Into the Mainstream (with catalog), Denver Art Mus & Pa Acad Fine Arts, 89; John Berggruen Gallery, San Francisco, 92; Clothing Metaphors, John Michael Kohler Arts Ctr, Sheboygan, Wis, 93; Fall from Fashion (with catalog), Aldrich Mus Contemp Art, 93; Am Art Today: Clothing as Metaphor, Art Mus, Fla Int Univ, Miami, 93; Figurative Contemp Sculpture, Albuquerque Mus, 93; The Rag Trade, InterArts Ctr, NY, 93; In the Garden, In the Galleries, Walker Art Ctr, 94; Ideas and Objects: Selected Drawings and Sculpture from the Permanent Collection, Whitney Mus Am Art, 94; and others. *Teaching:* Instr, Parsons Sch Design, New York, 79-86, New York Univ, 80-86; vis prof, Univ Calif Davis, 91; vis fac grad sculpture, Yale Univ, fall 92. *Awards:* Nat Endowment Arts Grant, 84 & 86; Solomon R Guggenheim Sculptor-in-Residence at Chesterwood, Mass, 89; Rome Prize Fel, Am Acad, Rome, Italy, 94. *Bibliog:* Peter Schjeldahl (auth), Metaphysics of skin, The Village Voice, Art, 99, 4/16/91; Roberta Smith (auth), Judith Shea, art in review, New York Times, 2/6/93; Charles Hagen (auth), In Connecticut, clothes, photos & Yale on Yale, New York Times, 7/23/93. *Mem:* Nat Acad (acad, 95-). *Media:* Bronze, Wood. *Publ:* Auth, Style: The art of clothing, Craft Horizons, 10/78; The original clothes, extra, extra, New York, spring 79; Beyond fashion: Mariano Fortuny, Art Am, 11/82; Valentino, Artforum, 12/82. *Dealer:* John Berggruen Gallery, San Francisco, CA. *Mailing Add:* Univ Pa Sch Design 102 Meyerson Hall 210 S 34th St Philadelphia PA 19104-6311

SHEAD, S RAY
PAINTER, PRINTMAKER
b Cartersville, Ga, Nov 27, 38. *Study:* Atlanta Art Inst, BFA, 60; Art Ctr Col Design, BPA, 63; Ga State Univ, MVA; Inst Allende, Mex; also with John Rodgers & Loser Fiedelson, Los Angeles. *Work:* Columbus Mus, Ga; Montgomery Mus, Ala; Opelika Art League, Ala; Atlanta High Mus, Ga; Southwest Ga Art Mus, Albany. *Comn:* Painting, Chrysler Corp, Atlanta, 60; sculpture, Dibco-Wayne Corp, Atlanta, 68; painting, Callaway Gardens, Ga, 70; C & S Bank; First Nat Bank. *Exhib:* Dixie Ann, Montgomery, Ala, 60; 6th Ann Callaway Gardens Exhib, Ga, 69; 49th Shreveport Art Exhib, La, 70; Ga Artists Exhib I & II, Atlanta, 71-72; SC Artists, 74. *Pos:* Art dir, Compton Advert, New York, 63-67; art dir, Marschalk Co, Atlanta, 67; creative dir, Storer Studio, 67. *Teaching:* Assoc prof art & head dept, LaGrange Col, 68-74; head dept art, Presby Col, 74-76; chmn commercial art, Dekalb Col, 77-86; head com art, Dekalb Tech Inst, 86-. *Awards:* Second Dixie Ann Award, 60; Southern Contemp Award, 69; 6th Ann Columbus Exhib Award, 70. *Mem:* Col Art Asn Am. *Media:* Acrylic, Epoxy; Etching. *Dealer:* Singlee Ltd, Atlanta, GA, 30507. *Mailing Add:* 5133 Strickland Rd Gainsville GA 30507

SHEAKS, BARCLAY
PAINTER, WRITER
b East Chicago, Ind. *Study:* Va Commonwealth Univ, BFA; Col William & Mary, teaching cert; Christopher Newport Univ, Va, Hon Dr. *Work:* Va Mus Fine Arts, Richmond; Butler Inst Am Art, Youngstown, Ohio; Columbia Mus Fine Arts, SC; Mobile Mus, Ala; Chrysler Mus, Norfolk, Va; and others. *Comn:* Portrait of USS Enterprise, comn by off of ship, 65; portrait of USS John F Kennedy, City of Newport News, 69; painting series, Exec Suite, Tenneco Corp, Newport News Shipyard, 72; space paintings, NASA, Langley Res Ctr, Hampton, Va; painting depicting surface of Mars, US Bicentennial Expo on Sci & Technol, Kennedy Space Ctr, 76; and others. *Exhib:* Nat Drawing Biennial (drawing selected for Smithsonian Inst Nat Traveling Exhib), Norfolk Mus, Va, 65; Butler Inst Am Art Mid-Year Show Am Painting, 65, 66 & 67; 99 Exhibition, Am Watercolor Soc, Nat Acad Design, NY, 66; Juried Art Exhib, Corcoran Gallery Art, Washington, DC, 67; Ten Top Realists SE, Gallery Contemp Art, Winston-Salem, NC, 69-70. *Pos:* lectr, Va Mus, Richmond, 70; artist-in-residence, Richmond Humanities Ctr, 71 & Va Mus, Richmond, 78; art consult & TV host, Painting with Acrylic with Barclay Sheake, PBS-TV, 85. *Teaching:* assoc prof art & distinguished res artist, Va Wesleyan Col, 69-, prof, 69-97. *Awards:* Va Comn Arts & Humanities Top Award, 79. *Bibliog:* Russel Woody (auth), chap, In: Painting in Synthetic Media & Complete Guide to Polymer Paintings, Van Nostrand Reinhold. *Mem:* Tidewater Artists Asn. *Media:* Acrylic, Polymer. *Publ:* Auth, Painting with Acrylics from Start to Finish, 72, Drawing and Painting the Natural Environment, 74, Painting with Oils, Davis & Drawing Figures and Faces, 87; The Acrylics Book, Watson Guptill, 95. *Dealer:* Chester Smith Seaside Art Gallery P O Box 1 Nags Head NC 27959. *Mailing Add:* 51 Hopkins St Newport News VA 23601

SHEARD, WENDY STEDMAN
HISTORIAN, EDUCATOR
b New Haven, Conn, July 24, 35. *Study:* Vassar Col, BA, 57; Yale Univ, with Charles Seymour Jr, MA, 65, PhD, 71. *Exhib:* Antiquity in the Renaissance (auth, catalog), Smith Col Mus Art, 78. *Teaching:* Asst prof art hist, Mt Holyoke Col, 78-79; vis asst prof, Univ Hartford, 79-80 & Boston Univ, 83-84; vis assoc prof, Boston Univ, spring 88; vis scholar in art, Wesleyan Univ, spring 90. *Mem:* Col Art Asn; Asn Independent Art Historians. *Res:* Relationships between sculpture and painting in Renaissance Venice. *Publ:* Ed, Collaboration in Italian Renaissance Art, Yale Univ Press, 78; auth, Asa Adorna: The Prehistory of the Vendramin Tomb, Jahrbuch Berliner Mus, Vol 20, 78; auth, Giorgione and Tullio Lombardo in Giorgione, Convegno Int Studi, Castelfranco, Italy, 79. *Mailing Add:* 693 Leetes Island Rd Branford CT 06405-3364

SHEARER, LINDA
MUSEUM DIRECTOR
b Long Island, NY, Feb 13, 46. *Study:* Sarah Lawrence Col, Bronxville, NY, BA, 68. *Pos:* Solomon R Guggenheim Mus, NY, 69-80; exec dir, Artists Space, NY, 80-85; cur, Dept Painting & Sculpture, Mus Mod Art, NY, 85-89; dir, Williams Col Mus Art, 89-2004; chmn bd, Am Fedn of Arts Exhib Comm, 94-2000; comt mem, Mus Loan Network, 98; dir, Contemp Arts Ctr, Cincinnati, 2004-. *Teaching:* Instr, Sch Visual Arts, NY, 73-79 & Williams Col Mass, 91-. *Mem:* Asn Art Mus Dirs. *Mailing Add:* Contemp Arts Ctr 44 E Sixth St Cincinnati OH 45202

SHEARER, RHONDA ROLAND
SCULPTOR, WRITER
b Aurora, Ill, June 12, 54. *Study:* Central Col, Chicago, Ill; Boston Univ, 70-74. *Work:* Hallmark Corp, Kansas City, Mo; Hartz Mountain Corp, New York, NY. *Comn:* Lifesize bronze horse, Goffs Bloodstock Sales Co, Kildare, Ireland, 84. *Exhib:* One-man shows, Am Asn Advan Sci, Washington, 90, James A Michner Art Mus, Doylestown, 93, Cheekwood Mus Art, Nashville, 93, Knoxville Mus Art, 94, Gibbes Mus Art, Charleston, 94, Jacksonville Art Mus, 94 & NY Botanical Gardens, 96; Ambiguous Figures, Feingarten Gallery, Los Angeles, Calif, 90. *Bibliog:* Lawrence Gowing (auth), Still Lifes in Bronze (exhib catalog), Wildenstein Gallery, 87; Jerzy Kosinski (auth), Sculptorids of Rhonda Roland Shearer (exhib catalog), Wildenstein Gallery, 90; Arlene Raven (auth), Fracturing Frames (exhib catalog), Wildenstein Gallery, 93. *Media:* Bronze, Mixed Media. *Res:* New science of chaos; fractal geometry's potential influence in art & culture. *Publ:* Auth, National Symposium: The Role of Horticulture in Human Well-Being and Social Development, Timber, 91 & 92; From flatland to fractaland: New geometries in relationship to artistic and scientific revolutions, Fractals, Vol 3, No 3, 95; Real or Ideal? DNA iconography in a new fractal era, Col Art Asn Art J, Vol 55 No 1, spring 96; The Flatland Hypothesis: How Artistic and scientific revolutions Work, Springer-Verlag, 97; A square in Fractaland, Springer-Verlag, 97. *Dealer:* Wildenstein Gallery 19 E 64th St New York NY 10021

SHECHET, ARLENE J
ARTIST
Study: NYU, BA; BA, Skidmore Col; RI Sch Design, MFA. *Exhib:* One-man shows incl Bernard Toale Gallery, Boston, 97, John Berggruen Gallery, San Francisco, 97, Mirror Mirror, Elizabeth Harris Gallery, 99, Galerie Rene Blouin, Montreal, 2000, Flowers Found, Elizabeth Harris Gallery, 2002, Harbor Cult Ctr, 2003, Out of the Blue, Shoshana Wayne Gallery, 2004, exhibited in group shows at Water, Water, Rotunda Gallery, 2003, Vessels, Greenwich House Poetry, 2003, Mystic, Mass Col Art, 2003, Adlrich Contemp Art Mus, 2004, pub collections, Brooklyn Mus Art, Fidelity Investments, Boston, NY Pub Libr, Drawings & Prints Collection, Banff Sch Fine Arts, Can. *Pos:* Artist-in-residence Pilchuck Glass Sch. *Awards:* Fel Guggenheim Mem Found, 2004; grantee NY Found for Arts, Artist Fel, 99. *Mailing Add:* 52 White St New York NY 10013

SHECHTER, BEN-ZION
PAINTER, ILLUSTRATOR
b Tel Aviv, Israel, Aug 7, 40; US & Israel citizen. *Study:* Bezalel Sch Art, Jerusalem, BFA, 66; Sch Visual Arts, New York, 67-69. *Work:* Whitney Mus Am Art & New York Pub Libr, NY; Mus Fine Art, Boston; Brooklyn Mus; Houghton Libr, Harvard Univ, Cambridge, Mass; Univ Iowa Mus. *Exhib:* Interiors-Exteriors: Figurative Artist, Brooklyn Mus, 80; solo exhibs, Wustum Mus, Racine, Wis, 82, Capricorn Gallery Bethseda, Md, 89 & FDR Gallery, NY, 93; Ark Art Ctr, Little Rock, 86 & 92; Carnegie Inst, Pittsburgh, Pa, 88; Hunt Inst, Pittsburgh, Pa, 88; Buther Inst; Squibb Gallery, Princeton, NJ, 94; and others. *Awards:* Purchase Award, West Publ, 80. *Bibliog:* Lawrence Alloway (auth), Park Slope: The Urban Subject, Brooklyn Mus, 80; Susan Paul (auth), Interiors/Exteriors, Phoenix, Brooklyn, 80; N Scott Marraday (auth), Recent Press Book, Fine Print, 81. *Media:* Gouache; Pen & Ink, Watercolor, Silverpoint. *Publ:* Illusr, Common Ground, Bieler Press, 80. *Dealer:* Biddingtons 425 # 50th St New York 10022. *Mailing Add:* 429 4th St Brooklyn NY 11215

SHECHTER, LAURA J
PAINTER, DRAFTSMAN
b Brooklyn, NY, Aug 26, 44. *Study:* Brooklyn Col, BA, 65. *Work:* Boston Mus Fine Arts, Mass; Brooklyn Mus, NY; Indianapolis Mus Art, Ind; Albright-Knox Art Gallery; Art Inst, Chicago, Ill. *Exhib:* One-man shows, Suffolk Mus, Stony Brook, NY, 71, Wuster Mus, Wis, 82, Greenville Co Mus Art, SC, 82, Univ Richmond, Va, 91, Rahur West Mus, Wis, 91 & Perlow Gallery, NY, 94, Pucker Gallery, Boston, 96 & 99; The New Am Still Life, Westmoreland Co Mus Art, Greenburg, Pa, 79; Am Drawing in Black & White, Brooklyn Mus, NY, 80 & 81; Still Life, Albright-Knox Art Gallery, Buffalo, NY, 81; West 81/Art & the Law, Minn Mus Art, St Paul, 81; Contemp Art-Gund Collection, Boston Mus, 82; Perspectives on Contemp Realism, Pa Acad Fine Art, 82 & Art Inst Chicago, 83; Am Realism, San Francisco Mus, 85;

Metal Point etc, Ark Art Ctr, 92; Loring Gallery, Sheffield, Mass, 02. *Teaching:* Instr, Parson Col, 84 & Nat Acad Fine Art Sch, New York, 85-88, 94-98, 02. *Awards:* Creative Artists Pub Serv Prog Grant, 81-82. *Bibliog:* Ralph Poweroy (auth), Laura Shechter, Arts Mag, 81; Eric Widing (auth), Laura Shechter, Am Artist, 83; Romen Cohen (auth), Laura Shechter (mus catalog, Wis & Va), 91. *Mem:* Artists Equity; Nat Acad Art, NY; Nat Acad (acad, 95-). *Media:* Oil, Watercolor; Pencil, Silverpoint. *Dealer:* Loring Gallery Sheffield MA; MA Doran Gallery 35-09 S Peoria Av Tulsa OK 74805. *Mailing Add:* 429 4th St Brooklyn NY 11215

SHECHTMAN, GEORGE HENOCH
DEALER
b Paterson, NJ, Dec 8, 41. *Study:* Rutgers Univ, BA(art hist), 64. *Pos:* Dir, Gallery Henoch, NY, currently. *Specialty:* Contemporary American paintings. *Dealer:* Gallery Henoch 555 W 25th St New York NY 10001

SHEDOSKY, SUZANNE
PAINTER
b Joliet, Ill, Sept 11, 55. *Study:* Brookwood Gallery/Merfeld Atelier with Gerald Merfeld, 76-92. *Work:* Ore Ill Pub Libr; Loveland Comm House, Dixon, Ill. *Exhib:* Allied Artists Am, NY, 84, 87, 88, 91 & 92; Am Artists Prof League, NY, 86; Midwest Pastel Soc, Chicago, Ill, 86 & 87; Catharine Lorillard Wolfe Art Club, NY, 86; Nat Small Oil Painting Exhib, Wichita Art Asn, 88; Oil Painters Am Nat, Chicago, Ill, 93, Regional Exhib, 93 & 94; My Favorite Place, Pueblo, Colo, 93; Happy Canyon Western Art Invitational, Pendleton, Ore, 97; Ann Art Sangres Invitational Exhib & Sale, Westcliffe, Colo, 97 & 98. *Pos:* Studio asst, Brookwood Gallery/Merfeld Atelier, 83-92. *Teaching:* Brookwood Gallery, 89-91; Sauk Valley Cmty Col. *Awards:* Ann & Richard Sauter Award for Pastel, Allied Artists Am, 84; Ella Shaw Mem Best of Show Award & Lucille Warner Award, Phidian Art Club, Dixon, Ill, 88 & 91; Best of Show, Oil Painters Am, 92; Silver Medal Honor, Allied Artists Am, New York, 92. *Bibliog:* Betty Harvey (auth), Suzanne Shedosky, Western Horseman Mag, 6/96. *Media:* All Media. *Publ:* The Best of Oil Painting & Flora Inspiriations, Rockport Publ. *Dealer:* Thum'prints Art Gallery Hilton Head Island SC; Brookwood Gallery Merfeld Atelier 2302 Muddy Rd Westcliffe CO 81252. *Mailing Add:* 1120 Hamilton Rd Rock Falls IL 61071

SHEEHAN, DIANE
CRAFTSMAN
b Elizabeth, NJ, Dec 22, 45. *Study:* Montclair State Col, BA, 68; Indiana Univ, MFA, 72. *Work:* Greater Lafayette Mus Art, Wis; Ctr Visual Arts, Ill State Univ; West Lafayette Mus Art, Ind; Univ Ore, Eugene; Elvehjen Mus, Madison, Wis. *Exhib:* Mano Galleries, Chicago, Ill, 76; Vatican Mus, Rome, Italy, 78; Univ Hawaii, Manoa, Hawaii, 81; Brainerd Art Gallery, State Univ Col Arts & Science, Potsdam, NY, 84; Indianapolis Mus Art, Ind, 85; Univ Art Mus, Univ Wis-Milwaukee, Wis, 86. *Teaching:* From asst prof to assoc prof, Purdue Univ, 72-85; prof, Univ Wis, Madison, currently. *Awards:* Lilly Endowment Fel, 80; Nat Endowment Arts Fel, 87 & 92; Grad Sch Grant, Univ Wis, 99. *Mailing Add:* 3452 Crestwood Dr Madison WI 53705

SHEEHAN, EVELYN
PAINTER
b Hymera, Ind, Dec 27, 19. *Study:* Scripps Col, with Jean Ames; also study with Phil Dike & Rex Brandt. *Work:* Lytton Collection, Los Angeles; Calif Bank, San Francisco; Mus Art, Univ Ore, Eugene; Tacoma Bank, Wash. *Exhib:* Spokane Ann Art Exhib, Cheney-Cowles Mus Art, Wash, 69; Watercolor USA, Springfield Art Mus, Mo, 70; 32nd Ann Northwest Exhib, Seattle Art Mus, Wash, 71; Dimensional Construction Exhib, Portland Contemp Craft Gallery, 77; Exhib of Paintings, Governor's Ceremonial Chambers, Salem, 77; one-man show, Mus Art, Univ Ore, Eugene, 71. *Awards:* Lytton Purchase Award, Watercolor USA, 67; Mo Award, 32nd Ann Nat Watercolor Soc, 71; Cash Award, 62nd Ann Nat Watercolor Soc, 82. *Mem:* Nat Soc Painters in Casein; Nat Watercolor Soc; Portland Art Asn. *Media:* Water Media, Collage. *Mailing Add:* 3935 SW Corbett Ave Portland OR 97201

SHEEHAN, MAURA A
SCULPTOR, PAINTER
b New York, NY, Dec 2, 1954. *Study:* Art Students League, 68-72; Carnegie-Mellon Univ, Pittsburgh, Pa, 72-74; San Francisco Art Inst, Calif, BFA, 74-76. *Work:* Art in Public Spaces, Hamden, Conn; The Weatherspoon, Univ NC, Greensboro. *Comn:* De Appel Foundation, Amsterdam, Hollan, 84; Urban Sited Sculpture, Comn The Seattle Arts Comn, 84; Art in Public Places, Hamden Plaza, Conn, 88 & Cermak Plaza, Chicago, 90; Percent for the Arts, Ceramic-Tile Frieze, W Queens High Sch, 93-95; The Bank, Lower Manhattan Cult Coun, 97; glass mural for Henry Feiwel, 2000. *Exhib:* Solo exhibs, Big Girls Don't Cry, Staller Art Ctr, State Univ NY, Stonybrook, 94, Pinkitude, Helen MZ Ceveran Gallery, NY, 94, The Half-Pipe, Art at the Anchorage, NY, 95, The Kitchen, Lausanne Biennale, Switz, 95, Open Mike at the Voice Box, State Univ NY Gallery, Plattsburgh, 96, Ocean Floor, Cristinerose Gallery, NY, 96 & Aerial Idea, Helsinki Mus, Finland, Art Gallery Ont, Toronto, Can & Old Yacht Club, Cobh, Cork, Ireland, 97; The Bearded Lady, Kunsthalle, Dusseldorf, Ger; Elapsed Time, Grey Gallery, NY Univ, 87; Orchard Gallery, Derry, Northern Ireland, 89; Insulation, Bruno Facchetti Gallery, NY, 90; Parcours-Prives, Paris, France, 10/90; Casino Fantasimo, Venice, Italy, 6/90; The New Metaphysical Art, Amy Lipton Gallery, NY, 9/90; Helen M Z Cevern Gallery, NY, 93; Percent for the Arts, Munic Art Soc, NY, 94; Queer Space, Storefront for Art & Archit, NY, 94; Strangers in the Arctic, Ultima Thule and the Modernity, The Rundetarn, Copenhagen, Denmark & the Porin Taidemuseo, Pori, Finland, 96; Scratch, Threadwaxing Space, NY, 96; Model Home, Clocktower, NY, 96; People in Glass Houses, Urban Glass, Brooklyn, NY, 96; Uncommon Sense, Mus Contemp Art, Los Angeles, 97; Boom, Art Fest, Cork, Ireland, 97; Art Walk, Benefit Auction, Puck Bldg, 97; Summer Reading, Printed Matter, 97; In the Name of the Place, Grand Arts, Kansas City, 98; Disappearing Act, Bound Unbound Gallery, NY, 98; Glass House, Nueberger Mus, State Univ NY, Purchase, 98; Vision Festival, Orensanz Found, NY, 98; Limerick Gallery Art, Ireland, 99; Veladura, Centro Anduluz De Arte Contemporaneo, Sevilla, Spain, 2000; Architectural Accupuncture, Urban Glass, Brooklyn, NY, 2000; and others. *Teaching:* Assoc prof art, Sch Visual Arts, New York, 88-. *Awards:* Painting Award, Nat Endowment Arts, 87; Sculptor Award, New York State Arts Grant, 91. *Bibliog:* Kin Levin (auth), Art Pick, Village Voice, 6/15/96; Linda Yablonsky (auth), rev & picture, Time Out, 6/26/96; Holland Cotter (auth), rev, NY Times, 5/98; Judy Collischan (auth), Glass Mag, 99. *Media:* Installation, Multimedia. *Dealer:* Helen M Z Cevern New York NY

SHEIKH, FAZAL
PHOTOGRAPHER
b New York, NY, 65. *Study:* Princeton Univ, BA, 87. *Work:* San Francisco Mus Mod Art, Calif; Sprengel Mus, Hanover, Ger; Art Inst Chicago; Int Ctr of Photog, NY; Philadelphia Mus Art, Pa; Metrop Mus Art, NY; Los Angeles Co Mus of Art; Mus of Fine Arts, Houston; and several others. *Exhib:* Syracuse Univ (auth, catalog), 93; Other Africans: Photographs by Max Belcher, Fazal Sheikh, and Vera Vidits Ward, Photog Resource Ctr, Boston, 94; Rhode Island Sch Design, Providence, 96; A Sense of Common Ground, Int Ctr Photog, NY, 96 & Nederlands Foto Institut, Rotterdam, The Neth, 97; Diggs Gallery, Winston-Salem State Univ, NC, 97; Houston Ctr Photog, Tex, 97; Sprengel Mus (auth, catalog), Hanover, Ger, 98; Fotomuseum, Winterthur, Switz, 99; solo exhib Art Inst of Chicago, 2000; Smithsonian Inst, 2000; Am Univ of Beirut, Lebanon, 2000; Northwestern Univ, Chicago, 2000; The Corcoran Gallery of Art, Washington (traveling), 01-04; and others. *Awards:* Fulbright Fel Arts, Kenya, 92; Photog Fel, Nat Endowment Arts, 94; Infinity Award, Int Ctr Photog, 95; Mother Jones Int Documentary Award, 95; Leica Medal of Excellence, 95; Mondriaan Found & Netherlands Fofo Inst Award, 99; and others. *Bibliog:* The Nature of Photography, Johns Hopkins Univ Press, Nat Pub Radio-Fresh Air, 3/96; Witness in our Time: Social and Documentary Photography, Smithsonian Inst Press, 98; Face Forward: Young African American Men in a Critical Age, Chronicle Books, 98; Vince Aletti (auth), Out of the past, The Village Voice, 12/29/98; Beyond Cliched Interpretations of Exile, Suffering & Death, The NY Times, 1/1/99. *Publ:* Auth, Herkunft, Winterthur Mus, Switz, 96; The Garden of Eden, Asn Aurora Borealis, Holland, 97; Linguna France, Encontras de Fotografia, Portugal, 97; The Victor Weeps, Afghanistan, Scalo, Zurich, Berlin, New York, 98; Innovation/Imagination: 50 Years of Polaroid Photography, Abrams/The Friends of Photography, 99; Documents: Artifacts of Modern Knowledge, Duke Univ Press, 01; In Response to Place, The Nature Conservancy's Last Great Places, Chronicle Books, 01; and others. *Mailing Add:* c/o Pace MacGill 32 E 57th St New York NY 10022

SHEIRR, OLGA (KROLIK)
PAINTER, PHOTOGRAPHER
b New York, NY, June 7, 31. *Study:* Art Students League, with Reginald Marsh, 48-50; Brooklyn Col, with Rothko, Reinhardt & Still, BA, 53; New York Inst Fine Arts, 54; Pratt Graphics Ctr, with Michael Ponce de Leon, 65-70; Art Students League, with Michael Ponce de Leon, 70-72. *Work:* Springfield Art Mus, Mo; Southeast Mo State Univ, Cape Girardeau, Mo; Greenville Co Mus, SC; Nat Mus Women Arts, Wash; Bank of Tokyo, NY; NY Artists Equity, Art Bank, NY; Mus City New York; St Vincent's Hospital, NY. *Comn:* Serigraph eds, Art Resources and Treasures, NY, 79 & Summit Fine Arts, NY, 79. *Exhib:* one-person shows, Noho Gallery, 75-92, New Sch Social Res, NY, 84, Barbizon Gallery, Greenwich, Conn, 84, Farleigh Dickinson Univ, 85 & 91, Kendall Gallery, NY 86, Passaic Co Community Col, Paterson, NJ, 90 & San Giorio Island, Venice, Italy, 94, Gallery Juno, NY, 96, 98 & 2002, The Jewish Ctr of the Hamptons, NY, 96, Paul Edward Gingras Gallery, Southampton, NY, 2001; Sharjah Art Mus, United Arab Emerates, 2000 & 2005; Pliedes Gallery, NY, 2003-2004 & 2006; Open Studio, WIHS Art Deco Bldg, Long Island City, NY, 2003-05; The Carriage Barn Art Ctr, Conn, 2005; Open Studios 2005, Wills Art Deco Bldg, Long Island City, NY, 2005; Art Students Open League, NY, 2006; Springs Improvement Soc, East Hampton, NY, 2006. *Collection Arranged:* Noho Gallery Invitational Exhib, 76 & Madness on Mercer, 86, NY; Twenty Three Artists at Ten Studios (auth, catalog), NY, 77; Six at the Arsenal (auth, catalog), NY, 78. *Pos:* Instr, art workshop, Fla Gulf Coast Art Ctr, Belleair, 87; Education Alliance, NY, 89; watercolor workshop, Barkly Art Ctr, Custer, SDak, 90; lectr, Rutgers Univ, New Brunswick, NJ, 90, Art Student's League, 93, NY Artists Equity, 95, Synagogue for the Arts, 96. *Awards:* First Prize Drawing, Md Fedn Art, 93; Patrons Purchase Award, Springfield Mus Art, 97; Best work on Paper, Guild Hall, 2004; Windsor Newton Watercolor Award, Silvermine Guild Arts Ctr, New Canann, Conn, 2005. *Bibliog:* Stephen DeLauro (auth), Am Artist Mag, 84; Sheriden Sansegundo (auth), article, East Hampton Star, 7/11/93; Mark Pilipski (auth), The Healing Art, Channel 26, 93; Ed McCormack (auth), article, Artspeak, 12/95; Ed McCormack (auth), article, Gallery & Studies, 4-5/2002. *Mem:* Women in Arts; NY Soc Women Artists; NY Artists Equity; EHampton Artist's Alliances; Southampton Artists Asn; Nat Arts Club. *Media:* Watercolor, Oil. *Dealer:* Aldona M Gobuzas 215 E 79th St 7D NY NY 10021. *Mailing Add:* 360 First Ave Apt 11G New York NY 10010

SHELLER, G A
PAINTER, INSTRUCTOR
b Altoona, Pa, June 20, 36. *Study:* Col New Rochelle, BFA, 58; Pa State Univ, 59; Visual Studies Workshop, Yale Univ, with Robert Reed, 81-83. *Work:* Xerox Corp, Stamford, Conn; IBM Corp, Armonk, NY; Chase Manhattan Bank, Eastman Kodak Co, PriceWaterhouse, Rochester, NY. *Comn:* Dyptich acrylic painting, Annandale, Va, 78; gum bichromate painting, Tokyo, Japan, 89; gum bichromate painting, Austin, Tex, 89; gum bichromate painting, Atlanta, Ga, 92; gum bichromate paintings, Rochester, NY, 94, 95, 96, 2002-2003. *Exhib:* Solo exhib, Arnot Art Mus, Elmira, NY,

83, Gum Bichromate Paintings, Nazareth Col, Rochester, NY, 94, 95, 96, 2000, others; Nat Exhib, Virginia Beach, Va, 88, 99; Under the Oaks Exhib, Ctr for Arts, Vero Beach, Fla, 90; Skaneateles Art Expo, Skaneateles, NY, 91; Ann Exhib, Mem Art Gallery, Rochester, NY, 93, 94, 95 & 96, 97, 98, 99, 2000, 2002-2004; Hilton Head Art League Ann, 94 & 95; Fac Exhib, mem Art Gallery, Univ Rochester, 97, 98, 99, 2000-2004; Insights Exhib, Bausch & Lomb Gallery, 2006; plus others. *Collection Arranged:* Memorial Art Gallery, Univ of Rochester, NY. *Pos:* artist-in-residence Irondequoit Schs, Rochester, NY, 2000; bd dir, Rochester Art Club, Rochester, NY, 2004-2006. *Teaching:* Instr adult drawing/painting, Studio Sch, Mem Art Gallery, 83-2006; instr painting, Inniemore Sch Art, Mull, Scotland, 92, Burren Painting Ctr, Co Clare, Ireland, 92-94 & 97, Province Workshop, France, 97 & 2000, Greek Island Workshop, 97, Santa Fe Workshop, 98 & Dingle, Ireland Workshops, 2000, 2003 & 2006; guest lectr Univ Rochester, NY, 99, Univ Galway, Ireland, 97, Memorial Art Gallery, Rochester, NY, 2000, Savannah, Ga, 2003, Blufftonm SC, 2005. *Awards:* Finalist, NY State Artisans Award, Southern Tier Arts Asn, 82; Merit, Ann Exhib, Mem Art Gallery, 93; Merit Award, Rochester Art Club, 96; Named one of 2000 Outstanding Artists of 20th Century, Internat Biograph Ctr, Cambridge, Eng; Merit Award, Sonnenberg, NY Nat exhib, 2004; 2nd place painting, NY State, 2005. *Bibliog:* Nancy Wellard (auth), Art League Show charms, Island Packet, 3/6/92; M Stephen Doherty (auth), Adding pattern and texture with light-sensitive materials, Watercolor, 2/97; Stuart Lowe (auth) Mixing Media - g.a. Sheller, Gannett Press, 4/13/97. *Mem:* Rochester Art Club, NY (prog chairperson, 78-85, 2004-2005); Pittsford Art Club, NY (vpres, 70 & libr liaison, 82-); advanced merit mem Atlanta Artists Club, Ga; Hilton Head Art League, SC; Print Club Rochester NY. *Media:* Gum Bichromate, Watercolor, Acrylic. *Mailing Add:* 106 Overbrook Rd Rochester NY 14618

SHELTON, PETER T
SCULPTOR

b Troy, Ohio, Jan 18, 51. *Study:* Pomona Col, BA(fine arts), 73; Hobart Sch Welding Technol, cert, 74; Univ Calif, Los Angeles, MFA, 79. *Work:* State Wash; Artpark, Lewiston, NY. *Comn:* Artpark, Lewistown, NY; Exposition Park, Los Angeles. *Exhib:* Solo exhibs, Chapman Col, Orange, Calif, 80 & Malinda Wyatt Gallery, Los Angeles, 81; Los Angeles Co Mus Art, 81; Open Space Gallery, Victoria, Can, 82; Artists Space, NY, 82; Mus D'Art Mod, Paris, 82; Ctr Contemp Art, Seattle, 83; Portland Ctr Visual Arts, 84; and others. *Teaching:* Lectr sculpture, Otis/Parsons Sch Art & Design, 80-; lectr sculpture, Claremont Grad Sch, 81-. *Awards:* Purchase Award, State Wash, 77; Fel, Nat Endowment Arts, 80. *Bibliog:* Christopher Knight (auth), Your Place or Shelton's, Los Angeles Herald Examiner, 81; Merle Schipper (auth), Peter Shelton's Places and Spaces, Images & Issues, 81; Melinda Wortz (auth), Peter Shelton at the Santa Barbara Contemporary Arts Forum, Artnews, 83. *Media:* Multi-Media. *Publ:* Contribr, Neckwall, Footscreen, Sleeper, Dreamworks, Human Sci Press, 82. *Dealer:* LA Louver 45 N Venice Blvd Venice California 90291. *Mailing Add:* c/o LA Louver Gallery 45 N Venice Blvd Venice CA 90291

SHELTON, ROBERT LEE
DESIGNER, EDUCATOR

b Memphis, Tenn, Apr 8, 39. *Study:* Memphis State Univ, BFA; Univ Ala, MA. *Work:* South Central Bell, Regional Off, Birmingham, Ala; First Nat Bank, Montgomery, Ala; Ambassadors Off, Fed Repub Ger. *Exhib:* Nat Small Painting Biennial, Purdue Univ, 66; Nat Black & White Prints, Kans State Univ, 66; Mid-South Ann, Memphis, Tenn, 69; Hunter Gallery Ann, Chattanooga, Tenn, 69; Graphics USA, Dubuque, Iowa, 70. *Teaching:* Asst prof drawing & design, Auburn Univ, Ala, 64-68; prof printmaking & design, Birmingham-Southern Col, Ala, 68-. *Awards:* First Prize, Macon Mus, 68; First Purchase Award, Columbus Mus Art, 69 & 72; First Purchase Award, Montgomery Mus Art, 70. *Bibliog:* Martin Hames (auth), Robert Shelton, 1975 Birmingham Festival of Arts Bull, 3/75. *Mem:* Birmingham Art Asn (bd mem, 74-75, pres, 81-); Tenn Valley Art Asn. *Media:* Crayon, Oil. *Publ:* Auth, Contemporary printmaking in the US, Birmingham Festival Bulletin, 73. *Dealer:* Courtyard Gallery 2800 Sixth Ave S Birmingham AL 35208. *Mailing Add:* Ten Fifth St Birmingham AL 35217

SHEMDIN, AZHAR H
PAINTER, INSTRUCTOR

b Can citizen. *Study:* Al-Hikma Univ Baghdad, BSc, 68; Am Univ Beirut, MA, 74; Univ Toronto, BEd, 77. *Work:* Oakville Munic Bldg, Ont; Westwood Sanitarium, Toronto. *Exhib:* Ann Juried Art Exhib, Mississauga City Hall, Ont, 87; Peace at Home - TV Wars, Oakville Munic Bldg, 91; Every War Brings Its Peace, Oakville Art Soc, Ont, 92; 32nd Toronto Outdoor Art Exhib, Toronto City Hall, 93; A Celebration of the Shemdin Women, Oakville Munic Bldg, 97. *Teaching:* Instr painting, Humber Col, Toronto, formerly; instr visual arts, Halton Bd Educ, Ont, 89-96; instr art hist, color theory & painting, Sheridan Col, Oakville, Ont, 97-2000. *Bibliog:* Dennis Smith (auth), World Art Tour, The Burlington Past, 10/24/99; Carol Baldwin (auth), Millennium Art Show, The Oakville Beaver, 12/10/99; Patricia Frazier (auth), Local Bronte Artist to Display Work at the Millennium Art Show, The Bronte Villager, vol 2, no 1, spring 2000. *Mem:* Oakville Art Coun; Burlington Fine Arts Asn. *Media:* Acrylic on canvas. *Dealer:* Anastasia Gallery Oakville Ont Canada. *Mailing Add:* 2316 Millward Ave Oakville ON L6L 1W4 Canada

SHEMESH, LORRAINE R
PAINTER

b Jersey City, NJ. *Study:* Boston Univ, BFA(magna cum laude), 71; Tyler Sch Art, Rome, 71-72; Tyler Sch Art, MFA(painting fel), 73. *Work:* Butler Inst Am Art, Youngstown, OH; DeCordova Mus, Lincoln, Mass; Mus RI Sch Design, Providence; Am Tel & Tel, Chicago; Mus City of New York; Boise Art Mus, Idaho; Novartis Corp, Basel, Switzerland; Morgan Stanley, NYC. *Exhib:* solo shows, Rhode Island Sch Design, 76, Alpha Gallery, Boston, 78, Allan Stone Gallery, NY, 83, 85, 88, 91, 95 & 2000; Am Realism: 20th Century Drawings, San Francisco Mus Mod Art, 85-86; Duke Univ, Mus Art, Durham, NC, 87; Akron Art Mus, Ohio, 87; Am Broadcasting Corp, NY, 90; Sotheby's, NY, 93; Musee de Carouge (Switz), 99; Tryon Ctr Visual Art, Charlotte, NC, 99; Frye Art Mus, Seattle, 2002; Invitational, Nat Acad Design, 2002; Nat Acad Design Mus, 2002 & 2006; Allan Stone Gallery, NY, 2004; Butler Inst Am Art, Youngstown, OH, 2006. *Teaching:* Asst prof fine arts, RI Sch Design, 73-80 & Amherst Col, 80-81; vis artist, Marie Walsh Sharpe Art Foundation, 2002. *Awards:* RI State Coun Arts Grant, 79; Distinguished Alumni Award, Sch Visual Arts, Boston Univ, 92; Painting finalist, Nat Endowment Arts/Regional Fels, 96; Yaddo Fel, 81. *Bibliog:* NY Times, 8/95, 5/2000, 4/2004; The New Yorker, 5/95, 5/2000; Art in America, 9/88, 12/95, 12/2000. *Mem:* Nat Acad (acad, 04-). *Media:* Oil. *Publ:* American Realism-20th C Drawings and Watercolors, Harry N Abrams, 86; auth, A Guide to Drawing-m Fourth Ed, Holt, Rinehart & Winston, 88; auth, A Decade of American Figure Drawing, Frye Art Mus, 2002; auth, Drawing Space Form & Expression, Prentice Hall, 2003; auth, Re-Presenting Representation, Arnot Art Mus, 95; Breaking the Surface-Lorraine Shemesh at the Butler Institute of American Art, 2006. *Dealer:* Allan Stone Gallery 113 E 90th St New York NY 10128. *Mailing Add:* 22 W 30th St # 4-5 New York NY 10001

SHEON, AARON
HISTORIAN, ADMINISTRATOR

b Toledo, Ohio, Oct 7, 37. *Study:* Univ Mich, AB, MA, 60; Inst d'Art et d'Archeolgie, Paris, 62; Princeton Univ, MFA, PhD, 66. *Teaching:* Assoc prof, Univ Pittsburgh, Pa, 66-78, prof, 78-; vis mem, Inst Advan Study, Princeton, 84-85. *Awards:* Bowman Fac Award, Univ Pittsburgh, 76; Hon Award, Pa Soc Architects, 82; Gould Found Fel, 86. *Mem:* Col Art Asn; Soc Fr Art Hist. *Res:* French 19th and 20th century art history; art and scientific thought; educational role of the museum. *Publ:* Auth, Monticelli, His Contemporaries, His Influence, 79; Organic Vision: The Architecture of Peter Berndston, 80; Octave Tassaert's Le Suicide, Arts, 81; Courbet, French realism and discovery of unconscious, Arts, 81; 1913: Forgotten cubist exhibitions in America, Arts, 83; Monticelli Centennial Exhib, Marseille, 86; Paul Guigou, 87. *Mailing Add:* Dept of History Art & Architecture Univ Pittsburgh Pittsburgh PA 15260

SHEPARD, LEWIS ALBERT
DEALER, HISTORIAN

b East Orange, NJ, May 24, 45. *Study:* Rutgers Univ, New Brunswick, BA, 67; Ind Univ, Bloomington, MA, 70. *Collection Arranged:* Cowboys, Indians, Trappers & Traders (with catalog), Mead Art Gallery, Amherst Col, 73 & Am Painters of the Arctic (with catalog), 75. *Pos:* Trainee catalog & dept head, Sotheby Parke Bernet, New York, 70-72; cur, Mead Art Gallery, Amherst Col, 72-77; proprietor, dealer & appraiser, pvt pract, Worcester, Mass, 77-; coord appraisers study program, RI Sch Design, 2001-2006. *Teaching:* Asst instr mod art, Ind Univ, Bloomington, 69-70; instr Am art, Amherst Col, 73-76, Clark Univ, 80 & 84, Worcester State Col, 95- & Bentley Col, 2002-2004. *Mem:* Worcester Heritage Preserv Soc (bd dir, 79-84); Appraisers Registry 80-92; Appraisers Asn of Am (mem, 2004-). *Res:* American 19th and 20th century painting; Western Americana; Arctic exploration; arts and crafts movement. *Specialty:* American and European 19th and 20th century art. *Collection:* American drawings 1830-1930. *Publ:* Auth, Willard Metcalf Exhibition--a Review, Am Art Rev, 77; American Art at Amherst Collage--a Summary Catalogue, Amherst Col, 78; The Diary of Anne Frank, Pennyroyal Press, 85. *Mailing Add:* 2 Rollingwood Dr Worcester MA 01609

SHEPARD, STEVEN L
PAINTER

b Port Arthur, Tex, Mar 23, 55. *Study:* Univ S Ala, BFA, 77. *Work:* Miss Mus Art, Jackson; Mobile Mus Art, Ala. *Comn:* J L Scott Marine Educ Ctr, Biloxi, Miss; George Ohr Mus, Biloxi, Miss. *Exhib:* Urgent Messages, Chicago Pub Libr, 87; Contemp Drawing Invitational, Wake Forest Univ, Winston-Salem, NC, 88; Exchange D'Experiences Culturelles Entre Le Burkina Faso et Les Estats-Unis, Poboye Konate et Steve Shepard, Am Cult Ctr, Ouagadougou, Burkina Faso, W Africa, 88; The Original Art, Mus Soc Bk Illustrs, NY, 91; 1996 Southern Arts Fedn/Nat Endowment Arts Regional Visual Arts Fels Painting, Drawing & Works on Paper, Southeastern Ctr Contemp Art, Winston Salem, NC, 97; Miss Mus of Art Invitational, 99; La State Univ Works on Paper Exhib, 2001; one-person exhib, Univ S Ala, 02; one-person exhib, Montogmery Mus of Art, 03. *Awards:* Nat Endowment Arts/Southern Arts Fedn Visual Arts Fel, 96-97; Miss Arts Commission Grant, 97; W T Neal Residency Grant, Blountstown, Fla, 97. *Bibliog:* C E Licka (auth), Steve Shepard: works on paper (catalog), Southeastern Mass, Univ, 90; Joe Adams (auth), The Missssissippi imagists: Steve Shepard and David Thomas Roberts, Raw Vision, winter 94-95; Tom Patterson (auth), Several works stand out, Winston-Salem J, 97. *Mem:* Nat Asn Independent Artists. *Media:* Mixed Media. *Publ:* Auth & illustr, Elvis Hornbill: International Business Bird, Henry Holt, 91. *Dealer:* America Oh Yes Gallery PO Box 3078 Hilton Head Island SC 29928. *Mailing Add:* PO Box 1295 Gautier MS 39553

SHEPHERD, HELEN PARSONS
PAINTER

b St John's, Nfld, Jan 16, 23. *Study:* Mem Univ Nfld, LLD, 41-42; Ontario Col Art, hons grad, 48. *Work:* Mem Univ Gallery, St John's Nfld, Can; Beaverbrook Gallery, Fredericton, New Brunswick, Can; Gov General Shreyer's Portrait, Readeau Hall, Ottawa, Ont, Can; Reader's Digest Coll, Can; Coll Northern Telecom, Can Ltd. *Comn:* Portraits, mayors, St John's, 73; portrait, Lord Taylor of Harlow, Mem Univ, 73; portrait, Prince Philip, Government House, St John's, Royal Canadian Legion, 76. *Exhib:* Maritime Art exhib, Beaverbrook Gallery, 64; Expo 67, Montreal; Montreal Mus Fine Arts Exhib, 68; Solo exhib, Mem Univ, Nfld, 75, Erindale Col, Toronto, 75, The Gallery-Mauskoph, St John's, Nfld, 85; Mem Univ Gallery 25th Ann Exhib, St

John's, 86; Helen Parsons Shepherd & Reginald Shepherd - Four Decades, Mem Univ Gallery, 89. *Pos:* Co-founder & teacher, Nfld Acad Art, 49-61. *Teaching:* Instr drawing & painting, Nfld Acad Art, 49-61. *Awards:* Royal Can Acad Arts; Mem Univ, Nfld, LLD. *Bibliog:* Rex Murphy (dir), Here & Now (film), Can Broadcasting Corp TV, 76; Neil Murray (auth), Profile, Nfld Herald, 79; Helen Parsons Shepherd & Reginald Shepherd, Four Decades, Peter Gard (art critic). *Mem:* Royal Can Acad Arts; St Michael's Print Shop. *Media:* Oil, Graphic Drawing. *Mailing Add:* 26 Oxen Pond Rd Saint John's NL A1B 3J3 Canada

SHEPHERD, REGINALD
PAINTER, PRINTMAKER
b Portugal Cove, Nfld, Can, Mar 28, 24. *Study:* Ont Col Art, Toronto, AOCA, 49; Mem Univ, Nfld, LLD, 88. *Work:* Mem Univ Gallery, St John's, Nfld, Can; Univ Ore, Corvallis; Art Gallery London, Ont; Dalhousie Art Gallery, Halifax, NS; Mt Allison Univ Gallery, Sackville, NB. *Comn:* Reredos, St Patricks Roman Cath Church, St John's, Nfld, 62; 12 watercolors, City of St John's, Nfld, 73; oil mural in Atlantic Pl, Crosbie & Co, St John's, Nfld, 75; Canada Postage Stamp Commemorating Canada's 125th Year of Confederation. *Exhib:* First Biennial Exhib, Nat Gallery Can, Ottawa, 55; Survey 64, Montreal Mus; solo exhibs, Mem Univ Gallery, St John's, Nfld, 72, Canada House Gallery, London, Eng, 83, Univ Leeds Gallery, Eng, 83 & Piazza Cardelli, Rome, Italy, 83-84; Traveling Print Exhib, Univ Ore, Corvallis, 76; Exhib Helen Parsons Shepherd & Reginald Shepherd, Four Decades, Memorial Univ, 89c. *Teaching:* dir & instr drawing & painting, Nfld Acad Art, 49-61; vis lectr art educ, Mem Univ, St John's, 51-61; specialist fine arts, Prince Wales Col, 62-80. *Awards:* Can Govt Fel for study in Holland, Royal Soc Can, 56-57. *Bibliog:* Rex Murphy (dir), Here & Now (film), Can Broadcasting Corp TV, 76; Neil Murray (auth), Profile, Nfld Herald, 79; Colleen Lynch (auth), Watercolours Reflect Human Values, Nfld Daily News, 1/84; Peter Gard (art critic), Helen Parsons Shepherd-Reginald Shepherd, Four Decades; James Wade (art critic), Evening Telegram, St John's, Nfld. *Mem:* Royal Can Acad Arts (provincial vpres, 78-83); fel Int Inst Arts & Lett. *Media:* Watercolor, Serigraphy. *Dealer:* The Topsail Art Gallery Topsail NF Canada; Contemporary Fine Art Services 411 Richmond St E Suite 103 Toronto ON M5A 355 Canada. *Mailing Add:* 26 Oxen Pond Rd Saint John's NL A1B 3J3 Canada

SHEPHERD, WILLIAM FRITZ
PAINTER
b Casper, Wyo, April 1, 43. *Study:* Univ Wyo, BA, MFA, 72. *Work:* Amoco Oil Co, Houston; Univ Wyo Art Mus, Laramie; IT&T, Basking Ridge, NJ; NMex Fine Arts Mus, Santa Fe; pvt collection of Mrs Joseph Hirshhorn, Washington, DC. *Exhib:* New Works New Mexico, Blaffer Gallery, Univ Houston, 81; Rosalind Constable Selects, Sweeney Ctr, Santa Fe, 81; Best of Decade, Hills Gallery, Santa Fe, 81; one-person show, Amarillo Art Ctr, Tex, 86; Boundless Realism, Rockwell Mus, Corning, NY, 87; The Face of the Land, Southern Alleghenies Mus Art, Loretto, Pa, 88; The Art Collection of Abassador and Mrs Keith Campham Brown, Am Embassy Residence, Copenhagen, Denmark, 90-92; Events About a Rectangle, Cedar Rapids Mus Art, Iowa, 91; Events About a Rectangle, Eiteljorg Mus, Indianapolis, Ind, 91. *Awards:* Spec Jurors Prize, Washington & Jefferson Col, 74. *Bibliog:* Harold Olejarz (auth), article, Arts Mag, 1/79; William Peterson (auth), Smoke Rings, Shinto Shrines, Doktor Thrill and the Snake Lady, Art News, 12/80; Carol Everingham (auth), Bi-lateral--bi-literal rocks, spring 83, Town & Country, 7/84 & Art & Antiques, 4/86, Artspace. *Media:* Oil on Canvas. *Mailing Add:* 1519 Canyon Rd Santa Fe NM 87501-6135

SHEPP, ALAN
GRAPHIC ARTIST, DIGITAL PHOTOGRAPHER
b Cleveland, Ohio, Nov 11, 35. *Study:* Bowling Green State Univ, BA, 57; Cleveland Inst Art, BFA, 58; Univ Wash, Seattle, MFA, 63. *Work:* Seattle Art Mus, Wash; Walker Art Ctr, Minneapolis, Minn; Univ Wis, Menomie; Cleveland Mus Art; Univ Notre Dame, Idaho. *Comn:* Marble relief, Mill Valley City Hall, Calif, 82; slate relief, Bank Am, San Francisco, 83; Pan Pac Singapore Hotel, Singapore, 86; IBM, Alameda, Calif, 86; Hewlett Packard, Mountain View, Calif, 86. *Exhib:* Seattle Art Mus, 63; one-man shows, Calif State Univ, Hayward, 74, AND/OR Gallery, Seattle, 75, 80 Langton St Gallery, San Francisco, 75, Univ Waterloo, Ontario, 77, Neill Gallery, NY, 78-79, Steven Wirtz Gallery, San Francisco, 82, 85, 90, 92 & 96 & Monterey Peninsula Mus Art, 91; Aesthetics of Graffiti, San Francisco Mus Mod Art, 78; Wax & Lead, Steven Wirtz Gallery, San Francisco, 90; Uncommon Objects, Richmond Art Ctr, Calif, 90; traveling show, West Art and the Law (with catalog), San Francisco, Raleigh & Tacoma, 92; Images in Bronze, China Basin Build Gallery, San Francisco; California Eclectic, TransAm Pyramid Lobby, San Francisco, 93; Galerie Sho, Tokyo, Japan, 94. *Teaching:* Instr, Goldsmiths Col, Univ London, 64-66; Minneapolis Col Art, 66-70; Univ Victoria, 70; Calif State Univ, Hayward, 71-. *Awards:* Fulbright Fel to Italy, 63-64; Nat Endowment Arts Fel, 79; Fulbright Travel Grant to Egypt, 91. *Bibliog:* Jane Ayers (auth), Times Tribune, Palo Alto, Calif, 3/20/88; Rick Deragon (auth), Stone Cool, The Herald, 12/6/91; Anita Decarlo (auth), Shepp's Stone Works are at MPMA, The Weekly Sun, 12/5/91. *Media:* Slate. *Publ:* Auth, 1968 Biennial of Painting and Sculpture, Walker Art Ctr, 68; RE-DACT, Willis, Locker & Owens, 84. *Mailing Add:* c/o Stephen Wirtz Gallery 49 Geary San Francisco CA 94108

SHEPPARD, JOSEPH SHERLY
PAINTER, SCULPTOR
b Owings Mills, Md, Dec 20, 30. *Study:* Md Inst Col Art, cert (fine art); also with Jacques Maroger. *Work:* Butler Inst Am Art; Fine Arts Mus, Mobile, Ala; Baltimore Mus Art, Md; Carnegie Inst; Westmoreland Art Mus, Greenburg, Pa; Midwest Mus of Am Art, Elkhart, IN; Natl Portrait Gallery, Washington, DC; Consiglio Regionale Delle Toscana, Florence, Italy. *Comn:* Murals, Police Dept Hq Bldg, Baltimore; bronze, Holocaust Mem, Baltimore; mural, Palmer House Hotel, Chicago, Ill; President Bush (portrait), comn by Presidential Libr, Col Station, Tex, 98; Archbishop J Foley (portrait), comn by Vatican City, 98; and others. *Exhib:* One-man shows, Butler Inst Am Art, 64 & 72, Westmoreland Co Mus, 66, 72 & 82 & Davenport Munic Art Gallery, Iowa, 67 & 83; consecutive shows, Florence, Italy, 77-; Walters Art Gallery, Balt, 2002-03; Forbes Gallery, NY, 2003; and others. *Pos:* Owner studio, Pietrasanta, Italy. *Teaching:* Instr painting & artist-in-residence, Dickinson Col, 56-57; instr drawing, painting & anat, Md Inst Col Art, 60-75. *Awards:* Prize for Figure Painting, 63 & Paul Puzinas Award, 84, Allied Artists; John J McDonough Prize, Butler Inst Am Art, 67; Gov Prize, Md Artists Exhib, Baltimore Mus, 71; Tallix Foundry Prize, 83, Agop Agopoff Mem Prize, 86, & C Percival Dietch Prize, 94, Nat Sculpture Soc; Award of Merit, Soc Animal Artists, 83. *Bibliog:* The Work of Joseph Sheppard, Arti Grafiche Giorgi & Gambi, Italy, 82; Joseph Sheppard-Sculpture, Arti Grafiche Giorgi & Gambi, Italy, 93; Joseph Sheppard-Portraits, Arti Grafiche Giorgi & Gambi, Italy, 96; Joseph Sheppard-50 Years of Art, Arti Garfiche Giorgi & Gambi, Italy, 2000; Uomo Di Penna (Beast of Burden), Polistampe, Italy, 2005; Legacy (The Tradition Lives On), Grafichegelli, Italy, 2005. *Mem:* Allied Artists Am; Nat Sculpture Soc; Soc Animal Artists; Knickerbocker Artists. *Media:* Oil; Bronze, Marble. *Publ:* Auth, Anatomy, 75, Drawing the Female Figure, 75, Drawing the Male Figure, 76, Learning From the Masters, 79 & Drawing the Living Figure, 84, Watson-Guptill; auth, Keeping Christmas, Stemmer House, 81. *Dealer:* Marin-Price Gallery 7022 Wisconsin Ave Chevy Chase MD. *Mailing Add:* 3908 N Charles St Baltimore MD 21218

SHER, ELIZABETH
VIDEO ARTIST, PRINTMAKER
b Washington, DC, Feb 13, 43. *Study:* Smith Col, Mass, 60-62; Univ Calif, Berkeley, BA, 64, MA, 67; San Francisco Art Inst, 65-66. *Work:* US Info Agency, Washington, DC; Oakland Mus; Calif Palace Legion Hon; Sierra Mus Art; Carnegie Mellon Univ. *Exhib:* Fifty-seven Calif Printmakers, Calif Palace Legion Hon; Edinburgh Int Film Fest, 82; First Int Video Fest, Montbeliard, France, 82; San Francisco Int Film Fest, 82 & 83; Athens Int Film & Video Fest, Mich, 83; AFI Women in Film III, John F Kennedy Ctr, Washington, DC, 83; Ann Arbor Film Fest, Mich, 83; Milan Fest Am Independent Cinema, 83; Video on the Rock, La Rochelle, France, 84; Calif Collection, Fortuny Mus, Venice, Italy, 84; New Music USA, Musee d'Art Moderne de la Ville de Paris, 85. *Collection Arranged:* Guest cur, Mixed Media on Paper, Berkeley Art Ctr, 78. *Pos:* Dir, IV Studios, Berkeley, Calif, 82-. *Teaching:* Assoc prof, Calif Col Arts & Crafts, 77-. *Awards:* Purchase Award, Seventh Nevada Ann, 80; Union of Independent Art Col Fac Grant, 82 & 83; Most Humorous Video, Hollywood Erotic Film & Video Fest, 84; Western Regional Media Arts Fel, 84. *Bibliog:* Articles, San Diego Mag, 81 & Artweek Mag, 82; Video, Ego Mag, 82; Showing a head for video, Chicago Tribune, 4/85; review, St Louis Post-Dispatch, 9/12/85; Totally tubular artists, Calif Living Mag, 9/15/85. *Mem:* Film Arts Found; Calif Soc Printmakers; Bay Area Video Coalition; Women's Caucus Art; Canyon Cinemateque Film Soc. *Media:* Mixed Media. *Publ:* Illusr, A Child's Library of Dreams, Celestial Arts, 78. *Mailing Add:* 985 Regal Rd Berkeley CA 94708

SHERBELL, RHODA
SCULPTOR, CONSULTANT
b Brooklyn, NY. *Study:* Art Students League, with William Zorach & Reginald Marsh, 50-53; Brooklyn Mus Art Sch, with Hugo Robies 59-61; study in Italy, France, Eng & Switz, with Mervin Honig, 56. *Work:* William Benton Mus Art, Conn; Colby Col Art Mus, Waterville, Maine; NY Pub Libr, Queens Mus & Brooklyn Mus, NY; Nat Arts Collection, Smithsonian Inst; Nat Portrait Gallery; Mus Mod Art, NY; Jewish Mus, NY; Nat Acad Mus; Hofstra Mus, NY; Heckscher Mus Art, Huntington, NY; Smithsonian Am Art Mus, Washington, D.C.; Nat Acad Design, NY. *Comn:* Marguerite & William Zorach Bronze, Nat Arts Collection, Smithsonian Inst, Washington, DC, 64; bronzes of Aaron Copland, Eleanore Roosevelt, & Yogi Berra, Montclair Art Mus; Casey Stengel, Country Art Gallery Long Island, Baseball Hall of Fame, Cooperstown, NY; Yogi Berra, comn by Percy Uris; Colonal Man (bronze), Hofstra Univ; The Am Baseball Family Group, Portland, ME, 2006. *Exhib:* Pa Acad Fine Arts, 60; Brooklyn Mus Art Award Winners Exhib, 65; Nat Acad Design, 67, 72, 80, 82 & 98; Jewish Mus, NY; Nat Arts Club, Allied Artists Am, William Benton Mus; solo exhibs, Brooklyn Mus, NY Cult Ctr & Bronx Mus Art, NY; and over 25 solo exhibs. *Pos:* Pres bd, Friends Emily Lowe Gallery; dir sculpture, Allied Artists; dir pub rels, Audubon Artists, currently. *Teaching:* Instr, Mus Mod Art, Art Students League, Nat Acad Design; prof art, Hofstra Univ, NY. *Awards:* Am Acad Arts & Lett Awards; Louis Comfort, Tiffany Found Award; Ford Found Award; Gold Medals, Audubon Artists Am, Allied Artists & Nat Asn Woman; and many others; Allied Artists Am; guest at Dept of State Embassy Prog, Prague, Czech Rep, 2003-04. *Bibliog:* Articles, Mus Mag, 4/82 & McCall's Mag, 8/82; Woman in Bronze (film), PBS TV; and many others. *Mem:* Allied Artists Am; Audubon Artists; life mem Art Students League; Am Inst Arts & Letters; assoc mem Am Watercolor Soc; Nat Acad (assoc, 79, acad, 82-); Nat Sculpture Soc (fellow); and many others. *Media:* Bronze, Pastel. *Collection:* Contemporary American realistic work, including M & R Soyer, W Zorach, Marguerite Zorach, Mervin Honig, Harry Sternberg, John Koch, Agostine, H Jackson, Margit Beck and others. *Mailing Add:* 64 Jane Ct Westbury NY 11590

SHERIDAN, HELEN ADLER
CURATOR
b Kansas City, Mo. *Study:* Ohio State Univ; Univ Kans, BA; Univ Calif Los Angeles, MA; Western Mich Univ, MLS. *Collection Arranged:* Super Realism from the Morton G Neuman Family Collection (ed, catalog), 81; New Image-Pattern & Decoration from the Morton G Neumann Family Collection (ed, catalog), 83; Kirk Newman Retrospective (ed, catalog), 84; A Century of Caring: American Realism, 1880's-1980's (ed, catalog), 86, Kalamazoo Inst Arts, Mich; The Cutting Edge, New Directions in Handmade Papers (ed, catalog), 88; Meetings in The Garden: The Art of

John Himmelfarb (catalog), 89; Richard Hunt: Sculpture Past, Present, & Future (catalog), 90; Stephen Hansen: Recent Sculpture (catalog), 92; Contemporary Children's Book Illustration (traveling exhib), 94; Hispanic Am Art: A Sacred Tradition (catalog), 95. *Pos:* Head librn & cur collections, Kalamazoo Inst Arts, Mich, 75-82, asst to dir collections & exhibs, 83-88; dir collections & exhib, 89- & 99-. *Teaching:* Instr arts of the 20th century, Western Mich Univ, 66-75. *Mem:* Col Art Asn; Midwest Mus Asn; Am Asn Mus; Mich Mus Asn. *Res:* Contemporary American art and artists; documentation of Mich artists and art collections. *Interests:* American arts of the twentieth century; regionalist art; photography. *Publ:* Co-ed, The Vagaries of Invention, 81. *Mailing Add:* c/o Kalamazoo Inst Arts 314 S Park St Kalamazoo MI 49006

SHERIDAN, SONIA LANDY
MEDIA ARTIST
b Newark, Ohio, Apr 10, 25. *Study:* Hunter Col, AB, 45; Columbia Univ, 46-48; Taiwan She Da Univ, 58; Yoshida Studio, Tokyo, 60; Calif Col Arts & Crafts, MFA, 60. *Work:* Art Inst Chicago; Fundacion Artey Technol, Madrid; San Francisco Mus Art; George Eastman House, Rochester, NY; Nat Gallery, Ottawa, Can; Tokyo Metrop Mus Photog; Hood Mus of Art, Dartmouth Daniel Langlois Foundation, Montreal, Canada; and others. *Exhib:* Two-person show, Projects, Mus Mod Art, NY, 74; Women of Photog, San Francisco Mus Art, 75; retrospective, Univ Iowa Mus Art, 76; Mus Mod Art, Paris, 83; Reine Sofia Mus, Madrid, 86; Photog & Art, Los Angeles Co Mus, 87; Am Women Artists: 20th Century, Knoxville Mus Art & Queensboro Community Art Col, NY, 89-90; Infinite Illusion, Smithsonian, 90; Tokyo Metrop Mus, 91; Vasarely Mus, Budapest, 92; Trivial Machines, Osthaus Mus, Hagen, Ger, 92; Circulo des Belles Artes, 92; Emblems, Yale Univ Art Gallery, 95; Moholy-Nagy Tribute, Magyar, Foto Grafia Mus, Hungary, 95; What Happened to the Pioneers?, Galerie Arts Technol, Montreal, 95; Kapieren, Scryption, Tilburg, The Neth, 98; Vidego Gallery, Hungary, 2000; Mus fur Communication, Frankfurt Ger, 2001; 2 NY Biennale Buenos Aries, Argentina, 2002; Lessaedra Bulgaria, 2005. *Pos:* Co-ed, Leonardo, Int J Art, Sci, Tech, currently; hon dir, Mus fur Fotocopie, Mulheim an der Ruhr; Honrary Dir, Leonardo. *Teaching:* Instr art educ & design, Calif Col Arts & Crafts, 60-61; founder, prof & area head generative systems, Sch Art Inst Chicago, 61-80, prof emer, 80-; artist in residence, 3M Co, St Paul, 70 & 76, Xerox Corp, 81. *Awards:* NEA Workshop Grant, 74, Union Independent Cols Art Grant, 75; Pub Media Grant, 76 & Artist Grant, 81-82; Nat Asn Sch Art & Design Citation, 2006. *Bibliog:* Raymond Synard (ed), Color Theory and Imaging Systems, Soc Photog Scientists & Engrs, 73; Diane Kirkpatrick (auth), Chicago the City and Its Artists, Univ Mich, 78; Richard Wickstrom (auth), NMex State Univ, Art Science, 78; The Computer Revolution in Art, Univ Fla Press, 3/88; Gardner's Art Through the Ages (auth, 10th ed), De la Croix, Tansey, Kirkpatrick; Visual Resources, 2006. *Mem:* Founding mem Int Soc Interdisciplinary Study Symmetry, Budapest, Hungary; Col Art Asn; ACLU; Dem for New Hampshire. *Media:* Electronic Imaging. *Publ:* Symmetry/Asymmetry: An Artist's View, Symmetry in a Kaleidoscope, Int Soc Interdisciplinary Study of Symmetry, Budapest, Hungary, 89; Guest ed & auth, New Foundations: Lessons in Art/Science/Technology, Leonardo: Int J Art, Sci, Tech, Vol 23, No 2/3 Pergammon Press, Berkeley, Calif, 90; Timescope: Patterns in Flow Symmetrically, Symmetry: Culture & Science, Budapest, Hungary, 92. *Mailing Add:* 80 Lyme Rd Apt 438 Hanover NH 03755-1225

SHERMAN, CINDY
PHOTOGRAPHER
b Glen Ridge, NJ, Jan 19, 54. *Study:* State Univ NY, Buffalo, BA, 76. *Work:* Mus Mod Art, Metrop Mus Art, & Brooklyn Mus, NY; Tate Gallery, London; Walker Art Ctr, Minneapolis, Minn; San Francisco Mus Art, Calif; Corcoran Gallery Art, Washington; and many others. *Exhib:* solo exhibs, Contemp Arts Mus, Houston, 80, Stedlijk Mus, Amsterdam, 82, St Louis Art Mus, 83, Baltimore Mus Art, 84, Aldrich Mus Contemp Art, 86, Wadsworth Atheneum, 86, Whitney Mus Am Art, 87, Inst Contemp Art, Boston, 87, Dallas Mus Art, 87, Nat Art Gallery, NZ, 89, Whitechapel Gallery, London, 91, Milwaukee Art Mus, 91, Walker Art Ctr, 91, San Francisco Mus Mod Art, 95 & Kunstmus Lucerne, 95, Studio Guenzani, Milan, 2001, Centerfolds, 1981, Skarstedt Fine Art, NY, 2003; Newport Harbor Art Mus & Israel Mus, Jerusalem, 91; Geementemus Arnhem, The Neth, Neth & Aarhus Kunstmus, Denmark, 93; Kunsthistorisches Mus, Vienna, Austria (with catalog), 93; Radical Images, 2nd Austrian Triennial on Photog 1996 (with catalog), Neue Galerie am Landesmus Joanneum, Graz, 96; Picasso: A Contemp Dialogue, Galerie Thaddeus Ropac, Salzburg/Paris, 96; Tableaux Vivants, Kunsthalle Wien, Vienna, 2002; Moving Pictures, Solomon R Guggenheim Mus, NY, 2002. *Awards:* MacArthur Found Fel, 95; NY State Gov's Arts Award, 2001; Nat Arts Award, 2002. *Bibliog:* Cindy Sherman, BT Mag, 10/96; David D'Arcy (auth), Screen romance, Art & Auction, 10/96; Robert Hirsch (auth), Exploring Color Photography, third ed, State Univ NY, Buffalo, 97; and others. *Publ:* Photog & auth, Fitcher's Bird, Rizzoli, New York, 92; coauth (with Andrea Dietrich), Cindy Sherman (exhib catalog), ACC Galerie Weimer, Ger, 94. *Mailing Add:* 9 Debrosses St #520A New York NY 10032

SHERMAN, CLAIRE RICHTER
HISTORIAN, EDUCATOR
b Boston, Mass, Feb 11, 30. *Study:* Radcliffe Col, BA(Fulbright Scholar), 51; Univ Mich, with Marvin J Eisenberg, MA(Am Univ Women Fel), 58; Johns Hopkins Univ, with Adolf Katzenellenbogen, PhD, 64. *Collection Arranged:* Writing on Hands: Memory & Knowledge in Early Modern Europe (auth, catalog), The Trout Gallery, Dickinson Col, 2000, The Folger Shakespeare Libr, 2000-01; Interpretation by Design: Contemp bookbindings by Stanley M Sherman, The Walters Art Mus, 2006. *Pos:* Sr fel, Ctr Advan Study Visual Arts, Nat Gallery Art, 81-82; consult, J Paul Getty Trust, 83; sr res assoc, Ctr Advan Study Visual Arts, Nat Gallery Art, 86-94. *Teaching:* Instr art hist, Univ Mich, 58-59; lectr art hist, Am Univ, 66-72; vis assoc prof of art, McIntire Dept of Art, Univ of Va, 76. *Awards:* Grant in Aid, Am Coun Learned Socs, 75 & 82; Grants, Am Philos Soc & Nat Endowment Humanities, 85. *Mem:* Col Art Asn Am. *Res:* Illustrations of Aristotle's Ethics & Politics in fourteenth and fifteenth century manuscripts; women scholars in the arts; the inscribed hand in medieval & Renaissance culture. *Publ:* Auth, The Portraits of Charles V of France (1338-80), 69; The Queen in Charles V's Coronation Book, Viator, Medieval & Renaissance Studies, Vol 8, 77; Some visual definitions of the illustrations of Aristotle's Nifchomachean Ethics and Politics in the French translation of Nicole Oresme, Art Bull, Vol 59, 77; ed & contribr, Women as Interpreters of the Visual Arts, 1820-1979, 81; Imaging Aristotle: Verbal and Visual Representation in 14th Century France, 95; and many others. *Mailing Add:* 4516 Que Ln NW Washington DC 20007

SHERMAN, LENORE WALTON
PAINTER, WRITER
b New York, NY, May 11, 20. *Study:* With Leon Franks, Hayward Veal, Orrin A White & Sergei Bongart, watercolor with James Couper Wright & portrait with Eignar Hansen. *Work:* San Diego Law Libr; var banks. *Exhib:* Southern Calif Expos, Del Mar, 70-72; Calif Fedn Women's Club Fine Arts Festival, 71; Southern NMex State Fair, 81 & 82; and others. *Pos:* Writer, Senior Living Newspaper, 98-. *Teaching:* Instr oil painting, San Diego Art Inst, 60-67, Foothills Art Asn, La Mesa, Calif, summer 72 & Las Cruces Arts & Crafts Asn, NMex, 80-81 & 88. *Awards:* First Award Oils, NMex State Fair, 82 & Best in Show, 82; and others. *Bibliog:* Ed Ainsworth (auth), The Cowboy in Art, World Publ, 68; articles in San Diego Union, 60-72; articles, Las Cruces Sun News, NMex, 80-81. *Mem:* Salmagundi Club, NY. *Media:* Oil. *Publ:* Auth, Impressionistic Flowers, Impressionistic Landscapes, Walter Foster Art Bks, 75 & 80. *Dealer:* Lundeen Inn of the Arts 618 S Alameda Blvd Las Cruces NM

SHERMAN, SARAI
PAINTER, SCULPTOR
b Philadelphia, Pa, 22. *Study:* Tyler Sch Art, Temple Univ, BFA, BS(educ); Barnes Found; Univ Iowa, MFA. *Work:* Whitney Mus Am Art, Mus Mod Art, NY; Hirshhorn Collection, Smithsonian Inst, Washington, DC; Uffizi Gallery Print Collection, Florence, Italy; Collection Mod Art, Southwestern Methodist Univ, Dallas; Univ Nebr, Lincoln; Wichita Mus, Kans; Okla Art Ctr. *Comn:* 18th Century Chapel, 10 murals, ceramic altar wall, sculpture, Capella Guzzetti, Cortona, Italy, 88-93; Sculpture installation, State Off Complex, Waterbury, Vt, 96. *Exhib:* Recent Painting USA: The Figure, Traveling Show, Mus Mod Art, NY, 62-63; Venice Biennial, Int Graphics: USA, Italy, 72; Childe Hassam Acquisition Fund, 75; 30 Yrs--Painting, Sculpture, Drawing, Palazzo Acad, Tod, Italy, 83; Forum Gallery, NY, 86; Idiomi Della Scuttura Contemp, Verona, 89; Carnera Pieta, Il, Bisonte, Florence, Italy, 97; Premio Suzzara, Italy, 98; Premio Biella, 99. *Pos:* Juror for Artists' Awards, Fulbright Comn, 89-91. *Awards:* Award for Painting, Nat Inst Arts & Lett, 64; Europ Community Prize, Premio Marzotto, 67; Ann Painting Award, Repub San Marino, 75; Proctor Prize, Nat Acad Design, 76. *Bibliog:* Bryant (auth) & Venturoli (auth), Painting of Sarai Sherman (monogr), Galleria Penelope, Rome, 63; Sarai Sherman, Edizioni Enrico Vallecchi, Florence, 83; Geske (auth), American Painting Collection, Sheldon Mem Gallery, Univ Nebr, 83; Bellini, Busignani & Krulike (auths), Camera Picta, Univ Wash Press, Seattle, Valecchi, Florence, Italy, Capella Guzzetti, Cortona, 94. *Mem:* Nat Acad (acad, 99-). *Media:* All; Ceramic Sculpture. *Dealer:* Forum Gallery 745 Fifth Ave New York NY 10151; Appiani Arte via Appiano 1 Milan Italy. *Mailing Add:* Forum Gallery 7445 Fifth Ave New York NY 10151

SHERMAN, Z CHARLOTTE
PAINTER
b Los Angeles, Calif. *Study:* Univ Calif, Los Angeles; Kann Art Inst; Otis Art Inst, scholar. *Work:* Munic Art Gallery, Los Angeles; Palm Springs Mus, Calif; Glass Container Corp Am; Winthrop Rockefeller Found, Ark; Laguna Art Mus; Vincent Price Gallery. *Comn:* Glass Container Corp; F Fuller Collection; Mr & Mrs Winthrop Rockefeller. *Exhib:* Downey Mus, 67; Gallery Rene Barel, Paris, France, 72; Heritage Gallery, Los Angeles, 63-94, 95, 97, 99, 2000, 01, 03 & 05; Habitant, Los Angeles, Calif, 2003; Metro Gallery, Bakersfield, Calif, 2006; plus others. *Teaching:* teacher, cult arts dept, Munic Arts Dept, City of Los Angeles, Calif, 65-80. *Awards:* Phelan Found Award, 61; Pasadena Mus Ann Award, 61; All City Exhib Award, Barnsdale, Los Angeles, 63 & 65; and others. *Bibliog:* Joseph Mugnaini (auth), Oil Painting Techniques, Van Nostrand, 63; Bertrand Sorlot (auth), article, La Rev Mod, Paris, 74; Don Rothenberg (producer), Z Charlotte Sherman, Portrait of a Woman Artist (film), 77, 79. *Mem:* Nat Watercolor Soc; signature mem Nat Watercolor Soc. *Media:* Oil, Watercolor, Acrylic, Prints, Sculpture. *Dealer:* Heritage Gallery 718 N La Cienega Blvd Los Angeles CA 90069. *Mailing Add:* 1300 Chautauqua Blvd Pacific Palisades CA 90272

SHERMAN-ZINN, ELLEN R
PAINTER, DESIGNER
b Newton, Mass, Mar 13, 45. *Study:* Syracuse Univ, BFA, 66; studies at Parsons Sch Design, 75; Montclair State Univ, MA(fine arts), 88. *Work:* Raritan Bay Med Ctr, Perth Amboy, NJ; Continental Airlines President's Club, Newark, NJ; Solomon A Berson Found, Long Island. *Comn:* Mural, comn by Mr & Mrs J Weisglass, West Orange, NJ, 94; mural, comn by Dr Linda & Mr Michael Stone, Greenbrook, NJ, 96; mural, comn by Mr & Mrs S Fromm, NY, 96. *Exhib:* Union Co Col Solo Invitational, Tamasulo Gallery, Cranford, NJ, 94; Warner Lambert Invitational, Morris Plains, NJ, 94; CAA Midlantic Open Juried Show, Ridgewood Art Inst, NJ, 94; Nat Juried Show, Art Ctr Northern NJ, Passaic, 94; Corp Art Prog Invitational, Johnson & Johnson Hq, New Brunswick, NJ, 95; Invitational exhib, Nabisco Foods, E Hanover, NJ, 97. *Pos:* Designers' group dir, New York City, 80-84; fashion dir, Nat Knitwear & Sportswear Asn, 80-84. *Awards:* Best Contemp Work, Kerygma Gallery, Ridgewood, NY, 94. *Bibliog:* Eileen Watkins (auth), Bergen exhibit confronts viewer with bold colors,

Sunday Newark Star Ledger, 92; Sally Friedman (auth), Ellen Sherman-Zinn born to paint, NJ Women Mag, 93; Michelle Morris (auth), Woman leaves corporate world to fulfill dreams as an artist, Echoes Sentinel, 94. *Mem:* NJ Ctr Visual Arts; Watchung Art Ctr, NJ. *Media:* Acrylic, Oil. *Publ:* Auth, Viewpoint, Knitting Times Mag, 80-84; contribr, Spokesman for the knit industry, Am Fabric & Fashion Mag, 82. *Dealer:* Everhart Gallery 117 S Maple Ave Basking Ridge NJ 07920

SHERR, RONALD NORMAN
PAINTER
b Plainfield, NJ, July 17, 52. *Study:* DuCret Sch Art, Plainfield, NJ; Nat Acad Design Sch Fine Art; also with Burton Silverman. *Work:* Phoenix Mus Art, Ariz; Nat Portrait Gallery, Washington, DC. *Exhib:* Ann Exhib, Nat Acad Design, NY, 78; Hassam Fund Exhib, Inst Arts & Letters, NY, 78; Painting & Sculpture Today, Indianapolis Art Mus, Ind, 78; Drawing Exhib, Univ NH, 79; A Heritage Renewed: Representational Drawing Today Traveling Exhib, 83. *Pos:* Instr painting seminar, Galeria San Juan, PR. *Teaching:* Instr painting, Nat Acad Sch Fine Art, & Art Students League, New York, currently. *Awards:* Benjamin Altman Figure Prize, Nat Acad Design, New York, 78; Award for Excellence, Int Ed Design Competition, 83; Allied Artists Am Gold Medal of Honor, New York, 86; Hubbard Art Award for Excellence, Ruidoso, NMex, 91. *Bibliog:* Smithsonian Mag, 7/88; Am Artist, 9/91; Southwest Art, 8/91. *Media:* Oil, Drawing. *Publ:* Illusr, Illusr 25, 29. *Mailing Add:* 1361 Madison Ave Apt 7B New York NY 10128

SHERRATT, HOLLY
Study: Univ Calif, Los Angeles, BA; Univ Calif, Irvine, MA. *Pos:* Trainee, Laguna Art Mus, Laguna Beach, Calif; staff, Nat Mus Am Art, Smithsonian Inst, Washington, DC; cur staff, Huntongton Beach Fine Arts Ctr, Calif; modern, contemp & Latin-American specialist, Bonhams & Butterfields, San Francisco, Calif, 2000-. *Mailing Add:* Bonhams & Butterfields 220 San Bruno Ave San Francisco CA 94103

SHERRILL, MILTON LEWIS
SCULPTOR, PAINTER
b New York, NY, May 30, 49. *Study:* Cooper Union, NY, 72; State Univ NY, BA, 74; Pratt Inst, NY, MFA, 76. *Work:* Studio Mus in Harlem, NY; Schomburg Collection, NY; City of NY; The Apollo Theater, NY. *Comn:* Monument (steel sculpture), City of Mt Vernon, NY, 78; bronze abstraction, Selchow & Righter Co, NY, 83; lifesize bronze figures, City of NY, 83 & Apollo Theater, NY, 87; One Child Our Village Found, Los Angeles, Calif; Nat Bar Inst, Washington, DC. *Exhib:* One-man show, SUNY Col at Old Westbury, Pratt Inst, Brooklyn, NY, Studio Mus in Harlem, NY, Countee Cullen Libr, NY, Mt Vernon Coop Col, NY, Interfaith Ctr, NY, Mt Vernon Pub Libr, NY, White Plains Libr, NY; Emerging Artists, Neuberger Mus, Purchase, NY, 80; 35 Under 35, Lever House, NY, 80; Ideas in Bronze, Los Angeles Co Mus, Calif, 83; two-man exhib (with Robert P Dilworth), Isobel Neal Gallery, Chicago, Ill, 88; UFA Gallery, NY, NY, 99; Mount Vernon Fine Art Gallery, 2000; Federal Mem Hall, New York; National Sculpture Soc, New York. *Collection Arranged:* Hosp for Joint Diseases Orthopedic Inst, NY; Apollo Theater, NY; Columbia Law Sch, NY; Ford Motor Co, Gary Found, Harris Bank, Chicago, Ill; Schomburg Collection, NY. *Teaching:* Teacher sculpture, State Univ NY, Mt Vernon Co-Op Col, 70-72; dir, Artists in Schs Prog, Mt Vernon, 73-74; teacher, Studio Mus Co-Op Sch Prog, 74-75; teacher Westcher Art Coun, 2000. *Awards:* Westchester Arts Council CETA, Adolph & Ester Gitllieb Found; Arts Council Arts Alive Grants, 2000, 01 & 02. *Bibliog:* C Gerald Fraser (auth), Guide going out, New York Times, 83; Terrie S Rouse (auth), From painter to sculptor, Rev African Am Art, 84; Frank Oliveri Monument for Dr Martin Luther King Jr, J News. *Mem:* Artists' Equity Asn; Orgn Independent Artists; Nat Sculpture Soc. *Media:* Bronze, Steel; Oil, Acrylic. *Mailing Add:* PO Box 2421 Mount Vernon NY 10551

SHERROD, PHILIP LAWRENCE
PAINTER, WRITER
b Pauls Valley, Okla, Oct 12, 35. *Study:* Okla State Univ, BS, 57, BA(painting), 59; Art Students League, Am Fed Arts & Lett Scholar, NY, 63; Jacques Seligman Col, Postgrad, 68; Carrol Reese Mus, Postgrad, 68. *Work:* Herbert Johnson Gallery, Cornell Univ, Ithaca, NY; Smithsonian Inst, Hirshhorn Mus & Sculpture Garden, Washington, DC; Worcester Fine Arts Mus, Mass; Mus City NY; Newark Mus, NJ; and others. *Exhib:* Inside Out, Newport Harbor Art Mus, Newport Beach, Calif, 81; one-man show, Herbert Johnson Mus, Cornell Univ, Ithacia, NY, 85; Hirshhorn Mus & Sculpture Garden, Smithsonian Inst, Washington, DC, 89; Street Painters, Cork Gallery, Lincoln Ctr, NY, 97-98; Instructor's Exhib, Art Students League, NY, 98; Nat Acad Sch Fine Arts, NY, 98, 99; The Artists Enterprets, NJ Ctr US Arts Summit, 98; Fed Mod Painters & Sculptors Exhib, Brooklyn Community Col, NY, 98; Art Students League, New York City, 99, 2000, 2001, 2002; NJ Ctr Visual Arts, Summit, 2000, 2001, 2002, 2003; Fedn Modern Painters and Sculptors, Fordham Univ, New York City, 2000, 2002, 2003; Cork Gallery, New York City, 2000, 2002; Nat Acad Sch Design Mus, New York City, 2001; Limner Gallery, New York City, 2003. *Pos:* Pres & founder, Street Painters, NY. *Teaching:* Instr color & design, Okla State Univ, 59; asst painting, Art Students League, 60 & instr, 84-99; instr, Morristown Art Asn, NJ, 73-74 & NJ Ctr Visual Arts, 77-99; Nat Acad Sch Fine Arts, 94, 98-99. *Awards:* Childe Hassam Purchase Award, Am Acad Arts & Letters 67, 69, 74; Adolph/Esther Gottlieb Found Grants, 81, 88, 96 & 2006; Nat Endowment Grant, 82; Prix de Rome Fel, Am Acad in Rome, 85-86; The Pollock-Krasner Found Grant, 89; Creative Public Serv Prog Grants, New York, NY. *Bibliog:* Barry Schwartz (auth), Arts in Society (Humanist Alternative), Univ Wis, 4/73; Barry Schwartz (auth) New Humanism: Art in a Time of Change, Praeger, 74. *Mem:* Nat Acad (assoc, 93, acad, 94-); Fel Am Acad in Rome. *Media:* Oil, Etching. *Publ:* Auth, 30 Mentaltalia (poems & paintings), Merging Media Publ, 80; Black Truck (poems), Mirronic Pub, 81; Mr Wigley Cums (poems), Mirronic Pub, 83; Images Below the Belt (poems & paintings), Carrousel Pub, 84; Sex (I) Con (poem), Carrousel Pub, 85. *Dealer:* Allan Stone Gallery 113 E 90th St New York NY 10128. *Mailing Add:* 41 W 24th St New York NY 10010

SHERWOOD , JAMES BLAIR
PATRON
b New Castle, Pa, Aug 8, 1933. *Study:* Yale Univ, BA, 1955. *Pos:* Mgr French ports, US Lines Inc, LeHavre, France, 1959-62, asst gen freight traffic mgr, New York, NY, 1962-63; gen mgr, CTI Inc, 1963-65; pres, Sea Containers Ltd, London, 1965-; chmn, Orient-Express Hotels Inc, 1987-; dir, Through Transit Marine Mutual Assurance Asn, Hamilton, Bermuda, Venice Simplon-Orient Express Ltd, London, Hotel Cipriani SPA, Venice, Italy, Isle of Man Steam Packet Co, Douglas; vpres, Transport Trust, London, Motor Neuron Disease Asn; bd dir, Peggy Guggenheim Mus, Venice, Italy, 1983-, Mus Modern Art, Oxford, Eng, 1987-; trustee, Solomon R Guggenheim Found, 1989-. *Mem:* Pilgrims, Hurlingham, Mark's, Annabel's, Harry's Bar (London). *Mailing Add:* Sea Containers Ltd 20 Upper Ground London United Kingdom

SHERWOOD, KATHERINE
PAINTER
b New Orleans, La, Oct 17, 52. *Study:* Univ Calif at Davis, BA, 75; San Francisco Art Inst, MFA, 79. *Exhib:* One-person shows, 8 BC, NY 85 & Gallery Paule Anglim, San Francisco, 88 & 92, DP Fong Gallery, San Jose, Calif, 94, Flora Lamson Hewlett Libr, Berkeley, Calif, 94, Fine Arts Gallery, Chiang Mai Univ, Thailand, 94, Univ de Concepcion, Chile, 94, Gallery Paule Anglim, San Francisco, 98, Adaline Kent Award exhib, San Francisco Art Inst, 99, Gallery Paule Anglim, San Francisco, 2001, Cole Pratt Gallery, New Orleans, 2002, Michael Kohn Gallery, Los Angeles, 2002, Locks Gallery, Philadelphia, 2003; Chain Reaction VII, San Francisco Art Comn Gallery, Calif, 92; Second Ann, Long Beach Arts, Calif, 93; Artist Coun Ann Exhib, Palm Springs Desert Mus, Calif, 94; Reverence, 313 Gallery, NY, 94; Likeness of Being, DC Moore Gallery, NY, 99; Medicine in Art, Col of Mainland, Texas City, 2000; Six Painters, Sonoma State Univ, Calif, 2000; Michael Kohn Gallery, Los Angeles, 2001; Kick Back, Univ Calif, Berkeley, 2001; Bay Area Now 3, Yerba Buena Ctr for Arts, San Francisco, 2002; and others. *Teaching:* Instr, San Francisco Art Inst, 79; adj prof, NY Univ, NY, 83-88; asst prof, Univ Calif, 98-. *Awards:* Nat Endowment Arts, 89; Univ Calif Fac Mentor Grant, 91 & 93; Adeline Kent Award, San Francisco Art Inst, Calif, 98; Pollack-Krasner Found Grant, 98. *Bibliog:* Kenneth Baker (auth), Katherine Sherwood at Paule Anglim, San Francisco Chronicle, 8/13/92; Maria Porges (auth), Katherine Sherwood/Gallery Paul Anglim, ArtForum, 11/95; Tom Patterson (auth), Five in show at WFU display new perspective on painting, Winston Salem J, 3/3/96. *Dealer:* Paule Anglim 14 Geary St San Francisco CA 94108. *Mailing Add:* 28 Pacific Ave Rodeo CA 94572

SHERWOOD, LEONA
PAINTER, INSTRUCTOR
b New York, NY. *Study:* Studied with John Chetcuti, New York, 46-48; workshop critiques with Philip Hicken, Mass, 58, Robert Gelinas, Fla, 65, Leon Berkowitz, New Col, 80, William Pachner, New Col, 81. *Work:* Hickory Mus Art, NC; Edison Col, Ft Myers, Fla; Collegiate Sch Boys, NY; Diamond Shamrock Co, Cleveland, Ohio; Barnett Bank, Sarasota, Fla; Town of Longboat Key, Fla. *Comn:* 42 paintings for Strathmore Co, Sarasota, Fla, 67-; painting, Lido Ambassador, Sarasota, 71; paintings, Thru Hang-up Gallery, Sarasota, Fla, 90; and others. *Exhib:* Metrop Art Mus, Miami, Fla, 77; one-person show, Hickory Mus Art, NC, 79 & Sarasota, Fla, 86; Boca Raton Art Mus, Fla, 83; Cornell Fine Arts, Rollins Col, 89; Polk Co Col, Winter Park, Fla, 90, Daytona, Fla, Racardi, Miami, Tampa; Sumner Mus, Washington, 92; Cork Gallery, NY, 94; and others. *Teaching:* Instr contemp painting & drawing, Longboat Ctr for the Arts, Fla, 69- & Art League Manatee, Bradenton, Fla, 74-89; instr workshops, NC & Fla Art Ctrs, 79-, Chateau de La Napoule Art Found, France, 86, 87, 89, 91 & 93, Corfu, 89, O'Neill Art Ctr, Ireland, Madeira, Port, 90, Wilson Art Ctr, Wales, 91 & Malta, 92. *Awards:* First in Painting, Nat League Pen Women State Biennial, 71, 72, 76, 78, 79, 91, 93; Am Artist Award Watercolor, Fla Suncoast Ann, 90; Best of Show & Merit Award, Nat Biennial Nat League Am Penwomen, Washington, DC, 92; Best in Show, watercolor and acrylic, Longboat Key Art Ctr, 94, 95. *Bibliog:* Sheila Scotter (auth), An artist, cook & gardener, Australian Women's Weekly & Tatler, London, Eng, 79; Jane Roehr (auth) Art for the Artists Sake, Sarasota Times, 89; Penwoman, biennial issue, 92; Dora Walters (auth), Painting - A Colorful Life, The Longboat Observer, 01. *Mem:* Fla Artist Group; Nat League Am Pen Women; Fla Watercolor Soc; Artists Fel, NY; Women Contemp Artists; Nat Mus Women in the Arts. *Media:* Multimedia, Watercolor. *Publ:* Auth, Learn to really see, not just look, Islander, 81; The Best of Watercolor, 95; The Best of Watercolor - Painting Textures, 97, Creative Inspirations, 98, Rockport Publ Inc, The Best of Watercolor, 99, The Collected Best of Watercolor, 02. *Mailing Add:* 915 Oasis Ct Southlake TX 76092-6339

SHESTACK, ALAN
MUSEUM ADMINISTRATOR, ART HISTORIAN
b New York, NY, June 23, 38. *Study:* Wesleyan Univ, Middletown, Conn, BA, 60; Harvard Univ, Cambridge, Mass, MA, 62; Zentralinstitut Fur Kunstgeschichte, Munich, 63-64; Wesleyan Univ, DFA, 78. *Collection Arranged:* Master E S (auth catalog), Philadelphia Mus Art, 67; Fifteenth-century Engravings (auth catalog), Nat Gallery Art, Washington, DC, 67-68; Graphic Art of the Danube School (with catalog), Yale Art Gallery, St Louis Art Mus, Philadelphia Mus Art, 68-69; Hans Baldung Grien (auth, catalog), Nat Gallery Art, Washington, DC, 81; Art for the Nation, Nat Gallery Art, Washington, DC, 2000. *Pos:* Mus cur graphic art, Nat Gallery, 65-67; cur prints & drawings, Yale Univ Art Gallery, New Haven, Conn, 68-71, dir, 71-85; bd dir, Am Fedn Art, 81-88; indemnification panel, Nat Endowment Arts, 80-84; pres, Asn Art Mus Dir, 83-84; dir, Minneapolis Inst Art, 85-87, Boston Mus Fine Arts, 87-93; dep dir, chief cur, Nat Gallery Art, Washington, DC, 94-. *Teaching:* Adj prof hist art, Yale Univ, 71-85. *Awards:* Woodrow Wilson Fel, 61-62; David E Finley Fel, Nat Gallery, 63-65; Ctr Advan Studies Visual Arts Sr Fel, 84. *Mem:* Visiting comt, Mus Mod Art; Internal Revenue Serv (art adv panel 84-88). *Res:*

Fifteenth and sixteenth century printmaking in Europe; German art of 15th and 16th centuries. *Publ:* Auth, The Complete Engravings of Martin Schongauer, 68; Master LCz & Master WB, 71; coauth, Hans Baldung Grien: Prints and Drawings, Univ Chicago Press, 81. *Mailing Add:* c/o Nat Gallery of Art 2000B S Club Dr Hyattsville MD 20785

SHIBATA, TOSHIO
PHOTOGRAPHER
b Tokyo, Japan, 49. *Study:* Tokyo Nat Univ Fine Art & Music, Japan, BFA, 72, MFA, 74. *Work:* Mus Contemp Art, Art Inst Chicago; Metrop Mus Art, Mus Mod Art, NY; Los Angeles Co Mus Art; Mus Fine Arts, Houston; Nat Gallery Can, Ottawa. *Exhib:* New Acquisitions, New Work, New Directions, Los Angeles Co Mus, 92; New Photog 8, Mus Mod Art, NY, 92; Art Inst Chicago, 93; Inside Out: Japanese Contemp Photog, Light Factory, Charlotte, NC, 94; Santa Monica Col, Los Angeles, 94; Landmark Tower Gallery, Yokohama City, Japan, 94; Fabulous Photos, Worcester Art Mus, Mass, 95; Gallery RAM, Los Angeles, 95; Halsted Gallery, Detroit, 95; Yokohama Portside Gallery, Japan, 95; Cleveland Mus Art, 95; Photog and Beyond in Japan, Los Angeles Co Mus Art & Corcoran Gallery Art, Washington, DC, 96; Denver Mus Art, 96; Landscapes/People, Tepper Takayama Fine Arts, Boston, 97-98; People and Landscapes, Fitchburg Art Mus, Mass, 97-98; Beyond the Familiar, Mus Contemp Art, Chicago, 97-98. *Awards:* Ministry Nat Educ Dutch Cult Fel, Belg, 75 & 76; Ihei Kimura Prize, Asahi Newspaper Publ Co, 92. *Bibliog:* Jane Brettle (auth), Liquid crystal futures, transcript I, part I, 1/94; Catherine Grout (auth), Variations on process in Japanese photography, Art Press 209, 29-32, 1/96; Charles Hagen (auth), Review, NY Times, 1/19/96. *Publ:* Auth, Photographs by Toshio Shibata, Asahi Shinbun Publ, Tokyo, 92; Terra: Photographs by Toshio Shibata (Essay by Yoshio Nakamura), Toshi Shuppan, 94; Landscape, Nazzaeli Press, Tucson, 96; View: Visions of Japan, Korinsha Press, Kyoto, 98. *Mailing Add:* c/o Tepper Takayama Fine Arts 20 Park Plaza Suite 600 Boston MA 02116

SHIBLEY, GERTRUDE
PAINTER
b Brooklyn, NY. *Study:* Brooklyn Col, BA; with Francis Criss, 42; Hans Hofmann Sch Fine Arts, 52-53. *Work:* Wichita State Univ Mus Collection, Kans; Guild Hall Mus, Easthampton, NY; Univ Ala, Birmingham; Provincetown Art Asn & Mus, Mass; St Vincent's Med Ctr, NY. *Exhib:* Nat Asn Women Painters, Nat Acad Design Gallery, 51; Prizewinners Village Art Ctr, Whitney Mus Am Art, NY, 54; NY WPA Art, Then & Now (with catalog), Parsons Sch Design, 77; Tenth St Days: The Co-ops of the 50s (with catalog), NY, 77; Abraham Rattner Ctr Arts, Sag Harbor, NY, 79-80; Provincetown Art Asn & Mus, Mass, 80-81; The Gathering of the Avante-Garde: 1948-70, Ken Keleba Gallery, NY, 85. *Pos:* Ceramist, Design Technics, 44-48. *Teaching:* Instr painting, Halloran Hosp, Staten Island, 42-44 & Ruth Ettinger Sch, New York, 55-56. *Awards:* Prize for One-man Show, Village Art Ctr, 49; Hon Mention, Terry Art Award, Miami, Fla, 52. *Mem:* Guild Hall; Provincetown Art Asn; Jimmy Ernst Artists Alliance Inc. *Media:* Acrylic, Oil. *Dealer:* Atlantic Gallery 475 Broome St New York NY 10012. *Mailing Add:* c/o Atlantic Gallery 475 Broome St New York NY 10012

SHIE & ACORD, SUSAN & JAMES
CRAFTSMAN, PAINTER
Shie: b Wooster, Ohio, Sept 28, 50; Acord: b Fairfield, Ill, Nov 26, 53. *Study:* Shie: Col Wooster, Ohio, BA, 81; Sch Art, Kent State Univ, Ohio, MFA, 86 Acord: Self-taught. *Exhib:* Mus Arte Sao Paulo, Brazil, 89; solo exhibs, Wasmer Gallery, Ursuline Col, Cleveland, 94, MOBILIA Gallery, Cambridge, Mass, 95, River Oaks Sq Art Ctr, Alexandria, La, 95, Wayne Ctr Arts, Wooster, Ohio, 96, Art Gallery Univ Wis, La Crosse, Adams Art Gallery, Dunkirk, NY, 99, Fitton Ctr Creative Arts, Hamilton, Ohio, 2000 & Mt Vernon Nazarene Col, Mont, 2001; Renwick Gallery, Nat Gallery Art, Washington, DC, 95; Celebrations, Art Quilt Network, Mansfield Art Ctr, Ohio, 97; Stitchers & Beaders: America's Best, Ohio Craft Mus, Columbus, 97; Up in the Air: UFO Invitational, Roswell Mus & Art Ctr, NMex, 97; Quilt Nat '97, Southeastern Ohio Cult Arts Ctr, Athens (2 1/2 yr world tour), 99; The Kiss, Eastern Wash Univ Exhib Touring Svcs, 98; Tiger on the Hearth, Mansfield (Ohio) Arts Ctr, 98; Art Quilts: A Haystack Faculty Survey, Maine Arts Comn and Haystack Sch, Blaine House, Augusta, Maine, 98; Ohio Craft Invitational, Mansfield Art Ctr, 98; Colander Girls, Qult Art Internet Group, 99; Quilt and basket Invitational, Peninsula Art Sch, Fish Creek, Wis, 99; Fine Focus touring exhib, 99; The Good Earth, Aullwood Audubon Ctr, Dayton, Ohio, 2000; The Best of 2000, Ohio Designer Craftsmen, Columbus, 2000; CraftSummer Faculty Exhib, Hiestand Gallery, Miami, Univ, Oxford, Ohio, 2000; Linda Schwartz Gallery, Cincinnati; Mitakuye Oyasin, Wayne Ctr Arts, Wooster, Ohio, 2000; Remnants: The Thread of Memory, Spruill Ctr Arts, Atlanta, 2000; Tell Me a Story - Chapter 1: Narrative Themes in Contemp Fabric Arts, Cahoon, Mus Am Art, Cotuit, Cape Cod, Mass, 2001; Thirteen Moons Gallery, Santa Fe, NMex, 2001; Alegre Retreat Art Show, Sweeny Ctr, Santa Fe, NMex, 2001; Fantastic Fibers, Yeiser Art Ctr, Paducah, Ky, 2001; Quilt National '01, Dairy Barn Arts Ctr, Athens, Ohio, 2001; Craftsummer (faculy exhib), Miami U, Oxford, Ohio, 2001, Parallel Threads, New Eng Quilt Mus, Lowell, Mass, 2001; WAGE group exhib, Lowry Ctr, Col Wooster, 2001; AQN Exhib, Fitton Ctr, Hamilton, Ohio, 2003; Dreaming the Garden, Touring Exhib, Laura Cater-Woods, Cur, 2003; group exhib, Claypool-Young Art Bldg, Morehead State Univ, Morehead, KY, 2004; and others. *Pos:* Founders, Turtle Moon Studios; Shie: founder, Green Quilts Proj, 89. *Teaching:* Mixed Media Healing quilts classes world wide; week long art camps, Turtle Moon Studios; workshops at craft schs, cols & mus; artist-in-residence, PS1, NY, 88 & Crafts Coun Ireland, 94; exchange artist to China, Ohio Arts Coun, 90; artist residency, Alfred Univ, NY, 97. *Awards:* Individual Artist Grants, Nat Endowment Arts, 90-91 & 94-95 & Ohio Arts Coun, 96 & 98; numerous other grants & awards. *Media:* Quilting, Mixed Media. *Mailing Add:* Turtle Moon Studios 2612 Armstrong Dr Wooster OH 44691-1806

SHIELDS, ANNE KESLER
PAINTER, ASSEMBLAGE ARTIST
b Winston-Salem, NC, Jan 27, 32. *Study:* Hollins Col, Roanoke, Va, BA, 54; studied with Hans Hoffman, Provincetown, Mass, 57; Univ NC, Greensboro, MFA, 59. *Work:* NC Mus Fine Art, Raleigh; Mint Mus, Charlotte, NC; Weatherspoon Gallery, Univ NC, Greensboro; Mus Fine Arts, Montgomery, Ala; Cornell Univ, Ithaca, NY. *Comn:* Portrait of James English, Conn Bank & Trust, Hartford, 70; urban wall mural, Arts Coun, Winston-Salem, NC, 75; portraits (4), Wake Forest Univ, Winston-Salem, NC, 80, 82, 83 & 88; portraits (3), Trinity Col, Hartford, Conn, 88 & 89. *Exhib:* Xylon IV, Int Exhib Woodcuts, Musee d'art et d'historie, Geneva, Switz, 65; 20th Nat Exhib Prints, Libr Cong, Washington, DC, 66; Printmakers, US Pavillion, Japan Expo, 70; solo exhibs, Silvermine Guild, New Canaan, Conn, 70 & Southeastern Ctr Contemp Art, Winston-Salem, NC, 77; 200 Yrs of Art in NC, NC Mus Art, Raleigh, 76; Five Winston-Salem Printmakers, Southeastern Ctr Contemp Art, NC, 83; After Her Own Image, Woman's Work, Salem Fine Arts Ctr, NC, 85. *Awards:* Atwater Kent Award, Soc Four Arts, Palm Beach, Fla, 64; E J Arden Prize, Boston Printmakers, Mass, 70; Va Ctr Creative Arts fels, 87, 88 & 90. *Bibliog:* Joanna L Krotz (auth), New traditions, Money Mag, 6/90; Genie Carr (auth), Face to face, portrait-group, Winston-Salem J, 8/25/91; Jean S Rodgers (auth), Women of letters, a group portrait of North Carolina writers, Winston-Salem, 3/18/92. *Mem:* Artworks Gallery (Artists Cooperative, Winston-Salem). *Media:* Oil on Canvas. *Publ:* Illustr, Whedbee--Legends of the Outer Banks & Tarheel Tidewater, Blair Publ Co, 66. *Dealer:* Portraits Inc 985 Park Ave New York NY 10028. *Mailing Add:* c/o Portraits South 105 S Bloodworth Raleigh NC 27601

SHIH, JOAN FAI
PAINTER, INSTRUCTOR
b Shantou, China. *Study:* Studied Chinese painting & calligraphy in Hong Kong, 49-52; Art Students League New York, 53; Kansas City Art Inst, BFA, 56, MFA, 61; Pa Acad Fine Arts, 57-59, 61-63. *Work:* ARCO Chemical Co, Newtown Square, PA, 91; Methodist Hosp, Philadelphia, PA; DW Newcomer's Sons, Kansas City, MO; Villanova Univ, PA, 2004. *Exhib:* Philadelphia Art Alliance, 66, 68, 79 & 83; Mus Philadelphia Civic Ctr, 70, 74, 79, 80 & 82; Nat Asn Women Artists Traveling Exhib, 78-80, 80-82, 83-85, 85-87; Nat Asn Women Artists Ann, Fed Bldg, NY, 79-83, 85; Woodmere Art Mus, Philadelphia, 79, 81 & 87; Peele Hoe Galleries, Pa Acad Fine Arts, 82; Bergen Mus, Paramus, NJ, 83; Plastic Club Ann Art Exhib, Philadelphia, 85, 88-91, 2000-02; solo exhib, Danville Mus Fine Arts, Va, 86, Connelly Art Gallery, Vaillanova Univ, PA, 2004; Art Inst Philadelphia, 87, 90 & 91; John Geiszel All Transparent Watercolor Ann Exhib, Philadelphia, 88-91; group shows, Wayne Art Ctr, Pa, 94, Plum Gallery, Paoli, Pa, 95 & 96, Philadelphia Watercolor Club Members Exhib of Works on Paper, Art Inst Philadelphia, Pa, 95 & 96, 16th Ann Philadelphia Sketch Club All Transparent Watercolor Exhib, Pa, 96, 1st ann-exhib by prof artists from the Tri-State Area, Philadelpia Art Alliance, Pa, 96, 96th Ann Int Exhib of the Philadelphia Watercolor Club, Berman Mus Art, Collegeville, Pa, 96, Main Line Art Ctr, Haverford, Pa, 1999 -2002, David David Gallery, Philadelphia, Pa, 1999-2003; Main Line Art Ctr, Haverford, Pa, 2005 & 06. *Teaching:* Instr, Kansas City Art Inst, Mo, 59-61; Converse Col, Spartanburg, SC, 66-67; lectr, Rosemont Col, Pa, 69-88; instr, Maine Line Art Ctr, Haverford, Pa, 98-. *Awards:* Marion Cohee Mem Award (First Prize), Plastic Club Open Juried Ann Art Exhib, Philadelphia, 89; George Dawson Mem Award for Flowers or Gardens, Philadelphia Watercolor Club 96th Anniversary Int Exhib, Berman Mus Art, Collegeville, Pa, 97; Grant, Female assn Philadelphia, Pa, 98. *Mem:* Nat Asn Women Artists; Philadelphia Watercolor Club; Hong Kong Art Club; Fel Pa Acad Fine Arts. *Media:* Watercolor, Oil. *Mailing Add:* 2014 Walnut St Apt 205 Philadelphia PA 19103-5778

SHIKLER, AARON
PAINTER
b Brooklyn, NY, Mar 18, 22. *Study:* Tyler Sch Fine Arts, Temple Univ, BFA, BSEd & MFA, 1948; Barnes Found, 1943; Hans Hofmann Sch, 1951. *Work:* Metrop Mus Art, NY; Mint Mus Art, Charlotte, NC; Sheldon Mus Art, Lincoln, Nebr; New Britain Mus Am Art, Conn; Brooklyn Mus, NY. *Comn:* Portraits of President & Mrs John F Kennedy for White House. *Exhib:* New Britain Mus Art, Conn, 64; Gallery Mod Art, NY, 65; Nat Acad Design, 65, 76 & 80; Brooklyn Mus, 71; Calif Palace Legion Honor, San Francisco, 71; one person exhibs, Meredith & Long Company, Houston, Tex, 72, 76 & 85, Davis & Long Company, NY, 83, 87, 90, 93 & 96, Tyler Alumni Gallery, Temple Univ, Philadelphia, Pa, 85, Lyme Acad Art Gallery, Old Lyme, Conn, 86, Galerie Laimbrock Langbroek, Utrecht, The Neth, 97; Sheldon Mem Art Gallery, Neb Art Asn, 79; Nassau Co Mus Fine Art, Roslyn Harbor, NY, 80; Nat Portrait Gallery, Washington, DC, 80; Rotunda Gallery, Brooklyn, NY, 83; The Forum Gallery, NY, 84; Hermitage Found Mus, Norfolk, Va, 85; Kunsthaus Buhler, Stuttgart, Ger, 94; and others. *Awards:* Thomas B Clarke Prize, 61; US Dept State Traveling Grant, 76; Benjamin Figure Prize, Nat Acad Design, 76; and others. *Bibliog:* articles, Am Artist, 9/71 & Current Biog, 12/71. *Mem:* Nat Acad (assoc, 62, acad, 65-); Century Asn. *Publ:* Contribr two chaps, In: Pastel Painting, 68. *Dealer:* Davis & Long Co 746 Madison Ave New York NY 10021

SHILSON, WAYNE STUART
PAINTER, ILLUSTRATOR
b Minneapolis, Minn, July 14, 43. *Study:* Univ Minn, BS(art educ), 71, MFA, 72; study with Katherine Nash, 68-70; Univ Minn, with GP Weisberg (prof), 87-89. *Work:* Parks Fine Art Gallery, Sycamore, Ill; Arthur's Int Gallery, Las Vegas, Nev; Meadowcreek Gallery, Edina, Minn; Framestyles Gallery, Kenwood, Minneapolis, Minn; Southdale/Hennipen Publ Libr, Edina, Minn; and many other permanent collections. *Comn:* Paintings, Bernard Picture Co, Stamford, Conn, 86; paintings, comn by William George, Minneapolis, 88; paintings, Arthur's Int, Honolulu, 88-90; paintings, Scafa-Tornabene, Nyack, NY, 90; Lake Harriet Bandshell (painting), comn

by Julie Andrews (actress). *Exhib:* One-man shows, Sky Gallery, St Paul, Minn, 76 & 79, Minn Inst Arts, Minneapolis, 79 & 80, Horizon Gallery, Bloomingdale, Ill, 86, Arthurs Int, Honolulu, Hawaii & Las Vegas, Nev, 87-90, Minn State Fair, St Paul, 90, The Stable Art Gallery, Maddens Resort, Gull Lake, Minn, 2001 & The Paul Bunyan Art Gallery, Bemidji, Minn, 2001; retrospectives, Normandale Cent Gallery, Bloomington, Minn, 87-89 & Lutheran Brotherhood, Minneapolis, 89; Eagan Auction, Eagan Rotary, Minn, 90; Minn State Fair, 90; N Country Mus Art, Park Rapids, Minn 93-96 & 2006. *Pos:* Artist & illusr, Honeywell, Minneapolis, Minn, 74-; pres, Household Landscapes, 87-; Judge, North Country Mus Art, 94; art dir & artist, Top Dog Productions, Park Rapids, Minn, 96; bd mem, N Country Mus Art, Park Rapids, Minn, 97-98; design layout artist, Bemidji Pioneer Newspaper, Minn, 98. *Teaching:* drawing, painting, art hist & caricatures, N Country Mus, Park Rapids, Minn,19 94-2000; painting & drawing, Park Rapids Comn Educ, Minn, 97-98; art teacher Pine Point Sch, White Earth Indian Reservation, Minn, 98-99, Remer-Longville Elem, Remer, Minn, 99-2000, Pine River/Backus Elem and High Sch, Minn, 2000-01. *Awards:* Award, Sky Gallery, St Paul, 76 & Art Ctr Minn, 80; Second prize, Eagan Rotary Club, 90; Artist grant McKnight Found, 98; Region Two Arts Grant, 99-2000. *Bibliog:* Liz Healy (auth), The Enterprise, Park Rapids, Minn, 1/92; Chelsey Johnson (auth), The Enterprise, Park Rapids, Minn, 8/94; Charmaine Barrawco (auth), Bemidji Pioneer Newspaper, 7/26/98. *Media:* Acrylic on Canvas. *Publ:* Park Rapids Enterprise, 11/91; illusr, Keyboard Classic, Sept-Oct, 92; Park Rapids Enterprise, 5/94, 8/94; The Maha-Leader, 9/93, 3/94; Summer Scene, 8/93, 8/94. *Dealer:* Marvin C Arthur 2613 High Range Dr Las Vegas NV 89134. *Mailing Add:* 17767 Emerald Island Cir Park Rapids MN 56470

SHIMIZU, YOSHIAKI
HISTORIAN, CURATOR
b Tokyo, Japan, Feb 27, 36. *Study:* Harvard Col, BA, 63; Univ Kans, MA, 68; Princeton Univ, MFA, 71, PhD, 74. *Pos:* Cur Japanese art, Freer Gallery Art, Smithsonian Inst, Washington, DC, 79-84; bd adv, Japan Soc NY, 81- & Arthur Sackler Gallery, Ctr Asian Art, Smithsonian Inst, Washington, DC, 84; ed bd, Arch Asian Art, 82-; consult cur, Nat Gallery Art, Washington, DC, 84-89; bd dir, Col Art Asn Am, 87-91; adv comt, Asia Soc Galleries, 92. *Teaching:* Asst prof art & archeol, Princeton Univ, 73-75, vis lectr, 81-84, prof, 84-, Marquand prof, 92-; asst prof Oriental art, Univ Calif, Berkeley, 75-78, assoc prof art hist, 78-79. *Awards:* Social Sci Res Coun Am Coun Learned Soc Grant, 78; Asian Cult Coun Grant, 95; Kajima Found Grant, 96. *Mem:* Japan Art Hist Soc; Col Art Asn Am; Asn Asian Studies. *Res:* Primarily Japanese art of the medieval period with reference to Chinese art. *Publ:* Coauth, Masters of Japanese Calligraphy: 8th-19th Centuries, Asia Soc-Japan Soc, New York, 84; auth, A Chinese album leaf from the former Ashikaga Collection in the Freer Gallery of Art, Arch Asian Art, Vol 38; Zen Art? Zen in China, Japan and East Asian Art, Swiss Asian Studies, Vol III, Peter Lang, Berne-New York, 85; ed & coauth, Japan: The Shaping of Daimyo Culture 1185-1868, Nat Gallery Art, 88; The Vegetable Nehan of Ito Jakuchu, in Sanford, LaFleur and Nagatomi, Flowing Traces: Buddhism in the Literary and Visual Arts of Japan, Princeton Univ Press, 92; and others. *Mailing Add:* Dept Art & Archeol McCormack Hall Princeton Univ Princeton NJ 08544

SHIMOMURA, ROGER
PAINTER, PERFORMANCE ARTIST
b Seattle, Wash, June 26, 39. *Study:* Univ Wash, BA(graphic design), 61; Syracuse Univ, MFA(painting), 69. *Work:* Seattle Art Mus; Nat Mus Am Art; Phoneix Mus Art; San Jose Art Mus; Denver Art Mus; Whitney Mus Am Art; Philadelphia Mus Art; and others. *Comn:* Mural (120″ x 420″), Westlake Station, Metro, Seattle, 90. *Exhib:* Pyramid Galleries Ltd, Washington, DC, 76; Morgan Gallery, Kansas City, Kans, 77, 79; Dobrick Gallery, Chicago, 77, 80; Elaine Horwitch Gallery; Steinbaum Krauss Gallery, NY, 89, 90, 92, 94 & 99; and many others. *Teaching:* Distinguished prof art, Univ Kans, Lawrence, 69-. *Awards:* Nat Endowment for the Arts Grant, 77, 89 & 91; seventeen gen res grants, Univ Kans; McKnight Fel, 95; and numerous others. *Bibliog:* Harold Haydon (auth), An unexpected sensation, Chicago Sun-Times, 5/17/74; JoAnn Lewis (auth), The American ethic, Washington Post, 6/3/76; David L Shirley (auth), Twitting the Samurai style, NY Times, 11/23/76. *Media:* Acrylic, Serigraphs. *Dealer:* Greg Kucera Gallery Seattle WA; Bernice Steinbaum Gallery Miami; Flomenhaft Gallery NYC. *Mailing Add:* 1424 Wagon Wheel Rd Lawrence KS 66049

SHIPLEY, ROGER DOUGLAS
SCULPTOR, EDUCATOR
b Cleveland Heights, Ohio, Dec 27, 41. *Study:* Am Sch Fontainebleau, France, with Monsieur Goetz, cert (painting), 62; Otterbein Col, Ohio, BA, 64; Cleveland Inst Art, painting & sculpture, 64-65; Cranbrook Acad Art, Mich, MFA, 67. *Work:* Nat City Bank, Cleveland, Ohio; Kalamazoo Inst Arts, Mich; Cranbrook Acad Art; Lock Haven Univ, Pa; M & T Bank; Penn Col, Williamsport, PA; Sterling Drug Inc, Philadelphia, Penn; Penn Col of Technol, Williamsport. *Comn:* Achievement award, comn by Williamsport/Lycoming Found, 91; recognition award, comn by N Cent Pa Conservancy, 91. *Exhib:* 31st Ann Mid-Year Show, Butler Inst Am Art, 66; A Plastic Presence, Milwaukee Art Ctr, 69-70; Henri Gallery, Washington, 86; Penn's Landing, Port Hist Mus, Philadelphia, 83; AAV/108 Nat Competition Metal Sculpture, Millerville Univ, PA, 84; B & S Galleries, Williamport, PA, 1985-2004; Extension Gallery, Johnson Atelier, Mercerville, NJ, 88; and many others. *Pos:* Prof of Art, Lycoming College; Logan Richmond Chair. *Teaching:* Prof painting, drawing, printmaking, two-dimensional design & color theory, Lycoming Col, coord Commercial Design Major, 67-,. *Awards:* Second Place Sculpture Award & Charlie Gohn Sculpture Award, William Penn Mus, Harrisburg, Pa, 83; May show, Cleveland Mus Art, 83; Cultural Enhancement Award, Williamsport/Lycoming Found, 93; Recognition Award, Williamsport, Lycoming Arts Council, 2002. *Bibliog:* Bringing the art of plastics into focus, Chicago Tribune, 2/70; The brightness of lesser lights, Cincinnati Enquirer, 10/73; Penns landing sculpture show, in doors and out, Philadelphia Inquirer, 8/83; Artist La; Artists Laudeo For Work, Williamport, Sun-Gazette, 99; and others. *Mem:* Lyco Co Hist Soc; Williamsport/Lycoming Arts Council; Bald Eagle Art League; Coalition Indpendent Artists & Artisans. *Media:* Cast Bronze, Plexiglass. *Publ:* Severin Roesen, Greater Williamsport Community Arts Coun, Bucknell Univ Press, 92; The Park Home Collection, 97 & The John Sloan Collection, Lycoming Co Hist Soc, Williamsport, Pa, 98; Beginning- Sculpture, Davis Pubications, Inc, 2005; The Sculpture Reference, Sculpture Books, Publishing, 2005. *Dealer:* B & S Gallery Williamsport Pa 17701; William Ris Gallery, Camp Hill, Pa 17011; Seaside Art Gallery, Nags Head, NC 27959; Faustina Gallery Lewsburg Pa 17837; Artist on the Green, Eagles Mere, Pa 17731. *Mailing Add:* 264 Lehman Dr Cogan Station PA 17728-9228

SHIRE, PETER
SCULPTOR, DESIGNER
b Los Angeles, Calif, Dec 27, 47. *Study:* Chouinard Art Inst, BFA, 70. *Work:* Mus Mod Art, Lodz, Poland; Art Inst Chicago; Los Angeles Co Mus Art; Brooklyn Mus, NY; Oakland Mus Art, Calif; Victoria & Albert Mus, London. *Comn:* Sculpture, McCarren Airport, Nev, 87; sculpture, Hokuden Electric, 94; sculpture, Sapporo Factory, Japan, 94; sculpture, Angels Point, Los Angeles, Calif, 94; sculpture, AIM Corp, Japan, 95; Colburn Sch Performing Arts, Los Angeles. *Exhib:* Seattle Art Mus, Was, 87; Los Angeles Munic Gallery, Calif, 88; Design Gallery, Milano, Italy, 89; Groninger Mus, The Neth, 90; Riva Yares Gallery, Ariz, 92; Ueda Gallery, Japan, 93; plus many others. *Teaching:* Calif State Univ, Los Angeles, 81-82; Hochschule Angewandte Kunst, Vienna, 83; Otis Parsons Sch Design, Los Angeles, 83; San Diego Univ, 85; Polytech Univ, Pomona, 86; Southern Calif Inst Arch, Santa Monica, 89-93. *Awards:* Design Team of XXIII Olympiad, Inst Architects, 84; Esquire Register, 85. *Bibliog:* Maria Porges (auth), Am Craft, 89; Peter Clothier (auth), Am Ceramics, 89; Hunter Drohojowska (auth), Ceramic Monthly, 89; Penny Smith (auth), Art & Perception, 2001. *Media:* Metal, Clay. *Publ:* Auth, Teatypes, Tea Garden Press, 80; Tempest in a Tea Pot, Rizzoli Int Publ, 91. *Dealer:* Modernism San Francisco; Frank Lloyd Gallery Santa Monica CA. *Mailing Add:* 1850 Echo Park Ave Los Angeles CA 90026

SHIRK, HELEN Z
CRAFTSMAN
Study: Skidmore Col, BS, 63; Kunsthaandvaerkerskolen, Copenhagen, Denmark, 63-64; Ind Univ, Bloomington, Ind, MFA, 69. *Work:* Carnegie Mus Art, Pittsburgh; Nat Mus Mod Art, Kyoto, Japan; Minnesota Mus Art, St Paul, Minn; Schmuckmuseum, Pforzheim, Ger; Univ Tex, El Paso. *Exhib:* Young Americans '62, Mus Contemp Crafts, NY, 62; Objects & Crafts, Indianapolis Mus Art, 73; Am Craft Mus, NY, 82; Galveston Arts Ctr, Galveston, Tex, 86; Wita Gardiner Gallery, San Diego, Calif, 87; Los Angeles Co Mus, 88; The Oriental Expression, Joan Robey Gallery, Denver, 90; Five in One Metals, Zoller Gallery, Penn State Univ, Pa, 90. *Teaching:* Asst prof art, Ind Univ, 71-73; instr jewelry & metalsmithing, Des Moines Art Mus, 73-75; lectr, Silversmithing Dept, Camberwell Sch Arts & Crafts, London, Eng, 83; prof art, San Diego State Univ, 75-. *Awards:* Fulbright Grant to Denmark, 63; Nat Endowment Arts, 78 & 88. *Bibliog:* Peter Dormer & Ralph Turner (auths), The New Jewelry: Trends & Traditions, Thames & Hudson, 85; Weidenfeld & Nicholson (auths), Craft Today: Poetry of the Physical, Am Craft Mus, 86; Barbara Mayer (auth), Contemporary American Craft Art: A Collector's Guide, Peregrine Smith Bks, 88. *Mem:* Soc N Am Goldsmiths; Am Crafts Coun. *Dealer:* Lisa Kurts Gallery 766 S White Station Rd Memphis TN 38117. *Mailing Add:* Sch Art Design Art Hist 5500 Campinile Dr San Diego CA 92182-4805

SHIRLEY, JON ANTHONY
COLLECTOR
b San Diego, Calif, Apr 12, 38. *Study:* Mass Inst of Technol, 57. *Pos:* Several Radio Shack div Tandy Corp, Ft Worth, 63-72, vpres, 72-83; pres, chief operating off, Microsoft Corp, Redmond, Wash, 83-90, bd dir, 83—; dir, Manzanita Capital, Seattle. *Awards:* Named one of Top 200 Collectors, ARTnews Mag, 2004. *Mem:* Asn Data Processing Serv Orgn (bd dir, 86-); Seattle Yacht Club. *Collection:* Vintage Ferrari Motor Cars; Modern & Contemporary Art

SHIVES, ARNOLD EDWARD
PAINTER, SCULPTOR
b Vancouver, BC, Dec 27, 43. *Study:* Univ BC, 62-64; San Francisco Art Inst, BFA, 66; Stanford Univ, MA, 69. *Work:* Achenbach Found Graphic Arts; Nat Gallery Ottawa; New York Pub Libr; San Francisco Mus Modern Art, State Univ New York, Buffalo, NY. *Comn:* Print ed, Visions of the North Shore, 2000; North Shore Arts Comn. *Exhib:* One-man shows, Pollock Gallery, Toronto, 75 & 76, Galerie Lindenthal, Cologne, Ger, 2000; World Print Competition, San Francisco Mus Mod Art, 77-79; New Acquisitions, 1940-1984, Achenbach Found, Calif Palace of Legion of Hon, San Francisco, 84; DeLeon White Gallery, Toronto, 96 & 98; DeLeon White Gallery, Denver, 01; Bond Univ Art Gallery, Queensland, Australia, 2004. *Teaching:* instr, 2 & 3 dimensional design, Trinity Wesleyan Univ, Langley, BC, Can, 2004. *Awards:* Distinguished Citizen Award, North Vancouver Centennial, 91; Fans Award, North Vancouver, 98; Nomination, Royal Can acad Art, 2006. *Bibliog:* John K Grande (auth), Arnold Shives, Art Forum, New York, 3/96; Fif Fernandez (auth), Arnold Shives Fans Award, 98; Rodgers Cable, Vancouver, 10/17/98; Trevor Carolan (auth) The Wilderness Sacraments of Arnold Shives, Image Mag, 2001. *Media:* Mixed Media on Panel, Relief Prints & Monotypes. *Publ:* Auth, Artist's Book: Mountain Journal, Prospect Press, Vancouver, 99. *Mailing Add:* 4217 Prospect Rd North Vancouver BC V7N 3L6 Canada

SHLIEN, HELEN S
CURATOR
b Kansas City, Mo. *Study:* Sarah Lawrence Col, BA, 41; Univ Chicago, MA, 64. *Collection Arranged:* Four Installations, Mobius, Boston, 87; Social Concerns, The Space, Boston, 88; Layerings, Newton Art Ctr, Maine, 89; I Want a Child, Westfield State Col, Maine, 89; Boston-Montreal, Artists Found, Boston, 90; Other Views, Danforth Mus Art, 94; Over Seventy, Boston's Honored Artists, Danforth Mus Art, 95; Still Life and Portraits, Danforth Mus Art, 97. *Pos:* Owner, Contemp Prints & Drawings Gallery, Chicago, 65-67; cur, Inst Contemp Art, Boston, Mass, 69-72; gallery dir, Boston Visual Artists Union, 74-75; owner, Helen Shlien Gallery, Boston, 78-85; independent cur, 85-; Appraiser, 20th Century and Contemp painting, sculpture and prints, 2001-. *Awards:* Nat Endowment Arts Grant, 77. *Mem:* Int Soc of Appraisers. *Specialty:* Contemporary painting and sculpture. *Publ:* Auth, Artists' Associations in the USA, A Descriptive Directory, pvt publ, 77; Ewa Kuryluk (auth), catalogue introduction, Fiberarts, vol 15, #2, 88; Gabrielle Rossmer (auth), catalogue introduction, Aspeckte der Gegenwartskunst; Virginia Gunter (auth), catalogue introduction, Revelations, 97. *Mailing Add:* 11740 Wilshire Blvd A2006 Los Angeles CA 90025

SHOEMAKER, INNIS HOWE
CURATOR
b Reading, Pa, Feb 7, 42. *Study:* Vassar Col, Poughkeepsie, NY, AB, 64; Columbia Univ, New York, MA, 68, PhD, 75. *Collection Arranged:* Paul Cezanne: Two Sketchbooks, Philadelphia Mus of Art, 89 (exhib & cat coauth); The Picture of Health: Images of Medicine and Pharmacy, William H Helfand Collection, 91; A Severe Selection: Modern Works on paper, A E Gallatin Collection, 94; Matisse's the Dance: The Barnes Found Mural, 94; New Art on Paper 2 (coauth, catalog), Hunt Manufacturing Co Collection, 96; Encounters with Modern Art (coauth, catalog), Selections from Rothschild Family Collection, 97; Mad for Modernism: Earl Horter and His Collection (auth, catalog), 99; Jacques Villon and His Cubist Prings, 2001. *Pos:* Cur, Vassar Col Art Gallery, Poughkeepsie, NY, 73-76; asst dir, Ackland Art Mus, Univ NC, Chapel Hill, 76-78, acting dir, 78, dir, 83-86; sr cur prints, drawings & photogr, Philadelphia Mus Art, 86-. *Teaching:* Vis lectr, dept art, Wesleyan Univ, Middletown, Conn, 75; adj prof, dept art, Univ NC, Chapel Hill; adj prof dept art history & archaelogy, Univ Pa, 2002-. *Awards:* Travel Grant, Samuel H Kress, 70; Rome Prize Fel, Hist Art, Am Acad Rome, 71-73. *Mem:* Am Asn Mus; Print Coun of Am; Col Art Asn Am. *Publ:* Contrib, Some Observations on the Development of FIlippino Lippi's Figure Drawings, Florentine Drawing at the Time of Lorenzo the Magnificent, Bologna, 255-264, 94; Philadelphia Museum of Art Handbook of the Collections, Philadelphia Mus, 95; Filippino Lippi and his Antique Sources, The Drawings of Filippino Lippi and his Circle, Metrop Mus Art, NY, 29-36, 97. *Mailing Add:* Philadelphia Museum of Art Philadelphia PA 19130

SHORE, ROBERT
PAINTER, ILLUSTRATOR
b New York, NY, Feb 27, 24. *Study:* Art Students League, New York; Boro Polytech, London, 46; Cranbrook Acad Art, Mich, 48 & 51. *Work:* Air & Space Mus, Washington; Newbury Libr, Chicago; Mus Univ Miss; NASA Space Ctr, Houston, Tex; Cranbrook Acad Art Mus, Bloomfield Hills, Mich; Smithsonian Inst, Washington. *Comn:* Drawings, Nat Broadcasting Co, NY, 57; Moby Dick (painting), MacMillan Co, NY, 62; paintings, USAF, Washington, 62-68; paintings, Nat Aeronaut Space Admin, Washington, 63-64; Heart of Darkness (paintings) & Billy Bud (paintings), Ltd Editions Club, NY, 69. *Exhib:* One-man show, Sch Visual Arts Gallery, NY, 50; Young Am Craftsman Show, Am House, NY, 51; Cranbrook Art, Detroit Inst Art, Mich, 51; Cooper Union Gallery Traveling Exhib, NY, 54; Permanent Collection, Houston Space Ctr, Tex, 60; Visions of Space, Nat Gallery Art, Washington, 63; Permanent Collection, Smithsonian Inst, Washington, 64-. *Pos:* Bd mem, Artists Equity, NY, 92-95. *Teaching:* Instr art, Cooper Union, 51-55, Sch Visual Arts, 53-75, Parsons Sch Design, 74-94, Art Students League, 75. *Awards:* First Prize Ceramic Sculpture, Young Am Craftsman Show, 52; Fulbright Fel (painting), US Govt, 52; Gold Medal, Soc Illusr, NY, 66. *Bibliog:* HL Cooke & JD Dean (auths), Eyewitness to Space, Harry N Abrams, New York, 71; FC Durant III (auth), Eyewitness to space (book review), Omni, 9/79; Elizabeth A Schultz (auth), Unpainted to the Last Moby Dick and 20th Century American Art, Univ Pr Kansas, 95. *Mem:* NY Artists Equity. *Media:* Acrylic, Oil. *Mailing Add:* 131 E 93rd St New York NY 10138

SHORE, STEPHEN
PHOTOGRAPHER
b New York, NY, Oct 8, 47. *Work:* Metrop Mus Art, Mus Mod Art & Whitney Mus Am Art, NY; George Eastman House, Rochester, NY; Mus Fine Arts, Boston; Art Inst Chicago; San Francisco Mus Mod Art; Los Angeles Co Mus Art; and others. *Exhib:* Solo exhibs, Nederlands Foto Inst, Rotterdam, 97, Photog Resource Ctr, Boston, 97, CRAF, Villa Cini, Spilinbergo, Italy, 98, Gallery Contemp Art, Mestre, Italy, 99, Musei Comunali, Rimini, Italy, 99, Palazzo Civico, Rubiera, Italy, 99, SK Stiftung Kultur, Cologne, Ger, 99 & Victorian Arts Ctr, Melbourne, Australia, 2000, Galerie Conrads, Ger, 2001, Galerie Rodolphe Janssen, Brussels, Belgium, 2002, 303 Gallery, NY, 2003; Flora Photographica, S Bank Art Ctr, London, Eng, 92; Am Studies, Aktions Forum Praterinsel, Munich, 95; Breuer's Whitney, Whitney Mus Am Art, NY, 96; Metrop Mus Art, NY, 97 & 98; Photog Innovators, 1840s-1990s, Victoria & Albert Mus, London, 99; Places as Landscape, Uffizi Gallery, Florence, Italy, 2000; Galerie Sprüth Magers, Cologne, Ger, 2005; Jeu De Paume, Paris, France, 2005; Hammer Mus, Los Angeles, Calif, 2005; Henry Art Gallery, Seattle, Wash, 2006; 303 Gallery, NY, 2006; Galerie Sprüth Magers, Munich, Ger, 2006. *Teaching:* Chmn photog dept, Bard Col, 82- & chmn arts div, 96-. *Awards:* Nat Endowment Arts Grants, 74 & 79; Guggenheim Fel, 75; Am Acad Rome, 80; MacDowell Colony Grant, 93. *Bibliog:* Tony Hiss (auth), The framing of Stephen Shore, Am Photog, 2/79. *Publ:* Auth, Uncommon places, 82 & The gardens at Giverny, 83, Aperture; Luzzara, Arcadia, Edizioni, 93; The Velvet Years, Pavilion Books, 95; Stephen Shore: Photographs, 1973-1993, Schirmer/Mosel, 95; The Nature of Photographs, Johns Hopkins, 98; American Surfaces, Schirmer/Mosel, 99; Uncommon Places, The Complete Works, Aperture, 2004; American Surfaces, Phaidon, 2005. *Dealer:* 303 Gallery 525 W 22d St Fl 1 New York NY 10011-1100. *Mailing Add:* c/o Bard Col Annandale-on-Hudson NY 12504

SHORES, (JAMES) FRANKLIN
PAINTER
b Hampton, Va, Nov 9, 42. *Study:* Pa Acad Fine Arts, Cresson Europe Traveling Scholar, Eakins Figure Painting Prize. *Work:* Pa Acad Fine Arts, Philadelphia; Camden Pub Libr, Maine. *Exhib:* Pa Acad Fine Arts Ann, 67 & 69; Philadelphia Watercolor Club Exhibs, 68-; Cabrini Col, 86. *Teaching:* Instr art, Pa Acad Fine Arts, 65-86. *Awards:* Harry Deitch Mem Prize, Philadelphia Watercolor Club, 78. *Mem:* Philadelphia Watercolor Club (hon pres, currently). *Media:* Watercolor, Oil. *Mailing Add:* 612 S Ninth St Philadelphia PA 19147

SHORR, HARRIET
PAINTER
b New York, NY, May 14, 39. *Study:* Swarthmore Col, BA, 60; Yale Sch Art & Archit, BFA, 62. *Work:* Bklyn Mus; Utah Mus Fine Arts, Salt Lake City; Citicorp, NY; Chemical Bank, NY; Estee Lauder Corp, NY. *Exhib:* Eight Women-Still Life, New Britain Mus, Conn, 82; Painterly Realism, 82 & Contemp Women Painters, 83, Rahr West Mus, Manitowac, Wis; Am Realism, William Sawyer Gallery, San Francisco, 85 & San Francisco Mus Fine Art, 85-86; Artists Choosing Artists, Artists Choice Mus, NY, 85; The Object Revitalized, Paine Arts Ctr, Oshkosh, Wis, 85-86; Contemp Am Still Life, One Penn Plaza, NY, 85-86; one-person exhibs, Evelyn Segal Gallery, Fort Worth, Tex, 93, 98, Editions Ltd, Indianapolis, IN, 93, Gallery of Contemp Art, Univ Colo, 93, Gallery Camino Real, Boca Raton, Fla, 94, Mus East Tex, Lufkin, 95, Neuberger Mus, Purchase, NY, 99, Purchase Col, SUNY, 99, Cheryl Pelavin, New York City, 2001, 2002; Bristol Meyers Squibb Gallery, Princeton, NJ, 97; Gischback Gallery, New York City, 97; Century Asn, New York City, 98; Univ NH, 98; Nat Acad Design, New York City, 98; Am Acad and Inst of Arts and Letters, New York City, 99; Qualita Gallery, Las Vegas, 99; Qualita Fine Arts, Las Vegas, 99; Erector Sq Gallery, New Haven, Conn, 2000; Del Ctr Contemp Arts, Wilmington, 2002. *Teaching:* retired, Prof painting, State Univ NY, Purchase, 79-2006. *Awards:* Nat Endowment Arts Grant, 80; Am Artist Achievement award, 94; Purchase Award, Am Acad of Arts and Letters, 99; Pollock-Krasner award, 2000. *Bibliog:* Nathan Kernan (auth), Review, Art in Am, 6/2005-7/2005; Ken Johnson (auth), NY Times, 2001; Faye Hirsch (auth), Review, Art on Paper, 3/2001-4/2001. *Mem:* Nat Acad. *Media:* Oil. *Publ:* Auth, A painter's reflections on real painting, Arts, 79; Auth, The Artist's Eye, Watson-Guptill, 91. *Dealer:* Cheryl Pelavin New York NY. *Mailing Add:* 117 Mercer St New York NY 10012

SHORR, KENNETH
PHOTOGRAPHER
Work: Calif Mus Photog; Ctr Creative Photog, Tucson; Mus Fine Arts, Houston; San Francisco Mus Mod Art; Nat Endowment Arts Arch, Smithsonian Inst, Washington. *Exhib:* Walker Art Ctr, 81; Whitney Mus Am Art Biennial, 83; San Francisco Mus Mod Art Biennial, 84; solo exhibs, Calif Mus Photog, Riverside, 92, Daniel Saxon Gallery, Los Angeles, 93, Ehlers Caudill Gallery, Chicago, 93, Bero Gallery, Tucson, Ariz, 97 & Gross Gallery, Univ Ariz, Tucson, 97; Arizona Artists, Nelson Fine Arts Mus, Ariz State Univ, Tempe, 96; Summer Show, Pace Magill Wildenstein, Beverly Hills, Calif, 96; Blindspot, Paolo Baldacci Gallery, NY, 96; A Glimpse of the Norton Collection, Site Santa Fe, 96; Making it Real, Aldrich Mus Contemp Art, traveling to Reykjavik Munic Mus, Iceland & Portland Mus Art, 97. *Awards:* Nat Endowment Arts Photog Fel, 79, 82, 84 & 94; Photog Fel, Nat Endowment Arts, 82, 84 & 94. *Bibliog:* Faye Hirsch (auth), Rethinking genres in contemporary photography, On Paper, Vol 3, No 3, 2/99. *Dealer:* Joseph Gross Gallery Dept Art Univ Ariz Tucson AZ 85721

SHOSTAK, ED (EDWIN) BENNETT
SCULPTOR
b New York, NY, Aug 23, 41. *Study:* Ohio Univ, 59-60; Cooper Union, 60-61. *Work:* Many pvt collections including: Phillip Johnson, New Canaan, Conn, Sydney Lewis, Richmond, Va & Mrs Horace Solomon, NY. *Exhib:* Am Exhib of Am Sculpture, 70 & Biennial, 73, Whitney Mus Am Art, NY; 76 Jefferson St, Mus Mod Art, NY, 75; Selections for New & Old Collections, Art Mus STex, Corpus Christi, 76; Non-Collectible Art from the Collection of Holly Solomon, Sarah Lawrence Col, Bronxville, NY, 77; A Collection, A Collector, Norman Fisher Collection, Jacksonville Art Mus, 79. *Awards:* Creative Artists Pub Serv Award, 73; Guggenheim Fel, 74. *Bibliog:* Robert Hughes (auth), In search of the new; Pursuit of the old, Time Mag, 1/71; Le Salon des Artists Independents, Grand Palais, Paris, France, 80; Decorative Sculpture, Sculpture Ctr, New York, 81; plus numerous others. *Media:* Wood, Metals. *Mailing Add:* 303 E Houston St New York NY 10002

SHUBIN, MORRIS JACK
PAINTER, LECTURER
b Mansfield, Wash, Feb 25, 20. *Work:* Utah State Univ, Logan; Las Vegas Art Mus, Nev; Home Savings & Loan, Calif; City La Mirada, Calif; Philip H Greene Collection; Glendale Federal Savings & Loan, Calif; Springmaid Beach Le Roy Springs Co, SC; and others. *Comn:* Painting (brochure), Robert Mondavi Winery, Calif, 90. *Exhib:* Nat Watercolor Soc Ann, Palm Springs Art Mus, Calif, 81; Art and the Law, Atlanta, 83; Utah State Univ, Logan, 83; 161st Ann Exhib, Nat Acad Design, 86, 88 & 92; Am Watercolor Soc Invitational, Museo de la Acurela Mexicana, Mexico City. *Teaching:* Instr watercolor workshops, Fla, Tex, NMex, Ore, Colo, Mo & Mex,

74-84, Spain, 85 & Canada, 90. *Awards:* Addeso Franklin Page Award, Owensboro Mus, Ky, 83; Samuel J Bloomingdal Mem Award, Am Watercolor Soc, 118th Ann Exhib, Canton Art Inst, 85; Crandall Norton Award, Downey Art Mus, 90. *Bibliog:* Gerald Brommer (auth), Transparent Watercolor, Davis, 73; Susan Meyer (auth), 40 Watercolorists and How They Work, Watson-Guptill; McClelland & Last (coauths, publ), The California Style, 85. *Mem:* Am Watercolor Soc (vpres, 87-89); Nat Watercolor Soc (treas, 70-72, 89-90, vpres, 72-73); WCoast Watercolor Soc; Pasadena Soc Artists; Watercolor USA Hon Soc. *Media:* Multimedia. *Publ:* Auth, Watercolor page, Am Artists, 8/74; producer, Nat Watercolor Soc Ann Catalog, 89-90; cover art, Your Research: Data Analysis for Criminal Justice and Criminology, West Publ Co, 92. *Dealer:* Eileen Kremen's Gallery 619 N Harbor Blvd Fullerton CA. *Mailing Add:* 313 N 12th St Montebello CA 90640

SHUEBROOK, RON (RONALD) LEE
PAINTER, EDUCATOR
b Ft Monroe, Va, July 29, 1943. *Study:* Haystack Mountain Sch, Maine, 65 & 67; Kutztown State Col, Pa, BS, 65, MEd, 69; Kent State Univ, Ohio, MFA, 72. *Hon Degrees:* Hon Doctorate, 2005 Ontario Col of Art and Design. *Work:* Art Gallery Ont, Toronto; Nat Gallery Can, Ottawa; Art Gallery Hamilton, Ont; Art Gallery, Windsor, Ont; Confederation Ctr PEI; and others. *Comn:* Cineplex, Odeon Corp, Tucson, Ariz, 88. *Exhib:* Olga Korper Gallery, Toronto, 80, 82, 83, 84, 87, 90, 92, 95, 97, 2001; Secession Mus, Vienna, 81; Select Acquisitions 1975-1988, Art Gallery Nova Scotia, Halifax, 88; 49th Parallel, NY, 89; Escapade a la conquete de la troisieme dimension, Mus des Beaux Arts, Sherbrooke, Que, 1990; Site Memory, Cleveland Ctr Contemp Art, 1991; A Century of Canadian Drawings, Dalhousie Univ, Halifax, Nova Scotia, 1999; Painters 15, Shanghai Art Mus, 2002, & MOCCA, North York, Ontario, 2003; Mendel Art Gallery, Saskatoon, Sask, & McLaughlin, Oshawa, ON, 2005; and others; Solo exhib, Recent work, Concordia Univ Art Gallery, Montreal, 86, Paintings, Drawings & Construction (catalog), Art Gallery Hamilton, traveled to Beaverbrook Art Gallery, Fredericton, NB, Kitchener-Waterloo Art Gallery, Ont, Mendel Art Gallery, Saskatoon, Saskatchewan, 87-88, Galerie Maghi Bettini, Amsterdam, 88 & 91, Forest City Gallery, London, Ont, 89, Galerie Beggini Marti Brummelkamp, Amsterdam, 1992, Ron Shuebrook Art Gallery, Univ Lethbridge, Alberta, 1996, MacDonald Stewart Art Centre, Guelph, Ontario, 1999, Galerie Graff, Montreal, 2000, NY Studio Sch, New York (with Charles Hewlings), others; Univ of Waterloo Art Gallery, ON, 2004; St Mary's Univ Art Gallery, Halifax, NJ, 2005; Olga Korper Gallery, Toronto, ON, 2005. *Pos:* Asst to dir, Provincetown Art Asn, 70. *Teaching:* Assoc prof, Nova Scotia Col Art & Design, 79 & 86-87, chmn studio div, 80-83, coordr painting & drawing, 83-84 & coordr drawing & fdn art, 84-85; exec dir, Ottawa Sch Art, Ont, 87-88; prof painting & Drawing, Univ Guelph, 88-, Chmn, Fine Art Dept, 88-93, coordr, MFA prog studio art, 94-95, joint coordr, 95-, Actg Chmn, Fine Art Dept, 96-99; vpres, Acad, Ontario Col Art & Design, Toronto, 1999-2000, pres, 2000-2005. *Awards:* Grants, Can Coun, 80, 81, 83, 85, 86, 88 & 90; Fel, McDowell Colony, Peterborough, NH, 81; Vis Art Critics Grant, Ont Arts Coun, 92; mem Royal Canadian Acad of Arts, 2000; Citation Alumni Award, Kutztown Univ, PA, 2003. *Bibliog:* Gloria Hickey (auth), Ron Shuebrook, Artsatlantic 30, winter 88; Kit Lort (auth), Interview with Ron Shuebrook, Artsatlantic, summer 88; Ingrid Jenkner (auth), Ron Shuebrook in Guelph, MacDonald Stewart Art Ctr, Guelph, Ont, 90. *Mem:* Univ Art Asn; Can Asn Univ Teachers. *Media:* Painting & Drawing. *Res:* Professional Art and Design Educ, & Abstraction in Painting & Sculpture. *Collection:* more than 60 public Art Galleries including Art Gallery of Ontario; Art Gallery of Nova Scotia; Nat'l Gallery of Canada. *Publ:* Thinking and Making: Notes for the Duration, Ron Shuebrook: Recent Work, Concordia Art Gallery, 3-4/86; Richard Gorman, Canadian Art, winter 87; John Greer, Vanguard, Vancouver, 9/87; Rockwell Kent at Dalhousie, Canadian Art, summer 87; Context and Paradigm, Ron Shuebrook in Guelph, MacDonald Stewart Art Ctr, Guelph, Ont, 90; Karen Wilkin, Partisan Review, Boston, Summer 2002; numerous others. *Dealer:* Olga Korper 17 Morrow Ave Toronto Ont M6R 2H9 Canada

SHUKMAN, SOLOMON
PAINTER, PRINTMAKER
b Bobr Prov, USSR, July 5, 27; US citizen. *Study:* Col Fine Arts & Theater Design, Moscow, BA, 49; Stroganoff Inst Art, Moscow, BA, 52. *Work:* Mankind and Work (monumental composition), Moscow; Energy/Metal (monumental composition), Paris; Summer, Spring, Autumn (monumental composition), Ehrfurt, EGer; Majakovski (collage), NY; Transport (3 decorative compositions), Prague. *Comn:* Mankind & Oil (mural), Art Found USSR, Moscow, 68; Morning, Union Soviet Artist, Moscow, 69; Cosmos, Union Soviet Artist, Moscow, 69; Country and Army (mural), Art Found USSR, Moscow, 71; Men and Cloth, Art Found USSR, Moscow, 72. *Exhib:* Solo exhibs, Loeb Rhode Market Gallery, 75, Panteon Gallery, 77 & Nathan Gallery, 78, San Francisco & Magnes Mus (with catalog), Berkeley, Calif, 78-79; Int Art Expo, NY Coliseum, NY & Los Angeles Convention Ctr, 85. *Awards:* First Praise, Int Expo, Moscow, 69 & 72, 2nd Praise, 73. *Bibliog:* Article, Best show of the year, Art in the USSR Mag, 72. *Mem:* Int Soc Artists; Graphic Arts Coun; Ctr Visual Arts; World Print Coun. *Media:* Murals, Graphics. *Mailing Add:* 554 Beresford Ave Redwood City CA 94061

SHULER, THOMAS H, JR
PHOTOGRAPHER, EDUCATOR
b Detroit, Mich, Apr 15, 49. *Study:* Princeton Univ, BA, 71; Univ Del, MA, 78. *Work:* Corcoran Gallery Art; Mus Francais Photog, Bievres, France; Bibliot Nat, Paris; Libr Cong, Washington, DC. *Exhib:* Recent Acquisitions, 77 & Still Life, 78, Corcoran Gallery Art; Focus Gallery, San Francisco, 79; MFA Gallery-The Platinotype, Rochester Inst Technol, 79; Photographer's Gallery, London, Eng, 79; Nuages, Bibliot Nat, Paris, 80; Invisible Light, Harvard Univ, 81; and others. *Teaching:* Instr photog, Smithsonian Inst, 75-76; chmn, asst prof & prog head photog, Northern Va Community Col, 76-. *Awards:* Medaille Verrieres Buisson, Mus Francais Photog, 78. *Bibliog:* Ben Forgey (auth), A sense of the moment when everything's right, Washington Star, 5/5/78; Time-Life Photo Annual, 79; Hafey & Shillea (auth), The Platinum Print, Graphic Arts Res Ctr, Rochester Inst Technol, 80; and others. *Mem:* Soc Photog Educ. *Publ:* Ed, Places, Infrared Photographs 1976-1978, pvt publ, 78. *Mailing Add:* 3715 Cardiff Rd Chevy Chase MD 20815

SHUMAKER, RITA LINDER
PAINTER, SCULPTOR
b Macon, Ga, Feb 27, 38. *Study:* Pfeiffer Univ, BA(magna cum lauda), 59; E Carolina Univ, MFA(painting), 83. *Work:* Z Smith Reynolds Found, Winston-Salem, NC; Georgia Governor's Coll, Atlanta; Squibb Corp; Rouch Industries Gastonia, NC; Eastern Airline Coll. *Comn:* Silk batik, comn by Marion Woodman, Toronto, 87; silk batik, comn by Robert Bly, Minneapolis, 87; silk batik sets, Ramanalla Dance Theater Co, Minneapolis, 94-95; Paintings, NC Nat Bank, Charlotte; Paintings, City Nat Bank, Charlotte. *Exhib:* Piedmont Crafts Exhib, Mint Mus, Charlotte, NC, 67, 69, 70, 71 & 72; Southeastern Crafts Invitational, Southern Ctr Contemp Art, Winston-Salem, NC, 72; Nat Print & Drawing Exhib, Davidson Col, NC, 72; Southeastern Drawing Exhib, Spartanberg Mus Art, SC, 83; United States Book Art Exhib, New Delhi, India, 87; Invitational Artist Exhib, Springfield Art Mus, Ill, 86 & 88. *Pos:* Artist-in-residence, SC Arts Comn 76-78, 2000- & Cent Col Univ Nebr, Lincoln, 78; consult, HBW Arts in Basic Educ, SC Arts Coun, 78-79; family prog asst, Mint Mus Art, Charlotte, NC, 2000-. *Teaching:* Adj prof art, Cent Piedmont Community Col, Charlotte, 74-81 & 2000-; prof art, Upper Sch Charlotte Co, NC, 83-95; asst prof art educ, Univ NC, Charlotte, 95-00. *Awards:* Gov Merit Award for Fiber, Atlanta Piedmont Art Fest, 71; Colortex Corp Merit Award, NC-SC Fiber Exhib, 84; Scholar in Schs, Charlotte World Affairs Council, 94-95 & summer study grant to Bali, 95. *Bibliog:* Interview (film), Art Scene, CCPC Pub TV, 92. *Mem:* Exhib mem Piedmont Craftsmen; Nat Art Educ Asn; NC Art Educ Asn. *Media:* Watercolor, Fiber; Ceramic. *Publ:* contrib, Batik and Tie Dye, Crown Publ, 73, Contemporary College, 74, Construction & Soft Sculpture, 74, The Comedy of Desire, Blue Sofa Press, 90, Walking Swiftly: The Life & Work of Robert Bly, Harper Perennial, 93, A Chemical History Tour, Arthur Breenbey, John Wiley & Sims, 2000

SHUTE, ROBERTA E
SCULPTOR
b Saskatoon, Sask. *Study:* Corcoran Mus Art Sch, 49-52; Am Univ, 52-53; study with Hans Hofmann, 53. *Work:* Alice Denny Collection; Henri Goetz Collection, Paris; Tremaine Collection, NY. *Comn:* Environ sculpture (with Maxine Cable), Noche Crist, engrs & technicians, Allied Chem, NY, 70; maj installation, Wolf Trap, summer 71. *Exhib:* Baltimore Mus, 53; Corcoran Mus, 53, 54, 56, 59, 65 & 67; Happening for Summers in the Park Prog, Nat Park Serv, Washington, 72; Installations, Textile Mus, Washington, 74; Sculpture on Grounds, Rockville City, 90; French Embassy, 95; Japanese Embassy, 96; and others. *Teaching:* Painting, Corcoran Mus Sch, 51-52; guest lectr plastic sculpture, Am Univ, 72; sculpture, Glen Echo Creative Adult Educ Prog, 73; pvt classes. *Awards:* Nathan Goodman Estate Award, 51; Second Prize, Wash Soc Artists, 62; First Prize, Art & Relig, 63. *Mem:* Wash Sculptor's Group; Int Sculpture Ctr; Gallery Ten. *Media:* Mixed Media, Poly-Adam Concrete System. *Dealer:* Gallery Ten 1519 Connecticut Ave NW Washington DC 20036-1115

SIAMIS, JANET NEAL
PAINTER
b Cleveland, Ohio, July 31, 38. *Study:* Rollins Col, Winter Park, Fla, 56-57; Antelope Valley Col, Lancaster, Calif, 78-81; study with Ralph Love, Temecula, Calif. *Work:* Home Savings Am; Fluor Corp, Irvine, Calif; Kaiser Permanente; Security Pac Bank; Embassy Suites Hotel; Marriott Hotel, Presidential Suites, New Orleans, La; Marriott Lincolnshire, Exec Suites, Chicago, Ill; Marriott Hotel, Ballrooms & Hospitality Suites, Anaheim, Calif. *Exhib:* All Media Exhib, Lancaster Mus, Calif, 85; Tallahassee City Hall Art Show, 88 & 89; Fla Watercolor Ann, St Petersburg, 91 & 96; Monotypes, Philbrook Mus, Tulsa, Okla, 95; Fla State Univ, Mus Fine Arts, 2003. *Awards:* Judge's Choice Award, Fla Watercolor Soc, 91. *Bibliog:* JS Ayres (auth), Brushes, Am Artist Mag, 86, Making Watercolor Monotypes, 88, Monotypes, Mediums & Methods, Watson-Guptill, 91; Dorothy Hoyal (auth), Taking oneself seriously as an artist, Am Artist Mag, 6/86; JS Ayres (auth), Printmaking Techniques, 93. *Mem:* Fla Watercolor Soc. *Media:* Watercolor. *Publ:* Illusr, A Christmas to Remember, Antelope Valley Press, 80; cover painting, Forecast Mag, Fla State Univ, 95; Flowers in Watercolor, Rockport Publ, 96. *Dealer:* Siamis Studios PO Box 1383 Crawfordville FL 32326. *Mailing Add:* Hwy 98 PO Box 1383 Crawfordville FL 32327

SIBERELL, ANNE HICKS
PAINTER, SCULPTOR
b Los Angeles, Calif. *Study:* Univ Calif, Los Angeles; Chouinard Art Inst, BFA; studied with John Wheat, Richard Lytle & Antonio Frasconi. *Work:* Fine Arts Mus, San Francisco; Cleveland Art Inst; Victoria & Albert Mus, London; Nat Mus Women Arts; Library of Congress, Washington, DC; Oakland Mus, Calif; Victoria & Albert Mus, London; and others. *Comn:* Ed 100 woodcuts, Silvermine Guild Art, Silvermine Col Art, 66. *Exhib:* Grad Theological Union, Berkeley, Calif, 2000; Unique Handmade Books, San Francisco Pub Libr, 2001; The Spirit of Handmade Prints, Triton Mus Art, Santa Clara, Calif, 2001; The Learning Curve, Ctr for the Book, San Francisco, 2001; 1st Ann Contemp Graphics Exhib, Galeria Nat, San Jose, 2002; Imagining the Book, Libr of Alexandria, Egypt, 2002; Imagining the Book 2, Libr of Alexandria, Egypt, 2005; plus many others. *Pos:* Asst art ed, Walt Disney Prods, Inc, 56-59; ed filmstrip prep from children's lit, Weston Woods Studios, Conn, 60; bd dir, Appletree Etchers, Inc, 72-74; artist-in-residence, Women's Graphics Ctr, Los Angeles & Nat Endowment Arts, 83 & Ragdale Found, Lake Forest, Ill, 90; panelists, Book Arts Conf & Exhib, San Francisco, 91; Invited lectr, Am Libr, Paris, 96; Invited auth

& illus, Rabat Am Sch, Morocco. *Teaching:* Art for Children, Silvermine Col Art, 66-68 & Martin Luther King, Jr Ctr, San Mateo, 68-70; woodblock printmaking, San Mateo Adult Educ, 70, illus children's lit, 74-75 & teaching, 76-78; guest lectr, Bakersfield Col, Calif, 77, Univ Ky, 80 & Mills Col, Oakland, Calif, 86 & Sonoma State Univ, 92; Advisor, Grad Studies Book Arts, Acad Art Col, San Francisco, 96. *Awards:* San Francisco Art Festival Award, Palo Alto Cult Ctr, 77; Grant, Nat Endowment Arts & Women's Graphic Ctr Bk Prod, 82; Peninsula Community Found Grant, Burlingame, Calif, 87; Artist-in-Residence, Ragdale Found, Lake Forest, Ill, 90. *Bibliog:* Design without Clients, Fortune Mag, 75; TV interview, Festival of Arts, San Carlos, Calif, 75. *Mem:* Calif Soc Printmakers; Appletree Etchers, Inc; Ctr Bk Arts, NY; Pac Ctr Bk Arts. *Media:* Oil Based Paint, Ink; Collage, Metals. *Publ:* Illusr, Emanuel Thayer's, Climbing Sun - The Story of a Hopi Indian Boy, Dodd, Mead, 80; auth & illusr, Whale in the Sky, EP Dutton, 82; coauth & illusr, Who Found America, 83 & Feast of Thanksgiving, 84, Children's Press; auth & illusr, A Journey to Paradise, Henry Holt, 90, Arabic translation, 2005; Bravo! Brava! A Night at the Opera, Oxford Univ Press, 2001. *Mailing Add:* 1041 La Cuesta Rd Hillsborough CA 94010

SIBONY, GEDI
SCULPTOR
b NYC, 73. *Study:* Brown Univ, BA, 1995; Student, Skowhegan Sch Painting & Sculpture, Maine, 1999; Columbia Univ, MFA, 2000. *Exhib:* Two Person Show, Gallery 16, San Francisco, 1998; Superimposition, Caren Golden Fine Art, NYC, 2001; Silent Takeover, Staedtische Gallerie, Baden, Switz, 2002; One Fine Day, Block Gallery, Sydney, Australia, 2003; Breaking Ground, White Columns, NYC, 2003; Playpen: Selections Summer, The Drawing Center, NYC, 2004; Slouching Towards Bethlehem, The Project, NYC, 2004; Floorplay, Brooklyn War Mem, 2004; The Qualities Depend Upon Other Qualities, 2004; Art Rev 25, Philips De Pury, NYC, 2005; Greener Pastures Contemp Art, Toronto, Can, 2005; Make it Now, The Sculpture Center, NY, 2005; Walls'n Things, Nicole Klagsbrun Gallery, NYC, 2005; Some Places Exist, London, 2005; The Wrong Galley, NYC, 2005; Poetry in the Backyard, Galerie Art: Concept, Paris, 2006; Whitney Biennial: Day for Night, Witney Mus Am Art, 2006. *Awards:* Grantee, Rema Hort Mann Found, 2004. *Mailing Add:* c/o Canada Gallery 55 Chrystie St New York NY 10002

SICHEL, KIM
HISTORIAN
b New York, NY, Dec 31, 55. *Study:* Yale Univ, MA, 81, PhD(art hist), 86. *Collection Arranged:* Brassai: Paris le jour, Paris la nuit, Mus Carnavalet, Paris, 88; Mapping the West: 19th Century Am Landscape Photos, 92; Philip Guston: Private & Public Battles, Boston Univ Art Gallery, 94; Black Boston: Documentary Photog & the African Am Experience, 94; From Icon to Ivory: Ger & Am Indust Photog, 95. *Pos:* Dir, Boston Univ Art Gallery, 92-98. *Teaching:* Adj lectr art hist, Yale Univ, New Haven, Conn, 85-86; asst prof, Smith Col, Northampton, Mass, 86-87; asst prof, Boston Univ, Mass, 87-99, assoc prof 2000-. *Awards:* Georges Lurcy fel, Lurcy Found, 84; Bunting fel, Radcliffe Col, 95; prof fel, NEH Univ, 95. *Mem:* Col Art Asn; Am Asn Mus. *Res:* History of Photography; European Interwar Modernism. *Publ:* Auth, Robert Demachy, Turn of the Century Photographer, Yale Univ Art Gallery, 83; Brassai: Paris Lejour, Paris LaNuit, Musee Carnavalet, Paris, 88; Black Boston, Documentary Photography & the African American Experience, Boston Univ Art Gallery/Univ Pa, 92; Philip Guston: Private & Public Battles, Boston, 94 & From Icon to Irony: German & American Industrial Photography, 95, Boston Univ Art Gallery/Univ Wash Press; Germaine Krull: Photographer of Modernity, MIT Press, 99

SICKLER, MICHAEL ALLAN
PAINTER, EDUCATOR
b Milwaukee, Wis, Aug 11, 45. *Study:* Layton Sch Art, Milwaukee, Wis, BFA, 70; Univ Wis-Milwaukee, MFA, 73. *Work:* Univ Potsdam, NY; Layton Sch Art, Milwaukee, Wis; Keith Corp, Salmon Brook, Conn; Oswego State Univ, NY. *Comn:* Painting mural, Keith Corp, Glastonbury, Conn, 84; 2 paintings, Birnbaum & Assoc, Syracuse, NY, 85; painting, comn by Sheraton Hotel, Liverpool, NY, 86. *Exhib:* Regional, 76 & New Paintings, 77, Everson Mus, Syracuse, NY; 42nd Ann, Munson-Williams-Proctor, Utica, NY, 79; Recent Paintings, Univ London, Ctr Related Arts, Eng, 83; Six Syracuse Painters, Skidmore Col, Saratoga, NY, 85; Retrospective: John Mulroy Civic Ctr, Syracuse, NY, 6/2000. *Collection Arranged:* Co-cur, Drawing Lives Exhibition, Lowe Gallery, Syracuse Univ, 2005. *Pos:* Art dir & sole auctioneer, WCNY, WXXI, WNPE & WNPI, NY State PBS, 83-, KTEH, San Jose, Calif, WSKG-Binghampton, NY; assoc editor Comstock Review; cur Point of Contact mag art holdings; panel moderator, Clement Greenberg: Memorial Exhib, Lowe Gallery, Syracuse Univ. *Teaching:* Assoc prof studio art & art hist, Syracuse Univ, NY, 73-, chair studio arts. *Awards:* Ford Found Grants, 79-83; First Prize, WCNY Invitational, PBS Sta, NY, 83; Golden Poet Award, World Poetry Press, 85, 86, 87 & 88; 3rd Place Defined Providence J Nat Poetry. *Bibliog:* Carmen Livingston (auth), Artist Draws on Various Styles, Auburn Citizen, 4/96; Bev Leesman (interview), 5 Yr New Times, 96; Katherine Rushworth (auth), Snapshot of An Artist, Herald Am Stars, 4/2000. *Mem:* Am Asn Univ Prof. *Media:* Acrylic on Canvas, Watercolor. *Publ:* Poetry, Salt Hill J, Syracuse Univ, 94; contribr, Defined Providence J, Ia, 95 & 96; Int Asheville Poetry Rev, 96-2004; Red Brick Rev, 96; Controlled Burn, poetry mag, 1997; Comstock Review, poetry mag, 2000-2005; Chapbook, Stereopticon, 2002; Threshold Press, Cathy Gibbons (ed). *Dealer:* Roberta Wood Gallery NC. *Mailing Add:* Art Dept Syracuse Univ 102 Shaffer Blds Syracuse NY 13210

SIDAWI, RAJA
PATRON
b Damascus, Syria. *Study:* Am Univ, Beirut, grad, 1962. *Pos:* Chmn, RWS Energy Servs, New York, NY, Energy Intelligence; trustee, Solomon R Guggenheim Mus; mem Wilson Coun, Woodrow Wilson Int Ctr for Scholars, Washington; mem, James Madison Nat Coun Libr of Congress. *Mailing Add:* Energy Intelligence 5 E 37th St New York NY 10016-2807

SIDEMAN, CAROL K
PAINTER
b Oakland, Calif, Feb 18, 25. *Study:* UC Berkeley, Calif, BA, 47; UC Berkeley (Erle Loran) Calif, Secondary Cred, 48; Grad Sch, Col Arts & Crafts (Harry Krell), 59. *Work:* Kaiser Permanente, Hospitals & Exec Offices, Oakland, Vallejo, CA; Glenborough Realtors, Corp Offices throuhgout US. *Exhib:* Collector's Gallery, Oakland Mus, Calif, 65-05; Annual Marin Soc Artists, Frances Young Gallery, Ross, Calif, 67; Featured Artist, OAA, Keith Gallery, St Mary's Col, Moraga, Calif, 71; California State Fair, Sacramento, Calif; Arts for the Parks, US Parks (Nat), Jackson Hole, WY. *Teaching:* Teacher art, Oakland PS, 49-52; teaching asst architectural rendering. *Awards:* First place, Marin Annual, Marin Soc Artists, 67; first place oils-figure, Alameda Co Fair, 75; first place, Kaiser Gallery Show, Oakland Art Asn, 2000. *Bibliog:* Kay Alexander (auth), Take 5 Art Prints-Teacher's Guide, Crystal Productions, 92-2005; Stacy Trevenson (auth), Art Reporter, Half Moon Bay Review, 2003. *Mem:* Oakland Art Asn, exhib coordr, 2003-2004; Marin Soc Artists, juror for numerous shows; Valley Art. *Media:* Oil, Watercolor. *Publ:* Prize Winning Art, Book IV, Allied Publ, 67; Art Education Resources, Take 5 Art Prints, Crystal Productions, 95-2005. *Dealer:* Sue Grim Langert, Langert Publishing, 300 Main St, Half Moon Bay, CA, 94019

SIDEN, FRANKLIN
DEALER, LECTURER
b Highland Park, Mich, Nov 16, 22. *Study:* Soc Arts & Crafts, 32-36; Meinzinger Art Sch, 40; Univ Ill, BS, 47; Wayne State Univ, MA(art hist), 77. *Pos:* Owner, Franklin Siden Gallery, Detroit, Mich, 64-72 & West Bloomfield, Mich, 72-82 & Bloomfield Hills, 82-. *Teaching:* Lectr art, Bloomfield Birmingham Art Asn, 74 & 76-77; lectr art & collecting prints, Univ Courses in Adult Educ, 78-80 & Jewish Community Ctr, 81-82. *Bibliog:* Six Detroit dealers who are serving a growing art market, The Art Gallery, 66; Kick out the jams: Detroit's cass corridor 1963-1977, Detroit Inst Arts, 80. *Mem:* Fel Founders Soc, Detroit Inst Arts; Friends of Mod Art, Detroit Inst Arts; Mus Mod Art, NY; Cranbrook Acad Arts, Bloomfield Hills. *Specialty:* Contemporary paintings, drawings, sculptures and prints

SIEBER, ROY
EDUCATOR, HISTORIAN
b Shawano, Wis, Apr 28, 23. *Study:* New Sch Social Res, BA, 49; Univ Iowa, MA, 51, PhD, 57. *Pos:* Mem foreign area fel prog, Africa Screening Comt, 59-63; cur primitive art, Ind Univ Fine Arts Mus, 62-; mem primitive art adv comt, Metrop Mus Art; mem joint comt Africa, Am Coun Learned Socs-Social Sci Res Coun, 62-70; trustee, Mus African Art. *Teaching:* From instr to asst prof art hist, Univ Iowa, 50-62; mem fac, Ind Univ, 62-64, prof art hist, 64-74, chmn fine arts dept, 67-70, Rudy Prof Fine Arts, formerly; vis prof, Univ Ghana, 64 & 67; vis prof, Univ Ife, Nigeria, 71; Benedict Distinguished Vis Prof, Carleton Col, 76-77. *Awards:* African-Am Univ Grant, 64; Ind Univ Int Studies Grant, 64 & 67; Nat Endowment for Humanities Sr Fel, 70-71 & 80-81; plus others. *Mem:* African Studies Asn; Col Art Asn Am; Am Asn Univ Prof; Midwest Art Asn (secy, 63). *Res:* African art. *Publ:* Auth, Sculpture of Northern Nigeria, Mus Primitive Art, NY, 61; co-auth, Sculpture of Black Africa, Los Angeles Co Mus Art, 68; auth, African Textiles & Decorative Arts, Mus Mod Art, NY, 72; auth, African Furniture and Household Objects, Am Fedn of Arts, 80. *Mailing Add:* 114 Glenwood E Bloomington IN 47408

SIEDMAN, SCOTT
PAINTER, ILLUSTRATOR
b Los Angeles, Calif, 48. *Study:* Calif Art Inst, Valencia, BS; studied with John Baldessari. *Work:* Secretariat, Manhattan Beach, Calif; mural, Giant Ramp, Rector Corp; Rene & Veronica di Rosa Mus, Napa, Calif. *Exhib:* Laguna Art Mus, Calif; Morphos Gallery, San Francisco, Calif, 94; Catherine Clark Gallery, San Francisco, Calif, 96; Six Calif Painters, Circle Elephant Art, Los Angeles, Calif, 2001; Solo exhib, Black Acre Gallery, Santa Rosa, Calif, 74, Catherine Clark Gallery, San Francisco, Calif, Horn Gallery, Vancouver, British Columbia, Can, Robert Berman Gallery, Santa Monica, Calif, 98. *Awards:* Bank Am Award Fine Arts; Scholarship, Chouinard Art Sch. *Mailing Add:* 2333 Chiselhurst Dr Los Angeles CA 90027

SIEG, ROBERT LAWRENCE
SCULPTOR, EDUCATOR
b Cement, Okla. *Study:* Cent State Univ, Okla, BA, 63; Inst Allende, Univ de Guanajuato, MFA, 68. *Work:* Ark Arts Ctr, Little Rock; Okla Art Ctr, Oklahoma City; Mus Art, Univ Okla, Norman; Okla Arts & Humanities Coun Collection, Oklahoma City. *Exhib:* Inter-D Exhib, McAllen Int Mus, Tex; Midwest Biennial Joslyn Art Mus, Omaha, Nebr; Monroe Ann, Masur Mus Art, La; Delta Art Exhib, Ark Art Ctr; Goddard Arts Ctr, Okla, 78; Since Statehood: Twelve Oklahoma Artists, Oklahoma City Art Mus, 96. *Teaching:* Asst prof art, ECent Okla State Univ, 66-86, chmn art dept, 90-2000, ret. *Awards:* Sculpture Award, 15th Mid-Am, Nelson Gallery Art, Kansas City, 65; Inter-Am Craft Alliance Award, McAllen Int Mus, Tex, 70; Purchase Award, Toys Designed by Artists, Ark Art Ctr, 74. *Bibliog:* BJ Smith (auth), Features artist, Cimarron Rev, 4/73. *Mem:* Individual Artists of Okla. *Media:* Wood, Metal. *Mailing Add:* 20669 County Rd #3 Dr Stonewall OK 74871

SIEGEL, BARBARA
PAINTER; ARCHITECT
b Baltimore, Md, Oct 26, 59. *Study:* U Wis, with Don Reitz, BA, 80; Univ Md, MArch, 85; Corcoran Gallery Sch Art, with Bert Schmutzhart and F L Wall, 85-92. *Work:* Children's Nat Med Ctr, Washington, DC. *Exhib:* One-woman show, Cafe Zino, Bethesda, Md, 95, Bethesda Regional Libr, 95, 97, 98, New Horizons Gallery, 98, 2000, Barnes and Noble, Bethesda, Md, 99; Then and Now: Twenty Yrs of A Salon, 98; Elements, Wilson Ctr Gallery, 99; Sweet and Sour, Wilson Ctr Gallery, 2000; Room with a View, Bethesda Artspace, 2000; Suburbanscape, Anne Arundel Community Col, 2000. *Awards:* Frederick Festival Arts Award of Merit, 98; Third Pl, Bethesda Row Arts Festival, 98; Individual Artists Award, Md State Arts Coun, 2000-. *Mem:* A Salon Ltd (vpres Bethesda Artspace, 98). *Media:* Pastel. *Dealer:* Marin-Price Gallery. *Mailing Add:* 7107 Exfair Rd Bethesda MD 20814

SIEGEL, (LEO) DINK
ILLUSTRATOR, CARTOONIST
b Birmingham, Ala. *Study:* Nat Acad Design; Art Students League; Am Sch Art; also with Robert Brackman. *Exhib:* Soc Illustrators, NY; Quilts & Illustrations: A Husband and Wife Exhib, 89; Dink Siegel - Pioneer in Cyberspace, Soc Illusrs, New York City, 00. *Mem:* Soc Illusr (life mem). *Media:* Ink, Computer. *Interests:* flute, sports. *Publ:* Illusr, Redbook, Cosmopolitan, Saturday Evening Post, Field & Stream, Ladies Home Journal, Good Housekeeping, New Yorker, Playboy & many others. *Dealer:* Illustration House Inc 110 W 25th St New York NY 10001. *Mailing Add:* 100 W 57th St New York NY 10019

SIEGEL, FRAN
PAINTER
b Mar 10, 60. *Study:* Tyler Sch Art, Temple Univ, BFA(magna cum laude), 82; Yale Univ Sch Art, MFA, 87. *Work:* Paine Webber; Brown Found; ITT Sheraton; Caddell & Conwell Found Arts; Alta Light Productions; and many others. *Comn:* West Hollywood Public Art. *Exhib:* Solo shows, New Gallery, Houston, Tex, 84, 86, 87, 89, 91, 93, 96, Genovese Gallery, Boston, Mass, 92, 94, 97, Margaret Thatcher Projs, NY, 97-98 & Mus Eds, NY, 2001; Art in General, NY, 94; Tricia Collins: Grand Salon, NY, 95; Corning Inc Gallery, New York City, Univ of RI; Kingston Mus Szuki; Lodz, Poland. *Teaching:* Painting, Fine Arts Dept, Pratt Inst, currently; Painting & Drawing, Calif State Univ, Long Beach. *Awards:* Yaddo, 95; Albee Found, 97; ED Found, 97; City Los Angeles Individual Artist Fel, 2005-2006. *Bibliog:* article in Artweek, 5/85; article in Boston Herald, 3/94; articles in Art New Eng, 6/94 & 10/94 & Rev, 5/97; article in Los Angeles Times, 10/99; article in Los Angeles Weekly, 10/99. *Mem:* CAA, Asn Colour Int. *Media:* Scrim & Glass. *Publ:* Light/Shadow, Art Mus Arad, Romania; Art in America, 01; Sculpture Magazine, 01; NY Times, 01. *Dealer:* Genovese Gallery Boston MA; Margaret Thatcher Projects New York NY

SIEGESMUND, RICHARD
MUSEUM DIRECTOR, EDUCATOR
b Jan 10, 51. *Study:* Trinity Col, Hartford, Conn, BA, 73; Univ Hawaii, Manoa, Honolulu, Hawaii, grad study, 73-75; Fel Arts Mgt, Visual Arts Prog, Nat Endowment Arts, Washington, DC, 81, Stanford Univ, MA 95, PhD, 2000. *Work:* Hawaii State Found Culture & Arts. *Exhib:* Artists of Hawaii, Honolulu Acad, 75; Kala Inst, Berkeley, Calif, 94; Univ Calif, Berkeley, 94; Blackhawk Mus, 94. *Pos:* assoc dir, Wash Proj Arts, 86-89; dir, The Fabric Workshop, Philadelphia, Pa, 89-90, San Francisco Mus Mod Art, 91-92; artist in residence, Kala Art Inst, 93-97; consult, guest cur, guest lectr, & panelist for numerous programs. *Teaching:* Asst, Stanford Univ, 95-98. *Awards:* Dissertation Fel, Getty Educ Inst for Arts, 99. *Mem:* The Photo Rev (bd mem, 89-97); Col Art Asn; Am Asn Mus; Nat Art Educ Asn; Am Educ Res Asn. *Media:* Printmaking, Painting. *Res:* cognition and creating visual art. *Publ:* Auth, The Context of Creativity, An Industrious Art: Innovation at the Fabric Workshop, 91; Wy do we teach art today, In: Studies in Education, 98; Teaching art as reasoned perception, In: Working Papers in Art Education, 98. *Mailing Add:* 2700 Guildford Ave Baltimore MD 21218-4415

SIEMS, ANNE
PAINTER
b Berlin, Ger, Feb 16, 65. *Study:* Hochschule der Kunste, Berlin, Ger, MFA, 91. *Work:* Boise Art Mus, Idaho; Am Airlines, Seattle, Wash; Hallmark Collection, NY; Microsoft Collection, Redmond, Wash; Ark Art Ctr, Little Rock. *Comn:* Spiral Screen, Ore Col Arts & Crafts, 95. *Exhib:* NW Juried Art Exhib, Cheney Cowles Mus, Spokane, Wash, 92; Figure 7, Bellevue Art Mus, Wash, 92; one-woman show, Calif State Univ Art Gallery, San Bernardino, 95; Seventh Nat Juried Exhib, Viridian, NY, 96; Botanical Vision, Boise Art Mus, Idaho, 96; Out of Eden, Kemper Mus Contemp Art, Kansas City, Mo, 97; Botanically Inspired, Holter Mus Art, Helena, Mont, 97; Since 1907, Ore Col Art & Craft, Portland, 97. *Teaching:* Ore Col Art & Craft, Portland, 97. *Awards:* First Prize Drawing, Artquake, Portland, Ore, 94; Alice Rooney NW Women Artist Stipend, Pilchuck Glan Sch, 95; Ore Col Arts & Crafts 90th Anniversary Award, 97. *Bibliog:* Michael Lawrence (auth), Visions, 94; Tracy Smith (auth), Anne Siems at PDG, Art Am, 96. *Mem:* Artista Trust. *Media:* Beeswax, Acrylic on Paper. *Dealer:* Grover Thurston Gallery 309 Occidental Ave S Seattle WA 98104. *Mailing Add:* 6548 21st Ave NW Seattle WA 98117

SIENA, JAMES
PAINTER
b Oceanside, Calif, Oct 28, 57. *Study:* Cornell Univ, BFA, 79. *Work:* San Francisco Mus Mod Art, Calif; Whitney Mus Am Art, NY, NY; Mus Modern Art, NYC. *Exhib:* San Francisco Art Institute, 2003; invited exhibitor Whitney Mus Art, 2004. *Teaching:* adj prof art, Va Commonwealth Univ, Richmond, 2000, 2002; adj prof art, San Francisco Art Inst, 2002; vis prof, New School, NYC, 2003. *Awards:* fel in painting NY Found for the Arts, 95; Tiffany Award, Louis Comfort Tiffany Found, 99; Acad Award in Painting, invitational, Am Acad Arts & Letters, 2000. *Bibliog:* Amy Michael (auth), James Siena at Cristinerose Gallery, Art in Am, 11/98; Goings on About Town/Galleries-Chelsea: James Siena at Gorney Bravin - Lee, The New Yorker, 10/29/2001; Ken Johnson (auth), Art in Review: James Siena at Gorney Bravin - Lee, NY Times, 10/26/2001; David Frankel (auth), Reviews: James Siena at Gorney Bravin - Lee, Artforum, 1/2001; Joe Fyfe (auth), Strange Loops, Art on Paper, Jan-Feb, 2003. *Dealer:* Daniel Weinberg 6148 Wilshire Los Angeles 90048; Gorney Bravin & Lee 534 W 26th New York NY 10001

SIGAL-IBSEN, ROSE
CALLIGRAPHER, PAINTER
b Bucharest, Romania, Aug 22; US citizen. *Study:* Fashion Inst Technol, 78; Parson Sch Design, 85-86; Koho Sch of Sumi-E, 79-90; Zhejiang Acad Fine Arts, China, 90. *Work:* NY Pub Libr; Manhattan Savings Bank, NY; Steinhardt Conservatory, Brooklyn Botanical Garden; Nat Mus Women in Arts, Washington DC; Chemical Bank, NY. *Exhib:* one-woman shows, China-Gallery Weizhi Schubert, Hanover, Ger, 91, Manhattan Savings Bank, NY, 93-94, Roumanian Cult Found, Bucharest, 98, World Fine Art Gallery, NY, 98, NY Pub Libr; China Nat Acad Fine Arts, Hangzhou, 94; Fine Arts Gallery, Huntington Beach, Calif, 95; Seaton Hall Gallery, S Orange, NJ, 96; Cork Gallery/Lincoln Ctr, NY, 98; Broome St Gallery, 99; Doizaki Gallery, 99; Group exhib, Art of Ink in Am, Newark Mus & Nat Taiwan Art Educ Inst, 2000, JACCC, Los Angeles, 99, Conn 98 Int Contemp Calligraphy Exhibit, Weslyan Univ, Middletown, Conn, 98, Seton Hall Univ, South Orange, NJ, 96, Golden West Col, Huntington Beach, Calif, 95, Gallery Korea, New York City, 94, Global Focus The Nat Mus of Women in the Arts, Washington, DC, 96; Contemp Art guild, Corg Gallery, 03; Romanian Cult Ctr, NY, 03; trav exhib, Art of INK in Am, 2004-2005; NY Artists Equity, Holiday Invitational Exhib, 2005; Am Soc Contemp Artists, 87th Ann Exhib, Broome St Gallery, 2005; JAA NY, Hammond Mus, 2005; One Woman Show, Berkeley College Gallery, 2006. *Pos:* Cur, Metrop NY Chap of Sumi-E Soc, 90-, vpres, 90-. *Teaching:* Lectr, Taiwan Art Edn Ctr, 2000, Bronx Sch Sci, 99. *Awards:* Manhattan Arts Award Cover Art Competition, NY, 92, 94, 95 & 97; Tenth Japanese Int Calligraphy Exhib Award, NY, 96; Emily N Hatch Mem Award, Pen and Brush Inc, 98; Nat Sumi-e Soc Shoe Ming Chiao Award, 99; Award of Excellence, Calligraphy Competition, Kampo Cult Ctr, NY, 96; Nat Sumi-e Soc Hallie Hazen Mem Award, 2001; Nat Sumi-e Soc Am Frame Award, 2004. *Mem:* Nat Mus Women in Arts; Artist Equity of NY; Am Soc Contemp Artists; Art of Ink Am; Oriental Brushwork Soc Am; Genesis 21 Am-Romania Artists; The Oriental Brushwork Soc Am; Am Soc Contemp Artists (ASCA); Artist Ink in Am; Contemp Artists Guild. *Media:* Watercolor. *Publ:* Newart International, pages 50-51, 2001; New Art, 54-55, 2003 & 144-145, 2005. *Mailing Add:* One Irving Pl Apt 222 B New York NY 10003-9741

SIGALA, STEPHANIE CHILDS
LIBRARIAN, EDUCATOR
b Berkeley, Calif, Nov 1, 47. *Study:* Univ Calif, Los Angeles, BA, 68, MA, 70; Univ Ill, MLS, 84. *Pos:* Slide cur, Univ Wisc, Milwaukee, 73-74; archit librn, Auburn Univ, 84-85; head librn, St Louis Art Mus, 85-2000, actg dir educ, 2000. *Teaching:* Instr art hist, Univ Wis, Whitewater, 71-73; asst prof, Ill State Univ, 78-83; adj prof libr sci, Univ Mo, 88-96; sr educ, St Louis Art Mus, 2001-. *Awards:* Kress Found Grant, 69; Fel, Univ Ill, 74-75. *Mem:* Art Libr Soc of NAm (chap pres, 88-90, exec bd, 94-96); Spec Libr Asn (chap dir, 89-90); Am Libr Asn. *Res:* Greek and Roman art; mus librarianship; history of the St Louis Art Mus. *Publ:* Auth, A Decade of Professional Literature for Slide Curators, VRA Bulletin, 85; Exhibition Catalogs on Exchange, Art Documentation, 88; Art of the Ancient World, St Louis Art Mus, 89; auth, The Museum Building: Inside and Out, St Louis Art Mus, 90; contribr, History of American Mass Market Magazines, Greenwood Press, 90. *Mailing Add:* 815 Brookside Dr Saint Louis MO 63122-1804

SIGEL, ANTHONY B
CONSERVATOR
Pos: Assoc conservator, objects Straus Ctr Conserv, Harvard Art Mus, Cambridge, Mass. *Awards:* Nat Educ Asn Rome Prize Fel for Historic Preserv and Conserv, 2004-05. *Mailing Add:* Straus Ctr Conserv Harvard Art Mus 32 Quincy St Cambridge MA 02138

SIGISMUND, VIOLET M
PAINTER, PRINTMAKER
b New York, NY. *Study:* Art Students League; also with Sidney Laufman & George Grosz. *Comn:* Many portrait comns. *Exhib:* Butler Inst Am Art, Youngstown, Ohio, 62; print show, Albany Inst Arts, 71; print show, Washington Co Mus, Md, 71-73; print show, Cayuga Mus, 73; one-woman show, Paul Kessler, Provincetown, Mass, 73; Nat Asn Women Artists Traveling Group Oil Show, US, 75-77, Israel & Egypt, 81-82 & Traveling Group Print Show, 79-81; NY Nat Acad, Audubon; and others. *Awards:* Sargent Prize, Nat Asn Women Artists, 63; Provincetown Art Asn, 83; Pen & Brush, 91; and others. *Mem:* Knickerbocker Artists; Nat Asn Women Artists; Provincetown Art Asn; NY Artists' Equity Asn (chmn mem, 60-73, mem bd dir, 81-82); Pen & Brush, NY. *Media:* Oil, Watercolor; Woodblock, Lithography

SIKANDER, SHAHZIA
PAINTER
b Lahore, Pakistan, 69. *Study:* Nat Col Arts, Lahore, Pakistan, BFA, 92; Rhode Island Sch Design, Providence, MFA, 95. *Exhib:* Solo exhibs, Pakistan Embassy, Washington, DC, 93, Veil: In Their Minds and on Our Heads, Rhode Island Sch Design, Providence, 94, Introduction 96, Barbara Davis Gallery, Houston, 96, Miniatures and Murals, Deitch Proj, NY, 97, Renaissance Soc, Univ Chicago, 98,

Kemper Mus Contemp Art & Design, Kansas City, Mo, 98-99, Hishorn Mus, Washington, DC, 99, Acts of Balance, Whitney Mus, Phillip Morris Br, NY, 2000, The Renaissance Soc at the Univ of Chicago (catalog), 01, Brent Sikeema, New York City, 03; Biennial Exhib (auth, catalog), Whitney Mus Am Art, NY, 97; Out of India (auth, catalog), Queens Mus Art, Flushing Meadows, NY, 97; On the Wall, Forum Contemp Art, St Louis, Mo, 98; I love NY (auth, catalog), Ludwig Mus, Austria, 98; Pop Surrealism (auth, catalog), Aldrich Mus Contemp Art, Conn, 98; Cinco Continentes y una Ciudad, Museo de Ciudad de Mexico (catalog), Mexico City, 99; Negotiating Small Truths, The Blanton Mus of Art, Austin, Tex, 99; Art-Worlds in Dialogue, Ludwig Mus (catalog), Koln, Ger, 99; Third Asia-Pacific Triennial of Contemp Art (catalog), Brisbane, Australia, 99; The Am Century, Whitney Mus (catalog), NY, 99; Greater New York, PSI, in collaboration with MOMA, Queens, NY, 2000; "00", Barbara Gladstone Gallery (catalog), NY, 2000; New Works: 01.1 Rivane Neuenschwander, Shahzia Sikander, Tony Villejo, Art Pace, San Antonio, Tex, 2001; Elusive Paradise, Nat Gallery of Can, Ottawa, Ont, 2001; Expanding Tradition, Deutsche Bank Lobby Gallery, NY, 2001; ARS 01, Mus of Contemp Art, Kiasma, Helsinki, 2001; Conversations with Traditions, Asia Soc, NY, 2001; Threads of Vision: Toward a New Feminine Poetics, Cleveland Ctr for Contemp Art, Ohio, 2001; Mus Mod Art, 02, 05; Weatherspoon Art Mus, Greensboro, NC, 02-03; Fabric Workshop and Mus, Phila, Pa, 06. *Pos:* co-cur The Stroke, an overview of contemp painting, Exit Art, 5/1-7/2, 99. *Awards:* Shakir Ali Award/Kipling Award, Nat Col Arts, Lahore, 93; Louis Comfort Tiffany Found Award, 97; Joan Mitchell Award, 98-99; South Asian Women's Creative Collective Achievement Award, 99; MacArthur Fellow, John D and Catherine T MacArthur Found, 2006. *Bibliog:* Thomas McEvilley (auth), Tracking the Indian Diaspora, Art Am, 74-79, 10/97; Edward Gomez (auth), Past is present, Art & Antiques, 60-66, 12/98; Phoebe Hoban (auth), The Mod Squad, NY Mag, 30-37, 1/11/99; Germaine Gomez-Haro (auth), Five Continents and a City-Museo de Ciudad de Mexico, Art Nexus, 8-10, 99; Francine Prose (auth), The Gallery: The Artist as Curator, The Wall St Jour, 5/20/99; Homi Bhabha (auth), Miniaturizing Modernity, Public Culture, Winter 99; Homi Bhabha (auth), Shahzia Sikander, a Happy dislocation, Elaine Kim and Margo Machida (eds), Fresh Talk: Daring Gazes, Univ of Calif Press, 99; Edith Newhall (auth), Installation, New York Mag, 4/24/2000; Holland Cotter (auth), Shahzia Sikander, Acts of Balance, The NY Times, 6/9/2000; Franklin Sirmans (auth), Shahzia Sikander, Acts of Balance, Time Out, 6/15/2000; Jonathan Goodman, Shahzia Sikander, Art Asia Pacific, 2001; Harriet Zinnes (auth), Projects 70, NY Arts, 1/2001; Jerry Saltz (auth), Good on Paper, The Village Voice, 57, 10-11/2002; The New Yorker, 1/27/2003; and many others. *Mailing Add:* c/o Deitch Projs 76 Grand St New York NY 10013

SILBERSTEIN-STORFER, MURIEL ROSOFF
ART EDUCATOR, INSTRUCTOR

b Brooklyn, NY. *Study:* Carnegie Inst Technol, BFA; Philadelphia Mus Art, with Hobson Pitman; Inst Mod Art, with Victor D'Amico, Donald Stacy, Jane Bland, Betty Edward, Paulus Berensohn. *Comn:* Prog drawings, Philadelphia Symphony Orch Children's Concerts, 49; murals & other projs, Mt Sinai Hosp & West Philadelphia Psychiat Hosp. *Exhib:* Jewish Community Ctr Group Show, 71-72; one-woman shows, Panoras Gallery, NY, 72, Pacem in Terris Gallery, NY, 75 & Gallery 84, 78 & 83. *Pos:* Assoc tech dir & scene designer, Pittsburgh Playhouse, 44-46; interior display designer, var Pittsburgh Dept Stores, 46-47; art educ consult, Staten Island Ment Health Schs, Head Start, Staten Island Community Col Mus Mod Art, Metrop Mus Art & others; founder & creative dir, Doing Art Together, Inc, 82; art ed adv bd, Binney Smith Inc, 86-91. *Teaching:* Instr, Inst Mod Art, Mus Mod Art, New York, 63-70, Int Playgroups Art Workshops, New York, 70-71, Victor D'Amico Institute of Art, Amagansett, NY, Staten Island Community Col, 70-71, Metrop Mus Art, 72-; guest lectr art educ, var univs, cols & community education groups, New York, 67-. *Awards:* Art Commission Serv Award, Mayor of NY, 85; New York City Sch Art League Award, 95; Very Spec Arts Mayors Award, 96; and others; Art Educator Award New York City Art Teachers Asn & United Fedn Teachers, 2000. *Bibliog:* The Museologist, Vol 47, No 169, winter 85; NY Mag, 1/88; Art News, Vol 88, No 6, summer 89. *Mem:* New York Art Comn (comnr, 70-85); Metrop Mus Art (trustee, 71-77 & emer trustee, 77-); Assoc Art Comn City New York (pres, formerly); Snug Harbor Cult Ctr (trustee, 76-87); Nat Art Educ Asn; and others. *Media:* Assemblage, All Media. *Res:* Art education; community arts projects. *Publ:* Auth, Parent-Child Workshops (pamphlet), Metrop Mus Art, NY; Doing Art Together, Simon & Schuster, 82, rev ed, Harry Abrams Inc, 97; Look What I See (CD-Rom), Mitsubishi Chemical Am, 96, new Look What I See! (CD-Rom), Metrop Mus Art. *Mailing Add:* 2500 Johnson Ave #16N Riverdale NY 10463-4944

SILER, PATRICK W
PAINTER, CERAMIST

b Spokane, Wash, 39. *Study:* Wash State Univ, Pullman, BA, 61; Univ Calif, Berkeley, MA(painting), 63. *Work:* Johnson's Wax, Racine, Wis; Utah Mus Fine Arts, Salt Lake City; Cranbrook Inst, Bloomfield Hills, Mich; many pvt collections; Seattle Art Comn Collection, Wash. *Comn:* painting, Wash State Dept Juvenile Correction; Mukilteo Sch, Wash; Wash State Comn. *Exhib:* Clays Rivisions Show, Seattle Art Mus, 87; Incisive Expressions, Woodcut Print Show, Univ Puget Sound, Tacoma, Wash, 91; Cup as Metaphor, Sybaris Gallery, Royal Oak, Mich, 91; Ceramic Show cur by Dean Moniz, Jennifer Pauls Gallery, 92; Dean Moniz Gallery, Sacramento, Calif, 93; Lorinda Knight Gallery, Spokane, Wash, 98; Dennis Ochi Gallery, Sun Valley, Idaho, 2000; John Natsoulas Gallery, Davis, Calif, 2001. *Teaching:* Artist-in-residence & instr, Univ SDak, Vermillion, 68; guest lectr, Col San Mateo, Calif, 69; instr ceramics, Univ Calif, Berkeley, 71; assoc prof found drawing & ceramics, Wash State Univ, Pullman, 73- & drawing instr, coordr, 89-. *Awards:* Medal of Excellence, Int Ceramic Expo, 72; Fel, Wash State Arts Comn, 86; Residency Award, Alternative Workspace, Omaha, Nebr, 86-87; Ceramic Sculpture Fel, Nat Endowment Arts, 90. *Bibliog:* Profile: Patrick Siler, Am Ceramics, Spring/84; Feature article, Ceramics Monthly Mag, 9/88 & 90; Susan Biskeborn (auth), Artists at work, Northwest Ceramists, 90; article, Craft Arts Int Mag, Sydney, Australia, 91; Kippy Stroud (auth), An Industrious Art, 92. *Mailing Add:* 325 NW Dillon St Pullman WA 99163

SILER, TODD (LAEL)
PAINTER, SCULPTOR

b Long Island, NY, Aug 21, 53. *Study:* Smith Col, with Leonard Baskin, 73-74; Bowdoin Col, BA(cum laude), 75; Mass Inst Technol, MS(visual studies), 81, PhD(intedisciplinary studies in psychol & art), 86. *Work:* The Solomon R Guggenheim Mus; Whitney Mus Am Art; Metrop Mus Art; Mus Mod Art; Pushkin Mus Fine Arts, Moscow. *Comn:* Sculpture, Alvin I Schragis, New York City, 88. *Exhib:* Schemes: A Decade of Installation Drawings, Mus D'Art Contemp, Montreal & traveling, 81; Revolutions Per Minute (The Art Record), Ronald Feldman Fine Arts, Tate Gallery, Documenta, Ger & Biennale De Paris, 82; Alea(s), Mus D'Art Mod, Paris, 82; Brainworks, Munic Art Gallery, Los Angeles, 85; Savoir-vivre, Savoir-faire, Savoir-etre, Centre Int D'Art Contemporain, De Montreal, Que, 90; solo exhibs, Humanature-A Turbulent Integration, Mus Mod Art, Belo Horizonte, Brazil, 91, Metaphorms, Turman Gallery, Ind State Univ, 92, Radical Futures, Ronald Feldman Fine Arts, 93, Artscience, Crossman Gallery, Univ Wis-Whitewater, 94, Mind Icons, Allen Ctr, Houston, Tex, 95, Metaphorming Civilization, Ronald Feldman Fine Arts, 95 & Metaphorming Worlds, Taipei Fine Arts Mus, Taiwan, 95, Mind Icons, The Allen Ctr, Houston, Tex, 95, Changing Minds, Ronald Feldman Fine Arts, NY, 97; Eighteen from NY, traveling Galerie Lohrl, Mochengladbach, Ger, 91; Blast 3, Remaking Civilization, X-Art Found, 93; The Unconscious at Work, Peyton Wright Gallery, Santa Fe, NMex, 93; traveling exhib, 25 Yrs: Light Space Time, 94-; Blast Art Benefit, The X-Art Found and Blast, NY, 94, 96; Withdrawing, Ronald Feldman Fine Arts, NY, 96; Baroque Bash: A Fan Fantasy, The John and Mable Ringling Mus Art, Sarasota, Fla, 98; Defining Structures, LaSalle Partners at NationsBank Plaza, Charlotte, NC, 98. *Pos:* Res fel, Ctr Adv Visual Studies, Mass Inst Technol, 81-; co-pres & consult, United Sciences & Arts, 83-; res affil, Computer-Aided Design Lab, Dept Mech Eng, Mass Inst Technol, 86-91; adv bd, Coun Art, Sci & Technol, Mass Inst Technol, Cambridge; founder, Psi-Phi Commun; founder, Art Sci Ctr, Mus Outdoor Arts, Greenwood, Colo. *Teaching:* Instr visual design, Mass Inst Technol, 82-83. *Awards:* Gold Medal Award, Int Book Fair, Jerusalem, 93; Grawemeyer Award Educ Nominee, Univ Louisville, 94; Artist of Yr Award, New York City Art Teachers Asn/United Fedn Teachers, 95; Colo Space Educ Distinguished Educator Award, Lt Gov Colo, 96. *Bibliog:* Gary Massaro (auth), This Genius Opens Minds, The Rocky Mountain News, 12/6/96; Robert Schwab (auth), Firm Sells Real Talent-Creativity, The Denver Post, 1/97; Helen Levin (auth), Try a little 'metaphorming', Staten Island Register, 5/5/98. *Media:* All. *Publ:* Healing and The Mind, Bill Moyer, Doubleday, NY, 93; METAPHORMERS: Connecting Our Work and Our World Through Metaphorms in R&D Innovator, 7/94; Metaphorming the Genetic Code, Art J, Col Art Asn, 95; Freeing Your Mind: Thresholds of ArtScience, Artsci Publ, 95. *Dealer:* Ronald Feldman Fine Arts Inc 31 Mercer St New York NY 10013; Pas-Phi Communications 7070-B S Tucson Way Englewood NY 80112. *Mailing Add:* c/o Ronald Feldman Fine Arts 31 Mercer St New York NY 10013

SILL, GERTRUDE GRACE
WRITER, CURATOR

b New York, NY. *Study:* Smith Col, with Oliver Larkin, BA, 48; Wesleyan Univ, with Samuel Greene & Richard Field, MA, 78. *Collection Arranged:* Amen Carter Mus, Houston, Tex, 85; John Haberle, Master of Illusion (auth, catalog), Mus Fine Arts, Springfield, Mass, 85-86; Whitney Mus Am Art, 86; Realism and Romanticism in 19th Century New England Seascapes, Whitney Mus Am Art, Stamford, Conn, 89; George Cope (auth), An Artists Life, Chester Co Hist Soc, West Chester, Pa, 2004. *Pos:* Writer & art critic, Connoisseur, Antiques, Art in Am, Portfolio, Art & Antiques & others, 68-; art critic, Brooks Community Papers, 86-90, Conn Post, 90-. *Teaching:* Lectr & consult, Metrop Mus Art, NY, 75-78; lectr, Southern Conn State Univ, New Haven, 80-81, Whitney Mus Am Art, 89, New Brit Mus Am Art, 89-95, Yale Univ, 89, 91, 93 & 98, Mus Fine Art, Houston, Tex, 90, Smith Col Sem, 91, Mus Fine Arts, Boston, Mass, 91 & 94, Portland Mus Art, Maine, 92 & Col Art Asn, 93; lectr, Fairfield Univ, Conn, 76-2003, Minneapolis Inst Art, 95 & Cummer Mus Art, 96, San Diego Art Mus, Yale Univ Art Mus & Cummer Mus Art, Jacksonville, Fla, 98, 99; adj prof, Fairfield Univ, Ct, 76-03; instr, Chester Co Hist Soc, 2004-. *Awards:* Nat Endowment Humanities Grant, 78; Nat Endowment Arts Grant, 85 & 86. *Mem:* Col Art Asn; Archives Am Art; Asn Am Art Historians. *Res:* John Haberle, American painter (1853-1933) monogr for publ; George Brainerd Burr (1875-1933) for exhib, Am Impressionists; John Haberle, Master of Illusion, 03-. *Interests:* John Haberle, 19th Century American trompe l'oeil panter; American Still life & Landscape painters. *Collection:* 19th century American still-life, landscape paintings & drawings. *Publ:* John Haberle: Master of Illusion, Mus Fine Arts, Springfield, Mass; George Cope: West Chester's Home Artist, Brandywine River Mus & UMI, 78; A Handbook of Symbols In Christian Art, Simon & Schuster/Touchstone, 96; Groves Dictionary of Art, Macmillan, London, 97; George Cope: An Artists Life, Chester Co Hist Soc, West Chester, Pa, 2004; article, Am Nat Biography, Oxford Univ Press, vol 10, Cary, NC. *Mailing Add:* 112 Southport Woods Dr Southport CT 06890

SILLMAN, AMY
PAINTER, EDUCATOR

b Oct, 55. *Work:* Whitney Biennial, Whitney Mus Am Art, NY, 2004. *Exhib:* exhib incl, Casey Kaplan Gallery, Manhattan, NY, 96 & 98, White Columns, 96, Postmasters Gallery, New York City, 97 Sixth@Prince Fine Art, 99, Exit Art, 2000; One-man shows incl Brent Sikkema Gallery, 2000. *Teaching:* Milton Avery prof arts, fac Milton Avery Grad; Sch Arts, Bard Col, 96—. *Awards:* Recipient Tiffany Found award, 99—2000; Guggenheim fel, 2001—02. *Mailing Add:* 59 Montgomery St Tivoli NY 12583

SILLMAN, AMY (DENISON)
PAINTER
b Detroit, Mich, Oct 6, 55. *Study:* Sch Visual Art, New York, BFA, 79; Bard Col, MFA, 94. *Work:* Art Inst Chicago; Baltimore Mus Art; Brooklyn Mus; NY Pub Libr; Jewish Mus. *Comn:* print, Jewish Mus, 2000. *Exhib:* solo shows, Kanoria Ctr Art, Ahmedabad, India, 88, Ledis Flam, NY, 91, Lipton Owens Co, NY, 94, Casey Kaplan, NY, 96 & 98, Brent Sikkema, NY, 2000 & 03, Galleria Marabini, Bologna, Italy, 2001, Susanne Vielmetter, Los Angeles, 2002 & Letters from Tex, Dartmouth Col, Hanover, NH, 2003; New Generations: NY, Carnegie Mellon Gallery, Pittsburgh, 91; Out West & Back East - New Work from NY & Los Angeles, Santa Monica Mus Contemp Art, Calif, 95; Imaginary Beings, Exit Art, NY, 96; Nu-Glu, Jospeh Helman Gallery, NY, 97; Team SHaG, Postmasters Gallery, NY, 97; Irredeemable Skeletons, Shillam & Smith, London, Eng, 97; Distraction, TBA Exhib Space, Chicago, 97; New York Drawers, Gasworks, London, Eng, 97; Current Undercurrent: Working in Brooklyn, Brooklyn Mus, NY, 97; Art on Paper, Weatherspoon Art Gallery, Univ NC, 97; Art and Provocation: Images From Rebels, Boulder Mus Contemp Art, 97; Drawings & Paintings, Wooster Gardens Gallery, NY, 97; The Secret Charts, Jonctions Festival, Brussels, 98; Drawings, Graham Mod Gallery, NY, 98; Codex USA, Entwistle Gallery, London, 98; Pop Surrealism, Aldrich Mus, Ridgefield, Conn, 98; From Here to Eternity: Painting in the 1990's, Max Protech Gallery, NY, 98; Commitment to Image, Univ NTex Art Gallery, Denton, 98; Personal Touch, Art in General, NY, 98; Cluster Bomb, Morrison-Judd, London, Eng, 98; The New Surrealism, Pamela Auchincloss Proj Space, NY, 98; Drawing in the Present Tense, Parsons Sch Design, NY, 99; James Van Damme Gallery, Brussels, 2000; Greater NY, PS1, 2000; Ghislaine Hussenot, Paris, 2001. *Pos:* Vis artist, Sch Art Inst Chicago, 93 & 95; vis critic, MFA/Fine Art Prog, Parsons Sch Design, 96-. *Teaching:* Instr painting, Bennington Col, Vt, 90-95; asst prof art, Bard Col, 96- & fac mem painting, MFA Prog, 96-. *Awards:* Nat Endowment Arts Fel, 95; Pollock-Krasner Found Fel, 99; Civitella Ranieri Found Fel/Residency, Umbria, Italy, 99; Louis Comfort Tiffany Award, 99. *Bibliog:* Thad Ziolkowski (auth), rev, Artforum, 98; Wayne Koestenbaum (auth), The best of-1998, Artforum, 98; Jonathon Goodman (auth), Medrie Macphee & Amy Sillman, Contemp Visual Art, 99; David Humphrey (auth), Bomb Mag, 2000; Gail Gregg (auth), Profile, Art News, 2001; Gregory Volk (auth), (catalog essays), Regarding Amy Stillman's Paintings, 1998; Gail Gregg, Art News, 2001; Helen Molesworth (catalog), 2002. *Media:* Gouache, Oil. *Dealer:* 530 W 22 St New York NY 10011. *Mailing Add:* 705 Driggs Ave Brooklyn NY 11211

SILVA, JUDE HUTTON
ARTIST
b Springfield, Mass, Dec 15, 39. *Study:* San Jose State Univ, BFA, 81; San Jose State Univ, MA, MFA, 91, 93. *Work:* Kaiser Hosp, Oakland, Calif, 82; Progressive Corp, Colo Springs, 98; Commerce Bank, Arvada, Colo, 02. *Exhib:* Installations, Univ Southern Colo, Pueblo, 02; Paradise Lost-Redefining, Univ Colo, Boulder, 98. *Teaching:* Artist in Residence, Sacred Heart Co Serv, 92, 94; Instr, Colo Mountain Col, 97-; Instr, Co Sch of Music & Art, 93-95. *Awards:* State of Colo Fel, Republic Plaza, 01. *Mem:* Bay Area Basketry Guild, pres, founding mem; Ark Valley Art Ctr. *Publ:* Donnaz Melack, Basketry Today, 79; Consuelo Underwood, Fiberarts, 90; Clint Driscoll, Fiber is Good for Your Art, Colo Central, 01. *Dealer:* Cultureclash 100 North F St Salida CO 81201. *Mailing Add:* 28875 County Rd 330 Buena Vista CO 81211

SILVER, LARRY ARNOLD
CURATOR, HISTORIAN
b Los Angeles, Calif, Oct 14, 47. *Study:* Univ Chicago, BA, 69; Harvard Univ, MA, 71, PhD, 74. *Pos:* Vis cur, St Louis Art Mus, 81-82; vis res cur, Art Inst Chicago, 81-84; vis cur, Block Gallery, Northwestern Univ, 89-97. *Teaching:* Asst prof Medieval & Renaissance art, Univ Calif, Berkeley, 74-79; prof Medieval, Renaissance & Baroque art & chmn dept, Northwestern Univ, 79-97; prof art hist, Univ Pa, 97-. *Awards:* Porter Prize, Col Art Asn, 75; Col Art Asn. *Mem:* Renaissance Soc Am; Soc Values in Higher Educ; Col Art Asn (vpres, 90-92, pres, 92-). *Res:* Painting and graphics in northern Europe, 15th and 16th century. *Publ:* Coauth, Flemish Dutch Paintings (catalog), Ringling Mus, 80; auth, Early Northern European Paintings (catalog), St Louis Art Mus, 82; Forest primeval: Albrecht Altdorfer and --- landscape, Simiolus, 83; The Paintings of Quinten Massys, 84; Rembrandt, 92; and others. *Mailing Add:* 7 Woodsworth Ct Wayne PA 19087

SILVER, RAWLEY A
EDUCATOR, PAINTER
b New York, NY. *Study:* Cornell Univ, BA, 39; Art Students League, with George Grosz, 48, 50; Columbia Univ, MA(fine arts educ), 64, EdD(fine arts educ), 66. *Exhib:* 16 solo invitationals, 55-92 & 2005; Hudson River Mus Invitational, Yonkers, NY, 76. *Collection Arranged:* Shout in Silence (auth, catalog), 69-77 & Art as Language (auth, catalog), 79-82, Smithsonian Inst Traveling Exhib. *Teaching:* Instr art, 61-73; adj assoc res prof art therapy, Col New Rochelle Grad Sch, 74-81. *Awards:* Ann Award Res, Am Art Therapy Asn, 76, 80, 92 & 96; Res Grants, US Off Educ, Nat Inst Educ & NY State Dept Educ. *Bibliog:* Alexander Kopytin (auth), The silver drawing test standardization in Russia, Am J Art Therapy v 40 (4), May 2002; CD Allessandrini et al (auth), SDT: the Brazilian standardization of the silver drawing test of cognition and emotion, ARTherapy, J of the Am Art Therapy Asn, vol 15 (2) 1998; Linda Jppfeiffer (auth), The Arts in Psychotherapy, vol 29 (1), 2003; Amelia C Joynes (auth), Natl Arts Ed Assn News, vol 45 (2), April, 2003; Donna H Kaiser (auth), Art Therapy, J of Am Art Assn, vol 20 (4), 2003. *Mem:* Hon life mem Am Art Therapy Asn; Hon life mem Art Therapy Asn Fla. *Media:* Watercolor, Oils. *Res:* Developing and assessing cognitive skills and adjustment nonverbally through drawing; assessing gender & age differences. *Publ:* Developing Cognitive and Creative Skills Through Art, 1Universe.com Ppubl, 2000; Art as Language, Brunner-Routledge, 2001 & 2002; Agression and Depression Assessed through Art Using Draw-A-Story to Identify Children and Adolescents at Risk, Brunner-Routledge (NY)/ Taylor & Francis (UK), Jan 2005; others. *Mailing Add:* 700 John Ringling Blvd No 1603 Sarasota FL 34236-1599

SILVER, SHELLY ANDREA
VIDEO ARTIST, FILMMAKER
b Manhattan, NY, July 16, 57. *Study:* Cornell Univ, Col Arts & Sci, BA, 79, Col Art & Archit, BFA, 79; Whitney Mus Am Art Independent Studio Prog, 80-81. *Work:* Mus d'Arte Moderne Centre Georges Pompidou, Paris, France; Long Beach Mus Art, Los Angeles, Calif. *Exhib:* New York Film Festival, NY, 94; Nat Film Theaters, London, Eng, 94; Filmladen Dokumentarfilm & Videofestival, Kassel, Ger, 94; Cinevideo Festival, Karlsrube, Ger, 94; Yokohama Mus Art, Japan, 94; and others; Yokohama Portside Gallery, 02; Singapore Int Film Festival, 02; Kunsthaus, Zurich, Switz, 02; Musee de L' Elysee, Switz, 01; Palm Beach Inst of Contemp Art, 01. *Collection Arranged:* The Mus of Modern Art, NYC; Mus of Broadcasting, NYC; Centre Georges Pompidou, Paris; Yokohama Art Mus, Japan. *Teaching:* Sch of Visual Arts, New York City; The Cooper Union, New York City. *Awards:* Nat Endowment Arts Fel, 89; Checkerboard Found Grant, 90; US/Japan Artists Exchange Fel, 93. *Mem:* Media Alliance; Asn of Independent Video and Filmmakers. *Dealer:* EAI 536 Broadway New York NY; Video Data Bank 37 S Wabash 10th Floor Chicago IL 60603. *Mailing Add:* 22 Catherine St No 6 New York NY 10038

SILVERBERG, JUNE ROSELYN
PAINTER
b Brooklyn, NY. *Study:* Brooklyn Col, BA, 56 cum laude, honors in design: Yale Univ, with Joseph Albers, 56-57 honors,; Art Students League, Concours honors, Pratt Inst, MS, 69. *Work:* Arthur Andersen Corp Collection, Minneapolis, Minn; Bryn Mawr Col Libr Collection, Pa; Art Students League, NY. *Exhib:* NY Univ 9th, 25th, 26th Ann Small Works, 80 Wash Sq E Galleries, NY, 85, 02, 03; Am Drawing Biennial II, Muscarelle Mus Art, Williamsburg, Va, 90; Int Exhib Miniature & Small Format Art, Metro Toronto Conv Ctr & Del Bello Gallery, Can, 90 & 91; Landscape Works by Women Artists, Bryn Mawr Col, Pa, 94; 25th Anniversary Show, Bowery Gallery, NY, 94: Bowery Gallery Solo Shows 3/83, 3/93: NY Group Shows 80-2005; Audubon Artists, Ann Exhib Nat Arts Club, NY, 91-95; Fed Hall, NY, 96; Salmagundi Club, NY, 97-03, 06; Butler Inst Am Art, 66th Nat Midyear Exhib, Youngstown, Ohio, 02; Life of the City, Moma, NY, 02. *Pos:* Dir oils, Audubon Artists, 98. *Awards:* Premier Prix, Salon du Portrait de Montreal, 91; Hon Mention, Audubon Artists Ann Exhib, 95, SCAC Small Works Exhib, 94; The Conn Acad of Fine Arts Graphic Award for Allied Artists of America Annual Exhib, 11/2004. *Bibliog:* Tallahassee Democrat 12/89- Betty Rubenstein; Archival Listing, Nat Mus Women Arts, Washington, DC, 93; The NY Sun, Pg 17, 1/6/2005- Work Cited with Photo. *Mem:* Audubon Artists; life mem Art Students League New York; Artists Equity; Bowery Gallery. *Media:* All media. *Mailing Add:* 32 Union Sq Rm 1205 New York NY 10003

SILVERMAN, BURTON PHILIP
PAINTER
b Brooklyn, NY, June 11, 28. *Study:* Pratt Inst; Art Students League, 46-49; Columbia Univ, BA, 49. *Hon Degrees:* Sch of Humane Letters, Acad Art Col, San Francisco, Calif, 2003. *Work:* Brooklyn Mus, NY; Philadelphia Mus Art; Butler Inst Am Art; Del Art Mus, Wilmington; New Britain Mus Am Art, Conn; Denver Art Mus, CO; Brigham Young Mus Art, Provo, UT; Nat Portrait Gallery, Smithsonian Inst Mus, Washington, DC. *Comn:* Portrait, Paul Moore, Jr, Episcopal Bishop of NY; portrait, Dr David Hamburg (chmn bd), Carnegie Corp; portrait, Robert McCormack Adams Retired Secy, Smithsonian Inst; portrait, Joseph Allbritton (chmn/CEO), Riggs Nat Bank; portrait, Barry Sullivan (retired trustee), Univ Chicago; Bruce Babbit, Former Secy Interior; Richard West, dir Mus Am Indian; Lewis Sharp, dir Denver Art Mus. *Exhib:* Butler Inst Am Art Ann, Ohio, 54-70, 71, 74, 76, 79, 82, 86, 90 & 92; Nat Acad 59-2001, 2003-2005; Am Watercolor Soc Ann, 79-99; Face of Am, W/C Portraits 150 Contemp, Old Forge Mus, NY, 94; Int Waters, 3 Nation Traveling Show, Us, Can & United Kingdom, 92-94; South Bend Mus, 94; Retrospective, Butler Inst Am Art & Brigham Young Mus, 99; Artists of Am, 94, 2000; Re-Presenting Representation, Arnot Mus, 2001-2002. *Pos:* asst treas, Coun Nat Acad Design; Membership subcomm Nat Acad Design. *Teaching:* Instr drawing & painting, Sch Visual Arts, New York, 64-67; lectr & workshops, Nat Acad Design, New York, 90-94, 2004-2005; distinguished vis prof, George Washington Univ, Washington, 92; Wkshops, Scottsdale Artists Sch, 2004; Lectr, The Creative Progressive, Scottsdale, 2005. *Awards:* Soc Illusrs Hall Fame, Pastel Soc Am, Hall of Fame, New York, 92; Isidor Gold Medal, Nat Acad Design, New York, 92; Silver Medal, Am Watercolor Soc, 94. *Bibliog:* Fredrick Whitaker (auth), Four realists, 10/64, Elizabeth Case (auth), Burton Silverman captures the moment, 6/71 & Pat Van Gelder (auth), Drawing the human figure, an interview with Burt Silverman, 7/81, Am Artist Mag; Robert McGrath (auth) & others, Sight & Insight: The Art of Burton Silverman, Madison Square Press, 12/98. *Mem:* Am Watercolor Soc; Nat Acad (assoc, 69, acad, 72-); Century Asn, New York, 2005. *Media:* Oil, Watercolor. *Publ:* Auth, A Portfolio of Drawings, 68; Painting People, 77 & Breaking the Rules of Watercolor, 83, Watson-Guptill; Realism rediscovered, Artist's Mag, 90; What makes art great, Am Arts Quart; and others. *Dealer:* Gallery Henoch, 555 W 25th St, NYC, 10001; Merrill Gallery, 315 Detroit St, Denver, Colo, 80206; Total Arts Gallery, 122A Kit Carson Rd, Taos, NM, 87571. *Mailing Add:* 324 W 71st St New York NY 10023

SILVERMAN, GILBERT B
COLLECTOR
Study: Univ Calif Berkeley. *Pos:* Chairman and chief exec office Silverman Companies, Bingham Farms, Mich, currently; owner Amurcon, currently; bd dirs Univ Cancer Found, On My Own, Mich, and The Greening, Detroit. *Awards:* Named one of top 200 collectors, ARTnews Magazine, 2004, 2005, 2006. *Mem:* Bldg Indust Asn (pres 96). *Collection:* Fluxus-realted material & conceptual art. *Mailing Add:* Silverman Companies Ste 220 32100 Telegraph Rd Bingham Farms MI 48025

SILVERMAN, LANNY HARRIS
DIRECTOR, CURATOR
b Philadelphia, Pa, Oct 16, 47. *Study:* Case Western Reserve Univ, BA, 69. *Collection Arranged:* Sowers of Myth (catalog), 91; Michiiko Itatani: Paintings Since 1984 (interview, catalog), 92; The Nature of the Machine (auth, catalog), 93; Con/textual: Art & Text in Chicago (catalog), 2001; Leon Golub: Works since 1947 (catalog), 2003; Kif Slemmons: Re: Pair & Imperfection (catalog), 2006; Nick Care: Soundsuits (catalog), 2006. *Pos:* Educ asst, Akron Art Mus, 80-81; cur educ & pub prog, Madison Art Ctr, Wis, 81-84; dir, NAME Gallery, Chicago, 85-87; asst dir, Evanston Art Ctr, 87-89; cur, Chicago Cult Ctr, 89-. *Teaching:* Instr art, poetry & performance, Cleveland Mus Art, 74-78. *Bibliog:* Barbara Newsom & Adele Silver (ed), The Museum as Educator, Univ Calif Press, 78. *Specialty:* Experimental art; mixed media; installations; performance art; new music. *Interests:* New Music and World Music. *Mailing Add:* Dept Cult Affairs Visual Arts Dept 78 E Washington 4th Fl Chicago IL 60602

SILVERMAN, RONALD H
EDUCATOR, WRITER
b Cleveland, Ohio. *Study:* Univ Calif, Los Angeles, BA, 52; Los Angeles State Col, MA, 55; Stanford Univ, EdD, 62. *Pos:* Consult, Nat Assessment Educ Progress Art; assoc dir, Getty Inst Educators Visual Arts. *Teaching:* Prof emer art, Calif State Univ, Los Angeles, 55-88. *Awards:* Bur Res grant, US Office Educ, 1967-69; Outstanding Prof Award, Calif State Univ, Los Angeles, 78; Award, Nat Art Educ Asn, 81; Distinguished Fel, Nat Art Educ Asn, 91; Best in Show, Artists Over 50, 2002. *Mem:* Life mem, Nat Art Educ Asn; Calif Art Educ Asn. *Media:* Acrylic, Oil. *Publ:* Auth, Spectrum of Music, Macmillan, 74; Goals and roles in art education of children, In: The Arts, Human Development and Education, McCutchan, 76; A comprehensive model for teaching art, In: Report of the NAEA Commission on Art Education, Nat Art Educ Asn, 77; ed, Art, Education and the World of Work, Nat Art Educ Asn, 80; The egalitarianism of discipline-based art education, Art Educ, 3/88. *Mailing Add:* 47 Hillgrass Irvine CA 92603

SILVERTOOTH, DENNIS CARL
SCULPTOR
b Killeen, Tex, Aug 20, 57. *Study:* Corpus Christi Community Art Ctr, with Maurice Schmidt & Ann Armstrong, 74. *Exhib:* Am Cowboy: Fact & Fiction, Eastman Kodak, NY, 75; Tex Art Classic, Tarrant Co Convention Ctr, Ft Worth, 76-79; Shidoni Summer Sculpture Show, Shidoni Foundry & Gallery, Santa Fe, NMex, 77-81; Philbrook Presents Sculpture, Philbrook Mus, Tulsa, Okla, 78; Midland Col Sculpture Show, Tex, 78-81; and others. *Awards:* Best Sculpture, Art About Town, Dallas Crippled Childrens Soc, 77; Best Sculpture, 34th Ann American Indian Artist Exhib, Philbrook Mus, Okla, 79; Artist of the Year, Santa Fean Mag, 80. *Bibliog:* Donn Puca (auth), A young artist working magic, Southwest Art Collector, 12/79; Marion Love (auth), article, Santa Fean Mag, 8/80; Joseph Cain (auth), article, Art Voices/South, 9-10/80. *Media:* Bronze, Plaster. *Mailing Add:* 3014 Pimlico St Corpus Christi TX 78418

SIMKIN, PHILLIPS M
SCULPTOR
b Philadelphia, Pa, Jan 19, 44. *Study:* Tyler Art Sch, Temple Univ, BFA; Cornell Univ, MFA; Univ Pa, post grad fel. *Comn:* Sculpture, Pub Ctr for Collection & Dissemination of Secrets, Inst Contemp Art, Univ Pa, 73; Displacement Proj I (with Doris Olafson), Inst Contemp Art, Boston, 74; Displacement Proj II (with Doris Olafson), Philadelphia Mus Art, 74; Artpark (with Thom Farmer), Lewiston State Arts Park, NY, 75. *Exhib:* Displacement Proj II-a Pub Event, Philadelphia, 74; Commodity Exchange, Human Puzzle, Lewiston, NY, 75; Choices Maze, Inst Art & Urban Resources, PS1, NY, 76; Project Looking Glass, Three Centuries of Am Art exhib, Philadelphia Mus of Art, 76; Proj--Is There Anything Else You Want to Tell Me?, Brooklyn Mus, 77; solo proj, Pa Acad of Fine Arts, Philadelphia, 78; Sculpture Performance Comn, Nat Fine Arts Comt, XIII Winter Olympics, Lake Placid, NY, 80; and others. *Pos:* Art dir, Earthweek Inc, Philadelphia, 71-73; co-dir (with John Formicola), The Luncheonette Inc Artist Ctr, Philadelphia, 75; adv bd mem, Dept Community Programs, Philadelphia Art Mus, 77-82. *Teaching:* Assoc prof studio fine arts, York Col, City Univ New York, 73-; adj asst prof studio fine arts, Moore Col Art, Philadelphia, 73-; artist-in-residence, Brooklyn Mus, 77. *Awards:* Nat Endowment Arts Artist Fel, 75-76; Creative Artists Pub Serv Sculpture Grant, New York, 76; Artist Fel Grant, Pa State Coun Arts, 80. *Mailing Add:* 1434 S Broad St Philadelphia PA 19146

SIMMONS, CLEDA-MARIE
PAINTER, MURALIST
b Douglas, Wyo, June 24, 27. *Study:* Univ NMex, Albuquerque, with Ralph Douglas & Raymond Jonson; studied seven yrs in Madrid, Spain. *Work:* Pan Am Gallery, San Antonio, Tex; Ateneo de Belles Artes, Madrid; San Diefo Central libr, San Diego, Calif. *Comn:* Mural, City Vista, Calif, 94; mural, City Carlsbad, Calif, 96; Mural, City of San Marcos, Calif, 2002-2004. *Exhib:* US Info Serv Traveling Show, Mus Mod Art, Paris & Madrid, 53; two-woman show, Jonson Gallery, Univ NMex, 56; Detroit Art Inst, 64; Denver Art Mus, 70; EQUUS, Denver, Colo, 77; RI Sch Design, Providence, 81; and others. *Collection Arranged:* Continental Waterways Corp, Boston, MA; Dannison Paper Co, Framingham, MA; WS & Allyn Malleu, Encinidas, CA; Eileen Monaghan Whitaker, La Jolla, CA. *Pos:* Graphic artist, ESA Women Int, Loveland, Colo, 69-70, art ed, 70-73, art dir, 73-77; assoc ed & art dir, Jonquil Mag, 77-78. *Teaching:* Workshops, Boston, Ma & Southern Calif. *Awards:* Purchase Award, Ateneo de Belles Artes, Madrid, Spain, 54. *Bibliog:* Mary Hagen (auth), The challenge of art, Southwest Art Mag, 1/77; article, Int Soc Artists Communicator, 7-8/78. *Mem:* Collection Orgn for Visual Arts; San Diego Visual Artists Guild. *Media:* Acrylic, Mixed Media. *Publ:* Illusr, Our Government, 69; coauth, Art of Editorship, ESA Women Int, 72; illusr, Beneath the Peaks, ESA Women Int, 73; This is Loveland, League of Women Voters, 76; auth & pub, Design and Your World, 94; auth & publ, The Art of Mixing Color, 2005. *Dealer:* The Art Collector, San Diego, CA. *Mailing Add:* 724 Osborne St Vista CA 92084

SIMMONS, DANNY, JR
GALLERY DIRECTOR
Exhib: Exhibs incl New York City Groove, Noel Gallery, Charlotte, NC, 99, Be Still & Listen, 2001, Represented in permanent collections Smithsonian Inst, Chase Manhattan Bank, March of Dimes, Schomberg Ctr for Black Cult, UN Gen Assembly, Warner Brothers/Black Pearl Entertainment. *Pos:* Found, pres, Rush Arts Gallery, New York City, Corridor Gallery, Brooklyn; co-found Rush Philanthropic Arts Found, New York City; found, dir, Def Poetry Jam. *Mailing Add:* Rush Art Gallery 526 W 26th St Ste 311 New York NY 10001

SIMMONS, JOHN HERBERT
EDUCATOR, HISTORIAN
b Springfield, Mo, Mar 23, 38. *Study:* Drury Col, BA, 60; Univ Ark, MA, 73; Univ Rome, DA, 78. *Collection Arranged:* All cataloged, Ernest Trova, Work by Contemp Sculptor, 71, Classical Greek Ceramics, Early Movement Through Gallo Rome, 75, Sung Dynasty Ceramics, Chinese Ceramics, 75, Egyptian Art, Works from the Duncan Collection, 78, Chinese Art, Neolithic Through Ching Dynasty, 79 & Alice Neel, 80. *Pos:* Chmn bd trustees, Springfield Art Mus, Mo, 79-80; art critic, Springfield News Leader, 87-. *Teaching:* Prof & chmn art dept, Drury Col, 69-83. *Mem:* Col Art Asn; Am Inst Archaeol; assoc Am Inst Archit. *Res:* Chinese art with papers published and read on Ku kai chih; also early printing in Europe. *Interests:* Chinese art, especially ceramics, and early European printed books. *Publ:* Auth, Ku kai chih, an Early Chinese Painter, 73, Ching-te-Chan, 74 & The Loud Brothers of Philadelphia, 75, Gallery. *Mailing Add:* 2059 S Mayfair Ave Springfield MO 65804

SIMMONS, JULIE LUTZ
PAINTER, SCULPTOR
b San Diego, Calif. *Study:* Murray State Univ, BS, 64, with Miles Batt, Ed Betts, Virginia Cobb, Maxine Masterfield, Barbara Nechis, Charles Reid, Frank Webb & Daniel Green; Southeast Mo State Univ. *Work:* Southwestern Bell, St Louis, Mo; Coca Cola Inc, Atlanta, Ga; Marriot Hotels, Atlanta, Ga; First Bank Fla; First Bank Tenn. *Comn:* sculptured reredos wall and baptismal, Hillside Village, Chapel of the Running Waters, Peoria, Ill; sculptured reredos wall, Trinity Lutheran Church, Bay City, Mich, 97; sculptured wire mesh tosos, comn by Dr Larry Shaw, Phoenix, 98; mural, Encian Meadows Chapel, Flagstaff, Ariz, 98; sculptured the wall Jesus speaks the Masses on the Sea of Galilee, Salen Lutheran Church, Peoria, Il, 2003; sculptured reredos wall, St Matthew Luthern Church, Sonora, Calif, 03. *Exhib:* Abstein Gallery, Atlanta, Ga, 86-90; Shawnee Col, Ill, 87; Barucci's Gallery, St Louis, Mo, 90; Sun Cities Mus, Sun City, Ariz, 92; Village Gallery, Scottsdale, Ariz, 96; Robb & Stuck, Phoenix, Ariz, 98; Postera 2004 Int Jazz Festival, Sedona, Ariz, 04. *Teaching:* Instr studio workshops watercolor, Charleston, Mo, 70-; instr, studio workshops, Medford, Ore, Monroe, La, 86 & 89, Sikeston, Mo, 86, Lighthouse Art Ctr, Crescent City, Calif, 88, 89 & 91, Geneseo Art League, Ill, 88 & 89, ECent Col, Union, Mo, 88, Ill Art League, Peoria, 89, Sun Cities, Ariz, 90-, Friends of Arts & Scis, Sarasota, Fla, 91 & Left Bank Art League, Moline, Ill, 91. *Awards:* First Prize, Midwest Watercolor Soc Seventh Ann Exhib, 83; Ky Watercolor Soc Exhib Award, 84; An Art Affair Award, St Louis, 85; Ga Watercolor Soc Award, 86; La Watercolor Int Award, 86; Ariz Watercolor Soc Award, 91 & 93. *Bibliog:* Article, The watercolor page, Am Artist, 1/86; articles in Phoenix Home & Garden, Am Artists & The Adelphean, 91-98; aricle, 101 North Magazine, 04. *Mem:* Soc Layerists Multi-Media; Ariz Watercolor Asn; Ariz Artists Guild; Sonoran Art League. *Media:* Watercolor; Mixed Media, Woven Wire Sculpture. *Publ:* Auth, article, The watercolor page, Am Artist, 1/86; Interior design, Southern Accents, 9/89; Architectural Design Collaborators 2, 91. *Dealer:* Xanadu Gallery Scottsdale Ariz. *Mailing Add:* 11783 E Becker Ln Scottsdale AZ 85259

SIMMONS, LAURIE
PHOTOGRAPHER
b Long Island, NY, Oct 3, 49. *Study:* Tyler Sch Art, Temple Univ, BFA, 71. *Work:* Metrop Mus Art, Mus Mod Art, Whitney Mus Mod Art, NY; Mus Art Contemp, Montreal, Can; Stajdelik Mus, Holland; Fogg Mus Art, Boston; Albright-Knox Gallery, Buffalo, NY; and many others. *Exhib:* Biennial Exhib, Whitney Mus Am Art, NY, 91; Pleasures & Terrors of Domestic Comfort, Mus Mod Art, NY, 91; More Than One Photog (with catalog), Mus Mod Art, NY, 92; solo exhibs, Galerie Rizzo, Paris, 93 & 95, Metro Pictures, 94 & 95, SL Simpson Gallery, Toronto, 95, Sprengel Mus, 95 & Savannah Col Art & Design, Ga, 96; Altered & Irrational, Whitney Mus Am Art, 96; Galerie Philippe Rizzo, Paris, 96; Metro Pictures, NY, 96 & 98; Baltimore Mus Art, Md, 97. *Teaching:* Asst prof grad photog, Yale Univ; adj prof grad fine arts, Columbia Univ. *Awards:* Nat Endowment Arts, 84; Guggenheim Fel, 97. *Bibliog:* Robert Sabbag (auth), The invisible family, NY Times Mag, 2/11/96; Modernism - Laurie Simmons (rev), San Francisco Examiner, 4/5/96; Vicki Golberg (auth), Laurie Simmons, NY Times, 7/4/97; and others. *Mailing Add:* c/o Metro Pictures 519 W 24th St New York NY 10011

SIMON, BARBARA R See Rothschild, Barbara R Simon

SIMON, C M
MUSEUM DIRECTOR
b Nov 23, 36. *Collection Arranged:* Standing Soldier Retrospective (photog), 91; Come Dance With Us (photog), 93; Robert Freeman (photog), 96; Roger Broer New Directions (photog), 98; Arthur Amiosk: Continuity & Diversity, 01; Donald Releaux: Betwwen Two Worlds. *Pos:* Dir, Heritage Ctr, Pine Ridge, SDak, 82-; bd mem, Buwechel Mus, currently. *Awards:* Governor Award Support Arts. *Mem:* Northern Plains Tribal Arts. *Mailing Add:* Red Cloud Indian Sch Heritage Ctr Pine Ridge SD 57770

SIMON, DAVID L
HISTORIAN, EDUCATOR
b Lawrence, Mass, June 14, 46. *Study:* Boston Univ, BA, 69, MA, 71; Courtauld Inst Art, Univ London, PhD, 77. *Teaching:* Chmn & assoc prof, State Univ NY Col, Cortland, 74-81; chmn & Ellerton M Jette prof art, Colby Col, 81-. *Awards:* Am Coun Learned Soc Travel Grant, 78; US-Spanish Comt Educ & Cult Affairs Res Fel, 78-79, 94; Mellon Found Fel, Metrop Mus Art, 80-81. *Mem:* Col Art Asn; Int Ctr Medieval Art. *Res:* Romanesque sculpture. *Publ:* Romanesque Sculpture in North American Collections, The Metrop Museum of Art, Gesta, XXIII, XXV, XXVI, 84, 86 & 87; El timpano de la Catedral de Jaca, Actas: XV Congreso De Historia De La Corona De Aragón, Vol III, 94; La Condesa Dona Sancha Y Los Orígenes De Aragón, Zaragoza, 95; Moses Capital at Jaca, Imagines y Promotores en el arte medieval: Homenaje Yaza Luaces, Bettatera, 01; Eastman Johnson's Lunchtime, Colby Quarterly, XXXIX, 2003. *Mailing Add:* Colby Col Art Dept Waterville ME 04901

SIMON, HELENE
SCULPTOR
b Bagdad, Iraq; US citizen. *Study:* Bedford Col, London; Am Univ, Beirut, Lebanon; Islamic Art with Mary Devonshire, Cairo, Egypt; painting with Anthony Toney & Jacob Lawrence; New Sch, sculpture with Lorrie Goulet. *Work:* Phoenix Art Mus, Ariz; Jewish Mus, NY; Hirshhorn Mus, Washington, DC; NY Univ Art Collection, NY; Fordham Univ Art Collection, Bronx; Pepsico, Purchase, NY. *Comn:* Merck & Co; Banca Nazional del Lavoro, NY. *Exhib:* One-man shows, Bodley Gallery, NY, 71 & 73, Fordham Univ, 75 & Haber Theodore Gallery, 80; Sculptors 9, Caravan House, NY, 71; Stable Gallery, Scottsdale, Ariz, 73; Habib Anavian Gallery, 81-83; Carolyn Hill, Soho, 86-90. *Bibliog:* Andrea Mikotajuk (auth), In the galleries, 12/71 & 1/72 & Gordon Brown (auth), In the galleries, 12/73, Arts Mag; article in Artworld, 2/80; articles in Artspeak, 2/80, 86, 87 & 4/88. *Mem:* Artists Equity Asn, NY. *Media:* Marble, Bronze. *Mailing Add:* 200 E 74th St No 18F New York NY 10021

SIMON, HERBERT BERNHEIMER
SCULPTOR
b Nashville, Tenn, Sept 20, 27. *Study:* Brooklyn Mus Art Sch; Hans Hofmann Studio, NY; Colorado Springs Fine Art Ctr; Hunter Col, study with Robert Motherwell; NY Univ, BA & MA, study with Philip Guston. *Work:* Everhart Mus, Scranton, Pa; Lehigh Univ, Bethlehem, Pa; Roberson Ctr Arts & Sci, Binghamton, NY; State Mus Pa, Harrisburg; Roberson Ctr for the Arts and Scis, Binghamton, NY; and others. *Comn:* Two Modules (sculpture), Coal St Park, Wilkes-Barre, Pa, 77; Facets (aluminum relief), Wilkes Col, Wilkes-Barre, Pa, 77; Aluminum Relief, Schaeffer Residence, Mountaintop, Pa, 78. *Exhib:* Drawings USA, Mus Mod Art, NY, 55; Fed Hall, NY, 82; 84 Sculptors for 1984, Rodger LaPelle Gallery, 84, 85, 86 & 90; Five Sides & Some Tops, Southern Ohio Mus & Cult Ctr, Portsmouth, Ohio, 85; Sordoni Art Gallery, Wilkes Col, Wilkes-Barre, Pa, 86; Susquehanna Regional Art Exhib, Roberson Mus, Binghamton, NY, 88 & 92; Mayfair Juried Art Exhib, Allentown Art Mus, Allentown, Pa, 89, 90 & 91; Katharina Rich Perlow Gallery, New York, NY, 89; Penn State Univ, 90, State Mus Pa, 91 & 92; Contemp Gallery, Marywood Col, Scranton, Pa, 90, 91 & 92; Bixler Gallery, Stroudsburg, Pa, 91; Riverwalk Juried Exhib, York, Pa, 92; Col Miseriocordia Dallas, Pa, 92; Places & Things, Wilkes Univ, 93; Art Marries Industry, Alumni Tech, Atlanta, 94; Contemp Pa Sculpture Southern Alleghenies Mus Art, Loretto, 95; and others. *Teaching:* Instr painting & drawing, Sch Design, NC State Col, Raleigh, 56-58; prof sculpture & 3-D design, Wilkes Univ, Wilkes-Barre, Pa, 69-92. *Awards:* Award, William Penn Mus, Harrisburg, Pa, 71; Purchase Prize Regional Art Exhib, Everhart Mus, Scranton, Pa, 76; Artist-in-Residence, Johnson Atelier, Mercerville, NJ, 86. *Bibliog:* William Sterling (auth), Herbert Simon: Metal Sculpture 1976-1980, Wilkes Col, Wilkes-Barre, Pa, 80. *Media:* Welded Steel, Aluminum; Cast Bronze. *Mailing Add:* 25 E Center St Shavertown PA 18708

SIMON, LEONARD RONALD
ADMINISTRATOR, WRITER
b Norristown, Pa, Dec 9, 36. *Study:* Ohio State Univ. *Collection Arranged:* Two Centuries of Black American Art (coauth, catalog), 75. *Pos:* Registr, Stanford Mus, 65-69; deputy dir, Calif Arts Coun, 77-80; vpres, Robert Brownlee Found, San Jose, Calif, 87-; pres, Celebration Theatre, Los Angeles, Calif, 92-. *Teaching:* Instr Black Am art, Univ Calif, Riverside, 76-77 & 80-. *Awards:* Oscar Micheaux Visual Arts Award, Int Black Writers & Artists, 94. *Mem:* Col Art Asn. *Res:* Black American artists. *Publ:* Auth, The American presence of the Black artist, Am Art Rev, 76; The sound of people, Arts in Soc, Vol 12, No 1. *Mailing Add:* 360 S Mills Ave Claremont CA 91711

SIMON, MICHAEL A
PHOTOGRAPHER
b Budapest, Hungary, June 20, 36; US citizen. *Study:* Budapest Tech Univ, 54-56; Pa State Univ, 57-58; Wis Arts Bd photog fel, 80, Rochester Inst Technol, MFA; Beloit Col, Wis, Hon BA. *Work:* Mus Mod Art, George Eastman House, Rochester, NY; Univ Kans, Lawrence; Minneapolis Inst Arts, Minn; Sheldon Mem Art Gallery, Lincoln, Nebr; Theodore Lyman Art Ctr, Beloit Col; Wis State Hist Soc, Madison. *Exhib:* Contemp Photog VII, George Eastman House, Rochester, NY, 72; Midwest Invitational, Walker Art Ctr, Minneapolis, 73; one-man shows, Wright Art Ctr, 77, 78 & 80, Minneapolis Inst Arts, Minn, 79, Write Art Ctr, Beloit Col, 80, TUBE Gallery, Write Art Ctr, Beloit Col, 83, Write Art Mus, Beloit Col, Univ Rochester, 85, Malone Gallery, Rochester, NY, 86 & The World is Beautiful, Wright Mus Art, 98; Recent Acquisitions, Minneapolis Inst Arts, Minn, 76; Madison Art Ctr, Wis, 83; Aspen Ctr Visual Arts, Colo, 83; Wright Art Mus, Beloit Col, 85; Univ Rochester, NY, 85; Malone Gallery, Rochester, NY, 86, The World is Beautiful, Wright Mus Art, 98; Wisconsin Sesquicentennial Re-Photog Project, Wisc State Hist Soc, 98. *Pos:* Cur photog, Wright Art Ctr, Beloit Col, currently; consult, Andre Kertes Retrospective exhib, Art Inst Chicago, 83-85; guest cur, exhib, Hungarian Photog from 1839 to Present, Fratelli Aliari, Florence, Italy, 87-89. *Teaching:* Assoc prof photog, Beloit Col, Wis, 69-; artist-in-residence photog, Univ Del, 74; vis artist photog, Art Inst Chicago, 78; artist-in-residence, Avila Col, Kansas City, Mo, 81; instr workshop, Chilmark Photog Workshop, Martha's Vineyard, Mass, 86; chmn dept art & art hist, Beloit Col, currently, emer prof art, 98-. *Awards:* Nat Endowment Arts Photog Survey Grant, 80; Nat Endowment Arts Exhib Grant, 81; grant, Wis Humanities Comt, 81; Purchase Awards, Mus Mod Art, NY, George Eastman House, Rochester, NY, Univ Kans, Lawrence, Minneapolis Inst Arts, Minn & Sheldon Mem Art Gallery, Lincoln, Nebr. *Bibliog:* Diaframma Italiana, Milan, Italy, 1-2/75. *Mem:* Soc Photog Educ (nat bd mem, 76-84, chmn nat bd dir, 79-81, chmn reg affairs comt, 81-83, chmn educ comt & mem steering comt, 83-84); Szechenyi Soc Hungary. *Res:* Mellon Foundation grant for the research of the history of photography in Hungary (76-80). *Publ:* auth, three Hungarian Photographers (exhib catalogue), Wright Mus Art, Beloit Col, Beloit, Wis; auth, article, Newslett Photog teachers, Polaroid Corp, summer 85; auth, essay in exhib catalogue for Contemp Hungarian Photogr, Allen Mus, Oberlin Col, Ohio, 89; auth, three Hungarian Photographers (exhib catalogue), Wright Mus Art, Beloit Col, Beloit, Wis; Jewish Photographers of Hungary, Mus Jewish Diaspora, Tel Aviv, Israel, 98

SIMON, MICHAEL J
CERAMIST
b Springfield, Minn, Dec 27, 47. *Study:* Univ Minn, BA, 70; Univ Ga, MFA, 80. *Exhib:* Solo exhibs, Baltimore Clayworks, Md, 89, Arvada Ctr Arts & Humanities, Denver, Colo, 89, Fla Gulf Coast Art Ctr, Belleair, Fla, 90; group shows, Pro Art Gallery, St Louis, Mo, 90; Expressive Teapot, Swidler Gallery, Royal Oak, Mich, 90; McKenzie Legacy, Manchester Craftsmen Guild, Pittsburgh, 91; Beyond the Body: Architectural Ceramics, LaCoste Gallery, Concord, Mass, 2000; Collaborating Couples, Ga Mus of Art, Athens, 2000; Color and Fire, Los Angeles Co Mus of Art, Calif, 2000; and many others. *Pos:* Many workshops & lectr including, Stetson Univ, Deland, Fla, 88, Fla Gulf Coast Art Ctr, Belleair, 90, Arrowmont Sch, Gatlinburg, Tenn, 91, Pa State Univ State Col, 91, Ga Mus of Art, 99, Baltimore Claywork, 2000. *Awards:* Fel, Ford Found, 81; Craft Fel, Nat Endowment Arts, 90. *Bibliog:* Michael Simon (auth), Old & New Pots: A Ceramics Monthly Portfolio, Ceramics Monthly, p 53-62, 6/83; Andy Nasisse (auth), A Coffee Bowl, Ceramics Monthly, p 63, 6/83; Am Craft, 92, 95, 97; Ceramics Monthly, 90, 95; Molded by Tradition, Atlanta Jour-Constitution, 96; Michelle Coaks (auth), Creative Pottery, Rockport Pub, 98; Don Davis (auth), Wheel Thrown Ceramics, 98; Karen Ann Wood (auth), Tableware in Clay: From Studio and Workshop, Croward Press UK, 99; Color and Fire: Defining Moments in Studio Ceramics, 1950-2000, Rizzoli Internat Pubs and Los Angeles Co Mus of Art, 2000. *Media:* Salt Glazed Stoneware. *Dealer:* Leslie Ferrin The Ferrin Gallery Lenox Mass Carr McQuistion; The Signature Shop Roswell Rd Atlanta Ga. *Mailing Add:* 2270 Crawford Smithonia Rd Colbert GA 30628

SIMON, NETTY D
PAINTER
Study: Escuela de la Bellas Artes, Lima, Peru; Utica Col; Art Students League; C W Post Col. *Work:* NY Tel Co; W C Grace Co, NY; Bethlehem Steel Co, NY; East Meadow Publ Libr, NY; Tower Mus, Philadelphia, Pa. *Exhib:* Solo shows, Steinhardt Gallery, Long Island, NY, 78, Sonnenberg Gallery, Rapperswil, Switz, 80 & 81, Halsten Gallery, Stockbridge, Mass, 81, Loring Gallery, Long Island, NY, 84 & Joy Berman Gallery, Philadelphia, 87; Audubon Artists, NY; Nat Acad Galleries, NY. *Awards:* First prize-oil, Locust Valley Art Show, 76 & 77 & St John's Univ, 80; Grumbacher Award, 78. *Bibliog:* articles in Interior Design, 8/78, Art Speaks, 8/81 & Uptown News, 1/90. *Mailing Add:* 487 Richmond Rd East Meadow NY 11554

SIMON, ROBERT BARRY
ART DEALER, HISTORIAN
b New York, NY, Nov 27, 52. *Study:* Columbia Col, BA, 73; Columbia Univ, MA, 75, MPhil, 76, PhD, 82. *Collection Arranged:* Sixteenth Century Portraits (auth, catalog), Soprintendenza, Florence, Italy, 80-82; US Info Agency Permanent Collection (auth, catalog), 82; Haggerty Mus, Marquette Univ (auth, catalog), 84; Discoveries in una nuova luce (auth catalog), 88 & Devotion and Delight (auth catalog), 89, Piero Corsini Gallery, NY; From Sacred to Sensual: Italian Paintings 1400-1750 (auth, catalog), Berry-Hill Galleries, New York, 98, Figure and Fantasy in French Painting 1650-1800 (auth, catalog), 99, Visions and Vistas: Old Master Paintings and Drawings (auth, catalog), 2000 & Old Master Paintings, 2001. *Pos:* Chester Dale Fel, Metrop Mus Art, New York, 76-78; dir, Fine Arts Group Crosson Dannis, 82-85 & Robert B Simon Fine Art Inc, 85-05; lectr, Fakes & Forgeries, Appraisal Inst Am, 97, Improving Old Masters & Mannerist Portraiture, Baylor Univ, 99, New Technology and Appraisal, Valuation, 2000 & Collecting Old Masters, Sotheby's Inst, 2000. *Teaching:* lectr appraisal old master paintings, Marymount Col, 91; lectr conservation & value, New York Univ, 94, El Greco in Venice, Univ Crete, 95 & Crivelli, Montreal Mus Fine Art, 95; Tracing Provenance in Old Master Paintings, 02; Bronzimo Working Methods, RSA, Toronto, 03; Building a Significant Art Collection, Palm Beach, 04; Art as an

Investment, Palm Beach, 05. *Mem:* Col Art Asn; Am Soc Appraisers; Am Asn Mus; Appraisers Asn Am (bd dir, 90, treas, 92, first vpres, 96, pres, 98-2000); Prv Art Dealers Asn & Antique Dealers League of N Am. *Res:* Bronzino, Salviati; American Impressionists; Mannerism; Richardsonian Romanesque architecture. *Specialty:* old master paintings. *Publ:* Auth, Bronzino's portrait of Cosimo I De'Medici, Burlington Mag, 83, Giulio Clovio's Eleonora Di Toledo, 89; Sofonisba Anguisciola, 86 & Dore in the Highlands, 89, Walters Art Gallery J; Yo Pontormo, J Art, 89; The Renaissance of the 16th Century, Sotheby's, 2001. *Mailing Add:* Satis House Tower Hill Rd Tuxedo Park NY 10987

SIMONDS, CHARLES FREDERICK
SCULPTOR, ARCHITECT
b New York, NY, Nov 14, 45. *Study:* Univ Calif, Berkeley, BA, 67; Rutgers Univ, Douglass Col, New Brunswick, NJ, MFA, 67. *Work:* Mus Mod Art, Guggenheim Mus & Whitney Mus Am Art, NY; Walker Art Ctr, Minneapolis; Mus Contemp Art, Chicago; Centre Georges Pompidon, Paris; Hirshhorn Mus, Washington. *Comn:* Dwellings, over 300 works constructed in the streets of NY for an imaginary civilization of little people migrating through the city, 70-; Project Uphill-La Placita (park playlot sculpture), Lower East Side Coalition for Human Housing, 74; full scale Dwellings, 74 & Growth House, 75, Art Park; Refuge (full scale work), 1988 Seoul Olympics; Olympiades des Arts, Seoul, Korea, 88. *Exhib:* Whitney Biennial, 75 & 77; Made by Sculptors, Stedelijk Mus, Amsterdam, The Neth, 78; Contemp Sculpture, Selections from the Collection of the Mus Mod Art, NY, 79; one-person shows, Projects: Picaresque Landscape, Mus Mod Art, NY, 76 & 77, Temenos, Albright-Knox Art Gallery, Buffalo, NY, 77, Floating Cities & Other Archit, Westfalischer Kunstverein, Munster, 78, Mus Sables D'Olonne, France, 79, Architekturmuseum, Basel, 85, Galerie Maeghtlelong, Paris, 86, Galerie Baudoin Lebon, Paris, 87, Corcoran Gallery, Washington, DC, 88 & Leo Castelli Gallery, NY, 89 & 92; Circles & Towers Growing, traveling exhib, Mus Contemp Art, Chicago, Los Angeles Co Mus Art, Ft Worth Art Mus & Contemp Arts Mus, Houston, Tex; Solomon R Guggenheim Mus, NY; House Plants and Rocks, Leo Castelli Gallery, NY, 84; retrospective, Charles Simonds, La Caixa, Barcelona, Spain & Jeu de Paume, Paris, 94; Retrospective, IVAM, Valencia, Spain, 2003. *Awards:* Artist-in-Residence Grant, 74 & Young Artists Grant, Nat Endowment Arts, 74-75; Nat Endowment Arts, 80; Mem, Soc Fels Am Acad Rome. *Bibliog:* John Beardsley (auth), Charles Simonds: Extending the metaphor, Art Int, Vol 22, No 9, 2/79; Mark Stevens (auth), The dizzy decade, Newsweek, 3/26/79; Kate Linker (auth), Charles Simonds' emblematic architecture, Art Forum, 3/79; and many others. *Publ:* Auth, Microcosm to macrocosm, 2/74 & Three peoples, 75, Art Forum. *Mailing Add:* 26 E 22nd St New York NY 10010

SIMONEAU, DANIEL ROBERT
PAINTER
b Lewiston, Maine, Aug 3, 62. *Study:* Univ of Southern Maine, BFA, 1984. *Work:* Toledo Mus of Art, Ohio. *Comn:* Bowling Mural, Holiday Lanes, Lewiston, Maine, 1979; Beethoven Mural, Lewiston High Sch, Maine, 1980. *Exhib:* Toledo Area Artist's Exhib: Toledo Mus of Art, Ohio, 1992, 1994; Northwestern Ohio Watercolor Soc, Toldo, Ohio, 1994; Salon De Refuses Exhib, Spectrum Gallery, Toledo, Ohio 1994; Artlink Mem Exhib, Artlink Gallery, Ft Wayne, Ind, 1995; Along the Waterfront, Seebeck Gallery, Kenosha, Wis, 2001; Wis Watercolor Soc Group Exhib, 2005 & 06. *Teaching:* Instr, Spectrum Gallery, Toledo, Ohio, 1993-94; instr, Auburn, Maine Adult Educ, 1989-90. *Awards:* Toledo Area Artists Exhib (third Judges Award, Purchase Award), 1992; Salon De Rufuses Exhib (Comt Award), 1994; Third Judges Award, Lewiston Art Festival, Maine, 1988, 90, & 91. *Mem:* Spectrum Friends of Art; Midwest Watercolor Soc; Transparent Watercolor Soc of Am; Northwestern Ohio Watercolor Soc; Wis Watercolor Soc; Am Soc Portrait Artists. *Media:* Watercolor, Acrylic. *Publ:* Expressions in Watercolor, LA Today Mag, 1991, Dan Simoneau. *Mailing Add:* 9507 74th St Kenosha WI 53142-8194

SIMONIAN, JUDITH
PAINTER, COLLAGE ARTIST
b Los Angeles, Calif, 45. *Study:* Calif State Univ, Northridge, BA, 67; MA, 74. *Work:* Chemical Bank, NY; Security Pac Bank, NY & Los Angeles; Prudential Savings Insurance Co, NJ, Kaufman & Broad, Los Angeles & Paris, France; Newport Harbor Mus, Calif; Mus Contemp Art, San Diego. *Comn:* Sculpture, Barbara Sinatra Children's Ctr, Palm Springs, Calif, 86; street installation, Washington Proj Arts, Washington, DC, 87; site sculpture, Art on the Beach, NY, 88; The Art Mall (dressing rooms), New Mus, NY, 92; 6 sculptures (installation), Long Island Univ, Brooklyn, NY, 94. *Exhib:* Fresh Paint, San Francisco Mus Mod Art, 82; one-person exhibs, Ovsey Gallery, Los Angeles, Calif, 82, 83, 84, 86, 88, 90, 91 & 94, Leila Taghinia-Milani, NY, 84, Newport Harbor Art Mus, Calif, 84, Peter Miller Gallery, Chicago, Ill, 84 & 91 & Jane H Baum Gallery, NY, 89; Hells Kitchen, Salon de Guerre, NY, 92; Am Embassy, Zurich, Switz, 94; FAO Gallery, NY, 96; NY Kunsthalle (installation), 96; Long Island Univ, Brooklyn, 97; Spensieri Contemp Art, San Francisco, 97-98; Chimeat, NY, 98; Jorgensen Gallery, NY, 99; The Passion/Passions of Art, Richard Anderson, NY, 99; Out of Y2k, Im n il, Greenpoint, NY, 99; NY/Arts Mag Collection, Artists Mus, Lodz, Poland, Emmanuel Heller, Tel Aviv, Isreal, Kulture Bahnhof, Ger, 2000; Facts and Figures, Margaret Bodell Gallery, 2000. *Teaching:* Instr drawing, Moorpark Community Col, 74-78; East Los Angeles Community Col, 78-82; instr color theory & graphic art, Calif State Univ, Long Beach, 80-81; instr drawings & painting, Otis Parson Sch of Design, Los Angeles, Calif, 81-85; vis artist, Clairmont Grad Sch, Calif, 83 & 88; instr, Cooper Union, 93-. *Awards:* Fel, Calif Confederation of Arts, 78; Fel, Nat Endowment Arts, 87; Site Installation Design Award, Dept Transportation, NY, 96. *Bibliog:* Kathy Norklon (auth), First Newport Biennial-Los Angeles, Newport Harbor Art Mus, 84; Robert L Pincus (auth), Art as Artifact, Flash Art, summer 85; Terry Bissell (auth), Art: Judith Simonian, Southern Calif Home & Garden, 11/88. *Media:* Acrylic, Mixed Media. *Mailing Add:* 231 E 5th St No 5 New York NY 10003

SIMONS, DONA
PAINTER
b Bryn Athyn, Pa, Aug 10, 53. *Study:* Univ of the Arts, 1974; Moore Col of Art, 1976; Pa Accad of Fine Arts, studied with Arthur DeCosta, Henry Pearson, Ben Kamahira, 1977-79. *Work:* Pub Libr, City of New Orleans, LA; New Orleans East Regional Libr. *Comn:* Portrait of Nat Hero, Dept of Culture, Gov of Curaco, Neth, Antilles, 1990; oil paintings, Shell Offshore, Inc, New Orleans, LA, 1998. *Exhib:* Contemporian, Monte Carlo, Monaco, 1985; Curacao Mus, Curacao, The Neth Antilles, 1991; Allentown Mus of Art, Allentown, Pa, 1998; Masur Mus of Art, Monroe, La, 2001; Alexandria Mus of Art, Alexandria, La, 2003. *Mem:* Pa Acad of the Fine Arts Fel. *Media:* Acrylic, Oil. *Publ:* Illus, Henry's Journey, Portals Press, 1992, The Gren and the Burning Alike, 1992, Cafe Millennium, 2000, Waterblind, 2002. *Dealer:* Sylvia Schmidt Gallery, 400 A Julia St, New Orleans, LA 70130

SIMOR, SUZANNA B
LIBRARIAN, GALLERY DIRECTOR
b Prague, Czech; US citizen. *Study:* Inst Fine Arts, NY Univ, MA, 74; Grad Sch Libr & Info Sci, Pratt Inst, MLS, 76. *Collection Arranged:* Italian Art--15th to 18th Century (auth catalog), Godwin-Ternbach Mus, Queens Col, 86. *Pos:* Head Art Libr, dir Art Ctr, Queens Col, City Univ NY, 80-. *Teaching:* Asst prof art librarianship, Queens Col, City Univ NY, 77-. *Awards:* Nat Endowment Arts Grant, 85; PSC/City Univ NY Grant, 86-87. *Mem:* Art Librs Soc NAM (chmn, 77, NY chap chmn, 90-); Col Art Asn; Special Librs Asn-Mus-Arts and Humanities Div; Am Libr Asn; Libr Asn City Univ NY (chmn, 77-). *Res:* Art librarianship; art bibliography and research methods; late medieval and Renaissance art; 20th century art. *Interests:* Medieval and Renaissance art; art of the 20th century contemporary art and artists. *Publ:* Auth, articles, Basic Materials for Reference & Research in Art History, Queens Col, 81-86; auth & ed, Art of E Africa Slide Collection, IFLA, Art Librs Sect, 84; ed, NY Membership Directory, ARLIS/NY, 85; coauth, Italian Art--15th to 18th Century, Queens Col, 86; auth, Necessary luxury: art exhibitions in academic libraries, 90; The Credo in Context: Endorsing Other Themes, Pensee - image et communication en Europe medievale, 91. *Mailing Add:* 13927 Coolidge Ave Jamaica NY 11435

SIMPER, FREDERICK
PAINTER
b Mishawaka, Ind, July 31, 14. *Study:* Self-taught. *Work:* Detroit Inst Arts; South Bend Art Mus, Ind; US Embassies Collection. *Exhib:* Detroit Inst Arts, 38-68; Art Inst Chicago, 48; Watercolor USA, Springfield, Mo, 65; Butler Inst Art, Youngstown, Ohio; Pa Acad Fine Arts, Philadelphia; one-man shows, Arwin Gallery, Detroit, 78 & Herman Frankel Orgn, W Bloomfield, 86. *Pos:* Art dir, D'Arcy, Macmanus Int, 49-80. *Teaching:* Instr watercolor, Soc Arts & Crafts, Detroit, 48-51; instr watercolor, Bloomfield Art Asn, Birmingham, Mich, 68-70. *Awards:* Robert Tanahill Award, 42; Baltimore Sun Award for Black & White Drawing, 45; Mich Watercolor Soc Award, 72. *Mem:* Mich Watercolor Soc. *Media:* Watercolor. *Mailing Add:* 4769 Golfview Dr Leland MI 49654

SIMPSON, BENNETT
CURATOR, CRITIC
Study: Univ Va, BA, 94. *Exhib:* Apex Art, NY, 99; Elysian Fields, Centre Pompidou, Paris, 2000; Shoot the Singer: Music on Video, ICA, Philadelphia, 2002; Make Your Own Life: Artists in and out of Cologne, 2004. *Pos:* former ed, ArtByte Mag, NY & Purple Mag, NY; Whitney Lauder cur fel, Inst Contemp Art, 2001-2002; assoc cur, Philadelphia, 2002-2003 & Boston, 2004-. *Publ:* contribr, articles in many professional journals. *Mailing Add:* ICA Boston 955 Boylston St Boston MA 02115

SIMPSON, BUSTER (LEWIS BUSTER C)
SCULPTOR
b May 29, 42. *Study:* Univ Mich, BA, MFA, 63-69. *Comn:* Moving Over, Miami Dade Metro, 94; Phase II, Anaheim Ctr Redevelopment Streetscape, 95; Water-Earth-Light, Pub Art Comn, 96; Brush with Illumination, City Vancouver, 98; Monolith, Turtle Bay, Redding, Calif, 2000. *Exhib:* one-man show, Western Front, Vancouver, BC, 80, Hirshorn Mus & Sculpture Garden, Washington, 89, Seattle Art Mus, 91 & Capp St Proj, San Francisco, 93, Henry Art Gallery, Univ Wash, Seattle, 2000; Fragile Ecologies, Queens Mus, NY, 92; Pub Introventions, Cent Intelligence Agency, Boston, 94; Reuse Refuse, Honolulu Art Acad, 94; Hello Again, Fashion Inst Technol Mus, NY, 94; Natural Dialogue, Pratt Manhattan Gallery, 94; Hello Again, Oakland Mus, Calif, 97-98; Biennial Exhibition of Pub Art, Neuberger Mus Art, Purchase, NY, 99. *Pos:* Comnr, Pike Pl Market Hist Dist Comn, Seattle, Wash, 83; artist, consult, Redondo Seawall, 88-92, New Denver Airport, Colo, 90-91, Central Artery/Tunnel, Bectel, Boston, Mass, 91-92, King Cross Railroad Lands, London, Eng, 94-96 & Amtrak King St Sta, Seattle, Wash, 98-99; artist/designer with Revy Design Painters, San Jose Int Airport, 94-95; mem design team, San Jose Int Airport Terminal, Calif, 95, Mid-Embarcadero, San Francisco, Calif, 96-97, Downtown Denny Regrade Master Plan, Seattle, Wash, 97-98 & Vine St Green, Seattle, Wash, 98-2000; lead landscape designer, Ellington, Intracorp Pub Plaza, 98-99. *Teaching:* Instr drawing & mixed media, Flint Jr Col, Mich, 69; artist-in-residence, Artpark, Lewiston, NY, 78; vis lectr, Univ NC, Chapel Hill, 92 & Deep Springs Col, Calif, 98; lectr, Deep Springs Col, 98. *Awards:* Urban Arboretum Proj Grant, Nat Endowment Arts, 84; Sculpture Fel, Nat Endowment Arts, 88 & Individual Artist Fel, 91; Howard S Wright Award, Seattle Arts Comn, 96; Visual Artist Award, Flintridge Found, 99; Distinguished Alumni Award, Univ Mich, 2000. *Bibliog:* Ned Rifkin (auth), Buster Simpson Works (exhib catalog, interview), Hirshorn Mus & Sculpture Garden, Smithsonian Inst, 89; Barbara Matilsky (auth), Fragile Ecologies (exhib catalog), Queens Mus/Rizzali Int, 92; Bailey Oakes (auth), Sculpting with the Environment, Van Nostrand Reinhold, 95. *Mailing Add:* 901 Yakima Ave S Seattle WA 98114

SIMPSON, DAVID
PAINTER
b Pasadena, Calif, Jan 20, 28. *Study:* Calif Sch Fine Arts, with Clyfford Still & others, BFA, 56; San Francisco State Col, MA, 58. *Work:* Panza Collection, Milan, Italy; Laguna Art Mus, Laguna Beach, Calif; Mus Contemp Art, Los Angeles; Muses Di Arte Moderna E Cont Empornea Di Trento E Roveret & Mart, Italy; Albright Knox Art Gallery, NMex. *Exhib:* Americans 1963, Mus Mod Art, NY, 63; retrospective, Oakland Mus, Calif, 78; Angles Gallery, Santa Monica, Calif, 91-92 & 94; Bemis Found, Omaha, Nebr, 92; Haines Gallery, San Francisco, 96 & 2002; Studio La Citta, Verona, Italy, 97 & 2001; Renate Schroder Galerie, Cologne, 2002; Charlotte Jackson Fine Arts, Santa Fe, NMex, 2005; Galerie Sonta Roesch, Houston, Tex, 2005. *Teaching:* Prof art emer, Univ Calif, Berkeley, 65-. *Awards:* Nat Endowment Arts Grant, 90. *Media:* Acrylic, Canvas. *Dealer:* Angeles Gallery Santa Monica CA; Haines Gallery San Francisco. *Mailing Add:* 565 Vistamont Berkeley CA 94708

SIMPSON, GAIL A
SCULPTOR, EDUCATOR
b Baltimore, Md. *Study:* Wash Univ, St Louis, Mo, BFA; Art Inst Chicago, MFA. *Work:* Chicago Title & Trust, First Nat Bank Chicago, Ill. *Exhib:* Two-person exhib, Cage Gallery, Cincinnati, Ohio, 90; Omnibus, Herron Gallery, Indianapolis, Ind, 91; three-person exhib, Abel Joseph Gallery, 92; Sequence of Forms, Ill Sculpture, State Ill Gallery, Chicago, 93; City Sculpture '94, Bellingham, Wash, 94; Linda Hodges Gallery, Seattle, Wash, 98; Lead Gallery, Seattle, Wash, 99; and others. *Teaching:* Asst prof sculpture, Ill State Univ, 89-93; instr art, Western Wash Univ, 93-. *Awards:* Nat Endowment Arts, 88-; Ill Arts Coun Proj Grant, 90. *Mem:* Col Art Asn; Int Sculpture Soc. *Mailing Add:* 673 Center Road Stoughton WI 53589-3917

SIMPSON, JOSH (JOSIAH) J L SIMPSON
GLASS BLOWER
b Aug 17, 37. *Study:* Hamilton Col, Clinton, NY, BA, 72. *Work:* Renwick Gallery/Smithsonian Inst, Washington, DC; Mus Fine Arts, Boston, Mass; Corning Mus, NY; Chrysler Mus Art, Norfolk, Va; Sphere Mus, Tokyo, Japan. *Comn:* Mega Planet, Nortel Inc, Tex, 97 & Moritex Corp, Japan, 98; Mega, Mega Planets, Royal Caribbean Cruise, Norway, 98. *Exhib:* New Glass, Corning Mus, NY, 79 & Heidi Schneider, Switz, 88; one-man show, Arnot Mus, Elmira, NY, 91; Int Exhib Glass, Kanazawa, Japan, 92; New Work, New Worlds, Hamilton Col, Fred L Emerson Gallery, NY, 94; White House Collection, White House, Washington, DC, 95; Visionary Landscapes, Bruce Mus, Conn, 98. *Teaching:* Glass, Penland Sch Crafts, NC, 89; Aichi Univ, Hirosawa, 93; Corning Mus, NY, 97. *Awards:* Humanitarian Award, Niche, 93; Achievement in Limited Series Design, Urban Glass, 96. *Bibliog:* S Frantz (auth), Contemporary Glass, 89; Artists look at earth, Smithsonian, 11/96; K Conover (auth), From a fiery inferno, Christian Sci, 4/6/97. *Mem:* Am Craft Enterprises, 84-85; Craft Emergency Relief Fund (pres, 85-92); life mem Glass Art Soc (pres, 92-94). *Media:* Glass. *Mailing Add:* Frank Williams Rd Shelburne Falls MA 01370

SIMPSON, MARIANNA SHREVE
HISTORIAN, CURATOR
b Washington, DC, Nov 17, 49. *Study:* Univ Pa, BA, 70; Johns Hopkins Univ, 71-72; Harvard Univ, PhD, 78. *Pos:* From asst to assoc dean, Ctr Advan Study Visual Arts, Nat Gallery Art, Washington, DC, 80-92; asst dir & cur Islamic Near Eastern art, Freer/Sackler Galleries, Smithsonian Inst, 93-95. *Teaching:* Lectr, Harvard Univ, Cambridge, Mass, 78 & 95-, Georgetown Univ, Washington, DC, 80-91; vis asst prof, Univ Calif, Los Angeles, 80, Princeton Univ, 93 & Johns Hopkins Univ, 97. *Awards:* Mus Intern Fel, Nat Endowment Arts & Fogg Art Mus, Harvard Univ, 76-77; Pre-Doctoral Fel, Smithsonian Inst, 77-78; Grant-in-aid, Am Coun Learned Soc, 79. *Mem:* Middle East Studies Asn; Col Art Asn. *Res:* Medieval Islamic art, with focus on problems in illustrated manuscript studies of fourteenth through sixteenth centuries. *Publ:* auth, The role of Baghdad in the formation of Persian painting, In: Art et Societe Dans le Monde Iranien, Paris, 82; L'art Islamique an Asic, 82

SIMPSON, MARILYN JEAN
PAINTER, INSTRUCTOR
b Birmingham, Ala, 29. *Study:* Univ Ala; Art Students League, NY; Inst Allende, San Miguel Allende, Mex; Madison Art Sch, Conn; with Robert Brackman; Am Univ Avignon, France; Rome & Florence, Italy. *Exhib:* Smithsonian Inst, Wash, DC; Pastel Soc Am, NY; Pastel Soc NMex; Pastel Soc West Coast; Pastel Soc N Fla; Arts in the Park, Decas Pastel Soc; Pastel Soc Southwest. *Pos:* dir, Sch Pastel Painting, Ft Walton Beach, Fla. *Teaching:* Dir & instr, Acad Fine Arts, Ft Walton Beach, Fla. *Awards:* Arts Speak, PSA Award, Edith Barow, PSA Award; Pres Award, PSWC; Richardson Award, PSNF, First Place, PSNF. *Mem:* Signature mem Pastel Soc Am, NY; Knickerbocher Artist, USA, NY; Pastel Soc N Fla (founder & pres), Ft Walton Beach, Fla; Int Asn Pastel Soc (vpres), NY; Decas Pastel Soc. *Media:* Pastel, Oil. *Specialty:* Fine Arts Gallery. *Interests:* Teaching and Reading. *Publ:* Auth, The Art of Pastel Portraiture; auth, 100 Arts for the Parks, Artists Int. *Dealer:* Gallery Fine Arts Hwy 98 East Destin FL. *Mailing Add:* 2991 W Highway 98 Mary Esther FL 32569-2336

SIMPSON, MERTON D
PAINTER, DEALER
b Charleston, SC, Sept 20, 28. *Study:* NY Univ; Cooper Union Art Sch, with Robert Motherwell & Baziotes; also with William Halsey. *Work:* James J Sweeney Collection, Guggenheim Mus; Howard Univ, Washington, DC; Scott Field Mus, Chicago; Atlanta Univ; Gibbs Art Gallery. *Comn:* painting, Black Portrait Study: Rev Daniel J Jenkins, Charleston, 84. *Exhib:* one person exhib: Ancestral Improvisation, Noid d'Ivoire Gallery, Paris, 92; Hale House Benefit Exhib: Tambaran gallery, NY, 1993; Rudolph E Lee Gallery, Clemson Univ, SC, 95; Nations Bank place, Columbia, SC, 95; Journey of an Artist, Gibbs Mus of Art, 95; group exhib: Jazz and Visual Improvisations, Katonah Mus, 01; Not Just February: Works by African Am Artist 1817-2002, Steve Turner Gallery, 02; Transatlantic Jazz: Herbert Gentry and Merton Simpson, Steve Turner Gallery, 02; No Greater Love: Abstraction, Tilton/Krustera Gallery, 02; Spirit of an Artist: Merton Simpson, a Retrospective, Merton Simpson Gallery, 03. *Collection Arranged:* perm col: Atlanta Univ, Univ of Mass, Rogers Engraving Company, NY, James J Sweeney Col, Detroit Art Inst; prvt col: Nelson D Rockerfeller, Dwight Eisenhowe, Helena Rubenstein, Spike Lee, Bill Cobsy, and others. *Pos:* Owner, Merton D Simpson Gallery, NY. *Awards:* Red Cross Exchange Exhib Award, Tokyo & Paris, 50; Atlanta Univ Awards, 50, 51 & 56; Oakland Art Mus Award, 52; Studio Mus of Harlem Award, 2002. *Publ:* Art & Antiques, Top 100 Treasures, 2001; Artist Portrait Series: Images of Contemporary African-American Artists, Fem Logan, Southern Ill Univ, 2001; St James Guide to Black Artsits, Thomas Riggs, Schomburg Ctr for Research in Black Culture, St James Press, 97; and many others. *Mailing Add:* 38 W 28th St Apt 5 New York NY 10001

SIMPSON, WILLIAM KELLY
HISTORIAN, EDUCATOR
b New York, NY, Jan 3, 28. *Study:* Yale Univ, BA, 47, MA, 48, PhD, 54; Ecole Practique Hautes Etudes, Paris. *Hon Degrees:* DHL, Am Univ, Cairo, 01. *Collection Arranged:* The Pennsylvania-Yale Expedition to Nubia, Peabody Mus, Yale Univ, New Haven, Conn, 63; Recent Accessions in Egyptian & Ancient Near Eastern Art & The Horace L Mayer Collection, 72, Mus Fine Arts, Boston; Metrop Mus, New York; Univ Pa Mus, Philadelphia. *Pos:* Cur Egyptian art & ancient Near Eastern art, Mus Fine Arts, Boston, 70-86. *Teaching:* Prof Egyptol, Yale Univ, 65-2004, chmn dept Near Eastern langs, 66-69-; vis prof Egyptol, Univ Pa. *Awards:* Guggenheim Found Fel, 65. *Mem:* Archaeol Inst Am; Am Oriental Soc; Am Res Ctr in Egypt; Int Coun Mus Mod Art, NY; and others. *Res:* Art, history, and literature of ancient Egypt. *Collection:* The Offering Chapel of Kayemnolnet, Mus Fine Arts, Boston, 92; The Inscribed Material from Pa-Yale Excavations, Abydos, 95; and others. *Publ:* Auth, Papyrus Reisner I-Records of a Building Project, 63; auth, Papyrus Reisner II-Accounts of the Dockyard Workshop, 65; auth, Papyrus Reisner III-Records of a Building Project in the Early Twelfth Dynasty, 69; coauth, The Ancient Near East: A History, 71; coauth, The Literature of Ancient Egypt, 72; auth, The Mastaba of Queen Mersyankh III, 74. *Mailing Add:* Katonah's Wood Rd Katonah NY 10536

SIMS, LOWERY STOKES
HISTORIAN, CURATOR
b Washington, DC, Feb 13, 49. *Study:* Queens Col, City Univ New York, BA, 70, MPhil, 90, PhD, 95; Johns Hopkins Univ, MA, 72. *Hon Degrees:* Md Inst Col Art, DHL, 88; Moore Col Art & Design, DArt, 91; Parsons Sch Design, DArt, 00; Atlanta Col Art, DArt, 02; Brown Univ, DFA, 03. *Exhib:* Romare Bearen: And Artists' Odyssey, (catalog essay & organizer), 86; Race and Representation, (catalog essay), Hunter Col Gallery, NY, 87; Art as a Verb, The Evolving Continuum, (co-cur & essay), Maryland Inst Col of Art, Baltimore, Md, 88-89; Next Generation, Southern Black Aesthetic, (catalog essay), Southern Ctr Contemp Art, Winston-Salem, NC, 90; Challenge of the Mod African-Am Artists, 1925-1945, 03; Curator's Choice: Install & Insight, Nat Gallery, Kingston, Jamaica, 2004; Legacies: Contemporary Artists Reflect on Slavery, New Hist Soc, 2006. *Pos:* Asst mus educ, Metrop Mus Art, NY, 72-75, assoc cur 20th century art, 75-95, & cur, 95-2000; dir, Studio Mus in Harlem, 2000-05; juror, guest cur, Queens Mus, Studio Mus in Harlem, Pratt Inst, Caribbean Cult Ctr, New York, Cooper Union, and others; panelist, mem bd numerous orgs; adj cur, SMH, 2006-. *Teaching:* vis critic, Md Inst, 87, Pa Acad Arts, 88, Univ Pa & Univ Tex, Austin; vis prof, Hunter Col, 2005, 06; vis prof, Queens Col, 2006; AD White prof at large, Cornell Univ, 2006-. *Awards:* Frank Jewett Award, Col Art Asn, 91; Lifetime Achievement in the Arts Award, Queens Mus Arts, 98; Distinguished Alumni, City Univ NY Grad Ctr, 02. *Mem:* Int Asn Art Critics; Asn Am Mus Dirs. *Res:* 20th century painting, sculpture and architecture especially of the last 30 years, with special interest in Afro-American, Latin American, Asian and Native American artists. *Publ:* Race Riots - Cocktail Parties - Black Panthers - Moon Shoots and Feminists: Faith Ringgold's Observations on the 1960's in America, (essay), Faith Ringgold: A 25 Year Survey, Fine Arts Mus Long Island, Hempstead, New York, 90; Beulahland (for Marilyn Monroe), An Icon for America, (essay), IDA Applebroog: Happy Families, A Fifteen-Year Survey, Contemp Arts Mus, Houston, 90; Cultural Diversity or the Americanist Canon: The Aesthetic Dialog of the 1990's, (catalog essay), The Decade Show, New Mus Contemp Art, Studio Mus Harlem & Mus Contemp Hispanic Art, New York, 90; Wifredo Lam and his contemporaries, 1938-1952, Studio Mus Harlem, 92; Stuart Davis, American Painter (exhib catalog), Metropolitan Mus Art, 91; Wifredo Lam and the International Avant-Garde, 1923-1982, 02; Challenge of the Modern African-American Artists, 1925-1945, 03. *Mailing Add:* 1125 Lexington Ave New York NY 10021

SIMS, PATTERSON
CURATOR
b Philadelphia, Pa, Nov 17, 47. *Study:* Chestnut Hill Acad, Philadelphia, Pa; Darrow Sch, New Lebanon, NY; Trinity Col, Hartford, Conn; New Sch Social Res, New York, BA, 72. *Collection Arranged:* Seven Decades of MacDowell Colony Artists, James Yu Gallery, 76; On Canvas, 76, 30 Years of American Art, Whitney Biennial Exhibition, American Art 1900-1950 & Selections from the Promised Gift of Mrs Percy Uris, 77 & American Art 1920- 1945, 77-78, Whitney Mus Am Art, NY; School of Visual Arts 1977 End of the Year Show, 77; American Art 1900-1950, 77, Jasper Johns: A Selected View, 89 & Made in New York: The New York School: 1945-1965, 89, Seattle Art Mus, Mark Tansey: Art and Source, 90, Documents Northwest Series: Buster Simpson, 91 & Dale Chihuly: Installations 1964-1992 (auth, catalog), 92, Seattle Art Mus; Jacob Lawrence: The Early Decades 1935-1950, Katona Mus, NY, 92; Art Chantry: Posters; Fred Wilson: The Museum Mixed Metraphors, Seattle Art

Mus, 93. *Pos:* Asst dir, O K Harris Works of Art, New York, 69-76; assoc cur permanent collection, Whitney Mus Am Art, 76-87; assoc dir art & exhibs & cur mod art, Seattle Art Mus, Wash, 87-. *Teaching:* Part-time instr, Sch Continuing Educ, New York Univ, 75-77 & 84-86. *Publ:* Auth, Alan Shields, Moore Col Art, Pa, 77; Jan Matulka: A Life in Art, Smithsonian Press, 79; Whitney Museum of American Art: Selected Works from the Permanent Collection, 86; Documents Northwest Series: CT Chew, 88, Figures of Translucence, 89 & Crossed Cultures, 89 (exhib brochures), Seattle Art Mus. *Mailing Add:* Director Montclair Art Museum 3 S Mountain Ave Montclair NJ 07042-1747

SIMSON, BEVLYN A
PAINTER, PRINTMAKER
b Columbus, Ohio, Sept 9, 17. *Study:* Ohio State Univ, BFA & MFA; mus in Europe & Japan. *Work:* Chase Manhattan Bank, NY; Kresge Collection, Detroit; Columbus Mus Art; JB Speed Mus, Louisville, Ky; Tyler Mus, Tex; Wichita Mus Art, Kans; Fordham Univ, Lincoln Ctr, NY; Capital Univ, Ohio. *Comn:* Nine paintings, Lobby, McCampell, Ohio State Nisonger Ctr; three-panel paintings, First Investment Co, 69 & First Community Bank, 81; Grant Hosp Med Ctr. *Exhib:* One-person shows, JB Speed Mus, Louisville, Ky, 70, City Hall, Columbus, Ohio, 73, Capital Univ, 77, Springfield Art Mus, 80, Franklin Univ, 81 & Collectors Gallery, Columbus Mus Art, 83; 37th Nat Painting Show, Butler Inst Am Art, Youngstown, Ohio, 73; Contemp Prints for Collectors, Columbus Mus Art, 74 & 75; Represented US at 2nd Int Art Exhib, Parimaribo, Suriname, 74; Ohio Women Artists: Past & Present, Butler Inst Am Art, 76; Legacy of Hoyt Sherman, Denver Mus Art & Ohio State Univ Gallery, 82; Centre Int d'Art Contemp, Paris, 83; 9th Ann Women Artists Expo, Seal of Ohio Girl Scout Coun, Columbus, Ohio, 96; 4th Biennial Alumni Exhib, Res Divists, Ohio State Univ, 97. *Pos:* owner, dir, Bevlyn Simion Gallery; art adv, 1st Community Bank, 1st City Bank. *Awards:* Dipl di Merito, Univ della Arte, Acad Ital, 82; Best of Show, State of Ohio Competition, Nat League Am PEN Women, 85; Shared Best of Show Award, 29th Ann Fall Exhib, Bexley Art League, Trinity Lutheran Sem, 90; and others. *Bibliog:* Jacqueline Hall (auth), Bevlyn Simson displays works internationally, Columbus Dispatch, 4/9/75; Mary Bridgman (auth), Bevlyn Simson rhymes colors & shapes, Columbus Dispatch, 12/11/77; Tricia & Mat Herban (auths), Bevlyn Simson neo-geometrics show a technique of modern art, Columbus Citizen-J, 5/16/83. *Mem:* Nat Mus Women in the Arts, Columbus Mus Art; Am Fedn Arts; Nat League Am Pen Women; Bexley Art League; Ohio Art League (past pres). *Media:* Acrylic; Lithograph, Silkscreen. *Publ:* Auth, Prints & Poetry, 69; Rare Book Room, Ohio State Univ Library. *Mailing Add:* Bevlyn Simson Gallery 289 S Roosevelt Ave Columbus OH 43209

SINA, ALEJANDRO
KINETIC ARTIST, SCULPTOR
b Santiago, Chile, May 10, 45. *Study:* Univ Chile, MBA, 73; Ctr Advan Visual Studies, Mass Inst Technol, with Gyorgy Kepes & Otto Piene, fel, 73-79. *Work:* Mus Sci & Indust, Chicago; Nat Mus Fine Arts & Museo Interactivo Mirador, Santiago; Nat Sci Mus, Veno Park, Tokyo; Saitama Childrens Mus, Higashi-Matsuyama, Japan; Bruce Mus, Greenwich, Conn. *Comn:* End of Redline/Alewife Station, Mass Bay Transit Authority, Cambridge, 85; Sprouts, Fidelity Investments, Boston, 89; Neon Veils & Double Sprouts, New Eng Development, Cambridge, 90; Coca Cola Hq with Jonathon Spiers, London, Eng, 93; Six Helicoils, The Trocadero, Sega Floor, London, Eng, 96. *Exhib:* Gaslight Phenomena, Inst Contemp Art, Boston, 77; Five Artists, Five Technologies, Grand Rapids Art Mus, Mich, 79; Art in Light and Illusion, Isetan Mus Art, Tokyo, 82; Color-Light-Motion, Wadsworth Atheneum, Hartford, Conn, 84; ARTEC 89, Inagural Bienal, Nagoya, Japan; Les Artistes et la Lumiere, Rheims, France, 91; Electrique, Mus de la Civilisation, Que, Can; Esculturas Luminicas, Sala de Arte, CTC, Santiago, Chile. *Teaching:* Instr, Ctr Advan Visual Studies, Mass Inst Technol, 73-77. *Awards:* Fulbright Fel, 73-75; Nat Endowment Arts Grant, 76-77; Lumen Award/Light Artists, NY Illuminating Eng Soc, Santiago, Chile, 95. *Bibliog:* Sixto Escobar (producer), The Art of Alejandro Sina, La Plaza Prog, TV Channel 7, Boston, 83; Michael Webb (auth), The Magic of Neon, Gibbs M Smith Inc, 83; Michael Webb (auth), Liquid Fire, Gibbs Smith, 90; Rudi Stern (auth), Contemporary Neon, Larry Fuersich Retail Reporting, 91; Christian Schiess (auth), The Light Artist Anthology, ST Publ, 93. *Media:* Neon, Electronics; Glass. *Publ:* Auth, Guide Internacional de Arts Electroniques, Guide Kanal, Paris, France. *Mailing Add:* 21 Andem Pl No 1 Brookline MA 02146

SINCLAIR, ROBERT (W)
PAINTER, SCULPTOR
b Saltcoats, Sask, Can, Feb 9, 39. *Study:* Univ Manitoba Sch Art, BFA, 61; Univ Iowa, MA, 65, MFA, 67. *Work:* Art Gallery, Windsor, Ont; Agnes Etherington Art Gallery, Queens Univ, Kingston, Ont; Confederation Art Gallery, Charlottetown, PEI; Glenbow Mus, Calgary, Alta; Edmonton Art Gallery, Alta; Royal Collection, Windsor Castle Libr, Eng. *Comn:* Foyer painting (acrylic stain), Oxford Develop Group, Royal Trust Tower, Edmonton, Alta, 79; Slumped Glass Landscape (sculpture), Brit Petroleum, Calgary, Alta, 89. *Exhib:* Changing Visions, Art Gallery Ont, Toronto, 76-77; one-man shows, Gallery-Stratford, Ont, 76 & Edmonton Art Gallery, Alta, 82-83; Pertaining to Space, Art Gallery Ont, Toronto, 76-77; Diamond Jubilee Collection, Royal Libr, Windsor Castle, Eng, 86; Spaces & Places, Alta Art Found, traveling China & Japan, 86-90; Heaven-and-Earth, Whyte Mus Can Rockies, Banff, Alta, 91; Artists in Wilderness: Images of a Vanishing Alberta, Provincial Mus, Edmonton, 92; A View of Nfld, Art Gallery Nfld & Labrador Univ, St Johns, 96. *Teaching:* Prof art painting & drawing, Dept Art & Design, Univ Alta, 65-97; vis artist, Univ Iowa, 73 & Banff Sch Fine Art, 76; prof emeritus. *Bibliog:* Four Prairie Artists (film), Can Broadcasting Corp, 85. *Mem:* Royal Canadian Acad Arts; Can Soc Painters Watercolour. *Media:* Watercolor, Acrylic Stain; Folded Paper, Oil Painting, Embossed Prints. *Specialty:* paintings, drawings, prints & sculpture photographs. *Dealer:* Gallery at Jasper Park Lodge Box 1651 Jasper Alberta TOEIEO; Willcok & Sax, Waterton Park Box 72 Alberta TOK 2MO; Ingram Gallery, 49 Ave Rd Toronto ON M5R 2G3; Scott Gallery, 10411-124st Edmonton AB T5N 3Z5; Gallery at Banff Springs Hotel, 405 Spray Ave Banff AB; Gallery at Chateau Whister, 4559 Chateau Blvd Whistler, BC Von 1B4. *Mailing Add:* 10819 52 Ave Edmonton AB T6H 0P2 Canada

SINDELIR, ROBERT JOHN
GALLERY DIRECTOR, ADMINISTRATOR
b Olivia, Minn, June 12, 32. *Study:* Univ Miami, Coral Gables, Fla, with Virgil Barker, AB, 57. *Collection Arranged:* Christo, Wrapped Coastline, 72; Lee Krasner, Selected Paintings, 73; Duane Michals, Photographs, 77; Philip Pearlstein, Selected Paintings, 78; Komar and Melamid, Monotype Prints, 90. *Pos:* Dir, Art Pub Places Prog, Miami, Fla, 74-76, Mitchell Wolfson Gallery, 83-90, Kendall Campus Art Gallery, 90-. *Teaching:* Instr humanities, Miami-Dade Community Col, 70-74. *Publ:* Auth, African Tribal Art (exhib catalog), Miami-Dade Community Col, 83; contribr, Journal of Decorative and Propaganda Arts, Wolfsonian Found, 86; auth, Susana Sori (exhib catalog), Thomas Ctr, 88; Julio Antonio (exhib catalog), Elite Fine Art, 89; Lynn Davison (exhib catalog), Miami-Dade Community Col, 91. *Mailing Add:* 10601 SW 74th Ave Miami FL 33156-3829

SINGER, ALAN DANIEL
PAINTER, PRINTMAKER
b Jun 19,1950. *Study:* The Cooper Union, BFA, 1972; Cornell Univ, MFA, 1975; Pratt, post grad. *Work:* Leigh Yawkey Woodson Art Mus, Wausau, WI; The US Postal Mus, Washington, DC. *Comn:* Birds and Flowers of 50 States, US Postal Service, Washington, DC, 1982; 5 Pathogens for Levaquin Johnson & Johnson, 2006; Everson Mus Art, Syracuse, NY, 2000, 06. *Exhib:* State Birds & Flowers, Smithsonian, Washington, DC, 1988; Finger Lakes Invitational, Memorial Art Gallery, Rochester, NY, 1992; Biennial, Everson, Syracuse, NY, 2000; Pushing the Envelope, Norman Rockwell Mus, Stockbridge, MA, 2000. *Pos:* pres, The Print Club of Rochester, Rochester, NY, 1995-2000. *Teaching:* vis artist, painting, Parson's School of Design (grad prog), 1986-87, Syracuse Univ, 2006; prof, fine art, Rochester Inst of Technology, 1987-. *Awards:* Purchase Prize, Watercolors, Nassau Community Col, 1983; S.O.S. Award, Slice of Life, Dyer Art Ctr, 2003. *Mem:* Print Club of Rochester, pres, 1995-2000; Col Art Assoc; Am Soc of Botonical Artists. *Media:* Oil, Watercolor, Print making, Art writer. *Publ:* Auth, Wildlife Art, Rockport Press, 1999; illusr, State Birds, Lodestar Books, 1986. *Dealer:* Mona Berman Fine Art 72 Lyon St New Haven CT 06511. *Mailing Add:* 3021 Elmwood Ave Rochester NY 14618

SINGER, CLIFFORD
PAINTER, PRINTMAKER
b Great Neck, NY. *Study:* Alfred Univ, BFA, 77; City Col New York, MFA, 90. *Work:* Mus Mod Art, New York Pub Libr, Chelsea Sch Art & Lincoln Ctr, NY; Aldrich Mus Contemp Art, Conn; Boca Raton Mus Art, Fla; Stanford Univ, Calif; and many others in US and abroad. *Comn:* Lemma III (three paintings), Mobil Oil Corp Hq, NY, 83; Didecameter Suite (paintings), AT&T, Atlanta, Ga, 85; List Art Posters, Lincoln Ctr, NY, 91. *Exhib:* Acquisitions Since 1980, Aldrich Mus Contemp Art, 86; one-man shows, Eisner Gallery, City Col, NY, 90, Art Res Ctr, Kansas City, Mo, 92, Compuserve Fine Arts Forum, 94, Eich Space, 96, NonEuclid World-Wide-Web Gallery, Rice Univ, Tex, 97, St Edmund Hall, Univ Oxford, Eng, 2000, Truly Virtual Web Art Mus, 2000; Gallery at Lincoln Ctr, 93; Art Res Ctr, Kansas City, Mo, 95; Cercle et Carre (Circle & Square), Vallejo, Calif, 96 & 98; Abstract - Art Repository, Portfolio Gallery, 97; Noneuclid World-Wide-Web Gallery, Rice Univ, Tex, 97; Directors Choice: New Acquisitions, Boca Raton Mus Art, Fla, 97; The President's Gallery, Darbeth fine Arts Ctr, Southwestern Col, Winfield, Kans, 98; Art & Mathematics Conf, Bechtel Ctr, Univ Calif, Berkeley, 98; Cercle et Carre, Gallery Fine Art, Vallejo, Calif, 98; The Mondriaanhuis/Archive '90 Reference Collection, Mondriaanhuis, Amersfoort, The Neth, 2000; Art & Mathematics 2000, Cooper Union, Albert Nerken Sch Eng, 2000; The Bridges: Mathematical Connections in Visual Art (auth, catalog), Holtzman Art Gallery, Towson Univ, Md, 2002. *Teaching:* Lectr, Cooper Union Adult Educ Prog, Art & Sci Collaboration Inc, Southwestern Col, Kans & Beech Sci Ctr, Univ Calif, Berkeley, 98, Univ Pais Vasco, San Sebastian, Spain, 99, Southwestern Col, Winfield, Kans, 99. *Awards:* Award, Summit Art Ctr, 85; Change Found Grant, Rober Rauchenberg, 89; IMPACT II Disseminator Grant, Teachers Network, 2001. *Bibliog:* Les Krantz (auth), New York Art Review, 88; Jill Hoffman (auth), Geometrical Clouds from the Seventies (gallery announcement), 96; Dennis Wepman (auth), Prints & Posters from Lincoln Center, J Print World, summer 96. *Mem:* Visual Artists & Galleries Asn, Inc; Orgn Independent Artists, Inc. *Media:* Acrylic; Silkscreen. *Publ:* Contbr, Entering the Fine Arts Forum on Compuserve reminds us of our visits to the Metropolitan Museum of Art, The Geometry of the Heart (color reproduction), 121-122, Net Guide - The Guide to Internet and Online Services, Cyberguide - Fine Arts, 2/95; Contemporary Art & Poetry, Mudfish 9 (front & back cover), Box Turtle Press, 96; VisMath, 99; Engineering a Visual Field, Smarandache Notions Jour (front cover), Vol 13, No 1-2-3, 13-15, spring 2002; auth, OCTAGON 8, Mathematical Mag, Vol 10, No 1, 365-369, April 2002

SINGER, ESTHER FORMAN
PAINTER, CRITIC
b New York, NY, Oct 14, 28. *Study:* Art Students League, 39-41; Temple Univ, 41-44; NY Univ, 47-49; New Sch Social Res, 68-70; Fairleigh Dickinson Univ, pvt study with Hans Hoffman, Brackman, George Gross & Tosun Bayrak. *Hon Degrees:* Hon degree, Univ dell'Arte Contemp, Parma, Italy. *Work:* NJ State Mus, Trenton; Finch Mus Contemp Art, Whitney Mus Permanent Collection, NY; Yonkers Mus, NY; Morris Mus Arts & Sciences, Morristown, NJ; Newark Mus, NJ; Libr Congress; private collections of Sen Nelson Stamler & Gov Richard J Hughes; State House,

Morven, NJ; and others. *Comn:* Many works in pvt & pub collections. *Exhib:* Chubb Art Gallery, Warren, NJ, 86; Shering-Plough, Madison, NJ, 88; Johnson & Johnson Corp Hq, 90; Governors Club, Palm Beach, Fla, 90; Aids Project, Hyacinth Fund, 91; Biennale Int Dell Arte Florence, Italy, Nov-Dec, 2005; and others. *Pos:* Guest panelist, Art Forms, WOR-TV, 67-68; ed, Newark News, 70-74; art critic, Am Artist Mag, 72-, Worrall Press, 74- & Suburban Life Mag, currently; art ed, Jersey Jour Newspaper, Suburban Mag, Newark Evening News; staff writer, Am Artist Mag; syndicated art column, Worrall Press. *Teaching:* Instr elementary art, Baird Community Ctr, South Orange, NJ, 69-; pvt instr at own studio, South Orange, NJ, 68-70. *Awards:* Gov Purchase Award, Art from NJ 10; Painting Prize, Mus Mod Art, Paris, 73; and others. *Bibliog:* Articles in NJ Suburban Life Mag, 3/70; article, New York Art Rev Mag, 87; Art Views (film), Ch 36, 10/91; and others. *Mem:* Artists Equity Asn, NJ & NY; Old Bergen Art Guild; Painters & Sculptors Soc, NJ; Am Veterans Soc Artists. *Media:* Acrylic. *Dealer:* Helander Gallery Palm Beach FL; Key Gallery Soho NY. *Mailing Add:* 3 Schindler Way Sterling Green Fairfield NJ 07004

SINGER, MICHAEL
SCULPTOR
b 1945. *Study:* Cornell Univ, BFA, 67; Rutgers Univ, New Brunswick, grad study, 68; Yale Univ, Norfolk Prog, 68. *Work:* Albright-Knox Art Gallery, Buffalo; Australian Nat Gallery, Canberra; Louisiana Mus Mod Art, Humrebaek, Denmark; Solomon R Guggenheim Mus, Mus Mod Art & Metrop Mus Art, NY; Yale Univ Art Gallery; and others. *Comn:* Urban renewal waterfront park, Long Wharf, New Haven, Conn; recycling center, Dept Pub Works, Phoenix, Ariz; Those Who Survived (sculptural garden), Stuttgart, WGer; sculpture & walkway, Grand River East Bank, Grand Rapids, Mich, 94; interior sculpture garden, New Denver Airport. *Exhib:* Solo exhibs, Galerie Zabriskie, Paris, 81, J Walter Thompson Art Gallery, NY, 83, Solomon R Guggenheim, NY, 84, Sperone Westwater, NY, 86, Michael Singer Ritual Series, Retelling, Fine Arts Ctr, Art Gallery, State Univ NY-Stonybrook & Michael Singer-Ritual Series, Santa Barbara Contemp Arts Forum, 87, Artworks: Michael Singer, Williams Col Mus Art, Williamstown, Mass, 90; Sculpture Inside Outside, Walker Art Ctr, Minneapolis, 88; Collage, Robinson Orange Gallery, Boston, 89; Arts on Paper, Weatherspoon Art Gallery, Univ NC, Greensboro, 90-91; The Transparent Thread: Asian Philosophy in Recent Am Art (travel), Hofstra Mus, Hofstra Univ, Hempstead, NY, 90 & many other mus, 90-92; Art for the Land, Five Points Gallery, E Chatham, NY, 91; Guggenheim's Ten Young Artists Theodorn Award Show, Documenta; The Kunsthaus Zurich's Mythos and Ritual; Sculpture in the Twentieth Century, Reihen, Switz. *Bibliog:* Patricia C Phillips (auth), Michael Singer: Williams College, Artforum, 131-132, 1/91; Michele Cone (auth), Baroque Nature, Arts Mag, 3/91; Ann Wilson Lloyd (auth), Michael Singer at Williams College Museum of Art, Art in Am, 4/91

SINGH, CAROLYN
PAINTER, CERAMIST
b St Paul, Minn, May 11, 47. *Study:* Univ Minn, BA(studio arts) & BFA(painting & drawing), 72. *Work:* Museo de Arte del INBA, CD Juarez, Chih, Mex; Dept Art & Prinkmaking, Univ Minn, Minneapolis; Nat Bank Com San Antonio, Tex; El Paso Mus Art, Tex. *Comn:* painting, comn by Hazel Johnson, Minneapolis, Minn, 80; watercolor painting, comn by Sean Jarem, Huntsville, Ala, 85; painting, comn by Elizabeth Jarem, Huntsville, Ala, 86; Lg Bowl, Comn by Rebecca Krasne, 97, 2000; paintings, comn by V. Ajay Singh & Morela Hernandez, Washington, DC, 2006; paintings, comn by Joseph & Irma Raseon, Phoenix, Ariz, 2006. *Exhib:* 16th Ann Exhib Western Fedn Watercolor Socs, Art Ctr Corpus Christi, Tex, 91; Ariz Aqueous VII, Tubac Arts Ctr, Ariz, 92; Artists on Art, El Paso Mus Art, Tex, 93; Seven Points of View, Americana Mus, El Paso, Tex, 93; Transpositions, Galerie M, Berlin, 96; Desert Echos: The DIVA Show (I),The Peoples Gallery, El Paso, Tex, 98, & The DIVA Show (II), El Museo de Arte del INBA, CD Juarez, Chih, Mex, 98; Desert Echo IV/Sacred Journey, Chamizal Nat Mem, Los Paisanos Galery, El Paso, Tex, 99; Apair Margo Gallery, El Paso, Tex, 2000; Desert Echo: Women Illuminate the Sacred, Women's Mus: An Inst fo the Future, Dallas, 2001; Keith Batchelor (photograph) and Carolyn Sigh (mixed media), Arts place Lexington, KY, 2002; The Other Nude Show, Miller Fine Art, 2003; Earth and Air Ceramics by Carolyn Singh, photographs by Leonor de Lohle, CTR Libr Gallery, Lexington, KY, 05. *Teaching:* Teacher drawing, painting & claywork, El Paso Mus Art Sch, 83-2000; instr figure drawing & sculpture, Dept Prof & Continuing Educ, Univ Tex, El Paso, 93-2000 & Sculpture Ctr Life Long Learning, 96-2000, Laudable Mud Studio, Lexington, KY, 2005-. *Awards:* Second Place, Rio Bravo Watercolorists Ann Exhib, 94 & 95; Juror's Selection Award, Close to the Border: Biennial Exhib, 94; Second Place, NMex Watercolor Soc, 92; Best in Mixed Media, Visual Expressions of Love Exhibit, Gallery on Main, Eastern Ky Univ, 2003. *Bibliog:* Betty Ligon (auth), The Women's Voices Heard Through the Eyes, El Paso Inc, 10/11-17/98; NEUE Bildende Kunst (auth), Berlin, Ger, 10/11/96; Jaime Castaneda Reyes (auth), Acuarelas del Rio Bravo, Seccion Cultural, Periodico Norte, Juarez, Mex, 10/94; Scott Wampler (ed), Contemporary American Oil Painting, Jilin Fine Arts Publ, Chang Chun, China, 99; Jacquelyn Stroud Spier (auth), Desert Echo: Women Illuminate the Sacred, Women's Mus, Dallas, Tex, 2000; Tuland Review, Dept of Art, Tulane Univ, New Orleans, LA, Fall, 2000. *Mem:* Signature mem Rio Bravo Watercolorists (pres, 87-88 & 93-94, vpres, 91-92); signature mem NMex Watercolor Soc; signature mem Tex Watercolor Soc; Southwestern Watercolor Soc; Purple Sage Soc. *Media:* Mixed Media; Clay. *Publ:* Auth, Artists, donors deserve contributions break, El Paso Times, 83; Guest speaker, Rio Bravo Watercolorists Newsletter, 90; David Milton (auth), In a High Traffic Area, Lexington Herald Leader, 8/11/02; Earth and Air (video), LPL Gallery, Lexington, KY, Jan/Feb, 2005. *Dealer:* Miller Fine Arts 501 High St Lexington KY 40502. *Mailing Add:* 4109 Kentucky River Parkway Lexington KY 40515

SINGLETARY, MICHAEL JAMES
PAINTER
b New York, NY, Jan 23, 50. *Study:* Art Student League; Vt Acad, 68; Univ Ghana, W Africa, 69; Guadalajara Univ, Mex, 70; Ecole De Beaux Art, Fountainbleau, France, 71; Syracuse Univ, BFA, 72; RI Sch Design, 73; Lehman Col, New York, 74; State Univ New York, 88; Bob Blackburn Printmaking Workshop, 88. *Work:* Pvt collections of Kim Alexis, Don King, Dizzy Gillespie, Nancy Wilson, and others. *Comn:* Eight painting ser, Am Contract Designers, New York, NY; 12 painting ser for Grand Paradise Island Hotel, Creative Concepts, NY; 7 painting ser for hotel chain, Sheraton Inn, Roanoke, Va; Tribute to Woodie Shaw, New York Jazz Committee; Martin Luther King, painting, Ariel Mgt Corp, Chicago, Ill; 23 portraits, New York City Basketball Hall of Fame. *Exhib:* solo exhibs, US Fed Court House, NY, 82-84, 112 Greene St Gallery, Soho, NY, 90 Jazz Series, Dalcour Fine Art, 90, Mercy Col, Dobbs Ferry, NY, 90, Iona Col, New Rochelle, NY, 90, Heritage Show, NY Univ, 90; Printmakers Show, Kent State Univ, 90; Edwin A Ulrich Mus Art, Wichita, Kans, 90; The Humanist Icon, NY Acad Art, NY & Univ Va, 90; Bayly Art Mus, 90; and others. *Pos:* Assoc dir, CBS Inc, 75-86. *Teaching:* Artist-in-residence, Bronx Mus Art, 72-73; master teacher mosaic, Cloister Mus, Metrop Mus Art, New York, 73; teacher art, New York City Bd Educ, 74; artist in residence, Studio Mus, 74; Sarah Lawrence Col Gallery Sch, Bronxville, NY, 89-90. *Awards:* First Prize Portrait, Bridgeport Art League Exhib, Bridgeport Mus, 85. *Bibliog:* Television appearances, Best Talk in Town, WPIX, New York, 88, Phil Donahue Show, WNBC, New York, 89 & State of the Art Show, WDMC, 90; Fine arts and collectibles, Emerge Mag, 10/89; numerous other mag & newspaper articles. *Mem:* Dir Guild Am; Writers Guild Am; Harrison Art League; Found Community Artists; New York Artist Equity ASN. *Media:* Acrylic, Oil. *Publ:* The artist life - A Master of Improvisation, Artist Mag, 3/91; The art of Basketball, Daily News, New York, 9/24/91; Inside Track Michael Singletary: Guilding Light Gets Jazzy, Soap Opera Digest; Own Way, Art Sect, Kenichi Ishizuka, Tokyo, Japan, winter 91. *Mailing Add:* 375 Hawthorne Terr Mt Vernon NY 10552

SINNARD, ELAINE (JANICE)
PAINTER, SCULPTOR
b Ft Collins, Colo, Feb 14, 26. *Study:* Art Students League, 48-49, with Reginald Marsh; NY Univ, 51, with Samuel Adler; also with Robert D Kaufmann, 51; Sculpture Ctr, 55, with Dorothea Denslow; Acad Grande Chaumiere, Paris, 56. *Comn:* Five wall hangings (with Mrs Cris Darlington, Marlin Studios), Scandinavian Airline, NY, 61; three oil paintings, Basker Bldg Corp 5660, Miami Beach, 70. *Exhib:* One-woman shows, Ward Eggleston Galleries, NY, 59, Fairleigh Dickinson Univ, NJ, 60 & Lord & Taylor Art Gallery, 63-78; Sinnard Art Studio, NY; Chevy Chase Gallery, Kensington, Md; Bergdorf Goodman, Nina's Choice Gallery, NY; Exodus Int, Orlando, Fla, 2000. *Bibliog:* Article in Art News, 54; James E Duffy (auth), article in World Telegram, 59; Fran Hepperle (auth), article in Times Herald Rec, 73, 83 & 86; Art in Am, 75. *Mem:* Nat Arts Club, NY. *Media:* Oil; All. *Dealer:* Fifth Ave at 57th St New York NY 10019. *Mailing Add:* PO Box 304 New Hampton NY 10958

SINNER, STEVE
SCULPTOR
b Omaha, 42. *Study:* Iowa State Univ, BS(industrial educ), 65. *Exhib:* Arrowmont Sch Arts and Crafts, Gatlinburg, Tenn, 2001; Minn Mus Art, St Paul, Minn, 2001; Univ Calif, Davis, 2001; Defining Craft: Collecting for the New Millenium, Davenport Mus Art, 2002; Put a Lid on It: Containinig Human Experience, Am Asn Woodturners, 2003; Turned Wood-Small Treasures, del Mano Galleries, LA, 2003-2005, Selected Works, 2006; Functional Art Exposition, NY City, 2003-2006; Beneath the Bark: 25 Years of Woodturning, BYU, 2004; Against the Grain: Contemporary Turned Wood Urns, Dubuque Mus Art, 2006; Our Turn Now: Artists Speak Out in Wood, 2006. *Mailing Add:* c/o del Mano Gallery 11981 San Vicente Blvd Los Angeles CA 90049

SIPHO, ELLA
PAINTER
b Kansas City, Mo, Aug 12, 64. *Exhib:* Small Works, Limner Gallery, NY, 2002; Legler Barn Mus, Fem Canvas, Womens Art Hist, Kans, 2003; Paradigms of Conception, Amsterdam Whitney, NY, 2003; group show, Galerie Gora, Montreal, Can, 2003; Regional River Market, Kansas City Artist Coalition, Kansas City, Mo, 2003; Lessedra World Print Ann, Lessedra Gallery Contemp Art Projects, Sofia, Bulgaria, 2004; Art Expo, NY, Sneak Preview Attraction Art, 2005; Int Experimental Film Festival, Florean Mus, Romania, 2005; Bohemian Gallery, 2005; The Mus Television & Radio, Beverly Hills, Calif, 2005; Int Videoart Festival, Sala Estense, Piazza Municipale, Ferrara, Italy, 2005. *Awards:* River Market Annual, Kansas City Artist Coalition, 2003; Frontice Piece Cover Award, New Art Int, 2003 & 2004; Manhattan Arts Award, 2003; ARTV Award, Venetion Resort Las Vegas, 2005. *Bibliog:* Peter Wiley (auth), Gallery & Studio, 2002; Jeremy Sedley (auth), New Art Int, Book Art Press, 2003; Tom Palmer (auth), Am Art Collection, Alcove Books, 11/2004; The View Grandview Parks, 2004; Int Encyclopedia Dictionary of Mod abd Contemp Artist, 2005/2006; Art Worls News, 1/2006. *Mem:* Chicago Artist Coalition. *Media:* Acrylic, Oil, Filmaker. *Publ:* Art Exposed, 2002; Art World News, 11/2002; Gallery & Studio, 2002-2003; Direct Art, 2003; Montreal Gallery Guide (catalog) 6/2003. *Mailing Add:* 8309 E 110th St Kansas City MO 64134

SIPIORA, LEONARD PAUL
MUSEUM DIRECTOR, MUSEOLOGIST
b Lawrence, Mass, Sept 1, 34. *Study:* Vanderbilt Univ; Univ Mich, Ann Arbor, AB(cum laude), 55, MA, 56. *Collection Arranged:* Ann Nat Sun Carnival Exhib; Biennial, Int Designer Craftsmen; W S Horton Retrospective, 70; Tom Lea Retrospective, 71; Walter Griffin Retrospective, 71; Kress Collection, 19 & 20th Cent Am Art, Mexican Colonial Coll, Art on Paper Coll. *Pos:* Co-founder & pres, El Paso Arts Coun, 69-70, dir, 71-; dir, El Paso Mus Art, 67-91; ret. *Teaching:* Ctr for Lifelong

Learning, Univ Tex, El Paso, Tex. *Awards:* Knight Grand Cross of Malta. *Mem:* Tex Asn Mus (pres, 77-79); Am Asn Mus; Am Fedn Arts; Am Platform Asn; Asn Art Mus Dir; Mt Plains Mus Asn (pres, 78-79); Appraisers Asn Am. *Res:* Nineteenth and twentieth century American painting. *Specialty:* American/European Fine Art. *Interests:* Am, European, Oriental Art. *Collection:* American paintings and graphics. *Publ:* Auth, The Universality of Tom Lea (catalog), 71; A Community Oriented Art Museum, Southwest Gallery Art Mag, 71; auth foreword, Biography of John Enneking, 72. *Mailing Add:* 1012 Blanchard El Paso TX 79902

SIPIORSKI, DENNIS M
CERAMIST, CURATOR
b June 23, 53. *Study:* Univ Wis at LaCrosse, BS, 76; Univ Wis at Superior, MA, 78; Univ Notre Dame, MFA, 80. *Exhib:* Lafayette Natural Hist Mus, 82; Int Expo, Belgium, 88; Alexandria Mus Nat Competition, La, 88; Meridian Mus Art Exhib, Miss, 93; San Diego Art Int Mus, 93; St Tammany Mus Art La Sculpture Biennial, Covington, 94; Natural His Mus, Lafayette, La, 94; Univ W Fla Nat, Pensacola, 98; Tex Artists Mus Photog Exhib, Port Arthur, 98; Southeastern Univ, Hammond, La, 98; and many others. *Collection Arranged:* Louisiana Photo Exhib (photog), 92; South Louisiana Artists, 93; Don Kraemer Exhibit, Bayou Animals, 93; Clay Only Exhibit (ceramics), 94; Notre Dame on the Bayou (ceramics), 94. *Pos:* Actg head dept art, Nicholls State Univ, 91, head dept art, 91-. *Teaching:* Instr ceramics & photog, Nicholls State Univ, Thibodaux, La, 80-. *Awards:* Award of Excellence, New Orleans Jazz & Heritage Festival, La, 90; Who's Who in Higher Education, 91; First Place, Tex Artists Mus, Port Arthur, Tex, 98. *Mem:* Bayou La fourche; Nat Coun Educ Ceramics Art; Am Crafts Coun; Col Art Asn; La Contemp Arts Asn. *Publ:* Contrib, Am Craft Mag, 88; A View from the Heart, Bayou Country Ecology, 91; J Am Asn Wood Turners, 9/91; Am Craft Mag, 3/94; Nat Coun Educators Ceramic Arts J: Hand building techniques, 94

SIRES, JONATHAN PAUL
SCULPTOR
b Savannah, Ga, 55. *Study:* Kent State Univ, BFA, 79; Cranbrook Acad Art, MFA, 82. *Work:* Ga State Univ, Atlanta; Butler Inst Am Art, Youngstown, Ohio; Weber State Col, Ogden, Utah; pvt collections include Glaxo Corp, Raleigh, NC, Hearst Corp, Charlotte, Mint Mus of Art, Charlotte, NationsBank, Charlotte, Northern Telecom, Research Triangle Park, NC, many others. *Comn:* NC Mus Natural Hist, NC Arts Coun, 88; Governor's Bus Awards, Governors Bus Coun on the Arts & Humanities; NC Arts & Sci Coun Endowment, Charlotte, 95; Trammel Crow, Charlotte, NC, 98; NationsBank, Charlotte, NC, 98; Savannah Col of Art & Design, Ga, 99; Tucson Devel, Charlotte, NC, 2000; Edifice Inc, Charlotte, NC, 2000; Elon Col, NC, 2000. *Exhib:* One-man shows, Canton Art Inst, Ohio, 79, Barry Merritt Gallery, Rochester, NY, 83 & Ctr Earth Gallery, Charlotte, NC, 96, 99 & 2000; Blue Spiral Gallery, Asheville, NC, 93; Mus York Co, 94; Nat Ceramics Invitational, 95; Green Hill Ctr, NC, 95; 10th Ann Rosen Outdoor Sculpture Competition, Appalachian State Univ, 96; Chester Springs Nat Invitational, Pa, 97; Somerhill Gallery 25th Ann Exhib, Chapell Hill, NC, 97; Fayetteville Mus of Art, NC, 98; Sculpture 99, Ctr of the Earth Gallery, Charlotte, NC, 99; Agitating Utopia, Craft and Folk Art Mus, La, 99; Terra Firma, Gallerie Dorita, Ga, 2000; Rosen Competition, Appalachian State Univ, NC, 2000; The Artists of Charlotte, Fayetteville Mus of Art, NC, 2000; Major Pub Art Comn for the Charlotte Arena, Charlotte, NC. *Pos:* Dir/artist-in-residence Clay Works, Spirit Sq Ctr Arts, Charlotte, NC, 83-89; dir studio prog Visual Arts Dept, Spirit Sq Ctr Arts, 89-92; co-owner, Ctr Earth Gallery, 90-; mem panel Arts Midwest Peer Rev, 94; bd dir, Tryon Ctr for Visual Arts, 99-2000; mem panel Arts Midwest, Nat Endowment for the Arts; peer review panelist Regional Visual Artists Fel Awards, Mid-Am Art Alliance/NEA Visual Artist Fel Awards, many others. *Teaching:* lectr large scale ceramics, Wayne State Univ, Detroit; lectr work and life as an artist, Univ of Mich, Ann Arbor. *Awards:* Individual Artist Fel Grant, Ohio Arts Coun, 83; NC Visual Artist Fel Grant, NC Arts Coun, 88; Nat Endowment Arts, 88. *Bibliog:* Terra Firma, Charlotte Observer, 3/2/87. *Media:* Ceramic, Stone. *Publ:* Auth, Artist Profile, Charlotte Mag, 2/86; Terra Firma, Charlotte Observer, 3/2/87; Nat Endowment Fel, Ceramics Monthly, 2/89; J Paul Sires, Studio Potter, 6/89; CITI Mag, summer 90; The Sign Post, Utah, 94; Standard Examiner, 3/5/94; Kevin Hluch (auth), Ceramics: Art & Perception, 96; Handbuilt Ceramics, 97; Sculpture 99, Charlotte Observer, 2/99; Peter King (auth), Architectural Ceramics, Lark B; Sculpture Mag, 5/99, Sculptural Ceramics, Lark Books, 2000; Making Ceramic Sculpture, Lark Books, 2000. *Mailing Add:* 7448 Valleybrook Rd Charlotte NC 28270

SIRLIN, DEANNA LOUISE
PAINTER, ENVIRONMENTAL ARTIST
b Brooklyn, NY, Mar 7, 58. *Study:* State Univ NY, Albany, BA, 78; Queens Col, City Univ NY, MFA, 80. *Work:* Macon Mus Arts & Sci, Ga; Ga Pac & Egleston Hosp, Atlanta; United Airlines Dalles Airport, Washington, DC; Penny McCall Found, NY; Woodruff Park, Atlanta, Ga; High Mus Art, Atlanta, Ga. *Comn:* Ceramic Tondos, Omni Hotel, Charlotte, NC, 91; Paintings, Omni Hotels, Miami, Fla, 94; Art on Digital Billboard, Arts Festival Atlanta, Ga, 96; Installation-Glass-Silkscreen & Etching, Fulton Co, Atlanta, Ga, 98; Atlanta Gas Light, Ga; Wells Corp, Minn; Hartsfield-Jackson Internat Airport, Atlanta, 2005. *Exhib:* Solo exhib, Arnot Art Mus, Elmira, NY, 83, Catholic Univ, Washington, DC, 86, Forecasts, Cheekwood Fine Arts Ctr, Nashville, Tenn, 95, Quarnity, Nexus Contemp Art Ctr, Atlanta, Ga, 96, High Mus Art, Atlanta, Ga, 99, Vanishing Point Installation, Univ Ca'Foscari Venezia, Italy, 2001 & Installation, Saltworks Gallery, Atlanta, Ga, 2003, Plus Gallery, Denver, 2006, Ctr 4 Recent Drawing, London, 2006, Ferst Ctr for Arts, Atlanta, 2006; Multiple World: An Int Survey of Artists Books, Atlanta Col Art, 94; Collaborating Couples, Ga Mus Art, Athens, 2000; New Orleans Triennial, New Orleans Mus Art, 2001; Kunsthaus Invitational, Heidenheim, Ger, 2002; Shenzhen Biennial, Guan Shanyue Art Mus, China, 2002; Shenzhen Biennial, 2002 & 2004; Antalya Cultural Ctr, Turkey, 2004; group shows, Color, Space 301, Mobile, Ala, 2006. *Awards:* Yaddo Found Fel, 83; Ga Women in the Visual Arts Honoree, Ga Dept Natural Resources, 97; Artist in Communities Grant, Fulton Co Arts Coun, Atlanta, Ga, 2002. *Bibliog:* Jerry Cullum (auth), On Meteorological & Meditative Conditions: Reflections on the paintings of Deanna Sirlin, Fay Gold Gallery, 95; Blake Leland (auth), Into the Blue, Solomon Projects, 98; Carrie Przybilla (auth) Retracings, High Mus of Art, 99; W Eric Martin (auth) Art on High, Modern Reprographics, 2000; John Vilani (auth), Catching the World's Emerging Art Voices, Sirlin's Vanishing Point in Venice, Art World News, 44, 9/2001; Frances Colpitt (auth), Report from New Orleans, Art in Am, 58-63, 11/2001; Nancy Staab (auth), Art on a Grand Scale, Southern Living Mag, 10/2004; Larry Qualls, Arton Paper Mag, 2005; Rebecca Cochran, Sculpture Mag, 2005. *Mem:* CAA. *Media:* Painting and Site Works and Installation. *Publ:* Auth, Disappearance, Fulton Co Arts Coun, 93; Into the Blue, Solomon Projects, 98. *Mailing Add:* 120 North Christopher's Run Alpharetta GA 30004-3100

SIRUGO, SAL (SALVATORE)
PAINTER
b Pozzallo, Italy; US citizen. *Study:* Art Students League, with Philip Guston, 48-49; Brooklyn Mus Art Sch, NY, with John Ferren, 50-51. *Work:* NY Univ; Pace Univ, NY; Vassar Col, Poughkeepsie, NY; Ciba-Geigy Corp, Ardsley, NY; Lannan Found Collection at Zimmerli Art Mus, New Brunswick, NJ; Woodstock Artists Asn, NY; Judith Rothschild Found, Museum Modern Art, NYC; and others. *Exhib:* Whitney Mus Am Art Ann, NY, 52; Pa Acad Fine Arts Ann, Philadelphia, 53; one-man exhibs, Tanager Gallery, 61, Great Jones Gallery, 66, Landmark Gallery, 76, 78 & 81, Thomas J Walsh Art Gallery, Fairfield Univ, Retrospective 1948-2000, CT, 2002, The Gallery At 6th & 6th, Tucson, Az, 2007; group exhibs, Gallery Asn NY, traveling exhib, 78-80, First Int Exhib Watercolor Painting, Korea, 91; Whitney Mus Am Art Philip Morris, 90; Sixth Asia Int Watercolor Painting, Nagoya, Japan, 91; Luebsdorf Gallery, Hunter Col, 94; Corcoran Gallery Art, Washington, DC, 94; Fischer Art Gallery, Univ Southern Calif, Los Angeles, 95; Portland Mus Art, Ore, 96; Gary Snyder Fine Art, Mod Am Art, 1930-1975, New York City, 2002. *Awards:* Longview Found Award, 62; Creative Artists Pub Serv Prog Fel, 79-80; Adolph & Esther Gottlieb Found, 82 & 84. *Bibliog:* Tram Combs (auth), Sirugo's miniature sublime, Woodstock Times, 2/19/81; Jeffrey Wechsler (auth), Abstract Expressionism: Other Dimensions 1940-1965 (catalog), Zimmerli Art Mus, Rutgers Univ, 89; Stuart Shedletsky (auth), Still Working (catalog), 89, Parsons Sch Design, NY, 94. *Mem:* Life mem Art Students League; Artists' Club. *Media:* Acrylic, Inks. *Mailing Add:* 321 W 24th St #2F New York NY 10011

SISCHY, INGRID B
EDITOR, CURATOR
b Johannesburg, SAfrica, Mar 2, 52; Brit citizen. *Study:* Sarah Lawrence Col, BA, 73; Moore Col Art PhD(hon). *Collection Arranged:* In the Twenties: Portraits from Photog Collection, Mus Mod Art, New York, 79 & 80; Florence Biennale, 96; Guggenheim Mus, New York, 97. *Pos:* Asst ed, Print Collector's Newslett, 75-76 & assoc ed, 76-77; curatorial intern, Dept Photog, Mus Mod Art, NY, 78-79; dir, Printed Matter Inc, 78-80; ed, Artforum, 80-88; critic & staff writer, New Yorker, 89-; ed-in-chief, Interview Mag, 89-; staff writer & consult ed, NY Mag, 87-97. *Bibliog:* Janet Malcolm (auth), The girl of the Zeitgeist, New Yorker, 10/86; Women we love (ann special issue), Esquire, 8/92. *Publ:* Contribr, Donna Karan, Assouline Eds, 6/98; Ellen Von Unwerth's, Couples, Teneues Publ, 1/99; and many others incl HG & NY Times. *Mailing Add:* c/o Interview Magazine 575 Broadway 5th Flr New York NY 10012

SISCO, ELIZABETH
CONCEPTUAL ARTIST, PHOTOGRAPHER
b Cheverly, Md, Aug 21, 54. *Study:* Univ Calif, San Diego, BFA(cum laude), 78, MFA, 81, teacher educ prog, 87; Southwestern Col, 92; Photoshop, digital imaging Macintosh, Univ Calif Exten, 92. *Work:* La Jolla Mus Contemp Art; Kans City Art Inst, Mo; Lynne Schutte, San Diego; Univ Wis, Milwaukee; Univ Calif, San Diego, La Jolla. *Exhib:* Solo shows, Ctr US-Mex Studies, La Jolla, Calif, 85 & SUSHI, San Diego, Calif, 85; John Michael Kohler Arts Ctr, Sheboygan, Wis, 92; Cameraworks, San Francisco, 92; Univ Art Gallery, Calif State Polytechnic Univ, Pamona, Calif, 92. *Pos:* Div Arts & Humanities, Southwestern Col, Chula Vista, Calif, currently. *Teaching:* Prof, Univ Calif, San Diego Exten, 80-88, lectr dept visual art, summer 82, 83, 84, 85, 87 & 88 & spring 85-88; prof, Southwestern Col, Chula Vista, Calif, currently. *Awards:* Artist-in-residence, Banff Ctr, 6-7/91; Art Matters Inc, 92; Artist Fel, Calif Arts Coun Arts, 92. *Bibliog:* Cylena Simmons (auth), Public Exposure, Vol 22, No 2, Afterimage, summer 94; John Welchman (auth), Bait or Tackle, No 48, A & T Art & Text, 5/94; Nina Felshin (ed), But is it Art, Art as Activism, Bay Press, 95. *Publ:* Coauth, NHI (bk), 92; (with D Small, L Hock & D Avalos), High School Art and Criticism Learning Guide, New Mus New York, in prep; auth, The Cultural Battlefield, Artist, Citizen, Taxpayer, Avocus Press, Washington, DC, 94; Art & Politics A Pre Election Symposium, Vol 80, No 10, Art Am, 10/92; NHI- No Humans Involved in Critical Conditions: Women on the Edge of Violence (Amy Scholder ed), City Lights Books, 94. *Mailing Add:* 903 26th St San Diego CA 92102

SISSOM, EVELYN JANELLE See Lee-Sissom, E (Evelyn) Janelle Sissom

SISSON, LAURENCE P
PAINTER
b Boston, Mass, Apr 27, 28. *Study:* Worcester Mus Sch, grad, 49; Yale Univ, summer sch, scholar, 48-49. *Hon Degrees:* Portland Sch Arts, Hon DFA, 92. *Work:* Mus Fine Arts, Boston; Portland Mus, Maine; Dartmouth Col; DeCordova Mus, Mass; Worcester Mus, Mass. *Comn:* Four murals, Boston Five Cent Saving Bank Br Offs, 55-67; mural, Worcester Polytech Inst, 66; mural, Carrick Agency, Whitinsville, Mass,

72. *Exhib:* Hallmark Int Exhib, 49; Ill Art Festival, 51; Am Watercolor Soc, 55-60; one-man shows, Gallery Mod Art, NY, 69 & Brockton Art Ctr, Mass, 72; Westbrook Col Gallery, Portland, Maine, 93; Thomasville Cult Ctr, Ga, 2000. *Pos:* Corporator, Worcester Art Mus, 72-. *Teaching:* Teacher & dir, Portland Art Mus Sch, Maine, 54-58. *Awards:* Fourth Am Prize, Hallmark Int Show, 49; First Prize, Boston Arts Festival, 56 & 64 & Boston Watercolor Soc, 57. *Bibliog:* Maine Harvesters of the Sea (film), Film Group, 69; W Caldwell (auth), The man and the artist, Down E Mag, 68. *Media:* Oil, Watercolor. *Interests:* golf, politics, croquet. *Publ:* Auth, Along Time River, 75. *Dealer:* Michael Wigley Galleries Ltd 1111 Paseo de Peralta Santa Fe NM 87501; Frost Gully, Freeport, Maine, 04032; Leslie Levy Fine Art Inc 7137 Main St Scottsdale AZ 85251. *Mailing Add:* 1408 Camino Amparo NW Albuquerque NM 87107

SKALAGARD, HANS
PAINTER, LECTURER

b Skuo, Faroe Islands, Europe, Feb 7, 24; nat US. *Study:* Royal Acad Art, Copenhagen; with marine artist Anton Otto Fisher, New York. *Work:* Constitution, Dudley Knox Libr & War of 1812 Constitution & Guerriere, Hermann Hall, Naval Post Grad Sch, Monterey, Calif; Casco, Reid Hall, Robert Louis Stevenson Sch, Pebble Beach, Calif; Frigate Ship United States, Salvation Army Hq & Savannah US Frigate, Allen Knight Maritime Mus, Monterey; Flying Cloud Clipper Ship, Carmel Community Hosp, 95; William P Frye, Petaluma Community Hosp, 2000; WWII North Atlantic Convoy Series, 11 Oils on Canvas; Pacific coast Lumber Schooner Series, 15 Oils on Canvas. *Comn:* Olivebank Deck View, comn by Dr Wm Rustad, Sea Cliff, San Francisco, 68; USN BB Maine, comn by Hal Whitten, Dean Witter & Assoc, San Mateo, Calif, 73; Anna Maerske, comn by Capt Olsen, Port Capt Maersk Line, San Francisco, 75; and other pvt collections. *Exhib:* Galerie De Tours, San Francisco, 72; Gallerie Vallombreuse, Biarritz, France, 75; New Los Angeles Maritime Mus, 80; Skaalegaard's Square-Rigger Art Gallery, Carmel, Calif, 66-97, 00-02; Stanton Hist Ctr, New Maritime Mus, Monterey, Calif, 92-95; 200 Yrs of USS Constitution, Maritime Mus, 97; Maritime Ventura Co Mus, 98; Monterey Stanton Ctr Maritime Mus, 99; Life Under Sail, Monterey Maritime Mus, 2006-; over 75 others. *Pos:* Dir, Skaalegaard's Square-Rigger Art Gallery, Carmel, 66-97, 2000-; Calif hist librn, Mayo Hayes O'Donnel Libr, Monterey Hist & Art Asn, 72 & 73; dir bd, Allen Knight Maritime Mus, 72-76; cult dir, Sons of Norway, Monterey, 74-76. *Teaching:* Studied Breifly with Anton Otto Fischer, In NY. *Awards:* Gold Medal & Title Master Painter, Tommaso Campanella Acad Arts, Lett & Sci, Rome, 72; Gold Medal, Academia Italia Delle Arti e Del Honoro, Parma, 80; Statua della Vittoria, Italian Premio Mondale dell Cultural, 85; and others. *Bibliog:* Judith A Eisner (auth), Carmel closeup, Pine Cone, Carmel, 9/14/72; and others; Salinas Weekend Living Full Page in 1985. *Mem:* Life hon Academia Italia Delle Arti e Del Honoro; US Navy League, Monterey chap; Am Coun Master Mariners, San Francisco chap (speaker). *Media:* Multimedia. *Specialty:* Sailing Ships thru the Ages and Variety of Seafaring Vessels. *Interests:* Martime History. *Collection:* Monterey's Historic Addbe Col. by 17 Artists Who donated their art to Monterey's Civic Club, Oldest Women Club House in America; Several latest 20 oils of Am Rev. War & US 200th Yr Constitution. *Publ:* Sea Classics 1992-93. *Dealer:* Currently shown at Winters Fine Art Galleries in Carmel, CA. *Mailing Add:* 602 Stony Point Rd Petaluma CA 94952-1048

SKELLEY, ROBERT CHARLES
EDUCATOR, PRINTMAKER

b Bellevue, Ohio, Jan 15, 34. *Study:* Ind Univ, AB & MFA; Studied with Rudy Pozzatti, Arthur Deshaies, Alton Pickets, Jack Twarkov, James McGarrell, Richard Barnes, Leon Golub, David Smith, Robert Laurant, Carl Martz, George Rickey, plus others. *Work:* Libr of Cong, Washington, DC; Mint Mus, Charlotte, NC; Montgomery Mus Art, Ala; Springfield Col, Mass; Southern Ill Univ, Carbondale; Rockford Col, Rockford, Ill; Calif Soc Etchers, San Francisco, Calif; Jacksonville U, Jacksonville, Fla; plus many others. *Exhib:* Dixie Ann Graphic Exhib, Montgomery Mus Art; Boston Printmakers, Mass; Mint Mus Ann Graphics; Libr Cong Print Ann; Am Graphics, Col of Pac, Stockton, Calif; One-person shows incl, Pensacola Jr Col, Pensacola, Fla, Brevard Jr Col, Cocoa Beach, Fla, Micanopy Mus Modern Art, Micanopy, Fla, Univ Fla Tchg Gallery, Gainesville, Fla, plus numerous others; Pacific Print Exhbn, Col of the Pacific, Stockton, Calif; Mint Mus Ann, Charlotte, NC; Dixie Ann, Montgomery, Ala; Savannah Art Festival, Savannah, Ga; Mercyhurst Col, Erie, Pa; plus many others. *Teaching:* Prof graphic design, Univ Fla, Gainesville, 61-81. *Awards:* Dixie Ann Best in Show Purchase, Montgomery Mus Art; Boston Printmakers Hon Mention, Boston Mus Art; Libr of Cong Purchase Award; Humanities Coun Res Grant. *Bibliog:* Graphic rev in La Rev Mod, 1/65 & Art Rev Mag, 4/66; Norman Kent (auth), Robert Skelley wood cuts, Am Artist Mag, 1/71; Lanny Sommesse (auth), Robert Skelley Woodcuts, Novum Gebrauchs Graphik, 10/76. *Mem:* Soc Am Graphic Artists; Southern Graphic Artist Circle. *Media:* Woodcut, wood sculpture. *Publ:* Auth, articles in Am Artist Mag, Novum Gebrauchs Graphic Mag & 30 Years of Am Printmaking. *Mailing Add:* Univ Fla Dept Art Gainesville FL 32611

SKLAR-WEINSTEIN, ARLENE (ARLE)
GRAPHICS ARTIST

b Detroit, Mich, Oct 25, 31. *Study:* Parsons Sch Design; Mus Mod Art, New York, scholar & study with Bernard Pfreim; Albright Art Sch; New York Univ, with Hale Woodruff, BS, 52, MA(art educ), 55; Pratt Graphics Ctr, with Andrew Stasik; Ctr for Understanding Media, 74; Col New Rochelle (cert prog, educ for gifted & talented), 75 & 81; Columbia Univ, 85-86. *Work:* Mus Mod Art, NY; NY Pub Libr Permanent Print Collection; Hudson River Mus Permanent Collection, Yonkers, NY; Metrop Mus Art, Slide Libr; Pepsico Art Collection. *Exhib:* Tirca Karlis Gallery, Provincetown, Mass, 67; The Visionaries, Easthampton Galleries, NY, 68-69; Manhattan Col, 75 & Neuberger Col, 75, Purchase, NY; Lending Art Gallery, Mus Mod Art, NY, 79; Boston Visual Artists Union Gallery, Mass, 80; Roundhouse, Copenhagen, Denmark, 80; Bridge Gallery, White Plains, NY, 82 & 84; Interchurch Ctr, NY, 95; Chappaua Libr Gallery, NY, 95 & 97; Contemp Textile, Rye Art Ctr, NY, 95 & 98; Left Bank Gallery, Bennington, Vt, 96; Northern Westchester Ctr Arts, Mt Kisco, Nt, 97; Peekskill Performing Arts Ctr, NY, 97; Columbia Univ Law Libr, NY, 97; Women Artists of the Hudson Valley, Howland Ctr, Beacon, NY, 98; Wave Hill/Glyndor Mansion Galleries, Riverdale, NY, 97-98; Solo exhib, Katonah Gallery, 75-96, South Church, Dobbs Ferry, NY, 94 & 98, Westchester Art Workshop Galleries, Peekskill, White Plains, NY, 95-96, Aisling Galleries, Durango, Colo, 95-96, Bloodroot Gallery, Bridgeport, Conn, 95 & NY Focus: Arle Sklar-Weinstein, The Gallery at Hastings on Hudson, 96 & Animazing Gallery, NY, 97; Columbus Mus of Art, Ohio, 2003; Katonah Mus Art, NY, 2003; Galerie du Bar Zinc, Paris, France, 2002; Cornell Mus, Del Ray Beach, Fla, 2001; Houston Int Quilt Festival, Tex, 01, 02, 03; San Diego Mus Hist, 99. *Collection Arranged:* Cur, Masks: The Alternative Self (40 artists), The Gallery of Hastings-on-Hudson, NY, 89-90. *Pos:* Visual arts coordr, Coun Arts Westchester, White Plains, NY, 69-70; co-found, Westbroadway Gallery, SoHo & NY, 72-79; bd mem, Hastings Creative Arts Coun, 73-93; artists adv bd, Katonah Mus Art, 92-; artist-in-residence, Washington ST Sch, Mt Vernon, NY, 94; lectr/workshop facilitator, Hudson River Mus, Westchester, Yonkers, NY, 94-95. *Teaching:* Art specialist, Hillside Sch, Hastings-on-Hudson, NY, 73-81; lower sch art specialist, Marymount Sch of NY, 81-87; Fieldston Lower Sch, NY Ethical Cult Soc, 87-94. *Awards:* Purchase Prize, Albright-Knox Galleries, Buffalo, NY, 51; First Prize, Hudson River Mus Regional, Yonkers Art Asn, 71; Print Competition Award, Gestetner Corp, 71; SOS Grant, NY Found for the Arts, 2002. *Bibliog:* Masters & Houston (auths), Psychedelic Art, Grove, 68; H H Arnason (auth), History of Modern Art, Abrams, 69; HH Arnason (auth), Contemporary Art, Abrams, 69. *Mem:* Manhattan Quilters Guild; Katonah Mus Artists Adv Bd; Textile Study Group. *Media:* Fabric Construction, Digital Photographs, Mixed Media. *Interests:* Computer Imaging, Photography, Travel. *Publ:* NY Sunday Times, 10/22/95, 11/97, 6/99, 11/01; Am Crafts Mag, 12/97; Oceanside Mus of Art Yardworks Catalog, Calif, 2001; Quilt 21 Catalog, 2002; Artnew, Westchester Arts Coun, 2000; Fiberarts Mag, 10/99; Fibrearts Design Book 6. *Dealer:* Katonah Museum Shop Katonah Mus of Art Rt 22 at Jay St Katonah NY 10536. *Mailing Add:* 18 Harvard Ln Hastings-on-Hudson NY 10706

SKOFF, GAIL LYNN
PHOTOGRAPHER

b Los Angeles, Calif. *Study:* Univ Calif, Berkeley, 67-69; San Francisco Art Inst, BFA, 72, MFA, 79. *Work:* Nat Mus Am Art, Smithsonian Inst; Bibliot Nat, Paris; Oakland Mus, Calif; Ctr Creative Photog, Tucson, Ariz; Smith Col Art Gallery. *Exhib:* Exchange, Ft Worth Mus Art & San Francisco Mus Mod Art, 75-76; Attitudes: Photog in the '70's, Santa Barbara Mus Art; Soc Encouragement Contemp Art Photog Invitational, San Francisco Mus Mod Art, 80; Contemp Hand-Colored Photographs, DeSaisset Mus, Univ Santa Clara, 81; Am Photogrs and the Nat Parks, traveling to NY Pub Libr, Los Angeles Co Mus, Amon Carter Mus, Corcoran Gallery, and others; In Color: Ten California Photographers, Oakland Mus, 83; Exposed and Developed, Nat Mus Am Art, Smithsonian Inst, Washington, DC, 84; The Colored Image: Hand Applied Color in Photog, Friend of Photog, Carmel, Calif, 85; one-person exhibs, Badlands, Robert Koch Gallery, San Francisco, Calif, 87 & Cecile Moochnek Gallery, Berkely, Calif, 97; The Painted Photograph, Robert Koch Gallery, San Francisco, Calif, 86; Eye of the Beholder, ICP, NY, 97; New Realities, Hand Colored Photographs 1839-Present, Univ Wyo, 97; French Roots, SK Josefsberg Gallery, Portland, Ore, 99. *Teaching:* Instr photog and hand-colored photog, Univ Calif Extension, San Francisco, 76-; instr photog, Univ Calif, Berkeley, summer 80. *Awards:* Nat Endowment Arts Photogr Fel, 76. *Bibliog:* Contemporary hand-colored photography, Picture Mag, 81; Dana Asbury (auth), Gail Skoff/Judy Dater, Popular Photog, 83; Kermit Lynch (auth), Adventures on the Wine Route, Farran Straus, 88. *Mem:* Friends of Photog, Carmel, Calif. *Publ:* Contribr, The young romantics, Newsweek, 79; New Landscapes & Untitled 24, Friends Photog, 81; Photography Year, Trends, Time-Life Books, 82; Cliches, Brussels, 84; Chez Panisse Cooking, Random House, 88. *Dealer:* Jones Troyer Gallery 1614 20th St NW Washington DC 20009; Terry Etherton Gallery 424 E 6th St Tucson Ariz 85705. *Mailing Add:* 717 The Alameda Berkeley CA 94707

SKOGLUND, SANDY
PHOTOGRAPHER, SCULPTOR

b Boston, Mass, Sept 11, 46. *Study:* Smith Col, BA, 68; Univ Iowa, MFA, 72. *Work:* Metrop Mus Art, Chase Manhattan Bank, NY; St Louis Mus Art, Mo; Art Inst Chicago; Brooklyn Mus, NY; Centre Georges Pompidou, Paris, France; Eastman House Int Mus Photog, Rochester, NY; Tampa Mus Art, Fla; Univ Mass Mus Art, Amherst; Walker Art Ctr, Minneapolis, Minn. *Exhib:* Solo exhibs, In the Last Hour (with catalog), Fred Jones Jr Mus Art, Univ Okla, Norman, Okla, 92, The Green House, Aspen Art Mus, 92, Radioactive Cats (with catalog), L'Espace Photog de la Ville de Paris, France, 92, Fundacio la Caixa, Sala Catalunya, Barcelona, Spain, 92, Columbus Mus Art, Ohio, 94, Miss Mus Art, Jackson, 95, Smith Col Art Mus, North Hampton, Mass, 98, Janet Borden Inc, NY, 98, Norton Mus of Art, Palm Beach, Fla, 2000 & Am Crafts Mus, New York City, 2000; Whitney Mus Am Art, NY; Biennale de Marseille, Musee de Marseille, France, 90; Lo Specchio/In/Fedele: Padiglione d'Arte Contemp di Milano, Milan, Italy, 91; Fotografia Am del Segle XX: Centre Cult de la Fundacio, Barcelona, Spain, 91; The Intuitive Eye: Photog from the David C I Sarajean Ruttenberg Collection, Art Inst Chicago, Ill, 91 & 92; Atomic Love, Body Limits & The Cocktail Party, Janet Borden Inc, NY, 92; The Wedding, Columbus Mus Art, Ohio, 94; Bathroom, Paul Morris Gallery, 98; Am Crafts Mus, NY, 2000; Raining Popcorn, Janet Borden, Inc, NY, 2001; and others. *Teaching:* Prof art, Univ Hartford, Conn, 73-76, vis prof, 92; prof, Rutgers Univ, Newark, NJ, currently. *Awards:* NY Found Arts, 88; The Bd of Trustees Award for Excellence in Res, Rutgers Univ, New Brunswick, NJ, 91; Richard Koopman Distinguished Chair in the Visual Arts, Hartford Art Sch, Univ Hartford, Conn, 92. *Bibliog:* Andy Grundberg (auth), Weekend

Reviews: Sandy Skoglund; The Green House at Janet Borden Inc, New York Times, 9/14/90; Nan Richardson (auth), Sandy Skoglund: Wild at Heart, Art News, 4/91; Gloria Picazo (auth), Paradoxes of Photography - On the work of Sandy Skoglund (catalog), Barcelona, Spain, 92, reprinted, Paris, France, 92. *Publ:* Auth, Spirituality in the Flesh, Artforum Int, 2/92. *Dealer:* Janet Borden Inc 560 Broadway New York NY 10012; PPOW Gallery 532 Broadway New York NY 10012. *Mailing Add:* c/o Janet Borden 560 Broadway New York NY 10012

SKOLER, CELIA REBECCA
CONSULTANT, GALLERY DIRECTOR
b Sioux City, Iowa, Apr 7, 31. *Study:* Syracuse Univ, NY, BFA (music & art), 76. *Work:* Syracuse Univ, Marine Midland Bank Cent, Crouse Irving Mem, Syracuse, NY; Savannah Col Art and Design, Ga. *Exhib:* Rochester-Finger Lakes, Univ Rochester Mem Art Gallery, NY, 70 & 73; Cooperstown Ann, Village Libr Bldg, NY, 72; Everson Mus Art Regional, Syracuse, NY, 73; one-women show, Assoc Artists, 73; Munson-Wms-Proctor Inst 38th Ann, Utica, NY, 75. *Pos:* Freelance artist, Syracuse, NY, 73-80; owner, dir & consult, New Acquistions, Syracuse, NY, 81-2003; orgn supervisor gallery management, Syracuse Univ Community Internship Prog, 81-93; contrib writer of art critiques in Syracuse newspapers, NY, 89-91; partner, Gallery Metro, Syracuse, NY, 91-93; fine arts appraiser, Syracuse, NY, 89-. *Awards:* Purchase Prize, NY Art Open, 70 & 71; Fine Arts Exhib First Prize, NY State Fair, 74; Purchase Prize, Arena '75 Regional. *Bibliog:* In celebration of women, Oswego City Messenger, 3/21/84; Linda M Herbert (dir), State of the Arts (film), Cooke Cablevision, 89; Lynn Zerschling (auth), Central Grad Records Album, Sioux City J, 9/19/98. *Mem:* Everson Mus Art (corp mem). *Specialty:* Contemporary. *Publ:* Auth, Sharply compelling contrasts, 89, Luck of the draw, 90, Artist struggles against setting, 90 & Exhibit challenges views, 91, Syracuse Herald-Am; Going to extremes, Syracuse New Times, 10/24/90. *Mailing Add:* 213 Scottholm Terr Syracuse NY 13224-1737

SKOLER, CELIA REBECCA
LIBRARIAN, WRITER
b Sioux City, Iowa, Apr 7, 31. *Study:* Univ Chicago, AM(art hist), 83, AM(libr sci), 85; Art Libr Fel, Univ Calif, Los Angeles, 84. *Pos:* Catalog maintenance, Ryerson Libr, Art Inst Chicago, 84-86; art & reference librn, Univ Ariz, Tucson, 86-90; art librn & bibliographer, Duke Univ, Durham, NC, 90-. *Awards:* Libr Scholar, H W Wilson Found, 84. *Mem:* Col Art Asn; Art Libr Soc N Am (exec bd, 89 & 97-, web adminr, 98-2000). *Res:* Art history, including bio-bibliographies of art historians. *Interests:* German expressionist art, Roman studies, art historiography. *Publ:* Auth, Art bibliographies: their history 1595-1821, Libr Quart 56, 86; Determined Donor: T E Hanley, Univ Ariz, 89; ed, Cambridge Dictionary of American Biography, Cambridge Univ, 95; auth, Bibliography of art, MacMillan Groves, 96; Dictionary of Art Historians, Duke Univ, 97-; auth, Art Reference Sources, ALA Guide to Reference Books, 2005. *Mailing Add:* Lilly Libr Duke Univ PO Box 90727 Durham NC 27708-0727

SKUPINSKI, BOGDAN KAZIMIERZ
PRINTMAKER, PAINTER
b Pabianice, Poland, July 16, 42. *Study:* Acad Fine Arts, Krakow, Poland, MFA (very good, with distinction), 1969; Ecole Nat Superieure Beaux Arts, Paris, cert, 1971; Pratt Graphics Ctr, cert, 1972. *Work:* Lib of Congress, Washington; Nat Gallery Art, Washington; State of NJ Dept Edn, Trenton; NY Pub Libr, NY; Nat Lib France, Paris. *Exhib:* Int Exhib of Graphic Art, Frechen Ger, 1978; one-man show, Atlantic Gallery, NY, 1980; X Int Exposition of Original Drawing, Mus Mod Art, Rijeka, Yugoslavia,1986; 9 Int Triennale of Graphic, Berlin, Ger, 1990; Boston Expo, Nat Exposition of Art, Boston, 1992. *Collection Arranged:* Libr Congress; Nat Gallery Art; NJ State Mus; NY Pub Libr; Nat Libr in Paris; Ministry of Cult, France; Salon D'Autome - Purchase, Paris. *Pos:* pres, Bogdan & Assoc, NY, 84-2002. *Awards:* Medal of Merit, Int Exhib of Graphic Art, Frechen Ger, 1976, Purchase award, 1978; Medal of Merit, Rep Presdl Task Force, 1990; Order of Merit, Rep Presdl Legion of Merit, 1994; Cannon prize for Graphic Art, Nat Acad Design, NY, 71; Acad prize for Print and Drawing, Conn Acad Fine Arts, 71. *Bibliog:* Boleslaw Wierzbianski, (auth), Bogdan Skupinski, New Horizon Polish American Review, 5/19/1976; Palmer Poroner (auth), Reality through ideas and symbols, Artspeak, Vol 3, No 7, 11/20/80; J.T. (auth), Exhibition reviews, Art/World, Vol 5, No 3, 11/20-12/20/80; Contemporary Prints of the World, 89; E Benezit, Dictionnaire, Critique and Documentaire, Fr, 99. *Mem:* Askart.com; Artprice.com. *Media:* Oil. *Res:* Life & work of John F Kennedy & Alber Michelson, 69-76. *Specialty:* Paintings, Graphics. *Interests:* Sports. *Collection:* Old Master Painting, 16c-19c. *Publ:* E Benezit, Dictionnaire, Critique and Documentaire, Paris, Fr, 99; Gwan Kim Chae (auth), Bk II Vol, Contemp Prints of the World, 89; Mark Ryden (auth), Bk, Blood, 2003; Lonnie Dunbier (auth), Bk, Artist Bluebook, 2005. *Dealer:* Art Commun Internat 210 W Rittenhouse Sq Ste 400 Philadelphia PA 19103. *Mailing Add:* PO Box 849 New York NY 10025

SKURKIS, BARRY A
PAINTER, SCULPTOR
b Chicago, Ill, Nov 21, 51. *Study:* Col Du Page, with Karl Owen; AA, 71; Sch Art Inst Chicago, With T Karpalis, R Yoshida & C Wirsum, BFA, 75; Univ Notre Dame, with Don Vogl, MA, 78. *Comn:* watercolor, Robert Malorny, DDS, Westmont, Ill, 82; oil painting, Edward Mazurowski, Westmont, 82; watercolor, Dean Bunting, Downers Grove, Ill, 82; St Francis Residence, 95; John Dicken, 98; and others. *Exhib:* Solo exhibs, Aurora Univ, Ill, 88, N Cent Col, Naperville, 88 & Rainy River Col, Minn, 94 & 98; Historical Crosscuts: Private Response to World Events Flint, Mich, 92; 42nd Spiva Ann Competition, Joplin, Mo, 92; Salon Exhib, Windham, NY, 94; Yosemite Renaissance, Calif, 94; Mini Print Int 14 (traveling), Spain, Eng, Repub Korea, 95, 96, 97 & 98; Anderson Art Ctr, Kenosha, Wisc, 98; and many others. *Collection Arranged:* The Holocaust: 1933-1945, 89. *Pos:* Gallery cur, N Cent Col, Naperville, Ill, 83-90; mem bd dir & vpres, Sch Art Inst Chicago Alumni Asn, 88; bd dir, Riverwalk Sculpture Garden, 88-89 & chmn, 89-90; pres, Chicago Soc Artists, 89-98. *Teaching:* Instr, Col DuPage, Glen Ellyn, Ill, 75-83; vis lectr painting, drawing & design, N Cent Col, 80-83, chmn, dept art, 83-91, assoc prof, 91. *Awards:* Third Place, Linoleum Print Competition, Chicago Soc Artists, 90; Daniel Smith Award, Nat Small Works, Schohaire Co Arts Coun, Cobleskill, NY; 11th Ann Juried Exhib of Soc Watercolor Artists, Ft Worth, Tex, 92. *Bibliog:* Mementy's, Featured Artist, Linoleum Prints, 88; Chicago Soc Artists Block Print Calendar, 86-. *Mem:* Chicago Soc Artists; Art Inst Chicago; Wedge Pub Cult Ctr Arts (bd mem, 78-84); Chicago Soc Artists (mem bd dir, 87-); Chicago Artists Coalition, 88. *Media:* Acrylics, Watercolor; Bronze, Wood. *Mailing Add:* N Cent Col 30 N Brainard St Naperville IL 60566

SKY, ALISON
ENVIRONMENTAL ARTIST
b New York, NY, Aug 1, 46. *Study:* Columbia Univ, 62; Adelphi Univ, with Peter Lipman-Wulf, BA(fine arts), 67; Art Students League, with Jose de Creeft & John Hovannes, scholar, 67-69. *Work:* Smithsonian Inst, Washington, DC; Mus Mod Art & Avery Libr, Columbia Univ, NY; and others. *Comn:* Formica Corp, 83; McDonald Corp, 83; NJ Transit Arts, Hoboken, 98; New York City Dept Cult Affairs, Bronx, 98; sculpture, Conn Comn Arts, Univ Conn, Avery Pt, 98; and others. *Exhib:* Louvre, Paris, 75; Cooper-Hewitt Mus, NY 78; Am Now, traveling, Hudson River Mus, NY & Wadsworth Atheneum, Hartford, Conn, 79; Mus Mod Art, NY 79; Va Mus Fine Arts, Richmond, Va, 80; 1984-A Preview, Ronald Feldman Fine Arts, NY 83; Opening Exhib, Mus Mod Art, NY, 84; Boiler House Projects, Victoria & Albert Mus, London, Eng, 84; High Styles: Twentieth-Century Am Design, Whitney Mus Am Art, NY, 85-86; Museum of the Future, Documenta 8, Kassel, W Ger, 87. *Pos:* Vpres & co-founder principal, SITE Projects Inc, 78-91. *Teaching:* Instr, Parsons Sch Design, New York, 94 & Cooper Union, New York, 95; vis artist, Purchase Col, State Univ NY, 94-95. *Awards:* Award, Progressive Archit, 80; Ward for Showroom Design, Interiors Mag, 83 & 85; Nat Endowment Arts Design Fel, 84. *Bibliog:* Jutta Fedderson (auth), Soft Sculpture & Beyond, G&B Arts Int, Australia, 93; Ellis Seebohm & Sykes (auths), At Home with Books, Crown, New York, 95. *Mem:* Fel Am Acad Rome. *Media:* Multi-Media. *Publ:* Auth, Sky Book, Profile Press, 72; ed, On SITE On Energy, SITE/Scribners, 74; co-auth, Unbuilt America, McGraw-Hill, 76; SITE: Projects and Theories 1969-78, Dedalo Libri, 78; SITE: Architecture as Art, Acad Ed & St Martin's Press, 81. *Mailing Add:* 60 Greene St New York NY 10012

SKY, CAROL VETH
PAINTER, PHOTOGRAPHER
b Cleveland, Ohio, Aug 30, 34. *Study:* Ohio State Univ, 52-53, Col of the Mainland, Texas City, Tex, 71-74, Slade Sch of Art, Univ Londong, Eng, 79, Univ Houston, BFA cum laude, 79, Univ Iowa, MA, 82, MFA, 83, Corcoran Sch Art, 86. *Work:* Nat Mus Women Arts, Washington; Univ Iowa, Iowa City; Univ St Thomas, Houston; Col Mainland, Texas City. *Exhib:* Nat Drawing & Sculpture, Del Mar Col, Corpus Christ, Tex, 75; Nat on Paper Show, Terrance Gallery, Palenville, NY, 83; Focus Int: Am Women in Art, United Nations World Conf, Nairobi, Kenya, 85; Visions, Westbeth Gallery, NY, 90; Nat Oceanic and Atmospheric Admin 25th Ann, 95; Nat Mus of Women in the Arts, 91, 96; Corcoran Gallery of Art, Washington, 92, 97; Nat Acad Art, New Delhi, India, 99. *Collection Arranged:* Con Fao, San Antonio, Col of the Mainland, 75, Orgn of Black Artists, 75, Primitive Art from Greenland, 76, The Art of Vodun, Sculpture and Dance from Haiti, 78; Washington Area Women in Surface Design, Md Col Art and Design, Silver Spring, MD, 91. *Teaching:* instr drawing, arts appreciation Col of Mainland, Texas City, 73-79; instr drawing, painting Capitol Hill Arts Workshop, Washington, DC, 87-89; instr drawing Md Col Art and Design, Silver Spring, MD, 87-88; instr drawing, painting, Smithsonian Resident Assocs Program, Washington, DC, 94-95; instr drawing, painting, Georgetown Univ, Washington, DC, 88, 92-95. *Awards:* 2nd prize Howard Fox, Arlington Art Ctr, 96; Best of Show, Laurie Hughes, Artists Equity, 96; Juror's Spl Award, Samuel Hoi, Touchstone Gallery, 97. *Bibliog:* Michael Welzenbach (auth), Landscapes of light & shadow, Wash Post, 7/11/92; John Dorsey (auth) School 33 shows work their way up, Baltimore Sun, Nov 11/94; Sara Wildberger (auth) Color it Brilliant, Washington Post, 12/22/99. *Mem:* Int Artists Support Group, Washington (bd dir, 99-); Corcoran Alumni Asn (steering com 94-); Nat Artists Equity (officers); Washington Chpt Artists Equity (pres 94-97); Women's Caucus for Art. *Media:* All. *Publ:* Auth, Brazilian Art & History; Focus on Modernism, Univ Iowa, 83; Ethical & political considerations of being an artist, Nat Artist Equity, 87; Art, Funding, Choice, Accountability & Censorship: Orienting Students to Issues & Realities, Nat Asn Schs Art & Design, 90; The Role of Art Colleges for the Artist, ACA/Inst Asn Art Critics, Pub Policy Forum, 88-92; Nat Artist Equity response to 1992 report of Lib Cong, J Copyright Soc USA, 92. *Dealer:* The Ralls Collection 1516 31st St NW Washington DC 20007; Rendezvous Gallery 5 Loudoun St SE Leesburg Va 20175. *Mailing Add:* 705 Pinon Dr Santa Fe NM 87501-1337

SLADE, GEORGE G
HISTORIAN, ADMINISTRATOR
b St Paul, Minn, Jan 2, 61. *Study:* Yale Univ, with Alan Trachtenberg, Tod Papageorge & Ben Lifson, BA, 83. *Collection Arranged:* Automotive Minnesota, pARTs, Minneapolis, 93; Local Color, pArts, 94; Democratic Processes, pArts, 96; Roger Mertin: In Minnesota 1991-2001, pARTs, 2001; Jerowe Liebling: Selected Photographs, Minn Ctr Photography, Minneapolis, 2006, Hand in Hand, 2006, Choreographic, 2006, Downriver, 2006. *Pos:* Librn, Walker Art Ctr, 92-95; lectr, Walker Art Ctr, Minneapolis Inst Arts, 93-98; ed, pARTs J, pARTs Photogr Arts, Minneapolis, 95-98; dir, McKnight Photog Fels, 98-; project adv, Minn Hist Soc, St

Paul, 95-2000; Artistic Dir Minnesota Ctr for Photography, Minneapolis, 2003-Present. *Mem:* Soc Photog Educ. *Publ:* Auth, Contact Sheet (article), Light Work, No 89, 96; editor, auth, Minnesota in Our Time: A Photographic Portrait, Minn Historical Soc Press, 2000. *Mailing Add:* Minn Ctr Photography 165 13th Ave Minneapolis MN 55413

SLADE, ROY
PAINTER, MUSEUM DIRECTOR
b Cardiff, Wales, July 14, 33. *Study:* Cardiff Col Art, NDD, 54; Univ Wales, ATD, 54. *Work:* Arts Coun Gt Brit; Contemp Art Soc; Nuffield Found; Westinghouse Corp; Brit Overseas Airways Corp. *Exhib:* Nat Print Club, Nat Col Fine Art, Washington, DC, 72; Pyramid Gallery, Washington DC, 76 & 77; Robert Kidd Gallery, Birmingham, Mich, 81; The Cranbook Vision, touring exhib, 86; Cranbook Contemp, touring exhib in Latin Am, 86; & others. *Pos:* Chmn, Comt Art in Pub Places, State of Mich, 83-85; comnr, Comn on Inst Higher Educ, NCentral Asn Col & Sch, 83-; chmn, Design Mich Adv Coun, 78-; mem, Mus Prog Overview Panel, Nat Endowment Arts, 90-93. *Teaching:* Sr lectr post-grad studies, Leeds Col Art, Eng, 64-69; prof painting, Corcoran Sch Art, Washington, DC, 67-68, dean, 70-77, dir, Gallery, 72-; pres, Cranbrook Acad Art, Bloomfield Hills, Mich, 77-95. *Awards:* Fulbright-Hays Scholar, 67; Knight, First Class, Order of the White Rose, Finland, 85; Knight, Order of the Polar Star, Sweden. *Mem:* Nat Soc of Lit & Arts; Nat Coun Art Admin (chmn, 81-); hon mem Asn Art Mus Dir; Nat Asn Schs Art & Design; Soc Bolivariana de Arguitectors, hon mem; Am Inst Architects (hon mem, Detroit chap); Asn of Art Mus Directors (hon mem). *Publ:* Auth, Report from Washington, Studio Int, 1/72; Studio Int; A new cultural center, Yorkshire Post, 2/69; Artist in America, Contemp Rev, 5/69; The Temple Flourishes, Nat Council of Art Administrators Publ, 80; Toward understanding and collaboration, Nat Asn Sch Art & Design Publ & Asn Art Mus Dir Publ, 82. *Dealer:* Robert Kidd Gallery 107 Townsend Birmingham MI 48011

SLAPO, DANIEL E
PAINTER
Study: studied with John Howard Sanden, David Leffel, Joe Hing Lowe and many others; City Col, NY, MA (art educ). *Exhib:* various group exhib's; Queens Mus, Nassau Co Mus; solo exhib, Mallette Gallery, Garden City, NY. *Teaching:* instr in art, New York City Sch Systems, currently; instr, pvt classes and adult educ, currently. *Awards:* Best in Show Awards; Excellence Awards; over 100 various awards. *Bibliog:* The Best of Pastels Vol I & II, by Rockport Publ. *Mem:* Pastel Soc Am (PSA) (bd mem, currently); Hudson Valley Art Asn; Am Artists Prof League; Art League Nassau Co, (pres, formerly); Art Student's League NY (lifetime mem). *Media:* Oils, Pastels and Charcoal. *Mailing Add:* 356 Nursery La Westbury NY 11590

SLATE, JOSEPH FRANK
WRITER, CONCEPTUAL ARTIST
b Holliday's Cove, WVa, Jan 19, 28. *Study:* Univ Wash, BA, 51; printmaking, Tokyo, Japan, 57; Yale Univ Sch Art & Archit, Alumni fel & BFA, 60; study of sumi-e painting, Kyoto, Japan, 75. *Hon Degrees:* Kenyon Col, hon DFA, 88. *Work:* Kenyon Col; Yale Univ; Newberry Collection Rare Books, Univ Chicago, Ill; Kerlan Col, Children;'s Lit, Univ Minn. *Exhib:* 12th Nat Print Show, Brooklyn Mus, 60; Whitney Mus, NY, 74; Cent Ohio Watercolor Soc, Schumacher Gallery, Columbus, 75; Hopkins Hall Gallery, Columbus, Ohio, 76; Mus Art, Port Huron, Mich, 78; Retrospective, 1956-1988, Olin Gallery, 88. *Pos:* Consult, studies on aesthet & perception, Yale Univ Dept Psychol, 60-65; mem exec comt, Kress Found Consortium Art Hist, 65-69; consult, Nat Endowment for the Arts, 77-78; Juror, Soc Children Book Writers & Illusrs, 86. *Teaching:* Prof Art, Kenyon Col, 62-88, chmn dept, 64-72 & 81-82, chmn fine arts div, 67-69, emer prof, 88-. *Awards:* Ohioana Libr Asn Award for Distinguished Contribution to Children's Lit, 88; 100 Best Books, New York Pub Libr, 88 &96; Blue Hen Award, Delaware, 97; Outstanding Md Auth Award, Asn Childhood Educ Int, 2001. *Bibliog:* Wash Alumnus, fall 82; numerous reviews in Publishers Weekly, NY Times, Horn Bk and others, 82-2006; Something about the author, vols 38 and 122, Contemp Auth, Vol 110, fall 88. *Mem:* Auth Guild; Soc Children Book, Writers & Illusr. *Media:* Conceptual, Acrylic. *Res:* The preconceptual eye; study on Aesthetics with Irvin L Child, Yale University. *Interests:* Illustration; travel; children's books. *Publ:* Miss Bindergarten Series, Dutton, 96, 98, 2000, 01, 02, 05 & 06; The Star Rocker, Harper & Row, 1982; What Star Is This? Putnam, 2005. *Dealer:* William Reiss John Hawkins & Associates Inc 71 W 23rd St Suite 1600 New York NY 10010. *Mailing Add:* 15107 Interlachen Dr Apt 701 Silver Spring MD 20906

SLATER, GARY LEE
SCULPTOR
b Montevideo, Minn, Oct 27, 47. *Study:* Univ Minn, BFA, 70; Ariz State Univ, MFA, 73. *Work:* Sky Harbor Int Airport, Phoenix, Ariz; Mus Fine Arts, NMex; City Monterey Park, Calif; City Palo Alto, Calif; Tucson Mus Art, Ariz. *Comn:* Ambassador Row Ctr, Lafayette, La, 86; Gwinett Com Ctr, Atlanta, Ga, 87; Ctr Park II, Calverton, Md, 88; Univ Ariz, Cancer Ctr, Tucson, 89; Chase Manhattan Bank, Tempe, Ariz, 92; and others. *Exhib:* Corten Steel: Contemp Sculpture, Bowers Mus, Santa Ana, Calif, 74; SW Fine Arts Biennial, Santa Fe, NMex, 76; Summer Outdoor Sculpture Exhib, Palo Alto, Calif, 77; Ariz Biennial, Tucson Mus Art, 80; NAm Sculpture Exhib, Golden, Colo, 83; and others. *Awards:* Nat Endowment Arts Grant, 73-74; Purchase Awards, 9th Ann Drawing & Sculpture Show, Del Mar Col, Corpus Christi, Tex, 75 & Ariz Outlook 76, Tucson Mus of Art, 76; Master of Southwest, Phoenix Home and Garden Mag; Architectural Excellence award, Art in Pub Places, Chandler, Ariz; Pred citation, Ariz AIA; Excellence award, Art in Pvt Develop, Tempe, Ariz. *Media:* Metal. *Dealer:* Victoria Boyce Gallery 7130 E Main Scottsdale AZ 85251. *Mailing Add:* 638 W Contessa Cir Mesa AZ 85201

SLATKIN, WENDY
HISTORIAN
b New York, NY, June 20, 50. *Study:* Barnard Col, Columbia Univ, with Barbara Novak, BA, 70; Villa Schifanoia Grad Sch Fine Arts, Florence, Italy, MA, 71; Univ Pa, with John McCoubrey, PhD, 76. *Teaching:* Asst prof art hist, survey & post-renaissance, Camden Col Arts & Sci, Rutgers Univ, 76-83; vis lectr, Univ Calif, Riverside, 83-85, Univ Redlands, 85- 90; prof, Calif Polytech, Pomona, Calif, currently. *Publ:* Auth, The genesis of Maillol's la Mediterranee, Art J, spring, 79; The early sculpture of Maillol, Gazette des Beaux Arts, 10/80; Reminiscences of Maillol: A conversation with Dina Vierny, Arts Mag, 2/80; Maternity and sexuality in the 1890's, Woman's Art J, spring 80; Women Artists in History, Prentice-Hall, 84, 2nd rev ed, 90. *Mailing Add:* Art Dept Univ Redlands Redlands CA 92374

SLATTON, RALPH DAVID
PRINTMAKER, GRAPHIC ARTIST
b Trumann, Ark, March 19, 52. *Study:* Ark State Univ, BFA, 81, MA, 86; Univ Iowa, MFA, 90. *Work:* Taiwan Mus Art, Taichung; Print Consortium, Kansas City, Mo; Proj Home, Baltimore, Md; Found Arts, Little Rock, Ark; Ark Artists Registry, Little Rock. *Exhib:* 15th Harper Nat, William Harper Raney, Palatine, Ill, 91; 35th Anne Steele Marsh, Hunterdon Art Ctr, Clinton, NJ, 91; 2nd Sapporo Int Print Biennale, Osawa Bldg, Japan, 93; 2nd Kochi Int Triennial, Ico-cho, Japan, 93; Mini Print Slovenija 93, Maribor Art Gallery, 93; Art Link, Contemp Art Gallery, Ind, 97; Nineth Ann Nat, Col Notre Dame, Md, 97; Pressed and Pulled, Ga Col State Univ, 97; Southern Graphics Asn traveling Exhib, 98. *Teaching:* Asst prof printmaking, E Tenn State Univ, Johnson City, formerly, assoc prof, chmn dept art and design, currently. *Awards:* Purchase Award, 17th La Ann, Sulzer Escher Wyss Serv Ctr, 90; Purchase Award, Henley Southeastern Spectrum, 91; Purchase Award, 21st Prints & Drawings, Ark Arts Found, 91. *Mem:* Print Consortium; Philadelphia Print Club; Asociacion Difusora Obra Grafica Int. *Media:* Etching. *Publ:* Best of Printmaking '97, Rockford Publ, 97. *Mailing Add:* 314 N Willow Ave Erwin TN 37650-1245

SLAVICK, SUSANNE MECHTILD
PAINTER, EDUCATOR
b South Bend, Ind, Apr 1, 56. *Study:* Yale Univ, with B Chaet, Samia Halaby, R Reed, G Peterdi, BA, 78; Tyler Sch Art, with David Pease, Margo Margolis & John Moore, Philadelphia, MFA, 80. *Work:* Madison Art Ctr, Wis; Prairie State Col, Chicago Heights, Ill; Wabash Col, Crawfordsville, Ind; Mercyhurst Col, Erie, Pa; Heinz Foundation, Pittsburgh. *Exhib:* Anderson, Lane, Slavick, Minn Mus Art, St Paul, 83; 80th Chicago Vicinity Exhib, Art Inst Chicago, 84; Wisconsin Directions 4, Milwaukee Art Mus, 84; solo exhibs, Pittsburgh Ctr Arts, Pa, 88, CAGE Gallery, Cincinnati, 89, Foster Art Gallery, Univ Wis, Eau Claire, 89, Denison Univ, 94, Mercyhurst Col, 94 & Otterbein Col, Westerville, Ohio, 95 & Rose Lehrmann Art Ctr, Harrisburg, Pa, 98; Anxious Nature, Univ Nebr, Lincoln, 91; Parteciparte, Venice, Italy, 93; Violent Violence, Arti et Amicitiae, Amsterdam, 2003; Six Painters, Art Acad Cincinnati, 96; Made in Heaven, Utrecht, The Neth, 97; Flesh and Blood, Hewlett Gallery, Carnegie Mellon Univ, Pittsburgh, 97; Aichi Prefectural Art Mus, Nagoya, Japan, 97; George Billis Gallery, NY, 98; WVa Univ, Morgantown, 99; Cult of Class, MICA, Baltimore, 2000; Univ Galleries, Murray State Univ, Ky, 01; and others. *Pos:* head Sch of Art, Carnegie-Mellon Univ, Pittsburgh, 2000-. *Teaching:* Instr art, Kutztown State Col, Pa, 80-81; asst prof, Univ Wis, Madison, 81-84; prof, Carnegie-Mellon, Pittsburgh, Pa, 84-; Andrew W Mellon prof of art, Carnegie-Mellon, Pittsburgh, 2001-. *Awards:* Broadus James Clarke Mem Prize, 80th Chicago & Vicinity Exhib, 84; Pa Coun Arts Fel in Painting, 84, 95 & 98; Nat Endowment Arts Grant, 87; SOS grant, Pa Coun Arts, 2000. *Bibliog:* Michael Bonesteel (auth), rev, Art Am, 10/87; Mary Jean Kenton (auth), Perspectives from Pa, New Art Examiner, 89; Richard Schindler (auth), Susanne Slavick (rev), New Art Examiner, 95. *Media:* Oil, Acrylic. *Publ:* Dinah Ryan (auth), Perspectives from Pa, Flesh & Blood, Art Papers, 2000; Phyllis Leverich Evans (auth), Susanne Slavick, Art Papers, 2000. *Mailing Add:* 14 Swan Dr Pittsburgh PA 15237-2375

SLAVIN, ARLENE
SCULPTOR
b New York, NY. *Study:* Cooper Union, BFA, 64; Pratt Inst, MFA, 67. *Work:* Brooklyn Mus, Metrop Mus Art, Hudson River Mus, Yonkers, NY; Fogg Art Mus, Cambridge, Mass; Allen Mem Art Mus, Oberlin, Ohio; Berkeley Univ Art Gallery, Calif; Norton Mus Art, Palm Beach, Fla; Chase Manhattan Bank. *Comn:* Cut-steel stair rail main stairway, Desoto Sch, NY, 95; ornamental steel fencing & posts, Kissena Park, Steel Plate animal art panels & gates, Ft Tryon Park, New York City Parks & Recreation, NY, 97-98; Paving inserts, etched glass, tree grates & seating (artist designed), Liberty State Park, NJ Transit Sta, 97-98; Entry Sculptures (4 large scale steel), Junction Plaza, Zoological Park, Asheboro, NC, 98-99; Gateway Sculptures & Terrazzo Floor (artist designed), Richard Stockton Col, NJ, Percents for Art, 98-99, Court St Development, Handy Holzman Heiffer Assocs ornamental fence, 99-00; designed steel benches, Town of Chapel Hill, NC, 2002; 8 carved glass windscreen murals, Hoboken Transit Terminal, NJ, 2003; Assunpink Wildlife, NJ, 2004. *Exhib:* Whitney Biennial Contemp Art, 73 & Am Drawings 1967-1973, Whitney Mus; solo exhibs, Alexander F Milliken Gallery, NY, 79-83, Am Embassy, Belgrade, Yugoslavia, 84, Painterly Panels, Heckscher Mus, NY, 87 & Simultaneous Landscapes, Rich Perlow Gallery, 88, Chauncey Gallery, Princeton, NJ, 90, The Gallery: Benjamin N Cardozo Sch Law, Screen Retrospect, NY, 91; Large Drawings, Santa Barbara Mus Art, Calif, 86; group exhib, Noahs Art, NY Parks & Recreation, Central Park, 89; Screen Retrospect, Norton Ctr Arts, Danville, Ky, 92; Karesh Gallery, Ketchem, Idaho, 93; Hebrew Union Col, 96-97; paintings, Fischbach Gallery, 2003. *Teaching:* Instr painting, Hofstra Univ, Long Island, NY, 71-72, Pratt Inst, 74 & Skowhegen Art Sch, Maine, 75 & 76; vis critic, Grad Sch, Univ Pa, 77; vis artist, Syracuse Univ, NY, 79 & Centre Col, Ky, 92. *Awards:* Printmaking Grant, Nat Endowment Arts, 77; Threshold

Foundation, 91. *Bibliog:* Helen Harrison (auth), Painterly Panels: Hybrid Art, NY Times, 8/23/87; Pat Van Gelder (auth), Animals as subjects in contemporary art, Am Artists Mag, 89; Gail Levin (auth), Arlene Slavin Screens (catalog essay), Yeshiva Univ, 91; Phyllis Braff (auth), Creatures, NY Times, 96; Carolee Thea (auth), Arlene Slavin Mediating Public Space, Sculpture Mag, 2001; Joyce Korotkin (auth), Arlene Slavin, NY Art World, 2003; City Art: NY % for Art Collections 2005, Merrell Publishers. *Mem:* Cent Womens Focus. *Media:* Metal sculpture, painting. *Interests:* Gardening. *Collection:* Metropolitan Mus of Art, New York, NY; Brooklyn mus of Art, Brooklyn, NY; Fogg Art Mus, Harvard Univ, Cambridge, MA; Allen Memorial Art Mus, Oberlin, OH; Readers Digest, Pleasantville, NY; Berkeley Univ Art Gallery, Berkeley, CA. *Mailing Add:* 119 E 18th St New York NY 10003

SLAVIN, NEAL
PHOTOGRAPHER
b New York, NY, Aug 19, 41. *Study:* Scholar, Lincoln Col, Oxford Univ, Eng, 61; Cooper Union, BFA, 63. *Work:* Metrop Mus Art, Mus Mod Art, Photog Arch, Int Ctr Photog, NY; Int Mus Photog, George Eastman House, Rochester, NY; Akron Art Inst, Ohio. *Comn:* The official cabinet portraits, Carter Administration, Nat Portrait Gallery, Washington, 80; official White House portrait of Pres & Mrs Clinton for their first White House Christmas card, 12/93. *Exhib:* One person exhibs, Allen St Gallery, Dallas, Tex, 86, Kennedy Gallery, Cambridge, Mass, 87, Photogr Gallery, London, Eng, 87, Foto Forum, Frankfurt, Ger, 87, Festival at Arles, Arles, France, 87, Chase Manhattan Corp Hq, NY, 87 & Centre National De La Photographie, Palais De Tokyo, Paris, 90; solo exhibs, Underground Gallery, NY, 65 & 71, Royal Ont Mus, Toronto, 71, Wadsworth Atheneum, Hartford, Conn, 76, Ctr Creative Photog, Tucson, Ariz, 76, Oakland Mus, Calif, 76, Light Gallery, NY, 76, Akron Art Inst, Ohio, 80, Nat Mus Photog, Film & TV, Eng, 86, Int Ctr Photog, NY, 86, Foto Forum, Frankfurt, Ger, 87 & Festival at Arles, France, 87; Rooms, Mus Mod Art, NY, 76; Venezia, The History of Polaroid, Venice, Italy, 79; Aspects of Am Photog, Galerie Spectrum, Hannover, W Ger, 81; The New Color, 81, Review, 86 & Legacy of Light, 87, Int Ctr Photog, NY; Color as Form: A History of Color Photog, Int Mus Photog & George Eastman House, Rochester, NY, 81; Va Mus Fine Arts, Richmond, 87; Zilkha Gallery Wesleyan Univ, Middletown, Conn, 92; Multiple Exposure: The Group Portrait in Photog, Zabriskie Gallery, NY, 92; plus many others. *Pos:* Lectr, Cooper Union Forum, New York, 75, Int Mus Photog, Rochester, NY, 75, Int Ctr Photog, New York, 77, Univ Calif, Los Angeles, 77, Milan workshops, Italy, 78, Ansel Adams Workshop, Yosemite, Calif, 77 & 80 & Smithsonian Inst, Washington, DC, 81. *Awards:* Nat Endowment Arts Grant, 72 & 76; Augustus Saint Gaudens medal for Art, Cooper Union Sch Art & Archit, 88; Recipient of Press & Poster Gold Lion, Cannes Festival, 92; Communications Arts Award, Water Country USA, 92. *Bibliog:* New frontiers in color, Newsweek, 4/76; Fox Style News, Fox Network, 91; Photo Dist News, 6/92. *Mem:* Am Soc Mag Photogrs; Dirs Guild Am. *Publ:* Auth, Britons, Andre Deutsch Ltd, London & Aperture, NY; Athletes: Photographs 1860, 86 Knopf, NY, 87; American Photography, Edward Booth-Clibborn, Rizzoli Int Publ Inc, 89; A Photographer's Source, 1989 by Henry Horenstein, Simon & Schuster; The Meaning of Life, Time Life Bks, 92. *Mailing Add:* 62 Greene St New York NY 10012

SLEIGH, SYLVIA
PAINTER, EDUCATOR
b Llandudno, Wales. *Study:* Brighton Sch Art, Eng. *Work:* Everson Mus Art, Syracuse, NY; Art Inst Chicago, Smart Mus, Univ Chicago; Milwaukee Art Mus; Va Mus Fine Arts, Richmond; St Louis Mus Art, Mo. *Exhib:* One-artist shows, Bennington Col, Vt, 63, Soho 20 Gallery, 73, Fine Arts Ctr, Univ RI, Kingston, 74, AIR Gallery, 74, 76 & 78, Milwaukee Art Mus, 90, Ball State Univ, Muncie, Ind, & Butler Inst, Youngstown, Ohio & Stiebel Mod, 92 & 94; Tokyo Int Biennial: New Image in Painting, 74; GW Einstein Co, Inc, 80 & 83; Zaks Gallery, Chicago, 85 & 95; Soho 20, NY, 85; Crossing The Threshold (traveling mus tour), 97-99; From Blast To Pop, David & Alfred Smart Mus Art, Chicago, 97; Not for Sale, Apet Art Co, NY, 98; Art Alliance, Philadelphia, 2001; Group exhibs, Realism Now, Vasser Col, Poughkeepsie, NY, 68, The Realist Revival, Am Federation Arts, NY, 72, Women Choose Women, NY Cult Ctr, 73, The Sister Chapel, PS 1, Long Island City, NY (traveling exhib), 78, Selections from The Dennis Adrian Collection, Mus Contemp Art, Chicago, 82, Emminent Immigrants, New House Gallery, Staten Island, NY, 86, Making Their Mark, traveling mus exhib, 89, Crossing the Threshold, Steinbaun-Krauss Gallery, NY (traveling mus exhib), 88, & Personal and Political, Guild Hall, East Hampton, NY, 2002; Critiques & New Works, Soho 20, New York City, 04; Portraits, Snug Harbor Cult Ctr, Staten Island, NY, 05. *Pos:* Selection Comt, Women Choose Women, New York Cult Ctr, 73; ann grants adv, Adolph & Ester Gottlieb Found, 88. *Teaching:* Instr life painting, New Sch Social Res, 74-80; Kreeger Wolf Distinguished Prof, Northwestern Univ, 77; vis artist, Baldwyn Seminar, Oberlin Col, Ohio, 82; Cornell Univ, Nancy C Dickinson, 87. *Awards:* Nat Endowment Arts Visual Artists Fel Grant, 82; Pollock-Krasner Found Grant, 85. *Bibliog:* Dennis Adrian (auth), Seeing the Figure Now; John Perreault (auth), Sylvia Sleigh; Stanley I Grand (auth), Drawing on the Figure; Donald Kuspir (auth), Stones and Flowers: Paintings and Watercolors by Sylvia Sleigh. *Mem:* Women's Caucus For Art; Col Art Asn. *Media:* Acrylic, Oil. *Publ:* Contribr, Anonymous was a Woman, 74 & Art: A Woman's Sensibility, 75, Feminist Art Prog, Calif Inst of the Arts; articles in Art News & Art Am. *Mailing Add:* 330 W 20th St New York NY 10011

SLEMMONS, ROD
MUSEUM DIRECTOR, EDUCATOR, CURATOR
Study: Univ Iowa, BA; Univ IA, MA in Eng; Rochester Inst Tech, MFA, 76-78. *Comn:* Cur Eye of the Mind/Mind of the Eye, 88, Water: The Renewable Metaphor, 97, Beyond Novelty: New Digital Art, 2000. *Pos:* Cur, prints and photog Seattle Art Mus, 82-96; dir, Mus of Contemp Photog, Columbia Col, Chicago, 2002—. *Teaching:* Teacher, hist photog and grad mus studies Univ Wash, Seattle. *Mailing Add:* Mus Contemp Photog Columbia Col Chgo 600 S Mich Ave Chicago IL 60605

SLENTZ, JACK RANDALL
SCULPTOR, EDUCATOR
b Oklahoma City, Okla, Nov 26, 63. *Study:* Univ the Ozarks, BA, 94; Univ Ark at Little Rock, MA, 96; Univ Memphis, MFA, 98. *Work:* Mint Mus of Craft & Design, Charlotte, NC; Minn Inst Art, Minneapolis; Am Crafts Mus, NY; Ark Arts Ctr, Little Rock; First Charter Ctr Bank, Charlotte, NC; Hendrix Col, Conway, Ark. *Comn:* steel sculpture, Univ the Ozarks, Clarksville, Ark, 94; Ceremonial Mace & Stand, Univ Ark at Little Rock, 96 & wood sculpture, 98; wood sculpture, Renwick Gallery, Smithsonian Am Art Mus, Washington DC, 99. *Exhib:* Best of Tennessee Crafts, The Parthenon, Nashville, 98; Lubbock Fine Arts Ctr Ann, Tex, 98; Allturnatives Form & Spirit, Berman Mus Art, Collegeville, Pa, 98; Am Woodturning: Emerging Contemp Art Form, Rochester Arts Ctr, Minn, 2000; Turned Wood 2000, Del Mano Gallery, Los Angeles; Redefining Craft, Am Crafts Mus, NY; A Way with Wood, The Signiture Shop & Gallery, Atlanta; New Artists, New Works, New Year, Blue Spiral 1, Asheville, NC. *Teaching:* instr/lab technician, Univ Cent Ark, Conway, 98-. *Awards:* Grand Award, Ark Arts Ctr, 99 & Artists Fel, 2000. *Bibliog:* Ray Lier, Jay Peters & Kevin Wallace (auths), Contemporary Turned Wood: New Perspectives In a Rich Tradition, Hand Books Press, Madison, Wis, 99; Terry Martin (auth), Collector's Choice at SOFA Chicago, Woodworth, 8/2000; Suzanne Ramljak & Michael W Monroe (auths), Turning Wood into Art: The Jane adn Arthur Mason Collection, Abrams Publ, New York, 2000; Arthur Mason (auth), Turnign Wood into Art, American Craft 8/2000; Werner Trieschmann (auth), Collecting a Life, John and Robyn Horn, American Craft, 1/2001. *Mem:* Int Sculpture Ctr; ACC. *Media:* Wood. *Publ:* contrib, Contemporary Turned Wood, Hand Books Press, 99, Living with Form, Bradley Publ, 99 & Turning Wood into Art, Herry N. Abrams Inc, 2000. *Dealer:* Blue Spiral 1 Gallery 38 Biltmore Ave Asheville NC 28801

SLETTEHAUGH, THOMAS CHESTER
PRINTMAKER, PHOTOGRAPHER
b Minneapolis, Minn, May 8, 25. *Study:* Univ Minn, BS, 49, MEd, 50, with Walter Quint, Peter Lupori, Malcolm Myers & John Rood; Pa State Univ, DEd, 56, with Viktor Lowenfeld; spec study, Williams Col, Univ SC, Univ Ga & Syracuse Univ, NY. *Work:* Bucharest Univ, Romania; Cult Ctr, Budapest, Hungary; Univ Belgrade, Yugoslavia; Univ Sao Paolo, Brazil; Cult Ctr Fjorde, Norway. *Comn:* Symbol of Excellence, Miss Univ Women, 70; Miss Univ Women Crest for Apollo 14, Alumni Asn, 71; Architectural Graphics, Newman Ctr, 86. *Exhib:* Taller Gallery, Barcelonia, Spain, 83-90; Centro Para Las Artes, Montevideo, Uruguay, 90; Arte Sella, Borgo Valsugana, Italy, 92 & 96; Mus de Arte Contemporanea, Sao Paulo, Brasil, 92; Culturehouse, Forde, Norway, 94; Acad Sci, Prague, Czech Repub, 96; Fine Arts Inst, Glasgow, Scotland, 97; La Sapienza, Mus Contemp Art, 1st Univ Rome, 98; New Sch Univ, NY, 2000; Reba & Dave Williams Coleection, NY, 2003; and others. *Collection Arranged:* Max Klager--Printmaker, Heidelberg Univ, WGer; John Jackson--Drawings, Cambridge Univ, Eng; Charlotte Strobele Graphics, Univ Vienna, Austria; Zheng Sheng Tian Paintings, Hangzhou, PRC; Juan Carlos Ferreyra Santos-Acrylics, Punta del Este, Uruguay. *Teaching:* Prof fine arts, Slippery Rock State Univ, Pa, 56-62, Frostburg State Univ, Md, 62-68 & Miss Univ Women, 68-70; assoc prof grad studies art educ, Univ Minn, 70-, psychoaesthetician, emer prof, 87-; vis prof, Kenyatta Univ, Kenya, 86-88; Centro Paralas Artes, Montevideo, Uruguay, 90; Kossuth Univ, Debrecen, Hungary, 90, Univ Sao Paulo, Brazil 92, culturehouse, Forde Norway, 94; Casa Strobele Gallery, Borgo, Italy, 96, Intercultural Educ Through Art. *Awards:* Minneapolis Arts Comn, 86-89; Minnesota Fine Arts, Color Photog, 88; Int Man of the Year Award for Aesthetics, Art & Educ, Int Biog Ctr, Cambridge, Eng, 97 & 98; Minneapolis Aquatennial Sculpture Award, 2002; 50 yr award, Minnesota State Fine Arts, 2003. *Bibliog:* Hans Stumbauer (auth), Art education in Austria, Art Sch Linz, 71; Paul Cornel Chitic (auth), articles in Tribune & Art Rev, Bucharest, Romania, 72; Rajztanitas, Aradi jeno, Budapest, Hungary, 1979. *Mem:* Int Soc Educ in Art; Int Soc Aesthet; Int Soc Art Hist; Int Soc Empirical Aesthet; Int Union Architects. *Media:* All Media, Serigraphs. *Res:* Visual, tactile stimuli and creative imagery, a stastical analysis. *Specialty:* Mixed Media. *Collection:* Children's art, original works in various media. *Publ:* Auth, The analysis & synthesis of psychoaestheics, Cambridge Univ, 75; Southern Hemisphere Research, Aboriginals in Australia and Maori in New Zealand, 78 & Oriental Seminar in People's Republic of China, Hong Kong, Japan and Philippines, Int Soc for Educ through Art, United Nations Educ, Sci & Cult Orgn, 79 & 81; Taller de la Flor, Centro Artistico Antesanal, Buenos Aires, Argentina, 84; Derivations of Psixel Modes of Visual Expression, Czech Acad Sci, Prague, Czech Repub, 96; Printworld Dir, 97; New University of Lisbon, Lisbon, Portugal, 2004. *Dealer:* The Picture Store 37 Clarendon St Boston MA 02116; North Shore Gallery, 16 Hillview Est Rd, Groveland, MA 01834. *Mailing Add:* 49 Williams Ave SE Minneapolis MN 55414-3449

SLIDER, DORLA DEAN
PAINTER
b Tampa, Fla, Sept 9, 29. *Study:* Study with Dr Walter Emerson Baum, 40-48. *Work:* Allentown Art Mus, Pa; Berman Art Mus, Collegeville, Pa; Lenfest Group Impressionist Am Artists; DuPont Corp, Del; Cedar Crest Col, Pa; Brandywine River Mus, Chadds Ford, Pa; Fla Keys Mus, Marathon, Fla. *Exhib:* Allied Artists of Am, Nat Acad Design, 67-77; Pa Acad Fine Arts, Philadelphia, 69; William Penn Mus, Harrisburg, Pa, 75; Watercolor USA, Springfield, Ohio; Butler Inst of Am Art, Ohio; Nat Watercolor Soc, 04; Adirondacks Nat, 2000-06; San Diego Watercolor Soc, 2006. *Pos:* Bd dir, Philadelphia Watercolor Soc, 96-2003; judge, juror, Nat & Regional Art Shows, currently. *Awards:* Old Forge Hardware Co Award, Adirondacks Nat of Am Watercolors, 2000; M Graham Award, Berman Art Mus, Pa, 2004; Bd Dir Award, PWCS, Widener Col, Delaware, 2005; MF Kratz Award PWCS, Berman Art Mus, Pa, 2006; San Diego Watercolor Soc, 2006; Viewer's Choice Award PWCS, Wallingford, Pa, 2006. *Bibliog:* Henry C Pitz (auth), Brandywine Tradition, Houghton Mifflin Co, Boston, 69; articles, Brandywine Bugle & Trade Mag, Pa, 71-74. *Mem:* Am Watercolor Soc & Nat Watercolor Soc; Nat Soc Painters in Casein & Acrylic; Artists

Equity Asn; Philadelphia Watercolor Soc; Audubon Artists. *Media:* Watercolor, Acrylic. *Publ:* Artists Fla, 89-90; Penna Artists, 95-96; Best of Watercolor: Painting Light & Shadows, 97, The Best of Watercolor, 3rd ed, 99, Rockport Publ & Collected Best of Watercolor, 2002, The Very Best of Watercolor, 2004; Daphne Landis (auth), Speaking for Themselves - The Artists of Southeastern Penna, 2005. *Dealer:* Chadds Ford Gallery Chadds Ford PA 19317; Hardcastles Gallery 5714 Kennet Pike Centerville Delaware 19807; Swan Gallery 215 Old York Rd Jenkintown PA 19046. *Mailing Add:* 268 Estate Rd Boyertown PA 19512

SLIGH, CLARISSA T
PHOTOGRAPHER, PAINTER
b Washington, DC, Aug 30, 39. *Study:* Hampton Inst, BS, 61; Howard Univ, BFA, 72; Skowhegan Sch Art, Maine, 72; Univ Pa, MBA, 73; Int Ctr Photog, New York, 79-80; Howard Univ, MFA, 99. *Work:* Mus Mod Art, NY; Nat Mus Women in the Arts, Washington, DC; Victoria & Albert Mus, London; Australian Nat Gallery, Canberra; Corcoran Gallery Art, Washington, DC; Philadelphia Mus; Int Mus Photog, Rochester, NY. *Comn:* Who We Are: Autobiographies in Art Traveling Collection, Washington State, 90; Malcolm X: Man, Ideal, Icon Installation, Walker Art Ctr, 92. *Exhib:* One-woman shows, Ctr for Photog in Woodstock, NY, 92, Art in General, NY, 92, Afro-Am Hist & Cult Mus, Philadelphia, 93, Toronto Photogrs Workshop, Toronto, 94, Univ Md, 2002; Malcolm X: Man, Ideal, Icon, Walker Art Ctr, Minneapolis & traveling, 92; The Subjecy of Rape (with catalog), Whitney Mus Am Art Film & Video Gallery, 93; The Visual Diary: Women's Own Stories, Houston Ctr for Photog & traveling, 94; Black Power Black Art: Political Imagery from the Black Arts Movement of the 1960s & 1970s, San Francisco State Univ, 94; History 101: The Re-Search for Family (with catalog), Installation at The Forum for Contemp Art, St Louis, 94; Imagining Families: Images & Voices (with catalog), Nat African Am Mus Project, Smithsonian Inst, Washington, DC, 94; Thinking Print: Books to Billbaords, 1980-95, Mus Mod Art, NY, 96; Am Families in Photographs, Nat Mus Am History, Smithsonian Inst, Washington, DC, 97; Developing Illusions, 1873-1998, Photographs from the Collection, Corcoran Gallery Art, Washington, DC, 98; Reflections in Black: A History of Black Photogrs, Smithsonian Ctr for African-Am History & Cult, Wash DC, 2000; Photographers, Writers and the Am Scene: Visions of Passage, Mus Photog Arts, San Diego, 2000; Mus Mod Art & Design, NY, 2003; Mus für Angewandte, Frankfurt, Ger, 2003; Screenings: Pub & Pvt, Noyes Mus Art, Oceanville, NJ, 2004. *Teaching:* Instr, City Col NY, 86-87; vis artist fac, Minn Col Art & Design, Minneapolis, Minn, spring term, 88-89; instr, Lower Eastside Printship, NY, winter 88-90; distinguished vis artist/teacher, Carlton Col, Northfield, Minn, spring term, 92; artist-in-residence/teacher, Tisch Sch Arts, NY Univ, 2003-04; adj prof, Sch Vis Arts, NY, 2002-. *Awards:* Nat Endowment Arts, 88; NY State Coun Arts, 90; Artiste En France Award, Greater NY Links, French Govt, Moet & Chandon, 92; Ann President's Award, Nat Women's Caucus for Art, 94; Jerome Found Grant for Women Artists of Color Leadership Workshops, 94; NY Found for the Arts fel in Photog, 2000; grant, Andrea Frank Found, 2000; Anonymous was a Woman Award, 2001. *Bibliog:* Naomi Rosenblum (auth), A History of Women Photographers, Abbeville Press, 94; Arlene Raven (auth), Well healed, Village Voice, 3/1/94; Carla Williams (auth), Reading Deeper: The Legacy of Dick and Jane in the Work of Clarissa Sligh, Image, Vol 38, 1995; Deborah Wills (auth), Clarissa Sligh, Aperture, #138, Winter 1995. *Mem:* Coast to Coast Nat Women Artists Color; Women's Caucus Art Col Art Asn. *Publ:* Auth, Reliving my Mother's Struggle, Liberating Memory: Our Work & Our Working Class Consciousness, Rutgers Univ Press, 94; The Plaintiff Speaks, Picturing Us: African American Identity in Photography, The New Press, 94; auth, Wrongly Bodied Two, Women's Studio Workshop Press, Rosendale, NY, 2004; auth, It Wasn't Little Rock, Vis Studies Workshop Press, 2005. *Dealer:* Robert Bain Joysmith Gallery 46 Huling Ave Memphis TN 38103. *Mailing Add:* 465 W Broadway New York NY 10012

SLIVE, SEYMOUR
HISTORIAN, MUSEUM DIRECTOR
b Chicago, Ill, Sept 15, 20. *Study:* Univ Chicago, AB, 43, PhD, 52. *Pos:* trustee, Solomon R Guggenheim Mus, New York City, 78-; trustee, Norton Simon Mus, 89-91; emer, Elizabeth & John Moors Cabot dir, Harvard Art Mus, 82; trustees' coun, Nat Gallery Art, Wash, currently. *Teaching:* Instr fine arts, Oberlin Col, Ohio, 50-51; asst prof art & chmn dept, Pomona Col, Calif, 52-54; mem fac, Harvard Univ, Cambridge, Mass, from 54, prof fine arts, from 61, Gleason prof fine arts, 73-91, emer, chmn dept fine arts, 68-71, dir, Fogg Mus, 72-82. *Awards:* Of of Order of House of Orange-Nassau, 62; Charles Rufus Morey Prize, Col Art Asn Am, 70; Award for Achievement in Art Hist, Art Dealers' Asn Am, 79. *Mem:* Fel Am Acad Arts & Sci; hon mem Karel van Mander Soc; Col Art Asn (dir, 58-62 & 65-69); Renaissance Soc; foreign mem Dutch Soc Sci; Corresp Fel Brit Acad. *Res:* Baroque art. *Publ:* Auth, Drawings of Rembrandt, 2 vols, Dover Publ, NY, 65; auth, Frans Hals, 3 vols, Phaidon Press, London, 70-74; Jacob van Ruisdael, Abbeville Press, NY, 81; Frans Hals, Prestel Press, Munich, 89; Dutch Painting, Yale Press, New Haven, Conn, 95; Jacob van Ruisdael: A Complete Catalogue of His Paintings, Drawings and Etchings, Yale Press, 2001. *Mailing Add:* Harvard Univ Sackler Art Mus Cambridge MA 02138

SLIVKA, DAVID
SCULPTOR
b Chicago, Ill. *Study:* Calif Sch Fine Arts. *Work:* Univ Pa, Philadelphia; Baltimore Mus; Rutgers Univ, Camden, NJ; Everson Mus, Syracuse, NY; Brooklyn Mus, NY. *Exhib:* Mus Mod Art, 62; Hirshhorn Collection Mod Sculpture, Guggenheim Mus, 62-63; Mus Fine Arts, Boston, 68; Selections from Chase Manhattan Bank Collection, 71; Albright-Knox Art Gallery, Buffalo, NY, 74; one-man shows, Southern Ill Univ, Carbondale, 68, Everson Mus, Syracuse, NY, 74 & Univ Pa, Philadelphia, 75; Corcoran Gallery Art, Washington, 94; Chicago Cult Ctr, 94; IBM Gallery, 95; Portland Mus Art, Ore, 96. *Teaching:* Prof sculpture, Univ Mass, Amherst, 64-67; artist-in-residence, Southern Ill Univ, Carbondale, 67-68; instr, Queens Col, NY, 71-73; prof, Pa Acad Fine Arts, Philadelphia, 72-94. *Awards:* Brandeis Univ Creative Arts Award for Am Sculpture, 62; Louis Comfort Tiffany Award-Sculpture, 77; Pollock-Krasner Found Award, 85-86 & 92. *Bibliog:* Georgine Oeri (auth), The sculpture of David Slivka, Quadrum, 63; Harold Rosenberg (auth), The anxious object, Illus, 65; Studio series, Art News, 12/94. *Media:* Miscellaneous. *Mailing Add:* 549 W 52nd New York NY 10019

SLIZYS, HAVILAND See Brown, Susan LT (Haviland Slizys)

SLOAN, JEANETTE PASIN
PAINTER, PRINTMAKER
b Chicago, Ill, Mar 18, 46. *Study:* Marymount Col, Tarrytown, NY, BFA, 67; Art Inst of Chicago; Univ Chicago, MFA, 69. *Work:* Nat Mus Am Art, Smithsonian Inst, Washington, DC; Cleveland Mus Fine Arts; Art Inst Chicago; Minneapolis Inst Art; Yale Univ Art Gallery; Metrop Mus Art, NY; and others. *Exhib:* G W Einstein Co, NY, 77, 79, 80, 83 & 85; Tatischeff Gallery, NY, 95, 97 & 99; Cline Fine Art, Santa Fe NMex, 98; Gierhard Wurzer Gallery, Houston, Tex, 98 & 2001; Frederick Baker Fine Art, Chicago, 98; J Cacciola Gallery, 2004 & 05. *Teaching:* instr Northwestern Univ, Chicago, spring, 2000, Anderson Ranch Arts Ctr, Snowmass, Colo, summer, 2001. *Awards:* Ill Arts Coun Fel, 86. *Bibliog:* Michele Vishney (auth), Still-Life and the Art of Jeanette Pasin Sloan, Arts, 3/83; Am Artist, New York, 1/94; Gerritt Henry (auth), Jeanette Pasin Sloan, Hudson Hills Press, New York, 2000; James Yood (auth) The Prints of Jeanette Pasin Sloan, 03. *Media:* Lithography, Oil. *Dealer:* Peltz Gallery Milwaukee WI; J Cacciola Gallery New York NY. *Mailing Add:* 301 Loma Arisco Santa Fe NM 87501

SLOAN, JENNIFER
SCULPTOR
b New York, NY, Jan 20, 58. *Study:* Empire State Col, State Univ NY, BA(photog, archeol), 78; Univ Paris, Nanterre, 79; Int Ctr Photog, New York, 83. *Work:* Brooklyn Mus, NY; Nat Mus Women Arts, Washington; NY Pub Libr, Media Libr, NY; Empire State Col, Saratoga Springs, NY; St Vincent's Med Ctr, NY. *Comn:* Photo Collages, Art on Film/Metrop Mus, NY, 89 & 90; photo sculpture, Francis Hauert, NY, 90; photo sculpture, Vasilli Kostoulas, Paris, France, 91; photo collage/sculpture, Julie Lipius/Steve Riskin, NY, 91; photo sculpture, Donna Cameron, NY, 92. *Exhib:* Solos exhibs, Photog Resource Ctr, Boston, NY, 89, Ctr Photog, Woodstock, NY, 91; Non-Traditional Photog, Robert Burge 20th Cent Photog, NY, 92; Earthly Virtues Window Installation, Art in Gen, NY, 92; Jennifer Sloan, Photo Sculpture, Kean Col, Union, NJ, 93; About Faces, Houston Ctr Photog, Tex, 94; AIDS Forum, Artists Space, NY, 94; Artist in the Marketplace, Bronx Mus Arts, NY, 94; Luminous Image, Alternative Mus, 96; The Tree Truck installation, Downtown Arts Festival, NY, 97; Glass Photo Blocks, Robert Burge 20th Century Photographers, NY, 99. *Collection Arranged:* The Self-Portrait Show, Art Initiatives, NY, 94. *Pos:* Pub prog audio visual technician, Int Ctr Photog, New York, 81-83; exhib developer, Station Island Children's Mus, NY, 93-96, Childrens Mus Manhattan, 96-97 & Web Master, WNYC radio, NY, 98-. *Teaching:* Artist/teacher art, Bronx Mus Arts, 93; artist/teacher art for kids, Franklin Furnace, New York, 94. *Awards:* Money for Women, Barbara Demming Mem Fund, 91; Artist Residency Program, Kean Col Residency, Mid-Atlantic Arts Found, 93; Residency & Grant, Sculpture Space, 96. *Bibliog:* William Zimmer (auth), A religous spirit vies with fun, NY Times, 7/31/94; Holland Cotter (auth), A showcase for artists learning their business, NY Times, 8/19/94; Craig Kellog (auth), Galleries to Go, Metropolis Mag, 12/97 & 1/98. *Mem:* Int Sculpture Ctr; Art & Sci Collab Inc. *Media:* Mixed Media. *Publ:* Coauth, Its News To Me, teaching activities, Staten Island Children's Mus, 94. *Mailing Add:* 105 Duane St No 15C New York NY 10007

SLOAN, MARK
MUSEUM DIRECTOR
b Durham, NC, Nov 16, 1957. *Study:* Univ Richmond, BA, 80; Va Commonwealth Univ, MFA, 84. *Exhib:* Photoglyphs: Rimma and Varleriy Gerlovin, 91; Intimate Technologies/Fictional Personas, 92; Dear Mr Ripley, 93; Self-Made Worlds: Visionary Folk Art Environments (with catalog), 97; PopLuxe: The Language of the Garment, (with catalog) 98; Right to Assemble (with catalog), 99; Palimpsest: Afghanisfan, 2002; Breath ona Mirror, 2002; No Man's Land, 2004; Alive Inside, 2005; Force of Nature. *Pos:* Asst dir, San Francisco Camerawork, 86-89; dir, Roland Gibson Gallery, Potsdam, NY, formerly & Halsey Inst Contemp Art, Col Charleston, SC, currently prof arts mgt. *Teaching:* Prof of Arts Mgt. *Specialty:* Contemp Art in all Media. *Publ:* Auth, Spirit in the Land: Photographs from the Bible Belt, Southern Accents; Spectacular Photographs: Unforgettable Faces, Facts and Feats, 1989; Hoaxes, Humbugs and Spectacles, Villard/Random House, 1990; Dear Mr Ripley, Bulfinch/Little, Brown & Co, 1993; Self Made World's Visonary Folk Art Enviroments (Aperture, 97); Wild, Weird and Wonderful: The American Circus 1901-1927 as Seen by F. W. Glasier, Quartuck Press, 2003; The Rarest of the Rare; Stories Behind the Treasures at the Harvard Mus of National History, Harper Collins, 2004. *Mailing Add:* Col of Charleston Halsey Inst School of Arts Charleston SC 29424-0001

SLOAN, RICHARD
PAINTER, ILLUSTRATOR
b Chicago, Ill, Dec 11, 35. *Study:* Am Acad of Art, Chicago, Ill. *Work:* Denver Mus Natural Hist; Ill State Mus, Springfield; Leigh Yawkey Woodson Art Mus, Wausau, Wis. *Comn:* The Raptors of Arizona (paintings), Ariz Wildlife Found, Ariz Game & Fish Dept, & Univ Ariz Press, 98. *Exhib:* Birds in Art, Leigh Yawkey Woodson Art Mus, 79-81, 83-89 & 91-2000; Wildlife in Art, 87; Cummings Nature Ctr, Rochester Mus Sci Ctr, Rochester, 88; Animals in Art, Soc Animal Artists, Jamestown, NY, 92, Art & The Animal, 93-2000; Natural Selections, Joan D McArthur State Park, Palm Beach, Fla, 93, 98-2000; Wildlife Art Am, James Ford Bell Mus, Minneapolis, Minn,

94; Soc Animal Artists, Disney's Animal Kingdom, 98. *Pos:* Staff artist, Lincoln Park Zoo, Chicago, 62-65. *Teaching:* Workshops, Jackson Hole Wyo, 95, Tucson Ariz, 96, Lighthouse Ctr for the Arts, Tequesta, Fla, 2001. *Awards:* Award of Excellence, Soc Animal Artists, 90 & 98; Master Wildlife Artist, Leigh Yawkey Woodson Art Mus, 94; Speical Guest Artist, Vancouver Int Wildlife Art Show, Can. *Mem:* Soc Animal Artists, NY; Inter Asn Nitrox & Tech Divers. *Media:* Acrylic. *Publ:* The Best of Wildlife Art, N Light Bks, 97; Modern Wildlife Painting, Yale Univ Press, 98; The Raptors of Arizona, UA Press, 98; Wildlife Art, Rockport Publ, 99; The Best of Wildlife Art 2, N Light Bks, 2000. *Dealer:* Images Gallery Naples FL; Geoffrey Smith Gallery Stuart Fla; Patricia Cloutier Galley Tequesta Fla. *Mailing Add:* 1623 SW Pineland Way Palm City FL 34990

SLOAN, ROBERT SMULLYAN
PAINTER
b New York, NY, Dec 5, 1915. *Study:* City Col New York, AB, 36; Inst Fine Arts, NY Univ, 37-39. *Work:* IBM Collection; Bradford Jr Col, Haverhill, Mass; Herbert F Johnson Mus, Ithaca, NY; Nat Portrait Gallery, Washington, DC; US Treas; Fogg Mus, Harvard Univ, Boston. *Comn:* Many covers & spec features, Time, Coronet & Colliers, 41-50; posters, Russian War Relief, 43 & Doing All You Can, Brother, US Treas, 43. *Exhib:* Soldier Art, Nat Gallery Art, Washington, DC, 45; Corcoran Biennial, 49; Portraits of Yr, Portraits, Inc, 49; one-man shows, Leger Galleries, White Plains, NY, 55, Herbert F Johnson Mus, Cornell Univ, 74, Capricorn Galleries, Bethesda, Md, 75 & Instituto Nacional de Bellas Artes, San Miguel de Allende, Mex, 99; Time Salutes Pennsylvania, Hist Soc Pa, 82; The Seasoned Eye III (traveling exhib), 90-91; Ending, Kennedy Ctr, Washington, DC. *Teaching:* Sch Visual Arts, New York, NY, 50, 51. *Awards:* Citation for Distinguished Serv, US Treas, 43; Watercolor Div Award, Nat Soldier Art Show, USA, 45; Distinguished Achievement Award, The Seasoned Eye III, Mod Maturity Mag, 90. *Bibliog:* George Wiswell (auth), Discovery of a Copley portrait, Am Heritage Mag, 60. *Mem:* Appraisers Asn Am; Mamaroneck Artists Guild (pres, 54). *Media:* Oil. *Interests:* physics, cosmology, music and history. *Publ:* Illusr, Army Educ Prog & other mags; Soldier Art, Infantry J, 45. *Mailing Add:* 290 Kingstown Way Unit 341 Duxbury MA 02332-4637

SLOAN, RONALD J
PAINTER
b Brooklyn, NY, Jan 8, 32. *Study:* Central State Univ, Edmond, Okla, MA(art educ), 65; Univ Albany, NY, MA, 75; Univ Ky, Lexington, MFA(painting), 79. *Work:* Mattatuck, Waterbury, Conn; Provincetown Mus, Cape Cod, Mass; Chase Manhattan Bank, NY; Gen Elec Corp, Conn; Northwestern Community Col, Winsted, Conn. *Exhib:* Canton Gallery on the Green, Canton, Conn, 96; New Arts Gallery, Bantam, Conn, 96; Alexandria Mus Art, La, 96; Patterns of Perception, Conn Comn Arts Gallery, Hartford, 96; Provincetown Art Asn, 96. *Awards:* Provincetown Fine Arts Work Ctr Fel, 84-85; Nat Endowment Arts, 87-88; Conn Grant, 98. *Mem:* Conn Acad Fine Arts; New Haven Paint & Clay. *Media:* Acrylic. *Mailing Add:* PO Box 361 Norfolk CT 06058-0361

SLOAN (KAY SLOAN), KAY
EDUCATOR
Mailing Add: Mass Col of Art Off of Pres 621 Huntington Ave Boston MA 02115

SLOANE, PHYLLIS LESTER
PAINTER, PRINTMAKER
b Worcester, Mass. *Study:* Carnegie-Mellon Univ, BFA. *Work:* Canton Art Ctr, Ohio; Rutgers Univ Archives, NJ; Mus Fine Art, Santa Fe, NMex; Cleveland Artists Found; Las Vegas Art Mus, Nev. *Comn:* Mural (on bldg side), Cleveland Area Arts Coun, Am Inst of Archit & NOVA, 74; ed of print La Nue, Univ Print Club, Cleveland, 77; 4 print eds, Transworld Art Corp, 79; presentation print, Cleveland Print Club, 83; portfolio, Image Resource Ctr, NOVA, Cleveland, 83. *Exhib:* Boston Printmakers Exhib, 79-81, 84 & 85; Cleveland Play House Gallery, 83 & 85; The Printed Image, Hudson River Mus, Yonkers, NY, 87; retrospective, Mansfield Art Ctr, 96; Midyear Exhib, Butler Mus, 98, 2000; Philadelphia Art Mus, Pa; NMex Mus Fine Art, Santa Fe; Cleveland Mus Art; others. *Awards:* Graphics Awards, Cleveland Mus Art May Show, 78; Cleveland Visual Arts Award, 82; First Prize, Miami Int Print Biennial, 84; Purchase Awards, NC Print & Drawing Ann & Anderson Ind Print Show, 85. *Bibliog:* Ruth Thompson (auth), The Multiple Methods of Phyllis Sloane, Am Artist, 2/93; Chas LeClair (auth), The Art of Watercolor, Watson Guptil, 94; H Daniel Butts III (auth), The Art of Phyllis Sloane, Ohio Artists Now, 96. *Mem:* New Orgn Visual Arts (bd trustees, 73-79); Print Club of Cleveland (chair publ comt); Artists Arch Western Reserve (bd trustees 96-2003); Santa Fe Print Club. *Media:* Watercolor; Miscellaneous Media. *Publ:* auth, The Relief Prints - Jour of the Print World, 91; auth, Retrspective Exhib, Las Vegas Art Mus, Robert Bell & James Mann, 2004. *Dealer:* Hand Graphics 2312 W Alemeda St Santa Fe NM 98501; Argos Gallery 821 Canyon Rd Santa Fe NM 87501

SLOAT, RICHARD JOEL
PAINTER, PRINTMAKER
b Easton, Pa, Sept 18, 45. *Study:* Univ Pa, BA, 69; Art Students League, 72. *Work:* Brit Mus, London; Israel Mus, Jerusalem; Fogg Mus, Cambridge, Mass; Mus City of New York; Portland Art Mus, Oreg; Nat Acad Mus, New York City; Library of Congress, Washington, DC. *Comn:* 5 Print Editions, NY Graphic Soc, Greenwich, 72-80. *Exhib:* solo-exhibs, Martin Sumers Gallery, NY, 87, Wood & Stone Gallery, Taipei, 90, FDR Gallery, NY, 93, Old Print Shop, NY, 95 & Ottendoreer Libr, NY, 96, Howard Salon, Taiwan, 98, 2001, Paul McCarron, NY, 2001, Safe-T-Gallery, NY, 2005, NY Transit Mus, 97, 2003, Springfield Art Mus, 2001, 05, MO; two person shows, Falken Stern Fine Art, NY, 90 & Gate Gallery, Kaoshiung, Taiwan, 94, Old Print Shop, NY, 2004, Michael Ingbar Gallery, NY, 2005; Contemp Prints from the US, Nat Mus Fine Arts, Hanoi, Repub Vietnam, Macau Mus Art, 2000; group shows, Michael Ingbar Gallery, NY, 93, 94, 96, 98, 2000, 06, Life of City, Mus Mod Art, 2002, Mus of the City NY, 82, 2002, UBS Paine Weber Art Gallery, 2002, Art Students League, 2002, 05, NY Hist Soc, NY, 2004, Susan Teller Gallery, NY, 2002, 04, Natl Acad Design, NY, 74, 86, 88, 94, 99, 2000, 01, 03, 04, 05; Reveal Haromonize, Macau Mus Art, 2000; Noble Maritime Collec, NY, 2006; many others. *Pos:* Prog dir, Alliance Figurative Artist, 82-85; Co-found, Sky Wheel Configurist Group, 84-90; cur, Contemp Block prints, Ten Worlds Gallery, NY, 88; pres, Soc Am Graphic Artists, 2003-. *Teaching:* Lectr drawing methods, Univ Calif, Berkeley, 96; adj instr printmaking, Fashion Inst Technol, NY; adj prof, FIT, NY, 98-99; master drawing inst, Nat Acad Design Sch Fine Arts, 2003. *Awards:* Leo Meisner Prize, Nat Acad Design, 86 & 94; Savoir Faire-Lana Paper Award, Audubon Artists, 96 & Art Students League Award in Graphics, 98; Art Students League Award, Audubon Artists, 98, 2002; AO Crimi Award, Audobon Artists, 99; JM Kaueney Award, Janet Turner Print Competition, 99; John Taylor Arms Award, Audubon Artists, 2001. *Bibliog:* Vivien Raynor (auth), Sunday New York Times, 3/6/88; Wu Jin Fa (auth), Min Chung Dailey News, Taiwan, 9/1/89; RJ Steiner (auth), Art Times, 3/98; Wendy Moonan (auth), New York Times, 5/3/02. *Mem:* Soc Am Graphic Artists (coun mem, 95-, vpres, 99, pres 2003-); Found Mod Painters & Sculptors (exec comt mem, 96, vp 99-2002); Boston Printmakers; Nat Acad (acad, 97-). *Media:* Etching; Watercolor. *Publ:* United Daily News Taipei, 89; Mythic City & Friends, Book by Artist, 91; article & illus, J Print World, 91, 98, 99 & 2000; The old print shop portfolio Vol LU No 4, 95, Vol LXI No 1, 2001, Vol LXI No 5, 2002; New York City Centenial Portfolio, vol LVII 6, 98; Marilyn Symmes (auth), Impressions of New York, Prints from the New York Historical Soc, 2004. *Dealer:* The Old Print Shop 150 Lexington Ave New York NY 10016. *Mailing Add:* 170 Second Ave No 7B New York NY 10003-5779

SLONE, SANDI
PAINTER, CONCEPTUAL ARTIST
b Boston, Mass, Oct 1, 39. *Study:* Mus Fine Arts Sch, Boston, diploma, 73; Wellesley Col, BA, 74 (Magna Cum Laude). *Work:* Mus Mod Art, NY; Rose Art Mus, Brandeis Univ; New Mus Contemp Art, Barcelona, Spain; Smithsonian Inst; Portland Mus Fine Arts, Oreg; Fitzwilliam Mus, Cambridge, England; and others. *Exhib:* The Uneasy Surface: Points of Turbulence, Univ RI, 96; Transfolk, Artists Mus, Lodz, Poland, 97; Ground Control, Lombard Freid Fine Arts, NY, 98; The 45th Corcoran Mus Biennial, 98; Masters of the Masters, Butler Inst Am Art, 98; Cristinerose Gallery, NY, 99; Savage Gallery, Portland, Oreg, 2001; Santa Fe Art Inst, NMex, 2002; Tower Gallery, Hong Kong, 2004; Art In General, Through Our Eyes, 2004; The Transformer Room, Belfast, Ireland, 2006. *Pos:* Dir & cofounder, Art/OMI Int Artists Found, 92. *Teaching:* Asst prof painting, Brandeis Univ, 76-77; MFA fac, Sch Visual Arts, New York, 89-90; prof painting grad fac, Sch of Mus Fine Arts, Boston, 75-; Triangle Int Artists Colony, 82, 87, 90, Art On, 1992; Santa Fe Art Inst, 92. *Awards:* Ford Found Grant, 81; Artist-in-Residence, City Hall, Barcelona, Spain, 87 & 89; Mus Fine Arts Sabbatical, China, 85-87. *Bibliog:* Dominique Nahas (auth), Sandi Slone at Crestinerose Gallery, Review Mag, 12/99; Lilly Wei (auth), Sandi Slone at Cristinerose, ARTNEWS, 3/00; Cristopher Chambers (auth), Eternitas Interruptus, Sandi Slone at Cristinerose Gallery, FLASH Art, 2/00; Robert C. Morgan (auth), review, 99. *Mem:* Col Art Asn; Wellesley Col Friends Art. *Media:* All Media. *Dealer:* Cristinerose Gallery New York NY. *Mailing Add:* 13 Worth St New York NY 10013

SLONEM, HUNT
PAINTER, MURALIST
b Kittery, Maine, July 18, 51. *Study:* Skowhegan Sch Painting & Sculpture, 72; Tulane Univ, BA, 73. *Work:* Metrop Mus Art, NY; Birmingham Mus Art, Ala; Kemper Mus, Kans; Va Mus Fine Arts, Richmond; Solomon R Guggenheim Mus, NY; Whitney Mus. *Comn:* Fan Dance (mural), World Trade Port Authority Ctr, NY, 80; Bryand Park Grill, NYC. *Exhib:* Figurative Drawings, Va Mus Art (with catalog), Richmond, 85; Feathers, Fur & Fin, Laguna Gloria Mus, Austin, Tex, 90; Menagerie, Mus Mod Art, 90; solo exhibs, Ben Shahn Galleries, William Paterson Col, Wayne, NJ, 90, Harcourts Contemp Art, San Francisco, Calif, 91 & Tenn State Univ Mus, Nashville; Marlborough Gallery, NY; Colby Mus, Waterville, Maine; plus many others. *Awards:* Fel, Millay Colony Arts, 82, 83, 84 & 86; Painting Grant, Nat Endowment Arts, 91; MacDowell Fel, Skowhegan Alumnae. *Bibliog:* Ken Johnson (auth), NY Times, 99; Brooks Adams (auth), Treasure Hunt, Elle Decor, 1/99; Vincent Katz (auth), Animal, Vegetable, Mystical, Art in Am, 99; Donald Kuspit (auth), Art Rich & Strange. *Mem:* Art Committe New School, NYC; Skowhegan Alumni. *Media:* Oil on Canvas. *Interests:* collecting 19th Century houses. *Publ:* Illusr of three textbook. *Dealer:* Robert McClain Inc Houston TX; Marlborough Gallery New York NY. *Mailing Add:* 87 E Houston New York NY 10012

SLOSBURG-ACKERMAN, JILL
SCULPTOR, JEWELER
b Omaha, Nebr, Aug 28, 1948. *Study:* Tufts Univ, BFA, 71, MFA, 83; Sch Boston Mus Fine Arts, dipl. *Work:* Mass Col Art, Boston; Boston Pub Libr; Cranbrook Acad Art Mus, Bloomfield Hills, Mich; Robert Lee Morris; Union Pac Railroad, NY; Daphne Farago; JL Brandeis & Sons, Omaha, Nebr; City of Cambridge, Mass; The Mary Ingraham Bunting Inst, Cambridge, Mass. *Exhib:* Solo exhibs, Harcus-Krakow Gallery, Boston, Mass, 78, 80 & 85, Helen Shlien Gallery, Boston, Mass, 80 & 82, Cohen Arts Ctr, Tufts Univ, Medford, Mass, 82, Van Buren/Brazelton/Cutting Gallery, Cambridge, Mass, 85, Genovese Gallery, Boston, 95, Conn Col, 95, Rose Art Mus, Brandis Univ, 96, Univ Mass, Dartmouth, 99, Judy Ann Goldman Fine Art, 99 & 2004 & Gallery at Green St, Jamaica Plain, Mass, 99; Amerricky Sperk, Mus Decorative Arts, Prague, 91; Of Power, Myth, and Memory, Bellevue Art Mus, Wash, 92; Crossroads, (with catalog), Artwear, NY, 92; Material Boundaries Between the Sexes, Genovese Gallery Albany, Boston, 92; Schmuckzene (with catalog), Munich, Ger, 93;

Inside/Out (with catalog), Starr Gallery, Jewish Community Ctr, Newton, Mass, 93; Boston Mus Fine Arts, Traveling Scholars, 98; Annual Exhib, DeCordova Mus & Sculpture Park, Lincoln, Mass, 2000; Judy Ann Goldman Fine Art, Boston, 02; Forest Hills Cemetary, Boston, 02 & 04; Mills Gallery, Boston, 04; Fuller Craft Mus, Brocton, Mass, 05. *Pos:* founder, mem, Boston Women's Action Coalition; bd dir, Cambridge Multi-Cult Ctr, Gallery at Green St, Mass, 93. *Teaching:* prof arts, Mass Col Art, 72-; artist in residence, Cranbrook Acad Art, 93. *Awards:* NEA Artists Grants, 74 & 86; Fel, Artist Found, 84 & 91; Prof Develop Grant, Mass Col Art, 87; 20 x 24 Photog Grant, Polaroid Corp, 88; Boston Mus Fine Arts Traveling Scholar, 98; New Eng Found for the Arts Fel, 98; Mass Cult Coun Artist's Grant, 99 & 2006; Artist's Resource Trust, 01; New Eng Art Critics Asn Award, 2004 & 2006. *Bibliog:* Christine Temin (auth), Making Room for artworks, Boston Globe, 7/20/90; Ron Glowen (auth), These art works can be worn, be expressive & evocative, Herald, Seattle, Wash, 5/15/92; William Baran-Mickle (auth), Of Magic Power & Memory: Contemporary & International Jewelry, Metalsmith, fall 92; Lewin, Susan Grant (auth), One of a Kind: Art Jewelry Today, Abrams, 94; Turner, Ralph (auth), Jewelry in Europe & Am: New Times New Thinking, Thames & Hudson Ltd, 96; Articles in Boston Globe & Boston Phoenix, 90, 98-2000 & 2004; Ann Wilson Lloyd (auth), Art in America (review), 6/2005. *Media:* Wood; Found Furniture. *Dealer:* Judy Ann Goldman Fine Art 14 Newbury St Boston MA 02116. *Mailing Add:* C415 One Fitchburg St Apt C415 Somerville MA 02143-2128

SLOSHBERG, LEAH PHYFER
MUSEUM DIRECTOR

b New Albany, Miss, Feb 21, 37. *Study:* Miss State Col Women, BFA, 59; Tulane Univ, La, MA, 61; Univ Pa, Bryn Mawr, grad studies. *Pos:* Cur arts, NJ State Mus, Trenton, asst dir, 69-71, dir, 71-; bd mem, Conserv Ctr Art & Artifacts, 79 & Trenton Hist Soc, 87. *Mem:* Am Asn Mus; Conserv Ctr Art & Artifacts; Mid-Atlantic Asn Mus; NJ Asn Mus; Trenton Hist Soc. *Res:* American art; museum management. *Mailing Add:* New Jersey State Mus 205 W State St CN 530 Trenton NJ 08625

SLOTNICK, MORTIMER H
PAINTER, EDUCATOR

b New York, NY, Nov 7, 20. *Study:* City Col New York; Columbia Univ. *Work:* In pvt collections of Mrs Harry S Truman, Mrs Cordell Hull, Robert Merrill and others; New Brit Mus Am Art, Conn; Nat Mus Am Art, Smithsonian Inst; Johnson Art Mus, Cornell Univ; Nat Archives; and others. *Exhib:* Whitney Mus Am Art, Riverside Mus, Hudson River Mus, New Rochelle Pub Libr, Nat Acad Design, NY; and others. *Teaching:* Adj prof art & art educ, City Col New York; supvr arts & humanities, City Sch Dist, New Rochelle, NY; adj prof art educ, Col New Rochelle; adj prof educ, Pace Univ; principal, Davis Elem Sch, New Rochelle, NY. *Mem:* Allied Artists Am; Am Artists Prof League; Artists Equity, NY; Am Vet Soc Artists; Knickerbocker Artists, NY; Salmagundi Club, NY. *Media:* Oil, Drawing. *Publ:* Works publ by Am Artists Group, Donald Art Co, Bernard Picture Co, Scafa-Tornabene Art Publ & McCleery-Cummings Co. *Mailing Add:* 43 Amherst Dr New Rochelle NY 10804

SLOVIN, ROCHELLE
DIRECTOR

b New York, NY, Sept 24, 40. *Study:* Cornell Univ, BA, 62; Columbia Univ, MS, 74. *Pos:* dir Cult Coun Found, CETA Artists Project, 77-80; dir Am Mus of Moving Image, 81-. *Awards:* NY State Govs Arts Award, 02; City of MY Mayor's Award of Honor for Arts & Cluture, 92. *Mem:* Am Asn Mus; Nat Acad TV Arts & Scis. *Mailing Add:* Am Mus of Moving Image 35th Ave at 36th St Astoria NY 11106

SLUSKY, JOSEPH
SCULPTOR, EDUCATOR

b Philadelphia, Pa, June 7, 42. *Study:* Univ Calif, Berkeley, BA(arch), MA(art), studied with James Prestini, Ibram Lassaw, James Melchert, Wilfred Zogbaum, Sidney Gordin, Harold Paris, Richard O'Hanlon, William King & Robert Hudson. *Work:* Hayward Area Festival of the Arts, Calif; City San Francisco; San Francisco Dept Water. *Comn:* Outdoor sculpture, City Berkeley, 81; interior lobby sculpture, San Francisco Dept Water, 84; interior lobby sculpture, Peerless Lighting Corp, Berkeley, Calif, 89; interior lobby sculpture, Ctr for Middle Eastern Studies, Univ Calif, Berkeley, 2000; outdoor sculpture, Bayer Corp, Berkeley, Calif, 2002; Restoration, City Berkeley, 2004. *Exhib:* Outdoor Sculpture Exhib, Oakland Mus, Oakland, Calif, 94; Maquette Exhib, Mus Val'Aosta, Italy, 95; Interpretations of Light: Menorah Invitational, Jewish Mus, San Francisco, 95; Drawings & Sculpture, Galerie Johannestrasse, Erfurt, Ger, 96; Sculpture Survey 78-98, Oakland Mus Sculpture Ct, Calif, 99; Making Change: 100 Artists Interpret the Tzedakah Box, Jewish Mus, San Francisco, 2000; Steel Dreams, City of Oakland Craft and Cult Arts Gallery, Oakland, Calif, 2001; Scents of Purpose: Artists Interpret The Spice Box, The Contemp Jewish Mus San Francisco, 2005; and many others. *Teaching:* instr sculpture & drawing, Ohlone Col, Fremont, Calif, 72-85; lectr sculpture, Calif State Univ, San Francisco, 78, and others; sr lectr visual studies dept archit Univ Calif, Berkeley, 80-. *Awards:* Purchase Award, Hayward Festival of the Arts, 75 & 79; First Place Award, Bay Arts, Belmont, Calif, 87 & 90; Sculpture Award, Calif State Fair, 85, 88, 91, 92, 93, 94, 95 & 96; and others. *Bibliog:* Victoria Powers (auth), Contrasts of concepts and form, Artweek, 3/29/86; Andy Brumer (auth), Joe Slusky: The fluidity of feeling & the solidity of form, Visions Art Quarterly, spring 94; Jack Foley (auth), Better Living Through Alchemy, The East Bay Express, 3/12/99; Philip Isaacson (auth), Pairing of Artists Provokes, Stimulates, Maine Sunday Telegraph, 11/19/2000; Jakob Schiller (auth), Calliope Shines Again at Marina Mall, Berkeley Daily Planet, 10/29/2005; others; Andy Brumer (auth), The Artist and the Dance, 360: Life From Every Angle, summer 2006. *Media:* Painted Steel; Drawing, Mixed Media. *Publ:* Art in The San Francisco Bay Area 1945-1980; Thomas Albright (auth), Univ of CA Press, 1980. *Dealer:* Sculpture Site Gallery Conv Plaza 201 Third St Ste 102 San Francisco CA 94103. *Mailing Add:* 1727 8th St Berkeley CA 94710

SMALL, DEBORAH
PAINTER

b Mariemont, Ohio, Oct 28, 48. *Study:* Univ Pa, BS, 70; Univ Calif, Irvine, BA, 80; Univ Calif, San Diego, MFA, 83. *Exhib:* IMAG(in)ING CULTURE/African Am and Chicano Visual Art, Univ Tex, Austin, 94; Does It Come in Another Colour?, Inst Contemp Art Cinematique, London, Eng, 94; History 101, Forum Contemp Art, St Louis, Mo, 94; The Box Show, Children's Mus, San Diego, Calif, 94; Timken Mus Art, San Diego, Calif, 94. *Pos:* Art ed, Fiction International, San Diego State Univ Press, Calif, 84-90. *Teaching:* Asst prof visual arts, Calif State Univ, San Marcos, 92-. *Awards:* Painting Fel, 87 & 89 & Interarts Grant, 90 & 91, Nat Endowment Arts; Art Matters Grant, 92; Headliner of the Year Award in Arts, San Diego Press Club, 93. *Bibliog:* Collette Chattopadhyay (auth), Two thousand miles of misery: A phenomenon called border art, Artweek, vol, 24, 93; Miguel Mora & Jesus Ruiz Mantilla (auths), En la Frontera, El Pais Int, 3/1/93; Deborah L Knaff (auth), A collection of cultures, The Press-Enterprise, 3/28/93. *Mailing Add:* Calif State Univ San Marcos CA 92096

SMALL, NEAL
CONCEPTUAL ARTIST, DESIGNER

b New York, NY, Aug 4, 37. *Study:* Tex A&M Sch Archit, 54-55; WVa Wesleyan, 56-57. *Work:* Mus Mod Art, NY; Brooklyn Mus; Philadelphia Mus Art; Albright-Knox Art Gallery, Buffalo, NY; Dallas Mus Fine Arts; Mus of Mus, Waregem, Belg; and others. *Exhib:* Excellence in Design, 67, 68 & 69, Brooklyn Mus, 67, Smithsonian Inst, DC, 68 & Mus Sci & Indust, Chicago, 69; Flint Invitational, Flint Inst Art, Dc Waters Art Ctr, Flint, Mich, 71; one-man show, Mus Univ SFla, 71; AIR Gallery, 81. *Collection Arranged:* Environment, St Louis Mus, 70; US Info Agency Show, Zagreb, Yugoslavia, 71, Bucharest, Romania, 72. *Pos:* Pres, Neal Small Designs, New York, 66-73 & Squire & Small, 74-79. *Awards:* Awards for excellence of design, An Design Revs, Indust Design, 68-70. *Mem:* St Simian Soc (pres, 81-). *Media:* Acrylic, Bronze and Collage. *Publ:* Articles, NY Times; articles, Industrial Design Mag; articles, Home Furnishings Daily; articles, Life Mag; Plastic as Design Form, Chilton. *Dealer:* George Beylerian 16 E 77 New York NY 10021

SMALLEY, DAVID ALLAN
SCULPTOR, EDUCATOR

b New London, Conn, Dec 17, 40. *Study:* RI Sch Design, 58-60; Univ Conn, with Antony Padovano, BFA, 63; Ind Univ with Jean-Paul Darriau, MFA, 65. *Work:* Lyman Allyn Mus & Conn Col, New London; State of Conn Superior Ct. *Comn:* Warlock III (cor-ten steel), Conn Commission Arts, New London, 73; State of Conn Ocean Clouds 35 ft suspended kinetic, Conn Comn on the Arts; Ad-Astra, stainless steel (10 ft), Conn Col. *Exhib:* Conn Painting, Drawing & Sculpture, Univ Bridgeport, New Britain Mus & Conn Col, 79; Penwith Gallery, Cornwall, Eng, 79; Krausaar Galleries, NY, 80-81; one-man show, Lyman Allyn Mus, New London, Conn, 81 & Kraushaar Galleries, NY, 84, 87, 90 & 93; Vangarde Gallery, New London, Conn, 87 & 90. *Pos:* Bd dir, Art Resources Conn, 75-80; pres, Vangarde Co-op Gallery, 86; co-dir, Ctr Arts Technol, Conn Col. *Teaching:* Prof sculpture & Henry B Plant prof art, Conn Col, 65-. *Awards:* Ingram Merrill Found Grant, 69; Research Grant, Dana Found, 80. *Bibliog:* Barbara Zabel (auth), Profile, Art Voices, 7-8/81 & review, Arts Mag, 4/84, review Sculpture Mag, 9/87. *Mem:* Mystic Art Asn; Vangarde Co-op Gallery. *Media:* Stainless Steel, Brass. *Dealer:* Kraushaar Galleries 724 5th Ave New York NY

SMALLEY, STEPHEN FRANCIS
EDUCATOR, PAINTER

b Rockville, Conn, Apr 14, 41. *Study:* Mass Col Art, BS, 63; State Col, Boston, MEd, 65; Pa State Univ, DEd, 70. *Work:* Bridgewater State Col, Mass; Mansfield State Col, Pa; RI Col. *Exhib:* Mass Col Art, Arnheim Gallery, 93; Touching All The Bases, Gallery 53, Cooperstown, NY, 96; The Word Is Art, Manchester Metrop Univ, 96; From Baseball Cards to Tutti Frutti, Univ Mass, Lowell, 98; Popular Celebrities & Personal Celebrations, Monmouth Univ, NJ, 2001; When I'm Sixty-four, Bridgewater State Col. *Teaching:* Fac art, Rindge Tech High Sch, Cambridge, Mass, 63-65; teaching asst design & printmaking, Pa State Univ, 65-67; assoc prof & chmn, Dept Art Educ, Tyler Sch Art, 67-72; chmn dept art, Bridgewater State Col, Mass, 72-84, prof, 72-05; fac assoc, Wadham Col, Bridgewater-at-Oxford, 96-; vis lectr, Bridgewater, Mass col, 2005. *Awards:* Outstanding Art Teacher Award, Mass Art Educ Asn, 85; Grant, Bridgewater State Col, Mass, 93, 98 & 2000; Mass Higher Educ Art Educator of Yr, 2000. *Mem:* Nat Art Educ Asn; Mass Art Educ. *Media:* Acrylics, Pen & Ink, pencil. *Interests:* British art, pop cult. *Publ:* Auth, Fungoes That Go Pop, A Teaching Compendium of Art Essays Tied to Pop Culture and the Classroom, 97; A Book of Yells (painting, poetry, & prose), 99; Lights Camera Cannes (painting, photog, poetry & prose); Coming Ashore (painting & prose), 2005. *Mailing Add:* 144 Atkinson Dr Bridgewater MA 02324

SMART, MARY-LEIGH
CONSULTANT, PATRON

b Springfield, Ill, Feb 27, 17. *Study:* Oxford Univ, dipl Extra Mural Delegacy, 35; Wellesley Col, BA, 37; Columbia Univ, MA, 39; also with Bernard Karfiol, 38-39. *Collection Arranged:* Art: Ogunquit, A National Exhibition of Artists Who Have Worked in Ogunquit (auth, catalog), 67, Peggy Bacon, A Celebration (auth, catalog), 79 & three exhibitions each season, 80-86, Barn Gallery, Ogunquit, Maine. *Pos:* Founding secy & prog dir, Barn Gallery Assocs, Ogunquit, Maine, 58-78; cur, Hamilton Easter Field Art Found Collection, 66-79, pres, 69-70 & 82-87, hon dir, 71-78, cur exhibs, 79-86, chair exhib comt, 87-94, vpres, 94-; founding mem bd adv, Univ Art Galleries, Univ NH, 73-89, vpres, 75-81, pres, 81-89; mem coun adv, Farnsworth Art Mus, 86-98; mem mus panel, Maine Arts Comn, 83-86; mem collections comt, Payson Gallery, Westbrook Col, Portland, Maine, 87-90; founder, Surf Point Found, a non-profit art found, York, Maine, 88; Mem, Maine Womens

Forum, 93-; corporator, Ogunquit Mus Am Art, 88-90 & 95-2000. *Awards:* Deborah Morton Award, Westbrook Col, Portland, Me, 88; Friend of Arts Award, Maine Art Dealers Asn, 93. *Bibliog:* Louise Balch Hatfield (auth), Art Foundation, Wellesley, summer 92; Alice Giordano (auth), A Foundation for New England artists, Boston Sunday Globe, 1/7/98; Virginia L Woodwell (auth), Artists colony to be patron's legacy, NY Weekly, 1/7/98. *Mem:* Fel Portland Mus Art, Maine; Nat Comt Friends Art, Wellesley Col. *Interests:* Contemporary art. *Collection:* Twentieth century New England painting and sculpture; American, European and Asian contemporary graphics; photography. *Publ:* Auth, Hamilton Easter Field Art Foundation Collection (catalog), 66; Ed, A Century of Color, Ogunquit, Maine's Art Colony, 1886-1986, Barn Gallery Assocs Pub, 87; J Scott Smart AKA, The Fat Man, pvt publ, 94; coauth (Beverly Hallam), Maine is their Mentor, Maine Arts Comn Mag, winter 2006. *Mailing Add:* 30 Surf Point Rd York ME 03909-5053

SMEDLEY, GEOFFREY
EDUCATOR, SCULPTOR
b London, Eng, Feb 24, 27. *Study:* Camberwell Sch Art, London; Slade Sch Fine Arts, London, 54. *Work:* Victoria & Albert Mus & Arts Coun Gt Brit, London. *Comn:* Sculpture Garden, Commune Pirano, Istria, Yugoslavia, 72; Southern Arts Asn Eng, Portsmouth, 74; set design, Freddy Wood Theatre; Rowingbridge, a 50 foot high kinetic sculpture, Expo 86. *Exhib:* Whitechapel Art Gallery, 72; Arts Coun, traveling, 73 & 76; Agnes Etherington Art Ctr, Queen's Univ, Kingston, Ont, 78; Nature as Material, traveling, Eng, 80-81; solo exhib, Vancouver Art Gallery, BC, 82; Vancouver Art & Artists, Vancouver Art Gallery (with catalog), 83; Canada Collects, Art Bank & traveling USA; Making Hist, Vancouver Art Gallery, 86; traveling show, Memory, Measure, Time and Numbers, 00; Pietro en tete: Meditation on Piero, 01; one man show, Memory, Measure, Time and Numbers, Suncy inst Art & Design, Univ Col, UK; Memory, Measure, Time & Numbers, Yorkshire Sculpture Park, UK. *Teaching:* Prof fine arts, Univ BC, 78-, emer prof, 92-. *Awards:* Proj Art Award, Arts Coun Great Brit, 72; Sculpture award, West Gate Plaza Expo 86; Materials Grant, 85 & Sr Grant, 87, Can Coun; Can Coun Travel Grant, 00; Can Coun A Grant, 01; Fel Anni and Josef Albers Found, Conn, 01; Daniel Langois Found Award, 02. *Bibliog:* Memory, Measure, Time & Numbers, Suncy Inst Art & Design, Univ College, 69 pp; Piero en Tete-Canadian Ctr for Architecture, Montreal, 63 pp. *Mailing Add:* RR 3 Gambier Island Gibsons BC V0N 1V0 Canada

SMEDSTAD, DEBORAH BARLOW
LIBRARIAN
b Cooperstown, NY, Dec 14, 58. *Study:* Univ San Diego, BA, 81; Simmons Col Grad Sch Libr & Info Sci, MS, 84; Boston Univ Grad Sch Arts Sci, MA, 85. *Pos:* Visual resources librn, Cooper Union Libr, 85-87; art librn, asst prof & cur, Queens Col, 87-90; reference librn, Univ SCalif, Archit Fine Arts Libr, 90-94; head librn, Los Angeles Co Mus Art, 95-2003; head librn, Mus Fine Arts, Boston, 2003-. *Mem:* Art Libr Soc NAm. *Interests:* Seventeenth-twentieth century western art, general western art & American art. *Publ:* contribr, Hendrick Goltzius and the Classical Tradition, Fisher Gallery, Univ SCalif, 92; Richard Diebenkorn: Prints from the Harry W and Mary Margaret Anderson Collection, Fisher Gallery, Univ SCalif, 93. *Mailing Add:* William Morris Hunt Libr Mus Fine Arts 465 Huntington Ave Boston MA 02115

SMIGOCKI, STEPHEN VINCENT
PAINTER, PRINTMAKER
b Washington, DC, Nov 20, 42. *Study:* Univ Md, BA(fine arts), 64, MA(drawing), 68; Univ SFla, Tampa; Fla State Univ, painting with Karl Zerbe, PhD(art educ). *Work:* Ringling Mus, Sarasota, Fla; Huntington Gallery, WVa; WVa Sci & Cult Complex, Sunrise Gallery, Charleston. *Exhib:* Dallas Summer Arts Festival Nat Competition, Tex, 71; Biennial I Six-State Painting Competition, Va Commonwealth Univ, 73; Drawings '74 Nat Exhib, Wheaton Col, Norton, Mass; Thirteen State Regional Exhib, Appalachian Corridors, Charleston, WVa, 75; All WVa Exhib, Charleston, 79, 81, 83, 85 & 89; Huntington Galleries, 79, 83 & 88. *Pos:* Graphic artist, Univ Md Ctr Adult Educ, 64-66. *Teaching:* Prof art, Fairmont State Col, WVa, 72-. *Awards:* Purchase Awards, Huntington Galleries Exhib 280, WVa, 72 & Appalachian Corridors, 75; merit award, All WVa Exhib, Charleston, 79. *Bibliog:* Art Pedagogy of Paul Klee and Wassily Kandinsky (dissertation). *Mem:* Los Angeles Printmaking Soc. *Media:* Etching; woodcut. *Publ:* Contribr, Echo Without Sound, Northwoods Press, 80; illus, Perspectives Mag Fairmont State Col, Fall, 91. *Dealer:* Bill Tomlinson Garo Gallery Morgantown WV. *Mailing Add:* 1205 Peacock Ln Fairmont WV 26554

SMIRA, SHAOUL
PAINTER
b Oct 10, 39. *Study:* Auni Art Inst, Tel-Aviv, 58-61; Acad Chomier, Paris, 65-66; Graphics study: etching & lythography, USA, 1969-72; The Art Paper Making, Belgium, 1975-79. *Work:* Tel-Aviv Mus, Israel; Rockefeller Art Ctr, NY; Fine Art Mus, Ostend, Belg; Fredrick Weisman Found, Los Angeles, Calif; Bank Paribas Collection, Bruselles, Belg. *Comn:* Sheraton Hotel, Tel-Aviv, 64; Beth Yeshuron Congregation, Houston, Tex 79; Collabr, Beth-El, Baltimore, Md, 82. *Exhib:* Contemp Israel Koninklijk, Belg, 85; The Concern Eyes, Port of Hist, Philadelphia, 86; Arbitrariness, Israeli Art, Ramat, Gan, 90; Collection, Skir Ball, Los Angeles, 91; solo exhib, Mus de la Nacion, Lima, Peru, 95, Gallereia et Museo, Bogota, Columbia, 2001, Gallery Guy Pieters, Knokke-Zoute, Belgium, 2003, July M. Gallery, Tel-Aviv, Israel, 2003, Galerie Guy Pieters, Saint-Paul de Vence, France, 2004 & 05, De Latemse Galerij, Sint-Martens-Latem, Belgium, 2006; Cahn Gal, New York, 2000; Anne Frank, Syracuse Univ, New York, 2001. *Bibliog:* Kuspit Donald (auth), Art of Moral Mission, Flash Art, 86; The desire of Planet Earth, Kunst & Colture, 93; Gerard Goodrow (auth), Creative Chaos, Am House, 95. *Media:* Multi Media. *Dealer:* Alex Kahan Medison New York NY. *Mailing Add:* 451 Broome St New York NY 10013

SMITH, AJ
PRINTMAKER
b Jonestown, Miss, Mar 10, 52. *Study:* Skowhogan Sch Painting & Sculpture, 73; Kansas City Art Inst, BFA, 74; Queens Col/CUNY, MFA, 77; Apprenticed with Robert Blackburn 77-82. *Hon Degrees:* Master Printer, Printmaking Workshop Inc, NYC. *Work:* Columbia Mus, SC; Philadelphia Mus of Art; Printmaking Workshop Inc, NY; Ark Arts Ctr Found Collection, Little Rock; Schomburg Res Ctr, New York City; Libr Congress, Washington, DC. *Comn:* Dream Microcosm Series, Henderson State Univ, Arkadelphia, Ark, 89; Dream Macrocosm Series, Southeast Ark Art Ctr, Pine Bluff, 90; Fellowship Edition, Brandywine Ctr Creative Arts, Philadelphia, 92; Life Series and Quiet Series, Cent Ark Pub Libr, Little Rock, 97; CALM Monoprint Series, Convention and Civic Ctr, Hot Springs, Ark, 98. *Exhib:* Impressive Expressions, Smithsonian Inst Traveling Exhib Series, 79-89; Prints of the City, Mus of the City of NY, 81; Way Down South Series, Ark Art Ctr, Little Rock, 83; In a Stream of Ink, Bronx Mus of Art, NY, 86; Acquisition Invitational, Philadelphia Mus Art, 94; Artist of Color, Albany Inst of History & Art, 95; 25th Anniversary Celebration, Longview Art Mus, Tex, 95; African-Am Artist, Carnegie Hall Mus, Lewisburg, WVa, 2000; 18th Southwest Comp Invitational, Mus African Am Art, Dallas, Tex; Black Romantic, Studio Mus, Harlem, NY, 02; Drawing VI, Koplin Gallery, Los Angeles, 02; In Print: The Language of Art, Fla State Univ Art Mus, Tallahassee, 03. *Pos:* Master printer Printmaking Workshop, Inc, NY, 78-82; Mentor Pratt Integrative Studies, Pratt Inst, Brooklyn, 79-80; Artist in Residence, Ark Arts Ctr, Little Rock, 82-83. *Teaching:* Adj prof art appreciation, Upper Montclair State Col, NJ, 79-82; Adj prof drawing, La Guardia Community Col, Long Island City, NY, 79-81; Prof drawing & printmaking, Univ Ark at Little Rock, 82-. *Awards:* Artist in Residence, Studio Mus in Harlem, 78-79; Mid-Am Arts Alliance/NEA, 84; Fel, Vt Studio Ctr, 97; Fel, Ark Arts Coun/NEA, 99. *Bibliog:* Xian Rang Yong (auth), Fine Art Society, Lu Xun Fine Art Inst Jour, 87; Xian Rang Yong (auth), Artist Anthology, Beijing Graphic Art Publishing House, 93; Halima Taha (auth) Collecting African American Art, Craven Publishing, Inc, 98. *Mem:* Ark Arts Ctr, Little Rock; Printmaking Workshop Inc, New York City; Kansas City Art Inst Alumni Asn; Skowhegah Sch of Painting and Sculpture Alumni Asn. *Media:* Drawing, Monoprint, Monotype, Lithography. *Res:* Traditional limestone lithography. *Dealer:* Mary Pauline 982 Broad St Augusta GA 30901; MCS Gallery 1110 Northampton St Easton Pa 18042. *Mailing Add:* 1709 S Arch St Little Rock AR 72206

SMITH, ALBERT E
PAINTER
b San Francisco, Calif, 1929. *Study:* Univ Calif, Berkeley. *Work:* Achenbach Found, Calif Palace Legion of Hon, San Francisco; Stanford Univ Art Mus, Calif; Triton Mus, Santa Clara, Calif; Oakland Mus, Calif; Univ Calif, Davis. *Exhib:* Marunouchi Gallery, Tokyo, Japan, 84, 86, 91; Anthony Ralph Gallery, NY, 87, 89; Roger Ramsay Gallery, Chicago, 89; 871 Fine Arts, San Francisco, 91-93 & 98; retrospective 1954-1994, Triton Mus, Santa Clara, Calif, 95-2005; Kurt Lidtke Fine Art, Wash, 96; solo exhibs, Kurt Lidke Gallery, Seattle, Wash, 96 & 871 Fine Arts, San Francisco, 98; Perimeter Gallery, Chicago, 2000. *Publ:* Asteion, Japan, 88; Art of California, 3-4/93; California Vistas: 10 Paintings by Albert Smith, 95. *Dealer:* Perimeter Gallery Chicago IL; Anne Berthoud Gallery London Eng. *Mailing Add:* 1425 Wendy Way Menlo Park CA 94025

SMITH, ALEXIS (PATRICIA ANNE)
COLLAGE ARTIST, CONCEPTUAL ARTIST
b Los Angeles, Calif, Aug 24, 49. *Study:* Univ Calif, Irvine, 66-70, BA (art), 70; study with Robert Irwin & Vija Celmins. *Work:* Whitney Mus Am Art; Mus Contemp Art, Los Angeles; Walker Art Ctr, Minneapolis. *Comn:* Monuments, MacArthur Park Pub Art Prog, Los Angeles, 86; Snake Path, Stuart Collection, Univ Calif, San Diego, La Jolla; South & West Lobby Terrazzo floors, Los Angeles Conv Ctr Expansion; mixed media, murals, Getty Ctr Restaurant; Terrazzo, Schotten Stein Arena, Getty Ctr, Columbus, Ohio. *Exhib:* Lowe, Munger, Smith, Wilson, Los Angeles Co Mus Art, 72; Four Los Angeles Artists, Corcoran Gallery Am Art, Washington, DC, 75; Whitney Biennial, Whitney Mus Am Art, NY, 75, 79, 81; solo exhibs, Whitney Mus Am Art, 75, Rosamund Felsen Gallery, 78, 80, 82, De Appel, Amsterdam, 79, Walker Art Ctr, 86, Inst Contemp Art, Boston, 86, Margo Leavin Gallery 82, 85, 88, 90, 95, 99, Aspen Art Mus, 87, Brooklyn Mus, 87-88, Wexner Ctr for the Arts, Ohio State Univ, 97, 98, Miami Art Mus, 00, Lawrence Rubin Greenbery Van Doren Fine Art, NYC, 01, Mus Contemp Art, San Diego, 01; Am Narrative/Story Art, Contemp Art Mus, Houston, Tex, 77, J Paul Getty Mus, 97; Holly Solomon Gallery, 77, 78, 79, 81, 83; Narration, Inst Contemp Art, Boston, 78; Mus as Site, Los Angeles Co Mus Art, 81; New Directions, Hirshhorn Mus & Sculpture Garden, 83; Verbally Charged Images, Independent Curators, 84-86; Mus Mod Art, NY, 84; Individuals, Mus Contemp Art, Los Angeles, 86-88; Josh Baer Gallery, 90; Retrospective exhib, Whitney Mus Am Art, Mus Cont Art, Los Angeles, 91-92; Whitney Mus Am Art, New York City, 01, Margo Leavin Gallery, Los Angeles, 02, Japanese Am Nat Mus, 02; and others. *Teaching:* Instr, Univ Calif, Los Angeles, 79-88, Skowhegan, 90 & Southern Methodist Univ, Tex, 93. *Awards:* New Talent Award, Contemp Arts Coun, Los Angeles Co Mus Art, 74; Nat Endowment Arts Fel Grant, 76-77, 87-88; Residency, Rockefeller Found Study Ctr, Bellagio, Italy, 95; Terrazzo Job of the Year, Nat Terrazzo & Mosaic Asn, 99, Epoxy Terrazzo Job of the Century, 00; COLA Individual Artist Fel, 02. *Bibliog:* Nancy Marmer (auth), Alexis Smith: The narrative act, Artforum, 12/76; Leo Rubinfien, Through western eyes, Art in Am, 9-10/78; Hunter Drohojowska (auth), Alexis Smith: The Public Works, Artspace, Summer 91; Richard Armstrong (auth), Alexis Smith (catalog Bk), publ Rizzoli, 91; Grace Glueck (auth), NY Times, B36, 4/6/2001. *Media:* Multimedia, Public Art. *Publ:* Contribr centerfold, Avalanche, fall 75; auth, Alone, 77; contribr, Italics, Paris Rev, spring 79; Shanghai Express, Los Angeles Herald-Examiner, 11/81; coauth, Past Lives,(with Amy Gerstler), 89. *Dealer:* Margo Leavin Gallery 812 N Robertson Blvd Los Angeles CA 90069. *Mailing Add:* 1907 Lincoln Blvd Venice CA 90291

SMITH, ANDREA B
PAINTER
b Detroit, Mich, June 29, 46. *Study:* Wayne State Univ, BA, 67. *Work:* Pearson Art Found Mus, Des Moines, Iowa; Pereslaul Mus, Russ; Univ Peace, San Jose, Costa Rica. *Comn:* Painting, Am Vet Vietnam War, NY, 87; Preuss Found, La Jolla, Calif, 88; Group Health Found, Seattle, 89; Writers Companion (painting), Prentice Hall, NY, 90; painting, Waokele Opuna-Rainforest, Hilo, Hawaii, 90. *Exhib:* Watercolor, Mich Watercolor Soc, Detroit, 79; 31st Ann Exhib, Knickerbocker Artists, NY, 81; Bakersfield Col, Calif, 83; Contemp Art, Am Mus, Williamsburg, Va, 86; Art for Peace, Womens Nat Bank, Washington, DC, 86, Irving Ctr Art Mus, 87 & Children's Russ Bibliotech, Moscow, 87. *Awards:* Best of Show, Mich Watercolor Soc, 79 & Musee de Duncan, 81. *Bibliog:* Jamie Forbes (auth), Sunstrom Mag, 86. *Media:* Watercolor, Acrylic. *Mailing Add:* 1590 Lokia St Lahaina HI 96761

SMITH, ANN Y
MUSEUM DIRECTOR, CURATOR
b Alma, Mich, Oct 7, 50. *Study:* Univ Mich, BA, 72; State Univ NY, MA, 73; Univ Conn Law Sch, JD, 91. *Collection Arranged:* Fiddlebacks and Crooked-backs, 82; Connecticut Masters, 86; Brass Valley, 86. *Pos:* Asst cur, Hist Soc York Co, Pa, 73-74; dir, Lyme Hist Soc, Conn, 74-76; Mattatuck Mus, Waterbury, Conn, 76-. *Teaching:* Adj fac, Univ Conn, Archit Hist. *Mem:* Conn Comn Arts (art selection panel); New Eng Mus Asn; Am Asn Mus; Conn Mus Asn (chair); New Eng Found Arts (bd mem). *Publ:* Ed, Minds and Machines: Waterbury at Work, Mattatuck Hist Soc, 80; William Merit Post (essay), 97; auth, AT Van Laer, 98. *Mailing Add:* Mattatuck Mus 144 W Main St Waterbury CT 06702

SMITH, ANNA DEAVERE
PATRON
b Baltimore, MD, Sept 18, 50. *Study:* Beaver Col, Pa, BA, 71; Am Conservatory Theatre, MFA, 77. *Hon Degrees:* Beaver Col, Pa, Hon Dr, 73; Univ NC, Hon Dr, 95; numerous hon degrees from US cols & univs, 95-97. *Pos:* Founding dir, Inst Arts & Civic Dialogue Harvard Univ, 98; trustee, Mus Modern Art, New York City. *Teaching:* artist-in-residence, Ford Found, 97; prof arts & drama, Ann O'Day Maples, Stanford Univ. *Awards:* Named One of Women of Year, Glamour Mag, 93; fel, Bunting Inst, Radcliffe Col; genius fel, The MacArthur Found, 96. *Publ:* Playwright, performer one-woman shows On the Road: A Search for American Character, 83, Aye, Aye, Aye, I'm Integrated, 84, Piano, 91, Fires in the Mirror, 89, Twilight: Los Angeles 92, House Arrest, 1997; writer, libretto for Judith Jamison, performer Hymn, 93; appeared in (films) Dave, 93, Philadelphia, 93, The American President, 95, Twilight: Los Angeles, 2000. *Mailing Add:* 1460 4th St Ste 212 Santa Monica CA 90401-3414

SMITH, B J
MUSEUM DIRECTOR, INSTRUCTOR
b Beaver, Okla, Aug 22, 31. *Study:* Okla State Univ, Stillwater, BFA, 55; Univ Okla, Norman, MFA, 59. *Work:* Joslyn Art Mus, Omaha, Nebr; Mus Art, Univ Okla, Norman; State Collection of Okla Artists & Craftsmen, Oklahoma City; Okla Art Ctr, Oklahoma City. *Exhib:* Ann Eight State Exhib, 63, 64, 68, 70 & 74, 13 Artists You Should Collect, 65, Okla Art Ctr, Oklahoma City; solo exhib, WNebr Arts Ctr, Scottsbluff, 83, Tex Wesleyan Col, Ft Worth, Tex, 86, WNebr Arts Ctr, Scottsbluff, 87, Western Okla Images, Pioneer Mus, Woodward, 87 & Ecent, Ada, Okla, 94; Pioneer Mus & Arts Ctr, Woodward, Okla, 83; Small Wonders, Kirkpatrick Ctr, Oklahoma City, 90; Okla Small Works 2, E Cent, Ada, 92; Tom Preston Mem Exhib, Alexandra, La, 92; 25th Ann, W Nebr Arts Ctr, Scottsbluff, 92; and others. *Pos:* Asst to dir, Okla Art Ctr, Oklahoma City, 61-65; dir, Gardiner Art Gallery, Okla State Univ, 65-94. *Teaching:* Assoc prof color & design, Okla State Univ, 65-81, assoc prof, 81-94; retired. *Awards:* Purchase Awards, Ninth Midwest Biennial, Joslyn Art Mus, Omaha, 66, Okla Biennial, Okla Art Ctr, Oklahoma City, 67 & Okla Artists Ann, Philbrook Art Ctr, Tulsa, 68. *Media:* Acrylic on Masonite. *Mailing Add:* 2132 W Sunset Dr Stillwater OK 74074

SMITH, BARBARA TURNER
VIDEO & PERFORMANCE ARTIST, EDUCATOR
b Pasadena, Calif, July 6, 31. *Study:* Pomona Col, BA, 53; Chouinard Art Inst, with Emerson Woelfer, 65; workshops with Alex Hay, 68 & Steve Paxton, 69; Univ Calif, Irvine, with Bob Irwin, Barbara Rose, Moira Roth & Larry Bell, MFA, 71. *Work:* Newport Harbor Art Mus, Newport Beach, Calif; Herbert F Johnson, Cornell Univ; Mus Mod Art; Frac des Pays De La Loire; Pomona Col Mus of Art. *Comn:* Capp Street Proj, Installation/Performance 84; SPARC, Community-Wide Performance, 89. *Exhib:* People Who Should Be Seen, Los Angeles Co Art Mus, Los Angeles, 65; Performance Conf, Womanspace & Woman's Bldg, 73,75, & 77; Retrospective (auth, catalog), Univ Calif, San Diego, 74; 60-80 Show Stedelijk Mus, Amsterdam, 82; Endurance, Exit Art, NY, 95; MAC galerie contemporaines des Musee de Marseilles l'art au Corpo, 96; Out of Action (with catalog), Mus Contemp Art, Los Angeles, 98 & Between Performance & the Object: 1949-1979 (with catalog), 98; Centre Georges Pompidou, Paris, (Los Angeles 1955-1985), 2006. *Pos:* Co-founder, F-Space Gallery, Santa Ana, Calif, 70-72; founding mem, Grandview I & II Gallery & The Women's Bldg, Los Angeles, 73-75; organizer, New Dimensions in Sci series, Los Angeles Inst Contemp Art, 75; Dir, New Gallery, Santa Monica, Calif, 94-96. *Teaching:* Fac fel art, Univ Redlands, Calif, 74-; vis performance artist, Univ Calif, San Diego, 77; vis artist, San Francisco Art Inst, 78, Ohio State Univ, 90; lectr, Univ Calif, Los Angeles, 79-82, Univ Calif, San Diego, 78, 86 & 93; vis artist design, Otis Col Art, 96. *Awards:* Nat Endowment Arts Grant, 74, 79 & 85; Woman's Bldg Vista Award, Los Angeles, 83; Nat Honorary Award, Women's Caucus Arts, 99. *Bibliog:* Moira Roth (auth), The Amazing Decade: Women in Performance Art 1970-1980, 83; Linda Burnham (auth), Performance Art in Southern Calif: an overview, High Performance Mag, Vol 2 No 3; Tom Marioni (auth), l'Art corporel et ses Origines eo Caliponie Internationoules, l'Art au Corps, 96; Laura Cottingham (auth), Are You Experienced (catalog essay), l'Art au Corps, 96. *Mem:* Los Angeles Contemp Exhibs; Women's Caucus Art; Mus Contemp Art; Santa Monica Mus Art. *Media:* Body and Video. *Publ:* Auth, Rope, pvt publ, 71; Burden case tried, dismissed, Artweek, 73; Women in industry, Los Angeles Inst Contemp Art J, 74; contribr, Buddha mind performance, In: Vision, Crown, 75; auth, Rachel Rosenthal performs Charm, Artweek, 2/77; Notes on Allan Kaprow, Mus Am O St Wall, Dortmund, Ger, 87. *Mailing Add:* 801 Coeur d'Alene Venice CA 90291

SMITH, BARRIE CALABRESE See Van Osdell, Barrie (Calabrese) Smith

SMITH, CARY
PAINTER
b Puerto Rico, 1955; US citizen. *Study:* Sir John Cass Art Sch, London, Eng, 76; Syracuse Abroad, Florence, Italy, 76; Syracuse Univ Art Sch, NY, BFA, 77. *Work:* Whitney Mus Am Art, NY; Brooklyn Mus, NY; Osaka Art Mus, Japan; Wadsworth Atheneum, Hartford, Conn. *Exhib:* Solo exhibs, Linda Cathcart Gallery, Santa Monica, 91, Stephen Wirtz Gallery, San Francisco, Calif, 91, Rubin Spangle Gallery, NY, 92, Roger Ramsay Gallery, Chicago, 93, Salvatore Ala Gallery, NY, 93-94, Galerie Paal, Munich, Ger, 95 & 97, Derek Eller, NY, 97, 99 & 2000; Whitney Biennial, Whitney Mus Am Art, NY, 89; Selection from the Collection: Art of the 80's, Whitney Mus Am Art, NY, 91; group exhibs, Wadsworth Atheneum, Hartford, Conn, 92, Rubin Spangle Gallery, NY, 92, August Confessions, Geoffrey Young Gallery, Great Barrington, MA, Boomerang, Collector's Choice, Exit Art, NY, 2001, Loss & Ardor, Geoffrey Young Gallery, Great Barrington, MA & Anna Appleby, Mala Breuer, Wes Mills, Cary Smith, Galerie Susan Albrecht, Munich, Ger, 2002; The Geometric Tradition in Am Art, Whitney Mus Am Art, NY, 93; The Uses of Geometry-Then and Now, Snyder Fine Arts, NY, 93; NY Abstract Painting, Salvatore Ala Gallery, NY, 94; Lawrence Markey Inc, NY, 96; Paol Gallery, Munich, Austria, 97. *Awards:* Nat Endowment Arts Fel, 91-92; Pollack Krasner Found Grant, 93-94; Artist Enhancement Prog, Wash Nat Airport, 94-97. *Bibliog:* Barry Schwabsky (auth), Carey Smith at Salvatore Ala, Art Forum, 4/94; Ken Johnson & Cany Smith (auths), Derek Eller, Art Guide, NY Times, 10/17/97; Faye Hirsch & Cary Smith (auths), Red Print Suite No 1, Rev of Prints, On Paper, 4/98; Holland Carter (auth), Bill De Lottie and Cary Smith at Derek Miller, New York Times, Art in Review, 6/18/99; Roberta Smith (auth), Cary Smith at Derek Miller, Art Guide, New York Times, 4/17/2000. *Dealer:* Lawrence Markey Inc 55 Van Dam New York NY. *Mailing Add:* PO Box 924 Farmington CT 06034

SMITH, CLARE
APPRAISER
Study: Oxford Univ. *Pos:* Specialist, Victorian Picture Dept, Christie's, NYC, 99; specialist, Sporting Art, currently. *Mailing Add:* Christie's 20 Rockefeller Plz New York NY 10020

SMITH, CLYDE
PAINTER
b Pa, June 20, 32. *Study:* Dartmouth Col, BA, 54; Art Ctr Col Design, BFA, 58. *Work:* Mus City of New York; Chrysler Mus, Norfolk; Harvard Col. *Teaching:* Instr painting, & drawing, Sch Visual Art, formerly. *Media:* Oil. *Publ:* Contribr, Painting Men's Portraits & Painting Women's Portraits, Watson-Guptill, 77. *Dealer:* Portraits Inc New York NY; Portraits Brokers Am Montgomery AL. *Mailing Add:* 29 West Way Old Greenwich CT 06870-2429

SMITH, DAVID LOEFFLER
PAINTER, EDUCATOR
b New York, NY, May 1, 28. *Study:* Bard Col, BA; Cranbrook Acad Art, MFA; also with Hans Hofmann & Raphael Soyer. *Work:* Munson Williams Proctor Inst, Utica, NY. *Exhib:* Seligman Gallery, NY; one-man shows, First St Gallery, NY, 72-73, 76-77,79, 82 & 85; M13 Gallery, NY, 86, 87 & 90; Water Street Gallery, Mass, 88; Nemasket Gallery, Fairhaven, Mass, 90; News as Muse, Baltimore, 91; Cherry Stone Gallery, 2004, 2005, 2006. *Collection Arranged:* Crapo Gallery; Swain Sch Design; Paul Resiwa; Leland Bell. *Teaching:* chmn dept art, Chatham Col; vis critic, New York Studio Sch, Md Art Inst, Queens Col, State Univ NY, Grad Sch Painting, Parson's Sch Design; prof painting, Southeastern Mass Univ, North Dartmouth, Mass, formerly; retired; dir Swain Sch Design, 62-66. *Awards:* Henry Posner Prize, Carnegie Inst, 61. *Media:* Oil. *Publ:* Auth, articles, Am Artist, 59-62, Antiques Mag, 11/67, Arts Mag, 3/68 & Art & Artists, 1/70 & 5/71. *Dealer:* Cherry Stone Gallery. *Mailing Add:* 122 Hawthorn St New Bedford MA 02740

SMITH, DENNIS V
PAINTER, SCULPTOR
b Murray, Utah, June 16, 42. *Study:* Brigham Young Univ, BA, 67; Danish Royal Acad, 68. *Work:* Springville Mus Art, Utah; LDS Church Mus & Utah Div Fine Arts Collection, Salt Lake City. *Comn:* The World of Children, Primary Children Hosp, Salt Lake City, 90; Campus Talk (bronze), Western Mich Univ, Kalamazoo, 96; Summer Series (bronze), comn by Steven & Eileen Simmons, Greenwich, Conn, 96; Stiltwalkers (bronze), Charity Hosp, New Orleans, 98; Two Airships, Yuma Int Airport, Ariz, 98. *Media:* Oil, Etchings; Clay, Wax. *Publ:* Auth, Meanderings, Clayhill, 96; contribr, New Genesis, Gibb Smith, 98

SMITH, DINAH MAXWELL
PAINTER, PHOTOGRAPHER
b New York, NY. *Study:* L'Academie Julian; RI Sch Design, BFA(painting), 63; Masters Prog, Santa Fe Inst Fine Arts, Wayne Thiebaud Workshop, 88. *Work:* Bank Rhode Island, RI; Bridgeport Mus Art, Science & Industry, CT; Chase Bank; O'Neals Lincoln Ctr, Rhode Island School of Design, RI; Union League Club. *Comn:* Dog

portraits, comn by: Carolyn Rockafellow Lopez-Balboa, Mr & Mrs Kevin Cronin, Mssr Peter Hallock & Craig Mowry, Mr & Mrs John Richey. *Exhib:* Solo exhibs, Paradise Cafe, Sag Harbor, NY, 02, Hampton Road Gallery, 03, Union League Club, NY, 88 & 92, Gallery Wessel, Hamburg, Ger, 90-98, 01, Lizan-Tops/AHI Gallery, NY, 95, Convent Sacred Heart, Greenwich, Conn, 95, Coach Gallery, E Hampton, NY, 96, New Light Arts, Water Mill, NY, 96 & Mecox Gardens, Water Hill, NY, 98, Cook-Pony Farm, Sag Harbor, NY, 01; Group shows, Local Color, Gallery North, Setauket, NY, 97-02, By-the-Sea, Lizan-Tops Gallery, E Hampton, NY, 96; Creatures, Elaine Benson Gallery, Bridgehampton, NY, 96; Potato Exhibit, Water Mill Mus, NY, 95 & Mem Show, 96; Artists' Registry, Dog Mus, St Louis, Mo, 92, 94, 96 & 98; Photog show, AKC/Dog Mus, St Louis, Mo; By-The-Sea, Lizan-Tops Gallery, 2000; Ron Cavalier Gallery, Nantucket, Mass, 2000; plus others. *Pos:* curator Art with a Heart Auction, Southampton, NY, 99. *Teaching:* Instr, Watercolor, Parrish Art Mus, Southampton, NY, 79; adult educ oil painting on paper, Southhampton, NY, 97-98, pvt oil on paper, 99. *Awards:* Nat Arts Club Graphics Prize, 72 & Special Award, 74; Fourth Prize, Five Towns M&A Found, 85; Third Prize, Photog Show, 89, First Prize, Painting Show, 89, East End Arts Coun. *Bibliog:* James R Genovese (auth), Light at the end of the island, 5/28/83 & Phyllis Braff (auth), From the studio, 9/22/83, Hamptons Newspaper Mag; Helen Harrison (auth), NY Times; Karen Frankel (auth), Exposed Lines and Sunfilled Colors, Am Artist Mag, 3/98; Mary Cummings (auth), Images that capture moments in time, Arts & Living, Southampton Press, 8/31/00; Dan's Papers Covers & Write-Ups; plus others. *Mem:* Artist Alliance East Hampton. *Media:* Oils; Black & White Photography. *Interests:* Photography, room-boxes (dioramas), gardening, tennis. *Dealer:* Hampton Road Gallery, Southampton, NY

SMITH, DONALD C
PAINTER
b Dexter, Mo, July 10, 35. *Study:* Univ Mo, BA & MA; Santa Reparata Ctr Graphic Art, Florence, Italy; also painting with Fred Conway & printmaking with Maricio Lasansky. *Work:* ABC Broadcasting Corp; Spiva Art Ctr, Joplin, Mo; Santa Reparata Stamperia d'Arte Grafica, Florence; Boston Pub Libr; Bank RI, Providence; Allan Stone Gallerys, NY; Wheeler Gallery, Providence, RI; Newport Mus Art, RI. *Exhib:* One-man shows, NW Mo State Univ, Maryville, 63, RI Col, 69 & 82, Wheelock Col, 71, Lowell State Univ, 83, Wheeler Gallery, Providence, RI, 92, 2003, Bannister Gallery, RI Col, 95; Boston Printmakers Ann, 75 & 76; Davidson Printmaking, 76; RI Painters Ann, RI Sch Design Mus, 82; Invitational Group, Duxbury Art Complex, Mass, 88; Bannister Gallery, RI Col, Providence, 96; Bromfield Gallery, Boston, Mass, 2001; Ctr for the Arts, Sarasota, Fla, 2002; Newport Mus Art, 2005. *Pos:* Dir, Spiva Art Ctr, Joplin, Mo, 60-64. *Teaching:* Prof painting & drawing, RI Col, 64-97, prof emeritus, 97-. *Awards:* Univ Fel, Univ Mo, 58; Faculty Res Grant, RI Col, 83-84 & 86-87; Emerson Award, Wheeler Gallery, Providence, RI, 87. *Media:* Oil, Watercolor. *Publ:* Auth, Edwin Dickinson, draftsman/painter, Arts New Eng, 7-8/82. *Mailing Add:* 12 Pine Hill Ave Johnston RI 02919

SMITH, ELIZABETH ANGELE
CURATOR
Study: Columbia Univ, Degree art hist. *Work:* Mus Contemp Art, Los Angeles, 1989, Urban Revisions: Current Projects for the Pub Realm, 1994, Cindy Sherman: Retrospective, 1997, At the End of the Century: One Hundred Yrs of Archit, 1998, The Archit of RM Schindler, 2001 (Named Best Archit or Design Exhib of Yr, Int Asn Art Critics/USA, 2001), Matta in Am: Painting and Drawings of the 1940s, Mus Contemp Art, Chicago, 2001, Donald Moffett: What Barbara Jordan Wore, 2002, Lee Bontecou: A Retrospective, 2003 (Named Best Monographic Mus Show Nationally, Int Asn Art Critics/USA, 2004). *Exhib:* Curator (exhib) Blueprints for Modern Living: Hist and Legacy of the Case Study Houses, Urban. *Pos:* Cur, Mus Contemp Art, Los Angeles, 83-99; James W Alsdorf Chief Cur, Chicago, 99-; bd overseers, Sch Archit, Ill Inst Tech, Chicago. *Teaching:* Adj prof, pub art studies prog Univ Southern Calif, 92-98; bd adv, Independent Cur Int New York City. *Awards:* Named Woman of Yr, Chicago Soc Artists, 2004. *Publ:* auth: (books) Techno Archit, 2000, Case Study Houses: The Complete CSH Prog 1945-66, 2002; co-ed: Lee Bontecou: A Retrospective of Sculpture and Drawing, 1958-2000, 2003. *Mailing Add:* Mus Contemp Art 220 E Chicago Ave Chicago IL 60611

SMITH, ELLIOT
DEALER, HISTORIAN
b St Louis, Mo, Sept 22, 42. *Study:* Washington Univ, St Louis, AB, 66; Univ Mo, MEd, 68. *Pos:* Founder & vpres, 87-88, St Louis Gallery Contemp Art; dir, Elliot Smith Gallery, St Louis, Mo & New York, NY, currently. *Teaching:* Assoc prof, English & speech, Washington Univ, St Louis, 68-73; assoc prof Am studies, St Louis Univ, 81-84. *Mem:* St Louis Gallery Asn (treas, 85-86 & vpres, 87); Friends Pub Art (founder & pres, 86-). *Res:* Early 20th century American architecture. *Specialty:* Paintings and sculpture of bold imagery and strong intellectual content. *Publ:* Auth, Louis Sullivan, The Last Romantic, St Louis Univ Press, 84. *Mailing Add:* Elliot Smith Contemporary Art 14 Horatio #14 H New York NY 10014

SMITH, FRANCES KATHLEEN
CURATOR, HISTORIAN
b Bolton, Eng, Nov 19, 13; Can citizen. *Study:* London Univ, Eng; Queen's Univ, Kingston, Ont, BA, 56; Oxford Univ, Eng, with Pope Hennessey, Italian sculpture, 56-57. *Collection Arranged:* Andre Bieler: 50 Years (auth, catalog), Retrospective, traveled, Can, 70-71; Heritage Kingston (contribr, catalog), 73; Painting Now 1976/77 (auth, catalog); Henry Moore, Sculpture, Prints, Drawings, 78; Daniel Fowler of Amherst Island, (auth, catalog), traveled, Can, 79; The Brave New World of Fritz Brandtner Traveling Show (coauth, catalog), 81-82; Kathleen Moir Morris (auth, catalog), 83; John Herbert Caddy (auth, catalog), 85; Andre Bieler in Rural Quebec (auth, catalog), 88-89. *Pos:* Cur, Agnes Etherington Art Ctr, Kingston, Ont, Can, 57-79, cur emer, 79-. *Awards:* Merit Award, Ont Asn Art Galleries, 80; Merit Award, Can Mus Asn, 81; Distinguished Serv Award, Queen's Univ, 87; Celebration 88, Cert Merit, Olympic Comt, 88. *Mem:* Can Mus Asn (nominating comt, 78); Ont Asn Art Galleries (secy, 68-69). *Res:* Canadian artists: Daniel Fowler, Andre Bieler, Fritz Brandtner, John Herbert Caddy and others. *Specialty:* Canadian Art, European 16h and 17th Century paintings, African sculpture. *Interests:* Reading, Art History, Writing. *Publ:* Coauth, A Permanent Collection of the Agnes Etherington Art Centre, 68; auth, George Harlow White 1817-1887, 75 & Daniel Fowler of Amherst Island, 79, Art Ctr, Queens Univ, Kingston, Ont; Andre Bieler: An Artist's Life and Times, Merritt Publ Co, Toronto, 80, Re-printed French translation, new intro & epilogue, Philippe Baylaueg (ed), 9/2006. *Mailing Add:* 404-174 Ypres Green SW Calgary AB T2T 6M2 Canada

SMITH, FRANK ANTHONY
PAINTER
b Salt Lake City, Utah, Aug 4, 39. *Study:* Univ Utah, BFA, 62, MFA, 64. *Work:* Univ Utah Mus Fine Art; Utah State Univ; Salt Lake Art Ctr; Nat Gallery, Washington, DC. *Comn:* design (dance pieces), Repertory Dance Theatre, 66, 71 & 73; stimuli sensory environ for children, Salt Lake Art Ctr, 70; mural, Univ Utah Biol Bldg, 72. *Exhib:* Look Again, Illusionist Painting, Taft Mus, Cincinnati, 76; Reality of Illustion, Univ Southern Calif, 79; Four Corners Biennial, Phoenix, Ariz, 81; Illusions, Faire Int D'art Contemp, Grand Palais, Paris, 82; solo exhib, Suellen Haber Gallery, NY, 82; and others. *Pos:* Illusr, Star Trek: The Movie, 77. *Teaching:* Prof painting & drawing, Univ Utah, 68-. *Awards:* San Francisco Art Dirs Gold Medal, 64; Purchase Award, 3rd Intermountain Biennial, 68. *Media:* Acrylic. *Dealer:* Osuna Gallery Washington DC; Phillips Gallery Salt Lake City UT

SMITH, GARY
SCULPTOR, GALLERY DIRECTOR
b Portland, Ore, Nov 25, 49. *Study:* Lewis & Clark Col, Portland, Ore, BA, 71; Univ Calif, Santa Barbara, MFA, 75. *Work:* Art Mus Santa Cruz Co, Calif; St Mary's Col, Moraga, Calif; Calif Polytechnic Inst, San Luis Obispo. *Comn:* Large scale granite sculpture, Nanao, Japan, 96. *Exhib:* Large Scale Sculpture, Univ Calif, Davis, 79; Recent Sculpture, Quay Gallery, San Francisco, 80; Departure Gallery, NY, 83-86; Summer Int, Keramik Studio, Vienna, Austria, 84; Recent Sculpture, Cuesta Col, San Luis Obispo, Calif, 85. *Collection Arranged:* Hartnell Col Farm Security Administration Photograph Collection (auth, catalog), 82; Leslie Fenton Netsuke Collection (auth, catalog), 85; Virginia Bacher Huichol Artifact Collection (auth, catalog), 86; Daniel Rhodes: The California Years (auth, catalog), 86. *Teaching:* Instr ceramics-art, Hartnell Col, Salinas, 76-, dir gallery, 76-. *Awards:* Harden Teaching Award, 92; Gleason Teaching award, 2004. *Mem:* Col Art Asn. *Media:* Clay. *Mailing Add:* c/o Hartnell Col 156 Homestead Ave Salinas CA 93901

SMITH, GARY DOUGLAS
DRAFTSMAN, PAINTER
b San Francisco, Calif, July 29, 48. *Study:* Calif Col Arts & Crafts, BFA(scholoarship), 71; extensive study in Mexico; Atelier 17, Paris; etching with S W Hayter, also engraving with George Ball, also Mezzotint with Yozo Hamaguchi. *Work:* Palm Springs Mus Art, Calif; Achenbach Found Graphic Arts, San Franicisco; De Saisset Mus, Santa Clara, Calif; Calif Acad Sciences, San Francisco; Calif Col Arts & Crafts, Oakland. *Exhib:* San Francisco Mus Mod Art, 70 & 77; Anchorage Hist & Fine Arts Mus, Alaska, 77; El Paso Mus Art, Tex, 77; World Print Competition & Traveling Show, 79; Krannert Art Mus, Ill, 79; Toledo Mus Art, Ohio, 79; Achenbach Found Graphic Arts, San Francisco, 83; solo exhibs, Historic Olema Inn, Calif, 83, Vorpal Galleries, Soho, NY, 85, Laguna Beach, Calif, 85 & San Francisco, 86, Inverness Studio, Calif, 87-90, Robert Mondavi Winery, Oakmille, Calif, 90; Inverness Ridge Assoc, Calif, 87; San Francisco Arts Comn, Calif, 88; Concordia-Argonaut Club, San Francisco, 88 & 89. *Teaching:* Lectr/demonstration, Fine Art Mus San Francisco, 85; lectr, Calif Col Arts & Crafts, Oakland, 87 & 88. *Awards:* Silver Prize, Calif Col Arts & Crafts, 69. *Bibliog:* Thomas Albright (auth), Landscapes in translation, San Francisco Chronicle, 7/7/71; John Marlowe (auth), interview, Currant Art Mag, 76; Carol A Hayes (auth), Profile of an artist, Bay View Mag, 9/81; Al Morch (auth), Too much of a good thing, San Francisco Chronicle, 11/9/81; Diana Freedman (auth), The catalyst in creation, Arts/Speak NY, 83. *Mem:* Graphic Arts Coun; World Print Coun. *Media:* Prismacolor Pencil, Silverpoint. *Publ:* Cover, Floating Island I, 76. *Dealer:* Claudia Chapline Gallery Stinson Beach CA; Waterworks Gallery Harbor Bay WA. *Mailing Add:* PO Box 244 Inverness CA 94937

SMITH, GIL R
ADMINISTRATOR, HISTORIAN
b Rochester, NY, Oct 18, 52. *Study:* State Univ NY, BA (art hist), 75; Pa State Univ, PHD (art hist), 87. *Teaching:* asst prof art hist, State Univ, Fredonia, NY, 84-85; assoc prof archit, Ball State Univ, 85-95; prof art hist, Eastern Ky Univ, 95-. *Mem:* Col Art Asn; SAH; NCAA; Am Soc 18th Century Studies; Mid-west Art Hists Soc. *Res:* 18th century architectural theory and practice, focusing on transition from baroque to neoclasssical. *Publ:* contribr, Projects & monuments in the Roman baroque, Penn State Press, 84; auth, Competitions Vol 2, Louisville, Ky, 92; auth, An architectural progress in the renaissance & baroque, Penn State Press, 92; auth, Architectural Diplomacy: Rome & Paris in the Late Baroque, Archit Hist Found, 93; contribr, The dictionary of art, Macmillan, London, 96. *Mailing Add:* 1104 Valley Run Dr Richmond KY 40475

SMITH, GREG
PAINTER, GRAPHIC ARTIST
b Easton, Pa, June 13, 51. *Study:* Duke Univ, BFA, 73; Pa Acad Fine Arts, 73. *Work:* Chemical Bank Corp Collection, NY. *Exhib:* Reagan: Am Icon, Bucknell Univ, Lewisburg, Pa, 89; Scenic Views, Willoughby Sharp Gallery, NY, 90; New Landscape Paintings, Willoughby Sharp Gallery, NY, 91; 25th Juried Show, Allentown Art Mus,

Pa, 96; Nat Soc Painters Casein & Acrylic, Salmagundi Club, NY, 96. *Pos:* Sr artist, Prodigy Videotex Servs, 87-93; graphic artist, Delphi Internet, 95. *Teaching:* 2D computer graphics, Pratt Inst, 92-95; visual founds, Muhlenberg Col, Allentown, Pa, 95-96. *Bibliog:* Patty Harris (auth), 4 summer art shows, Downtown, 9/90; Gary Azon (auth), Art Around Town, Downtown, 4/91; Geoff Gehman (auth), Juried show a vision of delights restored, Morning Call, Allentown, Pa, 1/96. *Mem:* Spec Interest Group Computer Graphics & Interactive Techniques, Asn Computer Machinery. *Media:* Oil, Acrylics; Computers. *Mailing Add:* 163 Main St Apt 1 Emmaus PA 18049-4038

SMITH, GREGORY ALLGIRE
EDUCATOR, ADMINISTRATOR
b Washington, DC, Mar 31, 51. *Study:* Johns Hopkins Univ, BA(art hist), 72; Williams Col-Clark Art Inst, MA(art hist), 74; Harvard Univ-Inst Arts Admin, cert, 74. *Exhib:* El Greco Toledo, Toledo Art Mus, 82-83; Impressionism & Post-Impressionism; The Courtauld Collection Nat Tour, Int Exhibs, 86-87; Malcolm Grear: The Art of Design (with catalog), Art Acad Cincinnati/Cincinnati Art Mus, 96. *Pos:* NEH intern, Walker Art Ctr, 75-76; asst dir, Akron Art Mus, 77-80; Asst dir admin, Toledo Mus Art, 80-86; exec vpres, Int Exhibs Fdn, 86-87; dir, Telfair Mus Art, 87-94; pres, Art Acad Cincinnati, 94-; adminstr asst, Washington Project for the Arts, 75. *Mem:* Asn Independent Cols Art & Design (trustee, 94-, exec comt mem, 99-); Greater Cincinnati Consortium Cols & Univs (exec comt mem, 96-99); Am Asn Mus. *Mailing Add:* Art Acad Cincinnati 1125 St Gregory Cincinnati OH 45202

SMITH, HARRY WILLIAM
ILLUSTRATOR, JEWELER
b Chicago, Ill, July 12, 37. *Study:* Wash Univ, St Louis; Command Mgt Art Sch, Ft Belvoir, Va; Chicago Acad Fine Arts; Gemological Inst Am. *Work:* Yorktown Mus, NY; Gibbes Art Gallery, Charleston, SC; Miniature Mus, Kansas City, Mo; Mus Miniatures, Los Angeles, Calif. *Comn:* Miniature Mus Kansas City, 89; Mus Miniatures, Los Angeles, 93; pair of torcheres, Mt Vernon, 97. *Exhib:* Solo exhib, Brown Co Art Gallery, Nashville, Ind, 71; Colby Coll Mus Art, 76; Coe-Kew Gallery, NY, 84; Mystic Seaport, Mystic, Conn, 84; Neiman Marcus, 87; Farnsworth Mus, 90; Landis Valley Mus; Abby Aldrich Rockefeller Art Ctr, Williamsburg, Va, 96; Naples Mus of Art, 00. *Pos:* Chmn, Maine Libr Comn, 79-83. *Awards:* Early American Life Craftsman Award, Acad of Honor; Am's Top 200 Traditional Craftsmen, CGA. *Bibliog:* Let it be wee, NY Mag, 83; article, Nutshell News, 90; article, Miniature Collector, 90, 93 & 94; article, Forbes; article, Silver Mag; article, Collector Editions; article, Washington Univ Mag; Traditional Crafts in America - Yankee Way with Wood. *Mem:* Copley Soc; life mem Brown Co Art Gallery Asn (bd dir, 70-71); Am Soc Marine Artists; Int Miniature Artists. *Media:* Watercolor; Precious Metals, Wood. *Publ:* Auth & illusr, Michael and the Mary Day, 79, ABC's of Maine, 80, Windjammers of the Maine Coast, 82, ABC's of New Hampshire, 84, Down East Books; The Art of Making Furniture in Miniature, Scott Publ, 92 & 98; Traditional Homes, McCall's Art in Action; Dutton, 82; Kalmbach, 93; Scott Pub, 98. *Dealer:* Barnstable Originals. *Mailing Add:* 50 Harden Ave Camden ME 04843

SMITH, J WELDON
MUSEUM DIRECTOR, HISTORIAN
b Richmond, Va. *Study:* Yale Univ, BA, 55; Cambridge Univ, 59 & 69; Northwestern Univ, PhD, 62. *Collection Arranged:* African Pragmatism (catalog), Boise Art Mus, Sonoma State Univ, 85; The Painter as Sculptor and Collector: John Haley, 90. *Pos:* Dir, Fiberworks-Ctr Textile Arts, 81-86, San Francisco Craft & Folk Art Mus, 86-. *Teaching:* Prof aesthetics, Mac Murray Col, 65-80; vis prof African art, Inst Allende, Mex, 76 & 80, San Francisco Art Inst, 85. *Mem:* Am Asn Mus. *Res:* Investigation of the socio-religious aspects of African traditional art. *Publ:* Various articles in African Arts; A Report: Journal of San Francisco Craft & Folk Art Mus, African Traditional Art: Haley Collection. *Mailing Add:* San Francisco Craft & Folk Art Mus Ft Mason Ctr Bldg A San Francisco CA 94123

SMITH, JACK RICHARD
PAINTER, PRINTMAKER
b Fremont, Mich, Aug 3, 50. *Study:* Columbus Col Art & Design, 68-69; Instituto Allende, San Miguel, Mex, 69-70; Thomas Jefferson Col, 70-71. *Work:* Muskegon Mus Art, Mich; De Pauw Univ, Indianapolis, Ind. *Comn:* Murals, comn by Thomas Worrell, at Dharma Holdings, 97, at Milagroo, Taos, NMex, 98 & at The Rectory, Delrey Beach, Fla, 98; Robert D Morgan (portrait), De Pauw Univ, Indianapolis, Ind, 98. *Exhib:* A Light from Within, Muskegon Mus Art, Mich, 89; one-man show, Denos Mus, Traverse City, Mich, 89; solo exhib, Henry Mathews, Curator, Deno Mus, Traverse City, Mich, 89; solo exhib, The Taos Portraits, Univ NM Harwood Mus. *Media:* Oil. *Publ:* Tom Collins, Visual Fetishization, Albuquerque Jour, 02; Las Casas de Los Valles, exhib catalog, Mongerson/Wunderlich Gallery. *Dealer:* Sullivan Goss Galleries, Santa Barbara and Monticito, Calif, Parks Galleries, Taos and Santa Fe. *Mailing Add:* 114 Las Cruces #B Taos NM 87571-6576

SMITH, JAMES MICHAEL
PAINTER, ASSEMBLAGE ARTIST
b Aug 18, 49. *Study:* Univ Kans, Lawrence, BFA, 71, Univ Ill, Champaign-Urbana, MFA, 73. *Work:* Chase Manhattan Bank, NY; Univ Tex Collection, El Paso; Saks Fifth Avenue, NY; John W Hechinger Col, Largo, Md; Cedar Rapids Mus of Art, Cedar Rapids, Iowa. *Comn:* The Realty Co, St Louis, Mo; Renaissance Fin St Louis, Mo. *Exhib:* Solo exhibs, Festival Gallery, Krannert Ctr Performing Arts, Univ Ill, Urbana, 77, Joy Horwich Gallery, Chicago, Ill, 80, 81, 82, 83, 84 & 89, Locus Gallery, St Louis, MO, 85, 87, The City Series, Group Exch Cedar Rapids Mus of Art, Cedar Rapids, Iowa, 98, The Sheldon Art Galleries, St Louis, Mo, 2000, Cedar Rapids Mus of Art, 2000, plus others; The NY Connection, Florissant Valley Community Col, St Louis, MO, 89; Locus Gallery, St Louis, MO, 90; Flora '90, Chicago Botanical Gardens, Ill, 90; Painted constructions, Fassbender Gallery, Chicago, 95, 97, 97 & 98, & Duane Reed Gallery, St Louis, Mo, 96, 97, Bentley Gallery, Scottsdale, Ariz, 95, 96 & 97. *Pos:* Juror, Ill Small Painting Competition, Western Ill Univ, Macomb, 87; panelist, Careers in the Arts Seminar, St Louis Community Col, Florissant, 88. *Teaching:* Vis artist lectr, Nat Philosophical Soc, Joy Horwich Gallery, 83; vis artist, Sch of Ozarks, Lookout Point, MO, 88. *Awards:* Honorarium, Mo Vis Arts Biennial, Mo Arts Coun, 87; Cash Award, The Louis E Sieden Mem Award, Chautagua 27th Ann Nat Exhib, NY, 84; Honorarium, Five Choose Five Exhib, First Street Forum Gallery, St Louis, Mo, 82; Art Forms Nat Exhib, Philadelphia, 99; 49th Ann Art Competition, Nat Exhib, Ft Smith, Ark, 99; Dishman Competition, 99; Nat Exhib, Lamar Univ, Beaumont, Tex, 99. *Publ:* Tools as Art: The Hechinger Collection, Abrams; New American Painting, Open Studio Press, Boston, Mass; Art News, NY; New Art Examiner, Chicago, Ill; plus others. *Dealer:* Crows Ink PO Box 19842 St Louis MO 63144. *Mailing Add:* 436 Bismark Saint Louis MO 63119

SMITH, JAMES MORTON
HISTORIAN
b Bernie, Mo, May 28, 19. *Study:* Southern Ill Univ, BEd, 41; Univ Okla, MA, 46; Cornell Univ, PhD, 51. *Pos:* Ed, Inst Early Am Hist & Cult, 55-66; dir, State Hist Soc Wis, 70-76; dir & dir emer, Winterthur Mus, 76-84. *Teaching:* Prof hist, Cornell Univ, 66-70; prof hist, Univ Wis, 70-76; prof hist, Univ Del, 76-89. *Mem:* Asn Art Mus Dirs; Am Hist Asn; Orgn Historians; Am Asn Mus. *Res:* Early American history and culture. *Publ:* Jefferson & Madison: Republican Correspondence Between Thomas Jefferson and James Madison 1779-1826 (Am Revolution Roundtable Award, 96)

SMITH, JAN
DIRECTOR
b Milwuakee, Wis, Aug 26, 55. *Study:* Univ Wis, BFA, 76, MA, 89, Cert in Mus Studies, 89. *Exhib:* Solo Exhib: Monroe Arts and Activities Cen, Monroe, Wis, 85; Plymouth Arts Foundation, Plymouth, Wis, 2005; Group Exhib: Unique Arts & Craft Gallery, Shorewood, Wis, 82; Madison Art Cen, Sales & Rental Gallery, 83. *Collection Arranged:* Paul Joseph Stankard, 20 year Retrospective, 1990; Contemporary Studio Glass, 40 pieces from pvt Col, 2000; Contemporary Studio Glass, An Internat Perspective, 02; Kemper Insurance Group; Marc Chagall: Le Cerque, 2003; A roal & ancient Game: Presening Golf, 2004; The Art of Assemblage. *Pos:* Wis Fedn of Mus, Bd Mem; Convention Bur Bd, Chair Visitor. *Awards:* Best of Show, Wis Biennial, Edna Carlsten Gallery, 76. *Mem:* Wis Painters and Sculptors; AAM; Wis Fedn of Mus; Wis Art Educ Asn; Nat Art Educ Asn. *Media:* Pastel, Watercolor. *Res:* Printmaking. *Specialty:* Coventry Glass Gallery, Appleton, WI; David Barnett Gallery, Milwaukee, WI; 19th & 20th Cen Am Art. *Publ:* Paperweight Bulletin, Paperweight Collectors Asn, 95; Brandwine River Mus Catalogue, 99; Paul Stankard Catalogue. *Dealer:* Barry Sautner, Cameo Carved Glass, Wisconsin Glass Makers. *Mailing Add:* 9251 Bomar Ave Neenah WI 54956

SMITH, JAUNE QUICK-TO-SEE
PAINTER, CURATOR
b St Ignatius, Indian Mission Flathead Reservation, Mont. *Study:* Framingham State Col, Mass, BA, 76; Univ NMex, MA, 80; Minneapolis Art & Design, Minn, Hon Dr, 92; Pa Acad Art, Philadelphia, Hon Dr, 98. *Work:* Birmingham Mus Art, Ala; Am Med Asn, Continental Bank, Chicago, Ill; Steinberg Mus, St Louis, Mo; Denver Art Mus, Colo; Nat Mus Am Art, Nat Mus Women in Arts, Washington; Mus Mod Art, NY; and many others. *Comn:* Sculpture Garden, Yerba Buena Park, Moscone Ctr, San Francisco, Calif; Northwind Fishing Weir Proj, Duwamish Tribe, King Co Arts Comn, Seattle, Wash, 92; artist on design team, Nat Mus of Am Indians, Smithsonian Inst, Washington, 93; and others. *Exhib:* Albright-Knox Gallery, Buffalo, NY, 81; Kornblee Drawing, Aldrich Mus Contemp Art, Conn, 81; Smithsonian Inst, Washington, 82 & 96; Western States Biennial, Corcoran Art Gallery, Washington, San Francisco Mus Mod Art & Brooklyn Mus, NY, 83; Grey Canyon, 83 & Other Voices: Mediating Between the Ethnic Traditions & the Modernist Mainstream, 91, Portland Mus Art, Ore; Western States Biennial, Corcoran Art Gallery, Washington, San Drancisco Mus Mod Art, Calif & Brooklyn Mus, NY, 83; Views Across Am, 86, Committed to Print, 88, Figuration, 88 & 91, Mus Mod Art, NY; solo exhibs, LewAllen Gallery, Santa Fe, NMex, 90, 91, 92, 93 & 94, Steinbaum Krauss Gallery, NY, 83, 85, 86, 87, 90, 92 & 95, Santa Fe Inst Fine Arts, NMex, 94, Jersey City Mus (traveling exhib, catalogue), NJ, 96, Austin Mus Art at Laguna Gloria (with catalogue), Tex, 96, Art Mus Missoula (with catalogue), Mont, 96 & 98, Subversions/Affirmations: Jaune Quick-to-See Smith, Survey, Jersey City Mus, NJ (traveling exhib with catalogue), Lehight Univ Art Galleries, Bethlehem, Pa, 98; Into the Forefront: Am Indian Art in the 20th Century, Denver Art Mus, Colo, 93; one-person retrospective, Chrysler Mus, Norfolk, Va, 93, Parameters Series (brochure), Smith Col Mus Art, Northampton, Mass, 93; Current Identities IV Biennal Int de Pintura 94-95 (traveling exhib with catalogue), South Am, 95; Art at the Edge: Social Turf (brochure), High Mus Art, Atlanta, Ga, 95; Am Kaleidoscope: Themes and Perspectives in Recent Art (with catalogue), Nat Mus Am Art, Smithsonian Inst, Washington, 96; Mouse: An Am Icon, The Alternative Mus, NY, 98. *Collection Arranged:* Our Land/Ourselves: American Indian Contemporary Artists (traveling exhib, auth, catalogue), 91; We, the Human Beings: 27 Contemporary Native American Artists (auth, catalogue essay), Wooster Col Art Mus (traveling exhib), 92-93; Biennial: The Land, Tacoma Art Mus, Wash, 95. *Pos:* Trustee, Inst Am Indian Art, Santa Fe, NMex, Mont Indian Contemp Arts, Bozeman; cur & juror for numerous mus & orgns. *Teaching:* Lectr, numerous cols, insts & mus, 79-94. *Awards:* Wallace Stegner Award, Ctr Am West, Univ Colo, Boulder, 95; Outstanding Achievement Award (visual arts), Women's Caucus Art, 97; Honorary Doctorate, Pa Acad Art Philadelphia, 98. *Bibliog:* Lydia Haustein (auth), Jaune Quick-to-See Smith und Vera Frenkel, ARTIS, 2-3/94; Fauntleroy (auth), Traveling Between Two Worlds, Pasatiempo, 11/4/94; Fred Camper (auth), Self-Expressionism,

Chicago Reader, 11/11/94; and many others. *Mem:* Col Art Asn (bd mem); ATLATL, Indian Orgn for the Arts, Phoenix, Ariz (bd mem); Am Indian Contemp Arts, San Francisco, Calif (bd mem). *Publ:* Contrib, Stand in the Center of Good: Interviews with Contemporary Native American Artists, Univ Nebr Press, Lincoln, 94; Mapping the Terrain: New Genre Public Art, Bay Press, San Francisco, Calif, 94; auth, Creating and Beyond, Getty Center for Education in the Arts, Los Angeles, 96; featured on numerous TV shows; and many more. *Dealer:* Steinbaum Krauss Gallery 132 Greene St New York NY 10012

SMITH, JEFFREY CHIPPS
HISTORIAN
Study: Duke Univ, BA(art hist), 73; Columbia Univ, MA, 75, MPh, 77, PhD, 79. *Teaching:* Vis asst prof, Univ Pittsburgh, 78; Ruth Head Centennial prof art hist, Univ Tex, Austin, 79-2000; Kay Fortson chair in european art, Univ Tex, Austin, 2000-. *Awards:* Alexander von Humbolt Stiftung Res Fel, Bonn, Ger, 85-86 & 92-93; Gordan Book Prize, Renaissance Soc Am, 96; John Simon Guggenheim Mem Found Fel, 98-99. *Mem:* Historians Netherlandish Art (bd dir, 89-94); Col Art Asn, (bd dir, 96-); Renaissance Soc Am (coun, 2000-, assoc ed Renaissance Quarterly, 2000-03, ed 2003-06); Sixteenth Century Soc and Conf (bd dir, 2004-07). *Res:* Northern Renaissance and Baroque art. *Publ:* Auth, Seventeenth-Century Landscape Drawings, Huntington Art Gallery, Austin, 82; Nuremberg A Renaissance City 1500-1618, Univ Tex Press, Austin, 83; ed, New Perspectives on the Art of Renaissance Nuremberg, Univ Tex Press, 85; auth, German Sculpture of the Later Renaissance, Princeton Univ Press, 94; Sensous Worship: Jesuits and the Art of the Early Catholic Reformation in Germany, Princeton Univ Pres, 2002; over 100 reviews & articles; The Northern Renaissance, 2004; The Art of the Goldsmith in Late Fifteenth Century Germany: The Kimbell Virgin and Her Bishop, 2006. *Mailing Add:* Dept Art & Art Hist Univ Tex 1 University Sta D 1300 Austin TX 78712

SMITH, JENNIE
ARTIST
b San Francisco, 81. *Study:* Student, Burren Col Art, Ireland, 2002; Mpls Col Art & Design, BFA, 2004. *Exhib:* Migration, 2003; Animal Its Habitat, 2004; Animals Slumber, 2004; Kite Wars, 2004; We'll Never Tell You Where We Have Gone, 2004; group shows at Made at MCAD, Mpls, 2005; Sr Exhib, Mpls Collection Art & Design, 2005; Drawing Show, Soo Vac Gallery, Mpls, 2005; Group Drawing Show, The Gen Store, Milwaukee, 2005; Four Color Drawing Show, Van Harrison Gallery, Chicago, 2005; Whitney Biennial: Day for Night, Whitney Mus Am Arts, 2006; Bull Bd Project 008, Calif, Collection Arts Wattis Inst Contemp Arts, San Francisco, 2006; Rena Bransten Gallery, San Francisco, 2006. *Mailing Add:* c/o Rena Bransten Gallery 77 Geary St San Francisco CA 94108

SMITH, JO-AN
PAINTER, DESIGNER
b Eugene, Ore. *Study:* Defense Lang Inst (span), 64; Indiana Univ, 65; Pvt studies in Buenos Aires, Arg, 66, San Salvador, El Salvador, 67, Panama, 68-70; Univ Tex, El Paso, BA(art), 71; NMex State Univ, MA(art), 75; Gemological Inst Am, 77; studied with Aleksander Titovets, 95, Albert Handel, 96 & Cheng Khee Chee, 2000. *Work:* Smithsonian Inst, Washington; Mem Med Ctr, NMex State Univ; Mesilla Valley Hospice; Branigan Cult Complex Permanent Collection. *Comn:* Roush Award Medallions, NMex State Univ, 1985-98; Borman necklace, 1994; Lovell painting, 1998; Medoff Jewelry, 1999-2000; Pres's Medal, NMex State Univ, 2000; Betty & Bobby Merit, 2001; Robert Jones, 2003; New Mexico Capital Art Foundation, Permanent Coll, NM Capitol Bldg, 2003. *Exhib:* Wearable Art, Potsdam Col, NY, 89; Ancient Space, Las Cruces, 96; New Orleans Nat Exhib, La, 97; Pittsburg Aqueous Open, 97; Salmagundi Club Nat Exhib, NY, 97; Nightwalker 97, Ft Collins, Colo, 97; solo exhib, Emerging, NMex, 1998, Up Close & Far Away, NMex, 1999, Explorations, NMex, 2001, Inner Light, NMex, 2002; Sierra Med Int Exhib, Tex, 98, 99, 2000; Masterworks 2000, NMex, 2000; Sun Bowl Art Exhib 2000, Tex; NMex Watercolor Soc, Fall, 2000; Up Close & Far Away, 2001, NM; Santa Fe Mus Art, 2004; New Harvest, NM, 2004. *Pos:* Proprietor & designer, JOS Studio, 71-2005; dir citywide art tour, Las Cruces Artshop, 1994-2003. *Teaching:* Instr design, NMex State Univ, 75-81 & Career Art Path, Las Cruces Sch (design), 94-97. *Awards:* Gamblin Merit Award, XVIII, New Orleans Nat Exhib, 97; Hon Mention, Nightwalker 97 Nat Exhib, 97. *Bibliog:* New Art International, Book Art Press, 96-98; Jo-An Smith, An Artist and Jewelry Designer, Ventanas Del Valle, New Mexico Mountain Dreams Publishing, Spring, 2001; Artist Molds Dwelling Around Her Environment, NMex Mag, Santa Fe, 5/98; Artist's Retreat, The Desert Home, Northland Press, 2002. *Mem:* Distinguished mem Soc NAm Goldsmiths; signature mem NMex Watercolor Soc; Nat Oil & Acrylic Painter's Soc; Dona Arts Coun; Border Artists. *Media:* Gold; Watercolor, Oil, Cloisonné Enamel. *Interests:* Southwest landscapes & cliff dwellings history. *Publ:* Contribr, Bead J, Craftsman's Gallery, Design, Golddust, Goldsmith's J & Working Craftsman; ed & contribr, Cutters comments, Las Cruces, 93-94; book cover illusr, Feroza Jussawala (auth), Chifon Saris, Writer Workshop Publ, India, 2003. *Dealer:* Glenn Cutter Jewelers & Gallery 2640 El Paseo Rd Las Cruces NM 88001; Dartmouth St Gallery, Albuquerque NM, www.dsg-art.com/s/smithjoan. *Mailing Add:* Box 786 Dona Ana NM 88032

SMITH, JOHN IVOR
SCULPTOR, EDUCATOR
b London, Eng, Jan 28, 27; Can citizen. *Study:* McGill Univ, BSc, 48; Montreal Mus Fine Arts; study with Arthur Lismer, Jacques de Tonnancour & Eldon Grier. *Work:* Art Gallery Ont, Toronto; Provincial Mus Que, Quebec City; Winnipeg Art Gallery, Manitoba; London Pub Art Mus, Ont; Edmonton Art Gallery, Alta. *Comn:* 20' Fiberglass chimeric figure, Expo '67, Montreal, 67; 9' Fiberglass female figure, Can Govt Exhib Comn, Ottawa, 67; 13' Fiberglas sculpture, Nat Capital Comn, Ottawa, 86. *Exhib:* Nat Outdoor Sculpture Show, Ottawa, Ont, 60; Can Sculpture, Dorothy Cameron Gallery, Toronto, Ont, 64; Sculpture '67, City Hall, Nat Gallery Can, Toronto, 67; Expo '67, Montreal; Can Sculpture, Rodin Gallery, Paris, France, 70; La Sculpture Au Quebec, Musee Du Quebec, Quebec, Canada, 92. *Teaching:* Assoc prof sculpture, Concordia Univ, Montreal, 66-84. *Awards:* First Prizes, Winnipeg Art Gallery, 59-61; Grand Centennial Award, Montreal Mus Fine Arts, 60; Senior Art Awards, Can Coun, 67, 69 & 73. *Mem:* Royal Can Acad. *Media:* Fiberglass reinforced epoxy. *Dealer:* Kingman Robinson Galleries 14 Hazelton Ave Toronto ON M5R 2E2; Buschlen-Mowatt Fine Arts Ltd 1445 W Georgia St Vancouver BC V6G 2T3

SMITH, JOHN W
DIRECTOR
Study: Southern Ill Univ, BA (in English), 1980. *Pos:* Founding cur special collections and archives, Chicago Park Dist, 1988-90; vis archivist, Royal Opera House, Covent Garden, London, 1991; chief archivist, Art Inst Chicago, 1990-94; cur archives, The Andy Warhol Mus, 1994-2000, dir, Archives Res Ctr, 1994-2000, interim dir, 1995-96, asst dir collections, exhibitions and rsch, 2000-06; dir, Archives of American Art, Smithsonian Inst, Washington, DC, 2006-. *Publ:* Auth, Strange Messenger: The Work of Patti Smith, 2002; auth, Andy Warhol's Time Capsule 21, 2003; auth, 365 Takes: The Andy Warhol Museum Collection, 2004; as well as others. *Mailing Add:* Archives American Art Smithsonian Inst PO Box 37012 Victor Bldg Ste 2200 MRC 937 Washington DC 20013-7012

SMITH, JOS(EPH) A(NTHONY)
ILLUSTRATOR, PAINTER
b Bellefonte, Pa, Sept 5, 36. *Study:* Pa State Univ, with Hobson Pittman, 55-57 & 60; Pratt Inst, BFA. *Work:* Lauren Rogers Mus, Miss; Univ Miss, Oxford; Kassel Documenta Arch, Ger; Coeln Ludwig Mus, Ger; Stuttgart Staatsgalerie Grafische Sammlung, Ger; Univ Conn, Storrs; and others. *Exhib:* Pa Acad Fine Arts, 61, 67 & 69; solo exhib paintings, drawings & sculpture, Staten Island Inst Arts & Sci, 66; Bethel Gallery, Conn, 78; Newhouse Gallery, Staten Island Cult Ctr, NY, 82; Adirondak Community Col, NY, 87; Artists Select Artists, Trenton City Mus, NJ, 92; The Art of Drawing VII, Staemfli Gallery, NY, 92; The Esther Allen Greer Mus, Ohio, 2000; Martin Art Gallery, Muhlinberg Coll, Allentown, PA, 01; The Art Inst of Chicago, 01; Gallery 20, NY, 01; OHR-O'Keefe Mus, Biloxi, MS, 02. *Pos:* Design consult, Brooks Bros, 70-75; exhib designer & consult, Staten Island Inst Arts & Sci, 70-75; mem bd dir, Staten Island Coun Arts, 71-76. *Teaching:* Prof fine art, Pratt Inst, 61-; asst prof fine art, Richmond Col, London, Eng, 84. *Awards:* Mary S Litt Award for Watercolor, 100th Ann Am Watercolor Soc, 67; Merit Award, NY Soc Illusr, 73, 74, 79, 82 & 98; Merit Award, Nat Works on Paper, Univ Miss, Oxford; and others. *Bibliog:* Jane Cottingham (auth), The imaginary drawings of Joseph A Smith, Am Artist, 7/81; Albert, Seckler & Albert (auth), Figure Drawing Comes to Life, 2nd ed, Prentice Hall, 86; Suzi Galik (auth), The Reenchantment of Art, Thames & Hudson, 91; and others. *Mem:* NY Visionary Artists. *Media:* Oil, Pencil, Pen & Ink. *Publ:* Eric Jong (auth), Witches, Abrams, 80; Susan Cooper (auth), Matthew's Dragon, McElderry Bks, 91; auth, Pen & Ink Book, Watson-Guptill Publ, 92; illusr, Goblins in Green, Nicholas Heller, 95; Clay Boy, Mirra Ginsburg, 97; and others; auth, Circus Trin, Abrams Pub, 2001; The Yellow House, Susan Goldman Rubin, Abrams Pub, 01; Audubon, Jennifer Armstrong, Abrams Pub, 02. *Mailing Add:* 381 Shawnee Dr Easton PA 18042

SMITH, KEITH A
PHOTOGRAPHER, PRINTMAKER
b Tipton, Ind, May 20, 38. *Study:* Art Inst of Chicago, BAE, with Aatis Lillstrom, Ken Josephson, Vera Berdich & Sonia Sheridan; Inst Design, Ill Inst Technol, MS(photog), with Aaron Siskind, Arthur Siegel & Misch Kohn; Guggenheim Fel in Photog, 72 & 80. *Work:* Mus Mod Art, NY; Art Inst of Chicago; Int Mus Photog, George Eastman House, Rochester, NY; Nat Gallery of Can, Ottawa, Ont; Houghton Rare Books Libr, Harvard Univ; and others. *Exhib:* Solo exhibs, Light Gallery, NY, 76, Chicago Ctr Contemp Photog, 78 & Stuart Wilber Inc, Chicago, 78, 79 & 80; Mirrors and Windows: Am Photog Since 1960, Mus Mod Art, 78 & traveling, 78-80; Am Photog of the Seventies, Art Inst Chicago, 79; Cliche Verre: 1939 to the Present, Detroit Inst Arts, 80; Hand-Colored Photographs, Philadelphia Col Art, 80; and others. *Teaching:* Instr photog, Univ Calif, Los Angeles, 70; instr photog generative systems, Sch of Art Inst Chicago, 71-74; coordr of printmaking, Visula Studies Workshop, Rochester, 74-. *Awards:* Guggenheim Fel, 72 & 80; Nat Endowment Arts Grant, 78; NY Found Arts Grant, 85. *Media:* Photography; Etching with Photoetching. *Publ:* Auth, When I Was Two, Visual Studies Workshop, 77; auth, Book 91, 82 & Book 89 Patterned Apart, 83, Space Heater Multiples; coauth (with Jonathan Williams), Lexinton Nocturne, A Poem by Jonathan Williams as Interpreted by Keith Smith, private publ, 83; auth, Book 95 Structure of the Visual Book, Visual Studies Workshop Press, 83. *Mailing Add:* 22 Cayuga St Rochester NY 14620

SMITH, KENT ALVIN
SCULPTOR
b White Earth Indian Reservation, Minn, Dec 23, 43. *Study:* Univ Minn, Minneapolis, with Katherine Nash, BA(sculpture), 71, MFA(sculpture), 75. *Work:* General Mills Inc, Univ Minn Galleries, Fed Reserve Bank, Minneapolis; Bemidji State Univ, Minn. *Comn:* Outdoor sculpture, Portfolio Management Corp, Minneapolis, 75. *Exhib:* Bois Fort Gallery, Ely, Minn, 74 & 75; Ojibwe Exhib, Bemidji State Univ & Minn State Hist Soc, St Paul, 74 & 75; Flatland Sculpture, Drake Univ, Des Moines, Iowa, 75; Drawing Show, Univ Minn, 75. *Pos:* Res asst, Ceramic Shell, Univ Minn, 68-69; sculpture asst to Katherine Nash, Minneapolis, 68-69; gallery technician, Univ Minn Galleries, 69-73; dir, Ojibwe Art Expo, 74-. *Teaching:* Artist in residence, Bemidji State Univ, 74-75, instr contemp Am Indian sculpture & painting, 74-. *Bibliog:* Gerald

Vizenor (auth), The Everlasting Sky, Collier-Macmillan, 70; Brian Anderson (auth), The present: Is there Indian art, Minneapolis Tribune, 10/22/72; Don Morrison (auth), Ojibwe art 1974, Minneapolis Star, 6/74. *Mem:* Col Art Asn; Ojibwe Art Asn. *Media:* Cast Metal, Wood. *Dealer:* Art Lending Gallery 2500 Groveland Terrace Minneapolis MN 55403

SMITH, KIKI
PAINTER, SCULPTOR
b Nuremberg, Ger, 54. *Work:* Art Inst Chicago, Ill; Brooklyn Mus Art, Metrop Mus Art, Mus Mod Art, Whitney Mus Am Art & NY Pub Libr, NY; Corcoran Gallery Art, Washington, DC; Fogg Art Mus, Harvard Univ, Cambridge, Mass; plus many others. *Exhib:* Modern Masks, Whitney Mus Am Art, NY, 84; Committed to Print, Mus Mod Art, NY, 88; Recent Acquisitions: 1986-1988, Mus Mod Art, NY, 88; Recent Acquisitions, Corcoran Gallery Art, Washington, DC, 90; The Unique Print: 70's into 90's, Mus Fine Arts, Boston, 90; The Interrupted Life, New Mus Contemp Art, NY, 91; Whitney Biennial, Whitney Mus Am Art, NY, 92 & 93; The Body Electric, Corcoran Gallery Art, Washington, DC, 92; Acquisitions of the 90's, Whitney Mus Am Art, NY, 92; Prints, Whitney Mus Am Art, NY, 92; Recent Aquisitions, Mus Mod Art, NY, 92; The Material Imagination, Guggenheim Mus SoHo, NY, 95-96; Being Human, Mus Fine Arts, Boston, 95-96; Feminin-Masculin: le sex de l'art, Mus Nat D'Art Mod Ctr, Georges Pompidou, Paris, France, 95-96; Everything that's interesting is new: The Dakis Joannou Collection, DESTE Found, Athens, Greece, Mus Mod Art, Copenhagen & Guggenheim Mus SoHo, NY, 96-97; Am Acad Invitational Exhib Painting & Sculpture, Am Acad Arts & Letts, NY, 97; Proof Positive: Forty Years of Contemp Am Printmaking at ULAE 1957-1997, Corcoran Gallery Art, Washington, DC, 97-98; Objects of Desire: The Modern Still Life, Mus Mod Art, NY, 97 & Hayward Gallery, London, 97-98; Beyond Belief: Modern Art and the Religious Imagination, Nat Gallery Victoria, Melbourne, Australia, 98; Giacometti to Judd: Prints by Sculptors, Mus Mod Art, NY, 98; Double Trouble: The Patchett Collection (traveling exhib), Mus Contemp Art, San Diego, Calif, 98; As Above, So Below: The Body at Work, Fabric Workshop & Mus, Philadelphia, Pa, 99; My Nature: Works with Paper by Kiki Smith, St Louis Art Mus, 1999; Kiki Smith: Telling Tales at the Int Ctr for Photog, 2001; Whitney 2002 Biennial, Whitney Mus of Am Art; John Berggruen Gallery, 2005; plus many others. *Awards:* Urban Glass Award, 96; Skowhegan Medal for Sculpture, 2000. *Bibliog:* Mercedes Vincente (auth), Un mundo natural, Lapiz, Spain, 2/98; Sarah Tanguy (auth), Kiki Smith: Night Sculpture, 9/98; Roberta Smith (auth), Galleries are labs of a sort, NY Times, 2/14/99. *Mailing Add:* c/o PaceWildenstein Gallery 32 E 57th St 2nd Fl New York NY 10022

SMITH, LAWRY
DIRECTOR, CURATOR
b Cleveland, Ohio, Aug 29, 52. *Study:* Baldwin Wallace Col, BA, 74; Cleveland State Univ, MFA, 77. *Collection Arranged:* Artist's Adopt, St Vincent Charity Hosp, 89; Ken Burgess (retrospective), La Mama La Galleria, 89, Danforth Mus, 90, Art Students League, 91. *Pos:* Dir & cur, Lamama Lagalleria, New York, 85-97, Citicorp Ctr, New York, 86-87, Cleveland Pub Theatre Ohio, 90; Nat Pub Radio, WBOE, 77-80; dir & cur, Marlen Gallery, NY, currently. *Awards:* Recepient Twyia M Conway Radio-TV Award; Hastings Grant. *Mem:* Screen Actors Guild; Am Fedn TV & Radio Artists. *Specialty:* Emerging artists. *Mailing Add:* La Mama-La Galleria 6 E First St New York NY 10003

SMITH, LAWSON WENTWORTH
SCULPTOR, EDUCATOR
b Havana, Cuba, Apr 20, 47; US citizen. *Study:* Okla State Univ, BFA, 70; Univ Nebr, MFA, 74. *Work:* Ctr Visual Arts Gallery, Ill State Univ, Bloomington & Normal; Sioux City Art Ctr, Sioux City, Iowa; and others. *Exhib:* One man shows, Contemp Arts Found, Oklahoma City, 71, Henri Gallery, Washington, DC, 75, 77, 79 & 82, Schweinfurth Art Mus, Auburn, NY, 88, Rome Art Ctr, NY, 89, Bartlett Art Ctr, Stillwater, Okla, 93, Pooke Mus, Natick, Mass, 94 & OK Harris Gallery, NY, 98; Rutgers Nat Drawing Exhib, 79 & 81; OK Harris Gallery, NY, 82; Nat Works on Paper, Great Falls, NDak, 87. *Teaching:* Instr sculpture, Wichita State Univ, Kans, 74-75; assoc prof, Syracuse Univ, NY, 76-. *Awards:* Purchase Award, 35th Ann Exhib, Sioux City Art Ctr, Iowa, 73; Purchase Award, Ball State Univ, 76; Sculpture Award, Fingerlakes Regional, Mem Art Gallery, Rochester, NY, 80; and others. *Media:* All. *Mailing Add:* Syracuse Univ Syracuse NY 13244

SMITH, LINDA KYSER
PAINTER, INSTRUCTOR
b Fort Worth, TX, Mar 16,42. *Study:* Univ N Tex, BA & MA, 1966; Studied under: Everett Raymond Kinstler, Aaron Shikler, Burton Silverman, Bettina Steinke, William Reese, Ned Jacob, 1972. *Work:* Nat Cowgirl Hall of Fame, Fort Worth, Tex; Musée de la Grande Vigne, Dinan, Brittany; Montgomery Mus of Fine Art, Montgomery, Ala. *Comn:* Portrait of Fern Sawyer, Nat Cowgirl Hall of Fame, Fort Worth, 1998. *Exhib:* Allied Artists, Butler Mus, 1999. *Teaching:* instr, Scottsdale Artists' Sch, Ariz; instr, Andreeva Portrait Academy, Santa Fe, NMex. *Awards:* Gold Medal for Oil, Knickerbocker Artists 45th Open, 2000; Everett Award, Allied Artists of Am, 2005. *Mem:* Nat Arts Club, NYC (artist mem); Salmagundi Club, NYC; Allied Artists of Am, NYC; Pastel Soc of Am, NYC; Artists Fel Inc, NYC. *Media:* Mixed Media. *Publ:* Coauth, Focus Santa Fe Cover & Feature Art, 1997, 2004; contribr (bk), Best of Portraits, Northlight Books, 1998; coauth, feature art, US Mag, 2002; coauth, Art Business News, 2002. *Mailing Add:* 233 Delgado St Santa Fe NM 87501

SMITH, LOWELL ELLSWORTH
PAINTER
b Canton, Ohio, Nov 20, 1924. *Study:* Miami Univ, Ohio, BFA, 48; Famous Artists Schs, dipl, 55. *Work:* Canton Art Mus, Ohio; Akron Art Mus; Frye Mus, Seattle; Cowboy Hall Fame, Oklahoma City. *Exhib:* Nat Acad Western Art, Cowboy Hall Fame, Oklahoma City, 78 & 81-83; The Oaxaca Experience, Frye Mus, Seattle, 80; Western Heritage Show, Houston, 81-85; Artists of Am, Colo Hist Soc, Denver, 82-85; Am Watercolor Soc Exhib, Nat Acad, NY. *Teaching:* Instr landscape & figure painting, privately, 60 . *Awards:* Gold Medal Watercolor, Nat Acad Western Art, 82 & 83; Prix West, Nat Acad Western Art Show, Cowboy Hall Fame, 83; Silver Medal, Watercolor, 85, Gold Medal, 88 & Silver Medal, Nat Acad Western Art, 90; Silver Medal, Nat Acad Western Art, 90. *Bibliog:* Don Blanchard (producer), The Mood, the Moment (TV film), Metrop Libr, Oklahoma City, 82; Mary Bowman (auth), article, Artists of Rockies, 82; Susan Dodd Whelan (auth), Light washed shadows, Southwest Art Mag, 83; article, Art West Mag, 89. *Mem:* Ohio Watercolor Soc; Am Watercolor Soc; Nat Acad Western Art; Northwest Rendevous Group. *Media:* Watercolor. *Dealer:* Pierce Gallery Scottsdale AZ; Shriver Gallery Taos NM

SMITH, LUTHER A
PHOTOGRAPHER
b Tishomingo, Miss, Mar 16, 50. *Study:* Univ Ill, Urbana, with Art Singabaugh & Bart Parker, BA, 72; RI Sch Design, with Harry Callahan & Aaron Siskind, MFA(photog), 74. *Work:* Portland Mus Art, Maine; Mass Inst Technol; Ark Arts Ctr, Little Rock; Monmouth Col, Ill; La Grange Col, Ga; Chicago Art Inst, Ill; Houston Mus Fine Arts, Tex; Amon Carter Mus, Ft Worth, Tex; Dallas Mus Art. *Exhib:* Photog, Kansas City Art Inst, Mo, 78; Black & White & Color, Mass Inst Technol, 79; Contacts, Western Heritage Mus, Omaha, Nebr, 80; Invisible Light, Smithsonian Inst Traveling Exhib, 80-83; Second Sight, Carpenter Ctr, Harvard Univ, 81; Road & Roadside, Chicago Art Inst, 87; one person exhib, Waco Art Ctr, Tex, 87, Springfield Art Mus, Mo, 91 & Amarillo Art Mus, Tex, 94. *Teaching:* Vis lectr, Univ Ill, Urbana, 74-75, instr art, 75-78, asst prof, 78-81, assoc prof, 81-; assoc prof art dept, Tex Christian Univ, 83; prof art, Tex Christian Univ, 92-. *Awards:* Purchase Prizes, Allied Arts Asn, 79, Chattahoochi Art Asn, 80 & Ark Art Ctr, 80; Sesquicentennial Award, Tarrant Co Works on Paper, Ft Worth, Tex. *Mem:* Soc Photographic Educ. *Media:* Photography. *Res:* Landscape Photogr of Texas and the Am South. *Interests:* Landscape Photography. *Publ:* Illusr, Camera, 75, The Trinity River, TCU Press, 77; illusr, Chicago Mag, 78; illusr, Darkroom Dynamics, 78, Electronic Flash Photography, 80 & Photographing Indoors With Your Automatic Camera, 81, Curtin-London. *Dealer:* William Campbell Contemporary Art, Fort Worth, TX. *Mailing Add:* Art Dept Tex Christian Univ PO Box 298000 Ft Worth TX 76129

SMITH, MICHAEL A
PHOTOGRAPHER, PUBLISHER
b Philadelphia, Pa, Feb 16, 42. *Study:* Self-taught. *Work:* Mus Mod Art, Metrop Mus Art, NY; Art Inst Chicago; Mus Fine Arts, Boston; Philadelphia Mus Art. *Comn:* To Photograph Toledo, Toledo Mus Art, 80; Study of Princeton NJ, Princeton Gallery Fine Art, 84; To Photograph New Orleans, Historic New Orleans Collection, 85; Art in Pub Places, Broward Co, Fla, 89. *Exhib:* Solo exhibs, Sheldon Mem Art Gallery, 76, Del Art Mus, 78 & Ringling Mus Art, 80; Landscapes 75-79, Stanford Univ Mus Art, 81, Toledo Mus Art, 81 & Norton Gallery Fine Art, West Palm Beach, Fla, 82; Foto Biennal Enschede, The Neth, 84; Lowe Art Gallery, Syracuse Univ, 86; Loyola Col, Baltimore, 87; Michael A Smith: A Visual Journey, Inter Mus Photo at George Eastman House, 92. *Teaching:* Vis prof, Philadelphia Col Art, 70-72, Bucks Co Community Col, 71-73. *Awards:* Photogr Fel, Nat Endowment Arts, 77; Best Photog Bk of Yr, Le Grand Prix DuLivre, Recontres Int dela Photog, Arles, France, 81; Photogr Fel, Pa Coun Arts. *Bibliog:* Estelle Jussim (auth), A dead straight picture: The landscapes of Michael A Smith, Boston Rev, 2/77; James Enyeart (auth), Intro to Landscapes 1975-1979, Lodima Press, 81; Richard Trenner (auth), A portrait of the artist, Ont Rev, fall-winter 82-83; John Bratnober (auth), A Visual Journey, Lodima Press, 92. *Media:* Photography. *Publ:* Auth & illusr, Twelve Photographs 67-69, pvt publ, 70; auth, On teaching photography, Exposure, J Soc Photog Educ, 76; auth & illusr, Landscapes 1975-1979 (exhib catalog), Lehigh Univ, 81; Landscapes 1975-1979 (monogr), Lodima Press, 81; Eight Landscape Photographs, Regnis Press, 83; illusr, Michael A Smith: A Visual Journey (monogr), Lodima Press, 92; auth & illusr, Tscany: Wandering the Backroads, Lodima Press, 2004; auth & illusr, The Stduents of Deep Springs College, Lodima Press, 2000. *Mailing Add:* PO Box 400 Ottsville PA 18942

SMITH, MIMI
SCULPTOR, CONCEPTUAL ARTIST
b Brookline, Mass, May 13, 42. *Study:* Mass Col Art, Boston, BFA, 1963; Rutgers Univ, New Brunswick, NJ, MFA, 1966. *Work:* Franklin Furnace, NY; The Getty Ctr, Santa Monica, Calif; Hosp Corp Am; The Inst Contemp Art, Tokyo; Mus Mod Art, NY; The Newark Mus; Spencer Art Mus, Lawrence, Kans. *Exhib:* Committed to Print, Mus of Modern Art, New York City, 1988; Television Apparatus, The New Mus, NY, 90; Div of Labor, Bronx Mus, La Mocha, 95-96; Art with Conscience, Newark Mus, NJ, 95-96; one-woman show, Inst of Contemp Art, Univ of Pa, 94; Addressing the Century, Hayward Gallery, London, 98-99; Representing a Show of Identities, Parish Art Mus, Southampton, NY, 2000; Gloria: Another Look at Feminist Art in the 1970's, White Columns, NY, Moore Col, Philadelphia, RISD Mus, Providence, 2002-2003; Critical Mass, Mead Art Mus, Amherst Col, Mass, 2003. *Awards:* Grant, Nat Educ Asn Artists Fel, 78; NYSCA Project Grant, Visual Studies Workshop, 82; Grant, Joan Mitchell, 98; Fel, NY Found of the Arts, 86. *Bibliog:* Roberta Smith (auth), Mimi Smith Knotted Thread Work from the 60's and 70's, NY Times, 1/15/99, Helen Molesworth (auth), Frieze, Mimi Smith, Issue 46, 5/99, Gretchen Kurtz (auth), The Works Curators Covet, 11/18/2001; others. *Publ:* auth, This is a Test, Visual Studies Workshop. *Dealer:* Anna Kustera at Tilton Kustera Gallery. *Mailing Add:* 451 W Broadway New York NY 10012-5300

SMITH, NAN S(HELLEY)
SCULPTOR, CERAMIST
b Philadelphia, Pa, Nov 10, 52. *Study:* Tyler Sch Art, Temple Univ, Philadelphia, BFA, 74; Ohio State Univ, Columbus, MFA, 77; Univ Ill, Japan House, with Shozo Sato, 79. *Work:* IDS/American Express Corp Hq, Minneapolis, Minn; Lamar Dood Art Ctr, La Grange Col, Ga; Wocek Int Ceramics Collection; Ichon Ceramics Ctr, Korea. *Exhib:* World Ceramics Exposition Korea, 2001; Taking Measure: Am Ceramic Art at the New Millenium, Yertu, Korea, 2001; Clay Body Rhetoric: Ceramic Figure of Speach, Marianna Kistler Beach Mus Art, Kans State Univ, Manhattan, 2002; Women Playing with Fire, Art Dept Gallery, Tex Womne's Univ, Denton, 2003; Rawspace Gallery, Sofa Chicago, 2004; 21st Century Ceramics in the US and Can, Canzani Ctr, Gallery, Columbus, Ohio, 2003; The Figure in Contemp Ceramics, Creative Alliance Gallery, Baltimore, MD, 2005. *Teaching:* Vis instr design & ceramics, Univ Ill, Champaign-Urbana, 77-79; assoc prof ceramics, Univ Fla, Gainesville, 79-96, prof, 96-, res found prof, 2000. *Awards:* Fla Arts Coun Artist Fel, 81-92-98; SAF-NEA Fel, 93; Scholar Enhancement Fund Award, Univ Fla, 98, 99, 2000, 2001, 2002 & 2004-06. *Bibliog:* Potters of Northern Florida, The Studio Potter, vol 26, 6/98; Susan Peterson (auth), Contemporary Ceramics, Watson and Cuptill Pub, 2000; Glen Nelson and Richard Burkett (coauth), Ceramics: A Potter's Handbook, 6th edit, Harcourtt Col Pub; Susan Peterson (auth), Working with Clay, Laurence King Pub, 2002; World Famous Ceramic Artists Studios, Hebei Fine Art Pub House, 2005. *Mem:* Nat Coun Educ Ceramic Arts; Fla Craftsmen Inc; Int Sculpture Ctr. *Media:* Clay; Gypsum Cement, Metal. *Publ:* Auth, Blending institution and logic, Ceramics Monthly Mag, fall 90; Flexible Molds for Ceramics, Ceramics Monthly Mag, 2/96; auth, Flexible Mold Making, The Studio Potter, 12/99; auth, Controlled Drying and Firing, Ceramics Monthly, 5/2000; auth, color, Air, Illusions & Ceramics, Technical, No 11, 2000. *Mailing Add:* 2310 NW 142nd Ave Gainesville FL 32609-4022

SMITH, NELSON DAVID
PAINTER, ENVIRONMENTAL ARTIST
b Detroit, Mich, Apr 29, 55. *Study:* Studies with Agnes Denes, New York, 76; Col Wooster, BA(art), 77; Cranbrook Acad Art, MFA, 80. *Work:* Detroit Inst Art, Mich; Ameritech Collection, Detroit, Mich; Neiman Marcus, Houston, Tex; Franklin Furnace, NY; Cleveland Inst Art, Ohio. *Comn:* Mural, Martin Luther King Ctr, Holtzman & Silverman, Detroit, Mich, 82; Fore Art (art golf), Detroit Artists Market, Mich, 94. *Exhib:* 11th Biennial of Mich, Kresge Mus, Lansing, Mich, 89; solo shows, Paint Creek Ctr Arts, Rochester, Mich, 95; Detroit Painters, Cent Mich Univ, Mt Pleasant, 93; Human Radiation, installation/performance, Performance Network, Ann Arbor, Mich, 96; Sweet Alchemy, Bunting Gallery, Mich, 97; Cleveland Performing Arts Fest, Pub Theater, 98. *Pos:* Co-dir, Contemp Art Inst Detroit, Mich, 90-93. *Teaching:* Instr foundations, Lawrence Technol Univ, 91-. *Awards:* Project Grant, The Missing Persons (performance), Art Matters, 89; Creative Artist Grant, Psychological Gravity (performance/installation), Mich Coun Art & Cult Affairs, Arts Found Mich, 93; First Prize, Celebrate Mich Artists, Arts Found Mich, 94. *Bibliog:* Marsha Miro (auth), Defining Michigan through its artists, Detroit Free Press, 9/4/94; Bruce Martin (auth), Flash and fizzle, Ann Arbor News, 10/11/96; Keri G Cohen (auth), Int Smith's World, Detroit Free Press, 7/16/97. *Mem:* Contemp Art Inst Detroit (pres, 90-93); Detroit Focus Gallery (exhib comt, 94-96); Detroit Artists Market. *Media:* Miscellaneous Media; Performance & Installation. *Publ:* Contribr, Sweat Bombs, Cranbrook Acad Art, 80; auth, Victims of Circumstance, Mich Coun Arts, 87

SMITH, PAUL J
MUSEUM DIRECTOR
b Sept 8, 31. *Study:* Art Inst Buffalo; Sch Am Craftsman; Parsons Sch Design; New Sch Social Res, Hon Dr Fine Arts, 87. *Collection Arranged:* Craft Today: Poetry of the Physical, 86; The Confectioner's Art; Designed for Production: The Craftmen's Approach; The Teapot, The Door; For the Body; Object for Preparing Food; Portable World; The Great American Foot; Objects for Use: Handmade by Design; cur adv, Objects USA, 69; cur adv, Craft, Art & Religion, Vatican, Rome, Ital, 78; cur adv, In Praise of Hands, Toronto, Can, 74; plus over 200 other exhibs, 63-. *Pos:* Bd dir, Louis Comfort Tiffany Found, currently; former adv trustee, Haystack Mountain Sch Crafts, Deer Isle, Maine; Nat Coun adv bd, Atlantic Ctr Arts; dir emer, Am Craft Mus, currently; former bd trustees, Penland Sch Crafts; int adv bd, Friends Fiber Art Int; trustee, LGT Foundation; mem prof comt, Friends of Art in Embassies. *Awards:* Hon Degree, Fine Arts, Parsons Sch Design New Sch for Soc Res, 87. *Mem:* Hon Fel Am Craft Coun; Hon Intl Mem Can Craft Coun. *Publ:* Craft Today: Poetry of the Physical Am Craft Mus, Weidenfeld & Nicholson, 86; Objects for Use: Handmade by Design; served as general ed for a 336 book pub by Abrams, 2001. *Mailing Add:* 1349 Lexington Ave New York NY 10128

SMITH, RAE
PAINTER
b New York, NY. *Study:* Franklin Sch Prof Arts, with V K Jonynas. *Exhib:* Solo exhib, Galleria Prova, Tokyo, Japan, Lois Richards Gallery Greenwich, Conn, Accent Gallery, Ocean City, NJ, Greene Art Gallery, Guilfard, Conn, Images Gallery, Briacliff Manor, NJ, Pen & Brush Inc, Gallery, New York City, Emelin Theatre Gallery Inaugural Exhib, Mamaroneck, NY, Mussavi Art Ctr, New York City; Butler Inst Am Art, Youngstown, Ohio; Charter Oak Gallery, Fairfield, Conn; Euro Pastel Exhib, St Petersburg, Russia; Xi'an Acad Fine Arts, China; SoHo Gallery 420, Nat Asn Women Artists, New York City; Cork Gallery, Avery Fisher Hall, Lincoln Ctr, New York City; Triton Mus Art, Santa Clara, Calif; Slater Mus, Norwich, Conn; Mus Contemp Masters, San Antonio; Noyes Mus, Oceanville, NJ; China Mus Art, Suzhou; Hammond Mus, North Salem, NY. *Teaching:* instr pastel and oil painting, Katonah Art Ctr, NY. *Awards:* Gold Medal Hon, Audubon Artists Inc; Pastel Soc Can Award, Pastel Soc Am; First Prize, Pastel, Mamaroneck Artists Guild, NY; Bd Dirs Award, Slater Mus, Norwich; Artistic Excellence in Oils Award, Mus Contemp Masters; Art du Pastel en France Award, Vernon; Cardman Award, CLWAC, Nat Arts Club, New York City. *Mem:* Pastel Soc Am, NYC (master pastelist); Am Artists Prof League, NYC (fellow); Catharine Lorillard Wolfe Art Club, NYC; Hudson Valley Art Asn, NY; Allied Artists Am NYC; Audubon Artists NYC. *Media:* Pastels, Oils. *Publ:* articles in Mitsukoshi Mag, Publ Tokyo, Japan, 98; articles in Best of Pastel 2, Rockport Publishers, Inc, 98; articles in Pastel J Mag, 11-12/99; Articles in Int Artists Mag, 5-6/2000, 7-8/2002. *Dealer:* Accent Gallery Ocean City NJ; Lois Richards Gallery Greenwich Conn; Peter McPhee Gallery Stone Harbor NJ; Corporate Art Group Chicago IL. *Mailing Add:* 513 W Country Club Dr Egg Harbor City NJ 08215

SMITH, RAECHELL M
DIRECTOR
Study: Univ Mo, BA, 84; Univ Kans, MA, 91. *Pos:* Curatorial Ast, Nelson-Atkins Mus of Art, 92-96; Dir, H&R Block Artspace at KC Art Inst, 96-; Co-cur, The Works Bldg, Kansas City, Mo, 98; Cur, Albrecht-Kemper Mus, St Joseph, Mo, 99; Cur, The Jewish Mus Gallery at Village Shalom, Overland Park, KS, 2001. *Mem:* Kansas City Visual Arts Com. *Mailing Add:* Kans City Art Inst H&R Block Artspace 16 E 43 St Kansas City MO 64111

SMITH, RALPH ALEXANDER
WRITER, EDUCATOR
b Ellwood City, Pa, June 12, 29. *Study:* Columbia Univ, AB, Teachers Col, MA & EdD. *Pos:* Ed, J Aesthetic Educ, 66-2000; Exec secy, Coun for Policy Studies Art Educ, 78-82; contrib ed, Arts Educ Policy Rev, 2000-. *Teaching:* Instr art hist & art educ, Kent State Univ, 59-61; asst prof art hist & art educ & chmn dept art, Wis State Univ-Oshkosh, 61-63; asst prof art hist & art educ, State Univ NY Col New Paltz, 63-64; asst prof aesthet educ, Univ Ill, Urbana, 64-67, assoc prof, 67-71, prof cult and educ policy, 71-96, emer prof cult & educ policy, 96-. *Awards:* Distinguished Univ vis Prof, Ohio State Univ; Distinguished sr scholar, Col Educ, Univ Ill; Disting lectr Studies in Art Edn Award, 91. *Mem:* Am Soc Aesthet; distinguished mem Ill Art Educ Asn; Nat Art Educ Asn. *Res:* Theoretical foundations of aesthetic and humanities education; cultural and educational policy analysis. *Publ:* Co-ed, Aesthetics and Arts Education, Univ Ill Press, 91; ed, The Sense of Art, 89, Cultural Literacy and Arts Education, Univ Ill Press, 91; coauth, Art Education: A Cultural Necessity, Univ Ill Press, 91; coed, The Arts, Education and Aesthetic Knowing, Univ Chicago Press, 92; Public Policy and the Aesthetic Interest, Univ Press, 92; General Knowledge & Arts Educating, 94; plus others. *Mailing Add:* 2909 Henthwood CT Champaign IL 61822

SMITH, RAYMOND WALTER
PHOTOGRAPHER, BOOK DEALER
b Newark, NJ, Oct 26, 42. *Study:* Stetson Univ, BA, 64; Yale Univ, MA, 66, MPhil, 68. *Work:* Yale Univ Art Gallery, New Haven; Univ Tex, Gernsheim Collection, Austin. *Exhib:* Conn Photography, Greater Hariford Arts Festival, Hartford, 74 & 75; Am As Found Photos by Ray Smith, Yale Univ Libr, New Haven, 75; Photographs by Ray Smith, Stetson Univ Art Gallery, Deland, Fla, 76; Beyond Documentary Four Photographers, John Slade Ely House, New Haven, 77. *Pos:* Cur, John Slade Ely House, New Haven, 85-95. *Mem:* Art Libr Soc-N Am; Antiqn Bksellers Asn Am. *Publ:* Articles in American Art Review, 75, Photographic Rev, 79-80; ed, 15 Painters & Sculptors (exhib catalog), John Slade Ely House, 85; auth, Artists From People's Republic of China (exhib catalog), 91, Architecture and Process (exhib catalog), 92, John Slade Ely House; John OC McCrillis: 50 Years in Art & Design, John Slade Ely House, 94; Surrealist Affinities (exhib catalog), John Slade Ely House, 94. *Mailing Add:* c/o RW Smith Bookseller 130 Cold Spring St New Haven CT 06511

SMITH, ROBERT CHARLES
DESIGNER, PAINTER
b Buffalo, NY, Jan 21, 26. *Study:* Albright Art Sch, Univ Buffalo, BFA, 50; Univ Cincinnati. *Work:* Morton D May Collection, St Louis, Mo; Wash Univ Gallery Art, St Louis, Mo; Butler Inst Am Art; Laumeier, Sculpture Park, St Louis. *Comn:* Fountain, Pub Libr Hamilton Co, Cincinnati, Ohio, 60; fountain, Temple Ark & Eternal Light, Glen Manor Temple, Cincinnati, 64; fountain, Munic Opera Asn Forest Park, St Louis, Mo, 74; fountain, Boone Co Nat Bank, Columbia, Mo, 75 & 86. *Exhib:* Fountains 69, Taft Mus, Cincinnati, 69; Multiples '80, Contemp Arts Ctr, New Orleans, La, 80; The Book, Peoria Art Guild, 98; Bookentics: Bob Smith, Book Artist, 98; Beyond the Fold, Gallery at S Orange, NJ, 99; one-man shows, Univ City Pub Libr, Schweig Gallery, St Louis, 81, Bonsack Gallery, 94 & Art Acad Cincinnati, 95, Typoetica: Kinetic Books, Washington Univ, Special Coll, 2002; Bob Smith, Eclectic Vision, Deer Isle, ME, 2002. *Teaching:* Instr design, Albright Art Sch, 50-52; instr design & drawing, Art Acad Cincinnati, 52-65; prof design, Sch Fine Arts, Wash Univ, 65-94, prof emer, 95. *Awards:* Community Arts Award, US Dept of Housing & Urban Develop, 73; Purchase Award, Ann Drawing Show, Ball State Univ Art Gallery, 74. *Bibliog:* K Hanna (auth), Fountains '69, Taft Mus, 69; S Pollack (auth), RC Smith--Waterworks, New Art Examiner, 81; Jan Garden Castro (auth), Bookonetics, Sculpture, 99. *Media:* Artists Books; Painting. *Publ:* Auth, Basic Graphic Design, Prentice-Hall, 86, 2nd ed, 92; Main By Line, 91, Sunrise-Sunset, 91 & Master's Pieces, 92, Eclectic Press. *Mailing Add:* 6316 Washington Ave St Louis MO 63130

SMITH, ROBERT LEWIS
DESIGNER, EDUCATOR
b Salem, Ohio, Aug 5, 40. *Study:* Univ Southern Calif; Univ Calif, Los Angeles, BA, 63, MFA, 66. *Collection Arranged:* Three Photographers--Bullock, Sommer, Teske, 68; Jud Fine, 72; Narrative Themes: Audio Works, 78; Sound, 79; Leroy Neiman-Andy Warhol, 81; Changing Trends: Content and Style, 82. *Pos:* Gallery dir, Calif State Univ, Northridge, 66-70 & Brand Lib Art Ctr, Glendale, Calif, 70-73; dir & founder, Los Angeles Inst Contemp Art, 74-86. *Teaching:* Prof & design, Calif State Univ, Nortridge, 66-. *Awards:* DAAD Fel, 85. *Bibliog:* Michael Auping (auth), Interview with Bob Smith, La Mamelle, Berkeley, Calif, 75; plus others. *Publ:* Auth & designer numerous exhib catalogs. *Mailing Add:* Dept Art Calif State Univ 18111 Nordoff St Northridge CA 91330-8300

SMITH, ROWENA MARCUS
PAINTER, COLLAGE ARTIST
b Bethel, Vt, June 6, 1923. *Study:* Syracuse Univ, BFA, 43; Hofstra Univ, MS, 66; studied with Rex Brandt, Joan Irving, Miles G Batt, Charles Reid, Barbara Nechis, Don Andrews, 77-2000. *Work:* Broward Co Libr Found, Ft Lauderdale; Oakland Park Libr, Oakland Park, Fla; Coral Springs Libr, Fla; Nat Asn Women Artists Collection, Zimmerli Mus, Douglass Col, Rutgers Univ; Hollywood Art Culture Ctr, 94; Fla Atlantic Univ, Ft Lauderdale Ctr, Fla; City of Pembroke Pines, Fla; Hope Ctr, Miami, Fla. *Comn:* Ltd ed print 4-color lithography, Floyd L Wray Found, Davie, 88; 2-Ltd Ed Prints-4 Color Lithography, Smart Art Co, Boca Raton, Fla. *Exhib:* Allied Artists Am Ann, NY, 94; Soc Experimental Artists, Ft Worth, Tex, 94; Ga Watercolor Soc 15th Traveling Exhib, 94; All Fla, Boca Raton Mus Art, Fla; Taos Nat Exhib Am Watercolor II, NMex; Mentor to Mentor Traveling Exhib, Duneden Art Ctr, Coral Springs Mus Art, Fla, 99 & 2001; Under the Influence 2/3 Exhib, Fort Lauderdale Mus Art, 2000; Gross Innovations, Cynon Valley Mus, Aberdore, Wales, 2004-05; and others. *Pos:* Coordr, Masters Degree Prog in Creative Arts Therapy, Hofstra Univ, 75; exec secy, Gold Coast Watercolor Soc, 85-91; mem, co-chmn, 2 plus 3 Artists Orgn; exec dir, Gold Coast Watercolor Soc, 94-2003. *Teaching:* Watercolor & collage, Broward Art Guild, 80-94, Floyd L Wray Found Flamingo Gardens, 87-; workshop leader painting & drawing, Art Adventures Inc, Ft Lauderdale, 84-89; Holiday Park Community Ctr, Ft Lauderdale, 91-93; Figure Workshop, Coral Springs Artists Guild, 93; Charlotte Maloney Workshops, 95-97; master workshop, Coral Springs Mus Art, 2001. *Awards:* Am Frame Award, Ga Watercolor Soc, 96; Am Artist Award, Western Colo Watercolor Soc 6th Nat Exhib, 96; Nautalus Fel, Int Soc Experimental Artists, 2000; and others. *Bibliog:* Joan Davenport (auth), Art Notes, Village Press, 3/92; City Link, Fort Lauderdale, Fla, 11/2000; Eastsider, Broward Co, Fla, 11/2000; Tamarac Forum, 3/21/03. *Mem:* Am Watercolor Soc; Nat Asn Women Artists; 2 + 3 Artists Asn, (co-chmn); signature mem Transparent Watercolor Soc Am; and others. *Media:* Watercolor, Acrylic; Collage. *Publ:* Complete Guide to Creative Watercolor, Creative Art Publs, 88; Artists of Fla, vol I and vol II; XS Mag, Sun Sentinal, 6/93; Watercolor - A Step by Step Guide & Showcase, Rockport Press, 96; Bridging Time and Space Essays on Layered Art, Markowitz Publ, 98; Collage in all Dimensions, 2005. *Dealer:* Ganymede Gallery New York NY; Light House Gallery Tequesta FL; Gallery 421 Fort Lauderdale FL; Carlton Fine Arts, Ft Lauderdale, FL; Boca Raton Museum of Art Artists Guild. *Mailing Add:* 5313 Bayberry Ln Tamarac FL 33319

SMITH, RUTH REININGHAUS See Reininghaus (Smith), Ruth

SMITH, SHERRI
WEAVER, EDUCATOR
b Chicago, Ill, Mar 21, 43. *Study:* Stanford Univ, Calif, BA, 65; Cranbrook Acad Art, Bloomfield Hills, Mich, MFA, 67. *Work:* Art Inst Chicago; Hackley Art Mus, Muskegon, Mich, Am Tel & Tel Co; Borg Warner Corp; Colorado Springs Fine Arts Ctr, Colo. *Comn:* Wall hangings, Detroit Plaza Hotel, 77; Fed Bldg, Ann Arbor, 78; Du Page Co Hosp, Ill, 78; Int Business Machines, Atlanta. *Exhib:* Mus Mod Art, NY, 69; Biennale of Tapestry, Lausanne, Switz, 71-77; Three-Dimensional Fibers, Govett-Brewster Art Gallery, New Plymouth, NZ, 74; Am Crafts 76, Mus Contemp Art, Chicago, 76; Fiberworks, Cleveland Mus Art, Ohio, 77; one-person show, Hadler Gallery, NY, 78; Mainstream, the Art Fabric Traveling Exhib; and others. *Teaching:* Instr weaving & textile design, Colo State Univ, Ft Collins, 71-75; prof weaving & textile design, Sch Art, Univ Mich, Ann Arbor, 75-. *Bibliog:* Larson & Constantine, Beyond Crafts, The Art Fabric, Van Nostrand, 75; Kuenzi (auth), La nouvelle tapisserie, Bonvent, 75; Waller (auth), Textile sculptures, Studio Vista, 77. *Dealer:* Jacques Baruch Gallery 900 N Michigan Ave Chicago IL 60611; Modern Masters Tapestries 11 E 57th New York NY 10022. *Mailing Add:* 1733 Jackson Rd Ann Arbor MI 48103

SMITH, SHIRLEY
PAINTER
b Wichita, Kans. *Study:* Kans State Univ, BFA; Provincetown Workshop Art Sch, Mass; Art Students League. *Work:* Whitney Mus Am Art, NY; Univ Calif Art Mus, Berkeley; Aldrich Mus Contemp Art, Ridgefield, Conn; Phoenix Art Mus, Ariz; Prudential Insurance Co Am, Newark, NJ; and others. *Exhib:* Am Painting 1970, Va Mus, Richmond; Lyrical Abstraction, Aldrich Mus Contemp Art, 70; Recent Acquisitions & Lyrical Abstraction, Whitney Mus Am Art, NY, 71; From the Mus Collection Art by Women, Univ Calif Art Mus, Berkeley, 73; Auditorium Installation Exhib, Everson Mus, Syracuse, NY, 76-79; Views by Women Artists, Women's Caucus Art, NY, 82; 161st Ann Exhib, Nat Acad Design, NY, 86; Animal Life, 87 & Nature in Art, 88, One Penn Plaza, NY; one-woman show, Wichita Art Mus, 78, Art/EX Gallery, Stamford Mus & Nature Ctr, Conn, 87, Aaron Gallery, Washington, DC, 87, Joan Hodgell Gallery, 87, John Jay Gallery, New York, NY, 2000; Am Acad Inst Arts & Lett Invitational, NY, 90 & 91; one-woman retrospective (auth, catalog), Beach Mus, Kans State Univ, Manhattan, 99. *Collection Arranged:* Mus Collections, Whitney Mus Am Art, NYC, Phoenix Art Mus, The Aldrich Mus Contemp Art, Conn, Ulrich Mus, Wichita State Univ, Univ Calif Art Mus, Berkeley, Everson Mus, NY, Telfair Mus, Savana, Ga, and others; Pub Collections, Chase Manhattan Bank, NYC, King Features Syndicate, MYC, Prudential Life Insurance, Newark. *Teaching:* Instr painting, Teamsters Local 237, New York, 88-95. *Awards:* Grumbacher Artists Mat Co Award Mixed Media, New Eng Exhib, Silvermine, 67; Acad Inst Award, Am Acad Inst Arts & Lett, New York, 91; Richard Florsheim Art Fund Grant, 998; Retrospective Opening Grant, 99. *Bibliog:* Rosemary Mayer (auth), article, Arts, 2/73; April Kingsley (auth), article, Art Int; The Longboat Observer, Oct, Animals, Joan Hodgell Gallery, Sarasota, FL; The Whichita Eagle Beacon, Artists forms Muslim into Paintings, Dorothy Beldon (auth); Art in Focus, Two Viewpoints, Dorothy Grafly, Philadelphia, PA. *Mem:* Artists Equity. *Mailing Add:* 141 Wooster St New York NY 10012

SMITH, SUSAN
PAINTER, COLLAGE ARTIST
b Greensburg, Pa. *Study:* Art Students League, 55-57, with Edwin Dickinson; Briarcliff Col, BS, 71; Hunter Col, New York, NY, MA, 76. *Work:* Weatherspoon Art Gallery, Univ NC, Greensboro; Copenhagen Handelsbank, Denmark. *Exhib:* Solo exhibs, Westmoreland Mus, Greensburg, Pa, 86 & Galerie Art In, Nürnberg, Ger, 93; Intericon 1986, Charlottenborg, Copenhagen, Denmark, 86; After Matisse, Traveling Exhib, Worcester Art Mus, Mass, Portland Mus Art, Maine, Queens Mus, Flushing, NY, Chrysler Mus, Norfolk, Va, Dayton Art Inst, Ohio & Phillips Collection, Washington, DC, 86-87. *Teaching:* Lectr art & painting, Sch Visual Arts, New York, 69-70; adj asst prof color, Pratt Inst, Brooklyn, NY, 74; asst prof art, Wagner Col, Staten Island, NY, 82-99. *Awards:* MacDowell Colony Fel, Peterboro, NH, 69; New York Creative Artists Pub Serv Prog Fel, 75-76; Artist Fel Grant, Nat Endowment Arts, Washington, DC, 81. *Bibliog:* Peggy Cyphers (auth), Susan Smith, Arts Mag, 9/91; Stephen Bann & William Allen (coauths), Interpreting Contemporary Art, 91; Yve-Alain Bois (auth), Susan Smith's Archeology, Edinburgh: Reakton Books & New York: Harper Collins Inc, 91; and others. *Media:* Oil. *Dealer:* Margarete Roeder Gallery 545 Broadway New York NY 10012. *Mailing Add:* 39 Bond St New York NY 10012

SMITH, TODD D
MUSEUM DIRECTOR
Study: Duke Univ, BA; Ind Univ, MA. *Pos:* with, Dayton Art Inst, Ohio, Mint Mus, Charlotte, NC; pres, Chief Exec Officer, Plains Art Mus, Fargo, Ndak; dir, Knoxville Mus of Art, Tenn, 2002-. *Mailing Add:* Knoxville Mus Art 1050 World's Park Fair Park Knoxville TN 37916-1653

SMITH, VALERIE
CURATOR
Work: Joan Jonas: Five Works, Queens Art Mus, 2003—04 (Award for Best Exhib of Time Based Art, Int Asn Art Critics/USA, 2005). *Exhib:* Cur, (exhibs) Sonsbeek Sculpture Exhib, Arnhem, The Neth, 1993 (Named one of the top 10 shows of the 1990s, Artforum mag). *Pos:* Cur, Artists Space, New York City; cur dir, exhibs Queens Mus Art. *Mailing Add:* Queens Mus Art NY City Bldg Flushing Meadows Corona Park Flushing NY 11368

SMITH, ZAK
ARTIST
b Syracuse, NY, Jul 16, 1976. *Study:* Cooper Union, NY, BFA, 94—98; Skowhegan Sch Painting & Sculpture, Maine, 99; Yale Univ, MFA, 99—2001. *Work:* Whitney Biennial, Whitney Mus Am Art, NY, 2004; Contemp Mus, Baltimore, 2004; Feeling Strangely Fine, Estrany De La Mota, Barcelona, Spain, 2005; Rep in permanent collections, Progressive Corp, Mayfield, Ohio. *Exhib:* One-man shows, 20 Eyes in My Head, Fredericks Freiser Gallery, NY, 2002, Paintings That Look Good and Were Hard to Make, 2003, Hope You Like It, Franklin Art Works, Minneapolis, 2004, Fredericks Freiser Gallery, NY, 2005; group shows, at I See You 2, 2001, Comic Release: Negotiating Identity for a New Generation, Carnegie Mellon Univ, Pittsburgh, 2002, Hello, My Name Is, 2002, Upstream Gallery, Amsterdam, 2004. *Mailing Add:* c/o Fredericks Freiser Gallery 504 W 22nd St New York NY 10011

SMITH-THEOBALD, SHARON A
CONSULTANT
b New Jersey, Feb 12, 42. *Study:* State Col NJ, BA; Hofstra Univ, MA. *Pos:* Dir, Bridgton Art Gallery, 69-75; exec dir, Greater Lafayette Mus Art, 78-89; bd mem, Ind State Coun, 82-92; pres, Theobald Co, West Lafayette, Ind, 92- & Appraisal Asn Int, 92-; ed, Am Soc Appraisers Quart; sr appraiser, fine art specialist. *Teaching:* Lectr commun, Wilfrid Laurier Univ Can, 75-77; instr art appreciation, Greater Lafayette Mus Art, 78-89. *Awards:* Estabrook Award, Hofstra Univ, 87. *Mem:* Am Asn Mus (chair, Small Mus Adminrs Comt, 87-89); Am Soc Appraisers, Ind Chap (pres, 92; state dir, 93, nat faculty mem); Contemporary Art Soc; Indianapolis Mus Art (personal property comt). *Res:* Women artists, specifically Laura Anne Fry and Alice Baber. *Publ:* Auth, Media, metaphor, manipulation, New Art Examiner, 81; Sculpture in the Space Age, 85 & Laura Anne Frye: Rookwood and Beyond, 86, Greater Lafayette Mus Art; Latin American Visions I, Am Express Found, 88; Arts Indiana, 88. *Mailing Add:* c/o Theobald Co 2167 Tecumseh Park Ln West Lafayette IN 47906

SMITHER, EDWARD MURRAY
DEALER, CONSULTANT
b Huntsville, Tex, July 23, 37. *Study:* Sam Houston State Univ, BS, 58; Dallas Mus Fine Arts Sch, 59. *Pos:* Dir, Cranfill Gallery, Dallas, 70-72; owner & dir, Smither Gallery, Dallas, 72-74; co-owner, Delahunty Gallery, Dallas, 74-82; pvt dealer & consult, 83-; adv, AH Belo Corp, Estates of Otis Dozier, Jerry Bywaters, Charles Taylor Bowling, Dallas; consult, currently. *Awards:* Legend Award, Dallas Visual Arts Ctr, 98. *Mem:* Dallas Mus Art. *Mailing Add:* 1934 Kessler Pkwy Dallas TX 75208

SMOKLER, STANLEY B
SCULPTOR, ASSEMBLAGE ARTIST
b Bronx, New York, Nov 27, 44. *Study:* Univ Pittsburgh, studio art with Virgil Cantini, BFA, 67; Pratt Inst, with George McNeil & Calvin Albert, MFA, 75; also, study with Anthony Caro, 85. *Work:* Morgan Trust, NY; Minskoff Realty, 88; NY Sports Clubs. *Comn:* Steel sculpture (abstract), comn by Nitkin Alkalay-Robbins, NY, 82; steel sculpture abstractions, Edelman Pub Relations, 84, Patterson-Schwartz, Wilmington, Del, Krapf Assoc, Newark, NJ; wall-relief sculpture (steel), Tanenbaum-Haber Co, NY, 85; Dansko Manfacturing, Pa; Del Horticulture, Wilmington. *Exhib:* Sculpture Exhib, Stroud Water, PA, 79, Salmagundi Club, NY, 81, Tenn Tech Univ, 98, Albright Col, VA, 2000, Blue Streak, DC, 2001, West Chester Univ, PA, 2001, Mira Mar

Gallery, Fla, 2001, Bloomsbury Univ, PA, 2002, Klein Gallery, PA, 2002, Kim Foster Lines, NY, 2002, Dartsmouth Col, Hanover, NH, 2003; Terminal Art Show, Brooklyn, NY, 83; In the Courtyard, PS 1, Long Island, NY, 83; Objects, Paulo Salvador, NY, 85; New Art in NY, Parsons Sch Design, NY, 85; Biennial, Everson Mus, Syracuse, NY, 85; Abstractions, Hudson Highland Mus, Cornwall, NY, 86; Case de Picos, Segovia, Spain, 86; one-person shows, Allegheny Col, 88 & Ledis Flam, NY, 89; Three Rivers Arts Festival, Pittsburgh, Pa; Bill Bace Gallery, NY, 91; Biennial, Delaware Art Mus, Wilmington, 93; one person exhib, Kim Foster Gallery, NY, 95. *Pos:* Artist-in-residence, Art Park, Nat Heritage Trust, Lewiston, NY, 85; guest lectr contemp art, IBM, NY, 85; fel, Triangle Artists, Pinc Plains, NY, 86. *Teaching:* Guest lectr mod art, NY Univ, 84 & Vsdan, 93-95; prof sculpture, Urban Ctr for the Performing Arts, 93-94; prof art, fundamentals 3D design, Del Col of Art & Design, 97-2005. *Awards:* NY Heritage Trust Grant, 85; City of NY Grant, 86. *Bibliog:* Susan Drew (auth), Art in public places (radio interview), WBAI, 8/83; The ladies mile, NY Times, 6/86; Vivian Raynor (auth), Blue Hill art exhibit, NY Times, 93; Koran Wilkin (auth), Partisan Rev. *Mem:* Found Community Artists; Col Art Asn Am; Int Sculpture Ctr. *Media:* Steel, Fabricated. *Dealer:* Kim Foster Gallery, NYC. *Mailing Add:* 873 Broadway No 401 New York NY 10003

SMOLAREK, WALDEMAR
PAINTER, PRINTMAKER
b Warsaw, Poland, Sept 5, 37; Can citizen. *Study:* Warsaw Sch Art, 52; Warsaw Acad Fine Arts, 57, with Zygmunt Tom-Kiewicz & Wincenty Sliwinski. *Work:* Miami Mus Mod Art; Mus Mod Art, Stockholm; Mus Nat, Warsaw, Poland; Artist Coop, San Francisco; Selected Artist Gallery, NY. *Exhib:* Langton Gallery, London, 77; Harrison Galleries, Vancouver, BC, 86; Osaka Found Cult, Japan, 91; 8th Int Graphic Exhib, Catania, Italy, 92; Montserret Gallery, NY, 92; and others. *Teaching:* Instr form & color composition, Warsaw Sch Art, 57-60; instr continuing educ, Univ BC, 72. *Awards:* Man of Year, Am Biog Inst, 96; Men of Achievement, Int Biog Ctr, Cambridge, Eng. *Media:* Oil, Watercolor; Serigraphy, Woodcut. *Publ:* North Star News, (article), 8/18/76. *Dealer:* Artbarbakan Muzeum Historycznym Rynek Starego Miast 28 Warsaw 00-272 Poland. *Mailing Add:* 311-1564 SW Marine Dr Vancouver BC V6P 6R6 Canada

SMUSKIEWICZ, TED
PAINTER, EDUCATOR
b Chicago, Ill, Sept 22, 32. *Study:* Am Acad Art, AA, 56-60. *Work:* Northern Indiana Public Service Co, Hammond, Ind. *Exhib:* one-man show, Freeport Art Mus, Ill, 79; Denver Rotary Club's Artists of Am, Denver, Colo, 88 & 90; Butler Inst of Am Art, 88 & 89; Salmagundi 11th Ann Exhib, NY, 88; 4th Ann Arts for the Parks Nat Competition, 90; Oil Painters Am, 1st Nat Exhibit, Chicago, Ill, 92; Am Art in Miniature, Gilcrease Mus, Tulsa, Okla, 93 & 94; Miniatures Exhibs, Albuquerque Mus, NMex, 93, 94, 96, 97, 98, 99 & 2000. *Teaching:* Instr oil & pastel painting, Am Acad Art, Chicago, 79-, chair fine art dept, 93-. *Awards:* Diamond Medal, Palette & Chisel Acad, 70 & Gold Medal, 97; Finalist, Am Artist Mag Competition, 78; 1st Place Award, Municipal Art League Chicago, 90. *Bibliog:* Article, Back of the yards artist, Chicago Back Yards J, 70; article, Midwest Art Mag, 5/87. *Mem:* Palette & Chisel Acad Fine Arts, Chicago, Ill. *Media:* Oil, Pastel. *Publ:* Auth, Creative Painting of Everyday Subjects, Watson-Guptill, 86; Oil Painting Step By Step, North Light, 92; contribr, Basic Oil Painting Techniques, North Light Books, 93; Basic Portrait Techniques, North Light Books, 94; Basic Still Life Techniques, North Light Books, 94. *Dealer:* Ottinger Gallery 670 N Wells St Chicago IL 60610. *Mailing Add:* 1356 Whitcomb Des Plaines IL 60018

SNEED, PATRICIA M
COLLECTOR, CONSULTANT
b Spencer, Iowa, Oct 24, 22. *Study:* Drake Univ, 40-42; Univ Cincinnati, 45-46. *Collection Arranged:* Fifty Artists for Fifty States (nat art exhib), 65-; Art in Other Media, 70. *Pos:* Founder & mem women's bd, Rockford Art Mus, currently. *Mem:* Am Fedn Arts. *Collection:* Contemporary American art. *Mailing Add:* 1311 Parkview Ave Rockford IL 61107

SNELL, ERIC
SCULPTOR
b Guernsey, Channel Islands, 53. *Study:* Birmingham Polytechnic, London, Eng, 72-73; Hornsey Col Art, London, 73-76, DAAD Artist-in-Berlin Prog, 85-86. *Work:* Univ E Anglia, Norwich, Eng; Mus Mod Art, Linz, Austria; Art Gallery of Hamilton, Ont; La Jolla Mus Contemp Art. *Exhib:* Solo exhibs, Galerie Work, Kaiserslauterm, WGer, 88, Galerie Bernard Jordan, Paris, France, 88, CREDAC, Centre d'Art Contemporain, Ivry, France, 88, Galerie Corla Feuhr, Munich, Ger, 89, Galerie Schoeller, Dusseldorf, Ger, 89, Galerie Fortlaan 17, Ghent, Belgium, 90; Distances, 86, Ephemerite, 87, Chapelle St Louis de la Salpetriere, Paris, France; Konstruktion, Kontemplation, Expression, Galerie im Trudelhaus, Baden, Switz, 87; Mathematik in der Kunst der letzen Dreizig Jahre, Wilhelm- Hack-Mus, Ludwigshafen, Ger, 87; Die Ecke, Kantonales Kunstmuseum, Sion, Switz & Austellungsraume, Ger, 88; 49th Parallel, NY, 89. *Bibliog:* John Bentley Mays (auth), Drawing's physical qualities focus of artist's work, Globe & Mail, Toronto, 12/16/88; Liliana Albertazzi (auth), Paris, Contemporanea, 1-2/89; Susan Freudenheim (auth), La Jolla: Eric Snell, Artforum Int, 1/89

SNELSON, KENNETH D
SCULPTOR, PAINTER
b Pendleton, Ore, June 29, 27. *Study:* Black Mountain Col, NC, 48-49; with Fernand Leger, Paris, 50. *Work:* Whitney Mus Am Art & Mus Mod Art, NY; Staedelijk Mus, Amsterdam, Holland; City Buffalo, NY; Storm King Art Ctr; Albright-Knox Art Gallery, Buffalo, NY; Hirshhorn Mus & Sculpture Garden, Washington; Japan Iron & Steel Fedn, Osaka. *Comn:* Baltimore Inner Harbor, Md, 80; Albright-Knox Art Gallery, 82; Stanford Univ, Calif, 82; Mus Mod Art, Shiga, Japan. *Exhib:* Int Sculpture Symp, Osaka, Japan, 69; one-man shows, Ger, 71, Wilhelm Lehmbruck Mus, Ger & Berlin Nationalgalerie, 77, Hirshhorn Mus, 81, Albright-Knox Art Gallery, 81, Nat Acad Sci, Washington, 90 & Maxwell Davidson Gallery, 94; Portrait of an Atom Traveling Exhib, 79-83; Addison Gallery Am Art, Phillips Acd, Andover, Mass, 84; Toledo Mus, Ohio, 84; Aldrich Mus Contemp Art, Ridgefield, Conn, 85; Cleveland Ctr Contemp Art, Ohio, 85; Contemp Sculpture Ctr, Tokyo, Japan, 91 & 95. *Awards:* Deutscher Akad Austauschdienst for Berlin Kunstlerprogram, 76; Am Inst Archit Medal, 81; Amer Acad & Inst Arts & Letts, Artist Award, 87; Lifetime Achievment Aeard, Int Sculpture Ctr, 99. *Bibliog:* Articles, Artforum, 5/77 & Art News, 2/81; Martica Sawin (auth), Kenneth Snelson: unbounded space, Arts Mag, 9/81; article, Print Collector's Newslett, 84. *Mem:* Am Acad Arts & Letts. *Media:* Mixed. *Publ:* Auth, A design for the atom, Indust Design, 2/63; auth, Continuous Tension, Discontinuous Compression Structures, 65 & A Model for Atomic Forms, 66 & 78, US Patent Off; Portrait of An Atom, 81. *Mailing Add:* 37 W 12th St New York NY 10011

SNIDOW, GORDON E
PAINTER, SCULPTOR
b Paris, Mo, Sept 30, 36. *Study:* Art Ctr Col Design, BA. *Work:* Nat Cowboy Hall Fame, Oklahoma City; Phoenix Mus, Ariz; Gilcrease Mus, Tulsa, Okla; Mont Hist Soc, Helena; Cowboy Artists Am Mus, Kerrville, Tex. *Exhib:* Cowboy Artist Am Ann Exhib, Nat Cowboy Hall Fame & Phoenix Art Mus, 65-75 & 78; two-man show, Nat Cowboy Hall Fame, 70; one-man show, C M Russell Gallery, Mont Hist Soc, 73; Cowboy Art Exhib, Grande Palais, Paris France, 80; Am Western Art Exhib, Beijing, China, 81; retrospective, Gilcrease Mus, Tulsa, Okla, 81; The American Cowboy, Libr Cong, 83; Hubbard's Mus of Am West, NMex; Smithsonian, Washington, DC. *Teaching:* Instr workshop, Cowboy Artists Am Mus, Kerrville, Tex, currently. *Awards:* Silver Medal for Watercolor, Cowboy Artist of Am, 74, Mem Award, 78; Gold Medal, 75, 77-79 & 81, Best of Show, 77, 78 & 82, Colt Award, 79, Silver, 84, Western Assoc, Phoenix Art Mus; and numerous other awards. *Bibliog:* Meigs (auth), The Cowboy in American Prints, Sage Swallow, 72; Broder (auth), Bronzes of the American West, Abrams, 74; Hassrick (auth), American Painting Today, Watson-Guptill, 75. *Mem:* Cowboy Artist Am (secy-treas, 67-68, vpres, 68-69, pres, 78-79 & 84-85). *Media:* Gouache. *Publ:* Contribr, Persimmon Hill, 70; auth, Gordon Snidow, Chronicler of the Contemporary West, 73; Hanging On: Gordon Snidow Portrays the Cowboy Heritage, Northland Press. *Mailing Add:* 1011 Hull Rd Ruidoso NM 88345-7703

SNODGRASS-KING, JEANNE OWEN (MRS M EUGENE KING)
CONSULTANT, WRITER
b Muskogee, Okla, Sept 12, 27. *Study:* Art Instr, Inc; Northeastern State Col; Okla Univ. *Collection Arranged:* 214 exhibs of Indian art & artifacts, Philbrook Art Ctr, 55-68; Am Indian Artists Nat Competition Ann, Philbrook Art Ctr, 55-68; Beaver-McCombs Mem Exhib; Oscar Howe Retrospective, 1979-1982; The James Bialec Collection, Heard Mus, 99. *Pos:* Asst to dir & cur Am Indian Art, Philbrook Art Ctr, 55-68; admin asst to pres, Educ Dimensions, Inc, 69-71; registr, Gilcrease Mus, 73-90; assoc, Am Indian Affairs & mem Arts & Crafts Adv Comt; juror, many nat & regional Indian Art Exhibs. *Teaching:* Lectr, American Indian painting. *Awards:* Outstanding Contrib to Indian Art Award, US Dept Interior, 67. *Mem:* Okla Mus Asn (charter secy); Tulsa Hist Soc; Am Asn Mus; Life mem Gilcrease Mus. *Publ:* Ed, American Indian Basketry, 64; auth, American Indian Painters: A Biographical Directory, Heye Found, 68; American Indian Painting, Amarillo Art Ctr, Tex, 81; contribr, Oscar Howe, A Retrospective Exhibition, 82; auth, articles, Gilcrease Mag, 73-82, Southwestern Art Mag, 82-85 & Am Indian Art Mag, 85. *Mailing Add:* 3931 S Madison Ave Tulsa OK 74105

SNOW, DASH
PHOTOGRAPHER
b NYC, 1981. *Exhib:* Group shows, Interstate, Nicole Klagsbrun Gallery, 2005; Whitney Biennial: Day before Night, Whitney Mus Am Art, 2006; Silence is the Only True Friend That Shall Never Betray You, Rivington Arms Gallery, NYC, 2006. *Mailing Add:* c/o Rivington Arms Gallery 4E 2nd St 1Fl New York NY 10003

SNOW, LEE ERLIN
PAINTER, INSTRUCTOR
b Buffalo, NY, Jan 2, 24. *Study:* Univ Buffalo, BA, 47; Otis Art Inst, with Joseph Young, scholar; Univ Calif, Los Angeles, with Neda Al-Hilali. *Work:* Skirball Mus, Los Angeles; Halls Crown Ctr, Kansas City; Craft & Folk Art Mus, Los Angeles. *Comn:* Mosaic portrait Bess Hawes, Folk Music Classes Univ Calif, Los Angeles; Mosaic portrait Rebecca Berman, Teaneck, NJ. *Exhib:* Solo shows, Southwest Craft Ctr Gallery, San Antonio, 75, Front Rm, Dallas, Tex, 76 & Galeria de Sol, Santa Barbara, Calif, 76; Art Rental Gallery, Los Angeles Co Mus Art, 76-80; Jewish Fedn Craft Show, Los Angeles, 83; Los Angeles Art Asn Exhib, Craft & Folk Art Mus; Santa Barbara Art Asn, 84-98; Juried Weavers Guild, 84 & 85; Gallery 113, Santa Barbara, Calif, 84-98; Adult Educ Fac, Faulkner Gallery, 85-98. *Pos:* Interviewer, Starship Earth, KHJ Radio, Los Angeles. *Teaching:* Instr multimedia fibre, Barnsdall Arts & Crafts Ctr, Los Angeles, 72-76 & Los Angeles Co Mus Art, 75; workshop leader non-loom weaving, World Crafts Conf, Toronto, Ont, 74; instr, Necklace Design-Adult Educ, Santa Barbara, 85-98; Beads, Santa Barbara Art Mus, 87. *Awards:* Third Prize Painting & Award Study, Westwood Art Asn, 63. *Bibliog:* Lois McAfee (auth), Oh, what a tangled web, Sun-Tel, San Bernardino, 1/75; article, Los Angeles Times Home Mag, 12/17/78; Santa Barbara News Press, 92. *Mem:* Los Angeles Art Asn; Am Crafts Coun; Southern Calif Weavers Guild; Santa Barbara Art Asn. *Media:*

Watercolor, Collage. *Publ:* Coauth (with Dona Mellach), Weaving Off-Loom, 73 & contribr, Creating Art From Fibers and Fabrics, 74, Regnery; contribr, How to Create Your Own Designs, Doubleday, 75; Exotic Needlework, 78 & Ethnic Jewelry, 81, Crown; coauth, Creative Stitchery with Dona Meilach, Regnery. *Mailing Add:* 775 Terni Lane Santa Barbara CA 93105-4431

SNOW, MARYLY A
LIBRARIAN, PRINTMAKER
b Oakland, Calif; Dec 1, 44. *Study:* Univ Calif, Berkeley, BA, 66, MLIS, 73. *Work:* Fine Arts Mus San Francisco; Achenbach Found for Graphic Arts, San Francisco; Librn, archit slide & photograph libr, Univ Calif Berkeley, 76-96. *Exhib:* Recent Acquisitions, Fine Arts Mus, San Francisco, 81; Paper: A Survey of Bay Area Printmakers, Hatley Martin Gallery, Calif, 88; Sapporo Int Print Biennial Event Hall Marui Imai, Japan, 91; Current Trends in Printmaking, Art Works, Sacramento, Calif, 92; Pulp Fictions, Austin Mus Art, Tex, 96. *Mem:* Calif Soc Printmakers Art Libr Soc (secy 95-97). *Media:* Prints & Photographs. *Res:* Image management, intellectual property, data base standards. *Interests:* Architectural History, Urbanism & design. *Publ:* Auth, Visual Depictions and the Use of MARC & coauth, Access to Diverse Collections in University Settings, Beyond the Book, G K Hall, 90; auth, Spiro at the University of California, Computer & the History of Art, 95; auth, SPIRO FAQ, Visual Resources Association Bulletin, 96; auth, Pedagogical Consequences of Photo Mechanical Reproduction in the Visual Histories from Copy Photograph to Digital Mnemonics, Visual Resources, 96. *Dealer:* Suzy Locke & Assoc 4254 Piedmont Ave Oakland CA 94611. *Mailing Add:* Archit Slide Libr 232 Wurster Hall Berkeley CA 94720-1800

SNOW, MICHAEL
PAINTER, FILMMAKER
b Toronto, Ont, Dec 10, 1929. *Study:* Ont Col Art, Toronto; Brock Univ, Ont, LLD, 75. *Work:* Mus Mod Art & Albright-Knox Art Gallery, NY; Art Gallery of Ont, Toronto; Montreal Mus Fine Arts; Nat Gallery Can, Ottawa; Univ Waterloo, Ont; many other pvt Am & Can Collections. *Comn:* Flightstop, Cadillac Fairview Comn, Toronto Eaton's Ctr, 79; Hologram Gallery, Round House, Expo '86, Vancouver, BC, 86; Audience, Skydome, Toronto, Ont, 88-89; photo mural, Reflections, Can Embassy, Wash, 89; Red, Orange & Green, Confederation Life, Toronto, 92. *Exhib:* Biennale of Can Painting, Nat Gallery Can, 57, 61 & 65; Walker Art Ctr, Minneapolis, Minn, 58, 75 & 90; Art Gallery of Ontario, Toronto, 59, 69, 70 & 83; JB Speed Art Mus, Louisville, Ky, 62; Gallery XII, Montreal Mus Fine Arts, Que, 63; Nat Gallery of Can Painting, Mus Mod Art, Paris, France, 67; Anti-Illusion: Procedures & Materials, 69 & Re-visions: Projects & Proposals in Film & Video, 79, Whitney Mus Am Art, NY; Another Dimension, Nat Gallery Can, 77-78; solo exhibs, Isaacs Gallery, 79, 82, 84, 86, 87, 88, 89 & 91, San Francisco Art Inst, Calif, 92, Galerie Claire Burrus, Paris, France, 92-93, SL Simpson Gallery, 93 & 94, Embodied Vision, The Power Plant, Toronto, Ont, 94, Art Gallery of Toronto, 94, Light, Surface & Sound, Presentation House Gallery, Vancouver, BC, 94; Photography & Art 1984-86, Los Angeles Co Mus Art, Calif, 87; Passages de l'image, Ctr Georges Pompidou, Paris, traveling, 90-92; SL Simpson Gallery, Toronto, Ont, 92; Crisis of Abstraction, Que Mus, traveling, 93; Wavelengths, 95; Whitney Biennial: Day for Night, Whitney Mus Am Art, NY, 2006; and many others. *Teaching:* Prof advan film, Yale Univ, 70; vis artist, Nova Scotia Col Art & Design, Halifax, 70 & 74 & Ont Col Art, Toronto, 73, 74 & 76; vis prof, Princeton Univ, 88. *Awards:* Guggenheim Fel, 72; Order of Can, 83; Best Independent Experimental Film, Los Angeles Film Critics' Asn, 83; Visual Arts Award, Toronto, 86; and others. *Bibliog:* Adele Freedman (auth), Michael Snow: Forty Years of Achievement, Can Art, Spring, 94; Susan Walker (auth), Michael Snow Drawings at SLSG, Toronto Star, 3/12/94; Pamela Young (auth), Snow Storm, Maclean's Mag, 3/21/94; and many others. *Mem:* Royal Can Acad Arts. *Publ:* Auth, Cover to Cover, Nova Scotia Series, NS Col Art & Design, Halifax, 75; High School, Impulse Ed, Isaacs Gallery, 79; illustr, diacritics: A Review of Contemporary Criticism, fall 84. *Dealer:* Samantha Scroggie. *Mailing Add:* 176 Cottingham St Toronto ON M4V 1Z5 Canada

SNOWDEN, GILDA
PAINTER, WRITER
b Detroit, Mich, July 29, 54. *Study:* Wayne St Univ, BFA, 77, MA, 78, MFA, 79. *Work:* Art Ctr of Battle Creek, Mich; Dayton Hudson Corp, Post/Newsweek Corp, Mich Bell Tel & Edward F Duffy Co, Detroit; Detroit Inst Arts. *Comn:* Painting/construction, Post/Newsweek, Detroit, 83. *Exhib:* View Point-Out of Square, 84 & Detroit Artist Update, 86, Cranbrook Acad Art Mus, West Bloomfield, Mich; Transformations, 88 & Signature Images, 90, Detroit Inst Art; Black Creativity, Mus Sci & Indust, Chicago, Ill, 88; Coast to Coast, Univ Mich Mus Art, Ann Arbor, 89. *Pos:* Dir, Detroit Repertory Theater; contribr, Detroit Focus Quarterly, Focus Gallery & New Art Examiner, currently. *Teaching:* Instr fine arts, Wayne State Univ, Detroit, 79-85; asst prof fine arts, Ctr Creative Studies, Detroit, 81-. *Awards:* Artists Grant, Mich Coun Arts, 82, 85, 88 & 90; Arts Midwest Award, Nat Endowment Arts, 90. *Bibliog:* Edsel Reid (dir) 15 Black Artists (video), 88; Jan Vander Marck (auth), Signature Images (exhib catalog), Detroit Inst Arts, 90. *Mem:* Nat Conf Artists; founders soc Detroit Inst Arts. *Media:* Painting, Drawing. *Publ:* Contribr, City Mag, Sutton Publ, 87; Detroit Artist Market J, 90; Chicago New Art Examiner, 92. *Dealer:* Paul Holoweski 430 N Washington Royal Oak MI 48067; Sherry Washington Gallery 1274 Library Detroit MI 48226. *Mailing Add:* c/o Fine Arts Ctr Creative Studies 201 E Kirby Detroit MI 48202-4048

SNYDER, HILLS
SCULPTOR, WRITER
b Lubbock, Tex, Dec 1, 50. *Study:* Univ Kans, Lawrence, 69-70; Tex Tech Univ, Lubbock, 70, 72-73; Univ Tex, San Antonio, MFA, 94. *Work:* Univ Tex, El Paso; Ucross Found, Ucross, Wyo; Austin Mus Art; Mont Arts Coun, Helena; Nicolaysen Mus Art, Casper, Wyo. *Exhib:* solo exhibs, Tyler Mus Art (with catalog), Tex, 85, Custer Co Art Ctr, Miles City, Mont, 87, Patrick Gallery, Austin, Tex, 87, Nicolaysen Art Mus, Casper, Wyo, 92, ArtPace, San Antonio, Tex, 96, Austin Mus Art, Tex, 96, Hand Not Hand, ArtPace, San Antonio, Tex, 96, Representative Material, Rrose Amarillo, San Antonio, Tex, 97, Gloville, Casino Luxembourg, 98, Suede Sandbox, DiverseWorks, Houston, Tex, 98, Neil Diamond's Greatest Hits, Sala Diaz, San Antonio, Tex, 98, The Incredible Shrinking Man, The Project Room, San Antonio, Tex, 99, Mercury Poisoning, Finesilver, San Antonio, Tex, 2000, The Wind Cries Mary, Project Space, Angstrom Gallery, Dallas, Tex, 2000, Tea For One, Three Walls, San Antonio, Tex, 2000, Jack, James Gallery, Houston, Tex, 2000. *Pos:* dir, Sala Diaz, San Antonio, Tex. *Teaching:* Artist-in-educ drawing & sculpture, Custer Co Art Ctr, Miles City, Mont, 86-87; Mont Arts Coun artist in Schs/Communities, 86-88; Lectr sculpture, Univ Tex, San Antonio, 92, 95-96. *Awards:* Fel, Art Matters Inc, 90 & 96; Fel (sculpture), Nat Endowment Arts, 95. *Bibliog:* Francis Colpitt (auth) Hills Snyder at The Austin Museum Art, Art in Am, 2/97; Michael Duncan (auth), Report from San Antonio, Artnet Mag, 8/2000; Dana Friis-Hansen (auth), Double Trouble: Mirrors/Pairs/Twins/Lovers, Blue Star Art Space, 96. *Media:* Mixed-media, Drawing. *Publ:* Auth, Predicaments: Elizabeth McGrath: Installations 94-96 (exhib catalog), Eugene Binder Gallery, Long Island City, NY, 96; Body and Site (exhib catalog), ArtPace, San Antonio, Tex, 96; Trajectory: How Am I? (exhib catalog), ArtPace, San Antonio, Tex, 96; Evidence of Play (exhib catalog), ArtPace, San Antonio, Tex, 96. *Mailing Add:* 19693 Bluehill Dr Helotes TX 78023

SNYDER, JILL
MUSEUM DIRECTOR
b Trenton, NJ, Jun 28, 57. *Study:* Wesleyan Univ, Middletown, Conn, BA, 1979. *Pos:* Exec assoc, Guggenheim Mus, New York City, 1983-88, educ assoc, 1989-91; adj fac, NY Sch Interior Design, 1988-92, Mary Schiller Myers Sch Art, Univ Akron; staff lectr, Mus of Modern Art, New York City, 1989-94, Guggenheim Mus, 1988-92; dir, cur, Freedman Gallery, Albright Col, Reading, Pa 1993-95; dir, The Aldrich Mus of Contemp Art, Ridgefield, Conn, 1995-96; mem cur rev panel, Abington Art Ctr, Jenkintown, Pa, 1995; exec dir, Mus Contemp Art Cleveland, 1996-. *Awards:* Shelby and Leon Levy fel, 1988; Milton and Sally Avery Found fel, 1990. *Mem:* Art Table; Am Asn Mus; Col Art Asn. *Mailing Add:* Cleveland Ctr Contemp Art 8501 Carnegie Ave Cleveland OH 44106

SNYDER, JOAN
PAINTER
b Highland Park, NJ, Apr 16, 40. *Study:* Douglas Col, BA, 62; Rutgers Univ, MFA, 66. *Work:* Phillips Collection, Washington; Mus Fine Arts, Boston, Mass; Jewish Mus, NY; Mus Mod Art, NY; Whitney Mus Am Art; and others. *Exhib:* exhibs incl Whitney Ann, 1972, Whitney Bienniel, 1974, 80, Corcoran Bienniel, 1975, 87, Mus Modern Art, New York City, Ann Jaffe Gallery, Bay Harbor Island, Fla, 1991, Cynthia Mcallister Gallery, New York City, Bixler Gallery, New York City, Parrish Art Museum, Southampton, NY, Acad Arts and Letters, New York City, Tribeca 148 Gallery, New York City; traveling one-woman show, San Francisco Art Inst, Grand Rapids Art Mus, Renaissance Soc, Univ Chicago, Anderson Gallery, Va Commonwealth Univ, Richmond, 1979-80; solo-exhibs, Wadsworth Atheneum, Conn, 81, Nielsen Gallery, Boston, 81, 83, 86, 91, 94 & 97, Hirschl & Adler Mod, NY, 85, 88, 90, 92, 94, 96 & 98, Allentown Art Mus, Pa, 93, Rose Art Mus, Brandeis Univ, Waltham, Mass, 94 & Brooklyn Mus Art, NY, 98; Biennial exhib, Whitney Mus Am Art, NY, 81 & Corcoran Gallery Art, 87; Robert Miller Gallery, NY, 2001, Elena Zang Gallery, NY, 2003, Betty Cuningham Gallery, 2004. *Teaching:* Yale Univ, New Haven, Conn, Atlanta Col Art, Princeton Univ, NJ, State Univ, NY, Stonybrook, 66-, Parsons Sch Design, NY, 90-, Vt Studio Sch, 90, 92 & Sch Visual Arts, NY, 96. *Awards:* Nat Endowment Arts Grant, 74; John Simon Guggenheim Fel, 83. *Bibliog:* Donald Kuspit (auth), Joan Snyder at Hirschl & Adler Modern, Artforum, summer 94; Roberta Smith (auth), Building on the bare, bare bones, NY Times, 94; Ted Perl (auth), Seeing & Time, The New Republic, 8/3/98; Robert M Murdock (auth), Rev, 5/1/98. *Mem:* Nat Acad (acad, 95-). *Media:* Oil, Acrylic

SNYDER, KIT-YIN
SCULPTOR, ENVIRONMENTAL ARTIST
b Canton, China; US citizen. *Study:* City Col, New York, BSEE; Univ Mich, Ann Arbor; Claremont Grad Sch, Calif, MFA. *Work:* Margaret Mitchell Square, Atlanta, Ga; White St Detention Ctr, NY. *Exhib:* Rome, Italy, 89 & 92; Kunstraum, Ger, 91; Reed Col, Portland, Ore, 91; State Univ NY, Brockport, 92; Gallery L'Eclisse, Rome, 94. *Awards:* Nat Endowment Arts Grant, 80, 82 & 86; NY Found Arts Fel Sculpture, 86 & 91; Award Excellence in Design, White St Detention Ctr, NY, 89. *Publ:* dir, Double Exposure: An Immigrants Journey (documentary film). *Mailing Add:* 80 Warren St Apt 13 New York NY 10007

SNYDER, RUTH (COZEN)
SCULPTOR, PAINTER
b Montreal, Que; US citizen. *Study:* Univ Calif, Los Angeles; Otis Art Inst. *Work:* Smithsonian Inst, Washington; Frederick S Wight Gallery, Univ Calif, Los Angeles; US State Dept, US Embassy, Lisbon, Portugal; US State Dept, US Embassy, Riyadh, Saudi Arabia; Coos Art Mus, Ore; Brigham Young Univ, Provo, Utah; and others. *Comn:* The Three Muses (bronze sculpture), Los Angeles Co Mus Art; Nat Mus Women Art, Washington, DC; Bone Jungle Gym (stainless steel), Orthopaedic Hosp, Los Angeles; Ghetto Wall (bronze), Sacramento, Calif; Emergence Structural Column, Santa Monica, Calif; installation, Bone Jungle Gym, Los Angeles; Bone Rainbow (bronze), Barnsdale Park; Curved wall series (bronze), Venice Art Walk, Pytka Studio. *Exhib:* Armand Hammer Mus, Los Angeles; Palm Springs Desert Mus, Calif; Laguna Beach Mus Art, Calif; Butler Inst Am Art, Youngstown, Ohio; Tokyo Metrop Mus, Osaka, Japan; Coos Art Mus; Nat Mus Women Art, Washington, DC; Threshold Gallery Sculpture, Pergamont Station, Santa Monica; Dept of Health and Human

Svcs, Washington, DC; Chicago Cult Ctr; UN Hqrs, NY; and others. *Collection Arranged:* Light, Illusion and Reality & Three from Los Angeles, Riverside Art Ctr & Mus, Calif; Merrill Lynch Corp, Newport Beach, Calif; First Beverly Bank, Beverly Hills, Calif; Dept State, US Embassy, Riyadh, Saudi Arabia; Lisbon, Portugal; Smithsonian Instn, Washington, DC; Frederick S Wight Galleries, Univ Calif, Los Angeles; Brigham Young Univ, Provo, Utah; Betty Ford Ctr, Eisenhower Hosp, Palm Springs, Calif; Coos Art Mus, Coos Bay, Oreg; Pacific Design Ctr, Los Angeles. *Pos:* Exec bd mem, Watercolor West, Riverside, Calif, 77-80; guest cur, Riverside Art Ctr, Calif, 85; juror, San Diego Int Water Color Soc, currently. *Teaching:* Lectr, Brigham Young Univ, Provo, Utah, 83, Southern Utah State Col, Cedar City, 84 & Golden West Col, Orange Co, Calif, 90. *Awards:* Walter Annenberg Award, Nat Watercolor Soc, 78; Scottsdale Ctr Arts Juror's Award; Sculpture & Watercolor Award, San Bernardino Mus Art; and others. *Bibliog:* Art in America, 9/84; Nancy Stapen (auth), Boston Globe, 7/93; Peter Frank (art critic), Ruth Snyder: Sculptor of the Human, 98. *Mem:* Nat Watercolor Soc; Artists Equity; Watercolor West; Womens Caucus Arts; Int Sculptor Soc. *Media:* Bronze; Watercolor. *Publ:* Contribr, Creative Seascape Painting, by Edward Betts, Watson-Guptill; and others. *Dealer:* Threshold Gallery Bergamont Station Santa Monica CA; Michael Himovitz Gallery Sacramento CA. *Mailing Add:* 550 Hanley Ave Los Angeles CA 90049

SNYDER, WILLIAM B
PAINTER, EDUCATOR
b San Francisco, Calif, Sept 26, 28. *Study:* Chouinard's Art Inst, 43; San Francisco State Col; Stanford Univ, fel, 61-62. *Work:* Oakland Art Mus, Calif; City Chico, Calif; Haggin Mus, Stockton, Calif; Richmond Art Ctr, Richmond, Calif; and others. *Comn:* Portrait, USS Posco Steel Mills, Korea/USA; portrait, John F Kennedy Univ, Calif; mural, Cretaceous period, Calif Acad Sci, San Francisco, 90. *Exhib:* Phelan Award Biennial De Young Mus, 65; Christmas Show, San Francisco Mus Mod Art, 70; one-man shows, Wooster Col, Ohio, 74, Sacramento State Univ, Calif, 77 & San Francisco Art Comn, 78; Jos Chowning Gallery San Francisco (Dealer), 80-; Comic Iconoclasm Show, ICA Gallery, London, Eng, 87-88; Les Misquetes Show, Courbevoie Cult Ctr, Courbevoie, France, 90; Columbus 500th Anniversary Show, Triton Mus, Santa Clara, Calif, 92; and others. *Pos:* Art teacher, Laney Col, Oak, Calif, 65-, Stamford Univ, 61-62 & Sonoma State Col, 80-81; illusr, Bay Area Illusr Tech, 84-. *Teaching:* Instr drawing, Stanford Univ, 61-62; instr art, Foothills Jr Col, 62-63; instr drawing & painting, Laney Col, Oakland, Calif, 64-. *Awards:* First Prize, San Joaquin Valley Regional Fall Arts Festival, Stockton Art League, Calif, 58; Teaching Fel, Stanford Univ, Chico, Calif, 61-62; Purchase Award, Chico Savings & Loan, 66 & Fairfield Art Comn, 74. *Bibliog:* Tom Albright (auth), $5,000: Study for nightwatch, Art Gallery Mag, 3/73 & Interview: William Snyder, Currant Art Mag, 8/75; Ralph Pomeroy (auth), Triumph of Disneyanity, Art & Artists, London, 8/74; Alfred Jan (auth), article, Flash Art, Italy, summer 84. *Media:* Oil, Watercolor. *Publ:* Illusr, Monterey Advocate, Panadero, 66-68. *Mailing Add:* 3121 Fruitvale Ave Oakland CA 94602

SOBEL, DEAN
MUSEUM DIRECTOR, CURATOR
Pos: Cur, contemp art Milwaukee Art Mus; dir, chief cur, Aspen Art Mus, Colo, 2000-. *Publ:* Auth: One Hour Ahead: The Avant-Garde in Aspen, 1945-2004. *Mailing Add:* Aspen Art Mus 590 N Mill St Aspen CO 81611

SOBOL, JUDITH ELLEN
FOUNDATION DIRECTOR, CURATOR
b Washington, DC, June 1, 46. *Study:* Univ Calif, Los Angeles, BA, 68; George Washington Univ, MA, 70. *Collection Arranged:* Intaglio: An Appreciation, 82; New Architecture-Maine Traditions (with catalog), Payson Gallery, 83; Len Jenshel: Photographs, 10/83; Guy Bourdin: Sighs & Whispers, 84; Mainers Away, 85; Sue Coe, Porkopolis, 90; Fire, Air, Earth and Water, 94; Rodin: A Magnificent Obsession, 2001; Rodin: In His Own Words. *Pos:* Asst cur Univ Collection, Georgetown Univ, 70-72; supvr interpretive serv, Minneapolis Inst Arts, 73-77; chair, div educ, Baltimore Mus Art, 77-78; exec dir, Don't Tear It Down, Washington, DC, 78-81; dir, Joan Whitney Payson Gallery Art, Westbrook Col, 81-91; dir Grand Rapids Art Mus, 91-95; dir Newport Art Mus, RI, 95-98; dir Ziegler Ctr, Los Angeles, Calif, 99-2001; exec dir, Iris & B Gerald Cantor Found, 2001-. *Teaching:* Lectr fine arts, Georgetown Univ, 70-72; instr Am art, Westbrook Col, 82-83, Elderhostel, Westbrook Col, 83-. *Mem:* Art Table; Am Asn Mus. *Res:* Contemporary art, impressionism and post-impressionism; American art and architecture, especially 1880-1920, art nouveau; Rodin sculpture. *Publ:* Auth, Gilbert Stuart Portrait, Bull, Minneapolis Inst Arts, 77; Neighborhood coalitions, Univ New Orleans, 82; Polly Brown: Drawings, Payson Gallery, 10/83; Land America Leaves Wild, Wilderness Society and Grand Rapids Art Mus, 99. *Mailing Add:* 1180 S Beverly Dr Ste 321 Los Angeles CA 90035-1153

SOFFER, SASSON
ENVIRONMENTAL ARTIST, CONCEPTUAL ARTIST
b Baghdad, Iraq, June 1, 25; US citizen. *Study:* Brooklyn Col, with Mark Rothko & others, 50-54. *Work:* Indianapolis Mus Fine Art; Albright-Knox Gallery, Buffalo; Rockefeller Inst, NY; Butler Inst Am Art, Youngstown, Ohio; Whitney Mus Am Art, NY. *Exhib:* Whitney Mus Am Art, NY; one-man shows, Betty Parsons Gallery, NY, 61-63, Corpus Christi Mus, Tex, 64, Portland Mus, Maine, 66, Montclair State Col, NJ, 74, Battery Park, NY, 75 & 76 & Grandstreet, NY, 95, 96 & 97; and others. *Pos:* Ford Found artist in residence, Portland Mus, 66. *Awards:* Ford Found Purchase Award, Whitney Mus Am Art, 62 & Portland Mus, Maine, 64; North Jersey Cult Coun, 74 & Nat Endowment Arts. *Bibliog:* Sasson Soffer in the City of New York, 85; Sasson Soffer, Metal Sculpture, 85; Art in Am, 96. *Media:* Stainless Steel, Glass. *Mailing Add:* 78 Grand St No 5 New York NY 10013

SOFTIC, TANJA
PAINTER, PRINTMAKER
Study: Acad Fine Arts, Univ Sarajevo, Bosnia & Herzegovina, BFA, 88; Old Dominion Univ/Norfolk State Univ, Va, MFA, 92. *Work:* Atlanta Col Art & Design, Ga; Cornell Mus Fine Arts & Olin Libr, Rollins Col, Winter Park, Fla; Orlando City Hall & Valencia Community Col, Fla; Univ Dallas, Irving, Tex; Rutgers Archive Printmaking Studios, New Brunswick, NJ; and others. *Exhib:* One-woman shows, Coker Col Art Gallery, Hartsville, SC, 95, Kendall Gallery, Miami-Dade Community Col, 96, Allen R Hite Art Inst, Univ Louisville, Ky, 96, Catherine J Smith Gallery, Appalachian State Univ, Boone, NC, 97, Scuola Int Grafica Venezia, Venice, Italy, 99, Kathy Caraccio Studio Gallery, NY, 2000, Sarratt Gallery, Vanderbilt Univ, Nashville, Tenn, 2000, Miramar Gallery, Sarasota, Fla, 2001, Va Ctr Contemp Art, Virginia Beach, Va, 2001, Cervini Haas Gallery, Scottsdale, Ariz, 2001, New Harmony Gallery Contemp Art, Virginia Beach, Va, 2001 & Brad Cooper Gallery, Tampa, Fla, 2001; Ninth Nat Parkside Small Print Exhib, Parkside Gallery, Univ Wis, Kenosha, 95; Halpert Biennial, Catherine D Smith Gallery, Appalachian State Univ, NC, 95; Second Printmakers Renaissance Nat Exhib, Rolling Stone Press, Atlanta, Ga, 96; Eight States, Lamar Dodd Sch Art, Univ Ga, Athens, 96; Sapporo Int Print Bienalle, Hokkaido Mus Mod Art, Japan, 96 & 2000; Carroll Gallery, Tulane Univ, New Orleans, La, 97; 1st Northern Ireland Int Small Print Exhibition, Townhouse Gallery, Belfast, 98; You Cannot Go Home Again: Exiled Artists in the United States, Philadelphia Arts Alliance, Pa, 2000; International Print Triennial, World Award Winners Gallery, Katowice, Poland, 2000; Hyundai Art Gallery, Kwangju City, Korea, 2001; and many others. *Pos:* Printer, Kathy Caraccio Printmaking Workshop, New York, 91. *Teaching:* Asst, Old Dominion Univ, Norfolk, Va, 89-92; adj instr, Norfolk State Univ, Va, 91-92; asst prof art, Rollins Col, Winter Park, Fla, 92-98, assoc prof art, 98-2000; assoc prof art, Univ Richmond, Va, 2001-. *Awards:* Artist Scholar, Acad Arts & Scis, Bosnia & Herzegovina, 90-91; Visual Artist Grant, Southeastern Col Art Conf, 92 & 94; Jack B Critchfield Grant Individual Fac Development, Rollins Col, 93-94; Individual Artist Fel, Fla Dept State, 96-97; Exhibition Support Grant, Open Soc Fund, 97; Residency Fel, Va Ctr Creative Arts, 98, Ucross Found, 98, McDowell Colony, 98, Pyramid Atlantic, 98, Scuola Int Grafica, 99 & Flemish Ministry Cult, 2001. *Bibliog:* Laura Stewart (auth), Tanja Softic at the Cornell Fine Arts Museum, Art Papers, 1/95; Elisa Turner (auth), Tanja Softic's Subtle Politics and Shadowy Pods, Miami Herald, 5/24/96; Lynne Allen, Phyllis McGibbon (auths), The Best of Printmaking, Rockport Publ, Inc; Mary Ann Marger (auth), Bicultural Identities, St Petersburg Times, 5/1/98; John Dorsey (auth), Collectors' at Evergreen, Baltimore Sun, 2/9/99; Deborah McLeod (auth), Tanja Softic at the Marsh Gallery, Art Papers, 2/2001. *Mailing Add:* Univ Richmond Modin Center Arts Dept Art and Art History Richmond VA 23173

SOKOL, DAVID MARTIN
HISTORIAN, MUSEOLOGIST
b New York, NY, Nov 3, 42. *Study:* Hunter Col, AB, 63; Inst for Fine Arts, NY Univ, MA, 66, PhD, 70. *Pos:* Cur, Terra Mus Am Art, 81-85; interim dir, Spertus Mus, 85-86; adj cur, Maier Mus Art, 88-90; dir mus studio, UIC, 2002-. *Teaching:* Instr art hist, Kingsborough Community Col, Brooklyn, NY, 66-68; asst prof art hist, Western Ill Univ, Macomb, 68-71; assoc prof art & archit hist, Univ Ill, Chicago, 71-82, chmn dept, 77-84 & 92-2002, prof, 82-, dir grad studies, 90-92; vis asst prof, New York Univ, 70; vis prof, Randolph-Macon Women's Col, 88-89; prof emeritus. *Awards:* Univ Scholar, New York Univ, 70; First Award for scholarship in contributions in the Arts in Ill, Ill Acad Fine Arts, 92. *Mem:* Col Art Asn (placement comt, 77 & prof practices comt, 91-94, chair, 95-98; Am Studies Asn (nat coun, 76-78); Am Asn Univ Prof (comt treas, 75-78); Asn Historians Am Art (treas, 79-89); Am Cult Asn (gov bd mem, 95-99, vpres 2001-2003, pres 2003-2005); Art & Archit (area chmn, bd mem, 95-, sec, 99-); fel Inst Humanities (exec comt). *Res:* American painting and decorative arts; relations between American and European art; history of art patronage in the US; F L Wright. *Publ:* Co-auth, Hist of Am Art, Abrams, 79; auth, Otto Neumann, 82 & Heidelberger Kunstverein, Solitude, 82, Terra Mus Am Art; ed, Cambridge Monographs on Am Artists; co-auth, Am Art: American Vision, Maier Mus Art, 90; Six Prairie Artists, portfolio, State of Ill Art Gallery, 97; Engaging with the Present, Spehus Musen, 2004. *Mailing Add:* 222 N Marion St Oak Park IL 60302-1962

SOKOLOW, ISOBEL FOLB
SCULPTOR, EDUCATOR
b Brooklyn, NY. *Study:* Silvermine Col Art, 65-68; Coll New Rochelle; Art Students League; Nat Acad Design; Educ Alliance Art Sch; Independent Study in Florence & Pietrasanta, Italy. *Work:* Westchester Community Col, Valhalla, NY, 85-88; Roosevelt High Sch, Yonkers, NY, 92-94. *Comn:* Private collections in US & Italy; Pan American Wall, Uruguay, SAm, 94. *Exhib:* Yonkers Art Asn, Hudson River Mus, Yonkers, NY, 80; solo exhibs, N Shore Sculpture Ctr, 80, Harkness House, 81, Musaui Gallery, 84, Atlanta Gallery, 88, 90, 92, 94 & 98; Sculptors Alliance, Lever House, NY 87; Am Soc Contemp Artists, Westbeth Gallery, NY, 88; Nat Asn Women Artists, Monmouth Mus, Red Bank, NJ, 88; Faustini Gallery, Florence, Italy, 2000; Bromme St Gallery, 2000; Atlantic Gallery, 2000. *Pos:* Dir, Westchester Art & Cult Asn, 80-92; co-dir fine arts in Venice, Pratt Sch Design, 85. *Teaching:* Instr art, Jewish Guild for the Blind, Home for the Aged Blind, Yonkers, NY, 74-76 & Clay & Marble Workshops, Pietrasanta, Italy, 84-86; producer & host, Art Scene through an Artists Eye (cable TV prog), 97-. *Awards:* Silver Medal, Audubon Artists; Best in Show, Am Soc Contemp Artists, 88 & 90; Tre Jolie des Arts, Nat Asn Women Artists. *Bibliog:* Enrico Moreti (critic), Il Progresso-An American Artist in Florence, 80; Malcom Preston (auth), Review, Newsday, 82; Angela Pegani (dir), Isobel Folb Sokolow (TV doc), 87; David Bourdon (critic), Art in America, Critics Diary, Sept, 92; Swiss/Italian

TV, 87; State of the Art (TV series), 89; and others. *Mem:* Am Soc Contemp Artists (dir, 79-80, vpres, 94-98); NY Artists Equity (dir, 75-80, vpres, 80-84); Nat Asn Women Artists, Art Students League. *Media:* Welded Steel, Raku. *Dealer:* Atlantic Gallery 475 Broome St New York NY 10013. *Mailing Add:* 95 Lexington Ave Apt 3E New York NY 10016-8936

SOKOLOWSKI, LINDA ROBINSON
PRINTMAKER, PAINTER
b Utica, NY, May 20, 43. *Study:* RI Sch Design, BFA(painting), 65; Univ Iowa, with Mauricio Lasansky & James Lechay, MA, 70 & MFA, 71. *Work:* State Univ NY, Potsdam; Libr Congress, Washington; Ball State Univ; Pepsico,; IBM. *Exhib:* Solo shows, Kraushaar Galleries, NY, 76, 79, 82, 86, 89, 91, 94 & 98; More than Land or Sky: Art from Appalachia, Nat Mus Am Art, Smithsonian Inst, 81; Realist Tradition in Central NY, Munson-Williams Proctor Inst; 43rd, 44th & 56th Ann Painting Exhib, Butler Inst Am Art; 154th, 161st & 165th Ann Exhib, Nat Acad Design; Artists Who Teach, Fed Reserve Bd, Washington, 87; Summer Pleasures, Kornbluth Gallery, Fairlawn, NJ, 89; The Art Show, Art Dealers Asn, NY, 89-2000; Works on Paper, Park Ave 7th Regiment Armory, 95-2000. *Teaching:* Prof Art, State Univ NY, Binghamton, 71-. *Awards:* Childe Hassam Purchase Award, Am Acad & Inst of Art & Lett, 78; Research grants, State Univ NY, Binghamton, 90. *Bibliog:* G Henry (auth), Art News (rev), 86; Wendy Beckett (auth), Contemporary Women Artists, Universe Bks, 88; John Driscoll & Arnold Skolnick (auths), The Artist and the American Landscape, Chameleon Bks. *Media:* Monotypes, Etching. *Publ:* Auth, The Original Prints and Restrikes from the Plates of Kaethe Kollwitz, Univ Iowa Press, 70. *Dealer:* Carole Pesner & Kathryn Kaplan Kraushaar Galleries 724 Fifth Ave New York NY 10028. *Mailing Add:* Binghamton Univ Art Dept Binghamton NY 13902-6000

SOKOV, LEONID
SCULPTOR, PAINTER
b Tver (Kalinin), USSR, Oct 11, 41; US citizen. *Study:* Sch Art, Moscow, 56-61; Stroganov Col Art & Design, Moscow, MFA, 69. *Work:* Metrop Mus part; Centre Gerges Pompidou, Paris; Guggenheim Mus; Pushkin Mus Fine Art, Moscow; Tretyakow Gallery, Moscow. *Comn:* 5 sculptures, comn by Pushino, 73; sculpture, Ashkhabad, Turkmenistan, 74. *Exhib:* La Biennale di Venezia la Nuova Arte Sovietica, Venezia, 77; Sots Art, New Mus contemp Art, NY, 86; Elvis & Marilyn 2 Immortal, traveling, 94-97; Art as Witness, Kwangju Beinnale Korea, 95; Russian Pavillion, 49th Venice Biennial (catalog), 2001. *Bibliog:* Margarita Tupitsyn (auth), Margins of Soviet art, Ginacarlo Politi Editore, 89; Tom Csasar (auth), Nonconformist vision, New Art Examiner, 96; Victor Tupitsyn, L'estetica della transparenza, Tema Celeste, 96; Victor and Ilva Kabakov, conversation with Leonid Sokov; Dan Cameron (auth), Comic Relief, Palace Editions. *Dealer:* Frediano Farsetti Via della repubblica Prato Italy. *Mailing Add:* 356 Broadway No 3A New York NY 10013-3927

SOLBERG, MORTEN EDWARD
PAINTER
b Cleveland, Ohio, Nov 8, 35. *Study:* Cleveland Inst Art. *Work:* Nat Gallery Art, Washington, DC; Cleveland Mus Art; Nat Acad Design, NY; Hunt Wesson Foods, Home Savings & Loan, Calif; Leigh Yawkey Woodson Mus Art, Wausau, Wis; Dunnegan Mus, Springfield, Mo; Smithsonian; and others. *Comn:* Painting of hist fountain, Marriott Hotels, Newport Beach, Calif, 75; painting of hist settings, Irvine Co, Newport Beach, 75; collector print, Am Artist Mag, NY. *Exhib:* Nat Acad Design, NY, 66 & 76; Am Watercolor Soc, NY, 68 & 74-76; Nat Watercolor Soc, Los Angeles, 70-75; Soc Animal Artists, NY, 79-94; Birds In Art, Wausau, Wis, 87-94; and others. *Pos:* Art dir, Am Greeting Corp, Cleveland, 58-68; art dir, Buzza Cardoza Corp, Anaheim, Calif, 68-71; pres, Calif Graphics, Design Studio, Orange, 71-73 & Graybear Publ, 92-93. *Teaching:* Instr, int workshops. *Awards:* San Bernardino Co Mus Award; Knickerbocker Artists, NY; Hall of Fame, US Art Mag, 93; and others; Purchase Award, Calif Bicentennial; Master Artist, Wildlife Art Mag; Purchase Award, Nat Acad of Design. *Bibliog:* Wildlife Art News, 5-6/87; Sporting Classic, 11-12/87 & 9-10/92; Southwest Art, 10/92; Wildlife Art, 5-6/2001. *Mem:* Soc Animal Artists, NY; Nat Watercolor Soc (ad hoc bd mem, 74, first vpres, 75); Knickerbocker Artists; Am Watercolor Soc; Artist Guild of The San Diego Mus of Art; Board Member Susan K Black Found. *Media:* All Media. *Collection:* Smithsonian; Cleveland Mus of Art; The White House; Hunt Wesson Foods; Wildlife Art Magazine; Dunnegan Mus of Art; Bennington Ctr for the Arts; The Irving Corp Commission; American Greetings Corp. *Dealer:* Toh-atin Publishing, Durango, Colo. *Mailing Add:* 621 Edgewater Ave Oceanside CA 92057

SOLDNER, PAUL EDMUND
SCULPTOR, CERAMIST
b Summerfield, Ill, Apr 24, 21. *Study:* Bluffton Col, BA; Univ Colo, MA; County Art Inst, Los Angeles, MFA; Wesminster Col, Hon DFA, 92. *Work:* Victoria & Albert Mus, London; San Francisco Mus Art; Oakland Art Mus, Calif; Emerson Mus, Syracuse, NY; Smithsonian Mus, Washington, DC; and others. *Comn:* Ceramic mural, Home Savings & Loan Asn, Los Angeles, 56. *Exhib:* Am Potters Today, Victoria & Albert Mus, London, 86; Poetry of the Physical, Am Craft Mus, NY, 86; Esther Saks Gallery, Chicago, Ill, 86 & 88; Cal Prifysgol Cymru, Aberyothwyth, Wales, 87; Eloquent Object, Oakland Mus, Calif, 88; Traveling retrospective exhib, 91-94; and others. *Teaching:* Prof ceramics, Scripps Col & Claremont Grad Sch, Calif, 55-66 & 70-92; vis prof ceramics, Univ Colo, Boulder, 66-67; prof ceramics, Univ Iowa, 67-68. *Awards:* Louis Comfort Tiffany Found Grant, 66 & 72; Purchase Award, Victoria & Albert Mus, 72; Craftsmen's Fel Grant, Nat Endowment Arts, 76. *Bibliog:* John W Conrad (auth), Contemporary Ceramics, Prentice-Hall, 77; Donald Campbell (auth), Using the Potter's Wheel, Van Nostrand Reinhold, 77; Paul Soldner, A Retrospective, Univ Washington Press, 91; & others. *Mem:* Am Craft Coun; Nat Coun Educ Ceramic Arts; Acad Int de Céramique. *Media:* Clay, Metal. *Mailing Add:* PO Box 90 Aspen CO 81612

SOLEM, (ELMO) JOHN
PAINTER, SCULPTOR
b St Paul, Minn, Aug 10, 33. *Study:* Minn Sch Art, 51-53; Wartburg Col, Waverly, Iowa, BA, 59; Univ Calif, Los Angeles, MA, 62. *Work:* Santa Barbara Mus Art, Calif; Atlantic Richfield Corp Art Collection, Los Angeles; US Embassy, Embassy Residence, Oslo, Norway; Los Angeles Printmaking Soc; Tex Tech Univ, Lubbock. *Comn:* Chapel communion serving set, CA Lutheran Univ, Thousand Oaks, 1991. *Exhib:* 14th Nat Print Exhib, Brooklyn Mus, 64; Artists-Teachers in Southern Calif, Santa Barbara Mus Art, Calif, 75; Los Angeles Bicentennial Exhib, Mus Sci & Industry, 81; Ojai Art Ctr, 93; Conejo Valley Art Mus, 94; Calif Lutheran Univ, Thousand Oaks, 2000 & 2003; Northridge Hosp, 2004. *Pos:* Fac Emer, Calif Lutheran Univ, currently. *Teaching:* Sr extension teacher art, Univ Calif, Los Angeles, 1963-80; prof painting, printmaking & drawing, Calif Lutheran Univ, Thousand Oaks, 67-95. *Awards:* Tiffany Found Grant, Graphics, 63; Purchase Awards, 5th Ann Colorprint, USA, Tex Tech Univ, 74 & Los Angeles Printmaking Soc 2nd Nat Exhib, 74. *Bibliog:* Louis Newman (auth), Recent works on paper, Monogr, 78; Betts Kimball (auth), John Solem: a portrait of the artist, Westlake Mag, 79; Sandy Roberts (auth), John Solem educator/artist.who looks for the challenge of climbing to the top, Conejo Mag, 1981. *Media:* Acrylic; Sculptor, Clay. *Interests:* beauty in fractal quality of nature. *Publ:* Illus, Gethsemai Poems, Vanguard Press, 1994 & Voices and Echoes, CA Lutheran Univ, 1995. *Mailing Add:* 43070 Wild Flower Ct Coarsegold CA 93614

SOLERI, PAOLO
ARCHITECT, SCULPTOR
b Torino, Italy, 1919. *Study:* Polytech Torino, Frank Lloyd Wright fel. *Work:* Mus Mod Art, NY. *Comn:* Dome House, Cave Creek, Ariz, 49; Native American Theater (amphitheater), Santa Fe, NMex, 68; II Donnone (sculpture), Phoenix, Ariz, 72; Glendale Community Col, Ariz, 96. *Exhib:* Corcoran Gallery Art, Washington, DC, 70; Whitney Mus Am Art, NY, 70; Mus Contemp Art, Chicago, 70; Nat Conf Ctr, Ottawa, Can, 71; Univ Art Mus, Berkeley, Calif, 71; Two Suns Arcology Exhib, Xerox Corp-sponsored, 76; NY Acad Sci, 89; Soleri Cities Architecture for the Planet Earth and Beyond, Scottsdale Ctr Arts, 93. *Teaching:* Distinguished vis lectr, Ariz State Univ, Sch Archit, currently. *Awards:* Graham Found, 62; Guggenheim Found, 64 & 67; Gold Medal, World Biennale Archit, Sofia, Bulgaria, 81; Governor's Arts Award, Ariz, 96; Nat Design Lifetime Achievement Award, 2006. *Mem:* Hon fel Brit Royal Inst Architects. *Publ:* Auth, Arcology: The City in the Image of Man, 69 & The Sketchbooks of Paolo Soleri, 71, Mass Inst Technol; The Bridge Between Matter & Spirit is Matter Becoming Spirit, Doubleday, 73; Fragments, Harper & Row; Paolo Soleri's Earth Casting, Peregrine-Smith, 84; Technology and Cosmogenesis, Paragon House, 86. *Mailing Add:* Cosanti Found 6433 Doubletree Ranch Rd Paradise Valley AZ 85253

SOLINAS, RICO
PAINTER
b Berkeley, Calif, Sept 13, 54. *Study:* Univ Calif, Santa Barbara, BA, 77; San Francisco Art Inst, MFA, 89. *Work:* Ft Worth Mus, Tex; Di Rosa Found, Peteluma, Calif. *Comn:* Illustrations, Richard Misrach, Emeryville, Calif, 90. *Exhib:* Hello Again, Oakland Mus, Calif, 97; Bravo 20, Ft Worth Mus, Tex, 98. *Pos:* installer, San Francisco Mus Modern Art, Calif, 87-2000. *Teaching:* tchr drawing, San Francisco Art Inst, Calif, 87; tchr design, De Anza Col, Cupertino, Calif, 94; prof drawiing, Diablo Valley Col, Calif, 96-98. *Bibliog:* A Ross (auth), Bravo 20, Documents, 92; Pete Hammil (auth), Tools As Art, Harry N. Abrams, 95; Mark Van Proyen (auth), New Issues, New Issues, 99. *Media:* Oil on Metal. *Publ:* Illusr, Bravo 20, The bombing of the Am west, Johns Hopkins, 90. *Dealer:* John Berggruen 228 Grant Ave San Francisco Calif 94108. *Mailing Add:* 2730 23rd St San Francisco CA 94110

SOLMAN, JOSEPH
PAINTER
b Vitebsk, Russia, Jan 25, 1909; US citizen. *Study:* Nat Acad Design, New York, 26-29; Art Students League, 29-30. *Work:* Whitney Mus Am Art, NY; Phillips Collection, Washington; Fogg Mus, Cambridge, Mass; Butler Inst Am Art, Youngstown, Ohio; Los Angeles Co Mus; Brit Mus; Wichita Mus, Kans. *Exhib:* Retrospective oils, Phillips Collection, Washington, 49; ACA Galleries, New York, NY, 50-; Whitney Mus Am Art Ann, 52, 53 & 55; retrospective, Wichita Mus, Kans, 84; Mercury Gallery, Boston, 1995, 96, 98, 99, 2000, 03; Eleonore Austerer Gallery, San Francisco, 2001, 03; several paintings. *Pos:* Treas, Nat Acad Design, 79-84. *Teaching:* Instr oil painting, Mus Mod Art, 52-54, New Sch Social Res, 64-66 & City Col New York, 67-75. *Awards:* Nat Inst Arts & Lett Award for Painting, 61; Isaac N Maynard Prize for Portrait, 69 & Saltus Gold Medal for Merit, 71, Nat Acad Design, 67-89. *Mem:* Fedn Mod Painters & Sculptors (pres, 65-67, vpres, 67-) (exec board 1968-89); Mem Nat Acad (treasurer, 79-85, acad, 74-); fel (life) Art Student League. *Media:* Monotype; Oil, Gouache. *Publ:* editor-in-chief, Art Front Mag, 1937-38; auth: books, Joseph Solman, Crown Publ, 1966, Monotypes of Joseph Solman, Da Capo Press, 1977, Mozartiana, 1990, Joseph Solman, Da Capo Press, 1995. *Mailing Add:* c/o Mercury Gallery 2nd Floor 8 Newbury St Boston MA 02116

SOLOCHEK, SYLVIA See Walters, Sylvia Solochek

SOLOFF, LAURA J
ADMINISTRATOR
Study: UCLA, BA in Eng, minor in Art Hist. *Pos:* Human resources position, Broadway Dept Stores; dir, career planning & placement Fashion Inst Design & Merchandising, Calif; campus dir, reg dir, dir student financial servs; dir human resources & admin, Sony Pictures Entertainment, Culver City; mem Educ Mgt Corp, 98-; pres, Art Inst Calif-Orange Co, 2000-03; reg vpres, Educ Mgt Corp, 2004-. *Mailing Add:* Art Inst Calif LA Off Pres 2900 31st St Santa Monica CA 90405-3035

SOLOMON, GERALD
ART DEALER, PAINTER
b Apr 3, 30. *Exhib:* Tyringham Gallery, Mass, 96. *Pos:* Pres-dir, Solomon & Co Fine Art, New York, currently. *Specialty:* 20th century American and European paintings, graphics, drawing and sculpture. *Mailing Add:* 372 Central Park W New York NY 10025

SOLOMON, RICHARD H
PUBLISHER, ART DEALER
b Boston, Mass, May 12, 34. *Study:* Harvard Col, AB, 56; Harvard Bus Sch, MBA, 58. *Pos:* Pres, Pace Editions Inc/Pace/Masterprints, Pace Primitive & Ancient Art, NY, currently; chmn, Pace/MacGill Inc 20th Century Photog Gallery, formerly; chmn, Overseers Vis Comt, Visual & Environ Studies Dept, Harvard Col, formerly. *Mem:* Art Dealers Asn Am (pres, currently); Primitive Art Dealers Asn Am; Int Fine Print Dealers Asn (vpres); Art Dealers Asn Am (bd dir 1990-92, pres, currently); Int Fine Print Dealers Asn (pres, formerly). *Specialty:* Contemporary and modern master prints and drawings, contemporary modern photography, African, Oceanic and Nepalese; Japanese woodcut prints. *Collection:* Contemporary art and primitive art. *Mailing Add:* c/o Pace Editions Inc 32 E 57th St New York NY 10022

SOLOMON, ROSALIND
PHOTOGRAPHER
Study: Goucher Col, Towson, Md, BA, 51; study with Lisette Model, 74-76. *Work:* Metrop Mus Art, Mus Mod Art, NY; Nat Portrait Gallery, Washington, DC; Eastman House, Rochester, NY; Musee de la Ville de Paris; Victoria & Albert Mus, London. *Exhib:* One-person show, Mus Mod Art, 86; PTI Gallery, Tokyo, 91; Inst de Estudios Norte Americanos, Spain, 92. *Awards:* John Simon Guggenheim Mem Fel, 80; Nat Endowment Arts, 88; Am Inst Indian Studies, 81-83; Art Matters Inc, 88. *Mailing Add:* 712 Broadway New York NY 10003

SOLOMON, (MRS) SIDNEY L
COLLECTOR
b Boston, Mass, May 15, 09. *Study:* Radcliffe Col, AB; Simmons Col, BS. *Exhib:* Sargent, Whitney Mus, NY. *Collection:* Sculpture of the twentieth century to contemporary, including Giacometti, Lipschitz, Marini, Nevelson, Dubuffet, Arp, Chadwick, Calder, Schmidt, Doris Cassar & Trova; painting collection includes Sargent, Vuillard, Tomayo, Leger, Giacometti, Monet and Matta; drawings of Maillol, Archipenko, Degas, Lachaise & many others; watercolors of Nolde & Marini; also a collection of pop art; Picasso Print 1907 Master Drawings. *Mailing Add:* 834 Fifth Ave New York NY 10021

SOLON, LISA H
PHOTOGRAPHER
b Brooklyn, NY. *Study:* NYU, BA, 81; NYU, MBA, 85. *Work:* The Libr of Mus of Modern Art, NY; The Libr of the Nat Gallery of Art, Washington; The Montclair Art Mus, NJ; Nat Art Libr, Victoria & Albert Mus, London; The Newark Mus. *Exhib:* solo shows incl Johnson & Johnson World Hq, New Brunswick, NJ, 96, Donnell Libr Ctr, NY, 97, Gallery of Sourth Orange, NJ, 2000; Body Traces, Marymount Manhattan Col Gallery, NY, 98; The NJ Fine Arts Ann, Montclair Art Mus, 98; A New View: Worked Images by Contemp Photogs, Noyes Mus, Oceanville, NJ, 2000; Photoworks 2000, Erector Square Gallery, New Haven, Conn, 2000; Smallworks, 80 Washington Sq E Galleries, NY, 2000. *Teaching:* instr photog, Newark Mus, NJ, 94-. *Awards:* Artist-in-Residence, Newark Mus, 96; Third prize Soho Photo An Exhbn, 98; NJ State Coun on the Arts Fel, 99. *Bibliog:* Self-Portraits, The Star-Ledger, 10/2/99; Corpus of work, The Star-Ledger, 3/10/2000; When color illuminates, The NY Times, 3/26/2000. *Dealer:* Sharon Gill 35 Godfrey Rd Montclair NJ 07043. *Mailing Add:* PO Box 8145 Glen Ridge NJ 07028

SOL'SAX
PAINTER, EDUCATOR
Study: Cooper Union, BFA, 92; Yale Univ, MFA, 96. *Work:* Represented in permanent collections Bronx Mus, Mus of City NY. *Exhib:* One-man shows, Recognize the Real, Silverstein Gallery, 95, The Wild Herb of Bushwick Presents: My Tea Blessed Heads of Kind Co, Rush Arts Gallery, 97, Hood Flags, New York City Libr, 2001, These Hands Me Down Black and Blue Jeans, PS 1, 2002, The Other Mainstream: Selections from the Collection of Mikki and Stanley Weithorn, Ariz State Univ Art Mus, 2005. *Teaching:* Lectr, art Medgar Evers Col, City Univ NY. *Awards:* Fel Guggenheim Mem Found, 2004. *Mailing Add:* c/o ASU Art Mus PO Box 872911 Tempe AZ 85287-2911

SOLWAY, CARL E
DEALER
b Chicago, Ill, Jan 12, 35. *Pos:* Dir, Carl Solway Gallery, Cincinnati. *Mem:* Art Dealers Asn Am. *Specialty:* 20th century American and European painting, sculpture and graphics; video installations; publisher of graphic works by John Cage, Buckminster Fuller, Richard Hamilton, Nancy Graves, Nam June Paik, Matt Mullican, Peter Nagy, Julia Wachtel & Vito Acconci. *Mailing Add:* 424 Findlay St Cincinnati OH 45214

SOMBERG, EMILIJA O K
PAINTER
b Utena, Lithuania, Feb 20, 24; US citizen. *Study:* Univ Hamburg, BA, 49; study with Hans Hofman, 61-62; Southern Conn State Col, MS, 62; NY Univ, 64. *Work:* Tweed Mus; Lithuanian Embassy & Libr Cong, Washington; Southern Conn State Col; Univ Minn, Minneapolis; Maison Baltique De Paris. *Exhib:* Green Ross Gallery, NY, 65; retrospectives, Normandale Community Col, 78, Nobles Co Art Ctr, Worthington, Mich, 78, Custer Co Arts Ctr, Miles City, Mont, 81 & Tweed Mus, 81 & Alternative Mus, Minneapolis, 85 & Murphy Art Gallery, St Paul, Minn, 87; Minneapolis Inst Art, 79; Minn Mus Art, 80; Invitational, Univ Minn, 86, 95 & 96; Moon Art Gallery, Minneapolis, Minn, 91; solo exhibs, Heath Found, Minneapolis, Minn, 93, Campus Club Art Gallery, Univ, Minn, 94. *Teaching:* Instr art, pub schs, New York, Conn & NJ, 64-74. *Awards:* Distinguished Serv Award, Mayor A Hofstede, Minneapolis, Minn, 79 & Mayor, Fraser, 91. *Bibliog:* Martin Keller (auth), Somberg achieves liberation through art, Insight, 9/78; Elizabeth Miller (auth), Somberg's retrospective, Univ Minn Rev, 3/79; Mary Scarvalone (auth), Somberg's art, Minn Daily, 5/79. *Mem:* Artists' Guild, West Palm Beach, Fla. *Media:* Oil. *Mailing Add:* 1131 Monroe St NE Minneapolis MN 55413

SOMERS, FREDERICK D(UANE)
PAINTER, INSTRUCTOR
b Omaha, Nebr, Feb 26, 42. *Study:* Univ Omaha, BFA, 65; Univ Iowa, MA(drawing), MFA(painting). *Work:* Univ Minn Hosp, Minneapolis; Nebr Mus Art, Kearny; Mayo Clinic, Rochester, Minn; Miller Art Mus, Sturgeon Bay, Wis Leigh Yawkey Woodson Mus, Wausau, Wis. *Comn:* Wausau Insurance, Wis; Radisson Hotels, Scottsdale, Ariz & Bloomington, Minn; Mayo Clinic, Rochester, Minn; Lutheran Brotherhood, Minneapolis; Grand Hotel, Mall of Am, 94. *Exhib:* Charles H MacNider Mus, 10th Ann Area Competition, Mason City, Iowa, 75; solo shows, Light in Tangent, Smoland Mus, Vaxjo, Sweden, 84, Am Swed Inst, Minneapolis, 84, Homeland, Am Swed Inst, 88 & Hyllningsfest, Birger Sandzén Mus, Lindsborg, Kans, 93; Contemp Realism, Nat Exhib, Yuma Art Ctr & Leslie Levy Gallery, Scottsdale, 85-86; Nebraska Artists Retrospective, Nebr Mus Art, Kearny, 90; Nat Wetlands Exhib, Yonkers, NY, 92; Birds in Art, Leigh Yawkey Woodson Mus, Wausau, Wis, 97; Int Pastel Soc, Kansas City, 97. *Teaching:* Instr drawing, painting & printmaking, Carleton Col, Northfield, Minn, 70 & 73 & St Olaf Col, 71, 72, 74, 75 & 80; Watercolor painting, Mus Folkhogskola, Sweden, 89 & pastel painting, 94. *Awards:* Various Peoples & Jurors Choice Awards. *Bibliog:* Article, US Art Mag, 3/89. *Mem:* Pastel Soc Am. *Media:* Pastels, Oils. *Mailing Add:* 9775 Dennison Blvd S Northfield MN 55057

SOMERS, H(ARRY) W
PAINTER, PRINTMAKER
b Zweibruecken, Ger, May 28, 22; US citizen. *Study:* Dookie Col, Australia; City Col New York, cert; Art Students League; Brisbane Art Ctr, Australia; also with Joseph Schwartz & S Greene. *Work:* Jewish Mus, NY; Univ Melbourne, Australia; Lowe Art Mus, Coral Gables, Fla; Metrop Mus & Art Ctr, Miami, Fla; Nat Art Gallery, Wellington, NZ; and others. *Exhib:* Vercel Gallery, NY & Paris, 70-78; Hilde Gerst Gallery, NY & Palm Beach, Fla, 78-85; Artworld Gallery, San Diego, 80-82; Frances Aronson Gallery, Atlanta, 83-89; Park Shore Gallery, Naples, 88; one man shows, Tokyo, London, Paris, Brussels, Dallas, Houston, San Francisco, Laguna Beach, Los Angeles, Caracas, San Diego, Phoenix, Washington & Palm Springs; Arthur James Gallery, Delray Beach, Fla, 90-93; DM Galleries, Calif, 96-97; and others. *Bibliog:* Charles Z Offin (auth), articles, 70, 71 & 72 & Beatrice Dain (auth), article, 3/74, Pictures on Exhibit; Lawrence Dame (auth), Somers the impressionist, Palm Beach Post, 1/78; and other Intl Publ. *Mem:* Am Artists Prof League; Artists Equity Asn. *Media:* Acrylic, Oil; Serigraphy, Silkscreen. *Publ:* Auth, The Art of Collecting, 63

SOMERSON, ROSANNE
CRAFTSMAN, EDUCATOR
b Philadelphia, Pa, June 21, 54. *Study:* RI Sch Design, BFA, 76. *Work:* Mus Fine Arts, Boston, Mass; Fuller Art Mus, Brockton, Mass; Huntsville Mus, Ala; RI Sch Design Mus; Nat Mus Am Art, Renwick Gallery Smithsonian. *Comn:* Kohn Pedersen Fox & Conway, NY. *Exhib:* Craft Today USA, Mus Decorative Arts, Louve Mus, Paris, France & traveling Europe, 89-90; New Am Furniture, Mus Fine Arts, Renwick Gallery, Smithsonian Inst, Washington, DC, 90 & Oakland Mus, Calif, 90; solo exhib, Peter Joseph Gallery, NY, 93 & 95. *Teaching:* Prof & dept head, Furniture Design Dept, RI Sch Design, 84-. *Awards:* Grand Prize Winner, Am Crafts Guild, 87; Nat Endowment Arts Visual Arts Fel, 84 & 88. *Bibliog:* Kulturweltspiegel: Furniture as Art, Ger Television Ard 1, 90; Mary Frakes (auth), Alphonse Martha, Rosanne Somerson, Am Craft, 12-1/94; Zoe Ingalls (auth), Designing woman, Chronicle Higher Ed, 95. *Mem:* Am Craft Coun; WARP. *Media:* Furniture Design. *Publ:* Auth, Looking Back & Forth & Furniture of the 90's (catalogue), Essay Conn Vis & Performing Arts, Tex Med Ctr; Perfect Sweep, Am Craft, June/July

SOMERVILLE, ROMAINE STEC
ADMINISTRATOR
b Scranton, Pa, May 24, 30. *Study:* Marymount Col, BA, 51; Columbia Univ, MA, 53; Yale Univ, 58-60. *Collection Arranged:* The Peale Collection of the Maryland Historical Society, 75 (coauth, catalog) & Life in Maryland in the 18th Century, Bicentennial Exhib, 76, Md Hist Soc; 200 Years of the Cath Church in Am, Md Hist Soc. *Pos:* Cur art, Everhart Mus, Scranton, Pa, 54-58; cur decorative art, Baltimore Mus Art, 60-63; exec dir, Baltimore City Comn Hist & Archit Preservation, 66-72; asst dir & chief cur, Md Hist Soc, 72-78, dir, 78-84; field consult, Nat Endowment Arts, 84-86; consult cur, Bicentennial Exhib, Roman Cath Archdiocese of Baltimore, 86-90; Admis Preserv Soc, Baltimore, 93-2000; pres, Baltimore Ci8ty Hist Soc Inc, 2002-05; chair, Peale Mus Restoration Coord Comt, 2002-. *Teaching:* Lectr art hist, Marywood Col, Scranton, Pa, 54-58; lectr Am decorative arts, Johns Hopkins Univ evening sch, 78-82, 2005. *Awards:* Douglas Gordon Award for distinguished hist presentation accomplishment, Baltimore Heritage Inc, 2004. *Mem:* bd mem, Baltimore City Hist Soc Inc; Decorative Arts Accessions Comt & Friends of Am Wing, Baltimore Mus Art; gallery comt, Maryland Hist Soc; bd mem, develop comt chair & furnishings comt, Hist Hampton Inc; bd mem & preserv planning comt Baltimore Hert Inc; bd mem, preserv advocacy comt & archit design review comt, Preserv Soc; ad hoc comt, review ordinance governing Baltimore Com, Hist & Archit

Preserv. *Res:* Nineteenth century American architecture, decorative arts and painting. *Publ:* The Perlman Bequest, BMA Quarterly, Fall 1961; Peale Collection at MHS, 11/75 & MHS Furniture Collection, 5/76, Antiques Mag; Contribr, Maryland Heritage, Five Baltimore Institutions Celebrate the American Bicentennial, Md Hist Soc, 76. *Mailing Add:* 118 W Lafayette Ave Baltimore MD 21217

SOMMA, THOMAS P
HISTORIAN, MUSEUM DIRECTOR
b Somerville, NJ, Sept 8, 49. *Study:* Marietta Col, Marietta, Ohio, BS, 1972; Rutgers Univ, New Brunswick, NJ, MA, 1983; Univ of Delaware, Newark, Del, PhD, 1990; Fel, US Capitol Historical Soc, 1987,1991. *Exhib:* Leon Golub: Solo Exhib of Paintings, 1998; Nancy Spero: Sheila Does Fredericksburg, 2000; Leonardo da Vinci: Artist, Scientist, Engineer, 2002; Reflections on American Salvery: Selected Objects from the US Nat Slavery Mus, 2004; All that is Glorious Around Us: Paintings from the Hudson River Sch, 2005. *Collection Arranged:* Paintings by Masters of the Hudson River School, 1995; Leon Golub: Solo Exhibition, 1998; Nancy Spero: Sheila Does Fredericksburg, 2002; Leonardo da Vinci: Artist, Scientist, Engineer, 2002; Reflections on American Slavery, 2004; Selected Works from the James Monroe Museum, 2005. *Pos:* Mus dir, Ithaca Col, Ithaca, NY, 1994-98; Administrative fac, Univ Mary Washington, Fredericksburg, Va, 1998-. *Teaching:* Adj fac am art hist, Georgetown Univ, Washington, DC, 2001-; instr art & archit, Ithaca Col, Washington, DC, 2001-; co-dir NEH landmarks am hist, Washington, DC, 2004-. *Awards:* Henry Luce Foundation Dissertation Year Grant, 1987-88; Univ Delaware Press Am Art Manuscript Competition Award, 1992. *Mem:* College Art Asn; Am Asn of Mus; Virginia Asn of Mus; Southeastern Mus Conference. *Media:* Sculpture, Public art. *Specialty:* 19th and 20th Century Am and European painting and drawing. *Interests:* Am sculpture; pub art, especially in Wash, DC; Fr-Am statues; Am landscape painting. *Publ:* Auth, The Apotheosis of Democracy 1908-1916: The Pediment for the Hose Wing of the US Capitol, Univ Del Press, 1995; contrib, Library of Congress: The Art & Archit of the Thomas Jefferson Bldg, W W Norton & Co, 1997; auth, Rodin's Am Connection, Cantor Arts Center Journal Vol III, Stamford Univ, 2002-2003; contrib, Perspectives on Am Sculpture before 1925, Metrop Mus of Art, 2003; Ed & contrib, Am Pantheon: Sculptural & Artistic Decoration of the US Capitol, Ohio Univ Press, 2004. *Mailing Add:* 11016 Naples Ct Fredericksburg VA 22407

SOMMER, FRANK H, III
HISTORIAN, ARCHEOLOGIST
b Newark, NJ, July 30, 22. *Study:* Yale Col; Yale Grad Sch; Corpus Christi Col, Cambridge Univ, Henry Fel, 47-48; Art Students League. *Work:* Yale Univ Art Gallery; Peabody Mus, Yale Univ; Brooklyn Mus, NY; Mus Mod Art, NY; Wintherthur Mus, Del. *Collection Arranged:* Pennsylvanian German Folk Art, 62; Recent Accessions, Winterthur Libr, 63-78 & Winterthur Mus. *Pos:* Keeper folk art, Winterthur Mus, 58-63, head of libr, 63-87. *Teaching:* Teaching asst, Yale Univ, 46-47; from instr to prof anthrop & art hist, Univ Del, 48-87 Pos, Coordr, Winterthur Prog, Univ Del, 52-55. *Res:* Design books, trade catalogues, architectural books; Anglo-American classicism and United States folk art. *Publ:* Auth, NW Argentine Archeology, 42, Excavations, 49 & Metamorphoses of Britannia, 76, Yale Univ; Triumph of Neptune, Warburg, 61; Thomas Jefferson's First Plan, Friends Independence Hall Nat Park, 76; Arts of the Pennsylvania Germans, Winterthur Mus, 83

SOMMER, SUSAN
PAINTER, PRINTMAKER
b Brooklyn, NY, Feb 23, 50. *Study:* studied Art Students League, 65-70, Moore Col Art & Design, BFA, 72; studied with Calvin J Goodman. *Work:* Univ Santa Clara, de Saisset Mus, Calif; Children's Hosp, Vanderbilt Univ; Moore Col Art & Design, Kimmel Ctr, Philadelphia; Govt House, St Vincent, West Indies. *Exhib:* Seven from the Seventies, Levy Gallery, Philadelphia, 97; 3d Ann Nat, Cerrs Gallery, NY, 99; On-Line Exhib, Nat Arts Club, NY, 2004; Art Students League, NY, 2004; Samuel Dorsky Mus, SUNY, New Paltz, NY, 2005; Susan Sommer's Improvisations, Kimmel Ctr, Philadelphia, Pa, 2005. *Awards:* Special Jurors Award, Nat Arts Club, 2004. *Bibliog:* Edward Feldman (auth), Two Arrel Soloists, Manhattan Arts, 97; Peter Frank (auth), Susan Sommer's Improvisations, Gee Tee Bee, 2005. *Mem:* Nat Art Club; Art Students League. *Media:* Monotype. *Publ:* auth, Susan Sommer Oils, Charcoal & Pastels, Maiden Lane Pub, 90; auth, Mystique, Maiden Lane Pub, 94. *Dealer:* Wooster Projects 418 W 15th St Ne w Yok NY 10011. *Mailing Add:* 91 Central Park W New York NY 10023

SOMMESE, LANNY BEAL
EDUCATOR, DESIGNER
b East Moline, Ill, May 14, 43. *Study:* Univ Fla, Gainesville, BD(graphics), 65, BFA(painting), 66; Univ Ill, Urbana, MFA(graphic design), 70. *Work:* Libr Cong; Zachata Art Gallery, Warsaw, Poland; Lahti Art Mus, Finland; Colo State Collection, Ft Collins; Moravian Gallery, Brno, Czech. *Exhib:* Warsaw Poster Biennale, Poland, 74, 76, 78, 80, 84, 86 & 88; NY Art Dirs Club, 76, 82 & 86; Colo State Biennale, Ft Collins, 79, 81, 83, 85 & 87; Lahti Poster Biennale, Finland, 79, 81, 83, 85 & 87; Brno Graphic Design Biennale, Czech, 80, 82, 84, 86 & 88; Toyama Triennial of Poster, Japan, 85. *Teaching:* Instr, Univ Ill, Urbana, 70; from instr to prof & head graphic design, Pa State Univ, 70-. *Awards:* Merit Award, New York Art Dirs Club, 76, 79 & 82; Gold Medal, Univ & Col Design Asn, 79. *Bibliog:* Gibbons & Kinser (auths), article, Graphis 202, 78; Fukuda (auth), article, Idea 176, 83; Neumeier (auth), article, Communication Arts, 5-6/83, Von Conta (auth) article, Novum Gebrauchsgraphik, 7/88; article, Design J, 4/88. *Mem:* Am Inst Graphic Arts. *Publ:* Auth, James McMullan, Graphis 213, 82; Tom Carnase, Ligature, 82; McRay Magleby, Print, 82; Design and technology, 7/83 & coauth, Design training USA, 9/83, Novum Gebrauchgraphik; auth, On Campus: Personal Motives and Publis Interest, Am Inst Graphic Arts J, Vol VII, 88; Design Resource 7/88, Mobium Corp for Design & Commun, 10/88, Novum Gebrauchsgraphic. *Mailing Add:* Dept Art Penn State Univ 207 Visual Arts Bldg University Park PA 16802

SONDAY, MILTON FRANKLIN, JR
CURATOR
b Hamburg, Pa, Dec 18, 39. *Study:* Wyomissing Inst Fine Arts, Pa, 55-61; Carnegie-Mellon Univ, Pittsburgh, Pa, 57-61, BFA(painting & design), 61; Penland Sch Crafts, NC, summer 66; ETenn State Univ (Penland Sch), summer 67; US Dept Agr Grad Sch, Washington, DC, fall 67; The Textile Mus (seminar), 67; The New Sch, New York, 68; Ctr Int d'Etude des Textiles Anciens, Lyon, France, 69. *Exhib:* Student Exhib, Carnegie Inst of Technol, 57-61; Reading Pub Mus & Art Gallery, Pa, 63; Gallery Mod Art, Fredricksburg, Va, 63. *Pos:* Mus assst & staff artist, Textile Mus, Washington, DC, 62-65, keeper of rugs, 65-67; asst cur textiles, Cooper Union Mus, New York, 67-68; cur textiles, Cooper-Hewitt Mus Design, Smithsonian Mus, New York, 68-. *Awards:* New York Home Fashion League Art Award, 72. *Mem:* Ctr Int d'Etudes des Textiles Anciens, Lyon, France. *Publ:* Illusr, Tiahnuaco Tapestry Design, 63 & Principles of Tixtile Conservation Science, 63-64, The Textile Mus; auth, Counterchange & New Color, Handweaver and Craftsman, summer, 69; coauth, with N Kajitani, A Type of Mughal Sash, 70 & A Second Type of Mughal Sash, 71, The Textile Mus J. *Mailing Add:* 35 Prospect Pl Brooklyn NY 11217

SONE, YUTAKA
ARTIST
b Shizuoka, Japan, 65. *Study:* Tokyo Geijutsu Univ, BFA, 88, MA, 92. *Work:* The Gift. Generous offering, insidious hospitality, Scotsdale Mus Contemp Art, Ariz, 2002; Metascape, Cleveland Mus Art, 2003; 100 Artists See God, Ind. Curators International, NY, 2004; Whitney Biennial, Whitney Mus Am Art, NY, 2004; Universal Experience: Art, Life & the Tourists Eye, Mus Contemp Art, Chicago, 2005. *Exhib:* One-man shows, One hand clapping, Yokohama Galleria, Japan, 93, Her 19th Foot, Contemp Art Ctr, Art Tower Mito, Japan, 93, Space Luxury Art, Hosomi Gallery, Tokyo, Japan, 94, Departures, Roentgen Kunst Inst, Tokyo, Japan, 95, Future Perfect, Bunkamura Gallery, Tokyo, Japan, 96, Scoop, Mitaka City Arts Found, Tokyo, Japan, 96, Amusement, Gallery Side 2, Tokyo, Japan, 97, At the End of All the Journeys, Shiseido Art House, Kakegawa, Japan, 98, David Zwirner, NY, 99, Double Six, Artpace, San Antonio, 2000, Travel to Double River Island, Toyota Municipal Mus Art, Toyota City, Japan, 2002, Yutaka Sone: Jungle Island, Mus Contemp Art, LA, 2003, Amusment Romana, David Zwirner, NY, 2004; group shows, Shinjuku Shonen Art, Tokyo, Japan, 94, Ripple Across the Water, Watari Mus Contemp Art, Watari-um, Tokyo, 95, Join Me! One Night Artist's Cafe, Spiral Wacoal Art Ctr, Tokyo, 96, Cities on the Move 1, Wiener Secession, Vienna, Austria, 97, Unfinished Hist, Walker Art Ctr, Minneapolis, 98, Cities on the Move 3, PS1 Contemp Art Ctr, Queens, NY, 98, Cities on the Move 5, Hayward Gallery, London, 99, From a Distance: Landscape in Contemp Art, Inst Contemp Art, Boston, 2000, Déjà Vu, Ctr Curatorial Studies, Bard Col, Annandale-on-Hudson, NY, 2000, New Works: 00.4, ArtPace, A Found for Contemp Art, San Antonio, 2001, Pub Offerings, Mus Contemp Art, LA, 2001, Is NY, David Zwirner, NY, 2001; Loop, PS1 Contemp Art Ctr, Long Island City, NY, 2002. *Mailing Add:* c/o David Zwirner 525 W 19th St New York NY 10011

SONFIST, ALAN
ENVIRONMENTAL ARTIST
b New York, NY, Mar 26, 46. *Work:* Mus Mod Art, Albright-Knox Mus, Mus Mod Art, NY; Boston Mus Fine Art; Oberlin Art Mus, Ohio; Wallarf-Richartz Mux, Koln, Ger; Power Inst, Sydney, Australia; Mus Contemp Art, Chicago; High Mus, Atlanta, Ga; J B Speed Mus, Louisville, Ky; Ludwig Found Mus, Auchen, Ger. *Comn:* Four Seasons (sculpture), Temple Univ, Pa; 5 Time Enclosures with Forrest Seeds, Grove Isle, Fla; Time Landscape: Dual History Forrest, St Louis, Mo; Time Landscape, Greenwich Village, NY; Time Landscape, Redhook, NY; Time Landscape, Tuscany; Hemlock Forrest, Bronx, NY; Towers of Growth, Louisville, Ky; Sun Monument, Kingston, RI; Earth Wall, Buffalo, NY; Rock Monument of Buffalo, NY; 100 Foot Column of Earth, Morgan City, La. *Exhib:* One-man shows, Smithsonian Inst, 78, High Mus Art, Atlanta, 79, Albright-Knox Mus, Buffalo, NY, 80, JB Speed Art Mus, Louisville, Ky, 81, Corcoran Mus, Wash, DC, 84, World's Fair, Osaka, Japan, 88 & Max Protetch Gallery, NY, 90, Retrospective Univ Iowa Art Mus, 96, Photo Collage Exhib, Am First Found, Chicago, 97, Natural/Cult Photo Collages, Goethe House, NY, 2000; The Artist As Social Designer, Los Angeles Co Mus, 85; World's Fair in Osaka, Japan, 88; Pub Sculpture Show, Whitney Mus Am Art, Downtown, NY, 90; Green, Max Protetch Gallery, NY, 91; Trilogi: Kunst, Natur, Vindeskab Kunsthallen Brandts, Klaedefabrik, Denmark, 96; .of Nature of., Arena Gallery, Chicago, 2000. *Awards:* Creative Artists Pub Serv Grant, 77; Nat Endowment Arts Grant, 78 & 79. *Bibliog:* Robert Hobbs (auth), Review, Sculpture Mag, 12/90; Regina Hackett (auth), Heavyweight artists discuss public works, stress collaboration, Seattle Times, 5/20/91; Giuliano Gori (auth), Living with art: Skeletons, stairways, and thunderbolts, ARTNews, 1/91. *Dealer:* Peter Rose Gallery 200 E 58th St # 20c New York NY 10022. *Mailing Add:* 205 Mulberry St New York NY 10012

SONNABEND, JOAN
ART DEALER, COLLECTOR
b Boston, Mass, July 9, 28. *Study:* Sarah Lawrence Col, BA, 50. *Specialty:* Contemporary American and European, drawings, painting, sculpture and prints. *Mailing Add:* 72 Mt Vernon St Boston MA 02114

SONNENBERG, FRANCES
SCULPTOR
b Brooklyn, NY. *Study:* With Prof Alfred Van Loen. *Work:* Hall of Fame. *Comn:* Five ft carved acrylic sculpture, Aquarius, Fla, 75. *Exhib:* One-woman shows, Stephan Gallery, NY, Buyways Gallery, Fla, Shelter Rock Gallery, NY, Cedar Crest Col, Pa & Adelphi Univ, NY; and others. *Teaching:* Sculpture classes in own studio, 72-. *Mem:* Nat Asn Women Artists; NY Soc Women Artists (secy, 73-74, rec secy, 74-); Metrop Painters & Sculptors (rec secy, 73-, secy, 74-); Am Soc Contemp Artists; Artist Craftsman. *Media:* Acrylic. *Mailing Add:* 1010 Paseo De La Luma Santa Fe NM 87501

SONNIER, KEITH
SCULPTOR, VIDEO ARTIST
b Mamou, La, July 31, 1941. *Study:* Rutgers Univ, NJ, MFA, 66. *Work:* Hara Mus Contemp Art, Tokyo; Mus Mod Art & Whitney Mus, NY; Australian Nat Gallery, Canberra; Sprengel Mus, Hannover, Ger; Mus Contemp Art, Los Angeles; Moderna Museet, Stockholm, Sweden; Dr Peter Ludwig Collection, Aachen, WGer; Mus Contemp Art, Los Angeles, Calif; Mus Haus Lange, Krefeld, WGer. *Comn:* Lichtweg (permanent indoor neon installation), City of Munich, Ger, 89; Pro Eco (permanent outdoor neon installation), City of New Orleans, 91; Lecon en Bouge, Ja'une et Bleu (permanent indoor neon installation), City of Paris, 93; DeRouge a Bleu (permanent indoor neon installation), City of Rouen, France, 94; Miami Heliotrope (permanent outdoor neon installation), City of Miami, Fla, 96. *Exhib:* Gravity & Grace, The Changing Condition Sculpture 1965-75; Postminimalism, Aldridge Mus, Ridgefield, Conn, 82; one-man shows, Hara Mus Contemp Art, Tokyo, 84, Mus Mod Art, NY, 86, Ceatre d'Art Contemporain du Kerguehennec, Rennes, 87, Chrysler Mus, Va, 88 & Hirschhorn Mus, Nat Gallery, Washington, 89; Galerie Montemy, Paris, 86 & 89; Blum-Helman Gallery, NY, 86 & 90; Tony Shafrazi Gallery, NY, 86 & 89; Domaine de Kerguehennec, Rennes, France, 87; Keith Sonnier/Lynda Benglis, Alexandria Mus, La, 87; solo exhibs Neon Sculpture, Chrysler Mus, Norfolk, Va, 88 & Expanded file series: 1969-1989, Stadtisches Mus, Abteiber; The New Sculpture 1965-75, Whitney Mus Am Art, 90; one-man retrospective traveling exhib (with catalog), 93. *Teaching:* Instr art & art hist, Rutgers Univ, NJ, 69-72, Sch Visual Arts, NY, 72-84 & Bard Col, Rhinebeck, NY, 84-86. *Awards:* Guggenheim Fel, 74; First Prize, Tokyo Prints Biennale, 74; Nat Endowment Arts, 86. *Bibliog:* Donald Kuspit (auth), Interim Shrines: The Sculptures of Keith Sonnier (catalog), 89; Lichtweg Keith Sonnier Lightway, Stuttgart Edition, Cantz, 93. *Dealer:* Leo Castelli Gallery 420 W Broadway New York NY 10012. *Mailing Add:* 145 Chambers St New York NY 10007

SONO, MASAYUKI
ARCHITECT
b Kobe, Japan, 71. *Study:* Univ Wash, Seattle, MArch, 96; Kobe Univ, Japan, MArch, 98. *Work:* Asia Soc and Mus renovation and addition, NY City; Univ Va Art Mus, Charlottesville; LaGuardia Internat Airport Control Tower, Queens, NY; Aspen Residence, Colo; World Trade Ctr Site Perimeter Enclosure, NY City; Ashiya Art Gallery, Hyogo, Japan; Shofu-den renovation and addition, Sullivan County, NY; Postcards: The Staten Island Sept 11th Mem, NY (Merit award, Small Project, NY Construct News, 2004. *Exhib:* over 60 exhibs. *Pos:* Architect, Voorsanger & Assocs, NY City, 1998-2003; principle architect, Masayuki Sono Architects, 2003-. *Awards:* Achievement in the Arts award, Coun on the Arts & Humanities for Staten Island, 2004. *Mailing Add:* Masayuki Sono Architects 308 Mott St Suite 3F New York NY 10012

SOPPELSA, GEORGE
PAINTER, COLLAGE ARTIST
b Youngstown, Ohio, July 16, 39. *Study:* Ohio State Univ, BFA, 61. *Work:* Mulvane Art Mus, Topeka, Kans; Conn Collection, Conn Comn Arts, Hartford. *Exhib:* One-man shows, Inter Art Galerie Reich, Cologne, 77, 81, 84, 87, 90, 94, 98, 2001 & 2005, Mulvane Art Mus, Topeka, 85, John Szoke Gallery, NY, 89, Univ Conn, 90, 91, & Randall Tuttle Fine Arts, Woodbury, Conn, 96; Dreamscapes-Aspects of Surreality in Conn, Mattatuck Mus, Waterbury, 88; ARCHA Soc Touring Mus Exhib, Ger, 93; Surrealist Affinities, John Slade Ely House Gallery, New Haven, Conn, 94; Investing In Dreams, Mattatuck Mus, Waterbury, Conn, 95; Landscape as Inspiration, Aldrich Mus Contemp Art, Ridgefield, Conn, 96; 64th Ann Midyear show, Butler Inst Am Art, Youngstown, Ohio, 2002; New Brit Mus Am Art, Conn, 99; Greater Hartford Jewish Community Ctr, W Hartford, Conn, 99; Wenniger Gallery, 95, 97; ADD Gallery, Hudson, NY, 99; Montserrat Col of Art, Beverly, MA, 2004. *Pos:* Vis Artist, Weir Farm Nat Hist Site, 95. *Teaching:* Instr, design theory, drawing, Fortman Studios, Florence, Italy, 1978-80. *Awards:* Nat Endowment Arts Fel, 87; Vt Studio Colony Fel, 88; Conn Comn on the Arts, Individual Artist Grant, 91. *Bibliog:* Christine Smith (auth), Classical Balance within the New Realist Idiom: George Soppelsa Inter Art Galerie Reich, Koln, 1981; Placido Torresi (auth) George Soppelsa Inter Art Galerie Reich, Koln, 1984; Leo Forte (auth), Bridges Between Two Worlds of Light, Inter Art Galerie Reich, Köln, 89; Klaus Tippmann (auth), Domhofgalerie im Aufwind, Zwickauer Zeitung, Zwickau, 7/31/93; Annette Schroeder (auth), Sprung ins Blau Kolnishe Rundschau, 9/30/94. *Media:* Acrylic. *Dealer:* Inter Art Galerie Reich Koln Cologne Germany; Brairton Stubbs Art Agents East Hartford CT. *Mailing Add:* 135 Central Ave Hartford CT 06108

SORCE, ANTHONY JOHN
PAINTER
b Chicago, Ill, Apr 30, 37. *Study:* Am Acad Art, dipl, 57; Univ Notre Dame, BFA, 61, MFA, 62. *Work:* Allen & Co, New York City; AT&T, Long Vines, Va; British Airways, New York City; Davis, Polk & Wardell, London, England; Pepiso, Purchase, NY. *Comn:* Sculpture, Wichita Art Mus, Kans, 70; painting, TRW, Linhurst, Ohio, 84-85; painting, Arby's Inc, Atlanta, Ga, 90. *Exhib:* Midyear Exhib, Butler Inst, Youngstown, Ohio, 62; Watercolor USA, Springfield Art Mus, Mo, 63; solo exhibs, Kalamazoo Inst Art, Mich, 66, Nazareth Coll, Rochester, NY, 68, Jewish Mus, NY, 70, Wichita Art Mus, Kans, 70, OK Harris Works Art, NY, 77, 79, 80, 82, 84 & 86, Lance Fung Gallery, NY, Joan Prats Gallery, NY & Sordoni Art Gallery, Wilkes Univ, Pa, 98, 2nd Flint Int, Flint Inst Art, Mich, 70, NY Gallery Showcase, Okla Art Ctr, Oklahoma City, 81, Roy Boyd Gallery, Chicago, 2001-6006; OK Harris Works of Art, NY, 2005; Wilson Adams Gallery, Denver, Colo, 2005. *Teaching:* Prof art, Nazareth Col, Kalamazoo, Mich, 62-67; Nazareth Col, Rochester, Mich, 67-68; Manhattan Community Col, City Univ NY, 71-. *Awards:* Guggenheim Fel, 68; Fac Res Award for Painting, City Univ, NY, 73-74, 96-98, 2003-04, State Univ, NY, 74-75. *Media:* Rhoplex, Acrylic. *Collection:* Wichita Art Mus, Wichita, Kans; The Speed Art Mus, Louisville, Ky; Snite Mus Art, Notre Dame, Ind; Newark Mus, Newark, NJ; Kalamazoo Inst Art, Kalamazoo, Mich; Maslow Collection, Wilkes-Barre, Pa. *Publ:* John Yau (auth), Anthony Sorce's Recent Work; Stanley I Grand (auth), Progess and Innovation: The Art of Anthony Sorce. *Dealer:* OK Harris Works of Art 383 West Broadway New York NY 10012; Roy Boyd Gallery 739 N Wells St Chicago IL 60610; Wilson Adams Gallery 1307 Bannock St Denver Colo 80204. *Mailing Add:* 939B 463 West St New York NY 10014

SOREFF, STEPHEN
SCULPTOR, ASSEMBLAGE ARTIST
b New York, NY, Feb 2, 31. *Study:* Brooklyn Col, BA, 54; Pratt Inst, BA, 60. *Work:* Mus Mod Art Libr & Whitney Mus Libr, NY; Hirshhorn Mus Libr, Washington; Nat Mus, Stockholm Sweden. *Exhib:* Projects for a New Millenium, Peabody Mus, New Haven, Conn; Artists of the Springs E Hampton, NY; Artist's Woods, E Hampton, NY; AAEH, E Hampton, NY; Arlene Bujese gallery, E Hampton, NY. *Pos:* Staff reviewer, Artworld, 74, 57th Street Rev, 74-75, Art Economist, 80-81; sr ed, Art & Artists, 81-83; ed & publ, Avant Garde Art Rev, 80-90. *Teaching:* Prof art & design, Long Island Univ, Brookville, NY, 70-2000. *Awards:* Res grants, Long Island Univ Res Comt, 80, 83 & 90; Residency, MacDowell Colony, Peterborough, NH, 83; Residency, Va Colony Arts, Sweet Briar, Va, 87. *Bibliog:* In the art galleries, New York Post, 64; The big thing show?, Seattle Times, 69; Clifford Pickover (auth), Mazes for the Mind, Art News, 92. *Media:* All Media. *Mailing Add:* 79 Mercer St New York NY 10012

SOREL, EDWARD
ILLUSTRATOR, WRITER
b New York, NY, Mar 26, 29. *Study:* Cooper Union, dipl, 51; Art Inst Boston, DFA. *Hon Degrees:* Art Inst Boston, DFA. *Work:* Unauthorized Portraits, 97; Nat Portrait Gallery, Washington. *Comn:* Men and Women of Progress, comn by Nat Portrait Gallery. *Exhib:* One-man shows, Graham Gallery, NY, 73, New Sch Social Res, 74 & Galerie Bartsch & Chariau, Munich, 86; Push Pin Style, Mus des Arts Decoratifs, Paris, 70; Susan Conway Galleries, Washington, DC, 92; Davis & Langsdale Galleries, 94; Nat Portrait Gallery, 97. *Pos:* Co-founder, Push-Pin Studios, New York, 53-56; art dir, CBS Promotion Art, New York, 56-57; syndicated cartoonist, King Features, 69-71; contribr, Atlantic Mag, 69-; contrib ed, New York Mag, 72-78 & GQ Mag, 84-; cartoonist, Village Voice, 74-78; cartoonist, The Nation, 85, New Yorker, 90-. *Teaching:* tchr, Parsons, New York, NY, 83-84. *Awards:* St Gauden's Medal, Cooper Union, 73; George Polk Award for Satiric Drawing, 81; Page One Award, Newspaper Guild, 88. *Bibliog:* Carlos C Drake (auth), Edward Sorel, Graphis, No 105, 63; Jerome Snyder (auth), Edward Sorel, Graphis, No 154, 71-72. *Mem:* Century Asn; Freedom From Religion. *Media:* Pen & Ink, Watercolor. *Specialty:* English Watercolors & Drawings. *Publ:* auth & illusr, Moon Missing, 72; Making the World Safe for Hypocrisy, 72; Superpen, 78; First Encounters, 94; Unauthorized Portraits, 97; The Saturday Kid, 2000. *Dealer:* Davis and Langdale 231 E 60th St New York NY 10022

SORELL, VICTOR ALEXANDER
HISTORIAN, ADMINISTRATOR
b Mexico City, Mex, Oct 31, 44. *Study:* Shimer Col, BA; Univ Chicago, with Joshua C Taylor and John Rewald, MA; Univ Chicago. *Collection Arranged:* Mexposicion I (with catalog in Eng & Span), 75 & Mexposicion II: Photographic Images of the Mex Revolution by Agustin Victor Casasola, 76, A Montgomery Ward Gallery, Univ Ill, Chicago Circle; Hispanic American Art in Chicago & Chilean Arpilleras, Univ Galleries, Chicago State Univ, 80. *Pos:* Co-ed, Abrazo (Embrace) J, 76-; prog admin, Park Forest Art Ctr, 78 & 79; coordr, Hispanic Am Cult Enrichment Progs, Chicago State Univ, 79-80 & 83; fac fel art hist & sr prog officer, Nat Endowment Humanities, 80-83. *Teaching:* Chmn art dept, Chicago State Univ, 75-80 & 83. *Awards:* Fac Scholar, Inst Bilingual Educ, Educ Prof Develop Act, 75; Grant, Ill Humanities Coun, 76; Grants, Ill Arts & Humanities Coun, 80. *Mem:* Col Art Asn Am; el Movimiento Artistico Chicano (chmn, 79). *Res:* Documentary investigation of modern (1900-present) Canadian, Mexican & US mural art; Chilean arpilleras and subject of human rights as reflected in visual arts. *Publ:* Auth, Barrio murals in Chicago: Painting the Hispanic-American experience on our community walls, In: Revista Chicano--Riquena, Ind Univ-Northwest, 75; co-reviewer articles in American studies sect, Am Quart, 69-73; transl, Jose David Alfaro Siqueiros (auth), Como se Pinta un Mural (How to Paint a Mural), 78; ed, Guide to Chicago Murals: Yesterday and Today, 1st ed, 78, 2nd ed, 79; auth, Hispanic American Art in Chicago (catalog), 80. *Mailing Add:* 10420 S Wood St Chicago IL 60643

SORGE, WALTER
PAINTER, PRINTMAKER
b Forestberg, Alta, Oct 25, 31. *Study:* Univ Calif, Los Angeles, BA, 54, MA, 55; Columbia Univ, EDD, 64; also with Stanley William Hayter, Paris, 61-62 & 68. *Work:* Victoria & Albert Mus, London, Eng; J B Speed Mus, Louisville, Ky; Sheldon Swope Art Gallery, Terre Haute, Ind. *Exhib:* One-man show, Inst Mex NAm Relationes Cult, Mexico City, 71; Sheldon Swope Art Gallery, Terre Haute, Ind, 71, Am Embassies,

Ankara, Izmir & Istanbul, Turkey, 74-75; Second Can Biennial, 57 & Canadian Watercolors, Drawings & Prints, 66, Nat Gallery Can; Smithsonian Inst Traveling Exhib, Washington, DC, 67; and others. *Pos:* Chmn dept painting, drawing & printmaking, Ky Southern Col, 64-69 & Hardin-Simmons Univ, Tex, 69-70; chmn dept, Eastern Ill Univ, Charleston, 70-75, prof art, 75-; exchange prof, Portsmouth Polytech Inst, England, 77. *Awards:* C W Jefferys Award, 26th Ann Exhib, Can Soc Graphic Art, 59; Jr League Purchase Award, Mid-States Art Exhib, Evansville Mus Arts & Sci, Ind, 67; Helen Van Aken Purchase Award, Fifth Ann Gulf Coast Exhib, Mobile Art Gallery, 70. *Media:* Watercolor, Mixed Media; Intaglio. *Mailing Add:* Eastern Ill Univ Art Dept 600 Lincoln St Charleston IL 61920-3099

SORKIN, EMILY
ART DEALER, GALLERY DIRECTOR
b New York, NY. *Study:* New York Univ, BS(art): Hunter Col, NY, MA(fine arts). *Collection Arranged:* New York to Bennington: Paintings (auth, catalog), 83 & Matter & Spirit, 85, Bennington Col, Vt; Seven Painters, State Univ NY, Purchase, 83; Ontogeny: Sculpture and Painting by 20th Century American Sculptors, New York Studio Sch, 85; Portraits and Self-Portraits, Sorkin Gallery, New York, 86. *Pos:* Dir, Robert Freidus Gallery, 76-77, John Gibson Gallery, 79-81, Sorkin Gallery, 85-90, New York & K & E Gallery, New York, 93-95; private dealer, 96. *Bibliog:* Peter Gallo (auth), rev, Rutland Herald, Vt, 10/85; Barry Schwabsky (auth), rev, Arts Mag, 6/86; Vivien Raynor (auth), rev, New York Times, 4/86. *Mem:* Fla Keys Council of the Arts (Advisory bd mem, 2003-06). *Specialty:* 20th century art. *Publ:* Auth, Intro to Bill Jensen Etching Portfolio, Universal Ed, 85; Matter & spirit, Bennington Col, Vt, 85; contribr, Bill Jensen Etchings (exhib catalog), Mus Mod Art, New York, 86; auth, The sculpture of Ronald Bladen, Arts Mag, 86; Introd to Margrit Lewczuk (exhib catalog), Heland Thorden Wetterling Galleries, Stockholm, Sweden, 87. *Mailing Add:* 150 Franklin St New York NY 10013

SORKIN, JENNI
CURATOR, CRITIC
Study: Scho of Art Inst of Chicago, BFA, 99; Bard Col, MA, 2002; Yale Univ, student in PhD prog in Hist of Art, 2004-. *Exhib:* High Performance: The First Five Yrs, 78-82, Bard Col, 2002, Los Angeles Contemp Exhibs, 2003, Judy Chicago: Minimalism, 65-73, LewAllen Contemp, Santa Fe, 2004. *Pos:* cur, res asst, proj coordr, Mus Contemp Art, LA, formerly; res asst, Dept Contemp Prog & Res Getty Res Inst, formerly. *Awards:* Recipient Art J Award for article Envisioning High Performance, Col Art Assoc, 2004. *Mem:* Queer Caucus for Art (co-chmn, 2004—). *Mailing Add:* Yale Univ Hist of Art Dept 56 High St New Haven CT 06520

SORMAN, STEVEN
PAINTER, PRINTMAKER
b Minneapolis, Minn, June 14, 48. *Study:* Univ Minn, BFA, 71. *Work:* Mus Mod Art, Whitney Mus Am Art, NY; Art Inst Chicago; Princeton Univ Art Mus; Walker Art Ctr, Minn; and others. *Comn:* Springhill Found, Minn; Prudential Insurance; IBM; Honeywell; Hyatt Regency. *Exhib:* Printmakers Midwest Invitational, Walker Art Ctr, Minn, 73; Corcoran Biennial, Corcoran Gallery Art, Washington, DC, 75; Paper as Medium, Smithsonian Inst, Washington, DC, 78; Painting and Sculpture Today, Indianapolis Mus Art, Ind, 78; 21st Nat Print Exhib, Brooklyn Mus, NY, 78; Artist and Printer, Walker Art Ctr, Minn, 80; Bienal Americana de Artes Graficas, Museo de Arte Moderno La Tertulia, Colombia, 81; 24th Nat Print Exhib, Brooklyn Mus, 86; First Impressions, Walker Art Ctr, 89; The 1980's: Prints from the Collection of Joshua P Smith, Nat Gallery, 89; Contemp Illus Books, Words & Image, 67-88, Independent Curators Inc, 90; Mind & Matter: New Am Abstract, World Print Coun, 90; 42nd Ann Acad Inst Purchase Exhib, Am Acad & Inst Arts & Lett, 90; 5th Int Biennial Print Exhib, Taipei, 91; Innovation in Collaborative Printmaking, Yokohama Mus Art, 92; Contemp Classics, The Illus Book Redefined, Minn Ctr Bk Arts, 93; Int Biennal Graphic Art, Ljubijana, 93 & 99; Printmaking in Am: Collaborative Prints & Presses, Zimmerli Art Mus, 95; Beyond Print, LaSalle, SIA Col Arts, Singapore, 96; Singular Impressions: The Monotype in Am, Nat Mus Am Art, 97; Printed Abstraction: Prints from Tyler Graphics Arch Collection, CCGA, Fukushima, Japan, 97; Contemp Arts Ctr, Cincinnati, 98; 175th Ann Exhib, Nat Acad Design, NY; many others. *Awards:* Bush Found Artist's Fel, 79; Merit Award, San Francisco Mus Mod Art, 80; Rockefeller Found, Am Ctr Artist in Residence, Paris, 82. *Bibliog:* Bernard Toale (auth), Basic Printmaking Techniques, Worcester, 92; Joanne Moser (auth), Singular Impressions, The Monotype in America, Washington, DC, 97; Marjorie Devon, Tamarind Forty Years, Albuquerque, 2000. *Mailing Add:* 2201 Rt 82 Ancram NY 12502

SOROKIN, JANET
ARTIST, PAINTER
b Hartford, Conn, Apr 2, 32. *Study:* Simmons Col, 50-52, Univ Hartford Art Sch, with Paul Zimmerman; courses at Trinity Col & Wesleyan Univ, Conn. *Work:* Mass Mutual Insurance Co, Springfield; Metrop Fed Bank, Nashville; Dewey Ballantine, NY; Lourde's Hosp, Padukah, Ky; Peat, Marwick & Main, New York & Danbury, Conn; more than 100 corp & pub collections; Univ Conn Health Ctr, Farmington, CT; Harvard Pilgrim Health Care, Kenmore Facility, Boston, MA; Prosser Public Library, Bloomfield, CT. *Comn:* 8 serigraphs chosen by Cesar Pelli & Assocs for the Cleveland Clinic, Ohio; cow, Cow Parade, NYC, 2000. *Exhib:* Nat Acad Design, NY, 81, 84 & 90; solo exhibs, Slater Mus, Norwich, Conn, 73 & 89 & Univ Conn, Storrs, 99; group shows, Nat Asn Women Artists, 83-88, New Brit Mus Am Art, 93 & 94 & Nat Soc Painters in Casein & Acrylic, 83-85 & 87, West Hartford Art League, 99; Slater Mus, Norwich, Conn, 92, 93 & 94; two-person exhib, Univ Minn at Morris, Humanities Fine Arts Gallery, 92; The Conn Vision 1990, Mattatuck Mus, Waterbury, Conn; Glass, Textiles, Prints, San Francisco State Univ, 92; Horizon Series, 2000, Small Work, 2002, Atrium Gallery, St Louis, Mo; one-person show, Univ Conn Health Ctr, 99 & 2006; featured artist, Serendipity, 2005-2006, & 10 at 20, twentieth celebration 20th Gallery anniversary. *Pos:* Mem, Coun Conn Acad Fine Art, 82-90. *Awards:* First Prize, The Slater Mem Mus Ann Exhib, 81 & 88; Binney & Smith Award, 83; Janet Turner Award, Nat Asn Women Artists Ann Exhib, 85; and over 58 other awards; Second Prize regional exhib, Mystic Art Asn, Conn, 01; CT Watercolor Soc, Univ Hartford Award, 2004. *Mem:* Conn Watercolor Soc; Conn Women Artists; Conn Acad Fine Arts; Nat Asn Women Artists; Essex Art Asoc. *Media:* Mixed Media. *Publ:* Illusr, The Other Side II (poster), Modern Art Ed, 85; poster, In: Room Design, House Beautiful, 6/85; Contemp Graphic Artists, Gale Res Co, New York, 88; greeting card, Glaucama Research Found. *Dealer:* Atrium Gallery St Louis MO. *Mailing Add:* 101 Mohawk Dr West Hartford CT 06117

SOROKIN, MAXINE ANN
PAINTER, EDUCATOR
b Brooklyn, NY, Dec 15, 48. *Study:* Kingsborough Community Col, AA, 67; Brooklyn Col, with Philip Pearlstein, Jimmy Ernst, Robert Wolff & Samuel Gelber, BA(cum laude), 70, MFA, 72. *Comn:* Window & portal paintings, Congregation of Kehillath Jacobs Synagogue, Newton, Mass, 73; paintings, Solomon Schechter Day Sch, Newton, Mass. *Exhib:* Invitational, Newton City Hall, Mass, 73-76; Meetinghouse Gallery, Boston, 73; Boston Visual Artists Union, 74 & 75; two-person exhibs, Goethe Inst, Boston, 80, Jewish Community Ctr Southern NJ, Cherry Hill, 80, Young Adult Ctr, Boston, 84 & Warner House Gallery, Univ Cincinnati, 86, and more; 30 yr retrospective, Perkins Gallery, Stoughton, Mass, 95; group exhibs, Wells Pub Libr, Maine, 2004, Shore Gallery, Ogunquit, Maine, 2006-. *Teaching:* Fel & grad asst painting, Brooklyn Col, 71-72; lectr art, Univ Mass, Boston, 72-73; assoc prof, Art Inst of Boston, 87-; visual arts coordr, Jewish Community Ctr, Stoughton-Newton, Mass, 87-90; art specialist, Schecter Day Sch, 90-2003, Harvard Hillel Children's Sch, 90 & The Rashi Sch, 91-95; prog supv, Grad Sch Dept of Creative Arts in Learning, Lesley Univ; adj fac, grad sch, Lesley Univ, 2003-. *Awards:* Eisler Award Painting Excellence, City Univ New York, 70. *Bibliog:* Lisa Taylor (producer), Woman 76, WBZ Television, 76. *Mem:* Boston Visual Artists Union; West Roxbury Artists Asn (vpres, 77-78); West Roxbury Hist Soc; Victorian Soc. *Media:* Oil, Pen & Ink. *Interests:* antiques; needlework. *Publ:* Auth, Harvard Hillel Children's Sch Curric, Cambridge, Mass, 90-91; cover illusr, Learning Disabilities, Houghton Mifflin Inc, 93; illusr, Burning Beds and Mermaids, Prentice-Hall, 93; It All Started in Kindergarten, Prentice-Hall, 93. *Dealer:* Shore Gallery, Ogunquit, Maine. *Mailing Add:* 61 Perham St West Roxbury MA 02132

SORRIN, MARY LOUISE
PAINTER
b Woodward, Okla, Mar 9, 46. *Study:* studied with Richard McDaniel, Elizabeth Mowry, John DiMestico, Rosalie Nadeau, Albert Handell. *Work:* Nat Vietnam Vets Art Mus, Chicago; Vietnam Women's Meml Project, Washington. *Exhib:* Int Asn of Pastel Soc, Albuquerque, NMex, 1998; Pastel Society of the West Coast 12 Ann Int Exhib, Roseville, Calif, 1998; LaFond Galleries Ann Exhib, LaFond Gallery, Pittsburgh, 1999; Pastel Painters Society Cape Cod, Creative Arts Ctr, Chatham, Mass, 2000; Pastels on High, Sierra Pastel Soc, Placerville, Calif, 2001. *Awards:* Canson Merit award, Pastel Soc SW, 2000; Mountain High award, Pastels on High, 2001. *Bibliog:* Eve Sinaiko (ed), Vietnam, Reflexes & Reflexions, 98. *Mem:* Pastel Painters Soc of Cape Cod; Sierra Paste Soc; Southwest Pastel Soc; Connecticut Pastel Soc; Independent Artists of Oklahoma

SOTH, ALEC
PHOTOGRAPHER
Study: Sarah Lawrence Col, NY, BA. *Work:* Rep in permanent collections, San Francisco Mus Modern Art, Los Angeles Co Mus Art, Mus Fine Arts, Houston, Walker Art Ctr, Minneapolis, Minneapolis Inst Arts, Odged Mus Southern Art, New Orleans, Carleton Col, Minn, NDak Mus Art. *Exhib:* One-man shows, The Middle Night, Minneapolis Photogr's Gallery, 93, Art at the Bar, Icebox Gallery, Minneapolis, 95-96, Minn Ctr Photog, 98, Portraits (From Here to There), Central Lakes Col Gallery, 2001, Sleeping By the Miss, Weitman Gallery of Photog, Wash Univ, St Louis, Mo, 2003; group shows, at Campus as Place, Photog Carleton, Carleton Col Art Gallery, Minn, 2002, Dog Days, Gallery T, Minneapolis, 2003, Summer Life, Alice Austen House Mus, Staten Island, NY, 2003, Picturing Bill - Portraits of William Eggleston, John Stinson Fine Arts, New Orleans, 2003, Sao Paulo Biennial, Sao Paulo, Brazil, 2004, Whitney Biennial, Whitney Mus Am Art, 2004. *Awards:* McKnight Photog Fel, 99 & 2004; Jerome Travel & Study Grant, 2001; Recipient Santa Fe Prize Photog, 2003. *Publ:* auth: (book) Sleeping by the Miss, 2004. *Mailing Add:* Alec Soth Photography 856 Raymond Ave Unit D Saint Paul MN 55114

SOTTUNG, GEORGE (K)
PAINTER, SCULPTOR
b Chicago, Ill. *Study:* Art Inst Chicago, grad; DePaul Univ; Brooklyn Mus Art, post grad study: apprentice to Haddon H Sundblom. *Work:* Bethesda Naval Hosp Rotunda, Washington; Princeton Univ, NJ; US Naval War Col, Newport, RI; US Military Acad, West Point; US Air Force Acad, Colorado Springs, 90; and others. *Comn:* First Atlantic Crossing, 75, Capt Healy, 78 & Invasion of Normandy, 79-80, US Govt; US Military History oil paintings series, United Technologies, 84-85; Hist Portrait, Lt Elmer Stone, 89; many portrait comns for pvt individuals and corps. *Exhib:* Grumbacher Exhib; Allied Artists Am Exhib, Nat Acad Galleries, NY, 75 & Am Watercolor Soc Exhib, ann; Am Painters in Paris Exhib, Palais des Cong, France, 75 & 76; Art Inst Chicago; Smithsonian Inst; Fogg Mus; Nat Acad Design, 167th Ann Exhib, 92. *Pos:* Illusr, Chicago Tribune Co, 54-62, Charles E Cooper Studios, New York, 62-64; freelance artist, painter & sculptor (style & technique, realism and abstraction), 64-. *Awards:* Art Students League Nat Sculpture Soc Award, New York, 83; Conn Watercolor Soc Award, 90; Seley Gold Medal & Abe Sharp Awards,

Salmagundi Club NY; and others. *Bibliog:* US Navy Artists (film), US Govt, 74; Ellen Anderson (auth), Meet George Sottung, North Light/Fletcher Art Serv, 76; Creative Watercolor, 95 & Best of Watercolor, 97, Rockport Publ. *Mem:* Salmagundi Club; Am Watercolor Soc; Soc Illusr; Chicago Press Club; Conn Watercolor Soc. *Media:* All Media. *Mailing Add:* 111 Tower Rd Brookfield Center CT 06804

SOUGSTAD, MIKE
GRAPHIC ARTIST, EDUCATOR
b Madison, SDak, June 18, 39. *Study:* Dakota Wesleyan Univ, Mitchell, SDak, BA, 61; Univ Wyo, MFA, 85. *Work:* Pioneer Mus, Wyo State Fairgrounds, Douglas, Wyo; Univ Wyo Art Mus, Laramie; Friends of the Middle Border Mus & Dakota Wesleyan Univ Collection, Mitchell, SDak. *Comn:* Old West Cattle Trails (murals), High Plains Heritage Ctr, Spearfish, SDak; educational murals (3), Hopkins Elementary Sch, Littleton, Colo; History of the Region (mural), The West in Miniature, Spearfish, SDak; Fulton Area History (mural), Fulton State Bank, Mitchell, SDak; murals, The Country Store, Robb's, Inc, Belle Fourche, SDak; regional historic murals & paintings, Mid Border Mus, Mitchell SD. *Exhib:* Rushmore Insurance Prof Artist Invitational Art Show, Rapid City, SDak, 84-89; Railroads in the West, Oscar Howe Art Ctr, Mitchell, SDak, 87; Town Hall Art Ctr, Littleton, Colo, 88; Mus of Pioneer Life, Douglas, Wyo, 89; Dakota Prix, High Plains Heritage Ctr, Spearfish, SDak, 90-91; Douglas Invitational Art Show, Wyo, 91-94; The West in Miniature, Spearfish, SDak, 92-99; Fulton Art Show, 98-; Heartdreams & Legends, Int Tour of Lakota Sioux & Australian Aboriginal Art, 2000-03; Ctr Western Studies Juried Show, Sioux Falls, SDak, 2003. *Pos:* Freelance artist & illusr, 57-; ed, Dakota West (mag), SDak Cowboy & Western Heritage Hall of Fame, 75; mgr, Dakota Western Art Gallery, Lead, SDak, formerly; founder & dir, Denkota Inst, Spearfish, SDak, 91-98, Fulton, SDak, 98-; cofounder & dir, The West in Miniature, Spearfish, SDak, 92-99; curator art, Middle Border Mus, Mitchell, 2001-. *Teaching:* Vis lectr art, Univ Wyo, Laramie, 84-86; dept head & prof graphic design & illus, Arapahoe Community Col, Littleton, Colo, 87-91; adj fac, Metrop State Univ, Denver, Colo, 92, Black Hills State Univ, Spearfish, SDak, 94-, Dakota Wesleyan Univ, Mitchel, SDak, 2000-; instr graphic design, Platt Col, Aurora, Colo, 92-93; dir & instr art, Denkota Inst, Spearfish, SDak, 93--98, Den Kota Inst, Fulton, SD, 98- & Mobridge, SD, 2000-. *Awards:* Juried Award, Coors Corp Show, Adolf Coors Corp, 85, Oscar Howe Art Ctr, Mitchell, SD, 98, 2000; Purchase Award, Wyo State Fair, State of Wyo, 84. *Bibliog:* Ruth Brennan & Jan Nanman (auths), Sougstad's art mixes railroads with paint, Rapid City J, 1/27/84; Susan Lanneborg, Artist puts small-town life to canvas, Mitchell Daily Repub, 5/8/98; Jerry Wilson (auth), Fulton Artists, SDak Mag, Apr-May/2000. *Media:* Acrylics, Pencil. *Publ:* Navy UDT Handbook, US Navy, 66; Buffalo, 73-74; Old West Trail Vacation Guide, Old West Trail Found, 81-86, Vistor Mag, 83-84 & 96-97; Heart Dreams and Legends, 2000; History & Art of the Middle Border, 2002. *Mailing Add:* 10314 Lakeland Dr Fishers IN 46038-9323

SOUSA, JOHN PHILIP
PHOTOGRAPHER, COLLAGE ARTIST
b Detroit, Mich. *Study:* Bradley Univ, BFA, 82. *Exhib:* Photographs, Findlay Univ, Ohio, 97, John Philip Sousa at ACME Art Co, Columbus, Ohio, 97; Art Bytes, Freeport Art Mus, Ill, 95; 1996 Regional Biennial, Ft Wayne Mus Art, Ind, 96; Invitational Group Exhib, Carnegie Arts Ctr, Kans, 96; Members Show, Dayton Visual Arts Ctr, Dayton, Ohio, 97; Flirting at a Distance: New Abstraction, Del Ctr Contemp Arts, Wilmington, 97; Abstraction Two to Three, Cleveland State Univ, Ohio, 99; Transcending Limits: Moving Beyond Mainstream, Tex Fine Arts Asn, Austin, 99. *Awards:* Nat Scholastic Art Merit Scholar, 78; Individual Artist Fel, Montogomery Co Regional Arts & Cult Dist, 94 & 97. *Bibliog:* Steven Litt (auth), Views on culture, The Plain Dealer, 12/10/94; Robert Schroeder (auth), 1996 Regional Biennial, Art Dialog, May/June 96; Scott Dowd (dir), Radio Interview with Artist, WFPK-WFPL, 1/96. *Media:* Conceptual Photography; Mixed Media. *Mailing Add:* 6783 Quarterhorse Dr Springboro OH 45066-7778

SOUTHEY, TREVOR J T
PAINTER, SCULPTOR
b Zimbabwe, Rhodesia, Jan 12, 40; US citizen. *Study:* Brighton Col Art, Eng, 59; Natal Technical Col, Durban, S Africa, 60; Brigham Young Univ, Provo, Utah, BFA, 67, MA, 69. *Work:* Utah State Mus, Salt Lake City & Springville Mus Art, Utah; Rhodes Nat, Zimbabwe; Brigham Young Univ; Mormon Mus, Salt Lake City. *Comn:* Painting, Brigham Young Univ, Provo, Utah, 75; mural, Salt Lake Int Airport, 81; life size sculpture, Univ Utah Medical Ctr, Salt Lake City, 81; Painter Freeze, Univ Scranton, Pa; Monumental Bronze, Trammell Crow Corp, Atlanta, Ga & Phoenix, Ariz; Nature Sunshine Prod Inc, Provo, Utah. *Exhib:* Utah State Mus, Salt Lake City, 79 & Ill Ctr, Chicago, 79; Twenty Utah Printmakers, traveling show, Utah Arts Coun, 82; solo exhibs, Salt Lake City Art Ctr, Utah, 97; Barbican Ctr, London, 89; Calif Soc Printmakers, San Francisco, 90; Kimball Arts Ctr, Park City, Utah, 91; Waterworks Gallery, Friday Harbor, Wash, 92; Salt Lake Art Ctr, Main Gallery, Utah, 92; Vorpal Gallery, San Francisco, 92; Belcher Street Gallery, San Francisco, 93 & 94; Alumni Exhib, Brigham Young Univ, Provo, Utah, 93; The Nude, Vorpal Gallery, San Francisco, 95; Richmond Art Ctr, Calif, 96; Beyond Boundaries Print Competition, 96; and others. *Teaching:* Asst prof drawing & painting, Brigham Young Univ, Provo, 69-76. *Bibliog:* Trevor Southey/Stephen Doherty, Images and Ideas, Am Artist, 80; Steven P Sondrup (auth), Trevor Southey - the art and the man, Artists of the Rockies and the Golden West, summer 82. *Mem:* North Mountain Artists Cooperative; Alpine Community Arts (chmn, 78-); Calif Print Makers Asn. *Media:* Oil, Etchings; Bronzes. *Publ:* Illusr, The Search, 69, Doubleday; The Growing Season, Bookcraft, 75; Marriage and Divorce, Deseret Book, 76; The Sex Book, Pelton, 78; A Widening View, Bookcraft, 83; and others. *Dealer:* Lowe Galleries Atlanta GA & Santa Monica CA. *Mailing Add:* 5366 Leona St Oakland CA 94619

SOWERS, MIRIAM R
PAINTER
b Bluffton, Ohio, Oct 4, 22. *Study:* Miami Univ, BFA; Art Inst Chicago; Univ NMex. *Work:* Tex A&M Univ; Mus of NMex Art Gallery; Sheldon Swope Gallery, Terre Haute, Ind; Nat Arch, Washington; Chicago Art Inst. *Comn:* Over 500 portraits. *Exhib:* Butler Inst Am Art; St Johns Col, Santa Fe, NMex, 85; Findlay Col, Findlay, Ohio, 87; Chicago Art Inst, 93; Chicago Art Inst, 93; Coriell Gallery, Albuquerque, NMex, 93; Blankley Gallery, Albuquerque, NMex, 93-94; Southwest Cornerhouse Gallery, Albuquerque, NMex, 94; and others. *Pos:* Owner, Symbol Gallery Art, 61-79; owner, Sowers Symbolic art Studios, currently. *Awards:* Prizes, Toledo Mus Art, Ouray Colo Nat & NMex State Fair; plus others. *Bibliog:* Mary Carroll Nelson (auth), Miriam Sowers, Art Voices, 9-10/81; articles, Encore Poetry Mag, 86; Article, Metro Plus-Albuquerque, 93. *Media:* Oil. *Specialty:* Oils on gold leaf; silver and copper; symbolism of man and nature. *Publ:* Auth, Parables from Paradise, Branden Press; The Suns of Man, Symbol, 81

SOWERS, RUSSELL FREDERIC
GALLERY DIRECTOR, MUSEUM DIRECTOR
b Kauai, Hawaii, Aug 1, 34. *Pos:* Dir, Ramsay Mus, Honolulu. *Mem:* Honolulu Acad Arts. *Specialty:* Artists of Hawaii. *Mailing Add:* Ramsay Museum 1128 Smith St Honolulu HI 96817-5194

SOWINSKI, STANISLAUS JOSEPH
PAINTER, ICONOGRAPHER
b Milwaukee, Wis, May 7, 27. *Study:* San Diego Sch Arts, 48-49; San Diego State Univ, BA, 52. *Hon Degrees:* Dept Defense, Interlligence sch, 1965. *Work:* Dept Defense, Pentagon; Univ Calif, La Jolla; San Diego State Univ; City Escondido, Calif. *Comn:* 25 Major icons, Sts Constantine & Helen Church, Solana Beach, Calif, 82-90 & Corpus Christi Church, Bonita, Calif, 94-98; 3 large paintings, City Escondido, Calif, 88; full length portraits, City Escondido, Calif, 88; numerous large paintings, Univ Calif, La Jolla, 89-93, 5 large corp paintings, Poway, Calif, 90; designer altar, 5 large paintings, St Marys Ch, Escondido, Calif, 99-2000; Large painting, St Stephen's church, Valley Ctr, Calif & Wisconsin Polish Ctr, Franklin, Wis, 2005. *Exhib:* Royal Watercolour Soc, London, 65 & 66; solo exhibs, US Embassy, London, 67 & Escondido Hist Mus, Calif, 83; Royal Soc Brit Artists, London, 67; Royal Acad, London, 67; solo exhib, A Huney Gallery & Thackeray Gallery, San Diego, Calif, 89-92, Brandon Gallery, Fallbrook, Calif, 2000, Santa Ysabel Gallery, Santa Yshbel, Calif, 2005, Bradley Fine Art, San Diego, Calif, 2004-2005, Wisconsin Polish Ctr, Franklin, Wis, 2006; Sparrow Fine Art Gallery, Solana Beach, Calif, 2002. *Pos:* Demonr watercolor, Grumbacher Inc, New York, 76-79 & Inveresk Paper Co, Bath, UK, 79-86. *Teaching:* Instr watercolor workshops, Calif, Ore & SDak, 71-76; watercolor painting, San Diego Art Inst, 76-77. *Awards:* Int Friendship Festival Best of Show Award, El Cajon, Calif, 2000; ir, Calif, 2001. *Bibliog:* Brand Book IV, San Diego Corral-Westerners, Calif, 76. *Mem:* San Diego Portrait Soc; San Diego Fine Arts Guild. *Media:* Oil, Watercolor, Acrylic, Tonal Impressionist. *Dealer:* Santa Ysabel Gallery PO Box 480 Santa Ysabel CA 92070; Kuhnly Fine Art 218 E Grand #4 Escondido CA 92025; Bradley Fine Art 2168 Chatsworth Blvd Sand Diego CA 92107. *Mailing Add:* 13040 Cedilla Pl San Diego CA 92128

SPAFFORD, MICHAEL CHARLES
EDUCATOR, PAINTER
b Palm Springs, Calif, Nov 6, 35. *Study:* Pomona Co, BA, 59; Harvard Univ, MA(art hist), 60. *Work:* Seattle Art Mus, Wash; Galeria de Inst Mexicano-Norte Americano, Mexico City; Undergrad Libr, Univ Wash; Tacoma Art Mus, Wash; Bellevue Art Mus, Wash. *Comn:* Mural, Kingdome, Seattle, Wash, 79; murals, House Chambers State Capitol Bldg, Olympia, Wash, 81; mural, Seattle Opera House, 85; Centrum Print, Ft Worden, Wash, 87. *Exhib:* One-man shows, Utah Mus Fine Arts, 75, Am Acad & Inst Arts & Letters Awards Selection Show, NY, 80 & 83 & Seattle Art Mus, 82 & 86; Focus Seattle, San Jose Mus Art, 87; Bellevue Art Mus, Wash, 91; Cheney Cowles Mus, Spokane, Wash, 94; Holter Mus Art, Helena, Mont, 97. *Teaching:* Instr painting, Mexico City Col, 61-62; assoc prof painting-drawing, Univ Wash, 63-78, prof, 78-95, retired. *Awards:* Award in Painting, Am Acad & Inst Arts & Lett, 83; The Neddy Artist Fel, Behnke Found, Seattle, 96. *Bibliog:* Bruce Guenther (auth), 50 Northwest Artists, San Francisco Chronicle Bks, 83; Barbara Johns (auth), Modern Art from the Pacific NW in the Collection of the Seattle Art Museum, Seattle, 90; Chris Bruce (auth), The Art of Microsoft, Henry Art Gallery, Seattle, 93. *Media:* Oil on Canvas. *Dealer:* Francine Seders Gallery 6701 Greenwood Ave N Seattle WA 98103. *Mailing Add:* 2418 E Interlaken Blvd Seattle WA 98112

SPAGNOLO, KATHLEEN MARY
PRINTMAKER, ILLUSTRATOR
b London, Eng, Sept 12, 19. *Study:* Bromley Art Sch; Royal Col Art, London, Royal scholar & Princess of Wales scholar, 39-42; Sch Design, with E W Tristram; Am Univ, with Robert Gates & Krishna Reddy. *Work:* Dept of Interior, Washington, DC; Univ Va, Charlottesville; George Washington Univ; Libr Cong, Washington, DC. *Comn:* Rendering (bench), Index Am Design, Nat Gallery Art, Washington, DC, 69. *Exhib:* Corcoran Gallery Art, Washington, DC, 62; Silvermine Guild Artists, 63; Soc Washington Printmakers, 69-75; one-man exhib, Va Mus Fine Arts, 78; All Hallows by the Tower, London, 82. *Mem:* Soc Washington Printmakers; Washington Watercolor Asn; Washington Print Club; Artist's Equity Asn. *Media:* Graphics. *Dealer:* Gallery 4 115 S Columbus Alexandria VA 22314. *Mailing Add:* 7401 Recard Ln Alexandria VA 22307

SPANDORFER, MERLE SUE
PAINTER, PRINTMAKER
b Baltimore, Md, Sept 4, 34. *Study:* Syracuse Univ, 52-54; Univ Md, BS, 56. *Work:* Metrop Mus Art, Mus Mod Art & Whitney Mus Am Art, NY; Libr Cong, DC; Philadelphia Mus Art; Baltimore Mus; Israel Mus; Reading Mus; Pa Acad Fine Arts. *Comn:* Fifty-four graphics, Inland Steel Corp, Alexandria, Va, 75; graphics, Thiokol

Corp, Newtown, Pa, 76; Mellon Bank, 83; Temple Univ, 84; Univ Pa, Inst Contemp Art, 91. *Exhib:* Md Regional, Baltimore Mus Art, 74; 30 one-woman shows incl RI Sch Design, Providence, 79, Yoseido Gallery, Tokyo, Japan, 81, Cabrini Coll, 99, Mangel Gallery, 2000; Gov's Residence, Harrisburg, Pa, 87; Wennizer Graphics Gallery, Provincetown, Mass, 89; Philadelphia Mus Art, 90; Mangel Gallery, 92, 96 & 99; Widener Univ, 95; Mangel Gallery, 2006; Mus Modern Art, Metropolitan Mus Art & Whitney Mus Am Art, NYC; and others. *Teaching:* Instr painting, Cheltenham Sch Fine Arts, 65-; instr printmaking, Tyler Sch Art, Philadelphia, 79-84 & Pratt Inst, New York, 85-86; lectr, Tokyo Nat Univ Fine Art & Sichuan Fine Arts Inst, China. *Awards:* Harry Rockower Mem Award, Cheltenham Ctr Arts, 88; Pa Coun Arts Grant Award, 89; Purchase Award, Berman Mus, 94; Pa Edu Assoc Outstand Art Educ Award; and others. *Bibliog:* Vivien Raynor (auth), New York Times, 9/13/92; Victoria Donohoe (auth), Philadelphia Inquirer, 5/10/92; Edward Sozanski (auth), Philadelphia Inquirer, 5/14/92, 12/19/93, 3/5/99 & 3/17/00. *Mem:* Artists Equity; Am Color Print Soc. *Media:* Acrylics, Water-based Printing Inks. *Publ:* Coauth, Making Art Safely, Van Nostrand Reinhold, 93. *Dealer:* Mangel Gallery 1714 Rittenhouse Sq Philadelphia PA 19103. *Mailing Add:* 8012 Ellen Ln Cheltenham PA 19012

SPANGENBERG, KRISTIN L
CURATOR, HISTORIAN

b Palo Alto, Calif, June 3, 44. *Study:* Univ Calif, Davis, AB, 68; Univ Mich, MA, 71. *Collection Arranged:* Cincinnati Collects Photographs (auth, catalog) & German Expressionist Prints (auth, catalog), Cincinnati Art Mus, 85. *Pos:* Asst cur prints, drawings & photographs, Cincinnati Art Mus, 71-73, cur, 74-. *Mem:* Print Coun Am. *Res:* prints of Paul Ashbrook; Stobridge lithography company posters. *Publ:* Auth, Eastern European Printmakers, 75, French Drawings, Watercolors & Pastels 1800-1950, 78, ed, Nineteenth Century Drawings from the Grand Duchy of Baden, 83 & auth, Photographic Treasures from the Cincinnati Art Mus, 89, Cincinnati Art Mus; Innovation & Tradition, Twentieth Century Japanese prints from The Howard & Caroline Porter Collection, 90; ed & contribr, Six centuries of master prints: Treasures from the Herbert Greer French collection, Cincinnati Art Mus, 1/93; compiled, organized, The Golden Age of Costume and Set Design, 2002. *Mailing Add:* c/o Cincinnati Art Mus 953 Eden Park Dr Cincinnati OH 45202-1596

SPANN, SUSANNA EVONNE
PAINTER, EDUCATOR

b Oakland, Calif, June 13, 43. *Study:* Ariz State Univ, BFA, 67 & MA, 69; Art Ctr col Design, 74-77. *Work:* Tampa Electric Co, Tampa, Fla; Disney World, Orlando, Fla; Santa Fe Community col, Gainsville, Fla; City Miami Beach, Miami Beach, Fla; Nations Bank, Charlotte, NC. *Comn:* portrait, Judge Roberta Knowles Manatee Co Courthouse, Bradenton, Fla, 80. *Exhib:* Am Watercolor Soc, New York City, NY, 79, 86 & 97; Watercolor US, Springfield, Mo, 92; Nat Watercolor, Soc, Riverside, Calif, 97; and many others. *Pos:* Susanna Spann Studios, Bradenton, Fla, 77-; Workshop Instr, all over US, 94-. *Teaching:* instr, illus, Ringling Sch Art & Design, Sarasota, Fla, 81-95. *Awards:* Key Mem Award, Am Watercolor Soc, 79; Holbein Award, Fla Watercolor Soc, Holbein Paints, 2003; Kanuga Award, Fla Watercolor Soc, Kanuga Workshop, 2003. *Bibliog:* Patrick Seslar (auth), Secrets of painting glass, The Artist's Mag, 3/93; Patrick Seslary (auth), Object lessons, The Artist's Mag, 11/98; Kristin Godsey (auth), Point-and-shoot sketchbook, Artist's Sketchbook, 7/2003. *Mem:* Am Watercolor Soc; Nat Watercolor Soc; Fla Watercolor Soc. *Media:* Watercolor. *Publ:* contribr, The Best of Flowers Painting, F&W Publ, 97; auth, Painting Crystal and Flowers in Watercolor, F&W Publ, 2001; contribr, 100 Ways to Paint People & Figures, Int Artist, 2004; contribr, Painting Light & Shade, F&W Publ, 2004; contribr, Splash 9 - Watercolor Secrets, F&W Publ, 2006. *Mailing Add:* 1729 8th Ave Bradenton FL 34205

SPARKS, JOHN EDWIN
PRINTMAKER, INSTRUCTOR

b Washington, DC, Sept 14, 42. *Study:* Richmond Prof Inst; Yale-Norfolk Summer Sch Art & Music; Md Inst Col Art, BFA; Univ Ill, Urbana, MFA. *Work:* Libr of Cong, Washington, DC. *Exhib:* 36th Int Exhib, Northwest Printmakers, Seattle, 65; Libr of Cong Print Exhib, Washington, DC, 66; 47th Exhib, Soc Am Graphic Artists, NY, 66; Maryland Artists Regional, Baltimore Mus Art, 68; one-man exhibs, L Katzenstein Gallery, Towson, Md, 69, Univ Md, Baltimore Co, Catonsville, 72, Watermark Gallery, Annapolis, Md, 81 & Catonsville Community Col, 83; 10th National Print Exhib, Silvermine Guild Artists, Conn, 74; Director's Choice, Albrecht Art Mus, St Joseph, Mo. *Pos:* Cataloger, George A Lucas Print Collection, Union of Independent Cols Art, 69; dir first restrike ed, Rodolphe Bresdin's etching Flight into Egypt, 70; art adv, Md Arts Coun, 70-71. *Teaching:* Instr lithography & intaglio, Md Inst Col Art, 66-, chmn, Printmaking Dept; instr intaglio & lithography, Lake Placid Summer Workshop, 71-75; instr intaglio, NS Col of Art & Design, 77. *Awards:* Printmaking Grant, Louis Comfort Tiffany Found, 67. *Media:* Intaglio, Lithography. *Mailing Add:* 2942 Guilford Baltimore MD 21218

SPEAR, LAURINDA HOPE
ARCHITECT

b Rochester, Minn, Aug 23, 50. *Study:* Brown Univ, BA, 72; Columbia Univ, 75; Mass Inst Technol, currently. *Work:* LA Entertainment Dist, Calif; Pan Am Games Study, Miami, Fla; Int Airport Terminal, Miami, Fla; Disney Cruise Terminal, Port Canaveral, Fla; Puerto Rico Trade & Convention Ctr Dist, San Juan. *Exhib:* Ctr for the Fine Arts, Miami, Fla, 84; Inst Contemp Art, Philadelphia, 86; Bass Mus, Miami Beach, Fla, 88; Chicago Athenaeum Mus Archit and Design, 98, 2000; Urban Land Inst, Miami Beach, Fla, 2000; The Skyscraper Mus, NY, 2000; many others. *Pos:* Principal, Arquitectonica, Miami, Fla, 77-; vis prof, Univ Miami, 75-77, 93-94, Harvard Univ, 94. *Awards:* Excellence Award, Fla AIA, 2000; Am Architecture Award, Festival Walk, 2000, Philips Arena, 2000; Founder's Award, Salvadori Ctr, 2000. *Mem:* Archit Club Miami; Dade Co Historic Preservation Bd; Am Inst Architects; Int Interior Design Asn; Nat Acad (assoc, 93, acad, 94-). *Mailing Add:* Arquitectonica 550 Brickell Ave Ste 200 Miami FL 33131

SPEAR, RICHARD EDMUND
EDUCATOR

b Michigan City, Ind, Feb 3, 40. *Study:* Univ Chicago, BA(art hist); Princeton Univ, MFA(art hist) & PhD(art hist). *Pos:* Dir, Allen Mem Art Mus, Oberlin Col, 72-83; pres, Intermuseum Conserv Asn, 75-77; ed-in-chief, Art Bulletin, 85-88. *Teaching:* Mildred C Jay prof art hist, Oberlin Col, 64-; distinguished vis prof, George Washington Univ, 83-84; Harn eminent scholar, Univ Fla, 97-98. *Awards:* Premio Daria Borghese Gold Medal, Rome, 72. *Mem:* Col Art Asn. *Res:* Seventeenth century painting. *Publ:* Auth, Caravaggio and His Followers, Cleveland Mus Art, 71 & Harper & Row, rev ed 75; Renaissance and Baroque Paintings from the Sciarra and Fiano Collections, Pa State Univ Press & Ugo Bozzi, Rome, 72; Domenichino, Yale Univ Press, 82; The Divine Guido, Religion, Sex, Money & Art in the World of Guido Reni, Yale Univ Press, 97. *Mailing Add:* Oberlin Col Dept Art Oberlin OH 44074

SPECTOR, BUZZ (FRANKLIN MAC SPECTOR)
CONCEPTUAL ARTIST, CRITIC

b Chicago, Ill, Mar 13, 48. *Study:* Southern Ill Univ, Carbondale, BA(studio art), 72; Univ Chicago, MFA, 78. *Work:* Mus Contemp Art, Chicago; Getty Res Inst, Malibu, Calif; Corcoran Gallery Art, Washington DC; Art Inst, Chicago; Los Angeles Co Mus Art. *Comn:* Los Angeles Co Metrop Transportation Authority. *Exhib:* Solo exhibs, Art Inst Chicago (with catalog), 88 & Spertus Mus of Judaica, Chicago, 88; Transgression (with Donald Lipski, with catalog), Corcoran Gallery Art, Washington, DC, 90; Newport Harbor Art Mus (with catalog), 90; Mattress Factory, Pittsburgh, Pa, 91; Cleveland Ctr Contemp Art (with catalog); Cranbrook Art Mus (with catalog), Bloomfield Hills, Mich, 98; List Art Gallery (with catalog), Swarthmore Col, 2001; and others. *Pos:* Ed, WhiteWalls, 78-87; bd dir CAA, 2004-. *Teaching:* Vis lectr art hist & criticism, Art Inst Chicago, 83-88; vis lectr, Art Ctr Col Design, Pasadena, Calif, 89-94; prof, Univ Ill, Urbana Champaign, 94 2001; Prof & Chair, Cornell Univ, 2001-. *Awards:* Fel for Drawing, Nat Endowment Arts, 82-83 & Fel for Artists Books, 85-86 & 91-92; Ill Arts Coun Fel, 88; Tiffany Fel, 91; NYFA Fel, 2005. *Bibliog:* Neal Benezra (auth), Buzz Spector: Library of Babel (exhib catalog), Art Inst Chicago, 88; Johanna Drucker (auth), The Century of Artists Books, Granary Bks, New York, 96; Renee Riese Hubert and Judd Hubert (auths), The Cutting Edge of Reading: Artists Books, Granary Bks, New York, 99. *Mem:* Col Art Asn. *Publ:* Objects and Logotypes (exhib catalog), Renaissance Soc, Chicago, Ill, 80; Jo Ann Callis: Objects of Reverie (exhib catalog), Des Moines, Art Ctr, 90; Ann Hamilton: Sao Paulo-Seattle (exhib catalog), Henry Art Gallery, Univ Wash, 92; Book Maker's Desire (essays), Umbrella Press, Los Angeles, 95; Beautiful Scenes (exhib catalog), Cranbrook Art Mus, 98; Details; Closed to Open (artists' book), 2001. *Dealer:* Zolla-Lieberman Gallery Chicago IL; Marsha Mateyka Gallery Washington DC. *Mailing Add:* 105 Horizon Dr Ithaca NY 14850-9791

SPECTOR, JACK J
HISTORIAN, EDUCATOR

b Bayonne, NJ, Oct 2, 25. *Study:* City Col New York, BS, 56; Columbia Univ, MA, 59, PhD, 64; Fulbright Fel, Paris, 60-61. *Pos:* Ed bd, Am Imag, 89-. *Teaching:* Prof art hist, Rutgers Univ, 62-79 & distinguished prof, 88; vis prof Romanticism, City Univ New York Grad Ctr, 79; vis distinguished prof, Columbian Col, George Washington Univ, Washington, DC, 85; vis scholar, Univ Queensland, Brisbane, Australia, 89. *Awards:* Am Coun Learned Socs Grant, 70; Sr Fel, Ctr Advanced Study Visual Arts, Nat Gallery Art, 85; Fel Rutgers Ctr Hist Analysis, 90-91. *Mem:* Col Art Asn. *Res:* Nineteenth century French Romanticism, chiefly Eugene Delacroix; psychoanalytic approaches to 19th and 20th century art. *Publ:* Freud-Ferenczi Brief Wechsel, Vol I, Boler Verlag, Vienna, 93; ed, New Directions in Art History, Vol 53 No 1 & 2, Am Imago; Delacroixs Liberty on the Barricade in 1815 & 1830, Vol XV, No 3, Source, spring 96; Medusa on the Barricades, Vol 53, No 1, Am Imago, spring 96; Surrealist Art and Writing 1919-39, The Gold of Time, Cambridge Univ Press, 11/8/96. *Mailing Add:* 28 Spring St Somerset NJ 08873

SPECTOR, NAOMI
WRITER

b Lynn, Mass, Mar 6, 39. *Study:* Brandeis Univ, BA, 60; NY Univ, MA, 66. *Pos:* Asst dir, Byron Gallery, New York, 63-64; mgr, Fischbach Gallery, New York, 67-70; dir, John Weber Gallery, New York, 73-75; pres, Greenwich Collection, Ltd, currently. *Res:* Contemporary art. *Specialty:* Minimal-conceptual. *Publ:* Auth, Robert Ryman (essay), Stedelijk Mus, Amsterdam, 2/74; Robert Ryman, Whitechapel Art Gallery, London, 9/77; Eva Hesse: anima and art, Galeries Mag, Int Ed, Paris, 12/92-1/93; Eva Hesse: the early years, 1960-1965, In: Eva Hesse: Drawing in Space - Paintings & Reliefs (catalog), Ulm Mus, Ger, 3/94; Forum: well defined enigmas/ordering chaos: an untitled drawing by Eva Hesse, Drawing, New York, 11/94. *Mailing Add:* 435 W Broadway New York NY 10012

SPEED, (ULYSSES) GRANT
SCULPTOR

b San Angelo, Tex, Jan 6, 30. *Study:* Brigham Young Univ, BS; also with Soloman Aranda. *Work:* Whitney Mus, Cody, Wyo; Diamond M Mus, Snyder, Tex; Devonian Found, Calgary, Alta; Repub Nat Bank, Dallas. *Comn:* Sculpture, Brigham Young Univ Animal Sci Dept, 75-76, 76-77 & 77-78; monuments, Charlie Goodnight, Mesa Petrolium, Amarillo, Tex, 79, Buddy Holly, city of Lubbock, Tex, 79 & John Wayne, comn by Ron Chamnis, Dallas, 80. *Exhib:* Ann Preview Exhib, Tex Art Gallery,

71-78; Phoenix Art Mus, 73-75; two-man show, Tex Art Gallery, Dallas, 75; Spec Exhib, Whitney Mus, Cody, 75; Montrail Galleries, Scottsdale, Ariz, 77. *Awards:* Achievement Award Art, Brigham Young Univ Animal Sci Dept, 72; Purchase Award, Men's Art Coun Phoenix, 73; Gold Medal Award/Sculpture, Cowboy Artists of Am Ann, 76. *Bibliog:* Ed Ainsworth (auth), Cowboy in Art, World, 68; Pat Broder (auth), Bronzes of the American West, Abrams, 74; Don Hedgpeth (auth), From Broncs to Bronzes, 79. *Mem:* Cowboy Artists Am (pres, 72-73, bd dir, 73-74 & 76-78). *Media:* Bronze. *Publ:* Auth, Hooked on cowboyin', Western Horseman, 70. *Dealer:* Tex Art Gallery 1408 Main St Dallas TX 75202; Main Trail Galleries Jackson WY 83001. *Mailing Add:* 139 S 400 E Lindon UT 84042

SPEIGHT, JERRY BROOKS
EDUCATOR, WRITER
b Murray, Ky, Nov 27, 42. *Study:* Murray State Univ, Ky, BS, 64, MA, 68; Memphis State Univ. *Comn:* YMCA Supergraphic, City of Somerset, Ky, 75. *Exhib:* Mid-States Art Exhib, Evansville Mus Arts & Sci, Ind, 70 & Mid-States Craft Exhib, 70 & 73; All Ky Drawing Competition, Univ Ky, Lexington, 78; one-man shows, Owensboro Mus Arts & Sci, Ky, 79, The Automobile in the Landscape, Watercolors, Evansville Indiana Street Rod Assoc Ann, Fairgrounds Exhib Ctr, Evansville, 97 & 98, Wyndham Resort, Nashville, Tenn, 97, Knoxville, Tenn, 98, Louisville Fairground Exhib Hall, Louisville, Ky, 98; Inagural Faculty Exhib, Murray State Univ, 95; Five Kentucky Artists, Coconino Ctr for Arts, Flagstaff, Ariz, 96. *Pos:* Regional corresp for Art Voices South Mag, Art Voices Publ Co, West Palm Beach, Fla, 78-. *Teaching:* Art dept chmn, Brescia Col, Owensboro, Ky, 70-74; instr art educ, Univ Ky, Lexington, 74-75 & Murray State Univ, Ky, 75-, prof, 92-. *Awards:* Merit Award, All Ky Drawing Competition, 78; Ky Art Educator Year, 80. *Mem:* Ky Art Educ Asn (vpres, 77-78); Nat Art Educ Asn. *Media:* Watercolor, Graphite. *Res:* Artists' work from a technical and conceptual standpoint. *Publ:* Auth, John Thomas Bensing, Sch Arts, 11/80; Wear an original painting, Fiberarts, 1/81; Richard Abrams, Art Voices, 4-5/81; Basic photography experiences, Sch Arts, 5/81; A shoe recall, Sch Arts, 10/81; and many others. *Mailing Add:* 1601 Loch Lomond Dr Murray KY 42071-3704

SPEISER, STUART M
COLLECTOR, PATRON
b New York, NY, June 4, 23. *Exhib:* Stuart M Speiser Collection of Photorealism, shown at 20 mus, incl, Addison Gallery Am Art, Andover, Mass, 74, Allentown Art Mus, Pa, 74, Witte Mem Mus, San Antonio, Tex, 74, Brooks Mem Mus, Memphis, Tenn, 75 & Krannert Mus, Champaign, Ill, 75; donated to Smithsonian Inst, 78. *Awards:* James Smithson Medal, Smithsonian Art Inst, 79. *Bibliog:* Judy Beardsall (auth), Stuart M Speiser Photo-Realist Collection, Art Gallery Mag, 10/73; Phyllis Derfner (auth), New York letter, Art Int Lugano Rev, 11/73; Gregory Battcock (auth), New York, Art & Artists, London, 3/74. *Interests:* Promoting new art movements and pioneering in law as it pertains to artists, in capacity as an attorney. *Collection:* Photorealism. *Mailing Add:* c/o Spelser Krause Madole & Nolan Two Grand Central Tower 140 E 45th St 34 New York NY 10017

SPELMAN, JILL SULLIVAN
PAINTER
b Chicago, Ill, Feb 17, 37. *Study:* Hilton Leech Art Sch, Sarasota, Fla, 55-57; and with Paul Ninas, New Orleans, 56-58. *Work:* Univ Mass, Amherst. *Exhib:* Watercolor USA, Springfield Art Mus, Mo, 67; Mainstreams '70, Marietta Col, Ohio, 70; Salon 72, Ward Nasse Gallery, NY, 72; one-man shows, Phoenix Gallery, NY, 73, 75 & 77 & Ward-Nasse Gallery, NY, 77; and others. *Pos:* Pres, Phoenix Coop Gallery, 72-74; assoc ed, Artists Rev Art, 77-78. *Teaching:* Lectr, Ringling Mus Art, Sarasota, 58-60. *Awards:* Sarasota Art Asn First Prize, Art Student Exhib, 57; Hamel Prize, Sarasota Art Asn Ann, 58; Grumbacher Oil Prize, Knickerbocker Artists Ann, 70. *Mem:* Asn Artist-Run Galleries. *Media:* Acrylic. *Dealer:* Rhodd Sande Gallery 61 E 57th St New York NY. *Mailing Add:* 22 W 96th St New York NY 10025

SPENCE, ANDREW
PAINTER
b Bryn Mawr, Pa, Oct 4, 47. *Study:* Tyler Sch Art, Temple Univ, Philadelphia, BFA, 69; Univ Calif, Santa Barbara, MFA, 71. *Work:* Metrop Mus Art; Hirshhorn Mus Sculpture Garden; Whitney Mus Am Art; Smithsonian Inst, Washington, DC; Carnegie Mus, Pittsburgh; and others. *Exhib:* One-man shows, Barbara Toll Fine Arts, NY, 82, 83, 85, 87, 88 & 90, Compass Rose Gallery, Chicago, 90, James Corcoran Gallery, Los Angeles, 90, Insights: Ann Messner & Andrew Spence, Wooster Art Mus, Mass, 91, Max Protetch Gallery, NY, 92 & 93 & Morris Healy Gallery, 96, Art Resources Transfer, NY, 2000 & Edward Thorp Gallery, NY, 2001, 02 & 06; group exhib, Generations of Geometry, Whitney Mus of Am Art at the Equitable Center, NY & The Fortieth Biennial Exhib Contemp Am Painting, Corcoran Gallery Art, Washington, DC, 87; group exhib, Whitney Biennial, Whitney Mus of Am Art, New Acquisitions, Hirshhorn Mus & Sculpture Garden, Smithsonian Inst, Washington, DC, 89; group exhib, The 1980s: Selections from the Permanent Collection, Whitney Mus Am Art, NY, 91; group exhib, Metropolitan Mus of Art, NY, 1993; group exhib, Specifically Painting, Edward Thorp Gallery, NY, 2001; group exhib, Painting by Design, Wayne State Univ, Detroit, MI, 2003; Ulrich Mus Art, Wichta, Kans, 2005; Two Friends and So On, Andrew Kreps Gallery, NY, 2006. *Teaching:* Prof painting, Bennington Col, Vt, 94-. *Awards:* Painting, Nat Endowment Arts, 87; Guggenheim Fel Painting, 94. *Bibliog:* Andrew Spence (monogr), Art Resources Transfer Inc, Los Angeles, 92; S Robert Orton (auth), Benevolence & Blasphemy, Turtle Point Press, 95; William S Bartman, Between Artists, Art Resources Transfer, Los Angeles, 96. *Media:* Oil Painting. *Dealer:* Edward Thorp Gallery 210 W 26th St New York NY 10001. *Mailing Add:* Six Varick St New York NY 10013

SPENCER, DEIRDRE DIANE
LIBRARIAN
b Indianapolis, Ind, Sep 28, 55. *Study:* Ind Univ, Bloomington, AB, 77, MLS, 85; Univ Chicago, MA, 84; Univ Mich, Ann Arbor, PhD candidate, 96. *Pos:* Asst art & archit librn, Univ Fla, Gainesville, 86-88; dir, Fine Arts Libr, Univ Mich, Ann Arbor, 88-; Reference Librn, Washteraw Community Col, Libr, 2000, Ann Arbor, Mich. *Teaching:* Instr hist art, Martin Ctr Col, Indianapolis, Ind, 83; adj instr hist art, Herron Sch Art, Ind Univ-Purdue Univ, Indianapolis, 84; Washtenaw Community Col, Ann Arbor, 2002-2003; Concordia Col, 2003, Ann Arbor Mich. *Awards:* Univ Mich Rackham Merit Fel Doctoral Study; Univ Mich Fel, Ctr Educ Women. *Bibliog:* Martha Keller (auth), Technology may radically alter the way art history is taught, Ann Arbor News, 2/12/89. *Mem:* Art Libr Soc NAm (chmn, Muehsam Award Comt, 90); Art Libr Soc Mich (pres, 90); Col Art Asn. *Res:* African ethnicity in 19th century art and visual culture; ancient art; computer usage and digitized images in art libraries. *Interests:* 18th & 19th century French and American art; race & gender in 19th and early 20th century visual culture. *Publ:* Auth, Lockefield gardens, Ind Preservationist, 81; Reviews of Oliver Harrington's Why I Left America and Other Essays & Dark Laughter: pub-in Inks: Cartoon & Comic Art Studies, 94. *Mailing Add:* Univ Mich Fine Arts Libr 260 Tappan Hall Ann Arbor MI 48109

SPENCER, HAROLD EDWIN
HISTORIAN, PAINTER
b Corning, NY, Oct 1, 20. *Study:* Art Students League, 41-42; Univ Calif, BA(highest hon art), 48 & James Phelan scholar, MA, 49; Harvard Univ (summer scholar), 58, Fac Arts & Sci Fel, 60-61 & Frank Knox Fel, 64, PhD, 68. *Work:* William Benton Mus Art; New Haven Paint & Clay Club, Inc; Homer Babbidge Libr, Univ Conn. *Exhib:* Mo Exhib, St Louis Art Mus, 52, 55, 59 & 61; Ann Drawing & Print Exhib, San Francisco Art Mus, 55-56; Washington Printmakers Soc, Smithsonian Inst, 57 & 62; Conn Acad Art Ann, Wadsworth Atheneum, Hartford, Conn, 76; Monotypes Today I-XIII, 77-96; solo exhib, Slater Mus, Norwich, Conn, 87 & Benton Mus, Storrs, Conn, 90; Jorgensen Gallery, Univ Conn, 98, 99, 2000; New Haven Paint & Clay Club Centennial Exhib, 2000. *Collection Arranged:* The American Earls, William Benton Mus, 72; Connecticut and American Impressionism, William Benton Mus, 80; Wilson Irvine and The Poetry of Light, Florence Griswold Mus, 98; A Connecticut Place: Weir Farm, An American Painter's Rural Retreat, Nat Park Ser & Weir Farm Trust, 2000. *Pos:* Chmn art dept, Blackburn Col, Carlinville, Ill, 49-62; coun overseers, Weir Farm Trust, 89-93, bd dir, vpres, 93-; bd trustees, Lyme Acad Fine Arts, 93-98; guest cur, Florence Griswold Mus, 95-98 & Weir Farm Nat Hist Site, 98-2000. *Teaching:* assoc prof, Occidental Col, Los Angeles, Calif, 62-68, chmn art dept, 63-68; assoc prof, Univ Conn, Storrs, 68-69, prof, 69-88, assoc dept head, 77-79, prof emer, 88-. *Awards:* Merit Award, 65th Ann Springfield Art League, 84; First Prize, Conn Artists Ann, Slater Mus, 87; Purchase Award, New Haven PCC, 95; and others. *Bibliog:* Roberta Capers (auth), Reviews of Readings in Art Hist, Art Bull, 71; Henri Dorra (auth), article in Art J, summer 78; William Zimmer (auth), Review of Wilson Irvine Exhib at Florence Griswold Mus, New York Times, 8/16/98. *Mem:* Col Art Asn; Conn Acad of Arts & Sci; Conn Acad Fine Arts; Weir Farm Trust. *Media:* Oil; Monotype. *Res:* Nineteenth Century European Painting and American Art. *Publ:* Auth, Reflections on Impressionism: It's Genesis & American Phase, in Connecticut & American Impressionism (exhib catalog), William Benton Mus Art, 80; ed, Readings in Art History, Scribner's 82 & 83; coauth (with Elizabeth Kornhauser), Pride of Place: The Artistic Heritage of Connecticut, 1790-1920 (exhib catalog), Wadsworth Atheneum, 89; auth, Wilson Henry Irvine and the Poetry of Light (exhib catalog), Florence Griswold Mus, 98; and others. *Mailing Add:* 294 Mansfield Rd Ashford CT 06278

SPENCER, JEFFREY PAUL
PAINTER
b Omaha Nebr, Oct 31, 62. *Study:* Univ Nebr, Omaha, BFA, 87; Univ Tenn, Knoxville, MFA, 90. *Work:* Ewing Gallery Art, Univ Tenn, Knoxville. *Exhib:* Solo exhib, Krantz Gallery, Louisville, Ky, 90; Salina Art Ctr Ann, Kans; Bemis Artworks, Omaha, Nebr, 93; Fete Nouvell I, Jackson Art Works, Omaha, Nebr 93; Art Alumni Exhib, Univ Tenn Ewing Gallery, Knoxville, 94; and others. *Pos:* Preparator, Ewing Gallery Art, 88-89, head gallery preparator, Knoxville Mus Art, 89-90. *Teaching:* Art, Metrop Community Col, Omaha, Nebr, 90- & Univ Nebr, Omaha, 96-. *Awards:* Visual Arts Fel, Nat Endowment Arts, 91; Best of Show, Salina Arts Ctr Ann, 92. *Bibliog:* Kyle MacMillan (auth), Grant winning artist does user friendly abstracts, Omaha World Herald, 6/10/92. *Mem:* Col Art Asn. *Media:* Oil on Canvas. *Dealer:* Anderson O'Brien Gallery. *Mailing Add:* 815 S 46th Ave Omaha NE 68106

SPENCER, MARK J
MUSEUM DIRECTOR, CURATOR
b Madison, Wis, June 8, 57. *Study:* Univ Wis, Stevens Point, BS, 79; Madison MA(art hist), 83. *Collection Arranged:* Alan Rath, Johnson Co Community Col, 93; Johnny Naugahyde, Random Ranch, Kansas City, Mo, 93; Johnny Naugahyde & Mike Corgiat, Kansas City Artists Coalition, Mo, 94; William Christianberry Retrospective, Albrecht-Kemper Mus, (coauth, catalog), 94, Lorna Simpson Wigs, 95, Native American Basketry-The Hartman Collection, (contribr, catalog), 96, William Wegmen Photographs & Paintings, 96 & William Wiley: 60 Prints for 60 Years, 97; Johnny Navgahyde, Dolphin Gallery, Kansas City, Mo, 99. *Pos:* Asst dir, Haggerty Mus Art, formerly; cur, Yellow Freight System, 89-94; dir, Albrecht-Kemper Mus Art, 94-. *Teaching:* Instr art hist, Univ Wis, Stevens Point, 84-86. *Mem:* Am Asn Mus; Midwest Mus Conf (gen co-chair, currently). *Res:* Contemporary art. *Publ:* Auth, Barry Moser: Original Wood Engravings, Exhibits USA, 90; Duane Hanson: Sculptures, Johnson Co Community Col, 91; Brininstool and Lynch: Architects, Inland Architect, 95. *Mailing Add:* c/o Albrecht-Kemper Mus Art 2818 Frederick Blvd Saint Joseph MO 64506

SPENCER, SUSAN ELIZABETH
PAINTER, INSTRUCTOR
b Buffalo, NY, Oct 31, 54. *Study:* Sullivan Co Community Col, AA(graphic art), 74, Onondaga Community Col, 79-83. *Work:* Kidder-Peabody Inc, NY; Trustmark Nat Bank, Jackson, Miss; Neville Public Mus, Green Bay, Wis; Agway Corp; Peerless Insurance, Neth. *Comn:* Historical sites of Clay, NY, Marine Midland Bank, Syracuse, 85; painting of Crouse Col, King & King Architects, Syracuse, 86; 5 paintings, Zausmer & Frisch Archit Firm. *Exhib:* Pa Watercolor Soc, Port Hist Mus, Philadelphia, 87; 17th Int Exhib La Watercolor Soc, World Trade Ctr, New Orleans, 87; Audubon Artists Exhib, Nat Arts Club, NY, 88; Midwest Watercolor Soc, Neville Pub Mus, Green Bay, Wis, 88 & 89; Watercolor West, Brea Civic Ctr Gallery, Calif; Adirondack Nat Exhib Am Watercolors. *Teaching:* Pvt classes in watercolor, Syracuse, NY, 84-; instr, workshops for var organizations & institutes throughout central NY. *Awards:* Trustmark Purchase Award, Miss Watercolor Show, 86; Mary Garrison Award, Cooperstown Nat Exhib, 87; Outstanding Adirondack Painting, Central Adirondack Show, Enchanted Forest, 88; Award of Distinction, Syracuse Art Festival. *Bibliog:* Sherry Chayat (auth), rev, Syracuse Herald-Am, 85; Stephen Doherty, article, Am Artist, Watercolor, 90. *Mem:* Cent NY Watercolor Soc (secy, 87-89); Onondaga Art Guild. *Media:* Watercolor, Pencil. *Publ:* Security Mag, Security Mutual Insurance, 86; Nat Catalogue Arts, Assoc Arts Orgn, 87; Artists Mag, 5/93; The Best of Watercolor & Painting Composition, Rockport Publ. *Dealer:* Gallery Luna 7 Jordan St Skaneateles NY 13158. *Mailing Add:* 306 Gordon Pkwy Syracuse NY 13219

SPERAKIS, NICHOLAS GEORGE
PAINTER, PRINTMAKER
b New York, NY, June 8, 43. *Study:* Pratt Inst, 60; Nat Acad Design Sch Fine Art, New York; Art Students League, 63; Pratt Graphic Art Ctr. *Work:* Kunst Mus, Fine Arts Mus Bern, Switz, Permanent Print Collection; The Ulmer Mus, ULM, WGer, Permanent Print Collection; The Australian Nat Gallery, Canberra, Australia, Permanent Print Collection; The Israel Mus, Jerusalem, Permanent Print Collection; Yale Univ Art Gallery, New Haven, Conn, Permanent Print Collection; Pratt Inst, The Schafler Gallery, Brooklyn, NY, Permanent Print Collection; The Stedman Art Gallery, Fine Arts Ctr State Univ NJ Rutgers, Camden, Permanent Print Collection; and many others. *Exhib:* Brooklyn Mus Biennials, 64, 66 & 70; Ann Print Exhib, Honolulu Acad Fine Arts, Hawaii, 71; Reading & Bucks Co Collect, Reading Mus Art, Pa, 77; Friends of Corcoran, Corcoran Gallery Art, 81; Ann Acquisition Exhib, Midwest Mus Am Art, Elkart, Ind, 81; one-man exhibs, Washington Irving Gallery, NY, 82, Galerie Taub, Philadelphia, 82-83, Arbitrage Gallery, NY, 83 & Retrospective of Woodcuts, Museo Universitario Del Chopo, Mexico City, 84, Univ Mass, Herter Art Gallery, 87, Leonardo Di Mauro Gallery, 88, Galerie Leopold, Hamburg, WGer, 88; Forum Gallery, NY, 84; and others. *Teaching:* Instr painting, New Sch Social Res, New York, 72-; teacher, Fashion Inst Technol, New York, 72-; adj asst prof, Long Island Univ, Brooklyn Campus, 85-86; adj asst lectr, Sch Painting & Sculpture of Columbia Univ, New York, 86-; and others. *Awards:* Lawrence & Hinda Rosenthal Fel, Am Acad Arts & Lett & Nat Inst Arts & Lett, 69; J S Guggenheim Mem Found Fel Graphics, 70; MacDowell Colony Summer Residency, Peterborough, NH, 76. *Bibliog:* Robert Henkes (auth), The crucifixion as depicted by contemporary artists, Nazarine Col, 72; Barry Shwartz (auth), 20th Century Humanist Art, Praeger, 73; articles, Arts Mag, 75-78 & 80. *Mem:* Am Fedn Modern Painters & Sculptors; Rhino Horn Orgn Humanist Art; Am Fedn Art; Soc Am Graphic Artists. *Dealer:* The Andrew Edlin Gallery 529 West 20th St 6th Fl New York NY 10011. *Mailing Add:* 245 W 29th St 12A New York NY 10001

SPERATH, ALBERT FRANK
MUSEUM DIRECTOR, SCULPTOR
b Philadelphia, PA, Feb 12, 44. *Study:* Ohio Univ, BFA, 73; Univ Nebraska, Lincoln, MFA, 76. *Work:* Friedman Gallery, Louisville, Ky. *Comn:* Vietnam shrapnel sculpture, comn by Richard Lennon, Louisville, Ky, 96. *Collection Arranged:* The Art of Ellis Wilson, (painting retrospect; coauth, catalog), Univ Art Galleries, Murray, Ky, 2000. *Pos:* dir univ art galleries, Murray State Univ, Ky, 90-. *Awards:* Fel, Ky Arts Coun, 94. *Mem:* Col Art Asn; Am Asn Mus; Asn Col and Univ Mus and Galleries. *Media:* Mixed Media. *Res:* art of Ellis Wilson. *Publ:* coauth The Art of Ellis Wilson, Univ Press Ky, 2000. *Mailing Add:* Murray State Univ Art Galleries 604 Price Doyle Fine Arts Ctr Murray KY 42071-3342

SPERO, NANCY
PAINTER, COLLAGE ARTIST
b Cleveland, Ohio, Aug, 24, 26. *Study:* Art Inst Chicago, BFA, 49; Atelier Andre L'Hote; Ecole des Beaux Arts, 49-50; Art Inst Chicago, Hon Dr Art, 91. *Hon Degrees:* Sch of the Art Inst of Chicago, DFA, 91; Williams Col, DFA, 2000. *Work:* Mus des Beaux Arts, Montreal; Ulmer Mus, Ulm, Ger; Mus Mod Art, NY; Australian Nat Gallery; Philadelphia Mus Art; Art Inst Chicago; plust others. *Comn:* Vulture Goddess and Chorus Line, Inst Contemp Art, Philadelphia, 91; The Ballad of Marie Sanders & Voices: Jewis Women in Time, Jewish Mus, NY; Premiere, Ronacher Theatre, Vienna, Austria; Black and The Red III, Malmo Konsthall, Swed, 94; To The Revolution, Am Ctr, Paris, 94. *Exhib:* Committed to Print, Mus Mod Art, NY, 88; Works on Paper 1981-1991, Salzburger Kunstverein, Kunstlerhaus Salzburg, Austria, 91; solo retrospectives Ulmer Mus, Ulm, Ger, 92 & Malmo Konsthal, Swed, 94; Allegories of Modernism: Contemp Drawing, Mus Mod Art, NY, 92; solo exhibs, Jack Tilton Gallery, NY, 96, Documenta X, Kassel, Ger, 97, Barbara Gross Galerie, Munich, 97-98, Crown Gallery, Brussels, 97-98 & Ikon Gallery, Birmingham, Eng, 97-98, Galerie Montenay-Giroux, Paris, 98, Miami Univ, Oxford, Ohio, 2000; Documenta X, Kassel, Ger, 97; The Whitney Mus Am Art, NY, 99; plus others. *Awards:* NY State Coun for the Arts Creative Artists Pub Serv Prog fel, 76-77; Nat Endowment for Arts grant, 77-78; Skowhegan Medal for Works on Paper, 95; NARAL/NY Pro-Choice Media Award, 95; Hiroshima Art Prize, Hiroshima, Japan, 96. *Bibliog:* Nancy Spero: Rebirth of Venus, Art Random, Kyoto Shoin, Japan, 89; Jon Bird (auth), Nancy Spero--Zwischen den Zeiel--Die Frau (catalog essay), Haus am Waldsee, Berlin, Ger, 90; Nancy Spero: Woman Breathing, Ulmer Mus (exhib catalog), Ed Cantz, Ostfildern, Ger, 92; Nancy Spero (auth), Phaidon Press Ltd, London, 96. *Mem:* Women's Caucus Art; Amer Acad Arts and Letters; Nat Acad (acad, 04-). *Media:* Collage on Paper. *Publ:* Co-ed, Rip-off file, Ad Hoc Comt Women Artists, 73; auth, Ende, Woman's Studies, England, 78; Sky goddess - Egyptian acrobat, Artforum, No 7, 3/88; contribr, The Discovered Uncovered, M/E/A/N/I/N/G, No 2, 11/87; auth, Tracing Ana Mendieta, Art Forum, 4/92. *Dealer:* Barbara Gross Galerie, Munich, Germany; Rhona Hoffman Gallery Chicago IL. *Mailing Add:* 530 La Guardia Pl New York NY 10012

SPEYER, JERRY I
COLLECTOR
b Milwaukee, Wis, Jun 23, 40. *Study:* Jerry: Columbia Col, BA, 62, MBA, 64; Katherine: Brown Univ, graduate, 71; Harvard Grad Sch Designs, MA(archit), 76. *Pos:* Jerry: Sr vpres, dir, Tishman Realty & Construction Co, Inc, 66-78; co-founder, pres, Chief Exec Officer, Tishman Speyer Properties, New York City, 78-; Katherine: Mgr bus develop E Asia Turner Construction; sr managing dir, Latin Am & Global Corp Marketing, Tishman Speyer Properties, New York City, 84-; vchmn Mus Modern Art, New York City, New York Presbyterian Hosp; co-chair, New York City Partnership. *Awards:* Named one of Top 200 Collectors, ARTnews Mag, 2004, 2005, 2006. *Collection:* Contemporary Art. *Mailing Add:* Tishman Speyer Properties 520 Madison Ave New York NY 10022

SPEYER, NORA
PAINTER
b Pittsburgh, Pa, Nov 24, 22. *Study:* Tyler Col Fine Art, Philadelphia, Pa. *Work:* Carnegie Inst, Philadelphia Mus Art, Pa; Corcoran Gallery, Washington, DC; Nelson Rockefeller Pvt Collection. *Exhib:* Darethea Speyer Gallery Paris, France, 70, 74 & 89; Landmark Gallery, NY, 78, 80 & 82; Longpoint Gallery, Provincetown, Mass, 82, 85, 88, 91 & 94; Emotional Impact, Art Mus Asn (traveling exhib), 84-86; Ingber Gallery, NY, 87; Relatively Speaking, Mothers & Daughters in Art (traveling exhib), Sweet Briar Col, New House Gallery, Rockford Mus, Rahr West Mus & Emily Loew Gallery, 94-; collage drawings, Denise Bibro Fine Art, NY, 96 & Trees & Flowers, 97; paintings, Galerie Dorthea Speyer, Paris, 96. *Bibliog:* Dore Ashton (auth), Nora Speyer, New York Times, 4/57; Judith Applegale (auth), Nora Speyer, Art Int, 10/70; William P Scott (auth), The Sensousness of Point-Nora Speyer, Am Artist, 5/84. *Mem:* Nat Acad (assoc, 91, 92). *Media:* Oil on Canvas. *Publ:* Auth, Painting the Landscape, Watson-Guptill, 86. *Mailing Add:* 178 Prince St New York NY 10012

SPICER, JEAN (DORIS) UHL
PAINTER, INSTRUCTOR, WRITER, AUTHOR
b Philadelphia, Pa, Nov 5, 35. *Study:* Philadelphia Col Art, dipl, 57; also with Domenic DiStefano, Charles Reid, Frank Webb, Judi Betts, Claude Crooney, 71 & Nita Engle. *Work:* Price Waterhouse, Pa; Haverford Sch Dist, Pa; Superior Models, Del; Stroemann Bread Co, Pa; John Sabatino Architects, Pa. *Comn:* Exhibitor/Flower Show, Philadelphia, 80; paintings, Havertown Sch Dist, Pa, 83. *Exhib:* Philadelphia Mus Art, 73; Bicentennial Cult Exchange Show, Wales, Gt Brit, 76; Salmagundi Club, NY, 79; Philadelphia Watercolor Club Ann, Pa, 89; Am Watercolor Soc, 95; Nat Watercolor Soc, 97. *Teaching:* Instr, Watercolor Workshop, Sydney, Australia, 86, Wayne Art Ctr, 86-2006, Naples & Ft Myers, Fla, 88 & 89, Bermuda & Cornwall, England, 1990-1994; instr, Wallingford Community Art Ctr, 2006, & Wayne Art Ctr, 87; instr, Somerset Art Asn, NJ, 2003, 2005; instr, Ocean Co, NJ, 2003, 2005; instr, Hudson River Valley, NY, 2003, 2006; instr, The Art Barn, Ind, 04; instr, Hawaii Watercolor Soc, 2006. *Awards:* Silver Medal, Art Dirs Club, 76; Gold Medal, Rittenhouse Sq, 83; Gold Medal, Philadelphia Sketch Club, 88; Gold Medal, Pa Watercolor Soc, 2005; Edgar Whitney Cash Award, Am Watercolor Soc, 95 & 2001; Watson-Guptill award, Pa Watercolor Soc, 02; Cash award, Philadelphia Watercolor Soc, 03; Cash award, Watercolor Mo, Nat, 04; Western Colo Watercolor Soc, 2006. *Bibliog:* Rachel Rubin Wolf (auth), The Best of Flower Painting #2, 99; Whyte (auth), Watercolor for the Serious Beginner, 97; Rachel Rubin Wolf (auth), Splash 5, 98. *Mem:* Pa Soc Watercolor Painters; Philadelphia Watercolor Soc; signature mem Am Watercolor Soc; signature mem Nat Watercolor Soc; Western Colo Water Soc; Catharine Lorillard Wolfe Art Club, NY. *Media:* Watercolor, Charcoal. *Res:* New Jersey Watercolor Soc, Juror, 2004; Jane Law Gallery, NJ, 2004. *Specialty:* All paintig media. *Interests:* Creates seashell designs for Sailor's Valentine's. *Publ:* Auth, Floral Painting-Watercolor, Am Artist Mag, Spring 94; auth, Landscape Painting, Int Artist Mag, 03; auth, Int Nat Artist Book (chap), 03; auth, Bright & Beautiful Flowes in Watercolor, for North Light Books, 04. *Dealer:* 11 Tenby Rd Havertown, PA 19083. *Mailing Add:* No 11 Tenby Rd Havertown PA 19083

SPIEGEL, EMILY JOY
COLLECTOR
b New York, NY. *Study:* Adelphi Univ, BA, 50. *Pos:* painting and sculpture comt Mus Mod Art, NY; collectors comt Nat Gallery Art, Washington, DC; contemp arts acquisitions comt Am Friends of the Israel Mus; honarary Trus, bd Moma, NY. *Mem:* Metrop Opera Assoc (bd mem). *Collection:* American & German contemporary art, 60's -present; photography; early modernism, pictorialism, contemporary. *Mailing Add:* 10 Broadlawn Ave Kings Point NY 11024

SPIEGEL, JERRY
COLLECTOR
b New York, NY. *Pos:* Collectors comt Nat Gallery Art, Washington, DC; contemp art acquisitions comt Am Friends of the Israel Mus. *Collection:* American and German contemporary art, 60's to present; photography, early modernism and pictorialism and contemporary. *Mailing Add:* 10 Broadlawn Ave Kings Point NY 11024

SPIEGEL, LAURIE
COMPUTER ARTIST, AUDIO-VISUAL ARTIST, PHOTOGRAPHER
b Chicago, Ill, Sept 20, 45. *Study:* Oxford Univ, 66-67; Shimer Col, BA, 67; Julliard Sch, 69-72; City Univ New York, MA, 75. *Work:* Over 80 works in public collections. *Exhib:* 2nd, 3rd & 4th Int Computer Arts Festival, NY, 74, 75 & 76; Fur Augen und Ohren, Akademie der Kunst, Berlin, Ger, 79; Crossovers, Just Above Midtown Gallery, NY, 81; Space Probes, Nexus, Atlanta, Ga, 81; Art by Computer and Video, Mus of the Surreal & Fantastique, NY, 82; Location 1 Gallery, NY; 3 Legged Dog Gallery, NY. *Pos:* designer, programmer various pioneering interactive computer programs for music and art, 73-. *Teaching:* Instr & dir computer music studio, Cooper Union, 80-82 & NY Univ, 82-83. *Awards:* Creative Artists Pub Serv Fel, NY State Coun Arts, 75-76 & 79-80; Artist-in-Residence Production Support Grant, Experimental TV Lab WNET-New York, 76; New York Found Arts Fel Award, 91-92. *Bibliog:* Evan Brubaker & Peter Wetzler (auths), Laurie Spiegel: technofolk, Ear Mag, 5/91; Cole Gagne (auth), Soundpieces 2: Interviews with American Composers, Scarecrow Press, 93; Vanessa Else (auth), EQ Mag, 5/94; Bode (auth), Soundpieces 1. *Mem:* ASCAP; ASCI; SEAMUS; ICMA. *Media:* Video, Graphics, Pencils & Pens on Paper, Digital display media. *Interests:* Compositional processes and structures. *Publ:* Auth, numerous articles on technol in the arts, Ear Mag, 78-86, Keyboard, Electronic Musician, Computer Music J, Organized Sound & others. *Dealer:* The Electronic Music Found. *Mailing Add:* 173 Duane St New York NY 10013

SPIEGELMAN, ART
CARTOONIST
b Stockholm, Feb 15, 48. *Study:* Student, Harpur Col (now State Univ of NY), Binghamton, NY. *Exhib:* exhibs incl NY Cult Ctr, Inst Contemp Art, London, Seibu Gallery, Tokyo, Mus Modern Art, New York City, 91, Galerie St Etienne, New York City, 92, Ft Lauderdale Mus Art, 93; creator Wacky Packages, Garbage Pail Kids and other novelties; contribr to numerous underground comics. *Pos:* Creative consultant, artist, designer, editor, writer Topps Chewing Gum, Inc, Brooklyn, 66-88; editor Douglas Comix, 72; contribr ed Arcade, the Comics Revue, 75-76; founding ed, Raw, 1980-; artist, contribr ed, New Yorker, 92-2003. *Teaching:* Instr, San Francisco Acad Art, 74-75, NY Sch Visual Arts, 79-87. *Awards:* Inkpot award San Diego Comics Convention, 87; Stripschappening award for best foreign comics album, 87; Alpha Art award Angoulerne, France, 93. *Publ:* Auth, illustrator: The Complete Mr. Infinity, 1970, The Viper Vicar of Vice, Villainy, and Vickedness, 1972, Ace Hole, Midge Detective, 1974, The Language of Comics, 1974, Breakdowns: From Maus to Now: An Anthology of Strips, 1977, Work and Turn, 1979, Every Day Has Its Dog, 1979, Two-Fisted Painters Action Adventure, 1980, Maus: A Survivor's Tale, 1986 (Joel M. Cavior award for Jewish Writing 1986, Nat Book Critics Cir. nomination 1986, Pulitzer prize 1992), Maus, Part Two, 1992 (Nat Book Critics Cir. nomination 1992, Pulitzer prize 1992), Open Me. I'm a Dog!, 1997; (with J.M. March) The Wild Party, 1994, Kisses from NY; (with F. Mouly) Read Yourself Raw, 1987, In the Shadow of No Towers, 2004 (named one of the 100 Notable Books of 2004, NY Times Book Review); contribr The Apex Treasury of Underground Comics, 1974; compiling editor (with B. Schneider) Whole Grains: A Book of Quotations, 1972; creator (with composer Phillip Johnston) Drawn to Death: A Three Panel Opera, Am. Repertory Theatre Co., Cambridge, Mass; ed (comic series) Little Lit

SPIESS-FERRIS, ELEANOR
PAINTER
b Las Vegas, NMex, July 3, 41. *Study:* Under Kenneth Adams, 59-60 & 64-67; Univ NMex, BFA, 60-62; Art Inst Chicago. *Work:* State of Ill Bldg, Chicago; Portland Art Mus, Ore; Ill State Mus, Springfield, Ill; Col of Du Page, Ill; Kemper Group Art Collection, Long Grove, Ill; and others. *Comn:* Prints, Plucked Chicken Press, Evanston, Ill, 85. *Exhib:* New Horizons, Chicago Cult Ctr, 73-74, 80-82 & 85-86; Still and Not-So-Still Lives, Marianne Deson Gallery, Chicago, 77; Chicago Drawing, Columbia Univ, 79; Am Drawing IV, Portsmouth Mus, Va, 82; one-person show, Van Straaten Gallery, Chicago, 84, Univ Wis, Green Bay, Wustum Mus, Racine, Zaks Gallery, 99, Zaks Gallery, Chicago, 2002; 80th and 81st Exhibition by Artists of Chicago and Vicinity, Art Inst Chicago, 84 & 85; Fetish Art, Rockford Art Mus, Ill, 86; Chicago Show, Chicago Cult Ctr; Sansker Kendra Mus, Ahmedebad, India; Watercolor '88, Springfield Arts Mus, Mo; Am Drawing IV, Portsmouth Mus, Va; Ill Women Artists, 2000-01; Evanston Art Ctr, Ill, 2002. *Collection Arranged:* Shelters, 83, Chicago 1984 Contemporary Furniture, 84, Alter Egos-Masks, 85, Indoor-Outdoor Sculpture: An Overview, 85 & Vernal Woods, 86, Evanston Art Ctr, Ill. *Teaching:* Instr figure painting, Evanston Art Ctr, Ill, 86 & 99-00, 2005. *Awards:* Ill Arts Coun Artists Fel Grant, 89, 2000; Arts Midwest Fel Grant, 91; Fel Grant, Ill Arts Coun, 99. *Bibliog:* James Bone (auth), Erotic dreams, The Reader, 84; Harry Boris, Art review, WTTW-FM Radio, 84; Estell Lauter (auth), Women as Mythmakers, Ind Univ Press; Stanely Marcus (auth), Exploring Imaginary Subjects, Am Artist Publ, 88; James Yood (auth), Eleanor Spiess-Ferris, Artforum, 91; and others. *Mem:* Arts Club Chicago; Art Inst Chicago (artists adv bd, 84-86). *Media:* Oil, Gouache. *Dealer:* Aaron Packer Gallery 118 N Peoria Chicago IL 60607. *Mailing Add:* 6551 N Ashland Ave Chicago IL 60626

SPINK, FRANK HENRY
PAINTER
Study: Univ Ill, Urbana, BArch, 58; Univ Wash, MUP, 64. *Work:* Chung Cheng Art Gallery, St John's Univ, Jamaica, NY; Benihana of Tokyo & Va Bankshares. *Exhib:* Soc Western Artists, DeYoung Mus, San Francisco, 67; Palace Fine Arts Dedication Festival, San Francisco, 67; 12th-42nd Ann Sumie Soc Shows, NY, 75-2006; Va Watercolor Soc Ann, 80-85, 91-92, 96, 2000, 02. *Pos:* Dir publ, Urban Land Inst, 72-88; dir, Non Residential Res, 83-88, vpres publ, 88-97; pub Urban Land Mag, 94-97. *Awards:* Summer Sketch Prize, Univ Ill, 55; Best of Show, Va Watercolor Soc, 81; Best of Show, Sumi-e Soc of Am, 91. *Mem:* Sumi-e Soc Am (treas, 2001-); Va Watercolor Soc; Potomac Valley Watercolorists; Kiln Club, Alexandria, Va. *Media:* Watercolor, Sumie, Clay. *Res:* Adaptive reuse of existing buildings, Shopping Centers, Suburban Activity Centers; Mixed Use Devel. *Interests:* Pottery, Community Svc Projects/Orgns. *Publ:* Ed, Community Builders Handbook Series, 75-96; contribr, Shopping Center Development Handbook, 1st ed, 77, 2nd ed, 85; Residential Develop Handbook, 78; Downtown Develop Handbook, 80; Shopping Centers USA, 81; Dollars and Cents of Shopping Centers, Series & Spl Reports, 78-87; Contbg auth Mixed Use Development Handbook, 2001; plus others; contrib auth, Professional Real Estate Development, 02; contrib auth, Resort Development, 2006. *Mailing Add:* 5158 Piedmont Pl Annandale VA 22003

SPINK, WALTER M
EDUCATOR, ADMINISTRATOR
b Worcester, Mass, Feb 16, 28. *Study:* Amherst Col, BA(summa cum laude), 49; Harvard Univ, MA(art hist), 50, PhD, 54; Fulbright grant, Dept Anthrop, Indian Mus, Calcutta 52-53. *Pos:* Cur, Brandeis Univ Art Collection, 56-61, acting chmn, Dept Fine Art, 59-60; dir, Asian Art Arch, Univ Mich, Ann Arbor, 62; dir, Photog Exped to India, 64-68. *Teaching:* Instr, Dept Fine Arts, Brandeis Univ, 56-61, assoc prof, 61-68; vis lectr, Dept Art, Brown Univ, 60; from assoc prof to prof art hist, Univ Mich, Ann Arbor, formerly; vis lectr, Dept S Asian Studies, Univ Chicago, summer 72. *Awards:* Fulbright Grant, 90-91; Guggenheim Grant, 91-92. *Mem:* Am Inst Indian Studies (trustee, 62-65 & 72-73); Asn Asian Studies, Indian Asn Art Historians, Col Art Asn, Am Comt S Asian Art (pres,72-76, dir color slide proj, 74-). *Publ:* Auth, Ajanta to Ellora, 67, Krishnamandala, 71, Ctr & Southeast Asian Studies, Univ Mich; The Axis of Eros, Schocken, 73 & Penguin, 75; Jogeswari, J Indian Soc of Oriental Art, 77; The Great Cave at Elephanta, with a study of sources, In: The Gupta Period, 77. *Mailing Add:* Dept Art Hist Univ Mich Main Campus 110 Tappan Hall Ann Arbor MI 48109

SPINKA, WILLIAM J
EDUCATOR, SCULPTOR
b Bridgeport, Conn, Oct 3, 20. *Study:* City Col New York, BS (art edn), 42, MS (art edn), 45. *Work:* Sharon Hosp, Sharon, Conn, Painting, 50. *Comn:* Col seal, Baruch Col, NY, 53, speaker stand, 53; MACE, 53; Pres chain and medal, City Col NY, 54, student life lounges, 66-68. *Exhib:* Concoran Gallery, Painting and others - Sculpture, Washington, DC, 46; Jersey City Mus, NJ, 64; One-man shows, Canton Artists' Guild, Conn, 79; Lever House Gallery, NY, 86, 95; Nat Gallery, Nat Acad Arts Club, Salmagundi Club, 76-99. *Teaching:* instr, assoc prof drawing, sculpting, 20th century art, City Col NY, 46-66, prof design sculpting, 20th cent art, 61-80, prof design theory & applies, 81-85, prof emer art, 86-; Instr 46-60 Art Hist, Drawing, Design, Metal, Wood; Asst Prof 61-66 Design, Interier, 20 Century Hist, Metal, Wood; Prof 81-85 Design Theory, Interior & Arch Des, Sculpture; Prof Emer, 86-. *Awards:* Gold Medal, Audubon Artists, Inc, 88 & Silver Medal, 92. *Bibliog:* Promotion To Full Prof-Critique-Louise Nevelson, 80. *Mem:* Audubon Artists, Inc (vpres sculpture, 87-93, sr vpres, 94-98), mem 80-present. *Media:* Mixed Media. *Publ:* auth, Wood Sculpture, Todays Art Mag, 11/62; contribr, Interiors, Contract Mag, 5/66; contribr, National Society of Interior Designers, Interior Design Mag, 3/66. *Mailing Add:* 4658 Grosvenor Ave Bronx NY 10471

SPINOSA, GARY PAUL
SCULPTOR
b Memphis, Tenn, Dec, 26, 47. *Study:* Yale Univ Summer Sch Art & Music, 70; Cleveland Inst Art, BFA(Agnes Gund Mem Traveling Scholar), 72, Edinboro Univ, Pa, MFA, 88. *Work:* Southern Alleghenies Mus Art, Pa; Cleveland Art Asn, Ohio; Butler Inst Am Art; Lockhaven Univ, Pa. *Comn:* Public sculpture, Ohio Arts Coun, 78. *Exhib:* May Show, Cleveland Mus Art, 71-82; Eight State Ann, Speed Mus Art, Louisville, 74; Butler Inst Am Art, 74-75; European Triannual Sculpture Exhib, Paris, 78; one-man shows, Kent State Univ, 80, Ashland Col, 81 & Sandusky Cult Ctr, 82; Canton Art Inst, 89. *Awards:* Fel Grant, Ohio Arts Coun, 79; First Place for Sculpture, May Show, Cleveland Mus Art, 81; Pa Coun Arts Fel, 88. *Media:* Clay, Mixed Media. *Dealer:* Riley Hawk Galleries 642 N High St Columbus OH 43215; Riley Hawk Galleries 2026 Murray Hill Rd Cleveland OH 44106. *Mailing Add:* 22778 Blystone Rd Venango PA 16440

SPINSKI, VICTOR
SCULPTOR, EDUCATOR
b Newton, Kans, Oct 10, 40. *Study:* Kans State Teachers Col, BSE, 63; Ind Univ, Bloomington, MFA, 67. *Work:* State Univ NY Potsdam; Haystack Mountain Sch Crafts, Deer Isle, Maine; Elmira Col, NY; Del Art Mus, Wilmington. *Exhib:* Coffee, Tea & Other Cups, Mus Contemp Crafts, NY, 71; Int Exhib Ceramics, Victoria & Albert Mus, London, Eng, 72; Soup Tureens, Campbell Mus, Camden, NJ, 76; Century of Ceramics in US, Everson Mus Art, Syracuse, NY, 79; Hot of the Press, The Craft Coun, London, Eng, 96 & 97; Food Glorious Food, Artists and Eating, Charles A Wustum Mus Fine Art, Nat Invitational Exhib, Racine, Wis, 97; Ceramic Still Life: The Common Object, Select Nat Exhib, Oakland, Calif, 97; Clay Realists, Nancy Margolis Gallery, NY, 98. *Teaching:* Grad teaching asst, Ind Univ, 67; prof ceramics, Univ Del, 67-; summer fac, Haystack Mountain Sch Crafts, 68 & 70, Brooklyn Mus Art Sch, 70 & Council Grove Craft Sch, Missoula, Mont, 74-76. *Bibliog:* Richard Zakin (auth), Ceramics: Mastering the Craft, Chilton Book Co, Radnor, Pa, 90; Paul Scott & Terry Bennett (auths), Hot of the press, Bellow Publ, 96; Robert Piepenburg (auth), The Spirit of Clay: A classical guide to ceramics, Pebble Press Inc, 98. *Mem:* Nat Coun Ceramic Arts; Am Crafts Coun; Int Acad Ceramics. *Media:* Ceramics; Photography. *Publ:* Auth, Ceramic Photo silk screening, Nat Coun Educ Ceramic Arts, 70; The New Yorker, New York, 87; The Craft and Art of Clay, Susan Peterson Prentice Hall, Englewood Cliffs, NJ, 92 & 95. *Dealer:* Theo Portnoy Gallery 56 W 57th St New York NY 10019. *Mailing Add:* Univ Del Art Dept Newark DE 19716

SPIRA, BILL
SCULPTOR, PHOTOGRAPHER
b Antwerp, Belg; US citizen. *Study:* Ill Inst Technol, with L Mies Van der Rohe, L Hillberseimer & Walter Peterhans, BS, 58. *Work:* Am Broadcasting Co, NY; Phillips Petroleum Co; also pvt collections of Richard Brown Baker, NY, Graham Gund, Boston & William King. *Comn:* Sculpture, Sheraton, Manhattan & New York, 93, 97. *Exhib:* Penthouse Group, Mus Mod Art, NY, 65; Play Ball (with catalog), Queens Mus, NY, 78; On-Off the Wall, Va Beach Arts Ctr, 86. *Bibliog:* Ellen Lee Klein (auth), Bill Sprira, Arts, 1/84 & 4/87; Edmund Leites (auth), rev, Art in Am, 4/84. *Media:* Photography, wood. *Publ:* Hasselblad Forum, Vol 35, no 2, 1999, no 4, 2001. *Mailing Add:* 30 Waterside Plaza Apt 28F New York NY 10010

SPITLER, CLARE BLACKFORD
ART DEALER
b Findlay, Ohio, Feb 2, 23. *Study:* DePauw Univ; Univ Mich, AB, 44. *Pos:* Owner & dir, Gallery One, Findlay, Ohio, 65-76, Gallery One, Ann Arbor, Mich, 77-81 & Clare Spitler Works of Art, Ann Arbor, Mich, 81-, Clare Spitler Fine Art, 2000-; art writer, bi-weekly column, Art Dealings, Ann Arbor News, Mich, 82-83. *Specialty:* Contemporary American paintings, sculpture, graphics and selected crafts, often featuring Midwestern artists; additional European & Japanese artists. *Mailing Add:* Clare Spitler Fine Art 2007 Pauline Ct Ann Arbor MI 48103

SPITZ, BARBARA S
PRINTMAKER, PHOTOGRAPHER
b Chicago, Ill, Jan 8, 26. *Study:* Art Inst Chicago; RI Sch Design; Brown Univ, AB. *Work:* Art Inst Chicago; Philadelphia Mus Art; Smart Gallery, Univ Chicago; DeCordova Mus, Lincoln, Mass; Los Angeles Co Mus, Calif; Mary & Leigh Block Collection, Northwestern Univ; pvt collections of Bank of Am, First Nat Bank of Boston, Price Waterhouse, Chase Manhattan Bank, IBM, Arthur Anderson & Co, Arthur Young & Co, Peat, Marwick & Mitchell, Std Oil of Ind, Union Nat Bank of Switzerland, others. *Comn:* First Ill Print Comn Prog, 73. *Exhib:* Libr Cong & Nat Collection Fine Arts, 73 & 74; Pratt Graphic Ctr, NY, 77; Nat Aperture, 86; Loyola Univ, Chicago, 88; Schneider Gallery, Chicago, 93; The Ctr Gallery, Southern Calif, 94; solo exhib incl Kunsthaus Buhler, Stuttgart, Ger, Elca London Studio, Montreal, Can, Tower Park Gallery, Peoria, Ill, Van Straaten Gallery, Chicago, Schneider-Bluhm-Loeb Gallery, Chicago, RST Galerie, Scottsdale, Ariz, Loyola Univ, Chicago, Ctr Gallery, Calif, Newport Beach Pub Libr, Benjamin Gallery, Chicago. *Teaching:* studio demonstrations, Univ Irvine; instr, Highland Park, High Sch. *Awards:* Childe Hassam Purchase Award, Am Acad of Arts & Lett, 73; First Prize, 77 & Purchase Award, 78, Ill Regional Print Show; Stuart M Egnal Prize, Int Biennial Print Exhib, Print Club, Philadelphia, 77; Decordova Mus Purchase Awards, Boston Printmakers; George May Internat Award, New Horizons, Chicago; Municipal Art League Prize, Art Inst of Chicago; Purchase Award, Nat Exhib of Prints & Drawings, Okla Art Ctr; Ill Print Commn Program Grant. *Bibliog:* Article, Printmaker in Illinois, Ill Educ Asn, 72, Illinois Printmakers I Proj, Ill Arts Coun, 74 & others. *Mem:* Artist Equity Asn; Arts Club Chicago; Los Angeles Printmaking Soc; Boston Printmakers; Soc Am Graphic Artists; Print Club Philadelphia. *Media:* Intaglio; Photography. *Dealer:* Schneider Gallery Chicago IL. *Mailing Add:* 1106 Somerset Ln Newport Beach CA 92660

SPIVY-ANDERSON, C ALEXANDRA
CRITIC, WRITER
b Boston, Mass, May 14, 42. *Study:* Sarah Lawrence Col, BA, 61; Sorbonne, France, 63. *Pos:* Art ed, Paris Rev, 73-78; art ed, Village Voice, 74-77; sr ed, Portfolio Mag, 79-83; ed in chief, Art & Antiques, 83-84; exec ed, Am Photogr, 85-87; arts ed & exec ed, Smart Mag, 88-89; contrib art ed, Esquire Mag, 90-94; reviews ed, Art J, 95-2001; ed, Interactive Bureau, 96-2000; editl dir, Circle.com, 2000-02. *Awards:* Nat Endowment Arts Critic Grant, 78; Prof Fel, Morgan Libr. *Mem:* Int Asn Art Critics (pres, US sect); Am Soc Mag Ed; Art Table; Colby Col Art Mus (bd govs, currently); Contemp Arts Coun, Mus Mod Art (vpres); Exhbns Internat (chair adv bd 1998-2005. *Res:* Contemporary art and artist's publications; 20th century art. *Interests:* Decorative & Fine arts. *Publ:* Co-auth, Anderson and Archer's Soho: The Essential Guide to Art and Life in Lower Manhattan, Simon & Schuster, 79; Living with Art, Rizzoli, 88; auth, Passions & Tenderness: Portraits of Olga by the Baron de Meyer, Graystone Books, 92; Gardens of Earthly Delight: The Art of Robert Kushner, Hudson Hills Press, 97; Foleage, The Art of Harold Feensteer, 1999. *Mailing Add:* 125 W 12th St New York NY 10011

SPOFFORD, SALLY
PAINTER, SCULPTOR
b New York, NY, Aug 20, 1929. *Study:* Swarthmore Col, BFA, 52; Art Students League, studied with Bernard Klonis & George Grosz, 53-54; The China Inst, New York, studied with Ya-Hung Wang, 53. *Work:* NJ State Mus, Trenton; Newark Mus, Newark, NJ; Owens Corning Fiber Glass, Corning, NY; AT&T Corp Hq, Basking Ridge, NJ; Morris Mus, Morristown, NJ; Bristol Myers, Squibb, Princeton, NJ; and others. *Exhib:* solo exhib, Morris Mus, Morristown, NJ, 89; Newark Acad, Livingston, NJ, 97; Monmouth Mus Art, Lincroft NJ, 98; Williams Gallery, 2000; Simon Gallery, Morristown, NJ, 2004. *Media:* Miscellaneous Media, Watercolor, Wood Sculpture. *Dealer:* Simon Gallery Morristown NJ. *Mailing Add:* PO Box 443 Bernardsville NJ 07924

SPOHN, FRANZ FREDERICK
PRINTMAKER, ILLUSTRATOR
b Columbus, Ohio, June 6, 50. *Study:* Ohio State Univ, BFA, 73, MFA, 75. *Work:* Glenbow Mus, Calgary, Alta; Ohio State Univ. *Comn:* Print, Philadelphia Art Alliance, 88. *Exhib:* The Confectioner's Art, Am Craft Mus, New York City, (3 yr traveling exhib); Collaboration: Printmaking in Philadelphia, Glen Vivian Mus, Swansea, Wales & Strozzi Palace, Florance, Italy; one-man show, Glenbow Mus, Calgary, Alta, 81; Collage & Assemblage Traveling Exhib, Miss Mus Art, Jackson, 81-83; Feast Your Eyes, Philadelphia Mus Art, 82; Material Illusions, Unlikely Materials, Taft Mus, Cincinnati, 83; and others. *Collection Arranged:* Eighteen Buys Twenty, Portico Gallery, Philadelphia, 83. *Awards:* Commissioned print by Philadelphia Art Alliance, Philadelphia, 88. *Bibliog:* Nancy Tousley (auth), Artist sweetens his biting satire, Calgary Herald, 2/12/81; Keith Morrison (auth), Realistic self portraits, New Art Examiner, 4/81; Jo Ann Lewis (auth), Artistic couples, Wash Post, 5/31/81. *Mem:* Col Art Asn; Print Club Philadelphia. *Media:* Serigraphy, Silkscreen

SPONENBURGH, MARK
HISTORIAN, SCULPTOR
b Cadillac, Mich, June 15, 16. *Study:* Cranbrook Acad Art, scholar, 40; Wayne Univ; Ecole Beaux-Arts, Paris, France; Univ London; Univ Cairo; Hon DFA, 70. *Work:* Detroit Inst Art; Portland Art Mus; Univ Ore; Willamette Univ; Ore State Univ. *Comn:* Architectural sculpture, McGruder Veterinary Hosp, 80; Fisherman's Mem, Newport, Ore, 88; Town & Gown, bronze group, Willamette Univ. *Exhib:* North Am Sculpture, Paris Salon, France; Mus Mod Art, Cairo; retrospective, 1940-1996, Triad Gallery, 96; and 35 one-man exhibs, sculpture. *Pos:* Consult, curator & museologist. *Teaching:* Assoc prof, Univ Ore, 46-56; vis prof, Royal Col Arts, 56-57; prof & dean, Nat Col Arts, Pakistan, 58-61; prof, Ore State Univ, 61-84, chmn art dept, 82-, emer prof, 84-. *Awards:* Distinguished Lectr, Phi Kappa Phi, 82; Distinguished Prof, Ore State Univ, 82. *Mem:* Int Asn Egyptologists; Royal Soc Arts; Royal Soc Antiquaries; Int Asn Art Historians; Am Res Ctr in Egypt; Oxford Soc. *Media:* Wood, Stone, Bronze. *Res:* Stylistic analogies in Coptic & Celtic; sculpture of Moukhtar; modular systems in Egyptian sculpture; the walking pose in Egyptian sculpture. *Publ:* Contribr, Arts Quart, J Inst Egypte, Rev Caire, Near E Bull & J Near E Studies; Royal Soc Antiquaries; and others. *Mailing Add:* 5562 NW Pacific Coast Hwy Seal Rock OR 97376-9619

SPRATT, FREDERICK R
GALLERY DIRECTOR, PAINTER
b Cedar Rapids, Iowa, June 15, 27. *Study:* Dallas Mus Fine Art, studied painting, 58; Iowa Wesleyan Col, BA, 51; Univ Iowa, MA, 56. *Work:* Iowa Wesleyan Col, Mt Pleasant; State Univ Iowa, Iowa City; De Saisset Mus, Univ Santa Clara, Calif; San Jose Mus Art; Coldwell-Banker Corp, Washington, DC. *Exhib:* Four Contemp Calif Artists, Calif Arts Comn, Humboldt, 68; California Landscape, Lytton Ctr Visual Arts, Los Angeles, 68; Biennial of Am Painting and Sculpture, Univ Ill, Urbana, 68; OK Harris Gallery, NY, 76; Janus Gallery, Los Angeles, 78; The Clocktower, Inst Art & Urban Res, NY, 79; Northern California Art of the Sixties, De Saisset Mus, Santa Clara Univ, San Jose, 82; Ten California Colorists, traveling exhib, Redding, San Jose & Palm Springs, Calif, 85-86. *Pos:* Owner/dir, Frederick Spratt Gallery, San Jose. *Teaching:* Prof art, San Jose State Univ, 56-; retired. *Bibliog:* Dorothy Burkhart (auth), Fred Spratt, Arts Mag, 78; Peter Frank (auth), Los Angeles Art, Art in Am, 78. *Specialty:* Contemporary American art with a focus on West Coast. *Publ:* Auth, Art Production in Discipline Based Art Education, J Paul Getty Educ Prog, 86. *Mailing Add:* 920 S First St San Jose CA 95110

SPRICK, DANIEL
PAINTER
b May 1, 53; US citizen. *Study:* Nat Acad Fine Arts with Harvey Dinnerstein, 76; Univ Northern Colo, BFA, 78. *Work:* Nat Mus Am Art, Smithsonian Inst, Washington, DC; Denver Art Mus, Colo; Hunter Mus Art, Chattanooga, Tenn; Evansville Mus Art & Sci, Ind; Williams Col Mus Art, Williamsburg, Mass. *Comn:* Large tripych, Holme, Robert & Owens, Denver, Colo, 89; large diptych, US Govt, 94. *Exhib:* The Tradition of Vanitas in Contemp Painting, Noyes Mus, Univ Ala Mus, 87-89; solo shows, Aspen Art Mus, Colo, 90 & Hunter Mus Art, Chattanooga, Tenn, 93; Colorado 1990, Denver Art Mus, Colo; Love & Charity, Contemp Painting, State Univ NY, Cortland & Potsdam, 90; Am Still Life Painting, Minn Mus Art, Minneapolis, 91-92; Contemp Self Portraits, Nat Portrait Gallery, Washington, DC, 93. *Teaching:* Adj fac figure drawing, Colo Mountain Col, 83-94. *Awards:* Gold Medal, Allied Artists Am, 83. *Bibliog:* PD Douslin (auth), Daniel Sprick, Art Gallery Int, 86; Peter Eichner Dixon (auth), Daniel Sprick, Am Artist, 87; Michael & Patricia Coronel (auths), Daniel Sprick: Realism, Art Space, 91. *Media:* Oil. *Dealer:* Merrill Gallery of Fine Art 1401 17th St Denver CO 81601. *Mailing Add:* 609 W Harvard Dr Glenwood Springs CO 81601-2860

SPROAT, CHRISTOPHER TOWNSEND
SCULPTOR
b Boston, Mass, Sept 23, 45. *Study:* Skowhegan Sch Painting & Sculpture, 69; Boston Univ; Boston Mus Sch Fine Arts; also with George Aarons. *Work:* US Govt; Hasbro; Hyatt Hotels; Bank of Am; Rayovac Corp; 600' Sculpture, Grand Cen Sta, NY Arts for Transit. *Comn:* Unibank Corp, San Francisco; Los Angeles Rapid Transit. *Exhib:* One-man show, Inst Contemp Art, Boston, 70; Elements of Art, Mus Fine Arts, Boston, 71-72 & Rohm/Sproat, 74; Whitney Mus Am Art Biennial, NY, 73; Hayden Gallery, Mass Inst Technol, Cambridge; Marian Goodman Gallery, NY, 80; Bette Stoler Gallery, NY, 83 & 85; Boston Athenaeum, Mass, 84; Barbara Krakow Gallery, Boston, Mass, 85, 95. *Awards:* Mass Arts & Humanities Found Fel, 75; Nat Endowment Arts Grant, 75,80 & 84; Grant, Nat Endowment Arts, 84-85; Grant, NY Found Arts, 85. *Bibliog:* Kenneth Baker (auth), Sproat & Samaras, Boston Rev Arts, 4/72; Carl Belz (auth), Deliberating with color, drawing with light, Art in Am, 5-6/72; and others; Robert Taplin (auth) Art in Am, 9/95. *Media:* Light. *Dealer:* Barbara Krakow Gallery 10 Newbury St Boston MA 02116. *Mailing Add:* 467 Holland Hill Rd Putney VT 05346

SPROUT, FRANCIS
ARTIST, EDUCATOR
b Tucson, Ariz, Mar 5, 40. *Study:* Univ Ariz, BFA; Univ Calif, San Diego, MFA(Ford Found Fel), 72; Univ Calif, Los Angeles, MA(African Studies), 90. *Work:* Exeter Co, Denver; Mountain Bell, Denver; Ariz State Art Mus, Tempe; Metro Media Corp, White Plains, NY; Neuberger Mus Art, Purchase, NY; Art Mus, Arizonia State Univ, Tempe, 1986; Corporate Collection, Pfizer Learning Ctr, Rye Brook, NY, 2001; and others. *Exhib:* Emerging Southern California Artists, Pollock Gallery, Art Mus, Southern Methodist Univ, Dallas, 72; 74th Western Ann, 73 & 2nd, 3rd, 5th & 6th All-Colo, 74-80, Denver Art Mus; Colo-Nebr Exchange, Joslyn Mus Art, Omaha, 73; Remnant Transpositions, Fine Arts Ctr, Univ Colo, Boulder, 79; Aboriginal Transpositions, Patio Gallery, Univ Northern Colo, Greeley, 88; Animals in Art, Art Mus, Ariz State Univ, 88; Poetic License, Staller Gallery, State Univ NY, Stony Brook, 90; Fantasy in Form, Rye Arts Ctr, NY, 95; Millennium Box Exhib, Neuberger Mus Art, 2000; Beyond the Pale, Neuberger Mus Art, Purchase, NY, 2002. *Teaching:* Asst prof painting, Univ Denver, 72-75; assoc prof painting, Metrop State Col, Denver, 76-87; adj prof, Ariz State Univ, West Campus, Phoenix, 87-90; adj prof, Manhattanville Col, Purchase, NY, 93-2004; adj assoc prof drawing, Pratt Inst, Bklyn, 95-2004; adj prof, Indian River Community Col, Fort Pierce, Fla, 2004-. *Awards:* African Inst Fel, Hamline Univ, summer 78. *Mem:* Col Art Asn Am; Westchester Arts Coun; Cult Coun & Indian River County; and others. *Media:* Acrylic, Graphite, Mixed Media. *Mailing Add:* 921 Oyster Shell Lane Vero Beach FL 32963

SPURGIN, JOHN EDWIN
ADMINISTRATOR, PAINTER
b Indianapolis, Ind, Dec 17, 32. *Study:* Ind State Univ, BS & MA; Mich State Univ, with Angelo Ippolito; Univ Cincinnati, with Robert Knipschild, MFA. *Work:* Mich Educ Asn, East Lansing; Hubbard Milling Co, Mankato, Minn; Gustavus Adolphus Col, St Peter, Minn; Southwest State Univ, Marshall, Minn; Univ Cincinnati, Ohio. *Exhib:* Biennial of Painting & Sculpture, Walker Art Ctr, Minneapolis, 66; Okla Art Ctr, Oklahoma City, 67; Minn Mus, St Paul, 70; Miami Univ, Oxford, Ohio, 72; Northeast La Univ, Monroe, 74; one-man shows, Univ Wis, Marshfield, 75, Southwest State Univ, Marshall, 77 & Art Ctr, Minn, 83; Pillsbury Competitive Exhib, Minneapolis, 81; and others. *Collection Arranged:* American National Bank Collection Exhibition, St Paul, Minn, 74; Mankato Clinic, Ltd, Minn, 81. *Pos:* Gallery dir, Gallery Five Hundred, Fine Arts, Inc, Mankato, 69-72 & Nichols Gallery, Mankato State Univ, 73-75. *Teaching:* Instr art educ, Flint Inst Art, Mich, 60-64; prof design, painting, Mankato State Univ, 65-, chmn art dept, 75-89; vpres acad affairs, Milwaukee Inst Art & Design, 89-. *Awards:* First Prize Painting, Rochester Area Artists, Rochester Art Ctr, Minn, 66; Best-in-Show, Southern Minn Art Exhib, Mankato Free Press, 67 & 72; Minn State Individual Artists Grant, 77-78. *Media:* Mixed Media. *Mailing Add:* 333 Pepperidge Ln Evansville IN 47711

SPURLOCK, WILLIAM
HISTORIAN, CRITIC
b Chicago, Ill, Oct 23, 45. *Study:* Trinity Univ, San Antonio, Tex, BA; Univ NMex, Albuquerque, MA; Union Grad Sch, PhD. *Collection Arranged:* Vito Acconci (auth, catalog), Wright State Univ Art Gallery, 76; Barry Le Va (auth, catalog), Stephen Antonakos, Dennis Oppenheim, 77; Larry Bell (auth, catalog), Laurie Anderson, William Wegman, Alice Aycock & Pat Steir, 76; Photo-Realist Painting in Calif (auth, catalog), Santa Barbara Mus Art, 80; Herbert Bayer: Sited Sculpture and the Environment (auth, catalog), Roland Reiss, Sam Richardson, 81; and others. *Pos:* Fine art consult, Atlantic Richfield Co, Los Angeles, 79-84; cur exhibs & contemp art, Santa Barbara Mus Art, 78-81. *Teaching:* Asst dir educ in art hist & admin, Des Moines Art Ctr, Iowa, 72-74; asst prof art hist & dir, Fine Arts Galleries, Wright State Univ, Dayton, 74-78; assoc prof art hist, 82-, chair dept art, Univ Tex at Arlington, 82-86. *Mem:* Int Asn Art Critics; Col Art Asn; Am Asn Mus; Int Coun Mus; Am Fedn Arts; Nat Coun Art Adminr; Nat Asn Sch Art & Design. *Res:* Modern and contemporary art forms; environmental arts; criticism & theory; museology. *Publ:* Auth, Social & Ecological Issues in Contemporary Art, National Arts Guide, 3-4/80; Cecile Abish, 78; Richard Fisher, Current Charts: Chosen Lands, 78; Federal Art Patronage in the State of New Mexico: 1933-1943 (catalog), Mus NMex, 78; Dialogue-Discourse-Research: Eleanor Antin, Helen and Newton Harrison, Fred Lonidier, Barbara Strasen, Santa Barbara Mus Art, 79; numerous articles & essays on contemp art & artists. *Mailing Add:* Dept Art & Art History Univ Tex Arlington TX 76019

SQUADRA, JOHN
PAINTER, RESTORER
b New York, NY, June 25, 32. *Study:* RI Sch Design, BFA, 53. *Exhib:* Artist's Showcase, Mus Art, Bridgeport, Conn, 78; one-man shows, Nonson Gallery, Soho, NY, 79, Gallery Lory, Norwalk, Conn, 88, Gallery-Musee des Duncan, Paris, 80 & Agape Ctr, Portlant, Maine, 97; Vered Int Art Gallery, East Hampton, NY, 80; People 81, Hudson River Mus, Yonkers, NY; Athena Gallery, Chicago, 98. *Teaching:* Oils, acrylics, watercolor, Rowayton Arts Ctr, Conn, 74-87. *Awards:* Top Ten, Irene Leache Mem, Norfolk Mus, Va, 55; Second Prize, Darien Art Show, 82; First Prize, Rowayton Arts Ctr, 85. *Bibliog:* Reviews in Le Nouveau J, Paris, 11/80 & Playboy Mag, 2/81; Hudson River Mus Show, New York Times, 10/81; and others. *Media:* Oil, Acrylic. *Publ:* Illusr, Songs from Silences, 76; auth & illusr, Dr Miraculous, 81; auth, This Ecstasy, 96; Compass Of The Rose (CD), 2000. *Dealer:* Bayview Gallery Camden ME. *Mailing Add:* 93 Knowlton Rd Brooks ME 04921

SQUIER, JACK LESLIE
SCULPTOR, EDUCATOR
b Feb 27, 27; US citizen. *Study:* Ind Univ, BS, 50; Cornell Univ, MFA, 52. *Work:* Mus Mod Art & Whitney Mus Am Art, NY; Houston Mus Fine Arts, Tex; Everson Mus, Syracuse, NY; Johnson Mus, Cornell Univ; Hirshhorn Mus, Washington, DC; Ithaca Col, NY; SUNY Potsdam Mus, NY; Castellani Mus, Niagara Univ, NY; Fogg Mus, Harvard, Univ,; Conn Conservancy. *Comn:* Disc (fiber glass & aluminum leaf sculpture), Ithaca Col, 68; Emerson Mus, Hamilton Col, NY. *Exhib:* Carnegie Inst, Pittsburgh; Brussels World's Fair; Recent Sculpture USA, Mus Mod Art; 30 Americans Under 35, Whitney Mus Am Art, 57; Hirshhorn Mus & Sculpture Garden, Washington; Los Angeles Co Mus Art; Art Inst Chicago; Denver Art Mus; Albright-Knox Art Gallery, Buffalo, NY; Addison Gallery, Phillips Acad, Andover, Mass; Houston Mus Fine Arts, Tex; Pa Acad Fine Arts, Philadelphia; St Louis Art Mus, Mo; Wadsworth Antheneum, Hartford, Conn; one-person exhib, Alan Gallery, NY, 56, 59, 62, 64, A D White Mus Art, Cornell Univ, 59, 64, 68, Inst de Arte Contemp, Lima, Peru, 63, Landau-Allan Gallery, NY, 66, 70 & 72; one-man retrospective, Herbert F Johnson Mus Art, Cornell Univ, Ithaca, NY, 93. *Teaching:* From instr to asst prof, 52-64, prof sculpture, Cornell Univ, 65-. *Bibliog:* William Lipke (auth), Disc, by Jack Squier, Cornell Univ, 68. *Mem:* Int Asn Art; Sculptors Guild. *Media:* Bronze, Fiberglass

SQUIERS, CAROL
WRITER, CRITIC
b Oak Park, Ill. *Study:* Univ Ill, Chicago, BA(art hist), 71; Hunter Col, NY. *Pos:* Cur photog, PS 1, Inst Art & Urban Resources, New York, 80-84; photog critic, Village Voice, New York, 82-83 & Vanity Fair, 83-84; assoc ed, Am Photogr Mag, 86-89; sr ed, Am Photog Mag, 89-. *Awards:* Nat Endowment Arts Fel, 81. *Bibliog:* Andy Grundberg (auth), Mixing art & commerce, NY Times, 5/81; Sharon Gill (auth), Curator as critic: Carol Squiers, New York Photo District News, 9/82; Brian Wallis (ed), Silvia Kolbowski, Discordant Voices, Blasted Allegories: An Anthology of Writings by Contemporary Artists, New Mus Contemp Art, New York & Mass Inst Technol Press, Cambridge, Mass, 87. *Res:* The politics of photographic representation. *Publ:* Diversionary (Syn)tactics: Barbara Kruger Has Her Way With Words, Art News, 87; Picturing Scandal: Iranscam, the Reagan White House, and the Photo Opportunity, The Critical Image: Essays on Contemporary Photography, Carol Squiers, ed, Bay Press, Seattle, 90; Entertainment and Distress: The Photographs of Sandy Skoglund, Sandy Skoglund: Reality Under Seige, Abrams/Smith Col Mus Art, 98; Class Struggle: The Invention of Paparazzi Photography and the Death of Diana, Princess of Wales, Overexposed: Essays on Contemporary Photography, New Press, NY, 99. *Mailing Add:* 218 Thompson St No 15 New York NY 10012

SQUIRES, GERALD LEOPOLD
PAINTER, SCULPTOR, PRINTMAKER
b Nfld, Nov 17, 37. *Study:* Danforth Tech Sch, graduate 1957; Ontario Col of Art (night courses), 1958 & 1959; mainly self-taught. *Hon Degrees:* Mem Univ of NL, DLitt, 1992. *Work:* Saidye & Samuel Bronfman Collection, Montreal; Govt Nfld; Hibernia Corp; Art Gallery of Nfld & Labrador Permanent Collection; Confederation Art Gallery, Prince Edward Island. *Comn:* painting for Hibernia poster, Dept Mines & Energy, Govt Can, 88; St John the Baptist Cathedral, ceramic wall mural, "Portrait of Bishop Lampert", comn by Basilica Parish, St John's, 2005; Mary Queen of the World Church, Mt Pearl, Nfld, 27 paintings, drawings, 14 stained glass windows, comn by MQWC Parish, 1983-2004; St Clare's Hosp Foyer, St John's, "For Mercy Has A Human Heart" (history of St Clares), 16X16 raku ceramic wall mural comn by the Sisters of Mercy, 2004; St John's Airport, 6X10 oil on canvas, "Caribou on the Barrens", commissioned by St John's Airport Authority; Boyd's Cove Beothuk Interpretation Centre, life-size bronze sculpture, "Shanawdithit", comn by Beothuk Institute of Newfoundland & Labrador, 2002. *Exhib:* one man shows, Portraits, 78, Ferryland Downs, 79-81, Cassandra Series, 83 (traveling exhib), Crucifixion-Resurrection, The Last Supper & St John's, Nfld, 87, Mem Univ, Nfld, Gerald Squires: A Retrospective, Atlantic Arts Gallery, St John's, Nfld, 81; No Fishing, RCA Gallery, St Johns, 1991; Cult Assets: Art From Newfoundland Corp Collections, AGNL, 1997; Gerald Squires: New Landscapes, RCA Gallery, St Johns, 1997; Gerald Squires: Journey - selections from 4 decades work, Art Gallery Newfoundland & Labrador, 1998; Whodunit, Ontario Col of Art & Design, Toronto, 2004; A Showcase of Four Canadian Artists, St Jeromes 2nd Ann Festival of Art and Spirit, Waterloo Univ Art Gallery, Ont, 2004. *Pos:* Artistic dir, Breakwater Books Publishing Co, St John's; bd dir, Artist's Coalition Nfld & Labrador. *Teaching:* Instr art, Mem Univ Nfld, 70-88; workshops and lectrs in pub schs & art asns throughout Nfld & Labrador. *Awards:* Can Coun Arts B Award, 87; Royal Canadian Acad Arts Award, 1999; Her Majesty Queen Elizabeth 11, Golden Jubilee Medal, awarded 2003. *Bibliog:* Joan Marie Sullivan (auth), Nfld roots nurture Squires work, Globe & Mail, Toronto, 88; James Wade (auth), A medieval saint in a secular world, The Nfld Herald, 10/1/88; Arnold Bennett (auth, film) The Newfoundland Passion, 1998, Cine Terre-Neuve/Sleeping Giant, 60 minute doc film on Squires and his Mary Queen of the World Church paintings shown on Vision TV; Caroline Stone, Elizabeth Kidd (cur, auth) Gerald Squires, Journey, a 1998 Art Gallery of Newfoundland publication to commemorate the exhib by the same title, containing reproductions from the exhib, essays and articles; Sean J McGrath (auth), The Newfoundland Quarterly, Vol 96 #4, Transformative Imagery The Landscape Art of Gerald Squires, 2003 & 04. *Mem:* Great Northern AUK Workshop; founding mem Oshawa Art Gallery; Can Drawing Soc; Royal Can Acad. *Media:* All Media. *Dealer:* Emma Butler Gallery 111 George St St John's Nfld; Christine Parker Contemporary Graphics 127 Queen's Rd St John's Nfld; Gerald Squires Gallery Art St John's. *Mailing Add:* Bennetts Rd Box 361 Holyrood NL A0A 2R0 Canada

SQUIRES, NORMA JEAN
PAINTER, SCULPTOR
b Toronto, Ont; US citizen. *Study:* Art Students League; Cooper Univ, BFA, 61; also spec studies with James Rosati; Calif State Univ, Northridge, MA, 83. *Work:* Warner Brothers, Burbank, Calif; V-Tek Corp, Santa Monica, Calif; Siemens Pacesetter Systems, Los Angeles; Redwood City Pub Libr, Calif; Perkins Bldg, City of Glendale; and others. *Comn:* Mural, pvt collector, Calabasas, Calif, 93. *Exhib:* Dimensions II,

Los Angeles Co Mus Art, 87; solo exhibs, Mendenhall Gallery, Whittier Col, Calif, 90, Walker & Walker Gallery, Santa Monica, 90, Contemp Images, Sherman Oaks, 90, Maturango Mus, Ridgecrest, 91, Los Angeles Artcore, Los Angeles, Calif, 91, 95 & 98 & Quarks to Quasars, Century Gallary, Sylmar, Calif; Mt St Mary's Col, Jose Drudi's-Biada Art Gallery, 90; Group 9, Calif State Univ, Northridge, 98; 8th Pyong Taek Int Arts Festival, Korea, 2000; Peace Show, Nagasaki Mus Art, Japan, 2000, 2002; and many others; 1st Int Art Festival, Jeju Cutural Ctr, Jeju Island, Korea, 2004; 14th Int Art Festival, Burapha Univ, Chon Buri, Thailand, 2005; LELA Int, Museo del Historico, Ensenada, Mex, 2005; Gwang Hwa Moon Int Art Festival, Seoul, Korea, 2006. *Pos:* Agent & partner, Contemp Fine Artists Reps, 85-; freelance poetry coordr, cur, lectr & writer; writer, art criticism, catalogs, artists profiles, press materials and editing, currently. *Teaching:* Instr sculpture, Lucinda Art Sch, Tenafly, NJ, 67-69. *Awards:* Sarah Cooper Hewitt Award Advan Sci & Art, Cooper Union, 61; Int Friends of Transformative Art Grant, 93; Hans & G Thordis Burkhardt Found Grant, 94. *Bibliog:* Gerald Hopman (auth), Visions Art Quart, fall 91; Review in Artscene, 12/91; Nancy Kapitanoff (auth), revs, LA Times, 95; and many others. *Mem:* Artists Professional Exchange (bd mem); Los Angeles Co Mus Art; Lantern of the East, Los Angeles, LELA (bd mem, currently). *Media:* Mixed. *Interests:* Flamenco daning, singing, reading. *Publ:* Illusr, three children's bks, Addie Ripple Co, 78; The Healing Power of Art, 93; Poem Into Life, XLibris Corp, 2006. *Dealer:* Film Art LA 1680 N Vine St Hollywood CA 90028. *Mailing Add:* 9347 Valjean Ave North Hills CA 91343

SQUIRES GANZ, SYLVIA (TYKIE)
PAINTER
b Southampton, NY, Oct 8, 32. *Study:* Cortland State Univ, 51-53; also with Helen A Del Grosso, 70-71. *Work:* Smithonian Inst Mus. *Comn:* Paintings, First Federal Savings Loan, Delray Beach, Fla, 79 & 81; poster, Isle Royale Nat Park, 96. *Exhib:* Nat Miniature Art Soc Fla Exhib, Clearwater, 77-2005; Nat Painters, Sculptors & Gravers Soc, Arts Club, Washington, DC, 78-2004; Nat Ann Miniature Art Exhib, Gallery La Luz, NMex, 79-2001; Miniature Art Asn traveling exhib; Mus Fine Arts, St Petersburg; St Petersburg Mus Art; Leigh, Yawkey Woodson Art Mus, 93; one-woman show, Hampton Bays Pub Libr, 2002; World Federation of Miniaturists, Smithsonians Int Gallery, Wash, DC, 2004; World Exhib of Miniatures, Tasmania, 2004. *Pos:* Artist-in-residence, Isle Royale Nat Park, 96; jurist & judge for many nat shows, incl Miniature Art Soc Fla Int Show, 98-99; show judge Seacoast Gallery, Nags Head, NC, 2004 & 06. *Awards:* First Prize (acrylic), Arts for the Parks Nat Competition, 96 & 99; Grumbacher Award, 96-99; Best in Show, Loxahatchee Nat Wildlife Refuge Yr Show, 02 & 03; Palm Beach Community Col First Nat Drawing, Painting & Printmaking Competition, Excellence Award. *Bibliog:* Timeless Treasures (video), Miniature Art Soc, Fla; Isle Royale (auth), The Island Within US, 97; Wildlife Art, vol XIV, no 7, 96. *Mem:* Assoc Miniature Painters, Sculptors & Gravers Soc, Washington, DC; Miniature Art Soc, Fla; Del Ray Art League; found mem Miniature Artists Am since 85. *Media:* Acrylic. *Interests:* woodcarving, conservation, hiking, gardening. *Publ:* Contribr, Arts for the Parks, 91, 92, 93, 96 & 99; The Island within Us, 2000. *Mailing Add:* 10290 Seagrape Way Palm Beach Gardens FL 33418

SRAGOW, ELLEN
GALLERY DIRECTOR
b New York, NY. *Study:* Hofstra Univ, BA, 64; New York Univ, MA, 66. *Pos:* Registr & asst cur, New York Univ Art Collection, 67-71; dir, Prints on Prince St Gallery, 74-76 & Sragow Gallery, 76-. *Mem:* Int Fine Print Dealers Asn; Art Table Inc; Appraisers Asn of Am. *Specialty:* American prints, drawings, paintings from the 1920's, 1930's & 1940's, including the WPA period; contemporary prints 1960's-1970's of the NY Sch, African Am Art. *Mailing Add:* 73 Spring St New York NY 10012

STACH, JUDY
PAINTER, INSTRUCTOR
b Long Branch, NJ, Feb 25, 47. *Study:* Mount Ida Chamberlain Col, AA, 1967; Art Students League with David LaFelle, 2000; Putney Painters with Richard Schmid, 2004. *Work:* Mount Ida Chamberlain Col, Newton, Mass; Parker Clinic, Red Bank, NJ; Gateway Nat Park, Sandy Hook, NJ; Patricia Turchyn Interiors, Little Silver, NJ; Osprey Partners Investment Management, Shrewsbury, NJ. *Comn:* Kroon Family Home, Richard Kroon, Rumson, NJ, 2001; Family Home, Patrick Barovian, Coral Gables, Fla, 2003; Loveladies NJ Marina, Mr & Mrs Michael Tierney, Shrewsbury, NJ, 2004; Rogers Family, Kevin Rogers, Naples, Fla, 2005; Child on Beach with Dog, Adam Fazackerly, Reston, Va, 2005. *Exhib:* Three Unique Perspectives, Poricy Park Nature Ctr, Middletown, NJ, 1996; 2002 Florida Invitational, Main St Gallery, Perry, Fla, 2002; Two Woman Show, Guild of Creative Art, Shrewsbury, NJ, 2002; Boulder Art Assoc Nat Juried Show, Boulder Art Assoc, Colo, 2003; Am Artists Prof League, Fla, NMex, NYC, 2004-05; Am Impressionists Soc, Fla, NMex, NYC, 2004-05; 19th Juried Show, Catherine Lorillard Wolf Art Club, NYC, 2005; one woman retrospective, Frederick Gallery, Allenhurst, NJ, 2006; Audubon Artists Nat Juried, Salmagundi Art Club, NY, 2006. *Collection Arranged:* Making Friends Around the World, Americorp Childrens Expo, 2002; Senior Citizens Council on Aging, Co Library, Freehold, NJ, 2004. *Pos:* vp bd trustees, Guild of Creative Art, Shrewsbury, NJ, 1996-2003; founder, pres, Plein Air Painters of the Jersey Coast, 2003-. *Teaching:* instr plein air materials, Freehold, NJ Artists Soc, 2003 & Studio, Little Silver, NJ, 2003-; instr, Marketing Yourself, Guild Creative Art, 2006. *Awards:* Second Place Landscape Div, Ann Contest, The Artists Mag, 1998; Honorable Mention, The Best of Florida Art, Best Of Books, 2005-06; Inclusion in Volume, Long Beach Island Rhapsody, George Valenti (publ), 2006. *Bibliog:* Paul Soderburg (auth), Richard Schmid Interview, Art Talk Mag, 8-9/2004; Paul Soderburg (auth), Gender Bias in the Arts, Art Talk Mag, 8-9/2005; Kathy Collins (auth), Painting at Disney World, Vero Beach Mag, 2005; Linda DeNicola (auth), Living the Dream, The Hub, Monmouth Co, NJ, 6/2006; Painting on Sandy Hook NJ, Workshop Mag, fall 2006. *Mem:* Salmagundi Club; sig mem Plein Air Painters of Fla; Plein Air Painters of the Jersey Coast (founder, pres); Guild of Creative Art, Shrewsbury, NJ (exhib mem & bd mem 1996-2003); Am Impressionist Soc; Audubon Artists Inc, NY. *Media:* Oil, Acrylic. *Interests:* Boating, golf, tennis, gardening. *Publ:* coauth, Living the Dream, Stinehour Wemyss, 2005; contrib, Long Beach Island Rhapsody, George Valenti, 2006. *Dealer:* Meghan Chandler/Findlay 1270 Hwy A1A Vero Beach FL 32963; Lambertville Gallery of Fine Art 20 Union St Lambertville NJ 08530; The Frederick Gallery 401 Spier Ave Allenhurst NJ 07760. *Mailing Add:* 15 Alwin Terr Little Silver NJ 07739

STACK, FRANK HUNTINGTON
PAINTER, PRINTMAKER
b Houston, Tex, Oct 31, 37. *Study:* Univ Tex, Austin, BFA; Art Inst Chicago; Univ Wyo, Laramie, MFA; Acad Grande Chaumiere, Paris, Lakeside Studio Print Workshops. *Work:* Sheldon Mem Gallery, Univ of Nebr; Madison Art Ctr, Wis; Mo Hist Soc, Columbia; Kalamazoo Art Inst, Mich; Mus Art Archaeology, Columbia. *Comn:* Outdoor mural, First Nat Bank, Columbia, Mo. *Exhib:* Ten Missouri Painters, 69; one-man show, Etchings, US Info Serv, US Embassy, Turkey, Prints, Kalamazoo Art Inst, Mich, 76 & Watercolors, Va Tech Univ, 86, Harwell Mus, Poplar Bluff, Mo, 87 & Frye Art Mus, Seattle; From Zap to Zippy, San Francisco, 89; Misfit Lit Show, Seattle, 91; Bingham Gallery, Univ Mo, 2000. *Pos:* Contrib ed, The Comics J, 88; ed bd, Inks. *Teaching:* prof art, Univ Mo-Columbia, 63-, Middlebush prof fine arts, 94-99, prof emeritus, 2000. *Awards:* Summer Res Fel, 68, 74 & 76 & Foreign Study Grant, 70 & 93, 98, Univ Mo Res Coun; Mo Arts Coun Awards, 86. *Bibliog:* Sidney Larson (auth), Etchings and Lithographs by Frank Stack, Singing Wind Publ, 76; exhib catalog, Watercolors by Frank Stack, Mo Arts Coun, 77; R C Harvey (auth), Naked Glory: Erotic Art of Frank Stack, Fantagraphics Book. *Mem:* Kans Watercolor Soc; Columbia Art League; Mo Watercolor Soc. *Media:* Oil, Watercolor; Etching, Cartoonist. *Res:* Comics History. *Collection:* European and Am Master Prints. *Publ:* assoc ed, Houston Chronicle, 59; Auth, A metal plate sketchbook, Am Artist, 10/75; New Adventures of Jesus, 69-73, Feelgood Funnies, 71, 84, Dorman's Doggie, Kitchen Sink Press, 90, Amazon, Fantagraphics, 90; ed, Alley Oop (3 Vols), 46-50, by V T Hamlin reprint of comic strip, 90-92; auth, Watercolor Wisdom, The Artist's Mag, 4/93; artist, Our Cancer Year, 93; ed, Alley Oop Mag, 96-99. *Dealer:* Denis Kitchen Art Agency, PO Box 2250, Northampton, MA 01004; Philip Slein Gallery, Washington Ave, St Louis, 63103. *Mailing Add:* 409 Thilly Ave Columbia MO 65203

STACK, GAEL Z
PAINTER, EDUCATOR
b Chicago, Ill, Apr 28, 41. *Study:* Univ Ill, Champaign, BFA; Southern Ill Univ, MFA. *Work:* Mus Fine Art, Houston; Solomon R Guggenheim Mus, NY; Dallas Mus Art, Tex; Menil Collection, Houston Tex. *Exhib:* 19 Artists-Emergent Americans: 1981 (catalog), Solomon R Guggenheim Mus, NY, 81; solo exhibs, Hadler-Rodriguez Galleries, NY, 85, Brown-Lupton Gallery, Fort Worth, Tex, 85, Janie C Lee Gallery, Houston, Tex, 83, 85, 87 & 89, Beitzel Fine Arts, NY, 88, Sarah Campbell Blaffer Gallery, Univ Houston, Tex, 89, Univ Ark, Little Rock, 89, Moody Gallery, Houston, Tex, 90; Emerging Artists 1978-1986: Selections from the Exxon Series (catalog), Guggenheim Mus, NY, 87; The Artist's Eye: Fourteen Collections Diverse Works, Houston, Tex, 89; Women View Women, RGK Found Gallery, Austin, Tex, 90; Tradition and Innovation: A Mus Celebration of Texas Art, Mus Fine Arts, Houston, Tex, 90; Northwest X Southwest: Painted Fictions (catalog), Palm Springs Desert Mus, Calif, 90; Art from Houston in Norway, Stavanger Mus, 82; New Art from a New City, Frankfurter Kunstverein, Ger, 82; New Orleans Trienniale, New Orleans Mus Art, 83; Fresh Paint, The Houston Sch, Mus Fine Arts, 85; Texas Currents, San Antonio Art Inst, 85; and others. *Teaching:* Instr, Univ Wis, La Crosse, 72-73; from asst prof to assoc prof, Univ Houston, 74-85, prof, 85-. *Awards:* Nat Endowment Arts Artists Grant, 82, 89; Cult Arts Coun Houston Award Visual Arts, 85; Tiffany Found Award, 86. *Bibliog:* Michael Ennis (auth), Gael's Force, Domain, 5-6/89, 12, 14, 16; Elizabeth McBride (auth), Gael Stock, Artspace, 9-10/89, 65-65; Ann Holmes (auth), What artists collect, Houston Chronicle, 11/14/89, Sect D, 1, 4. *Dealer:* Condeso Lowler Gallery 524 Broadway New York NY 10012. *Mailing Add:* c/o Moody Gallery 2815 Colquitt Houston TX 77098

STACK, MICHAEL T
PAINTER, SCULPTOR
b Chicago, Ill, Oct 30, 41. *Study:* Univ Ill, BFA, 64; Univ Fla, MFA, 66. *Work:* Okla Art Ctr; Olivet Univ; Nelson-Atkins Mus Art; Yellow Freight Corp, NCAA Headquarters, Overland Park, Kans; Hallmark Collection, Twentieth Century Investments, Dean Witter Reynolds, Kansas City, Mo; and others; Cindy Pritzker, San Diego, CA. *Comn:* Garden of Earthly Delights (painting), KCRF Inc, Hayworth, Ill, 69; painting, MLLJN Inc, Bloomington, Ill, 73; Tensegrity structure, Metrop Life Insurance, Overland Park, Kans, 83; Dancin' (serigraph), Kansas City Arts Coun & Crown Ctr Redevelopment Corp, Kansas City, Mo, 83; mural, Sharon & John Hoffman, Kansas City, 86; bronze sculpture, Pauline & Patrick Dolan, Kansas City, Mo; Gould Evans Goodman Architects, Kansas city, MO, 96; Cerner Corp, North Kansas city, MO, 97; sokkia Corp, Lenexa, KS, 2000; Blue Ridge Bank, Indepenence, MO, 2003. *Exhib:* Ultimate Concerns, Ohio Univ, Athens, 65; Art Across Am, Knoedler Gallery, NY & traveling, 65-66; Fla State Fair Fine Art Exhib, Tampa, 65 & 66; 72nd Chicago & Vicinity Exhib, Art Inst Chicago, 69; Nat Print & Drawing Exhib, Western Ill Univ, 70; Mid-Four Painting Exhib, Nelson-Atkins Mus Art, 80; Three Painters, Mulvane Art Ctr, Topeka, Kans, 83. *Teaching:* Instr painting, Ill State Univ, 67-70; vis artist, NS Col Fine Arts, 69 & Kansas City Art Inst, 76, 87. *Awards:* Third Prize, Chicago Fine Arts Exhib, 63; Merit Award, Fla State Fair, 65; Third Prize, Mid-Four Painting Exhib, 80; Award of Merit, Kansas City Artists Coalition Exhib, 88. *Bibliog:* Mary King (auth), Fishbowl taxicab, Stack-ed deck, St Louis Post Dispatch, 4/11/80; Mary Sprague (auth), article, New Art Examiner, 7/80; Donald

Hoffmann (auth), 4 articles in Kansas City Star, 10/9/83 & 11/23/86; Ellen Goheen (auth), Parton Prompts painter, Forum, Vol 15, No 4, 90; Janet Majure (auth), Whirling dancers cast in bronze, Kansas City Star, 4/22/90. *Mem:* Col Art Asn; Kansas City Artists Coalition. *Media:* Acrylic, Oil; Bronze. *Mailing Add:* 2023 W Carroll Ave Chicago IL 60612

STACKHOUSE, ROBERT
SCULPTOR
b Bronxville, NY, 42. *Study:* Univ S Fla, Tampa, BA, 65; Univ Md, College Park, Mass, 67. *Work:* Exxon Corp, Citicorp, Philip Morris, Mus Mod Art, NY; Art Inst Chicago, Mus Contemp Art, Chicago; Walker Art Ctr, Minneapolis; Baltimore Mus Art, Md; Hirshhorn Mus & Sculpture Garden, Phillips Collection, Corcoran Gallery Art, Washington, DC; and others; John & Maxine Belger Family Found; Ctr Creativity-Univ Mo, Kansas City. *Comn:* Bronze, On the Beach Again, Australia Nat Gallery, Canberra; painted wood, St Louie Bones, Laumeier Sculpture Park, St Louis; Prudential Instalation, Prudential Ins, Plymouth, Minn, 81; Oliver Ranch Project/Russian River Bones (painted wood), Geyserville, Calif, 89; extruded red brass, Delaware Passage, Del Art Mus, Wilmington, 91; Divers (extruded red brass), Marine Sci Bldg, Univ Hawaii, Manoa, 91; Mo Bones, Albrecht-Kemper Mus, St Joseph, 97. *Exhib:* New Sculpture: Baltimore, Washington & Richmond (with catalog), Corcoran Gallery Art, Washington, DC, 70; 20 Yrs of Washington Art (with catalog), Baltimore Mus Art, Md, 70; solo exhibs, Corcoran Gallery Art, Washington, 73 & 88, Honolulu Acad Arts, Hawaii, 90, Va Mus Fine Arts, Richmond, 90, Univ Denver Art Gallery, 93, Struve Gallery, Chicago, 93, Morgan Gallery, Kansas City, 93 & Baumgartner Galleries Inc, Washington, DC, 93; North, East, West, South, Middle, traveling exhib to Corcoran Gallery Art, Washington, DC & Ft Worth Art Mus, Tex, 75; Scale and Environment, Ten Sculptors, Walker Art Ctr, Minneapolis, 77; Drawings of the 70's (with catalog), Art Inst Chicago, 77; Working Drawings, Hunter Mus Art, Chattanooga, Tenn, 81; Deep Swimmers (with catalog), traveling exhib to Huntsville Mus Art, Ala & Hunter Mus Art, Chattanooga, Tenn, 84; Monumental Drawings: Works by Twenty Am Artists (with catalog), Brooklyn Mus, NY, 86; Am Masters-Works on paper from the Corcoran Gallery Art, traveling exhib to Oklahoma Mus Art, Oklahoma City & Corcoran Gallery Art, Washington, DC, 87; The Boat Show: Fantastic Vessels, Fictional Voyages, Nat Mus Am Art, Smithsonian Inst, Washington, DC, 89; Projects & Portfolios, The 25th Nat Print Exhib (with catalog) Brooklyn Mus, NY, 89; New Editions, Pace Prints, NY, 90 & 91; 5th Int Biennial Print Exhibit, Taipei, Tawain, 91; Voyages of the Modern Imagination, William A Farnsworth Libr & Art Mus, Rockland, Maine, 90; 43rd Ann Purchase Exhib, Am Acad & Inst Arts & Lett, NY, 91; Pace Prints, New York City, 92; Outdoor Sculpture, Univ Wyoming Art Mus, 93; Morgan Gallery, Kansas City, Mo, 93 & 99; Sameways, Albrecht-Kemper Mus, St Joseph, Mo, 98; Morris Mus, Augusta, Ga, 99; Kalamazoo Inst Art, Mich, 99; Resurgent Hartford Sch Art, Conn, 2000; Univ Ariz, Mus Art, Tucson, 2001; many others. *Teaching:* Vis artist & lectr, Univ Hawaii, Manoa, 90, Univ S Fla, Tampa, 91, Univ Denver, Colo, 92; prof emer, Corcoran Sch Art; Leo Block Distingguished chair, Univ Denver, Colo, 93; Lamar Dodd Distinguished chair, Sch Art, Univ Ga, 2000-; Koopman Distinguished chair, Hartford Sch Art, Univ Hartford, Conn, 2001. *Bibliog:* Sidney Lawrence (auth), Sculpting the Land at Oliver Ranch, Garden Design Mag, 12/91; Stackhouse Commission Dedicated at University, Hawaii Artreach, Nov/Dec, Vol 7, No 5, 91; Ina Pasch (auth), Artist's Passage: Printmaker Enjoys Journey's to Tandem, Wis State J, 2/6/92

STACY, DONALD L
PAINTER, EDUCATOR
b West Paterson, NJ, Sept 3, 25. *Study:* Newark Sch Fine Art; Art Students League; Univ Paris Sch Art & Archeol; Univ Aix-Marseille; Pratt Graphic Art Ctr; New Sch Social Res. *Hon Degrees:* Fulbright. *Work:* Print Dept, Mus Mod Art; Birla Acad Art, Calcutta; Casa de Xilogravra, Sao Paulo, Brazil. *Comn:* Three decorative wall panels, US Plywood. *Exhib:* Documenta II, Kassel, Ger; Kyoto Gallery, Japan; Grenchen, Switz; Philadelphia Print Club; Knoedlers, York. *Collection Arranged:* Ann Exhibs Stacy Studio. *Pos:* Dir, Stacy Studio Workshop, 69-. *Teaching:* Mem fac, Dept Art, Inst Mod Art, Mus Mod Art, 57-69, Dept Art, Sch Visual Arts, New York, 69-70 & Dept Art, New Sch Social Res, 67-. *Awards:* Fulbright Grant, 53-55. *Bibliog:* Michael Lastnite (dir), Don Stacy--Art & the Autonomy of the Psyche (video), On the Otherhand Productions, 90. *Mem:* Am Inst Conserv Hist & Artistic Works; Engadiner Kollegium, Zurich; Am Inst Conservation, 82-. *Media:* Acrylic, Oil. *Publ:* Auth, The Runaway Dot: A Concept Book for Children, Bobbs, 69; contribr, articles in: Main Currents in Mod Thought, 69-74; Emergent Man, Gordon & Breach, 73; auth, Experiments in Art, Scholastic, 75; Drawing and Painting from Imagination, Stravon Press, 80. *Dealer:* Stacy Studio Workshop. *Mailing Add:* 17 E 16th St New York NY 10003

STACY, JOHN RUSSELL
ILLUSTRATOR
b Denver, Colo, Mar 18, 19. *Study:* Denver Art Inst, dipl, 39; Univ Wash, 47. *Work:* Boy Scouts Am Hq, Cimarron, NMex; Arches, Canyonlands, Yellowstone & Grand Teton Nat Parks, Wyo; Libr Cong, Washington. *Comn:* Painting, Izaac Walton League Am, Denver, Colo, 39; illusr, Colo Sch Mines, Golden, 60-70; illusr, Geological Soc Am, Boulder, Colo, 60-70. *Pos:* Illusr, US Geological Survey, Denver, Colo, 50-74; dir & illusr, Rocky Mountain Nature Asn, Estes Park, Colo, 74. *Awards:* O'Brien Faceting Trophy, Calif Fedn Mineralogical Soc, 84; Meritorious Serv Award, Dept Interior, 86. *Mem:* Life Santa Cruz Art League (bd dir, 81-82). *Media:* Oil. *Publ:* Auth & illusr, Terrain Diagrams in Isometric Projection--Simplified, Annals Asn Am Geographers, 58; illusr, Philmont Country, Professional Paper 505, 64, Geologic Story of Yellowstone National Park, 73, Geologic Story of Canyonlands National Park, 74 & Geologic Story of Arches National Park, 75, US Geological Survey. *Mailing Add:* 12681 SW Peachvale St Portland OR 97224-2194

STAFFEL, DORIS
PAINTER, EDUCATOR
b New York, NY, 1921. *Study:* Tyler Sch Art, 39-44; Iowa Univ, MA, 45; Hans Hoffman Sch, 45-47. *Work:* Iowa Univ; Tylor Woodruff, London, Eng; Wills Eye Hosp; Cigna Mus. *Exhib:* One-woman shows, Chatham Col, Pittsburgh, Pa, 65, Tyler Abroad, Rome Gallery, Italy, 68 & Gross McCleaf Gallery, Philadelphia, Pa, 79 & 82; Broad Spectrum, Allentown Art Mus, Pa, 81; Ann Drawing Exhib, Beaver Col, Glenside, Pa, 81. *Teaching:* Assoc prof painting, Philadelphia Col Art, 61-. *Awards:* Purchase Prize, Beaver Col, 78. *Media:* Oil, Watercolor. *Mailing Add:* 210 Locust St Apt 3A Philadelphia PA 19106

STAHANOVICH, KOLBA TAMARA See St Tamara, Kolba Tamara Stahanovich

STAHL, ALAN M
CURATOR, HISTORIAN
b Providence, RI, Aug 7, 47. *Study:* Univ Calif, Berkeley, BA, 68; Univ Pa, MA, PhD, 77. *Collection Arranged:* The Beaux-Arts Medal in America, loan exhib, Am Numismatic Soc, NY, 87-88; USA Exhib, Int Fedn Medal, Helsinki, Finland, 90, British Mus, 92 & Budapest, Hungary, 94 & Neuchatel, Switz, 96. *Pos:* Cur medals, Am Numismatic Soc, 80-. *Mem:* Am Medallic Sculpture Asn (pres, 83-87); Fedn Int de la Medaille, (USA delgate, 85-); Nat Sculpture Soc (coun, 91-96). *Res:* History of the medal in USA & abroad; art of medieval coinage of Europe. *Publ:* Auth, The American Industrial Medal, The Numismatist, 84; Lauffer's Medal Cabinet, Medallic Sculpture, 85; coauth, The Beaux Art Medal in America, Am Numismatic Soc, 87; ed, The Medal in America, New York, 88; American Indian Peace Medals of the Colonial Period in Money of Pre-Federal America, New York, 92. *Mailing Add:* Am Numismatic Soc 155th St & Broadway New York NY 10032

STAKE, PETER
EDUCATOR
Study: Arizona State Univ, BFA; Calif State Univ, Long Beach, MFA. *Exhib:* Ctr Art & Design, Univ Wales Inst. *Pos:* Chmn art & art hist dept Skidmore Col, Saratoga Springs, Calif. *Mem:* Bd trustees, Hyde Col. *Mailing Add:* Skidmore Col Art Dept 815 N Broadway Sasselin 200 Saratoga Springs NY 12866

STALLER, ERIC P
PHOTOGRAPHER, SCULPTOR
b Mineola, NY, Sept 14, 47. *Study:* Univ of Mich, BArch, 71. *Work:* Mus Mod Art, NY; Everson Mus, Syracuse; Int Mus Photog, Rochester; Nat Acad Sci; State Univ NY, Stony Brook. *Comn:* lighting installations, Int Ctr of Photog, NY, 79, City Univ NY, 79 & Md Inst Col Art, Baltimore, 79; light sculptures, Port Authority NY & NJ, 83; Three Rivers Art Festival, Pittsburgh, 85; Anchorage Performing Arts Ctr, Alaska, 86. *Exhib:* Biennials, Indianapolis Mus, 76 & Taft Mus, Cincinnati, 76; Samual Wagstaff Collection, Corcoran Gallery, Washington, DC, 79; Nat Acad Sci, Washington DC, 81; Lightmobile, City Univ Grad Ctr, NY, 85; City Lights, Int Ctr Photog, NY, 86. *Awards:* Creative Arts Pub Serv Prog Grant, 77; Nat Endowment Arts Grant, 78. *Bibliog:* Owen Edwards (auth), Tripping the light fantastic, Am Photog Mag, 4/78; article, The New York Times, 4/22/84; article, Wall St Jour, 8/8/85; article, Darkroom Mag, 11/85. *Media:* Light. *Mailing Add:* c/o Virginia Miller Galleries 169 Madeira Ave Coral Gables FL 33134

STALLWITZ, CAROLYN
PAINTER, PHOTOGRAPHER
b Abilene, Tex, Apr 27, 36. *Study:* WTex State Univ, with Clarence Kincaid, Jr, BS(art); also with Emilio Caballero, Stefan Kramer, Lee Simpson & Chris Gikas. *Work:* Pioneer Natural Gas Co, First Nat Bank, Amarillo, Tex; Sun Bank, Dumas, Tex; Cliff Dwellers, Los Alamos, NMex. *Exhib:* Tex Watercolor Soc Exhib, 70; Wichita Centennial Nat Art Exhib, 70; Best Southwest, 71; Amarillo Fine Art Asn Citation Show, 73; Denver Audubon Wildlife Art Show, 77; African Wildlife, Crabb Art Ctr, Dumas, Tex. *Teaching:* Instr drawing, Amarillo Art Ctr, 73-74, instr watercolor, 74-75; Crab Art Ctr, 80-2003. *Mem:* Moore Co Arts Asn (pres, 69-70 & 89-2000). *Media:* Watercolor, Pencil, Acrylics, Oils, Gouache. *Publ:* Window on the Prairie, Feather Press, 81. *Dealer:* Stallwitz Studio 5958 Stallwitz Rd Dumas TX 79029; Crabb Art Center 234 W 1st Dumas TX. *Mailing Add:* PO Box 1225 Dumas TX 79029

STALOFF, FRED
PAINTER
b Jersey City, NJ, 24. *Study:* Newark Sch Fine & Ind Art, Newark, NJ, 46-49; Acad de la Grande Chaumiere & Atelier Zadkine, Paris, 49-50. *Work:* Butler Inst Am Art, Youngstown, Ohio; James A Michener Art Mus, Doylestown, Pa; Kunstzall Polder, The Hague, Holland; Atelier Decima, Paris, France. *Exhib:* solo exhib, Kunstzall Polder, Th Hague, Holland, 65; Bicentennial Exhib, Jersey City Mus, Jersey City, NJ, 76; Ann Exhib, Nat Acad Design, NY; 40 Years in Retrospect, Butler Inst Am Art, Youngstown Ohio, 96 & James A Michener Art Mus, Doylstown, Pa, 97; Allied Artists of America, Invitational Traveling Exhib, Tex, Ala, Wis, Va & Mich, 2003-2005. *Awards:* Allied Artists Gold Medal, Ann Allied Artist Am, Allied Artist Am, 97; Stefan Hirsh Mem Award, 97 & The Ralph Fabri Medal, 2000, Ann Audubon Artists, Audubon Artists. *Mem:* Allied Artists Am (mem chmn, 94-97); Audubon Artists (treas, 70s); Artists' Fel. *Media:* Oil. *Mailing Add:* 2108 Harmon Cove Towers Secaucus NJ 07094

STAMATY, CLARA GEE KASTNER
PAINTER
b Piqua, Ohio, May 15, 19. *Study:* Art Acad Cincinnati, 43; Art Students League, NY City, 59; Pratt Graphic Workshop, NY, 69; Prints Div Libr, NY City, 90. *Work:* Ford Times Collection Am Art, Detroit, Mich; Monmouth Reform Temple, Tinton Falls, NJ; United Methodist Church, Red Bank, NJ; Turbeville Collection, Emerson Col,

Boston, Mass; Libr Graphic Arts & Commun, Ohio State Univ, Columbus, Ohio. *Comn:* Paintings for windows & interio displays, Giddings, Cincinnati, Ohio, 42, Lawtons, 43, Rollman & Sons, etc. *Exhib:* Artists of Cincinnati & Vicinity, Cincinnati Art Mus, Ohio, 41; Annual New Year Show, Butler Art Inst, Youngstown, Ohio, 44 & 45; Artists of Dayton & Vicinity, Dayton Art Inst, Ohio, 45; NJ Watercolor Soc, Ann Juried Shows, Monmouth Mus, Lincroft, NJ 74-77; Am Watercolor Soc, 107th Ann Nat Acad Galleries, New York City, 74; Art for Reflection, Avery Fisher Hall - Lincoln Ctr, New York City, 2000; Artists Studio, Monmouth Mus, Lincroft, NJ, 2001. *Pos:* Artist, Air Serv Command/Paterson Field, Dayton, Ohio, 43-45; superv, art Colony Surf Club, West End, NJ, 60-66. *Teaching:* instr, Stamaty Studios, Elberon, 62-81; many seminars & worshops on printmaking, collage & mixed media, 60-2000. *Awards:* Recipient 8, 1st prize Awards Three Arts Club, 39-42; Special award, Dayton Art Inst, 45; Gold medal, Long Branch Community Ctr, 62; First Prize, Ann Exhib, Middletown, NJ, 72; First Prize, Mixed Media, Monmouth Arts Found, 74; and many others. *Bibliog:* Herman Landau (auth), Clara Gee Stamaty Exhibit is a Delight, Red Bank Register, 5/6/88; Kisha Ciabattari (auth), Tooned in Artist, Asbury Park Press, 5/15/89; Ronnie Gardstein (auth), Centerfold - No Title, State of Art, 7-8/2002. *Mem:* Nat Cartoonist Soc (honorary Lifetime mem, 79-); Guild of Creative Art (secy, 67—68, vpres, 74 & 75); Monmouth Co Arts Coun (adv bd, 96-2001); Monmouth Arts Found (bd mem, 65-80); Art Alliance NJ. *Media:* Watercolor, printmaking, monotype & Mixed Media. *Publ:* co-auth, Life's Little Miracles, Am Mag, 48-50; co-auth, Budget Busters, Better Homes & Gardens, 50-51; auth, illustr, Sitter Sue, Christian Sci Monitor, 58-61; auth, Making the Rounds, NY Cartoon News, 3/59; Auth, illustr, Ginny, Scholastic book Serv; and freelance cartoons & illustrations for over 50 magazines, 41-70. *Dealer:* Guild of Creative Art 620 Broad St & Rt 35 Shrewsbury NJ 07702. *Mailing Add:* 1019 Woodgate Ave Long Branch NJ 07740-4631

STAMELOS, ELECTRA GEORGIA MOUSMOULES
PAINTER, EDUCATOR
b Jersey City, NJ. *Study:* Corcoran Mus Sch, study with Aurelius Battaglia & Heinz Warneke, 43-45; Nat Art Sch, 45-48; Magda Sch Design, Am Univ, Washington, DC, 46; work with Margaret Cramer, 61-63; Univ Mich, study with Guy Palazola, 64; Ctr Creative Studies, with Russell Keeter, 65-68 & 79; Wayne State Univ, BA (painting), 70, Eastern Mich Univ, MFA(watercolor), with Kingsley Calkins, 76. *Work:* Nat Watercolor Soc, Calif; Dennos Mus, Travis City; Flint Mus Art, Mich; Brown& Lund, Washington, DC; Eastern Ill Univ; Jessie Bessard Mus, Alpena; and others; Univ of Mich- Dearborn. *Comn:* Hardedge acrylic, Northwest Br, YWCA, Detroit, 70; Lithograph, Ctr for Creative Studies; Beaumont Hosp. *Exhib:* Source Detroit, Cranbrook Art Mus, Birmingham, Mich, 76; Butler Inst Am Art, Youngstown, Ohio, 76-77 & 79-80; Watercolor USA, 77, 79 & 86, Springfield Art Mus, 77, 80 & 2002; Nat Watercolor Soc, Fine Arts Gallery, Calif State Univ, Northridge, 77-81; Watercolor USA, Honor Soc, 93, 95, 97 & 2000; Detroit Realist, Oakland Univ, 79; Slusser Gallery, Univ Mich, 85; Springfield Art Asn, Ill, 86; Rocky Mountain Nat Watermedia Exhib, Foothills Art Ctr, Golden, Colo; Uni Quincey, Quincey, Ill, 2000; Retrospective, Univ Mich, 2001; Biennial, WC Invitational, Parkland Univ, Champaign, Ill, 2003. *Pos:* Dir art exhibs, Acquisitions, Univ Mich. *Teaching:* Instr drawing & painting, Nat Art Sch, Washington, DC, 45-48; instr drawing & painting, Northwest Br, YWCA, Detroit, 68-72; instr watercolor, Ann Arbor Asn, Mich, 77-78; instr, Birmingham Bloomfield Art Asn, 79-, lectr, Applied Arts, Univ Mich, Dearborn, 80-92. *Awards:* Purchase Award, Nat Watercolor Soc, 76, 90, 91, 92 & 2003; Purchase Award, 7 for 76, Eastern Ill Univ, 76; Purchase Award, Battle Creek Art Ctr. *Bibliog:* Watercolor Expressions, Betty Lou Sibleman, 99. *Mem:* Nat Watercolor Soc, Calif; Mich Watercolor Soc; Birmingham-Bloomfield Art Asn; Ann Arbor Art Asn; Watercolor USA, Honor Soc. *Media:* Watercolor, Acrylic; Pencil, Pastel. *Res:* Georgia O'Keefe. *Interests:* Photography. *Publ:* Illusr, The Tree House (24 drawings), 76; SE Michigan Calendar, 82; Splash I & II, Northlight Books, 90 & 92; Breaking Watercolor Rules, Artist's Mag, 91; Understanding Watercolor, G Brommer, 93 & Watercolor Magic, 2003. *Dealer:* Gallery 100 Saratoga Springs NY; Paloma Gallery, Ann Arbor, Mich. *Mailing Add:* 38131 N Vista Dr Livonia MI 48152

STAMSTA, JEAN
PAINTER
b Sheboygan, Wis, Nov 2, 1936. *Study:* Univ Wis, Milwaukee, BS, 58; Haystack Mountain Sch Crafts, 66; Fiberworks Ctr Textile Research, 81; Banff Ctr, Alta, Can, 86; Leighton Artist Colony, Banff, Alta, Can, 87. *Work:* Cleveland Mus Art, Ohio; Am Craft Mus, NY; Milwaukee Art Mus, Wis; Mus Fine Arts, Columbus; US Vice President's House, Washington, DC; Wustum Mus, Racine, Wis; Ark Art Ctr, Little Rock. *Comn:* Woven panels, Bank of Commerce, Milwaukee, 78; wall hanging, Sentry Insurance, Wis, 78; wall hangings, Miller Brewing Co, Milwaukee, 79; fiber sculpture, Ohio Bell, Cleveland, 84; painting, Johnson Hill Press, Ft Atkinson, Wis, 93; Painting, Kursel Family Coll, 2005. *Exhib:* Fiberworks (with catalog), Cleveland Mus Art, Ohio, 77; Fiber R/Evolution(with catalog), Milwaukee Art Mus, 86; Wis Triannual (with catalog), Madison Art Ctr, 87 & 90; Paper (with catalog), Fine Arts Mus, Budapest, Hungary, 92; USA-Today (with catalog), Textile Mus, Tilburg, The Neth, 93; Spirit in the Land, Mem Union Gallery, Univ Wis, Madison, 94; solo exhibs, Univ Wis Ctr, Sheboygan, 98, Wis Luth Coll, Milwaukee, 99, Rendering Smbols and Codes, West Band Mus Art, Wis, 2000; Paper Show, Bergtrom Mahler Mus, Neenah, Wis, 98; solo exhib, Carroll College, Waukesha, Wis, 2006; and others. *Pos:* Guest cur, Fiber R/Evolution exhib, 86. *Teaching:* Instr weaving, Alverno Col, Milwaukee, Wis, 65-72, Mt Mary Col, Milwaukee, Wis, 70-73, Univ Northern Mich, summer 77, Rochester Inst Technol, New York, summer 80 & Univ Wis, Milwaukee, 84. *Awards:* Purchase Award, Columbus Mus Fine Arts, 72; First Prize, Marietta Col Crafts Nat, 74; Nat Endowment Arts Craftsman Fel, 74. *Bibliog:* Elizabeth A Bard (auth), Great Lake series, Fiberarts, 4/83; Randy Bitter (auth), Papermaking using Wisconsin Effigies-The Art of Jean Stamsta, Progress in Paper Recycling, 5/94; Kevin Lynch (auth), Art show ties environment to human growth, The Capital Times, Madison, Wis, 6/30/94. *Mem:* Int Asn Handpaper Makers & Artists; Friends of Dard Hunter Paper Mus. *Media:* Paper, Fabric, acrylic paint. *Publ:* Coauth, Fiber R/Evolution (exhib catalog), 86. *Dealer:* Tory Folliard Gallery 233 N Milwaukee St Milwaukee WI 53202. *Mailing Add:* W 299 N 9313 Center Oak Rd Hartland WI 53029

STANBRIDGE, HARRY ANDREW
PAINTER, PRINTMAKER
b Quesnel, BC, July 23, 43. *Study:* Vancouver Sch Art, dipl(hons), 68; Univ BC, BA(art educ), 74, MA, 82. *Work:* City of Vancouver, BC; Seattle Art Mus; Nat Gallery Can Libr, Ottawa; Provincial Collection, Victoria, BC; Univ Alta Libr, Edmonton; Art Gallery of Greater Victoria; Can Coun Art Bank, Ottawa; Can Embassy, Australia. *Exhib:* Woman, Burnaby Art Gallery, BC, 72; Kinesis, Art Gallery Victoria, BC, 76; Victoria Artist, Art Gallery Victoria, BC, 86; Come Zion, Art Gallery of Greater Victoria, BC, 87; two-person show (with P Coupey), Surrey Arts Ctr, BC, 88; and others. *Teaching:* Instr drawing & painting, Spectrum Community Sch, Victoria, BC, 74-. *Awards:* Grant, Can Coun, 69; Purchase Award, Northwest Printmakers 40th Ann, Seattle Art Mus, 69. *Bibliog:* Charles Shere (auth), Four days from a diary, Arts Can, 75; Frank Nowasad (auth), Moments of cocksure bravado, Monday Mag, 86; N Tuele (auth), Come Zion, Recent Paintings by H Stanbridge (exhib catalog), Art Gallery of Greater Victoria. *Media:* Acrylic, Oil. *Publ:* Auth & illusr, Mirrored Barriers, Takao Tanabe (publ), 68; Great Works, Contemporary BC Artists, Melanie Gold, (publ), 96. *Dealer:* Bau-Xi Gallery 3045 Granville Vancouver BC V6H 3J9 Canada. *Mailing Add:* 4526 Hughes Rd Victoria BC V8X 3X1 Canada

STANCZAK, JULIAN
PAINTER, EDUCATOR
b Borownica, Poland, Nov 5, 28; US citizen. *Study:* Uganda, Africa & London, Eng; Cleveland Inst Art, BFA, 54; Yale Univ, with Albers & Marca-Relli, MFA, 56. *Work:* Carnegie Inst, Pittsburgh; Albright-Knox Art Gallery, Buffalo; San Francisco Mus Art; Corcoran Art Mus, Washington, DC; Nat Gallery, Washington, DC; Tulsa Mus, Okla; Hirshhorn Mus, Washington, DC; and others. *Comn:* Altar piece, St John's Unitarian Church, Cincinnati, 68; mural, Cleveland City Canvasses, 74; flag, City of Rottweil, Ger, 74; atrium layout, Dracket Co, Cincinnati, 84; Case Western Reserve Biomedical Building, Cleveland, Ohio, 93 & 94; and others. *Exhib:* One-man exhibs, Dayton Art Inst, 64, Akron Art Inst, 69, Concoran Art Gallery, Washington, DC, 72, Canton Art Inst, 74, Ohio State Univ, Columbus, 76, Int Monitary Fund, Washington, DC, 78, Butler Inst Am Art, 80, Nat Mus, Warsaw, Poland, 81, Standard Oil Co World Hq, Cleveland, Ohio, 87, Boca Raton Mus Art, 89 & Dennos Mus Ctr, Traverse City, Mich, 93, Columbus Mus Art, Ohio, 99, Asheville Mus Art, Ohio, 2000, Midland Ctr for the Arts, Midland, Mich, 2001, Eckert Fine Art Naples, Inc, Fla, 2002; retrospective, Butler Inst Am Art, Youngstown, Ohio, 98, Lowe Art Mus, Univ Miami, Coral Gables, Fla, 2001, Frederick R Weisman Mus Art, Pepperdine Univ, Malibu, Calif, 2001, Cleve Inst Art, Ohio, 2001, Washington State Univ Mus Art, Pullman, Wash, 2002, Naples Mus Art, Fla, 2002; Art in the Embassies, Madrid, 87; Galleria Zacheta, Warsaw, Poland, 91; Baum Gallery Art, Univ Ctrl Ark, Conway, 2000; Cleve Artists Found, Beck Ctr Arts, 2001; Bertha and Karl Leubsdorf Art Gallery, Hunter Col, New York City, 2003. *Teaching:* Instr, Art Acad Cincinnati, 57-64; prof painting, Cleveland Inst Art, 64-95; artist-in-residence, Dartmouth Col, 68 and others. *Awards:* Cleveland Fine Arts Award, 70; Outstanding Educ Am, 70; Ohio Arts Coun Award, 72; Medal of Excellence Award, Cleve Inst Art, 2001. *Bibliog:* Art/Search & Self Discovery, 68; Jean Lipman (auth), Provocation Parallels: Naive Early American/International Sophisticates, Dutton Inc, New York, 75; Decades of Light, 40 years of works by Julian Stanczak, State Univ New York at Buffalo, 90; Elizabeth McClelland (auth), Julian Stanczak, Retrospective: 1948-1998, Butler Inst Am Art, 98; and others. *Mem:* Am Abstract Artists; Am Int Platform Asn. *Media:* Acrylic. *Res:* Pioneer in optical art. *Dealer:* Stefan Stux Gallery 529 W 20th St New York NY 10011; McClain Gallery 2242 Richmond Ave Houston TX 77098; Eckert Fine Art Naples Inc 390 12th Ave S Naples FL 34102. *Mailing Add:* 6229 Cabrini Ln Seven Hills OH 44131

STANFORD, GINNY C
PAINTER
b Lamar, Mo, Sept 3, 1950. *Study:* St Olaf Col, Northfield, Minn, 67; Southwest Mo State Col, 68. *Work:* Ft Smith Art Ctr, Ark; Nat Portrait Gallery, Smithsonian Inst, Washington,; Duke Univ, Durham, NC; Butler Ctr for Arts, Little Rock. *Comn:* Two paintings, Kaiser Hosp, Santa Rosa, Calif, 89 & 90; three paintings, Kaiser Permanente Med Group, Santa Rosa, Calif, 89-91; painting, Bronson, Bronson & McKinnon, Santa Rosa, Calif, 91; two paintings, Duke Univ, Durham, NC, 96; two paintings, Carolina Cent Bank, Durham, NC, 96; 2000-one painting, Duke Univ, Raleigh, NC, 2000; portrait of Hillary Rodham Clinton, Nat Portrait Gallery, Smithsonian Institution, 2006. *Exhib:* New Acquisitions, Nat Portrait Gallery, Washington, 93; Chroma (with catalog), Fla State Univ, Tallahassee, 93; Emulations, Riverside Art Mus, Calif, 95; Recent Paintings, Saginaw Art Mus, Mich, 95; Recent Paintings, Pensacola Jr Col, Fla, 95; A Brush With History: Notable Americans from the Collection of the Nat Portrait Gallery (with catalog), NC Mus Art, Raleigh, 2001; Tennessee State Mus, Nashville, 2001; Nat Mus Western Art, Tokyo, 2001; JB Speed Art Mus, Louisville, 2001-; Montgomery Mus Fine Arts, Ala, 2002-; A Brush with History, New Orleans Mus Art, La, 2002; Nat Portrait Gallery, London, Eng, 2002; Outwin Boochever Portrait Competition (with catalog), Nat Portrait Gallery, Washington, DC, 2006. *Awards:* Western States Art Fedn Corp Collectors Project Award, Nat Endowment Arts, 90; Sonoma Co Found, Ind Artists Fel, Nat Endowment Arts, 90; Sonoma Found Grant, Individual Artist Fel, Sonoma Co Found & Nat Endowment Arts, 91. *Bibliog:* Laurie Cohn (auth), An American painter, KFTY Television, Santa Rosa, Calif, 4/91; James Carroll (auth), The Paper, Study of an Assassination: Ginny Stanford's Poem Mourning John F Kennedy, 5/91; Julie Allen (auth), Studio View, KRBC Television, 92; Carolyn Kinder Carr & Ellen G Miles

(auths), A Brush With History, Smithsonian Inst, 2001; Allys Paladino Craig (auth), Chroma: Comtemporary Luminist Painting, Florida State Univ, 94; Alison Guss, auth & producer, A Brush With History, History Channel, A&E Network, 2004. *Media:* Acrylic on Canvas. *Publ:* Illusr, Victory Over Japan, Little Brown & Co, 86; Mr Bridge/Mrs Bridge, N Point Press, 88; Remember Me, Mercury House, 91; The Light the Dead See, Univ Ark Press, 91; auth, Requiem: New Orleans Review, Loyola Univ, 12/94. *Dealer:* Portraits Inc 985 Park Ave New York NY 10028; Somerhill Gallery 3 Eastgate E Franklin St Chapel Hill NC 27514-5816. *Mailing Add:* PO Box 2014 Sebastopol CA 95473

STANFORD, LINDA OLIPHANT
ADMINISTRATOR, HISTORIAN
b Hollis, NY, Feb 11, 46. *Study:* Hunter Col, AB, 67; Indiana Univ, MS, 68; Univ NC, Chapel Hill, PhD, 76. *Pos:* Mem, State Mich Hist Preserv Rev Bd, 79-91; assoc chairperson, Mich State Univ, 85-89; assoc dean, Col Arts & Letts, Mich State Univ, 90-92, chair, Dept Art, 93-99, asst to provost, 99, registrar and asst to provost, 2000-02, asst provost acad servs and registrar, 2002-. *Teaching:* Asst prof art hist, design, Campbell Univ, Buie's Creek, NC, 68-75; from instr to prof, Mich State Univ, East Lansing, 75-. *Awards:* Fel, Am Coun on Educ, 89-90; Hall Fame, Alumni Asn, Hunter Col, City Univ NY, 94. *Mem:* Col Art Asn; Soc Archit Historians; Nat Trust Hist Preserv. *Publ:* Auth, WK Kellogg and His Gull Lake Home, Mich State Univ, 83; Railway designs by Fellheimer and Wagner, Queen City Heritage, 85; The Powerless and the Powerful: A Look at Rape by Kathe Kollwitz, Kresge Art Mus Bull, 85; Art and the Elem Sch Experience, Inst for Res on Teaching, Mich State Univ, 90; Women Art Historians, In: The Oxford Companion to Women's Writing in the US, 95; Coauth 98-99 Faculty Ext Lectr Series MSU, 98 & MSU Campus: Buildings, Places, Spaces, 2002. *Mailing Add:* Mich State Univ 216 Administration East Lansing MI 48824-1046

STANFORTH, MELVIN SIDNEY
EDUCATOR, PAINTER
b Tuscaloosa, Ala, Sept 22, 37. *Study:* Univ Ala, BFA; Wayne State Univ, MFA. *Work:* Duke Univ Med Ctr; R J Reynolds; Kaiser Permanente, Raleigh, NC; East Carolina Univ, Greenville, NC; Burroughs-Wellcome Corp; and others. *Exhib:* Regional Painting Exhib, 73-76 & Regional Drawing & Prints Exhib, 73-77, Southeastern Ctr Contemp Arts, Winston-Salem, NC; Ball State Univ Nat Drawing Exhib, Muncie, Ind, 74; Potsdam Nat Drawing Exhib, NY, 75; Piedmont Graphics, Greenville Co Mus, Greenville, SC, 77-78; Award Winners Exhib, NC Mus of Art, Raleigh, 79; NC Artists Exhibit, Rutgers Gallery, 80; Works on Paper, National-Weatherspoon Gallery, 87; Drawing/Photog, WVa Juried Show, 87; Outerbanks to Infinity (Nat Photog Show), 87-88; three man show, East Carolina Univ, 88, Boykin Gallery, Wilson, NC, 89; solo exhibs, Art Ctr, Goldsboro, 91, Greenville Mus Art, Spirit Sq Ctr, Charlotte, NC, 92; Community Ctr for the Arts, Kinston, NC, 99; Coastal Bend Col, Beeville, Tex, 99; Nat Juried Exhib, Kinston, NC, 98 & 99; Semi-Pub Gallery, Asheville, NC, 2001; Nat Juried Exhib, Rocky Mountain Art Ctr, 2002. *Teaching:* Prof emer & painting, E Carolina Univ, Greenville, NC, 69-. *Awards:* Second Purchase Award, NC Artists Exhib, NC Arts Coun, 71; Purchase Awards, Regional Painting Exhib, 73 & Regional Drawing & Prints Exhib, 73, Southeastern Ctr Contemp Arts, Winston-Salem, NC; NC Artists Fel, NC Arts Coun, 99; NC Mus of Art Award, 74; NC Art Fel, Weatherspoon Gallery, Greensboro, NC, 2000, Fayetteville Mus of Art, NC, 2000 & Platinum Gallery, Greenville, NC, 2000. *Mem:* Durham Art Guild. *Media:* All Media. *Publ:* Contribr, Art Papers, 5-6/88, 8-9/90. *Mailing Add:* 2205 E Fifth St Greenville NC 27858

STANICH, NANCY JEAN
PHOTOGRAPHER, PRINTMAKER
b Pittsburgh, Pa, July 26, 39. *Study:* Parsons Col, BA, 63; Ohio State Univ, MA, 67; State Univ NY, New Paltz, grad study printmaking, 82, 96. *Work:* Canal Lock Mus, High Falls, NY; Monhegan Mus, Monhegan Island, Maine; Pemiquid Point Mus, Maine; North Star Bank, Syracuse, NY. *Exhib:* Printmaking Traveling Exhib, Nat Asn Women Artists, 78-92; 155th Nat Acad Design Exhib, NY, 80; Audubon Artists Open Exhib, Audubon Artists Asn, NY, 86 & 89; Salmagundi Open Exhib, Salmagundi Club, NY, 86 & 89. *Teaching:* Instr serigraphy, Woodstock Sch Art, NY, 85 & Round Top Ctr Arts, Damarisotta, Maine, 93. *Awards:* First Place Graphics, Mt St Mary's Col, 83 & 85; Jeffery Childs Willis Mem Award, Nat Asn Women Artists, 92; First Place Graphics, Northeast Art Festival, Caldwell Col, 93. *Mem:* Nat Asn Women Artists; Woodstock Artist Asn; North Shore Artists Asn; Maine Coast Artists Asn. *Media:* All Media. *Dealer:* Nancy Starich 362 SR 32 N New Paltz NY 12561. *Mailing Add:* 362 Rte 32 N New Paltz NY 12561

STANKIEWICZ, MARY ANN
EDUCATOR
b Keene, NH, May 5, 48. *Study:* Syracuse Univ, BFA(art educ), 70, MFA(art educ), 76; Ohio State Univ, PhD(art educ), 79; Phi Kappa Phi. *Pos:* Consultant Getty Ctr for Educ in Arts, Los Angeles, 84-; servs at, Pa State Univ incl, adv, Pa Art Educ Asn student chap, 2000-01. *Teaching:* prog off, Getty Ctr for Educ in Arts, Santa Monica, Calif, 90-92; asst vpres, acad affairs Ringling Sch Art and Design, Sarasota, Fla, 92-94; assoc prof, art educ, Sch Visual Arts Pa State Univ, Univ Park, Pa, 1999-2000, 2000-2004; prof, art educ, Penn State Univ, 2004. *Awards:* Grantee Nat Endowment of the Humanities, 1986, Spencer Found, 1987; recipient Kenneth Marantz Distinguished Alumni award Grad Students Dept Art Educ, Ohio State Univ, 1992; Grad. Fel, 1976-77, Grad Student Alumni Research award, 1978; summer res fel, Ore Ctr for Humanities, Univ Ore, 1995. *Mem:* Coun Policy Studies in Art Educ, Nat Art Educ Asn (pres women's caucus 1984-85; June King McFee award, 2003, historian/archivist 1980-88, Maine Art Educator of Yr 1983, pres-elect 2001-03, pres, 2003-, Maine Art Educator Yr, and Maine Art Educ Asn, 1983), Philosophy of Educ Soc, Hist of Educ Soc. *Publ:* Co-ed: Framing the Past, 90; co-ed with Patricia M Amburgy, Donald Soucy, Brent Wilson & Marjorie Wilson, History of Art Education: Proceedings from the Second Penn State Conference, Reston Va: Nat Art Educ Asn, 1992; ed, Art Education, Nat Art Educ Asn, 95-98; auth, Roots of Art Education Practice, 2001; ed, books and monographs; contribr articles to prof jour & book chap. *Mailing Add:* Pa State Univ Art Educ Prog 207 Arts Cottage State College PA 16802-2905

STANLEY, CHRISTOPHER P
CERAMIST
b Boston, Mass, July 8, 54. *Study:* Wittenberg Univ, BFA, 77; Kans City Art Inst, Special Student, 77-78; Alfred Univ, MFA, 80. *Work:* Victoria & Albert Mus, London, Eng; Wichita Art Mus, Wichita Art Asn, Kans; Daniel Jacobs, NY; Lannon Found, Fla; Garth Clark Gallery, NY. *Exhib:* One-man shows, George Ciscle Gallery, Baltimore, Md, 88, Garth Clark Gallery, NY, 85, 87, 88, 91 & 96, Pro Art Gallery, St Louis, Mo, 87 & 89, Fla Gulf Coast Art Ctr, Belleair, Fla, 91, NHCC Fine Art Gallery, Houston, Tex, 91, Manchester Craftsmens Guild, Pittsburgh, Pa, 92; Craftsman's Gallery, Rhode Island Sch Design, 83; Clay USA 1984, Radford Univ, Va, 84; Works Gallery, Group Invitational, Philadelphia, 85; Archie Bray Found Show, Maveety Gallery, Portland, Ore, 90; The Expressive Teapot, Swidler Gallery, Royal Oak, Mich, 91; Clay Coast to Coast, Trisolini Gallery Ohio Univ, Athens, Ohio, 91; A Decade of Crafts, Auction, Am Craft Mus, NY, 91; Nat Ceramic Invitational Exhib, West Chester Univ, Pa, 92; Garth Clark Gallery, NY, 96; Smithsonian, Washington, DC, 98. *Pos:* Lectr and workshops at many cols, universities, and institutions, 80-92. *Teaching:* Summer Sch fac, RI Sch Design, 82, 84, 85, ceramic technician, 80-82, adj prof, 82-85; asst prof, Wichita State Univ, 85-89, Penn State Univ, currently; artist-in-residence, Archie Bray Found, Mont, 89-90; head, Ceramic Dept, Pa State Col, currently; prof, Pa State Col, 98-. *Awards:* Award for Excellence, Clay USA 1984, 84; Nat Endowment Arts Fel Grant, 86 & 88; Governor's Arts Award, Kans, 89; Pa Artist Grant, State of Pa, 94. *Bibliog:* Richard Zakin (auth), Ceramics, Mastering the Craft, Chilton Bk Co, 90; American Ceramics (rev), 9/91; Janet Mansfield (auth), Salt Glazed Ceramics, An Int Perspective, Chilton Bk Co, 91. *Mem:* Nat Coun Educ for the Ceramic Arts (bd dir, 88); Col Art Asn Am. *Dealer:* The Works Gallery 319 South St Philadelphia PA 19147. *Mailing Add:* 1269 Pennfield Rd State College PA 16801

STANLEY, M LOUISE
PAINTER
b Charleston, WVa, Aug 28, 42. *Study:* La Verne Col, BA, 64; Calif Col Arts & Crafts, BFA, 67, MFA, 69. *Work:* Triptych, Oakland Mus. *Exhib:* Solo shows, Univ Art Mus, Univ Calif, Berkeley, 78, PS1, Queens, NY, 78, Quay Gallery, San Francisco, 83, Rena Bransten Gallery, 86, Calif State Hayward, 94, Cal State, Haywood, Calif, 96 & SFMOMA Rental Gallery, San Francisco, 99; Drawings by Painters, Long Beach Mus Art, Calif, 82; Second Sight: Biennail IV, San Francisco Mus Mod Art, 86; Myth and Magick, Fetterly Gallery, Vallejo, Calif, 98; Art the Other Industry, Emeryville, Calif, 99; Watercolor, City Col, San Francisco, 99; Wood St Gallery, Chicago, 99; New Acquisitions: Permanent Collection, Triton Mus, Santa Clara, Calif, 2000; (solo) "M Louise Stanley' San Francisco Mus Mod Art, 99; (solo) "M Louise Stanley: Classics Illustrated," Reese Bullen Gallery, Humbolt St Univ, Arcata, Ca, 2000; (group) "The Lighter Side of Bay Area Figuration," San Jose Mus of Art, 2000. *Collection Arranged:* Public Art Project, City of Emeryville, CA, 2003. *Pos:* Tour Leader, Art Lovers Tour of Italy, currently. *Teaching:* Instr painting & drawing, San Francisco State Univ, Calif, 77-78; asst prof painting, drawing & watercolor, La State Univ, Baton Rouge, 78-79; instr painting, San Francisco Art Inst, Calif, 82-; vis artist, Univ NC, Chapel Hill, 84; instr painting, Univ Calif, Berkeley, 85-86; prof art, Vista Coll, Berkeley, 2002. *Awards:* Nat Endowment Arts Grant, 83 & 89; Fleishhacker Grant S F; Fleishhacker Grant, San Francisco; Adolph and Esther Gottlieb Found Grant, 97 & 2005. *Bibliog:* Yasmin Anwar (auth), Mary, Mary quite contrary, Oakland Tribune, 4/1/97; Michelle Paisley (auth), The many faces of Mary, Contra Costa Sun, 3/26/97; Darwin Marable (auth), Mary exhib inspires and incites, Catholic Voice, 4/7/97. *Mem:* Charter mem Calif Fedn Art Teachers Local 1. *Media:* Oil, Gouache. *Interests:* Founder, dir, "Art Lovers Tours" to Italy, 1994-. *Publ:* Auth, portfolio, Paris Review, Winter 84; Modern Myths: Regarding Art: J of Exploration, Winter/Spring, 98. *Dealer:* Michael Himovitz Gallery 1616 Del Paso Blvd Sacramento CA 95815. *Mailing Add:* 1420 45th St Apt 29 Emeryville CA 94608

STANTON, HARRIET L
PAINTER
b New York, NY, Mar 27, 24. *Study:* Cornell Univ, 41; Richmond Prof Inst, Col William & Mary, Cert, 44; Art Student's League, 46-47. *Work:* Milwaukee Art Ctr, Wis; Yale Univ Art Gallery, New Haven, Conn; C W Post Col Mus, Brookville, NY; US Embassy, Paris, France; Univ NC, Chapel Hill. *Exhib:* San Francisco Mus Art, Calif, 63; Artists Use of Paper, Suffolk Mus, Stony Brook, NY, 74; New Talent, Gimpel & Weitzenhuffer, NY, 74; Graphics, Albright-Knox Mus, Buffalo, NY, 78; Art in Bloom, Mem Art Mus, Univ Rochester, NY, 78; Am Printmakers, Tokyo Central Mus, Japan, 78; Elaine Benson Gallery, Bridgehampton, NY, 90 & 91; Gallery Emanuel, NY, 93; Adelphi Univ, Garden City, NY, 97; Nassau Co Mus Exhib, NY, Shelter Rock Libr, 97 & Great Neck Libr, 98. *Teaching:* Instr drawing & painting, Nassau Co Mus, Roslyn, NY; NY Univ, NY, 67-71 & Hofstra Univ, Hempstead, NY, 68-75. *Awards:* Art Honor Award, Richmond Prof Inst; Emily Lowe Found Award; Premier Prix Int, Cannes, France. *Mem:* Nat Drawing Asn; Nat Asn Women Artists. *Media:* Oil. *Dealer:* Szoke Koo 164 Mercer St New York NY 10012. *Mailing Add:* 119 Malverne Ave Malverne NY 11565

STANTON, PHIL
CONCEPTUAL ARTIST, KINETIC ARTIST
b Tex, Nov 16, 59. *Study:* Evangel, theatre, 83. *Work:* New Mus Contemp Art (performance), NY; Milwaukee Art Mus (performance), Wis; Contemp Art Ctr New Orleans (performance), Fla. *Pos:* Founder & creator, Blue Man Group. *Awards:* Obie, Tubes, Village Voice, 91; Drama Desk, Tubes, 92; Lucille Lortel Found Award, Tubes, 92. *Bibliog:* Alisa Soloman (auth), Pissing on propriety, Village Voice, 1/15/91; Vicki Goldberg (auth), Hi tech meets God with Blue Man Group, NY Times, 1/17/91; Thomas M Disch (auth), Blue Man Group: Tubes, Nation, 1/20/92. *Media:* Performance

STANTON, SYLVIA DOUCETT
PAINTER
b New Orleans, La, Sept 21, 35. *Study:* Newman, New Orleans, La, 52; Univ NMex, 62. *Work:* City of New Orleans, Permanent Collection, La; Sarah Gillespie Gallery, William Carey Col, Biloxi, Miss; Lucille Parker Gallery, William Carey Col, Hattiesburg, Miss. *Exhib:* group exhib, Montserrat Gallery, Broadway, NY, 2001; one woman show, Joze de Vie, Lucille Parker William Carey Col, Hattiesburg, Miss, 2005. *Pos:* pres, owner, Millbrook Art Gallery, Picayune, Miss, 2001-; pres, owner, French Salon Gallery, Bay St Luis, Miss, 2004-. *Teaching:* instr, oil painting, NMex Art League, 62-67; instr, oil painting, Millbrook Gallery, Picayune, Miss, 2001-; instr, oil painting, French Salon Gallery, Bay St Louis, Miss, 2004-. *Awards:* First Place Award, Pirates Alley Show, New Orleans Art League, 2002; First Place Award, Brew House Show, New Orleans Art League, 2003; First Place, Primate Center Show, St Tammy Art Assn; Best of Show, Fort Pike Show. *Mem:* New Orleans Art League, La; Audubon Artists, NY; Allied Artists Am, NY; Biloxi Art Asn, Miss. *Media:* Oil, Instructor, Art Dealer. *Specialty:* Show my own work; students work and New Orleans Artists; Realistic & impressionist. *Dealer:* Lott Stanton Gallery 1800 N State St Jackson MS 39202; French Salon In Serenity Place 126 N Main Bay St Louis, MS. *Mailing Add:* 615 E Lakeshore Dr Carriere MS 39426

STAPEN, NANCY
CRITIC, WRITER
b New York, NY, Dec, 3, 50. *Study:* Brandeis Univ, BA(fine art, magna cum laude), 72. *Collection Arranged:* Robert Henry Logan Retrospective, 84. *Pos:* Asst dir, Clark Gallery, Lincoln, Mass, 81-84; coordr, Mus Goers Month, var Boston mus, 83; sr art critic, Boston Herald, 84-90; exclusive Boston rep, Artforum, 85-88; feature writer, Christian Sci Monitor, Artnews & ELLE, 87-; Boston corresp, Artnews, 88-, Town & Country, 93-; art critic, Boston Globe, 90-. *Teaching:* Chmn fine arts, Belvoir Terrace Fine Arts, Lenox, Mass, summers 76-78; instr sculpture, Concord-Carlisle High Sch, Mass, 79-80; instr learning through art, De Cordova Mus, 81-83; lectr numerous univs & mus, 82 ; dir, Docent Prog, DeCordova Mus, 83-84. *Awards:* Hon Mention Best Visual Arts Critic, Boston Mag, 86; Chemical Bank Award for Distinguished Newspaper Art Criticism, 87, 90 & 92. *Mem:* Am Asn Art Critics; Women's Caucus Art; PEN, New Eng; Nat Writers Union; Art Table; and others. *Res:* Visual arts; specializing in contemporary art. *Publ:* Auth, John Imber, Paintings, 78-89 (catalog essay), Fitchburg Art Mus, 9-11/90; Annette Lemieux, Recent Work, Paris Exhib, 9/91; Kiki Smith, Prints and Multiples 1985-1993, 1/94; Jake Berthot, Paintings (catalog essay), Dartmouth Col, 96. *Mailing Add:* 25 Euston St Brookline MA 02146

STAPLETON, BENJAMIN F, III
PATRON
b Newport News, Va, 43. *Study:* Harvard Univ, BA, 65, Yale Univ, LLB, 69. *Pos:* Assoc, Sullivan & Cromwell, New York City, 69-77, partner, 77-, mem, mergers & acquisitions group, 78-, sr partner; bd trustees, Amon Carter Mus, Ft Worth. *Mem:* Bar: NY 1972. *Mailing Add:* Sullivan & Cromwell 125 Broad St New York NY 10004-2498

STAPRANS, RAIMONDS
PAINTER, SCULPTOR
b Riga, Latvia, Oct 13, 26; US citizen. *Study:* Sch Art, Esslingen, Stuttgart, 46; Univ Wash, BA, 52; Univ Calif, MA, 55; also with Archipenko. *Work:* Calif Palace Legion Hon, San Francisco; Oakland Mus, Calif; Santa Barbara Mus, Calif; Los Angeles Co Mus; Phoenix Art Mus; Anderson Collection, San Francisco. *Exhib:* Portland Art Mus, Ore, 56 & 57; Oakland Art Mus, 57; Calif Palace Legion Hon Winter Invitational, 57, 59 & 60; Litton Industs, 62; Am Acad Arts & Lett, NY, 70; and many one-man shows, in US, Can & Europe incl San Jose Mus of Art, Pasadena Mus Art, Calif, 2006, Latvian State Mus, 2006, Hackett-Freeman, 2006. *Teaching:* Instr, Univ Alaska, 78 & 81. *Awards:* San Francisco Art Festival. *Bibliog:* California Canvas (film), KRON, San Francisco, 66; Artists Eye (film), Motion Media, 67; Color in Contemporary Painting. *Mem:* Z Lazda Mem Found (past chmn). *Media:* Oil, Acrylic; Plastic. *Publ:* Raimonos Staprans, Univ Washington Press. *Dealer:* Hackett-Freedman Gallery 250 Sutter St San Francisco CA 94108. *Mailing Add:* 2052 20th St San Francisco CA 94107

STARK, BRUCE GUNSTEN
CARTOONIST, ILLUSTRATOR
b Queens, NY, Feb 17, 33. *Study:* Sch Visual Arts, New York, 55-58. *Work:* Everett Dirksen Libr; L B Johnson Libr; Baseball Hall of Fame, Cooperstown, NY; Basketball Hall of Fame, Mass. *Exhib:* One-man shows, Art Inst Pittsburgh, 68, Univ Kutztown, Pa, 70 & NY Bank for Savings, NY, 71; Nat Art Mus Sport, NY, 71. *Pos:* Artist, cartoonist, New York Daily News, 60-82. *Awards:* Nat Cartoonist Soc Reuben Awards, 66, 68 & 75; Page One Award for Best Sports Cartoon, 70, 71 & 73; Most Outstanding Achievement Award, Sch Visual Arts, 82

STARK, KATHY
PAINTER
b Croton-on-Hudson, NY. *Study:* Univ NMex; NY Univ; Art Student's League, NY; Printmaking Workshop, NY. *Work:* Smithsonian Inst; Bibliotheque Nat; Neuberger Mus, Purchase, NY; Southeast Ark Art Ctr, Pine Bluffs; Chase Manhattan Bank; Chemical Bank; Bell Labs. *Comn:* Painting, comn by Mr R Kanofsky, NY 87; painting, Genesys Software Systems, Inc, 88; painting, comn by Dr & Mrs R Riechers, Mt Kisco, NY, 89; painting, comn by Mr D Masters, Nantucket, Mass, 90; painting, comn by Pamala Killen, Nantucket, Mass, 92. *Exhib:* One-man shows, Kenneth Taylor Gallery, Nantucket, Mass, 89, Sun Gallery, Nantucket, Mass, 90, 91 & 92, Art Source, Cleveland, Ohio, 91, Little Gallery, Nantucket, Mass, 91, de Havilland Gallery, Boston, 92 & New Hampton Gallery, NH, 93; Copley Soc, Boston, 91; Left Bank Gallery, Wellfleet, Mass, 93; Hooper Mus, Nyack, NY, 93; Nat Asn Women Artists Ann Exhib, Javits Ctr, NY, 93; Main Street Gallery, Nantucket, Mass, 93-99; West Branch Gallery, Vt, 2004-2006; SoHo 20, Chelsea, NY, 2006; Spheris Gallery, Vt, 2006. *Awards:* Target Presentations Grant, Found Community on Artists, 79-80; Independent Exhib Grant, Artists Space, 83 & 86; 1st Prize, Temple Arts Festival, 2005. *Mem:* Nat Asn Women Artists; Copley Soc; Artists' Asn Nantucket. *Media:* Acrylic. *Interests:* Gardening & reading. *Dealer:* SoHo 20 NY; West Branch Gallery Vt

STARK, LINDA
PAINTER
b San Diego, Calif, 56. *Study:* San Diego State Univ, Calif, 75; Grossmont Col, El Cajon, Calif, 76; Univ Calif, Davis, BA, 78; Univ Calif, Irvine, Regents Fel, 83, Laguna Beach Arts Fel, 84, MFA, 85. *Exhib:* Newport Harbor Art Mus, 86; solo exhibs, Cirrus, Los Angeles, 90, 91 & 93, Jack Shainman Gallery, NY, 94 & 96, Feigen Inc, Chicago, 95, Marc Foxx, Santa Monica, Calif, 95, Runaway Love, Jack Shainman Gallery, NY, 96 & 97 & Angles Gallery, Santa Monica, Calif, 98; Aldrich Mus Contemp Art, 94; Skew: The Unruly Grid, Gallery 400, Sch Art & Design, Univ Ill, Chicago, 95; Sexy: Sensual Abstraction in California Art 1960s-1990s, Temporary Contemp Gallery, Las Vegas, 95; And the Verdict Is, Jack Shainman Gallery, NY, 95; Untitled, Jack Shainman Gallery, NY, 96; Pop Surrealism (catalog), Aldrich Mus Contemp Art, Ridgefield, Conn, 98; Precious, Jan Baum Gallery, Los Angeles, Calif, 98; Ecstasy, Jack Shainman Gallery, NY, 98. *Awards:* Vis Artist Fel Grant, Nat Endowment Arts, 95-96; Vis Artist Fel, Calif Arts Coun, Sacramento, Calif, 98. *Bibliog:* Michael Kimmelman (auth), In Los Angeles, the makings of a better mood, NY Times, 1/14/96; Michael Cohen (auth), Linda Stark at Mark Foxx, Flash Art, 1-2/96; Frederick Ted Castle (auth), Linda Stark at Jack Shainman, Rev, 4/1/96. *Dealer:* Jack Shainman Gallery 560 Broadway 2nd Floor New York NY 10012; Angles Gallery 2230 & 2222 Main St Santa Monica CA 90405. *Mailing Add:* 3456 Atwater Ave Los Angeles CA 90039

STARK, ROBERT
PAINTER, PHOTOGRAPHER
b Sidney, NY, Mar 27, 39. *Study:* Studied photog with Minor White, 61-64; also painting restoration with Robert Scott Wiles, Corcoran Gallery of Art, 71-74. *Work:* Mus Modern Art, NY; Phillips Collection, Corcoran Gallery Art. *Comn:* Sullivan & Cromwell, Washington, DC, 89. *Exhib:* One-person shows, Corcoran Gallery, 69, Phillips Collection, Washington, DC, 79 & Cheekwood Fine Arts Ctr, Nashville, 82; retrospective, Southern Alleghenies Mus Art, Loretto, Pa, 94. *Pos:* Visual arts adv panel, Pa Coun on the Arts, 89-91. *Awards:* Belin Arts Scholar, 88. *Mem:* Cosmos Club, Wash, DC. *Media:* Oil. *Mailing Add:* Main St PO Box 21 Union Dale PA 18470

STARK, RON
PAINTER, PHOTOGRAPHER
b Sidney, NY, June 27, 44. *Study:* Univ Denver, Colo; NY State Univ, Oneonta, BA, 68; Int Inst Educ(Fulbright-Hayes Found fel), 74. *Work:* Baltimore Mus, Md; Smithsonian Inst, Phillips Collection, Corcoran Gallery Art, Washington; Bibliot Nat, Paris; Mus Photog, Bievres, France; Metrop Mus Art Libr, NY. *Comn:* Two portraits, comn by Leanne Rees, Bethesda, Md, 78; two portraits & painting, comn by J Forstmann, McLean, Va, 79; landscape painting, comn by Merceile Hayes, Mendocino, Calif, 82; two portraits, comn by Peter Palmer, Jacksonville, Fla, 87; landscape painting, comn by Steve Lawrence, Wilkes Barre, Pa, 88. *Exhib:* One-man shows, Phillips Collection, Washington, 73, San Francisco Mus Art, 74, Mus Art, Zurich, 76, Va Mus Art, Richmond, 80, Corcoran Gallery Art, Washington, 81; Artists of America, Pompidou Ctr, Paris, 77; Harmon Gallery, Sarasota, Fla, 81; one-man retrospective, Mus Photog, Bievres, France, 96; Rebis Galleries, Denver, 96-97; Summit of 8 Exhibition 97, 17 one man and group ehxibs; Santa Fe, NMex Klebau Gallery, Chambrelain-Stark, Canyon Road Fine Art Studio, Gerald Peters Gallery, Shidoni & St Johns Col, 96-2005; Ghost Ranch & Smithsonian Traveling Exhib, 2006; Albuquerque NMex Mus, Biennial. *Pos:* Master printer, Reginald Marsh Photog, NY, 74; guest cur, Edward S Curtis Exhib, Corcoran Gallery Art, Washington, 76; consult, Gallerie Die Brucke, Vienna, Austria & Nuance Gallery, Tampa, Fla. *Teaching:* Lectr art & photog, Smithsonian Inst, Washington, DC, 69-78. *Awards:* Va Mus Grant, 74. *Bibliog:* Werner Marz (auth), Collectable Photographers, pvt publ, Vienna, Austria, 74; Alan Porter (auth), Ron Stark - nudes, Camera Mag, 75; Mark Power (auth), Washington photographers, Washingtonian Mag, 75; article, eight page featured article, Int Pastel Artist Mag, 2001. *Media:* Pastel, Landscape; Large Format Photography. *Publ:* Auth, Delicacies, William & Morrow, NY, 78; Logotypes, 94, 2nd ed, 95. *Mailing Add:* PO Box 31252 Santa Fe NM 87594

STARKWEATHER-NELSON, CYNTHIA LOUISE
PAINTER
b Moline, Ill, July 29, 50. *Study:* Northern Ill Univ, BFA, 72; Univ Minn, Minneapolis, MFA, 76. *Work:* Gen Mills, NY; Bank Am, San Francisco; Prudential Insurance Co, Northwestern Life Insurance, Faegre & Benson Law Firm, Minneapolis; Champion Paper Co, Washington, DC. *Comn:* WCCO-TV, Minneapolis.

Exhib: One-woman show, Am Gallery, Bern, Switz, 81; Drawing, Minneapolis Inst Arts, 81; Works on Paper, Davis-McClain Gallery, St Louis, 82; Of, On, Or About Paper, USA Today, Arlington, Va, 82; New Am Paperworks, US & Far East, 82-84; and others. *Pos:* Printer, Vermillion Ed Ltd, Minneapolis, 76-79. *Teaching:* Instr drawing, St Thomas Acad, 95-97. *Awards:* Minn State Arts Bd Grants, 78 & 80. *Bibliog:* Mary A Martin (auth), Landscape portraiture, Twin Cities Mag, 80. *Dealer:* Peter M David Gallery 430 Oak Grove Minneapolis MN. *Mailing Add:* 666 Apache Ln Mendota Heights MN 55120

STARR, SYDNEY
LIBRARIAN, EDUCATOR
b Grand Rapids, Mich, Nov 12, 39. *Study:* Wellesley Col, BA(art hist), 61; Simmons Col, MS(libr sci), 64; Rutgers Univ, PhD(libr & info sci), SLA Plenum Scholar, 83. *Pos:* Fine arts librn, Boston Pub Libr, Mass, 62-66. *Teaching:* Prof art & archit dept, Pratt Inst Libr, Brooklyn, NY, 66-91, lectr art info & picture resources, 68-80 & info resource for designers, 97, asst dean libr, 91-94, chmn, Libr Fac, 94-98, acting dean librs, 98-99, chmn libr fac, 99-. *Mem:* Special Libr Asn (pres, NY chap, 73-74); Art Librn Soc NAm; Art Librn Soc NY (chmn, 77); NY Libr Club (pres, 95-96); Am Libr Asn. *Res:* Methods in art and architecture research. *Interests:* Modern art, architecture and American art. *Publ:* Auth, American Painting: An Information Guide, 74 & ed, Art and Architecture Information Guide Series, 74-80, Detroit, 14 vols; Contemporary Art Documentation, Scarecrow Press, 86. *Mailing Add:* Pratt Inst Libr Brooklyn NY 11205

STASACK, EDWARD ARMEN
PAINTER, PRINTMAKER
b Chicago, Ill, Oct 1, 29. *Study:* Univ Ill, BFA 55' with High Honors, MFA, 56. *Work:* Libr Cong, Washington, DC; Honolulu Acad Arts; Mus Mod Art, NY; Metrop Mus Art, NY; Art Inst Chicago. *Comn:* Precast concrete murals, City Honolulu, Fort St Mall, 68 & Honolulu Community Col, 72; Captain Cook Series (print portfolio), Hawaii State Found Cult & Arts; outdoor sculpture & wall sculpture, Hawaii State Intake Serv Ctr, Honolulu. *Exhib:* One-man show, Honolulu Acad Arts, Hawaii, 76-78; Amfac Exhib Rm, Honolulu, 77; Ryan Gallery, Kailua, Hawaii, 81; Honolulu Acad Arts, 88; Volcano Art Ctr, 98. *Pos:* President & Founder, Rock Art Asn Hawaii, 88-90; prin investigator Rock Art of Hawaii, Volcanos Nat Park. *Teaching:* Prof art, Univ Hawaii, 69-88, chmn dept, 69-72; emer prof, 88. *Awards:* Rockefeller Found Fel, 59; Award of Last Days of Capt Cook, Hawaii State and US Bicentennial Comm Grant, 76; Hawaii Community Found Grant, 2000. *Bibliog:* George Tahara (dir), Drawing-Painting-Stasack (film), 67; Neogy & Haar (auth), Artists of Hawaii, 74. *Mem:* Soc Am Graphic Artists; Am Rock Art Research Asn; Sharlot Hall Mus Asn; Soc Hawaiian Archeol; Austalian Rock Art Asn. *Media:* Acrylic, Oil; Collagraph, Printmaking. *Res:* Recording reports on 20 rock art sites on Hawaii Island. *Publ:* reviews, Honolulu Star-Bull, 68 & 74; coauth, Hawaiian petroglyphs, Bishop Mus, 70; Petroglyphs of Kahooawe, Hawaii, 93; Rock Art of Hawaii Volcanoes Nat Park, 95-2000; coauth, Spirit of Place, Easter Island Found, 99. *Dealer:* Volcano Art Ctr. *Mailing Add:* 1623 Morning Stone Dr Prescott AZ 86305-1102

STATMAN, JAN B
PAINTER, SCULPTOR
b New York, NY. *Study:* Hunter Col, with William Baziotes, Bernard Klonis & Richard Lippold, AB. *Work:* Mus Mod Art Alto Aragon, Huesca, Spain; Civic Mus Contemp Art, Sasso Ferrato, Italy; Longview Mus & Arts Ctr, Tex. *Exhib:* Solo exhibs, McAllen Int Mus, Tex, 85, Wichita Falls Art Asn, Tex, 90, Longview Art Mus, 94; Milam Gallery, Dallas, Tex, 95, Marshall Visual Arts Ctr, Marshall, Tex, 2000, Art Gallery 100, Tex, 2005; Barnwell Art Ctr, Shreveport, La, 2002. *Pos:* Auth, Art Notes (weekly column), Longview News, 65-70, Artists World (weekly column), Gtr Longview Post, 70-77 & Final Word (weekly column), Dallas Morning News, 81-82. *Teaching:* Instr painting, Longview Mus & Arts Ctr, Tex, 72- & Kilgore Col, 82-84; artist-in-residence, Tex Comn Arts, State of Tex, 85; instr Marshall Visual Art Ctr, Marshall, Tex, 1999-. *Awards:* First Prize Painting, 33rd Ann Cedar City Nat Art Exhib, Utah, 73; Jr League Purchase Award, 25th Ann Exhib, Longview Mus & Arts Ctr, 83; Second Prize Painting, 19th Ann Juried Competition, Masur Mus Art, Monroe, La, 92; and others. *Bibliog:* Ruth Winegarten (auth), A New York Yankee in Longview Texas, Equal Times, Dallas, Tex, 76; Donna Berliner (auth), Jan B Statman, Art Voices-South, 12/78. *Mem:* Nat Asn Women Artists NY. *Media:* Acrylic, Watercolor. *Publ:* The Battered Woman's Survival Guide, Taylor Publ Co, Dallas, Tex, 90; co-auth, Living With Environmental Illness, Taylor Publ Co, Dallas, 98; Raisins & Almonds - and Texas Oil, Eakin Press, 2003 & 2004. *Dealer:* Art Gallery 100 100 W Tyler St Longview TX 75601. *Mailing Add:* 461 Country Pl Longview TX 75605-9707

STAUDINGER, BERNICE MARIE
CERAMIST, SCULPTOR
b Paterson, NJ, Apr 22, 54. *Study:* Moore Col Art, BA, 76. *Comn:* Tile murals (3 ceramic), Merck Chemical, Edison, NJ, 92; tile murals (2), Conn Med Ctr, Hartford, 93. *Exhib:* Artist as Outsider Exhib, Newark Mus, NJ, 92; La Femme Exhib, William C William Ctr Arts, NJ, 92; Lotsa Clay III, The Clay Studio, Philadelphia, 92; Sommerfest Exhib, Arts Ctr NJ, Demerest, 92; CAA 1993 Tri-State Exhib, Ridgewood Art Ctr, NJ, 93; and others. *Pos:* Judge sculpture, North Jersey Student Craftman, 91 & 92. *Awards:* First Place Sculpture, Northern NJ Art Exhib, 90, 91 & 92. *Mem:* Salute to Women in Arts (pres, 92-94); Nat Asn Women Artists; Women in Arts Networking Internationally, London; Allied Artists Am Inc; Federated Art Asn NJ. *Media:* Ceramics. *Publ:* Contribr, Garden State Home & Garden - Gallery, Robin Pearson, 12/90; Ceramics Monthly - Up Front, 9/91; Ceramics Monthly - Up Front, Tile Nat, 9/91; Art Speak NY - Art in NJ is cosmopolitan, 4/92. *Dealer:* Nathans Gallery West Paterson NJ

STAVANS, ISAAC
PAINTER
b Tampico, Mex, Aug 25, 31. *Study:* Mexico City Col, BA, 52; Brooklyn Col, MA, 53; apprentice to Arnold Belkin, 56-60. *Work:* Pedagogical Mus, Mex Inst Cult Relations, Mexico City; Centro Asturiano de Mexico. *Exhib:* Solo exhibs, Recent Works, Misrachi Gallery, Mex City, 79, Univ Ariz, 81, Mus Art & Hist, Ciudad Juarez, Mex, 83, Lourdes Chumacero Gallery, Estocolmo, Mex, 86, Centro Asturiano, 2/90 & Fragments, Gallery Torre del Reloj, 91, Centro Asturiano, 97 & Lourdes Chumacero Gallery, Mex, 99. *Teaching:* Instr painting, CDI Art Sch, 65-74, Hispanic-Mex Univ, 65-74 & privately, 74-. *Awards:* New Values Contest, Gallery CDI, 63; Artist of Yr, Mexico This Month Mag, 70. *Bibliog:* Alfonso de Neuvillate (auth), Stavans: Reminiscences and evolations, Novedades Newspaper, 2/5/76; Berta Taracena (auth), Art: Recent shows, Tiempo Mag, 7/19/76; Bryan Johnstone (auth), Stavans inner landscapes, Ariz Daily Wildcat Newspaper, 1/23/81; Alfonso de Neuvillate (auth), Stavans: An opalescent beauty, Novedades Newspaper, 4/4/86. *Mem:* Mex Soc Visual Artists. *Media:* Oil, Mixed Techniques. *Dealer:* Misrachi Gallery Genova No 20 Mexico 6 DF Mex 06600; Lourdes Chumacero Gallery Estocolmo 34 Mexico 6 DF 06600. *Mailing Add:* Bosque Minas 55B Apt 1104 Bosques Herradura Mexico 53920 Mexico

STAVEN, LELAND CARROLL
PAINTER
b Milwaukee, Wis, Dec 17, 33. *Study:* Univ Wis-Milwaukee, BFA, 56; Layton Sch Art, 57; Calif Col Arts & Crafts, MFA, 60; Ill Inst Technol, 63. *Work:* Univ Ga Art Mus; Ga Tech Univ Art Gallery; S DeKalb Col; LaGrange Col; State Mutual Insurance Co; and others. *Exhib:* 18th Southeastern Ann Exhib, Atlanta, Ga, 63; Contemp Southern Art Exhib, 64; 1st S Cent Exhib, Nashville, Tenn, 66; 1st Ann Greater Birmingham Arts Alliance Exhib, Ala, 75; 2nd Ann Nat Dogwood Festival Art Show, Atlanta, 75; Georgia Artists Show, 86; Carrollton Regional Exhibition, III, 86. *Pos:* Vchmn, Ga Comn Arts, Atlanta, 67-72. *Teaching:* Chmn dept painting, drawing & printmaking, Berry Col, 60-68 & Mercer Univ Atlanta, 68-69; assoc prof painting, drawing & printmaking & cur, Dalton Galleries, Agnes Scott Col, 70-89; retired. *Awards:* Purchase Awards, Asn Ga Artists, 61 & Fourth Ann Callaway Gardens Art Exhib, 67; Achievement Award, Appalachian Corridors: Exhib I, 68. *Mem:* Southeastern Col Art Conf; Southern Graphics Coun; Georgia Poetry Soc. *Media:* Acrylic. *Interests:* Profl Jazz Musician/trumpet. *Collection:* Ga State Art Collection. *Publ:* Auth, poetry in: Motive, Discourse & Odessa Poetry Rev; Reach of Song, 86-2002, 2005-2006, Midwest Poetry Rev, 88-98. *Mailing Add:* 31 View Dr Rome GA 30161-8911

STAVITSKY, GAIL BETH
CURATOR, WRITER
b Cleveland, Ohio, 1954. *Study:* Univ Mich, Ann Arbor, AB, 76; Inst Fine Arts, NY Univ, MA(cert curatorial studies), 78, PhD, 90. *Collection Arranged:* Precisionism in America 1915-1941: Reordering Reality (auth, catalog), Montclair Art Mus, NJ & other venues, 94-; The Montclair Art Colony: Past and Present, 97; Steve Wheeler: The Oracle Visiting the Twentieth Century (auth, catalog), 97-98; Waxing Poetic: Encaustic Art in America, (auth, catalog), Montclair Art Mus, 99; Paris 1900: The American School, The Universal Exposition (project dir, catalog contribr), 1999-2000; Will Barnet: A Timeless World (curator, auth, catalog), 2000-01; Conversion to Modernism: The Early Works of Man Ray (co-cur, contbr catalog); A Translation in Paris, 1918-39: Albert Gallantirand The Paris-NY Connection (auth, essay); Univ Calif, Press and Musee D'arr Am Giverny, 2003; The Unseen Cindy Sherman: Early Tranformations, Montclair Art Mus, 2004; Roy Lichenstein: American Indian Ecnounters (co-auth, catalog), Montclair Art Mus, 2005. *Pos:* Supervisor docent progs, Carnegie Mus Art, Pittsburgh, Pa, 79-80, asst cur fine arts, 81-83; lectr, Mus Mod Art, 83-; contractual lectr, Metrop Mus Art, 84-; art critic, Arts, 85-87; independent cur & scholar, 90-94; cur collections & exhibs, Montclair Art Mus, NJ, 94, chief cur, 98-. *Awards:* Chester Dale Fel Twentieth Century Art, Metrop Mus Art, 87-88; Andrew W Mellon Fel Twentieth Century Art, Metrop Mus Art, 88-89. *Mem:* Col Arts Asn; Am Asn Mus. *Res:* American modernism; private and public patronage of modern art; A E Gallatin; American abstract artists. *Publ:* auth, Waxing Poetic: Encaustic Art in America, 99; auth, Will Barnet: A Timeless World, 2000; auth, essay on Francis Criss in the 1930s: A Rare Synthesis of Realism and Abstraction, Corcoran Gallery of Art, 2001; co-auth, Montclair Art Mus Selected Works, 2002; auth, The Unseen Andy Shermans Early Transformations, 2004; auth, The Unseen Any Shermans Early Transformations, 2004. *Mailing Add:* 23 Macopin Rd Upper Montclair NJ 07043

STEADMAN, DAVID WILTON
MUSEUM DIRECTOR
b Honolulu, Hawaii, Oct 24, 36. *Study:* Harvard Col, BA(magna cum laude), 60; Harvard Univ, MAT, 61; Univ Calif, Berkeley, MA(art hist), 66; Princeton Univ, PhD, 74. *Collection Arranged:* P P Rubens before 1620 (with catalog), Princeton Art Mus, 71; Selections from the Norton Simon, Inc Mus Art (with catalog), 73; Graphic Art of Francisco Goya (with catalog), Galleries of Claremont Cols, 75, 18th Century Drawing from California Collections (with catalog), 76 & Works on Paper 1900-1960 from Southern Calif Collections (with catalog), 77. *Pos:* Lectr, Frick Collection, New York, 70-71; asst dir, Art Mus, Princeton Univ, 71-72, actg dir, 72-73, assoc dir, 73; dir, Galleries of Claremont Cols, 74-80; res cur, Norton Simon Mus, Pasadena, Calif, 77-80; dir, Chrysler Mus, Norfolk, Va, 80-89; dir, Toledo Mus Art, 89-. *Teaching:* Asst prof 17th & 18th centuries art, Pomona Col, 74-78, assoc prof, 78-80. *Awards:* Nat Defense Educ Act fel, 66-69; Chester Dale Fel, Nat Gallery Art, 69-70. *Mem:* Am Asn Mus Dirs; Col Art Asn; Art Mus Asn (trustee). *Res:* 17th and 18th century drawings. *Publ:* Auth, Abraham van Dipenbeeck, UMI Res Press, 82; coauth, A Tricentennial Celebration: Norfolk 1682-1982, 82. *Mailing Add:* Toledo Mus Art PO Box 1013 Toledo OH 43697

STEARNS, ROBERT
CURATOR, ADMINISTRATOR
b Los Angeles, Calif, Aug 28, 47. *Study:* Calif State Univ, San Luis Obispo, 68; Univ Calif, San Diego, BFA, 70. *Collection Arranged:* Robert Wilson: Knee Plays for the Civil Wars, 85 & Trisha Brown & Nancy Graves: Lateral Pass, 86, Tokyo Arts Festival; Art in Europe and America: The 1950s and 1960s, Art in Europe and America: The 1960s and 1970s, 90, New Works for New Spaces: Into the 90s, Wexner Ctr for the Arts, 91; Labyrinth of the Spirit: Robert Smithson, Terry Fox, Bill Viola, Andres Serrano (catalog), Hammond Gallery, 94; Personal Stories: A History of the Universe, Jennifer Bartlett, Ilya Kabakov, Yasumasa Morimura; Photography & Beyond in Japan: Space Time & Memory (catalog), Hara Mus & Abrams, 95; In Person: Ourselves, Friends & Others, Hammond Gallery & Ohio Arts Coun, 95; En Las Calles: Artists in Mexico City, Hammond Gallery, 96; Mexico Ahora: Punto de Partida (auth catalog), Ohio Arts Coun & Inst Fine Arts, Mexico City, 97; Illusions of Eden, Visions of the Am Heartland, Columbus Mus of Art, 2000; Aspirations: Toward a Future in the Middle East, Ohio Arts Coun, 2001. *Pos:* Asst dir, Paula Cooper Gallery, NY, 70-72; dir, Kitchen Ctr for Video & Music, NY, 72-78; bd dir, Haleakala Inc, Kitchen Ctr Video & Mus, 73-96, Minn Independent Choreographers Alliance, 83-88, Wexner Ctr Found, 90-93 & Trisha Brown Dance Co, 90-93; founding dir & pres, Artists Television Network, NY, 76-77; dir, Contemp Arts Ctr, Cincinnati, 78-82, Wexner Ctr for the Arts, Ohio State Univ, Columbus, 88-93 & Stearns & Assocs Contemp Exhibs Servs, 92-; dir performing arts, Walker Art Ctr, Minneapolis, 82-88; sr prog dir, Arts Midwest, Minneapolis, 97-. *Teaching:* Lectr, performance art & alternative media, var US cols & univs; assoc dean & adj asst prof, Dept Art, Col Arts, Ohio State Univ, 88-92. *Awards:* Rank of Chevalier, Order of Arts and Letters, the French Cult Ministry, 88. *Mem:* Minn Independent Choreographers Alliance; Wexner Ctr Found; Trisha Brown Dance Co; Asn Art Mus (dir, 90-93); Am Asn Mus (dir). *Publ:* Contribr, Video Art: An Anthology, Harcourt Brace, 76; Robert Wilson: From Theater of Images, Contemp Arts Ctr & Harper & Row, 82; auth, The Wexner Center for the Visual Arts: The Ohio State University (essay), Rizzoli Int, 89; exec ed & forward, Breakthroughs: Avant Garde Artists in Europe and America: 1950-1990, Rizzoli Int, 91; Robert Wilson: Scenografie e Installazione, Octavo, Florence, Rizzoli, New York, 97; Illusions of Eden, Arts Midwest, Minneapolis, 00; The View From Here, Arts Midwest, 02. *Mailing Add:* Art Midwest/Columbus 2761 Kensington Pl E Columbus OH 43202

STEARNS, THOMAS ROBERT
SCULPTOR, EDUCATOR
b Oklahoma City, Okla, Sept 4, 36. *Study:* Memphis Acad Art, Tenn, 55-57; Cranbrook Acad Art, 57-60; Acad Belli Arti, Venice, Italy, 60-61. *Work:* Minn Mus Art, St Paul; Philadelphia Mus Art; Mus Art, Iowa City, Iowa; Ringling Mus, Sarasota, Fla; Victoria & Albert Mus, London. *Comn:* Sculpture, J Huston Collection, Gaughwell, Ireland, 61-62. *Exhib:* Venice Biennale, Venice, Italy, 62; Glass: Czechoslovakia & Italy, Mus Contemp Crafts, NY, 64; Am Oil Painting & Sculpture, Pa Acad Fine Arts Mus, 66; Johnson Collection, Objects, Smithsonian Inst, Washington, 69; Drawing USA, Minn Mus, St Paul, 71; Pacemakers and Trendsetters, Detroit Inst Art, Mich, 73; Venini Retrospective Renwick, Nat Mus Am Art, Washington, 81. *Pos:* Guest research designer, Venini Glass, Venice, Italy, 60-62. *Teaching:* Assoc prof sculpture, Philadelphia Col Art, 70-. *Awards:* Fulbright Travel Grant, 60; Italian Govt Award Fel, 60-61; John Simon Guggenheim Fel, 65-66; Nat Inst Arts & Letters Grant, 65-66. *Bibliog:* Domas (auth), Thomas Stearns per Venini, Domasmagazine, Italy, 62; New York Commentary, Thomas Stearns, Willard Gallery, Studio Int, 64. *Media:* Mixed, Charcoal. *Mailing Add:* 2121 Walnut St Philadelphia PA 19103

STEBBINS, THEODORE ELLIS, JR
HISTORIAN, ADMINISTRATOR
b New York, NY, Aug 11, 38. *Study:* Yale Univ, BA, 60; Harvard Univ Law Sch, JD, 64, Harvard Univ, PhD, 71. *Collection Arranged:* Luminous Landscape, Fogg Art Mus, 66; Martin Johnson Heade, Whitney Mus Am Art, 69; New Haven Scene, New Haven Colony Hist Soc, 70; Richard Brown Baker Collects, Yale Univ, 75; Am Landscapes at the Wadsworth Atheneum, Hudson River Sch, 76; Am Master Drawings, Whitney Mus, 76. *Pos:* Assoc cur, Garvan Collections, Yale Univ Art Gallery, 68-77, cur Am painting & sculpture, 71-77; cur Am painting, Mus Fine Arts, Boston, Mass, 77-. *Teaching:* Instr hist art, Smith Col, 67; asst prof hist art, Yale Univ, 69-75, Morse fel, 72, assoc prof, 75-77; vis prof, Boston Univ, 78, prof art hist, 82-. *Awards:* Chester Dale Fel, Nat Gallery Art, Washington, 66; Joseph Coolidge Shaw Soc Medal, Boston Univ, 85; Minda Da Gunzberg Prize, 93; and others. *Mem:* Col Art Asn Am; Am Fedn Arts. *Res:* American landscape painting of the nineteenth century; history of American drawings and watercolors. *Collection:* Nineteenth and twentieth century American art. *Publ:* Coauth, Boston Collects: Contemporary Painting and Sculpture, 86 & Charles Sheeler: The Photographs, Mus Fine Arts, Boston, 88; Introductory Essay in a Book by Anselm Kiefer, George Braziller Inc & Mus Fine Arts, Boston, 88; auth, Weston's Westons: Portraits and Nudes, 89; The Lure of Italy: American Artists and the Italian Experience, 1760-1914, 92; Weston's Westons: California & the West, 94; coauth, John J Audubon: The Watercolors for The Birds of America, 94; John Singleton Copley in America, 95; The Lure of Italy: American Artists and the Halian Experience, 1760-1914, 92; Weston's Westons: California & the West, 94; coauth, John J Audubon: The Watercolors for The Birds of America, 94

STECHER, PAULINE
PAINTER, INSTRUCTOR
b Brooklyn, NY. *Study:* Studied painting with Paul Puzinas, 61-63; Self taught. *Comn:* oil paintings, Caesarea Gallery, Boca Raton, Fla. *Exhib:* Am Artists Prof League Grand Nat, Salmagundi Club, NY, 91, 94, 97, 99, 2001, 2003; Hudson Valley Art Asn Ann, Westchester Co Ctr, NY, 91, Newington/Cropsey Found, Hastings-On-Hudson, NY, 98, 2002, 2004 & Salmagundi Club, NY, 2000; Art League Nassau Co Open Show, Nassau Co Mus Art, Roslyn, NY, 93. *Teaching:* instr oil painting, various adult educ ctrs in New York, 60-85. *Awards:* Isabel Steinschneider Mem Award, Hudson Valley Art Asn, 91; John R Grabach Mem Award, Am Artists Prof League, 94; Dumond Meml Award, Hudson Valley Art Asn, 98; Georgie Read Barton Mem Award, 2002; Jane Peterson Still Life Mem Award, 2004; other national awards. *Mem:* Am Artists Prof League Inc (bd dir, 85-); Hudson Valley Art Asn Inc; Art League of Nassau Co Inc; Nat Art League. *Media:* Oil. *Publ:* auth, Teacher Feature, Palette Talk, 83, I'm Hooked on Oil Painting, 87 & The Alluring but Elusive Aspects of Oil Painting, 90; contrib, The Literary Cyclist, Breakaway Books, 97. *Dealer:* Caesarea Gallery Gallery Center 608 Banyan Trail Boca Raton Fl 33431; Gallery Matisse 1170 Third St S Suite C-106 Naples Fl 34102. *Mailing Add:* 80-30 250th St Bellerose NY 11426

STECHER, RUTH (RUSTY) L
PAINTER, INSTRUCTOR
b Washington, DC. Sept 14, 24. *Study:* studied with Harold Landaker - 1950; Art Students League with Daniel Greene, 1979, with David Leffel, 1981-83. *Pos:* class monitor to David Leffel, Art Students League, New York City, 1981-83. *Teaching:* instr oil & pastel, Union Square Studio, New York City, 1984-94; instr workshops NY, Pa, Ore, NMex. *Awards:* Philip Isenberg Award, Salmagundi Club, pastel & oil pastel 1991 & pastel & oil acrylic 1991; Martin Harmon Mem, Salmagundi, 1991; Alice B. McReynolds Award, Salmagundi Club, 1990. *Mem:* life mem Salmagundi Club (vpres & art comt); Pastel Soc of Am (dir & co-chr); Nat Asn of Women Artists; Hudson Valley Art Asn. *Media:* Oil, Pastel. *Mailing Add:* 1582 Glengang Dr Palm Harbor FL 34684

STECKEL, ANITA
COLLAGE ARTIST, PAINTER
b New York, NY. *Study:* Cooper Union; Art Students League, with Edwin Dickenson; Alfred Univ. *Exhib:* Whitney Mus, 70, Portland Mus, 74, Bronx Mus, 76 & 77; Aldrich Mus, 74; one-person exhibs, Art in Gen, NY, 84, Rutgers, NJ, 85, Gallery 410, NY, 88, Kingsboro Col, NY, 88, Beacon St Gallery, Chicago, 89 & 90, Kenkeleba Gallery, 91 & Ann Harper, 94; Parsons, 94; Bryn Mawr, 94; Rutgers, 96; Art Students League, 96; Westbeth Women at Aud Art, 97; And I quote, Mary Delahoyt Gallery, 98; Radford Mus, Va, 99; Attleboro Mus, Mass, 2000; Mitchell Algus Gallery, NY, 2000-2001, 2004 & 2006. *Teaching:* Lectr, Sarah Lawrence Col, NY Univ, Rutgers, New Rochelle Col, Univ RI & Queens Col; instr, Parson Sch Design, SVA, 79- & Art Students League, 85-. *Awards:* Nat Endowment Arts Grant Painting, 83; Pollack-Krasner Award, 2006. *Bibliog:* Ntozake Shange (auth), Ridin the Moon in Texas, St Martins Press, 87; Eileen O'Neill (auth), IKON #7, 87; Lucy R Lippard (auth), The Pink Glass Swan, New Press, 95. *Media:* Collage, Oil, Drawing. *Publ:* Contribr, Feminist Art Criticism, an Anthology, Arlene Raven (ed), Univ Microfilms Inc Press; New Feminist Criticism, Arlene Raven (ed), Harper-Collins, 94; Womens Almanac, Louie Bermkow, 98; Women Artists Self Portraits, 2000; "Not for Sale", Laura Cottingham, 99; Most Excellent Female Artists, 2003; Aldrich Museum, 2005. *Dealer:* Mitchell Algus Gallery, NY

STECYK, CRAIG R
SCULPTOR, CURATOR
b Ocean Park, Calif. *Study:* Calif State Univ, Los Angeles, MFA, 86. *Work:* New Zealand Nat Gallery, Wellington; Oakland Mus, Calif; Calif Mus Photog, Riverside; Smithsonian Inst, Washington, DC; Laguna Art Mus, Laguna Beach, Calif. *Exhib:* Comstock Column, Sierra Nev Mus Art, Reno, 87; Papa Moana, Laguna Art Mus, Laguna Beach, Calif, 89, Emerald Avenue Modesto, Oakland Mus Art, Calif, 97; Ocean View, Calif Mus Photog, Riverside, 97; solo exhib, Ibero-Cuban Inst Photog, Havana, Cuba, 98. *Collection Arranged:* Kustom Kulture, Laguna Art Mus, Laguna Beach, Calif & Md Inst Contemp Art, 94; retrospective, RW Simmons, Int Surfing Mus, Huntington Beach, Calif, 94; Don James, Laguna Art Mus, Laguna Beach, Calif, 97. *Media:* Sculpture. *Publ:* Auth, Kustom Kulture, Last Gasp, 93; San Onofre to Point Dume 1936-1942, Adler Bks, 96; Malicious Resplendence, Fanta Bks, 97; Dysfunctional, Moway Press, 98. *Dealer:* Copro Nason Gallery 3606 Veteran Ave Los Angeles CA 90034. *Mailing Add:* 22818 Ave San Luis Woodland Hills CA 91364

STECZYNSKI, JOHN MYRON
DRAFTSMAN, EDUCATOR
b Chicago, Ill, June 22, 36. *Study:* Art Inst Chicago; Craft Ctr, Worcester, Mass; Univ Notre Dame, BFA(magna cum laude), 58; Yale Univ, MFA, 61; Acad Fine Arts, Warsaw; and with Umberto Romano. *Work:* McMullen Mus Art, Boston Col; Marriott Corp; Hilton Corp; The Arts Visionary Col. *Comn:* Dossals for Easter, 71, Christmas, 71, Lent, 73, Pentecost, 75, & Easter, 93-94, Univ Lutheran Church, Cambridge, Mass; drawing, Hilton Hotel, West Palm Beach, Fla, 84; drawings, Marriott Corp, 86; Lithographs, NY Plaza Hotel, 94; Drawing, Eventide Arts Festival, Dennis, Mass, 97; and others. *Exhib:* Newport Art Mus, RI, 89; Kunsthalle Exnergasse, Vienna, 89; Greek Inst, Cambridge, Mass, 92; Fuller Art Mus, Brockton, Mass, 94; Fowler Gallery, Providencetown, Mass, 98; and others; Univ Scranton Art Gallery, 00; Creighton Univ, Liet Gallery, 99. *Teaching:* Instr studio art, Worcester Art Mus Sch, 61-64; instr art hist, Boston Mus Fine Arts Sch, 64-67 & Tufts in Italy, Naples, 67-68; asst prof & chmn dept studio art & art history, Newton Col Sacred Heart, 68-75; asst prof studio art, Boston Col, 75-79, asst chmn dept fine arts, 77-81, assoc prof, 79-88, acting chmn, 81-82, assoc chmn, 85-88, prof, 88-, chmn, 93-96. *Awards:* Woodrow Wilson Found Fel, 58; Mellon Found Grant, 82; Finalist Drawing, Artists Found, 87; and others. *Bibliog:* Pierrina Rohde (auth), John Steczynski: Artists Yes/Beatnick No, WORC Telegram, 4/26/64; Christine Temin (auth), John Steczynski: a figure outside the gallery scene, Boston Globe, 10/24/85; Christine Iemin (auth), The Art of Resurrection: IWO Local Artists Find New Life in Easter Themes, Boston Sunday

Globe, 4/7/96. *Media:* Pen & Ink, Acrylic. *Publ:* Auth, Visual thinking in education, In: Inscape: Studies Presented to Charles F Donovan, SJ, 77; Tradition, Creativity and the Liturgical Artist, Religion Arts, Vol I, No 4, 98; Gay Archetypes: Visual Expression, White Crane J, summer 98; A Study of the Iconographic Program of Blessed Sacrament Church, Church of the Blessed Sacrament, Jamaica Plain: Historic Structure Report: Historic Boston Inc, 89; Pleasure, Sex and Salvation, White Crane Jour, 02; On Envisioning The Book of Revelation, Text, Context and Image, The Plume and The Palette, Essays in Honor of Josephine von Henneberg, 2001. *Dealer:* Ginsburg Hallowell & Assoc Fine Art 125 Newbury St Boston MA 02116; Dragonfly Gallery PO Box 2608 Oak Bluffs Marthas Vineyard MA 02557. *Mailing Add:* 140 Commonwealth Ave Chestnut Hill MA 02167-3809

STEEL, VIRGINIA OBERLIN
GALLERY DIRECTOR, CURATOR
b Pa, Sept 27, 50. *Study:* Carnegie-Mellon Univ; Univ Hartford, BA, 73; Univ Mass-Amherst, MA, 75. *Pos:* Dir, Stedman Art Gallery, Rutgers Univ, Camden, NJ, 76-. *Teaching:* Mus Studies Prog, Rutgers Univ, Camden, NJ, 79-. *Mem:* Am Asn Mus. *Mailing Add:* c/o Stedman Art Gallery Rutgers Univ The State Univ of NJ Camden NJ 08102

STEELE, BENJAMIN CHARLES
PAINTER, EDUCATOR
b Roundup, Mont, Nov 17, 17. *Study:* Cleveland Inst Art, dipl; Kent State Univ, BS; Denver Univ, MA; Univ Ore; Ill State Univ; Mont State Univ. *Work:* Univ Mont; Mont Inst Arts, Permanent Collection; Brown Univ, Providence, RI; Mont State Univ, Billings. *Comn:* Arts of the West (mural), Denver Univ; Indoor and Outdoor Sports (mural), Mont State Univ, Billings; and pvt collections. *Exhib:* Mont Arts & Crafts Exhib, Senate Caucus Room, Wash; Mont Inst Arts Little Festival, 75-; Stillwater Soc Shows; one-man shows, CM Russell Mus & Minneapolis VA Med Ctr, WWII POW Collection, Mont State Univ, Billings, Univ Mont, 86-87, Truman Lib, 92 & US Air Force Acad, 96; Spirit of Modernism, Paris Gibson Ctr, Great Falls, Holter Mus, Helena, 87-88; Stillwater Soc Shows; Ctr for Arts, Scottsdale, Ariz. *Collection Arranged:* WWII Japanese POW Collection, Montana Hist Soc Mus, Ben Steele Wing, Lewistown, Mont. *Teaching:* Art teacher, New London, Ohio High Sch, 51-52; crafts dir, Ft Riley, Kans, 53-54; staff crafts dir, Mil District Wash, 54-56 & Fort MacPherson, Ga, 54-59; prof art & head dept, Mont State Univ, Billings, 59-82, prof emer, 82-. *Awards:* Ben Steele Day, Proc Gov, 77; Distinguished Prof Award, Mont State Univ, 80; Mont Governors Award, Outstanding Achievement Arts, 92. *Bibliog:* Dorothy Larsen (auth), Man of gentle fiber & Nancy Olson (auth), Briefly biographical, Mont Arts Mag; also feature art in Washington Post, Altanta Const, Kansas City Star & many others. *Mem:* Am Defenders Bataan & Corregidor; Stillwater Soc; First United Methodist Church; Golden Kiwanis Club; Am Ex Prisoners of War. *Media:* Oil, Watercolor. *Publ:* Cover designs & illus, A Long March Home, 98, Footprints of Courage, 2002, Silent Tears, 2002 and others; Soldier of Bataan, Prisoner of Hope, Corregipor, Paradise to Hell, Cabanatuan Japanese Death Camp, WC Refused to Die, The Long March Home, Sochow of 4th Marines, Bataan Diary. *Mailing Add:* 2425 Cascade Ave Billings MT 59102

STEELE, LISA
VIDEO ARTIST
b Kansas City, Mo, Sept 22, 47. *Study:* Univ Mo, Kansas City, 65-68; Hon Dr, Ontario Col Art & Design, 2003. *Work:* Art Gallery of Ont, Toronto; The Kitchen, NY; Mus Mod Art, New York City; National Gallery Can, Ottawa; Ctr Georges Pompidou, Paris. *Exhib:* A Response to the Environment, Rutgers Univ Art Gallery, New Brunswick, NJ, 75; Video Int, Aarhus Mus of Art, Denmark, 76; Videotapes, Mus of Mod Art, NY, 77; Southland Video Anthology, Part 4, Long Beach Mus of Art, Calif, 77; Kunsthalle, Basel, Switz, 78; Venice Biennale, 80; Documenta 8, Kassel, Ger, 87; Four hours & thirty-eight minutes, Art Gallery Ontario, Toronto, 89; The Enn, Chisenhale Gallery, London, 2000; Oberhausen Short Film Festival, 2001; Ctr Contemps de Basse, Normandie, France, 2003; Before I Wake., Can Cult Ctr, Paris, 2003. *Pos:* Video coordr, A Space Gallery, Toronto, 72-74, creative dir, 80-. *Teaching:* lectr, Ontario Col Art & Design, 1981-2002; lectr, Univ Toronto, Dept Fine Art, 2002-. *Awards:* Award for Excellence in Video Art, Bell Can, 93; Gov Gerard's Award for Visual & Media Arts, Lifetime Achievement, 2005. *Bibliog:* Eric Cameron (auth), Structural videotape in Canada, In: Video Art, Harcourt, Brace & Jovanovich, 76. *Media:* Videotape. *Publ:* editor, UK/Canadian Video Exchange, 2003-04; auth, Persistence of Vision: Recent videoworks from the UK; guest editor, Felix: A Journal of Media & Culture, 2000. *Dealer:* Vtape 401 Richmond St W Suite 45 Toronto Canada M5V 3A8. *Mailing Add:* 287 Claremont Toronto ON M6J 2N1 Canada

STEEN, CAROL J
PAINTER, SCULPTOR
b Highland Park, Mich, Nov 6, 43. *Study:* Mich State Univ, BA, 65; Cranbrook Acad Art, MFA, 71. *Work:* Printmaking Workshop, NY; Smithsonian Archives Am Art; Am Craft Mus, NY; Detroit Inst Arts; Robert McLaughlin Gallery, Oshawa, Ont; Libr Congress; Univ Waterloo, Ont, Can. *Exhib:* Brody's Gallery, Washington, DC, 88 & Philadelphia Mus Art, 89 & 90; B4A Gallery, NY, 91; C A Wustum Mus, Racine, Wis, 92; Cleveland Inst Art, Ohio, 92; Joel Starkman Gallery, Toronto, Ont, 92; Kouros Gallery, NY, 95; and others; 55 Mercer Gallery, New York City, 81, 82, 85, 87, 89, 93, 95, 97; La Frontera, New York City, 93. *Pos:* co-founder, bd mem, Am Synesthesia Asn, Inc. *Teaching:* Ford Found vis lectr studio art, Univ Mich, 75; asst prof studio art, William Paterson Col, 77-82 & Touro Col, 83-. *Awards:* Grant, Printmaking Workshop, New York, 82; NY Found Arts Fel, 86-87; Materials for the Arts, New York, 87; MacDowell Colony, 80. *Bibliog:* doc films, BBC Horizon, UK, 12/94, CNN, 11/95 & 60 Minutes Australia, 4/98; Brad Lemley (auth), Do You See What They See, Discover Mag, 12/99; Beyond Human Senses (doc film), BBC, 7/11/2000; 6th Sense, 60 Minutes II doc, 02; The Infinite Mind, Nat Pub Radio, 1/12/2005; Short Circuit, Radio Netherlands, 1/12/2003. *Mem:* Col Art Asn, NY. *Media:* Alkyd, Oil; Metal. *Publ:* auth, Visions Shared: A First Hand Look Into Synesthesia and Art, MIT Press, in press; Leonardo, MIT Press, Vol 34, No 3, 203-208, 2001. *Dealer:* Stephen Rosenberg Gallery 115 Wooster NY 10012. *Mailing Add:* 39 Bond St New York NY 10012

STEFAN, ROSS
PAINTER
b Milwaukee, Wis, June 13, 34. *Study:* Primarily self-taught; collab with Dan Muller, Milwaukee, Dale Nichols, Antigua, Guatemala & Frederic Whitaker, La Jolla, Calif. *Work:* Ford Motor Co; Milwaukee Jour; Harmsen's Western Americana, Denver; Gilcrease Inst Am Hist & Art, Tulsa; Amerind Found, Dragoon, Ariz. *Exhib:* Our Western Heritage, Univ Ariz, 62; one-man shows, Rosequist Galleries, Tucson, 70-82 & 83-86; Grand Central Art Galleries, NY, 72; 42nd Ann Ariz Exhib, Rosequist Galleries, 90; Stefan's Southern Eng, Rosequist Galleries, Tucson, Ariz, 93; Paloma Art, Tuscon, Ariz, 98. *Awards:* Artist of the Yr, Tucson Festival Soc Award, 78; Artist Am, Denver, Colo. *Bibliog:* Sen Barry Goldwater (auth), Ross Stefan 1975, Wollheims' Rosequist Galleries; John K Goodman (auth), Ross Stefan: An Impressionistic Painter of the Contemporary Southwest, Northland Press, 77; Jon Stefan (auth), article, Artists of the Rockies, fall 79. *Media:* Oil on Canvas. *Res:* Painters of the Southwest as it is today; since 1948, Southern Arizona, Navajo and Hopi country, the Rio Grande North to Santa Fe and Taos, New Mexico. *Publ:* Articles in Ariz Highways, Reader's Digest, Ford Times, Am Artist, Southwest Art. *Mailing Add:* 10541 N Desert Mirage Way 7643 Girard Ave Tucson AZ 85737

STEFANELLI, JOSEPH JAMES
PAINTER
b Philadelphia, Pa, Mar 20, 21. *Study:* Philadelphia Mus Col Art, 38-40; Pa Acad Fine Arts, 40-41; New Sch Social Res, New York, 49-50; Art Students League, 50-51; Hans Hofmann Sch Painting, New York, 51-52. *Work:* Whitney Mus Am Art; Walker Art Ctr; Norfolk Art Mus; Baltimore Mus; NY Univ; and others. *Comn:* Mural, Brooklyn Bd Educ, 77. *Exhib:* Whitney Mus Am Art; Mus Mod Art, NY; Pa Acad Fine Arts; Walker Art Ctr, Minneapolis; Corcoran Gallery Art; Carnegie Inst Int; Art Inst Chicago; one-man shows, Westbeth Galleries, 71, New Sch Social Res, 72, Ingber Gallery, 84, Armstrong Gallery, 88 & Cyrus Gallery, 89; M 13 Gallery, 91; Olaf Clasen, Ger, 92 & 94; Peter Baumler, Regensburg, Ger, 93; and others. *Teaching:* Instr, Univ Calif, Berkeley, summers 60 & 63; vis critic, Cornell Univ; artist in residence, Princeton Univ, 63-66; vis critic, Univ Ark; instr, Columbia Univ, 66-74; instr, New Sch Social Res, 66-, Wash Univ, St Louis, 89. *Awards:* Am Res Ctr Egypt Fel, 66-67; NY State Coun Arts Award, 71; Adolph & Esther Gottlieb Found, 86, 88; Pollock & Krasner Found, 91. *Mem:* Fel Am Research Ctr Egypt; Nat Acad of Design (academician 1995-). *Dealer:* Olaf Clasen Cologne Ger. *Mailing Add:* 463 West St D1006 New York NY 10014

STEG, JAMES LOUIS
PRINTMAKER, SCULPTOR
b Alexandria, Va. *Study:* Rochester Inst Technol, cert; State Univ Iowa, BFA & MFA. *Work:* Libr Cong, Washington, DC; Smithsonian Nat Collection, Washington, DC; Brooklyn Mus, NY; Mus Mod Art, NY; Fogg Mus, Cambridge, Mass; Metropolitan Mus. *Exhib:* One-man shows, Weyhe Gallery, 45 & Assoc Am Artists, 64, NY; Big Prints USA, State Univ NY Col New Paltz, 68; USIS Cult Ctr, Ankara, Turkey, 75; 30 Yr Retrospective Traveling Exhib, New Orleans Mus Art, 78; Marguerite Oeftreicher Fine Arts, New Orleans, La, 97-; and others; Aldridge- Leatherman, 2005. *Teaching:* Instr drawing & painting, Cornell Univ, 49-51; prof drawing & printing, Tulane Univ La, 51-92. *Awards:* Purchase Prize, Eighth Int Print & Drawing Exhib, Lugano, 64; Purchase Prizes, State Univ NY Col Potsdam Print Exhib, 64-68; Printmaker emeritus, Southern Graphics Art Coun, 90. *Bibliog:* Barry Schwartz (auth), Humanism in Art. *Mem:* Am Color Print Soc. *Media:* Wood. *Publ:* Auth, article, Artists Proof, 66

STEGEMAN, CHARLES
PAINTER, EDUCATOR
b Ede, Neth, June 5, 24: US citizen. *Study:* Acad Beeldende Kunst, The Hague; Acad Royale Beaux Arts, Brussels; Inst Nat Superieur Beaux-Arts, Antwerp. *Work:* Nat Gallery Can, Ont Art Gallery; Vancouver Art Gallery, Art Gallery Gtr Victoria; Univ BC. *Exhib:* Toronto Art Gallery, 61; Winnipeg Biannual, 61; Montreal Mus Fine Arts, 62; Chicago Centennial Exhib, Ill, 63; Stratford Art Festival Exhib, Ont, 70; Vancouver Art & Artists 1931-1983, 83; First Int Invitational, Anniversary Israel, Baltimore, 88. *Pos:* Founding pres, Asn Villard de Honnecourt, Medieval Technol, Sci Art, 84-90. *Teaching:* Prof painting, Art Inst Chicago, 62-69; prof painting & chmn dept fine arts, Haverford Col, 69-. *Awards:* Purchase Award, 76 & Merit Grant, 78, Belg Govt; Humanities Fel, Med Col Pa, 81-83; Fedn Field Res Grant, Calif & Chartres, France, 90. *Bibliog:* Scott Watson (auth), Art in the fifties, Design, Leisure and Painting in the Age of Anxiety, Vancouver Art & Artists, 1931-1983, Vancouver Art Gallery, 83; Marie-Therese Zinner (auth), Charles Stegeman, The Vigil of Spring (exhib catalog essay), Cantor Fitzgerald Gallery, Harverford Col, Pa, 97. *Mem:* Int Ctr Medieval Art, New York, 85-. *Media:* Oil, Acrylic. *Mailing Add:* Fine Arts Dept Haverford Col 370 Lancaster Ave Haverford PA 19041

STEGLICH, DAVID M.
MUSEUM ADMINISTRATOR
b Wis. *Study:* St Olaf Col, BA (math and philosophy), 1989; student in economics and political theory, Trinity Col, Dublin, Ireland, 1990; Yale Univ, JD, 1995. *Pos:* Law clerk for Chief Judge Paul A. Magnuson, US Dist Ct, St Paul, 1995-97; atty, Corp Law Dept, Dorsey & Whitney, Minn, 1997-2000; with McKinsey & Co, Minneapolis, 2000, assoc principal; chief operating officer, Walker Art Ctr, Minneapolis, 2006-. *Mailing Add:* Walker Art Ctr 1750 Hennepin Minneapolis MN 55403

STEGMAN, PATRICIA
PAINTER, PRINTMAKER
b San Antonio, Tex, Nov 27, 29. *Study:* Kansas City Univ, Mo, 48-49; Kansas City Art Inst, Mo, BFA, 52; Art Students League, study with Reginald Marsh, Will Barnet, Vaclav Vytlacil & Morris Kantor, 54-57. *Work:* Paintings (Banners), Kansas City Art Inst, Kansas City, Mo. *Comn:* Paintings (Backdrops for plays, Him & Freud, Circle Repertory Company, NYC, 1974, 1975; Backdrop for play, Confrontation on Atlantic Avenue, Big Apple Theatre Company, Brooklyn, NY, 1975. *Exhib:* Drawings, Atlantic Gallery, NY, 77, 79, 84; Landmark Gallery, NY; Tenth St Days--Retrospective of Art of the 50s, Fourteen Sculptors Gallery, NY, 77; one-artist shows, paintings & drawings, Brata Gallery, NY, 61 & 63 & Gallery 91, Brooklyn, 75 & 76; Atlantic Gallery, NYC, 1988, 1993, 1995, 1997. *Pos:* staff writer, Artists Review Art, New York & Phoenix (newspaper), Brooklyn, 76-80. *Teaching:* Instr painting & drawing, Kansas City Art Inst, 52. *Mem:* Art Students League, NYC; East End Arts Counc, Riverhead, NY. *Media:* Oil, Watercolor; Etching, Lithography. *Dealer:* RVS Fine Art 20 Job's La Southampton NY. *Mailing Add:* 245 Dean St Brooklyn NY 11217

STEIGMAN, MARGOT See Robinson, Margot Steigman

STEIN, CLAIRE A
ADMINISTRATOR
b New York, NY, Sept 19, 23. *Study:* Art Students League; Adelphi Col, BA; sculpture with Robert Cronbach. *Collection Arranged:* Nat Sculpture Soc Ann, 68-86; North Shore Community Art Ctr Exhib, 60s. *Pos:* Bd dir, North Shore Community Art Ctr, 57-62; exec dir, Nat Sculpture Soc, retired. *Mem:* Art Table. *Publ:* Contribr, Nat Sculpture Rev, fall 73, winter 74 & 75 & spring 75; contribr sculpture suppl, Grolier Encyclopedia, 70-73. *Mailing Add:* Six Dorchester Dr Manhasset NY 11030

STEIN, JUDITH ELLEN
HISTORIAN, CURATOR
b New York, NY, June 27, 43. *Study:* Barnard Col, Columbia Univ, BA(art hist), 65; Univ Pa, MA(art hist), 67, PhD(art hist), 81. *Collection Arranged:* Red Grooms: A Retrospective, 1956-1984, (auth, catalog), 85; Betye Saar: Sentimental Sojourn, 87; The Figurative Fifties: New York Figurative Expressionism, (auth catalog), 87; I Tell My Heart: Horace Pippin, (auth catalog), 94. *Pos:* Staff lectr, Philadelphia Mus Art, 66-71; arts reviewer, Art in Am, 74-99 & Nat Pub Radio, Philadelphia, 79-83; coordr, Morris Gallery, Pa Acad Fine Arts, 81-94; asst cur, Pa Acad Fine Arts, 83-85, assoc cur, 85-88, cur, 88-91, adjunct cur, 91-94. *Teaching:* Instr, Tyler Sch Art, Philadelphia, 71-78; Univ PA, 80; Md Inst Col Art, 90-93. *Awards:* Fel Literary Nonfiction, Pew, 94. *Mem:* Col Art Asn (bd mem, 95-96); Int Art Critics Asn (treas, 96, pres, 98); Fabric Workshop. *Publ:* Collaboration, Power of Feminist Art, Abrams, 94; Space & place (Maya Lin), Art in Am, 12/94, The word made image (Hammond & Ashberry), 10/95 & Report on Australia: the Asia Pacific Triennial and the Sydney Biennale, 6/97, Art Am; John Kane(auth), Self-Taught Artists of the 20th Century: An American Anthology, Mus Am Folk Art & Chronicle Bks, 98. *Mailing Add:* 2400 Waverly St Philadelphia PA 19146

STEIN, LEWIS
CONCEPTUAL ARTIST
b New York, NY. *Study:* Mass Inst Technol, 64-66; Univ Calif, Berkeley, 66-68. *Work:* Mus de Stadt, Aachen, Ger; Greenville Mus Art, SC; Ludwig Mus, Cologne, Ger; Yale Univ Art Mus, New Haven, Conn; Univ Art Mus, Berkeley, Calif. *Exhib:* Whitney Biennial, Whitney Mus Am Art, NY, 69. *Bibliog:* Pratt J Archit, 88. *Media:* Photography, Sculpture. *Mailing Add:* 450 Broome St New York NY 10013

STEIN, LUDWIG
PAINTER, EDUCATOR
b Wyoming, Del, Mar 20, 38. *Study:* Kutztown State Col, BFA, 64; Tyler Sch Art, with Steve Green, David Pease & Charles Schmitt, MFA, 69. *Work:* Sheldon Mem Gallery Art, Univ Nebr, Lincoln; Everson Mus Art, Syracuse, NY; Philadelphia Mus Art; Univ Belfast, Ireland; Long Beach Art Found, NJ. *Exhib:* One-man shows, Barbara Gillman, Miami, Fla, 86, Adele M Gallery, Dallas, Tex, 86, John Christian Gallery, NY, 86, Basel Art Fair, Switz, 87, Schoeneck Gallery, Basel, Switz, 90; and many others. *Teaching:* Instr, Wis State Univ, Eau Claire, 69-71; Univ Calif, Northridge, 71-72; prof, Syracuse Univ, NY, 72-. *Awards:* Best Show, Waterloo Regional, Iowa, 71; Jurors Award, Tyler Alumni, 76; Grant, Northern British Arts Coun, 77. *Mem:* Col Art Asn. *Media:* Oil. *Mailing Add:* c/o Barbara Gilman Gallery 939 Lincoln Rd Miami Beach FL 33139

STEIN, ROGER BREED
HISTORIAN, EDUCATOR
b Orange, NJ, Mar 29, 32. *Study:* Harvard Univ, AB, 54, AM, 58, PhD, 60. *Collection Arranged:* Susquehanna: Images of the Settled Landscape (with catalog), Roberson Ctr, Binghamton, NY; Seascape & American Imagination (with catalog), Whitney Mus Am Art; The View & the Vision: Landscape Painting in 19th Century Am (with catalog), Univ Wash; Shaping the Landscape Image 1865-1910: John Douglas Woodward (with catalog), Univ Va Art Mus; Picturing Old New England: Image & Memory (with catalog), Nat Mus Am Art. *Teaching:* Assoc prof & prof, State Univ NY, Binghamton, 70-86; Sr Fulbright lectr, Gt Brit, 76-77; prof art hist, Univ Va, 86-98; professor emeritus, Univ Va. *Awards:* Prize in Humanities, Am Acad Arts & Sci, 60; Guggenheim Fel, 68-69; Smithsonian Fel, Nat Collection Fine Arts, 77-78; Dan Walker Prize, Western Lit Asn, 85; Outstand Publication, Am Hist Print Collectors Soc, 97; Int Ctr Jefferson Studies Fel, 99. *Mem:* Am Studies Asn; Mod Lang Asn; Col Art Asn. *Res:* 17-19th Century American painting and art in its cultural context; Winslow Homer; interpretive strategies in museum exhibitions; regional approaches to American art, literature and culture. *Publ:* Auth, John Ruskin & American Aesthetic Thought, 1840-1900, 67; Copley's Watson and the Shark and Aesthetics in the 1770's, Discoveries and Considerations, State Univ NY Press, 76; Charles Willson Peale's expressive design, Prospects, No 6, 81; Thomas Smith's self-portrait: image/text as artifact, Art J, No 44, 84; Packaging the Great Plains: the role of the visual arts, Great Plains Quart, No 5, winter 85; Artifact as Ideology: The Aesthetic Movement in American Cultural Context, in: Pursuit of Beauty: Americans & the Aesthetic Movement, Metrop Mus Art, NY, 86; Picture & the Text, The Literary World of Winslow Homer, in: Winslow Homer: A Symposium, Nat Gallery Art, 90; In Search of Jacob's Ladder, Colby Quarterly 29, 3/2003. *Mailing Add:* 110 Holly Ct Charlottesville VA 22901

STEIN, RONALD JAY
PAINTER, SCULPTOR
b New York, NY, Sept 15, 30. *Study:* Cooper Union, cert fine art, with Will Barnet; Yale Univ, with Joseph Albers, BFA; Rutgers Univ, MFA. *Work:* Carnegie Inst, Pittsburgh, Pa; Guggenheim Mus, NY; Joseph H Hirshhorn Collection, Washington; Wadsworth Atheneum, Hartford, Conn; Finch Col Mus, NY. *Comn:* Sculpture, Playboy Mag; sculpture, Debeers Ltd, 70; Am Cyanamid; Ford Corp; Special Minister of the Eucharist, Roman Catholic Church, 92. *Exhib:* Art Inst Chicago Int, 60; Art in the Mirror, Mus Mod Art, NY, 70; Bologna & Landi Gallery, E Hampton, NY, 83; Bensen Gallery, Bridgehampton, NY, 88; Benton Gallery, Southampton, NY, 88 & 89; Odeon Gallery Sag, Harbor, NY, 93; group show, Arlene Bujese Gallery, E Hampton, NY, 94, 95, 96, 97 & 98. *Bibliog:* article, New York Newsday, Long Island, NY, 88; article, Country Magazine, Long Island, NY, 96; article, NY Times, Long Island section, 96. *Mem:* Yale Club. *Media:* All. *Dealer:* Marlborough Gallery 40 W 57th St New York NY 10019; Arlene Bujese Gallery E Hampton NY

STEINBACH, HAIM
SCULPTOR, CONCEPTUAL ARTIST
b Israel, Feb 25, 44; US citizen. *Study:* Pratt Inst, BA, 68; Yale Univ, MFA, 73. *Work:* Mus Contemp Art, Chicago, Ill; Los Angeles Co Mus Art, Calif; Israel Mus, Jerusalem; Centre Georges Pompidou, Paris, France; Milwaukee Art Mus, Wis. *Comn:* Coat of Arms, mixed media construct, Gruppo GFT, Torino, Italy, 88. *Exhib:* Brokerage of Desire, Otis Art Inst, Los Angeles, 86; Les Courtiers du Desir, Centre Georges Pompidou, Paris, 87; Documenta 8, Kassel, W Ger, 87; one-man show, Cape Mus D'Art Contemporain, Bordeaux, 88; Binational, Mus Fine Arts, Boston & Kunsthalle, Dusseldorf, W Ger, 88. *Teaching:* Instr, Middlebury Col, 73-77 & Cornell Univ, 77-80. *Awards:* CAPS Award, NY State Coun on the Arts, 83. *Bibliog:* Germano Celant (auth), Haim Steinbach's Wild Wild Wild West, Artforum, 87; John Miller (auth), The Consumption of everyday life, Artscribe, 88; Holland Cotter (auth), Haim Steinbach shelf life, Art in Am, 88. *Media:* Mixed. *Dealer:* Sonnabend Gallery 420 W Broadway New York NY 11222; Jay Gorney Modern Art 100 Greene St New York NY 10012. *Mailing Add:* 85 Quay St No 3A Brooklyn NY 11222

STEINBER, BLEMA
COLLECTOR
Study: BA, McGill Univ, BA, 55; Cornell Univ, MA; McGill Univ, PhD, 61. *Teaching:* Assoc prof McGill Univ, prof, 96-2001, prof eme, 2001-. *Awards:* Named one of Top 200 Collectors, ARTnews Magazine, 2004. *Bibliog:* (auth): Shame & Humiliation: Pres Decision Making on Vietnam, 96 (Quebec Writers Federation award, 96, QSPELL First Book award, 96), co-editor: Superpower Involvement in the Middle East, 85; contributor articles to professional journals. *Collection:* Modern & contemporary art. *Mailing Add:* McGill University Political Science Depa 855 Sherbrooke St W Montreal PQ H3A 2T7 Canada

STEINBERG, ARNOLD See Steinberg, H Arnold

STEINBERG, H ARNOLD
COLLECTOR
b Montreal, Canada, Oct 25, 33. *Study:* McGill Univ, B Commerce, 54; Harvard Univ, MBA, 57; McGill Univ, LLD(hon). *Pos:* Exec vpres, Chief Financial Officer, dir & mem exec comt Steinberg Inc, Montreal, Can, 58-89; princ, retail & investment banking Cleman Ludmer Steinberg Inc, Can, 89-; Mem, Can Council, 79-85, mem, exec comt, 81-85; chmn bd gov McGill Univ-Montreal Children's Hosp Research Inst, 72-91; mem bd, gov McGill Univ, 80-90; chmn, interim bd McGill Univ Health Ctr, 95-97, chmn bd, 97-2000; bd mem, McGill Univ Health Ctr Found, 2000-, McGill Univ Health Ctr Res Inst, 2000-; chmn adv bd, McGill Univ Faculty of Medicine; chmn, Can Health Infoway, 2003-. *Awards:* Named one of Top 200 Collectors, ARTnews Mag, 2004, 2005, 2006. *Mem:* Order of Canada. *Collection:* Modern & Contemporary art. *Mailing Add:* Cleman Ludmer Steinberg Inc 2 Place Alexis Nihon 3500 de Maisonneuve Montreal PQ H3Z 3C1 Canada

STEINBERG, LEO
EDUCATOR, HISTORIAN
b Moscow, USSR, July 9, 20; US citizen. *Study:* Slade Sch Art, Univ London, dipl(fine arts), 40; Inst Fine Arts, NY Univ, PhD, 60; Philadelphia Col Art, PhD (hon) 81; Parsons Sch Design, PhD (hon) 86; Mass Col Art, PhD (hon) 87; Bowdoin Col, PhD (hon), 95. *Hon Degrees:* Philadelphia Col Art, Hon Dr, 81; Parsons Sch Design, Hon Dr, 86; Mass Col Art, Hon Dr, 87; Bowdoin Col, Hon Dr, 95. *Teaching:* Prof art hist, Hunter Col & Grad Ctr City Univ NY, 61-75, Univ Pa, 75-91, prof emer, 91-; Norton vis prof, Harvard, 95-96. *Awards:* Mather Award for Art Criticism, 56 & 84; Am Acad Arts & Sci Fel, 78; Univ Col Fel, London, 79; Award in Literature, Am Acad & Inst Arts & Letters, 83; MacArthur Found Fel, 86. *Mem:* Col Art Asn; Col Art Asn Am (bd mem, 1969-71, recipent Frank Jewett Mather award for Distinction in Criticism, 84, Distinguished Scholar award 2002). *Publ:* Resisting Cezanne: Picasso's three women, Art in Am, 11 12/78; The Line of Fate in Michelangelo's Painting, Critical Inquiry 6, spring 80; A Corner of the Last Judgment, Daedalus, spring 80; The sexuality of Christ in Renaissance Art & in Mod Oblivion, rev ed, 96; Leonardo's Incessant Last Supper, 2001. *Mailing Add:* 165 W 66th St New York NY 10023

STEINBERG, RUBIN
COLLAGE ARTIST, PAINTER
b Chicago, Ill, May 31, 34. *Study:* Chicago Teachers Col, BE, 52-57; Art Inst Chicago, MFA, 52- 68; Roosevelt Univ, ME, 60-61; IIT, Inst Design, 59-60. *Work:* Southern Ohio Mus, Portsmouth; Ill State Mus, Springfield; Spertus Mus Judaica, Borg Warner, Chicago, Ill; McDonalds Corp, Oakbrook, Ill; and others. *Comn:* Sudler & Co, Chicago, Ill, 65; Malow Cordage Corp, Irving Malow, Mt Prospect, Ill, 68; Madison Steel Co, LA Morgan, Skokie, Ill, 70-75; also pvt collections of Mr & Mrs Elton Herrick, Park Ridge, Ill, Louise D Yochim, Evanston, Ill, Ardis Krainik, Lyric Opera, Chicago, Mr & Mrs Haskell Schiff, Evanston, Ill, Dr Robert Selman, Boca Raton, Fla; and others. *Exhib:* Art Inst Chicago, Chicago & Vicinity Show, 68-73; Mask, Southern Ohio Mus, Portsmouth, 83; Chicago Soc Artists Reprospective, Mus Science & Industry, 83; one-man shows, Bernard Horwich Jewish Community Ctr, Chicago, 4 Arts Assoc, Evanston, One Ill Ctr, Chicago, Monroe Gallery, Chicago, Oak Park Libr, Park Forest Art Ctr, Northbrook Racquet Club No 2, Chicago Cult Arts Ctr and many more; ARC Gallery, Chicago, Ill; Chicago Cult Ctr, 96; Balzekas Mus, Chicago, 96; Blue Moon Gallery, 96; Taipei Fine Arts Mus, Taiwan, 99; Marshall Fields Stores, Chicago area, Ill. *Pos:* bd dir, Chicago Soc Artists, 78-99 & Am Jewish Art Club, 78-99. *Teaching:* Teacher art, Curie High Sch, Chicago Bd Educ, formerly. *Bibliog:* Michael Karzen (auth), Rubin Steinberg one of Chicago finest, Sch Art Mag, 87; Laura Nilges-Matias (auth), Artist uses bits, pieces in a big way, Pulitzer-Lerner Newspaper, 4/6/88; Michael Bonesteel (auth), Assemblage Artist, Pioneer Press; and others. *Mem:* Chicago Soc Artists; Am Jewish Artists Club; Chicago Artists Coalition. *Media:* Collage, Acrylic Painted Sculptural Weaving. *Publ:* Auth, The art of mosaic masks, 87, Repousse - metal embossing, 88, Janus Masks - a metal sandwich, 89, Applique Owls - and a few other birds, 89, Dreaming Transformed, 90, Arts & Activities; 50 articles, 85-98. *Dealer:* Marshall Fields Chicago IL. *Mailing Add:* 3127 W Jerome Ave Chicago IL 60645

STEINER, CHARLES K
MUSEUM DIRECTOR, PAINTER
b Champaign, Ill, Apr 27, 51. *Study:* Cornell Univ, BFA, 1973; George Wash Univ, MFA, 1976. *Work:* 3-M, Minneapolis, Minn; NY Health & Hosp Corp; Montgomery Co Md Govt, Rockville, Md; George Washington Univ, Washington, DC; Empire Bank, Wichita, Kans. *Exhib:* Col Art Asn Drawing Show, Corcoran Mus, Washington, DC, 75; The Working Process, Org of Independent Artists, NY Dept Cult Affairs, 81; New Talent Outside of Calif, Delphine Gallery, Santu Borbara, Calif, 87; Architecture; Artist Interpretations; Braituwaite Fine Arts Gallery, Southern Utah Univ, Cedar City, Utah, 93; one-man shows, 10 Downtown, NY, 1981, Educ Testing Serv, Princeton, NJ, 93; Wichita Ctr for the Arts, Wichita, Kans, 2001. *Pos:* from asst mus educ to assoc, The Metropolitan Mus Art, NY, 86; from asst dir to assoc, The Art Mus Princeton Univ, 86-99; mus dir, Wichita Art Mus, 2000-. *Teaching:* Princeton Adult Sch, 97-98, Drawing & Design. *Awards:* Vis Painter, Edward Albee Found, 77 & 78; Rockefeller Found Fel, Metrop, Mus of Art, 77 & 78; Metrop Mus Art travel grantee, Europe, 1981; Spears Travel Grants, Princeton Univ, 95 & 98. *Bibliog:* Meryl Secrest, Galleries: A Fusion of Sensibility, Washington Post, 75; Artists Liaison Exhibitions, Santa Monica, Ca, 87; Vivian Raynor, A Show by 28 Artists & Solong Their Judge, NY Times, 93. *Mem:* Asn of Art Mus (dir, 2001-). *Media:* Acrylic. *Specialty:* American Art. *Publ:* auth, Art museums & visually handicapped consumers, J Visual Impairment and Blindness, 83; auth, Design comes to Whitney, Arts, Nat. *Mailing Add:* Wichita Art Mus 1400 Museum Blvd Wichita KS 67203

STEINER, JEFFREY JOSEF
ADMINISTRATOR, COLLECTOR
b Vienna, Austria, Apr 3, 37. *Study:* Univ London, Student textile design, 56; Bradford Inst Tech, London, Student textile manufacturing, 57. *Hon Degrees:* Yeshiva Univ, HHD(hon), 96. *Pos:* Bd dir, Copley Fund, Fall River, Mass, Comms Intelligence Corp, Corp Express, Inc; trustee, Montefiore Med Ctr, New York City; bd dir, Israel Mus, Yeshiva Univ Bus Sch; mgt trainee, Metals & Controls div Texas Instruments, Attleborough, Mass, 58-59, mgr int, 59-60, pres, Arg, Brazil, Mex, Switzer, France, 60-66, Burlington Tapis, Paris, 67-72; chmn, pres, Cedec SA Eng Co, 73-84; chmn, Chief Exec Officer, Fairchild Corp, New York City, 85-, Banner Aerospace, 93-. *Awards:* Recipient Mayor's Medal, City of Paris, 90; Decorated Knight of Arts (France), knight Industrial Merit of France, chevalier de L'Ordre des Arts et des Lettres, 90, chevalier de L'order National du Merite (France), commandatore de la Republica (Italy); Named one of Top 200 Collectors, ARTnews Mag, 2004, 2005, 2006. *Mem:* City Athletic Club; Racing Club & Polo Club. *Collection:* Impressionism, contemporary & modern art. *Mailing Add:* The Fairchild Corp 1750 Tysons Blvd Ste 1400 Mc Lean VA 22102

STEINER, MICHAEL
SCULPTOR, PAINTER
b New York, NY, 1945. *Work:* Storm King Art Ctr; Boston Mus Fine Arts; Mus Mod Art; Solomon R Guggenheim Mus; Denver Art Mus; Mass Inst Technol Mus; Edmonton Art Gallery; Walker Art Ctr; Musee d'Art Moderne et d'Art Contemp. *Exhib:* Whitney Mus Am Art, 70 & 72; Edmonton Art Gallery, Alta, 72; solo exhib, Andre Emmerich Galleries, 75-87, Martha White Gallery, Louisville, Ky, 83, Meredith Long & Co, Houston, Tex, 85, Galerie Elca London, Montreal, Que, 83, Douglas Drake Gallery, Kansas City, 85, Salander-O'Reilly Galleries, NY, 90, 97, 99, 01, Helander Gallery, Palm Beach, Fla, 90, Galerie Piltzer, Paris, 00; Mus Contemp Art, Chicago, Ill, 85; Sierra Nevada Mus Art, Reno, 86; Meredith Long & Co, Houston, Tex, 89; Bruce Mus, Greenwich, Conn, 89; Security Pacific Gallery, Costa Mesa, Calif, 89; Steven Scott Gallery, Baltimore, Md, 90; Univ Mich Art Mus, 90; Grounds for Sculpture, Hamilton, NY, 98; Pier Walk, Chicago, 01. *Collection Arranged:* Bank Am, San Francisco; Denver Art Mus; Des Moines Art Ctr; Guggenheim Mus; Mus Fine Arts, Boston; Mus Mod Art; Mus Fine Arts, Houston; Whitney Mus Am Art. *Teaching:* Instr, Emma Lake Workshop, Univ Sask, Regina, 69; vis artist, Cranbrook Art Inst, Bloomfield Heights, Mich, 69. *Awards:* Guggenheim Award, 71. *Bibliog:* Anthony Haden-Guest (auth), Alternate States: City & Country Addresses of Michael & Phyllis Steinen, Architectural Digest, 7/86; Susan Gill (auth), Michael Steiner at Andre Emmerich, Artnews, 11/87; Ann E Berman (auth), Sculptors - in Progress, Town & Country, 9/87; Robert Dahlin (auth), Noted Sculptor Michael Steiner of Bridgewater: Master of Steel, The Litchfield Co Times, 5/25/1990; Robert Taplin (auth), Patterns of Mind, Art in America, 148-49, 4/2000. *Media:* Steel, Aluminum. *Dealer:* Salander-O'Reilly 20 E 79th St New York NY 10021

STEINER, PAUL
WRITER, CRITIC
b Ger; US citizen. *Study:* NY Univ, BS. *Work:* Calif Mus Photogr. *Exhib:* Reinhold & Brown, NY; Karl Junghans & Galerie Michael Schultz, Berlin; multiples show, Frankfurt, Berlin, Switz, Japan, Can, 90. *Pos:* Assoc ed, Esquire, Inc, 47-52; feature writer & columnist, NAm Newspaper Alliance, Women's News Serv, 60-80; writer, Pop Scene Serv (syndicated rev of NY mus exhibs), 67-72; contrib ed, Nat Jeweller, 76, 77 & 78; columnist, Murray Hill News, 77-79, NY Entertainer, 79-82, Stagebill, 81-, Artspeak, 81-, TV Today, 82-83, Jewish J, 83-86, Reuters, 83-, NY Sunday News, 84-, USA Today, 84-, Cable TV World, 84-, Theater Week, 87-90, Cover Arts & Jewish Herald, Greenwich Village Press, 92-95, 50-Plus Sr News, Forum of Queens, 99-; corresp, NY Post, 77-82, NY Mag, Star Mag, US Mag, 78-, People Mag, NY Daily News, 81-, Omni, 81-90, Broadway Mag, 85-86 & Metrop Home, 91, Ad Week, 94-96 & In Style Mag, 94-96; contrib ed, Metrop Jewish Life, Show Illus, 81-83; NY Business News, 89-90, Jewish Post NY 94-; media work, Clinton Chronicle, NY, 95-99, Crains NY, 96- & Modern Collage, 98-99; Jewish Post, 2006. *Awards:* Columnist Award, 69 & Press Award, 70 & 94, Bk Author Award, 91, Beaux Arts Soc NY; Int Press Award, NY, 81; World Cult Prize, Italy Centro Studi Recherche dell Nazione, 85. *Publ:* Auth of 17 books; interviews with Chagall, Warhol, LeRoy Neiman & O'Keefe, Artspeak, 81-96. *Mailing Add:* 161 W 54th St New York NY 10019

STEINER, RAYMOND JOHN
CRITIC, WRITER
b Brooklyn, NY, May 1, 33. *Study:* State Univ NY, New Paltz, BA, 66, MA, 71. *Exhib:* Natl Arts Club, Impressions: Oils by RJ Steiner; Hudson Valley Landscapes, Woodstock Artists Asn, 2006. *Pos:* Ed, art critic & reviewer, Art Times, CSS Publ Inc, 84-. *Awards:* Award for Governors Office, 94. *Mem:* Int Asn Art Critics; Nat Arts Club; Am Soc Aesthetics; Nat Press Club; Artists Fel Inc (vpres 89-92); Salmagundi Club NY. *Publ:* Heinrich J Jarczyk: Toward a Vision of Wholeness, Laumann Verlag, 92; Frank Mason (exhib catalog), Art Students League, 93; The Four Hearts of Chen Chi, Chen Chi Studio, 93; Feld-Am See: Etchings of Robert Angeloch, 96, Heinrich J Jarczyk: Etchings-1968-1998, 98, Phantom Press; The Art Students League of New York: Hist, CSS Publ, 99. *Mailing Add:* c/o Art Times PO Box 730 Mt Marion NY 12456

STEINER, SHERRY L
PAINTER, WRITER, INSTRUCTOR, GALLERY DIRECTOR
Study: Sch of Visual Arts, NYC, 72. *Exhib:* Mobius, Boston, Berkshire Pub Theatre, Pittsfield, Mass, Ctr for the Arts, Northhampton, Mass, 87; first night Pittsfield, Mass, 94-95; Front St Gallery, Housatonic, mass, 1996-97; East West Fusion, Sharon, Conn, 97; Warehouse Gallery, Lee, Mass, 98; Norman Rockwell Mus, 99; and others. *Pos:* founder, Artists Action Group, Binghamton, NY, 74-76, The Mus of Teen Art, Housatonic, Mass, 99-; artist in residence Cummington Community, Mass, 86, 92, & 93; founder, owner, Le Petit Musee, Wild Sage, Pittsfield, Mass, 92-; artist in residence, Palenville Interarts Colony, Palenville, NY, 94; artist in residence, Doset Writer's Colony, Vt, 96-2005; owner, Albany Ctr Galleries, NY. *Teaching:* instr, creative arts, YM-YWHA, Flushing, NY, 66-70, Girls Club, Endicott, NY, 72-74, Hillel Acad, Vestal, NY, Riverbrook Sch, Stockbridge, Mass, 82-83, Acad for Myotherapy, Lenox, Mass, 85-86, Eden Hill Summer Prog, Stockbridge, Mass, 88-91,; instr, Private Studio Workshops, Binghamton, Mass, 75-77, Housatonic, Mass, 86-88; instr, studio art, art hist, & mixed media, De Sisto Sch, Stockbridge, Mass, 88-89; instr, graphic arts, So Berkshire Educ. Collaborative, Pittsfield, Mass, 79-81; instr, studio, drama, writing, music, film, & art history, John Dewey Acad, Great Barrington, Mass, 89-; instr, studio art & creative writing, Main Street Human Resources, Great Barrington, Mass, 80-85. *Awards:* Pittsfield & N Berkshire Arts Lottery, 1991, 92, 95; Berkshire Taconic Foun, Mus of Teen Art, 99-00; Nass Cult Coun Award, Finausr, Playwriting & New Theatre World, 2003. *Mem:* Great Barrington Arts Lottery Coun; Berkshire Writers Room (pres, currently). *Publ:* profiled, WomanArt Mag, NY, 77, 78; profiles, The Eagle, The Paper, Sp Union, 86-99; publisher/editor, In The Arts, 89; and others. *Mailing Add:* PO Box 556 Housatonic MA 01236

STEINHARDT, ALICE
DRAFTSMAN, PAINTER - ACRYLIC, OIL
b New York, NY, Feb 9, 50. *Study:* Univ Miami, Coral Gables, BA, 72; Int Ctr Photog, New York, 75. *Work:* Ctr Creative Photog, Tucson; Corcoran Gallery Art; Los Angeles Co Mus Art; Portland Mus Art, Ore; Santa Barbara Mus Art, Calif. *Exhib:* Solo exhib, Photog Gallery, La Jolla, Calif, 82, G Ray Hawkins Gallery, Los Angeles, Calif, 84, Leighton Gallery, Blue Hill, Maine, 88 & 89, Dean Velentgas Gallery, Portland, Maine, 89 & 92, Maine Coast Artists, Rockport, Maine, 93 & Icon Gallery, Maine, 96; Round Top Ctr Arts, Maine, 95; James A Michner Art Mus, Pa, 97; Portland Mus Art, Maine, 98; Bowdoin Col, Maine, 2001; June Fitzpatrick Gallery, Maine, 2005; Aucocisco Gallery, Maine, 2005. *Collection Arranged:* Bowdoin Col Mus Art, Brunswick, Maine; Corcoran Gallery Art, Wash, DC; Los Angeles Co Mus Art, Calif; Santa Barbara Mus Art, Calif; Farnsworth Mus Art, Rockland, Maine.

Awards: Purchase Prize, LaGrange III, 77; Millay Colony Arts Award, Austerlitz, NY, 94. *Bibliog:* Article, Photo Bulletin, 80. *Mem:* Friends Photog; Los Angeles Ctr Photog Studies. *Media:* Drawing & Painting. *Publ:* auth, Photography Yr 1982, Time Life Books; Suzette McAvoy (auth), Interstices, Farnsworth Mus, Rockland, 89; Edgar Allen Beem (auth), Maine Art Now, Dog Ear Press, Brunswick, 90; Liv Kristin Robinson (auth), Beyond Black and White, Farnsworth Mus, Rockland, 90; Wolff Theodore (auth), On the Edge: Forty Years of Maine Painting, Maine Coast Artists, Rockport, 92. *Dealer:* Aucocisco Galleries 157 High St Portland Maine 014101; AIR Gallery 511 West 25th St ny 01001

STEINHARDT, MICHAEL H
COLLECTOR
b Brooklyn, 40. *Study:* Univ Pa Wharton Sch Finance, BS, 60. *Pos:* Founding partner, Steinhardt Partners LP, 67-95; chmn, Jewish Life Network/Steinhardt Found, NY City, 94-, Jewish Media Renaissance, Birthright Israel; managing mem, Steinhardt Mgt LLC, 96-; trustee & chmn investment comt NY Univ, currently; trustee, Brandeis Univ, Brooklyn Botanical Garden, Mus Jewish Heritage, Wildlife Conservation Soc, currently; mem vis comt dept Greek & Roman art, Metrop Mus Art, NY City, currently. *Awards:* Named one of Top 200 Collectors, ARTnews mag, 2003-06; Recipient Medallion, Univ Albany, 2004. *Collection:* Classical antiquities & modern art, especially drawing. *Publ:* Author: No Bull: My Life In and Out of the Markets, 2001. *Mailing Add:* Jewish Life Network 6 E 39th St 10th fl New York NY 10016

STEINHOFF, MONIKA
PAINTER, PRINTMAKER
b Swinemuende, Ger, Oct 19, 41. *Study:* Univ Calif, Los Angeles, BA, 64, MA, 66; Univ Munich, 65; Univ Calif, Berkeley, 69; Master Class: Henriette Wyeth, 90; Monoprint Workshop, Col Santa Fe, Goldleaf Master Class, 94. *Work:* Smithsonian Inst, Washington; IBM, NY; Mus NMex Fine Arts; Roswell M - Art Ctr, Albuquerque, N Mex. *Comn:* Santa Fe Youth Mural Program, May the Forest be with you (interior painting), comn by Julian Heldman, 86, Denillos Garden, comn by Don Meredith, family portrait, comn by Eugene Talbert, Tyler, Tex, Old Mexico Grill comn lg oil for hwy billboard, Las Supper after DeVinci, commn by Rob Weiland. *Exhib:* one-person shows, Dewey Gallery, 87, Zaplin-Lampert Gallery, Santa Fe, 88, Peyton Wright, 92, Turner Carroll, 94, Hand Artes, Truches, NMex, 96 & Galerie am Havelufer, Berlin, 96 & Roswell Mus, NMex, 99, Univ NMex, Los Alamos Gallery, 2005; Fine Arts Mus SW, 90 & 96; Galerie Marstella, Mexico City, 94; Gallery im Adlon, Berlin, Ger, 98; El Museo de Cult Matrix; Lewallen Gallery, 98 & 05; Austrian Biennal, 02; Taos Mus, Water Media Soc, 04; Berkley Art Ctr, Member Show, 05; Masur Mus, Twin Cities, Monroe, Los Angeles, 2006; Women in the Arts, Mus Fine Arts, 2005, 2006. *Collection Arranged:* Ricky Medlock, Dan Lynch, Sam Baller. *Pos:* curator Sanctified and Censored Sanctuario de Gueadalupe, July 2000; curator Panacea on the Plaza, Oct/Nov 2000. *Teaching:* Instr, Col Santa Fe & Univ Calif, Berkeley, formerly. *Bibliog:* Pase Tiempo, NMex, 10/97; Focus Mag, 12/96; Am Talk, 10/96; Santa Fe, NMex, 12/1/99, 3/17/2000; ABQ Jour 3/23/2000; plus others. *Mem:* Soc Egg Tempera Painters; Asn Socially Engaged Artists (founder, pres); NMex Print Makers (gallery mem). *Media:* Egg Tempera; Aquatint, Casein, Monoprints. *Specialty:* Hand pulled prints. *Interests:* Buddhism, swimming, skiing. *Dealer:* Hand Artes Truchas NM; Galerie Im Adlon Berlin Germany. *Mailing Add:* 1298 Lejano Ln Santa Fe NM 87501

STEINHOUSE, TOBIE (THELMA)
PAINTER, PRINTMAKER
b Montreal, Que. *Study:* Sir George Williams Univ; Art Students League, NY, with Morris Kantor & Harry Sternberg, 46-47; Ecole Beaux-Arts, Paris; Atelier 17, Paris, France, with W S Hayter, 61-62. *Work:* Nat Gallery Can, Ottawa; Montreal Mus Fine Arts, PQ; Confederation Art Gallery, Charlottetown, PEI; Ministry of External Affairs of Can, Moscow Embassy, USSR; McMichael Conserv Collection, Kleinburg, Ont. *Comn:* Ed 250 prints, Carousel, Heuga Co, 81; ed 110 prints, Paysage de Rue, Sheraton Hotel, 82; ed 75 prints, Pastorale Quebecoise, Int Conf Opthamology-Sherbrooke, Que. *Exhib:* Solo exhibs, Galerie Lara Vincy, France, 57, Montreal Mus Fine Arts, 59, 63 & 78, Galerie du Parc, Trois-Riviellres, 83, 92, L'Equivoque Gallery, Ottawa, 80, 86, 90, Gallery Arts Sutton, Que, 91 & Galerie de la ville, Montreal, 96; Montreal Mus Fine Arts, 59 & 63; Japanese Calligraphy Exhibs, 65-99; 1st & 3rd Brit Int Print Biennial, Bradford, Eng, 68 & 72; 9th Int Biennial Art, Menton, France, 72; 50 Yr Retrospective of Atelier 17, Elvehem Art Centre, Wis, 77; Biennial de Grabado de Am, Venezuela, 82; Museo de la Estampa, Mex, 92; NY-Montreal Printcollectors Exhib, 97; Mus Que, Collection of Mus, 96-99; Royal Canadian Acad Arts Exhib, Mus Quebee, 98; Japanese Calligraphy, Los Angeles, 98. *Awards:* Sterling Trust Award, Soc Can Painter-Etchers & Engravers, 63; Jessie Dow First Prize Award, Montreal Mus Fine Arts, 63; Govt Can Centennial Medal of Honor, 67; and others. *Bibliog:* Guy Viau (auth), La Peinture Moderne au Canada Francais, Ministere Affaires Cult, PQ, 64; Guy Robert (auth), Ecole de Montreal, Collection Artistes Can, 65; V Nixon (auth), Tobie Steinhouse-artist, Vie des Arts Mag, summer 72; L'Estampe Originale au Québec - 1980-1990, Bibliotheque National du Québec, 91; and others. *Mem:* Royal Can Acad Arts; Can Group Painters (pres, 66-68); L'Atelier Libre Recherches Graphique; Soc Can Painter-Etchers & Engravers; life mem Art Students' League; and others. *Media:* Oils & Watercolours; Etching & Engraving. *Publ:* Songes et Limiére, portfolio of eight prints, La Guilde Graphique, Montreal, Que, 72; Into my Green World, portfolio of six prints, La Guilde Graphique, 75; and many other editions of prints, 70-92. *Dealer:* La Guilde Graphique 9 St Paul St W Montreal PQ H2Y 1Y6 Can; Galerie L'autre Equivoque 333 Cumberland Ottawa Can K1N 7J3. *Mailing Add:* 208 Cote St Antoine Rd Montreal PQ H3Y 2J3 Canada

STEINMAN, BARBARA
CONCEPTUAL ARTIST, PHOTOGRAPHER
b Montreal, Que. *Work:* Nat Gallery Can, Ottawa, Ont; Art Gallery Ont, Toronto; Musee d'art Contemporain, Montreal; Vancouver Art Gallery, Ont; Maison Europeenne de la Photographie, Paris; Seoul Metropolitan Mus, Seoul. *Comn:* reflecting pool, sculpture & benches, Concord Pac Develop Corp, Vancouver, 96-97; urban park & walkway design, East of Bay Develop Corp, Toronto, 98-2003; Large Format Photographic Work, O & Y Properties, Inc, Toronto. *Exhib:* Mus Mod Art, NY, 90; Nat Gallery Can, Ottawa, 90; Biennale de la Imagen en Movimiento, Reina Sofia Centro de Arte, Madrid, 90; Places with a Past, Charleston, SC, 91; Setagaya Art Mus, Tokyo, 95; Recent Art of the Americas, Art Inst Chicago, 95; Notion of Conflict (with catalog), Stedelijk Mus, Amsterdam, The Neth, 95; ICA/VITA Brevis, Boston, Mass, 98; Mus Fine Art, Montreal, 2004. *Awards:* Governor General's Award in Visual and Media Arts, Can, 2002. *Bibliog:* Gillian Mackay (auth), Governor General's Awards, Visual & Media Arts, Ottawa 2002; Peggy Gale (auth), Toutle Temps, Le Biennale, Montreal, 2002; Jill Medvedow (ed) ICA/Vitra Brevis, 1998-2003: History, Landscape and Art, Boston, 2004. *Media:* Multimedia. *Dealer:* Olga Korper Gallery 17 Morrow Ave Toronto ON M6R 2H9 Canada. *Mailing Add:* c/o Olga Korper Gallery 17 Morrow Ave Toronto ON M6R 2H9 Canada

STEINWORTH, SKIP (WILLIAM) EUGENE, JR
GRAPHIC ARTIST
b St Paul, Minn, May 2, 50. *Study:* St Cloud State Univ, Minn, BA, 74, MA, 79. *Work:* Springfield Civic Collection, Ill; Plains Mus, Moorhead, Minn; Minneapolis Inst Art; Kemper Insurance Corp Collection, Chicago; City of Winter Park, Fla. *Exhib:* Contemp Still Lifes, Riverside Art Mus, Calif, 91; Parkersburg Art Ctr, WVa, 95; Drawings Midwest, Minn Mus Art, St Paul, 97; Amarillo Mus Art, Tex, 98; Evansville Mus Art, Ind, 99. *Teaching:* St Columbia's Col, Melbourne, Australia, 74-77. *Awards:* Minn State Arts Bd Fel, 99. *Bibliog:* Betsy Goldman-Schein (auth), Skip Steinworth, Am Artist, 6/89; Deborah Gimelson (auth), Contemporary realist drawings, Archit Dig, 7/95; Bill Lasarow (auth), Skip Steinworth, Art Scene, 5/98. *Media:* Pencil. *Dealer:* Hackett/Freedman Gallery 250 Sutter St San Francisco CA. *Mailing Add:* 13460 51st St N Stillwater MN 55082

STEIR, PAT
PAINTER
b Newark, NJ, 1940. *Study:* Boston Univ, 60; Pratt Inst, BFA, 62. *Hon Degrees:* Pratt Inst, DFA, 91. *Work:* Mus Mod Art, Metrop Mus Art, NY; Nat Gallery Art, Washington, DC; Walker Art Ctr, Minneapolis, Minn; Brooklyn Mus, NY; Tate Gallery, London; Phila Mus Art; Whitney Mus Am Art, NY; Albright-Knox Art Gallery, Buffalo, NY; The Art Mus, Princeton Univ; The Hirshorn Mus, Washington; Irish Mus Mod Art, Dublin; Lyon Mus d'Art Moderne, France; Malmo Mus, Sweden; and numerous others. *Exhib:* Brooklyn Mus, NY, 84 & 92; Baltimore Mus Art, Md, 87; First Impressions (traveling exhib), Walker Art Ctr, Minneapolis, Minn, 89-90; Musee d'Art Contemporain, Lyon, 90; Nat Gallery Art, Washington, DC, 90; solo exhibs, Galerie Franck & Schulte, Berlin, 93, Galleria Allessandra Bonomo, Rome, 93, Guild Hall Mus, East Hampton, NY, 93, Irish Mus Mod Art, Dublin, 94, Jaffe Baker Blau, Boca Raton, Fla, 94 & Anders Thornberg Gallery, Lund, Sweden, 94, Kunstwerke Berlin, Ger, 95, Baldwin Gallery, Aspen, Colo, 96, Robert Miller Gallery, NY, 95, 97, Irish Mus Mod Art, Dublin, 96, Dorothy Blau Gallery, Bay Harbor Islands, Fla, 96, Brooklyn Gallery, 97, Galerie Deux Co Ltd, Japan, 97, Rhona Hoffman Gallery, Chicago, 98, 2000, Baumgartner Galleries, Washington, 98, Whitney Mus Am Art, NY, 98, Weatherspoon Art Gallery, 99, Butler Inst Am Art, Youngstown, Ohio, 2000, Sherman Gallery, Boston U, 2001, Galleria Bonomo, Bari, Italy, 2001, Galerie Simonne Stern, New Orleans, 2001, Contemp Arts Mus, Honolulu, 2001, many others; Black & White & Read All Over, LaSalle Lobby Gallery, Nationsbank Plaza, Charlotte, NC, 95; American Art Today: Night Paintings, Art Mus, Int Univ, Miami, 95; Inspired by Nature, Neuberger Mus, Purchase, NY, 94; Dialogue with the Other, Kunsthallen Brandts Klaedefabrik, Odense, Denmark, 94; A Room with Some Views, Sonnabend Gallery, NY, 94; Va Mus Fine Arts, 95; From Picasso to Woodrow, Suite of Prints, Long Vertical Falls, Tate Gallery, London, 95; Nuevas Abstracciones, Palacio de Velazquez, Museo Nacional Centro de Arte Reina Sofia, Madrid, Spain, 96; Museo de Arte Contemporaneo, Barcelona, Spain, 96; Original Visions: Women, Art and the Politics of Gender, Boston Col Mus Art, 97; A Thought Intercepted, Calif Mus Art, Santa Rosa, 97; Mus Mod Art, 97; Likity Split Installation, Whitney Mus Art, NY, 98; The Am Century, Whitney Mus Am Art, 99; Nat Gallery of Art, 2000; Pat Steir, Brice Marden & Michael Mazur, Boston Univ, 2001; and numerous others. *Awards:* Nat Endowment Arts, 74, 76; Guggenheim Fel, 82; Boston Univ Sch for the Arts Disting Alumni Award, 2001. *Bibliog:* John Howell (auth), A Bloom of one's own, Elle Mag, 2/88; Pat McCoy (auth), Pat Steir: Knoedler, Artscribe, 2/88; Michael Kimmelman (auth), This American in Paris kept true to New York, New York Times, 4/17/88. *Mailing Add:* 80 McDougal St New York NY 10012

STELLA, FRANK
PAINTER
b Malden, Mass, May 12, 36. *Study:* Phillips Acad, with Patrick Morgan; Princeton Univ, with William Seitz & Stephen Greene; Princeton Univ, Hon DA, 84; Dartmouth Col, Hanover, NH, hon degree, 85. *Work:* Solomon R Guggenheim Mus, Metrop Mus Art & Whitney Mus Am Art, NY; Hirshhorn Mus & Sculpture Garden, Nat Collection Fine Art, Smithsonian Inst, Nat Gallery Art & Nat Mus Art, Washington, DC; Art Inst Chicago, Ill; Los Angeles Co Mus Art & Mus Contemp Art, Calif; Milwaukee Art Ctr, Wis; Walker Art Ctr, Minneapolis, Minn; Brooklyn Mus, NY; Musée d'Art Moderne, Paris; and many others. *Exhib:* 30th Biennial Contemp Am Painting, 66 & 37th Ann Exhib Contemp Art Am Painting (with catalog), 81, Corcoran Gallery Art, Washington, DC, 66; Am Abstract Painting: Selections from the Whitney Mus Collection, 75 & Biennial Exhib, 79, Whitney Mus Am Art, NY, 75; Second Am

Exhib, 76 & 73rd Am Exhib, 79, Art Inst Chicago, Ill; Acquisition Priorities: Aspects of Postwar Painting in Am, 76 & The NY Sch: Four Decades, Guggenheim Mus Collection, Major Loans, 82, Solomon R Guggenheim Mus, NY; Am Painting of the 1970's, Albright-Knox Art Gallery, Buffalo, NY, 78; Selections from the Meyerhoff Collection, Baltimore Mus Art, Md, 78; Stella Since 1970, Ft Worth Art Mus, Tex, 78; Emergence & Progression, Milwaukee Art Ctr, 79; Morton G Newmann Family Collection, Nat Gallery Art, Washington, DC, 80; Changes, Aldrich Mus Contemp Art, Ridgefield, Conn, 83; Selections from the Twentieth Century Art Collection, Los Angeles Co Mus Art, Calif, 83; solo exhibs, Resource/Response/Reservoir: Stella Survey 1959-1982 (with catalog), San Francisco Mus Art, Calif, 83, Frank Stella 1970-1987 (with catalog), Mus Mod Art, NY, traveling, 87-89, Frank Stella: Prints from the Collection, Hirshhorn Mus & Sculpture Garden, Smithsonian Inst, Washington, DC, 92, Richard Meier/Frank Stella: Arte e Architettura (with catalog), Palazzo della Esposizioni, Rome, Italy, 93, Moby Dick Series, Engravings, Domes & Deckle Edges (with catalog), Ulmer Mus, Stadthaus Ulm, Ger, 93, Space in Progress (with catalog), Kawamura Mem Mus Art, Sakura, Japan, 94 & Imaginary Places, New Work: Painting, Relief & Sculpture, Waddington Galleries, London, Eng, 94, Bernard Jacobson Gallery, London, Eng, 99, Sperone Westwater Gallery, NY, 99, Frank Stella at 2000: Changing the Rules, Mus of Contemp Art, N Miami, Fl, 2000; Nine Printmakers & the Working Process, Whitney Mus Am Art Fairfield Co, Stamford, Conn, 85; Seven Master Printmakers: Innovations in the Eighties, Mus Mod Art, NY, 91; Four Centuries of Drawing 1593-1993, Kohn Abrams Gallery, Los Angeles, Calif, 93; Isamu Wakabayashi, Frank Stella, Jannis Kounellis, Richard Serra, Akira Ikeda Gallery, Nagoya, Japan, 94; Inaugural Exhib, Kemper Mus Contemp Art & Design Kansas City Art Inst, Mo, 94; and many others. *Pos:* vis critic, dept art, Cornell Univ, 1965. *Teaching:* Lectr, numerous cols, univs & orgns; Rep, by Leo Castelli Gallery, 1959; artist-in-residence, Dartmouth Coll, 1963; instr, art Univ Saskatchewan, 1967, Brandeis Univ, 1968; instr, Brandeis Univ, 1969; Charles Eliot Norton prof, poetry Harvard Univ, Cambridge, Mass, 1983. *Awards:* Charles Eliot Norton Professorship of Poetry, Harvard Univ, Cambridge, Mass, 83-84; NY Univ Resident Fel, Soc Fels; Award Am Art, Pa Acad Fine Arts, Philadelphia, 10/25/85; Hon Degree, Brandeis Univ, 86; Hon Degree, Dartmouth Col, 85; NH Award of Am Art, 85; NJ Bernard Medal of Distinction, 85. *Bibliog:* Suzanne Stephens (auth), Portrait: Frank Stella, Blurring the Line Between Art & Architecture, Archit Digest, 7/94; Robert Smith (auth), Frank Stella (review: Knoedler), New York Times, 10/21/94; Judd Tully (auth), Art: Frank Stella at Knoedler Fine Arts in October, Cover, 10/94; and many others. *Mem:* Coun US and Italy; Fel Soc Fel (NY Univ); Nat Acad (assoc, 90, acad, 94-). *Publ:* Auth, On Caravaggio, New York Times Mag, 2/3/85; Working Space, Harvard Univ Press, 86. *Dealer:* Leo Castelli Gallery 420 W Broadway New York NY 10012. *Mailing Add:* Bernard Jacobson Gallery 6 Cork St London United Kingdom W1S 3EE

STELZER, MICHAEL NORMAN
SCULPTOR, INSTRUCTOR
b Brooklyn, NY, Jan 6, 38. *Study:* Pratt Inst, 56; Art Students League, 60-62; Nat Acad Sch Fine Arts, Edward Mooney traveling scholar, 66 & Nat Sculpture Soc Joseph Nicolosi grant, 67; and with Nathaniel Choate, 64, Michael Lantz, 64-67 & Donald DeLue, 68 & 69. *Comn:* 12 ft relief, Worcester Polytech Inst, 64. *Exhib:* Am Artists Prof League Grand Nat, 63, 76 & 77; Nat Arts Club, 63-64; Nat Acad Design, 64-67, 70-71 & 74-77; Allied Artists Am, 67 & 71-81; Nat Sculpture Soc Ann Exhib, 68-81. *Pos:* Team mem, Restoration Leonardo Da Vincis 24 ft Horse Sculpture, 98. *Teaching:* Instr sculpture, Fashion Inst Technol, New York, 79. *Awards:* Helen Foster Barnett Prize, Nat Acad Design, 66; Gold Medal, Hudson Valley Art Asn, 76; Gold Medal, Grand Nat Exhib, Am Artists Pro Prof League, 76; Allied Artists Am Award, 81; Hudson Valley Art Asn Award, 85. *Bibliog:* Article in, Pen & Brush, 66; Opportunities offered the young sculptor, 67 & Interpreting the human figure, 68, Nat Sculpture Rev. *Mem:* Nat Sculpture Soc; Hudson Valley Art Asn; Allied Artists Am; Am Artists Prof League. *Mailing Add:* 8 Everit St Brooklyn NY 11201

STENT, TERRY & MARGARET
COLLECTOR
Study: Yale Univ, BA, 61; Harvard Univ, MBA, 68. *Pos:* Pilot, Delta Air Lines, 70-97; dir, Callanwolde Fine Arts Ctr, Atlanta, 83-86; mem, Art Collectors group High Mus Art, Atlanta, 93—, dir, 97—, chmn, collections comt, 99-2001, bd chmn, 2001—; bd comnr & Art Forum Smithsonian Am Art Mus, Wash, chmn bd comnr, 99-2003. *Awards:* Decorated nine Air Combat medals; named one of Top 200 Collectors, ARTnews Mag, 2004. *Collection:* 19th & 20th century art, especially Hudson River Sch & Ashcan Sch; American Realism. *Mailing Add:* High Mus Art 1280 Peachtree St NE Atlanta GA 30309

STEPHAN, GARY
PAINTER, EDUCATOR
b Brooklyn, NY, 42. *Study:* Parsons Sch Design, NY, 60-61; Art Students League, NY, 61; Pratt Inst, 61-64; San Francisco Art Inst, MFA, 67. *Work:* Whitney Mus Am Art, Metrop Mus Art, Guggenheim Mus, NY; Mus Contemp Art, Los Angeles; Mus Contemp Art, Miami. *Exhib:* Aldrich Mus Contemp Art, Ridgefield, Conn, 87; solo shows, Hirschl & Adler Mod, NY, 88, Galeria Lino Silverstein, Barcelona, Spain, 89, Mary Boone Gallery, NY, 90 & 93, Fuller Gross Gallery, San Francisco, 90, Baumgartner Galleries, Washington, DC, 90 & 92, Galleria in Arco, Torino, Italy, 93 & Revolution Gallery, Detroit, Mich, 95; Cristinerose Gallery, NY, 95; Galerie Fernando Alcolea, Barcelona, Spain, 95; Margulis Kaplan Gallery, Coral Gables, Fla, 96; Attitudes, Soma Gallery, San Diego, 96; Alternate Art Show, Pierogi 200, NY. *Teaching:* Grad prof, Sch Visual Arts, NY, currently. *Awards:* Nat Endowment Arts; Guggenheim Found Fel; NY Arts Found. *Bibliog:* Stephen Westfall (auth), Gary Stephen at Marlborough, Art in Am, 11/84; John Yau (auth), Gary Stephan at Marlborough, Artforum, 12/84; Peter Haaren (auth), Feigning the visonary: Gary Stephan, Arts Mag, 12/84. *Dealer:* Baumgartner Galleries 2016 R St NW Washington DC 20009. *Mailing Add:* 530 Canal St New York NY 10013

STEPHANSON, LORAINE ANN
PAINTER
b Edmonton, Alta, Apr 19, 50. *Study:* Univ Alta, BED & MVA, 78; Univ Sask, Emma Lake Workshops with Friedl Dzubas, John Elderfield & Kenworth Moffett, 79-80; Triangle Workshop, New York, wtih Larry Poons & Michael Fried, 86; Triangle Workshop, New York, NY, with Karen Wilkin, Willard Boepple, Michael Chisholm, Alexei Worth, 2000. *Work:* Univ Alta, Edmonton; Prov of BC Collection; Air Canada, Montreal; Royal Trust, Vancouver; Triangle Trust, NY. *Exhib:* Solo exhib, Univ Art Gallery & Mus, Edmonton, 78; Grand Forks Art Gallery, 92, Barton Leier Gallery, Victoria, 94 & CAC Gallery, Victoria, 2000; Emma Lake '79, 79-80, Alberta Now, 80 & Canadian Contemp Art, 83, Edmonton Art Gallery; The Joy of Form, Burnaby Art Gallery, Vancouver, 86; Celebrations, Univ Art Gallery, Edmonton, 87; 16X one, Gallery One, Toronto, 96; Arts 2000, Gallery Stratford, 2000. *Pos:* Illusr, Brit Inst Archeol-Univ Alta Classics Dept, Gravina, Italy, 70-71. *Teaching:* Lectr painting, Univ Alta, Edmonton, 78-80, asst prof, 85; extension fac, Univ Victoria, 90; Contemp Artforum, Victoria, 98. *Awards:* Univ Alta Prize Art & Design, 76; Heinz Jordan Mem Scholar, Heinz Jordan Co, Toronto, 77; Can Coun Grant, 80. *Bibliog:* R Lawrence (auth), Review, Vanguard Mag, 85; R. Amos (auth), Review, Victoria Times Colonist, 9/10/2000. *Media:* Acrylic on Canvas, Watercolor. *Dealer:* Virginia Christopher Galleries Ltd 1134 8th Ave SW Calgary Alberta T2P 1J5 Can; Art Placement Inc 228 3rd Ave S Saskatoon SK S7K 1L9. *Mailing Add:* 608 Oliver St Victoria BC V8S 4W3 Canada

STEPHANY, JAROMIR
PHOTOGRAPHER, EDUCATOR
b Rochester, NY, Mar 23, 30. *Study:* Rochester Inst Technol, AAS, 56, with Ralph Hattersley, Miner White & B Newhall, BFA, 58; Ind Univ, with Henry Holmes Smith, MFA, 60. *Work:* George Eastman House; Univ Md, Baltimore Co; Detroit Inst Arts; Mus Fine Arts St Petersburg, Fla; Baltimore Mus Fine Arts. *Exhib:* Mus Mod Art, NY, 60; Smithsonian Inst, Washington, DC, 69; Baltimore Mus Art, 70; Addison Gallery Am Art, 75; one-man shows, Dundalk Community Col, Md, 77, Mus Without Walls, Md, 75-76, Catskills Ctr Photog, 79, Int Ctr Photog, 80 & Dalsheimer Gallery, 81; and others. *Pos:* Series writer, Developing Image, Extended Learning Inst, Channel 53-TV, Va. *Teaching:* Lectr hist photog, Md Inst Col Art, 66-77; assoc prof, Dept Visual Arts, Univ Md, Baltimore Co, 72-. *Awards:* Univ Md Baltimore Co Summer Fel, 83 & 97. *Mem:* Soc Photog Educ. *Mailing Add:* 786 Creek View Rd Severna Park MD 21146

STEPHEN, FRANCIS B
JEWELER, SCULPTOR
b Dublin, Tex, Mar 7, 16. *Study:* Fine Art Ctr, Colorado Springs, Colo; Univ Okla, study with Jean Charlot & Robert von Neumann, MFA. *Work:* Witte Mem Mus, San Antonio, Tex; Okla Art Ctr; Hallmark Collection, Mo. *Exhib:* The Patron Church, Mus Contemp Crafts, NY, 61; 11th Mid-Am Exhib, Nelson Gallery, Kansas City, Mo, 61; Craft Exhib, Dallas Mus Fine Arts, 71-74 & 78; South Central States Crafts Exhib, Denver Art Mus, Colo, 73; Contemp Crafts of The Americas, Denver Art Mus, 74; Lake Superior Int Crafts Exhib, Tweed Mus Art, Univ Minn, Duluth, 74-75; The Metalsmith, Phoenix Art Mus, Ariz, 77; one-man show, Mus of Art, Okla Univ, 79; and others. *Teaching:* Asst prof jewelry & sculpture, North Tex State Univ, Denton, 64-67; prof jewelry, Tex Tech Univ, Lubbock, 67-83. *Awards:* Swarovski Award, Great Designs in Jewelry, Swarovski & Co, 67; Grand Award, 15th Tex Crafts Exhib, 71; Purchase Award, Miniature Works, Tex Tech Mus Art, 75. *Mem:* Soc of NAm Goldsmiths. *Media:* Miscellaneous Media. *Dealer:* Schneider-Bluhm-Loeb Gallery Inc 230 W Superior St Chicago IL 60610. *Mailing Add:* 4610 29th St Lubbock TX 79410

STEPHENS, CURTIS
EDUCATOR, DESIGNER
b Athens, Ga, Dec 13, 32. *Study:* Univ Ga, MFA. *Work:* Objects USA, Johnson's Wax Collection; Ill State Mus, Springfield. *Exhib:* Designed for Production, Mus Contemp Crafts, 64; Objects USA, Johnson's Wax Collection, Smithsonian Inst, 69; 24th & 25th Ill Exhib, Ill State Mus, 71 & 72. *Pos:* Designer, Callaway Mills, LaGrange, Ga, 63-66; photogr, 1960 Pandora (Popular Photog Award-Winning Yearbk, Univ Ga). *Teaching:* Asst prof art, LaGrange Col, 61-63 & Univ Northern Mich, 66-68; assoc prof art & design, Univ Ill, Champaign-Urbana, 68-, assoc dir sch, 75-90. *Bibliog:* Lee Nordness (auth), Objects: USA, Viking Press, 70; Jay Hartley Newman & Lee Scott Newman (auth), Plastics for the Craftsman, Crown, 72. *Media:* Papers, Plastics. *Mailing Add:* 2604 Natalie Dr Champaign IL 61822-7372

STEPHENS, ELISA
EDUCATOR
Study: Vassar Col, BA; Univ San Francisco Sch Law, JD. *Pos:* With Cellular Holdings, San Francisco; in-house coun Acad of Art Univ (formerly Acad of Art Col), San Francisco, 89-92, pres, 92-. *Mailing Add:* Acad Art Univ 6th Fl 79 New Montgomery St San Francisco CA 94105-3410

STEPHENS, THOMAS MICHAEL
KINETIC ARTIST, DESIGNER
b Elkins, Ark, Feb 21, 41. *Study:* Univ Kans, 59-63; pvt study & travel. *Exhib:* New Tendencies 4 & 5, Galeria Grada Zagreba, Zagreb, Yugoslavia, 69 & 73; 20th Century Am Photog, Nelson-Atkins Mus, Kansas City, Mo, 74; Cybernetic Symbiosis, Lawrence Hall Sci, Berkeley, Calif, 79; Critica I, Mus Graphics, Terme, Italy, 81; Univ Ctr Gallery, Lawrence, Kans, 81; one-man shows, Lawrence Gallery, 81, Rockhurst Gallery, 82 & Batz Gallery, 83. *Pos:* Principal, T M Stephens Design Assoc, currently. *Teaching:* Instr sculpture, Kansas City Art Inst, 86-87. *Awards:* Proclamation of Commendation by Mayor of Kansas City, 85. *Bibliog:* Peter Von Ziegesar (auth), article, Kansas City Mag, 7/86; Virginia Hillix (auth), article, New Art Examiner, 10/86. *Mem:* Comput Art Soc; assoc Hypergraphics Int Alliance; Kansas City Art Gallery Asn. *Mailing Add:* 7676 High Dr Shawnee Mission KS 66208

STEPHENS, WILLIAM BLAKELY
EDUCATOR, PAINTER
b Corpus Christi, Tex, June 8, 30. *Study:* Univ Tex, BFA, 56, with Hiram Williams, MEd, 57, MFA, 66; Univ Fla, EdD, 72. *Work:* Mus ETex, Lufkin; Tyler Mus Art. *Exhib:* 23rd Ann Tex Painting & Sculpture, Dallas Mus Fine Arts, 61; Art on Paper, Weatherspoon Gallery, Greensboro, NC, 67; Super Graphics, Brooks Mem Art Mus, Memphis, Tenn, 74; one-man show, Emerging Figures, Univ Tex, Tyler, 82; Contemp Art of the USA, Hamburg, WGer, 89 & Bonn, WGer, 90; USAid Mission, Tegucigalpa, Honduras, 91; and others. *Pos:* Art ed, New Voices in Educ, 71-72. *Teaching:* Asst occup ther, Univ Fla, 70-71; assoc prof art educ, Memphis State Univ, 72-76; prof art, Univ Tex, Tyler, 76- & chmn dept, 76-84 650 Watercolors. *Awards:* Univ Tex at Tyler Fac Res Grants, 78, 80, 90 & 94. *Mem:* Life mem Tex Fine Arts Asn. *Media:* Watercolor. *Res:* Artists' personality types; monuments and myths; the family saga in the south. *Publ:* Auth, Blue Ridge Studies, Fac Publ, Appalachian State Univ, 5/69; On creativity and teaching: talk with Hiram Williams, Art J, summer 71; Relationship between selected personality characteristics, Studies in Art Educ, spring 73; University art departments and academies of art: The artists' psychological types to their specialities and interests, Bull of Res in Psychological Type, summer 77; Hiram Williams, Memphis State Univ, 78. *Mailing Add:* Univ Tex Dept Art Tyler TX 75701

STEPHENSON, JOHN H
SCULPTOR, CERAMIST
b Waterloo, Iowa, Oct 27, 29. *Study:* Univ Northern Iowa, BA; Cranbrook Acad Art, MFA. *Hon Degrees:* Grand Valley State Univ, Hon DFA, 92. *Work:* Int Mus Ceramics Faenza, Italy; Everson Mus, Syracuse, NY; Portland Art Mus; Detroit Inst Arts; Cranbrook Mus; Keramon, Frechen, Ger. *Comn:* Champion No 3 (sculpture), Mich Mall, Battle Cree, Mich, 76. *Exhib:* retrospective, Sustained Visions, Detroit, 88; Waterloo Mus Art, 90; Revolution Gallery, Ferndale, Mich, 96; Univ Mich Mus Art, 94; Detroit Mus Art, 9650; Nanfeng Mus, Foshan, China, 2000; World Ceramics Ctr, Icheon, Korea, 2004. *Teaching:* Instr ceramics, Cleveland Inst Art, 58-59; prof art, Univ Mich Sch Art, Catherine B Heller Distinguished prof, 89, interim dean, 91-93, prof art emer, 95. *Awards:* Artists Fel, NEA, 86; Artist Fel, Mich Coun, 89. *Bibliog:* Century of Ceramics in the USA, Objects USA; John H Stephenson: After the Fire, A Retrospective. *Mem:* Nat Coun Educ Ceramic Arts; Mich Potters Asn; Int Acad of Ceramics Asn (IAC); Founders Soc Detroit Inst Art; Friends, Mus Art, Univ Mich. *Media:* Ceramic, Mixed. *Res:* Chinese ceramic folk art. *Publ:* Auth, Form & Color, Studio Potter, 83; Perception/Inner & Outer Vision, Studio Potter, 88; Time, Place and a Taste of Clay, Studio Potter, 92. *Mailing Add:* 4380 Waters Rd Ann Arbor MI 48103

STEPHENSON, SUSANNE G
CERAMIST, EDUCATOR
b Canton, Ohio, Nov 5, 35. *Study:* Carnegie-Mellon Univ, BFA; Cranbrook Acad of Fine Art, Bloomfield Hills, Mich, MFA. *Hon Degrees:* D of Arts, Grand Valley State Univ, Allandale, Mich. *Work:* Victoria & Albert Mus, London; Everson Mus Art, Syracuse, NY; Detroit Inst Arts, Mich; Int Ceramics Mus, Bechyne, Czech Repub; Los Angeles Co Mus, Calif. *Comn:* Ceramic Planters, Burroughs Corp, Detroit, Mich, 70, Grosse Pointe Br, Nat Bank of Detroit, 72 & Harper Hosp, Detroit, 72; Liturgical Vessels, Lutheran Chapel, Eastern Mich Univ, Ypsilanti, 72. *Exhib:* Garth Clark Gallery, NY, 86; solo exhib, Carnegie Inst Mus Art, Pittsburgh, Pa, 85; Fletcher Challenge Award Exhib, Auckland, NZ, 94; 4th Int Ceramic Competition, Mino, Japan, 95; Ist Ceramic Biennale Korean Int Competition, 2002, 03; 21st century ceramics, Columbus, Ohio, 2003; Visceral Vessal, San Antonio, Tex, 2005. *Teaching:* Instr ceramics, Univ Mich, Ann Arbor, 60-61; prof ceramics, Eastern Mich Univ, 63-91. *Awards:* Mich Ceramics Award, 78, 81, 85 & 88; Best in Ceramics, Beaux Arts Designer Craftsmen Exhib, Columbus, Ohio; Regional Visual Arts Fel, 87; Mich Coun Arts Grant, 87. *Bibliog:* Garth Clark & Margie Hughto (coauths), Century of Ceramics, E P Dutton, 79; Garth Clark (auth), American Potters, Watson Guptill, 81; Janet Koplos (auth), Alternations--the ceramics of Susanne Stephenson, Am Crafts, 1/83; Susan Crowell (auth), Together in Clay, Ceramics Art and Perception, No 7, 94. *Mem:* Am Craftsmen's Coun; Mich Potters Asn; Nat Coun Educ for Ceramic Arts; Internat Acad Ceramics; Pewabic Soc. *Media:* Porcelain, Earthenware. *Dealer:* Clay Place Gallery 5416 Walnut St Pittsburgh Pa 15232; Adam Whitney Gallery Omaha Nebr. *Mailing Add:* 4380 Waters Rd Ann Arbor MI 48103

STERLING, COLLEEN
PAINTER
b Sterling, Ill, Dec 17, 51. *Study:* Mus Sch of the Art Inst, Chicago, Ill - 1975-76; Massachusetts Col of Art, Boston, Mass - 1985; John C Campbell Folk Sch, Brasstoun, NC, cert, 2003. *Work:* Hunter Mus of Am Art, Chattanooga, Tenn; City of Atlanta, Dept Aviation, Atlanta, Ga; City of Atlanta, Rotating Art Collection, Atlanta, Ga. *Comn:* Site specific artwork (wall), Hyatt Roissy, Paris, France, 1992; Site specific artwork (wall), Dept Aviation, City of Atlanta, Ga, 1999; site specific artwork (wall) YMCA, Sterling, Ill, 2000; Fulton Co Arts Coun, public art prog, Sr Ctr, Palmetto, Ga, 2003. *Exhib:* Overlays, GSU Gallery, Boston Univ, Boston, Mass, 1986; Works on Paper, Berkshire Art Mus, Pittsfield, Mass, 1988; Basically Balck & White, Riverside Art Mus, Riverside, Calif, 1992; Inaugural Exhib, Contemporary Mus of Art, Buford, Ga, 1992; Urban Flashes, Amarillo Art Ctr & Mus, Amarillo, Tex, 1993; Mapping the Self, Telfair Mus of Art, Savannah, Ga, 1994; Nat Juried Exhib, Brenau Univ, Gainesville, Ga, 1994; Intermix, Sarratt Gallery, Vanderbilt Univ, Nashville, Tenn, 1995; Artstravaganza, Hunter Mus of Am Art, Chattanooga, Tenn, 1998; Soho Gallery, Los Angeles, Calif, 2004; Silver Fox Gallery, NC, 2005. *Pos:* freelance critic, Art Papers, Atlanta, Ga. *Teaching:* Instruc art, private lessons in studio, 1998- & Inst for Continuing Learning, Young Harris, Ga, 1999- & Blue Ridge Mt Arts Assoc, Blue Ridge, Ga, 2006-. *Awards:* AVA II, nominee, SECCA, Winston Salem, 1991; Ga Women in the Visual Arts, Nexus Contemp Art Ctr, State Rep Lewis Massey, 1997; 2nd level award, Artstravaganza, Hunter, Mus, Donald Kuspit, 1998. *Bibliog:* Bill Alexander (auth), Art Papers, Vol 18, No 5, 9-10/94; Donald Locke (auth), Creative Loafing, Vol 24, No 39, 2/17/96; Jerry Cullum (auth), Atlanta Journal & Constitution, 1/9/98. *Mem:* Blue Ridge Mt Arts Asn (member at large). *Media:* Charcoal paste "drawing" with plexiglas overlays. *Publ:* Auth, David Fraley, 1993 & Robert Rauschenberg, A Print Survey, 1993 & Charles Burchfield, 1994 & Lee Bontecou, Sculpture & Drawings of the 60's, 1994 & William Dooley (review), 2001, Art Papers Mag. *Dealer:* Bonnie Rash c/o Silver Fox Gallery, 508 North Main St Hendersonville, NC 28792. *Mailing Add:* 3529 Mason Rd Blairsville GA 30515-5256

STERMER, DUGALD ROBERT
ILLUSTRATOR, WRITER
b Los Angeles, Calif, Dec 17, 36. *Study:* Univ Calif, Los Angeles, BA, 60; printmaking with John Paul Jones. *Comn:* Designer, Olympic Games Official Medals, 84. *Exhib:* One-man show, Andre's, San Francisco, 69 & Jernigan Wicker Gallery, San Francisco, 96; group show, Greengrass Gallery, 78; Mus Exhib, Calif Acad Sci, 86. *Teaching:* Lectr advan design, Acad Art, San Francisco, 78; instr illus, Artists in Print, San Francisco, 78-79, inst advanced illus, Calif Col Arts Crafts, San Francisco, chair, Illus Dept, 94-. *Awards:* Excellence Award, Ann Exhibs, Soc Illustrators; Illustr Ann, Communication Arts, 76-90; Am Illusr Awards; plus others. *Bibliog:* 50 Important US Designers, Idea, 78; Steven Heller (auth), Call of nature, Print, 89; profile, Creation (Japan), 91. *Mem:* Am Inst Graphic Design; Am Inst Graphic Arts (bd dir, 89-91). *Media:* Watercolor, Graphite. *Publ:* Auth, The Art of Revolution, McGraw-Hill, 71; ed, The enviroment, Richard Coyne, 72 & ed & illusr, Vanishing creatures, 80, Communication Arts; auth & illusr, Vanishing Creatures, Lancaster-Miller, 80; Vanishing Flora, Harry N Abrams, 95; Birds & Bees, Harper Collins, 95. *Mailing Add:* 600 Embarcadero San Francisco CA 94107

STERN, ARTHUR I
STAINED GLASS ARTIST, SCULPTOR
b June 18, 50. *Study:* Dept Archit, Univ Ill, 68-72; Calif Col Arts & Crafts, BFA (environ design), 73, MFA, 75. *Comn:* Las Vegas Temple, LDS Church, Las Vegas, Nev, 88; Leader glass, LDS Church, Bountiful, Utah, 94; sculpture & leaded glass windows, Fed Courthouse, Baton Rouge, 94; Christ Church Episcopal, Portola Gallery, Calif, 94; St Matthews Lutheran Church, Walnut Creek, Calif, 94; and others. *Exhib:* One-man shows, Bank Am Gallery, San Francisco, 83 & Calif Col Arts Crafts Gallery, 83, Calif Coun Am Inst Archit Conv, San Diego, 83, Frank Lloyd Wright: In the Realm of Ideas, Marin Co Civic Ctr, San Rafael, Calif, 90, Am Inst Archit Gallery, San Francisco, Calif, 94; Nat AIA Col, Phoenix, 84, San Francisco, 85 & NY, 88; Image, Light & Structure, Pontiac, Mich, 84; Nat Glass, Downy Art Mus, Los Angeles, 86; Design 1987, Galleria Design Ctr, San Francisco, 87; Calif Design 2000, San Francisco, 99. *Collection Arranged:* CCAIA, Arch Glass, 81; AIA Nat Conv, Arch Craft, 85. *Teaching:* Instr sculpture, Calif Col Arts & Crafts, Oakland, Calif, 87 & instr glass, 88. *Awards:* IFRAA, Art in Archit Award, 87 & 90; Am Inst Arts Design Award, 96. *Media:* Architectural Glass. *Publ:* Auth, Stained Glass, fall 94. *Mailing Add:* 1075 Jackson St Benicia CA 94510

STERN, H PETER
COLLECTOR
Study: Harvard Univ, AB(magna cum laude), 50; Columbia Univ, MA, 52; Yale Univ Law Sch, LLB, 54. *Pos:* Pres, Storm King Art Ctr, Mountainville, NY; vchmn, World Monuments Fund, NY; pres, Ralph Ogden Found, Mountainville, NY; hon dir, Friends of Vassar Art Gallery, Poughkeepsie, NY; chmn bd, Star Expansion Co, Mountainville, NY; pres, Star Expansion Indust Corp, Mountainville. *Collection:* Contemporary paintings, graphics and sculpture; Indian & Turkish art. *Mailing Add:* PO Box 330 Mountainville NY 10953

STERN, LOUIS
DEALER, CONSULTANT
b Jan 7, 45; US citizen. *Study:* Calif State Univ, Northridge, BA. *Pos:* Pres, Wally Findlay Galleries, Beverly Hills, Calif, 80-82; pres, Louis Stern Galleries, Beverly Hills, Calif, 82-93, Louis Stern Fine Arts, Los Angeles, Calif, currently. *Awards:* Chevalier de L'ordre des Afts et des Lettres, French Ministry of Culture, 2001. *Mem:* Los Angeles Co Mus Art; Los Angeles Art Coun; Int Found Art Res, NY; Friends of French Art; Am Friends of Blerancourt; Art Dealers Asn Calif; Fine Arts Dealers Asn (FADA) (sec bd of dirs). *Specialty:* Impressionist, important Modern, Latin American, 19th and 20th century American and European painting and works on paper, 20th Century Hungarian Avantgarde. *Publ:* Janos Mattis Teutsch and The Hungarian Avant Garde, 1910-1935, Louis Stern Fine Arts, 2002; Transmigrations, Sculpture by Cecilia Miguez, Louis Stern Fine Arts, 2002; Lorser Feitelson and the Invention of Hard Edge Painting, 1945-1965, Louis Stern Fine Arts, 2004; Frederick Wight, Visions of California, Louis Stern Fine Arts, 2005; Lorser Feitelson, The Kinetic Series - Works from 1916-1923, Louis Stern Fine Arts, 2005; Lucien Clergue, Fifty Years of Photography, Vintage & Recent Works, Louis Stern Fine Arts, 2006; Claire Falkenstein, Structure and Flow, Works from 1950-1980, Louis Stern Fine Arts, 2006. *Mailing Add:* 9002 Melrose Ave Los Angeles CA 90069

STERN, LOUISE G
PRINTMAKER, PAINTER
b New Haven, Conn, Apr 24, 21. *Study:* Syracuse Univ, 39-42; Boston Univ, BA, 43; Mus Mod Art, 60-62; Art Students League & Roberto DeLamonica & Edgar A Whitney (watercolor); study with Don Stacy & Reiji Kimura. *Work:* Gen Foods Corp, Tarrytown, NY; Cabrini Med Ctr, Dobbs Ferry, NY; Brown Chemical Corp, NY; Morani Art Gallery, Med Col Pa, Philadelphia; Pfizer Collection, Westchester, NY; and others. *Comn:* Dr Barbara Melamed; Ellen Lazarus; Dr & Mrs Giancarlo Ginanangeli. *Exhib:* Prints Int 1990, 1992 & 1996, Silvermine Guild Artists, New

Canaan, Conn; Heaton Gallery, Rockland Ctr Arts, West Nyack, NY; Adelphi Univ, Manhattan Ctr, 91; Grass Roots Alumni, Gallery Hastings, 91; Union Am Hebrew Congregations, NY, 92; The Printed Image, Gallery Hastings, 92; solo exhibs, Banco Popular, NY, 93, Silvermine Guild Arts Ctr, New Canaan, Conn, 94 & Broome St Gallery, Soho, NY, 96; Manhattan Borough Pres Off, Women's Hist Month, Working Artists Katonah Mus Artists, Mt Kisco, 2003. *Teaching:* Children's class, Mamaroneck Artists Guild, 90; instr, watercolor, Learning in Retirement Inst, Iona Col, 94-; instr, home studio, 95-2005. *Awards:* First Prize: Mixed Media, New Rochelle Art Asn, 97, 2000; Louise H Renwick Mem Award, Graphics Art Show, Bedford, NY, 99; Dermont Gale Award, New Rocelle Art Asn, 2002; Katonan Mus Artists' Asoc Juried Exhib, Third Place; first place, Active Members Award Show, MAG 2004; first place, Mixed Media, New Rochelle Art Asn, 2004. *Bibliog:* Manhattan Arts Int, 96. *Mem:* Artist Equity NY; Nat Asn Women Artists, NY (chmn, print jury, 88-90 & chmn, nominating committee, 90-92); Silvermine Guild Artists, New Canaan, Conn; Mamaroneck Artists Guild, Larchmont, NY (exhib chmn); New Rochelle Art Asn, NY (exhib co-chmn); Am Asn Univ Women. *Media:* Watercolor, Graphics. *Interests:* playing the recorder. *Collection:* Pfizer Collection, Westchester Metro Media Corp, White Plains, NY; Marion Stein, Scarsdale, NY. *Dealer:* Marla Passarelli 43 Irenhy Ave Portchester, NY, 10573, web: www.m.p.artsales.com. *Mailing Add:* 120 Lakeshore Dr Eastchester NY 10707

STERNE, HEDDA
PAINTER
b Bucharest, Romania, Aug 4, 16; US citizen. *Study:* Pvt study in Paris, Bucharest & Vienna. *Work:* Va Mus Fine Arts, Richmond; Metrop Mus Art, Mus Mod Art, Whitney Mus Am Art, NY; Albright-Knox Art Gallery, Buffalo, NY; Pa Acad Fine Arts, Philadelphia; Art Inst Chicago; and many others. *Exhib:* Solo exhibs, Mortimer Brandt, NY, 45, Betty Parson Gallery, NY, 47-78, Lee Ault & Co, NY, 75, Fairweather Hardin Gallery, Chicago, 75, Montclair Art Mus, NJ, 77, ICL Gallery, East Hampton, 80, CDS Gallery, NY, 82, 84, 87, 90, & 92 & The Queens Mus, 85; 58th Exhib Am Painting & Sculpture, Art Inst Chicago, 47; 143rd-145th Ann Exhib of Painting & Sculpture, Pa Acad Fine Arts, Philadelphia, 48, 49 & 50; 21st Biennial Exhib 1949, Corcoran Gallery Art, Washington, DC, 49 & 50; Ann Exhib Contemp Am Painting, Whitney Mus Am Art, NY, 49; Contemp Painting in the US, Los Angeles Co Mus Art, 51; 61st Am Exhib: Paintings & Sculpture, Art Inst Chicago, 54; 50 Ans d'Art aux Etats-Unis: Collections fu Mus of Modern Art de NY, Musee National d'Art Moderne, Paris, 55; Am Artists Paint the City, Art Inst Chicago, 56; 62nd Exhib Am Painting & Sculpture, Art Inst Chicago, 57; Ann Exhib: Sculpture, Paintings, Watercolors, Whitney Mus Am Art, 57; 26th Biennial Exhib, Corcoran Gallery Art, 59; Ann Exhib--Contemp Am Painting, Whitney Mus Am Art, 59; 155th Ann Exhib Am Painting & Sculpture, Pa Acad Fine Arts, 60; 64th Am Exhib: Painting, Sculpture, Art Inst Chicago, 61; 65th Am Exhib: Some Directions in Contemp Painting & Sculpture, Art Inst Chicago, 62; 28th Biennial Exhib, Corcoran Gallery Art, 63; 159th Ann Exhib Am Painting & Sculpture, Pa Acad Fine Arts, 64; Ann Exhib Contemp Am Painting, Whitney Mus Am Art, 67; Vintage Artists, Penn Plaza, NY, 83; CDS Gallery, NY, 82, 84, 86, 88, 90 & 92. *Teaching:* Instr art hist, Carbondale Col, 64; conducted workshop for art teachers, NY State Coun Arts, 68. *Awards:* Fulbright Fel, painting, Venicer, 63; Childe Hassam Purchase Award, Am Acad Arts & Lett, NY, 71; Hassam & Speicher Purchase Fund Award, Am Acad Arts & Lett, 84. *Bibliog:* Robert Motherwell & Reinhardt (ed), Modern Artists in America, Wittenborn, 51; Nathaniel Pousette-Dart (ed), American Painting Today, Hastings, 56; Herbert Read (auth), The Quest and the Quarry, Rome-New York Art Found Inc, 61; and others. *Mailing Add:* c/o CDS 76 E 79th St New York NY 10021

STERRITT, COLEEN
SCULPTOR, EDUCATOR
b Morris, Ill, Jan 8, 53. *Study:* Univ Ill, BFA, 76; Otis Art Inst, MFA, 79. *Work:* Mus Contemp Art, Los Angeles. *Exhib:* Solo exhibs, Karl Bornstein Gallery, 84 & 86, Seaver Col Art Gallery, Pepperdine Univ, Malibu, Calif, 87, Santa Monica City Col, Santa Monica, Calif, 88, Cal State Univ, Los Angeles, 90, Claremont Grad Sch, Calif, 96 & Los Angeles Seoul Contemp Arts, 96; Selections from the Permanent Collection: 75-91, MOCA, Los Angeles, 91; Sexy: Sensual Abstraction in California Art, 1950's-1990's, Contemp Artists Collective/Temporary Contemp, Las Vegas, Nev, 95; Armory Ctr Arts, Pasadena, Calif, 96; Drawn from LA, Armory Ctr Arts, 96; The Empowered Object, Hunsacker/Schlesinger Gallery, Santa Monica, Calif, 96; and others. *Pos:* Bd dir, Los Angeles Contemp Exhibs, 86-92, treas, 88-90, chmn, 91-92. *Teaching:* Vis artist, Claremont Grad Sch, 85- 99, Calif State Univ, Fullerton, 86-87 & Pepperdine Univ, 87-88; instr drawing, Univ Southern Calif, 85-86, instr sculpture, 89; instr sculpture, Otis Art Inst, Parsons Sch Design, 87-93; Long Beach City Col, instr, sculpture, 96-98; head sculpture program, Long Branch City Coll, 98-. *Awards:* Fel, Nat Endowment Arts, 86; Artist Fel, Art Matters Inc, 94; Artist-in-Residence Grant, Roswell Mus & Art Ctr, NMex, 94; JP Getty Trust Fel, Calif Community Found, 96. *Bibliog:* Charlotte Streifer Rubenstein (auth), American Women Sculptors, A History of Women Working in Three Dimension, GK Hall & Co, Boston, 90; Peter Frank (auth), Pick of the week, LA Weekly, 10/18/90; Michal Reed (auth), Coleen Sterritt at LASCA, Artweek, 12/96. *Mem:* Int Sculpture Ctr; Los Angeles Contemp Exhib; Col Art Asn. *Media:* Mixed. *Publ:* Charlotte Streifer, Rubenstein, American Women Sculptors, A History of Women Working in Three Dimension, GK Hall & Co, Boston. *Mailing Add:* 3101 N Raymond Ave Altadena CA 91001

STETSON, DANIEL EVERETT
MUSEUM DIRECTOR, CURATOR
b Oneida, NY, Jan 3, 56. *Study:* State Univ NY Col Potsdam, BA, 78; Syracuse Univ, NY, MFA(grad asst), 81. *Collection Arranged:* Focus 1 Michael Boyd (auth, catalog), Focus 3 The Art of Haiti: A Sense of Wonder (auth, catalog), 89, Focus 6 Contemp Developments in Glass (auth, catalog), 90, Stieglitz and 40 other Photographers: The Development of a Collection (auth, catalog), 91-92, New Works: Featuring Austin and Central Texas Artists (auth, catalog), 92. *Pos:* Actg dir, Picker Art Gallery, Colgate Univ, Hamilton, NY, 80-81; dir, Gallery Art & cataloger, Permanent Collection, Univ Northern Iowa, Cedar Falls, 81-87, Davenport Mus Art, Iowa, 87-91; exec dir, Austin Mus Art, Tex, 91-96, Polk Mus, Lakeland, Fla, 96-. *Teaching:* Museology, Colgate Univ, 80-81; Univ Northern Iowa, 81-87; Mem adv comt MBA Course of Study Styles & Strategies Non-Prof Orgn, St Ambrose Univ, 89-91. *Awards:* Fel, Northeast Mus Conf, 79; Scholar ALI-ABA, 84. *Mem:* Am Asn Mus; Tex Asn Mus; Fla Art Dir Asn; Fla Asn Mus; and others. *Mailing Add:* Polk Mus Art 800 E Palmetto Lakeland FL 33801-5529

STETTNER, LOUIS
PHOTOGRAPHER
b New York, NY, Nov 7, 22. *Study:* Princeton Univ, 42-44; Inst Hautes Etudes Cinematographiques, BA, 49. *Work:* Victoria & Albert Mus, London; Bibliotheque Nat, Paris; Mus Mod Art, Int Ctr Photog & Metrop Mus Art, NY; Nat Mus Am Art; Mus de Elysee, Switzerland; Chicago Art Inst; San Francisco Mus Art; Smithsonian Inst, Washington, DC; Carnaualet Mus, Paris; and others. *Exhib:* Bibliotheque Nat, Paris, 49; Photog in the Fine Arts, Chicago Inst Art, 61 & traveling exhib; Photo League, Int Ctr Photog, NY, 81; Critics Choice, Victoria & Albert Mus, London, 83; Subjective Photog, San Francisco Mus Mod Art, 84; Neikrug Gallery, NY, 85; Daniel Wolf Gallery, NY, 86; Ctr Photog, Geneva, 86; Retrospective Early Work Photofind Gallery, NY, 88; NY Trilogy, Union Sq Gallery, 88; Comptoir de la Photographie, Paris, 89; Kate Heller Gallery, London, 90; Vision Gallery, San Francisco, 90; Gallery Spectrum, Zaragoza, Spain, 90; Recent Work Howard Greenberg Gallery, 92 & 96; Bonni Benrubi Gallery, 96 & 2006; Suermondt Ludwig Mus Aachen, 97; Marion Mayer Gallery, 98; Mus Belle Artes, Santiago, Chile, 2000; Woerdsdoff Gallery, Paris, 2004 & 06; Camera Wovll Gallery, Berlin, 2006; Whitney Museum, NY, 2006. *Awards:* Photog Fel, Yaddo, 56; Creative Photog Grant, NY State Coun Arts, 73 & Nat Endowment Arts, 74. *Bibliog:* Norman Hall (auth), The Indestructable Image, Brit Photog, 67; Alan Porter (auth), monograph, Swiss Camera, 72; Ken Poli (auth), Delights of the Quiet Eye, Popular Photog, 83. *Media:* Black and White. *Publ:* Auth, Paris Street Scenes, Two Cities Publ, 49; Weegee the Famous, Knopf Publ, 78; Sur Le Tas, Cercle D'Art, 79; Streetwork, Symbax Inc, 81; photgr, Poster Series by Flammarion, Flammarion Publ, 86; Early Joys Photographs from 1947-72, J Iffland, Pub, 86; Photo Poche #76 Louis Stettner, Nathan, 1994; Louis Stettner's New York, Rizzoli, 1996; Wisdom Cries Out in the Streets Editions, Flammarion, 1999; Edmund White (auth), Recent Work, Flammarion, 2000; Penn Station, Editions, Camera Work, 2006. *Dealer:* Howard Greenberg Gallery New York NY 10012. *Mailing Add:* 172 W 79th St No 6G New York NY 10024

STEVANOV, ZORAN
PAINTER, SCULPTOR
b Novi Sad, Yugoslavia, June 25, 45; US citizen. *Study:* Fla Atlantic Univ, Boca Raton, BA, 68; Wichita State Univ, Kans, MFA, 70. *Work:* Wichita State Univ; Emporia State Univ, Kans; Ft Hays State Univ, Kans. *Comn:* Sculpture fountain, State Kans, Emporia State Univ Libr, 71-73. *Exhib:* Nat Exhib Drawing & Sculpture, Muncie, Ind, 67; Nat Ann Exhib, Monroe, La, 71; Kans Biennial Art Exhib, Lindsborg, 72; Eight State Ann Exhib, Oklahoma City, 74; three-man show, Lynn Kottler Gallery, NY, 75. *Teaching:* Instr sculpture & design, Emporia State Univ, 70-73; assoc prof design, Ft Hays State Univ, 73-, assoc prof art, currently. *Awards:* Second Prize Ann State Exhib, Fort Lauderdale, Fla, 67; First Prize Ann State Exhib, Hollywood, Fla, 68; Third Prize Nat Art Exhib, Winter Park, Fla, 68; and others. *Mem:* Col Art Asn. *Mailing Add:* 1208 Donald Dr Hays KS 67601-2607

STEVENS, ANDREW RICH
CURATOR, HISTORIAN
b Dubuque, Iowa, Feb 1, 56. *Study:* Iowa State Univ, BA, 78, MA, 80; Univ Kans, MA(art hist), 88. *Collection Arranged:* American Color Woodcuts: Bounty from the Block, 1890s-1990s (with James Watrous, auth, catalog), 93; Tandem Press Five Years of Collaboration and Experimentation (auth, catalog), 94; Henry Moore: Prints and Maquettes from the William S Fairfield Collection (auth, catalog), 95; Hogarth and The Shows of London (auth, catalog), 96; 150 Years of Wisconsin Printmaking (auth, catalog), 98. *Pos:* Cur of Prints, Drawings and Photographs, currently. *Mem:* Print Coun Am; Am Asn Mus. *Res:* History and aesthetic of printed art. *Publ:* Contribr, The World in Miniature: Engravings By the German Little Masters (exhib catalog), Spencer, 88; Visions and Revisions: Works on Paper by Robert Cumming (exhib catalog), Elvehjem Mus, 91. *Mailing Add:* c/o Elvehjem Mus Art Univ Wis Madison WI 53706

STEVENS, ELISABETH GOSS
WRITER, PRINTMAKER
b Rome, NY, Aug 11, 29. *Study:* Wellesley Col, BA, 51; Columbia Univ, MA(high hons), 56. *Exhib:* Corcoran Gallery Art, Washington, DC; Towson State Univ, Baltimore; Atelier A/E, NY; one woman show, Col Notre Dame, Md, 97, Galerie Francoise, Lutherville, Md, 2000, Univ Minn at Morris, 2001; Katharine Butler Gallery, Sarasota, Fla, 2004. *Pos:* Ed assoc, Art News, 64-65; art critic, Washington Post, 65; free lance art critic & writer, 65-78; columnist, The Gallery, Wall St J, 69-71; Sunday art columnist, Trenton Times, 74-77; art & archit critic, Baltimore Sun, 78-86; Sarasota Herald Tribane Free Lance Art Critic, 2005. *Awards:* Prizewinner First Fiction Contest, Maryland Poetry Reviews, 93, Second Fiction Contest, 94; Prizewinner, Fiction Contest, Lite Circle, 94-96; Prizewinner, Playwriting Contest, Baltimore Writers Alliance, 95. *Mem:* Col Art Asn; Soc Graphic Artists; Women Contemp Artists of Sarasota, Fla; Fla Printmakers; Southern Graphics Council. *Media:* Etching. *Collection:* Baltimore Mus of Art; Brown Univ; Cornell Univ; Harvard Univ; New York Public Libr; Princeton Univ; School of the Art Inst of Chicago; Univ of

Texas at Austin. *Publ:* Artist of Delight: A Retrospective of the Works of Keith M Martin, 1911-83 (exhib, catalog), Ciscle Gallery, 87; Horse and Cart: Stories from the Country, Wineberry Press, 90; The Night Lover, 94, In Foreign Parts, Nine Stories, 97, Birch Brook Press; Household Words, Three Conditions Press, 2000; Eranos, Goss Press, 2000; Cherry Pie and Other Stories, Lite Circle, 2001. *Dealer:* Katharine Butler Gallery, 1943 Morrill St, Sarasota, FL, 34236. *Mailing Add:* Bards Castle 5353 Creekside Trail Sarasota FL 34243

STEVENS, JANE ALDEN
PHOTOGRAPHER, EDUCATOR
b Rochester, NY, 52. *Study:* St Lawrence Univ, BA, 1974; Rochester Inst Technol, MFA, 1982. *Work:* Int Mus Photog, Rochester, NY; Mus da Imagem e do Som, Mus de Arte Contemporanea, Sao Paulo, Brazil; Camera Club, NY; Cincinnati Art Mus; Ctr Photog as Art Form, Bombay, India. *Exhib:* One-man show, Galerie Greisinghaus, WGer, 1983 & Ctr for Photog Woodstock, NY, 1990 & ARC Gallery Chicago, 1994, Blue Sky Gallery, Portland, Oreg, 2002; Rochester: An Am Ctr of Photog, Int Mus Photog, Rochester, NY, 84; Photovisions, Contemp Arts Ctr, Cincinnati, 87; Extended Image, Photo Central Gallery, Hayward, Calif, 89; Pan Horama, Tampere, Finland, 91 & 97. *Teaching:* Asst prof photog, Univ Cincinnati, 83-88, assoc prof, 88-96, prof fine arts, 96-. *Awards:* Individual Artist Grant, Ohio Arts Coun, 1990 & 1992; Travel/Res Grant, English-Speaking Union, 2000; Artists Projects Grant, Ohio Arts Coun, 2000. *Bibliog:* Adirondack Life Mag, 10/97; Jane Stevens Swing-Lens Photographs Absorbing, Arts & Entertainment section, Pittsburgh Post Gazette, 2/96; Jane Alden Stevens, Kamera-Lehti Mag, Helsinki, Finland, 8/95. *Mem:* Col Art Asn; Soc Photog Educ; Int Asn Panoramic Photog. *Media:* Photography. *Publ:* Contribr, Solos do Imagem: Visao American-Janelos Brasilei (exhib catalog), 82; Camerawork of Jane Alden Stevens, Adirondac Mag, 88; All-embracing camera, The World & I, 1/92, pp 282-287; Fotografia Pensante, pub Sao Paulo, Brazil, 97, pp 80-81, 204, 210-111; auth, Tears of Stone: World War I Remembered, Cincinati, Ohio, 2004. *Mailing Add:* 515 Terrace Ave Cincinnati OH 45220-1916

STEVENS, JANE M
PHOTOGRAPHER, ADMINISTRATOR
b Chicago, Ill, Oct 1, 47. *Study:* Univ Ill Chicago, BA(anthopology), 72; Sch Art Inst Chicago; State Univ New York, Buffalo, MA(experimental video), 81; Univ Mass, Amherst, arts mgt cert, 94. *Work:* Visual Arts Collection Pensacola Col, Fla; Ill State Mus, Springfield; McCartney Award Portfolio, Women in Photography, London, Eng; Ill State Mus; Pensacola Col Visual Arts Collection; pvt collections. *Exhib:* Positive/Negative, Coos Art Mus, Coos Bay, Ore, 89; 7th Nat Exhib, Alexandria Mus Art, La, 88; The Toronto/Chicago Exchange, Toronto, Canada, 92; Jane Stevens/Robert Walker, Univ Ariz, Tucson, 92; solo show, ARC Gallery, 93; and others. *Pos:* Asst cur, Chicago Hist Soc, 78-85; asst admin, Ill Art Gallery, Chicago, 85-. *Teaching:* Instr photogr, Morton Col, Cicero, Ill, 87-90 & 94-2005; coord, fine arts seminar, Chicago Metrop Ctr, 99-. *Awards:* Project Completion, Solitude, Ill Arts Coun, 81; Purchase Award, Pensacola Portrait Exhib, Pensacola Col, 84; Award Portfolio, McCartney Award, Women in Photography, 88; Rocke feller Fel Humanities, The Newberry Lib, Chicago, 2002. *Bibliog:* Catharine Reeves (auth), Jane Stevens, transformations, Chicago Tribune, 3/31/89; Abigail Foerstner (auth), Artists Residents Chicago Gallery, Burke/Stevens, Chicago Tribune, 4/12/91; Abigail Foerstner (auth), Array of images, Chicago Tribune, 3/12/93. *Mem:* Artists Residents Chicago (pres, 92-93, grants 91-92); Chicago Artists Coalition; Soc Photg Educ; Col Art Asn; Am Asn Mus. *Res:* 50 years of Powwows at Newberry Library & Am Indian Ctr Chicago. *Publ:* Contribr, Zoom, Int Mag, 90; Computer Art: Pushing the Boundaries, Ill State Mus, 92; Camera & Darkroom Mag, 1/92; Visions From Within: Art from prison, Ill State Mus, 95; Artists using Science and Technology, YLEM, 9-10/96; From the Reservation to Urban Life, 2002; Chicago's 50years of Powwows, Arcadia publishing, 2004. *Dealer:* Artists Residents Chicago Gallery 1040 W Huron Chicago IL 60622; Ceres Gallery 584 Broadway New York NY 10011. *Mailing Add:* 1631 N Nagle Ave Chicago IL 60707

STEVENS, MARK WHITNEY
CRITIC
b New York City, Aug 14, 1951. *Study:* Princeton Univ, AB, 1973; Cambridge Univ, MA, 1975. *Pos:* Art critic, Newsweek, New York City, 1977-87, The New Republic, Washington, DC, 1986-94, Vanity Fair, New York City, 1988-92, New York Magazine, New York City, 1994-. *Publ:* auth, Richard Diebenkorn, 1984; auth, Summer in the City, 1984; co-auth, de Kooning: An American Master, 2004 (Nat. Book Critics Guild Prize for Biography, 2004, Pulitzer Prize for Biography, 2005); contribr numerous articles and essays on art. *Mailing Add:* NY Magazine 444 Madison Ave New York NY 10022

STEVENS, MAY
PAINTER
b Boston, Mass, June 9, 24. *Study:* Mass Col Art, BFA, 46; Art Students League, 48; Acad Julian, Paris, 48. *Work:* Whitney Mus Am Art, New Mus Contemp Art, Metrop Mus Art, NY; Brooklyn Mus; Herbert F Johnson Mus, Cornell Univ; San Francisco Mus Art; Ohio State Univ; Boston Mus Fine Arts. *Exhib:* Recent Acquisitions & Women Artists From Permanent Collection, Whitney Mus Am Art, 70; Rutgers Univ, NJ, 96; solo exhibs, Mary Ryan Gallery, NY, 96, 97 & 99, Univ Art Mus, Univ NMex, 96, SoHo 20, NY, 97, Lew Allen Contemp, Santa Fe, 98 & Mus Fine Arts, Boston, 99; Nassau Co Mus Art, Roslyn Harbor, NY, 97; Bernice Steinbaum Gallery, NY, 97; Mary Ryan Gallery, NY, 97 & 98; Crossing the Threshold, Brevard Mus Art & Sci, Fla, Spencer Mus Art, Kans, Mus Arts & Sci, Ga, Muscarelle Mus Art, Va, McAllen Int Mus, Tex & others, 97-; Fear & Desire, Cline Lew Allen Contemp, Santa Fe, 97; Feminine Image, Nassau Co Mus Art, NY, 97; and others. *Teaching:* Instr painting, Sch Visual Arts, 62-; vis artist, Cornell Univ, 73, Rhode Island Sch Design, 77, Cal State Univ, Long Beach, 90; Skowhegan Sch Printing & Sculpture, 92; Vt Studio Ctr, 97. *Awards:* Nat Endowment Arts Grant for Painting, 83; Yaddo Artists Colony Award, 85; Fel Painting, Guggenheim Found, 86; Fel, Bunting Inst, Radcliffe, 88. *Bibliog:* Donald Kuspit (auth), Crowding the picture, Artforum, 5/88; Carol Jacobsen (auth), Two Lives: Ordinary Extraordinary, Art Am, 2/89; Whitney Chadwick (auth), Women, Art and Society, Thames & Hudson, 90; Norma Broude & Mary Garrard (ed), The Power of Feminist Art, Abrams, 94; Patricia Mathews (auth), Rudolf Baranik & May Stevens at Exit Art, Art Am, 9/94; auth, Pomegranate, Pathius, 2005. *Mem:* Col Art Asn; Nat Acad (acad, 03-). *Media:* Oil, Acrylic. *Publ:* Auth, Working It Out, Pantheon, 77; Between Women, Beacon Press, 84; Fire Over Water, Tanam Press, 86; Visibly Female, Camden Press, 87; Voicing our Visions, Universe, 94. *Mailing Add:* c/o Mary Ryan Gallery 24 W 57th St New York NY 10019

STEVENS, MICHAEL KEITH
SCULPTOR
b Gilroy, Calif, July 14, 45. *Study:* Am River Col, 63-65; Calif State Univ, Sacramento, BA, 67, MA, 69; Univ Guadalajara, Mex, 66. *Work:* Squadron Press, Kansas City, Mo; Persis Corp, Honolulu, Hawaii; CSC Index, San Francisco; Livingston & Mattesich, Sacramento; Crocker Art Mus, Sacramento. *Comn:* Bronze sculpture, Cherry Island Golf Course. *Exhib:* Solo exhibs, Braunstein-Quay Gallery, NY, 78, Braunstein Gallery, San Francisco, 77, 79, 82, 84, 86, 89, 92, 94 & 97 & Betsy Rosenfield Gallery, Chicago, 81, 83, 85 & 88; Ovsey Gallery, Los Angeles, 90; Against The Grain: Contemp Wood Sculpture, Oliver Art Ctr, Calif Col Arts & Crafts, Oakland, 90; Michael Stevens & Suzanne Adan: A Survey, Mem Union Gallery, Univ Calif, Davis, 90; California Eccentrics, Ill Union Art Gallery, Univ Ill, Urbana-Champagne, 90; Discovery Contemp Calif Narrations, Am Cult Ctr, Brussels, Belgium, 92; From The Studio: Recent Painting & Sculpture By 20 California Artists, Oakland Mus, 92; Mr & Mrs Michael Stevens & Suzanne Adan, Michael Himovitz Gallery, Sacramento, Calif, 93; The Michael Himovitz Gallery, Crocker Art Mus, Sacramento, Calif, 94; Here and Now: Bay Area Masterworks From The Di Rosa Collections, Great Hall High Bay, Oakland Mus, Calif, 94; The Art of Collecting: The Artist As Collector, Mem Union Gallery, Univ Calif, Davis, 94; and many others. *Awards:* Phelan Award, Sculpture, San Francisco Found, 82; Indiv Fel Award, Calif Arts Coun. *Bibliog:* Albert Stewart (auth), Contemporary American Wood Sculpture, Crocker Art Mus, 84; Phil Linhares (auth), From the Studio: Recent Painting & Sculpture by 20 California Artists, Oakland Mus, 92; Phil Linhares (auth), Here & Now: Bay Area Masterworks From The Di Rosa Collections, 94. *Media:* Wood, Mixed Media. *Dealer:* Braunstein/Quay Gallery 250 Sutter St San Francisco CA 94108. *Mailing Add:* 3977 Rosemary Cir Sacramento CA 95821

STEVENS, THELMA K
EDUCATOR, DEALER
b New York, NY, Dec 4, 32. *Study:* Pratt Inst, Brooklyn, NY, BS, 54; Queens Col, Flushing, NY, MS, 59; Fordham Univ, NY, PhD, 80. *Pos:* Owner & pres, Isis Gallery, 82-. *Teaching:* Art instructor, painting & sculpture, various NY State schs, grades K-12, 54-; instr reading & art, Fordham Univ Grad Sch, 79. *Awards:* Art Educator of the Year, NY State, 83; Award, Innovative curriculum design, Cromacyl Paint Co, 83. *Mem:* Nat Art Educ Asn (dir secondary educ, Eastern Region USA & Canada, 86-88); Int Soc Educ through Art (NY State Rep, 88-); US Soc Educ Art; NY State Art Teachers Asn; Long Island Art Teachers Asn. *Res:* Cognition and art. *Specialty:* Contemporary paintings and sculpture. *Publ:* Coauth, Super sculpture, Using Science and Technology, Van Nostrand Reinhold, 74; contribr, Art theory, In: Tapestry, Collegium Book Publ, Inc, 79; auth, articles in Clearing House, Sch Arts. *Mailing Add:* 17 Harriman Dr Sands Point NY 11050

STEVENS, WILLIAM ANSEL, SR
PAINTER, CARTOONIST
b Akron, Ohio, Sept 6, 19. *Study:* Kent State Univ; NMex State Univ; also with E Ladislaw Novotny, Fredric Taubes, Gerry Pierce, Kenneth Barrack & Ramon Froman. *Work:* US Naval Air Station Corpus Christi, Tex Hist Collection; White Sands Missile Range, NMex; US Forest Serv; White Sands Nat Monument; CofC, Alamogordo. *Comn:* Various oil portraits & landscapes throughout the US, Ger, Japan and Australia. *Exhib:* NMex State Fair, Albuquerque, 65; Llano Estacado Art Exhib, Hobbs, NMex, 67-68; Sun Carnival Art Exhib, El Paso, Tex, 68-69; Nat Wild Turkey Fedn Show, 78; Law West Exhib, 78, Ballut Abyad Shrine Temple, Albuquerque, NMex, 83 (permanent). *Pos:* Owner, Art Enterprises, Alamogordo, 60-; ed cartoons for three newspapers, 67-69; ed & illusr, Mgt Digest, 74-75. *Awards:* Grand Champion Art Award, Otero Co Fair, Alamagordo CofC, 62; Grand Champion Art Award, US Forest Serv, White Sands, NMex, 64 & 71; First Place Art Award, CofC Banquet, Alamogordo, 71. *Bibliog:* B Schwartz (auth), Sun dial, El Paso Times Sunday Mag, 5/75; J Baldwin (auth), articles in art sect, Alamogordo Daily News; E White (auth), article in Missile Ranger, White Sands Missile Range, Dept Defense Publ. *Mem:* Black Range Artists Inc; NMex Desert Arts League (pres, 69-70). *Media:* Oil, Watercolor, Pen & Ink. *Publ:* Illusr, Capabilities of the White Sands Complex, 75 & 77; auth, Dear Smudge (weekly art column), 79-80. *Mailing Add:* 1416 Taft Ave Alamogordo NM 88310

STEVENSON, A BROCKIE
PAINTER, EDUCATOR
b Montgomery Co, Pa, Sept 24, 1919. *Study:* Pa Acad Fine Arts, Philadelphia; Barnes Found, Merion, Pa; Skowhegan Sch Painting & Sculpture, Maine. *Work:* Corcoran Gallery Art & Nat Mus Am Art; State Univ NY, Potsdam; Woodward Found, Washington, DC; Phillips Collection, Washington, DC; Brown Univ Libr Military Col, Providence, RI; Dept Defense, Washington DC; Mariners Mus New Port News, Va. *Comn:* Am Artists Report the War, Nat Gallery, London, 44. *Exhib:* Eight Washington Artists, Columbia Mus Art, SC, 71; Pyramid Galleries, Washington, DC, 73; Our

Land, Our Sky, Our Water, Spokane World's Fair, 74; retrospective, Northern Va Community Col, Annandale, 74; Images of the '70s: Nine Washington Artists, Corcoran Gallery Art, DC, 80; one-man shows, Fendrick Gallery, Washington, DC, 78, 84 & 88; Villanova Univ, Pa, 02; Strathmore Hall, Bethesda, Md, 04. *Pos:* War artist corresp, European Theater Operations, 43-45. *Teaching:* Instr compos, Sch Fine Arts, Washington Univ, 60-62; prof design, drawing & painting, Corcoran Sch Art, Washington, DC, 65-98. *Awards:* Penn Acad Fine Arts Fel, Philadelphia, Pa. *Bibliog:* Paul Richard (auth), article, Washington Post, 4/29/78 & 5/28/88; Benjamin Forgey (auth), articles, Washington Star-News, 5/7/78 & Washington Post, 5/12/84; David Tannous (auth), article, Art Am, 9-10/78; Florence Gilbard (auth), Mus & Arts Washington, 5-6/98; Lincoln Kirstein (auth), Mag of Art, 5/44; Samuel Young (auth), Southern Accents, 7-8/89. *Media:* Acrylic, Silkscreen Prints. *Mailing Add:* 6106 Yale Ave Glen Echo MD 20812

STEVENSON, HAROLD, JR
PAINTER
b Idabel, Okla, Mar 11, 29. *Study:* Univ Okla, Norman; Univ Mex, Mexico City; Art Students League, New York. *Work:* Whitney Mus, NY; Ctr George Pompidou, Paris. *Comn:* Tennessee Williams gold medallion, comn by Nat Comt Literary Arts, 81; Stations of the Cross, Cathedral St John Divine, 90; mural, NY Eye & Ear Infirmary, 91. *Exhib:* One man shows in San Francisco, 49, Univ Oklahoma, 49, Oklahoma Art Ctr, 49, Galerie Le Cour d'Ingres, Paris, 60, Le Sensuel Fantastique, Galerie Iris Clert, 62, Richard Feigen Galleries, NY, 64, Sculptures in Crystal, Knoedler and Co, Murano, Italy, 70; Group shows include Ann Exhib, Whitney Mus Am Art, NY, 62, New Realists, Sidney Janis Gallery, NY, 62; Galleria La Medusa, Rome, 73; Americans in Paris, Mus Nat Art Mod, 79; La Famille des Portraits, Louvre Mus Portrait of Francois de Menil, 79-80; and many others. *Teaching:* Artist-in-residence, Austin Col, Sherman, Tex, formerly. *Bibliog:* Andy Warhol (dir), Harold (film), New York, 64; Lucy Lippard (auth), Pop Art, New York, 66; Iris Clert (auth), Iris-Time l'artventure; Andre Morain (auth), Le Milieu de L'Art. *Media:* Oil. *Dealer:* Mitchell Algus Gallery511 W 25th St New York NY 10001

STEVENSON, RUTH CARTER
COLLECTOR, PATRON
b Ft Worth, Tex, Oct 19, 23. *Study:* Sarah Lawrence Col, BA, 45. *Pos:* Pres bd trustees, Amon Carter Mus; founder, Ft Worth Art Coun; vpres, Int Coun Mus Mod Art, 67-72; nat chmn collector's comt, Nat Gallery of Art, 74-95; mem vis comt, Fogg Mus, Cambridge, Mass, 77-83; trustee, Nat Gallery Art, 79-97 & chmn, 93-97, trustee emer, currently; pres, Amon G Carter Found, 82-; chmn, Ft Worth Cult Dist Comt, 86-89; trustee, Nat Trust Hist Preserv, 89-93; co-chair, Ft Worth Water Gardens Conservancy,currently. *Awards:* Gertrude V Whitney Award, Skowhegan, 95. *Mem:* Nat Endowment of the Arts; Ft Worth City Art Comn (chmn, George Rickey Sculpture Comt, 74-75). *Interests:* Am 19th and 20th Century Sculpture. *Collection:* American sculpture and graphics. *Mailing Add:* Amon Carter Mus 3501 Camp Bowie Blvd Fort Worth TX 76107

STEVOVICH, ANDREW VLASTIMIR
PAINTER, PRINTMAKER
b Salzburg, Austria, July 2, 48; US citizen. *Study:* RI Sch Design, BFA(painting; Sydney Richmond Burley Award; Presidential Fel Travel in Europe), 70; Mass Col Art, MFA(painting), 80. *Work:* Fuller Art Mus, Mass; Danforth Mus, Framingham, Mass; Portland Mus Art, Maine; Mus Fine Arts, Boston, Mass; New Brit Mus Am Art, Conn. *Exhib:* Triennial, Brockton Art Mus, 78 & 81; one-man show, Clark Univ Art Gallery, 80, Coe Kerr Gallery, NY, 83, 85, 87 & 90, Tatistcheff-Rogers Gallery, Santa Monica, Calif, 89 & 93 & Adelson Gallery, NY, 92 & 95; 20th Anniversary Exhib, Corcoran Gallery Art, 81; Boston Artists Work on Paper, Boston Univ Art Gallery, 81; Realistic Directions, Pa State Univ, University Park, 83; New Eng Impression, The Fitchburg Art Mus, Mass. *Bibliog:* Ronny Cohen (auth), review, Artforum, 4/90. *Media:* Oil, Pastel; Etchings. *Dealer:* Adelson Gallery 25 E 77th New York NY 10021

STEWARD, ALETA ROSSI
PAINTER, GRAPHIC ARTIST
b Bethpage, NY, Dec 18, 57. *Study:* Art Students League, W 57th St, New York, NY, with Frank Mason (figure painting) - 1976; Paul Wood Studios, Port Washington, NY, (abstract painting) -1976; Lassen College, Susanville, Calif, with Sophie Sheppard, (drawing & compos) - 1986. *Work:* Modoc Med Ctr, Alturas, Calif; San Bernadino Co Mus, Redlands, Calif; Cape Cod Mus of Natural Hist, Brewster, Mass; Mass Audubon Soc, Marshfield, Mass. *Comn:* wildlife mural, State of Calif 34th Dist Agr Asn, Cedarville, Calif, 1976. *Exhib:* The Still Wild West, Cape Cod Mus of Natural Hist, Brewster, Mass, 1989; Annual Wildlife, San Bernadino Co Mus, Redlands, Calif, 1990; Wyoming Centennial, Wyoming State Capitol Bldg, Cheyenne, Wyo, 1990; Annual Art in Nature, Vt Inst of Natural Sci, Woodstock, Vt, 1992; Faculty Exhib, Cape Mus of Fine Arts, Dennis, Mass, 1993. *Teaching:* instr wildlife drawing, Cape Cod Mus Art, summer 94. *Awards:* 2nd Best in Show, New Eng Woodcarving & Wildlife Art Show, 1993; Visitors Choice, Mass Audubon Soc, 1994; Best in Show, Annual New Eng Woodcarving & Wildlife Art Show, 1997. *Bibliog:* Marcia Monbleau (auth), Ah Wilderness!, The Review, 1990; Member of the Issue, North Light Magazine, 1992; Emerging Artists of the Cape & Islands, Cape Cod Life, 1996. *Mem:* Copley Soc Boston, 91-98; Soc Animal Artists, NY, 2004-. *Media:* Acrylic, Oil. *Publ:* auth, Cape Cod Gems (series of 4 art), Cape Cod Oracle, 1990. *Dealer:* Trees Place Julian Baird Rt 6A at 28 Orleans Mass 02653. *Mailing Add:* 57 Colonial Way Harwich MA 02645

STEWARD, JAMES
MUSEUM DIRECTOR, EDUCATOR
b Nov 15, 59. *Study:* Univ Va, BA, 81; Inst Fine Arts, NY Univ, MA, 88; Oxford Univ, England, DPhil, 92. *Collection Arranged:* Edvard Munch and His Models: 1912-1944, 92; Gertrude Jekyll: Private Gardens, Vanishing Arts, 93; Innocence and Experience in German Expressionist Prints and Drawings, 96; The Mask of Venice: Masking, Theater and Identity in the Art of Tiepolo and His Time, 96; Masterworks of Greek & Roman Art from the Hearst Mus, 96; Hogarth and His Times: Serious Comedy, 98; When Time Began to Rant & Rage: Figurative Painting from Twentieth-Century Ireland, 98; In Human Touch: Photographs by Ernestine Ruben, 2001; Donald Sultan: Smoke Rings, 2001; The Romanovs Collect: European Art for the Hermitage, 2003. *Pos:* chief curator, Berkeley Art Mus, 92-98; dir, Univ Mich Mus Art, 98-. *Teaching:* instr, Univ Va, 81-83; adj asst prof, hist of art, Univ Calif, Berkeley, 92-98; asst prof hist of art, Univ Mich, 98-2001, assoc prof, 2001-2003, prof, 2003-; vis asst prof art history, State Univ NY, 91-92. *Awards:* Exhibition Grant, NEH, 94 & 97; Exhibition Grant, Am Ireland Fund, 97; Exhibition Grant, Robert Gore Rifkind Found, 96; Chancellor's Award Distinguished Service, Univ Calif, Berkeley, 96; British Coun Res Fel, 94 & 95; Mellon Fund Fel, The Huntington Libr, San Marino, Calif, 93-94; Art His Fel, Va Mus Found, 90-91; Arnold, Bryce and Read Trust Award, Oxford Univ, 1991; Exhibition Grant, Samual H Kress Found, 2002 & 2003. *Mem:* AAM; Asn Art Mus Dirs; Col Art Asn; Mich Mus Asn (bd dir, 99-, vpres 2001-); Asn Col and Univ Mus and Galleries; Asn Art Historians; Am Soc Eighteenth-Century Studies; The Walpole Soc; The London Libr; Va Club of NY. *Res:* 18th and 19th century European art; Irish art 1900 to present; Contemporary photography; history of patronage; landscape history. *Publ:* The Mask of Venice, Univ Washington Press, 96; When Time Began to Rant & Rage, Merrell Holberton, 98; In Human Touch: Photographs by Ernestine Ruben, Nazraeli Press, 2001; The Romanovs Collect: European Art from the Hermitage, Merrell, 2003; Betye Soar: Extending the Frozen Moment, Univ Calif Press, 2005. *Mailing Add:* 1070Univ Michigan Mus Art Rackham Bldy 915 E Washington St Ste 0540 Ann Arbor MI 48109-1354

STEWART, BILL
SCULPTOR, CERAMIST
b Plattsburgh, NY, June 21, 41. *Study:* State Univ NY Col, Buffalo, BS(art educ), 63; Ohio Univ, MFA, 66. *Work:* San Angelo Mus Fine Arts, Tex; Mint Mus Art, Charlotte, NC; Ark Mus Art, Little Rock, Ark; Mus Am Crafts, NY; Mem Art Gallery, Rochester; Racine Art Mus, Racine Wis; Burchfield Penney Art Ctr, Buffalo, NY. *Comn:* Environmental sculpture, Greater Rochester Int Airport, NY, 91. *Exhib:* Clayworks--20 Americans, Mus Contemp Crafts, NY, 71; Figure and Fantasy, Renwick Gallery, 74; Clay, Whitney Mus, 74; Clay USA, Fendrick Gallery, Washington, DC, 75; Sculptureens USA, Campbell Mus, Camden, NJ, 76; Contemp Ceramic Sculpture, Achland Mem Art Ctr, Univ NC, Chapel Hill, 77; Tribute to Josiah Wedgewood, Philadelphia Mus Art, 80; Ancient Inspirations--Contemp Interpretations, Roberson Ctr, Binghamton, NY, 82; solo exhibs, Dawson Gallery, Rochester, NY, 87 & Munsom Williams Proctor Mus Art, Utica, NY, 89; Expressions in Color: Ceramics, NJ Ctr Visual Arts, Summit, NJ, 88; Contemp NY State Crafts, NY State Mus, 97; Okla City Mus Art, 97; Nancy Margolis Gallery, NY, 97; Western Heritage Mus, Omaha, Nebr, 97; Craft Alliance, St Louis, Mo, 98; John Elder Gallery, NY, 98; Works Gallery, Philadelphia, 98; Dorothy Weis Gallery, San Francisco, 98; Clockwork, Ctr Contemp Arts, Mo, 98; 12th San Angelo Nat Ceramic Competition, San Angelo Mus Fine Arts, Tex, 98; solo, Bernice Steinbaum Gallery, Miami, 2005; solo, R Duane Reed Gallery, NY, 2005. *Teaching:* Prof art, State Univ NY, Brockport, 66-, prof emeritus. *Awards:* Nat Endowment Arts Res Grant, 76; Lillian Fairchild Award, Univ Rochester, 79; Chancellor's Award Excellence in Teaching, State Univ NY, 82; United Univ Prof Award, Outstanding Comm Serv, 90; Lillian Fairchild Award, Univ Rochester, NY, 90. *Bibliog:* Leon Nigrosh (auth), Sculpting Clay, Davis Publ Inc, Mass, 92; Richard Zakin (auth), Electric Kiln Ceramics, Chilton Bk Co, Radnor, Pa, 94; Johnathon & Angela Fina Fairbanks (auths), The Best of Pottery, Rockport Publ, Mass, 96; Suan Peterson (auth), Contemporary Ceramics, Watson Guptill, NY, 2000; 500 Figures in Clay Ceramic Artist Celebrate the Human Form, Lark Books, 2004; Mathias Osterman (auth), The Ceramic Narrative, Univ Penn Press, Philadelphia, 2006; and many others. *Media:* Ceramics. *Mailing Add:* 245 Hinkleyville Rd Spencerport NY 14559

STEWART, DOROTHY S
PAINTER, PRINTMAKER
b Brooklyn, NY. *Study:* Art Students League; Nat Acad Sch Fine Art, New York; NY Univ. *Comn:* In pvt collections. *Exhib:* Catharine Lorillard Wolfe Art Club 68-93rd Ann, 68th-105th ann exhib, 65-01; Allied Artists Am 56-89th Ann, 69-02; Academic Artists, 88; Hudson Valley Art Asn, 89, 90, 91; Allied Artists Am, Butler Inst Am Art, 2001. *Teaching:* Instr art, Malverne Sr High Sch, NY, 65-66. *Awards:* Catharine Lorillard Wolfe Club Award, 74, 79, 83, 85, 87, 89, 94, 95 & 99; Brookhaven Art Coun Award of Excellence, 98; Winsor & Newton Painting Award, Arts Coun East Islip, 2004. *Mem:* Catharine Lorillard Wolfe Art Club (dir, 70, 2nd vpres, 71-74); Allied Artists Am (asst corresp secy, 78-79); N Shore Art Asn; Kent Art Asn (pres, 77-78); life mem Art Students League; among others. *Media:* Oil, Watercolor. *Publ:* Contribr, Prize-winning art book 7, Allied Publ, Inc, Ft Lauderdale, Fla, 67. *Dealer:* Phoenix Fine Arts Gallery 139 Main St Bellport NY 11713. *Mailing Add:* 39 Idle Hour Rd Oakdale NY 11769

STEWART, DUNCAN E
COLLAGE ARTIST
b St Paul, Minn, Sept 30, 40. *Study:* Calif State Univ, San Diego, BA, 67, MA, 69; Fla State Univ, 74. *Work:* Pensacola Mus Art, Fla. *Exhib:* Solo exhibs, Fla State Univ-Florence Study Ctr, Italy, 82, LeMoyne Art Found, Fla, 84 & Univ New Orleans, 86; The Glove Invitational, Valencia Jr Col, Orlando, Fla, 87; The Box, SE Ctr Contemp Artists, Raleigh, 85; Pensacola Mus Art, Fla, 88; Fla A & M Univ, 89. *Pos:* Dir, Univ West Fla Art Gallery, Pensacola, currently. *Awards:* Fla Arts Coun Individual Artists Fel, 82. *Mem:* Col Art Asn; Southeastern Col Art Asn. *Dealer:* Mario Villa Gallery 3908 Magazine St New Orleans LA 70115. *Mailing Add:* 321 W DeSoto St Pensacola FL 32501

STEWART, F CLARK
DRAFTSMAN, PAINTER
b Evansville, Ind, July 18, 42. *Study:* Univ Redlands, Calif, BA(art), 64; Claremont Grad Sch & Univ Ctr, Calif, MFA(painting), 66. *Work:* Mint Mus Art, Charlotte, NC; Tenn State Mus, Nashville; Knoxville Mus Art, Tenn; Austin Peay State Univ, Clarksville, Tenn; Clemson Univ, SC. *Exhib:* Solo exhibs, Hunter Mus, Chattanooga, 82, WVa Univ, Morgantown, 87 & Cheekwood Fine Arts Ctr, Nashville, 88; More Than Earth & Sky, Nat Mus Am Art, Washington, 81; Art Quest 86, Video Exhib, Los Angeles; Fact, Fiction, Fantasy-Recent Art in the Southeast, Touring Exhib, Univ Tenn, 87; Clemson Print & Drawing Show, Lee Hall Gallery, Clemson Univ, SC, 87; Festival Int de Louisiane, Lafayette Art Gallery, 91; and others. *Teaching:* Prof drawing, Univ Tenn, Knoxville, 66-. *Awards:* Purchase Prizes, Tenn Asn Mus, 76, Marietta Nat Print & Drawing Show, 81 & Clemson Nat Print & Drawing Exhib, 85; AAVW Prize, Northern Nat Art Exhib, Rhinelander, Wis, 90. *Bibliog:* Dale Cleaver (auth), illus rev, Art Express, Vols 1 & 2, 82; Fred Moffat (auth), illus rev, Art Papers, Vols 4 & 6; Susan Knowles (auth), rev, New Art Examiner, Vol 16, No 10, 6/89. *Mem:* Col Art Asn. *Media:* Works on Paper; Mixed Media on Panels. *Publ:* Illusr, The Marriage of Heaven and Hell, Darkpool Press, Tenn, 72. *Mailing Add:* Dept Art Univ Tenn 1715 Volunteer Blvd Knoxville TN 37996

STEWART, JACK
PAINTER, EDUCATOR
b Atlanta, Ga, Jan 27, 26. *Study:* With Steffen Thomas, Atlanta; Yale Univ Sch Fine Arts, under Albers & deKooning, BFA; Columbia Univ Sch Archit; NY Univ, MA, PhD. *Work:* Yale Univ Art Gallery; Columbia, SC, Mus Fine Arts; Greenville Mus, SC; New York Univ; Mus City NY; Nat Acad Mus, NY; SEMO Mus, Md. *Comn:* Six mosaic murals on SS Santa Paula, Grace Lines, 57; mosaic mural on facade of Hotel Aruba Caribbean, Netherlands Antilles, 58; two mosaic murals in Pub Sch 28, Manhattan, NY, 58; stained glass, Cinerama, Inc, NY, 60; cloth mosaic mural, Cluett Peabody, Inc, NY, 88. *Exhib:* Pa Acad Fine Arts, Philadelphia, 53; Collegeo Raffaello, Urbino, Italy, 73; NY Univ, 75; one-man shows, Grippi Gallery, 63-64, Wash Sq East Galleries, NY, 75, Woods Gerry Gallery, Providence, RI, 76, 97 & 99, Blue Hill Cult Ctr, Pearl River, NY, 89 & The Broome St Gallery, NY, 91-92 & 2001; Nat Acad Mus, 95,97, 99, 2001 & 2003. *Pos:* Pres, Stewart Studio, NY, 51-. *Teaching:* Lectr art & archit, New Sch Social Res, 53-58; instr design, Pratt Inst, 55-61; lectr drawing & painting, Columbia Univ, 67-76; instr drawing & painting, Cooper Union Sch Art & Archit, 60-71, assoc prof & chmn dept, 71-74; instr graphics & drawing, Queens Col, NY, 74-76; instr painting & drawing, NY Univ, 74-76; provost & vpres acad affairs, RI Sch Design, 76-77; prof art & chmn dept, Ind State Univ, Terre Haute, 78-80. *Awards:* Academician, Nat Acad. *Bibliog:* Regina S. Stewart (auth), Jack Stewart, Drawings Looking Into the 21st Century, 2000. *Mem:* Artists Equity Asn, NY (pres, 87-89); Nat Soc Mural Painters (pres, 96-2000); Fine Arts Fed NY (vpres, 2000-, pres, 2003-). *Media:* Acrylic, Watercolor. *Publ:* Contribr, Mosaic Art Today, 59; ed, Modern Mosaic Techniques, Watson Guptill, 67; auth, short articles on drawing & mosaic, In: Jefferson Encycl, World, 69; contribr, Art of Mosaic, 69; article on Richard Meier's New Harmony Atheneum, In: USA Today, 1/84; Subway Graffiti: Anesthetic study of graffiti on the subway system of NYC, 70-78; MTA-Mass transit art of Dc Kunst Van Het Massavercoer; In coming from the subway, 91; American graffiti, 97. *Dealer:* Broome St Gallery New York New York. *Mailing Add:* 31 E Seventh St New York NY 10003

STEWART, J(OHN) DOUGLAS
HISTORIAN
b Kingston, Ont, Jan 28, 34. *Study:* Queen's Univ, Kingston, Ont, BA(hons), 55; McGill Univ, BLS, 56; Courtauld Inst, Univ London, PhD, 68. *Teaching:* Lectr art hist, Univ Toronto, 64-65; asst prof art hist, Queen's Univ, Kingston, Ont, 65-70, assoc prof, 70-80, prof, 80-, acting head, 85 & 94-95; guest lectr, Kunstgeschichtliche Gesellschaft zu Berlin, 94. *Awards:* Best Local Hist Award, Can Hist Asn, 74; Leave Fels, Can Coun, 74-75 & 81-82. *Res:* 17th century English painting & Flemish painting, sculpture and architecture; 19th century Canadian architecture. *Publ:* Auth, Sir Godfrey Kneller, Nat Portrait Gallery, 71; coauth, Heritage Kingston, Agnes Etherington Art Ctr, 73; English Portraits of the Seventeenth and Eighteenth Centuries, W A Clark Mem Libr, 74; auth, Sir Godfrey Kneller and the English Baroque Portrait, Oxford Univ Press, 83. *Mailing Add:* Queen's Univ Dept Art Kingston ON K7L 3N6 Canada

STEWART, JOHN LINCOLN
EDUCATOR, WRITER
b Alton, Ill, Jan 24, 17. *Study:* Denison Univ, AB, 38; Ohio State Univ, MA, 39, PhD, 47; Denison Univ, hon DA, 64. *Pos:* Assoc dir, Hopkins Art Ctr, Dartmouth Col, 62-64; dir, Mandeville Ctr for Arts, Univ Calif, San Diego, 75-76. *Teaching:* From asst prof to prof, Dartmouth Col, 49-64; prof Am lit & provost, John Muir Col, Univ Calif, San Diego, 64-87. *Awards:* Howard Found Fel, 53-54; Dartmouth Fac Fel, 62-63. *Res:* Contemporary American and British literature. *Publ:* Auth, John Crowe Ransom, Univ Minn, 62; Burden of Time, The Fugitives and Agrarians, Princeton Univ, 65; co-auth, Horizons Circled, Univ Calif, 74; Ernst Krenek, Calif Univ Press, 91. *Mailing Add:* 2361 E 29th St Oakland CA 94606-3511

STEWART, JOHN P
PAINTER, PRINTMAKER
b Ft Leavenworth, Kans, Mar 11, 45. *Study:* Univ Colo, with Roland Reiss & Wendel Black, BFA, 67; Univ Calif, Santa Barbara, MFA, 69. *Work:* Corcoran Gallery Art, Washington, DC; Whitney Mus Am Art, NY; Ponce Mus, PR; New Orleans Mus of Art, La; Mint Mus, NC; Cincinnati Art Mus. *Comn:* Painting, Rubloff Inc, Bicentennial, Cincinnati, 88; paintings, Wright Patterson Air Force Base, Dayton Ohio, 94. *Exhib:* Recent Acquisitions, Whitney Mus, NY, 72; Foire Int D'Art Contemporain, Grand Palais, Paris, 82; Carl Solway Gallery, Cincinnati, Ohio, 85; Works of the Figure, Allegheny Col, Pa, 86; Landscapes, Southern Ohio Art Mus, 91, An Infinite Adjustment, 2001; Atmospheres, AB Closson Co, Cincinnati, Ohio, 93; and others; Art of the American West, Oglebay Institute, Wheeling, WVa, 2002. *Teaching:* Prof, Univ Cincinnati, 73-. *Awards:* Individual Artist Grant, Ohio Arts Coun, 78 & 82; Prof of Yr, DAAP, 2000. *Media:* Oil. *Dealer:* A B Closson Art Gallery 401 Race St Cincinnati OH 45202. *Mailing Add:* 3836 Barker Rd Cincinnati OH 45229

STEWART, JOHN STEWART HOUSTON
DEALER
b Orange, NJ, Dec 24, 45. *Study:* Miami Univ, BA, 68. *Collection Arranged:* Works by Van Selm, Barnwell Art Ctr, Shreveport, La, 78; Sculpture of Russell Jacques, Abilene Fine Arts Mus, 79; Watercolors by Jo Taylor, El Dorado Art Ctr, Ark, 80; Figurative Works by Charles Campbell, Univ Tex, Dallas, 81; Mardi Gras by Arie Van Selm, Dallas City Hall, 81, Int House, New Orleans, 81 & touring in Europe; Nathan Jones Touring Exhib, Randall Gallery, New York, 81, Fed Reserve Bank, Cleveland, 81, Fed Reserve Bank, Cincinnati, 81, Univ Tex, Arlington, 81, Univ Calif, Los Angeles, 82 & Fisk Univ, 82; Landscapes by Jeff Tabor, Tex Womens Univ, 82; Artists from the Stewart Gallery, Abilene Christian Univ, 83; Black Heritage Today, Longview Mus, Tex, 83; Landscapes by Four American Artists, Coninck Gallery, Holland. *Pos:* Designer & planner, Galleria des Bellas Artes, Phoenix, 71 & White Gallery, Westlake Village, Calif, 80; founder & dir, Stewart Gallery, Dallas, 72-; dir & mgr, Artists Courtyard, 76-; partner, Jones-Houston Graphics, currently. *Specialty:* Art by young, contemporary artists. *Mailing Add:* 7139 Azalea Ln Dallas TX 75230

STEWART, LORELEI
CURATOR, ADMINISTRATOR
b Hattiesburg, Miss, Sept 3, 66. *Study:* Smith Col, MAss, BA, 87; Corcoran Sch Art, Wash, DC, BFA, 92; Bard Col, Ctr for Cur Studies, NY, 98-2000. *Collection Arranged:* At the Edge:L Innovative Art Chicago, 2002, 2003 & 2004; Jenny Perlin: A worry Free Life or your Money, 2004; Impure Beauty: Ruben Ortiz to Pres, 2003; Revolutions Per Minute, 2001; Inside the City, 2001. *Pos:* Dir, Gallery 400, 2000-; cur, Mus Cont Art, Los Angeles, Calif, 99; prog dir, New Langton Arts, San Francisco, Calif, 94-98. *Publ:* Contribr, New Langton Arts, 97. *Mailing Add:* Coll Arch & Arts UIC Gallery 400 1240 W Harrison St (MC 034) Chicago IL 60607-7034

STEWART, NORMAN
PRINTMAKER, PUBLISHER
b Detroit, Mich, Mar 31, 1947. *Study:* Univ Mich, BFA, 69, MA, 72; Cranbrook Acad Art, studied with Irwin Hollander & Sewell Sillman, MFA, 77. *Work:* Brooklyn Mus, NY; Cleveland Mus Art, Ohio; Detroit Inst Art, Mich; Univ Ariz Mus Art, Tucson; Toledo Mus Art, Ohio; Kalamazoo Inst Arts, Mich. *Comn:* Print comn, PBS, WTVS, Detroit, Mich, 75; Creative Artist Grant, Mich Coun Arts, Detroit, 81; print comn, Detroit Inst Arts, Founders Soc, Detroit, Mich, 82 & 96; collaborative print comns, Univ Mich Sch Art, Ann Arbor, 84 & Mt Holyoke Col, South Hadley, Mass, 87; print comn, General Motors, Detroit, Mich, 98; Stewart & Stewart Screenprints, river Gallery, Chelsea, MI, 2002; Cranbrook Art Mus, Bloomfield Hills, MI, 2003. *Exhib:* 21st & 22nd Nat Invitational Print Exhib, Brooklyn Mus, NY, 78-79 & 81-82; 20th Century Prints & Drawings, Detroit Inst Arts, Mich, 81-82; New Am Graphics Two Invitational, Madison Arts Ctr, Wis, 82; Cabo Frio Int Print Biennial-82, Brazil, 82-83; Gene Baro Collects, Brooklyn Mus, 83; On the Leading Edge, Gen Elec Hq, Fairfield, Conn, 85; A Graphic Muse, Mt Holyoke Col Art Mus, Mass, Yale Univ Art Gallery, Conn, Santa Barbara Mus Art, Calif, Va Mus Fine Arts, Nelson-Atkins Mus Art, Mo, 87-88; Collaboration in Print, Stewart & Stewart Prints, 1980-1990 (with catalog), touring 91-93; Print Fest, Milwaukee Art Mus, Wis, 93 & 95; IFPDA Print Fair, NY, 94-98; Fine Print Fair, Cleveland Mus Art, Ohio, 96. *Pos:* Partner & master printer, Stewart & Stewart, Bloomfield Hills, Mich, 80-. *Teaching:* Guest artist screenprinting, Wayne State Univ, Detroit, Mich, 79-80; adj asst prof screenprinting, Sch Art, Univ Mich, Ann Arbor, 79-85; guest artist & lectr screenprinting, numerous art schs & museums across USA, 79-. *Awards:* Disting Svc Award, Univ of Mich Sch of Art and Design, Ann Arbor, MI, 2000. *Bibliog:* Reviews, The Print Collector's Newslett & Art On Paper, Stewart & Stewart Fine Print Publ, 84-96; reviews, J of the Print World, Stewart & Stewart Fine Print Publ, 91-98; Janet Fish in Detroit, Printable News, Detroit Inst Arts, fall 96. *Mem:* Int Fine Print Dealers Asn; Nat Educ Asn; Mich Educ Asn; Detroit Inst Arts Founders Soc. *Publ:* Contribr, Screenprint in the making: Sondra Freckleton collaborates with Norman Stewart (video), Stewart & Stewart Printer/Publisher of Fine Prints, 85; Collaboration in Print-Stewart & Stewart Prints; 1980-1990, Washtenaw Community Col Found, Ann Arbor, Mich, 90; coauth, John Himmelfarb, Contemporary Impressions, The J of Am Print Alliance, fall 94; Ink on Paper, Quad/Collection, Milwaukee Art Mus, Wis, 96. *Mailing Add:* c/o Stewart & Stewart 5571 Wing Lake Rd Bloomfield Hills MI 48301-1250

STEWART, PAUL LEROY
PRINTMAKER, EDUCATOR
b Cleveland, Ohio, June 28, 28. *Study:* Cleveland Inst Art, 46-48; Albion Col, BA, 53; Univ Mich, Ann Arbor, MA, 59. *Work:* Detroit Inst Art; Libr Cong; Metrop Mus Art, NY; Minneapolis Inst Art; Cleveland Mus Art, Ohio. *Comn:* Bicentennial print, Mich Workshop Fine Prints, Detroit, 75. *Exhib:* Solo exhibs, DeWaters Art Ctr, Flint, Mich, 79, Lill Street Gallery, Chicago, Ill, 87, Deutsch-Amerikanisches Inst, Tubingen, Ger, 87, Gallery Nishiazabu, Tokyo, Japan, 91, Fuji Cult Ctr, 94 & Gallery Otowa, Tokyo, 95 & 96; Between Nature & Cult: Am Prints, Felix Jenewein Gallery, Czech Republic, 99; 14th Premio Int Biella Per L'Incisione, Italy, 99; Int Print Triennial-Cracow 2000-Bridge to the Future, Poland; Int Print Triennial Colour in Graphic Art, Torun, Poland, 2000; many others. *Teaching:* Assoc prof art, Albion Col, 59-72; Catherine C Heller prof art emer, Univ Mich, Ann Arbor, 73-; guest instr lithography, Univ NMex,

Albuquerque, summer 79. *Awards:* Special Award, 13 Premio Int Biella Per L'Incisione, Italy, 96; 4th Prize, 3d Kochi Int Triennial Exhib of Prints, Japan, 99; Spl Prize, Int Print Triennial, Cracow, Poland, 2000; others. *Bibliog:* C Overvoorte (auth), article, For the Time Being Fine Arts Mag, Vol II, No 2, 73; Artists in Michigan of the 20th Century, Smithsonian Inst Arch Am Art; Artists in Michigan, 1900-1976, Wayne State Univ Press. *Media:* All Media. *Publ:* AXIS World Design J, No 44, Tokyo, Japan, summer 92; The Best of Printmaking, An International Collection, Allen & McGibbon, Rockport Publ, 97. *Dealer:* Art Search 717 W Huron Ann Arbor MI 48103. *Mailing Add:* 4040 Danford Rd Ann Arbor MI 48105

STEWART, REGINA
PAINTER, WRITER
b Passaic, NJ, 42. *Study:* Cooper Union; Hunter Col. *Work:* Columbia Mus of Art, SC; Greenville Co Mus, SC; Aldrich Mus of Contemp Art, Ridgefield, Conn; Mus Savannah Col Art & Design, Ga; Jacqueline Casey Hudgens Ctr for Arts, Duluth, Ga; SE Mo Univ Mus, Cape Girardeau, Mo. *Exhib:* Collegeo Raffaello, Urbino, Italy, 73; Columbus Mus Art, Columbus, Ohio, 85; Ann Broome St Gallery Exhib, NY, 1996-2002; Voices through Vision: Eight Women Artists, Gwinnett Fine Arts Ctr, Deluth, Ga, 97; Radford Art Mus, Va, 2000; SE Mo Univ Mus, Cape Girardeau, Mo, 2002; One-woman show, 25 Yr Retrospective, NY, 2002, Jacqueline Casey Hudgens Ctr Arts, Duluth, Ga, 2005. *Pos:* Promotion for art & antiques, Channel 13 TV Sta, NY, 76; treas, NY Artists Equity, 90-91; pres, 91-93; exec dir, 93-; mem adv bd, Steffen Thomas Mus & Arch, 97-; mem adv bd, Fine Arts Fedn NY, 2000-. *Teaching:* Instr painting & drawing, NY Univ, 76-. *Awards:* First Prize/Painting, Ann John Roebling Exhib, John Roebling Found, 60; NEA Matching Purchase Funds Award. *Bibliog:* Notable Americans, Hist Preserv Am, 76; Regina Stewart: The Sweep of History, Gallery & Studio, 2003. *Mem:* Art Spaces (adv, 60-); Artists Equity Asn; The Art Club, NY, 98. *Media:* Acrylic. *Publ:* Auth, Richard Meier's building: The Athenaeum at New Harmony, USA Today, 1/84; co-auth, Golden Series of Books of Collectibles: American Stoneware, Kitchenware, carnival glass & bottles, The Artists Proof News Mag, New York Artists Equity Asn, NY, 92-; auth, Henry Ryan McGinnis: American Impressionist 1875-1962, 2000; auth, Jack Stewart Drawings: Looking Into the 21st Century, 2000; auth, Broome Street Gallery, 15th Anniversary Exhib, 2005. *Mailing Add:* 31 E Seventh St New York NY 10003

STEWART, SHEILA L
DIRECTOR, CURATOR
Study: Ga Southern Col, BA, 76; Southern Ill Univ, MFA, 81. *Work:* Univ Mus, Carbondale, Ill; Alexandria Art Mus, La; Art Mus Southeast Tex, Beaumont. *Collection Arranged:* Laughing to Keep from Crying, Alexandria Mus, 85; Southeast Tex Collects Am Art (auth, catalog), 87; 500 Main: Installations (auth, catalog), Art Mus Southeast Tex, 85; Curator's Choice (auth, catalog), 88; James Surls, Art Mus Southeast Tex, 88. *Pos:* Cur, Alexandria Art Mus, 81-83, exec dir, 83-86; exec dir, Art Mus Southeast Tex, 86-. *Awards:* Alexandria Mus Art, 84; Special Exhib Award, Nat Endowment Arts, 85 & 87; Art Mus Southeast Tex, 89. *Publ:* Laughing to Keep from Crying (catalog), 85; Annual Report (catalog), 87-92; John Alexander (catalog), 90; Paths to Grace (catalog), 91; Paul Maness (catalog), 92. *Mailing Add:* Brevard Art Ctr 1463 Highland Ave Melbourne FL 32936

STEWART, WILLIAM
PAINTER, EDUCATOR
b Waco, Tex, Aug 18, 1938. *Study:* Univ Tex, BFA, 60, MFA, 62, int artists seminars, Fairleigh Dickinson Univ, Madison, NJ, summers 61 & 62. *Work:* Fordham Univ, Bronx, NY; Fairleigh Dickinson Univ, Madison, NJ; Mus Mod Art, Vienna, Austria. *Exhib:* One-man shows, OK Harris Gallery, NY, 69, Rudolf Zwirner Gallery, Cologne, Ger, 70, Pergola Gallery, San Miguel de Allende, 78, Regional Mus, Oaxaca, Mex, 79, Bonnafont Gallery, San Francisco, Calif, 79, Old Jail Art Mus, Albany, Tex, 85; Thomas Moore Chapel, Fordham Univ, Bronx, NY, 76; Charles Furr Gallery, Sante Fe, Mex, 85; Munson Gallery, Santa Fe, NMex, 96; Collins Pettit Gallery, Taos, NMex, 96; Water Currents, Kouros Gallery, NY, 05. *Teaching:* Asst dir educ dept & instr, San Francisco Mus Art, Calif, 63-64; art instr, Baleares Int Sch, Palma de Mallorca, Spain, 66-67; instr, Dept Art, Fairleigh Dickinson Univ, Madison, NJ, 68-70, City Col NY, 71 & Ed Dept, Newark Mus, NJ, 73-74; instr drawing & painting, Instituto Allende, San Miguel de Allende, Guanajuato, Mex, 77-78; vis artist, dept art & art hist, Univ Iowa, Iowa City, 81; art instr, Taos Valley Sch, NMex, 85; instr, Dept Art, Northern NMex Community Col, 90-93 & Univ NMex, Taos, 93-; instr watercolor workshops, Taos Inst Arts, NMex, 93-97; instr drawing and painting, Univ NMex, currently; instr workshops, Taos Art Sch, summer, fall, 2000; instr, State Univ NY, Dutchess, Community Col, Poughkeesie, NY, 2002; lectr, for art students, Relationship of Artist to Subject Matter, 2002. *Bibliog:* Rosalind Constable (auth), New sites for new sights, NY Mag, 12/70; William Stewart at Zwirner Gallery, Kölner Kulturspiegel, 9/70; Colin Naylor (ed), Contemporary Artist, St James Press Ltd, London, 77; Eric Somers (auth), video documentary. *Media:* Oil, Watercolor, pastel, charcoal. *Mailing Add:* 4161 NDCBU Taos NM 87571-6007

STEYNOVITZ, ZAMY
PAINTER
b Liegnitz, Poland, Jan 1, 51; US citizen. *Study:* Avni Inst, Tel-Aviv, 70-72; Royal Acad, London, 72-75; Art League, New York, 76-80. *Work:* Museo Simon Bolivar, Caracas, Venezuela; Ana Frank Mus, Amsterdam, Holland; Nat Mus Art, San-Jose, Costa-Rica. *Comn:* Medal, Judaic Heritage Soc, NY, 79; mural, Mus Simon Bolivar, Caracas, Venezuela, 83. *Exhib:* One-man shows, Ramat-Gan, Israel, 70, Jewish Mus, Cleveland, Ohio, 80 & Nat Mus Art, San-Jose, Costa-Rica, 83; Tribute to John Lennon, Abraham-Goodman House, NY, 81; Homage to Bolivar, Simon Bolivar Mus, Caracas, Venezuela, 83; Centrum Judaica, Berlin, 95. *Bibliog:* Saul Mayzlish (auth), Zamy Steynovitz, Revivim Publ, 80; Alex Meilichson (auth), Zamy Steynovitz, Kshatot Arts, 92. *Media:* Oils, Litographe. *Publ:* Auth, Peace Litographe between Israel & Egypt, NY Times & Harold Tribion Int, 79; Art Book of Steynovitz in Colors, Revivim Israel, 80 & Kshatot Israel, 92; Medal Ana Frank, NY Times, sunday 80. *Mailing Add:* c/o ISART - Israli Art Ctr 6721 N Corie Lane Westhills CA 91307

STICKER, ROBERT EDWARD
PAINTER
b Jersey City, NJ, Dec 26, 22. *Study:* Art Students League, with Frank Reilly. *Work:* IBM Corp & AT&T. *Exhib:* Mystic Maritime Gallery; Grand Cent Art Gallery. *Pos:* Mem bd control, Art Students League, 59-. *Awards:* Gold Medal, Franklin Mint Nat Marine Competition, 74; Award of Excellence, Mystic Int, 89. *Media:* Oil, Watercolor. *Publ:* Illusr, Famous small boat voyages, 69-72 & Classical work boats of America, 73- (ser of paintings), Yachting Mag; Steam on the Rivers (prints), Janus Lithograph. *Dealer:* Mystic Maritime Gallery. *Mailing Add:* RD 1 Pleasant Mount PA 18453

STIEBEL, GERALD G
DEALER
b New York, NY, Sept 28, 44. *Study:* CW Post Col, BA, 65; Courtauld Inst, London, 65-66; Study Centre Fine & Decorative Arts, London, dipl, 66; Columbia Univ, MA(art hist), 67. *Collection Arranged:* Grand Gallery Exhib, Metrop Mus Art, New York, 74-75; Experts Choice, Va Mus Art, 83; Chez Elle Chez Lui: At Home in 18th Century France, 87; Collecting at the top, 88; Of Knights & Spires: Gothic Renewal in France & Germany, 89; Louis XV and Madame de Pompadour: A Love Affair with Style, 90. *Pos:* Treas, Rosenberg & Stiebel Ltd, 68-71, vpres, 71-85, pres, 85-2000; Art Adv Panel, Internal Revenue Serv, 81-84; Pres's Cult Property Adv Comt, 94-99; pres, Stiebel Ltd, 2000-; dir, Diamond Point Theater Co, 2000. *Teaching:* Lectr, numerous universities & museums incl Guggenheim Mus & Metrop Mus Art, NY. *Mem:* Nat Antique & Art Dealers Asn Am (secy, 71-73, vpres, 73-77, pres, 77-79, bd dir, 71-84); La Confederation Int Negociants Oeuvres d'Art (permanent deleg, 72-, pres, 81-84, counr, 84-85, life councillor, 90-, bd dir, 97-, chmn internet com, 99-); Art Dealers Asn Am (bd dir, 80-89, 97-98, chmn pub rels com, 81-86, chmn internet com, 96-2000); Syndicat Nat des Antiquaires (France). *Specialty:* Old master paintings and drawings; important French 18th century furniture; renaissance bronzes. *Publ:* Auth, The Passionate Collector, Designer Mag, 72; Collector's Handbook, Cincinnati Art Mus, 78. *Mailing Add:* 252 E 68th St New York NY 10021

STIEBEL, PENELOPE HUNTER See Hunter-Stiebel, Penelope Hunter Stiebel

STILLMAN, DAMIE
HISTORIAN, EDUCATOR
b Dallas, Tex, July 27, 33. *Study:* Northwestern Univ, BS, 54; Univ Del, MA, 56; Columbia Univ, PhD, 61. *Collection Arranged:* Architecture & Ornament in Late 19th Century America (ed, catalog), 81. *Teaching:* Asst prof art hist, Oakland Univ, 61-65; assoc prof, Univ Wis, Milwaukee, 65-67, prof, 67-77, chmn dept, 75-77; prof, Univ Del, 77-89, chmn dept, 81-86 & 93-98, John W Shirley prof emeritus, art hist, 89-00. *Awards:* Nat Endowment Humanities Fel, 70-71 & 86-87; Founders Award, Soc Archit Historians, 75; Gottschalk Prize, Am Soc for 18th Century Study, 88. *Mem:* Col Art Asn Am; Soc Archit Historians (mem bd dir, 75-78 & 84-87, second vpres, 78-80, first vpres, 80-82, pres, 82-84); NE Am Soc for 18th Century Studies (exec bd, 87-93, vpres, 94-95 & pres, 95-96); Vernacular Architectual Forum; Soc Early Americanists. *Res:* American and British architecture with special emphasis on neo-classicism. *Publ:* Auth, The Decorative Work of Robert Adam, Tiranti, 67; ed, Architecture & Ornament in Late 19th Century America, Univ Del, 81; auth, English Neo-classical Architecture, Zwemmer, 88; auth, The United States Capitol: Icon of the Republic, in: Capital Drawings: Architectural Designs for Washington DC, Johns Hopkins Univ Press, 2005, 59-86; auth, Six Houses for the President, Pa Magazine of History & Biography, Vol 129, No 4, 10/2005, 411-431. *Mailing Add:* Dept Art Hist Univ Del Newark DE 19716

STILLMAN(MYERS), JOYCE L
PAINTER, LECTURER
b New York, NY, Jan 19, 43. *Study:* New York Univ, BA, 64, Art Students League, 66; Pratt Inst, 72; Long Island Univ, MA, 75; Calif Inst Integral Studies. *Work:* Aldrich Mus Contemp Art, Ridgefield, Conn; Byer Mus Art, Evanston, Ill; Hillwood Gallery, C W Post Col, Greenvale, NY; Randolf Macon Women's Col, Lynchburg, Va; Greater Lafayette Mus, Indianapolis, Ind. *Comn:* Time Life poster, Time Life Inc, NY, 77; Christmas card, Mus Mod Art, NY, 78 & 94. *Exhib:* Out of the House, Whitney Mus Downtown, NY, 76 & 78; Illusion and Reality, Australian Nat Gallery, Canberra, Australia, 77; Caps at the State Mus, NY State Mus, Albany, 81; What's New, Byer Mus, Evanston, Ill, 84; Holiday Show, New Mus, NY, 84; Art of Seventies and Eighties, Aldrich Mus, Ridgefield, Conn, 85; Traveling show Wassav Co Mus, NY, and others across US; 100 Women Artists, Arnot Art Mus, Elmira, NY, 91. *Collection Arranged:* Kemper Insurance; Joyce & Harvey Gladstein Coll; Fingerlakes School Art. *Teaching:* Assoc prof painting, Towson Univ, 82-88; prof art hist, Tompkins-Cortland Community Col, Dryden, NY, 88-90; lectr art, Cornell Univ, 90-. *Awards:* Creative Artist Pub Service Grant, 79; Distinctive Merit for Poster, Art Dir's Club, 79. *Mem:* Nat Asn Women Artists; Inst Noetic Sci; Literacy Vol; Arts if Southern tier, NY. *Media:* Paint, Pastel. *Dealer:* Allan Stone Gallery E 96th St New York NY. *Mailing Add:* 112 Brooklyn Tr Odessa NY 14869

STINGEL, RUDOLF

STINGEL, RUDOLF
ARTIST
b Merano, Italy, 57. *Exhib:* One-man shows: pittura austriae - Positionen aus Osterreich I/III, Galerie Elisabeth & Klaus Thoman, Innsbruck, 2000; Monochrome/Monochrome? Florence Lynch Gallery, NYC, 2001; Stanze, Museo d'arte moderna e contemporanea, 2001; Collector's Choice, Neue Galerie Graz am

Landesmuseum, Joanneum, 2002; Penetration, Friedrich Petzel Gallery, NYC, 2002; Int Landscape, Galerie Rololphe Janssen, Brussels, 2002; Dreams & Conflicts: The Dictatorship of the Viewer, La Biennale di Venezia, Venice, 2003; Walk Ways, Univ S Fla, Contemp Art Mus, 2003; Invite - Silver Convention, Galerie Giti Nourbakhsch, Berlin, 2003; Ruina - Aesthetic of Desstruction, Galeria Helga de Alvear, Madrid, 2004; Miradas y conceptos en la Coleccion Helga de Alvear, 2005; Home Depot, Mus fur Moderne Kunst, Franfurt, 2004; Art Underfoot - Carpeting the Walker Entry, Walker Art Center, Mpls, 2004; Sadie Coles HQ London, 2004; None of the Above, SI Swiss Inst, NYC, 2004; Singular Forms (Sometimes Repeated): Art from 1951 to the Present, Solomon R Mus, NY, 2004; Power, Corruption & Lies, Roth Horowitz, NYC, 2004; Mus fur Kunst, Frankfurt, 2004; Galleria Massimo de Carlo, Milan, 2004; EURAC Tower, Bolzano, Italy, 2005; MART, Roverto, Italy, 2005; Hayward Gallery, London, 2005; Universal Experience: Art, Life & the Tourist's Eye, Mus Contemp Art, 2005; The Red Thread, Howard House Contemp, Seattle, 2005; Group shows: Examining Pictures, Mus Contemp Art, Chicago, 1999; GOOD TIMING, George Kargl Fine Arts, Vienna, 2005; Whitney Biennial: Day for Night, Whitney Mus Am Art, NYC, 2006. *Mailing Add:* 46 Stuyvesant St New York NY 10003

STINNETT, HESTER A
PRINTMAKER
b Baltimore, Md, June 29, 56. *Study:* Hartford Art Sch, Univ Hartford, Conn, BFA, 78; Tyler Sch Art, Temple Univ, Philadelphia, MFA, 82. *Work:* Walker Art Ctr, Minneapolis; West Chester Univ, Pa; Philadelphia Mus Art, Pa. *Exhib:* Fleisher Art Mem, Philadelphia, 82; 16th National, Potsdam State Univ, NY, 82, Rutgers National, Stedman Art Gallery, Camden, NJ, 84; Solo exhibs, Denison Univ, Ohio, 85 & Haverford Col, Pa, 86; Prints from Blocks: 1900-1985, Assoc Am Artists, NY, 85; Cassa di Risparmio di Biella, Biella, Italy, 87; Pertainting to Philadelphia, Philadelphia Mus Art, 92. *Pos:* Dir, Philadelphia Col Art printmaking workshop, 84-86. *Teaching:* Adj lectr printmaking, Philadelphia Col Art, 82-86; lectr printmaking, Bryn Mawr, Col Pa, 85-86; asst prof printmaking, Tyler Sch Art, Temple Univ, Philadelphia, 86-92, assoc prof & assoc dean, 92-. *Mem:* Col Art Asn; Philadelphia Print Club. *Media:* Woodcut. *Publ:* Water-based Inks: A Screenprinting Manual for Studio and Classroom, Univ Arts, Philadelphia, Pa, 87. *Mailing Add:* Tyler Sch Arts Temple Univ 7725 Penrose Ave Elkins Park PA 19027

STINSMUEHLEN-AMEND, SUSAN
COLLAGE ARTIST, PAINTER
b Baltimore, Md, Nov 5, 48. *Study:* Hood Col, Indiana Univ & Univ Tex, 66-72. *Work:* Leigh Yawkey Woodson Mus, Wausau, Wis; Wagga Wagga City Art Gallery, New South Wales, Australia; Renwick Gallery Nat Mus Am Art, Smithsonian Inst, Washington, DC; Corning Mus Glass, NY; Detroit Inst Arts, Mich; and others. *Comn:* leaded glass mural, Christ Church Cathedral, Houston, Tex, 91; illuminated glass wall, AT&T NY, 93; glass inlaid concrete crosswalk & wrought iron fence, Pub Art, Hollywood, Calif, 94; Crosswalk painting, West Hollywood, Calif, 96-97; pedestrian scape, Community Redevelop Agency, Canoga Park, Calif, 96-97; and others. *Exhib:* Texas Crafts, Dallas Mus Fine Arts, 81; solo exhibs, Mattingly Baker Gallery, Dallas, 84, Kurland Summers Gallery, Los Angeles, 85, 88, 90 & 92, Traver Sutton Gallery, Seattle, 86, Habatat Galleries, Detroit, 91 & Nest Gallery, Ojai, Calif, 97; Light Interpretations, Jewish Mus, San Francisco, 95; Miller Gallery, NY, 95; Breaking Tradition: The Art of Fine Glass, Wignall Mus, Rancho Cucamonga, Calif, 95; Calido, Tucson Mus Art, 97; California Glass Today, Fresno Art Mus, Calif, 98; Loveland Mus Gallery, Colo, 98; Huntsville Mus Art, Ala, 98; Narration in Contemp Glass, Holters Mus Art, Helena, Mont, 98; The Quality of Glass: Heat and Light, Santa Cruz Mus Art & Hist, Calif, 99; The Inspired Vessel, Los Angeles Munic Art Gallery, Los Angeles, Calif; Invisibility, Reynolds Gallery, Richmond, VA; Nouvelle Nuptials, San Francisco Mus of Art & Design, 2005. *Collection Arranged:* Los Angeles Co Mus of Art; Detroit Inst of the Arts; Mus of Arts & Design, NY; Oakland Mus of Calif; The Renwick Gallery of the Nat Mus of Am. *Pos:* Owner & designer, Renaissance Glass Co, Austin, Tex, 73-87; lead artist, Hollywood Blvd Streetscape Team, Design for Pub Art in Hollywood, Calif, 91-92. *Teaching:* Guest artist & lectr Pilchurch Glass Sch, 80, 97, 2005, Glass Art Soc Conference, 81, 87 & 90, Calif Col Arts & Crafts, 85, 89 & 92, Santa Monica City Col, 88 & 92, Calif State Univ, Fullerton, 91, Cleveland Art Inst, 91, San Francisco Art Inst, 92, Penland Sch Crafts, NC, 96- & RI Sch Design, 96-; and many others. *Awards:* Nat Endowment Arts Fel, 82 & 88; Tex Home Design Competition Honor Award, 86. *Bibliog:* Galleries, Los Angeles Times, 2/2/90; Patricia Conway (auth), Art for Everyday: The New Craft Movement; Lloyd E Herman (auth), Art That Works: Decorative Arts of the Eighties Crafted in America, Univ of Was Press, Seattle, 90; Rick Mashburn (auth), The new gleam in stained glass, Diversion, 90, p145-47 & 228-29; Ben Marks (auth), Short reviews, Artweek, 2/1/90; Showcase: Screens and dividers, Professional Stained Glass, The Edge Publishing Co, Brewster, NY, 8/91; Shawn Waggoner (auth), Southern California's glass artists: Diversity defined, Glass Art, 1-2/92; Ben Marks (auth), Susan Stinsmuehlen-Amend and the aesthetics of anarchy, Glass, summer 92, No 48; Between Abstraction and Revelation, Jo Lauria, writer; Ojai Studio Artists Group, 2002-2005, publicity chair; mem of Ats comn, city of Ojai, CA, 2000-2005. *Mem:* Hon life mem, Glass Art Soc (bd dir, 82-84, pres, 84-86); Am Craft Coun (bd trustee, 88-92). *Media:* Glass, Mixed Media. *Interests:* Hiking, Golf, Gardening. *Dealer:* Ann Cohen, D&A Fine Arts, Los Angeles, 12750 Ventura Blvd, Ste 201, 91604. *Mailing Add:* c/o Impresa Inc 291 Avenida del Recreo Ojai CA 93023

STIRNWEIS, SHANNON
PAINTER, ILLUSTRATOR
b Portland, Ore, Feb 26, 31. *Study:* Univ Ore, 49-50; Art Ctr Col Design with John Lagatta, BFA, 50-54; Study with Joseph Henniger & Reynold Brown, 56. *Work:* Parks Dept, US Dept Interior, US Air Force Hist & Mus Collection, US Army Hist Mus Collection, Washington, DC; Univ Wyo, Laramie; Calif Fed Savings Collection. *Comn:* Reindeer Being Loaded on Coast Guard Ship, US Coast Guard, 88; Jennings-All American (portrait), US Air Force Acad, Colo; portrait, US Air Force, Lt Gen De Cox, 2004. *Exhib:* Soc Illustrators Ann Exhib, Mus Am Illus, NY, 68-75; 200 Yrs of Am Illustration, Mus City NY, 76; Governors Show, Cheyenne, Wyo, 85; Hubbard Mus, NM, 2005 & 06. *Teaching:* instr, Western Conn State Col; instr, Sharon (NH) Arts Ctr. *Awards:* Best Dog Book of Year, Dog Writers Asn, 65; Award of Merit, Soc Illus Ann Exhib, 68-75 & 86. *Bibliog:* R Bolivar (auth), An artist who has returned to the West, SW Art, 10/77; Samuels (auth), Contemporary Western artists, SW Art; Walt Reed (auth), Illustrator in America 1880-1980, Madison Sq Press. *Mem:* Soc Illus, NY; Western Artists Am, Ariz; Have Brush Will Travel, Inc (pres); Sharon Arts Ctr, NH; New Ipswich Artists League, NH. *Media:* Oil. *Publ:* Illusr, Dogs of the World, Whitman, 65; Ah, Wilderness, Ltd Editions Club, 72; Auth, Art of Painting the Dog, 77, Art of Painting the Cat, 77 & Art of Painting the Wild West, 78, Grumbacher. *Dealer:* JW Art Gallery Hurley NM. *Mailing Add:* 116 Perry Rd New Ipswich NH 03071

STIRRATT, BETSY (ELIZABETH) ANNE
PAINTER, GALLERY DIRECTOR
b New Orleans, La, Sept 22, 58. *Study:* La State Univ, BFA, 80; Ind Univ, MFA, 83. *Exhib:* Dark Ages, Indianapolis Mus Art, 91; Language & Symbol in Contemp Art, Greater Lafayette Mus Art, Ind, 92; Salon Show, Art in General, NY, 92; Primarily Paint, Laguna Gloria Art Mus, Houston, Tex, 92; Gallery Artists, Carl Hammer Gallery, Chicago, Ill, 94; Solar Exhib; and others. *Pos:* Dir, Sch of Fine Arts Gallery, Univ of Ind, Bloomington. *Awards:* Master's Fel, Ind Arts Comn, 89; Fel, Arts Midwest, 89; Visual Arts Fel, Nat Endowment Arts, 90; Ind Arts Comn Masters Fel, 99. *Mailing Add:* 2504 Poplar Ct Bloomington IN 47401

STITT, SUSAN (MARGARET)
MUSEUM DIRECTOR, ADMINISTRATOR
b East Liverpool, Ohio, Jan 24, 42. *Study:* Col William & Mary, AB; Univ Pa, MA. *Pos:* Asst to dir, Hist Soc Pa; dir, Mus Albemarle; adminr, Mus Early Southern Decorative Arts; asst to dir, Brooklyn Mus; proj dir surv placement & training, Old Sturbridge Village, Mass; dir, Mus at Stony Brook, 74-88; consult, Mus Historical Gallery, 88; pres & chief exec officer, Hist Soc Pa, 90-98. *Teaching:* Adj assoc prof, State Univ NY, Stonybrook, 75-78. *Awards:* Women of the Year in Art, Village Times, 87; Kathleen Coffey Award, Mid-Atlantic Asn Mus, 87; Ward Melville Community Award, Three Village Historical Soc, 88. *Mem:* Am Asn Mus (vpres, 85-86); Mid-Atlantic Asn Mus, (vpres, 82-86); NY State Asn Mus (pres, 85-87); and others. *Publ:* Auth, The will of Stephen Charlton & Hungars Parish, Va Mag Hist & Biog, 7/69; Today's labor practices, the search for equality, Mus News, 9-10/75; Trustee orientation: A sound investment, Mus News, 5-6/81; Bryant F Tolles, Jr (ed), The Diamond Link: The Director as Internal Communicator and Human Resources Manager, in Leadership for the Future: Changing Directoral Roles in American History Museums and Historical Societies, 89; A Reference for Stewardship, Forum, Issue 11, May/June, 94. *Mailing Add:* c/o Historical Soc Pa 1300 Locust St Philadelphia PA 19107

STOCKHOLDER, JESSICA
SCULPTOR AND EDUCATOR
b Seattle, 1959. *Study:* Univ Victoria, BFA, 82; Yale Univ, New Haven, Conn, MFA, 85. *Exhib:* Contingent Realms: Four Conemp Sculptors, Whitney Mus Am Art, NY City, 90; Whitney Biennial, 91; Perfume, Dia Ctr Arts, NY City, 95; La Biennale di Venezia: 47th Esposizione Internazionale d'arte, Venice, Italy, 97; Blaffer Gallery, Art Mus Houston, 99, 2004. *Teaching:* Instr dept sculpture NY Univ, 92, Bard Col, 93. *Awards:* Nat Endowment Arts Award for Sculpture, 88; NY Found Arts Grant in Painting, 89. *Mailing Add:* c/o Blaffer Gallery 120 Fine Arts Bldg Univ Houston TX 77204

STOCKMAN, JENNIFER BLEI
PATRON
b Philadelphia, Dec 5, 1954. *Study:* Univ Md, BS, 1976; George Washington Univ, MBA in Finance, 1983. *Pos:* Systems engineer, IBM Corp, 1976-78, marketing rep, 1978-81, staff marketing mgr, 1981-83; dir tech trade, Sears World Trade, 1983-84, vpres tech investment, 1984-85; founder, Stockman & Associates Inc, Greenwich, Conn, 1985, past pres, chief exec officer; nat co-chair, Rep Majority for Choice (formerly Rep Pro-Choice Coalition); Bd trustees, Solomon R Guggenheim Mus, 2003-. *Mailing Add:* 1850 Henry Cowgill Rd Camden Wyoming DE 19934

STODDARD, ELIZABETH JANE
PAINTER
b Buffalo, NY, June 20, 40. *Study:* State Univ NY, Buffalo, 82-85; studied with Zoltan Szabo, 87, with Frank Webb, 90. *Work:* Albright Knox Art Gallery; Brea Cult Ctr Gallery, Calif; Broome Street Gallery, NY; Neville Mus, Green Bay; World Trade Ctr Gallery, New Orleans. *Comn:* Watercolor, Moog & Co, Buffalo, NY, 82; watercolor, Lockport Savings Bank Inst, Buffalo, 95; watercolor, Austin Develop, Erie, Pa, 98; watercolor, Roswell Park Mem, Buffalo, 98; watercolor, Henry & Henry Co, Buffalo, 98. *Exhib:* Adirondack Mus Nat Exhib, Old Forge, NY, 85; Grand Central Gallery, NY, 85; Albright-Knox Art Gallery Members Show, Buffalo, NY, 85-98; Midwest Watercolor Soc Exhib, Neville Mus, Green Bay, Wis, 96; La Int Show, World Trade Ctr, New Orleans, 96-98; Nat Watercolor Show, Brea Cult Ctr, Calif, 96; Realism, Parkersburg Art Mus, WVa, 97; Northeast Watercolor Soc, Harness Racing Mus, Goshen, NY, 97. *Awards:* Am Pen Women Award of Excellence, Lincoln Ctr Gallery, 93; Grumbacher Gold Medal, Pa Nat Watercolor Show, 95; William Roth Mem Award, Northwest Watercolor Show, 95. *Bibliog:* E Jane Stoddard (auth), From oil to water, Artist Mag, 97. *Mem:* Nat Watercolor Soc; Northwest Watercolor Soc; Am Artists Prof League; Pa Watercolor Soc; Ga Watercolor Soc. *Media:* Watercolor. *Mailing Add:* 123 Wellingwood Dr East Amherst NY 14051

STOEVEKEN, ANTHONY CHARLES
PRINTMAKER, EDUCATOR
b Milwaukee, Wis, Oct 28, 38. *Study:* Univ Wis-Milwaukee, BS(art educ), 60, MS(art), 66; Tamarind Lithography Workshop, Los Angeles, Master Printer(Ford Found Fel), 68. *Work:* Mus Mod Art, NY; Gruenwald Graphic Arts Found, Univ Calif, Los Angeles; Los Angeles Co Mus Art; Nat Gallery Art, Washington; Crocker Nat Bank, San Francisco, Calif; San Diego Fine Arts Gallery, Calif; plus others. *Comn:* Ed of prints, Edgewood Orchard Galleries, Fish Creek, Wis, 74; exterior mural, John Michael Kohler Art Ctr, Sheboygan, Wis, 77; mural, Wis Art Bd's Percent for Art, 85. *Exhib:* Northwest Printmakers 41st Int Exhib, Seattle Art Mus & Portland Art Mus, Ore, 70; 42nd Ann Seattle Print Int, Seattle Art Mus, 71; IX Salon de Grabado, Inst Cult Peruana--Norte Americano, Lima, Peru, 73; 74th Exhib by Artists of Chicago & 77th Exhib, Works on Paper, Art Inst Chicago, 73 & 78; Wis Directions Two, Milwaukee Art Ctr, 78; 50 Artists-50 Printers, Univ NMex Art Mus, 85; Contemp Realism, K Gingrass Gallery, 89; 35 Contemp Artists, Univ Nebr, Lincoln, 93; Mount Mary Col, 2003, Milwaukee, Wis. *Pos:* Asst studio mgr, Tamarind Lithography Workshop, Los Angeles, 68; tech dir, Graphicstudio, Univ Fla Tampa, 68-70. *Teaching:* Asst prof art, lithography, Univ SFla, Tampa, 68-70; prof art & lithography, 70-98, & prof emer, 98-, Univ Wis, Milwaukee. *Awards:* Univ Wis-Milwaukee grad sch grant, aluminum plate & lithography, 75 & 86; Wis Arts Bd res grant, Chine-Colle, 79. *Bibliog:* Donald Key (auth), Graphic by University of Wisconsin-Milwaukee teacher, Milwaukee J, 72; Barbara Manger (auth), Tucholke and Stoeveken at the Kohler Art Center, Mid-West Art, Gary Pizarick, 76; James Auer (auth), Fantasy in the family, Milwaukee J, 80. *Mem:* Col Art Asn; Mid-America Col Art Asn (pres, 81); Mid-Am Print Coun. *Media:* Lithography, Drawing. *Res:* Aluminum plate lithography. *Interests:* Pastel drawings. *Dealer:* Edgewood Orchard Gallery Fish Creek Wis 54212. *Mailing Add:* 8535 W Mequon Rd Mequon WI 53097

STOEVEKEN, CHRISTEL E See Tucholke, Christel-Anthony

STOFFEL, PAUL T
COLLECTOR
Study: Harvard Bus Sch, MBA. *Pos:* various positions to bd dirs, Centex Corp; chmn, Triple S Capital Corp, Paul Stoffel Investments; bd dirs, Holly Corp, Dallas, Dallas Symphony Asn, Dallas Symphony Found; co-founder, Gayle and Paul Stoffel Found; bd mem, Dallas Symphony Orchestra, Southwestern Med Found, Zale Lipshy Hosp, St. Paul Univ Hosp. *Mailing Add:* 5949 Sherry Ln Suite 1465 Dallas TX 75225

STOFFLET, MARY
CURATOR, CRITIC
b Long Branch, NJ, Dec 23, 42. *Study:* Skidmore Col, BA, 64; NY Univ, MA, 69; M H de Young Mem Mus, San Francisco, Rockefeller-Nat Endowment Arts Fel Mus Educ, 75-76. *Collection Arranged:* International Rubber Stamp Art Exhibition, La Mamelle Arts Ctr, San Francisco, 76; Cityscapes, 77 & Yosemite, 79, Fine Arts Mus San Francisco, Downtown Ctr; Construction, San Francisco Int Airport, 82; Dr Seuss from Then to Now, 86, More Then Meets the Eye, 87, Cultural Currents, 88, San Diego Mus Art, 88; Faberge: The Imperial Eggs, 89, Li Huai: An Artist in Two Cultures, 89, Latin American Drawings Today, 91, San Diego Mus Art; Calif Cityscapes, 91 & The Frederick R Weisman Collection of Contemporary California Art, 91, San Diego Mus Art; Silver/Clay/Wood/Gold, San Diego Crafts, San Diego, Mus Art, 93; Andy Goldsworthy Two Stones, San Diego, Mus Art, 94; Deborah Butterfield (auth, catalog), San Diego Mus Art, 95. *Pos:* Newsletter ed, Western Asn of Art Mus, Oakland, 74-77; contrib ed, Artweek, 74-81; assoc ed, La Mamelle, 75-77; ed, Front, 76-; coordr intern prog, M H de Young Mem Mus, 77-80; contrib ed, Images & Issues, 80-; asst cur, San Francisco Int Airport, 82-84; cur educ, San Diego Mus Art, 85-88, cur mod art, 88-97; asst dir, Education & Publications, San Francisco Airport Mus, 98-. *Teaching:* Instr art hist, Oakland Mus, Calif, 77-; lectr art hist, San Francisco State Univ, 77 & 81, Univ Calif San Diego Extension, 87. *Awards:* Critic's Fel, Nat Endowment Arts, 81. *Mem:* Col Art Asn; Am Asn Mus; Int Asn Art Critics; Art Table Inc; Modern Lang Asn. *Publ:* Auth, American Women Artists: 20th Century, Slides & Notes, 78 & Women Artists: Sculptors-Photographers, Slides & Notes, 79, Harper & Row; ed, Correspondence Art: Sourcebook for the Network of International Postal Art Activity, Contemp Arts Press, 84; auth, Dr Seuss From Then to Now, San Diego Mus Art, 86 & Random House, 87; essayist & coordr ed, Latin American Drawings Today, San Diego Mus Art & Univ Wash Press, 91; auth & coordr ed, California Cityscapes, San Diego Mus Art & Universe, 91. *Mailing Add:* 1520 California St No 9 San Francisco CA 94109

STOIANOVICH, MARCELLE
PAINTER, PRINTMAKER
Study: Col d'Art Applique a l'Industrie, Paris, France. *Work:* Work in pvt collections. *Comn:* Window display, Guerlain, Paris; book jacket designs for Doubleday & Co. *Exhib:* Salon des Artistes Francais, Paris; Galerie Pierre Hautot, Paris; Assoc Am Artists, NY; Mitsukoshi Galerie, Paris; FAR Galleries & Weyhe Gallery, NY; Venable Galleries, Washington; France Garo, Tokyo; Zimmerli Art Mus, New Brunswick, NJ; Mason Gross Sch Arts, New Brunswick, NJ. *Awards:* Hon Mention for Watercolor, Beaux-Arts, Paris, 50; Selected Film Credits, Festival Am Films, Deauville, France, 75. *Bibliog:* New York Art Review, 89; Chicago Art Review, 89. *Mem:* Metrop Mus Art, New York City; Artists' Asn Nantucket/Mass. *Media:* Miscellaneous Media, Lithography. *Dealer:* Mitsukoshi Paris France. *Mailing Add:* 60 Rector St Metuchen NJ 08840

STOKSTAD, MARILYN
HISTORIAN, EDUCATOR
b Lansing, Mich, Feb 16, 29. *Study:* Carleton Col, BA, 50; Mich State Univ, MA, 53; Univ Mich, PhD, 57; Hon LHD, Carleton Col, 97. *Pos:* Cur, Spencer Mus Art, 67-95; res cur medieval art, Nelson-Atkins Mus Art, Kansas City, 69-2002. *Teaching:* Prof hist art, Univ Kans, 58-79, chmn dept, 61-72, dir, Mus Art, 61-67, assoc dean, Col Arts & Sci, 72-76, Univ Distinguished Prof, 79-2002. *Awards:* Dumbarton Oaks Fel, 81-82; Smithsonian Fel, 86, 90; Kans Gov's Arts Award, 97; Lifetime Achievement Award, WCA. *Mem:* Midwest Col Art Conf (pres, 64-65); Col Art Asn Am (pres, 78-80); Am Asn Univ Prof; Soc Archit Historians; Int Ctr Medieval Art (vpres, 90-93, pres, 93-96). *Res:* Medieval art; Spanish art; art of the British Isles. *Publ:* Auth, Renaissance art outside Italy, Art Horizons, 68; ed & auth, Hortus Imaginum: Studies in Western Art, Humanistic Series 45, Univ Kans, 74; auth, Santiago de Compostela in the Age of the Pilgrimages, Okla Univ, 79; Scottish Culture, Abrams, 81; ed & auth, Museums, Humanities and the Educated Eye, Univ Kans, 82; Medieval Art, Harper & Row, 86; Art History, Abrams/Prentice Hall, 95, 98 & 2002; Art a Brief History, Prentice Hall, 2000. *Mailing Add:* 4703 Balmoral Dr Lawrence KS 66047

STOLL, GEORGE
ARTIST
b Baltimore, MD, 54. *Exhib:* Solo exhibs, Tupperware, A/B Gallery, Los Angeles, 94, Newspaper & Plywood Drawings, Paper Towel Paintings, Fast Food Wrappers, TRI Gallery, Los Angeles, 94, Sculpture, Morris Healy Gallery, New York City, 95, New Sculpture, Paintings, and Drawings, 97, Toilet Paper, Dan Bernier Gallery, Santa Monica, 95, Snowflakes, 96, 161 Tumblers 2 Ways, Daniel Weinberger Gallery, San Francisco, 95, Windows, Bruxelles, Belgium, 97, New Work, Thomas Healy Gallery, New York City, 98, Gallery Paule Anglim, San Francisco, 99, George Stoll: Thinking of Christmas, Angles Gallery, Santa Monica, 2004-05. *Awards:* John Armstrong Chaloner Rome Prize Fel in Visual Arts, Am Acad in Rome, 2004-05

STOLOFF, CAROLYN
PAINTER, COLLAGE ARTIST
b New York, NY. *Study:* Univ Ill; Columbia Univ, BS; Art Students League; Atelier 17; with Xavier Gonzalez, Eric Isenburger & Hans Hofmann. *Work:* Norfolk Mus Arts & Scis; Canadian Imperial Bank Commerce; Roslyn Willett; Lester Klepper; Sonya Hess; and others; Ruth Unterberg. *Exhib:* Whitney Mus Am Art, 51; Pa Acad Fine Arts; Audubon Artists; Oakland Art Mus; one-person shows, Dubin Gallery, Pa, Manhattanville Col, NY, Donnell Libr, 88, Open Studios, 84 & 87, Atlantic Gallery, 85, Pine Pub Libr, Fairlawn, NJ, 89 & Tom Kendall Gallery, 90; Pine Pub Libr Gallery, Fairlawn, NJ, 89; Kendall Gallery, NY, 90; Silvermine Guild; ACA Gallery; Nat Asn Women Artists; City Ctr Gallery; Atlantic Gallery; Krasner Gallery; New Talent Show, Laurel Gallery; Knickerbocker Artists; Long Island League Painters & Sculptors; NJ Soc Painters & Sculptors; Arthur Brown Gallery; Bowery Gallery. *Pos:* Prof, 57-74 & chmn dept art, Manhattanville Col, 61-65. *Teaching:* Asst prof painting & drawing, Manhattanville Col, 57-74, lectr, Eng, 69-74; vis writer, Stephens Col, 75 & Hamilton Col, 85. *Awards:* Daler-Rowney Award for Oil Painting, 94; Art Students League Award for Oil Painting, 95; Grumbacher Gold medal, 98; and others; Emily Lowe Award for Oil Painting, 00; Silver Anniversary Medal, Audubon Artists Annual, 67; Michael M Engel Sr Mem Award, Audubon Artists Annual, 82; Robert Phillips Mem Award for Painting, Audubon Artists Annual, 90. *Bibliog:* Jean Gould (auth), Modern American Women Poets, Dodd Mead & Co, 85, 349; Robert Peters (auth), 2 collages reproduced, Caliban No 7; The Great Am Poetry BakeOff II. *Mem:* Poetry Soc Am; Audubon Artists. *Media:* Oil, Collage, Drawing. *Collection:* Norfolk Mus; Can Imperial Bank of Com; Roslyn Willett; Lester Klepper; Sonya Hess. *Publ:* Auth, Stepping Out, Unicorn Press, 71; Dying to Survive, Doubleday & Co, 73; Swiftly Now, Ohio Univ Press, 82; A Spool of Blue: New and Selected Poems, Scarecrow Press, 83; You Came to Meet Someone Else, Asylum Arts Press, 93; Reaching for Honey, Red Hen Press, 03. *Mailing Add:* 32 Union Sq E Ste 911 New York NY 10003

STOLPIN, WILLIAM ROGER
PRINTMAKER
b Flint, Mich, June 25, 42. *Study:* Kettering Univ, Flint, Mich, BME, 65; Charles Stewart Mott Community Col, Flint, Mich, AA, 78; Studied lithography with Emil Weddige, 69-70, Robert Nelson, 81 & Japanese woodblock with Akira Kurosaki, 86; Eastern Mich Univ, Ypsilanti, Mich, 92; Studied collaborative printmaking, NY Univ, 98; studied intaglio printmaking, Crown Point Press, San Francisco, 2000. *Work:* Smithsonian Inst Nat Air & Space Mus, Washington, DC; Flint Inst Arts, Mich; Kettering Univ, Flint, Mich; Nat Trust, London, Eng; Brit Interplanetary Asn, London, Eng; Delta Col, Midland, Mich. *Comn:* Serigraph, Genesis Corp, Flint, Mich, 94; Serigraph, Mott Found, 2000; Serigraph, Mass Transportation Asn, Flint, Mich, 2002. *Exhib:* Ann Print Competition, Ann Arbor Art Asn, Mich, 95 & 2003; Ann Print Competition, Flora Beck Gallery, Mich, 96-2000 & 2002, 2003, 2004; All Media Competition, Birmingham Bloomfield Art Asn, Mich, 96; Planetfest, Pasadena Convention Center, Calif, 97; Mich Asn printmakers, Left Bank Gallery, Flint, Mich, 2000,2003, 2004; SAGA Nat Mems Exhib, Stephen Gang Gallery, NY, 2000 & 2002; Mich Directions, Flint Inst Arts, 2000; Scarab Club, Detroit, Mich, 2003; Festival of the Masters, Downtown Disney, Lake Buena Vista, Fla, 2006; Am Color Print Soc, Art of Printmaking, Spring Bull Gallery, Newport, RI, 2006; Two-man show, Starkweather Gallery, Romeo, Mich, 2006. *Pos:* art dept adv bd, Alma Col, Mich, 98-2000; bd dir/adv & pub relations chmn, Greater Flint Art Coun, 98-; accessions & collections comt, Flint Inst Arts, Mich, 2000-; lectr printmaking, Univ Mich, 99-2001 & Ctr for Creative Studies, 2001. *Teaching:* lectr color serigraphy, Cent Mich Univ, 99; art dept, printmaking, Flint Inst Arts, Mich, 2006. *Awards:* First in Graphics, Internat Platform Asn, 69; First Prize, Left Bank Gallery, 98; Purchase Prize, Saginaw Art Mus, Mich, 98; Notable Mention, Friends of Mod Art, 2001; First Prize Flint Art Fair, 2004; Third Prize, Flint Art Fair, 2006. *Bibliog:* Michelle Harrison (auth), Art of the matter, On the Town/McVey Marketing, 94; Selma Smith (auth), William R Stolpin, Internat printworld Dir, 98-present; Rachelle Richert (auth), Michigan Directions, J of Printworld, 2000. *Mem:* Soc Am Graphic Artists; Mich Asn Printmakers; Asn Sci Fiction & Fantasy Artists; Int Asn for Astronomical Arts; Detroit Inst Arts; Mich Guild Artists and Artisans; Flint Inst Arts; Greater Flint Arts Coun;

Shiawassee Arts Coun; Detroit Artists Market; Mich Renaissance Festival; Buckham Fine Arts Project; Left Bank Gallery. *Media:* Printmaking. *Dealer:* Detroit Artists Market 4719 Woodward Ave Detroit Mich 48201; Blue Heron Gallery 133 Ames St Elk Rapids Mich 49629. *Mailing Add:* 12201 Gage Rd Holly MI 48442-8339

STOLTENBERG, DONALD HUGO
PAINTER, PRINTMAKER
b Milwaukee, Wis, Oct 15, 27. *Study:* Inst Design, Ill Inst Technol, BS(visual design). *Work:* Boston Mus Fine Art & Boston Nat Hist Park, Mass; Addison Gallery Am Art, Andover, Mass; DeCordova Mus, Lincoln, Mass; Portland Mus Art; Cape Mus Fine Arts, Dennis, Mass. *Exhib:* Venice Observed, Fogg Mus, Cambridge, Mass, 56; Boston Arts Festival, 56-61; Corcoran Gallery Art Exhib, Washington, 63; Landscape, DeCordova Mus, 71; Am Art Exhib, Art Inst Chicago; Mass Open, Worcester Art Mus, 77; Am Watercolor Soc, 90, 94, 98, 2000 & 05. *Teaching:* Instr painting & printmaking, DeCordova Mus Sch; vis critic, RI Sch Design; Instr drawing & printmaking, Cape Cod Conservatory. *Awards:* Grand Prize, Boston Arts Festival, 57, First Prize in Painting, 59; First Purchase Prize, Portland Mus Arts Festival; High Winds Medal, Am Watercolor Soc, Exhib, 2005. *Bibliog:* Painting with the White of Your Paper, 94 & Splash #1, 2 & 4 Painting from Photographs, 99, North Light Bks, 94,; The Best of Watercolor, 95 & Abstracts in Watercolor, 96, Rockport Publ Inc; A Gallery of Marine Art, 98, Rockport Publ, Inc; Bound for Blue Water Contemp Am Marine Art, Greenwich Workshop Press, 2003. *Mem:* New Eng Watercolor Soc; Am Watercolor Soc; Fel Am Soc Marine Artists. *Media:* Oil, Watercolor. *Interests:* Maritime & Industrial History. *Publ:* Auth, Collagraph Printmaking, 75 & The Artist and the Built Environment, 80, Davis. *Dealer:* Mystic Maritime Gallery Mystic CT. *Mailing Add:* 947 Satucket Rd Brewster MA 02631

STOMPS, WALTER E, JR
EDUCATOR, PAINTER
b Hamilton, Ohio, July 13, 29. *Study:* Miami Univ, BFA; Art Inst Chicago, with Boris Anisfeld, Paul Weighardt, Isabelle MacKinnon & Edgar Pillet, MFA; Syracuse Univ. *Work:* Cleveland Mus Art; Miami Univ; 4 works, TransFinancial Bank, Bowling Green, Ky. *Comn:* Ctr City Murals Proj, Nat Endowment Arts, Dayton, 72; Gen Motors (Frigidaire), Dayton; Bicentennial Poster Proj, Dayton. *Exhib:* Mid-States Exhib, Evansville, Ind, 77, 79 & 80; Cent S Exhib, Nashville, Tenn, 77; 1st Ann Mid-Am Exhib Art, Owensboro Mus Art, Ky, 79; Eight States Exhib, Speed Mus Art, Louisville; Print Invitational, Univ Kans, Lawrence, 80; and others. *Teaching:* Prof painting & drawing, Western Ky Univ, 75-. *Awards:* James Nelson Raymond Award, Art Inst Chicago, 59; Purchase Awards, Dayton Art Inst, 66 & 68, Owensboro Mus Art, Ky, 79 & Evansville Mus Art & Sci, Ind, 86; and others. *Media:* Acrylic, Watercolor. *Publ:* Illusr, Dayton USA, 72. *Mailing Add:* 837 Nutwood St Bowling Green KY 42103

STONE, DON
PAINTER
b Council Bluffs, Iowa, Mar 27, 29. *Study:* Vesper George Sch Art, Boston, 52. *Work:* Marietta Col, Ohio; Mobile Art Mus, Ala; Charles Greenshield Collection, Montreal; Peabody Maritime Mus, Salem, Mass. *Comn:* Large Egg Tempera, Univ NH, Durham, 79. *Exhib:* Nat Acad Design & Am Watercolor Soc, NY; Boston Soc Watercolor Painters, Boston Mus Fine Art, 71; Winter, 77 & New Eng Painters, 78, DeCordova Mus, Lincoln, Mass. *Pos:* Juror, of selection Am Water color Soc, New York City, 1977. *Teaching:* Instr art, Vesper George Sch Art, Boston, 60-65; instr, New Eng Sch Art, Boston, 60-65; Monhegan Island Workshop, Maine, 1970-. *Awards:* Gold Medals, Franklin Mint, 74 & 75 & Hudson Valley Art Asn, 80. *Mem:* Nat Acad (assoc, 68, acad, 94-); Am Watercolor Soc; Guild Boston Artists; New Eng Watercolor Soc; Hudson Valley Art Asn. *Media:* Egg Tempera, Watercolor. *Publ:* Auth, Watercolor page, Am Artist, 62. *Dealer:* Whistlers Daughter Art Gallery 88 S Finley Ave Basking Ridge NJ 07920. *Mailing Add:* 7 Hartman Pl Exeter NH 03833

STONE, GEORGE H
SCULPTOR
b Los Angeles, Calif, Aug 9, 46. *Study:* Orange Coast Col, Costa Mesa, Calif, 66-69; Calif State Univ, Long Beach, BA, 72; RI Sch Design, MFA, 74. *Comn:* Temporary site proj, City West Hollywood, 86; temporary site proj, Community Redevelop Asn, City Los Angeles, 87; Art for Rail Transit, Los Angeles Co Transportation Comn, 90-92. *Exhib:* Solo exhibs, Otis/Parsons Gallery, 81, East Gallery, Claremont Grad Sch, Calif, 85, Univ Art Mus, Calif State Univ, Long Beach, 86, Meyers/Bloom Gallery, Santa Monica, Calif, 88 & 91, Laguna Art Mus Satellite, Costa Mesa, Calif, 90, New Langton Arts, San Francisco, Calif, 91, Capp Street Project, San Francisco, 91, Ruth Bloom Gallery, Santa Monica, Calif, 93 & Pittsburgh Ctr Arts, 94; La Next, Contemp Arts Ctr, New Orleans, 93; I Am The Enunciator, Thread Waxing Space, NY, 93; Home Show 2, Contemp Arts Forum, Santa Barbara, Calif, 96; Scene of the Crime, UCLA Armand Hammer Mus Art & Cult Ctr, Los Angeles, 97. *Teaching:* Part-time instr sculpture, Portsmouth Abbey Sch, RI, 73-74; instr, Wayne State Univ, Detroit, 74-75; lectr, Ohio Univ, Athens, 76-77; part-time instr, Found Dept, Otis/Parsons Sch Design, Los Angeles, 82-83; asst prof sculpture, Art Inst Southern Calif, 89-, chmn, Found Dept, 89-90. *Awards:* Project grant, Capp Street Proj, San Francisco, Calif, 91; Artists fel, J Paul Getty Trust Fund Visual Arts, 91-92; Individual Artist Grant, Nat Endowment Arts, 93. *Bibliog:* Nicole Johnson (auth), Body and machine, Offramp Mag, Issue Technol, 91; Robert Miller, Renee Petropoulos, George Stone & anonymous (auths), Visions, fall 92; Robot Redux, Artforum, 11/92. *Mailing Add:* 1815 Laurel Canyon Blvd Los Angeles CA 90046

STONE, GWEN
PAINTER, COLLAGE ARTIST
b New York, NY, Feb 1, 1913. *Study:* Col Marin, Kentfield, Calif; San Francisco Art Inst, Calif, BFA, 1936; Univ Calif, Berkeley, teaching cert; also with Walt Kuhlman. *Work:* San Francisco Art Comn, Calif; Univ Calif, Berkeley, Libr; Standard Oil; Univ Tex at Austin; Levi Straus; and others. *Comn:* Siskiyou Arts Coun Grant, Res & 5 lectrs with slides, Yreka Community Theatre, 87; Yreka City Partial Grant (video), The Eye, the Paint and the Brush, 88-89. *Exhib:* San Francisco Mus Mod Art Ann, 59-67; one person shows, Calif Palace Legion Honor, San Francisco, 66 & 67, The Pillowbook Series (collage), Redding Mus, 83 & Rogue Gallery, Medford, Ore, 90; Four Views (collage), Shasta Col Art Gallery, Calif, 83; Col Marin Invitational, 84; Mandela Series (collage & sculpture), Coos Art Mus, Coos Bay, Ore, 93; Four Northcoast Artists, Redding Mus, 94; Sacred Mountain Sumi-e Drawings, Asian Art Ctr, Ashland, 96; Schneider Mus Art, Ashland, Oreg, 2002. *Pos:* Guest cur, More Blue is Bluer, Shasta Col, Redding, Calif, 89; guest inst, collage workshop, Sitka Art Ctr, Otis, Ore, 90-92 & 94-96. *Teaching:* Instr life drawing, Col Marin, Kentfield, 67-79, instr design, 67-70, instr collage & assemblage, 75-79; instr collage, Art Sch, Belvedere, 77-79. *Awards:* Painting Ann Award, Redding Mus, 85; 5,000 Grant award, Pollock-Krasner Found, NY, 90, 10,000 Grant award; Grant, Pollock-Krasner Found, 2001. *Bibliog:* E M Polley (auth), East Bay, 65 & Marilyn Hagberg (auth), San Diego, 65, Artforum; Lynn Grant (auth), article, Visual Dialog, Vol 2 (1976); Maggie Hazell-Rosen (auth), Artweek, 73; Stone, Center Visual Arts Newsletter, Oakland, Calif, 88. *Mem:* Life mem, Marin Soc Artists (signature). *Media:* All. *Publ:* Auth, Conversation with Robert Arneson, 76, Eleanor Bender talks with Gwen Stone, 76, Women Artists: Realities, 77 & Conversation with Wayne Thiebaud, 77, Visual Dialog; dir, The Eye, the Paint and the Brush (video), grant by Siskiyou Arts Coun, 88. *Dealer:* Davis and Cline Gallery 525 A St Ashland OR 97520. *Mailing Add:* 17530 Pilar Rd Montague CA 96064

STONE, JEFFREY INGRAM
PAINTER, INSTRUCTOR
b Richmond, Va, Mar 14, 45. *Study:* Univ Calif, Northridge, BA, 67; Pratt Inst, MFA, 69. *Work:* Mus Mod Art, NY. *Exhib:* Eighteenth Nat Print Exhib, Brooklyn Mus, 73; Fourth Ann Nat Print Exhib, Atlanta Art Mus, 73; Second Ann Int Norwegian Biannale, Norway Nat Arts Mus, 74; Premio Int Biella Per I'Incisione, Biella's Art Mus, Italy, 80; NMex Univ, 83; Gallery of the Royal Melbourne Inst, 87. *Teaching:* Adj assoc prof printmaking, Pratt Inst, Brooklyn, NY, 70-; guest instr, Yale Univ, 74-75; Head Art & Film Dept, Loyola Sch, 87-. *Awards:* Purchase Award, Fourth Ann Nat Print Exhib, Ga, 73. *Bibliog:* Fletcher Kastner (auth), Jeffrey Ingram Stone Graphics, Galaxy Press, 79. *Mem:* Artist Equity NY. *Media:* Oil, Watercolor. *Publ:* Illusr, The psychiatric holocaust, Penthouse Mag, 79; Sweet songs of spring, New York Mag, 78

STONE, JEREMY PATRICIA
CONSULTANT, APPRAISER, CURATOR
b Boston, Mass, Nov 15, 57. *Study:* Cooper Union, 1974-75; Univ San Francisco, Exec Cert in Nonprofit Orgn Mgmt, 1993, BS in Organization Behavior (summa cum laude),1995; Prog Appraisal Studies, Univ Calilfornia, Irvine, 2005. *Exhib:* Curated over 90 exhibs. *Pos:* Spec activities coordr, Commonwealth Cult Preservation Trust, Boston, 79; res coordr, Anne Kohs Asn, San Francisco, 81-82; owner & dir, Jeremy Stone Gallery, San Francisco, 82-91; exec dir, Learning Through Educ in Arts Proj, 92; consult, Jewish Mus, San Francisco & Nestle Bevaerage Co, 93-94; dir career servs, San Francisco Arts Inst, Career Resources Prog, 94-97; founder & principal, Business Matters in the Visual Arts, San Francisco, 97-. *Teaching:* Vis lectr, Univ Wash, Pullman, 84, Calif Col Arts & Crafts, Oakland, 84-86, Univ Calif, Berkeley, 84 & 86, Sanford Univ Sch Law, 85, This Business of Art, Calif Lawyers for Arts, Hastings Col Law, 9/89; guest lectr, Calif Arts Coun, 96; vis fac, San Francisco Art Inst, 96-2000; Talking Art, The Players, San Jose Inst of Contemp Art, San Jose, Jan 11, 2005 panel. *Bibliog:* Leah Garchik (auth), Pricing Yourself Into The Art market, San Francisco Chronicle, p 8, 8/10/97; Cay Lang (auth) Taking the Leap: Building a Career as a Visual Artist, 98; Andrea Siegel (auth), Open and Clothed, Agapanthus Books, Woodside, NY, 99; Linda Franklin (auth), Doing What Comes Naturally, The Calif Executive, 12/1988; Alice Marquis (auth), The Art Biz, Contemp Art Books, Inc, Chicago, 91; George Lauer, Eclectic Couple, The Press Democrat, Santa Rosa, CA, D1 & D6, 2/20/05; Catherine Bigelow, Swells, SF Chronicle, 11/7/04, p. D12; Ilana DeBare (auth), Artists mix business with pleasure, Seattle Post-Intelligencer, 1/16/2006; and many others. *Mem:* ArtTable, Inc (mem nat bd, co-chmn mem com No Calif chap 1995-97, mem exec com, 1995-2002, mem nat bd, 2000-02); Am Soc Appraisers (accredited senior mem); The Oxbow Sch, San Francisco Art Inst (bd trustees 87-2005). *Publ:* Auth, Honoring Ruth Asawa, Asake Bomani and Rudy Nothenberg, Bridging the Community Through Art (exhib catalog), Jewish Mus San Francisco, 93; Working artist: The purpose of work, Artweek, Vol 26, No 1, p 37, 1/95; Relationships are created and built, not bought, Artweek, Vol 26, No 6, p 32, 6/95; Thirty Years of Box Construction, Sunne Savage Gallery, Boston, MA, 11/79. *Mailing Add:* Bus Matters in Vis Arts PO Box 460190 San Francisco CA 94146-0190

STONE, JIM (JAMES) J
PHOTOGRAPHER, WRITER
b Los Angeles, Calif, Dec 2, 47. *Study:* Mass Inst Technol, with Minor White, SB, 70; RI Sch Design, with Harry Callahan & Aaron Siskind, MFA, 75. *Work:* Corcoran Gallery Art & Nat Mus Am Art, Washington; Fogg Art Mus, Harvard Univ, Cambridge, Mass; Int Mus Photog, Rochester, NY; Los Angeles Co Mus Art; Polaroid Collection, Offenbach, Ger & Cambridge, Mass; Mus Mod Art, NY; and others. *Exhib:* Photovision, Boston Ctr Arts, 72; New Eng Experience, De Cordova Mus, Lincoln, Mass, 72; Photog Unlimited, Fogg Art Mus, Harvard Univ, 74 & Contemp Photog, 76; Still Life, Corcoran Gallery Art, Washington, 79; Venezia '79, Venice, Italy, 79; Boston Now: Photog, ICA, 85; Photographs Beget Photographs, Minn Inst Arts, 87; Twelve Photogs Look at US, Philadelphia Mus Art, 87; Future of Photog, Corcoran Gallery Art, Washington, 87; Between Home and Heaven, Nat Mus Am Art, 92; Commodity Image, Int Ctr Photog, NY, 93; City of Las Vegas Cultural Ctr, 96; Innovation / Imagination, Friends of Photog, San Francisco, 99; Point of View, Silver Eye Ctr for Photog, Pittsburgh, 2000; Photog in Boston, DeCordova Mus, Lincoln,

Nebr, 2000; Idea Photog, Mus Fine Arts, Santa Fe, NMex, 2002. *Pos:* Artist-in-residence, Lightwork, Syracuse, NY, 84, Visual Studies Workshop, Rochester, NY, 85, Nat Col Arts, Lahore, Pakistan, 86 & Ariz Western Col, Yuma, Ariz, 88; ed, PhotoEducation: A Polaroid Newsletter for Teachers of Photography, 88-. *Teaching:* Instr, Boston Col, 73-88; instr, RI Sch Design, 75-78 & 93-98; asst prof, Univ NMex, 98-2002, assoc prof, 2002-. *Awards:* Mass Arts & Humanities Found photog fel, 76 & 88; New Eng Found Arts, 93. *Bibliog:* Channing (ed), Art of the State/State of the Art, Addison House, 78; Shamlian (auth), article in Philadelphia Photo Rev, 78; Hughes (ed), Photography Annuals, Popular Photog, 80 & 86; Photovision, Sevile, Spain, 94; Riverstyx, 97; View Camera Mag, 2000. *Mem:* Boston Photog Resource Ctr (bd dir, 84-96, bd pres, 94-96); Soc Photog Educ. *Media:* Photographs, Digital Prints. *Publ:* Ed, Darkroom Dynamics: A Guide to Creative Darkroom Techniques, Focal Press, 79; auth, A User's Guide to the View Camera, Harper Collins, 87, second ed, Addison Wesley Longman, 97, 3rd Prentice Hall, 2004; Stranger than Fiction, Light Work, 93; Historiostomy, Pittdown Press, 2001; coauth, A Short Course in Photog, 3rd ed, Addison Wesley Longman, 96, 4th ed, Prentice Hall, 2000 & 5th ed, 2003 & 6th ed, Prentice Hall, 2006. *Mailing Add:* 1044 Stanford Dr NE Albuquerque NM 87106

STONE, JUDITH ELISE
COLLAGE ARTIST, EDUCATOR
b Boston, Mass, Sept 15, 1940. *Study:* Vassar Col, BA(magna cum laude), 62; Harvard Univ, MAT, 65; Univ Colo, Boulder, MFA, 77. *Work:* Univ City Sci Ctr, St Joseph's Univ, Philadelphia; Baltimore Gulf & Electric; Toyoda Int Sales, The Design Studios, Tokyo; Idaho Nat Bank, Boise. *Exhib:* One-woman shows, C Grimaldis Gallery, 85, Hinoki Gallery, Tokyo, 1987, St Joseph's Univ Mem Exhib, 96, Lancaster Mus Art, 96, l'Espace 234, Montreal, 2002, Caelum Gallery, NY, 2003 & 2005, Southern VT Art Ctr, 2003; Art of the State, Pa State Mus, Harrisburg, 94; John Cage Retrospective, Philadelphia Mus Art, 95; Gallery BAI, NY, 97; Pa State Univ, Harrisburg, 98; Art on Campus, Southern Vt Art Ctr, 2002. *Collection Arranged:* Solomon & Barbara Wank; John & Sheila Paulos. *Teaching:* Adj prof humanities, Temple Univ, Philadelphia, 79-86; adj prof eng & drawing, St Joseph's Univ, Philadelphia, 83-96; asst prof humanities, Temple Univ, Japan, 86-87; vis instr, Middlebury Col, 99; senior lectr, Univ Vt, Contemp Art Hist, currently. *Awards:* Resident Fel, MacDowell Colony, 1992; Grand (first) Prize, San Diego 41st Int Juried Competition, 1996. *Bibliog:* Edward Sozanski (auth), The art of drawing is thriving nicely, Philadelphia Inquirer, 84; Daina Savage (auth), Landscapes abloom in steel & grit, Intelligencer J, 96; Tom Weisser, Works Out, Baltimore Arts Newsletter, 1985; Henry Lehmann, Books and Visual Arts, The Gazette, Montreal, 2002. *Mem:* AAUP; ACLU. *Media:* Drawing, Collaged With Photo & Japanese Paper, transparent plexi & hardware. *Res:* German Satiric Art of the 1920's and 30's; Oxford Round Table, The Two Cultures: The Literary Moderns Revisited, 2006. *Specialty:* Contemporary American, European; Japanese art: old master prints. *Interests:* Holocaust Studies: International Film. *Publ:* Auth, Part-time pathos, Temple Univ Fac Herald, 84; Discord in a Japanese sculpture garden, Vassar Quart, 89; Charlotte Solomon: Life or Theater, Holocaust Studies Bulletin, Univ Vt, 2001. *Dealer:* Caelum Gallery, New York, Nicholas Bergman & Misuzu Takemoto, Dirs. *Mailing Add:* 68 Richardson St Burlington VT 05401

STONE, M LEE
ART DEALER
b Chicago, Ill, Apr 11, 37. *Study:* Univ Ill, BS, 58; Univ Ill Col Med, MD, 62. *Pos:* Pvt dealer, M Lee Stone Fine Prints, 75. *Mem:* IFPDA. *Specialty:* American artists, 20th Century. *Mailing Add:* 2101 Forest Ave Suite 130 San Jose CA 95128

STONEBARGER, VIRGINIA
PAINTER, INSTRUCTOR
b Ann Arbor, Mich, Mar 9, 26. *Study:* Antioch Col, BA, 50; Colorado Springs Fine Arts Ctr, 50-51; Art Students League, 51-52; Hans Hofmann Sch, 54; NY Univ, 54 & 56; Univ Wis-Milwaukee, MS, 72. *Work:* Mrs Harry Lynde Bradley, Milwaukee, Wis. *Comn:* Painting & reproduction of bldg, Nat Bank of Tucson; two paintings, Arlington Race Course, Arlington Heights, Ill. *Exhib:* Univ Wis, 59; Milwaukee Art Ctr, 59-61; one-woman shows, Lakeland Col, 69, Univ Wis, 71, Jewish Community Ctr, Milwaukee, 78 & Galleria Simon, 79; Tucson Int Airport, Ariz, 99; plus many others. *Teaching:* Instr art, Univ Lake Sch, Hartland, Wis, 59-62, Waukesha Co Tech Inst, 70-72 & Milwaukee Area Tech Col, 73-77; instr painting, Univ Wis, Milwaukee Exten, 82-; lectr art, Univ Ariz, 83-99; Painting Instr, Casas Adabes Fine Arts Acad, Tucson, AZ, 2000-05. *Awards:* Danforth Found Fel, 69; Merit Award, Nat League of Am Pen Women, Tucson; Awards, Southern Ariz Watercolor Guild, 86, 90 & 2006. *Mem:* Southern Ariz Watercolor Guild; Nat League Am Pen Women. *Media:* Watercolor, Acrylic. *Dealer:* Cobalt Fine Arts 5 Camino Otero Tubac Ariz 85646. *Mailing Add:* 855 E River #35 Tucson AZ 85718

STONEHAM, JOHN
LIBRARIAN
b Eng, Oct 1, 29; US citizen. *Pos:* Co-ed, The Lively Arts, Baltimore, 59-61; head librn, Md Inst, 65-96; Librn Emer, Decker Libr, Md Inst. *Teaching:* Teacher lit, Md Inst. *Mem:* Founding mem Worst Verse Conspiracy Baltimore; Art Libr Soc NAm. *Res:* Bad verse; military costume; curiosa; Chaucer; Malory

STONEHOUSE, FRED A
PAINTER, COLLAGE ARTIST
b Milwaukee, Wis, June 30, 60. *Study:* Univ Wis, Milwaukee, BFA, 82. *Work:* Tacoma Art Mus, Wash; Milwaukee Art Mus & Marquette Univ, Haggerty Mus Art, Wis; Madison Art Ctr, Wis; Univ Ariz, Tempe. *Exhib:* 10 Yr Survey, Madison Art Ctr, Wis, 92; In the Light of Goya, Univ Calif, Berkeley, 95; The Mythic Narrative, Palo Alto Cult Ctr, Calif, 96; Reality Bites, Kansas City Art Inst, Kemper Mus Contemp Art & Design, 96; Devotional Rescue, Contemp Arts Ctr, Cincinnati, Ohio, 97; Surreal Wisconsin, Madison Art Ctr, Wis, 98. *Awards:* Midwest Nat Endowment Arts Fel, 91; Penny McCall Found Fel, 92; Wis Arts Bd Fel, 93. *Bibliog:* Garret Holg (auth), Review, Art News, 9/94; David Ebony (auth), Fred Stonehouse at M-13, Art in Am, 12/95; Ken Johnson (auth), Review, NY Times, 4/24/98. *Publ:* Illusr, Playboy Mag, 90-97; Milwaukee Mag, 93. *Dealer:* Dean Jensen Gallery Milwaukee WI 53219. *Mailing Add:* 8327 W Rogers West Allis WI 53219

STONER, (DR) JOYCE HILL
CONSERVATOR, EDUCATOR
b Washington, DC, Oct 9, 46. *Study:* Col William & Mary, BA(fine arts; summa cum laude); NY Univ, Inst Fine Arts, Conserv Ctr, MA(fine arts) & dipl conserv, spec grad study with Bernard Rabin (Metrop Mus) John Brealey; Getty Mus, with Mr Andrea Rothe; Univ Del, PhD(art hist), 95. *Work:* Freer Gallery Art; Winterthur Mus, Del; Va Mus Fine Arts, Richmond; Del Art Mus; and others. *Comn:* Edward Laning murals, NY Pub Libr; NC Wyeth mural treatments, WSFS, Wilmington, Del, 98. *Collection Arranged:* Know What You See, a traveling exhib organized by Louis Pomerantz, Found Am Inst Conserv & Smithsonian Inst Traveling Exhib Serv, 76; Flaking, Foxing and Fine Works, conserv exhib, Del Art Mus, 77; Factory Work: Warhol, Wyeth, and Basquiat, Brandywine River Mus, Farnsworth Art Mus, 2006. *Pos:* Managing ed, Art & Archeol Tech Abstracts, 69-86; consult conserv paintings, Freer Gallery Art, 75-76 & 88-92; exec dir, Found Am Inst Conserv, 75-79; paintings conservator, Winterthur Mus, Del, 76-82, supv conserv section, 81-82; vis scholar painting conserv, Metrop Mus Art, 80; guest scholar, Getty Mus Painting Conserv, 85; trustee, Williamstown Regional Art conserv lab, 89-95. *Teaching:* Assoc prof intro art conserv, Va Commonwealth Univ, 75-76; asst prof paintings conserv, Univ Del, 76-79, assoc prof, 79-, assoc dir, Art Conserv Prog, 80-82, dir, 82-97, chair, 90-97, prof, 96-; dir, Preserv Studies Doctoral Prog, Univ Del, 2005-. *Awards:* Getty Guest Scholar Grant, 85; Del State Arts Coun Grant, 91, 92 & 94; Del Humanities Forum, 95 & 96; Am Inst for Conserv Lifetime Achievement Award, 2003. *Mem:* Fel Int Inst Conserv Historic & Artistic Works; Fel Am Inst Conserv Historic & Artistic Works; Int Coun Mus; Nat Mus Act Advisory Coun, 81-84; Nat Inst for Conserv Proj Dir; Col Art Asn (bd 2000-04, vpres 2004-05). *Media:* Conservation of Oil & Tempera Paintings. *Res:* History of art conservation in America; the technique of contemporary artists Whistler, J McNeill, Andrew & Jamie Wyeth. *Interests:* Musical Theatre; Cabaret. *Publ:* Andy Warhol and Jamie Wyeth (co-auth), Interactions, America Art, vol 12, no 3, fall 99; Are There Great Women Art Conservators, Int Inst for Conservation Bulletin, no 1, 2/2000; Climbiing Toward an Ideal: Andrew Wyeth's Portrait of Henry Francis du Pont, Winterthur Mag, 12/2001; Hell vs. Ruhemann: The Metaphysical and the Physical, Controversies about the Cleaning of Paintings, Brit Mus, 12/2001; The Debate Over Cleaning Paintings: How Much is Too Much, Int Found Art Research Tour, vol 5, no 3, 2002; plus others. *Mailing Add:* Univ Del 303 Old College Newark DE 19716

STONES, MARGARET ALISON
EDUCATOR, HISTORIAN
b Eng, Mar 11, 42. *Study:* Univ London, BA, 64, PhD(art hist), 70. *Teaching:* Assoc prof Medieval art, Univ Minn, 69-81, prof, 81-83; vis prof, Univ Reading, 75; prof, Univ Pittsburgh, 84-; vis fel, All Souls Col, Oxford, 99, Magdalen Col, Oxford, 2001 & Corpus Christi Col, Cambridge, 2002. *Awards:* APS Grant, 71, 79 & 93; Am Coun Learned Soc Grant, 73; Nat Endowment Humanities Grant, 73, 77, 78, 82, 85, 92-93 & 2001-; Andrew W Mellon Found Grant, 2001-2002. *Mem:* Medieval Acad Am; Brit Archaeol Asn; Int Arthurian Soc; Soc Nat des antiquaires de France; Fel Soc Antiquaries London. *Res:* Manuscript illumination. *Publ:* Auth, Images of Temptation, Seduction and Discovery in the Prose Lancelot: a Preliminary Note, Festschrift Gerhard Schmidt, Wiener Jahrbuch fur Kunstgeschichte, 46-47, pp 93-4; Les Manuscrits de Chriton de Troyes, ed, earth, 93; Madame Marie's Picture-Book: a precursor of Flemish Painting around 1400, In: Flanders in a Europan Perspective, ed Maurits Smeyers, pp 429-43, Leuven: Peeters, 95; Qui a lu le Guide du plerin? (with Jeanne Krochalis), In: Plerinages et croisades, ed Leon Pressouyre 118e Colloque du Comite des travaux historiques et scientifiques, Pau, 93, Paris, pp 11-36, 95; Stylistic Associations, Evolution and Collaboration: Charting the Bute Painter's Career, The J Paul Getty Mus J, Vol 23, pp 11-29, 95; The Codex Calixtinus and the Iconography of Charlemagne, In: Roland and Charlemagne in Europe: Essays on the Reception and Transformation of a Legend, ed Karen Pratt King's Col London Medieval Studies XII, London, pp 169-203, 96; The Pilgrams Guide to Santiago de Compostela, (with Jeanne Krochalis), ed, 98; Lelived Images de Madame Marie, Paris, 97; Seeing the Grail on the Grail: A Casebook (with D. Mahoney), ed, 2000; and others. *Mailing Add:* Dept Fine Arts Univ Pittsburgh 104 Frick Fine Arts Bldg Pittsburgh PA 15260

STOPPERT, MARY KAY
ADMINISTRATOR, GALLERY DIRECTOR
b Flint, Mich, Aug 19, 1941. *Study:* Western Mich Univ, Kalamazoo, BS, 64; Sch Art Inst Chicago, MFA, 68. *Work:* Mus Contemp Art & Northeastern Ill Univ, Chicago; Michael Rockefeller Art Ctr, State Univ NY, Fredonia; Northern Ill Univ, DeKalb; Kemper Insurance Co, Long Grove, Ill; Corcoran Gallery, Washington, DC. *Exhib:* Solo exhib (with catalog), New Mus Contemp Art, NY, 82; Painting and Sculpture Today, Indianapolis Mus Art, Ind, 76; Works on Paper, Art Inst Chicago, 78; Detroit and Chicago Art of the 70s, Detroit Inst Arts, 78; Art Inst Chicago, 74, 77 & 79; Museo de Arte Contemporanea, Sao Paolo, Brazil, 80; Chicago: Some Other Traditions, San Francisco Mus Art, 83; The Figure in Chicago Art, Mus Contemp Art, Chicago, 85. *Teaching:* Prof art, Northeastern Ill Univ, Chicago, 70-. *Awards:* Frank G Logan Award, 75th Chicago and Vicinity Show, 74, John G Curtis Jr Award, 77th Chicago and Vicinity Show, 78, Art Inst Chicago; President Merit Award, Northeastern Ill Univ, Chicago, 79; Nat Endowment of Arts Visual Artist Fel, 86.

Bibliog: Grace Glueck (auth), rev, in: New York Times, 6/18/82; Christopher Lyon (auth), rev, in: Chicago Sun Times, 3/11/84. *Mem:* Col Art Asn; Women's Caucus Art (bd adv 76-79, 81-85); Chicago Women's Caucus Art (pres, 79-83); Int Sculpture Ctr. *Dealer:* Phyllis Kind Gallery 136 Greene Street New York NY & W Superior Chicago IL 60610. *Mailing Add:* Northeastern Ill Univ Chicago IL 60625

STOREY, DAVID
PAINTER
b Madison, Wis, 1948. *Study:* Univ Calif-Berkeley, 66-68; Univ Calif-Davis, BA, 70 & MFA, 72. *Exhib:* Solo exhibs, Concord Contemp Art, 81, 83 & 84, Jay Gorney Mod Art, 85, Hirschl & Adler Mod, NY, 87, 91 & 92, Lino Silverstein Gallery, Barcelona, Spain, 89, Jorge Albero Arte Contemporaneo, Madrid, Spain & Davis-McClain Gallery, Houston, Tex, 90, Betsy Senior Contemp Prints, NY, 91; Surface Printing in the 80's, Zimmerli Art Mus, Rutgers Univ, NJ, 90; 42nd Ann Purchase Exhib, Am Acad & Inst Arts & Letts, NY, 90; The Unique Print 70s into 90s, Mus Fine Arts, Boston, 90; A Bestiary, Paula Cooper Gallery, NY, 91; Hirschl & Adler Gallery, NY, 92. *Awards:* NY State Found Arts Grant, 89; Nat Endowment Arts Fel, 91. *Bibliog:* Susan Tallman (auth), Many Monotypes, Arts Mag, 1/91; Peggy Cyphers (auth), review, Arts, 9/91; Lisa Liebmann (auth), review, Artforum, 10/91. *Publ:* Contribr, Bestiary, Brad Morrow (auth), 90. *Mailing Add:* 134 W Broadway New York NY 10013-3328

STORM, HOWARD
PAINTER, SCULPTOR
b Newton, Mass, Oct 26, 46. *Study:* Denison Univ; J Ferguson Stained Glass Studio, Weston, Mass, apprenticeship; San Francisco Art Inst, BFA, 69; Univ Calif, Berkeley, MA, 70, MFA, 72. *Work:* Roswell Mus, NMex; Denison Univ; Mt St Joseph Col, Ohio; Ky Arts Comn, Frankfort; Baylor Univ. *Comn:* Pioneer Award, Northern KY Chamber Commerce. *Exhib:* One-man shows, Berkeley Mus, 72 & Baylor Univ, 73; Huntington Galleries, 72-74; Univ Cincinnati, 74; Cincinnati Art Mus, 75; plus others. *Pos:* Artist-in-residence, Roswell Mus, 71-72. *Teaching:* Prof art, Northern Ky Univ, 72-, chmn art dept, currently. *Awards:* Eisner Prize, Univ Calif, Berkeley, 72; Purchase Award, Preview '73; Purchase Award, Huntington Galleries. *Media:* Acrylic, Oil; Wood. *Publ:* Left Alone, Logan Elm Press, Ohio State Univ, 85. *Mailing Add:* 90 Hawthorne Ave Newport KY 41075

STORM, LARUE
PAINTER
b Pittsburgh, Pa. *Study:* Univ Miami, AB & MA; Art Students League, Woodstock; also printmaking with Calvaert Brun, Paris. *Work:* Lowe Mus, Coral Gables, Fla; Columbia Mus Art, Ga; Norton Gallery Art, West Palm Beach, Fla; Peabody Col, Nashville, Tenn. *Exhib:* Corcoran Gallery Art Biennial, Washington, DC, 57; Butler Inst Am Art, Youngstown, Ohio, 58-60; Miami Six, El Paso Mus, 65; Fla Creates, var mus Fla, 71-; one-man show, Lowe Mus Art, Norton Gallery Art & Columbia Mus Art; and others. *Teaching:* Adj asst prof drawing & design, Univ Miami, 67-84. *Awards:* Purchase Award, Columbia Mus Art, SC. *Media:* Collage, Assemblage. *Publ:* Auth, Jose Guadalupe Posada: Guerrilla Fighter of the Throwaways, Carrell, 70. *Mailing Add:* Coconut Grove 3737 Justison Rd Miami FL 33133

STORR, ROBERT
CURATOR, PAINTER
b Portland, Maine, Dec 28, 1949. *Study:* Swarthmore Col, BA, 1972; Sch Art Inst Chicago, postgrad, 1975-78; Skowhegan Sch Painting and Sculptor, MA, 1978. *Exhib:* Betty Cuinningham Gallery; Andre Zarre Gallery; Jack Tilton Gallery; NY Studio Sch; Nelson Atkins Mus; Mus Modern Art, 1991, 93-96; Inst Contemp Art, Phila, 1991. *Pos:* Sr cur painting and sculptor, Mus Modern Art, NY City, 1991-2002; dean, Yale Sch Art, 2006-; vis artist, Cooper Union, NY City, 1988-89; vis artist, critic, RI Sch Design, Providence, 1988; ed bd, Art Journal, 1985-95. *Teaching:* Assoc dean, NY Studio Sch, NYC, 1987-88; asst prof, Tyler Sch Art, Phila, 1989; Avery prof, Bard Col, Annandale on Hudson, NY, 1990-91; Rosalie Solow prof modern art, New York Univ Inst Fine Arts, 2002-06; lectr art mus, univs and art schols in US and abroad. *Awards:* Penny McCall Found grantee, 1988; Peter Norton Family Found grantee, 1990. *Publ:* Auth, Philip Guston, 1986; co-auth Chuck Close, 1987; co-auth (with Lars Hitue), Susan Rothenberg 15 Years a Survey, 1990; co-auth (with Kirk Varnedoe) From Bauhaus to Pop: Masterworks Given by Phillip Johnson, 1996; contrib ed, Art in America, 1981-, Grand Street; bimonthly columnist, Frieze, London. *Mailing Add:* Yale Univ Sch Art Holcombe T Green Jr Hall 1156 Chapel St New Haven CT 06511-8921

STORRS, IMMI CASAGRANDE
SCULPTOR
b Aug 2, 45. *Study:* Univ Denver, BA, 68. *Work:* group shows incl Fleming Mus, Burlington, Vt, 73, Artist Choice Mus, NY City, 83, Nat Accad Mus, NY City, 88, 92, 94, 95, 97, 99, 2001, 2003, Provincetown Art Asn & Mus, Mass, 88, Nat Scultpure Soc, NY City, 89, 91, Elaine Benson Gallery, Bridgehampton, NY, 93, Sculptors Guild, Kyoto, Japan & Wash, 93, NY City, 94, Cline Fine Art Gallery, Sante Fe, 94, 95, Stamford Mus, Conn, 96, Bachelier-Cardonsky Gallery, 96, The White House, Wash, 96, 97; represented in permanent collections at The Nat Mus Women in Arts, Wash, The Snite Mus, Nat Accad Mus, The Herbert Johnson Mus at Cornell, numerous private collections. *Exhib:* One-woman shows, Gallery 2, Woodstock, Vt, 73, Fairwinds Gallery, Ferrisburg, Vt, 74, Congress Hall, Timmendorferstrand, Ger, 76, Amerika Haus, Hamburg, Ger, 76, Cambridge Art Asn, Mass, 1978, Goethe Inst, Boston, 80, 83, Sutton Gallery, New York City, 81, 82, 83, 86, Madison Gallery, 87, Bologna-Landi Gallery, Easthampton, NY, 87, 93, Vorpal Gallery, New York City, 89, 91, 92, La Posada, Santa Fe, 89, Ruth Volid Gallery, Chicago, 90, Bachelier-Cardonsky Gallery, Kent, Conn, 96, Hurlbutt Gallery, Greenwich, Conn, 97, Dillon Gallery, New York City, 97 & 2000. *Awards:* Nessa Cohen grantee, 1981, 82, ED Found grantee, 1989, 96; recipient Purchase award, Art Students League NY, Chaim Gross Found award, 1989, Nat Acad Mus Speyer prize, 1992. *Mem:* Nat Acad (assoc, 93, acad, 94-); Century Asn, Sculptors Guild. *Mailing Add:* 169 E 78th St New York NY 10021-0485

STORY WILSON, MARTHA REDY
CONCEPTUAL ARTIST, MUSEUM DIRECTOR
b Philadelphia, Pa, Dec 18, 47. *Study:* Wilmington Col, Ohio, BA; Dalhousie Univ, Halifax, NS, Can, MA & studies for PhD. *Exhib:* Circa 7500 (traveling exhib of women conceptual artists), 73-74; Autogeography, Downtown, Whitney Mus Am Art, NY, 75; Four Evenings, Four Days, Whitney Mus Am Art, NY, 76; Performance for Tipper Gore, Cooper Union, NY, 94. *Pos:* Found & dir, Franklin Furnace Archives Inc, 76-. *Teaching:* Lectr lit, NS Col Art & Design, 72-74; lectr 20th century art, Brooklyn Col, NY, 75. *Awards:* Grants, Nat Endowment Arts Fel, Performance Art, 78 & 83. *Bibliog:* Moira Roth (auth), The Amazing Decade: Women's Performance Art in America 1970-1980, Astro Artz, Los Angeles, 83; Heresies: Acting Up: Women in Theatre and Performance, Heresies Collective, NY, 84, Vol 5, No 1, Issue 17; Randy Rosen & Catherine C Brower (auths), Making Their Mark: Women Artists Move into the Mainstream 1970-1985, Abbeville Press, NY, 89. *Mem:* Col Art Asn; Gallery Asn NY State. *Media:* Mixed. *Publ:* ed, Art Jour, Col Art Asn, Vol 56, No 4, 98

STOTT, DEBORAH
HISTORIAN
b Minneapolis, Minn, June 11, 42. *Study:* Wellesley Col, BA, 64; Columbia Univ, MA, 66, PhD, 75. *Pos:* Assoc dean undergrad studies, Sch Arts & Humanities, Univ Tex, Dallas, 94-. *Teaching:* Instr art hist, Wheaton Col, Mass, 70-75; asst prof, Intercollegiate Ctr Classical Studies, Rome, 75-76; assoc prof, Univ Tex, Dallas, 76-. *Awards:* Am Acad Rome Fel, 80-81; Delmas Found Grant, 80 & 82; Bunting Inst Fel, Radcliffe Col, 82-83. *Mem:* Col Art Asn Am; Midwest Art Hist Asn; Soc Fels Am Acad (regional rep). *Res:* Style and theory in Italian Renaissance reliefs. *Publ:* Auth, Jacques Lipchitz and Cubism, Garland Publ, 78; auth, Jacopo Sansovino's Bronze Reliefs and Venetian Colorism, Hofstra Univ, 82; auth, Fatte a sembianza di pittura: Jacopo Sansovino's bronze reliefs in San Marco, Art Bulletin, spring 82. *Mailing Add:* Sch Arts & Humanities Univ Tex PO Box 830688 Richardson TX 75083-0688

STOUFFER, DANIEL HENRY, JR
PAINTER, DESIGNER
b Paulding, Ohio, Sept 26, 37. *Study:* Ohio State Univ, BFA, 59. *Work:* Ohio State Univ, Columbus; Amoco Oil Co, Houston; Pub Serv Co, NMex; Sandia Fed Savings & Loan Bank, Albuquerque; Fed Reserve Bank, Denver. *Comn:* Ann commemorative painting, Pub Serv Co NMex, Albuquerque, 76; painting, Sandia Fed Savings, Albuquerque, 86; ann commemorative poster, NMex Arts & Crafts Fair, 88; ann commemorative poster, Weems Artfest, 90 & 94. *Exhib:* Albuquerque Mus, 82 & 83; Two Watercolorists, Carlsbad Mus, NMex, 84; Watercolor USA, 87, 93, 94, 98, 2000, 2001, 2003, 2004; Rocky Mountain Nat Watermedia Exhib, 87, 88, 93, 97, 2000, 2002-2006; Nature Conservancy Show, Gingrass Gallery, Milwaukee, 90; Governor's Show, Albuquerque, 92; Arts for the Parks, Jackson Hole, Wyoming, 94, 96, 2000, 2002-2006 (Nat Traveling Show). *Pos:* Artist & dir design, Charles Merrill Publ, Columbus, Ohio, 60-72; art dir, Univ NMex Press, Albuquerque, 72-79. *Awards:* Grumbacher Gold Medallion, NMex State Fair, 95; Award of Merit, Rocky Mtn Nat, 97; Strathmore Award, Watercolor USA, 2004; Region II Award, Arts for the Parks, 2004 & 2005. *Bibliog:* Article, Watercolor Mag, summer 97; Article, Southwest Art Mag, Feb 2003; Article, Watercolor Magic, Dec, 2004,. *Mem:* Rocky Mtn Nat Watercolor Soc; Watercolor USA Honor Soc. *Media:* Watercolor. *Publ:* Acoma: Pueblo in the Sky, 76, This Shining Land, 82, The Galaz Ruins: Mimbres Pottery, 83, Univ NMex Press; illusr & collabr, In Celebration of The Book, NMex Book League, 82; Who's Who In The West, Marquis (23rd ed), 92. *Dealer:* Weems Gallery 2801 M Eubank NE Albuquerque NM 87112. *Mailing Add:* 1190 Calle del Oro Bosque Farms NM 87068

STOUT, DONNA PHIPPS
PAINTER
b McCraken Co, Ky, 44. *Study:* Georgetown Col, Ky, BA, 62-66; Ind Univ, Bloomington, MFA; studied with William Bailey. *Exhib:* Jerald Melberg Gallery; Valley House Gallery, Dallas, Tex, 88-2001; Solo exhib, Quincy Art Ctr, Ill, Univ Tulsa, Okla, Valey House Gallery, Jerald Melberg Gallery, 2001. *Teaching:* instr, painting, Univ Ark; instr, painting, John Brown Univ; instr, painting, Murray State Univ, Ky; instr, painting, Berea Col, Ky. *Awards:* Farman Still Life Prize, Salon Biennial, Paris, France; Millay Colony for Arts; Reader's Digest Fel. *Media:* Acrylic, Oil. *Specialty:* Still lifes. *Mailing Add:* c/o Jerald Melberg Gallery 625 S Sharon Amity Rd Charlotte NC 28211

STOUT, FRANK J
PAINTER, SCULPTOR
b Lynn, Mass, Feb 17, 26. *Study:* Boston Mus Sch, 49-50; San Gimignano, Siena, Italy, painting & sculpture, 82-84; Marlboro Col sch yr abroad, Italy, 85. *Work:* Springfield Mus, Mass; Wichita Art Mus, Kans; Sheldon Swope Art Gallery, Terre Haute, Ind; Vermont State House, Montpelier; Univ Vt, Burlington; Am Embassies in Peru & Brazil. *Comn:* Members portrait, Nat Acad Design, NY, 79; portrait, Ex-Gov Emerson, Montpelier, Vt, 80; monumental sculpture, Burlington, Vt, 81; plaza fountain, Burlington, Vt. *Exhib:* Solo exhibs, Landmark Gallery, NY, 79 81 & Mercer Price Gallery, Putney, Vt, 83; By the Sea, Queens Mus, NY, 79; Vermont Landscape, Fleming Mus, Burlington, Vt; Nat Acad Design, NY, 83; Vermont Skies, Brattleboro Mus, Vt, 86. *Pos:* Mem, Vt Coun Arts, 75-80, New Eng Found Arts, 79-81. *Teaching:* Chmn dept arts, drawing, painting & sculpture, Marlboro Col, Vt, 66-90. *Awards:* H

W Ranger Award, Nat Acad Design, New York, 82. *Bibliog:* Rev, Art News, 2/65; The Brattleboro Reformer, Vt, 69-91; Wolf Kahn (auth), the subject matter in new realism, Am Artist, 11/79. *Media:* All. *Dealer:* William Price 1205 Bolton St Baltimore MD 21217. *Mailing Add:* Butterfield Rd PO Box 75 Marlboro VT 05344

STOUT, RICHARD GORDON
PAINTER
b Beaumont, Tex, Aug 21, 34. *Study:* Cincinnati Art Acad, 52-53; Sch Art Inst Chicago, BFA, 57; Univ Tex, MFA, 69. *Work:* Mus Fine Arts, Houston; Dallas Mus Fine Arts; Marion Koogler McNay Art Mus, San Antonio; Rice Univ; Univ Houston. *Exhib:* One Hundred Contemp Am Draftsmen, Univ Mich, 63; Marion Koogler McNay Art Inst, 64 & 71; Contemp Arts Mus, Houston, 75; Jurgen Schweinebroden, Berlin, 80; Barbara Davis Gallery, Houston, 94-96. *Pos:* Mem adv bd, Mus Fine Arts, Houston, 73-. *Teaching:* Instr painting, Mus Fine Arts, Houston, 58-67; assoc prof drawing & painting, Univ Houston, 69-96. *Awards:* Longview Purchase Prize, Jr Serv League, 65 & 72; Tex Fine Arts Asn Awards, 66 & 71; Houston Area Exhib First Prize, Blaffer Gallery, Univ Houston, 75; and others. *Media:* Acrylic. *Dealer:* Graham Gallery 1431 W Alabama Houston TX 77006; Davis McLain Gallery 2627 Colqoitt Houston TX 77098. *Mailing Add:* 1213 Bonnie Brae Houston TX 77006

STOVALL, LUTHER MCKINLEY
PRINTMAKER
b Athens, Ga, Jan 1, 37. *Study:* RI Sch Design; Howard Univ, BFA, 65. *Work:* Corcoran Gallery Art, Nat Mus Am Art, Wash Post Co, Washington; Howrey & Simon; Ropes & Gray. *Comn:* Silkscreens, Smithsonian Inst Resident Assoc Prog, 85, 87 & 88; silkscreens, Spalding-Amers, 86-; Right (silkscreen ed), Amnesty Int, 89; Breathing Hope (silkscreen ed), Howard Univ, 96; silkscreen ed Sam Gilliam's Think Tank, Joint Ctr Political & Econ Study, 96. *Exhib:* Impressionisms/Expressionisms: Black Am Graphic Exhibs (traveling), Smithsonian Inst, 80-81; Art in Washington & its Afro-Am Presence: 1940-1979, Washington Proj for Arts, 85; The Art of Black Americans in Japan, Tokyo, 87; Heroes and Teachers (auth, catalog), African-Am Atelier, Greensboro, NC, 91; Heroes, Teachers and Friends, Corcoran Gallery Art, 92; Art Silkscreen Printmaking, Howard Univ Gallery, 2001; Art, Strathmore Hall, 2004. *Pos:* Dir, Workshop, Inc, 68-; mem, Corcoran Bd Overseers, DC Comn Arts & Humanities, Georgetown Arts Comn, Pen Faulkner Bd Dir & Washington Nat Cathedral Arts Coun, Washington, currently. *Teaching:* Master printmaking & silkscreen, Workshop, Corcoran Gallery Art, 69-72. *Awards:* Stern Grant, 68-72; Individual Artist Grant, 72 & Workshop Grant, 72-76, Nat Endowment Arts; Fourth Ann Mayor's Art Award, Washington, DC, 85; Bd Dir Award, Source Theatre Co, Washington, DC, 88. *Bibliog:* Lou Stovall, Printmaker (film), Smithsonian Inst, 83; Patricia Dane Rogers (auth), A workshop atelier comes to life in NW Washington, Wash Post, 3/26/87; Ken Oda (auth), Lou Stovall, on how people make a difference, Koan, 3/93. *Mem:* DC Comn Arts & Humanities. *Media:* Silkscreen. *Publ:* Auth, Of the Land, 73. *Mailing Add:* Workshop Inc 3145 Newark St NW Washington DC 20008

STOVER, DONALD LEWIS
CURATOR
b Staunton, Va, Jan 8, 43. *Study:* Va Polytechnic Inst Col Archit, 61-65; St Marys Univ, BA, 72; Univ Del Winterthur Prog, 75-77. *Collection Arranged:* Early Texas Furniture and Decorative Arts (auth, catalog), 72 & Tischlermeister Jahn (auth, catalog), 75, San Antonio Mus Asn; Art of Louis C Tiffany (auth, catalog), 81, American Sculpture (auth, catalog), 82 & Pennsylvania German, 83, Fine Arts Mus San Francisco. *Pos:* Cur furniture, San Antonio Mus Asn, 72-75; cur-in-charge, Decorative Arts & Sculpture, Fine Arts Mus San Francisco, 81-83, cur-in-charge, Am Decorative Arts & Sculpture, 83-. *Mem:* Soc Winterthur Grads; Decorative Arts Trust; Am Decorative Arts Forum Northern Calif; Western Region Arch Am Art (chmn, currently). *Res:* Nineteenth century Texas cabinetmakers; mid-19th century emmigrant cabinetmakers, New York; Louis Comfort Tiffany; American sculpture. *Publ:* Coauth, Early Texas Furniture, Trinity Press, 74; auth, American decorative arts: Recent acquisitions, Apollo Mag, 80. *Mailing Add:* 15 Buena Vista Ave E San Francisco CA 94117

STRAIGHT, ELSIE H
LIBRARIAN, SCULPTOR
b Cumberland, Eng. *Study:* Art Inst Pittsburgh, dipl(illus), 39; New York Sch of Applied Design for Women, with Kimon Nicholaides, dipl(des), 41; Roger Williams Col, BA, 66; Univ RI, MLS, 72. *Pos:* Librn, Ringling Sch Art Libr, 74-, retired; rare books & libr res, Univ So Fla. *Mem:* Art Libr Soc NAm, Southeastern Region (chmn, 80); Sch Libr Asn (secy, 70); Nat Sculpture Soc. *Media:* Stone, Clay. *Res:* John Simmons Collection of French Revolutionary Statesmen and military leaders; 17th century prints. *Interests:* Portrait artists, painters and sculptors; Pre-Columbian art. *Mailing Add:* 435 Edward Sarasota FL 33580

STRAIGHT, ROBERT L
PAINTER
b Halstead, Kans, Apr 19, 46. *Study:* Calif State Univ, Longbeach, 69; Cranbrook Acad of Art, MFA, 71. *Work:* Del Art Mus, Wilmington; Downey Art Mus; Cranbrook Acad Art Mus, Bloomfield Hills, Mich. *Comn:* Painting, Met Life, Philadelphia, 97. *Exhib:* Robert Straight, Del Art Mus, 97; Contemplation, Abington Art Center, Jenkintown, Pa, 99; Group Exh, The Painting Center, NY, 01; Biomorphix, Del Ctr for Contemp Art, Wilmington, 02. *Teaching:* Ast Prof, Conn Col, 73-80; Prof, Univ Del, Newark, 80-. *Awards:* Artists Grant, Del State Arts Coun, 85-86; Artist in Residence, YADPO, 76; Block Grant, Univ Del, 02. *Publ:* auth, Nancy Miller-Batty, Robert Straight New Paintings, Del Art Mus, 97; auth, Virgina Fabbri Butera, The Fan as Form and Image in Contemporary Art, Arts, 81. *Dealer:* Schmidt/Dean Gallery, 1710 Sonsom St, Philadelphia, 19103. *Mailing Add:* 2600 Newport Gap Pike Wilmington DE 19808

STRAND, SALLY ELLIS
PAINTER, INSTRUCTOR
b Denver, Colo, Oct 11, 54. *Study:* Am Acad Art, Chicago, 75-77; Denver Univ, BFA, 78; Art Students League, New York, 81-82. *Work:* IDAK, Am Express, Minneapolis; Goldman-Sachs, NY; Grand Hyatt Hotel, NY; Hunter Mus, Chattanooga, Tenn. *Exhib:* Am Watercolor Soc, Salmagundi Club, NY, 83; All Media '83 Exhib, Laguna Beach Mus Art, Calif, 83; Pastel Soc Am, Nat Arts Club Gallery, NY, 83, 85, 89-93, 95-2000; Pastel Soc Am, Special Invitation, Hermitage Mus, Norfolk, Va, 85; Pastel Soc Am, Special Invitation, Monmouth Mus, NJ, 85; Pastel Soc W Coast, Sacramento Fine Arts Ctr, 92; and others. *Teaching:* Fac color theory, Colo Inst Art, Denver, 78-79; fac pastel/mixed media, Scottsdale Artist's Sch, Ariz, 90-; Nat & Local workshops, The Color of Light. *Awards:* Master Pastellist Title, Pastel Soc of Am, 97, Hahnemuhle Pastel Award, 97 & Joseph v Giffuni Memorial Award, 98; Thomas & Margery Leighton Mem Award, Pastel Soc West Coast, 92; Bd Dirs Award, Pastel Soc Am, 93; Canson Talens Award, Pastel Soc Am, 95; Joseph V Giffuni Found Award, Pastel Soc Am, 99, Sauter-Margulies Award, 2000. *Bibliog:* Carole Katchen (auth), Ordinary people, great paintings, Artist's Mag, 9/87; Jacqueline M Pontello (auth), Sally Strand, Southwest Art Mag, 6/89; Martin Parsons (auth), The singular glory of pastel, Artspeak, 9/90; Georgina Kelnam (auth), Symbolic Gestures, Am Artists Mag, 9/99. *Mem:* Pastel Soc Am. *Media:* Pastel, Mixed Media. *Publ:* Auth, Pastels Masterclass, Harper Collins Publ, 93; Artist's Manual, Harper Collins Publ, 95; The Best of Pastel, 96 & The Best of Pastel 2, 98, Rockport Publ; Guide to Materials and Techniques, Northlight, 96; The Artist's Guide, Darling Kindersley, 98; and others. *Dealer:* J Cacciola Galleries 501 W 23rd St New York NY 10011; Telluride Gallery of Fine Art 130 E Colorado Ave Telluride CO 81435; Diana Nelson Fine Art 435 Ocean Ave Laguna Beach CA 92651. *Mailing Add:* 33601 Moonsail Dr Dana Point CA 92629-4483

STRASEN, BARBARA ELAINE
PAINTER, CONCEPTUAL ARTIST
b Brooklyn, NY, Aug 12, 48. *Study:* Yale Univ Sch Art, summer 68; Carnegie-Mellon Univ, BFA, 69; Univ Calif, Berkeley, MFA, 71. *Work:* Nat Gallery Art, Washington; Best Products Collection, Richmond, Va; Callas, Powell, Rosenthal & Bloch Advert, Lafayette, Calif; Dorothy & Herman Vogel pvt collection, NY; Allen Mem Art Mus, Oberlin, Ohio. *Comn:* Visions LA 1992 (painting & videotape composite), Los Angeles Arts Recovery Grant. *Exhib:* Biennial Contemp Art, Whitney Mus Am Art, 75, AIR Gallery, 83, NY; About Face, Munic Art Gallery, Los Angeles, 96; Gallery Group, Adamar Fine Art, Miami, 96; Codpiece, Griffin Linton Gallery, Venice, Calif, 96; Light Abberations, Univ Tex San Antonio Art Gallery, 96; solo-exhibs, Angels Gate Cult Ctr, Los Angeles, 96, Forum Gallery, San Diego, Calif, 97, Galeria Soloblu, Milan, 98, Adamar Fine Art, Miami, Fla, 98 & Layers of Perception, Galerie Budapest, 98; Gallery Artists, Adamar Fine Art, Miami, Fla, 97; In Response, Marc Arranaga Contemp Art, Los Angeles, 97; New Art Los Angeles, Coast Contemp Art, Los Angeles, 97; Generations, AIR Gallery, NY, 97; House Party, Long Beach Mus Art, Calif, 98; Five Artists, Rico Gallery, Santa Monica, Calif, 98; Contempo-Italianate, Laband Gallery, Loyola Marymount Univ, Los Angeles, 98. *Pos:* Bd dir, Angels Gate Cult Ctr, San Pedro, 94-; asst cur, Hammer Mus, Univ Calif, Los Angeles, 98. *Teaching:* Instr visual arts, Cabrillo Col, Calif, 69-70, Southwestern Col, Calif, 72-75; asst prof visual arts, Univ Calif, San Diego, 75-80. *Awards:* Artist Fel Grant, Nat Endowment Arts, 75-76; Acad Senate Res Grant, Univ of Calif, San Diego, 76-77; Arts Recovery Grant, Los Angeles, 92-93. *Bibliog:* Lynn Crandell (auth), The Paintings of Barbara Strasen: Visual Metaphors for Leadership and the New Science, Southern Calif Bus J, 11/94; Peter Frank (auth), Solo Series: Works by Barbara Strasen, Marie Thiebault and Kathryn Tubbs, Long Beach Press-Telegram, 3/13/96; Robert L Pincus (auth), Layers on layers: Barbara Strasen, San Diego Union Tribune, 11/27/97. *Mem:* Inner City Arts (artist adv bd, currently); Angels Gate Cult Ctr, San Pedro, Calif (bd dir, 95-97); Los Angeles Cult Affairs Dept, Vis Art Div (panelist, 96). *Media:* Acrylic, Mixed; Photography. *Publ:* Auth, The Immigrants, J Los Angeles Inst Contemp Art, 75; Desert Notes, Santa Barbara Mus Art, 80; Women and Ecology, Heresies, winter, 82; Changing at Will Chapter of the Book Animal Art: The Animal as a conveyor and medium of art, Steirischer Herbst, Graz, Austria, 87. *Dealer:* Space Gallery 305 Main St Santa Monica CA. *Mailing Add:* 1724 S Pacific Ave San Pedro CA 90731

STRASSBERG, ROY I
CERAMIST, SCULPTOR
b Brooklyn, NY, Sept 18, 50. *Study:* State Univ NY Col, Oswego, BA, 72; Univ Mich, MFA, 74. *Work:* Tenn State Mus, Nashville; SDak Mem Art Ctr, Brookings; Mint Mus Art, Charlotte, NC; Sourwood Regional Art Ctr, Jonesboro, Tenn. *Exhib:* J B Speed Mus, Louisville, Ky, 76; Mint Mus Art, Charlotte, NC, 76; Mus Contemp Crafts, NY, 78; Ft Wayne Mus Art, Ind, 80; Wichita Mus Art, Kans, 81; Plains Art Mus, Moorehead, Minn, 81; and others. *Teaching:* Fel ceramics, Univ Mich, 73-74; instr, Memphis State Univ, 74-76; asst prof, Mankato State Univ, 76-. *Awards:* Grand Prize, Miss River Crafts, Brooks Mem Art Gallery, 75; Second Prize, Midwest Craft Exhib, Rochester Art Ctr, Minn, 77; Purchase Award, Plains Art Mus, 79. *Mem:* Nat Coun Educ Ceramic Arts. *Media:* Clay. *Publ:* Contribr, Ceramics Monthly, 5/76-5/80 & Am Craft Mag, 8/76-12/81. *Dealer:* Cooper/Lynn Gallery 54 Seventh Ave S New York NY 10014; Robert L Kidd & Assocs 107 Townsend St Birmingham MI 48011. *Mailing Add:* 2004 Midwood Pl Charlotte NC 28205-3649

STRASSHEIM, ANGELA
PHOTOGRAPHER
b Bloomfield, IA, 69. *Study:* Mpls Col Art & Design, BFA, 1995; Forensic & Biomedical Photog Cert, Metro-Dade Co, Forensic Imaging Bureau, Miami, Fla, 1997; Yale Univ, MFA, 2003. *Exhib:* One-woman shows: Photog Thesis Exhib, Yale Univ, 2003; Black Milk, Marvelli Gallery, NYC, 2004; Factory Direct, Artspace Inc,

New Haven, Conn, 2005; Traces & Omens, Noorderlicht Photofestival, Neth, 2005; Left Behind, Marvelli Gallery, 2005; reGeneration, Aperture Found, NYC, Marvelli Gallery, 2006; Group show, Whitney Biennial: Day for Night, Whitney Mus Am Art, NYC, 2006. *Pos:* Forensic photogr, Miami, Fla, NYC. *Awards:* Jerome Fel Emerging Artist Grant; Artist Initiative Grant, Minn State Arts Bd; Bush Found, Artist Fel, St Paul, Minn. *Mailing Add:* Marvelli Gallery 526 W 26th St 2Fl New York NY 10001

STRATAKOS, STEVE JOHN
CRAFTSMAN, TAPESTRY ARTIST
b Chicago, Ill, Nov 26, 54. *Study:* Italian Univ, Perugia, Italy, 74-75; Sch Art Inst Chicago, BFA, 77. *Work:* DuSable Mus African/American Art, Chicago, Ill; Chicago Public Libr, Chicago, Ill. *Comn:* Five banners, DeVry Tech Inst, Chicago, Ill, 85; 2 appliques, Brookfield Zoo, Brookfield, Ill, 87; bedspread, rug, wallpaper design, Univ Chicago, 87; 7 applique banners, Ruby Mem Hosp, Morgantown, WVa, 88. *Exhib:* New Horizons in Art, Chicago Pub Libr Cult Ctr, Chicago, Ill, 84; Artist as Quiltmaker, 84 & 86 and Fantasies in Fabric, 87, F A V A Gallery, Oberlin, Ohio; At the Table, Soc Arts & Crafts, Boston, Mass, 88; Manmade Quilts, Geneva Courthouse, Ill, 90. *Pos:* Banner designer & fabricator, Advert Flag & Banner, Chicago, Ill, 79-82; sr artist/designer, Brookfield Zoo, Ill, 83-90. *Bibliog:* Dimeta Karis (auth), First Prize Quilts, Simon & Schuster, 84; Roberick Kiracofe, The Quilt Digest 5, Quilt Digest Press, 87; The Guild, Sourcebook, Kraus Sikes, 87 & 88. *Media:* Fabric. *Dealer:* Sandy Friedman 107 Edinburgh South Cary NC 27511. *Mailing Add:* 800 W Annie St Austin TX 78704-4106

STRATMAN, DEBORAH
FILMMAKER
Study: Univ Ill, 85—86; Sch of the Art Inst of Chicago, BFA, 86-90; Calif Inst of the Arts, MFA, 92—95. *Pos:* staff, audio visual dept, Mich & Adams, 90-91; projectionist, The Film Ctr Art Inst Chicago, 90-92; co-op & tech dir, Chicago Filmmakers, 91-92; 35 mm projectionist, Cal Arts, Valencia, Calif, 92-95; dir prodr, Ind Film/Video Production, Pythagoras Productions, 95-2002. *Teaching:* vis instr, live action film/video Calif Inst Arts, Valencia, 2002; adj asst prof, dept film, video & new media Sch Art Inst, Chicago, 98-2003; adj asst prof, art & archit dept Univ Ill, 2003-. *Awards:* Community Arts Assistance Grants, 1999, 2000, 2001; Cal Arts Deans Coun Grant, 2002; Guggenheim Fel, 2003. *Publ:* Prodr.: (films) My Alchemy, 1990, Upon a Time, 1991, A Letter, 1992, Possibilities, Dilemmas, 1992, the train from l.a. to l.a., 1992, In Flight: Day No. 2,128, 1993, Palimpsest, 1993, Waking, 1994, Iolanthe, 1995, On the Various Nature of Things, 1995 (Ann Arbor Film Festival, 1996), From Hetty to Nancy, 1997 (Athens International Film/Video Festival: best experimental, 1998), The BLVD, 1999 (Athens Inter Film/Video Festival: best documentary, 2000), Untied, 2001, In Order Not to Be Here, 2002 (THAW Film/Video Festival: best of festival, 2002, Chicago Underground Film Festival: best experimental, 2002, Film Festival: Gecko Award, 2002, Media City Film Festival: hon. mention, 2003, Ann Arbor Film Festival: best experimental & best narrative integrity, 2003), Meet Adiljan, 2003. *Mailing Add:* Pythagoras Productions PO Box 6167 Chicago IL 60680

STRATTON, DOROTHY
PAINTER, PRINTMAKER
b Worcester, Mass, Dec 21, 08. *Study:* Pratt Inst, cert, 42; Brooklyn Mus Sch, 42-43; Acad Grande Chaumiere, with Andre Lhote, Paris, 47-48; Univ Calif, Los Angeles, with Rico Lebrun, 56-57; Univ Calif, Los Angeles, 61; Univ Calif, San Diego, 66-67. *Work:* Los Angeles Munic Art Collection, City Hall; Art in Embassies, Dept of State, Washington; Acadia Univ, Nova Scotia, Can; Univ San Diego, Calif; Pushkin Mus Art, Moscow, Russia; and others. *Comn:* Painted Wall Murals, City is for People, San Diego Mus Art, Contemp Company. *Exhib:* Solo shows, Pasadena Art Mus, 59, La Jolla Mus Contemp Art, 62, Univ San Diego, 73, 80 & 94, San Diego State Univ, 79, 30-yr retrospective, Wash Printmakers Gallery, 85, 88 & 92, Barry Gallery, Marymount Univ N Va, 90, Acadia Univ, Nova Scotia, Can, 91; Art in Embassies Prog, 65-96; Smithsonian Inst, 69-; Calif Soc Printmakers Nat Traveling Shows, 72-74 & 82-90; Pratt Graphics Ctr, NY, 80-83; Int Exchange Printmakers Coun Gt Brit, Los Angeles Print Soc, 88-90. *Pos:* Special effects decorator, Paramount Studios, George Pal Productions, Hollywood, 45-47; gallery receptionist & ed publicity, Munic Art Dept, Los Angeles, 52-61; registr & mem secy, La Jolla Mus Art, 64-65, vol art ref libr, 66-74; mem, Contemp Art Comt, San Diego Mus Art, 72-82. *Teaching:* Instr seminars printmaking, Univ Calif, 67, 73-75, 76 & 80-83. *Awards:* 40 Awards through 1997. *Bibliog:* Dorothy Stratton (auth), An exciting future, a romantic past, J Printworld, Vol 12, No 4, 89; San Diego Res Mus Art, taped interview, 90; Calif Soc Printmakers Quart, 90. *Mem:* Calif Soc Printmakers; Artists Equity Asn; Mingei Int; Wash Printmakers Found; Art & Art Guild, Calif. *Media:* Etching, Painting. *Mailing Add:* c/o Heather Hicks-Beach 417 Hampton Ct Falls Church VA 22046

STRATTON, MARGARET MARY
PHOTOGRAPHER, EDUCATOR
b Seattle, Wash, Nov 12, 53. *Study:* Evergreen State Col, BA (art), 77; Univ NMex, MA (art), 83 & MFA (art), 85. *Work:* Video Data Bank, Chicago, Ill; Chicago Art Inst, Ill; Hampshire Col; Univ Ill, Chicago; George Eastman Ho, Int Ctr Photog and Film, Rochester, NY. *Comn:* Light box installation, Seattle Art Comn, 91. *Exhib:* First Nat Bank, Minneapolis; Camera Works, San Francisco; Eyes on Pub Art, Portable Works Collection, Seattle Ctr Pavilion, Wash, 94; Mapping: Identities, Mus Contemp Photog, Chicago, Ill, 94; Int Women's Day Video Festival, Boston, Mass, 94; one-woman shows, Cedar Rapids Mus Art, Iowa, 98, Art Inst Chicago, Ill, 99, James Worrell Photog, NY, 2000, Media Arts Center, Univ Arts, Philadelphia, Pa, 2001, Southeast Mus Photog, Daytona Beach, Fla, 2001, Robert Menchal Gallery, Syracuse, NY, 2001; Mus Contemp Photog, Chicago, Ill, 98; Hand Art Gallery, Richmond, Va, 99; William Benton Mus Art, Storrs, Conn, 2000. *Pos:* Nat bd mem, Soc Photo Educ, Dallas, 90-94; New Forms Grant Adv, Regional NEA, Arts, Midwest, 90-; chmn, Nat Conf, Soc Photog Ed, 92-93; artist in residence, UCross Artists Found, Ucross, Wyo, summer, 94 & Villa Montalvo, Saratoga, Calif, 2000. *Teaching:* asst prof, Univ Iowa, Iowa City, 81-86, assoc prof, 86-91 & prof, 92-; vis prof photog, Sch Art Inst, 92-93; vis artist, Univ Ill, Chicago, 94. *Awards:* Jerome Rockefeller Video Award, 94; Nat Award Arts, Nat Endowment Arts, 95; Fac Scholar Award, Univ Iowa, 95 & Arts and Humanities Initiative Grant, 99; Individual Artist Grant, Iowa Arts Coun, 2000 & Individual Fel, 2001; Avid Editing Residency, Wexner Center, Ohio State Univ, 2001. *Bibliog:* David McCraken (auth), Exhib has fun/serious side, Chicago Tribune, 89; Helen Slade (auth), Courting the Mammoth, Reflex, 91; Regina Hackett (auth), 9 Artists Link Vision, Seattle Times, 92; Dorota Kozinska (auth), 101 bites of the apple, Montreal Gazette, 5/23/98. *Mem:* Col Art Asn; Soc Photog Educ (bd mem). *Media:* Video. *Publ:* Auth, Taking it to the Streets, 90 & Images In Action, 91, Afterimage; Nuclear Matters-Camerawork Quarterly, Camerawork, San Francisco, 91; Robbie Steinback's Women-XS Gallery, Western Nev Col, 91; New Feminist Photography, Temple Univ Press, 93; Lesbian Art in America, Rizzolli Press, 2000. *Mailing Add:* 1611 E Court St Iowa City IA 52245

STRAUS, MARC JOSHUA
EDUCATOR
b NY City, 43. *Study:* Franklin & Marshall Col, AB, 64; State Univ of NY, MD, 68. *Pos:* co-found (with Livia Straus) Hudson Valley Ctr for Contemp Art, Peekskill, NY, 2002-. *Awards:* Yaddo fel in poetry, 93. *Mailing Add:* Hudson Valley Ctr Contemp Art 1701 Main St PO Box 209 Peekskill NY 10566

STRAUS, SANDY
PAINTER
b Omaha, Nebr, Mar 15, 48. *Study:* Art Inst Chicago, BFA, 76. *Comn:* Jessica Hahn (mural), The Tunnel, NY, 88; Billy Boggs (billboards), Mars Steel Corp, NY, 88; Clarence Darrow (billboard), D Fiedler, 89; Salmon Rushdie (poster), C Carson, NY, 90; Prejudice, Beat It Billboards, W Giles, NY, 93. *Exhib:* Nat Gallery Mod Art, New Delhi, India; NY State Mus, Albany; Documenta Kessel, Ger; Mus De Art Contemporanee, Sao Paulo, Brazil; Solo exhibs, Smart Gallery, Univ Chicago, 76, M Deson, Chicago, 80, 55 Mercer, NY, 82, Germans Van Eck, NY, 83, Sensory Evolution, 86-87, Air Gallery, NY, 95 & St Peter's Church, NY, 96; I Arose, Nat Arts Club, NY, 98; Rockford Mus, Ill; Mass Mus Contemp Art; Nat Arts Club, 2004-2005; Gallery 128, New York, NY, 2004; Ellenville Mus & Libr, NY, 2006. *Collection Arranged:* Nat Arts Club; Actors Inst; Mars Steel Corp; for John Bergman, Jean Louis Bourgeois, Will & Elena Barnet, Jerry Wenzel, Anthony Cueto, Trudy Craney Germans & Blake Benton. *Awards:* First Prize, Nat Arts Club Exhib Mems, 98, 01. *Bibliog:* Newsweek Mag, 11/24/86; Sharon Churcher (auth), Art imitates death, Reuters Ltd, 1/14/88; Art & Artists Cover, Vol 17, 1/89. *Mem:* Nat Arts Club; Artists Fel. *Media:* Oil, Charcoal, Pastel. *Publ:* (photos), France Soir, NY Post, NY Times Art Forum, Arts. *Dealer:* Blake Benton Fine Arts. *Mailing Add:* 124 Thompson St Apt C New York NY 10012-3131

STRAUSS, ZOE
PHOTOGRAPHER
b Philadelphia, Pa, 70. *Work:* Philadelphia Mus Art. *Exhib:* One-women shows: Under I-95, S Philadelphia, 2001; The Ramp Project, Inst Contemp Art, Philadelphia, 2006; Whitney Biennial: Day for Night, Whitney Mus Am Art, NYC, 2006; This is America: Visions of the American Dream, Centraal Mus, Utrecht, Holland, 2006. *Pos:* Found, Philadelphia Pub Art Project, 1995; Mem advert comt, Leeway Found, Philadelphia. *Teaching:* Instr artist, Rosenbach Mus & Libr, Philadelphia. *Awards:* Pew Visual Arts Fel, 2005. *Mailing Add:* 1313 Dickinson St Philadelphia PA 19147-6217

STRAWN, BERNICE I
SCULPTOR
b Vallejo, Calif. *Study:* Univ Calif, Berkeley, BA, MA, 52. *Work:* Adrian Col, Mich; Western Mich Univ, Kalamazoo; McDonald's Corp, Chicago, Ill; Kaiser Permanente Corp. *Comn:* Bas relief, Christ on the Mountain Church, Denver, Colo, 81; crucifix, St Michael's Church, Aurora, Colo, 82; crucifix, Holy Family cast bronze, life size, St Francis & Mother Cabrini relief, St Joseph's Church, Golden, Colo, 85. *Exhib:* Nat Religious Art Exhib, Nat Cathedral, Washington, DC, 83; Colorado 3D Invitational, Arvada Ctr, Denver, 85; Kalamazoo Inst Art, Mich, 87; one-person shows, Mesa Col Gallery, Grand Junction, Colo, 90 & Western State Col, Gunnison, Colo, 92; two-person show, Sangre de Cristo Art Ctr, Pueblo, Colo, 91, Western Mich Univ Space Gallery, Kalamazoo, 95; and others. *Teaching:* Art video instr, Adams Cty Sch Dist #12, Northglenn, Colo, 80- 87. *Media:* Wood, Bronze. *Publ:* New Lines, Portfolio of Drawings with Mel Strawn, Kalamazoo Press, 57. *Dealer:* Clay & Fiber Taos NM; Inkfish Denver CO. *Mailing Add:* c/o William Havu Gallery 1040 Cherokee St Denver CO 80204

STRAWN, MARTHA (A)
PHOTOGRAPHER, EDUCATOR
b Washington, Apr 29, 45. *Study:* Fla State Univ, Tallahassee, BA, 67; Brooks Inst Photog, Santa Barbara, Calif, basic tech cert, 68; Ohio Univ, Athens, MFA, 70. *Work:* Indira Gandhi Nat Ctr Arts, New Delhi, India; Art Mus, Princeton Univ, NJ; Southeastern Ctr Contemp Art & RJ Reynolds Co, Winston-Salem, NC; St Petersburg Mus Art, Fla; Mint Mus Art, Charlotte, NC. *Comn:* Photog, NC Gov Bus Awards Comn, 82. *Exhib:* Fulbright Art Exhibition, Woodrow Wilson Ctr, Smithsonian Inst, Washington, 86; Southeast Seven 10, Southeastern Ctr Contemp Art, Winston-Salem, NC, 87; solo exhib, Sol Mednick Gallery, Univ Arts, Philadelphia, 87; Threshold Diagrams of India, Richard F Brush Art Gallery, St Lawrence Univ, Canton, NY, 96; Alligators, Prehistoric Presence in the Am Landscape, Mint Mus Art & Discovery Pl Sci Mus, Charlotte, NC, 97; Artist as Activist: Ecological Concerns in the '90's, Wellington B Gray Gallery, Sch Art, East Carolina Univ, Greenville, NC, 97; The

Swamp: On the Edge of Eden, The Samuel P Harn Mus Art, Univ Fla, Gainesville, Fla, 2000-2001; After the Dinosaurs, The Science Mus Minn, St Paul, 2000-2001; The Swamp: On the Edge of Eden, Cummer Mus Art & Gardens, Jacksonville, Fla, 2001; Peter C Bunnell Collection Exhib, Princeton Art Mus, NJ, 2002; When Crocodiles Ruled, The Milwaukee Co Zoo, WI, 2003, Carnegie Mus Nat History, Pittsburgh, PA, 2001-2002, San Diego Mus Nat History, Calif, 2002, Oregon Mus Sci and Indust, Portland, Ore, 2002, Nat Geographic Soc Mus, Washington, DC, 2001. *Pos:* Photogr, Goleta Gazette, Calif, 67-68. *Teaching:* Instr art, Fla State Univ, Tallahassee, 69-70; asst prof & mem grad fac, NE La Univ, Monroe, 70-71; courtesy prof, Univ Fla, Gainesville, 85; prof & women's studies fac, Univ NC, Charlotte, 71-2004. *Awards:* Photogr fel, Nat Endowment Arts, Washington, 80; Sr res fel, Fulbright, India, 84; Individual Artist Fel, 10th Ann SE7 Southeastern Ctr Contemp Art/RJ Reynolds, 86-87. *Bibliog:* The New York Art Review, Third Edition: Artist Profile, American References Publishing Corporation, Chicago, Ill, 88; Images from India Portfolio: Untitled, 1986, Chromogenic color print, 16x20 inches, Exploring Color Photography, Robert Hirsch, Brown, and Benchmark Publishers, page 109, 2nd ed, 89; Transient Acts and Permanent Records of Female Mark Making: Martha Strawn Documents the Art of Indian Threshold Drawing, English Knowles, ARTVU, pages 28-31, Vol 5, No 2, Fall, 91; Nicholas Drake (auth), Indian Culture Depicted in Halsey Gallery Exhibit (review), The Post and Courier, Charleston, SC, 9/1995; Alligators, Prehistoric Presence in the American Landscape, Forecasts, Publishers' Weekly, 3/1997; Peter N. Spotts, Know Your Neighbors Well, The Christian Science Monitor, books from University Presses, Section B1, page 1, 4/1997; Elaine Morgan (auth), Gators Lure Author Across the Country, The Tampa Tribune Newspaper, 1/1999; William E. Parker (auth), Martha Strawn, Alligators, Prehistoric Presence in the American Landscape, EXPOSURE (Photographic Arts Prof Jour), Vol 32.1, pages 90-91, 9/1999; and others. *Mem:* Ctr Am Places, Harrisonburg, Va (bd trustees, 93-); Friends Photog, San Francisco (bd trustees, 86-94 & exec bd mem, 88-90); Soc Photog, Educ (nat bd dir, 77-85, chmn, 82-83, 83-85 & adv bd liaison, 85-86); Light Factory, Inc (non-profit photog orgn), Charlotte, NC (co-founder, 73, dir, 74-76, 77-78, bd, 78-79, 82-85, chmn 84-85 & adv bd, 88-); Fulbright Alumni Asn, 84-. *Media:* Photography. *Specialty:* Contemporary Art. *Publ:* Coauth (with Jane Gibson, PhD, J Whitfield Gibbons PhD & LeRoy Overstreet), Alligators, Prehistoric Presence in the American Landscape, Johns Hopkins Univ Press (in prep), Baltimore, Md, 97; and others. *Dealer:* Hodges Taylor Gallery, Charlotte, NC. *Mailing Add:* PO Box 936 Davidson NC 28036-8792

STRAWN, MELVIN NICHOLAS
PAINTER, SCULPTOR

b Boise, Idaho, Aug 5, 29. *Study:* Chouinard Art Inst; Los Angeles Co Art Inst; Jepson Art Inst; Calif Col Arts & Crafts, BFA & MFA. *Work:* Columbus Mus Art; Antioch Col; Colo State Univ; Colo Springs Fine Arts Ctr; Western Mich Univ; Ohio State Univ; Ottowa Univ; Colo Hist Soc; Sangre de Cristo Community Center; Univ Denver; plus many corporate & pvt collections. *Comn:* Environ design (sculpture), Ottawa Col, Kans, 72. *Exhib:* Colo State Univ Centennial Exhib, 70; Cedar City Nat, Utah, 72; I-25 Artists Alliance, Colorado Springs Fine Arts Ctr, 72; Colorado Springs Biennial, Colorado Springs Fine Arts Ctr, 81; Major Retrospective, Denver Central Libr, Colo, 2006; and others. *Teaching:* Instr art, Midwestern Univ, Mich State Univ, Antioch Col & Univ Denver, 56-72; chmn dept art, Antioch Col, 66-69 & Western Mich Univ, 85-88; prof & dir, Sch Art, Univ Denver, 69-85, emer prof, 85-. *Awards:* First Purchase Award, Centennial Exhibs Colo State Univ, 70. *Bibliog:* Nathan Goldstein (auth), The Art of Responsive Drawing, third ed, Prentice Hall, 84; Harold Linton (auth), Color Consulting-A Survey of International Color Design, Van Nostrand Reinhold, New York, 91. *Media:* Oil, All; Computer-Direct Digital Prints. *Interests:* Art theory, digital technology & environmental studies. *Publ:* Transitions (Book-traditional to digital art), 98. *Dealer:* Sandra Phillips Gallery Denver Colo; Trembling Aspen Gallery Buena Vista Colo. *Mailing Add:* 8905 Hwy 285 Salida CO 81201

STREETER, TAL
SCULPTOR, WRITER

b Oklahoma City, Okla, Aug 1, 34. *Study:* Univ Kans, BFA & MFA; Colorado Springs Fine Arts Ctr, with Robert Motherwell; Colo Col; with Seymour Lipton, 3 yrs. *Work:* Mus Mod Art, NY; San Francisco Mus Art; Corcoran Gallery Art, Washington; National Mus Contemp Art, Seoul, Korea; Newark Mus, NJ; Storm King Art Ctr, Mountainville, NY; Wadsworth Athenaeum, Hartford, Conn; Neuberger Mus, Purchase, NY; Smith Col Mus, North Hampton, Mass; Hood Mus, Hanover, H; Milwaukee Art Ctr, Wis. *Comn:* High Mus Art, Mem Arts Ctr, Atlanta, Ga; Ark Art Ctr, Little Rock, 70; Hong-Ik Univ, Seoul, Korea, 74; Morris Col, Morristown, NJ, 81; Libr for the Blind, Trenton, NJ, 81-83; Kaywon Col Art & Design, 91; Total Cont Art Mus, Seoul, Korea, 93; Il-San Lake Park Sculpture, Seoul, Korea, 96. *Exhib:* Whitney Ann, 65, NY World's Fair, 65; Cool Art & Highlights of the Season, Aldrich Mus, 68 & 70; American Sculpture, Sheldon Art Mus, 70; Drawings by Sculptors, Corcoran Gallery, 78; Sky Art, Mass Inst Technol, 80 & 81; Bruckner Festival, Linz, Austria, 82; Minimal Line, Milton Avery Mus, Bard Col, NY, 85; Dayton Art Inst, Ohio, 90; Total Mus, Seoul, Korea, 93; Like a Shadow on the Sky, Fairfield Art Ctr, Calif, 97; Indianapolis Art Mus, 98; Art Kites, Hudson River Mus, Yonkers, NY; Wiesman FA Mus, Minneapolis, Minn, 2004; solo exhib, Amel Gallery, NY, 66-67, Minami Gallery, Tokyo, 71, Neuberger Mus, Purchase, NY, 77, Univ Ky Mus Art, 82, Total Mus, Seoul, Korea, 93, Like a Shodow on the Sky, Fairfield Art Ctr, Calif, 98, Longhouse Reserve, EHampton, NY, 2000, Am Craft Mus, NY, 2001, Crissy Field, San Francisco, Calif, 2001, Smithsonian Nat Air & Space Mus, Washington, DC, 2003, Streckler/Nelson Gallery, Manhattan, Kans, 2006, and many others. *Collection Arranged:* cur, Art of the Japanese Kite, Japan Soc, NY, 80; co-cur, Art That Flies, Dayton Art Inst, OH, 90. *Pos:* Cur, Feather on the Wind, EPCOT Ctr, Orlando, Fla, 85; Ice & Air Show, Lake George, NY, 90; master artist & dir, Atlantic Ctr Arts, New Smyrna, Fla, 2003. *Teaching:* vis artist-in-residence, Dartmouth Col, Hanover, NH, 63 & Sun Valley Ctr for Arts, Idaho, 86; vis artist, Univ NC, Greensboro, 70 & 72-73 & Penland Sch Crafts, NC, 74-76; Fulbright prof, Seoul, Korea, 71; vis lectr, US Info Serv, Japan, 72; adj prof, Queen's Col, 73; founder, prof Sculpture/III-D/media dept, Sch of Art & Design, State Univ NY Col Purchase, 71-2001, prof emer, 2001-; assoc fel & prof, Ctr Advan Visual Studies, Mass Inst Technol, 84-; Sun Valley Ctr Arts, Idaho, 86; prof, Univ NY, Punchase; assoc prof & fel, advan vis studies, Mass Inst Technol, 84-93. *Awards:* State Univ NY Int Studies Grant, Japan, 69; Collaborations in Art, Sci, & Technol, New State Coun Arts Grant, 78; Artpark Artist, Lewisboro, NY, 78; and others. *Bibliog:* G A Ruda (auth), Kitesmanship: Tal Streeter, Craft Horizons, 74; Carter Ratcliff (auth), Tal Streeter: Beyond absolutes, Arts Mag, 77; article, Sky painting, Newsweek, 8/80; Nam Jun Palk (coauth), Sky, Moon, Dragons, Kites and Smiles: Am American Artist in Asia, 93; Susan Boetger (auth), Endless Columns, Sculpt Magazine, 94; Earth, Sky, and Sculpture, Storm King Art Ctr, Mountainville, NY, 2000. *Media:* Multimedia, Welded Metal, Cloth & Paper. *Res:* Kite inventions & kite origins. *Specialty:* Fine Art. *Interests:* Street photography. *Publ:* Heavenly Humors: The Modern Kite, Am Craft, 79; Art That Flys, Dayton Art Inst Press, 90; A Kite Journey Through India, Weatherhill, 96; The Philosopher's Kite, 2002; and others. *Dealer:* Gallerie Bhak, Seoul, Korea. *Mailing Add:* 14 Verbank Village Rd Verbank NY 12585

STREETMAN, JOHN WILLIAM, III
ADMINISTRATOR

b Marion, NC, Jan 19, 41. *Study:* Western Carolina Univ, AB; Lincoln Col, Oxford Univ, cert. *Collection Arranged:* The Eye and The Heart: Watercolors of John Stuart Ingle, 87-88; Two American Realists: William Bailey and DeWitt Hardy, 73 & 74; Simplicity, A Grace: Jacob Maentel in Indiana, 89; Beverly Hallam: The Flower Paintings, 90. *Pos:* Founding dir, Jewett Creative Arts Ctr, South Berwick, Maine, 66-70; exec dir, Polk Pub Mus, Lakeland, Fla, 70-75; dir, Mus Arts & Sci, Evansville, Ind, 75-. *Awards:* Mayor's Arts Award, Evansville, Ind, 90. *Mem:* Am Asn Mus; Midwestern Mus Conf. *Mailing Add:* 411 SE Riverside Dr Evansville IN 47713

STREETT, TYLDEN WESTCOTT
SCULPTOR, INSTRUCTOR

b Baltimore, Md, Nov 28, 22. *Study:* Johns Hopkins Univ; St John's Col; Md Inst Col Art, with Sidney Waugh & Cecil Howard, BFA & MFA; also asst to Lee Lawrie; Rinehart Sch Sculpture. *Work:* bronze, John O'Donnel; bronze, Firefighter's Mem. *Comn:* medal, Johns Hopkins Univ; Kuwait Embassy; Eisenhower's Class Mem; GBMC, Lifesize garden figure; Kirk in the Hills; Md State Courthouse; Nat Cathedral; portraits, St. John's Col, Annapolis, Md. *Exhib:* Corcoran Gallery Art, Washington, DC, 60; Baltimore Mus Art, 69. *Collection Arranged:* Mr & Mrs WM Downey; Mr & Mrs George Udel; Ms Jody Albright; Mr & Mrs Kurt Lederer; Mr & Mrs Lawrence Holdridge. *Teaching:* Prof sculpture, Md Inst Col Art, Baltimore, 59-, dir, Grad Studies, 66-72; instr sculpture, Jewish Community Ctr, Baltimore, 63-65; prof, Figurative Sculpture. *Awards:* John Gregory Award, 62; Union Independent Col Art Grant, 71; Ford Found Grant, 80; and others. *Mem:* Fel, Nat Sculpture Soc; Artists Equity Asn; Sculptors Inc. *Media:* Bronze, terr cotta, wood, stone. *Interests:* history of sculpture, bronzes, carvings, plastics and flying. *Publ:* Auth, Plaster Casting Using a Waste Mold (film), 70. *Mailing Add:* 4622 Keswick Rd Baltimore MD 21210

STRICK, JEREMY
CURATOR

Study: Univ Calif, Santa Cruz, BA(hist art), 77. *Collection Arranged:* Nat Gallery Art, Washington, DC, 87 & 90-96; St Louis Art Mus, Mo, 93, 94 & 96; NY Interpreted Joseph Stella and Alfred Stieglitz, Nat Gallery Art, 87; Milton Avery, 90; Mark Rothko The Spirit Myth, 90-95; A Century of Modern Sculpture The Patsy and Raymond Nasher Collection, 87; Twentieth Century Art Selections for the Tenth Anniversary of the East Building, 87; Brice Marden A Painting, Drawings, Pritns, St Louis Art Mus, 93; Currents 58 Susan Crile The Fires of War, 94; Currents 60 Jerald Ieans, 94; Masterworks from Stuttgar The Romantic Age in German Art, 95; others. *Pos:* asst cur 20th century art Nat Gallery Art, Washington, 86-89, assoc cur, 89-93, acting cur, 92-93; cur Nat Sculpture Garden proj, 89-93; Cur mod art, St Louis Art Mus, Mo, 93-96; Frances & Thomas Dittmer cur twentieth century painting & sculpture, Art Inst Chicago, 96-99; dir, Los Angeles Mus of Contemp Art, 99-. *Teaching:* Lectr, St Louis Art Mus, 97, Allen Mem Art Mus, Oberlin Art Col, 97, Art Club Chicago, 97 & 98, Art Inst Chicago, 98. *Awards:* Samuel H Kress Found Instnl Fel, 83-85; Mrs Giles Whiting Found Fel, 85-86. *Bibliog:* James Bishop (auth), St Louis Post-Dispatch, 2/94. *Publ:* contrib auth Works by Antonie-Louis Barye in the Collection of the Fogg art Mus Vol IV, 82

STRICKLAND, BARNABAS LAND
SCULPTOR, KINETIC ARTIST

b Attapulgus, Ga, Jan 2, 60. *Study:* Ringling Sch Art & Design, Sarasota, Fla, BFA, 87; Univ S Fla, MFA, 91. *Work:* Zoetropia, Zeum Ctr Art & Technol, San Francisco, Calif. *Comn:* Earthday piece (site specific), MLK Plaza, Tampa, Fla, 90; Wind Powered Zoetrope, City of Houston, Tex, 93; Marble carvings, City of Houston, Tex, 95. *Exhib:* Battery, Univ S Fla, Tampa, 91; Texas Art Celebration, Cullen Ctr, Houston, Tex, 93, 94 & 95; Muscle, Art League Houston, Tex, 95; Member show, World Arts Asn, Eng, 98; Bytes of Art, Ctr Visual Arts, Oakland, Calif, 98; Zoetropia, Zeum Ctr Art & Technol, San Francisco, Calif, 99. *Pos:* Studio asst, Art Systems Unlimited, 87-88; lectr photog, SE Regional Photog Soc, 91; lectr art & technol, Bath Royal Lit & Sci Inst, UK, 98. *Teaching:* Adj prof drawing, sculpture & photog, Univ S Fla, 90-91; instr photog, Orange Show, Houston, Tex, 96; instr art, Futures Explored, Lafeyette, Calif, 96-. *Awards:* Ga Gov Honors Award, Wesleyan Col, Ga, 76; Pub Art Award, City of Houston, Tex, 94 & 96. *Mem:* Leonardo Int Soc Arts Sci/Technol; Col Arts Asn; World Arts Asn (vpres, 97-). *Media:* Mixed Media, Digital. *Dealer:* Robinson Galleries 2800 Kipling Houston TX 77098

STRICKLAND, THOMAS J
PAINTER
b Keyport, NJ, Dec 28, 32. *Study:* Newark Sch Fine & Indust Arts, NJ; Am Art Sch & Nat Acad Fine Arts, New York, with Robert Philipp & Gordon Samstag. *Work:* Elliott Mus, Stuart, Fla; St Hugh Catholic Church; Salem Col; St Vincent Col; and others. *Exhib:* Butler Inst Am Art Fine Arts Festival, Youngstown, Ohio, 63; 7th Grand Prix Int Peinture Cote d'Azur, Cannes, France, 71; Martin Co Hist Soc, Elliott Mus, Fla, 74; Am Painters in Paris, 75; Am Artists Prof League, NY, 97; Audubon Artists Ann Exhib, NY, 97 & 98; and others. *Awards:* Charles Hawthorne Mem Award, Nat Arts Club, 77; Self Portrait Contest, Winner, Hahnemuhle Paper, 97; 1st Prize, Lafayette Art Asn, 98; plus others. *Bibliog:* Ann D Browne (auth), Personality of the month, Directions, 12/73; The Best of Pastel, Quarry Books, 96; Portrait Inspirations, Rockport Publ, 97. *Mem:* Pastel Soc of Am; Fla Pastel Asn; Am Artists Prof League; Pastel Soc SW. *Media:* Oil, Pastel. *Publ:* Auth, A painting demonstration by Thomas J Strickland, Directions, 5 & 7/74; The impressionistic pastels of Thomas J Strickland, 5/76, Painting self-portraits, 7/76 & How Thomas Strickland paints a still life, 3/77, Today's Art. *Mailing Add:* 2595 Taluga Dr Miami FL 33133

STRICKLER, SUSAN ELIZABETH
CURATOR, HISTORIAN
b Baltimore, Md, Jan 23, 52. *Study:* Ecole du Louvre, Paris, 1st yr cert, 72; Mt Holyoke Col, BA, 73; Univ Del, MA, 77. *Collection Arranged:* John Ritto Penniman 1782-1841: An Ingenious New England Artist, 82; John Frederick Kensett: An American Master, 85; American Traditions in Watercolor: The Worcester Art Mus Collection (with catalog), 87; Heritage of the Land: Contrasts in Native American Art & Life, 94; Impressionism Transformed: The Paintings of Edmund C Tasbell (with catalog), 2001; Andrew Wyeth: Early Watercolors (with catalog), 2004. *Pos:* Res assoc, Toledo Mus Art, Ohio, 78-79; spec proj dir, Va Mus, Richmond, 79-80; cur Am art, Worcester Art Mus, Mass, 81-95, dir curatorial affairs, 87-95; dir, Currier Mus Art, Manchester, NH, 95-. *Mem:* Am Asn Mus Dirs; Am Asn Mus; New Eng Mus Asn. *Res:* American painting, especially eighteenth & nineteenth centuries. *Specialty:* American and European Art. *Publ:* auth, American paintings (catalog), Toledo Mus Art, 79; ed, John Frederick Kensett; An American Master, Worcester Art Mus & W W Norton, 85; auth, American Portrait Miniatures: The Worcester Art Mus Collection, 89; co-auth, The Second Wave: American Abstraction of the 1930s & 1940s: Selections from the Penny & Elton Yasuna Collection, 91; auth, ed, Impressionism Transformed: The Paintings of Edmund C Tarbell, 2001; auth, Andrew Wyeth, Early Watercolors, 2004. *Mailing Add:* Currier Museum Art 201 Myrtle Way Manchester NH 03104

STRIDER, MARJORIE VIRGINIA
SCULPTOR, PAINTER
b Okla. *Study:* Kansas City Art Inst, Mo; Okla Univ, BFA. *Work:* Guggenheim Mus, NY; Albright Knox Mus, Buffalo, NY; Wadsworth Atheneum, Hartford, Conn; Larry Aldrich Contemp Art Mus, Conn; Hirshhorn Mus, Washington, DC; and others. *Comn:* Carnegie Ctr, Princeton, New Jersey. *Exhib:* Pace Gallery, NY, 63-64; Whitney Sculpture Ann, Whitney Mus Am Art, 70; Nancy Hoffman Gallery, 74-75; one-woman shows, The Clocktower, NY, 77, Grad Ctr, City Univ NY, 77 & Bernice Steinbaum Gallery, NY, 83 & 84; 10 Yrs Work Traveling Exhib, C W Post Ctr, Long Island Univ, Sculpture Ctr, NY, Joslyn Art Mus, Omaha, McNay Art Inst, San Antonio & elsewhere, 82-85; Andre Zarre Gallery, NY, 93 & 95. *Teaching:* Prof sculpture, Sch Visual Arts, New York, 68-, Univ Iowa, summer 70 & Univ Ga, summer 72; also lectr var univ & col throughout US. *Awards:* Nat Endowment Arts Grant, 74 & 80-81; Pollack-Krasner Grant, 90; Florsheim Fund, 92. *Bibliog:* Lucy Lippard (auth), Six Years, Praeger, 73; Lawrence Alloway (auth), Great Drawings of the Western World, Shorewood Publ, 80; Robert Pincus-Witten (auth), Post Minimalism, Out of London Press, London, 80. *Mem:* Salmagundi Club; Nat Arts Club. *Media:* Bronze; Acrylic. *Publ:* Auth, Moving out-moving up, Art News, 1/71; Radical scale, Art & Artists, 1/72; illusr & contribr, Modern American Painting & Sculpture, Abrams, 72; M Strider Dramatic Gestures, Hardwood Press, 2006. *Dealer:* Andre Zarre. *Mailing Add:* 170 Clint Finger Rd Saugerties NY 12477

STRIKER, CECIL L
HISTORIAN, EDUCATOR
b July 15, 32. *Study:* Oberlin Col, AB, 56; Inst Fine Arts, NY Univ, MA, 60, PhD, 68; Univ Pa, Hon MA, 73. *Pos:* Field archeologist, Dumbarton Oaks Ctr Byzantine Studies, 66-. *Teaching:* From instr to asst prof medieval art, Vassar Col, 62-68; from assoc prof to prof Byzantine & Medieval art & arch, Univ Pa, 68-2006, chmn dept art hist, 79-86, prof emeritus, 2006-. *Mem:* Col Art Asn Am; Archeol Inst Am; Am Res Inst Turkey (pres, 78-84); Coun Am Overseas Res Ctrs (chmn, 81-84); corresp mem Ger Archaeol Inst; Koldewey Gesellschaft. *Res:* Byzantine architecture and archeology; medieval architecture. *Publ:* Coauth, Work at Kalenderhane Camii in Istanbul: Preliminary reports, Dumbarton Oaks Papers, 67-74; auth, The Myrelaion (Bodrum Camii) in Istanbul, Princeton Univ Press, 82; coauth, Tree ring dating in the Aegean & neighboring regions, J Field Archeol, 84 & 88; ed, Architectural Studies in Memory of Richard Krautheimer, Philipp-von-Zabern, Mainz, 96; coauth & ed, Kalenderhane in Istanbul: The Buildings, Philipp-von-Zabern, Mainz, 97; and others. *Mailing Add:* Univ Pa Dept Art Hist Philadelphia PA 19104-6208

STRINGER, MARY EVELYN
EDUCATOR, ART HISTORIAN
b Huntsville, Mo, July 31, 21. *Study:* Univ Mo, AB; Univ NC, AM; Harvard Univ, univ traveling fel, 66-67, with Ernst Kitzinger, PhD, 73; studied at Syracuse Univ, 80. *Teaching:* Prof art, Miss Univ Women, 47-91, emer prof, 91-. *Awards:* Fulbright Scholar, 55-56; Danforth Found Grant, 59-60 & 64-65; Harvard Travel Grant, 66-67. *Mem:* Int Ctr Medieval Art; Southeastern Col Art Conf; Nat Mus Women Art; Am Birding Asn; Nature Conservancy. *Res:* Stained glass windows in America. *Publ:* Auth, Review of Andrew Martindale, Gothic Art, 69; auth, Composite nativity-adoration of English medieval alabasters, NC Mus Art Bulletin, 70; auth, Three Faces of A-T-AH: Artist-Teacher-Art Historian, Southeastern Col Art Conf Rev, 80; auth, Review of Avril Henry, Biblia Pauperum, Facsimile and Edition, SE Col Art Conf Rev, 89. *Mailing Add:* Rocky Branch Rd Columbia MS 39429

STROH, CHARLES
PRINTMAKER, PAINTER
b Aberdeen, SDak, Feb 20, 43. *Study:* Minneapolis Sch Art, with Eugene Larkin, BFA, 65; Univ Wis, Milwaukee, with T Stoeveken, MS, MFA, 72; US Peace Corps, Kabul, Afghanistan; Northern State Univ. *Work:* Milwaukee Art Mus, Wis; Washington Co Mus Fine Arts, Md; Roanoke Mus Fine Arts, Va; Sioux City Art Ctr, Iowa; Mulvane Art Mus, Kans; Marianna Kistler Beach Mus Art, Kans; Spencer Mus Art, Kans. *Exhib:* Va Mus, Richmond, 76; Spiva Art Ctr, Joplin, Mo, 77, 89, 91 & 94; Bharat Bhavan Int Biennial Prints, 89; exhibs in various locations in India, 89 & 90; Sioux City Art Ctr, 93 & 94; Greater Midwest Int, 94; Cheekwood Nat, 94; and others. *Collection Arranged:* The Hand-Printed Lithograph (auth, catalog), traveling, Iowa Arts Coun, 80-81; Prints from Kans State Univ Permanent Collection, 81 & Gordon Parks: Photographer (auth, catalog), Kans State Univ, 81; Gordon Parks: Photographer, Miami-Dade Community Col, 82 & traveling exhib US, 84-85; Contemp Printmaking in India, Mt Kailash Meets Mt St Victoire, traveling exhib (auth, catalog), 87-89. *Pos:* Art writer, Cedar Rapids Gazette, Iowa, 78-80; bd dir, Manhattan Arts Coun, 80-84; dir, Kans State Univ Friends of Art, 80-89; regional rep, FATE, 96. *Teaching:* Instr, Northern Mich Univ, Marquette, 72-73; asst prof, Roanoke Col, Salem, Va, 73-76; assoc prof & chmn dept, Coe Col, Cedar Rapids, Iowa, 76-80; prof & head dept, Kans State Univ, Manhattan, 80-89, prof, 89-96; lectr at various art schs in India, 85, 89 & 90; prof & dept chmn, Western Mich Univ, 97-99, prof, 99-. *Awards:* Fulbright to India, 89-90; Kans Artists Fel, 93; Nat Endowment Arts Fel, Mid Am Arts Alliance, 96; AIIS/Smithsonian Fel India, 85. *Mem:* Found: Art, Theory & Educ; Nat Coun Art Adminrs; Col Art Asn. *Media:* Lithography, Acrylic. *Publ:* Auth, articles, Art Educ, 74, 81, 83, 97 & 99, New Art Examiner, 80, Midwest Quarterly, 82, Print Collectors Newslett, 86, Tamarind Papers, 87, Print News, 87 & 89, Arts of Asia, 88, Design for Arts Educ, 89 & Span Mag, 90. *Mailing Add:* 8225 East H Ave Kalamazoo MI 49048-5869

STROMSDORFER, DEBORAH ANN
PAINTER, GRAPHIC ARTIST
b Aurora, Ill, Dec 18, 61. *Study:* Northern Ill Univ, BFA(painting), 84, MFA(drawing), 89. *Work:* Arlington Heights Mem Libr, Ill; Schaumburg Township Libr, Ill; Kelley-Williamson Corp & Swed Am Hosp, Rockford, Ill; Sycamore Munic Hosp, Ill; Alexian Brothers Medical Ctr, Elk Grove Village, Ill. *Comn:* Triptych (44″h x 60″w) Lasalle Consult Ltd, 89; Growth (3 panels), Rockford Clinic, Ill, 91. *Exhib:* 25th Ann Exhib, San Bernardino Co Mus, Redlands, Calif, 90; Women Artists of Am, Chautauqua Art Asn Galleries, NY, 90; Inter Art Exhib, Helio Galleries, NY, 91; 6th Inter Small Works Exhib, Del Bello Gallery, Toronto, Can, 91; Nat Art Competition Winners, UND, Witmer Art Ctr, Grand Forks, NDak, 92; NAm Invitational, Mus Without Walls Inter, Bemus Point, NY, 92; Gray Gallery, Quincy Col, Ill, 92; one woman exhibs, Clack Art Ctr, Alma, Mich, 92, Schaumburg Prairie Ctr Arts, Ill, 93 & Tullibody Fine Arts Gallery, Ala State Univ, Montgomery, 93; Phoebus Abroad, Phoebus Gallery, Athens, Greece, 93; Stateline Vicinity Exhib, Rockford Art Mus, Ill, 94; Union League Club of Chicago, 95; Village Gallery, Rockford, 96; Ill Artisans Shop Chicago, 2000; Wachovia Securities, Rockford, 2003. *Pos:* Graphic designer, Northern Ill Univ, DeKalb, Ill, 83-87 & Univ Ill Col Med, Rockford, Ill, 87-90; graphic designer, Univ Ill Col Med, Rockford, Ill, 87-90. *Teaching:* Art instr design/drawing, Rock Valley Col, Rockford, Ill, 1990-1998, 2001-2002. *Awards:* Best of Show, Rockford Vicinity Exhib, Gallery Ten, 88; Best of Show, Art Ctr '91, Elk Grove Village, IL, Talman Home Fed, 91; Best of Show, 2nd Ann Mem Juried Exhib, Colored Pencil Soc Am, Chicago, 96; Peoples Choice Award, Bernina Univ Fashion Show & Competition, Long Beach, Calif, 99. *Bibliog:* Bebe Raupe (auth), 1986 Floral Competition Winners (2nd place), Artist's Mag, 12/86; The Best of Colored Pencil Two, Rockport Publishers, 94; Vicki Anderson (auth) Sew News Mag, 12/99. *Mem:* Colored Pencil Soc Am; Chicago Artists' Coalition; Nat Asn Women Artists. *Media:* Colored Pencil, Wearable Art. *Dealer:* Robert Galitz Fine Art 166 Hilltop Dundee IL 60118. *Mailing Add:* 3602 Grenoble Ct Rockford IL 61114

STRONG, BEVERLY JEAN See Jean, Beverly (Beverly) Jean Strong

STRONG, LESLIE (SUTTER)
SCULPTOR, CERAMIST
b Newport News, Va, Dec 1, 53. *Study:* Skidmore Col, Saratoga Springs, NY, BS(art), 76; Syracuse Univ, NY (Univ Fel), MFA, 85. *Work:* President's Collection, Skidmore Col, NY; Roland Gibson Collection, State Univ NY, Potsdam; Richard Brush Art Gallery, St Lawrence Univ, Canton, NY; North Ga Col Art; also pvt collection of Dr Ralph Lillford, London. *Comn:* Exterior wall sculptures, State Univ NY, Cobleskill, 82. *Exhib:* Solo exhib, Work in Transition, St Lawrence Univ, NY, 85; Clay Nat, Upton Hall Gallery, State Univ NY, Buffalo, 85; Artist's Cent NY, 89 & 91; The Clay's the Thing, St Lawrence Univ, 93; Northern Clay Invitational, Potsdam Col, State Univ NY, 96. *Pos:* Consult & in-house conservator, Brush Gallery, St Lawrence Univ, Canton, NY, 85-88. *Teaching:* Art teacher, Burnt Hill Jr High Sch, NY, 81-83; instr, Skidmore Col, 84-88 & Potsdam High Sch, 87-. *Awards:* Hon Mention, AEIOU Exhib, Massena, NY, 86; Roland Gibson Award, N Co Regional Exhib, Gibson Gallery, Potsdam, NY, 88; First Prize, Small Sculpture Exhib, NGeorgia Col, Delongena, Ga, 90. *Mem:* Col Art Asn. *Media:* Clay, Bronze. *Publ:* Auth, Handformed Ceramics, Zakin. *Dealer:* Sodarco Gallery Montreal PQ Can. *Mailing Add:* 11 New St Norwood NY 13668

STRONG-CUEVAS
SCULPTOR, KINETIC ARTIST
b St Germain en Laye, France, Jan 22, 1929; US citizen. *Study:* Vassar Col, Sarah Lawrence Col, AB, 52; Art Students League, 63-67 studied with John Hovannes, 63-73, with Toto Meylan, 75-83. *Work:* Bruce Mus, Greenwich, Conn; Heckscher Mus, Huntington, NY; Guild Hall Mus, East Hampton, NY; Grounds for Sculpture, Hamilton, NJ. *Comn:* Obelisk & Head V, comn by Evan Frankel, East Hampton, NY, 83; wall relief, comn by Mr & Mrs Lewis Cullman, NY; solo shows include Grounds for Sculpture, Hamilton, NJ, 99. *Exhib:* The Art Show, Femgarten Galleries, NY, 90; Marisa del Re Biennale III & IV, Marisa del Re Gallery, Monte Carlo, Monaco, 91 & 93; Mirrors, Parrish Mus, Southampton, NY, 94; Fall/Winter 94-95 Exhib, Grounds for Sculpture, Hamilton, NJ, 94-95; Arch I, Arch II, Set II, Shidoni, Tessaque, NMex, 95-96; and others. *Awards:* 1984 Award, 46th Ann Mem Exhib, William Woolfenden, with Guild Hall Mus, East Hampton, NY, 84. *Bibliog:* Robert Becker (dir), Ancient Visions Through Modern Eyes (video), 88; Christopher French (auth), The dichotomy of the profile (exhib catalog), Marisa del Re Gallery, 92; Lana Pih Jokel (video), 96; Dorothy Kosinski (auth), Ancient Visions Through Modern Eyes (catalog) Bruce Mus, Greenwich, Ct, 84; Alexander Russo (auth), Profiles on Women Artists, Univ Pubs of Am, Inc, 85; Brooke Barrie (auth) Contemporary Outdoor Sculpture, Rockport Pubs, Inc., Gloucester, Mass, 99; Strong-Cuevas Scultpure (video-DVD by Laura Jokel), 2002; plus others. *Mem:* Art Students League, NY; Nat Acad Design NY. *Media:* Bronze, Steel. *Collection:* Bruce Mus Greenwich CT,; Grounds for Sculpture, NJ. *Publ:* Auth, John Hovanes: A remarkable man, Art Students League, 73; Auth, A farewell to Michael Lekakis, Art Students League, 88. *Dealer:* Kouros Gallery 23 E 73d St New York NY 10021; Island Weiss Gallery, NY. *Mailing Add:* PO Box 7067 Amagansett NY 11930

STRONGHILOS, CAROL
PAINTER
b New York, NY. *Study:* Empire State, BFS, Art Students League; Brooklyn Mus Art Sch, study with Reuben Tam. *Exhib:* NJ State Mus, 72; Monmouth Col, 72; Brooklyn Mus, 74; Larry Aldrich Mus, 75; Women in the Arts, 76 & 77; Newark Mus, 77; Art in Pub Bldg, NY Orgn of Independent Artists, World Trade Ctr, 77; Women 78, Women's Caucus for the Arts, City Univ NY, 78; one-woman shows, Brooklyn Mus, 71, Whitney Mus, 75, Bernice Steinbaum Gallery, 83, Kingsborough Community Col, 88, Ctr Gallery, 2000; group show, Madylon Jordon Gallery, 94. *Pos:* Founder, NY Feminist Art Inst, NY; consult, Am the Beautiful Fund, 76-77; dir, Art Sch-Mid Westchester, 83. *Teaching:* Instr painting, Brooklyn Mus Art Sch, 71-77 & Brooklyn House of Detention, 74-77; instr painting & drawing, Five Towns Music & Art Ctr, 74-76, Feminist Art Inst, 79-80, Old Church Cult Ctr, 86-2000. *Awards:* Fac & Alumni First Prize, Brooklyn Mus, 70; Grant, Adolph Gottlieb, 86. *Mem:* Women in the Arts; Woman's Caucus for Art, Col Art Asn. *Media:* Acrylic, Oil. *Mailing Add:* 13-17 Laight St New York NY 10013

STROPPEL, BETTY MACNAIR
PAINTER, INSTRUCTOR
b Woodbridge, NJ, Feb 26, 27. *Study:* Miami Univ, Oxford, Ohio, BFA, 48. *Hon Degrees:* Delta TAU Delta- National Art Fraternity. *Work:* Stone & Wood Silos of NJ, NJ State Council on the Arts, 78. *Exhib:* Am Watercolor Soc, Nat Acad Art & Salmagundi Club, NY, 77-84 & 95, 2000; Grand Nat, Salmagundi Club, NY, 90 & 92; The Tree-An Artists Gift, Bergen Mus, Paramus, NJ, 91; Audubon Artists, Nat Arts Club, NY, 92; Philadelphia Watercolor Club, Berman Mus Art, Collegeville, Pa, 96; and others. *Teaching:* Instr watercolor, studios & classrooms, NJ, 71-2001; Union Co Col, Cranford, NJ, 74-86; Du Cret Sch Arts, Plainfield, NJ, 79-80. *Awards:* Gehner Watercolor Award, Nat Asn Women Artists, 91; Catharine L Wolfe Seascape Award, 96; Daler-Rowney Award, Essex Watercolor Club-2005. *Mem:* Am Watercolor Soc; Audubon Artists; Philadelphia Watercolor Club; Hudson Valley Art Asn; NJ Watercolor Soc. *Media:* Watercolor. *Publ:* Best of Watercolor-Painting Composition & Best of Watercolor-Painting Textrue, Rockport Publ, 97. *Mailing Add:* 115 Sweetbriar Lane North Plainfield NJ 07060

STROUD, BILLY
PAINTER, COLLECTOR
b Peoria, IL, Mar 23, 69. *Study:* Univ Ill U-C, BFA (sculpture) 1994; MA (art educ) 2003. *Exhib:* Studio Show 2002; Gallery Studio 402, New York City, 2002; Skin Deep, I-Space, Chicago, Ill, 2005. *Pos:* Bd dir, McLean Co Art Ctr, 2005-. *Teaching:* Univ Ill, Urbana-Champaign, 2002-2003; instr, McLean Co Art Ctr, 2004-. *Awards:* Kotteman Sculpture Award, Bradley Univ, Peoria, Ill, 92-93. *Media:* Acrylic on Canvas & Paper. *Collection:* Karl Moehl, Ben Gardner & Tara McArthy. *Mailing Add:* 605 E Washington St Bloomington IL 61701

STROUD, PETER ANTHONY
PAINTER, EDUCATOR
b London, Eng, May 23, 21. *Study:* Teacher Training Col, London Univ, Central Hammersmith Schs Art, 48-53. *Work:* Tate Gallery, London; Guggenheim Mus, NY; Los Angeles Co Mus; Detroit Inst Fine Arts; Pasadena Art Mus; Mus of Modern Art, NY; Whitney Mus, NY. *Comn:* Mural, Int Union Archit Congress Bldg, London, 61; mural, State Sch Leverkusen, Ger, 63; mural, Mfrs Hanover Trust Co, NY, 69. *Exhib:* Nat Gallery Victoria, Melbourne, Australia, 70; Univ Calif, Santa Barbara, 70; Ulster Mus, Belfast, Northern Ireland, 71; Finch Col, NY, 72; Retrospective New Jersey, State Mus, Trenton, NJ, 90; Central Academy, Bejing, 92; East China, Normal Univ, Shang Hui, 94; Abstraction and Immanence, Hunter Coll, NY, 02. *Teaching:* Prof visual studies, Bennington Col, 63-68; prof painting, Grad Sch, Rutgers Univ, New Brunswick, 68-. *Awards:* Pasadena Mus Fel, 64. *Bibliog:* Dore Ashton (auth), Peter Stroud's relief-paintings, Studio Int, 66; John Coplans (auth), Interview with Peter Stroud, Artforum, 66. *Mem:* American Abstract Artists. *Media:* Acrylic. *Res:* Philosophy & Art. *Publ:* Paul Cumming (interview), Archives of American Art, 90; Chris Benencasor (tv interview), New Lansyon The Arts, Dec, 04. *Mailing Add:* 59 Harriet Dr Princeton NJ 08540

STRUCK, NORMA JOHANSEN
PAINTER
b West Englewood, NJ. *Study:* NY Phoenix Sch Design, 47-50; study with Paul Burns, 69; Art Students League, NY, 76-77; master class, John Sanden, 78. *Work:* Pentagon, Navy Hist Mus, USN Combat Mus, Coast Guard Art Collection, Washington; Governor's Island, NY; Portrait of Sonja Henie, Henie-Onstad Mus, Oslo, Norway; Portrait of Sonja Henie, World Figure Skating Hall Fame, Colorado Springs, Colo. *Comn:* First Woman Line Admiral, Washington, 82, US Navy; Admiral Wayne Caldwell, 84 & Vice Admiral Paul Yost, Commandant, 86, US Coast Guard, Governor's Island, NY; Vice Admiral Donald C Thompson, US Coast Guard, 88; Vice Admiral James Irwin. *Exhib:* Navy Combat Art, Navy Combat Art Gallery, Washington, 77-86 & Salmagundi Club, NY, 77-82; Catherine Lorillard Wolfe, Nat Arts Club, NY, 78; Am Artist Prof League, World Trade Ctr, NY, 79; Coast Guard Traveling Art Show, 80-86. *Collection Arranged:* Navy Art Prog; Coast Guard Art Prog; Paintings Tour the Country, since 1970's, arranged by Hq in Wash, DC. *Pos:* Comt mem, Navy Art Coop & Liaison, 80-96. *Awards:* Louis E Seley Award, US Navy Art Prog, 79; George Gray Award, US Coast Guard, 82 & 89; Second Coast Guard Award, Governors Island, 89. *Bibliog:* John Pangburn (auth), People, the Record, 82; Linda Bruhn (auth), Guard duty, Profile Mag, 83. *Mem:* Hudson Valley Art Asn (bd dir, 85-88); Am Artists Prof League; life mem Art Students League; Coast Guard Art Prog (comt mem, 80-96); Soc Illustrators & Salmagundi Club; charter mem, Nat Mus Women in Arts. *Media:* Oil, Acrylic. *Interests:* Painting the natural beauty of all nationalities. *Publ:* Illusr, World Trade Ctr News, 79; Sea Power, Navy League USA, 82, 84; contribr, Profile: Art for Your Country, Am Portrait Soc, 83; illusr, Retiree News, US Coast Guard, 86. *Mailing Add:* 910 Midland Rd Oradell NJ 07649

STRUEKEN-BACHMANN, MARION
PAINTER, CURATOR
b Ger. *Study:* Nat Acad Design, (art), 70-74; New Sch of Social Res, cert, 76. *Exhib:* Am Painters in Paris, Palais Des Congres, Paris, 75; Pastel Soc, Hermitage Mus, 82; Pastel Soc, Copley Soc, Boston, 83; Pastel Paintings, Pen & Brush Club, NY, 85 & 87; Pastels, Nelson Rockefeller Art Ctr, NY, 86; Women in Art, Women Art Gallery, NY, 86. *Awards:* Blick Award, Pen & Brush Club, 90; Alice McReynolds Award, Salmagundi Club, 91; Hazel Witte Mem Award, Nat Asn Women Artists, 91; and others. *Bibliog:* Hamburger Abendblatt, Ger, 88; Artspeak, 9/92; Christel Vollmer (auth), Erfolgreiche Deutsche in New York, Ullstein Verlag, Berlin, Ger, 93; and others. *Mem:* Pastel Soc Am (bd dir); Salmagundi Club, NY; Nat Asn Women Artists; assoc mem Allied Artist Am; Nat Arts Club. *Media:* Pastel. *Publ:* Contribr, Contemporary Women Artists, 89. *Dealer:* Leader Assocs 66 Madison Ave New York NY 10003. *Mailing Add:* 444 E 86th St New York NY 10028

STRUNCK, JUERGEN
PRINTMAKER
b Ger, 43. *Study:* State Univ NY, Cortland, BS(chemical), 70; State Univ NY, Buffalo, BFA, 73; Yale Univ, MFA(printmaking), 75. *Exhib:* One-man shows, Martha Gault Art Gallery, Slippery Rock Univ, Pa, 90, Slocumb Galleries, Eastern Tenn State Univ, 93, Warehouse Living Arts Ctr, Corsicana, Tex, 93, Dutch Phillips & Co Fine Art, Fort Worth, Tex, 94, Univ Art Gallery, Baylor Univ, Waco, Tex, 94, Univ Tex, Tyler, 95, Museu Nacional de Bellas Artes, Rio de Janeiro, Brazil, 95, Spring Creek Gallery, Collin Co Community Col, Plano, Tex, 96; group exhib, 10th Norwegian Int Print Triennale, Fredrikstad, Norway, 92, Southern Graphics Council, Univ Tenn, Knoxville, 92, Md Inst Col of Art, Baltimore, 93, Nat Ctr for Fine Arts of Egypt, Giza, 93, 1st Int Print Triennale Colour in Graphic Art, District Mus, Old Town Hall, Torun, Poland, 94, San Angelo Mus Fine Arts, Tex, 94, 170th Ann Exhib, Nat Acad of Design, New York City, 95, La Societe Int des Beaux-arts, Trammell Crow Ctr, Dallas, 96, ArtCentre of Plano, Tex, 2003; others; workshop presenter, lectr, panelist, juror. *Teaching:* Artist-in-residence, Univ Pa, Philadelphia, 78-88; instr, Tyler Sch of Art, Elkins Park, 79, Pratt Graphics Ctr, New York City, 83, Kutztown Univ, Pa, 84-85, asst prof, 87-91, assoc prof, 91-. *Awards:* Recipient Berthe von Moschzisker prize, 82; Silver medal, 10th Norwegian Internat Print Triennial, Fredrikstad, Norway, 92; Leo Meissner prize, Nat Acad of Design, 99. *Mem:* Boston Printmakers, Int print Triennial Soc, Nat Acad (acad, 94-). *Mailing Add:* Art Dept Univ Dallas 1845 E Northgate Dr Irving TX 75062

STUART, DONALD ALEXANDER
GOLDSMITH, SILVERSMITH
b Toronto, Ont, Aug 25, 44. *Study:* Ont Col Art; Sch Am Craftsmen, Rochester Inst Technol, MFA. *Work:* Massey Found, Nat Mus Can; Jean A Chalmers Nat Craft Collection, Can Crafts Coun; Chalmers Collection, Ont Crafts Coun. *Comn:* sterling chalice, Reverend Ron Raab, South Bend, Ind, 83; altar cross, Rosedale Presbyterian Church, Toronto, 84; silver medal, Victoria Col, Univ Toronto, 84; sterling presentation bowl, Glenn Gould Mem Found, 86; Benton St Baptist Church, Kitchoner, 89; Imperial Oil Ltd, 90; First Unitarian Congregation, Toronto, 93 & 96; Govt Ontario, 99-; First Romanian Baptist Ch, Waterloo, 99; Islington United Church, Rotonto, 99, 2000. *Exhib:* solo exhib, Brampton Art Gallery, 81 & Craft Gallery, Toronto, 82; Electrum Gallery, London, Eng, 88; Cambridge Gallery, 89; Koffler Gallery, Toronto, 90; Pro-Art, St Louis, 92; McLaren Art Gallery & Nat Tour, 93-94; Craft Gallery, Toronto, 95; Breckenridge Gallery, Colo, 96; Montgomery Col, Rockville, Md, 96; Mus da Pampulha, Belo Horizonte, Brazil, 97; Seafirst Gallery,

Seattle, 98. *Pos:* Mgr, Weaving indust in Pangnirtung, Baffin Island, for Eskimo women, 69-72. *Teaching:* prof jewelry & design, Georgian Col, Barrie, Ont, 72-; instr in various workshops in USA & Can. *Awards:* Visual Artist Award, 81, Craftsman Grant, 85 & 88, Ont Arts Coun; Diamonds Today Award, 93 & 95; Jean A Chalmers Award Craft, 94. *Bibliog:* article, Ont Craft, summer 94; A Barros (auth), Ornament and Object, Boston Mills Press, 97; G Crawford (auth), A Fine Line, Dundurn Press, 98. *Mem:* Ont Crafts Coun (bd dir, 74-78 & pres, 82-85); Can Crafts Coun (bd dir, 83-85, 88-90); Soc NAm Goldsmiths (conf chmn, 84-85, bd, 1992-2000, pres, 97-99); hon life mem Metal Arts Guild; Royal Can Acad (bd dir, 87-90 & 95-97). *Media:* Jewelry, Holloware. *Publ:* Contribr, The wonderful world of crafts, Toronto Star, 76; auth, Teaching contracts, Craftsnews, 77; The technique of inlaying, Craftsman, Ont Crafts Coun, 81; Pangnirtung weavers, Shuttle, Spindle & Dyepot, fall 85. *Dealer:* Ontario Crafts Coun 170 Bedford Rd No 300 Toronto ON MSR 2K9

STUART, JOSEPH MARTIN
PAINTER, MUSEUM DIRECTOR
b Seminole, Okla, Nov 9, 32. *Study:* Univ NMex, BFA, 59, MA, 62. *Work:* Art Mus, Univ NMex, Albuquerque; Salt Lake Art Ctr, Salt Lake City; Col of Idaho, Caldwell; Sioux City Art Ctr, Iowa; Civic Fine Arts Ctr, Sioux Falls, SDak. *Exhib:* Northwest Artists 50th & 52nd Ann, Seattle Art Mus, 64 & 66; Midwest Biennial, Joslyn Art Mus, Omaha 74 & 76; Drawings USA, Minn Mus of Art, St Paul, 77; Nat Drawings, Rutgers Univ, Camden, NJ, 77; solo exhib, The Canyon Suite, WTex State Univ, Canyon, 82; Ritz Gallery, SDak State Univ, Brookings, 92; Minimalist Painting, Ruhlen Gallery, Santa Fe, NMex, 97. *Collection Arranged:* Jannis Spyropoulos: Paintings, Roswell Mus & Art Ctr, NMex, 62; Edward Kienholz: Sculpture, Boise Gallery Art, Idaho, 67; Art of South Dakota, 74, The Calligraphic Statement, 77, Berry Collection of Asian Arts & Crafts, 79, Sioux Art Collections, 86, Art for a New Century, 89 & Seiferle Collection of American Art, 92, SDak Art Mus, Brookings; Utah painting & sculpture, Utah Mus Fine Arts, Salt Lake City, 90. *Pos:* Cur, Mus Art, Univ Ore, 62-63; dir, Boise Gallery Art, 64-68, Salt Lake Art Ctr, 68-71 & SDak Art Mus, 71-93. *Teaching:* Lectr art, Univ Utah, 69; prof art hist, SDak State Univ, 71-93; retired. *Awards:* First Prize in Painting, Cheney Cowles Mem Mus, Spokane, 65; Salt Lake Art Ctr Purchase Award, 67; Purchase Award, Sioux City Art Ctr, 73. *Media:* Acrylic. *Res:* Art history of South Dakota, Native American Tribal Art. *Publ:* Auth, Stimuli, Utah Archit, fall 69; Art of South Dakota, SDak State Univ, 74; Architecture of Harold Spitznagel, Brookings, 75; South Dakota Collection, 88; The Legacy of South Dakota Art, Pierre: Robinson Mus, 90. *Mailing Add:* 18 Gavilan Rd Santa Fe NM 87505

STUART, MICHELLE
PAINTER, SCULPTOR
b Borrego Springs, Calif, Feb 10, 40. *Study:* Chouinard Art Inst, Los Angeles; apprenticed to Diego Rivera, Mex; New Sch Social Res. *Work:* Mus Mod Art, Brooklyn Mus & Whitney Mus Am Art, NY; Walker Art Ctr, Minneapolis, Minn; Nat Collection Australia, Canberra; Mod Museet, Stockholm, Sweden; Kaiser-Wilhelm Mus, Krefeld, Ger; and others. *Comn:* Painting, Union Cent Life Insurance, Forest Park, Ohio, 87; painting, Security Pac Nat Bank, 87; bronze sculpture & corresponding painting, Col Wooster, Ohio, 87-88; Battery Park City, NY, 92; Tochigi Ctr, Japan, 96-97; and others. *Exhib:* One person shows, Haags Gemeentemuseum, Hague, The Neth, 83, Walker Art Ctr, Minneapolis, Minn, 83, Neuberger Mus, Purchase, NY, 84, Brooklyn Mus, NY, 86, Rose Art Mus, Waltham, Mass, 88 & Wadsworth Atheneum, Hartford, Conn, 88; Mus Mod Art, 76 & 84; Nat Mus Mod Art, Kyoto, Japan, 83; Mus Contemp Art, Chicago, Ill, 84; Moderna Museet, Stockholm, Sweden, 85; San Francisco Mus Mod Art, Calif, 86; Cleveland Mus Art, Ohio, 86; Biennial, US Pavilion, Cairo, Egypt, 94; and many other group & one person shows. *Awards:* Nat Endowment Arts Fel Individual Artists, 74, 77, 80, & 89; Award for Excellence in Design, Arts Comn, New York, 90; Am Acad in Rome, 95; and others. *Bibliog:* Carey Lovelace (auth), Michelle Stuart's silent gardens, Arts Mag, 9/88; Susan L Stoops (auth), Michelle Stuart: Silent Gardens: The American Landscape (catalog), Rose Art Mus, Brandeis Univ, 88; Joseph Ruzicka (auth), Essential Light: The Skyes of Michelle Stuart, Art in Am, 6/2000. *Mem:* Nat Acad. *Media:* Encaustic; Bronze. *Publ:* Auth, The Fall, Printed Matter Inc, New York, 76; A Complete Folk History of the United States at the End of the Century, Wright State Univ, Ohio, 78; From the Silent Garden, Williams Col, Mass, 79; I-80 Series: Michelle Stuart, Joslyn Art Mus, Omaha, Nebr, 81; Sacred Precincts: From Dreamtime to the South China Sea, Neuberger Mus, State Univ, New York, 84; auth, Natural Histories, Essay, Richard Foreman, NY, 96; auth, Butterflies & Moths, Dadadog Press, NY, 2006. *Dealer:* Diane Villani Editions 271 Mulberry St #D New York New York 10012; Emily Goldstein The Drawing Room 16R Newton Lane East Hampton NY 11937. *Mailing Add:* 152 Wooster St New York NY 10012

STUART, SHERRY BLANCHARD
PAINTER
b Newport, Ark, Feb 19, 41. *Study:* Minneapolis Col Art & Design, BFA, 64; studied painting with Richard Lack Atlier, 70; Scottsdale Artists Sch with Wilson Hurley, 89. *Work:* Tucson Mus Art, Ariz; Desert Caballeros Western Art Mus, Wickenburg, Ariz; 3M Co; Bureau Engraving, Minneapolis, Minn. *Comn:* Paintings comn by Mr & Mrs Graves, 89, Mr & Mrs Beede, 93, Mr & Mrs Rod Boggs, 97, Scottsdale, Ariz, Sharon Bracken, Scottsdale, 2002. *Exhib:* Mountain Oyster Club Exhib, Tucson, 1993-2004; Women Artists of the West, Tucson Mus Art, 94-96; Oil Painters of Am, Long Grove Invitational, Ill, 94; Top 200 Arts for Parks, Nat Art Show, Jackson, Wyo, 94 & 98; Horses in Motion, Kentuck Derby Mus, Louisville, 96; Am Acad Women Artists, Ariz His Soc, 98; Am Plains Artists, 2002-2004; Oil Painters Am, 2003-2004. *Teaching:* Instr at various art schs, 64-98. *Awards:* 1st Place Oil Painting & Gold Medal Purchase Award, Western Acad Women Artists, Desert Caballeros Western Art Mus, 97; Peoples Choice Award, Am Acad Women Artists, Cauley Gallery, 98; 1st Place Ariz Cowboy Classics, 2001; 1st Place Best of Show Award Am Plains Artists, 2002. *Bibliog:* A Contrad Posz (auth), Art of Sherry Blanchard Stuart, Illustrator, Vol 6, No 2, 83. *Mem:* Am Acad Women Artists (bd dir, 1994-2003); juried mem Ariz Artists Guild; found mem Creative Women Pinnacle Peak (print dir, 98, found mem); Oil Painters Am (signature mem); sign mem Oil Painters of Am, Am Plains Artists. *Media:* Oil on Canvas. *Publ:* Auth, articles in Midwest Art Mag, Dorn Commun Inc, 5-6/85; Equine Images Mag, Heartland Commun Group, 88; Am Artist Mag, 12/94; Cowboys & Indians Mag, 96; Art of West Mag, Duerr & Tierney, Ltd, 96; Southwest Art Magazine (featured), March, 2005; and many others. *Dealer:* The Gold Nugget Art Gallery 274 E Wickenburg Way Wickenburg AZ 85358; Nichols Fine Art Gallery Taos NM; El Presidio Gallery Tulson Arizona. *Mailing Add:* 8402 Country Club Tr Scottsdale AZ 85255

STUART, SIGNE NELSON See Nelson, Signe

STUBBS, LU
SCULPTOR
b New York, NY, Aug 16, 25. *Study:* Sch Boston Mus Fine Arts, MA, 64, studied with Harold Tovish & Nathaniel Neujean; L'Accademia di Belle Arti, Perugia, Italy, 71. *Work:* Brita (bronze), New Eng Med Ctr, Boston, Mass, 88; Happy Frog (bronze), Post Office Sq, Sharon, Mass, 96; US Eagle, Sharon high Sch, Mass, 99; Torso (life-sized bronze), Women's Div Greater Springfield Chamber Com, Mass, 77; Foxtale Family, Boyden Libr, Foxboro, Mass, 2000. *Comn:* Deborah Sampson, life-sized bronze, Sharon Pub Libr, Mass, 89; Sundial, with life-sized children (bronze), Browne Fund/City of Boston, Charlestown, Mass, 90-91; Pregnant Woman II (bronze), Cooley Dickinson Hosp, Northampton, Mass, 01; Mt Holyoke Col Libr, Mass, 2006; and others. *Exhib:* One-person shows, Attleboro Mus, Mass, 73, Brockton Art Mus, 73-74 & DeCordova Mus (with catalog), Lincoln, 77; Art in Transition-A Century of the Mus Sch, Mus Fine Arts, Boston, 77; Sculpture Outdoors, Schulman Sculpture Forum, White Plains, NY, 80-82; Nat Sculpture Soc Celebrates the Figure, Port Hist Mus, Philadelphia, 87; group show, 100 yrs of Am Sculpture, America's Tower, NY, 93-94; group show, Sculpture in the Center, Stamford, Conn, 94; 2 person show, Forms & Views of Nature, Audubon Gallery, Sharon, Mass, 94. *Teaching:* Instr sculpture, Boston Ctr Adult Educ, 63-77, Milton Acad, 67-68 & Boston Univ, 76-77. *Awards:* Exhib grant, Nat Endowment Arts & Humanities, 77; First Prize, New Eng Artist Showcase, Univ Mass, 81; Best of Show, New Eng Sculptors Asn, 86. *Bibliog:* Marty Carlock (auth), A Guide to Public Art in Greater Boston, 93; Marty Carlock (auth), Nature adds form to art of sculptor, Boston Globe, 9/25/94; Pattie Hainer (auth), You gotta have art, Patriot Ledger, 9/7/96; Amy Guerrero (auth), Pulling up Stakes, Sharon Advocate, 8/25/00. *Mem:* Nat Sculp Soc; New Eng Sculptors Asn; Northampton Arts Coun. *Media:* Bronze, Wood, Oil Painting, Marble. *Interests:* Creative writing. *Publ:* Auth, The Happy Frog Speaks, Sharon Advocate, 8/22/97; auth, Studying Language and Life in Italy, Boston Sunday Globe, 7/31/00. *Mailing Add:* 11 Trumbull Rd Northampton MA 01060

STUCKEY, CHARLES F
HISTORIAN, CURATOR
b Teaneck, NJ, Mar 14, 45. *Study:* Yale Univ, BA, 67; Univ Pa, MA, 70 & PhD, 72. *Collection Arranged:* Georgia O'Keeffe, Art Inst Chicago, 88, Andy Warhol: A Retrospective, 89, Degenerate Art: The Fate of the Advant-Garde in Nazi Germany, 91, Magritte, 93, Max Ernst, Dada and the Dawn of Surrealism, 93 & Claude Monet 1840-1926, 95; The Art of Paul Gauguin, Nat Gallery Art, Washington, DC, Art Inst Chicago & Mus d'Orsay, Paris, 88; Cezanne: The Early Years, London Royal Acad, Mus d'Orsay, Paris & Nat Gallery Art, Washington, DC, 88-89; The Chicago Show, Chicago Cult Ctr, 89; The Rudolf Staechelin Family Foundation Collection of Basel, Switzerland, Kimbell Art Mus, 97 & Renoirs Portraits: Impressions of an Age, 98. *Pos:* Contrib ed, Art Am, 80-; cur mod painting, Nat Gallery Art, Washington, DC, 85-87; cur 20th century painting & sculpture, Art Inst Chicago, 87-95; cur paintings & sculpture after 1800, Minneapolis Inst Arts, 95-97; spec cur consult, Salvador Dali Mus, St Petersburg, Fla, 95-98; sr cur, Kimbell Art Mus, Ft Worth, Tex, 97-. *Teaching:* Asst prof art hist, The Johns Hopkins Univ, Baltimore, 72-77; visiting prof, Sch Art Inst Chicago, 79; visiting asst prof, Dept Visual Arts, State Univ, NY, 80-81; adj prof fine arts, NY Univ, 83. *Awards:* Outstanding Scholar, Ill Acad Fine Arts, 93; Chevalier de l'ordre des arts et des lettres, 97. *Mem:* The Turner Soc. *Res:* 19th and 20th century European and American art. *Publ:* Auth, Monet: Water Lilies, 88 & French Painting, 91, Hugh Lauter Levin Assocs Inc; contribr, Vance Kirkland 1904-1981: a Colorado painter without geographical boundaries, In: Vance Kirkland, Vance Kirkland Found & Mus, 98; Love, money and Monet's debacle paintings of 1880, In: Monet at Vetheuil: The Turning Point, Univ Lithoprinters Inc & Univ Mich Mus Art, Ann Arbor, 98. *Mailing Add:* 5823 N Magnolia Ave #1 Chicago IL 60660-3498

STUDSTILL, PAMELA
CRAFTSMAN
b San Antonio, Tex, Sept 27, 54. *Study:* Univ Tex, San Antonio, BFA, 78. *Work:* Bank South, IBM Corp & High Must Art, Atlanta, Ga; Fidelity Financial Services, Boston, Mass; Jack Lenor Larsen, NY; Bank San Antonio, San Antonio Arts Coun; Helen Allen Collection, Univ Wis, Madison; and many others. *Exhib:* Solo exhibs, Contemp Quilts and Sewn Paper, 86, Art Quilts and Sewn Paper Pieces, 87, Masterworks, Connell Gallery & Great Am Gallery, Atlanta, Ga, 90, Quilt Constructions, Joanne Rapp Gallery, 90 & Quilts and Collages, Connell Gallery, 93; Quilts Now, Zephr Gallery, Louisville, Ky, 92; Color, Light and Motion, The Works Gallery, Philadelphia, Pa, 92; Contemp Am Quilts (catalog), Craft Coun Gallery, London, 93-94; Studio Quilts, An Invitational Exhib Contemp Quilts, Kurts Bingham Gallery, Memphis, Tenn, 94; KPMG Peat Marwick Collection of Am Craft (catalog), Renwick Gallery, Nat Mus Am Art & Smithsonian Inst, 94; and many others. *Awards:* Nat Endowment Arts Visual Arts Fel, 83 & 88; Quilt Nat 91 Award Excellence,

Southeastern Ohio Cult Arts Ctr, 91. *Bibliog:* Nat Objects Invitational (exhib catalog), Ark Arts Ctr Decorative Arts Mus, 89; Lone Stars, Vol II: A Legacy of Texas Quilts, 1936-1986, Univ Tex Press, Austin, 90; Katherine Pearson (auth), American Crafts: A Sourcebook for the Home, Stewart, Tabori & Chang, New York, NY, 93; and many others

STUHL, MICHELLE
SCULPTOR, ENVIRONMENTAL ARTIST
b Toledo, Ohio, 57. *Study:* Univ Wis-Madison, BS, 78; RI Sch Design, MFA, 82. *Work:* Corning Mus Glass, NY. *Comn:* The McDowell Arch (large pub gateway), Phoenix Arts Comn, Ariz, 91. *Exhib:* New Glass Traveling Exhib, Corning Glass Ctr, Metrop Mus Art, NY, Smithsonian Inst, De Young Mem Mus, Victoria & Albert Mus, and others, 79; Mass Col Art, Boston, 80; List Art Ctr, Brown Univ, 81; Mus Fine Art, Providence, 82; Sculpture Invitational, Barrington Col, RI, 82; Ctr for the Arts, State Univ NY at Purchase, 84; Mid Hudson Art Ctr, 89; Joann Rapp Gallery, Scottsdale, Ariz, 96, 97. *Teaching:* Vis artist sculpture, Ariz State Univ, Tempe, 87. *Bibliog:* Suzanne K Frantz (auth), Contemporary Glass, 89

STULER, JACK
PHOTOGRAPHER, EDUCATOR
b Homestead, Pa, Aug 30, 32. *Study:* Phoenix Col, 57; Ariz State Univ, BA, 60, with Van Deren Coke, MFA, 63; workshop with Ansel Adams, 66. *Work:* George Eastman House, Rochester, NY; Gen Aniline Films, NY; Univ Collections, Ariz State Univ, Tempe; Yuma Art Ctr, Ariz; Phoenix Col; Bibliotheque Nationale, Paris; San Francisco Mus Mod Art. *Exhib:* George Eastman House, 63; Photog In Twentieth Century, Nat Gallery Can, 67; Am Photog: The Sixties, Sheldon Mem Art Gallery, Univ Nebr, Lincoln, 66; Photog USA, DeCordova Mus, Lincoln, Mass, 68; Celebrations, Hayden Gallery, Mass Inst Technol, 74; Ariz Arts Showcase, John F Kennedy Ctr for the Performing Arts, Washington, DC, 74; First Light, Focus Gallery, San Francisco, Calif, 75; one-man show, Univ of Ore, Eugene, 76. *Teaching:* Asst prof photog art, Ariz State Univ, 66-72, assoc prof, 73-75, prof, 75-, currently. *Awards:* First Award Biennial Photog, Phoenix Art Mus, 67; Southwestern Art Best of Show, Yuma Fine Arts Asn, 68; Summer Fel, Ariz State Univ, 68. *Bibliog:* Helmut Gernsheim (auth), A Consise History of Photography, Dover Publ Inc, New York, 86; Jack Stuler in the Nature of Things (monogr), Nazraeli Press, Munich, Ger, 90; Jack Stuler A Retrospective, 1962-1997 (monogr), Les Work Publ, Portland, Ore, 97. *Mem:* Soc Photog Educ; Inst Cult Exchange Through Photog (mem adv bd, 66-). *Publ:* Contribr, Photography in the Twentieth Century, Horizon, 67; Being without clothes, Aperture, 15:3, 70; Camera, Lucerne, Switz, 11/71; Concise History of Photography, Dover Publ. *Mailing Add:* Dept Art Arizona State Univ Tempe AZ 85287

STULL, JEAN HIMROD
PAINTER
b Waterford, Pa, Jan 30, 29. *Study:* Edinboro State Col, BS(art educ); Pa State Univ. *Work:* Mus Fine Arts, Springfield, Mass; Frye Mus, Seattle; Time Equities, NY; Erie Insurance Exchange, Pa; Erie Art Mus, Pa; and others. *Comn:* Pa Wild Plants of Concern Poster, Wild Resource CF. *Exhib:* Watercolor USA, Springfield, Mo, 66-68 & 75; Pa Soc of Watercolor Painters Ann 80 & 81; Pa Artists, Capitol Bldg, Harrisburg, 81-82; Invitational for Pa Govs Mansion, Harrisburg, 81-82; solo shows, Erie Art Mus, 88; Remembering Africa, KADA Gallery, 99, 2004; Without Walls: From the Tundra to the Tropics; and many others. *Teaching:* Teacher art, Bessemer Sch Dist, Pa, 49-51 & Ft LeBoeuf Sch Dist, Waterford, Pa, 56-84; retired. *Awards:* Rocky Mountain Nat Watermedia Award, 75 & 81; Best of Show, Cincinnati Mus Nat Hist, 82; Distinguished Alumni, Arts & Humanities, 90 & Art Achievement Award, 91, Edinboro Univ, Pa; and others. *Bibliog:* Meyer (auth), Forty Watercolorists and How They Work, Watson-Guptill, 76. *Mem:* Am Watercolor Soc; Northwestern Pa Artists Asn. *Media:* Watercolor. *Publ:* Contribr & illusr, The Sandpiper, 56-64; auth & illusr, untitled weekly column in Erie Times-News, 57-58; Finding Birds on Presque isle, 65; auth, The Watercolor Page, Am Artist, 1/75; coauth & illusr, Birds of Erie County, Pa, 85. *Mailing Add:* 661 Benson Rd Waterford PA 16441

STUMP, M PAMELA
SCULPTOR
b Detroit, Mich, July, 8, 28. *Study:* Cranbrook Acad Art, 47; Univ Mich, BA, 50-51, MA, 51; Oakland Univ & Univ Mich, 69. *Work:* Rochester Hills Libr, Mich; Saginaw Civic Ctr, Mich; Univ Mich Alumni Ctr, Ann Arbor. *Comn:* six bronze sculptures, Cranbrook Educational Community, Bloomfield Hills, Mich, 90; bronze fountain, Grosse Ile Presbyterian Church, 93; Cross-Sacred Heart Church, Grosse Ile, Mich, 94; Baptismal Font, All Saints, E Lansing, Mich, 96; Theodore Roethke Univ Ctr, 98. *Exhib:* Ceceile Gallery, NY, 56; Pa Adac Fine Arts, Philadelphia, 58; Mich/Pa Artist Show, Pa Acad Fine Arts, Philadelphia, 59; Outdoor Sculpture II & III, Southfield, 90 & 91; NY Acad Fine Arts, 91; NY Acad Scis, 91; Arc Gallery, Chicago, 92; Jr League Traveling Show, 92; one-person, Womens Hist Ctr, Hall of Fame, Lansing, Mich, 94 & Swann Gallery, 97; and others. *Teaching:* Instr ceramic sculpture, Saginaw Mus Art, 59-64; instr design, Washtenaw Community Col, 66; instr sculpture, Cranbrook Kingswood, 69-90. *Awards:* 3rd Prize, First Int Cult & Artistic Exhib, 59; Jurors Award, Mich Fine Arts Competition, 87; Distinguished Alumna Medal, Cranbrook Kingswood, 88; Award of Excellence in Teaching, Crawbrook, Kingswood, 90. *Bibliog:* Virginia Watson-Jones (auth), Contemporary American Women Sculptors, Oryx Press, 86; C Stokes (auth), Odyssey, Artspeak, New York, 91. *Mem:* Founders Soc Detroit Inst Arts; Int Sculptors; Nat Asn Women Artists; Nat Mus of Women in Arts. *Media:* Cast Metal, Welded Metal. *Publ:* Auth, Michigan Voices (poems), Mich Voices, 50; Mich Alumnus Quarterly Rev, Univ Mich, 56-60; The Moment in Time, pvt publ, 70; auth & illusr, Cranbrook Rev, Cranbrook Sch, 85-92. *Mailing Add:* 19629 Park Ln Grosse Ile MI 48138

STURGEN, WINSTON
PHOTOGRAPHER, PRINTMAKER
b Harrisburg, Pa, Aug 27, 38. *Study:* Pa State Univ, BS, 60, MF, 64; studied with Gerhard Bakker, 80-83; Univ Oreg, 66-68. *Work:* Helene Wurlitzer Found, Taos, NMex; Carlsbad Mus, NMex. *Comn:* Photo mural, Sta Rite Industries, Delavan, Wis, 84; photo mural, Phelps Dodge Corp, Phoenix, Ariz, 92. *Exhib:* Beyond Photog, Tex Fine Arts Asn, touring, 91-93; Nat Art Show, Epilepsy Soc, NY, 92-94; 2nd Sapporo Int Print Biennale, Japan, 93; An Am Collection Int Touring Exhib, 93-95; Caje 94; America's Cult Diversity, Ctr Contemp Art, St Louis, 94; Art & Soul, An Int Celebration Arts, Disability & Cult, Los Angeles, 99; The Aesthetic Contribr Photogrs with Disabilities, Int Photog Mus, Okla City, 99. *Pos:* Certified prof photogr, Prof Photogrs Asn Am, Des Plains, Ill, 83-88; various bd offs, Prof Photogrs Asn, NMex, 85-88. *Teaching:* Art photog, Western NMex Univ, 88-91; image photog, Silver City, 89-91; color photog, NMex, 90-91. *Awards:* Award Merit, Int Exposition Photog, Prof Photogrs Asn Am, 83-84 & 86-87; Residency Grants, Wurlitzer Found, 87-89; Third Place, Sister Kenny Int, 92. *Bibliog:* Francis de Buda (auth), Art Photography Show, 89 & Metamorphosis Reviewed, 89, Wilderness Outlook; Pete Szilagyi (auth), Photgraphy's Fuzzy Edges Explored, Austin Am Statesman, 91. *Mem:* Resources Artists Disabilites; Enabled Artists United; Disabled Artists Network; Fuller Lodge Mus Art Ctr. *Media:* Assemblage. *Publ:* auth, Park Cafe, est 1932 (poem), Single Life, 84; Art, artists and photography, 86, Is Photography an Art Form?, 87 & What if?, 87, Prof Photogrs Asn NMex; Death is Not the Parting Way (poetry book), Singing Wings, 89; Kaleidoscope Mag, Akron, Ohio, 99. *Dealer:* Cecilia Torres, New Directions Gallery, 107-B N Plaza, Taos, NMex, 87571

STURGEON, JOHN FLOYD
VIDEO ARTIST
b Springfield, Ill, Jan 6, 46. *Study:* Yale Univ, Yale-Norfolk fel, 67; Univ Ill, BFA, 68; Cornell Univ, MFA, 70. *Work:* Mus Mod Art, NY; Los Angeles Co Mus Art; Long Beach Mus Art; Kunstmuseum, Bonn, WGer; Biennale Venice, Italy; and others. *Comn:* No Earth-No Earth Station (video performance), Los Angeles Mus Art, 83; I Will Take You (video installation), Long Beach Mus Art, 84; Trap/bat (video installation), Mus Mod Art, NY, 93; Narkose (video installation), Contemp Art Ctr, Cincinnati, Ohio, 94; Blooming, While We Are Sinking (video installation), Braemen, Ger, 96. *Pos:* Video artist, Los Angeles Inst Contemp Art, 78-79; vis artist, Sch Art Inst Chicago, 80 & 83; Univ Iowa, 82. *Teaching:* Instr, Univ Calif, Los Angeles, 79-80; vis artist fac, Claremont Grad Sch, Calif, 80, Art Inst Chicago, 80, 82 & 83; assoc prof, Rensselaer Polytechnic Inst, 83-91; mem art fac, State Univ New York, at Purchase, 85-91; guest prof, Hochschule für Künste, Bremen, Ger; assoc prof art, Carnegie Mellon Univ Pittsburgh, Pa, 91-, assoc dept head, 96-. *Awards:* Nat Endowment Arts, Individual Artists Fels, 75, 77 & 80, Video Production Grant, 84; Guggenheim Found Fel, 81; Nat Endowment Arts Mid Atlantic Region Media Fel, 92 & 94; and others. *Bibliog:* Louise Lewis (auth), Art as alchemy, Artweek, 7/28/79; Barbara London (auth), Independent Video: The first fifteen years, Artforum, 9/80; Michael Nash (auth), Present tense rights of passage, Art-Com, fall 83; Kathy Huffman (auth), The Second Link (exhib catalog) & Video Art Personal Medium; Margot Lovejoy (auth), Postmodern Currents, Art & Artists in the Age of Electronic Media, UMI Press, 89, Prentice Hall, 2nd ed, 97. *Publ:* Contribr, Video Art, Harcourt Brace Jovanovich, 76; Two Video Installations, Long Beach Mus Art, 78; auth, Spinning dream, Dreamworks, fall 80; US Film & Video Festival (catalog), 83; Polulism--Report from the Field, Art-Com, spring 83; and others. *Dealer:* L A Louver Gallery 55 North Venice Blvd Venice CA 90291; Data Bank Sch of the Art Inst of Chicago Columbus at Jackson Blvd Chicago IL 60603. *Mailing Add:* Univ Maryland Dept Visual Art 1000 Hilltop Cir Baltimore MD 21250

STURGEON, MARY C
EDUCATOR, HISTORIAN
b Los Angeles, Calif, Dec 6, 43. *Study:* Univ Minn, BA(summa cum laude), 65; Bryn Mawr Col, MA, 68, PhD(classical archaeol & Greek), 71; Am Sch Class Studies in Athens, 68-70 & 70-71. *Teaching:* Asst prof Greek & Roman Art, Oberlin Col, 72-77; assoc prof Greek art, Univ NC, Chapel Hill, 77-85, prof, 85-, chair, 93-; Whitehead Prof, Am Sch Classical Studies, Athens, 98-99. *Mem:* Archaeol Inst Am; Col Art Asn; Am Sch Classical Studies in Athens; Am Philological Asn. *Res:* Greek sculpture. *Publ:* Auth, The reliefs of the Theatre of Dionysus in Athens, Am J Archaeol, 77; Corinth IX 2: Sculpture, The reliefs from the theater, Princeton-Am Sch, 77 & Isthmia IV; Sculpture I, 1952-1967, 87; The Corinth Amazon: Formation of a Roman Classical Sculpture, Am J Archaeol 99, 95; co-ed, Stephanos Studies in honor of Brunilde Sismondo Ridgeway, Philadelphia, 98; auth, A Peloponnesian Aphrodite, The Corinth Theater Type, Stephanos, 98. *Mailing Add:* Dept Art Univ NC Chapel Hill NC 27514

STURGES, HOLLISTER
CURATOR, HISTORIAN
b Kingston, NY. *Study:* Cornell Univ, BA, 62; Univ Calif, Berkeley, MA, 69. *Pos:* Dir, Univ Mo Art Gallery, Kansas City, 76-78; cur European art, Joslyn Art Mus, 80-; Dir, Springfield Mus Fine Arts & George Walter Vincent Smith Art Mus, Mass, 88-95; Dir, Bruce Mus, Greenwich, Conn, 95-2000. *Teaching:* Instr, Univ Mo, Kansas City, 72-80; lectr, Univ Nebr, Lincoln, 83. *Mem:* Col Art Asn; Asn Art Mus Dirs; Am Asn Mus. *Res:* 18th and 19th century French painting with emphasis on social themes; contemporary American. *Publ:* Auth, Chicago abstractionists: Romanticized structures, Univ Mo, Kansas City, 78; Angels and urchins: Images of children at the Joslyn, 80, I-80 series: Mario Merz, 81 & Jules Breton and the French Rural Tradition, 82, Joslyn Art Mus; coauth, Art of the Fantastic: Latin America, 1920-1987, 87; Collection Handbook, Indianapolis Mus Art, 88; auth, New Art from Puerto Rico, Springfield Mus Fine Arts, 90. *Mailing Add:* 91 Putnam Park Greenwich CT 06830

STURMAN, EUGENE
SCULPTOR, PAINTER
b New York, NY, Jan 28, 45. *Study:* Alfred Univ, BFA, 67; Univ NMex, MFA, 69; Tamarind Lithograph Workshop, 70. *Work:* Metro Media Studios, Hollywood, Calif; Warner Bros Records, Universal City, Calif; Los Angeles Co Mus; Newport Harbor Mus. *Comn:* Pub sculpture, City of Los Angeles, 85. *Exhib:* LA Six 74, Los Angeles Co Mus, 74; 24 from Los Angeles, Barnsdall Munic Gallery, Los Angeles, 74; Basel Art Fair, Switz, 74 & 75; Whitney Mus Am Art Biennial, 75; Chicago Art Fair, 82; Los Angeles Co Mus, 83. *Teaching:* Instr printmaking, Long Beach State Univ, 72-74; lectr printmaking, painting & drawing, Univ Calif, Los Angeles, 73-78; instr, Otis-Parsons Sch Design, Los Angeles, 84-91; lectr, Pepperdine Univ, 92, 94-95. *Awards:* Michael Levins Award, Alfred Univ, 66; New Talent Award, Los Angeles Co Mus, 74; Nat Endowment Arts Grant, 75. *Media:* Copper, Lead. *Mailing Add:* 190 Loma Metisse St Malibu CA 90265

STURTEVANT, E
PAINTER, SCULPTOR
b Lakewood, Ohio, Aug 23, 30. *Study:* Univ Iowa, BA, 47; Columbia Univ, MA, 74; Chicago Art Inst; Art Students League; Univ Zurich. *Work:* Mus Mod Art, Paris, France; Mus Contemp Art, Los Angeles, Calif; Everson Mus, Syracuse, NY; Stedelijk Mus, Amsterdam, Holland; Staats Galerie, Stuttgart, Ger; Mus Fur Moderne Kunst Franfurt Am Main, 2004. *Exhib:* Art in the Mirror, Mus Mod Art, NY, 67; solo exhibs, Everson Mus (with catalog), Syracuse, NY, 73, Kunstverein (with catalog), Stuttgart, Ger, 92, Diechtorhallen, Hamburg, Ger, 92, Villa Arson, Nice, France, 93 & Ecole Regionalle des Beaux-Arts (auth catalog), Le Mans, France, 96; Saut Vide, Centre De Exhib, Moscow, Russia, 94; Magritte (auth catalog), Montreal Mus Fine Arts, Montreal Kunstsammulung Nordhein-Westfalen, Dusseldorf, Ger, 96; La Criee (with catalog), La Criee Ctr d'Art Rennes, France, 96; L'Art du Plastique, Ecole Nat Supérieure des Beaux-Arts, Paris, 96; Now/Here (auth, catalog), La Mus Mod Art, Humleback Denmark, 96; solo shows, Galerie Six Friedrich, Munic, 97, Galerie Thaddaeus Ropac, Paris, 98 & Air de Paris, 98; Wiener Secession, Vienna, 98; Wiemar Neues Mus, Weimar, 98; City Art Mus, Helsinki, 98; Gallerie Ropac, Paris, 2002, I Love Arlette; Gallerie Mezzanin, Vienna, 2003; Mus Fur Moderne Kunst Frankfor, 2004; The Brutal Tiluth Perry Rubenstein Gallery, NY, 2005, List, Visual Arts Ctr, MIT, Cambridge, 2005; Anthong Reynolds Gallery, London, 2006; Unlimited, Basel, Switz, 2006; Biennial, Whitney Mus Am Art, 2006. *Pos:* Harvard Univ, Visiting prof, 99-2000. *Teaching:* Vis prof dialectics of thinking (art philosophy), Huchsch Kunste, Berlin, 95; Akad Bildennden Kunste, Munich, Ger, 96; Royal Danish Acad Fine Arts, Copenhagen, 97; Rijkakademie, Amsterdam, 97; vis prof Harvard Univ, Cambridge, Mass, 99-2000, Getty Rsch Inst, Los Angeles, Calif, 2001; MIT Sch of Architecture, Cambridge, Visiting Prof, 2002. *Awards:* Beux Arts; Best International Exhib, 2005; Prix de la Melleure Exposition Internationale, 2005. *Bibliog:* W Arning (auth), Sturtevant, Uwe Krauss GmbH, 92; Herbert Besacier (auth), Sturtevant, Arte Factum, 93; Sturtevant, Video Mag, Zapp, 94; Brue Haunley (auth) Erase and rewind, Frieze, June/July/Aug 2000; April Lamm (auth), Art Review, 2005; Bruce Hainley (auth), Art Forum, 2005; Nancy Princenthal (auth), Art in Am, 2006; plus many others. *Publ:* Auth, Goya, 93; Blocknotes, 93; Original, Cantz Verlag, Ger, 95; International Avant-guard Since 1960, Vol I & II, 98; plus others; The Brutal Truth Exhib Catalogue Mus Fur Modern Kunst, Cantz Verlaz, Ger, 2004; Sturevant Catalogue Ralsonne, MMK Cantz, 2005; Push and Shove Exhib Catalogue Perry Rubenstein Gallery, New York, NY, 2005; Shifting Mental Structures Neuer Berliner Kunstuerein 2002 Kantz. *Dealer:* Galerie Thaddaeus Ropac Paris; Perry Rubenstein Gallery, New York, NY; Galerie Hans Mayer Berlin Germany; Gallerie Mezzanin, Vienna; Gallery Anthony Reynolds London. *Mailing Add:* 23 rue des Lombards Paris 75004 France

STURTZ-DAVIS, SHIRLEY ZAMPELLI
PAINTER, EDUCATOR
b Lewistown, Pa. *Study:* Penn State Univ, BS, 59, MA (studio art), 61. *Work:* Penn State, Univ Park, Pa; Pa Dept Educ, Harrisburg, Pa; Shriner Burn Inst, Boston; Wash Co Mus Fine Arts, Hagerstown, Md. *Comn:* Still Life Series, Mellon Bank, State Col, Pa, 80s; watercolors, comn by private individuals, 80s-90s. *Exhib:* one-woman show, Mus Art, Indiana Univ Pa, 88 & Watercolor Still Lifes, Mus Fine Arts Wash Co, Hagerstown, Md, 2001-03; Art of State Juried Exhib, State Mus Pa, Harrisburg, 93, 94, 95 & 97; Southern Alleghanies Trien Invitational, Southern Alleghanies Mus Art, Loretta, Pa, 93-94 & 99-2000; San Diego Watercolor Soc Int, Poway Ctr Performing Arts, Calif, 94, 98 & 99; Watercolor USA Nat, Springfield Art Mus, Mo, 96; Phildelphia Water color Soc Int, Berman Mus Art, Pa, 96, 97, 98 & 99; Miss Grand Nat Exhib, Miss Mus Art, Jackson, 98 & 99; Watercolor Hon Soc, 2003. *Collection Arranged:* Shippensburg Univ Fashion Archives Exhibs, 1990-1996; William D Davis Retrospective, 2004. *Pos:* dir arts in educ, Cent Intermedia Unit 10, Penn State, 76-89; dir fashion archives, Shippensburg Univ, 90-96. *Teaching:* instr art, pub sch Pa, 59-66; adj prof, Penn State Univ, 62-76 & Shippensburg Univ, 96-98. *Awards:* Jack Richeson Award, Jack Richeson Co, 94; First Place, Baltimore Watercolor Soc, 98; Grumbacker Gold Medal, 93 & 99; Gold Sable Award for Excellence in Watercolor, 2001. *Bibliog:* Paula Banks Mitchell (auth), Portrait of an Organized Artist, State Col Mag, 86; Stanley Marcus (auth), There's Always Time to Paint, Watercolor Mag of Am Arts, 96; Terry Di Domenico (auth), Passionate About Painting, VISTA, Shippensburg Univ, 99. *Mem:* Watercolor Honor Soc USA (bd mem, 98-); Tex Watercolor Soc; La Watercolor Soc; Ga Watercolor Soc; Pa Watercolor Soc; Ala Watercolor Soc; Baltimore Watercolor Soc; Phildelphia Watercolor Soc. *Media:* Watercolor. *Res:* The use of creative dramatic techniques as a stimulus to the artist. *Interests:* Gardening, raising Bonsai trees, Ikebana, antiquing, reading, collecting. *Publ:* contribr, Watercolor Sketching on the Move, Am Artists Mag, 98, Fifty Years of Excellence, Tex Watercolor Soc, 99, Watercolor Expressions & The Best of Watercolor Vol 3, Rockport Publ, 99. *Mailing Add:* 1427 Curtin St State College PA 16803

STUTESMAN, CEZANNE SLOUGH
PAINTER
b Bucks Co, Pa, Dec 25, 56. *Study:* Univ State of NY, BS, 85; Pima Community Col, Ariz, AS; studied under Dr William Kuchler, Philadelphia, Pa. *Work:* BloodHorse Inc, Lexington; The Am Quarter Horse Asn, Amerillo, Tex; Nat Park Serv, Ariz; City of Beverly Hills; Univ Ariz, Tucson. *Comn:* SeaCove, GrandPrix horse, Belynda Bond; Clover Hills Trinity Champion horse, L MacMillan; Disco Lemonade champion horse, J Jensen; Paxton champion horse, K Herberger. *Exhib:* Solo-exhib, Military History of the SW, US Army Mus, Ft Huachuca, Az; Paradise Horses, Paradise Race Track, Phoenix; The Am Air Craft, Tucson Int Airport; 25 one-man shows. *Pos:* illustrative artis, Sears; textile designer, Quaker Lace; dir, Cezanne's Gallery, Ariz. *Awards:* Equine Artist of the Yr, NA Horsemens Asn, 03. *Mem:* USA Equestrian; British Horse Soc; Am Cattle Women; Az Cowbelles. *Publ:* PBS Feature, 95; Lisa Sheehy, CS Stutesman, Equine Images, 00; Lisa Sheehy, CS Stutesman, Polo Players Edition, 02; Gwen Rizzo (editor), Players Ed, 02; N Am Horsemen's Asn, 03. *Mailing Add:* c/o HorsesInOil dot com PO Box 562 Bowie AZ 85605

STUX, STEFAN VICTOR
ART DEALER, DIRECTOR
b Timisoara, Romania, Oct 28, 42; US citizen. *Study:* New York Univ, PhD, 75. *Pos:* Pres & dir, Stux Gallery, Boston, 80-, Stux Gallery, New York, 86-, Stux Art Ltd, New York, 94 & Stefan Stux Gallery, 96. *Teaching:* Instr, Brandeis Univ, 75-78 & Harvard Univ, 79-84. *Specialty:* Contemporary, modern master, and impressionist. *Mailing Add:* 520 W End Ave Apt 9 New York NY 10024-3240

SUBA, SUSANNE (MRS BERTAM BLOCH)
PAINTER, ILLUSTRATOR
b Budapest, Hungary; US citizen. *Study:* Pratt Inst, grad. *Work:* Metrop Mus Art, NY; Brooklyn Mus, NY; Art Inst Chicago; Mus City of NY; Hyde Collection, Glen Falls, NY. *Exhib:* Ansdell Gallery, London, Eng; Hammer Gallery, NY; Kalamazoo Inst Art; Art Inst Chicago; Mus Mod Art, NY; Works on Paper, Weatherspoon Gallery, Chapel Hill, NC. *Pos:* Teacher, Nelson Univ, Nelson, BC & Community Col, NY. *Awards:* Awards, Am Inst Graphic Art, Art Dirs Club New York & Art Dirs Club Chicago. *Media:* Watercolor, Black Ink. *Publ:* A Rocket in My Pocket; The Monkeys and the Pedlar; The Man with the Bushy Beard

SUBLETT, CARL CECIL
PAINTER
b Johnson Co, Ky, Feb 4, 19. *Study:* Western Ky Univ, 40; Univ Study Ctr, 45, Florence, Italy; Univ Tenn, 56. *Work:* Nat Acad Design, NY; Hunter Gallery Art, Chattanooga, Tenn; Mint Mus, Charlotte, NC; Springfield Art Mus, Mo; Tenn Arts Comn, Nashville; Knoxville Mus Art, Tenn. *Comn:* Five watercolor paintings, Kimberly Clark Corp Off, Knoxville, Tenn. *Exhib:* Southeastern Art Ann, Atlanta, Ga; Paintings of Yr, Atlanta; New Painters of South, Birmingham, Ala; Watercolor USA, Springfield, Mo, 64-72; Am Watercolor Soc, NY, 72; one-man retrospective, Tenn State Mus, Nashville, 83 & Knoxville Mus Art, Tenn, 91. *Pos:* Indust eng, draftsman Enterprise Wheel & Car Corp, Bristol, Va, 1946-49; artist, asst mgr Bristol Art Engravers, 1952-54; art dir, Charles S Kane Co, Knoxville, Tenn, 1954-65; juror, Watercolor Soc Ala, Birmingham, 1979, Jacksonville Univ Ann, 1980; Juror, Bristol Art Guild 8th ann juried exhib, 1993. *Teaching:* staff artist Bristol, Va-Tennescan & Herald Courier, 1950-52; Prof art, Univ Tenn, emer, 66-82-. *Awards:* Art Embassies Prog State Dept, 68-83, 87-90, 90-; Lifetime Achievement Award, Mayor's Art Celebration, Knoxville Art Ctr; Inaugural Distinguished Fac/Alumni/Student Award, Univ Tenn Sch Art, 2000. *Bibliog:* Prize Winning Watercolors, Allied Publ, Inc, 65; Invitational Carl Sublett Exhibition Catalog, Tenn State Mus, 83; A Visual Odyssey: The Art of Carl Sublett, U T Ewing Gallery, 2000; Watercolor Expressions, Rockport Publ, 99. *Mem:* Nat Acad (assoc, 77, acad, 94-); Knoxville Watercolor Soc; Tenn Watercolor Soc; Port Clyde Arts & Crafts Soc, Maine; Watercolor USA Hon Soc. *Media:* Watercolor, Oil. *Publ:* Illusr, (exhib catalog), Tenn State Mus, 83. *Dealer:* Collector's Gallery Nashville TN; Bennett Galleries Knoxville TN. *Mailing Add:* PO BOx 101 Port Clyde ME 04855

SUBRIN, ELISABETH A
VIDEO ARTIST, FILMMAKER
b Boston, Mass, Dec 13, 64. *Study:* Mass Col Art, with Tony Oursler, BFA, 90; Art Inst Chicago, MFA, 95. *Exhib:* Chicago Retrospecitve, Mus Contemp Art, Chicago, 97; Art & Technol, Wexner Ctr for the Arts, Columbus, Ohio, 98, 2001; Boston Now, Inst Contemp Art, Boston, Mass, 98; Int Film Festival Rotterdam, The Neth, 98, 2001; Cineprobe: Elizabeth Subrin Recent Works, Mus Mod Art, NY, 98; Women in Film, Walker Art Ctr, Minneapolis, Minn, 99; The Cool World: Film & Video in Am Art 1950-2000, Whitney Mus Am Art, NY, 2000; 2000 Biennial, Whitney Mus Am Art, NY, 2000. *Collection Arranged:* The Failure to Assimilate: Cecilia Dougharty, Thread Waxing Space, New York, 98; Acting Out: Video Artists Mess with Mass Media, Mt Holyoke Col, 98; No More Sweets for You: New Film & Video, Anthology Film Arch, ICA, Boston, SUNY, Buffalo. *Pos:* producer, The Judy Spots, MTV, 95; res coord, The File Room, Randolph St Gallery, 94-95. *Teaching:* vis instr film/video, Sch Art Inst Chicago, 95-97; asst prof film/video, The Five Col Inc, Amherst Col, 97-. *Awards:* First Pl Experimental, USA Film Festival, 96; LA Film Critics Award for Best Experimental Film, 99; Best Experimental Film, New Eng Film and Video Festival, 2000. *Bibliog:* Jonathan Rosenbaum (auth), Remaking history, Chicago Reader, 98; B. Ruby Rich (auth), Chick Flicks: Theories and Memories of the Feminist Film Movement, Duke Univ Press, 98; Lia Gangitano (auth), File Under Heroes, Thread Waxing Space, 2000. *Mem:* Col Arts Asn; Independent Features Proj. *Media:* Film, Video. *Mailing Add:* 231 Frost St Apt 1R Brooklyn NY 11211

SUDBRACK, ELI
ARTIST
b Rio de Janeiro, Brazil, 68. *Study:* Pontificia Unive Catolica, Rio de Janeiro, Bachelor, 92; Int Ctr Photog, Degree, NY, 99. *Work:* Walking on Thin Ice, peres projects, LA, 2002, canopy, Skate Cir, Central Park, NY City, 2004, avaf8 (floorscape), 2004. *Exhib:* group shows, GNS: Global Navigation Systems, Palais de Tokyo, Paris, 2003, K48 Teenage Rebel: The Bedroom Show, galerie du jour, 2003, Popstraction, Deitch Projects, NY, 2003, Whitney Biennial Am Art, Whitney Mus Am Art, 2004, Videodrome: 27 Int Artists, Santa Barbara Contemp Arts Forum, Calif, 2005; one-man shows, Midway Contemp Gallery, Saint Paul, Mich, 2003, Resodiversion, Paris, 2003, Galeria Triângulo, São Paulo, Brazil, 2004. *Mailing Add:* c/o Santa Barbara Contemp Arts Forum 653 Paseo Nuevo Santa Barbara CA 93101

SUDLOW, ROBERT N
PAINTER, PRINTMAKER, SCULPTOR
b Holton, Kans, Feb 25, 20. *Study:* Univ Kans, BFA; Univ Calif, Berkeley; Calif Col Arts & Crafts, Oakland, MFA; Acad Grande Chaumiere, Paris; Acad Andre L'Hote, Paris. *Work:* City Art Mus, St Louis, Mo; Yellow Freight Collection, Kansas City, Mo; Joslyn Art Mus, Omaha; Sheldon Art Mus, Lincoln, Nebr; Menninger Found, Topeka, Kans; Spencer Art Mus Univ of Kans, Lawrence, Kans; Beach Mus KS State Univ, Manhattan, Kans. *Comn:* Mural Com State Bank, Topeka, Kans. *Exhib:* One man show, Beauchamp Gallery, Topeka, 84-90, 94 & 2003, Am Legacy Gallery, Kansas City, Mo, 90-94 & 2003; Kansas Landscapes, traveling show, 85 & 87; one man Retrospective, Wichita Art Mus Kans, 94; Beyond the Horizon, Nat Traveling Show, 98; Spiritual Journeys Traveling Show Exhib, 2002-; retrospective, Lawrence Arts Ctr, Kansas, 2002. *Pos:* Prof Emer, 87. *Teaching:* Prof art, Univ Kans, 47-87; ret. *Awards:* Gov Artist, 76; Baker Univ Citation, 90; Native Son of Kans Award, 96. *Bibliog:* Sunflower Journey, Channel II KTWU. *Media:* Oil, Watercolor; Lithography; Wood. *Specialty:* Landscape Painting. *Interests:* Poetry. *Collection:* Spencer Univ Art Mus, Univ of KS, Lawrence KS; Spiritual Jouneys The Art of Robert Sudlow. *Publ:* Landscapes in Kansas, Kans Univ Press, 87. *Dealer:* Am Legacy Gallery 5911 Main Kansas City MO 66103; Beauchamp Frame Shop 3113 Huntoon Topeka KS; Roy Gallery 1410 Kasold Dr. Lawrence, KS, 66049. *Mailing Add:* 886 E 1050th Rd Lawrence KS 66047

SUFFOLK, RANDALL
MUSEUM DIRECTOR, CURATOR
Study: Conn Col, BA; Columbia Univ, MA in higher educ admin; Bryn Mawr Col, MA in art hist. *Pos:* Assoc, W Graham Arader III Galleries, Philadelphia, New York City; Mem strategic planning comt Univ Art Mus, State Univ of NY, Albany; consultant Arts Corp, Ltd, Philadelphia; review panel mem for Special Opportunity Stipend Grants NY State Coun on Arts; cur, The Hyde Collection, Glen Falls, NY, 1995-1998, deputy dir, 1998-1999, acting dir, 1999-2000, dir, 2000. *Mailing Add:* The Hyde Collection Art Mus 161 Warren St Glens Falls NY 12801

SUGGS, DON
PAINTER, PHOTOGRAPHER
b Ft Worth, Tex, Mar 16, 45. *Study:* Univ Calif Los Angeles, MA, 71, MSA, 72. *Work:* San Diego Mus Contemp Art, Calif; Univ Calif, Los Angeles. *Exhib:* Clearing, Los Angeles Co Mus, Calif, 89. *Teaching:* Instr painting & drawing, Univ Calif Los Angeles, 83-. *Awards:* Artist Fel, Nat Endowment Arts, 91. *Mailing Add:* 423 Molino St Los Angeles CA 90013

SUGGS, PAT(RICIA) ANN
PAINTER, CONCEPTUAL ARTIST
b Reedley, Calif, Mar 17, 36. *Study:* Old World Acad Training; Leighton Fine Art Acad, with Thomas & Margery Lester Leighton, San Francisco, 74-81; extensive travel & study at the great art centers of Europe, London, Paris, Rome, Florence, Dresden & Prague, etc. *Comn:* Pastel portrait painting, comn by Melody Grey, Santa Rosa Calif, 86; Pastel floral painting, comn by Elaine Clarke, Grants Pass, Ore, 91; Pastel landscape painting, comn by James & Helen Riley, Saratoga, Calif, 92; Pastel rose floral, comn by Jean Afonso, 93 & 96. *Exhib:* Hayward Arts Coun, Calif, 98; Pure Pigment,Los Gatos, Calif, 98; Degas Pastel Soc Exhib, Lauren Rogers Mus Art, Miss; IAPS Open Exhib, Dartmouth St Gallery, Albuquerque, NMex, 99; Nat Exhib, Fort Walton Beach Mus Art, 2000-02; Pastel Soc of Am Thirteenth Ann Juried Exhib, 03 & Renaissance in Pastel, Slater Mem Mus, 2006; The Butler Inst of Am Art, Youngstown, Ohio, 03; one-woman group shows, Gadabout Gallery, Los Gatos, Calif, 86, Pure Pigment, Los Gatos Mus of Art, 98; Leighton Studio Exhib, Triton Mus Fine Art, Santa Clara, Calif, 2001-2002; Binney & Smith Gallery, Banana Factory, Bethlehem, PA, 2004; Triton Mus Fine Art, Santa Clara, Calif, Allied Artists West, 2005. *Pos:* Judge fine arts, Arts Clubs, The Peninsula, Northern Calif & San Joaquin Valley, 84-94 & 94-96 & Sonoma Co, Alameda Co & Santa Clara Co Fairs, 89-91; judge, SWA 50th Ann, 2000; judge, Santa Clara Co Fair, 2000 & Alameda Co Fair, 2003. *Teaching:* various workshops, Calif, NMex. *Awards:* Two Grumbacher Gold Medals, SWA Annual Show, 98; Award of Excellence, South Bay Fine Arts Festival, Santa Clara, Calif, 2000; Best Floral Award, Nat Pastel Art Show, Lone Star Pastel Soc, 2003; Canson Award, Pastel Soc Oreg, 2003; Master Circle Gold Medallion Award, Int Asn Pastel Soc, 2005. *Bibliog:* John Lehman (auth), Three Native Daughters' Show, The New Outlook, 6/6/83; Urania Tarbet (auth), Art Revue, winter 95/96; Pratt & Monato (auths), Best of Pastel, Rockport Publ, 96. *Mem:* Pastel Soc Am, NY; Pastel Soc WCoast, Carmichael, Calif (adv bd, 86-2006); Soc Western Artists (trustee, 86-96); Allied Artists West (dir, exhibs, 91-92); The Nat League Am Pen Women, Las Artes Br; Int Asn Pastel Soc (treas 94-2006). *Media:* Pastel, Oil. *Publ:* Luminous Trnaslucence Mag, 50-57, 1/2000; Floral Inspiration, 72, 97 & Best of Pastel, 130, 96, Rockport Publ. *Dealer:* Carol A Dabb 41 Sunkist Lane Los Altos CA 94022. *Mailing Add:* 4127 Beebe Cir San Jose CA 95135-1010

SUGIMOTO, HIROSHI
PHOTOGRAPHER
b 1948. *Study:* Art Ctr Coll, La, 72. *Exhib:* Solo shows include Nat Mus Art, Cleveland, Ohio, 89, Mus Contemp Art, La, 94-95, Mus Modern Art, NY City, Metrop Mus Art, 95, La Caixa, Madrid, Spain, 98, Beilefeld Mus, Ger, Kitakyushu Project Gallery, Moderna Museet, Sweden, Deutsche Guggenheim, Berlin, 2000, Soanbend Gallery, NY City, Robert Klein Gallery, Boston, Mass, 2006; group shows include Lion Biennale, Lion, France, 96; Palazzo delle esposioni, Rome, 96; Mus Contemp Art, Chicago, 96; Wexner Ctr Arts, 96; By Night, Found Caltier pour l'art contemporain, Paris, France, 96; Johannesburg Bienna, South Africa, 97; At the End of the Century: One Hundred Years of Architecture, Mus Brazil, 98; Terra Incognita, Neues Mus Weserburg, Bremen, Ger, 98; Photographer's Gallery, London, Eng, 98; Int Ctr Photography, NY City, 99. *Awards:* Hasselblad Award, 2001. *Mailing Add:* c/o Robert Klein Gallery 4th Floor 38 Newbury St Boston MA 02116

SUGIURA, KUNIE
PHOTOGRAPHER, PAINTER
b Naqoya. *Study:* Art Inst Chicago, BFA, 67. *Work:* Mus Mod Art, NY; Mus Fine Arts, Boston; Denver Art Mus; George Eastman House, Rochester, NY; Va Mus Art, Richmond. *Comn:* photog, JGS, New York City, 03. *Exhib:* Selections From the Collection, Aldrich Mus Art, Ridgefield, Conn, 72; Painting & Sculpture Today, Indianapolis Mus Art, 72; Ann Exhib Painting, Whitney Mus Am Art, NY, 72; Fossilization: Imprinted Light, Mus Mod Art, Saltama, Japan, 97; New Photog 13, Mus Mod Art, NY, 97-98; Attractants: Kunie Sugiura, Aichi Pretectural Mus Art, Japan, 98. *Awards:* Robert Scull Found Grant, 85; Catalogue Project Grant, NY Found Arts, 97 & Artist Fel, 98. *Bibliog:* Julia Scully (auth), CKO, Mod Photog, 68; Janet Koplos (auth), Shadow Play, Art in Am, 4/02; Michael Klein (auth), Lucid Encounters, World Art, Spring 99. *Dealer:* Leslie Toukonow 535 W 22nd St 6th fl New York NY 10011. *Mailing Add:* 7 Doyers St 4th fl New York NY 10013

SUGIYAMA, AKIKO
COLLAGE ARTIST, ASSEMBLAGE ARTIST
b Noheji, Aomori Prefecture, Japan. *Study:* Joshibi Daigaku, Tokyo, BA, 1974. *Work:* Fla Gulf Coast Art Ctr, Belleair, Fla; Polk Mus Art, Lakeland, Fla; Daytona Beach Arts & Scis Ctr, Daytona Beach, Fla; Deland Mus Art, Deland, Fla. *Comn:* Wall hangings, Holland & Knight Law Firm, Tampa, Fla, 1988; wall hangings, Daytona Beach Int Airport, 1993; wall hangings, Coca-Cola Co, Atlanta, Ga, 1993; wall hangings, Bert Fish Med Ctr, New Smyrna Beach, Fla, 1996; wall hangings, Volusia Co Courthouse, Deland, Fla, 2001. *Exhib:* One-woman show, Paper Play, Gulf Coast Art Ctr, Belleair, Fla, 1997; Craft Show, Philadelphia Mus Art, 2000 & 2004-2005; Craft Show, Smithsonian, Wash, 2002 & 2005-2006; Incarnations, Gayle Wilson Gallery, South Hampton, NY, 2001; Visual Art Fel Exhib, Lowe Art Mus, Coral Gables, Fla, 2004; two-person show, Gallery Camino Real, Boca Raton, Fla, 2005; Am Craft Expos, 2001-2005. *Awards:* Merit award in fiber decoration, Smithsonian Craft Show, 2002; Grainger Best of Fiber award, American Craft Exposition, 2002; Visual Arts fellow, State of Fla, 2002. *Bibliog:* Paper Play, The Georgia Review, spring 91; Portfolio, American Craft, 4/5/94; Barbara Wylan Sefton (auth), In touch with studio artists, American Style, summer 97. *Mem:* Am Craft Coun; Fla Craftsmen. *Media:* Paper; Fiber decorative. *Dealer:* Blue Spiral 1 38 Biltmore Ave Ashville NC 28801. *Mailing Add:* 5 Bay Hill Dr Ormond Beach FL 32174

SUHRE, TERRY L
DIRECTOR
b Ft Benning, Ga. *Study:* Univ Ill-Urbana-Champaign, BFA, 1976; So Ill Univ, Carbondale, MFA, 1980. *Comn:* BiState Devel, St Louis Circulation, St Louis, Mo, 2002; Arts-in-Transit, At West Co Transfer Ctr, 2002. *Collection Arranged:* So Ill Univ - Carbondale Univ Mus; Of Earth and Cotton (installation), Jackie Brookner, 1998; sculptors prints, James Surls: Embracing Paradox, 1999; video installation, Waves Face: Jeff Carter and Susan Giles, 2002. *Pos:* assoc cur, Ill State Mus, Springfield, 80-90; dir, Catherin Smith Gallery, Appalachian State Univ, Bonne, NC, 90-96; dir, Gallery 210, Univ Mo St Louis, 96-. *Teaching:* teacher arts & tech, Univ Mo St Louis, 96-. *Awards:* Best Cur Award, Gallery 210 Season 1999-2000. *Mem:* Am Asn Mus. *Res:* contemporary. *Specialty:* contemporary. *Interests:* Contemporary, Bauhaus. *Publ:* (ed-auth) James Surls: Embracing Paradox, 99; (ed-coauth with Phyyllis Brramson, Uera Klensnt & Micniko Itatani) Locations of Desire, 90, (ed-auth) Moholy-Nagy: A New View for Chicago, 91. *Mailing Add:* Univ Missouri Gallery 210 8001 Natural Bridge Rd Saint Louis MO 63121

SUJO, CLARA DIAMENT
GALLERY DIRECTOR, ART DEALER, CURATOR, WRITER
b Argentina. *Study:* Studied with Jorge Romero Brest & Pierre Francastel. *Exhib:* Vision of Venezuelan Art, Nat Gallery, Caracas, 95. *Pos:* cur New Acquisitions, Mus Bellas Artes Caracas, 58-63; dir, Documentary Films on Art, 63-67, Estudio Actual, Caracas, 68-91 & CDS Gallery, New York, 81-. *Teaching:* Prof art hist & fine Arts, Cristobal Rojas Sch Fine Arts, Caracas, 58-65; prof art hist & art appreciation, Neumann Found Inst Design, 67-70. *Awards:* Order Andre Bello list class, Venezuelan Govt. *Mem:* Int Asn Art Critics; Art Table Inc; Art Dealers Asn Am. *Specialty:* International contemporary art. *Publ:* Auth, Art in Latin America Today, Panamerican Union, 62; coauth, Joseph Albers, Kellar Velag, 67; contribr, The Emergent Decade, Cornell Univ, 65. *Mailing Add:* 74 E 79th St New York NY 10021

SULKOWSKI, ELIZABETH BRANDON
PAINTER
b Oct 09, 52. *Study:* Calif Col of Arts & Crafts, summer 1973; Univ of Ga, BFA Interior Design, 1974; Art Students League of NY, 1974-1979. *Exhib:* Women Artists, Cheekwood Mus, Nashville, Tenn, 1994; AAPL Grand Nat, Nat Arts Club, NYC, 1995; Women of the West, Tucson Mus of Art, Tucson, Ariz, 1996. *Media:* Oil. *Mailing Add:* 4685 Everal Ln Franklin TN 37064

SULKOWSKI, JAMES M
PAINTER, INSTRUCTOR
b Pittsburgh, PA, Dec 10, 51. *Study:* Pa Academy of the Fine Arts, 1969-71; Carnegie Mellon Univ, 1971-72; Art Students League of NY with Frank Mason & Robert Beverlyhale, 1974-79. *Work:* PNC Bank, Pittsburgh, Pa; Golden Eagle Resort, Stowe, Vt; Mercy Hospital, Pittsburgh, Pa; Metropolitan Opera, New York City; George H. W. Bush Presidential Library, Tex. *Comn:* Ikhwan Revolt of 1929, comn by King of Saudi Arabia, Jeddah, Saudi Arabia, 1979-80; Court of Baghdad 9th Century, comn by King of Saudi Arabia, 1979-80; 3 landscape murals, St. Francis Health Sys, Pittsburgh, Pa, 1986; mural Gen Lafayette, Nemacolin Woodlands Resort, Pa, 2000; portrait Richard White, Washington Fed Bank, Washington, Pa, 2006. *Exhib:* Art in Am, Denver Mus, Colo, 1994; The Nude in Fine Art, Vanier & Roberts Fine Art, Scottsdale, Ariz, 1994; Art in Am, Denver Mus, Colo, 1995; Art in the Mountains, Nemacolin Woodlands Resort, Pittsburgh, Pa, 1996; Art in the Garden, Washington Co Hist Soc, Washington, Pa, 2005. *Collection Arranged:* Opera Art, Chautauqua Inst, NY, 1984; Opera Art of James Sulkowski, Metropolitan Opera of NY, 1984; Art of James Sulkowski, Laroche Col, Pa, 1995; Opera Art, Stifel Fine Arts, Wheeling WVa, 2002; Beyond the Sea, Sulkowski Fine Art Gallery, 2005; Looking Back-A Retrospective 1966-2006, Sulkowski Fine Art Gallery, 2006. *Pos:* Artist in res, Pittsburgh Opera, Pittsburgh, Pa, 1981-83; owner & inst, Sulkowski Acad of Fine Art, Houston, Pa, 1994-2001; owner, Sulkowski Fine Art Gallery, Canonsburg, Pa, 2003-. *Teaching:* Classical still life painting, Sweetwater Art Ctr, Sewickley, Pa, 1987-1994; portrait painting, Sulkowski Acad of Fine Art, Houston, Pa, 1994-2001; figure drawing, Sulkowski Academy of Fine Art, Canonsburg, Pa, 1994-2001. *Awards:* Helen de Cozen Award, Am Artists Prof League; Best of Show, 30th Annual Exhib of Printing Indus of Western Pa, 1996; People's Choice Award, Art in the Mountains, US Art Magazine, 1997. *Bibliog:* David Templeton (auth), A Fine Day for the Fine Arts, Pittsburgh Post Gazette, 1994; Stephen Doherty (auth), Turning to Floral Still Lites, Am Artist Mag, 1996; Kathryn Kipp (auth), The Best of Flower Painting, North Light Books, 1997; The Best of Flower Painting 2, North Light Books, 1997. *Mem:* Nat Soc of Mural Painters; Nat Arts Club of New York; Am Artist Prof League; Art Students League of New York. *Media:* Oil. *Mailing Add:* 329 Hawthorne St Canonsburg PA 15317

SULKOWSKI, JOSEPH H
PAINTER
b Pittsburgh, Pa Dec 10, 51. *Study:* Pa Acad of the Fine Arts, 1969-1971; Art Students League of NY with Frank Mason, 1974-1979. *Work:* King Abdul Aziz Naval Mus, Jedda, Saudi Arabia; Tenn State Mus, Nashville, Tenn. *Comn:* The Ikhwan Revolt of 1929, The Court of Baghdad in the 9th Century, Saudi Arabian Royal Family, Jedda, Saudi Arabia, 1980. *Awards:* Grumbacher Gold Medallion, AAPL Show, 1990. *Bibliog:* Katherine A Sulkowski (auth), Master and Hands, Washington/Green, 2004. *Mem:* Art Students League of NY (life mem); Nat Arts club, NY; Nat Soc of Mural Painters; Am Artists Prof League; Artwatch Int. *Media:* Oil. *Publ:* A Joyous Process, Sporting Classics, 1997; The Sporting Art of Joseph Sulkowski, Canine Images, 2001. *Dealer:* Halcyon Gallery London England. *Mailing Add:* 4685 Everal Ln Franklin TN 37064

SULLIVAN, ANNE DOROTHY HEVNER
PAINTER, PRINTMAKER
b Boston, Mass, Mar 17, 29. *Study:* Northeastern Univ, Boston, Mass, 72-74; Univ Lowell, Mass, BA (magna cum laude), 77; DeCordova Mus, with King Coffin, Carlton Plummer, Glen Bradshaw & K Chang Liu and others. *Work:* The New Eng Permanent Collection, Boston, Mass; Shawmut Bank, Boston, Mass; Bay Banks of New Eng, Boston, Mass; Sheraton Corp, Boston, Mass; Amoskeag Banks, Manchester, NH; and others. *Exhib:* Whistler House Mus (2 person invitational), Lowell, Mass, 95; Nat Asn Women Artists traveling graphics, 96; Nat Asn Women Artists 107th Ann, NY, 96, 97 & 98; NAm Open Competition, Boston, 1992,1994, 1996,1998, 2000, 2002, 2004; C Lorillard Wolfe 100th Exhib, NY, 96; Int Soc of Experimental Artists, Sarasota, Fla, 98, 99, 2002; DeVos Mus, N Mich Univ, New Bedford, Mass Mus, 2006; and numerous others. *Collection Arranged:* Emerging Boston Artists, Brush Gallery, Urban Internat Park, Lowell, Mass, 90. *Pos:* Vpres, Whistler Mus, 77-79; chmn, Lowell Arts Lottery Coun, 79-81; bd mem, Mass Arts & Humanities Adv Comt, 81-82; consult, pvt & pub collections, 88-90; dir, Abbey Art Gallery, Boston; pres, Monotype Guild New Eng, 92-93. *Teaching:* Dir & instr art program, Whistler House Mus Art, Lowell, Mass, 75-76, instr, 96 & 98; dir & instr AID Prog, Univ Lowell, Mass, 76-84; instr, Brush Gallery, Urban Nat Park Lowell, Mass, 96. *Awards:* MM Rines Award for outstanding contemporary painting, NAm Open Competition, Boston, 94; Am Artist Mag Award, Catherine Lorillard Wolfe Art Club, NY, 96; Hon Mention, Nat Open Competition, RI Watercolor Soc, 2002; Martha Reed Mem Award, 98; Hon Mention, 63rd Nat Open Competition, Exptl Artists Ala, 2004; and others. *Bibliog:* Ann Schecter (auth), Sun Art critics review, Lowell Sun, Mass, 4/8/79 & 4/6/84; Marie Geary (auth), Art is, Chelmsford Weekly, Mass, 4/3/80; Boston Globe, 12/3/95. *Mem:* New Eng Watercolor Soc (bd dir, 82-92); Nat League Penwomen, Washington; Internat Soc Experimental Artists, Fla; Monotype Guild of Northeast (pres, 92-93); Copley Soc Boston; Nat Asn Women Artists. *Media:* Mixed Media, Monotype. *Publ:* Contribr, Abstracts in Watercolor (cover & p 61), Rockport Publ, 96; Painting Composition, pg 56 & Best of Watercolor 2, pg 77, 97 Rockport Publ. *Mailing Add:* 28 Rindo Pk Dr Lowell MA 01851

SULLIVAN, BARBARA JEAN
PAINTER, INSTRUCTOR
b Indianapolis, Ind. *Study:* Howard Terpning, Cowboy Artists of Am, student. *Comn:* paintings (22), Virgins River Hotel / Casino. *Exhib:* Auction of Original Western Art, C M Russel Mus, Great Falls, Mont, 84; Mem Westert Art Show, George Phippen Mus, Prescott, Ariz, 84; Women Artists Am West, PaJo's Gallery, Pinedale, Wyo, 85; 8th Ann Nat Western Art Show, Burk Gallery, Boulder City, Nev, 85; Artists Invitational Exhib, C M Russel Mus, Great Falls, Mont, 86; Native Am Indian Art Competition, Las Vegas Art Mus, Nev, 94; 43rd Ann Art Roundup, Las Vegas Art Mus, Nev, 95; Nat Fine Arts Competition, Braithwaite Fine Arts Gallery, Cedar City, Utah, 99; Navarro Gallery, Sedona, Ariz, 2002; Providence Gallery, Scottsdale, Ariz, 2006. *Collection Arranged:* White House, Washington, DC; Nev Nat Bank, Las Vegas; Virgin River Casino/Hotel, Msquite, Nev. *Teaching:* instr oil pianting, Las Vegas Art Mus, Nev, 83-85. *Awards:* Best of Show award, Native Am Indian Art Inst, Las Vegas, Nev, 94; Judges award, 43rd Ann Art Roundup, Las Vegas, Nev, 95; Gold Medal Award, Best Oil, Bosque Conservatory 16th Ann Art Competition, 2001. *Bibliog:* illusr, Winter Rage, 91 & The Horsemen, 92, Putnam Berkley. *Mem:* Oil Painters Am. *Media:* Oil. *Publ:* Vivian Woods (auth), Arts & Artists, Las Vegas Sun, 82; Vivian Woods (auth), Artist Thrives on Diet of Travel, Paint, LAs Vegas, Review J, 86; Bill Hollis (auth), Emerging Artists, Southwest Art Mag, 96. *Dealer:* LMR Gallery 2470 Silver Sage Dr Pahrump Nev 89060; Navarro Gallery Tlaquepaque Ste D103 336 Hwy 179 Sedona AZ 86336; Tribal Treasures Gallery Green Tree Inn 14173 Green Tree Blvd Victorville CA 92392; Inspirations Gallery 165 N Main St Lakeport CA 95453. *Mailing Add:* 2470 Silver Sage Dr Pahrump NV 89060

SULLIVAN, BILL
PAINTER, PRINTMAKER
b New Haven, Conn, Sept 10, 1942. *Study:* Silvermine Col Art, 60-65; Univ Pa Grad Sch Fine Arts, MFA, 68. *Work:* Cleveland Mus Art, Ohio; Mus City New York; Reading Mus, Pa; Metrop Mus Art, NY Pub Libr, NY; Hudson River Mus, NY, Albany Inst of History & Art. *Exhib:* Solo exhibs, Siegal Contemp Art, 81, David Findlay Jr Gallery, 84, G W Einstein, 86 & 89 & Schreiber Cutler, 86, NY; Painting Calif: Five NY Artists Look at Los Angeles & Plein Air Painting: Capturing the Moment, Tatistcheff Gallery, Santa Monica, Calif, 90; Land/Sea/Air, Steven Scott Gallery, Baltimore, Md, 90; Pa Prints: 30 Yrs of Printmaking at the Univ Pa, Arthur Ross Gallery, Philadelphia, Pa, 90; Uptown Gallery, NY, 96; Sch House Ctr, Provinceton, Mass, 99; St Charles Gallery, Hudson NY, 2002; Roxbury Art Group Roxbury NY, 2005; Albany Inst of Hist & Art, (retrospective exhib 2006). *Awards:* Premio Quirama, Inst de Integracion Cult, Medelin, Colombia, 79; Ingram Merrill Found Fel, 81; Nat Endowment Arts Fel, 90; Futhermore Found, 2006. *Bibliog:* John Arthur (auth), The Spirit of Place: Am Landscape Painting, 90; Lori Simmons Zelinko (auth), Bill Sullivan's Reality, Am Artist, 10/90; Ilene Miles (auth), Art in Am, 12/96; Jamie Mamtique (auth) Bill Sullivan, The Ground water Press 2006. *Media:* Oil on Canvas, Pastel. *Mailing Add:* 526 Prospect St Hudson NY 12534-2218

SULLIVAN, BILLY
ARTIST
b NYC, 46. *Study:* Sch Vis Arts, NY, Ed, 1968. *Exhib:* One-man shows: Fischbach Gallery, NY, 1986, 1989, 1990, 1992, 1997; Rebecca Ibel Gallery, 1994, 1998, 2000, 2001; Photographs, New Mus Contemp Art, NY, 2002; New Work, Nicole Klagsbrun, NY, 2003; North Fork/South Fork: EastEnd Art Now, Parrish Art Mus South Hampton, 2004; Galleria Francesca Kaufmann, Milan, Italy, 2005; group shows: Face Value: Am Portraits, Parrish Art Mus, 1995; Summer 1996; Rebecca Ibel Gallery, 1996; Sex/Industry Stefan Stux Gallery, NY, 1997; Summer, Lennon, Weinberg, Inc, NY, 1998; Couples, Cheim & Read Gallery, NY, 2000; Reflection, 2001; Summertime, 2002; Ten Years in Columbus: Part 3, 2003; Fabulous, 2005; Whitney Biennial: Day for Night, Whitney Mus Am Art, NY, 2006. *Mailing Add:* c/o Rebecca Ibel Gallery 1055 N High St Columbus OH 43201

SULLIVAN, CONNIE C
PHOTOGRAPHER
b Cincinnati, Ohio. *Study:* Manhattanville Col, BA, Purchase, NY. *Work:* Mus Nat D'Art Mod, Ctr Georges Pompidou, Paris, France; Mus Photog Arts, San Diego; Denver Art Mus; Boston Mus Fine Arts; Munchner Stadtmuseum Fotomuseum, Munich, Ger; and many others. *Exhib:* Solo exhibs, Cleveland Ctr Contemp Art, Ohio, 82, Fogg Mus, Harvard Univ, Cambridge, Mass, 83 & 90, Contemp Arts Ctr, Cincinnati, Ohio, 83, Evanston Art Ctr, Ill, 87, Silver Image Galler, Ohio State Univ, Columbus, 88, David Winton Bell Gallery, Brown Univ, Providence, RI, 89 & Rochester Inst Technol, NY, 91; Univ Ky Art Mus, Lexington, 93; Checkwood Mus Art, Nashville, Tenn, 94; Inst d'Estudis Fotografics de Catalunya, Barcelona, Spain, 94; Univ Notre Dame Photog Gallery, Ind, 95; Louisville Visual Art Asn, Water Tower, Ky, 95; Mus Damy di Fotografia Contemp, Brescia, Italy, 95; Jean-Pierre Lambert Gallerie, Paris, France, 96; Ctr Photog Art Form, Bombay, India, 97; Mus Damy, Milano, Italy, 97; Miami Univ Art Mus, Oxford, Ohio, 98; and many others. *Teaching:* Lectr, Univ Kentucky Art Mus, Lexington, 93; Dennison Univ Sch Art, Gambier, Ohio, 93; El Instituto de Estudios Norte Americanos, Barcelona, Spain, 94. *Awards:* National Endowment for the Arts Fel Midwest, 89-90; Purchase Award, Pres Coun Arts, Manhattanville, Col, NY, 91; 1996 Person of the Year, Hyde Park Living, Cincinnati, 96. *Bibliog:* National Centre for the Performing Arts Programmes (exhib catalog), Bombay, India, 11/97; Article in Cincinnati Enquirer, 11/1/98; Guide de la Photographie'en France et en Europe, Photographie a Paris, 11/96. *Publ:* Auth, Petroglyphs of the Heart, Photographs by Connie Sullivan, Morgan & Morgan, 83. *Dealer:* Jean-Pierre Lambert Galerie Paris France; Witkin Gallery New York NY

SULLIVAN, DAVID FRANCIS
PAINTER, PRINTMAKER
b Stoughton, Mass. *Study:* Univ NH, 57-61; Chouinard Sch Fine Arts, Los Angeles, Calif; Boston Mus Fine Arts Sch. *Work:* Addison Gallery Am Art, Andover, Mass; Montreal Mus Art; Philadelphia Mus Art, Pa; Cleveland Mus, Ohio; Minn Mus Art, St Paul; Fogg Art Mus, Cambridge, Mass. *Exhib:* Twenty-Fifth Nat Exhib Prints, Smithsonian Inst, 77; Nat Print Exhib, Trenton State Col, NJ, 78; Art of the State, Hayden Gallery, Mass Inst Technol, Cambridge, 78; Printmaking Biennial, Brooklyn

Mus, NY, 78; Recent Trends in Am Printmaking, Mitchell Mus, 79; New Am Still Life, Westmoreland Co Mus Art, Greensburg, Pa, 79; Genovese Gallery, Boston, 94. *Awards:* Purchase Awards, De Cordova Mus, 76 & Trenton State Col, 78; Stuart M Egnal Prize, Philadelphia Mus Art, 77; Blanche E Coleman Found Grants, 80, 81 & 82. *Bibliog:* Pamela Allara (auth), New Editions, Artnews, 9/82. *Media:* Oils; Silkscreens, Drawings. *Dealer:* Genovese/Sullivan Boston MA. *Mailing Add:* 94 N Main St Andover MA 01810-3515

SULLIVAN, FRANCOISE
PAINTER, SCULPTOR
b Montreal, Que, June 10, 25. *Study:* Ecole des Beaux Arts de Montreal; modern Dance, New Dance Group, New York City. *Hon Degrees:* Hon Doctorate, York Univ, Toronto, 1998; Hon Doctorate UQAM, 2000. *Work:* Nat Gallery, Ottawa; Le Mus d'Art Contemporain, Montreal; La Banque d'Art du Can; Univ Sask; and others. *Comn:* Sculpture, Toronto City Hall, comn by City of Toronto, Ont, 67; sculpture, Expo '67, & Les Jeux Olympiques (artwork), 76, comn by City of Montreal; Corridart 1976-; UQAM 1995 for the Science Bldg. *Exhib:* Art and Engineering, Art Gallery Ont, Toronto, 65; 11th Biennial, Middleheim, Anvers, Belg, 71; Su Proust, Arte Studio, Brescia, Italy, 74; Chi E Pandora, Galleria Unimedia, Genova, Italy, 81; retrospective (with catalog), Mus d'Art Contemporain, Montreal, 81; Montreal Painting, A Second Look, Mem Univ Art Gallery, St Johns, Nfld, 85; Le Musée Imaginaire, Saidye Bronfman Ctr, Montreal, 86; Station, Centre Int d'Art Contemp, 87, Consenses et Contestation, 92, L'Anarchie resplendissaute de la peinture, Galerie de l'UQAM, Montreal, 92; Kunst aus Canada, Galerie Clara Maria Sels, Dusseldorf, Ger, 92; Presence quebecoise, Chateau de Biron, Dordogne, France, 92; La Ferme du Buisson, Marne La Vallee, France, 92; Naissauce et persistance de la sculpture, Mus de Que, 92; Ten yrs of painting, traveling exhib, Quebec, 96; solo exhibs, Univesite Libre de Brussels, Belg, 97 & Lillian Rodriquez Gallery, 98, UQAM Gallery, 98; Saint-Hilaire and the automatistes, Mus Mont Saint-Hilaire, 97; Epopee automatistle, Monteal Contemp Mus, 98; Ecstasy, Jack Shainman Gallery, NY, 98; Eclat de Rouge Gallery, UQAM, 1998; Sullivan/Ferron, Domaine Cataraqui, Quebec City, 99; Mirages Du Nord, Maisons Hamel-Bruneau, Quebec City, 99; Retrospective, Mus des Beaux Arts de Mtl, 2003; Le Touche de la Picture UQAM Gallery, 2004; Ron Moore Gallery, Toronto, 2004; Bruxelles Univ Libre, 2005. *Pos:* Instructor; York Univ 1998, anniversary of the Refus Global Concordia & UQAM on the force of Painting; Goodby Monsieur Duchump, The Royal Soc, 2004. *Teaching:* Conf presenter, conceptual art, Univ Que, Montreal, 75; instr drawing & painting, Concordia Univ, Montreal, 77-. *Awards:* Maurice Cullen Prize 1943-Prixdu Que for sculpture 1963; Martin Lynch Staunten Award, Can Coun, 84; Prix Borduas, 87-; Royal Acad Arts, 92; The Govenor General Prize, 2005. *Bibliog:* Manon Lapointe (auth), Francoise Sullivan: Renouer avec la presence du passe, ETC, spring, 88; Claire Gravel (auth), Francoise Sullivan: La parole retrouvee, Vie des Arts, 03/88; Gilles Daigneault (auth), L'Art au Quebec depuis Pellan-une histoire des prix Borduas, Mus du Que, 05/88; Les Femmes du Refus global Patricia Sniayt; Borduas, Sullivan, Riopelle, Louise Vignaut; From Automatism to Modern Dance, FS; With Franziska Boas in New York, 2003, by Allana Lindgren. *Mem:* Vehicule Art Inc; Montreal Art Coun-Beena Ellen Gallery Concordia Univ. *Media:* All media, Painting. *Specialty:* Painting. *Interests:* Art, Conversation, Friends, Swimming. *Publ:* Auth, Poeme, Da Vinci, Montreal, No 2, p 64, 74; Peiripheiries (exhib catalog), Mus d'Art Contemp-Vehicule Art Inc, Montreal, 74; Francoise Sullivan & David Moore (auths), Textes de F Sullivan et de D Moore, et Texte Commun des Deux Artistes (exhib catalog), Galerie Vehicule Art, Montreal, 77; Good by Monsieur Duchamp, Les Ecrits, 2005. *Dealer:* Ron Moore, Toronto. *Mailing Add:* 2358 Hingston Montreal PQ H4A 2J2 Canada

SULLIVAN, JIM
PAINTER
b Providence, RI, Apr 1, 39. *Study:* RI Sch Design, BFA, 61, Stanford Univ, 62-63. *Work:* Whitney Mus Am Art, NY; Wadsworth Atheneum, Hartford, Conn; Metrop Mus, NY; Amerado Hess, NY; Owens Corning, Toledo, Ohio; Phillip Morris, NY. *Exhib:* NY Painting Today, Three Rivers Festival, Pittsburgh, 83; Dart Gallery, Chicago, 84; Bayly Art Mus, Charlottesville, Va, 88; Queens Mus, NY, 88; Anne Jaffe Gallery, Bay Harbor Islands, Fla, 90; Nancy Hoffman Gallery, New York City, 2004; and others. *Teaching:* Prof painting, Bard Col, 65-95, now prof emeritus. *Awards:* Fulbright Fel, Paris, 61-62; Guggehiem Award, 72; Rosenthal Award, Am Acad Arts & Letters, 73; Nat Endowment Arts Grant, 83. *Bibliog:* Kay Larson (auth), article, NY Mag, 1/19/81; Vivian Raynor (auth), article, NY Times, 1/9/81; Gerrit Henry (auth), Rev, Art in America, 10/86; and others; Ken Johnson (auth), Rev NY Times, 12/24/04. *Mem:* Schoharie Land Trust. *Media:* Oil on Canvas, wood panel & aluminum. *Publ:* Empire State Collection, Art for the Public, Tiffany Bell, 87; American Still Life, Linda Cathcart, 83; New York Painting Today, Donald Kuspit, 83; Diamonds are Forever, Peter Gordon, 87. *Dealer:* Nancy Hoffman 429 W Broadway New York NY 10012. *Mailing Add:* 59 Wooster St New York NY 10013

SULLIVAN, JUNEANN MARGARET
PAINTER, GALLERY DIRECTOR
b Princeton, NJ. *Study:* Winthrop Col, BFA, 63; NY Univ, MFA, 65; studies with Betty Lou Schlemm, 74-76 & Frank Webb, 84-85. *Exhib:* Artworks, Ellarslie Mus, Trenton, NJ, 88; Nat Arts Club 89th Ann Open Watercolor, NY, 89; NW Pastel Soc Juried Exhib, Seattle, Wash, 90; Women History Month, Paterson Mus, NJ, 91; Nat Asn Women Artists Exhib, NY, 91 & 92; Catherine Lorillard Wolfe Ann Exhib, NY, 93; NE Watercolor Soc Ann Exhib, Goshen, NY, 94. *Pos:* Porcelain designer, Edward Marshall Boehm Co, Trenton, NJ, 64-68; chmn bd dir, Piermont Fine Arts Gallery, NY, 93-; co-founder & art consult, Cat Sullivan Gallery, Suffern, NY, 94-. *Teaching:* Arts & crafts, Hopewell Valley Sch, Pennington, NJ, 75-78. *Awards:* Board of Directors Award, Catherine Lorillard Wolfe, 89; Irwin Zlowe Mem Award, Nat Asn Women Artists, 91; President's Award, Northeast Watercolor Soc, 91. *Bibliog:* Elizabeth Case (auth), June Sullivan translates life into art, Tuckerton Times-Beacon, 8/94. *Mem:* Nat Asn Women Artists; NE Watercolor Soc; Oil Pastel Asn Int; United Pastelists Am; Arts Coun Rockland Co, NY. *Media:* Watercolor, Monoprints. *Publ:* Contribr, The Encyclopedia of Printmaking Techniques, Quatro Publ, 93; cover artist, The Literary Review, Fairleigh Dickinson Univ, 95. *Mailing Add:* 115 Water St Tuckerton NJ 08087

SULLIVAN, PATRICE MAUREEN
ARTIST
b Portland, Ore, Aug 25, 53. *Study:* Mass Col Art, BFA, 83; Univ Pa, MFA, 86. *Exhib:* one-woman show, Somerville Mus, Mass, 90; Domestic Landscape, Sullivan Co Mus, Hurleyville, NY, 95; Boston Printmakers Show, Duxburg Art Mus, Mass, 97. *Teaching:* Lectr, Harvard Univ, Cambridge, Mass, 89-91; Prof Painting, Colo State Univ, 91-. *Awards:* World Trade Ctr Residency, Lower Manhattan Cult Coun, 1997-98. *Mem:* The Boston Printmakers. *Publ:* Diane Sophrin (auth), Reconstructing of Femenist, 98; Visions and Voices of Our Time, Harvard Libr Rev, 98. *Mailing Add:* PO Box 974 Estes Park CO 80517

SULLIVAN, RONALD DEE
SCULPTOR, EDUCATOR, LECTURER
b Norman, Okla, Feb 6, 39. *Study:* Univ Okla, BFA, 63; Calif State Univ, Sacramento, MA, 69; ETex State Univ, postgrad. *Work:* NY Pub Libr; Art Mus South Tex; Calif State Univ; Delmar Col, Tex; Mary and Kathleen Kenned Collection. *Exhib:* Retrospective exhib, Joseph A Cain Gallery, 2000; Philbrook Art Inst, Temple Univ, 2000; Cheltewham Art Ctr, Phila; Art Mus South Tex, Corpus Christi. *Pos:* Conservator, var pub & pvt collections, 89-; designer, lectr, writer, currently. *Teaching:* Prof sculpture, drawing, Del Mar Col, Corpus Christi, 69-2001. *Awards:* Fac Develop Grant, Del Mar Col, 89-92; NISOD Excellence Award, Univ Tex, Austin, 93. *Bibliog:* The Mystery and Magic of Glass, Channel 16, Corpus Christi, Tex, 78; Ron George (auth), Red Earth Images, Caller-Times, 92; Carey Rote (auth) Caller-Times, 93; Leakey Star (auth), Penny McGuire, 2005. *Media:* All Media. *Specialty:* Repesntational, abstract sculpture, painting and drawing. *Publ:* Auth, Hillabee to Weogufkee, Del Mar Col, 89; Jane Beckman, restoring a queen, The Rotarian, 1/92; Projection into Imagery (video tape), 1980; Del Mar Col Sculpting a Portrait in Clay, 1998. *Dealer:* Connie L Sullivan

SULLIVAN, RUTH WILKINS
CURATOR, AUTHOR
b Boston, Mass, Nov 20, 26. *Study:* Wellesley Col, AB. *Collection Arranged:* Chinese Export Porcelain, 65; American Painting from 1830 (with catalog), 65; Chinese Art from the Cloud Wampler Collection (with catalog), 68; Wealth of the Ancient World: The Nelson Bunker Hunter & William Herbert Hunt Collections (with catalog), 83. *Pos:* Admin asst, Everson Mus Art, 58-60, registr, 60-62, cur & ed publ, 63-70, cur collections, 66-70; consult, Mus Am China Trade, 71; cur educ, Kimbell Art Mus, 71-82, res cur, 83-2006, emeritus res cur. *Awards:* Woman Achievement Arts, Post Stand, 68. *Mem:* Col Art Asn. *Res:* Early Italian painting. *Publ:* Auth, Saints Peter & Paul: Some Ironic Aspects of Their Imaging, Art Hist, 94; Hospitality to the Divine Stranger in Jacopo Bassano's Supper to Emmaus, Source, 94; Cracking the Egg: Jacopo Bassano's Supper at Emmaus, Source, 95; Three Ferrarese panels on the theme of 'Death Rather than Dishonor' and the Neapolitan connection, Zeitschrift fur Kunstgeschichte, Vol 57, No 4, 610-625, 94; The Wilton Diptych: mysteries, majesty, and a complex exchange of faith and power, Gazette des Beaux-Arts, 1-17, 1/97. *Mailing Add:* 5031 Pershing Ave Ft Worth TX 76107-4897

SULLIVAN, SCOTT A
HISTORIAN, EDUCATOR
b Cleveland, Ohio, May 22, 47. *Study:* John Carroll Univ, BA, 69; Case Western Reserve Univ, MA, 72, PhD, 78. *Teaching:* Asst prof art hist, Univ NTex, 75-81, assoc prof, 81-87, prof, 87-96, chmn dept, 87-92, actg dean, 92-93, assoc dean, 93-96; dean fine arts, Kent State Univ, 96-99. *Mem:* Historians of Netherlandish Art; Col Art Asn Am; Midwest Art Hist Soc (secy-treas, 85-87, pres, 87-89); Am Asn Netherlandic Studies; Nat Coun Art. *Res:* 17th century Flemish and Dutch painting, especially still life. *Publ:* In the Shadow of Caravaggio: Pietro Paolini's Bacchic Concert, Dallas Mus Art Bull, 85; Abraham van Beyeren's Visserij bord at the Groote Kerk, Maassluis Oud Holland, 87; Auth, Still Life with a Dead Hore by Jan Weenix & Pantry Scene with a Serving Figure, 90; Dictionary of Art and Artists, Vol 2, St James Press, London, 90; Auth, Dictionary of Art, MacMillan Publ, Ltd, London, 96. *Mailing Add:* Kent State Univ Dean Fine & Prof Arts 204 Taylor Hall Kent OH 44242

SULTAN, ALTOON
PAINTER
b Brooklyn, NY, Sept 29, 48. *Study:* Brooklyn Col, BA, 69, MFA, 71, study with Phillip Pearlstein; Boston Univ at Tanglewood, 69; Skowhegan Sch Painting & Sculpture, study with Gabriel Laderman, 70. *Work:* Hunter Mus, Chattanooga, Tenn; Yale Univ Art Gallery; Metrop Mus Art, NY; Nat Acad Design, NY; Hunter Mus, Chattanooga, Tenn; Metrop Mus Art, NY; Mus Fine Arts, Boston; Nat Mus Women in the Arts, Washington, DC. *Exhib:* One-woman shows, Marlborough Gallery, 77, 79, 81, 84, 85, 88, 90, 93, 95 & 98, Middendorf Gallery, Washington, 87 & Hokin-Kaufman Gallery, Chicago, 90; A Private Vision: Contemp Art from the Graham Gund Collection, Boston Mus Fine Arts, Mass, 82; Lower Manhattan from Street to Sky, Whitney Mus Am Art, 82; Small Pictures, New Brit Mus Am Art, 82; Painted Light, Reading Pub Mus, Butler Inst Am Art, 83; Am Realism: 20th Century Drawings & Watercolors, San Francisco Mus Mod Art, 85; The Landscape in 20th Century Am Art: Selections from the Metrop Mus Art, Philbrook Mus Art, Tulsa, Okla; and others; Community of Creativity: A Century of MacDowell Colory Artists, Wichita Art Mus, nat Acad Design, 96-97; Post-Pastoral: New Images of New Eng

Landscape, Hood Mus Art, 98; Green Woods and Crystal Waters: The Am Landscape Tradition, Philbrook Mus Art, Ringling Mus Art, Davenport Mus Art. *Teaching:* Vis critic, Univ Pa, Philadelphia, 85-88; Resident fac, Skowhegan Sch Painting & Sculpture, 88; asst prof, San Jose State Univ, Calif, 91-94; vis prof, Dartmouth Col, 98-2001. *Awards:* Yaddo Fel, 75 & 76; Nat Endowment Arts Fel Grant, 83 & 89; Acad Award in Art, Am Acad Arts & Letters, 99; Docde Valverde d'Ayala Valva Prize, Found Vionaco, 99. *Bibliog:* John Arthur (auth), The remembrance of tranquility: Altoon Sultan's new paintings, Arts Mag, 3/84; Articles and reviews in NY Times, Art News & Art Week, 85-98. *Mem:* Nat Acad (acad, 95-). *Media:* Oil, Egg tempera. *Publ:* Culture/Cultivation: Thoughts on Painting the Landscape, Art Jour, 98; the Luminous Brush: Painting with ESS Tempera, Watson-Guptill Pubs, 99. *Dealer:* Tibor de Nagy 724 Fifth Ave New York NY 10019. *Mailing Add:* PO Box 2 Groton VT 05046

SULTAN, DONALD K
PAINTER, PRINTMAKER

b Asheville, NC, May 5, 51. *Study:* Univ NC, Chapel Hill, BFA, 73; Art Inst Chicago, MFA, 75. *Hon Degrees:* Corcoran Sch Arts, D (fine arts); PhD, Corcoran Sch of Art, Washington, DC, 00; PhD NY Acad Art, 02. *Work:* High Mus Art; Dallas Mus Fine Arts; Albright-Knox Art Gallery, Buffalo, NY; Whitney Mus Am Art, Guggenheim Mus, Mus Mod Art, NY; La Jolla Mus, Calif; Walker Art Ctr, Minneapolis; Art Inst Chicago; Kitakyushu Munic Mus Art, Tobataku Kitakyushu, Japan. *Comn:* Absolut Sultan ad, Absolut Vodka; Artótel Budapest, Park Plaza Worldwide, 2000. *Exhib:* Prints from Blocks--Gaugin to Now, Mus Mod Art, NY, 83; Boston Mus Fine Arts, 83; Boston Collects: Contemp Painting & Sculpture, Mus Fine Arts, Mass, 86; New Romantic Landscape, Whitney Mus Am Art, Stanford, Conn, 87; solo exhib, Mus Mod Art, 88; Projects and Portfolios: 25th Nat Print exhib, Brooklyn Mus, NY, 89; Art Inst Chicago (with catalog), 92; Nassau Co Mus (with catalog), Roslyn Harbor, NY, 92; Tucson Mus Art, Ariz, 92; Bibliotheque Nationale (with catalog), Paris, France, 92; Nat Galerie, Berlin, Ger, 93; Nat Mus Art, Smithsonian Inst, Washington, DC, 95; Thinking Print (with catalog), Mus Mod Art, NY, 96; Jewish Mus, NY, 98; one-man show, Brooke Mus, Memphis, Tenn, 2000, Corcoran Gallery Art, Washington, DC, 2000, Kemper Mus Contemp Art, Kansas City, Mo, 2000, Polk Mus Art, Lakeland, Fla, 2000, Scottsdale Mus Contemp Art, Ariz, 2000; Baldwin Gallery, Aspen, Colo, 01; Louise Wells Cameron Mus, Wilmington, NC, 02; Knoedler & Co, NY, 03. *Teaching:* Lectr, Greenberg Gallery, St Louis, Mo, 89; lectr, Meadows Sch Arts, 89; lectr, Hirshhorn Mus & Sculpture Garden, Washington, DC, 89. *Awards:* Creative Artists Pub Serv Grant, 78-79; Nat Endowment Arts State Grant, 80-81. *Media:* Tar, Spackle. *Dealer:* Knoedler & Co Inc 19 E 70th St New York NY 10021; Ameringer Yohe Fine Art, 20 W 57th St, NY, 10019. *Mailing Add:* 74 Franklin St New York NY 10013

SULTAN, LARRY A
PHOTOGRAPHER, EDUCATOR

b New York, NY, July 13, 46. *Study:* Univ Calif, BA, 68; San Francisco Art Inst, MFA, 73. *Work:* Chase Manhattan Bank, Mus Mod Art & Metrop Mus Art, NY; Art Inst Chicago; Birmingham Mus Art; J Paul Getty Mus, Los Angeles; Bibliotheque Nationale, Paris, France; and others. *Comn:* Plexiglas map, Atlantic Richfield Co, Los Angeles, 79; Constitution Wall, Calif State Arch Found, 92-93; Market Street Art in Transit Prog, San Francisco Art Comn, 92-93; DeFremery Pool Enhancement, City of Oakland, Calif, 92-93. *Exhib:* Contemp Photog, Fogg Art Mus, Harvard Univ, Cambridge, 76; San Francisco Mus Mod Art, 77; one-man shows, Fogg Art Mus, Harvard Univ, Cambridge, 78, San Jose Mus Art, 92, Mus Contemp Art, 94, Chicago Cult Ctr, 94, Corcoran Gallery Art, Washington, 94 & 95, Scottsdale Ctr Arts, 95 & Bronx Mus Art, 96; Beyond Color, San Francisco Mus Mod Art, 82; Color As Form: A Hist of Color Photog, Corcoran Gallery Art, Washington, 82; Photog in Calif: 1945-1975 (with catalog), San Francisco Mus Mod Art, 84; Signs of the Times, San Francisco Mus Mod Art, 85; New Color Photog, Mus Mod Art, NY, 85; Calif Photog: Remaking Make-Believe (with catalog), Mus Mod Art, NY, 89; Real Life Fictions: Photographs of Bill Dane, John Harding & Larry Sultan, San Francisco Mus Mod Art, 89; Re: Memory, The Work of Lorie Novak, George Krause, Larry Sultan & Anne Turyn, Birmingham Mus Art, Ala, 90; Pleasures & Terrors of Domestic Comfort (with catalog), Mus Mod Art, NY, 91; Summer Selection, Metrop Mus Art, NY, 91; Photog As Idea: Conceptual Photog of the 60's & 70's, San Francisco Mus Mod Art, 91; Death & the Family, Presentation House Centre Visual & Performing Arts, Vancouver, 95; We Look & See, Univ Art Mus, Berkeley, 95; A Selection of Photog by Gallery Artists, Stephen Wirtz Gallery, San Francisco, 95; Home Is Where, Weatherspoon Art Gallery, Greensboro, NC, 95; To Keep Her Countenance, Stephen Wirtz Gallery, San Francisco, 96; The Familial Gaze, Hood Mus Art, Dartmouth Col, Hanover, NH, 96; People in Real Life, Stoneridge Mall, Pleasantville, Calif, 97. *Teaching:* Instr photog, Univ Calif, Berkeley, 73-78 & San Francisco Art Inst, 78-; asst prof art, Lone Mountain Col, 74-78; prof, Calif Col Arts & Crafts. *Awards:* Photog Fel, Nat Endowment Arts, 86 & 92; Pub Arts Award, Oakland Cult Arts, 90; Louis Comfort Tiffany Fel, 91. *Bibliog:* Vicki Goldberg (auth), The snapshot, history's modest helper, NY Times, 6/16/96; Jolene Thym (auth), A perfect exhibit for an imperfect world, Valley Herald, 8/9/97; Donna Graves (auth), People in real life suburbia, Sculpture, 4/98. *Publ:* Pictures From Home, Harry N Abrams Inc, New York, 92. *Mailing Add:* c/o Stephen Wirtz Gallery 49 Geary St San Francisco CA 94108

SULTAN, TERRIE FRANCES
MUSEUM DIRECTOR

b Asheville, NC, Oct 28, 52. *Study:* Syracuse Univ, BFA, 73; John F Kennedy Univ, MA, 85. *Collection Arranged:* Corcoran Biennial #42, 91; #43, 93: #44, 95; Ida Apple Broog, 10 yr survey, 98, DAP; Corcoran Biennial #45, Retrospective of works collected, 98; Radcliffe Bailey: Tides, 2002; Chuck Close Prints, Retrospective of 30 yr career, Book PU Press, 2003; Angela Graverholz: Reading Room, 2003; Jessica Stockholder, 15 yr survey, 2004, DAP. *Pos:* Cur Contemp Art, Corcoran Gallery Art, Washington, DC, 88-99; Dir Blaffer Gallery, Art Mus Univ Houston, Tex, 2000-. *Teaching:* Critique, Md Inst, Baltimore, 98. *Awards:* Chevalier Order Arts and Letters, 2003. *Mem:* AAM; Coll Art Asn; Internat Asn Art Critics. *Res:* preparation of survey 20 year survey of work by James Surls. *Publ:* Donald Lipski: Brief History of Twine, Madison Art Ctr/DAP, 2000; Seeing & Believing: Art of Nancy Burson, Twin Palms Press, 2002; Chuck Close Prints: Progress & Collaboration, Princeton Univ Press, 2003; Bob Knox: Non Fiction Paintings, Blaffer Gallery, 2003; Jessica Stockholder: Kissing the wall, Blaffer Gallery/DAP, 2004. *Mailing Add:* Univ Houston Blaffer Gallery 120 Fine Arts Bldg Houston TX 77204-4018

SUMMER, (EMILY) EUGENIA
PAINTER

b Newton, Miss, June 13, 23. *Study:* Miss Univ for Women, BS; Columbia Univ, MA; Art Inst Chicago; Calif Col Arts & Crafts; Penland Sch Crafts, NC; Seattle Univ. *Hon Degrees:* Hon Doc Art & Humane Letters, Mississippi Univ Women, 2005. *Work:* Miss Mus Art & First Nat Bank, Jackson; Nat Bank Commerce Collection, Columbus, Miss; First Nat Bank, Laurel, Miss; First Miss Nat Bank, Hattiesburg; Missssissippi Mus Art, Jackson, MS; Personal Col Wilhelmina Cole Holladay, bd chair, Nat Mus, Women in the Arts. *Exhib:* Delta Ann Exhib, Ark Art Ctr, Little Rock, 60, 62-63, 74 & 82; Art in Embassies Prog, US State Dept, Rio de Janeiro, Brazil, 66-67; Eighth Decade: Painters Choice, Ga Col Milledgeville, 71; 5th Greater New Orleans Int Art Exhib, 75; Nat Asn Painters Acrylic & Casein, Nat Arts Club, NY, 80. *Pos:* Bd dir, Southeastern Col Art Conf, 81-83. *Teaching:* Prof art, Miss Univ Women, 50-, head div fine & performing arts, 82-86, emer prof, 86-. *Awards:* Dumas Milner Purchase Award, Nat Watercolor Exhib, Jackson, 62, Jurors Award, 68; Purchase Prizes, Lauren Rogers Mus Exhib & Miss Southern Univ Exhib; Award of Merit, Miss Mus Art, 83. *Bibliog:* Patti Carr Black (auth), Art in Mississippi, Heritage Miss series, Vol I), Univ Miss Press, 1998. *Mem:* Col Art Asn Am; Phi Kappa Phi; Miss State Comt; Nat Mus Women in the Arts. *Media:* Acrylic, Watercolor, Alkyd. *Mailing Add:* 915 5th Ave S Columbus MS 39701

SUMMER, EVAN D
ARTIST

b Buffalo, NY, Sept 26, 48. *Study:* State Univ of NY, Cortland, BS in Chemistry, 70; State Univ of NY, Buffalo, BFA, 73; Yale Univ, MFA in Printmaking, 75. *Exhib:* Exhib in group shows at Chongqing and Tianjin Arts Col, Tianjin, People's Republic of China, 1986, Pa Acad Fine Arts, 1987, Brooklyn Mus, 1989, Hewlett Gallery, Carnegie-Mellon Univ, Pittsburgh, 1991, Int Print Triennale and Intergrafia, Krakow, Poland, Katowice, Poland, 1991, 1st Egyptian Int Print Tirennale, 1993, Corcoran Gallery of Art, Washington, DC, 2005; solo shows, Corcoran Gallery Art, Washington, DC, 99-2000, State Univ NY, Col at Cortland, NY, 2000, Reading Public Mus, Reading, Pa, 2001 & 2005, The Arts Club of Washington, Washington, DC, 2003, Cosmos Club, Washington, DC, 2003; Rep in permanent collections Nat Gallery Art, Wash, Corcoran Gallery Art, Brooklyn Mus, Taipei City Mus Fine Arts, Nat Acad of Design, New York City, Metrop Mus Art, NY, Pa Acad Fine Arts, Philadelphia, Nat Mus Am Art, Washington, DC & many others. *Teaching:* Artist-in-residence, Univ Pa, Philadelphia, 1978-88; instr, State Univ NY, Buffalo, 77 & 79, Wesleyan Univ, Middletown, Conn, 78, Tyler Sch Art, Elkins Park, 1979, Pratt Graphics Ctr, New York City, 1983, Kutztown Univ, Pa, 1984-85, asst prof, 1987-91, assoc prof, 1991-94, prof, 1994-. *Awards:* Recipient Berthe von Moschzisker prize, 1982, Juror's award; Pacific States Nat Biennial Print Exhib, Univ Hawaii, 1992; Silver medal, 10th Norwegian Internat Print Triennial, Fredrikstad, Norway, 1992; Tai-he Masterpiece Award, Int Print Biennial, Beijing, 2003; Henry Legrand Cannon Prize, 178th Ann Exhib, Nat Acad Design, 2003. *Mem:* Boston Printmakers, Inter print Triennial Soc, Nat Acad (assoc, 93, acad, 94-). *Media:* Printmaker - Etching, Engraving & Calligraphy. *Collection:* Metropolitan Museum of Art and Achenbach Foundation. *Mailing Add:* Sharadin Art Studio 2AG Kutztown Univ Kutztown PA 19530

SUMMERS, CAROL
PRINTMAKER

b Kingston, NY, Dec 26, 25. *Study:* Bard Col, BA, 51, PhD, 75. *Hon Degrees:* PhD Fine Arts, Bard Col, 74. *Work:* Corcoran Gallery Art, Libr Cong, Nat Gallery, Washington, DC; Metrop Mus Art & Mus Mod Art, NY; Kunstmuseum, Malmö, Sweden; and many others. *Comn:* Posters NY Film Festival, US Park Serv, Ojai Festival, Venice Biennial and many others. *Exhib:* One-person shows, Mus Mod Art, NY, 64-66, AAA Gallery, NY, 67 & Bard Col, 68; Retrospective, San Francisco Mus Art, Calif, 67; 20th Nat Print Exhib, Brooklyn Mus, 77; ADI Gallery, 77; plus others. *Pos:* folk art and textiles tour leader, to Rajasthan, India, winters 1995-2004. *Teaching:* Instr, Brooklyn Mus Sch Art, 54, Pratt Graphic Art Ctr, 62, Hunter Col, 63, Sch Visual Arts, New York, 65, Pa State Univ, 68, Columbia Univ, New York, 69 & San Francisco Art Inst, 73; US Info Serv tour of India, 74 & 79. *Awards:* Louis Comfort Tiffany Found Fels, 55 & 60; Guggenheim Found Fel, 59; Coun Int Exchange Scholars Grant, res India, 93-94; Artist of Yr, Santa Cruz Co Arts Comn, 2001; Outstanding Printmaker award, Mid Am Print Coun, 2004. *Mem:* Print Coun Am (artist adv bd); Print Club Philadelphia; Calif Soc Printmakers; Nat Acad (assoc, 90, acad, 94-); Boston Printmakers. *Media:* Wood. *Publ:* Carol Summers Catalogue Raisonne, 88; Carol Summers Woodcuts, 50 yr Retrospective, 99; A Treasury of Indian Folk Textiles, La Casa de Espiritus Alegres, 02. *Dealer:* Peggity's. *Mailing Add:* 2817 Smith Grade Santa Cruz CA 95060

SUMNER, STEPHEN CHARLES
ADMINISTRATOR, EDUCATOR

b New Haven, Conn, Sept 8, 40. *Study:* Univ Mich, BS(design), 63; Univ Mass, MFA, 67. *Work:* Mills Col, Oakland, Calif; Colgate Univ, Hamilton, NY; Nelson Atkins Mus, Kansas City, Mo; Brooklyn Mus, NY; Potsdam Col, NY. *Exhib:* 15th Nat Print Exhib, Brooklyn Mus, NY, 66; Nat Print Exhib, Providence Art Club, RI, 69;

Albright-Knox Graphic Ann, Albright-Knox Art Gallery, Buffalo, NY, 69; 31st Ann, Munson-Williams-Proctor Mus, Utica, NY, 72; Artist Space Gallery, NY, 77; Peripheral-Vision, Amarillo Fine Arts Ctr, Tex, 91; Philbrook Mus Art, Tulsa, Okla, 94. *Pos:* Dir, Sch Art, Univ Tulsa, 89-94 & Div Fine & Performing Art, 94-2001; Pres, Rocky Mountain Coll Art & Design, Co. *Teaching:* Prof photog, State Univ NY, Potsdam, 68-89; Provost, New World Sch Art, Miami, 2001-03. *Awards:* Fel, Orgn Am States, Guatemala, 74; Fulbright Fel, Peru & Bolivia, 80; The Makers Exhib, State Arts Coun Okla, 91. *Mem:* Found Art, Theory & Educ (pres, 84-93); Col Art Asn Am; Nat Asn Art Adminr; Art Dirs Club Tulsa. *Mailing Add:* Rocky Mountain Coll Art & Design Off of Pre 1600 Pierce St Denver CO 80214

SUN, MAY
SCULPTOR
Study: Univ Calif, Los Angeles, BFA, 76; Otis Art Inst, Los Angeles, MFA, 78-79. *Work:* Mus Contemp Art, Los Angeles, Calif; Ore Art Inst, Portland. *Exhib:* Solo exhibs, B-1 Gallery, Santa Monica, Calif, 89, Mus Contemp Art, Los Angeles, Calif, 89 & 93, Los Angeles Festival, 90, Capp Street Proj, San Francisco, 91, List Visual Arts Ctr, Mass Inst Technol, 91 & Robert Berman Gallery, Santa Monica, 92-93; Southern Calif: The Conceptual Landscape, Madison Art Ctr, 94; Collaborations, Armory Ctr Arts, Pasadena, Calif, 94; Los Angeles Mind Quakes, De Beyerd Ctr Contemp Art, Breda, The Neth, 94; Equal Rights and Justice: Thirty Years and Counting, High Mus Art, 94; Asian Soc Galleries, NY, 94; Pub Interventions, Inst Contemp Art, Boston, 94. *Awards:* Silver Award, Corp Pub Broadcasting, 90; Calif Arts Coun Fel, 92; Nat Endowment Arts Fel, 93. *Bibliog:* Jan Breslauer (auth), Past, present and pc, Los Angeles Times, 12/20/92; James Scarborough (auth), May Sun and her persistence of memory, Visions Art Quart, summer 93; Betty Brown (auth), The color weal, a new American art in Los Angeles, Visions Art Quart, fall 93. *Mailing Add:* 18741 S Bechard Pl Cerritos CA 90703

SUNDBERG, CARL GUSTAVE
ENAMELIST, DIRECTOR
b Erie, Pa, June 23, 28. *Study:* Albright Art Sch, Univ Buffalo, grad; study with Joseph Plavcan, Virginia Cuthbert, Albert Blaustien, Letterio Calipia & Robert Bruce. *Work:* Butler Inst Am Art, Youngstown, Ohio; Tyler Mus Art, Tex; Erie Pub Libr; Erie Art Mus; Albright-Knox Rental Art Gallery; Metropolitan Mus Art, NY; Hunterian Art Gallery, Glasgow, Scotland. *Comn:* Six porcelain panels (mod motif with coins), Mellon Bank, Erie, 69; three porcelain enamel panels, Gannon Resource Ctr, Erie, 73; three enclosure set (Plexiglas-enamel), St Vincent Hosp, Erie, 74. *Exhib:* NPAA Exhibs, 1968-2005; The Cutting Edge, Frye Mus, Seattle, Wash, 92; Am, Can & Europ Enamelist, Kent State Univ & Glass & Ceramic Mus, Toronto, Can, 94; Int Enamel Exhib, Coburg Mus, Ger, 95; Enameling Art in Japan, Tokyo, 96; one-person shows, Hallwalls Contemp Art Ctr, Buffalo, NY, 90, Nina Freudenheim Gallery, Buffalo, NY, 94, Binghamton Univ Art Mus, NY, 97, Milton Weil Gallery, NY, 97, David Anderson Gallery, Buffalo, NY, 2004; group shows, Mona Bismark Found, Paris, 2003, Univ Alberta Print Ctr, Edmonton, Can, 2004, Vose Galleries, Boston, 2004, Susan Teller Gallery, NY, 2005. *Pos:* Art dir, Erie Ceramic Arts Co, 53-; dir, Galerie 8, Erie, 67-74. *Teaching:* Instr painting, Erie Art Ctr, 64-78; enamel screen print workshop, Kent State Univ, 90. *Awards:* Purchase Prize & Hon Mention, Butler Inst Am Art Mid Year Show, 70 & 81; Purchase Prize, Tyler Mus Art 7th Nat Exhib, 70 & Int Enamelist Exhib, Newport, KY, 80; Prize for Non-Traditional, Chautauqua Exhib, 72 & 76; Jurors' Choice Award, Pittsburgh North Hills Exhib, 87; Purchase Award, Int Enamelist Exhib, Newport, Ky, 89. *Bibliog:* Clyde Singer (auth), article, Youngstown Vindicator, 6/28/70; Ada C Turner (auth), article, Chautauqua Daily, 8/17/70; Peggy Krider (auth), Art Demonstration (film), Villa Maria Col, 70. *Mem:* Erie Art Ctr (pres, 67-69); Erie Arts Mus (vpres, 70-71); Pittsburgh Soc of Artists; Northwestern Pa Artist Asn (co-dir); Enamelist Soc, 88. *Media:* Porcelain Enamel, Graphic. *Mailing Add:* 5518 Bondy Dr Erie PA 16509

SUNDBERG, WILDA (REGELMAN)
PAINTER, INSTRUCTOR
b Erie, Pa, Oct 5, 30. *Study:* Albright Art Sch, Univ Buffalo, 49-51; Gannon col, 64-66; Mercyhurst Col, Pa, 78-79; with Al Broulette, Harrisburg, 82; Edinboro Univ, 85 & 86; Tony Couch, Union Deposit, Pa, 86. *Work:* Thiel Col, Greenville, Pa; Erie Pub Libr; Erie Art Mus; Regional Cancer Res Ctr, Erie, Pa; Eat n Park Restaurant Chain, Pa; and others. *Exhib:* Albright-Knox Mem Gallery, Buffalo, 71-2000; one-women show, Waterford Community Ctr, Pa, Thiel Col, Pa, 77, Gannon Univ, Eric, Pa, 76,79,81, & Erie Art Mus, 84; Butler Inst Am Art, Ohio; Counterpoint II, Pittsburgh, Pa, 81; Pa Gov Mansion, Harrisburg, 81-82; McClelland Gallery, Melbourne, Australia, 83; La Roche Col, Pittsburgh, Pa, 85; Access to the Arts, Dunkirk, NY, 85; North Hills, 86-88; Jamestown Community Col, NY, 87; St Vincent Col, Latrobe, Pa 88; Blair Co Arts Festival, Altoona, Pa, 88 & 2000; Aqueous 89 & 91 Nat Watercolor; Lahaina Arts Soc, Maui, Hawaii, 90; one person exhibs, Erie Art Mus, 84 & 92, Gannon Univ, Erie, Pa, 76, 79, 81, Thiel Col, Greenvilla, Pa, 77; Northwest Pa Artist Asn Exhibs, 93-2000. *Teaching:* Instr art, Erie Art Mus, 64-90; instr drawing & painting, Mercyhurst Col, 79-90; Behrend, Pa State Instr Watercolor, Erie Art Mus, 64-2000; Harbor Creek Pub Sch, Enrichment Prog, 90. *Awards:* Chautauqua Nat Watercolor Award, Chautauqua Art Asn, 70; Nat Scholastic Scholar; Award Purchase, North Hills Pittsburgh, Pa. *Mem:* Pittsburgh Watercolor Soc; NW Pa Artist Asn; Watercolor Soc, Pa. *Media:* Transparent Watercolor. *Dealer:* Textures W 8th Erie PA 16503; Kada Gallery 2632 N 8th St Erie PA 16505. *Mailing Add:* 5518 Bondy Dr Erie PA 16509

SUNDBLAD, EMILY
ARTIST, DIRECTOR
Study: Parsons Sch Design, NYC, BFA, 2002. *Exhib:* One-women shows: 1000 Drawings, Artists Space, NYC, 2001; Fine Arts Thesis Exhib, Parsons Sch Design, 2002; Alicia McCarthy New Works, Rare Gallery, NYC, 2002; You're Just a Summer Love But I'll Remember You When Winter Comes, Priska Juschka Fine Art, Brooklyn, 2002; group shows: Whitney Biennial: Day for Night, Whitney Mus Am Art, NYC, 2006. *Pos:* Co-dir, Reena Spauldings Fine Art Gallery, NYC. *Mailing Add:* Reena Spaulings Fine Art 165 E Broadway 2nd Fl New York NY 10002

SUNDERLAND, NITA KATHLEEN
EDUCATOR, SCULPTOR
b Olney, Ill, Nov 9, 27. *Study:* Duke Univ; Bradley Univ, BFA & MA. *Work:* Fed Plaza, Chicago; Civic Ctr, Peoria, Ill. *Comn:* Archit sculpture, Bradley Univ Bookstore, 64, monumental sculpture, Williams Hall Mall, 67; archit sculpture, St John's Cath Church, Woodhull, Ill, 69; stone and bronze sculpture, Ill State Univ, State Ill capital develop bd, 90. *Exhib:* Chicago Mus Without Walls, 78; 31st Ill Invitational, 79; Selections from the Collection of George M Irwin, 80; 30 Yrs of Pub Sculpture in Ill, 81; Eighteen Ill Sculptors, 83. *Teaching:* Prof art, Bradley Univ, 56-86, emer prof, 86-. *Bibliog:* Three Illinois Artists (film), Ill Arts Coun, WCBV-TV, Peoria, 79. *Mem:* Am Soc Testing & Materials. *Media:* Bronze, Stone. *Publ:* Contribr, Contemporary American Women Sculptors, Watson-Jones, Oryx Press, 86. *Mailing Add:* 22225 Grosenbach Rd Washington IL 61571

SUNDIN, ADELAIDE TOOMBS
CERAMIST, SCULPTOR
b Boston, Mass, May 8, 1915. *Study:* Mass Col Art, with Cyrus Dallin & Raymond Porter, BS(educ), 38; Mass Inst Technol, 42-47. *Work:* Mass Inst Technol. *Comn:* Bronze bas-relief, comn by family of Dr Otis Airfield, Mass, 36; silver medal of Amandus Johson, Am Swed Hist Mus, Philadelphia; var pvt comn bas-relief portraits in Parian Porcelain, 36-96. *Exhib:* Pa Acad Fine Arts Ann, 41 & 42; Corcoran Gallery Art Ann Exhib, 42; solo exhib, Centerville Gallery, Wilmington, 77 & Hudiksvall Mus, Sweden, 80; Women at MIT, Boston Athenaeum, 77 & Mass Inst Technol, 81; Am Medallic Sculpture Asn, Am Numismatic Soc, NY, 83; Pen & Brush, NY, 92; Portraits Inc & Portraits South, NY, 92; Somerville-Manning Gallery, Wilmington, Del, 92. *Awards:* Pen & Brush Ann Sculpture Exhib, New York, 95. *Bibliog:* Jane Guernsey (auth), An ancient art revived, Philadelphia Inquirer, 79; Elaine Leotti (auth), The American Woman Medalist, A Critical Survey, 88; Marsha Mah (auth), Face Value, Delaware Today, 5/98. *Mem:* Portraits Inc NY; Am Medallic Sculpture Asn. *Media:* Parian Porcelain, Bronze; Bas-Relief. *Mailing Add:* 132 Hedge Apple Ln Wilmington DE 19807

SUPERIOR, MARA R
CERAMIST
b New York, NY, Dec 1, 51. *Study:* Hartford Art Sch, Univ Conn, 70-71; Univ Conn, Storrs, BFA(painting), 75; Univ Mass, Amherst, MA, MAT, 80. *Work:* Charles A Wustrum Mus Fine Arts, Racine, Wis; White House Collection Am Crafts & Renwick Gallery, Smithsonian Inst, Washington; Los Angeles Co Mus. *Exhib:* Solo shows, DeCordova Mus, Lincoln, Mass, 91 & Ferrin Gallery, Pinch Pottery, Northampton, Mass, 91; Creative Arts Workshop, New Haven, Conn, 91; Am Craft Mus, NY, 91; John MichaelKobler Art Ctr, Sheboygan, Wis, 91; Ceramic Nat, Everson Mus, Syracuse, NY, 94; Re: Form, Fuller Mus, Brockton, Mass, 99; Clay Nat Exhib, Columbus, Ohio, 99; Defining Moments in Studio Ceramics: 1950-2000; Sofa Chicago/NY Exhib of Sculptured Objects & Function Art, Ferrin Gallery, Hudson, NY, 2001; and others. *Pos:* Co-owner, Contemp Craft Shop/Gallery, Pinch Pottery, Northampton, Mass, 79-99; founder, East St Clay Studios, Hadley, Mass. *Teaching:* Grad teaching assoc design, Univ Mass, Amherst, 79, 80; instr ceramics, Pinch Pottery, Northampton, Mass, 81. *Awards:* Fel, Mass Artists Fel, 88, 91; Fel, Nat Endowment Arts, 90; Mass Cult Coun Grant, 92. *Bibliog:* Angela Finn (auth), rev, Am Ceramics, 4/90; Philadelphia Craft Show Portfolio, Ceramics Monthly, 5/90; Randi Danforth (auth), Pride of the Yankees, Bon Appetit, 11/91; Tommy Simpson (auth), Hand in Home, 98; Leslie Ferrin (auth), T- Pots Transformed, 2000; and others. *Mem:* Am Crafts Coun; Asparagus Valley Potters Guild. *Mailing Add:* 8 Williams St Box 230 Williamsburg MA 01096

SURES, JACK
CERAMIST, EDUCATOR
b Brandon, Man, Nov 20, 34. *Study:* Univ Man, BFA, 57; Mich State Univ, MA, 59. *Work:* Montreal Mus Fine Arts; Can Coun Art Bank, Ottawa; Sask Art Bd, Regina; Burlington Cult Ctr, Ont; Can Guild Potters, Toronto; Pecs Mus, Hungary; Norman Mackenzie Art Gallery; Tajimi Mus, Japan. *Comn:* Clay mural, Sch Archit, Winnipeg, Man, 64; clay mural, Col Veterinary Med, Saskatoon, Sask, 69; 2900 square foot mural, Province Sask, Saskatoon, 79; clay wall, Waterloo Potters Workshop, Ont, 86; mural, Mus Civilization, Holl, Que, 89. *Exhib:* Nat Gallery, Ottawa, Ont, 67; Kunstnerforbundet, Oslo, Norway, 83; Rosemont Art Gallery, Regina, 85; Moose Jaw Art Mus, 87; Franklin Silverstone Gallery, Montreal, 87-89; Ashton's, Toronto, ll/91; and others. *Pos:* Chmn, Can Craftsman's Asn, 68-70; bd mem, Can Coun Arts, 69-71 & Sask Craft Coun. *Teaching:* Prof ceramics, Univ Regina, 65-. *Awards:* Senior Award, Can Coun Arts, 72; Grand Prix Mino, Tajimi, Japan, 89; Order Can, 92; and others. *Mem:* Hon mem Waterloo Potters Guild; Nat Coun Educ Ceramic Arts; Ceramics Can. *Media:* Clay. *Publ:* Coauth, Down to Earth, Nelson, 80; auth, Spirit of Place, In: Ceramic Art & Perception, No 14, CG Driscoll, 93. *Mailing Add:* 2237 Rae St Regina SK S4T 2G1 Canada

SUSSMAN, ARTHUR
PAINTER
b Brooklyn, NY, Mar 30, 27. *Study:* Syracuse Univ, BFA; Brooklyn Mus Sch Art. *Work:* NMex Mus Fine Art, Santa Fe; Okla Art Ctr; Skirball Mus; Univ NMex; Albuquerque Mus Fine Art; Jewish Mus NY; Am Mus Jewish Hist, Philadelphia; Okla Art Ctr; Albuquerque Mus Purchase of Joseph & Coat of Many Colors, 2000; Bernalillo Co Courthouse Purchase of Eye of the Sunflower, 2000; Albuquerque Mus Fine Art Purchase of David's Dance, 2004. *Comn:* Ethicon; Joe G Maloof Corp; Pub Serv NMex; stained glass windows, Monte Vista Christian Church & Congregation Albert, Albuquerque, NMex; Stained Glass Window, Las Padillos Community Ctr, Bernalillo Co, NMex, 98; portrait, Gov Richardson, NMex, 2004. *Exhib:* One-man shows, Univ NMex, 67, 77 & 97, Nat Acad Desgn, NY, 69, NMex Mus Fine Arts Biennials, 72 & 74, Univ Judaism, Los Angeles, 88, Nat Fedn Temple sisterhoods, NY, 89; Gallery 16, NY, 86; Albuquerque Mus Fine Arts Miniatures Shows, 91-93; Nat Christian Art Exhib, Farmington, NMex, 99; From Realism to Abstraction: Art in NMex 1917-2002, NMex Mus Fine Art, 2002-03. *Collection Arranged:* Babel, Albuquerque Mus Fine Art, 2004. *Pos:* Art & film ed, KOAT TV, Albuquerque, formerly; pub TV film critic, indust art consult & courtroom sketch artist, currently; owner, A Sussman Gallery, Albuquerque, NMex, currently; writer art articles, "Prime Time" newspaper, NMex, currently. *Teaching:* Adj prof, Univ Albuquerque, formerly. *Awards:* Oriental Studies Found Grant, 62; Prize Award, NMex So West Invitational Arts & Craft Show, 78; Prize Award, Nat Christian Fine Arts Exhib, 99. *Bibliog:* Station KNME, PBS (TV doc); Colores, 89; NMex Bus J, 94; American Jewish Archives; ABC TV (arts editor), 73-79. *Mem:* Nat Mural Painters Soc. *Media:* Oil, Mixed. *Specialty:* biblical old testament painting. *Publ:* Albuquerque Jour, West Side Jour, 2001; Santa Fe New Mexican, 2003. *Dealer:* Arthur Sussman Gallery. *Mailing Add:* PO Box 13493 Albuquerque NM 87192

SUSSMAN, BARBARA J
ART APPRAISER, CONSULTANT,
b Hackensack, NJ, Apr 14, 55. *Study:* RI Sch Design, 72-73; Art Students League, study with Richard L Seyffert, 72-77; studies at George Washington Univ, 2002; Skowhegan Sch Painting & Sculpture, 77; Skidmore Col, BS, 2005. *Work:* Susan Blanchard Gallery, NY; Union Mutual, Portland, Maine; Hoglund & Pearce, Portland, Maine; Md Inst, 99; Bond Market Asn, New York City; Sloan Kettering, New York City; and other pvt collections worldwide. *Exhib:* solo exhib, Hobe Sound Gallery, Hobe Sound, Fla, 85, Nat Acad of Design, New York City, 2000 & Southern Vermont Artists, Highlands of Scotland, 2002; Southern Vt Art Ctr, Manchester, 88; Albany Biennial, 92; Pub Securities Asn, NY, 94; Kunstsalon Wolfsburg, Zürich, Switz, 96; Southern Vt Art Ctr, Manchester, 2004; Salander O'Reilly, New York City, 2004. *Awards:* Best Oils, State Show, Somerset, NJ, 78; Jay Hall Connoway Landscape Award SVA, 90. *Bibliog:* Rev, Art Critic, Maine Times, 12/16/83; Schenectady Gazzette, 90; Manchester News, 7/22/92. *Mem:* Kent Art Asn; Life mem Art Students League; So Vt Art Ctr; Am Soc of Appraisers, Designated Fine Arts. *Dealer:* Newman Galleries, Philadelphia, Pa. *Mailing Add:* 173 Fog Hill Rd Hoosick Falls NY 12090

SUSSMAN, BONNIE KAUFMAN
DEALER, CONSULTANT
b Minneapolis, Minn. *Study:* Univ Minn, BS. *Pos:* Bd dir, Goldstein Gallery, Univ Minn, St Paul, formerly; dir-owner, Peter M David Gallery, Minneapolis, 70-. *Mem:* Arts Consortium (for religions art), Minneapolis/St Paul. *Media:* Works on paper. *Specialty:* Contemporary American and English paintings, sculpture, prints, drawings, watercolor, photography, handmade paper. *Dealer:* Pvt Dealer, Consult. *Mailing Add:* 7639 Harold Ave Golden Valley MN 55427

SUSSMAN, GARY LAWRENCE
SCULPTOR, DIRECTOR
b New York, NY, Feb 15, 52. *Study:* Art Students League, apprentice to Jose de Creeft, 71-75; Ecole des Beaux Arts, Paris, France, 74; Academy, Florence, Italy, 74. *Work:* Sunnyside State Park, Tarrytown, NY; Storm King Sch, Mountainville, NY; Mt Carmel Sch, Ridgewood, NJ; Art Students League, NY; Mus Art & Sci, Los Angeles, Calif. *Comn:* large relief sculpture, Rockefeller Ctr, 88; bronze cloisonre, Radio City Music Hall, NY, 88; temple doors, Bethel Synagogue, Bennington, Vt, 89; marble bust of Giomatti, Yale Univ, 91; Rainforest Steamroom, comn by Marlo Thomas, Gymnasium Southport, Conn, 96. *Exhib:* Solo exhibs, Art Students League, NY, 74, Bergen Co Mus, Paramus, NJ, 77 & St Gaudens Nat Hist Park, Cornish, NH, 87; Newark Mus Invitational, NJ, 78; Discovery, Rediscovery, 82, Toys by Artists, 84 & Drawings by Artists, 84, Sculpture Ctr, NY; Skowhegan Artists, Colby Mus, Waterville, Maine, 83 & 84; Portraits by Artists, Bethune Gallery, State Univ NY, Buffalo, 84. *Pos:* Pres, Fine Arts Studio, Hoosick Falls, NY, 76; dir, Sculpture Ctr Studio, Sculpture Ctr, Inc, New York, 79-88. *Teaching:* Sculpture technician, Skowhegan Sch Painting & Sculpture, Maine, 76 & 77, dean, 83-84; prof sculpture, Sculpture Ctr, 79-89; adj lectr, City Col NY, 83-84; sculpture, Art Students League, NY, 92-. *Awards:* McDowell Fel, Art Students League, NY, 73; William Zorach Mem Scholar, NY, Bd Control Scholar, ASC, NY; Am Artist in Residence 90, Musie Roche, Fort en Terre, Brittany, France, 90. *Mem:* Life mem Art Students League, NY; Artists Equity; Nat Sculpture Soc (fel); Audubon Artists; Artist Fel Inc. *Media:* All Media. *Dealer:* Fog Hill & Co Inc. *Mailing Add:* Fine Arts Studio Fog Hill Rd Hoosick Falls NY 12090

SUSSMAN, JILL
GALLERY DIRECTOR
b New York, NY, June 29, 54. *Study:* RI Sch Design, 75; State Univ Alfred, NY, BA, 76. *Pos:* Cur asst, Whitney Mus Am Art, New York, 77-81; dir, Marian Goodman Gallery, New York, 81- & Multiples Inc, New York, currently. *Specialty:* Contemporary American and European painting, sculpture, photos & prints. *Mailing Add:* One Irving Pl No 324D New York NY 10003

SUSSMAN, WENDY
PAINTER
b Brooklyn, NY, June 3, 49. *Study:* Empire State Col, State Univ NY, BA, 77; Brooklyn Col, MFA, 79. *Exhib:* An Appreciation of Realism, Munson-Williams-Proctor Inst, Utica, NY, 82; Painted Light, Queens Mus Art, Flushing, NY & Butler Inst Am Art, Youngstown, Ohio, 83; NY Award Candidates, Am Acad Arts & Letts, NY, 84; Artists Choice Mus, NY, 84; Ann Exhib in Rome, Italy, Am Acad Rome, NY, 87; John Buggruen Gallery, San Francisco, 92; Platt Gallery, Univ Judaism, Los Angeles, 95; Paul Anslim Gallery, San Francisco, 96; Jan Baum Gallery, Los Angeles, 96; Jewish Mus, San Francisco, 96; Boulder Mus Contemp Art, Colo, 96; Seduced by Surface, Univ Calif Art Gallery, San Diego, 97; About Face, TransAm Pyramid, San Francisco, 97; Gallery Panle Anghim, San Francisco, 98, 99. *Teaching:* Asst prof, Univ Calif, Berkeley, 89-96, assoc prof, 96. *Awards:* Grant, Nat Endowment Arts, 89; Max & Sophie Adler Award, 96; Guggenheim Fel, 98. *Media:* Oil. *Mailing Add:* 4934 Telegraph Ave Oakland CA 94609

SUTTENFIELD, DIANA
PAINTER
b Washington, DC, Nov 20, 44. *Study:* Md Inst Col Art, Baltimore, BFA(painting), 72. *Work:* Washington Co Mus Fine Arts, Hagerstown, Md; United Airlines; Fidelity Investments, Boston; Sunrise Mus, Charleston, WVa; Art in embassies Program, US Dept State, 99, 2001-2006. *Comn:* Univ Md Hosp, Physicians Complex, Baltimore, 86; Peat Marwick Main & Co, Baltimore, 87; AT&T, Martinsburg, WVa 89; Westfield Corp, Ohio, 93 & 94; Brunswick Corp, Chicago, 96; Nat Conservation Tng Ctr, The Land Where We Were Dreaming, 02. *Exhib:* Midyear Show, Butler Inst Am Art, Youngstown, Ohio, 81; USArtists 92, Pa Acad Art, Philadelphia, Pa, 92; Pastel Soc Am, NY, 93 & 94; Md Pastel Soc, 94; Audubon Artists, New York City, 2000; and others; Md Fedn of Art, Am Landscapes, 2001-. *Collection Arranged:* United Stes Dept of the Interior, Natl Training Ctr, Shepherdstwon, WV; United Stes Dept of the Interior, Chesapeake & Ohio Canal Natl Historical Park; Fidelity Investments, Boston, MA; S.A.S., NC; United Airlines; Johns Hopkins Univ Hospital; Wash County Mus Fine Arts, Md; AT&T; C&P Telephone, NJ; Marshall Univ, WVa; Univ Charleston, WVa; Univ WVa; McDonald's. *Awards:* Carolyn Griffuni Award, Pastel Soc Am, 93 & 94; Best Show, Wash Co Mus Fine Arts, Hagerstown, Md, 91 & 94. *Media:* Pastel, Oil. *Publ:* Auth, Shepherdstown Sketchbook, 76; Martinsburg Sketchbook, 79; Pen & Ink Drawings of Harpers Ferry, 80; C and O Canal: An Illustrated History, 81; illus, The Language of Literature & BlackBerry Cove Herbal, 2000; Elegy for Barns, 02. *Dealer:* Mary Bell Galleries 714 N Franklin St Chicago IL; AIIA, Shepherdstown, WV. *Mailing Add:* PO Box 832 Shepherdstown WV 25443

SUTTER, JAMES STEWART
SCULPTOR, EDUCATOR
b Milwaukee, Wis, Feb 12, 40. *Study:* Univ Wis, BA(art educ), 64; Univ Iowa, MA(sculpture), 65; Univ Mass, univ fels, 65-67, MFA(sculpture), 67. *Work:* St Lawrence Univ, Canton, NY; Del Mar Col, Corpus Christi, Tex; Mus Fine Arts, Springfield, Mass; Hoyt Inst Fine Arts, New Castle, Pa; Millersville Univ, Pa; and others. *Exhib:* RK Parker Gallery, NY, 82 & 83; Peter Drew Gallery, Palm Beach, Boca Raton, Fla, 83-89; Tenth Anniversary Drawing Invitational, Artist Space Gallery, NY, 84; Sodarc Gallery, Montreal, Can, 94; La Grange Nat XIX, Ga, 96; and others. *Teaching:* Drawing asst, Univ Mass, 66-67; assoc prof sculpture, State Univ NY Col Potsdam, NY, 67-79, prof art, 79 ; guest prof sculpture & drawing, Skidmore Col, Saratoga Springs, 79-88. *Awards:* First Prize, 5th Ann Arena Nat, Binghamton, NY, 78; Sculpture Prize, Cooperstown Nat, NY, 84; Prize, Nat Metal Sculpture Compt, Millersville Univ, Pa, 84; Prize for Sculpture, Nat Small Works Exhib, Schoharie Arts Coun, Cobleskill, NY, 85; Artist Fel, NY State Found Arts, 87. *Mem:* Col Art Asn. *Media:* Bronze, Aluminum. *Publ:* Coauth, with Dr Frank Seiberling, The Role of Sculpture in Modern Architecture, Univ Iowa, 65. *Dealer:* Peter Drew Gallery Worth Crocke Ctr Boca Raton FL; Judith Posner Associates Milwaukee WI. *Mailing Add:* 11 New St Norwood NY 13668

SUTTON, CAROL (LORRAINE)
PAINTER
b Norfolk, Va, Sept 3, 45. *Study:* Richmond Prof Inst, BFA, 67; Univ NC, MFA. *Work:* Mus Fine Arts, Boston; Nat Collection Fine Art, Smithsonian Inst; Mus Contemp Art, Barcelona, Spain, 87; Can Coun Art Bank, Ottawa, Can; Agnes Etherington Gallery, Kingston, Ont. *Comn:* The Eye of the Oval, (painting 8 by 18) Cineplex Oleon Corp, Sand Lake Seven Cinemas, Orlando, Fla, 87. *Exhib:* Barcelona Triangle 1987 Exposicio, Centre de Creacio Contemporania, Inst NAm Studies, Brit Coun, Ambassador Can, Barcelona, Spain, 87; Silhouette-Grill-Balcony, Gallery One, Toronto, Can, 89; A Spanner in The Works Ethos and Spirituality in Abstract Painting, Terrance Sulymko Fine Art & Oakham House, Ryerson Col, Toronto, Can, 89; Ideas For A Collection-A Spanner in The Works, Randwood, Niagara Inst, Niagara-on-the-Lake, Can, 91; Recent Paintings, Kathleen Laverty Gallery Ltd, Edmonton, Can, 92. *Teaching:* Lectr, Alfred State Col, NY, 90. *Awards:* Adolph & Esther Gottleib Found Grant, NY, 92. *Bibliog:* James Clark (auth), The Problem of Fundamental Ontology Book, Limits Bk Co, 81; Karen Wilkin (auth), Toronto: Fans, flickers & penny arcades, Art News, 2/82. *Media:* Acrylic on Canvas. *Dealer:* Gallery One Toronto Ont Can. *Mailing Add:* 27 Davies Ave Toronto ON M4M 2A9 Canada

SUTTON, PETER C
CURATOR, HISTORIAN
b Mar 30, 49. *Study:* The Gunnery, Washington, Conn, 68; Harvard Col, AB, 72 (Fel 72); Yale Univ, (Fel 73-76) MA, 75, PhD, 78. *Collection Arranged:* Masters of Seventeenth-Century Dutch Genre Painting (auth, catalog), Philadelphia Mus Art & tour to West Berlin & London, 84; Renoir, 85-86 & Manet to Matisse, 86, Mus Fine

Arts, Boston; Masters of Seventeenth-Century Dutch Landscape Painting (auth, catalog), Rijksmus Amsterdam & tour to Boston & Philadelphia, 87-88; Prized Possessions: European Paintings from Private Collections, Mus Fine Arts, Boston, 92; Age of Rubens, Boston & Toledo, 93-94; The Golden Age of Dutch Landscape Painting, Thyssen-Bomemisza collection, Madrid, Spain, 94. *Pos:* Asst cur Europ paintings before 1900, Philadelphia Mus Art, 79-83, assoc cur, 83-85; Mrs Russell Baker cur Europ paintings, Mus Fine Arts, Boston, 85-94; sr dir, Old Master Paintings, Christies, New York, 94-96; dir, Wadsworth Atheneum, Hartford, Conn, 96. *Awards:* Kress Travel Grant Summer, 75; David E Finley Fel, Nat Gallery Art, 76-79; Alfred Barr Award Most Distinguished Mus Pub of 1984, Col Art Asn, 86. *Publ:* Auth, Pieter de Hooch (1629-1684): Complete Edition, Phaidon Press 80; Masterpiece Paintings from the Museum of Fine Arts, Boston, Abrams Press, 86; Dutch Art in America, Eerdmans Publ Co, 86; Dutch & Flemish Seventeenth-Century Paintings, The Harold Samuel Collection, Cambridge Univ Press, 92. *Mailing Add:* Wadsworth Atheneum 600 Main St Hartford CT 06103-2990

SUZEN, SUSAN R RUBINSTEIN
PHOTOGRAPHER, DESIGNER
b New York, NY, May 17, 46. *Study:* Brooklyn Mus Art Sch; Am Univ, BA(fine arts & graphic design); Art Ctr Col Design, Los Angeles, with Todd Walker. *Work:* Denver Mus Art; Yale Univ Art Gallery; Exchange Nat Bank Chicago; Mus Art & Hist, Fribourg, Switz; Het Sterckhof Mus, Antwerp, Belg; Libr of Cong, Washington, DC; Santa Barbara Mus; Bibliotheque Nat, Paris. *Exhib:* Solo exhibs, Herbert F Johnson Mus, Ithaca, NY, 77, Bertha Urdang Gallery, NY, 80, Canon Photo Gallery, Geneva, Switz, 81, Galerie Karin Steins, Frankfurt, WGer, 82, Howard Univ, Washington, DC, 82 & Mus Ludwig, Cologne, WGer, 84; Fac Exhib, Int Ctr Photog, NY, 80; Independent Am Photog, Warsaw, 80; Live from NY, Lowe Gallery, Syracuse, NY, 82; Works in Progress, Heller Gallery, NY, 83; Spirit of Spring Festival of the Arts, Performance, at Port Authority, NY, 84. *Pos:* Founder/dir, Art for the People. *Teaching:* Instr photog, Hunter Col, 78-79, Marymount Manahattan Col, 78-, Int Ctr Photog, 79-82 & Asphalt Green/Murphy Ctr, 85-90, NY; artist-in-residence, Apeiron Workshops, Millerton, NY, 79, NY Found Art/Guggenheim Mus, 85. *Awards:* NY State Coun Arts grant, 84; Nat Endowment Arts/Inter Arts grant, 85. *Bibliog:* John Hunter (auth), Ironic reality, Art Week, 1/75; Jacques J Halber (auth), Brief vit Belge, Foto, 3/77; Arthur Secunda (auth), article, Visual Dialogue, winter 77-78; article, Kolner Stadt-Anseiger, WGer, 84; article, New York Daily News, 11-12/84. *Mem:* Soc Photog Educators; NY Mac User Group. *Media:* Light. *Publ:* Illusr, The Love Story of Sushi & Sashimi: A Cat Tale, Capra Press, 90. *Mailing Add:* 155 Banks St New York NY 10014-2010

SUZUKI, JAMES HIROSHI
PAINTER
b Yokohama, Japan, Sept 19, 33. *Study:* Sch of Fine & Appl Art, Portland, Maine, 52; Corcoran Sch Art, 53-54; privately with Yoshio Markino. *Work:* Corcoran Gallery of Art, Washington, DC; Wadsworth Atheneum, Hartford, Conn; Rockefeller Inst, NY; Nat Mus Mod Art, Tokyo, Japan; Toledo Mus Art, Ohio. *Exhib:* Corcoran Gallery Art, 56, 58 & 60; Whitney Mus Am Art; Baltimore Mus Art, Md; Contemp Painters of Japanese Origin in Am, Inst Contemp Art, Boston; Everson Mus Art, Syracuse, NY, 58; Wadsworth Atheneum, 59; Waning Moon and Rising Sun, Mus Fine Arts of Houston, 59; San Francisco Mus Art, 63 & 64; solo exhibs, Quay Gallery, 73, Braustein Quay Gallery, 76 & 78 & Sacramento State Univ, 78; Aesthetics of Graffiti, San Francisco Mus Mod Art, 78. *Teaching:* Instr, Univ Calif, Berkeley, 62-63 & Univ Ky, 66-68; assoc prof art, Sacramento State Univ, currently. *Awards:* Eugene Weiss Scholar, Corcoran Gallery Art, 54; John Hay Whitney Fel, 58; Larry Aldrich Prize, Silvermine Guild, 59. *Dealer:* Braunstein Quay Gallery 254 Sutter St San Francisco CA 94108. *Mailing Add:* 1319 Brown Dr Davis CA 95616

SUZUKI, TARO
SCULPTOR, PAINTER
b New York, NY, Nov 17, 53. *Study:* Syracuse Univ, 71-72; Sch Visual Arts, 72-73; Cooper Union, BFA, 76. *Comn:* Installation, comn by Schorr, Aspen, Colo, 80; installation, comn by J Shore, Cincinnati, 82; installation, comn by M Sklar, NY, 82; installation, comn by C Cameron, NY, 83. *Exhib:* Marta Cerveras Gallery, NY, 90; White Columns, NY, 90; Fay Gold Gallery, Atlanta, 91; Rempire Gallery, NY, 91; Fogg Mus, Cambridge, Ma, 94; Rushmore Festival, Woodbury, NJ, 94; Fawbush Gallery, NY & Charles Cowles Gallery, NY, 94; and others. *Pos:* Dir, Space Force, NY, 80-84 & 92-; mem bd dir, Ocean Earth Construct & Develop, NY, 80-. *Teaching:* Teacher sculpture, RI Sch Design, 85. *Awards:* Nat Endowment Arts Grant, 82; Pollock Krasner Grant, 89 & 2006; Elizabeth Found for the Arts, Studio Award, 2006. *Bibliog:* Alan Jones (auth), article, Arts Mag, 89; Roberta Smith (auth), NY Times, 89; and others. *Mem:* White Columns. *Media:* All. *Mailing Add:* 323 W 39th St New York NY 10018

SVEDLOW, ANDREW JAY
ADMINISTRATOR, PAINTER
b Stamford, Conn, Dec 9, 55. *Study:* George Washington Univ, BA (fine arts), 77; Bank Street Col, MS, 82; Pa State Univ, PhD (art educ), 85. *Work:* Mus City New York; Whistler House Mus Art, Lowell, Mass; Mulvane Art Mus, Topeka, Kans; The Bruce Mus, Greenwich, Conn; NH Inst Art; Hallmark Collection, Kansas City, Mo; Ossorio Collection, Greenwich, Conn. *Exhib:* Realism Today, Stamford Mus, Conn, 80; Stamford Loft Artists, Stamford Mus, Conn, 83; Recent Prints, Washburn Univ Gallery, Topeka, Kans, 84; Fire & Air, Pa State Univ Gallery, 85; Voices of Poverty, Kans State Univ Gallery, 88; solo shows: Beowulf & Fragments, Dalton Gallery, Rock Hill, SC, 2001, Freedom, Gaston Col Gallery, Gastonia, SC. *Pos:* Dir, Mulane Art Mus, Topeka, Kans, 86-89; asst dir, Mus City New York, 90-93; pres, NH Inst Art, 93-; Dean, Col Visual & Performing Arts, Winthrop Univ, 2000-2005; dean, Col Performing & Visual Arts, Univ Northern Colo, 2005-. *Teaching:* Vis assoc prof art educ, Univ Southern Miss, Hattisburg, 84; adv & adj fac mus leadership, Bank Street Col, New York, 89-; adj fac art educ, Parsons Sch Design, New York, 90-93. *Mem:* NH Visual Arts Coalition (pres, 94-96); New York City Mus Educators Roundtable (chair, 92-94); Nat Art Educ Asn (task force chair, 87); Col Art Asn; Int Soc Educ Through Art. *Publ:* Auth, Heartland of the here & now, New Art Examiner, 6/87; Reading Prints, Mulvane Art Mus, 87; Within the mask, Kans Quart, 88; Rare prints & drawings: A case study, Acume J, 88; A World Together: Korean Art, Korean Cult Serv, 92. *Mailing Add:* 3337 New Castle Dr Loveland CO 80538

SVENSON, JOHN EDWARD
SCULPTOR, MEDALIST
b Los Angeles, Calif, May 10, 23. *Study:* Claremont Grad Sch, Calif. *Work:* Ahmandson Ctr, Los Angeles; San Bernardino Co Mus; Skagway, Alaska Sch Dist; Civic Ctr, Garden Grove, Calif; Smithsonian Air Mus; Foothill Ranch, Laguna Hills, Calif; and others. *Comn:* Gold portrait medallions of King Hussein, Jordan & Ibn Saud Saudi Arabia; bronze porpoise fountain, Ritz Carlton, Laguna Niguel, Calif; hist panels, San Gabriel Mission Chapel, Calif; bldg facade & sculpture, Purex Corp, Lakewood, Calif; Alaska Tlingit Medal, Soc Medallists An Issue; hist sculptures Anchorage, Valdez and Skagway, AK; Fleischer Mus, Scottsdale, Ariz; Brookgreen Gardens, NC; 22 Ft 17 Ton Redwood Sculpture, Ranchero, Pomona, CA; 8 Ft Bronze Sculpture, George Chaffey, City Hall, Uplano, CA. *Exhib:* Los Angeles Co Mus Art, 62; Newman Galleries, Philadelphia, 71; Kennedy Galleries, NY, 72; Alaska State Mus; Svenson Arts Gallery, Haines, Alaska; and others. *Pos:* Trustee, Alaska Indian Arts, Inc, Port Chilkoot, 67-. *Awards:* Awards for Excellence in Sculpture, Am Inst Archit, 57 & 61; Sculpture Award, City of Garden Grove, Calif, 80; Gold Medal & Hester Prize, Nat Sculpture Soc, New York, 96. *Bibliog:* Nat Sculpture Rev, 77; Inland Empire Mag, 8/82 & 10/98; Elan Mag, 3/90; Beautiful Things Art Book, 2000. *Mem:* Fel Nat Sculpture Soc; Soc Medalists, NY; Chaffey Art Asn (trustee). *Media:* Wood, Bronze. *Mailing Add:* c/o Svenson Arts Gallery 2480 Vista Dr Upland CA 91784

SVERDLOVE, ZOLITA
PAINTER, PRINTMAKER
b New York, NY, Feb 21, 36. *Study:* Art Students League, 49-52; Cooper Union Art Sch, cert, 56, BFA, 77; San Francisco State Univ, 59-60; Calif Sch Fine Arts, 60; Pratt Graphic Arts Ctr, 67; Southern Methodist Univ, 70-74. *Work:* Owens-Corning Collection, Toledo Mus, Ohio; Dallas Mus Fine Arts, Tex; Purdue Univ, Ind; Marymount Col, NY; plus many others. *Comn:* Grand Hotel, Houston, 79; Patron Print, Los Angeles Printmaking Soc, 82. *Exhib:* one-person shows, Hooks-Epstein Gallery, Houston, 78, Longview Mus, Tex, 79, Brand Libr Art Gallery, Glendale, Calif, 81, Orlando Gallery, Sherman Oaks, Calif, 95, The Subject is Water, Maturango Mus, Ridgecrest, Calif, 01; Pasadena Art Alliance Gallery, 91-97; group show, Valley House Gallery, Dallas, Tex, 82, Arroyo Landscape, Occidental Col, 92, Platt & Borstein Galleries, Univ Judaism, Bel Air, Calif, 01; Unatural Landscapes, Century Gallery, Sylmar, Calif, 94; Landscapes, Dallas (Tex) Mus Fine Art, 98; Old Town Gallery, Austin, Tex, 99; The Orginals, Triage Gallery, Pasadena, Calif; Highways & Byways, Pierce Col, Los Angeles. *Pos:* art exhibs dir, Univ Tex, Dallas, 72-73. *Awards:* Purchase Prize, Purdue Univ, 70; Top Prize, Dallas Mus Fine Arts, 72; Nat Endowment Arts Grant, 73-74; and others. *Bibliog:* Women in Art (TV-video), Women's Caucus for Art, 89; Review, Los Angeles Times, 4/29/94, 4/97 & 1/28/2000; Peter Frank (auth), Landscape & Cityscapes (catalog with essay), 2006. *Mem:* Los Angeles Printmakers Soc; Painting and Drawing Coun. *Media:* Monotype, Oil, Watercolor. *Specialty:* Plein-Aire. *Publ:* Designed & publ five booklets for Nat Endowment for Arts grant, 73-74; contribr, Mundus Artium, Univ Tex, Dallas, 76. *Dealer:* Valley House Gallery 6616 Spring Valley Rd Dallas TX; Tirage Gallery 1 W California Pasadena CA; Larry Warnock Prints San Francisco CA. *Mailing Add:* 1445 Indiana Ave South Pasadena CA 91030

SWAIN, ROBERT
PAINTER
b Austin, Tex, Dec 7, 40. *Study:* Am Univ, Washington, DC, BA. *Work:* Corcoran Gallery of Art, Washington, DC; Walker Art Ctr, Minneapolis; Denver Art Mus, Colo; Albright-Knox Mus, Buffalo, NY; Everson Art Mus, Syracuse, NY. *Comn:* Painting (8 1/2ft x 20ft), Schering Labs, Bloomfield, NJ, comn by Skidmore, Owings & Merrill, NY, 70; painting (5ft x 10ft), Phillip Mallis of Kahn & Mallis Assocs, NY, 72; painting (4ft x 27ft), IBM, Charlotte, NC, 81; painting (5ft x 9ft), Tupperware World Headquarters, Kissimmee, Fla, 81. *Exhib:* The Art of the Real, Mus of Mod Art, NY, 68; one-man shows, Susan Caldwell Gallery, 74, 76, 78 & 81, Everson Art Mus, Syracuse, 74 & Columbus Gallery of Fine Arts, Ohio, 76; 31st Biennial, Corcoran Gallery of Art, 69; The Structure of Color, Whitney Mus of Am Art, 71; Painting & Sculpture Today, Indianapolis Mus of Art, Ind, 74; Color as Language (traveling exhib, Latin Am), Mus of Mod Art, NY, 74-75; Nina Freudenheim Galley, Buffalo, NY, 78; Toni Birckhead Gallery, Cincinnati, Ohio, 80. *Teaching:* Prof fine arts, Hunter Col, NY. *Awards:* Guggenheim Fel, 69; Nat Endowment for Arts Grant, 76. *Bibliog:* Scott Burton (auth), Light from Aten to Laser, MacMillan Co, 69; B Wasserman (auth), Modern Painting, Davis Publ, 70; Roberta Smith (auth), Artforum, 76. *Media:* Acrylic. *Mailing Add:* 57 Leonard St New York NY 10013

SWAIN, ROBERT FRANCIS
GALLERY DIRECTOR
b Halifax, NS, Oct 25, 42. *Study:* Carleton Univ, BA. *Collection Arranged:* Joan Frick, 74; Robert Sinclair, 76; Made Glorious: 25 Years of Stratford Design, 76; A History of Children's Book Illustrations, 77; Fantastic Shakespeare; Coasts: The Sea and Canadian Art. *Pos:* Dir, Agnes Etherington Art Ctr, Kingston, Ont. *Mem:* Int Comt Mus; Ont Asn Art Galleries (dir); and others. *Publ:* Auth, many exhib catalogs. *Mailing Add:* 43 Jorene Dr Kingston ON K7M 3X5 Canada

SWAN, BARBARA
PAINTER
b Newton, Mass, June 23, 22. *Study:* Wellesley Col, BA; Boston Mus Sch. *Work:* Philadelphia Mus Art; Boston Mus Art & Boston Pub Libr, Boston; Worcester Mus; Fogg Art Mus. *Exhib:* Carnegie Ann, 49; Contemp Am Painting, Univ Ill, 50; View 1960, Inst Contemp Arts, Boston, 60; Brooklyn Mus Biennial Print Exhib, 65; New Eng Women, De Cordova Mus, 75; Eight New Eng Artists, Works on Paper, Boston Mus Fine Arts, 77; New Eng Realists, Danforth Mus, 80. *Teaching:* Instr painting, Wellesley Col, 46-49; instr art, Milton Acad, 51-54; instr painting & drawing, Boston Univ, 60-65. *Awards:* Assoc Scholar, Inst Independent Study, Radcliffe Col, 61-63; George Roth Prize, Philadelphia Print Club, 65; Lifetime Achievement Award, Wellesley Col, 96. *Media:* Oil. *Dealer:* Alpha Gallery 122 Newbury St Boston MA 02116. *Mailing Add:* 808 Washington St Brookline MA 02146

SWANSON, CAROLINE
PAINTER
Work: Columbia Mus of Art, SC; Gertrude Herbert Inst Art, Augusta, Ga; Int Cult Ctr, Takarazuka, Japan; Nat Arts Club, NY; Deland Mus Art, Fla. *Collection Arranged:* Pvt and Corp Collections. *Awards:* Leila Gardin Sawyer Mem Award, AAPL, NY; Best in Watercolor, New Horizons Arts Festival, Augusta, Ga; Purchase Award, Visual Arts Ctr Mus, Panama City, Fla. *Mem:* Nat Asn Women Artists; Nat Watercolor Soc; Philadelphia Watercolor Soc; Tex Watercolor Soc; Western Colo Watercolor Soc. *Mailing Add:* 612 Brae Burn Dr Augusta GA 30907

SWANSON, CHARLES
CRAFTSMAN, EDUCATOR
Study: Kent State Univ, BBA(magna cum laude), 76; Wendell Castle Sch, AOS, 86; RI Sch Design, MFA, 89. *Exhib:* Solo exhibs, Snyderman Gallery, Philadelphia, 92 & 95; Donald Brecker Gallery, Miami, Fla, 95; Rochester Inst Technol, NY, 96; Virginia Lynch Gallery, Tiverton, RI, 96; Soc Arts & Crafts, Boston, 96. *Pos:* Juror, Maine Crafts Asn, Deer Isle, Maine, 92, Mass Cult Coun, Boston, 92 & Marblehead Festival Arts, Mass, 93. *Teaching:* Instr woodworking & furniture design, RI Sch Design, undergrad prog, 89- & grad prog, 91-92; instr woodworking, Haystack Mountain Sch Crafts, Deer Isle, Maine, 90 & 96 & Anderson Ranch Sch Crafts, Snowmass, Colo, 96; pub slide lectr, Stone Boat, Nemasket Gallery, New Bedford, Mass, 93; pub slide lectr & visual design workshop, Alaskan Woodworkers Asn, Anchorage, 94. *Awards:* New Eng Found Arts/Nat Endowment Arts Fel, 93; Soc Arts & Crafts Award, Boston, 94; Nat Endowment Arts Fel, Washington, 94. *Bibliog:* Boston Herald, 3/19/93; Am Craft, 6/93; New Bedford Standard Times, Mass, 8/1/93. *Media:* Wood. *Dealer:* Snyderman Gallery 303 Cherry St Philadelphia PA 19186. *Mailing Add:* 32 Wadsworth Ln South Dartmouth MA 02748

SWANSON, J N
PAINTER, SCULPTOR
b Duluth, Minn, Feb 4, 27. *Study:* Col Arts & Crafts, Oakland, Calif; Carmel Art Inst; also with Donald Teague & Armin Hansen. *Work:* Read Mullin Collection, Phoenix; Sunset Mag Collection Art; Leaning Tree Mus, Boulder, Colo; Diamond M Mus, Tex; Cowboy Artist Am Mus, Kerrville, Tex; and others. *Comn:* Pvt comn only. *Exhib:* Monterey Co Fair Prof Div, Calif, 67; Springville Regional Show, Utah; Cowboy Artists Ann Show, Hall Fame, Okla, 70-75; Soc Western Artists, De Young Mus, San Francisco, 71. *Teaching:* Horse anat, Cowboy Artist Mus, Kerrville, Tex. *Awards:* San Francisco Best of Show Award, Monterey Co Fair, 67; Soc Western Artists Atelier Award, De Young Mus, 71. *Bibliog:* Ainsworth (auth), Cowboy in Art, World, 68; Paul Weaver (ed), Cowboy Artists Ann Exhib Bks, Northland, 69-75; Broder (auth), Bronzes of the American West, Abrams, 74. *Mem:* Cowboy Artists Am (vpres, 70). *Media:* Oil; Plastilene Clay. *Res:* Complete Western library for research into historical Western painting; first hand knowledge of the cowboy subject of present day. *Dealer:* Kyle Gallery Los Olivus CA. *Mailing Add:* 18865 Cachagua Rd Carmel Valley CA 93924

SWANSON, RAY V
PAINTER
b Alcester, SDak, Oct 4, 37. *Study:* Northrop Inst, BS, 60. *Work:* Indianapolis Mus Art; Riverside Art Collection Mus, Calif. *Exhib:* Wichita Nat Art Exhib, Kans, 70; Franklin Mint Gallery Am Art, 73-74; Capitol Bldg, Phoenix, Ariz, 75; Nat Acad Western Art, Cowboy Hall of Fame, 76. *Awards:* Silver Medal, Water Solubles, Cowboy Artists Am, 90 & Gold Medal, 92; Bronze Medal, Am Watercolor Soc, 91. *Bibliog:* J & J Ward (auth), Renaissance of Western Art, Franklin Mint Gallery, 74; Tom Cooper (auth), The Best of Arizona Highways, Ariz Hwys, 75; Royal B Hassrick (auth), Western Painting Today, Watson-Guptill Publ, 75. *Mem:* Prescott Fine Arts Asn; signature mem Am Watercolor Soc; Western Art Asn (bd mem, 91-92); Cowboy Artists Am (vpres, 92-93, pres, 93-94). *Media:* Oil; Watercolor. *Publ:* Contribr, Artist of the Rockies, Colo Publ, 75; contribr, Illuminator, Grand Cent Publ, 75. *Dealer:* Husberg Fine Arts Gallery 330 Hwy 179 Sedona AZ 86336. *Mailing Add:* PO Box 937 Carefree AZ 85377

SWANSON, VERN GROSVENOR
MUSEUM DIRECTOR, HISTORIAN
b Central Point, Ore, Feb 4, 45. *Study:* Brigham Young Univ, Provo, Utah, BA, 69; Univ Utah, Salt Lake City, MA(art hist), 75; Univ London, Courtauld Inst Art, PhD(art hist), 94. *Collection Arranged:* An Exhibition of British and American Paintings (auth, catalog), 76, Auburn Univ; The Unknown Alma-Tadema (auth, catalog), Brigham Young Univ, Utah, 79; Permanent Collection (auth, catalog), 81 & National April Salon (auth, catalog), 81-89, Springville Mus Art; Soviet & Russian Impressionism, Fleischer Mus, 94; When Art Was Popular - European Masters of 19th Century Art, Springville Mus, 96; Retrospective - Art of John Wilson Godward 1976-1997, Richard Green Fine Art, London, Eng, 97; over 25 other temporary exhibs at the Springville Mus Art. *Pos:* Mus aide supervisor, Nat Gallery Art, Washington, 69-70; gallery dir, House Fine Arts, Provo, Utah, 70-71; art consult British classical art, major auction houses, 73-; mus dir, Springville Mus Art, Utah, 80-; art hist, Brigham Young Univ, 87-88; art consult to Australian Collector. *Teaching:* Asst prof art hist, Auburn Univ, Ala, 71-75; guest lectr, Sotheby's, NY. *Awards:* Research grant, Paul Mellon Inst Studies Brit Art, 88 & Am Acad Art, 88; George S & Delores Dore' Eccles Found, 89; Gov Award, Dir Art Mus Utah, 94. *Mem:* Am Asn Mus; Victorian Soc Am; Art Mus Asn; Utah Mus Asn (vpres, 86-87); Grand Cent Art Galleries Educ Asn (bd dir, 88-92). *Res:* The fine arts among the Mormons in Utah; Catalogues Raisonnies on John William Godward & John Hapen; editing and preperation of the volume work on Soviet socialist realist art with Matthew Brown; Editing and writing encyclopedia of Utah art. *Publ:* The Life and Works of Sir Lawrence Alma-Tadema, Garton & Co, 90; The Biography & Catalogue Raisonne of the Paintings of Sir Lawrence Alma-Tadema, Garton & Co, 90; Utah Art, Peregrine-Smith, 91; Mormon art & belief movement, Southwest Art Mag, 12/91; Hidden Treasures: Russian & Soviet Impressionism 1930-1970's, 1/94; auth, Artists of Utah, 2000 & Soviet Working Class Impressionism, 9/2001; coauth, Utah Art - Utah Artists, 2001. *Mailing Add:* 1305 E Hobble Creek Dr Springville UT 84663

SWARD, ROBERT S
WRITER, EDITOR
b Chicago, Ill, June 23, 33. *Study:* Univ Ill, BA(hons), 56; Univ Iowa, MA, 58; Univ Bristol, Eng, 60-61; post grad studies, Middlebury Col, 56-60. *Work:* Archive Collection, City Hall, Toronto, Ont; Provincial Mus Collection, BC Provincial Govt; Santa Cruz Libr Archive, Univ Calif; McHenry Libr, Santa Cruz, Calif; Wash Univ Libr Arch, St. Louis, Mo. *Comn:* Earthquake collage, loma Prieta, Santa Cruz, Calif, 89; Earthquake Cabrillo Col, Aptos, Calif, 89 & 2000. *Exhib:* Traveling Exhib, The Toronto Islands (auth, catalog), Toronto City Archive, Can, 80-83. *Pos:* Ed, Soft Press Publ, Victoria, BC, 70-79 & Business to Business Network, Santa Cruz, 86-88; ed-in-chief, Hancock House Publ, Vancouver, BC, 75-79; vis artist poetry & bk-making, Ont Arts Coun, Toronto, 81-85; vis artist poetry, bk-making & illus, Cult Coun Santa Cruz, 86-; freelance writer, ed & consult, currently; founder, Uncle Dog Audio, currently. *Teaching:* Instr creative writing, Univ Calif Ext, currently; instr creative writing, Foothill Col; Eng prof, Monterey Peninsula Col, Calif, 85-87; instr, Univ Calif, Santa Cruz Extension, 86-; prof eng, Cabrillo Col, 87-2000. *Awards:* Guggenheim Fel Poetry, 65; D H Lawrence Fel Poetry, Univ NMex, 66; Grants, Can Coun, Ontario Arts Coun & Ontario Heritage Found, 81-84; Villa Montalvo Literary Arts Award, 90. *Bibliog:* John Malcolm Brinnin (auth), NY Times Book Review; Tina Barr (auth), Harvard Rev, 6/92; Contemporary Poets, ed by Janice Jorgenson, 6th ed, St. James Press, 94-95; Contemporary Authors: A Bio-Bibliographical Guide, Gale Thomson, vol 206, 2003; Collected Poems, 1957-2004, Black Moss Press. *Mem:* Nat Writer's Union; fel Yaddo, MacDowell Colony & Djerassi Found, 60-92; Poetry Santa Cruz; League pf Canadian Poets. *Media:* Book-Making, Mixed Media; Printed Word Illustrations. *Res:* Small Press Publications in the USA and Canada (bks & mags) Emily Carr: The Untold Story, 78 & The Art of the Haida, Argillite, 80, Hancock House. *Interests:* computers, multi-media, books and book making. *Publ:* Four Incarnations, New & Selected Poems, 1957-1991, Coffee House Press, 91; Contemp Authors Autobiography Series, Gale Research, vol 13, 90; CD-ROM, Discovering Authors Canada, ed by James Draper, 94; Family, Select Poet Series, 94; A Much-Married Man, A Novel, Ekstasis Eds, Can, 96; Rosicrucian in the Basement, New & Selected Poems, Black Moss Press, 2001; Heavenly Sex & Other Poems, Black Moss Press, 2002; Collected Poems: 1957-2004, Black Moss Press, 2004; God is in the Cracks, A Narrative in Voices, Black Moss Press, 2006. *Mailing Add:* PO Box 7062 Santa Cruz CA 95061-7062

SWARTZ, BETH AMES
PAINTER
b New York, NY, Feb 5, 36. *Study:* Art Students League; Cornell Univ, BS, 57; NY Univ, MA, 60. *Work:* Jewish Mus, NY; Nat Mus Am Art, Washington, DC; Phoenix Art Mus; San Francisco Mus Art; Mus Fine Art, Santa Fe, NMex. *Exhib:* Solo exhibs, Elaine Horwitch Galleries, Scottsdale, Ariz, 79, 80, 82, 84, 86 & 88, A Moving Point of Balance, traveling show, 85-92, Plaka Art Gallery, Athens, Greece, Nafplion Art Gallery, Greece, 89, Galeria Yolanda Rios, Sitges, Barcelona, Spain, 89, New Gallery, Houston, Tex, 89 & Elaine Horwitch Galleries, Palm Springs, 89; Paper: Surface and Image, Rutgers Univ, touring, 81-82; Artists in the Am Desert Touring Show, 81-82; Artist as Shaman, Women's Bldg, Los Angeles, 86; Artists of the Western States Biennial, Elaine Horwitch Galleries, Palm Springs, 87; New Sacred Art: Prayers for Peace, White Light Gallery, NY, 87; Newhouse Ctr Contemp Arts, Staten Island, NY, 88; The Transformative Vision, Phyllis Weil & Co, NY, 89; A Moving Point of Balance, Ariz Cancer Ctr, 98. *Teaching:* Assoc, Exten Dept, Ariz State Univ, 63-74. *Awards:* Nat Endowment Arts Grant, 75; Ariz Comn Arts & Humanities Educ Grant, 77. *Bibliog:* Lynn Pyne (auth), Artist approaches life from a different angle, Phoenix Gazette, 4/20/88; Victoria Beaudin (auth), Artist's work depicts heavenly inspiration, Scottsdale Progress Weekend Mag, 5/6/88; Jodie Snyder (auth), Valley Artist Hopes Work Helps Cancer Patients, Ariz Repub, A1 & A8, 1/12/98. *Mem:* Nat & Ariz Art Educ Asns. *Media:* Fire on Paper; Mixed-Media. *Publ:* Are we stifling our children's creativity?, Point West Mag, 63; Help your child create, Art Handbook for Parents, 65; auth, Inquiry into fire, Ariz Artist, fall 77. *Mailing Add:* 5346 E Sapphire Ln Scottsdale AZ 85253

SWARTZ, JULIANNE
ARTIST
b Phoenix, Airz, Apr 29, 67. *Study:* Univ Ariz, BA(photog & creative writing), 89; Skowhegan Sch for Painting and Sculpture, Postgrad, 99; Bard Col, MFA, 2002. *Work:* Brooklyn Mus Art, 1997 Bronx Mus for the Arts, 1999, Bellevue Art Mus, Seattle, 2000, Mus Contemp Art, Tucson, 2003, New Mus Contemp Art, New York

City, 2004, Whitney Biennial, Whitney Mus Am Art, NY, 2004. *Exhib:* One-woman shows, Numinious, Lombard Freid Fine Arts, NY, 97, NY Biennial Glass, Robert Lehman Gallery, Brooklyn, 99, Shadow House, Ricco/Maresca Gallery New York City 2000, Piot Brehmer Landing the Bubble, 123 Watts, New York City, 2001, Shroeder-Romero Gallery, Brooklyn, 2002; group shows, Weatherspoon Art Gallery, Univ NC, Chapel Hill, 96, Robert Lehman Gallery at Urban Glass, Brooklyn, 98, Ellen Kim Murphy Gallery, Santa Monica, Calif, 99, Tulane Univ, New Orleans, 99, 123 Watts Gallery, New York City, 2000, Let's Get To Work, Univ Arts, Philadelphia, 2001, Plant Life, KS Art, New York City, 2001, clenchclutchflynch, Paul Rogers Gallery, New York City, 2001, Mixed Greens, Space 101, Brooklyn, 2001, Sculpture Ctr, New York City, 2001, Brooklyn!, Palm Beach (Fla) Inst Contemp Art, 2001, Periphera, Murray Guy Gallery, New York City, 2002, PS 1 Inst for Contemp Art, Queens, NY, 2000, Christinerose/Josee Bienvenu Gallery, New York City, 2003, Line Drawing, Artist's Space Project Room, New York City, 2003, Grant Selwyn Fine Art, Los Angeles, 2003, Still/Motion, Hosfelt Gallery, San Francisco, 2003, Muller Dechiara Gallery, Berlin, 2004, ARCO, Spain, 2004, Catharine Clark Gallery, San Francisco, 2004. *Awards:* Special Editions Grant, Lower East Side Printshop, 98; Richard Kelly Found Grant, 99; Cite Internationale des Arts, Paris, 2000. *Mailing Add:* c/o Josee Bienvenu Gallery 529 W 20th St New York NY 10011

SWARTZMAN, ROSLYN
PRINTMAKER, SCULPTOR
b Montreal, Que, Aug 17, 31. *Study:* Montreal Artists Sch; Montreal Mus Fine Arts; Ecole des Beaux Arts, with Albert Dumouchez. *Work:* Nat Gallery Can, Ottawa, Ont; Montreal Mus Fine Arts, Que; DeCordova Mus, Boston; Brooklyn Mus, NY; NY Pub Libr; and many others. *Comn:* Aluminium bas-relief sculpture, Arctic Forms, Montreal, 83-84; aluminium wall sculpture, Oiseau de Feu, Place Bonaventure Entrance Lobby, St Antoine & Univ, Montreal, 90-91. *Exhib:* 2nd Int Graphics Biennial, Miami, 75; Jewish Experience in the 20th Century, Mt St Vincent Univ, Halifax, NS; Can Landscape through Drawings & Prints, Mus Fine Arts, Montreal; Boston Printmakers, 78; one-man show, Burnaby Art Gallery, BC, 80 & Saidye Bronfman Ctr, 81; and others. *Teaching:* Teacher & dir graphics dept, Sayde Bronfman Ctr, Montreal, 71-; printmaking instr, Univ Haifa, Israel, 88; art instr, Israel Painting Workshop Tour, 89; founder & coordr comprehensive art prog, Saidye Bronfman Centre, Montreal, Que, 90-. *Awards:* two patron selection awards, Boston Printmakers 30th Exhib; Thomas Moore Purchase Award, Montreal, 80; Travel Grant to Israel, Can-Israel Cult Found, 88; and others. *Bibliog:* Nicole Malenfant (auth), L'Estampe - La Documentation Québécoise, 79; Gilles Daigneault & Ginette Deslauriers (auths), La Gravure Au Québec - 1940-1980; Elyse (auth), Musée du Québec, 81; Marcel Broquet (auth), Musée du Québec, 86; Idea of North, Royal Can Acad Arts, 83. *Mem:* Royal Can Acad; Graphic Arts Coun Can; Print & Drawing Coun Can; Graphics Soc NH. *Media:* Intaglio; Bas-Relief. *Dealer:* La Guild Graphique 9 St Paul Ouest Montreal Can. *Mailing Add:* 4174 Oxford St Montreal PQ H4A 2Y4 Canada

SWEENEY, J GRAY
HISTORIAN, CURATOR
b Jacksonville, Fla, Nov 20, 43. *Study:* Univ NMex, BA, 66; Ind Univ, MA, 69, PhD, 75. *Collection Arranged:* Themes in American Painting (auth, catalog), Grand Rapids Art Mus, 77; Artists of Grand Rapids: 1840-1980 (auth, catalog), 81; Great Lakes Marine Painting of the 19th Century (auth, catalog), Muskegon Mus Art, 83, Artists of Michigan from the 19th Century (auth, catalog), Muskegan Mus Art, 87. *Pos:* Cur, Themes in Am Painting, Grand Rapids Art Mus, 75-77, Tweed Mus, 80, Grand Rapids Art Mus, Mich, 81 & Muskegon Mus Art, 83 & 86. *Teaching:* Asst prof 19th & 20th century Am painting, Grand Valley State Univ, 71-78, assoc prof, 78-85; assoc prof, Ariz State Univ, 86-88, prof, 89-. *Awards:* Fels, Carnegie Found, 67 & 70 & Samuel H Kress Found, 70-71; Senior fel, Smithsonian Inst, Nat Mus Am Art, 84-85. *Mem:* Col Art Asn; Asn Hist Am Art. *Res:* Nineteenth century American landscape painting; influence of Thomas Cole; Regional and Western Am Art. *Publ:* The Nude of Landscape Painting: Emblematic Personification in the Art of the Hudson River School, Smithsonian Studies in Am Art, fall 89; A very peculiar picture: Martin J Heades Thunderstorm over Narragansett Bay, Archs Am Art J, #4, 88; Masterpieces of Western American Painting, 91; The Columbus of the Woods: Daniel Boone & Manifest Destiny (catalog), 92; Racism, Nationalism & Nostalgia in Cowboy Art, Oxford Art J, 92; and others. *Mailing Add:* c/o Sch of Art Ariz State Univ PO Box 871505 Tempe AZ 85287-1505

SWEENEY, SPENCER
ARTIST
Study: Pa Acad Fine Arts, BA, 1993-1997. *Exhib:* Free Coke, Greene Naftali Gallery, NYC, 1999; Legal Paper Work, Beyond Baroque, 2000; Paintings, Gavin Brown's Enterprise, 2002; Today's Man, John Connely, NY, 2003; Subway Series, Bronx Mus Arts, NY, 2004; Modern Inst, Glasgow, Eng, 2005; Whitney Biennial: Day for Night, Whitney Mus Am Art, NY, 2006. *Awards:* Lewis S Ware Mem prize exceptional work; Jimmy C Leuders painting prize; Angelo Pinto Mem prize exceptional work; Cuff/Sammack prize abstract art; Lucile Sorgenti scholar artistic excellence. *Mailing Add:* c/o Gavin Brown Enterprise 620 Greenwich St New York NY 10014

SWEET, FRANCIS EDWARD
PAINTER
b Watertown, NY, Oct 16, 38. *Work:* Leigh Yawkey Woodson Art Mus, Wausau, Wis; Hirem Blauvelt Art Mus, Oradel, NJ; Roger Tory Peterson Inst, Jamestown, NY; Bennington Ctr for the Arts, Bennington, Vt; Joseph Hardy Collection, Farmington, Pa. *Exhib:* SAA Exhibs, Cleveland Mus Nat Hist, Cleveland, Ohio, 1991; SAA Exhibs, Witte Mus, San antonio, Tex, 1996; SAA Special Exhib, Nat Geographic Asn, Washington, DC, 2002; Nature Defined, Roger Tory Peterson Inst, Jamestown, NY, 2005. *Pos:* Pres, Soc of Animal Artist, NY, 2000-2003. *Awards:* Award of Excellence, SAA, 1991-1996, 1998-2004; Patricia Bott Award, Blauvelt Mus, SAA, 2003. *Bibliog:* Kay Johnson (auth), How Sweet it is, Wildlife Art News Mag, 1996. *Mem:* Soc Animal Artists, NY (pres 2000-2003); World Wide Nature Artists Group, Canada. *Media:* Oil & Scratchboard. *Publ:* Illusr, Ecology & Management of the Mourning Dove (bk), 1993; illusr, Ecology & Management of the Woodduck (bk), 1994; illusr, Best of Wildlife Art II (bk), 1999. *Dealer:* Francis E Sweet Studios 1402 Port Echo La Bowie Maryland 20716. *Mailing Add:* 1402 Port Echo Ln Bowie MD 20716

SWEET, MARSHA (MARSHA) SWEET WELCH
PRINTMAKER, PAINTER
b Cleveland, Ohio, Dec 11, 36. *Study:* Miami Univ, studied with Douglas Huebler, BFA, 58; Baldwin Wallace Col, 70; Cleveland Inst Art; Case Western Reserve Univ, MA, 81. *Work:* Akron Art Mus Archive, Ohio; ADOGI, Cadaques Municipal Mus Art, Spain; Nat Mus Fine Arts, Hanoi, Vietnam; Artists Archive of the Western Reserve, Cleveland. *Comn:* Limited Edition Patron Print, Baycrafter Gallery Inc, Bay Village, Ohio, 75; Int traveling displays, Bruel & Kjaer, Copenhagen, Denmark, 79-80; Presentation print, Cleveland Arts Festival, Ohio, 83. *Exhib:* The May Show, Cleveland Mus Art, Ohio, 71, 75, 83 & 86; Print Int, ADOGI, Taller Gallerie Fort, Barcelona, Cadaques, Spain, 88-99; Int Prints, Mus Nat de la Estampa, Mex, 89; Boston Printmakers Nat Exhibs, Mass, 89-99; 2003-2005; Saga 90, Grand Palais, Paris, France, 90; Indochina Arts Proj, Nat Mus Fine Arts, Hanoi, Vietnam, 91; Society of Wood Engravers 54th Exhib, various mus UK, 91-92; Int Print Triennial, Contemp Art Gallery, Cracow, Poland, 94; Mid-Year Painting Exhib, Butler Inst Am Art, Youngstown, Ohio, 99; Xylon Argentina, Buenos Aires, 2000; Chongqing Print Exhib, China, 2000; A Shared Journey, Greater Lafayette Mus Art, Lafayette, Ind; Cleveland Biennial, CSU, Cleveland, 2001; A Century of Portraiture, Cleveland Artists Found, 2002; Face to Face, FAVA Gallery, Oberlin, Ohio, 2003; We Just Met, AAWR Gallery, Cleveland, Ohio, 2003; Ohio Artists After Surrealism, Cleveland Artists Found Cleveland, Ohio, 2003; Buddha Project At Cleveland State Univ Art Gallery, 2004; Sacred Images, Scarab Club Gallery, Detroit, MI, 2004; A Selection of Contemp Prints, Studio 18 Gallery, NY, 2005. *Pos:* Bd trustees, Baycrafter Gallery Inc, Ohio, 69-79, chmn, 77-78; asst dir visual arts, Interlochen Arts Acad Summer Prog, Mich, 78; juror, 10th Int Small Print Competition, Barcelona, Cadaques, Spain, 90. *Teaching:* Instr printmaking, Interlochen Arts Acad Summer, Mich, 76-78; lectr, Case Western Reserve Univ, Cleveland, Ohio, 86-87. *Awards:* May Show Spec Mention Graphics, Cleveland Mus Art, 83; 8th Mini Print Int Selection Award, ADOGI, Taller Gallery, Barcelona, Cadaques, Spain, 88-89; Boston Printmakers Show Award, Duxbury Art Complex, 89-90. *Bibliog:* Tisa, Empresa Editora, El Minigrabado Int, La Vanguardia, Barcelona, Spain, 1/7/89; Simon Brett (auth), An Engraver's Glove: Wood Engraving World-Wide in the Twenty-First Century, Primrose Hill Press, London, 2002; Elizabeth McClelland (auth), Marsha Sweet: Prints (Woodcuts and Wood Engravings), 2003. *Mem:* New Orgn Visual Arts; Wood Engravers Network; Boston Printmakers; Performers & Artists Nuclear Disarmament; Philadelphia Print Club. *Media:* Woodcut, Wood Engraving; Oil, Watercolor. *Mailing Add:* 29700 Osborn Rd Cleveland OH 44140-1852

SWEET, MARY (FRENCH)
PAINTER, PRINTMAKER
b Cincinnati, Ohio, Oct 10, 37. *Study:* Stanford Univ, with Daniel Mendelowitz, AB(art), 59, MA(art), 60. *Work:* Carlsbad Art Mus, NMex; La Posada Hotel & Menninger Clinic, Albuquerque NMex; First Nat Bank, Albuquerque, NMex; NMex Educ Credit Union; NMex Dept Transportation, Espanola Off. *Comn:* Painting, USS Barb Submarine, 63; NMex Educ Credit Union, Albuquerque, 88; Damsite, Elephant Butte State Park, NMex, 91 & 94. *Exhib:* Magnifico, Albuquerque, NMex, 91-97; Western Fedn Watercolor Soc 17 traveling exhib, Albuquerque Mus, NMex, 92; Main Street, Fort Worth, Tex, 93; Monothon, Col Santa Fe NMex, 93, 95, 96; 21st Ann San Antonio & Traveling Exhib, Western Fedn Watercolor Soc, 96; Moku Hanga Traveling Exhib: Contemp Japanese Woodcuts NAm, Walla Walla Col, Wash, NW Print Coun Galleries, Portland, Ore, Columbia Arts Ctr, Vancouver, Wash & Japanese Cult Soc, San Francisco, Calif, 97; Handpulled Prints XI, Stone Metal Press, San Antonio, Tex, 97, 03; Kyoto Int Woodprint Asn, Exhibits, Kyoto, Japan, 98-2000, 2003; Janet Turner 4th Nat Print Competition, Calif State, Chicago, 02; Western Federation Watercolor Ann, Tex, 2004, Ariz, 2005; Harwood Art Ctr, Albuquerque, NMex, 2005; WFS 22nd Ann, Tucson Mus Art, Ariz; Landscapes of NMex, Manitou Galleries, Santa Fe, 2006. *Collection Arranged:* Art in the Embassies program, US State Dept, 2000. *Teaching:* Teacher, watercolor & acrylics, YWCA, Greater Vallejo, CA, 67, Albuquerque, NMex, 78; instr, Workshop in Traditional, Japanese & Expirimental Woodblock Printing, State Fair Fine Arts Gallery, Albuquerque. *Awards:* Lena Newcastle Award, Am Watercolor Soc, 88; Merit Award, Tubac Ctr Arts, 90; Best of Show, Western Fedn Watercolor Soc, 96; and others; Yosemite Renaissance XIV, 99; Best of Show, NMex Watercolor Soc, fall 2005. *Bibliog:* SPLASH, America's Best Contemporary Watercolors, North Light Books, 91; Phil Metzger (auth), Enliven Your Paintings with Light, North Light Books, 93; Rachel Wolfe (auth), The Acrylic Painter's Book of Styles & Techniques, 97; Gary Greene (auth), Artist's Photo Reference Landscpaes, North Light Books, 2001; Douglas Bullis (auth), 100 Artists of the Southwest, 2006; Suzan Campbell & Suzanne Deats (coauths), Landscapes of New Mexico, Unum Press, 2006. *Mem:* NMex Watercolor Soc; Escribiente; Western Federation Watercolor Soc, signature mem; NMex Printmakers Soc. *Media:* Acrylics, Miscellaneous Media; Monotype, Woodcut, Watercolor, Artist Books. *Publ:* Watercolor, Am Artist, fall 96; Artists Photo Reference Landscapes, Northlight Books, 01; The Acrylic Painter's book of Styles and Techniques, Rachel Wolf, North Light Books, 97. *Dealer:* Weyrich Gallery 2935D Louisiana NE Albuquerque NM 87059; THe Johnsons of Madrid, 2843 Hwy 14, Madrid, NM, 87010; Dartmouth St Gallery 510 14th St SW Albuquerque, NM 87507. *Mailing Add:* PO Box 280 Tijeras NM 87059

SWEET, ROGER
SCULPTOR, CERAMIST
b Huntington Park, Calif, Jan 22, 46. *Study:* Orange Coast Col, Costa Mesa, Calif, AA, 70; Whitney Mus Independent Study Prog, New York, 73; Univ Calif, BFA, 72, MFA, 75. *Work:* Univ NMex, Albuquerque; Santa Fe Arts Mus, NMex. *Exhib:* Solo exhibs, Bowers Mus, Santa Ana, Calif, 75, Fuller Lodge Art Ctr, Los Alamos, NMex, 82, Ctr Contemp Art, Santa Fe, NMex, 85, Fine Arts Gallery, Tex Tech Univ, Lubbock, 87, Johnson Gallery, Univ NMex, Albuquerque, NMex, 88 & Graham Gallery, Albuquerque, NMex, 90; Fac Exhib, Univ NMex, Los Alamos, 91; New Aquisitions 1982-1990, Univ NMex, Johnson Gallery, Univ Art Mus, Albuquerque, 91; Artists of the 20th Century New Mexico, Mus Fine Arts, Santa Fe, 92; Cafe Gallery, Albuquerque, NMex, 92; and many others. *Pos:* Vis artist, Los Angeles State Univ, Calif, 76, San Francisco Art Inst, Calif, 79, Tex Tech Univ, Lubbock, 82; vis lectr, Univ Calif, Irvine, 76-79. *Teaching:* Instr ceramics & sculpture, Univ NMex, Albuquerque, 75-80; fine arts coodr, Univ NMex, Los Alamos, 83-. *Awards:* NMex Humanities Grant Scholar, Socorro Co Rephotographed, 80; Artist Award Grant, Nat Endowment Arts, 89; NMex Humanities. *Bibliog:* Jill Sweet (auth), Dances of the Tewa Pueblo Indians, Sch Am Res Press, Santa Fe, NMex, 85; Robert S Cauthorn (auth), Works have parallel views of man has wrought, Ariz Daily Star, 10/26/86; Artists of 20th Century NMex, Mus NMex Press, 92. *Mailing Add:* PO Box 272 Jemez Springs NM 87025

SWEET, STEVE (STEVEN) MARK
COLLAGE ARTIST, GRAPHIC ARTIST
b Boston, Mass, Mar 13, 52. *Study:* Antioch Col, with Paul Sharits, Allan Jones & Tony Conrad, BA(visual arts), 74. *Work:* Pan-Am Life Insurance Corp, New Orleans; United Media Enterprises, NY; New Orleans Mus Art; Contemp Arts Ctr; Russel Wright Household Designs. *Comn:* The Appliance Giant Mural, comn by Tony Campo, New Orleans, 83; City of New Orleans, 89; New Orleans Int Airport, 90. *Exhib:* Louisiana Major Works, Contemp Arts Ctr, New Orleans, 79; New Orleans Triennial, New Orleans Mus Art, 80 & 86; Focus, Ft Worth Art Mus, 81; Art of New Orleans, Southeast Ctr Contemp Arts, Winston-Salem, NC, 84; New Music Am 83, Hirshhorn Mus & Sculpture Garden, 83; Birmingham Biennial, Birmingham Mus Art, 85; Corcoran Biennial, Corcoran Gallery, Washington, DC, 89. *Pos:* Artist-in-residence, La Superdome, 86; Webmaster, The Historic New Orleans Collection, 97. *Awards:* Services to the Field, Contemp Arts Ctr & Nat Endowment Arts, 80; Nat Endowment Arts Fel, 81 & Interarts grant, 85; Rockefeller Grant, Southeastern Interdisciplinary Fund, 89. *Bibliog:* Roger Green (auth), Flattened people: Portraits in depth, Times Picyunne-States Item, 1/83; Jeff Zeldman (auth), Picture perfect, City Papers, Washington, DC, 10/14/83; David Rive (auth), SteveSweet, Art Papers, 5/87. *Mem:* Contemp Arts Ctr. *Mailing Add:* 16 S Park Pl New Orleans LA 70124

SWEITZER, CHARLES LEROY
MURALIST, PAINTER
b Brownsville, Pa, Mar 23, 39. *Study:* Univ NC, BA, 76; NC Cent Univ, MA, 88; NC Cent Univ, MA(clin psychology), 91. *Comn:* History of North Carolina, comn by Dwight Phillips, Charlotte, NC, 68; Man's Relationship to God, Douglas MacArthur Acad, Tex Baptist, Brownwood, 72; Nashville Civil War Cyclorama, comn by Sam Fleming, Franklin, Tenn, 79; Place in Time, Othal Brand, Loma Linda, Calif, 85. *Pos:* pres, Educ Training Serv, Inc. *Teaching:* Instr visual art, Sweitzer Sch Art, 85-87 & Cent Piedmont Col, 80-82. *Bibliog:* Judith Sands (dir), Making a Mural (film), Media Consultants, 72; Carrol DeWhit (auth), The cyclorama at Franklin, Southern Living Mag, 79. *Mem:* Nat Soc Mural Painters, NY; NC Coun Arts; Wake Co Visual Artists. *Media:* Oil on Canvas. *Mailing Add:* 1302 Timber Dr Garner NC 27529-4730

SWENSEN, J(EAN) MARY JEANETTE HAMILTON
GRAPHIC ARTIST, CALLIGRAPHER
b Laurens, SC, June 25, 10. *Study:* Columbia Univ, with Hans Mueller, BS, 56, with Arthur Young, MA(graphic arts), 60; Fine Arts Sch for Am, Fountainbleau, France, with Lucien Fontanerosa; Ariz State Univ, with Arthur Hahn, 5 summers. *Work:* Metrop Mus Art, NY; Nat Graphic Arts Collection, Smithsonian Inst, Washington, DC; Graphic Arts Collection, NY Pub Libr; Laurens Pub Libr, SC. *Exhib:* Soc Western Artists, M H de Young Mus, San Francisco, 64; Nat Art Roundup, Las Vegas, Nev, 65; Fine Arts Bldg, Colo State Fair, Pueblo, 65; Duncan Gallery, Paris, 74; Co Fed Savings & Loan Asn, Denver, Colo, 78. *Awards:* Honorable Mention for Drawing, Soc Western Artists, 64; Duncan Gallery Prix de Paris, 74. *Mem:* Delta Phi Delta

SWENSON, ADA PEREZ
PAINTER
b New York, NY Jan 9, 1931. *Study:* Studies at NY Art Student League, 51-53; Studies at Stony Brook Univ, 75-77; Studies at Indian River Community Col, 2000-2002; Studied with John Seerly-Lester & Joyce Pike, 2006. *Work:* Univ Fla Res Ctr, Ft Pierce; Vero Beach Mus Art; AE Backus Gallery & Mus, Ft Pierce; Martha Lincoln Gallery, Vero Beach; Count Down Studio, NY; Indian River Community Col Gallery; Everglades Nat Park, Fla. *Comn:* watercolor resort, Harbour Village Resort, Bonaire, 1998; watercolor resort, Port de Palisance, St Maarten, 1999; watercolor seascape, Bahia Redonda Hotel, Venezuela, 1999; oil seascape, Mares Mares Hotel, Venezuela, 1999; oil Florida wildlife, comn by Mr & Mrs H Steward, North Hutchinson Island, Fla, 2000. *Exhib:* Ann 4 county juried show, A E Backus Mus, Fort Pierce, 1999 & 2000; Under the Oak Int Show, Vero Beach, 2001 & 2002-05; Down by the Sea, Vero Beach, 2001; one-woman show, Vero Beach Main Lib, 2001; Vero Beach Invitational, Vero Beach Mus Art, 2002-03; Gayle Smith Board Room, Vero Beach Mus Art, 2002-2003; Vero Beach Libr, 2001-2003; group show, Indian River Community Col & Vero Beach Mus Art, 2005-06; Everglades Nat Park Mus. *Pos:* Landscape painter, muralist, furniture colorist, 99-2006; acting coord, Vero Beach Main County Libr, 2005-06. *Teaching:* Artist in residence, Little Pee Dee State Park, Dillion, South Calif, 2004 & Everglades Nat Park, 2005. *Awards:* Hon award for oil, Vero Beach Invitational, Vero Beach Mus, 2000; 1st Place in oil, 4 Co Juried Show, AE Backus Mus, 2001, 2nd Place monoprint; Scholastic Scholarship Award, Pratt Univ Sch of Design, 49. *Bibliog:* The News, 2000; Vero Beach Press Jour, 2002; Home Town News, 2004-06. *Mem:* Nat Watercolor Soc; Fla Watercolor Soc; Ctr Arts; State of Fla Occupational Licenses; Soc Am Impressionist. *Media:* Oil, Watercolor. *Collection:* antique furniture; lamp tiffiny. *Dealer:* Megan Chanle Gallery Vero Beach FL; Art Direct Naples FL. *Mailing Add:* 256 Marina Dr Hutchinson Island FL 34949

SWENSON, ERICK
PAINTER
Study: Univ N Tex, BFA, 99. *Work:* Rep in permanent collections, Dallas Mus Art, Modern Mus Art, Ft Worth, Tex; Out of the Ordinary: New Art From Tex, Contemp Arts Mus, Houston, 2000; Swallow Swenson, Mus Contemp Art, Sydney, Australia, 2001; New Orleans Triennial, New Orleans Mus Art, 2001; Whitney Biennial, Whitney Mus Am Art, NY, 2004; Natural Hist: Realism Revisited, Scottsdale Mus Contemp Art, Ariz, 2004. *Exhib:* group shows, el clumsio, Angstrom Gallery, Dallas, 96, Mad, Good/Bad, and Dangerous to Know, Good/Bad Art Collective, Denton, Tex, 96, Popo y Lupe, 96, Isolation Chamber, 96, Gay Art/Straight Play, 97; The Big Id, James Cohan Gallery, NY, 2001, Summer, 2002, Air, 2003, Erick Swenson & Ricky Swallow, Karen Lovegrove Gallery, Los Angeles, 2003, Summer Show, James Cohan Gallery, NY, 2004; One Person Show, Strange Loops, 97, Hallowmas, 97, Wee Coma, 97, Very Fake, but Real, Diverse Works Art Space, Houston, 97, Welcome to Important Town, Conduit Gallery Annex, Dallas, 98, Tex Dialogues Parallels, Blue Star Art Gallery, San Antonio, 98, Its a Peeece in Itself, Good/Bad Art Collective, Denton, Tex, 98, Fire Sale 2000, Angstrom Gallery, Dallas, 99. *Awards:* Arch & Anne Giles Kimbrough Fund, Dallas Mus Art, 99. *Mailing Add:* c/o James Cohan Gallery 533 26th St New York NY 10001

SWERGOLD, MARCELLE M
SCULPTOR
b Antwerp, Belg; US citizen. *Study:* NY Univ, painting with Aaron Berkman & Henry Kallem; sculpture at Art Students League, with John Hovanes & Jose deCreft; wax with Harold Caster. *Work:* Yad Vashem-Sculpture Garden & Shaare Zedek Med Ctr, Jerusalem, Israel; City Park Ma' Aleh Adumim, Israel; Fairlawn Jewish Ctr, Fairlawn, NJ; The Jewish Ctr, NY; Mudge, Rose, Guthrie, Alexander & Feldon, 82; and others. *Exhib:* Fairleigh Dickenson Univ, NJ, 72; Union Carbide Gallery, Park Ave, NY, 78; Cork Gallery, Lincoln Ctr, NY, 90, 91 & 94; Leaver House Gallery, Park Ave, NY, 80, 88, 90, 93, 94 & 98; Allied Artists of Am, Nat Acad Galleries, NY, Bankers Trust Co, Park Ave, NY; Broom St Gallery, 91, 92, 93, 94 & 95; Betty Barker Gallery, Carriage Barn Art Ctr, New Canaan, Conn, 98-. *Awards:* First Prize, Womanart Gallery, New York, 77 & Stanley Richter Asn Arts, Danbury, Conn, 85; Vincent Glinsky Mem Award, Audubon Artists, 86; Union Carbide, First Prize. *Bibliog:* Article, Museum collection grows again, The Herald, New Britain, Conn, 12/80; articles, Jerusalem Post, 10/90 & The News Times, Danbury, Conn; Mizrachi Magazine (Amit), 82. *Mem:* NY Soc Women Artists (corresp secy, 77-79, pres, 79-81, exec vpres, 81-); Artists Equity Asn, NY; Contemp Artist Guild. *Media:* Bronze, Stone. *Dealer:* 246 W 80th St New York NY 10024; 43 Paul St Danbury CT 06810. *Mailing Add:* 450 West End Ave New York NY 10024

SWETCHARNIK, SARA MORRIS
PAINTER, SCULPTOR
b Shelby, NC, May 21, 55. *Study:* Schuler Sch Fine Art, 73-79; Art Students League, 80-82. *Work:* Haussners Restaurant & Mus, Baltimore, Md. *Comn:* Portrait sculpture, comn by Walter Finch Esq, 78. *Exhib:* Nat Sculpture Soc Gallery, NY, 95; Am Medallic Sculpture Asn Invitational Exhib, Am Numismatic Mus, Colorado Springs, 95; East Meets West: Old & New, Delaplaine Visual Arts Ctr, Frederick, Md, 95; Juried Exhib, Delaplaine Visual Arts Ctr, 96; Canine Art, Dog Mus, St Louis, Mo, 96. *Pos:* Resident fel, Va Ctr Creative Arts, Sweet Briar, Va, 90, Am Numismatic Asn Conf, Am Numismatic Mus, Colo Springs, 94; juror, Nat Sculpture Exhib (V Concurso de Escultura y Ceramica Dante Lazzaroni Andino), Inst Honduren de Cult Interamericana, Tegucigalpa, Honduras, 95. *Teaching:* Monitor for Robert Beverly Hale, Art Students League, 79-80, fel, 81; instr, Frederick Acad Arts, Md, 81-82 & workshop, Landon Sch, Washington, DC, 91-96. *Awards:* Artist's Residency Fel, Va Ctr Creative Arts, Sweet Briar, Va, 90; Juror: Biennial Nat Sculpture & Ceramics Exhib, V VI Concursos de Escultura y Ceramica, Instituto Hondureno de Cultura Interamericana, Tequcigalpa, Honduras, 95 & 97; Artist's Residency fel, Am Numismatic Asn Conf, Am Numismatic Mus, Colorado Springs, 94 & 98. *Bibliog:* Dena Crosson (auth), Artists in residence, Frederick Mag, 6/94; Karen Gardner (auth), Sculptor gives life to zoo animals, Assoc Press, 94; George Baumann (interviewer), Interview of Sara Morris Swetcharnik on Maryland by George, Channel 7 News, Baltimore, 95. *Mem:* Fulbright Asn, Washington, DC; Delaplaine Visual Art Ctr, Frederick, Md. *Media:* Bronze, Terracotta. *Publ:* Portrait Medals of the Renaissance at the Nat Gallery, 94; Romeo's offering, 96; Spanish & English in Guacamaya: Revista Historico, Cultural de Honduros, 96. *Mailing Add:* Swetcharnik Studio 7044 Woodville Rd Mount Airy MD 21771

SWETCHARNIK, WILLIAM NORTON
PAINTER, SCULPTOR
b Philadelphia, Pa, Oct 18, 1951. *Study:* RI Sch Design, 69-71; Univ Calif, San Diego, 73-76; Towson State Univ, Md, BS, 77. *Work:* Art Mus, Fla Int Univ, Miami, Fla; Cintas Found, NY; Comm Cult Exchange between United States & Madrid, Spain; Salisbury St Hosp, Salisbury, Md. *Exhib:* Solo exhibs, Weinberg Ctr Arts, Frederick, Md, 80, Mt St Mary's Col, Emmitsburg, Md, 81, Harbor Gallery, NY, Cold Spring

Harbor, Foxhall Gallery, Washington, DC, John Pence Gallery, San Francisco, Calif, Md Col Art & Design, Silver Spring, Md, 86, Washington Co Mus Art, Hagerstown, Md, 93; Foxhall Gallery, Wash, DC, 82-84; Md Art Place, Baltimore, 90; Nat Acad Design, NY, 90. *Pos:* Resident artist, Hood Col, Fred, Md. *Awards:* Cintas Found Fel, Inst Int Educ, 85-86; Yaddo Residency, 87; Fulbright Int Fel, Spain, 87-89 & Honduras, 94-95. *Bibliog:* Robin Longman (auth), Emerging artists, Am Artist, 84. *Mem:* Delaplaine visual Art Ctr; Fulbright Asn. *Media:* Oils. *Mailing Add:* 7044 Woodville Rd Mount Airy MD 21771

SWICK, LINDA ANN
SCULPTOR
b Bedford, Ohio, Sept 9, 48. *Study:* Kent State Univ, BA, 70; Fla State Univ, MFA, 77. *Exhib:* Solo show, Washington Proj Arts, Washington, DC, 79; Rutgers Univ, Camden, NJ, 79; Laguna Gloria Art Mus, Austin, 80; Middendorf Lane, Washington, DC, 80; Corcoran Gallery, Washington, DC, 81; Lawndale, Univ Houston, 82. *Pos:* Set designer for animated films, Broadcast Arts, Washington, DC, 80-. *Awards:* Fel, City Washington, DC, 82. *Bibliog:* Sylvia Shauck (auth), interview, Art & Craft Mag, 6/80; Charlotte Moser (auth), Washington art, Art News, 10/81. *Media:* Wood. *Dealer:* Gallery K 2032 P St Washington DC. *Mailing Add:* 1728 S St NW Washington DC 20009

SWID, STEPHEN CLAAR
COLLECTOR
b NY City, Oct 26, 40. *Study:* Ohio State Unive, BS, 62. *Pos:* trustee, Horace Mann Sch, New York City, formerly; exec vpres bd dir, Lenox Sch NY, formerly; Mgt trainee, Alside Aluminum Co, Akron, Ohio, 62-63; securities analyst, Dreyfus Fund, New York City, 63-66; sr investment off, Oppenheimer Fund, 66-67; gen partner, City Assoc, 67-69, Swid Investors, New York City, 70-78; co-chmn, bd Gen, Felt Industries Inc, Saddle Brook, NJ, 74-86, Knoll Int, 77-86; chmn bd, Chief Exec Officer, SBK Entertainment World, Inc, New York City, 86-89; chmn, Chief Exec Officer, SCS Commun, 89-, SESAC, 92-; vis comt, 20th century art Metrop Mus Art, currently; dir, Munic Art Soc, currently; trustee, Solomon R Guggenheim Mus,currently; bd dir, Bally Fitness Corp, currently; New Sch Univ, currently. *Mem:* Coun Foreign Relations. *Mailing Add:* SESAC Inc 152 W 57th St New York NY 10019

SWIGART, LYNN S
PHOTOGRAPHER
b Kansas City, Mo, Aug 22, 30. *Study:* Bradley Univ, Peoria, Ill, BS(psychol, philos); also photog with Minor White & George Tice. *Work:* Carpenter Ctr for Visual Arts, Harvard Univ, Cambridge, Mass; Stanford Univ; Ill State Mus; Lakeview Mus; Petry Collection; Cape Ann Mus, Gloucester, Mass. *Exhib:* Radius, 76, Burpee Art Mus, Rockford, Ill, 76; one-man shows, Univ Conn, 77, Stanford Univ, 78, Univ Iowa, 78, Ill State Mus, 78, Art Inst, Chicago, 78, Lakeview Mus, Peoria, Ill, 80, Cape Ann Hist Mus, Glouchester, Mass, 81; Twelfth Biennial Michiana Regional, 82; Arts Works Nat Photog Exhib, Brattleboro, Vt, 82; Camera Movements, Moore Col Art, Philadelphia, Pa, 82; Ill Photogr, 85; Ill State Mus, 85; Arts Center, Westport, Conn, 91, 92, 93; Retrospective, Cape Ann Mus, Gloucester, Mass, 2005. *Teaching:* Instr photog, Multi-Media Arts Inst, Bradley Univ, summer 73 & 74. *Publ:* Contribr, Olson's Gloucester, LSU Press, 80, The Best of Photog Ann, 82 & NDak Quart, 85. *Dealer:* Wenniger Gallery, Rockport, Mass. *Mailing Add:* 13 Marble Rd Gloucester MA 01930

SWOFFORD, BETH
COLLECTOR
Pos: Motion picture agent, Creative Artists Agency (Civil Aeronautics Admin), Beverly Hills. *Awards:* Named one of Top 200 Collectors, ARTnews Mag, 2004. *Mem:* Mus Contemp Art, LA (Board Trus). *Collection:* Contemporary Art. *Mailing Add:* Creative Artists Agency 9830 Wilshire Blvd Beverly Hills CA 90212

SYLVAN, RITA M
PHOTOGRAPHER, PAINTER
b Minneapolis, Minn, Mar 21, 28. *Study:* Minneapolis Sch Art, Univ Minn with Ralston Crawford & Paul Burlin, BA, 48; Columbia Univ, MA, 67; Fine Arts Inst; Penland Sch; Bennington Col with Stuart Davis. *Work:* Rose Mus, Brandeis Univ, Waltham, Mass; Columbia Univ, NY; Boca Raton Mus Art. *Exhib:* Regional Exhib, Minneapolis Inst Art, 48; 50 NJ Artists, Newark Mus, 65; US State Dept, Nat Asn Women Artists Traveling Exhib, India & Pakistan, 65-66; Philharmonic Hall Invitational, NY, 69; NJ State, Biennial, NJ State Mus, Trenton, 69; Ann Artists Guild Exhib, Norton Gallery Art, Palm Beach, Fla, 84-89; All Fla Exhib, Boca Raton Mus Art, Fla, 86, 87, 88 & 89; 32nd Ann Hortt Exhib, Ft Lauderdale Mus Art, Fla, 90; one-man show, Art in Pub Places, Boca Raton Nat Endowment for the Arts, Bergen Mus, Pembroke Pines Millennium; Retrospective, Boca Mus, Pinecrest Sch, 97. *Pos:* Asst cur photog, Brooklyn Mus, NY, 50-51; asst to dir photog, Mus Mod Art, New York, 52-53. *Teaching:* St Andrews Sch, Boca Raton, Fla; instr & dir art, Art Ctr of Northern NJ, Tenafly High Sch, 68-73, Boca Raton Mus. *Awards:* Ann Award, Nat Asn Women Artists, 66; Best 2-D, Prof Artists Guild Ann Exhib, 89-94; First Prize, Norton Gallery, 92; and others. *Bibliog:* Bruce Weber (auth), Artcetera (auction catalog), Broward Art Guild, 90. *Mem:* Prof Artists Guild (admin chmn, 86-90); Women's Caucus Art; 2 plus 3--Artists Orgn, Ft Lauderdale, Fla; Broward Art Guild. *Media:* Color Photography; Mixed Media, Watercolor. *Publ:* Contribr, Edward Steichen: A memoir, Connoisseur, 2/88

SYLVESTER, ROBERT
EDUCATOR
b New York City, NY. *Pos:* dir, cult affairs Western Wash Univ; dean, Sch Fine & Performing Arts; pres, Portland State Univ, 1997-. *Mailing Add:* Portland State UnivSch Fine & Performing Art 349 Lincoln Hall Portland OR 97207-0751

SYLVESTRE, GUY
CRITIC, WRITER
b Sorel, Que, May 17, 18. *Study:* Col Ste Marie, Montreal; Univ Ottawa, MA. *Pos:* Ed, Gants du Ciel, 43-46; nat librn, Nat Libr, Ottawa, 68-83. *Mem:* Can Libr Asn; Soc Ecrivains Can; Royal Soc Can (pres 73-74); Acad Can Francaise. *Publ:* Auth, Anthologie de la Poesie Canadienne-Francaise, Beauchemin, 64 & 74; Panorama des Lettres Canadiennes Francaises, 64 & Literature in French Canada, 67, EOQ; Ecrivains Canadiens, HMH, 64 & McGraw, 67; Structures Sociales du Canada Francais, Laval, 66; and many others. *Mailing Add:* 2286 Bowman Rd Ottawa ON K1H 6V6 Canada

SYROP, MITCHELL
CONCEPTUAL ARTIST
b Yonkers, NY, Dec 21, 53. *Study:* Pratt Inst, Brooklyn, NY, BFA, 75; Calif Inst Arts, Valencia, MFA, 78. *Work:* Los Angeles Co Mus, Calif; Newport Art Mus, Newport Beach, Calif; La Jolla Mus Contemp Art, Calif; Lannan Found, Los Angeles, Calif; Tampa Mus Art, Fla. *Comn:* Seattle Arts Comn, Washington, 89; Peter & Eileen Norton, Santa Monica, Calif, 89; Progressive Corp, 89; Times Square spectacular lightboard, Pub Art Fund, NY, 89; Los Angeles Central Libr, Calif, 90. *Exhib:* Video: A Retrospective/Long Beach Mus Art, 1974-1984 (with catalog), Long Beach Mus Art, 84; Avante-Garde in the Eighties (with catalog), Los Angeles Co Mus Art, 87; The Photog of Invention: Am Pictures of the Eighties, Nat Mus Am Art, Washington, DC, Mus Contemp Art, Chicago, Walker Art Ctr, Minneapolis, 89; one-person exhibs, Kuhlenschmidt Simon, Los Angeles, 88, Lieberman & Saul Gallery, NY, 89 & 90, Univ Art Mus, Univ Calif, Santa Barbara, 89, Galeria Oliva Arauna, Madrid, Spain, 90 & 93, Rosamund Felsen Gallery, Los Angeles, 92 & 93 & Santa Monica Mus Art, 94, Rosamund Felsen Gallery, Santa Monica, Calif, 96, 98, Galeria Olivia Arauna, Madrid, Spain, 97; Spec Collections The Photog Order from Pop to Now, Int Ctr Photog, NY, 92; LA Stories, Jack Rutberg Fine Arts, Los Angeles, 93; X-Treme Research, Calif State Univ, Los Angeles, 93. *Teaching:* Minneapolis Col Design, Minn, 85; Art Ctr Col Design, Pasadena, Calif, 87-90; Otis Art Inst/Parsons Sch Design, Los Angeles, 89-91; Univ Calif, Santa Barbara, 89-90; instr, Calif Inst Arts, Valencia, 90-91. *Awards:* Nat Endowment Arts Fel, 87. *Bibliog:* Michael Duncan (auth), Review, Art in Am, 12/93; David Pagel (auth), Syrop's dead: chilling, mind boggling, Los Angeles Times, 4/7/94; Lee Carter (auth), Review, Visions, fall 94. *Publ:* Auth, Tortured Thoughts, 80; Be careful around these people, LightWorks Mag, No 13, fall 80; Demenstruation, Los Angeles Inst Contemp Art J, 85 & 89; Loaded (exhib catalog), Richard Kuhlenschmidt Gallery, Santa Monica, Calif, 89. *Dealer:* Rosamund Felsen Gallery 8525 Santa Monica Blvd Los Angeles CA 90069. *Mailing Add:* 1640 Point View Los Angeles CA 90035

SZABO, JOSEPH GEORGE
CARTOONIST, EDITOR
b Budapest, Hungary, Feb 4, 50; US citizen. *Study:* Sch Masters Typography, cert, 69; Hungarian Acad Journalism, BA(summa cum laude), 74; Sch Com, cert, 78. *Work:* Cult Ctr Scharpoord, Knokke-Heist, Belg; Yomiuri Shimbun, Tokyo; Cartoon Art Mus, San Francisco. *Exhib:* Humorfoto '82-'86, Cult Ctr Scharpoord, Kuokke Heist, Belg, 82-86; Man and His World, Int Salon Cartoons, Montreal, 84-86; Yomiuri Int Cartoon Contest, Tokyo, 85-86; Everything is Cabaret, World Cartoon Gallery, Skopje, Yugoslavia, 86; South Africa, Montevideo, Uruguay, 86; Int Simavi Cartoon Competition, Istanbul, Turkey, 86. *Pos:* Assoc art dir, Nôk Lapja (weekly), Budapest, Hungary, 75-78; managing graphics ed & ed cartoonist, Magyar Nemzet (daily), Budapest, Hungary, 78-80; art dir & cartoonist, Sting (satirical mag), Ctr Sq, Philadelphia, 84-85. *Awards:* Press Prize, Humorfoto '84, Belg, 84; Bronze Medals, Yomiuri Int Cartoon Contest, Tokyo, 85 & 86. *Bibliog:* Istvan Molnar (auth), article, Magyar Grafika, 2/80; Gloria Sipes Paleveda (auth), Hungarian political cartoonist, Philadelphia Inquirer, 6/23/85; Ann Whiteside (auth), Cartoonist's sketches span the globe, Montgomeryville Spirit, 4/30/86. *Mem:* Nat Cartoonists Soc; Asn Am Ed Cartoonists. *Media:* Coated Cardboard, Marker. *Publ:* Auth, Photo-Cartoon Calendar, self-publ, 83; Illus, Animal Farm, by George Orwell, Rainbow Publ, 84; auth, Never pointing a different way, Target, 85; ed, WittyWorld, Int Cartoon Mag, 87; Finest International Political Cartoons of our Time, 92, Witty World Books, 92. *Mailing Add:* 214 School St North Wales PA 19454

SZABO, STEPHEN LEE
PHOTOGRAPHER
b Berwick, Pa, July 17, 40. *Study:* Art Ctr Col Design, Los Angeles, Calif; Pa State Univ. *Work:* Int Ctr Photog, Mus Mod Art, NY; Corcoran Gallery Art, Libr Cong, Washington, DC; Int Mus Photog, George Eastman House, Rochester, NY; Nat Mus Am Art, Washington, DC; Fine Arts Mus S, Mobile, Ala. *Exhib:* Old Techniques by Young Photographers, Eastern Shore, Phillips Collection, Washington, DC, 73, Springfield Art Mus, Mo, 77, Hunter Mus Art, Chattanooga, Tenn, 77, Int Ctr Photog, NY, 77, Fine Arts Mus of the South, Mobile, Ala, 77 & Baltimore Mus Art, Md, 77; one person exhibs, Kathleen Ewing Gallery, Washington, DC, 78, 86, 91 & 96, Madison Art Ctr, Wis, 79, The Mariner's Mus, Newport News, Va, 82, Sheldon Mem Art Gallery, Lincoln, Nebr, 95; Acad Arts, Easton, Md, 78; Auto as Icon, Int Mus Photog, George Eastman House, Rochester, NY, 79; Three Washington Photographers, Kathleen Ewing Gallery, Washington, DC, 80, The First Nine Yrs, 85; Environment Urbain, Charleroi, France, 82; Hommage a la Terre Natale, Hungarian Nat Mus, Budapest (with catalog), 83; The Washington Show, Corcoran Gallery Art, Washington, DC, 85; A Breath of Light, The Contemp Platinum Print, NJ State Mus, Trenton, 86. *Teaching:* Instr, Corcoran Sch Art, Washington, DC. *Awards:* Nat Endowment Arts, 86. *Bibliog:* Paul Richard (auth), Of time and the photograph, Washington Post, 72; A dialogue with the present to document the past, Camera, 76; Mark Power (auth), Washington photographs and the contact print, Washington Rev Arts, 77. *Publ:* Illusr, Where We Live, Fed Home Loan Mortgage Corp, 73; auth-illusr, The Eastern Shore, Addison House, 76. *Mailing Add:* c/o Kathleen Ewing Gallery 1609 Connecticut Ave NW Washington DC 20009

SZARKOWSKI, T(HADDEUS) JOHN
ADMINISTRATOR
b Ashland, Wis, Dec 18, 25. *Study:* Univ Wis, BS, 48; Philadelphia Col Art, BS, 72; Minneapolis Col Art & Design, BS, 74. *Work:* Auth: The Idea of Louis Sullivan, 1956, The Face of Minnesota, 1958, The Photographer & the Am Landscape, 1963, The Photographer's Eye, 1966, Walker Evans, 1971, Looking at Photographs, 1973, Mirrors & Windows: Am Photography Since 1960, 1978, Irving Penn, 1984, Photography Until Now, 1990, Ansel Adams at 100, 1991, Atget, 2000, Photographs, 2005; co-auth (with Alfred Stieglitz): Alfred Stieglitz at Lake George, 1995. *Pos:* Photog Walker Art Ctr, Minneapolis, 48-51; dir, dept photog (emeritus) Mus Modern Art, New York City, 62-. *Teaching:* instr, Albright Art Sch, Univ Buffalo, 51-53; instr in photog, Univer Minn, 50. *Awards:* Fel John Simon Guggenheim Found, 54, & 61. *Mailing Add:* Mus Modern Art 11 W 53rd St New York NY 10019-5498

SZEITZ, P RICHARD
EDUCATOR, SCULPTOR
b Budapest, Hungary, Jan 5, 30; US citizen. *Study:* St Anselm Univ, Rome, 50-53; Layton Sch Art, BFA, 57; Univ Wis-Madison, MS & MFA, 59. *Work:* Dallas Mus Fine Arts, Tex; Herman Otto Mus, Miskole, Hungary; Minn Mus, St Paul; Rourke Gallery, Moorhead State Univ, Moorhead, Minn. *Comn:* St Albert (sculpture), Dominican Priory, Irving, Tex, 63; Fountain of Abundance (sculpture), W Acres Shopping Ctr, Fargo, NDak, 72; Assumption of the Virgin (sculpture), Assumption Church, Barnsville, Minn, 78; three-story fountain with 6 figures, First Bank, Robbinsdale, Minn, 83; Minnesota Flora and Fauna (six fountains series), Centennial Lakes Condominium Courtyards, Edina, Minn, 91. *Teaching:* From instr to assoc prof, Univ Dallas, 60-66; prof sculpture, art & law & dept chmn, Moorhead State Univ, 66-94. *Awards:* Fulbright Hayes Lectureship, US Govt, 65. *Media:* Metal, Cast Bronze. *Mailing Add:* 1220 S 12th Ave Moorhead MN 56560-3719

SZESKO, JUDITH CLARANN See Jaidinger, Judith C Clarann Szesko

SZESKO, LENORE RUNDLE
PAINTER, PRINTMAKER
b Galesburg, Ill, Mar 13, 33. *Study:* Art Inst Chicago, BFA(drawing, painting, illus), 61, MFA(painting), 66; wood engraving with Adrian Troy. *Work:* Standard Oil Co, Chicago; NJ State Mus; Jayell Publ House, Miami, Fla; Springfield Col; Kemper Ins Co Collection, Long Grove, Ill. *Exhib:* Conn Acad Fine Arts 62nd Ann, Wadsworth Atheneum, Hartford, Conn, 72; Cedar City Ann Fine Art Exhib, Utah, 72-75; Contemp Am Graphics, Old Bergen Art Guild, Bayonne, NJ (traveling exhib), 72-80; Soc Am Graphic Artists 52nd Nat Print Exhib, NY & Chicago, 73; NH Print Club 1st & 2nd Int, Nashua, 73-74. *Awards:* James R Marsh Mem Purchase Prize, Hunterdon Art Ctr 16th Print, Clinton, NJ, 72; Muth Award, Miniature Painters, Sculptors & Gravers Soc of Washington, DC, 73; Award Highest Merit-Drawing, Miniature Art Soc of Fla Nat Exhib, 76; and others. *Mem:* Audubon Artists, Inc, NY; Painters & Sculptors Soc NJ; Boston Printmakers, Mass; Miniature Art Soc NJ; La Watercolor Soc. *Media:* Multimedia. *Collection:* American Indian and Pre-Columbian, some African art; antique furniture and dolls. *Mailing Add:* 5728 N Austin Ave Chicago IL 60646-6231

SZILVASY, LINDA MARKULY
PAINTER, WRITER
b Granite City, Ill, Oct, 7, 40. *Study:* Lindenwood Col Women, St Charles, Mo, BA, 61; George Peabody Col, Nashville, Tenn, MA, 62. *Work:* Eden Theol Sem, Webster Groves, Mo; US Army Chaplain Mus, Ft Hamilton, NY; Lindenwood Col Women; George Peabody Col. *Comn:* Paintings used for official Christmas cards, First Cavalry Div, Ft Hood, Tex, 72, III Corps, Ft Hood, Tex, 73 & 75 & Officer Wives Club, Ft Leonard Wood, Mo, 75; jeweled ostrich shells painted symbols of longevity, comn by Charlene Franz for Premier Sun Yun-hsuan & Pres Chiang Ching-kuo, Taiwan, 78; jeweled egg by Am Egg Board for First Lady Nancy Reagan, 80. *Exhib:* One-woman show, Petite Pigalle Gallery, St Louis, Mo, 62; 10th Ann Arts & Crafts Festival, Killeen, Tex, 73; jeweled eggs, Galeria de las Artes, Las Cruces, NMex, 80; Centennial Mus, Univ Tex El Paso, 86; Glorietta's Gallery, El Paso, Tex, 86-90; Sun Bowl Exhib, juried show 3 paintings, Int Mus Art, El Paso, Tex, 2004 & 05; Fall Show, juried show 3 paintings, El Paso Art Asn, 04; Arts Int Exhib, juried show, juror's recog award, Int Mus Art, El Paso, 2005; June Artistry, Rio Bravo Watercolorists, Int Mus Art, merit award, El Paso, 2005; Spring Show, El Paso Art Asn, juried show, third place, Basset Pl, 2005; The Arts of March, Rio Bravo Watercolorists, int Mus Art, juried 3 paintings, 2006; Patriotic Art Exhib, El Paso Art Asn, merit award, Crossland Gallery, El Paso, 2006. *Pos:* Co-chmn Arts Comt, Metamora Woman's Club, 91-92; 1st vpres, Rio Bravo Watercolorists, El Paso, Tex, 2004-07. *Teaching:* Art instr, Omaha Pub Sch System, Nebr, 63-66, Killeen Independent Sch Dist, Tex, 72-73 & var eggs-ibits, Dallas, Mich & Md, 75-. *Awards:* Sweepstakes Winner, 10th Ann Arts & Crafts Festival, Killeen, Tex, 73; Best in Show Eggs-ibits: Dallas, 75, New Carrollton, Md, 75 & 76 & Oklahoma City, Okla, 76; Best Depicting Texas History, Tex Guild Egg Shell Artists, 86. *Bibliog:* Eggs $250 a dozen and up, El Paso Today Mag, 4/80; Barbra Brabec (auth), The jeweled egg, Artisan Crafts, 4/75; The egg and leather, Make It With Leather Mag, 1/77. *Mem:* Am Crafts Coun; Artists' Equity Asn; Tex Guild Egg Shell Artists (1st vpres, 85-86); Nat Egg Art Guild; Rio Brave Watercolors Asn; Woman's Club of El Paso; El Paso Art Asn; Rio Bravo Watercolorists (1st vpres 2005-07). *Media:* Jeweled Egg Shells, Paintings and Sculptures Inside; Paintings on Canvas. *Publ:* Contrib, A bit of the woods, Creative Crafts Mag, 6/75; auth, The Jeweled Egg: A Handbook for Beginning and Advanced Craftsmen, Assoc Press, 76; contrib, Barbara Brabec's Creative Cash: How to Sell Your Crafts, Countryside Bks, 79; Aline Becker (auth), Almost Everything about Heirloom Eggs, 80; illus, Dottie Miller's Around the World in 99 Beds, Eden Pub House, 73. *Mailing Add:* 9006 Belk St El Paso TX 79904

SZNAJDERMAN, MARIUS S
PRINTMAKER, PAINTER
b Paris, France, July 18, 26; US citizen. *Study:* Sch Plastic Arts, Caracas, Venezuela, with Rafael Monasterios, Ramon Martin Durban & Ventrillon-Horber, 47-48; Columbia Univ, BS, with printmaker Hans Mueller, BS, 53; T C Colombia, MFA, 58. *Work:* Mus Mod Art, Jewish Heritage Mus, NY Pub Libr, Yeshiva Univ Mus, Yivo Inst, NY; Rayo Mus, Roldanillo, Colombia; Yad Washem Mus, Jerusalem, Israel; Nat Gallery, Mus Contemp Art, Caracas, Venezuela; B'nai B'rith Klutznick Mus, Washington, DC; Fine Arts Mus, Caracas, Venezuela; Libr Cong, Washington; N J State Mus, Trenton; Tel Aviv Univ, Ramataviv, Israel. *Comn:* Prints, Agrupacion Grafica Pan Americana, 78-86; Carton de Venezuela, 86; Holocaust, brass monument, Temple Bethel, Hackensack, NJ. *Exhib:* Galeria Venezuela, NY, 76; One-man shows, Estevez Vilas Gallery, Cincinnati, 82-84, Rayo Mus, Colombia, 82 & Galeria Borkas, Lima, 82, Mus Contemp Hispanic Arts, NY, 89 & Corinne Timsit Int Gallery, San Juan, PR, 90; Jewish Community Ctr Palisades, Tenafly, NJ, 90; Mus Contemp Art, Caracas, Venezuela, 91; The Venezuelan Ctr Gallery, NY, 99; Nat Yiddish Book Ctr, Amherst, Mass, 2005-06; and others. *Pos:* Dir, Galeria Venezuela, New York, 74-83. *Teaching:* Instr art hist & painting, Sch Visual Arts, New York, 65-71; lectr, Fairleigh Dickinson Univ, Madison, NJ, 69-73; artist-in-residence, AIM Prog, NJ Pub Sch, 74-77. *Bibliog:* Hispanic Culture in New Jersey (film), NJ Pub TV, 78; Carlos Silva (auth), Historia De La Pintura en Venezuela, Tomo III, Caracas, 89. *Media:* All. *Publ:* Illusr, Magicismos, Colleccion Rasgos Comunes, Caracas, 89; Who were the Precolombians, New World Art, Pinehurst, NC, 92. *Mailing Add:* 242 Summit Ave Hackensack NJ 07601

SZOKE, JOHN
DEALER, PUBLISHER
Study: NY Univ, BS, 72; Grad Sch Bus Admin, MBA, 73. *Pos:* Owner, John Szoke Editions, NY. *Teaching:* Asst prof, Baruch Col, City Univ NY, 75-79; bus sem, Gallaudet Univ, Washington. *Awards:* Personal Citation, Int Olympic Comt, 66, 96; Recognition Award, Am Anorexia/Bulimia Asn, 93. *Bibliog:* There Are Miracles-Twelve American Careers, Bolgar-Fazekas, 93; The Life & times on an art dealer, SunStorm Fine Art Mag, winter 96. *Mem:* Fine Art Publ Asn; Gallaudet Univ, Washington (mem bd assoc). *Media:* Prints, Works on Paper. *Mailing Add:* 591 Broadway 3rd Flr New York NY 10012-3232

SZOLD, LAUREN G
PAINTER, SCULPTOR
b New York, NY, Nov 26, 57. *Study:* RI Sch Design, 81. *Comn:* Ca-Ca Poo-Poo, Udo Kittelmann, Kolnischer Kunstverein, Koln, Ger, 97; Threshold/Recent American Sculpture, Serralves Found, Oporto, Portugal, 95; Heaven's in the Back Seat of My Cadillac, NAME, Chicago, Il, 95; Wild Friendzy, comn by Paula Hayes, NY, 94; Dyad, comn by Annie Herron, Sauce, Brooklyn, NY, 94. *Exhib:* Skin Deep, New Mus Contemp Art, NY, 93; Out Of Town: The Williamsburg Paradigm, Kranert Art Mus, Champange, Ill, 93; Pieces ou Sol, Le Consortium, Centre d'Art Contemporain, Dijon, France, 93; 44th Biennial Exhib Contemp Am Painting: Painting Outside Painting, The Corcoran Mus Art, Washington, DC; Sharpe Studios, Marie Walsh Sharpe Art Found, NY, 96; Show and Tell, Lauren Whittel Gallery, NY, 96; Bronwyn Keenan Gallery, NY, 96; Auto-Portrait: The Calligraphy of Power, Exit Art, NY, 97; Do Paintings Dream of Veronese Green?, Elga Wimmer Gallery, NY, 99; Artists to Artists, New York City, 02. *Awards:* award, Marie Walsh Sharpe Art Found, 96; award, Yado, Syracuse, NY, 93. *Bibliog:* Ynglingagatenl, Zapp Mag, Vol 4, 4-95; Gregory Volk (auth), Lauren Szold Transgressing Borders, Artnews, 105, 10/94; Roberta Smith (auth), Review, The NY Times, C22, 2/25/94. *Media:* All media. *Publ:* Artists to Artists, a Decade of the Space Prog. *Mailing Add:* 375 New Rochelle Rd Bronxville NY 10708

T

TABACK, SIMMS
ILLUSTRATOR, DESIGNER
b New York, NY, Feb 13, 32. *Study:* Cooper Union, BFA; Sch Visual Arts. *Exhib:* Soc Illusr Ann Exhib, 63-86; Art Dir Club Show; Am Inst Graphic Arts; Soc Publ Designers; Type Dir Club. *Teaching:* Instr illus & design, Sch Visual Arts, New York, 67-82, Syracuse Univ Grad Program, 94. *Awards:* Cert of Merit, Soc Illusr Show, Ten Best Illus Children's Books, New York Times, 67 & 99; Louie Award, Greeting Card Asn; Caldecott Honor Bk, 98, Medal, 2000; Graphic Artists Guild Lifetime Achievement Award, 99; Cooper Union-Augustus St Gaudens Medal, 2000. *Mem:* Soc Illusr; Illusr Guild (pres, 75-76); Graphic Artists Guild (pres, 79-80 & 90-91). *Media:* Pen & Ink; Watercolor; Mixed Media. *Res:* Simms Taback; 2005 DVD & Video Weston Scholastic. *Publ:* Illusr, Ruggy Riddles, Dial, 86; Roadbuilders, Viking, 94; Sam's Wild West Show, Dial, 95; Two Little Witches, Candlewick Press, 96; There was an Old Lady Who Swallowed a Fly, Viking, 97; When I First Came to This Land, Putnam, 98; Joseph Had a Little Overcoat, Viking, 99; This is the House that Jack Built Putnam, 2002; Kibitzers & Fools, Viking, 2005. *Mailing Add:* 2747 Channel Dr Ventura CA 93003

TABAK, CHAIM
PAINTER, SCULPTOR
b Bamberg, Ger, Nov 13, 46, US citizen. *Study:* Brooklyn Col, 70-71; Art Students League NY, cert, 75. *Work:* Brooklyn Mus; Wichita Art Mus, Kans; Weatherspoon Art Gallery, Univ NC; Samuel Dorsky Mus, State Univ NY, New Paltz; Fred F French Investment Corp; Nielson Corp. *Exhib:* On Radioactive Waste, Harvard Univ, 77 & Yale Univ, 78; Art and the Law, Landmark Ctr, Minneapolis, 82; HRCA 67th Ann,

Hudson River Mus, Yonkers, NY, 82; The Radwaste and Stonehenge Series (with catalog), Wichita Art Mus, Kans, Carnegie Ctr Arts, Kans, Mulvane Art Ctr, Washburn Univ, Topeka, Pittsburg State Univ, Kans, Emporia State Univ, Kans, Samuel Dorksy Mus State Univ NY, New Paltz, Nelson Fosdick Gallery, State Univ NY, Alfred Tyler Art Gallery, State Univ NY, Oswego, 85-89; one-man show, Dorsky Galleries, NY, 86; Contemp Bestiary, Islip Art Mus, NY, 89; Recent Acquisitions, Samuel Dorsky Mus, State Univ NY, 92. *Bibliog:* Anthony S Maulucci (auth), Radioactive waste as a subject of art, New Haven Register, 2/5/78; Nancy Pate (auth), Books are art with a message, Wichita Eagle Beacon, 4/7/85. *Media:* Mixed Media; Sculptural Relief. *Dealer:* Mixed-Media Gallery 10 Main St Ste 324 New-Paltz NY 12561. *Mailing Add:* 41 Hornbeck Ridge Poughkeepsie NY 12603

TABASCO, EVANGELINE See Wiener, Sam Evangeline Tabasco

TABOR, VIRGINIA S
PAINTER, PRINTMAKER
b Putnam, Conn, Mar 28, 26. *Study:* Bethany Col, BA, 47; Cornell Univ, MA, 50; Pa Acad Fine Arts, 66-70; also critiques with Myron Barnstone, 88-92. *Exhib:* Boston Printmakers, 87; Provident Nat Bank, Philadelphia, Pa, 87; Philadelphia Art Show, Philadelphia, Pa, 90 & 91; Exhib of the Fel Pa Acad Fine Arts, 93; Barnstone Studio Group Show, Marywood Col, 94; and others. *Teaching:* Vis instr painting & design, Lehigh Univ, fall, 72 & 73; instr painting & drawing, Lehigh Co Community Col, 75-84. *Awards:* Pen & Brush Award, Salmagundi Club, New York, 83; Purchase Awards, Printmaking Coun NJ, Red Devil Corp, 83 & 85-87; 1st Place Pastels, Rittenhouse Sq Fine Arts Ann, 92. *Bibliog:* Jill Stewart Narrow (auth), Virginia Tabor-Artist & Printmaker, Theatrical Faces Mag. *Mem:* Lehigh Art Alliance (pres, 78-80); fel Pa Acad Fine Arts; Artists Equity; Philadelphia Watercolor Club. *Media:* Pastel; Silkscreen. *Dealer:* Tabor Studio 46 Covington Pl Catasauqua Pa 18032. *Mailing Add:* 46 Covington Pl Catasauqua PA 18032

TACHA, ATHENA
SCULPTOR, EDUCATOR
b Larissa, Greece, Apr 23, 36; nat US. *Study:* Nat Acad Fine Arts, Athens, MA(sculpture), 59; Oberlin Col, Ohio, MA(art hist), 61; Univ Paris, PhD(aesthetics), 63. *Hon Degrees:* Col Wooster, Ohio, FA, 90. *Work:* Mus Fine Arts, Houston; Nat Col Fine Arts, Washington, DC; Albright-Knox Art Gallery, Buffalo, NY; J B Speed Art Mus, Louisville; Hirshhorn Mus, Washington, DC; and others; Cleveland Mus Art; Nelson-Atkins Mus Art, Kansas City, MO. *Comn:* sculpture, Dept Environ Protection, Trenton, NJ; sculpture, Case Western Reserve Univ, Cleveland, Ohio; sculpture, Low Water Dam Riverfront Park, Tulsa, Okla; sculpture, Dept Transportation, Hartford, Conn; sculpture, Strathmore Music Ctr, Bethesda, MD; sculpture, Am Airlines Plaza, Dallas, TX; sculpture, Franklintown Park, Philadelphia, PA; sculpture, Metrorail, Miiami; sculpture, Newark, NJ; and many others. *Exhib:* One-woman shows, Zabriskie Gallery, NY, 79 & 81, Max Hutchinson Gallery, NY, 84, High Mus Art, Atlanta, 89, Franklin FUrnace, NY, 94 & Beck Ctr, Cleveland, Ohio, 98-99; many others worldwide, 66-; Found for Hellenic Cult, NY, 2001; M Mateyka Gallery, Washington, DC, 2004; Am Univ Mus/Katzen, Wash, DC, 2006. *Pos:* Cur mod art, Allen Art Mus, Oberlin, Ohio, 63-73. *Teaching:* Prof art, Oberlin Col, Ohio, 73-2000; adj prof art, Univ Md, College Park, 99-. *Awards:* Fel, Ctr Advan Visual Studies, Mass Inst Technol, 74; Artist's Grant, Nat Endowment Arts, 75; Artist's Grant, Ohio Arts Coun, 91; resident fel, Bogliasco Foundation, Genoa, 2003; resident fel, Bellagio Study Ctr, 2007. *Bibliog:* Articles, Landscape Architecture, 5/78, Artforum, 1/81, Arts Mag, 10/88, Sculpture, 11/2000; E McClelland (auth), Cosmic Rhythms: Athena Tacha's Public Sculpture, 98; Dancing in the Landscape: The Sculpture of Athena Tacha, 2000. *Mem:* Int Sculpture Asn; Col Art Asn Am (dir, 73-76). *Media:* Sculpture, Photography. *Res:* Art history. *Interests:* Nature & science. *Publ:* ed, Art in the Mind, 70; auth, Athena Tacha: Public Works, 70, 88 & 89; auth, Athena Tacha: Public Sculpture, 82; Forms of Chaos: Drawings by Athena Tacha, 88; Vulnerability: New Fashions, 94. *Dealer:* Marsha Mateyka Gallery, Washington, DC. *Mailing Add:* 3721 Huntington NW Washington DC 20015-1817

TACLA, JORGE
PAINTER, MURALIST
b Santiago, Chile, 58. *Study:* Univ de Chile, Santiago, BFA, 79. *Work:* Archer M Huntington Art Gallery, Univ Tex, Austin; High Mus Art, Atlanta; Walker Hill Art Ctr, Seoul, South Korea; ECO Art, Rio de Janeiro, Brazil. *Comn:* Mural, Bronx Housing Ct, Percent Arts, NY, 91-92. *Exhib:* Myth & Magic in the Americas, Museo de Monterrey, Mex, 91; Cruciformed, Ctr Contemp Art & Travel, Cleveland, 91-92; solo exhibs, High Mus, Atlanta, 91 & Lehman Col, Bronx, 92; Migrations, RI Sch Design, Providence, 92; and others. *Awards:* Grant, NY Found Arts, 87 & 91; Grant, J S Guggenheim Found, 88. *Bibliog:* Donald Kuspit (auth), Jorge Tacla: Hemispheric Problem, 91 & Bruce Guenther (auth), Jorge Tacla-Borders, 92, Nohra Haime Gallery; Carrie Pryzbilla (auth), Art on the Edge: Tacla, High Mus Art, 91. *Media:* Oil on Canvas. *Mailing Add:* 245 E 50th St Apt 3A New York NY 10022-7752

TAFEL, EDGAR
ARCHITECT
b NY City, Mar 4, 12. *Study:* NYU, student, 32; State Univ NY, Geneseo, DFA (hon), 2001. *Pos:* Sr fel, Frank Lloyd Wright's Taliesin Fels, Spring Green, Wis, 32-41; practice archit, New York City, 46-; fac, Smithsonian Inst, 78; co-prod, actor (video), The Frank Lloyd Wright Way. *Teaching:* Lectr, USIS, Eng, Israel, India, Neth, 72-73; New Sch for Social Res, New York City, 74. *Awards:* Award of merit for Presbyterian Church Fifth Ave; Asn, New York City, service citation State Univ NY Coll at Geneseo, 70. *Mem:* Fel Am Inst of Archits; Nat Accad Arts (assoc), Taliesin Fels (coun), Fallingwater (adv comt); Nat Acad (assoc, 57, acad, 94-). *Publ:* Author: Yrs with Frank Lloyd Wright, 1993, Frank Lloyd Wright, 1993; contribr articles to prof j

TAFT, FRANCES PRINDLE
EDUCATOR, PAINTER - WATERCOLOR
b New Haven, Conn, 21. *Study:* Vassar Col, AB 42; Yale Univ, grad sch, MA (art history), 48; with George Heard Hamilton, George Kubler & Sumner McKnight Crosby. *Exhib:* Print Club Exhib, Cleveland Artist Archives, 2004; South Wing Gallery St Paul's Church, Cleveland Heights, 2004. *Collection Arranged:* Collection of Artists of Northeast Ohio. *Pos:* Prof art hist, Cleveland Inst Art, 50-, actg dean, 73-74; trustee France Lehman Loeb Art Ctr, Eleanor Roosevelt Ctr, Val-Kill, NY, Laurel Sch, Cleveland Mus Art, Cleveland Arts Prize; Chmn liberal arts, 19th & 20th century art, Pre-Columbian art, Cleveland Inst Art, 50-. *Teaching:* instr, Cleveland Col, Case Western Reserve Univ, Cleveland Mus Art, Brandeis Univ; freelance lect, 20th century art, archit hist, Primitivism, Pre-Columbian art & European Megaliths. *Awards:* Medal of Excellence, Cleveland Inst Art, 94; Cleveland Arts Prize, 95. *Mem:* Col Art Asn Am; Western Reserve Archit Historians (pres, 71-72); Art Asn Cleveland; Cleveland Mus Art (prog chmn, 72, trustee, 72-); Womens Coun, Cleveland Mus Art; Cleveland Artist's Archives; Cleveland Archaeological Soc. *Media:* Watercolor. *Res:* Pre-Columbian art in Mesoamerica & Peru; study of Megaliths of Western Europe. *Collection:* Small pre-Columbian collection and collection of painting, sculpture & prints with a focus on northeastern Ohio artists. *Mailing Add:* 6 Pepper Ridge Rd Cleveland OH 44124

TAGGART, WILLIAM JOHN
PAINTER, SCULPTOR
b Buffalo, NY, Aug 8, 40. *Study:* Art Inst Chicago, BFA; Univ NMex, MFA. *Work:* Int Arrivals Bldg, JFK Airport, NY; Installation, Pub Sch 3, NY; Univ NMex, Albuquerque; Art in the Embassies Prog, Bonn, Ger & New Delhi, India; Mus Contemp Art, Chicago. *Comn:* Sculpture, Port Authority, NY, 73. *Exhib:* Whitney Mus Am Art, NY, 74; Off the Wall, Pace Univ, NY, 74; Hokin Gallery, Chicago, 80; Nina Freudenheim Gallery, Buffalo, NY, 81; Betty Parsons Gallery, NY, 81; Appalachian State Univ, Boone, NC, 82; and others. *Pos:* Vis artist, Sch Art Inst Chicago, 78-. *Teaching:* Instr printmaking, Cooper Union, New York, 68-71; instr visual fundamentals, York Community Col, 75; instr, Montclair State Col, NJ, 77-

TAHEDL, ERNESTINE
STAINED GLASS ARTIST, PAINTER
b Vienna, Austria, Oct 10, 40; Can citizen. *Study:* Acad for Appl Arts, Vienna, Austria, with Franz Herbert, MA in Graphic Arts, 61; with Prof Heinrich Tahedl, collab in design & execution of stained glass works, 61-63. *Work:* Paintings represented in public galleries in Vienna, Japan, Montpellier, France, London, Ont & Mus de Que, Can. *Comn:* Stained glass murals, Fed Revenue Bldg, Quebec, Que, 71, Bibiotheque Varennes, Quebec, 81, Greenfield Park Libr, Quebec, 82 & Ctr D'Accueil, St Bruno, Quebec, 82, Annunciation Church, Ottawa, 87, St Peters Church, Toronto, 90, 94 & Restoration, Chriskoenigs Church, Klagenfurt, Austria, 89-90. *Exhib:* Third & Fourth Int Print Biennale, Korea, 81 & 83; solo exhibs, Gallery Quan, Toronto, 83-93, Tudor Collection, Montreal, 83, Bugera-Kmet Gallery, Edmonton, Alta, 90-2005 & Trias Gallery, Toronto 97-2005; 15th Int Biennial Graphic Art, Ljubljana, Yugoslavia, 83; Hanga Int Print Exhib, Metrop Mus, Tokyo, Japan, 85-87; 3rd Int Biennal Print Exhib, Taipei, Taiwan; Agora Gallery, NY, 2006; Retrospective 1946-2006, Karley Art Gallery, Markham, Ontario. *Pos:* Vpres, Royal Can Acad Arts, formerly; Pres, Ontario Soc Artists, currently; Chmn, Mgt Committee, currently; JB Aird Gallery Toronto, Ontario, 2001-2006. *Awards:* Can Coun Arts Award, 67; Gov Gereral's 125th Anniversary Medal; 2000 Arts and Letters Award; In Celebration of Women, Arts, Long-Term Achievement Award, 2004; President's Medal, Ontario Soc Artists, 2006. *Bibliog:* Guy Robert (auth), Art Actuel au Quebec, Iconia, Quebec, 83; Joel Russ & Lou Lynn (auth), Contemporary Stained Glass, Doubleday, Toronto, 85; Guy Simard (auth), Verriers du Quebec, Ed Broquet, Ottawa, 89; Nancy Townshend (auth), A History of Art in Alberta 1905-1970, Bayeux Arts Inc, Calgary Can, 2005. *Mem:* Royal Can Acad Arts; Ont Soc Artists (past pres); Arts and Letters Club (Toronto chpt). *Media:* Acrylic Painting; Stained Glass; Printing. *Collection:* Albert Art Found; Art Gallery, Hamilton; Kanagawa Prefectural Gallery, Japan; Mus De Quebec; Publ Gallery City of Vienna, Austria. *Publ:* Ltd ed portfolio etchings, Circle of Energy, Art World Int, 81; Contemporary Stained Glass Artists, ABC Black Publ Ltd, London, Eng, 2006. *Dealer:* Hubert Gallery 1046 Madison Ave New York NY 10021; Trias Gallery 80 Spadina Ave Toronto Ontario Can M5V 2J3; Elliot Louis Gallery 1540 W 2nd Ave Vancouver BC V6J 1H2. *Mailing Add:* 79 Collard Dr King City ON L7B 1E4 Canada

TAHIR, ABE M, JR
CONSULTANT
b Greenwood, Miss, Feb 18, 31. *Study:* Univ Miss, BBA; George Washington Univ, MBA. *Exhib:* With Nothing On: Prints and Drawings of the Nude by Am Artists, New Orleans Mus Art, 2-3/90; Gerald L Brockhurst: A Retrospective of Prints and Drawings, New Orleans Mus Art, 9-10/91. *Pos:* Dir, Tahir Fine Arts, currently. *Specialty:* Original prints & drawings. *Publ:* Auth, Jacques Hnizdovsky, Woodcuts and Etchings, 87. *Mailing Add:* Tahir Fine Arts PO Box 8805 Metairie LA 70011

TAI, JANE S
ADMINISTRATOR
b Poughkeepsie, NY, May 14, 44. *Study:* Syracuse Univ, BA, 67. *Pos:* Exhib coordr, Everson Mus Art, Syracuse, NY, 67-69; exhib coordr, Am Fedn Arts, New York, 70-75, asst dir, exhib dir, 75-78, assoc dir prog, 78-83, assoc dir & exhib prog dir, 83-87; owner, Tai Assoc, Int Inc, NY, Exhib Serv, currently. *Mailing Add:* 529 E 87th St No 1W New York NY 10028-1322

TAIRA, MASA MORIOKA
GALLERY DIRECTOR, CONSULTANT
b Kagoshima City, Japan, Nov 25, 23; US citizen. *Study:* Studio Prog, Honolulu Acad Arts, with Joseph Feher & Ron Kowalke, studied gallery mgt with David Asherman & Tom M Klobe; materials tech, Univ Hawaii Art Dept with Don Dugal; painting with Helen Gilbert, Advanced Painting with John Wisnosky & intermediate & adv drawing with Ron Kowalke, Univ Hawaii; Life Drawing with Sara Frankel & Kenneth Bushnell; Sculpture with Rick Mills & David Landry. *Comn:* Human Form: From Egypt to the Renaissance, Queen's Med Ctr/Hawaii Med Libr. *Exhib:* Wu Shih Tung Tang, Five Generations in Hawaii, 87; Na Inoa Na Ali'i: First Homage to Manamana, 87-02. *Collection Arranged:* Human Form: From Egypt to the Renaissance, Queen Emma Gallery, 84, traveling, 84-86 & exhib, pub lecture & traveling, 97-98; Monouri: Street Vendors of Old Japan, Queen Emma Gallery, 85 & traveling, 86; Kumulipo: Hawaiian Chant of Creation, Visual Perspectives traveling, 88. *Pos:* Founder & chmn, Queen Emma Gallery, Honolulu, 76-85, dir, 85-02. *Mem:* Nat Mus Women Arts; Contemp Mus Art; Honolulu Acad Arts. *Publ:* Auth, Human Form: From Egypt to the Renaissance, Humanities News, 84. *Mailing Add:* Queen Emma Gallery PO Box 861 Honolulu HI 96808

TAIT, WILL(IAM) H
PAINTER
b Edinburgh, Scotland, Apr 1, 42; nat US. *Study:* Art Students League NY, 69-71; San Francisco Art Inst, 74. *Work:* Achenbach Found, Calif Palace Legion Honor, San Francisco. *Comn:* Painted mural, Mt Tamalpais State Park, Mill Valley, Calif, 93. *Exhib:* Northwest Regional, Grants Pass, 76; Berkeley Nat Show, Berkeley Art Ctr, 84; Contemp Prints, Western NMex Univ, Silver City, 84; San Francisco Mus Mod Art Rental Gallery; Dow & Frosini Gallery, Berkeley, Calif. *Pos:* Coordr, Berkeley Art Ctr, Calif, 83-85; digital artist, Intuit. *Teaching:* Instr life drawing, painting, Rogue Community Col, Oreg, 76-77 & Monterey Peninsula Col, Calif, 81-82; instr interface design, San Francisco State Univ, 93-94; instr computer animation/multimedia develop, Ohlone Col, Fremont, Calif, 94. *Bibliog:* Feature article, Printing J, Mar/89. *Mem:* Int Soc Art, Sci & Tech; Asn Computing Machines; Siggraph. *Media:* Painting, Digital Multimedia. *Publ:* Coauth, Official Microsoft Image Composer Book & Photodraw by Design, Microsoft Press. *Dealer:* The Digital Pond 50 Minna St San Francisco CA 94105. *Mailing Add:* c/o Digital Pond 88 Arkansas St San Francisco CA 94107

TAKAMORI, AKIO
CERAMIST
b Nobeoka, Miyazaki, Japan, 50. *Study:* Musashino Art Col, Tokyo, Japan, 69-71; Koishiwara-ware, Fukuoka, Japan, 72-74; Kansas City Art Inst, Mo, BFA, 76; NY State Col Ceramics, Alfred Univ, MFA, 78. *Work:* Carnegie Inst Art Mus, Pittsburgh, Pa; Los Angeles Co Mus, Calif; Victoria & Albert Mus, London; Kansas City Art Inst; RI Sch Design Mus. *Exhib:* Nelson-Atkins Mus Art, 83 & 89; Smits Collection, Los Angeles Co Art Mus, Calif, 87; solo exhibs, Everson Mus, Syracuse, NY, 89, Garth Clark Gallery, NY, 91, 93, 97 & 2000, Garth Clark Gallery, Los Angeles, 92 & 94, Garth Clark Gallery, Kansas City, 94, Tempe Arts Ctr, Ariz, 96, Frank Lloyd Gallery, Los Angeles, Calif, 98 & 2001, Grover Thurston Gallery, Seattle, Wash, 99 & 2000; The Collection of Anne Davis (with catalog), El Paso Mus Art, Tex, 93; Beth Urdang Gallery, Boston, 93; Europe Ceramic Work Ctr, 's-Hertogenbosch, The Neth, 93; Material Vision: Image & Object (with catalog), Tarble Arts Ctr, Eastern Ill Univ, Charleston, 93; Emigres: Cult References in Contemp Clay (with catalog), New Orleans Mus Art, 94; Crack Pots from the Collection of Donna Moog, Forum Contemp Art, St Louis, Mo, 99; Allan Chasanoff Ceramic Collection, Mint Mus Craft & Design, Charlotte, NC, 2000. *Teaching:* Instr, Sheridan Col Appl Art & Technol, Mississauga, Ont, 81, NS Col Art & Design, Halifax, Can, 81, Emily Carr Col Art, Vancouver, 82, Mont State Univ, Bozeman, 83-84, Kansas City Art Inst, Mo, 86, RI Sch Design, Providence, 86, Univ Wash, Seattle, 88-89 & 93-; resident artist, Archie Bray Found, Helena, Mont, 58-88; vis asst prof, Alfred Univ, NY, 93. *Awards:* Fel, Nat Endowment Arts, 86 & 88; Keramisch Werkcentrum Fel, 's-Hertogenbosch, Neth, 93 & 96. *Bibliog:* The Book of Cups, Abbeville Press, NY, 90; Susan Biskeborn (auth), Artists at Work: Twenty-five Northwest Glassmakers, Ceramists & Jewelers, Alaska NW Bks, Seattle, 90; Norma Tirrell (auth), The Archie Bray legacy-four decades of American ceramic art, Ceramics Monthly, 12/93; Coletta Chattoadhyay (auth), Akio Takamori at Frank Lloyd Gallery, World Sculpture News, Spring/98; Will Levi Marshall (auth), Head, heart and hand, Ceramic Review, 5-6/98. *Publ:* Auth, Artists at Work, Alaska Northwest Books, 90; Art Random, Ceramic Art: 7 Individuals, Kyoto Shoin, 90; Clay Today, Los Angeles Co Mus Art, 90; Out of the Cage, Studio Potter, 12/92. *Mailing Add:* 2618 30th Ave W Seattle WA 98199

TAKASHIMA, SHIZUYE VIOLET
ILLUSTRATOR, PAINTER
b Vancouver, BC, June 12, 28. *Study:* Ont Col Art, BA, 53; Fine Arts Inst, San Miguel, Mex (weaving), 65; Pratt Art Ctr Graphic Arts, New York, 66. *Work:* Nat Gallery, Ottawa, Can; Imperial Oil; Can Titanium Pigments Ltd, Montreal; Montreal Standard Publ Co, Montreal; Midland Computer Bldg, Syracuse, NY. *Comn:* Four Posters, Midwestern Regional Libr, Kitchener, Ont, 78. *Exhib:* Hamilton Art Gallery, Ont, 61; Hart House, Univ Toronto, 61; VI Biennial Exhib, Nat Gallery Ottawa, 65; Mystic Circle Traveling Show, Burnaby Art Gallery, 74; five-man show, Montreal Mus Fine Arts, 65; four-man show, Art Gallery Ont, Toronto, 60; one-man shows, Burnaby Art Gallery, BC, 65 & 78 & Japanese Can Cult Ctr, Toronto, 74. *Pos:* Assoc ed, Rika Mag, 76-79, Inner City Angels, Toronto, 79-84. *Teaching:* Instr drawing & painting, Forest Hill Learning & Ont Col Art, 71-94, Resources, 71 & Ont Col Art, Toronto, 76-95. *Awards:* Can Coun Grant, 71 & 73; Bronze Award, Can Asn Children's Libr Asn, 72; Sankai Shinbun Ann Literary Award, Tokyo, 74; VI Premio Europeo di Litteratura Gioranite Award, Padua, Italy, 76. *Bibliog:* Robin Mathews (auth), Young Artists, Can Forum, 61; David P Silcox (auth), Young Artists, Can Art Mag, 62. *Media:* Oils, Watercolor. *Publ:* A Child in Prison Camp, Tundra Books, Montreal, 71; illusr, Watercolors: Kenji and the Cricket, Adele Wiseman Porcupine & Quill Inc, 88. *Mailing Add:* 5438 Larch St Vancouver BC V6M 4C8 Canada

TAKAYAMA, MARTHA TEPPER
GALLERY DIRECTOR, PUBLISHER
b Cambridge, Mass. *Study:* Boston Univ, BA, 65; Boston Col, MAT, 74. *Exhib:* People and Landscape: Hiromi Tsuchida, Toshio Shibata, Fitchburg Art Mus, Mass, 97-98. *Pos:* Dir, Martha Tepper Fine Arts, 78-94 & Tepper Takayama Fine Arts, 94-; cur & co-publ no-print workshops. *Specialty:* Contemporary paintings, prints and photographs. *Interests:* Latin American and Japanese art. *Mailing Add:* 20 Park Plaza Suite 600 Boston MA 02116

TAKEMOTO, HENRY TADAAKI
CRAFTSMAN, SCULPTOR
b Honolulu, Hawaii, July 23, 30. *Study:* Univ Hawaii, BFA; Los Angeles Co Art Inst, MFA. *Work:* Smithsonian Inst. *Exhib:* Int Exhib Contemp Ceramics, Ostend, Belg, 59; 3rd Int Exhib Contemp Ceramics, Prague, Czech, 62; Studio Potter Exhib, Victoria & Albert Mus, London, Eng, 66-70; Objects: USA, Johnson Wax Collection Contemp Crafts, Smithsonian Inst, Washington, DC, 70-73; Contemp Ceramic Art, US, Can, Mex, Japan, 71-72. *Pos:* Designer & glaze chemist, Wedgewood of Eng, 69-. *Teaching:* Instr ceramics, Calif Sch Fine Arts, San Francisco, formerly; instr ceramics, Scripps Col, 65-69; instr ceramics, Otis Art Inst, formerly. *Awards:* Double Purchase Prize, Wichita Art Asn, 59; Silver Medal for Sculpture, Ostend, Belg, 59; Bronze Medal, Mus Contemp Crafts, NY, 60; and others. *Media:* Ceramics. *Mailing Add:* 3209 Landa St Los Angeles CA 90039

TALABA, L (LINDA) TALABA CUMMENS
SCULPTOR, PRINTMAKER
b Detroit, Mich, July 15, 43. *Study:* Detroit Inst Technol, with Maxwell Wright; pvt instr with Lois Pety; Ill Wesleyan Univ, with Fred Brian, BFA; Southern Ill Univ, with David Folkman & Lewis Brent Kington, MFA; Phi Kappa Phi. *Work:* Henry Ford Found Print Collection, Detroit; Can Arts Coun; Albion Univ Print Collection; Leopold Schepp Found Collection, NY; Detroit Art Inst Rental Collection; St John's Univ Prints; and others. *Comn:* Painting, Waterford Twp Bd Educ, 61; Isaac E Crary Jr High Sch, 63; Burton Title & Abstract Co, Detroit, 67; bronze door ornaments, Little Grassy Mus, Southern Ill Univ, 70; bronze sculpture, Dir & Bur Budget, State of Ill, Springfield, 75; and other comn by individuals. *Exhib:* one-woman shows, Renee Gallery, Detroit, 68, Lewis Towers Gallery, Loyola Univ, 75 & Deerfield Courts Gallery, 84-85, Kraft Corp, Cook Meml Libr, Highland Park City Hall Rotunda, Chicago, 96, others; Rotunda City Hall, Highland Park, 85 & 96; Cook Mem Libr Gallery, 88; Kraft Co Gallery, 89; Body Politic Gallery, Chicago, 93; Dittmar Gallery, 98; Koho Gallery, 2000-04. *Pos:* Dir, sch art, Suburban Fine Art Ctr, 84-85, Gallery des Refuses, 97-2000, Seebeck Gallery, 99, Koho Gallery, 2000-02 & New Zone Gallery, 2003. *Teaching:* Guest artist, sculpture, Springfield Art Asn, 74-78, Sangamon State Univ, 75-78, Col Lake Co, 80-85, Suburban Fine Art Ctr, Highland Park, Ill, 83-86 & 96, Dist #113 Continuing Educ, 83-96, Westmorebud Sch, 2000-05; art fac, Park Dist Highland Park, 86-96 & Caruso Jr High, 86-96. *Awards:* Beacon St Gallery, Chicago Women's Caucus Award, 90, Northern Ill Art Mus, 90-91; Recent Works Award, Col Lake Co, 91, 93 & CLC Invitational Exhib; Dittmar Gallery-Parallel Visions, Northwestern Univ, 98; Awards Maude Kerns and Group Show 97-; Group Show Award, Florence, Ore, 2004. *Mem:* Symphony Guild; Leff Coast Crime Writers; Sisters in Crime Writers; Willanette Writers Asn; Lifetime mem, AAUW. *Media:* Bronze; Graphics, Handmade Paper. *Res:* Smithsonian Research Grant 1976; Cooper Hewett Museum Grant. *Interests:* Playing recorders, bass, tenor, alto & soprano, Hiking, Writing; Poetry and mystery novels. *Collection:* Burfon Title and Abstract Company, Henry Ford Private & Public Art Collections; St John's Univ, New Foundland, Calif; Akron University, Ill, Wesleyan University, Roper Foundation, Cranbrook Art Academy. *Publ:* Illusr, Lakeland's Paradise, Bd Educ Oakland Co, Pontiac, Mich, 61; art ed, Argus Newspaper, 62 & illusr, Black Book (literary mag), 63-65, Ill Wesleyan Univ; illusr, Experimental Math Books, Cent Mid-Western Regional Educ Labs, 70; illusr & co-auth, Helping Your Doctor - A Children's Self-Healing Guide, 84; Brochures, spot illusr, cartoon art, art from junk for kids & no budget art for teachers, 96-. *Mailing Add:* 3415 Timberline Dr Eugene OR 97405

TALBERT, RICHARD HARRISON
PAINTER, ARCHITECT
b Rockville Centre, NY, Apr 23, 57. *Study:* RI Sch Design, 75-77; Sarah Lawrence Col, BA(philos), 80; Inst for Archit & Urban Studies, 82-83; Univ Cambridge, cert, 86; Univ Miami, BA(archit), 92, MA(archit), 93. *Work:* Dana Roth Collection, Ft Lauderdale, Fla; Susie & Robert Lafer Collection, NY; Hyundai Motor Co, Seoul, Korea; Robert Scull Collection, NY; Michael & Katherine Karolyi Mus Collection, Vence, France. *Comn:* City Scapes Mural, Hoboken Arts Coun, NJ, 84; Water Tower Mural, 85, Banners, 85, Karolyi Found, Vence, France; mixed media/oil on canvas/neon, Mrs Dana Roth, Ft Lauderdale, Fla, 90; exterior mural, comn by Dr Harry Sanchez, Coral Gables, Fla, 95; Exterior Mural, EWALK, 42nd St Redevelopment, Times Sq, NY. *Exhib:* Solo exhibs, Michael Karolyi Found, Vence, France, 85, Esta Robinson Gallery, NY, 86, Gallery des Artiste, West Palm Beach, Fla, 90, Bonwit Teller's Atrium Gallery, Bal Harbor, Fla, 90, La Gallerie Presidence, Bordeaux, France, 91 & Santarella Mus & Gardens, Sky Gallery, Tyringham, Mass, 96; Summer Exhibition, Royal Acad Arts Mus, London, Eng, 86; Image Gallery, Stockbridge, Mass, 89; Berkshire Artisans, Pittsfield, Mass, 91; 80 Washington Sq E Galleries, NY, 93. *Pos:* Artist in Residence, Santarella Mus & Gardens, Studio of Sir Henry Hudson, Kitson, Tyringham, Mass, 2000. *Teaching:* Asst to Vincent Scully, hist of archit, Univ Miami, 92. *Awards:* Jane B W Whitney Award, Whitney Found, NY,

78; Michael Karolyi Fel, Karolyi Found, Vence, France, 85; Hon Travel Fel, Kettle's Yard Art Gallery, Univ Cambridge, Eng, 85. *Mem:* NY Artist Equity; Am Inst Archit. *Publ:* Auth, Art on Madison Avenue, Art Speak, 83; article in Views, RI Sch Design, 90; auth, Mural Maker, Sunday NY Times, 6/95. *Mailing Add:* 410 W End Ave New York NY 10024

TALBOT, JONATHAN
PAINTER, COLLAGE ARTIST
b New York, NY, Nov 14, 39. *Study:* Brandeis Univ; New Sch Social Res; San Francisco Acad Art. *Work:* Smith Col Mus, Northampton, Mass; torun Mus, Torun, Poland; Everhart Mus, Scranton, Pa; Beach Mus Art, Manhattan, KS; Newark Mus, NJ; Musée Artcolle, Sergines, France; Montclair Art Mus, NJ; San Diego Mus Art; Housatonic Mus of Art, Bridgeport, Conn; Coos Art Mus, Oreg; Longview Mus of Fine Arts, Tex; and others. *Exhib:* solo exhibs, Res & Devel, Gallery Contemp Art, Sacred Heart Univ, Fairfield, Conn, 90; Mus Managerie, Mus Mod Art, NY, 76; Recent Am Works on Paper, Smithsonian Inst Traveling Exhib Serv, 85-87; Surrealism After Surrealism, Ark Arts Ctr, Little Rock, Ark, 86; The Humanist Icon, Bayly Art Mus, Univ Va, Charlottesville, NY Acad Art, NY & Ulrich Mus Art, Wichita, Kans, 90; In This Time & Place, State Univ NY, New Paltz, 96; and others; Florence Biennial, Italy, 02; Jonathan Talbot: Collage Paintings 1980-2000, Housatonic Mus, Bridgeport, Conn, 2000 (solo exhib); The Artist as an Explorer, Coos Art Mus, Oreg, 02 (solo exhibit). *Awards:* Ranger Fund Purchase Award, Nat Acad, 82; Audubon Artists Award, 41st Ann Exhib, Nat Arts Club, 83; C R Gibson Award, Art of Northeast USA, 83; Career Achievement Award, Florence Biennial, Italy, 02; Ranger Fundn Purchase Award, Nat Acad, 82; and others. *Bibliog:* Amy Goldberger (auth) Collage of Conscience, Orange Mag, 89; Gerald Brommer (auth), Collage Techniques, Watson-Guptill, 94. *Publ:* Auth, Collage: A New Approach, 5th edit, Talbot Arts, 01. *Mailing Add:* 7 Amity Rd Warwick NY 10990

TALBOTT, SUSAN LUBOWSKY
DIRECTOR
b Brooklyn, NY, Jan 16, 49. *Study:* Pratt Inst, BFA, 70, MFA, 75. *Collection Arranged:* Constructivism and the Geometric Tradition, McCrory Corp, traveling exhib, 77-80; Yasuo Kuniyoshi, 86; George Ault (1891-1948), 88; Artist and the Community, 94-98; Heroic Painting, 98; Vincent Desiderio, 98; Almost Warm & Fuzzy: Childhood and Contemporary Art, 99; My Reality: Contemporary Art and the Culture of Japanese Animation, 2001-02. *Pos:* Asst cur, McCrory Corp, NY, 77-80; asst dir, Queens Mus, 80-82; branch dir, Whitney Mus at Philip Morris, 82-88 & Whitney Mus at Equitable Ctr, 87-88; dir, Visual Arts, Nat Endowment Arts, 89-92, Southeastern Ctr Contemp Art, Winston-Salem, NC, 92-98; dir, Des Moines Art Ctr, 98-. *Teaching:* Instr art hist & gallery dir, State Univ NY, Brockport, 75-77; adj prof art, New York Univ, 86-88. *Awards:* Distinguished Service Award, Nat Endowment Arts, 91; Alumni Achievement Award, Pratt Inst, 93. *Mem:* Asn Art Mus Dirs; Am Asn Mus; Int Coun Mus. *Res:* 20th century American art, specialization in the 1920s, 1930s and contemporary art. *Publ:* Auth, Figures of Mystery (exhib catalog), Queens Mus, 82; Three American Families: A Tradition of Artistic Pursuit, 83, Alexander Calder: Selections from the Permanent Collection, 84, The Surreal City, 1930s-1950, 85, coauth, Yasuo Kuniyoshi, 86 (all exhib catalogs), Whitney Mus & auth, George Ault, Sculpture Since the 60's, 88; Spaces '88, Mus d'Arte Contemporanea, Prato, Italy, 88; coauth, Yasuo Kuniyoshi, Nat Mus Mod Art, Kyoto, Japan; Artist and Community Series: Donald Lipski, Tim Rollins, Fred Wilson, Hope Sandrow, Willie Birch, Eleanor Antin, Heroic Painting. *Mailing Add:* Des Moines Art Ctr 4700 Grand Ave Des Moines IA 50312

TALIAFERRO, NANCY ELLEN TAYLOR
PAINTER
b Richmond, Va, Feb 16, 37. *Study:* Va Commonwealth Univ, BFA, 59. *Comn:* portrait Richmond Ct Clk for Manchester Co Ct House, Richmond, Va, 00; other pvt commns. *Exhib:* Charter Mem Uptown Gallery, Richmond, Va, 92; Nat Asn Women Artists Exhib, Du Pont Art Gallery, Washington & Lee Univ, Lexington, Va, 93; 32nd Irene Leache Mem Exhib, Chrysler Mus, Norfolk, Va, 94; Nat Asn Women Artists Traveling Exhib, Greater Lafayette Mus Art, Ind & Sordoni Art Gallery, Wilkes Univ, Wilkes Barre, Pa, 96, Midwest Mus Am Art, Elkhart, Ind, Gannon Gallery, Bismark State Col, NDak & NW Art Ctr, Minot State Univ, NDak, 97, Charleston Heights Art Ctr & Reed Whipple Cult Ctr, Las Vegas, Nev & Longview Art Mus, Tex, 98; Va Portrait Painters, Peninsula Fine Arts Ctr, Newport News, Va, 97; Peninsula Fine Arts Ctr, Newport News, Va, 2002. *Awards:* Artists Mag Award, 92; Medal Honor & Audrey Hope Shirk Mem Award, Nat Asn Women Artists, 95; Doris Kreindler Mem Award, Nat Asn Women Artists, 2004. *Mem:* Nat Asn Women Artists; James River Art League; Univ Painters. *Media:* Oil. *Publ:* Photo of painting in The Artists Mag, 92. *Mailing Add:* 6724 Forest Hill Ave Richmond VA 23225

TALLEY, DAN R
CURATOR, WRITER
b Hogansville, Ga, Jan 6, 51. *Study:* Atlanta Col Art, BFA, 73; Univ Hartford, MFA(art), 76. *Pos:* Asst ed, Contemp Art-Southeast, Atlanta, 76-77; ed, Art Papers, 79-82; gallery dir, Nexus Contemp Art Ctr, Atlanta, 87-89; visual arts initiative, Forum Gallery, Jamestown, NY, 89-91, dir, 91-96; dir, Sharadin Art Gallery, Kutztown Univ, Pa, 96-; contrib ed, Art Papers, 98-. *Teaching:* Issues in contemp art, Jamestown Community Col, 92-96; Paris Its Art & People, Jamestown Community col, 95-96; instr, business art, 2005-, Digital Photog & Electronic media for Artist, 2006- Kutztown Univ. *Mem:* Col Art Asn. *Publ:* Virgil Marti at the Pa Acad of Fine Arts, Art Papers Mag, 01; Photography at Larry Becker Contemp Art, Art Papers Mag, 02; Color, Culture, Complexity, Mus Contemp Art of GA, Atlanta, 02; Accelerating Sequence: Artists Consider Time and Aging, Mus Contemp Art Ga, Atlanta, 05. *Mailing Add:* 496 W Walnut St # 2 Kutztown PA 19530

TALMOR, LIHIE
PRINTMAKER, SCULPTOR
b Tel-Aviv, Israel, Sept 9, 44; Israeli & Venezuelan citizen. *Study:* Technion, Technol Inst Israel, BSc, 69; Tel-Aviv Univ, 71; Studio Luis Camnitzer, Italy, 89. *Work:* Nat Art Gallery, Caracas, Venezuela; NY Pub Libr; Cult Inst PR; Reina Sofia Ctr, Madrid, Spain; Nat Mus Prints, Mexico City. *Exhib:* Readings in National Art, Nat Art Gallery, Caracas, 87; Venezuelan Graphics, Nat Mus Mexico City, 90; Homage to Vladimir Horowitz, Robert Fisher Hall, Jerusalem, 92; La Habana Biennial, Wifredo Lam Prints Ctr, Havana, Cuba, 94 & 96; Estampa 95, Reina Sofia Mus, Madrid, Spain, 95; The Creativity of Evil, Sofia Imber Mus Contemp Art, Caracas, 96. *Awards:* Int Award for Printmaking, Biella, Italy, 93; Honorable Mention, Int Biennale Small Graphic Forms, Poland, 97; San Juan Biennale of Prints Honorary Prize, PR, 98; and others. *Mem:* Int Asn Art; Taller de Artistas Graficos Asociados; Painters & Sculptors Asn-Israel. *Mailing Add:* Bamco CCS-113-000 PO Box 025322 Miami FL 33102-5322

TAMBURINE, JEAN HELEN
PAINTER, SCULPTOR
b Meriden, Conn, Feb 20, 30. *Study:* Traphagen Sch, New York, 48-49; Art Students League, New York, with Jon Corbino & John Groth, 48-50; also with Elizabeth Gordon Chandler, Harry R Ballinger. *Work:* Middletown Pub Libr & State Libr, Middletown, Conn; Nashville Pub Libr, Tenn; Strong Sch, Hartford, Conn; and others. *Comn:* Heritage (bronze sculpture), Wallingford Pub Libr, 86. *Exhib:* Town & Country Club Exhib, West Hartford, Conn, 69; George Walter Vincent Smith Art Mus, Springfield, Mass; one-woman show, L'Heure Joyeux, Paris, France, 69; Pearl S Buck Found Exhib, Meriden Pub Libr, 72; Ellsworth Gallery, Simsbury, Conn, 76; and others. *Pos:* Comnr, Conn Comn on Arts, State Conn, 63-65; chmn & organizer, Cult Comn for Art Appointments to Pub Bldg, 66-70. *Awards:* Asn Members Prize, Academic Artists Asn, Inc, Springfield, Mass, 81; Martha Moore Mem Award for Excellence in Portrait, Rockport Art Asn, 83; Margaret Fitzhugh Brown Award Excellence in Painting, North Shore Arts Asn, 93. *Mem:* Acad Artists Asn; Am Artists Prof League; Salmagundi Club; Am Medallic Sculpture Asn; North Shore Arts Asn; Rockport Art Asn; FIDEM (internat medallic sculpture orgn). *Publ:* Auth & illusr, How Now, Brown Cow, Abingdon Press, 67; illusr, It's Nice To Be Little, Rand-McNally, 65; The Complete Peddlers Pack, Univ Tenn Press, 67; Something Was Missing, Follett, 69; Five Busy Bears, Rand-McNally, 69; and others; auth & illusr, Almost Big Enough, Abingdon Press; auth & illusr, I Think I Will Go to the Hospital, Abingdon Press; illusr, The Five Busy Bears by Sterling North, Rand McNally. *Mailing Add:* c/o The Bertolli Studio 73 Reynolds Dr Meriden CT 06450

TAN, LIQIN
EDUCATOR
b Hengshan, Hunan, P.R. China, Feb 17, 57. *Study:* Hengyang Teachers Col Fine Arts, China - 1981; Central Acad Fine Arts, Bejing, China - 1984; Concordia Univ, Montreal, Can, MA, 1993. *Hon Degrees:* Sheridan Col, Computer Animation, Canada - 1996. *Work:* Shanghai Duolun Mus Mod Art, China; Emin Hekimgil Art Gal, Turkish-Am Asn, Ankara, Turkey; Sing Tao Art Gal, Toronto, Can; The Noyes Mus Art, Oceanville, NJ. *Exhib:* Nat Int Contemp Prints Exhib, Lancaster Mus Art, Pa, 2004; one-man show, Digital & Primitive, Shanghai Duolun Mus Mod Art, China, 2005 & Animation Permeates Rawhides, Stedman Art Gal, Rutgers Univ, Camden, NJ, 2004; 5th Dig Art & Anima Juried Competition, Beecher Ctr Art & Technol, Youngstown, OH, 2005; Threading Time, Digital Art Gal Siggraph, Los Angeles, Calif, 2005; Award Winning Artists, Gallery Int, Baltimore, MD, 2005; Path of Technol & Cosmology, Noyes Mus Art, Oceanville, NJ, 2006. *Pos:* exec art ed, Hunan Art Publ House, China, 1/1985-8/1987; art dir, 12 Sources Arts Inc., Mississauga, Can, 1/1991-12/1996; juror, Siggraph 2006 Art Gallery, Boston, 2/2006-8/2006. *Teaching:* art instr painting, Hengyang Teachers' Col, China, 1981-85; lectr 3D animation, Ngee Ann Polytechnic, Singapore, 1997-2000; asst prof 3D animation, Rutgers Univ, Camden, NJ, 2000-. *Awards:* Gold Medal, Ann Members Exhib, Da Vinci Art Alliance, 2004; Best of Show, iDEAa Int, Int Digital Media & Arts Asn, 2004; First Place, 5th Digital Art & Animatiion Competition, Beecher Ctr Art & Technol, Youngstown State Univ, 2006. *Bibliog:* Edward McCormack (auth), Uniting Nature & Technol, Gallery & Studio, New York City, 2005; Robert Baxter (auth), Revolutionary Artist, Courier-Post, 2005; William Zimmer (auth), The Collaboration Between Artists, The Noyes Mus Art, 2006. *Mem:* ATC Asn Softimage/XSI, 1998-; Am Asn Univ Prof, 2000-; ACM Siggraph, 2000-; Asn Calligraphic Art, 2003-; Philadelphia Da Vinci Art Alliance, 2004-. *Media:* Animation Installation, Digital Media. *Publ:* auth, A future Vision of China's Art (The Trend of Art Thought), Hubei Art & Littera Asn, 1985; auth, Art Criticism Approaches: A Scattered Sense & Theory, The Theory of Contemp Art, Hunan Art Publ House, 1988; coauth, Animating Art History for Teaching, Conf Abstracts & Applications, ACM Siggraph, 2002; coauth, Animating Art History-Building a Bridge Between Disciplines, Conf Select CD-ROM, ACM Siggraph, 2003; auth, Digital-Primitive Art: Animation Permeates Centuries Old Rawhides, IV04 Int Visualization, IEEE, 2004. *Mailing Add:* 1712 Independence Ln Cherry Hill NJ 08003

TANCOCK, JOHN LEON
APPRAISER
b London, Eng, June 11, 42. *Study:* Downing Col, Cambridge Univ, Eng, MA, 63; Courtauld Inst Art, Univ London, PhD, 77. *Collection Arranged:* Multiples the First Decade (auth, catalog), Philadelphia Mus Art, 71. *Pos:* Assoc cur, Philadelphia Mus Art, 67-73; head, Contemp Art Dept, Sotheby Parke Bernet, 73-78, dir, Impressionist & Mod Art Dept, 78-, worldwide dir scholar & res, 91-. *Publ:* Auth, The influence of Marcel Duchamp, In: Marcel Duchamp, Philadelphia Mus Art & Mus Mod Art, New York, 73-74; The Sculpture of Auguste Rodin, Philadelphia Mus Art & David Godine, 76. *Mailing Add:* c/o Sotheby's 1334 York Ave New York NY 10021

TANENBAUM, JOEY
COLLECTOR
Hon Degrees: Ryerson Univ, PhD (hon), 2003. *Pos:* Chmn, Chief Exec Officer, Jay-M Enterprises Ltd, Jay-M Holdings Ltd; trustee, Royal Ontario Mus, Art Gallery of Ontario, currently; hon chmn, Can Psychiatric Res Found, currently. *Awards:* Named one of Top 200 Collectors, ARTnews Mag, 2003-06; Recipient Order of Can. *Collection:* 19th century European art; Cycladic & Neolithic art. *Mailing Add:* 981 Longboat Club Rd Longboat Key FL 34228

TANGER, SUSANNA
PAINTER, WRITER
b Boston, Mass, June 9, 42. *Study:* Boston Mus Sch; Univ Colo; Univ Calif, Berkeley. *Exhib:* Post Washington NY Cent Hall Gallery, 75; City of Paris Mus Mod Art, 75; PS 1, NY, 76; Hal Bromm Gallery, NY, 76; Galerie Rencontres, Paris, France, 76; Moore Col of Art Gallery, Philadelphia, 77; and others. *Mailing Add:* 141 Wooster St No 8C New York NY 10012

TANKSLEY, ANN
PAINTER, PRINTMAKER
b Pittsburgh, Pa, Jan 25, 34. *Study:* Carnegie Inst Technol, with Samuel Rosenberg & Balcomb Green, BFA; Art Students League, with Norman Lewis; New Sch Social Res, with Robert Conover; Bob Blackburn Printmaking Workshop. *Work:* Johnson Publ Co, Chicago; Studio Mus In Harlem, NY; Maitland Art Ctr, Fla; City Col NY; Medgar Evers Col, NY; Nat Mus Women Arts, Washington, DC. *Comn:* Book Jacket, The Power of the Porch (Trudier Harris, auth), Univ Ga Press; New Yorker Mag; Time-Life Bks Inc, Va; Pepsi Cola Co, NY; Coors Brewing Co. *Exhib:* Solo exhibs, Acts of Art, NY, 73-74, Dorsey Gallery, 86, Campbell Gallery, Sewickley, Pa, 87, Jamaica Arts Ctr, NY, 87, Spiral Gallery, NY, 88, Isobel Neal Gallery, Chicago, Ill, 90 & Maitland Art Ctr, 94; Carnegie Inst, Pa; Queens Mus, NY; Hudson River Mus, Yonkers, NY; Salmagundi Club, NY; Am Women in Art, Nairobi, Kenya; Indianapolis Mus Art; Langston Hughes Libr, Queens, NY; Christie's, NY; Savacou Galleries, NY. *Pos:* Consult, NY State Coun Arts. *Teaching:* Adj art instr, Suffolk Co Community Col, 73-75. *Awards:* Harlem Cult Coun Grant, 81. *Bibliog:* Arna Alexander Bontemps Stephenson (auth), Forever Free: Art by African-American Women, 1862-1980; Elton C Fax (auth), Black Artists of the New Generation, Dodd, Mead & Co, 77; Clara Heron (auth), In Celebration of Black History, Pittsburgh Post Gazette, 2/5/87; Robert Henks (auth), The Art of Black American Women-Works of Twenty-Four Artists of the Twentieth Century, McFarland & Co, 93; Leslie King-Hammon (intro), Gumbo Ya Ya: Anthology of Contemporary African American Women Artists, Mid March Arts Press, 95; Perspectives Authentic Voices of African Americans, Curriculum Assoc Inc, 96. *Mem:* Artists Equity Asn. *Media:* Oil, Charcoal. *Dealer:* Cinque Gallery 560 Broadway 5th Floor New York NY 10012; Sragrow Gallery 67-73 Spring St New York NY 10012. *Mailing Add:* 18 Carlton Rd Great Neck NY 11021

TANNENBAUM, BARBARA LEE
CURATOR, HISTORIAN
b Chicago, Ill, Aug 15, 52. *Study:* Reed Col, Portland, Ore, BA, 75; Univ Mich, Ann Arbor, MA, 77, PhD, 93, Getty Leadership Inst Mus Mgt, 97. *Exhib:* The Art of Seymour Rosofsky, Krannert Art Mus, Champaign-Urbana, Ill, 84 & Cultural Ctr, Chicago, Ill, 85; Hollis Sigler, Akron Art Mus & Cult Ctr, Chicago, Ill, 87; SeeTV: An Exhibition of Video Art, Akron Art Mus, 87; Aminah Robinson: Painting and Sculpture, 87, Susan Shie: Diary Quilts, 87, Ohio Perspectives: New Work in Clay, Glass, Textiles and Metals (auth, catalog), 88 & The Cuyahoga Valley: Photographs by Robert Glenn Ketchem (traveling exhib), 89, Akron Art Mus (catalog), Akron Art Mus, 88-89; Ralph Eugene Meatyard: An American Visionary (co-cur), Akron Art Mus, San Francisco Mus Mod Art & Traveling, 91; A History of Women Photographers (co-cur), Akron Art Mus, New York Pub Libr & Traveling, 96. *Pos:* Cur, Seymour Rosofsky Mem Found, 81-85; cur, Akron Art Mus, 85-96, chief cur, 96-, head pub prog, 97-. *Teaching:* Vis instr art hist, Univ Ill, Chicago, 82; vis prof art hist, Univ Wyo, Laramie, 83; inst art hist, Oberlin Col, Ohio, 83-85; NE Ohio Univ Col Med, 88-96. *Awards:* Marion Talbot Endowed Fel, Am Asn Univ Women, 80; Henry Luce Found Grant, Univ Mich, 88; Northern Ohio Live Achievement Award, 98; 100 Women of Distinction Award, Summit Co YWCA, 01. *Mem:* Art Table; Nat Adv Bd of Photo Lucida Asn. *Res:* Contemporary art, photography, outsider art. *Publ:* Auth, Politics, economics and personality as media: the art of the Christos, Nat Arts Guide, 80; ed, The Edwin C Shaw Collection of American Impressionist and Tonalist Painting, Akron Art Mus, 86; The soul cannot exist without the body: contemporary artists' books, In: Artists' books-Illinois: A Traveling Exhibition, 87; ed & contribr, Akron Art Mus: An Introduction to the Collection, 2001, Ralph Eugene Meatyard: An American Visionary, 91. *Mailing Add:* c/o Akron Art Mus One South High Akron OH 44308

TANNENBAUM, JUDITH E
CURATOR, CRITIC
b Bronx, NY, Oct 26, 44. *Study:* Douglass Col, Rutgers Univ, New Brunswick, NJ, BA(Eng), 66; Hunter Col, City Univ New York, MA(art hist), 73. *Collection Arranged:* Concept, Narrative, Document: Recent Photographic Works from the Morton Neumann Family Collection & Three Dimensional Painting, Mus Contemp Art, Chicago; Landscape in Sculpture, Day In/Day Out: Ordinary Life as a Source for Art, Art in Public Places & The Ceramics of Betty Woodman (auth, catalog), 81, Freedman Gallery, Albright Col; Peter Campus: Selected Works 1973-1987, Investigations, 86-89, Innst Contemp Art, Philadelphia. *Pos:* Ed-in-chief, Noyes Art Books, New York, 75-77; acting cur, Mus Contemp Art, Chicago, 78-79; contrib ed, Arts Mag, New York, 73-81; dir, Freedman Gallery, Albright Col, Reading, Pa, 81-86; asst dir, Inst of Contemp Art, Univ of Pa, 86-. *Mem:* Col Art Asn Am. *Res:* European and American modern and contemporary art. *Publ:* Auth, Ilya Bolotowsky, 74, Arts Mag; auth, Blythe Bohnen: The kinesthetic of form, 77, Arts Mag; ed, New York Art Yearbook, Noyes Art Books, 76; contribr, Handbook of the Guggenheim Museum Collection, S R Guggenheim Mus, New York, 80. *Mailing Add:* 220 E 78th St New York NY 10021

TANNER, JAMES L
CRAFTSMAN
b Jacksonville, Fla, July 22, 41. *Study:* Fla A&M Univ, BA, 64; Aspen Sch Contemp Art, summer 64; Univ Wis-Madison, MS, 66, MFA, 67; also studied with Harvey Littleton, Donald Reitz, Hal Lotterman & Amos White. *Work:* Renwick Gallery Nat Mus Am Art, Smithsonian Inst, Washington; Am Craft Mus, NY; Mus Contemp Crafts, NY; Everson Mus, Syracuse, NY; Charles A Wustum Mus Fine Arts, Racine, Wis; and others. *Exhib:* Objects USA, circulated by Smithsonian Inst, 69-70; Brooks Mem Art Gallery, Memphis, Tenn, 79; The Eloquent Object, circulated US & Japan, Philbrook Mus Art, Tulsa, Okla, 87-89; Craft Today - USA, circulated Europe, Am Craft Mus, NY, 89-91 & Breaking Barriers: Recent Am Craft, circulated US, 95-96; 28th Ceramic Nat Exhib, Everson Mus, NY, 90; Figures in Ceramics, La State Univ, Baton Rouge, 90; SDak Art Mus, Brookings, 90; Eight McKnight Artists, Minneapolis Col Art & Design, 92; solo show, Minneapolis Inst Art, 95; plus many others. *Pos:* Bd Trustees, Am Craft Coun, 93-94; bd dir, Nat Coun Educ Ceramic Arts, 91-93 & 94-96. *Teaching:* Prof art ceramics, Mankato State Univ, Minn, 68-. *Awards:* Nat Endowment Arts Fel, 84 & 90; McKnight Found Fel, 91-92; Minn State Arts Bd Fel, 93. *Bibliog:* Lee Nordness (auth), Objects USA, 70; Ray Grover & Lee Grover (coauth), Contemporary Art Glass, Crown Publ Co Inc, 75; Paul Donhauser (auth), The History of American Ceramics--Studio Potter, WC Brown, Kendall/Hunt Publ, 78. *Mem:* Nat Coun Educ Ceramic Arts; Am Craftsman Coun; Minn Craftsman Coun (bd dir, 72-77); Am Craft Coun; Nat Coun Educ Ceramic Arts (pres, 96-98). *Media:* Ceramics, Mixed Media. *Dealer:* Maurine Littleton Gallery 1667 Wisconsin Ave NW Washington DC 20007. *Mailing Add:* Rte 3 Box 189 Janesville MN 56048

TANSEY, MARK
PAINTER
b San Jose, Calif, 1949. *Study:* Art Center Col Design, LA, Calif, BA, 1972; grad studies in painting, Hunter Col, NY, 1975-78. *Exhib:* One man shows, Grace Borgenicht, 1982, 1984, John Berggruen Gallery, San Francisco, 1984, Contemp Arts Mus, Houston, Tex, 1984, Curt Marcus Gallery, NY, 1986, 1990, 1993, 1997, 2000, Walker Art Center, Minn, 1990, Kohn/Abrams Gallery, LA, 1993, Mus Fine Arts, Boston, 1994, Galleri Faurschou, Copenhagen, 1995, Gagosian Gallery, NY 2004, Mus Kurhaus Kleve, Germany, 2005; Recent Acquisitions, Mus Modern Art, NY, 1983; Biennial Exhib, Whitney Mus Am Art, NY, 1983, 1991; Aperto 86, Venice Biennale, Italy, 1986; Color and/or Monochrome, Nat Mus Modern Art, Tokyo, 1989; 10+10: Contemp Soviet & Am Painters, Corcoran Gallery Art, Washington, DC, 1989; The Charade of Mastery: Deciphering Modernism in Contemp Art, Whitney Mus Am Art, 1990; Mountains of the Mind, Aspen Art Mus, Colo, 1994; Am Kaleidoscope, Nat Mus Am Art, Washington, DC, 1996; Double Trouble: The Patchett Collection, Mus Contemp Art, San Diego, Calif, 1998; Reality and Desire, J??Miro Found, Barcelona, 1999; The Burbs, DFN Gallery, NY, 2003; Perspectivesat25: A Quarter Century of New Art in Houston, Contemp Arts Mus, 2004; Am Art of the 1980s, Washington Univ Gallery Art, St Louis, Mo, 2004. *Media:* acrylic, oil. *Mailing Add:* 90 Warren St New York NY 10007

TAPER, GERI
PAINTER, ENVIRONMENTAL ARTIST
b Pittsburgh, Pa, Dec 5, 29. *Study:* Carnegie Mus Sch, 37-47; Univ Pittsburgh, BS(summa cum Laude), 51; Carnegie-Mellon Grad Studies, 70-72. *Work:* Allentown Mus Art, Pa; Carnegie Mus Art, Pittsburgh; Pittsburgh Nat Bank; Chase Manhattan Bank & Citibank NAm, NY. *Comn:* The Seasons, Pittsburgh Nat Bank, 73; Dancers (triptych), Carnegie Libr, Pittsburgh, 74; Lobby, 401 N Broad Bldg, Philadelphia, 81; Public Spaces, Ctr Bldg, NY, 85; interior & exterior art work, Redstone Bldg, NY, 86; The Falchi Bldg, NY, 87-90; creator of banner sculpture, Colorfield, MTA Transit Prog, NY, 89; Celebrating the Boroughs Van Project, Bronx Community Col, NY, 90; Seniors Early Childhood Mural, Sunnyside Communicty Childhood Ctr, NY, 91. *Exhib:* Westmoreland Mus, Greensburg, Pa, 73-75; William Penn Mem Mus, Harrisburg, Pa, 75; Springfield Art Mus, Mo, 75; solo exhibs, Carnegie Mus Art, Pittsburgh, 76, Movement in Space and Time, 5-year retrospective, NY, 82, Sculpted Paintings Accessible to the Blind and Visually Impaired, NY, 84, Space, Time and Infinity, 20-year retrospective, 1971-1991, NY, 91; Bicentennial Invitational, Madden Galleries, London, 76; Nancy Poole Int Exchange, Toronto, 79; Grey Art Gallery Invitational, NY, 81; and others. *Pos:* Artist in residence, Indust Complexes, Long Island City, NY, 80-90. *Teaching:* Instr adult educ, Univ Pittsburgh, 69-70; instr, Duquesne Univ, 71-72 & Laroche Col, 72-73; community educator handicapped audiences, Metrop Mus Art, NY, 84; environ art teacher in community, NY, 86-90. *Awards:* Carnegie Mus Friends of Art Award, 72; Juror's Award, Carnegie Mus Art, 76; Alcoa Corp Award, 76. *Bibliog:* Harry Schwalb (auth), Taking it to New York, 8/77 & New York, New York, 6/82, Pittsburgher Mag; Rachel Chodorov (auth), Geri Taper, Arts Mag, 2/82. *Mem:* Found Community Artists NY; Artists Equity, NY; charter mem Nat Mus Women in the Arts, Washington, DC. *Media:* Acrylic, All. *Publ:* Lynx, J for Linking Poets of Renga & Tanka, Vol 9, No 3, 10/94; In the Desert Sun, Nat Libr Poetry, 94; Haiku Newsletter, Am Haiku soc, Vol Xiii, No 4, 98. *Dealer:* Harold Hart 156 W 86th St New York NY 10024

TAPIES, ANTONI
PAINTER, SCULPTOR
b Barcelona, Spain, Dec 13, 23. *Study:* Royal Col Art, London, Hon Dr Art, 81; Univ Barcelona, Dr, 88; Univ Galsgow, Dr, 90. *Work:* Albright-Knox Art Gallery, Buffalo, NY; Baltimore Mus Art; Mus d'Art Mod de la Villa de Paris; Mus Mod Art, NY; plus many others. *Comn:* Monument to Picasso, City of Barcelona, 83; large mosaic, Plaza

Cataluña, Sant Boi, Barcelona, 83; Núvol i Cadira (sculpture), Fundació Antoni Tàpies, Barcelona, 90; mural, Catalan pavilion, Seville World Fair, 92; mural, Int Olympics Compt pavilion, Seville World Fair, 92. *Exhib:* Fifty Yrs of Collecting: An Anniversary Selection Painting Since World War II, Solomon R Guggenheim Mus, NY, 87; Aspects of Collage, Assemblage and the Found Object in Twentieth-Century Art, Solomon R Guggenheim Mus, NY, 88; one-man show, Palacio Mudejar, Seville, 92, Mus Mod Art, NY, 92-93, Detroit Inst Arts, Mich, 92-93, Detroit Inst Arts, Mich, 92-93, Mus de Arte Contemporáneo, Caracas, 93, Galerie Adriana Schmidt, Stuttgart, 93, Galerie Lelong, Paris, 94, Lunds Konsthall, Lund, 94; Sculpture, Waddington Galleries, London, 92; Antoni Tàpies & Eduardo Chillida, Schirn Kunsthalle, Frankfurt, 93; Magic Blue, Galerie Beyeler, Basel, 94; Chillida, Tàpies, Nitsch, Baselitz, Poliakoff, Kirkeby: large prints, Galerie Biedermann, Munich, 94; Antoni Tapies, the 90's, Musee d art Moderne, Ceret, France, 95; Antoni Tapies: Uma Antologica 59-95, Centro Cult de Belem, Lisbon, 96; Antoni Tapies, Museo Nacional Centro de Art Reina Sofia, Madrid, 2000; Antoni Tapies: Retrospective, Mus d Art, Contemporanide Barcelona, 2004. *Awards:* Guggenheim Found Award, 64; Peace Prize, Span Asn for UN, 84; Picasso Medal, UNESCO, 93. *Bibliog:* Antoni Tàpies et l'oeuvre complète, Michel Tapié, 56; Clovis Prevost (dir), Antoni Tàpies' Works, Fondation Maeght, 69. *Mem:* Royal Acad Arts, Stockholm; hon mem Gesellschaft Bildener Kustler Österreichs, Vienna; hon mem Kunstlerhaus, Vienna; hon mem Royal Acad Arts, London; hon mem Am Acad Art & Sci, Cambridge, Mass. *Publ:* Auth, Memoría Personal, 78. *Mailing Add:* c/o Pace Wildenstein 32 E 57th St 4th Fl New York NY 10022

TARADASH, MERYL
ENVIRONMENTAL ARTIST, KINETIC ARTIST
b Passaic, NJ, Jan 25, 1953. *Study:* Conn Col, New London, 70-71;Banff Sch Fine Arts, Alta, Can, 71; Pratt Inst, New York, BFA, 74, MFA, 78. *Work:* Newark Mus, NJ; Colgate-Palmolive Co, NY; AT&T Longlines, Bedminister, NJ; Bellevue Hosp Ctr, NY; NY State Legislature, Albany; Cold Spring Harbor Labs, NY. *Comn:* Light Dance (suspended installation), State NJ, Rutgers Med Sch, 84; Waves (suspended installation), ARAMARK Corp, Philadelphia, 89; Wind Dancing, (wind-driven outdoor sculpture), David Bermant Found, Santa Barbara, Calif, 92; Rhodes/Nadler Collection (suspended sculpture), McLean, Va, 02; Music of Light (suspended installation), Music Ctr at Strathmore, North Bethesda, Md, 04. *Exhib:* Personal Patterns, Elaine Benson Gallery, Bridgehampton, NY, 89; Kinetic Sculpture Show, Hastings Gallery, Hastings-on-Hudson, NY, 90-91; Wind Dancing, Art Mus Univ Calif, Santa Barbara, Calif, 92-93; Jacksonville Art Mus, Jacksonville, Fla, 93; solo exhibs, James A Michener Art Mus, Doylestown, Pa, 97, Elaine Benson Gallery, Bridgehampton, NY, 98, 02, Fordham Univ, Lincoln Ctr Campus, New York City, 01; Strokes of Genius, Artists' Miniature Golf Course, Montclair Art Mus, NJ, 98; and others. *Teaching:* Vis specialist contemp art, Montclair State Col, NJ, 88-03, life drawing I-IV, 89, art & civilization I, 90, drawing II, 96, 3D design, 03-06; Sch Visual Arts, Int Prog, NY, 97-03, Summer Residency Publ Art Prog, 2005-2006. *Awards:* Ford Found Grant, 78; Post-Production Video Funds for Documentary Light Dance, NJ State Coun Arts, 85; Fel Panelist Sculpture, NJ State Coun Arts, 92. *Bibliog:* Vivien Raynor (auth), Art from state buildings, NY Times, 85; Kent Kiser (auth), Commissions, Int Sculpture, 86; Jessica Althoz (auth), Commissions, Sculpture Mag, 88; Mila Andre (auth), Sculptures Take to Great Outdoors, Daily News, 5/4/01; Erica-Lynn Gambino, Sculpture, Vol 18, No 2, 3/99; Dickson Mercer (auth), Strathmore Hall, Frederick News Post, 2/3/05; Deborah Dietsch (auth), Strathmore a Great Hall of Suburbia, Washington Times, 2/5/05. *Mem:* Int Sculpture Ctr; Col Art Asn. *Media:* Rotating Acrylic, Aluminum within Stainless Steel, Reflected Light. *Mailing Add:* 300 Mercer St #23H New York NY 10003

TARBET, URANIA CHRISTY
PAINTER, WRITER
b Dec 19, 31. *Study:* Pasadena Col, 78; Otis Art Inst, 79-81; Sergei Bongart Sch Art, 81-83. *Work:* Loomis, Sayles Co Inc, Pasadena, Calif; South Gate Art Asn Collection, Calif; World Trade Ctr, San Francisco, Calif. *Comn:* pastel portraits, comn by Mr Lyn Nofziger, communication dir to Pres Reagan, Washington, DC, 90; pastel floral painting, comn by Ms M Burton, Casablanca Fan Corp, Newport Beach, Calif, 92; Unison Pastels, Jack Richesson, Kimberly, Wis; Prints from Pastel Original Paintings, Ronad Regan Pres Libr, Simi Valley; Ruth Cameron (portrait), Residential Living Senior Ctr, Cameron Park, Calif. *Exhib:* Pastel Society of Am, Ashland Art Mus, Ky, 90; Pastel Society of Am, Quincey Art Mus, Ill, 90; Degas Pastel Society, Lauren-Rogers Mus Art, Laurel, Miss, 90; Women Artists of the West, Chinese Cult Mus, Visallia, Calif, 92; Am Contemp Outstanding Masters, Dr Sun Yat Sen Mem Mus, Taiwan; Int Asn Pastel Soc Mus Exhib, Denver Hist Mus, Colo. *Pos:* Co-founder & vpres, Pastel Soc West Coast, 84-85; pres & founder, Cassatt Pastel Soc/A Nat Soc Prof Artists, 88-90; co-found & pres, Int Asn Pastel Soc; ed, Pastel Artist Int Mag. *Teaching:* Instr oil, pastel, art marketing, art workshops throughout US, Mex & Europe, 83-92; instr, Hillcrest Art Ctr, 83-98; instr oil, pastel, St Mary's Art Ctr, 91-92 & St Mary's Art Ctr, 91-98. *Awards:* Fred & Mary Trump Award, Pastel Soc Am; Award Excellence, Degas Pastel Soc, 90; Award Excellence, Women Artists West, 91. *Bibliog:* Patricia Seligman (auth), Trees, Flowers and Foliage, Bastsford Publ; Hazel Harrison, Pastel Sch, Reader's Digest; 200 Painting Ideas for the Artist, Int Artists Mag, North Light, Australia, 12/98. *Mem:* Pastel Soc Am; Knickerbocker Artists; Calif Art Club; Soc Western Artists; pres Sacramento chap, Nat League Am Pen Women; Int Asn Pastel Soc (pres, 94-2001); Salmagundi Club. *Media:* Pastel, Oil. *Publ:* Auth, One artist's experience, Am Artist Mag, 7/89; Urania's Artistic Universe, The Mountain Democrat (weekly column), Placerville, Calif; auth, Flowers Always, Art Revue Mag, summer 95; Everett Raymond Kinstler, Art Revue Mag, Anniversary Issue, 95. *Dealer:* Helen Jones Gallery Sacramento CA; Gallerie Iona Stockton CA. *Mailing Add:* PO Box 567 Pollock Pines CA 95726-0567

TARBOX, GURDON LUCIUS, JR
MUSEUM DIRECTOR, ADMINISTRATOR
b Plainfield, NJ, Dec 25, 27. *Study:* Mich State Col, BS, 52; Purdue Univ, MS, 54. *Pos:* Trustee, Brookgreen Gardens, Murrells Inlet, SC, 59-, dir, 63 & pres, 90. *Publ:* Contribr, A Century of American Sculpture - Treasures of Brookgreen Gardens, Abbeville Press, 81. *Mailing Add:* 644 Crooked Oak Dr Pawleys Island SC 29585

TARDO, RODULFO
SCULPTOR
b Matanzas, Cuba, Feb 18, 19; US citizen. *Study:* Nat Fine Arts Sch, Havana, Cuba, prof(sculpture & drawing); Clay Club & Art Students League, scholar. *Work:* Nat Mus Cuba; Sch Archit, Havana; Sch Pedagogy, Havana Univ; Art Gallery Matanzas; Cathedral of St John the Divine, NY. *Comn:* Image, Nat Shrine Immaculate Conception, Washington, 75-76; outdoor & indoor bronze sculptures, Church Immaculad Corazon Maria, NJ; bas relief, comn by Father Varelo, Church Transfiguration, NY, 88; Virgen Altagracia (bust), Church St Peter & St Paul, Union City, NJ, 90; and others in US & Cuba. *Exhib:* Philadelphia Mus Art, 49; Mus Nat D'Art Mod, Paris, France, 51; Bienal Hispanoamericana de Arte, Madrid, Spain, 52; Brooklyn Mus, NY, 73; Metrop Mus Art, NY, 76; one-man shows, Galerie Int, NY, 71, Cisnero Gallery, NY, 73 & Horizon Galleries, NY, 82. *Pos:* Dir, Art Mag, Matanzas, 50-52. *Teaching:* Prof drawing, Sch Plastic Arts, Matanzas, 41-51, dir, 44-49, prof sculpture, 51-61. *Awards:* Gold Medals, Tampa Univ, 52 & Acad Italia Delle, 80. *Bibliog:* Articles, Art News, 2/70 & Arts Mag, 11/70; Jeanne Paris (auth), Rodulfo Tardo, Long Island Press, 71. *Mem:* Artisti Contemp Acad Italia. *Publ:* Auth, Tendenze e Testimonianze dell Arte Contemporanea, Nicole Panepinto & Calogero Panepinto, 83. *Mailing Add:* 5012 41st St Long Island City NY 11104

TARGAN, JUDY
PRINTMAKER, PAINTER
b New York, NY, Oct 12, 31. *Study:* Smith Col, BA(magna cum laude, Ph Beta Kappa), 53; Rutgers Univ, 55; Fairleigh Dickinson Univ, 56-59. *Work:* State Mus, Trenton, NJ; Newark Mus, NJ; Libr Cong, Washington; Univ Pa, Philadelphia; and many corporate collections. *Comn:* Women's Div, Jewish Community Fedn, Metropolitan, NJ, 80; Nat Women's Div, Albert Einstein Col Medicine, NJ, 81; UNICEF greeting cards. *Exhib:* State Mus, Trenton, NJ, 78; Boston Mus Fine Arts, Mass, 78; Newark Mus, NJ, 79; Outstanding Women Artists of NJ, YMHA & YWHA, 79; Unspoken Seasons, NJ Ctr Visual Arts, 95; Wood Works, Hutchins Gallery, Maplewood, NJ, 96; Earth Tapestries, Gallery South Orange, NJ, 98. *Pos:* Art comt, Montclair Mus, NJ; adv coun, Col Visual & Performing Arts, Kutztown Univ; vis comt, Smith Mus Art. *Awards:* Roth Award, Nat Asn Women Artists, 77; Purchase Award, Irvington Art Asn, NJ, 78; First Prize, Summit Art Ctr Regional Show, 79. *Bibliog:* Paintings from New Jersey Collections, The Judith Targan Collection, NJ Visual Arts Ctr; Edward J Nygren (auth), Smith Collects Contemporary, Smith Col, Northampton, Mass, 92. *Media:* Mixed Media, Oil on Wood. *Collection:* Contemporary painting and sculpture. *Publ:* Four commerative stamps, United Synagogues Am, 76; UNICEF notecards, New York Botanical Garden, 78. *Mailing Add:* 40 Glenside Rd South Orange NJ 07079

TARRELL, ROBERT RAY
EDUCATOR, PAINTER
b Oct 18, 56. *Study:* Univ Wis, Platteville, BS, 80; Univ Iowa, MA, 83; Univ Wis, MFA, 95. *Pos:* Ed, Art Times Newsletter, Wis Art Asn, 98-99. *Teaching:* Prof drawing & painting, Edgewood Col, Madison, Wis, 90-. *Awards:* Wisconsin Art Educator of the Yr, 2003. *Mem:* Nat Art Educ Asn; Wis Art Educ Asn (pres, 1999-2001); Wis Painters & Sculptors Inc; Wis Alliance Arts Educ; Nat Asn Schs Art & Design. *Media:* Oil. *Publ:* Coauth, Wisconsin Art Curriculum Guide, Wis Dept Pub Instr. *Mailing Add:* 4318 Tokay Blvd Madison WI 53711

TARSHIS, JEROME
WRITER
b New York, NY, June 27, 36. *Study:* Columbia Col, AB, 57. *Awards:* Nat Endowment Arts Art Critic's Fel, 79. *Res:* Hist art mus & exhibs. *Publ:* Contribr, Art in Am & Christian Sci Monitor. *Mailing Add:* #424 25 Sanchez San Francisco CA 94114-1142

TASCONA, ANTONIO TONY
PAINTER, PRINTMAKER
b St Boniface, Man, Mar 16, 26. *Study:* Winnipeg Sch Art, dipl, 50; Univ Man Sch Fine Arts, 50-53; Univ Winnipeg, LLD, 94. *Work:* Winnipeg Art Gallery, Man; Confederation Art Gallery & Mus Charlottetown, PEI; Art Gallery Ont, Toronto; Nat Gallery Can, Ottawa; Can Coun Art Bank; S J Drake Collection, Univ Man Law Sch; Vancouver Art Gallery. *Comn:* Aluminum bas relief, Man Centennial Art Ctr, 67-68; epoxy resin disks, in steel rings, Fed Dept Pub Works for Freshwater Inst, Univ Man, 72; hanging stabiles, Law Courts Bldg, Winnipeg, 84 & St Boniface Hosp Med Res Bldg, Winnipeg, 86; mural, lounge of Assinaboine Dome Car for Via Rail, Park Cars Proj, Montreal, 88. *Exhib:* One-man shows, Carman Lamana Gallery, Toronto, 68, La Gallerie Int, Ribe, Denmark, 76 & The Dynamics of Tony Tascona (traveling exhib), 84-85; Manitoba Mainstream, Nat Gallery Can (traveling exhib), 72; Manitoba Artists Overseas, Winnipeg Art Gallery (traveling to London, Paris & Brussels), 84; and others. *Pos:* Bd trustees, Nat Gallery, Can, Ottawa, 97-. *Awards:* Arts Medal, Royal Archit Inst Can, Ottawa, 70; Can Silver Jubilee Medal, Govt Can, 77; Gold Medal, Accademia Italia, Parma, Italy, 80; Premio D'Eccellenza Award, Ital Can League Manitoba Inc, 89; Mem, Order Can, Ottawa, 96; and others. *Bibliog:* Virgil Hammock (auth), Tony Tascona: Le succes interieur, Vie Des Arts Mag, winter 75; Visions: A Definition of Space-Prairie Visual Artists, TV Ontario, 83; Arthur Kroker & Kenneth J Hughes (auths), Technology and emancipatory art: The Manitoba vision, Can J Political & Social Theory, 2/86. *Mem:* Royal Can Acad Art (vpres, Prairie Region, 79-81); Can Conf Arts. *Media:* Aluminum Construction. *Mailing Add:* 208 Provencher Blvd Winnipeg MB R2H 0G4 Canada

TASENDE, JOSE MARIA
GALLERY DIRECTOR, DEALER
b Bilbao, Spain, 1932; US citizen. *Study:* Inst Bilbao, Basque Country, BA, 48. *Collection Arranged:* Francisco Zuniga: Exhibit of Drawings & Sculpture, Fine Arts Gallery San Diego, 71 & Everson Mus, 77; Jose Luis Cuevas: An Exhibition of Recent Works, Phoenix Art Mus, 75 & Calif Palace Legion Hon, 75; Jose Luis Cuevas Drawings, Brigham Young Univ, 77; Giacomo Manzu: Exhibition of Sculptures & Drawings, Springfield Mus Art, Mo, 78; Roberto Matta: Paintings & Drawings, Metrop Mus, Coral Gables, Fla, 81; Henry Moore Sculptures & Drawings, Blanden Mem Art Gallery, Ft Dodge, Iowa, 82; An Irreverent Approach (exhib), The Meadows Mus, Southern Methodist Univ, Dallas, 90; Pasadena City Col, Calif, 92; Univ Iowa Mus Art, Iowa City, 93. *Mem:* Art Mus Asn Am; Art Dealer Asn Am. *Publ:* Image and Specter (exhib catalog), Jose Luis Cuevas Letters, Tasende Gallery, 81; Personal Approach (exhib catalog), Figure, Space, Image, Tasende Gallery, 85; The American Factor (exhib catalog), Andres Nagel, Tasende Gallery, 90. *Mailing Add:* Tasende Gallery 820 Prospect St La Jolla CA 92037

TASSE, M JEANNE
HISTORIAN, CALLIGRAPHER
b Worcester, Mass, Mar 25, 25. *Study:* Anna Maria Col, AB, 55; Univ Notre Dame, MA, 62; Boston Univ, PhD (Spec Study) with Sheila Waters, 72. *Work:* Hymns to the Suns; The Gospel According to Luke; An Old Irish Prayer; Dinner Custons ont eh Frontier; Psalm XCII. *Comn:* Calligraphy, comn by The Mountain State Co, Easter Seals and pvt comns; Marietta Col; Pyles Communs, Anna Maria Col. *Exhib:* By Women's Hands, ECC & MC Faculty Art Show; All Calligraphy Exhib, Town House Gallery, Marietta Calligraphy; and others. *Collection Arranged:* Marietta Col Permanent Coll, By Women's Hands, Peoples Art Coll. *Pos:* Dir Inst Learning Retirement; coordr Peoples Art Collection, Marietta, Ohio, 2000. *Teaching:* Prof art & music, Anna Maria Col, 55-75; prof art, Marietta Col, 75-92; chmn, Art Dept, 77-82. *Awards:* Art Teacher Award, Artsbridge, 91; Outstanding Prof Achievement, Anna Maria Col, 2001; Zonta Woman of the Yr, 2006. *Bibliog:* Calligraphy, The Marietta Times; Beautiful writing, Marietta Col Mag; Ex-teacher promotes art in area, Parkersburg News. *Mem:* Nat Soc Arts & Lett (nat pres); founding mem Marietta Calligraphy Soc (pres formerly); Nat Mus for Women in the Arts; Parkersburg Art Ctr; Campus Martius Mus; and others. *Media:* Pen and Ink. *Res:* Medieval period. *Specialty:* Scultpure. *Interests:* Relationship between art and physics; Needlework. *Collection:* Medieval manuscript folios; miniature prints and paintings. *Publ:* Career Award Winners for NSAL, 94. *Mailing Add:* 100 Becker Ln Marietta OH 45750

TATE, BLAIR
TAPESTRY ARTIST, EDUCATOR
b New York, NY, Aug 28, 52. *Study:* RI Sch Design, BFA, 74; Haystack Mountain Sch Crafts, studied with Jack Larsen, 78. *Work:* Mass Inst Technol, Cambridge; Boston Trade Bank. *Comn:* Inset (tapestry), Rocky Mountain Energy Co, Broomfield, Colo, 81; Crossover (tapestry in two parts), Conn Comn for Arts Stamford, Conn, 83-85; Revisions (tapestry), Southeastern Mass Univ, N Dartmouth, 89; Seton Hall Sch Law, Newark, 92. *Exhib:* Contemp Crafts Americas, Colo State Univ, Ft Collins & traveling, 75; Am Acad, Rome, 77; Three Dimensional Possibilities, Rose Art Mus, Brandeis Univ, Waltham, Mass, 79; National Miniature Textile Exhib, Textile Mus, Washington, DC & traveling, 79-81; Crafts of the Commonwealth, Berkshire Mus, Pittsfield, Mass & traveling, 80-81; Skidmore Col Invitational, Saratoga Springs, NY, 84; Fiber R/Evolution, Univ Art Mus, Milwaukee & traveling, 86-87; one-person show, La Jolla Mus Contemp Art, 87, Am Craft Mus, NY, 91; 25 for the 25th, Browngrotta Arts, Wilton, Conn, 99. *Pos:* Studio artist, 75-. *Teaching:* Lectr textiles & weaving, Mass Col Art, Boston, 83 & RI Sch Design, 83-87; instr weaving, Sch Art Inst Chicago, 87. *Awards:* Fel, Mass Artists Found, Crafts, 80 & Project Completion Award, 82; Bunting Fel, Bunting Inst, Radcliffe Col, 83-84. *Bibliog:* Jack Larsen & Mildred Constantine (auths), The Art Fabric: Mainstream, Van Nostrand Reinhold, 81 & 85; Barbara Mayer (auth), Contemporary American Craft - A collectors guide, Peregrine Smith Bks, 88. *Mem:* Am Craft Coun. *Media:* Fiber. *Publ:* Auth, The Warp: A Weaving Reference, Van Nostrand Reinhold, 84. *Dealer:* Browngrotta Arts 276 Ridgefield Rd Wilton CT 06897. *Mailing Add:* 209 Clinton St Apt 2R Brooklyn NY 11201-6268

TATE, GAYLE BLAIR
PAINTER
b Abilene, Tex, Apr 3, 44. *Study:* Univ Wyo, Laramie, 62-64; Fla State Univ, Tallahassee, BS, 67; Loch Haven Art Ctr, Orlando, Fla, 71-72. *Comn:* Trompe l'oeil paintings, comn by Robert Smith, Tampa, Fla, 87 & 88 & Ken Allen, Hendersonville, NC, 88-90, 93-98; Ron Hall, Dallas, 90; Robert Griffin, Charlotte, NC, 91-92. *Exhib:* Ann Jacob Gallery, Highlands, NC; S & S Dillon, Clayton, Ga; The Picture House, Charlotte, NC; M Kenneth Allen Fine Arts, Hendersonville, NC; Creighton Davis Gallery, Washington, DC, 93-94; and others. *Pos:* Pres, Tate Gallery, Tallahassee, 72-; pres, Interarts Inc/Tate Galleries, Tampa, 73-83; pres, Southeast Prof Art Dealers Asn, 80-83; dir, Upper Room Gallery, Biltmore Village, NC, 93-98. *Teaching:* Lectr art & Christianity, 77-; guest lectr, Univ Tampa, 82; Biblical Principles, 85-; art & internet marketing, 98-. *Awards:* First & Third in Painting, Charlotte Spring Show, 91; Exhibitor's Award, Merrimon Galleries, Asheville, NC, 92; Prize, Ann Mus Show, Asheville Art Mus, 94. *Bibliog:* American Artists, Illustrated Survey 1986, New York Art Review, 89; Men of Achievement 1986, Internationale Biographie, 85. *Mem:* Founding mem The Seven, Artist Alliance, Asheville, NC (pres, 92-). *Media:* Oil, Watercolor. *Publ:* Auth, Miro, The Early Works, Interarts Inc, 78; auth, Chapter One, Verse One, Living Waters Press, 89. *Dealer:* M Kenneth Allen Fine Arts 225 N Main St Hendersonville NC 28792; Creighton-Davis Gallery 3300 M St NW Washington DC 20007

TATHAM, DAVID FREDERIC
HISTORIAN
b Wellesley, Mass, Nov 29, 32. *Study:* Univ Mass, AB; Syracuse Univ, MA & PhD. *Teaching:* Prof hist art, Syracuse Univ, 68-2002; Prof Emer Fine Arts, Syracuse Univ. *Awards:* Am Art J Award, 84; H A Moe Prize, NY State Hist Asn, 91; J B Show Prize, 95. *Mem:* Col Art Asn; Am Antiq Soc; life fel Athenaeum Philadelphia. *Res:* American painting and graphic arts of the nineteenth and twentieth centuries. *Publ:* Auth, Winslow Homer's Drawings, Lowe Art Gallery, 79; Winslow Homer in the 1880's, Everson Mus, 83; ed, Prints and Printmakers of New York State 1825-1940, Syracuse Univ Press, 86; Winslow Homer and the Illustrated Book, Syracuse Univ Press, 92; Fishing in the North Woods: Winslow Homer, Mus Fine Arts, Boston; Winslow Homer in the Adirondacks, 96 & Winslow Homer and the Pictoral Press, 2003, Syracuse Univ Press; North American Prints 1913-1947, Syracuse Univ Press, 2006. *Mailing Add:* Dept Fine Arts Syracuse Univ 308 Bowne Syracuse NY 13244

TATISTCHEFF, PETER ALEXIS
DEALER, GALLERY DIRECTOR
b New York, NY, Dec 12, 38. *Study:* Yale Univ, New Haven, Conn. *Collection Arranged:* New Images, Figuration in American Painting, Queens Mus, NY, 74, New Figurative Painting Tour, 77, First Charleston Ann Tour, 77. *Pos:* Pres & dir, Tatistcheff & Co Inc, New York & Tatistcheff/Rogers Gallery, Inc, Los Angeles. *Specialty:* Contemporary American painting, drawing. *Mailing Add:* 529 W 20th St New York NY 10011

TATRO, RONALD EDWARD
SCULPTOR, INSTRUCTOR
b Kankakee, Ill, Jan 12, 43. *Study:* Southern Ill Univ, BA & MFA. *Work:* San Jose Mus Art, Calif; Southwestern Col; Fluor Corp, Irvine, Calif; Saddleback Col, Mission Viejo, Calif; Coleman Col, La Mesa, Calif. *Comn:* Shape Mountain No 4 (12' high), Co San Diego, Health Servs Complex, Calif, 89; Cube On Point (12' high), Paragon Gateway, Mariner Sq Loop, Alameda, Calif, 91; Shadows and Squiggles (8' h x 6' w x 18" d wall sculpture), Technimed-Vernon, Calif, 92; Still Life No 3, Luce, Foward, Hamilton & Scripps, San Diego, Calif, 92; Laguna Sunrise (10' high), AT&T Global Information Solutions, San Diego, Calif, 94. *Exhib:* Fourteenth Ann Purchase Prize Competition, Riverside Art Ctr & Mus, Calif, 76; Calif Hawaii Biennial, San Diego Mus Art, 76; San Jose Mus Art, Permanent Collection Exhib, Calif, 85; New Art Forms-Chicago Int Expos, Nave Pier, Ill, 88; Art 17, 86, Art 19, 88, Art 20, 89, Art 21, 90, Basel Art Fair, Switz, 87; solo exhibs, Lever Meyerson Gallery, NY, 87, David Zapf Gallery, San Diego, Calif, 93 & Wylie & May Louis Jones Art Gallery, Bakersfield Col, Calif, 98; Erika Meyerovich Gallery, San Francisco, Calif, 93, 94, 95, 96, 97 & 98; Artwalk at the Paladion, San Diego, Calif, 94; Artwalk San Diego, David Zapf Gallery, Calif, 95 & 96; LA Current: The Fall Spectrum, Art Rental & Sales Gallery, Armand Hammer Mus Art & Cult Ctr, Calif, 96, Full Spectrum, 96, New View, 97, A Media Fusion, 97, Looking at the Light-3 Generations of Los Angeles Artists, 98; and others. *Teaching:* Instr basic art, Southern Ill Univ, Carbondale, 66-67; asst prof art, Va State Col, 67-68; instr sculpture, Grossmont Col, 68-95, instr art, 95-, dept chmn, 95-. *Awards:* Third Prize in Sculpture, San Diego Art Inst, 75; Juror's Award, Crafts-Sculpture-Painting-Graphics, Orange Co Art Asn, 76; Muckenthaler Cult Ctr, Fullerton, Calif, 79. *Media:* Steel. *Dealer:* Meyerovich Gallery San Francisco CA. *Mailing Add:* 202 Highline Tr El Cajon CA 92021

TAUBES, TIMOTHY EVAN
CRITIC, CURATOR
b New York, NY, June 6, 55. *Study:* Ohio Univ, BA, 77; Hunter Col, art history with Rosalind Krauss & E C Goosens, MBA, 79. *Work:* Artists' Choice Mus, NY. *Exhib:* Abstractscapes, Longboat Key, Fla, 88. *Collection Arranged:* Frederic Taubes Memorial Retrospective, Butler Inst Am Art, Youngstown, Ohio, Canton Art Inst, Ohio & Westmoreland Mus, Greensberg, Pa, 83; Frederic Taubes-Paintings & Drawings, Marymount Manhattan Col Art Gallery, New York, 84; Realist Antecedents, Artists' Choice Mus, New York, 85. *Pos:* Exec dir, Artists' Choice Mus, New York, 83-86; dir, Gallery Educ Ctr, Longboat Key, Fla, 87. *Teaching:* The Educ Ctr, Longboat Key, Fla, 87. *Bibliog:* Article in Art World Mag, 10/84, 3/85. *Res:* 20th century American painting. *Publ:* Contribr, J Artists' Choice Mus, Vols 5-8, 84-86; Chronicles, 3/93; Art & Philosophy, Prometheus Books, 93. *Mailing Add:* 585 Barrack Hill Rd Ridgefield CT 06877

TAULBEE, ANN
DIRECTOR
b Hamilton, Ohio, Aug 23, 59. *Study:* Miami Univ, Oxford, Ohio, BFA, 81; Univ Mass, Amherst, MFA, 84. *Work:* Nelson Atkins Mus, Kansas City, MO; Harvard Univ, Cambridge; Univ Az, Mesa; Univ Wis, Maidson. *Comn:* Wine Label, Benziger Family Winery, Sonoma, Calif, 01. *Mem:* Col Art Asn. *Mailing Add:* Miami Univ Hiestand Galleries Art Dept Oxford OH 45056

TAVENNER, PATRICIA
VIDEO ARTIST
b Doster, Mich. *Study:* Mich State Univ, BA; Calif Col Arts & Crafts, Oakland, MFA. *Work:* San Francisco Mus Art; J Paul Getty Mus, Los Angeles; Royal Mus Fine Arts, Antwerp, Belgium; Sackner Mus, Miami, Fla; Mus Mod Art, NY. *Comn:* Facade, Mus Contemp Crafts, NY, 71; sect of wall, Can Nat Res Libr, Ottawa, 73; Univ Calif, San Francisco, 95 & 98. *Exhib:* Inst Environ, Paris, France, 74; solo exhibs, Mills Col, Oakland, 74, OHS Parsens, Los Angeles, Calif, 82, Atkins Mus Fine Arts, Kansas City, Mo, 85, Mus Mod Kunst, Weddel, Ger, 87, Univ Calif, Berkeley Exten, 85, 89, 92 & 97; Mus Fine Arts, Budapest, Hungary, 87; Am Hist, Atlanta Col of Art, 88; Davidson Gallery, Seattle, Wash, 89. *Teaching:* Instr, Univ Calif, Berkeley Exten, 67-. *Awards:* Acquisitions, San Francisco Mus Mod Art; Residency, Centrum Frans,

Belgium. *Bibliog:* Thomas Albright (AUTH), Bay Area Art, Univ Calif Press. *Mem:* Womens Caucus for Art. *Media:* Collage; Monoprint. *Publ:* Contribr, Art: A Womans Sensibility, 75; A Point of View, D Balator, Nat Ctr Contemp Art, Moscow, 98. *Mailing Add:* PO Box 11032 Piedmont CA 94611

TAWNEY, LENORE
WEAVER, ASSEMBLAGE ARTIST
b Lorain, Ohio. *Study:* Univ Ill, 43-45; Inst Design, Ill, with Archipenko, 46-47; also with Martta Taipale, Finland, 54, with Lili blumenau, 61. *Hon Degrees:* Md Inst Col Art, DD, 92. *Work:* Mus Arts & Design, NY; Mus Mod Art, NY; Kunstegwerbe Mus, Zurich; Art Inst Chicago; Brooklyn Mus; Metropolitan Mus Art, NY; Philadelphia Mus Art, PA; Renwick Gallery, Washington, DC; Am Crafts Mus, NY, 90. *Comn:* Santa Rosa Fed Building, Calif, 77-78; Frank J Lausche State Office Building, Cleveland, 81. *Exhib:* Art Inst Chicago, 79; one-person show, Md Inst Col Art, Baltimore, 92, Tenri Gallery, New York City, 94 & 98, Perimeter Gallery, Chicago, 95, Contemp Mus, Honolulu, 96, Donahue/Sosinski Art, New York City, 96 & 98, Michael Rosenfeld Gallery, New York City, 97 & Allentown Art Mus, Pa, 97; Fiber 82, Hunterdon Art Ctr, Clinton, NJ, 82; Katonah Gallery, NY, 82; Port Hist Mus, Philadelphia, 83; 75th Int Bienniale Tapestry Exhib, Lausanne, Switz, 84; Am Craft Mus, NY, 86-89; Milwaukee Art Mus, Wis, 86-88; Monmouth Mus Art, Lincroft, NJ, 86-88; and others. *Teaching:* artist in residence, Univ Norte Dame, Ind, 78 & Fabric Workshop, Philadelphia, 82; guest lectr, Barff Ctr Arts, Alberta, Can, 83; dist lectr, Univ Ariz, Tucson, 87. *Awards:* Women's Caucus for Arts Honor Award for Outstanding Achievement in Visual Arts, Port of Hist Mus, Philadelphia, 83; Gold Medal, Am Crafts Coun, 87; Mast of Medium Award, Renwick Alliance, 99. *Bibliog:* Charlotte Streifer Rubenstein (auth), American Women Artists, Avon Books, 82; Hiolland Cotter (auth), Lenore Tawney, Signs on the Wind, Pomegranate, 2002; James Schuyler (auth), Selected Art Writings, Black Sparrow Press, 98. *Media:* Linen, Collages. *Mailing Add:* 32 W 20th St New York NY 10011

TAY, ENG
PAINTER
b Kedah, Malaysia, 1947. *Study:* Sch Visual Arts, NY, 67-72; Art Students League, NY, 68; Pratt Graphic Ctr, NY, 72-78. *Work:* Alor Seter Art Mus, Kedah, Malaysia; NY Univ; Pratt Graphics Ctr, NY; Singapore Develop Bank, Singapore; US Embassy Malaysia, Kuala Lumpur. *Exhib:* One-man shows, Nan Gallery, Taipei, Taiwan, 85, FAO Gallery, Fla, 86, Hsiung Shih Gallery, Taipei, 87, JRS Fine Art, RI, 87 & 90, Galerie Du Monde, Hong Kong, 88, Gallery Citra, Malaysia, 90 & Art Base Gallery, Singapore, 90; Multiple Impressions Gallery, NY, 91; Parkshore Gallery, Fla, 91; Premier Gallery, Va, 91; Portfolio Gallery, Eng, 91; Ginger Gallery, Eng, 91; John Sewell Fine Art, Eng, 91. *Publ:* Contribr, Eng Tay Illustrated Graphics, 87; Hsiung Shih, Art Mag, 11/87; Better Life Monthly, 1/88; The Works of Eng Tay, Sunstorm Arts Mag, 3/90; Eng Tay, World tour, Art Bus News, 10/90. *Mailing Add:* c/o Russell Klatt Gallery 33644 Woodward Birmingham MI 48009

TAYLOR, ANN
PAINTER
b Rochester, NY, Mar 23, 41. *Study:* Vassar Col; New Sch Univ, BA, in Englsh, 62; self-taught painter; legal assisting program, Phoenix Col, 94-95. *Work:* Bank Am, Houston; Bausch & Lomb Inc & Xerox, Rochester; Palm Springs Desert Mus, Calif; Honeywell Inc, Minneapolis; and others. *Comn:* Paintings, Central Trust Co, Cincinnati, Ohio, 75; Third Nat Bank, Dayton, Ohio, 79; A C Neilson Corp, Northbrook, Ill, 85. *Exhib:* Butler Inst Am Art, Youngstown, Ohio, 66; Gallery Mod Art, NY, 67; Saginaw Art Mus, 68 & 84; Mem Art Gallery, Univ Rochester, 70; Scottsdale Ctr Arts, Ariz, 82 & 84; Rochester Mus & Sci Ctr, 84; Palm Springs Desert Mus, 84; Yuma Fine Arts Ctr, 84; Reed Whipple Cult Ctr, 84; Beaumont Art Mus, 85; CG Rein Galleries, Scottsdale; Gallery vander woude, Palm Springs, Calif, 86; Oxford Gallery, Rochester, NY, 87 & 95; Marilyn Butler Fine Art, Scottsdale, 87; Perry Sherwood Fine Art, Petoskey, 94; one person shows Scottsdale Ctr Arts, 85, Beaumont Art Mus, 85, Gallery Vander Woude, Palm Springs, Calif, 86, Oxford Gallery, Rochester, 87 & 95, Marilyn Butler Fine Arts, Scottsdale, 87, Rochester Mus & Sci Ctr, 92, Perry sherwood Fine Art, Petoskey, 92; Indianapolis Ctr Contemp Art; Gallery Mod Art, NY; Everson Mus, Syracuse, NY; Janet Fleischer Gallery, Philadelphia; and others. *Pos:* asst to commercial photogr, Jack Cowley Studios, NY, 66 70. *Teaching:* pvt tutor English, NY, 65-70; pvt tutor, substitute teacher in language arts & humanities, creative writing, rsch, hist & social studies, grades 7-12, Scottsdale, Ariz, 95-98. *Awards:* Commemorative Lithograph Competition, Scottsdale Ctr for the Arts, 85. *Bibliog:* Donna Marxer (auth), Painting the very air, Southwest Art, 2/78; Carol Kotrozo (auth), Ann Taylor, Artspace, 4/81; Donald Locke (auth), Ann Taylor, Arts Mag, 2/83 & 3/84; Barbara Cortright (auth), The Reach of Solitude: The Paintings of Ann Taylor, Paul S Eriksson Publ, 83. *Mem:* Las Villas Homeowners Asn (property mgr, treas bd dir, 81-87, 94-98). *Media:* Oil, Lithographs. *Publ:* researcher, ed, designer, pub, documentary, All of Us: A Biographical History of John Jacob Bausch and his descendants, 1830 to 1978, 75-78; ed, co-designer, The Reach of Solitude: The Paintings of Ann Taylor, Paul S Erikson, pub, 1981-82; researcher, ed, designer, Rollie McKenna: A Life in Photography, Alfred A Knopf, Inc, 91. *Mailing Add:* 7209 E McDonald Dr No 30 Scottsdale AZ 85250

TAYLOR, BRIAN DAVID
PHOTOGRAPHER, EDUCATOR
b Tucson, Ariz, June 14, 54. *Study:* Univ Calif, San Diego, BA(visual arts, cum laude), 75; Stanford Univ, MA, 76; Univ NMex, studied with Beaumont Newhall, MFA(art), 79. *Work:* San Francisco Mus Mod Art, Calif; Bibliot Nat, Paris; Int Mus Photog, Rochester, NY; Australian Photog Soc, Victoria; Victor & Albert Mus, London, Eng. *Exhib:* Solo exhibs, Nagase Photo Salon, Tokyo, 85, Triton Mus, 90 & Ctr Photog Arts, 95; Facets of the Collection, San Francisco Mus Mod Art, 87; The Human Vessel, Antwerp Mus Photog, Belg, 88; Picturim Calif, Oakland Mus, 89; Recent Acquisitions, Int Mus Photog, 89; Sneak Previews, Ansel Adams Ctr, 90. *Teaching:* Art & design, photog, San Jose State Univ, 79-. *Awards:* Visual Arts Fel, Santa Clara Co, 90 & 96; Polaroid Artists Grant, New York Studio, 90; Regional Fel, Nat Endowment Arts, 91. *Bibliog:* Robert Hirsch (auth), Photographic Possibilities, Focal Press, 90; Stewart Tabori (auth), The Painted Photograph, Pa State Univ, 95; John P Schaefer (auth), The Ansel Adams Guide: Basic Techniques of Photography, Book 2, Little Brown Co Publ, 98. *Mem:* Soc Photog Educ (chair, West Coast region, 89); Col Art Asn; Phi Kappa Phi. *Media:* Photography. *Publ:* Auth, Places of Magic, Darkroom Photog Mag, Vol 9, No 8, 12/87. *Dealer:* Chris Winfield Gallery Carmel CA. *Mailing Add:* 17341 Valley Oak Dr Monte Sereno CA 95030

TAYLOR, BRIE (BENJAMIN DE BRIE)
EDUCATOR, PAINTER
b Paris, France, Mar 5, 23; US citizen. *Study:* Harvard Univ, BS, 47; Art Students League NY, dipl, 55. *Work:* Johnson Mus, Cornell Univ; Mus Mod Art Miami, Fla. *Exhib:* Butler Inst Biennial, 57; Am Artists, Dallas Mus Fine Arts, 57; Brooklyn and Long Island Artists, Brooklyn Mus, 58 & 60-62; solo exhib, Mus Mod Art Miami, Fla, 59; Contemp Am Painting, Whitney Mus, 60; Corcoran Gallery Biennial, 61; West Side Artists, Riverside Mus, NY, 66; Indiana Artists, Indianapolis Mus Art, 71. *Pos:* Dean, Parsons Sch Design, 68-70 & Herron Sch Art, Ind Univ, 70-73; dir, Inst Design, Ill Inst Technol, 73-75. *Teaching:* Instr painting & drawing, Pratt Inst, 60-68; instr drawing & visual communications, Parsons Sch Design, 67-70; prof drawing & art hist, Inst Design, Ill Inst Technol, 73-87, prof emer, 87-. *Awards:* Fels, MacDowell Colony, 62 & Yaddo, 62. *Bibliog:* James R Mellow (auth), In the galleries, Arts Mag, 10/58; Dore Ashton (auth), Art, NY Times, 10/3/58; Henry Butler (auth), New Herron dean, Indianapolis News, 10/30/70. *Mem:* Col Art Asn; Art Students League; S Co Art Asn (pres, 92-96). *Media:* Oil, Watercolors. *Publ:* Auth, Towards a plastic revolution, Art News, 64; A problem in painting, Sch Arts, 67; John Heliker, Arts Mag, 68; articles, Art, Crowell-Collier, 62, 63, 64, 67, 68, 69 & 70; Design Lessons From Nature, Watson-Guptill, 74. *Mailing Add:* 26 Wild Goose Rd Wakefield RI 02879-6702

TAYLOR, DAVIS
EDUCATOR
Study: Sch Mus Fine Arts, Diploma in Fine Arts; Tufts Univ, BS(educ); Milton Avery Grad, Sch Arts Bard Col, MFA. *Exhib:* Whitney Biennial, Whitney Mus Am Art, 2004; Triple Candle, NY; Inst Contemp Art, Boston; Green Street Gallery, Bonston; Chicago Arts Coun. *Teaching:* Asst prof, Mass Col Art, 99-; fac mem, Milton Avery Sch Arts Bard Col, 2003-. *Awards:* Recipient Artist Prize, Inst Contemp Art, 2001; Asn Int Arts Critics Award, 2002; grant St Botolph Found Grant, 2003. *Mailing Add:* Bard College Milton Avery Graduate Sch Arts PO Box 5000 - 30 Campus Rd Annandale On Hudson NY 12504-5000

TAYLOR, GAGE
PAINTER, ILLUSTRATOR
b Ft Worth, Tex, Jan 20, 42. *Study:* Univ of Tex, BFA, 65; Mich State Univ, MFA, 67. *Work:* Haggin Mus, Stockton, Calif; Jamaica Nat Gallery Art; US Embassy, Georgetown, Guyana; US Info Agency, Washington, DC. *Comn:* 12 watercolors, Hyatt Regency Hotel, Waikoloa, Hawaii, 88; 2 oil paintings, Hyatt Regency Hotel, Kavai, Hawaii, 90; 7 murals, Casa Madrona Hotel, Sausalito, Calif, 93; mural, comn by Dr Anthony Elite, San Francisco, 97. *Exhib:* Divergent Representation, Smithsonian Inst, Washington, DC, 73; Extraordinary Realities, Whitney Mus of Am Art, NY, 73; Our Land, Our Sky, Our Water, Expo 74, Spokane, Wash, 74; Baja, San Francisco Mus of Art, Calif, 75; Paris Biennale, Mus of Mod Art, Paris, 75; Alternative Realities, Mus of Contemp Art, Chicago, Ill, 76; Calif Painting & Sculpture, Mus of Mod Art, San Francisco, 76 & Nat Collection of Fine Arts, Washington, DC, 77; Artists of the Bay Area 1945 to Present, Oakland Mus, 85; Rosicrucian/Egyptian Mus, San Jose, Calif, 93. *Teaching:* Instr landscape painting, San Francisco Art Inst, 71; instr painting & drawing, pvt studio, 72-85; lectr, US State Dept, Caribbean Islands, 87. *Awards:* Kirkus Award, 96; Parents Circle Award, 98. *Bibliog:* Mary Rourke (auth), Fantastic voyages, Newsweek, 7/77; Walter Hopps (auth Introd), Visions I, Pomegranate, 77; articles in Art Voices S, 80, Artweek, 85 & New Realities, 85; Thomas Albright (auth), Art of the Bay Area, 85. *Media:* Oil, Gouache. *Publ:* Auth & illusr, Bears at Work: A Book of Bearable Jobs, Chronicle Bks, 95; auth, Music with the Code, Sirius Art Newsletter

TAYLOR, HUGH HOLLOWAY
HISTORIAN, EDUCATOR
b Charlottesville, Va, July 18, 41. *Study:* Col of William & Mary, Williamsburg, Va, AB(art hist), 63; George Washington Univ, MA(art hist & theory), 65, with Lawrence Leite. *Collection Arranged:* Dir cataloging of collection of Washington Co Hist Soc, Pa, 76-77. *Pos:* chmn & dir, Olin Art Gallery, currently. *Teaching:* Prof art hist, Washington & Jefferson Col, Washington, Pa, 65-, Edith M Kelso Chair Art Hist, currently. *Awards:* Distinguished Professor Award, 90; Sears & Roebuck Leadership Award, 90. *Mem:* Soc Archit Historians; Nat Trust Hist Preserv; Washington Co (Pa) Hist & Landmarks. *Res:* Nineteenth century architecture of western Pennsylvania

TAYLOR, JANET R
TAPESTRY ARTIST, WEAVER
b Lima, Ohio, Jan 19, 41. *Study:* Cleveland Inst Art, dipl, 63; Syracuse Univ Sch Art, MFA, 65. *Comn:* Tapestries, Morris Knudson hq, Boise, Idaho, 81; tapestries, Corpus Christi Bank, Tex, 82; tapestry, Neshaminy Complex, Trevose, Pa, 85; tapestries, The Boulders Resort, Carefree, Ariz, 86; tapestries, Westcourt in the Buttes, Tempe, Ariz, 86. *Exhib:* Solo exhibs, Swan Gallery, Philadelphia, 83 & Willingheart Gallery, Austin, Tex, 85; The Creative Spirit, Maier Mus Art, Lynchburg, Va, 85; Woven

Works, Univ Wis, Green Bay & traveling, 85; Fiber and Clay, Augustana Col, Rock Island, Ill, 85; The Hand and the Spirit Gallery, Scottsdale, Ariz. *Teaching:* Asst prof fiber art, Kent State Univ, Ohio, 69-76; prof fiber art, Sch Art, Ariz State Univ, Tempe, from 77, prof emeritus, currently. *Bibliog:* Tapestries by Janet Taylor, Fiberarts Mag, 9-10/82; Contemporary tapestry, Interior Design, 11/85; Commissions, Am Craft Mag, 4-5/86. *Mem:* Am Craft Coun. *Media:* Tapestry. *Mailing Add:* Sch Art Herberger College Fine Arts Ariz State Univ PO Box 871505 Tempe AZ 85287-1505

TAYLOR, MAGGIE
PHOTOGRAPHER
b Cleveland, Ohio. *Study:* Yale Univ, BA (Philosophy), 83; Univ Fla, MFA, 87. *Work:* Fogg Art Mus, Harvard Univ, Cambridge, Mass; Mus Fine Arts, Houston, Tex; Princeton Univ Art Mus, NJ; Mobile Mus Art, Ala; Mus de la Photog, Charleroi, Belgium; High Mus, Atlanta, Ga; Santa Barbara Mus Art, Calif. *Exhib:* What Photographs Look Like, Art Mus, Princeton Univ, NJ, 95; Common Elements, Islip Art Mus, NY, 97; solo exhibs, New Image Gallery, James Madison Univ, Harrisonburg, Va, 97, Univ N Fla Gallery, Jacksonville, 97, Univ Ctr Gallery, Univ Ala, Huntsville, 98, Bassetti Fine Art Photogs, New Orleans, 98 & Space Gallery, W Mich Univ, Kalamazoo, 98, Lawrence Miller Gallery, NYC, 2005; group exhibs, Jackson Fine Arts, Atla, 92, Creadle Sch Art, Fla, 94, Irvine Fine Arts, Calif, 97, The Equitable Gallery, NY, 99, Laurence Miller Gallery, NY, 2000, Halsey Gallery, Charleston, 2002; plus many others. *Collection Arranged:* Ctr for Creative Photography, Tucson; City of Orlando, Fla; Davidson Col Art Gallery, Davidson, NC; Mobile Mus Art, Ala; Musee de la Photographie, Charleroi, Belgium; Museet for Fotokunst, Odense, Denmark; Mus Fine Arts, Houston; NationsBank, Charlotte, NC; Purdential Insurance Co, Newark, NJ; Art Mus, Princeton Univ, NJ; Fogg Art Mus, Harvard Univ, Cambridge, Mass; Univ Nev, Las Vegas. *Awards:* Individual Artists Grant, State of Fla, 96, 2001; Grand Prize, Photo Distric News/PIX Mag Ann Digital Imaging Competition, 2000; Project Competition winner, Santa Fe Ctr Photog, 2004. *Bibliog:* Amy Standen (auth), Maggie Taylor's Landscapes of Dreams, Peachpit Press. *Mem:* Soc Photog Educ. *Media:* Photography, Digital Imagery. *Dealer:* Laurence Miller Gallery 20 W 57th St New York NY 10019

TAYLOR, MICHAEL D
HISTORIAN
b Philadelphia, Pa. *Study:* Swarthmore Col, BA, 63; Princeton Univ, MFA, PhD, 70. *Teaching:* Asst prof art hist, Univ Chicago, 66-74; assoc prof & chmn, Univ Mo, St Louis, 74-84; prof & chmn, Univ Houston, 84-89; prof, 89- & dean, 89-98, Univ Mass, Dartmouth. *Mem:* Col Art Asn; Nat Asn Schs Art & Design; Int Coun Fine Arts Deans. *Res:* Medieval and early Renaissance imagery. *Publ:* Auth, Prophetic scenes at Orvieto, Art Bull, 72; A historiated tree of Jesse, Dumbarton Oaks Papers, 80-81; The pentecost at Vezelay, Gesta, 80; Gentile la fabriano shame, J Family Hist, 82. *Mailing Add:* Univ Mass Col Visual & Performing Arts North Dartmouth MA 02747

TAYLOR, MICHAEL (ESTES)
INSTRUCTOR, SCULPTOR
b Lewisburg, Tenn, May 10, 44. *Study:* Middle Tenn State Univ, BS, 1967; E Tenn State Univ, MA, 1968; Univ Wis, Post Grad Fel, 1970; E Tenn State Univ, MFA, 1977. *Work:* Corning Mus Glass, NY; Smithsonian Inst; Mus fur Kunsthandiwerk, Frankfurt, W Ger; Vanderbilt Univ, Tenn State Mus & Metrop Govt, Nashville; Speed Art Mus, Louisville, Ky; Chrysler Mus of Art, Norfolk, Va; and others. *Comn:* Sculpture, Bella Mare Towers, Miami, Fla; Awards, NY Gov Arts Awards, Albany; Sculpture, Nmseoul Univ, Seoul, Korea; Sculpture, Kanazawa Grand Hotel, Kanazawa, Japan; Sculpture, Seasons Hotel, Dobra, Qatar. *Exhib:* Boise Gallery of Art, Rosenthal Gallery Art, Caldwell, 80, Idaho; Contemp Art Glass Gallery, Toronto, Ont, 82; Elaine Potter Gallery, San Francisco, Calif, 84-85; Glass Now 85, Yamaha Nippon Gakki, Hamamatsu, World Glass Now '85, Hokkaido Mus Mod Art, Sapporo, Shimonoseki City Art Mus, 85, Japan; Sculptural Glass Invitational, Erie Art Mus, Pa, 85; Renwick Gallery, Smithsonian Inst, Washington, 94; The Studio, Corning Mus of Glass, Corning, NY; Resources Exhib, Bevier Gallery Art, RIT, Rochester, NY; Eighteenth Ann Int Invitational Glass Exhib, Habatat Galleries, Boca Raton, Fla; Glass Am '02, Heller Gallery, NY, 2001; Hodgell Gallery, Sarasota, Fla, The Furnace Found, Istanbul, Turkey, Gallery Artists, Sandra Ainsley Gallery, Toronto, Ontario, Can, 2002; Leo Kaplan Mod Gallery, NY; Clearly Influential Contemp Am Glass Art Educ; Tittot Mus Art, Taipei Tiwan, Repub China; Contemp Glass, 20th Ann Int Invitational Habatat Galleries, Boca Raton, Fla; Racine Mus Art, Racine, Wis, 2003; Hodgell Gallelry, Sarasota Fla; Sandra Ainsley Gallery, Toronto, Ontario, Can; Nat Liberty Mus, Philadelphia, Pa; Four Seasons Hotel, Dobra, Qatar, 2004; Prints & Glass Sculpture (solo), Ky Mus Art & Craft, Louisville, Ky, 2005; Cadence Sculptural Installation, WCI Bella Mare Communities, N Miami, Fla; Contemp Glass 22nd Ann Int Invitational, Habatat Galleries, Boca Raton, Fla & Berrington, Mass, 2005; and others. *Pos:* Chmn arts fac, George Peabody Col, 76-79; chmn art dept, Col Idaho, Caldwell, 80-81; bd gov's NY State Found for Arts; nat screening com, Inst Int Educ, 95-98; juror, New Glass Review, The Corning Mus Glass. *Teaching:* Assoc prof, Vanderbilt Univ, Nashville, 71-79, chairperson, 75-79; vis artist, glass, Konfax Skolen, Stockholm, Sweden, 74 & Gerrit Rietuield Akad, Amsterdam, Holland, 74; chmn art dept, Col Idaho, 79-81; prof, head of glass prog, Rochester Inst Technol, 81-; instr, Pilchuck Sch Glass, 96. *Awards:* Visual Artist Exhib Grant, NY State Coun Arts, 85-86; Visual Arts Fel, NY State Coun for the Arts, 86; Grand Prize, The Int Exhib Glass, Kanazawa, Japan, 88; Grand prize, Int Glass Exhib, Kanazawa, Japan, 89; Cultural Specialist Award Grant, US Dept Info Svcs, Monterey, Mexico, 95. *Bibliog:* Richard Skull (dir), Michael Taylor: Glass (film), Micki Colman, 68; Rusty Chapman (dir), Glass Craft (film); Glass Art Soc J, 88 & 90. *Mem:* Tenn Artists-Craftsmen Asn (pres, 70-71); Am Crafts Coun; Glass Art Soc (bd dir, 78-82); Am Asn Univ Prof; Asn Portugesa Vidizo. *Media:* Glass, Graphics. *Publ:* Auth, A Geometry of Meaning, Hudson Hills Press, NY, 2006. *Dealer:* Leo Kaplan Modern Gallery 41 E 57th St NY 10022; Habatat Gallery 608 Banyan Trail Boca Raton FL 33431; Hodgell Gallery 46 Palm Ave S Sarasota FL 34236; Holsten Gallery 1 Elm St Stockbridge MA 01262. *Mailing Add:* 41 French Road Rochester NY 14618-3825

TAYLOR, ROBERT
CRITIC, WRITER
b Newton, Mass, Jan 19, 25. *Study:* Colgate Univ, AB, 47; Brown Univ Grad Sch, 48. *Pos:* Art critic, Boston Herald, 52-67; Boston corresp, Pictures on Exhib, 54-59; mem staff, Boston Globe Mag, 68-72, art critic, 72-, arts ed, 73-76, columnist, 76-82, chief bk & art critic, 82-. *Teaching:* Prof Eng, Wheaton Col, 60-; lectr art hist, Boston Univ, 72-74. *Mem:* St Botolph Club, Boston; Mass Hist Soc. *Publ:* Auth, In Red Weather, 61; ed, publs, Inst Contemp Art, Boston, 67; auth, Treasures of Massachusetts, 72; Saranac, 86; Fred Allen, 89. *Mailing Add:* 1 Thomas Cir Marblehead MA 01945

TAYLOR, ROSEMARY
CERAMIST, SCULPTOR
b Joseph, Ore. *Study:* Cleveland Inst Art; NY Univ; Greenwich House; Arrowmount Col. *Work:* Westchester Col. *Exhib:* Hudson River Gallery, NY, 81; Am Crafts, Cleveland, Ohio, 85-94; Guild Gallery, Princeton, NJ, 85-90; Sign of the Clef, Savannah, Ga, 91-94; James Michener Mus, Pa, 95-96; and others. *Pos:* pottery consult, McCall's Mag, 62-72; Juror, Fulbright Award & Grants, 81-82; standards chmn, NJ Designer-Craftsman, 92-94. *Teaching:* Instr, Rahway Art Ctr, 50-60. *Bibliog:* Arthur Williams (auth), Sculpture, Craft Report Mag. *Mem:* NJ Designer-Craftsman; Am Craft Coun. *Media:* Stoneware. *Publ:* Contribr, McCall's Needlework, Craft Mag & Craft Report; and others. *Mailing Add:* Box 282 Stockton NJ 18559

TAYLOR, SANDRA ORTIZ
ASSEMBLAGE ARTIST, SCULPTOR
b Los Angeles, Calif, Apr 27, 36. *Study:* Univ Calif, with William Brice & Sam Amato, BA; Iowa State Univ, with Byron Burford, MA; Chicano & Latino Lit Studies Grad Prog, Univ Calif, Irvine. *Work:* Univ Iowa; Macy's Corp, NY; Univ Calif Res Libr, Los Angeles; Oakland Mus. *Exhib:* Paper Stars: Nat Women's Exhib, San Francisco Artist Gallery, Calif, 94; Selections, Acad Art Col Gallery, 96; Le Petit Three, Alder Gallery, Eugene, Ore, 96; Pulp Fiction Works on Paper, Tex Fine Arts Asn, 96; Works from Imaginary Parents (auth, catalog), Galeria Dos Damas, San Diego, Calif, 96; Glean, Four Walls, San Francisco, 96; solo exhibs, 871 Fine Arts, San Fran, 97, Oakland Int Airport, Calif, 2003, Sonoma Co Mus, Santa Rosa, Calif, 2003, San Francisco Main Libr, 2004, Motazabu Gallery, Tokyo, 2004, Nexus Gallery, Philadelphia, 2005, Glass Curtain Gallery, Columbia Col, Chicago, 2005; 6th Int Shoebox sculpture, Univ Hawaii Art Gallery, Honolulu; 19th Ann solo mujeres exhib, Mission Cultural Ctr Latino Arts, San Francisco, Calif, 2006; Artfully Reclaimed 2nd Ann Exhib, art League N Calif, Norato, 2006; 3rd ann nat juried exhib, Art League N Calif, Norato, 2006; Con(text) Koelsch Gallery, Houston, TX, 2006. *Pos:* Gallery asst, John Bolles Gallery, 70-71; guest curator, Sonoma Mus Vis Arts, Santa Rosa, Calif, 2001. *Teaching:* Instr, San Francisco Community Col, 66-2001 & Indian Valley Col, Marin, Calif, 74. *Awards:* Jurors Award, Calif Small Works, 92; Barbara Deming Mem Fund Grant, 96. *Bibliog:* Article in Art Monthly, 93; Randal Davis (auth), article, Artweek, 93; Chiori Santiago (auth), article, Oakland Tribune, 93; Timothy Don Adams (auth), Light Writing & Life Writing, Photography in Autobiography, Univ NC Press, 2000; Debra Castillo & Maria Socorro Tabuenca Cordoba (auths), Border Women, Writing From LA Frontera, Univ Minn Press (chap 4), 2003; Laura E Perez (auth), Altarities: Chicana Art, Politics & Spirituality, Duke Univ, 2006. *Media:* Mixed Media; Found Objects. *Publ:* Contr, Imaginary Parents, Sheila Ortiz Taylor (auth), Univ Nex Mex Press, 1996. *Dealer:* Franny Koelsh Koelish Gallery Houston TX; Adrienne Fish 871 Fine Arts San Francisco, CA. *Mailing Add:* 2200 23rd St San Francisco CA 94107

TAYLOR, SUSAN M
MUSEUM DIRECTOR
Pos: Dir, Davis Mus and Cult Ctr, Wellesley Col, Mass, Princeton Univ Art Mus, NJ, 2000—. *Mailing Add:* Princeton Univ Art Mus McCormick Hall Princeton NJ 08544

TAYSOM, WAYNE PENDELTON
SCULPTOR, EDUCATOR
b Afton, Wyo, Oct 10, 25. *Study:* Univ Wyo; Columbia Univ; Univ Utah, BFA, 48; Ecole Beaux-Arts, Paris; Teachers Col, Columbia Univ, MA, 50; Cranbrook Acad Art. *Work:* Ore State Univ Mem Union; Corvallis Clin, Ore; Univ Ore Erb Mem Union; US Nat Bank Ore, Portland. *Comn:* Archit sculpture, Lane Co Courthouse, Eugene; Corvallis Br, US Nat Bank Ore; fountain & doors, Ore State Univ Libr; coun chamber doors, Salem Civic Ctr, Ore; St Mary's Cath Church, Corvallis; and others. *Exhib:* One-man show, Portland Art Mus, 54, Paper Works, 72; Seattle World's Fair, 62; Am Crafts Coun, Western Craftsmen, 64; Hunnicutt Art Gallery, Hawaii, 67; and others. *Teaching:* Instr sculpture, Univ Ore, 51-52; prof sculpture, Ore State Univ, 53-88, prof emer, currently. *Awards:* Purchase Prize, Portland Art Mus, 56. *Mem:* Portland Art Asn; Corvallis Art Asn

TEACHOUT, DAVID DELANO
PAINTER
b Santa Monica, Calif, Nov 16, 33. *Study:* NC State Univ, BA(landscape archit), 63. *Work:* Occidental Col, Los Angeles, Calif; Univ Calif, Santa Cruz. *Exhib:* James D Phelan Awards, Palace Legion Honor 65-67; 85th Ann Exhib San Francisco Art Inst, San Francisco Mus Art, 66; 15th Painting Ann, Richmond Art Ctr, 66; 30th Biennial Exhib Contemp Am Painting, Corcoran Gallery Art, Washington, 67; 14th Ann Exhib, Laguna Beach Mus Art, 68; Real Colorists, Richmond Art Ctr, Richmond, Calif, 69;

Occidental Col Centennial Exhib, Los Angeles, Calif, 87. *Bibliog:* Constance Perkins (auth), Critical Review of Teachout Painting Retrospective, Occidental Col, 75; Art Forum Mag, 75. *Media:* Acrylic, Oil. *Publ:* Co-auth, Jazz 4 Linguis, Jazz Press, 79; co-auth, Jazz 5, Jazz Press, 80; illusr, An Occassional Suite, Jazz Press, 81. *Mailing Add:* 315 McAmant Dr Santa Cruz CA 95060

TEAGUE, EDWARD H
LIBRARIAN, EDUCATOR
b Lenoir, NC, Jan 5, 52. *Study:* Univ NC, Chapel Hill, BFA, 73, MSLS, 78; Univ Ga, MA(art hist), 76. *Pos:* Reference librn, Valdosta State Univ, Ga, 78-80; head reference dept, Univ NC, Charlotte, 82-84; archit & fine arts librn, Univ Fla, Gainesville, 84-2000, art & archtl libr, Univ Oreg, 2000-. *Bibliog:* Henry Moore (auth), Bibliography and Reproductions Index, McFarland, 82. *Mem:* Art Libr Soc NAm (pres, 95-96); Asn Archit Librns; Asn Archit Sch Librns; Am Libr Asn. *Res:* Reference and research services for design disciplines. *Interests:* Architecture, modern art, ancient art, landscape architecture, interior design, building construction. *Publ:* Auth, World Architecture Index, Greenwood Press, 91; Index to Italian Archit, Greenwood Press, 92; Webmaster, Art Libr Soc NAm, 96-98

TECZAR, STEVEN W
EDUCATOR, PAINTER
b St Joseph, Mo, Aug 8, 48. *Study:* Univ Mo, Columbia, AB, 70, AM, 72; Washington Univ, St Louis, MFA, 86. *Work:* Greenville Co Mus Art, SC; Southeastern Ctr Contemp Art, Winston-Salem, NC; Va Mus Fine Arts, Richmond; Suwa Munic Art Mus, Japan; Nanjing Sch Fine Arts, China. *Comn:* Sculpture, Southern Bankshares Inc & Va Commonwealth Univ Child Care Cooperative, Richmond, Va, 75; sculpture, RF&P RR Co, Richmond, Va, 76; play sculpture, Ethical Soc Nursery Sch, St Louis, Mo, 81. *Exhib:* 1940-80 Fellowship Recipients, Va Mus, Richmond, 80; The Next Juried Show, Va Mus, Richmond, 83; Currents 29: Drawing in St Louis, St Louis Art Mus, 85; Four Square Feet, Sazama/Brauer Gallery, Chicago, Ill, 88; New Work on Paper & Constructions, BZ Wagman Gallery, St Louis, 89; New Constructions and Drawings, Atrium Gallery, St Louis, 91; London Summer 94; Works on paper and Sculpture, Family resource Ctr, Gorham, NH, 2001; Autobiographical Fragments, A Gallery Installation, Maryville May Found Gallery, 2002. *Pos:* Prin, Design Collaborative Richmond, Va, 74-78. *Teaching:* Asst prof drawing & design, Va Commonwealth Univ, Richmond, 72-79; instr, Southside Va Community Col, Alberta, 74; chair art & design, Maryville Univ St Louis, 79-99; prof art, Maryville Univ, St Louis, 99-. *Awards:* Residency, Cite Int des Arts, Paris, 95; Prof Develop Grants, Maryville Univ, 95-2003; Sabbatical Sculpture and Mixed-Media Works, 2000. *Bibliog:* Alexandra Bellos (auth), Sea Views, Riverfront Times, St Louis, 1/91; Karen Schmitendorf (auth), Teczar's Trailing Lines, St Louis Post-Dispatch, 2/2/91; Eddie Silva (auth), In the Realm of Possibility, Riverfront Times, St louis, 1/98. *Mem:* Col Art Asn Am; Art St Louis. *Media:* All Media. *Publ:* American Drawings, St Louis Art Mus, 76; Drawing in St Louis, 85; St Louis Contemporary Works: An International Exchange, 87; Art St Louis V, 89. *Mailing Add:* 315 S Gore Ave St Louis MO 63119-3603

TEFFT, ELDEN CECIL
SCULPTOR, EDUCATOR
b Hartford, Kans, Dec 22, 1919. *Study:* Univ Kans, BFA, 49, MFA, 50; Cranbrook Acad Art, 51-52; with Bernard Frazier, William McVey. *Comn:* Franklin D Murphy (bronze), Sculpture Garden, Univ Calif, Los Angeles, 69; Moses (bronze), Kans Sch Religion, Lawrence, Kans, 82; Ida B Wells (bronze bust), Wells Journalistic Ann Award, 83; Buddy Award, a bronze sculpture presented ann by the Kans Univ Dept Theatre & Media Arts & the Univ Theatre, 87-; Keepers of the Universe (limestone triptych), City of Lawrence, Kans, 88. *Exhib:* One-man show, Philbrook Art Ctr, Tulsa, Okla, 48; San Francisco Mus Art, Calif, 50; Carnegie Mus, Philadelphia, Pa, 50; The Midwest Show, Joslyn Art Mus, Nebr, 52; 58th Ann Exhib for Western Artists, Denver Art Mus, Colo, 53; Mid-Am Invitational, William Rockhill Nelson Gallery Art, Kansas City, Mo, 55; Missouri Show, City Art Mus, St Louis Art Mus, 59; Kans Sculptors Asn Outdoor Ann Exhib, Lawrence, Kans, 88-89 & 91-92; two-man show with Kim T Tefft, Baker Univ, Baldwin, Kans, 92. *Pos:* Chmn, Nat-Int Sculpture Conf, 60-78; dir, Nat Sculpture Ctr, Lawrence, Kans, 67-77, Int Sculpture Ctr, Lawrence, Kans, 77-80, Sculpture Research Ctr, Univ Kansas, Lawrence, 80-90; dir emer, Int Sculptor Ctr, Washington, DC, 80-; prof emer, Univ Kans, 90-. *Teaching:* Prof sculpture, Univ Kans, 50-90; vis prof, Univ Philippines, Quezon City, 64, Univ Ore, Eugene, 64, Univ Costa Rica, San Jose, 71, Cent Inst Fine Art Beijing, Shanghai Jiao Tong Univ, China, 86 & Ateno Paraquayo, Asuncion, Paraguay, 88; workshop, Baker Univ, Baldwin, Kans, 92. *Awards:* 17th Mo Show, City Art Mus St Louis, 59; First Award Arch Sculpture Competition, Fidelity State Bank, Topeka, Kans, 67; Nat Sculpture Conf, Jonesboro, Ark, 77. *Bibliog:* Dennis Kowal & D Meilach (auths), Sculpture Casting, Crown Publ, Inc, NY, 72; Robert Rose (cinematographer), Moses, The Creation of a Heroic Sculpture, Sculpture Research Ctr, Lawrence, Kansas, 85. *Media:* Bronze, Stone. *Res:* World sculpture founding techniques and their effect on the creative process. *Publ:* Auth, Bronze Casting of Sculpture (film), Int Film Bureau, Chicago, 60; Lost Wax Sculpture Foundry Equipment & Design: Ceramic Shell Supplement, Sculpture Res Ctr, 83; Lost Wax Sculpture Founding, An Exploration, Sculpture Res Ctr, Univ Kans, 92. *Mailing Add:* Tefft Terra Studios 1333 E 1600 Rd Lawrence KS 66046

TEICHMAN, MARY MELINDA
PRINTMAKER, CALLIGRAPHER
b Newark, NJ, Sept 8, 54. *Study:* Cooper Union, New York, BFA, 76. *Work:* Corcoran Gallery, Washington; Brooklyn Mus, NY; Mus City NY; Mus Art Carnegie Inst, Pittsburgh; Duxbury Art Complex Mus; Nat Mus Women in Arts, Washington; Jane Voorhees Zimmerli Art Mus, Rutgers Univ, N Brunswick, NJ; Newark Pub Libr, Newark, NJ. *Comn:* Recollection (ed 150 prints), Presentation Print Artist, Print Club Albany, 93. *Exhib:* Soc Am Graphics Artists Competition, NY, 79, 86, 88, 91, 92, 93 & 2002; Print Club, Philadelphia, 80-81; Brooklyn Mus, NY, 81; Hunterdon Art Ctr, NJ, 81, 83 & 85; Assoc Am Artists, NY, 82, 84, 85, 87, 89, 92 & 96; Contemp Images, Mus City NY, 82-92; Boston Printmakers Int, De Cordova Mus, Lincoln, Mass, 82, 83, 84, 86, 89, 90, 91, 93 & 2005; Contemp Images of the City, Mus City NY, 92; Recent Acquisitions, Mus City NY, 94; Delta Nat Small Prints Exhibn (auth catalog), Ark State Univ, 69, 99, 2000 & 01. *Awards:* Boston Printmakers Award, 88, 93 & 97; Chancellor's Purchase Award, 62nd Nat Print Exhib, Univ Wis, 89; Merit Award, Purdue Univ, Ind, 90; K Caraccio Color Intaglio Purchase Awards, SAGA, New York, 2000 & 01; and others. *Bibliog:* Robin Longman (auth), Emerging artists-Mary Teichman, Am Artist Mag, 8/84; Nicole Plett (auth), The new mexican, prints take you to.,Pasatiempo Mag, 7/85; Presentation print, Mary Teichman, the print club of Albany, Jour of print world, Vol 16, No 3, Summer 93; Mary Teichman, journal of the print world, Vol 28, No 1, Winter, 2005. *Mem:* Boston Printmakers; Soc Am Graphic Artists; Print Club Albany; Soc Scribes; Soc Egg Tempera Painters. *Media:* Color Etching. *Dealer:* The Old Print Shop New York. *Mailing Add:* 14 Hooker Ave Northampton MA 01060

TEIGER, DAVID
COLLECTOR
b Newark, June 13, 29. *Study:* Cornell Univ, BS, 51. *Pos:* served to lt, USA, 51-53; Partner, Samuel Teiger & Co, Newark, 53-59, Ira Haupt & Co, NY City, 59-64, Bache & Co, NY City, 64-65; exec vpres, Shearson, Hammill & Co, Inc, 65-73; chmn, Chief Exec Officer, United Res Co, Morristown, NJ, 73-90; chmn, Gemini Consulting, 90-95; hon trustee, Mus Modern Art, NY City. *Awards:* Named one of Top 200 Collectors, ARTnews mag, 2006. *Mem:* Meadowood; Mountain Ridge

TEILHET-FISK, JEHANNE HILDEGARDE
HISTORIAN, EDUCATOR
b Palo Alto, Calif, May 16, 39. *Study:* Univ Calif, Los Angeles, BA, 62, MA, 67 & PhD(art hist), 75. *Collection Arranged:* Arts of East Africa, Los Angeles Mus Sci & Indust, 67; Dimensions of Black (auth, catalog), La Jolla Mus Art, 70; Dimensions of Polynesia (auth, catalog), San Diego Fine Arts Gallery, 73; Gauguin: Polynesian Sources, Mus A Gauguin, Tahiti, 81. *Pos:* Asst cur, Jos Mus, Nigeria, 67-68; consult ed, Tofua Press, San Diego, Calif, 75-77; filmmaker, Tapa Production in Tonga, 76-. *Teaching:* Prof non-western art hist, Dept Visual Arts, Univ Calif, San Diego, 68-94; prof art hist, Fla State Univ, Tallahassee, 94-. *Awards:* Kress Found & Nat Endowment Arts Awards, Dimensions of Polynesia, 73; Univ Research Grants, 87 & 88; Distinguished Teaching Award, Univ Calif, 90. *Res:* Focus on non-Western arts of Oceania, Native American & Afro-Am with special interests in woman's art forms & folk art. *Publ:* Auth, The Role of Women Artists in Polynesia and Melanesia, Dunmore Press, 83; Paradise Review: An Interpretation of Gauguin's Polynesian Symbolism, UMI Press, 83; Tongan Grave Art: Indicators of Social Change, Univ Hawaii, 90; To Beat or Not to Beat; A Study on Acculturation and change in an Art Making Process, Pacific Studies, 91; Clothes in Tradition: The Ta'ovala and Kiekie as Social Text and Aesthetic Markers of Custom and Identity in contemporary Tongan Society, Part I & II, Pacific Arts, 92. *Mailing Add:* Fla State Univ Art Hist Dept 220 D Fine Art Bldg Tallahassee FL 32306-1151

TELLER, DOUGLAS H
PAINTER, EDUCATOR
b Battle Creek, Mich, June 1, 33. *Study:* Western Mich Univ, BA, 56; Mich State Univ, George Washington Univ, MFA, 62. *Work:* Corcoran Gallery Art, State Dept, George Washington Univ, Smithsonian Inst & Libr of Cong, Washington, DC. *Exhib:* Corcoran Gallery Touring Show, 59 & 60; Relig Arts Show, Smithsonian Inst, DC, 61; Provincetown Art Asn, Chrysler Mus, Mass, 63; Soc Washington Printmakers Int Show, Nat Collection Fine Arts, DC, 64; one-man show, Corcoran Gallery Art, 65; Massillon Mus Invitational, Ohio, 69; two-man show, Dimock Gallery, George Washington Univ, DC, 79; George Washington Univ, ann; Cosmos Club, 87; and others. *Teaching:* Prof Design & watercolor, George Washington Univ, DC, 63-, Prof Emer, 95. *Awards:* 1st Prize Printmaking, Corcoran Gallery Art, 59; Best of Show, Rapaitannock Regional Show, 92; Several Awards, Fla Suncoast, 99 & 2000. *Mem:* Fla Watercolor Soc; Southern Watecolor Soc; Suncoast Watercolor Asn; Fla Artists Group Inc. *Media:* Watercolor. *Publ:* Auth, Art and Design, George Washington Univ, 60. *Dealer:* Serendipity Gallery 321 Park Ave PO Box 453 Boca Grande FL 33921

TELLIER, CASSANDRA LEE
MUSEUM DIRECTOR, EDUCATOR
Study: Ohio State Univ, MA, 79, PhD, 84. *Collection Arranged:* Ancient Art, 87; Petersburg/Perestroika: Contemp Russian Art from Ohio Collections, 90; Sakura in Buckeye Country: Japanese Artists in Ohio, 91; The Far North: Works of the Inuit & Northwest Indians, 95; African Art Revealed, 96; Selected Works by Modern Masters, 99; Tempus Fugit, 2000; African American Artists of WPA, 2001; African American Artists of Central Ohio, 2003. *Pos:* Prog dir arts, Ga Tech, 80-81; dir, Schumacher Gallery, Capital Univ, Columbus, Ohio, 89-. *Teaching:* Vis asst prof art, Kent State Univ, 84-86; asst prof, Capital Univ, 89-. *Mem:* Am Asn Mus; Ohio Mus Asn; Asn Col & Univ Mus & Galleries. *Res:* Egypt, Africa & the ancient Mediterranean world. *Publ:* Auth, What you see & what you get: frame of reference in museum exhibits, Curator, 86; The significance of the history museum as a resource for art appreciation, Res Abstracts, 86; auth, Imhotep, Cult of Isis, Anchient Ghana, Saharan Rock Art, Alwa & Makouria, in: Encyl Ancient World, Salem Press, 2001; auth, Warfare of African empires, Military Arts in the Cultures of African People, Moscow State Univ Press, 2001; auth, Ezana & the fourth century kingdom of Aksum, the Meroitic empire, rock art of the Sahara, Great Events From History: The Ancient World, Salem Press, 2003. *Mailing Add:* c/o Capital Univ Schumacher Gallery 2199 E Main St Columbus OH 43209

TEMES, MORT (MORTIMER) ROBERT TEMES
CARTOONIST, DESIGNER
b Jersey City, NJ, Apr 15, 28. *Study:* Art Students League, with William McNulty, Jon Corbino, Frank Reilly & Robert B Hale, 47-49; NY Univ, BA, 53. *Pos:* Prof free lance cartoonist, 50-; dir spec serv, NJ Inst Technol, 58-88; dir off serv, 88-91. *Teaching:* Newark Col Eng, 60-65. *Mem:* Nat Cartoonists Soc; Life mem, Art Students League. *Media:* Pen, Ink; Pencil, Watercolor. *Publ:* Illusr, Engineers & Engineering--Some Definitions, 68; Making Tomorrow Happen, 70; cartoons have appeared in many nat mags & cartoon anthologies

TEMPEST, GERARD FRANCIS
PAINTER, SCULPTOR
b San Donato, Italy, Feb 23, 18; US citizen. *Study:* Mass Sch Art (studio art), 39; Tufts Univ, Mus Sch, Boston, Mass, 45; pvt study with Giorgio de Chirico, Rome, 48; Univ NC, BA, 49. *Work:* Vatican Mus Art, Vatican City, Italy; Akiraniasaki Collection, Tokyo, Japan; NC Mus, Raleigh; La Fondation Michelange, Venaco, Corsica; Monte Cassino Mus, Cassino, Italy. *Comn:* Empress Farah Diba (HIM), comn by Shah of Iran, Teheran, 74. *Exhib:* Newport Art Soc Mus, 59; Salon D'Automne de Lyon, France, 67; Mus Fine Arts, Boston, 68; solo exhibs, Duke Mus Art, Durham, NC, 78 & Bergen Co, NJ, 91; NY Cult Ctr, 72. *Awards:* Purchase Award, NC Mus Art, Raleigh, 49; Gold Medal, II Biennale Azureen, Cannes, France, 67. *Bibliog:* Donald Kuspit (auth), Gerard Tempest: Abstract Spiritualism, Bergen Mus, 91; M Stephen Doherty (auth), Gerard Tempest: Giving form to spiritual notions, Vol 55, Am Artists, 10/91; Carol Volk (auth), On the Edge, Vol VIII, No 8, Art & Antiques, 10/91. *Media:* Oil on Canvas; Cast Metal. *Publ:* Illusr (cover), Vol 58, No 1, J Am Planning Asn, winter 92. *Mailing Add:* 1307 N Magnum St Durham NC 27701

TEMPLE, BYRON
CERAMIST
b Ind, 33. *Study:* Ball State Univ, 51-52. *Work:* State Mus NJ; Harrison Mus Art; Ball State Univ Mus; Am Craft Mus; Peat Marwick Montvale Art Collection. *Exhib:* One-man shows, Indianapolis Mus Art, 92, The Gallery, Bloomington, Ind, 93, Ceramic ART, Sydney, 94, Clay Feat, Auckland, 94, Contemp Craft, Portland, Ore, 94, Boymans-van Beuningen, Rotterdam, 95 & Anton Gallery, Washington, 95; Soc Arts & Crafts, Boston, 95; Ceramics Ky, 95; Jane Hartsook Gallery, NY, 95; Scripps Ann, Calif, 96. *Pos:* Independent studio potter. *Bibliog:* Dawna Richard-Hyde (auth), Byron Temple's Quest for Beauty and Utility, Ceramics Art & Perception, No 6, 91. *Mailing Add:* c/o The Works Gallery 303 Cherry St Philadelphia PA 19106

TEMPLE, LESLIE ALCOTT (LESLIE JANE ATKINSON)
SCULPTURE, WRITER
b Oklahoma City, Okla, 51. *Study:* Univ Denver, 69-70; Oklahoma City Univ, BS (ed & art), 73; grad work, Univ Central Okla, 73-74; studied with Bruno Lucchesi & Jon Zahourek. *Work:* Monumental Work, Mus Outdoor Art, Englewood, Colo; Denver Pub Libr Permanent Collection, Western Hist Dept, Colo; Founders Corp, NY; Serrano Corp, Mexico City; City & County of Denver Auditor's Office; Project Safeguard, Denver, Colo; Nat Jewish Medical & Research Ctr, Denver; Pvt collections of Dr Patricia Ellison, Denver, Colo, Denny LeRoux J Friedman, NY. *Comn:* Nude Female, marble statue, Mus Outdoor Art, Englewood, Colo; Mother & Child, bronze statue, Consortium for Community Centered Comprehensive Child Care, Tanzania, Africa; Bronze portrait, Child, comn by Dr David Clausen, Denver, Colo; Bronze portrait, Pres, Founders Corp, NY. *Exhib:* NAm Sculpture Exhib, Golden, Colo, 82, 83 & 84; Greeley Invitational, Greeley, Colo, 83; High Plains Sculpture Exhib, Loveland, 84, 86, 87 & 88; Catherine Lorillard Wolfe, 92nd Ann, Nat Arts Club, NY, 88; Am Artists Prof League, 60th Grand Nat Exhib, Salmagundi Club, NY, 88; Mus Outdoor Arts, Englewood, Colo, 2001; Denver Int Airport, 2001; Univ Denver, Mus Anthropology & Penrose Libr, 2002. *Pos:* Pres, SLA Arch/Couture Inc-An Environmental Enrichment Design Co, 90-; SLA Concrete Construction Inc, 90-93; adv comt, Colo Dept Transportation, 92-93; adv, Native Am, Denver Indian Ctr, 83-93; bd dir, Construction Women Owners & Exec, 90-93; bd trustees, Denver Art Mus, 92, mem marketing & ed, audience develop comt, 93; mem Artists Am Marketing Comt, Colo Hist Mus, Denver, Colo, 99. *Teaching:* Art, Oklahoma City Fin Arts Mus, 71-72; art & art hist, Our Lady of Lourdes Sch, Denver, 85-87. *Awards:* Drawing I, Best of Show, Greely Invitational, 83; Hon Mention, Sculpture, Nat Jewish Community Ctr, 86; Judges Merit Honor, Prof Fine Art Photog, Hayes Kans Art Coun, 15th Ann Nat Competition, 99. *Bibliog:* American Artists, An illustrated Survey of Leading Contemp, 90; Sculptor's Resistance Mirrors Her Withdrawal, Sunday Oklahoman, 7/8/84; The Mus Outdoor Arts(bk & film), Englewood, Colo. *Mem:* Denver Art Students League (82-94). *Media:* All Media. *Publ:* Coauth, with George Carlson, The Tarahumara, pvt publ, 76; auth, A Body of Work, pvt publ, 82; documentary film, Art in Process, produced by Mus of Outdoor Art, copyright, 90; Primitive Tarahumara Indian Tribe (5 bk series & photog exhib), in prep; Outstanding People of 20th Century, Biographical 2000 Data Ctr, Cambridge, Eng. *Dealer:* Belleli Antiques & Fine Art Gallery Denver CO. *Mailing Add:* 2088 S Pennsylvania Denver CO 80210-4034

TEN
PAINTER
b Marienberg, Neth, June 8, 1930. *Exhib:* Newark Mus, 61; one-man shows, Flemington Studio Arts, NJ, 71, Upstairs Gallery, Somerville, NJ, 72 & Papermill Playhouse, Milburn, NJ, 72; Plainfield Regional Art Mus, NJ, 79; Ctr Int D'Art Contemporain, Paris, France, 84; Mandragore Int Galerie D'Art, Paris, France, 86; Art Philadelphia, 2003; Int Festival Erotic Art, Montreal Calif, 2004; and others. *Pos:* Art dir, NJ Print Coun, 92-95. *Awards:* Wally's Award, Plainfield Art Asn, 66, First Prize in Oils, 69; Tracy Long Mem Award, Summit Art Ctr, 66. *Bibliog:* Doris Brown (auth), Surrealist's exhibit opens, 5/3/70, Franklin artist, 8/8/71 & Dutch-born artist, 6/25/72, Sunday Home News. *Mem:* Hunterdon Mus Art; NJ Print Coun; Artists Equity. *Media:* Oil, Ceramics. *Publ:* Erotic Art by Living Artists, Art Network Press, Renaissance, Calif. *Dealer:* Gallery of Surrealism 395 S End Ave #2YM New York NY 10280. *Mailing Add:* 2346 Amwell Rd Somerset NJ 08873-7217

TENENBAUM, ANN
ADMINISTRATOR, COLLECTOR
b Savannah, Ga, June, 1961. *Study:* Sarah Lawrence Col, grad. *Pos:* Mem vis comt dept photographs, Metrop Mus Art, 1996-2005, trustee, 2005-; vchmn bd trustees, Dia Art Found, NY City, 1994-2006; co-pres bd trustees, Film Soc Lincoln Ctr for Performing Arts, currently; founding mem bd govs, Bard Col Ctr Curatorial Studies; bd dirs, Sarah Lawrence Col, Channel 13/WNET, Studio Mus, Harlem, NY, Second Stage Theatre, Guild Hall East Hampton; mem chmn's coun, Mus Modern Art. *Awards:* Named one of Top 200 Collectors, ARTnews Mag, 2003-06; Leo award, Independent Curs Int, 2003; Child Advocacy award, NY Univ Child Study Ctr, 2003. *Collection:* Contemporary & Modern art; Egyptian art. *Mailing Add:* c/o Metrop Mus Art 1000 5th Ave New York NY 10028

TENNANT, DONNA KAY
WRITER, EDITOR
b Waynesburg, Pa, Nov 28, 49. *Study:* Univ Rochester, NY, BA(art hist), 71; Univ NMex, Albuquerque, MA(art hist), 79; also with Beaumont Newhall. *Pos:* Art critic, Houston Chronicle, Tex, 79-81; Jeremy Stone Gallery, San Francisco, 82-84 & 89-91, Sherry French Gallery, New York, 84-85; assoc ed, Mus Fine Arts, Houston, 85-86; adminr, Houston Art Dealers Asn, 87-89 & 91-; ed, Mus & Arts Mag, 93 94; managing ed, Houston Life Mag, 94-95; sr ed, Southwest Art, 96-98; ed, Polo Mag, 98-99. *Teaching:* Adj lect, Art History, Univ of Houston, Downtown, 2001-. *Res:* Second-generation abstract expressionism thesis; 19th & 20th century art, history of photography, contemporary art. *Publ:* Ibsen Espada (catalog), McMurtrey Gallery, 89; Nine in Fiber, Artspace, 90; Jacob Lawrence, Painter, Mus & Arts Mag, 92; Lydia Bodnar Balahutrak (catalog), Nave Mus, 95; Dianne L Reeves, Art Papers, 96. *Mailing Add:* 2603 Parana Houston TX 77080

TENZER, (DR & MRS) JONATHAN A
COLLECTORS
b New York, NY, May 21, 40. *Study:* Dr Tenzer, Univ Vt, BA, 62; Univ Pa, DMD, 66. *Collection:* A Wyeth, Moses (Anna Robertson), Rockwell; Michele Delacroix. *Mailing Add:* 625 N 29th St Allentown PA 18104-4237

TEPFER, DIANE
CURATOR, HISTORIAN
Study: Brooklyn Col; Univ Wash, BA (art hist), 68, MA (art hist), 72; Univ Mich, PhD, 89. *Collection Arranged:* Am Artists Look at Chinese Culture, Beijing, Am Embassy, 96; A Vision of Am, (auth catalog) The Berlin Embassy, Berlin and Vienna, 99; Art fromthe Palouse and Beyond, The Cameroon Embassy Collection, Yaounde and Vienna, 99; Celebrating the Am Family, (auth catalog) The Copenhagen Embassy Collection, Denmark, 99; The Healing Spirit, (auth catalog) the Dar es Salaam Collection, Tanzania, 2000; Am Visions, the Ukraine Collection, Kiev, 2001; The Spirit of the Midwest, the Vilnius Embassy Collection, Latvia, 2001; From the Gulf States to the Caribbean, the Venezuela Embassy Collection, Caracas, 2001. *Pos:* asst cur prints and photographs div, Libr Congress, Washington, DC, 91-94; cur, Art in Embassies Program, US Dept State, 95-2001, curatorial cons, 2001-. *Teaching:* instr, Oberlin Coll, Ohio, 80 81; instr, Colby Coll, Waterville, Maine, 82 83; adj assoc prof humanities, Univ Md, Univ Col ONLINE, 2002-. *Awards:* Fel Am Art, Rockefeller Found, 77-78; Res Fel, Smithsonian Inst, Nat Mus Am Art, 81-82; Fel Am Art Hist, Luce Found, 87, 89. *Mem:* Col Art Asn; Smithsonian Material Culture Forum; Wash Indep Writers Art Table. *Res:* Am art patronage, dealers, crafts; Samuel and Edith Halpert. *Publ:* Edith Gregor Halpert and the Downtown Gallery Downtown 1926-1940 & A Study in Am Art Patronage, UMI, 90; Edith Gregor Halpert, Impresario of Jacob Lawrence's Migration Series, The Phillips Collection, Wash, 93; Times Square, Pont Neuf, Lake Mahopac, and More; the Art and Life of Samuel Halpert (1844-1930), 2001; Ukrainian Roots: American Visions: The Ameican Embassy Collection, Kyiv and Vienna, 2002; Janet Sobel 1894-1968, Art in America, 7/2002. *Mailing Add:* 1737 Willard St NW Apt 1 Washington DC 20009-1753

TERAOKA, MASAMI
PAINTER, SCULPTOR
b Onomichi, Japan, Jan 13, 36. *Study:* Kwansei Gakuin Univ, Kobe, Japan, BA(esthetics), 59; Otis Art Inst, BA, MFA, 68. *Work:* Oakland Mus; Achenbach Found Graphic Arts, Fine Arts Mus San Francisco; Los Angeles Co Mus Art; Nat Mus Am Art, Washington, DC; Minneapolis Inst Arts. *Comn:* Cover illus, Time Mag, 3/30/81. *Exhib:* Solo exhibs, Masami Teraoka: AIDS Ser, Grey Art Gallery, NY Univ, 90, Henry Art Gallery, Seattle, Wash, 91, Schmidt/Dean Gallery, Philadelphia, Pa, 91, Macquarie Galleries, Rushcutters Bay, Australia, 92, Rebecca Hossack Gallery, London, Eng, 92 & Pamela Auchincloss Gallery, NY, 90, 92 & 94; All for Love, Tyler Galleries, Temple Univ, Pa, 91; In the Looking Glass, Mint Mus, Charlotte, NC, 91; Parallel Visions: Modern Artists & Outsider Art, Los Angeles Co Mus Art, 92; From Media to Metaphor: Art About AIDS, organized by Independent Cur Inc (traveling), 92; Paintings by Masami Teraoka, Arthur M Sackler Gallery, Washington, DC & Asian Art Mus, San Francisco; and others. *Pos:* Lectr, Art Gallery New South Wales, Victorian Col Arts, Melbourne, Australia, 89 & San Francisco Art Inst, Calif, 89. *Teaching:* Artist-in-residence, Victorian Col Arts, Melbourne, Australia. *Awards:* Artists Fel, Nat Endowment Arts, 80 & 89; Kay Nielsen Mem Purchase Award, Los Angeles Co Mus Art, 78. *Bibliog:* Howard Link (auth), Waves & Plaques: The Art of Masami Teraoka, Contemp Mus, Honolulu, 88; Paintings by Masami Teraoka, Weatherhill Press; From Tradition to Technology: The Floating World Comes of Age, Univ Wash Press. *Media:* Watercolor, Oil

TERMES, (DICK A)
PAINTER, SCULPTOR
b San Diego, Calif, Nov 7, 41. *Study:* Black Hills State Col, BS, 64; Univ Wyo, Laramie, MA(art), 69; Otis Art Inst, Los Angeles, MFA, 71. *Work:* Denver Art Mus; Sphere Mus, Tokyo, Japan; Coca Cola Corp, Atlanta, Ga; Doene Col, Crete, Nebr; Univ Cent Fla, Orlando. *Comn:* 5 1/2 ft centennial sphere for State of SDak; Pull to the North (sphere), North Pole, Alaska; Order/Disorder (sphere), Law Enforcement Acad, Wyo; Univ Cent Fla, Orlando, 93; Against the Current, SD Humanities Coun, 2003; Porthole to the Past, Deadwood SD, 2002. *Exhib:* Spherical Thinking and Total Photos, Col Archit Gallery, Ariz State Univ, 82 & Univ Ky, Lexington, 83; Mus of Fun (15 cities), Japan, 84; Air & Space Mus, Smithsonian Inst, 87; Montana Moon Gallery, Chicago, Ill, 88; Gallery on the Green, Lexington, Mass, 89; San Francisco State Univ, 90; Univ Ill; MS Escher Centennial Congress, Univ Rome, 98; Extrasensory Mus, Japan, 99. *Teaching:* Instr art, Henley High Sch, Klamath Falls, Ore, 64-66, Sheridan High Sch, 66-68 & Black Hills State Univ, 71-72. *Awards:* SDak Arts Coun Fel, 76, 80 & 94; Artistic Achievment Citation, SDak Mus Art, 86; Gov's Award for Creative Distinction, 99. *Bibliog:* Susan O'Neill (auth), Six point perspective--the total view, Denver Post, 77; David Miller (auth), Total photographer has whole world in his hands, 80, Mod Photog, 80; Daralice Boles (auth), Termes total photo, Progressive Archit, 83; Shaping Space, 88; Rochelle Newman (auth), Malleable Matter and Stretchable Space, Pythagorean Press, 2000. *Media:* Lexan Plastic Globe Canvas, Acrylic. *Publ:* Art Gallery Int Mag, 8/89; Art & Man, MC Escher Scholastic, 92; The Visual Mind, Art and Math, Mass Inst Technol Press, 94; Psycological Perspectives, 92 & 96; Homage to Escher, Leonardo Mag, Vol 33, 1, 2000. *Mailing Add:* 1920 Christensen Dr Spearfish SD 57783

TERMINI, CHRISTINE See Genute, Christine Termini

TERRASSA, JACQUELINE
MUSEUM DIRECTOR
Study: MFA, Univ Chgo, 94. *Pos:* Staff mem, Columbia Col, Chgo; educ dir, Hyde Park Art Ctr, David and Alfred Smart Mus Art, Univ Chgo, 98-, interim dir, 2004-. *Mailing Add:* Smart Mus Art Univ Chgo 5550 S Greenwood Ave Chicago IL 60637

TERRIS, ALBERT
SCULPTOR, EDUCATOR
b New York, NY, Nov 10, 16. *Study:* With Aaron J Goodelman, 33; Works Progress Admin Art Sch, New York; Beaux Arts Inst Design, New York 33-34; City Col New York, with George W Eggers, BSS, 39; Inst Fine Arts, New York Univ, with Walter Friedlander, Richard Krautheimer & Goldwater, A Phillip McMahon, 39-42. *Comn:* Signature piece (with Jimmy Ernst), for Pontiac Hour, Television, Playwrights 56, comn by Nat Broadcasting Co, 56; Sun (for Wide, Wide World), comn by Abe Liss of Electra Films, 58; Words: Strong, Weak, Argonne Nat Lab, Downers Grove, Ill, comn by Dr Ted Novy, 62; In the Beginning Was the Word, Dr Bill Gerhard, 63; 50 Years, Brooklyn Col Anniversary, 80. *Exhib:* One-man shows, Duveen-Graham, 58, Allan Stone, 62, Artist Space, 75 & Gloria Cortella Gallery, NY, 77; Brooklyn-Long Island Artists Biennale, Brooklyn Mus, NY, 60; Sculpture Show, Mus Mod Art, NY, 62; Bundy Int Sculpture Exhib, Waitsfield, Vt, 63; Treasures of 20th Century Art, Maremont Collection, Wash Gallery Mod Art, Washington, 64; Critics Choice, Sculpture Ctr NY, 72; Artist in the Civil Service, Brooklyn Col Gallery, 85; and others. *Pos:* Deputy chmn in charge of Dept Art, Sch Gen Studies, Brooklyn Col, NY, 58-70, emer prof, 86. *Teaching:* Prof sculpture & theory of art, Dept Art, Brooklyn Col, NY, 47-86. *Awards:* First Prize, Long Island Artists Biennale, Brooklyn Mus, 60. *Bibliog:* Sidney Geist (auth), Month in review, Arts Mag, 1/58; Irving Sandler (auth), Am construction sculpture, Evergreen Review, Vol 2, No 2, spring 59; James A Schinneller (auth), Search & Self Discovery, Int Textbook Co, 68. *Media:* Steel Welded. *Publ:* Contribr, Artists on the Current Scene, Arts Yrbk 4, 60; The Private Myth, Tanager Gallery, 60; auth, Retrospective 1950-1975, Metal Sculpture, Freeport Mem Libr, 77. *Mailing Add:* 280 S Ocean Ave Freeport NY 11520

TERRY, CHRISTOPHER T
PAINTER, DRAFTSMAN
b Stamford, Conn, Jan 8, 56. *Study:* RI Col, BA, 78; Univ Wis-Madison, MFA, 81. *Work:* Mus der Kreisstadt, Ahrweiler, Rheinland-Pfalz, Ger; Ger Fulbright Kommission, Berlin; Nora Eccles Harrison Mus Art, Logan, Utah; Springville Mus Art, Utah; Park Hyatt Corp Coll, San Francisco. *Exhib:* Solo show,Hackett/Freedman Gallery, San Francisco, 2000, Enigmatic Ritual, Nicolaysen Mus, Casper, Wyo, 2000, Interior Landscapes, Plains Mus Am Art, Fargo, ND, 2000 & Marshall Art Gallery, Scottsdale, Ariz; Charlotte Int,Spirit Sq Ctr for Arts, NC, 93; Contemp Still Life, Riverside Mus Art, Calif, 94; Nachbar Am, Altes Synogogue, Ahrweiler, Rheinland Pfalz, Ger, 95; Still Life, Contemp Realist Gallery, San Francisco, 96; Utah Art, Utah Artists, Springfield Mus Art, Utah, 2001. *Teaching:* Lectr drawing & painting, Calif State Univ, Long Beach, 85-88; prof painting, Utah State, Univ, 88-; guest prof, Univ Essen NRW, Ger, 94-95; vis artist, Am Acad, Rome, Italy, 2000; guest prof, Univ Essen NRW, Germany, 2002-03. *Awards:* Westaf/Nat Endowment Arts Regional Fel in Painting, 95; Alumnus of Yr Award, RI Col Art Dept, 2001; Fulbright Scholar, Univ Essen, Ger, 2003. *Bibliog:* Roberts Carasso (auth), Realism through a Modern Lens, Orange Co Register, 12/7/2000; Wesley Pulkka (auth), Contemporary Realism, Southwest Art, 3/2000; Bonnie Gangelhoff (auth), Contemporary Realism in California, Southwest Art, 1/2001; Amy Abrams (auth), Looking Beyond Oil, Canvas, Get Out Mag, Ariz Republican, 3/22/2001; Vern Swanson (auth), Utah Art, Utah Artists, Springville Mus of Art, 2002. *Media:* Oil on Canvas. *Dealer:* Hidell, Brooks Gallery 1910 South Blvd Charlotte NC 28203. *Mailing Add:* Utah State U Art Dept 4000 Old Main Hill Logan UT 84322

TERRY, HILDA
CARTOONIST, WRITER
b Newburyport, Mass, June 25, 14. *Study:* Art Students League; Nat Acad Design; NY Univ. *Work:* Boston Univ; Univ Ohio; Salisbury Hist Mus; Newburyport Hist Mus. *Comn:* Fulton Fish Market (acrylics), comn by Sam Marg, NY, 71; Woolworth Bldg, 71; Information Bd, AT&T Info Ctr, 84. *Pos:* Creator, Teena (comic strip), King Features Syndication, 41-63; Dir, Hilda Terry Gallery, NY; Pioneer computer graphics for electronic score boards, 69-88; founder & dir, 8 Henderson Place Found Inc. *Teaching:* Instr cartooning, New Sch Social Res, 68 & NY Phoenix Sch Art & Design, 69-71, & Art Students League, 90-. *Awards:* Wohelo Award, Camp Fire Girls; Best Waste-Not Cartoon, New York Times, 42; NCS Best Animations Cartoonist, 80. *Bibliog:* Cartoonist Profiles No 39, Judd Hurd Pub, 78; Old Troubadour, Walker & Co, 87; Trina Robbins (auth), Century of Women Cartoonists, Kitchen Sink Publ, 93. *Mem:* Nat Cartoonists Soc; NYMUG; Nat Women Writers Guild. *Media:* Pen, Ink, Computer. *Publ:* assoc ed Matusow's, Art Collectors Almanac, 65; Baseball Lights Up, 86; Does God Eat Us?, 90; Strange Bod Fellows, 93; God's DNA, 96. *Mailing Add:* 8 Henderson Pl New York NY 10028

TESFAGIORGIS, FREIDA
PRINTMAKER, EDUCATOR
b Starkville, Miss, Oct 21, 46. *Study:* Graceland Col, Lamoni, Iowa, AA, 66; Northern Ill Univ, De Kalb, BS, 68; Univ Wis, Madison, with Ray Gloeckler & Robert Grilley, MA, 70, MFA, 71. *Work:* Grad Sch, Univ Wis, Madison; Du Sable Mus of African & Afro-Am Art, Chicago; S Side Community Art Ctr, Chicago; Afro-Am Ctr, Univ Wis. *Comn:* Mixed-media drawing, Afro-Am Arts Inst, Univ Ind, Bloomington, 76; prints & drawings, Wis Arts Bd, 78. *Exhib:* Sixth Concours Int de la Palme d'Or des Beaux Arts, Palmares, Monte Carlo, France, 74; Prints & Drawings, MAMA Gallery, Madison, Wis, 76; Beloit Vicinity Ann Exhib, Wright Art Ctr, Wis, 76; 15th Nat Print Exhib, Art Gallery, Bradley Univ, Peoria, Ill, 76; Midwestern Black Artist, Performing Arts Ctr, Milwaukee, Wis, 76. *Pos:* Artist-in-residence, Univ Wis, Madison, 71-72. *Teaching:* Asst prof African/Afro-Am art, Univ Wis, Madison, 72-77, assoc prof African/Afro-Am art, 77-. *Awards:* Wis Arts Bd Art Grant, 77; City Arts Grant, Prints & Drawings, Off of the Mayor, Madison, 77. *Bibliog:* Interest in African art is on the increase in US, Capital Times, 7/75; James Auer (auth), PAC surveys midwestern Black art, Milwaukee J, 2/76; Shirley Carley (auth), Starkville native making name in field of art, Starkville Daily News 3/76. *Mem:* Wis Women in the Arts; Nat Conf of Artists (regional coordr, 74); Nat Coun for Black Studies. *Media:* Woodcut. *Publ:* Illusr (cover), Ba Shiru, Univ Wis, 71 & 76-77; contribr, Center debut: A Black artist's view, Milwaukee J, 11/75. *Dealer:* Assoc Am Artist 663 Fifth Ave New York NY 10022. *Mailing Add:* 6109 Piping Rock Rd Madison WI 53711

TETHEROW, MICHAEL
PAINTER
b Tacoma, Wash, 1942. *Study:* San Francisco Art Inst, BFA. *Work:* Dallas Mus Art, Dallas, Tex; Seattle Mus Contemp Art, Seattle, Wash; Syracuse Univ Art Collection, NY; Neuberger Mus Art, Southampton, NY; Whitney Mus Am Art, NY; Brooklyn Mus, NY; New York Pub Libr; Albright-Knox Art Gallery, Buffalo, NY. *Comn:* comn by SI Newhouse, NY, Richard Brown Baker, NY, Mr & Mrs Cargill MacMillan, Minneapolis, Minn, Phil Schrager, Omaha, Nebr. *Exhib:* Konstallen Gotaplatsen, Goteborg, Swed, 82; Parrish Art Mus, Southampton, NY, 83; Baskerville & Watson, NY, 86; Nina Freudenheim Gallery, Buffalo, NY, 89-90; Vital Forces: Nature in Contemp Abstraction, Heckscher Mus, Huntington, NY, 91; NY Collection 1991-92, Albright-Knox Art Gallery, Buffalo, NY, 91; Palm Beach Community Col Mus Art, Fla, 92; Totem Paintings, Jason McCoy Inc, 94, Works on Paper, 96; and others. *Awards:* Fel, Nat Endowment Arts, 79 & 87; Engelhard Found Award, 85. *Bibliog:* Ken Johnson (auth), Michael Tetherow, Art Am, 10/91; Charles Hagen (auth), Inspiration from Dreams, Spirits and the Center of the Earth, Times, 11/8/91; Gary Schwan (auth), NY Exhibition Intentive, Cheeky, Palm Beach Post, 1/31/92; Grace Glueck (auth), Michael Tetherow, New York Observer, 11/92; Donald Kuspit (auth), Michael Tetherow Review, ArtForum, 12/92. *Mailing Add:* PO Box 1811 Bridgehampton NY 11932

TETTLETON, ROBERT LYNN
PAINTER, EDUCATOR
b Ruston, La, Dec 23, 29. *Study:* La Polytech Inst, BA, 50; La State Univ, Baton Rouge, MEd, 53; studied painting with Louis Guglielmi, 53 & Hale Woodruff, 63; New York Univ, 63-64. *Exhib:* Mid-South Art Show, Brooks Mem Art Gallery, Memphis, Tenn, 69; one-man shows, Little Theater, Monroe, La, 54, Mary Buie Mus, Oxford, Miss, 70, Sardis Pub Libr, Miss, 79, Univ Gallerie, Univ Miss, 81; Teacher's Touch, Miss Mus Art, Jackson, 83; plus others. *Pos:* Interior designer, Sears Roebuck & Co, Shreveport, La, 59-61; local site coordr, Very Special Arts, 78-88. *Teaching:* Instr art, Port Arthur Independent Sch Dist, 50-51 & Northeast La State Col, 55-56; asst prof art, Univ Fla, 61-65; prof art, Univ Miss, 65-95, chmn art dept, 65-76. *Awards:* Hon mention, La Art Comn Exhib, 54; Governors Award, Volunteers, 87. *Mem:* Nat Art Educ Asn; Southeastern Col Art Asn; Col Art Asn; Miss Art Educ Asn (pres, 79-82); Am Soc Interior Designers; and others. *Media:* Oil, Acrylic, Collage. *Mailing Add:* 137 Leighton Rd Oxford MS 38655-2009

TEWES, ROBIN J
PAINTER
b Queens, NY, Sept 16, 1950. *Study:* Hunter Col, BA(fine arts), 78. *Work:* Prudential Life Insurance; Cabrini Nursing Home; Incarnation Children's Ctr, Artist & Homeless Collaborative. *Comn:* Tent Project for Artist & Homeless Collaborative, Henry St Settlement, NY, 93; Facade of One City Cafe, Artist & Homeless Collaborative & the Food & Hunger Hotline, NY, 94; Art in Gen, Window Installation, 95; Pyramid Atlantic Book & Printmaking Proj (5 rooms), Riverdale, Md, 96. *Exhib:* Situations,

Mus Modern Art, NY, 85; The Human Figure in Cont Art, (with catalog) Contemp Art Ctr, New Orleans, La, 82; Portraits on a Human Scale (with catalog), Whitney Mus Art, NY, 83; Situations, Mus Mod Art, NY, 85; The Subject of Rape (with catalog), Whitney Mus Art, NY, 94; The New Portrait, PSI Inst, NY, 84; The Return of the Cadavre Exquis (with catalog), The Drawing Ctr, 93; solo exhibs, John Weber Gallery, NY, 94 & 98, Bill Maynes Gallery, NY, 94, 95 & 97 & Faggonato Fine Arts, London, 98; Mary Dana Women Series, Rutgers Univ, 96; Girls, Girls, Girls: Grand Salon; Realism After Seven AM: Realist Painting After Edward Hopper (with catalog), NY, 96; Pop Surrealism (with catalog), Aldridge Mus, Ridgefield, Conn, 98. *Teaching:* Parsons Sch Design, New York, 97 & 98; Bard Univ, MFA Prog, New York, 97 & 98. *Awards:* Mid Atlantic Arts Found, 96; Pyramid Atlantic Residency, 96; Djerassi Artist Residency, 97; and others. *Bibliog:* Roberta Smith (auth), The New Galleries of the 90's, New York Times, 4/23/94 & 12/5/97; David Humphrey (auth), New York Fax, Art Issues #34, 94; Ingrid Schaeffner (auth), article, Artforum Mag, 4/96; and others. *Media:* Acrylic, Oil; All. *Publ:* Auth, Art for the Eighties (catalog), Scott Cook, 80 & Episodes (catalog), Carter Ratcliff, 81, Borgenicht Gallery; 26 paintings-Robin Tewes, Hanging Loose Press, 82; Collins & Milazzo & Sandro Chia (catalog), Elvis Has Left The Building, 93; R Honda Lieberman (catalog), Wild Kingdom, Bill Maynes Gallery, 94; Parnassus Poetry in Review, Vol 23, 98. *Dealer:* Bill Maynes Gallery New York, NY

TEWI, THEA
SCULPTOR
US citizen. *Study:* Nat Acad Fine Arts, Berlin; Art Students League; Greenwich House; New Sch Social Res. *Work:* Nat Collection Fine Arts, Smithsonian Inst, Washington, DC; Cincinnati Art Mus; Chrysler Mus, Norfolk, Va; Univ Notre Dame; Am Ins Co Corp Collection, Galveston, Tex; Citicorp, NY; City of New York, Dept of Parks; Brooklyn Botanic Garden, NY; plus many others. *Exhib:* 18th-20th Ann New Eng Exhib, Silvermine Guild Artists, 65 & 67-69; Nat Arts Club Exhib Relig Art, 66; one-person shows, La Boetie Gallery, NY, 66, 68 & 70, Hallway Gallery, Washington, DC, 76 & 80, Randall Gallery, NY, 77, 79, 81 & 83, Vorpal Gallery, NY, 85 & NY Acad Sci, 92 & 93; Erie Summer Festival Arts, Pa State Univ, 68; 6th Bienniale of Sculpture, Carrara, Italy, 69; and many others. *Awards:* First Prize for Sculpture, Am Soc Contemp Artists, 71, 75, 76 & 79; Nat Arts Club Medal of Merit, 74 & 75; Sculpture Prize, Nat Asn Women Artists, 75 & 76; and others. *Bibliog:* D Meilach (auth), Contemporary Stone Sculpture, Crown, 70; Prize Winning Art, Harold Publ, 67; Art in Public Places, Bowling Green Press, 68. *Mem:* Am Soc Contemp Artists; Sculptors League (pres, 71-); Nat Asn Women Artist. *Media:* Stone

THACHER, ANITA
INSTALLATION ARTIST, FILMMAKER
b New York, NY, Apr 4, 40. *Study:* Antioch Col; New Sch Social Res, BA, 64; New York Studio Sch Drawing, Painting & Sculpture, 65-66; Millennium Film Sch, 67. *Work:* Metrop Mus Art, NY; Chicago Art Inst; Neuberger Mus, State Univ NY, Purchase; SC Art Inst, Columbia; Inst Arts, Rice Univ Mus; Mus Mod Art. *Comn:* Painted Earth, The Art of the Mimbres Indians (Film), Metrop Mus Art & Getty Mus, 89. *Exhib:* Mus Mod Art, 91; Anthology Film Arch NY, 91; JM Kohler Arts Ctr, Sheboygan, Wis, 93; Los Angeles Co Mus, 93; Lumen-essence, Westbeth Gallery, NY, 96; The Luminous Image III Velan, Torino, Italy; Am Century 1950-1999, Whitney Mus Am Art, 2000; Arts for Transit, MTA, Greenpoint, NY, 20031. *Awards:* Nat Endowment Arts, 77, 78, 80 & 87; Martin E Segal Award, Lincoln Ctr, 88; Jerome Found; and others. *Bibliog:* Marion Boulton Stroud (auth), An Industrious Art, Innovation in Pattern and Print at the Fabric Workshop, WW Norton & Co, 91; Jill Conner (auth), Sculpture Mag, 10/2002; Hellen Harrison (auth), New York Times, 5/12/2002. *Mem:* NY Women in Film; Filmmakers Co-op (bd dir, 85-86); MacDowell Colony (mem bd dir, 80-85); Civitelli Renigri, 2002. *Media:* Film, Video, Installation. *Publ:* Contribr, Frames, 78, Cover Mag, summer 80, Idiolects J, 83 & Film as Installation Catalog, 83; Millenium Film Jour, 2000. *Dealer:* Art Resources Transfer 511 W 33 St New York NY. *Mailing Add:* Cooper Sta PO Box 1625 New York NY 10276

THACKSTON, R KING
PAINTER, CURATOR
b Greenville, SC, Dec 21, 48. *Study:* Atlanta Col Art, BFA, 74. *Work:* Albany Mus Art, Ga; State Ga, Atlanta; SC Nat Bank, Greenville. *Comn:* Illusionary graphic mural, Bur Cult Affairs, Atlanta, Ga, 84; 200' Street of Shops, Dewar's Fine Foods, Atlanta, Ga, 89. *Exhib:* Ga Artists, High Mus Art, Atlanta, 73; Piedmont Graphics Exhib, Greenville Mus Art, SC, 75; Murders & Miracles, Albany Mus Art, Ga, 93; Arts Festival, Atlanta, 94; New Drawings, Blue Spiral I Gallery, Asheville, NC, 96; Testosterone, Vaknin Schwartz Gallery, Atlanta, Ga, 98. *Collection Arranged:* Johnny Detroit's Brunch (40 placesettings by males), 89-90; The Cross Show (70 interpretations of the cross), 90; Taboo's Angry Love, Arts Festival Atlanta, 92; Taboo Confessions, Atlanta, 95; Taboo's Gone With the Wind, Chastain Gallery, Atlanta, 96; Taboo's Requiem, Nexus Contemp Art Ctr, Atlanta, 99. *Pos:* Found mem, TABOO Curatorial Group, 88-. *Awards:* First Award Drawing, Arts Festival Atlanta, 76; Artist Initiated Grant, Bur Cult Affairs, 83; Art Acquisition Prog, Ga Coun Arts, 86-88. *Media:* Drawing. *Publ:* Illusr (2), The Heart of Healing, Turner Publ; Five Points, Ga State Lit Mag, 98

THALL, BOB
PHOTOGRAPHER
b Chicago, Ill, Dec 6, 48. *Study:* Univ Ill, Chicago, BA(photog design), 72, MFA(photog), 86. *Work:* Libr Congress, Washington, DC; Mus Contemp Photog, Art Inst Chicago, Chicago Hist Soc & Lasalle Bank Collection, Chicago; Mus Mod Art, Paine-Weber Collection & Seagram Collection, NY; Victoria & Albert Mus, London, Eng; plus many others. *Comn:* Co Courthouses (photographs), Seagram Bicentennial Proj; Historic Buildings (photographs), Hist Am Bldgs Survey, US Park Serv; Central Manufacturing District (photographs), Photog Collection, Art Inst Chicago; Route 40 in Indiana and Ohio (photographs), Johns Hopkins Univ Press; plus many others. *Exhib:* Court House (auth catalog), Mus Mod Art, NY, 77, Art Inst Chicago, 78 & Amon Carter Mus, Ft Worth, Tex, 79; Luminescence, Truman Col, Chicago, 80; Evanston Art Ctr, Ill, 80; Calif Mus Photog, Riverside, 81; Bronfman Ctr, Montreal, Can, 81; Dittmar Gallery, Nwestern Univ, Evanston, Ill, 81; Swen Parson Gallery, N Ill Univ, DeKalb, 82; Landmarks Reviewed, Pensacola Mus Art, Fla, 83; Bob Thall Photographs, Chicago Ctr Contemp Photog, 83; Chicago, the Architectural City, Art Inst Chicago, 83; Landscape Starts Here, Visual Studies Workshop, Rochester, NY, 83; Film and Foto, Santa Fe Ctr Photog, NMex, 83; solo exhibs, Edwynn Houk Gallery, Chicago, 84, N Ky Univ, Highland Heights, 95, Ehlers Caudill Gallery, Chicago, 95, Mus Contemp Photog, Chicago, 99 & Carol Ehlers Gallery, Chicago, 99; Tarant Col Gallery, Ft Worth, Tex, 84; Univ Kans Gallery, Lawrence, 84; River Edges, Loyola Univ Gallery, Chicago, 84; Recent Acquisitions, Art Inst Chicago, 85; Chicago Photographers, Mus Contemp Photog, Chicago, 85; Road, Roadside, Art Inst Chicago & Ill State Univ Mus, Normal, 87; Changing Chicago, Art Inst Chicago & Chicago Cult Ctr, 89; Site Work, Photogr Gallery, Halina House, London, Eng, 91; Systems of Vision, Ehlers Caudill Gallery, Chicago, 92; The Perfect City: Photographs of Chicago by Bob Thall (auth catalog), Art Inst Chicago, 94; Art in Chicago, 1945-1995 (auth catalog), Mus Contemp Art, Chicago, 96; From Corporate Collections, Gallery 312, Chicago, 98; Streets of Chicago, Ehlers Caudill Gallery, Chicago, 98; Under construction, Milwaukee Art Mus, Wis, 99; Photog's Multiple Roles (auth catalog), Mus Contemp Photog, Chicago, 98; Landmarks, Chicago/NY, Chicago Cult Ctr, 99; plus many others. *Teaching:* Vis artist, Univ Ill, Chicago, Summer 75 & adj asst prof art, 80; prof photog, Columbia Col, 76-. *Awards:* Columbia Col Fac Develop Grant, 93 & 98; Graham Found Grant, 98; John Simon Guggenheim Mem Found Fel, 98. *Bibliog:* Numerous book & exhib revs in Exposure & New Art Examiner, 80-83; Abigail Foerstner (auth), Perfect City, rev, Chicago Tribune, 10/10/94. *Publ:* Auth, The New American Village, Johns Hopkins Univ, 99. *Dealer:* Carol Ehlers Gallery Chicago IL. *Mailing Add:* Art Dept Columbia Col 600 S Michigan Ave Chicago IL 60605

THAW, EUGENE VICTOR
DEALER, COLLECTOR
b New York, NY, Oct 27, 27. *Study:* St John's Col, BA, 47; Columbia Univ (art hist), 47-49. *Hon Degrees:* Hartwick Col, Oneonta, NY, Hon Dr Art, 90. *Exhib:* Pvt collection, Pierpont Morgan Libr, Cleveland Mus, Art Inst Chicago & Nat Gallery Can, 75-76; Part II, Thaw Collection, Pierpont Morgan Libr, 85 & Mus Fine Arts, Richmond, Va, 86; New Acquisitions, Pierpont Morgan Libr; Royal Acad, London, 96; Nomadic Art of the Eastern Eurasian Steppes, Eugene V Thaw and other NY Col, Metrop Mus Art, NY, 2002. *Pos:* Art dealer & pres, E V Thaw & Co, Inc, 50-; writer, Spectator, London, 76-77 & Times, London, 77-78; vchmn, Artemis, S A, 76-; contrib ed, New Republic, 83-; trustee, St John's Col, Annapolis & Santa Fe, 75-83, Glimmerglass Opera Theater, Cooperstown, NY, 83, Hartwick Col, Oneonta, NY, 86-89, Pierpont Morgan Libr, NY, 88 & World Monuments Fund, 90-96; pres, Pollock-Krasner Found Inc, NY; Trustee, Pierre & Maria-Gaetana Matisse Found, 2001-. *Teaching:* Vis lectr fine art, St John's Col, 73, Asn Art Mus Dirs, 83, Nat Gallery, Washington, DC, 83, Mus Fine Arts, Boston, 83, Pierpont Morgan Libr, 84-85 & Ft Worth Art Mus, 86. *Awards:* Gertrude Vanderbilt Whitney Award, Outstanding Patronage of the Arts, 2001; Medal for Distinguished Philanthropy, Asn Mus, 2002; Hadrian Award, World Monuments Fund, 2003. *Mem:* Art Dealers' Asn Am (bd dir, 64-, secy & treas, 66-68, vpres, 68-70 & pres, 70 72); IRS Art Adv Panel, 68-71; fel perpetuity, Pierpont Morgan Libr, NY; Grolier Club, NY; Century Asn, NY. *Collection:* Master drawings. *Publ:* Coauth, Jackson Pollock: A Catalogue Raisonne, Yale Univ Press, 78; auth, articles, New York Review of Books, 80, New Criterion, 83 & New Republic, 83; Am Scholar, 83-84 & New York Times Bk Rev, 84; The Abstract Expressionists, Metrop Mus Art, Bulletin, winter 86/87. *Mailing Add:* 726 Park Ave New York NY 10021

THEA, CAROLEE B
WRITER, SCULPTOR
b Brooklyn, NY, Dec 13, 47. *Study:* Skidmore Col, Saratoga Springs; Columbia Univ, BA, 64; Hunter Col, City Univ NY, MA, 76. *Work:* Hofstra Univ Mus, LI, NY; Fla Int Univ Mus, Miami; AMOCO, Denver, Colo; Best Products, Va; and others. *Comn:* Gullivers Blocks, environ sculpture, Md Inst Art, Baltimore, 80; Hellgate Maze, earth work, AREA, Ward Island, NY, 81; site sculptures, Morristown Mus, NJ, Wastson Gallery, Wheaton Col, Queens Mus, Hofstra Univ Mus, Nicholas Alexander Gallery & Douglas Col, Rutgers Univ. *Exhib:* Solo-exhibs, Frank Marino Gallery, NY, 80 & 81, Morristown Mus, NJ, 81, Douglas Col Rutgers Univ, New Brunswick, NJ, 84, Adam L Gimbell Gallery, NY, 84, Wastson Gallery, Wheaton Col, Norton Mass, 86, Gallery Ninety Nine, Miami, Fla, 87, Queens Mus, Flushing, NY, 89, Anne Jaffe Gallery, Miami, Fla, 90, Hofstra Univ Mus, 91, La Frontera Gallery, NY, 93 & Nicholas Alexander Gallery, NY, 95; Out of Square, Cranbrook Acad Mus, Bloomfield, Mich, 84 & 85; Intermedia, Aldrich Mus, Ridgefield, Conn, 84; Cranbrook Acad Mus, Bloomfield, Mich, 86; Still Life, EHCCA, East Hampton, NY, 90; Songs of Retribution, Richard Anderson Gallery, 93; Nicholas-Alexander Gallery, NY, 94; Tribeca 148 Gallery, NY, 94; Friends and Family, Lombard Fried Gallery, 2002; and others. *Pos:* Educ rep to UN Women's Year, 75; fac mem, Parsons Sch Design, formerly, Col New Rochelle, formerly; coordr arts, Sch New Resources, formerly; distinguished vis artist, Bard Col, Syracuse Univ, Skidmore Col, State Univ NY, Stonybrook, Purchase, Fla Int Univ & City Univ NY; contrib ed, Sculpture Mag; lectr & vis critic, Rhode Island Sch Design, 2002; co-founder, Westchester Chap of Artists and Writers: Nat Orgn for Women: Edu Rep to the UN "International Year of the Women" Urban League-Housing Volunteer. *Teaching:* Instr & coordr art dept, Sch of New Resources, Col New Rochelle, NY, 73-78; assoc prof, Parsons/New Sch, NY, 81-92, Pratt Inst, Brooklyn, 95-98; adj fac, City Univ NY, 81; distinguished vis artist,

Bard Col, 85, Syracuse Univ, 87-88 & Skidmore Col, 87. *Awards:* Nat Endowment Arts Award, 90; CAPS Finalist, 77, 78 & 79; Athena Found Award, 88. *Bibliog:* Revs in, New York Times, Schjeldahl, Braff, Washington Post, The Nation, Artforum, Arts, Soho News, New York Art J, East Hampton Star, Bomb Mag, Int Sculpture Mag, Arts Mag, and others. *Mem:* Nat Orgn Women Artists & Writers (co-founder & chmn, Westchester Co, NY, branch, 74-76); Womens Action Coalition; Int Sculptors Asn; Col Art Asn; Womens Caucus Art. *Media:* All Media. *Publ:* Contribr, Eve's idle hand, Art J, 75; Masks power & sisterhood in African Society, Heresies, 78; auth, Self Portraits (catalog essay), Skidmore Col, 88; auth, FOCI: Interviews with Ten International Curators, Apexart Curatorial Prog, 2001. *Dealer:* Jaffe Baker Blau Gallery Boca Raton FL 33431; Nicholas Alexander Gallery 155 Spring St New York NY 10012. *Mailing Add:* 534 LaGuardia Pl New York NY 10012

THENHAUS, PAULETTE ANN
PAINTER, WRITER
b St Louis, Mo, Nov 8, 48. *Study:* Webster Univ, St Louis, Mo, BA, 71; San Francisco Art Inst, with Perkle Jones, Calif; Southern Ill Univ, Carbondale, Ill, MFA(Phi Kappa Phi), 87. *Work:* Tarble Art Ctr, Eastern Univ, Charleston, Ill; Woodstock Sch Art, NY; Granite City Steel Collection, Ill; Giant City State Park Ctr, Makanda, Ill; Fleming Collection, Peoria, Ill; Evansville Mus, Ind. *Comn:* Trailing the American Dream (painting), pvt collector, San Francisco, Calif, 84; Percent for Art (2 paintings), Ill State Grant City State Parklodge, 87. *Exhib:* One-woman shows, In the Field, Seghi Gallery St Louis, Mo, 86, The Land with Additions, Northeast Mo State, Kirksville, 90; Watercolor: Illinois '89, Tarble Art Ctr, Charleston, Ill, 87; Horizontal Traditions, New Harmony Contemp Gallery, Ind, 87; 44th Ann Wash Valley Exhib, Sheldon Swope Gallery, Terra Haute, Ind, 88; 20th Joslyn Biennial, Joslyn Mus, Omaha, Nebr, 88; Seven State Art in the Woods, Overland Park, Kans, 94; Thirteenth & Fifteenth Biennial Watercolor & Drawing Exhib, Eastern Ill Univ, Charleston; Seasons, Galesburg Civic Art Ctr, 2003; Buchanan Center Arts, Monmouth, Ill, 2006. *Collection Arranged:* Pressworks Ill Printmakers (catalog), 91; Collage/Assemblage (catalog), 92. *Pos:* Asst dir, Peoria Art Guild, Ill, 87-88; mus ed, Blanden Mem Mus, Iowa, 89-90; dir, Galesburg Civic Art Ctr, Ill, 90-94; gallery/studio proprietor, Art, Naturally; owner, Studio T, 99-. *Teaching:* Art educator studio art, Branson Sch, Marin, Calif, 78-84; artist-in-residence, Dorland Colony, Temecula, Calif, 85 & Woodstock Studio Space, NY, 87; instr painting, Carl Sandburg Community Col. *Awards:* Best Show (mus purchase), 38th Mid-States Exhib, 86; Award, 20th Joslyn Biennial, 88; Best Show (purchase), Tarble Art Ctr, 89. *Bibliog:* Celeste Rehm & Paulette Thenhaus (auths), New Art Examiner, 89; Suitcase is worth seeing, Peoria J Star, 91; Art Talks, Radio interview, 3/18/99; Exhibit focuses on two women, Register Mail, 2/6/2003. *Mem:* Am Asn Mus; Chic Artists Coalition. *Media:* Acrylic, Oil. *Res:* website creation, History of Public Art in Knox County. *Publ:* Auth, Form beyond function, New Art Examiner, Vol XIII, No 13, 6/86; Paul Flexner, 88 & James Fritz/Lisa Sheets, 89, New Art Examiner; Auth, Drawing From Life art column, Zephyr, 93-; Mark Barone, Southern Arts Fedn, 10/94; NewArt Examiner, 11/94; Art Review, The Zephyr; auth, A Century of Public Art in Knox County, privat publ, 2006. *Dealer:* Studio T Galesburg Civic Art Ctr Galesburg, IL. *Mailing Add:* 1431 Maple Ave Galesburg IL 61401

THEOBALD, GILLIAN LEE
PAINTER, LITHOGRAPHER
b La Jolla, Calif, Nov 17, 44. *Study:* Byam Shaw, Sch Art London, 64-65; San Diego State Univ, BA, 67, MA, 71. *Exhib:* Solo exhib, Cirrus Gallery, Los Angeles, 83, 86, 88, 89, 90, 93, 94, 96, 99 & 2001, 2005; Patty Aande Gallery, San Diego, 85-87, Palomar Col, San Marcos, 88, Mark Quint Gallery, La Jolla, 93, Linda Hodges Gallery, Seattle, 97, 98, 2000, 2001, 2002 & 2003, 2006, Rocket Gallery, London, 98, Polarities: A Retrospective, Port Angeles Fine Art Center, Port Angeles, WA, 2002; Spectrum Los Angeles (with catalog), Gallery Akmak, Berlin, Ger, 85; Scapes (with catalog), Univ Art Mus, Univ Calif, Santa Barbara, 85; Reaching the Summit: Mountain Landscape, Laguna Beach & Saddleback Col, 86; On the Horizon: Emerging Art in Calif, Fresno Mus, 87; Lines of Vision; Drawings by Contemp Women (with catalog), Long Island Univ, NY, 89 & Blum Helman, NY, 89; Waterfall as Image, Occidental Col, Los Angeles, 90; Soul Survivors; The Courage to go Beyond (with catalog), Beacon St Gallery, Chicago, Ill, 90; The Contemp Drawing: Existence, Passage & the Dream (with catalog), Rose Art Mus, Brandeis Univ Mass, 91; The Spirtual Landscape, Biota Gallery, Los Angeles, 91; Eye of the Creator; Artist's Self Portraits, Bush Art Ctr, Salem, Ore, 92; Summer, 92, Cirrus Gallery, Los Angeles, Calif, 92; Made in LA, Los Angeles Co Mus Art, Calif, 95 (catalog); Utopian Visions, Port Angeles Fine Art Ctr, Wash, 96; New Work, Linda Hodges Gallery, Seattle, Wash, 97; Nine Painters Plus One, Emmanuel Gallery, Univ Colo, Denver, 97; In Over Our Heads: The Image of Water in Contemp, San Jose Mus Art, 98; Bumber Biennale Bumbershoot Festival Arts, Seattle, WA, 2004; plus numerous others. *Bibliog:* Nancy Stapen (auth), Drawings at Brandeis Ask Profound Questions, The Boston Globe, 3/91; Dr Judy Collischan Van Wagner (auth), Lines of Vision: Drawings by Contemporary Women, Hudson Hills Press, NY, 89; Jan Butterfield (auth), The Art Collection of Pacific Enterprises, Pacific Enterprises, Los Angeles, Calif, 91; Bruce Davis (auth), Made in LA: The Prints of Cirrus Editions, Los Angeles Co Mus Art, 1995. *Media:* Oil; Mixed Media. *Dealer:* Cirrus Gallery 542 S Alameda St Los Angeles CA 90013; Linda Hodges Gallery Seattle WA. *Mailing Add:* 6041 Palatine Ave N Seattle WA 98103-5350

THEOFILES, GEORGE
HISTORIAN, DEALER
b Reading, Pa, July 28, 47. *Study:* Md Inst Col Art, BFA(graphics), 69. *Pos:* Owner, catalog publ & seller, Miscellaneous Man, Vintage Graphics, New Freedom, Pa, 70-. *Awards:* Gold Medal Poster Design, Baltimore Md Art Dir Club, 70-. *Mem:* Co Military Historians; Poster Soc (bd); Ephemera Soc. *Specialty:* American and European poster art and communication graphics, 1850-1960. *Publ:* Publ, Catalog of Original Poster Art and Graphics (tri-ann), 71-; auth, American Posters of World War I, Dafran House, 72. *Mailing Add:* PO Box 191 New Freedom PA 17349-0191

THEROUX, CAROL
PAINTER
b Cardwell, Mo, Aug 10, 30. *Study:* Cerritos Col Calif, with Donald Putman, Gerome Grimmer, life teaching credential, 76; Scottsdale Art Sch, 90; Scholar Art Ctr Design, La, 48. *Work:* Northwestern Bell Corp, Omaha, Nebr. *Comn:* Drawing of Borglum Statue, Prescott C of C, Ariz, 86; Buffalo Child (painting to celebrate NE Indian Arts Show), State of Nebr, Omaha, 88. *Exhib:* Ten one-woman shows, Mammen Gallery, Scottsdale, Ariz, 81-91; Wilcox Gallery, Sedona, Ariz, 92-96; Classic-Am Art Show, Invitational, Beverly Hills, Calif, 89-94; C M Russel Art Show & Auction, Great Falls, Mont, 90-93; Pastel Soc Am, NY, 91; The Albuquerque Miniatures, Albuquerque Mus, NMex, 91-94; and others. *Teaching:* Artist, drawing & painting, S Calif Studios, 63-78; artist, demonstrations, All S Calif Art Asns, 70-80; artist, Bellflower High Sch, 75-77. *Bibliog:* Susan Vreeland (auth), Dancing the ancient steps, Southwest Art Mag, 4/83; Vicki Stavic (auth), One on One, 87 & Artists to watch, 89, Art West Mag. *Mem:* Charter mem Pastel Soc Am; Pastel Soc W Coast; Pastel Soc Southern Calif; Nat Mus Women Arts. *Media:* Pastel. *Interests:* Collectable dolls and porcelain plates. *Mailing Add:* 17825 Canehill Ave Bellflower CA 90076-7119

THERRIEN, ROBERT
SCULPTOR, PAINTER
b Chicago, Ill, Nov 17, 47. *Work:* Mus Mod Art & Whitney Mus Am Art, NY; Walker Art Ctr, Minneapolis, Minn; Dallas Mus Art; High Mus Art, Atlanta; Los Angeles Co Mus Art, Mus Contemp Art, Los Angeles; Tate Gallery, London; Pompidou Mus, Paris; Kemper Mus, Kansas City. *Exhib:* Biennial Exhib, Whitney Biennial, 85; solo exhib, MOCA Los Angeles, Calif, 86 & Museo Nat Reina Sofia, Madrid, Spain, 91-92; Documenta Invitational, Kassel, Ger, 92 & San Diego, Calif, 94; Carnegie Int, Carnegie Mus Art, Pittsburgh, 95-96; Contemp Art Ctr, Cincinnati, Ohio, 97. *Bibliog:* Margit Rowell (auth), Robert Therrien, Nat Reina Sofia, 91; William Hackman (auth), Sunshine & Noir, In: Art in Los Angeles, 97; Margit Rowell (auth), Objects of Desire: The Modern Still Life. *Media:* Miscellaneous Media. *Publ:* Illusr, 7 plus 6 (Michael Butor & Robert Creely, auths), Use Hoshour, 89; Mesa Verde (Evan Connell, auth), Whitney Mus, 93. *Mailing Add:* c/o Maureen Mahony 139 N 6th St Brooklyn NY 11211

THIBAULT, ANDRE (TEABO)
PAINTER
b Quebec, Can, 48. *Study:* Boston Univ, BS, 72-76; pupil & asst, Romare Bearden, 80-88. *Work:* Owenboro Mus Fine Art, Ky; Kelly Springfield Tire Co, Great Falls, Va; Boston Univ, Mass; AT&T, Basking Ridge, NJ. *Exhib:* 22nd Nat Sun Carnival Art Exhib, El Paso Mus Art, Tex; 32nd New Eng Exhib Paintings, Drawings & Sculpture, Silvermine Ctr for Arts, New Canaan, Conn; Montclair Art Mus, NJ; Nat Gallery Art, Wash, DC, 2000; Solo exhib, Nabisco Hq, NJ, Warehouse Gallery, Lee, Mass, Seraphim Gallery, NJ, 85-91, Wycoff Gallery, NJ 96-99. *Pos:* Asst, to the famous black artist, Romare Bearden. *Awards:* 41st Nat Exhib Award, Salmagundi Club, NY; 32nd Silvermine New Eng Exhib Award, Conn; Mid Am Biennial Purchase Award. *Bibliog:* Myron Schwartzman (auth): A Bearden-Murray Interplay, Callaloo, Vol 11, No 3, John Hopkins Univ Press, 1988, Romare Bearden - His Life & Art, Harry N Abrams Publ, NY, 1990, Entering the World of Romare Bearden: Bostonia, Alumni Quart Boston Univ, spring 2001. *Mem:* NJ Artist Guild; Modern Artist Guild; NJ Art Coun. *Media:* mixed, collage. *Specialty:* Collages, landscapes, portraits & abstracts. *Interests:* Serious cyclist. *Mailing Add:* 453 Fort Lee Rd Leonia NJ 07605

THIBERT, PATRICK A
SCULPTOR, EDUCATOR
b Windsor, Ont, Feb 25, 43. *Study:* Univ Windsor, Ont, BFA, 72; Fla State Univ, Tallahassee, MFA, 74. *Work:* McIntosh Art Gallery, Univ Western Ont, London; Can Coun Art Bank, Ottawa; London Regional Art & Hist Mus, Ont; Art Gallery of Ont, Toronto; Kitchener-Waterloo Art Gallery, Ont. *Exhib:* Solo shows, Art Gallery of Hamilton, Ont, 86, Kitchener-Waterloo Art Gallery, Ont, 86 & 95, Forest City Gallery, London, 87 & 94, London Regional Art & Hist Mus, London, Ont, 92, Locating Identity: Patrick Thibert, McIntosh Gallery, Univ West Ont, 93, Art Gallery At Windsor, Ont, 94 & Robert McLaughlin Gallery, Oshawa, Ont 95, In the Mind of the Viewer: An Epilogue, Thames Art Gallery, 2000, Gallery Lambton, Sarnia, Ont, 2000, Woodstock Art Gallery, Woodstock, Ont, 2001; Sculpture Tour, Univ Tenn, Knoxville, 83-85, 87-88; Outdoor sculpture exhib, Burlington Cult Ctr, Ont, 87; Artists & Portraits, McIntosh Gallery, Univ West Ont, London, 89; Open Doors, Centre Contemp Art, St Thomas, Ont, 92. *Teaching:* Grad teaching asst, Fla State Univ, Tallahassee, 73-74; instr, St Clair Col Applied Art & Technol, Windsor, Ont, 74-75; prof, Fanshawe Col Applied Art & Technol, London, Ont, 75-. *Awards:* Ont Arts Coun Mat Grants, 75-83 & 92. *Bibliog:* David Burnett (auth), Patrick Thibert-Sculpture, 86; Judith Maclean Rodger (auth), Patrick Thibert: Transitions 1979-1987, London Regional Art & Hist Mus, London, Ont, 92-93; Ihor Holubizky & Robert McKaskell

(auths), Locating Identity: Patrick Thibert, 93; Ted Fraser, In the Mind of the Viewer: An Epilogue, 2000, plus others. *Mem:* Forest City Gallery, London, Ont. *Media:* Metal, Mixed Materials. *Dealer:* Olga Korper Gallery 157 Morrow Ave Toronto ON Canada M6R 2H9. *Mailing Add:* 8952 Irish Dr RR 1 Mount Brydges ON N0L 1W0 Canada

THIEBAUD, WAYNE MORTON
PAINTER, EDUCATOR
b Mesa, Ariz, Nov 15, 1920. *Study:* Calif State Univ, Sacramento, BA(art), 51, MA, 52. *Hon Degrees:* Calif Col Arts & Crafts, Oakland, Hon Dr, 72, Hon MFA, 1975; Dickinson Col, Carlisle, Pa, Hon Dr, 83; San Francisco Art Inst, Hon Dr, 88; Art Inst Southern Calif, Laguna Beach, Hon Dr, 93; Calif State Univ, Sacramento, Hon DFA, 98. *Work:* Mus Mod Art; Whitney Mus Am Art; Libr Cong; Albright-Knox Art Gallery; Washington Gallery Mod Art; plus many others. *Comn:* Fountain mobile structure, Calif State Fair, 52; mosaic mural, Munic Utility Dist Bldg, Sacramento, 59; producer 11 educ motion pictures, Bailey Films, Hollywood, Calif; Time, Inc; license plate design, Calif Arts Coun, 93. *Exhib:* Solo exhibs, MH De Young Mem Mus, 62, San Francisco Mus Mod Art, 65, 68, 78 & 85, Walker Art Ctr, 68 & 81, Portland Ctr Visual Arts, Ore, 73, Newport Harbor Art Mus, Calif, 86, Milwaukee Art Mus, 86, Nelson-Atkins Mus Art, 86, Calif Palace Legion Honor, 91 & Nat Mus Am Art, Smithsonian Inst, Washington, 91; Int Contemp Art, Houston, Tex; San Francisco Mus Art; Kompas 4-West Coast USA, Stedlijk Abbemuseum, Eindhoven, The Neth, 69; Documenta 5: Inquiry into Reality--Today's Image, Kassel, Ger, 72; Los Angeles Munic Mus, Calif, 73; Delphian Gallery, Sheridan, Ore, 77; Contemp Realism, Palo Alto Cult Ctr, 87; retrospective, Hearst Art Gallery, St Mary's Col, Moraga, Calif, 90; and many others. *Pos:* Animation dept, Walt Disney Studios, Los Angeles, 36-37. *Teaching:* Instr art, Sacramento City Col, 51-60 & chmn art dept, 54-56 & 58-60; guest instr, San Francisco Art Inst, 58; instr art, Univ Calif, Davis, assoc prof, 63-67, prof, 67-92 & prof emeritus, 92-; prof art & artist-in-residence, Cornell Univ, 66; NY Studio Sch, Paris, 69-70; vis artist, UC Davis, 69-70; artist-in-residence, Yale Univ, 74 & Rice Univ, 75; weekend seminar, Nat Acad Design, Sch Fine Arts, NY, 95. *Awards:* Pres Nat Medal Arts, Pres Bill Clinton, 94; Gold Award for bk illus (Yosemite and the Mariposa Grove), Western Art Dirs Club, 94; Distinguished Artistic Achievement Award, Calif Soc Printmakers, Berkeley, 95; Grumbacher Gold Medallion Award for Painting, Am Acad of Design, NY, 93; Nat Acad of Design Award, 2001. *Bibliog:* Lucy R Lippard (auth), Pop Art, Praeger, 66; Allen S Weller (auth), The Joys and Sorrows of Recent American Art, Univ Ill Press, 68; Perils of a thank-you speech, NY Times, late ed, 5/25/2001. *Mem:* Am Acad & Inst Arts & Lett, NY; Nat Acad (assoc, 85, acad, 87-); fel Acad Arts & Sci, Boston. *Publ:* Auth, American Rediscovered, 63 & Delights, 65; Wayne Thiebaud: Private Drawings-The Artist's Sketchbook, Harry F Abrams Publ, 87; illusr, The Physiology of Taste (JA Brillat-Savarin, auth), Aaron Press, San Francisco, 94 & Invisible Cities, Arion Pres, 99

THIES, CHARLES HERMAN
PAINTER, PRINTMAKER
b Poplar Bluff, Mo, Aug 22, 40. *Study:* SE Mo State Univ, BS(fine arts educ), 63; Kans State Univ, MA(drawing & painting), 70; also studied at Washington Univ, St Louis, Kans Univ, Lawrence & Univ Northern Colo, Greeley. *Work:* St Louis Art Mus; Nelson-Atkins Art Mus, Kansas City, Mo; Springfield Art Mus, Mo; Wichita Art Mus, Kans; Utah Mus Fine Arts; and others; Minn Art Mus; Margaret Harweil Art Mus, Poplar Bluff, Mo. *Comn:* Exterior mural, Ford Found Sponsored Prog, Kans State Univ, 69; six canvases, Marriott Hotel, Ft Collins, Colo, 85. *Exhib:* Thirty Miles of Art, Nelson Gallery-Atkins Mus, Kansas City, Mo, 76; Western Ann Nat Drawing Exhib, Western Ill Univ, 76; Drawings/USA, Minn Art Mus, St Paul, 77; Joslyn Biennial, Joslyn Art Mus, Omaha, Nebr, 78; one-man exhibs, Margaret Harwell Art Mus, Popular Bluff, Mo, 82 & 88 & Univ Art Mus, Cape Girardeau, Mo, 87; All Colo Art Exhib, 86, 88, 91 & 92; Expo 93, Boston, Mass; and others; CPCC, Charlotte, NC, 2002. *Pos:* Asst dir admis, Kansas City Art Inst, Mo, 76-77. *Teaching:* Instr drawing, design & figure drawing, Florissant Valley Col, St Louis, Mo, 69-76; instr 3-D design, Johnson Co Community Col, Overland Parks, Kans, 76. *Awards:* Painting Award, Exhib 70, St Louis, N Co Art Asn, 70; Drawing Award, Quincy Ill Fine Arts Asn, 71; Purchase, Drawings/USA 1977, Minn Mus Art. *Bibliog:* Int Personalities, Parma, Italy, 81. *Media:* Oil; Etching, Lithography. *Interests:* Religious Art and Nostaligic Sports Art (by comn); painting, classical music. *Dealer:* Studio 37, 8518 E Thunderbird Rd, Parker, Colo, 80134. *Mailing Add:* 8518 Thunderbird Rd Parker CO 80134

THIEWES, RACHELLE R
JEWELER
b Owatonna, Minn, Jan 11, 52. *Study:* Western Ill Univ, 70-72; Southern Ill Univ, BA, 74; Kent State Univ, MFA, 76. *Work:* Evansville Art Mus, Ind; Univ Tex, El Paso; Art Inst Chicago; Am Craft Mus; Smithsonian Inst Renwick Gallery. *Exhib:* Solo shows, CDK Gallery, NY, 89, Jewelers' Werk Galerie, Washington, 89 & 94 Dartmouth Col, 91, Galveston Arts Ctr, Tex, 93, El Paso Mus Art, Tex, 93, Susan Cummins Gallery, Mill Valley, Calif, 96 & Joanne Rapp Gallery, Scottsdale, Ariz, 97, Jeweler's Werk, Wash, DC, 2000; The Art of Jewellery, Setagaya Art Mus, Tokyo, 93; One of a Kind: Am Art Jewelry Today, Mobilia Gallery, Cambridge, Mass, 94; One of a Kind, Joanne Rapp Gallery, 95; Jewelry: Selections from the Permanent Collection, Am Craft Mus, NY, 95; Ring of Thorns, Adair Margo Gallery, El Paso, Tex, 96; Am Revelations, Shipley Gallery, Newcastle, Eng, 96; Chain Gang, Soc Nam Goldsmiths 1996 Nat Jewelry Show, Target Gallery, Alexandria, Va, 96; Artists Choose Artists, Peter Joseph Gallery, NY, 96; Jewelry in Europe and Am: New Times, New Thinking, Crafts Coun London & Nat Mus & Gallery, Cardiff, 96; Rachelle Thiewes: Ring of Thorns, Susan Cummins Gallery, Mill Valley, Calif, 96; Jewelers' werk Galerie Exhib, Sch Fine Arts, Chicago, 96, Sch Fine Arts, NY & Chicago, 98; Gold and Silver: 1996, Am Craft Mus, NY, 96; 3 Generations, Mobilia Gallery, Cambridge, Mass, 96; Uniqueness from the Hand, Univ Tex San Antonio Art Gallery, 97; Rachelle Thiewes: New Jewelry, Joanne Rapp Gallery, Scottsdale, Ariz, 97; Centennial Metals, Soc Arts & Crafts, Boston, Mass, 97; The Renwick at 25, Renwick Gallery, Washington, DC, 97; The Body Eclectic, Spruill Ctr Arts, Atlanta, Ga, 97; Formulations: A Metals Invitational, Reese Mus, E Tenn State Univ, 97; Revelations, Nat Ornamental Mus, Memphis, Tenn, 97; Four Jewelers: Holiday Show, Nancy Sachs Gallery, 97; Inventing Am: Am Metalanguage - Rachelle Thiewes, Barbican Ctr, London, Eng, 98; Jewellery Moves, Nat Mus Scotland, Edinburgh, 98; El Paso Mus of Art, Tex, 2001; Musee D'Art Et D'Histoire, Switz, 2002; Ark Arts Ctr, 2002; Gallery Yu, Tokyo, Japan, 2002; Beyond the MinesL The Art of Gold, Crocker Art Mus, Calif, 2003; group exhibs: Sofa, Chicago, Ill, 2002, Univ Place Art Gallery, Lincoln, Nebr, 2002, Arrowmont, Gatinburg, Tenn, 2002, The Soc of Arts and Crafts, Boston, Mass, 2002, El Paso Int Airport, Tex, 2002. *Teaching:* Instr art, Univ Tex, El Paso, 76-80, from asst prof to assoc prof, 80-89, prof art, 89-; Master Class, Royal Col Art, London, 95. *Awards:* Vpres Award Acad Excellence, Univ Tex, El Paso, 83; Visual Artist Fel, Nat Endowment Arts, 88; Lib Arts Outstanding Achievement Fac Award, Univ Tex, El Paso, 97; El Paso Energy Found Fac Acheivement Award for Teaching Excellence, 99. *Bibliog:* David Watkins (auth), The Best in Contemporary Jewelry, Quatro Publ, London, 93; Beverly Penn (auth), From the fire (rev), Metalsmith, winter 94; Susan Grant Lewin (auth), One of a Kind, American Art Jewelry Today, Harry N Abrams Publ, 94. *Mem:* Bridge Ctr Contemp Art, El Paso (bd dir, 87-90 & vpres, 88-89); Soc N Am Goldsmiths (bd dir, 88-90). *Dealer:* Adair Margo Gallery 415 E Yandell El Paso TX

THISTLETHWAITE, MARK EDWARD
EDUCATOR, HISTORIAN
b Baton Rouge, La, Jan 26, 48. *Study:* Univ Calif, Santa Barbara, BA, 70, MA, 72; Univ Pa, Kress Found Fel, PhD, 77. *Collection Arranged:* The Artist as Interpreter of American History (auth, catalog), Pa Acad Fine Arts, Philadelphia, 76; Ed Blackburn, Tex Christian Univ, Ft Worth, 82 & co-cur, Dan Rizzie, Kimbell Art Mus, 90; Peter Rothermel Exhib, Brandywine River Mus, 95; Ed & Linda Blackburn, Contemp Art Ctr, Ft Worth; Celebrating Early Texas Art, Fort Worth Arts Complex, TX, 2005. *Pos:* Trustee, Mod Art Mus Ft Worth; Kay & Velma Kimbell chair art hist, Tex Christian Univ; Cardin Chair in Humanities, Loyola Col, Md, 2000. *Teaching:* Lectr mod art, Univ Pa, Philadelphia, 74-75; lectr Am & mod art, Philadelphia Col Art, 74-76; from asst prof to prof, Am & mod art & archit, Tex Christian Univ, Ft Worth, 77-. *Awards:* Tex Christian Univ Grants, 79, 81, 84-85, 88-89 & 90-91, 95, 98-99, 03-04; NEH Summer Institute Fel, 85, 95; Chancellor's Award Distinguished Teaching, 90. *Mem:* Col Art Asn; Midwest Art Hist Soc; Southeastern Col Art Conf. *Res:* American art and architecture, especially 19th century history painting and contemporary art. *Publ:* Coauth (with W Gerdts), Grand Illusions: History of Painting in America, 88; William Ranney: East of the Mississippi, Brandywine River Mus, 91; Painting in the Grand Manner: Art & PF Rothermel, 95; plus numerous articles, exhibition reviews and criticism. *Mailing Add:* Tex Christian Univ TCU Box 298000 Ft Worth TX 76129

THOLLANDER, EARL
ILLUSTRATOR, GRAPHIC ARTIST
b Kingsburg, Calif, Apr 13, 22. *Study:* Univ Calif, BA. *Work:* Sanoma State Univ; City San Francisco Art Comn Collection; Napa Heritage Fund Collection; Nut Tree Collection, Vacaville, Calif; US Air Force Art Collection. *Exhib:* Fifty-nine one-man shows. *Teaching:* Life drawing, landscape painting, Napa Col, 72-73. *Bibliog:* Diana Klemin (auth), The Illustrated Book, Clarkson N Potter, 70; The Quietude of Paths Less Taken, The Art of Calif, 6/93; Through the Eye of Thollander, Napa Valley Register, 9/25/96. *Media:* Drawing; Acrylic, Watercolor. *Publ:* Auth & illusr, Backroads of California, Sunset Books, 71; Barns of California, Calif Hist Soc, 74; Back Roads of New England, rev ed, Potter, 82; Back Roads of Texas, 90 & Arizona's Scenic Byways, rev ed, 92, Northland Press; Back Roads of Washington, rev ed, 92, Earl Thollander's Back Roads of California, rev ed, 94 & Earl Thollander's San Francisco, rev ed 94, Sasquatch. *Mailing Add:* 19210 Hwy 128 Calistoga CA 94515

THOMAS, C DAVID
PRINTMAKER
b July 15, 46. *Study:* Portland Sch Art, Maine, dipl, 68; Tufts Univ, BFA, 72; RI Sch Design, MFA, 74. *Work:* Brooklyn Mus; Mus Fine Art, Boston; DeCordova Mus, Lincoln, Mass; Philadelphia Mus Art; Portland Mus, Maine. *Exhib:* Thirty Yrs of Am Printmaking, Brooklyn Mus, 78; Recent Prints, Gallery Nat Asn Graphic Artists, Boston, 83. *Teaching:* Asst prof art, Emmanuel Col, 78-. *Awards:* Bort Award, Boston Mus Sch, 72; Emmanuel Col Fac Develop Grant, 83. *Mem:* Boston Printmakers (exec bd, 79-); Philadelphia Print Club; Los Angeles Print Soc; Nat Asn Graphic Artists (chair, 80-). *Media:* Lithography. *Dealer:* Gallery Nat Asn Graphic Artists 67 Newbury St Boston MA 02116. *Mailing Add:* Emanuel Col Dept Art 400 Fenway Boston MA 02115

THOMAS, ELAINE FREEMAN
EDUCATOR, ADMINISTRATOR
b Cleveland, Ohio, July 21, 23. *Study:* Northwestern Univ, Evanston, 44; Tuskegee Inst, BS(magna cum laude), 45; Black Mountain Col, 45, with Josef Albers & Robert Motherwell; NY Univ, Bodden fel, MA, 49, with Hale Woodruff; Mexico City Col, 56; Berea Col, 61; Univ Paris, 66; Southern Univ Workshop, 68; Columbia Univ, 70. *Collection Arranged:* One-man exhib, Winston-Salem State Univ, 70; Discovery 70, Univ Cincinnati; George Washington Carver Exhib, White House, 71; Ala Black Artists Exhib, Birmingham Festival Art, 72; plus others. *Teaching:* Asst prof art & chmn dept, Tuskegee Inst, 45-89; retired. *Awards:* Distinguished Participation, Am Artists Prof League, 68; Beaux Arts Festival Award. *Mem:* Am Asn Mus; Col Art Asn Am; Nat Art Educ Asn; Nat Conf Artists; Ala Art League. *Mailing Add:* 202 Rush Dr Tuskegee AL 36083

THOMAS, KATHLEEN K
SCULPTOR, ASSEMBLAGE ARTIST
b Jan 1, 1940; US citizen. *Study:* Wichita State Univ, BA (art educ), 75, BA (art hist, cum laude), 76; Ind Univ Masters Prog, 77; Helena Rubenstein Fel, Whitney Mus Am Art, 77. *Work:* Chase Bank, NY; Deste Found Contemp Art, Athens; pvt collections, Ms Anne Dayton, Mr & Mrs Saul Skolar & others; and others. *Exhib:* Solo exhibs, Barbara Gladstone Gallery, NY, 81 & 84, Fashion Moda Gallery, Bronx, NY, 81 & Civilian Warfare Gallery, NY, 86; Beelden/Sculpture 83 (with catalog), Rotterdam Arts Coun, The Neth, 83; Materialisms (with catalog), Visual Arts Gallery, State Univ NY, Purchase, 84; Preview: 1984 (with catalog), Ronald Feldman Gallery, NY, 84; Precious (with catalog), Grey Art Gallery & Study Ctr, NY Univ, 85; Int High Tech Art Festival (with catalog), Seibu Mus, Tokyo, 85; Solo exhib, Studio Bergemeinde, Frankfurt, W Ger, 88, Max Fish, NY, 90, 92, 96, 2000. *Collection Arranged:* Co-cur, Outside New York (contribr, catalog), 78, Sustained Visions (contribr, catalog), 79, In a Pictorial Framework (contribr, catalog), 79, Ree Morton Retrospective: 1971-1977 (coauth, catalog), 77 & traveling, 80-81, New Mus Contemp Art. *Pos:* Assoc cur, New Mus Contemp Art, NY, 77-79. *Awards:* Helena Rubenstein Fel, Whitney Mus Am Art, 77; Deste Found Contemp Art Fel, 86. *Bibliog:* Ronnie H Cohen (auth), rev, Artforum Mag, 9/80; Jamie Gambrell (auth), Kathleen Thomas, East Village Eye, 10/84; Annelle Pohlen (auth), Skulptur '85, Kunstforum, 5-6/85; Jamie Gambrell (auth), rev, Art in Am Mag, 5/86. *Media:* Contemporary electronic, industrial, military, automotive and often unidentified machine-made components. *Collection:* JP Morgan Chase Bank, Anne Dayton, Sol & Laura Skolar, Deste Foundation, Athens. *Publ:* Coauth, The 1970's: New American Painting, US Info Agency, 80. *Mailing Add:* 198 E 7 St Apt 1 New York NY 10009

THOMAS, LARRY W
PAINTER, PRINTMAKER
b Memphis, Tenn, Oct 29, 43. *Study:* Memphis Acad Arts, BFA, 66; San Francisco Art Inst, MFA, 79. *Work:* Oakland Mus, Calif; San Francisco Mus Mod Art, Calif; Achenbach Found Graphic Arts, Palace Legion Hon, San Francisco, Calif; Nat Mus Am Art, Washington, DC; Whitney Mus Am Art, Metrop Mus Art, NY; and others. *Comn:* Series of monotypes, Achenbach Found Graphic Arts, San Francisco, Calif, 86; edition of lithographs, Fairmont Hotels, Chicago, Ill, 87; large scale drawing, No 44 Montgomery St, San Francisco, 87. *Exhib:* Solo exhib, San Francisco Mus Mod Art, 84, Fuller Goldeen Gallery, San Francisco, 87, Susan Cummins Gallery, Mill Valley, Calif, 92 & Marti Koplin Gallery, Santa Monica, Calif, 92; Recent 20th Century Acquisitions, Oakland Mus, 85; Pub and Pvt: Am Prints Today, Brooklyn Mus (and traveling), 86-87; Graphica Creativa, Alvar Aalto Mus, Jyvaskyla, Finland, 87; A Drawing Show, San Francisco Art Inst, Calif, 87; Recent Acquisitions, Works on Paper, Nat Mus Am Art, Washington, DC, 91; Macau Printmaking 92 (catalog), Cult Inst Macau, 92; Ann Painting & Sculpture Invitational, Am Acad Arts & Letters, NY, 96. *Pos:* Dean acad affairs, San Francisco Art Inst, 94-. *Teaching:* Instr drawing, Santa Rosa Jr Col, 81-84; instr drawing & printmaking, San Francisco Art Inst, 83- & Stanford Univ, Palo Alto, Calif, 89-, chair, dept print, 92-. *Awards:* Individual Fel, Nat Endowment Arts, 80-81 & 87-88 & Djerassi Found, 86; SECA Art Award, San Francisco Mus Mod Art, 84. *Bibliog:* Thomas Albright (auth), An etcher stands out, San Francisco Chronicle, 7/9/80; Judith Dunham (auth), Larry Thomas, Vanguard Mag, 4/84; Donna Graves (auth), Larry Thomas, San Francisco Mus Mod Art, 84. *Dealer:* Susan Cummins Gallery 12 Miller Ave Mill Valley CA 94941; Experimental Workshop PO Box 77504 San Francisco CA 94107. *Mailing Add:* 601 Chenery St San Francisco CA 94131

THOMAS, THALIA ANN MARIE
PAINTER, EDUCATOR
b Wilkes Barre, Pa, Apr 22, 35. *Study:* Col Misericordia, BA, 56; Columbia Univ, MA, 62; Pius XII Inst, dipl, 63; Univ Guanajuato, MFA, 76; Marywood Col, MA, 87. *Work:* Gallery, Col Misericordia, Dallas, Pa; Contemp Gallery, Marywood Col, Scranton, Pa; Galerie Internationale, NY. *Comn:* Painting, Col Misericordia, Dallas, Pa, 87. *Exhib:* Retrospective, Windsor Studio, Scranton, Pa, 82; one-woman shows, United Penn Bank, Forty Fort, Pa, 83 & Wyoming Seminary, Kingston, Pa, 84; Retrospective, Penn State Univ, Scranton, 86; Retrospective, Col Misericordia, Dallas, Pa, 87; Art as Therapy, John Heinz Ctr, Wilkes Barre, Pa, 88; Kappa Pi & Alumni Show, Marywood Col, Scranton, Pa, 88; Pennsylvania Educators, William Penn Mus, Harrisburg, Pa. *Teaching:* Asst prof art, Marywood Col, 62 85; asst chmn art, Scranton, Pa, 77-85. *Awards:* Cor Mariae Pro Fide et Cultura, Marywood Col, 82; Melvin Medal, Marywood Col, 85; Alumni Achievement award Col Misericordia, Dallas, Pa, 96; Presdl Scholarship Marywood Univ, 99. *Bibliog:* Artists, USA, 76; Women Artists of America-18th Century to the Present, 80; International Directory of the Arts, 86. *Mem:* Northeastern Pa Creative Arts Therapy Asn (pres, 87-88); Inst Sr Learners (pres-elect); Am Asn Univ Profs; Wyoming Valley Art League & Hist Soc; Am Art Therapy Asn. *Media:* Acrylic, Watercolor. *Publ:* ed, Contemporary Art, Degree Studies, ICS, 85. *Mailing Add:* 18 Welles St Forty Fort PA 18704

THOMAS, YVONNE
PAINTER
b Nice, France. *Study:* Cooper Union; Art Students League; studied with Hans Hoffman, Amedee Ozenfant, B Neurman & Robert Motherwell. *Work:* Guggenheim Mus; Corcoran Gallery; Atlantic Richfield, Los Angeles; Brandeis Univ; Loeb Ctr, NY Univ; Nat Gallery Art, Washington, DC; Ciba-Geigy, Greensboro, NC. *Exhib:* Am Abstract Artists, 48; Eleven Americans, Riverside Mus, NY, 55; Women in the Arts, NY Cult Ctr, 73; Brooklyn Mus, 75; The Magic Circle, Bronx Mus, 77; Acad & Inst Arts & Lett, NY, 82; Fond Nat D'Art Contemp, Paris, France, 88. *Teaching:* Instr painting & drawing, Colo Mountain Col, summers 67-72 & La State Univ, 73. *Bibliog:* Lawrence Campbell (auth), article, Art News, Vol 72, 3/73; Grace Glueck (auth), article, NY Times, 5/12/78; Kim Levin (critic), article, Art News, Vol 64, 5/65; Gerrit Henry (critic), article, Art Am, Vol 74, 12/86. *Media:* Oil, Acrylic. *Mailing Add:* 147 W 15th St New York NY 10011

THOMASON, MICHAEL VINCENT
PHOTOGRAPHER, CURATOR
b West Palm Beach, Fla, June 20, 42. *Study:* Univ South, Sewanee, Tenn, BA, 64; Duke Univ, MA, 66, PhD, 68. *Exhib:* Work & Leisure in Turn Century Mobile, Fine Arts Mus South, Mobile, 80; Allied Arts Competition, 77, Mobile, 77; The Image of Progress: Alabama Photographs 1877-1917, Birmingham Mus Art, Ala, 81; Buildings Reborn: Adaptive Re-use Proposals, traveling exhib, Ala, 80. *Collection Arranged:* Work & Leisure Turn Century Mobile (auth, catalog), 80; The Image of Progress (auth, catalog), Birmingham, Ala, 81; Mobile's Black Heritage in Photographs, 83; Mardi Gras from the Gay Nineties to the Great Depression, 83; Trying Times: Alabama Photographs, 1917-1945 (auth, catalog), 85. *Pos:* Dir, Photo Archives, Univ South Ala, Mobile, 78-. *Teaching:* Prof, Univ S Ala, 78-. *Awards:* First Prize, Allied Arts Competition, 77. *Media:* Black & White. *Res:* Uses of photography in history; the photography as a historical source. *Publ:* Coauth, Mobile: American River City, Easter, Mobile, 75; coauth, Mobile: The Life and Times of a Great Southern Seaport, Windsor, Calif, 81. *Mailing Add:* 1548 Deerwood Dr E Mobile AL 36618-3073

THOMASOS, DENYSE
PAINTER, SCULPTOR
b Trinidad, 64. *Study:* Univ Toronto, Ont, BA(painting & art hist), 87; Skowhegan Sch Painting & Sculpture, Maine, 88; Yale Sch Art, Yale Univ, New Haven, Conn, MFA(painting & sculpture), 89. *Exhib:* Alpha Gallery, Boston, Mass, 89; A Space, Toronto, Ont, 92; Vox Populi, Philadelphia, Pa, 93; solo exhibs, Fleisher Art Mem Gallery, Philadelphia, Pa, 93, Olga Korper Gallery, Toronto, Ont, 94 & 98, Lennon Weinberg, NY, 97 & Queens Mus Art, Bulova Corp Ctr, NY, 97; Mud, Toronto, Ont, 94; Mercer Union, Toronto, Ont, 94; Practice Ground, Ottawa Art Gallery, Ont, 94; Summer Exhib: Mitchell, Jaffe, Westerlund Roosen, Morales, Jaudon, Korman, Hill, Workman, Thomasos, Lennon Weinberg Gallery, New York, 96; Deliberate Hand: Four Paintings, Banyan Tree - Proj Room, NY, 96; After the Fall, Newhouse Ctr Contemp Art & Snug Harbor Cult Ctr, Staten Island, NY, 97; New Jersey Arts Ann: Choosing New Jersey (with catalog), Newark Mus, 97; Really, Unfinished, Brooklyn, NY, 97; NY, N York: Canadian Artists in the Big Apple, Art Gallery N York, Ont, Can, 97-98; Basically Black and White, Neuberger Mus, Purchase, NY, 97-98; UTZ: A Collected Exhib, Lennon Weinberg, NY, 98; Paintings, Lennon Weinberg, NY, 98; Unlocking the Grid: concerning the grid in recent painting, Fine Arts Ctr Galleries, Univ RI, Kingston, 99; Immediacies of the Hand, Recent Abstract Painting in NY, Hunter Col & Times Sq Gallery, NY, 99. *Collection Arranged:* Crossing Lines, Gallery 6, New York, 98-99. *Teaching:* Asst prof painting, Tyler Sch Art, Temple Univ, Philadelphia, Pa, 90-95 & Visual & Performing Arts, Rutgers Univ, Newark, NJ, 95-. *Awards:* Mid-Atlantic Regional Grant Painting, Nat Endowment Arts, 94; Pew Recipient, Am Acad Rome, NY, 95; Guggenheim Found Fel Award, 97. *Bibliog:* Dominique Nahas (auth), Denyse Thomasos, rev, 6/15/97; Edith Newhall (auth), Talent, Denyse Thomasos, NY, 7/7/97; Tom Moody (auth), Denyse Thomasos, Artforum, 11/97. *Mailing Add:* Rutgers Univ Fine Arts Dept 110 Warren St Newark NJ 07102

THOMPSON, CAPPY (CATHERINE)
PAINTER
b Jan 22, 52. *Study:* Fairhaven Col, Bellingham, Wash, 70-71; Factory Visual Arts, Seattle, Wash, 71-72; Evergreen State Col, Olympia, Wash, BA, 76. *Work:* Art Gallery W Australia, Perth; Chrysler Mus Art, Norfolk, Va; Hokkaido Mus Mod Art, Sapporo, Japan; Davis, Wright, Tremaine, Seattle, Wash; and others. *Comn:* Stained glass entryway, South Bay Elem Sch, Olympia, Wash, 84; stained glass panels, Mount Lake Terrace Pub Libr, Wash, 86. *Exhib:* Betsy Rosenfield Gallery, Chicago, Ill, 92; Leo Kaplan Gallery, NY, 93; Am Craft Mus, NY, 93; Hokkaido Mus Mod Art, Sapporo, Japan, 94; Seattle Art Mus, Wash, 95; Breaking the Mold: New Directions in Glass, Huntsville Mus Art, Ala, 96; Celebrating the Figure, Penland Gallery, Penland Sch Crafts, NC, 96; Solo shows, Leo Kaplan Mod, NY, 97, New Works, Grover/Thurston Gallery, Seattle, Wash, 97, Habatat Galleries, Boca Raton, Fla, 98, R Duane Reed Gallery, Chicago, 99, William Traver Gallery, Seattle, 02, Carnegie Mus Art, Pittsburgh, 02; Glass Today by Am Studio Artists, Mus Fine Art, Boston, Mass, 97; Telling Compelling Tales: The Narrative in Contemp Glass, Holter Mus Art, Helena, Mont, 98; The Dimensional Canvas: Painted Studio Glass, Dorothy Weiss Gallery, San Francisco, Calif, 98; Smithsonian Inst, 98-2000; Contemp Art Ctr Va, Va Beach, 99; Margo Jacobsen Gallery, Portland, Ore, 2000; Habatat Galleries, Boca Raton, Fla, 2000-01; Ky Art & Craft Found, 2000-01; Heller Gallery, NY, 2001; and others. *Collection Arranged:* Am Craft Mus, NY; Birmingham Mus Art, Ala; Hokkaido Mus Mod Art, Sapporo, Japan; Microsoft Corp, Redmond, Wash; Montgomery Mus Art, Ala; Nordstrom Inc, Seattle; Tacoma Art Mus, Wash; Wash State Arts Comn, Olympia; Toyama City Inst Glass Art, Japan. *Pos:* Studio coordr, Pilchuck Sch, Stanwood, Wash, 87, printmaker, 90; designer, Juanita Kreps Award, JC Penney Co, 95-00. *Teaching:* Artist-in-residence, Pilchuck Sch, Stanwood, Wash, 84, fac, 88, 89, 92, 96, Penland Sch Crafts, NC, 96; fac, Pratt Fine Arts Ctr, Seattle, Wash, 90, 91, master arts workshop, 01; Int Conf Workshop, Glass Art Soc, Monterey, Mex, 92; Int Conf Workshop, Auglass, Camberra, Australia, 93; workshop instr, Centro del Arte Vitro, Monterrey, Mex, 92 & Canberra Sch Art, Australia, 93; workshop, Toyana City Inst Glass Art, Japan, 95, Calif Col of Arts & Crafts, Oakland, 01, Sch Art, Rochester Inst Tech, NY, 01; Fac, Penland Sch Crafts, NC, 96 & Col Fine Arts, Jacksonville Univ, Fla, 97. *Awards:* Nat Endowment Arts Fel Visual Arts, 90; Artist in Res, Toyama City Inst Glass Art, Japan, 95; Fel, Artist Trust, Seattle, Wash, 97; John H Hauberg Fel, Pilchuck Glass Sch, Stanwood, Wash, 01; selected for a Univ Wash Artist Images Series Bookmark, 98. *Bibliog:* Tina Old Know (auth), Pilchuck: A Glass School, Univ Wash Press, 96; Cappy Thompson: Narrative, Mythopoesis and the Vessel Form, Glass Art, 1-2/97; Karen Chambers (auth), Cappy Thompson, Leo Kaplan Modern, through July 4, 1997, World Art Rev, 97; William S Ellis (auth), Glass: From the First Mirror to Fiber Optics, The Story of the Substance that Changed the World, 98; Geoffrey Wichert (auth), What Happened to Stained Glass?, Glass 86, 02. *Mem:* Glass

Art Soc (bd dir, 89-92, secy, 90-92); Pilchuck Glass Sch (artistic adv comt, 92). *Media:* Blown Glass, Stained Glass. *Dealer:* Leo Kaplan Modern 965 Madison Ave New York NY 10021; Gover/Thurston Gallery 309 Occidental Ave S Seattle Wash 98104. *Mailing Add:* 707 S Snoqualmie No 4A Seattle WA 98108

THOMPSON, COLIN (H)
PAINTER
b London, Eng, 49. *Study:* Lake Forest Col, Ill, BA, 71; Skowhegan Sch Painting & Sculpture, Maine, 74; New York Studio Sch, 72-75; Yale Univ, New Haven, Conn, MFA, 77. *Work:* Albright-Knox Mus; Centro Cult, Arte Contemporaneo, Mexico City; Chase Manhattan Bank; Chemical Bank; Equitable Life Assurance Soc; M&T Bank; and others. *Exhib:* Solo shows, Nine Freudenheim Gallery, Buffalo, NY, 87, 88 & 92 & Lieberman & Saul Gallery, NY, 89 & 91; Int Sculpture Ctr, Washington, 88; Nina Freudenheim Gallery, Buffalo, NY, 88 & 91; Lieberman & Saul Gallery, NY, 92; David Beitzel Gallery, NY, 92; and others. *Pos:* Dir, Painewebber Art Gallery, currently. *Awards:* Nat Endowment Arts Fel, 91-92. *Bibliog:* William Wilson (auth), Review, LA Times, 6/9/87; Richard Huntington (auth), Review, 6/9/87 & 5/6/88 & Elizabeth Licata (auth), The other side of summer, 7/5/91, Buffalo News; Justin Spring (auth), Review, Artforum, 113, summer 91; and others. *Dealer:* Dinaberg FIne Art 49 W 24th St New York NY 10011; Art Resources Inc 210 11th Ave Ste 403 New York NY 10001. *Mailing Add:* 142 Henry St 1FW New York NY 10022

THOMPSON, DONALD ROY
PAINTER, EDUCATOR
b Fowler, Calif, Mar 2, 36. *Study:* Calif State Univ, Sacramento, BA, 60, MA, 62. *Work:* Oakland Mus, Calif; Seattle First Nat Bank; Crocker Art Mus, Calif State Univ, Sacramento, Calif; Art Mus Santa Cruz Co, Calif; Santa Clara Univ Law Sch. *Exhib:* West '81/Art and the Law, Minn Mus Art, St Paul; Smith Andersen Gallery, Palo Alto, Calif, 86; D P Fong & Spratt Galleries, San Jose, Calif, 92, Frederick Spratt Gallery, San Jose, Calif, 02, 03; Composer's Choice: Selections from the Collection of Lou Harrison, Octagon Mus, Santa Cruz, Calif, 92; Frederick Spratt Gallery, San Jose, Calif, 93; solo show, Frederick Spratt Gallery, San Jose, Calif, 95, 98, 01 & Cabrillo Col Gallery, Aptos, Calif, 00; and others. *Teaching:* emeritus Instr art, painting & drawing, Cabrillo Col, 71-2000. *Awards:* Purchase Award, West '81/Art & the Law, West Publ Co, 81. *Bibliog:* Mark Levy (auth), Vital fabrications, Artweek, 12/18/1982; Claude Lesuer (auth), Rare summer pleasures, Artspeak, 6/23/1983; Jack Fischer (auth), Artist Subverts Expectations, San Jose Mercury-News, 7/29/2001. *Media:* Acrylic. *Dealer:* Frederick Spratt Gallery San Jose CA. *Mailing Add:* c/o Frederick Spratt Gallery 920 S First St San Jose CA 95110

THOMPSON, ERNEST THORNE, JR
SILVERSMITH, PAINTER
b South Bend, Ind, Nov 9, 28. *Study:* Huguenot Sch Art, with Courtney Allen, Charles R Kingnan, Ernest T Thompson, Sr, dipl; Sch Mus Fine Arts, Boston, with Joseph L Sharrock, Sr & Hazel Olsen Brown, dipl, independent study in Japan. *Work:* Mus Sci, Boston, Mass; USAF Chapel, Bien Hoe, Vietnam; Corp Plate, Boston, Gt Brit. *Comn:* Industrial comns & pvt collections; chapel & altar pieces, Miles Mem Hosp Chapel. *Pos:* Trustee, Soc Arts & Crafts, 61-64; juror, Sterling Silver Design Competition, 75; owner & partner, Thompsons Studio Inc. *Teaching:* Dept head jewelry & silversmith, Boston Mus Sch, 61-70 & Portland Sch Art, 69-80. *Bibliog:* Bill Cauldwell (auth), Stop, silversmith at work, Ford Times Mag, 10/69; Richard Stilwell (auth), Ernest Thompson unselfish in silver, Maine Guide Dir, 74; article in House Beautiful Mag, 2/80; Damon Ripley & Lawrence Willard (auths), Thompson's silversmith studio, Yankee Mag, 12/81. *Mem:* Pemaquid Group of Artists. *Media:* Gold, Silver; Oils, Watercolor. *Mailing Add:* 401 Back Meadow Rd Damariscotta ME 04951

THOMPSON, JACK
SCULPTOR, EDUCATOR
b Los Angeles, Calif, May 25, 46. *Study:* Calif State Univ, Northridge, BA, 70; San Francisco Art Inst, 71; Tyler Sch Art, Temple Univ, MFA, 73. *Work:* Int Acad Ceramics, Calgary; John Michael Kohler Arts Ctr Mus, Sheboygan, Wis; Los Angeles Co Art Mus, Calif. *Comn:* Ltd ed teapots, Garth Clark Gallery, NY, 84 & 91; Sculpture, Caesars Palace, Las Vegas, Nev, 90; Sculpture, Riverwack Piers 3 & 5, Philadelphia, Pa, 90. *Exhib:* Hot off the Press (auth catalog), Tulie House Mus, Carlisle, Eng; The Animal Image, Renwick Gallery, Smithsonian Inst, 81; Am Clay Artists, Port of Hist Mus, Philadelphia, Pa, 89; one-man shows, Viaje Despues De LaVida, LaGaleria, San Cristobal De Las Casas, Mex, 97, Recent Work, Sande Webster Gallery, 92, Animal Love, Sacred or Profane, Jasuta Gallery, Philadelphia, Pa, 94 & Clay Studio, Philadelphia, 96; Bucks Biennial, James Michener Mus, Doylestown, Pa, 94; Transformations, 4 Bucks Co Artists, James A Michener Art Mus, Doyalstown, Pa, 95; ICA: 1 Singular Sensation, Inst Contemp Art, Univ Pa, Philadelphia, 95; and others. *Teaching:* Prof, Moore Col Art, Philadelphia, Pa, 74-96; vis Lectr, Princeton Univ, 93-94. *Awards:* Fel, Pa State Coun Arts, 81, 83 & 87; Purchase Award, JM Kohler Art Mus, 89; Fulbright Fel, Mex, 96-97. *Bibliog:* Susan Peterson (auth), The Art & Craft of Clay, Prentice Hall, New York, 91; Arthur Williams (auth), Sculpture Technique form & Content, Davis Publ, Worcester, Mass, 91; Leon Nigrosh (auth), Sculpting Clay, Davis Publ, Worcester, Mass. *Mem:* Bucks Co Coun Arts; Int Sculpture Ctr. *Media:* Ceramic, Cement. *Dealer:* Ferrin Gallery Northampton MA. *Mailing Add:* 705 Almshouse Rd Doylestown PA 18901

THOMPSON, JEAN DANFORTH
PHOTOGRAPHER
b Baltimore, Md, May 3, 33. *Study:* Md Inst Art, 50; Univ Md, BA, 54; Wright State Univ, MA, 72. *Work:* Univ Md; Am Embassy, Bonn, WGer; US Cent Intelligence Agency, McLean, Va; US Dept of State; Marriott Corp, Washington, DC; Sheraton Hotel, Baton Rouge, La. *Comn:* Xerox, Arlington, Va, 80, Nat Rural Electric Coop Asn, Washington DC, 80, McDonalds Corp, Fairfax, Va, 81, Am Apparel Asn, Rosslyn, Va, 83 & Paffrather Raiffeisen Bank, Cologne, WGer. *Exhib:* Solo exhib, Geilsdorfer Gallerie, Cologne, WGer, 82-84 & 86; Gayle Wilson Gallery, Southampton, NY, 83; Arverne Art Int, Ltd, NY, 83; Leighton-Richey Gallery, Columbia, 92; Bell-Atlantic, Washington, DC, 95; and others. *Collection Arranged:* Art USA, London, 80. *Mem:* Torpedo Factory Artists Asn (pres, 79-80, bd mem, 76-86); Fiber Workshop; Artists Equity. *Media:* Digital Photography. *Mailing Add:* Studio 16 Torpedo Factory Art Ctr 105 N Union St Alexandria VA 22314

THOMPSON, JUDITH KAY
PAINTER
b Kansas City, Kans, May 28, 40. *Study:* William Jewell Col, Liberty, Mo, 60; Kans City Art Inst, Wilbur Neiwald, BFA, 65; Univ Cincinnati & Art Acad, MFA, 67. *Exhib:* Nat Assoc of Women Artists, Millenium Collection, United Nations, Washington, DC, Works on Paper, Fairleigh Dickinson Univ, Hackensack, NJ, 75 & Brooklyn Mus, NY, 75; 96th Ann Nat Exhib Asn, Jacob K Javits Fed Bldg, NY, 85; Nat Asn Women Artists (traveling), 2000. *Pos:* Admin Asst. *Teaching:* Instr drawing, Cincinnati Art Mus, 66; instr draw, 2-D & 3-D design, St Cloud State Univ, Minn, 69; instr painting & draw, St Benedict's Col, Minn, 69. *Awards:* Goldie Paley Award, Celebration Bicentennial, Nat Asn Women Arts, 76. *Bibliog:* Notable Women of Tex, 84; New York Art Review, 87. *Mem:* Nat Asn of Women Artists, NY, 1976-2005; Nat Mus of Women in the Arts, Washington, DC, 1987-2006. *Media:* Oil. *Res:* 74-traveled to Europe to res women painters in hist. *Interests:* walking, pets. *Mailing Add:* 9337 Westwood Village Dr Houston TX 77036

THOMPSON, LYNN P
PAINTER, PHOTOGRAPHER
b Plainfield, NJ, July 22, 1922. *Study:* Bennett Jr Col, 39-40; Douglas Col, BA, 43; Cornell Med Col, MD, 46; Nat Acad Design; Art Students League, Maine Coast Workshops, Schlemm & Wagner, 97-98. *Work:* New York Hosp; Khanbegian Gallery, Sonogee, Bar Harbor, Maine; Inglemoor, Englewood, NJ; Kodak Artcart Collection, 86-. *Comn:* El Molino (oil), comn by George Moore, Sotogrande, Spain, 80; seascape, comn by Dr Eibl, Vienna, 80; Maine seascape, Drawing Room, Pennsula, Ohio, 81; painting (oil), New York Hosp, 83; Series Watercolors, David Elliott; plus many others. *Exhib:* Solo exhib, Bergen Mus, Paramus, NJ, 74 & El Molino, Spain, 79; Federated Art Asn, NJ State Mus, Trenton, 75; NY Physicians Art Asn Ann, Union Carbide, 76; NY Physicians Art Exhib, NY Acad Med, 76-79; Oil Painting & Watercolors Exhib, Col Atlantic, Bar Harbor, Maine, 98. *Collection Arranged:* The David Elhots, Dean Lambertson, Anthony Swan; Collections with the George Moore Family of Spain and NYC, and Peter Thompson. *Pos:* Dir, New York Hosp Art Comn, 66-74 & 77-80 & Child Life Ctr, New York, 82-; dir & adv, Circulating Art Cart Prog, 78; coordr, Hosp Audiences, New York, 82-; 300 progs underway in 31 states, Que, Can & Am Hosp, Paris; exec comm assoc, Healthcare Art Admin, 89-. *Teaching:* Instr watercolor, Sonogee, Bar Harbor, Maine, 79-, Mainescape Gallery, Bar Harbor, Maine. *Awards:* Prix Etats-Unis, Duncan Gallery, New York & Paris, 75; First & Second Awards, New York Physicians Art Asn Ann, 76-79; Bocour Award, Orange Art Asn, 78; Volunteer of Yr Award for Art in Nursing Homes, Am Health Asn, 88. *Bibliog:* Marguerite Logan (auth), Circulating Art Program Brings New Vistas to Facility Life, Am Health Care Asn J, 85; Judy Haberek (auth), Nursing Home Volunteers Circulate Art & Heart in Bergen County, Voluntary Action Leadership, winter 86; Marian (auth), Doctor Finds Art the Best Medicine, Lancet, Art in Health care facilities, 12/88. *Mem:* Salmagundi Club; Catharine Lorillard Wolfe Club; Allied Artists Am; New York Physicians Art Asn (dir, 78-); Bergen Co Artists Guild. *Media:* Watercolor, Oil. *Res:* Cancer research with Dr. George Snell (Nobel Prize Winner) at the Jackson Lab in Bar Harbor, ME, 1940; Research on the development of Sanddollar embryos at MDIBL in Bar Harbor, ME, 1964. *Specialty:* Watercolors. *Interests:* Love to paint and facilitate a sense of well being at hospitals and nursing homes through work with the Circulating Art Program. *Publ:* Contribr, Cornell Medical College Alumni News, 81 & 84. *Dealer:* Mainescape Gallery 54 West St Bar Harbor ME 04609. *Mailing Add:* 8 Heritage Ln Cumberland Foreside ME 04110-1306

THOMPSON, MALCOLM BARTON
PAINTER, FILM MAKER
b Coraopolis, Pa, Dec 25, 16. *Study:* Pratt Inst, grad; Art Students League; also illus with Nicholas Riley. *Comn:* US Army in Action Ser, Pentagon, 49. *Exhib:* Soc Casein Artists, NY, 70; Slater Mem Mus, Norwich, Conn, 71; Conn Watercolor Soc, Hartford, Conn, 71; Mainstreams '71, Marietta, Ohio, 71; Am Watercolor Soc Traveling Exhibs, 72 & 73; 18 one-man shows, Lord & Taylor, NY, 3 one-man shows, Marshall Fields, Chicago. *Teaching:* Instr watercolor & anat, McLane Art Inst, New York, 38-40. *Awards:* Marjorie Salembier Award, Conn Classic Arts, 68; First Prize, New Canaan Art Show, 70; Grumbacher Acrylic Award, Am Artists Prof League, 71 & 75. *Mem:* Am & Conn Watercolor Soc; Silvermine Guild Artists; Am Artist Prof League. *Media:* Acrylic-Oil, Watercolor. *Dealer:* Newman Galleries 1625 Walnut St Philadelphia PA 19103; Settlers West Galleries 6420 N Campbell Ave Tucson AZ 85718. *Mailing Add:* 40 Honey Hill Rd Wilton CT 06897

THOMPSON, MARK L
SCULPTOR
b Ft Sill, Okla, 50. *Study:* Va Polytech Inst, 68-70; Univ Calif, Berkeley, BA, 72, MA, 73. *Work:* Berkeley Art Mus, Calif; Hartnell Col, Salinas, Calif; Newberger Berman Corp, San Francisco. *Exhib:* Invocations, Whitechapel Art Gallery, London, 90; Dance of the Honeybees: An Exploration of San Francisco's Mission District, Exploratorium, San Francisco, Calif, 92; Walk with Backpack I Live (performance), Japan-US friendship Comn, Kurobane, 92; solo exhib, Hartnell Col Art Gallery, Salinas, Calif, 93; Color in the Shadows: Bay Area Cyberart, Oliver Ctr, Calif Col Arts & Crafts, Oakland, 94; Tiniest Show on Earth, Boulder Mus Contemp Art, Col, 96; Animalia,

Stadtgalrie Wellerdeler, Berlin, Ger, 97; Out of Actions: Between Performance and the Object, 1949-1979, Los Angeles, 98-99; 25/25, Southern Exposure, San Francisco, 99; The Boy Mechcanic, Yerba Buena Ctr for Arts, San Francisco, 99; Essence of Composition, Gallery Paule Anglim, San Francisco, 2001. *Pos:* Artist-in-residence, Hartnell Col, Salinas, Calif, 77; artist-in-residence proj mgr, Headlands Ctr Arts, Ft Barry, Calif, 86; panel mem, Going Public: Western Regional Pub Art Forum, San Francisco, 88, Earth Day: Artists Respond to the Environmental Crisis, Palo Alto Cult Ctr, Calif, 90 & Installation Art, Discussion with Chris Burden and Mark Thompson, Whitechapel Art Gallery, London, Eng, 90. *Teaching:* Var lect-film presentations, 77-92; lectr art-conceptual design, San Francisco State Univ, 88 & 89, lectr sculpture, 91-93, grad workshop, 92; vis lectr sculpture, Univ Col London, Slade Sch Fine Art, 90; grad workshop, Univ Colo, Boulder, 94; adj prof sculpture, Calif Col Arts & Crafts, 93-96, assoc prof, 96-2000, prof, 2000-. *Awards:* New Genre Artists Fel, Calif Arts Coun, 92; Creative Arts Fel, Cult Arts, City Oakland, Calif, 94; Visual Artists Award, Flintridge Found, 98; NEA Fel Grant, 89, 90; Civitella Ranieri Ctr Fel, Umbertide, Italy, 2001. *Bibliog:* George Gessert (auth), Notes on genetic art, Vol 26, No 3, Leonardo, 93; Barrett Watten (auth), Science Fair, Vol 25, No 4, Artweek, 2/17/94; Bill Berkson (auth), The Salon at Mission & Third, Art in Am, 6/94; and others. *Publ:* Animalia: Stellvertreter (catalog), Haus am Waldsee, Berlin, Ger, 90; Seven Obsessions (catalog), Whitechapel Art Gallery & Performanc Mag, No 63, London, Eng, 11/90; Performance-Ritual-Process, Elisabeth Jappe, Prestel-Verlag, Munich, NY, 93; In Out of the Cold (catalog), Ctr Arts, Yerba Buena Gardens, San Francisco, Calif, 93; Visions of America: Landscape as Metaphor In The Late 20th Century (essays by Martin Friedman, et al), Denver Art Mus, 94; and others. *Mailing Add:* 4 Valley View Orinda CA 94563

THOMPSON, NANCY KUNKLE
JEWELER, EDUCATOR
b Marion, Ind, Dec 30, 41. *Study:* Ball State Teachers Col, BS(art), 63; Ind Univ, MFA(jewelry design & metalsmithing), 68. *Work:* Ind Univ Mus Art, Bloomington; Greenville Co Mus Art, SC. *Exhib:* Extraordinary Vehicles, J M Kohler Arts Ctr, Sheboygan, Wis, 74; Southeastern Crafts, Greenville Co Mus Art, SC, 74; Bicentennial Craft Invitational, Ind Univ Art Mus, 76; Wearables, Renwick Gallery, DC, 79; The Next Juried Show, Va Mus Fine Arts, 83; New Art Forms: Virginia, Hand Workshop, 88. *Teaching:* Prof jewelry & metalwork, Va Commonwealth Univ, 73-. *Awards:* Exp Metalwork, Carnegie Found, 68; Slide Doc of Hist Jewelry-Ornamental Devices, Va Commonwealth Univ, 71, Fac Grant-in-Aid, 76. *Bibliog:* Geff Reed (auth), Thompson/Kerrigan, Craft Horizons, 72. *Mem:* Am Crafts Coun; Col Art Asn; Soc NAm Goldsmiths. *Media:* Precious Metals, Nonmetallic Materials. *Mailing Add:* Dept Crafts Va Commonwealth Univ 325 N Harrison St Richmond VA 23284

THOMPSON, RENA
WEAVER, PAINTER
b New York, NY, Jan 22, 50. *Study:* Moore Col Art, BFA, 78; Tyler Sch Art, Temple Univ, MFA, 80. *Work:* Provident Mutual Life Insurance Co, Philadelphia, Pa; Chase Manhattan Bank, NY; First Am Bank Va, Richmond; Cent Trust Bank, Jefferson City, Mont; Bristol-Myers, NJ. *Exhib:* Solo exhibs, Marian Locks Gallery, Philadelphia, Pa, 87, Leedy-Voulkos Gallery, Kansas City, Mo, 87 & Del Ctr Contemp Art, Wilmington, 92; Fiber Chronicals (with catalog), Moore Col Art, Philadelphia, Pa, 88; Out of the Woods, Fairmount Park, Philadelphia, 90; Bucks Biennial I, James Michener Art Mus, Doylestown, Pa, 92; Threads in Common, Philadelphia Art Alliance, Pa, 92; Artfront, Philadelphia, Pa, 96-97; and others. *Teaching:* Artist-in-residence, State of Pa, 88-92. *Awards:* Visual Arts Fel, Nat Endowment Arts, 80 & 87; Pa Coun Arts Fel, 83, 88 & 91; 1st Prize, State of the Art, State Mus Pa, Harrisburg, 94. *Media:* Fiber; Acrylic, Canvas. *Mailing Add:* 705 Almshouse Rd Doylestown PA 18901

THOMPSON, RICHARD CRAIG
PAINTER
b McMinnville, Ore, June 27, 45. *Study:* Ore State Univ, 63-65; Univ NMex, BFA, 67, MA, 72; painting with John Kacere; also lithography with Garo Antresian. *Work:* San Antonio Mus Art, Tex; Roswell Mus, NMex. *Comn:* Twenty Sculpture Pieces, Univ Md, 69; Impermanent Sculpture, Mich Arts Coun, Detroit, 74; Cowboy Nights, Warehouse Living Arts Ctr, Corsicana, Tex. *Exhib:* Solo exhibs, Roswell Mus, NMex, 81, Monique Knowlton Gallery, NY, 81, 82 & 84, Art Mus STex, Corpus Christi, 84, Harris Gallery, Houston, 85; Biennial of Contemp Am Art, Whitney Mus, NY, 75; Space Gallery, Los Angeles, 80 & 84; Fresh Paint, Mus Fine Arts, Houston; Hill's Gallery, Santa Fe, NMex, 75-78; Scottish Arts Festival, Edinburgh, Scotland, 80; and others. *Teaching:* Lectr painting & drawing, Univ Albuquerque, 72-75; vis lectr color, Wayne State Univ, spring 74; instr design-color, Univ NMex, 75-78; vis prof, Univ Tex, San Antonio, 84; asst prof, Univ Tex, Austin, 84-. *Awards:* Nat Endowment Arts Fel, 78; Artist-in-residence, Australia Arts Coun, 82; Mid-Am Art Alliance Award, 86; artist-in-residence grant, Roswell Mus, NMex. *Bibliog:* Charlotte Moser, New Mexico, open land and psychic elbow room, ARTnews, 12/77; article in New America, Univ NMex, 79; Portfolio, Paris Review, Summer 79. *Mem:* Col Art Asn; Nat Watercolor Honor Soc. *Media:* Acrylic, Oil. *Dealer:* Harris Gallery 1100 Bissonnet Houston TX 77005; Space Gallery 6015 Santa Monica Blvd Los Angeles CA 90038. *Mailing Add:* c/o Robischon Gallery 1740 Wazee St Denver CO 80202

THOMPSON, RICHARD E, JR
DEALER, COLLECTOR
b Oak Park, Ill, Dec 30, 39. *Study:* Univ Wis; Wayland Acad. *Collection Arranged:* Richard Thompson, Sr, 77. *Pos:* Dir, Richard Thompson Gallery, San Francisco, 77-. *Specialty:* Twentieth century American impressionists. *Collection:* American impressionists

THOMPSON, TAMARA
ASSEMBLAGE ARTIST, PAINTER
b Anderson, Ind, Apr 8, 35. *Study:* Univ Ky, BA(art); Ind Univ, MFA; study with Leon Golub & Creighton Gilbert. *Work:* Ind Univ, Bloomington; Colgate Univ; Univ Ky; Syracuse Univ. *Comn:* Mural, Children & Sports, Albuquerque Pub Schs, 85. *Exhib:* 17 Conn Artists, Wadsworth Atheneum, Hartford, 60; Arts of Cent NY 36th & 38th Ann, Munson-Williams-Proctor Inst, Utica, 73 & 75; solo exhibs, Picker Art Gallery, Colgate Univ, 78, Photogenesis, Albuquerque, 81 & Hoshour Gallery, Albuquerque, 83; Electroworks, Int Mus of Photog, George Eastman House, Rochester, 79-80; Mutiples 80, Contemp Arts Ctr, New Orleans; Spring Arts Festival, Taos, 85; On the Wall-Off the Wall, Ctr for Contemp Arts, Santa Fe, 85; Statements 88 Invitational, Albuquerque, 88; Magnifico, Albuquerque, 91. *Pos:* Dir art classes, Wadsworth Atheneum, 59-61; vis artist in residence, Univ Ky, 65, Everson Mus, Syracuse, 79 & Int Mus Photog, George Eastman House, Rochester, 80. *Teaching:* Instr art, Univ Ky, 65-66; instr fine arts, Colgate Univ, 72-80, asst prof, 80; art specialist, The Montessori Sch, Albuquerque, 86-95; Art Specialist & Teacher, Mountain Shadows Montessori School, Boulder, CO, 95-2004. *Awards:* First Prize, Hartford Soc Women Painters, 60 & 61; Colgate Univ Fac Develop Fund Grant, 77-78, Res Coun Grant, 79-81. *Bibliog:* Catherine Lord (auth), Women and photography, Afterimage, 1/80 & Modern photography, 9/80; Ellen Land-Weber (auth), Processes: Copying Machines, Afterimage. *Mem:* Col Art Asn Am; Albuquerque United Artists. *Media:* Multi. *Publ:* Contribr, Drawings of the Italian Renaissance, Ind Univ Press, 58. *Mailing Add:* 1255 3rd Ave Longmont CO 80501-5300

THOMPSON, VIRGINIA ABBATE
PAINTER, INSTRUCTOR
b Brooklyn, NY. *Study:* Univ Miami, BA, 60; Miami Dade Community Col, AS, 72. *Exhib:* Fla Watercolor Soc Ann, Mus Fine Arts, St Petersburg, 96; Audubon Artists Ann, Salmagundi Club, NY, 98; Lancaster Mus Art, Pa, 99; Magnificent Eleven, Schacknow Mus Fine Arts, Plantation, Fla, 2000; Int Watercolor Biennial, Lat Am Mus, Coral Gables, Fla, 2000. *Teaching:* instr, Miami Dade Community Col, 2001-02. *Awards:* Jane Peterson Mem Award, Audubon Artists, 95; Merit Award, Pa Watercolor Soc, 99; 2d Place Int Watercolor Biennial, Latin Am Mus, 2000. *Bibliog:* Mary Ann Beckwith (auth), Creative Watercolor, Rockport Publ, 95; Sara M Doherty (ed), Painting Light & Shadow, Rockport Publ, 97. *Mem:* Nat Watercolor Soc; Audubon Artists; Pa Watercolor Soc; Fla Watercolor Soc; Gold Coast Watercolor Soc. *Media:* Watercolor. *Mailing Add:* PO Box 835394 Miami FL 33283

THOMPSON, WADE S
PAINTER, EDUCATOR
b Moorhead, Minn, July 30, 46. *Study:* Macalester Col, BA, 68; Bowling Green State Univ, MA, MFA, 72; Pratt Inst, 85. *Work:* IBM Corp, Kansas City, Mo; M-Bank Corp, Houston, Tex; Freeport-MacMahon Corp, New Orleans, La; Provincetown Art Asn, Mass; Hoyt Institute of Fine Arts, New Castle, Pa; Jena Int, Washington; Univ Art & Design, Helsinki, Finland. *Comn:* Aerialscape 2000 (painting), Springfield Branson Regional Airport, Springfield, Mo, 92. *Exhib:* Am Drawing 1976, Smithsonian Inst Traveling Exhib, Portsmouth Arts Ctr, Va, 76; one-man shows, Hansen Galleries, NY, 77, Mary Bell Gallery, Chicago, 84, 85, 87, 88 & 89, Jack Meir Gallery, Houston, Tex, 85, 87, 88, 91, 93, 94 & 97, Martin Schweig Gallery, St Louis, 86, Still-Zinzel New Orleans, 90 & Parthenon Mus, Nashville, Tenn, 95; Washington Collectors: One Plus One, Watkins Gallery, Am Univ, 93; Gala '94 Nat, Brenau Univ, Gainesville, Ga, 94; Krasl Art Mus, St Joseph, Mich, 95; Millikin Univ, Decatur, Ill, 96; Keyes Gallery, Springfield, Mo, 99; Malton Gallery, Cincinnati, Ohio, 2001. *Collection Arranged:* Centennial Art Exhib; Springfield Art Mus, Feb 18-Mar 13, 2005. *Pos:* Designer, Assoc Design, St Paul, Minn, 70-71; co-chmn, Art, Design & Psychology Interest Group, Inter-Soc, Color Coun, 88-94, chmn, 94-96, bd dir, 96-98; organizing chmn, Color & Tech Conf, ISCC, Williamsburg, Va, 98. *Teaching:* Asst prof art, Tyler Sch Art, Temple Univ, 75-79; prof art and design, Mo State Univ, 79-91, distinguished scholar, 92-97, asst head dept art and design, 99-2001, acting dept head, 2001-2002; vis prof, Summer Design Inst, Univ Minn, Minneapolis, 95. *Awards:* Award for Acrylic, 27th Ann Chautauqua Nat Exhib Am Art, 84; Best of Show, Brenau Univ Gala 94 Nat Invitational, Gainesville, Ga; Vis Arts Prog Grant, Miss Arts Coun, St Louis, 98. *Bibliog:* Camille Howell (auth), Artists Enjoy Their Work, Springfield News Leader, Mo, 4/7/94; Kay Dillon (auth), Two Worth While Exhibits, The Oaks Ridger, Tenn, 12/19/95; Christopher Willard (auth), How to set up a still-life, Am Artist Mag, NY, 11/97. *Mem:* Inter-Soc Color Coun (bd dir); Col Art Asn; and others. *Media:* Acrylic on Canvas. *Res:* color theory and practice. *Publ:* Auth, Wade S Thompson, Color Light and Temperature: A General Studies Component for Fine Arts Painting; Aspects of Colour (ed by Harald Arnkil & Esa Hamalainen, Publ Series, Univ Art & Design, Helsinki, Finland, 95; Colour Illusion in Painting, Colour Anthology, Scandinavian Colour Inst, Stockholm, 97; Dimensional Form Through Color and Light, Colour Between Art and Science, Inst of Colour, Oslo, Norway, 98; Digitally Manipulated Images and Painting, 2001. *Dealer:* Malton Gallery, Cincinnati, OH. *Mailing Add:* Mo State Univ Springfield MO 65804

THOMSON, CARL L
PAINTER, ART APPRAISER
b Brooklyn, NY, Mar 6, 13. *Study:* Pratt Inst. *Work:* Salmagundi Club; Burr Artists Group. *Exhib:* Salmagundi Club Ann Watercolor & Oil Shows, 59-72. *Pos:* Advert designer, C Thomson Assoc, 47-59; art dir, Am Home Prod Corp, 59-70; owner, Thomson Gallery; pres, Equitable Appraisal Co, Inc, New York, 73-. *Teaching:* Instr drawing, Salmagundi Club, 61-63. *Awards:* Graphic Arts Award, Printing Industs Am, 69; Cert Spec Merit, Printing Industs Metrop New York, 70. *Mem:* Salmagundi Club (pres, 81-83); Dutch Treat Club; Appraisers Asn Am. *Media:* Watercolor, Oil; Pastel. *Mailing Add:* 19 E 75th St New York NY 10021-2608

THOMSON, DAVID K.R.
COLLECTOR
Awards: Named one of Top 200 Collectors, ARTnews Magazine, 2004. *Collection:* Contemporary art. *Mailing Add:* Thomson Corp Toronto-Dominion Bank Tower 66 Wellington St W Toronto ON M5K 1A1 Canada

THORNE, JOAN
PAINTER, EDUCATOR
b New York, NY. *Study:* New York Univ, BS, 65; Hunter Col, MFA, 68. *Work:* Albright Knox Art Gallery, Buffalo, NY; Aldrich Mus Contemp Art, Ridgefield, Conn; Brooklyn Mus, NY; Dallas Mus Art; Krannert Mus, Univ Ill, Champaign. *Exhib:* Solo exhib, Corcoran Gallery of Art, Wash, DC, 73, Graham & Sons, NY, 90, Ramapo Col, NJ, Museo Voluntariado De Las Casas Reales (retrospective), Casa de Bastedas, Santo Domingo, Dominican Repub & Museo Patronato Plaza, de la Cultura (retrospective), Santiago Apostol, Dominican Repub, 98, Mus de Las Americas, San Juan, PR, 2000; Whitney Annual, Whitney Mus Am Art, NY, 72, 1981 Biennial Exhib, 81; Spring Ann, Adrich Mus Contemp Art, Ridgefield, Conn, 72, Tenth Anniversary Exhib, 74, The Art of the 1970's & 1980's, 85; An Affair of the Heart, Albright-Knox Art Gallery, Buffalo, NY, 85; Graham Modern Selections, NY Stock Exchange, 91; Abstract Painting of the 90's, Andre Emmerich Gallery, 91; Altos de Chavon, Los Artislas Residentes (with catalog), Dominican Republic, 93; Through Thick & Thin, Andre Zarre Gallery, 94, The Exuberant 80's, 94. *Teaching:* assoc prof, Borough of Manhattan Community Col, NY. *Awards:* Painting Fel, Nat Endowment Arts, 79 & 83; Grant Painting, NY State Coun Arts, 80; Grant Painting, Prix de Rome, Am Acad Rome Pollock Krasner Found, 86. *Bibliog:* Richard Vine (auth), Art In America Mag, 6/98; Stephen Westfall (auth), Wild Beauty, essay in catalogue Mus de Las Americas, March/April 2000; Robert C Morgan (auth), PAINTED In New York City: The Presence of the Past, essay for catalogue Joe and Emily Lowe Art Gallery, 2001. *Mem:* Col Art Asn; Am Acad in Rome (fellow). *Media:* Oil Paint on Linen. *Mailing Add:* 169 Mercer St New York NY 10012

THORNE-THOMSEN, RUTH T
PHOTOGRAPHER, EDUCATOR
b New York, NY, May 13, 43. *Study:* Colubia Col, Mo, FA (dance), 63; Southern Ill Univ, Carbondale, BFA (painting), 70; Columbia Col, Chicago, BA (photog), 73; Art Inst Chicago, MFA (photog, John Quincy Adams fel), 76. *Work:* Art Inst Chicago; San Francisco Mus Mod Art; Santa Barbara Mus Art, Calif; Walker Art Ctr, Minneapolis; Hallmark Photog Collection, St Louis; Mus Fine Arts, Houston. *Exhib:* Solo exhibs, Allan Frumkin Gallery, Chicago, 80, Art Inst Chicago, 81, Marcuse Pfeifer Gallery, NY, 83 & Jones Troyer Gallery, Washington, DC, 84, Cleveland Mus Art, 93, Within This Garden, Mus Contemporary Photography, Chicago, 93-95, Journey, Special Photographers Co, London, Eng, 95, Univ Wyoming Art Mus, 96, Mythologies, St Louis Art Mus, Mo, 97, Jackson Fine Art, Atlanta, Ga, 98, Schmidt Dean Gallery, Pa, 98, John Oulman Gallery, Minneapolis, 98, Orphans, Schmidt Dean Gallery, Philadelphia, 2000, Catherine Edelman Gallery, Chicago, 2002; The Photographer and the City, Mus Contemp Art, Chicago, 77; Landscape Images, La Jolla Mus Contemp Art, Calif, 80; Midwest Photog (with catalog), Walker Art Ctr, Minneapolis, 81; Timed and Spaced, Alchemic Gallery, Boston, 83; Extending the Perimeters of Twentieth Century Photog & Sign of the Times, San Francisco Mus Mod Art, 85; Photographs from the Getty Mus & City Light, Int Ctr Photog, NY, 85; Photog Fiction (with catalog), Whitney Mus Fairfield Co, Stamford, Conn, 86; Defining Eye: Women Photographers of the 20th Century, St Louis Art Mus, 97; Years Ending in Nine, Mus Fine Arts, Houston, Tex, 98; Resurrections, Brussels, Belgium, 98; Egypt of the Mind, Denver Art Mus, 98; The Cultured Tourist, Leslie Tonkonow Gallery, NY, 98; Fabulists: Fictions in Word Image by Philadelphia Artists, Levy Gallery, Moore Col Art, Philadelphia, 99; Ancient History: Photographs of the Ancient World 1851-1997, Yancey Richardson Gallery, NY, 99; What's New: Recent Acquisitions in Photography, Sondra Gilman Gallery, Whitney Mus Am Art, NY, 2000. *Pos:* Staff photographer, Chicago Sun-Times, 78. *Teaching:* Instr photog, Columbia Col, Chicago, 74-83; asst prof, Univ Colo, Denver, 83-87, chair dept fine arts, 88, assoc prof, 87-89. *Awards:* Nat Endowment Humanities Fel, Paris, 79; Nat Endowment Arts Fel, 82; Lifetime Achievement Award, Columbia Col, Chicago, 95; Bessie Berman Award for Photography, Leeway Found, Philadelphia, 96; Fellowship, Pa Council on Arts, 2001. *Bibliog:* Discoveries, In: Photography Year 1980, Time-Life Bks, 80; Jon Cook, The marvelous journey: Photographs of Ruth Thorne-Thomsen, Nits & Wits Mag, 3-4/82; Owen Edwards (auth), Tripping the light fantastic, Am Photographr, 3/84; Lisbeth Morano (auth), Ruth Thorne-Thomsen at Marcuse Pfeifer, Art in Am, 4/84; Lauren Smith (auth), The Visionary Pinhole, Peregrine Smith Bks, Salt Lake City, 85. *Mem:* Soc Photog Educ

THORNS, JOHN CYRIL, JR
DESIGNER, PAINTER
b Denver, Colo, Apr 14, 26. *Study:* Ft Hays State Univ, BA; Ind Univ, with Henry Hope & George Rickey, MA(art hist); Univ Iowa, with John Schulze & Lester Longman, MFA(archit design). *Work:* Hastings Col, Nebr; Friends of Art Collection, Kans State Univ; Marian Col, Wis; Hansen Mus, Logan, Kans; Ft Hays State Univ, Hays, Kans. *Comn:* Bldg design, First Presby Church, Hays, Kans, 74; campanile design, Campus, Ft Hays State Univ, 75. *Exhib:* Am Craftsman Coun Exhib, Mus Contemp Crafts, NY, 62 & 63; Watercolor USA, Springfield Art Mus, Mo, 63 & 64; Kans Watercolor Exhib, 71, 74, 76 & 85-88; Smoky Hill, 80, 83, 85-2005; Kans Nat Small Paintings, Drawings, Prints, 91-94; numerous one-man exhibs; Kans Watercolor Mem Show, 90-95; Great Plains Nat, 95. *Pos:* Pres, Hays Arts Coun, Kans, 72-74. *Teaching:* Mem fac, Ft Hays State Univ, 54-72, prof art hist & design & chmn dept art, 72-90; consult, Hays Med Ctr, 93-2006. *Awards:* Governor's Artist, Kans, 85-86; Moss-Thorns Gallery Art, 87; Best Kans, Ft Hays State Names Art Gallery, 88; and others. *Bibliog:* Prarie Romantic: story of John C Thorns Jr, Kans Quart, Vol 24, No 1, Kans State Univ. *Mem:* Col Art Asn Am; Delta Phi Delta (pres, 70-73); Kans Watercolor Soc; Kans Art Educ Asn; Nat Coun Art Adminr; and others. *Media:* Collage; Acrylic, Watercolor. *Res:* Kans Artists. *Specialty:* 2 dimensional work. *Interests:* collecting art. *Publ:* Illusr, Frontier Mag, 57-62; contribr, Ft Hays Studies, Ser 1 & 2, Ft Hays State Univ, 60 & 66; ed, Palette, spring 66-70 & 73. *Dealer:* History Dept of Art 75 Hays State Univ Madd Matter Gallery 112 E 11th St Hays Kans 67601. *Mailing Add:* 500 W 36th St Hays KS 67601

THORNTON, RICHARD SAMUEL
EDUCATOR, WRITER
b Columbia, Mo, Aug 5, 34. *Study:* Univ Mo, BA, 56; Cranbrook Acad Art, MFA, 57. *Collection Arranged:* cur, New Japanese Graphics, London Design Mus, 91. *Teaching:* Prof graphic design, Wash State Univ, 60-77, chmn art dept, 72-76; head art dept, Univ Conn, Storrs, 77-87, prof graphic design, 77-, interim dean, Sch Fine Arts, 89-90, interim head art dept, 97. *Awards:* Teacher of the Yr, Wash State Univ, 77-78; Fulbright Scholars Award, Japan, 90-91. *Mem:* Fulbright Assocs; Graphic Design Educ Asn; Conn Art Dirs Club; Conn Acad Arts & Sci. *Res:* Japanese graphic design history. *Publ:* Auth, Education of the Japanese designer, Graphis, 69; New generation Japanese graphic designers, Print Mag, 84; SEVEN, seven graphic designers, Grapha-Sha, 85; Japanese Posters: The First 100 Years, Design Issues J, 89; Essay, Best 100 Japanese Posters 1945-1989, Tokyo, Kodansha 90; Graphic Spirit of Japan, Van Nostrand Reinhold, 91. *Mailing Add:* Dept Art Univ Conn Storrs CT 06268

THORNYCROFT, ANN
PAINTER
b Petersfield, Hampshire, Eng, Feb 29, 44. *Study:* Central Sch Art, London, BA, 66; Chelsea Sch Art, London, Dipl(art), 68. *Work:* Los Angeles Co Mus Art, Calif; Pepsico, NY; Transamerica, Los Angeles, Calif. *Exhib:* Drawings by Painters, Long Beach Mus Art, Calif, 82; Michael & Dorothy Blankfort Collection, Los Angeles Co Mus Art, Calif, 82; Coastal Abstraction: Transcendence, Calif, Los Angeles, 98. *Teaching:* Instr painting, Santa Monica Col Design, Art & Archit, 96-99, Brentwood Art Ctr, 96-2001. *Awards:* Individual Artist Grant, Nat Endowment Arts, 82. *Media:* Oil, Watercolor. *Specialty:* Contemp Art. *Dealer:* George Billis Gallery 2716 S La Cienega Blvd Los Angeles CA 90034. *Mailing Add:* 12229 Palms Blvd Los Angeles CA 90066

THORPE, JAMES GEORGE
DESIGNER, ILLUSTRATOR
b Fort Dix, NJ, May 4, 51. *Study:* Univ Md, College Park, BA, 73, MFA, 75; studied painting with Frank Bunts, sculpture & design with Claudia Demonte. *Work:* Poster Collection, Libr Cong, Washington, DC; Lahti Poster Mus, Finland; Warsaw Poster Mus, Poland; Musee de la Publicite, Paris, France; Hiroshima Mus Art, Japan. *Comn:* Hiroshima Appeals '85 (poster), Shoshin Soc Am, Washington, DC, 85. *Exhib:* 22nd Ann Irene Leache Exhib, Chrysler Mus, Norfolk, Va, 74; Maryland Biennial, Baltimore Mus Art, 76; 1st Triennial Toyama Poster Exhib, Toyama Mus Art, Japan, 85; Lahti Poster Biennale Int, Lahti Poster Mus, Finland, 85; Hiroshima Appeals '85 Invitational, Hiroshima Mus Art, Japan, 85; Colo Int Poster Biennial, Univ Colo Mus, Ft Collins, 85; 10 yr retrospective, Univ & Col Designers Assoc, Chicago, Ill, 85; Warsaw Poster Biennale, Warsaw Poster Mus, Poland, 86; Lahti Poster Bienale, Lahti, Finalnd, 87; Moscow Int Peace Poster Exhib, USSR, 87; one-man exhib, posters, Am Cult Ctr, Brussels, Belgium, 88. *Pos:* Designer-illusr, US Army European Command, 77-78 & Md Nat Capital Park & Planning Comt, 78; freelance designer-illusr, James Thorpe Graphic Design, 77. *Teaching:* Lectr graphic design-illus, Univ Md, College Park, 80-85, asst prof graphic design, 85-. *Awards:* Design Excellence Award, Nekoosa Paper Corp, 81. *Bibliog:* Walter Herdeg (auth), Graphis Posters, 84 & Glenn Beal (auth), Images for Survival, 12/85, Graphis Press; Ann & Ha Hanna (auths), the art of peace, ID Mag, 12/85. *Mem:* Univ & Col Designers Assoc. *Media:* Montage, Posters. *Publ:* Contribr, Print Mag-Reg Design Ann, R C Publ, NY 83 & 84; American Illustration Ann, Abrams, NY, 84; Graphis Poster Ann, Graphis Press, Zurich, 84; ID Mag, 85. *Mailing Add:* Univ Md Art Dept Mount Hall College Park MD 20742

THORSON, ALICE R
EDITOR, CRITIC
b Hinsdale, Ill, Sept 22, 53. *Study:* Western Ill Univ, BA, 75; Northern Ill Univ, MA, 81; Univ Chicago, PhD prog, 80-82. *Pos:* Managing ed, New Art Examiner, Chicago & Washington, DC, 82-90; Art Critic, Washington Times, Washington, DC, 87-90, Kansas City Star, Mo, 91-. *Teaching:* Adj Prof, Corcoran Sch Art, Washington, DC, 89-91 & Univ Mo, Kansas City, 98-99. *Res:* Contemporary visual art. *Publ:* Contribr, The Earthly Chimera & The Femme Fatale (exhib catalog), Univ Chicago, 81; auth, Hirshhorn's content swamps issues, 85 & 49th Carnegie International sets the record straight, 86, New Art Examiner; Morris Yarowsky: Paintings 1971-1991 (exhib catalog), McLean Project for the Arts, 91. *Mailing Add:* c/o Kansas City Star 1729 Grand Ave Kansas City MO 64108

THORSTON, LUDLOW
PAINTER
b Irvington, NJ, 27. *Study:* Newark Sch Fine and Indstrial Arts, 49; NY Univ, BA, MA, 59; student of Hans Weingartner, STanley Turnbull, Syd Browne & others. *Work:* Ludlow Thorston Galleries; Mural, US Army Comn. *Exhib:* Am Watercolor Soc; Ludlow Thorston Galleries. *Mem:* NJ Watercolor Soc (pres, formerly); Salmagundi Club, NY; others. *Media:* Watercolor, aquarelle. *Specialty:* Eastern US Figuratives. *Mailing Add:* PO Box 1047 10 Central Ave Island Heights NJ 08732

THRALL, ARTHUR
PRINTMAKER, PAINTER
b Milwaukee, Wis, Mar 18, 26. *Study:* Univ Wis, Milwaukee, BS & MS; Univ Wis, Madison; Univ Ill, Urbana; Ohio State Univ. *Work:* Brit Mus, London, Eng; Libr Cong, Washington, DC; Art Inst Chicago; Brooklyn Mus, NY; Tate Gallery, London, Eng. *Comn:* 50 print ed, Wis Arts Found, 84. *Exhib:* Carnegie Inst Int Print Exhib,

Pittsburgh, 51; Young Am Printmakers, Mus Mod Art, NY, 53; one-man show, Smithsonian Inst, 60; 160th Ann, Pa Acad Art, Philadelphia, 64; 143rd Ann, Nat Acad Design, NY, 67; 43rd Ann, Audubon Artists, NY, 85. *Teaching:* Assoc prof art, Milwaukee-Downer Col, 56-64; prof art, Lawrence Univ, 64-, chairperson, Art Dept, 81-86; vis prof art, Univ Wis-Madison, 66-67 (retired 90). *Awards:* Louis Comfort Tiffany Found Fel Graphics, 63; Purchase Award, Brooklyn Mus 14th Ann, 63; Cannon Prize, Nat Acad Design 143rd Ann, 67. *Bibliog:* M Fish (auth), Arthur Thrall, Wis Architect, 65; D Anderson (auth), The Art of Written Forms, Holt Rinehart & Winston, 69; J Watrous (auth), A Century of American Printmaking, Univ Wis Press, 84. *Mem:* Soc Am Graphic Artists; Boston Printmakers; Audubon Artists. *Media:* Etching; Miscellaneous Media. *Mailing Add:* 4225 N Woodburn Shorewood WI 53211

THRELKELD, DALE
PAINTER
b Mo, Apr 11, 44. *Study:* Northeast Mo State Col, BS, 66; Ball State Univ, MA, 70; Southern Ill Univ, Edwardsville, MFA, 75. *Work:* Brooklyn Mus Art, NY; Arco Collection Los Angeles; Ill State Mus; Northern Ill Univ Collection. *Exhib:* New Talent Exhib, Gimpel & Weitzenhoffer Gallery, NY, 74; Los Angeles Print Soc Nat Print Exhib, 74; 28th Ann Ill Invitational, Ill State Mus, 75; Unique Works on Paper, Frank Marino Gallery, NY, 75-79; Arco Collection, Los Angeles; Peoria Contemp Art Ctr, 96. *Teaching:* Prof drawing & painting, Belleville Area Col, Ill, 71-. *Awards:* Purchase Awards, Dulin Gallery Art, 70, Ark Arts Ctr, 71, Ill State Mus, 75 & Brooklyn Mus, 75. *Media:* Mixed, Oil on Canvas. *Mailing Add:* Dept Humanities & Soc Scis Belleville Area Col 2500 Carlyle Belleville IL 62221

THROCKMORTON, SPENCER S, III
ART DEALER, CONSULTANT
b South Boston, Va, Oct 29, 48. *Study:* Va Community Univ, BFA, 72; San Carlos Univ, Guatemala, MFA, 76. *Collection Arranged:* Valdir Cauz: Faces of the Rain Forest (auth, catalog), Denver Art Mus; Photography of Frida Kahlo, Diego Rivera, at Fon cation Pierre Granaddar, 98. *Pos:* Owner & pres, Throckmorton Fine Art Inc, currently. *Mem:* Friends of Columbia; Nat Asn Dealer's Inc; Antique Tribal Art Dealers Asn; Asn Int Photog Art Dealers. *Publ:* Auth, Mario Algaze, Hector Garica - Icono's Photography (exhib catalog), 83

THURMAN, CHRISTA CHARLOTTE MAYER
CURATOR
b Darmstadt, Ger, Dec 12, 34; US citizen. *Study:* Finch Col, NY, BA, 58; NY Univ Inst Fine Arts, MA, 66. *Collection Arranged:* Masterpieces of Western Textiles: A Handbook on the Art Institute of Chicago's Western Textile Collection (auth, catalog), Art Inst Chicago, 69; Coverlets: a Handbook on the Collection of Woven Coverlets in the Art Institute of Chicago (coauth, catalog), 73, Raiment for the Lord's Service: a Thousand Years of Western Vestments (auth, catalog), 76 & Claire Zeisler: a Retrospective (auth, catalog), 79; Ancient Textiles from Nubia (coauth, catalog), Art Inst Chicago & Univ Chicago, 79. *Pos:* Conserv apprentice, New York, 59-61; asst cur dept textiles, Cooper Union Mus, New York, 61-67; assoc cur dept textiles, Art Inst Chicago, 67-68 & cur, 68-82, cur chrmn, 92. *Teaching:* Vis asst prof hist archit & art, Univ Ill, Chicago Circle, 74. *Awards:* Charles F Montgomery Prize, Most Distinguished Contribution, Am Decorative Art; George Wittenborn Mem Book Award, Best of Art Publ. *Bibliog:* Alan G Artner (auth), The department of textiles, 1/16/78 & Peter Gorner (auth), Nubian textiles, 5/24/79, Chicago Tribune; Christa Thurman (auth), Textiles, Art Inst Chicago; Christa Thurman (auth), Museum Studies, Vol 23, No 1, Rooted in Chicago: Fifty Years of Textile Design Traditions, The Art Inst Chicago, 98. *Mem:* founder, The Textile Soc Am; Int & Nat Prof Asn related to textiles & conser; vpres, Centre Int d'Etude des Textiles Anciens Int & North American Rep; Int Comt Mus & Collections Costumes & Textiles; Costume Soc Am. *Publ:* Auth, Design in America: The Cranbrook Vision, 1925-1940

THURMER, ROBERT
SCULPTOR, GALLERY DIRECTOR
b Vienna, Austria, Oct 8, 53; US citizen. *Study:* Syracuse Univ, Col Visual & Performing Arts, BFA, 77; Univ Nebr, Lincoln, RI Sch Design, MFA, 81. *Work:* Cleveland Mus Art, Ohio; Everson Mus Art, Syracuse, NY; RI Sch Design Mus, Providence; Annmary Brown Mem, Providence, RI; B K Smith Gallery, Lake Erie Col, Painesville, Ohio. *Comn:* Indoor monumental installations, numerous pvt individuals, Cleveland, NY, San Diego & Chicago, 86-92; indoor monumental installation, Jacobs/Visconci/Jacobs, Cleveland, 90. *Exhib:* May Show, Cleveland Mus Art, 86-88; Int Selected Group Show, Lucia Gallery, NY, 89; Int Art Horizons, Art 54 Gallery, NY, 89-90; Sculpture Survey, Metro Gallery (Tri-C), Cleveland, 92; Body and Soul, Beck Ctr Mus, Lakewood, Ohio, 93; and others. *Collection Arranged:* Nature in Art, Cleveland Mus Art, 85; North Coast-New Imagery, Beck Ctr Mus, 86; Sculpture Exposed essay, Everson Mus Art, 89; Metaphysical Vistas, Cleveland State Art Gallery, 91; Vision Quest, Cleveland State Art Gallery, 92; Celia Rabinovitch, The Grotto Cycle, Beck Ctr Mus, 92; GAIA Coughs, Cleveland State Art Gallery, 93; A Place in Time: Great Lakes Regional Painting 1913-1958 (auth, catalog), Cleveland State Art Gallery, Ctr Creative Studies, Detroit, Mich, 94; Body of Evidence: The Figure in Contemporary Photography, 95. *Pos:* Exhib specialist, Cleveland Mus Art, 83-83, gallery dir, 90-; cur educ, Everson Mus Art, Syracuse, 88-90; gallery dir, Cleveland State Univ Art Gallery, 90-; mem, visual arts & craft review panel, Ohio Arts Coun, 92. *Teaching:* Lectr 3-d design, State Univ NY, Oswego, 82-83; instr 3-d design, Cazenovia Col, NY, 88-90; acad appointment 3-d design & sculpture, Cleveland State Univ, 90-; exhib design, Univ Calif Berkeley Exten, San Francisco, 94; instr museology, Cleveland State Univ, 94-, drawing, 95-. *Mem:* Col Art Asn; SPACES; New Organization Visual Arts; Am Asn Mus. *Media:* Miscellaneous. *Publ:* Auth, New World Folk Art 1492-1992, Cleveland State Univ, 92. *Mailing Add:* Cleveland State Univ Art Gallery 2307 Chester Ave Cleveland OH 44114

THURSTON, JACQUELINE BEVERLY
EDUCATOR, ARTIST, WRITER
b Cincinnati, Ohio, Jan 27, 1939. *Study:* Carnegie-Mellon Univ, BFA(painting), 61; Stanford Univ, MA(painting), 62. *Work:* Libr Cong; San Francisco Mus Mod Art; Oakland Mus, Calif; St Louis Mus Art; Henry Gallery, Univ Wash, Seattle; Los Angeles Co Art Mus, Calif; Carnegie Mus Art, Pittsburgh; Int Mus Photog, George Eastman House, Rochester, NY; Bibliotheque National; and other pub & pvt collections. *Exhib:* Observations/Translations--Four Photogr, Oakland Mus, Calif, 72; Two Photogr, Oakland Mus, 75; Photog 2 (exhib catalog), Jack Glenn Gallery, Newport Beach, Calif, 75; Am Photogr: Past into Present (exhib catalog), Seattle Mus Art, Wash, 76; one-person show, Susan Spiritus Gallery, Newport Beach, 77, 80, 94, 95 & 2002; Graham Nash Collection (exhib catalog), Univ Santa Clara, Calif, 79, San Francisco Mus Mod Art, 80; La Photographie Creative (exhib catalog), Pavillon des Arts, Paris, France, 84; Univ NMex Mus Art, Albuquerque, 2002; San Jose Mus Thirty-Fifth Anniversary Exhib (catalogue), 2004; San Jose Mus of Art Vital Signs, One Person Show, 2005. *Teaching:* Lectr, Stanford Univ, Calif; prof art, San Jose State Univ, Calif, 65-; lectr, CG Jung Inst, San Francisco, 89, San Francisco Psychoanalytic Inst, 92 & 94, Southern Calif Psychoanalytic Inst & Ctr Psychoanalytic Studies Creativity & Art, 96 & Am Inst Med Educ, Santa Fe, China, 98 & 2002; International Federation for Psychoanalytic Education, 2003; Dream Inst of Northern CA, 2004; Visiting Scholars, Sonoma State Univ, 2004. *Awards:* Nat Endowment Art Fel, 76 & 78; Fac Artist Residence, Arts Fac Inst, 88; Meritorius Performance & Prof Promise Award, San Jose State Univ, 89; CSU Summer Arts Exchange, 92; and others. *Bibliog:* Thomas Albright (auth), Observations/translations - four photographers, 9/11/72 & Two photographers, 8/6/75, San Francisco Chronicle; Joan Murray (auth), Observations/translations - four photographers, 9/23/72, Dorothy Burkhardt (auth), rev, 76 & Rebecca Palmer (auth), Dioramas, 86, Artweek; Ann Elliott Sherman (auth), Don't squeeze the shaman, Metro, 1/99; Jack Fisher (auth), Exploring myth & metaphor through her art, San Jose Mercury News, 1/24/99; Shari Kaplan (auth), Montalvo exhibit features 10 years of expression, Los Gatos Weekly-Times, 1/20/99. *Media:* All. *Res:* Nature of the creative process and artists' memories and dreams as sources for works of art. *Interests:* Hiking, Gardening. *Publ:* Coauth (with Ronald Carraherr), Optical Illusions and the Visual Arts, Van Nostrand Reinhold, 66; auth, Geoff Winningham & Jacqueline Thurston (exhib catalog), Calif Inst Technol, Pasadena, 78; Individual Visions (exhib catalog), 82 & A Show of Hands (exhib catalog), 82, San Francisco Mus Mod Art; contribr, The Voice of the Image, Cameraworks, 89. *Mailing Add:* San Jose State Univ Dept Art San Jose CA 95192-0089

TICE, GEORGE (ANDREW)
PHOTOGRAPHER, WRITER
b Newark, NJ, Oct 13, 38. *Study:* Newark Vocational & Tech High Sch, NJ, 55. *Hon Degrees:* William Patterson Univ, LHD, 2003. *Work:* Metrop Mus Art, NY; Mus Mod Art, NY; Art Inst Chicago; Bibliot Nat, Paris, France; Nihon Univ Art Mus, Japan. *Comn:* Two 55ft photog murals, Field Mus Natural Hist, Chicago, 75; photog, Liberty Park, Mus Mod Art, NY, 79; photog, Bank Archit, Mus Fine Arts, Houston, 90. *Exhib:* One-man shows, Metrop Mus Art, NY, 72, NJ State Mus, 76, Witkin Gallery, NY, 81 & Photo Gallery Int, Tokyo, 82, Nat Mus Photog, Film & Television, Bradford, Eng, 91, Newark Mus, 2006; Photog in Am, Whitney Mus, 74; Mirrors & Windows, Mus Mod Art, 79; and others. *Teaching:* Instr master class photog, The New Sch Social Research, New York, 70-98. *Awards:* Grand Prix, Festival d'Arles, France, 73; Nat Endowment for Arts Fel, 73; Guggenheim fel, 73-74; Fel, Nat Mus Photog & Bradford & Ilkley COl, Bradford, England, 90-91. *Bibliog:* Gerry Badger (auth), Recent books, British J Photog, 3/77; Barbara Lobron, Romantic notions, Camera Arts, 6/83; Peggy Sealfon (auth), Meet the masters, Peterson's Photographic, 10/83. *Publ:* Auth, Artie Van Blarcum, Addison House, 77; Urban Romantic, The Photographs of George Tice, Godine, 82; Hometowns, Graphic Soc, 88; Stone Walls, Grey Skies, Nat Mus Photog Film & Television, Eng, 91; Fields of Peace, Godine, 98; George Tice: Selected Photographs, 1953-1999, Godine, 2001; George Tice: Urban Landscapes, W.W. Norton & Co, 2002; Common Mementos, Lodima Press, Revere, Pa, 2005; Paterson II, Godine, 2006. *Dealer:* The Witkin Gallery 415 West Broadway New York NY 10012

TICHICH, RICHARD
EDUCATOR, ADMINISTRATOR
b Minneapolis, Minn, Jan 3, 47. *Study:* Univ Iowa, MA, 71; Univ Tex, MFA, 79. *Work:* Ga Coun Art, Atlanta; Maine Photog Workshop, Rockport; Minneapolis Inst Art, Minn. *Exhib:* Cult Olympics, Ga Coun Art, Atlanta, 93; one-man show, OK Harris Gallery, NY, 85. *Pos:* Photogr, Galveston Arts Ctr, 72-80, dir, 80-82; dept chmn, Ga Southern Univ, 82-. *Teaching:* Prof photog, Ga Southern Univ, 82-, dept chmn, 82-. *Awards:* Am Coun Educ Fel, 96. *Mem:* Col Art Asn; Nat Coun Art Admn (bd, 94-97). *Mailing Add:* Dept of Art Ga Southern Univ PO Box 8032 Statesboro GA 30460

TIEGREEN, ALAN F
PAINTER, ILLUSTRATOR
b Boise, Idaho, July 6, 35. *Study:* Univ Southern Miss, AB, 57; Art Ctr Col Design, 61. *Work:* High Mus Art, Atlanta, Ga. *Comn:* Painting, Atlanta Bur Cult Affairs, Ga, 75; mural, Simmons Corp, Atlanta, 76; paintings, Hilton Hotels, Knoxville, Tenn, 81. *Exhib:* Nat Drawing Exhib, High Mus, Atlanta, 65; Prof Art Am, Smithsonian Inst, Washington, DC, 66; SEastern Ann Exhib, 67 & Ga Artists Exhib, 68, High Mus, Atlanta; SEastern Regional, Columbus, Ga, 70. *Teaching:* Prof, Ga State Univ, 65-. *Awards:* First Award, Nat Drawing Soc, 65; Purchase Prize, Atlanta Arts Festival, Ga, 68; 1st Award, Decatur Sesquicentennial, Ga, 72. *Bibliog:* Clyde Burnette (auth), Charcoal drawings, Atlanta Newspapers, 2/80; article, Art Voices, 7/81; article, American Illustrators, Dell, 81. *Media:* Acrylic; Ink, Charcoal. *Publ:* Illusr, Doodle &

the Go-Cart, Viking, 72; illusr, Ramona the Brave, Morrow, 75; illusr, Silver Woven in my Hair, Atheneum, 77; illusr, Kelly's Creek, Crowell, 77; illusr, Ramona Age 8, Morrow, 81. *Dealer:* Artists Assocs Gallery 3261 Roswell Rd Atlanta GA 30305. *Mailing Add:* 4279 Wieuca Rd NE Atlanta GA 30342

TIEMANN, ROBERT E
PAINTER, SCULPTOR
b Austin, Tex, Jan 12, 36. *Study:* Univ Tex, Austin, BFA, 58; Univ Southern Calif, MFA, 60. *Work:* Los Angeles City Collection; San Antonio Mus Art, Tex; Am Tel & Tel Collection, NY; Univ Tex & Laguna Gloria Mus, Austin; Museo Cantonale d'Art, Lugano, Switz. *Comn:* Voyage to Cythera (mural), Charles Butt Found Hemisfair, San Antonio, Tex, 68; mural, Citizens Nat Bank, Austin, Tex, 74; Joffrey Ballet Program Cover, Soc Performing. *Exhib:* Invitational Texas Artists Show, Dallas Mus Fine Arts, 72; Laguna Gloria Art Mus, Austin, Tex, 74; San Antonio Mus Art, Tex, 82; Mus Dhond Dhgenens, Deurle, Belgium, 91; Panza DiBiumo: The Eighties & Nineties from the Collection, Mus Cantonale d'Arte, Lugano, Switz, 92. *Pos:* Art therapist, Audie Murphy Veterans Hosp, San Antonio, 75-77; design consult, Chumney-Urrutia Archit Firm, San Antonio, 85-. *Teaching:* Prof art, Trinity Univ, San Antonio, 65-, chmn dept, 82-88; prof art, Harvard Univ, summers, 82-85, Univ Tex, San Antonio, 81, Hanover Col, 86. *Awards:* Nat Endowment Arts Grant, 68; Fac Res & Develop Grant, Trinity Univ, San Antonio, 78. *Bibliog:* Susan Platt (auth), rev, Artforum, 4/80; Frances Colpitt (auth), Robert Tiemann/Annabelle & Robert Tiemann, A Survey: Twenty Years (catalog & essay), Blue Star Art Space, 92; Frances Colpitt (auth), article, Artspace, 9/92. *Mem:* Col Art Asn; The Blue Star-Contemp Art for San Antonio (bd mem, 86 & 93-94). *Publ:* Auth, art criticism column, San Antonio Express-News, Tex, 78. *Mailing Add:* Dept Art Trinity Univ 715 Stadium Dr San Antonio TX 78212

TIERNEY, PATRICK LENNOX
HISTORIAN, EDUCATOR, LECTURER
b Weston, WVa, Jan 28, 14. *Study:* Univ Calif, Los Angeles, EdB(cum laude), 36; Columbia Univ, New York, MA, 44; Sogetsu-Ryu, Tokyo, Japan, Seizan I, 52. *Pos:* Cur, Asian Art, San Diego Mus Art, 74-82; mem & cur Asian art, Mingei Mus, San Diego, 77-; Art Dir, Japanese Friendship Garden, San Diego. *Teaching:* Chmn arts fac, Pasadena City Col, Calif, 46-71; lectr, Univ Calif, Los Angeles & San Diego, 52-71; assoc dean col fine arts & prof hist Oriental art, Univ Utah, 71-94, emeritus, 94-; prof, Univ Pittsburgh, 89-90, 90-91. *Awards:* Emmy, Acad Television Arts & Sci, 67; Hons Citation, Resolution of Bd Trustees, Pasadena City Col, Calif, 71. *Mem:* Royal Asiatic Soc, Seoul, Korea; Pacificulture Found, Pasadena, Calif (dir, mus div, 61-70, mem bd dir, Asian Mus, 61-); Acad Television Arts & Sci; Salt Lake Art Ctr (mem bd dir, 71-); Japan-Am Soc, Southern Calif (dir, 72-); Asian Art Mus, San Francisco; and others. *Media:* Sumi-e. *Res:* Folk arts of Japan. *Collection:* Japanese Folk Arts, Painting, Prints, Ceramics and Textiles. *Publ:* Coauth, Japan, Int Publ, 58; coauth, Chanoyu, as a form of non literary art criticism, Chanoyu J, Kyoto, 76; coauth, Cambodia, Khmer Remains, 79; auth, Wabi Sabi, A New Look at Japanese Design, 2000. *Mailing Add:* 3758 Adonis Dr Salt Lake City UT 84124

TIGERMAN, STANLEY
PAINTER, ARCHITECT
b Chicago, Ill, Sept, 20, 30. *Study:* Mass Inst Technol, 48-49; Inst Design, 49-50; Yale Univ, BArch, 60 & MArch, 61. *Work:* Art Inst Chicago; Metrop Mus Art, NY; Mus Mod Art; Deutshes Arch Mus. *Comn:* Modular structure, Metrop Structures, Chicago, 71. *Exhib:* Eight Chicago Artists, Walker Art Ctr, Minneapolis, Minn, 65; one-man shows, Evanston Art Ctr, Ill, 69, Art Res Ctr, Kansas City, Mo, 69 & Springfield Arts Asn, Ill, 70; IBA, Deutches Architekus Mus, Frankfurt, WGerm, 86; Chicago Arch 1872-1922, Art Inst, Chicago, 89; Gulbenkian Found, Lisbon, Portugal, 89. *Pos:* Prin, Stanley Tigerman & Assocs, Chicago, 62-. *Teaching:* Prof archit & art, Univ Ill, Chicago Circle, 65-71, dir, Sch Arch, 80-; archit-in-residence, Am Acad in Rome, 80. *Awards:* AIA-DBA Suburban Village, 91; AIA Interior Archit Award Excellence, Am Standard, 92; AIA Int Archit Award, The Ernest Graham Study Ctr Art Inst Chicago, 92; AIA INT Archit Award, The Arts Club Chicago, Ill Acad Fine Arts, 92. *Bibliog:* R A M Stern (auth), New Directions in American Architecture, Braziller, 69; Faulkner & Ziegfield (auth), Art Today, Holt, Rinehart & Winston, 69; Dahinden (auth), Urban Structures of the Future, Praeger, 72. *Mem:* Am Inst Architects; Yale Art Asn; Ill Arts Coun; Yale Club NY; Arts Club Chicago. *Media:* Acrylic. *Publ:* VERSUS: An American Architect's Alternatives, 82; Chicago's Architectural Heritage: A Romantic Classical Image--Work of the Current Generation of Chicago Architects, Arquitectura, 79; Stanley Tigerman Architoons, 88; The Architecture of Exile, 88; Stanley Tigerman: Buildings & Projects 1966-1989. *Mailing Add:* 910 N Lakeshore Dr No 2916 Chicago IL 60611

TILESTON, JACKIE
ARTIST
b Manila, Phillippines, 60. *Study:* Yale Univ, BA in fine arts (painting), 83; Ind Univ, Bloomington, MFA(painting), 88. *Work:* Mus Fine Arts, Houston; Dallas Mus Art, Tex; JP Morgan Chase. *Exhib:* Solo exhibs, Introductions, WA Graham Gallery, Houston, 90, New Work, 92, New Work, Lawing Gallery, Houston, 95, New Paintings, 97, Jackie Tileston: New Paintings, Satellite Space, Univ Tex, San Antonio, 98, Jackie Tileston, Univ NMex, Albuquerque, 2000, Empty and Full, Barbara Davis Gallery, Houston, 2003, Cures for Cosmophobia, Philadelphia Art Alliance, 2003, Heterotopia, Zg Gallery, Chicago, 2005, Not Always So, Barbara Davis Gallery, Houston, 2006, Surface Tension, The Painting Center, NY, 2006; numerous group shows. *Teaching:* taught, Univ Houston, Rice Univ; asst prof, painting Univ New Mex; from asst prof to assoc prof, fine arts, Univ Pa, 2000-. *Awards:* Mid-Am Arts Alliance/Nat Endowment for the Arts, 94; Pew Fel in the Arts, 2004; Bellagio Residency, Rockefeller Found, Italy, 2004; Guggenheim Fel, 2006. *Bibliog:* review, Art in America, 5/98; review, Art News, 12/2003. *Mem:* Col Art Asn. *Dealer:* Zg Gallery 300 W Superior St Chicago Ill 60610; Holly Johnson Gallery 1411 Dragon St Dallas Tex 75207; Barbara Davis Gallery 4411 Montrose Blvd Houston Tex 77006

TILLENIUS, CLARENCE INGWALL
PAINTER, WRITER
b Sandridge, Man, Aug 31, 1913. *Study:* Teulon Col, with A J Musgrove; Univ Winnipeg, hon LLD, 70. *Work:* Pavilion Gallery, Winnipeg, Manitoba; Whyte Mus, Banff, Alta, Govt Manitoba. *Comn:* Collection of wildlife painting, North American Life Assurance Co, Winnipeg, 54-80; dioramas, habitat groups, Nat Mus Can, Ottawa, Ont, 60-72, BC Mus, Victoria, 65-70 & Mus Alta, Edmonton, 72-74; dioramas, paintings, Man Mus Man & Nature, Winnipeg, 69-79. *Exhib:* Two one-man shows, London Art Gallery, London Shute Inst, 54; one-man exhibs, Monarch Life Bldg, 62, Whitney Gallery Western Art, Cody, Wyo, 64, Man Mus Man & Nature, 74 & Glenbow-Alta Inst, 75; Soc Wildlife Art Nations Opening Exhib, Eng, 88; Retrospective, Mus Man & Nature, 98. *Pos:* Diorama dir, Nat Mus Can, Ottawa, 62-72. *Teaching:* Lectr art appreciation, Man, 50-52; lectr wildlife painters, Glenbow Inst, 70; dir wildlife drawings, Okanagan Summer Sch Arts, Penticton, BC, 73-82. *Awards:* Man Centennial Medal Honor, Gov Gen, Prov Man, 72; Seton Medal, 85. *Bibliog:* Peter Kelly & Paul Guyot (coauth), Tillenius on the Prairies (film), Can Broadcasting Corp, 63; Eric Mitchell (auth), Clarence Tillenius, Nature Can Mag, 73; Richard Savage (auth), Tokens of Myself--Tillenius, the Man and the Art (film), Wilderness Trail Motion Picture Co, 78, rev and copyrighted by artist, 84. *Mem:* Explorers Club, NY; Soc Animal Artists; life mem Man Naturalist Soc; Royal Geographical Soc, London, Eng; Soc Wildlife Art Nations, Eng. *Media:* Oil, Watercolor. *Res:* Lifetime study of wild animals, wilderness travels across North America into Yukon and the arctic. *Publ:* Illusr, Little Giant, 51, Orphan of the North, 58, Days of the Buffalo, 98; illusr & auth, Fur Bearers of Canada, 51, Buffalo, 92; Monarchs of the Canadian Wilds, 54-75; auth, Sketchpad Out of Doors, 56 & 62, Tillenius, 98. *Dealer:* Loch and Mayberry Fine Art Inc 306 St Marys Rd Winnipeg Manitoba Canada R2H 158. *Mailing Add:* 121 Parkside Dr Winnipeg MB R3J IMI Canada

TILLEY, LEWIS LEE
PAINTER, VIDEO ARTIST
b Parrott, Ga, May 17, 21. *Study:* High Mus Sch Art, 37-39; Emory Univ, 37-39; Univ Ga, BFA, 42; Colorado Springs Fine Arts Ctr, with Boardman Robinson, Adolph Dehn & John Held, 42-45; Inst Allende, Mex, MFA, 68; British Film Inst, 72-75, Univ Ga, Cortona, Italy, 85. *Work:* Post Card No 2, Colorado Springs Fine Arts Ctr, Colo; Ga Art Asn; Southern States Art League; Cañnon City Art Ctr, Colo. *Comn:* Mural, Broadmoor Cheyenne Mountain Zoo, Colorado Springs, 58; dragon wall mural, Victor Hornbein House, Denver, 59; mural, First Nat Bank, Colorado Springs, 59; four polyester resin sculptures, Colorado Springs Eye Clinic, 60; exterior wall mural, Horace Mann Jr High Sch, Colorado Springs, 62. *Exhib:* Am Fedn Arts; Graphic Arts Chicago; Denver Ann & Biennial; Artists West of Mississippi; Washington Cathedral Relig Exhib; Southern State Art League; Dallas Print & Drawing Show. *Pos:* Producer & dir, Alexander Film Co, 58-62; artist-in-residence, Univ Ga, Cotona, Italy, 85; columnist, Your Amiga, London. *Teaching:* Instr painting, life drawing & design, Colorado Springs Fine Arts Ctr, 45-51; prof art, Univ Southern Colo, 65-86, prof emer, currently. *Awards:* First Purchase Award for oil, Canon City Blossom Festival, 69; First Purchase Award for oil, Colo State Fair, 70. *Bibliog:* Discovery No 49, Mod Photog, 58; Info 64, 9/85. *Media:* All Media, Computer Graphics. *Publ:* Auth, History of writing and painting, 63; illusr, English with the twins, 63; History of medicine, 63; ed, The story of Nok culture, 63. *Mailing Add:* 241 Huckaby St NE Parrott GA 31777

TILLMAN, PATRICIA ANN
SCULPTOR
Study: Univ Tex, Austin BFA(painting, drawing), 76; Univ Okla, Norman, MFA(painting, mixed media constructions), 78. *Exhib:* Solo shows, Koehler Cult Ctr, San Antonio Col, Tex, 80, Brown-Lupton Gallery, Tex Christian Univ, Ft Worth, Tex, 84 & Ft Worth Gallery, Tex, 85, 87 & 90; Texas Exhibit (auth catalog), Nat Mus Arts, Washington, DC, 88; A Century of Sculpture in Texas, 1889-1989 (auth, catalog), Archer M Huntington Gallery, Univ Tex Austin, 89; Austin Visual Arts Asn, Tex, 90; and others. *Teaching:* Adj lectr art dept, Baylor Univ, Waco, Tex, 82, part-time adj lectr, 83-89; part-time instr art dept, McLennan Community Col, Waco, Tex, 83-85, adj instr, 85 & 90; lectr, var univ & col, Tex. *Awards:* Nominee, Awards Visual Arts, 86, 87; Nat Endowment Arts Fel Grant, 86. *Bibliog:* Annette Carlozzi (auth), 50 Texas Artists, A Critical Selection of Painters and Sculptors, Chronicle Bks, San Francisco, 98, 99, 86; Mark Smith (auth), Laguna Gloria exhibit embodies substance of women's souls, Austin Am-Statesman, F4, 3/23/89; Janet Kutner (auth), Figurative art: Patricia Tillman's sculpture evolves, Dallas Morning News, 5C-6C, 5/5/90; and others. *Mailing Add:* 920 Simon Dr Cedar Hill TX 75104

TILTON, JOHN ELLSWORTH
CERAMIST
b Red Bank, NJ, Nov 8, 44. *Study:* Univ Fla, MS in Maths, 1970; Univ South Fla, MFA in Ceramics, 1972. *Work:* Lowe Art Mus, Miami; City of Winter Park, Fla; Cigna Corp, Philadelphia; Walt Disney Corp, Orlando; Blue Cross/Blue Shield NJ. *Mailing Add:* 16211 Northwest 88 Terr Alachua FL 32615

TIMMAS, OSVALD
PAINTER, LECTURER
b Estonia, Sept 17, 19; Can citizen. *Study:* Tartu State Univ, Atelier Sch Tartu & Tallinn, Estonia, with Nicholas Kummits & Gunther Reindorff. *Work:* London Art Mus, Ont; Art Gallery Hamilton; Art Gallery Windsor; Rodman Hall Art Ctr, St Catharines, Ont; Art Gallery Ont, Toronto. *Exhib:* Can Watercolors, Drawings &

Prints, Nat Gallery Can, Ottawa, 66; Audubon Artists, 66-69, Am Watercolor Soc, 66, 67 & 69 & Nat Acad Design, 67, 68 & 71, NY; Royal Can Acad Arts, Nat Gallery Can, 70; OSA Image (circulating show), Ont Pub Galleries, 75-77 & 79; Watercolour Painting in Canada, A Survey, Univ Waterloo, 79; one-man shows, Pollock Gallery, Merton Gallery, Univ Toronto & St Mary's Univ; and others. *Awards:* CSPWC Hon Award, Sarnia Art Gallery, 81; Award, Adirondacks Nat Exhib, Am Watercolors, 82, 88, 91 & 92; Medal Hon, AWS Both Ann Int Exhib, NY, 97. *Bibliog:* Anthony Ferry (auth), A floating world, 2/20/65 & It's now time for Timmas, 11/11/65, Toronto Star; Stevens (auth), Osvald Timmas, La Rev Mod, 11/66. *Mem:* Royal Can Acad Arts; Am Watercolor Soc; Can Soc Painters Watercolor; Ont Soc Artists (vpres, 71-75). *Media:* Watercolor, Acrylic. *Dealer:* Harbour Gallery 1697 Lakeshore Rd West Mississauga Ontario LSJ 1J4. *Mailing Add:* 776 Marlee Ave Toronto ON M6B 3J9 Canada

TIMMS, PETER ROWLAND
MUSEUM DIRECTOR
b Philadelphia, Pa, Aug 26, 42. *Study:* Brown Univ, Providence, RI, BA, 64; Harvard Univ, MA, 69 & PhD(anthrop), 76. *Pos:* Dir, Fitchburg Art Mus, Mass, 73-; trustee, Applewild Sch, Fitchburg, Mass, 82-92, Nashua Arts & Sci Ctr, 83-86 & Nat Plastics Mus, Leominster, Mass, 86-97. *Teaching:* Instr, Int Col, Beirut, Lebanon, 68; teaching fel, Harvard Univ & Mass Inst Technol, 69-73; vis lectr, Fitchburg State Col, 78; instr, Applewild Sch, 78-79. *Mem:* Am Asn Mus (chmn, State Comt Energy, 78); Applewild Sch (trustee, 82-); Nashua Arts & Sci Ctr (trustee, 83-). *Publ:* Auth, Flint Implements of the Old Stone Age, Shire Publ, United Kingdom, 74, 2nd ed, 79; consult ed & illusr, Human Biology & Ecology, Albert Damon, WW Norton & Co, New York, 77; auth, Accreditation and the small museum, Mus News, 7-8/80. *Mailing Add:* c/o Fitchburg Art Mus 185 Elm St Fitchburg MA 01420

TIMOTHY, GROVER See Whiten, Tim (Timothy) Grover

TIMPANO, ANNE
MUSEUM DIRECTOR, HISTORIAN
b Osaka, Japan; US citizen. *Study:* Col William & Mary, Williamsburg, Va, BA, 72; George Washington Univ, Washington, DC, MA, 83. *Collection Arranged:* William Christenberry: A Southern Perspective, 87; A Select View: American Paintings from Columbus Museum, (auth catalog), 87; Paintings and Sculpture from the Permanent Collection, 91; Starstruck: Images from Hollywood's Golden Age, (auth catalog), 92; Enriching the Future (auth, catalog), Univ Cincinnati Fine Arts Collection, Ohio, 95; A Different Drummer: Benny Andrews, the Music Series (auth, catalog), 99; Focus 2000: Juried Photography Exhib, 2000; William Christenberry: Architecture/Archetype (auth catalog), 2001; John Walker: Recent Painting and Prints, 2002; Katherine Kadish: Paintings and Monotypes, 2005; Univ Cincinnati Fine Arts Collection permanent installation, 2005; Making an Impression: Etchings & Engravings from Permanent Collection, 2006. *Pos:* Docent prog coord, Nat Mus Am Art, Washington, DC, 77-80, res asst, 80-83 & prog mgt asst, 83-86; dir, Columbus Mus, Ga, 86-93; dir DAAP Galleries, Univ Cincinnati, 93-. *Teaching:* Adj prof Mus Mgt, Univ Cincinnati, 97-; dir Mus Studies Prog, Univ Cincinnati, 2000-. *Awards:* David Lloyd Kreeger Prize in the History of Art. *Mem:* Am Asn Mus; Col Art Asn. *Res:* American art & architecture. *Mailing Add:* DAAP Galleries Univ Cincinnati PO Box 210016 Cincinnati OH 45221-0016

TIMS, MICHAEL WAYNE See Bronson, A A (Michael Wayne Tims)

TING, WALASSE
PAINTER
b Wuxi, China, Oct 13, 29. *Work:* Rockefeller Univ, Mus Mod Art, Metrop Mus Art & Solomon R Guggenheim Mus, NY; Chicago Art Inst, Ill; Carnegie Inst, US Steel & Gulf Oil Corp, Pittsburgh; Albright-Knox Art Gallery, Buffalo; Mus of Fine Arts, Boston; and others. *Exhib:* Paul Facchetti, Paris, France, 54; Martha Jackson Gallery, 60; Carnegie Inst Int, 61, 64, 67 & 70; Galerie Birch, 63; Galerie France, 68; Lefebre Gallery, 71; solo exhibs, P Gallery, Hamburg, 93 & 94, Luc Pieters Gallery, Knokke, Belgium, 93, Galerie l'Orangerie, St Paul-de-Vence, 93, Lung Men Gallery, Taipei, 94, Kunstforum, Belgium, 94, Tresors, Singapore, 94 & Shanghai Art Mus, 97; and many others. *Awards:* Guggenheim Fel, 77. *Publ:* Auth, Rice Paper Painting, 84; Jolies Dames, 88; Blue Sky, 93; Dream, 95; A Very Hot Day, 97; and others. *Dealer:* Lefebre Gallery 47 E 77th St New York NY 10028. *Mailing Add:* 463 West St New York NY 10014

TINKLER, BARRIE KEITH
PAINTER
b Tyler, Tex, 35. *Study:* Univ Houston, BFA, 62; pvt study with Guido Fulignot; Mus Fine Arts, Houston (scholor); study with Emil Bisttram. *Work:* Canvas murals, Historic Garcia Opera House, Socorro, NMex; Hotel Plaza, Liberty Bank & Banker's tile Bldg, Houston, Tex; H E Stratagraph Inc, Lafayette, La. *Comn:* Portrait, comn by R C Gorman, 83. *Exhib:* Art Ctr for Southwestern La & La Landmarks Soc Exhib of La Artists, Lafayette; Taos Festival of Arts, NMex, 80; Art Expo, NY, 84; Daffodil Arabian Horse Asn, Washington, DC, 84. *Awards:* Purchase Prize, Brazosport Art League, Tex; First Prize, J K Ralston Mus & Art Ctr, Sidney, Mont, 82; Second Place, 11th Ann Nat Small Painting Exhib, 83, NMex Art League. *Publ:* John Gaines (auth), article, Astrology J, 5/70; Houston Scene Mag, 8/76; Prime Times, Albuquerque, NMex, 82

TINSLEY, BARRY
SCULPTOR
b Roanoke, Va, Feb 19, 42. *Study:* Col William & Mary, Williamsburg, Va, BA, 64; Sch Art & Hist, Univ Iowa, Iowa City, MA, 67, MFA, 68. *Work:* S W & B M Koffler Found Collection, Nat Mus Am Art, Washington, DC; Lakeview Mus, Peoria, Ill; Ctr Visual Arts Gallery, Normal, Ill. *Comn:* Jetty (corten steel), comn by City of Chicago, Ill, 80; Silver Oak, (stainless steel & painted aluminum), Green Co, Miami, Fla, 85; Silver Blade (stainless steel relief), Borg Warner Corp, Chicago, Ill, 84; Urban Moraine, comn by State of Ill, Chicago, 84. *Exhib:* Solo exhibs, Ill State Mus, Springfield, 79, Piedmont Arts Asn, Martinsville, Va, 84 & Ordean Ct, Tweed Mus, Duluth, Minn, 86; Mayor Byrne's Mile of Sculpture, Int Art Expo, Navy Pier, Chicago, Ill, 82; Festival of the Arts, Arts Coun Oklahoma City, 85; Chicago Sculpture, Rockford Col, Ill, 85; Sculpture Campus Tour, Univ Tenn, Knoxville, 85-86; Traveling Exhib, New Traditions in Sculpture, Ill Grant, 86. *Pos:* Treas, Chicago Sculpture Soc, 82-; vis artist, Visual Arts Ctr Alaska, 83; bd mem, Sculpture Chicago, Burham Park Planning Asn, 84-. *Teaching:* Instr art & sculpture, Eastern Ky Univ, Richmond, 68-70; assoc prof art & sculpture, Ill State Univ, Normal, 70-78. *Awards:* Dick Blick Mem Award, Galex X, Galesburg, Ill, 76; Chicago Sculpture Syposium Award, 83. *Mem:* Ill Arts Coun (visual artist panel); Chicago Artists Coalition (adv bd, 86). *Mailing Add:* c/o Thomas McCormick Gallery 835 West Washington Blvd Chicago IL 60607

TIRAVANIJA, RIRKRIT
SCULPTOR
b Buenos Aires, Arg, 61. *Study:* Ont Col Art, Toronto, 81; Banff Ctr Sch Fine Arts, Can, 84; Art Inst Chicago, 85; Whitney Independent Studies Prof, New York, 86. *Exhib:* Solo exhibs, Paula Allen Gallery, NY, 90, Randy Alexander Gallery, NY, 91, 303 Gallery, NY, 92 & 95, Randolph St Gallery, Chicago, 93, Jack Hanley Gallery, San Francisco, 94, Schipper & Krome, Ger, 94, The Modern Inst, Glasgow, Eng, 99, The Land, Galerie Changtal Crousel, Paris, 2001, He Promised, Secession, Vienna, Austria, 2002, In the Future Everything Will Be Chrome, Gavin Brown's enterprise, NY, 2003, Retrospective, Mus Bomans Van Beuningen, Rotterdam, Netherlands, 2004, ARC, Mus d'Art Moderne de la Ville de Paris, 2005; Simply Made in Am, Aldrich Mus Contemp Art, Conn, 93; Sleepless Nights, PS1 Mus, Queens, NY, 93; L'Hiver de l'Amour, Musee d'Art Moderne de la Ville de Paris, France, 94; Whitney Mus Am Art Biennial, NY, 95; Wexner Ctr, Columbus, Ohio, 99; Points of Departure, San Francisco Mus Modern Art, 2001; En Route, Serpentine Gallery, London, 2002; Elephant Juice, Kurimanzutto, Mexico City, 2003; Perfect Timeless Repetition, Alte Gerhardsen, Berlin, 2003; Small: The Object in Film, Video and Slide Installation, Whitney Mus Am Art, NY, 2004; Nothing Big, Inst Contemporary Art, Philadelphia, 2004; Peace Tower, Day for Night, Whitney Biennial, 2006. *Pos:* Pres The Land Foundation; adv bd mem New Media Inst, Univ Chiang Mai, Thailand, 2003, Tokyo Wondersite Cultural Arts Center, Tokyo, 2003, Carnegie Int, 2002-04. *Teaching:* Guest prof and vis artist Nat Acad Fine Arts, Oslo, Norway, 2001; guest prof Stadelschule Staalich Hochschule Bildende Kunst, Frankfurt, 2001, Royal Danish Art Acad, 2001-02; adj asst prof Columbia Univ, 1999-2000; assoc prof, Univ Venice, 2003-04, Columbia Univ, 2001-. *Awards:* Hugo Boss Prize; Lucelia Artist Award, Smithsonian Am Art Mus; Goron Matta Clark Grant; Louis Comfort Tiffany Award. *Bibliog:* Rainald Schumacher (auth), Koln Kritik, Flash Art, 51, summer 94; Gavin Brown (auth), Otherthings Elsewhere, Flash Art, 102, summer 94; Bruce Hainley (auth), Reviews, Artforum, 86, 1/95

TISCHLER, GARY
CRITIC
Study: Arts and entertainment critic Wash Diplomat, Wheaton, Md; art and entertainment critic Georgetowner, Wash. *Mailing Add:* Georgetowner 1054 Potomac St Washington DC 20007

TISCH SUSSMAN, LAURIE
GALLERY DIRECTOR
Study: Duke Univ; Catholic Univ, MFA. *Pos:* Chmn, Ctr Arts Educ Inc, Children's Mus Manhattan; pres, Laurie Tisch Found; cmnr, New York City Dept Cult Affairs; Secy, Whitney Mus Am Art, currently; bd dir, Mattel Entertainment, Food & Agr Orgn Schwartz, currently. *Mem:* NY State Coun Arts. *Mailing Add:* c/o Witney Mus Am Art 945 Madison Ave New York NY 10021

TOBIA, BLAISE JOSEPH
PHOTOGRAPHER, EDUCATOR
b Brooklyn, NY, Jan 20, 1953. *Study:* Brooklyn Col, with Walter Rosenblum, George Krause, Bob D'Allesandro & Philip Pearlstein, BA, 74; Univ Calif, San Diego, with David Antin, Allan Kaprow & Newton Harrison, MFA, 77. *Work:* Archives City of New York; Delaware Mus Art; World Lomographic Soc; many pvt collections. *Comn:* Many commissioned photographic works as well as documentations of artist-performances. *Exhib:* Encampments, Randolph St Gallery, Chicago, 89; Biennial '91, Delaware Art Mus, 91; Surveillance: 6 Days, CEPA Gallery, Buffalo, 91; Am Pie: Myth Representation, Abington Arts Ctr, Philadelphia, 92; Crimes & Punishments, Philadelphia Art Alliance, 95; New Means, Silicon Gallery, Philadelphia, 96; Contemp-Italianate, Loyola Mary Mount Univ, Los Angeles, Calif, 98; Cult Syntax: Recent Work of Blaise Tobia, Drexel Univ, 2000, Tulane Univ, 2001; Blaise Tobia, Oskar Friedl Gallery, Chicago, 2002; Direct Objects, Delaware Ctr for Contemp Art, 2005. *Pos:* Prof Media Arts, Drexel Univ. *Teaching:* Vis photogr, Univ Calif, San Diego, 79, Wayne State Univ, Detroit, 81; prof photog, Drexel Univ, 85-. *Awards:* Ford Found Grant, 77; Fac Res Award, Drexel Univ, Philadelphia, 86; Nat Endowment Humanities Res Fel, 88. *Bibliog:* Miles Orvell (auth), Democracy, Disorder, and the New Political Art, American Pie (exhib catalog), Abington/CEPA, 92; Wit on Wry: Humor in Photography, NY Times, 93; New Means, Philadelphia Inquirer, 96; Joseph Gregory (auth), Some Notes on Interpretation; exhbn catalog, Design Arts Gallery, Drexel; Joseph Gregory (auth), Dangerous Curves: Poetry and Politics in the work of Blaise Tobia, 2003. *Mem:* Col Art Asn; Soc Photog Educ. *Media:* Photography, Digital and Chemical. *Interests:* Image and text; panoramic imagery; social and political issues. *Publ:* Undermining Documentary, Afterimage, 90; auth, From Resistance to Embrace: Text/Image Relationships in 20th-Century

Fine-Art Photographic Practice, Word & Image, fall 92; Art & Society- Monthly Colum Co-auth with Virginia Maksymowicz, The Witnes, 1993-94; Change of Scenery, Silicon Gallery, 2000; Digital Printmaking, Photography, London & UK, 2001; Digital Photography Encyclopedia of 20th Century Photographers, 2005. *Dealer:* TandM Arts, Philadelphia PA. *Mailing Add:* c/o T and M Arts 3719 Lancaster Ave Philadelphia PA 19104-2415

TOBIAS, RICHARD
PAINTER
b New York, NY, 52. *Study:* Philadelphia Col Art, Pa, 72-74; Independent Study Prog, Whitney Mus Am Art, 73-75; Pratt Inst, BFA, 75. *Exhib:* Solo exhibs, Brooke Alexander, 84, 86, 87 & 91; Black & White, Art Advisory Serv, Mus Mod Art, NY, 86 Abstract Painting, Asher Faure Gallery, Los Angeles, 87; Generations of Geometry, Whitney Mus Am Art, NY, 87; Logical Foundations, Art Advisory Serv, Mus Mod Art, NY, 88; Visiting Artists, Ewing Gallery, Univ Tenn, Knoxville,88; Columnar, Hudson River Mus, Yonkers, NY, 88; Geometric Abstraction, The Private Side, Real Art, NY; Vis Artists 10th Anniversary Exhib, Ewing Gallery, Univ Tenn, Knoxville, 92. *Teaching:* Vis artist, Univ Tenn, Knoxville, 88, Ill State Univ, 92. *Awards:* Edward F Albee Found, Montauk, NY, 83; Pollock-Krasner Found, New York, 86; Nat Endowment Arts, 87. *Bibliog:* Jed Perl (auth), Versions of pastoral, New Criterion, 6/86; Margaret R Lazzri (auth), Evasion of abstraction, Artweek, 5/9/87; Jed Perl, Where do we come from? Where are we going?, Mod Painters, autumn 91. *Media:* Acrylic, Oil. *Dealer:* Brooke Alexander Inc 59 Wooster St New York NY 10012

TOBIAS, ROBERT PAUL
PAINTER, SCULPTOR
b Reading, Pa, Dec 14, 33. *Study:* Ariz State Univ, BS(appl arts, ceramics), 64, MFA(sculpture), 69. *Work:* Matthews Ctr, Ariz State Univ, Tempe; Univ Ariz Mus Art, Tucson; Ariz Western Col, Yuma; Phoenix Art Mus, Ariz. *Comn:* Monumental sculpture, La Placita, City of Tucson, 74. *Exhib:* Painting, 1973 Four Corners Exhib, Phoenix & 1974 Mainstreams, Marietta Col, Ohio; sculpture, Nelson Art Mus, Kansas City, Mo, 70, Yuma Invitational, 73 & Arizona's Outlook '74, Tucson Art Ctr. *Teaching:* Instr design, Univ Kans, Lawrence, 69-71; assoc prof sculpture & design, Univ Ariz, Tucson, 71-. *Awards:* Sculpture Purchase Award, Wis State Univ, Platteville, 67; Painting Award, 1972 Yuma Invitational, Ariz Western Col; Sculpture Exhib Award, Tucson Art Mus, 74. *Bibliog:* Tobias show in Lawrence, Kansas City Star, 3/22/70; Darrell Dobraus (auth), Artists review, Desert Silhouette, Tucson, 10/75. *Dealer:* Gekas/Nicholas Gallery 6538 East Tangue Verde Rd Tucson AZ 85715. *Mailing Add:* 5600 W Moore Rd Marana AZ 85653-4109

TOBIN, NANCY
DESIGNER, EDITOR
b New York, NY, Aug 31, 43. *Study:* Syracuse Univ Sch Art, BFA, 65; SUNY, Buffalo, MA, 92. *Pos:* Art dir, Buffalo Mag, 65-75, asst ed, 65-69; art critic, Courier Express, Buffalo, 71-77, ed, Sunday Mag, 78-81; news art dir, Buffalo Courier Express, formerly; freelance writer, Art News, New York Times & Progressive Archit; design dir, Asbury Park Press, 87-89; dir publ, Univ at Buffalo, 89-92; managing ed, Albany Times-Union, 93-95; pres, Tobin Paperworks, 95-. *Teaching:* asst prof, S I Newhouse Sch Pub Commun, Syracuse Univ, 85-87. *Awards:* Awards for Ed Content & Visual Content for Buffalo Mag, Am Asn Com Publ, 66-71; Merit Award for Criticism, Am Newspaper Guild, 75; 1st & 2nd Place Awards, newspaper design & headline writing, Am Newspaper Guild; Award of Excellence, Soc Newspaper Design, 84, 87, 88, 89 & 90. *Mem:* Soc Newspaper Design (bd mem, pres, 93); Albright-Knox Art Gallery Coun for the Support & Advan Educ. *Publ:* Auth, Understanding changes in the growth and shape of newspaper art departments, Soc Newspaper Design, 10/85

TOBLER, GISELA ERNA MARIA
PAINTER, ARCHITECT
b Hamburg, Ger, Mar 29, 39; Swiss citizen. *Study:* Kunstgewerbeschule, Zurich, Switz, scholar grafique designer, 56-59. *Work:* Museo de Arte de La Universidad, Mexico City; Univ Tex, Austin. *Exhib:* 15 one-woman shows, 36 collective expositions; Museo de Arte dela Universidad, Mexico City, Los Colores en el Piensamento, Museo-Casa Diego Rivera, Guanajuato, Mex, 97; Mujeres y Sus Colores, Tallera-de Alfaro Sigueiros, Cuernavaca, Estado de Morelos, 98. *Media:* Oil. *Publ:* Contribr, Cien Mujeres en La Plastica Mexicana, UNAM-Muca, 97; Demos-Carta Demografica Sobre Mexico, UNAM-Raul Benitez Zenteno, 98 & Mujeres de Colores. *Mailing Add:* Otono 17 Col Merced Gomez Mexico DF Mexico

TODD, MICHAEL CULLEN
SCULPTOR, PAINTER
b Omaha, Nebr, June 20, 35. *Study:* Univ Notre Dame, BFA, 57; Univ Calif, Los Angeles, MA, 59; Woodrow Wilson Fel, 59; Fulbright Fel, France, 61. *Work:* Whitney Mus Am Art, NY; Los Angeles Co Mus Art; Oakland Mus; Hirshhorn Mus & Sculpture Garden, Washington; Metrop Mus, NY; and others. *Comn:* Pac Mutual Insurance, Costa Mesa, Calif. *Exhib:* Whitney Mus Am Art Sculpture Ann, 64-70; Sculpture of 60's, Los Angeles Co Mus Art, 65 & Philadelphia Mus, 66; Living Am Art, Maeght Found, France, 71; Exhibs Large Scale Sculpture, Lippincott Corp; Charles Cowles Gallery, NY, 81; and others. *Collection Arranged:* Sculpture Garden, City of Hope, Duarte, Calif. *Teaching:* Instr sculpture, Bennington Col, 66-68; asst prof sculpture, Univ Calif, San Diego, 68-76. *Awards:* Nat Endowment Arts. *Bibliog:* Catalog: 25 Year Survey, Palm Springs Desert Mus. *Media:* Steel, Aluminum, Bronze, Ceramics. *Publ:* 25 year survey, Palm Springs Desert Mus, Calif. *Dealer:* Stremmel Gallery Reno NV; Gremillion & Co Fine Art Houston TX; Bentley Gallery Phoenix AZ. *Mailing Add:* 2817 Clearwater Los Angeles CA 90039

TODT
SCULPTOR, CONCEPTUAL ARTIST
b New York, NY. *Work:* Metrop Mus Art, NY; Brooklyn Mus, NY; Middendorf Gallery, Washington, DC; New Sch for Social Res, NY; ERA Int/Club Gold, Tokyo, Japan. *Exhib:* Occupied Territory, Mus Contemp Art, Chicago, 92; Aperto: Open Emergency, XLV Venice Biennale, Italy, 93; Womb Wars, Galerie am Pariser, Berlin, Ger, 94; Miami Univ Heistand Galleries, Oxford, Ohio, 96; Indianapolis Mus Art, Ind, 96; Mechanical Man, Gallery Green, Oxford, Ohio, 97; Group show, Gallery Green, Oxford, Ohio, 96, PPOW Gallery, NY, 98 & Erie Art Ctr, Pa, 97; Inagural show, David Tipiskey Gallery, Denver, Colo, 98; TODT, Scanned posters, The Loft, Cincinnati, Ohio, 98; TODT, Schick Art Gallery, Skidmore Col, Saratoga Springs, NY, 98; TODT, Arts Consortium, Linn Street Gallery, Cincinnati, Ohio, 99; TODT, Spaces, Cleveland, Ohio, 99. *Awards:* Fel, Media Arts Award, Ohio Arts Coun, 95; Fel, Visual Arts Award, Ohio Coun, 95 & 96. *Bibliog:* Robert Braiser (auth), Dialogue (p 19), 95; Joan Robinson (auth), ARTForum, 12/95; TODT, Zero-Sum (auth, catalog), Lightborne Commun, Inc, Cincinnatti, Ohio, 96. *Media:* Mixed Media. *Publ:* Contribr, Zone: Fragments for the History of the Human Body, Zone, 93; XLV International Exhibit of Art (exhib catalog), XLV Venice Biennale, Venice, Italy, 93

TOKER, FRANKLIN
HISTORIAN, EDUCATOR
b Montreal, Que, Apr 29, 44; US citizen. *Study:* McGill Univ, BA, 64; Oberlin Col, AM, 66; Harvard Univ, PhD, 73. *Exhib:* Poussin en detail, Fogg Art Mus, Harvard Univ, 67. *Pos:* Archeol dir excavations, Cathedral of Florence, Italy, 69-74 & 80. *Teaching:* A W Mellon vis prof fine arts, Carnegie-Mellon Univ, Pittsburgh, 74-76, assoc prof, 76-80; assoc prof hist art & archit, Univ Pittsburgh, 80-87, prof, 87; vis prof hist art, Univ Florence, Italy, 89; vis prof hist archit, Univ Rome, Italy, 91; vis prof hist archit, Univ Reggio Calabria, Italy, 96. *Awards:* Interpretive Res Grant, Nat Endowment Humanities, 92-94; Residency, Bellagio Study Ctr, Italy, 94; Graham Found Advanced Studies in Visual Arts Fel, 95. *Bibliog:* Ada Louise Huxtable (auth), The current age of rediscovery, 11/27/77 & Henry Tanner (auth), Florence cathedral credited to sculptor, 5/7/80, New York Times; Brendan Gill (auth), Skyline, New Yorker, 1/9/89. *Mem:* Life mem Medieval Acad Am; Inst Advan Study, Princeton; life mem Col Art Asn; life mem Soc Archit Historian (dir, 85-88, vpres, 90-93, pres, 93-94); Archaeological Inst Am. *Res:* Medieval art; American and 19th century architecture and urban design; Early Christian archaeology. *Publ:* Arnolfo's S Maria del Fiore, J Soc Archit Hist, 83; Alberti's ideal architect, Renaissance Studies honoring Craig Hugh Smyth, Florence, 85; auth, The Church of Notre-Dame in Montreal, McGill Univ Press, rev ed 91; Building on Paper: The Role of Architectural Drawings in Late-Medieval Italy, Actes du XVIIe congres International de l'Histoire de l'Art, Strasbourg, 92; auth, Pittsburgh: An Urban Portrait, Univ Pittsburgh Press, rev ed 95. *Mailing Add:* Dept Hist Art & Archit Univ Pittsburgh Pittsburgh PA 15260-7610

TOLL, BARBARA ELIZABETH
DEALER, CURATOR
b Philadelphia, Pa, June 8, 45. *Study:* Goucher Col, Towson, Md, AB, 67; Radcliffe Col, 67; Pratt Inst, New York, MFA, 69. *Collection Arranged:* Focus: Donald Judd Furniture, Parrish Art Mus, 96; Curator David Rockefeller Col, 77-81; Friendships in Arcadia: Writers and Artists at Yaddo in the 90's, Art in General, MY; Follies: Fantasy in the Landscape, Parrish Art Mus, 01; Reconfiguring Space: Blueprints for Art in General, 03. *Pos:* Dir, Hundred Acres Gallery, New York, 70-77; freelance cur & dealer, 77-81 & 94-; owner & dir, Barbara Toll Fine Arts, New York, 81-94. *Teaching:* New York Univ Sch Continuing Educ, 79-81. *Mem:* Art Table; Corp Yaddo; trustee, Independent Cur Int. *Specialty:* Contemporary works of art in all media. *Mailing Add:* c/o Barbara Toll Fine Arts 138 Prince St New York NY 10012

TOLLES, BRYANT FRANKLIN, JR
EDUCATOR, HISTORIAN
b Hartford, Conn, Mar 14, 39. *Study:* Yale Univ, BA, 61, MAT, 62; Boston Univ, PhD, 70. *Pos:* Asst dir & libr, NH Hist Soc, Concord, 72-74; exec dir & librn, Essex Inst, Salem, Mass, 74-84; dir, Mus Studies Prog, Univ Del, 84-2005. *Teaching:* Asst dean & instr hist, Tufts Univ, Medford, Mass 65-71; prof art history & hist, Univ Del, 84-2005, prof emeritus, 2005-. *Mem:* Orgn Am Historians; Soc Archit Historians; Nat Trust Hist Preserv; AAS. *Res:* New England architectural history, late 18th to early 20th century; White Mountain illustrators, 1820-1910; Architecture of tourism, 1800-1950. *Interests:* American architectural history; American portraiture, 1750-1900; American landscape art, 19th century. *Publ:* The Evolution of a Campus: Dartmouth Col Archit Before 1860, Hist NH, 87; The Grand Resort Hotels of the White Mountains, David R Godine, Publ Inc, 98; Summer Cottages in the White Mountains, Univ Press of New Eng, 2000; Resort Hotels of the Adirondacks, 2003; NH Archit: A Guide, Univ Press of New Eng, 2004; Archit in Salem: An Illustrated Guide, 2004. *Mailing Add:* 1002 Kent Rd Wilmington DE 19807

TOLLIVER, MOSE
PAINTER
b Pike Road, Ala, 1915. *Study:* Self-taught. *Work:* Montgomery Mus Art, Ala; Mus Am Folk Art, NY; Philadelphia Col Art, Pa; Anton Haardt Pvt Collection, Montgomery, Ala. *Exhib:* Black Folk Art in Am, Corcoran Gallery Art, Washington, DC, 80; one-man retrospective, Mus Am Folk Art, NY, 93; Passionate Visions, New Orleans Mus Art, 93; Orphans in the Storm, Tucson Mus Art, 94. *Bibliog:* Anton Haardt (auth), Mose Tolliver goes to Washington, Raw Visions Mag, summer 95. *Media:* House Paint on Plywood. *Dealer:* Anton Haardt Gallery 2714 Coliseum St New Orleans LA 70130. *Mailing Add:* 1220 S Hull St Montgomery AL 36104

TOLPO, CAROLYN LEE
PAINTER, TAPESTRY
b Detroit, Mich, 40. *Study:* Wayne State Univ, Detroit, BA, 62. *Work:* Highland Col Art Collection, Freeport, Ill; Amaco Art Collection, Denver, Colo; Digital Corp, Denver, Colo; Joslyn Art Mus, Omaha, Nebr. *Comn:* Alamo Ctr, Colorado Springs, 83; atrium fiber mural, Cumberland Bldg, Denver, 85; fiber mural, Mega Bank, 86 & Tishman West Inc, 89, Denver, Colo; fiber mural, Hamilton Standard Corp, Colorado Springs, 92; mural, Marina Hotel, Jacksonville, Fla, 93; sculpture, Mesa Co Libr, Grand Junction, Colo, 95. *Exhib:* Stanley Gallery, Muscatine, Iowa, 80; Women's Caucus Art Group Show, Western Ill Univ, Macomb, Ill, 81; Women's Caucus for Art Show, Quad City Arts Ctr, Rock Island, Ill, 81; Sculptour, Gunnison, Colo, 94, 95 & 96; Art on the Corner Sculpture Exhib, Grand Junction, Colo, 94, 95 & 96; Steam Plant Art Ctr, Salida, Colo, 1999-2002; Convergence, World Fiber Convention, Exhib Shawnee Mountain Gallery, 2004. *Pos:* Gallery dir, Shawnee Mountain Gallery, Shawnee, Colo, 81-; owner, Shawnee Mountain Gallery, Colo. *Teaching:* Art teacher/coordr, Freeport Catholic Sch, 71-76. *Awards:* Best Show Watercolor, Nat Orchid Soc Art Exhib, 81. *Bibliog:* Art Today Mag, 92; Fiberarts Mag, Nov/Dec, 92. *Mem:* Woman's Caucus Art, Midwest Chap (founding pres, 79-81); Cult Coun Park Co, Colo (founding bd mem); Rocky Mountain Weavers Guild. *Media:* Wrapped Fiber, Watercolor, Jewelry. *Publ:* The Guild 5, 6, 7 & 8: Artist Sourcebook, Krause Sikes Inc, Madison, Wis; Profiles in American Craft, Rosen Inc, Baltimore, Md, 93. *Dealer:* 21st Century Gallery Denver Colo; Earthwood Artisans Estes Park Colo; Klay Gallery Nyack NY; Cross/Harris Gallery NY; Stonehenge Gallery Georgetown Colo; Campbell Steele Gallery Marion Iowa; Peoria Art Guild Gallery Peoria Ill. *Mailing Add:* PO Box 134 Shawnee CO 80475

TOLPO, VINCENT CARL
PAINTER, SCULPTOR
b Chicago, Ill, Apr 26, 50. *Study:* Univ Wyo, Laramie, 69-69, Am Acad Art, Chicago, 70-71; Ariz State Univ, Tempe, BFA, 74; studied with Carl & Lily Tolpo, 69-76. *Work:* Freeport Art Mus, Ill; Augustana Hosp Portrait Gallery, Chicago; Park Co Libr, Ft Carson, Colo; Joselyn Art Mus, Omaha Nebr. *Comn:* Fiber murals (collab with Carolyn L Tolpo), Alamo Ctr, Colorado Springs, Colo, 83; atrium metal sculture, Glenarm Bldg, Denver, 92; metal wall sculpture, Regel Riverfront Hotel, St Louis, Mo, 93-; Moon Over Red Rocks (oil painting), Park Meadow Village, Denver, Colo, 96; Peaks & Valleys, metal & stoneware mural, Commercial Bank, Buena Vista, Colo, 97; metal wall sculpture, Elkhorn Conf Ctr, Colorado Springs, Colo, 2001; metal wall sculpture, Health Partners, Colorado Springs, Colo, 2004; Metal wall sculpture, Exempla Hosp Lafayette, Colo, 2005. *Exhib:* Scottsdale Ann, Scottsdale Fine Art Ctr, Ariz, 73; 14th Ann, Stanley Gallery, Muscatine, Iowa, 80; sculpture exhib, Art on the Corner, Grand Junction, Colo, 90-96; Sculptour, Gunnison, Colo, 93-96; Real West, Denver Art Mus, Colo, 96; Steamplant Art Ctr, Salida, Colo, 2000-03. *Pos:* owner, Shawnee Mountain Gallery, Colo. *Teaching:* Ceramics, art appreciation, Highland Col, Freeport, Ill, 75-77. *Awards:* Co-visions, Colo Arts Coun, 92. *Bibliog:* Art Today Mag, 92; Fiber Arts Mag, Nov/Dec 92. *Mem:* Am Craft Coun; Park Co Cult Coun; Colo Metalsmith Asn; Rocky Mountain Weavers Guild. *Media:* Oil, Welded Metal, Ceramics. *Specialty:* Contemp Art; Ceramics; Jewelry. *Publ:* Guild 5, 6, 7 & 8: Artist Sourcebook, Krause/Sikes Inc, Madison, Wisc; Profiles in American Craft, Rosen Inc, Baltimore, Md, 93. *Dealer:* 21st Century Gallery Denver Colo; Old Town Gallery Colorado Springs Colo; Cross/Harris Gallery New York NY; Klay Gallery Nyack NY; Eartwoods Artisans Estes Park Colo; Walker Fine Arts Denver Colo; Stonehenge Gallery, Georgetown Colo; Campbell Steele Gallery Marion Iowa; Peoria Art Guild Gallery Peoria Ill. *Mailing Add:* c/o Shawnee Mountain Studios PO Box 134 Shawnee CO 80475

TOMASELLI, FRED
ARTIST
b Santa Monica, Calif, 56. *Study:* Calif State Univ, Fullerton, BA in Painting and Drawing, 82. *Work:* Whitney Mus Am Art, 1997, Whitney Biennial, Whitney Mus Am Art, NY, 2004. *Exhib:* One-man shows incl Contemp Arts Ctr, Cincinnati, 97, White Cube, London, 2001, Alright-Knox Gallery Art, New York City, 2003, James Cohan Gallery, 2003; exhib in group shows at The Barbican Gallery, London, 2001, Malborough Gallery, New York City, 2003. *Awards:* recipient Art Commission award for excellence in design, City Hall, New York City, 93; Joan Mitchell Grant, 98; Named Invited Exhib, Biennial Exhib, Whitney Mus Am Art, New York City, 2004. *Publ:* co-auth (with Michael Rush, Amy Cappellazzo): Fred Tomaselli: Ten Yr Survey, 2003; co-auth: (with Franz Ackerman, Eija-Liisa Ahtila, Dan Graham, John Boc) Parkett #68: Eija-Liisa Ahtila, 2003; co-auth: (with Peter Buchanan-Smith and Rick Mooty) The Wilco Book, 2004. *Mailing Add:* c/o James Cohan Gallery 533 W 26th St New York NY 10001

TOMASINI, WALLACE J
ADMINISTRATOR, HISTORIAN
b Brooklyn, NY, Oct 19, 26. *Study:* Univ Mich, AB, 49, AM, 50, PhD, 53; Univ Florence, Fulbright grant, 51-52; NY Univ Inst Fine Arts, 54-57. *Teaching:* Instr hist of art, Finch Col, 54-57; asst prof art hist, Univ Iowa, 57-61, assoc prof, 61-64, prof, 64-, dir, Sch Art & Art Hist, 72-93. *Awards:* Am Numismatic Soc Grant, 57; Am Philos Soc Grant, 58. *Mem:* Am Numismatic Soc; Mid-Am Col Art Conf; Int Exchange Scholars; Sixteenth Century Studies; Midwest Art Hist Soc; Haviland collectors int found pres. *Res:* Social and economic determinants of Italian Renaissance art; Late Imperial and Barbaric numismatics. *Publ:* Auth, Report on Visigothic Numismatic Research, 62; Exhibition Catalogue:Drawing & the Human Figure 1400-1964, 64; The Barbaric Tremissis in Spain & Southern France, Anastasius to Leovigild (numismatic notes & monogr 152), 64; contribr, 17th Century Art Essay (CIC Exhib Catalogue), 73; Paintings of Eve Drewelowe, 85; Catalogue of Haviland china: celebrating 150 yrs, 92. *Mailing Add:* 610 Beldon Ave Iowa City IA 52246

TOMCHUK, MARJORIE
PRINTMAKER, PAINTER
b Manitoba, Can, Oct 16, 33; US citizen. *Study:* Univ Mich, BA, 57, MA, 61; Long Beach State Col, 62; Sophia Univ, Japan; Pratt Graphics Ctr, NY. *Work:* Nat Air & Space Mus, Smithsonian Inst, Washington, DC; DeCordova Mus, Mass; Butler Inst of Am Art, Youngstown, Ohio; Mus of Native Am Cult, Spokane, Wash; Nelson Gallery, Kansas City, Mo; Newark Mus, NJ. *Comn:* Xerox Corp; General Electric; Northern Telecom; West Point Military Acad, NY. *Exhib:* World Art Exposition, Boston, 79; one-man shows, Art Expo NY, 79-98, Art Washington, 79-83 & Art Expo Calif, 81-93; Isetan Art Gallery, Tokyo, 86; Fayetteville Mus Art, NC, 89; West Point Military Acad, 93; Silvermine Guild Art Ctr, 99; Am Mus Papermaking, Atlanta, Ga. *Awards:* Boston Nat Print Show, Purchase Prizes, DeCordova Mus, 71 & 73; Nat Arts Club Award, New York, 72; Stamford Art Club First Prize, 73; Best Print Award, Art Trends Mag, 2000. *Bibliog:* Ellen Kaplan (auth), A Collectors Guide, Prints, 83; Franz Geierhaas (auth), M Tomchuk Graphic Work, 1962-89, 89; Interview, PaintingsDirect.com, 12/21/99; Personal visions, the handmade look, Art Trends Mag, 8/2000; Marjorie Tomchuk, Printmaker, Embossings on Handmade Paper (video), Curtis/Cromwell Productions, 8/2000. *Mem:* Silvermine Guild Artists (bd mem, 73-78); Philadelphia Print Club; Pratt Graphics Ctr; Int Artists & Papermakers Asn; NY Artists Equity; Friends Dard Hunter. *Media:* Collage, Embossing, Handmade paper. *Publ:* Contribr, article, J Print World, Vol 5, No 4 & Vol 17, No 4, 94; article, Prints, 7-8/82. *Mailing Add:* 44 Horton Lane New Canaan CT 06840

TOMCIK, ANDREW MICHAEL
EDUCATOR, DESIGNER
b Cleveland, Ohio, June 18, 38; Can citizen. *Study:* Cleveland Inst Art, Diploma, 60; Somerakadmie der Bildende Kunst, Salzburg, with Oskar Kokoschka, Cert, 61; Yale Univ Sch Art & Archit, BFA, MFA, 65. *Comn:* Loretto Col Infirmary Chapel, 89. *Exhib:* Westlake Print Biennale, Zhejiang, China, 87; Sense of Place: Photographs, Founders Col, York Univ, Toronto, 88; Ekoplagat, Sch of Nature Protection, Gbel'any, Czechoslovakia, 90. *Pos:* Designer: The Carborundum Co, Niagara Falls, NY, 65-67; sr design assoc, Hauser Assoc Inc, Atlanta, Ga, 67-74; chmn, dept of visual arts, York Univ, Toronto, Ont, 81-84 & 90-91. *Teaching:* Assoc prof visual arts, Ga State Univ, Atlanta, 67-74; prof fine arts, York Univ, Toronto, 74-; master, Winters Col, 95-; prof emer, 2001. *Awards:* Fac Asn Award, Ont Coun Univ, 86; Gen Excellence Design Award, Can Church Press, 94. *Mem:* Soc Graphic Designers of Can (nat vpres educ, 85-87, secy, 87-90); Registered Graphic Designers, Ont. *Media:* Graphic Design, Print. *Res:* Design history, criticism. *Publ:* Auth, Art in Everyday Life: Aspects of Canadian Design, 67-87; Benchmarks, The Best of the Eighties, 85; From inspiration to imitation: How close can we come to our sources of inspiration before the work cannot be said to be ours?, Scan, summer 86; Exhib Rev, Ontario Craft, 88; Pol Posters, 89 & The Depreciation of Originality, Azure Mag, 90; Aspects of Color, Assorted art & design periodicals, Univ Art & Design, Helsinki, 1995. *Mailing Add:* 48 Parkhurst Blvd Toronto ON M4G 2C9 Canada

TOMKINS, CALVIN
WRITER
b Orange, NJ, Dec 17, 25. *Study:* Princeton Univ, BA. *Pos:* Staff writer, The New Yorker, Mag, 61-. *Publ:* Auth, The Bride and the Bachelors, Viking Press, 65; Merchants and Masterpieces: The Story of the Metropolitan Museum of Art, EP Dutton, 70; Living Well Is the Best Revenge, 71 & auth, The Scene: Reports on Post-Modern Art, 76, Viking Press; Off the Wall: Robert Rauschenberg and the Art World of Our Time, Doubleday & Co, Inc, 80; Duchamp: A Biography, Henry Holt & Co, Inc, 96. *Mailing Add:* c/o The New Yorker 4 Times Square New York NY 10036

TOMPKINS, ALAN
PAINTER; EDUCATOR
b New Rochelle, NY, Oct 29, 07. *Study:* Columbia Univ, BA; Yale Univ, BFA. *Hon Degrees:* Univ Hartford, Hon DFA, 87. *Work:* New Britain Mus Am Art, Conn. *Comn:* Mural paintings comn by US Treas Dept for post off at Indianapolis, Ind, 36, Martinsville, Ind, 37 & Boone, NC, 40; mural painting, Gen Elec Co, Bridgeport, Conn, 44; mural painting, Cent Baptist Church, Hartford, Conn, 58. *Exhib:* Ind Artists Ann, 37-38; Art Inst Chicago Ann, 38; Conn Acad Ann, 52-81; one-man shows, Canton, Conn, 84 & Hartford, Conn, 86, 92, 97, 01. *Pos:* Dir, Hartford Art Sch, Univ Hartford, 57-69, vchancellor, 60-74; comnr, Fine Arts Comn, Hartford, 59-69. *Teaching:* Instr painting, Cooper Union Art Sch, 38-43; lectr painting, Columbia Univ, 46-51; prof painting & art hist, Univ Hartford, 51-74. *Awards:* First Prize for painting, Conn Acad, 68-70 & 73; Painting Awards, Beth-El Regional Exhib, 72 & 79 & Canton Open Show, 77, 80, 81, 85 & 88. *Mem:* Conn Acad (vpres, 70-72). *Media:* All Media. *Mailing Add:* 60 Loeffler Rd Bloomfield CT 06002

TOMPKINS, BETTY (I)
PAINTER, PRINTMAKER
b Washington, DC, June 20, 45. *Study:* Syracuse Univ, BFA, 66; Central Wash State Col, BEd, 69, MA, 69. *Work:* Aldrich Mus, Conn; Chase Bank, NY; Oberlin Col, Ohio; Marvin Sackner Archives, Miami Beach, Fla; Rutgers Univ; Stamford Mus, Conn; Zimmerli Mus, NJ; Paterson Mus, NJ; Mus of the City of New York, NYC; Islip Mus Art, East Islip, NY. *Exhib:* Solo exhibs, Fairleigh Dickenson Univ, NJ, 87, White Columns, NY, 91, Margulies Taplin Gallery, Boca Raton, Fla, 91, Fridholm Fine Arts, Asheville, NC, 91, Alan Brown Gallery, Hartsdale, NY, 91, Fridholm Fine Arts, NC, 93 & 94 & Drew Univ NJ Charleston Gallery, RI, 95, Juniata Mus, Huntingdon, Pa, 98, Egizio's Project, New York City, 2000, Mitchell Algus, New York City, 2002; Selections from the Collection, Aldrich Mus, Conn, 88; Lines of Vision (traveling show), US, Pan Am & Europe, 89-90; The Living Object: The Art Collection of Ellen H Johnson, Allen Mem Art Mus, Oberlin, Ohio, 92; Yale Univ, Conn, 95; Ctr Book Arts, NY; Berta Walker, Mass, 96; Juniata Mus Art, Huntington,

Pa; Salvadore Park Mus, Miami, Fla, 2001; Mus Mod Art, New York City, 2002; Lyon Biennale, 2003. *Collection Arranged:* Animals in the Arsenal (auth, catalog), Central Park Zoo, 81. *Pos:* Contrib ed, Appearances Mag, 79-. *Teaching:* Painting, Sch Visual Arts, NY, 91-. *Awards:* NY Found Arts Grant, 88; Fel, MacDowell, 82, 83, 88 & 90; Artist in Residence, Weir Farm Heritage Trust, Branchville, Conn, 99. *Bibliog:* Joanne Barkan & Jon Friedman (auth), The beast in question, Arts Mag, 81; Sande Zorn (auth), Cows in the gallery, Holstein World, 82; Vivien Raynor (auth), Painter's work in a singular show, NY Times, 1/19/86; Robert Mahoney (auth), Betty Tompkins, Arts Mag, 88. *Media:* Acrylic, Watercolor; Etching. *Dealer:* Mitchell Algus NYC. *Mailing Add:* 101 Prince St New York NY 10012

TOMPKINS, MICHAEL
PAINTER
b Chester, Pa, 55. *Study:* Cabrillo Col, Aptos, Calif, AA, 78; Univ Que, Montreal, 79; Univ Calif, Davis, BA(studio art), 81, MFA(painting) 83. *Work:* L Price Amerson, Deborah Born, Woodland, Calif; Gary Anderson, Carmichael, Calif; Dr Joseph Baird, San Francisco; Mr & Mrs Edward Grebitus, Sacramento, Calif; Robert Hudson, Cotati, Calif. *Exhib:* Solo exhibs, Richard L Nelson Gallery, Univ Calif, Davis, 83, Artworks Gallery, Fair Oaks, Calif, 85, Davis Art Ctr, Calif, 85, Artists Contemp Gallery, Sacramento, 86 & 88-90, William Sawyer Gallery, San Francisco, 87 & 89, Worden Gallery, San Francisco, 88 & Campbell-Thiebaud Gallery, San Francisco, 90, 91 & 93; California Figuration-Then and Now, Natsoulas/Novelozo Gallery, Davis, Calif, 90; Artists of Contra Costa Co, Hearst Gallery, St Mary's Col, Moraga, 90; Rodeo: A Contra Costa Studio Community, Bedford Gallery, Walnut Creek, 92; Landscapes: Paintings and Works on Paper, Wayne Thiebaud & Michael Tompkins, Artists Contemp Gallery, Sacramento, 92; and many others. *Teaching:* Teaching asst color, figure drawing & art appreciation, Univ Calif, Davis, 81-83; instr drawing, color theory, painting, printmaking & art hist, Sierra Col, Rocklin, Calif, 84-86; instr landscape painting, Am River Col, Placerville, 85; vis lectr drawing & descriptive drawing, Univ Calif, 86-88, painting, San Francisco Art Inst, 88-89. *Awards:* Fel, Nat Endowment Arts, 87 & 89; Am Acad & Inst Arts & Letts, 89; Richard & Hinda Rosenthal Found Award, 89; and others. *Bibliog:* Charles Shere (auth), Introductions '87, Oakland Tribune, 7/14/87; Victoria Dalkey (auth), Varying Visions, Sacramento Bee, 3/20/88; Teri Bachman (auth), Art at UC Davis, Univ Calif, Davis, Mag, summer 88; Ann Seymour (auth), Gallery reviews, Nob Hill Gazette, 4/89; Victoria Dalkey (auth), Invitation to contemplation, Sacramento Bee, 3/26/89; and others. *Dealer:* Campbell - Thiebaud Gallery San Francisco CA. *Mailing Add:* c/o Campbell-Thiebaud Gallery 645 Chestnut St San Francisco CA 94133

TONELLI, EDITH ANN
MUSEUM DIRECTOR, HISTORIAN
b Westfield, Mass, May 20, 49. *Study:* Vassar Col, NY, BA, 71, Helen Squier Townsend Fel, 71; Hunter Col, City Univ New York, with Vincent Longo & Robert Morris, MA (creative arts), 74; Boston Univ, Doctoral Fel, 74-79, with Patricia Hills, PhD, 81; Antioch Univ, MA (clinical psychology), 92. *Collection Arranged:* Homer to Hopper: 60 Years of American Watercolor (auth, catalog), 76; By the People, For the People: New England (auth, catalog), 77; Non-Conformists: Contemporary Commentary from the Soviet Union (auth, catalog), 80; Louis Faurer: Photographs of Philadelphia & New York, 1937-1973 (auth, catalog), 81; Ralston Crawford: Photographs/Art and Process (auth, catalog), 82; Involvement: The Graphic Art of Antonio Frasconi (auth, catalogue), 88; Chicano Art: Resistance and Affirmation, 1965-1985, 89. *Pos:* Cur, DeCordova Mus, Mass, 76-78; dir, Univ Md Art Gallery, 79 ; dir, Frederick S Wight Art Gallery, Univ Calif, Los Angeles, 82-91; dir, Art Mus, UCLA. *Teaching:* Instr Am material culture, Boston Univ, Mass, 76; asst prof, Univ Md, College Park, 80-82; adj asst prof, Univ Calif, Los Angeles, 82-92; adj instr art therapy, Antioch Univ, 93. *Awards:* Smithsonian Fel, 79. *Bibliog:* Jane Holtz Kay (auth), Boston, Art News, 12/77. *Mem:* Am Asn Mus; Col Art Asn; Art Mus Asn; Am Asn Col Univ Mus Galleries; Asn Art Mus Dirs (trustee, 87-); and others. *Res:* Twentieth century American art; American prints. *Publ:* Auth, The Avant-Garde in Boston: The WPA's federal art project, Archives Am Art J, 80; contribr, Frank Mechau, Aspen Ctr Visual Arts, 81 & City Life, Whitney Mus Amer Art, 86. *Mailing Add:* 1910 Parnell Ave Los Angeles CA 90025

TONEY, ANITA KAREN
PRINTMAKER
b New York City, NY. *Study:* Syracuse Univ, BFA; San Francisco State Univ, MA. *Exhib:* Exhib in group shows at Nancy Dodds Gallery, Carmel, Calif, Le Celle Gallery, San Anselmo, Calif, Andrea Schwartz Gallery, San Francisco, Images Gallery, Briarcliff, NY, exhibs incl with father, Anthony Toney, Col of Marin, 2003. *Teaching:* Instr printmaking City Col San Francisco, 1979-. *Mem:* Calif Soc Printmakers; Nat Acad (acad, 95-). *Mailing Add:* Printmaking City Coll San Francisco 50 Phelan Ave San Francisco CA 94112

TOOGOOD, JAMES S
PAINTER, INSTRUCTOR
b Sept 26, 54. *Study:* Pa Acad Fine Arts - 1973-76. *Work:* The Woodmere Art Mus, Phila, Pa; The Noyes Mus, Oceanville, NJ; The Masterworks Mus Bermudian Art, Hamilton, Bermuda; Rowan Univ, Glassboro, NJ; Pa Acad Fine Arts Fellowship, Phila. *Comn:* Painting of Corporate Headquarters, CIGNA, Phila, Pa, 1982; Fireworks Over the City (painting), Oceangate Twp, NJ, 1994; painting, The Woodere Art Mus, Phila, Pa, 1994; historic landmarks (paintings), Cherry Hill Twp, NJ, 1996, 98 & 2000. *Exhib:* Dreams/Realities, Delaware Ctr for Contemp Arts, Wilmington, 1985; one man retrospective, Woodmere Art Mus, Phila, Pa, 1986; juried exhib, Nat Acad of Design, New York City, 1994; Two Centuries of Inspiration: Works from Recent Work, Masterwork Mus of Bermudian Art, Phila, Pa, New York City & Toronto, Can, 2000; juried exhib, Nat Watercolor Soc, Brea, Calif, 2003; A Collectors View, Noyes Mus, Oceanville, NJ, 2005; traveling juried exhib, Am Watercolor Soc, various cities, 2006-07. *Collection Arranged:* Co-cur, A Collectors View, Noyes Mus, Oceanside, NJ, 2005. *Awards:* The Artist's Magazine Award, Am Watercolor Soc, 1990; Dagmar Tribble Award Best in Show, Garden State Watercolor Soc, The Tribble Family, 1992; Best in Show, Phila Sketch Club, 2006. *Bibliog:* Lynn Kosek Brown (producer), The Art of James Toogood (film), State of the Arts, NJNTV, 1990; Charles Nicol (auth), Toogood To Be True, Bermuda Mag, 1996; Stephen Doherty (auth), Watercolor as a Personal Language, Am Artist Watercolor, 2001. *Mem:* Am Watercolor Soc; Nat Watercolor Soc; Pa Acad of Fine Arts Alumni & Fel; Northeast Watercolor Soc; NJ Watercolor Soc. *Media:* Watercolor. *Publ:* Auth, Behind The Scenes, The Artists Mag, 2001; coauth, Expressing the Visual Language of the Landscape, Int Artist Books, 2002; auth, Incredible Light & Texture in Watercolor, Northlight Books, 2004; auth, The Simple Truth, Watercolor Magic, 2005; auth, Five Techniques Every Watercolorist Should Know, Watercolor Magic, 2006. *Dealer:* Rosenfeld Gallery Richard Rosenfeld 113 Arch St Phila PA 19106; Desmond Fountain Gallery The Emporium Bldg 69 Front St Hamilton Bermuda. *Mailing Add:* 920 Park Dr Cherry Hill NJ 08002

TOOKER, GEORGE
PAINTER, PRINTMAKER
b Brooklyn, NY, Aug 5, 1920. *Study:* Phillips Acad, 38; Harvard Univ, AB, 42; Art Students league, with Reginald Marsh, Kenneth Hayes Miller & Harry Sternberg, 43-44. *Work:* Whitney Mus Am Art, Metrop Mus Art & Mus Mod Art, NY; Walker Art Ctr, Minneapolis; Addison Gallery Am Art, Phillips Acad, Andover, Mass; Brooklyn Mus Art; Va Mus Fine Arts, Richmond; Nat Mus Am Art, Smithsonian, Wash; and others. *Comn:* The Seven Sacraments & The Stations of the Cross, St Francis of Assisi, Windsor, Vt. *Exhib:* One-man exhibs, Durlacher Brothers, NY, 67, Fine Arts Mus San Francisco, Calif, Palace Legion Honor, San Francisco, Mus Contemp Art Chicago, Whitney Mus Art, NY, Indianapolis Mus Art, 74-75, Marisa Del Re Gallery, NY, 85, 88 & 92 Gibbs Art Gallery, Charleston, SC, 87, Robert Hull Fleming Mus, Univ Vt, Burlington, 87, Marsh Gallery, Univ Richmond, Va, 89 & Addison Gallery Am Art, 94, Ogunquit Mus, Maine, 96 & DC Moore Gallery, 98, 2000; Contemp Artists in Vt, Robert Hull Fleming Mus, Univ Vt, Burlington, 84; Surreal City, 1930-1950, Whitney Mus Art at Philip Morris, NY, 85; Modern Am Realism, Sara Roby Found Collection, Nat Mus Am Art, Wash, 87; Cadmus, French & Tooker: The Early Yrs, Whitney Mus Am Art at Philip Morris, NY, 90; Close Encounters: The art of Paul Cadmus, Jared French and George Tooker, Midtown Galleries, NY, 2/20-4/7/90; Art What Thou Eat: Images of Food in Am Art, traveling, Edith C Blum Art Inst, Bard Col, Annandale-on-Hudson, NY, 90; Contemp Surrealism, NJ Ctr Visual Arts, Summit, 91; The Am Century 1900-1950 Whitney Mus Am Art, 99; Making Choices 1929-55, Mus Mod Art, NY; Cadmus French Tooker, Columbus (Ohio) Mus Art, 2001. *Teaching:* Instr, Art Students League, 65-68. *Awards:* Nat Inst Arts & Lett Grant, 60; Gov Award Excellence Arts, Montpelier, Vt, 83. *Bibliog:* Thomas H Garver (auth), George Tooker, Clarkson N Potter Inc, Publ, 85. *Mem:* Nat Acad (assoc, 68, acad, 70-); Am Acad Arts & Letters. *Media:* Egg Tempera; Lithography. *Dealer:* DC Moore Gallery 724 Fifth Ave New York NY 10019. *Mailing Add:* c/o D C Moore Gallery 724 Fifth Ave New York NY 10019

TOOLE, LOIS SALMON
PAINTER, WATERCOLOR
b New Brunswick, NJ. *Study:* Douglass Col, Rutgers Univ, BA(fine arts), 52; watercolor instr with Florian K Lawton, 77 & Claude Croney, 80. *Work:* Key Bank, Cleveland, Ohio; Brit Petroleum, Scotland; TRW, Cleveland, Ohio; Hi Techmetal Group, Cleveland, Ohio; Signal Financial Corp, Pittsburgh, Pa; Evans Printing Co, Solon, Ohio. *Comn:* Dir covers-Collection regional, Chagrin Valley, Chamber Com, Ohio, 82, 90 & 05; Pres Off Greeting Card, Am Bar Asn, Cleveland, Ohio, 85; painting, EG Baldwin Corp, Cleveland, Ohio, 87; paintings, Antenna Specialists Allen Group, Solon, Ohio, 88. *Exhib:* Ky Watercolor Soc, Ky Mus, Bowling Green, 79, 80, 81, 84, 86, 88, 89, 93, 94, 97, 99 & 05; Rocky Mountain Nat Watermedia Exhib, 2006, Foothills Art Ctr, Golden, Colo, 82, 85, 88, 90, 93, 94, 95, 99 & 03; Allied Artists Am, 2005, Nat Arts Club, NY, 86, 89, 92, 97, 98, 99, 02-04, Butler Inst, 98 & 00; Watercolor USA, Springfield Mus, Mo, 87, 92 & 96; 50th Anniversary Signature Mem Invitational, NJ Watercolor Soc, Montclair Mus, 88; Mary H Dana Women Artists Series, Douglass Col of Rutgers Univ, 99; World Fedn of Miniature Art, London, Eng, 95, Tasmania, Australia, 2000, Smithsonian Inst, Washington, DC, 2004; Am Watercolor Soc, NY, 01; plus others. *Pos:* Trustee bd dir, Valley Art Ctr, 87-93, adv bd, 93-; coordr, Art in Park, Chagrin Valley Chamber Comm, 83-98; founding artist, Blue Moon Gallery, 93-. *Teaching:* pvt teacher, lectr in field. *Awards:* Pearl Fine Arts Award, Rocky Mountain Nat Watermedia Exhib, 93; NJ Watercolor Soc Award, 96; M Grumbacker Award, Miniature Painters, Sculptors, Gravers Soc, Wash, DC,97; Finalist Am Artist Realism Today Competition, 2000; Mary K Karasick Memorial Award National Assoc of Women Artist, 2002; Winsor & Newton Award, Allied Artists Am, 2005; and numerous others. *Bibliog:* article, American Society of Marine Artist, 02; interview, Artist Magazine, website, 03; Verticle File, Smithsonian Am Art Mus Libr, 2006. *Mem:* Nat Watercolor Soc; Rocky Mountain Nat Watermedia Soc; Transparent Watercolor Soc of Am; Allied Artists Am, NY; Miniature Artists Am; Am Soc Marine Artists; Nat Asn of Women Artists; Watercolor Soc; Catharine Lorillard Wolfe Art Club; and numerous others. *Media:* Transparent Watercolor. *Publ:* Auth, NWS Conf Report, Ohio Watercolor Soc, 88; contribr, Splash III: Ideas & Inspirations, North Light Bks, 94; Best Watercolor, Rockport Publ, 95; Painting Ships, Shores and the Sea, North Light Bks, 97; Landscape Inspiration, Rockport Publ, 97; Best of Watercolor III, 99; Splash 7: A Celbration of Light, North Light, 02; Watercolor Skies & Clouds Techniques of 23 International Artists, Internet Artist Pub, 04. *Mailing Add:* 16880 Knolls Way Chagrin Falls OH 44023

TOPALIS, DANIEL P
PAINTER
b Norwich, Conn, Sept 3, 55. *Study:* Three Rivers Col; Univ Arts. *Work:* Slater Mem Mus, Norwich, Conn; Martin Luther King Ctr, Norwich, Ct; Quest Diagnostics, Teterborough, NJ. *Comn:* Peter Woodward, Caribbean Cruiseline, Heneley on The Thames, England; Dr and Mrs F Carter; Dr Shiela Tabakoff. *Exhib:* Conn Artist Show, Slater Mem Mus, 98, 99, 2000; 43rd Regional Exhib, Mystic Art Asn, 99, NAC Gallery 44th Regional Exhib, 2000; Conn Artist Show, 2001; Agora Gallery So Ho, NY; solo exhib, Slater Memorial Mus, John Slade Eli House, New Haven, Conn, Hunting House Mus, Windsor, Conn & Emporium Gallery, Mystic, Conn; Hygenic Galleries, New London, Conn; Agaat Salatte Gallery, Norwich, Conn; NAC Gallery, Norwich, Conn; Ct Commn Arts, Hartford, Conn. *Pos:* mem bd, Norwich Arts Coun, 96-2001; mem bd, Agaat Salatte Gallery, Norwich, CT. *Awards:* Artist Fel Award, Conn Comn of The Arts, 2000; Margaret Darrin Found Grant; Fel, Conn Comn Arts, 2004. *Mem:* NAC Artist Co-perative, Mystic Art Asn; Agaat Salatte Co-Operative. *Media:* Acrylic, Canvas. *Publ:* Eleanor Charles (auth), Deadly Art, New York Times, 4/2001 & People in art, New York Times, 7/2002. *Mailing Add:* 72 Briar Hill Rd Norwich CT 06360

TOPERZER, THOMAS RAYMOND
MUSEUM DIRECTOR, PAINTER
b Homestead, Pa, Aug 12, 39. *Study:* Sterling Col, 59-61; Southwestern Col (Kans), BA, 63; Univ Nebr-Lincoln, Woods fel, 69-70, MFA, 70. *Work:* Des Moines Art Ctr, Iowa; Springfield Art Mus, Mo; Rochester Art Ctr, Minn; Blanden Art Mus, Iowa; Ill State Univ; Bethel Col & Sem, Minn. *Exhib:* Iowa Artists, Des Moines Art Ctr; New Horizons, Chicago; Nat Drawing, San Francisco Mus Art; Nat Prints & Drawings, Okla Art Ctr, Mid-Am, Kansas City-St Louis, 74. *Pos:* Dir, Blanden Art Mus, 70-71, Rochester Art Ctr, 71-72; asst dir, Mus & Galleries, Ill State Univ, 72, dir, Univ Galleries, Ctr Visual Arts Gallery, 73-82, ed, Univ Mus Newslett, 75-76; coordr fine arts, Bethel Col, St Paul, Minn, 82-84 & Fred Jones Jr Mus Art, Univ Okla, 84-. *Mem:* Am Asn Mus; Col Art Asn; Art Mus Asn. *Publ:* Auth, Current Issues in University Art Museums, Southern Ill Univ. *Mailing Add:* 5700 Berget Dr Amarillo TX 79106-4804

TOPOL, ROBERT MARTIN
COLLECTOR
b New York, NY, Mar 9, 25. *Collection:* Frescos, oils and sculptures. *Mailing Add:* 825 Orienta Ave Mamaroneck NY 10543

TOPPER, DAVID R
EDUCATOR, HISTORIAN
b Pittsburgh, Pa, Jan 1, 43. *Study:* Duquesne Univ, BS, 64; Case Inst Technol, MS, 66; Case Western Reserve Univ, MA, 68; & PhD, 70. *Pos:* Int co-ed, Leonardo Jour Arts, Sci & Technol, currently. *Teaching:* Prof art hist, Univ Winnipeg, Man, 70-. *Awards:* Clifford J Robson Mem Award for Excellence in Teaching, Univ Winnipeg, 81; 3M Teaching Fel, 87. *Mem:* Int Soc Arts, Sci & Technol. *Res:* Historical perspectives on visual perception of images and the interrelationship with science. *Publ:* Perspectives on perspective: Gombrich and his critics, Gombrich on Art & Psychology, 96; Trajectories of blood: Artemesia Genitleschi and Galileo's parabolic path, Woman's Art J, 96; The Neutrino and the Sydney Opera House, Leonardo, 97; On Anamorphosis, Leonardo, 2000; Visual Arts & Nat Sciences: Annotated Bibliography, Leonardo-online, 2003. *Mailing Add:* Univ Winnipeg Hist Dept Winnipeg MB R3B 2E9 Canada

TORAK, ELIZABETH
PAINTER
b NY City, April 12, 59. *Study:* Art Students League, NY. *Exhib:* numerous solo exhib's, two person & group exhib's; Butler Inst Am Art; Sna Diego Art Inst; Arlington Mus Art, Tex. *Awards:* Honorable Mention, Butler Inst Am Art, Midyear Exhib; John Spiegel Mem Award, Am Artists Prof League; Marguerite Sinaly Mem Award, Salmagundi Club. *Bibliog:* Article Am Artist Mag, 8/94. *Media:* Oil, Acrylic. *Publ:* Contribr, Creative Oil Painting, Techniques from 15 Master Painters, Stephen Doherty (auth). *Dealer:* Tilting at Windmills Gallery Manchester VT; Principle Gallery Alexandria VA; Sylvan Gallery Clinton Conn. *Mailing Add:* 360 Beaver Brook Rd Pawlet VT 05761

TORAK, THOMAS
PAINTER
b Pottstown, PA, Sept 7, 53. *Work:* Masur Mus Art, Wallace found. *Exhib:* Butler Inst of Am Art; Nat Acad Mus; Springfield Mus Fine Art; Nat Arts Club; Bergstrom, Mahler Mus, Masur Mus Art, San Diego Art Inst, Huntsville Mus Art, Krasl Art Ctr; and many others. *Awards:* Medal of Honor, Am Artists Prof League, 66th Grand Nat Exhib; Gold Medal of Honor, Audubon Artists, 59th Annual Exhib; Honor Award for Oil, Acad Artists Asn, 50th Nat Exhib, Contemp Realism. *Mem:* Salmagundi Club; Am Artists Prof League; Allied Artists of Am; Audubon Artists; Oil Painters of Am (signature mem, currently). *Media:* Oil. *Dealer:* GC Lucas Gallery Clington Conn; Gardner Colby Gallery Martha's Vineyard; Anderson Fine Art St Simons Ga; Fox Hall Gallery, Washington DC; GC Lucs Gallery Indianapolis Ind; Sylvan Gallery, Clinton, Conn; Christina Gallery, Edgartown, Mass; Four India st Gallery nantucret Mass; VT Fine Art Gallery Stowe Vt. *Mailing Add:* 360 Beaver Brook Rd Pawlet VT 05761

TORBERT, STEPHANIE BIRCH
PHOTOGRAPHER, ILLUSTRATOR
b Wichita Falls, Tex, May 31, 45. *Study:* Univ NMex, BFA, 68; Sch for Am Craftsman, Rochester Inst Technol, NY, 68; Visual Studies Workshop, State Univ NY, Buffalo, MFA, 71. *Work:* Weisman Mus Art, Minneapolis Inst Arts, Minn; Int Mus Photography, George Eastman House, Rochester; Ctr for Creative Photog, Tucson, Ariz; Mus NMex, Santa Fe. *Exhib:* Minn Survey: Six Photogrs, Minneapolis Inst Arts & Nat Endowment Arts, 78; one-person shows, Minneapolis Inst Arts, 70, Walker Art Ctr, Minneapolis, 73, Int Mus Photog, George Eastman House, Rochester, NY, 78 & Friends Photog, Carmel, Calif, 79; and others. *Collection Arranged:* Libr of Congress, Ctr for Creative Photog, Tuscon, Ariz, Walker Art Ctr, Minneapolis Inst of Art, Frederick R. Weisman Art Mus, Mus of NMex, Santa Fe, and others. *Pos:* Visual arts panel, Minn State Arts Bd, 76-. *Teaching:* Asst prof, N Hennepin Community Col, Minneapolis, 74-75 & Minneapolis Col Art & Design, 77-78 & 88-89. *Awards:* Bush Found Artists Fel, Minneapolis, 76-77; Nat Endowment Arts Grant, Minn Survey: Six Photogr, 77; Mckning Artist Fel, 84; MacDowell Colony Fel, 83, 84, 92; Nadine Blacklock Mem Award for Women Photgr, 99; Hand Hallow Found, NY, 99. *Mem:* Guild Natural Sci Illusrs. *Media:* Cibachrome, Pastel; Ink, Acrylic, Digital. *Interests:* Gardens of the World. *Publ:* The New Color Photography, Abbeville Press; Parks and Wildlands, Nodin Press; The Walk Book, Nodin Press; The Clay that Breathes, Milkweed Eds. *Dealer:* Alinder Gallery, Gualala, Calif, Flanders Contemp Art, Minneapolis, Minn, Alan Klotz, Photo Collect, NY. *Mailing Add:* 3824 Harriet Ave Minneapolis MN 55409

TORCOLETTI, ENZO
SCULPTOR
b Fano, Italy, May 1, 43; US citizen. *Study:* Inst Statale D'Arte A Apolloni, Fano, Italy, 54-58; Univ Windsor, Ont, BFA(sculpture), 69; Fla State Univ, MFA, 71. *Work:* Sculpture (40 ft site specific), Koger Properties, Jacksonville, Fla; Fla Nat Guard, Camp Blanding; Fla Artists Hall Fame, The Capital, Tallahassee; Waynesville Country Club, NC; Barnett Bank, Tampa, Fla. *Comn:* Aluminum wall relief, Fla Sch for Deaf, St Augustine, 90; granite site-specific sculpture, Kings' Hill, Kent, Eng, 92. *Exhib:* Solo exhibs, WGa Col, Carrollton, 73, Oklaloose-Walton Jr Col, Niceville, Fla, 76, Univ NFla, Jacksonville, 81 & 86, Sandestin, Destin Beach, Fla, 86, Embry-Riddle Aeronautical Univ, Daytona Beach, Fla, 88, Cummer Gallery Art, Jacksonville, 90-91; Brest Mus Gallery, Jacksonville Univ, 81, 82 & 84; Boca Raton Ctr Arts, Fla, 82; Jacksonville Collects, Jacksonville Art Mus, 84; Flagler Col, St Augustine, Fla, 90. *Teaching:* Asst, Fla State Univ, Tallahassee, 69-71; prof visual arts, Flagler Col, St Augustine, Fla, 71-; guest artist/lectr, Okaloosa-Walton Jr Col, Niceville, Fla, 72, Fla Jr Col & Univ NFla, Jacksonville, 80 & 81, Univ Fla, Gainesville, 81, Jacksonville Art Mus, 83, 84 & 87, Sandestin, Destin Beach, Fla, 86 & Douglas Anderson Sch Art, Jacksonville, 90. *Awards:* Purchase Award, Mint Mus Art, Charlotte, NC, 72; First Prize in Sculpture, Titusville Spring Art Show, Fla, 75; Hilton Leach Mem Award, Mus Arts & Sciences, Daytona Beach, 79. *Bibliog:* Susan Lynn Lester (auth), mag article, Jacksonville, 6/86; Diane Edwards (auth), mag article, 10/1/87; Arthur Williams (auth), Sculpture: Technique-Form-Content, 89. *Mem:* Fla Artists Group; Int Sculpture Ctr. *Media:* Stone, Bronze. *Dealer:* Agnes Gallery Birmingham AL; Moultrie Creek Studios Gallery St Augustine FL. *Mailing Add:* 120 W Genung Ave Saint Augustine FL 32086-7055

TORF, LOIS BEURMAN
COLLECTOR, PUBLISHER
b Boston, Mass, Sept 20, 26. *Study:* Univ Mass, Amherst, BA, 46. *Hon Degrees:* U Mass, Hon DFA, 84; Art Inst Boston, Hon DFA, 95. *Exhib:* Two Women Collect, Wellesley Col Mus Art, Mass, 76; The Modern Art of the Print, Williams Col Mus Art, Williamstown, Mass & Mus Fine Arts, Boston, 84; 70's into 80's: Printmaking Now, Mus Fine Arts, Boston, 87; Faces & Figures in Contemp Art, Mus Fine Arts, Boston, 96; one-woman show, Univ Mass, 97; Photo Image Printmaking 60's-90's, Mus Fine Arts, 98, Des Moines Art Ctr, 99; Sets, Series & Suites: Contemporary Prints (with catalog), 2005, David Hockney Portraits, 2006, Facets of Cubism, 2006, Degas to Picasso, 2006, Mus Fine Arts, Boston, Mass. *Pos:* VPres, Inst Contemp Art, 70-87. *Bibliog:* Deborah Menaker (auth), The Modern Art of the Print: Selections from the Collection of Lois & Michael Torf, Mus Fine Arts, Boston, 84; Pilgrims & Pioneers: New England Women in the Arts, Midmarch Arts Press, New York, 87. *Mem:* Int Coun ArCA, (trustee 70-); Mus Fine Arts, Boston (trustee 84-); Univ Mass Chancellor's Exec Comt, currently; hon mem Fine Arts Ctr, Univ Mass. *Collection:* 20th century graphic expressionism, pop & contemporary prints. *Mailing Add:* 15 Young Rd Weston MA 02193

TORLAKSON, JAMES DANIEL
PAINTER, FILMMAKER
b San Francisco, Calif, Feb 19, 51. *Study:* Calif Col Arts & Crafts, BFA, 73; San Francisco State Univ, MA, 74. *Work:* San Francisco Mus Mod Art; Oakland Mus, Calif; Brooklyn Mus; Carnegie Inst, Pittsburgh, Pa; Libr of Cong. *Exhib:* One-man shows, Calif Palace Legion of Hon, Achenbach Found, San Francisco, 76 & San Jose Mus Art, Calif, 79; VX Inst Sao Paul Biennial, Int Communications Agency, SAm, 79; Recent Trends in Am Printmaking, Mitchell Mus, Mt Vernon, Ill, 79; Am Realism, 20th Century Drawing & Watercolors, San Francisco Mus Mod Art, Calif, 85; Mainstream Am, The Collection of Phil Desind, Butler Inst Am Art, Youngstown, Ohio, 87; New Horizons in Am Realism, Flint Inst Arts, Mich, 91; and others. *Teaching:* Instr, Skyline Col, San Bruno, Calif, Col San Mateo, Calif & San Francisco City Col, Calif. *Awards:* Airport Purchase Award, San Francisco Int Airport Painting Competition, 77; Purchase Awards, 17th Nat Print & Drawing Exhib, Bradley Univ, 79 & Boston Printmakers 31st Nat Exhib, 79. *Bibliog:* Peter Frank (auth), New York Reviews, Artnews, 10/75. *Media:* Watercolor; Oil. *Publ:* Contemporary Am Realism, Since 1960, NY Graphics Soc, 81; Mendelowitz's Guide to Drawing, Holt Rinehart Winston, 82; Contrib, Am Realism, 20th Century Drawings & Watercolors, Abrams, 86; auth (with Judith Gordon), Deeping the third dimension, The Artist's Mag, 4/89. *Dealer:* John Berggruen 228 Grant Ave San Francisco CA 94108. *Mailing Add:* 433 Rockaway Beach Ave Pacifica CA 94044

TORLEN, MICHAEL ARNOLD
PAINTER, EDUCATOR
b San Diego, Calif, Feb 28, 40. *Study:* Cranbrook Acad Art, Bloomfield Hills, Mich, BFA, 62; Ohio State Univ, Columbus, fel 63-64, with Hoyt Sherman, MFA, 65. *Work:* Aldrich Mus, Ridgefield, Conn; Neuberger Mus & Roy Neuberger Collection, Purchase, NY; Prudential Insurance Co, Newark, NJ. *Comn:* Symbolic portraits, Arlene Sarapa, Wingate Paine & Buford Pippin, NY, 76; Meditation Mandala, Growth Ctr, NY, 77 & Goldleaf Omega Cross, 78. *Exhib:* Weatherspoon Ann, Univ NC, Greensboro, 67, 69 & 83; Aldrich Mus, Ridgefield, Conn, 72 & 73; one-man shows, Neuberger Mus, Purchase, NY, 79 & Cathedral St John the Divine, NY, 83; Artists Space, NY, 83; Luise Ross Fine Art, NY, 83; and others. *Teaching:* Asst prof painting & drawing, Univ Ga, 65-70; assoc prof & dept head painting & drawing, State Univ NY Col, Purchase, 72-. *Awards:* Purchase Award, Ga Comn Arts, 69; State Univ NY Res Fel & Grant, 78; Visiting Artist Traveling Grant, Vis Arts Bd, Australia Coun, 82. *Bibliog:* Robert Yoskowitz (auth), article, Arts Mag, 9/81. *Mem:* Col Art Asn; Lindisfarne Asn. *Dealer:* Luise Ross 162 56th St New York NY. *Mailing Add:* Purchase Col Suny Dept Visual Arts 735 Anderson Hill Rd Purchase NY 10577-1400

TORN, JERRY (GERALD J)
DRAFTSMAN, PHOTOGRAPHER
b Burlington, Iowa, Mar 16, 33. *Study:* Univ Iowa, studied printmaking with Mauricio Lasansky, BA(fine arts), 58. *Work:* Art Inst Chicago, First Nat Bank Chicago, Ill; Ill State Mus, Springfield; Portland Art Mus, Ore; Kemper Insurance Co, Long Grove, Ill; Va Mus Fine Arts, Richmond; Mus Fine Art, Univ Iowa, Iowa City. *Comn:* Drawings for exec dining room, First Nat Bank Chicago, London Branch, 81; Lithograph Suite, Plucked Chicken Press, Chicago, 83. *Exhib:* New Figurative Work, Univ Ind, Gary, 80; Drawings of David, Univ Wis, Marshfield, 81; 62nd Ann Exhib, Arts Club Chicago, 82; Dancers, Univ Wis, Marinette, 82, Art Guild, Burlington, Iowa, 82 & 94 & Fairweather Hardin Gallery, Chicago, 82 & 85. *Teaching:* Instr design, Loyola Univ, Chicago, 70-71. *Bibliog:* Alan Artner (auth), Jerry Torn, Chicago Tribune, 7/25/80; Margaret Hawkins (auth), Jerry Torn, New Art Examiner, 11/80; Les Krantz (auth), The Chicago Art Review, Am References, 89. *Mem:* Arts Club Chicago. *Media:* Graphite. *Mailing Add:* 216 S Marshall Burlington IA 52601

TORNHEIM, NORMAN
SCULPTOR
b Chicago, Ill, Sept 16, 42. *Study:* Art Ctr Col Design, BS, 66; Calif State Univ, San Diego, MA, 75. *Work:* Las Vegas Art Mus, Nev; Marietta Col, Ohio; Smith Col, Northampton, Mass; Ind Univ. *Comn:* Sculpture, comn by Mr & Mrs Stern, Calif, 76; sculpture, comn by Mr & Mrs Lewis, Calif, 77; sculpture, comn by Dr I Mori, Calif, 77. *Exhib:* Mainstreams 76, Marietta Col, Ohio, 76; Calif Craftsmen, Monterey Mus Art, Calif, 76; Designer-Craftsmen 76, Richmond Art Ctr, Calif, 76; Nat Competition 77, Dahl Fine Arts Ctr, 77; Calif Craftsmen, E B Crocker Art Mus, Sacramento, 77; Goldsmiths USA, Univ Wash, Seattle, 77; Musical Instruments, The Smithsonian Inst, Washington, DC, 78-80. *Collection Arranged:* Golden West Col Invitational, 78. *Teaching:* Instr wood, metal & leather, San Diego State Univ, Calif, 72-75; instr wood, metal, leather & clay, Golden West Col, Huntington Beach, Calif, 75-. *Awards:* Jurors Award, Las Vegas Art Mus, 75; Purchase Award, Ark Art Ctr, 76; Merit Award, Nat Competition 77, Dahl Fine Arts Ctr, 77. *Bibliog:* Dona Z Meilach (auth), Wood Objects as Functional Sculpture, Crown, 76. *Media:* Clay, Porcelain. *Publ:* Contribr, Artweek, 76-77. *Mailing Add:* Dept Art Golden West Col 15744 Golden West St Huntington Beach CA 92647

TORREANO, JOHN FRANCIS
PAINTER, SCULPTOR
b Flint, Mich, Aug 17, 41. *Study:* Cranbrook Acad Art, BFA, 63; Ohio State Univ, MFA, 67; also with Robert King & Hoyt L Sherman. *Work:* Whitney Mus Am Art, NY; Aldrich Mus Contemp Art, Ridgefield, Conn; Michener Collection, Univ Tex; The Corcoran Gallery Art, Washington, DC; Denver Art Mus; Indpls Mus Art; Contemp Mus Fine Arts, Houston; Honolulu Mus Contemp Art. *Comn:* Found Villa Rufolo, Amalfi, Italy; Ghost Gems, McCarran Int Airport, Las Vegas, Nev, 92. *Exhib:* Solo exhibs, Scott Hanson Gallery, NY, 89, Shea & Beker Gallery, NY, 89 & 90, The Corcoran Gallery, Washington, DC, 89, Susanne Hilberry Gallery, Birmingham, MI, 90, Shea & Beker Gallery, NY, 90, Dart Gallery, Chicago, Ill, 90 & Hypo Bank, NY, 92; Post Minimalsim 1979-1990 An Extended Harvest, Genouese Gallery, Boston, MA, 90; Painting Between the Paradigms Part IV: A Category of Objects As Yet Unnamed, Penine Hart Gallery, NY; With the Grain: Contemp Panel Painting, Whitney Mus Am Art, Stamford, Conn, 90; group show, Margo Leavin Gallery, Los Angeles, Calif, 90; Laforet Mus, Havajuku, Japan; Pleasure, Hallwalls, Buffalo, NY, 91; Glass: Material in the Service of Meaning, Tacoma Art Mus, Wash, 91; Cruciformed: Images of the Cross Since 1980, Cleveland Ctr Contemp Art, Ohio, 91. *Pos:* prog dir, NY Univ, 92-05. *Awards:* Nat Endowment Arts Grant & Creative Artists Pub Serv Grant, 78-79; Nat Endowments Arts Fel, 82-83 & 89-90; John Simon Guggenheim Mem Found Fel, 91; New York Found Arts Fel, 91. *Bibliog:* Michael Welzenbach (auth), rev, The Washington Post, 89; Goings On About Town, The New Yorker, 5/21/90; Theodore F Wolff (auth), The Art of Painting Plywood, The Christian Science Monitor, 8/17/90; Brook Adams (auth), Scarred Diamonds, ArtNews, 2/91. *Media:* Plywood. *Dealer:* Susanne Hilberry Gallery Birmingham MI; Margo Leavin Gallery Los Angeles CA. *Mailing Add:* 103 Franklin St New York NY 10013

TORRES, FRANCESC
VIDEO ARTIST, SCULPTOR
b Barcelona, Spain, Aug 8, 48. *Study:* Massana Art Inst, Barcelona, Spain(graphic design & painting), 64-67; Fine Arts Sch, Paris, France, cert(etching), 67-68. *Work:* Book Collection, Mus Mod Art, NY; Cooper-Hewitt Mus, NY; Everson Mus Art, Syracuse, NY; Mus Art, Carnegie Inst, Pittsburg, Pa; Museo Nacional Centro de Arte Reina Sofia, Madrid, Spain; Los Angeles Inst Contemp Art; Mus of Contemp Art, Sao Palo, Brazil. *Exhib:* This Is An Installation That Has A Title, Fundacio Joan Miro, Barcelona, 79; Residual Regions, Los Angeles Inst Contemp Art, Calif, 80; The Head of the Dragon, Whitney Mus Am Art, NY, 81; Field of Action, Herbert F Johnson Mus Art, Ithaca, NY, 82; Tough Limo, Mus Art, Carnegie Inst, Pittsburgh, Pa, 85; The Dictatorship of Swiftness, La Jolla Mus Contemp Art, Calif, 86; plus Ultra, Nat Galerie, Berlin, WGer, 88; La Cabeza del Dragon (with catalog), Muse Nacional Centro de Arte, Reina Sofia, Madrid, Spain, 91; Too Late for Goya (with catalog), Ariz State Univ Art Mus, Tempe, 93; one-man shows: Gallery 21, St Petersburg, Russia, 95, MIT, List Visual Arts Ctr, Cambridge, Mass, 98, Univ Salamanca, Palacio de Maldonado, Spain, 99, Fundación Telefónica, Madrid, 00, Ctr Cult Tecla Sala, Hospitalet, Spain, 00, Rafael Inst Contemp Art, Barcelona, 01, Sala Metrónom, Barcelona, 01; Gallery 21, St Petersburg, Russia, 95; MIT List Visual Art Ctr, Cambridge, Mass, 98; Fundacio Rafael Tous d'Art Contemporani, Barcelona, Spain, 01; Garage: imágenes del automóvil en la pintura española del siglo XX, Ctr Gallego de Arte Contemp, Santiago de Compostela, Spain, 01; Darrera Escena, Casal Solleric, Ajuntament de Palma, Palma de Mallorca, Spain, 02; Fragments, Mus de la Univ d'Alacant, Alicante, Spain, 02; Desesculturas, Círculo de Bellas Artes de Madrid, 02; Granada de Fondo, Colección de Arte Contemp de la Diputación de Granada, Ctr José Guerrero y Palacio de los Condes de Gabia, Granada, Spain, 03. *Collection Arranged:* NY Pub Libra Video Collection, Donnell Libr; LA Inst Contemp Art; Centro de Arte Reina Sofia, Madrid; La Jolla Mus Contemp Art; Mus Art, Carnegie Inst; Mus Mod Art; High Mus Art, Atlanta. *Teaching:* Instr mixed media & installations, Sch Visual Arts, NY, 86. *Awards:* Sponsored Projects Grant, NY State Coun Arts, 83-84; Spanish-Am Joint Com Cult & Educ Cooperation, 85; Individual Artist Fel, DAAD Berliner Kunstleprogramm, 86; NEA Video Prod Grant, 86-87, 93-94; NY Found for Arts, 1986-87; NEA Individual Artist Fel, 93-94; NY Found for the Arts, Individual Artist's Fellowship on Multidisciplinary Work, 01-02; Fundación Picasso, Casa Natal, Málaga, Spain, 02. *Media:* Mixed. *Dealer:* Elba Benitez Gallery, Madrid, Spain. *Mailing Add:* 38 N Moore St New York NY 10013

TORREY, ELLA KING
ADMINISTRATOR
b Vauxhall, NY, June, 57. *Study:* Germantown Friends Sch, 75; Yale Univ, New Haven, Conn, BA(art hist, cum laude), 80; Univ Miss, Oxford, MA(art hist), 84. *Collection Arranged:* The History of the Hasty Pudding Theatricals, Harvard Univ Librs, Mass, 78; Toying With The Times: A Critical Analysis of the Barbie Doll, 1959-1980, Yale Univ, New Haven, Conn, 79-80; Ten Afro-American Quilters (coauth with Maude Wahlman, catalog), toured US & Africa, Univ Miss, Oxford, 81-83. *Pos:* Cur & designer, Harvard Theatre Collection, Harvard Univ Librs, Cambridge, Mass, 78; asst cur, Whitney Mus Am Art, NY, 78; educ coordr, curatorial asst, Art Resources Conn, New Haven, 78-79; cur, Yale Ctr Am Art & Mat Cult, Yale Univ, New Haven, Conn, 79-80; asst cur, designer, John David Williams Libr, Univ Miss, Oxford, 81-82; cur, educational coordr, Ctr Study Southern Cult, Univ Miss, 81-83; spec proj consult, Robert Hull Fleming Mus, Univ Vt, Burlington, 83; sr mem, Pew Charitable Trusts, Philadelphia, Pa, 85-94; founding dir, Pew Fel Arts, Pa, 91-95; pres, San Francisco Art Inst, 95-. *Teaching:* Instr, Univ Miss, Oxford, 81-83, Univ Pa, Philadelphia, 94; lectr, Drexel Univ, Philadelphia, Pa, 85-95. *Awards:* Nancy Ann Thorpe Award Fine Arts, 75; David L Stokes Award Hist, 75; Irving C Poley Award Dramatic Arts, 75. *Publ:* Coauth (with Maude Wahlman), Quilts, Craft Int, New York, fall 82; Afro-American Quilts, Art Papers, Atlanta, Ga, fall 82; auth, Confessions/Confusions of a Private Funder: Arts Support within the American Philanthropic System, Orcas Conference: Creative Support Creative Artist, New York, 88; coauth (with Maude Wahlman), Theora Hamblett & Afro-Am Quilts, Encyl Southern Cult, Chapel Hill, NC, 89; auth, Artists-Art: The Role of Artists' Organizations in the National Arts Community, forward to 1989 Nat Asn Artists Orgn Directory, Washington, 89; and others. *Mailing Add:* San Francisco Art Inst 800 Chestnut St San Francisco CA 94133

TOSCAN, RICHARD ERIC
EDUCATOR
b New York, NY, Jul 1, 41. *Pos:* Adv bd, Int Contemp Art Fair, Los Angeles, 89-91, Tygres Heart Shakespeare Co, Portland, 92-, Portland Ctr Performing Arts, 92-, Image Theatre Mask Ensemble, 94-; mem, theatre panel Cult Affairs Dept, Los Angeles, 90-92; mem, selection comt Javits fel US Dept Educ, Wash, 90-93; dean, sch fine and performing arts Portland (Ore) State Univ, 92-96; dean, sch arts Va Commonwealth Univ, Sch of Arts, Richmond, Va, 96-. *Teaching:* Postdoctoral teaching resident Nat Endowment of the Humanities, 67-69. *Awards:* Woodrow Wilson Found fel, 63-64; Univ Ill fel, 64. *Mem:* Fel (Assoc) East Asian Study Ctr; Am Soc Theatre Res, Int Coun Fine Arts Deans. *Mailing Add:* Va Commonwealth Univ Sch of Arts 325 N Harrison St Richmond VA 23284

TOSCANO, DOLORES A
PAINTER, SCULPTOR
b Ft Worth, Tex. *Study:* Studied with Bruno Lucchesi (sculpture) & Daniel Green (pastel painting), 85. *Work:* San Juan Col, NMex; Benson Park, Loveland, Colo; and others. *Comn:* Life size bronze St Walburga, Walburga Convent, Boulder, Colo, 85-86; twelve ft marble figure of Christ, Risen Christ Church, Denver, Colo, 87; life size bronze Mary & Jesus, Blessed Heart Jesus, Boulder, Colo, 88. *Exhib:* Pioneer's Mus Show, Colorado Springs Mus, 85; Society de Pastellistes de France, Salon Int Du Pastel, Paris, 87; Miniature Show, Albuquerque Mus, 91 & 92; Women Who Paint the West, Tucson Mus, Ariz, 91-93; Rotary Invitational, Loveland, Colo, 92-95; and others. *Teaching:* Pastel instr portraits, Scottsdale Art Sch, Ariz, 87-88 & Denver, Colo Art Student League, 90-91. *Awards:* Gold Medal, Catherine L Wolfe, NY, 78-79; Gold Medal, Pastel Soc Southwest, 87; Master Pastelist, Flora Guffino, Pastel Soc Am, 87; and others. *Bibliog:* Toscano Southwest Art, 79-87; Mary C Nelson (auth),

Pastels by Toscanco, Am Artist, 83; Vicki Stavig (auth), I had the want to's, Art West, 91; and others. *Mem:* Pastel Soc Am, NY; Catherine Lorrillard Wolfe Club, NY. *Media:* Pastel; Bronze. *Publ:* Contribr, American Artist of Renown, Wilson Pub, 81; Contemporary Western Artists, Harold Samuels, 82

TOSCHIK, LARRY
PAINTER, WRITER
b Milwaukee, Wis, July 17, 22. *Study:* Wis Art Acad, scholar; Layton Art Sch, Milwaukee. *Work:* Ariz State Univ Col Bus Admin; Riveredge Found, Calgary; US House of Rep; US Dept of Interior; Soc Wildlife Art Nations, London. *Comn:* Battlefield monument, 361st Inf 91st Div Mil Cemetery, Florence, Italy, 44; 30 paintings (wildlife), Hallmark Permanent Collection, 69-71; 20 silver medallions, Ducks Unlimited Inc, Chicago, 74; four wildlife lithographs, Franklin Mint; painting, 50th Anniversary of Ducks Unlimited, 86-87; two paintings for collector ed, Waterfowl of North Am, Can, 87. *Exhib:* Nat Cowboy Hall of Fame, Oklahoma City, 73; Waterfowl Festival, Easton, Md, 73; Pac Flyway Show, Santa Rosa, Calif, 75; Retrospective, Scottsdale Ctr for Arts, 78; Inaugural Exhib, Soc Wildlife Art for the Nations, London, Eng, 85; and others. *Awards:* 3M Co Design Award, 62; Ducks Unlimited Inc Artist of the Year, 75-76; two awards, Printing Indust Am, 77; Flyway Artist of Year, Ducks Unlimited, 92-93. *Mem:* Audubon Soc; Soc for Wildlife Art for the Nations, London, Eng (vpres). *Media:* Miscellaneous Media. *Publ:* Auth & illusr, Whispering skies of Arizona, 3/73, Shadowed trails, 2/76, Prowlers of the clouds, 2/79 & Shorebirds, 2/82, Ariz Highways Mag; illusr, Wildlife Techniques Manual; and thirty juvenile books on wildlife subjects. *Dealer:* Troys Gallery Main St Scottsdale AZ 85251. *Mailing Add:* 13840 N Desert Harbor Dr Apt 153 Peoria AZ 85381

TOSK, MARSHA
SCULPTOR
b NY, Apr 27, 48. *Study:* Herbert H Lehman Col, NY, BA; Art Students League, NY; Nat Acad Sch Fine Arts, NY; Cathedral St John the Divine, Greg Wyatt Sculpture Studio, NY; studied with Anthony Antonios, Peter Rubino & Michael Keropian. *Exhib:* Nat Acad Sch Fine Arts, Acad Mus, NY, 95; Riverdale Country Sch, Festival of Arts, Bronx, NY, 96-98; North Am Sculpture Exhib, Foothills Art Ctr, Golden, Colo, 98; 57th Ann Audubon Artists Exhib, Salmagundi Club, NY, 99; Allied Artists Am, 87th Ann Exhib, Salmagundi Club, NY, 2000; Round & Round, Am Carousel Figures, Brookgreen Gardens, Murrells Inlet, SC, 2001; Catharine Lorillard Wolfe Art Club, 106th Ann Open Juried Exhib, Nat Arts Club, NY, 2002. *Awards:* Salmagundi Club Award, 54th Annual Sculpture & Medallic Art Exhib, Pen & Brush Inc, NY; Elliot Liskin Mem Award, 57th Annual Audubon Artists Exhib, Salmagundi Club, NY; Artists Showcase Award Winner, Manhattan Arts Int, NY, 99. *Bibliog:* Barbara Byrnes (auth), Lenarcic, Showcase a Mix of Artistic Forms, Westminster Window, 6/11/98; Jeff Bradley (auth), Tradition Lifts Golden Show to Top of Form, Denver Post, 5/30/98. *Mem:* Am Artists Prof League; Nat Sculpture Soc (assoc mem, currently); Allied Artists Am (assoc mem, currently); Catharine Lomllard Wolfe (bd dirs). *Media:* Bronze. *Mailing Add:* 115 Central Park W Apt 3B New York NY 10023

TOTH, CARYL
PHOTOGRAPHER
b Cleveland, Ohio, Dec 7, 47. *Study:* Rochester Inst Technol, AAS, 68; State Univ NY, Buffalo, with Donald Blumberg, BA Eng, 70, MFA, 72. *Work:* Int Mus Photog at George Eastman House, Rochester, NY; Visual Studies Workshop, Rochester; Mus Mod Art, NY; Australian Nat Gallery, Canberra; San Francisco Mus Mod Art, Calif. *Exhib:* Ctr for Creative Photog, Tucson, 81; Northlight Gallery, Tempe, Ariz, 81; Corcoran Gallery Art, Washington, DC, 82; Cleveland Inst Art, 85; Los Angeles Ctr for Visual Studies Workshop, 85 & Photg Studies, 87; Mus Mod Art, Mexico City, 87; and others. *Teaching:* Head dept photog, Cranbrook Acad of Art, Bloomfield Hills, Mich, 72-; instr artistically gifted, Putnam Sch, WVa, 80-. *Awards:* Photogr Fel, Nat Endowment Arts, 75, 80 & 86; Mich Coun for the Arts, 83, 85 & 90. *Bibliog:* Photography Year, Time Life Books, 73; Exhibition Review, Artforum, 1/75 & 10/85. *Mem:* Soc Photog Educ; Col Art Asn. *Publ:* Auth, Caryl Toth: Recent Works, Cranbrook Acad Art, 83; Latent Images: Great Lakes Arts Alliance, Nat Endowment Arts, 86; Under Construction: New Photomontage, Cranbrook Acad Art, 88. *Dealer:* MacGill Pace 32 E 57th New York NY; The Art Store Charleston WV. *Mailing Add:* c/o The Art Store 1013 Bridge Rd Charleston WV 25314

TOTH, GEORGINA GY
ART LIBRARIAN
b Budapest, Hungary, Aug 28, 32; US citizen. *Study:* Eotvos Lorond Univ, Budapest, MA, 56; Case Western Reserve Univ, MSLS, 62. *Pos:* Cataloger, Cleveland Mus Art Libr, 62-69, reference librn, 69-75, assoc librn for reference, 75-; book reviewer, Art Documentation, 81-. *Mem:* Art Libr Soc NAm, Ohio chap, (vchmn, 88, chmn, 89). *Interests:* Art Research; Methodology; Collectors and Collecting; Bibliography. *Mailing Add:* 2574 Dysart Rd University Heights OH 44118

TOULIS, VASILIOS (APOSTOLOS)
PRINTMAKER, EDUCATOR
b Clewiston, Fla, Mar 24, 31. *Study:* Univ Fla, with Fletcher Martin & Carl Holty, BDes; Pratt Inst, with Richard Lindner, Fritz Eichenberg, Jacob Landau & Walter Rogalski, BFA. *Work:* US State Dept, Washington, DC; Mus Arte Mod, Mexico City, Mex; Caravan House, NY. *Comn:* Portfolio of prints, Ctr for Contemp Printmaking, 68. *Exhib:* Brooklyn Mus, NY, 66; Fleishcer Mem, Philadelphia, 66; Mus Arte Mod, Mexico City, 67; Int Miniature Print Exhib, 68; New Paltz Nat Print Exhib, 68; and others. *Teaching:* Lectr serigraphic printmaking, Univ RI, 67 & Pratt Inst Seminar, 69; head graphic workshops, Pratt Inst, 66-, instr printmaking, 69-71, assoc prof & head undergrad printmaking, 71-; dir silk screen workshops, The Artists Collective, Hartford, Conn, 73-. *Awards:* Tiffany Found Grant in Printmaking, 67. *Mem:* Am Asn Univ Prof; United Fedn Col Teachers; Screen Printers Asn. *Mailing Add:* 76 Oscawana Heights Rd Putnam Valley NY 10579

TOURLENTES, STEPHEN C
PHOTOGRAPHER, SCULPTOR
b Galesburg, Ill, 59. *Study:* Knox Col, BA Art, 82; Mass Col Art, MFA Photography, 88. *Work:* Art Inst Chicago; Metrop Mus of Art, NY; Mus of Fine Arts, Boston; Harvard Univ, Cambridge, Mass. *Exhib:* Family and Friends, Mus of Contemp Photog, Chicago 88; Retraining Nature, Art Inst Chicago, 97; Panoramic Vision, Addison Gallery of Am Art, Andover, Mass, 98. *Teaching:* Vis assoc prof Mass Col of Art, Boston, 89-; Faculty mem, Island Ctr Arts, Skopeles, Greece, 95-. *Awards:* Fel New England Found for the Arts, 94; McDowell Fel, 98, 99, 2000; Guggenheim fel, 2000. *Dealer:* Revolution 23257 Woodward Ave Ferndale MI 48220. *Mailing Add:* 195 Summer St Apt K Somerville MA 02143

TOUSIGNANT, CLAUDE
PAINTER, SCULPTOR
b Montreal, Que, Dec 23, 32. *Study:* Sch Art & Design, Montreal. *Work:* Nat Gallery Can; Phoenix Art Mus, Ariz; Larry Aldrich Mus, Ridgefield, Conn; York Univ; Mus Contemp Art, Montreal & Quebec; and others. *Exhib:* The Responsive Eye, traveling, 65; Biennale, Nat Gallery Can, Ottawa, 65 & 68; Trois cents ans de peinture Canadienne, Nat Gallery Can, Ottawa, 67; Panorama de la peinture au Québec, 1940-1966, Mus d'Art Contemporain, Montreal, 67; Forme-Couleur, Nat Gallery Can, Ottawa, 69; Panorama de la Sculpture au Québec 1945-1970, Mus d'Art Contemporain, Montreal & Mus Rodin, Paris, 70; Dix ans de Propositions Géométriques, Mus d'Art Contemporain & traveling, 79-81; Reflects, Nat Gallery Can, Ottawa, 84; Les vingt ans de Graff, Mus d'Art Contemporain, Montreal, 86; solo exhibs, 49th Parallel, NY, 87, Galerie Waddington Gorce, Montreal, 89, Vancouver Art Gallery, 90, Drabinsky Gallery, Toronto, 91, Mus de Québéc, traveling, 94, Galerie Christiane Chassay, Montreal & Christopher Cutts Gallery, Toronto, 95, and many more; La crise de l'abstraction au Canada, Les annéles 1950, traveling, 92-93; Recent Acquisitions, Montreal Mus Fine Arts, 95. *Awards:* Prize, Centennial Exhib, 67; Rome Prize, 73; Borduas Prize, 89. *Bibliog:* David Burnett & Marilyn Schiff, Contemporary Canadian Art, Edmonton: Hurtig, 83; James D Campbell, Abstract Practices (exhib catalog), Toronto, The Power Plant, 91; After Geometry: The Abstract Art of Claude Tousignant, Montreal: ECW Press, 95. *Mailing Add:* 181 Bourget Montreal PQ H4C 2M1 Canada

TOUSIGNANT, SERGE
PHOTOGRAPHER, CONCEPTUAL ARTIST
b Montreal, Que, May 28, 42. *Study:* Ecole des Beaux-Arts de Montreal, dipl, 62; studied at Slade Sch Fine Art, London, Eng, 67. *Work:* Nat Gallery Can, Ottawa; Victoria & Albers Mus, London, Eng; Bridgestone Art Gallery, Tokyo, Japan; Mus d Art Contemporain, Montreal, Can; Conseil des Arts de Val-de-Marne, Credac, Paris, France; Musée des Beaux-Arts de Montreal, Can; Art Gallery Ontario, Toronto; Tate Gallery, London. *Exhib:* New Images, Que' Photog, 49 Parallel Gallery, NY, 83; Canadian Impressions, Contemp Art Ctr, Osaka, Japan, 84; Lumieres: Projections, Can Indian Artcrafts, Montreal, Can, 85; Les Temps Chauds, Mus Asn Can, Montreal, 88; Montreal/Berlin, Saydie Bronfman Ctr/TIP Berlin, Montreal, Can, 89; Constructed Spaces, Photog Resource Ctr, Boston Univ, 90; Phases in Photog (coauth catalog), Can Mus Contemp Photo, Ottawa, Can, 92-96; Cutting Edge, Arco, Madrid, 98; Art Paris, Carousel du Louvres, 2000; Le Cadres, Le Site, La Scene, Centro de La Imagen, Mexico City, 2000; Toronto Int Art Fair, Convention Ctr, Can, 2004; The Sixties in Can, The Sixties: The Question of Photog, Nat Gallery Can, Ottawa, 2005. *Teaching:* Prof art & photog, Univ Montreal, Que, Can, 78-2005. *Awards:* Tokyo Print Biennale Lithography Prize, Bridgestone Art Gallery, Mus Contemp Art, Japan, 65; 200th Anniversary, 1789-1989: Image Pour la Revolution (participant), Credac, Paris, 89; nominee, Royal Acad Arts Can, 2004. *Bibliog:* Sylvain Campeau (auth), Chambres Obscures, Ed Trois, Montreal, Can, 95; Indices, Études et Maquettes: Serge Tousignant, Eds Graff, Montreal, 2000. *Media:* Photography. *Specialty:* Contemp art. *Publ:* Auth, Monography of the Artist, Yvan Boulerice, Montreal, Can, 78. *Dealer:* Galerie Graf 963 ru Rachel est Montreal Quebec Canada H2J 2J4. *Mailing Add:* 4060 boul St Laurent App 606 Montreal PQ H2W 1Y9 Canada

TOVISH, HAROLD
SCULPTOR
b New York, NY, July 31, 21. *Study:* Columbia Univ, 40-43; Ossip Zadkine Sch Sculpture, Paris, 49-50; Acad Grande Chaumiere, Paris, 50-51. *Work:* Whitney Mus Am Art & Mus Mod Art, NY; Philadelphia Mus Art; Hirshhorn Mus, Washington, DC; Boston Mus Fine Art, Mass; Walker Art Ctr, Minneapolis, Minn; and others. *Comn:* Epitaph (sculpture), State of Hawaii, 70. *Exhib:* Metrop Mus Art, 42; Twenty-Eighth Venice Biennial, Italy, 56; Carnegie Inst Int, 58; Recent Sculpture: USA, Mus Mod Art, NY, 59; Chicago Art Inst, 59; Whitney Mus Am Art Ann, 66; retrospectives, Watson Gallery, Wheaton Col, 67 & Addison Gallery Am Art, Andover, Mass, 88; solo exhib, Guggenheim Mus, 68; Int Award Exhib, Guggenheim Mus, 68; Inst Contemp Art, Boston, 76, 77 & 84; Boston Mus Fine Art, 77; Nat Mus Am Art, Washington, DC, 87; Muscarelle Mus, William & Mary Col, Williamsburg, Va, 90. *Teaching:* Asst prof sculpture & drawing, Univ Minn, 51-54; vis prof sculpture, Univ Hawaii, 64-70; prof art, Boston Univ, 71-84, prof emer, 86-. *Awards:* Am Inst Arts & Lett Grant, 60 & 71; Guggenheim Fel, 67; Fel, Ctr Advanced Visual Studies, Mass Inst Technol, 68. *Bibliog:* H Harvard Arneson (auth), New talent, Art in Am, 54. *Mem:* Nat Acad (assoc 1981-90, acad 1990-). *Media:* Bronze, Mixed Media. *Publ:* Sculpture: The sober art, Atlantic Monthly, 61. *Dealer:* Howard Yezersky Gallery 186 South St Boston MA; Martin Sumers Graphics 50 W 57th St New York NY. *Mailing Add:* 380 Marlborough St Boston MA 02115

TOWNER, MARK ANDREW
ADMINISTRATOR, PHOTOGRAPHER
b Evanston, Ill, 1956. *Study:* Visual Studies Workshop, Rochester, NY, 78; Columbia Col, Chicago, BA, 78; Cranbrook Acad Art, MFA, 81; Int Ctr Photog, 82; Metrop Mus Art, New York, 88; Am Law Inst-Am Bar Asn, Boston, 2000. *Work:* Detroit Inst Arts; Ill State Mus; Cranbrook Acad Art Mus; Davenport Mus Art, Iowa; Univ Iowa. *Comn:* The Law Sch, Univ Mich. *Exhib:* Solo exhibs, Southeastern Ohio Series, Photog Gallery, Southern Ill Univ, Carbondale, 84, Anima/Animals: New Figurative Photographs, Photogr's Collective, South Bend, Ind, 85, Post Industrialization, P A C A Gallery, NY, 87, The Illuminated Ones, Trabia-MacAfee Gallery, NY, 89, Evolution of the Crucifix, Quad City Arts Gallery, Rock Island, Ill, 90, On Aesthetics, Mt Mercy Col, Cedar Rapids, Iowa, 93, Arresting Images From Popular Cult Arts, Iowa City, Iowa, 95, Oakland Co Arts Ctr, Pontiac, Mich, 95 Quad City Arts Gallery, Rock Island, Ill, 95; 20/20 Vision, Cranbrook Acad Art, Bloomfield Hills, 92; The Search for Color, Detroit Inst Arts, Mich, 93; Iowa Artists 1994, Des Moines Art Ctr, 94; Art as Healing, Pyramid Arts Ctr, Rochester, NY, 94; Spirit In Art and History, Andover Historial Soc, Andover, Mass, 2001; Digital City, New Squirts for Now People, NESAD at Suffolk Univ, Boston, Mass, 2003; Endicott Faculty Reaches Out, Aberjona River Gallery, Winchester, Mass, 2004; Annual Spring Exhib, Small Works Gallery, Haverhill, Mass, 2004 & 06; Cranbrook to Lancaster and Back, Cranbrook Art Mus, Bloomfield Hills, Mich, 2005 & 06; Creative Arts, Dana-Farber Cancer Inst, Boston, Mass, 2006. *Collection Arranged:* Richard Bolton: Photographs, Gallery 681, Wayne State Univ, 82; Four Women Photographers, St Mary's Col Photog Gallery, Notre Dame, Ind, 85; The Painted Spirit: Selected Works from the Permanent Collection, Davenport Mus Art, Iowa, 89; Three Decades of Midwestern Photography: 1960-1990, Davenport Mus Art; The Moving Wall: Vietnam War Mem, Frejervary Park, Davenport, Iowa, 91; Wellness Disease & Visual Art, Arts Iowa City, 97; Art By Healers, Broudo Gallery, 2004. *Pos:* Photogr, Metrop Mus Art, NY, 82-83; dir, Circlework Visions Ltd, NY, 85-87; chief preparator & exhib designer, Am Craft Mus, NY, 87-88; asst dir, Davenport Mus Art, Iowa, 89- & NE Doc Conserv Ctr, Andover, Mass; dir, proj art, Univ Iowa Hosp & Clinics, Iowa City, 94-98; Dean of Art & Design, Endicott Col, Beverly, Ma, 2000-. *Bibliog:* Celeste Olalquiaga (auth), Megalopolis: Contemporary Cultural Sensibilities, 92; Arts In Healing, Butler Inst, 95; Sex Wars: Photography on the Frontlines, Exposure, 95. *Mem:* Am Asn Mus; Col Art Asn; Am Art Therpy Asn; Col Art Asn. *Media:* Collage Art, Photography. *Publ:* Nathan Lerners Maxwell Street, River Cities Reader, 12/93; Featured Artist, ArtsBeat, 3/93; National Exposure, New City, Chicago, 6/10/93; Iowa Artists: 1994, Des Moines Art Ctr, 9/94; Offset: ARTS Iowa City, River Cities Reader, 10/95; Printed Pleasure: Published Pain, Iowa City Press, 9/95; Complex Collages Capture Culture, Moline Dispatch, 6/96; Iowa City: Views & Reviews, River Cities Readers, 2/94; Paper/Fiber XVII, Iowa City Press-Citizen, 4/20/94; Ralph Eugene Meatyard: An American Visionary, River Cities Reader, 5/94; Creating With Others, by Shaun Mcnitt, 2003. *Mailing Add:* Endicott College 376 Hale St Beverly MA 01915

TOWNLEY, HUGH
SCULPTOR, PRINTMAKER
b Lafayette, Ind, Feb 6, 23. *Study:* Univ Wis, 46-48; also with Ossip Zadkine, Paris, 48-49; London Co Coun Arts & Crafts, 49-50. *Hon Degrees:* MA, Brown Univ, 64. *Work:* Mus Mod Art; Whitney Mus Am Art; Boston Mus Fine Arts; Fogg Mus Art, Harvard Univ; Los Angeles Co Mus Art; Mus Fine Art, Houston, TX. *Comn:* Three concrete pieces, Class of 65, Brown Univ, Providence, RI, 70; three concrete pieces, State of Ky Comprehensive Training Ctr, Somerset, Ky, 72; eleven concrete pieces, Northwest Sculpture Advocates, Inc, Eugene, Ore, 74; designed 14 benches for City of Providence, RI, 79; Relief Lunar Migration, Luis Muñoz Airport, Am Airlines Admirals Club, San Juan, Puerto Rico, 91. *Exhib:* New Talent Show, Mus Mod Art, 55; Exhib Drawings & Sculpture, Whitney Mus Am Art, 62 & 63; 65th Am Painting & Sculpture Exhib, Art Inst Chicago, 64; Univ Calif Santa Barbara, CA, 68; solo exhibs, DeCordova & Dana Mus, Lincoln, Mass, 69; Monumenta, Newport, RI, 74; State Univ NY, Albany, 80; Worcester Art Mus, Worcester, Mass, 80; Contemp Am Prints, Philadelphia Art Alliance, 85; Inst Contemp Art, Boston, 77; US Information Service, Leningrad, Soviet Union, 85-86; Int Small Sculpture Exhib, Budapest, 87; Virginia Lynch Gallery, Tiverton, RI, 88 & 92; Univ Wis, Milwaukee Fine Arts Gallery, 89, Dartmouth Col Artist in Residence, 91; St Gardens Nat Hist Site Gallery, Cornish NH, 2002; TW Wood Gallery, Montpelier Vt, 2004; H Townley with Edward Koren Exhibition, Washington Depot, CT, 2004; Chaplin Gallery, Norwhich Univ, Northfield, Vt, 2005; Big Town Gallery, Rochester, Vt, 2006; Governor's Off Gallery, Montpelier, Vt, 2006. *Collection Arranged:* cur, George Herriman's Krazy Kat Exhib, Brown Univ, 84; cur, Some Photographic Uses of Color Exhib, Brown Univ, 84. *Pos:* Prof Emer, Brown Univ, Providence, RI. *Teaching:* Instr sculpture & drawing, Layton Sch Art, Milwaukee, 51-56; asst prof sculpture, Beloit Col, 56-57; asst prof sculpture & drawing, Boston Univ, 57-61; prof art, Brown Univ, 61-89; vis prof, Univ Calif, Berkeley, 61, Santa Barbara, 68; vis lectr, Harvard Univ, 67; artist in res, Dartmouth Col, 91. *Awards:* Yaddo Found, Saratoga Springs, 64; Nat Inst Arts & Letters, 67; Tamarind Lithography Found, Los Angeles, Fel, 69; Gov Award, State of RI Coun Arts, 72; Ore Sculpture Symposium, Eugene, 74. *Media:* Wood, Concrete; Lithography. *Dealer:* Anni Mackay Rochester Vt. *Mailing Add:* 228 River St Bethel VT 05032

TOWNSEND, GAVIN EDWARD
HISTORIAN, EDUCATOR
b Santa Monica, Calif, June 16, 56. *Study:* Hamilton Col, Clinton, NY, BA, 78; Univ Calif, Santa Barbara, MA, 81, PhD, 86. *Collection Arranged:* The Linens of R H Hunt: drawings by Chattanooga's Foremost Architect, Univ Art Gallery, Univ Tenn, 88. *Pos:* Asst cur archit drawing, Univ Calif, Santa Barbara, 82-86; gallery coordr, Univ Tenn, Chattanooga, 87-92, asst dir hons prog, 92 -97, dir hons prog, 97-2003. *Teaching:* Instr art hist, Univ Calif, Santa Barbara, 79-86; asst prof art hist, Univ Tenn, Chattanooga, 86-93, assoc prof, 93-2001, prof, 2001-. *Awards:* Kress Found Fel, 82-84. *Mem:* Soc Archit Hist; Hist Zoning Comn, Chattanooga, Tenn; Tenn State Hist Comn. *Res:* Anglo-American architecture 1865-1945. *Publ:* Auth, Airborne Toxins and the American House 1865-1895, Winterthur Portfolio, 89; The Tudor House of the Prairie Sch, Arris, 92; Frank Forster and the French Provincial Revival in America, Arris, 95; Lamb and Rich in Robert Mackay ed, Long Island Country Estates and Their Architects, 1860-1940, NY, Norton, 97; Reuben Harrison Hunt: A History of Tennesse Arts, Univ Tenn Press, 2004; contribr, Encyclopedia of 20th Century Architecture Chicago, Fitzray-Dearborn. *Mailing Add:* 1631 Rock Bluff Rd Hixson TN 37343

TOWNSEND, JEAN (MRS SAUL FIELD)
PAINTER, PRINTMAKER
b Toronto, Ont, July 23, 21. *Study:* Art Gallery Ont, studied with Arthur Lismer, 29-38; Ont Col Art, studied with Franklin Carmichael, John Alfsen & Rowley Murphy, 38-43; Instituto Allende, Mexico, 59; post-grad study with Nicholas Hornyansky, Guillermo Silva & J W G MacDonald; Inst Allende, Mexico, 88-90. *Work:* Montreal Mus Fine Art; Nat Libr Can, Ottawa; Art Gallery Hamilton, Ont; Art Gallery Peterborough, Ont; Univ Toronto; Thomas Fisher Rare Bks Libr. *Comn:* Wind Among the Reeds (print portfolio), Upstairs Gallery, Toronto, 72; Blue Jean Series (portfolio), Galerie Int, Ribe, Denmark, 77; Tales of Heritage II (portfolio & book collaboration with Saul Field), Can Govt/York Univ, 83 & 86. *Exhib:* Ontario Society of Artists, Art Gallery Ont, Toronto, 43-45; Canadian Soc Graphic Art, Art Gallery Ont, 64-65, Canadian Painters-Etchers, Montreal Mus Fine Art, 67; Juxtaposition of Joyce & Yeats, Print Club, Philadelphia, 72, Canada House, London, 83, Art Alliance, Philadelphia, 85; Pioneers in the Collograph Print, Wenninger Gallery, Boston, 79; Yeats Summer Sch, Sligo, Ireland, 82; Print Biennale, Palace of Sport & Cult, Varna, Bulgaria, 83; Expo 67, Montreal. *Pos:* Dir, Upstairs Gallery, Toronto, 58-66. *Teaching:* Printmaking fel, Sheridan Col, 73 & York Univ, Toronto, 74-79. *Awards:* Governor-General's Medal, Ont Col Art, 42; Ontario Arts Coun Grants, 77 & 85; Artist-in-Residence Grant, Can Coun, 84; and others. *Bibliog:* Life & Work of Jean Townsend & Saul Field (film), Brilliant Films, 88. *Mem:* Ont Soc Arts (exec, 79-82); Heliconian Club; Arts & Letters Club. *Media:* Oils, Watercolour. *Publ:* Illusr, Mozaic Mag, Univ Man, 74; Celtic Twilight (by W B Yeats), Colin Smythe, 82; Tales of Heritage II, York Univ, 86; J Mod Literature (cover), Temple Univ, Philadelphia, 88; Yeats' Irland (by David Pierce), Yale Univ Press, 94, J Mod Literature, Temple Univ, Philadelphia Cover, 88

TOWNSEND, JOHN F
SCULPTOR, PAINTER
b La Crosse, Wis. *Study:* Carroll Col, Waukesha, Wis, BS, 51; Minneapolis Sch of Art, 53-55; Univ of Minn Grad Sch, MFA, 59. *Work:* Mus Fine Art, Boston, Mass; Rose Mus, Brandeis Univ, Waltham, Mass; Allentown Art Mus, Pa; Chase Manhattan Bank, NY; World Bank, Washington, DC. *Exhib:* Art for US Embassies, Inst Contemp Art, Boston, 66; Optical Art Traveling Exhib, Mus Mod Art, NY, 66-68; Small Paintings for Mus Collections, Am Fedn of Art Traveling Exhib, 67-68; one-man shows, Eleanor Rigelhaupt Gallery, Boston, 67, Ward-Nasse Gallery, Boston, 70, Danco Gallery, Florence, 79, Berkshire Artisans, Pittsfield, 81 & Zone, Springfield, 85, Mass; and others. *Pos:* Dir art exhibs, 60-64 & dir grad art prog, 71-74, Univ Mass, Amherst; bd dir, Zone Art Ctr, Springfield, Mass, 86-. *Teaching:* Instr sculpture & painting, Eastern NMex Univ, Portales, 59-60; from instr to full prof sculpture, drawing & design, Univ of Mass, Amherst, 60-; part-time instr painting, Mt Holyoke Col, South Hadley, Mass, 61-62. *Awards:* First Award Sculpture, Second Ann Univ Arts Faculty Exhib, Argus Gallery, Madison, NJ, 63; Crane Co Award, 17th Ann Exhib of Painting & Drawing, 68; President's Award, Springfield Art League 66th Nat Exhib, Mus Fine Arts, Mass, 85. *Bibliog:* Dona Z Meilach (auth), Contemporary Art with Wood, Crown Publ Inc, New York, 68; Gloria Russell (auth), review, The Sunday Republican, Springfield, Mass, 4/21/85. *Media:* Wood & Bronze; Acrylic. *Mailing Add:* 118 Aubinwood Rd Amherst MA 01002-1690

TOWNSEND, STORM D
SCULPTOR, INSTRUCTOR
b London, Eng, Aug 31, 37. *Study:* London Univ, NDD, ATC, Goldsmiths' Col Art, 6 yrs, with Harold Parker & Ivor Roberts Jones. *Hon Degrees:* Nat Diploma in Design and Art Tchg Cert, NDD, ATC, London. *Work:* Fine Arts Mus NMex, Santa Fe; Genesee Co Mus, Rochester. *Comn:* Life-size portrait in bronze, comn by David Cargo, Gov NMex, 67; To Serve & Protect (life-size bronze to honour the police force), comn by City of Albuquerque; Charlie Pride Int Sr Golf Classic (bronze trophy design), 87 & Tres Culturas del Rio Grande (bronze figures), 88, Sunwest Bank, Albuquerque, NMex. *Exhib:* One-person shows, Gallery Marquis, Denver, Colo, 75, Gallery Eleven, Lubbock, Tex, 77 & Am Inst Architects, Albuquerque, NMex, 90; Survey of Contemp NMex Sculpture, NMex Mus Fine Art, Santa Fe, 76; Santa Fe Festival Arts, 79; Great Garden Exhib, Sculptural Arts Mus, Atlanta, 82; Circle of Art Gallery, Scottsdale Village, Albuquerque, NMex, 97; plus others. *Collection Arranged:* NMex Mus of Fine Art, Santa Fe; Sunwest Bank Albuquerque, NMex; Genesee Country Mus, Rochester, NY. *Pos:* Moulder/caster prep lab fossils, Mus Nat Hist, Albuquerque, NMex, 87-89. *Teaching:* Instr sculpture, Pojoaque Art Ctr, Santa Fe, 65-66, Col of Santa Fe, 73-75, Univ Albuquerque, NMex & adult educ prog Univ NMex, currently. *Awards:* Jajasan Siswa Lokantara Resident Fel to study the arts in Indonesia, 60-61; Resident Fels, Huntington Hartford Found, Calif, 63 & Helene Wurlitzer Found, Taos, NMex, 64. *Bibliog:* Robert M Powers (auth), NMex Mag, 78; Mary Carroll Nelson (auth), articles, Am Artist, 79, Art Voices S, 80 & Southwest Art Mag, 86. *Mem:* Albuquerque Arts Alliance. *Media:* Clay to Cast Bronze, Concrete. *Mailing Add:* PO Box 1165 Corrales NM 87048

TOWNSEND, TERYL
PAINTER, EDUCATOR
b Coronado, Calif, May 9, 38. *Study:* Ray Froman Sch Art, Univ Tex, study with Millard Sheets, Chen Chi, Charles Reid, Edgar Whitney, Carl Molno & Glenn Bradshaw. *Work:* Foothills Art Ctr, Golden, Colo; US Navy. *Comn:* Painting, USN, US Bristol Co, 68; painting, Grumman Int Corp Off, 76; painting, Rawson Int Corp Off; 400 pvt collections. *Exhib:* Mus Albuquerque Western Fedn Group Show, 75; Watercolor Soc Group Show, Birmingham Mus Art, Ala, 76; Western Fedn Group Show, Tucson Mus Art, Ariz, 76; Butler Inst Am Art Mid-Yr Ann, Youngstown, Ohio, 77; Watercolor USA Ann, Springfield, Ill, 77; Checkwood Art Ctr, Southern Watercolor Soc Group Show, Tenn, 77; one-man show, Stephen F Austin State Univ, Tex, 78; and others. *Pos:* Art experience facilitator, Tex Inst Child Psychiat, 75-76. *Teaching:* Instr water media painting, Canary Hill Galleries, Houston, Tex, 74-77, Tex Art Supply Inc, Houston, 75-77 & pvt studio, Houston, 78-, Nantucket, Mass, 80-90. *Awards:* Director's Award, Southern Watercolor Ann Exhib, 77; Art League Houston Dimension Award, 82; Southwestern Watercolor Soc Award, 83; New Canaan Soc for the Arts Award, 96, 97. *Bibliog:* Pat Lasher (auth), Seeing the ordinary in a special way, Southwest Art Mag, 9/77; Naomi Brotherton (auth), Spotlight on the artist, The Scene, Southwestern Watercolor Soc, 1/78; Watercolor Energies, Frank Webb, 82. *Mem:* Am Watercolor Soc; Nat Watercolor Soc; Rocky Mountain Nat Watermedia Soc; Vero Beach Mus Art; New Canaan Soc Arts. *Mailing Add:* Teryl Townsend Studio 28 Vitti St New Canaan CT 06840

TRACHTMAN, ARNOLD S
PAINTER
b Lynn, Mass, Oct 5, 30. *Study:* Mass Sch Art, BFA; Sch Art Inst Chicago, MFA. *Work:* Fogg Art Mus, Harvard Univ, Cambridge, Mass; Addison Gallery Am Art, Andover, Mass; Wiggin Collection, Boston Pub Libr, Mass; Boston Mus Fine Arts; Mus Nat Ctr of Afro-American Artists, Roxbury, Mass; Lynn Mus, Lynn, MA; Decordova Mus, Lincoln, MA; Fla Holocaust Mus, St Petersburg. *Exhib:* One-man shows, Inst Contemp Art, Boston, 70 & Addison Gallery Am Art, Andover, Mass, 76, Brockton Art Ctr, Mass, 79, Montserrat Sch Visual Art, Beverly, Mass, 85; AAMARP Gallery, Boston, 81; Bradford Col, Mass, 82; Cambridge Mult Cult Art Ctr, Cambridge, Mass, 1999; Lynn Mus, Lynn Mass, 2000; group shows, Staatliche Kunsthalle, Berlin, WGer, 83, Royal Festival Hall, London, UK, 85, Gallery Naga, Boston, Mass, 88, Arvada Art Ctr, Colo, 90 & Boston Univ Art Gallery, Mass, 91; Newton Art Ctr, Newtonville, Mass, 92; Mus Am Art, St Paul, Minn, 95; Absence/Presente Univ of Minn, 99; 1850-1950 Lynn Mus, Lynn Mass, Lynn's Jewish Community, 2004. *Teaching:* Instr art, Lynnfield High Sch, Mass, 71-80, Cambridge Sch, Weston, 80-81; assoc prof, Mass Col Art, 81-. *Bibliog:* Indochina Arts Proj Inc (auth), As Seen By Both Sides, Univ Mass Press, 91; Approaching a Horrible Truth: 2 Artists Painting the Holocaust, Newton Arts Ctr, 92; Witness & Legacy, Lerner Publ, 95. *Mem:* Boston Visual Artist Union; Mass Cult Alliance. *Media:* Acrylic, Watercolor, Mixed Media. *Publ:* Alone Stands the Artist, Boston Globe, 72. *Dealer:* Howard Yezersky Gallery Boston Mass. *Mailing Add:* 27 Dana St Cambridge MA 02138

TRACY, MICHAEL
SCULPTOR, PAINTER
b Bellevue, Ohio, Sept 30, 43. *Study:* St Edward's Univ, Austin, BA, 64; Cleveland Inst Art, 64-67; Univ Tex, Austin, MFA, 69. *Work:* Art Mus STex, Corpus Christi; San Antonio Art Mus & McNay Art Inst, San Antonio, Tex; Mus Fine Art, Houston; Dallas Mus Art, Tex; Metrop Mus Art, NY. *Comn:* Emmanuel Chapel, Corpus Christi, Tex, 85; Santuario San Miquel Archangel, Our Lady of Guadalupe Cath Church, Alice, Tex. *Exhib:* Works on Paper: Eleven Houston Artists, Houston Mus Fine Arts, Tex, 85; Tex Landscape 1900-1986, Houston Mus Fine Arts, Tex, 86; Seventy-Fifth Am Exhib, Art Inst Chicago, Ill, 86; Escultures Diversos, La Quinsonera, Mexico City, 89; The Bleeding Heart (with catalog), Inst Contemp Art, Boston, 91; solo exhibs, Zolla/Lieberman Gallery, Chicago, 91, Blue Star Art Space, (with catalog), San Antonio, Tex, 92, St Clemens Cath Church (with catalog), Hanover, Ger, 93, Raab Gallery, London, 93, Moody Gallery, Houston, Tex, 93, Gallery Paule Anglim, San Francisco, 94 & Mattress Factory, Pittsburgh, 94-95; Maler/Bildhauer--Painter/Sculptor, Raab Gallery, Berrlin, 91; After the Apocalypse: A Different Humanism, Southeastern Ctr Contemp Art, Winston-Salem, NC, 91; Sanctuaries: Recovering the Holy in Contemp Art, Mus Contemp Relig Art, St Louis, Mo, 93; and others. *Awards:* Awards in Visual Arts, 87. *Bibliog:* Mark Durant (auth), Michael Tracy, Shift, 36-39, 2/90; John Yau (auth), Michael Tracy, Arts Mag, 3/90; Richard Lacayo (auth), Prophet of the River Pierce, Metrop Homes, 5/91. *Media:* Acrylic, Oil. *Publ:* Coauth, Terminal Privileges (exhib catalog), PS1, Inst Art & Urban Resources Inc, Long Island City, NY, 87; The River Pierce: Sacrifice II, River Pierce Found, San Ygnacio, Tex, 92; Smoking Mirror (exhib catalog), Blue Star Art Space, San Antonio, Tex, 92. *Dealer:* Gallery Paule Anglim 14 Geary St San Francisco CA 94108. *Mailing Add:* PO Box 235 San Ignacio TX 78067

TRACY, ROBERT H
EDUCATOR, CURATOR
b Alameda, Calif, March 14, 48. *Study:* Calif State Univ, Hayward, BA, 70; Univ Calif, Los Angeles, MA, 77, PhD, 82. *Collection Arranged:* Palaces of Finance (co-cur), Spring St Hist Dist, 82; Architecture of Modern Olympiad: 1896 to Present (co-cur), 84; John & Donald Parkinson, Architects (auth, catalog), 89-90. *Pos:* Bd dir, Preservation Asn Clark Co, 84-, Las Vegas Neon Mus, 88- & Nev Inst Contemp Arts, 89-; Cur, Parkinson Arch, Los Angeles, 84-; chmn, dept art, Univ Nev, Las Vegas, 89-. *Teaching:* Assoc prof art hist, Chapman Col, Orange, Calif, 79-84 & Univ Nev,Las Vegas, 84-; cur, Parkinson Arch, Los Angeles, 84-; Univ London, spring, 93. *Awards:* Nevada Humanities Comt, 85-89 & 92; Las Vegas Chap Am Inst Architects, 85-89, 92 & 96; Nev State Coun Arts, 96. *Mem:* Soc Archit Historians; Col Art Asn; Semiotic Soc Am. *Res:* Late 19th century to 20th century business architectural imagery. *Mailing Add:* Univ Nevada Las Vegas Dept of Art 4505 Maryland Pkwy Las Vegas NV 89154-5002

TRAGER, NEIL C
MUSEUM DIRECTOR, PHOTOGRAPHER
b Aug 14, 47. *Study:* City Col New York, BA, 69. *Work:* Mus Mod Art, NY; Neuberger Mus, Purchase, NY; Harry Ransom Humanities Res Ctr, Univ Tex, Austin; Ctr for Photo, Woodstock, NY. *Comn:* Ok Harris Works of Art; Brooklyn Mus of Art; Ctr for Photograph at Woodstock; Sante Fe Ctr of Photography; Nikon House. *Exhib:* Hot Spots: America's Volcanic Landscape, Hudson Valley Artists Series. *Collection Arranged:* George Bellows Lithographs; A Kind of History; Mark Goodman; Ctr for Photography at Woodstock Permanent Print Collection; SDMA Historic & Contemp Metal Work. *Pos:* Assoc cur, Catskill Ctr Photog, Woodstock, NY, 78-81, mem bd dir, 86-; trustee, Klyne Esopus Mus, Port Ewen, NY, 82-84; dir, Samuel Dorsky Mus Art, State Univ NY, New Paltz, currently; adv bd, Ctr Photog Woodstock, currently. *Teaching:* Adj lectr photog & art, La Guardia Community Col, Queens, NY, 76-78; lectr photog, State Univ NY, New Paltz, 79-81. *Awards:* Creative Artists Pub Serv Fel, NY State Coun Arts, 81; Chancellors Award for Excellence in Service, State Univ NY; United University Professions Award for Excellence. *Mem:* Gallery & Mus Asn, State Univ NY; Am Asn Mus. *Res:* Contemporary and historical photography. *Specialty:* AM Works on Paper; Hudson Valley-Caskill Mt. *Interests:* 19 & 20 Century Photographs, Metal works. *Publ:* Bolton Coit Brown; A Retrospectire; Don Nice: The Nature of Art. *Mailing Add:* Samuel Dorksy Mus of Art Suny New 1 Hawk Dr New Paltz NY 12561

TRAGER, PHILIP
PHOTOGRAPHER
b Bridgeport, Conn, Feb 27, 35. *Study:* Wesleyan Univ, BA, 56; Columbia Univ Sch Law, JD, 60. *Work:* Mus Mod Art, Metrop Mus Art, NY; Corcoran Gallery Art; Bibliot Nat, Paris; Smithsonian Inst; Can Ctr Archit. *Comn:* Photog study Wesleyan Univ, Bd Trustees, 80; Photog study Birmingham, Birmingham Mus Art, 88; Photog study Wave Hill, Bd Dirs, 90; Photog study, Saline Royale, Found Ledoux, 91. *Exhib:* Solo exhibs, Davison Art Ctr, Middletown, Conn, 70, 74, 81, 92 & 2000, Witkin Gallery, NY, 72, 77, 80 & 87, Mus Art, Univ Ore, 89 & Julie Saul Gallery, 92 & 2000, The French Embassy, Washington, 2000, Mus Photog Arts, San Diego, Calif, 94, plus others; Portfolio Gallery, London, 89; Brooklyn Mus, 89; Found Ledoux, 91; and others in the US and France. *Teaching:* Instr masterclasses & workshops. *Awards:* Distinguished Alumnus Award, 81; 1987 Book Award, The Villas of Palladio, Maine Photog Workshops; Finalist Grant Prix Award, Int Festival Photog, Arles, France. *Bibliog:* Eve Auchincloss (auth), Connoisseur, 2/87; C J Dickinson (auth), Am Photog, 3/87; Ziva Freiman (auth), In print, Metropolis, 7-8/87; Barbara L Michael (auth), Art on Paper, Nov/Dec 2000; Ken Johnson (auth) The New York Times, 5/2000; plus others. *Media:* Silver & Platinum photographs. *Publ:* Contribr, Creative Camera 20th Ann Catalog, London, 88; Flatiron, A Photographic History of the World's First Steel Frame Skyscraper, Am Inst Architects Press, 90; Charles Hagar, New York Times, 91; photogr, Wave Hill Pictured, 91; Dancers, Bulfinch Press, 92; and others; contrib auth The Body, 94, Hope Photographs, 98, Architecture et Grande Travaux, 97, others. *Dealer:* The John Stevenson Gallery 20 Rolling Ridge Rd Fairfield CT 06430

TRAINES, ROSE WUNDERBAUM
SCULPTOR, LECTURER
b Monroeville, Ind, Sept 13, 28. *Study:* Indiana State Teacher's Col, 1946-48; Mich State Univ, 1948-49; Central Mich Univ, BS, 1950-51. *Work:* Elliott Mus, Stuart, Fla; Blake Library Art Collection, Stuart, Fla; Alden Dow Science & Art Mus, Midland, Mich; Boston Col Club Art Collection, Mass; Norman Cousins Office Art, Los Angeles, Calif. *Comn:* Walt Kuhn Gallery, Ms. Kuhn, Cape Neddic, ME, 1988; Central Mich Comm Hospital, 50th Anniversary, Brd Trustees, Mt. Pleasant, Mich, 1999; "Donny" Hersee Collection, Mt Pleasant, Mich, 2000; 50th Anniv Rollie/Olga Denison, Detroit, Mich, 2001; Lewis Johnsons, Naples, Fla, 2002. *Exhib:* With This Torch I Thee Weld, Elliott Mus, Stuart, Fla, 1983-1988, 1993, 1998, 2006; Self Family Performing Arts, Performing Arts Ctr, Hilton Head, SC, 1999; With This Torch I Theee Weld, Copley Soc of Boston, Mass, 2001; 2001 Ann Exhib, Allied Artists of Am, New York City, 2001; Photograph & Sculpture, Salmagundi Club, New York City, 2001; Month-of-March, Gallery Five, Tequesta, Fla, 2002; Central Mich Art Exhib, Alden Dow Science Art, Midland, Mich, 2002; With This Torch I Thee Weld, Glick Community Ctr, Indianapolis, Ind, 2004; This Torch I Thee Weld & All's Weld That Ends Weld, Art Reach of Mid-Michigan, Mt Pleasant, 2006. *Pos:* Guest presenter & teacher with majority of exhibitions/lectures at art galleries, museums, art centers, univ & school classes (gr 1-12), Indianapolis, Ind, Hiltonhead, SC & Mich cities, 1964-2007. *Teaching:* lectr & sculptor in res, Northwood Univ, W Palm, Fla & Midland, Mich, 1988; Elliott Mus, Stuart, Fla, Dec 2005-Jan 06 & Art Reach of mid-Mich, May-June 2006. *Awards:* Alumni Recognition, Homecoming, Central Mich Univ, Mt Pleasant, 1991; Lifetime of Creative Excellence, Performing Arts Ctr, Hilton Head, SC Art League, 1998; Members Memorial, Ann Summer Exhib, Salmagundi Club, NYC, 2003. *Bibliog:* Videografic dept (dir), With This Torch I Thee Weld, CMU Media Ctr Publicity, 2002; Heitman Audio Visual (dir) With This Torch I Thee Weld, distrib to sculptor owners, schools, galleries, museums & art ctrs, 2003-2006. *Mem:* The Salmagundi Club, NYC; Allied Artists of America Inc, NYC; The Copley Soc of Art, Boston, Mass; Alden Dow Science & Art Mus, Midland, Mich; Mus of Art, Vero Beach, Fla. *Media:* Metal, Welded, Acetylene Torch. *Interests:* Family, friends, community activities, presenting lectures, tennis & drums. *Publ:* Junkyard Junkie, Mich Journal, E. Berley, May/June 1981; contrib, Treasure Coastline

- Coastal Currents, Dorothy Yates, Stuart, Fla, Mar 1998; contrib, Mt Pleasant Magazine, Naseem Stecker, 1996; contrib, Niche, Magazine for Progressive Retailers, Susan York, Baltimore, Md, spring 2001; contrib, Centralite CMU Magazine, Mary Lu Fleming, summer 2002. *Mailing Add:* 1217 North Dr Mount Pleasant MI 48858-3226

TRAINOR, JIM
FILMMAKER
Study: Columbia Univ, BA, 83. *Teaching:* Asst prof, -film, video & new media Sch Art Inst Chicago, 2000-. *Awards:* San Francisco Film Festival; Black Maria Film Festival; NY Underground Film Festival. *Publ:* Dir.: (films, screening), Whitney Biennial; (films) From Microbe to Man, 1974, Antrozous, 1976, Torn Up, 1994, The Bat & the Virgin, 1997, The Fetish, 1997, The Bats, 1998, The Ordovicians, The Magic Kingdom, Sun Shames Headhunting Moon: Story of Nazr, Serene Velocity, The Skulls & the Skulls, the Bones & the Bones, The Moschops, 2000, A Net, 2000, Harmony, 2004, Could Be Tropical Fish, 2005, Leafy, Leafy Jungle, 2005, Blood, 2005, New Diagonal Symphony, 2005. *Mailing Add:* Sch Art Inst Chicago 37 S Wabash Chicago IL 60603-3103

TRAKAS, GEORGE
SCULPTOR
b Quebec, Que, May 11, 44. *Study:* Brooklyn Mus Art Sch; Hunter Col, New York Univ, BS. *Work:* Solomon R Guggenheim Mus. *Comn:* Omaha Opportunities Industrialization Ctr, 80; Nat Oceanic and Atmospheric Admin, Seattle, 83. *Exhib:* Projects: Pier 18, Mus Mod Art, NY, 71; Ten Young Artists: Theodoron Awards, Guggenheim Mus, NY, 71; Route Point, Scale and Environment: 10 Sculptors, Walker Art Ctr, Minneapolis, Minn, 77; El, 1979 Biennial, Whitney Mus Am Art, NY, 79; Pacific Union, San Diego Mus Contemp Art, La Jolla, Calif, 89; Routes from the Heart, La Mus, Humlebaek, Denmark, 89; Le Pont d'Epee au Creux de l'Enfer, Thiers, France, 89; Todd Terrace, Wash State Univ, Pullman, 90; Constructions, Wall Pieces and Drawings, Quint Krichman Projs, San Diego, Calif, 92; and others. *Teaching:* Lectr, Boston Mus, 72; lectr, Cooper Union, 78; lectr, Yale Univ, 80. *Awards:* Nat Endowment Arts Fel, 79; Guggenheim Fel, 83. *Bibliog:* Paul Stimson (auth), article, Art Am, 9-10/75; Kate Linker (auth), George Trakas & the syntax of space, Arts Mag, 1/76. *Media:* Steel, Wood. *Publ:* Contribr, Outcrops, Avalanche, fall 71; catalogue essays, Projects in Nature, 75 & Artpark, 76. *Mailing Add:* c/o Quint Contemp Art PO Box 1172 La Jolla CA 92038-1172

TRAKIS, LOUIS
SCULPTOR, EDUCATOR
b New York, NY, June 22, 27. *Study:* Cooper Union, BFA; Columbia Univ; Art Students League; Politechneion, Athens, Greece; Fulbright grants, Acad Fine Arts, Rome, Italy, 59-60 & 60-61. *Work:* Guild Hall Mus, East Hampton, NY; Village Kournas, Crete, Greece; Revco Corp, Southampton, NY. *Comn:* War hero monument (bronze), Crete, Greece, 88. *Exhib:* Pa Acad, Philadelphia; Corcoran Gallery, Washington, DC; Brooklyn Mus, NY; Feingarten Gallery, NY; Benson Gallery, Bridgehampton, LI, NY; Manhattanville Col, Purchase, NY; Benton Gallery, Southampton, NY; New Sch, Social Res, New York, NY; and others. *Pos:* Emer prof, Manhattanville Col, Artist's Equity Asn NY, Audubon Artists & Fulbright Asn. *Teaching:* Instr sculpture, Philadelphia Col of Art, Columbia Univ, New Sch for Social Res & Southhampton Col; prof ceramics & sculpture, Manhattanville Col, 65-, adminr, Summer in Crete Prog, 80-85. *Awards:* Sculpture Award, Parrish Art Mus, Southampton, NY; Sculpture Award, Guild Hall Mus, E Hampton, NY; Sculpture Award, Audubon Artists Exhib, NY; Tiffany Award, Louis Comfort, 61 & 63. *Bibliog:* Interview (TV prog), Carlson Int, 84. *Mem:* Artists Equity, NY; Am Asn Univ Profs; Audubon Artists. *Publ:* Contribr, Prize Winning Sculpture (bks I & II), Allied Publ. *Dealer:* Vorpal Gallery 459 West Broadway New York NY 10012. *Mailing Add:* 532 16th St Brooklyn NY 11215

TRAN, TAM VAN
PAINTER
b Kontum, Vietnam, 66. *Study:* Pratt Film Inst, BFA in painting, 1990; UCLA, Grad Film & TV Prog, 1996. *Work:* UCLA Hammer Mus, 2003; Whitney Biennial, Whitney Mus Am Art, NY, 2004; Knoxville Mus Art, Tenn, 2005. *Exhib:* One-man shows incl Turkey Diesel, Dirt Gallery, Los Angeles, 1999, Cold Frost, Irvine Fine Arts Ctr, Calif, 2000, Susanne Vielmetter Los Angeles Projects, 2000, 2001, Beetle Manifesto, 2002, Project Room: Lover of Air, Cohan Leslie & Browne, NY, 2002, Vegetarian Summer, 2003, Lord of Hot Butter, Anthony Meier Fine Arts, San Francisco, 2003; exhib in group shows at Kassel Ducumenta Archiv, Ludwig Mus, Cologne, 1990, House of Styles, Tri Gallery, Los Angeles, 1995, Asian Am Art Ctr, NY, 1998, Other Paintings, Huntington Beach Art Ctr, Calif, 1999, Pierogi 2000: Flat Files, Yerba Buena Ctr Arts, San Francisco, 2000, Luminous, Ikon Fine Art, Santa Monica, Calif, 2000, Radar Love, Gallery Marabini, Italy, 2000, Car Pooling from Los Angeles, Asian Am Art Ctr, NY, 2000; New Work: LA Painting, Hosfelt Gallery, San Francisco, 2001, Black Dragon Soc, Los Angeles, 2001, Panorama, Room Interior Products, 2002, Cohan Leslie & Browne, NY, 2002, Drawing Biennial, Weatherspoon Art Gallery, NC, 2002; In the Making: Drawings from a Pvt Collection, Univer Mass Amherst, 2003, Int Paper, Around About Abstraction, Weatherspoon Art Gallery, NC, 2005. *Awards:* Creative Fel Visual Arts, Colo Coun Arts & Humanities, 1991; Ucross Artists Residency, Ucross, Wyo, 1993; Pollock Krasner Fel, 2000; Recipient Joan Mitchell Found Award, 2001. *Mailing Add:* c/o Cohan Leslie & Browne 138 Tenth Ave New York NY 10011

TRAUB, CHARLES H
EDUCATOR, PHOTOGRAPHER
b Louisville, Ky, Apr 6, 45. *Study:* Univ of Ill, Urbana, BA, 67; Inst of Design, Ill Inst of Technol, MS(photog), 71. *Work:* Int Ctr Photog, NY; Mus of Mod Art, NY; Art Inst of Chicago, Ill; Fogg Mus, Harvard Univ, Cambridge, Mass; Int Mus of Photog, Rochester, NY; and others. *Comn:* Olympic Arts Found, 84; New York City Parks Dept, 89. *Exhib:* Photographs of Charles Traub, Art Inst of Chicago, 75; The City, Mus of Contemp Art, Chicago, 77; one-man shows, Light Gallery, NY, 77, Looking in Color, Light Gallery, NY, 84, Nudes, Marcuse Pfeifer Gallery, NY, 84, In Decent Exposure, Van Straaten Gallery, Chicago, 83, Beach, Art Directors Guild of NY, 83, Recognitions, Faces and Places: Photographs by Charles Traub, Hudson River Mus, NY, 82; Contemp Photog, Fogg Mus, 77; Color in the Streets, Calif Mus Photog, Univ Calif, Riverside, 83; 10 Photographers: Olympic Photographs, LAOOC Mus Contemp Art, Los Angeles, Traveling, 85; Family Portraits (with catalog), Univ Art Gallery, Wright State Univ, Dayton, 87. *Pos:* Freelance photogr, 69-; pres, Photog Adv Group, Chicago, Ill, 75-77; dir, Light Gallery, NY, 77-80; sr ed, Matrix Publ; chmn, Sch visual arts, NY; partner, Wayfarer Photography Inc, 82-. *Teaching:* Vis artist, Franconia Col, NH, 73-74 & Tyler Sch Art, Philadelphia, Pa, 81; prof photog & chmn dept, Columbia Col, Chicago, Ill, 71-; instr, Sch Visual Art, NY, 85, dir grad dept photogr, 87-. *Mem:* Soc of Photog Educ; Col Art Asn. *Publ:* Auth, Some Other Pictures of Italy, Porfolio Camera Int, No 11, Paris, France, 87; Nudes, Portfolio, Zoom, Paris, France, 12/87; Am Photography Annuals No 1 & 2, NY, 85-86; Italy Observed, Rizzoli, 88; An Angler's Album, Rizzoli, 90. *Dealer:* Light Gallery 724 Fifth Ave New York NY 10019; Howard Greenberg Photo Find, New York, NY. *Mailing Add:* 39 E 10th St New York NY 10003

TRAUERMAN, MARGY ANN
PAINTER, INSTRUCTOR
b Sioux Falls, SDak. *Study:* Univ Iowa, Iowa City, BFA; Am Acad Art, Chicago; Art Students League, New York; Los Angeles City Col. *Exhib:* Am Watercolor Soc Ann, 53-68; NY Figurative Painting & Traveling Exhib, 71; one-man shows, Chatham Col, Pittsburgh, 61, First Street Gallery, NY, 72, 74, 77, 79, 82 & 84 & Landmark Gallery, McAllen, Tex, 75. *Teaching:* Instr art, Art & Design High Sch, New York, 52-77; instr art, Queens Col, New York, spring 75. *Bibliog:* David Loeffler Smith (auth), Celebrated women artists, 1/62 & Heritage of the thirties, 10/62, Am Artist; Watercolor page, Am Artist, 7/74. *Mem:* Am Watercolor Soc. *Media:* Watercolor. *Mailing Add:* 2 W 67th St New York NY 10023

TRAUSCH, THOMAS V
PAINTER, EDUCATOR
b Chicago, Ill, Sept 4, 43. *Study:* Univ Ill, BFA, 66; Am Acad Art, with Irving Shapiro, 74-77, Art Study, Giverny, France with Gale Bennett, 97. *Work:* Elmhurst Fine Arts Mus, Ill; Smith-Barney, Chicago; Burlington Northern Railway, Ill; Nissei-Sanyo; Blue Cross-Blue Shield Ins Co; Northern Trust Bank; Oprah Winfrey pvt collection. *Comn:* mural, Home State Bank, Woodstock, Ill, 99. *Exhib:* Transparetn Watercolor Soc Am, 90, 94, 97, 2000, 03 & 06; Am Watercolor Soc, NY, 86; one-man show, Lakeshore Gallery, Milwaukee, Wis, 98, 99 & 2000; Oil Painters of Am, 94, 98, 2004 & 06; Bosque Conserv Art, Tex, 98 & 2003; Color 2002, Nat Exhib, Downers Grove, Ill; Salon Int 2002, San Antonio. *Pos:* Guest instr, Am Acad Art, 88-90 & Giverny & Normandy, France, 98; pvt instr watercolor & oil, US and Europe, currently. *Teaching:* instr workshops, Giverny & Normandy, France, 98, 99 & 2000, Great Smoky Mts Nat Park, 95, 96, 97 & 2004, Okla Art Guild, Oklahoma City, 2000, St Remy, Provence, France, 2001 & 2002; Cincinatti Arts Club, 2005, Ireland, 06. *Awards:* Spec Merit Award, Midwest Watercolor Soc, 85; Artists Choice Award, Glen Ellyn, Ill, 2000; Color 2002 Award, Downers Grove, Ill; Master Status Award, Transparent Watercolor Soc Am, 2006. *Bibliog:* Danielle Aceto (auth), Couple finds painting adds to art of marriage, Northwest Herald, 88; William Stanek (auth), McHenry County artists, Chicago Tribune, 94; and many others. *Mem:* Transparent Watercolor Soc Am (signature mem, 85-2005, master 2006); Oil Painters Am. *Media:* Oil, Watercolor. *Interests:* Photography; Travel. *Publ:* Splash III, North Light Publ, Cincinnati, Ohio, 94; Victorian Sampler, Sambler Publ, St Charles, Ill, 95; The Best of Watercolor, 96 & The Best of Watercolor II, 97, Rockport Publ; Portraist Inspirations, Rockport Pub; Plein Air Mag, 12/2005; and others. *Mailing Add:* 2403 Mustang Trail Woodstock IL 60098-8423

TRAVANTI, LEON EMIDIO
PAINTER, DESIGNER
b Kenosha, Wis, Aug 5, 36. *Study:* Cranbrook Acad of Arts, MFA, 60; Layton Sch of Art, BFA, 59. *Work:* Milwaukee Art Mus; Bergstrom Mus, Neenah, Wis; Rahr Art Ctr, La Crosse, Wis; Univ Mo; Univ Wis; Northern Ill Univ. *Comn:* Paintings & drawings, Ansul Int, Brussels, Belg, 74, Lane Ltd, Sydney, Australia, 74-75 & Malaysia Ancom, Kuala Lumpur, Malaysia, 75; painting, First Wis Nat Bank, 76; posters, comn by Wis Great Circus Parade, 88-92; Design House, Milwaukee Mural Comn, 91. *Exhib:* Detroit Inst Art, 60; Columbia Col, Mo, 78; Pillsbury Nat, 81-82; West Art & The Law Nat, 83; one-man shows, Charles Allis Art Mus, Milwaukee, 83 & Posner Gallery, Milwaukee, 90, Michael Lord Gallery, Milwaukee, 2003, Mt Mary Col, Milwaukee, Wis, 2005; Technology in Art Invitational Exhib, Milwaukee Art Mus, 86; Rahr-West Mus, Manitowoc, Wis, 88. *Pos:* Art dir, Wis Archit & Milwaukee Mag, 60-64; dir graphic design, Sch Fine Arts, Univ Wis, 64-74. *Teaching:* Prof art & design, Univ Wis, Milwaukee, 64-, dir design program; vis lectr graphic design, Parsons NY Sch of Design, summer 77 & 79; vis lectr, Pratt Inst, Manhattan Campus, 78-79, Parsons Sch Design, 79-80. *Awards:* Purchase Prizes, Milwaukee Renaissance, 60, Wis Invitational, 65 & Pillsbury Co, Minneapolis; and others. *Bibliog:* Walter Herdig (ed), Ann report paintings, Graphis Ann, 66-67 & 75-76; Paintings in reports, Print Mag, 76 & Current Am Paintings, La Revue Moderne, Paris, 60. *Mem:* Am Inst Graphic Arts; Graphic Arts Guild; Am Ctr Design; and others. *Media:* Acrylics & Collage. *Specialty:* Paintings, Sculpture, Constructions, Prints & Drawings. *Interests:* Works with directs children, teachers in annual art exhib at Villa Terrace Museum, Milwaukee, Wis. *Dealer:* Michael Lord Gallery Milwaukee WI. *Mailing Add:* 1425 N Prospect Ave Milwaukee WI 53202

TRAVER, DONALD
CONCEPTUAL ARTIST
b Poughkeepsie, NY, Feb 3, 57. *Study:* Art Students League, 76; Empire State Col, NY, 77; SUNY, New Paltz, 80. *Exhib:* Solo exhibs, Massimo Audiello Gallery, NY, 85 & 86, Hillman Holland Fine Art, Atlanta, Ga, 86 & Elizabeth McDonald Gallery, NY, 88; Pictures From the Inner Mind, Palladium, NY, 86; Abstraction, Dart Gallery, Chicago, Ill, 86; Emerging Artists 1986, Cleveland Ctr Contemp Art, 86; Abstraction Rediscovered, Rosa Esman Gallery, NY, 86; Romantic Science, One Penn Plaza, NY, 87; 3X4, Galeria Fucares, Madrid, Spain, 87; Inaugural Exhib, Elizabeth McDonald Gallery, NY, 87; Group Show, Massimo Audiello Gallery, NY, 87; Barbara Toll Gallery, NY, 88; Grey Art Gallery, NY, 88; Krygierr-Landau Gallery, Los Angeles, 89. *Awards:* Nat Endowment Arts, 87; NY State Found, Arts, 87. *Bibliog:* Dan Cameron (auth), In the realm of the hyper-abstract, Arts, 11/86; E S, Smith, Suzuki y Traver: El arte joven de Nueva York, No 16, Diario, 6/12/87; Jose Luis Loarce, 3X4, No 44, Lapiz Mag, Spain, 87

TRAVERS-SMITH, BRIAN JOHN
PAINTER, INSTRUCTOR
b Tangshan, North China, June 26, 31; Can & UK citizen. *Study:* Ont Col Art, Toronto, 49-50; self-taught in watercolor. *Work:* Art Gallery Greater Victoria, BC; Provincial Collection BC; Dofasco Collection, Hamilton, Ont; Chevron Standard Collection, Calgary, Alta; Hiram Walker Collection, BC; Royal Collection, Windsor, UK. *Exhib:* One-man show, Art Gallery Greater Victoria, BC, 62; Allied Artists Am, NY, 69, 71, 72 & 81; Am Watercolor Soc, ann & traveling, 71, 76, 77 & 81; Can Soc Painters Watercolour, Toronto, 76 & 77; BC Through the Eyes of Its Artists, Govt BC, traveling Europe, 79. *Pos:* Bd dir, Art Gallery Greater Victoria, BC, 63-70, pres, bd dir, 69-70; bd dir, Emily Carr Col Art & Design, 80-82. *Teaching:* Instr, Studios in Victoria, BC, 65-75. *Awards:* First Prize, Vancouver Island Ann, 62; Royal Jubilee Medal, Can, 77. *Bibliog:* Margaret Harold (auth), Brian Travers-Smith, Prize-Winning Watercolors, 63; R Ashwell (auth), Brian Travers-Smith, Westworld Mag, 4/78. *Mem:* Am Watercolor Soc; Allied Artists Am (hon). *Media:* Watercolor. *Mailing Add:* 1405 St Patrick St Victoria BC V8S 4Y5 Canada

TRAVIS, DAVID B
CURATOR, HISTORIAN
b Omaha, Nebr, Jan 31, 48. *Study:* Univ of Chicago, BA(art hist), Smithsonian Inst, res fel, 72. *Collection Arranged:* Exhibitions of photography, Art Inst of Chicago, 73-; Starting with Atget (auth, catalog), 77; Photographs from the Andre Jammes Collection: Niepce to Atget (ed, catalog), 77; Photography Rediscovered: American Photographs 1900-1930 (auth, catalog), 79; Photographs in Chicago Collections (auth, catalog), 82. *Pos:* Asst cur photog, Art Inst of Chicago, 74-77, assoc cur photog, 77-78, cur photog, 79-. *Teaching:* Lectr hist of photog, Sch of the Art Inst of Chicago, 74. *Mailing Add:* Art Institute Chicago Michigan Ave and Adams St Chicago IL 60603

TRAYLOR, ANGELIKA
STAINED GLASS ARTIST
b Munich, Ger, Aug 24, 42; US citizen. *Study:* Private Handelsschule Morawetz, Munich, WGer, 58; studied with Gil Reynolds & Tim McCreight. *Work:* Holmes Regional Med Ctr, Melbourne, Fla, 98; White House Christmas Ornament Collection, Washington, DC, 93 & 97; William Childs Hospice House, Palm Bay, Fla. *Comn:* White House Christmas Ornament Collection, 93 & 97; Holmes Regional Med Ctr, Melbrurne, Fla, 98; William Childs Hospice House, Palm Bay, Fla; and many others. *Exhib:* Fla Craftsmen Exhibit, 81, 83, 86, 87, 89 & 93; Ann Assoc Exhib, Stained Glass Asn Am, 84, 85, 89, 90, 91 & 94; Vitraux des USA, Chartes, France, 85; Ann Assoc Exhib, Stained Glass Asn Am, Nora Eckles Harrison Mus, Logan, Utah, 89; Artists Forum Ann Exhib, Brevard Art Ctr & Mus, Melbourne, Fla, 90, 91, 93 & 96. *Awards:* 2nd Place, Non-figurative Composition, Vitraux des USA, 85; Best of Show, Stained Glass Asn Am, 89; Historic Woman of Brevard, Brevard Cult Alliance, 91; One of 200 Best Craftsmen, Early Am Life Mag, 94, 95 & 97; and others. *Bibliog:* Melbourne Times, 94; The Orbiter, 96; Glass Collector's Digest, 96; Women's Day Mag, 99; Space Coast Press, 99; Sterling Publ, 00; Crative Stained Glass, Lark Books, 04. *Mem:* Stained Glass Asn Am; Nat League Am Pen Women; Fla Craftsmen; Pa Guild of Craftsmen. *Media:* Stained Glass. *Dealer:* Dennison-Moran Gallery Naples FL; Nancy Markoe Gallery St Petersburg Beach Fla. *Mailing Add:* 100 Poinciana Dr Indian Harbor Beach FL 32937

TRAYNOR, JOHN C
PAINTER
b Morristown, NJ, 61. *Study:* Paier Col Art, New Haven, Conn, 77-80; Art Students League, NY; studied with Jerome Cox, Carol Jones & Frank Mason. *Work:* Sony Music Corp; Mural, Ironbound Cult Art Ctr, NJ. *Exhib:* Salmagundi Club, NY; Hudson Valley Art Asn; Noroton Gallery, Darien, Conn; many others 1984-2000; Copley Soc, 2001. *Awards:* Frank DuMond Award, Best Light & Atmospheric effect painting, Hudson Valley Asn; Frederick S Church Award, Salmagundi Club, NY; Award for Excellence, Fanklin Mint. *Mem:* Salmagundi Club, NY; Copley Soc, Boston, Mass; Hudson Valley Art Asn; Nat Soc Mural Painters, NY. *Media:* Acrylic, Oil. *Specialty:* Landscapes, Still lifes, figures & portraits. *Mailing Add:* PO Box 553 West Swanzey NH 03469

TRECARTIN, RYAN
FILMMAKER
b Webster, Tex, 81. *Study:* RI Sch Design, BFA, 2000-2004. *Exhib:* Group shows: Sympathetic Magic, 2005; Performer: Alternative Theatre Endings, 2005,; Nothing Wrong with August, 2005; One-man show, I Smell Pregnant, QED, Los Angeles, Calif, 2006; Schindler House, 2006; Whitney Biennial: Day for Night, Whitney Mus Am Art, NY 2006; Reckless Behavior, Getty Center, Los Angeles, 2006; Pictures, The Moore Space, Miami, 2006; USA Today, Royal Acad Arts, Burlington Gardens, 2006; Screenings, A Family Finds Entertainment, NY Underground Film Festival, 2006; Chicago Underground Film Festival, 2006; Valentine's Day Girl, Multiplex, Smack Mellon, Brooklyn, NY, 2006. *Mailing Add:* c/o Elizabeth Dee Gallery 545 W 20th St New York NY 10011

TRECHSEL, GAIL ANDREWS
DIRECTOR
b Washington, DC, Nov 4, 53. *Study:* Col William & Mary, Va, BA, 74; Cooperstown Grad Prog, NY, MA(mus studies), 76; Winterthur Summer Inst, 77; Attingham Summer Sch, 81. *Collection Arranged:* Black Belt to Hill Co: Ala Quilts, Birmingham Mus Art, 81; Alabama Quilts & Southern Quilts: A New View, Hunter Mus Art, 90. *Pos:* Nat Endowment Humanities Intern, Colonial Williamsburg, Va, 75-76; cur decorative arts, Birmingham Mus Art, Ala, 76-82, asst dir, 83-85, actg dir, 91-92, asst to dir, 92-. *Teaching:* Adj prof, Univ Ala, Birmingham, 83-87, dir, 96-. *Awards:* Nat Endowment Arts Fel, 86. *Publ:* Coauth, Index to American Coverlet Weavers, Univ Va Press, 78; auth, Lamprecht collection of cast iron art, 2/83 & Beeson collection of wedgwood in Birmingham Museum of Art, 6/83, Mag Antiques; Southern Quilts: A New View, EPM Press; contribr, Pictured in My Mind: Contemporary Self-Taught Art, Birmingham Mus Art, 96. *Mailing Add:* Birmingham Mus Art 2000 8th Ave Birmingham AL 35203-2278

TRECKER, STANLEY MATTHEW MATTHEW
ART COLLEGE PRESIDENT
b Manning, Iowa, July 15, 44. *Study:* Ind Univ, Bloomington, MBA, 68; Columbia Col, Chicago, BA, 75; Sch Art Inst Chicago, MFA, 78. *Work:* Art Inst Chicago; George Eastman House. *Exhib:* Arles Festival, France, 75; Calif Inst Fine Arts, Valencia, 77; Moming Gallery, Chicago, 78; ARC Gallery, Chicago, 78; Art Inst Chicago, 78; Artist Coop, Toronto, Can, 79. *Pos:* Cur, Moming Gallery, Chicago, 77-80; dir, Photog Resource Ctr, Boston, 80-91; pres, Art Inst Boston, 92-. *Teaching:* Instr photog, Columbia Col, Chicago, 78-80. *Awards:* Ill Art Coun Grant, 79; Artists' Found Proj Grant, 83. *Mem:* Soc Photog Educators (bd dir, 83-87); Col Art Asn. *Media:* Photography. *Mailing Add:* c/o Art Inst Boston 700 Beacon St Boston MA 02215

TREDENNICK, DOROTHY W
EDUCATOR, LECTURER
b Bristol, Conn, Oct 5, 1914. *Study:* Norwich Art Sch, 32-34; Berea Col, AB, 46, Univ Mich, Gen Educ Bd fel, MA(art hist), 51. *Exhib:* Art by Women's Hands Berta Arts Coun. *Pos:* Assoc dir, Slater Mem Mus, 39-43. *Teaching:* Instr art, Norwich Art Sch, 33-34; prof art hist & humanities, Berea Col, 46-70, Morris Belknap prof art, 70-87, co-chmn dept art, 54-70, teaching consult, 85-87; lectr, US & Asia; Elderhostel Instr, 87-94. *Awards:* Seabury Award for Excellence in Teaching, Berea Col, 62; Fulbright Award, Chinese Civilization, 63; Nat Endowment Humanities Grant, Univ Calif, 77; Fel, Ctr Ecumenical & Cult Studies, St John's, Minn, 83-84. *Mem:* Southern Humanities Conf; Asn Gen & Liberal Studies; Interfaith Task Force for Peace; Berea Arts Coun. *Media:* Watercolor. *Publ:* Co-auth, This is Our Best, 55; Kress Study Collection, 61; auth, Living by Design, 63; Art & The Protestant Church Today, 66; Design for Living, 68; Two Worlds Meet: The Religious Dimensions of Art, 84. *Mailing Add:* 216 Peach Bloom Hill Rd Berea KY 40403-1819

TREISTER, KENNETH
PAINTER, SCULPTOR
b New York, NY, Mar 5, 30. *Study:* Univ Miami; Univ Fla, BArch, 53. *Work:* Norton Gallery, Palm Beach, Fla; Miami Mus Mod Art, Fla; Fla Supreme Ct, Tallahassee. *Comn:* Family of God (limited ed bronze menorahs), 69 & six bronze plaques depicting hist of Jews, United Jewish Appeal; ten paintings depicting 4,000 yr hist of Jews, Temple Israel, Miami; Eternal Light, Great Miami Rabinical Asn, 4/86; Niel Schiff Mem Bust, Univ Miami, 4/86; In Memory of the Six Million (sculpture), Mem Holocaust City of Miami, 4/86. *Exhib:* Greenwich Gallery, NY; Mus Fine Arts, Columbus, Ga; Lowe Art Gallery, Coral Gables, Fla; Contemp Art Mus, Houston, Tex; High Mus, Atlanta, Ga; and several one-man shows. *Teaching:* Guest lectr art & archit, Mass Inst Technol, Univ Syracuse, Univ Pa, Fla Atlantic Univ, Dade Jr Col/South Campus, Univ Miami, Univ Fla, Jewish Fedn, Univ Chile & Qinghua Univ, Beijing, China. *Awards:* First Prize for Four Conversations (sculpture), Nat Ceramic Exhib, Lowe Art Gallery, 53. *Mem:* Blue Dome Soc, Miami; Fla Sculptural Soc; Southern Asn Sculptors. *Publ:* Contribr, Fla Architecture (40th edition), Nat Mall Monitor, 10/81, FDQ-Design South, 5/85, Interiors, 12/85 & Fla Municipal Record, 2/86; auth, A Sculpture of Love and Anguish, 97; auth, Habaneros, 99; auth, Chapel of Light, 2001. *Mailing Add:* 1600 Island Way Winter Haven FL 33884-3606

TREITLER, RHODA CHAPRACK
PAINTER
b New York, NY. *Study:* Bennington Col, AB; Artists in America, studied with Paul Feeley, Moselsio, Eugene Goosen & Jerry Okimoto; Adelphi Univ, grad study in psychology. *Work:* Equitable Life, NY; private and corp collections. *Exhib:* First Open Exhib, Nassau Co Mus Fine Arts, Roslyn, NY, 88; Ten Bennington Graduates Exhib, Huntington Libr, NY, 88; Marbella Gallery, NY, 89; The Tree An Artist's Gift, Bergen Mus Art & Sci, NJ, 91; Gallery 395 Juried Show, NY, 94; Hutchins Gallery, CW Post Col, 1983, 1984, 1990; Federal Bldg, NY, 1982-1994; Concordia Gallery, NY, 1992; Adelphi Univ, 1993; Drake Co Ctr for the Arts, Ohio, 1993; Marcella Geltman Gallery, Art Center, NJ, 1995; Gallery Art 54, Soho, NY, 1997; New World Art Ctr, Soho, NY, 1998-1999; Gallery, Boynton Beach, Fla, 1998; Wisser Mem Libr, NY Inst Tech, 1998; Chelsea Ctr for Cult Arts, NY, 1996-99; Atelier 14, NY, 2000; Elizabeth Found, NY, 2001; The Banana Factory, Bethlehem, Pa, 2002; Binney & Smith Gallery, 2002; NAWA Gallery, 2003; 88 Greenwich Street, NY, 2004; The Karpeles

Libr Mus, 2006; Port of Call Gallery, Warwick, NY, 2006. *Pos:* Exec bd, Nat Asn Women Artists, 80- & Vaali, 96-98; pres, Aquarelle Watercolor Group, Long Island, 84-86; adv bd, Coun Celebration Arts, 84-86; juror, Long Island Arts League, 88-89. *Awards:* Nat League Am Pen Women Award, 97; Chelsea Ctr Peacock Showcase Award, 98; Sarah Winston Mem Award, 2002. *Mem:* Nat Asn Women Artists; Aquarelle Watercolor Group Long Island. *Media:* Watercolors, Acrylics on Canvas. *Mailing Add:* 81 Finch Dr Roslyn NY 11576

TREJOS, CHARLOTTE (CARLOTA) MARIE
PAINTER
b Trout Lake, Mich, Jul 5, 20. *Study:* Hawthorne Christian Col, Calf, MA, 1975; No Light Art Sch, Cinncinnati, Ohio, 1998-99. *Work:* Mus of Latin Am Art, Long Branch, Calif; Nat Mus of Women in the Arts, Washington, DC. *Comn:* Floral painting - Oil, BA Price, Bay City, 1986; Ukelele with Hibiscus, Eugenia Carpenter, Hemet, Calif, 1990. *Exhib:* So Bay Regional Art Show, Carson, Calif, 1980-87; Several Firsts, Redondo Beach Juried Art Show, Calif, 1985; Mus of Latin Am, Long Branch, Calif, 1986; Nat Mus of Women in Art, Washington, DC, 1990. *Awards:* Third prize, Am Legion, Prescott, Va, 2003. *Mem:* Nat Mus of Women in Arts, 10 yrs; Mus of Latin Am Art, 12 yrs. *Media:* Acrylic, Oil. *Mailing Add:* 3872 Roxbury Dr Hemet CA 92545

TRENTON, PATRICIA JEAN
HISTORIAN
b Los Angeles, Calif, 27. *Study:* Univ Calif, Berkeley & Los Angeles, BA, MA(art hist), PhD, 80. *Exhib:* The Rocky Mountains: A Vision for Artists in the Nineteenth Century (auth, catalog), Buffalo Bill Hist Ctr, Cody, Wyo, 83; Native Faces: Indian Cultures in Am Art (coauth, catalog), Southwest Mus, Los Angeles, 84; California Light 1900-1930 (coauth, catalog), Laguna Art Mus, Laguna Beach, 90; Independent Spirits: Women Painters of the Am West 1890-1945 (with catalog), Autry Mus Western Heritage, Los Angeles, 95-97. *Pos:* Cur Am art, Denver Art Mus, Colo, 69-74; art dir, The Los Angeles Athletic Club, 82-. *Awards:* Nat Am Publ Award in Humanities, 83; Nat Hon Merit, Am Asn Mus, 84; Humanities Award, Nat Am Publ, 83; Western Heritage Wrangler Award, Nat Cowboy Hall of Fame & Heritage Ctr Outstanding Art Book of 1995; Caroline Bancroft Award for Outstanding Book on Western Art, 97. *Bibliog:* Joseph Klitsch (auth), A Kaleidoscope of Color, Irvine Mus, 2006. *Mem:* Col Art Asn. *Res:* Feminist research. *Publ:* Coauth, The Rocky Mountains: A Vision for Artists in the Nineteenth Century, Univ Okla Press, Norman, 83; Native Faces: Indian Cultures in American Art, Southwest Mus in Asn with LAACO Ltd, 84; Southwest Mus in Association with LAACO, Ltd, 84; Native Americans: Five Centuries of Changing Images, Harry N Abrams Publ, 89; California Light, Laguna Art Mus, 90; co-auth, The Not-So-Still-Life: a Century of California Painting and Sculpture, UC Press, 2004. *Mailing Add:* 10112 Empyrean No 303 Los Angeles CA 90067

TRESS, ARTHUR
PHOTOGRAPHER
b Brooklyn, NY, Nov 24, 40. *Study:* Bard Col, NY, BA, 62. *Work:* Metrop Mus Art, NY; San Francisco Mus Mod Art; Los Angeles Co Mus Art; Art Inst Chicago; Ctr Nat D'Art Cult Georges Pompidou, Paris, France. *Exhib:* Talisman (auth, catalog), Mus Mod Art, Oxford, Eng, 86; Fish Tank Sonata, Santa Barbara Contemp Arts Forum, Calif, 94; Warlitzen Trilogy, Ctr Photog, Tucson, 95; Fantastic Voyage, Singapore Mus Art, 95; Requiem for a Paperweight, Univ Art Mus, Calif State Univ, Long Beach, 95; Retrospective, Taipei Mus Art, Taiwan, 97. *Bibliog:* A D Coleman (auth), A Grotesque in Photography, Summit Books, 77; Allen Ellenzweig (auth), Homoerotic Photograph, Columbia Univ Press, 92. *Publ:* Auth, Dream Collection, Avon Publ, 72; Theater of the Mind, Morgan & Morgan, 76; Facing Up, St Martin's Press, 80; Arthur Tress, Stemmle, 95. *Mailing Add:* 2705 Marlborough Ln Cambria CA 93428

TRIBUSH, BRENDA
PAINTER, INSTRUCTOR
b New York, NY, Nov 5, 1939. *Study:* AAS, Fashion Inst Tech, NY; Adelphi Univ, NY, BA, 1981, MA, 1983; studied with Isaac Soyer & Ruben Tam, Brooklyn Mus of Art, NY; NY Art Students League. *Exhib:* Ruth Harely Univ Ctr Gallery, Garden City, NY, 83; Union League Club, NY, 92; Pen & Brush Club, NY, 95; Louisa Melrose GAllery, Holicong, Pa, 99; group exhib, Butler Inst Am Art, Ohio, John Brown Univ, Alaska, Huntsville Mus Art, Ala, Dansville Mus Art, Va, Mus Tex Tech Univ, Tex A&M Univ, Peter Paul Fortress Mus, Russia, Nassau County Mus Fine Arts, NY, Allied Artist Am, NY, 1988-2006, Pastel Soc Am, NY, 87-2006, Cetnre Cultural, France, 2002-05 & 2006, Europastel, Italy, 2003 & Xi'an Acad Fine Arts, China, 1997. *Collection Arranged:* Union League Club; DuPont Pharmaceutical Co. *Pos:* Juror, Alliance Queens Artist, NY, 1994, Annual Fine Arts Show, Long Beach, NY, 2001 & 02. *Teaching:* instr, pvt classes, Studio Manhattan, NY & Long Island Arts Coun, Freeport, NY, 1993 & 94; Ernest Crichlolo instr, NY Art Students League; instr workshop, Terence Cardinal Cooke Health Ctr, NY, 2003. *Awards:* William Alfred White Award, Salmagundi Club, NY & Jane Impastatd Award, 2002; Award, Allied Artists Am, 2001; Klimberger Meml Award, Pastel Soc Am, 2001. *Mem:* Allied Artists Am (bd dir, currently); NY Artists Equity (vpres, currently); Pastel Soc Am (bd dir, currently); Pen & Brush Asn; Salmagundi Club. *Media:* Pastels. *Publ:* auth, Best of Pastels 2, 1998, Allied Artists Am, 2001, Butler Inst Am Art, Am Art Mag, 2001, Jour Pastello Contemporano en Europa, 2003 & L'Art du Pastel, 2005. *Mailing Add:* 41 Union Sq W New York NY 10003

TRIEFF, SELINA
PAINTER, INSTRUCTOR
b Brooklyn, NY, Jan 7, 34. *Study:* Art Students League, study with Morris Kantor; Hans Hofmann Sch, study with Hofmann; Brooklyn Col, BA, study with Rothko & Reinhardt, 55. *Work:* Brooklyn Mus; NY Pub Libr; Inst for Human Develop; Prudential Life Insurance Co; Bayonne Jewish Ctr; Smite Mus, Norte Dame Univ; and others. *Comn:* Lithograph, Bayonne Jewish Ctr. *Exhib:* Contemp Am Figure Painting, Wadsworth Atheneum, 64; Work on Paper, Brooklyn Mus, 75; Butler Inst Ann, 77; Artes Gallery, Olso & Cassandra Gallery, Orobak, Norway, 84; Graham Modern Gallery, 86, 87 & 88; Ruth Bachofner Gallery, Santa Monica, 87, 90, 92 & 94; Katharina Rich Perlow Gallery, NY, 91, 93 & 94; Berta Walker Gallery, Provincetown, 92 93; and others. *Teaching:* Instr drawing, New York Inst of Technol, 75-; vis artist painting, Notre Dame Univ, Ind, 76; instr painting, New York Studio Sch, formerly; instr painting, Pratt Inst, formerly, Nat Acad Design. *Awards:* Second Prize, Goddard Col Ann, 76; Purchase Prize, View from the Ctr, Bayonne Community Ctr, 78; Thomas B Clarke Prize, Nat Acad Design, 79; and others. *Bibliog:* Corinne Robins (auth), Selina Trieff, Arts, 78; Hilton Kramer (auth), article, New York Times, 82; Maureen Mullarky (auth), article, 84 & Joan Marter (auth), article, 6/86, Arts Mag; John Rusgell, New York Times; Vivian Raynol, New York Times. *Mem:* Women in the Arts; Womens Caucus Art; Col Art Asn. *Media:* Oil, Charcoal. *Mailing Add:* c/o Ruth Bachofner Gallery 2525 Michigan Ave G2 Santa Monica CA 90404

TRIEN, MAY ROLSTAD
PAINTER, GRAPHIC ARTIST
b Oslo, Norway. *Study:* Univ Madrid, Spain; Bath Acad of Art, Eng; studied with Howard Hodgkin, Harvey Dinnerstein; Art Students League, NY; degree in textile design, Norway. *Exhib:* Salmagundi Club, New York City, 90 & 97; Catharine Lorillard Wolfe Art Club, 91-97, 99-01, 04 & 05; Audubon Artists, New York City, 93, 97-01 & 2005; Allied Artists Am, 96, 98, 99, 2001, 04 & 05; Nat Acad Design, New York City, 2000; NY Artists Equity, Invitational Sm Works Exhib, 2002; Art Students League of New York, Juried Mem Exhib, 2004. *Teaching:* instr art, Oslo Jr High Sch; instr art, United Nations Int Sch, NY; instr crafts prog, Riverside Church, NY. *Awards:* Gold Medal of Hon, Am Artists Prof League; Gold Medal, Catharine Lorillard Wolfe Art Club; First prize award, Pen & Brush Inc. *Mem:* Allied Artists Am; Audubon Artists (bd mem, currently); Am Artists Prof League; Salmagundi Club; Catharine Corillard Wolfe Art Club (bd dirs). *Media:* Oil; Graphite Pencil. *Publ:* Adressavisen, Trondheim, Norway; Fiberarts Mag; Viking Mag; The Artful Mind. *Mailing Add:* 90 Riverside Dr New York NY 10024

TRIMM, H WAYNE
ILLUSTRATOR, PAINTER
b Albany, NY, Aug 16, 22. *Study:* Cornell Univ, 40; Augustana Col, BS, 48; Kans State Univ, 49; Col Forestry, Syracuse Univ, MS, 53. *Comn:* Dioramas, Springfield Mus Art; three ecol dioramas, Augustana Col, 67; World Wildlife Fund, Int Stamps for Congo, Bolivia, Bangladesh, 74; mural, Alley Pond Environ Ctr, Douglaston, NY, 80; mural of summer pond, 5 Rivers Environ Educ Ctr, Delmar, NY; and others. *Exhib:* Am Bird Artists Traveling Exhib, Audubon Artists; Joslyn Mus Art; Buffalo Mus Sci; one-man show, Remington Mus; SAA Show, San Francisco Acad Arts & Sci; Philadelphia Mus Art; and others. *Pos:* Art dir, Conservationist Mag, Div Educ Serv, NY State Dept Environ Conserv, 53-, sr ed, 53-73; ed, Outdoor Communicator Mag, formerly; vpres, Soc Animal Artists, NY, The Catasus (animal art), currently; ed, Catasus, Jour Soc Animal Artists, currently; leader Fed Duck Stamp workshops, 96, 97, 98; judge Fed Duck Stamp Competition, Washington, DC. *Teaching:* Lectr conserv & wildlife painting, currently; instr nature & sci illus, State Univ NY, Albany & Col St Rose, Nat Wildlife Fedn Summits, Sagamore Inst, Raguette Lake, New York, Adirondack Ctr Arts, Blue Mt Lake, New York, Asa Wright Ctr, Trinidad; Asa Wright Nature Ctr, 81; Fed Duck Stamp Workshop, Old Forge, NY; Outdoor World for Learning, Hoosick Falls, NY; art groups in Albany & Troy, NY; Peconic Dunes Environ Ctr, Peconic, NY. *Awards:* The Trad Award, NY State Dept Environmental Conservationist; The Golden Award, NYSOEA; Artist of the Year 1988, WNPE/WNPI, Watertown, NY; Purchase Award, Blauveld Mus. *Bibliog:* Glenn Goff (interviewer), Cabin Country, WNPE-TV, 87. *Mem:* Columbia Co Arts & Crafts; Soc Animal Artists (vpres); hon mem Tuscarora Indian Tribe; Am Ornithologists Union; Guild Nat Sci Illusr. *Media:* Watercolor, Acrylic, Oil; Marble, Wood. *Publ:* Illustr, The Guild Handbook of Scientific Illustration, Smithsonian Inst; Illustrators Annual--Nature Drawing, No 27 & Nature Sketching, Claire Leslie Walker; auth, Dr Phyllis Busch, Back Yard Satariis. *Mailing Add:* 64 High St Hoosick Falls NY 12090

TRIMPIN
CONCEPTUAL ARTIST
b Ger, 50. *Pos:* Co-chair, Electronics Music Dept, Sweelinck Conserv, Amsterdam, 85-87; composer, Composer Conf, Telluride, Colo & Brooklyn Acad Music, 89. *Awards:* Guggenheim Found Fel, 97; MacArthur Fel, 97. *Mailing Add:* 1131 36th Ave Seattle WA 98122-5220

TRINCERE, LI
PAINTER
b New York, NY, May 7, 59. *Study:* Southampton Col, Long Island Univ, NY, BFA(printing, printmaking), 81; Hunter Col, New York, CW Post Univ, Long Island NY, MFA, 83. *Work:* Exon Corp; Am Express. *Exhib:* Cologne Art Fair, Galerie Ricke, Ger, 88, 89, 90, 91 & 92; Shaped Paintings, Julian Pretto, Berland Hall, NY, 89; one-woman shows, New Shaped Paintings, Julian Pretto, NY, 89, New Paintings, Galerie Rolf Ricke, Cologne, Ger, 89, Paintings/Drawings, Galerie Ranate Kammer, Hamburg, Ger, 90, New Paintings, Berland/Hall Gallery, NY, 90; Aus Meiner Sicht, Kolnisher Kunstverein, Cologne, Ger, 90; Kinder, Macht Neues, Galerie Rolf Ricke, Cologne, Ger, 92. *Awards:* Pollock/Krasner Found, 86 & 88; NY State Fel Arts, 89; Nat Endowment Arts Fel, 91. *Bibliog:* Farben und Flachen Kulurberichte, Die Konstuktivistin, Cologne, Ger, 10/89; Peter Frank (auth), Reconstructive painting, Artspace, 3/90; Art reproduction, Bomb Mag, p 81, 10th Year Issue, summer 91

TRIPP, JAN PETER
PAINTER, PRINTMAKER
b Oberstdorf, Bavaria, Ger, May 15, 45. *Study:* Acad Art, Stuttgart, sculpture, 68; Acad Art, Vienna, Austria, painting, 69-73; Masters class at Rudolf Hausner. *Work:* Staatsgalerie, Stuttgart, Ger; Kunsthalle, Hamburg, Ger; Albertina, Vienna, Austria; Frac, Strasbourg, France. *Exhib:* Graphic Biennales, Krakow, Ljubljana, Segovia, Bradford & Frechen, 72-90; 7 Ger Realists, Triennale, New Delhi, India, 78; 20 Ger Painters & Drawers, Warzowa, Poland, 79; Man and Landscape in Contemp Painting and Graphic in BRD, Moscow, Leningrad, Russ, 83; 25 Ger Painters, Lissabonn Iporto, Port, 84; and others. *Mem:* Deutscher Kunstlerbund. *Media:* Acrylic, Egg Tempera; Etching. *Publ:* Contribr, Die Kehrseite der Dinge, Gehring Gallery, Frankfurt, 85. *Mailing Add:* John Szoke Editions and Graphics 591 Broadway New York NY 10012-3232

TRIPP, SUSAN GERWE
MUSEUM DIRECTOR
b Baltimore, Md, Dec 28, 45. *Study:* Univ Md, BS, 67. *Work:* Evergreen House, Johns Hopkins Univ; Homewood Mus, Baltimore, Md; Old Westbury Gardens, NY. *Pos:* Cur art, Johns Hopkins Univ, 74-79, dir univ collections, 79-91; exec dir, Old Westbury Gardens, 91-96; mus & hist restoration consult, 96-; trustee, Columbia Co Hist Soc, 96-, pres & bd dir, 97-2002, 2003-bd dir & secy; Regional & Comty Hist Preservation Benefit 2002-; bd trustee AM Numismatic Soc, 2003-; Judge Hist Hudson Preservation Awards, 2000-; chmn Vanderpael House restoration Columbia Co Hist Soc, 2002. *Teaching:* Lectr art hist, Sch Continuing Educ, Johns Hopkins Univ, 78-. *Awards:* Mus Fel, Nat Endowment Arts, 80; Hist Preserv Award, Baltimore, Heritage, 88 & 91; Hist Preserv Award, ASID, 91. *Mem:* Oriental Ceramic Soc; Am Asn Mus; Oriental Ceramic Soc; Furniture Hist Soc; Am Numismatic Soc (mem, standing Comt, Libr & Archives). *Res:* Japanese minor arts, emphasis on history of lacquer and adaptation of theater masks to netsuke; Leon Bakst; 18th and 19th century domestic economy; 19th century textiles and carpets; federal pd America. *Publ:* Auth, Bakst, Johns Hopkins Mag, 84; contribr, A Taste of Maryland, Walters Art Gallery, 85; auth, Chinese Collections in Evergreen House (exhib catalog), Baltimore Antiques Show, 85 & A Gentleman from Baltimore, Southeby's Great Sales, Barrie and Jenkins, Ltd, London, 89; coauth (with N K Davey), The Garrett Collection of Japanese Art, Dauphin Publ, 92; auth, Homewood in Baltimore, Maryland, Mag Antiques & Evergreen House, Baltimore, Md. *Mailing Add:* PO Box G Stuyvesant NY 12173

TRISSEL, JAMES NEVIN
PAINTER, PRINTMAKER
b Davenport, Iowa, Nov 7, 30. *Study:* State Univ Iowa, BA; Colo State Col, MA; State Univ Iowa, MFA. *Work:* Univ Wis; Beloit Col; Colo Col; Colorado Springs Fine Arts Ctr; Libr Congress. *Exhib:* One-man show, Beloit Col, 57, & Colorado Springs Fine Arts Ctr, 66 & 72, Ankrum Gallery, Los Angeles, 76; Wis Salon, 58; El Paso Biennial, 64 & 66. *Pos:* Actg dir, Wright Art Ctr, Beloit Col, 58-59; dir, Univ Exten Prog in Art, Univ Calif, Los Angeles, 62-64; proprietor, The Press, Colo Col, 78-. *Teaching:* Instr art, Beloit Col, 58-60; asst prof art & art theory, Univ Calif, Los Angeles, 60-64; assoc prof art & art hist, Colo Col, 64-70, prof art, 70-, chmn dept art, 71-77. *Media:* Oil; Letter Press Book Printing. *Dealer:* Califia Books San Francisco CA; Joshua Heller Roll Books Washington DC

TRIVIGNO, PAT
PAINTER, EDUCATOR
b New York, NY, Mar 13, 22. *Study:* Tyler Sch Art; NY Univ; Columbia Univ, BA & MA. *Work:* Solomon R Guggenheim Mus, NY; New Orleans Mus Art, La; Everson Mus, Syracuse, NY; NY Times; Gen Elec Corp. *Comn:* Murals, Lykes Steamship Lines & Cook Conv Ctr, Memphis, Sports Arena, New Orleans. *Exhib:* Whitney Mus Am Art Ann; Art Inst Chicago; Pa Acad Fine Arts; Am Acad Arts & Lett; Univ Ill Biennial; retrospective, (with catalog), New Orleans Mus Art; S Stern Gallery, New Orleans; Contemp Art Ctr, New Orleans. *Collection Arranged:* AETNA Life Ins Co, New Orleans; Acquarium of Americas, New Orleans; Brooklyn Mus; Guggheim Mus; Los Angeles Land & Exploration Co; Canizaro Interests, New Orleans; Neuberger Mus, NY; New Orleans Mus Art; Alton Ochnsner Medical Found; Touro Infirmary-Ogden Mus Southern Art. *Teaching:* Prof art, Tulane Univ La, 50-, chmn art dept. *Bibliog:* Articles in New York Times, 10/8/50 & 1/10/60; R Pearson (auth), Modern Renaissance in American Art, Harper. *Media:* Acrylic, Oil. *Dealer:* Simone Stern Gallery New Orleans LA. *Mailing Add:* 1831 Marengo St New Orleans LA 70115

TROMBETTA, ANNAMARIE
PAINTER, PRINTMAKER
b Brooklyn, NY, Aug 5, 63. *Study:* Parsons Sch Design; NY Acad Art, cert; Nat Acad Sch Fine Art, cert; Studies with Everett Raymond Kinstler, Wayne Thiebaud; Painting group, with Aaron Shikler & David Levine, Soho, NY. *Work:* off Mayor R Guiliani, NY; Nat Acad Design, NY. *Comn:* mural, State Island Mall Ctr, NY, 81; Croquet Game (painting), commn. by treas US Croquet Asn, NY, 94; Madonna of Maternity (painting), Daniel's Restaurant, NY, 95; portrait, commn by Dir Metrop Mag, NY, 99; conservancy garden, commn by Mark Boyle, NY, 98. *Exhib:* Solo show, Liederkrantz Club, NY, 93, Dana Ctr Artworks of Ctrl Park NY, 03, Historic Richmondtown Mus, 01, Garibaldi-Meucci Mus, 02, Wagner Col, 03, Junefest award, Citibank, Staten Island, NY, 2005; 1st St Gallery Nat Competition Exhib, NY, 94; Catherine Lorillard Wolfe Art Club Competition Exhib, NY, 94; Am Artist Prof League Competition Exhib, NY, 94; Gallery on 2d Nat Juried Competition Figurative Art, NY, 96; PSA 25th Ann Exhib, NY, 97; Print exhib Pakistan Mission, NY, 98; Audubon Artists 58th Int Ann Exhib, NY, 2000; Godwin-Ternbach Mus Ital Am Women, 01; Arnot Mus, 03; Plain Air Painting, The Staten Island Mus, 2004; Bendheim Gallery, Greenwich, Conn, 2006; 64th Audubon Artists, NY, 2005 & 06; Yellow Gallery, Cross River, NY, 2006. *Teaching:* teacher, NY Acad Art, The Snug Harbor Cult Ctr. *Awards:* Inga Denton Award, 97; Milton Avery Award, 98; Ogden M Pleissner Award, 2000; Robert Lehman Award, 2001; Coashi Grant, 2001, 2003 & 2004; Pollack-Krasner Grant, 2004; Plein Air Painting Grant, 2005, Traveling Grant, 2006, Richmond Co Savings Bank. *Bibliog:* Raymond J Steiner (auth), profile, Art Times, 1/96; Frank Mazza (auth), The Artist Who Paints (video), CTV, Staten Island, NY, 98; Plain Air Painting Video, 2001; Cent Park to Staten Island, 2004 (video). *Mem:* Pastel Soc of Am; Nat Orgn of Italian Am Women. *Media:* Oil, Watercolor. *Interests:* Running; Hindo Buddist Philos. *Publ:* auth, Poetry in Pastel, Pastelagram, Spring 99; auth, Future of Figurative Art, Art Times, July 99; Italian Tribune, 2002; Staten Island Advance, 2001- 2004. *Mailing Add:* 175 E 96th St Apt 14P New York NY 10128

TROMEUR, ROBYN LORI
CURATOR, DIRECTOR
b Ridgewood, NJ, Oct 19, 66. *Study:* Muhlenberg Col, BFA (art hist, summa cum laude), 88. *Hon Degrees:* Rutgers Univ, MFA, 92, cert mus studies, 92. *Collection Arranged:* The World of Faberge (Russian gems and jewels), Houston Mus Natural Sci, 94; Artifacts of an Assassination (hist manuscripts), Forbes Mag Galleries, 95; Treasures of the Czars, Mus Fine Arts, St Petersburg, Fla, 95; La Belle Epoque, Nassau Co Mus Art, Roslyn Harbor, NY, 95; Faberge: Juwelier des Zarenhofes, Mus fur Kunst und Gewerbe, Hamburg, Ger, 95; Small Wonders: The Fantastic Voyage into Miniature Worlds, Margaret Woodbury Strong Mus, Rochester, NY, 95-97; Faberge Silver from the Forbes Magazine Collection, Mus Natural Hist & Sci, Albuquerque, NMex, 95-96; First Families (hist manuscripts), Forbes Mag Galleries, 95-97; And If Elected.200 Years of Presidential Elections (hist manuscripts), San Diego Mus Art, 96; Faberge and Finland: Exquisite Objects, Corcoran Gallery Art, Washington DC, 96-97; Faberge in America, Metrop Mus Art, NY, H.M. De Young Mem Mus, San Francisco, Mus Fine Art, Richmond, Va, New Orleans Mus Art, Cleveland Mus Art, 96-97; Philadelphia and the American Revolution (hist manuscripts), Franklin Inst, 96-97; Faberge: Loistavaa Kultasepantaidetta, Lahti Art Mus, Finland, 97; Maryland Blossoms in the Arts, Govt House, Annapolis, Md, 97; Carl Faberge: Goldsmith tothe Tsar, Nat Mus, Stockholm, Sweden, 97; Highlights from the Forbes Magazine Collection, 97-2000; The Glitter and the Gold: Faberge at Biltmore Estate, Asheville, NC, 98; Peterhof: Treasures of Russia, Rio All-Suites Hotel and Casino, Las Vegas, 98-99; Regal Splendor: Masterpieces from the House of Faberge: Ronald Reagan Presidential Libr, Simi Valley, Calif, 98-99; Nicholas & Alexandra: The Last Imperial Family of Tsarist Russia, 1st USA Riverfront Arts Ctr, Wilmington, Del, 99. *Pos:* curator, Forbes Mag Collection, New York, 92-2000; exec dir, Somerset Art Asn, Bedminster, NJ, 2000-. *Mem:* Nat Asn Corp Art Mgt (newsletter ed). *Publ:* auth, Faberge Treasures, Harry N Abrams, 98; co-auth, Faberge: The Forbes Collection, 99. *Mailing Add:* Somerset Art Assn 2020 Burnt Mills Rd Bedminster NJ 07921

TRONCALE, FRANK THOMAS
DEALER, COLLECTOR
b Birmingham, Ala, Aug 11, 41. *Study:* Birmingham Southern Col, BA, 65. *Pos:* Docent (tour guide), John & Mable Ringling Mus Art, 77-79; dir, Hang-Up, Sarasota, Fla, currently. *Specialty:* Contemporary graphics. *Collection:* Contemporary graphics of Dali, Nierman, Nieman, Paul Maxwell, Picasso, Calder, Paul Jenkins, Thornton Utz, Frank Hopper, Dorothy Gillespie, P Mackie, Calzado & Jack Dowd

TROP, SANDRA
DIRECTOR
b Brooklyn, NY. *Study:* NY Univ, BS(cum laude); Everson Mus Art; Inst Arts Admin; Harvard Univ. *Pos:* Cur traveling exhibs, Everson Mus Art, Syracuse, NY, 72, asst to dir, 73, actg dir, 74, asst dir, 74-. *Teaching:* Adj prof, Syracuse Univ Museology, 74. *Awards:* Women in Bus award, 2002; Spirit Women award; Northeast Baptist Scholarship award. *Mem:* Int Coun Mus (int comt mus & collections mod art); Am Asn Mus. *Media:* Newspaper. *Specialty:* Ceramics, video, contemp art. *Mailing Add:* Everson Mus Art 401 Harrison St Syracuse NY 13202

TROSKY, HELENE ROTH
PRINTMAKER, PAPERMAKER
b Monticello, NY. *Study:* New Sch Social Res, with Kuniyoshi Egas; Manhattanville Col, BA, with Al Blaustein, John Ross & Garner Tullis. *Work:* Wichita Mus of Art; Sheldon Swope Mus of Art, Terre Haute, Ind; Staten Island Mus; Hudson River Mus, Paine-Webber. *Comn:* Comn by Konigsberg & Wolf, 84, The Eggers Grp, 85, Am Ultramar, 85 & Pepsico, 86; Reader's Digest, 89. *Exhib:* Silvermine Guild, 68-70; Alan Brown Gallery, Hartsdale, NY, 80, 86, 90 & 92; Westchester Community Col, 81; Mus Gallery, White Plains, 87; Hammond Mus, Yorktown, NY, 92; Paramount Ctr Arts, Peekskill, NY, 92. *Pos:* Columnist, Muse Roundup, Harrison Independent Greenburgh Rec & Yonkers Rec, 60-76; art consult, Westchester Libr Syst, 65-70; dir, Second Regional Plan, New York, 65-. *Teaching:* Art dir, Westchester Co Music & Art Camp, 65, 66, 71 & 72; lectr art hist, Brandeis Univ Women, 66-85; instr printmaking, Manhattanville Col, 71-76; adj prof art hist, Westchester Community Col, 81-; lectr, Marymount Col, 87. *Awards:* Northern Westchester Award, 68; Nat Asn Women Artists Award, 69 & 82; Coun Arts Westchester Award, 86. *Bibliog:* Marna Elyea Kern (auth), The Complete Book of Hand Crafted Paper, Coward McCann & Geoghegon. *Mem:* Silvermine Guild; Nat Asn Women Artists; Am Soc Contemp Artists; Hudson River Contemp Artists; Katonah Gallery; and others. *Media:* All. *Publ:* Auth, art columns & revs for Women's News, Harrison Independent & North Castle News, Pleasantville Post & Chappaqua J, 82-. *Dealer:* Alan Brown Gallery Hartsdale NY

TROTMAN, BOB
SCULPTOR
b Winston-Salem, NC, June 25, 47. *Study:* Wash & Lee Univ, BA(magna cum laude), 69; Penland Sch, 76-77; Sculpture Ctr, New York, 88. *Work:* Vpres Residence, Washington, DC; Va Mus Fine Arts, Richmond; Mint Mus Art, Charlotte, NC; Smithsonian Inst; Mus Art, RI Sch Design, Providence; NC Mus Art, Raleigh. *Exhib:*

one-man exhibs, Hodges/Taylor Gallery, Charlotte, NC, 1989, Franklin Parrasch Gallery, NY, 1994, 1996, 1998 & 2001, Mint Mus Art, Charlotte, NC, 95-96 & Weatherspoon Art Gallery, Greensboro, NC, 01; Mus, Union Arts Decoratifs, Paris, 89; Mus Appl Arts, Moscow, 90; Mus Arts Decoratifs, Lausanne, Switz, 90; one-man retrospective, NC State Univ, 94; Conservation by Design, Renwick Gallery, Smithsonian Inst, Washington, DC, 96; Four Decades of Discovery: The 40th Anniversary Am Craft Mus, NY, 96; Model Citizens, Hand Workshop Art Center, Richmond, 2002. *Pos:* panelist, Gov Awards Art, NC Arts Coun, 83, Grants in Visual Arts, 86, Ill Arts Coun, 86, Artist Proj Grants, NC Arts Coun, 88 & Craft Fels, Arts Midwest, Minneapolis, Minn, 89; lectr, RI Sch Design, 90, NC Mus Art, Raleigh, 90 & Renwick Gallery, Washington, DC, 97. *Teaching:* Eng, Christchurch Sch, Va, 69-70, Lake Forest Acad, Ill, 70-72; Penland Sch Crafts, NC, 80, 81, 85, 93, 96 & 2000, Haystack-Mountain Sch, Deer Isle, Maine, 90 & 95, San Diego State Univ, Calif, 96, Anderson Ranch Arts Ctr, Snowmass, Colo, 96 & Renwick Gallery, Washington, DC, 97. *Awards:* Nat Endowment Arts Fel, 84 & 88; NC Artists Fel, 84, 95 & 2000; Cohn Family Trust Prize Excellence in Design, Philadelphia, Pa, 90. *Bibliog:* Charlotte V Brown & Nina Stritzler (coauths), Bob Trotman: A Retrospective of Furniture & Sculpture (exhib catalog), NC State Univ; Mark Richard Leach (auth), Artcurrents 20: Bob Trotman, Mint Mus Art; Bob Trotman: Woodworker Plus, NC Homes & Gardens, 3/91; Art in Am, (by Janet Koplos), Oct 2001; Sculpture, (by Dina Ryan), Dec 2002. *Mem:* Penland Sch Crafts (bd trustees). *Media:* Wood, Miscellaneous. *Publ:* Auth, Wearing Water/Eating Cement, Art Papers, 7/90; Amateur Hour (Ned Cooke, ed), Yale Univ, 97. *Dealer:* Franklin Parrasch Gallery 20 W 57th St New York NY 10019; Hodges Taylor Gallery 401 N Tryon St Charlotte NC. *Mailing Add:* 368 Quince Rd Casar NC 28020

TROUTMAN, JILL
PAINTER
b Newton, Iowa, July 20, 38. *Study:* Univ Va, EdB(art hist), 69; Cleveland Inst Art, Lacoste, France, 83; Art Studios Int, Florence, Italy, 84. *Work:* NC Nat Bank, Charlotte, NC; R J Reynolds Collection, Winston-Salem, NC. *Comn:* Lobby collection, Guilford Neurological, Greensboro, NC; lobby collection, Cent Carolina Bank, Burlington, NC; lobby collection, York Properties, Raleigh, NC; lobby collection, WFMY-TV, Greensboro, NC; cancer unit, Duke Med Ctr, Durham, NC. *Exhib:* 37 one-woman shows, 72-94. *Teaching:* Instr painting, Ctr Creative Arts, Greensboro, NC, 81-86; instr, 50 adult art students, currently. *Mem:* High Point Fine Art Guild (pres, 78-79); NC Watercolor Soc (pres, 80-81); High Point Arts Coun; Alamance Co Arts Ctr. *Media:* Acrylic, Acrylic Collages. *Specialty:* Harrison's in Burlington, NC. *Interests:* Taking Jazz piano lessons. *Mailing Add:* 1089 Foxcliff Dr Mebane NC 27302

TROVA, ERNEST TINO
SCULPTOR, PAINTER
b St Louis, Mo, Feb 19, 27. *Work:* Hirshhorn Mus, Washington, DC; Guggenheim Mus, Mus Mod Art, Metrop Mus Art & Whitney Mus Am Art, NY; Boca Raton (Fla) Mus Arts Lococo, St. Louis. *Exhib:* One-man exhibs, Hokin Gallery, Miami Beach, 88 & 90, Mangel Gallery, Philadelphia, 89, Galeria Freites, Caracas, Venezuela, 89 & 90, Hanson Galleries, San Francisco & Beverly Hills, 89, ACA Galleries, NY, 90, Philharmonic Ctr for the Arts, Naples, Fla, 91, Boca Raton Mus. Art, 99; Guggenheim Mus, NY, 64, 65, 67 & 84; Whitney Mus Mod Art, NY, 66, 68, 69 & 78; Mus Mod Art, NY, 68; Hirshhorn Mus & Sculpture Garden, Smithsonian Inst, Washington, DC, 74 & 83; Hanson Galleries, LaJolla, Calif, 89, Miami, 90; ACA Galleries, NY, 90; Galaria Freites, Caracas, Venezuela, 90; Philharmonic Ctr for the Arts, Naples, Fla, 91; Art Chicago, 91; Dorothy Blau Gallery, Bay Harbor, & Miami, Fla, 2000, Laumeier Sculpture Park Celebration, Sunset Hills, Mo, 2001, New Iris Paintings, Lococo, St Louis, 2001. *Awards:* Nat Humanitarian Award, Nat Recreation & Park Asn, 79; Utsukushi-ga-hara Open Air Mus Award, 83; Excellence in Arts, Arts and Edn Coun of St Louis, 2000. *Bibliog:* Ellen Post (auth), Ernest Trova: New Works, Laumeier Sculpture Park, 86; Riva Yares (auth), Ernest Trova: Falling Man-Poets-Pyramids-Gox, Yares Gallery, 86; Andrew Kagan (auth), Trova, 2nd Ed, Trova Found, St Louis, Mo, 87; Ernest Trova, Paintings, Sculptures and Communications, Lococo Publs, St. Louis. *Media:* All. *Dealer:* Lococo-Mulder 9320 Olive Blvd St Louis MO 63132. *Mailing Add:* 6 Layton Terr Saint Louis MO 63124

TROY, NANCY J
HISTORIAN
Study: Wesleyan Univ, BA (magna cum laude), 74; Yale Univ, MA (twentieth century European art), 76, PhD (Kress Found Travel Grant, Fulbright-Hays Grant), 79. *Pos:* Guest cur, Yale Univ Art Gallery, New Haven, Conn, 79; mem fine arts accessions com, com collections, Baltimore Mus Art, Md, 79-82; cons, Walker Art Center, Minneapolis, MInn, 82 & Art Inst Chicago, Ill, 84-85; mem vis com, Harvard Univ Art Mus, Cambridge, Mass, 92-98; series co-ed, Histories, Cultures, Contexts, Reaktion Books. *Teaching:* Asst prof, Johns Hopkins Univ, Baltimore, Md, 79-83; asst prof, Northwestern Univ, 83-85, assoc prof, 85-92, acting chairperson, 88, chairperson, 90-92, prof, 92-93; vis prof, Univ Calif, Los Angeles, 94; vis prof, Univ Southern Calif, Los Angeles, 94-95, prof, 95-, chairperson, 97-; scholar-in-residence, Getty Res INst History Art and Humanities, 93-96. *Awards:* Grant, Am Coun Learned Soc, 81, 91 & 98-99; Fel, John Simon Guggenheim Mem Found, 98-99; Zumberge Fac Res and Innovation Fund, Univ Southern Calif, 98-99; Distinguished Alumna Award, Wesleyan Univ, 99. *Bibliog:* Linda Dahlrymple (auth), The Fourth Dimension and Non-Euclidian Geometry in Modern Art, Design Bk Rev, fall 84; Kenneth E Silver (auth), Esprit de corps: The art of the Parisian avant garde and the first world war, Art Bulletin, LXXIII, 3/1/91. *Mem:* Nat Comn Hist Art (bd dir, 98-). *Publ:* Auth, The De Stijl Environment, Mass Inst Technol Press, Cambridge, 83; Modernism and the Decorative Arts in France: Art Nouveau to Le Corbusier, Yale Univ Press, New Haven, 91; The logic of function, Decorative Arts Soc J, 95; Domesticity, Decoration and Consumer Culture: Selling Art and Design in Pre-World War I France, Not at Home the Suppression of Domesticity in Modern Art & Archit, Thames & Hudson, London & New York, 96; co-ed, Architecture and Cubism, Mass Inst Technol Press, Cambridge, Mass & London, 97. *Mailing Add:* Dept Art HIstory Univ Southern Calif Watt Hall 104 Los Angeles CA 90089-0293

TRUBY, BETSY KIRBY
PAINTER, ILLUSTRATOR
b Winchester, Va, Nov 8, 26. *Study:* Hiram Col; Cleveland Sch Art; NMex Inst Mining & Technol; Univ NMex; also with David Moneypenny, Oden Hullenkramer & Joe Morello. *Work:* Int Moral Re-Armament Ctr, Mackinaw Island, Mich; Cancer Res & Treatment Ctr, Albuquerque; Truth or Consequences Geronimo Springs Art Mus, NMex; Sheraton Hotel, Santa Fe, NMex; La Quinta Mus, Albuquerque. *Comn:* Portrait, Congressman Albert G Simms, 64; Indian child portrait, NMex Easter Seal Soc, 69; paintings, First Presby Church, Albuquerque, 72-74; historical portrait, Synod Southwest, Presby Church, 75; paintings, Cystic Fibrosis Found, NMex, 76 & 77; paintings reproduced, Southwest Arts & Graphics, 84, 85, 86, 87, 88, 89 & 90. *Exhib:* Fine Arts Gallery, Carnegie Inst, Pittsburgh, 46; NMex Fiesta Biennial, State Mus, Santa Fe, 64 & 68; Nat Art Show, Lawton, Okla, 74; Nat League Am Pen Women Mid-Ad Cong, Phoenix, Ariz, 75; One-woman show, Hiram Col, Ohio, 87; Nat League Am Pen Women Nat Show, Kansas City, Mo, 90. *Pos:* exhib chmn, Yucca Art Gallery, Albuquerque, Old Town, NMex, 70-72; Photogr, Nat League Am Pen Women-Yucca Branch, 92-2006. *Teaching:* Instr ceramics, US Pub Health Hosp, 48-49, Ohio Pub Sch Syst, 49-50; instr ceramics, Ohio Pub Sch Syst, 49-50. *Awards:* Nat League Am Pen Women State Show, First Premium Pastel, Third Premium Oil, Secorro, NMex, 10/89; Third Premium-Pastel, Juried Exhib, Pastel Soc NMex, Albuquerque, 91; Second Premium Pastel, Nat League Am Pen Women, NMex, 95, 99; Nat League Am Pen Women Show, Juried, Best of Show, Albuquerque, NMex, 2003; Nat Show, Master Works, 2nd award, Albuquerque, NMex, 2004; 2nd Place Pastel, Nat League Am Pen Woman State Show, Socorro, NMex, 2005. *Bibliog:* J Bonnette (auth), The Creative Process, KNME TV, Univ NMex, 73. *Mem:* Nat League Am Pen Women; charter mem, Pastel Soc NMex. *Media:* Pastel, Watercolor. *Publ:* Cover illusr, Flags, 73 & Let Our Light Shine, 74. *Dealer:* Pastel Soc NMex Box 3571 Albuquerque NM 87190; Bardean Gallery PO Box 3055 Albuquerque NM 87190. *Mailing Add:* 6609 Loftus Ave NE Albuquerque NM 87109-2721

TRUDEAU, GARRY B
CARTOONIST
b New York, NY, 48. *Study:* Yale Univ, BA & MFA. *Work:* Graphics Arts Collection, Libr Cong, Washington. *Pos:* Creator, Doonesbury (comic strip). *Awards:* Pulitzer Prize, 75; Nominated for Acad Award, 77 & Drama Desk Awards, 83; Special Jury Prize, Cannes Film Festival, 77. *Publ:* Auth, Adjectives Will Cost You Extra, 82, Gotta Run, My Government is Collapsing, 82 & Cartoons from In Search of Reagan's Brain, 82, Fawcett; Ask for May, Settle for June, 82 & Unfortunately, She Was Also Wired for Sound, 82, Holt, Rinehart & Winston; Doonesbury (play), 83; articles in various publ incl, Harper's, Rolling Stone, New Yorker, Wash Post. *Mailing Add:* c/o Universal Press Syndicate 4520 Main St Suite 700 Kansas City MO 64111

TRUDEAU, YVES (CM)
SCULPTOR
b Montreal, Que, Dec 3, 30. *Study:* Ecole Beaux Arts Montreal, sr matriculant with Marie Mediatrice. *Work:* Mus Quebec; Galerie Nat Can; Mus Art Contemp Montreal; Mus Art Prague, Czech; Mus Plein Air D'Ostrava, Czech. *Comn:* bronze relief doors, Teleglobe Can, Mtl, 81; aluminium relief doors, Place Alcan, Mtl, 83; Place de la Decouverter (large aluminium sculpture, Gaspe, Que, 84; 2 large reliefs, Metro Station Cote, Vertu, Mtl, 1986; Place de l'an 2000, Ville St-Laurent, Que, 2000. *Exhib:* Int Symp Sculpture, Ostrava, 69; Biennale Middleheim, Anvers, Belg, 71; Premiere Biennale Petite Sculpture, Budapest, Hungary, 71; one-man show, Mus Quebec, 70, Contemp Mus Montreal, 78; and others. *Teaching:* Prof sculpture, Ecole Beaux-Arts Montreal, 67-69; prof sculpture concept & metal, Univ Que, Montreal, dir, visual art dept, 79-81, ex-prof of UQAM, retired from teaching. *Awards:* Can Coun Awards, 63 & 69; Ministere Educ Quebec Award, 70-71. *Bibliog:* Robert Guy (auth), Yves Trudeau, sculptor, Asn Sculpteurs Quebec, 71; Jacques De Roussan (ed), Yves Trudeau, Works from 1959-80, Broquet. *Mem:* Royal Can Acad Arts (vpres, 75-83); Can Conf Arts (vpres, 82-83); Int Conf Mus; Int Asn Plastic Art; Order Can. *Media:* Multimedia. *Res:* Polarized light. *Publ:* Auth, article in Metiers D'Arts Quebec, 63; coauth, Catalogue, Galerie Nat Can, 66; auth, Confrontation 67 (catalog), 67. *Dealer:* Madeleine Lacerte, Quebec City Gallery Orange Mtl Gallery Bernard. *Mailing Add:* 5429 Ave Durocher Outremont Montreal PQ H2V 3X9 Canada

TRUE, DAVID
PAINTER
b Marietta, Ohio, 42. *Study:* Ohio Univ, BFA, 66, MFA, 67. *Work:* Whitney Mus Am Art, NY; Metrop Mus Art, Mus Mod Art, NY; Munson-Williams-Proctor Inst, Utica, NY; Henie-Orstad Art Ctr, Hoevikodden, Norway; Va Mus Fine Arts, Richmond. *Exhib:* Solo shows, Va Mus Fine Arts, Richmond, 84, Barbara Krakow Gallery, Boston, 86, Mangel Gallery, Philadelphia, 87 & Blum Helman Gallery, NY, 87, 88 & 90; Crown Point Press, San Francisco, 89; Walker Art Ctr, Minneapolis, 89; Blum Helman Gallery, NY, 91; The Other Side of Modernism, 2000. *Teaching:* Cooper Union, Columbia Univ, NY. *Awards:* Painting Grant, Nat Endowment Arts, 82-83 & 91. *Bibliog:* John Yau (auth), Reviews: David True Blum Helman, Artforum, 113-114, 12/87; Eleanor Heartney (auth), David True at Blum Helman, Art Am, 150, 3/88; David E Loper (auth), Scorched earth, Scis, 22-28, 9-10/90. *Mailing Add:* 457 Broome St New York NY 10013

TRUE, WILLIAM L
COLLECTOR
b Apr 54. *Pos:* Chmn, Chief Exec Officer, Gull Industries, Inc, Seattle; mem adv bd, Seattle Arts & Lectures; mem Betty Bowen com, Seattle Art Mus, 2004; co-founder, Western Bridge Gallery, Seattle; bd dirs, Pike Place Market Found, Seattle. *Awards:* Named one of Top 200 Collectors, ARTnews mag, 2003-06. *Collection:* Contemporary art. *Mailing Add:* 832 37th Ave E Seattle WA 98112-4326

TRUEBLOOD, EMILY HERRICK
PRINTMAKER
b Alexandria, Va, Aug 13, 42. *Study:* Beloit Col, Wis; Univ Wis, Madison, BA, 65; Columbia Univ Sch Libr Serv, MS, 69. *Work:* Mus Mod Art, Haifa, Israel; Portland Mus Art, Ore; Trenton State Col, NJ; Newark Pub Lib, NJ; NY Pub Libr; Brit Mus; Cleveland Mus Art. *Comn:* pvt commissions. *Exhib:* Traveling exhib, Va Mus Fine Arts, Richmond, 86; Contemp Am Printmaker, Fairfield Univ, Conn, 94; Centennial Portfolio, Old Print Shop, NY, 98; Xylon 13, 98, 01; Int Miniature Print Exhib, Conn Graphic Arts Ctr, New Canaan, 2005; Artists Revisit the Chrysler, Michael Ingbar Gallery, NY, 2000-2001, 2006; Silvermine Guild, New Canaan, Conn, 2000; Up on the Roof, NY Hist Soc, NY, 01; Miniprint Finland, 2001; 6th Int Miniature Art Biennial, Salle Augustin-Chenier, Ville-Marie, Que, 2002; two-person show, Old Print Shop, NY, 2003, 2005-2006. *Pos:* Co-chmn graphics, Pen & Brush, NY, 88-92, chmn graphics, 92-2002; vpres, Soc Am Graphic Artists, 2003-. *Teaching:* vis artist various classes. *Awards:* Purchase Prize, Nat Print Exhib, Trenton State Col, 82; E Weyhe Gallery Purchase Award, SAGA 64th Nat, 91; Silver Medal of Honor for Graphics, Audubon Artists, 99, 01; Catharine Lorillard Wolfe Art Club "Anna Hyatt Huntington Bronze Medal, 2002; Takayo Noda Award, Nat Arts Club, 2004. *Bibliog:* Helen Harrison (auth), Urban themes are a source for imagery in two shows, NY Times, 2/5/95; Eleanor Charles (auth), article, NY Times, 11/10/96; New York Centennial Exhibition at the Old Print Shop, Art Times, 3/98; William Zimmer (auth), A Commitment.to Good Things in Small., NY Times, 4/15/01; Ariella Bodick (auth), Up on the Roof, Newsday, 7/10/01; Mary Jane Fine (auth), Form & Function - Rooftop Water Tanks, Newsday, 11/8/01; William Behnken & Emily Trueblood, Jour of the Print World, winter, 2003. *Mem:* Salmagundi Club; Special Libr Asn; Pen & Brush; Soc Am Graphic Artists; Nat Arts Club; Nat Asn Women Artists; Catharine Lorillard Wolfe Art Club. *Media:* Woodcut, Linocut. *Interests:* Swimming. *Dealer:* The Old Print Shop. *Mailing Add:* 20 E Ninth St No 18C New York NY 10003-5944

TRUEBLOOD, L'DEANE
SCULPTOR, PAINTER
b Norman, Okla, Dec 26, 28. *Study:* Univ Okla, BFA, 45; Okla City Univ, MA, 70; study under Charles Reid, Bruno Lucchesi, Kenn Bunn, Sandy Scott & Sherrie McGraw; Scottsdale Artists Sch, with Richard Schmid. *Work:* City of Springville, Springville Art Mus, Utah; Dixie Col Art Mus, St George, Utah; Latter Day Saints Church Art Mus, Salt Lake City; pvt collection of Armand Hammer. *Comn:* bust of Pres Doug Alder, Dixie Col, St George, Utah, 89; bust of Armand Hammer, Huntsman Chem Corp, Salt Lake City, 90; bust of Val Browning, Browning Arms Corp, Odgen, Utah, 91; children's fountain, Morinda Corp, 2002; children's collection, Lake George Meml Hosp, Ill, 2002. *Exhib:* Springville Salon Ann, Springville Mus Art, Utah, 75-95; Sculptors of Utah, Springville Mus Art, Utah, 85; Int Latter Day Saints Church Ann Exhib, Latter Day Saints Church Art Mus, Salt Lake City, 89; Braithwaite Invitational, Braithwaite Mus Art, Cedar City, Utah, 90; Okla Watercolor Soc, Kirkpatrick Mus, Oklahoma City, 91; Utah Watercolor Soc, Pioneer Theatre Mus, Salt Lake City, 92; Pen & Brush Sculpture Ann, Pen & Brush Club, NY; one-woman show, Meyer Gallery, Santa Fe, NMex, 98, 99, 2000 & 2003; Sculptures in the Park, Loveland, Colo, 98-2003; one-person show, St George Art Mus, 99, Hilligoss Gallery, Chicago, 2003. *Pos:* Secy/pres, Southwest Utah Arts Coun, 85-86; mem bd dir, Utah Arts Coun, 86-97; bd dir, Pioneer Arts Heritage Found, 2000-2001. *Awards:* Religious Art Merit Award, 2000; Named Utah Top 100 Artists, 2002; Governor's Invitational Show, 2003. *Bibliog:* Cheryl Koeven (auth), Capturing the inner light, St George Mag, 92; Kimberly Perkins (dir), Images, KTVX TV, Salt Lake City, 92; feature article, Oklahoma Living Mag, 99 & 2000. *Mem:* Nat Sculpture Soc; Okla Sculpture Soc; Utah Watercolor Soc; Nev Watercolor Soc. *Media:* Bronze, Watercolor. *Publ:* Illusr, cover, Am Mothers Mag, spring 94 & winter 94. *Dealer:* Meyer Gallery 225 Canyon Rd Sante Fe NM 87501; Coda Gallery 73-151 El Paseo Palm Desert CA 92260

TRUETTNER, WILLIAM H
CURATOR
Pos: Cur eighteenth and nineteenth century painting & sculpture, Nat Collection Fine Arts, currently. *Mailing Add:* 6702 Hillcrest Pl Chevy Chase MD 20815

TRUMBLE, BEVERLY (JANE)
PAINTER
b Milwaukee, Wis. *Study:* Univ Colo, 60; Art Students League, 76-83; Daniel E Greene Workshop, 84. *Work:* Nationwide Cellular Serv Inc, Valley Stream, NY; Strategic Resource Group Inc, East Norwalk, Conn. *Comn:* Terri & Jerry (oil portrait), Comn by Mr & Mrs Forrest Newton, Littleton, Colo, 86; 4 paintings, Comn by Mr & Mrs Thomas Keller, White Plains, 90; Brian (oil portrait), Comn by Lt Col & Mrs Orville Hays, Breckenridge, Colo, 91; Taos Pueblo on Christmas Eve (oil painting), comn by Mrs William Webster, Taos, NMex, 98. *Exhib:* solo exhib, Univ Denver, Colo, 93; Northern Ariz Univ Mus & Galleries, Flagstaff, 94; Western NMex Univ, Silver City, 96; Nightwalker Nat Juried Exhib, Colo State Univ, Ft Collins, 97; Great Plains Nat, Hays State Univ, Hays, Kans, 98; St Johns Coll, Sanfa Fe, NMex, 2000; La Chaleppe des Penitents, Gourdes, France, 2000. *Collection Arranged:* WSAC, Broadway Mall Gallery (coauth, catalog), 87-88; Riverside Arts Festival, City of New York, 88; Westside Arts Coalition (auth, catalog), Lever House Gallery, 88; Premiere Soho Exhib (auth, catalog), West Side Artists Pleiades, 88; Painting & Sculpture-WSAC, Pen & Brush, 89. *Pos:* Guided tours Artists Studios, NY, 88-90. *Teaching:* Drawing & pastel workshops, The Balance Sheet, Frisco, Colo, 91. *Awards:* Solo Exhib Award, Pen & Brush Inc, 85; Artist Guild Award, Mamaroneck Artist Guild, 88; First Prize, Summit Co Arts Coun, 92. *Bibliog:* T Alex Miller (auth), article, Summit Daily News, Colo, 4/20/93; Sonya Ellingboe (auth), article, Littleton Independent, Colo, 8/25/94; Ann Hartley, Susan McGarry, Mary Carroll Nelson (eds), Bridging Time & Space, Essays on Layered Art, Markowitza Publ, 11/98. *Mem:* Pastel Soc Am; Soc Layerists Multi Media; Art Students League NY; NY Artist's Equity; Taos Art Asn. *Media:* Oil, Pastel Aqua Media. *Mailing Add:* c/o Gail Newton 6851 S Forest St Centennial CO 80120

TRUPP, BARBARA LEE
PAINTER, DESIGNER
b Scottsbluff, Nebr, Nov 17, 50. *Study:* Studied with Ilda Lubane, Banff Ctr Arts, Alta, Can, 68-70; Univ Puget Sound, Tacoma, Wash, 69-70; Univ Mich, Ann Arbor, BFA, 71-74, MAC Univ, 2000. *Work:* Ill State Mus, Springfield; Fermi Nat Accelorator Lab, US Dept Energy, Batavia, Ill; Ore State Mus, Portland; Am Mus, Bath, Eng; Banff Ctr Arts, Alta, Can; Mary & Leigh Block Gallery, NWestern Univ, Evanston, Ill; Krannert Mus, Univ Ill, Champaign; Ruttenberg Art Found, Chicago, Ill; Univ Nev, Reno. *Comn:* Prints, Plucked Chicken Press, Evanston, Ill, 88. *Exhib:* Selections from the Permanent Collection, Banff Ctr, traveling throughout Can, 75; 2nd Ann Great Lakes Show, Ill St Gallery, Chicago, Ill, 88; Chicago Int New Art Forms Expos, Navy Pier, Chicago, Ill, 88, 90 & 92; Selections from Permanent Collection, Ill State Mus, Springfield, Ill, 88-89; Am & Int Craft Exhib, World Trade Ctr, Boston, Mass, 90; Multiple Images, Ill State Mus, Springfield, 91; one-person shows, Vignettes, 92, The New Collection, 94 & Prehistoire, 96, Citywoods, Highland Park, Ill; Fine Art of Fiber, Chicago Botanic Gardens, Highland Park, Ill, 97; Flights of Imagination, Chicago Cult Center, Ill, 2003. *Pos:* Owner, Pixelswest, Evanston, Ill, currently. *Teaching:* Instr painting, Evanston Art Ctr, 87-96; Instr painting, digital media, art & design, 98-. *Bibliog:* Barbara Buchholz (auth), The tile revival, Chicago Tribune, 10/9/94. *Mem:* Nat Asoc Photoshop Profs; Windy City Arts; Chicago Soc Artists; Chicago Artists Coalition. *Media:* watercolor, digital media. *Dealer:* Deer Path Gallery Lake Forest IL 60045. *Mailing Add:* 625 Deerfield Rd Apt 205 Deerfield IL 60015-3236

TRUTTY-COOHILL, PATRICIA
EDUCATOR, HISTORIAN
b Uniontown, Pa. *Study:* Univ Toronto, BA, 62, Pa State Univ, MA, 68, PhD, 82. *Pos:* Assoc prof art hist, Western Ky Univ, 83-. *Teaching:* Lectr, art dept, Western Ky Univ, 80-82, asst prof, 82-86, assoc prof, 86-. *Mem:* Col Art Asn; Raccolta Vinciana; Leonardo Soc. *Res:* School of Leonardo da Vinci. *Publ:* Auth & illusr, La Eminentia in Antonello de Messina, Antichità viva vol XXI/4, 82; Narrative to Icon, Achademia Leonardi Vinci, vol 1, 88; The Drawings of Leonardo da Vinci and his Circle in America, Giunti, 93 with Carlo Pedretti; Visualizing Tyminenięcka's Poetica nova, Analecta Hüserliana, 52, Jean-Claude Novaro, 96. *Mailing Add:* Western Ky Univ Art Dept Bowling Green KY 42101

TSAI, HSIAO HSIA
PAINTER, SCULPTOR
b China; US citizen. *Study:* Nat Col Art China, BFA; Univ Okla, MFA(scholar); Hamilton State Univ, Hon PhD, 78. *Exhib:* White Mus, San Antonio, 65, 66 & 80; Jess Besser Mus, Pensacola Art Ctr, 75; Everhart Mus, Pa, 75; Dallas Mus Fine Arts, 76; Brick Stone Mus, 77; Corpus Christi Mus, 78-81; and many others. *Awards:* Gold Medal, Italy Competition, 83; Corpus Christi Mus Award, 86; Award, Art Mus S Tex, 91-94; and many others. *Mem:* Hon mem Int Asn Art. *Publ:* Principles Chinese Painting Adapted to Modern Needs and Treaties, Mustard Seed Garden Treaties; articles in Today's Art, Arts Mag, Art News, J Am, New York & Sund Mag, Houston. *Mailing Add:* Hsiao-Hsia Tsai Gallery Fine Art 1437 Casa Verde Dr Corpus Christi TX 78411

TSAI, WEN-YING
SCULPTOR, PAINTER
b Xiamen, China, Oct 13, 28; US citizen. *Study:* Univ Mich, ME, 53; Art Students League, 53-57; grad fac polit & social sci, New Sch Social Res, 56-58. *Work:* Tate Gallery, London; Centre Nat d'Art Contemporain, Paris; Kaiser Wilhem Mus, Krefeld, Ger; Albright-Knox Art Gallery, Buffalo, NY; Whitney Mus Am Art, NY; and others. *Comn:* Gloucester Tower (cybernetic water sculpture), Palmer & Turner Archits, Hong Kong, 80; Raffles Tower Fountain, Singapore Land Pte Ltd, Singapore, 82; Dancing Menorah with Lotus, Israel Mus, Jerusalem, 82; Spatial Dynamic Hydro-Cybernetic Systs, Musee National des Science, des Techniques et des Industries, La Villette, Paris, 86 (Concept and Fabrication). *Exhib:* Group shows, The Responsive Eye, 65 & The Machine as Seen at the End of the Mechanical Age (with catalog), Mus Mod Art, NY, 68; Pittsburgh Int, Carnegie Inst Mus Art, 70; one-man shows, Hayden Gallery, Mass Inst of Technol, Cambridge, Corcoran Gallery of Art, Washington, Mus d'Art Contemporain, Montreal, Que, Hong Kong Mus Art, 79, Isetan Mus, Tokyo, 80 & Nat Mus Hist, Taipei, 89, Taiwan Mus Art, 90 & Nat Mus Fine Art, Beijing, 97; Electra-1983, Mus D'Art Mod, Paris, 83; 42nd Int Exhib Art, La Biennale di Venezia, 86; Computer Art, IBM Gallery Sci & Art, NY, 88; Images Du Futur 90, Montreal, 90; Artec 91, Int Biennale, Nagoya, 91; Kwangju Biennale, Korea, 95; Osaka Triennial, Japan, 95. *Pos:* Proj eng, Guy B Panero Engineers, New York, 56-60; proj mgr, Cosentini Assocs Engineers, New York, 62-63. *Awards:* Ctr Advan Visual Studies Fel, Mass Inst Technol, 69-71; Design in Steel Award, Best Fine Art in Steel, Am Iron & Steel Inst, 71; Artec Grand Prix, 91. *Bibliog:* Vilem Flusser (auth), Aspects and prospects of Tsais work, Art Int, London, 3/74; Art & Sci-Innovation (film), WNET-TV, 88; Cynthia Goodman (auth), Digital Visions, Computers and Art, Harry N Abrams, New York, 87; Frank Popper (auth), Art of the Electronic Age, Harry N Abrams, New York, 93. *Mem:* Nat Arts Club, NY. *Media:* Water, Fiber Optics, Fiberglass and Stainless Steel. *Dealer:* Galerie Denise Rene Paris

TSARIKOVSKY, VALERY (TSAR)
PAINTER, MURALIST
b Kiev, Ukraine, May 29, 52; US citizen. *Study:* Kiev Tech Col Construct, Ukraine, diploma, 70. *Work:* Salmagundi Club Ctr Am Art, Metrop Opera Asn & Lincoln Ctr Performing Arts, NY; Contemp Mus Art, Atlanta, Ga. *Comn:* Ranch, Rockefeller Ctr Main Off, NY, 97. *Exhib:* Salmagundi Art Club Ann Exhib, 87-91; Miami Int Art Expos, Miami conv Ctr, 92-93; Palm Beach Int Art Antique Fair, 97; Fine Arts Dealers Asn, Univ Calif, Los Angeles, 97 & 98; Committed To Improving The State of the World, World Econ Forum, Davos, Switz, 98; Hilde Gerst Gallery, 91-. *Pos:* Architect asst, Kiev Tech Col Construct, Ukraine, 75. *Awards:* 1st Prize, Salmagundi Art Club, 87; Lee M Loeb Mem Award for a Traditional Landscape, 91; Frank B Williams Found Award, 91. *Bibliog:* Article in NY Times, 6/91; CNN Internet (TV doc), 1/98; CNN, Business Unusual (TV doc), 2/98. *Media:* Oil. *Dealer:* Hilde Gerst Gallery 987 Madison Ave New York NY 11235. *Mailing Add:* 4564 Bedford Ave Brooklyn NY 11235

TSE, STEPHEN
PAINTER, EDUCATOR
b Hong Kong, Oct 20, 38; US citizen. *Study:* Washburn Univ, Topeka, Kans, BFA; Univ Idaho, MFA; also with Jack Tworkov. *Work:* Wenatchee Valley Col, Wash; Yakima Valley Col, Wash; Spokane Falls Community Col, Wash; Rainier Nat Bank, Olympia, Wash; First Nat Bank Idaho, Boise; Seattle First Nat Bank; Mus Art, Eugene, Ore; Univ Ore, Eugene, Ore; many others. *Comn:* Sculpture panels with painting, Student Union, Univ Idaho, 65. *Exhib:* One-man shows, Gallery-76, Wenatchee Valley Col, Wash, 78 & Kirsten Gallery, Seattle, 77, 78, 80, 82 & 85, Prichard Art Gallery, Univ Idaho, 86 & Still Water Art Gallery, Seattle, 91; Nat Painting Exhib, Grover M Hermann Fine Art Ctr, Marietta Col, Ohio, 79; Nat Small Painting Purchase Exhib, Western Ill Univ, Macomb, 79; Compton Gallery, Wash State Univ, Pullman, 83; Alcoa/Gallery 76 Art Exhib, Wenatchee, Wash, 84-86 & 89; Mus of Art, Univ Oreg, Eugene, Oreg; Big Bend Cmty Col, Moses Lake, Wash; Watcom Mus History and Art, Bellingham, Wash; Yakima Valley Col, Yakima, Wash; plus many others. *Teaching:* Prof emer, Big Bend Community Col. *Awards:* Painting Award, 28th Ann Centennial Wash Artist Exhib, Larson Gallery, Yakima, 84; Merit Award, Carnegie Ctr, Walla Walla, Wash, 85 & 87; Painting Award, Carnegie Ctr, Walla Walla, Wash, 90, Third Painting Award, 93. *Mem:* Wash Art Asn; Oriental Ceramic Soc, London. *Media:* Oil and Watercolor; Clay. *Dealer:* Kirsten Gallery 5320 Roosevelt Way NE Seattle WA 98105. *Mailing Add:* 1302 Evergreen Point Rd Medina WA 98039

TUCHMAN, MAURICE
MUSEUM CURATOR
b Jacksonville, Fla, Nov 30, 36. *Study:* Nat Univ Mex; City Col NY, BA(art hist), 57, Fel, 58; Columbia Univ, MA(art hist), 59, studies with Theodore Reff, George Collins & Julius Held; Fulbright Scholar, Freie Univ, Berlin, 60 61. *Collection Arranged:* Five Younger Calif Artists, 65; Edward Kienholz, 66; Irwin-Price, 66; John Mason, 66; Am Sculpture of 60's (with catalog), 67; Soutine (with catalog), 68; Art & Technol (with catalog), 71; 11 Los Angeles Artists, 1971 Traveling Exhib (with catalog), Sidney Janis Gallery, 72; European Paintings in the 70's (with catalog), 75; Richard Diebenkorn: Paintings and Drawings, 77, Mus Mod Art, 89; Italo Scanga, 83; Susan Rothenberg, 83; The Artist as Social Designer: Aspects of Public Art Today, 85; in prep: Hidden Meanings in Modern Art: Abstract Painting and Mysticism, 1891-1986, 86; David Hockney A Retrospective, Metrop Mus Art, New York, 88 & Tate Gallery, London, 88; Chain Soutine Centenary Retrospective (with catalog), Odakyu Mus, Tokyo, 92. *Pos:* Art ed mod art sect, Columbia Encycl, 62; mem curatorial & lect staff, Guggenheim Mus, 62-64, organizer, summer 64; sr cur mod art, Los Angeles Co Mus Art, 64-94, emer sr cur, 94-; mem art adv panel to the comnr Internal Revenue Serv, 75-78; mem bd dir, Am Asn Mus/Inst Coun Mus, 79-83; mem adv comt & contribr, Random House Libr Painting & Sculpture, 81; mem adv comt, Skowhegan Sch Painting, New York, Archives Am Art, San Marino, Calif; mem int comt, Int Coun Mus & Collections of Mod Art, Int Coun Mus/CIMAM; mem int res & exhanges bd, Princeton Univ, NJ, 89; dir, Int Coun Artec Biennale, Nagoya, Japan, 92. *Awards:* Fulbright Scholar, 60-61. *Mem:* Am Arts Alliance, (bd dir, 77-80); Nat Endowment Arts, 77-79; Am Fedn Arts (nat exhib comt); Los Angeles Design Alliance, (bd gov, 84); Int Adv Comt, Mus Art Carnegie Inst, 85. *Publ:* Chaim Soutine (1893-1943) (essay, catalog), Kunstmuseum Lucerne, 82; The Avant-Garde in Russia, 1910-1930: New Perspectives, 82; Artists Look at Los Angeles, Am Illustrated, No 331, 6/84; The Spiritual in Art: Abstract Painting 1890-1985, Second Christensen Lect, Art Gallery Western Australia, 88; Chaim Soutine Catalogue Raisonné, Gay Loudmer & Perls Galleries Publ, Paris, 93. *Mailing Add:* 2210 Astral Pl Los Angeles CA 90046

TUCHMAN, PHYLLIS
CRITIC, CURATOR
b Passaic, NJ, Jan 4, 47. *Study:* Sarah Lawrence Col Summer Session in Florence, 67; Boston Univ, BA(distinction in fine arts), 68; Inst of Fine Arts, NY Univ, MA, 73, with Robert Goldwater, Robert Rosenblum & William S Rubin. *Collection Arranged:* Six in Bronze, Williams Col Mus Art, 84; Big Little Sculpture, Williams Col Mus Art, 88; Venezuela: The Next Generation, Baruch Col Gallery, 90; Drawing Redux, San Jose Mus Art, 92; Norte del Sur: Venezuelan Art Today, Philbrook Art Mus, 97. *Pos:* Mem ed bd, Marsyas, NY, 71-74; vpres, Art Table, 87-88; contribr, NY Newsday, 1985-94, Town & Country, 1995-, Smithsonian Mag 1998-, artnet.com and mag, 2000-; pres, AICA USA, 1986-90. *Teaching:* Instr art hist, Sch of Visual Arts, NY, 72-75; adj lectr art hist, Hunter Col, 76-79; vis prof art, Williams Col, 81-83. *Awards:* Nat Endowment Arts art critic's grant, 78-79; Nat Endowment Humanities fel, 80. *Mem:* Inst Asn Art Critics (pres Am sect, 86-90, vpres Int parent body, 89-91); Art Table; Col Art Asn. *Publ:* Auth, George Segal, Abbeville Press, 83; contribr,Town & Country, Smithsonian, Art in Am, artnet; contribr, Artnet, Bloomberg News. *Mailing Add:* 340 E 80th St New York NY 10021

TUCHOLKE, CHRISTEL-ANTHONY
PAINTER
b Poland, Mar 2, 41; US citizen. *Study:* Univ Wis, Milwaukee, BS, 65 & MS, 65; Tamarind Lithography Workshop, Los Angeles, 68. *Work:* Milwaukee Art Mus, Wis; Miller Brewing Co Hq, Milwaukee, Wis; Charles Wustum Mus Art, Racine, Wis; Bradley Univ, Peoria, Ill; Kans State Univ Art Mus, Manhattan; Wis Bell Co Hdqtrs, Milwaukee; plus others. *Comn:* Exterior mural, John Michael Kohler Art Ctr, Sheboygan, Wis, 77; four paintings, Northwestern Mutual Life Insurance Co, Milwaukee, Wis, 79; telephone bk cover, Wis Telephone Co, 81; mural, Percent for Art Prog, Wis Art Bd, 85; Artists Limited Editions, Kohler Co, Wis, 89. *Exhib:* 74th, 76th, 77th & 80th Exhibs by Artists of Chicago & Vincinity, Chicago Art Inst, Ill, 73, 77, 78 & 84; Wis Directions Two, Milwaukee Art Mus, 78; Wis Biennale, Madison Art Ctr, 80 & 82; State of the Art: Wisconsin Painting and Drawing, J Michael Kohler Art Ctr, Sheboygan, Wis, 82; Belk Gallery, Western Carolina Univ, NC, 85; Wis-Minn Interface, Minn Mus Art, St Paul, Minn & Milwaukee Art Mus, 86; Edgewood Orchard Gallery, Fish Creek, Wis, 98; and others; Mount Mary College, Wauwatosa. *Awards:* Top Award, Madison Art Ctr, 80; Purchase Award, Wright Art Ctr, 80; Purchase Award, Bradley Univ, 81; Purchase Award, Wustum Mus, 85 & 89. *Media:* Acrylic, Pastel. *Dealer:* Edgewood Orchard Galleries Fish Creek WI 54212. *Mailing Add:* 8535 W Meguon Rd Mequon WI 53097

TUCK, NORMAN VICTOR
KINETIC ARTIST, SCULPTOR
b Lebanon, Pa, Aug 14, 45. *Study:* Univ Fla, with Geoffrey Naylor, BFA, 67; Pa State Univ, MFA, 72. *Work:* Science Mus Minn, St Paul; New York Hall Sci, Queens, NY; Sci Mus Barcelona, Spain. *Comn:* Lariat Chain, Exploratorium, San Francisco, 87; Lariat Chain II, Sci Mus Hong Kong, 89; Pendulum Clock, Exploratorium, San Francisco, 89; Ch-Ch-Ch Chainges, Technorama, Winterthur, Switz, 90. *Exhib:* Solo exhibs, O K Harris Gallery, NY, 74 & 77, Liberty Sci Ctr, NJ, 93, Technorania, Winterthur, Switz, 93 & Exploratorium, San Francisco, 94; Labor Intensive Abstraction, Clock Tower, NY, 84; Mechanisms, PS-1, Queens, NY, 84; Clockwork, List Art Ctr, Mass Inst Technol, Cambridge, Mass, 88. *Pos:* Gallery dir, Wake Forest Univ Art Gallery, 80-81; artists-in-residence, New York Hall Sci, 86 & Exploratorium, San Francisco, 87 & 89. *Teaching:* Asst prof sculpture, Wake Forest Univ, Winston-Salem, NC, 85-86; instr sculpture, Univ Minn, Minneapolis, 78-79. *Bibliog:* Jeffrey Wechsler (auth, catalog), Norman Tuck, Rutgers Univ Art Gallery, 78; Michael Brewson (auth), Norman Tuck, NY Times, 85; Richard Craven (auth, catalog), Mindless Mechanisms, Southeastern Ctr Contemp Art, 92; Margaret Shearin (auth), Art Machines, City Gallery, Raleigh, NC, 92. *Media:* Kinetic Sculpture

TUCKER, ANNE WILKES
CURATOR, HISTORIAN
b Baton Rouge, La, Oct 18, 45. *Study:* Randolph-Macon Women's Col, Lynchburg Va, BA (art hist), 67; Rochester Inst of Technol, AAS (photog), 68; Visual Studies Workshop, SUNY Buffalo, NY, MFA, 72; photo hist and mus procedure with Nathan Lyons & Beaumont Newhall, 70. *Collection Arranged:* American Prospects: The Photographs of Joel Sternfeld (travelling), 87, Evocative Presence: Twentieth-Century Photographs in the Museum Collection, 88, American Classroom: The Photographs of Catherine Wagner (travelling), 88, The Private Eye, 89, Czeck Modernism 1900-1945 (travelling), 89 & Money Matters: A Critical Look at Bank Architecture (travelling), 90, Houston Mus Fine Arts, Tex; Martin Luther King and the Civil Rights Movement, Mus Fine Arts, Houston, 1991, travel to Baltimiore Mus Art; Brassai, Mus Fine Arts, Houston, 1996; Myths, Dreamn and Realities: Contemporary Argentine Photography, Pan Am Cultural Exchange Houston, 1996, toured US & Mexico, 1997-1999; Postwar Italian Photography, Mus Fine Arts Houston, 2002; Japanese Photography in the Manfred Heiting Collection, Lower Brown Gallery, Mus Fine Arts, Houston, 2003; Aaron Sisking: Centennial Celebration, Cameron Found Gallery, Mus Fine Arts, Houston, 2004; 94th Ann Exhib, Documenting Poetry: Contemporary Latin Am Photography, Maier Mus Art, Randolph Macon Women's Col, Lynchburg, Va, 2005; and many others. *Pos:* Res asst, Int Mus Photogr, George Eastman House, Rochester, NY, 68-70; res assoc, Gernsheim Collection, Univ Tex, Austin, 69 & 79; cur intern, NY State Coun Art Grant, Photogr Dept, Mus Mod Art, NY, 70-71; photogr consult, Creative Artists Pub Serv Prog, NY, 71-72; dir, Photo Lecture Series, Cooper Union Forum, NY, 72-75; cur photogr, Mus Fine Arts, Houston, Tex, 76-, Gus & Lyndall Wortham cur, 84-. *Teaching:* Vis lectr, New Sch Soc Research, NY, spring 73 & Philadelphia Col Art, 73-75; lectr, Cooper Union Advan Arts & Sci, NY, 72-75; affliate artist, Univ Houston, Tex, 76-80; lectr, panelist numerous workshops, univs and confs, 1973-. *Awards:* Guggenheim Fel, 83; Nat Endowment Arts, 76, 86 & 90; Rsch Support Grant, Getty Center History of Art & the Humanities Resource Collections, 1995; Golden Light Awards Book fo Yr, Maine Photogr Workshops, 1996; Selected Best Cur, Time mag, 9/17/2001; The 100 Most Important People in Photography, Am Photo Mag, 2005; Focus Award for Lifetime Achievement, Griffin Mus of Photography, 2006. *Mem:* Soc Photog Educ (secy, nat bd 77-79); Col Art Asn; Visual Studies Wkshp (bd trustees, 80-); Visual Arts Panel, Houston Fest, 81-83; Randolph-Macon Woman's Col Art Gallery (adv bd, 82-84); Art Table, Inc, 83-; Houston Ctr for Photog (adv bd 1980-90, 1994-95, bd trustees 1990-93, sec 1990-93); Am Leadership Forum (bd trustees 1992-94, co-chair selection com 1993-94); others. *Res:* Concentrated on 20th century American photographs. *Interests:* Absences and gaps in current photographic history. *Publ:* The Blue Man'a Photographs, Rice Univ Press, 90; Czeck Modernism 1900-1945, Bolfinch Press & Mus Fine Arts, Houston, 90; Money Matters: A Critical Look at Bank Architecture, McGraw-Hill & Mus Fine Arts, Houston, 90; Carry Me Home, Smithsonian Press, 90; George Krause, Rice Univ Press, 92; Crimes and Splendors: The Desert Cantos of Richard Misrach, with essay by Rebecca Solnit, Bulfinch Press & Mus Fine Arts Houston, 1996; auth essay, When the Whole is Undecipherable, in: David Maisel: Terminal Image, Paul Kopeikin Gallery, Los Angeles, 2005; auth intro, Dave Anderson, Dewi Lewis Publ, Eng, 2006; and many others. *Mailing Add:* Mus Fine Arts PO Box 6826 Houston TX 77265-6826

TUCKER, JAMES EWING
CURATOR, PAINTER
b Rule, Tex, Aug 13, 30. *Study:* Midwestern Univ; Univ Tex, Austin, BFA; Univ Iowa, MFA. *Work:* NC State Univ, Raleigh; Weatherspoon Art Gallery; Miller Brewing Co; Pine Bluff Art Ctr, Ark; Witte Mus, San Antonio. *Collection Arranged:* Art on Paper, Cone Collection & Dillard Collection, Weatherspoon Art Gallery, 65-. *Pos:* Cur, Weatherspoon Art Gallery, 59-, ed, Bulletin, 65-. *Media:* Mixed. *Dealer:* Ingber Gallery 460 West Broadway New York NY 10012. *Mailing Add:* 632 Scott Ave Greensboro NC 27403

TUCKER, LEATRICE YVONNE See Edwards-Tucker, Yvonne Leatrice

TUCKER, MARCIA
MUSEUM DIRECTOR, CURATOR
b New York, NY, Apr 11, 40. *Study:* Ecole du Louvre & Acad Grande Chaumiere, Paris, France, 59-60; Conn Col, BA(fine arts), 61; NY Univ Inst Fine Arts, MA, 69; San Francisco Art Inst, Hon Dr, 5/83. *Exhib:* New Mus Contemp Art, 77-91; Markus Raetz: In the Realm of the Possible, 88; Picture This: An Introduction to Interim, Mary Kelly INTERIM (with Norman Bryson, Griselda Pollok, & Hal Foster), 90; Late 20th Century Still Lifes (work of Manuel Pardo), 91; Bad Girl, New Mus Contemp Art, NY, 93; and others. *Collection Arranged:* Anti-Illusion: Procedures/Materials, Whitney Mus of Am Art, 69, Robert Morris, 70 (with catalog), The Structure of Color, 71, James Rosenquist & Bruce Nauman (with catalog), Retrospective Exhibs, 72 & 73, Lee Krasner, 74, Al Held, 74, Joan Mitchell, 75, Richard Tuttle, 75. Two Hundred Years of American Sculpture (with catalog), 77, 1977 Biennial: Contemporary Art (with catalog) & many other solo exhib; The Invisible Image, Sch Visual Arts Gallery, New York, 70; John Baldessai, New Mus Contemp Art, 1980, Not Just For Laughs: The Art of Subversion, 81, Early Work, 82, Earl Staley: 1973-1983, 84, US Comn 41st Venice, Biennale, 84, Choices: Making an Art of Everyday Life, 86, Markus Raetz: In the Realm of the Possible (auth, catalog), 88, Bad Girls, 94, A Labor of Love, 96 & The Time of Our Lives, 99; Critical Perspective In American Art, Univ Mass at Amherst, 76; Twentieth-Century American Sculpture: A Northeast Region Exhibition, The First Lady's Garden, The White House, Washington DC, 96; Prejaume 'Dis-Exhibit' (with catalog), MACBA, Barcelona, 99. *Pos:* Cur, William N Copley Collection, 63-66; ed assoc, Art News, 65-69; cur painting & sculpture, Whitney Mus Am Art, NY, 69-77; founder & dir, The New Mus, New York, 77-99; adv bd, Am Fedn Mus; bd dir, Jerome Found, Minneapolis, 99-; free-lance art critic, writer & lectr, New York, 2000-. *Teaching:* Instr art, Univ RI, 66-68, City Univ New York, 67-68 & Sch Visual Arts, 69-73; Columbia Univ Grad Sch Arts & Sci, New York, 77; guest lectr, cols, univs & inst; Maine Col of Art, Summer 99, RI Sch Design, Spring 2000. *Awards:* Penny McCall Found Award, 88; Asian Cult Coun Fel, 89; City Arts Award, 94; Chevalier de L'Order des Arts et des Lettres, French Govt, 97; Bard Col Award for Curatorial Achievement, 99; Art Table Award for distinguished service to visual arts, 2000. *Bibliog:* Celia McGee (auth), Profile, NY Times, 1/15/93; Kristi Vaughan (auth), Interview, Conn Col Mag, 3-4/93; Ladies who launch, Mirabella, 6/94; Edith Newhall (auth), Art for Argument's Sake, New York, 3/24/97; Kay Larson (auth), We've Come a Long Way.Maybe, ArtNews, 3/97; Mastering the Art of Pragmatism, Crain's New York Business, 4/20/98; The New Museum, ArtNews, 5/98; Regine Basha (interview), Doyen of the New Museum, aRUDE, 11/10/98; Randy Kennedy (auth), After a Life in Art, a Quest for the Art of Life, NY Times, 9/30/99; Lucy Lethbridge (auth), Meet Miss Mannerist, Art News, summer 99. *Mem:* Int Art Critics Asn; Am Asn Mus; Asn Art Mus Dirs (chair, External Affairs Comm, 89-90, trustee, 90-95, secy, 92-94); Am Fedn Mus (adv bd, 90-95); Art Mus Asn; Mass Coun on Arts and Humanities; Am Civil Liberties Union Found; Col Art Asn; Int Asn Art Critics. *Publ:* Auth, Nancy Dwyer makes trubble, Artforum, 11/89; Common ground, Mus News, 7-8/90; introduction, Mary Kelly Interim, New York Mus Contemp Art, 90; Discourses: Conversations in Postmodern Art and Culture & Out There: Marginalization and Contemporary Cultures, The New Mus Contemp Art in conjunction with Mass Inst Technol Press, 90; Out There: Marginalizations and Contemporary Cultures, New Mus Contemp Art & Mass Inst Technol Press, 90; auth, The New Museum: Documentary Sources in Contemporary Art, Am Art Review, 95, Questing for New Definitions of Contemporary Art, NY Times (Arts & Leisure Sec), 3/29/98, Museums Experiment with New Exhibitions Strategies, 1/10/99 & Talking Visions: Multicultural Feminism in a Transnational Age, MIT Press with New Mus Contemp Art, 99

TUCKER, WILLIAM EDWARD
PATRON
b Charlotte, NC, June 22, 1932. *Study:* Barton Col, BA, 1953. *Pos:* Ordained to ministry Disciples of Christ Church, 1956; prof, Barton Col, 1959-55, chmn dept religion & philosophy, 1961-66; mem fac, Brite Divsn Sch, Tex Christian Univ, 1966-76, prof church hist, 1969-76, dean 1971-76, chancellor 1979-98, chancellor emer, 1998-; pres, Bethany Col, WVa, 1976-79; dir, RadioShack Corp, 1985-2003, Brown and Lupton Found; mem gen bd, Christian Church (Disciples of Christ), 1971-74, 75-87, admin comt, 1975-81, chmn theological educ comn, 1972-73, mem exec comt, chmn bd higher educ, 1975-77; dir, Christian Church Found, 1980-83; moderator, Christian Church (Disciples of Christ), 1983-85. *Mem:* Trustee, Amon Carter Mus; Phi Beta Kappa, Exchange Club; bd dir, Van Cliburn Found, 1981-, Ft Worth Symphony Orchestra. *Mailing Add:* 777 Taylor St Ste P2J Fort Worth TX 76102

TUCKER, WILLIAM G
SCULPTOR
b Cairo, Egypt, Feb 28, 35; US citizen. *Study:* Oxford Univ, BA(mod Hist), 58; Cent Sch Art & St Martin's Sch Art, London, 59-60. *Work:* Tate Gallery, London; Guggenheim Mus, NY; Mus Mod Art, NY; Metrop Mus Art, NY; Rijksmuseum Kroller-Muller, Otterlo, Holland; Kroller-Muller Mus, Holland; Tate Gallery, London; and others. *Comn:* Journey, Dag Hammarskjold Plaza, NY, 82-83; Victory, Doris C Freedman Plaza, NY, 83; Arc & Fear, Springs Mills Building, Citicorp Ctr, NY, 84; Guardian I, St Peter's Church, Citicorp Ctr, NY, 84; Rhea, Greenwich Plaza, Conn, 86; Large-scale sculptue, Bilbao, Spain, 96. *Exhib:* II Biennale de Paris, Nat Mus Mod Art, Paris, 61; London - The New Scene, Walker Art Ctr, Minneapolis, Minn, 65; Guggenheim Int Sculpture Exhib, Solomon R Guggenheim Mus, NY, 67; Orpheus II, (1965 exhib British Artists) Mus Mod Art, NY, 68; British Painting and Sculpture, 1960-1961, Nat Gallery Art, Washington, DC, 71; Contemp Sculpture, Mus Mod Art, NY, 79; NY on Paper I, Mus Mod Art, NY, 81; Working in Brooklyn - Sculpture, Brooklyn Mus, NY, 85; Recent Acquisitions, Mus Mod Art, NY, 86; one-man exhibs, Pamela Auchincloss Gallery, Santa Barbara, Calif, 87, Tate Gallery, London, 87, Annely Juda Gallery, London, 87, David McKee Gallery, NY, 87, 89, 91, 92, 94, 95 & 96, The Am Decade 1978-1988, Storm King Art Ctr, Mountainville, NY, 88, Fla Int Univ, Miami, 88, Gallery Paule Anglim, San Francisco, Calif, 89 & 99, Williams Ctr Arts, Lafayette Col Art Gallery, Easton, Pa, 92, Maak Gallery, London, 93 & Aldelphi Univ Ctr Gallery, Long Island, NY, 93, Arts Coun of Gt Brit (traveling), 95, Davidson Col, NC, 99, Bethel Col, St Paul, 2000, Tate Gallery, Liverpool, Eng, 2000, Bothy Gallery, Yorkshire Sculpture Park, Wakefield, Eng, 01; Innovations in Sculpture, Aldrich Mus, Ridgefield, Conn, 88; NY Beijing Art Inst (traveling exhib), 88; Art Mus, Fla Int Univ, Miami, 89; Yorkshire Sculpture Park, Eng, 95; Am Acad Arts & Lett, NY, 96; Butler Inst Am Art, Youngstown, Ohio, 98; Am Acad Art and Letters, NY, 2000; Herter Art Gallery, Univ Mass, 01; William Tucker, Bothy Gallery, Yorkshire Sculpture Park, Wakefield, UK, 2001; solo exhibs, The Sleep of Reason, the Olson Gallery, Bethal Coll, Minn, 2000, Drawings, NY Studio Sch, NY, 2002, Arts on the Point, Healey Libr Gallery, Univ Mass, 2003. *Teaching:* Goldsmith's Col, London, 62-66; St Martin's Sch Art, London, 63-74; Univ West Ontario, Can, 76; Nova Scotia Col Art & Design, Halifax, Can, 77; NY Studio Sch Painting & Sculpture, 78-92; Columbia Univ, NY, 78-82; Bard Col, Legrand Ramsey Prof in Sculpture, formerly. *Awards:* Guggenheim Fel, 80-81; Nat Endowment for the Arts Fed, 86; Sculpture Ctr Award, Distinction in sculpture, 91; Rodin-Moore Mem Prize, 2d Fujisankei Biennale, Hakone Open-Air Mus, Japan, 95; NY Studio Sch Award, 99. *Bibliog:* Grace Glueck (auth), William Tucker, The NY Times, Dec 3, 99; Mario Naves (auth), What sculpture might have looked like on day 1, The NY Observer, Dec 13, 99; Ken Johnson (auth), Invitational exhib, The NY Times, Mar 31, 2000. *Media:* Mixed. *Publ:* Auth, Early Modern Sculpture, Oxford Univ Press, 74; Modernism, freedom, sculpture, Art J, winter 77-78; The Gonzalez exhib, The New Criterion, 5/83; Rodin in the round, The New Criterion, 3/94. *Dealer:* David McKee Gallery 745 5th Ave New York NY 10151

TUCKERMAN, JANE BAYARD
PHOTOGRAPHER, EDUCATOR
b Boston, Mass, June 11, 47. *Study:* Art Inst Boston, 68-71; RI Sch Design, MFA, 73-75. *Work:* Metrop Mus Art & Mus Mod Art, NY; Minneapolis Inst Art, Minn; Detroit Inst Arts; Boston Mus Fine Arts; RI Sch Design; Addison Gallery Am Art; Univ Mass. *Comn:* New Work's Portfolio, Boston Photog Resource Soc, 81. *Exhib:* Invisible Light, Smithsonian Inst Traveling Exhib, 80-84; solo exhibs, Addison Gallery Am Art, 76 & Photogalerie Pennings Edinhoven, The Neth, 81; Inst Contemp Art, Boston, 85; Ateneo de Caracas, Venezuela, 90; Photographers on Ellis Island, 1900-1990, Nat Park Ellis Island, 91; An Historical Preview 30 Woman Photographers, Silver Image Gallery, Seattle, 92; Looking at Death, Harvard Univ, 93; Mus de Chopo, Mexico City, 95; plus many others. *Collection Arranged:* Second Sight: Exhib of Infrared Photog (auth, catalog), traveling in US, Canada & Europe, 81-84. *Teaching:* Asst prof photog, Wellesley Col, 76-77; assoc prof & dir photog prog, Harvard Univ, 78-; guest instr & lectr, Maine Photog Workshop, Rockport, Factory Visual Arts, Seattle, 79; guest instr, Chulalongkoin Univ, Bangkok, 85, Yale Univ, 86; vis prof, Northeastern Univ, 90-91; Prof, Art Inst Boston, 90-; Harnish vis artist, Smith Col, 95-97. *Awards:* Polaroid Exhib Grant for Second Sight, 81; New Works Fel, Traveling Exhib in New England, Mass Coun Arts & Boston Photog Resource Ctr, 81-82; Individual Artists Fel, Nat Endowment Arts, 82-83; Smithsonian, Nat Endowment Arts, Benares proj, 85; Mass Artists Found Fel, 86. *Bibliog:* Allen Porter (auth), Camera Mag, 74, 80 & 81; Pamela Allara (auth), The scope of Boston art is much broader than it would appear, Art News, 11/81; Photography Year 1982, Time/Life Bks, 82. *Publ:* Contribr, Self Portrayal, Friends Photog, 78; Darkroom Dynamics, Curtain & London, 79; contribr & illusr, American photographer, CBS Publ, 82; contribr, Aperture Mag, 83; The Making of a Collection, Hartwell-Aperture, 85; auth, India: Ritual & the River, Aperture Mag, 87; Invisible Light, Univ Mass, 87. *Dealer:* Witkin Gallery 415 W Broadway New York NY; Pierce St Gallery 217 Pierce St Suite 206 Birmingham MI 48011. *Mailing Add:* Main St Box 399 Dublin NH 03444

TUEGEL, MICHELE BECKMAN
CRAFTSMAN, ADMINISTRATOR
b Pittsburgh, Pa, Sept 26, 52. *Study:* Univ S Fla, Tampa, MFA, 77; Int Inst Experimental Printmaking, Calif, papermaking cert, 76; independent study at Dieu Donne Paper Mill, NY, 86. *Work:* Walt Disney World Productions, Orlando, Fla; Hyatt Regency Hotel, Aruba; Southern Progress Corp Birmingham Ala; City of St Petersburg, Fla. *Comn:* Lobby installation (paper), AmeriFirst Bank, Boca Raton, Fla, 84; framed paperworks, SW Bell Telephone Co, St Louis, Mo, 86, Jewish Hosp, St Louis, 87; Landowne Conf Ctr, Washington DC, 90; Children's Presbyterian Hosp, Plano, Tex, 91; Fossil Park, City of St Petersburg Pub Art Comn, 97. *Exhib:* Paper As Medium, Smithsonian Inst, Washington, DC, 78-80; Papermaking & Paper Using, Southeastern Ctr Contemp Art, Winston-Salem, 79; Paper: New & Renewed Art, Tampa Mus, 87; A New Era of Paper, DeLand Mus Art, 90; Paper: US/Finland, WCarolina Univ, NC, 92-95. *Pos:* Spec proj coordr, Fla Gulf Coast Art Ctr, Belleair, 83-87; dir, Fla Craftsmen Inc, St Petersburg, 88-04; spec proj, Pinellas Co Arts Coun, 04-; independent cur, 2004-. *Teaching:* Asst design & silkscreen, Univ S Fla, Tampa, 76-77; workshop leader papermaking, Jacksonville Art Mus, Fla, and other cities, 79-;

adj asst prof papermaking, Eckerd Col, St Petersburg, 84-85; lectr & juror papermaking workshops across US. *Awards:* Friends of the Arts Award, Pinellas Co Arts Coun, 87; Award of Excellence, Fla Craftsmen 36th Ann, Zelo Mag, 87; Distinguised Alumni Award Fine Arts, Univ of SFla, 93; Women Honoring Women Award, Soroptomist Int, 2005. *Bibliog:* MaryAnn Marger (auth), Fiber Arts, Fiber Arts Mag, 86; Heart on Paper, Creative Ideas for Living Mag, 87. *Mem:* Am Craft Coun; Fla Craftsmen; Fla Cult Action & Educ Alliance; Craft Org Dirs Asn. *Media:* Handmade Paper. *Mailing Add:* 433 Monte Cristo Blvd Tierra Verde FL 33715

TUER, DOT (DOROTHY) J
CRITIC, CURATOR
b Toronto, Ont, Aug 28, 57. *Study:* Queen's Univ, BA, 81; Univ Toronto, MA, 94; Univ Toronto, PhD, 99. *Collection Arranged:* Perspectives of Women, Funnel Film Theatre, 88; Imaging Labor, Ont Ministry Cult, 91; Retrospective: Festival of Festivals, Can Cinema, 92; Images Film Spotlight: Retrospective of Vera Frekel, 97. *Pos:* Prog coordr, Funnel Experimental Film Ctr, 85-86; residency leader/consult, Banff Ctr Arts, 94; bd mem, Fuse Mag, 94-96 & The Power Plant, 91-95. *Teaching:* lectr art theory & hist, Ont Col Art & Design, 91-; lectr contemp art, Art Gallery Ont, 92. *Awards:* B Grants, Can Coun, 86, 87, 88, 91, 93 & 97; Best Curatorial Essay, Ont Art Gallery Asn, 94. *Mem:* Cinemateque Ont (bd mem, 91-97). *Res:* Contemporary new media art; Latin American art; issues of technology, identiy and post colonialism. *Publ:* Contribr, Sightlines: Reading Contemporary Art, Artextes, 94; But is it Art? Spirit of Art as Activism, Bay Press, 94; Dara Birnbawn, Kuntshalle Vienna, 95; Robert Lehman Lectures in Contemporary Art, DIA Centre NY, 96; contribr, Ephemere: Char Davies, Nat Gallery Can, 98. *Mailing Add:* 143 Marlbourough Pl Toronto ON M5R 3J5 Canada

TUFT, THOMAS E
PATRON
Pos: Exec, diversified financial serv co, formerly; inst, salesman, Goldman Sachs, vchmn, managing partner, currently. *Mem:* Whitney Mus Am Art, NY, (trustee, currently); Boys & Girls Harbor Asn (bd dir, currently). *Mailing Add:* Goldman Sachs 85 Broad St New York NY 10004

TULLIS, GARNER H
PUBLISHER, PRINTMAKER
b Cincinnati, Ohio, Dec 12, 39. *Study:* Univ Pa, BFA, 64; Accademia Di Belli Arte, Italy, Fulbright Scholar, 64-65; Stanford Univ, MA(Carnegie Fel), 67. *Work:* Cleveland Mus Art, Ohio; Philadelphia Mus Art, Pa; San Francisco Mus Mod Art, Calif; Mus Mod Art, NY; Brooklyn Mus Art, NY. *Exhib:* Ann Invitational, Pa Acad Fine Arts, 64; 49th Ann, Cleveland Mus Art, Ohio, 65; Nat Ann, San Francisco Mus Mod Art, Calif, 66; Albright-Knox Gallery, Buffalo, NY, 72; one-man show, Cleveland Art Inst, Ohio, 75; Works in handmade paper, Mus Mod Art, NY, 76; 30 Yrs, 30 Printmakers, Nat Collection Fine Arts, Washington, DC, 78; Paper as Medium Traveling Exhib, Smithsonian, 78-82. *Pos:* Dir, Inst Experimental Printmaking, 73-; founder, Garner Tullis Workshop, New York, NY, Santa Barbara, Calif & Pietrarubbia, Italy, 86-. *Teaching:* Foundry supervisor sculpture, Univ Calif, Berkeley, 67-69; artist-in-residence papermaking, Bennington Col, 76; assoc prof printmaking, Univ Calif, Davis, 76-84; artist-in-residence, Harvard Univ, 92. *Awards:* Nat Endowment Arts Grant, 76. *Bibliog:* Jules Heller (auth), Papermaking Today, Watson-Guptill, 78; Paper: Art & Technology, World Print Coun, 79; Patricia Newman (auth), Experimental workshop of Garner Tullis, Smithsonian Mag, 8/80; Charles Millard (auth), Garner Tullis, Print Quart, 6/89. *Mem:* Life mem, The Print Club, Philadelphia; Calif Soc Printmakers; Col Art Asn; Fulbright Alumni Asn. *Media:* Monotype. *Dealer:* Rosenberg & Kaufman Gallery 115 Wooser St New York NY 10012. *Mailing Add:* 200 E 10th St #302 New York NY 10003-7702

TULLOS, MARK A, JR
ADMINISTRATOR, CURATOR
b Baton Rouge, La, Jan 19, 61. *Study:* La State Univ, Baton Rouge, BFA, 84; Stephen F Austin State Univ, Nacogdoches, Tex, 88-90. *Collection Arranged:* Some Past is Present, Janet Turner, 90; Nature in Ornament, Newcomb Pottery, 91; The Spiritual in Nature, Will Stevens/Walter Anderson, 92; Salvation on San Mountain: Jim Neel & Melissa Springer, 97; Louisiana Artist Alumni Retrospective, 98. *Pos:* Exec dir, Mus ETex, Lufkin, 87-90, Walter Anderson Mus Art, Ocean Springs, 91-92 & Alexandria Mus Art, La, 92-. *Awards:* Nancy Hanks Mem Award for Prof Excellence, Asn Mus, 95; Paul Harris Fel, Rotary Int. *Mem:* Am Asn Mus; SE Mus Asn; La Asn Mus (vpres, 96). *Mailing Add:* c/o Alexandria Mus Art 933 Main St PO Box 1028 Alexandria LA 71309

TULLY, JUDD
WRITER, CURATOR
b Chicago, Ill, Apr 13, 47. *Study:* Am Univ, Washington, BA, 69; Univ Ore, Eugene. *Collection Arranged:* Vintage New York (auth, catalog), 83-84, One Penn Plaza, New York; Reuben Kadish Survey: 1935-1985 (auth, catalog), Artists' Choice Mus, New York, 86; The New Sculpture Group - A Look Back: 1957-1962 (auth, catalog), New York Studio Sch, 88; Made in NY: Encounters with contemporary sculpture (auth, catalog), Williams Ctr for Arts, Easton, Pa, 89; Lost and Found (auth, catalog), Sculpture Ctr, NY, 91; The Convergence of Art & Poetry, Mus at Fashion Inst of Technology, 2003. *Pos:* Lectr contemp art, NY Bd Educ, 84-; interviewer, Archives of Am Art, Smithsonian Inst, 88-; Editor at Large, Art & Auction Mag, 98; Chmn, The Reuben Kadish Art Found, 2000-. *Teaching:* NY Studio Sch Drawing, Painting & Sculpture, 95-. *Awards:* Arts & Culture reporting award, 98; Asn for Women in Communications 26th annual Clarion Awards, 98. *Mem:* Int Asn Art Critics; Authors Guild Inc. *Res:* Cultural reportage on contemporary painting and sculpture. *Publ:* Auth, Red Grooms and Ruckus Manhattan, George Braziller, NY, 77; Troubled times for artists' foundations, Art & Auction, 11/94; Who owns NY museums old masters?, Wash Post, 1/12/95; Posthumous sculpture casts-the messiest subject alive, Artnews, 12/95; Outside, inside or somewhere in between, Artnews, 5/96; When is a Calder Not a Calder, Art News, 2/97; The Floor is Theirs, The NY Times Mag, 97; Michel Cohen: The Con & the Pros, Art & Auction, 3/2001; Special Report: The Taubman Trial, Art & Auction, 2/2002; High and Inside, Marlborough Chelsea, May, 2003; Reuben Kadish; Metaunorphosis, Pollock-Kuasner House and Study Center, Aug, 2004; Market Spice; Modern Indian Art & Auction, April, 2005. *Mailing Add:* 187 Chrystie St New York NY 10002-1221

TULUMELLO, PETER M
CONSULTANT, DESIGNER
b Welland, Ont, Apr 15, 54. *Study:* Damaen Col, Buffalo, NY, 73-74; Univ Waterloo, Ont, BA(fine arts, hon), 78; Univ Regina, Sask, MFA, 80. *Work:* Univ Waterloo, Ont; Univ Regina. *Pos:* Dir & cur, Estevan Nat Exhib Ctr, 81-83, Mus Northern Hist, Ont, 84-85 & Art Gallery Northumberland, Cobourg, Ont, 85-89; pres, Corp Image Art & Design Consult Inc, 89-2000; pres, Wavelight Web Dimensions Inc, 2000-. *Teaching:* Lectr, Univ Regina, 79-83 & Niagara Col, 96. *Awards:* Prov Sask Grad Scholar, 79; Proj Cost Grant, Can Coun Award, 82. *Mem:* Can Mus Asn; Ont Mus Asn. *Collection:* University of Regina, University of Waterloo, Bazette Newspaper. *Mailing Add:* 66 State St Welland ON L3B 4K5 Canada

TULVING, RUTH
PAINTER, PRINTMAKER
b Estonia; Can citizen. *Study:* Ont Col Art, 62; Royal Can Acad Art. *Work:* Can Govt; Nat Gallery, Bejing, China; Nat Art Mus Estonia; and many pub and corp collections. *Comn:* murals, Washington Univ, St Louis, Mo. *Exhib:* Many mus and pub gallery individual exhibs in NAm, Europe & Asia. *Pos:* artist-in-residence, Washington Univ, St Louis, Mo. *Teaching:* Instr painting & printmaking, Ont Col Art, Toronto. *Mem:* Royal Can Acad Art; Ont Soc Artists (pres, 83-84). *Media:* Acrylic; Embossing, Etching. *Interests:* Opera History. *Publ:* Auth, Ruth Tulving, Estonian TV, 94. *Mailing Add:* 45 Baby Point Crescent Toronto ON M6S 2B7 Canada

TUNIS, ROSLYN
CURATOR, GALLERY DIRECTOR
b Montreal, Que; US citizen. *Study:* State Univ NY, Binghamton, BA(studio art & art hist), 72, MA(art hist & anthrop), 80. *Collection Arranged:* Festival of Mexico (auth, catalog), 73; The Fine Art of Craftsmanship (auth, catalog), 74; William Bingham: America a Good Investment (auth, catalog), 75; Artistic Spirit of the North American Indian (auth, catalog), 76; Treasure House: Museums of the Empire State (auth, catalog), 79; Charles Eldred: Sculpture and Drawing (auth, catalog), 80; Fusing Traditions: Transformations in Glass, Native Am Artists Mus Craft and Folk Art, San Francisco (auth, catalog); The Art of Research: Nelson Graburn and the Aesthetics of Inuit Sculpture, Phoebe Hearst Mus Anthrop, UCLA Berkeley; Silent Voices Speak: Remembering the Holocaust, Paintings by Barbara Shilo, San Francisco Presidio (auth, catalog); The Pan American Unity Multi-Media Exhib: An Exploration of the Mural by Diego Rivera, DeYoung Mus, San Francisco; Art As a Reflection of Eskimo / Inuit Culture: Tradition and Change in the 20th Century, Gallery Concord, Calif; The Artistic Spirit: Selections from the Phoebe A Hearst Mus Anthrop, UCLA Berkeley (auth, catalog), 90-93; and many others. *Pos:* Cur art, Roberson Ctr for Arts & Sci, Binghamton, NY, 72-84; dir, Carlyn Gallery, Madison Ave, New York, 84-89 & Danville, Calif, 90-93; chief cur & deputy dir curatorial servs, Univ Calif/Berkeley Mus, Blackhawk. *Teaching:* adj prof, John F Kennedy Univ, 94. *Mem:* Am Crafts Coun; Art Table Inc; Friends Ethnic Art (bd mem); Western Mus Asn (bd mem); Am Asn Mus. *Res:* Art of the Iroquois, contemporary American crafts; anthropology-Native American; Eskimo; ethnic art and folk art. *Mailing Add:* 5727 La Salle Ave Oakland CA 94611

TUPITSYN, MARGARITA
CRITIC, CURATOR
b Moscow, Russia, Mar 23, 55; US citizen. *Study:* Grad Sch, City Univ New York, with Rosalind Krauss & R C Washton-Long. *Collection Arranged:* SOTS Art (auth, catalog), New Mus, 86; Between Spring & Summer: Soviet Conceptual Art (auth, catalog), 90 & Montage & Modern Life (auth, catalog), 92, Inst Contemp Art, Boston; The Great Utopia (auth, catalog), Guggenheim Mus, 92. *Teaching:* Lectr Russ, Avanta-Garde New Sch, 87-87 & Avant-Garde State Univ NY, 87-88. *Mem:* Col Art Asn. *Publ:* Auth, Margins of Soviet Art: Socialist Realism to the Present, Giancarlo Politi Editore, 89; Between art & politics: Gustave Klutsis, Art Am, 91. *Mailing Add:* PO BOX 67 Cragsmoor NY 12420-0067

TURCONI, SUE (SUSAN) KINDER
PAINTER, PHOTOGRAPHER
b Teaneck, NJ, Feb 26, 39. *Study:* William Paterson U, Wayne, NJ, BA, 74; Pratt Inst, Brooklyn, MFA, 76. *Work:* NJ State Mus, Trenton; Newark Mus, NJ; Pratt Inst, Brooklyn; City Hall of Venice, Fl; Rutgers Univ, New Brunswick, NJ. *Comn:* Hackensack (photog pub), Hackensack Chamber of Com, NJ, 76. *Exhib:* Bergen Mus Art & Sci, Paramus, NJ, 90 Exhib, 92 Solo Exhib; Robeson Gallery, Rutgers Univ, Newark, NJ, 92; Barrier Island Ctr Arts, Big Arts Mus, Sanibel, Fla, 94; Nanjing Arts Col, Nanjing, China, 97; Boca Raton Mus Art, Boca Raton, Fla, 98; Curator's Choice: Legacy II, Mus Art & Sci, Melbourne, Fla, 99; Tampa Mus Art, Tampa, Fla, 2004. *Collection Arranged:* Jersey City Mus Exhib & Benefit Invitational, 02. *Pos:* Art critic, Suburban Trends, Riverside Publ Co, 74-80; writer column, Prof Women Photographers Times, 81-82; NJ correspondent, Art Express, 82; print librn, Soho Photo, New York, 86-87. *Teaching:* Instr photog, Passaic Coun Community Col, Paterson, NJ, 84-86, Bergen Community Col, Paramus, NJ, 85-93, Manatee Community Col, Venice, Fla, 94- & Edison Community Col, Ft Meyers, Fla, 96; artist

teacher studio art, Vt Col, Norwich Univ, Montpelier, 98, photography, printmaking, Venice (Fla) Art Ctr, 99-2000. *Awards:* NJ State Coun Arts Fel, 85-85; Grumbacher Medal, Venice Art Ctr, Venice, Fla, 98; combined talents, Fla Int 2004, Fla State Univ Mus Fine Arts, Tallahassee. *Bibliog:* John Zeaman (auth), Fine Arts, Sunday Record, 92; Mitchell Siedel (auth), Photography, Sunday Star Ledger, 92; Joan Altabe (auth) Fine Arts, Sunday Sarasota Herald Tribune, 2000. *Mem:* Womens Caucus Art; Fla Artists' Group. *Media:* All Media. *Publ:* Auth, Getting started, 84 & Ghosts, 85, Strategies Mag; Historical Composition & Teaching & Learning Strategies, Ilford Photo Instructor Newsletter, 91; Notes on Photography, Sweet & Bitter Fruit, Bergen Community Col, Paramus, NJ. *Dealer:* Grass Roots Gallery 411 West Dearorn St Englewood Fla 34223. *Mailing Add:* 1220 Sleepy Hollow Rd Venice FL 34292-1441

TURK, RUDY H
MUSEUM DIRECTOR, PAINTER
b Sheboygan, Wis, June 24, 27. *Study:* Univ Wis, 46-49; Univ Tenn, 49-51; Ind Univ, 52-56; Univ Paris, Fulbright Scholar, 56-57. *Work:* Bank One, Ariz. *Exhib:* Solo exhibs, The Store, Berkeley, Calif, 66, Udinotti Gallery, San Francisco, 79, Ariz Western Col, 81, Alwun House Found, Phoenix, 99; invitational group exhibs, Fac Art Exhibs, Ariz State Univ, 68, 69 & 70, Works by Wanda and Rudy Turk, Missoula Art Ctr, 75, Two Edges on a Line: A Comparative Migration of Images Between Ariz-NMex, ASA Gallery, Univ NMex, 77, Retributive Justice, Simms Art Ctr, Albuquerque, NMex, 77, Masks and Self-Portraits, Udinotti Gallery Scottsdale, 79-98, Valley Nat Bank (Tempe Off), Selected Works of Ariz State Univ Artists, 80 & Scholder Collects, Ariz State Univ Art Mus, 87; Spec Traveling Exhib, Scholder by Scholder and Others, Western Assoc Art Mus, 79; retrospective New Sch for the Arts, Scottsdale, Ariz, 98. *Collection Arranged:* The Works of John Roeder, Richmond Art Ctr, Calif, 61-62; Contemp Glass, San Diego Mus Fine Arts, 67; The World of David Gilhooly, Ariz State Univ, 69; Henry Strater Retrospective, 79; The World of Viola Frey, 82; Edward Jacobson collection of Am wood bowls, 85 & 90; Sculpture by John Paul Jones, 87; City Phoenix Ceramics Collection, 98. *Pos:* Art historian & dir art gallery, Univ Mont, 57-60; dir, Richmond Art Ctr, 60-65 & Univ Art Mus, Ariz State Univ, 67-; asst dir, San Diego Mus Fine Arts, 65-67; dir, Art Mus, Ariz State Univ, Tempe, 67-92, dir emer, 92-. *Teaching:* Prof art, Ariz State Univ, 67-77. *Awards:* Hon fel, Am Craftsman Coun, 88; Governor's Art Award, Arts of Ariz, 92. *Mem:* Friends Mex Art; Asn Am Mus; Col Art Asn Am. *Media:* Oil, Acrylic. *Res:* Contemporary art; Eighteenth century French art; humanities; American history & contemporary ceramics. *Collection:* Eighteenth century French prints; contemporary American ceramics; New Guinea Sculpture. *Publ:* Auth, IL Udell, Univ Art Collections, 71; coauth, Scholder/Indians, Northland, 72; The Search for Personal Freedom, William C Brown, Vols I & II, 4th ed 72, 5th ed 77, 6th ed 81, 7th ed 84; auth, Monumental Landscapes of Merrill Mahaffey, Northland, 79; auth, Scholder, New York, Rizzoli Press, 266, 82; plus critical studies, art catalogues & art reviews. *Dealer:* Udinotti Gallery 4215 N Marshall Way Scottsdale AZ 85251. *Mailing Add:* 760 E Courtney Ln Tempe AZ 85284

TURLINGTON, PATRICIA R
PAINTER, SCULPTOR
b Washington, DC, Sept 14, 39. *Study:* Washburn Univ, 62-63; NC State Univ Sch Design, spec study with Joe Cox, 69-71; Atlantic Ctr Arts, spec study with Audrey Flack, 86. *Work:* Mint Mus, Charlotte, NC; Duke Univ Med Ctr, Durham, NC; Univ NC, Chapel Hill; Wachovia Bank & Trust Co, Winston Salem, NC; Blue Cross-Blue Shield, Chapel Hill, NC. *Comn:* Brick sculpture murals, (first brick sculpture in a pub sch in the US), Goldsboro City Sch, NC, 75; brick sculpture mural, City of Sanford, NC, 80; brick sculpture mural, McDonald's Corp, Oak Brook, Ill, 90; brick sculpture mural, Rowan Mem Hosp, Salisbury, NC, 91; brick sculpture mural, New York City Transit Authority, 92. *Exhib:* Artist's Political Statements, Southeastern Ctr Contemp Art, Winston Salem, NC, 86; A Feminest Odyssey, Wake Forest Univ Fine Arts Ctr, Winston Salem, NC, 87; Am Herstory, Atlanta Col Art Gallery, Ga, 90; Women and Art: Creating the Feminine Icon, Winthrop Col Fine Arts Ctr, Rock Hill, SC, 91; Women's Issues as Art, Salem Col Fine Arts Ctr, Winston Salem, NC, 92. *Teaching:* Prof studio art & art hist, Wayne Community Col, Goldsboro, NC, 86-2005. *Awards:* Collaborating Arts Award, NC Chap Am Inst Architects, 78; Cash Award, Tex Fine Arts Asn Nat Exhib, 84; First Prize: Works on Paper, Nat Asn Women Artists, Morris J Heiman, 85. *Bibliog:* Norman Farley (dir), Sculptured Brick (film), Brick Inst Am, 89; Kathryn Gleason (auth), Brick Added to McDonald's drive thru menu, BIA News Mag/Brick Inst Am, 1/90; Norman Farley (auth), Brick sculpture: art becomes architecture, Archit Mag, 12/90. *Mem:* Nat Asn Women Artists. *Media:* Watercolor; Brick. *Publ:* Auth, North Drive Elementary School Intaglio Brick Sculptures, NC Architect, 77. *Mailing Add:* 709 Park Ave Goldsboro NC 27530

TURNBULL, BETTY
CURATOR
b Hollywood, Calif, Aug 4, 24. *Study:* Los Angeles Valley Col (art hist, design, drawing & painting), 56-59. *Collection Arranged:* Art of the Northwest Indian & Alaska Eskimo, Fine Arts Patrons of Newport Harbor, 68; Directly Seen; New Realism, 70 & Art of the Indian Southwest, 71, Newport Harbor Art Mus & Pasadena Mus Art; Mary Cassatt (auth, catalog), 74; The Flute and the Brush: Indian Miniature Paintings, 76; The Last Time I Saw Ferus (auth, catalog), 76; David Park Retrospective (auth, catalog), 77; The Prometheus Archives-A Retrospective of the Work of George Herms, 79; Via Celmins Survey (intro catalog), 79; California, The State of Landscape 1827-1981 (auth, catalog), Newport Harbor Art Mus, 81; Perpetual Motion (auth, catalog), Santa Barbara Mus Art, 87-88; and others. *Pos:* cur art, Newport Harbor Art Mus, Calif, 69-72 & 73-77, actg dir, 72-73, cur exhibs & collections, 77-81; dir, Turnbull, Lutjeans, Kogan (TLK) Gallery, 81-85; speaker/adv, Art Forum Prog, Rancho Santiago Col, 83-85. *Teaching:* Asst prof, Mus Studies Prog, Calif State Univ, Long Beach, 86-87. *Specialty:* Contemporary painting, sculpture & graphics. *Mailing Add:* 2328 Vista Huerta Newport Beach CA 92660-4042

TURNBULL, LUCY
MUSEUM DIRECTOR, EDUCATOR
b Lancaster, Ohio. *Study:* Bryn Mawr Col, Pa, AB, 52; Am Sch Classical Studies, Athens, Greece, 55-57; Radcliffe Col, Cambridge, Mass, AM, 54, PhD, 60. *Collection Arranged:* Yoknapatawpha Through Other Eyes, 83, O Look Heaven is Coming to Earth, paintings of Theora Hamblett (auth, catalog), 84, Three Southern Photographers, 84, Images of the Southern Woman, 85, Mr McCrady of La-Fay-Ette Co, 86, Univ Mus, Univ Miss, Treasures from Oxford Homes I & II, 87. *Pos:* Mus asst, Mus Fine Arts, Boston, 58-60; cur, classical antiq, Univ Mus, Univ Miss, 77-, dir, 85-90. *Teaching:* From asst prof classical archaeol, to assoc prof, Univ Miss, 61-66, prof classics, 74-81, prof classics & art, 81-90, emer prof, 90-. *Mem:* Am Asn Mus; Archaeol Inst Am; Asn Col & Univ Mus & Galleries. *Res:* Iconography of Greek mythology, especially in vase-painting; influence of other arts on vase-painting; topical themes in iconography. *Publ:* Contribr, Art, Myth & Culture; Greek Vases from the Southern Collections, New Orlean Mus, 81; Poets and Heroes, Emory Univ, Atlanta, 86. *Mailing Add:* 714 S 8th St Oxford MS 38655

TURNER, A RICHARD
HISTORIAN, EDUCATOR
b New Bedford, Mass, July 28, 32. *Study:* Princeton Univ, PhD, 59. *Hon Degrees:* Univ Puget Sound, LHD, 2001. *Pos:* Chairperson, Inst Fine Arts, NY, 79-82; dir, NY Inst Humanities, NY Univ, 86-93. *Teaching:* Prof Renaissance art, Princeton Univ, 60-68; prof & chmn Renaissance art, Middlebury Col, Vt, 68-75; pres & prof art, Grinnell Col, 75-79, NY Univ, 79-2000. *Mem:* Col Art Asn Am. *Res:* Historiography and criticism of Renaissance art. *Publ:* Auth, The Vision of Landscape in Renaissance Italy, Princeton, 66 & 73; coauth, Art of Florence, Abbeville, 88; auth, Inventing Leonardo, Knopf, 93; auth, Florence: The Invention of a New Art, 1997; auth, Pietra: Florence, A Family and A Villa, 2002. *Mailing Add:* PO Box 2322 Cape May NJ 08204

TURNER, ALAN
PAINTER, PRINTMAKER
b New York, NY, July 6, 43. *Study:* City Col New York, BA, 65; Univ Calif, Berkeley, MA (painting), 67. *Work:* Whitney Mus Am Art, Mus Mod Art, NY; Mus Fine Arts, Boston; Minneapolis Inst Fine Art; MIT. *Comn:* Lithograph, Kunstvereine, Hamburg, Ger, 71; Painting, Third Nat Bank, Toledo, Ohio, 79. *Exhib:* Whitney Mus Am Art Biennial, 75 & 95; The Am Artist as Printmaker, 23rd Nat Print Exhib, Brooklyn Mus, NY, 84; Mus Fine Arts, Boston, 84; solo exhibs, Jason McCoy Gallery, NY, 87, Everson Mus Art, 88, Koury Wingate Gallery, NY, 88, 90, Tyler Gallery, Temple Univ, Elkins Park, Pa, 89, Ealan Wingate Gallery, NY, 91, Allez Les Filles Gallery, Columbus, Ohio, 95, Lennon, Weinberg Gallery, NY, 96, 2000, 2003; Inst Contemp Art, Boston, 89; Who Chooses Who, The New Mus, NY, 94; Lennon Weinberg Inc, NY, 94, 98, 02; Oeuvres Choisis, Allez Les Filles Gallery, Columbus, Ohio, 94; Jay Gorney Mod Art, NY, 94; Barbara Gladstone Gallery, New York City, 2000; Mathew Marks Gallery, New York City, 2000; Islip Art Mus, East Islip, NY, 02; and many others. *Awards:* Nat Endowment Arts Fel Grant, 77, 81, 87; Spoleto Choice, Spoleto, USA, 80; John Simon Guggenheim Mem Found Fel, 88; Pollock-Krasner Found Grant, 01. *Bibliog:* Stuart Servetar (auth), Alan Turner: Recent paintings, NY Press, 1/17-23/96; Robert Mahoney (auth), Alan Turner, Time Out NY, 1/17-24/96; Pepe Karmel (auth), Alan Turner, NY Times, 2/2/96; and many others. *Media:* Oil. *Publ:* Auth, Etchings, Parasol Press, 78; Lithos & Etchings, Brooke Alexander, 80; Ilene Kurtz Editions, 90. *Dealer:* Lennon Weinberg Inc 560 Broadway Suite 308 New York NY 10012. *Mailing Add:* 114 Franklin St New York NY 10013

TURNER, (CHARLES) ARTHUR
PAINTER, INSTRUCTOR
b Houston, Tex, Nov 17, 40. *Study:* NTex State Univ, BA, 62; Cranbrook Acad Art, Bloomfield Hills, Mich, MFA, 66, with Zoltan Shepeshy. *Work:* Mus Fine Arts & Houston Ind Inc, Houston; McNay Art Inst, San Antonio; Beaumont Art Mus, Tex; McAllen Int Mus, McAllen, Tex; Lord Fairfax Community Col, Middletown, Va. *Exhib:* One-man show, Moody Gallery, Houston, 78, 82, 87, 92, 96 & 99, Patricia Moore Gallery, Aspen, 83 & 86 & Moody Gallery, 99, 2006; Recent Acquisitions, Mus Fine Arts, Houston, 78; Kunst Fra Houston I Norge, Stavanger Mus, Norway, 1982; Pecos River Suite, Moody Gallery, Houston, Tex, 96; Contemplating Translucence, Allen Ctr, Houston, 96; Flora Bella, Galveston Arts Ctr, Tex, 97; Watercolor USA, Springfield, Mo, 2000; Reserved Light, Mus Fine Arts, Houston, 2001; Spirit of the Planet, Residence of the US Amb to UN, Vienna, Austria, 2003; Recent Watercolors, Lew Allen Contemp, Santa Fe, 2002. *Teaching:* Asst prof painting, Madison Col, Va, 66-68; instr painting, Glassell Sch Art, Mus Fine Arts, Houston, 69-; guest instr, Univ Houston, 73; instr, Hill Country Arts Found, Ingram, Tex, 84, 89 & 90 & Anderson Ranch Art Ctr, Snowmass, Colo, 85; instr watercolor workshop, James Madison Univ, Orkney Springs, Va, 90 & Malakad Schloss Goldegg, Austria, 96, 99, 2003. *Awards:* First Purchase Award, Beaumont Art Mus 20th Ann, 71; First Award, Art Found Ann, Art Mus South Tex, 73; First Place, Clear Lake Arts Alliance, Tex, 2000. *Bibliog:* Edwy B Lee (auth), Arthur Turner, drawings, Art Voices/South, 3/78; Elanor Freed (auth), Texas roundup, Art Am, 11/68; Jana Vander Lee (auth), Arthur Turner, Grand Mesa Mask, ie Mag, summer 92. *Mem:* Tex Watercolor Soc; Col Art Asn Am. *Media:* Acrylic, Watercolor, Collage. *Publ:* Color perception (video), Crystal Productions, Aspen, Colo. *Dealer:* Moody Gallery 2815 Colquitt Houston TX 77098. *Mailing Add:* 2419 Julian Houston TX 77009

TURNER, BONESE COLLINS
PAINTER, DESIGNER
b Abilene, Kans. *Study:* Univ Idaho, BSEd, 53, MEd, 54; Univ Calif, Los Angeles, 67; Calif State Univ, Northridge, MA, 74. *Work:* Smithsonian Inst, Washington, DC; Nebr Libr, Lincoln; Home Savings & Loan; Ore Coun Arts, Newport; Hartung Performing Arts Ctr, Moscow, Idaho; Brand Libr Permanent Collection, Robert Fulton Mus Art,

Calif State Univ San Bernardino; San Bernardino Sun Telegram Newspapers, Calif; Springfield Art Mus, Springfield, Mo. *Comn:* Mural, mosaic, tile & glass, Indust Tile Corp, Lincoln, Nebr, 60-61; paintings & drawings, Harding Realty, Lincoln, Nebr, 60-61; paintings, Delta Gamma House, Moscow, Idaho, 69-70; paintings, Alsa Distributing Co, Denver, Colo, 81-82; interior environment, Los Angeles Pierce Col, Woodland Hills, Calif, 85-86. *Exhib:* Los Angeles Co Mus Art, 57 & 58; Va Mus Art, Richmond, 74 & 75; Laguna Gloria Art Mus, Austin, Tex, 78; Birmingham Mus Art, Ala, 78-80; one-man exhibs, Brand Libr, 78, 88, 93, 2000, Orlando Gallery, Sherman Oaks, Calif, 80, 86, 93, 98, 2002, 2005, Univ Nev, Reno, 87, Coos Art Mus, Coos Bay, Ore, 88 & Angel's Gate Gallery, San Pedro, Calif, 89, Village Square Gallery, Montrose, Calif, 2002, 2005; Rocky Mountain Nat Exhib, Golden, Colo, 81, 82 & 85; National Egg Design Invitational, White House & Smithsonian Inst, Washington, DC, 84-85; Hollywood and the Muse, Olympic Arts Celebration, Palos Verdes Art Mus, Calif, 84; Art of the 80's, Calif State Univ, Northridge, 85. *Collection Arranged:* Traditional Concepts of Quilting in the US, Los Angeles Pierce Col, Woodland Hills, Calif, 76. *Pos:* Lens consult, Warner Bros & 20th Century Fox, Calif, 67-68; Instr, Coordr, Interior/Environ Design Prog, Los Angeles Pierce Col, Woodland Hills, Calif, 68-; bd dir & consult, Preserve Bottle Village, Simi Valley, Calif, 84-. *Teaching:* Adj prof, art, Los Angeles Pierce Col, Woodland Hills, Calif, 64-; adj instr art structures, Fashion Inst, Los Angeles, 84; adj prof 3D art, design & interior design, Calif State Univ, Northridge, 86-88; adj prof, art hist & drawing, Los Angeles Valley Col, Van Nuys, Calif, 87-89; adj prof, drawing, Moorpark Col, Calif, 89-. *Awards:* Cash Awards, 45th Ann Watercolor USA, 89, 2002, Butler Inst 53rd Ann, 89 & Nat Acrylic Painters Asn, Long Beach, Calif, 96, Brand Libr Purchase Prize, 1998 & 2004; First prize graphics, Pasadena Soc Artist Diamond Jubilee (catalog), 2002. *Bibliog:* Steve Harvey (auth), Only in LA, Los Angeles Times, 89; Louise Moore (auth), Celebrating women's art, Artweek, Vol 15, No 23, 6/4/84; Shirle Gottlieb (auth), Press Telegram, 11/10/96. *Mem:* Life mem Nat Watercolor Soc (jury, 80, pres, 89-90, chmn: jury, 91); Pa Watercolor Soc; Univ Idaho Col Art & Archit (adv bd); Watercolor West; Watercolor USA Honor Soc; Women Painters/West. *Media:* All Media, Mixed. *Specialty:* Contemporary Western Art, African Art. *Collection:* Native American; Contemporary such as Helen Lundeberg, Marvin Hardin, Irving Block & Kent Twitchell with Lita Albuquerque Albuquerque American folk art & quilts. *Publ:* Contrib, The great cover-up, Images & Issues, 7/8/83; TV interview, The Sushi Series, Asahi Cable Systems, 89; TV interview, Multi-Media Works, Am Cable Systems, 89; Psychological Perspectives, Issue 23, 90; Best of Drawing & Sketching, Rockport Publ, 98; Josef Woodard (auth), Girls' Power, Valley B9, LA Times, 65/19/2000; Josef Woodard (auth), 4Perspectives, B6 Gallery, LA Times, 9/18/2000. *Dealer:* Orlando Gallery 14553 Ventura Blvd Sherman Oaks CA 91403. *Mailing Add:* 4808 Larkwood Ave Woodland Hills CA 91364

TURNER, BRUCE BACKMAN
PAINTER
b Worcester, Mass, Oct 28, 41. *Work:* Sloan-Kettering Cancer Ctr, NY; Cheshire Pub Libr, Conn; also pvt collections throughout the US, Can, Eng, France, Belg, Swed, Saudi Arabia and Australia. *Exhib:* North Shore Arts Asn Ann, East Gloucester, Mass, 72-99; 2nd Greater New Orleans Nat Exhib, La, 72; Rockport Art Asn, 72-99; Attleboro Mus Ann, Mass, 75; Am Fortnight Exhib, Hong Kong, China, 75; Mainstreams, Marietta Col, Ohio, 76; Mid Yr Show, Butler Inst Am Art, Ohio, 78 & Hope Show, 80; A Tribute to Harry R Ballinger, Ellsworth Gallery, Simsbury, Conn, 80; New Eng Impressions, Painting From Life, Attleboro Mus, Mass, 80; Mary Bryan Mem Gallery, Jeffersonville, Vt, 96-98; and many others. *Teaching:* Pvt classes oil painting, Rockport, Mass, 71-72; workshops, Rockport, Mass, Carmel, Calif, Antigonish, NS, Knoxville, Tenn, Ridgewood, NJ, Cheshire, Conn, Sturbridge, Mass, Port Clyde, Maine. *Awards:* Shumaker Award, Rockport Art Asn, Mass, 76; Seley Purchase Prize, 76 & Arthur T Hill Mem, 79, Salmagundi Club, NY; Harriet Lumis Award, Acad Artists Asn, 78. *Mem:* Am Artists Prof League; Rockport Art Asn; North Shore Arts Asn; Acad Artists Asn; Salmagundi Club. *Media:* Oil. *Publ:* Contribr, Am Artist Mag, 1/86; Monhegan - The Artist Island, Down E Publ, 95; Best of Oil Painting, 96, Portrait Impressions, 97 & A Gallery of Marine Art, 98, Rockport Publ. *Mailing Add:* Four Story St Rockport MA 01966

TURNER, DAVID
MUSEUM DIRECTOR, EDUCATOR
b Houston, Tex, Dec 1, 48. *Study:* Southern Methodist Univ, Dallas, BBA, 71; Univ Ore, Eugene, MA, 74. *Collection Arranged:* Approaches to Photography (auth, catalog), 79; Amarillo Earthworks, 81; Touring the World (auth, catalog), 81; Early French Moderns, (auth, catalog), 82. *Pos:* Asst registrar, Mus Fine Arts, Houston, Tex, 71-72; cur educ, Amarillo Art Ctr, Tex, 77-80, dir, 80-; dir, Mus Fine Arts, Mus NMex, formerly; dir, Colo Springs Fine Arts Ctr, currently. *Teaching:* Instr art hist & photog, Umpqua Community Col, Roseburg, Ore, 74-77; instr art history, Colorado Coll, 99. *Mem:* Am Asn Mus; Soc Photog Educ; Asn Art Mus Dirs. *Publ:* Auth & ed, American Images (video tape), 79 & auth, Amarillo Landmarks, 81, Amarillo Art Ctr; auth, Jack Boynton, Artspace, 81. *Mailing Add:* Colo Springs Fine Arts Ctr 30 W Dale St Colorado Springs CO 80903

TURNER, EVAN HOPKINS
MUSEUM DIRECTOR
b Orono, Maine, Nov 8, 27. *Study:* Harvard Univ, AB, MA & PhD. *Hon Degrees:* Sir George Williams Univ, LHD, 65; Swarthmore Col, LHD, 67; Temple Univ, hon DL, 74l; Cleveland State Univ, hon DLA, 92. *Pos:* Lectr & res asst, Frick Collection, New York, 53-56; gen cur & asst dir, Wadsworth Atheneum, Hartford, Conn, 55-59; dir, Mont Mus Fine Arts, 59-64, Philadelphia Mus Art, 64-77, Ackland Art Mus, 78-83 & Cleveland Mus Art, 83-93. *Teaching:* Adj prof art hist, Univ Pa, 70-78 & Univ NC, Chapel Hill, 78-83; distinguished vis prof, Oberlin Col, Ohio, 91-94. *Bibliog:* Ray K Metclur (auth), Landscapes, Aperture, 2000. *Mem:* Am Asn Mus; Asn Art Mus Dirs (pres, 75-76); Benjamin Franklin fel Royal Soc Arts; Am Fedn Arts; Century Club. *Res:* Thomas Eakins; 19th century American sculpture. *Mailing Add:* 2125 Cypress St Philadelphia PA 19103

TURNER, HERBERT B
PAINTER
Study: Lehigh Univ, Bethlehem, Pa, 45; US Military Acad, West Point, NY, BA (sci), 49; Naum Los Sch Art in Sculpture, 50. *Exhib:* Solo exhib, World Art Res Gallery, Del Mar, Calif, Pub Access Channel 37, Del Mar, Calif, Laguna Beach Art Mus, Calif, La Jolla Art Asn, Calif, San Diego Art Inst, La Jolla, Calif, Mathes Cult Ctr Invitational, Escondido, Calif, Boehm Art Gallery, Palomar Col, San Marcos, Calif, Anaheim Mus, Calif; group exhib, Artists Guild San Diego, Calif, San Diego Fine Arts Gallery, Calif, Audubon Artists, New York City, Allied Artists, NY, 50th Nat Soc of Painters in Casein & Acrylic, Tex Fine Arts Asn, Austin, Tex, Butler Art Inst, Youngstown, Ohio, Perdue Univ. *Bibliog:* Janice Lovoos (auth), American Artists Mag, 2/62. *Mailing Add:* 606 Zuni Dr Del Mar CA 92014

TURNER, JANET SULLIVAN
PAINTER, SCULPTOR
b Gardiner, Maine, Nov 15, 35. *Study:* Chicago Acad Fine Arts (Scholarship), 53; Mich State Univ, BFA (cum laude), 56; Haystack Mountain Sch Arts & Crafts, Deer Isle, Maine, 64. *Work:* La Salle Univ Art Mus, Phila; Noyes Mus, Oceanville, NJ; Nat Liberty Mus, Phila; Kimmel Ctr; and many others. *Comn:* Painting, Univ Maine, Farmington, 80; Painting, Systems & Computer Tech Corp, Malvern, Pa, 82; painting, Teradyne Cent Inc, Deerfield, Ill, 83; paintings, Del Investment Adv, Philadelphia, 86. *Exhib:* Solo exhibs, St Joseph's Univ, Philadelphia, 81, Villanova Univ, Villanova, 82, Pa State Univ, Middletown, 85, Temple Univ, Philadelphia, Pa, 86, Suzanne Gross Gallery, Philadelphia, 88, Gloucester Co Col, NJ, 90, Newark Mus, Newark, NJ, 93 & Rosemont Col, Pa, Sande Webster Gallery, Philadelphia, 98, 2000; Am Women in Art, UN World Conf Women, Nairobi, Kenya, 85; Widener Univ Art Mus, Chester, Pa, 87 & 94; 4 person, Trenton City Mus, NJ, 90; 3 person, Del Ctr Contemp Arts, Wilmington, 92; Noyes Mus, NJ, 95, 97, 2000; and others; 50 Year Retrospective, Widener Univ Art Gallery, Chester, Pa, 2005. *Collection Arranged:* Per Collections State Mus of PA Harrisburg; Noyes Mus, NJ; Kresge Art Mus, Mich; Natl Liberty Mus; La Salle Univ Art Mus, Philadelphia, PA. *Pos:* Bd dir, Artists Equity, 85-86, 1st vpres, Philadelphia Chap, 86-, pres, 87 & 88. *Teaching:* Guest lectr, Cult Events Prog, Pa State Univ, 85, Rosemont Col, Pa, 95, Noyes Mus, NJ, 95. *Awards:* Hon Mention, Nat Artists Equity Traveling Show, Stedman Gallery, Rutgers Univ, 85; Third Prize, Katonah Art Mus, 92; Purchase Award, State Mus Pa, Harrisburg, 92. *Bibliog:* Victoria Donohoe (auth), critiques in Philadelphia Inquirer, 6/2/85, 1/10/86, 4/17/87, 5/14/88, 10/2/94 & 11/20/2005; Burton Wasserman (critic), article, Art Matters, 9/94, 9/95, 2/96, 2/98, 5/2000, 6/2000, 11/2005; Robin Rice (critic), Philadelphia City Paper, 8/2000; TV news, Dick Sheeran's World, Philadelphia, Channel 3, 5/1/2002. *Mem:* Philadelphia Watercolor Club (bd dir, 92); Artists Equity Philadelphia, Pa; Philadelphia Tri-State Artists Asn (life hon). *Media:* Mixed, Acrylic, Sculpture. *Specialty:* Contemparary Art. *Publ:* Contemporary Women Artists, Cedco Publ, 92; Woodmere Art Museum, Philadelphia Sculptors 2000, Colorcraft Ltd, 2000. *Dealer:* Sande Webster Gallery 2018 Locust St Philadelphia PA 19103. *Mailing Add:* 88 Cambridge Dr Glen Mills PA 19342

TURNER, JUDITH ESTELLE
PHOTOGRAPHER, VIDEO ARTIST
b Atlantic City, NJ. *Study:* Boston Univ, Sch Fine Arts, BFA. *Work:* Libr Cong; J Paul Getty Mus, Santa Monica, Calif; Brooklyn Mus; Bibliot Nat, Paris, France; Tokyo Metrop Mus Photg, Japan; Whitney Mus, NY. *Comn:* Photogs, Philip Morris, Richmond, Va, 82; Becton Dickinson, Franklin Lakes, NJ, 86; Spiral, Tokyo, Japan, 87; Tepia, Tokyo, Japan, 89; Peoples Bank, Bridgeport, Conn, 89; Republic Nat Bank, NY, 90; Kajima Corp Tokyo, Japan, 91 & 94. *Exhib:* Solo exhibs, Sites/Insights, Int Ctr Photog, NY, 80, Int Cult Ctr, Antwerp, Belg, 81, Portland Mus Art, Maine, 83, White City (traveling exhib), Tel Aviv Mus, Israel, 84, Axis Gallery, Tokyo, Japan, 86 & City Arts Ctr, Oklahoma City, 95; Inside Spaces, Mus Mod Art, NY, 81; Site Work (traveling exhib), Photogrs' Gallery, London, Eng, 91; George Eastman House, Rochester, 93; Recontres Int de la Photographie, Arles, 94; Tokyo Metrop Mus Photog, 95; Marlborough Gallery, NY, 96; and others. *Awards:* Lila Acheson Wallace Fund, The Capitol in Albany, Reader's Digest Asn, 84; Asian Cult Coun Fel, 85; Honor Award, Am Inst Architects, 94. *Bibliog:* Albert Champeau (auth), Creatis, Publico, Paris, 79; A Busch (auth), The Photography of Architecture, Van Nostand, Reinhold Co, 86; William Kennedy (auth), The Capitol in Albany, Aperture, 86. *Publ:* Illusr, Judith Turner Photographs Five Architects, Rizzoli Int Publs, 80; White City, Tel Aviv Mus, 84; Annotations on Ambiguity, Axis Gallery, 86; Spiral Book, Wacoal Art Ctr, 88; Parables & Pieces, Kafka/Turner, After, Feingold/Turner V FitzGerald & Co, 91 & 93. *Dealer:* Vincent FitzGerald 11 E 78th St New York NY 10021. *Mailing Add:* 323 W 82nd St New York NY 10024

TURNER, NORMAN HUNTINGTON
PAINTER, WRITER
b Storm Lake, Iowa, July 11, 39. *Study:* New York Studio Sch, 64-65; Empire State Col, BA, 79. *Exhib:* Drawing Each Other, Brooklyn Mus, 71; one-man shows, Green Mountain Gallery, 72-75 & Ingber Gallery, 77 & 79, NY, New Paintings from the Del Water Gap, Hopper House Nyak, 77, Bowery Gallery, NY, 89; Younger Artists', Artists Choice Mus, 83; Bowery Gallery, NY, 89-96; NY Studio Sch, 2003; Wash Art Asn, 2005; The Coutinuous Mark, NY Studio Sch, 2005. *Teaching:* Adj lectr, Queens Col, 82-85, dir summer painting pro, 85-89 & adj asst prof, 86-; instr painting, NY Studio Sch, 82-84 & 94-2003. *Awards:* Painting Fel, NJ State Coun Arts, 80. *Bibliog:*

Lawrence Campbell (auth), rev in Art News, 11/72; Laura Schwartz (auth), rev, 2/73, Ellen Lubell (auth), rev, 4/75 & Allen Ellenzweig (auth), rev, 4/77, Arts Mag; Jed Perl (auth), rev, Art in Am, 5-6/77; John Caldwell (auth), review, NY Sunday Times, 10/26/80. *Media:* Oil on Canvas, Drawing. *Publ:* Auth, Subjective Curvature in late Cezanne, Art Bull, 12/81; Stella on Caravaggio, Arts, summer 85; Some Questions About EH Gombrich on Perspective, J Aesthetics & Art Criticism, spring 92; The Semantic of Linear Perspective, Philosophical Forum, summer 96. *Mailing Add:* 71 Prospect St New Paltz NY 12561-1143

TURNER, RALPH JAMES
SCULPTOR, PAINTER
b Ashland, Ore, Oct 24, 35. *Study:* Reed Col, with calligrapher, Lloyd Reynolds, BA, 58; Portland Art Mus Sch, with painter, Louis Bunce, dipl, 58; Portland State Col, 59; Univ Ore, with Jan Zach & Gerald di Guisto, MFA(sculpture), 62; Univ Ariz, 65, 72 & 73. *Work:* Catalina Observatory, Univ Ariz, Tucson; Flandrau Planetarium, Tucson; Hayden Planetarium, NY; Nat Aeronautical & Space Admin-Ames, San Francisco; Phoenix (five ft limestone), Syracuse Univ, NY, 66; also many pvt collections. *Comn:* Jupiter (two planetary models), NASA/Ames, Mt View, Calif, 74 & 76; Dr Gerard Kuiper (bronze bust), Univ Ariz, 75; Phobos (planetary model), Smithsonian Inst, 78; Seer (marble carving), M & J Shapiro, Beverly Hills, Calif, 80; mural of athletes, Multnomah Athletic Club, Portland, Ore, 81; four Northwest Indian motif wood carvings, Hyland Hills Ctr, Beaverton, Ore, 82; Athletic Figures (mural), Multnomah Athletic Club, Portland, Ore, 82; Factory Workers (mural), Norwest Publ Co, Greeley, Colo, 85; Medieval Figures (mural), The Knight's Castle Apts, Wilsonville, Ore, 90; Athletic Figures Witham Oaks Recreation Ctr (mural), Corvallis, Ore, 87; Brix Maritime Mural, Portland, Ore, 94; Mt Hood Community Col Donor Wall, 99; The Columbia (mural), Tidewater Cove Condominiums, 2003. *Exhib:* Ralph J Turner, Sculpture, Tucson Art Ctr, 63 & Univ Ariz, Tucson, 64; three-man exhib, Space & Art, Rainbow Gallery, Cannon Beach, Ore, 76; Planets & Progs: A Retrospective, Delphian Found, Sheridan, Ore, 77 & Willamette Sci & Technol Ctr, Eugene, 77; Hexagon Galaxies, Delphian Found, 80; Electro Arts Gallery, San Francisco, 81. *Pos:* Res assoc planetary models, Lunar & Planetary Lab, Univ Ariz, Tucson, 64-73; co-dir/designer, Rock Creek Experimental Sta, 73-. *Teaching:* Instr sculpture, Univ Ariz, Tucson, 62-65; asst prof design & drawing, Syracuse Univ, NY, 66-69; art coordr graphics, humanities & sculpture, Pima Col, Tucson, 70-72; instr design & calligraphy, Chemekta Community Col, Salem, Ore, 75-78. *Awards:* Nat Endowment Humanities Fel, 72-73. *Bibliog:* Fred Crafts (auth), Is it art or science, Eugene Register Guard, 77; Mary Rash (auth), Ralph Turner: Renaissance Man, The Sun, Sheridan, Ore, 12/5/2001; The Artists of Yam Hill Co, McMinnville, Ore, 99, 2001, 2002. *Mem:* Int Sculptur Ctr; Int Soc Art & Technol; Oregon Art Inst. *Media:* Stone, Wood; Acrylic on Plexiglas. *Interests:* photography. *Publ:* Auth, The Northeast Rim of Tycho, Lunar & Planetary Commun, 70; Extraterrestrial landscapes through the eyes of a sculptor, Leonardo, 72; A model of the eastern portion of Schroter's Valley, Lunar & Planetary Commun, 73; A model of Phobos, Icarus, Cornell Univ, 78; Modeling and mapping Phobos, Sky & telescope, 77-78. *Mailing Add:* 14320 SW Rock Creek Rd Sheridan OR 97378

TURNER, WILLIAM EUGENE
PAINTER, EDUCATOR
b Dallas, Tex, Oct 15, 28. *Study:* Southern Methodist Univ, BA, 52; Univ NMex, summer 53; La State Univ, MA, 54. *Work:* Portsmouth Arts Ctr, Va; Ark Arts Ctr, Little Rock; Atlantic Richfield Corp, Dallas, Tex & Anchorage, Alaska. *Comn:* Hallway murals, Dallas Middle & High Sch (with Bill Hendricks, archit), comn by STB Archit & Planners, Tex, 77. *Exhib:* Drawing Invitational, Emporia State Univ, Kans, 82; Smithsonian Inst traveling exhib, 82-83; Art in the Metroplex, Tex Christian Univ, Ft Worth, 83; Delta States Art Ann, Ark Art Ctr, Little Rock, 83; Works on Paper, SW Tex State Univ, San Marcos & Rutgers Univ, Camden, NJ, 83. *Teaching:* Prof painting & design, Univ Tex, Arlington, 59-92. *Awards:* Purchase Awards, Works on Paper, Portsmouth Art Ctr, 82 & Delta States Exhib, Ark Art Ctr, 83. *Mem:* Col Art Asn. *Media:* Oil, Pencil. *Mailing Add:* 1116 Mockingbird Ln Arlington TX 76013

TURNURE, JAMES HARVEY
EDUCATOR, HISTORIAN
b Yonkers, NY, July 8, 24. *Study:* Princeton Univ, AB, MFA(art hist), PhD. *Teaching:* Instr, Cornell Univ, Ithaca, NY, 53-58, asst prof, 58-64, assoc prof, 64-68; prof, Bucknell Univ, Lewisburg, Pa, 69-, Samuel H Kress Prof art hist, 74-92; retired. *Mem:* Archeol Inst Am. *Res:* Interpretation of evidence in archaeology and art history. *Publ:* Auth, Statuette of Imhotep, Rec of Art Mus, 52 & Princeton's enigmatic relief, 63, Princeton Univ; auth, Late style of Ambrogio Figino, Art Bulletin, 65; contribr, Il Duomo di Milano, Edizioni La Rete, 69. *Mailing Add:* RR 1 Lewisburg PA 17837

TUSTIAN, BRENDA HARRIS
PAINTER, PUBLISHER
b Birmingham, Ala, Jan 20, 43. *Study:* Univ Tenn, studied with Kermit Ewing, 63. *Work:* Coca-Cola Corp, Dow Chemical Corp, IBM Corp, Cox Broadcasting Corp, Atlanta; Reinhardt Col, Waleska, Ga. *Comn:* official 1996 poster, Semco Productions Inc, Atlanta, 96; official 1996 print, Atlanta Dogwood Festival, 96; 34″ x 42″ dogwood painting, Northside Hosp, Atlanta, 98. *Exhib:* Festival of the Masters, Walt Disney World, 80; Yellow Daisy Festival, Stone Mountain, Ga, 89-98; Cent Pa Art Asn Festival of Art, Pa State Univ, 91; City of Ann Arbor Art Festival, Mich, 96-98; one-woman show, Reinhardt Col, Waleska, Ga, 97. *Bibliog:* Christine Antolik & Mike Kendrick (auths), Art Trends, 96 & Watercolor Magic, 98. *Mem:* Southern Watercolor Soc; Am Watercolor Soc; juried mem Atlanta Artists Club; assoc mem Ga Watercolor Soc. *Media:* Watercolor. *Mailing Add:* 1579 Julius Bridge Rd Ball Ground GA 30107

TUTTLE, LISA
CONCEPTUAL ARTIST, CURATOR
b Little Rock, Ark, Sept 25, 51. *Study:* New Col, Sarasota, Fla, BA, 74. *Comn:* Video installations, Memphis Contemp Art Ctr, Tenn, 88, New Visions Gallery, IMAGE Film/Video, Atlanta, Ga, 88, New South Group, NY, 89, Arts Festival, Atlanta, Ga, 90 & High Mus Art, 91. *Exhib:* Solo exhibs, Running Diana, Seven Stages, Atlanta, Ga, 88, Vindication of Lilith, Albany Mus Art, Ga, 89 & Ga Mus Art, Athens, Ga, 93; Between Myth and Reality: New Southern Photog, Aperture Found, NY, 89; Rethinking the Sacred Image, Ga State Univ Gallery, 90; Artists on the Discovery of the New World, Agnes Scott Col, Decatur, Ga, 92; Constitutions, Spelman Col, Atlanta, Ga, 93; and others. *Collection Arranged:* Small scale sculpture, 87, 1938-88: The Work of Five Black Women Artists, 88, The Assembled Object, 89, Ecos del Espiritu, 90; New History: Buchanan/Edwards/Hassinger, 90, Oh, Those four white walls, Gallery as Context, 90; Contemporary Bronze: Process and Object, 91; Cross-Cultural Explorations, 92; The Metaphorical Machine, 93; Money Changes Everything, Or Seeking the Souk, 94. *Pos:* Assoc cur, Nexus Contemp Art Ctr, Atlanta, Ga, 83-85; gallery dir, Nexus Contemp Art Ctr, Atlanta, 85-86; gallery dir, Atlanta Col Art, Ga, 86-93; visual arts dir, Arts Festival Atlanta, 93-. *Teaching:* Adj fac, Atlanta Col Art, 89-. *Awards:* Bur Cult Affairs, Artist Proj, Atlanta, 87; Fel Sculpture, Southern Arts Fedn, 91; Individual Artists Award, Ga Coun Arts, 93. *Bibliog:* Jerry Cullum (auth), catalog essay, New S Group, 89; Peter Doroschenko (auth), essay, Albany Mus Art, 89; Carrie Przybilla (auth), Southern expressions: tales untold (catalog essay), 91. *Mem:* Nexus Studio Artist, 82-88; Atlanta Gallery Asn (adv bd, 85-86); Atlanta Arts Festival (adv bd, 89); Fulton Co Pub Art Committee. *Media:* Video Installation. *Dealer:* Sandler Hudson Gallery 1831-A Peachtree Rd NE Atlanta GA 30309. *Mailing Add:* 1088 Amsterdam Ave NE Atlanta GA 30306

TUTTLE, RICHARD
PAINTER
b Rahway, NJ, 41. *Study:* Trinity Col, Hartford, Conn, BA, 63. *Work:* Fogg Art Mus, Harvard Univ, Cambridge, Mass; Metrop Mus Art, NY; Mus Mod Art, NY; Seattle Art Mus, Wash; Whitney Mus Am Art, NY; Stedekijk Mus, Amsterdam, Neth; City Art Mus, St Louis, Mo; and numerous pvt collections. *Exhib:* solo exhibs, Calif State Long Beach Art Mus, 97, Art Gallery York Univ, Ont, 97, Kunsthaus Zag, Switz, 97, 98-99, Fabric Workshop & Mus, Philadelphia, 98, Ludwig Forum fur Int Kunst, Ger, 98-99, Arts Club Chicago, Ill, 99 & Stiftung Schleswig-Holsteinische Landesmuseum, Schloss Gottorf, 2000; La Biennale di Venezia, XLVII Esposizione Int d'Art, Venice, 97; Circa 1968, Museu de Serralves, Museu de Arte Contemp, Portugal, 99; Landesmuseum, Schloss Gottorf, Schleswig-Holsteinische, 2000; Stiftung Schleswig, 2000; Sperone Westwater, NY, 2000, 03; Extreme Connoisseurship, Fogg Art Mus, Cambridge, Mass, 2001. *Awards:* Fel, Nat Endowment Arts, 68; Skowhegan Medal for Sculpture, NY, 98; Aachen Prize, Ludwig Forum for Int Art, 98. *Bibliog:* James Narwocki (auth), twistfoldlayerflake, New Art Examiner, 5/99; Michael Kimmelman (auth), Richard Tuttle: Two with any to, NY Times, 1/28/2000; Kenneth Baker (auth), Great Art from Humble Means, San Francisco Chronicle, 1/20/2001. *Publ:* Contribr, Art Int. *Mailing Add:* c/o Sperone Westwater 415 W 13th St #2 New York NY 10014-1104

TWADDLE, RANDY
PAINTER
b Elmo, Miss, 1957. *Study:* Univ Mo, Columbia, 75-76; NW Mo State Univ, Maryville, BFA, 80. *Work:* Mus Fine Arts, Houston, Tex; Dallas Mus Art, Tex; Mod Art Mus Fort Worth, Tex; Brooklyn Mus, NY; New Orleans Mus Art, La; Addison Gallery Am Art, Andover, Mass. *Exhib:* New Orleans Triennial (with catalog), New Orleans Mus Art, La, 86; Monumental Drawing: Works by 22 Contemp Americans (with catalog), Brooklyn Mus, NY, 86; SPECTRUM: Drawn Out (with catalog), Corcoran Gallery Art, Washington, DC, 86; solo exhibs, DW Gallery, Dallas, Tex, 88, Damon Brandt Gallery, NY, 89, 91, Southwest Craft Ctr, San Antonio, Tex, 89, Barry Whistler Gallery, Dallas, Tex, 89, 92, Moody Gallery, Houston, Tex, 90, 92 & 95, Univ Gallery, Univ NC, Chapel Hill, 91, Steven Wirtz Gallery, San Francisco, Calif, 91; Awards in the Visual Arts 9 (with catalog), New Orleans Mus Art, traveling, 90; Drawn to Scale-Cynthia Carlson, Michael Glier & Randy Twaddle (with catalog), Addison Gallery Am Art, Phillips Acad, Andover, Mass, 90; The State I'm In: Texas Artists at the DMA, Dallas Mus Art, Tex, 91; Point of View-Landscapes from the Addison Collection (with catalog), Addison Gallery Am Art, Phillips Acad, Andover, Mass, 92; Seeing the Forest Through the Trees, Contemp Arts Mus, Houston, Tex, 93; Texas Selections from the Art Mus of Southwest Tex, Dishman Art Gallery, Lamar Univ, Beaumont, Tex, 94; Texas Art Celebration, Cullen Ctr, Houston, Tex, 94; Stories, Moody Gallery, Houston, Tex, 94; and many others. *Teaching:* Lectr, Kimbell Art Mus, Fort Worth, Tex, 85, Univ NC, Chapel Hill, 90, Glassell Sch Art, Mus Fine Arts, Houston, Tex, 94; vis artist, Univ NC,Chapel Hill, 90; vis asst prof, Univ Houston, Tex, 93-94. *Awards:* Fel, Nat Endowment Arts, 87; Awards in the Visual Arts 9, SECCA, Winston-Salem, NC, 90. *Bibliog:* Susan Chadwick (auth), 3 Artists Present Provocative Exhibits, The Houston Post, 9/29/92; Mary Sherman (auth), New Faces Exhibit Reflects Different Moods, The Boston Herald, 8/6/93; Nancy Stapen (auth), Summer Brings Nature into the Galleries, The Boston Globe, 8/12/93; and many others. *Media:* Charcoal on Paper. *Mailing Add:* 808 Ridge St Houston TX 77009-7420

TWARDOWICZ, STANLEY JAN
PAINTER, PHOTOGRAPHER
b Detroit, Mich, July 8, 17. *Study:* Meinzinger Art Sch, Detroit, 40-44; Skowhegan Sch Painting & Sculpture, Maine, summers 46 & 47. *Work:* Mus Mod Art, NY; Los Angeles Co Mus Art; NY Univ; Fogg Art Mus; Vassar Col Art Gallery; Hirshhorn Mus. *Exhib:* Art Inst Chicago, 54, 55 & 61; one-man shows, Peridot Gallery, NY, 56-70; five exhibs, Mus Mod Art, 57-69; Mus Fine Arts, Boston, 66; retrospective,

Heckscher Mus, Huntington, NY, 74; 30 Yr Retrospective Photog, Emily Lowe Gallery, Hempstead, NY, 79; Mitchell Algus Gallery, NY, 94, 96, 97, 1998-2000. *Teaching:* Instr art, Ohio State Univ, 46-51; assoc prof, Hofstra Univ, 65-87. *Awards:* Guggenheim Found Fel, 56-57. *Mailing Add:* 133 Crooked Hill Rd Huntington NY 11743

TWAROGOWSKI, LEROY ANDREW
DRAFTSMAN, EDUCATOR
b Chicago, Ill, Sept 12, 37. *Study:* Art Inst Chicago, 55-59; Univ Kans, Lawrence, BFA, 61, MFA, 65. *Work:* Denver Art Mus, Colo; Ft Hays State Univ, Hays, Kans; Hastings Col, Nebr; US Nat Bank, Omaha, Nebr; Mountain Bell Corp, Denver, Colo; Colo State Univ, Fort Collins. *Comn:* Colo Coun Arts & Humanities, 78. *Exhib:* Second All-Colo Competitive Exhib, Denver Art Mus, 74; 2nd Brit Int Drawing Biennale, Middlesbrough, Eng, 75; Drawings USA-75 Biennale, Minn Mus of Art, St Paul, 75; Spree-Colo Celebration of the Arts, Denver, 76; Rocky Mountain Drawing & Painting Exhib, Aspen Found for the Arts, Colo, 77; Denver Art Mus, 78. *Teaching:* Prof drawing, Colo State Univ, 67-. *Media:* Graphite

TWIGG-SMITH, THURSTON
COLLECTOR
b Honolulu, Hawaii, Aug 17, 21. *Study:* Yale Univ, BE, 42. *Awards:* Whitney Award, Skowhegan, 91. *Mem:* Yale Art Gallery, New Haven (trustee); Skowhegan, NY & Maine (trustee); Contemp Mus, Honolulu (trustee); Honolulu Acad Arts (trustee); Whitney Mus Am Art (nat comt). *Collection:* Contemporary art, emphasis on the 80s and 90s. *Publ:* Hawaiian Sovereignty, Do the Facts Matter, Goodale Publ, 98

TWIGGS, LEO FRANKLIN
PAINTER, EDUCATOR
b St Stephen, SC, Feb 13, 34. *Study:* Claflin Univ. *Work:* Herbert F Johnson Mus, Cornell Univ; Gibbes Mus, Charleston, SC; Columbia Mus, SC; SC State Mus; Greenville Mus Art, SC. *Comn:* Winston Salem State Univ, NC; Nations Bank. *Exhib:* Salute to Black Artists, NJ State Mus, Trenton, 72; Directions in Afro-Am Art, Cornell Univ, 74; Studio Mus, New York, NY; US Art in Embassies Prog, Dakar, 84; Palazzo Venezia, Rome, Italy, 86; SC State Mus, 89; Uncommon Beauty Traveling Exhib, Am Craft Mus, Renwick Gallery, Wash, 94; Hampton III Gallery, Greenville, SC, 98; Milton Rhodes Gallery, Winston-Salem, NC, 98. *Pos:* Consult African Am art, Art Ed, currently. *Awards:* Award of Distinction, Smith Mason Gallery, 71; Merit Prize, Guild SC Artists, 75; Governor's Trophy, 80; Regional Award for Distinction, Nat Art Educ Asn, 81; Nat Distinguished Alumni, 86. *Bibliog:* M Carnell (auth), article in Art Craft Mag, 79; Rhoda McKinney (auth), Ebony mag, 88; African Am Lit, 92; Rosalina Ragin (auth), Art Talk, 94. *Mem:* Col Art Asn Am; Nat Art Educ Asn; Nat Conf Artists; Guild SC Artists (vpres, 74); SC Mus Comn; African Am Mus Asn (vpres, 84). *Media:* Batik. *Publ:* Auth, articles in Design Mag, 72, Negro Educ Rev, 72, Sch Arts, 72, Mus News, 72, Hist News, 81, Arts in Educ, 86 & Art, Culture & Ethnicity, 90. *Dealer:* Hampton III Gallery Taylors SC 29678; Chuma Gallery Charleston SC 29403. *Mailing Add:* 420 Woodlawn Dr Orangeburg SC 29118

TWOMBLY, CY
PAINTER
b Lexington, Va, Apr 25, 28. *Study:* Boston Mus Sch Fine Arts, 48-49; Washington & Lee Univ, 50; Art Students League, 51; Black Mountain Col, with Frank Kline & Robert Motherwell, 52. *Work:* RI Sch Design; Mus Mod Art, Whitney Mus Am Art, NY; also pvt collections in NY, Chicago, Washington, DC & Europe. *Exhib:* Contemp Drawings, 64, Twentieth Century Am Drawing: Three Avant-Garde Generations, 76 & The NY Sch: Four Decades, 82, Solomon R Guggenheim Mus, NY; Ann Exhib Contemp Am Painting & Sculpture, 67, 69, 73 & 91, The Sculpture of Color, 71, Am Drawings 1963-1973, 73 & 20th Century American Art: Highlights of the Permanent Collection, 83, Whitney Mus Am Art, NY; one-man exhibs, Milwaukee Art Ctr, Wis, 68, Whitney Mus Am Art, NY, 79, Thomas Ammann Fine Art, AG Zurich, 94, A Retrospective, Mus Mod Art, NY, 94, Photog, Mathew Marks Gallery, NY, 94, Gagosian Gallery, NY, 94, C&M Arts, NY, 94; Highlights of the Art Season, Aldrich Mus Contemp Art, Ridgefield, Conn, 68; Am Art Since 1945, traveling, 75, Drawing Now, 76 & In Honor of Toiny Castelli: Drawings from the Toiny & Leo Castelli Collection, 88, Mus Mod Art, NY; Word as Image, Am Art 1960-1990, Milwaukee Art Mus, Wis, traveling, 90-91; Utopia-Arte Ital 1950-1993 (with catalog), Sulzburger Festspiele, 93; Drawing the Line Against AIDS, Biennale di Venezia & AmFar Int, 93; Abstract Works on Paper, Robert Miller Gallery, NY, 94; C&M Arts, NY, 94; Sculpture (with catalog), Anthony d'Offay Gallery, London, 94-95. *Teaching:* Head dept art, Southern Sem & Jr Col, Buena Vista, Va, 55-56. *Awards:* Va Mus Fine Arts Fel for Travel in Europe & Africa, 52-53; Praemium Imperiale Award, Japan Art Assoc, 96; Herbert Boeckl Award, 96. *Bibliog:* Mark Stevens (auth), After the Heroes, New York Mag, 100-102, 10/3/94; Jed Perl (auth), Twombly Time, The New Repub, Vol 211, No 20, 28-32, 11/14/94; Dorothy Spears (auth), Moment to Moment, Arts & Antiques, Vol VXII, No 10, 87, 12/94; and many others. *Mailing Add:* Cy Twombly Gallery 1511 Branard Houston TX 77006

TYE, WILLIAM ROY
SCULPTOR
b Harlan, Ky, Jan 25, 39. *Study:* Western Mich Univ, BS, 63, MFA, 77; Wayne State Univ, MA, 67. *Work:* Sturgis Coun Arts, Sturgis, Mich; Douglas Community Ctr & Western Mich Univ, Kalamazoo, Mich. *Comn:* Fighting Gamecock (bronze), Sr Class 1969, Univ SC, Columbia, 69; Cyclists (three bronze figures), City of Battle Creek, Mich, 76; J Fetzer (portrait relief), Western Mich Univ, 82; 10' Bronze Seal, Western Mich Univ, 93. *Exhib:* One-man show, Kalamazoo Inst Arts, 77; All State Competition, Battle Creek Art Ctr, 80 & 81; Mich Fine Arts, Birmingham Art Ctr, 83; Kalamazoo Bronzecasting Co, Krasl Art Ctr, St Joseph, Mich & Cain Gallery, Oak Park, Ill, 85; Mich Outdoor Sculpture, Southfield, 87; Sturges-Young Civic Ctr, 93; and others. *Pos:* Proprietor, Alchemist-Tye Studio (foudry), Kalamazoo, 83-. *Teaching:* Teacher high sch art, South Redford Pub Sch, South Redford, Mich, 63-66, Clarenceville Schs, Livonia, Mich, 66-68 & Mattawan Conserv Sch, Mattawan, Mich, 70-78; art instr, Univ SC, Columbia, 68-70; head sculpture dept, Kalamazoo Inst Arts, Kalamazoo, Mich, 78-83. *Awards:* Hon Mention, All State Competition, Mich Nat Bank, 81. *Bibliog:* Linda Fortino (auth), Marriage of arts, Kalamazoo Gazette, 4/30/78. *Mem:* Int Sculpture Ctr; Chicago Artists' Coalition. *Media:* Bronze. *Dealer:* Cain Gallery 1016 North Blvd Oak Park Ill 60301. *Mailing Add:* 701 N Berkeley Kalamazoo MI 49007

TYLER, RON C
ART HISTORIAN, MUSEUM DIRECTOR
b Temple, Tex, Dec 29, 41. *Study:* Abilene Christian Col, BS(educ), 64; Tex Christian Univ MA, 66, PhD, 68. *Hon Degrees:* Austin Col, DHL, 86. *Collection Arranged:* The Wild West, Amon Carter Mus Western Art, 70; The Big Bend (auth, catalog), 75; The Image of America in Caricature & Cartoon (auth, catalog), 75; Posada's Mexico (ed, catalog), Libr Cong, 79; Alfred Jacob Miller: Artist on the Oregon Trail (ed, catalog), 82; Views of Texas: Watercolors by Sarah Ann Lillian Hardings, Amos Carter Mus, 87; Nature's Classics: John James Audubon's Birds and Animals, 92; Audubon's Great National Work: The Royal Octavo Edition of the Birds of America, 93; Prints of the West, 94. *Pos:* Asst dir collections & prog, Amon Carter Mus Western Art, 69-86; dir, Tex State Hist Asn, 1986-2005; dir Amon Carter Mus, 2006-. *Teaching:* Asst prof, Austin Col, Sherman, Tex, 67-69; prof hist, Univ Tex, Austin, 1986-2006. *Mem:* Am Antiquarian Society; Tex Inst of Letters. *Res:* 19th century American & Western American art & prints; Mexican art & printmakers. *Publ:* Auth, The Mexican War: A Lithographic Record, Tex State Hist Asn, 73; The Rodeo Photographs of John A Stryker, Encino Press, 78; Visions of America: Pioneer Artists in a New Land, Thames & Hudson, 83; Nature's Classics: John James Audubon's Birds and Animals, 92; Prints of the West, 94. *Mailing Add:* Amon Carter Museum 3501 Camp Bowie Blvd Fort Worth TX 76107-2695

TYLER, VALTON
PRINTMAKER, PAINTER
b Texas City, Tex, Mar 30, 44. *Study:* Dallas Art Inst, Tex, 67. *Work:* Tyler Mus Art, Tex. *Exhib:* First Fifty Prints, Pollock Galleries, Southern Methodist Univ, Dallas & Tyler Mus Art, 72; 8th Ann New Talent in Printmaking, Assoc Am Artists, NY, 72; one-man shows, Galerie Claude Jongen, Brussels, Belg, 77 & Vallery House Gallery, Dallas, 79; Rosa Esman Gallery, NY, 85. *Awards:* Second Place, Art in the Metroplex, 88. *Bibliog:* Reynolds (auth), The fifty prints--Valton Tyler, Southern Methodist Univ Press, 72. *Media:* Aquatint; Oil on Canvas. *Publ:* Auth, Jalons et Actualites des Arts, 1/77; Un Artiste de 33 Ans, Hebdomadaire, 2/24/77; Ultra, 12/81. *Mailing Add:* 4021 Cole Ave No 201 Dallas TX 75204

TYNG, ANNE GRISWOLD
ARCHITECT
b Kuling, Kiangsi, China, Jul 14, 20. *Study:* Radcliffe Col, AB, 42; Harvard Univ, Master Archit, 44; Univ Pa, PhD, 75. *Comn:* prin works incl Walworth Tyng Farmhouse, builder (with G Yanchenko) Probability Pyramid, 84. *Exhib:* work incl in Smithsonian Traveling Exhib, 79-81, 82, Louis I Kahn: In the Realm of Archit, 90-94, Mus Contemp Art Traveling Exhib, LA, 98-. *Pos:* vis distinguished prof Pratt Inst, 79-81; asst leader, People to People Archit del to China, 83; panel speaker, Nat Convention Am Inst Archits, New York City, 88; Baltic Summer Sch, Archit and Planning, Tallinn, Estonia, Parnu, Estonia, 93. *Teaching:* lectr, Archit Assoc, London, Xian Univ, China, Bath Univ, Eng, Mex City, Hong Kong Univ, 89; instr, Barcelona Univ, Spain, 97, also numerous univs., throughout US & Can; adj assoc prof, archit Univ Pa Grad Sch Fine Arts, 68-96; vis critic, archit Rensselaer Poly. Inst, 69 & 78; vis artist, Am Acad, Rome, 95. *Awards:* Fel Graham Found for Advanced Study in Fine Arts, 65, 79-81. *Bibliog:* Subject of films Anne G. Tyng at Parsons Sch of Design, 1972, Anne G. Tyng at Univ of Minn, 1974, Connecting, 1976, Forming the Future, 1977; Number is Form and Form is Number, interview by Robert Kirkbride, 2005. *Mem:* Fel Am Inst of Archit (Brunner grantee NY chap, 64 & 83, dir, mem exec bd dir Philadelphia chap 76-78); Nat Acad (assoc, 75, acad, 94-),CG Jung Ctr Philadelphia (planning comt, 79-97), Form Forum (co-founder, planning comt, 78-85). *Publ:* author, editor: Louis Kahn to Anne Tyng, The Rome Letters 1953-1954, 1997; contribr articles to prof publi. *Mailing Add:* 2511 Waverly St Philadelphia PA 19146-1049

TYRRELL, LILIAN
CRAFTSMAN, TAPESTRY ARTIST
b London, Eng, 44. *Comn:* Designs for Tapestries (pastel on paper, 30″ x 50″), Jabob Visconi & Jacobs, Cleveland, Ohio; Long Sky/Impending Destruction (tapestry, wool, linen & cotton, 22' x 10'), Pepper Pike Place Assocs Atrium, Cleveland, Ohio; Asbury Hill (wool & Linen, 6 1/2' x 18'), Nationwide Ins Development Co Lobby, Columbus, Ohio. *Exhib:* Solo exhibs, Media Images, Richmond Art Mus, Ind, 93, Abandoned Heroes and Other Works from the Disaster Blanket Series, Va Ctr Craft Arts, Va, 93, Cleveland Mus Art Invitational, 94, Tapestries and Other Works from the Disaster Blankets, Slippery Rock Univ, Pa, 95, Maine Col Art, Portland, 95, Urban Evidence: Contemp Artists Revealed, Spaces Gallery, Cleveland Ctr Contemp Art & Cleveland Mus Art, Ohio, 96, New Work Out North, Visual Art Ctr Alaska, Anchorage, 98; Am Tapestry Invitational, Ohio State Univ, Lima, 94; Conceptual Textiles (auth, catalog), J M Kohlar Art Ctr, Sheboygan, Wis, 95; The Spirit of Cleveland (auth, Catalog), Cleveland Inst Art, Canton Mus Art, Artspace, Lima, Riffe Gallery & Beck Ctr Cult Arts, Cleveland, 95 & 96; Viewpoint/Art as Message, Craft Alliance Ctr Visual Art, St Louis, 96; Howing at the Edge of a Renaissance, Spaces Gallery, Cleveland, 98. *Publ:* Auth of numerous exhib catalogs, 84-98. *Mailing Add:* 7908 State 88 Ravenna OH 44266-9194

TYSER, PATRICIA ELLEN
STAINED GLASS ARTIST, ASSEMBLAGE ARTIST
b Rochester, NY, July 1, 52. *Study:* St John Fisher Col, BA, 74; studies with Katay Bunnel & Dan Fenton, Oakland Calif, 83, Johannes Schreiter & Lutz Haufschild, Toronto, Ont, 84, Norm Dobbins, Albuquerque, NMex, 87, Kathy Bradford & Dan Fenton, Colo, 88, Ken von Roehn & Tim O'Neill, Toronto, Ont, Boyce Lundstrum, 91, 92, Virginia Gabaldo, Toas, NMex, 93, Newy Fagan, Cocoa, Fla, 95-96. *Work:* Rochester Lead Works; Collection of Paul DuFour, La State Univ Glass Dept. *Exhib:* Solo exhibs, Wilson Gallery, Rochester, 77-79, B Forman Invitational, Rochester, 83, Gallery at 15 Stops, Ithaca, NY, 84, Philadelphia Art Show, Pa, 85, Huntington Galleries, WVa, 86 & Philadelphia Port Hist Mus, Pa, 87; Street of Glass, NY, 83; Crafts Western, Burchfield Penney Gallery, Buffalo State Col, NY, 94; Earth, Sand & Fire, Niagara Community Col, 96; Guilford Glass Biennial, Conn, 96; and others. *Pos:* Mgr, Stained Glass Works, Rochester, NY, 74-78; prin, Patricia Tyser Glass Studio, Rochester, NY, 78-85; dir, Archit Glass Designs, Rochester, NY, 85-94. *Teaching:* Instr, State Univ NY, Brockport, 87-88, Norman Howard Sch, Rochester, 88-92. *Awards:* Best of Show Crafts, Quaker Arts Festival, 94; First Place Glass, Colden Valley Art Show, 96; Second Place Glass, Allentown Art Festival, Buffalo, NY, 96. *Mem:* Stained Glass Asn Am; Nat Asn Female Exec. *Publ:* Professional Stained Glass, 89, 90 & 91. *Mailing Add:* 1826 S Yucca Mesa AZ 85202-5748

TYZACK, MICHAEL
PAINTER, EDUCATOR
b Sheffield, Eng, Aug 3, 33. *Study:* Sheffield Col Art & Crafts, Eng MEd(arts & crafts), 52; Slade Sch Fine Art, Univ Col, London, with Victor Pasmore, William Townsend & Anthony Gross, DFA, 55. *Work:* Tate Gallery, London, Eng; Victoria & Albert Mus, London; Sao Paulo Mus, Brazil; Peau de Lion Collection, Zurich, Switz; Indianapolis Mus Art. *Comn:* Multiple, Documenta Found, Kassell, WGer, 68; mural scale paintings, Univ Hospital Wales, Cardiff, 71; designs for proposed mural, comn by Albert Simons, Ctr for Fine Arts, Charleston, SC, 77; design for wall hanging, SC State Ports Authority, Charleston, 79. *Exhib:* New Shapes of Color, Stedelijk Mus, Amsterdam, 66-67; Documenta 4, Kassell, WGer; Troisieme Salon Int des Galeries Pilotes, Mus Cantonal des Beaux Arts, Lausanne, Switz & Mus Art Mod, Paris, France, 70; 56-Group-Wales, a 20 Yr Retrospective, Nat Mus Wales, Cardiff, 76; Art-Patron-Art, Southeast Ctr for Contemp Art, Winston Salem, NC, 79-80; and others. *Pos:* Consult, News & Courier, Charleston, SC, 79-. *Teaching:* Assoc prof painting, Univ Iowa, 71-76; prof fine arts, Col Charleston, SC, 76-. *Awards:* French Govt Fine Art Scholar, 56; First Prize, John Moores Liverpool Exhib 5, 65; Comn Award, Arts Coun Great Britain, 69. *Bibliog:* Edward Lucie Smith & Patricia White (auth), Art in Britain, 1969-1970, Dent, London, 71; Anthony F Janson (auth), Profile-Michael Tyzack, Art Voices South, 80. *Mem:* Artists Int Asn, London (vchmn, 64-66, exec comt, 64-68); Col Art Asn Am. *Dealer:* Gillain Jason Gallery 42 Inverness St London NW1 England

U

UBANS, JURIS K
PAINTER, EDUCATOR
b Riga, Latvia, July 12, 38; US citizen. *Study:* Yale Univ, with William Bailey & Bernard Chaet, 65; Syracuse Univ, BFA, 66, with Ainslee Burke & Frederick Hauck; Pa State Univ, MFA, 68, with Enrique Montenegro & Eugenio Battisti. *Work:* Yale Univ; Syracuse Univ; Pa State Univ; Univ Southern Maine; and pvt collections. *Comn:* A Season in Hell (ballet visuals), Syracuse Univ, NY, 66; Good Woman of Setzuan (theater visuals), Univ Maine, Portland-Gorham, 72, Renascence (planetarium visuals), 75 & From Morn Till Midnight (theater visuals), 76; Photography Maine 1973 (poster, catalog & cert design), Maine State Comn on Arts & Humanities, 73. *Exhib:* Everson Mus Art, Syracuse, 66; Nat Exhib Prints & Drawings, Okla Art Ctr, Okla, 69-70; Statements in Media, Haystack Traveling Exhib, 72-73; solo shows, Univ Maine, Augusta, 74 & Univ of the South, Sewanee, Tenn, 78; First Light Traveling Show, Calif, 75-76; Grand Valley State Col, Allendale, Mich, 79; and others. *Collection Arranged:* As It Was (auth, ed, catalog), 74, Ben Shahn-Photographs (auth & ed, catalog), 76 & Walker-Evans-Photographs, 78, Univ Southern Maine. *Pos:* Dir art gallery, Univ Southern Maine, 68-, chmn art dept, 74-; pres bd dir, Film Study Ctr, Portland, 72-. *Teaching:* From asst prof to prof painting, film, photog & drawing, Univ Southern Maine, 68-; coordr Soleri sem, Haystack Mountain Sch, Deer Isle, Maine, summer 71. *Awards:* Helen B Stoeckel Fel, Yale Univ, 66; Hiram Gee Fel, Lowe Art Ctr, Syracuse, NY, 65; Gregory Batcock Prize, Independent Filmmakers, 68. *Mem:* Col Art Asn; Nat Asn Sch Art; Am Film Inst; and others. *Media:* Oil, Mixed Media. *Mailing Add:* One Thomas St Portland ME 04102

UBOGY, JO
SCULPTOR
b Hartford, Conn, Mar 7, 40. *Study:* Univ Wis, BS, 61; self-taught sculptor. *Work:* Bedford Executive Hotel, Stamford, Conn; Landmark Bldg, Stamford, Conn. *Exhib:* Silvermine Art of NE USA, Silvermine Galleries, New Canaan, Conn, 82, 86, 89 & 90; Pindo Gallery Invitational, Soho, NY, 83; Sidney Rothman, The Gallery, Barnegat Light, NJ, 79-90. *Mem:* Nat Asn Women Artists; Silvermine Guild Artists. *Media:* Welded Steel, Polyester Resins. *Publ:* Contribr, Encyclopedia of Gardening-Foliage Houseplants, Time-Life, 80. *Mailing Add:* 319 Cognewaugh Rd Cos Cob CT 06807

UCHELLO, PATRICIA MILLER
PAINTER, EDUCATOR
b New Orleans, La, Apr 19, 54. *Study:* Tulane Univ, BFA, 76; Pratt Inst, MFA, 78. *Exhib:* Art League, 90-00; Have a Seat, Nat Inst Health, Bethesda, Md, 94; One-Woman Show, Shenandoah Valley Art Ctr, Waynesboro, Va, 95; Twenty for Tea, Nat Inst Health, Bethesda, 96; Landscape Invitational, 97; Gallery West Juried Exhib, 99; LMI, McLean, Va, 00; BTG, Fairfax, Va, 00; Realism Invitational, The Athenaeum 2000. *Pos:* Visual arts panelist, Alexandria Comn Arts, Va, 89-92; artist, Winsor-Newton Demonstr, 96. *Teaching:* Instr art, Studio, 90-00, Northern Va Community Col, Alexandria, Va, 94-95. *Awards:* First Prize Purchase Award, Am Ital Renaissance Found, 83; Equal Merit Award, Art League, 93; Art League, 94 & 99. *Mem:* Art League; Arts Coun Fairfax Co; Md Art Place. *Media:* Oil Paint. *Publ:* Illusr, Seaport Savories, The Twig, 94. *Dealer:* The Art League 105 N Union St Alexandria VA 22314; EC May & Co Alexandria VA. *Mailing Add:* 2001 Shiver Dr Alexandria VA 22307

UDVARDY, JOHN WARREN
SCULPTOR, EDUCATOR
b Elyria, Ohio. *Study:* Skowhegan Sch Painting & Sculpture, scholar, summer 57; Cleveland Inst Art, scholar, 55-58, BFA, 63; Yale Univ, scholar, 64-65, MFA, 65. *Work:* Newport Art Mus, RI; Columbia Broadcasting Syst, NY; Fogg Mus, Cambridge, Mass; Wellesley Col Mus, Mass; Mus of Art, RI Sch of Design. *Comn:* Outdoor site sculpture, Wellesley Col, Mass, 86. *Exhib:* Addison Gallery Am Art, Andover, Mass, 84; Newport Art Mus, RI, 89, 2002; Clark Univ, Worcester, Mass, 91; Virginia Lynch Gallery, Tiverton, RI, 92 & 96; Lenore Gray Gallery, Providence, RI, 96; Mus Art, RI Sch Design, 96, 98, 99, 2000, 2001-; Virginia Lynch Gallery, 98, 2000, 2001-2003, plus others; The Edmund Mauro Collection, Providence, RI; Wellesley Col Mus, Wellesley, Mass. *Pos:* Artist-in-residence, Dartmouth Col, Hanover, NH, fall 82; juror, Fel Awards, RI State Coun Arts, 85; vis artist, Wellesley Col, Mass, fall 86; nat screening comt, Fulbright Awards, Inst Int Educ, NY, 91, 92 & 93. *Teaching:* Instr drawing, Cleveland Inst Art, 62-63; asst printmaking, Yale Univ, 64-65; asst prof painting & design, Brown Univ, 65-73; chmn, Freshman Found Div, RI Sch Design, 73-77 & 79-82, prof design, 78-92, dir, summer transfer prog, 73-82; prof of design, RI Sch of Design, 78-. *Awards:* Distinguished Alumnus Award, Cleveland Inst Art, Ohio, 70; First Prize, Silver Medal, Centennial Sculpture Show, Providence Art Club, 80; Silver Medal, RI Sch Design, Providence, 90. *Mem:* Warren Preservation Soc. *Media:* Wood, Natural Materials. *Publ:* Illusr, Los, fall 68 & spring 70, Art J, winter 73, Art in Am, 3-4/75, Mich Quart Rev, spring 79. *Dealer:* Virginia Lynch Gallery 3883 Main Rd Rt 77 Tiverton RI 02878; Lenore Gray Gallery 15 Meeting St Providence RI 02903. *Mailing Add:* 60 Croade St Warren RI 02885

UELSMANN, JERRY
PHOTOGRAPHER
b Detroit, Mich, June 11, 34. *Study:* Rochester Inst Technol, with Ralph Hattersley & Minor White, BFA, 57; Ind Univ, with Henry Holmes Smith, MS, 58, MFA, 60. *Work:* Mus Mod Art, NY; Philadelphia Mus Art; Art Inst Chicago; Nat Gallery Can, Ottawa; Int Mus Photog, George Eastman House, Rochester, NY; Moderna Museet, Stockholm, Sweden; Nat Gallery Australia, Melbourne; and many others nat & int. *Exhib:* Photog in Am 1850-1965, Yale Univ Art Gallery, 65; Photog in the Twentieth Century, George Eastman House in collab with Nat Gallery Can, 67; one-man shows, Telluride Gallery Fine Arts, Colo, 95, Oasis Gallery, Marquette, Mich, 96, Northwest Mo State Univ Art Gallery, Maryville, 96, Hankins Gallery, Lansing, Mich, 96, Photographer's Gallery, Palo Alto, 96, US Embassy, Vienna, Austria, 96 & Yosemite Mus, Calif, 96; Nat Gallery Australia, Melbourne; Nat Gallery Can, Ottawa, Ont; Nat Mus Mod Art, Kyoto, Japan; Victoria & Albert Mus, London, Eng. *Teaching:* Instr photog, Univ Fla, Gainesville, 60-64, from asst to prof, 64-74, grad res prof, 74-; vis prof, Nihon Univ Art, Tokyo, Japan, 79. *Awards:* Guggenheim Fel, 67; Univ Fla Fac Develop Grant, 71; Nat Endowment Arts Fel, 72; Teacher/Scholar of the Year, Univ Fla, Gainesville, 75; Bronze Medal, Zagreb, Yugoslavia; Medal, City of Arles, France. *Bibliog:* James L Enyeart (auth), Jerry N Uelsmann twenty five years: a retrospective, NY Graphic Soc, 82; and others. *Mem:* Nat Endowment Arts (Photog Fel), 72; Fel Royal Photog Soc, Gt Brit; Soc Photog Educ (found mem & bd dir); The Friends of Photog (adv trustee); Kodak Educ Adv Coun, 87-90; and others. *Publ:* Auth, Silver Meditations, Morgan & Morgan Inc, Dobbs Ferry, NY, 75; Jerry N Uelsman-Photography from 1975-79, Columbia Col, Chicago, Ill, 80; Uelsmann: Process and Perception, 85, Jerry Uelsmann: Photo Synthesis, 92 & Uelsmann/Yosemite: Photographs by Jerry N Uelsmann, 96, Univ Fla Press, Gainesville; Museum Studies, 99 & Approaching the Shadow, 2000, Nazraeli Press; Referencing Art, Nazraeli Press, 2003; Other Realities, Bulfinch Press, 2005. *Dealer:* Laurence Miller Gallery New York NY. *Mailing Add:* 5701 SW 17th Dr Gainesville FL 32608

UGLOW, ALAN
PAINTER
b Luton, England, 41. *Study:* Cent Sch Art, BA, 64. *Work:* Fundacion Cult Televisa, Mexico City, Mex; McCrory Corp, NY; NY Pub Libr; Nat Gallery, Reykjavik, Iceland; San Jose Mus Contemp Art; Cin Art Mus; Mus de Beaux Arts, La Chaux de Fonds, Suisse; Nat Gallery, Reykjavik, Iceland; Staatliche Mus. Zu, Berlin; Stedlijik Mus, Amsterdam. *Exhib:* Biennial Exhib, Whitney Mus Am Art, 75; Une Autre Affaire, Le Consortium, Dijon, France, 89; The Red Show, Galerie Christine & Isy Brachot, Brussels, 90; solo-exhibs, Galerie Nordenhake, Stockholm, 93, Stadium Series Prints, Galerie Ars Nova, Goteborg, Sweden, 94, Second Floor Exhib Space, Reykjavik, Iceland, 94, Neue Arbeiten, Galerie Andreas Binder, Munich, 94, Gimpel Fils, London, Eng, 95, Galerie Bob Van Orsouw, Zurich, Switz, 96 & Paolo Baldacci Gallery, NY, 97, Stark Gallery, NY, 98, Galerie Onrust, Amsterdam, The Neth, 2000, Greidervonputkamer Galerie, Berlin, 2000; Silent Echoes, Tennisport Arts/Christian Haub, Long Island City, NY, 93; Phukn A, Reimission Gallery, NY, 93; Gallery Artists, Galerie Onrust, Amsterdam, 94; Galerie Tommy Lund, Odense, Denmark, 94; Galerie Sophia Ungers, Cologne, 94 & 95; Radikale Malerei, Galerie Paal, Munich, 96; High Precision, Halles Gallery & 172 Deptford High St, London, 97; Alan Uglow and Peter Holm, Galleri Tommy Lund, Denmark, 98; and others. *Bibliog:* Lily Wei (auth), Rev, Art in Am, 1/94; Andrea Edel (auth), Die Bespiegelung des Betrachters,

Kolner Stadt Anzeiger, 10/21/94; Justin Hoffmann (auth), Aktuell in Munchner Galerien, Suddeutsche Zeitung, 11/11/94; Martin Coomer (auth) Alan Uglow, London Time Out, 95; Ken Johnson (auth) Alan Uglow, New York Times, 98. *Media:* All Media. *Dealer:* Stark Gallery 113 Crosby St New York NY 10012-3301. *Mailing Add:* 103 Bowery New York NY 10002

UHLENBECK, ERICA
PHOTOGRAPHER
b Djakarta, Indonesia. *Study:* San Francisco Art Inst, BFA, 77, MFA, 79. *Work:* Munic Collection, Parliament Bldg, The Hague, Neth; Silver Image Gallery, Seattle; Stedlijk Mus, Amsterdam, Neth; Artotheek Amsterdam, Neth; Rijksdienst Beeldende Kunst. *Exhib:* Solo exhibs, Torch Gallery, Amsterdam, The Neth, 87, ZEBRA Gallery, Antwerpen, 88, Simon Lowinsky Gallery, NY, 90, Van Kranendonk Gallery, Den Haag, The Neth, 92, 94 & 97 & Gulf & Western Gallery, NY Univ, NY, 93; Kunsthalle Bielefeld (with catalog), Ger, 89; Rijkmus Twenthe Te Enschede, The Neth, 90; Ehlers Caudill Gallery, Chicago, 90; Revelation/Transformation, Rena Bransten Gallery, San Francisco, 92; Dutch Manneristic & Constructed Photog, Photofest, Houston, 92; Alan Chasanoff Photog Collection (with catalog), Mus Fine Arts, Houston, 94; Wall Gallery, John Jay Col Criminal Justice, NY, 96. *Awards:* Photog Grant, Amsterdam, Neth, 92; Nat Endowment Arts Fel, 94; Arts Stipendium, Neth, 95. *Bibliog:* Constructed for Photographs, Dutch Art Coun, 83; Amsterdam Purchases Art: Municipal Art Acquisitions Still Life in Photography, Rotterdam Art Coun, 84; Gottfried Jager (auth), Bildgebende Fotografie: Ursprunge, Konzepte und Spezifika einer Kunst form, 87. *Mailing Add:* 80 Wooster St Apt 4 New York NY 10012

UKELES, MIERLE LADERMAN
ENVIRONMENTAL ARTIST, SCULPTOR
b Denver, Colo, Sept 25, 39. *Study:* Barnard Col, New York, BA (history & int relations)', 61; New York Univ, MA (inter-related arts), 74; Studies in Colorado, 58-63; Pratt Inst, undergrad (studio studies in painting & sculpture), 62-64; Univ of Denver, cert (art), 66. *Work:* Flow City, New York City Dept Sanitation, 59th Marine Transfer Station; Tri-Met Westside Loght Rail Extension, Metropolitan Arts Comn Portland, Oreg; Flow Through, Maine Col Art, Portland; Flow Thru Out, Maine Col Art, Portland; Schuylkill River Partk, Schuylkill River Develop Coun, Philadelphia, Pa; Int Invitational, Hiriya, Nat Landfill Project and Exhib, Israel; GLORIA: Another Look at Feminist Art in the 1970's, White Columns, NY. *Comn:* Fresh Kills Landfill & Sanitation Garage No 2, Percent-for-Art Prog, NY; Tri-Met Westside Light Rail Extension, Metrop Arts Comn, Portland, Ore; Re-Spect, Inst Art & the City, Givors, France; Ceremonial Arch Honoring Service Workers in the New Service Economy, Olympia & York, NY; Vuilniswagendans, City Rotterdam, Holland. *Exhib:* Garbage The History & Politics of Trash in New York City, NYPub Libr; Methanogenesis, Mt Lake Workshop, Va Polytech Univ; Fragile Ecologies Traveling Exhib, Queens Mus, NY; Pit/Egg: A New Low for Holland, Zoetermeer, The Neth; Kunst-Kultur-Okologie, Bea Voigt Galerie, Ger; Ronald Feldman Fine Arts, 84 & 98; Mikva: The Place of Kissing Waters, Jewish Mus, NY, 86; Pit/Egg: A New Law for Holland, Floriade the Hague, Zoetermeer, The Neth, 92; Barge and Towboat Ballet, Three Rivers Arts Festival, Pittsburgh, Pa, 92; A Blizzard of Released and Agitated Materials in Flux, Taejon Int Expo, Republic Korea, 93; Garbage Ceremonial Arch, Version III, NY Pub Libr, 94-95; City Speculations, Fresh Kills: Imaging the Landfill/Scaling the City, Queens Mus, NY, 97; Uncommon Sense, Unburning Freedom Hall, Los Angeles Mus Contemp Art, Calif, 97; Mierle Laderman Ukeles, Matrix Gallery Wadsworth Antheneum, Hartford, Conn, 98; Hiriya in the Mus: Artists' and Architects' Proposals for Rehabilitation of the Site, Helena Rubinstein Pavilion for Contemp Art, Tel Aviv, Israel, 99; Measurement, State Univ NY, Long Island, 11/9-12/4/99; Artworkers, Newlyn Art Gallery, Penzance, Eng, 2/19-3/18/2000; Infrastructure Interface, 78-; Truck-Washing Fountain. *Pos:* Artist-in-residence, New York City Dept Sanitation, 82-, mem exec comt. *Teaching:* Lectr, Tate Gallery London, Kunsthallen Brands Klaedefabrik, Odense, Denmark, Off Arts, Harvard Univ & Radcliffe Univ, Cambridge, Mass, Rising Above Our Garbage, Exploratorium, San Francisco, Calif; symp organizer & post symp lectr, Weber State Univ, Ogden, Utah; pub art, The New Sch, NY, 2003; Univ of Washington, Seattle, 2003; lect at reception celebrating the first decade of pub art in Fulton Co, Atlanta Contemp Art Ctr, Atlanta, 2002. *Awards:* Grant, Joan Mitchell Found, 96; Grant, Anonymous was a Woman Found, 2001; Grant, Nat Found for Jewish Cult, 2003; Fel, Joanne Stolaroff Cotsen Mem Artist, 97; Permanent Pub Artwork Award, Maine Col of Art, 97; New York City Percent Award for Art Comn, Engine 75, Bronx, NY, 2000. *Bibliog:* James Barron (auth), Art Work is (Yes, Really) Garbage, NY Times, 6/10/93; Robin Cembalest (auth), Talking Trash with Mierle Laderman Ukeles, Forward, 11/25/94; Martha Schwendener (auth), Eleanor Antin, Portraits of 8 New York Women, 70 & Mierle Laderman Ukeles, Maintenance Art Works, 1969-1979, Timeout New York, 6/4-11/98; and others; Re-Spect, Inst for Art and the City, Givors, France, 93; Network Earth, Cable News Network (CNN), 93. *Publ:* Auth, Sanitation Manifesto, The Act, 90; Stretching the Canvas: Flow City, Environ Action, 7-8/91; A Journey: Earth/City/Flow, Art J, Col Art Asn, summer 92; with Anne Doran, Flow City, Grand Street 57, 96. *Mailing Add:* c/o Ronald Feldman 31-33 Mercer St New York NY 10013

ULLBERG, KENT
SCULPTOR
b Goteborg, Sweden, July 15, 45. *Study:* Swedish State Sch Art, cert(drawing & sculpture); Swedish Mus Natural Hist, anat, 4 yrs; Mus Des Sci Naturelles, Orleans, France. *Work:* Swedish Mus Natural Hist, Goteborg; Exhib Palace, Peking, China; Corpus Christi Mus, Tex; Los Angeles Co Mus; Denver Mus Natural Hist; City Ft Lauderdale, Fla. *Comn:* Monumental sculptures, Lincoln Ctr, Dallas, 81, Corpus Christi Nat Bank, Tex, 81, City Corpus Christi, 83, Corp Plaza, Boca Raton, Fla, 83, Lywam Art Mus, Wausau, Wis, 83, Genesee Mus, Rochester, NY, 84, Acad Natural Sci, Philadelphia, 87 & Nat Wildlife Fedn, Washington, DC, 89; First Nat Nabe, Omaha; Laeso, Denmark, 2002. *Exhib:* Ann Exhib, Nat Acad Design, NY, 75-94; Artists of Am, Colo Heritage Ctr Mus, 1981-2000; Art Mus S Tex, 85; Biologiska Museet, Stockholm, Sweden, 89; Munic Art Gallery, Luxemburg, 89; Gilcrease Mus, Tulsa, Okla, 91; Fleischer Mus, Scottsdale, Ariz, 2000; STX Inst for Arts, Corpus Christi, Tex, 2002; Nat Geographic, DC, 2002. *Pos:* Cur, Nat Mus & Art Gallery, Botswana, Africa, 71-74; cur/consult, Denver Mus Natural Hist, 74-76. *Teaching:* Instr, Scottsdale Artists Sch, 86, Loveland Art Acad, 93. *Awards:* Soc Animal Artists, 96; Rungius Medal, Am Wildlife Mus, 96; Prix De West Award, Nat Cowboy Hall Fame, 98. *Bibliog:* Article, Artists of the Rockies, winter 83; Kent Ullberg-Sculptor (film), PBS, 84; Kent Ullberg: Moments to Nature, 98; and others. *Mem:* Nat Sculpture Soc; Nat Acad Western Art; Nat Cowboy Hall Fame; Nat Acad (assoc, 81, acad, 90-); Soc Animal Artists & Nat Arts Club, NY; and others; Am Soc Mairne Artists. *Media:* Bronze, Steel. *Dealer:* C C Art Connection 3850 S Alameda Corpus Christi TX 78411; Trailside Gallery 105 N Ctr Jackson Hole Wyoming 83001. *Mailing Add:* Padre Island 14337 Aquarius St Corpus Christi TX 78418

ULLMAN, (MRS) GEORGE W
COLLECTOR
b Aug 23 1907, St Louis Mo. *Study:* Ariz State Univ, Hon PhD(humanities), 94. *Mem:* Costume Soc Am; Am Fedn Arts; Ariz Costume Inst; Desert Botanical Garden of Phoenix; Taliesin West. *Collection:* French furniture and paintings, Louis XV and Louis XVI periods; Haitian paintings; contemporary paintings of Philip Curtis; Spanish paintings, seventeenth and eighteenth century on painted furniture & glass. *Mailing Add:* 4642 N 56th St Phoenix AZ 85018

ULLRICH, POLLY
CRITIC
Study: Univ Wis, Madison, BA (jour), MA; Theory and Criticisim, Sch Art Inst, Chicago, MA in Art History. *Teaching:* Lectr in field; served on panels and juried and cur exhib. *Mem:* Chicago Art Critics Asn. *Publ:* Independent art critic, freelance journalist for NY Times, Newsweek, Chicago Mag, Chicago Sun-Times and the Milwaukee Journal, written analyses and reviews on contemp art for Sculpture Mag, frieze, Am Craft, KeramikMagazin, Bridge, Metalsmith, Fiberarts, Surface Design Journal, New Art Examiner, Ceramics Art and Perception. *Mailing Add:* 852 W WolframSt Chicago IL 60657

ULM-MAYHEW, MARY LOUISE
PAINTER, INSTRUCTOR
b Milwaukee, Wis. *Study:* Cardinal Stritch Univ, BFA, 81; workshops with Charles Movalli, Gregg Kreutz, Ann Templeton, 96, Matt Smith, Kevin McPhearson, 99-2000, Dan Gerhartz, 2002-03. *Work:* Courtland Med Ctr & St Mary's (Seton Corp), Milwaukee, Wis; New Visions Gallery, Marshfield, Wis; West Bend Mutual, West Bend, Wis; Nature Conservancy, Madison, Wis; Wausau Ins & Northwestern Mut Ins; Acuity Ins, Kohler, WI. *Comn:* Oil painting, Univ Wisc, 98. *Exhib:* Northern Nat Art Competition, LRC Gallery Nicolet Col, Rhinelander, Wis, 93; two-person invitational, New Visions Gallery, 95; Six Counties, John Michael Kohler Art Mus, Sheboygan, Wis, 94; OPA 4th Nat, San Antonio, Tex, 95; Nightwalker 96, Colo State Univ, Ft Collins, 96; OPA Regional, Chicago, 2000; Best and Brightest, Scottsdale Artists Sch, Scottsdale, Ariz, 99-2000; Solo exhib Henderson Art Center, Farmington NMex; Birds in Art, Leigh Yawkey Woodson Art Mus, WI, 2004; Edna Carlston Gallery, UW Stevens point, WI. *Teaching:* Instr oil painting fundamentals, West Bend Art Mus, 89-; plein air painting workshops, San Juan Islands, Washington, 95 & Minocqua, Wis, 96-2000; instr, oil painting, Dillmans Art Found, 99. *Awards:* 1st Place, Artists Mag Cover Competition, 94; Second Nat Cover Award-First Place, North Light Mag, 95; Third Place - FarEuropa Int Painting Competition, Stroncone, Italy, 98; Second Place - People Competition, Int Artist Mag; Cash Award, Flein Air Competition, Cedarburg, WI, 2000-2004. *Bibliog:* Glory McLaughlin (auth), First prize winner, North Light Mag, 3/95; Marsha Tuchscherer (auth), On site painter-teacher, Art Wis, 6-7/95; featured in Contemporary women artists, Cedco Publ, 96 & 99; Cynthia Marsh (auth), Painting nourishes artists soul, West Bend Daily News, 4/23/97; Prime Time, Sheboygan, 8/98. *Mem:* Wis Painters & Sculptors; Oil Painters Am; Alla Prima Int; Wis Women in the Arts; Tucson Plein Air Painters; Laguna Plein Air Painters. *Media:* Oil Paint. *Publ:* 100 Ways to Paint Florals, Intl Artists Pub, 2004. *Dealer:* Edgewood Orchard Galleries 4140 Peninsula Players Rd Fishcreek WI 54212. *Mailing Add:* 6871 Hickory Rd West Bend WI 53090

ULRICH, DAVID ALAN
PHOTOGRAPHER, EDUCATOR
b Akron, Ohio, Apr 18, 50. *Study:* Studied with Minor White, 70-76; Sch of Mus of Fine Arts, Tufts Univ, BFA, 74; RI Sch Design, MFA, 77. *Work:* Minor White Archives, Princeton Univ, NJ; Mass Inst Technol, Cambridge; RI Sch Design, Providence; The Photog Place, Philadelphia; Photogenesis, Columbus, Ohio; and others. *Comn:* Kahoolawe Proj, 93-95. *Exhib:* Recent Work of Twelve Photographers, Addison Gallery Am Art, Andover, 77; Second Sight-An Exploration Into Infrared Photog, Carpenter Ctr Visual Arts, Harvard Univ, 80; One-man exhibs, Hawaii: Landscape of Transformation, Gallery East, Boston, MA, 89, Bishop Mus, Honolulu, HI, 90, Hui No'eau Visual Arts Ctr, 91 & India Gandhi, Nat Ctr Arts, 94; Perspectival Multiples (catalog) Mus de Arte Contemp Gallery Caralas, Venezuela, 90; Image XVIII, Amfal Plaza, Honolulu, 91; Artists of Hawaii, Honolulu Acad Arts, 92; Contemp Mus, Honolulu, Hawaii, 93. *Pos:* Dir, Prospect Street Gallery, Cambridge, 73-74; exec dir, Hui No'eau Visual Arts Ctr, Maui, Hawaii, 91-93, Pacific Imaging Ctr, Honolulu, Hawaii, 93-. *Teaching:* Assoc prof photog, Art Inst Boston, 77-, co-chmn, photog dept, 80-84, chmn, 84-91. *Bibliog:* Fernando de Trazegnies G (auth), El sonido de una sola mano, El Comercio, Lima, Peru, 78; Stu Cohen (auth), The art

of making a point, Boston Phoenix, 79. *Mem:* Soc Photog Educ; Photog Resource Ctr. *Publ:* Contribr, Aura, Mag of Contemp Photog, Buffalo, 76; Parabola vol XIV, No 3, 89, NY; Manoa vol 2, No 1, Univ Hawaii Press, 90; The Burning Island, Sierra Club Bks, 91; Parabola, Vol XVIII, No 2, 93. *Mailing Add:* 2841 Baldwin Ave Makawao HI 96768

UMLAUF, KARL A
PAINTER, SCULPTOR
b Chicago, Ill, May 16, 39. *Study:* Univ Tex, Austin, BFA, 57-61; Yale Univ, fel, summer 60; Cornell Univ, MFA, 63. *Work:* New Orleans Mus Art, La; Everson Mus, Syracuse, NY; Joslyn Art Mus, Omaha; Mod Mus Art; Dallas Mus Art; IBM Corp, NY, Austin, Dallas; Fogg Art Mus; Cornell Univ, NY; Okla Art Ctr, Oklahoma City; Ark Arts Ctr, Little Rock; El Paso Mus; Longview Mus; Metrop Mus & Mus Mod Art, New York City; Philadelphia Mus Art; and many others. *Exhib:* Ann Nat Painting & Sculpture Exhib, Longview Mus, Tex, 76, 79, 82, 84, 86, 87, 89, 90 & 91; Works on Paper Southwest '78, Dallas Mus Art; The First 20 Yrs, Tyler Mus Art, Tex, 83; Tex Art Celebration, Houston, 86, 88, 90 & 91; Totally Tex, Dallas, 86; Univ Tex, Permain Basin, 87; North East Missouri Univ, 90; solo shows, Univ Tex, Tyler, 95, William Campbell Contemp Art Gallery, Fort Worth, 96, Martin Mus Art, Baylor Univ, Waco, Tex, 97, Okla State Univ, Stillwater, 98, Art Mus Southeast Tex, 99, Mus Southwest, Midland, Tex, 99, El Paso Mus Art, 99, Imago Gallery, Palm Desert, Calif, 2000; Harris Gallery, Houston, 94, 97, 2001, 2003 & 2006; Martin Mus, Waco, Tex, 91, 96, 2002 & 2005; Longview Mus, Longview, Tex, 77, 86, 91 & 2003; Cline Gallery Santa Fe, Scottsdale, 2003-2005; Roswell Ctr for the Arts, 2004; Irving Arts Ctr, Irving Tex, 2004; Art Ctr, Waco, Tex, 96 & 2002; TCU Art Mus, Fort Worth, Tex, 2006; and others. *Collection Arranged:* 20 works, Hall Art Collection, Frisco, Tex; 10 works, Midwestern State Univ, Wichita Falls, Tex; 35 works, Tex A&M Univ, Commerce Tex; 60 works, Baylor Univ, Waco, Tex; 6 works, Longview Mus, Longview, Tex. *Pos:* Vis artist, Tex Tech Univ, 74, 85 & 87; Colo State Univ, 73, Austin College, Sherman, Tex, 74, Baylor Univ, Waco, Tex, 75 & 85, Ball State Univ, 75, Ariz State Univ, 79, Univ of Tex, Tyler, 86, Univ Tex, Arlington, 91, Emporia State Univ, Kans, 94, Okla State Univ, Stillwater, 98. *Teaching:* instr Art, Univ Pa, Philadelphia, 63-66; asst prof art, Univ Northern Iowa, 66-67; Prof art, E Tex State Univ, Commerce, 67-89; prof, Ind Univ, Bloomington, 74-75 & 80; artist-in-residence, Baylor Univ, Waco, Tex, 89-. *Awards:* Third Prize, Tex Celebration, Houston, 91; First Prize 49th Ann Competition, Abilene Mus, Tex, 93; Purchase Prize, 23rd Prints Drawing Competition, Ark Art Ctr, 95; Pres Award & Purchase Prize, 28th & 30th Bradley Nat Drawing Exhib, Ill, 01 & 03; Special Award, Tex, Artist Celebration, Houston, 2005; Merit Award, 23rd Ann Dakota's Works on Paper Int, Vermillion, SDak. *Bibliog:* Review, Houston Chronicle, Art Scene, 86; Lifestyles, Perspective, Ft Worth Star Telegram, 88; Artists Turn Memories Into Reality, Waco Tribune, 91; Karl Umlauf at DUAC, Dallas Morning News, 93; Janice McCullagh (auth), Shrines, Mus Art, Waco, Tex, 94; Joe Kagle (auth), Salvage Series, Waco Art Ctr, 96; Art & Soul, Curatorial Review, Hall Art Collection, Frisco, Tex. *Mem:* Tex Sculpture Asn; Tex Fine Arts Asn; Tex Asn Col Teachers; Col Art Asn; Dallas Art Mus; The Mac, Dallas, Tex; Mod Art Mus, Fort Worth. *Media:* Mixed Media on wood & canvas. *Res:* Grants in fiberglass plastic & cast paper, A&M Univ, Commerce, 69, 71, 73, 75, 80 & 85; Grants in Independant Research, Baylor Univ, 91, 93, 96, 98, 2001-2002 & 2005-2006. *Specialty:* Am & Int Contemp Art. *Interests:* Taking trips to mountain regions, fishing; Building modified & classic cars. *Collection:* 19th & 20th Century Prints, Paintings & Drawings by 20th Century Artists. *Publ:* Auth, The First Twenty Years (catalog), Tyler Mus Art, 83; Karl Umlauf (catalog), 86; Karl Umlauf-Transitions (catalog), 89-91; Monograpg Ill Touring Retropective Exhib, 03; Recent Works in Cast Paper, Mark Thistle Waite (catalog); Transitions, William Wadley (catalog); Recent Works, Jan McCullagh, LongView Mus (catalog). *Dealer:* Imago Gallery Palm Desert CA; Parchman Stremmel Gallery San Antonio; Harris Gallery Houston Tex; Cline Gallery Santa Fe Scottsdale. *Mailing Add:* 307 S Borden St Lorena TX 76655-9778

UMLAUF, LYNN (CHARLOTTE)
SCULPTOR, PAINTER
b Austin, Tex, Jan 8, 42. *Study:* Art Students League, 61-62; Acad Fine Arts, Florence, 65-66; Univ Tex, Austin, MFA, 68. *Work:* Chase Manhattan Bank; PS 1, Long Island City, NY; Fox & Horan, NY; Reading Pub Mus, Pa; Pacesetter Corp, Omaha. *Exhib:* Whitney Mus Am Art Biennial Exhib, 75; Painting and Sculptur Today, Indianapolis Mus Art, 78 & 86; Seven Artists, Neuberger Mus, Purchase, NY, 85; solo exhibs, Hal Bromm Gallery, NY, 78-80 & Young & Hoffman Gallery, Chicago, 83; Oratorio Installation, Spinea (Ve), Italy, 92; Turchett Plurima Gallery, 85-2000; Basanese Studio Art, 82, 90, 2000; Galerie Biederman, Munich, Ger, 88, 92, 2003; Gallery Miralli, Chigi Palace, Viterbo, Italy, 2000; Revoltella Mus, Trieste, Italy, 2000; Eric Stark Gallery, NY, 2002. *Teaching:* Instr, Fairleigh-Dickinson Univ, 71-72, Philadelphia Col Art, 79, Kutztown State Col, 80-81 & Sch Visual Arts, NY, 81-2003; Ohio State Univ, 2004; instr painting & scuplture. *Awards:* Artists residency, Villa Waldberta, Feldafing, Ger, 2002. *Bibliog:* Carmelo Strano (auth), Europe-USA Unimplosive Art, Osterio Magno Palace, 98; Serena Bellini (auth), Umlavf and Vecchiet: So Close, So Far, Il Piccolo, 6/15/2000; Robert C Morgan (auth), Local Papers-A Quick Look at Williamsburg, NY Arts, vol 5, 23, no 4; Robert C. Morgan (auth), Lynn Umlauf, Edition Peccolo, Livorno, Italy, 2001. *Media:* Acrylic, Wire, Plexiglas, Sheet Metal. *Publ:* Auth, The question of gender in art, Tema Celeste, autumn 92. *Mailing Add:* 222 Bowery Apt 6 New York NY 10012

UNDERHILL, LINN B
PHOTOGRAPHER
b Oakland, Calif, Aug 8, 36. *Study:* Univ Calif Berkeley, 53-56; San Francisco Art Inst, with Dorothea Lange & John Collier Jr, 56-57; Univ Rochester, NY, hist 19th century photog with Robert Sobieszek, 77; Col Ceramics, Alfred Univ, NY, BFA(photog), 78; State Univ NY Buffalo, MFA(photog studies), 82; Visual Arts Studies Workshop, Rochester, NY, 82. *Exhib:* Solo shows, Light Work, Syracuse, NY, 84, CEPA Gallery, Buffalo, NY, 89 & Mednick Gallery, Univ arts, Philadelphia, Pa, 92; Toronto Photogs Workshop, Ont, 92; 494 Gallery, NY, 92; RIT, 93; Xenophobia, Ohio Univ, Athens, 95; 1995 Light Work Grant Recipients, Light Work Gallery, Syracuse, NY, 95; The Exquisite Corpse, Kirkland Art Ctr, NY, 98; and others. *Pos:* Edited & compiled photogs, The Buses Roll, W W Norton & Co Inc, 73-74; coordr, Copy Ctr, Visual Studies Workshop, 79-81, conserv tech, res ctr print collection, 81-82, coordr res ctr, 82-84. *Teaching:* Lectr & vis artist at var univ & cols, 83-92; asst prof, Dept Visual Arts, Mason Gross Sch Arts, Rutgers Univ, New Brunswick, NJ, 88-89; asst prof, Dept Art Media Studies, Col Visual Performing Arts, Syracuse Univ, NY, 89-92, instr photog, Div Int Prog Abroad (Florence, Italy), 90; vis asst prof, Dept Art & Art Hist, Colgate Univ, Hamilton, NY, 92-95 & asst prof, 95-; vis artist/instr, Carleton Col, Northfield, Minn, 94. *Awards:* Artist-in-residence, Light Work, Syracuse, NY, 83; Nat Endowment Arts, Visual Artists Fel, 84 & 90; New York Found Arts, Photogr's Fel, 89, Catalog Grant, 97. *Bibliog:* Esther Parada (auth), Women's vision extends the map of memory, Mich Quart Rev, winter 87; Marilyn Rivchin (auth), An interview with Linn Underhill, Q: A J Art, Dept Art, Cornell Univ, 89; Marion Faller (auth), Lost and found: an interview with Linn Underhill, Afterimage, 2/90. *Publ:* Auth, The National Endowment reviewed: a panelist speaks out, Exposure, Vol 26, No 4, 89. *Mailing Add:* 622 Oregon Hill Rd Lisle NY 13797

UNDERHILL, WILLIAM
SCULPTOR
b Berkeley, Calif, 33. *Study:* Univ Calif, Berkeley, BFA, 60, MFA, 61. *Work:* Am Craft Mus, Cooper Hewitt Mus, New York, NY; Oakland Mus Art; Johnson Wax Collection Contemp Am Crafts, Racine, Wis; Carnegie-Mellon Mus, Pittsburgh; Phillip Morris Co. *Comn:* Ursa Major Welded Steel, Bradley Sculp Garden, Milwaukee, Wisc, 66; King Alfred Statue, Alfred Univ, 88. *Exhib:* Solo exhibs, Blumenthal Gallery, NY, 63, Fosdick-Nelson Gallery, Alfred Univ, NY, 78, Garth Clark Gallery, NY, 89, Los Angeles, 90; Our Ladies of Art, Kohler Arts Ctr, Sheboygan, Wis, 90; The Gold Show, Garth Clark Gallery, Los Angeles, 91; The Ritual Object, Dworkman Gallery, Sarasota, Fla, 92; Art Alliance Gallery, Philadelphia, 92; Contemp Am Metalsmiths, Shalin Gallery, Los Angeles, 92; New Bronze Age, Pittsburgh Mus Contemp Crafts, 92; Contemp Cast Iron-Four Artists, Lithgow Gallery, Seattle, Wash, 93; Selections from Permanent Collection, Mus Contemp Crafts, NY, 93. *Teaching:* Instr, Pratt Inst, Brooklyn, 64-65, Columbia Teacher's Col, NY, 66-67 & NY Univ, 68-69; assoc prof, NY State Col Ceramics, Alfred Univ, NY, 69-97, ret. *Awards:* Purchase Prize, Oakland Art Mus, Calif, 61; Grant, Louis Comfort Tiffany Found, 64; Visual Artists Fel, Nat Endowment Arts, 86; NY State Found Arts fel, 88; Kohler Art Ctr & Co Artist-in-Residence Prog, Wis, 88. *Bibliog:* Oppi Untract (auth), Metal Techniques for Craftsmen, 68; Lee Nordness (auth), Objects: USA, 70; Ed Lebow (auth), William Underhill, Metalsmith, Winter, 87. *Mem:* Am Crafts Coun. *Media:* Bronze. *Mailing Add:* 312 W State St Wellsville NY 14895

UNTERSEHER, CHRIS CHRISTIAN
SCULPTOR
b Portland, Ore, May 14, 43. *Study:* San Francisco State Col, BA, 65; Univ Calif, Davis, MA, 67. *Work:* Objects USA, Johnson Wax Collection, Racine, Wis; Allan Stone Galleries Collection, NY; Jim Newman Found, San Francisco, Calif; Oakland Mus, Calif. *Comn:* Vet Admin Hosp, Reno, Nev. *Exhib:* Objects USA, Johnson Wax Collection, int traveling show, 69-73; 20 Americans, Mus Contemp Crafts, NY, 71; one-man shows, Hansen-Fuller Gallery, San Francisco, 67-70 & De Young Mus, San Francisco, Calif, 68 & 77; Clay, Whitney Mus, NY, 74; Quay Ceramics Gallery, San Francisco, 75 & 77; Los Angeles County Mus Art, 2000; Cantor Arts Ctr, Stanford Univ, 2005-06. *Teaching:* Instr ceramics, Univ Calif, Davis, 68-69; instr ceramics, Univ Cincinnati, 69-70; chmn ceramics dept, Univ Nev, Reno, 70-, assoc prof art, 78-. *Awards:* Purchase Award, Mem Union Art Gallery, Univ Calif, Davis, 68; Sr Fel, Nat Educ Assn, 81. *Bibliog:* Jo Lauria (auth), Color and Fire, Rizzoli Publs; Charlotte Speight and John Toki (auths), Make It in Clay, Mayfield Publ; Charlotte Speight (auth), Hands in Clay, Alfred Publ. *Mem:* Am Crafts Coun. *Mailing Add:* 1360 Burbank St Alameda CA 94501

UPTON, JOHN DAVID
EDUCATOR, CURATOR
b Des Moines, Iowa, May 4, 32. *Study:* Calif Sch Fine Arts; Univ Rochester, with Minor White & Beaumont Newhall; Univ Calif, Berkeley; Calif State Univ Long Beach, BA & grad study art hist. *Work:* Mass Inst Technol Creative Photog Collection, Cambridge; Fine Arts Collection, Metrop Mus Art. *Exhib:* 15 Am Photogrs, Houston Mus Contemp Art, 64; one-man shows, Mass Inst Technol Creative Photog Gallery, Cambridge, 65 & Camerawork Gallery, Costa Mesa, Calif, 68; Light 7, Mass Inst Technol Art Gallery, Cambridge, 68. *Collection Arranged:* The Photograph as: Metaphor, Object & Document of Concept (auth, catalog), 74 & The Photograph as Artifice (auth, catalog), 78, Calif State Univ Long Beach; Color as Form: A History of Color Photography, Corcoran Gallery Art, Washington, DC, 82. *Pos:* Chmn dept of photog & chmn div of fine arts, Orange Coast Col, Costa Mesa, Calif, 63-; vis cur, Int Mus Photog, George Eastman House, Rochester, NY, 79-82. *Teaching:* Prof hist of photog & creative photog, Orange Coast Col, Costa Mesa, Calif, 63-; vis lectr hist photog, Univ Calif, Los Angeles, 75, Calif Inst Arts, Valencia, 83-85; Calif State Univ Fullerton, 75-91. *Awards:* Ann Award for Contributions to Photog Ed and the Hist of Photog, Calif Mus Photog, Univ Calif, Riverside, 88. *Bibliog:* Minor White (auth), Photographers Northwest, Aperture, Vol 11, No 3, 64. *Mem:* Soc for Photog Educ (mem bd trustees, 75-79); Friends Photog (mem bd trustees, 74-80). *Res:* History of photography since 1900, especially Alfred Steiglitz, Minor White & Edward Neston. *Publ:* Contribr, New Vision of the 70's, Photographers Choice, Addison House, 75; coauth, Photography, Little, Brown & Co, 76, revised, 84, revised, 92 by Addison Wesley & Longman. *Mailing Add:* 3020 Via Buena Vis Unit N Laguna Woods CA 92637-3054

UPTON, RICHARD THOMAS
PAINTER, PRINTMAKER
b Hartford, Conn. *Study:* Univ Conn, BFA; Ind Univ, MFA; Ecole des Beaux Arts. *Work:* Nat Collection of Fine Arts, Smithsonian Inst, Washington; Mus Mod Art, NY; Victoria & Albert Mus, London, Eng; Bibliot Nat, Paris, France; Montreal Mus Fine Art, Can; and others; Metrop Mus of Art, New York City. *Comn:* Eros Thanatos Suite (German poem & woodcuts), Interlaken Corp, Providence, RI, 67; Salamovka Poster (limited ed silkscreen), Okla Art Ctr, Oklahoma City, 74; River Road Suite (lithographs), Salmagundi Mag for the Humanities, 76 & Robert Lowell at 66 (suite of drawings), 77; Ballingen Landscape, Rutgers Center for Innovative Print & Paper, NJ. *Exhib:* The Delaware Water Gap, Corcoran Gallery Art, Washington, 75; Nat Collection Prints & Poetry, Libr Cong, Washington, 76-77; Retrospective of prints from Elvehejm Art Ctr, Atelier 17, France, 77; Okla Art Ctr, 77; Weatherspoon Art Gallery, Greensboro, NC, 77; Tweed Mus Art, Duluth, Minn, 77; Paysage Demoralise--Landscape at the End of the Century, Grey Art Gallery, NY Univ; solo shows, List Gallery, Swathmore Col, Ben Shahn Gallery, William Patterson Univ, Georgia Mus f Art, Krannert Art Mus, Everson Mus Art, New Britain Mus Am Art & James A Michener Art Mus; The Artist in Rural Ireland: Images of North Mayo, Philadelphia Art Alliance; plus many others; Cooper Union, New York City; Nat Acad of Design, NY. *Collection Arranged:* Salamovka Series and Other New Paintings (auth, catalog), Oklahoma Art Ctr, Oklahoma City, 74; Bibliotheque Nationale, Paris; Metropolitan Mus Art, NYC; Nat Mus Art Inst, Washington, DC; Rose Art Mus, Brandes Univ; Montreal Mus Fine Art; Mus Mod Art, NYC; and others. *Awards:* Fulbright Fel; Nat Educ Asn Grant, Artists for Environ; Interlaken Corp Designer Award, Providence, RI, 67; Richard A FlorsheimFoundation Award, Nat Acad Design, 95. *Bibliog:* Sherry Chayat (auth), Richard Upton: Museum American Art, Art News, 92; Kenneth E Silver (auth), Richard Upton: Ten Years of Italian; Landscapes/Michener Museum, Art in America, 94; David Shapiro (auth), Landscape as God: The New Drawings of Richard Upton, 96; Umbria Rediscovered-The Chronicles of Richard Upton, Everson Mus Art, Syracuse, NY, 91; Michael Brenson (auth), article, Defining nature by it's battle scars, Grey Art Gallery, NY; Paul Hayes Tucker (auth), Univ Wash Press, 91, Richard Upton and the Rhetoric of Landscape (monogr); Robert Boyers (auth), The Drawings of Richard Upton, David Shapiro (monogr), Skidmore Col - Salmagundi, 97; Kim Smkapkh (auth), Landscape & Memory: The Tuscan Landscapes of Richard Upton, Cooper Union, 97; Richard Howard (auth), A Table of Green Fields: Richard Upton's Cortona Landscapes, Salmangundi, 2000; Fred Licht (auth), Richard Upton's Cortona Landscapes, Cur Peggy Guggenheim, Venice. *Mem:* Nat Acad (acad, 95-). *Media:* Oil, Water Based Media; Lithography, Intaglio. *Publ:* Auth, Impressions-A Paris Suite, 64, co-auth, Credo, 68 & Eros Thanatos, 68, Interlaken Corp; coauth & illusr, Models, 75 & River Road (with Stanley Kunitz), 75, Erebus Press. *Mailing Add:* One North Ln Saratoga Springs NY 12866

URAM, LAUREN MICHELLE
CONCEPTUAL ARTIST, ILLUSTRATOR
b Hartford, Conn, Nov, 9, 1957. *Study:* Pratt Inst, BFA, 80. *Work:* NBC & AT&T, New York, NY; Pacific Bell, San Francisco; Johnson & Johnson, New Brunswick, NJ. *Comn:* Collage of Golden Gate Bridge (pieces of ripped paper), Random House, Inc, NY, 85; relief portrait of Thomas Edison, Rupert Jensen Assocs, Atlanta, Ga, 85; collage of five portraits, Live for Life, Johnson & Johnson, New Brunswick, NJ, 85. *Exhib:* Student Scholarship Exhib (nat), 78 & 79 & 28th Ann Nat Exhib, 86, Mus Illus, NY. *Awards:* Art Directors Annual Award, 83; Commun Arts Illus Annual Award, 82 & 85; Print's Regional Design Annual Award, 86. *Mem:* Found Community Artists. *Media:* Paper. *Mailing Add:* 838 Carroll St No B Brooklyn NY 11215-1702

URQUHART, TONY (ANTHONY) MORSE
SCULPTOR, PAINTER
b Niagara Falls, Ont, Apr 9, 34. *Study:* Yale Univ, Norfolk, Conn, 55; Albright Art Sch, Buffalo, dipl, 56; Univ Buffalo, NY, BFA, 58. *Work:* Nat Gallery Can, Ottawa; Art Gallery Ont, Toronto; Mus Mod Art, NY; Victoria & Albert Mus, London; and others. *Comn:* Mural, Govt Ont, 68, bas-relief, 78; Sculpture magic wood (site specific), Macdonald Stewart Art Ctr, Guelph, Ont, 86; Sculpture our house, Rim Park Waterloo, Ont, 2003. *Exhib:* Carnegie Int, Philadelphia, 58; Guggenheim Int, NY, 59; solo shows, Winnipeg Art Gallery, Man, 59 & Walker Art Ctr, Minneapolis, 60; Am Acad Arts & Lett, NY, 60; Nat Gallery Can, Ottawa, 75; Mus Mod Art, Paris, 76; retrospective, Kitchener-Waterloo Gallery, traveling, 78-80; Thematic Retrospective, Art Gallery Windsor traveling, 88-89; Power of Invention: Drawing in Seven Decades, Tour, 03. *Collection Arranged:* MOMA, Nat Gallery, Ottawa Can, Walker Art Ctr, Canada Council Art Bank, Victoria & Albert London Eng, Art Gallery, Toronto ON. *Pos:* Artist-in-residence, Univ Western Ont, 60-65 & Kitchener-Waterloo Art Gallery, 81-83; Artist-in-residence, City of Kitchener, 2005; Cur Walte Allward Drawings 1910-1955, Ont, 2005-2006. *Teaching:* From asst prof to assoc prof, Univ Western Ont, London, 67-72; prof, Univ Waterloo, 72-, chmn, 77-79, 82-85 & 94-99; Retired, 99. *Awards:* First Prize, Albright-Knox Art Gallery, 58; Baxter Award, Art Gallery Ont, 60; Fel, Can Coun Sr Arts, 79-80. *Bibliog:* Dorothy Cameron (auth), Tony Urquhart: Reunion, 71, J Vastokas (auth), Archtypal imagery in the work of Tony Urquhart, 74 & Joe Bodelai (auth), Tony Urquhart: The story so far, 76, Artscan; J Vastokas (auth), Worlds Apart: The Symbolic Landscapes of Tony Urquhart, Winsor Art Gallery, Ont, 88 & Dialogues of Reconciliation: The Imagination of Tony Urquhart, 91; Michael Ondaatje (ed), The Broken Ark: Book of Beasts, Oberon Press, Ont, 69, reprinted 78; Terrance Heath: Tony Urqumart Power of Invention: Drawings in Seven Decades, 2003. *Mem:* foun mem Can Artists Rep/Front Artists Can (nat secy, 67-71); Jack Chambers Mem Found (chmn bd govs, 78-85); Can Conf Arts (vpres, 71-72); Order of Can. *Media:* Mixed Media; Oil. *Res:* French graveyards. *Publ:* Auth, The Urquhart Sketchbook, Isaacs Gallery, Toronto, 62; I Am Walking in the Garden of Your Imaginary Palace, AYA Press, Toronto, 82; Cells of Ourselves, 50 drawings chosen & annotated by G M Dault, Porcupines Quill Press, 89. *Dealer:* Moore Gallery 80 Spadina 4th Floor Toronto ON; Thielsen Gallery 1038 Adelaide St London ON Can; Harbinger Gallery 20 Dupont E Waterloo ON. *Mailing Add:* Univ Waterloo 200 University Ave Waterloo ON Canada

URSO, JOSETTE
PAINTER
b Tampa, Fla, June 5, 59. *Study:* Univ S Fla, BFA, 80, MFA, 83. *Work:* Springfield Mus Art, Springfield, Ohio; Mint Mus Art, Charlotte, NC; Tampa Mus Art, Fla; GE Fairfield, Conn; US Dept of State, Washington, DC. *Comn:* Fabric collage: Hillsborough Co Courthouse, Plant City, Fla, 96. *Exhib:* The Drawing Ctr, NY, 88; Bronx Mus Arts, NY, 90; Bernice Steinbaum Gallery, NY, 92; Galerie A-16, Zurich, Switz, 94; Galerie Industria, Wuppertal, Ger, 2000; solo shows, Kathryn Markel Gallery, New York City, 2000 & Museo de Las Americas, Old San Juan, PR, 2000, Lyons Wier Gallery, New York City, 02, Gescheidle Gallery, Chicago, 03; Leepa Rattner Mus of Art, Tarpon Springs, Fla, 2005. *Teaching:* Instr painting, Chautauqua Sch Art, NY, 84-90, The 92nd St Y, New York, 88-90, Art New England, 99-2003 & Cooper Union, 98-05. *Awards:* Grant, Pollock-Krasner Found Inc, 96; Award Ballinglen Arts Found, Co Mayo, Ireland, 2000, 2002; Basil H Alkazzi Award, 2000. *Bibliog:* The Message in the Media, Phyllis Braff (auth), NY Times, April 95; City Focus, Chicago Cutting Edge Hip to Blue Chip, Magaret Hawkins, ARTNews, April 2003; One View/ Two Visions, Melissa Kuntz (catalog essays), 2005. *Media:* Mixed Media. *Dealer:* Galerie Industria Wuppertal Ger; Sears-Peyton Gallery New York NY

URSO, LEONARD A
SCULPTOR, PAINTER
b Rome, NY, May 21, 53. *Study:* State Univ New York, New Paltz, BA, 75, MFA, 77. *Work:* Art Inst Chicago; Mem Art Gallery, Rochester, NY; Shanghai Univ Technol, Japan. *Comn:* MACE, Tri-State Univ, Angola, Ind, 90; 78 inch sculpture, Garth Fagan Dance, Rochester, NY, 90; 5 ft sculpture, Hansford Manufacturing, Rochester, NY, 91; Open Form, USA Today & Rochester Inst Technol, Rochester, NY, 92; Bauch & Lomb World Hq, 94. *Exhib:* Kanazawa Grand-Pris, Kanazawa Mus Art, Japan, 91; Dawson Gallery, Rochester, NY, 92; Chelsea Gallery, Cleveland, Ohio, 93; Brenden Walter Gallery, Santa Monica, 94. *Teaching:* Assoc prof fine art, Rochester Inst Technol, NY, 83-. *Bibliog:* Ron Netsky (auth), Sculptor Shapes Flowing Figures, Democrat & Cronicle, 88. *Media:* Metal; Acrylic, Oil. *Mailing Add:* 50 Rochester St Scottsville NY 14546-1343

USHENKO, AUDREY ANDREYEVNA
PAINTER, EDUCATOR
b Princeton, July 28, 45. *Study:* Sch Art Inst, 64; Ind Univ, BA, 65; Norhtwestern Univ, MA, 67, PhD, 79. *Work:* Bacchus & Ariadne III, 87 (Clark Prize, Nat Acad); Social Security, 87 (Purchase Prize, 89); Conviviality, 97 (Isidor Medal, Nat Acad, 97). *Exhib:* Gruen Gallery, Chicago, 83; Denise Bibro gallery, NY, 93; Yvonne Rapp Gallery, Louisville, 89; Chicago Art Expo, 96; Marriage Project, 96 (traveling); Fort Wayne Mus Art, 98. *Teaching:* Instr Valparaiso Univ, Ind, 68-73, asst prof, 78-79; instr Alan R Hite Inst Univ Louisville, 73-74; asst prof Northwestern Univ, Evanston, Ill, 74-75; vis faculty Columbia Col, 80-88; assoc prof Ind Univ-Perdue Univ, Ft Wayne, Ind, 88. *Mem:* Nat Acad (assoc, 93, acad, 94); Am Asn Univ Prof. *Media:* oil

USHER, ELIZABETH REUTER (MRS WILLIAM ARTHUR SCAR)
LIBRARIAN, LECTURER
b Seward, Nebr. *Study:* Concordia Teachers Col, Seward, dipl, DLitt(hon)Concordia Univ, 81; Univ Nebr, BScEd; Univ Ill, LSc; Cranbrook Acad of Art, Bloomfield Hills, Mich; NY Univ. *Pos:* Librn, Cranbrook Acad of Art, Bloomfield Hills, 45-48; catalog/reference librn, Metrop Mus of Art, NY, 48-53, head cataloguer, 53-54, actg head of libr, 54-57, chief, Art Reference Libr, 57-68, chief librn, 68-80; chief librn emer, Thomas J Watson Libr, 81-. *Awards:* Special Libr Asn Hall Fame, 80. *Mem:* Spec Libr Asn; NY Libr Club; Art Libr Soc NAm; Archons Colophon. *Res:* Art librarianship; bibliography. *Interests:* Modern art history; Bibliography. *Publ:* Auth, Rare Books and the Art Museum Library, Spec Libr, 1/61; Continuing Bibliography for the Fine Arts in the United States, Colloques Int, Paris, 3/69; The Metropolitan Museum of Art Library (Research & Reference) (Memorial Name: The Thomas J Watson Library), In: Allen Kent & Harold Lancour, ed, Encyclopedia of Library & Information Science Vol XVII, Dekker, 76; Staffing the Musuem Library, In: Mus Librarianship, ed, by John C Larson Libr Prof Publ, Chap 2, 85. *Mailing Add:* 517 NW Hope Ln Lees Summit MO 64081

UTKIN, ILYA See Brodsky, Alexander Ilya Utkin

UTTECH, THOMAS MARTIN
PAINTER, EDUCATOR
b Merrill, Wis, Oct 27, 42. *Study:* Layton Sch Art, BFA; Univ Cincinnati, MFA. *Work:* Milwaukee Art Mus; Univ Wis-Madison; Philbrook Art Ctr, Tulsa, Okla; Mus Contemp Art, Honolulu. *Comn:* Milwaukee Athletic Club, Carron & Black, Milwaukee, Wis; Northwestern Mutual Life Insurance Co. *Exhib:* Directions, Milwaukee Art Ctr, 75; Whitney Mus Art Asn, 75, Monique Knowlton Gallery, 85, Maxwell Davidson Gallery, 88, Schmidt-Bingham Gallery, 88, 93, 95, 97 & 99, Sherry French Gallery, NY, 88; Visions from the Northwoods, Milwaukee Art Mes, 77; Arthur Rogers Gallery, New Orleans, La, 89; 100 yrs Wis Art, Milwaukee Art Mus, 82; Mind & Beast, Leigh Yankey Woodson Art Mus, Wausau, Wis, 93; Am Realism & Figurative Art, 1952-1990, Miyagi Mus Art, Sendai, Miyagi, Japan, 93; Am Realism & Figurative Art, Cline Fine Art Gallery, Santa Fe, NMex, 94; Tony Folliard Gallery, 94, 96 & 98. *Awards:* Peninsula Sch Art Grant, Fish Creek, Wis, 73; Nat Endowment Arts, 88; Wis Arts Board, 89 & 94. *Bibliog:* Ellen Lee Klein, Arts,

12/85; Gerrit Henry, Art in Am, 3/86; John Arthur (auth), Spirit of Place: Contemp Landscape Painting & Am Tradition, 89. *Media:* Oil, Photographs. *Publ:* Illusr, A roadless area revisited, Audubon Mag, 75; Earth Care, Sierra Club & Audubon Soc, 75. *Dealer:* Schmidt-Bingham New York; Struve Gallery Chicago IL. *Mailing Add:* 4305 Hwy O Saukville WI 53080

UZILEVSKY, MARCUS
PAINTER, PRINTMAKER
US citizen. *Work:* Bezalel Aca Art & Design, Jerusalem, Israel; New Britain Mus Art, Conn; Tucson Mus Art, Ariz; Washington Co Mus Fine Arts, Hagerstown, Md; Hood Mus Art, Dartmouth Col, Hanover, NH; Cleveland Orchestra, Cleveland, Ohio; New England Ctr for Contemp Art, Brooklyn, Conn; Portland Art Mus, Portland, Ore. *Comn:* Musical Manuscripts, Chemers Gallery, Tustin, Calif. *Exhib:* Nat Print Competition, Edinboro, Pa, 83; Alexandria Mus, La, 84; 27th Nat Print Exhib, Hunterdon Art Ctr, Clinton, NJ, 86; Wesleyan Int Exhib Prints & Drawings, Wesleyan Col, Macon, Ga, 87. *Collection Arranged:* Nat Wildlife Federation, Washinton, DC; Environ Protection Agency, San Francisco, Calif; Berlin Philharmonic Orchestra, Berlin, Ger; Nat Audubon Soc, NY. *Awards:* Rapides Gen Hosp Purchase Award, Alexandria Mus, La; Purchase Award, Edinboro State Col, Pa; Purchase Award, 19th Bradley Nat Print & Drawing Exhib. *Bibliog:* Marja Eloheimo (auth), Marcus Uzilevsky - where music and art meet, 11/1/84; Larry Sibley (auth), Uzilevsky's art, Eternity, 10/86; Ruth Thompson (auth), Screen Printing, Artist of Sight and Sound, 3/88. *Mem:* Marin Art Coun. *Media:* All. *Dealer:* Oaksprings Impressions PO Box 572 Woodacre CA 94973. *Mailing Add:* PO Box 166 Woodacre CA 94973

V

VAADIA, BOAZ
SCULPTOR
b Israel, 51. *Study:* Pratt Art Inst Brooklyn, NY, 76; Avni Inst Fine Arts, BFA, 71. *Work:* Metro Mus Art, Jewish Mus, NY; Tel Aviv Mus, Israel Mus, Israel; Mus Mod Art, San Francisco; Philharmonic Ctr Art; Ravinia Sculpture Garden, Chicago; and pvt collections. *Comn:* Sculpture, Paine Webber, Puerto Rico, 87; Related Companies, NY, 88 & 93; LaSalle Partners, Roslyn, Va, 89. *Exhib:* One-man shows, OK Harris, NY, 86, 88, 89 & 92, Jewish Mus, NY, 88-89, Hokin Kaufman, Chicago, 89 & 90, Helander Gallery, Palm Beach, Fla, 91, Fay Gold Gallery, 93 & 97, Jaffe Baker Gallery, Fla, 96 & 97, Imago Gallery, Palm Desert, Calif, 97, Elaine Baker Gallery, Boca Raton, Fla, 2000, 02, Miriam Shiell Fine Art, Toronto, Can, 2004, Courcoux & Courcoux, Eng, 2005, Caldwell Snyder, San Francisco, Calif, 2005, Connaught Brown, London, Eng, 2006, Eckert Fine Art, Naples, Fla, 2006, Galerie Terminus, Munich, Ger, 2006; Utsukushi-ga-hara Open Air Mus, Japan, 92; Hakone Open-Air Mus, 94; First Lady's Sculpture Garden, White House, 95; Philharmonic Ctr Arts, Naples, Fla, 96. *Awards:* Ariana Found Arts Grant, 86; Nat Endowment Arts Grant, 88; Utsukushi-ga-hara Open Air Mus Award, 92. *Bibliog:* Jan Sjostrom (auth), Sculptor draws from earth, Palm Beach Daily News; Bernie Gould (auth), Sculptor harvests Brooklyn boulders, NY Times, 7/2/2000. *Mem:* Int Sculpture Ctr. *Media:* Stone. *Publ:* Boaz Vaadia, Stone Sculpture, 92. *Dealer:* Elaine Baker Gallery 608 Banyan Tr Boca Raton FL 33431; Imago Galleries 45-450 Highway 74 Palm Desert CA 92260. *Mailing Add:* 104 Berry St Brooklyn NY 11211

VACCARINO, ROBIN
SCULPTOR
b Seattle, Wash, Aug 14, 28. *Study:* Univ Calif, Los Angeles; Otis Art Inst, MFA(magna cum laude), 66. *Work:* Santa Barbara Mus; Library of Congress, Washington; De Cordova Mus; Los Angeles Co Mus. *Comn:* Hyatt Regency, Dallas, Tex, 78; Progressive Savings & Loan, Beverly Hills; Security Pac Nat Bank, Los Angeles; Koll Ctr, Irvine, Calif; IBM; Bank America; and others. *Exhib:* Otis Mus 50th Anniv Exhib, Los Angeles; Libr of Congress Nat Print Exhib, Washington; Univ of Calif, Santa Cruz; Santa Barbara Mus; Los Angeles Municipal Gallery, Barsdale Park: Los Angeles Bicentennial; Security Pacific Nat Bank Exhib. *Teaching:* Otis Art Inst, Parsons Sch Design, Los Angeles & Paris & Art Ctr Col Design; JP Getty Mus, Artists POV Series, Currently. *Awards:* Calif Arts Coun Grant, 79; Nat Endowment Arts Individual Fel, 80-81; and others. *Bibliog:* Joseph Mugaini (auth), Drawing, A Search for Form, Reinholt, 66; Innovative printmakers in Southern Calif, Southwest Art Mag, 73; article in Art Forum. *Media:* Metals, Resin, Concrete. *Mailing Add:* 3593 Berry Dr Studio City CA 91604

VACCARO, LUELLA GRACE
CERAMIST, PAINTER
b Miles City, Mont, June 2, 34. *Study:* Univ Wash, Seattle; Univ Calif, Berkeley; workshops with Peter Voulkas. *Work:* Antonio Prieto Collection, Mills Col, Oakland, Calif; Ceramics Monthly Collection, Columbus, Ohio; Spencer Art Mus Collection, Lawrence, Kans; Butler Mus Am Art, Youngstown, Ohio. *Exhib:* 32nd & 33rd Int Print Exhib, Seattle Art Mus, Wash, 61-62; Latitude 53 Gallery, Edmonton, Alta, 79; Mail Art Expo '80, Santa Cruz, Calif, 79; one-artist shows, Univ of Kans, 66 (125 pieces) & Lawrence City Libr, 67 (40 pieces); Kellas Gallery, Lawrence, Kans, 81 & 82; two-persons show, Lawrence Art Ctr, Kans, 86. *Awards:* Laguna Gloria Award, Tex Fine Arts Asn, Austin, 61; Kans Designer Craftsman Award, Kans Univ Art Mus, Lawrence, 68; Ceramic Monthly Award, Ceramics Monthly, Columbus, Ohio, 71. *Bibliog:* Luella Vaccaro and Her Pottery, Sunflower Cablevision interview, 79; Lynn Bretz (auth), Nick and Lu: A Couple of Artists, Lawrence J World, Sunday Arts Section, 5/3/81. *Media:* Stoneware, Clay; Acrylic, Oil. *Mailing Add:* 535 Kansas St Lawrence KS 66046

VACCARO, PATRICK FRANK
PRINTMAKER, PAINTER
b New Rochelle, NY. *Study:* Ohio State Univ; Youngstown State Univ. *Work:* Butler Inst Am Art, Youngstown, Ohio; Physicians Insurance Co, Ohio; Indianapolis Mus Art, Emmanuel Col, Boston; Nat Mus Fine Arts, Hanoi, Vietnam; Duxbury Art Complex Mus, Mass; East River Savings Bank, NY; and others. *Comn:* Presentation Print, Friends Am Art, Youngstown, 69; Honor Print commemorating first solar church, St Paul's, Ore, 80. *Exhib:* Boston Printmakers Ann, Boston Mus Fine Arts, 55-; Am Colorprint Soc Ann, Philadelphia, 59-; Butler Inst Am Art Midyears, Youngstown, 62-67; Carrier Found, NJ; Audubon Artists Exhib, NY; Italian Cult Ctr, Chicago; Exeter Academy, RI; one-man show, Butler Inst Art, Youngstown, Ohio, 94; Mus Mod Art; Butler Inst; Seattle Art Mus; Oakland Mus; Bethesda Art Gallery, Washington, DC. *Teaching:* Youngstown Univ, Ohio. *Awards:* Graphics Awards, Butler Inst Am Art; Acad Italy with Gold Medal, Parma, Italy; Dipl Merit, Univ Art, Salsomaggiore, Italy; and others. *Mem:* Boston Printmakers; Am Colorprint Soc. *Media:* Serigraphy; Watercolor & Acrylics. *Publ:* Illusr, Christian Herald; Together, Methodist Monthly, 69; Presby-Westminster Press, 71-72. *Mailing Add:* 7078 Oak Dr Poland OH 44514

VADIA, RAFAEL
PAINTER
b Havana, Cuba, Nov 27, 50; US citizen. *Study:* Miami-Dade Jr Col, AA, 71; Ecole des Beaux Arts, Paris, France, 73; Fla Int Univ, BFA, 76. *Work:* Greater Miami Pub Librs; Mus Modern Art at the Orgn of Am States, Washington, DC; Metro-Dade Govt Ctr, Art in Pub Places Trust, Miami, Fla; Citibank International; Visa International. *Exhib:* 49th, 50th, 51st & 60th Ann Nat Competition Contemp Am Painting Soc Four Arts, Palm Beach, Fla, 87-89 & 98; Drawing 1990 Nat Competition, Harris Fine Arts Ctr, Brigham Young Univ, Provo, Utah, 90; Broward Community Col, South Campus Art Gallery, Hollywood, Fla, 92; The Cult Resource Ctr/Metro Dade Govt Ctr, Miami, Fla, 93; Aqueous Open, Pittsburgh Ctr Arts, Penn, 95. *Pos:* Artist keynote speaker, Fla Art Educ Conf, Naples, 91; speaker, Miami Int Art Fair, 92; lectr, Broward Community Col, Hollywood, Fla, 92; North South Ctr, Cuban Nat Heritage (panel head), Coral Gables, Fla, 95; Acad Adv Miami-Dade Col, 2002-. *Awards:* Judge's Recognition Award, 31st Competition & Exhib, Broward Art Guild, Ft Lauderdale, 83; John Gordon Mem Award, 49th Ann Nat Exhib Contemp Am Paintings, Soc Four Arts, Palm Beach, Fla, 87; Cintas Found Fel, Inst Int Educ, New York, 91-92; and others. *Bibliog:* Helen L Kohen (auth), Bright days for art in South Florida, 12/80 & The Nation, 6/81; Joanne Butcher (auth), Art Papers, Reviews, Art News, 1/88; Giulio V Blanc (auth), Arts Mag, 11/90; Show Honors Artists from FLU (auth) Elisa Turner, The Miami Herald, 10/97. *Media:* Mixed on Canvas and Paper. *Publ:* Auth, Modern & Colonial Latin American Paintings, Sotheby Parke-Bernet, New York, 80; Rafael Vadia: New Drawings, De Armas Publ, Miami; auth, Art of Cuba in Exile, Jose Gomez Sicre, Munder Press, Miami, 87; Selections From Art Bank, Metro-Dade Govt Ctr: 27 Artists from Collection of Art in Public Places Trust, North Miami Ctr Contemp Art, Fla, 89. *Mailing Add:* 3130 Center St Miami FL 33133

VAILLANCOURT, ARMAND
SCULPTOR, PAINTER
b Quebec, Can, Sept 3, 29. *Study:* Ottawa Univ, 49-50; Ecole des Beaux Arts, Montreal, 51-55. *Work:* Banque d'oeuvres d'art du Can; Banque d'oeuvres d'art du Qué; Maison des Assemblées, Guernica, Espagne; Ville de Montréal; Ecole des Arts et Métiers, Asbestos; and others. *Comn:* Vaillancourt Fountain, Embarcadero Plaza, San Francisco, 67-71; Justice, Fountain, Palais de Justice de Qué; El Clamor, monumental sculpture-fountain, Santa Domingo, Dominican Repub, 85; Drapeau blanc, exterior monumental sculpture, Université Laval, Qué, 87; Passerelle Vaillancourt, pedestrian bridge (200 ft), Ville de Plessiville, 90; and many others. *Exhib:* Salon de mai, Musée d'Art Moderne, Paris, 62; First Ibero Am Symposium, Santo Domingo, Dominican Repub, 85; Contemp Outdoor Sculp at the Guild, Toronto, 82; Mus Fine Art Can, 90; La Sculpture au Québec (1946-61), Musée du Qué, 92; Collection au Musée, Musée d'Art Contemporain, Montréal, 92; Expos itinéiante a Travers le Canada, Musée des Beaux-Arts au Can, 92; solo shows, Galerie Maximum, Montréal, 84, Galerie Espace Global Montréal, 86, Caisse Pobulaire de Victoriaville, 87, Galerie d'Art Contemporain, Montréal, 90, Galerie Le Lieu et Mail Saint-Rock, Québec, 92; plus many others; and many other group & solo exhibs. *Awards:* First Prize, interior sculpture, 63 & exterior monumental sculpture, 63, Ecole des Arts & Métiers; First Prize, Int Competition for sculptural fountain, San Francisco, 69; and others. *Bibliog:* David Miller (auth), Vaillancourt sculptor (film), ONF, 63-64; Jean-Gaétan Séquin (auth), L'Univers d'Armand Vaillancourt (video), Radio Qué, Betacam, 84; Yvon Laurendeau (auth), Armand Vaillancourt, guercier de la paix (video), 92; Martial Lapointe (auth), Pierre et paix, J de Quebec, 7/24/87; A M Richard et C Robertson (auth), Performance in Canada, 1970-90, Inter ed, 91; Jocelyne Lepage (auth), A Vaillancourt, L'irréductible, La Presse, Montréal, 3/28/92; Pradel (auth), L'Art, la Résistance, L'Evénement du Jeudi, Paris, 10/23/86. *Mem:* Conseil de la Sculpture du Qué (founder); Conseil des Arts Visuels du Qué(founder). *Media:* All Media; Acrylic. *Mailing Add:* 4211 avenue del'Esplanade Montreal PQ H2W 1T1 Canada

VALADEZ, JOHN
PAINTER
b Los Angeles, Calif, 1951. *Study:* Calif State Univ, Long Beach, BFA, 76. *Comn:* Mural, Fed Bldg at border crossing, El Paso, Tex, 93; mural, Fed Bldg, downtown El Paso, Tex, 93; mural, Atrium at new Central Libr Bldg, Los Angeles, 93. *Exhib:* Solo Exhibs, John Valadez: Early/Recent Works, New Directions Gallery, Los Angeles, 83, Mark Taper Forum, 84, Simard Gallery, 84, Mus Contemp Hispanic Art, NY, 86, Lizardi/Harp Gallery, Pasadena, 87 & 89, Condenados, Saxon-Lee Gallery, Los Angeles, 90, New Visions & Ventures in Latino Art, Rancho Santiago Col, Santa Ana, Calif, 90, New Pastels, Daniel Saxon Gallery, Los Angeles, 90 & Domestic Allegories,

Galeria de la Raza, San Francisco, 91; Only Los Angeles Contemp Variations, Munic Art Gallery, Los Angeles, 86; Made in Aztlan, Centro Cult de la Raza, San Diego, 86; Symbolic Realities: John Valadez/David Baze, Dominguez Hills, 86; Primer Espacio de Identidad Cult, El Barrio, Centro Cult Tijuana, Baja, 86; Hispanic Art in the United States: Thirty Contemp Painters & Sculptors, Corcoran Gallery Art, Washington, DC and traveled, 87-89; From the Back Room, Saxon-Lee Gallery, Los Angeles, 88; Chicano Art/Resistance & Affirmation, 1965-85, Wight Art Gallery, UCLA, traveling through 1993 to Denver Art Mus, Albuquerque Mus, Nat Mus Am Art, San Francisco Mus Mod Art, Tucson Art Mus & Fresno Art Mus. *Bibliog:* Shauna Snow (auth), New Visions: Positive images through Latino art, Los Angeles Times, 3/11/90; Lynn Pyne (auth), Post-Chicano' art tries to 'break boundaries', Phoenix Gazette, 9/90; Susan Kandel (auth), LA in review, Arts Mag, 12/91. *Mailing Add:* c/o Daniel Saxon Gallery 552 Norwich Dr West Hollywood CA 90048

VALDES, KAREN W
DIRECTOR, EDUCATOR
b Los Angeles, Calif, May 25, 45. *Study:* Univ Calif, Irvine, BFA, 68; Nat Univ Mex, Mexico City, 69; Univ Chicago, Ill, 72; Fla State Univ, Tallahassee, MFA, 74; NY Univ, 83. *Collection Arranged:* Lynda Benglis 1968-1978 (with catalog), Lowe Art Mus, Univ Miami, 80; Vito Acconci: Installation, Miami Dade Community Col, 83; A Separate Reality: Florida Eccentrics (with catalog), Mus Art, Ft Lauderdale, 87; Suzanne Giroux: Video Installation, Univ Fla, 89; The Great American Lawnscape: Yard Art (with catalog), Univ Gallery Fla, 92. *Pos:* Cur exhibs, Art Mus STex, 75-76, Mus Art, Ft Lauderdale, Fla, 85-89; dir, Miami-Dade Community Col, Campu Art S Gallery, 76-85, Gloria Luria Gallery, Miami, 84-85, Univ Galleries, Univ Fla, 89-. *Teaching:* Assoc prof art & humanities, Miami-Dade Community Col, 76-84; assoc prof mus studies, Univ Fla, 89-. *Bibliog:* Elisa Turner (auth), A separate reality, Florida eccentric, Art News, 10/87. *Mem:* Col Art Asn; Am Asn Mus; Fla Art Mus Dirs Asn; Hispanic Fac Asn, Univ Fla. *Res:* Contemporary art and outsider art. *Publ:* Contribr, The Eye of the Beholder: SFla Collects Essay (catalog), Mus Art, Ft Lauderdale, 86; Styles, Strands & Sequences: American Painters & Drawing (catalog), Univ Fla, 90; auth (article), Coral castle, Forecast: Pub Artworks J, 92. *Mailing Add:* 1130 Bayshore Dr Niceville FL 32578-3007

VALDEZ, VINCENT E
SCULPTOR
b Mora, NMex, Mar 15, 40. *Study:* Univ Wyo, 67-70. *Work:* Nat Morgan Horse Asn Mus, Shellburn, NJ; Wyo State Mus, Cheyenne; Benson Park (outdoor sculpture), Loveland, Colo. *Comn:* Morgan Horse, comm by Anne Mears, Laramie, Wyo, 85; Monument of the Chase (bronze), Loveland High Plains Art Coun, Colo, 88; bas-relief, Tree of life, Ivinson Mem Hosp, Laramie, Wyo, 88. *Awards:* Best of Show, Western Regional Art Show, 87; Award of Merit, Anchorage Audubon Soc, 87; 2nd Place Bronze, George Phippen Mem Soc, 87. *Bibliog:* Anne Mears (auth), The magnificent Morgan, Today's Morgan, 5/85; Judy A Hughes (auth), Bronze: The rock of ages, Wildlife Art News, 1/88; Christina Leimer (auth), Metamorphic man, Art of the West, 11/88. *Mem:* Wyo Coun on the Arts. *Media:* Bronze. *Mailing Add:* PO Box 581 Laramie WY 82070

VALDEZ GONZALEZ, JULIO E
PAINTER, PRINTMAKER
b Santo Domingo, Dominican Republic, Jan 10, 69. *Study:* Nat Sch Fine Arts, Dominican Repub, 84-86; Altos de Chavon/Parsons Sch Design, Dominican Repub, 86-88. *Work:* Museo Omar Rayo, Roldamillo, Columbia; Museo de Arte Moderno, Las Casas Reales Mus, Santo Domingo, Dominican Repub; Altos de Chavon Cult Ctr Found, Bob Blackburn's Printmaking Workshop, NY; The Robert Blackburn Print Collection, NY; Brandywine Workshop, Philadelphia, Pa. *Comn:* Wood mural, Batista-Morera-Valdez Arq, Santo Domingo, 89. *Exhib:* Solo show, Instituto de Cultura Puertorriquena, San Juan, PR, 93, La Era del Mito, Galeria San Juan Bautista, Casa Alcaldia, San Juan, PR, 95, Transpositions, Museo de las Americas, San Juan, PR, 97, Toomey Tourell Fine Arts, San Francisco, Calif, 98 & 99, Museo de las Casas Reales, Santa Domingo, Dominican Repub, 99, Maison des Arts et de la Cult, St-Jean-sur-Richellieu, Que, Can, 99; Artist in the Marketplace, Bronx Mus Arts, NY, 94; Int Triennial Graphic Art, Bitola, Repub Macedonia, 94; II Painting Biennial of Latin Am & Caribbean, Mus Mod Art, Santo Domingo, 94; A Tribute to Bob Blackburn, Wilmer Jennings Gallery, NY, 94; Shades of the Spirit: Contemp Explorations in Printmaking and Drawing, Painted Bride Art Ctr, Philadelphia, Pa, 95; Art in Transit: A Dominican Experience, Intar Latin Am Gallery, NY, 96; Artist In the Marketplace, Benefit Gala, Bronx Mus Art, NY, 96; Invitational Exhib, DNA Gallery, Provincetown, Mass, 96; Small, Gallery Juno, SoHo, NY, 96; Inaugural Exhib, Toomy Tourell Fine Arts, San Francisco, Calif, 97; Small Works '97, Studio Sch Asn Inc, NY, 97; From the Studio: Artist-in-residence Ann Exhib, Studio Mus Harlem, NY, 98; New Strokes, Taller Puertorriqueno, Philadelphia, Pa, 98; Caribbean Connections, Discovery Mus, Bridgeport, Conn, 98; Inter-Actions: Urena, Cofone, Valdez, Julia de Burgos Latino Cult Ctr, NY, 98; 22nd National Print Biennial, Silvermine Guild Art Ctr, New Canaan, Conn, 98; Onani: The African presence in Contemp Latin Am and Caribbean Visual Arts, Taller Puertorriqueno, Philadelphia, Pa, 99; Papeles Preciosos, Galeria Ada Balcacer, Santa Dominto, Dominican Repub, 99; The S Files, Site Specific Installation, El Museo del Barrio, NY, 99. *Pos:* Admissions comt mem, Parsons Sch Design, Dominican Repub, 90-93. *Teaching:* Instr printmaking, illus, drawing, two dimensional design, Altos de Chavon/Parsons Sch Design, 90-93. *Awards:* Fel, Bob Blackburn's Print Shop, NY, 94; Mus Mod Art First Prize Printmaking, XIX Nat Art Biennial, 94. *Bibliog:* Marianne de Tolentino (auth), Julio Valdez: fresh air, 8/89. *Media:* Acrylic, Silkscreen. *Publ:* Co-auth, Impresiones de la computadora, Royal Houses Mus, 93. *Mailing Add:* 176 E 106th Street 4th Fl New York NY 10029

VALDOVINO, LUIS HECTOR
VIDEO ARTIST, EDUCATOR
b Bahia Blanca, Arg, June 7, 61. *Study:* Ohio Univ, with Arnold Gassan, BFA, 85; Univ Ill, Urbana, with Bea Nettles, MFA, 87. *Work:* Mus Mod Art, Rio de Janeiro, Brazil; Donnell Media Ctr, New York Pub Libr; APCLAI, Venice, Italy; Inst Cooperacion Iberoamericana, Buenos Aires, Arg; Univ San Diego, Calif; Mus Mod Art, NY. *Comn:* video, Cocteau Cento, Naropa Univ Audio Archive Preserv and Access Project, 2003. *Exhib:* II Cabo Frio Print Biennial, Mus Mod Art, Rio de Janeiro, 85; Dallas Video Festival, Dallas Mus Art, Tex, 90; Chicano Art: Resistance & Affirmation, San Francisco Mus Mod Art, Calif, 91; D'Ghetto Eyes, Kitchen, NY, 92, Committed Visions, Mus Mod Art, NY, 92; Black Maria Film Festival, Hirshhorn Mus, Washington, DC 93; Videonale Intermezzo, Kuntsmuseum, Bonn, Ger, 93; World Wide Video Festival, Stedelijk Mus, Amsterdam, The Neth, 97; Geme Biennale Int du Film surlant, Centre Georges Pompidou, Paris, France, 98; Third World Newsreel Retrospective, Mus Mod Art, NY, 98; Idea del Lugar, Museo Nacional Centros de Arte Reina Sofia, Madrid, Spain, 98; La Bienale di Venezia, Venice, Italy, 2000; BAC Int Film/Video Festival, Metrop Mus Art, NY, 2001. *Pos:* Assoc Prof, Art & Art History Dept, Univ of Colo, Boulder, Colo. *Teaching:* Prof video/computer, Carnegie Mellon Univ, Pittsburgh, Pa, 92-93; from asst prof to assoc prof video art, Univ Colo, Boulder, 93-. *Awards:* Individual Artist Fel, Nat Endowment Arts, 93; Film/Video Grant, Am Film Inst, 93; Ger Award Video Art, ZKM, Karlsruhe, Ger, 94. *Bibliog:* Coco Fusco (auth), Hybrid State Films, Anthology Film Arch, 91; Laura Marks (auth), Small pleasures in the dark, Afterimage, 93; Robert Koehler (auth), Society's outsiders get, Los Angeles Time, 93. *Mem:* Col Art Asn; Independent Film & Video Asn; Univ Film/Video Asn; Friends of Photog; Film Arts Found. *Media:* video. *Res:* Latina/o video art. *Interests:* visual anthropology; video art. *Collection:* The mus of Modern Art, New York, NY. *Publ:* The Photo Review National Photographic Competition, The Photo Review, 85; contribr & illusr, Winners of Photographer Forum Photo Contest, 87 & Photographs Luis Valdovino, 88, Photographer's Forum; Dimensions of Discovery, Krannert Art Mus, 89; contribr, Festival Internacional de Video del Cono Sur, Mus Image & Sound, 93; Blanco y Negro y de Color, Mus Nacional Centro de Arte Reina Sofia, Madrid, 2001. *Dealer:* Video Data Bank 37 Wabash Ave Chicago IL 60603. *Mailing Add:* Univ Colo Campus Box 318 Fine Arts Dept Sibell-Wolle Bldg N196A Boulder CO 80309

VALENCIA, CESAR
PAINTER, MURALIST
b Quito, Ecuador, Apr 2, 18; US citizen. *Study:* Archit & Fine Arts Sch, Quito, Ecuador, BA, 40. *Work:* Pan Am Union, Washington, DC; Mus Mod Art, Buenos Aires, Arg; Mus Art, Lima, Peru; Mod Art Gallery, Quito, Ecuador. *Comn:* ceramic mural, Dompe's Archit Assts, Mar del Plata, 52. *Exhib:* solo exhibs, Mus Mod Art, Buenos Aires, Arg, 62 & Pan Am Union, Washington, DC, 63; Mus Art, Lima, Peru, 45; Mus Nat Bellas Artes, Buenos Aires, 49; 1964 Pittsburgh Int, Pa, 64; Jason Gallery, NY, 65. *Awards:* First Prize, Mariano Aquilera, Ann Fine Arts Show, Mariano Aquilera Found, 44; First Prize, XXXLV Salon Watercolor, Mus Nat Bellas Artes, 48. *Bibliog:* E Ramallo (auth), Art ecuatoriano in bellas artes, La Prensa, Arg, 12/62; Bernardo Grauier (auth), Valencia: vital painter, El Comercio, Ecuador, 1/63; Leslie Judd Ahlander (auth), Ecuadorian has strong show, Washington Post, 11/63. *Media:* Encaustic. *Mailing Add:* 7855 Boulevard E Apt 191 North Bergen NJ 07047

VALENSTEIN, SUZANNE GEBHART
CURATOR
b Baltimore, Md, July 17, 28. *Pos:* Assoc cur Far Eastern art, Metrop Mus Art, New York, formerly, res cur, Asian Art, currently. *Teaching:* Vis lectr Chinese ceramics, Princeton Univ, NJ, fall 76. *Mem:* Oriental Ceramic Soc London; Oriental Ceramic Soc Hong Kong. *Publ:* Auth, Ming Porcelains: a Retrospective, China Inst in Am, 70; A Handbook of Chinese Ceramics, 75, revised & enlarged, 89 & Highlights of Chinese Ceramics, 75, Metrop Mus Art; coauth, Oriental Ceramics: The World's Great Collections, Vol XII, The Metropolitan Museum, Kodansha Int, 77; auth, Chinese celadons reclaimed from the sea, Oriental Art Mag, spring 79; The Herzman Collection of Chinese Ceramics, 92. *Mailing Add:* Metrop Mus Art Fifth Ave at 82nd St New York NY 10028

VALENTI, THOMAS
PAINTER, INSTRUCTOR
b New York, NY, May 5, 1953. *Study:* Newark Sch of Fine & Indust Art, Cert of Fine Art, 1971-1974. *Exhib:* Am Artists Prof League 71st Grand Nat Juried Exhib, Salmagundi Club, NY, 1999; 32nd Ann Juried Exhib, Garden State Watercolor Soc, Trenton City Mus, NJ, 2001; 62nd Ann Open Juried Exhib, NJ Water Color Soc, Monmouth Mus, NJ, 2004; 63rd Ann Juried Exhib, Audubon Artists of Am, Manhattan, NY, 2005; Comtemp Realism 2005, Cavalier Gallery Int Juried Exhib, Manhattan, NY, 2005. *Collection Arranged:* Lipton Tea Co; Hoffman LaRoche Inc; Rutgers Univ; Bellemead Construct Co; Indian Head Corp. *Pos:* Juror Fort Lee Art Asn, NJ, 2000. *Teaching:* Instr, Art Ctr Northern NJ & Ridgewood Sch Continuing educ, 2005. *Awards:* Am Artist's Prof League Award, Salmagundi Club, NY, 1999; Forbes Mag Award, NJ Water Color Soc, Monmouth Mus, NJ, 2004; Best in Show Award, Ridgewood Art Inst 25th Regional Open Juried Show, 2005. *Bibliog:* The Tonal Technique in Watercolor, Thomas Valenti, Artist's Mag, 1985; Bert Braham (auth), Design for Publishing, Graphic Arts Studio Manual, 1986; Local Artist Finds Inspiration from City Streets, Community of Life, 2005. *Mem:* Watercolor Club, NJ (pres, 1980); NJ Watercolor Soc; Am Artist's Prof League, NY; Allied Artist's Am, NY; NE Watercolor Soc, NY. *Media:* Watercolor. *Publ:* Auth, The Tonal Technique for Watercolor, Artist's Mag. *Mailing Add:* 345 Howard St Washington Township NJ 07676

VALENTIN, JEAN-PIERRE
DEALER
b France, Jan 31, 49; Can citizen. *Study:* Paris Business Sch, MBA(int trade), 71. *Bibliog:* A Gascon (auth), J P Valentin et galerie, Le Collectionneur, 78; G Robinson (auth), L' Art Francais Montreal, Can Art Investor's Guide, 80. *Mem:* Prof Art Dealers' Asn Can (pres, 81-85). *Specialty:* Prominent Quebec artists and Canadian artists; works by European masters of the 20th century. *Mailing Add:* Galerie L' Art Francais 1434 Sherbrooke W Montreal PQ H3G 1K4 Canada

VALENTINE, DEAN
COLLECTOR
Study: Univ Chicago, AB, 76. *Pos:* Pres, Walt Disney TV/Touchstone TV; pres, Chief Exec Officer, United Paramount Network, Los Angeles, 97-2002; with, Europlay Capital Adv, LLC, 2002-03; pres, First Family Entertainment, Beverly Hills, 2004. *Awards:* Named one of Top 200 Collectors, ARTnews Mag, 2004, 2006. *Collection:* Contemporary art. *Mailing Add:* Symbolic Action LLC 1888 Century Park E 18th Fl Los Angeles CA 90067

VALENTINE, DEWAIN
SCULPTOR
b Ft Collins, Colo, Aug 27, 36. *Study:* Univ Colo, BFA, 58, MFA, 60; Yale-Norfolk Art Sch, Yale Univ Fel, 58. *Work:* Whitney Mus Am Art, NY; Los Angeles Co Mus Art; Atlantic Richfield Corp, Washington, DC; Fed Reserve Bank, San Francisco; Stanford Univ Art Mus; Contemp Arts Ctr, Honolulu, Hawaii. *Comn:* Sky Gate (major outdoor work), comn by Frederick R Weisman; Open Diamond Double Diagonal (major outdoor work), comn by State Office Bldg, Van Nuys, Calif; Curved Waterwall (major indoor work), comn by Pacific Enterprises, Los Angeles; Diamond Waterwall (major outdoor work), comn by Metropolitan, Los Angeles. *Exhib:* Los Angeles Co Mus Art, 79; Pub Sch 1, Inst for Art & Urban Resources, NY, 81; Laumeier Int Sculpture Park, St Louis, Mo, 82; Madison Art Ctr, Wis, 83; Honolulu Acad Arts & the Contemp Arts Ctr, Hawaii, 85; Cartier Found for Contemp Art, France, 85-86. *Teaching:* Instr design & drawing, Univ Colo, 58-61 & 64-65; instr plastics, Univ Calif, Los Angeles, 65-67. *Awards:* John Simon Guggenheim Fel, 80; National Endowment for the Arts, 81. *Bibliog:* Peter Plagens (auth), Sunshine Muse, Praeger, 74; John Lloyd Taylor (auth), cover article in Art Int, Vol 17, No 7 & Jean Luc Bordeaux (auth), DeWain Valentine, Light Explored, Vol 67, No 8, 12/79, Art in Am; Jane Livingston, Artists Dialogue: DeWain Valentine, Archit Digest, 2/86. *Media:* Glass, Bronze, Steel, Stone. *Mailing Add:* 17921 S Western Ave Gardena CA 90248

VALERIO, JAMES ROBERT
PAINTER, EDUCATOR
b Chicago, Ill, Dec 2, 38. *Study:* Art Inst Chicago, BFA, 66, & MFA(Anne Louis Raymond Fel), 68; spec study with Seymour Rosofsky. *Work:* Ill Bell Telephone Co; Univ Iowa Mus Art; Prudential Insurance Co; Albuquerque Mus Art; Metrop Mus Art; Guggenheim Mus Art; Whitney Mus. *Exhib:* One-man shows, Frumkin-Struve Gallery, Chicago, Ill, 81-84, Del Art Mus, Wilmington, 83, Allan Frumkin Gallery, NY, 87 & 90 & Frumkin/Adams Gallery, NY, 91, 93 & 95; Painting & Sculpture in California: The Mod Era, Nat Col of Fine Arts of the Smithsonian Inst, Washington, DC & San Francisco Mus of Art, 76-77; Contemp Am Realism Since 1960, Pa Acad Fine Arts, 81; Drawings, Koplin Gallery, Santa Monica, Calif, 91; Am Narrative Painting & Sculpture: The 1980's, Nassau Co Mus Art, Roslyn Harbor, NY, 91; Am Realism & Figurative Art, 1955-1990 (traveling exhib), Miyagi Mus Art, Sendai, Japan, 92; Intimate Views (traveling), Glenn C Janss Collection of Am Realism; Recent Paintings, Univ Iowa Mus Art, 94; Art in Chicago 1945-1995, Mus Contemp Art, Chicago, 97; Still Life: The Object in Am Art 1915-1995 Traveling Exhib (auth, catalog), Metrop Mus Art, NY, 97-98; and others; Twentieth Century Am Drawing from the Ark Arts Ctr Found Collection (traveling exhib), 1998-2000; Contemp Am Realist Drawing: The Jalane & Richard Davidson Collection, The Art Inst of Chicago, 11/6/00-1/2/00. *Teaching:* Asst prof art, Rock Valley Col, Rockford, Ill, 68-70; assoc prof art, Univ Calif, Los Angeles, 70-79; assoc prof, Cornell Univ, 79-82; prof art, Northwestern Univ, Evanston, Ill, 85-. *Awards:* Purchase Award, Long Beach Mus of Art, 70; Creative Arts Award Fel, Univ Calif, Los Angeles, 76; Nat Endowment Arts Grant, 86. *Bibliog:* John Arthur (auth), Realists at Work, Watson-Guptill Publ, NY, 83; Charles Jencks (auth), Post-Modernism: The New Classicism in Art & Architecture, Rizzoli, 87; Edward Lucie-Smith (auth), Art Today, Phaidon Press, 95; and others. *Dealer:* George Adams Gallery 525 W 26th St 1st Fl New York NY 10001. *Mailing Add:* 1308 Gregory Wilmette IL 60091

VALERO, MARIA TERESA
PHOTOGRAPHER, EDUCATOR
b Venezuela. *Study:* Univ Kans, BFA in graphic design & art hist; Univ Kans, Master art hist. *Exhib:* Exhib incl, Kans, Mo, Okla, Ariz, Tex, Ark, Venezuela, Beauty of the Levant (Images of Lebanon & Syria Through Western Eyes), Syria. *Pos:* Dir, Sch Art, Univ Tulsa; found & dir Third Floor Designs (a student run design studio). *Teaching:* Prof, Gallery Dir, Alexandre Hogue Gallery. *Awards:* Recipient Graphex Award, Tulsa Addy, Creativity Today Award. *Mailing Add:* Univ of Tulsa Phillips Hall 104 600 S College Ave Tulsa OK 74104

VALESCO, FRANCES
MURALIST, PRINTMAKER
b Los Angeles, Calif, Aug 3, 41. *Study:* Univ Calif, Los Angeles, BA, 63; Sacramento State Univ, 64-65; Calif State Univ, Long Beach, MA, 72. *Work:* New York City Pub Libr; Oakland Mus, Calif; Readers Dig Corp; Clorox Corp; Boston Children's Hosp. *Comn:* Desert Mural, 82; Buffalo Sky Mural, 82; North Beach Fish Mural, 87; Quilt Mural, Dept Housing & Urban Develop, Off Community Develop, San Francisco, 93; Magic Carpet, Neighborhood Beautification Fund, San Francisco, 96. *Exhib:* 162nd Ann Exhib, Pa Acad Fine Arts, 67; Emerging Expression Biennial, Bronx Mus, 87; Recent Acquisitions, Achenbach Found, Fine Arts Mus, San Francisco, Calif, 91; Diversity & Vision of the Printed Image, Triton Mus Art, Santa Clara, Calif, 92; Miniatures, Bolinas Mus, 95; Clemson Nat Print Drawing Exhib, Clemson Univ, SC, 96; East/West Print Exchange (traveling), 96; Am Cult Ctr, Taipei, Taiwan, 99; McAllen Int Mus, Tex, 2000. *Pos:* Community artist, San Francisco Art Comn, 75-80; artist-in-residence in the community, Calif State Arts Coun, 80-85. *Teaching:* Lectr etching & screen printing, Univ Calif, Berkeley, 75-76 & 79; lectr screen printing, drawing & mural painting, Sonoma State Univ, 77-80; instr printmaking, Textiles & photog, San Francisco Acad Art, 82-96; lectr printmaking, San Francisco State Univ, 84 & 93-97 & San Francisco Art Inst, 93-96, San Francisco City Col, 97-. *Awards:* Print Purchase for Embassies, Beirut, Lebanon & Kuala Lumpur, Malaysia, US Info Agency, 67; Cert Hon, San Francisco City, 87; Proclamation, State of Calif, 94. *Bibliog:* Judith Anderson (auth), San Francisco's splashy outdoor art, San Francisco Chronicle, 82; Vivien Raynor (auth), Computer Reigns at Bronx Mus of Art, The NY Times, 87; William Zimmer (auth), East/West Print Exchange, NY Times, 96. *Mem:* Calif Soc Printmakers (historian, 78-80, pres, 94-96); San Francisco Mural (adv bd, 82-89); YLEM; Surface Design Asn; Am Print Alliance (vpres, bd dir, 95-97). *Media:* Mixed. *Publ:* Ed & illusr, Media Mixed, Joined Arts, 67; illusr, Music of the Whole Earth, Scribners, 76; coauth, Combining color xerography with the technique of silk screen and intaglio, Leonardo, 84; San Francisco Murals, Tim Drescher, 91; Zyzzva, 96. *Mailing Add:* 1901 Schiller St Alameda CA 94501

VALETTA
PAINTER
b Brooklyn, NY, Jan 17, 40. *Study:* Pratt Inst, BS(art educ), 61; Tyler Sch Fine Art; Univ Pa. *Work:* Delaware Theatre Co, Wilmington; Widener Univ Mus, Chester, Pa; Private collection of Pres Anwar Sadat Family, Egypt; Regional Ctr Women in Arts. *Exhib:* National Drawing Competition, Univ ND, 80, In the Guise of Reality, West Chester Univ, Pa, 2000; Am Embassy, Brussels, Belg, 90; Italian Am Women Artists, Campagnia Del Paiolo-Galleria, Florence, Italy, 94; Syne, Beyond Language, Kalmar Mus Art, Sweden, 96; By Mutual Consent (2 person), Widener Univ Gallery, Chester, Pa, 98, Five Times Two, Allentown Art Mus, Pa, 2001; Six Months Since September, Blue Streak Gallery, Wilmington, DE, 2002; Parallel Visions, traveling exhib, DE Ctr for Contemp Arts, Wilmington, DE, 2005; Affinities, Freedman Gallery, Albright Col, Reading, Pa, 2005; Craftforms, Wayne Art Ctr, 2005. *Pos:* Bd dir & co-chairperson collections comt, Afro Am Mus, Philadelphia, Pa, 82-88; Contemp Women Artists, Philadelphia Community Arts Ctr, Wallingford, Pa, 85-86; dir, Muse Gallery, Philadelphia, Pa, 89-90; cur, founder & dir, Regional Ctr for Women in Arts, West Chester, Pa, 98. *Teaching:* instr, painting, Widener Univ, Life Long Learning Prog, currently. *Awards:* Fisher Mem Award, 87; Harcum Jr Col Award, Arts in Progress Gallery, Philadelphia, Pa, 87; Second Prize, Delaware Ctr Contemp Arts, Wilmington, Del, 93; Merit and Purchase awards, Reading Art Mus, Pa, 2001. *Mem:* Artists Equity Asn; Del Ctr Contemp Arts; Sister Cities of Wilmington. *Media:* Oil, Pastel. *Mailing Add:* PO Box 510 Westtown PA 19395

VALIER, BIRON (FRANK)
PAINTER, PRINTMAKER
b W Palm Beach, Fla, Mar 13, 43. *Study:* Art Student's League, Woodstock, NY, 63-65; Cranbrook Acad Art, BFA, 67; Yale Univ, MFA, 69. *Work:* Achenbach Found, Calif, Palace Legion Hon, San Francisco; Los Angeles Co Mus Art; Metrop Mus Art, NY; Mus Fine Arts, Boston; Norton Gallery Contemp Collection, West Palm Beach, Fla. *Exhib:* 62nd Ann Int, Print Club, Philadelphia, Pa, 86; Brenau Nat Invitational, Brenau Col, Gainesville, Ga, 89; Acquisitions 1984-1990, Univ Art Mus, Univ of Queensland, Brisbane, Australia, 90; Urban Insights, Claremont Sch Art, Perth, West Australia, 92; Flagging The Republic, RMIT Gallery, Melbourne, Australia, 96; Along the Roadside, Stonemetal Press Gallery, San Antonio, Tex, 2002. *Pos:* Artist-in-residence, Mass Arts & Humanities Found, 77; head found yr, Sch Art & Design, PCAE, Melbourne, 77-79; publs consult, Australian Bicentennial Authority, Sydney, 87-89. *Teaching:* Instr art, Wheelock Col, Boston, Mass, 69-72; instr printmaking, DeCordova Mus Sch, Mass, 74-77; lectr corp art collections, City Art Inst, Univ of NSW, Sydney, 87-90. *Awards:* Bicentennial Comn, Boston City Hall, Boston 200, 75; Mardsen's Open Acquisitive, Campbelltown City Festival, NSW, Marsden Solicitors, 88; Best of Show, Hand Pulled Prints VI Int'l Exhib, San Antonio, Tex, 98. *Bibliog:* Bradford F Swan (auth), Valier at RI Col exhibition, Providence Sunday J, 1/7/73; Robert Taylor (auth), Famous Boston potholes, Boston Globe, 3/14/78; Jennifer Moran (auth), Valier charts images of urban life, West Australian, 6/1/92. *Mem:* Col Art Asn; Art Deco Soc Western Australia; 20th Century Heritage Soc NSW. *Publ:* Auth, Twenty Photographs, pvt publ, 67; Famous Boston Potholes, South Wind Graphics, 77; Luna and Metal, Namba Wan Arts, 82; Corporate sponsorship of the visual arts in Australia, Art Monthly Australia, 89; contribr, International Directory of Corporate Art Collections, ARTnews, NY, 90. *Dealer:* Wenniger Gallery 19 Mt Pleasant St Rockport MA 01966. *Mailing Add:* 303/12 Macleay St Potts Point NSW 2011 Australia

VALINCIUS, IRENE
PAINTER, PRINTMAKER
b Bonn, Ger, Feb 21, 48. *Study:* Mass Col Art, Boston, 75-77; Sch Mus Fine Arts, Boston, 78; Univ Mass, BA(magna cum laude), 78. *Work:* Mus Fine Arts, Boston Pub Libr; Rose Art Mus, Waltham, Mass; Huntsville Mus Art, Ala; Trenton State Col, NJ; DeCordova Mus Art, Lincoln, Mass; Graham Gund Collection, Cambridge Mass. *Comn:* Babson Col, Babson, MA, 99; Rose Art Mus, Visual Memories, 2000; Decordova Mus, 2000, 2002; Gallery NAGA, 2002. *Exhib:* Restive Visions, Rose Art Mus, Waltham, Mass, 89; solo exhibs, Gallery NAGA, Boston, 89, 91, 93, 94 & 97, Scott Alan Gallery, NY, 91, Louis Newman Gallery, Beverly Hills, 92 & Horwitch Newman Gallery, Scottsdale, Ariz, 95; Metaphor as Reality, Danforth Mus Art,

Framingham, Mass, 93; Timely and Timeless, Aldrich Mus Contemp Art, Ridgefield, Conn, 93; Landscape not Landscape, Gallery Camino Real, Boca Raton, Fla, 94; Manifest Destiny, Harns Mus Art, Gainesville, Fla, 96. *Pos:* Bd mem, Brickbottom Arts Asn, 91-94; adv bd mem, Somerville Arts Coun, 93-95. *Teaching:* Teacher art & printmaking, Rugg Rd, 91-93, Monserrat Sch Art, 93, Mass Col Art, 94-2005; Art New England Workshops, Bennington, Vt, 2003-2004. *Awards:* Dorchester Arts Coun Grant, 83; Somerville Arts Coun Grant, 90; Blanche Coleman Award, 94; Yaddo Visual Arts Fel, 82; Somerville Arts Grant, 99. *Bibliog:* Painting in Boston, 50-2000; DECordova Mus, 2002; New Am Paintings VII, Open Studio Press; Basic Printmaking Techniques, Bernard toale, 92. *Mem:* Brickbottom Arts Asn; Somerville Arts Coun. *Media:* Oil Painting; Monotypes. *Specialty:* Contemp Art. *Interests:* Study of light. *Collection:* Au Bon Pain Corp, Boston, MA, NYC, NY; Bank of Lowell, Lowell, MA; Bershire Partners, Boston, MA; The Boston Globe, Boston. *Publ:* Boston Globe, 94, 96, 97, 2002; Art New England, 91, 97, 81, 2002; Boston Phoenix, 91, 98; Bay Windows, 91, 89, 2002. *Dealer:* Gallery NAGA 67 Newbury St Boston MA 02116. *Mailing Add:* One Fitchburg St C107 Somerville MA 02143

VALLA, TERESSA MARIE
PAINTER, KINETIC SCULPTURE

b Lynchburg, VA. *Study:* Univ Vt, BS, 1979; NY Univ, Grad Studies, 1982; Art Students League, Leo Manso, Ponce de Leon, 1986-1989; Studio Art School of the Aegean, Samos Greece (Andrew Forge), 1987. *Work:* Mus of the City of NY; NY Pub Libr, NY; Libr of Cong, Wash DC; New Eng Ctr for contemp Art, Brooklyn, Conn; Paterson Mus, Paterson, NJ. *Comn:* Tree of Life, City Arts, NY, 1994; NY Cares (Pub Figurative Mural), NY Cares, 1996; Graffiti Alternative, NYC Housing Authority, 1997. *Exhib:* Women of the World: Diverse Perspectives, Am Mus of Natural Hist, NY, 1999; Snapshot, Contemp Mus, Baltimore, Md, 2000; Life of the City, Mus of Modern Art, NY, 2002; Considering Peace, Sato Mus, Tokyo, Japan, 2003; War is Over, Sideshow Gallery, NY, 2006. *Pos:* Visiting Artist, Workshop (Abstraction of Art through Music, Nature & Mathematics), Carnegie Hall NY, 1994. *Teaching:* Lectr, Workshop, Experimental Drawing, Cooper Union, 2001; instr, Annenberg artist in res, 2000-01. *Awards:* Ezra Jack Keats Mem Award, Lincoln Ctr, NYC, 1988-89 & 1990; Artist in Residence, Santa Fe Art Inst, 2001; NY Found Arts & NY Arts Recovery Fund, 2002; Recovery Grant, Gottlieb Found, 2002; Artist in Residence (Mojacar, Spain), Found Valparaiso, 2006. *Bibliog:* Brazilian TV Global Network (Diario de Perambuco), 1999; Dan Rather (auth, ABC News) Santa Fe Art Inst, Dan Rather 6PM News, 2001; Gary Shapiro (auth), The Pleasures of Urban Gardening, The NY Sun, 2005. *Mem:* Artists Circle; Int Wildlife Asoc; College Art Asoc. *Media:* Miscellaneous Media. *Interests:* Dance, poetry, rainforest-ecology, faith, music. *Dealer:* Hopkins Fine Art Scottsdale AZ

VALLANCE, JEFFREY K R
SCULPTOR, PAINTER

b Torrance, Calif, Jan 25, 55. *Study:* Calif State Univ, Northridge, BA, 79; Otis Inst Parsons Sch Design, MFA, 81. *Work:* Australian Nat Gallery, Canberra. *Comn:* Man and Dog (mural), Fallbrook Sq Mall, Woodland Hills, Calif, 73; Dinosaurs (mural), Powelle Butte Grocery, Ore, 77; Space (mural), Crippled Childrens Soc, Woodland Hills, Calif, 77; Blinky (gravestone), Los Angeles Pet Cemetery, Calabasas, Calif, 78. *Exhib:* Solo exhibs, Washington Proj Arts, 78, Daniel Sorano Hall Nat Treasure, Dakar, Senegal, 80, Univ Art Mus, Santa Barbara, 82; The Living Art Mus, Reykjavik, Iceland, 86; One-man shows incl: The US Senate: A Survey on the Arts, Wash Project for Arts, 78, Machines and Other Articles, Rosamund Felsen Gallery, 81, Icelandic Women and the King of Tonga, 87, The Throne Room: Icelandic Women and the King of Tonga Part II, 98, The Nixon Mus, Galerie Praz-Delavallade, Paris, 94, Clown Stains, Univ Tex, 2002, The Shape of Tex, Majestic Ranch, Boerne, Tex, 2002, Relics from LBJ's 66 Visit to Australia, Tasmanian Mus and Art Gallery, 2002, Saami and Aboriginal Flags, Black Kettle Mus, 2002, exhibited in group shows at Faith, Dynamite Gallery, 2000, Off the Grid, Lehmann Maupin, 2002, Five by Seven by X, The Jones Ctr for Contemp Art, 2002, A Thousand Clowns, Robert Berman Gallery, 2002, To Whom it May Concern, Logan Galleries, Calif Col Arts and Crafts, 2002. *Pos:* Art dir, Crippled Childrens Soc, Woodland Hills, Calif, 76-77; host, Cutting Edge, MTV, Los Angeles, 83. *Teaching:* Prof, Univ Calif, Los Angeles, 84-85; Vis prof art; instructor Los Angeles, Pierce Col, Woodland Hills, Calif, 87, Parsons Sch Design, 87-92, Community Col of Southern Nev, Las Vegas, 96, Univ Nev, 95-98; prof inte contemp art Umea Univ, Sweden, 99-2002; vis artist Chicago Art Inst, 99, Cranbrook Acad of Art, Detroit, 2001; artist-in-residence Majestic Ranch, Univ Tex, San Antonio, 2002, Univ Tasmania, Australia, 2002. *Awards:* Grantee Guggenheim Memorial Foundation, 2004. *Bibliog:* Peter Schjeldahl (auth), Los Angeles demystified, Village Voice, 81; Howard Singerman (auth), article, 81 & Bob Pincus (auth), article, 84, Artforum. *Media:* Enamel, Electronics. *Res:* Polynesian myth of Tiki; Symbols of Iceland; The King of Tonga. *Publ:* Auth, Blinky the Friendly Hen, private publ, 79. *Dealer:* Rosamund Felsen Gallery 669 N La Cienega Los Angeles CA 90069. *Mailing Add:* UCLA Dept Art 11000 Kinross Ave Ste 245 Los Angeles CA 90095

VALLEE, WILLIAM OSCAR
PAINTER, GRAPHIC ARTIST

b South Paris, Maine, June 18, 1934. *Study:* Univ Alaska. *Work:* Many in pvt collections. *Exhib:* Anchorage Fur Rendezvous, 63; Easter Arts Festival, 63; Alaska Festival Music & Art, 63 & 64; one-man shows, Anchorage Petrol Club, 63 & Anchor Galleries, 63. *Pos:* Instituted (in coop with Am Artists Prof League), Am Art Wk, 63; treas, Soc Alaskan Arts, 63; co-founder, Alaska-Int Cult Arts Ctr; bd dir & co-founder, Anchorage Community Art Ctr, currently; pres & chmn bd, Alaska Map Serv, Inc, currently. *Awards:* Anchorage Fur Rendezvous, 63; Easter Art Festival, 63; Artist of the Month, Alaska Art Guild, 63. *Mem:* Alaska Art Guild (pres & chmn, 64); Alaska Watercolor Soc (pres, 63); Am Soc Photogrammetry; Am Artist Prof League. *Media:* Watercolor. *Mailing Add:* 4118 Irene Dr Anchorage AK 99504

VALLILA, MARJA R
SCULPTOR

b Prague, Czech, Oct 20, 50; US citizen. *Study:* Hampshire Col, BA, 72; Cornell Univ, MFA, 75. *Work:* Johnson Mus; Everson Mus; Kennedy Airport, McCory Corp, NY; Gen Mills Corp, Minneapolis; Herbert F Johnson Mus, Ithaca, NY; and others. *Exhib:* Solo exhibs, Zabriskie Gallery, NY, 77, 80 & 89, Mus Fine Arts, Springfield, Mass, 79 & Tulane Univ, 81; View From Upstate, AIR Gallery, NY, 82 & 98; Zabriskie Gallery, 89, 99; Newark Mus, 91; Haenah-Kent Gallery, NY, 91; UBU Gallery, NY, 95; Ceramich Fanny, Deruta, Italy, 99; Antica, Derata, Italy, 99; Sofa, NY, 2000; Nancy Margolis Gallery, NY, 2000; U Prstenu Gallery, Prague, CZ, 01. *Teaching:* Asst prof sculpture, Cornell Univ, 79-80, mem adv coun, 81-; asst prof, Bard Col, 80 & State Univ NY, Albany, 81- & assoc prof, 90-. *Awards:* State Univ NY Res Grant, 83, 85, 86, 89, 99; Julia and David White Artists Colony, Costa Rica, 01. *Bibliog:* David L Shirley (auth), article, New York Times, 7/14/77; Sally Jessup (auth), article, Art World, 5/21/80; Alan Singer (auth), article, Arts Mag, 4/85; Brenson (auth), article, New York Times, 6/29/89. *Mem:* Col Art Asn. *Media:* Ceramics, Sculpture. *Dealer:* Nancy Margolis Gallery 560 Broadway New York NY

VAN ALSTINE, JOHN RICHARD
SCULPTOR

b Johnstown, NY, Aug 14, 52. *Study:* St Lawrence Univ, 70-72; Kent State Univ, BFA, 74; Cornell Univ Sch Art & Archit, MFA, 76. *Work:* Nat Mus Am Art, Smithsonian Inst; Hirshhorn Mus & Sculpture Garden; Denver Mus; Carnegie Inst Mus Art; Mus Mod Art, Gulbenkian Found, Lisbon, Portugal; Baltimore Mus Art; Corcoran Mus Art, Washington; Del Mus Art, Wilmington; Herbert F Johnson Mus, Cornell Univ, Ithaca, NY; Newark Mus Art, NJ; and many others. *Comn:* Pub Comn, Billings, Mont, 82 & Luck Stone Corp, Richmond, Va, 83; outdoor public sculptures, Austin Col, Sherman, Tex, 86; Inst Defence Analyses, Washington, DC, 88-89. *Exhib:* Solo exhibs, Grimaldis Gallery, Baltimore, 84, 92, 95, 97 & 2000, Univ NH, Durham, 94, Troyer Fitzpatrick, Lassman Gallery, Washington, 94, Cleveland State Univ, Ohio, 94, Nohra Haime Gallery, NY, 94, 96, 98 & 2000, Dartmouth Col, Hanover, NH, 95 & DeCordova Mus & Sculpture Garden, Lincoln, Mass, 96-97; 2nd Fujisankei Biennale, Hakone Open-Air Mus, Ninotaira, Japan, 94; Semaphore, Art Initiatives, NY, 95; New Acquisitions, Phillips Collection, Washington, 95; Tudor Place Exhib, Int Sculpture Ctr, Washington, 95; Sculptors Drawings, NJ Ctr Visual Arts, 95; Cerrillos Cult Ctr, NMex, 96. *Teaching:* Asst, Cornell Univ, 74-76; asst prof, Univ Wyo, Laramie, 76-80 & Univ Md, College Park, 80-86; vis prof, Md Art Inst, Baltimore, 88. *Awards:* Yaddo Fel, 85; Individual Artist Fel, Nat Endowment Arts, 86; Individual Artists Fel, NJ State Coun Arts, 88. *Bibliog:* Christine Tenin (auth), Boston Globe (rev), 7/31/96; Miles Unger (auth), Sculpture Mag (rev), 10/96; NicK Capasso (auth), Bones of the Earth, Spirit of the Land, 2000. *Media:* Stone, Welded Metal. *Specialty:* Contemporary Art. *Dealer:* Nohra Haime Gallery New York NY. *Mailing Add:* Van Alstine Studios S Main St PO Box 526 Wells NY 12190

VAN BRUGGEN, COOSJE
ARTIST, AUTHOR

b Groningen, The Netherlands, June 6, 42. *Study:* Art Hist, Rijks Univ of Groningen, DRS, 67. *Hon Degrees:* Calif Col Art and Craft, DFA(hon), 96; Univ Teesside, Middlesbrough, England, DLitt(hon), 99; DFA: Nova Scotia col Art & Design, Halifox & col creative studies, Detroit, 2005. *Work:* Univ Las Vegas; Minneapolis Sculpture Garden, Walker Art Center, Minneapolis; Rincon Park, San Francisco, Newmarket Gallery, Cheongyeon Stream, Seoul, Korea. *Exhib:* two-person shows (with Claes Oldenburg) No Ctr Contemp Art, Sunderland, 88, Leeds City Art Gallery, 88, Palais des Beaux-Arts, Brussels, 88, IVAM Ctr Julio Gonz?z, Valencia, 88, Galleria Christian Stein, Milan, 90, Leo Castelli Gallery, New York City, 90, Pace Gallery, 94, Museo Correr, Venice, 99, Museu Serralves, Porto, 2001, Metrop Mus Art, New York City, 2002, PaceWildenstein, 2002, Frederik Meijer Gardens and Sculpture Park, Grand Rapids, Mich, 2002; Paula Cooper Gallery, 2004, Pace Wildenstein, 2005, Konrad, Fischer Gallery, 2005, Exhibited in group shows at Guggenheim Mus, New York City, 93, Venice Triennale 97, Nat Gallery, London, 2000, others. *Pos:* Ast cur, Stedelijk Mus, Amsterdam, The Netherlands, 67-71; prof Acad Fine Arts, Enschede, The Netherlands, 71-76; sr critic landscape archit, Harvard univ, 1993; sr critic dept sculpture Yale Univ, New Haven, 96-97; Co-editor Catalogue Sonsbeek, 71; mem selection comt, Documenta 7, Kassel, Ger, 82; cur (with Dieter Koepplin) Bruce Nauman: Drawings, 65-86, Basel, Switzerland, 86-88. *Awards:* Recipient Distinction in Sculpture, Sculpture Ctr, New York City, 84, Nathaniel S Saltonstall award, Int Coop Admin, Boston, 96; Nat Medal Award, sch Mus Fine Arts, Boston, 2004. *Bibliog:* (auth): Mouse Mus/Ray Wing, 79, Bruce Nauman, 89, John Baldessari, 90, Frank O. Gehry: Guggenheim Mus Bilbao, 97; co-author (with Claes Oldenburg): Claes Oldenburg: Sketches and Blottings Toward the European Desk Top, 90, Just another room, 91, Large-Scale Projects, 94, Claes Oldenburg Coosje van Bruggen, 99, Down Liquidambar Lane: Sculpture in the Park, 2001; co-author: (with Claes Oldenburg and Frank O. Gehry) Il Corso del Coltello, 85;. *Dealer:* Pace Wildenstein Gallery & Paula Cooper Gallery, NY. *Mailing Add:* 556 Broome St New York NY 10013-1517

VAN CALDENBORGH, JOOP
COLLECTOR

Awards: Named one of top 200 art collectors, ARTnews mag, 2004. *Collection:* Achievements include collection of complete graphic works of Marcel Broodhaers; Modern & Contemporary Art, especially Conceptual, photography. *Publ:* Co-auth: Imagine You Are Standing Here In Front of Me, Caldic Collectie, 2003. *Mailing Add:* c/o Rotterdam CofC Blaak 40 PO Box 450 Rotterdam AL 3000 Netherlands

VANCO, JOHN LEROY
ADMINISTRATOR, CURATOR
b Erie, Pa, Aug 21, 45. *Study:* Allegheny Col, BA(art hist); Whitney Mus Am Art. *Collection Arranged:* Teco: Art Pottery of the Prairie School; In Harmony with The Earth; Paperthick: Forms and Images in Cast Paper; Images of War and Artists Respond to the Gulf War; A Peculiar Vision: The Work of George Ohr, The Mad Potter of Biloxi; Loud & Clear: Resonator Guitars and the Dopyera Brothers Legacy to American Music; Art & Life in Erie, Pa; From Mickey to the Grinch: Art of the Animated Film; Archaeology at the Dawn of History: the Khirbet Iskander Coll. *Pos:* Dir, Erie Art Mus, 68-. *Mem:* Pa Humanities Council; Am Asn Mus. *Interests:* Photography, ceramics, folk art, popular culture. *Publ:* Auth, What Ever Happened to Louis Eilshemius?, 67; A Roycroft Desktop, 94; illusr, Roger Misiewicz: Wolfman of the Blues, 72. *Mailing Add:* Erie Art Mus 411 State St Erie PA 16501

VAN DE BOVENKAMP, HANS
SCULPTOR
b Barneveld, Holland, June 1, 38. *Study:* Archit Sch Amsterdam, 57; Univ Mich, Ann Arbor, BScDes, 61. *Work:* Sculpture Garden, Nebr Bicentennial; State Capital Plaza, Lansing, Mich; Lowe Mus, Coral Gables, Fla; Boca Raton Mus, Fla; Youngstown Mus, Ohio; Stony Brook Univ, NY; Univ Missoula, Mont. *Comn:* Neiman Marcus, 95-97; Lighthouse (sculpture), Haverstraw Marina, 86; fountain, Amli Realty Co, Chicago, 88; sculpture, Marina Village, Alameda, Calif, 90; Tex A&M Univ; Mt Sinai Hosp, Miami; City of Ormond Beach; City of Toledo; Corporate Business Park, Columbia, Md. *Exhib:* Sculpture Ctr, NY, 79; Bologna Landi Gallery, East Hampton, NY, 82-92; Moosart Gallery, Miami, Fla, 85-87; Nina Owen Ltd, Chicago, Ill, 87-90; Shidoni, NMex, 88-92; Lowe Gallery, Atlanta, Ga, 89-92; Camenoreal, Boca Raton, Fla, 91; Cavalier Gallery, Greenwich, Conn, 94; Dietrich Contemp Arts, NY, 94; Lumina Gallery, Taos, NMex, 95-96; Stamford Mus, Conn, 96; Michener Mus, Doylestown, Pa, 96; Grounds for Sculpture, Hamilton, NJ; City of Ft Lauderdale, 00. *Awards:* Emily Lowe Award, 64; I-80 Nebr Award, 76. *Mem:* NY Sculptors Guild; Int Sculpture Ctr; Royal Soc Brit Sculptos; Cen Park Hist Soc; Omeage Inst. *Media:* Stainless Steel, Bronze. *Publ:* A Guide to Sculpture Parks & Gardens in the US

VANDEN BERGE, PETER WILLEM
SCULPTOR, MURALIST
b Voorburg, Zuid-Holland, Neth, Oct 16, 35; US citizen. *Study:* Art Acad, The Hague, Neth; Calif State Univ, Sacramento, BA; Univ Calif, Davis, MA. *Work:* Henry Gallery, Univ Wash, Seattle; Mus Contemp Crafts, NY; Johnson Collection Am Crafts, Racine, Wis; Crocker Art Mus, Sacramento; Oakland Art Mus, Calif. *Comn:* Three glazed relief tile murals, San Francisco City Col, 71; pub murals, San Francisco Arts Comn, City of San Francisco; glazed tile relief, Contra Costa Jr Col Dist Off, John F Gordon Educ Ctr, Martinez, Calif, 75; tile mural, Sacramento Metrop Arts Comn, 79. *Exhib:* Four Ceramic Sculptors from California, Alan Frumkin Gallery, NY, 73, Calif Ceramic Sculptors I & II, 74, Five Ceramic Sculptors from Calif, Chicago, 75; Clay, Whitney Mus Am Art, NY, 74; Fendrick's Gallery, Washington, DC, 76; Campbell Mus Contemp Crafts, Cranbrook Acad Art, Bloomfield Hills, Mich, 76; A Century of Ceramics in the United States, Everson Mus Art, Syracuse, NY, 79; Craft Today-USA, Mus Decorative Arts, Paris, France (traveling exhib through Europe); Poetry of the Physical, Am Craft Mus, NY; Contemp Am: 20 Americans, Newport Harbor Art Mus, Newport Beach, Calif; Tri Ann Int Craft Exhib, Art Gallery Western Australia, Perth. *Teaching:* Asst prof ceramics & sculpture, San Francisco State Univ, 66-73; prof ceramics & sculpture, Calif State Univ, Sacramento, 73-. *Awards:* Madeleine Cortese Williams Found Award, 63 & 66; Comn Awarded, Sacramento Metrop Arts Comn, Art in Pub Places Prog, 78-84; Nat Endowment for the Arts Fel Grant, 81. *Bibliog:* D Zack (auth), Mythology, California ceramics, Art & Artist Mag, London, 9/69, Nut art in quake time, Art News, 70 & Laugh in clay, Craft Horizon Mag, 71. *Media:* Stoneware, Porcelain; Clay, Terra Cotta. *Dealer:* Natsoulas/Novelozo Gallery 140 F St Davis CA 95616. *Mailing Add:* c/o John Natsoulas Gallery 140 F St Davis CA 95616

VANDERLIP, DIANNE PERRY
GALLERY DIRECTOR, EDUCATOR
b Toledo, Ohio, Apr 20, 41. *Study:* Ohio Univ, BFA; NY Univ; Pratt Inst. *Collection Arranged:* Recorded Activities (with catalog), 70; Artists Books (with catalog), 73; N, E, W, S & Middle (with catalog), 75; Alphons Schilling Stereoptics, 75; John Sloan/Robert Henri: Their Philadelphia Yrs, 76; Alan Shields' Environments, 77; Robert Hudson, 77; Poets & Painters, 79; Lucas Samaras Pastels, 81. *Pos:* Dir, Vanderlip Gallery, Philadelphia, 66-68; dir, Moore Col Art Gallery, 68-78; cur & consult, Dechert, Price & Rhoads, Philadelphia, 74-; panelist & consult, Nat Endowments Arts, Washington, DC, 74-; cur of contemp art, Denver Art Mus, 78-. *Teaching:* Prof aesthetics, Moore Col Art, 68-. *Awards:* Award of Excellence, Philadelphia Art Dir Club, 71. *Bibliog:* Dore Ashton (auth), Beyond literalism, Art Mag, 69; Lucy Lippard (auth), Dematerialization of Art, Praeger, 73; Dianne Kelder (auth), Artists books, Art in Am, 74. *Mem:* Am Asn Mus; Am Fedn Arts; Soc Arts & Lett. *Collection:* Contemporary paintings and drawings by American artists. *Publ:* Ed, More Ray Gun Poems by Claes Oldenburg, 74; ed, Hopi Kachina Dolls, 75. *Mailing Add:* Denver Art Mus 100 W 14th Ave Pkwy Denver CO 80204

VANDERPOOL, KAREN
WEAVER, EDUCATOR
b Troy, NY, July 14, 46. *Study:* State Univ NY, BS, 68; Tyler Sch Art, MFA, 70; Haystack Mt Sch Crafts; Sch Am Craftsmen. *Work:* Ball State Univ, Muncie, Ind; First Nat Bank, Boston. *Exhib:* Weaving Unlimited, De Cordova Mus, Lincoln, Mass, 71; Bodycraft, Portland Art Mus, Ore, 73; 3rd Int Exhib Miniature Textiles, Brit Craft Ctr, London, Eng, 78; Art in Crafts, Bronx Mus, NY, 78; Felting, Mus Am Craft, NY, 80; Art Fabric: Mainstream, San Francisco Mus Mod Art, 81; 30 Americans, Galveston Art Ctr, Tex, 81; Fiber Nat '85, Adams Mem Gallery, Dunkirk, NY, 85. *Teaching:* Asst prof weaving & fiber arts, Univ Wash, Seattle, 76-81; prof, Calif State Univ, Chico, 81-. *Awards:* First Award Fibers, Mass Artists-Craftsmen, 71 & Calif Works '84, 84; First Award Crafts, Pac Northwest Arts & Crafts, 72. *Bibliog:* Betty Scholossman (auth), Reviews: Clay, fiber, metal by women artists, Art J, Vol 37, No 4, summer 78; Betty Park (auth), Felting, Fiberarts, 11-12/80. *Mem:* Am Craft Coun; Handweavers Guild Am. *Media:* Papermaking, Computer Assisted Textile Design. *Dealer:* Dept Art & Art History. *Mailing Add:* Calif State Univ Dept Art Chico CA 95929-0820

VANDERSALL, AMY L
HISTORIAN, EDUCATOR
b West Newton, Pa, Oct 9, 33. *Study:* Col Wooster, Ohio, BA, 55; Mt Holyoke Col, South Hadley, Mass, MA, 58; Yale Univ, MA, 62, PhD, 65. *Teaching:* Asst prof medieval art hist, Smith Col, 66-72; assoc prof, Univ Colo, 73-81, prof, 81-95. *Mem:* Int Ctr Medieval Art (bd of dirs, 75-78 & 85-88); Col Art Asn; Medieval Acad Am. *Res:* Carolingian ivory carving, Anglo-Saxon art and Romanesque sculpture. *Publ:* Auth, Two Carolingian ivories in the Metropolitan Museum of Art, 72 & Five Romanesque Portals: Questions of Attributions and Ornament, 83, New York, Metrop Mus J; Date and provenance of the Franks casket, Gesta, 73; Homeric myth in early medieval England: The lid of the Franks casket, Studies Iconography, 75; Relationship of sculptors and painters at the court of Charles the Bald, 76 & Romanesque sculpture in American museums: The west, 80, Gesta. *Mailing Add:* 360 20th St Boulder CO 80302-8011

VANDERWEG, PHILLIP DALE
ADMINISTRATOR, SCULPTOR
b Benton Harbor, Mich, Aug 16, 43. *Study:* Albion Col, 61-63; Univ Mich, BS(design), 65, MFA, 68. *Work:* Tenn State Mus, Nashville; Butler Mus Art, Dayton, Ohio; NY State Univ, Potsdam; Kean Col NJ, Union; Albion Col, Mich. *Comn:* Figure grouping (sculpture), Columbia State Univ, Tenn, 81; exterior sculpture, Pargos Restaurant, Nashville, Tenn, 87; seated figure (double sculpture), Vanderbilt Univ, Nashville, 87; Welcome site sculpture I-65, Tenn Arts Comn, Mitchelville, 88. *Pos:* Founding mem, Foundations in Art: Theory & Educ, 76; mem visual arts rev panel, Tenn Arts Comn, 86-89; region 5 rep, Mich Artist Prog, Detroit Inst Arts, 90-92. *Teaching:* From instr to prof, Mid Tenn State Univ, 68-89; prof & chair, Western Mich Univ, 89-. *Mem:* Nat Asn Schs Art & Design; Nat Coun Art Adminrs; Col Art Asn; Mid-Am Col Art Conf. *Media:* All Media. *Mailing Add:* 6791 Penny Ln Kalamazoo MI 49009

VAN DOMMELEN, DAVID B
WRITER, FIBER ARTIST
b Grand Rapids, Mich, Aug 21, 29. *Study:* Harrington Interior Design Inst, cert; Mich State Univ, BA & MA; also with Abraham Rattner & Mariska Karasz. *Work:* Mich State Univ Mus Art, ELansing; Arrowmont Sch of Crafts, Gatlinburg, Tenn; Am Home Econ Asn Collection, Washington; Marshall Field Permanent Collection, Chicago; Portland Mus Fine Arts, Maine. *Exhib:* Group Traveling Show, Smithsonian Inst, Washington, 57-78; Invention with Thread, Montclair Art Mus, NJ, 61; one-man shows, Portland Mus of Art, Maine, 63, Kalamazoo Art Ctr Mus, Mich, 66, Univ Iowa, Iowa City, 67 & WVa State Univ Mus, Institute, 75; retrospective 56-68, Pa State Univ, 68; and many others. *Teaching:* Prof & head art educ, Pa State Univ, 59-88, prof emer, currently; summer instr, Haystack Sch Crafts, 62, 63 & 74; guest prof, Univ Iowa, 66-69; summer instr, Arrowmont Schs Crafts, 70-81. *Awards:* Fishburn Award, Int Understanding, Educ Press Am, 73. *Bibliog:* John Peter (auth), Sewing machine art, Look Mag, 8/61; Ruth Bunker (auth), David Van Dommelen, Cross-Country Craftsman, 10/62. *Mem:* Nat Art Educ Asn; Nat Craftsman's Asn; Am Craft Coun. *Media:* Fiber. *Publ:* Auth, Decorative Wall Hangings, 62 & Walls: Enrichment and Ornamentation, 65, Funk & Wagnalls; Designing and Decorating Interiors, John Wiley, 65; New Uses for Old Cannonballs, Funk & Wagnalls, 66; Doughboy Letters, 77 & Allen Eaton: Dean of American Crafts, 2003, Local History Company, Pitts. *Mailing Add:* 14320 Alan Seeger Rd Petersburg PA 16669

VAN DUINWYK, GEORGE PAUL
GOLDSMITH, SILVERSMITH
b New York, NY, Sept 30, 41. *Study:* Calif State Univ, Northridge, with Frederick Lauritzen, BA, 64; Calif State Univ, Long Beach, with Alvin A Pine, MA, 71; RI Sch of Design, with John A Prip, MFA, 72; Southern New Eng Sch Law, JD, 95. *Work:* Oakland Mus, Calif. *Exhib:* Mod Am Metalsmithing & Jewelry, Corcoran Gallery of Art, Washington, 72; Jewelry Invitational, Albright-Knox Mus, Buffalo, NY, 74; World Silver Fair, Mexico City, Mex, 74; Univ Colo, 74; 275 Yrs of Am Metalsmithing, Mus of Contemp Crafts, NY, 75; Goldsmiths 77, Phoenix Art Mus, Ariz, 77; Profiles of US Jewelry, Tex Tech Univ, Lubbock, 77; and others. *Pos:* Craftsman-in-residence, RI State Coun on the Arts, 76-77; dir tech resources, Jewelry Inst, Providence, RI, 77-79; dir, Southeast Asia Sch of Jewelry Arts, Bangkok, Thailand, 91, 92; freelance designer/craftsman. *Teaching:* Assoc prof metalsmithing, Calif State Univ, Long Beach, 72-73; adj prof metalsmithing, RI Sch of Design, 73-74; asst prof, Kent State Univ, 79-82. *Awards:* Purchase Award, The Metal Experience, Oakland Mus, 71; Design Award, Designer/Craftsman 77, Richmond Art Ctr, Calif, 76; Nat Endowment for the Arts Grant, Slide Jury Proj, 77. *Bibliog:* Ralph Turner (auth), Modern Jewelry, Eng publ, 76; Thelma Newman (auth), The Container Book, Chilton, 77; Oppi Untracht (auth), Jewelry Techniques, Doubleday 77. *Mem:* Soc NAm Goldsmiths; Am Crafts Coun; life mem Worshipful Co Goldsmiths, London, Eng; ABA; Mass Bar Asn. *Media:* Precious & Nonprecious Metals. *Publ:* Auth, Ralph Turner, Modern Jewelry, Crown Publ Jewelry, Oppi Untracht, Doubleday Publ. *Mailing Add:* 358 Boulevard 358 Boulevard Middletown RI 02842-5467

VANESS, MARGARET HELEN
PHOTOGRAPHER, WRITER
b Seattle, Wash, Nov 6, 19. *Study:* Univ Wash, BFA(painting), 70, BFA(printingmaking), 71, MAT & MFA, 73; Drexel Univ, cert(prof educ women in bus), 75; spec study with Francis Cellentano, Glen Alps, George Tsutakawa, Freeman Patterson & Robert Stahl; Boeing Co, management training, 78-81; Soc Tech Commun, 81-83. *Work:* US Embassies in Athens, Bogata, Caracas, Copenhagen, Seoul, Managua, Lima, Lagos, Dar es Salaam & Tanzania; Cheney-Cowles Mus, Spokane, Wash; Pratt-Manhattan Ctr Gallery, NY; World Print Orgn, San Francisco, Calif; Evergreen State Col Libr Collection, Olympia, Wash; and others. *Comn:* Two ed of ten prints each, US Info Agency, 73; mural, Med Ctr, Boeing Co, Philadelphia, Pa, 74; mural, Gem & Minerals Mag, 90. *Exhib:* Northwest Ann, Seattle Art Mus, Wash, 65 & 67; Judkin Mem Am Mus, Bath, Eng, Pratt Manhattan, NY, 72-74; 60th Ann, Del Art Mus, Wilmington, 74; Philadelphia Art Alliance, Pa, 75; one-person show, Greenhill-Lower Merion, Philadelphia, Pa, 76; Nat Print Exhib, Cheney-Cowles Mus, Spokane, Wash, 77; Gov Invitational, Olympia, Wash, 78; Gallery Soho, 2000; and others. *Collection Arranged:* Sari Robinson, Special Exhibit, Walnuts Gallery 73, Philadelphia, PA. *Pos:* Instr, Univ Washington, 71-73 & 84; audio-visual illusr, Boeing Co, Seattle, Wash, 72-73 & 78-84; tech illusr, Du Pont Co, Wilmington, Del, 73-74; consult, 80-; ed, Cable Releases, 85-90 & PSA Puget Soundoff (newsletter), 98; news ed & columnist, Photog Soc Am J, 96-98. *Teaching:* Instr painting & drawing, Burien Arts Gallery Sch, Seattle, Wash, 68-69; asst printmaking, Univ Wash, Seattle, 71-73; lectr, Abbotsford Can Photo-arts, 94; lectr at various other organizations 94-99. *Awards:* Progress/Serv Award for Advancement, Art & Photog, 89; Bronze Stars (4), Photogr Soc Am, Journalism, 91 95; Honor Award, Photog Soc Am, 93, Silver Star, 96 & 99; many others. *Bibliog:* Carolyn Wright (auth), Master of Fine Arts, Thesis exhibit at Henry Gallery, Univ Washington Daily, 6/73; Andrew Seraphin (auth), Four printmakers in Gallery F, Art Alliance Bull, 4/75; Karen Klamm (auth), Sound-Off, Soc Northwest Tech Commun, 12/83. *Mem:* charter mem Burien Arts Asn (trustee, 65-69); Photog Soc Am (zone dir, 94-98, dist rep, 88-94); charter mem Nat Mus Women in Arts, Washington, DC; Bellevue Art Mus; Boeing Employees Photog Soc (educ dir, 95-99). *Media:* Photography, Watercolor. *Res:* Visual Commun. *Specialty:* Painting; Photog (as painting); Natural Phenomena. *Interests:* Books; Gardens; Slide programs (Gemology, Geology & Gems); Visual Imagery. *Publ:* Contribr, Creativity, 4/91 & In persuit of contemporary images, 7/92, Photog Am Soc J; Eye & mind/minds-eye, summer 91 & Abstraction, beginnings, summer 92, NWCCC Newletter; Articles, Photog Soc Am J, 91-96, 98, 99 & 2000; Try a New Angle-Make It Soft, Aesthetic Experience, 2001

VAN GINKEL, BLANCHE LEMCO
ARCHITECT, EDUCATOR
b Can. *Study:* McGill Univ, BArch; Harvard Univ, MCP. *Hon Degrees:* Univ Aix-Marseille, Hon Dr, 2005. *Work:* Can Ctr Archit, Montreal. *Exhib:* Plan for Old Montreal, Place Ville Marie, Montreal, Que, 63; Midtown Manhattan Plan Exhib, Art Dir Club & NY Cult Ctr, 72; Work of van Ginkel Assoc, Columbia Univ, NY, 73; Spectrum Can, Royal Can Acad Arts, Montreal, 76; Earthworks, JB Aird Gallery, Toronto, 98; and others; Cur of exhib at Royal Cenadia Acad of Arts, Ital Cult Inst, Toronto; Univ Toronto Sch of Archit. *Pos:* Partner, van Ginkel Assocs, Montreal, Toronto, 57-; rep, Can Conf Arts, Ottawa, Royal Archit Inst Can, 71-74; mem adv comt on design, Nat Capital Planning Comn, 77-82; chmn, Massey Awards, Ottawa, Ont, 77-; bd, Asn Col Schs Archit, 81-84, vpres, 85-86, pres, 86-87. *Teaching:* Asst prof archit, Univ Pa, Philadelphia, 51-57; vis prof, Harvard Univ, Univ Montreal & McGill Univ; dean, Sch Archit, Univ Toronto, Ont, 77-82, prof archit, 77 . *Awards:* Asn Col Schs Archit Distinguished Professor, 89; Citizenship Citation, Govt Can, 91; Alumni Award, 91; Hon Fel, Am Inst Architects, 95; Order of Can Mem, 2000. *Bibliog:* Article, New patterns for a metropolis, Archit Forum, 10/71; Les effets Reels--, Archit Concept, 5/73. *Mem:* Royal Can Acad Arts (bd, 92-); Fel Royal Archit Inst Can. *Publ:* Auth, The form of the core, J Am Inst Planner, 2/61; ed & contribr, Automobile Issue Can Art, 62; Expo 67 Archit Design, 67; contribr, Phenomenon of Pollution, Harvest House, 68; contribr, Aesthetic Considerations, In: Urban Problems, Holt Rinehart & Winston, 71. *Mailing Add:* 38 Summerhill Gardens Toronto ON M4T 1B4 Canada

VAN HAAFTEN, JULIA
CURATOR, WRITER
b Lancaster, Pa, Nov 3, 46. *Study:* Barnard Col, BA, 68; Columbia Univ, MLS, 70. *Collection Arranged:* Original Sun Pictures (with catalog), 77 & 96 Images: Talbot to Stieglitz (with catalog), 81, New York Pub Libr Col; Francis Frith in the Middle East, 84; Clarence Kennedy, 87; The View From Space (sites), 89; Berenice Abbott: Modern Vision (with catalog), 89; Yosemite: Photography's Lanscape, 90; 400 Years of Native American Portraits, 92; A J Russell and the Union, Pacific RR, 94. *Pos:* Contribr, Libr J, Portfolio Mag, Hist Photog, 73-; dir photog collections, New York Pub Libr, 79-. *Teaching:* Instr, Rare Book Sch, Columbia Univ, 86-87. *Awards:* Summer stipend, Nat Endowment Humanities, 94. *Bibliog:* Article, AB Bookmen's Weekly, 1/12/82, Darkroom Photogr, 1/83, Photography Year, Time-Life, 82 & Portfolio, 1/2/82. *Res:* Documentary photography; illustrated books, albums, other forms of publications of photographs. *Publ:* Contribr, Guide to the literature of art history, Am Libr Asn, 81; coauth, Egypt and the Holy Land: 77 Views by Francis Frith, Dover, 81; The View From Space: American Astronaut Photography, 88. *Mailing Add:* NY Pub Libr Fifth Ave at 42nd St New York NY 10018

VAN HARLINGEN, JEAN (ANN)
ENVIRONMENTAL ARTIST, PAINTER
b Dayton, Ohio, Feb 12, 47. *Study:* Ohio State Univ, BS, 70; Tyler Sch Art (univ fel), MFA, 75. *Work:* Hallmark, Kansas City, Mo; Am Century Investments, Kansas City, Mo; AT&T, Kansas City; IBM, Detroit; Arrowmont's Sch of Arts and Crafts, 50th Ann Traveling Col, 97. *Comn:* Pet Inc, St Louis, Mo, 86; Laumeier Sculpture Park, St Louis, Mo, 95; Paper in the Millennium, Robert C Williams Am Mus of Papermaking, Atlanta, Ga, 2000. *Exhib:* 12th Int Biennial Tapestry, Mus Cantanol des Beaux Arts, Lausanne, Switz, 85; Int Biennial Paper Art, Leopold-Hoesch Mus, Duren, WGer; 13th Outdoor Sculpture Show, Shidoni Gallery, Santa Fe, NMex, 87; solo show, Leedy-Voulkos Gallery, Kansas City, 90 & 97, Western Mich Univ, Kalamazoo, 90, Park Col, Parkville, Mo, 98, Eastern Wash Univ, Chaney, 98; Liberties Expressions, 14th Int Sculpture Conf, Philadelphia, 92. *Pos:* Coordr, Visual Arts Pub Serv Prog, Brandywine Graphic Workshop, 78-80 & Women's Caucus Art, 80-81, Philadelphia, Pa. *Teaching:* Vis artist, Univ Mo, Kansas City, 86-94; adj prof, Park Univ, Parkville, Mo, 94-. *Awards:* Grant, Pa Coun Arts, 74; Second Prize, Paper Fiber XII, Iowa City/Johnson Co Arts Coun. *Bibliog:* Milena Lamarova (auth), Textile sculpture: The 12th international biennial of tapestry, Am Craft, 10-11/85; Greg Field (auth), Subtle Process Deserves a Second Look, 89; Susan Powers (auth), Pulp Art, Kansas City Mag, 6/96. *Mem:* Kansas City Artists Coalition (bd dir, 86); Int Sculpture Ctr; Int Asn Hand Papermakers; Robert C Williams Am Mus of Papermaking. *Media:* All. *Dealer:* Sherry Leedy Contemporary Art 2004 Baltimore Ave Kansas City MO. *Mailing Add:* 8142 1/2 Troost No 27 Kansas City MO 64131

VAN HORN, DANA CARL
PAINTER
b San Diego, Calif, Nov 19, 50. *Study:* San Diego State Univ, BFA, 72; Yale Univ, MFA, 74. *Work:* Metrop Mus Art, NY; Allentown Art Mus, Pa; Art Inst Chicago. *Comn:* Mural, Cathedral St Cath Siena, Allentown, Pa, 82; painting, St Bernards Church, Easton, Pa, 85; mural, Holy Ghost Church, Bethlehem, Pa, 90. *Exhib:* Local Heroes, Allentown Art Mus, Pa, 88. *Teaching:* Baum Sch Art, Allentown. *Bibliog:* Judd Tully (auth), article, Am Artist, 87; Tom Bolt (auth), article, Arts Mag, 87. *Media:* Oil on linen. *Mailing Add:* 1144 N 33rd St Allentown PA 18104-2674

VANIER, JERRE LYNN
ART DEALER, DIRECTOR
b Phoenix, Ariz, June 11, 57. *Study:* Ariz State Univ, BA (art hist, magna cum laude), 78, MA (humanities); studied with Frederic G Renner. *Exhib:* Dan Namingha: Pueblo Symbolism & Landscapes, Vanier Galleries on Marshall, 2000, Scholder 2000: New Works by Fritz Scholder, 2000, Francoise Gilot: 60 Yrs of Her Art, 2000, The Art of Janet Fish, 2001 & The Art of Dale Chihuly, 2002. *Pos:* dir, Joy Tash Gallery, Scottsdale, Ariz, 96-97; dir Estate Art, Vanier Fine Art on Main, Scottsdale, Ariz, 98-99; dir, Vanier Galleries on Marshall, Scottsdale, Ariz, 99-2001; dir of Client Relations 2001-2004; pres, Jerre Lynn Vanier, Fine Arts Ltd, 2004-. *Mem:* Nat Soc Arts & Letters (bd mem, 88-); Int Friends of Transformative Art (vchmn, 90-92 & chmn, 92-96); Scottsdale Cult Coun, Pub Arts Adv Bd; Adv bd, Friends of Sch Art, Ariz State Univ; Nat Art Chair for the Nat Soc of Arts and Letters 2001; Nat Art Competition 2001; Pres Elect for the Katherine Herberger Friends of the Sch of Art Ariz State Univ, 2004. *Specialty:* contemporary art; nineteenth & twentieth century estate art; Art of the American West. *Interests:* Collector of Contempory Art

VAN LAAR, TIMOTHY
PAINTER, WRITER
b Ann Arbor, Mich, Mar 7, 51. *Study:* Calvin Col, BA, 73; Wayne State Univ, MFA, 75. *Work:* Detroit Inst Art; Krannert Art Mus, Champaign, Ill; Herman Miller Inc, Zeeland, Mich; Valparaiso Univ, Ind; Steelcase Inc, Grand Rapids, Mich; Ill State Mus, Springfield. *Exhib:* Chinese Nat Fine Art Mus, Beijing, 87; Amalgama, Thessaloniki, Greece, 94; Fassbender Gallery, Chicago, 97, 2000; Univ Hertfordshire, Hatfield, Eng, 2000; Karl Gesellschaft, Berlin, Ger, 2002; Sheldon Memorial Gallery, Univ Nebraska, Lincoln, 2003; Grand Rapids, Art Mus, MI, 2004; Galerie Stella A, Berlin, Ger, 2006. *Pos:* Printer lithography, Mich Workshop Fine Prints, Detroit, 74-76; resident artist, Urban Inst Contemp Art, Grand Rapids, Mich, 78; ed bd, Art & Academe: A journal for the Humanities & Sciences in the Education of Artists, 88-; US Coordr, Burren Col Art, Ballyvaughn, Ireland, 94-99. *Teaching:* Instr painting & printmaking, Calvin Col, 77-81; asst prof painting, Univ Ill, Urbana-Champaign, 81-87, assoc prof, 87-97, prof, 97, painting program chair, 2000-2002; vis lectr, Glasgow Sch Art, 88-89. *Awards:* Yaddo Fel, 85; Ill Artists Fel, 87; Fulbright, 88; Arts Am Grant, 94; Howard Found Fel, 2001. *Bibliog:* Buzz Spector (auth), Natural Color Aerial Views (exhib catalog), Berlin, 1997; James Elkins (auth), The Exact Moment of Relaxation (exhib catalog), Chicago, 2001; Daniel A, Siedell (auth), Finding Our Way by Losing the Instructions (exhib catalog)., Lincoln, NE, 2003. *Media:* All Media. *Publ:* Coauth, Active Sights: Art as Social Interaction, Mayfield Press, 98; co-auth, Art with a Difference: Looking at Difficult and Unfamiliar Art, Mayfield Press, 2000. *Mailing Add:* Univ Ill Sch Art & Design Champaign IL 61820

VAN LEUNEN, ALICE LOUISE
SCULPTOR,TEXTURE & PAPER ARTIST
b Evansville, Ind, Feb 7, 43. *Study:* Smith Col, BA, 65; Ind Univ Fine Arts Dept, 66-67. *Work:* Seattle City Light Portable Works, 85; Atlantic Co Off Bldg, 85; Western Ore State Col, 89; Justice Servs Bldg, Hillsboro, Ore, 92; Napavine Wash Sch Dist, 2000; 8 NW 8th Bldg, Portland, Ore, 2004. *Comn:* Clackamas Community Col, Oregon City, 92; PT Mulia Bank Tower, Djakarta, Indonesia, 93 & 94; sculpture (in collab with Walter Gordinier), Nat Hig Magnetic Field Lab, Fla State Univ, Tallahassee, 95; sculpture (in collab with Walter Gordinier), Portland Community Col, Cascade Libr, 95; sculpture (in collab with Walter Gordinier), Minn High Security Hosp, St Peter; and others, 91-2000; Fairview Auditorium, Okla, 02; Paper Cuts, Nat'l Traveling Exhib under auspies of Exhibs USA, 2004-2007. *Exhib:* Works in Fabric, Renshaw Gallery, Linfield Col, Ore, 79; three-women exhib, Seattle Pac Univ, 79; Duo Exhib, Univ Ore Mus of Art, 78; one-woman shows, Contemp Crafts Gallery, Portland, 79 & The Lawrence Gallery Salishan, Gleneden Beach, Ore, 80; Smithsonian Inst, Washington DC, 80; Univ Evansville, Ind, 85. *Pos:* Asst dir, Delphian Gallery-Delphian Found, 77; exhib asst, Contemp Crafts Gallery, Portland,

78-79. *Teaching:* Seminar instr, Dept Fine Arts, Univ Ore, 78-; lectr textiles, Portland State Univ, 80-91. *Awards:* Cash Award, 76 Traveling Exhib Competition, Univ Ore Mus of Art, 6/76; Honorable Mention, 6th Ann Exhib, Corvallis Art Ctr, 11/76; Individual Arts Fel, Ore Arts Comn, 94. *Bibliog:* The state of the crafts--a visual review, Frank Petock & Assoc, 1980, Interweave Mag, summer 80; The Guild, Kraus Sikes, Inc, NY, 86, 88, 89, 90, 91, 92, 94, 95, 96, 97, 2000-2004. *Mem:* Am Crafts Coun, NW Region; Nexus. *Media:* Mixed Media, Sculpture. *Dealer:* Portland Art Mus Rental/Sales Gallery Portland OR. *Mailing Add:* 9025 SE Terrace View Ct Amity OR 97101

VANN, SAMUEL LEROY
PAINTER
b Ithaca, NY, Sept 16, 52. *Study:* Ft Lewis Col, BA, 73; State Univ NY, Brockport, MS(educ). *Work:* Everson Mus Art; Menninger Fund, Topeka, Kans; Joan Kennedy; Dr Benjamin Spock; Corporate and private collections throughout the US. *Exhib:* Watercolors USA, Springfield Art Mus, Mo, 77; Chautauqua 20th Nat Show, CAA Gallery, NY, 78; Second Int All on Paper Show, Assoc Art Orgn Western NY, Buffalo, 80; Rivers, Gorges, Canyons Traveling Exhib, 82-82; Midwest Watercolor Soc First 100 Exhib, Tweed Mus Art; Butler Inst Am Art 82, Midyear Show, Youngstown, Ohio, 82; NMex Int Art Show, Clovis; one-man shows, Prouty-Chew Mus, Geneva, NY, 82, Rome Art Ctr, NY, 82, Arnot Art Mus, Elmira, NY, 82, Schweinfurth Mem Art Gallery, Auburn, NY, 81, Sheldon Mem Art Gallery, Lincoln, Nebr, 82, Everson Mus Art, Suracuse, NY, 82, Albright-Knox Art Gallery, Buffalo, NY, 82. *Teaching:* Asst dir painting, Chautauqua Inst Ctr Arts, 79-80. *Awards:* First Prize Graphics, Twelfth Ann Western Art Show, 77 & Third Ann Nat Miniature Show, 77; First Prize Painting, Second Int All on Paper Show, 80. *Media:* Watercolor. *Dealer:* Bishop Gallery 7164 Main Scottsdale AZ 85251. *Mailing Add:* 5271 Cold Springs Rd Trumansburg NY 14886

VAN OSDELL, BARRIE (CALABRESE) SMITH
PAINTER, INSTRUCTOR
b Baton Rouge, La. *Study:* Self taught. *Work:* Pickens Co Art Mus, SC; SC Arts Comn. *Comn:* 17 pen & ink works, Am Bank Op Ctr, Baton Rouge, La, 82; 4 oil paintings, La Heritage Galleries, Baton Rouge, 85; 4 oil paintings of Clemson Univ, Campus Heritage Inc, Anderson, SC, 87; 22 oil paintings, Wachovia Bank, Winston-Salem & Charlotte, NC, 92-98. *Exhib:* Hudson Valley Art Asn, Hastings-on-Hudson, NY, 95 & 99; Nat Oil & Acrylic Painters Soc, Osage Beach, Mo, 95, 97 & 99; Am Artists Prof League, Salmagundi Club, NY, 95-2000; Oil Painters Am, Nat & Regional Exhib, 95-98, 2002 & 2006; Arts for the Parks Int Competition, Fed Nat Parks, Jackson, Wyo, 95, 96 & 98. *Teaching:* Pvt classes, 76-84; instr, painting workshops. *Awards:* Suppliers Award, Dick Blick Art Materials, 95; Award of Excellence, Oil Painters Am, 98; Medal Hon, Am Artists Prof League, 99. *Bibliog:* Don Marvine (auth), Design basics, Plate Collector Mag, 1/86; interview with Sumter Mus Art (TV doc), PBS, SC, 5/90. *Mem:* Oil Painters Am (signature mem); Am Artists Prof League (fel); Nat Oil & Acrylic Painters Soc (signature mem); Hudson Valley Art Asn (elected mem); Anderson Art League. *Media:* Acrylic, Oils. *Publ:* Art From the Parks, North Light Books, 9/2000. *Dealer:* Taylor Clark Gallery Baton Rouge LA 70806; Fountainside Gallery Wilmington NC. *Mailing Add:* 609 Horseshoe Rd Honeapath SC 29654

VAN RIPER, PETER
PRINTMAKER, CONCEPTUAL ARTIST
b Detroit, Mich, July 8, 42. *Study:* Univ NC, BA(art hist, Far Eastern hist); Univ Tokyo, MA(Far Eastern art hist); Univ Mich. *Work:* Everson Mus Art, Syracuse, NY; Mus Mod Art, NY; Los Angeles Inst Contemp Art; Mus Mod Art, Oxford, Eng; Stedelijk Mus, Amsterdam. *Exhib:* One-man shows, US Info Serv Japan Performance Tour, 74, Video & Graphics Exhib, Everson Mus, 75 & Washington Proj Arts, 79; Kunst Bleibt Kunst, Kunstverein Art Mus, Cologne, Ger, 74; Holography 75 First Decade, Int Ctr Photog, NY. *Teaching:* Teacher multi-media art, Calif Inst of Arts, Valencia, 70-73. *Awards:* Traveling Exhib Award, Western Asn of Art Mus, 74. *Mem:* Editions/Sch of Holography, Ann Arbor, Mich & San Francisco (pres); Fluxus, NY. *Publ:* Auth, It, 75. *Dealer:* Upstairs Gallery 1457 Grant Ave San Francisco CA 94133. *Mailing Add:* 73 Calyer St Brooklyn NY 11222

VAN SANT, TOM R
SCULPTOR, PAINTER
b Los Angeles, Calif, Feb 26, 31. *Study:* Stanford Univ, BA, 53; Otis Art Inst Los Angeles Co, MFA, 57; also studied with Herb Jepson, Peter Voulkos & Millard Sheets. *Work:* Davies Pac Ctr, Honolulu; Pac Design Ctr, Los Angeles; Libr Cong; Smithsonian Inst; Inst Contemp Art, London. *Comn:* Sculptured concrete walls, Irvine Co, Newport Beach, Calif, 68; sculptured concrete mural, Honolulu Int Airport, 73; mural, Taipei Int Airport, Taiwan, 74; fountain sculpture, City of Los Angeles, 75; bronze sculpture, Warmington Co, Newport Beach, Calif, 82. *Exhib:* One-man exhibs, Inst Contemp Art, London, 76, Myer Galleries, Melbourne & Sydney, Australia, 77, Stedelijk Mus, Amsterdam, The Neth, 77, Honolulu Hale, City Hall, 77 & Pac Design Ctr, Los Angeles, 80. *Teaching:* Instr design & drawing, Otis Art Inst Los Angeles Co, 60-66; instr creativity, Omega Sem, Fall City, Wash, 66-68; fel, Ctr Advan Visual Studies, Mass Inst Technol, 81-. *Awards:* Art in Architecture Award, Am Inst Archit, 56, 61 & 68; Award of Merit, First Ann Exhib Illus West, 59; Purchase Award, Int Sculpture Symposium, Calif State Univ, Long Beach, 74. *Bibliog:* Fundaburk (auth), Art in Public Places in the US, Popular Press, 75; Piene (auth), Sky Art Conf, Ctr Advan Visual Studies, Mass Inst Technol, 81-83. *Publ:* Co-dir, Flight Forms (film), Ed Spiegel Co, 76. *Mailing Add:* 146 Entrada Dr Santa Monica CA 90402

VAN SCHAACK, ERIC
HISTORIAN, EDUCATOR
b Evanston, Ill, June 10, 31. *Study:* Dartmouth Col, AB, 53; Columbia Univ, PhD, 69. *Pos:* Prof of Art and Art Hist, Emer Colgate Univ. *Teaching:* Lectr & research asst, The Frick Collection, NY, 60-62; from asst prof to prof, Goucher Col, Baltimore, 64-76, chmn, Dept Visual Arts, 73-76; prof, Dept Art & Art Hist, Colgate Univ, 77-96, chmn, 77-83, prof emer, 96-. *Awards:* Italian Govt Grant & Fulbright Travel Grant, 62-63, Ford Found Grant Humanities, 72-73; Colgate Univ Humanities Fac Development Fund Grant, 79-80 & 93. *Mem:* Col Art Asn Am; Soc Archit Historians. *Res:* Italian Renaissance & Baroque art; American architecture. *Publ:* An unpublished letter by Francesco Albani, Art Bull, 69; coauth, The music in Van Dyck's Rinaldo and Armida, Baltimore Mus Art Ann III, 69; contribr, Italian Paintings, Baltimore Mus Art, 81; Francesco Albani's Guida di Bologna, Acts of the 24th International Congress of the History of Art, Bologna, 82; other articles publ in Arte Antica e Moderna, Apollo and Picker Art Gallary Ann Report/Bull. *Mailing Add:* Dept Fine Arts Colgate Univ Hamilton NY 13346

VAN SUCHTELEN, ADRIAN
PRINTMAKER, EDUCATOR
b Semarang, Indonesia, June 18, 41; US citizen. *Study:* El Camino Col, Calif; Otis Art Inst, Los Angeles, BFA, MFA, 66. *Work:* Indianapolis Mus Art; De Cordova Mus, Lincoln, Mass; Cleveland Mus Art; Riverside Mus, Calif; Milwaukee Art Ctr; and others. *Comn:* Art work on film Young Lovers, Samuel Goldwyn Studios, Los Angeles, 64. *Exhib:* Drawing Soc Nat Exhib, Am Fedn Arts, NY, 70-72; Colorprint USA, Tex, 74; Davidson Nat Print & Drawing Exhib, NC, 75; Pratt Graphics Ctr Int Print Exhib, NY, 75; one-man show, Northern State Col, SDak, 83; and others. *Teaching:* Prof drawing & grad dir, Utah State Univ, 67-. *Awards:* Purchase Award, NMex State Univ, 71; Ben & Abbey Grey Found Purchase Award, Salt Lake Art Ctr, 72; Purchase Prize, Boston Printmakers, 81. *Mem:* Graphics Soc; Boston Printmakers Soc. *Publ:* Contribr, Drawing A Search for Form, 65; auth & illusr, Lifetime Career Schools, Correspondence Art Course, 67; contribr, Oil Painting, Techniques and Materials, 69; The Hidden Elements of Drawing, 73. *Dealer:* Sylvesters Art Studio 61 E 320 S Salt Lake City UT 84111. *Mailing Add:* 655 E 1800 N Logan UT 84341

VAN VLIET, CLAIRE
PRINTMAKER, PUBLISHER
b Ottawa, Ont, Aug 9, 33. *Study:* San Diego State Univ, AB, 52; Claremont Grad Sch, MFA, 54. *Hon Degrees:* Univ Arts, Hon Dr, 93; San Diego State Univ, Hon DFA, 2002. *Work:* Philadelphia Mus Art; Montreal Mus Fine Arts; Cleveland Mus Art; Victoria & Albert Mus, London; NDak Mus Art, Grand Forks. *Exhib:* Paper as Medium, Smithsonian Traveling Exhib, 78-80; The Janus Press 1975-80, Fleming Mus Traveling Exhib, 82-84; Dolan/Maxwell Gallery, Philadelphia, 84 & 91; Mary Ryan Gallery, NY, 86; Univ Arts, 89, 2001; Bates Col Mus Art, Lewiston, Maine, 94 & 99; Victoria & Albert Mus, London, 94; NDak Mus of Art, 95; Rosenwald-Wolf Gallery Univ Arts Philadelphia 2001; The Grolier Club New York City 2006; Nat Gallery Art Libr 2006; Humanities Gallery, Scripps Col, 2006; Group exhibitions include Brooklyn Nat, Philadelphia Arts Festival, Kunst zu Kafka, Germany, Paper as Medium, Smithsonian Inst, Washington, Paper Now, Cleveland Mus Art, 1986, Boyle Arts Festival, Ireland, 1993, Libr Congress, 1997-, ND Mus Art, 1999. *Pos:* Proprietor, Janus Press, 54-. *Teaching:* Asst prof printmaking, Philadelphia Col Art, 59-65; vis lectr, Univ Wis, 65-66, Univ Vt, 74-75, Univ Ala, 83, US Info Agency, Arts Am Prog to NZ, 95. *Awards:* Ingram Merrill Fel, 89; Mac Arthur Prize, Fel, 89-94; Ballinglen Fel, Ireland, 93; Paton Prize, Nat Acad Design, 2001. *Bibliog:* Lehrer (auth), The Janus Press 1955-75 & Fine (auth), Claire Van Vliet: Landscape Paperworks, Dolan-Maxwell, Pa, 84; McLean (auth) In Black & White: Landscape prints by Claire Van Vliet, Maine, 99; Fine, Ruth (auth) The Janus Press - Fifty Years 2006. *Mem:* Soc Printers Boston; Nat Acad (acad, 95-); Vt Acad Arts and Scis. *Media:* Relief, Lithography; Paper, Book Arts. *Collection:* Nat Gallery of Art Wash DC; Libr Cong; Winnipeg Art Gallery; Flemming Mus UVM Burlington Vt; Philadelphia Mus Art; Cleveland Mus Art; New Orleans Mus Art; Bates Col Mus Art; Univ Maine Machias Gallery; Nat Mus the Philippines; Tate; Wiggin Gallery Boston Pub Libr. *Publ:* Illusr & ed, Sky and Earth-Variable Landscape, Janus Press, 70; auth & illusr, Satellite, Mus Mod Art, 71; designer, Aunt Sallies Lament, Chronicle Bks, 93; Woven and Interlocking Book Structures - Janus/Gefn Unlimited 2002. *Dealer:* Dolan-Maxwell 2046 Rittenhouse Sq Philadelphia Pa 19103; Mary Ryan 24 W 57th St New York NY 10019. *Mailing Add:* 101 Schoolhouse Rd Newark VT 05871

VAN WINKELEN, BARBARA
PAINTER, ILLUSTRATOR
b Waban, Mass. *Study:* Yale Univ Sch Fine Arts, BFA, 43. *Work:* Windsor Hist Soc; Nantucket Hist Soc; Shaker Mus, Hancock Shaker Village Inc, Mass. *Exhib:* 82nd Ann, Catharine Lorillard Wolfe Art Club, NY, 78; Conn Watercolor Soc, 78-86 & Conn Acad, 80-86, Wadsworth Atheneum, Hartford, Conn; Slater Mem Mus, Norwich, Conn, 78-81; Conn Acad Fine Arts, Olde State House, Hartford, Conn, 81; Springfield Acad Assoc & Springfield Art League Mus Show, 86; New Haven Paint & Clay Club; Nat Watercolor Soc Members Show, Colo; NAm Juried Shows, NE Watercolor Soc, 90, 92, 94, 96 & 98, Windsor Hist Soc, 98. *Pos:* Staff asst, Mus Mod Art, New York, 43-44; tech illusr, United Technol, 53-71. *Teaching:* Children's art, Wadsworth Atheneum, Hartford, Conn, 48-50. *Awards:* First Prize, Conn Watercolor Soc, 85 & 86; Best Show, Conn Women Artists, 83 & 84 & Acad Artists Assoc, 86. *Bibliog:* Maureen O'Sullivan (auth), Nantucket Artist Barbara van Winkelen (film), 79; J Merrick-Windsor (interviewer), On Camera (1 hour interviews), WWEU, 86 & 87. *Mem:* Conn Acad Fine Arts; Conn Watercolor Soc; Conn Women Artists (bd dir, 80-82); Nantucket Artists Asn; New Haven Paint & Clay Club; New Eng Watercolor Soc; Acad Artists Asn. *Media:* Egg Tempera; All Media. *Publ:* Illusr, Escape from the

Chanticleer, Classic Collections Fine Arts Catalogues, 92-96; feature article, Nantucket Mag, autumn 93; Winds & Dragons Publ, 95. *Dealer:* Spindrift Gallery 11 Old S Wharf Nantucket MA 02554; Jay Whitney 405 Queen St Southington CT. *Mailing Add:* 1864 Poquonock Ave Poquonock CT 06064

VAN WINKLE, LESTER G
SCULPTOR, EDUCATOR
b Greenville, Tex, Jan 11, 44. *Study:* ETex State Univ, BS; Univ Ky, MA; also sculpture with Michael D Hall. *Work:* Arrowmont Sch Arts & Crafts, Gatlinburg, Tenn; Dade Co Jr Col, Miami. *Exhib:* Sculpt 70, Corcoran Gallery Art, Washington, DC, 70; Whitney Biennial of Painting & Sculpture, Whitney Mus, NY, 73; one-man shows, Henry Gallery, Washington, 73-75 & Webb Parsons Gallery, Bedford, NY, 74-75; Waves Exhib, Cranbrook Acad Art Galleries, 74. *Teaching:* From asst prof to assoc prof sculpture, Va Commonwealth Univ, 69-. *Dealer:* Henri Gallery 1500 21st St NW Washington DC 20036. *Mailing Add:* VCU Sculpture Dept PO Box 843005 1000 W Broad St Richmond VA 23284-3005

VARGAS, JOSEPHINE
ILLUSTRATOR, PAINTER
b New York, NY, July 31, 46. *Study:* Fashion Inst Technol, 64-65; Sch Visual Arts, 78-79. *Work:* Mus de la Historia, Ponce, PR. *Exhib:* Invitational, William Deford III Gallery, Citicorp, NY, 93; Fashion Inst Technol Mus, NY, 93-96; Flushing Coun on Arts, 93 & 94; Atelier 14, New York City, 2000; Gallery Emanuel, Great Neck, NY, 2000; Mus at the Fashion Inst Tech, New York City, 93-03; and others. *Pos:* Trustee, Nat Art League, Douglaston, NY, 87-. *Teaching:* adj, asst prof, Fashion Inst Tech, 92-; instr, Parsons Sch Design, 97-. *Awards:* Peacock Showcase Award, Visual Art Alliance of Long Island, 91; First Place Watercolor, Nat Art League, 91; Purchase Award Ponce Pinturoso Open Competition, Ponce, PR, 92. *Mem:* Nat Asn Women Artists (Marion de Sola Mendes award, 2000); Nat Art League (advisor). *Media:* Computer Artist; Watercolor, Mixed Media. *Publ:* contribr, Portfolio for Fashion Designers, 03. *Mailing Add:* 83-40 Austin St Kew Gardens NY 11415

VARGO, JOHN
EDUCATOR, PAINTER
b Cleveland, Ohio, Aug 9, 29. *Study:* Cleveland Inst Art, with Paul Riba & Louis Bosa. *Work:* Cleveland Mus Art; Syracuse Univ; Munson-Williams-Proctor Inst, Utica, NY; LeMoyne Col, Syracuse. *Comn:* The Erie Canal (mural), First Fed Savings Syracuse, 60. *Exhib:* Cooperstown 35th Ann Exhib, NY, 70; Rochester Finger Lakes Exhib, NY, 71; Artist as a Journalist, Soc Illusr, 77; one-man shows, LeMoyne Col, 71 & Everson Mus, 78; and others. *Pos:* Illusr, Advance Art, Cleveland, 51-58. *Teaching:* Prof illus & serigraph, Syracuse Univ, 58-. *Awards:* Eagan Pres Plaza Award & Popular Prize, 64, NY State Fair; First Prize for Portrait Painting, Cooperstown Art Asn, 70; Award for Painting, Mem Art Gallery, Univ Rochester, 71. *Media:* Tempera, Watercolor. *Publ:* Illusr, covers, Michael Brown's Laying Waste, 1/81 & Roger Shattuck's The Forbidden Experiment, 1/81, Washington Sq Press; illusr, cover, Daoma Winston's The Lotteries, Pocket, 4/81; illusr, Jacobo Timmerman's Prisoner Without a Name, Cell Without a Number, Reader's Digest, 11/81. *Mailing Add:* 6319 Danbury Dr Jamesville NY 13078

VARNAY JONES, THEODORA
PRINTMAKER, PAINTER
b Budapest, Hungary, Feb 26, 42; US citizen. *Study:* Univ Fine Art, Budapest, BA, 69, MA, 70. *Work:* Achenbach Found Graphic Arts, Fine Arts Mus of San Francisco, Calif; Bank Am Corp Art Collection, San Francisco; New Canaan Libr Permanent Collection, Conn; Kyoto Seika Univ, Japan. *Comn:* Color etching, Fine Arts Mus, San Francisco, 86; 12 large scale mixed media works, Sak's Fifth Ave, 89 & 90. *Exhib:* Contemp Calif Prints, San Jose Mus Art, Calif, 82; Mid Am Biennial, Mus Fine Art, Owensboro, Ky, 84; Prints USA, Nat Mus, Singapore, 84; Mini Print Int, Taller Galeria Fort, Cadoques, Spain, 84; Prints USA, Amerika Haus, Berlin, Ger, 85; The Hanga Ann, Metrop Art Mus, Tokyo, Japan, 85; Int Print Biennial, Mus de Arte Contemporanea, Cabo Frio, Brazil, 85; 3rd Biennial Exhib of Prints, Mus Mod Art, Wakayama, Japan, 89; Tamura Gallery, Tokyo, Japan, 90. *Teaching:* Guest lectr on prints, Oakland Mus Asn, 85; Guest lectr on prints, Kyoto Seika Univ, Japan. *Awards:* Purchase Award, Prints USA, Pratt Graphics Ctr, 82; Prof Prize, International Competition, 83; First Place, Cabo Frio Inter Print Biennial, 85. *Bibliog:* Miyagi Television Rev, Japan, 90. *Mem:* Calif Soc Printmakers; Graphic Arts Coun, Fine Arts Mus San Francisco; The Print Club of Philadelphia; Boston Printmakers. *Media:* Mixed media. *Dealer:* Don Soker Contemporary Art 251 Post St San Fancisco CA 94108. *Mailing Add:* 2180 Bryant St San Francisco CA 94110

VARNEY, EDWIN
CONCEPTUAL ARTIST, PRINTMAKER
b New Rochelle, NY, Oct 16, 44. *Study:* Syracuse Univ, BA, 65, MA, 66; Univ Vancouver, PhD, 76. *Work:* Vancouver Art Gallery, BC; Smith Col Art Gallery, Northampton, Mass; Alta Col Art, Calgary; Rotterdam Acad, Holland; Univ Colo, Boulder; Smithsonian, Washington DC: Art Bank, Ottawa; Allen Mus, Ohio; National Postal Mus, Ottawa. *Comn:* Wood sculpture, Burnaby Art Coun, BC, 71; concrete sculpture, BC Sculptor's Soc, 77. *Exhib:* Space Window, RI Sch Design, Providence, 78; Artists' Stamps, Mus Art & Hist, Geneva, Switz, 79; Mail Etc, Univ Colo, Boulder, Tyler Sch Art, Philadelphia & Fla State Univ, Tallahassee, 79; Post-Art, San Diego Univ Art Gallery, 88; The Nude, Vancouver Art Gallery, 93; Searching For the Hidden, Queens Col, Cambridge, Eng, 94; Outpost Biennale, Venice Biennale, Italy, 95; Arte Correo, Mus de Bellas Artes, Argentina, 97; and others. *Pos:* Artist/poet-in-residence, Intermedia, Vancouver, BC, 71-73, publ, ed & designer, 73-88; dir, Mus Int de Nuevo Art, 81-; pub art consult, Gibson & Varney, Vancouver, BC, 94-99; bd dir, Roundhouse Arts Ctr, 97-2001. *Awards:* Can Coun Grant, Environ Opera, 89. *Mem:* Cent Visual Arts Asn (bd dir, 79-); Ave des Arts; West Coast Surrealists. *Media:* Conceptual Art, Printmaking, Sculpture. *Publ:* Openings, 69, Human Nature, 74, ed, First, Second and Third International Artists' Stamp Edition, 76, 78 & 80, ed, Four Canadian Poets, 78 & ed, Contemporary Surrealist Prose, 79, Intermedia Bks; Auth, What the Wind Said, Caitlin Press, 91; Solar Eclipse, 93, Nothing Ever Changes, 95 & Entering The World, 97, The Poem Factory. *Mailing Add:* 4426 Island Hwy S Courtenay BC V9N9TI Canada

VARO, MARTON GEZA
SCULPTOR
b Szekelyudvarhely, Hungary, Mar 15, 43. *Study:* Ion Andreescu Art Acad, univ grad, 60-66. *Work:* Stedelijk Mus, Amsterdam; Nat Gallery, Budapest; Deri Mus, Debrecen, Hungary; Mora Ferenc Muzeum, Szeged, Hungary; Muzeul Tarii Crisurilor, Oradea, Romania. *Comn:* Civic Ctr, City of Brea, Calif, 90; Pereira Sculpture Garden, Univ Calif, Irvine, 91; Peace Memorial, City of Palm Desert, Calif, 92; Plaza of the Americas, Dallas, 92; Angels, Performing Arts Hall, Ft Worth, Tex, 95. *Exhib:* Studio of Young Artists, Grand Palais, Paris, 78; 4th Int Exhib Small Sculpture, Budapest, 78; Mucsarnok Exhib Hall, Budapest, 81; Bronzetto Piccola Sculptura, Padua, Italy, 86; Muckenthaler Cult Ctr, Fullerton, Calif, 90. *Awards:* Studio of Young Artist Award, 76; Munkacsy Award, 84; Fulbright Scholar, 88-91. *Media:* Marble, Stone. *Mailing Add:* 2 Charity Irvine CA 92612

VASA
SCULPTOR, EDUCATOR
b Otocac, Yugoslavia, April 25, 33; US citizen. *Study:* Sch Applied Arts, Belgrade, Yugoslavia, 47-51, Acad Applied Arts, Univ Belgrade, 51-54. *Work:* Hirshhorn Mus & Sculpture Garden, Smithsonian Inst, Washington; Mus Royaux des Beaux-Arts de Belgique, Art Mod, Brussels; Mus Mod Art, Belgrade; Phillips Collection, Washington; San Francisco Mus Mod Art, Calif. *Comn:* Sculpture, Toyota Auto Indus, Nagoya, Japan, 72; sculpture, Dallas Hyatt Regency, Tex, 78; sculpture, Cedars Sinai Med Ctr, Los Angeles, 79; sculpture, Tishman West Management Corp, Los Angeles, 86; sculpture, Olivetti, Ivrea, Italy, 86. *Exhib:* One-man shows, Palm Springs Desert Mus, Calif, 80, Mus Mod Art, Belgrade, 85 & 72, Gallery West, Los Angeles, 91, Hokin Gallery, Bay Harbor Islands, Fla, 91, John Mallon Gallery, Indianapolis, Ind, 92, Imago, Palm Springs, Calif, 92 & TR Yangle Gallery, Tokyo, 95. *Teaching:* Prof design, Univ Calif, Los Angeles, currently. *Media:* Laminated Acrylic. *Mailing Add:* 2243 Linnington Ave Los Angeles CA 90064-2339

VASELL, CHRIS
ARTIST, FILMMAKER
b Chicago, Ill, 74. *Exhib:* One-man shows: It Puts the Lotion in the Basket, Boom, Oak Park, Ill, 2002; Don't go Outside they're waiting for you, Blum & Poe, Los Angeles, 2005, 2006; Group shows: Whitecaps, Grand Rapids Art Mus, Mich, 1997; Nippon Steel, Chicago, 1999; Chicago Drawing, Forcefield Exhib Space, Chicago, 1999; Stray Show, Chicago, 2002; I See a Darkness, Blum & Poe, Los Angeles, 2003; On Paper, Nicole Klagsburn, NY, 2004; Trials & Terrors, Mus Contemp Art, Chicago, 2005; Having New Eyes, Aspen Art Mus, Colo, 2006; Whitney Biennial: Day for Night, Whitney Am Art Mus, NY, 2006. *Mailing Add:* c/o Blum and Poe 2754 S La Cienega Blvd Los Angeles CA 90034

VASQUEZ, EMIGDIO CHAVEZ
PAINTER, MURALIST
b Jerome, Ariz, May 25, 39. *Study:* Santa Ana Col, AA (art), 73; Calif State U, BA (art), 1978, MA (art), 79. *Work:* Laguna Art Mus, Laguna Beach, Calif; Bowers Mus Cult Arts, Santa Ana, Calif. *Comn:* La Educacion y El Trabajo (mural) Irvine Valley Col, Irvine, Calif; Un Pueblito en Mexico (mural), Disney Imagineering, Anaheim, Calif, 93; Ninos del Mundo (mural), City of Fullerton, Calif, 93; The Legacy of Cesar Chavez (mural), Santa Ana Col, 97; Faces of Fullerton, Fullerton (Calif) Mus, 99. *Exhib:* Our Own Artists in Orange Co, Newport Harbor Art Mus, Newport Beach, Calif, 79; The Real Thing: Southern Calif Realist painting, Laguna Beach (Calif) Mus Art, 82; Imagenes de La Raza, Amerika Haus Berlin US Cult Ctr, Berlin, 82; Vasquez in the Community, Irvine Gallery Bowers Mus, Santa Ana, Calif, 86; Paintings & Murals of Emigdio Vasquez, Anaheim Mus, Calif, 94; Cuentosy Retratos, Maria Elias Ctr Arts, Santa Ana, 98. *Teaching:* instr mural painting, City of Anaheim, 77-85; instr, Santa Ana Col, 86-87; artist-in-residence, Bowers Mus, 85-88. *Awards:* First Place Realist Painting, Twentieth la Mirada Fiesta de Artes, 81; First Place Realist Painting Twenty-First la Mirada Festival of Arts, 82; Chmn Spec Award, Anaheim Arts Coun, 90. *Bibliog:* Herman Wong (auth), Latino draws on Life, Los Angeles Times, 12/23/82; Jim Dobbs (auth), Art for the Community: An interview with Emigdio Vasquez, The Ear, spring/91; Kinney Littlefield (auth), Art for the Street, The Orange Co Register, 4/6/93. *Media:* Oil. *Mailing Add:* 1745 E Fairway Dr Apt 105 Orange CA 92866-3362

VASSDAL ELLIS, ELSI M
GRAPHIC ARTIST, EDUCATOR
b Fallon, Nev, June 9, 52. *Study:* Western Wash State Col, BS, 74; Western Wash Univ, MEd, 77; Univ Wash, PhD, 83. *Work:* Hunt Libr, Carnegie-Mellon Univ; Moravian Gallery, Brno, Czech Repub; Nat Mus Women in Arts, Washington; St Bride Printing Libr, London; Musee de la Publicite, Paris. *Exhib:* Off the Shelf, Tempe, Ariz, 94; Books-Objects of Art, Somerville, Mass, 94; Inky Fingers, NY, 94; Shape-Shifting: Transformations, Greely, Colo, 96; Turning the Page, Honolulu, 96. *Teaching:* Prof book arts, Western Wash Univ, 94-. *Awards:* Best of Category-Offset Design, Bumbershoot, 90; Best of Category-Typographic Excellence, NC & Pa Ann, 91. *Mem:* Alliance Contemp Book Arts; Ctr Book Arts; Guild Book Workers; Pac Ctr Book Arts; Type Dir Club. *Media:* Offset, Letterpress. *Publ:* Auth, Type '87, J Fûr Drucksgesichichte, Pts 1 & 2, 88-89; contribr, An Introduction to Book Design, Writer's NW Handbk, 91; auth, Artist's statement, Artweek, 1/95. *Dealer:* Edwina Legget-Califia San Francisco CA. *Mailing Add:* Dept Art Col Performing Arts Western Wash Univ MS 9068 516 High St Bellingham WA 98225

VATANDOOST, NOSSI MALEK
EDUCATOR, PAINTER
b Teheran, Iran, May 22, 35. *Study:* Persian Acad Art with Persian Miniatures Masters, 57-61; Western Ky Univ, BA, 70. *Work:* Wayland Baptist Col, Plainview, Tex; Nossi Col Art, Goodlettsville, Tenn; Persian Acad Art, Tehran, Iran; Blue Field State Col, WVa. *Exhib:* Central South, Parthenon, Nashville, Tenn, 75; Greater Madison Arts & Crafts Festival, Madison CofC, Tenn, 76. *Teaching:* Educ dir com & fine arts, Nossi Col Art, Goodlettsville, Tenn, 73-; Pres, Art Resources of Tenn-Sumner. *Awards:* Outstanding Young Artist, Persian Acad Art, 60-61; Business of the Year, Goodlettsville CofC, 98. *Mem:* Int Coun Design Sch (pres, 96-97); Nat Asn Schs Art & Design; Nashville Advert Fedn; Goodlettsville CofC; Nat Mus Women Arts. *Media:* Acrylic, Oil. *Mailing Add:* Nossi Col Art 907 Rivergate Pkwy Ste E-6 Goodlettsville TN 37072

VATER, REGINA VATER LUNDBERG
CONCEPTUAL ARTIST, LECTURER
b Rio De Janeiro, Brazil, May 11, 43. *Study:* Frank Schaeffer's Studio, Rio de Janeiro, 59; Sch Archit, Univ FED Rio de Janeiro, 60; Ibere Camargo's Studio, Rio de Janeiro, 62; Pratt Inst, Manhattan, NY, 74; Downtown Video Community Ctr, New York, 82. *Work:* Benson Latin Am Collection, Univ Tex, Austin; Video Annex, Long Beach Mus Art, Calif; Bibliotheque Nat Paris; Mus Contemp Arts, Univ Sao Paulo, Brazil; Jua Harfers, NY. *Comn:* Snake Nest, Laguna Gloria Arts Mus, Austin, 88; Light Poem, Women Studio Workshop, Rosendale, NY, 89; Amanaje, Clocktower Gallery, NY, 89; NikaUnikana, Ikon Gallery, Birmingham, Eng, 90; Mongarayba, Ctr Contemp Arts, Sante Fe, NMex, 90. *Exhib:* Biennale Des Jeunes, Paris, 67; Int Biennial Sao Paulo, 69; Venice Biennial, Italy, 76; solo show, Eugenia Cucalon Gallery, NY, 81; Montbeliard Int Video Festival, France, 84; Latin Am Women Artists, Bronx Mus, NY, 82; First Tex Triennial, Contemp Arts Mus, Houston, 88; The Revered Earth, Pratt Inst, NY, 90. *Collection Arranged:* Comtemp Brazil Works on Paper, 49 Artists, Nobe Gallery, New York, 79; Brazil Super-8 Films, Millenium, New York, 82; Latin Am Contemp Art, 83; Latin Am Visual Thinking, Art Awareness, Lexington, NY, 84. *Teaching:* Lectr, Univ Tex, Austin, 85, Mus Contemp Art, Univ Sao Paulo, 88 & S Eastern Mass Univ, 90. *Awards:* Travel abroad, Mod Art Nat Show, Ministery Cult Brazil, 72; Guggenheim Fel, 80; Fel on Film, NJ Coun Arts, 85. *Bibliog:* Robert C Morgan (auth), 3 South American women artists, High Performance-Astro Arts, Los Angeles, 86; Steve Kolpan (auth), The Amazon flows into--, Woodstock Times, 5/25/89; Guy Brett (auth), Transcontinental (exhib catalog), Ikon Gallery/Verso, London, 90. *Media:* Installation, Photography. *Publ:* Auth, Dreams That Money Can Buy, Artes Visuales Mus of Mod Art, Mexico City, 81; coauth, Latin American Contemporary Art Flue, Vol III, Now, Franklin Furnance, 83; auth Ecological art is alive and well in Los Angeles, High Performance Astro Artz, 88; Notes of ambition, High Performance Astroartz, 88; Women Artists Tell Her Own Stories-Regina Vater, Gallerie Publ, Vancouver, Can, 89. *Dealer:* Mexic-Arte Mus Austin TX. *Mailing Add:* 4901 Caswell Austin TX 78751

VAUX, RICHARD
PAINTER, PRINTMAKER
b Greensburg, Pa, Sept 15, 40. *Study:* Miami Univ, Ohio, BFA, 63; Northern Ill Univ, MFA, 69. *Work:* Wash Co Mus; Museu de Arte Contemporanea, Sao Paulo, Brazil; Gallery Robe, Ltd, Tokyo; NY State Mus Art, Albany, NY; Maier Mus, Lynchburg, Va; Heckscher Mus Art, Huntington, NY. *Exhib:* Butler Inst Am Art, Youngstown, Ohio, 68; Minn Mus Art, St Paul, 71; James Yu Gallery, Soho, NY, 74-76; Guild Hall Mus, East Hampton, NY, 78; Hudson River Mus, 77 & 79; Long Beach Mus Art, 79; Silvermine Guild, Conn, 80; Heckscher Mus, Huntington, NY, 88; Nippon Int, Tokyo, 97; NY State Mus, 98; Phillips Gallery, Sanibel, Fla, 2001; Jain Marunouchi Gallery, 2002; Alpan Gallery, Huntington, NY, 2002; Exposicion Binacional Arte, Asuncion, Paraguay, 2002; Hafnarborg Inst of Cult, Iceland, 2003. *Teaching:* Prof art, Adelphi Univ, 69. *Bibliog:* Irma B Jaffe (auth), Selected Silent Poems, Art News, 93; Jan Marunouchi (auth), Selected Silent Poems (catalog), 94; Article in Asian Art News, 1/95 & Archit Digest, 5/96; Helen A Harrison (auth), Monumental landscapes, NY Times, 8/97; Europ 'Geneve Art, L'Arten Toute Liberté, 4/01; Helen A Harrison (auth), Monumental Landscapes. *Mem:* Art Leagus Long Island; Heckscher Mus Art. *Media:* Acrylic, Oil, Charcoal. *Publ:* The New York Art Review, American References, 88. *Dealer:* Jain Marunouchi Gallery New York NY; Alpan Gallery Huntington NY. *Mailing Add:* 4 Lloyd Lane Huntington NY 11743

VAZQUEZ, PAUL
PAINTER
b Brooklyn, NY, Sept 19, 33. *Study:* Ohio Wesleyan Univ, BFA, 56; Univ Ill, MFA(Kate Neal Kinley Fel), 57. *Work:* Univ Ill, Urbana; Ball State Teachers Col, Muncie, Ind; New Britain Mus, Conn; Butler Inst Am Art, Ohio. *Exhib:* One-man shows, Paley & Lowe Gallery, 71-73, shows in Koln Ger & Madrid, Spain, 75, David Findlay Gallery, NY, 76-80; Kipa Contemp Art (catalog), London Eng, 87-88; Galerie LaMaiginere, Paris, 90; Barnard-Biderman, NY, 96; Andre Zarre Gallery, New York City, 2004-05; and others. *Teaching:* Instr art hist, Bennett Col, 63-66; asst prof humanities, Western Conn State Col, 66-69; prof drawing & painting, Univ Bridgeport, 69-89. *Awards:* Purchase Award, Butler Inst Am Art, 58; Conn Comn Arts Grant for Painting, 74; Artist Sponsorship Prog, NY Found Arts, 92-05. *Bibliog:* Virginia Mann (auth), article, Arts Mag, 2/78; Robert Sievert (auth), article, Arts Mag, 2/80; Lilly Wei (auth), essay, exhib catalog, critic, Art Am, Art News. *Media:* Acrylic oil, Watercolor. *Publ:* From Irony to Laughter, An Art Book of Images and Poems, Upstream Press, 2005. *Mailing Add:* 100 Bank St Apt 3H New York NY 10014-2123

VECSEY-ZSOLNAY, ESTHER BARBARA
EDUCATOR, MUSEUM DIRECTOR
b Pecs, Hungary, May 23, 44; US & Hungarian citizen. *Study:* Univ Calif, Los Angeles, with William Brice, John Paul Jones, Oliver Andrews, BA, 61, with Carlo Pedretti, MA, 75; Academia Di Belle Arti, Rome, cert, 66; Mus Mgt Inst, Univ Calif, Berkeley & J Paul Getty Trust, 85, PhD prog (theology & art history), 87-. *Collection Arranged:* Variants: Drawing by Contemporary Sculptors (auth, catalog), 81, Sewall Gallery, Rice Univ; David Hockney Graphics, 82; Italian Old Master Drawings, Houston Collections, 86; Gold & Silver treas Hungary from 9th-19th Century, 87; and many others. *Pos:* Res asst to dir, Los Angeles Co Mus, Calif, 76-77; coordr, Ace Gallery, Venice, Calif, 77; cur collections, Col Art Mus, Wooster, Ohio, 79-80; dir, Sewall Art Gallery, Rice Univ, Houston, Tex, 80-83; dir, Blaffer Gallery, Univ Houston, 83-87; curatorial & freelance critic, Bay Area Mus, 87-90; Budapest, Hungary, 90-91, Mus Fine Arts, 91-92 & Italian Cult Inst, Budapest, 92-93. *Teaching:* Instr mus studies practicum, Col Wooster, Ohio, 79-80; instr mus studies practicum, Rice Univ, Houston, Tex, 80-81, asst prof art hist, 81-83; instr mus methodology, Univ Houston, 84-86. *Awards:* Travel grant, Irex Princeton, Hungary, 90-91. *Mem:* Am Asn Mus; Mem, Univ Calif, Berkeley Art Mus, 87; Asn Univ & Col, Mus & Galleries; Col Art Asn Am. *Res:* Art, architecture, Italian Renaissance; Contemporary art and interdisciplinary topics; Hungarian architecture and ceramics. *Publ:* Articles in Budapest Sun & Budapest week newspapers; Artweek, 88-90

VEERKAMP, PATRICK BURKE
EDUCATOR, CERAMIST
b Joplin, Mo, Nov 22, 43. *Study:* Adams State Col, BA, 66; Univ Denver, MA, 76; Colo State Univ, MFA, 81. *Work:* Colo State Univ, Ft Collins; E Tenn State Univ, Johnson City; Abilene Fine Art Mus; Southwestern Univ. *Exhib:* Rutgers National Drawing '79, Rutgers Univ, Camden, NJ, 79; 37th Ann Painting Competition, Abilene Fine Arts Mus, Tex, 81; Seventh Ann Ceramic Invitational, Weber State Col, Ogden, Utah, 81; Works on Paper, E Carolina State Univ, Greenville, NC, 81; Kansas Sixth National, Ft Hays State Univ, Kans, 81; two-person show, Univ Wis, Parkside, 83; Positive-Negative, Slocumb Gallery, E Tenn State Univ, 85; Marriage a la Mode: The Aesthetics of Mating, Wustum Mus Fine Art, Racine, Wis, 86; Form / Function Invitational, Univ Tex, 98; The Earthmen Vessel III, Baylor Univ, 99; Attachments 2000, San Angelo Mus; Northern Exposure: Texas Clay, Univ Dallas, 2002. *Pos:* Assoc dir, Spec Visual Arts Prog, Colo State Univ, Ft Collins, 81-82. *Teaching:* Instr art, Mesa Col, Grand Junction, Colo, 73-78 & N Idaho Col, Coeur d'Alene, 82-83; prof art, Southwestern Univ, Georgetown, Tex, 83-. *Mem:* Nat Coun Art Adminrs; Col Art Asn. *Media:* Drawing; Ceramics. *Mailing Add:* Southwestern Univ Dept Art 1001 E University Ave Georgetown TX 78626

VEGA, EDWARD
SCULPTOR, EDUCATOR
b Deming, NMex, Oct 13, 38. *Study:* NMex State Univ, Las Cruces, BFA, 68; Univ NMex, Albuquerque, MA, 70; lithog with Garo Antreasian; drawing with Ilya Bolotowsky; sculpture with Charlie Mattox. *Work:* Eastern NMex Univ, Roswell; St Joseph Hosp, Albuquerque; Mus Albuquerque; Roswell Mus. *Comn:* City of Albuquerque, NMex. *Exhib:* Graphics '73, Western NMex Univ, Silver City; 50th Regional Art Exhib, Shreveport, La, 73; Gov Gallery, Santa Fe, NMex, 78; Roswell Mus, 79; Santa Fe Festival of the Arts, 79; and others. *Pos:* NMex Arts Comn chmn, 79. *Teaching:* Asst prof sculpture, drawing, Univ Albuquerque, 76-86. *Awards:* Third Place Purchase Award Sculpture, Univ NMex, 75; Res Grant Sculpture, NMex State Univ, 75; Artist-in-Residence Fel, Roswell Art Ctr; Finalist, five major sculpture comns, 85-86. *Media:* Steel, Wood. *Mailing Add:* 618 Roehl Rd NW Albuquerque NM 87107

VEKRIS, BABIS A
KINETIC ARTIST, SCULPTOR
b Tripolis, Greece, Aug 10, 50; US citizen. *Study:* NY Studio Sch (Ford Found grant), 79-82; Studies in US and Europe, 87-88. *Work:* Reading Pub Mus, Pa; Goulandris Mus Art, Andros, Greece; Hunterdon Mus Art, Clinton, NJ; Mus Moderner Kunst, Passau, Ger; Egon Schiele Art Centrum, Krumlov, Czech Republic; scuplture, Haffmann La Roche, Basel, Switzerland, 96. *Comn:* sculpture, Leube Group, Gartenau, Austria, 95; monument, Sanyo-Carrefour Plaza, Athens, Greece, 99; monument, City of Athens, 2000. *Exhib:* The Digital Series, Museo Del Chopo, Mexico City, Mex, 91; Artec '95 Int Biennale, Mus Sci, Nagoya, Japan, 95; NJ Arts Ann, Newark Mus, 97; Forces, Contemp Art Mus Va, Virginia Beach, 97; Art for the End of the 20th Century, Bellevue Art Mus, Wash, 98; 9th Int Contemp Art Competition, Mydome Osaka, Japan, 98; The Kinetic Spectrum, Mus Moderner Kunst, Passau, Ger, 99; Modern Odysseys, Queens Mus, NY, 99. *Media:* Electronic components, Light sound; Metal. *Mailing Add:* PO Box 1175 New York NY 10013-1175

VELASQUEZ, OSCAR
PAINTER, ILLUSTRATOR
b Pharr, Tex, Apr 5, 45. *Study:* Cooper Sch Art, AA, 65. *Work:* Joslyn Art Mus, Omaha; Nat Acad Design-Henry Ward Ranger, NY; Erskine Col, Due West, SC; Opera House, Abbeville, SC. *Comn:* Lion & Lamb Peace Ctr, Bluffton, Ohio; Erskine Col, Due West, SC; BEMIS Art Ctr, Omaha, Nebr. *Exhib:* Ga Watercolor Soc, High Mus, Atlanta, 79; SC Watercolor Soc, Greenville Mus Art; Am Watercolor Soc, Columbia Mus Art, SC, 79; Camden Art Mus, SC, 83; Sumter Art Mus, SC, 83; Cannon Bldg, Capitol, Washington, DC, 83; and others. *Awards:* High Winds Medal, 75 & Silver Medal of Honor, 77, Am Watercolor Soc; Georgia Gold Award, Watercolor Soc, 81. *Mem:* Am Watercolor Soc; SC Watercolor Soc; Southern Watercolor Asn; Ga Watercolor Soc. *Media:* Watercolor, Acrylic; Oils. *Publ:* The New Spirit of Watercolor, Northlight Books; Exploring Color, Northlight Books. *Mailing Add:* 2250 Rd R Bluffton OH 45817

VELEZ, EDIN
VIDEO ARTIST
b Arecibo, PR, Sept 3, 51. *Study:* Univ PR, 69-70; Inst Bellas Artes, 70; Inst Puerto Rican Cult Sch Fine Arts. *Work:* Mus Mod Art, NY; Stedjelik Mus Art, Amsterdam, Neth; Ithaca Mus Art, NY. *Comn:* Oblique Strategist Too, 85 & Naruhodo (installation), 87, NY State Coun Arts, NY; AS IS (video essay), 85, Meaning of the Interval (video doc), 87 & Dance of Darkness (video doc), 88, Nat Endowment Arts, Washington, DC. *Exhib:* III Festival Int D'Art, Locarno, Switz, 82; Whitney Mus Am Art Biennial, NY, 83; Video Art: A History, 84 & Video Viewpoint, 86, Mus Mod Art, NY; Cinema Du Reel, Pompidou Ctr, Paris, France, 85; Arts for Television, Stedjelik Mus Art, Amsterdam, 87-88; Int Pub Television Conf, Granada, Spain, 87 & Philadelphia, Pa, 88; Image Forum Film & Video Festival, Tokyo, Japan, 89; Nagoya Mus, Japan, 89; Video and the Computer, Mus Mod Art, NY, 89; Louvre Mus, Paris, France, 90; Elected Affinities, Cronis Gallery, NY, 90; and others internationally. *Awards:* Fel, Guggenheim Found & US/Japan Friendship Comn; Grants, Nat Endowment Arts, Jerome Found & NY State Coun Arts; First Prize, First Latino Film & Video Festival, 88; Maya Deren Award, Am Film Inst, 90. *Bibliog:* Victor Ancona (auth), Edin Velez: In essence a romantic realist, Videography, 83; Image Forum (auth), Edin Velez, video artist, Video Culture, Japan, 86; John Wallace (auth), Innovation: It's a primary color on the video, NY Times, 87. *Mem:* Asn Independent Video & Filmmakers. *Dealer:* Electronic Arts Intermix 536 Broadway New York NY 10012; Tape Connection Via P Querini 3 Roma Italy

VELICK, BRUCE
CURATOR
b Los Angeles, Calif, Jan 29, 49. *Study:* Univ Calif, Davis, BA(design), 71. *Pos:* Dir, Bruce Velick Eds, Mill Valley, Calif & New York, currently. *Specialty:* Contemporary art. *Mailing Add:* 39 Vestry St New York NY 10013

VELICK & SHISHIM, PAUL & BOB
PERFORMANCE ARTISTS
b Santa Monica, Calif, May 8, 53 & P Velick, b Detroit, Mich, Feb 8, 52. *Study:* P Velick, Art Ctr Col, Antioch Col, BFA, 75; F Shishim, Art Ctr Col, BFA, 75; both with Tom Wudl, Llyn Foulkes & Lorser Feitelson. *Work:* Ace Gallery, Toronto, Can. *Exhib:* Sex is Stupid, Los Angeles Inst Contemp Art, 79; Nature Is Perfect, Animals Are Perfect, What Are Humans?, Washington Hall Performance Gallery, Seattle, 80; Bob to Bob, Marianne Deson Gallery, Chicago, 82; We're All Lucky, Mus Contemp Art, Los Angeles, Calif, 85; retrospective (with catalog), Otis/Parson, 86; Philadelphia Mus Art, Pa, 98. *Awards:* Golden Turkey Award, Young Turks, DTLA Administration. *Bibliog:* Alyson Pov (auth), Across America, Art Papers, 1/81; Alyson Pov (auth), Retrospective rev, Los Angeles Times, 86; California Stories, KCET PBS-TV, Los Angeles. *Mem:* The Young Turks, Los Angeles. *Publ:* Contribr, High Performance/Public Spirit, Astro Arts, 79; Performance Anthology, Carl Loeffler, 80; Across America (record), MITB Records, Beverly Hills, 81; The Least I Can Do (record), MITB Records, Beverly Hills, 82; We Know You're Alone (record), Polydor Records, 83; and many other forms of technological reproduction. *Mailing Add:* PO Box 6461 Beverly Hills CA 90212

VENA, DANTE
EDUCATOR, PRINTMAKER
Study: Univ Wis, BS, 57, MS, 60; Univ Iowa, PhD, 76. *Work:* Milwaukee Art Ctr; Montgomery Mus, Ala; Bellarmine Col, Louisville; Nazareth Col, Ky; Ball State Univ, Ind. *Comn:* Wall mural (map), Customs House, New Orleans, 58; illus, Motive Mag, Nashville, 60; Keenland (illus), Ford Times Mag, 63; A Child is Born (cover illus), Companion Mag, 63; wall mural, Ohio Univ, Portsmouth, 68. *Exhib:* 14th Nat Exhib Prints, Libr Congress, Washington, DC, 56; 152nd Ann Exhib, Pa Acad Fine Arts, 57; 29th Int Exhib Northwest Printmakers, Seattle Art Mus, 57; 24th Ann Mid-Year Show, Butler Inst Am Art, 59; 65th Ann Western Artists, Denver Art Mus, 59; Nat Mus Wales, Cardiff, S Wales, 66; solo exhib, Bell Gallery, Belfast, N Ireland, 66; Southeastern Mass Univ Art Gallery, 72-91; group shows, Visual Images Gallery, New Bedford, 91 & 92; Hundred Languages of Children, Univ Mass, Dartmouth, 97. *Collection Arranged:* Alfred Sessler Retrospective Show, 61; A Town and its Artists, Portsmouth, 68; Artists Inmates, Portsmouth Gallery, 69. *Pos:* Framework curric comt, Mass Dept Educ, 93-96; exec coun, Mass Art Educ Asn, 94-95, Mass Alliance for Arts Educ; chairperson, Art, Music, Technol and Educ Conf, 94; dir, Art Educ Summer Inst, Nat Workshop Teachers, 98. *Teaching:* Art dir, Bellarmine Col, Louisville, Ky, 61-67; chmn art educ dept, Univ Mass, Dartmouth, 81-97. *Awards:* Fulbright to Italy, 53; Mrs Arthur Osborn Purchase Award, Ball State Univ, 63; New Bedford Arts Coun, 89; Research Fel, Edith Cowan Univ, Perth, Western Australia, 91. *Bibliog:* Cottie Burland (auth), Dante Vena-Artist Own Gallery, Arts Rev, 1/22/66. *Mem:* Nat Acad NY; Nat Art Educ Asn; Fairhaven Arts Coun (chmn, 81-83); Mass Asn Sch Comts; Bd Educ Fairhaven, Mass (chmn, 87-88). *Publ:* Auth, Contemporary Art, Irish-Am, 63; Learning Out There: A Program, Art Educ, 75; Integrated Arts in the Elementary Classroom, Charles Thomas Pub; Video Project, Integrated Arts in Schools, 91-92. *Mailing Add:* 738 Westminster Rd Brooklyn NY 11230

VENABLE, SUSAN C
SCULPTOR, PAINTER
b Calif, Dec 30, 44. *Study:* Calif State Univ, BFA, 82; Univ Calif, Los Angeles, MFA, 85. *Work:* Horoko Nakamotn, Tokoyo, Japan; Payden & Rygel, Los Angeles, Calif; Bear Stearns & Co, Los Angeles, Calif; Sudler-Marlins, Chicago, Ill; US Army, Honolulu, Hawaii. *Comn:* Lobby installations, Pac Plaza, Walnut Creek, Calif, 87, Hotel Nikko, Chicago, Ill, 87, Metroplex Wilshire, Los Angeles, 89, Western Digital Corp, Irvine, Calif, 90; auditorium installation, IBM, Atlanta, Ga, 88. *Exhib:* Group shows, Fiber Revolution, Witchita Art Mus, 87, Boulder Ctr Art, 89, SITE, Los Angeles, 89, Off the Wall, Los Angeles Co Mus Art, 90, Monotypes, Ariz State Univ Mus, 90; solo shows, New Work, Tally Richards, NMex, Mahoney/Butler, Calif, 89, Square & Square, Scottsdale Ctr Arts, Ariz, 90 & Sun Art Mus, Phoenix, Ariz, 92. *Awards:* Dean's Discretionary, 82, Fishbaugh Mem, 83, Univ Calif, Los Angeles. *Bibliog:* Michel Thomas (auth), Textiles/Art/Language, Architecture 85, France; Michael Webb (auth), Poetry in Concrete, Inside Mag, Japan, 6/90; Cover & Feature Article: Seasons Mag, 8/2004; Feature Article, TRENDS Mag, 4/2005. *Media:* Mixed; Encaustic, Oil. *Dealer:* Sherwood Gallery, Laguna Beach, CA. *Mailing Add:* 2323 Foothill Ln Santa Barbara CA 93105

VENEGAS, HAYDEE E
CONSULTANT
b Arecibo, PR, Mar 4, 50. *Study:* Univ PR, BA(art hist), 73; Fla State Univ, MA(mod art), 78. *Collection Arranged:* Francisco Oller: A Realist Impressionist, 83; La Moda en Puerto Rico, 85; Obra Uica sobre papel, 85; 25 anos de pintura Puertoriquena, 86; Quijano & Roche, 88; Irene Delano, 89; Antonio Nania, 92. *Pos:* Dir, Mus Fundacion Arqueologica, 76-79, Permanent Fund for Arts, 92-; asst dir, Ponce Art Mus, 80-88; pres, Concultura, 88-92. *Teaching:* Vis prof Puerto Rican art, Inter-Am Univ, summer 75, Escuelade Artes Plasticas, 90-91 & Escuela Hotelera, 92. *Awards:* Leon de Oro Award, 84. *Bibliog:* Connie Underhill (auth), The museum as a place, San Juan Star, Sunday Mag, 12/30/79; Mario Alegre (auth), Voluntades que Convergen, El Nuevo Dia, 4/14/90; Puerto Rican Art Phasing the End of the Century, Caribbean Art, Badajoz, Spain, 98. *Mem:* Int Comt Mus; Col Art Asn; Asn of Latin-Am Historians; Int Asn Art Critics (bd dir, 92, 95-96, vpres, 97-). *Res:* Puerto Rican art; Francisco Oller, 19th century painter. *Publ:* Contribr, Juan Ramon Valazquez, El Mundo, 78; El Velorio: Propuesta para una reinterpretacion, Plastica, 79; auth, Francisco Oller: Profile of a Puerto Rican Painter, Mus Art Ponce, 83, Oller in Cuba: Horizontes, 85, Irene Delano, 89. *Mailing Add:* Miramar Towers 4-F Santurce PR 00907

VENET, BERNAR
SCULPTOR, CONCEPTUAL ARTIST
b France, Apr 20, 41. *Study:* Sch Villa Thiole, Nice, France, 57-58. *Work:* Mus Nat Art Mod, Ctr Georges Pompidou, Paris; Neue Galerie Alten Kurhaus, Aachen, WGer; La Jolla Mus Contemp Art; Akron Art Inst, Ohio; Musee du Quebec, Can. *Comn:* tallest steel sculpture, France, 86; sculpture, Goodmann Gegar Hogan, Norfolk, Va, 87; sculpture, French Gout & Air France, Berlin, WGer, 88; Acropolis, Nice, France; Beijing Silver Tower Real Estate Develop Co, China. *Teaching:* Instr, La Sorbonne, Paris, France, 73-75. *Awards:* Grand Prix des Arts de la Ville de Paris, 90; Commandeur dans l'ordre des Arts et Lettres, awarded by the Minister of Culture, France, 1996; Chevalier de la Légion d'honneur, France, 2005. *Bibliog:* Catherine Millet (auth), Bernar Venet, Chene, France & Prearo, Italy, 75; J Pierre Mirouze (producer), film, WDR, WGer, 75; Seth Schneidman (producer), film, Seven Hills Productions, 83. *Media:* Wood Reliefs, Corten Steel. *Dealer:* Robert Miller Gallery 524 West 26th St New York NY 10001. *Mailing Add:* 117 W 21st St New York NY 10011

VENEZIA, MICHAEL
PAINTER
b Brooklyn, NY, July 23, 35. *Study:* State Univ NY, Buffalo, BS, 63; Univ Mich, Ann Arbor, MFA, 68. *Work:* Mus Mod Art, NY; Nat Gallery Can, Ottawa; Mus Modbuer Kunst, Otterndorf, Ger; Solomon R Guggenheim Mus, NY; Detroit Inst Arts; Australian Nat Gallery, Canberra; Kunstmuseum Winterthur, Switz; Hartford Atheneum, Conn. *Exhib:* Works on Paper, Mus Mod Art, NY, 74; one-man shows, Paintings, Bykert Gallery, NY, 73, Sperone Westwater Fisher Inc, NY, 79, Fred Hoffman Gallery, Santa Monica, Calif, 91, Umberg Rictveld, Ameusfoout, The Neth, 95, paintings 1970-1995 (with catalog), Kunstmuseum, Winterthur, Switz, 96 & Galericmeert-Rhioux, Brussels, 96; Two Artists: Dan Hill & Michael Venezia, Whitney Mus Art, NY, 77; Artists & Friends: Dan Flavin & Michael Venezia, Contemp Arts Ctr, Cincinnati, Ohio, 77; Drawings About Drawing Today, Acklund Art Mus, Chapel Hill, NC, 79; Selected Paintings 1969-1980, Detroit Inst Arts, 80; Carol Taylor-Art Inc, Dallas, Tex, 81 & 84; Paintings 1972-1983, Dia Found, Dan Flavin Art Inst, Bridgehampton, NY, 83; Biennale Artumbra, Foligno, Italy, 86; New Paintings, Margaret Roeder Gallery, NY, 87; Margaret Roeder Gallery, NY, 88; Frankfurt Art Fair, Ger, 89; Surface in Proportion, Margaret Roeder Gallery, NY, 90; Fred Hoffman Gallery, Santa Monica, Calif, 91; Michael Venezia, Rubin Spangle Gallery, NY, 92; Michael Venezia, Glan Enzo Sperone, Rome, Italy, 92; Westfalischeu Funstuenein, Munsten, Ger, 97; Heike Curtze, Dusseldorf, Ger, 98. *Teaching:* Vis lectr fine arts, Guildford Col, Surrey, Eng, 66-67, London Col Printing, 66-67; from asst prof to prof fine arts, Univ Rochester, NY 68-; prof art, Univ Rochester, 85-. *Awards:* Creative Artists Pub Serv Award, NY Coun Arts, State Univ NY, Fredonia, 75; Tiffany Found Award for Painting, 79; Artist Fel Painting, Nat Endowment Arts, 81-82. *Bibliog:* Helen A Harrison (auth), His paintings stress the paint, NY Times, Long Island Weekly, 11/27/83; David Carrier (auth), Michael Venezia, Tema Celeste, 80, spring 93; Alfred Corn (auth), Art in America, 1/97. *Media:* Powdered Metals, Glass and Pigments on Wood and Paper. *Dealer:* Stark Gallery 113 Crosby St New York NY 10012. *Mailing Add:* 20 N Moore St New York NY 10013

VENTIMIGLIA, JOHN THOMAS
SCULPTOR, EDUCATOR
b Augusta, Maine, Jan 12, 43. *Study:* Skowhegan Sch Paint & Sculpture, 64, Sch Art, Syracuse Univ, BFA, 65; Rinehart Sch, Md Inst Art, MFA (sculpture), 67. *Work:* Portland Mus Art; Portland Pub Libr; Mt Holyoke Col; Chateau de Rochefort-en-Terre, France. *Comn:* Agavney Johnson Mem Sculpture, Portland Pub Libr, 81; The Cedars Home, Tree of Life, Portland, Maine, 91; Terzian Meml Sculpture, Mt Holyoke Col Libr, South Hadley, Mass, 95. *Exhib:* Barn Gallery, Ogunquit, Maine, 77; Maine Coast Artists, Rockport; Barridoff Galleries; Round Top Ctr for Arts, Damariscotta, Maine; Icon Galleries, Brunswick, Maine. *Pos:* Chmn

Sculpture Dept, Portland Sch Art, 1972-98; cur, Outdoor Sculpture Exhib Series, Portland Sch Art, 1973-78; adv panelist, Maine State Comn Arts & Humanities, 1981-85; restoration adv, Simmons Civil War Monument, Portland, Maine, 1997. *Teaching:* Prof sculpture, 3D design & drawing, Maine Col Art, Portland, 1972-. *Awards:* Scholar, Showhegan Sch Painting & Sculpture, 64; Artist Residency in Brittany, Klotz Found, Rochefort-en-Terre, France, 1997. *Bibliog:* 76 Maine Artists (exhib catalog), Maine State Bicentennial Comn, 76; Maine Art Now, Beam, 90. *Media:* Bronze, Mixed Materials, Wood. *Dealer:* Icon Gallery Brunswick ME. *Mailing Add:* 41 Pleasant Ave Portland ME 04103-3217

VENTURA, ANTHONY
PAINTER
b Southampton, NY, Jan 24, 27. *Study:* Acad Arts, Newark NJ, BFA, 51; Pratt Inst, Brooklyn, NY, 52-53; Art Students League, NY, 54-55; studied with Robert Brackman, Ivan Olinsky, Edgar Whitney, Edmond Fitzgerald & Avery Johnson. *Work:* Ft Schlyer Maritime Mus, Bronx, NY; Am Can Co, Chicago, Ill; Hershey Corp, Pa; Winsor-Newton Co, Secaucus, NJ; Zhejiang Mus, China. *Exhib:* Tweed Mus, Duluth, Minn, 77; Am Watercolor Soc, NY, 82; Frye Mus, Seattle, 83; Am Artist Prof League, NJ, 87, 95, 96, 97, 98, 99, 2001-06; Salmagundi Club, NY, 96, 97, 98, 99, 2001-06; NJ Watercolor Soc, 96, 98, 99, 2001-05. *Pos:* Adv Comt Guild, Guild Creative Art, Shrewsbury, NJ, 80-84; pres, NJ Watercolor Soc, 86-87; off artist for US Coast Guard. *Teaching:* Workshops, demonstrations and lectures to art organizations throughout New Jersey and at own studio-gallery. *Awards:* Silver Medal Honor, NJ Watercolor Soc, 95, 98, 2002; Am Artists Prof League Awards, 99-2006; Salmagundi Club Awards, NY, 96, 98-2006. *Bibliog:* Listed in-Judge and Jury Selector of Federated Art Asn, NJ & Who's Who in the East, Who's Who in America, Who's Who in American Art; COGAP, Artist for US Coast Guard. *Mem:* NJ Watercolor Soc (pres, 86-87); Knickerbocker Artist; Salmagundi Club; N Shore Art Asn; Hudson Valley Art Asn; Am Artist Prof League; Garden State Watercolor Soc. *Media:* Watercolor, Oil. *Specialty:* Traditional landscapes, seascapes, still lifes. *Interests:* Reading, hiking, photography. *Collection:* Many private collections. *Publ:* Watercolor 95, 98, Am Artists Publ, fall ed; Best of Watercolor, Light & Shade, Rockport Publ, 97; Int Artist Pub, 99. *Dealer:* Guild Creative Art 620 Broad St Rte 35 Shrewsbury NJ 07702; Lambertville Gallery of Fine Art 20 N Union St Lambertville NJ 08530; Anchor & Palette Gallery 40 Mount St Bay Head NJ 08742; Sea Holly Art Gallery 718 Union Ave Brielle NJ 08730. *Mailing Add:* 3430 Hwy 66 Neptune NJ 07753

VENTURI, ROBERT
ARCHITECT
b Philadelphia, Pa, June 25, 25. *Study:* Princeton Univ, AB, 1947, MFA, 1950; Rome Prize Fel, Am Acad in Rome, 1954-56. *Hon Degrees:* Oberlin Col, Hon DFA, 1977; Yale Univ, Hon DFA, 1979; Univ Pa, Hon DFA, 1980; Princeton Univ, Hon DFA, 1983; NJ Inst Technol, Hon LHD, 1984; Philadelphia Col Art, Hon DFA, 1985; Univ NC Chapel Hill, LHD, 1989; Philadelphia Col Textiles & Sci, LHD, 1992; Laurea honoris causa in Architettura, Univ Rome, La Sapienza, 1994. *Comn:* Gordon & Virginia MacDonald Med Res Labs, Payette Assocs & UCLA, 86; Charles P Stevenson Libr, Bard Col, 89; Sainsburg Wing, Nat Gallery, London, Eng, 91; Hotel Midparque Resort Complex, Nikko, Kirifuri, Japan, 97; Hótel du Département de la Haute-Garonne, Toulouse, France, 99; amd many others. *Exhib:* Work of Venturi & Rauch, Whitney Mus Am Art, NY, 71 & Pa Acad Fine Arts, Philadelphia, 75; Venturi, Rauch & Scott Brown, Accademia delle Arti del Disegno, Firenze, Italy, 81; Buildings & Drawings, Max Protetch Gallery, NY, 82; A Generation of Architecture, Krannert Art Mus, Univ Ill & traveling, 84-86; High Styles: 20th Century Am Design, Whitney Mus Am Art, NY, 85-86; About Archit, Inst Contemp Art, Univ Pa, 93; Barnes Found Restoration & Renovation, Merion, Pa, 93; Disney Celebration Bank, Celebration, Fla, 93; Out of the Ordinary: Robert Venturi, Denise Scott Brown & Assoc-Architecture, Urbanism, Design, Philadelphia Mus Art, 2001. *Pos:* Partner, Venturi & Rauch, 1964-80; Venturi, Rauch & Scott Brown, 1980-89; Venturi, Scott Brown & Assoc, 1989-; architect-in-residence, Am Acad Rome, 66, trustee, 69-74. *Teaching:* From asst to assoc prof archit, Univ Pa, 57-65; Davenport Prof archit, Yale Univ, 66-70; bd adv, Princeton Univ, Dept Art & Archeol, 77-81; Walter Gropius lectr, Harvard Univ, Grad Sch Design, 82; Eero Saarinen vis prof archit design, Yale Univ, Sch Archit, 86-87. *Awards:* Pritzker Archit Prize, Hyatt Found, 91; Man Yr, Order Sons Italy & Coun City Philadelphis, 92; US Presidential Award, Nat Medal Arts, 92; and others. *Bibliog:* Stanislaus von Moos (auth), Venturi, Scott Brown, and Associates: Buildings and Projects, 1986-1997, Monacelli, 2000; David Brownlee, David G. De Long & Kathryn B. Hiesinger (coauths), Out of the Ordinary: Achitecture/Urbanism/Design, Yale Univ Press, 2001; and many others. *Mem:* Fel Am Acad Rome; Fel Am Inst Archit; Fel Accademia Nazionale di San Luca; Fel Am Acad Arts & Sci; Hon Fel Royal Incorp Architects Scotland; and others. *Publ:* Complexity & Contradiction in Architecture, 66, 2nd ed, 77; coauth (with Denise Scott Brown & Steven Izenour), Learning from Las Vegas, 72, 2nd ed, 77; coauth (with Denise Scott Brown), A View from the Campidoglio: Selected Essays 1953-84, 84; Iconography & Electronics Upon a Generic Architecture, 96; Architecture as Signs & Systems for a Mannerist Time, 2004; and others. *Mailing Add:* Venturi Scott Brown & Assoc 4236 Main St Philadelphia PA 19127-1696

VERENE, CHRIS
MULTIMEDIA ARTIST
b Galesburg, Ill, Oct 29, 69. *Study:* Ga State Univ, MFA, 96. *Work:* The Whitney Mus Am Art, NY; The High Mus Art, Atlanta, Ga; Metrop Mus Art; Walker Mus Art; Mus of Contemp Photog; J.Paul Getty Mus Art; Jewish Mus Art; Mus Contemporary Art Los Angeles. *Comn:* Jewish Mus, NY. *Exhib:* The Whitney Biennial, NY, 2000; Do You Hear What We Hear, Paul Morris Gallery, NY, 2000; Camera Club, Reflex Modern Art Gallery, Amsterdam, 2000; Uneasy, Howard Yezerski, Boston, 2001; A Way With Words, Whitney Mus Am Art at Phillip Morris, NY, 2001; Photographs, Cherry Street Temporaty Gallery, Galesburg, Ill, 2001; What's New, Whitney Mus Am Art, NY, 2001; Vereni, Escapista!, Times Square, NY, 2001; Where We Live, Getty Mus, 2006. *Teaching:* adj prof, Atlanta Col Art, 98-99, MFA Photog and Related Media, Sch Visual Art, NY, 2001; prof, Int Ctr Photog, NY, 2001; guest lectr, Bard Col, NY, 2001. *Awards:* Jackson Pollock / Barbra Krasner award, 2002. *Bibliog:* Catherine St Louis (auth), What They Were Thinking, NY Times Mag, 6/17/01; Rachel Kushner (auth), Opeanings: Chris Verene, Artforum, 2001; Johanna Lehan (auth), The Great Verene, Photo District News, 2001; Parkett, AM Homes (auth), 2002. *Mem:* Soc for Photog Educ. *Media:* Narrative Photography, Costumes, video performance. *Dealer:* Alona Vagan Gallery. *Mailing Add:* Box 118 442-D Lorimer St Brooklyn NY 11206

VERGNE, PHILIPPE
CURATOR
Collection Arranged: Shake Rattle and Roll: Christian Marclay; How Latitudes Become Forms: Art in a Global Age, 2003; Walk Around Time: Selections from the Permanent Collection; Let's Entertain; Herzog & de Meuron: In Process; Art Performs Life: Merce Cunningham/meredith Monk/BillT Jones; Huang Yong Ping: A Retrospective, 2005; co-cur, Whitney Biennial, 2006. *Pos:* Dir, Mus d'Art Contemporain, Marseille, France, 1994-97; cur, visual arts, Walker Art Ctr, 1997-2003, sr cur, 2003-05, dep dir and chief cur, 2005-. *Teaching:* Vis critic, Cranbrook Art Acad, Univ Ill, Sch of Art Inst, Chicago. *Awards:* Medal of Chevalier of Order of Arts and Letters, French Govt, 2004. *Publ:* Contribr to Artforum, Parkett, Asia Pacific mag, as well as other periodicals. *Mailing Add:* Walker Art Center 1750 Hennepin Minneapolis MN 55403

VERHOEVEN, RUDI
PAINTER
b Bladel, Neth, Sept 18, 49. *Study:* Acad Indust Design, BFA, 70; Jan van Eyck Acad, Maastricht, Holland, study under J C J van der Heyden, MFA, 73. *Work:* Mus Fine Arts, Santa Fe, NMex. *Exhib:* Paintings, Ariel Gallery, NY, 87; New Work, Tokoro Gallery, Los Angeles, Calif, 90; Numbers: Who's Counting, Spirit Arts, Santa Fe, NMex, 93; New Mexico 1993, Mus Fine Arts, Santa Fe, NMex, 93; Paintings, Cafe Gallery, Albuquerque, NMex. *Teaching:* Vis Artist, Inst Am Indian and Alaska Native Cult and Arts Development, Santa Fe, NMex. *Awards:* WESTAF/Nat Endowment Arts Grant, 92; Purchase Award, Mus NMex, Mus NMex Found, 93. *Bibliog:* Shirle Gottlieb (auth), Rudi Verhoeven, Artscene Los Angeles, 1/90; Marlene Donohue (auth), Lowlander in the highlands, Los Angeles Times, 2/9/90; Tom Nakashima (auth), Rudi Verhoeven, WESTAF/Nat Endowment Arts Catalog, 92. *Mem:* Albuquerque United Artists (bd mem, 88-90). *Media:* Mixed Media on Canvas. *Dealer:* Tokoro Inc 320 N Robertson Blvd Los Angeles Calif 90048

VERMEULE, CORNELIUS CLARKSON, III
HISTORIAN, WRITER
b on Atlantic Ocean, Aug 10, 25; US citizen. *Study:* Harvard Univ, AB, 47, MA, 51; Univ Col, Univ London, PhD, 53; Boston Col, DHL, 96. *Work:* Mus Fine Arts, Boston; Nat Mus, Pylos, Hellas; Morphou-Omorfo Mus, Cyprus. *Collection Arranged:* Many exhibs, Fogg Mus Art, 50-72; Sir John Soane's Mus, London; Mus Fine Arts, Boston; Art Ctr Plainfield, NJ. *Pos:* Asst, Sir John Soane's Mus, 51-53; cur classical art, Mus Fine Arts, Boston, 57-96, actg dir, 72-73, cur emer, 96-; cur coins, Mass Hist Soc, Boston, 69-. *Teaching:* Asst prof fine arts, Univ Mich, Ann Arbor, 53-55; asst prof archaeol, Bryn Mawr Col, 55-57; prof classics, Yale Univ, 68-69 & 72-73; prof fine arts, Boston Col, 78-98. *Awards:* Boston Col US Bicentennial Medal, 76. *Mem:* Life mem Col Art Asn Am; fel Royal Numismatic Soc; life fel Am Numismatic Soc (mem coun, 60-78); life mem Archaeol Inst Am; life mem Hellenic & Roman Soc. *Res:* European painting, Greek and Roman art; Renaissance sculpture and medals. *Interests:* Classical and Neo-classical style, Greek sculpture technique. *Publ:* Auth, Greek Sculpture & Roman Taste, 77; Art of Antiquity, Greek and Roman Art, Vols II-V, 79-86; Greek and Roman Sculpture in America, 82; Philatelic Art in America, 87; European & Am Medallic Art, 90

VERNON, KAREN
PAINTER, PRINTMAKER
b El Dorado, Ark, June 11, 48. *Study:* N Tex State Univ Denton, BFA, 72; private study with Robert Wood, 85. *Work:* Corpus Christi Mus, Tex; Crete City Hall, Ill; Walt Disney Corp, Orlando, Fla; Delta Airlines Crown Club, Orlando, Tex; Amoco Corp, Chicago, Ill; Nat PGA Hdqtrs, jacksonville, Fla; Gallery at Chateau de Vullievens, Switzerland; plus others. *Comn:* Quilt Series (watercolor), Burd Clinic, Beaumont, Tex, 85 & comn by Frank Macher, Ann Arbor, Mich, 86 & 87; Palmestry (watercolor), ECPI Inc, Va Beach, 86; Oriental Suite (watercolor), comn by Gloria Young, Waco, Tex, 87 & Congressman Leath, Washington, DC, 88; Royal Family, Saudi Arabia, 95. *Exhib:* Solo exhib, Corpus Christi Mus, Tex, 79, S Ark Art Ctr, El Dorado, 86 & Kershaw Co Art Ctr, Camden, 87; Watercolor Art Soc Houston, traveling exhib, 83; S Ark Art Ctr, El Dorado, 84; 65th Nat Springfield Exhib, 85; Art Alliance Int, El Paso Art Alliance, 85; WASH Int Spring Exhib, 2000. *Pos:* Pres, Portland Art Asn, 76-77; vpres & pres, Humble Art League, 84-86; Sr bd mem, Tex Arts & Craft Found, 85-. *Teaching:* Art dept dir, Frisco ISD, Tex, 73-74; instr watercolor, Amarillo Art Ctr, Tex, 85; Hill Country Art Found, Ingram, Tex, 87-88; instr watercolor throughout the US, 80-2000. *Awards:* Murt Hill Award, S Ark Art Ctr, Amarillo, Tex, 85; Best Floral, Vizcaya Days, Vizcaya Mus & City of Miami, 85; 1st Place Watercolor, Corsicana Nat Art Exhib, Corsicana Art Asn, 86. *Bibliog:* Cover, Tallascope, 6-8/93; Cover, Metrop Woman, 7/95; Video, Unleashing Dynamic Color in Watercolor, Ampersand Art Supply, Austin, Tex. *Mem:* Sign mem, Tex Watercolor Soc; Western Fedn Watercolorists; Watercolor Art Soc Houston. *Media:* Watercolor, Acrylic, Oil. *Mailing Add:* 2251 FM 50 Rd Brenham TX 77833

VERNON, KAREN
PAINTER, INSTRUCTOR
b El Dorado, Ark, June 11, 48. *Study:* N Tex State Univ, BFA, 72. *Work:* Chateau De Vullievens, Switz; Corpus Christi Mus, Corpus Christi, Tex; The City Crete, Crete, Ill. *Comn:* 3 40X60 paintings, Royal Family Saudi Arabia, 97; 3 48X60 paintings, Nat PGA HQ, Jacksonville, Fla, 98; 3 22X30 paintings, Delta Airlines, Orlando, Fla, 99; 1 48X60 painting, Avatar, Orlando, Fla, 2000; 3 4X6 paintings, Moody Gardens Resort, Galveston, Tex, 2000. *Exhib:* Nat Plein Aire Competition, Miami, Fla, 2003; Water Media 2003, FWS Exhib, Houston, Tex, 2003; Sea to Shining Sea, Traveling/multiple Mus, 2003-2006; Int Water Media XIV, Colorado Springs, Colo, 2005; Reo River Valley Nat juried, Red River Valley Mus, Vernon, Tex, 2006; Tex Watercolor Soc juried, Lubbock Art Ctr, Lubbock, Tex, 2006. *Pos:* dir, Coconut Grove Gallery, 2002-2005; consult/demonstr, Ampersand Art Supply, 2002-. *Teaching:* teacher, Art, Frisco ISD, Frisco, Tex, 78-79; teacher, Art Therapist & MHMR, Corpus Christi, Tex, 79-84; instr, Painting, Watercolor Orgn, 80-. *Awards:* 2nd Place, Wash Int, 2003; Best Show, Bosron Mills Art, 2005; Honorable Mention, Tex Watercolor Soc, 2006. *Mem:* Watercolor Art Soc, Houston, Tex; Tex Watercolor Soc; Birmingham Watercolor Soc. *Media:* Oil, Watercolor. *Interests:* Working currently in watercolor on claybord; Focus is luminosity in realism. *Collection:* Traditional watercolors dealing with archiotonic, floral & figurative work - some oil & acrylic. *Dealer:* The Gallery at Round Top PO Box 311 203 E Austin Round Top Tex 78954. *Mailing Add:* 2251 FM 50Rd Brenham TX 77833

VEROSTKO, ROMAN JOSEPH
PAINTER, HISTORIAN
b Tarrs, Pa, Sept 12, 29. *Study:* Art Inst Pittsburgh, dipl; St Vincent Col & Seminary, Latrobe, Pa, BA, 55; Pratt Inst, MFA, 61; New York Univ; Columbia Univ; Atelier 17, Paris. *Work:* Ariz State Univ, Tempe; Minneapolis Inst Art; Walker Art Ctr; Mus der Stadt Gladbeck, Ger; Minneapolis Col Art & Design. *Comn:* Mural, Frey Sci & Eng Ctr, Univ St Thomas, St Paul, Minn, 97; Mural, Spalding Univ, Louisville, Ky. *Exhib:* Siggraph Art Shows, Dallas, 90, Chicago, 92 & 96, Los Angeles, 95 & 97, ComputerKunst, Gladbeck, Ger, 2000 & 2002, San Diego, 2003; Int Symp Elec Art, Sydney, 92, Minneapolis, 93, Helsinki, 94 & Manchester, UK, 98; NY Digital Salon, 93, 95 & 96; Artec 95, Nagoya, Japan; Digital Art Mus, Berlin, 2005. *Pos:* Staff ed art & archit, New Catholic Encyclo, Catholic Univ, Washington, DC, 64-68; acad dean, Minneapolis Col Art & Design, 75-78; prog dir, Fourth Int Symp Electronic Art, 93. *Teaching:* Prof art hist, Minneapolis Col Art & Design, Minn, 68-94, emer prof, 94. *Awards:* Bush Fel, 69; Hon Mention, ars Electronica, 93; First Prize, Golden Plotter, 94. *Bibliog:* CJ McNaspy (auth), Art & the New Catholic Encyclo, Am, 3/67; F Debuyst (auth), Sculptures de Ciment, Roman Verostko, Art D'Eglise, 68; Roman Verostko in Visual Proceedings, Siggraph 97, ACM, Oxford, 52, 97; L Candy & E Edmonds (auths), Explorations in Art & Technology, 2002; Pearl Park Scriptures, Digital Art Gallery, Berlin, 2005. *Mem:* Col Art Asn; Am Asn Univ Prof; Asn Computing Machinery; Int Soc Elec Art. *Media:* Computer Code, Paper. *Res:* Changing roles of the artist in our society. *Publ:* Auth, Experience in Community: The New Art, Liturgical Arts, 72; Le Sacre et la Profane, Art D'Eglise, 75; A futures outlook on the role of artists and designers, Futurics, 80; Epigenetic Painting: Software As Genotype, Leonardo, 1/23/90; computer illus, Derivation of the Laws, St Sebastian Press, Minneapolis, 90; and others; Epigenetic Art Revisited In Code The Language of Our Time, Art Electronica, Linz Austria, 2004. *Dealer:* Mary Lou Bock, The Williams Gallery Princeton NJ 08542; Wolfgang Leiser, Digital Art Mus Tucholsky Strasse, Berlin. *Mailing Add:* 5535 Clinton Ave S Minneapolis MN 55419

VERZAR, CHRISTINE B
EDUCATOR
b Basel, Switz, Sept 05, 40; US citizen. *Study:* Courtauld Inst, London Univ, 63; Univ Florence, 63-64; Univ Basel, PhD, 66. *Teaching:* Asst prof hist art, Boston Univ, 66-69, Princeton Univ, 69-76; asst prof, Univ Mich, 73-84; prof/chmn hist art, Ohio State Univ, 84-94, prof hist Art, 9-. *Awards:* Phi Kappa Phi. *Mem:* Col Art Asn; Int Ctr Medieval Art (bd dir, 85-89); Medieval Acad Am. *Res:* Italian medieval art; Connections East-West. *Publ:* Auth, Die Romanischen Skulpturen der Abtei Sagra San Michele, Bern, 68; coauth, The Meeting of Two Worlds, Ann Arbor, 81; Portal & Politics in the Early Italian City/State, Parma, 88. *Mailing Add:* Dept Hist Art Ohio State Univ 100 Hayes Hall 108 N Oval Hall Columbus OH 43210

VERZYL, JUNE CAROL
DEALER, COLLECTOR
b Huntington, NY, Feb 5, 28. *Study:* Parsons Sch of Design. *Pos:* Co-dir, Verzyl Gallery, 66-. *Bibliog:* Jane Margold (auth), Galleries struggle with an image, Newsday, 3/31/67; Kevin Hayes (auth), Gallery almost set to re-open, Northport Observer, 10/29/81. *Mem:* Northport Hist Soc. *Specialty:* Contemporary American painting, graphics and sculpture. *Collection:* Contemporary American work, including Filmus, Refregier, Benda, Twardowicz, Clawson and Christopher; also a large collection of New England gravestone rubbings. *Mailing Add:* 25 Bevin Rd Northport NY 11768

VESERY, JACQUES
SCULPTOR, INSTRUCTOR
b Westwood, NJ, Jan 29, 60. *Work:* Detroit Inst Art Michican/Bohlen Collection. *Exhib:* Bohlen Collection Fine Art of Wood at the Millenium, Detroit Inst Art, 2000; Turned Wood 2000 & 1999, Delmano Gallery, Los Angeles, 2000, Small Treasures 2000 & 1999, 2000. *Awards:* Maine Art Comn fellow 2000. *Bibliog:* J. Vesery-A Craftsman's Path, Am Asn Woodturners, 99. *Mem:* Am Asn Woodturners (demonstrator 98-99); Am Craft Coun; Main Crafts Asn (bd 99-); Collectors of Wood Art. *Media:* Wood. *Publ:* auth, A Celebration of Thinking, Am Asn Woodturners, 99; auth, The Fine Art of Wood/Bohlen Collection, Abbeville Press, 2000. *Mailing Add:* 71 Lessner Rd Damariscotta ME 04543

VESSA See Meserole, Vera (Vessa) Stromsted

VESTAL, DAVID
PHOTOGRAPHER, WRITER
b Menlo Park, Calif, 24. *Study:* Art Inst Chicago, 41-44; studied photog with Sid Grossman, 47-55. *Work:* Mus Mod Art, NY Pub Libr, Metrop Mus & Whitney Mus Am Art, NY; Art Inst Chicago; George Eastman House, Rochester; Mus NMex, Santa Fe; High Mus Art, Atlanta; Nat Gallery, Ottawa; Univ Louisville, Ky; and others; Mus Art, Columbus, Ohio; Nat Gallery, Wash, DC. *Exhib:* Solo exhib, Witkin Gallery, NY, 71, East Street Gallery, Grinnell, Iowa, 75, Tom Zimmermann Fine Arts, New Hope, Pa, 85, Galeria del Bosque, Guadalajara, Mex, 87 & Daytona Beach Community Col, Fla, 89; Photog Crossroads: The Photo League, Nat Gallery Can, Ottawa, Int Ctr Photog, NY Mus Fine Arts, Houston & Minneapolis Inst Arts, 78; The Great West: Real/Ideal, Univ Colo, Boulder, 79 & Smithsonian Inst Traveling Exhib; NY Sch, Corcoran Gallery, Washington, DC, 85; Robert Mann Gallery, NY, 1996, 2001; Univ Louisville, Ky, 96; Foto Riografia, Rio de Janeiro, Brazil, 96; and others. *Pos:* Contrib ed, Popular Photog, 75-86 & Photo Tech, 89-. *Teaching:* Pvt instr photog, 56-; vis artist, Art Inst Chicago, 72-73; instr, Parsons Sch Design, 84-94, Sch Visual Arts, 86-93 & Pratt Inst, 87-01. *Awards:* Guggenheim Fel, 66 & 73-74; Fulbright Scholar Award, Brazil, 97. *Bibliog:* David Vestal, Photog Ann, 62; Vision and Expression, 69; David Vestal, Photog Ann, 76. *Media:* Black and White. *Specialty:* Photography. *Publ:* ed, US Camera Annual 1971, 70; ed, Leica Manual, 72; auth, The Craft of Photography, 75 & The Art of Black-and-White Enlarging, Harper & Row, 84; non-newsletter, Grump, 88-2005, Finity, 2006; column, Phot Techniques, 95-; auth, Picture Book, 2003; MCMNY, 2006. *Dealer:* Robert Mann Gallery 210 11th Ave New York NY 10001; Sandra Berler 7002 Connecticut Ave Chevy Chase Md 20815. *Mailing Add:* PO Box 309 Bethlehem CT 06751

VETROCQ, MARCIA E
EDITOR
Study: Princeton Univ, NJ, BA; Stanford Univ, Calif, PhD. *Pos:* Profe, fine arts, Univ New Orleans, 82-98; sr ed, Art in Am Mag, New York City, 98-. *Awards:* Grantee, Andrew and Marian Heiskell Vis Fel in Criticism, Am Acad, Rome, 2004. *Publ:* Coauth, The Founders & the Architects: Design of Stanford Univ, 76; coauth, Domenico Tiepolo's Punchinello Drawings, 79. *Mailing Add:* Art in America Brant Publications 575 Broadway New York NY 10012

VEVERS, TABITHA
PAINTER
b Mt Kisco, NY, May 4, 57. *Study:* Skowhegan Sch Painting & Sculpture, Maine, 78; Yale Univ, New Haven, Conn, BA(cum laude), 78. *Work:* LaSalle Univ Art Mus, Philadelphia; McNay Art Inst, San Antonio, Tex; Provincetown Art Asn & Mus, Mass; Decordova Mus, Lincoln, Mass. *Exhib:* Art--Made in the USA (auth, catalog), Stadtische Galerie Regensburg, Ger, 88, Contemp Provincetown (auth, catalog), Pac Design Ctr, West Hollywood, Calif, 89; Crosscurrents: The New Generation (auth, catalog), E Hampton Ctr Contemp Arts, NY, 90; solo exhibs, Kraushaar Galleries, New York, 92, 94, 97, 2000, 03; Relatively speaking: Mothers & Daughters in Art (traveling show, catalogue), Snug Harbor cult Ctr, Staten Island, NY; DNA Gallery, 96, 97, 98, 99, 2000, 2001, 2002, 2003, 2004; Immortalized (catalog), Art Complex Mus, Duxbury, Mass, 98; Painting in Boston 1950-2000 (book), DeCordova Mus, Lincoln, Mass, 2002-03; Pepper Gallery, Boston, 2004 & 2006; artSTRAND, Provincetown, Mass, 2005-2006; and others. *Collection Arranged:* Couples, Words and Pictures, 86, Laughter and Tears: a Show of Emotion, 88, Allegory, 89, Young Artists, 89, Provincetown Art Asn & Mus, Mass. *Pos:* Bd mem, Provincetown Art Asn & Mus, 85-91, mem exhib com, 86-91, 2004-; juror, Va Ctr Creative Arts, 98-; mem artists' adv bd, Castle Hill Ctr for the Arts, 98-. *Teaching:* Instr, Castle Hill Ctr Arts, 95-2003. *Awards:* VA Ctr Creative Arts Fel, Sweet Briar, Va, 86, 91 & 93; Oberpfaltzer Kunstlerhaus Painting Fel, Schwandorf, Ger, 93; fel, Fine Arts Work Ctr, Provincetown, Mass, 95-96; painting fel, MacDowell Colony, 83; grant, George & Helen Segal Found, 2005; Sea Grant, Univ RI, 2005; painting fel, Ballinglen Arts Found, Ireland, 2006. *Bibliog:* Lise Motherwell (auth), The Eye of the Beholder: The Art of Tabitha Vevers, Provincetown Arts Magazine, 2004. *Mem:* Am Asn Mus; Provincetown Art Asn & Mus. *Media:* Oil, Mixed Media. *Publ:* Tabitha Vevers: Flying Dreams, DNA Editions, 2002; Painting in Boston: 1950-2000, DeCordova Mus & Sculpture Park, 2002; New American Painting, Open Studio Press, 2003 & 2005. *Dealer:* Pepper Gallery 38 Newbury St Boston MA 02116; artSTRAND 494 Commercial St Provincetown Mass 02657. *Mailing Add:* 75 Richdale Ave No 4 Cambridge MA 02140

VEVERS, TONY
ASSEMBLAGE ARTIST, EDUCATOR
b London, Eng, May 20, 26; US citizen. *Study:* Yale Univ, BA, 50; Acad di Belle Arti, Florence, Italy, 50-51; Hans Hofmann Sch, New York, 52-53. *Work:* Isaac Delgado Mus, New Orleans; Univ Mass, Amherst; Purdue Univ, Lafayette, Ind; Chrysler Mus, Norfolk, Va; JH Hirshhorn Mus, Washington; Metrop Mus, NY; De Cordova Mus & Sculpture Park, Lincoln, Mass; Provincetown Art Asn & Mus, Mass. *Exhib:* One-man shows, Roko Gallery, NY, 65, Babcock Galleries, NY, 69, Artist's Space, Nk, 76, NY & Contemp Art Workshop, Chicago, 84; one-man retrospective, Lafayette Art Mus, 86; fifty yr retrospective, Provincetown Art Asn & Mus, Mass, 2000; Abstract Landscapes, Acme Fine Arts, Boston, 2003. *Pos:* vis artist, Caribbean Art Search Found, St Lucia, 84. *Teaching:* Lectr painting, Univ NC, Greensboro, 63-64; prof painting & art hist, Purdue Univ, Lafayette, Ind, 64-88, prof emer, 88-; vis staff, Fine Arts Work Ctr, Provincetown, Mass, 70-71, consult, 71-76. *Awards:* Grants, Nat Endowment Arts, 67 & Purdue Univ, 70; New Eng Painting & Sculpture Prize, 71. *Mem:* Col Art Asn; Art Asn Provincetown (vpres, 71-). *Media:* Acrylic, Oil. *Specialty:* Fine Art Galleries. *Interests:* art history. *Publ:* Auth, Alvin Ross, 7/78, The Sun

Gallery, 7/81 & Expressionism, 7/85; The Beginnings of the Provincetown Art Association and Museum, 8/90 Provincetown Art Asn; Provincetown Abstract Painting 1915-1950, 9/94. *Dealer:* Long Point Gallery Provincetown MA 02657. *Mailing Add:* 250 Bradford St Provincetown MA 02657

VICK, CONNIE R
CONSULTANT
b Philadelphia, Pa, Oct 17, 47. *Study:* Pa State Univ, BFA, 69; Cornell Univ, 70; Philadelphia Col Art, 72. *Pos:* Owner & dir, Vick Gallery, Philadelphia, Pa, 73-79; lectr painting, Neumann Ctr, Philadelphia, 76-80 & Manor Jr Col, 80-84; asst to dir, Fischbach Gallery, New York, 82-84; corp art adv, Vick Corp Art Adv, 84-. *Mailing Add:* 253 73rd St Apt 4D New York NY 10023-2752

VICKREY, ROBERT REMSEN
PAINTER
b New York, NY, Aug 20, 26. *Study:* Yale Univ, BA; Art Students League; Yale Sch Fine Arts, BFA; also with Kenneth Hayes Miller & Reginald Marsh. *Work:* Nat Mus Am Art, Corcoran Gallery Art, Washington, DC; Metrop Mus Art, Whitney Mus Am Art, NY; Butler Inst Am Art; and 60 others. *Comn:* Covers for Time Mag; also portraits & bk jackets. *Exhib:* Whitney Mus Am Art; 50 one-man shows, Santa Barbara Mus, Calif; Mus Fine Arts, Houston; Neuberger Mus, Purchase, NY; Chrysler Mus, Norfolk, Va; Lyrical Realist Traveling Exhib, 82-83. *Awards:* Am Audubon Artists; Int Hallmark Competition, Windsor; Newton Mem Award; 21 awards at AWC; 3 National Acad Awards. *Mem:* Am Watercolor Soc; Audubon Artists; Nat Acad (assoc, 61, acad, 64-). *Media:* Egg Tempera. *Publ:* Coauth, New Techniques in Egg Tempera & auth, Robert Vickery--Artist at Work, Watson-Guptill, The Affable Curmudgeon, Parnassus. *Dealer:* Kennedy Galleries 40 W 57th St New York NY. *Mailing Add:* 8231 Bay Colony Dr #1202 Naples FL 34108

VIDAL, FRANCISCO
PAINTER, PRINTMAKER
b Barranquilla, Columbia, July 22, 46. *Study:* Univ Altantico, Barranquilla, Columbia, 61-63, Art Students League, 69-71; printmaking workshop(scholarship), NY, 83-85. *Work:* Mus del Barrio, NY; Mus Modern Art, Cantagena, Columbia; Mus Contemp Art Monterrey, Marco, Monterrey, Mex; Adogi, Miniprint Intl, Cadaguez, Spain; Latin America Exhibit, Credit Swiss, NY. *Exhib:* Solo show, Mus Alternative, NY, 85, Gallery Frau, Soho, NY; Bass Art Mus, Miami, Fla, 88; Los Angeles Munic Art Gallery, Calif, 88; Centro Colombo Americano, Bogota, Columbia, 88; First Festival of Art, Barranquilla, Columbia, 89; E Hampton Ctr for Contemp Art, NY, 90; Mus Contemp Art, Monterrey; Int Contemp Art Biennial, Firenza, Italy, 2001; Ninth anniversary Latin Am Mus, Coral Gables, Fla, 2002; and others; Florence Biennal, Frienza, Italy. *Teaching:* Prof drawing, Col Barranquilla for Ladies, 63-68. *Awards:* Selected for 84/86 Nat Studio Prog; Fel painting, Mid Atlantic Arts Found, Baltimore, Md, 92. *Bibliog:* Fred Stern (auth), Artists with Latin American Roots, Mizue Art Mag, Tokyo, Japan, 89; Susana Torreulla Leval (auth), Identity and Freedom, Decade Show, 90; Phyllis Braff (auth), Expirimentation in the Still Life, NY Times, May 90. *Media:* Oil on Canvas, Miscellaneous Media. *Publ:* Contribr, Carnival on New York, 89 & En la brecha de la image, 90, El Tiempo, Columbia; article, Experimentation in still life, NY Times, 5/90; contribr, From the studio, East Hampton Star, 5/90; Miami Herald, 7/92; Ihalo mag, Bogots, Columbia, 10/94. *Mailing Add:* 143-16 Barclay Ave #2G Flushing NY 11355

VIDITZ-WARD, VERA LOUISE
PHOTOGRAPHER, HISTORIAN
b Buffalo, NY, May 24, 52. *Study:* Hartford Art Sch, Univ Hartford, BFA, 75; Sch Fine Arts, Ind Univ, MFA(Fulbright Hayes Res Grant), 88. *Work:* Smithsonian Inst, Nat Mus African Art; Visual Studies Workshop; Nat Mus Sierra Leone, WAfrica; Ga Coastal Hist Mus, St Simons Island, Ga; Penn Ctr of Sea Islands, St Helena Island, SC. *Exhib:* Paramount Chiefs of Sierra Leone, Smithsonian Inst, 90-91; Recent Work, Avery Ctr African Am Cult, Charleston, SC, 92; Recent Work, Sierra Leone Nat Mus, Freetown, W Africa, 93; Other Africas, Photog Resource Ctr, Boston, 93; Paramount Chiefs, Newark Mus, NJ, 95; The Trans-Atlantic Linkage Traveling Exhib, Ga Coastal Hist Mus, 95-97. *Pos:* Photogr volunteer, US Peace Corps, Sierra Leone, 77-79; photogr/stringer, Assoc Press, WAfrica, 86-88. *Teaching:* Assoc prof photog, Bloomsburg Univ, Pa, 88-. *Awards:* WAfrica Res Asn Fel Photog, Howard Univ, 96. *Bibliog:* J Kaplan (auth), West African Gullah traditions alive, Los Angeles Trib & Chicago Tribune, 91; C Kratz (auth), Paramount chiefs of Sierra Leone, African Arts, 10/91; M Sidell (auth), Exhib rev, The Star Ledger, Newark, 2/95. *Mem:* Soc Photog Educ; Arts Coun of African Studies Asn; WAfrican Res Asn; Col Art Asn. *Media:* Black & White Photography. *Res:* History of photography of Black Africa. *Publ:* Auth, Alphonso Lisk-Carew: Krio photographer, African Arts/Univ Calif Los Angeles, 85; Paramount chiefs of Sierra Leone: photographs by VV-W, Smithsonian, 91. *Mailing Add:* Bloomsburg Univ Dept Art Bloomsburg PA 17815

VIELEHR, WILLIAM RALPH
SCULPTOR
b Chicago, Ill, Jan 6, 45. *Study:* Univ Colo, 63-66; Colo State Univ, BFA, 69. *Work:* Crossroads Mall, Boulder, Colo; Byers Mus & Mus Contemp Art, Chicago; Prudential Bache, Boulder, Colo; Northern Ill Univ; Cherry Creek Plaza, Denver; and others. *Comn:* Interaction, Boulder Reservoir, Colo, 86; Digital, Colorado Springs, Colo, 86; Monument to Mining, Boulder Co Court House, Colo; Pub Art, City of Flagstaff, Ariz; Sch of Mines, Golden, Colo. *Exhib:* Denver Art Mus, 72; N Am Sculpture Exhib, 81 & 98; Art on the Corner, Grand Junction, Colo, 93-98; Boulder Art Ctr Invitational, Colo 93; Boulder Flow, Univ Colo, 93; Sculpture in the Park, Littleton, Colo, 94; Artyard Show, Denver, Colo, 94, 2000; Dairy Ctr for Arts, Boulder, Colo, 99. *Pos:* Dir, Form Sculpture, 81-; juror, Leonardo Di Vinci Award, 84, 86, 88, 90, 92, 94, 96 & 98. *Teaching:* Vis artist sculpture workshop, Jefferson Co Schs, 71-72 & Colo State Univ, 73; speaker, Art Week, Univ Colo, Colorado Springs, 88; workshops, Boulder Pub Schs, 89. *Awards:* City Arts Grant, Boulder, Colo, 81, 85, 88 & 98; Addison Grant, Neo Data, 98; Lou Wille Award for Excellence, Grand Junction, Colo, 2000. *Bibliog:* Art from the Soul, Taos Mag, 8/96; In Search of the Mark, Broomfield Enterprise, 4/97; Life of an Artist, Ariz Daily Sun, 6/99. *Mem:* Bully Boys Beer Club (pres 77-); Loon Rafting (rear admiral 85-2001). *Media:* Cast & Fabricated Bronze & Aluminum. *Dealer:* Shidoni-Bishops Lodge Rd Tesugeue NM 87574; Lumina Gallery 239 Movada Ln Taos NM 87571. *Mailing Add:* PO Box 19734 Broomfield CO 80308-2734

VIERA, CHARLES DAVID
EDUCATOR, PAINTER
b Dartmouth, Mass, Feb 21, 50. *Study:* Swain Sch Design, BFA, 72; Skowhegan Sch Painting & Sculpture; Brooklyn Col Grad Sch, with Philip Pearlstein, MFA, 74. *Work:* Pvt collection of A Hess, NY. *Comn:* Murals, Am Renaissance Festival, Brooklyn Mus, 79. *Exhib:* Brooklyn 1976, Brooklyn Mus; Nat Arts Club, NY, 77; 153 Ann, Nat Acad, NY, 78; solo shows, Animal Drawings, Long Island Univ, 80 & Paintings, Nassau Co Mus, 81; retrospective, Charles Viera 1972-1982, Brooklyn Mus Art Sch, 82; Works on Paper, Adam Gimbel Gallery, NY, 83. *Pos:* Coordr exhibs, Long Island Univ, Brooklyn, NY, 84 & 85, coordr fine arts, continuing educ prog, 86. *Teaching:* Instr painting & drawing, Brooklyn Mus Art Sch, 75- & Parsons Sch Design, 79-; assoc prof, Long Island Univ, 79-. *Bibliog:* Show of contrast, Phoenix, New York, 76; Inmates try art, 76 & Performers recreate art, 79, New York Times. *Media:* Mixed. *Mailing Add:* 10 Stacey Rd Flemington NJ 08822

VIERA, RICARDO
PAINTER, PRINTMAKER
b Ciego de Avila, Cuba, Dec 15, 45; US citizen. *Study:* Sch of the Mus of Fine Arts, Boston, dipl, 72; Tufts Univ, BFA, 73; RI Sch of Design, Providence, MFA, 74. *Work:* Allentown Art Mus, Pa; Tel Aviv Mus, Israel; Canton Art Inst, Ohio; Cleveland Mus; Fed Soc Arts & Humanities, Lagos, Nigeria; and others. *Exhib:* One-man shows, Inst Contemp Art, Boston, 73 & Canton Art Inst, Ohio, 80; Transitions in Art, Boston Mus of Fine Arts, 77; The Kadishman Connection, Israel Mus, Jerusalem, 79; Instituto de Cultura Puertorriquena, San Juan, 81; Alfred O Deshong Mus, Chester, Pa, 82; and many others. *Collection Arranged:* American Figure Drawing, Lehigh Univ & Victorian Col of Art, Melbourne, Australia, 76; Intentions & Techniques (auth, catalog), 79, 26th Ann Contemp Am Art Exhib (auth, catalog), traveling, 81 & Computer Art (auth, catalog), 82, Wilson Gallery, Lehigh Univ, Bethlehem, Pa; Michael Smith, Landscape Photography (auth, catalog), traveling, 81; and others. *Pos:* dir & cur, Lehigh Univ Art Galleries, 74-, chmn pro-tempore, 77-78; community arts coordr & discussion leader, Baum Sch Art, Allentown, Pa, 79-; consult, Cuban Mus Art & Cult, Miami, 81-; bd dir, Pa Citizens Arts, 79-, ARTS, Washington, DC; bd dir, Valley Art Coun. *Teaching:* Instr, Lehigh Univ, 74-78, assoc prof, 78. *Awards:* Elizabeth H Bartol Scholarship, Boston Mus of Fine Arts Sch, 71-72; Cintas fel, Cintas Found, Inst of Int Educ, 74-75; Mellon Found Grant, 78-80; and others. *Bibliog:* Ricardo Viera/Illustraciones Enlace, Nueva Revista Hispanoamericana, 76; Keith Schneider (auth), Capturing the intensity of life, Times Leader, Wilkes-Barre, Pa, 9/13/79; Norma Niurka (auth), A box of surprises, Miami Herald, 10/7/81. *Mem:* Pa Counc Arts; Print Club Philadelphia; Am Asn of Mus; Am Asn Mus/NEastern Conf. *Media:* Oil, Acrylic; Enamel Spray, Oil Crayon. *Publ:* Illusr, Dr Fernando Ortiz, auth, Los Negros Brujos, Ed Universal, Miami, Fla, 73; illusr, Libro Quinto de Lectura Gramatica y Ortografia, Leal & Sanchez Boudy, Miami, 75; illusr, Introduccion al Estudio de la Civilizacion Espanola, Barroso, Miami, 76; auth, Arte Visual en la Palabra de Lydia Cabrera, Festschriften/Ed Universal, 77; auth, From Limestones to aluminum plate lithography, RI Sch of Design Bull, 77. *Dealer:* Forma Hispanic Arts Dealers 305 Alcazar Coral Gables FL 33134. *Mailing Add:* Art Gallery Lehigh Univ Zoellner Arts Ctr 420 E Packer Ave Bethlehem PA 18015

VIERTHALER, BONNIE
COLLAGE ARTIST, LECTURER
b Milwaukee, Wis, Sept 11, 41. *Study:* Univ Wis-Madison, BS(art educ), 63; Univ Ga, MFA(fiber arts), 72. *Work:* City of Seattle, Seattle First Nat Bank, Wash; IBM, White Plains, NY; Prudential Insurance Co, NY. *Comn:* Fiber & dyed fabric hanging, comn by Richard Wimer, Atlanta, Ga, 71; works in rubber, Seattle Arts Comn, Wash, 76; Pollutius Conglomeratus (wearable art), Seattle Arts Comn & Seattle Aquarium, Wash, 79. *Exhib:* Solo exhibs, Polly Friedlander Gallery, Seattle, Wash, 74 & 76; Invitational, Seattle Art Mus, 76, Foster White Gallery, Seattle, 78; Works in Rubber (traveling), Smithsonian Inst, 79-80; The Joy of Smoking - A Spoof on Cigarette Advertising (traveling), Rotunda of Russell Senate Office Bldg, Washington, 86-90. *Pos:* Artist & pres, BADvertising Inst, Ithaca, NY, 86-; presenter, NJ Assist Prog, 88-. *Teaching:* Lectr hist fabrics, Emory Univ, Atlanta, 73-74; weaving teacher, Factory Visual Arts, Seattle, 76-77. *Awards:* Craftman's Fel, Nat Endowment Arts, 77 & Artist-in-Residence Grant, 78; Giraffe Award, Giraffe Proj, 90. *Publ:* Contrib articles in NJ J Med, 87

VIGNES, MICHELLE MARIE
PHOTOGRAPHER
b Reims, France, May 13, 26. *Study:* Studied philos in Reims. *Work:* Affaire Culturelles, Bibliot Nat, Mus Carnavalet, Paris, France; Centre Photographie, Geneva, Switzerland. *Exhib:* Trail of Broken Treaties, Oakland Mus, Calif, 71-73; Les Concierges, French Inst, NY, 76; The Blues, FNAC, 83 & Galarie Agathe Gaillard, 86, Paris, France; Jazz & Photog, Mus Mod Art, Paris, France, 83; Retrospective, Ctr Photog, Geneva, Switz, 87, FNAC, Paris, 90; Vision Gallery, San Francisco, 91-; Musee Carnavalet, Paris, 92. *Teaching:* Instr doc photog, Univ Calif, 78-, San Francisco, Calif, 85-; Paris Univ, France, 88-; instr photog & ethnology, Acad Arts,

San Francisco, 90-92. *Awards:* Media Alliance Award for Photogr of the Year, 83. *Mem:* Media Alliance (bd mem, 79-85); Camerawork (bd mem, 83-87); Mother Jones Int Fund for Doc Photog (founder). *Publ:* Auth, The Blues, North Beach Press, 85; Oakland Blues, Ed Marval, 90; Bay Area Blues, Pomegranate, Calif, 93. *Dealer:* Vision Gallery 2300 Polk St San Francisco CA; Agence Rapho 8 rue d'Alger Paris 75001

VIGTEL, GUDMUND
DIRECTOR
b July 9, 25; US citizen. *Study:* Isaac Grunewald's Sch Art, Stockholm, 43-44; Univ Ga, BFA, 52, MFA, 53. *Hon Degrees:* Atlanta Col Art, 91. *Collection Arranged:* The New Tradition, 63; The Beckoning Land, 71; The Modern Image, 72; The Dusseldorf Academy & the Americans, 73; A Retrospective, Harvey K Littleton, 84; Art in Berlin, 1815-1989, 89-90; The Sacred Art of Russia, 95; 9 Women in Georgia, 96. *Pos:* Admin asst, Corcoran Gallery Art, 54-57, asst to dir, 57-61, asst dir, 61-63; dir, High Mus Art, 63-91. *Awards:* Chevalier des Arts et Lettres, 86; Order of Merit, First Class, Fed Repub Ger, 89; Lifetime Achievement Award, Ga Asn Mus & Galleries, 90. *Mem:* Am Asn Mus; Asn Art Mus Dirs. *Publ:* Auth, 100 Years of Painting in Georgia, Alston & Bird, Atlanta, 92; 9 Women in Georgia, 96. *Mailing Add:* 2082 Golfview Dr NW Atlanta GA 30309-1210

VIKAN, GARY KENT
MUSEUM DIRECTOR
b Fosston, Minn, Nov 30, 46. *Study:* Carleton Col, BA, 67; Princeton Univ, MA, 70; Princeton Univ, PhD, 76. *Pos:* Art mus admin, cur, Byzantine art Dumbarton Oaks, Wash, 75-84; assist dir cur, affairs, cur, medieval art Walters Art Mus, Baltimore, 85-94, dir, 94-. *Teaching:* Adj prof, Johns Hopkins Univ. *Awards:* Woodrow Wilson Found fel, 1967-68. *Mem:* Byzantine Studies Counf (gov bd 89-), US Nat Comt for Byzantine Studies (exec comt, 88-92). *Mailing Add:* Walters Art Gallery 600 N Charles St Baltimore MD 21201

VILLA, CARLOS
PAINTER
Study: San Francisco Art Inst, BFA, 61; Mills Col, MFA, 63. *Exhib:* de Young Mus, San Francisco, 72; Whitney Mus Am Art Ann, NY, 72; San Francisco Mus, 74; San Francisco Art Inst, 76; Calif Show: The Mod Era, San Francisco Mus, Calif & Nat Collection Fine Arts, Washington, DC, 76-77; Calif Bay Area Art--Update, Huntsville Mus Art, Ala, 77; New in the Seventies, Univ Tex, Austin, 77; and many others. *Teaching:* Asst, Mills Col, 61-63; asst, Studio 1, Oakland, Calif, 61-63; instr, Telegraph Hill Neighborhood Ctr, Urban Arts, San Francisco, 69-70; chmn inter-dept studies, San Francisco Art Inst, currently; asst prof art, Calif State Univ, Sacramento, currently. *Awards:* Adeline Kent Award, San Francisco Art Inst, 73; Nat Endowment Arts Grant, 73; Visual Artists Award, Flintridge Found, 98. *Bibliog:* Article, 12/70 & Emily Wasserman (auth), article, 1/71, Artforum. *Mailing Add:* San Francisco Art Inst Col 800 Chestnut St San Francisco CA 94133

VILLA, MARIO
ART DEALER, ARCHITECT
b Managua, Nicaragua, Mar 16, 56. *Study:* Univ New Orleans, BA, 77, Tulane Univ, archit lic, 81. *Work:* Bellas Artes & Nat Art Expo, Managua, Nicaragua. *Comn:* Rotunda Condominium Complex, Entrance Gate, Warehouse Dist, New Orleans, La, 89; Princess Caroline Monaco, Dining Rm, Principality Monaco, 89-90; Karl Lagerfield, bedroom, Rome; Country House, LeMee, Monte Carlo; Villa Karl, Hamburg; LeRocMer, Monaco, 89-90; sconce design, front entrance Contemp Arts Ctr New Orleans, Artists & Architects Collab, New Orleans, La, 90; renovation, Ocshner Clinic Plastic Surgery Dept, New Orleans, La, 91; and others. *Exhib:* Odyssey Ball, New Orleans Mus Art, 85; Art for Arts Sake, Contemp Arts Ctr, New Orleans, La, 85 & 86; The Useful Arts, Contemp Arts Ctr, New Orleans, La, 87; Art in Bloom, New Orleans Mus Art, 88; Nat Convention, Am Inst Architects, NY, 88; and others. *Collection Arranged:* Helena Rubenstein Religious Collection, Graphic Editions, New Orleans, La, 79. *Pos:* Dir, Graphic Editions, New Orleans, La, 81; pres/owner, Mario Villa Inc, Beverly Hills, Calif; co-owner/dir bd, Mario Villa, Chicago, Ill; pres/owner, Mario Villa Inc, New Orleans, La, currently. *Teaching:* Prof archit, Nat Univ, Nicaragua, 75-76. *Awards:* Design 100 Award, Metrop Home, 90 & 92; Apaulso Awards Arts, Aqui New Orleans Bilingual Newsletter, 92; Man Yr Arts, Que Pasa Publ, New Orleans, La, 92; and others. *Bibliog:* Articles, Times Picayune, 79 & States-Item, 82; article, Mario Villa, Beaux Arts Mag, 84 & Times-Picayune, 9/86. *Mem:* Contemp Arts Ctr, New Orleans (bd mem); New Orleans Ballet Asn (bd mem, 92); Newcomb Sch Arts, Tulane Univ (adv bd, 92); Preserv Resource Ctr (hon chmn, 92); Sch Lib Arts, Univ New Orleans (adv bd, 91-); and others. *Media:* Bronze. *Res:* The formation of the British Museum. *Specialty:* Contemporary art. *Collection:* Pre-Columbian Latin America; 16th century Spanish. *Publ:* Auth, New Orleans Neighborhood, Tulane Univ, 81; Elegance and Decadence, Archit Digest, New Orleans, 99

VILLA, THEODORE B
PAINTER
b Santa Barbara, Calif, Sept 28, 36. *Study:* Santa Barbara City Col, AA, 61; Univ Calif, Santa Barbara, BA, 63, MFA, 74. *Work:* Inst Am Indian Mus, Santa Fe, NMex; Calif State Univ, Los Angeles; Univ Gallery, Univ Calif, Santa Barbara; Millicent Rogers Mus, Taos, NMex; Oakland Mus, Calif; Mus Northern Ariz, Flagstaff. *Comn:* Mus N Ariz, Flagstaff; Wigwam Resort & Country Club, Phoenix, Ariz; Desert Mountain Properties, Phoenix, Ariz; Phoenix Cardinals, Ariz; Stanford Univ Children's Hosp, Palo Alto, Calif. *Exhib:* solo exhibs, Sun Valley Ctr Arts, Ketchum, Idaho, 83, Taylor Mus, Colorado Springs Fine Arts Ctr, Colo, 87 & Mus Inst Am Indian Art, Santa Fe, NMex, 88, Millicent Rogers Mus, Taos, NMex, 90; No Beads, No Trinkets, Palais De Nations, Geneva, Switz, 84; Visage Transcended, Am Indian Contemp Arts, San Francisco, 86; Four Sacred Mountains, 2 yr traveling exhib, Ariz Arts Comn, 88-90; Decolonizing The Mind: End of a 500 Yr Era, Ctr Contemp Art, Seattle, Wash, 92; Centro Wash Irving, USIS, Madrid, 93; Fenderson Collection, Heard Mus, Phoenix, 93; 3 Visions, 3 Missions, Mus NAriz, 95. *Collection Arranged:* Grupo Larios, Madrid, Spain; AT&T, San Francisco, Calif; Root Corp, Daytona Beach, Fla; US West, Denver, Colo; Wigwam Resort & Country Club, Phoenix, Ariz; Indian Wells Country Club, Los Angeles, Calif; Mus Inst Am Indian Arts; Calif State Univ, Los Angeles; Millicent Rogers Mus, Taos, NMex; many others. *Teaching:* Instr design-watercolor, life drawing, Santa Barbara City Col, 75; lectr watercolor, Univ Calif, Santa Barbara, 83-86; Sun Valley Ctr Arts & Humanities; AHAA Sch, Telluride, Colo. *Bibliog:* Charles Clouse (auth), Doubletake, Southwest Art, 2/86. *Media:* Watercolor. *Publ:* Ya, Madrid, Spain & Valley Mag, Ketchum, ID, 2/8/93. *Dealer:* Broschofsky Galleries PO Box 1538 Ketchum ID 83340. *Mailing Add:* 1371 Santa Rita Cir Santa Barbara CA 93109

VILLARREAL-CASTELAZO, EDUARDO
ARCHITECT, PAINTER
b Mexico, DF Mex, Apr 14, 44. *Study:* Studied painting with Prof Alfredo Guati Rojo, 58 & Prof Carlos Medina, 63; Iberoamericana Univ, Archit, 68; Nat Univ Mex, MA, 78. *Work:* Mus Arzobispado Ministry Finance, Mex; Fla Mus Hispanic Latin Am Art, Miami; Mus Mod Art, Aquitaine, Lot et Garone, France; Gallery Mex Art, Seattle, Wash; Santa Cruz Parrish Complex XVI Century, Mex. *Comn:* Christmas decorations, Monterrey Insurance Corp Bldg, Monterrey Insurance Co, Mexico City, 65; Fountain Corp Bldg Proj, Mex Inst Social Security, Mexico City, 71; Fountain of Complex, Blessed Martyrs of Korea, Mexico City, 96; Mural Direction, Asuncion High Sch, Ixaltepec, Oaxaca, Mex, 87 & Corp Sculpture, 89. *Exhib:* Beams of Light, Salon Du Viex Colombier, Paris, France, 93; Winter Int Competition, Fla Mus Hispanic Latin Am Art, Miami, 93; 3rd Visual Dialogue, World Coun Visual Artists, Asis, Italy, 95; DAP 94, Pinacoteca Virreynal, Mex, 94; Museo Inconografico de Quijote, Guanajvato, VTO, 94; Top 70, Art 95, Gallery Art 54, NY, 95; Formalidades, Nat Univ Mex, Mexico, 96. *Pos:* Coordr cur, Nat Univ Mex, Acatlan Campus, 93-97; dir, Univ Exchanges World Coun Visual Artists, 95-97. *Teaching:* Archit contruct, Nat Univ Mex, Acatlan Campus, 80-98, precast in archit, 82-98, dipl art course coordr, 96-98. *Awards:* Jury Prize, Expos Flambouance, Paris, France, 93. *Bibliog:* Blanca Cecilia Puebla (auth), De Toro un Poco, Excelsior Newspaper, 11/29/93; Jorge Luis Berdeja (auth), El Centro Nacional de Las Artes, El Universal, 10/27/94; Maria Cecila Pontes (auth), Anniversary Enep Acatlan, El Universal Zona Norte, 10/20/95. *Mem:* World Coun Visual Artists; Colegio de Arquitectos de Mex; Sociedad de Arquitectos Mexicanos; Comn Univs (directorio de las artes plasticas, 96-). *Media:* Acrylic, Oil; Mixed Media. *Res:* application of construction materials in visual arts; quality in visual arts. *Publ:* Auth, Emergency Housing, CIDIV-INDECO, 81. *Mailing Add:* Jilquerds 39 Lomas Verdes Mexico 53120 Mexico

VILLINSKI, PAUL S
SCULPTOR, PAINTER
b York, Maine, May 28, 60. *Study:* Mass Col Art, 80-82, Cooper Union, 82-84, BFA, 84. *Work:* Cleary, Gottlieb, Steen & Hamilton, Attys, Mound, Cotton & Wollan, Attys, Nomura Securities Int, Ctr Reinsurance & John A Levin Co, NY; Brooklyn Union Gas Co, NY; Ogunquit Mus Am Art, Maine; and others. *Comn:* McCann Erickson Co, NY, 90; NY Life Insurance Co, Parsippany, NJ; Univ Wyoming Art Mus, Laramie, 99; Miller Gallery, Carnegie Mellon Univ, Pittsburgh, 01; Morgan Lehman Gallery, Lakeside, NY, 02. *Exhib:* Solo-shows, St Peter's Church, Citicorp Ctr, NY, 89, Midtown Payson Galleries, NY, 89 & Queens Mus Art, Bulova Corp Ctr, NY, 90, 3-D Lab, New York City, 97, Three Rivers Arts Festival Gallery, Pittsburgh, Pa, 2000; Brookworld, Soho Arts Festival, NY, 96; A Large Show of Small Works, Cooper Union, NY, 96; Suture, Rotunda Gallery, Brooklyn, NY, 97; On Air, St Peter's Church, NY, 97; The Alternative Mus, NY, 97; Artspace, New Haven, Conn, 98; Zoon Gallery, New Haven, Conn, 98; Islip Art Mus, East Islip, NY, 99; Scope, Miami, 2004; and many others. *Teaching:* Adj lectr, LaGuardia Community Col, City Univ NY, Long Island City, 90-93. *Awards:* Michael S Vivo Prize for Excellence, Cooper Union, 84; Nat Endowment Arts Grant, 87; Agnes Bourne Fel Painting, Djerassi Found, Woodside, Calif, 88. *Bibliog:* Belle Elving (auth), The language of gloves, Washington Post, 10/16/97; Ellen Lubell (auth), Common threads, Newark Star Ledger, 2/3/97; Donimique Naas (auth), Review of On Air, Rev, 3/1/97; and others. *Mem:* St Peter's Church Art & Archit (rev comt, 91-98), NY. *Media:* All. *Dealer:* Morgan Lehman Gallery, Lakeside, NY. *Mailing Add:* 9-01 44th Dr Long Island City NY 11101

VINCENT, CHRISTINE
ADMINISTRATOR
Study: Ill State Univ, BA in visual arts. *Pos:* Founder Community & cult Resource Develop Inc, New York City; deputy dir, Ford Found, 91-2001; pres Maine Col Art, Portland, 2001-. *Mailing Add:* Main Col of Art Off of Pres 97 Spring St Portland ME 04101

VINCENT, CLARE
CURATOR, HISTORIAN
b Jersey City, NJ, Aug 30, 35. *Study:* Col William & Mary, AB, 58; Inst Fine Arts, NY Univ, MA, 63; Inst Fine Arts & Metrop Mus Art, cert, 63. *Collection Arranged:* A Sure Reckoning, 68, Northern European Clocks in NY Collections, 72, Nineteenth Century French Sculpture, 80, Rodin: The Gates of Hell, 82; Rodin: The B Gerald Cantor Collection, 86, Metrop Mus Art, NY; Rodin's Monument to Victor Hugo, 99. *Pos:* Asst to cur decorative arts, Cooper Union Mus, 60-61; curatorial asst western Europ arts, Metrop Mus Art, New York, 62-67, asst cur, 67-72, assoc cur Europ sculpture & decorative arts, 72-; consult to catalogue of antique sci instruments, Adler

Planetarium, Chicago, 85-. *Teaching:* Curatorial Studies I, Metrop Mus Art & Inst Fine Arts, 95-96. *Mem:* Col Art Asn; Furniture Hist Soc; Antiquarian Horological Soc (vpres Am sect, 77-89). *Res:* European clocks and timekeeping instruments; European metalwork; European Renaissance enamels; 19th century European sculpture. *Interests:* Ballet, opera, concert going. *Publ:* auth, Rodin at the Metrop Mus Art: A Hist of the Collection, Metrop Mus Art, 81; Renaissance Decorative Arts, Leichtenstein: The Princely Collections, Metrop Mus Art, 85; A Beam Compass by Christoph Trechsler the Elder and the Origin of the Micrometer Screw, Metrop Mus J, Vol 24, 209-222, 89; coauth, A Watch for Monsieur Hesselin, Metrop Mus J, Vol 28, 103-119; coauth An Extravagant Jewel: The George Watch, Metro Mus J, Vol 35, 137-149; auth, Seventeenth Century French Painted Enamel Watchcases, Metrop Mus J, Vol 37, 89-106. *Mailing Add:* 326 E 85th St New York NY 10028

VINE, RICHARD
EDITOR
Study: Univ Chicago, PhD. *Pos:* Ed-in-Cief, Chicago Rev, Dialogue: An Art Journal, Ohio; editor, Art in Am, New York City. *Publ:* Old Nerdrum: Painting, Sketches and Drawings, 2001; Burhan Doancay: Works on Paper, 1950-2000, 2003. *Mailing Add:* Art in America Brant Art Publications 575 Broadway New Yor NY 10012

VINELLA, RAY (RAIMONDO) JOHN
PAINTER, SCULPTOR
b Bari, Italy, April 6, 33. *Study:* Art Ctr Col Design, with Lorsor Fietleson, Harry Carmean, John Lagatta & Reynold Brown, BPA, 59, BFA, 68. *Work:* Diamond M Found Mus, Snyder, Tex; Mansato Int, NY; Carlsbad Mus, NMex. *Exhib:* First Exhib Southwest Art, People's Republic China, 81; Mus Native Am Cult, Spokane, Wash, 82; Colo Sch Mines. *Pos:* Art comt, Harvard Found Mus, Taos, NMex. *Teaching:* Instr painting, Taos Acad Fine Art, 71-72 & Taos Art Workshops, 82-; fac dean, Taos Sch Fine Art, 77-78. *Awards:* B Altman Award, 51; Prof Award, Painting Competition, NMex State Fair, 71 & 73. *Bibliog:* Peggi Ridgway (auth), Southwest Art, 3/84; Roberta McIntyre (auth), Western Art Digest, 1-2/86; Today Show, 7/31/87; Nancy Ellis (auth), Southwest Profile, 1/89; Southwest Profile, 9/96. *Mem:* Soc Am Impressionists; Monac Art Soc. *Media:* Oil, Egg Tempera; Watercolor. *Publ:* Auth, Masterworks of Impressionism: Arlene Doran Kirkpatrick. *Dealer:* Brazos Fine Art. *Mailing Add:* c/o Brazos Fine Art 119 Bent St Taos NM 87571

VINOLY, RAFAEL
ARCHITECT
b Montevideo, Uruguay, 44. *Study:* Univ Buenos Aires, Argentina, Grad in Archit, 1969. *Exhib:* Principal works incl John Jay Col Criminal Justice, 1988, Tokyo Int Forum, 1996, Univ Chicago Grad Sch Bus, Howard Hughes Medical Inst Janelia Farm Research Campus, Virginia, Porter Neurosci. Research Ctr at Nat Inst of Health, Md, Cleveland Mus Art; author: Rafael Viñoly, 2003. *Pos:* Found partner, Estudio de Arquitectura, Argentina, 1964-78; found, prin Rafael Viñoly Archits PC, New York City, 1982-. *Teaching:* guest lectr, Univ Wash, Harvard Univ. *Awards:* Recipient Medal of Hon, Am Inst of Archit NY Chap, 1994. *Mem:* Fel: Am Inst of Archits; Nat Acad of Design (acad 1994-), Japan Inst Archit. *Mailing Add:* Rafael Vinoly Architects 50 Vandam St New York NY 10013

VIOLA, BILL
VIDEO ARTIST
b New York, NY, Jan 25, 51. *Study:* Syracuse Univ, BFA, 73, Hon Dr Fine Arts, 95; Art Inst Chicago, 97; Calif Col Arts & Crafts, 98. *Hon Degrees:* Syracuse Univ, DFA (hon), 95; Art Inst Chicago, 97; Calif Col Art & Crafts, 98; Mass Col Art, 99; Calif Inst Arts, 2000; Sunderland Univ, Eng, 2000. *Work:* Mus Mod Art, NY; Ctr Georges Pompidou, Paris, France; San Francisco Mus Mod Art; Mus Fur Mod Kunst, Frankfurt, Ger; Mus Contemp Art, Los Angeles. *Comn:* The Stopping Mind (video/sound installation), Mus fur Mod Kunst, Frankfurt, Ger, 91; Nantes Triptych (video/sound installation), Ministry Cult, France, 92; Slowly Turning Narrative (video/sound installation), Inst Contemp Art, Va Mus Fine Art, 92; Tiny Deaths (video/sound installation), Biennale d'Art Contemporian de Lyon, France, 93; Deserts (film), ZDF/ARTE Television & VARA-VPRO, Vienna, 94; The World of Appearances (video/sound installation), Helaba Main Tower, Frankfort, 00. *Exhib:* Biennial Exhib, Whitney Mus Am Art, NY, 75-87; solo exhibs, Mus Mod Art, NY, 79, Mus Mod Art (with catalog), NY, 87, Mus d'Art Contemp de Montreal (catalogue), 93, Buried Secrets, 46th Venice Biennale, Venice, Italy, 95, Savannah Col Art & Design, Ga, 96, Durham Cathedral, Eng, 96 & Chapelle Saint Louise de las Salpetriere, 96; Video Spaces: Eight Installations, Mus Mod Art, NY, 95; Rites of Passage, Tate Gallery, London, 95; Mus d'art Contemp, Lyon, 95; By Night, Found Cartier pour l'art contemp, Paris, 96; Bill Viola, A 25 Yr Survey (with catalog), Whitney Mus Am Art, travels to seven venues in the US & Europ, 97-; Along the Frontier (traveling), Int Ctr Photog, NY, 96; Islands: Contemp Installations from Australia, Asia, Europe & Am, Nat Gallery Australia, Canberra, 96. *Teaching:* Scholar in residence, Getty Res Inst, Getty Ctr, Los Angeles, 98. *Awards:* Rockefeller Found Video Artist Fel, 82-83; John Simon Guggenheim Mem Fel Video Art, 85-86; John D & Catherine T MacArthur Found Award, 89-94. *Bibliog:* Barbara London (auth), Bill Viola: Installations and Videotapes, Mus Mod Art, New York, 87; Marie Luise Syring (auth), Bill Viola: Unseen Images, Stadtische Kunsthalle Dusseldorf, Ger, 92; Alexander Puhringer (auth), Bill Viola: Salzburger Kunstverein, Austria, 94; David A Ross (ed) Bill Viola, Whitney Mus of Am Art, NY, 97. *Mem:* Am Acad Arts and Scis. *Media:* Videotapes, Video Installations. *Publ:* Auth, Sight Unseen-Enlighted squirrels & fatal experiments, No 4, spring 82 & Will there be condominiums in data space?, No 5, fall 82, Video 80; contribr, Video: A retrospective 1974-1984, Long Beach Mus Art, Calif, 84; Dan Lander & Micah Lexier (eds), Sound by Artists, The sound of one line scanning, Art Metropole, Toronto & Walter Phillips Gallery, Banff, 90; Video Black-The Mortality of the Image, Illuminating Video: An Essential Guide to Video Art, Aperture/Bay Area Video Coalition, 90; Reasons for Knocking at an Empty House: Writings 1973-95. *Dealer:* James Cohan Gallery 533 W 26th St, NY, 10001. *Mailing Add:* 282 Granada Ave Long Beach CA 90803

VIOLET, ULTRA
PAINTER, WRITER
b La Tronche, Isere, France, Sept 6, 35; Fr & Am citizen. *Study:* Sacred Art Sch, La Tronche Isere, France. *Work:* Mus Mod Art, Medzilaborce, Czech; Petit Palais Collection, Paris, France; Mus Art, Paterson, NJ; Espace Giletta Mus, Nice, France; HRH Prince Albert of Monaco. *Comn:* Portrait, Mr Toubon, French Minister of Cult. *Exhib:* Les Anges Apocalyptiques, French Inst, Bratislava, Czech, 92; L'art dams la Rue, La Rotonde, Beaulieu, France, 92; L'Art Influence les Artists, Found Sofia Lafitte, Antipolis, 92; Warhol et Moi, Inst Etudes Sup Arts, Paris, 92; Amherst Fine Arts Ctr, Mass Univ, 93; Galerie Olaf Clasen, Cologne, Allemagne, 93. *Pos:* Master of aprentis, Union Libre des Travailleurs Artistiques, 91-92; critic, New York Times. *Teaching:* Lectr, Arts Dept, Brigham Young Univ, currently & Del Univ, currently; New Jersey City Univ. *Awards:* Award for best bookwriting, pictures & graphics, Frankfurt, Deutsh Bibliothek, 89. *Bibliog:* Grace Gluck (auth), We Threw Andy Out, NY Times, 88; Frederick Mitterand, du Cote' de Chez Fred (film), TV, French, 89; Pavel Vojir (auth), Fialovy Andel, Reflex, 92. *Mem:* Union Libre des Travailleurs Artistiques (pres, 92). *Media:* All Media. *Res:* American pop art; Andy Warhol; Spiritual Christian belief, Scriptures; Angelogy (study of Angels). *Collection:* John Graham, Edward Ruschia, Andy Warhol. *Publ:* Auth & contrib ed, Diplomatic Corner, Diplomatic World Bulletin, 85; Famous for 15 Minutes, My Years with Andy Warhol, 88, 89, 90, 91 & 92; coauth, Kiki's Paris, J Art, 89; auth, Le Revers du Reve, Ancrage, 89; Goodbye Dali, It's Been Surreal, NY Times, 1/30/89; Tiffany, Warhol Christmas Boom, 2004. *Dealer:* Galerie du Cirque Paris 8e France; Galerie Ferrero Nice France 06 300; Galerie Guy Peters St Paul France Vence. *Mailing Add:* 19 E 88th St New York NY 10028

VIOLETTE, BANKS
PAINTER, SCULPTOR
b Ithica, NY, 1973. *Study:* Sch Visual Arts, NY, BFA, 98; Columbia Univ, MFA, 2002. *Work:* Rep in permanent collections, Whitney Mus Am Art, NY, Frederick R Weisman Art Found, Los Angeles, Mus OverHolland, Amsterdam, Mus Modern Art, NY, Mus Contemp Art, Los Angeles, Mus Art Moderne et Contemporain, Geneva; Diversity Plus: Emerging Artists in a Rapid World, Visual Arts Mus, NY, 2001; Whitney Biennial, Whitney Mus Am Art, NY, 2004. *Exhib:* One-man shows, Team Gallery, NY, 2000, 2002, 2004, LISTE, Basel, Switz, 2003, MW Projects, London, 2004, Galerie Rodolphe Janssen, Brussels, 2005; group shows, Lower East Side Community Ctr, NY, 97, Visual Arts Gallery, NY, 97, 98, Momenta Art, Brooklyn, 99, Two Friends and So On, Andrew Kreps Gallery, NY, 2000, Summer with Friends, Team Gallery, NY, 2000, Dirty Deeds Done Dirt Cheap, Contemp Arts Ctr, Atlanta, 2001, Ghost Stories, Sandroni-Rey Gallery, Venice, Calif, 2001, Learned Am, PPOW, NY, 2001; Back in Black, Cohan Leslie and Browne, NY, 2003; Return of the Creature, Kunstlerhaus Palais Thurn und Taxis Gartnerhaus, Austria, 2003; Screem, Anton Kern Gallery, NY, 2004; Noctambule, Alternative Space, Paris, 2004, Liverpool Biennial, Liverpool, Eng, 2004; Liverpool Biennial, Liverpool, Eng, 2004. *Awards:* Rema Hort Mann Found Grant, 2000. *Mailing Add:* c/o Team Gallery 527 W 26th St New York NY 10001

VIRGONA, HANK (HENRY) P
PAINTER, PRINTMAKER
b Brooklyn, NY, Oct 24, 29. *Study:* Pratt Inst Evening Sch, 54. *Work:* Metrop Mus Art, NY; Arch Am Art, Smithsonian Inst; Mus City New York; Wichita Mus, Kans; Pub Libr, NY. *Exhib:* New Am Still Life, Westmoreland Co Mus, Pa, 79; The Presidency: Relevant & Irrelevant Traveling Exhib, 80; West and the Law Traveling Exhib, 80-82; Prints USA, Pratt Inst, NY, 82; Subtle Observations-Subway Portraits by Hank Virgona, Transit Mus, Brooklyn, NY, 92. *Pos:* Co-founder, 41 Union Sq Open Studios, 80-. *Teaching:* Instr etching, pvt lessons, 82-; instr drawing, Pratt Graphic Ctr, NY. *Awards:* Gold Medal, Soc Illusr, 70; Purchase Prizes, Nat Acad Art, 79 & Prints USA, Pratt Inst, 82; Art Grant, NY Found Arts & Kanter-Plaut Found, 98. *Bibliog:* Ellyn Bloom (auth), Hank Virgona: The art of social satire, Am Artist Mag, 73; Paul Peter Piech (auth), Hank Virgona, Graphic Satirist, Idea Mag, 91; Unturned Corners, Recent Work by Hank Virgona, J Stefan Cole, 2002. *Mem:* Artists Equity, NY. *Media:* Watercolor; Etching. *Specialty:* Modern and contemporary art. *Publ:* Auth, The System Works The Etchings and Random Notes of Hank Virgona, Da Capo Press, 77; illusr, Ivan the Terrible, Ivan the Fool, G Putnam Sons, 80. *Dealer:* Galerie Mourlot 16 East 79 St New York NY 10021; Weber Fine Art 17 Boniface Cir Scarsdale NY 10583; The Old Printshop 150 Lexington Ave NY NY 10016. *Mailing Add:* 41 Union Sq W New York NY 10003

VISCO, ANTHONY SALVATORE
EDUCATOR, SCULPTOR
b Philadelphia, Pa, Sept 13, 48. *Study:* Fleischer Art Mem, Philadelphia, 64-66; Skowhegan Sch Painting & Sculpture, Maine, 69; Philadelphia Col Art, BFA, 70; Acad delle Belle Art, Florence, Italy, 70-71; Univ Pa, archit studies, 83. *Comn:* Stations of the Cross, Old St Joseph's Nat Shrine, Philadelphia, 81, Religious Freedom, 85; Resurrection altarpiece & bronze Assumption relief, Church of Assumption, Atco, NJ, 86; Raredose relief panels, bronze, Bryn Mawr Presby, 87-89; Stations of the Cross, St Joseph's Univ Chapel, Philadelphia, 93; Sanctuary wall & relief sculpture with mosaic, Our Lady of Mt Carmel, Berlin, NJ, 94; and others. *Exhib:* Solo exhibs, First Street Gallery, NY, 80, Lace Gallery, Philadelphia, Pa, 81, Cabrini Col, Radnor, Pa, 81, Bourse Bldg, Philadelphia, 81, Pa Acad Fine Arts, 83 & Bryn Mawr Presby Church, 84 & 89; In the Religious Spirit, Nat Sculpture Soc, 90; In

Conference, Fourteenth Int Sculpture Conv, Philadelphia, 92; Figurative Philadelphia, Woodmeere Mus, Philadelphia, 93; Acad Artists, Contemp Realist Gallery, San Francisco, 93; and others. *Pos:* Art instr, Recreation Ctr for Older People, Philadelphia, summer 68; apprentice, Waler Erlbacher, Elkins Park, Pa, summer, 70; sculpture technician, Skowhegan Sch, Maine, summer, 75. *Teaching:* Instr sculpture, Philadelphia Col Art, 76-85 & Creuzberg Ctr, Radnor, Pa, 76-78; instr anat, Pa Acad Fine Arts, 85-, chmn, Sculpture Dept, 86-92. *Awards:* Greenshields Award, Pvt Studio Work, Can, 75-76; Arthur Ross Award for Sculpture, Classical Am, 84; Greater Harrisburg Arts Festival Drawing Award, State Mus Pa, 89. *Bibliog:* Anthony Apesos (auth), New Art Examiner, 1/84; Victoria Donohoe (auth), Philadelphia Inquirer, 8/17/84 & 6/21/86; Robin Longman (auth), Am Artist, 9/84. *Media:* Wax, Bronze. *Mailing Add:* 1426 Christian St Philadelphia PA 19146

VISO, OLGA
MUSEUM DIRECTOR
b Fla. *Study:* Emory Univ, MA (art hist), 92. *Collection Arranged:* Distemper: Dissonant Themes in the Art of the 1990s, 96; Regarding Beauty: A View of the Late Twentieth Century, 1999-2000. *Pos:* Positions in dept moder & contemp art, office of registrar and office of dir, High Mus Art, Atlanta, 89-93; asst cur Norton Mus Art, West Palm Beach, Fla, 93; asst cur, Hirshhorn Mus and Sculpture Garden, Washington, DC, 95, assoc cur, 98, cur contemp art, 2000-03, dep dir, 2003-2006, dir, 2006-; mem Federal Adv Comt Int Exhibitions; co-comnr US Pavilion, Venice Biennial, 2001. *Res:* contemporary Latin American Art. *Mailing Add:* Smithsonian Inst PO Box 37012 Hirshhorn Mus MRC Code 350 Washington DC 20013

VITALE, DAVID J
PATRON
Pos: With First Nat Bank Chicago subsidiary First Chicago NBD Corp, 68-, exec vpres, 86-, First Chicago NBD Corp, 86-, also bd dir, 92-; vchmn, pres, First Nat Bank Chicago, 95-99; Chief Exec Officer, Chicago Bd Trade, 2001-02; chief admin off, Chicago Pub Sch, 2003-; Treas, mem bd trustees, Art Inst Chicago; vchmn bd trustees, Ill Inst Tech

VITALE, MAGDA
PAINTER
b New York, NY, July 20, 39. *Study:* Barnes Found, Marion, Pa, 77; Found Todays Art, Intern, Philadelphia, 78; Skowhegan Sch Painting & Sculpture, Maine, 79; Moore Col Art, Philadelphia, BFA, 80. *Work:* Carnegie Ctr, Princeton, NJ; Best Products Inc, Richmond, Va; NJ Power & Light; Del Co Community Col, Media, Pa; Am Embassy, Dublin, Ireland; Wheat, First, Butcher, Singer, Philadelphia; Duane, Morris & Hecksher, Philadelphia; Islip Art Mus, NY; Ballinglen Art Foundation, Ballycastle, Ireland. *Exhib:* Solo exhibs, Paintings, Chambers Gallery, Penn State Univ, University Park, 84, Abstraction, Univ Pittsburgh Gallery, 87, New Paintings, Camden Col, Blackwood, NJ, 88 & Paintings, Henri Gallery, Washington, DC, 92 & 95, The Nothern Indiana Arts Asn, Munster, 92, Leabharlann, Belmullet, Ireland, 99; New Am Talent 88, Laguna Gloria Art Mus, Austin, Tex, 88; Henri Gallery, Washington, DC; Biennial 89, Del Art Mus, Wilmington, 89; Am Embassy Cult Ctr, Brussels, Belg, 89; Nat Small Works Exhib, Schoharie Arts Coun Gallery, Cobleskill, NY, 90; Gallery Artists, J Lawrence Gallery, Melbourne, Fla, 90; Nat Works on Paper Exhib, Univ Tex, Tyler, 90; Metamorphosis of a Butterfly, Erie Art Mus, Pa, 92; group exhib, Moore Col Art, Philadelphia, 89, Cabrini Col, Radnor, Pa, 89, Henri Gallery, Washington, DC, 89, Zenith Gallery, 89, Trenton City Mus, NJ, 89. *Awards:* Scholarship Award, Skowhegan Sch Painting & Sculpture, 79; Expo V Award Winner, Northport Galleries, NY, 86; Grant, Ballenglen Art Found, Bally Castle, Ireland, 92. *Bibliog:* Mark Woodruff (auth), An Increase of Life, Paintings of Magda Vitale, Camden Co Col, Blackwood, NJ, 88; Francoises Andre (auth), Contemp Women Artists (exhib catalog), Am Embassy Cult Ctr, Brussels, Belg, 89; John Perreault & Jenine Culligan (coauths), Biennial 89 (exhib catalog), Del Art Mus, 89. *Mailing Add:* 12 Springton Lake Rd Media PA 19063

VITALE, VINCENT
PAINTER, TAPESTRY ARTIST
b Jersey City, NJ, Apr 23, 47. *Study:* Rutgers Univ, BA, 69; Art Students League. *Work:* Cooper-Hewitt Mus, NY; Smithsonian Inst, Washington, DC; Museo de Arte Contemporanea. *Comn:* Fan Composition (mixed media), Cooper-Hewitt Mus, NY, 86. *Exhib:* Papelarte, Inst Int Contemp Art, Bahia, Brazil, 85; Fans, Cooper Hewitt Mus, NY, 86 & Smithsonian Inst Washington, DC, 86; Cooper-Hewitt Mus, NY, 87. *Awards:* Hon Mention, Photovision '72, Boston Ctr Arts, 72. *Bibliog:* Second wind for the fan, Town & Country Mag, 6/87; Decorative fans painted or printed by hand, NY Times, 2/26/87. *Mem:* Orgn Independent Artists; Artists Equity Asn; Found Community Artists. *Media:* Photography; Textiles. *Publ:* Auth, Photographic Fans, Bull of Fan Circle Int, No 33, summer 86

VITALI, JULIUS M
PHOTOGRAPHER, PAINTER
b July 1, 52. *Study:* Nassau Col, Long Island, NY, 70-72; SUNY at Fredonia, BA, 74. *Work:* Bibliotheque Nationale, Paris, France; Polaroid Collection, Boston, Mass; Il Diaframma Galeria, Milan, Italy; Penn State Berks Campus, Reading, PA; Lehigh Univ Mus, Bethlehem, PA. *Comn:* Photo mural, Lawrence High Sch, Lawrence, NY, 85; mural, Weaversville Intensive Treatment Unit, Northampton, PA, 99. *Exhib:* Erronique, Crucial Gallery, London, United Kingdom, 87; Fashion & Surrealism, Victoria & Albert Mus, London, United Kingdom, 88; Tremplin Pour Les Images, Ctr Nationale de Photographie, Paris, France, 89; The Political Landscape, C W Post Mus, Greenvale, NY, 90; Hair Sculpture & Its Roots, Lehigh Univ Mus, Bethlehem, Pa, 91; Puddle Art: A Retrospective, Col Misericordia, Dallas, Pa, 94; Perfecting Art of Errors, Open Space Gallery, Allentwon, Pa, 97; Ground Zero, Mus of New Arts, Detroit, Mich; solo show, Digital Photog, Eric Art Mus, Erie, Pa, 2000. *Collection Arranged:* From the Ashes, Open Space Gallery, Allentown, Pa, 2002; Ground Zero, Mus New Art, Detroit, 2002. *Pos:* Gallery dir, Discovery Gallery, Glen Cove, NY, 82-85; exec dir, Open Space Gallery, Allentown, Pa, 96-02. *Teaching:* Instr photog, Pa Govt Sch Arts, Erie, 7-8/92; art instr, Weaversville Intensive Treatment Unit, Northampton, PA, 98-02. *Awards:* Nat Endowment Arts Forum Grant, Visuals & Music of Avante Disregarde, US Govt, 90; Spec Projs Award, At the Corner of Error & Perfection, Pa Coun Arts, 87, 91 & 93; Res Photog Award, Kodak Co, 92. *Bibliog:* Liana Bortolon (auth), The World in a Puddle, Grazia, Italy, 79; George Schaub (auth), Photography With a Splash, Photogrs Forum, 82; Lorenzo Santamaria (auth), Photography After the Rain, Fotopractica, Italy, 84. *Media:* Digital & Experimental Photography. *Publ:* Illusr, feature article/cover, Brit J Photog Art, 86; auth, Erronique, L'ARCA, Italy, 88; illusr, Art Images & Ideas Book, Davis Publs, 92; auth, Puddle Art, Sch Arts; Fine Artists Guide to Marketing & Self-Promotion, Allworth Press, 96, rev edit, 03. *Dealer:* Mistretta Galleries 394 Forest Ave Locust Valley NY 11560. *Mailing Add:* 612 Broad St Emmaus PA 18049

VIVOT, LEA
SCULPTOR
b Czechoslovakia; Can & Czech citizen. *Study:* Art Sch Stage Design, Prague, with Svoboda, 64-68; Acad Brera, Milan, 68; Ont Col Art, Toronto, with Erick Freifeld, 69-73; Art Students League, NY. *Work:* St Joseph's Health Ctr, Toronto; NY State Mus Holocaust; Montreal Botanical Gardens, Que; Madison Sq Garden, NY; Ottawa Parliament Hill, Nat Libr Can; and others. *Comn:* Unity, News Time; Toronto Sun; Finatial Post. *Exhib:* Solo exhib, Kar Gallery, Toronto, 79; Summer Exhib, Royal Acad Arts, London, 79; Sculpture of the 1980s, McMichael Collections, Kleinburg, Ont, 80; Sculptor's Soc Can, Pt Claire, Que, 82; Toronto Waldorf Sch, 82; Whitten Gallery, King City, Ont, 83; Central Park, NY, 86; and others. *Teaching:* Creative artist in sch, Kleinburg Pub Sch, Ont, 79. *Bibliog:* Sculpture Bronzing (film), City TV, Toronto, 12/6/82; Barbara McLeod (interviewer), Romance Factor/Sculpture (film), Can Broadcasting Corp, 12/14/82; The endless bench, Toronto Star 3/22/83; Numerous articles in Newsweek, NY Times, Toronto Star, Globe & Mail, Toronto Sun, Ottawa Citizen, Ottawa Hill Times, Rude01 Pravo, NY Post, J & Global News. *Mem:* Sculpture Soc Can; Royal Acad Arts; Ont Col Art, Toronto; Art Students League. *Media:* Bronze. *Publ:* Sculpture Review, 3rd Quarter, Vol 38, 89; Le Medicine ju Quebec, 9/89; Working toward the future, Metrop Toronto, 90; Miami Tropic, 3/91; New Yorker, 5/92

VIZNER, NIKOLA
ART DEALER, GALLERY DIRECTOR, PHD
b Bezdan, Yugoslavia, Nov 9, 45; US citizen. *Study:* Belgrade Univ, BA(art hist), 70, MA(hist mod art), 74; Univ of Zadar, Croatia, PhD, 05. *Pos:* Dir, Wiesner Gallery, Brooklyn & New York, NY, currently. *Teaching:* Prof art hist, Touro Coll, New York, currently. *Mem:* Nat Art Dealers Asn; Coll Art Assoc. *Specialty:* American and international contemporary art. *Dealer:* Art of Maxo Vanke The Mitchener Mus Bucks County PA. *Mailing Add:* 730 57th St No 4D Brooklyn NY 11220

VO-DINH, MAI
PAINTER, PRINTMAKER
b Hue, Vietnam, Nov 14, 33; US citizen. *Study:* Sorbonne, Fac Lett, 56; Acad Grande Chaumiere, 57; Ecole Nat Superieure Beaux-Arts, 59. *Work:* Mus d'Art Mod de la Ville de Paris; Mus Rouen; Schiedam Mus, Holland; Nashville Mus, Tenn; Wash Co Mus Fine Arts, Md. *Exhib:* One-man shows, Wash Co Mus Fine Arts, Md, 78 & Univ Md, 80; Arts Club Washington, Touchstone Gallery & Paul Rosen Gallery, Washington, 83; George Mason Univ, Va, 84 & 87; Les Jardins du Boise, Montreal, Can, 92; Pean Studio Savigny le Temple, Paris, 2000. *Teaching:* Instr watercolor painting, Hood Col, 78-79; artist-in-sch, Md State Coun, 86-87, 90 & 92. *Awards:* Christopher Award, Christopher Found, New York, NY, 75; Literature Prog Fel, Nat Endowment Arts, 84. *Bibliog:* Libbie Powell (auth), International recognized artist, The Daily Mail, Hagerstown, Md, 11/74; Henry Scarupa (auth), An artist's odyssey, Baltimore Sun, 7/80; Helen Hammond (auth), article, Diversions Mag, 3/90. *Media:* Oil, Acrylic; Woodblock. *Publ:* Sao Co Tieng Song; esssais, Van Nghe, 91; Sky Legends of Vietnam, Harper Collins, NY, 93; Lau Xep, Van Nghe, 97; Rung Mam, Van Nghe, 2000; Huyetuyet, Van Nghe, 2002; May Cho Thvdmd, 2004. *Mailing Add:* Mai-Hong Studios PO Box 211-626 Royal Palm Beach FL 33421-1626

VOELKER, ELIZABETH
PAINTER, COLLAGE ARTIST
b Pittsburgh, Pa, 1931. *Study:* Carnegie Inst Technol, BFA, 53. *Work:* Phillips Collection, Nat Mus Am Arts & Nat Mus Women Arts, Washington; Art Mus, Carnegie Inst, Pittsburgh, Pa; San Francisco Mus Mod Art; Santa Barbara Mus Art; Detroit Inst Arts; San Jose Mus Art. *Exhib:* Solo exhibs, San Jose Mus Art, 82 & Santa Barbara Mus Art, 82; Allport Gallery, 83 & 84; Hewlett Packard Gallery, 86; San Francisco Mus Mod Art, 90; Susan Conway Carroll Gallery, Washington, 90. *Teaching:* Lectr, Univ Calif Exten, San Francisco, 72. *Awards:* Carnegie Scholar, 49-51; Rockefeller Found Grant, 88; Pollock-Krasner Found Grant, 89-90, 96 & 98-99; Am Acad Rome Residency, 92 & 94; Gottlieb Found Grant, 96. *Bibliog:* David Burdon (auth), There's a new kid in town, Village Voice, 77; Judith Weiner (auth), Oriental ideas enrich paintings, collages, Oakland Press, 81; Andrea Liss (auth), A deceptive simplicity, Artweek, 83. *Mem:* MacDowell Colony Fels, Col Art Asn; Soc of Fels; Am Acad Rome. *Media:* Oil, Collage. *Dealer:* Susan Conway Carroll Gallery 1058 Thomas Jefferson St NW Washington DC 20007; Ebert Gallery 49 Geary St San Francisco CA 94108. *Mailing Add:* 301 Bloomfield Rd Burlingame CA 94010

VOELKER, JOHN
PAINTER, DESIGNER
b Givens, Ohio. *Study:* Columbus Col Art & Design, Ohio, 53-57; design workshop with Canzani; advan painting with Kuehn. *Work:* Columbus Gallery Fine Arts, Ohio; Abilene Mus Fine Arts, Tex. *Comn:* Posters, Cerebral Palsy Found, 56; Tex Fine Arts Asn, Dallas, 71 & Logo Design Bicentennial with Tex Fine Arts Asn, 75. *Exhib:* Ultimate Concerns, Prints & Drawings, Ohio Univ, 63 & 64; Artists of Gulf States & Tex, Delgado Mus, New Orleans, 64 & 66; Chautauqua Exhib Am Art, NY, 67; 11th Ann Prints & Drawings, Okla Art Ctr, Oklahoma City, 69; Southwest Painting Ann, Albuquerque, NMex, 70. *Pos:* Art coordr, Coronet Packaging, Dallas, 61-75. *Awards:* Permanent Collection Choice, Ultimate Concerns, Ohio Univ, 63; Haydon Calhoun Gallery Award, Painting & Sculpture Ann, Dallas Mus Fine Arts, 64; Best of Show, Tex Fine Arts Asn, 72. *Bibliog:* Article, Columbus Sunday Mag, Dispatch, 3/56; article, Dallas Times Herald, 10/76. *Mem:* Artists Equity, Dallas; Tex Fine Arts Asn; Artists Coalition of Tex. *Dealer:* Adelle Taylor 3317 McKinney Dallas TX

VOGEL, (MR & MRS) HERBERT
COLLECTORS
Mr Vogel b New York, NY, Aug 16, 22; Mrs Dorothy Vogel b Elmira, NY, May 14, 35. *Study:* Mr Vogel, NY Univ Inst Fine Arts; Mrs Vogel, Syracuse Univ, BA, 57; Univ Denver, MA, 58. *Exhib:* Painting, Drawing & Sculpture of the 60's and 70's, from the Dorothy and Herbert Vogel Collection, Inst Contemp Art, Univ Pa & Contemp Arts Ctr, Cincinnati, 75-76; Drawings from the Collection of Dorothy and Herbert Vogel, Univ Ark, Little Rock, 86; Beyond the Picture, Works from the Collection of Dorothy & Herbert Vogel, Kunsthalle, Bielefeld, Ger, 87; From the Collection of Dorothy & Herbert Vogel, Arnot Art Mus, Elmira, NY, 88; Poetry of Form: Richard Tuttle Drawings from the Vogel Collection, Inst Valenciano de Arte Mod, Valencia, Spain, 92; Indianapolis Mus Art, 93; From Minimal to Conceptual Art Works from the Dorothy & Herbert Vogel Collection, Nat Gallery Art, Washington, 94; and others. *Bibliog:* Paul Gardner (auth), Look It's the Vogels, Art News, 3/79; Meg Cox (auth), Postal clerk and wife amass art collection in a New York flat, Wall Street J, 1/30/86; Catherine Barnett (auth), A package deal, Art & Antiques, Summer 86; Paul Gardner (auth), Mesmerized by Minimalism, Contemporanea, 12/89; Sara Rimer (auth), Collecting priceless art, just for the love of it, NY Times, 2/11/92; and others. *Collection:* Contemporary drawing, sculpture and painting. *Mailing Add:* c/o Modern & Contemporary Art Nat Gallery Art 200 B South Clif Dr Landover MD 20785

VOGL, DON GEORGE
PAINTER, PRINTMAKER
b Milwaukee, Wis, July 22, 29. *Study:* Art Inst Chicago & Univ Chicago, BAE, 57; Univ Wis, Milwaukee, MS(art educ), 58. *Comn:* collage prints, IM Pei Building, Boston, 82 & Van Straaten Gallery, Chicago, Ill, 84; mural, Art in the Classroom, Math-Sci Auditorium Purdue U, 97. *Exhib:* solo shows, Quincy Col, Ill, Connections, Women's Art League Gallery, Century Ctr, S Bend Ind, 89, 16 Watercolors of Western Landscapes, W Ga Col Art, Carrolton, 91, Sense of Place, Snite Mus, Univ Notre Dame, 93 & Summer-Winter, Women's Art League Gallery, S Bend Reg Mus Art, 97; Annual Salon Show, Munster, Ind, 1984-98; Mus Art and Sci, Evansville, Ind, 11/91; W Ga Col Art, Carroton, 91; Sense of Place, Snite Mus, Univ Notre Dame, 93 & Summer-Winter, Women's Art League Gallery, S Bend Reg Mus Art, 97. *Pos:* Vis guest artist, Univ WVa, Morgantown, 75, Univ NC, Charlotte, 86 & W Ga Col, Carrollton, 91 & 96. *Teaching:* Instr art, Marygrove Col, Detroit, 61-63; assoc prof, Univ Notre Dame, 63-, prof emer, 94-. *Awards:* Best of Category, 86, Award of Distinction (second prize), 89 & Best of Show, Surovek Family Award of Excellence, 90, Salon Show Ann, Munster, Ind; Merit Award, Delicate Arch (watercolor), W Wash Art Fair, S Bend, Ind, 91; Best of Show, 14th Ann Elkhart Reg, Midwest Mus of Am Art, Ind, 92; Renee Denmark Meml Award Salon Show, Northern Ind Artists, Munster, Ind, Sept-Oct, 2000; Best of Show Award, Cross Currents Blank Ctr for the Arts, Mich City, Ind, 2000. *Bibliog:* Rudy Pozatti (auth), Indiana printmakers, Ind Art Educ Asn, 12/74. *Mem:* Am Col Art Asn. *Media:* Acrylic, Oil; Constructions. *Dealer:* Brunner Gallery Covington LA 70433

VOLID, RUTH
DEALER, CONSULTANT
b Chicago, Ill. *Study:* Art Inst Chicago; Chouinard Art Sch, Los Angeles; Otis Art Inst; Univ Chicago; Am Acad Art. *Pos:* Pres, Ruth Volid Gallery Ltd, 70-91. *Teaching:* Corp Art Roundtable, 88. *Awards:* Am & Int Soc Interior Designers Distinguished Serv Award; Indust Found Award. *Bibliog:* Barbara Varro (auth), A new start at midlife, Sun Times, 10/77; Special places, special people, Chicago Tribune, 12/83; Rivernorth News, 8/86. *Mem:* Arch of Am Art; Arts Club Chicago; Am Soc Interior Designers (bd mem). *Collection:* Henry Moore, Rauschenberg, Thomas Hart Benton, George Segal, Robert Natkin, Matta & Lofstutter. *Publ:* Auth, Art/an added dimension, Designer, 10/79; Threads of tradition, Studio 40, 10/79 & Picking a corporate art curator, 10/80, Collector Investor; Great Poems of the Western World, Vol II. *Mailing Add:* 89 East Ct New Buffalo MI 49117

VOLKERSZ, WILLEM
SCULPTOR, PAINTER
b Amsterdam, Neth, Aug 3, 39; US citizen. *Study:* Univ Washington, BA, 65; Mills Col, MFA, 67. *Work:* Seattle Art Mus, Seattle, Wash; Univ Arts, Osaka, Japan; Nanjing Col Arts, China; Kansas City Art Inst, Mo; Paris Gibson Sq Mus Art; Northwest Mus Arts & Cult; Bozeman Sr High Sch. *Comn:* Paris Gibson Square Mus Art, Great Falls, Mont, 88. *Exhib:* Solo exhibs, Plains Art Mus, 94, Mont State Univ, 94, Salt Lake Art Ctr, 95, Nicolaysen Art Mus, 98, Mus Northwest Art, 99, Univ Puget Sound, 2000 & Ind State Univ, 2001, Mus of Neon Art, 2002, Art Mus of Missoula, 2002, Beall Park Art Ctr, 2003, Mondak Heritage Ctr, 2004, Custer co Art Ctr, 2005, Holter Mus Art, 2006; Bags & Baggage, Arrowmont Sch Arts & Crafts, 96; Changing Horizons, Leedy Voulkos Gallery, 96; NW Neon (with catalog), Cheney Cowles Mus, 97; Pac NW Ann, Bellevue Art Mus, 98; The View From Here, Seafirst Gallery, 98; Drawing Retrospective, Mont State Univ, 99; Hsinchu Int Glass Art Festival, Taiwan, 99; Neon: Current (auth, catalog), Reed Whipple Cult Ctr, Las Vegas, 2000. *Collection Arranged:* Word & Image in American Folk Art, Mid-Am Arts Alliance Travelling Exhib, 86-88; The Radiant Object, Mont State Univ Travelling Exhib, 94-98. *Pos:* Dir admiss, Kansas City Art Inst, 81-83; dir, Sch Art, Mont State Univ, 86-91 & 94-95; vis fel, Univ Kansas, 1986; vis scholar, Univ Kent, Eng, 1991. *Teaching:* Prof found studies, Kansas City Art Inst, 68-86; prof art, Mont State Univ, 86-2001; Pilchuk Glass Sch, 99; prof emeritus, Mont State Univ, 2002-. *Awards:* Fulbright Award, Folk Art Res, Coun Int Exchange Scholars, 91; Anna Krueger Fridley Award, Mont State Univ, 96, Exceptional Opportunities Grant, 98, Wiley Fac Award for Meritorious Res, 98 & Provost's Award for Excellence, 99; Indiv Artists Fel, Mont Arts Coun, 98. *Bibliog:* Christian Schiess (auth), Willem Volkersz in The Light Artist Anthology, ST Publ, 93; Alan Goldman (dir), Glowing in the Dark (film), 97; Arthur Williams (auth), The Sculpture Ref, 2005. *Mem:* Phi Kappa Phi Hon Soc; Mus Am Folk Art; Folk Art Soc Am (nat bd, 90). *Media:* Neon, Wood. *Res:* Outsider Art and Environments. *Interests:* Am Popular Culture and Folk Art. *Collection:* Contemp Am folk and outsider art. *Publ:* Contribr, The Folk, Univ Kans, 89; auth (article), Private Spaces/Public Places, Pub Art Rev, 92; This is Art, This is Dream, This is Energy, Folk Art Messenger, 92; The Plastic Madonna, Phi Kappa Phi Nat Forum, 96; Roger Cardinal on Outsider Art, Raw Vision, 98. *Mailing Add:* 12299 Portnell Rd Bozeman MT 59718-9552

VOLKIN, HILDA APPEL
SCULPTOR
b Boston, Mass, Sept 24, 33. *Study:* Mass Col Art, BS, 54; Radcliffe Col, MA, 56. *Work:* Cleveland Mus Art, Ohio; Univ NMex, Albuquerque Mus Art & Albuquerque Int Airport; Los Alamos Nat Lab, NMex; Massillon Mus, Ohio. *Comn:* Rose Med Ctr, Denver, Colo, 90; St Joseph Med Ctr, Albuquerque, NMex, 94; Penrose Hosp, Colorado Springs, Colo, 95; Morris View Nursing Home, Morris Plains, NJ, 95; Lehigh Valley Hosp, Allentown, Pa, 96; and others; NW Watercolor Arts Comn, 2001; Los Badillas Aquatic Ctr, Albuquerque, NMex. *Exhib:* Here and Now: 35 Artists in New Mexico, Mus Albuquerque, 80 & 90 Walton Art Ctr, Fayetteville, Ark, 94; Paper--The Continuous Thread, Cleveland Mus Art, Ohio, 82; Bergen Community Mus, Paramus, NJ, 83; one-person retrospective, Mass Col Art, Boston, 84. *Pos:* Dir, Fuller Lodge Art Ctr, 77-80; art dir, EFA Studio, Albuquerque, NMex, 80-. *Teaching:* Instr painting, Univ NMex, Los Alamos, 74-. *Awards:* Purchase Award for Watercolor, Massillon Mus, 66; Graphics Awards, Cleveland Mus Art, 74 & Nat Asn Women Artists, 79. *Bibliog:* Laurie Volkin (auth), Albuquerque artist produces first acrylic silkscreen sculpture, The Link 9/88; Mary Carroll Nelson (auth), Year of the woman brings five artists to public eye, Albueuerque J, 1/3/93; Woman's memorial a labor of love, Albuquerque J, 1/16/93. *Mem:* Soc Layerists Mult-Media, Albuquerque Mus. *Media:* Metal. *Publ:* Auth, Paper, the continuous thread, Cleveland Mus Art & Ind Univ Press, 82; Cover Artist of month, Take Five, 1/87. *Mailing Add:* 14329 Skyline Rd NE Albuquerque NM 87123

VOLLMER, DAVID L
MUSEUM DIRECTOR
Pos: Dir, Janice Mason Art Mus, Cadiz, Kentucky, Swope Art Mus, Terre Haute, Ind, 2001-. *Mailing Add:* Swope Art Mus 25 S 7th St Terre Haute IN 47807

VON BARGHAN, BARBARA
EDUCATOR, WRITER
b Washington, DC, Feb 5, 49. *Study:* Univ Iowa, BA, 70; New York Univ, with Jose Lopez-Rey & Charles Sterling, MA, 72, with Jonathan Brown, Egbert Haverkamp-Begemann & Colin Eisler, PhD, 79. *Collection Arranged:* Contributor to exhibition, Pre-Columbian Ceramics, Dimock Gallery, George Washington Univ, 81, among others. *Pos:* Dir, Von Braghahn Gallery, Washington, DC, 74-78; Lectr, Embassy of Spain & Smithsonian Inst. *Teaching:* Instr, Sweet Briar Col, 73-74; asst prof, George Washington Univ, 74-82, assoc prof, 83-. *Awards:* Research Grant, George Washington Univ, 78-86. *Mem:* Am Soc of Hispanic Historical Studies; Renaissance Soc of Am; Soc for Spanish & Portuguese Historical Studies; Col Arts Asn. *Res:* Spanish, Portuguese and Latin American Art, Northern Baroque court art, architecture and gardens, Mannerism in the North, Primitive art. *Publ:* Auth, Philip IV and the Golden House of the Buen Retiro: In the Tradition of Caeser, 86; Age of Gold, Age of Iron: Renaissance Spain and Symbols of Monarchy, 86; co-auth (with Annemarie Jordan), The Torreao of the Lisbon Palace and the Escorial Library, 86; and many others. *Mailing Add:* Art Dept/George Washington Smith Hall Art Rm A 101 801 22nd St NW Washington DC 20052

VON BETZEN, VALERIE
PAINTER
b Providence, RI. *Study:* studied, Art Students League, NYC, Bard Col, Annandale-on-Hudson, NY. *Exhib:* Salmagundi Club, NY, 1990; One-woman shows, Plant Drawings, NY Botanical Soc, Bronx, NY, 1991, The Light of Day, Stover Mill Gallery, Erwinna, Pa, 1992, Am Towns, Katharina Rich Perlow Gallery, New York, 1997, Nocturnal Cityscapes, 2000 & Urban Twilight Scenes, 2002, A Limited Exhib of Recent Paintings, Morpeth Gallery, Hopewell, NJ, 2002; Philadelphia Sketch Club, 1997; Palm Springs Desert Mus, Calif, 1997; Albright-Knox Art Gallery, Buffalo, NY, 1998 & 99; Artsbridge, Stockton, NJ, 1998; Allentown Art Mus, Allentown, Pa, 1998; Palm Beach Art Fair, Fla, 1999; Morpeth Gallery, Hopewell, 2000; Coryell Gallery, Lambertville, NJ, 2002; Butler Inst Am Art, 2003; Michener Art Mus, Newhope, Pa, 2005. *Awards:* juror award, Small Works at 50 Washington St E Galleries, New York City, 95; Juror's award, Hunterdon Art Mus, Clinton, NJ, 95; The Artist Loofs at Hunterdon Co 91, 95; spec patrons' award for painting, Phillips Mill Ann Fall Exhib,

New Hope, Pa, 87, 92, 94, 96-97, 99, 2003; Vt's Studio Ctr Grant, Johnson, 97; Elizabeth Greenshields Found Grant, Montreal, Can, 99. *Bibliog:* Cathy Viksjo (auth), Gallery Hosts Classic Study in Contrasts, Times, Trenton, NJ, 12/12/1993; Doris Brandes (auth), Artist in Focus, New Hope Gazette, Pa, 11/1995; Doris Brandes (auth), Artists of the River Towns, River Arts Press, New Hope, Pa, 2000. *Mem:* New York Artists Equity; Michener Art Mus. *Media:* Oil. *Dealer:* Coryell Gallery 8 Coryell St Lambertville NJ 08530; Morpeth Gallery 43 W Broad St Hopewell NJ 08525. *Mailing Add:* PO Box 6986 FDR Station New York NY 10150

VON BOTHMER, DIETRICH FELIX
CURATOR, EDUCATOR
b Eisenach, Ger, Oct 26, 18; US citizen. *Study:* Friedrich Wilhelms Univ, Berlin, Ger; Oxford Univ, dipl(class archaeol); Univ Chicago; Univ Calif, PhD. *Hon Degrees:* Emory Univ, LHD, 2006. *Pos:* Asst cur, Dept Greek & Roman Art, Metrop Mus Art, 46-51, assoc cur, 51-59, cur, 59-73, chmn, 73-90, dist res cur, 90-. *Teaching:* Adj prof Greek art, Inst Fine Arts, New York Univ, from 65. *Awards:* Guggenheim Fel, 67. *Mem:* Archaeol Inst Am; Soc Promotion Hellenic Studies; Vereinigung der Freunde antiker Kunst; Deutsches Archaeol Inst; Acad Inscriptions & Belle-Lettres. *Res:* Greek and Roman art and archaeology. *Publ:* Auth, Ancient Art from New York Private Collections, 60; coauth, An Inquiry into the Forgery of the Etruscan Terracotta Warriors, 61; auth, Corpus Vasorum Antiquorum USA, Fascicule 12, 63, Fascicule 16, 76; Greek Vase Painting, 72; Greek Art of the Aegean Islands, 79; and others. *Mailing Add:* Distinguished Research Curator c/o Metrop Museum Art 1000 Fifth Ave New York NY 10028-0198

VON DER GOLZ, JAN See Mehn, Jan (Jan Von der Golz)

VON RECKLINGHAUSEN, MARIANNE BOWLES
PAINTER, SCULPTOR
b Munich, Ger, Jan 24, 29; US citizen. *Study:* Self taught. *Work:* Smithsonian Inst. *Exhib:* One-woman shows, Hudson River Mus, Yonkers, 63 & 84 & Katonah Mus Art, 82, NY, Islip Mus Art, 87, NY, Univ Mass, Lowell, 90; 19th Area Exhib, Corcoran Gallery Art, Washington, DC, 74; The Animal Image, Renwick Gallery, Smithsonian Inst, Washington, DC, 81; Assemblage & Collage Traveling Exhib, Miss Mus Art, Jackson, 81-83; Germans in New Eng, Goethe House, Boston, 83; Catholic Univ Art Gallery, Washington, DC, 83. *Teaching:* Lectr, Katonah Gallery, 82 & 86, Univ Lowell, Mass, 83 & 90. *Awards:* Painting Award, Charles of the Ritz Found, New York & 16th Ann New England Exhib, 65; First in Painting Award, Westchester Art Soc, 65-66; First in Painting Award, Lowman Mem Award, Art of the Northeast, 34th Ann Exhib, Silvermine, 83. *Bibliog:* Les Krantz (auth), American Artists; an illustrated survey of leading contemporary americans, Facts on File, New York & Oxford, England, 85; Virginia Watson-Jones (auth), Contemporary American Women Sculptors, Oryx Press, 86; Miles Under (auth), Darkness and Light Visible: Recklinghausen's Works, The Boston Globe, 12/90. *Mem:* Artists Equity; Silvermine Guild. *Media:* Acrylic on Wood; Sequential Painted Contructions. *Publ:* Dir, Mark Sadan & Lawrence Miller (film makers) Legends From Life: 12 Constructions from Paradise (film), Film & Video Workshop, NY, 86. *Mailing Add:* c/o Uptown Gallery 1194 Madison Ave New York NY 10128

VON RINGELHEIM, PAUL HELMUT
SCULPTOR
b Vienna, Austria. *Study:* Brooklyn Col, BS, 56; Fairleigh Dickinson Univ, MA, 58; Art Students League, 58-59; Acad Fine Arts, Munich, 60-61. *Work:* Welton Becket Assoc; Mus Mod Art, Whitney Mus Am Art, NY; Mus Mod Art, Tel Aviv; Mus Mod Art, Tokyo; Fairleigh Dickinson Univ; Time & Life collections, NY. *Comn:* World Peace Monument, US Pavilion, Worlds Fair, 64; Interstate 80 Bicentennial Sculpture Project, Houston Ctr, Tex Eastern Corp; sculpture (40 ft), Darby, Eng, 95; sculpture, Int Fair Year 2000, 95; bronze bust, Leonard Bernstein, Opera House Around the World, 95; sculpture (300 ft), Paris, 2000; sculpture (85ft), London, 2001. *Exhib:* Whitney Mus Am Art, 63 & 65; Mus Mod Art, NY, 64, 67 & 69; Jewish Mus, NY, 66 & 68; Cleveland Mus, 66; Albright-Knox Gallery, Buffalo, 67; Frick Mus, Pittsburgh, 68; solo exhib, O K Harris Gallery, NY, 71-73, 76, 78, 80 & 82. *Teaching:* Instr printmaking, Brooklyn Mus Sch, 57-58; prof sculpture, Sch Visual Arts, NY, 67-71. *Awards:* Fulbright Scholar, 74-75. *Mem:* Archit League City New York. *Mailing Add:* c/o Ro Gallery 47-15 36th St Long Island City NY 11101

VON RYDINGSVARD, URSULA
SCULPTOR
b Deensen, Ger, July 26, 42. *Study:* Univ Miami, Coral Gables, Fla, BA, 64, MA, 65; Univ Calif, Berkeley, 69-70; Columbia Univ, New York, MFA, 75. *Work:* Metrop Mus Art & Whitney Mus Am Art, NY; Brooklyn Mus, NY; Detroit Art Inst, Mich; Walker Art Ctr, Minneapolis, Minn; Nat Mus Women Arts; Madison Art Ctr, Wis. *Comn:* City Col, Staten Island, NY; Laumeier Sculpture Garden, St Louis, Mo; Capp St Proj, San Francisco, Calif. *Exhib:* Corcoran Gallery, Washington, 75; Contemp Reflections, Aldrich Mus Contemp Art, Ridgefield, Conn, 76; Selections from the Collection, Aldrich Mus Contemp Art, Ridgefield, Conn, 85; group shows: Metrop Mus Art, NY, Walker Art Ctr, Minneapolis, Minn, Brooklyn Mus, NY, Woman's Mus, Washington, Out of Wood, Whitney Mus Contemp Art, NY, 90 & Landscape as Metaphor; Denver Art Mus, 94-95; one-person exhibs, Univ Wyo Art Mus, Laramie, 95, Socks on My Spoons, Univ Gallery, Univ Mass, Amherst, 95, Mus Art, RI Sch Design, Providence, 96, Galerie Lelong, NY, 96, Yorkshire Sculpture Park, Wakefield Eng, 97, Madison Art Ctr, Wis, 98, Nelson-Atkins Mus Art, Kansas City, Mo, 98-99, Hood Mus Art, Dartmouth Col, NH, 98, Chicago Cult Ctr, 99, The Contemp Mus, Honolulu, 99, Barbara Krakow Gallery, Boston, 99, Indianapols Mus Art, 99-2000, Galerie DeLong, Zurich & New York, 2000, Cranbrook Art Mus, Bloomfield Hills, Mich, 2000, Hill Gallery, Birmingham, 2000 & The Butler Gallery, Kilkenny, Ireland, 2001; Body As Metaphor, Procter Art Ctr, Bard Col, Annandale-on-Hudson, NY, 95; Crossing State Lines: 20th Century Art from Pvt Collections in Westchester and Fairfield Counties, Neuberger Mus Art, Purchase Col, NY, 95; Am Sculpture: A Contemp Perspective, Univ Wyo Art Mus, Laramie, 95; Beyond Gender: In Three Dimensions; Women Sculptors of the Nineties Snug Harbor Art Ctr, Staten Island, NY, 95; The Shape of Sound, Exit Art, NY, 96; A Moveable Feast, David Klein Gallery, Birmingham, Mich, 97; Wood Work, Fisher Landau Ctr, Long Island City, NY, 97; 20/20, Contemp Arts Forum, Santa Barbara, Calif, 97; Masters of the Masters: MFA Faculty Sch of Visual Arts, NY, 1983-98, Butler Inst Am Art, Youngstown, Ohio, 98; Sculptors and Their Environments, Pratt Inst, NY, 98; KolnSkulptur 2, Cologne, Ger, 99-2000; Doris C Freedman Plaza, Central Park, NY, 2000; Drip, Blow, Burn: Forces of Nature in Contemp Art, The Hudson River Mus, Yonkers, NY, 99; The End: An Independent Vision of Contemp Cult, 1982-2000, Exit Art, NY, 2000. *Teaching:* Asst prof, Pratt Inst, Brooklyn, NY, 78-82; instr, Sch Visual Arts, 81-82; asst prof, Fordham Univ, Bronx, NY, 80-82; assoc prof, Yale Univ, New Haven, Conn, 82-86; prof, Sch Visual Arts, Grad Div, New York, 86-. *Awards:* Sculpture Award, Am Acad Arts & Lett, 94; Joan Mitchell Award, 97; 2nd Prize, Best show in a Commercial Gallery, Int Asn Critics, 2000. *Bibliog:* Paul Zelanski & Mary Pat Fisher (auths), Shaping Space, Harcourt Brace Col Publ, New York, 95; Arthur Williams (auth), Sculpture: Technique-Form-Content, Davis Publ Inc, Worcester, Mass, 95; Dore Ashton (auth), The Sculpture of Ursula von Rydingsvard, Hudson Hills Press, New York, 96; Horace Brockington (auth), Ursula von Rydingvard @ Galerie Lelong, NY Arts, Int edit, 4/2000; Zbigniew Basara (auth), Ursula von Rydingsvard, Wysokie Obcasy, 9/2000. *Media:* Wood. *Publ:* Review, Art Forum, Vol 33, No 2, 10/94; 15 Sacks for Cortazar (5 drawings), Point of Contact, fall/winter, 94; Arts of Wyoming: Into the Woods; Challenging art on display, Casper Star-Tribune, 4/95; Art, Roughly Hewn, Brooklyn Bridge, Vol 1, No 3, 1/96; Studio Visits: Pleasure, Pain and Protocol, ARTnews, Vol 95, No 3, 3/96; articles, The New Yorker,4/3/2000 & New York Contemporary art Report, 3-4/2000

VON SCHMIDT, ERIC
PAINTER, HISTORIAN
b Bridgeport, Conn, May 28, 31. *Study:* Art Students League, 50; Farnsworth Sch Art, Fla, 50-51;. *Work:* Ulrich Mus Art, Wichita, Kans. *Exhib:* Am Frontier: The Saga of Westward Expansion, Ulrich Mus Art, Wichita, Kans, 77; Remembering the Alamo, Witte Mus, San Antonio, 86; Legacy, L'Atelien Westport, Conn, 89; Last Stands, Mus Sci & Hist, Corpus Christi, Tex, 92; Von Schmittmen, Westport, Conn, 94; Rhythm & Blues, Discovery Mus, Bridgeport, Conn, 96. *Awards:* Fulbright Scholar, painting, 55-86; Nat Endowment Arts Grants, 87; ASCAP Lifetime Achievement Award in Folk Music, NY, 2000; 9th Annual Westport, Ct, Visual Arts Award, 2002. *Media:* Acrylic; Bronze. *Res:* The battle of Hue, 68. *Publ:* Auth, Custer, dying again, Smithsonian Mag, 86; How is the Alamo remembered?, Smithsonian Mag, 86; Sunday at the Little Big Horn with George, Univ Nebr Press, 89; Mont Mag, 92. *Dealer:* Minglewood Press PO Box 638 Westport CT 06880; JN Bartfield Gallery 30 W 57th St New York NY. *Mailing Add:* 38 Evergreen Ave Westport CT 06880

VON ZUR MUEHLEN, BERNIS SUSAN
PHOTOGRAPHER
b Philadelphia, Pa, Apr 10, 42. *Study:* Univ Pa, BA(lit), 63. *Work:* Corcoran Gallery Art, DC; Baltimore Mus Art, Md; B'nai B'rith Nat Jewish Mus, Washington, DC; Houston Mus Fine Arts, Tex; New Orleans Mus Art, La; Wesleyan Univ, Davidson Art Ctr, Middletown, Conn. *Exhib:* Va Mus Fine Arts, Richmond, 75 & Va Photogr, 75 & 78; Nation's Capital Photogr, Corcoran Gallery Art, DC, 76 & Recent Acquisitions, 79 & 80; one-woman shows, Baily Mus Art, Univ Va, Charlottesville, 80, Del Mus Art, Wilmington, 81, Osuna Gallery, 81, 84 & 89, Photoworks Gallery, Richmond, Va, 84, Corcoran Gallery Art, Washington, DC, 90, B'nai Brith Klutznick Nat Jewish Mus, 92, Narratives or Desire, Troyer, FitzPatrick, Lassman Gallery, Washington, DC, 98, Troyer Gallery, Washington, 2001; Invisible Light: An Exhibition of Infrared Photog, Smithsonian Inst, Washington, DC, 80 & 82; 35th Anniversary Area Show, Corcoran Gallery Art, Washington, DC, 82; From the Collection, Photographs by Women, Corcoran Gallery Art, 82; Recent Acquisitions in Photog, Corcoran Gallery Art, 87; Image of the Male Nude, Frankfurter Kunstverein, Fed Rep Ger, 88; Behold the Man, Photog's Gallery, London, Eng & Stills Gallery, Scotland, 88; Landscape Photographs from the Permanent Collection, Corcoran Gallery Art, 89; Jones Troyer Fitzpatrick Gallery, Washington, DC, 91; Triennial Exhib, New Orleans Mus Art, La, 92; B'nai B'rith Nat Jewish Mus, 92; Transformations: Spirit and Icon, www.Mastersofphotography.com, 2000; Evanescence, Troyer Gallery, Washington, DC, 2001; WPA, Corcoran Curated Exhib & Auction, Washington, DC, 2006. *Teaching:* Lectr, Baltimore Mus Art, Md, 78, Cath Univ, Washington, DC, 78, Corcoran Sch Art, Washington, DC, 81 & Univ Va, 87-. *Awards:* Three Judges' Awards, Womansphere, Glen Echo, Md, 75; Purchase Award, Corcoran Gallery Art, 76. *Media:* Chrome, Silver. *Publ:* Contribr, The Story of American Photography: an Illustrated History for Young People, Little Brown, 79; SX-70, Lustrum Press, 79; The Male Nude in Photography, Vermont Crossroads Press, 80; Frauen Sehen Manner, Frankurter Kunstverin, Verlag Photographie, 88; Male Nudes by Women: An Anthology, Eds Stemlag, AG, 95; Male Nude Now, Universe Publ, 2001; Male Bodies: A Photographic History of the Nude, Prestel, 2004; Male Nudes: Index, Feierabend Verlag, Berlin, 2006. *Dealer:* Osuna Gallery Bethesda Md. *Mailing Add:* 10435 Hunter View Rd Vienna VA 22181

VON ZUR MUEHLEN, PETER
PHOTOGRAPHER
b Berlin, Ger, Mar 10, 39; US citizen. *Study:* Washington Univ, St Louis, BA, 61; Princeton Univ, PhD, 72. *Work:* Corcoran Gallery. *Pos:* Economist, Fed Reserve Bd, Washington, DC. *Awards:* Cert Distinction, Va Photographers, Va Mus Fine Arts, 75. *Bibliog:* David Tannous (auth), article, 7/78 & Capital art: in the major leagues?, 7/79, Art Am; Emmanuel Cooper (auth) Male Bodies: A Photographic History of the Nude, London Prestel, 2004. *Media:* Chrome, Silver. *Publ:* Contribr, One of a Kind: Polaroid Photography, Polaroid Corp, 78. *Dealer:* Suna Gallery Bethesda Md. *Mailing Add:* 10435 Hunter View Rd Vienna VA 22181

VOORHEES, DONALD EDWARD
PAINTER, PRINTMAKER
b Neptune, NJ, May 6, 26. *Study:* Acad Arts, Newark, NJ; Art Students League, New York, Studied with Ed Whitney, John Pike, Mario Cooper & Don Stone. *Work:* Am Int Group, NY; Metrop Life, NY; Pfizer Chem Co, NY; Sun Oil Co, Tulsa, Okla; USA Today, & US Air, Arlington, VA; and others; Pfizer Pharmaceuticals; Chilian Embassy, Washington, DC; numerous privatre comns. *Comn:* Ed of prints, Sheraton Hotels, Tulsa, Okla, 84; ed of prints, Dallas Athletic Club, Dallas, Tex, 86; ed of prints, Buick Div Gen Motors, Flint, Mich, 88; ed of Prints, AlG, NY, 90; prints, Cambridge Sports Int, Washington, 91. *Exhib:* Frye Mus, Seattle, Wash; Edward Dean Mus, Cherry Valley, Calif; Cent Mus Wyo; Martello Mus, Key West, Fla. *Teaching:* Instr watercolor, Guild Creative Art, 1965-1975. *Awards:* Hudson Valley Art Asn Award; NJ Watercolor Soc Award; Salmagundi Club Award; plus others. *Mem:* NJ Watercolor Soc (Life Fel, pres, 75-76); Artists Fel; Salmagundi Club. *Media:* Watercolor. *Publ:* Collectors Mart, 6/84, The Artist's Mag, 4/84, Gems of New Jersey, 86, & Golf Week Mag, 10/88, PGA Mag, 1/91, US Art 5/91, Art Business News 4/94; auth, Secrets from a Lifetime of Watercolor Painting, Northlight Publ, 2006. *Dealer:* Donald Voorhees Studio Box 182 Atlantic Highlands NJ 07716. *Mailing Add:* 10 Ocean Blvd 4E Atlantic Highlands NJ 07716

VOORSANGER, BARTHOLOMEW
ARCHITECT
b Detroit, Mich, Mar 23, 37. *Study:* Princeton Univ, AB (cum laude), 60; Diplome, Fontainebleau, 60; Harvard Univ, MArch, 64. *Hon Degrees:* Univ Archit & Urbanism, Romania, Hon Dr. *Work:* Le Cygne Restaurant; Neiman houseboat; New York Univ Midtown Ctr; New York Univ Business Sch Libr; La Grandeur housing; New York Univ dormitories; Hostos Community Col, NY; Wethersfield Carraige Mus, Amenia, NY; Riverdale Jewish Ctr, NY; Port Authority NY/NJ Air Traffic Control Towers; Univ Art Mus, Univ Va; Asia Soc & Mus, NY; Olana Mus, Hudson, NY; Elie Tahari Offices, NJ; numerous pvt residences in NY, Va, Calif, Ariz, Mont & Wyo. *Exhib:* New York Univ; Archit Asn, London; Harvard Grad Sch Design; Vacant Lots Housing Study, NY; Deutsches Architeckur Mus, Frankfurt; Mus Finnish Archit; Avery Libr, Centennial Exhib, Columbia Univ; Helsinki, Brooklyn Mus. *Pos:* Assoc, Vincent Ponte, Montreal, Can, 64-67; IM Pei & Partners, 68-78; dir, Iran, 75-78; co-chm, Voorsanger & Mills, NY, 78-90; chmn bd advs, Study Am Archit, Columbia Univ, N, 89-; founder & prin, Voorsanger & Assocs, 90-; founder, Taylor/Voorsanger Urban Designers, 91; pred, NY Found Archit, 2000-2001; mem archit rev panel, Port Authority NY & NJ; adv, Samsung Corp, Korea; chmn bd advs, Temple Hoyne Buell Ctr; adv bd, Parsons Sch Archit; bd dirs, Worldesign Found. *Teaching:* lectr, Bennington Col, Vt, Univ Pa, Columbia Univ & Harvard Univ; guest critic & lectr, Yale Univ, Pratt Inst, CUNY, RI Sch Design, Univ Cincinnati, Syracuse Univ & Univ Tex, Arlington; mem adv bd, Parson Sch Archit. *Awards:* finalist, Brooklyn Masterplan Competition; finalist, Pierpont Morgan Libr Masterplan; winner, competition for Nat WWII Mus, New Orleans; Cannon Prize, Nat Accad Design; and many others. *Mem:* NAD (fel); AIA (fel & former pres NYC chap); J Pierpont Morgan Libr, NY (fel); Harvard Grad Sch Design Alumni Coun; Wadawanuck Club; Century Asn; Sir John Soane Mus Found; Archit LEague, NY (bd dirs); Ellis Island Yacht Club (commodore, 2001-); Port Authority NY/NJ Ground Zero Archive; NY Hist Soc; NY State Regent's Comt Schs. *Mailing Add:* 246 W 38th St Fl 14 New York NY 10018-5805

VOOS, WILLIAM JOHN
ADMINISTRATOR, PAINTER
b St Louis, Mo, July 2, 30. *Study:* Wash Univ Sch Fine Arts, BFA, 52; Univ Kans, MFA, 53; NY Univ, US Arts & Humanities Art Admin fel, 67. *Work:* Rend Lake Col Collection, Mt Vernon, Ill; Mus Contemp Art, Recife, Brazil; Ga Coun Arts. *Comn:* Mural, Army Educ Ctr, Ft Bragg, NC, 54; playground mural, Ferguson Park Comn, Mo, 60. *Exhib:* One-man shows, Lafayette Art Ctr, Ind, 66 & Northern State Col, 74; Fac Shows, Steinberg Hall, Wash Univ, 68-72; Atlanta Col Art Fac Show, High Mus Art, 75; Mus Contemp Art, Recife, Brazil, 75; Herron Gallery, 85-95. *Pos:* Dean, Atlanta Col Art, 73-75 & pres, 75-85; dean, Herron Sch Art, Indiana Univ-Purdue Univ, Indianapolis, 85-95, dean & prof emer, 95-. *Teaching:* Assoc prof art & chmn humanities div, Florissant Valley Community Col, 64-68; assoc prof art & assoc dean Sch Fine Arts, Wash Univ, 68-73. *Mem:* IUPUI Senior Academy, Indianapolis Mus of Art; Washington Univ Century Club; Commuity Church of Greenwood (Deacon); Univ of Kansas Gold Medal Club. *Media:* Acrylic, Watercolor. *Mailing Add:* 3899 Honey Creek Blvd Greenwood IN 46143-9316

VOS, CLAUDIA
PAINTER, PHOTOGRAPHER
b New York, NY, Mar 2, 63. *Study:* Art Students League, 77-81; State Univ NY, Col Purchase, BFA, 81-85; Copper Union, 90-92. *Work:* Libr Cong; Nat Mus Women Arts, Washington. *Comn:* Stage set, Residents Theatre Group, Cologne, Ger, 91; painting for book "The New Covanent", Outerlimits, NY, 93; painting, Japan Network Group, Inc, NY, 94. *Exhib:* Tower Gallery, NY, 93; Weapons and Shields (with catalog), Art Gallery Brocades, The Neth, 93; Claudia Puusep, Estonia House, NY, 95; Global Focus, Nat Mus Women Arts, Beijing, China, 95; Shifting Identities, CB's Gallery, NY, 96; Estonia House, 97; Artists Space, NY, 97, 98. *Awards:* Dealers Selectee, Art Initiatives, New York, 94. *Bibliog:* Susan Rutman (auth), All points bulletin, Photo District News, 8/91; Alfonso Manosalves (ed), Portfolio, Ark-Angel Rev, spring/summer 93; Delft Times (illus), p 15, sect A. *Mem:* Nat Mus Women in Arts; Art Students League, New York. *Media:* Oil, Acrylic. *Mailing Add:* 3340 81st St Apt 2 Jackson Hts NY 11372-1336

VOURVOULIAS, JOYCE BUSH See De Guatemala, Joyce Bush Vourvoulias

VOURVOULIAS-BUSH, ALBERTO
EDITOR
Study: Yale Univ, PhD. *Pos:* Program Assoc, Latin Am Coun Fgn Rels; staff, Time Mag; dept ed, Latin Am Bur; mng ed, ARTnews Mag; coed: The City & the World: New York's Global Future, 97. *Mailing Add:* ARTnews Magazine 48 W 38th St New York NY 10018-0042

VROOM, STEVEN M
INSTRUCTOR, CURATOR
b Dearborn, Mich, Feb 26, 61. *Study:* Cornell Col, BPh, BSS, 82; Sch Art & Art Hist, Univ Iowa, MA, 89. *Pos:* Asst cur, Off Visual Mat, Sch Art & Art Hist, Univ Iowa, 87-90; exhib dir, Iowa City Arts Ctr, 91-93; bd mem, Iowa City/Jefferson Co Arts Coun, 91-93; dir, Univ Gallery, Univ South Sewanee, 93-96; Ind cur, Seattle, 96-; cur visual resources, Cornish Coll Arts, Seattle, 96-. *Teaching:* Instr colloquium, Sch Art & Art Hist, Univ Iowa, 89-93; vis assoc prof mod art, Knox Col, Galesburg, Ill, 93; instr mod art, Univ South, 93-96; instr, Cornish Col Arts, 96-. *Awards:* Tenn Asn Mus Award, Imogen Cunningham, The Breath of All Things, 94, Romantic Visions of Johannes Oertel, 96. *Mem:* Col Art Asn; Am Asn Mus; Tenn Asn Mus; Iowa City/Johnson Co Arts Coun; Univ Iowa Art Hist Soc (pres, 89-90); Cornish Fedn Teachers. *Publ:* Contribr, Louise Noun: Art by Women, Univ Iowa Press, 90; auth, Six Americans Catalog, Manik Verlag, 93; ed, Texts from the Marlowe Room, Univ Gallery, 94; The Romantic Visions of Johannes Oertel, Univ South Press, 95; New Sculpture by Geof Bowie, Univ South Press, 96

W

WACHENHEIM, EDGAR, III
PATRON
b NY City, Oct 14, 37. *Study:* Williams Col, BA, 59; Harvard Univ, MBA, 59. *Pos:* trustee, Arthur Ross Found, New York City, 78-; chmn investment comt, trustee UJA Fedn Jewish Philanthropies, New York City, 85-97; mem fin comt, trustee Rye Country Day Sch, NY, 85-97, pres, 85-93; chmn, Greenhaven Assoc Inc, 87-; trustee, treas, NY Found, 93-; trustee, Skidmore Col 93-2001, trustee emer, 2001-; Bd dir, Cenro Corp, New York City, Sejak, New York City, Central Nat Gottesman, Inc, New York City; bd dir, Miriam & Ira D Wallach Found; trustee, Mus Modern Art New York City, currently; chmn, Sue & Edgar Wachenheim Found, currently. *Mem:* NY Soc Security Analysts. *Mailing Add:* Greenhaven Assocs Inc 3 Manhattanville Rd Purchase NY 10577-2116

WACHS, ETHEL
EDUCATOR, COLLECTOR
b New York, NY, Dec 26, 23. *Study:* Brooklyn Col, with Philip Pearlstein, A D Reinhardt & Jimmy Ernst, BS, MA & MS. *Exhib:* Nat Asn Women Artists, Federal Bldg, NY, 80-92; Nat Acad Design, NY, 80 & 82; Audubon Artists, Nat Arts Club, NY, 81-92; Bergen Community Mus, Paramus, NJ, 83; solo exhib, New Sch for Soc Res, 90-92. *Teaching:* Teacher fine arts, High Sch Health Professions & Human Serv, New York, 58-; instr adult educ, Brooklyn Col, New York, 68-96. *Awards:* Martha Reed Mem Award, 91; Philip Isenberg Award, 96; Savoir Faire Paper Award, Audubon Artists, 99. *Mem:* New York Artists Equity; New York Soc Women Artists; Nat Asn Women Artists; Audubon Artists; Am Soc Contemp Artists. *Media:* Watercolor. *Collection:* Contemporary American art. *Dealer:* Voltaire's Rte 2 New Milford CT 06776. *Mailing Add:* 20 E 9th St New York NY 10003

WACHTEL, JULIE
PAINTER
b New York, NY, July 24, 56. *Study:* Middlebury Col, BA, 78; independent study prog, Whitney Mus, 79. *Work:* Brooklyn Mus, NY; Chase Manhattan Bank, NY; Progressive Corp, NY; Am Bar Asn, NY. *Exhib:* Solo exhib, Mus Contemp Art, Chicago, 91; Pittura Immedia, Neue Galerie am Landesmuseum Joanneum Graz, Graz, Ger, 95. *Bibliog:* Joshua Dechter (auth), Julia Wachtel, Mus Comtemp Art, 91; Paul Ardenne (auth), Julia Wachtel: For an Ethics of Vision & Julia Wachtel: Expositions in France, Ondes de Pierre, Calif, 95. *Media:* Oil on canvas. *Dealer:* Sandra Gering Gallery Wooster St New York Ny 10012. *Mailing Add:* 85 Quay Brooklyn NY 11222-2016

WADA, YOSHI
SCULPTOR
b Kyoto, Japan, 1943. *Study:* Kyoto Univ Fine Arts, BA(sculpture), 67. *Exhib:* Carnegie Mellon Univ (installation), 94; Santa Barbara Mus Art (sound installation), 94. *Awards:* Grants, Nat Endowment Arts, 77, 79, 87 & 93; Guggenheim Fel, 91. *Mailing Add:* 1424 10th Ave San Francisco CA 94122

WADDELL, JOHN HENRY
SCULPTOR, PAINTER
b Des Moines, Iowa, Feb 14, 21. *Study:* Art Inst Chicago, BFA, MFA, 48, BAE & MAE, 51; Univ Chicago; Eureka Col, Eureka, Ill. *Hon Degrees:* Nat Col Educ, Evanston, Ill, Hon DFA, 79. *Work:* Phoenix Art Mus, Ariz; Univ Ariz Mus Art, Tucson; Kenyon Col, Gambier, Ohio; Nat Louis Univ, Evanston, Ill; Ravinia Park,

Highland Park, Ill; First Unitarian Universalist Church, Phoenix, Ariz; Pub installation: Flinn Found: "Compassion" bronze figure, Phoenix, 2000; and many others. *Comn:* Dance (sculpture), City of Phoenix, Herberger Theater, 74; I Am That I Am (sculpture), Temple Beth Israel, Phoenix, 82; Backwalkover (sculpture), Ctr Sports Med & Orthopedics, Phoenix, 85; Touchstone (stone sculpture), Boswell Mem Hosp, Sun City, Ariz; Dedication (sculpture), Carver Mus, 98; Sedona Cult Park, "Generations" 14 figure bronze composition, 2000-; 12 figure bronze sculpture grouping City of Phoenix. *Exhib:* Phoenix Art Mus, 60, 62 & 64; Northern Ariz Univ Art Mus & Gallery, 73, 82, 91-98; One man shows, Unitarian Church, Phoenix, 77, 85, 90, Verde Valley Artists Asn, Jerome, Ariz, 77, Nat Col Educ, Evanston, Ill, 79 & Sedona Arts Ctr, 80; Coconino Ctr Arts, Flagstaff, 82 & 91; Robert Mondavi Winery, 82, 86 & 94; Scottsdale Ctr Arts, 84; Tempe Arts Ctr, Ariz, 90; Sun Cities Art Mus, 91-92; Restrospective Gallery, San Diego, Calif, 91; solo shows, New Sch for Arts, Tempe, Ariz, 2000, 02, 05, Barbara Aronsen SEdona Artist Invitational, 2002, Cattle Track Compound Gallery, Scottsdale, 2004, Desert Bot Gardens, Phoenix, 2004. *Pos:* Sculptor. *Teaching:* Instr art & art educ, Nat Col Educ, Evanston, Ill, 49-55; asst prof art, Inst Design, Chicago, 55-57; prof art, Ariz State Univ, 57-61 & 63-64; founder & dir, Master Apprentice Prog, Waddell Sculpture Fel, 72-92. *Awards:* Alumni Award Merit, Eureka Col, Ill, 82; Artist of Year Award for Cult ural Contributions, Scottsdale, Fine Arts Comn, Ariz, 85; Artist of Year, Governor's Awards for Arts, 95. *Bibliog:* Alan Baker (dir), The Beauty of Individual Differences, Ariz State U; Amy Waddell (dir), The Reluctant Muse, 95; Michel F Sarda (auth), John Henry Waddell, the Art & the Artist, Bridgewood Press, Phoenix, Ariz, 96; Michael Sarda (auth), Faces of Arizona, 99; Univ Chgo Mag, 2005; Sedona Mag, 2003. *Mem:* Phoenix Art Mus; Detroit Med Ctr; US Tennis Assoc, Flushing Meadows, NY; Nat Louis Univ, Evanston, Ill. *Media:* Figurative Bronze, Stone; Pastel, Watercolor. *Publ:* Dir, Discovering Sculpture, 58 & Discovering Drawing and Painting (films), 61; auth, The Beauty of Individual Differences, Master Apprentice Programs, 85. *Dealer:* John and Ruth Waddell 10050 E Waddell Rd Cornville AZ 86325-6010. *Mailing Add:* 10050 E Waddell Rd Cornville AZ 86325-6010

WADDELL, THEODORE
PAINTER
b Billings, Mont, Oct 6, 41. *Study:* Brooklyn Mus Art Sch, 62; Eastern Mont Col, Billings, Mont, BS, 66; Wayne State Univ, Detroit, Mich, MFA, 68. *Work:* Eastern Mont Col & Yellowstone Art Ctr, Billings, Mont; Sheldon Mem Art Gallery, Univ Nebr, Lincoln, Nebr; City of Great Falls, Mont; Dallas Mus Art; San Jose Mus, Calif. *Exhib:* 38th Corcoran Biennial, Corcoran Gallery, Washington, DC, 83; solo exhibs, Univ Calif, San Diego, 84, Cheney Cowles Mem Mus, Spokane, Wash, 85; The New West, Colorado Springs Fine Arts Ctr, Colorado Springs, 86; Bernice Stein Baum Gallery, NY, 92. *Bibliog:* Gordon McConnell (auth), Theodore Waddell, Yellowstone Art Ctr, 84. *Media:* Oil on Canvas. *Mailing Add:* c/o Stremmel Gallery 1400 S Virginia St Reno NV 89502

WADDY, PATRICIA
HISTORIAN
b Cannelton, Ind, July 29, 41. *Study:* Rice Univ, BA, 63; Tulane Univ, MA, 65; New York Univ, PhD, 73. *Teaching:* Vis lectr, Carnegie-Mellon Univ, Pittsburgh, Pa, 70-71 & asst prof, 71-77 & Cornell Univ, Ithaca, NY, 77; vis assoc prof, Cornell Univ, Ithaca, NY, 80; assoc prof archit hist, Syracuse Univ, New York, 77-91 & prof, 91-. *Awards:* Am Acad in Rome Fel, 68-70; Guggenheim Fel, 98; NEH Fel, 98-99. *Mem:* Soc Archit Hist (bk rev ed J, 85-88, ed, 90-93, second vpres, 93-94, first vpres, 94-96 & pres, 96-98); Col Art Asn; Renaissance Soc Am; Italian Art Soc. *Res:* Roman 17th century houses and palaces. *Publ:* Auth, Seventeenth-Century Roman Palaces: Use and The Art of the Plan, 90; co-auth, Palazzo Pallavicini Rospigliosi e la Galleria Pallavicini, Umberto Allemandi, 2000. *Mailing Add:* Syracuse Univ Dept Architecture Syracuse NY 13244

WADE, ROBERT SCHROPE
PAINTER, SCULPTOR
b Austin, Tex, Jan 6, 43. *Study:* Univ Tex, Austin, BFA, 65; Univ Calif, Berkeley, MA, 66. *Work:* Menil Collection, Houston, Tex; Groningen Mus, Holland; Beaubourg Mus, Paris, France; NMex State Capitol; Royal Palace, Monaco; Nat Cowgirl Mus, Ft Worth, Tex; Dallas Mus, Austin Mus. *Comn:* Giant Iguana, Lone Star Cafe, NY, 78; Biggest Cowboy Boots, Washington Art Site, DC, 79; Giant Sax, Billy Blues, Houston, Tex, 93; Photo Canvas Murals, Torch Corp, Trucks for Tex, New Truck Makeover, Chevey, General Motors, 04. *Exhib:* one-man shows, Kornblee Gallery, NY, 71 & 74, Paris Biennale, Paris, France, 77, Jan Turner Gallery, Los Angeles, 78 & Elaine Horwitch Galleries, Santa Fe, NMex, 87, 90, 93 & 95; Sky Art Festival, Anchorage, AK, 89; Stremmel Gallery, Reno, Nev, 95; M D Mod, Houston, Tex, 98; William Campbell Contemp Art, Ft Worth, Tex, 2000, 2003; Nat Cowgirl Mus & Hall of Fame, Ft Worth, Tex, 2003; Am Pavillion Expo, Aichi, Japan 2005. *Teaching:* Instr, McLennan Col, 66-70; artist in residence & dir, Northwood Exp Art Inst, Dallas, 70-73; asst prof, NTex State Univ, Denton, 73-77; vis artist, Kansas City Art Inst, 79 & 92. *Awards:* Nat Endowment Grants, 73, 74 & 84. *Bibliog:* Kim Goad (auth), Bob Wade, A Portrait of the Artist as a Thoroughly Texas Icon, Dallas Morning News, 91; Jutta Feddersen (auth), Soft Sculpture (book), Gordon & Breach Int, London, NY, 93; Jeff Guinn (auth), Whats Up Daddy-o?, Ft Worth Star Telegram, 98; Karen Dinitz (dir) Too High Too Wide Too Long (documentary film), 99; Susie Kalil (auth), Bob Wade interview, Artlies Mag, Houston, Tex, Spring 2000; Vikki Loving (auth), Wildly Austin, Austins Landmark Art, Wildly Austin Press, 2004. *Media:* Miscellaneous Media. *Publ:* Article, Art Press Int, Paris, France, 10/77; coauth, Daddy-O: Iguana Heads and Texas Tales, St Martins Press, 95; Bob Wades Cowgirls, Gibbs Smith Pub, Salt Lake City, 2003. *Dealer:* William Campbell Contemporary Art Fort Worth Tex. *Mailing Add:* 3502 Winsome Ct Austin TX 78731

WADLER, RONNI
PAINTER, ILLUSTRATOR
b New York, NY, Feb 26, 46. *Study:* Queens Col, BA(fine arts), 67; Univ Wis-Madison, MA(painting), 69. *Work:* Queens Col. *Exhib:* 82nd Ann Exhib, Allied Artists Am, 95; 16th & 18th Ann Faber Birren, Nat Color Award Show, Mus Stamford, Conn, 96 & 98; Int Colored Pencil Exhib, San Diego, 95, 96, 97, 2001; Art Exhib, Athens, Greece, 96; 17th, 18th, 19th Ann Non-mems Exhib, Salmagundi Club, NY, 94, 95, 96; 56th Ann Exhib, Audibon Artists, 98; Realism Today, John Pence Gallery, San Francisco, Calif, 2000; Catherine Corilland Wolfe Art Club, Int Exhib, New York City, 98, 2000. *Pos:* Film ed, Wis Bur Pub Instr, 68-69; freelance illusr with var publ, 88-96. *Teaching:* Asst instr drawing, Univ Wis, 68-69; teacher art, NY Pub Schs, 69-76; guest lectr Luoyang Univ Teachers Col, Luoyang, China, 99; instr Colored Pencil Painting, Greenwich, Conn, 98-99. *Awards:* Finalist, Realism Today, American Artist, 2000; Daniel SMith Awrd, Expirimental Colored Pencil Exhibition, 2001; Yarka Art Materials Award, Audibon Artists, 98; and others. *Bibliog:* Colorful Additions, Artists Mag, 93; Sixteenth Anniversary Art Competition Finalist, Am Artist, 10/28/97; Realism Today, Am Artist, 10/2000; plus others. *Mem:* Nat Asn Women Artists; Mamaroneck Artists Guild (vpres, formerly; pres, 94-96); Colored Pencil Soc Am. *Media:* Colored Pencil, Pastel, Monotypes, Oil Painting. *Publ:* Contribr, The Best of Colored Pencil, 93, The Best of Colored Pencil 2, 94, Creative Colored Pencil, 95, The Best of Colored Pencil 3, 96, The Best of Colored Pencil 4, 97 & The Best of Colored Pencil 5, 99, Rockport Publ; illusr, Design Libr, Rockport Publ, 95; Sixtieth Ann Competition Finalists, American Artist, Oct, 97; Realism Today, American Artist Magazine, Oct 2000; Coping Through Art, American Artist Magazine, March 2005. *Dealer:* Steve Demus Bon a Tirer Gallery NY; Erlich Fine Arts Marblehead Mass. *Mailing Add:* 4 Ellsworth Rd Larchmont NY 10538

WADSWORTH, JOHN SPENCER, JR
PATRON
b Ft Thomas, Ky, Sept 12, 1939. *Study:* Williams Col, BA, 1961; U Chgo, MBA, 1963. *Pos:* Exec vpres & bd dir, First Boston Corp, NYC, 1963-78; joined Morgan Stanley, NYC, 1978, mng dir, various positions US investment banking divsn, 1978-87; pres, Morgan Stanley Japan, Tokyo, 1988-93; chmn, Morgan Stanley Asia Ltd, 1993-2000, hon chmn; adv dir, Morgan Stanley, currently; ptnr, Manitou Ventures. *Mem:* Bd dir, Pixar Inc, 2002-; chmn bd, Littleford Bros Inc, Forence, Ky; trustee, Asia Soc, Williams Col & Solomon R Guggenheim Mus; Asia Am MultiTechnology Asn (charter mem). *Mailing Add:* Morgan Stanley 1585 Broadway New York NY 10036

WAGNER, CATHERINE
PHOTOGRAPHER
b San Francisco, Calif, Jan 31, 53. *Study:* Inst Art, San Miguel de Allende, Mex, 71; San Francisco Art Inst, 71; San Francisco State Univ, BA(art, photog, cum laude), 75, MA, 77. *Work:* Mus Fine Arts, Houston; San Francisco Mus Mod Art, Calif; Oakland Mus Art, Calif; Nat Mus Am Art, Smithsonian Inst, Washington, DC; Metrop Mus Art, NY; and others. *Comn:* Construction of Louisiana, World Expos Can Centre Archit, Quebec City, Que, 84; photograph of Civic Ctr Plaza, Am Inst Archit, 85; Bank Archit, Parnassus Found, Houston, Tex, 87; rephotograph of the George Moscone Conv Ctr, Houston, 88; Louisiana World Expos, Libbie Rice Gallery, Houston, 88. *Exhib:* Retrospective 1976-1986 (with catalog), Min Gallery, Tokyo, Japan, 87; solo exhibs, Mus Fine Arts (with catalog), Houston, Tex, 88, Mus Contemp Photog, Columbia Col, Chicago, 88, Fraenkel Gallery, San Francisco, 89, Ansel Adams Ctr, San Francisco, 89, Laurence Miller Gallery, NY, 90, Home & Other Stories, Los Angeles Co Mus Art, 93, Fraenkel Gallery, San Francisco, 93, Mus fur Moderne Kunst, Frankfurt, Ger, 94 & Ctr Creative Photog, Tucson, Ariz, 94, Art and Sci: Investigating Matter (with catalog), Wash Gallery Art, St Louis, Mo, 96, Fraenkel Gallery, San Francisco, 96, Int Ctr Photog, NY, 97, Visual Arts Fel, Weizmann Inst, Rehovot, Israel, 98, Realism and Illusion: Catherine Wagner Photographs the Disnet Theme Parks, Nelson Atkins Mus, Kansas City, 2000, Cross Sections + Annotations: Can Jose Mus of Art, 2001; Several Exceptionally Good Recently Acquired Pictures VI, Fraenkel Gallery, San Francisco, 92; Home and Other Stories (with catalog), Corcoran Mus Art, Washington, DC, 94; Absolute Landscape: Between Illusion and Reality, Yokohama Mus Art, Japan, 97; group exhibs, Paradise Now: Creating the Genetic Revolution, Exit Art, NY, 2000, Beyond Boundries: Contemp Photog in California, traveling, 2001. *Teaching:* Lectr photog, San Francisco State Univ, 79-85; assoc prof art, Mills Col, Oakland, Calif, 79-94; prof of art, Mills Col, Oakland, Calif, 95-. *Awards:* Photog Fel, 81 & 90, Vis Artists Fel in Photog, 90 & 91, Nat Endowment Art; Guggenheim Found Fel, 87; Fel, San Jose Mus Art Visual Arts, 97. *Bibliog:* Jeanette Ross (auth), Organizing Meaning, Artweek, 12/21/89; Hilda Bijur (auth), Bodies and Classrooms, Chelsea Clinton News, 3/22/90; A D Coleman (auth), The New York Observer, 3/26/90; Andy Grundberg (auth), the New York Times, 3/30/90. *Mem:* Soc Photog Educ; Bay Area Consortium Visual Arts. *Publ:* Auth, To Collect the Art of Women: The Jane Reese Williams Collection of Photography, Mus NMex, Santa Fe, 92. *Dealer:* Stephen Writz Gallery San Francisco CA; Jack Shainman Gallery New York NY. *Mailing Add:* 308 Precita Ave San Francisco CA 94110

WAGNER, CHARLES H
ADMINISTRATOR, INSTRUCTOR
b Baltimore, Md. *Study:* Md Inst Col Art, BFA; Johns Hopkins Univ; Yale Univ, MFA. *Work:* Md Inst Col Art; Western Md Col, Westminster; Towson State Univ. *Exhib:* Baltimore Watercolor Club, Md, 73-75; Western Md Col, 75; Lindwood Gallery, 83; Rehobeth Art League, 83; Revelations Gallery, Baltimore, 83; Towson State Univ. *Teaching:* Instr drawing, painting & Art Hist, Md Inst Col Art, Baltimore, 50-; dept chmn sec art, Baltimore Co Pub Schs, Md, 55-70; instr design & watercolor, Towson State Univ, Md, 72-; instr drawing & painting, Howard Community Col, 82-; instr,

Essex Community Col, 87-. *Awards:* Bronze Medal Figure Painting, Md Inst, 55; John Hay Fel, Yale Univ, 60-61; First Prize Design, Nat Educ Asn, 65. *Publ:* Illusr, Baltimore County Serves the Nation, 59; auth, Classroom Discipline, 60; auth, Team Teaching in Art, 74; contribr, art curric guides, 82. *Mailing Add:* 1042 W Seminary Ave Lutherville Timonium MD 21093

WAGNER, MERRILL
PAINTER
b Seattle, Wash, June 12, 1935. *Study:* Sarah Lawrence Col, BA, 57; Art Students League, NY, with Edwin Dickenson, George Grosz & Julian Levy, 59-63. *Work:* Chase Manhattan Bank, NY; Seattle Arts Comn, Wash; Tacoma Art Mus, Wash; Weatherspoon Art Gallery, Univ NC, Greensboro. *Exhib:* one-person shows, The Clocktower, Inst Art & Urban Resources, NY, 79, Watson DeNagy Gallery, Houston, 82, Traver Gallery, Seattle, 87, 89, 91, 96, 97 & 99, Gemeentemuseum, The Neth, 91, Stark Gallery, NY, 92 & L Gray Gallery, Providence, RI, 91; Larry Becker Gallery, Philadelphia, 93; Outdoor installation, CW Post Campus, Long Island Univ, 93; Impermanence, Aldrich Mus, Ridgefield, Conn, 93; Painting Outside Painting (with catalog), Corcoran Gallery Art 44th Biennial Exhib Contemp Am Painting, 95; Better Color through Chemistry, Islip Mus, NY, 97; Merrill Wagner & Scott Reynolds, Workspace Gallery, NY, 98; Painting with an Edge: Four Contemp Artists, Hunterdon Mus Art, Clinton, NJ, 98; Substance, Tricia Collins Contemp Art, NY, 98; Hands on Color, Bellevue Art Mus, Wash, 98; Copper Drawings, Garner Tullis Workshop, New York City, 98; Works on Slate, William Traver Gallery, Seattle, 99, Recent Paintings on Steel, 2001; Nicolaysen Art Mus, Caspar, Wis, 2000; Freedman Gallery, Reading, Pa, 2000; Univ of Wyom, Laramie, 2001; Univ of Puget Sound, Kitteridge Gallery, Tacoma, WA, 2002; William Traver Gallery, Tacoma, Wash, 2001-03; Sundaram Tagore Gallery, New York City, 2004; group exhib incl: Beyond the Surface, Sundaram Tagore Gallery, New York City, 2004, Theories, Abstract NY Recent Paintings, LICK Lte, Fine Art, LI City, NY, 2003, 25th Anniversary Exhib, William Traver Gallery, Seattle, Wash, 2002, Ann Messner & Merrill Wagner, Lenore Gray Gallery, Providence, RI, 2001; Kiyo Higash Gallery, Los Angeles, Calif, 2003; New Arts Program, Kutztown, Pa, 2005; Renate Bender, Munich, Ger, 2006. *Collection Arranged:* Rose Art Mus, Brandeis Univ, MA; Gemeente Mus, The Hague, Holland; Richard Gluckman Architects, NYC; Microsoft Corp, Redmont, CA; Tacoma Art Mus, Tacoma, WA. *Teaching:* Vis lectr in the humanities, drawing & painting, Princeton Univ, 83-91, prof advan painting, 83-; instr drawing, Univ Puget Sound, summer 85 & 86 & Parson's, 92-97. *Awards:* Nat Endowment Arts Visual Artists Fel Grant, 89; Nat Endowment Arts Award Artists Bks, 90; AIGA Book Show Cert of Excellance, 91; Northwest Design Award, 92; Hassam Purchase Award, Am Acad of Arts & Lett, 2002. *Bibliog:* Tiffany Bell (auth), Article in Arts Mag, 5/86; Matthew Kangas (auth), Time Travellers, Seattle Weekly, 11/18/87; Lois Nesbit (auth), Merrill Wagner: Fanbush Gallery, Artforum, 10/89. *Mem:* Am Abstract Artists (pres, 82-85). *Media:* Multi. *Publ:* A Calendar, September 1982-December 1983, Magna Color Press, Inc, 82; auth, Notes on Paint, pvt publ, 90; Time and Materials, pvt publ, 95; Painted Sun Trails, pvt publ, 96; Oil & Water, pvt publ, 2001; Roger Boyce (auth), Art in Am, Merrill Wagner at Startk, 2002; ART Press, Merrill Wagner, 2003; Public and Private, pvt publ, 04. *Dealer:* Traver Gallery Seattle WA; Larry Becker Contemporary Art. *Mailing Add:* 17 W 16th New York NY 10011

WAGNER, RICHARD ELLIS
PAINTER
b Trotwood, Ohio, 1923. *Study:* Antioch Col; Dayton Art Inst, Ohio; Univ Colo, BFA & MFA. *Work:* Denver Art Mus, Colo; Libr of Cong, Washington; Dartmouth Col, Hanover, NH; DeCordova Mus, Lincoln, Mass; Rochester Mus, NY; Ford Motor Co, Univ of Wyo. *Comn:* Murals, Horizon House, Naples, Fla, 71. *Exhib:* Recent Drawings USA, Mus Mod Art, NY, 56; Boston Arts Festival, Mass, 58, 60 & 62; Youngstown Art Festival, Butler Inst Am Art, 70; Art USA, W Colo Ctr Arts, Grand Junction, 86 & 89; Artists of the West, Colo Springs Rotary, 90-96; State of the Art, NE Fine Arts Inst, 93; one-man show, Arts for Parks, 93 & Darvish Collection, Naples, Fla, 95; 62 one-man shows 53-; Bay City Art Ctr, Oreg, 2000, 01, 02; one-man show, Valley Art, Forest Grove, Ore, 2004. *Pos:* Jury for art shows, Grand Junction, Colo, 87, Delta, Colo, 88 & Glenwood Springs, Colo, Art Guild, 89. *Teaching:* Instr, Univ Colo, 52 & 55; assoc prof art, Dartmouth Col, 53-66; Castle Hill Art Ctr, Ipswich, Mass, 54 & 56. *Awards:* Purchase Prizes, Denver Art Mus, 50, Libr of Cong, 52 & De Cordova Mus, Mass; jurors award, Colo Springs Art Guild, 89; 1st Place, Pinon Arts, Cortez, Colo, 92. *Media:* Oil, Acrylic. *Collection:* 52 paintings, Johnson Collection, Tyler, Tex. *Publ:* Illusr, Ford Times, 58-70; Sketches in San Juans, 76; Sketches in Southwest Seasons, 82; article in: Palette Talk, 83. *Dealer:* Darvish Collection Naples Fla; Ryan Gallery Lincoln City OR; Valley Art Forest Grove Ore. *Mailing Add:* 5615 Castle Dr NW Tillamook OR 97141

WAGNER, TOM
PAINTER
b Kingston, Pa, 1953. *Study:* E Stroudsburg Univ, Pa, BS, 92; Marywood Univ, Scranton, Pa, MA, 95, MAT, 98. *Exhib:* Main Street Mus, Wayne Co Hist Mus, Honesdale, Pa, 93; Regional '94, Everhart Mus, Scranton, Pa, 94; Second Ann Nat, Dept Fine Arts, St John's Univ, Jamaica, NY, 96; Within & Without: The Intimate Moment, Muskingum Col Art Dept, New Concord, Ohio, 96; Mono-Production II, Dept Art, Auburn Univ, Ala, 97; Inside/Outside, Arts Coun, Fayetteville, NC, 97; Rituals of Dance, Marywood Univ, Scranton, Pa, 97, Bismark State Col, NDak, 99 & Ark River Valley Art Ctr, Russellville, Ark, 99; The Natural Figure, Nat Figure Art Asn, Stockholm, NJ, 97; Member's Ann, Nat Col Soc, Lorain Co Community Col, Elyria, Ohio, 97; Male Image, Fowler Gallery, Provincetown, Mass, 98; Shockoe Bottom Arts Ctr, Richmond, Va, 2000; Dutot Mus, Del Water Gap, Pa, 2000; Bridgewater Coll, Va, 2000. *Pos:* Contrib Ed, Village Life, NY, 92; gallery asst, Contemp Gallery, Marywood Col, Scranton, Pa, 94-95; artistic consult, Westmoreland Club, Wilkes-Barre, Pa, 96-98. *Teaching:* art tchr Hayfield Sec Sch, 2000-. *Awards:* Best of Show, Here & Now, Marywood Col, Scranton, Pa, 95. *Bibliog:* Pam Booker (auth), Synergism speaks volumes, The Crown, 2/18/93; Wagner exhibit at Misericordia, Citizen's Voice, 4/5/96; Henry Munoz (auth), Energy of Anthracite: colors and contrasts on exhibit, The Stroud Courier. *Mem:* Nat Figure Art Asn; Berkeley Art Ctr Asn; Col Art Asn; Nat Art Educ Asn; Caucus Soc Theory Art Educ. *Publ:* Illus, Treatment Today Mag, 96

WAGONER, ROBERT B
PAINTER, SCULPTOR
b Marion, Ohio, July 13, 28. *Study:* With Burt Procter & Olaf Weighorst. *Work:* Leanin' Tree Publ Mus, Boulder, Colo; Winthrop Rockefeller Collection. *Exhib:* Death Valley 49ers, Calif, 61; two-man shows, Scottsdale, Ariz, 72 & 73 & three-man show, 74; Mont Hist Soc, Helena, 74; Previews, Tex Gallery, Dallas, 75-79. *Pos:* Dir, Death Valley 49ers, 69-. *Awards:* First Award & Top Artists Award, Death Valley 49ers, 72 & 73 & First Award, 74, 75 & 76. *Bibliog:* James Serven (auth), Cattle, guns and cowboys, Ariz Hwys Mag, 70; Robert Wolenik (auth), Colorful west of Robert Wagoner, Westerner, 1-2/73; Portrait of a Westerner, Sierra Life Mag, 81. *Media:* Oil, Watercolor; Canvas, Masonite. *Dealer:* Texas Art Gallery Dallas TX; Saddleback Western Art Gallery Santa Ana CA. *Mailing Add:* 2710 Highland Dr Bishop CA 93514

WAHLING, JON B
SCULPTOR, WEAVER
b Council Bluffs, Iowa, Apr 14, 38. *Study:* Kansas City Art Inst & Sch Design, BFA, 62; Haystack Mountain Sch Crafts, Deer Isle, Maine, summers 63-65; Cranbrook Acad Art, MFA, 64; also with Maija Grotell & Glen Kauffman. *Work:* Columbus Mus of Art, Ohio; Yager Gallery, Hartwick Col; Univ Art Mus, Univ Tex, Austin; Ohio Arts Coun; Huntington Mortgage Co, Columbus, Ohio. *Comn:* Fiber sculpture hanging, Merchants & Mechanics Fed Loan & Savings Bank, Springfield, Ohio, 79. *Exhib:* Packard Gallery, Columbus Mus Art, Ohio, 77; Fiber Directions, Grunnier Gallery & Mus, Iowa State Univ, Ames, 82; In the Round, Southern Ohio Mus & Cult Ctr, Portsmouth, 83; The Works, Statewide Touring Exhib, Ohio Found Arts, 83-84; Five Sculptors, Springfield Art Ctr, Main Gallery, Ohio, 87; solo shows, Fiber Art, Eells Gallery, Blossom/Kent Festival, Blossom Music Ctr, Ohio, 87 & Gallery 200, Columbus, Ohio, 88 & 90; Disciples of Reenchantment: Jon Wahling, Paulus Berenshn, Ted Hallman, Mel Someroski, Columbus Cult Arts Ctr, Columbus, Ohio, 97; Coming of Age: The Ohio Arts Coun Fellowship Recipents, Rife Gallery, Columbus, Ohio, 2001. *Collection Arranged:* Lenone Davis and Bill Helwig: Surface Design and Enamels, Columbus Cultural Art Ctr, Ohio. *Pos:* Cur, artistic coordr, Garment Design: In Celebration of Body & Soul, Columbus Cult Arts Ctr, Ohio, 87. *Teaching:* Instr weaving, Columbus Cult Arts Ctr, Columbus Recreation & Parks Dept, Ohio, 64-; instr weaving, Penland Sch Crafts, NC, summers 66, 67 & 71. *Awards:* Craftsmen USA Nat Merit Award, Mus Contemp Crafts, New York, 66; Ten Outstanding Young Men Award, Columbus Jaycees, 72; Bordens Award for Outstanding Design in Fibre, 7th Beaux Arts Designer/Craftsmen Exhib, 73. *Bibliog:* Maryann Reilly (auth), Commissions opportunities for today's artists, Ohio Arts J, 7/80; Carla Peterson (auth), Technical virtuosity, Ohio Arts J, 1/85. *Mem:* Am Crafts Coun; hon mem Cent Ohio Weavers Guild; Ohio Designer Craftsmen; Ohio Designer Craftsmen (secy, 82-83); Surface Design Asn (North regional rep, Ohio rep). *Media:* Fiber, Metal. *Mailing Add:* 44 Stimmel St Columbus OH 43206

WAHLMAN, MAUDE SOUTHWELL
ADMINISTRATOR, HISTORIAN
b New York, NY. *Study:* Colo Col, BA(art), 69; Northwestern Univ, MA(anthrop), 69; Yale Univ, PhD(art hist, teaching fel), 80. *Collection Arranged:* Contemp African Arts, 73-75; Contemporary African Fabrics, Mus Contemp Art, Chicago, 75; Ten Afro-American Quilters, 82-; Gifts of the Spirit, 84-85. *Pos:* Consult African ethnology, Field Mus Nat Hist, Chicago, 71-74. *Teaching:* Asst prof art hist & southern studies, Univ Miss, 80-85; assoc prof & chmn art dept, Univ Cent Fla, Orlando, 85-98; Dorothy & Dale Thompson, Missouri Endowed Prof Global Arts, Art & Art History Dept, Univ Mo, Kansas City, 98. *Awards:* Res Grant Southern Folk Arts, Nat Endowment Humanities, 81-84; Nat Endowment Arts Grant, 82; Resident Research Fel, Harvard Univ African Am Art, 98. *Mem:* African Studies Asn; Am Folklore Soc; Soc Folk Arts Preservation; Women's Caucus Art. *Media:* Photography. *Res:* Historical roots of Afro-American Folk. *Publ:* Auth, Ceremonial Art of West Africa, Mich State Univ, 79; Traditional Art of West Africa, Colby Col, 80; co-ed, Spirit of Africa, Memphis State Univ, 82; auth, Afro-American Quiltmaking, Ind Univ (in prep); Religious Symbols in Afro-American Folk Arts, New York Folklore, Phillp Stevens, Vol 12, No 1-2. *Mailing Add:* 9700 Overbrook Rd Leawood KS 66206

WAID, JIM (JAMES) E
PAINTER
b Elgin, Okla, Nov 2, 42. *Study:* Univ NMex, with Morris Kantor & John Kacere, BFA, 65; Univ Ariz, MFA, 71. *Work:* Univ Ariz Mus Art; Metrop Mus Art, NY; Yuma Art Ctr, Ariz; IBM, Montvale, NJ; Chemical Bank, NY. *Comn:* Santa Cruz (mural), Tucson Pub Libr, 77. *Exhib:* 35th Biennial, Corcoran Gallery Art, 77; First Western States Biennial, Nat Collection Art, Washington, DC, 79-80; Four Corners States Biennial Exhib, Phoenix Art Mus, 81; Solo exhibs, Mus Art, Univ Ariz, Tucson, 85, Riva Yares Gallery, Scottsdale, Ariz, 86 & 88, Linda Durham Gallery, Santa Fe, NMex, 87, Southwest Tex State Univ, San Marcos, 87 & Shoshana Wayne Gallery, Santa Monica, Calif, 88; Phoenix Biennial, Phoenix Art Mus, 87; Large Scale Paintings, Riva Yares Gallery, Scottsdale, Ariz, 88; The New/Old Landscape, Mus Art, Uniz Ariz, Tucson, 89. *Teaching:* Instr art, Pima Community Col, 71-80. *Awards:*

Purchase Prizes, Arizona's Outlook, Tucson Mus Art, 80 & 14th Southwestern Invitational, Yuma Art Ctr, Ariz, 80; Nat Endowment Visual Arts Fel Grant, 85. *Mem:* Artists Equity; Dinnerware Artists Coop (treas, 79-82). *Dealer:* Riva Yares Gallery 3625 Bishop Lane Scottsdale AZ 85251. *Mailing Add:* c/o Riva Yares Gallery 3625 Bishop Ln Scottsdale AZ 85251

WAINWRIGHT, ROBERT BARRY
PAINTER, PRINTMAKER
b Chilliwack, BC, June 29, 35. *Study:* Vancouver Sch Art, dipl, 62; Atelier 17, Paris, with S W Hayter, Emily Carr Travel Study Scholar, 62. *Work:* Nat Gallery Can; Art Gallery Ont; Mus Fine Arts, Mus Art Contemp, Montreal; Can Indust Ltd, Toronto. *Exhib:* Premio Int Biella L'Incisione, Italy, 71, 73 & 76; solo exhib, Galerie Martal, Montreal, 72, Concordia Univ, Montreal, 76 & 80 & Mazelow Gallery, Toronto, 77; Galerie Elca London, Montreal, 84. *Teaching:* Assoc prof printmaking, Concordia Univ, Montreal, 66-. *Awards:* Can Coun Grants, 63-64 & 67-68; Erindale Col Purchase Prize, Int Exhib Graphics, Montreal, 71. *Mem:* Royal Can Acad Arts; Can Artists Rep. *Dealer:* Galerie Daniel 2159 Mackay St Montreal PQ H3G 2J2

WAISBROT, ANN M
ADMINISTRATOR, CURATOR
b Wausau, Wis, Oct 12, 43. *Study:* Univ Wis, Stevens Point, BS (art educ), 70. *Collection Arranged:* New Visions' Culture & Agriculture, (Nat Invitational Exhib) 89-98; Tradition & Innovation: Japanese Prints from the Collection; Ira Moskowitz (original drawings, painting, prints), 91 92; India: A Sense of Form & Color (art artifacts from pvt collections), 92; Memories of New Guinea, Medicine & Art, 96; Wahid Nahle: The Vibrant Canvas, 98. *Pos:* Exec dir, New Visions Gallery Inc, Marshfield, Wis, 86-. *Mem:* Am Asn Mus; Midwest Mus Conf; Wis Fed Mus; Am Coun Arts; Am Crafts Coun. *Mailing Add:* New Visions Gallery 1000 N Oak Ave Marshfield WI 54449

WAITZKIN, STELLA
SCULPTOR, PAINTER
b New York, NY. *Study:* NY Univ; Columbia Univ; also with Meyer Shapiro & Hans Hofmann. *Work:* Nat Gallery Fine Arts; Patrick Lanon Col, Fla; Walker Art Ctr; Tel-Aviv Mus, Israel; Everson Mus, Syracuse; NY Pub Libr. *Comn:* Con Ed Bldg, NY, 92. *Exhib:* One-woman show, Serious Lit, Calhoun Col, Yale Univ, 74; Potsdam Plastics, NY Univ, 75; Contemp Am Sculpture, Va Mus Downtown Gallery, 75; James Yu Exhib, 75; Renwick Gallery, Smithsonian Inst, Washington, DC; Nat Collection Fine Arts, Washington, DC; Selected Work, 1973-1983, Everson Mus, Syracuse, 83; Terminal Invitational, NY, 83; Witkin Gallery, NY, 87; Patricia Carrega Gallery, Wash, DC, 88; Anita Shapolsky Gallery, 88; Galerie Caroline Corre, Paris, 88, 89 & 90; State Mus, Trenton, NJ, 90; Corcoran Gallery Art, Washington, DC, 94, traveling USA through 96. *Pos:* Lectr, NY Univ. *Teaching:* Guest lectr, Columbia Univ Grad Sch, 73. *Awards:* Yaddo Found Fels, 73-76; MacDowell Found Fels, 74-83; Louis Comfort Tiffany Grant, 77. *Bibliog:* Taylor Mead, Studio Art (film); D Holmes (auth), article in Arch Am Art, 71; articles in Arts Mag, 73 & 74. *Mem:* Artist Equity. *Media:* Sandstone, Polyester Resin. *Publ:* Reproductions & articles in art publs; film work; reproduction, Washington Post, 94. *Dealer:* Anita Shapobry Gallery 99 Spring St New York NY; Witkin Gallery West Broadway New York NY. *Mailing Add:* 222 W 23rd St New York NY 10011

WAKEHAM, DUANE ALLEN
PAINTER, WRITER
b Port Huron, Mich, May 2, 31. *Study:* Mich State Univ, with Abraham Rattner, BA, 59; Stanford Univ, with Daniel Mendelowitz & Matt Kahn, MA, 61. *Work:* Galleries of Claremont Col, Calif; Port Huron Mus Art. *Exhib:* Artists of Hawaii, Honolulu Acad Art, Hawaii, 54; Mich Artists Ann, Detroit Inst Art, Mich, 59; Drawings of the Human Head (contribr, catalog), Metrop State Col, Denver, Colo, 89; solo exhib, Triton Mus Art, Santa Clara, Calif, 90; Pastels Only, Pastel Soc Am, NY, 92-2000; Pastels USA, Pastel Soc W Coast, Sacramento, Calif, 93-2000. *Teaching:* Instr drawing & painting, Stanford Univ, Calif, 60-62 & 64-65; prof art hist & painting, Col San Mateo, Calif, 65-87. *Awards:* Pastel Soc of Am Hall of Fame, 2000; Master Pastellist, Pastel Soc Am, 95; Distinguished Pastellist, Pastel Soc W Coast, 95. *Bibliog:* Jean McCord (auth), Duane Wakeham: Sharing a way of seeing Am Artist, 11/77; Bruce Nixon (essay), Duane Wakeham-Recent Paintings, 97; Kristina Feliciano (ed), The Best of Pastel 2, Rockport, 98; John Driscoll & Arnold Skolnick (auth), The Artist and the American Landscape, First Glance Books, 98; Maggie Price (auth), Duane Wakeham, The Pastel Jour, Sept/Oct, 2000. *Publ:* Auth, Joe Price: Serigraphs in light and tone, Am Artist, 10/77; coauth, Mendelowitz's Guide to Drawing, Harcourt Brace, rev ed 82, rev ed 88 & rev ed 92; Contemporary landscape painting, Artweek, 9/3/92; auth, Arriving at representation through abstraction, Am Artist, 8/94. *Mailing Add:* 218 Hoffman Ave San Francisco CA 94114

WAKSBERG, NOMI
PAINTER
b Ger, July 16, 47; US citizen. *Study:* Ohio State Univ, Columbus, BFA & BSci, 69; Md Inst Art, Baltimore, 70; Rutgers Univ, New Brunswick, NJ, MA & MFA, 72. *Work:* Ohio State Univ, Columbus; Continental Life Insurance Co, NY; Continental Group Investors, New Haven, Conn; First Nat Bank, Chicago; Japanese Embassy, Washington, DC; and others. *Exhib:* One-person show, Lehigh Univ, Bethlehem, Pa, 80 & Morris Mus; Artists Books, Philadelphia Art Alliance, 81; Rutgers Invitational, State Mus, Trenton, NJ, 82; Alternative Mus, NY, 82; Condeso/Lawler, NY, 82; Muse Found, Philadelphia, 83; State Mus, Trenton, NJ, 86; Lemieux Gallery, New Orleans, 2005; Islip Mus Contemp Art, NY, 2006; and others. *Pos:* Coordr & cur, Women Artists Series, Douglass Col Libr, 72-76; project dir, Her Own Space, Muse Foud, 82. *Teaching:* Instr art hist, Trenton State Univ, NJ, 80-81. *Awards:* Bea Camhi Award, Hudson River Mus, 80; NJ Arts Fel, 82-83; NJ Arts Coun Award, 82 & 84; Nat Endowment Award, Her Own Space, 83. *Bibliog:* Kay Larson (auth), Small talk, Village Voice, 2/11/80; Victoria Donahue (auth), rev, Philadelphia Inquirer, 5/81; Judith Stein (auth), article, Art Express, 11-12/81; Benjamin Genocchio (auth), NY Times, 7/23/2006. *Mem:* Women's Caucus Art (steering comt, 79-81); Col Art Asn, 2005-. *Media:* Acrylic, Oil Pastel, Photography. *Publ:* Contribr, Lehigh University Fall Collections, Lehigh Univ, 80. *Dealer:* Condeso/Lawler 119 West 25th St New York NY; Van Straaten Gallery 646 N Michigan Ave Chicago IL. *Mailing Add:* PO Box 21 Flemington NJ 08822-0021

WALBURG, GERALD
SCULPTOR, EDUCATOR
b Berkeley, Calif, May 5, 36. *Study:* Calif Col Arts & Crafts, 54-56; Calif State Univ, San Francisco, BA, 65; Univ Calif, Davis, MA, 67. *Work:* Storm King Art Ctr, Mountainville, NY; San Francisco Mus Art, Calif; Oakland Mus; Metrop Mus Art, NY; City of San Francisco. *Comn:* Sculptor, City of Sacramento, McCven & Steele, Calif. *Exhib:* San Francisco Mus Art, 67 & 69; Joslyn Art Mus, Omaha, Nebr, 70; Oakland Mus, Calif, 71 & 74; Baltimore Mus Art, Md, 73; Storm King Art Ctr, Mountainville, NY, 73-74; Crocker Gallery, Sacramento, 73 & 79; Soc of the Four Arts, Palm Beach, Fla, 74; NY Cult Ctr, 75; Bank of Am World Hq, San Francisco, 82. *Teaching:* Prof art, Calif State Univ, Sacramento, 68-. *Bibliog:* Gerald Nordland (auth), Gerald Waldbrug Recent Works, Oakland Mus, 79; David Collen & H Peter Stern (coauth), Sculpture at Storm King, NY, 80; Thomas Albright (auth), articles, San Franciscio Chronicle, 4/17/76 & 12/19/78. *Mem:* Int Sculpture. *Media:* Metal, Welded. *Mailing Add:* Art Dept Cal State Univ Sacramento 6000 J St Sacramento CA 95819-6061

WALD, CAROL
PAINTER
b Detroit, Mich, Jan 21, 35. *Study:* Art Sch Soc Arts & Crafts, Detroit, 58; Skowhegan Sch Painting & Sculpture, Maine, 63; Cranbrook Acad Art, Bloomfield Hills, Mich, 69. *Work:* Dennos Mus Ctr, Traverse City, Mich; Detroit Inst Arts, Mich; Utah Mus Fine Arts, Salt Lake City; Minneapolis Mus Art, St Paul, Minn; Mus of Am Illustration, NY; Butler Mus Am Art, Youngstown, Ohio; plus others. *Comn:* Mural, New Spirit of 76, Nat Bicentennial Comt, 76; murals, New Detroit, First Federal Savings & Loan, Detroit, Mich, 78; Ronald Reagan, Man of the Year, Time Mag, NY, 82; Towers of Grain, Fortune, NY, 82. *Exhib:* Arts & Crafts in Detroit 1906-1976, Detroit Inst Arts; Impression & Dreams, Gallery Gevik, Toronto, Can, 98, Arrival & Departures, 95 & Possible Dreams, 97, Kennedy Galleries, NY; Small Works of Art, Harmon-Meek Gallery, Naples, Fla; West Art and the Law Invitationals, Mineaspolis, Minn; Two Yr Traveling Exhib, 82, 93, 94 & 95; Contemp Color, The Monmouth Mus, Lingroft, NJ, 98; Distinguished Can Artists, Gallery Gevik, Toronto, 96; Art Show at Armory, NY, 96; A Woman's Place, Monmouth Mus, Lincroft, NJ, 96; Solo exhbns incl Retrospective, Flint Inst Arts, Mih, 64, collages, Cranbrook Mus Art, Bloomfield Hills, Mich, 81, Transformations, SI Mus Am Illus, 86, Sequences & Transformations, Recent maj paintings, Butler inst Am Art, Ohio, 91, Dennos Mus Ctr, Traverse City, Mich, 91, others. *Awards:* Grant, Mich Coun Arts, 89; Visual Arts Award, Arts Found Mich, 90; Ontario Art Coun, 96 & 98; Fel Yaddo Saratoga Springs, NY 71; Fel Huntington-Hartford, Pacific Palisades, Calif, 65. *Bibliog:* Maurice Horn (auth), Wald Biography, Gale Research, 88; William J Withrow (dir emer), Carol Wald, Sequences & Tranformations, Art Gallery, Ont, 91; Sequences & Transformations, Recent Paintings, Acad Chicago Publ, Ill, 92. *Mem:* Fel, MacDowell Colony, 68, 71 & Yaddo, 72. *Media:* Oil. *Publ:* The Metaphysical World of Hughie Lee-Smith, Am Artist, 78; illusr, Great Illustrators of our Time, Rizzoli Publ, New York, 82; Gorbachev's Russia, Business Week (cover), 85; Art for Survival, Graphis Press, 92; auth, Myth America, Picturing Women 1900-2000, US Male, Pictures Men 1900-2000, Stewart, Tabori & Chang Publ, 2000. *Dealer:* Kennedy Galleries Inc 730 Fifth Ave New York City NY 10019 (dir Lawrence A Fleishman). *Mailing Add:* 805-5280 Lakeshore Rd Burlington ON L7L 5R1 Canada

WALD, SYLVIA
PAINTER, SCULPTOR
b Philadelphia, Pa. *Study:* Moore Inst Art, Philadelphia. *Work:* Mus Mod Art, Metrop Mus Art & Whitney Mus Am Art, NY; Guggenheim Mus; Nat Gallery Art, Washington; Brooklyn Mus, NY; plus others. *Exhib:* one-woman shows, Knoll Int, Munich, 79 & Contruction & Sculpture, Aaron Berman Gallery, NY, 81, Tenri Cult Inst, 2004; Hirschl & Adler Gallery, NY, 93; New Brit Mus Am Art, 94; Dongah Art Gallery, Seoul, Korea, 95; Dong Shin Univ, Kwangiu, Korea, 96; Mus of Art, Chousun Univ, Kwangju, 2002; group show, Tenri Cult Inst, 2005. *Bibliog:* Zigrosser (auth), Prints and Their Creators--A World History, 74; Una E Johnson (auth), American Prints and Printmakers, 80; James Watrous (auth), A Century of American Printmaking 1880-1980, 84. *Mem:* Am Fedn Arts. *Media:* Miscellaneous. *Mailing Add:* 417 Lafayette St New York NY 10003

WALDMAN, LOUIS A
EDUCATOR
b Wyandotte, Mich, Oct 29, 65. *Study:* Hunter Col, BA, 89; NY Univ, MA, 93, PhD, 99. *Teaching:* lectr renaissance art, Syracuse Univ, Florence, NY, 99; sr lectr renaissance art, Univ Tex, Austin, 2000, asst prof, 2000-. *Awards:* Fel, Kunsth Inst, Fla, 95-97; Postdoctoral Fulb, 99-200; I Tatti, 2005-2006. *Mem:* Col Art Asn, Renaissance Soc Am. *Res:* Italian painting, sculpture, architecture, theory and criticism, 1400-1600. *Publ:* auth, Baccio Bandinelli and Art at the Medici Court, Philadelphia, Am Provincial Soc. *Mailing Add:* Univ Tex Dept Art & Art History Campus Mail Code D1300 Austin TX 78712-0337

WALDMAN, PAUL
PAINTER, SCULPTOR
b Erie, Pa, 1936. *Study:* Brooklyn Mus Art Sch; Pratt Inst. *Work:* Mus Mod Art, Solomon R Guggenheim Mus & NY Univ, NY; Los Angeles Co Mus Art, Calif; Smithsonian Inst & Hirshhorn Mus, Washington, DC; Denver Art Mus, Colo; Baltimore Mus Art, Md; Brooklyn Mus, NY; and many others. *Exhib:* 15th Nat Print Show, Brooklyn Mus, NY, 66; New Expressions in Fine Printmaking, Smithsonian Inst, traveling, 67-68; Painting Ann, Whitney Mus Am Art, NY, 67; Recent Gifts & Purchases, 77, Painting from the Collection, 79 & Recent Aquisitions, 84, Solomon R Guggenheim Mus, NY; one-man shows, Blum-Helman Gallery, NY, 78, Kunsthalle Tranegarden, Copenhagen, Denmark, 81, Norbyllands Kunstmuseum, Aalborg, Denmark, 81, Castelli Graphics, NY, 84, Farideh Cadot Gallery, Paris, 87, 88 & 91, Phyllis Kind Gallery, Chicago, 88 & Joseph Helman Gallery, 97, 98, 2000; Natural Wonders, Williams Col Mus Art, Mass, 90; Lennon Weinberg, NY, 93, 2002; Leo Castelli Gallery, NY, 73, 75, 78, 81, 88, 91, 96; and many others; Paint on Metal, Tucson Mus Art, Ariz, 2005. *Awards:* Artist-in-residence, Ford Found Grant, 65 & The Clamworks Studio Workshop, New York, 82. *Bibliog:* Liz Doup (auth), Boca Mus Lets Art Take a Flight of Fancy, Miami Herald, 6/3/93; Lydia Rebac (auth), Boca Flocks to Exhibit That's Strictly for the Birds, The News, Boca Raton, 6/9/93; MM Cloutier (auth), For the Birds, Palm Beach Life, 10/93; Lynn Gamwell, Dreams 1900-2000: Science, Art, and the Unconscious Mind. Cornell Univ Press, 2000; Edward Leffingwell (auth), Art in America, 9/2002; Donald Kuspit (auth), The End of Art, Cambridge Univ Press, 2004. *Media:* All. *Dealer:* Lennon Weinburg Broadway, NY. *Mailing Add:* 38 W 26 St New York NY 10010

WALETZKY, TSIRL (CECELIA) GROBLA
ASSEMBLAGE ARTIST, STAINED GLASS ARTIST
b New York, NY, Feb 12, 21. *Study:* Art Student League, NY, 42-43; Pratt Graphics, NY, 71; Parson's, 76-78. *Work:* Yeshiva Univ Mus, Cooper Hewitt Mus (Smithsonian), Jewish Mus, NY; Wolfson Mus, Jerusalem, Israel; Judaica Mus, Riverdale, NY. *Comn:* stained glass panel (with David Nulman), Hebrew Tabernacle, NY, 80; stained glass, 9 windows (with David Nulman), Cong Chofetz Chayim, Tucson, 88; stained glass scroll (with David Nulman), Cong Har Shalom, Potomac, Md, 89; cut-paper assemblage, Riverdale Temple, NY, 90; stained glass windows (with D Nulman), Cong B'nai Jacob, Phoenixville, Pa, 92-95, stained glass backlit panels (with D Nulman) Temple Emanuel, Lynbrook, NY, 96; Cut-paper Assemblage, Temple Shalom, Lawrence, NY, 98. *Exhib:* paper-cuts, Tower of David Mus, Jerusalem, Israel, 81; paper-cuts, Cooper Hewitt Mus, NY, 86; Stained glass (with David Nulman), Yeshiva Univ Mus, NY, 86; contemp paper-cuts, Judaica Mus, Riverdale, NY, 88; Expressions of Faith, Santuario de Gualalupe, Sante Fe, NMex, 90; Cut-paper Assemblage: Abrams Art Ctr Henry St, NY, 97; Castellani Mus, Niagra Falls, NY, 98; cut-paper and watch parts assemblage, Yeshiva Univ Mus, Ctr for Jewish Hist, 2004; plus others. *Teaching:* Judaic paper cutting, Hebrew Arts Sch, 85-87. *Bibliog:* From Editors, Papercuts by Tsirl Waletzky, Lilith, 78; Alice Greenwald (auth), The Mizrah, Hadassah Mag, 79; Lillian Wachtel (auth), Aus Kulturallem Interesse, Aufbau, 90. *Mem:* NY Artists Equity; Pomegranate Guild Judaic Needlework (bd mem, 76-94); Guild Am Papercutters. *Media:* Cut-Paper Assemblage; Stained Glass Design. *Publ:* illustr The New Book of Yiddish Songs, 72 & Pearls of Yiddish Songs, 88, Workmen's Circle; The Art of Judaic Needlework, Charles Scribners, 79; Eight Tales for Eight Nights, Jason Aronson, 90; The Jewish Wedding Book, Scripps Howard, 91; illustr, Yiddish Literature in America (two covers) 1870-2000, Vol 1, 99; Rememberings by Pauline, Wengeroff, Univ Md Press, 2000. *Mailing Add:* 80 Knolls Crescent Bronx NY 10463-6312

WALFORD, E JOHN
HISTORIAN, EDUCATOR
b London, Eng, Feb 16, 45. *Study:* Vrije Universiteit, Amsterdam, Kandidaats(hons), 76; Wolfson Col, Cambridge Speelman Fel (Dutch & Flemish art), 76-80; Univ Cambridge, Eng, PhD, 81. *Teaching:* Assoc prof & dept chmn art hist, Wheaton Col, Ill, 81-. *Mem:* Col Art Asn; Historians Netherlandish Art; Asn Art Historians, Gt Brit. *Publ:* Auth, Art and the Christian today, Messiah Col, 85; Jacob Van Ruisdael and the Perception of Landscape, Yale Univ Press, New Haven, London, 91; also occasional paper series. *Mailing Add:* Wheaton Col 501 E College Ave Wheaton IL 60187

WALGREN, FRANCES J
APPRAISER
Study: Art Hist, Queens Col, NY, MA, 85; Attended, Parsons Sch Design, NY; Attended, Am Col, Paris. *Pos:* With Christie's, NYC, 91—, specialist in books and manuscripts, department head, North America. *Awards:* Catalogued and auctioned the Fox-Bute Set of Audubon's Birds of America (2000) for $8 million, a world auction record for any printed book. *Mailing Add:* Christie's/NY 20 Rockefeller Plz New York NY 10020

WALKER, BERTA
ART DEALER
b New York, NY. *Study:* Univ Colo, 59-61; Burdett Col Bus, AA, 64. *Pos:* Founding dir mus progs, Opportunity Resources Arts, New York, 76-79; corp relations-spec events, Whitney Mus Am Art, New York, 79-81; assoc dir, Marisa del Re Gallery, New York, 81-83; founding dir, Graham Mod Gallery, New York, 84-89; owner, Berta Walker Gallery, Provincetown, Mass, 90- & Walkers Wonder Gallery. *Mem:* Fine Arts Work Ctr Artists Colony, Provincetown, Mass (chair, bd & trustee, formerly); Art Table, NY; Am Fedn Arts; Am Asn Mus; Provincetown Repertory Theatre, Mass (trustee). *Specialty:* Provincetown affiliated art, folk and functional art. *Mailing Add:* 208 Bradford St Provincetown MA 02657

WALKER, EDWARD (RUSTY) D
PAINTER
b Danville, Ill, Oct 31, 46. *Study:* Queensland Inst Technol, Brisbane, Australia, BFA, 66; Greenwich Univ, New Zealand, MFA, 89, PhD(art educ), 91. *Work:* Pres Gerald R Ford, Rancho Mirage, Calif; San Francisco Mus Mod Art; Charles & Emma Frye Art Mus, Seattle; Bender Room, Special Collections, Stanford Univ, Calif; Harcourt Brace Jovanovich Publ, NY. *Comn:* Robert L Montgomery (oil portrait), Alta Bates Hosp, Berkeley, Calif, 83; Donald P McCullum, Superior Court Judge, Oakland, Calif, 84; Int Posters, Leslie Levy Gallery Publishers, 90-92; Deer Dance, oil, comn by Bart Starr, 2000; Dr Jan Rosenquist, Midnight Mustangs, oil, 2005. *Exhib:* Crocker Kingsley Ann, E B Crocker Art Mus, Sacramento, 76; Am Watercolor Soc, Nat Acad Design, NY, 77; Art and the Law, Nat Invitational, West Publ, 85. *Pos:* Artist, US Air Force, Strategic Air Command Hq, Offutt Air Force Base, Nebr, 67-71; artist, fine Arts, 71-; vpres, provost, Collins Col, Ariz, 2005-. *Teaching:* Instr watercolor, Asilomar Watercolor Workshops, Monterey, Calif, 77-80, Hewitt Workshops, San Miguel De Allende, Mexico, 83; instr oils & watercolor, Fresno Watercolor Workshop, 77. *Awards:* Emily Lowe Mem Award, Am Watercolor Soc, Nat Acad, NY, 77; Teacher of the Year, Ariz Pvt Sch Asn, 91. *Bibliog:* Cover & feature article in Southwest Art, 6/80; feature article, Am Artist Mag, 10/80; feature article, Ariz Repub, 5/92; and others. *Mem:* Nat Watercolor Soc; Am Mensa. *Media:* Watercolor, Oils. *Interests:* Shuri-Ryu Karate Black Belt, 95, Am Karate Alliance, musician, blues harmonica player. *Publ:* Auth, Transparent Watercolor, Northlight Publ, 85; Contemporary Western Artists, Southwest Art Publ. *Dealer:* Leslie Levy Galleries Main Street Scottsdale AZ 85251

WALKER, HERBERT BROOKS
SCULPTOR, DESIGNER
b Brooklyn, NY, Nov 30, 27. *Study:* Art Students League, with Harry Sternberg & Robert B Hale, 43; Yale Sch Fine Arts, BFA, with R Eberhardt, R Zallinger, Graziani, J Albers & W De Konning. *Work:* Photographs of Antonio Gaudis Work, Mus Mod Art, NY; Barbados Mus, BWI; Walker Mus. *Comn:* Paintings, movie, photographs, Gahagan Dredging, Orinoco River, Venezuela, 53-54; paintings & photographs, US Steel, Cerro Bolivar, Venezuela; earth sculpture, Walker Mus, 60. *Exhib:* One-man shows, Stony Brook Mus, Long Island, NY, 52, Barbados Mus, 54 & IORC, Abadan, Iran, 58; Walker Mus, 60-; Rodin Mus, 70; Don Graziani Mem, Avesa, Italy, 94. *Collection Arranged:* Oil Exhibs, IORC, Abadan, Iran, 58 & 59; spec exhibs for pub schs, 60-72 & Walker Mus, Fairlee, Vt, 60-. *Pos:* Materials prod head, IROC, Abadan, Iran, 58-59; dir, Walker Mus, 59-. *Teaching:* Instr art, Thetford Acad, 64-. *Awards:* Gold Medal, ANCR, Verona, Italy, 74. *Bibliog:* H Brooks Walker, 1951, Eye Mag, Yale Univ, 67. *Mem:* Life mem Art Students League; Yale Arts Alumni Asn. *Media:* Sheet Metal, Bronze. *Res:* Arawak Carib, 54; Iran, 60; Italy, 70-. *Collection:* Justin Colin, Ted Leach, et alia in Japan Iran, Venezuela, France, Iceland, USA, Italy, Great Britain (private). *Publ:* Illusr, Gaudi, Mus Mod Art, 57. *Dealer:* Noel, Fairlee, VT 05045. *Mailing Add:* PO Box 6 Fairlee VT 05045

WALKER, JOHN SEIBELS
PAINTER
b Columbia, SC, Nov 12, 1960. *Study:* Univ South, BA (Studio Arts) 1983; apprentice study in classical realism, Atelier Lack, Minn, 1991. *Pos:* 19th and early 20th cent art dealer; instr, Charles Cecil Studios, Florence, Italy, 1991-; portraitist and fine artist, Charlotte, NC, 2000-. *Mem:* Am Soc Classical Realism; Am Soc Portrait Artists. *Media:* acrylic, oil. *Mailing Add:* John Seibels Walker Studios Ste 30 118 East Kingston Ave Charlotte NC 28203

WALKER, KARA
PAINTER, PRINTMAKER
b Stockton, Calif, Nov 26, 1969. *Study:* Atlanta Col Art, BA(painting & printmaking), 91; RI Sch Design, MFA(painting & printmaking), 94. *Exhib:* Into the Light-1992 Nexus Biennale, Nexus Contemp Arts Ctr, Atlanta, Ga, 93; An Historical Romance, Sol Koffler Gallery, Providence, RI, 94; Selections 1994, Drawing Ctr, NY, 94; Summer Group Show Plus 2, Stienbaum/Krauss Gallery, NY, 94; Now is the Time, Tony Shafrazi Gallery, NY, 95; Drawing Show, Bernard Toale Gallery, Boston, Mass, 95; Inaugural Show, Paul Morris Gallery, NY, 95; Landscapes, Borders, Boundaries, Nexus Contemp Arts Ctr, Atlanta, Ga, 95; La Belle et La Bete, Mus d'Art Mod de la Ville de Paris, France, 95; Real, Bass Mus, Miami, Fla, 96; Gone With the Wind: The Fabrication and Denial of Southern Cult, City Gallery, Atlanta, Ga, 96; Body Language, Mills Gallery, Boston, Mass, 96; No Doubt, Aldrich Mus, Ridgefield, Conn, 96; Conceal/Reveal, Site Santa Fe, NMex, 96; New Histories, Inst Contemp Art, Boston, Mass, 96; Pagan Stories: The Situations of Narrative in Recent Art, Apex Art, NY, 97; The Gaze, Momenta Art, Brooklyn, NY, 97; Civil Progress: Life in Black Am, Greg Kucera Gallery, Seattle, Wash, 97; no place (like home), Walker Art Ctr, Minneapolis, Minn, 97; Whitney Biennial, Whitney Mus Am Art, NY, 97; solo exhibs, Vienna State Opera House, Austria, 98, Print Ctr, Philadelphia, Pa, 98, Galleri Index, Stockholm, Sweden, 99, Contemp Arts Mus, Houston, Tex, 99, Calif Col Arts & Crafts, Oliver Art Ctr, Oakland, 99, Brent Sikkema, NY, 99 & 2001, McKinney Ave Contemp, Dallas, Tex, 99, Disturbing Allegories, Vanderbilt Univ Fine Arts Gallery, Nashville, 2001 & The Emancipation Approximation, Tel Aviv Mus Art, 2001, Kunstverein Hannover, Germ, 2002; Kara Walker/Charles Gaines, Inst Res African Diaspora Am & Caribbean, City Col NY, 98; Pierre Molinier, Kay Rosen, Kara Walker, Wooster Gardens/Brent Sikkema, NY, 98; Arturo Herrera and Kara Walker, Stephen Friedman Gallery, London, Eng, 98; Postcards From Black Am, De Beyerd, Breda & Frans Hals Mus, Harlem, The Neth, 98; Strange Days, Art Gallery New S Wales, Sydney, Australia, 98; Global Vision, New Art from the 90's, Deste Found, Athens, Greece, 98; Secret Victorians, Contemp Artists and a 19th Century Vision Traveling Exhib, 98; Looking Foward, Looking Back, Elaine L Jacob Gallery, Wayne State Univ, Detroit, Mich, 99; Istanbul Biennial: The Passion and the Wave, 99;

Re/Righting Hist: Counternarratives by Contemp African-Am Artists, Katonah (NY) Mus Art, 99; Other Narratives, Contemp Art Mus, Houston, 99; Au-Dela, Galerie Klosterfeide, Berlin, 2000; Glen Ligon & Kara Walker, Brent Sikkema, NY, 2000; 00, Barbara Gladstone Gallery, NY, 2000; Now is Not the Place, Ramapo Col, Mahwah, NJ, 2000; Age of Influence: Reflections in the Mirror of Am Cult, Mus Contemp Art, Chicago, 2000; Strength & Diversity: A Celebration of African-Am Artists, Carpenter Ctr Visual Arts, Harvard Univ, Cambridge, Mass, 2000; Drawing on the Figure: Works on Paper of the 1990's from the Manilow Collection, Mus Conemp Art, Chicago, 2000; Point of Reference, Frederick Hayes, Glen Ligon, Gary Simmons, Kara Walker, Addison Gallery of Am Art, Andover, Mass, 2000; Blurry Lines, John Michael Kohler Art Ctr, Sheboygan, Wis, 2000; The Power of Narration, Espal d'Art Contemp de Castello, Spain, 2000; Das Gedaschifnis der Kunst: History and Memory in Contemp Art, Historic Mus Frankfurt, 2000; The Americans, Barbican Art Galleries, 2001; Form Follows Fiction, Castello di Rivoli Museo d'Arte Contemporanea, 2001; Moving Pictures, Solomon R Guggenheim Mus, NYC, 2002; Telling Tales: Narrative Impulses in Recent Art, 2002; Tempo, MoMAQNS, NYC, 2002; Black Pres: The Art and Legacy of Fela Anikulapo-Kuti, New Mus, NYC, 2003; Comic Release: Negotiating Identity for a New Generation, Carnegie Mellon U, 2003; Monument to Now, DESTE Found Contemporary Art, Athens, Greece, 2004; Fairy Tales Forever: Int Homage to HC Andersen, Copenhagen, 2005; Kiss the Frog! The Art of Transformation, Nat Mus Art, 2005; Getting Emotional, Inst Contemporary Art, Boston, 2005; The Shadow, Vestsjaellands Kunstmuseum, Denmark, 2005; The World is a Stage, Mori Art Mus, Tokyo, 2005; Trials and Terrors, Mus Contemporary Art, 2005; Metrop Mus Art, NY, 2006. *Awards:* Presidental Scholar, Atlanta Coll Art; Art Matters Inc, Individual Artist's Fel; John D & Catherine T MacArthur Found; Lucelia Artist award, Smithsonian Am Art Mus, 2004. *Bibliog:* Mike Daniel (auth), Dividing lines, Dallas Morning News, 1/8/99; Annabelle Massey Helber (auth), Paper views, Met, 1/27-2/3/99; Pamela Newkirk (auth), Pride or prejudice, Artnews, 3/99. *Mailing Add:* c/o Sikkema Jenkins & Co 530 West 22nd St New York NY 10011

WALKER, KELLEY
PAINTER
b Columbus, Ga, 69. *Study:* Univ Tenn, BFA, 1995. *Exhib:* Group shows: Paula Cooper Gallery, NYC, 2003; Curious Crystals of Unusual Purity, PSI Contemp Art Center, 2004; Tuesday is Gone, Club 22, Tbilisi, Ga, 2004; La Lettre Volée, FRAC Franche-Comté Musée des Beaux-Arts de Dole, 2004; Galerie Peter Kichmann, Zurich, Switz, 2004; Last One On is a Soft Jimmy (curated by Kelly Walker), Paula Cooper Gallery, NYC, 2004; La Salle de Bains, Lyon, France, 2005; Situational Prosthetics, New Langton Center for the Arts, San Francisco, Calif, 2005; Log Cabin, Artists Space, NYC, 2005; 7th Shorjah Biennial, United Arab Emirates, 2005; Invisible Hands & the Common Good Champion Fine Art, Los Angeles, 2005; Bridge Freezes Before Road, Barbara Gladstone Gallery, 2005; Crash/Cars, Museo de Arte Contemporanea de Vigo (MARCO), Vigo, Spain, 2005; Whitney Biennial, Whitney Mus Art, 2006

WALKER, LARRY
PAINTER, EDUCATOR
b Franklin, Ga, Oct 22, 35. *Study:* High Sch Music & Art, New York; Wayne State Univ, Detroit, BS, 58, MA, 63. *Work:* Haggin Art Mus, City Hall & San Joaquin Delta Col, Stockton, Calif; Univ of the Pac, Stockton; Oakland Mus, Calif; City Atlanta; Studio Mus in Harlem; Buckhead Libr, Atlanta Life Insurance Co, Apex Mus, Hammonds House, Contel Corp, Atlanta; and others. *Comn:* Mural, Univ of the Pac, 65; mural comn by Benjamin Holt Found for San Joaquin Delta Col, 74; and others. *Exhib:* West Coast 74: The Black Image, E B Crocker Mus, Sacramento & Los Angeles Munic Art Gallery, 74; Northern Calif Arts Ann, Univ of Pac, Stockton; Atlanta Life Nat Exhib, Ga; Festival of Arts & Cult, Lagos, Nigeria, 77; Black Artists South, Huntsville Mus, Ala; Artists in Georgia, Athens, 85; Nat Black Arts Festival, 88 & 90, Hammonds House Mus & Galleries, Artspace Gallery, Chastain Gallery, Atlanta, 92; Lander Col, Greenwood, SC, 88. *Teaching:* Prof painting, drawing & art educ, Univ of the Pac, 64-, chmn art dept, 73-80; art critic, Stockton Record, Calif, 81-83; prof & dir, Sch Art & Design, Ga State Univ, Atlanta, 83-. *Bibliog:* Samella Lewis & Ruth Waddy (auths), The Black Artist on Art, Vol I, Contemp Crafts Publ, 69; article in Black Art, summer 77. *Mem:* Nat Coun Art Adminrs (bd dir, 76-79, 84-88, chmn, 78-79, 86-87); Nat Asn Sch Art & Design (bd dir, 89, 90-93); DeKalb Coun for the Arts (bd dir, 87-92, pres, 89-90); Marta Arts Coun. *Media:* Acrylic, Charcoal. *Publ:* Auth, The Visual Arts in the Ninth Decade, NCAA, 80; numerous revs of local & regional art exhibs, Stockton Record, Calif, 81-83; The State of the Arts in San Joaquin County, Walker & Watanabe. *Dealer:* Temme Barkin Leeds Barkin Leeds Ltd Fine Arts Management 2880 Vining Way Atlanta GA 30339; Artspace Gallery Atlanta GA. *Mailing Add:* School Art & Design Ga State Univ University Plaza Atlanta GA 30303-3083

WALKER, LARRY
PAINTER, EDUCATOR
b Newark, NJ, Mar 31, 52. *Study:* Jersey City State Col, NJ, BA, 73; Denver Univ, Colo, grad study, 75-76; Montclair State Col, NJ, MA, 80. *Exhib:* New Jersey Parks & Recreation Comn, Newark, 80; Rutgers Univ, Newark, NJ, 81; Transport NY-NJ, 82; Prudential Insurance Co, Newark, NJ, 82; Emerging and Established, Newark Mus, NJ, 83; Jersey City Mus, NJ, 83; Metro Show, City Without Walls Gallery, Newark, NJ, 84; Atrium Gallery, Morristown, NJ, 95. *Pos:* Treas, Northern NJ Chap, Nat Coun Artists, 81-; district coordr, Union Teen Arts Festival, Union, NJ, 84-86. *Teaching:* Art teacher, Newark Bd Educ, 76-78, Elizabeth High Sch, NJ, 80-; adj instr art, Jersey City State Col, NJ, 83-. *Awards:* Grant, NJ State Coun Arts, 85; Geraldine R Dodge Found Artist/Educ Grant, 98. *Mem:* Nat Conf Artists; Art Educators NJ. *Media:* Mixed Media. *Mailing Add:* 55 Randolph Place No 101 South Orange NJ 07079

WALKER, LAURIE ANN
SCULPTOR, CONCEPTUAL ARTIST
b Montreal, Que, Feb 2, 62. *Study:* Mount Allison Univ, BFA(distinction), 84; NS Col Art & Design, MFA, 87. *Work:* Musée Dárt Contemporain de Montréal, Que; Can Coun Art Bank, Ottawa, Ont; Banque Nationale, Montreal, Que. *Exhib:* Eye of Nature, Walter Phillips Art Gallery, Banff, Alta, 89; solo shows, Southern Alta Art Gallery, Lethbridge, Alta, 90, Oakville Galleries, Oakville, Ont, 94, Musée Dart Contemporain, Montreal, Que, 94; Rise & Fall, MacDonald Stewart Art Ctr, Guelph, Ont, 96 & Agnes Etherington Art Ctr, Kingston, Ont, 96; Voir, Savoir, Croire, Musée Régional De Rimouski, Que, 97. *Awards:* Joseph F Stauffer Prize, Can Coun, 89. *Dealer:* Galerie Christiane Chassay Catherine St W Suite 372 Montreal PQ H3B1A2. *Mailing Add:* 202 Saint Zotique W No C-2 Montreal PQ H2V 4S9 Canada

WALKER, MARIE SHEEHY
PAINTER
b Glen Cove, NY, May 23, 52. *Study:* Rosemont Col, BFA, 74; Art Students League, with Robert Brackman, 74-77. *Work:* Rosemont Col. *Comn:* Heffernan Hall (watercolor), Rosemont Col, 74. *Exhib:* Nat Acad Design Ann Exhib, NY, 82; Pastel Soc Am Ann Exhib Pastels Only, Nat Arts Club, NY, 82 & 83; Nassau Co Mus Ann Show, Roslyn, NY, 82 & 83; Nat Asn Women Artists Exhib, Bergen Community Mus, Paramus, NJ, 83; Nat Asn Women Artists Traveling Painting Exhib, 83-85; Huntington Libr, NY, 2003. *Awards:* Pastel Soc Am Award, Salmagundi Show, 80; Charlotte Winston Mem Award, Nat Asn Women Artists Exhib, 83; Gold Medal Oil Painting, Nat Art League, 83; Pastel Society Award, Suburban Art League Open Juried Show, 2003; Silver Medal, National Arts Club Members Show, 2003; Award of Excellence, Professional Art League, Suburban Art League Open Show, 2004; Bronze Medal Nartional Arts Club, Members Show, 2004. *Mem:* Pastel Soc Am; Nat Asn Women Artists; Art Students League; Nat Art League; Catharine Lorillard Wolfe; Art League of Long Island; Suburban Art League of Long Island. *Media:* Pastel, Oil; Watercolor. *Dealer:* Huntington Art Gallery Main St Huntington. *Mailing Add:* 3 Huxley Dr Huntington NY 11743

WALKER, MARY CAROLYN
CRAFTSMAN, JEWELER
b Lancaster, Pa, Oct 24, 38. *Study:* Pa State Univ, BS(home art); Rochester Inst Technol Sch for Am Craftsmen, with Don Drumm & Eleanor Moty. *Comn:* Maya Schock Award to Women in the Arts, Doshi, 85. *Exhib:* Young Americans, Mus Contemp Crafts, NY, 62; Southern Tier Arts & Crafts Show, Corning, NY, 73; First World Silver Fair, Mexico, 74; Spec Exhib for Nat Gov Conf, 76; one-person show, Pa Designer Craftsmen Gallery, Bushkill, 82; and others. *Pos:* Own, Tamcraft Products Co, Mechanicsburg, Pa, 60-. *Awards:* First Prize Metals, Harrisburg Arts Festival, 72; Best in Show, 73 & Fine Work in Precious Metals, 90, Pa Guild of Craftsman; and others. *Bibliog:* R Stevens (auth), Arts decoratifs, La Revue Mod des Arts et de la vie, France, 12/72. *Mem:* Am Crafts Coun (secy, Northeast Region, 71-74); Pa Guild Craftsman (treas, 70-71, pres, 72, vpres, 73); Harrisburg Craftsmen (pres, 70, secy, 72, treas, 73); Doshi Ctr Contemp Art (bd dir, 82-86). *Media:* Sterling Silver

WALKER, MELANIE
PHOTOGRAPHER
Study: San Francisco State Univ, BA, 72; Fla State Univ, MFA, 75. *Work:* Nat Endowment Arts, Washington, DC; Princeton Art Mus, NJ; Los Angeles Co Mus Art; San Francisco Mus Art; St Petersburg Mus Art, Fla; Chrysler Mus Art, Norfolk, Va; Polaroid Corp, Cambridge, Mass. *Exhib:* One person exhibitions, Lightwork Gallery, Syracuse Univ, NY, 78 & 88, Intersection for the Arts, San Francisco, 91, Rhode Island Sch Design, Providence, 92, Myopic Mythologies, Griffin Fine Arts, Costa Mesa, Calif, 95 & Personifications, Mus Art, Univ Ore, Eugene, 96; Hiroshima: From Me to You, Fukuya Gallery, Hiroshima, Japan, 95; Codpiece Project, Griffin Linton Contemp Exhibitions, Venice, Calif, 96; Electronic Mail, Anderson Ranch, Aspen, Colo, 96; Light Abberations, Univ Tex at San Antonio Art Gallery, 96; Group Hanging, Griffin-Linton Gallery, Costa Mesa, Calif, 96. *Teaching:* Asst prof, State Univ NY, Albany, 75-78, NY Col Ceramics at Alfred Univ, 86-88, Univ Ky, Lexington, 90-92 & Univ Colo, Boulder, 92-; lectr & vis artist, San Francisco State Univ, 78-86 & 88-90. *Awards:* GCAH Grant, Univ Colo, Boulder, 94; Photog fel, Nat Endowment Arts, 95; Colo Coun Arts CoVisions fel, 96. *Bibliog:* Henry Horenstein (auth), The Photography Source Book, Cambridge, Mass, 89; Leah Ollman (auth, review), Los Angeles Times San Diego Edition, 9/91; David Pincus (auth, review), San Diego Union. *Publ:* Auth, History of Photography Coloring Book, Thumbprint Press, 74; BEO, Senoj, 78. *Mailing Add:* Univ Colo Campus Box 318 Boulder CO 80309

WALKER, MORT
CARTOONIST
b El Dorado, Kans, Sept 3, 23. *Study:* Univ Mo, BA; Wm Penn Col, Hon LLD, 81. *Work:* Bird Libr, Syracuse Univ; Boston Univ Libr; Kans State Univ; Montreal Humor Pavilion; Smithsonian Inst; Int Mus Cartoon Art; and others. *Exhib:* Metrop Mus Art, NY, 52; Brussels Worlds Fair, 64; Mus Louvre, Paris, 65; NY Worlds Fair, 67; Expo, Montreal, 69; Int Mus Cartoon Art, 2000. *Pos:* Creator of Beetle Bailey, King Features Syndicate, 50-, Hi & Lois, 54-, Sam's Strip, 61-63, Boner's Ark, 68-, Sam & Silo, 77, The Evermores, 82 & Gamin and Patches, 87; chmn, Int Mus Cartoon Art, New York, NY, currently; pres, Comicana Corp, currently. *Teaching:* Scholar-in-Residence, Univ Mo, 92. *Awards:* Inkpot Award, 79; Wordsmith Award, 90; Gold T-Square Award, Nat Cartoonists Soc, Lifetime Achievement, 99; and others. *Mem:* Nat Cartoonists Soc (pres, 60); Newspaper Features Coun; Artists & Writers Asn (pres, 96-); Cartoonists Guild; Soc of Illustr. *Media:* Ink. *Publ:* Ed, Nat Cartoonists Soc Album, 61, 65 & 72; auth, Most, 71; Land of Lost Things, 72; auth & illusr, Backstage at the Strips, 76, Lexicon of Comicana, 81 & Best of Beetle Baily, 84; The Coconut Crew, 96; ed, Inklings Magazine; and others. *Mailing Add:* 61 Studio Rd Stamford CT 06903

WALKER, RONALD C
ARTIST
b Oxnard, Calif, Sept 3, 58. *Study:* Ctrl Mo State Univ, MA; Univ Kans, MFA; studied with Gerdkoch Margaret Peterson. *Exhib:* 12 Batavian Int Exhib, Richmond Meml Libr, Batavia, NY, 2001; 6th Nat, cincinnati Art Club, Cincinnati, 2001; Sanchez Art Center, Pacifica, Calif, 2004; Brown & Scurlag Galleries, Beaumont, Tex, 2004; Upstream People Gallery, Omaha, Nebr, 2005; Invitational Salon Exhib Small Works, New Arts Prog, Kutztown, Pa, 2006; Santa Cruz Art League, Santa Cruz, Calif, 2006. *Collection Arranged:* Cent Mo State Univ, Warrensburg; Art City Gallery, Ventura, Calif; Learning Tree Univ, Thousand Oaks, Calif. *Teaching:* Art Instr, Tacoma Com Coll, Gig Harbor, Calfi, 93-95; Art Instr, San Juan Sch Dist, 95-. *Awards:* Honorable Mention, 9th Internat Expo, Larado Ctr for the Arts, TX, 01; Second Place, Internat Juried Competition, Pindar Gallery, NY, 92; Hon Mention, Roseville Nat Open Expo, Calif, 04. *Bibliog:* Leo Smith (auth), Lighter Side of Art, Los Angeles Times, 1992. *Mem:* Calif Art Edn Asn; Nothern Calif Artist Inc. *Media:* Gouache, acrylic. *Publ:* Lisa McKinnon, Deciphering Methods, Press Courier, 92; Leo Smith, No Drawbacks, Los Angeles Times, 92. *Dealer:* Samantha Ridgeway Fine Art in Vegas Las Vegas NV. *Mailing Add:* Smiling Carrot Gallery 9413 Bullion Way Orangevale CA 95662

WALKER, SANDRA RADCLIFFE
PAINTER
b Milton, Pa, Aug 25, 37. *Work:* Conv Ctr, Nat League of Cities & Nat Geographic Hg, Washington, DC; US Mint; Feren Mus, Hall, United Kingdom; Wall Street Journal. *Comn:* Design, Simon Weisenthal Congressional Medal, 80; pvt comn, painting & prints of Houses of Parliament, comn by Lady Margaret Thatcher, London, Gt Brit. *Exhib:* Biennial, Corcoran Gallery Art, Washington, DC, 74 & 81; Va Mus Biennial, Richmond, 79; Duncan Miller Fine Arts, London, 90; Pierre Cardin Gallery, Paris, 92; Royal Watercolour Soc, London, 89-96; Galerie Atelier Mensch, Hamburg, Ger, 94; Royal Soc Brit Artists, London, 94. *Awards:* Best British Watercolour, Singer & Friedlander & London Times, 89; Salon Ind de la Peniture L'Eau-Grand Prix, Tregastel, France, 91; Royal Watercolour Soc Daler Rowner Award, London, 93. *Bibliog:* The Watercolor Page-Sandra Walker, Am Artist, 2/77; Art that catches the English heart, London Sunday Times, 89; Coming to America, US Art, 3/92. *Mem:* Nat Watercolor Soc; Washington Watercolor Soc. *Media:* Watercolor. *Publ:* Hazel Harrison (auth), Painting Shapes and Edges, Sandstone Books, 8/96; Hazel Harrison (auth), Watercolour Step by Step, Harper Collins, UK, 8/93; Hazel Harrison (auth), Encyclopedia of Watercolour Techniques, Headline Press, 90; Martin Davidson (auth), How to Draw and Paint Texture, Harper Collins, London, 93; Ian Simpson (auth), Collins Complete Painting Course, Harper Collins, London, 93. *Dealer:* Alresford Gallery Winchester UK. *Mailing Add:* 26A The Square Winchester S023 9EX United Kingdom

WALKER, SHARYNE ELAINE
PAINTER, SCULPTOR
b Vallejo, Calif, Sept 3, 49. *Study:* Self-educated. *Exhib:* Reve D'Artistes 90, Salon du Vieux Colombier Mus, Paris, 90; L'aura des Createurs, Chapelle de la Sorbonne Mus, Paris, 90; Women Artists of the West 1st Int, LJ Williams Theater Conv Ctr, Visala, Calif, 90; 17th Ann Non-Members Exhib, Salmagundi Club, 94; USA 1st Int, Nat Acrylic Painters Asn, 96; Seaside Gallery Int Christian Art Show, NC, 2000; 4th Nat Miniature & Small Works Show, Sulphur Springs Valley, Ariz, 2000; Int Miniature Art Exhib, Placerville, Calif, 2002; Art of Imagination, Cork Street Gallery, London, 2003; Brave Destiny, Kirkcudbright, Scotland, 2003; Williamsburg Art Center Mus, 2003; Diego Victorio Gallery, Miami, Fla, 2004. *Teaching:* private classes. *Awards:* Francesca Amato Kaulum Award, LRC Gallery, 89; City of Paris Laureat, Exposition Int d'Arts Plastiques, 90; Dorothy Roatz Myers Award, Salmagundi Club 17th Ann Non-Members Exhib, 94; Artists Mag Award, NAPA-USA 1st Int, 96. *Mem:* Signature mem NAPA; Soc Art Imagination. *Media:* Acrylic; Paperclay, Resins. *Publ:* Contribr, The Calif Art Review, 2nd ed, Am References Pub, 89; Le Petit Bleu, 10/90; Manhattan Arts, Renee Phillips, 90; The Best of Portrait Painting, Northlight Bks, 98; The Kali Guide, Zenprint, 2002; The Clay Palm Review, 2000 & 2001. *Mailing Add:* 2575 S Willow Ave #14 Fresno CA 93725

WALKER, STEVEN EDMUND
PRINTMAKER, PAINTER
b Brooklyn, NY, Mar 1, 55. *Study:* Wagner Col, New York, BA, 1978; Arts Students League of NY study under R Goetz & M Pellettieri - 1983-; Hunter Col, NY - 1998-2000; Landscape Workshop with Wolf Kahn -2000. *Work:* Housatonic Mus Art, Bridgeport, Conn; New York Hist Soc; Mus of City of New York; New York Public Library; Art Students League of NY; Brooklyn Mus, New York; John A Noble, Maritime Collection. *Comn:* paintings for pvt clients. *Exhib:* New York by New Yorkers, Mus of City of NY, 2002; 89th Annual Juried Exhib, Allied Artists of Am, New York City, 2002; Transit Views, NY Transit Mus Grand Cent Station, New York City, 2003; Trace 2003 Marie de 4ce, L'Hotel de Ville, Paris, France, 2003; Impressions of New York, NY Historical Soc, 2004; Hecho en New York, Instituto Cult Peruano N Americano, Lima Peru, 2005; Innovations in Contemp Printmaking, Housatonic Mus, Bridgeport, Conn, 2005; Tidelines, John A Noble Maritime Coll, Snug Harbor, Staten Is, NY, 2006. *Pos:* graphic artist, CVS Graphics Inc, New York City, 1987-2000; art handler/matter, The Old Print Shop, New York City, 2004-; designer, Random House Inc, New York City, 2005-. *Teaching:* instr drawing & painting, Forest Hills High Sch Adult Ctr, NY, 2002-; instr drawing, painting, design & color, Wagner Col, Staten Island, NY, 2003-; private drawing instr, currently. *Awards:* Tilden Award, 22nd Student Exhib, Nat Arts Club, New York City, 1997; Best in Show, Millburn (NJ) Outdoor Art Show, Chamber Commerce, 2005; First Prize (graphics), Wash Sq Outdoor Art Show, WSOAE Comt, New York City, 2005. *Bibliog:* Helen A Harrison (auth), Winners Circle Review, The New York Times, 1/20/2002; Bernard Rittersporn (auth), New York by New Yorkers, Journal of the Print World, spring 2002 & summer 2006; Marilyn Symmes (auth), Impressions of New York, Princeton Archt Press, NY, 2005. *Mem:* Soc of Am Graphic Artists; NY Soc of Etchers (bd mem 2004-); life mem Art Students League of NY. *Media:* Etching, Lithography, Oil, Woodcut. *Publ:* auth, It's Beyond Me, LINEA, Art Students League of NY, 2001; auth, Transit Views (catalog) & The Evocative Power of the Railroad, NY Soc of Etchers, 2003. *Dealer:* The Old Print Shop Inc 150 Lexington Ave New York NY 10016; Gallery of Graphic Arts 1601 York Ave New York NY 10028. *Mailing Add:* 34-50 30th St #1F Long Island City NY 11106

WALKER, WILLIAM BOND
PAINTER, LIBRARIAN
b Brownsville, Tenn, 30. *Study:* Bisttram Sch Fine Art, Taos, NMex & Los Angeles, with Emil Bisttram, 48-49; Univ Iowa, Iowa City, with Mauricio Lasansky, Howard Warshaw, James Lechay & Stuart Edie, BA, 53; Rutgers Univ Grad Sch Libr Serv, MSLS, 58. *Work:* ABC-TV, NY; Heller Ehrman LLP, Washington, DC. *Exhib:* Retrospective Exhib, Truffles & Such, Pittsfield, Mass, 96-97; solo exhibs, Chatham, NY, 97, 98, 2000 & 2005, Hudson, NY, 98, Old Chatham, NY, 2000-, Becket, Mass, 2002, Rochester, NY, 2003; group shows, Hudson, NY, 97, 2000, 2001, 2002, 2003 & 2004, Pittsfield, Mass, 97, 2001, Spencertown, NY, 97, 98, 2000, Canaan, NY, 98, 99 & West Stockbridge, Mass, 2000, New Lebanon, NY, 2001. *Pos:* Cataloger & reference librn, Libr Metrop Mus Art, New York, 57-59; chief librn, Art Reference Libr, Brooklyn Mus, 59-64, Libr Nat Collection Fine Arts & Nat Portrait Gallery, Smithsonian Inst, 64-80 & Thomas J Watson Libr, Metrop Mus Art, New York, 80-94; retired, 94. *Teaching:* Art bibliog, Columbia Univ, Sch Libr Serv, 87-88. *Awards:* Distinguished Serv Award, Art Libr Soc NAm, 91. *Mem:* Am Libr Asn; Art Libr Soc NAm (pres, 75). *Media:* Acrylic; Casein. *Interests:* Twentieth century American prints and twentieth century painting. *Publ:* Bibliography on American Sculpture, Eighteenth to Twentieth Century, Washington, Smithsonian Inst Press, 80. *Dealer:* Carrie Haddad, 622 Warren St, Hudson, NY 12534. *Mailing Add:* PO Box 237 Canaan NY 12029

WALKINGSTICK, KAY
PAINTER, GRAPHIC ARTIST
b Syracuse, NY, Mar 2, 35. *Study:* Beaver Col, Glenside, Pa, BFA, 59; Pratt Inst, Brooklyn, MFA, 75. *Work:* Metrop Mus Art, NYk; Albright-Knox Art Gallery, Buffalo, NY; Nat Gallery Can, Ottawa; Israel Mus, Jerusalem; Herbert F Johnson Mus, Cornell Univ; many others. *Comn:* A Retrospective, comn by Hillwood Gallery, Univ Long Island, Greenvale, NY, 91; print, Krege Art Mus, East Lansing, Mich, 98. *Exhib:* Solo shows, Wenger Gallery, Los Angeles, 84 & 88, M-13 Gallery, NY, 87 & 90, Heard Mus, Phoenix, Ariz, 92, Calumet Gallery, Heidelberg, Ger, 93, June Kelly Gallery, NY, 94, 99 & Atlantic Ctr Arts, New Smyrna Beach, 95; Am Acad Arts & Letts, NY, 87 & 88; Decade Show, New Mus, 90; Land Spirit Power, Nat Gallery Can, 92; Cairo Biennial, 95; Rose Art Mus, Boston, 96; Kendall Campus Gallery, Miami Univ, 99. *Pos:* Gallery dir, William Ctr Arts, Rutherford, NJ, 86 & 88. *Teaching:* Instr painting & drawing, Upsala Col, East Orange, NY, 75-79; artist-in-residence, Ft Lewis Col, Durango, Colo, 84 & Ohio State Univ, Columbus, 85; assoc prof art, Cornell Univ, Ithaca, NY, 88-90; asst prof art, State Univ NY, Stony Brook, 90, prof, 92-. *Awards:* NJ Coun Arts Fel, 81-82, 85 & 86; Nat Endowment Arts Grant, 83; Joan Mitchell Fel, painting, 96; and others. *Bibliog:* David Penney (auth), History of American Indian Art, 94 & Native American Art Masterpieces, 96; Anthony Janson (auth), Janson's History of Art, 5th ed, Abrams Publ, 95, rev ed, Prentiss Hall Publ, 97. *Mem:* Cherokee Nation, Okla. *Media:* Oil; Wax, Charcoal. *Dealer:* June Kelly Gallery 591 Broadway New York NY; Jan Cicero Gallery Chicago IL

WALL, BRIAN
SCULPTOR
b London, Eng, Sept 5, 31; US citizen. *Work:* Tate Gallery, London; Nat Gallery, Dublin; Art Gallery NSW, Sidney; Oakland Mus; Univ Art Mus, Berkeley; Seattle Art Mus; Sheldon Mem Art Gallery, Univ Nebr. *Comn:* Thornaby (sculpture), New Town Ctr, Thornaby, Eng, 68; Ali (sculpture), Univ Houston, Tex, 78. *Exhib:* 2nd Paris Biennale, Mus Mod Art, 61; Sculpture of the Sixties, Tate Gallery, 65; one-man shows, Seattle Art Mus, 82, San Francisco Mus Mod Art, 83, Jon Berggruen Gallery, San Francisco, 83, Simon Lowinsky Gallery, NY, 87 & 98, Francis Graham-Dixon Gallery, London, 92, Sheldon Mem Art Gallery & Sculpture Garden, Univ Nebr, 95 & Jernigan Wicker Fine Art, San Francisco, 95; St Ives 1939-64, Tate Gallery, London, 85; The Mansion House, Ilkley, Eng, 94; Sixteen California Artists, Galerie Sho, Tokyo, 94; Iris Gallery, Eng, 95; Flowers East, London, 95 & 96. *Teaching:* Chmn sculpture dept, Cent Sch Art & Design, London, 64-72; prof sculpture, Univ Calif, Berkeley, formerly, emer prof, currently. *Bibliog:* Charles Spencer (auth), Brian Wall, sculptor of simplicity, Studio Int, 3/66; G S Whittet (auth), Question and artist: Brian Wall, Sculpture Int, 10/69; Hilton Kramer (auth), article, 5/13/77 & John Russell (auth), articles, 1/79 & 4/24/81, New York Times. *Mem:* Int Sculpture Ctr, Washington, DC. *Media:* Steel. *Dealer:* Flowers Gallery, 1000 Madison Ave, New York, NY. *Mailing Add:* 306 Lombard St San Francisco CA 94133

WALL, BRUCE C
PAINTER, INSTRUCTOR
b Dallas, Tex, Feb 14, 54. *Study:* Univ Tex, Austin, BFA(with honors); RI Sch Design, Providence, RI, MFA; Fulbright-Hayes Grant, India, 79-80. *Work:* Aldrich Mus Contemp Art, Ridgefield, Conn; Best Products Corp, Richmond, Va; City Col, City Univ New York; Zale Products Corp, Dallas; Frederick R Weisman Found Art, Los Angeles, Calif. *Exhib:* New York City New Work, Del Art Mus, Wilmington; East Village Artists, Va Mus Fine Art, Richmond; East Village Galleries, Saidyre Bronfman, Montreal, Can; Selection from Weisman Collection, Utah Mus Fine Arts, Salt Lake City; The Art of the 70s & 80s, Aldrich Mus Contemp Art, Ridgefield, Conn; This Way/This Way, Thorpe Intermedia Ctr, Sparkhill, NY; Cross Currents,

Sande Webster Gallery, Philadelphia, Pa; Art & Ego, NY Acad Art, NY. *Teaching:* Adj prof art, painting, drawing, design & art hist, Northampton Community Col, Bethlehem, Pa, 93-. *Bibliog:* John Howell (auth), Bruce Wall, Artforum, 11/85; Holland Cotter (auth), Bruce Wall, Arts Mag, 9/85; Yivian Raynor (auth), Bruce Wall, NY Times, 5/86. *Mem:* Col Art Asn. *Media:* All Media. *Mailing Add:* 509 Mixsell St Easton PA 18042-1611

WALL, RALPH ALAN
PAINTER
b Hobart, Ind, Aug 1, 32. *Study:* Studied with Tom Lovell. *Work:* Bimson Collection, Valley Nat Bank, Phoenix, Ariz; Fidelity Bank Collection, Oklahoma City; Mountain Oyster Club, Tucson, Ariz; Goddard Ctr, Performing & Visual Arts, Ardmore, Okla; Frost Bank, San Antonio; Leanin Tree Mus, Boulder, Colo. *Comn:* Southland Corp, Dallas; and others. *Exhib:* One-man shows, Goddard Ctr, Ardmore, Okla & Ponca City Art Ctr, Okla, 72; Mus of the SW, Midland, Tex, 76; O S Ranch Show, Post, Tex, 79 & 81; Western Heritage Horse, Cattle & Art Auction, Houston, Tex, 79; Zuni Gallery, Dusseldorf, WGer, 87; Marshall, Gonzalez & Carlson, Houston, Tex, 91. *Pos:* Dir, Spirit of 76, Hist Orgn. *Awards:* Am Inst Graphic Art Award (packaging), 67; Gold Medal, 1974 Portfolio Western Art, Franklin Mint, 74; Gold Award, Texas Ranger Hall of Fame, 79; Purchase Award, Okla City Art Festival, 83. *Bibliog:* Freddie Steve (auth), Franklin Mint paint, Paint Horse J, 11/74; Susan Hallsten McGarry (auth), This life is but a shadow, Southwest Art Mag, 10/81; Gretchen Schmitz (auth), The artist, Ralph Wall, Prints Mag, 7-8/82. *Mem:* Hon mem Mountain Oyster Club, Tucson. *Media:* Multimedia. *Publ:* Illusr, American Horseman, 9/73, Paint Horse J (cover), 1/75 & 11/75; Okla Today, summer 76 & spring 79; Leanin Tree Greeting Card Series, 77, 78 & 82; Dean Krakel's Adventures in Western Art, 77; Quarterhorse J (cover), 1/80. *Dealer:* Guildhall Inc 3507 NW Loop 820 Ft Worth TX 76107. *Mailing Add:* 1540 Riada Dr New Braunfels TX 78132-3276

WALL, RHONDA
PAINTER, INSTRUCTOR
b Boston, Mass, Jan 26, 56. *Study:* RI Sch Design, BFA, 78; Vt Col, Montpelier, MFA, 95. *Work:* Aldrich Mus Contemp Art, Ridgefield, Conn; City Col, Univ NY & Needham Harper Steers, NY. *Exhib:* UFO Show, Queens Mus, NY, 82; solo exhibs, Beulah Gallery, 84, Limbo Gallery, 84, Sensory Evolution Gallery, 84 & B Side Gallery, 85, NY; Art & Ego, NY Acad Art, NY, 84; Art of the 70's and 80's, Aldrich Mus Contemp Art, Ridgefield, Conn, 85; USA and then India, Lehigh Univ, Bethlehem, Pa, 96; Life Is a Dada Fashion Show at the Bauhaus, Cedar Crest Col, Allentown, Pa, 96; Mind and Machine, Allentown Art Mus, 99. *Teaching:* Instr painting, RI Sch Design, 90-92; instr painting, design & art hist, Northampton Community Col, Bethlehem, Pa, 96-; asst prof, 2D & 3D Design, Kutztown Univ, Pa, 97-2001. *Bibliog:* Mark Frisk (auth), Rhonda Wall (essay), Arts Mag, 1/85; Ken Sofer (auth), Present pop, Art News, 5/85; Vivian Raynor (auth), This way, this way, NY Times, 11/10/85. *Mem:* Col Art Asn. *Media:* All Media. *Mailing Add:* 509 Mixsell St Easton PA 18042

WALL, SUE
PAINTER, PRINTMAKER
b Cleveland, Ohio, Feb 18, 50. *Study:* Ohio Univ, BFA, 72, MFA, 74. *Hon Degrees:* hon degree Cleveland Institute Art, 1990. *Work:* Cleveland Mus Art; Canton Art Inst Mus, Ohio; Butler Inst Am Art, Youngstown, Ohio; Zanesville Art Ctr, Ohio; Kennedy Mus Am Art; The Hague, The Netherlands; Univ Iowa Mus Art; Ohio Nat Plaza Co Collection; Kenneth Beck Ctr for Cult Arts; Trisolini Gallery; Marie Selby Botanical Gardens Collection; Southwest Mus; George Streeter Circulating Collection; Nat Arts Club; Aurora Nat Bank Collection; Mondak Heritage Ctr; Richard Brown Baker Collection; Yale Univ Art Collection; Philip Desind Collection; The Zanger Collection. *Exhib:* One-person shows, Gallery Madison 90, NY, 74, 76, 78, 80, 82, 84, 86, 88, 90 & 92, Zanesville Art Ctr, Ohio, 75, 86, 89 & 95, Strong's Gallery, Cleveland, 75, 77 & 79, Canton Art Inst, Ohio, 76, Gallery 200, Columbus, 75, 77, 84 & 86, Piccolo Mondo, Palm Beach, Fla, 76 & 78, Bonfoey's, Cleveland, 75, 77, 79, 81, 83, 85, 87, 89 & 91, Foster Harmon Gallery, Sarasota, Fla, 82, 84, 86, 89, 91 & 93, First Church Gallery, Springfield, Mass, 98, Cleveland Botanical Garden, Ohio, 99, Mondak Historical and Art Soc, Sidney, Mont, 99; Butler Ann Mid-Year Show, Youngstown, Ohio, 75-77; Sandusky Cult Ctr, Ohio, 78, 90 & 93; Holden Arboretum, 93, 97, 2000, 2004; Uptown Gallery, NY, 95, 2005; Loring Gallery, Sheffield, Mass, 94 & 95; Ziegonfuss Gallery, Sarasota, Fla, 95; Cleveland Inst Art, Ohio, 95; Capricorn Galleries, Bethesda, Md, 97; Gallery E, E Hampton, NY, 97; SW Mus, Los Angeles, Calif, 98; First Church Gallery, Springfield, Mass, 98; Gallery One, Mentor, Ohio, 2001; Cleveland Ctr for Information and Technolocy, 2003. *Awards:* Nat Acad, 150th Annual Exhib, SJ Wallace Truman Award, NY, 75; 1st place, painting, Zanesville Arts Ctr, Zanesville, Ohio, 97; Spec Mention Award, Jane Law's Long Beach Island Galley Miniature Exhib, Surf City, NJ, 2004. *Bibliog:* Am Artist, Watercolor Mag, 2002; Artists and Graphic Designer's Market, 98; American Artist, Watercolor Magazine, 2002. *Mem:* New Orgn Visual Arts; Audubon Artists; Nat Soc Painters Casein & Acrylic; Miniature Art Soc NJ; Allied Artists Am Inc; Catherine Lorillard Wolfe Art Club; Nat Hist Preservation; Knickerbocker Artists; Am Artistists Professional League; Am Craft Coun; Miniature Painters, Sculptors, & Gravers; Soc Washington, DC; Miniature Soc Fla; Garrison Art Ctr; Cider Painters Am. *Media:* Acrylic on board. *Interests:* dancing; music; opera; theater; travel. *Publ:* Contribr, New York Art Rev. *Dealer:* The Uptown Gallery 1194 Madison Ave New York NY 10023; Gallery One Mentor Ohio. *Mailing Add:* 11 Riverside Dr Suite 8JE New York NY 10023-2304

WALLACE, CAROL ANN (BRUCKER)
PAINTER, ILLUSTRATOR
b Doylestown, PA, Aug 2, 44. *Work:* Posters & note cards (collected for research & educ purposes) Nat Mus of Am, Smithsonian Inst, Washington, DC, 1997-2006; Country Stores of Vermont & Historic Bucks Co (posters), Libr of Cong, Washington, DC; US Coast Guard Permanent Traveling Art Collection, Washington, DC; Rhinestone Prancers, New England Carousel Mus, Bristol, Conn; Angel Delgadillo Hist Route 66, Barbershop Mus, Seligman. Ariz. *Comn:* Eight drawings & paintings, James Biddle (past pres Nat Trust for Hist Preserv), Andalusia, Pa, 1997; The Library Collection (watercolor painting), Univ of Conn, 1998; pen & ink drawings (20), Adirondack Mus, Blue Mountain Lake, NY, 1999; Ellis Island (painting), Statue of Liberty, Ellis Island Found, NY, 2001; Nat World War II Mem (pen & ink drawing & watercolor painting), Am Battle Monuments Comn, Washington, DC, 2004. *Pos:* founder & adminr, Preserve America; exec producer, Better Yet Connecticut; gubernatoral appointment, Conn Gov William O'Neill, Vacation & Travel Council, 83-85; freelance artist, 83-. *Awards:* Conn Tourism Award, 82; US Coast Guard Serv Award, 2002; Best NY Artists, Kennedy Promotions, 2005; Best Am Watercolor Artists, Kennedy Promotions, 2006. *Bibliog:* Rosemary Jette (auth), From Barns to Barbershops, History in a Small Format, NY Times, 2000; Pamela Graves (auth), Class of 2003, Giftware News, 2003; Pamela Bellows (auth) Carol Wallace on the Move, Pen Women Mag, 2006. *Mem:* Salmagundi Art Club (elected mem); Nat League of Am Pen Women (elected mem); Am Watercolor Soc (assoc mem); Nat Watercolor Soc (assoc mem). *Media:* Watercolor, Acrylic, Pen & Ink. *Res:* Independent research & extensive travels across America for Preserve America, 2000-2006. *Publ:* Illusr, Litchfield Co Times, 1984-1990; illusr, Litchfield Hills Touring Guides, Litchfield Hills Visitors & Conv Bur, 84-2006; illusr, The History of Pierce Pond, Knowlton & McLeary, 1992; contribr, The Artistic Touch 3, Creative Art Press, 1999; illusr (cover of sheet music), Cape May Preludes, SDG Press, 1999. *Dealer:* Umbrella Arts 317 E 9th St New York NY 10003. *Mailing Add:* 48 W West Hill Rd Barkhamsted CT 06063

WALLACE, GAEL LYNN
PAINTER
b Ft Worth, Tex, Aug 5, 41. *Study:* Okla State Univ, with Dale McKinney & David Allende, BA, 64; independent study with Don Fusco & Tom Owen. *Comn:* Old west storefront murals, Graden Elementary Sch, Kansas City, Mo, 78. *Exhib:* 60th Ann Nat Watercolor Soc, Laguna Beach Mus Art, Calif, 80 & 82; Rocky Mountain Nat Aquamedia, 82; Colorado 83 Biennial, Colo Springs Fine Art Mus, 83; San Diego Watercolor Soc Int Exhib, 85; State Watermedia Exhib, Colo Watercolor Soc, 93; Pike's Peak Watercolor Soc Invitational, 94; Contemp Art Exhib, Colo, 98. *Awards:* Purchase Awards, Nat Watercolor Soc, 80 & Glenwood Springs Fall Art Festival, Colo, 85; Honorable Mention, Colo State Fair, 80 & San Diego Watercolor Soc Int Exhib, 86. *Bibliog:* Diane Wengler (auth), The beauty of nature, Gazette Telegraph, 12/13/80. *Mem:* Nat Watercolor Soc. *Media:* Acrylic. *Mailing Add:* 23 Kris Ln Manitou Springs CO 80829

WALLACE, JOHN
PAINTER
b St Louis, Mo, Dec 29, 29. *Study:* Washington Univ, with Paul Burlin & Carl Holty, BFA, 53; Ind Univ, with Alton Pickens, MFA, 57: Skowhegan Sch Painting & Sculpture, with Henry Varnum Poor, 53. *Work:* St Louis Art Mus; Detroit Inst Arts; Roswell Mus, NMex. *Comn:* Fresco mural, South Solon Meeting House, Maine, 54; bronze sculpture panel, Aquatic House, St Louis Zool Gardens, 59. *Exhib:* 101st Am Painting Ann, Pa Acad Fine Arts, 52; 7th Ann Nat Print Exhib, Brooklyn Mus, 53; one-man shows, artist-in-residence exhib, Roswell Mus, NMex, 68, Green Mountain Gallery, NY, 79 & Blue Mountain Gallery, NY, 93, 95, 98 & 2000, 2003; Bertrand Russell Centenary, Nottingham, Eng, 73; Provincetown Art Asn, 78 & 86; The Figure in the Landscape, Artists' Choice Mus, NY, 85; Fresco: A Contemp Perspective, Snug Harbor, Newhouse Ctr Contemp Art, Staten Island, NY 93; plus many others. *Pos:* Co-ed, New Art Asn Newslett, 71; co-chmn, New directions in studio teaching, Col Art Asn Ann Meeting, 71. *Teaching:* Prof painting & drawing, Prairie State Col, Chicago Heights, Ill, 68-79 & chmn art dept, 71-74; vis artist, Truro Ctr Arts, 76-80, Silvermine Guild Art, 82, Stamford Mus, 82; prof painting & drawing, Western Conn State Univ, 81- & chmn art dept, 87-91; Co-Coord of Master of Fine Arts Degree Program in Painting, 2000-. *Awards:* Margaret Tiffany Blake Mural Fel, Skowhegan Sch, 54; Huntington Hartford Found Fel, 60; Artist-in-Residence Grant, Roswell Mus, 68. *Bibliog:* Mildred H Cummings (auth), South Solon; The Story of a Meeting House, 59; Helen Thomas (auth), article, Arts Mag, 5/79; Robert Bunkin (auth), Fresco: A Contemporary Perspective, 93; Richard Whelan (auth), The Sun, the Moon and the Stars, First Glance Bks, 98. *Mem:* Col Art Asn. *Media:* All Media. *Publ:* Auth, Fresco Workshop, Yankee Mag, 7/77; Art education: A consumer's viewpoint, Art Worker's News, 82. *Dealer:* Blue Mountain Gallery 530 W 25th St 4th Flr NEw York NY 10001. *Mailing Add:* PO Box 231 Washington Depot CT 06794

WALLACE, KENNETH WILLIAM
PAINTER, EDUCATOR
b Penticton, BC, July 7, 45. *Study:* Calgary Col Art, Alta, cert, 71; Vancouver Sch Art, BC, cert, 73; Banff Sch Fine Arts, 73. *Work:* Nat Art Gallery, Ottawa; Art Gallery Ont, Toronto; Vancouver Art Gallery, BC; Winnipeg Art Gallery, Man; Burnaby Art Gallery, BC. *Exhib:* One-man shows, Alternate Space, Vancouver Art Gallery, 74, Burnaby Art Gallery, BC, 80, Lefebvre Gallery, Edmonton, Alta, 81, Robert Lawrence Int, Bellingham, Wash, 82, Teck Gallery, Simon Fraser Univ, Bau-Xi Gallery, Vancouver, BC, 92; Pac Northwest Ann, Seattle, Wash, 73; Current Energies, Saydie Bronfman Arts Centre, Montreal, Que, 74-75; Three Directions in Painting, Fine Arts Gallery, Univ BC, Vancouver, 75; Canadian Canvas, Time Exhib, 11 maj Can cities, 76; New Abstract Art in Am, Edmonton Art Gallery, Alta, 77; Affinities, 79,

Vancouver Art & Artists, 1931-83, 83, Painted Gardens, Atilier Gallery, Vancouver, BC, 92; Canadian Painters, Can House, London, Eng, 79; Bienal De Arte Medellin, Columbia, SAm, 81; Current Concerns, Sarnia Art Gallery, Ont, 81; Living Nature 1987, Nat Mus Natural Sci, Ottawa, Ont, 87; Bau Xi Gallery, Vancouver, BC, 92, Image/ Mirage, Bau XI Gallery, Vancouver, BC, 2000; Wetlands Reclaimation BauXi Gallery, Vancouver BC, 2001; BauXI Gallery, Toronto, Ont, 2002; Kimzeymillar Gallery, Seattle WA, USA, 2002; Aqua Illumine Bau-XI Gallery, Vancouver, BC, 2003; Agnes Bugera Gallery, Edmonton, AB, 2003; Aqua Sanctum, Bau-XI Gallery, Vancouver, BC, 2005; Faculty Exhib, Concourse Gallery, Emily Carr, Institute of Art and Design Toronto Air Fair, Toronto, Ont, 2004; Northwest Landscapes Kimzey Miller Gallery, Seattle, WA, 2005. *Collection Arranged:* Images of Women (auth, catalog), Winnipeg Art Gallery, 75; Canadian Painters in Watercolor (auth, catalog), Glenbow Inst, Alta, 76; Olympic Exhibition of British Columbian Artists (auth, catalog), Montreal, Que, 76; West Coast on Canvas (auth, catalog), Birmingham Art Gallery, Ala, 79. *Teaching:* Instr painting & drawing, Univ BC, 76-78, instr painting, Dept Fine Arts, 77-80, Emily Carr Inst Art & Design, 80-2005 assoc Prof. *Awards:* Int Critics Award, Annecy Film Festival, France, 75; Can Coun Art Awards, 75-79. *Bibliog:* Mary Fox (auth), Images from the inside outside, Western Living, 76; Pat Fleisher (auth), interview in Arts Mag, Toronto, Ont, 76; Karen Wilken (auth), Vancouver scene, Art News, New York, 79. *Media:* Painting, Acrylic, Oil. *Mailing Add:* 125 N Slocan St Vancouver BC V5K 3M3 Canada

WALLACE, PATTY A
PAINTER, PHOTOGRAPHER
Study: Ctr Media Study, State Univ NY, Buffalo, study with Paul Sharits, Tony Conrad, Ernie Gehr, Hollis Frampton & Jack Goldstein, MAH, 86. *Work:* Burchfield Ctr Buffalo, NY; Albright-Knox Gallery, Buffalo; Tenn Fine Art Gallery & Botanical Gardens, Cheekwood, Nashville; Castellani Art Mus, Lewiston. *Exhib:* 42nd Western NY Exhib, Albright-Knox Art Gallery, Buffalo, 88; Women Depict Men, Ward-Nasse Gallery, NY, 92; Other Color, 55 Mercer Gallery, NY, 93; Art Expo '93, Mus Fine Arts, Boston, 93; Women's Art, Womens Lives, Women's Issues, Tweed Gallery, NY, 93; NY, Andrea Pintsch Contemp Art, Munich, Ger, 96. *Pos:* Libr clerk, Albright-Knox Art Gallery, 85- & curatorial researcher, 88; mus technician, Brooklyn Mus, 88-; photogr, Andy Warhol Found, 92-95; residency, Light Works-Syracuse Univ, 95. *Teaching:* Instr digital art, Albright-Knox Art Gallery, Buffalo, 85-86, instr bookmaking & video, 86-88. *Awards:* Res Grant, State Univ NY, Buffalo, 85. *Bibliog:* Anthony Bannon (auth), Small photo shines forth, Buffalo News, 1/11/83; John F Swed (auth), Childhood's ends, Village Voice, New York, 2/25/85; Ron Netsky (auth), Transformations, Rochester Democrat & Chronicle, 6/18/85; Elizabeth Hess (auth), Presumed guilty, Village Voice, 9/27/88; Arlene Raven (auth), Suffer the little children, The Village Voice, 10/24/89; Richard Huntington (auth), Burchfield shows off its new works, GUSTO Buffalo News, 8/11/89; Vince Aletti (auth), Other Color, Village Voice, 8/24/93. *Media:* Paint, Photography. *Publ:* Contribr, The Imagemaker (by Anthony Bannon), AAO Gallery, Buffalo, 85

WALLACE, PAULA S
ADMINISTRATOR
Study: Furman Univ, BA; Georgia State Univ, MEd; Georgia State Univ, EdS. *Pos:* Co-found, Savannah Col Art and Design, 79, pres, 2000—. *Awards:* Recipient Oglethorpe Bus and Prof Women award, James T Deason Human Relations award; named Outstanding Young Woman of Am, Kentucky Colonel; named to Savannah Business Hall of Fame. *Bibliog:* Auth of children's books. *Mailing Add:* Savannah Coll Art and Design PO Box 3146 622 Drayton St Savannah GA 31402-3146

WALLACE, RICHARD WILLIAM
EDUCATOR, HISTORIAN
b Rochester, NY, Oct 4, 33. *Study:* Williams Col, BA, 55; Princeton Univ, MFA, 61, PhD, 64. *Teaching:* Instr art hist, Princeton Univ, 60-61; from asst prof to prof, Wellesley Col, 64-. *Awards:* Fulbright Fel, 62-64; Nat Endowment Arts Summer Stipend, 67; Am Coun Learned Soc Fel, 69. *Res:* Italian baroque art. *Publ:* Contribr, Salvator Rosa (exhib catalog), Arts Coun Gr Brit, 73; auth, The Etchings of Salvator Rosa, Princeton Press, 79; Salvator Rosa in America (exhib catalog), Wellesley Col, 79; contribr, The Illustrated Bartsch, Abaris Books, 82; Italian Etchers of the Renaissance and Baroque (exhib catalog, with Su Welsh Reed), Boston, Cleveland & Washington, DC, 89. *Mailing Add:* 27 Service Dr Wellesley MA 02181-7315

WALLACH, ALAN
CRITIC, HISTORIAN
b Brooklyn, NY, June 8, 42. *Study:* Columbia Col, BA, 63; Columbia Univ, PhD, 73. *Teaching:* Assoc prof art hist, Kean Col Union, NJ, 74-88; vis prof, Univ Calif, Los Angeles, 82-83, Stanford Univ, 86-87, Univ Mich, 89; Ralph H Wark prof art & art hist & Am studies, Col William & Mary, 89-. *Awards:* Smithsonian Sr Post-Doctoral Fel, 85-86. *Mem:* Col Art Asn Am; Am Studies Asn; Am Soc Aesthetics; Art Historians Asn (Gt Brit). *Res:* Nineteenth century American art; history of museums; criticism of 20th century art. *Publ:* Coauth, Thomas Cole: Landscape into History, Cyale, 94; auth, Exhibiting Contradiction: Essays on the Art Museum in the United States, Univ Mass Press, 98; numerous articles. *Mailing Add:* 2009 Belmont Rd NW Suite 203 Washington DC 20009

WALLER, AARON BRET
MUSEUM DIRECTOR, ART HISTORIAN
b Liberal, Kans, Dec 7, 35. *Study:* Univ Kans, Lawrence, 53-56; Kansas City Art Inst & Sch of Design, BFA, 57; Univ Kans, Lawrence, MFA, 58; Univ Oslo, Norway, Fulbright Grant, 63-64; Univ Kans, 64-67. *Collection Arranged:* School for Scandal: Thomas Rowlandson's London (co-auth, catalog), 67 & The Waning Middle Ages (ed, catalog), 69, Univ Kans; Images of Love & Death in Late Medieval and Renaissance Art (ed, catalog), 75, Works from the Collection of Dorothy & Herbert Vogel (auth, catalog), 77, & The Crisis of Impressionism/1878-1882 (co-auth, catalog), 80, Univ Mich; The Fine Art of Funiture Maker (co-auth, catalog), 81 & Artists of La Revue Blanche, (co-auth, catalog), 84, Mem Art Gallery, Univ Rochester; South Bend Mus, Ind; Tucson Mus; Indianapolis Mus of Art, Ind. *Pos:* Dir, Mus Art, Univ Kans, Lawrence, 64-71; head, Dept Pub Educ & Higher Educ, Metrop Mus Art, NY, 71-73; dir, Univ Mich, Mus Art, 73-80; dir, Mem Art Gallery, Rochester, NY, 80-85; chmn mus educ comt, Col Art Mus, 81-82; assoc dir educ & pub affairs, J Paul Getty Mus, Malibu, Calif, 85-90; dir, Indianapolis Mus Art, Ind, 90-2001, dir emer, 2001; trustee, Asn Art Mus Dirs, 92-95. *Teaching:* Asst prof art hist, Univ Kans, Lawrence, 64-71; vis asst prof, Dept Art, City Col, 71-73; assoc prof art hist, Sch Art & chmn grad prog mus practice, Univ Mich, Ann Arbor, 73-80; adj assoc prof fine arts, Col Arts & Scis, Univ Rochester, 80-85. *Awards:* Nat Endowment Arts Prof Develop Grant, Int Art Market, 80; NY Governor's Award, Mem Art Gallery, 85; Int Citizen of the Yr, Int Ctr, Indianapolis, Ind, 98. *Mem:* Intermus Conserv Lab (vpres, 76-77, pres, 77-78); Am Asn Mus Dirs (treas, 80-81); NY State Asn Mus; Col Art Asn; Asn Art Mus Dirs; Am Asn of Mus. *Res:* Graphic arts; 20th century art. *Publ:* Sowing the Dragon's Teeth, Bull, Mus Art & Archeol, Univ Mich, Vol III, 50-57, 80; Museums in the groves of academe, Mus News, 1-2/80; Contribr, Rouault's Abandonne: Transformations of an Image, Porticus, J Mem Art Gallery, Univ Rochester, 84; Auth, Aping their betters: art appreciation and social class, Penn State Univ, 10/89; Looking, but not seeing, J Mus Educ, spring 90. *Mailing Add:* 4035 N Pennsylvania St Indianapolis IN 46205

WALLER, SUSAN
GALLERY DIRECTOR, WRITER
b Newton, Mass, July 28, 48. *Study:* Brown Univ, BA, 70; Boston Univ, MA(art hist), 75. *Collection Arranged:* At Issue: Art and Advocacy, St Louis Gallery Art, 87; Artists' Books, Book Arts, 89, Swiss School: Late to Post Modern Graphic Design, Other Voices, Baxter Gallery, 91 & Imperiled Shores, 92, Baxter Gallery. *Pos:* Asst cur, Cranbrook Acad Art Mus, 81-84, cur, 84-86; asst dir, St Louis Gallery Contemp Art, 87-88; dir, Baxter Gallery, Maine Col Art. *Teaching:* Instr art hist, Ctr Creative Studies, 79-81 & Main Col Art, Maine, 89-. *Mem:* Col Art Asn; Am Asn Mus. *Publ:* Auth, The artist, the writer and the queen, Women's Art J, 83; Strong-minded critics, Women Artists News, 85; Michael Hall: reasoned to believe (exhib catalog), St Louis Gallery, 88; Robert Stackhouse: St Louis bones (exhib, catalog), Laumeier Sculpture, 88; ed, Women Artists in the Modern Era, Scarecrow, 91. *Mailing Add:* c/o Horizons Unlimited 1636 Parkview Cir Salisbury NC 28144-2461

WALLIN, LAWRENCE BIER
SCULPTOR, PAINTER
b Norwalk, Conn, Apr 23, 44. *Study:* Los Angeles City Col, 62; Otis Art Inst Los Angeles Co, BFA & MFA, 66. *Work:* Otis-Parsons Art Inst, Los Angeles. *Comn:* Rock Resorts, Maui, Hawaii, 79; Two cityscapes, Bank of Am, Long Beach, Calif, 82; western scene, Wells Fargo, Palm Desert, Calif, 81; skyscape mural, Northrup Corp, Hawthorn, Calif, 82. *Exhib:* Current Concerns, Part II, 75 & Imagination, 76, Los Angeles Inst Contemp Art; Book Show, Inst Mod Art Brisbane, Australia & traveling, 78; solo exhibs, Brand Libr Art Ctr, Glendale, Calif, 85, Peter Nahum, London, Eng, 87, Carnegie Art Mus, Oxnard, Calif, 89, Art Angles Gallery, Orange, 95, Oliver & Espig, Santa Barbara, 96, & Svit Ozor Studio Channel Art Ctr, 2nd Invitational, 2000 & 2001; Karpeles Manuscript, Libr Mus, Santa Barbara, Calif, 94. *Bibliog:* Calvin J Goodman (auth), Return to regional art, Am Artist, 6/82; A survey of contemporary art of the figure, Am Artist, 2/85; Best of Acrylic Painting, Rockport Publ, 6/96; Landscape Inspirations, Rockport Publications, 11/97; Portrait Inspirations, Rockport Publications, 11/97. *Mem:* Artist Equity Asn (vpres, bd dir, 81-82); Santa Barbara Studio Artist, 2002-2003. *Media:* Acrylic. *Publ:* Auth, The Adventure, 70 & The Model, 77, pvt publ; Lightfastness in colored pencils, Los Angeles Equity News, 82; contribr, Photographing your artwork, Am Artist, 84. *Mailing Add:* 895 Toro Canyon Rd Montecito CA 93108

WALLIN, LELAND DEAN
PAINTER, EDUCATOR
b Sioux Falls, SDak, Oct 14, 42. *Study:* Columbus Col Art & Design, Ohio, 61; Kans City Art Inst, Mo, BFA, 65; Univ Cincinnati & Art Acad, Ohio, MFA fel, 67; Aspen Sch Contemp Art, Colo, 68; Sabbatical Study, Philip Pearlstein's Studio, NY, 76. *Exhib:* Brooklyn 79, Brooklyn Mus, NY, 79; Greenville Co Mus Art, SC, 1983; 30th Int Open Exhib, San Bernardino Co Mus, 95; Int Show, NJ Ctr Visual Arts, 95; Int Open Exhib, Sacramento Fine Arts Ctr, Calif, 97; Landscape and Still Life: A New Look, Downey Mus Art, Calif, 98; Palm Springs Desert Mus, 99; San Diego Art Inst, 2000; Bellevue Art Mus, Wash, 2001; Morris Mus Art, Ga, 2001; Mississippi Mus Art, 2001; Huntsville Mus Art, 2002; New Directions, Barret Art Ctr Galleries, Paughkeepsie, NY, 2003. *Collection Arranged:* cur, New Realism 70 (auth, catalog), St Cloud State Univ, Minn, 70, Philip Pearlstein Retrospective, Marywood,Univ, Scranton, Pa, 88. *Pos:* Juror Panelist, ann $8000 F Lamont Belin Grant for Northeast Professionals, PA, 86-89; Juror, Northern Nat Art Competition, Wis, 94. *Teaching:* Prof painting, E Carolina Univ, Greenville, NC, 92-2001. *Awards:* Fac res grants, East Carolina Univ, NC, 94, 96, 97, 2000 & 05; Outstanding Scholar-Teachers Awards, 94, 95 & 2004; Int First Prize Oil Painting Awards, Laredo Ctr Arts, Tex, 97 & 99. *Bibliog:* Gerrit Henry (auth), exhib catalog, Harold Reed Gallery, 83; Philip Pearlstein (auth), exhib catalog, Gallery Henoch, 91; Realism today, American Artist Mag, special issue, 2000; Ralph Pomeroy (auth), Exhib Catalog, Gallery Heroch, 91; and others. *Mem:* Col Art Asn. *Media:* Oil. *Publ:* Auth, The evolution of Philip Pearlstein, Art Int Mag, Part I, summer 79, Part II, fall 79; A twenty year cast of nudes in bronze: Richard McDermott Miller's retrospective, Arts Mag, 5/84; Toys take a holiday, play the theater, and travel through time, Arts Mag, 3/87; Rescuing Vermeer: Seeing Human Values and Virtues in Direct Observation, Am Arts Quar, Fall, 2002; Harnett's Hidden Constellation, American Arts Quarterly, Summer, 2004. *Mailing Add:* 218 York Rd Greenville NC 27858

WALP, SUSAN JANE
Study: Mt Holyoke Col, BA, 70; Attended, Boston Univ Sch Fine Arts, 68; Attended, NY Studio Sch Drawing, Painting and Sculpture, 69-71; Attended, Skowhegan Sch Painting and Sculpture, 71; Attended, Brooklyn Col, 72-79. *Exhib:* Exhib in group shows at Metrop Show, Denver Art Mus, 74, Artists Choose Artists, Lake George Arts Project, 82, Nature Morte: A Current View, NY Studio Sch, 93, Objects of Personal Significance, Knoxville Mus Art, 96-98, Texas Tech Lubbock, 89-98, Hunter Mus Art, 96-98, Tarble Art Center, 96-98, Am Acad Invitational Exhib of Painting & Sculpture, Am Acad of Arts and Letters, 99, Intimate Visions, State Univ NY, Cortland, 2001, one-man shows incl Victoria Munroe Fine Art, NY, 1994 Fischabach Gallery, 1996, Hackett Freedman Gallery, San Francisco, 1999, 2000. *Pos:* Faculty member painting International School Art, Montecastello di Vibio, Italy, 79—99; visiting assistant professor Dartmouth Coll, Department Studio Art, Hanover, New Hampshire, 98—. *Awards:* Recipient Soc Illustrators Award, 84, Am Illus Award, 84; fel Guggenheim Mem Found, 2004. *Mailing Add:* Dept Studio Art Dartmouth Coll Hanover New Hampshire NH 03755

WALSH, JAMES
PAINTER, SCULPTOR
b Newark, NJ, Aug 6, 1954. *Study:* Livingston Col, Rutgers Univ, NJ, BA, 76; Syracuse Univ, NY, MFA, 80. *Exhib:* First Biennial-New Jersey Artists, Newark Mus, 77; New Works in Clay III, Everson Mus Art, Syracuse, NY, 81-82; two-man show, Edmonton Art Gallery, Alberta, 85; Pre-Post Modern, Brush Art Gallery, St Laurence Univ, Canton, NY, 85; Assoc Am Artists, NY, 90. *Bibliog:* Valentin Tatransky (auth), The new avant-garde, Art Int, 4/84 & James Walsh, Arts Mag, 10/85; Russell Bingham (auth), James Walsh-John King, Update, 11-12/85. *Media:* Acrylic, Oil; Metal, Welded. *Dealer:* Galeria Joan Prats 24 W 57th St New York NY 10019; Associated American Artists 20 W 57th St New York NY 10019. *Mailing Add:* Four Great Jones St No 1 New York NY 10012

WALSH, JANET BARBARA
PAINTER
b Philadelphia, Pa, Aug 11, 39. *Study:* Art Students League, with Mario Cooper, Daniel Greene, cert, 69; Sch Visual Arts, with Francis Criss, Robert Frankenberg, Burton Silverman. *Work:* Progresso Corp; Mus de la Acuarela, Mex; Springmaid Found; St Antonin, Noble Val, France; Pfizer Corp. *Comn:* Avon Products Inc; Doran-Smith Adv Co. *Exhib:* Anchorage Hist & Fine Arts Mus, Alaska; Nat Acad Design, Salmagundi, Club, World Trade Ctr, Art Students League, Nat Arts Club, NY; Mus Arts & Hist, Port Huron, Mich; Columbus Mus Arts & Sci, Ga; Owensboro Mus Fine Arts, Ogunquit, Mass; Grants Pass Mus Art, Ore, 80; Columbus Mus Art; Albrect Art Mus, St Joseph, Mo; Charles & Emma Frye Mus, Seattle; QE2, Maruzen, Tokyo; Mus de la Acuadrela, Mex. *Pos:* pres, Am Watercolor Soc. *Teaching:* Workshops throughout the US & Europe; New York Horticutural Soc; Salmagundi Club. *Awards:* Bronze Medal Hon, Am Watercolor Soc; Edgar A Whitney Award, 92, Dixie Warehouse & Cartage Co Award, Ky Watercolor Soc, 94; and others. *Mem:* Am Watercolor Soc (pres); Allied Artists; Catharine Lorillard Wolfe Art Club; Ky Watercolor Soc; Royal Soc Arts, London; Nat Arts Club; Salmagundi Club. *Media:* Watercolor, Pastel, Printmaking. *Interests:* Gardening, kyacking, travel. *Publ:* Auth, Watercolor Made Easy, Watson-Guptill. *Mailing Add:* 6140 Beverly Hills Rd Coopersburg PA 18036-1865

WALSH, J(OHN) MICHAEL
DEALER, PRINTMAKER
b Peoria, Ill, July 16, 53. *Study:* Univ Iowa, printmaking with M Lazansky & U Meyers, BFA, 77; Bradley Univ, with W A S Hatch, MA, 80. *Exhib:* Davenport Munic Gallery, Iowa, 78; Minot State Col Mus, NDak, 79 & 81; Univ SDak Mus, Vermillion, traveling, 79 & 80; Dulin Gallery Art, Knoxville, Tenn, 80; Okla Arts Ctr, Oklahoma City, 81; Bradley Nat Exhib, Peoria, Ill, 83. *Pos:* Asst dir, Tower Park Gallery, Peoria, Ill, 78-; cur exhibs, Peoria Art Guild, Ill, 80-82; dir, Walsh Fine Arts, 83-. *Teaching:* Instr papermaking workshop, Peoria Art Guild, 81-. *Awards:* Purchase Award, Univ SDak, Vermillion, 80; First Place, Junction City Arts, Peoria, Ill, 82. *Mem:* Col Art Asn; World Print Coun. *Dealer:* Van Stratten Gallery 361 W Superior St Chicago IL 60610

WALSH, NAN
PAINTER - MISCELLANEOUS MEDIA, SCULPTURE
b NY, Nov 4, 32. *Study:* Fordham Univ, BS(elementary educ), 54; VK Jonynas, Long Island, NY, 88; Art Life Studio Inc, White Plains and Portchester, NY, 94; Art Ctr No NJ, 96—2002; Nat Accad Sch Fine Arts. *Work:* Sumner Mus, Washington, DC; Lehman Brothers, NY; Neiman Marcus, White Plains, NY; Pound Ridge Mus, NY; Westchester Beaux Arts Finale, NY; Katonah Mus Art. *Comn:* Central Park, Mayor & Mrs John Lindsay, NY, 72; Lazy Afternoon, Mr & Mrs Temple Buell, Denvet Colo, 73; Still Life Impression, Dr & Mrs Austin Murphy, Mamaroneck, NY, 76; April Bouquet, Mr & Mrs Randolf Guggenheimer, NY, 78; Large Triptyck, Mr & Mrs Ken Carlin, Weston, Conn, 85. *Exhib:* Solo exhib, For Arts Sake, Hilton Hotel, NY, 73, Nan Walsh at Rockefeller Ctr, NY, 76, Nan Walsh says it with Flowers, Womens Club Bronxville, NY, 78, Abstract, Ward Nasse Gallery, NY, 80, Semi Abstract Expressionism, MAG Gallery, Larchmont, NY, 84; Mamaroneck Artist Guild Nat Open Juried Exhib, White Plains, NY, 78, 81, 83, 84, 86, 87, 88, 91, 94 & 96; On the Cutting Edge, Broome Street Gallery, NY, 96; Nat League Am Pen Women, Sumner Mus, Washington, DC, 96. *Collection Arranged:* Gracie Mansion, Gracie Mansion for the Pub, 72; Studio XII Juried Exhib, Cork Room Gallery, Avery Fisher Hall, 78; Mamaroneck Artists' Guild, Nat Open Juried Exhib, 80; Studio XII, Art Show, Off of the Mayor, 80; Mag Gallery, 8 yrs 15 shows a year, 88-96. *Awards:* Award of Excellence, Sumner Mus, Wash, DC; First Prize, Beaux Arts Finale, Westchester, NY; Outstanding work, 11th Annual Sculpture Open, Salmagundi Club, NY. *Bibliog:* VK Jonynas (auth), About the Artist, The Villager Publ Co, 78; Lorraine Lange, Nan Walsh, The Artist, The Villager Publ Co, 78. *Mem:* Nat Mus of Women in Arts; Mamaroneck Artists Guild Inc (vpres, 80-); Allied Artists Am; NY Artists Equity; Nat League Am Pen Women (mem chmn, 92-96). *Media:* Oil, printmaking (monotypes), Clay & metal. *Interests:* Jurying art shows, art consultants & help legislate better laws for artists. *Collection:* Realistic painting, semi abstract paintings, expressionistic paintings, monotypes and sculptures. *Publ:* auth, Hist of the Mamaroneck Artists Guild (article), Gannett Westchester Newspaper, 88; ed, Mamaroneck Artists Guild Publicity, Gannett Westchester Newspaper, Review Press Reporter, Soundview News, Art Times, 88-96. *Mailing Add:* 3 Windward Way Red Bank NJ 07701

WALSH, PATRICIA RUTH
PAINTER
b Cleveland, Ohio. *Study:* Col Mt St Joseph, Cincinnati, BA; Art Students League; Syracuse Univ, NY, MFA. *Comn:* Four paintings, St Timothy's Church, Trenton, Mich; design for altar furnishings, St Mary's Church, Oakland, Calif. *Exhib:* Northwest Printmakers Int, Seattle Art Mus, 65; Pollution Show, Oakland Mus, 70; Three Watercolorists, San Jose Civic Art Ctr, 73; Spaces & Places, Palo Alto Cult Ctr, 75; Walnut Creek Civic Arts Ctr, 80. *Pos:* Liturgical designer, Holy Names Col, Oakland, Calif & St Clement's Church, Hayward, Calif & Christ the King Catholic Community, Las Vegas, Nevada; consult, St Francis de Sales Cathedral, Oakland, Sacred Heart Cath Community, Hollester, St Jerome's Church, El Cerrito, Calif. *Teaching:* Asst prof fine arts, Nazareth Col, Rochester, NY, 57-65; prof fine arts, Calif Col Arts & Crafts, 65-. *Awards:* Bene Award, Modern Liturgy Mag, 88; Hon Mention Mod Liturgy Mag, 92. *Mem:* Arch Mod Christian Art (bd mem). *Media:* Oil, Watercolor. *Mailing Add:* 1999 Gaspar Dr Oakland CA 94611

WALSH-PIPER, KATHY A
MUSEUM DIRECTOR, EDUCATOR
b Oak Park, Ill, Aug 17, 47. *Study:* Washington Univ, St Louis, AB, 69, MA, 73. *Pos:* head DET, Nat Gallery of Art, 88-95; dir educ & pub prog, Dallas Mus Art, 95-2002; dir, Univ Ky Art Mus, 2002-. *Teaching:* coordr educ, St Louis Art Mus, 76-80; assoc dir mus educ, Art Inst Chicago, 80-85; dir educ, Terra Mus Art, 85-88. *Awards:* Nat Mus Educator of Yr, NAEA, 84; Mus Guest Scholar, J Paul Getty Mus, 98; Robert Smith fel, Nat Gallery of Art, 96. *Mem:* Mem Nat Art Educ Asn (reg mus educ 1984, nat mus educ 1985, di mus division 1992-), Am Asn Mus (chair midwest educ ccom, 1983-84). *Interests:* Inquiry teaching and creative writing, based on art. *Publ:* Image to Word: Art and Creative Writing, Scarecrow Press, 2002; Handbook of Museum-Based Lesson Plans, St. Louis Art Mus, 79; Teachers Planning Guide to the Art Institute of Chicago, 84; Museum Education and the Aesthetic Experience, Jour of Aesthetic Educ, fall 94. *Mailing Add:* 307 Dudley Rd Lexington KY 40502

WALTEMATH, JOAN
PAINTER, EDUCATOR
b Nebr, Oct 6, 53. *Study:* Rhode Island Sch Design, BFA, 76; Hunter Col, MFA, 93. *Work:* Fogg Mus, Harvard Univ, Boston, Mass; Muse de Beaux Arts, La Chaux De/Fonds, Switz; Sears Merchandise, Ill; Yale Univ Art Gallery, New Haven, Conn; Harvard Univ Art Mus, Cambridge, Mass; NY Pub Libr; Nat Gallery Art, Washington, DC; Mus Modern Art, NY. *Comn:* Installation in lobby, Howco Investment Co, Metro Park, NJ, 87; St Canisius Ch, Berlin, 02. *Exhib:* Solo exhibs: White Skins, White-Out Studio, Knokke, Belgium, 2003; Two & Three, Victoria Munroe Fine Arts, Boston Mass, 2005; Infinity, notes on the sublime, Galerie Nivon, 2006; and others; Art on paper, Weatherspoon Gallery, Univ, NC, 2000; Fifteen Yrs of Painting, Stark Gallery, NY, 2001; Drawing, Victoria Munroe Fine Art, Boston, 2001; Immanance, Hunter Col, NY, 2001; Patient Process, Grinnell Col, Iowa, 2001; Math-Art Art-Math, Ringling Col, Sarasota, Fla, 2002; The Rhythm of Structure, Firehouse 5 Gallery, NY, 2003; Small Epiphonics, Victoria Munroe Fine Art, Boston; Paint it Black, B Cunningham Gallery, NY, 2006; Take Off, Basel Switz, 2006; The Rhythm of Structure, Firehouse 5 Gallery, NY, 2003; Resonance, The Work Space, NY, 2003; The Incredible Lightness of Being, Black and White Gallery, Brooklyn, NY, 2003; and others. *Collection Arranged:* Nat Gallery Art, Washington, DC; NY Pub Libr; Fondation Leschot, Bern, Switzerland; Hood Mus, Dartmouth, NH; Yale Univ Art Gallery, New Haven, Conn; Harvard Univ Art Mus, Cambridge, Mass; S Moody Gallery, Univ Ala; Weatherspoon Art Gallery, Univ NC; Krannert Art Mus, Univ Ill; Mona, Univ Nebr. *Teaching:* vis lectr, I S Chanin Sch Archit, Cooper Union, New York, 97-2001, adj asst prof, 2001-; vis lectr, Princeton Univ, 00-02; instr, Sch Art, Cooper Union, 02-03. *Awards:* BRA Arch Award, City of Berlin, 2003; Edward Albee Found Award, 2003 & 06; Jentel Found Award, 2005; Change Found Avard, 2006. *Bibliog:* William Zimmer (auth), Matters of Scale, NY Times, 3/8/98; Michael Brennan (auth), Painters Journal, artnet.com, 10/29/99, 9/27/2000; Roberta Fallon (auth), Math Works, Philadelphia Weekly, 11/21/2001; Peter Frank (auth), Pick of the Week, LA Weekly Times, 10/2/1998, 2/1/2003; Kim Levin (auth), Art in Brief, The Village Voice, 79, 5/10/1994; Roberta Smith (auth), NY Times, C26, 7/7/1996; Stephen Westfall, Art in America, 108, 7/1992. *Mem:* AM Abstract Artists. *Media:* Oil on Canvas, Graphite or Mylar. *Publ:* Blast, X Art Found, 91; A Decade of Collecting, Harvard Univ Art Mus, Cambridge, Mass, 2000; Art on Paper (exhib catalog), Weatherspoon Art Gallery, Univ NC, Greensboro, 2000; Babel, babble., Gugenheim pub, Venice, Italy, 3/2000; Patient Process, Grinell Col, Los Angeles, 2001; Thinking in Line, Univ Galleries, Univ Fla, 2003. *Dealer:* Victoria Munroe Fine Arts Boston MA; Nikios van Bartha London England. *Mailing Add:* 131 Bowery 4th Fl New York NY 10002

WALTER, ELIZABETH MITCHELL
ADMINISTRATOR, HISTORIAN
b Decatur, Ala, Feb 19, 36. *Study:* Florence State Col, BA, 57; Univ Ala, MA, 69; Univ Ga, PhD, 78. *Pos:* Consult, Kennedy Douglas Ctr Arts, 77-88. *Teaching:* Instr art hist, Univ Ga, 76; lectr, Hambidge Ctr, Rabun Gap, Ga, 77; prof, Univ NAla, 75-98, chair, Art Dept, 85-98. *Mem:* Col Art Asn; Nat Coun Art Adminirs; Southeastern Col Art Conf (bd dir, 85-88); Nat Asn Schs Art & Design. *Res:* Art and artists in Alabama; Pier Luigi Nervi; W Eugene Smith; Hans Namuth. *Publ:* Frank Lloyd Wright in Alabama, Apelles, 81; Mimi Holmes, Art Papers, 88; auth, William Aiken Walker: Paintings 1879-1915 (catalog), 90

WALTER, MARK R
PATRON
Study: Northwestern Univ, JD. *Pos:* Managing partner, Liberty Hampshire Co; Chief Exec Officer, Guggenheim Capital LLC, Chicago; trustee, Solomon R Guggenheim Mus, New York City. *Mailing Add:* Guggenheim Capital LLC 227 W Monroe St Chicago IL 60606

WALTER, PAUL F
COLLECTOR, PATRON
b Mt Vernon, NY, 35. *Study:* Oberlin Col, Ohio; Columbia Univ, New York. *Collection Arranged:* Indian Paintings, Morgan Libr; Indian Drawings from Paul Walter Collection, Los Angeles Co Mus; photographs, Mus Mod Art. *Pos:* Mem photog comt, Mus Mod Art, NY, 79, Metrop Mus Art; Friends Morgan Libr, NY, currently. *Mem:* Int Coun Mus Mod Art. *Interests:* Art education, avant garde theatre music and dance. *Collection:* Collection of Indian art; avant garde paintings, drawings and sculpture; photographs; African Art. *Mailing Add:* 450 E 52nd St New York NY 10022

WALTERS, BILLIE
CERAMIST
b Colman, Tex, Mar 12, 27. *Study:* Univ Colo; Univ NMex, BFA, 79, MA, 81. *Work:* Univ Calgary; Ariz State Univ; Southern Conn State Col; Western NMex Univ. *Exhib:* Ceramics Int, Calgary, Alta, 73; Mus Albuquerque, 79; Los Angeles Folk Art Mus, 79; Lange Gallery, Scripps Col, Claremont, Calif; and others. *Pos:* Crafts Rep, Bd NMex Arts & Crafts Fair, 74-; Southwest cur, Women's Caucus for Art Exhib, Bronx Mus, NY, 78. *Teaching:* Instr ceramics, Univ NMex, 79-81. *Awards:* Purchase Awards, Ceramics Int, 73 & Mus Albuquerque, NMex, 79. *Bibliog:* W R Mitchell (auth), Ceramic Art of the World 1973, Govt Can, Alta, 73; Elsbeth Woody (auth), Handbuilding Ceramic Forms, Farrar Straus Giroux, New York, 79. *Mem:* Albuquerque United Artists; NMex Potters Asn; Albuquerque Designer-Craftsman. *Mailing Add:* 3835 Rio Grande Blvd NW Albuquerque NM 87107-3093

WALTERS, ERNEST
PAINTER
b Elizabethtown, Ky, Nov 11, 27. *Study:* Univ Louisville; Univ Miami; French Studio Schs. *Work:* Mus Mod Art, NY; Israel Mus, Jerusalem; Frankfurt Mus, Ger; Albertina, Vienna, Austria; Mus d'Art Mod, Brussels, Belg. *Exhib:* IFA Galleries, Washington, DC; Galerie Richter, Wiesbaden, Ger; Siemens, Overbeck Gallery, Lubeck; Galerie Kumar, Vienna, Austria; Daedal Fine Arts, Baltimore; and others. *Teaching:* teacher, Baltimore Pub Schs. *Mem:* Print Consortium; MD Writers Asn; Philadelphia Writers' Conf. *Media:* Oil. *Publ:* Auth, Wiener Schwarzweiss, 68; An Astonished Survivor, 73; The Beast Within; Thorns of Life. *Dealer:* IFA Galleries 2623 Connecticut Ave NW Washington DC 20008; Daedal Fine Arts Fallston Mall Fallston MD 21047. *Mailing Add:* 257 Foster Knoll Dr Joppa MD 21085

WALTERS, SYLVIA SOLOCHEK
PRINTMAKER, EDUCATOR
b Milwaukee, Wis, Aug 24, 38. *Study:* Univ Wis, Madison, BS, MS, MFA. *Work:* St. Louis Art Mus; Achenbach Found Graphic Arts; Oakland Mus; Milwaukee Art Mus; Magnes Mus; Chazen Art Mus; and others. *Exhib:* 3rd Graphics Biennial, Metrop Mus & Art Ctr, Miami, 77, 80; 34th Ann Boston Printmakers, DeCordova Mus, 82; Prints from Blocks, Assoc Am Artists, NY, 85; California Prints in Japan, Tokyo Mus, 85; Drake Univ 8th Biennial PRWTA Symposium Exhibit; 150 Yrs of Wisconsin Printmakers, Elvejhem Mus Art; Cuts: Contemp Woodcuts, Kala Art Inst, 2003; Am Relief Prints, Univ Place Art Ctr, Lincoln, NE; 5th Minn Nat Print Biennial, 2004; Boston Printmakers Biennial, 2005. *Pos:* Graphic & bk designer, Univ Wis Press, 64-67; dir, Gallery 210, Univ Mo, 74-; chmn dept art, Univ Mo, 77-81; chmn, Dept Arts, San Francisco State Univ, 84-2004, actg dean, Col Creative Arts, 93-94 & 96-97. *Teaching:* Instr printmaking, Layton Sch of Art, 63-64; instr drawing, Doane Col, 67-68 & St Louis Univ, 68-69; prof printmaking & drawing, Univ Mo, St Louis; prof printmaking & drawing, San Francisco State Univ, 84-2004. *Awards:* Purchase Awards, Colorprint USA, 79, Vermillion, 79, 4th Miami Int Print Biennial, 80, 8th Univ Dallas Nat, 83, NDak Print & Drawing Show, 84; Best of Show Award, N Calif Print Competition, 86; Colorprint USA, 88; 42nd North American Boston Printmakers, 90. *Bibliog:* Marlene Schiller (auth), article, Am Artist 10/79; Julia Ayres (auth), Printmaking Techniques, Watson-Guptill, 93; James Watrous & Steven Andrews (auths), American Color Woodcuts: Bounty From the Block 1890's-1990's, Univ Wis, 93. *Mem:* Col Art Asn; Women's Caucus for Art; Boston Printmakers, Print Club; Calif Printmakers Soc. *Media:* Woodcut and Relief Prints, Watercolor. *Publ:* Auth, American Women Printmakers, Gallery 210, Univ Mo, St Louis, 75; Art on the Mississippi, 4/76 & Place, race & rights in St Louis, summer 76, Women Artist News; California Printmaker Quarterly J #3, 90. *Mailing Add:* 5217 Harbord Dr Oakland CA 94618

WALTNER, BEVERLY RULAND
PAINTER
b Kansas City, Mo. *Study:* Yale Univ, with Joseph Albers; Univ Miami, BA, 55; Kent State Univ, Blossom Kent Art Prog with Richard Anuszkiewiez, 68; Northern Ill Univ, MFA, 68. *Work:* Northern Ill Univ, De Kalb; also numerous pvt collections. *Comn:* Paintings, Alexander Muss & Sons, Equitable Life Assurance Soc, Zuckerman-Vernon Corp & Gen Development Corp. *Exhib:* Tenth Mid-Western Biennial, Joslyn Art Mus, Omaha, Nebr, 68; Chautauqua Exhib Am Art, Chautauqua Art Asn, NY, 68-73 & 78; Ann Exhib, Nat Soc Painters Casein & Acrylics, NY, 69, 70, 72 & 73; 35th Ann Mid Yr Show, Butler Inst Am Art, Youngstown, Ohio, 70; Ark Nat Art Exhib, Univ Ark, Little Rock, 70; Ann Exhib Am Painting, Soc Four Arts, Palm Beach, Fla, 71 & 74. *Teaching:* Instr art, Barry Col, Miami Shores, Fla, 69-70. *Awards:* Top Award, New Horizons in Painting, N Shore Art League, 66; First Place, 68 & Louis E Seldon Mem Award, 72, Chautauqua Art Asn. *Bibliog:* Donald L Hoffman (auth), The color image, Kansas City Star, 1/19/69; Bill van Mauer (auth), Colors get her vivid messages across, Miami News, 2/8/72. *Mem:* Chautauqua Art Asn; Prof Artist Guild (treas, Miami area, 77-78, vpres, 78); Artists Equity Asn; Visual Arts Coalition. *Media:* Acrylic, Oil. *Mailing Add:* 24500 142nd Ave SW Homestead FL 33032

WALTON, ALICE LOUISE
PATRON
b Newport, Ark, Oct 7, 49. *Study:* Trinity Univ, BBA, 1971. *Hon Degrees:* Southwest Baptist Univ, D of Bus Admin, 1988. *Pos:* Investment analyst, First Commerce Corp, New Orleans, 1972-75; dir, vpres investments, Walton Enterprises, Bentonville, Ark, 1975; retail & investment broker, EF Hutton Co, 1975-79; vice chair, investment dir, Walton Bank Group, 1982-88; founder, former pres, chair, chief exex officer, Llama Co/Llama Asset Mgt Co; Mem dean's adv coun, Univ Ark Coll Bus Adminstrn, 1989-90; Bd trustees, Amon Carter Mus, Ft Worth, Tex. *Awards:* Named Distinguished Bus Lect Cent State Univ, Edmond, Okla, 1989; Arkansan of Yr, Ark Easter Seals Soc, 1990; named one of Top 100 Women in Ark, Ark Bus, 1995; #13 on Forbes' World's Richest People List, 2005; named one of Top 200 Collectors, ARTnews mag, 2006. *Mem:* Northwest Ark Coun

WALTON, GUY E
WRITER, EDUCATOR
b New York, NY, Oct 18, 35. *Study:* Wesleyan Univ, BA, 57; NY Univ, MA, 62, PhD, 67. *Collection Arranged:* Versailles a Stockholm (auth, catalog), Paris, 85. *Teaching:* Prof Baroque art & archit, NY Univ, 72-2002 & prof emer, 2002-. *Awards:* Nat Endowment Humanities Grant, 84-85; Pub Grant, J Paul Getty Trust, 85. *Mem:* Col Art Asn; Soc Archit Historians; Soc l'Hist l'Art Francais. *Res:* Seventeenth century French and Italian sculpture; architecture and decor of palaces. *Publ:* Auth, Pierre Puget in Rome: 1662, Burlington Mag, 69; Lievin Cruyl, In: Essays for H W Hanson, Abrams, 81; The abduction of Helen, a 17th century French bronze, Bulletin Detroit Mus, 83; Louis XIV's Versailles, Univ Chicago Press, 86; ed, Gifts to the Tsars, Abrams, 2001. *Mailing Add:* 693 Route 519 Belvidere NJ 07823

WALTON, HARRY A, JR
COLLECTOR
b Covington, Va, Sept 24, 18. *Study:* Univ Va, 37; Columbia Univ, 39; Lynchburg Col, AB, 39. *Exhib:* Works have been exhibited in libraries at: Trinity Col, Washington, DC, Col William & Mary, Norfolk Mus Art & Sci, Univ Va & Lynchburg Col. *Mem:* Past-Fel Pierpont-Morgan Libr, NY; Univ Va Bibliog Soc. *Collection:* Early books and manuscripts, Bibles, fine binding, Aldinae and first editions. *Mailing Add:* White Oak Dairy PO Box 790 Covington VA 24426

WALTON, M DOUGLAS
PAINTER, INSTRUCTOR
b Alva, Okla, June 23, 42. *Study:* Okla State Univ, BA, 65; study with Edgar Whitney, Robert E Wood & Milford Zornes; Tech Rome Prog, Italy. *Teaching:* Assoc prof archit & watercolors, La Tech Univ, Ruston, 72-84; instr workshops, throughout US; Watercolor Encounter & Journey Encounter, US and abroad, 77-. *Mem:* Southwestern Watercolor Soc (signature mem); La Watercolor Soc; Southern Watercolor Soc; Mid-Southern Watercolorists (signature mem); Watercolor Art Soc, Houston. *Media:* Watercolor. *Publ:* Auth, A Special Kind of Silence, in prep. *Mailing Add:* 150 Encounter Point Ruston LA 71270

WALTZER, STEWART PAUL
DEALER, PAINTER
b New York, NY, Mar 17, 48. *Study:* NY Univ, BA, 69, MA, 70; Columbia Univ; New York Studio Sch; also with Irving Sandler, Audrey Flack, Chuck Close & Kenneth Noland. *Exhib:* City Univ NY; Gallery Don Stewart, Montreal; Waddington & Shiell, Toronto; Gallery 99, Miami, Fla; Eva Cohon Gallery, Chicago. *Pos:* Dir, Andre Emmerich Gallery Downtown, 72-74, Tibor de Nagy Gallery, 74-77 & Meredith Long Contemp, 77-79; pres, Waltzer & Assocs, 79-. *Specialty:* American 20th. *Dealer:* Galeria Joan Prats 29 W 57th St New York NY. *Mailing Add:* Stewart Waltzer Co 200 W Houston St New York NY 10014-4828

WANDEL, SHARON LEE
SCULPTOR, PAINTER
b Bemidji, Minnesota, Mar 19, 40. *Study:* Gustavus Adolphus Col, BA, 62; Columbia Univ, MSW, 65; State Univ NY, Purchase, Cert inArts Mgt, 93. *Work:* works in permanent collections at Art Students League, 89, Westinghouse Corp Collection, Pittsburgh, 90, Nat Acad, 94, Housatonic Mus, Conn, 98, CofC, Toyamura, Japan, 99; Pfizer Corp Collection, Armonk, NY, 2000; commns incl two 8' bronze figures for Ihilani Resort, Kapolei, Hawaii, 93, 2 5" figures Silvermine Galleries, 93. *Exhib:* One-person shows, at Silvermine Guild of Artists, New Canaan, Conn, 93, 97, 2001,

Pen and Brush, New York City, 94, Clark Whitney Gallery, Lenox, Mass, 94, James Cox Gallery, Woodstock, NY, 94, 96, Cortland Jessup Gallery, Provincetown, Mass, 98 New York City, 2000, 02, Gallery Marya, Osaka, Japan, 99, Laura Barton Gallery, Westport, Conn, 2000, Firehouse Gallery, Damaviscotta, Maine, 2000, Gallery Irohane, Osaka, Japan, 2001; Craven Gallery, Martha's Vineyard, Mass, 2002-2006, Berta Walker Gallery, Provincetown, Mass, 2002, Elan Fine Arts, Rockland, Maine, 2003-2006, Clarke Galleries, Stowe, Vt, 2003-2006, Palm Beach, Fla, 2003-2004, New York City, 2003-2004, Westchester Arts Council, White Plains, NY, 2004; group shows, most recently Nat Acad Design, New York City, 88, 90, 92, 94, 95, 97, 98, 99, 2000, 04, 06, Cortland Jessup Gallery, Provincetown and New York City, 98-2002, Canyon Ranch, Lenox, Mass 99-2003, Chesterwood, Lenox, Mass, 2000, 2001, Butler Inst Am Art, Youngstown, Ohio, 2000 Cavalier Gallery, Nantucket, Mass, 2001, Berkshires Botanical Garden, Mass, 2001, Paesaggio Gallery, W Hartford, Conn, 2001-04, Leighton Gallery, Blue Hill, ME, 2001-06, Munson Gallery, Chatham, Mass, 2002-04, Sakai (Japan) City Mus, 2002-06. *Pos:* Caseworker, Manhattan State Hosp, New York City, 63-64; caseworker/reseacher, Community Serv Soc, 65-67; mem adv, bd Lamia, Inc, New York City, 99-2003. *Teaching:* teaching assist, dept med NY Univ Med Ctr, 67-70. *Awards:* Nat Am Sculpture Exhib 2d place, 91; 1st place, Nat Competition Sundance Gallery, Bridgehampton, NY, 97; Vt Studio Ctr fel, 2000; and others. *Mem:* Silvermine Guild of Artists; NY Soc Woman Artists (pres, formerly); Knickerbocker Artists USA; Nat Acad; Nat Sculpture Soc. *Media:* Metal, Cast; All Media. *Dealer:* Elan Fine Arts Rockport ME; Munson Gallery Chatham NY. *Mailing Add:* PO Box 314 Croton On Hudson NY 10520-0314

WANDS, ROBERT JAMES
EDUCATOR, PAINTER
b Denver, Colo, June 24, 39. *Study:* With Alfred Wands, 56-60; Univ Denver, BFA, 61, MA, 63; Cleveland Art Inst; Western Reserve Univ. *Work:* Univ Denver; Colo Womens Col; Western Colo Ctr Arts, Grand Junction; Univ Southern Colo; Colo State Fair Collection. *Comn:* Painting, Fine Am Art Calendar, Cleveland, 70; murals, Cleopatra Health Spa, Pueblo, Colo, 76 & YMCA, Estes Park, Colo, 77; paintings, United Bank, Pueblo, Colo, 78, Dain Bosworth, Pueblo, 84, Colo Nat Bank-Belmont, Pueblo, 86 & Pueblo Teachers Credit Union, Colo, 86; mural, Colo State Vet Ctr, Homelake, Colo, 95. *Exhib:* solo exhib, Sangre de Cristo Art Ctr, Pueblo, Colo, 73 & 96, Western Colo Ctr Arts, Grand Junction, 74 & Univ Southern Colo, 81, Sabbatical Exhib, USC, 89, Nemick Thompson Gallery, 2004; two-man exhibs, Sangre de Cristo Art Ctr, Pueblo, Colo, 84, retrspective Exhib, Sangre de Cristo Art Ctr, 2001; Fac Exhib, S Colo Univ, 92, 93 & 94; Colo State Fair Art Exhib, 93; The Rockies Show, Sangre de Cristo Art Ctr, 94; Aqua Media Exhib 2000; Sangre de Cristo Art Ctr, 2000. *Pos:* Artist-in-residence, Asn Camp, Estes Park, Colo, summers 74-78. *Teaching:* Instr painting, Univ Denver, 63; assoc prof, Univ Southern Colo, 63-96. *Awards:* Purchase Prize, 65 & Meritorious Award, 72, Colo State Fair; Best of Show, Own Your Own Art Show, Sangre Cristo Art Ctr, 79 & Purchase Award, 96; Mayors Choice Award, Estes Park Plein Air Show, 2006. *Bibliog:* Carol Kronwitter (auth), Pueblo Chieftain, 2/28/81 & 9/30/84; Jeff Rennicke (auth), Colo Mountain Ranges, 86. *Mem:* I-25 Artist Alliance; Oil Painters Am; Pike Peak Pleain Air Painters. *Media:* Acrylic, Oil, Watercolor. *Dealer:* Wands Art Studio Gallery P O Box 2093 Estes Park CO 80517; Patrons Art Gallery Denver CO; Nemick-Thompson Gallery Pueblo CO

WANG, GAR
PAINTER
Study: Princeton Univ, BA(cum laude), 76; Hunter Col, MA(painting), 83. *Exhib:* Hunter Col Art Gallery, NY, 86; Mus Hudson Highlands, Cornwall on Hudson, NY, 86; solo exhibs, 55 Mercer, NY, 86 & 87; Vorhees Campus, Univ, NY, 89; Asian Am Arts Ctr, NY, 90; Physicality, Color Dimensionality, Hunter Col Gallery, NY, 91; Lycian Performing Arts Ctr, NY, 93. *Pos:* Panelist, NY Found Arts, 94. *Teaching:* Lectr, Visual Arts Dept, Princeton Univ, 88-89, City Univ NY, Hunter Col, 84-90. *Awards:* Frances Le Moyne Page Award, Princeton Univ, 76; Tony Smith Fund Award, Hunter Col, 83; Visual Artists Fel Grant, Nat Endowment Arts, 87-88. *Media:* Oil, Acrylic. *Mailing Add:* 71 Drew Rd Warwick NY 10990

WANG, SAM
PHOTOGRAPHER
b Peking, China, Apr 4, 39; US citizen. *Study:* Augustana Col, Sioux Falls, BA, 64; Univ Iowa, MFA, 66. *Work:* SC State Collection; Chase Manhattan Collection & Metrop Mus Art, NY; Ctr For Creative Photography, Ariz; Herbert F Johnson Mus Art, Ithaca, NY; and others. *Exhib:* Portrait of the South, Palazzo Vinizia, 84; Silver & Silk, Mus of Hist & Technol, Smithsonian Inst, 75-77; Translations: Photog in New Forms, Herbert F Johnson Mus, 79; one-man shows, Mint Mus Art, 70, Greenville Co Mus Art, 72, 77 & 81, Light Factory, 79, RI Sch Design Photog Gallery, 79 & Fay Gold Gallery, 83; Counterparts, Metrop Mus Art, San Francisco Mus Mod Art & Corcoran Gallery Art, 83. *Pos:* Acquistions Adv Panel, SC State Mus, 84-92; chmn, State Art Collections Comm, SC, 77-78. *Teaching:* Prof photog, Clemson Univ, SC, 66-; vis artist photog & computer graphics, Penland Sch of Crafts, NC, summers 70, 74, 79, 89 & 91; vis artist printmaking workshop, Univ Notre Dame, 79. *Awards:* Unicolor Artist Support Award, 83; Prof Award of Merit, AAUP, 85; SAF/NEA Photography Fel, 87. *Bibliog:* David Featherstone (auth), Art Week, 73. *Mem:* Soc Photog Educ (bd dir, 73-77); Southeastern Col Art Conf. *Media:* Digital & Analog Photography. *Res:* Alternative Printing Process. *Publ:* Illusr, South Carolina Architecture 1670-1970, SC Tricentennial Comn, 70; New Am Nudes, Morgan & Morgan, 81; Beyond the Zone System, Focal Press, 88. *Dealer:* Kiang Gallery, Atlanta

WANLASS, STANLEY GLEN
SCULPTOR, PAINTER
b American Fork, Utah, Apr 3, 41. *Study:* Brigham Young Univ, BFA, 66, MA, 68. *Work:* Lewis & Clark Nat Monument, Ore; Mus'ee Nat De 'Automobile Raamsdonkveer, Holland; Hutchings Mus, Lehi, Utah; Mus Western Expansion, St Louis, Mo; Blackhawk Mus, Danville, Calif. *Comn:* Heroic sculpture, Wash State Arts Comn, Everett, 76; heroic bronze statue, Nat Park Serv, 83; heroic Lewis & Clark (bronze sculpture), City Seaside, Ore, 90; heroic sculpture, City Longbeach, Wash, 90; heroic bronze sculpture (founder), Muhlenberg Col, Allentown, Pa, 91. *Exhib:* Meadow Brook Concours D'Elegance, Rochester, Mich, 81-2003; Russo Bianco Mus, Aschaffenburg, Ger, 83-92; Los Angeles Co Mus, 85 & 94; Whitehouse, Wash, 88; Campbell (Soup) Mus, Philadelphia, 90; retrospective, Canton Art Inst, 90; Kodak-Japan, Toyko, 92. *Teaching:* Instr, Brigham Young Univ, Provo, Utah, 65-70, Europ Art Acad, Paris, 65; prof, Univ Grenoble, France, 69-70, Medicine Hat Col, Univ Calgary, Alta, 70 & 71 & Clatsop Col, Astoria, Ore, 71-86. *Awards:* Best of Show, Ore Trail Nat, 81; Silver Medal, Springville Art Mus, Utah, 81; Blue Ribbon Concours d'Elegance, Oakland Univ, Detroit, Mich, 83; Grand Prize & First Place, Auburn-Cord, Duesenberg Mus, Auburn, Ind, 85. *Bibliog:* Articles, SW Art Mag, 82, Automania, 84, Automobile Quarterly, 84 & Forbes Mag, 90. *Mem:* Automotive Fine Arts Soc. *Media:* Bronze; Acrylic, Oil. *Publ:* Auth, Dictionary of American Automobiles 1900-1930, Dover Publ, 73; An Artist's Viewpoint, Knightsbridge Publ Inc, 94; auth, Se-Deuce-Ing (automotive Design Pricinples) Buckaroo Comn, 2005. *Mailing Add:* c/o Rennaissance Int 10770 S Wasatch Blvd Sandy UT 84092

WARASHINA, M PATRICIA
CERAMIST, EDUCATOR
b Spokane, Wash. *Study:* Univ Wash, Seattle, BFA, MFA. *Work:* Everson Art Mus, Syracuse, NY; Nelson Gallery Art, Kansas City, Mo; Detroit Art Inst, Mich; Henry Art Gallery, Seattle, Wash; John Michael Kohler Arts Ctr, Sheboygan, Wis. *Exhib:* Int Exhib of Ceramics, Victoria & Albert Mus, London, Eng, 72; Sensible Cup Int Exhib, Sea of Japan Expos, Kanazawa, Japan, 7; Clay, Whitney Mus Am Art, NY, 74; 1st World Crafts Exhib, Ont Sci Ctr, Toronto, 74; The Collector, Mus Contemp Crafts, NY, 74; NW 77 Exhib, Mod Art Pavilion, Seattle Ctr, Wash, 77. *Teaching:* Instr art, Wis State Univ, Platteville, 64-65; instr art, Eastern Mich Univ, Ypsilanti, 66-68; prof art, Univ Wash, Seattle, 70-. *Media:* Clay. *Mailing Add:* 120 E Edgar St Seattle WA 98102

WARBURG, STEPHANIE WENNER
PAINTER, INSTRUCTOR
b Kalamazoo, Mich, Dec 29, 41. *Study:* Univ Mich Col Archit & Design, BS(drawing & design); and with Guy Palazzola & Milton Cohen; Columbia Univ Teachers Col, MA(fine arts & fine arts educ). *Work:* Earthwatch, Atrium Schools, Watertown, Mass. *Comn:* Curtin House/Baliceaux, Mustique, WI. *Exhib:* Slater Mus, Norwich, Conn, 69; Gilman Gallery, Chicago, 72; Lord & Taylor Gallery, NY, 69-79; Flora & Fauna of Madeira, Funchal, Madeira, Portugal, 73; Bermuda Soc Arts, 84; St Botolph Club, Boston, 85; Gallery Nakazawa, Hiroshima, Japan, 86; Oda Gallery, Hiroshima, Japan, 87; Nena's Choice Gallery, Bergdorf Goodman, NY, 90; Gallery Nakazauia, Hiroshima, 2001; Saks Fifth Avenue, 2002; Treasure Boutique, Mustique, West Indies, 2003; Marion Art Assoc Exhib, 2005; Lunnarts Juried Show, 2006; Framingham Art Assoc Juried Show, 2006. *Pos:* vis artist Bermuda Soc Arts, 85. *Teaching:* Chmn, Dept Art, Latin Sch Chicago, 70-72; instr watercolor & freehand drawing, Chamberlayne Jr Col, Boston, 75-81. *Awards:* Am Cancer Soc Art Awards, 67 & 68; Lyme Art Asn Second Prize for Painting, 68. *Bibliog:* Susan Croce Kelly (auth), It's all in the family: Sister artists display work here, St Louis Globe Dem, 70; On exhibit, Where Mag, 12/72. *Mem:* Bermuda Soc Arts. *Media:* Oil Wash, Oil on canvas. *Specialty:* Contemporary sea & landscapes. *Dealer:* Treasure Boutique Mustique West Indies; Northeast Fine Arts Northeast Harbor ME; Rogers Gallery Fairham MA. *Mailing Add:* 360 Beacon St Boston MA 02116

WARD, ELAINE
PAINTER
b Boston, Mass, June 4, 29. *Study:* Ecole Des Beaux Arts, France, BA, 53; Art Students League, 57-61. *Hon Degrees:* Hon Diploma, Asn des Beaux Arts de Cannes, 74. *Work:* New Eng Contemp Art Ctr, Brooklyn, Conn; Daytona Beach Mus, Fla; Ardan Asn, NY; Coastal Steel Co, Carteret, NJ; Pandora Co, Conway, NH; Zimmerli Mus, Rutgers Univ, New Brunswick, NJ; Daytona Beach Mus, Fla; Mus Roxbury, Conn. *Comn:* Portrait, comn by Barbara Andreadls, NY, 86; acrylic on canvas, Arthur Dann & co, NY, 88; acrylic on canvas, Design Decisions, NY, 89; mural on canvas, comn by Senor Louis Carraquillo Vieques, PR, 89. *Exhib:* Viewpoint Gallery, NY, 91; Phoenix Gallery, NY, 92; Elaine Benson Gallery, Bridgehampton, NY, 92; Barnes & Noble, Union Sq, NY; Guild Hall Mus, East Hampton, NY; solo show, Phoenix Gallery, New York City, 2006. *Teaching:* teacher/artist various schs San Miguel de Allende, Mex. *Awards:* First Prize, Munic Casino Cannes, 77; Jeffrey Childs Willis Mem Award, 96; East End Arts Coun Award, 96; NAWA Award, recipient Muriel E Halpern Mem Award, 2003. *Bibliog:* Deanna Freedman (auth), Enlarging the viewers experience, Artspeak, 2/89; Mary Jo Godwin (auth), Exotic Star, Wilson Libr Bull, 4/89; Charles Ditlefsein (auth), Women Artists, Cedco Publ Co, 90. *Mem:* Nat Asn Women Artist; Art Studio Club (treas, 88-90); Nat Art Club. *Media:* Watercolor, Acrylic. *Specialty:* Fine Arts. *Publ:* Illusr, cover, Wilson Libr Bul, 4/89; auth, articles in Manhattan Art Mag & Artspeak, 90; Art review, NY Times, Helen A Harrison (cur), 9/29/02. *Dealer:* Phoenix Gallery 568 Broadway New York NY 10012. *Mailing Add:* 175 E 62 St New York NY 10021

WARD, JOHN LAWRENCE
HISTORIAN, PAINTER
b East Orange, NJ, Feb 6, 38. *Study:* Hamilton Col, BA, 60; Yale Univ, MA(art hist), 62; Univ NMex, MFA(painting), 66; Boston Univ, PhD(art hist), 84. *Work:* Univ NMex; Ala Power Co, Birmingham; Astronomy Dept, Univ Fla; McGraw-Hill Corp Headquarters, NY; Cornell Fine Arts Mus, Rollins Col. *Exhib:* The Human Presence, Jacksonville Art Mus, Fla, 74; one-man shows, Fla Tech Univ, Orlando, 76, Univ Fla, Gainesville, 76 & 86, Stetson Univ, DeLand, Fla, 92, & Univ N Fla, 01; Southeast Juried Exhib, Fine Arts Mus S, Mobile, Ala, 87; 59th Ann Cooperstown Art Asn Nat,

94; Charlotte Co Nat Art Show, Punta Gorda, Fla, 98; group shows, Southeastern Ctr for Contemp Art, Winston-Salem, NC, 79; Southern Realism, Miss Mus Art, traveling, 79, & Corporealities, Cornell Fine Arts Mus, Rollins Col, 2002; and others. *Teaching:* Prof art hist and painting, Univ Fla, 62-64 & 66-. *Awards:* Best of Show, 5th Ann N Fla Art Competition, Fla State Univ, 90; First Prize, 59th Ann Cooperstown Art Asn Nat, 94; Best in Show, Charlotte Co Nat Art Show, Punta Gorda, Fla. *Mem:* Col Art Asn; Hist Netherlandish Art. *Media:* Oil. *Res:* Flemish painting, American Realist painting. *Publ:* Auth, The criticism of photography as art: The photographs of Jerry Uelsmann, 70; Hidden symbols in Jan Van Eyck's Annunciations, Vol LVII, 75, Art Bulletin; The Perception of Pictorial Space in Perspective Pictures, Vol IX, Leonardo, 76; American Realist Painting, 1945-1980, UMI Res Press, 89; Disguised symbolism as enactive symbolism in Van Eyck's Paintings, Artibus et Historiae, 94; Edwin Dickinson: A Critical History of His Paintings, Univ Del Press, 2003. *Mailing Add:* Sch of Art and Art History Univ Fla PO Box 115801 Gainesville FL 32611-5801

WARD, JOSEPH MARSHALL
PAINTER, EDUCATOR
b Phoenix, Ariz, Feb 11, 22. *Study:* Univ Ky, Lexington, with Edward Warder Rannells, BA, 46; Philadelphia Col Art, with Henry C Pitz, dipl, 49; E Tenn State Univ, Johnson City, MA(art educ), 65. *Work:* Charleston Southern Univ; Bank of Murray, Ky; Va Intermont Col; City Hall, North Charleston. *Comn:* Oil painting, City of North Charleston, SC, 96. *Exhib:* Young Am Paints, Smithsonian Inst, Washington, 40; Ann Mid-South Exhib, Watkins Inst, Nashville, 50; Ann Guild SC Artists, Gibbes Art Gallery, Charleston, 76; Ann Coastal Carolina Fairs. *Pos:* Artist, Baptist Sunday Sch Bd, Nashville, 49-53, artist-illusr, 53-59. *Teaching:* Instr applied art, Va Intermont Col, Bristol, 59-68; assoc prof art & chmn dept, Charleston Southern Univ, Charleston, SC, 68-87. *Awards:* Second Place Oil Painting, Mid-South Exhib, Nashville, 50; Third Place Watercolor, Nationwide Sears Art Shows, Bristol, Tenn, 61; Merit Awards, Coastal Carolina Fair, Watercolors, 84, 86 & 93. *Mem:* Charleston Artist Guild (mem bd, 75-77, vpres, 76 & chmn scholarship comt, 83-89). *Media:* Watercolor, pastel

WARD, NARI
SCULPTOR
Exhib: One-person exhibs, Amazing Grace, Harlem Firehouse Space, New York & Carpet Angel, New Mus, New York, 93, Idle Drift, Le Magasin, Centre National d'Art Contemporain, Grenoble, France, 94 & Happy Smilers: Duty Free Shopping, Deitch Proj, New York, 96; Artists in Residence 1992-1993, Studio Mus, Harlem, NY, 93; Heart of Darkness, Kroller-Muller Mus, Neth, 94; Whitney Mus Am Art Biennial, New York, 95, 2006; Pusuit of the Sacred: Evocations of the Spiritual in Contemporary African American Art, Betty Rymer Gallery, Art Inst Chicago, 97; Projects: How to Build and Maintain the Virgin Fertility in our Soul, PS1 Mus, Long Island, 97; Edge of Awareness, World Health Orgn, Geneva, Switz, 98; Am Acad Arts & Letts Exhib, New York, 98; and others. *Awards:* John Simon Guggenheim Fel, New York, 92; Nat Endowment Arts, Washington, DC, 94; Pollack Krasner Found, New York, 96; Willard L Metcalf Award, Am Acad Arts & Letters, 98. *Bibliog:* Jeffrey Deitch (auth), Nari Ward: Aperto, Flash Art, 97, summer 93; Holland Carter (auth), Bob Rivera, Michelle Talibah, and Nari Ward, NY Times, C12, 12/17/93; Leslie Camhi (auth), Other rooms, Village Voice, 83, 10/9/96; and others. *Mailing Add:* 307 W 141st St Apt 180 New York NY 10030

WARD-BROWN, DENISE D
SCULPTOR
Study: Tyler Sch Art, Temple Univ, Philadelphia, Pa, BFA(cum laude, painting), 75; Howard Univ, Washington, DC, MFA(summa cum laude, sculpture), 84. *Exhib:* Other Rooms, Kunstrum, Washington, DC, 90; Encore Show, Montgomery Col, Tacoma Park, Md, 90; Gathered Visions, Smithsonian-Anacostia Mus, Washington, DC, 90; Next Generation: Southern Black Aesthetic, Contemp Arts Ctr, Cincinnati, Ohio, Orlando Mus Art, Fla, Contemp Arts Ctr, New Orleans, La, Hunter Mus Art, Chattanooga, Tenn, Samuel P Harn Mus, Gainesville, Fla & SE Ctr Contemp Art, Winston-Salem, NC, 90-92; Lost & Found, Art St Louis, Mo, 92; Sculptors Invitational, Lindenwood Col, St Louis, Mo, 93; New Blood, Murray State Univ, Eagle Gallery, Ky, 93; Girlfriends, Portfolio Gallery, St Louis, Mo, 94; History & Memory-Pictures & Objects, Univ Wis, Eau Claire, 94; Sources: Multi-Cult Influences on the Art of African-Am Sculptors, Univ Md, College Park, 94; wild dreams/domestic obsessions, St Louis Design Ctr, 96; Seeing Jazz, Smithsonian Inst Traveling Exhib Serv, 96; Currents 62, St Louis Art Mus, 97; Old Forms, New Rhythms, Ghanain Nat Mus, 99; one-woman show, De Paul Univ, 2000. *Teaching:* Assoc prof sculpture, dir grad studies, Wash Univ, currently. *Awards:* Individual Artist Grant, Washington DC Comn on the Arts & Humanities, 86, 87, 89 & 91; Mbari, Ritual & Rememory, Regional Artists' Projs Grant, 94; Fulbright Scholar, African Res Prog, Ghana, 97-98. *Bibliog:* Neal Lerner (auth), Artist/educator, Wash Univ Record, 9/9/96; Robert Duffy (auth), Six artists in search of a curator, St Louis Post-Dispatch, 10/20/96; Must see, Riverfront Times, St Louis, Mo, 10/23/96. *Publ:* auth, Isolation/Saturation: Washington, DC/Montana Artists Exchange, WPA Newsletter, Washington, DC, Vol 1, 87; ed, Am Weaver, Gumbo Ya Ya, 96. *Mailing Add:* Dept Sculpture Sch Art Washington Univ St Louis MO 63130-4899

WARDEN, P GREGORY
ADMINISTRATOR, WRITER
b Florence, Italy, Nov 28, 50; US Citizen. *Study:* Univ Pa, BA, 72; Bryn Mawr Col, MA, 76, PhD, 78. *Pos:* assoc dean, Meadows Sch Arts, 98-; interim dir, Meadows Mus, 2001-03. *Teaching:* prof, art hist, Southern Meth Univ, Dallas, 82-. *Interests:* Mediterranean Art & Archaeology. *Publ:* The Metal Finds from Poggio Eivitate (Murlo), Bretschneider, 85; Classical Near Eastern Bronzes in the Hilprecht Collection, Univ Pa, 97; Foru, Figure, and Narrative in Greek Vase Painting, Dallas, Ohio. *Mailing Add:* Southern Meth Univ Meadows Mus Meadows Sch of Arts Dallas TX 75275

WARDLAW, GEORGE MELVIN
PAINTER, SCULPTOR
b Baldwyn, Miss, Apr 9, 27. *Study:* Memphis Acad Arts, BFA, 51; Univ Miss, with David Smith & Jack Tworkov, MFA, 55. *Work:* Memphis Brooks Mus Art, Tenn; Milwaukee Art Mus, Wis; Wichita Art Mus, Kans; Yale Art Gallery, New Haven, Conn; Mus Fine ARts, Springfield, Mass; Memphis Brooks Mus Art, Tenn; Wichita Art Mus, Wichitka, Kans. *Comn:* Wall relief sculpture, 76 & sculpture, 76, Mt Sinai Med Ctr; specific sculpture, Johnson Wax Corp, Racine, Wis. *Exhib:* Yale Art Gallery, New Haven, Conn, 66; Abstract Paintings, 71 & solo exhib, 78-79, DeCordova Mus, Lincoln, Mass; Chicago Art Inst; Metrop Mus Art, NY; Nat Gallery; Portland Mus Art, Maine; Yeshiva Univ Mus, NY, 2002. *Teaching:* Asst prof art, State Univ NY Col, New Paltz, 56-63; assoc prof painting & exec off, Yale Univ, 64-68; prof painting & chmn dept, Univ Mass, 68-90, prof emer, 90-. *Awards:* Miss Inst Arts & Lett Award, 83; Univ Mass Fac Res Fel, 83. *Bibliog:* auth, Hugh Davies, Paintings in the Round (exhib catalog), DeCordova Mus & Sculpture Park, Lincoln, Mass, 78-79; auth & others, Transitions (exhib catalog), Memphis Brooks Mus Art, Tenn, 88. *Media:* Acrylic on canvas, Metal and wood. *Dealer:* Perimeter Gallery, Chicago, Ill. *Mailing Add:* 47 Morgan Cir Amherst MA 01002

WAREHALL, WILLIAM DONALD
GLASS BLOWER, CERAMIST
b Detroit, Mich, July 12, 1942. *Study:* Wayne State Univ, BFA, 68; Univ Wis, Madison, MFA, 71. *Work:* Chrysler Mus Art, Norfolk; Bergstrom Mahler Mus, Neenah, Wis; W Baton Rouge Hist Mus, Port Allen; La State Univ, Baton Rouge; Ariz State Univ, Tempe; and others. *Comn:* Reproduction of Ancient Maritime Glass Vessels, Tex A&M Univ, College Station, Tex, 90. *Exhib:* 20 Americans, Mus Contemp Art, NY, 71; Phases of New Realism, Lowe Art Mus, Coral Gables, Fla 72; California Design, Los Angeles Design Ctr, 76; one-man show, Anhalt Gallery, Los Angeles, 76; Tea Pot-24 Concepts, Rodell Gallery, Los Angeles, 82; New Glass, Heller Gallery, NY, 85; Southern Calif Glass, Scalar Gallery, Morristown, NJ 86; Calif, Elaine Potter Gallery, San Francisco, 86. *Teaching:* Instr art, Univ Minn, 71-73; from asst prof art to assoc prof, Calif State Univ, San Bernardino, 73-81, prof, 81-, chairperson, 88-90 & 95-97; asst prof, La State Univ, Baton Rouge, 78-79; exchange prof ceramics, Va Commonwealth Univ, Richmond, 86; Artist in residence, Buckingham Col Art & Design, UK, 94 & Southern Ill Univ, Edwardsville, 98-. *Bibliog:* Paul Donhauser (auth), History of Am Ceramics, Kendall & Hunt, 78. *Mem:* Am Craft Coun; Southern Calif Designer Craftsman; Glass Soc; Col Art Asn; Nat Coun Art Adminr. *Media:* Cast Glass, Pate de Verre; Clay. *Dealer:* Sandy Webster Gallery Philadelphia PA; Craft Alliance Gallery St Louis MO. *Mailing Add:* Calif State Univ Art Dept 5500 State College Pkwy San Bernardino CA 92407

WARK, ROBERT RODGER
ADMINISTRATOR, HISTORIAN
b Edmonton, Alta, Oct 7, 24; US citizen. *Study:* Univ Alta, BA & MA, LLD; Harvard Univ, MA & PhD. *Pos:* Cur art, Huntington Libr & Art Gallery, 56-90, sr res assoc, 90-. *Teaching:* Instr art, Harvard Univ, 52-54 & Yale Univ, 54-56; lectr art, Calif Inst Technol, 60-90 & Univ Calif, Los Angeles, 65-80; retired. *Res:* English art of the Georgian period. *Publ:* Ed, Sir Joshua Reynolds, Discourses on Art, 59; auth, Early British Drawings in the Huntington Collection 1700-1750, 69; Drawings by John Flaxman in the Huntington Collection, 70; Ten British Pictures 1740-1840; Drawings by Thomas Rowlandson in the Huntington Collection, 75; plus others. *Mailing Add:* Henry E Huntington Libr & Art Gallery 1151 Oxford Rd San Marino CA 91108

WARKOV, ESTHER
PAINTER
b Winnipeg, Man, Oct 12, 41. *Study:* Winnipeg Sch Art, 58-61. *Work:* Nat Gallery, Ottawa; Mus Fine Arts, Montreal; Vancouver Art Gallery; Winnipeg Art Gallery; Beaver Brook Art Gallery, Fredricton, NB. *Exhib:* Expo '67, Montreal; Marlborough Godard Exhib, 73; Mus Mod Art, Paris, 73; Albright-Knox Art Gallery, Buffalo, 74. *Awards:* Can Coun Bursaries, 67-72; Can Coun Grant, 73-74. *Bibliog:* Esther Warkov, Can Broadcasting Corp, 73. *Mem:* Royal Can Acad Arts. *Media:* Oil. *Dealer:* Marlborough Godard Ltd 1490 Sherbrooke W Montreal PQ Can. *Mailing Add:* 341 Matheson Ave Winnipeg MB R2W 0C9 Canada

WARNECKE, JOHN CARL
ARCHITECT
b Oakland, Ca, Feb 24, 19. *Study:* Stanford Univ, AB, 41; Harvard Univ, MA 42. *Comn:* Works incl US Naval Acad Master Plan, Michelson and Chauvenet Halls, Annapolis, Md, Univ Calif at Santa Cruz Master Plan and Libr, Lafayette Sq, Wash, Georgetown Univ Libr, Wash, Kaiser Ctr for Technol, Pleasanton, Calif; bldgs, Stanford Univ, Hawaii State Capitol, Honolulu, Philip A. Hart Senate off bldg, USSR Embassy, Hennepin Govt Ctr, Minneapolis, JF Kennedy Mem Grave, Arlington Nat Cemetery, Va, Neiman Marcus and Bergdorf Goodman Stores, Logan Airport, Boston, Am Hosp, Paris, The Sun Co. Hdqrs, Radnor, Pa, King Abdulaziz Univ Med Ctr, Jedda, Saudi Arabia, Yanbu Town Ctr Master Plan, Hilton Hotel & Casino, Atlantic City. *Pos:* Assoc, Miller & Warnecke, archit, 44-46; partner, Warnecke & Warnecke, 54-62; pres, dir, design John Carl Warnecke & Assoc, 58-. *Awards:* Recipient Arnold Brunner prize in archit Nat Inst Arts and Letters, 57; also 70 nat, regional awards for excellence. *Mem:* Fel Am Inst of Archits; Nat Acad (assoc, 58-94, acad, 94-). *Mailing Add:* 300 Broadway St San Francisco CA 94133-4587

WARNER, DOUGLAS WARFIELD
PAINTER, COLLAGE ARTIST
b Tulsa, Okla, June 8, 30. *Study:* Okla State Univ, BFA, 53; Univ Wis, MS(art), 57. *Work:* Brit Mus, London; Smithsonian Inst & Libr Cong, Washington; Cleveland Mus Art, Ohio; Calif Palace Legion Honor, San Francisco; Univ NC, Chapel Hill. *Comn:* Nine Sculptures, Flint Bd Educ, Mich, 75; Public Canvas I (billboard), Michelob Lite,

Flint, Mich, 81; painting, Perfusions Services Inc, Brighton, Mich. *Exhib:* 154th Ann Drawing Exhib, Pa Acad Fine Arts, Philadelphia, 59; Mich Artists' Ann, Detroit Inst Art, 59, 60, 61 & 65; Drawing USA, St Paul Art Ctr, Minn, 63; Six Printmakers, Univ Nev, Reno, 79; Mich Watercolor Soc, 80 & 81; Denver Mus Art; Tsukubu Tokyo, 84; Springfield Mus, Ill, 85; plus 40 solo exhib. *Teaching:* Instr drawing & design, C S Mott Community Col, Flint, Mich, 57-86, chmn dept art, 63-67, 86 (retired). *Awards:* Purchase Awards, Philbrook Art Ctr, 53, Okla Art Ctr, 77 & Mich Coun Arts, 78; Creative Artists Grant, Mich Coun Arts, 87 & 90. *Bibliog:* S Gordon Gapper (auth), Flint profile, Flint J, 4/3/66; Sam Olkinetzky (foreword), Exhib Catalog, Xochipilli Gallery, 2/81; John Dempsey (foreward), Subtle Reminders (exhib catalog), Buckham Gallery, 10/91. *Mem:* Buckham Gallery, Flint, Mich. *Media:* Mixed Media Constructions on Canvas & Board. *Mailing Add:* 2721 Coventry Ct Flint MI 48503

WARNER, HERBERT KELII, JR
PRINTMAKER
b Honolulu, Hawaii, July 29, 43. *Study:* Univ Hawaii, BFA, 67; Pratt Inst, MFA, 72. *Work:* Rutgers Univ, Camden, NJ; Honolulu Acad Arts, Honolulu, Hawaii. *Exhib:* Purdue Univ, West Lafayette, Ind, 77; Okla Nat Drawing & Prints, Oklahoma City, 77; Asn Am Artists, NY, 77; Libr Cong, Washington, 77; Trenton State Mus, NJ, 80. *Pos:* Prod mgr, Philadelphia Forum, 96. *Teaching:* Asst prof, Rutgers Univ, Camden, NJ, 72-79; teacher design, Art Inst Philadelphia, 80-82. *Awards:* Purchase Awards, Purdue Univ, 77 & Honolulu Acad Arts, 77; Fel, State NJ, 78. *Media:* Etching, Lithography. *Mailing Add:* 5425 Walker St Philadelphia PA 19124

WARNER, JACK
COLLECTOR
b Decatur, Ill. *Study:* Culver Military Acad, Ind, 1936; Washington & Lee Univ, BA, 1936-40. *Pos:* Chmn emer, Gulf States Paper Corp, Tuscaloosa, Ala, currently. *Awards:* Distinguished Achievement Award, President's Cabinet, Univ Ala, 1999; Howell Heflin Statesmanship Award, Arts & Humanities, 2000; Alabama Preservation Alliance Exemplary Award, 2001; West Alabama Community Hall of Fame, Chamber Com, 2003; Patron of Arts Award, Arts & Humanities Coun Tuscaloosa, 2003; Named one of Top 200 Collectors, ARTnews Mag, 2004. *Mem:* Decorative Arts Trust (bd gov); Univ Ala Nat Advisory Bd; Mt Vernon Advisory Com. *Collection:* Late 18th to early 20th Century American Art. *Mailing Add:* Westervelt Warner Mus of Am Art 2700 Yacht Club Way NE Tuscaloosa AL 35406

WARNER, MARINA
WRITER, CRITIC
b London, Eng, Nov 9, 46. *Study:* Lady Margaret Hall, Oxford Univ, MA, 67; Univ Exeter, DLitt, 95; Univ York, DLitt, 97; Univ St Andrews, DLitt, 98; Sheffield Hallam Univ, Hon Doc, 95; Univ N London, Hon Doc, 97. *Pos:* Vis scholar, Getty Ctr Hist Art & Humanities, 87-88. *Teaching:* Tinbergen prof Frasmus, Univ Rotterdam; vis prof, Queen Mary & Westfield Col, Univ London & Univ Ulster, 95-, Univ York, 96-; vis prof, Univ York, 96-; Mellon prof art hist, Univ Pittsburgh, spring 97. *Awards:* Short Term Fel, Coun Humanities, Princeton, 96; Harvey Darton Award, 96; Mythopoeic Fantasy Award, 96. *Mem:* Fel Royal Soc Lit, Eng. *Res:* Female symbols; the body as sign; the construction of female identity in imagery; fairy tales. *Publ:* Auth, Six Myths of Our Time, 95; contribr, Zarina Bhimji (exhib catalog), Cambridge, 95; Visual Display Culture Beyond Appearances (Lynne Cooke & Peter Wollen, eds), New York, 95; Helen Chadwick Stilled Lives, Edinburgh, 96; David Nash: Forms into Time, London, 96. *Mailing Add:* 10 Dunollie Pl London NW5 2XR United Kingdom

WARREN, DAVID BOARDMAN
CURATOR
b Baltimore, Md, Mar 11, 37. *Study:* Princeton Univ, AB(cum laude), 59; Univ Del, MA, 65. *Collection Arranged:* Bayou Bend Collection (auth, catalog), Mus Fine Arts, Houston, 65-, Southern Silver (auth, catalog), 68, Gothic Revival style in America 1830-1870 (auth, catalog), 76, nineteenth century American landscape: Selections from the Thyssen-Bornenisza Collection (auth, catalog), 82; Marks of Achievement: Four Centuries of American Presentation Silver (auth, catalog), 87; The Masterpieces of Bayou Bend (1620-1870) and the Voyage of Life, Bayou Bend Mus Americana Tenneco, 91; The Grandeur of Viceregal Mexico: Treasures from the Museo Franz Mayer, 2002, Mus Fine Arts, Houston, 2002, Winterhven Mus, 2002-2003, San Diego Mus Art, 2003 (co-auth catalog). *Pos:* Cur, Bayou Bend Collection, Mus Fine Arts, Houston, 65-, assoc dir, 74-; trustee, Henry Francis Du Pont Winterthur Mus, 77-; dir, Bayou Bend Collections and Gardens, 87-. *Teaching:* Lectr, Am Decorative Arts, Rice Univ, 66-73. *Publ:* Coauth, Texas Furniture: The Cabinetmakers and Their Work 1840-1870, Univ Tex Press, 75; contribr, A Guide to the Collections, Mus Fine Arts, Houston, 81; Harry N Abrams (auth), Marks of Achievement: Four Centuries of American Presentation Silver, 87; American Decorative Arts and Paintings in the Bayou Bend Collection & Gardens, Princeton Univ Press, 98. *Mailing Add:* Mus Fine Arts Houston 1001 Bissonnet St PO Box 6826 Houston TX 77005

WARREN, JACQUELINE LOUISE
PAINTER, EDUCATOR
b National City, Calif, Nov 3, 46. *Study:* Southwest Mo State Univ, BFA, 67; Ariz State Univ, MFA, 71; Stanford Univ, 89. *Work:* Hallmark Corp; Quaker Oats; IBM; Pepsi Cola; Blue Cross; Price Waterhouse; Seven Up Corp; May Corp. *Exhib:* Works of Paper Nat Competition, 80; Paper Nat Competitive, Columbia Col, Mo, 81; Watercolor, USA, Nelson-Atkins Mus Art, Kansas City; Morgan Gallery, Kansas City; Ruth Bachofner Gallery, Antsource Los Angeles, Calif; William Shearburn Gallery, St Louis. *Collection Arranged:* Art on Paper, Cox Gallery, Drury Col, 81. *Teaching:* Prof painting & drawing, Southwest Mo State Univ, Springfield, 75-79; prof design, Drury Col, Springfield, Mo, 79-; prof art & design, Drury Univ, currently. *Awards:* First Prize, Ariz State Fair, 70; Best of Show, Spiva Mus, Joplin, Mo, 78; First Prize, Sch Ozarks, Branson, Mo, 79; Best of Show, Mid Four Exhib, Nelson Alkins Art Mus, Kansas City; Fel painting, Nat Endowment Arts; Herword Cook Fel Painting. *Bibliog:* Edgar Albin (auth), Artist profile, Art Voices South Mag, 80; New Art Examiner. *Mem:* Col Art Asn; Watercolor Nat Hon Soc. *Media:* Mixed Media. *Dealer:* Morgan Gallery Kansas City MO; Vanstraaten Gallery Chicago IL; William Shearburn St Louis. *Mailing Add:* 918 S Weller St Springfield MO 65802

WARREN, JULIANNE BUSSERT BAKER
PHOTOGRAPHER, HISTORIAN
b Lima, Ohio, May 8, 16. *Work:* Pub Libr Cincinnati & Hamilton Co; Truman Libr & Johnson Libr, Austin, Tex; Smithsonian Inst. *Comn:* Photographs of eight US Presidents; Prime Minister Wilson, London; Princess Margaret. *Exhib:* Cincinnati Art Mus, 59; Shillito's Dept Store, Cincinnati, 61; Jewish Community Ctr, Cincinnati, 70; Cincinnati Woman's Club, 74; one-man shows, Pub Libr Cincinnati & Hamilton Co, 67 & Exhib of Collection, 78; Asn Am Ed Cartoonist Collection, Libr Commun Graphic Arts, Ohio State Univ, 84. *Pos:* Mgr, Photo-finishing Co, Cincinnati, 41-48; Photogr radio station, 50-52; news photogr, Cincinnati Post, 52-68; archivist, Asn Am Edit Cartoonist, Ohio State Univ, 84-. *Awards:* First Prize, Nat Heirloom Contest, 59; First Prize, Newspaper Guild's Page-One Ball, 61; Two Prizes, Best Women's Page Photog, Univ Mo, 65. *Mem:* Asn Am Edit Cartoonists (archivist 71-92, historian, 71-). *Publ:* Contribr & illusr, Press Photography, Macmillan, 61; coauth, Cincinnati in Color, Hastings House, 78. *Dealer:* B Alden Olson Corp Art Concepts The Loft Mt Adams St Cincinnati OH 45202. *Mailing Add:* 1815 William Howard Taft Rd Unit 203 Cincinnati OH 45206

WARREN, LYNNE
CURATOR, WRITER
b Lowell, Mass, Mar 12, 52. *Study:* Sch Art Inst Chicago, BFA, 76. *Collection Arranged:* Kenneth Josephson: Photographs (auth, catalog), 83; DOGS, 84; Alternative Spaces: A History in Chicago (auth, catalog), 84; Jon Kessler: Sculpture (auth, catalog), 86; Donald Sultan: Paintings (auth, catalog), 87; Starn Twins, 88; Julia Wachtel, 90; Art in Chicago, 1945-1995 (auth, catalog). *Pos:* Cur spec projs, Mus Contemp Art, Chicago, Ill, 90-95. *Awards:* Catalog Auth Award, DOGS, Art Mus Asn, 84. *Publ:* Auth, Mies in Chicago (brochure), Mus Contemp Art, 86. *Mailing Add:* 1554 N Hoyne Ave Chicago IL 60622-8840

WARREN, PETER WHITSON See Whitson, Peter Whitson Warren

WARREN, RUSS
PAINTER
b Washington, DC, Dec 29, 51. *Study:* Univ St Thomas, Houston, Tex, 69-71; Univ NMex, BFA, 73; Univ Tex, San Antonio, MFA, 77. *Work:* Chase Manhattan Bank, NY; Gen Elec Co, Fairfield, Conn; Sydney & Francis Lewis Found, Richmond, Va; Princeton Univ, NJ; Gibbs Art Mus, Charleston, SC. *Exhib:* Biennial, Whitney Mus Am Art, NY, 81; Painting & Sculpture Today, Indianapolis Mus Art, Ind, 82; Painting in the South (with catalog), Va Mus Art, Richmond, 83; Southern Fictions, Contemp Art Mus, Houston, 83; USA Portrait of the South, Palazzo Venezia, Rome, 84; Venice Biennale, Italy, 84; solo exhibs, Emblems of the Unseeable (with catalog), Knight Gallery, Charlotte, NC, 84 & NC Mus Art, Raleigh, 85; Looking South-A Different Dixie, Birmingham Mus Art, Birmingham, Ala, 88; 1989 Corcoran Biennial, Corcoran Mus, Washington, DC, 89. *Teaching:* Prof art, Davidson Col, Davidson, NC, 78-. *Awards:* Southeast Cent Contemp Art Fel, 84; NC Artist Fel, 85. *Bibliog:* Richard Flood (auth), Russ Warren, Artforum, 9/81; Ronny Cohen (auth), Russ Warren, Art News, 2/83; Vivian Raynor (auth), Russ Warren, New York Times, 12/28/85; Barry Schwabsky (auth), Russ Warren's magic theater, Arts Mag, 85. *Media:* Acrylic. *Dealer:* Hodges-Taylor Gallery 227 N Tryon Charlotte NC 28202; Les Yeux du Monde Gallery 115 S First St Charlottesville VA 22902. *Mailing Add:* PO Box 991 Davidson NC 28036

WARREN, TOM
PHOTOGRAPHER, CONCEPTUAL ARTIST
b Cleveland, Ohio, Aug 23, 54. *Study:* Kent State Univ, BS, 77. *Work:* Art Inst Chicago, Ill; Mus of the City of NY; Fales Libr & Bobst Libr, NY Univ, NYC; Queens Mus Art, Flushing, NY. *Comn:* New Heritage Theater, Youth Portraits, Harlem, NY, 2005. *Exhib:* Portrait Studio, Semaphore Gallery, NY, 83; No Portraits, Greathouse Gallery, NY, 85; Portrait Studio, Spaces Gallery, Cleveland, 90; Flash, Willoughby Sharp Gallery, NY, 91; Lessons in Life, Art Inst Chicago, Ill, 94; East Village USA, New Mus Contemp Art, NY, 2004; Queens Int, Queens Mus Art, Flushing, NY, 2004, 2006. *Pos:* Photogr, Sotheby's, 83-86 & freelance, 90-2003. *Teaching:* Instr photog, Case Western Reserve, Univ Cleveland, 88-90. *Awards:* Project Grant, NY State Coun on the Arts, 82. *Bibliog:* Judd Tully (auth), No portraits review, East Village Eye, 6/85; Lynn Padwe (auth), Artistic endeavors, Photo Dist News, 9/86; Helen Cullinan (auth), Performance Artists Exposes Nuances of Photog, Cleveland Plain Dealer, 1990. *Mem:* Spaces, Cleveland, Ohio; New York Artist Pass; MoMA, New York, NY; Harlem Arts Alliance, New York, NY; DIA Found, NY. *Media:* Photography. *Res:* music, sound, audio, film. *Interests:* Art, Music, Lit. *Collection:* Small works by young contemporary artists, and many others. *Publ:* Contribr, Just Another Asshole No 7, Thought Objects, Barbra Ess, 87; East Village Guide, Portraits of Art Dealers, Roland Hagenberg, 86; Life Lessons, Martin Edelston; East Village USA, New Mus, Cameron, Kiwin, Moore, 2004. *Dealer:* Abaton Garage 100 Gifford St Jersey City NJ 07304; Studio 323 W 39th St New York NY 10018. *Mailing Add:* 39-40 52nd St Apt 6D Woodside NY 11377

WARREN, WIN (WINTON) W
PAINTER, LECTURER
b Jakin, Ga, Nov 13, 1914. *Study:* Univ Ga, LLB & JD; US Dept Agr Grad Sch, 67; Cath Univ Am, 68 & 69; Univ Md Grad Sch, with Nicholas Krushenick, Jerry Clapsaddle & Helen Van Wyk, 77-82. *Work:* Univ Md; Sons of the Am Revolution Mus; Pioneers of Flight (painting), Hall of Fame Mus, 98; South Md Hosp Ctr;

Airport Mus, Col Park, Md. *Comn:* Equestrian portraits of George Washington & Lafayette, Johnston & Lemon Brokerage Firm, Washington, 76; mural, Community Ctr, Md-Nat Capital Park & Planning Comn, 79; portrait, Sons of the Am Revolution Mus, 92. *Exhib:* Artists Today Exhib, Md-Nat Capital Park & Planning Comn, 79; one-man shows, Montpelier Cult Arts Ctr, Laurel, 80 & Md Univ Club, 85; Art Barn Asn-Nat Park Serv Exhib, 83; Alpha Gallerie, Rockville, Md, 86. *Pos:* Lect & tours Am Art, Nat Mus Am Art, Smithsonian Inst, Washington, DC, 79-96; adv & selection bd, Montpelier Cult Arts Ctr, 79-93. *Awards:* Nat Capitol Area Artists Award, United Way, 85. *Bibliog:* article, Washington, DC Artists News, 3/84; article, Camilla Enterprise, 11/15/85 & 6/28/2000; article, College Park Gazette, Md, 3/18/99. *Mem:* Artists' Equity Asn; Col Art Asn; Prince George's Art Asn; Washington Soc Landscape Painters. *Media:* Acrylic, Oils. *Mailing Add:* 3112 Gracefield Rd #617 Silver Spring MD 20904-1896

WARRINER, LAURA B
ASSEMBLAGE ARTIST, COLLAGE ARTIST
b Tulsa Okla, Jan 18, 43. *Study:* Okla Baptist Univ; Oklahoma City Univ, 61-64 & 79-81. *Work:* Skidmore Col Art Gallery, Saratoga Springs, NY; Henry Ward Ranger Fund Purchase through Smithsonian Inst Nat Gallery, Washington, DC; Okla Univ Found, Norman; Univ Okla Med Ctr, Okla City. *Exhib:* Solo exhibs, Firehouse Art Ctr, Norman, Okla, 86, Hulsey Gallery, Norick Art Ctr, Okla City Univ, Okla, 91; Dimensions '87: Lenexa's National 3-Dimensional Art Show, Lenexa, Kans, 87 & North Lake Col, Irving, Tex, 94; The Painted Photographs, Cent State Univ Mus Art, Edmond, Okla, 89; Flash Points, Goddard Art Ctr, Ardmore, Okla, 89; Small Works Invitational, M A Doran Gallery, Tulsa, Okla, 88 & 90; Okla Visual Arts Coalition Invitational 12 x 12 Exhib, Okla City, 91, 92, 93, 94, 96, 97 & 98; Woman's Work, Invitational Exhib, City Arts, Okla City, 94; Cafe City Art Invitational, City Arts Ctr, Okla City, 95 & 96; Continued renovation and documentation of 1920's warehouse, 97, 98 & 99. *Pos:* Adv bd, Norick Art Ctr, Okla City Univ, 89-; bd trustees, 88-94. *Teaching:* Instr, Okla Mus Art, Okla City, 74-78; instr regional workshops, Norman, Okla, Stillwater, Okla, Okla City, Okla, Edmond, Okla & Red River, NMex, 75-; instr, Okla Arts Inst, Okla City, 77-81; instr artists-in-residence, Okla State Arts Coun, 81-85; instr, Goddard Art Ctr, Ardmore, Okla, 83. *Awards:* Award for Watercolor, Allied Artists Am 60th Ann Exhib, 74; Barbara Vassilieff Award for Flowers-Still Life, Allied Artists Am 61st Ann Exhib, 75; Century Award of Merit, Rocky Mountain Nat Watermedia Exhib, 75. *Bibliog:* Ralph Fabri (auth), Flower painting in all media, 2/74 & Can you succeed in art without really trying, 9/74, Today's Art; Barbara Nechis (auth), Watercolor the Creative Experience, Northlight; Flash Points (catalog), Central Univ, Edmond, Okla. *Mem:* Okla Visual Arts Coalition (vpres, 88- & bd trustee, 89-94). *Media:* Multimedia. *Mailing Add:* One NE Third St Oklahoma City OK 73104-2205

WARRIOR, DELLA C
ADMINISTRATOR
Study: Northeastern State Univ, BA(sociology); Harvard Univ, MA(educ). *Pos:* Pres, Inst Am Indian Arts, Santa Fe, develop dir; Chief Exec Officer, Otoe-Missouria Tribe, 89-92; exec bd mem, World Indigenous Nations Higher Educ Consortium; mem US Pres Bd Adv, on Tribal Col & Univ, 2002-. *Mailing Add:* Inst Am Indian Arts 83 Avon Nu Po Rd Santa Fe NM 87508

WARSHAW, ELAINE N
SCULPTOR, DIRECTOR
b New York, NY, Apr 11, 24. *Study:* Pratt Inst, 41-44; Art Students League, 45; studied with Jose de Creeft, 70 and Elaine Rapp. *Comn:* Holocaust Mem, Limestone, Temple Israel, Jamaica, Queens, NY, 80, Long Beach, 82; Garden Sculpture, comn by Dr & Mrs S Pion, Md. *Exhib:* Nat Asn Women Artists, Bergen Community Mus, NJ, 80, Equitable Galleries, New York, 82 & Lever House, NY, 82; Nat Acad Galleries, NY, 82; Family of Man, N Shore Sculpture Ctr, Great Neck, Long Island, NY, 85; Hecksher Mus, Long Island, 85. *Pos:* Dir sculptor, Merrick, NY, 72-90. *Teaching:* Instr stone carving, Sculpture Ctr, 70-72. *Mem:* Nat Asn Women Artists. *Media:* Stone, Wood. *Mailing Add:* 2164 Seneca Dr S Merrick NY 11566

WARSHAW, LARRY
PAINTER, PHOTOGRAPHER
b New York, NY, June 18, 36. *Study:* Showhegan Sch Painting & Sculpture, 57-58; NY Univ, BA, 58, MA, 59. *Work:* Boston Mus Fine Arts; Kunsthalle, Cologne, Ger; Contemp Art Mus, Houston; Worchester Art Mus, Mass; Philadelphia Mus Art; NY Life Insurance Co Collection; Lincoln Ctr Collection, NY; and others. *Comn:* Sculpture, Gen Servs Admin, NY, 75; wall relief & paintings, Swedish Metal Corp, Gottensburg, 78; wall murals, Hochschuler Gemeinshaft, Ger, 78, Giotto Restaurant, NY, 79 & Cunard Ship Lines Inc, 80. *Exhib:* Corcoran Biennial Exhib, 63 & Color Surfaces: New Poetics, 79, Corcoran Mus Art, Wash; Spirtual Forms in Painting, Philadelphia Mus, 80; Paint as Poetic Surface, Worchester Mus, 83. *Teaching:* Instr, Queens Col, H Lehman Col & Rockland Community Col. *Awards:* Ford Found Purchase Award, 64; MacDowell Colony Fel, Edward MacDowell Asn, 64; Edna St Vincent, Colony, NY, 91. *Bibliog:* Diana Morris (auth) Summer group show, Arts Mag, 10/83; Keneth Duncan (auth), Color field painting, Fine Arts Rev, 10/84. *Mem:* Comn Art & Antiquties. *Media:* Acrylics. *Mailing Add:* Canal St Post Off PO Box 1528 New York NY 10013

WARSINSKE, NORMAN GEORGE
SCULPTOR, PAINTER
b Wichita, Kans, Mar 4, 29. *Study:* Univ Mont, BA; Kunstwerkschule, Darmstadt, Ger; Univ Wash, BA. *Comn:* Brass & steel screen, Yellowstone Boy's Ranch, Billings, Mont, 69; gold leaf steel stabile, IBM Bldg Lobby, Seattle, 71; bronze & plexiglass fountain, J Hughes Home, Mauna Kea, Hawaii, 79; steel sculpture, comn by TC Swartz, Seattle, 92; and others; steel tower, W Ovens Garden, Bellevue, Wash, 99. *Exhib:* Northwest Ann, Seattle Art Mus, 59-65; Santa Barbara Invitational, Calif, 63; Sculpture, Los Angeles Co Mus Art, 64; Woodside Seattle, 73; Snohomish Arts Coun Gallery, 88; Univ Unitarian, 92; St Thomas, Bellevue, 2003. *Awards:* First Prize for Sculpture, Bellevue Art Festival, 60; Best of All Categories, Henry Art Gallery, 66. *Bibliog:* Louis Redstone (auth), Art in Architecture, McGraw, 68; MR Heinley (auth), Norman Warsinske--metal artistry, Designers W, 6/70; Sarah Clark-Langager (auth), Sculpture in Place, 2002. *Mem:* Northwest Craft Ctr (pres, 65-70). *Media:* Bronze, Steel; Acrylic. *Publ:* Illusr cover, Am Inst Architects J, 8/71. *Mailing Add:* 3823 94th NE Bellevue WA 98004-1321

WASHBURN, JOAN T
ART DEALER
b New York, NY, Dec 26, 29. *Study:* Middlebury Col, BA. *Pos:* Dir, Washburn Gallery, NY. *Awards:* RI Sch Design Fel. *Mem:* Art Dealers Asn Am. *Specialty:* Nineteenth and twentieth century American painting and sculpture. *Mailing Add:* 20 W 57th St New York NY 10019

WASHBURN, STAN
PRINTMAKER, PAINTER
b New York, NY, Jan 2, 43. *Study:* Calif Col Arts & Crafts, Oakland, BFA, 67 & MFA, 68. *Work:* Chicago Art Inst; Brooklyn Mus, NY; Calif Palace of Legion of Honor, San Francisco; Libr Cong, Washington; Mus Fine Arts, Boston. *Exhib:* 24th Nat Exhib Prints, Libr Cong, Washington, 75; Hassam Fund Purchase Prize Exhib, Am Acad of Arts & Lett, NY, 75 & 76; one-man show, Achenbach Found for Graphic Arts, Calif Palace of Legion of Honor, 77; Boston Printmakers Ann, 77-79, 81 & 85; 7th Brit Int Print Biennale, Bradford, Eng, 82; Western States Print Invitational, Portland Art Mus, Ore, 85; and others. *Awards:* Pennell Fund Purchase, Libr 75; Purchase Award, Int Miniature Print Collection, Pratt Graphics Ctr, New York, 77. *Bibliog:* One-half hour spec, KQED-TV, San Francisco, 75; Matthew Gurewitsch (auth), Against the grain, Connoisseur Mag, 2/86. *Media:* Etching; Oil. *Publ:* Auth & illusr, True History of the Death by Violence of George's Dragon, 74; auth & illusr, The Moral Alphabet of Vice & Folly Arbor House, 86; Intent to Harm, Pocket Books, 93; Into Thin Air, Pocket Books, 96. *Dealer:* North Point Gallery 250 Sutter St San Francisco CA. *Mailing Add:* 2010 Virginia St Berkeley CA 94709

WASHINGTON, JAMES W, JR
SCULPTOR, PAINTER
b Gloster, Miss. *Study:* Nat Landscape Inst; also with Mark Tobey; Grad Theological Union Ctr Urban Black Studies, Berkeley, Calif, Hon DFA, 75. *Work:* Seattle Art Mus, Wash; San Francisco Art Mus. *Comn:* The Creation (series 7-10), Seattle First Nat Bank Main Br, 68; bust of hist men, Progress Plaza, Philadelphia, 69; the Creation (series 5), Meany Jr High Sch, Seattle, 70; Woodchuck Sunning (sculpture), Frankfurt, WGer, 74; Children's Touchstone With Eagles (stone sculpture at Bailey Gatzert Elem), King Co Arts Comn, Seattle, Wash, 91; Bird From the Plane of Enlightenment (sculpture in stone), comn by John L & Dora E Smith, Seattle, Wash, 92; and others. *Exhib:* Expo '70, Osaka, Japan, 70; Art of the Pac Northwest, Nat Collection Fine Arts, Washington, 74; one-man exhibs, Foster-White Gallery, Seattle, Wash, 68, 78 & 80 & Mus Hist & Indust, Seattle, 80, Foster/White Gallery (with catalog), Seattle, Wash, 89; retrospective, Frye Art Mus, Seattle, 80; Fest Sundiata, Seattle, 80; Portopia, 81, Kobe, Japan, 81; retrospective (with catalog), Bellevue Art Mus, Wash, 89. *Pos:* Secy, Seattle Chap, Artists Equity Asn, 49-53, pres, 60-62; mem gov coun art, State of Wash, 59-60, state art comnr, 61-66. *Awards:* Gov Sculpture Award, 70; Wash State Centennial Hall Honor, Wash State Hist Soc, 84; Studio & Home of James W Washington Jr, Designated an Historic Landmark, Landmarks Preservation Bd, Seattle, Wash, 91; and others. *Bibliog:* Ann Faber (auth), James Washington's stone sculpture excellence, Seattle Post Intelligence, 56; Pauline Johnson (auth), James Washington speaks, Art Educ J, 68; Arch Am Art, Smithsonian Inst, 83. *Mem:* Int Platform Asn. *Media:* Oil, Tempera; Granite, Marble. *Mailing Add:* 1816 26th Ave Seattle WA 98122

WASHMON, GARY BRENT
PAINTER, PRINTMAKER
b Lake Charles, La, Nov 5, 55. *Study:* Yale Summer Sch Music & Art, 75; Univ NMex, BFA, 76; Univ Ill, MFA, 78. *Work:* Yale Univ; Univ Dallas; Pa State Univ; Visual Art Ctr Alaska, Anchorage; Ark Art Ctr, Little Rock; Tex Women's Univ. *Comn:* Art billboard, Patrick Billboard Co, Austin, Tex, 88. *Exhib:* Texas, Mus Gallery-San Francisco Mus Art, 87; Art of the New West, Eiteljorg Mus, Indianapolis, 90; House, Laguana Gloria Art Mus, Austin, Tex, 91; Chicago Art Expo, McCormick Ctr, 91; Natural Phenomena, Irving Art Ctr, Tex, 93; Fort Worth Community Art Center, Tex, 2005; Cinema Gallery, Champaign, Ill, 2006; solo exhib, Tex A&M Univ, 94, Tarleton State Univ, 2003, Ross State Univ, 2004, 416 West Gallery, 2005. *Pos:* Exhib comt, Denton Visual Arts Ctr, 89-; bd mem, Tex Asn Sch Art, 2002-05. *Teaching:* Asst prof painting & drawing, Univ Tex, Austin, 78-85; assoc prof, 86-94, Tex Womans Univ, interim chmn, 97-00, prof, 01-. *Awards:* Res Enhancement Grant, Tex Womans Univ, 92, Fac Develop Grant, 94; Fac Develop Leave, 2001. *Bibliog:* Edward Lucie-Smith (auth), American Art NOW, William Morrow & Co, 85; Edward Lucie-Smith (auth), Art of the Eighties, Phaidon Universe, New York, 90. *Media:* Acrylic, Oil, Etching. *Mailing Add:* 2297 Wood Hollow Rd Denton TX 76208

WASKO-FLOOD, SANDRA JEAN
PRINTMAKER, SCULPTOR
b Flushing, NY, Mar 12, 43. *Study:* Univ Calif, Los Angeles, Life Drawing with Gordon Nunes, Painting with Ray Brown & Charles Garabedian, BA, 65-69; UCLA, studied with Isabel Pons, Parque Lage, Rio de Janeiro, 72; Univ Wis, grad etching with Warrington Colescott, 77-78. *Work:* Mus de Arte Mod, Buenos Aires, Argentina;

Nat Mus Women Arts & Libr Cong, Washington; St Mary's Col, Md; Pushkin Mus, Moscow; and others; Cultural Found of Russia; Corcoran Gallery Art, Washington. *Comn:* Labyrinth Meditation Wheel, Kinetic Sculpture, Potomac Hosp, Woodbridge, 2000. *Exhib:* Boston Printmakers: 39th N Am Print Exhib, Danforth Mus, Framingham, Mass, 86; Printed Image 72nd Ann, Hudson River Mus, Yonkers, NY, 87; Seventh Ann Faber Birren Color Show Nat Juried Open Competition, Stamford, Conn, 87; Solo exhibs, St Peter's Church, NY, 89, Wash Printmakers Gallery, 86, 88 & 91, Mont Gallery, Alexandria, Va, 91, Montpelier Cult Arts Ctr, Laurel, Md, 92, Gallery 10 Ltd, Wash, 94 & 96, Sch 22 Art Ctr, Baltimore, 97; group exhib, Alternatives 88, Nat Juried Photog Competition, Univ Ohio, Athens, 88, Int Prints, 88, Silvermine Gallery, Stamford, Conn, 88, Stockton IV Prints & Drawings, Haggin Mus, Stockton, Calif, 88, Va Comn Arts Fel Winners, Peninsula Fine Arts Ctr, Newport News, Va, 95. *Pos:* pres, Wash Area Printmakers, 85-86; workshop coordr, Arlington Co Dept of Parks, Recreation & Community Resources, Lee Arts Ctr, 89-94; dir, Labyrinths for Peace, Exhib at Cannon Rotunda of House of Reps, 2000; cur, Common Ground: Labyrinth Designs, Past and Present, Charles Sumner Sch Mus, Washington, 2000; cur, Hist Part, Wash Women Artists Marching into the Millennium, Wash, 2001; founder/pres, Living Labyrinths for peace, Inc. *Teaching:* Instr printmaking, Wash Women's Arts Ctr, 83 & Arlington Co Art Prog, 89; artist-in-residence lithography, Univ Md, spring 84; prof printmaking, St Marys Col, spring 85; printmaking instr, Alexandria Studio, 87-; Labyviuths for cveativty & Peace, workshops Elementary sch, performing arts soc, Washington. *Awards:* Artist Grant, Friends Torpedo Factory Art Gallery, Alexandria, Va, 1989, Friends, The Torpedo Factory Art Gallery, Alexandria, Va; Va Comn Arts Fel Grant, 95; Best Show Cash Prize, Artists Equity, Wash, DC, 97; Hon Mention, Artists Equity: Coast to Coast, Harmony Hall Regional Art Ctr, Ft Wash, Md, 2001. *Bibliog:* Paul Franklin Pilato (auth), Printmakers: Cycles, Arlington Cable TV, 87; Lily Pond (auth), Yellow Silk Mag featured artist, Verygraphics, fall 87; Dance of the Labyrinth: An Installation by Sandra Wasko-Flood (video), Kelley Ellsworth Productions, 94; Al Kamen (auth), In the Loop: East Lawn, Right Brain, May Turns, Washington Post, 3/8; Julia Duin (auth), Spiritually Focused Labyrinth Coming to US Capitol Lawn, Washington Times, 3/3; Dash Robinson (auth), Labyrinthe Camp, City Paper; Jessica Dawson (auth), Mus of the Muses, Washington Post, 2001; Mina Cheon (auth), NY Arts Mag, 2002; many others. *Mem:* Wash Area Printmakers (pres, 85-86); Southern Graphics Coun, Pensacola, Fla; Internat Labyrinth Soc (founding mem); Ylem, Artists Using Sci & Tech. *Media:* Installation Sculpture, Prints, Photo Etchings, Monotypes. *Interests:* Creative writing, classical music, hiking. *Publ:* Nasca Tongue Iconography, El Dorado, Vol I, 77; Auth, The Role of Art in Feminist Spirituality, Women Artists News, spring 86; Unloose the Snake: One Artist's Labyrinth, Caerdroia, 94. *Mailing Add:* 2229 Lake Ave Baltimore MD 21213

WASSERMAN, ALBERT
PAINTER, DESIGNER
b New York, NY, 20. *Study:* Art Students League, with Charles Chapman, 37-39; Nat Acad Design, Pulitzer Prize scholar, 38-40; with Sidney Dickinson; Biarritz Am Univ, France, 45. *Work:* portrait, William R. Leigh, Traphagen Collection, Ariz; Aimee Ornstein Mem Libr, Adelphi Univ, NY, 83; Anne SK Brown Military Collection, Brown Univ, RI; Private collections Gibbs Smith, Utah, Frank J Oelshlager, Fla. *Comn:* Many private portrait commissions. *Exhib:* Nat Acad Design, NY, 40-42; Allied Artists Am, NY, 41-2005; NJ Painters & Sculptors Soc, 41-; Am Watercolor Soc, NY, 53-69 & 86; Audubon Artists, NY, 1960, 1990, 2000, 2002-2005. *Pos:* Graphic design consult, portrait painter, var agencies, 48-. *Teaching:* Instr & lectr, Jackson Heights Art Asn, 55- & Nat Art League, 67-69; instr painting, Educational Alliance, 2003-. *Awards:* Obrig Prize, 41, Nat Acad Design; Grumbacher Award, Allied Artists, 85, Gilmore-Romans Award, 95; S.T. Shaw Mem Award, Salmagundi Club, 2005. *Bibliog:* Ethel Traphagen (auth), article, Fashion Digest, 54. *Mem:* Salmagundi Club; Allied Artists Am; Audubon Artists; assoc Am Watercolor Soc; Nat Art League; and others. *Media:* Oil, Watercolor; Gouache. *Interests:* Painting, Music (classical & pop), cooking, animations & architecture. *Mailing Add:* 34-24 82nd St Jackson Heights NY 11372

WASSERMAN, BURTON
PAINTER, EDUCATOR
b Brooklyn, NY, Mar 10, 29. *Study:* Brooklyn Col, with Burgoyne Diller & Ad Reinhardt, BA; Columbia Univ, MA & EdD. *Work:* Philadelphia Mus Art, Pa; Munson-Williams-Proctor Inst, Utica, NY; Del Art Ctr, Wilmington; Montreal Mus Fine Arts; NJ State Mus, Trenton; and others. *Comn:* Relief triptych, comn by Mr & Mrs Herbert Kurtz, Melrose Park, Pa, 71; var indust & residential relief construction projs, Philadelphia area, 74-79. *Exhib:* 21st Am Drawing Biennial, Norfolk Mus Arts & Sci, 65; Art Alliance, Philadelphia, 66-80; USA Pavilion, Int Expos, Osaka, Japan, 70; Color Prints of the Americas, NJ State Mus, 70; Int Graphics Exhib, Montreal Mus Art, 71; Silkscreen: History of a Medium, Philadelphia Mus Art, 71-72; Benjamin Mangel Gallery, Philadelphia, Pa, 72-82; and others. *Teaching:* Emer Prof Art, Rowan Univ, Glassboro, NJ, 60-. *Awards:* Brickhouse Drawing Prize, 21st Am Drawing Biennial, Norfolk Mus Arts & Sci, 65; Ryan Purchase Prize, Art from NJ Ann Exhib, NJ State Mus, 67; Esther-Philip Klein Award, Am Color Print Soc Ann, 70; and others. *Mem:* Artists Equity Asn (nat pres, 71-73); Am Color Print Soc (mem exec coun, 65-81). *Media:* Oil. *Interests:* travel. *Publ:* Auth articles in Leonardo, Am Artist, Art Educ, Sch Arts, & many more, 59-72; auth, Modern Painting: The Movements, the Artists, Their Work, 70 & co-auth, Basic Silkscreen Printmaking, 71, Davis, Mass; Bridges of Vision: The Art of Prints & the Craft of Printmaking; Exploring the Visual Arts, Davis, Mass, 76. *Mailing Add:* 204 Dubois Rd Glassboro NJ 08028

WASSERMAN, CARY (ROBERT)
PHOTOGRAPHER, CONCEPTUAL ARTIST
b Los Angeles, Calif, Nov 27, 39. *Study:* Univ Calif, Los Angeles, BA, 61, MA, 63; Ind Univ, with Henry Holmes Smith, 67-70. *Work:* Mus Fine Arts, Boston; Smith Col Mus Art; Wellesley Col Mus Art; Portland Mus Art, Maine; Polaroid Collection, Cambridge, Mass. *Comn:* Charlestown: In Progress, Polaroid Corp, Cambridge, Mass, 74; A Call To Arts, Cambridge Arts Coun, Mass, 75; Large Totem (sculpture), WBZ-TV, Boston, 81. *Exhib:* Photographs: 1970-1974, Portland Mus Art, Maine, 74; Private Realities, Mus Fine Arts, Boston, 74; Color Photog Now, Wellesley Col Mus Art, 75; Color Photog Retrospective (with catalog), Williams Col Mus, 78; Aspects of the 70s, DeCordova Mus, 80; Polaroid Photographs in Historic Perspective, Brown Univ, 80; Proj Arts Ctr, Cambridge, 83; Galerie Texbraun, Paris, France, 86; Eiffel Tower & All That Jazz, French Libr, Boston, 86; Brooks Inst Photog, Santa Barbara, 90. *Collection Arranged:* Color in Photography, Soc Photog Educ, 75; Art Month, Clarence Kennedy Gallery, 76; Photo-Media, BVAU Gallery, 77; Color Photography: National Exhibit (auth, catalog), 81 & Seven Artists, 83, Boston Visual Artists Union. *Pos:* Creative dir, Art Consults Group, Cambridge, Mass, 73-88; sec gen, BVAU, 78 & 80; trustee, Inst Contemp Art, Boston, 83-85; dir, The Artists Orgn, 88-; coordr, Amiga Video Group, 90. *Teaching:* Instr, Photog, Univ Lowell, Mass, 77-79 & 82-83; Univ Southern Maine, 76-77; Art Inst Boston, 70-73; New England Sch Photogr, Boston, 83-84; Instr, Filmmaking, Phillips Acad Andover, Summer 73 & 79; vis lectr, Univ Lowell, 77-79 & 82-83; instr photog, NE Sch of Photog, 84-85; vis asst prof, computer design, Mass Col Art, 90. *Awards:* Polaroid Corp, Cambridge, Mass, 74; Cambridge Art Coun, Mass, 75; Change, Inc, 81; Blanche E Colman Found Grant, Boston, 82, 89. *Bibliog:* Susan Dodge Peters (auth), The Color Photographs of Cary Wasserman, Williams Col, 78; Kelly Wise: Wasserman At Large & /Wasserman's Enhanced SX-70, Boston Globe, 83 & 86; Stuart Cohen: Cary Wasserman, Contemp Photogr, St Martins Press, Chicago, 83-88. *Mem:* Boston Visual Artists Union, 74 (secy-gen, 78-80); Boston Visual Artists Union Federal Credit Union (vpres 76-77); Inst Contemp Art, Boston, Trustee, 83-85. *Media:* Bookworks, Computer Work. *Publ:* Contribr, Private Realities: Recent American Photography, New York Graphic Soc, 74; The Photographers Choice, Addison House, 75; auth, SX-Manipulation, Petersens Photog, 76; contribr, Creative Camera International Yearbook, 77; auth, Color Toning & SX-70 Image Manipulation, Darkroom Techniques, 81 & 83

WASSERMAN, JACK
EDUCATOR
b New York, NY, Apr 27, 21. *Study:* Wash Sq Col, NY Univ, BA; NY Univ Inst Fine Arts, with Karl Lehman & Richard Krautheimer, MA & PhD. *Teaching:* Instr art, Univ Conn, 53-60; asst prof art, Ind Univ, Bloomington, 60-62; prof Renaissance art, Univ Wis-Milwaukee, 62-75; dean, Tyler Sch Art, Temple Univ, Philadelphia, 75-77, prof art hist, 75-92, prof emer, 92-. *Awards:* Am Coun Learned Soc Grant, 70; Am Philos Soc Grant, 71; Kress Found Grant, 75, 96 & 2002. *Bibliog:* Observations on Two Statues in the Museo dell'Opera del Duomo and the Porta della Mandorla in Florence.Artibus et His, 1988. *Mem:* Col Art Asn Am; Soc Archit Historians (bd dir, 70-); Royal Soc Arts; Amici de Brera; Inst per la Storia dell'Arte Lombarda, Milan, Italy (mem bd councellors, 82-85); Acad Benemirito, Acad D San Luca in Rome. *Res:* Ital Renaissance Art and Archit. *Publ:* Auth, The dating & patronage of Leonardo's Burlington House cartoon, Art Bulletin, 71; Michelangelo's Virgin & Child with St Anne at Oxford, Burlington Mag, 69; Leonardo da Vinci, Abrams, 75; The Genesis of Raphael's Alba Madonna, Studies in History of Art, Nat Gallery Art, Wash 78; Reflections on Leonardo's Last Supper, Arte Lombarda, 83. *Mailing Add:* 409 Pine St Philadelphia PA 19106

WASSERMAN, MURIEL
PAINTER
b New York, NY, May 27, 35. *Study:* Queens Col, BFA & BA Art Hist, 78; Adelphi Univ, grad studies; Pratt Inst, MFA, 84; Studied at Brooklyn Mus, Five Town Music & Arts Found, NY, Newark Sch Art, NJ, Brookyln Col; Studied with Phillip Guston, Rudolf Nakien, Richard Bove, Arhtur Coppedge & Jack Rabinowitz. *Comn:* many pvt commissions. *Exhib:* Brooklyn Mus Exhib, 78; Old Westbury Gardens, Long Island, 88-90; Bergen Co Mus, NY, 89; Sands Point Mus, NY, 90-91; East End Arts Coun, NY; and others. *Pos:* Craftsperson (potter), craft shows & exhibs, 70-91; docent & cataloger, Nassau Co Mus System, 75-77; monthly columnist, Sunstorm Long Island Arts Newspaper, 82-84. *Teaching:* Instr painting & drawing, Long Island Adult Prog, NY, 77-98, & St Johns Univ, Queens, NY, 79-98. *Awards:* Am Artists Mag, 77; Town of Hempstead, NY, 80; Fed Plaza Exhibs, Nat Asn Women Artists, 80. *Mem:* Nat Asn Women Artists; Long Island Crafts Guild; Long Beach Art League, NY; Palm Beach Watercolor Asn, Fla. *Media:* Acrylic, Watercolors. *Interests:* Gardening, writing. *Publ:* Columnist, Sunstor, Long Island Arts Newspaper. *Mailing Add:* 70 Brentwood Ln Valley Stream NY 11580

WATERHOUSE, CHARLES HOWARD
ILLUSTRATOR, PAINTER
b Columbus, Ga, Sept 22, 24. *Study:* Newark Sch Fine & Indust Art; also with Steven R Kidd. *Work:* USMC Mus, US Navy Combat Art Collection & USAAF Collections, Washington, DC; Rutgers Univ, New Brunswick, NJ; NJ Bell Tel Co, Newark. *Comn:* Marines in the Revolution, 74, Vietnam Refugees, 75 & Marines in Mexican War, USMC, 75-76; Hamilton's Battery, Class of 24, Rutgers Univ, 74; Tarawa Beach Head, L P H Tarawa, US Navy, 75. *Exhib:* One-man shows, NJ State Mus, Trenton, US Naval Acad, Annapolis, Md, Los Angeles Mus Nat Hist, San Francisco City Hall & Soc Illusrs, NY, 75. *Pos:* Staff artist, Prudential Ins Co, 50-55; free-lance illusr, Nat Publ & Books, 55-73; artist-in-residence, USMC, 73. *Teaching:* Instr, lectr & demonstr illus, Newark Sch Fine & Indust Art, 55-73. *Bibliog:* Norman Kent (auth), Vietnam drawings, Am Artist, 68; Ed Fleming (auth), Vietnam Sketchbook, AP News Features, 68; F B Nihart (auth), Paintings by Charles Waterhouse, Marine Corps Publ,

75. *Mem:* Soc Illusr; Salmagundi Club; Nat Soc Mural Painters; USMC Combat Corresp; Naval Air Cooperation & Liaison Comt Artists. *Media:* Acrylic, Ink. *Publ:* Illusr, Outdoor Life, Argosy, Saga, Reader's Digest & others, 55-; illusr, Grosset, Dunlap, Viking, Am, & Rutgers Press, 55-; auth & illusr, Vietnam Sketchbook from Delta to DMZ, 68 & Vietnam War Drawings, Air, Land & Sea, 70; illusr, Marines in the Revolution, 75; auth & illusr, Marines and Others, 94

WATERHOUSE, RUSSELL RUTLEDGE
PAINTER, ILLUSTRATOR
b El Paso, Tex, Aug 11, 28. *Study:* Tex A&M Univ, BS, 50; Art Ctr Col Design, Pasadena, Calif, 54-56. *Work:* Tex Tech Univ Mus Art, Lubbock; El Paso Mus Art; Tex A&M Univ, College Station; Univ Tex, El Paso. *Exhib:* One-man shows, Wichita Falls Tex Cult Ctr & Mus Art, 72, Tex A&M Univ, 77, Dallas Safari Club, 83, Americana Mus, El Paso, 84 & 86 & Int Mus Art, El Paso, 2000; Game Conservation Int, San Antonio, 83, 85, 87, 89; El Paso Mus Int Art, 01. *Pos:* Mem, Tex Comn Arts & Humanities, 70-75. *Awards:* El Paso's Mayor's Award, 89; Invitational Art Exhib, El Paso Mus Art, 89; Inductee El Paso Artists Hall of Fame, 2000. *Media:* Watercolor, Oil. *Publ:* Illusr, Goodbye to a River, Knopf, 60; The Legal Heritage of El Paso, 63 & Pass of the North, 68, Tex Western Press. *Mailing Add:* PO Box 6 Lincoln NM 88338-9999

WATERS, JACK
FILMMAKER, CONCEPTUAL ARTIST
b Philadelphia, Pa, Oct 14, 54. *Study:* Julliard Col, BFA, 79. *Work:* Libr Cong, Washington; New York Libr Performing Arts, Lincoln Ctr; Paterson Mus, NJ. *Exhib:* ABC No Rio, NY, 83-; Limbo Gallery; NYCDCA Gallery, 85; Whitney Mus, 94. *Collection Arranged:* ABC No Rio Archival (contribr, catalog), NYCDCA City Gallery, 85. *Pos:* Founder & pres, Allied Productions, Inc, NY, 82-; co-dir, ABC No Rio, New York, 83-; consult & mem, Collaborative Projs, Inc, 84-87; dir, Naked Eye Cinema, 87-. *Teaching:* Instr dance, Univ City Arts League, Philadelphia, Pa, 78 & Univ Settlement, New York, 84-. *Awards:* Louis Horst Award for Choreography, Juillard, 79. *Bibliog:* Robert Gautier (auth), New form on the Lower East Side, NY Times, 3/84; ABC No Rio Dinero: The story of a Lower East Side art gallery, 84. *Mem:* Film/Video Arts; Millenium Film Group. *Publ:* Auth, On notational methods, Ear Mag, 12/83; film critique, Jumpcut Mag, spring 91; Social comment, Color Life Mag, summer 91; film critique, Fuse Mag, fall 91. *Mailing Add:* PO Box 20260 New York NY 10009

WATERSTREET, KEN (JAMES KENT)
PAINTER, INSTRUCTOR
b Ogden, Utah, July 18, 40. *Study:* Calif State Univ, Sacramento, BA, 63, MA, 69. *Work:* E B Crocker Art Mus, Sacramento; Southern Ill Univ; Stuart M Speiser Collection, Smithsonian Inst; San Francisco Mus Mod Art; Oakland Mus, Calif; Butler Inst Am Art; South Tex Mus Art; Yale Univ. *Exhib:* Human Concern-Personal Torment, Whitney Mus of Am Art, NY, 69; one-man shows, Louis K Meisel Gallery, NY, 74 & 77 & Zara Gallery, San Francisco, 79; Hue & Far Cry of Color, Ft Wayne Mus, Ind, 76; E B Crocker Art Mus, Sacramento, 80; Joseph Chowning Gallery, San Francisco, 81, 83, 86, 88, 91, 92 & 96; California A-Z and Return, Butler Inst Am Art, Youngstown, Ohio, 90; Solomon Dubnick Gallery, Sacramento, Calif, 96, 98, 2000, 2003 & 2006. *Pos:* Comnr, Sacramento Metrop Arts Comn, 77 & 78; bd mem, Ctr Contemp Art, Sacramento, Calif, 94-2000. *Teaching:* Chmn, Dept Visual & Performing Art, Mira Loma, High Sch, Sacramento, Calif 65-96; instr summer session, Calif State Univ, Sacramento, 90, 91 & 96-98. *Awards:* Fulbright-Hayes Study Tour, China, 88; Tap Award, Marie Walsh Sharpe Art Found, 95. *Mem:* Nat Art Educ Asn; Calif Art Educ Asn. *Media:* Oil on Canvas. *Dealer:* Solomon Dubnick Gallery 2131 Northrop Ave Sacramento CA 95825. *Mailing Add:* 3218 Tobari Ct Sacramento CA 95821

WATIA, TARMO
PAINTER, PRINTMAKER
b Detroit, Mich, May 11, 38. *Study:* Univ Mich, BS (design), 60, MFA, 62. *Work:* Boise Cascade & Boise Art Gallery, Idaho; Harrett Mus, Twin Falls, Idaho. *Exhib:* Boise State Col, Idaho; Rogue Valley Art Asn, Medford, Ore; Southern Ore Col, Ashland; Mont State Univ, Bozeman; Minot State Col, NDak; Rackham Galleries, Ann Arbor; Mich State Univ, East Lansing; Detroit Inst Art; AAA Gallery, Detroit; Raven Gallery, Detroit. *Teaching:* Instr art, Southern Ore Col, Ashland, 66-69; assoc prof, Boise State Univ, Idaho, 69-86. *Awards:* Second Place Award, Rock Springs, Wyo, 72; Purchase Award, Boise Art Gallery, Idaho, 74; Cash Award/Painting, Ninth Ann Arts & Crafts Festival, Coeur D'Alene, Idaho. *Media:* Oil; Woodcuts. *Mailing Add:* 1015 N Tenth St Boise ID 83702

WATKINS, EILEEN FRANCES
CRITIC
b Long Island, NY, Nov 22, 50. *Study:* Marywood Col, BA. *Pos:* Art ed, Newark Star-Ledger, currently. *Awards:* Citation, NJ Soc of Architects. *Publ:* Auth, articles, Air brush Action, Am Artist & Equine Images. *Mailing Add:* Newark Star-Ledger One Star-Ledger Plaza Newark NJ 07101

WATKINS, LEWIS
SCULPTOR, PAINTER
b Beckley, WVa, July 24, 45. *Study:* WVa State Col, BS(art educ), 78; Univ Southern Fla, MA, 82; St Leo Col, Fla, hon degree, 83. *Work:* Fla State Mus, Gainesville; WVa Fine Arts & Cult Ctr, Charleston; Vatican Mus, Rome, Italy; Leslie Stephens Fine Arts Ctr, Birmingham, Ala; Hyatt Regency Hotel, Atlanta, Ga. *Comn:* Limestone sculpture, Hernando Co, Brooksville, Fla, 81; Solidarity (steel sculpture), Brandon, Fla, 82; Crosses of Life (steel sculpture), City Atlanta, Ga, 83; Youth of Today (stone sculpture), Hernando Co, Fla, 83; St Leo (steel sculpture), St Leo Col, Fla, 83; Winning (steel sculpture), US Football League, 84; The National Memorial for the American Farmer (steel & bronze), 86. *Exhib:* Tools of Life, John W Davis Fine Art Gallery, Institute, WVa, 81; Leslie Stephens Fine Art Ctr, Samford Univ, Birmingham, Ala, 82; and others. *Teaching:* Vis artist series, Samford Univ, Birmingham, Ala, 82; vis artist, St Leo Col, Fla, 82, Univ Tampa, Fla, 83 & Univ SFla, Tampa, 83. *Awards:* Distinguished Serv Art Award, Atlanta, Ga, 83; Cert Recognition Art, State Ga, 83; Pub Serv Cult Award, Hernando Co, Fla, 83. *Bibliog:* Terry Misfeldt (auth), article, Future Mag, 6/83; Tom Kuennen (auth), article, Rock Products Mag, 6/83; John Levine (auth), article, Pit & Quarry Mag, 9/83; articles in: Agri- View, Country Today, Hog Farm Mgt, Western Art Digest, Art Papers, Kanas Square, Today's Farmer & Kansas City Corp Report, 86; and many others. *Media:* Watercolor, Acrylic; Marble, Steel. *Publ:* Coauth, Creating a year book, Instructor Mag, 80. *Mailing Add:* 22319 Powell Rd Brooksville FL 34602-5705

WATKINS, RAGLAND TOLK
CURATOR, DEALER
b San Francisco, Calif, Oct 31, 48. *Study:* Lake Forest Col, BA, 72; NY Univ, MA, 82. *Collection Arranged:* Bochner, Le Va, Rockburne, Tuttle (ed & contribr, catalog) Contemp Arts Ctr, Cincinnati, 75. *Pos:* Cur, Contemp Arts Ctr, Cincinnati, 73-75; field rep, New York State Coun Arts, 76-77; assoc dir exhibs, Artists Space, New York, 77-81; dir, Concord Contemp Art, New York, 81-85; dir, Jason McCoy Inc, New York, 85-88, Blum Helman Gallery, New York, 90-91, Stux Gallery, New York, 91-92 & James Graham & Sons, New York, 92-93. *Mailing Add:* 169 Sullivan St New York NY 10012

WATKINSON, PATRICIA GRIEVE
MUSEUM DIRECTOR, CURATOR
b Surrey, Eng, Mar 28, 46. *Study:* Bristol Univ, Eng, BA(hons), 68. *Collection Arranged:* A Partial View: Photographers in the Northwest (auth, catalog), 78; Contemporary Metals: Focus on Idea (auth, catalog), 81; British Prints: Highlights of Four Decades (auth, catalog), 81; Living with the Volcano: The Artists of Mount St Helens (auth, catalog), 85; Gaylen Hansen: The Paintings of a Decade (auth, catalog), 85; Patrick Siler: Recent Works (auth, catalog), 88; Facts of the Imagination, 89. *Pos:* Adminr, Mayfair Fine Arts, London, 69-71 & Bernard Jacobson Print Publ, 71-73; freelance cur & writer, Irish Arts Coun, Kilkenny Design Ctr & Trinity Col, Dublin, 75-76; cur, Mus Art, Wash State Univ, 76-83, dir, 84-. *Teaching:* Asst prof art hist, Wash State Univ, 78-79. *Bibliog:* Ron Glowen (auth), A partial view, 78 & Gaylen Hansen, 86, Artweek. *Mem:* Art Mus Asn Am (Wash State rep, 86-88); Wash Mus Asn (mem bd, 85-87); Int Coun Mus, CIMAM; Asn Col & Univ Mus & Galleries (western rep, 86-89); Am Asn Mus. *Res:* 20th Century prints; contemporary art, Northwest & Am. *Publ:* Auth, Mount St Helens: An Artistic Aftermath, Art J, fall 84; A Decade Apart: A Curatorial View, Glass Art Soc J, 84-85; Drawing on the American Dream-Patrick Siler, Am Ceramics, summer 88 & Patti Warashina, spring 92. *Mailing Add:* Ft Wayne Mus Art 311 E Main St Fort Wayne IN 46802

WATRISS, WENDY
PHOTOGRAPHER, CURATOR
b San Francisco, Calif, 1943. *Study:* Univ Madrid, 63; New York Univ, BA, 65. *Work:* Amon Carter Mus, Fort Worth; Mus Fine Arts, Houston; The Menil Collection, Houston; Humanities Res Ctr, Univ Tex, Austin; Bibliot Nat, Paris; var pvt collections. *Collection Arranged:* Image & Memory, Photography from Latin America (ed, catalog), Rice Univ Press, 94. *Pos:* Cofounder & officer, Live Oak Fund for Change, currently; juror & panelist photog grants, Nat Endowment Arts, Wis Arts Coun, Houston Ctr Photog, Laguna Gloria Arts Mus & Tex Photog Soc, currently; found mem, Fotofest, 84, art dir & cur, 90-. *Awards:* Women's Int Democratic Found Award, 83; Int Interpress Photo Award, 83; Nat Endowment Arts/Mid-Atlantic Arts Alliance, 87. *Bibliog:* Articles in Life, Stern (Ger), Geo, Photoreportages (France), NY Times, Smithsonian Mag, Historic Preserv, Village Voice, Mother Jones, Newsweek, Sci Digest, Southern Exposure, Tex Observer, Christian Sci Monitor, Camerawork, Bild (Sweden), & numerous other int publ. *Mem:* Tex Photog Soc (adv bd); fel Am Leadership Forum. *Publ:* Coauth, Coming to Terms, The German Hill Country of Tex, Tex A&M Univ Press, 91. *Mailing Add:* 1405 Branard St Houston TX 77006-4803

WATSON, ALDREN A
DESIGNER, ILLUSTRATOR
b Brooklyn, NY, May 10, 17. *Study:* Yale Univ, 35; Art Students League, with George Bridgman, Charles Chapman, Robert Brackman, William Auerbach-Levy & others. *Work:* Illus bks in libr, US, Can, Europe & pvt collections. *Comn:* Mural, SS Pres Hayes, Thomas Crowell Co Off, 64. *Exhib:* Fifty Bks Shows, Soc Illusr Ann; New Eng Textbk Shows. *Pos:* Textbk designer, D C Heath & Co, Boston, 65-66; chief ed curric oriented mat, Silver Burdett Co, Morristown NJ, 66-68; official NASA artist, Apollo 8, 68; consult art dir, Houghton Mifflin, Boston, 68-72. *Teaching:* Pvt instr, hand bookbinding. *Awards:* Prize, Domesday Bk Illus Competition, 45. *Bibliog:* Chap in Forty Illustrators & How They Work. *Mem:* Author's Guild. *Publ:* Auth & illusr, My Garden Grows, 62 & Maple Tree Begins, 70, Viking; auth & illusr, Hand Bookbinding, 63, 68 & 75; auth & illusr, Hand Tools: Their Ways and Workings, Norton, 82; coauth, Furniture Making Plain & Simple, Norton, 84; and others. *Mailing Add:* Old Clay Rd North Hartland VT 05052

WATSON, CLARISSA H
DEALER, WRITER
b Ashland, Wis. *Study:* Layton Art Sch, Milwaukee; Univ Wis-Milwaukee; Milwaukee-Downer Col, BA with spec hon; Country Art Sch, with Harry Sternberg. *Collection Arranged:* Long Island Artists Washington, DC, 67; The Collectors' Collections, Adelphi Univ, Garden City, Long Island, 68; Gabriel Spat (1890-1967)

Retrospective, Fine Arts Asn Willoughby, Cleveland, Ohio, 70; Nobility of the Horse in Art--to Save America's Wild Horses, Washington, DC, 71; Salon de Normandie (50 Norman painters honoring 50th Anniversary D-Day), Locust Valley, NY, 94; and others. *Pos:* Dir-founder, Country Art Sch, Westbury, Long Island, 53-68; dir & co-founder, Country Art Gallery, Locust Valley, Long Island, 53-90; art consult, Adelphi Univ, 67-69; dir film festivals, 7 Village Arts Coun, Locust Valley, 69-71; dir-producer, Medieval Christmas Festival, Locust Valley, 70-73; trustee, Nassau Mus Fine Arts, 77-83, Roslyn & Hechsher Mus, Huntington, NY, 84-87. *Specialty:* Nineteenth and twentieth century American realism and American and European naifs. *Publ:* Auth, The art virus, This Wk Mag, 64; ed, The Artists' Cookbook, Stevenson, 71; auth, Fourth Stage of Gainsborough Brown, McKay, 77; The Bishop in the Back Seat, 80 & Runaway, 84, Atheneum; Last Plane from Nice, Atheneum, 87; Somebody Killed the Messenger, Atheneum, 88; Last Plan from Nice, Atheneum, 86; Somebody Killed the Messenger, Atheneum 88; and others. *Mailing Add:* 30 Pearsall Ave Apt 4E Glean Cove NY 11542-3010

WATSON, DARLIENE KEENEY
PAINTER
b Amarillo, Tex, Mar 16, 29. *Study:* Univ Colo, BFA; Art Inst Chicago; Malden Bridge Sch Art, NY; also with Dick Goetz, Okla, Lui-Sang Wong, Calif, Ho Nien Au, Taiwan, Yue-kee Wo, I Hsiung Ju, Va, Chen Chi, Val Thelin & Tom Hill. *Work:* St John's Univ, Jamaica, NY. *Comn:* Numerous comns for pvt collections. *Exhib:* Columbus Mus Arts & Sci, Southern Watercolor Soc, 78; Meridian House Int, Sumi-e Soc Am, Washington, DC, 84; Univ Va Art Mus, Va Watercolor Soc, 84; Potomac Valley Watercolorists, Arts Club, Washington, DC, 85; Salmagundi Club, NY, 84, 85 & 87. *Pos:* Pres, Herndon Old Town Gallery, Herndon, Va, 88. *Teaching:* Instr, Oriental brush painting, Northern Va Community Col, Manassas, 80-81. *Awards:* First Prize, Sumi-e Soc Am, 73 & 75; Equal Merit Award, Potomac Valley Watercolor Soc, 77; Dick Blick & Wayne Shaffer Awards, Sumi-e Soc Am, 84, 85 & 87. *Bibliog:* Widening Horizons in Creative Arts, Ada King Wallis Calif. *Mem:* Sumi-e Soc Am (chap pres, 75-77); Potomac Valley Watercolor Soc; Va Watercolor Soc; Southern Watercolor Soc; Ga Watercolor Soc. *Media:* Watercolor, Acrylic. *Publ:* Contribr, Frozen Stream, Anima, Vol VII, No 1, 80. *Dealer:* Watercolor Room 314 Mill St Occoquan VA 22125. *Mailing Add:* 9617 Jomar Dr Fairfax VA 22032

WATSON, DONNA
PAINTER
b San Rafael, Calif, 49. *Study:* Western WA Univ, MA, 68-75; studied with Alex Powers & Katherine Chang Liu. *Work:* WA Publ Power Supply Systems, Richland; Edmonds Community Col, Wash; Evergreen Hosp, Kirkland, Wash; GTE, Seattle, Wash. *Exhib:* Lawrence Gallery, Sheridan, Ore, 95-99; Northwest Watercolor Soc Invitational Group Exhib; Frye Mus, Seattle, Wash; Lakeshore Gallery, Kirkland, Wash; Earthenworks Gallery, Wash, 93-2000; Solo exhib, Sutherlin Publ Libr, Ore, Umpqua Valley Art Ctr Gallery, Roseburg, Ore, Eileen Enck Gallery, Kirkland, Wash, Earthenworks Gallery, La Connor, Wash, 2000. *Teaching:* instr, painting 5-day workshops, currently. *Awards:* Award of Excellence, San Diego Int Watermedia Exhib; First place, Kirkland Art Ctr; Best of Show, Waterolor Soc Ore, 2000. *Mem:* Am Watercolor Soc; Northwest Watercolor Soc (pres, formerly); Nat Watercolor Soc (vpres, currently). *Media:* Acrylic, Oil. *Specialty:* Abstracts, 2-D, Asian Themes, Collages. *Mailing Add:* 1141 Cavalero Rd Camano Island WA 98282

WATSON, HOWARD N(OEL)
PAINTER, PRINTMAKER
b Pottsville, Pa, May 19, 29. *Study:* Pa State Univ, 47-49; Tyler Sch Fine Arts, 53-55; Mus Col Art, dipl, 60. *Work:* White House, Art in Embassies, Washington, DC; Temple Univ; private collections of Richard Manogian & Walter Mondale; Pres Jimmy Carter. *Comn:* Logan Square (mural), Archdiocese Philadelphia, 75; Betsy Ross Making Flag, Upholsterer Int Union NAm, Philadelphia, 76; 50 watercolor painting Independence Blue Cross, Philadelphia, Pa; 10 large paintings pvt collection, ARCO Chemical. *Exhib:* Pa Acad Fine Arts, 62-68; Denver's Artists of Am, 81-82; Audubon Artist Show, NY; Am Watercolor Soc Exhibs, NY; Allied Artists Am Exhibs, NY; Knickerbocker Artists Exhibs, NY; Nat Acad, NY; Philadelphia Watercolor Club Shows. *Teaching:* Instr watercolor, Hussian Sch Fine Arts, 61-63, Philadelphia Col Art, 63-70 & Abington Art Ctr, 71-; int watercolor workshops, including Austria, Switz, & Can. *Awards:* Super Achiever Award Art, Juvenile Diabetes Found, 78; Distinguished Pennsylvanians Award Art, State Pa, 80; Thornton Oakley Mem Award, Philadelphia Watercolor Club, 92. *Bibliog:* Article, Forbes Mag, 80; TLC Mag, 87. *Mem:* Philadelphia Watercolor Club (pres, 82-93); Am Watercolor Soc; Allied Artists Am; Knickerbocker Artists. *Media:* Watercolor. *Publ:* Philadelphia Watercolors, Barre Publ, 70; Old Philadelphia Impressions, Heritage Publ, 76; Proud Past, 77. *Dealer:* Newman Art Gallery 1625 Walnut St Philadelphia PA. *Mailing Add:* 348 Sinkler Rd Wyncote PA 19095

WATSON, KATHARINE JOHNSON
HISTORIAN, CONSULTANT
b Providence, RI, Nov 11, 42. *Study:* Duke Univ, BA, 64; Univ Pa, MA(art hist), 67, PhD(art hist), 73. *Pos:* Instr & cur of exhibs, Univ Pittsburgh, Pa, 69-70; cur art before 1800, Allen Mem Art Mus; co-ed, Allen Mem Art Mus Bull, 74-77; dir, Peary-MacMillan Arctic Mus, Bowdoin Col, Brunswick, Maine, 77-85, Bowdoin Col Mus Art, 77-98; trustee, Mus Art Ogunquit, 77-90, Williamstown Regional Art Conserv Laboratory Inc, 78-90 & Surf Point Found Victoria Mansion; mem Smithsonian Coun. *Teaching:* Instr Ital sculpture & Europ Baroque art, Univ Pittsburgh, 69-70; lectr mus sem, Oberlin Col, Ohio, 73-79; instr mus sem, Bowd. *Awards:* Kress Found fel, Univ Pa, 67-68; Fel, Harvard Univ Ctr Ital Renaissance Studies, 77-78; Nat Endowment Arts Grant, 81; and others. *Mem:* Asn Art Mus Dirs; Col Art Asn; Am Asn Mus; New Eng Mus Asn. *Res:* Sixteenth and seventeenth century Italian sculpture; art patronage in eighteenth and nineteenth century America. *Publ:* Auth, A Bronze Mercury after Giambologna, Allen Art Mus Bulletin, 75-76; Sculpture in the Allen Art Museum, Hellenistic to the Twentieth Century, Apollo, 76; Sugar sculpture for grand ducal weddings from the Giambologna Workshop, The Connoisseur, 78; contribr, Giambologna 1527-1608: Sculptor to the Medici, Arts Coun Gt Brit, 78; auth, Pietro Tacca, Garland Press, 83; coauth (with Anthea Brook), Pietro Tacca, In: Il Seicento Fiorentino, Vol III, Florence, 86; contribr to prof jour and/ mus catalog. *Mailing Add:* 10 Boody St Brunswick ME 04011

WATSON, MARY ANNE
PRINTMAKER, PAINTER
b Can; US citizen. *Study:* Ont Col Art; NY Univ, BSc, 71. *Work:* Nat Art Gallery, Ottawa; Nat Asn Women Artists Collection; Rutgers Univ, New Brunswick, NJ; Univ Toronto Libr, Univ Col Art Collection, Univ Toronto, Art Inst Ont, Imperial Oil Awards Collection & Toronto Dominion Bank Collection; Printmaking Workshop Collection; pvt collections throughout US & Can; plus others. *Exhib:* Catherine Lorillard Wolfe Show, Nat Arts Club, NY; Salmagundi Club; Audubon Show, Nat Arts Club, 89-91 & 93; Nat Asn Women Artists Show, ARC Gallery, Chicago, 92; Nat Asn Women Artists traveling print show, 92-93; Artists Equity Gallery, Soho, NY, Burr Artists Show, 92; Tom Thompson Mem Mus & Art Gallery, Owen Sound, Ont, 93, 95 & 96; Nat Asn Women Artists Ann Show, Soho, NY, 94, 97-98; solo show, Georgetown Art Ctr, Ont, 97, Safe Harbour Gallery, Owen Sound, Ont, 99, Hands to Work, Elora, Ont, 1999 & 2000; Southampton Mus, Southampton, Ont, 99; plus others. *Pos:* Printmaker, Bob Blackburn Workshops, NY, formerly. *Teaching:* instr art, Central YMCA, Toronto, Can, 60-61 & 66-. *Awards:* First Place, Individual Artists Showcase, 86; Warren E Bower Mem Award, Salmagundi Club, 88; Dr & Mrs IC Gaynor Award, Nat Asn Women Artists, 91; and others. *Bibliog:* Sun Times, Owen Sound, Ont, 3/14/98; Brucedale Family Reader, Brucedale Press, 99; Who's Who in Am Art, 90-present. *Mem:* Nat Asn of Am Women Artists; Nat Pen Women of Am; Bruce Peninsula Soc of Artists; Toronto Arts & Letters Club. *Media:* Acrylic, Oil, Etching, Watercolors. *Publ:* Brucedale Family Reader, Brucedale Press, 99. *Dealer:* Olga Domjan, 220 Smith St, Elora, Can, N0B 1S0; Bruce Peninsula Soc of Artists Co; Op Gallery. *Mailing Add:* 48 Spry Lake Rd Wiarton ON N0H 2T0 Canada

WATSON, RONALD G
PAINTER, EDUCATOR
b Grand Island, Neb, Oct 9, 41. *Study:* Univ Neb, Lincoln, BFA, 64, MFA(Woods Painting Fel), 67. *Work:* Grand Rapids Art Mus, Mich; Nat Collection Fine Arts, Washington, DC. *Comn:* Outdoor steel sculpture, City of Grand Rapids, Mich, 74; sculpture garden, Veterans Admin, Washington, DC, 81. *Exhib:* One-man exhibs, Grand Rapids Art Mus, Mich, 73, Ohio State Univ Art Gallery, 78, Dobrick Gallery, Chicago, 82, San Antonio Art Inst, 87, Tex Christian Univ, 91 & Midwestern Univ, Wichita Falls, Tex 99; Ft Worth Gallery, 83 & 86; Adams-Middleton Gallery, Dallas, 85; The Patrick Gallery, Austin, 86; William Campbell Contemp Art, Ft Worth, Tex, 88; and others. *Teaching:* Prof drawing & painting, Aquinas Col, Grand Rapids, Mich, 68-82, chmn dept art, 71-81; prof drawing & painting, Tex Christian Univ, 82-, chmn dept art & hist, 82-89, dir grad studies, Col Fine Arts & Commun, 91-94, Chmn, Dept Art & Art Hist, 94-. *Awards:* Artist Fel, Nat Endowment Arts, 75. *Bibliog:* Margaret Robinette (auth), Outdoor Sculpture, Watson-Guptill, 76; Fay L Hendry (auth), Outdoor Sculpture in Grand Rapids, Michigan, Iota Press, 76; Donald Thalacker (auth), Art in World of Architecture, Chelsea House, 80; Howard Smagula (auth), Currents: Contemporary Directions in the Visual Arts, Prentice-Hall, 83. *Mem:* Col Art Asn. *Media:* Acrylic, Oil. *Publ:* Auth, The challenge of public sculpture, Mich Art J, 76; Art in public places, Ferris State Col, 79; Angels on High, Tex Christian Univ Press, 99. *Dealer:* William Campbell Contemp Art 4935 Byers Ave Ft Worth TX 76107. *Mailing Add:* 4712 Driskell Blvd Ft Worth TX 76107-7213

WATSON, ROSS
CURATOR
b Bangor, N Ireland, July 29, 34. *Study:* Pembroke Col, Cambridge, BA(hist with hon), 56, MA, 59; Courtauld Inst Art, London, dipl (hist art, with distinction), 63. *Collection Arranged:* Brit Coun Exhib 18th Century English Watercolors (auth, catalog), Rijks Mus, Amsterdam, Albertina, Vienna, 66; J M W Turner from Mellon Collection, Nat Gallery Art, Washington, DC, 69; John Constable from Mellon Collection, 69; Joseph Wright Derby, from Mellon Collection, 69-70; William Hogarth from Mellon Collection, 70-71; Eye of Thomas Jefferson, Bicentennial Exhib, 76. *Pos:* Asst keeper, City Mus & Art Gallery, Birmingham, Eng, 63-66; asst cur, Paul Mellon Collection, Washington, DC, 66; cur, Nat Gallery Art, Washington, DC, 66-77; admin asst dir, Tudor Pl Found, Washington, DC, 88-. *Mem:* Walpole Soc; Asn Irish Art Hist; Palladian Soc Am, Decorative Arts Trust. *Res:* Eighteenth century European, particularly British painting. *Publ:* Coauth, Renaissance furniture, Antiques Int, 66; auth, Guardi and the visit of Pius VI to Venice in 1782, Nat Gallery Art Report & Studies Hist Art, 67; Irish portraits in American Collections, Irish Georgian Soc Bull, 69; National Gallery of Art, Washington, DC, 79

WATT, ROBB
ARTIST
b Denver, Colo, Nov 12, 55. *Study:* Colo Col, BA, 78; Colo State Univ, Ft Collins, BFA, 81. *Work:* Colo Springs Fine Art Center. *Exhib:* Intimate Expressions in Thread, Thirteen Moons Gallery, Santa Fe, NM, 2002; Fiber/Fabric Art, Curtis Arts Center, Greenwood Village, Colo, 2001; Art Market Show & Sale, Arvada Ctr for Arts, Colo, 2001-2002; Threads of Memory, Metro Ctr for Visual Arts, Denver, 2002. *Awards:* 1st Place, Celebrate Colo Artists, 02; Artist Fel, Colo Coun on Arts, 98. *Publ:* Fiberarts Design Book Six, Lark Books, 2000. *Mailing Add:* 770 Pontiac St Denver CO 80220

WATTENMAKER, RICHARD JOEL
ADMINISTRATOR, HISTORIAN
b Philadelphia, Pa, Feb 22, 41. *Study:* Univ Pa, BA; New York Univ, Inst Fine Arts, MA, PhD. *Collection Arranged:* The Art of William Glackens (with catalog), 67; The Art of Charles Prendergast (with catalog), 68; The Art of Jean Hugo (with catalog), 73; The Fauves (with catalog), 75; Puvis de Chavannes and The Modern Tradition (with catalog), 75; The Dutch Cityscape in the 17th Century and its Sources (with catalog), 77; European Tools from the 17th to the 19th Century (with catalog), 81; Jean Hugo Dessins des années de guerre (1915-1919), 94. *Pos:* Dir, Rutgers Univ Art Gallery, 66-69; chief cur, Art Gallery Ont, Toronto, 72-78; dir, Chrysler Mus, 79-80; dir, Flint Inst Arts, 80-88, Archives Am Art, Smithsonian Inst, 1990-2005, trustee, Intermus Conserv Asn, Oberlin, 82-88. *Teaching:* Adj prof, Univ Mich, Flint, 84-85, Univ Mich, Ann Arbor, 88 & The Barnes Found, Merion, Pa, 91-92. *Awards:* Founders Day Award, New York Univ, 72. *Mem:* Artist Blacksmith Asn Am. *Res:* 19th and 20th century European painting; Renaissance and Post-Renaissance European painting; American painting and decorative art. *Publ:* Auth, William Glackens Beach Scenes at Bellport, Smithsonian Studies in Am Art, 88; Maurice Prendergast at the Whitney, New Criterion, 90; Dr Albert C Barnes & the Barnes Foundation, Knopf, 93; Maurice Prendergast, Harry N Abrams, 94; Jean Hugo Retrospective, Mus Fabre & Reunion des musées nationaux, 95; Objects of Contemplation and Pleasure, Wrought Iron European Cokking & Fireplace, Untensils of the Early Modern Era, Five Continents, 2004

WATTS, R MICHAEL
MUSEUM DIRECTOR
b Quincy, Ill, July 2, 51. *Study:* Western Ill Univ, BS, 73, BA(art hist), 75; Univ Tex Austin, MFA, 77. *Collection Arranged:* Antique Quilts c 1830-1930, Paducah Art Guild Gallery, 82; New Wood/New Ways, with Paul Sasso co-curator, (with catalog), Southern Arts Fedn, 83; American Scene Prints, 87 & Illinois Traditions: Folk Arts, 90, Tarble Arts Ctr; Paul Sargent, Robert Root & the Brown Co Artist Colony (with Rachel Perry), Tarble Arts Ctr, 95. *Pos:* Dir, Paducah Art Guild, Ky; Eagle & Curris Galleries, Murray State Univ, Ky, 83-86; Tarble Arts Ctr, Eastern Ill Univ, 86-. *Teaching:* Instr art, Paducah Community Col, Ky, 81-82; asst prof, Murray State Univ, Ky, 83-86. *Mem:* Am Asn Mus; Col Art Asn; Asn Col/Univ Galleries & Mus; Midwest Mus Conf; Cong Ill Hist Soc & Mus. *Res:* Twentieth century American art, particularly contemporary folk art. *Publ:* Contribr, James A Michener Collection: 20th Century American Painting, Univ Mus, Univ Tex, Austin, 77; ed, African Arts: Beauty In Utility (catalog), Eagle Gallery, Murray State Univ, Ky, 83; Collecting outside the mainstream (folk art), Dialogue, 88; Virgil Grotfeldt: Recent Paintings (catalog), 90 & American Scene Prints (catalog), 91, Tarble Arts Ctr, Eastern Ill Univ, 91. *Mailing Add:* Eastern Ill Univ Tarble Arts Ctr 600 Lincoln Ave Charleston IL 61920

WAUFLE, ALAN DUANE
MUSEUM DIRECTOR
b Hornell, NY, Feb 11, 51. *Study:* Col William & Mary, BA; Duke Univ, MA. *Collection Arranged:* Antique Quilts & Coverlets of Gaston Co, 77, Textile History of Gaston Co, 78, Frank Creach: Retrospective, 78, The Christmas Doll, 79, Wheels & Runners: 18th Century America on the Move, 83, Gaston Co Mus Art & Hist. *Pos:* Dir, Gaston Co Mus Art & Hist, Dallas, NC, 76-. *Mem:* NC Mus Coun; Am Asn State & Local Hist; Am Asn of Mus; SE Mus Conf. *Res:* Iconography of works celebrating the 1571 Battle of Lepanto. *Publ:* Auth, Sitings/Sightings, Guide to mus, galleries & craft shops in NC. *Mailing Add:* 3308 Sherwood Cir Gastonia NC 28056

WAX, JOHN M
PAINTER, COLLAGE ARTIST, MIXED MEDIA ARTIST
b Philadelphia, Pa, Nov 1, 48. *Study:* Pa State Univ, 66-69; George Washington Univ, BA(fine arts), 71, MFA, 72. *Work:* Embassy of Norway, Washington, DC; Univ Konstanz, WGer; Nat Inst Health, Bethesda, Md. *Comn:* Aluminum cast sculptures, BKI Alloys, Birmingham, Eng, 70; wall sculpture, Crowell & Moring, Washington, DC, 78; wood assemblage, Rogovin, Stern & Huge, Washington, DC, 79; wood assemblage, A Sarowitz & Assoc, Philadelphia, Pa, 82. *Exhib:* 19th Area Exib, Corcoran Gallery Art, Washington, DC, 74; one-man shows, Wax Paper and Wood Too, Univ City Sci Ctr, Philadelphia, Pa, 81, Collages & Constructions, Hull Gallery, Washington, DC, 83, Artifacts, Pa State Univ, Abington, 86, Alter-Images, Charles Co Col, LRC Gallery, La Plata, Md, 91 & Icons & Apparitions, Nat Inst Health, Bethesda, Md, 93; Collage & Assemblage, Miss Mus Art, Jackson, 81; Shelter '85, Nat Exhib, traveling, Washington, DC & US, 85; Recent Am Works on Paper, Int/Nat Exhib, sponsored by Smithsonian Inst, US & 6 mo Europe, 85-88; Archaeology of the Spirit, Gallery Brocken, Tokyo & Provincetown, Mass, 96. *Teaching:* Instr art & design, NVa Col, Anandale, 78-79 & George Mason Univ, Fairfax, Va, 90-91. *Awards:* Individual Artists Fel, DC Commission on Arts, 82; Cecille R Hunt Mem Award, Geroge Washington Univ Art Exhib, 86. *Bibliog:* Val Lewton (auth), article, Washington Review, 12/15/77; Joseph Adcock (auth), Environment of inagination, The Bulletin (Philadelphia), 5/14/81; Roger Piantadosi (auth), John Wax: Art from the Litter of Life, Washington Post, 5/8/82; John Wax From Paper to Print (film), 97-98. *Mem:* Artists for Equal Justice. *Media:* Mixed; Miscellaneous. *Mailing Add:* 4336 River Rd NW Washington DC 20016

WAYNE, CYNTHIA M
CURATOR, HISTORIAN
b St Louis, Mo, Aug 16, 58. *Study:* Univ Mo, Columbia, BA, 80, MA, 83; Cornell Univ, Ithica, NY, 86-87. *Collection Arranged:* Masters of Contemporary Art in Poland (co-auth, catalog), 86; Dreams, Lies & Exaggerations: Photomontage in America (auth, catalog), 91; Masterworks from the Photography Collections, UMBC, 92; Alice Harold Murphy: Rediscovering the Female Perspective in American Art 1920-1950, 93; Masters of Contemporary Art in Poland (coauth, catalog), Herbert F Hohnson Mus Art, Cornell Univ, 86, New York State Artists V (with catalog), 86, Elements of Nature: Watercolors by Kenneth Evett, 87; Dreams, Lies and Exaggerations: Photomontage in American (with catalog), Art Gallery, Univ Md, College Park, 91; Alice Harold Murphy: Rediscovering the Female Perspective in American Art 1920-1950 (with catalog), Montpelier Cult Art Ctr, Laurel, Md, 93; Fields of Vision: Women in Photography (with catalog), Univ Md Baltimore Co, 95-96, Visual Groits: Works by Four African American Photographers (with catalog), 96, Word & Image: Swiss Poster Design 1955-1997 (with catalog), 98, Imprints: Photographs by David Plowden, 98, Eye of the Storm, Photogs by Mildred Grossman (with catalog), 99. *Pos:* Actg dir/asst dir, Art Gallery, Univ Md, College Park, 87-92; exec dir, Pyramid Atlantic, 92-93; coordr exhib, Albin O Kuhn Libr & Gallery, Univ Md, Baltimore Co, 94-. *Mem:* Am Asn Mus; Col Art Asn; Hist Photog Group. *Res:* History of photography, especially manipulated photography in Europe and United States. *Mailing Add:* Univ Maryland Albin O Kuhn Library & Gallery 1000 Hilltop Cir Baltimore MD 21250

WAYNE, JUNE
PAINTER, PRINTMAKER
b Chicago, Ill, March 17, 1918. *Study:* Atlanta Col Fine Arts, DFA, 88; Calif Col Arts & Crafts, San Francisco, DFA, 88; Moore Col Art & Design, Philadelphia, Pa, DFA, 91; RI Sch Design, Providence, DFA, 94. *Work:* Bibliot Nat, Paris, France; Brit Mus, London, Eng; Mus Mod Art, NY; Grunwald Ctr Graphic Arts, Los Angeles, Calif; Australian Nat Gallery, Canberra; and others. *Comn:* Tapestry, comn by KCET, Los Angeles, 76; lithography, comn by Music Ctr Los Angeles, 86. *Exhib:* Tidal Waves & Visas: Tapestries & Lithography, June Wayne La Demeure, Paris, 75; From Lurcat to Today: Masterpieces of Tapestry, La Royale Belge, Bruxelles, Belg; Tapisseries, Lithographies, traveling show in Europe, Cult Affairs, Am Embassy, Paris, France, 76-79; The Dorothy Series, traveling, Art Mus Asn, 80-84; solo-exhibs, Cult Affairs Dept, Am Embassy, France, 76-79, Art Mus Asn, 81-83, Fresno Mus Art, Calif, 88, Fresno Art Mus, Calif, 88, Print Coun Australia Melbourne, Macquarie Galleries, Sydney, 89, Assoc Am Artist, NY, 91 & Neuberger Mus, Purchase, NY, 93; Turning the Tide, Santa Barbara Mus Art, Calif, 90; and others. *Pos:* Founder & dir, Tamarind Lithography Workshop, 60-70; mem bd dir, Grunwald Graphic Arts Found, Univ Calif, Los Angeles, 65-75, adv to Arts Mgt Prog, Grad Sch Admin, 69-; mem overseers comt, Sch Visual & Environ Arts, Harvard Univ, 74-76; adv, Univ Calif, Long Beach, 87-; emer printmakers, Los Angeles Printmakers Soc, 88, Southern Graphics Coun, 94. *Awards:* Acad Award Nomination; Nat Endowment Arts Visual Arts Fel, 80; Southern Graphics Coun, Printmakers Emer, 95; Woman of Yr, Palm Springs Desert Mus, 99; Zimmerli Lifetime Achievement Award. 2003; Mason Gross Sch Distinguished Service in the Arts Award, 2004. *Bibliog:* R Barrett, P Gilmour, B Kester & A Raven (auths), June Wayne: The Djuna Set, Fresno Art Mus, 5&8/88; P Gilmour (auth), A Love Affair with Lithography: The Prints of June Wayne, Vol 9, No 2, 92; A Kirker (auth), Always the Artist's Advocate, Imprint, Vol 29, No 2, winter 94; plus others. *Mem:* Art Table New York; Art Table Los Angeles; Women Film; The Forum New York; The Forum Los Angeles; hon mem Printmaker Soc Washington; hon mem Printmaker Soc Los Angeles. *Media:* All Media. *Publ:* Auth, The creative process: Artists, carpenters and the Flat Earth Society, Craft Horizons, 76; The male artist as stereotypical female, Col Art J, 73; Avant-Garde Mindset in the Artist's Studio, HUUC '86, Hofstra Univ, 85; Seeing the Unseeable: Space from Earth, Pac Design Ctr Westweek, 86. *Mailing Add:* 1108 N Tamarind Ave Los Angeles CA 90038

WEALE, MARY JO
PAINTER, EDUCATOR
b Lexington, Ky, Feb 26, 24. *Study:* Univ Ky, BS, 45; Famous Artists Sch, cert graphic arts, 58; Fla State Univ, MS, 63, PhD, 68; studied with over 50 watercolorists incl Ed Whitney & Robert Wood. *Work:* Kennedy-Douglass Ctr Arts, Florence, Ala; Ed Ball Wakulla Springs State Park, Fla; Consulate General Iceland, Columbia Hosp, Champion Chevrolet, & Univ Chevolet Tallahassee, Fla; Miller Brewing Co; Walt Disney World; NCNB & Fla First Fed, Tampa; Barnett Bank Corporate Collection; 1st Fla Savings & Loan, Panama City; Savannah Col Art & Design; Fla's Gov Mansion. *Comn:* Large watercolors, Kozyak, Tropin & Throckmorton, Miami, Fla, 88, Tallahassee & Tampa, 88-92, Fla Gov Mansion, 99, Med & Dental offices, 98, 99; St Mark's Light House, Fla State Univ, Tallahassee, 88-89; Judge BK Roberts & Judge Parker McDonald; Wakulla Springs State Park; numerous corp & pvt comns. *Exhib:* Southern Watercolor Soc Ann, Okla Art Ctr, 83 & 86; Ga Watercolor Soc Open Show, Mus Arts & Sci, Macon GA, 86; Beaux Arts Exhib, Lowe Mus, Coral Gables, Fla, 87, 88 & 89; Ga Watercolor Soc Mus Show, Valdosta Art Mus, 88; Panama Nat Transparent Show Civic Ctr, Fla, 88; Mt Dora Art Festival, 89; one-person exhibs, The Fragile Moment, 89, Fla State Univ Command Performance Gallery, 92, Fine Art Galleries of Hawaii, 92, Southern Women, 94, Chez Pierre, 96 & numerous others. *Pos:* Artist-in-residence, Ed Ball Wakulla Springs State Park, 87, 90 & 91. *Teaching:* Chmn interior design, Fla State Univ, 73-85, prof watercolor, 73-90, serv prof, 85-90; vis prof watercolor, Int Inst of Foreign Study, London, 81; vis prof watercolor, Winthrop Col, 85, Savannah Col Art, 88; Walt Disney World Design & Eng Dept, 90; demonstr, St Cuthbert's Paper Mill, Eng at Fla Watercolor Soc Ann Mtg, 91. *Awards:* Best of Show, 86 & First Place, 88, Tallahassee Regional Watercolor Soc, 86; Award of Merit, Ga Watercolor Soc, 88; First place, watercolor, Mt Dora Art Fest, 89. *Bibliog:* Margaret Mitchell (auth), feature article, Tallahassee Mag, 90; Alan Wendt, news feature, WTVT (CBS) Tampa, 90; Andy Blount (auth), Florida Wildlife, 1-2/91; International Year Book, Wildlife Art News, 92. *Mem:* Southern Watercolor Soc (secy, 81-83); Fla Watercolor Soc sig mem (newsletter ed, 89-92, secy, 92-95); Ga Watercolor Soc; Founder 10 Artists Ltd. *Media:* Watercolor. *Res:* water color techniques; contemporary furniture design; historic costume1860-1920; orchids (greenhouse); contemporary watercolorists, painters and sculptors. *Specialty:* Wild Life, shore birds, Wet lands. *Interests:* Artists, green house, orchid, sewing, Music. *Collection:* Walkulla Springs State Park. *Publ:* Environmental Interiors, Macmillan, 82 & 96; Numerous articles in Interior Design, Contract, Journal of Interior Design

Education Research, The Designer, Lithographs, Egrets have no regrets, 88; diptych, Transparent Watercolor Techniques & Creative Applications for Walt Disney World, priv pub, 90; Transparent Watercolor for Elderhostel, Fla State Univ, 90 & 91; Ethics & the Artist, Fla Watercolor Soc, 96. *Dealer:* Nuance Gallery 720 S Date Mabry Tampa FL 33609; Gallery of Art Panama City FL. *Mailing Add:* 1102 Sarasota Dr Tallahassee FL 32301-5727

WEARE, SHANE
PRINTMAKER
b Eng, Aug 29, 36. *Study:* Royal Col Art, London, Eng, ARCA(printmaking), 63; Univ Iowa, asst etching, 63-64. *Work:* Brit Mus, London; Lib Libr Cong, Washington, DC; Brooklyn Mus, NY; Art Inst Chicago; San Francisco Mus Art. *Exhib:* Int Exhib Graphic Art, Ljubliana, Yugoslavia, 66; Brit Int Print Biennale, 68; 22nd Ann Print Exhib, Boston Mus, 70; World Print Competition, San Francisco Mus Art, 73; one-man show, Calif Palace of Legion of Honor, San Francisco, 73; 20th Nat Print Exhib, Brooklyn Mus, NY, 77. *Pos:* prof art emeritus, Sonoma State Univ. *Awards:* Purchase Awards, Los Angeles Soc Printmakers, 68-74, City of San Francisco, 72, City of Palo Alto, 74 & Univ Colo, 74; Spaces Between Prog Award, KQED-TV, San Francisco, 75. *Bibliog:* John Brunsden (auth), Technique of Etching & Engraving, Batsford, 66. *Mem:* Calif Soc Printmakers (vchmn, 72-73). *Media:* Pastel. *Dealer:* Printworks 311 West Superior St Suite 105 Chicago IL 60610. *Mailing Add:* 2663 Bennett Ridge Rd Santa Rosa CA 95404

WEAVER, AM
ADMINISTRATOR, HISTORIAN
b Philadelphia, Pa, Jul 31, 54. *Study:* Univ Arts, Philadelphia, Pa, BFA; Md Inst Col, Hoffberger Sch Painting, MFA. *Exhib:* Retrospective (auth, catalog), Univ Pa, Contemp Inst Art, Philadelphia, Pa, James E Lewis Mus Art, Baltimore, Md, Lehigh Univ, Bethlehem, Pa, Ft Lauderdale Mus, Fla. *Pos:* fac, alternative art ctr, Philadelphia, Pa, formerly; dir, Visual & Media Arts, formerly; exec dir, Art Santuary, formerly; cur, exhibs & collections, Noyes Mus Art, NJ, currently; Independent Cur, currently. *Media:* Photography. *Interests:* African Aesthetics, traditional & contemporary; photography. *Publ:* auth, Black Artists, St James Press; many essays, catalog essays & jour. *Mailing Add:* Noyes Mus Art Lily Lake Rd Oceanville NJ 08231

WEAVER, JOHN BARNEY
SCULPTOR
b Anaconda, Mont, Mar 28, 20. *Study:* Art Inst Chicago, dipl(Albert Kuppenhiemer Scholar), 46; monumental sculpture with Albin Polasek, Emil Zettler, Edward Chasang & Egon Weiner. *Hon Degrees:* Univ Arts, Parma, Italy, dipl merit, 81, Univ Alta, LLD, 84. *Work:* Bronzes, Charles Russell, Statuary Hall, Washington, Double Equestrian, Fort Walsh, Sask, Archaic Indian, NY State Mus, Albany & Govt House, Edmonton, Alta; Astokimake (portrait bust), Rideau Hall, Ottawa; heads & figures, Anthrop Hall, Smithsonian Inst. *Comn:* medal design, World Univ Games, 83; Expo '86 Commemorative Collection, 86; Edmonton Merchant (bronze), Edmonton CofC, Alta, 89; Ukrainian Pioneers (2 bronze figures), comn by Walter Dowhaniuk family, Two Hills, Alta, 92; Piper, James C Richardson, VC, for Chilliwack, 2003. *Exhib:* Chicago & Vicinity, Art Inst Chicago, 47; 68th Exhib Soc Wash Artists, Natural Hist Bldg, Wash, 61; Steel to the West (bronze), US, Toronto, London, Paris & Brussels, 78; Media Ctr, Robson Sq, Vancouver, BC, 80; Salon Nations, Paris, 83; Beijing, China, 2003-04. *Pos:* Sculptor, Mont Hist Soc, 55-60, Smithsonian Inst, 61-66 & Provincial Mus & Archives, Alta, 66-71. *Teaching:* Instr life drawing, Layton Sch Art, Milwaukee, 46-51; instr sculpture, Fraser Valley Col, Abbotsford, BC, 84-89. *Awards:* Alta Achievement Award for Excellence in Sculpture, 77; Gold Medal, Int Parliament Security & Peace, 82; Premio Milano Capitale Dell'Arte, Artista Dell'Anno, 88. *Bibliog:* Ruth Bowen (auth), Alberta art in bronze, My Golden West, 70; Mario Monteverdi & Calogero Panepinto (auth), The history of international art, Univ Arts, Parma, Italy, 82; Arthur Williams (auth), The Sculpture Reference, Sculpture Books Publishing. *Mem:* Italian Acad Art, Parma; Acad Europe; Acad Nations; life mem Univ Mont Mus Rockies; life mem Mont State Hist Soc. *Media:* Bronze. *Res:* Art history. *Specialty:* Univ Alberta, Ring Gallery. *Interests:* Sports, science, history. *Collection:* Artist copy collection of commissioned bronzes. *Publ:* Sculpture of John Weaver; Weaver Fine Art Bronze; Returning Art to the Free Market; Perspectives. *Mailing Add:* PO Box 1723 Hope BC V0X 1L0 Canada

WEBB, ALEX(ANDER) (DWIGHT)
PHOTOGRAPHER
b San Francisco, Calif, May 5, 52. *Study:* Harvard Univ, BA (hist and lit), 74; Apeiron Photog Workshop, with Charles Harbutt, 72. *Work:* Fogg Art Mus, Cambridge, Mass; Whitney Mus Am Art, NY; Int Ctr Photog, NY; Mus Photog Arts, San Diego, Calif; Brooklyn Mus, NY. *Comn:* Picturing the South, High Mus Art, Atlanta, Ga. *Exhib:* Contemp Photographers V, 75 & Color Photog, 80, Fogg Art Mus, Cambridge, Mass; 3 Color Photogrs, Amsterdam Photo 84, The Neth, 84; On the Line: The New Color Photojournalism (with catalog), Walker Art Ctr, Minneapolis, Minn, 86; solo shows, Calif Mus Photog, Riverside, 86 & Torino Fotogratia, Torino, Italy, US-Mex Border, FotoMassan, Gothenburg, Sweden, 97, Leica Gallery, NY, 98, Zentrum fur Photog, Berlin, Ger, 98 Under a Grudging Sun and Beyond, Int Fototage Herten, 99 & Amazon, Sky Harbor Gallery, Phoenix, Ariz, 99; group shows, Masters of the Streets & Haiti: Revolution in Progress, Mus Photog Arts, San Diego, Calif, 89, This & Other Worlds, Mus Contemp Photog, Chicago, Ill, In Our Time, Magnum Photos, Int Ctr Photog, NY, 89, Palats de Tokyo, Paris, France, 89 (traveling) & Minneapolis Mus Art, 90; This & Other Worlds, Mus Contemp Photog, Chicago, Ill; Atrium Gallery, Univ Conn, Storrs, 91; Whitney Mus Am Art, NY Biennial Exhib, 91; Civilians in War, Art Inst Boston, 95; India: A Celebration of Independence, Philadelphia Mus Art, 97; World Views, Southeast Mus Photogr, Daytona Beach, Fla, 2000; many others. *Pos:* Photogr, Magnum Photos, NY, 76-, vpres, 85-86. *Awards:* NY Found Arts Grant, 86; Nat Endowment Arts Grant, 90; Hasselblad Found Grant, 98; Leica Medal of Excellence, 2000. *Bibliog:* Andy Grundberg (auth), Photojournalism: It's back with a new face, Mod Photog, 80; Gary Walther (auth), In the heat of the light, Camera Arts, 83; M Johnstone (auth), The active streets, Art Week, 83; Haiti, Photo Mag, France, 4/88; Max Kozloff (auth), Picturing the Killing Fields, Art in Am, 6/90. *Publ:* Auth, Hot Light/Half-Made Worlds: Photographs from the Tropics, 86 & Under a Grudging Sun: Photographs from Haiti Libere, 89, Thames & Hudson; auth, From the Sunshine State: Photographs of Florida, 96 & Amazon: From the Floodplains to the Clouds, 97, Monacelli Press; auth, Dislocations, Harvard Univ, 98-99. *Dealer:* Catherine Edelman Gallery Chicago; Etherta Gallery Tucson

WEBB, FRANK (FRANCIS) H
PAINTER, INSTRUCTOR
b North Versailles, Pa, Sept 14, 27. *Study:* Art Inst Pittsburgh, with Edgar A Whitney. *Work:* Butler Inst Am Art, Youngstown, Ohio; PPG Found, Pittsburgh; Tweed Art Mus, Duluth, Mich; Ford Times Collection, Detroit; Taiwan Art Educ Inst; Palmer Mus Penn State Univ. *Comn:* Soc Naval Architects & Marine Engineers, 88. *Exhib:* Am Watercolor Soc Ann, Nat Acad, NY, 71-80; Nat Arts Club, NY, 71-81; Butler Inst Am Art, Youngstown, Ohio, 73; Audubon Artists, Nat Arts Club, NY, 73-83; Allied Artists, Nat Arts Club, NY, 73-80; Nat Acad Ann, NY, 77; Midwest Watercolor Soc Ann, Rawr-West Mus, Manitowac, Wis, 79-83; and many others. *Pos:* Pres, Phillips Studio, Pittsburgh, 57-80. *Teaching:* Guest lectr painting throughout N Am, Cent Am & Europe, 73-. *Awards:* Sizek Award, Butler Midyear Ann, Butler Inst Am Art, Youngstown, Ohio, 73; Bronze Medal of Honor, Am Watercolor Soc, 76; Walser Greathouse Medal, Am Watercolor Soc, 89; Gold Medal of Honor, Audubon Artists, 95; Philadelphia Watercolor Soc Medal for Achievement in the Arts. *Bibliog:* Webb on Watercolor (film/video); Using your Head, Heart and Hand (film/DVD); Frank Webb's Painting by Design (film/DVD); Frank Webb's Expression in Painting (film/DVD). *Mem:* Am Watercolor Soc, Dolphin Fel, (3rd vp, chmn mems, 01-); Rocky Mountain Nat Watermedia Asn; Allied Artists of Am; Audubon Artists. *Media:* Watercolor. *Publ:* Auth, Watercolor Energies, 83, North Light Publ; Webb on Watercolor, 90; Strengthen Your Paintings with Dynamic Composition, 94. *Dealer:* Harbor Square Gallery Rockland ME. *Mailing Add:* 5 Grandview Ave Apt 401 Pittsburgh PA 15211

WEBB, JEFFREY R
PAINTER, EDUCATOR
b Mineola, NY, Sept 29, 52. *Study:* Pratt Inst, Brooklyn, NY, BFA, 74; studied with John Koch Nat Acad, 74-78; C W Post Col, Long Island Univ, Old Brookville, MA, 76. *Work:* Heckscher Mus, Huntington, NY; Bayville Mus, NY. *Comn:* portrait, Dr G Perry, Mercy Hosp, Rockville Centre, NY, 86; portrait, Dr Robbins, South Oaks Hosp, Amityville, 86; historical portrait, Capt T Cook, City Glen Cove, NY, 86; mural, Wizard of Oz, Village Green Golf, Lake Ronkonroma, NY, 92; portrait, Maury Povitch and Connie Chung. *Exhib:* Pastel Soc Asn Ann Exhibs, Nat Arts Club, NY, 73-92; one-man show, Harbor Gallery, Cold Spring Harbor, NY, 78; Pastel Exposition Int, Maison Lafitte, Paris, France, 88; Master Pastellists, Quincy Art Mus, Ill, 90; Featured Show, Z Gallery, NY, 91; and others. *Pos:* Historian, bd dir, Pastel Soc Am, NY, 75-; vpres, Nat Drawing Asn, Garden City, NY, 88-90; art comt, Salmagundi Club, NY, 90-. *Teaching:* Instr painting, Huntington Township Art League, NY, 76-; instr pastel painting, Queensborough Community Col, Bayside, NY, 89-; instr art hist, Nassau Community Col, Garden City, NY, 88-; adj fac, SUNY, Farmingdale, NY. *Awards:* Knickerbocker Award for Oil, Knickerbocker Artists Ann, 78; Master Pastellist, Pastel Soc Am Exhib, 85; Grumbacher Gold Medal, Pastel Soc Am Ann Exhib, Grumbacher Artists Mats, 91. *Bibliog:* Domenique Sennelier (auth), The Sennelier Pastel Portrait Set, Sennelier Artists Mat, 91; Linda Price (auth) Creating Luminous Pastels The Paintings of Long Island Artist Jeff Webb, Am Artist Mag, 7/97; Kristina Feliciano (editor), The Best of Pastels 2, Rockport Press, 98. *Mem:* Pastel Soc Am (bd dir, 75-); Nat Drawing Asn (vpres, 88-90); Salmagundi Club (art comt, 90-); Nat Art League (exhib chmn, 92); Huntngton Township Art League. *Media:* Pastel, Oil. *Publ:* Illusr, Introduction to Meditation, 78 & Fundamentals of Jain Meditation, 79, Dodd-Mead; auth, Artists and models, Encore Plus, 89. *Dealer:* Owl 57 Gallery Woodmere NY. *Mailing Add:* 270 Lowndes Ave No 117 Huntington Station NY 11746

WEBB, PATRICK
PAINTER, MURALIST
b New York, NY, July 20, 55. *Study:* Md Inst/Col Art, BFA, 76; Skowhegan Sch Painting & Sculpture, 77; Yale Univ, MFA, 79. *Work:* Fred Alger & Co & Chemical Bank, NY; Boston Pub Libr & Shearson Lehman, Boston, Mass; Univ Wis, Oshkosh; Housatonic Mus, Bridgeport, Conn; Queensboro Col Mus, NY. *Comn:* Painting, Glickenhaus & Co, NY, 86; paintings, Sharf Marketing Group 87 & 88; portraits, Art Matters 2 Lithographs; Landscapes, 99 & 2002. *Exhib:* Solo shows, Forum Gallery, Minneapolis, Minn, 90, Group Gallery, Provincetown, Mass, 92, Amos Eno Gallery, NY, 93, Figuring it out, Daniel Quinn Gallery, Long Island, NY, 92, Mercer Gallery, 95, Punchinello Goes West (with catalog), Julie Heller Gallery, Provincetown, Mass, Punchinello Works Out (PWO), Cortland Jessup Gallery, NY, 98, Punchinello Undressed, Julie Heller Gallery, 99, Punchinello Young, Julie Heller Gallery, Mass, 2001, Punchinello's City, CJG Projs, NY, 2002, Home, Julie Heller Gallery, Mass, 2003, Punchinello Inside and Out, CJG Projs, NY, 2004; Mementomori, Open Space Gallery, Allentown, Pa, 93; Unexpected Courage, Multimedia Gallery, NY, 94; Tongue 'n Cheek, 450 Gallery, NY, 94; group exhibs, Transformations, Sakia City Mus Gallery, Osaka, Japan, 2002, Pratt Responds to 9/11, Schaffler Gallery, Pratt Inst, NY, 2002, The Body and its Dangers, The Painting Ctr, NY, 2003; Chaet Julieheller Gallery, 2005. *Teaching:* Lectr, Univ Wis, 79-81; asst prof, Cornell Univ, 81-83; vis artist, Yale Univ, 85, Brandeis Univ, 88, Minneapolis Col Art & Design, 89, 90 & 92,

Cranbook Acad, 92 & 94, NY Acad Art, 93-94, Fla Int Univ, 93 & RI Sch Design, 93, Pratt Inst, 95-; adj assoc prof, Pratt Inst, 2000-2004; assoc prof, Pratt Inst, 2004-. *Awards:* Fel, Nat Endowment Arts, 83, 85 & 87; Ingram Merrill Award, 89-90 & 95; Thomas B Clarke Award, Nat Acad, NY, 98. *Bibliog:* Phil Gambone (auth), Eros & Angst, Bay Windows; Nancy Grimes (auth), Punchinello Paintings (catalog), 93; and others. *Mem:* Col Art Asn; NY Artists Equity; Provincetown Art Asn; Brooklyn Waterfront Artist Asn; Art Group Inc. *Media:* Oil & Miscellaneous Frescoe. *Publ:* Cover, Public Speaking, Beebe Prentice Hall, 91; American Law Yearbook (reproduction & article by ed), 90; cover, Bar Asn J, Mass, 92; Punchinello Works Out, Weinsberg, Asn Am Mus. *Dealer:* Julie Heller Gallery Provincetown MA; Cortland Jessup Gallery New York NY. *Mailing Add:* Old Chelsea St PO Box 903 New York NY 10011

WEBB, SARAH A
PAINTER
b Nashville, Tenn, Feb 19, 48. *Study:* Univ Tenn, Ba, 78; Vanderbilt Univ, 79-80. *Work:* Holiday Corp, Memphis, Tenn; First Tenn Bank, Gallatin, Tenn. *Exhib:* Ann Cent South Art Competition, Parthenon Gallery, Nashville, Tenn, 82, 87 & 92; solo exhibs, Leu Gallery, Belmont Univ, Nashville, 83, 99, Nashville Int Airport, Metro Arts Comn, 94 and others; Am Artist Nat Art Competition, Grand Central Gallery, NY, 85; Ann Exhib, Soc Women Artists, Westminster Gallery, London, Eng, 89, 90, 91, 94, 98-01. *Awards:* Best of Show, 22nd Central South Art Competition, 87; Athena Award, 27th Central South Art Competition, 92. *Bibliog:* Clara Hieronymns (auth), Oh, how she loves Paris, 12/27/87 & Sarah Webb Works to Show in London, 5/17/89, Tennessean; Tennessee Crossroads: Profiling International Artist Sarah Webb in London (film), WDCN-PBS TV, Nashville, 94; Susan Chappell (auth), Nashville artist Sarah Webb breaks ground in Britain, Nashville Banner, 3/18/94; Alan Bostic (auth), Get real, Webb paints it like it is, The Tennessean, 9/12/99. *Mem:* Soc Women Artists, London, Eng. *Media:* Oil. *Mailing Add:* PO Box 50134 Nashville TN 37205

WEBER, IDELLE LOIS
PAINTER, EDUCATOR
b Chicago, Ill, Mar 12, 32. *Study:* Scripps Col, 51; Univ Calif, Los Angeles, BA & MA, 54-55. *Work:* Art Inst, Chicago; Fogg Mus, Harvard Univ, Cambridge, Mass; Albright-Knox Art Gallery, Buffalo, NY; San Francisco Mus Art, Calif. *Comn:* Pac Bell, San Ramon, Calif. *Exhib:* Contemp Am Realism Since 1960, Pa Acad Fine Arts, 81; Traveling Exhib, Woodson Art Mus, Wasau, Wis, 95-97; Santa Barbara Mus Contemp Art, Calif, 95; Harn Mus, Fla, 96; Solo exhibs Bertha Schaefer, NY, 1963-1964, Hundred Acres Gallery, NY, 1973-1977, OK Harris Gallery, NY, 1979-1982, Ruth Siegel Gallery, NY, 1984-1989, Anthony Ralph, NY, 1989-1992, Arts Club Chicago, 1989, Gerald Peters Gallery, Santa Fe, NMex, 1994, Schmidt Bingham Gallery, 1994-1998, others; Nat Acad mem exhib, 2003; Nassau Co Mus Art, NY, 2004. *Teaching:* Asst prof art, Harvard Univ, 1989-91; master prog, Long Island Univ, Southampton, NY; adj assoc prof art NY Univ Grad Sch, 1974-89; Melbourne Univ, Australia, 1995, Nat Acad, 2002 & 05. *Awards:* Distinguished Alumna Award, Scripps Col; Artist-in-Residence, Victoria Col Art, Melbourne, Australia; Recognized in various publ incl: Arts Mag, 1979, 82, 84, 86, Photo Realism (L Meisel), 1980, San Antonio Mus Catalogue (L Nochlin), 1981, Art in Am (E Lubell), Am Women Artists (CS Rubenstein), 1982, Wall St J, 1985, Christian Sci Monitor, 1985, 86, Art in Am, 1986, Wash Post, 1986, Chicago Tribune, 1986, Wash Post, 1986, 87, Art Examiner, 1986; subject of work: Am Realist Painting, 1945-1980 (John L Ward), 1989; Scholastic Arts magazine scholar, 1950. *Bibliog:* Alloway, Jan Ernst, Idelle Weber, The, Oct, 1994; Grace Glueck (auth), article, NY Times, 96; Whitney Chadwick, Women, Art and Society, Thames & Hudson, 1997; Gary Miles Chassman (auth), In the Spirit of Martin, the Living Legacy of Dr Martin Luther King, Jr, 2001; Jennifer New (auth), Drawing From Life: The J as Art, 2005. *Mem:* Col Art Asn; Women's Caucus Art; Poets House; Nat Acad (acad, 02-). *Media:* Oil, Watercolor, Pastel & Photography. *Interests:* Poetry, Photography and Music. *Mailing Add:* 429 W Broadway New York NY 10012

WEBER, JOHN PITMAN
MURALIST, PRINTMAKER
b Washington, DC, Dec 6, 42. *Study:* Harvard Col, BA(cum laude), 64; Atelier 17, Paris, with S Hayter & Jean Helion, Fulbright-Hays Scholar, 64-66; Ecole des Beaux Arts; Art Inst Chicago, with Yoshida & Halsted, MFA(painting), 68. *Work:* Cohen Libr, City Col, City Univ NY; Norris Ctr, Northwestern Univ, Evanston, Ill; Valparaiso Univ Mus Art, Ind; Spertus Mus, Chicago; Elmhurst Col, Ill. *Comn:* polychrome concrete relief mural, City Arts, NY, 84; mural, Valley Cities Jewish Community Ctr, Los Angeles, Calif, 93; mosaics (with N Cain), Beth-Anne Ctr, Chicago, 98-99; mosaic, The Gathering, Millenium Mosaic Plaza, Spencer, IA, 2000; play sculpture & mosaic (with Henri Marquet), A Place for Children, Sabin School, Chicago, 2005. *Exhib:* Murals for the People, Mus Contemp Art, Chicago, 71; Mural Art USA, Royal Mus, Bruxelles, Belgium, 78; SubCult, Group Material, IRT Subway, NY, 83; Committed to Print, Mus Mod Art, NY, 88; Kunst und Krieg, Kongreshalle, Berlin, 90; Chicago Crossings, Spertus Mus, Chicago, 94; Healing Walls, Ill State Art Mus, Springfield, 95; Retrospective, Valparaiso Univ Art Mus, Ind, 91; Bridges & Boundaries (traveling), Jewish Mus, New York City; A Shenere Velt Gallery, Los Angeles, 2002; Fences, Arc Gallery, Chicago, 2005; Lamentation, St Xavier Univ Gallery, Chicago, 2005; solo shows, Night Scenes, Chicago State Univ Gallery, 97; 10 Yrs of Printmaking, Taller Mestizarte, Chicago, 98; and others. *Pos:* Dir & founder, Chicago Pub Art Group, Chicago, 70-81. *Teaching:* prof art, Elmhurst Col, Ill, 68-; vis artist mural workshop, Univ NDak, Grand Forks, 75 & Dartington Col Art, Eng, 80. *Awards:* Beautiful Chicago, City of Chicago donor, 73 & 76; Pub Art, Chicago Bar Asn, 91. *Bibliog:* Shifra Goldman (auth), John Pitman Weber, (catalog), Valparaiso Univ, 91; Victor Sorell (auth), John Pitman Weber (catalog), Col Dupage Art Ctr Gallery, 94; Harpaz & Piazza (co-auth), John Pitman Weber-Glancing Back, Oakton Col, 2000. *Mem:* Col Art Asn; Chicago Pub Art Group; Community Built Asn; Chicago Artists Coalition; Piece Process Art Group. *Media:* Acrylic, Mosaic; Woodcut. *Publ:* Toward a People's Art, The Contemporary Mural Movement, Dutton, 77 & Univ NMex Press, rev 98; Murals as People's Art, Theories & Documents of Contemporary Art, Stiles & Selz, VCA, 96; Carlos Cortez, Catalog Essay, Dittmar Gallery, Northwestern Univ, 95; auth, Art in public spaces & public art, Art J, winter 90; Community Sculpture, Art & Artists, Feb. 83. *Mailing Add:* c/o Elmhurst Col Art Dept 190 Prospect Ave Elmhurst IL 60126

WEBER, SUZANNE OSTERWEIL
PAINTER, PRINTMAKER
b Brooklyn, NY, June 22, 40. *Study:* Pratt Inst, BS, 61, MFA, 64, with Richard Lindner, Jacob Landau, Fritz Eichenberg, Federico Castellon & Philip Pearlstein; Pratt Graphic Ctr, with Vasilios Toulis; NY Univ, with Lawrence Alloway. *Work:* US Info Agency (prints); Nat Art Mus Sport. *Comn:* Loral Corp, comn by Bernard Schwartz, NY, 75; Cent Rigging Corp, comn by Monroe Myerson, NY, 77; US Info Agency, Washington, DC, 78; portraits, comn by Spyros Niarchos; regular portrait comns since 1998. *Exhib:* Wagner Col Gallery, Staten Island, NY, 92; Thompkins Park Visitors Ctr Gallery, Lincroft, 95; Monmouth Festival of the Arts, Tinton Falls, NJ, 95-; Owl 57 Gallery, Woodmere, NY, 95-; Art Forms Gallery, Red bank, NJ 2002-; Renée Fossmer Gallery, Millburn, NJ, 2003; Blue Bay Inn, Atlantic Highlands, NJ. *Pos:* Graphics juror, Nat Asn Women Artists, 68-; bd trustees, Nat Art Mus Sport; interviewer, Bennington Rev; juror, Pratt Inst Student Exhib. *Teaching:* Instr painting, Brooklyn Mus, NY (formerly); asst prin art, High Sch Art & Design, NY, 79-90; principal, Port Richmond High Sch, Staten Island, NY, 90-94 & Monomouth Regional High Sch, Tinton Falls, NJ, 94-98. *Awards:* Janet E Turner Prize, 74 & Dorothy Seligson Prize, 80, Nat Asn Women Artists; Leadership in Art Educ, NYCATA/UFT, 85; Fac Appreciation Award, HS of Art & Design, 90, Port Richmond HS, 94. *Media:* Acrylics on Canvas; Serigraphy. *Specialty:* Comtemp painting, sculpture & graphics. *Interests:* photography. *Dealer:* Owl 57 Gallery 1074 Broadway Woodmere NY 11598; Beauregard Gallery Rumson NJ. *Mailing Add:* 39 Stonehenge Dr Ocean NJ 07712

WEBSTER, LARRY
PAINTER, PRINTMAKER
b Arlington, Mass, Mar 18, 30. *Study:* Mass Col Art, BFA; Boston Univ, MS. *Work:* DeCordova Mus, Lincoln, Mass; Grand Rapids Art Mus, Mich; Munic Gallery, Davenport, Iowa; Springfield Art Mus, Mo; Art Mus, Colby Col, Waterville, Maine; and others. *Exhib:* Am Watercolor Soc, NY, 61-88; Nat Acad Design, NY, 66-81; Rocky Mountain Nat Watermedia Exhib, 78-81. *Pos:* Package designer, Union Bag & Paper Corp, 53-54; illusr, USA, 54-56; graphic designer, vpres & dir, Thomas Todd Co, Boston, 56-78. *Teaching:* Asst prof typographic design, hist type & watercolor painting, Mass Col Art, 64-65. *Awards:* Obrig Prize, Nat Acad Design, 67 & 70; Silver Medal, Am Watercolor Soc, 68 & 72; High Winds Medal, Am Watercolor Soc, 82; and others. *Bibliog:* Gerald F Brommer & Nancy K Kinne (auths), Exploring Painting, Davis Publ, 88; Gerald F Brommer (auth), Understanding Transparent Watercolor, Davis Publ, 93; Betty Lou Schlemm & Tom Nicholas (auths), The Best of Watercolor, Rockport Publ Inc, 95, second ed, 96. *Mem:* Nat Acad Design; Am Watercolor Soc. *Media:* Watercolor, Mixed Media

WEBSTER, SALLY (SARA) B
HISTORIAN
b Hammond, Ind, May 24, 38. *Study:* Barnard Col, BA, 59; Harvard-Radcliffe Prog in Business Admin, cert, 60; Univ Cincinnati, MA, 74; Grad Ctr, City Univ New York, PhD(Am art), 85. *Pos:* Dir educ, Taft Mus, Cincinnati, Ohio, 74-75; dir, AIR Gallery, NY, 79-81; partner, Rose Web Proj, NY. *Teaching:* Instr hist art, Col Staten Island, fall 83; instr hist art, Lehman Col, 83-85, asst prof, 85-90, assoc prof, 90-95, prof, 95-; fac, Grad Ctr, City Univ NY, 94. *Mem:* Heresies Collective, NY; Col Art Asn; Arch Am Art; Asn Hist Am Art. *Publ:* Joyce Kozloft: Public decoration, Art America, 2/87; William Morris Hunt, Cambridge Univ Press, 91; co-ed, Critical Issues in Public Art: Content, Context and Controversy, Harper Collins, 92; Public Art in the Bronx, Lehman Col Art Gallery, 93; Mary Cassatt & Mary Fairchild MacMonnies: The Search for Their Woman Building Murals, Am Art, Spring 94. *Mailing Add:* 158 W 94th St New York NY 10025-7055

WECHSLER, JUDITH GLATZER
HISTORIAN, FILMMAKER
b Chicago, Ill, Dec 28, 40. *Study:* Brandeis Univ, BA, 62; Columbia Univ, MA, 67; Univ Calif, Los Angeles, PhD, 72. *Work:* Film, Daumier, Paris and the Spectator (with Charles Eames), 77, Pissarro, at the Heart of Impressionism, 81, Edouard Manet: Painter of Modern Life, 83, Mus Mod Art, Cézanne: The Late Work, 78 (with Charles Eames), Jasper Johns: Take an Object (with Hans Namuth), 90, Aaron Siskind, Mus Mod Art, 91, Harry Callahan, 93, Flora Natapof, 99 & Cézanne; Rachel of the Comédie, Frangaise, 2003; Film, The Training of Painters, 87, Portraits, 88, The Arrested Moment, 88, Painting and the Public, 88, Abstraction, 89. *Comn:* Titian: Venus & Adonis, Getty Mus, 94; Drawing: The Thinking Hand, Louvre, 96; Image and Enterprise: The Photography of Adolph Braun, RI Sch Design Mus, 98; Honoré Daumier, One Must be of One's Time, R'eunion des Musees Nation aux, 99. *Collection Arranged:* Robert Moskowitz (cataloged), Mass Inst Technol Hayden Gallery, 71; Daumier: Parisian Types, Brandeis Univ, 79; Rachel, Une vie pour le théâtre, Mus d'art et d'hist dur judaýme, Paris, 2004. *Pos:* Asst ed, Schocken Books Inc, NY, 63-65; consult, off of Charles and Ray Eames, Venice, Calif, 76-78; res fel, Ctr for Advanced Visual Studies, Mass Inst Technol, 77-79. *Teaching:* asst prof, MIT, 70-78; Lectr, Harvard Univ, 81-82; from assoc prof to prof, RI Sch Design, 81-89; vis prof, Harvard Univ, spring 89; NEH prof & chmn, dept art & art hist, 90-95, Tufts Univ, 89-; vis prof, Hebrew Univ, Jerusalem, 94 & 96; vis prof, Univ Paris, 98; prof, Nat Endowment Humanities, currently; vis prof, Ecole Normale Superieure, Paris,

2003. *Awards:* Nat Endowment for Humanities fel grants, 73, 75, 81, 83-84, 84-85, 85-86, 87-89 & 88-90; Nat Endowment for the Arts, 81, 87-89; Cine Golden Eagle Award for Manet Film, 84 & The Artist and the Nude, 85, The Arrested Moment, 89, and Portraits, 88; Am Film Festival Red Ribbon Award for Portraits, 89. *Mem:* Col Art Asn; 19th French Art Hist Asn; Int Coun Mus; SCAM. *Res:* 19th and 20th century art; Film; Publ. *Publ:* Ed introd, Cézanne in Perspective, Prentice-Hall Inc, 75; auth, Gyorgy Kepes, 78, MIT Press & ed introd, On Aesthetics in Science, 78, Mass Inst Technol Press; The Interpretation of Cézanne, UMI res Press, 81; A Human Comedy: Physiognomy and Caricature in 19th Century Paris, Thames & Hudson Ltd, Univ Chicago Press, 82; articles in Daedalus, Art Bulletin, Aperture, Artforum, Art J, Art News, Gazette des Beaux Arts & Studies in Visual Commnications; Les Cabinets des Dessins, Daumier, Flammarion, 99. *Mailing Add:* Dept Art History 11 Talbot Ave Medford MA 02155

WECHSLER, SUSAN
EDITOR, WRITER
b Neptune, NJ, Sept 15, 43. *Study:* Douglass Col, Rutgers Univ, BA, 65; Teachers Col, Columbia Univ. *Exhib:* Marietta Crafts Nat, 75; solo exhib, Queens Mus, NY, 76; Women Artists: Clay, Fiber and Metal, Bronx Mus, 78 & traveling. *Collection Arranged:* Is Anybody Home? (auth, catalog), Esther Saks Gallery, Chicago, Ill, 85; The Raw Edge: Ceramics of the 80's (auth, catalog), Hillwood Art Gallery, CW Post College, Greenvale, NY. *Pos:* Photo ed, 66-; writer, 77-. *Teaching:* Instr ceramic hist, Cooper Hewitt Mus/Parsons Sch Design, New York, 85-86, thesis adv, 86-87; critic-in-residence, Sch Art, Univ Tasmania, Australia, 85; vis fac, Banff Centre Sch Fine Arts, Alta, Can, 86. *Awards:* Artpark Fel, Nat Heritage Trust, 77; Nat Endowment Arts Award, 81. *Bibliog:* Mikail Zakin (auth), New York clay, Craft Horizons, 76; Elisabeth Woody (auth), Hand Building Ceramic Forms, Farrar Straus, 78; Elaine Levin (auth), A History of American Ceramics, Abrams, 88. *Mem:* Int Asn Art Critics. *Res:* Contemporary & historical ceramics; design; photography. *Publ:* Auth, Low-Fire Ceramics: A New Direction in American Clay, Watson-Guptill, 81; Views on the figure, Am Ceramics, Vol 3, No 1, 84; New breed, Am Craft, 10-11/84; The new American ceramics, ID, 5/85; Power over the clay: American Studio Potters, Detroit Inst Arts, 89. *Mailing Add:* 420 West End Ave New York NY 10024

WECHTER, VIVIENNE THAUL
EDUCATOR, PAINTER
b New York, NY. *Study:* Jamaica Teachers Col, with Hunter, BP; Columbia Univ; NY Univ; Pratt Inst; Sculpture Ctr, New York; Art Students League; with Robert Beverly Hale & de Creeft; Morris Davidson Sch Mod Art; Union Grad Sch, NY, PhD. *Work:* Corcoran Gallery Art, Washington; Everson Mus, Syracuse, NY; Johnson Mus, Cornell Univ, Ithaca, NY; Notre Dame Mus, South Bend, Ind; Mus Fine Art, Houston & Ft Worth, Tex. *Comn:* The Tradition of Caring (250 bronzes), Miami Jewish Home for Aged & Hosp & Gerontology Inst; colored lithographs, comn by Atelier Eleanor Ettinger; stainless steel & brass sculpture, comn by Richard Kluger; painting, Fac Bldg NY Univ Med Ctr, 92; paintings, Wechter Room, Hebrew Home Riverdale, NY, 92. *Exhib:* Mus Mod Art, NY; Works on Paper, Pavilion D'Exposition, Paris, 75; Invitational Biennale, Mus Mod Art, Rijeka, Yugoslavia, 76, 78 & 80; solo shows, Franklin & Marshall Col, Pa, 79, Kornblatt Gallery, Baltimore, Md, Long Island Univ, 88, 45 paintings on paper, New Eng Mus Contemp Art, 91, recent works on paper, Miami Jewish Home & Hosp for the Aged, combined with Poetry Reading (Wechter Poetry), 12/92 & The Silver Dream, Provincetown Art Mus, plus Poetry Reading; Regional Invitational, City Univ NY Grad Ctr; Contemp Issues Women, traveling throughout US, Everson Mus, 80, and many others. *Pos:* Int vpres, Int Biennale, Malta; moderator weekly broadcast arts & humanities, Today's World, formerly; vpres, IAA-US Comt, UNESCO, currently; chmn & moderator symposium Influences in Art, 88. *Teaching:* Artist-in-residence, Fordham Univ, 64-, chmn acquisitions & exhibs, 64-, prof inter-arts, 67-; vis artist, Kansas City Art Inst, Marist Col, Md Inst Col Art & others; lectr, Univ Malta. *Awards:* Am Soc Artists; Jersey City Mus; Am Acad Arts & Letts. *Bibliog:* G Brown (auth), article, 68, R Gurin (auth), article, 68 & Ronald Kuchta (auth), article, 81, Arts Mag. *Mem:* Col Art Asn Am; Fedn Mod Painters & Sculptors (vpres, currently); Am Soc Artists; Kappa Pi. *Media:* All. *Publ:* Illusr, The Park of Jonas, 67; ed, Five Museums Come to Fordham, 68; ed, Visual Fordham, 69 & 70; auth, A View From the Ark, Barlenmir House, 75; Philosophical Aspects of Thanatology, Arno Press; Art-Where Are We Today-And Why, Arts Interaction, Inc, NY. *Mailing Add:* Fordham Univ Fac Mem Hall Bronx NY 10458

WEDDING, WALTER JOSEPH
CERAMIST, EDUCATOR
b Saginaw, Mich, Feb 17, 52. *Study:* Arrowmount Sch Crafts, 69; Art Inst Chicago, 72; Mich State Univ, BFA, 76, MFA, 79. *Work:* Kresge Art Ctr, East Lansing; Mich Mus Asn, Detroit. *Comn:* Commemorative Pieces, Planters Bank, Salina, Kans, 82; Raku wall mural, City of Salina, Kans, 83. *Exhib:* Mid- Mich Arts, Midland Art Ctr, 79; Kansas Artists, Governor's Mansion, Topeka, 81. *Pos:* Coordr photog, Salina Arts Comn, Kans, 85. *Teaching:* Instr clay, Mich State Univ, East Lansing, 79-80; asst prof photog, Marymount Col, Kans, 80-86. *Mem:* Col Art Asn; Nat Asn Ceramic Educ. *Media:* Clay. *Mailing Add:* 9130 NW Benson Ct Portland OR 97229

WEEDMAN, KENNETH RUSSELL
PAINTER, SCULPTOR
b Little Rock, Ark, Sept 26, 39. *Study:* Memphis Acad Art; Univ Tulsa, BA & MA. *Work:* Cincinnati Mus Art, Ohio; Masur Mus Art, Monroe, La; Ark Art Ctr, Little Rock; Baldwin-Wallace Art & Drama Ctr, Berea, Ohio; Mus de Arte Contemporanea International, Salvador, Brazil; Museu de Arte Contemporanea, Salvador, Brazil; Internacional De Gravure Arte, Cabo Frio, Brazil. *Exhib:* Artist of Southeast & Tex Biennials, New Orleans City Art Mus, 66, 71 & 75; Past Jurors, Okla Art Ctr, Oklahoma City, 69; solo exhib, Gallery BAI, NY, 96, Bienville Gallery, New Orleans, 71 & Art & Drama Ctr Galleries, Baldwin-Wallace Col, 73, Maryville Col, Tenn, 98; Prints: Made in Kentucky, Louisville Art Gallery, 83; Cabo Frio Int Print Biennial, Brazil, 85-86; Papelarte Int, Brazil, 86; Showcase '87, Water Tower Gallery, Louisville, Ky, 87; Cumberland Col Gallery, 2003. *Pos:* Ed, Sculpture Quart, Southern Asn Sculptures, 74-75; cur, Cumberland Col, 81-. *Teaching:* Instr sculpture, Sul Ross State Col, Alpine, Tex, 65-66; prof sculpture, Cumberland Col, Williamsburg, Ky, 68-2003; vis artist, Nicholls State Univ, Thiobodaux, La, 70-71. *Awards:* Award of Merit for Sculpture, Univ Tulsa, 64 & Nebr Wesleyan Univ, 66; Andrew Mellon Found Grant, 98; Lilly Found Grant, 89. *Bibliog:* Les Kantz (ed), Am Artists, Kantz Publ, 85; Miyako Yoshinaga (auth), Nikkei Art, Kenneth Weedman, 8/96; Vivien Raynor (auth), Kenneth Weedman, Gallery BAI, 96; James McCormick (auth), Dialogue, Kenneth Weedman, 5-6/97. *Mem:* Col Art Asn of Am. *Media:* Plastic, Steel; Acrylic, Oil. *Publ:* Contribr, Sculpture Quart, 74 & 75; Dialogue, 7-8/88. *Mailing Add:* 81 Mano'war Tr Corbin KY 40701

WEEGE, WILLIAM
PRINTMAKER, EDUCATOR
b Milwaukee, Wis. *Study:* Univ Wis-Milwaukee; Univ Wis Madison, MA, 67, MFA, 68. *Work:* Akron Art Inst; Brooklyn Mus; Art Inst Chicago; Frankfurt Libr, Ger; Mus Mod Art, NY; plus many others. *Exhib:* Mechanics in Printmaking, 70 & Artist as Adversary, 70, Mus Mod Art, NY; Large Print Show, Whitney Mus Am Art, NY, 71; Works on Paper, Alice Simsar Gallery, Ann Arbor, Mich, 79, Inst for Experimental Printmaking, San Francisco, 79 & Circle Campus, Chicago, 79; Artrain, Mich Arts Coun, 79; Jones Road Print Shop, Univ of Mich, Kalamazoo, Mich, 79; Paper as Medium, Smithsonian Inst, 79-80; and many others. *Teaching:* From instr lettering to assoc prof art, Univ Wis-Madison, 67-80. *Bibliog:* Article, Arts, 1/78; article, Art News, 2/78. *Mailing Add:* 7046 Reiman Rd Arena WI 53503

WEEMS, CARRIE MAE
PHOTOGRAPHER
Study: Calif Inst Arts, Valencia, BA, 81; Univ Calif, San Diego, MFA, 84; Univ Calif, Berkeley, Grad Prog Folklore, 84-87. *Exhib:* One-person exhibs, Inst Contemp Art, 91, Matrix Gallery, Wadsworth Atheneum, Hartford, Conn, 91, Mus Mod Art, NY, 95, J Paul Getty Mus Art, Malibu, Calif, 95, Contemp Arts Mus, Houston, 96, Whitney Mus Am Art, Philip Morris, NY, 97, Va Mus Fine Arts, 97, Rhona Hoffman Gallery, Chicago, 99, Santa Barbara Mus Art, 99, Williams Col Mus Art, Williamstown, Mass, 2000-2002, Zora Neale Hurston Nat Mus Fine Arts, Etonville, Fla, 01, Parrish Art Mus, Southampton, NY, 2001, Palmer Mus Art, Univ Park, Pa, 2002, SC State Univ, Orangeburg, 2002, Sheppard Fine Arts Gallery, Reno, Nev, 2002; Inclusion/Exclusion, Steirischer Herbst, Graz, Austria, 96; Nat Gallery Can, Calgary, 99; Tretyakov Gallery, Moscow, 2000; UCLA Hammer Mus, 2001; Studio Mus in Harlem, NY, 2001; Jan Weiner Gallery, Kansas City, Mo, 2002; Tang Mus, Skidmore Col, Saratoga, NY, 2002. *Teaching:* San Diego City Col, Calif, 84; asst prof, Hampshire Col, Amherst, Mass, 87-91, Calif Col Arts & Crafts, Oakland, 91; vis prof, Hunter Col, NY, 88-89, Williams Col, Williamstown, Mass, 2000, Harvard Univ, Cambridge, Mass, 01; artist in res, Vis Studies Workshop, Rochester, NY, 86, RI Sch Design, 90, Art Inst Chicago, 90, Atlantic Ctr for the Arts, New Smyrna, Fla, 01, Wellesley Col, Mass, 01, Western Wash Univ, Bellingham, 01. *Awards:* Engelhard Grant, 90; Nat Endowment for the Arts Vis Arts Grant, 94; Alpert Award for Vis Arts, 96. *Bibliog:* Berta Sichel (auth), Carrie Mae Weems retrata a diáspora negra, Terra-Feira, Sao Paulo, Brazil, 96; Grady T Turner (auth), rev, Art Am, 6/96; Diane Neumaier (auth), Reframings: New American Feminist Photographies, Temple Univ Press, Philadelphia, 96

WEGMAN, WILLIAM
PAINTER, PHOTOGRAPHER
b Holyoke, Mass, Dec 2, 43. *Study:* Mass Col Art, Boston, BFA, 65; Univ Ill, Urbana-Champaign, MFA, 67. *Work:* Brooklyn Mus, Mus Mod Art, Whitney Mus Am Art, Chrysler Mus, NY; Mus Mod Art, Paris; Los Angeles Co Mus Art; Int Mus Photog, Rochester, NY; Honolulu Acad Arts; Albright-Knox Gallery, Buffalo; Carnegie Inst, Mus Art, Pittsburgh; Corcoran Gallery Art, Washington, DC; Minneapolis Inst Art, Walker Art Ctr, Minneapolis; Mus Fine Art, De Meril Collection, Houston; Newport Harbor Mus, San Francisco Mus Mod Art, Stewart Collection, Univ Calif, San Diego, Calif; St Louis Mus Mod Art; and others. *Comn:* Semi-buffet color video tape, WGBH, Boston, 74-75; video tape rev, Channel 13, WNET, NY, 75. *Exhib:* one-man exhibs, Honolulu Acad Arts, 87, McIntosh/Drysdale Gallery, Washington, DC, 87, Solo Gallery, NY 88, San Francisco Mus Mod Art, 88, Galerie Durand-Dessert, Paris, 89, Neuberger Mus, State Univ NY, 91, Galerie Andreas Binder, Munich, 92, Mus Mod Art, NY, 93, The Art Embodied, Musee de Marseilles, France, 96 & Isetan Mus Art, Tokyo, 97, Strange But True, Mass Col Art, Boston & Springfield Mus, Mass, 98, SOMA Gallery, La Jolla, Calif, 99, Return of the Weimaraner, ACC Gallery, Weimar, Ger, 99, William Wegman, Durant-Dessert Gallery, Paris, France, 99, William Wegman: Fashion Photographs, Birmingham Mus Art, Ala, 99, The MacKinney Ave Contemp, Dallas, Tex, 99, Miami Art Mus, Fla, 99, William Wegman, Orange Co Mus Art, Newport Beach, Calif, 2000, Pillbury & Peters Gallery, Washington, DC, 2000, Grant Selwyn Fine Art, Calif, 2003, David Adamson Gallery, Wash DC, 2003, Sperone Westwater, NY, 2003, Pace-Macgaill Gallery, NY, 2003, many others; Animal Farm, James Corcoran Gallery Art, Santa Monica, Calif, 94; Reconsidering the Object of Art: 1965-1975 (with catalogue), Los Angeles, Calif, 95; A Century of Projection and More, Cinematheque Quebecoise, Montreal, Can, 97; The Am Century, 1950-2000, The Whitney Mus Am Art, NY, 99; PS 1, Long Island City, NY, 2003; The RISD Mus, 2003. *Teaching:* Univ Wis, 68-70; Cal State Univ, Long Beach, 70. *Awards:* Guggenheim Fel, 75 & 86; Nat Endowment Arts Grant, 75-76 & 82; Creative Artists Pub Serv, 79; NY Found for the Arts Hon, 99; Bailey House Key Hon, 99. *Bibliog:* Christopher Knight (auth), William Wegman goes back to the future, Los Angeles Times, 4/11/90; William Wegman, Pace Wildenstein

MacGill, 98; William Wegman: Fashion Photographs, Abrams, 99. *Publ:* ABC, Hyperion, NY, 94; What Do You Do?, Hyperion, 99; Pups, Hyperion, 99; The Night Before Christmas, Hyperion, 2000; Chip Wants a Dog, Hyperion, NY, 2003. *Dealer:* Holly Solomon Gallery 172 Mercer St New York NY 10012; Pace/MacGill Gallery 32 E 57th St New York NY 10022. *Mailing Add:* 239 W 18th St New York NY 10011

WEGMANN, M (MARY) K (KATHERINE)
CONSULTANT, ADMINISTRATOR
b New Orleans, La, Sept 18, 48. *Study:* Spring Hill Col, BA, 70; Univ New Orleans, MA, 72. *Pos:* Assoc dir, Contemp Arts Ctr, New Orleans, 77-91; managing dir, Junebug Prod, 93-97. *Awards:* Mayor's Arts Award, Arts Coun New Orleans, 90. *Mem:* Nat Asn Artists Orgns (pres, 82-85); Cult Communs (treas, 82-89); Junebug Productions (treas, 82-90); Alternate Roots (chairperson, 88-90); Dog & Pony Theatre Co (treas). *Publ:* Auth, Fostering the Process, Art & Artists, 84; Non Profit Thinking, Art Papers, 87; Artists' Organizations Involvement in the Arts Community as a Whole, NAAO Bull, 88; Grantmakers in the Arts, Non Profit Structure in the Art Community, 92. *Mailing Add:* 2019 Chartres St New Orleans LA 70116

WEGNER, NADENE R
GOLDSMITH, CONSULTANT
b Sheboygan, Wis, Feb 18, 50. *Study:* Univ Wis-Milwaukee, BFA, 72; Tyler Sch Art, Temple Univ, MFA, 75. *Work:* Tyler Sch Art, Temple Univ, Philadelphia, Pa; Kentucky Fried Chicken, Louisville, Ky. *Exhib:* Craftwork 76, Metrop Mus & Art Ctr, Miami, Fla, 76; Intent: Jewelry-Metal, Edinboro, Pa, 76; Women's Art Symp, Terre Haute, Ind, 77; Copper, Brass & Bronze Competition Tucson, Ariz, 77; Profiles of US Jewelry, Lubbock, Tex, 77; and others. *Teaching:* Asst prof metalsmithing & jewelry, Louisville Sch Art, Ky, 75-83; art dir, Bruce Fox, Inc, New Albany, Ind, currently. *Awards:* First Prize, Second & Third Nat Ring Show, Athens, Ga; Award, Copper II Exhib, 80. *Bibliog:* Metalsmithing USA, 75 & New York Metal, 76, Craft Horizons; Marcia Chamberlain (auth), Metal Jewelry Techniques, Watson-Guptill, 76. *Mem:* Am Crafts Coun; distinguished mem Soc NAm Goldsmiths. *Media:* Precious Metals, Precious Woods. *Mailing Add:* Bruce Fox Inc PO Box 89 New Albany IN 47150

WEIDA, DONNA LEE
PAINTER, PHOTOGRAPHER
b Logansport, Ind, Oct 29, 39. *Study:* Calif Coast Univ, BS, 92. *Work:* Security Fed Savings Bank, Holiday Inn, Logansport, Ind; Bryant Products, Ixonia, Wis; Lewis Cass High Sch, Walton, Ind; Leading Edge Motor Sports, San Clemente, Calif. *Comn:* Portrait of Autumn, comn by David Smith, Springfield, Ill, 97; portrait of Emilee, comn by Deborah Delaplane, Logansport, Ind, 98; portrait of Torin, comn by Jill Jackson, Marco Island, Fla, 98; portrait of Christian, comn by Barb Mason, Springfield, Ill, 98; portrait of mother & child, comn by Deborah & Marla Spencer, Logansport, Ind, 98. *Exhib:* Niagara Frontier Nat Exhib, Kenan Ctr Gallery, Lockport, NY, 98; Aqueous '98, Actor's Theatre of Louisville, Ky, 98; Grand Exhib, Sheraton Suites, Cuyahoga Falls, Ohio, 98; Sixth Biennial NAm Open Show, Fed Reserve Bank of Boston, 98; Watercolor USA, Springfield Art Mus, 98; and others. *Awards:* Award of Excellence, Watercolor Soc Ind, 97; Edward Dupont Mem, La Watercolor Soc, 97; Merit Award, E Wash Watercolor Soc, 98; Outstanding Watercolor Award, Southside Art League, Greenwood, Ind, 2000. *Mem:* Hon life mem St Louis Watercolor Soc; Midwest Watercolor Soc; assoc mem Am Watercolor Soc; assoc mem Brown Co Art Guild; Ga Watercolor Soc; La Watercolor Soc; Watercolor Soc Ind. *Media:* Watercolor. *Specialty:* photography; investing; all arts. *Publ:* Best of Watercolor Series-People in Watercolor, Rockport Publ, MAss, 12/95; SPLASH 6, Northlight Books, 2000. *Dealer:* Hoosier Salon Gallery 6434 College Ave No C Indianapolis IN 46220; Reflections of the Heart-Tea Room 722 E Broadway Logansport IN 46947. *Mailing Add:* 625 Lakeview Dr Logansport IN 46947-2202

WEIDMAN, JEFFREY
LIBRARIAN, HISTORIAN
b New York, NY, Feb 17, 45. *Study:* Hamilton Col, Clinton, NY, AB, 67; Ind Univ, Bloomington, with Albert Elsen & John Jacobus, MA(art hist), 69, with Louis Hawes, PhD(art hist, Samuel H Kress Fel), 82, MLS, 82. *Collection Arranged:* H P Lovecraft, Lilly Libr, Ind Univ, Bloomington, 82; William Rimmer: A Yankee Michelangelo (auth, catalog), Brockton Art Mus, Mass, 85-86; William Rimmer, Cleveland Mus Art & Brooklyn Mus, 86. *Pos:* Art librn, Clarence Ward Art Libr, Oberlin Col, Ohio, 83-98; assoc librn, Access Serv & Collection Develop, Spencer Art Reference Libr, Nelson-Atkins Mus Art, Mo, 98-2000, sr librn, 2000. *Teaching:* Assoc instr art hist, Ind Univ, Bloomington, 68, 72-74 & 76; Art Dept, Oberlin Col, 93-96; adj prof art hist, UMO-KC, 2003-04. *Awards:* Gerd Muehsam Award, Art Libr Soc NAm, 83. *Bibliog:* Milo M Naeve (auth), A picture and sculpture by William Rimmer, Bull Art Inst Chicago, 77; Lewis Shepard (auth), American Art at Amherst, Wesleyan Univ Press, 78; Brockton's Artistic Heritage, Brockton Art Mus, 81. *Mem:* Art Libr Soc NAm; Asn Hist Am Art; Catalogue Raisonne Scholars Asn; Col Art Asn. *Res:* Nineteenth century American art, especially the work of William Rimmer. *Interests:* Classical, Baroque, British and American eighteenth to twentieth century art, especially American painting and sculpture of the nineteenth century; art reference materials. *Publ:* Auth, Reclassification of the Hamilton College Portraits, Hamilton Col, 67; contribr, Seymour Lipton, Harry Abrams, 70; The Art Institute of Chicago Centennial Lectures, Contemp Bks, 83; (co-auth), William Rimmer: A Yankee Michelangelo, United Press New Eng, 85; Researching your art object, Personal Property J, 97-98. *Mailing Add:* Nelson-Atkins Mus Art Spencer Art Reference Libr 4525 Oak St Kansas City MO 64111

WEIDNER, MARILYN KEMP
CONSERVATOR, LECTURER
b Floral Park, NY, Jan 10, 28. *Study:* Pratt Inst; Hofstra Univ, BA; Univ Pa; Metrop Mus Art; Freer Gallery Art. *Pos:* Asst registrar, Mus Mod Art, NY, 51-56; registrar, Brooklyn Mus, 56-58; conservator, pvt practice, Philadelphia, 60-79 & 84-; dir, Conserv Ctr Art & Hist Artifacts, Philadelphia, 77-84; adj conservator, Art Mus, Princeton Univ, 86-; chair, Conservators/Collections Care Network. *Teaching:* Adj prof conserv art on paper, NY State Univ, Cooperstown Grad Progs, 71-74; lectr, Univ Fine Arts & Music, Tokyo, Japan, Univ Del, Winterthur Mus & Am Inst Conserv Ann Meeting. *Awards:* Cert Conservator Hist & Artistic Works on Paper, 75; Rutherford John Gettens Merit Award, Am Inst Conserv, 90; Am Inst Conserv Univ Products Award Distinguished Achievement, 96. *Bibliog:* George W Cooke (auth), Marilyn Kemp Weidner pioneer paper conservator, Conserv Admin News, 7/92. *Mem:* Fel Int Inst Conserv Art & Hist Artifacts; Am Inst Conserv Art & Hist Artifacts (hon); Inst Paper Conserv, London; Mus Coun Philadelphia; Nat Inst Conserv Cult Property. *Media:* Art on Paper. *Res:* Moisture Chamber/Suction Table System (patent) and related techniques for the conservation treatment of art on paper. *Publ:* Contribr, Damage and deterioration of art on paper, Studies in Conservation, Int Inst Conserv Art & Hist Artifacts, 67; Repair of Wall Charts from Cloister Edhrata, Pa Conserv & Restoration of Pictorial Art, Butterworth's, 76; Water Treatments and Their Uses with a Moisture Chamber on the Suction Table, Am Inst Conserv Arts & Hist Artifacts Preprints, 85; Conservation Management, Getty Conserv Inst, 88; Symposium 88, Conservation of Historic & Artistic Works on Paper, Can Conserv Inst, 94. *Mailing Add:* 576 Brighton Way Phoenixville PA 19460-5718

WEIDNER, MARY ELIZABETH
PAINTER, EDUCATOR
b St Louis, Mo, June 10, 50. *Study:* Sch Fine Arts, Washington Univ, St Louis, Mo, BFA(fel), 72, MFA, 75. *Work:* Papercraft Corp, F B Foster Corp & Carnegie-Mellon Univ, Pittsburgh. *Exhib:* Butler Inst Am Art, Youngstown, Ohio, 77, 79 & 80; William Penn Mem Mus, Harrisburg, Pa, 80; Broussard Mem Galleries, Baton Rouge, La, 80; Carnegie Inst Mus Art, Pittsburgh, 81; Coos Mus Art, Coos Bay, Ore, 81; Herman Fine Arts Ctr, Marietta, Ohio, 81; and many others. *Teaching:* Lectr, Grinnell Col, Iowa, 75-76; prof, Carnegie-Mellon Univ, Pittsburgh, 78-. *Bibliog:* The Art of Drawing, Purdue Univ, 79. *Mem:* Col Art Asn; Women's Caucus Art; Assoc Artists Pittsburgh. *Media:* Oil, Colored Pencil. *Mailing Add:* Carnegie-Mellon Univ Sch Art Rm 312 5000 Forbes Ave Pittsburgh PA 15213

WEIHS, ERIKA
PAINTER, ILLUSTRATOR-CHILDREN BOOKS
b Vienna, Austria, Nov 4, 1917; arrived in US 1940. *Study:* Graphiche Lehr und Versuchsanstalt, Vienna, 34-37. *Work:* Mus City New York, New York Hist Soc, Schomberg Ctr Res Black Cult, & Yeshiva Univ Mus, NY; Butler Inst Am Art, Youngstown, Ohio; Slater Mem Mus, Norwich, Conn; Cape Ann Hist Asn, Gloucester, Mass; Jane Voorhees Zimmerli Mus, Rutgers, NJ. *Exhib:* Solo show, Pleiades Gallery, 89 and numerous others; Small Works, NY Univ Washington Square E Gallery, 89; Mus Nat Arts Found, 89; retrospective 1941-1991, Pleiades Gallery, NY, 91; The Embassy of Austria, Washington, 96; Aspects of Eve, Pleiades Gallery, NY, 96 & Memories, 98; Hudson Guild Gallery, New York City, 2001; Peace and Wars Past and Present, Pleiades Gallery, 2002; and others. *Awards:* Charlotte Whinston Prize, 84 & Elizabeth Stanton Blake Award, 87 Nat Asn Women Artists; Philip Reisman Award, ASCA, 92; Grumbacher Gold Medal, Audubon Artists, 95. *Bibliog:* Roy Moyer (auth), The Paintings of Erika Weihs, 91. *Mem:* Nat Asn Women Artists; Audubon Artists; ASCA; NY Artists Equity. *Media:* Oil. *Publ:* Illusr, How a Shirt Grew in the Field, Clarion Books, 92; Two Very Little Sisters, Clarion, 93; Bar Mitzvah, Viking, 95; Bat Mitzvah, Viking, 95; The Story of Passover, Harper Collins, 97; An Elmtree and Three Sisters, Viking, 2001. *Dealer:* Denise Bibro 529 W 20 St NYC 10011. *Mailing Add:* 41 Union Sq W Studio 1526 New York NY 10003

WEIL, LISL
ILLUSTRATOR, WRITER
b Vienna, Austria; US citizen. *Pos:* Auth & illusr of over 140 children's books; concert illusr with major symphony orchestras, US; concert illus on nationwide TV specials, movie films & schs. *Mailing Add:* 349 W End Ave No 3 New York NY 10024

WEIL, MARIANNE
SCULPTOR
b Mt Kisco, NY, Aug 2, 52. *Study:* Syracuse Univ, with Alan D'Arcangelo, 68; L'ecole des Beaux-Arts, Fontainebleau, France, 69; Goddard Col, BA, 74; Sch Visual Arts, MFA, 86. *Work:* Millhouse-Bundy Mus, Waitsfield, Vt; Commune di Pietrasanta "Mus dei Bozzetti", Pietrasanta, Italy. *Comn:* Bronze bust, comn by Frederick Ellwanger, Richmond, Va, 74; bronze sculpture, comn by Lawrence Lader, NY, 78; bronze sculpture, comn by Ed Weinberger, NY, 85 & 87; bronze sculpture, comn by Lenox Black, Philadelphia, Pa, 89 & 92; bronze sculpture, comn by Judy Woodard, NY, 91 & 96. *Exhib:* 12" x 12" x 12", Islip Art Mus, NY, 94; Goldstrom Gallery, NY, 97 & 98; Goodheart Fine Arts, Sag Harbor, NY, 98; one-woman show, Beatrice Conde Gallery, NY, 99; East End Arts Coun, Riverload, NY, 2000. *Pos:* artist in residence, US Dept Interior, Washington, 98. *Teaching:* Instr fine arts, Suffolk Community Col, NY, 90-; instr, Long Island Univ, CW Post, 93; prof sculpture, Univ Bridgeport, Conn, 94-95, State Univ NY, Stony Brook, 97-. *Bibliog:* Alistair Gordon (auth), Islip Mus, Newsday, 2/10/90; Helen Harrison (auth), NY Times, 9/96; Phyllis Braff (auth), NY Times, 4/19/98; Helen Harrison, NY Times, 6/4/00; Shari Narine, The Lethbridge Herald, 8/1/00. *Mem:* Col Art Asn; NY Artist Equity Asn; United Univ Prof. *Media:* Wax, Cast Bronze. *Dealer:* Beatrice Conde Gallery 529 West 20th St New York NY; Arlene Bujese Gallery East Hampton NY. *Mailing Add:* PO Box 341 Orient NY 11957

WEIL, REX
CRITIC
Work: Art critic ARTnews. *Pos:* Dir, art program for handicapped children; instr Corcoran Col Art & Design, Wash. *Mailing Add:* ARTnews 48 W 38th St New York NY 10018

WEIL-GARRIS, KATHLEEN See Brandt, Kathleen Weil-Garris

WEILER, JOSEPH FLACK
PHOTOGRAPHER, WRITER
b Rockville Ctr, NY, 43. *Study:* With Minor White, 65; Rochester Inst Technol, Sch Printing, AAS, 63, RIT Sch Photog, Syracuse Univ, BFA, 72. *Exhib:* Faces of Afghanistan, Berkshire Mus, Pittsfield, Mass, 81; 25-Year retrospective, Gordon Col, Wenham, Mass, 91. *Pos:* Dir, Flack Studio, Watertown, Mass, 68-. *Teaching:* Instr photog, NEng Sch Photog, Boston, Mass, 78 & Weiler Gallery, Gloucester, Mass, 92-. *Awards:* New Eng Book Show Award, Reprise, 75 & Encore, 76; First Place Award, 9th Open Photog, Salmagundi Club, 90. *Bibliog:* Photographer, Gloucester Times, 7/16/96; Faces of Afghanistan, Cambridge Chronicle, 12/26/2001. *Media:* Photographic Gelatin Silver Print. *Publ:* auth, Winslow Homer: Marine Painter, J Print World, 90; A Gift from Mr Alfred Stieglitz, J Print World, 91; Tarmarind Workshop at Thirty, J Print World, 91; The Tachach Press, J Print World, 92; Charles Sheeler: Photographer or Painter?, Jour Print World, 2003. *Dealer:* Weiler Gallery 77 Rocky Neck Ave East Gloucester MA 01930. *Mailing Add:* 288 Lexington St Watertown MA 02472

WEILER, MELODY M
ADMINISTRATOR, EDUCATOR
b Santa Monica, Calif, Mar 4, 47. *Study:* State Univ NY, Buffalo, BFA; Ohio Univ, MFA; also with Harvey Breverman, Seymour Drumlevitch, Donald Roberts & Harvey Daniels; Kala Inst, Berkeley; Calif Col Arts & Crafts, Oakland. *Work:* Ohio Univ, Athens; Kemper Gallery, Kansas City, Mo. *Comn:* Ceramic & screened mural, Ohio Univ, Athens, 70-71; cover design, Glass Eye Productions, Los Angeles, 76; posters, Hollins Col, Va & Murray State Univ, Ky, 76-77. *Exhib:* Western NY Art Exhib, Albright-Knox Art Gallery, Buffalo, 69; Nelson-Atkins Art Mus, Kansas City, Mo, 74; Huber Gallery, Washington, DC, 79; Lake Placid Sch Art, NY, 79; Imagery Gallery, Jacksonville, Fla, 79; Southeastern Ctr for Contemp Art, Winston-Salem, NC, 79; Appalachian Ctr for Crafts, Cookeville, Tenn, 80; and others. *Pos:* Pres-elect, Ky Arts Adminrs, 88-89, pres, 89-90; prog evaluator, Nat Asn Schs Art & Design, 92-. *Teaching:* Instr printmaking/design, Atlanta Sch of Art, Ga, 71-72; instr found design, Kansas City Art Inst, Mo, 72-73; asst prof printmaking, Murray State Univ, 75-78, assoc prof, 78-91; prof undergrad/grad sem, Tex Tech Univ, 91 . *Awards:* Res grant, Hand Papermaking, Murray State Univ, 76-77, 77-78, 90-91; Ky Arts Coun Grants, 77 & 78. *Mem:* Col Art Asn; Nat Asn Schs Art & Design; Nat Coun Art Adminr (bd dir, 92-); Tex Asn Schs Art; Nat Art Educ Asn. *Media:* Papermaking; Serigraphy. *Publ:* Contribr, Exploring Printmaking for Young People, Van Nostrand Reinhold, 72; photogr, The Painted Vega, 75 & illusr, cover design, Southern Exposure, 76, Glass Eye Productions; contribr, Washingtonian Mag, 78 & Art Craft, 2-3/80. *Mailing Add:* Dept of Art Tex Tech Univ Box 42081 Lubbock TX 79409-2081

WEIMER, DAWN
SCULPTOR
b Denver, Colo, 43. *Work:* Am Quarter Horse Mus, Amarillo, Tex; Westminster Munic Sculpture Garden, Colo; Fort Morgan Mus & Libr, Colo; Fort Collins Pub Libr, Colo; Colo State Univ, Fort Collins; Smithsonian Nat Mus Am History, Washington, DC, 2001. *Comn:* bronze sculpture, Colo State Univ, Fort Collins, 99, Loveland Good Samaritan, Colo, 2000, Shaner Hotel Group, Des Moines, Iowa, 2000 & Morgan Community Col, Fort Morgan, Colo, 2000, Univ of No Colo, 2004, The Ranch Larimer Co Fairgrounds and Event Ctr, 2004; sculpture, Mountain View High Sch, Loveland, Colo, 2000. *Exhib:* Am Artists Prof League, Salamagundi Club, NY, 93, Audubon Artists Exhib, Nat Arts Club, NY, 94; Catharine Lorillard Wolfe, Nat Arts Club, NY, 92-97; Califonia Species, Oakland Mus, Calif, 97; Artists in Colorado, Colo Hist Mus, Denver, 97; two-person show, Old West Mus, Cheyenne, Wyo, 97; one-person show, Fort Morgan Mus, Colo, 98; Western Spirit Exhibit, Old West Mus, Cheyenne, Wyo, 95-2000. *Awards:* Leila Gardin Sawyer Award, Catharine Lorillard Wolfe Art Club, 92; Anna Hyatt Huntington Award, Am Artists Prof League, 93; Philip Isenberg Award, Pen & Brush Sculpture Show, 94. *Bibliog:* Judy L Stewart (auth), Caressing the bronze, Wildlife Art, 97; Coleman Cornilius (auth), Bronze ram stands proud, Denver Post, 8/17/99; Betty Harvey (auth), Gallery sect, Western Horseman, 12/99; Arlene Ahlbrandt (auth), Annie-The Railroad Dog, 1998; Karen Derrico (auth), Unforgettable Mutts, 1999; Ahlbrandt & Hagan (auths), Women to Remember, 2001; Art of the West Guidebook, 2001; Lonnie Pierson (ed), The Artists Bluebook, 2003; Arthur Williams (auth), The Sculpture Ref, 2005. *Mem:* Catharine Lorillard Wolfe Art Club; NSS; Women Artists of West; Nat Asn Women Artists; Nat Mus Women in Arts. *Media:* Bronze. *Mailing Add:* 2727 Eldorado Springs Dr Loveland CO 80538-5321

WEINBAUM, JEAN
PAINTER, SCULPTOR
b Zurich, Switz, 1926. *Study:* Zurich Sch Fine Arts, 42-46; Acad Grande Chaumiere; Ecole Paul Colin; Acad Andre L'Hote, 47-48. *Work:* Mus Mod Art, Paris, France; Nat Collection Fine Arts, Washington; Univ Art Mus, Berkeley, Calif; Stanford Univ Mus, Calif; Calif Palace Legion Hon, San Francisco. *Comn:* Eleven stained glass windows, Chapelle de Mosloy, 51; rosette stained glass, Berne sur Oise, 55; 22 stained glass windows, St Pierre du Regard, 57; Wall of Light (monumental stained glass window), Escherange, 62; eight windows, Lycee de Jeunes Filles, Bayonne, France, 66. *Exhib:* Mus Mod Art, Paris, 62, 63 & 65; one-man shows, Galerie Smith-Andersen, Palo Alto, Calif, 70-73, 76 & 79, Calif Palace Legion Hon, 71, Mus Arts Decoratifs, Lausanne, Switz, 72, Bildungszentrum, Gelsenkirchen, Ger, 72 & San Francisco Mus Mod Art, 81; Michael Dunev Fine Arts, San Francisco, 86; Rado Int, Hong Kong, 87; Frank Bustamante Gallery, NY, 89; Fota Gallery, Old Town Alexandria, Va, 90 & 91; Alliance Francaise, San Francisco, 95; Kismet Gallery, San Jose, Calif, 96; Louvre Gallery, San Francisco, Calif, 2000; Rizzoli Gallery, San Francisco, Calif, 2000; www.nart-intl.com, 2000; Elizabeth Rice Fine Art, Sarasota, Fla, 2002 & 2003. *Awards:* Art Award, Inst for Aesthetic Develop, 87. *Bibliog:* Francois Mathey & others (auth), Vitrail Francais, In: Tendances Modernes, Ed Deux Mondes, Paris, 58; Robert Sowers (auth), Stained Glass: An Architectural Art, Universe Bks, New York, 65; Shuji Takashina (auth), Stained glass works by Jean Weinbaum, Space Design, Tokyo, 9/67. *Mem:* Mus of Modern Art Project Artaud. *Media:* Watercolor, Oil, Stained Glass, Mixed Media. *Dealer:* Elizabeth Rice Fine Art 1467 Main St Sarasota FL 34236. *Mailing Add:* 499 Alabama St No 223 San Francisco CA 94110-1353

WEINBERG, ADAM D
MUSEUM DIRECTOR
b New York City, Dec 10, 1954. *Study:* Brandeis Univ, BA, 77; State Univ NY, Buffalo, MFA, 81. *Pos:* dir educ, asst cur, Walker Art ctr, Minneapolis, 81-88; dir, equitable ctr, Whitney Mus Am Art, New York City, 88-90; artistic & program dir, Am Ctr, Paris, 90-92; sr cur, cur permanent collection, Whitney Mus Am Art, New York City, 93-99, mus dir, 2003-; dir, Addison Gallery of Am Art, Andover, MA, 99-2003. *Mem:* Am Asn Mus; Col Art Asn. *Publ:* Auth, On the Line: The New Color Photojournalism, 86; Vanishing Presence, 89; Aldo Crommelynck: Master Prints with Am Artists, 89; Contingent Realms, 90. *Mailing Add:* Whitney Museum of American Art 945 Madison Ave New York NY 10021

WEINBERG, EPHRAIM
ADMINISTRATOR, PAINTER
b Philadelphia, Pa, Apr 28, 38. *Study:* Philadelphia Col Art; Univ Pa. *Pos:* Dean, Pa Acad Fine Arts, 77-82; dir, Schs, 82-84; dir, Grand Rapids Art Mus, 84-86, dir, Nat Mus Am Jewish Hist, 86-88; pres, Art Sch & gallery mus consult, 88-. *Awards:* Hon Fel, Nat Mus Am Jewish Hist. *Mem:* Cult Arts Found (chmn); Urban Inst Contemp Art; Nat Asn Sch Art & Design (bd dir); Munic Arts Adv Comn, Grand Rapids (chmn); Abington Art Ctr, (bd mem, currently); and others. *Publ:* Auth, Who teaches art, In: Art Education: Junior High School, Nat Art Educ Asn, 73; (co-auth) (with Donald J Irving), The master of fine arts program, In: The Status of the Arts in Higher Education, 76 & auth, Venerable institutions in an age of conservation, In: The Visual Arts in the Ninth Decade, 80, Nat Coun Arts Adminr; auth, The school of the Pennsylvania Academy of the Fine Arts, Antiques, 3/81; School and Museum: The Pennsylvania Academy of the Fine Arts: A Case Study, Asn Art Mus Dirs, 82. *Mailing Add:* 19355 Turnberry Way Apt PHK Aventura FL 33180

WEINBERG, H BARBARA
CURATOR, EDUCATOR
b New York, NY. *Study:* Barnard Col, BA; Columbia Univ, MA, PhD(art hist, archeol). *Pos:* Alice Pratt Brown cur Am paintings & sculpture, Metrop Mus Art, NY. *Teaching:* Emer prof art hist, Queens Col, City Univ NY & Grad Sch. *Res:* Nineteenth century American painting. *Publ:* Auth, The Decorative Work of John La Farge, Garland, 77; The American Pupils of Jean-Leon Gerome, Amon Carter Mus, 84; The Lure of Paris: 19th Century American Painters & Their French Teachers, Abbeville, 91; (co-auth), American Impressionism & Realism: The Painting of Modern Life, 1885-1915, 94, Thomas Eakins and the Metropolitan Museum of Art, 94, Metrop Mus Art; (co-auth), Am Drawings and Watercolors in the Metrop Mus Art: John Singer Sargent, Met Mus Art, 2000; (co-auth), Am Impressionists Abroad and at Home, Am Fedn Arts, 2000; (co-auth), Child Hassam, Am Inpressionist, Metrop Mus Art, 2004; Americans in Paris, 1860-1900, Nat Gallery, London, 2006. *Mailing Add:* Metropolitan Mus Art 1000 Fifth Ave New York NY 10028-0198

WEINBERG, JONATHAN EDMAN
PAINTER, HISTORIAN
b Passaic, NJ, Sept 10, 57. *Study:* Yale Univ, BA, 78; Harvard Univ, PhD, 90. *Work:* Metrop Mus, NY; Montclair Art Mus, NJ; Jersey City, NJ. *Exhib:* 1980's: A New Generation, Metrop Mus Art, NY, 88; Divergenes, Montclair Art Mus, NJ, 90; Fun City, Jersey City Mus, NJ, 96; Still Life: The Object in Am Art, 1915-1955 (with catalog), Soc Four Arts, Palm Beach, Fla, 98; Later, Yale Univ Art Gallery, New Haven, Conn, 98; Alphabet, Nova Sch Fine Art, Vancouver, Can. *Teaching:* Assoc prof 20th century art, Yale Univ, 89-99. *Bibliog:* Vincent Scully (auth), Jonathan Weinberg, Cortland Jessup, 97. *Mem:* Col Art Asn; Gay & Lesbian Caucus (co-chair, 95-96). *Res:* Gay & Lesbian studies, Stieglitz circle. *Publ:* Auth, Speaking for Vice: Homosexuality in the Art of Charles Demuth & Marsden Hartley & the First American Avant-Garde, Yale Univ, 93. *Dealer:* CSJ PO Box 616 Provincetown MA 02657. *Mailing Add:* 41 Lawrence St New Haven CT 06511

WEINER, LAWRENCE CHARLES
SCULPTOR
b Bronx, NY, Feb 10, 42. *Work:* Mus Mod Art & Guggenheim Mus, NY; Vanabbe Mus, Eindhoven, Neth; Staatiches Mus Monchengladbach, Ger; Centre Georges Pompidou, Paris; Nat Gallery of Australia, Canberra; and others. *Comn:* Wexner Ctr, Columbus, Ohio; Pub Art Fund, NYC. *Exhib:* Information, Mus Mod Art, NY, 70; Idea & Image in Recent Art, Art Inst Chicago, Ill, 74; Tate Gallery, London, Eng, 82; Mus Contemp Art, Los Angeles, Calif, 83; one-man shows, Hirshhorn Mus & Sculpture Garden, Washington, DC, 90, San Francisco Mus Mod Art, Calif, 92, Stadtische Galerie Chemnitz, Ger, 94, Philadelphia Mus Art, Pa, 94, Radio Dusseldorf, Ger, 94, Leo Castelli Gallery, NY, 94 & 95 & NY Pub Libr, 95, Marian Goodman Gallery, Paris, 00, Kunstmus Wolfsburg, Ger, 2000-01, Mus Nat Ctr de Arte Reina Sofia, Madrid, 01, Birmingham Mus Art, Ala, 01-02, Galerie Roger Pailhas, Marseille, France, 02, Synagogue Stommeln, Ger, 03, Wexner Ctr for the Arts, Columbus, 02-; Fragments and Form: Conjunctions in the Permanent Collection, Mus Contemp Art, Los Angeles, 93; Rosebud, Kunstbau Lenbachhaus, Munich, 94-95; 10 Yrs Parkett 63 Artists' Editions, Peter Blum, NY, 94; For 25 Yrs-Brooke Alexander Editions, Mus Mod Art, NY, 94; The Tradition of the New: Postwar Masterpieces

from the Guggenheim Collection, Guggenheim Mus, NY, 94; From Minimal to Conceptual Art: Works from the Dorothy and Herbert Vogel Collection, Nat Gallery Art, Washington, DC, 94; Visible Means of Support, Wadsworth Atheneum, 94; Installations: Selections from the Permanent Collection, Mus Contemp Art, Los Angeles, 94; Ars 95, Mus Contemp Art, Finnish Nat Gallery, Helsinki, 95; 1968 SMS, IC Editions Inc, NY, 95; Neuger Riemschneider, Berlin, 00, Casino Luxembourg-Forum d'art Contemp, Luxembourg, 2000-2001, Northern Gallery for Contemp Art, Sunderland, Eng, 2001, Galeria André Viana, Porto, Port, 2001, Mus Contemp Art, LA, 2001, Mus d'Art Contemp, Bordeaux, France, 2002, New Sharjah Arat Mus, United Arab Emirates, 2002, Ctr de Arte de Salamanca, Spain, 2002-2003, Marian Goodman Gallery, New York City, 2003; and others. *Awards:* Nat Endowment Arts Fel, 76 & 83; Arthur Kopcke Prize, Copenhagen, Denmark, 91; John Simon Guggenheim Fel, 94; Skowhegan Medal for Painting/Conceptual Art, 99; Wolfgang Hahn Prize, Ludwig Mus, Cologne, Ger, 95; and others. *Dealer:* Marian Goodman Gallery New York NY. *Mailing Add:* 297 W Fourth New York NY 10014

WEINGARTEN, HILDE (KEVESS)
PAINTER, PRINTMAKER
b Berlin, Ger; US citizen. *Study:* Art Students League; Cooper Union Art Sch, with Morris Kantor, Robert Gwathmey & Will Barnet, cert, 47, BFA, 76; Pratt Graphics Ctr. *Work:* Brooklyn Mus; Herbert F Johnson Mus, Cornell Univ; Israel Mus, Jerusalem; NY Pub Libr Print Collection; Fogg Art Mus, Harvard Univ; and others. *Exhib:* Albright Art Gallery, Buffalo, 55; Dallas Mus of Fine Art, 56; Brooklyn Mus, NY, 58, 63, 71, 74, 76, 77 & 80; NY World's Fair, 65; Graphics 71 Print Exhib, Western NMex Univ, Silver City, 71; Audubon Artists, Nat Acad Design, NY, 71, 73, 75, 77-90; Palazzo Vecchio, Florence & Pompeiian Pavilion, Naples, Italy, 72; Pratt Graphics Ctr Ann, 72 79; plus many other group & six one-artist shows. *Awards:* Akston Found Prize, Nat Asn Women Artists, 80; Silver Medal Creative Graphics, Audubon Artists, 81; Doris Kreindler Memorial Award for Graphics, Am Soc Contemp Artists, 89; and many others. *Bibliog:* J L Collins (auth), Women Artists in America II & Contemporary Biography--Women, Vol I, Part II. *Mem:* Artists Equity Asn, NY (bd dir, 64-72, 90-92); Nat Asn Women Artists; Am Soc Contemp Artists (bd dir, 82-); Audubon Artists (bd dir, 85-87). *Media:* Oil, Acrylic; Etching, Collagraph. *Publ:* Illusr, Tune of the Calliope, 58; Collection of Poems by Aaron Kramer, Thomas Yoseloff Ltd; German folksongs, 68; 51 Songs, translated by Arthur Kevess, Oak Publ. *Mailing Add:* c/o Soho Grafic Arts Workshops 433 W Broadway New York NY 10012

WEINSTEIN, JOYCE
PAINTER
b New York, NY, June 7, 31. *Study:* City Col New York, 48-50; Art Students League, 48-50. *Work:* Mus Mod Art, NY; Pa Acad Fine Arts; Edmonton Art Gallery, Alta; NJ State Mus, Trenton; Weatherspoon Mus, Greensboro, NC; and many others. *Exhib:* Works on Paper, Women Artists, Brooklyn Mus, 75; New Abstract Art, Edmonton Art Gallery Mus, 83; New Acquisitions, Mus Mod Art, NY, 81; solo exhibs, Martin Gerard Gallery, Edmonton, Alta, 81-82, Gallerie Wentzel, Cologne, WGer, 82, Gallery One, Toronto, 83, 02, Haber Theodore Gallery, NY, 85, Flanders Contemp Art, Minneapolis, 99 & 2005 Harmon Meek Gallery, Naples, Fla, 2000; Meredith Long & Co Gallery, Houston, Tex & NY, 88 & 90; Alena Adlung Gallery, NY, 89. *Awards:* Lambert Fund Award, Pa Acad Fine Arts, 53. *Bibliog:* Hilton Kramer-Review NY Times, 76; Grace Glueck (auth), article, New York Times, 12/14/79; Valentin Tatransky (auth), Joyce Weinstein at Haber Theodore Gallery, Arts Mag, 5/83; Nancy Tousley (auth), article, Calgary Herald, 5/85; Karen Wilkin (auth), rev, Partisan Rev, 2/90. *Mem:* Women Arts Found Inc (bd mem, 71-83, exec coordr, 78-82, exec bd mem, 83-90). *Media:* Oil & Mixed Media on Canvas, Monotypes. *Dealer:* Flanders Contemporary Gallery Minn MI; Gallery One, Toronto, CA. *Mailing Add:* 46 Fox Hill Rd Ancramdale NY 12503

WEINSTEIN, RAYMOND
ARTIST
b Alexandria, VA, Jan 6, 20. *Study:* Pratt Inst - 1945-99; Educational Alliance Art Sch with Chaim Gross -1976-91. *Work:* Gallery One, New York City; Pace Col, New York City; Educational Alliance, New York City. *Comn:* scuptures, Michael Goodman, New York City, 2003. *Exhib:* Knickerbocker Artists, Nat Art Club, New York City, 1982; Audubon Artists, Salmagundi Club, New York City, 1989, 93, 94, 95; Den Invitational, Salmagundi Club, New York City. *Pos:* master wood carver, Gallery One, NY. *Teaching:* asst instr wood sculp to Chaim Gross, Edu Alliance Art Sch, 1985-91. *Awards:* Alice McReynolds Award, 1990, Doris Kriendler Award, 2002, Leggieri Award, 2003, Salmagundi Club. *Bibliog:* Susan Josephs (auth), Model for Future, Jewish Week, 8/2/1996; Claude Leisuer (auth), Gallery One Artists, Art Speaks, 1/4/1994; Andrew Margolis (auth), Broome St Gllery, Manhattan Arts, 11/1999. *Mem:* Auduban Artists; Am Soc of Contemp Artists (dir 1998-); Sculptors Alliance (pres 1989-98). *Media:* Sculpture. *Interests:* Nature, travel, Italian & French art. *Mailing Add:* 453 FDR Dr Apt# 1805 New York NY 10002-5907

WEINSTOCK, ROSE
PAINTER
b New York, NY. *Study:* Wellesley Col, BA; Nat Acad Design, with Harvey Dinnerstein; Queens Col, with Charles Cajori; privately with Shirley Gorelick. *Exhib:* Ann Long Island Exhib, Heckscher Mus, Huntington, NY, 85-87 & 90-93; one-woman shows, Recent Paintings, Art Upstairs Gallery, East Williston, NY, 87, Memories of Summer, Oakeside-Bloomfield Cult Ctr, NJ, 90, Archit Paintings, Pen & Brush Club, NY, 96, I Do Windows, Pen & Brush Club, 99, Mini Windows, Arts Club Wash, DC, 2001, Mini Windows Revisited, Interchurch Ctr, NY, 2002 & Windows, a Retrospective, Port Washington Libr, NY, 2006; 100 Yrs/100 Works, Traveling Exhib, 89; Longview Art Mus, Tex, 89; 171st Ann Exhib, Nat Acad Design, NY, 90 & 96; Queens Col Art Ctr, Benjamin Rosenthal Libr, City Univ NY, 91; CW Post Col, Brookville, NY, 93 & 98; Wellesley Col, Mass, 93 & 98; State Univ NY, Stonybrook, 94; Travling Painting Exhib, Sheldon Swope Mus Art, Terre Haute, Ind, Longview Art Mus, Texas, Greater Lafayette Mus Art, Ind, and others, 96-98; NJ Ctr Visual Arts; group shows, Fresh Paint, Flinn Gallery, Greenwich Libr, Conn; Windows, Min/Maxi, Blue Mountain Gallery, New York, NY. *Collection Arranged:* Larry Rivers Artist, D Porthault Inc, Clarion Partners, New York, NY. *Awards:* Gladys Serv Award, Heckscher Mus, 85 & 90; First Prize, Pindar Gallery, 87; Medal of Honor & Audrey Hope Shirk Mem Award, 91, Beatrice Jackson Mem Award, 95, Nat Asn Women Artists; and others; Medal of Honor & Elizabeth Blake Stanton Blake Mem Awrd, Nat Asn Women Artists, May, 2003, NY. *Bibliog:* Sean Simon (auth), Rose Weinstock: A realist master of light & shadow, Art Speak, 11/95; Steven Zevitas (ed), New American Paintings X, Open Studios Press, NY; Timothy Morrison (auth), The Poetry of Windows in the Paintings of Rose Weinstock, Gallery Studio, March/April, NY. *Mem:* Nat Asn Women Artists, NY; Audubon Artists, NY; Catherine Lorillard Wolfe Arts Club, NY; Artist's Equity, NY. *Media:* Oil, Pastel. *Dealer:* Blue Mountain Gallery 530 West 25th St 4th Fl New York New York 10001. *Mailing Add:* 35 E 75th St New York NY 10021

WEINTRAUB, ANNETTE
DIGITAL ARTIST, EDUCATOR
b New York, NY, July 2, 46. *Study:* Cooper Union, BFA, 67; Univ Pa Grad Sch Fine Arts, MFA, 70. *Work:* Aldrich Mus Contemp Art, Ridgefield, Conn; Prudential Insurance Co; Cooper Union Sch Art, NY; WTex Mus Asn; Wichita Art Mus; Peat Marwick Inc; and others. *Comn:* Sampling Broadway (website), comn by Turbulance & Jerome Found Grant. *Exhib:* Contemp Reflections, 1975-76, Aldrich Mus Contemp Art, 76; Members' Gallery, Albright-Knox Art Gallery, Columbus Art Mus, Ohio, 80; Third Int Symp Electronic Art, Gallery Arts Multiplicata, Sydney, Australia, 92; solo exhib, Annette Weintraub, Digital Composites: Disintegration/Reconstruction, Fine Arts Mus Long Island, 92; Picture Element Art Initiatives, NY Law Sch, 93; Night Light, Int Symp Elec Art, Mus Contemp Art, Helsinki, Finland, 94; The Art & Design Show, SIGGRAPH, Orlando, Fla, 94; Metamorphoses: Photog in the Electronic Age, Fashion Inst Technol Mus, 94; Image Electronic, Euphrat Mus Art, De Anza Col, Cupertino, Calif, 95; CODE, Ricco/Maresca Gallery, 95; Technoseduction, Cooper Union Sch Art, 97; Biennial, Whitney Mus Art, Bypaths, Moving Image Gallery, NY, 2000; plus others. *Collection Arranged:* Aldrich Mus; Best Products, FMC Corp; Peat Marwick; Prudential Ins; Wichita Mus; AT&T; Cooper Union; Euphrat Mus Art; LeHigh Univ; The West Texas Mus. *Teaching:* asst prof advert design & computer graphics, City Col, City Univ NY, 83, assoc prof, 89; prof, City Col, NY, 93; prof art, electronic design and multimedia, City Col, NY. *Awards:* PSC-City Univ NY Res Found Grant, Visual Arts, 90, 93, 95, 97 & 98, 2000, 2001; NY Found Arts, Artists Fel, Printmaking/Drawing/Artists Bks, 91; ID Mag Silver Award, Interactive Media Rev, 98; and others. *Bibliog:* State of the art, Computer Graphics World, 3/93; Not painting by numbers, Newsweek, 7/25/94; Psycho Geography, Intelligent Agent, Vol 2, No 2, spring 98; Bennial Angst, NY Mag, 3/2000; New York, Chaos Inspires Web Art, NY Times online, 7/2000; Whitney Biennial, ArtByte, May/June/2000. *Mem:* Women's Caucus Art (adv bd NY chap, 79-80); Spec Interest Group for Computer Graphics (bd dir, 88-90 & 90-92); Col Art Asn; Int Symp Electronic Art. *Media:* Photography, Internet, Digital Media. *Res:* multmedia narrative. *Publ:* Mapping the Learning Curve, Educators Tech Exchange, fall 94; Artice, Artifact: The Landscape of the Constructed Digital Environment, Leonardo 28:5, 95; When Worlds Collide: Live Action Footage & Computer-Generated Animation Sequences Learn to Get Along, FPS, Mag Computers & Animation, 96; Art on the Web, the Web as Art, Commun of one ACM, 10/92. *Mailing Add:* Two Bond St New York NY 10012

WEINTRAUB, JACOB D
ART DEALER
b Austria; US citizen. *Study:* Law degree. *Pos:* Owner & dir, Weintraub Gallery, New York, currently. *Mem:* Appraisers Asn Am. *Specialty:* 20th century masters: Henry Moore, Picasso, Chagall, Leger, Matisse, Arp, Miro, Calder, Marini, Botero, Giacometti, Zuniga, Lipschitz. *Collection:* Major works by: Moore, Shahn, Grosz, Botero, Marini, Klee, Pomodoro, Chagall, Epstein, Nolde, Magritte, Tamayo, & Feininger

WEINZAPFEL, CONNIE A
GALLERY DIRECTOR, CURATOR
b Evansville, Ind, Aug 8, 56. *Study:* Univ Southern Ind, BS, 78; Southern Ill Univ, MFA, 81. *Pos:* Coordr, Chicago Int Art Expo, Ill, 81-85; dir, New Harmony Gallery Contemp Art, Ind 85-. *Mailing Add:* Historic New Harmony PO Box 579 New Harmony IN 47631

WEISBERG, GABRIEL P
HISTORIAN, EDUCATOR
b New York, NY, May 4, 42. *Study:* New York Univ, BA, 63; Johns Hopkins Univ, MA, PhD, 67. *Collection Arranged:* Against the Modern, Dagnan-Boureret and the Transformation of the Academic Tradition, 2002. *Pos:* Cur art hist, Cleveland Mus Art, 73-81; asst dir, Nat Endowment Humanities, 83-85. *Teaching:* Asst prof art hist, Univ NMex, 67-69; assoc prof art hist, Univ Cincinnati, 69-73; Mellon prof art hist, Univ Pittsburgh, 81-82; prof art hist, Univ Minn, 85-. *Awards:* Guggenheim Found Fel, 81-82; Advan Study Visual Arts, Nat Gallery Art, Washington, DC, 83; Regents Fel, Smithsonian Inst, Nat Mus Am Art, 92; Chevalier de l'ordre des Arts et des lettres, Republique Francaise, Le Ministre de La Culture, Paris, 95. *Mem:* Print Coun Am; Decorative Arts Soc; Col Art Asn Am (bd dir, 80-). *Res:* Study of 19th century realism, Japonisme and art nouveau as a formalistic concern and as an example of social history. *Publ:* Art Nouveau Bing, 86; coauth, Japonisme Comes to America, 90; Beyond Impressionism: The Naturalist Impulse, 92; Collecting in the Gilded Age, Art

Patronage in Pittsburgh, 1890-1910, 97; Art Nouveau Research Guide for Design Reform in France, Belg, Eng & US, 98; Overcoming All Obstacles: The Women of the Academic Julian, 2000. *Mailing Add:* Univ Minn Dept Art History 348 Heller Hall 271 19th Ave South Minneapolis MN 55455-0121

WEISBERG, RUTH ELLEN
PAINTER, EDUCATOR
b Chicago, Ill, July 31, 42. *Study:* Acad di Belli Arte, Perugia, Italy, Laurea; Univ Mich, BS & MA; Atelier 17, Paris, with S W Hayter. *Hon Degrees:* DHL, Hebrew Union Col, 2001. *Work:* Bibliot Nat, France; Chicago Art Inst; Los Angeles Co Mus of Art; NY Pub Libr; Norwegian Nat Collection; Am Mus Art, Smithsonian; Oakland Mus, Calif. *Comn:* Together Again (ed of 150 lithographs), Midwest Regional Orgn for Rehabilitation & Training, 75; The Gift (ed of 60 lithographs), Univ Synagogue, Los Angeles, 75; Interlude, Los Angeles Co Mus of Art, 75; The Open Door Haggadal, Cen Conf of Am Rabbs. *Exhib:* Philadelphia Print Club, 85; Univ Richmond, Va, 85; Fisher Gallery, Univ Southern Calif, Los Angeles, 86; solo shows, Jack Rutberg Fine Arts, Los Angeles, 83, 85, 88, 91, 2006, The Scroll, Hebrew Union Col, NY, 87 & 88, Assoc Am Artists, NY, 87 & 90, Realms of Desire-A Print Retrospective, Fresno Art Mus, Calif, 90, Bethel Col, North Newton, Kans, 91 & Gwenda Jay Gallery, Chicago, Ill, 91 & 92; Her Story: Narrative Art by Contemp Calif Artists (catalog), Oakland Mus, 91; Passing Over, Sculptural Installation for, Passover and Passion, Leband Gallery, Loyola Marymount, Los Angeles, 91; 500 Yrs Since Columbus (catalog), Triton Mus, Santa Clara, Calif, 91; Presswork: The Art of Women Printmakers (traveling exhib, catalog), Nat Mus Women Arts, Washington, DC, Univ Art Mus, Univ Minn, Minneapolis, Elvehjem Mus Art, Univ Wis, Madison, Butler Inst Am Art, Youngstown, Ohio, 91-93. *Pos:* Dean, Univ Southern Calif, 74-75, 76-77 & dept chmn, 86-; dir, Kelyn Press, currently; lectr, demonstr, juror, cur Univ Mich, 87, 88, Univ Hi, Honolulu, 88, Pa Acad, Philadelphia, 87, Queens Col, New York City, 87, City Col of NY, 87, Univ Iowa, 78, 87, Univ N Dakota, Grand forks, 87, Fresno (Calif) Arts Ctr and Mus, Carnegie Mellon Univ Pittsburgh, 86, 87, Univ Tenn, Knoxville, 86, Univ Calif, Santa Cruz, 85, Univ Wash, Seattle, Univ Kans, Lawrence Skirball Mus Hebrew Union Col, Los Angeles, Calif Inst Arts, Valencia, Otis Art Inst, Los Angeles, Mass Col Art, Boston, Norwegian Graphic Atists Asn, Oslo Col Art Asn Conference, Detroit, many others. *Teaching:* Asst prof fine arts, Eastern Mich Univ, Ypsilanti, 66-67; from assoc prof to prof fine arts, Univ Southern Calif, Los Angeles, 70-. *Awards:* Third Ann Vesta Award, Visual Arts, Women's Bldg, Los Angeles, 84. *Bibliog:* Lydia Matthews (auth), Stories history didn't tell us, Artweek, 2/14/91; Lisbet Nilson (auth), Loyola Gallery puts its faith in religious exhibit, Los Angeles Times/Calendar, 3/24/91; Suvan Geer (auth), Weisberg's family album, Los Angeles Times, 3/1/91. *Mem:* Col Art Asn (bd dir & pres, 90-92); Western Regional Nat Women's Caucus Art (vpres & co-chair, 85); Nat Adv Bd Tamarind Inst; Los Angeles Artists Equity (adv bd). *Media:* Lithography. *Publ:* Illusr, Tom O'Bedlam's Song, 69 & auth & illusr, The Shtetl, A Journey and A Memorial, 72, Kelyn Press. *Dealer:* Assoc Am Artists New York NY; Gwenda Jay Gallery Chicago IL. *Mailing Add:* Sch Fine Arts US Calif Watt Hall 104 Los Angeles CA 90089-0001

WEISEL, THOMAS W
PATRON
Pos: Founder, chmn & CEO, Montgomery Securities, San Francisco, 78-98; owner, Thomas Weisel Partners, San Francisco, 99—; trustee, Mus Modern Art, New York City & San Francisco, currently. *Publ:* Coauth, (with Lance Armstrong & Richard Bryant) Capital Instincts: Life As an Entrepreneur, Financier & Athlete, 2003. *Mailing Add:* Thomas Weisel Partners 1 Montgomery St San Francisco CA 94104

WEISER, KURT D
CERAMIST
b Lansing, Mich, July 17, 50. *Work:* Nat Mus Hist, Taipei; Los Angeles Co Mus Art, Los Angeles, Calif; Victoria & Albert Mus, London, Eng; Mus Contemp Ceramics. *Exhib:* Solo exhib, Garth Clark Gallery, Los Angeles, Calif, 94, 95, 96, 2000, 02, Frank Lloyd, Calif, 2001; Ancient China, Modern Clay, Phoenix Art Mus, Ariz, 94; The Collections of Shigaraki Ceramics Mus, Contemp Ceramics Mus, Shigaraki, Japan, 94; Am Craft Mus, NY, 2000; Dolphin Gallery, Kansas City, Mo, 2002. *Teaching:* Assoc prof, Ariz State Univ, 89-. *Awards:* Nat Endowment Arts, 88 & 92; Asian Cult Counc, Artist Fel, 98; Res and Creative Activity Award, Ariz, State Univ, 98; Arizona Comm on the Arts, Artist Fel, 99; Regents Prof, Ariz State Univ, 99. *Dealer:* Garth Clark Gallery New York NY; Garth Clark Gallery Los Angeles CA. *Mailing Add:* 1130 S Ash Ave Tempe AZ 85281

WEISMAN, GARY MICHAEL
SCULPTOR, EDUCATOR
b Chicago, Ill, May 19, 52. *Study:* Art Inst Chicago, 73-74; Leslie Posey student of Charles Grafley & A Polacheck, 73-78; Columbia Col, BFA, 76;. *Work:* Michael Reese Hosp, Union League Club, Chicago, Ill; Cigna Corp, Philadelphia, Pa; Ralph Lauren Corp, NY; Chicago Pub Libr, Ill. *Comn:* Lifesize sculpture, Burroughs Pharmaceut, Chicago, Ill, 89; outdoor sculpture plaza, City Duluth, Minn, 90; lifesize sculpture, Pepsico/Elmira Col, NY, 94; pub outdoor sculpture, City Chicago, Ill; outdoor pub sculpture, City Philadelphia, Pa. *Exhib:* Juried show, State Mus Pa, Harrisburg, Pa, 92, Nat Acad Design, NY, 92, Berman Mus, Collegeville, Pa, 93, Mus Am Art, Philadelphia, Pa, 94; invitational, Arnot Mus Art, Elmira, NY, 94; one-man shows, Prince Gallery, Chicago, Ill, 91, Sande Webster Gallery, Philadelphia, Pa, 93, 96, 98 & 2000, Berry-Hill Galleries, NY, 95, 97 & 98, Am Cult Ctr, Taipei, Taiwan, 98 & Alter & Gil Gallery, Los Angeles, 2000; Arnot Art Mus, Elmira, NY, 93, 95 & 99; Sentec Int Ctr, Signapore, 96; solo exhibs, Fred Baker Gallery, Chicago, Ill, 2003, Galerie Yoram, Los Angeles, Calif, 2003, Chen Gallery, Seoul, Korea, 2003; many others. *Teaching:* Fac sculpture, Pa Acad Fine Arts, 86-. *Awards:* Sculpture Award, Nat Acad Design, 92; Purchase Award, Fel Pa Acad, 93; Pa Acad Fine Arts Fel, 93, 94, 96 & 97. *Mem:* Nat Sculpture Soc. *Media:* Bronze. *Mailing Add:* 376 Barnes Hill Rd Newfield NY 14867

WEISS, CLEMENS
CONCEPTUAL ARTIST, SCULPTOR
b Dusseldorf, Ger, Sept 26, 55. *Study:* Studies in medizin, philos & art, Vienna & Düsseldorf, Ger, 73-78. *Work:* Anderson Gallery, Va Commonwealth Univ, Richmond; Mus Mod Art, Pub Libr, NY; Pushkin Mus, Moscow, Russia; Folkwang Mus, Essen, Ger. *Comn:* UN, Geneva, Switzerland, 98; stage set, Bochum, Ger, 96; stage design, Sylf, Bremen, Hamburg, Germany, 2002. *Exhib:* Buchstablich, Von der Heydt Mus, Wuppertal, Ger, 91; Transparenz/tranzendenz, Gainesville Samuel Pham Mus, 92; Transparenz/tranzendenz, Miami Art Ctr, Fla, 92; Transparenz/tranzendenz, Univ SFla Mus, Tampa, 92; Fdkwag Mus, Essen, Ger, 95; the XX Century, a century of art in Ger, Berlin; plus others. *Bibliog:* Uli Bohnen (auth), Quintessenz, Kunstforum, 89; Friedemann Malsch (auth), To the Art of C Weiss, Katalog Aachen, 90; Steven High (auth), Towards Knowledge, Katalog neuer Aachener Kunstverein, 90. *Media:* All Media. *Publ:* Auth, Konzepte, Objekte und Fragmente Inst No 1, Galerie Lohrl, 89; illusr, The Complaint of the Art, Juni Verlag, 90; auth, Installation & Logic-Fragment & Object, R Feldman Gallery, 91; auth & ed, Eighteen from New York (exhib catalog), Juni Verlag, 91; auth & illusr, Fragmentarische Logik-Logische Fragmente, Juni Verlag, 95; auth drawings-series 1990-1997. *Dealer:* Ronald Feldman Fine Arts 31 Mercer St New York NY 10013. *Mailing Add:* 31 E 31st St #9g New York NY 10023

WEISS, DICK J
ENAMELIST, STAINED GLASS ARTIST
b Everett, Wash, June 24, 46. *Study:* Yale Univ, New Haven, Conn, BA, 68. *Work:* Corning Mus Glass, NY; Victoria & Albert Mus, London, Eng; City of Seattle Pub Art, Wash; 1 Percent-Wash State, Seattle; Pilchuck Glass Sch, Stanwood, Wash. *Comn:* Marine Sciences Bldg, Univ Wash, Seattle, 85; Kent Sr Citizen Ctr, City Kent, Wash, 86; Sea-Tac Airport, Port Seattle, Wash, 88; Kenai Community Col, State Alaska, Homer, 90; Opera House, Seattle, Arts Comt, Seattle, 90. *Exhib:* 4 Leaders in Glass, Craft & Folk Art Mus, Los Angeles, 80; Colorful Romances, Henry Art Gallery, Seattle, 81; Pilchuck Glass, Bellevue Art Mus, Wash, 88; Master Works, Bellevue Art Mus, Wash, 91; Clearly Art, Whatcom Mus, Bellingham, Wash, 92; Bellevue Art Mus, Wash, 93 & 94; William Traver Gallery, Seattle, Wash, 94, 98 & 99; Glorious Glass, Owensboro Mus Fine Arts, Ky, 97; 3-Dimensional Canvas, Dorothy Weiss Gallery, San Francisco, Calif, 98; Painting on Glass, Morgan Contemp Glass, Pittsburgh, Pa, 98; The Fluid Canvas, Chappell Gallery, Boston, Mass, 98 & Sch Fine Arts, Chicago, 98; Battle Creek Fine Arts Ctr, Mich, 98; 25th Anniversary Exhib, William Traver Gallery, Seattle, Wash, 2002. *Pos:* Co-cur, Bellevue Art Mus, Wash, 94; cur, Holter Mus Art, Helena, Mont, 97. *Teaching:* Fac, Univ Calif, Los Angeles, 80, Pilchuck Glass Sch, Stanwood, Wash, 83-84 & 93, Bild-Werk, Frauenau, Ger, 96, Haystack Mountain Sch Arts & Crafts, Deer Isle, Maine, 97; instr workshop, Pratt Fine Arts Ctr, Seattle, Wash, 94; Fac, Pilchuck Glass Sch, Stanwood, Wash, 2000. *Awards:* Craftsman Grant, 81 & 87, Nat Endowment Arts; Second Annual Hauberg Fel, Pilchuck Glass Sch, 2001,02. *Mem:* Glass Art Soc. *Dealer:* William Traver 110 Union St Seattle WA 98101-2028. *Mailing Add:* 811 N 36th St Seattle WA 98103

WEISS, HARVEY
SCULPTOR, WRITER
b New York, NY, Apr 10, 22. *Study:* Nat Acad Design; Art Students League; also with Ossipe Zadkine, Paris. *Work:* Albright-Knox Art Gallery; Krannert Mus; Silvermine Guild Collection; Nelson Rockefeller Collection; Joseph H Hirshhorn Collection; plus others. *Comn:* Menorah, Temple B'nai Zion, Shreveport, La, 67; reliefs, Mt Vernon Synagogue, NY, 69 & Conn Off Bldg, Westport, 71; reliefs, Danbury Courthouse, 88. *Exhib:* Five one-man shows, Paul Rosenberg & Co, 59-70; one-man show, Silvermine Guild, 68 & 83, Art Place, 90; retrospective, Fairfield Univ, 70; Am Inst Arts & Lett, 70; Sculptor's Guild Ann Shows; Cast Iron Gallery, 92. *Teaching:* Prof emer, Adelphi Univ, Garden City, NY, Silvermine Art Sch. *Awards:* Olivetti Award, New Eng Ann Exhib, 69; Nat Inst Arts & Lett Grant, 70; Alex J Ettl Grant, Nat Sculpture Soc, 93; and others. *Mem:* Sculptors Guild (pres, 70-71); Silvermine Guild Artists (bd trustees, 68-70); Auth Guild; Nat Sculpture Soc; Nat Acad (assoc, 93, acad, 94-). *Media:* Bronze, Welded Brass. *Publ:* Auth & illusr, Collage & Construction, 70, Gadget Book, 71, Lens & Shutter, 71, Machines & How They Work, 83 & Submarines, 90; Strange & Wonderful Aircraft, 95; and many others. *Mailing Add:* 42 Maple Ln Greens Farms CT 06436

WEISS, JEROME NATHAN
PAINTER, INSTRUCTOR
b NJ, Oct 21, 59. *Study:* Metrop Art Ctr, Miami, study with Roberto Martinez, 78; Art Students League, 79-83; Nat Acad Design, New York, 81-83. *Work:* Abraham Art Found, Canadian, Tex; New Britain Mus Am Art, New Britain, Conn; Northeastern Univ, Boston, Mass. *Comn:* Univ NC, Chapel Hill; Harvard Club of NYC; Brigham and Women's Hosp, Boston, Mass; Debevoise and Plimpton, NY; Conn Superior Courthouse, New London, Conn. *Exhib:* 159th, 163rd & 167th Ann Exhibs, Nat Acad Design, NY, 84, 88 & 92; Fel Exhib, Monmouth Mus, Lincroft, NJ, 88; Amarillo Mus Art, Tex, 00; Wayland Baptist Univ, Plainview, Tex, 00; Tomasulo Gallery Union Co Col, Cranford, NJ, 01; Arnot Art Mus, Elmira, NY, 2005; Univ Bridgeport, Conn, 2005. *Teaching:* Figure & Landscape Painting, Lyme Acad Fine Art, Old Lyme Conn; Silvermine Sch Art, New Canaan, Conn; Loveland Acad Fine Arts, Colo; NY Acad Art, NY. *Awards:* Best in Show, Hortt Ann, Ft Lauderdale Mus, 85; Painting Fel, NJ Coun Arts, 88; Julius Hallgarten Prize, 167th Ann Exhib, Nat Acad Design, 92; and others. *Bibliog:* Theodore F Wolff (auth), Portrait of the artist as a young master, Christian Sci Monitor, 7/25/85; John A Parks (auth), Jerry Weiss; Observe, Think & Practice, Am Artist Workshop Mag, winter 2005; Lynne Moss Perricelli (auth), Beyond Expectations & Monarchival Drawing Surfaces, Am Artist Drawing Mag, spring 2006. *Media:* Oil. *Dealer:* Portraits Inc New York NY; The Cooley Gallery Old Lyme CT. *Mailing Add:* 30 S Wig Hill Rd Chester CT 06412

WEISS, JOHN JOSEPH
PHOTOGRAPHER, EDITOR
b Philadelphia, Pa, Jan 31, 41. *Study:* Temple Univ, BS, 63; Mass Inst Technol, 69-73; RI Sch Design, MFA, 73. *Work:* Mus Mod Art, NY; Addison Gallery Am Art, Andover, Mass; Princeton Univ, NJ; Del Art Mus, Wilmington; Photog Place, Philadelphia. *Exhib:* Addison Gallery Am Art, Andover, Mass, 73; Mass Inst Technol Creative Photog Gallery, Cambridge, 76; Photopia, Philadelphia, 79; G H Dalsheimer Gallery, Baltimore, 83; The Photographers' Gallery, London, 83; Andover Gallery, Mass, 85; Book Trader Gallery, Philadelphia, 86. *Pos:* Coordr photog, Mass Inst Technol, 76-. *Teaching:* Instr photog, Mass Inst Technol, 69-73; asst prof photog, Univ Del, Newark, 75-79, assoc prof, 79-. *Publ:* Contribr, Portraits, Mod Photog, 77; auth, A darkroom philosophy, Camera 35, 77; ed, Venus, Jupiter and Mars--The Photographs of Frederick Sommer, Del Art Mus, 80; Philadelphia Photog Rev, 81; auth, Biography of Frederick Sommer, Collier's Encycl; article in Photo Review, 86. *Mailing Add:* Univ Del Dept Art Newark DE 19716

WEISS, LEE ELYSE C
PAINTER
b Inglewood, Calif, 28. *Study:* Calif Col Arts & Crafts, 46-47; also with N Eric Oback, 57 & Alexander Nepote, 58. *Work:* Nat Mus Am Art; Nat Mus Women in Arts, Wash; Phillips Collection, Wash; Exec Residence, State Wis; Springfield Mus Art, Mo; NASA Space Art Collection, Cape Canaveral, Fla; Davenport Munic Mus Art, Iowa; Hickory Mus, NC; US Dept of the Interior, Smithsonian Nat Air & Space Mus, Wash; Milwaukee Art Mus. *Comn:* Am Artist & Water Resources, one of 40 Am artists chosen for Bur Reclamation Art Proj, US Dept Interior, 71; artist for space shuttle launch, NASA, 84; comn artist, 2004 Gov's Awards, Support of Arts, Wis. *Exhib:* One-woman shows, Walker Art Ctr, Minneapolis, 60, Calif Place Legion Hon, San Francisco, 62, Milwaukee Art Mus, 65, West Bend Gallery Fine Art, Wis, 88, Chicago Botanic Garden, 88 & 89 & Neville Publ Mus, Green Bay, Wis, 96, Uihliein Peters Gallery Milwalkee Wis 2004, 05; Wisconsin Painters & Sculpters, Milwaukee Art Mus; Oakland Art Mus; Penn Acad Fine Art, Philadelphia; San Francisco Art Mus; Setagaya Mus Art, Tokyo, Japan, 88, 89, 90 & 94; Nat Invitational Watercolor Exhib, Northern Ariz Univ, 89; State of the Art Nat Invitational Watercolor Exhib, Parkland Col Art Gallery, Champagne, Ill, 89 & Biennial East/West Int Invitational, 97; Wis-Ill Art Exch, Art Asn, Springfield, Ill, 89; Meguro Mus, Tokyo, Japan, 91 & 92; Am Watercolor Invitational, Taipei Fine Arts Mus, Taiwan, 94; Shinjuku Cult Ctr, Toyko, Japan, 95, 96 & 97; Charles Allis Art Mus, Milwaukee, 2003; Saitama Mus of Contemp Art, 2002. *Teaching:* Artist-in-residence, Rhinelander Sch Arts, 7/89; Dillman's Creative Workshops, Lac du Flambeau, Wis, 90, 92, 93 & 94, Arrowmont Sch Arts & Crafts, Gaitlinburg, Tenn, 95; Washington Studio Sch, DC, 98. *Awards:* First Award, Watercolor Wis, 82, 84, 87 & 2005; Adirondack Wilderness Award with Rouse Gold Medallion, Adirondack Nat Exhib Am Watercolors, 90; First Award, WASH 17th Ann, Houston, Tex, 93; 2nd award WASH, 2002. *Bibliog:* Watercolor 91 (feature article), Artist's Mag, 9/91; Watercolor Am Artist Publ, 94 & 96. *Mem:* Dolphin fel, Am Watercolor Soc; Nat Watercolor Soc; life mem Wis Painters & Sculptors; Watercolor USA Hon Soc (vpres, 86, pres, 87-88); Rocky Mountain Water Media Soc; Fel Wis Acad Sci, Arts & Lett. *Media:* Watercolor. *Publ:* Lee Weiss, Watercolors II, the Seventies, Am Printing & Publ Co, 81; Lee Weiss, Watercolors III, Straus Printing Co, 90; contribr, Creative Watercolor, Rockport Publ, 96; contribr, Cutting Across Time, Schroeder Hist Soc, 99; Famous Wisconsin Artists & Architects, Badger Books, Oct 2004. *Dealer:* Fanny Garver Gallery 230 State St Madison WI 53703. *Mailing Add:* 106 Vaughn Ct Madison WI 53705

WEISS, MADELINE
PAINTER
b New York, NY. *Study:* Studies with Lillian Orlowski and William Freed. *Work:* State of Fla, Cocoa; Palm Beach Co Home, West Palm Beach, Fla; Good Samaritan Hosp, West Palm Beach, Fla. *Comn:* Signage tubes installation, JFK Med Ctr, Edison, NJ, 91; tubular installation, Children's Rehabilitation Hosp, Tustin Health Fac, Calif, 92; tubular installation, Froedtert Mem Lutheran Hosp, Milwaukee, Wis, 98; tubular installation, Skywalk Restaurant, Milwaukee, Wis, 98; tubular installation, Devonshire Life Care, Palm Beach Gardens, Fla, 2000. *Exhib:* One-woman exhib, Bronx Mus Arts, NY, 85, State Capitol Bldg, Tallahassee, Fla, 86 & Palm Beach Co Coun Arts, West Palm Beach, Fla, 86; Art in Pub Places, West Palm Beach, Fla, 92; Northwood Univ, West Palm Beach, Fla, 95 & 96; Armory Art Ctr, West Palm Beach, Fla, 96; 45th Ann All Fla, Boca Mus, Fla, 96. *Pos:* Mem chair, Phoenix Gallery, New York, 84-90; mem prof artists comt, Palm Beach Co. *Teaching:* Instr fine arts, Jewish Community Ctr, West Palm Beach, 92-. *Awards:* First Place Acrylics, YWCA, 88; First Place, Artists Guild, 90; Merit Award, Jewish Community Ctr, 94. *Bibliog:* Kiki Arco (auth), Palm Beach Panorama, WPBT, Miami, 6/21/86; Betsy Hutton (auth), Catch that color, Sun-Sentinel/News, 8/28/88; Joseph Picconi (dir), Artist Scene WPB, Channel 20, 5/92; Candace Russell, City Link, 9/99. *Mem:* Nat Asn Women Artists (pres, Fla branch); Norton Artists' Guild (pres, 89-90 & 92-93); Nat Artists Equity; Boca Mus Artist Guild. *Media:* Acrylic. *Dealer:* Hodgell Gallery 46 Palm Ave S Sarasota FL 34236; Akontempo Gallery 508 E Atlantic Ave Delray Beach FL 33483. *Mailing Add:* 117 Lake Gloria West Palm Beach FL 33411

WEISS, MARILYN ACKERMAN
COLLAGE ARTIST, PAINTER
b Brooklyn, NY, Sept 4, 32. *Study:* NY Univ, BS(magna cum laude), 53; Studied with Anthoney Toney, 66, Paul Margin, 67-72, Ruth Leaf, 78-79, Lynn Forgach, 92, Audrey Flack, 93 & Donna Karetsky, 95. *Work:* Mus Southwest, Midland, Tex; Fred Leighton Madison, Ltd, NY; CMF Colonial Inc, Hyannis, Mass; Bob Zimmerman, Inc, Boca Raton, Fla; Sarah Lawrence Col, Bronxville, NY; Sloan Kettering Art Collection, NY; Nat Mus Women in the Arts, Washington. *Exhib:* Solo exhibs: Bodley Gallery, 83; NY, Discovery Gallery, Glen Cove, NY, 90; Z Gallery, NY, 95; Allen Sheppard Gallery, Piermont, NY, 95 & 97; Sundance Gallery, Bridge Hampton, NY, 98; West Hampton Libr, Westhampton Beach, NY, 99 & 2001; Downstairs Gallery, Hewlett, NY, 1999-2000; Shelter Rock Art Gallery, Manhasset, NY, 2000; Omni Gallery, Uniondale, NY, 2003; Gayle Wilson Gallery, Southampton, NY, 2003, 04, 05; Madelle Hegeler Semerjian Gallery, Southampton, NY, 2005; Interchurch Ctr, NY, 2005; Harvest Gallery, Dennis, Mass, 2006; First Open Exhib, Fine Arts Mus Nassau Co, Roslyn, NY, 88; National Printmaking Exhib, Mus Southwest, Midland, Tex, 91; Quiet Reaction, Richmond Art Mus, Ind, 92; Global Focus-Women in Arts & Cult, Beijing, China & Women's Mus, Wash, 95; Cork Gallery, Lincoln Ctr, New York City, 99 & 2003; Broome St Gallery, New York City, 99, 2002, 2004-2006; Ise Art Found, New York City, 2000; Elizabeth Found for Arts, New York City, 2001; Frey Berger Gallery, Pa State Univ, Reading, 2002; Long Beach Art League, Long Beach, NY, 2003; Art-trium, Melville, NY; East End Art Coun Gallery, Riverhead, NY, 2004; Manhattan Boro Hall, NY, 2005; Google Works, Reading, Pa; Shelter Rock Art Gallery, Manhasset, NY, 2006. *Awards:* Canady-Karasik Mem Award, 97; Miriam E Halpren Mem Award, 91; Harriet FeBland Workshop Award, Am Soc Contemp Artists, 93; Irving H Silver Award for Innovative Collage, 2000; Donald Pierce Mem Award, 2000; Merit Award Long Beach Art League; Award for Excellence, Long Beach Art League, 2002-2004; Cleo Hartwig Award, Sculpture, NAWA Ann, 2004. *Bibliog:* Salon des Femme Artists de NY, La Revue Moderne, France, 71; John & John Digby (auths), The Collage Handbook, Thames & Hudson Ltd, 85; Helen Harrison (auth), New York Times, 99; Pat Rogers (auth), Southampton Press, 2003; Valerie Kellogg (auth), Newsday, 2003; Marion Wolberg Weiss (auth), Dan's Paper, 2003-2004; Pola Rosen, ED.D (auth), Education Update, 2005. *Mem:* Nat Asn Women Artists; Contemp Artists Guild; Am Soc Contemp Artists; Long Beach Art Asn; Artists Equity; Art League Long Island. *Media:* Hand Made Paper; Acrylic. *Dealer:* Gayle Wilson Gallery 51A Job's Ln Southampton NY 11968; PaintingsDirect.com (online gallery); Harvest Gallery 776 Main St Rte 6A Dennia MA 02638. *Mailing Add:* 1100 Park Ave Apt 14B New York NY 10128

WEISS, RACHEL
CURATOR
b Paterson, NJ, Sept 22, 54. *Study:* Marlboro Col, BA, 76; Mass Col Art, MFA, 80. *Work:* Ctr Georges Pompidou, Paris; Nat Mus Sci & Technol, Ottawa, Ont. *Exhib:* The Nearest Edge of the World: Art and Cuba Now, var mus, 90-93; Ante Am, Biblioteca Luis Angel Arango, Bogota, Colombia; Among Africas/In Americas, Banff Ctr, 91. *Pos:* Coordr, Vis Artists Prog, Mass Col Art, 84-89; pres, Polarities, Inc, 85-; chairperson, Arts Inst, Chicago. *Teaching:* Asst instr holography, Mass Col Art, Boston, 79-80, spec prog asst, 78-81; asst instr holography, Brown Univ, Providence, RI, 80-81. *Awards:* Numerous pub & pvt grants in support of pub art prog organized since 1983. *Publ:* Auth, Boycotting the truth, Black New York Mag, 88; Creating freedom, Tres Mundo, 88; Necessity and Invention: New Cuban Art, Wolgan Misul Mag, Seoul, 90; ed, Being America, White Pine Press, 91; contribr, Territories of Difference (chapt), 92. *Mailing Add:* c/o Sch Arts Inst Chicago 37 S Warbash Chicago IL 60603-3103

WEISSMAN, JULIAN PAUL
DEALER
b New York, NY, June 28, 43. *Study:* Hobart Col, Geneva, NY, BA. *Pos:* Art Critic, The Press, 73-77; ed assoc, writer & reviewer, Art News Mag, New York, 74-79; mgr, Susan Caldwell Gallery Inc, New York, 74-75; mgr, Gloria Cortella Inc (gallery), New York, 76-77; dir, Alexander F Milliken Inc (gallery), New York, 78-79; dir, Gruenebaum Gallery Inc, New York, 79-87; assoc dir, M Knoedler & Co, 87-89; dir, Mod Europ Art, Hirschl & Adler Galleries, New York, 89-91; dir & vpres, ACA Galleries, New York, 93-95; Owner, Jullian Weissman Fine Art, LLC, 95-Present. *Res:* Impressionism; German expressionism; the Bauhaus; 20th century sculpture; contemporary art and artists who live and work in New York; 20th Century European and Am and Contemp Art. *Specialty:* Contemporary American art and European modern. *Publ:* Auth, Standoff in Soho, Art News Mag, 74; What's wrong at the Whitney?, The Press, Vol 3, No 3, 75; Master Atget--& Portraits of the Artists, Art News Mag, 76; Here comes the taxman, Soho Weekly News, 76; Dazzling drawings are redefining the art, The Press, Vol 4, No 1, 76. *Mailing Add:* 26 Beaver St No 14 New York NY 10004

WEISSMAN, WALTER
PHOTOGRAPHER, SCULPTOR
b Brooklyn, NY, Dec 9, 46. *Study:* Kingsborough Community Col, with Gregory Battcock, AA, 67; Brooklyn Col, with Harry Holtzman, BA(hon; arts), 70; Hunter Col, with Robert Morris, MA(fine arts), 75. *Work:* Mus Mod Art, Whitney Mus & Guggenheim Mus, NY; Tate Mus, London, Eng; Va Commonwealth Univ. *Comn:* Alliance in the Park (outdoor/indoor collaborative work), Philadelphia Art Alliance, Pa, 87; Committed to Print, Mus Mod Art, NY, 88. *Exhib:* Contemp Reflections No 4, Aldrich Mus Contemp Art, 75; Open Studios at PS1, Queens, NY, 77; Centennial Exhib Sculpture, NJ Inst Technol, Newark, 81; solo exhibs, Structures and Shelters, 83 & 87 & De-Archit, 84, 14 Sculptors Gallery, NY; Artists Call, Hudson Mem Church, NY, 84; Art Works: Three Dimensions, Beaver Col, Glenside, Pa, 85; Art Against Apartheid, Boricua Col, Brooklyn, 85; 13-state traveling exhib, 87-89. *Collection Arranged:* Drawings, Models and Sculpture: A Re-Opening: Season's Premier, 14 Sculptors Gallery, 82. *Pos:* Sr ed, Art & Artists, NY, 78-89; adv, Artists Cert Cult Affairs, NY, 80-86; moderator, Artists Talk on Art, NY, 81-84; pres, 14 Sculptors Gallery, 85-88. *Teaching:* Asst instr photog, Yale Univ, 68; instr painting & drawing, Brooklyn Col, 71; artist-in-residence, PS 1, Long Island City, NY, 77. *Bibliog:* Burton Wasserman (auth), Exhibitions in sight, Art Matters, Pa, 6/85; Robert Metzger (auth), A 2nd Palette, In: Aldrich Mus catalog, 85; Michael Brenson (auth), article, New York Times, 12/28/86. *Mem:* Artists Meeting Cult Change (secy, 76-78); Found Community Arts (pres, 80-84); Graphic Artists Guild; Globe Photos Inc. *Specialty:* Contemporary

sculpture & photography. *Publ:* (co-auth), An Anti-Catalog, Artists Meeting Cult Change, 77; auth, Interview with John Perreault, 4/80, Automata and autonomy: Sculpture now, 11/81 & ed, Special Supplement, 11/81, Artworkers News; ed, Special Supplement, 82, auth, The terror of bureaucracy, 5/85 & View from a coop, 3/86, Art & Artists Mag; (co-auth), The Village, 87. *Mailing Add:* 463 West St Suite B-332 New York NY 10014

WEITZMAN, EILEEN
PAINTER, SCULPTOR
b Chicago, Ill, Feb 28, 51. *Study:* Self taught. *Work:* Pierogi 2000, Brooklyn. *Exhib:* 2-person show, 101 Wooster Gallery, NY, 91; Monumental Propaganda (traveling), 93; solo exhib, Jamaica Arts Ctr, NY, 93, Kentler Int Drawing Ctr, Brooklyn, 95; Contemp Am Artists, Windows Gallery, Birobijan, Russia, 94; Three Rivers Festival, Carnegie Mus Art, 96. *Awards:* Nat Endowment Humanities grant, 77; Honorable Mention, Int New Talent Competition, Lucia Gallery, 89; Artist Grant, Artists Space, 91. *Bibliog:* Basile Duodoumis (auth), Imagination and reality, The Reporters, 4/28/91; L Ulbyanenko (auth), 3 Americans at Windows Gallery, Press-fact, Birobijan, Russia, 12/21/94; Erin Kelly (auth), Using odds and ends to redefine clichés, NY Times, 3/5/95. *Mem:* Brooklyn Waterfront Artist Coalition; Millenium Film Workshop. *Publ:* Auth, Tony Moore at Salena Gallery, Art Initiatives, 92; Supermodern art, Art Initiatives, 93. *Mailing Add:* 784 Manhattan Ave No 4L Brooklyn NY 11222

WELCH, CHARLES D
PAINTER, SCULPTOR
b Kearney, Nebr, Oct 5, 48. *Study:* Kearney State Col, BA(art educ), 70, MS(art educ), 74; tuition fel, 84-87, Sch Mus Fine Arts, Boston, MFA, 87. *Work:* Chicago Art Inst; Tate Gallery, London; Mus Mod Art, NY; Arch Small Press & Commun, Antwerp, Belg; Nebr Art Collection; Getty Found Collection; Libr Congress. *Exhib:* Printmaking 1985, Northeastern Univ Gallery, Boston; Gallery II, Tufts Univ, Medford, Mass, 87; Paper Press Gallery, Chicago, 88; Int Stamp Invitational, Davidson Gallery, Seattle, 89; Aerial Gallery, NY, 89. *Pos:* Proprietor, Sandbar Willow Handmade Paper Mill, Omaha, 78-84, Lebanon, NH, 88-. *Teaching:* Chmn art dept, Bellevue Sr High Sch, 74-84 & Bellevue W High Sch, 77-84; instr, Bellevue Col, 78-80; teaching asst, Tufts Univ, 86-87; instr, AVA Gallery, 88-89. *Awards:* Fulbright Hayes Recipient, 76; Medal, Art 54 Gallery, 87; Special Artistic Excellence, Tokyo Metrop Mus, 90. *Bibliog:* Judith Hoffberg (auth), article, Umbrella Mag, 83; David Cole (auth), The Adventures of the Cracker Jack Kid, aka Chuck Welch, Lightworks Mag, 87. *Mem:* Nat Educ Asn; Bellevue Educ Asn; Int Soc Copier Artists; Friends Dard Hunter Soc. *Media:* Paper, Mail Art. *Publ:* Auth, Networking Currents, Sandbar Willow Press, 85; Whole Earth Review, Mail Art Glasnost, winter 89; ed, Eternal Network: A Mail Art Anthology, Univ Calgary Press, 95. *Dealer:* Benta West AVA Gallery Hanover NH; Rebecca McDonald Davidson Galleries Seattle WA. *Mailing Add:* 28 Evergreen Hill Rd Hancock NH 03449-5417

WELCH, JAMES EDWARD
PAINTER
b Nora, Va, July 14, 43. *Study:* Art Sch Soc Arts Crafts, 1963-1964. *Work:* McLaren Regional Med Ctr, Flint, Mich; Marshfield Clinic, Wis; Saginaw Township City Hall, Mich; Bank of Commerce, Hamtramck, Mich; Old Kent Bank SW, Niles, Mich. *Comn:* portrait founding pastor, Judson Baptist Church, Burton, Mich, 84; portrait founding pastor, Grace Emmanuel Baptist Church, Flint, Mich, 86; Children at Play (painting), McLaren Regional Med Ctr, 85 & pastel paintings, 98; Bankard Portraits, Sue and Miss Em, 86. *Exhib:* Midwest Regional Art Competition, Kendall Sch Design, Grand Rapids, 86; Five State Pastel Competition, Art Ctr Battle Creek, Mich, 86; Extended Media, Fresh Visions, Detroit Inst Arts, 87; Saginaw Art Mus, Mich, 88; Jackson Area Competition, Ella Sharp Mus, Mich, 90; 2-D 3-D Regional Art Competition, S Bend Art Ctr, Ind, 90; All Media State Wide Competition, Left Bank Gallery, Flint, 95; Our Town, State Competition, Birmingham, Mich, 97; Holiday Exhib, Lansing Art Gallery, Mich, 98; All Area Exhib, Saginaw Art Mus, Mich, 98; Greater Flint Arts Coun Ann Mem Exhib, 99; solo exhib, Saginaw Twp City Hall, Mich, 1993; Extended Media/Fresh Visions, Detroit Inst Arts, 1987; Ella Sharp Mus, 1990; NE Mich Artists Exhib, Jesse Besser Mus, 2004. *Awards:* Purchase Award & Views Choice Award for Krasl Art Ctr, All Mi, All Media, 90; Our Town Exhib Sponsor's Award, Chrysler Fund, 98; Outstanding Award of Merit & Viewers Choice Award, Midland Ctr Arts, 95; Award of Merit, Manhattan Arts Int, 99; Citizens Banking Corp Sponcer Award, 2003. *Bibliog:* Jean Spenner (auth), Artist portrays Bill Pless, Brighton Argus, 84; Cheryl Roof (auth), Tapping the surface in art, Independent, 86. *Mem:* E Shore Art Guild; hon mem Saginaw Artists Guild, Mich; Survivors Art Found NY. *Media:* Oil, Pastels, Acylic, Egg Tempera, Watercolor. *Specialty:* Liberty Gallery; Blue Bear Gallery. *Interests:* Hiking. *Publ:* Contribr, Best of Pastel, 96 & Portrait Inspirations, 97, Rockport Publs. *Mailing Add:* 585 S US 23 Harrisville MI 48740

WELCH, JAMES WYMORE
PAINTER, MURALIST
b Omaha, Nebr, June 7, 28. *Study:* George Washington Univ, BA; Univ Omaha, study with Anna C Myers; Acad Fine Arts, Tokyo, Japan, with Shiguru Yamamoto; Keio Univ, Hiyoshi, Japan, study with Daisuke Sakai; Sch of Fine Arts, Seoul, Korea, study with Kim Il Han; study with Mark Rothko; Harvard Univ, MBA, 66. *Work:* Nat Mus, Seoul; Joslyn Mem Mus, Omaha; Nat Mus Mod Art, Tokyo; Whitney Mus Am Art, NY; Fed Reserve Bank, Richmond, Va. *Comn:* Poster panel designs, US State Dept Arts Abroad Prog, Washington, DC, 63; acrylic mural, Univ Panama, Repub Panama, 59; acrylic paintings, McDonald's Corp, NY, 79; acrylic paintings, IBM Corp, NY, 81; acrylic paintings, Xerox Corp, NY, 82. *Exhib:* Oriental Art Trends for Today, Fine Arts Pavilion, Osaka, Japan, 50; Ann Invitational, Palacio de Bellas Artes, Panama City, Republic Panama, 59-60; Presidential Fine Arts Show, Duk-Soo Palace, Seoul, 63; 13th Biennial Show, Valentine Mus, Richmond, 74; Corcoran Gallery Art Biennial, DC; Minimal Arts of the 70's, Hirshhorn Mus, Washington, DC, 79; and others. *Pos:* Pres, Metrop Artists Asn, Richmond, Va,; bd dir, Richmond Pub Libr, Va. *Teaching:* Guest instr abstract painting, Univ Panama, 58-60; guest lectr Western US art, US State Dept-Korean Govt, Seoul, 63-64. *Awards:* Presidential Award, Presidential Fine Arts Show, Seoul, 63; Purchase Award, Shockoe Slip Art Fair, Xerox Corp, 76; Purchase Award, Federated Arts Show, Richmond, 82. *Bibliog:* B Green (auth), Artists works have deceptively simple sophistication, 81, Minimal art receives critical acclaim, 82, Artist works receive nat recognition, 86, Richmond News Leader. *Mem:* Metrop Artists Asn, Richmond; Federated Arts Coun, Richmond; Accademia Italia Delle Arti E Del Lavoro; Int Soc Artists; Va Mus Fine Arts, Richmond; Am Artists Prof League. *Media:* Oil, Acrylic. *Mailing Add:* c/o Welch Studio Inc 1500 Park Ave Richmond VA 23220

WELCH, MARSHA SWEET See Sweet, Marsha (Marsha) Sweet Welch

WELCH, ROGER
SCULPTOR, CONCEPTUAL ARTIST
b Westfield, NJ, Feb 10, 46. *Study:* Miami Univ, Ohio, BFA, 69; Whitney Mus Independent Study Prog, 70-71; Art Inst Chicago, MFA, 71. *Work:* Ga Mus Art, Athens; Rufino Tamayo Mus, Mexico City; Boston Mus Fine Arts; Mus Bellas Artes, Caracas, Venezuela; Chase Manhattan Collection, Mus Mod Art, NY; and other pvt and pub collections; Guggenheim Mus, NY; Reina Sofia Mus, Madrid. *Comn:* The OJ Simpson Project (multi-media work), Albright-Knox Art Gallery, 77; The Voice of Clint Eastwood (videotape), Process & Konstruktion, Munich, Ger, 85. *Exhib:* One-man shows, Milwaukee Art Ctr, 74, Albright-Knox Art Gallery, 77, Mus Nac, Havana, 81, Mus Bellas Artes, Caracas, Venezuela, 81, Whitney Mus Am Art, 82, Ted Greenwald Gallery, NY, 86 & 87, Ewing Gallery, Univ Tenn, 90, Liverpool Gallery, Brussels, Belg, 91 & Galerie Art Matters, Noerdwijk, The Neth, 93; Am Narrative Art, 1967-77, Contemp Art Mus, Houston, Tex, 77; Photog & Art since 1946, Los Angeles Co Mus, 87; Specs, Annina Nosei Gallery, NY, 92; Site Seeing, Islip Art Mus, NY, 92; Concept Art, Mus D'Art Mod, Saint-Etinne, France, 93; Conceptual Art of the 70's, Boston Mus Fine Arts, 93; Galleria Milano, Milan, Italy, 2000; Neuberger Mus, Purchase, NY, 2001. *Collection Arranged:* The Solomon Collection, Sarah Lawrence Col, 76; The Carter Collection, Ga Mus Art, 77; Vicky Remy Collection, Mus Modern Art, St Etienne, France. *Teaching:* Guest lectr many univs, 76-81; Sr instr, Univ Tex, Austin, 88 & 90; adj asst prof, SW Tex State Univ, 1998-99, assoc prof. *Awards:* Creative Artists Pub Serv Grant, 73 & 76; Nat Endowment Arts Grants, 74 & 80. *Bibliog:* William Zimmer (auth), A Genre comes into its own, New York Times, 8/2/92; Helen A Harrison (auth), For 12 artists, maps fill a role as raw material, NY Times, 10/18/92; Lucy Lippard (auth), Lure of the Local, The New Press, 97. *Mem:* Col Art Asn; Artists Equity Asn. *Media:* Multi-media & Sculpture. *Publ:* Contribr, Tracks J, spring 75; Unbuilt America, McGraw-Hill, 76; The Big Jewish Book, Doubleday, 78; Wide Angle Film Quarterly, Vol 5, No 3, Ohio Univ Press, 83; Photography & Art since 1946, Abbeville Press, 87; Installation Art, Thames & Hudson, 94. *Dealer:* Mary Delahoyd Gallery New York NY; John Gibson Gallery New York NY; Galleria Milano Milan Italy. *Mailing Add:* 87 E Houston St New York NY 10012

WELCH, STUART CARY
CURATOR, HISTORIAN
b Buffalo, NY, Apr 2, 28. *Study:* Harvard Col, AB, 50. *Pos:* Cur, Near Eastern & Indian Art, Fogg Art Mus, Harvard Univ, cur manuscripts, Harvard Col Libr; consult in charge of dept Islamic Art, Metrop Mus Art, NY. *Teaching:* Lectr, Near Eastern & Indian Art, Harvard Univ. *Res:* Safavid art (Iran); Mughal Decani and Rajput art (India). *Publ:* Coauth, Gods, Thrones and Peacocks: Northern Indian Painting from Two Traditions, Asia Soc, 65; auth, A King's Book of Kings: The Shahnameh of Shah Tahmasp, Metrop Mus Art, NY, 72; Room for Wonder: Indian Painting under the British Raj, Am Fedn Arts, 78; coauth, The Houghton Shahnameh, Harvard Univ Press, 80; auth, Annemarie Schimmel: A Pocketbook for Akbar, 83, The Emperor's Album, 87 & The Islamic World, 87, Metrop Mus Art, NY. *Mailing Add:* Harvard Univ Mus Art 485 Broadway Cambridge MA 02138

WELD, ALISON G
PAINTER
b Ft Knox, KY, Jun 10,1953. *Study:* Suny col of Ceramic Art & Design Alfred Univ, BFA (painting) 1975; School of the Art Institute of Chicago, MFA (painting) 1980. *Work:* Jersey City Mus, NJ; New Jersey State Mus, Trenton, NJ; Jane Voorhees Zimmerli Art Mus, New Brunswick, NJ; Newark Pub Library, Newark, NJ; Springfield Mus Art, Springfield, Ohio; Deskoba Inc, Olympia, Wash. *Exhib:* New Painterly Abstraction, Jersey City Mus, NJ, 1988; Hunterdon Mus of Art, Hunterdon, NJ, 1998; Different Ways of Seeing, Noyes Mus of Art, Oceanville, NJ, 2005-06; Abstraction Now: Scratching the Surface, Delaware Ctr of Contemp Art, Wilmington, DE, 2005; Pattern & Pulse,Cazenovia College Art Gallery, Cazenovia, NY, 2005; Allegories of Strife: The Diptychs of Alison Weld 1990-2005, 2006; Springfield Mus Art, Ohio; The Figurative Impulse in Abstraction, Rider Univ Art Gallery, Lawrenceville, NJ, 2006. *Pos:* asst cur, NJSM, 88-99. *Bibliog:* Jonathan Goodman (auth), Marks and Materials, William Paterson Univ, 2003; Domingue Nahas (auth), The Emotional Life of Inanimate Things, Robert Steele Gallery, 2003; Donald Kripit (auth), Discordis Concors, The Diptychs of Alison Weld, Springfield Museum of Art, 2006. *Mem:* College Art Asn. *Media:* Acrylic, Oil. *Specialty:* Abstraction. *Publ:* Springfield Mus Art (exhib catalog), 2006. *Dealer:* Robert Steele Gallery 511 W 25th St, New York, NY 10001

WELDEN, DANIEL W
PRINTMAKER, PAINTER
b New York, NY, Oct 22, 41. *Study:* Adelphi Univ, BA, 64, MA, 67; Acad Fine Art, Munich, Ger, 69-71. *Work:* Guild Hall Mus, East Hampton, NY; Greater Mus Art, Lafayette, Ind. *Comn:* Portfolio, Southampton Hosp, NY, 80-82. *Exhib:* Solo exhibs, Southwest Tex Univ, Canyon, 79, Long Beach Mus, NY, 81, Galerie Kausch, Kassel, Ger, 81, Port Washington Pub Libr, NY, 83, Macey Gallery, Columbia Univ, NY, 84, Hempstead Harbor Gallery, Glen Cove, NY, 86 & Parasol Gallery, Sag Harbor, NY, 86; Traveling exhib, Prints from the workshop of Dan Welden, Gallery North, Setauket, NY, Cent Conn State Univ, Print Coun NJ; Clarke Col, Dubuque, Iowa; Western Va Community Col, Roanoke, Va; Benton Gallery, Southampton, NY. *Pos:* Own & dir, Hampton Ed Ltd, 72-. *Teaching:* Prof art & printmaking, State Univ NY, Stony Brook, 77-85; artist-in-residence, Cent Conn State Univ, 86-87; asst prof art, Cent Conn State Univ, 87-88; adj asst prof, Suffolk Community Col, Riverhead, NY, 87-; adj assoc prof, Long Island Univ, 89. *Awards:* First Prize, Work on Paper, Guild Hall Mus, 86; and others. *Mem:* Jimmy Ernst Artists Alliance, East Hampton, NY; World Print Coun, San Francisco, Calif; Long Island Printmakers Soc, NY (pres, 77-84); Soc Am Graphic Artists, NY (vpres, 83-86); SAGA Artists/Printmakers (pres, 89; Soc Am Graphic Artists (hon pres, formerly). *Media:* All. *Publ:* Coauth, Understanding Prints, Long Island Printmakers Soc, 80; auth, Journal of the Print World, Lane, 81. *Dealer:* Benton Gallery 365 County Rd 39 Southampton NY 11968

WELDON, BARBARA MALTBY
PAINTER
b Yuma, Ariz. *Study:* San Diego State Univ, 50-52; Univ Calif, San Diego, 70-73. *Work:* Bank of San Francisco & Bank Am World Hq, San Francisco; San Diego Mus Art, Calif; Copley Mem Libr & Salk Inst, La Jolla, Calif; San Jose Mus Art, Calif; City of Santa Fe Springs, Calif; Utah State Univ; Gen-Probe, Inc, San Diego, CA; Oprah Winfrey; Saks Fifth Ave, New York, NY; Strauss Collections, Rancho Santa Fe, CA. *Comn:* Paintings, VRC Parkway Radiology Ctr, Escondido, Calif, 89; Peabody Hotel, Orlando, Fla, 88; Grossmont Hospital Women's Ctr, La Mesa, Calif, 90; Mason & Elizabeth Phelps Collection, La Jolla, Calif; Imperial Hotel, Tokyo, Japan, 96; Nikko Hotel, Tokyo, Japan, 96. *Exhib:* Solo exhibs, Thomas Babeor Gallery, La Jolla, 80-84, 86, 88, 90, 92, 96, 93 & 95, Ivory/Kimpton Gallery, San Francisco, 82, 83, 86 & 89, Patty Ande Gallery, San Diego, 84, Triangles, continuing rotation of artist's work, San Diego, 93-96, Tasende Gallery, Calif, 99, 2001, I Wolk Gallery, St Helena, Calif, 2003; Sheila Nussbaum Gallery, 84, 86, 92 & 96; Citizens Gallery, Yokohama, 92; Gallery 30, Calif, 96 & 97; Susan St Gallery, Calif, 97; Tasende Gallery, LaJolla, Calif, 99-01, Los Angeles, 2000-2001. *Pos:* Adv bd mem, Pub Arts, San Diego, Calif, 86 & 87; juror art exhibs (example: San Diego Del Mar Fair); commemorative artist for KPBS 25 yr Anniversary Poster, 92. *Teaching:* Guest Lecturer; Contemp Arts comt, SDMA, Feb, 2005. *Awards:* First Award, Nat Watercolor Soc, 74; Second Prize, San Diego Mus Art, 75; William A Paton Prize, Nat Acad Design, 79; Outstanding Achievement in the Arts Women Together Orgn, San Diego, 97. *Bibliog:* Les Krantz (auth), Calif Art Rev, 88 & 89; Robert Pincus (auth), rev, San Diego Union Tribune, 3/18/93, 12/23/93, 9/14/95; Johnathan Seville (auth), San Diego Reader, 8/95; and others. *Mem:* Mus of Contemp Art SD San Diego, Mus of Art; Mingei Int'l mus Kappa Alpha Theta (fratenity) Myeloma Research Found for a cure MRFC bd mem (Little Rock, AR); Children Home Soc of CA. *Media:* Oil, Encoustic, Acrylic. *Res:* Mythology; Medieval art; Symbolism; Ancient religious art pieces. *Specialty:* Tasende Gallery shows blue chip art with no specialty. *Interests:* Folk & Religious Art; my paintings are not restricted to religious art, Mythology, Symbolism, but are often influended by music, I listen to classical & jazz while working & my work evolves from one series to another. Also influenced by my interest in world travel What I absorb from other cultures. *Collection:* David Copley, La Jolla; Mason & Elizabeth Phelps, La Jolla, Strauss Collection. *Publ:* Martin Petersen (profile), Applause Mag, 9/79; Phyllis Van Doren (profiie), SD Home and Garden, 2/2002; Richard Reilly (rev), San Diego Union, 1/81; Robert McDonald (rev), Los Angeles Times, 4/15/86; Holly Myers (rev), LA Times, 10/2001; Robert Perine (bk, profiles of 40), San Diego Artists, Artra Publ, 88; Kathleen Mc Millen (profile) Decor and Style Mag, 2004. *Dealer:* Tasende Gallery La Jolla CA 92037. *Mailing Add:* 6131 Romany Dr San Diego CA 92120

WELLBORN, J(EANETTE) D(ARLEEN)
PAINTER
b Carlsbad, NMex, June 15, 43. *Study:* Univ NMex, BFA, 65. *Exhib:* Watercolor Southwest, Mus Tex Tech Univ, Lubbock, Tex, 80; West '83, Greenville Mus Art, Greenville, SC, 83; West '84, Minn Mus Art, St Paul, Minn, 84; Am Watercolor Society Traveling Exhib, Charles & Emma Frye Mus Art, Seattle, Wash, 84 & 88; Western Federation of Watercolor Societies Juried Exhibition, Mus Albuquerque, NMex, 84; Rocky Mountain National Watermedia, Foothills Art Ctr, Golden, Colo, 85; Solo exhib, Carlsbad Art Mus, 89. *Awards:* Western Fedn Watercolor Socs Exhib, Best of Show, 81 & 88; High Winds Medal, Am Watercolor Soc Exhib, 86 & 88; Nat invited juror, Am Watercolor Soc, 89. *Bibliog:* Mary Carrol Nelson (auth), J D M Welborn, Southwest Art, 2/87; Mike Ward (auth), New Spirit of Watercolor, F & W Publ, 89; Cris Parrington (producer, ed) Colores, KNME TV, 2/90. *Mem:* NMex Watercolor Soc (bd dir, 79-80); Albuquerque Mus Found; Dolphin Fel AWS; Am Watercolor Soc. *Media:* Acrylic, Watercolor. *Dealer:* Concetta D Farley 50 First Plaza Albuquerque NM 87110. *Mailing Add:* 3819 La Hacienda Dr NE Albuquerque NM 87110

WELLER, LAURIE JUNE
PAINTER
b Warsaw, NY, May 18, 53. *Study:* Univ Ill, Urbana, BFA, 76; Tyler Sch Art, Philadelphia, MFA, 80. *Work:* Tambrands Inc, Lake Success, NY; Steak & Ale Corp, Dallas, Tex; Mischer Corp Collections, Houston, Tex; Prudential Insurance Co Am, Newark, NJ; Transco Corp Collection, Houston, Tex; and others. *Comn:* Sybaritica (watercolor on paper), comn by Thomas Wright, San Antonio, Tex, 84; Fiesta (watercolor on paper), comn by Dr Evelyn Hammon, Austin, Tex, 88; Rivulets Triptych (watercolor on paper), comn by Intellicall Corp, Dallas, Tex, 89; Grazioso Forza, acrylic on wood, Crossroads, TX. *Exhib:* Elements and Environments, Univ Ark, Little Rock; Watercolor All-ways, Col Mainland Gallery, Texas City, Tex; solo shows, Mountian View Col, Dallas, Tex, 93, Tex Woman's Univ Gallery, 94, Richland Col, Dallas, 95 & Univ Wis, Platteville, 96, Bimorphia, Oklahoma Univ, Norman, Okla, 2003, Eccentric Boundaries, Harris Col, Housto, Tex, 2004, Ensemble, Hardin Simmons Univ, Albilene, Tex, 2006; Wood's Edge, Brookhaven Col, Dallas, Tex, 93; Woods Edge II, North Lake Col, Irving, Tex, 94; The Big Picture: Large Scale Watercolor, Meadows Gallery, Visual Arts Ctr, Denton, Tex, 94; Laurie Weller: Transformed by Nature, Nature Transformed (with catalog), Weil Gallery, Tex A & M, Corpus Christi, 97; Penrose Gallery, Tyler Sch Art, 2000; Eccentric Boundaries, Tex Christian Univ, Ft Worth, 02; Scratching the Surface, Austin Col, Sherman, Tex, 01. *Pos:* Vpres, Austin Contemp Visual Arts Asn, 84-84. *Teaching:* Lectr watercolor & drawing, SW Tex State Univ, San Marcos, 81-88; painting & drawing, Tex Woman's Univ, Denton, 88-90, adj asst prof, 90-; vis asst prof art, Tex A&M Univ, Corpus Christi, spring 97, Austin Col, Sherman, Tex, spring 99 & 2006. *Awards:* Cash Award, Tex Fine Arts Asn Juried Exhib, 82; Plaque of Distinction, Marietta Nat 15th Ann Painting & Sculpture, 82; Resident Visual Artist Fel, Va Ctr Creative Arts, 82 & 84. *Bibliog:* Marcie J Inman (auth), Artists' works convey responses to nature, Artimes, 9/93. *Mem:* Greater Denton Arts Coun (exhib comt chmn). *Media:* Acrylic on wood. *Dealer:* William Campbell Contemp Art 4935 Byers Ft Worth TX 76107; Cinema Gallery, 120 W Main, Urbana, IL 61801. *Mailing Add:* 2297 Wood Hollow Rd Denton TX 76208

WELLER, PAUL
PHOTOGRAPHER, PAINTER
b Boston, Mass, Dec 20, 12. *Study:* Nat Acad Design, 32-33; Art Students League, 45. *Work:* Metrop Mus, NY; San Francisco Mus, Mod Art, Calif; Philadelphia Mus Art, Pa; Baltimore Mus Art, Md; Wolfson Found Mus, Miami, Fla. *Comn:* Mural, US Post Off, US Treasury Dept, Baldwinsville, NY, 41. *Exhib:* Ann Show, Chicago Art Inst, 39; Ann, Philadelphia Art Alliance, Pa, 40; one-man show, Paul Weller Photos, Brooklyn Mus, NY, 50; Ann, Univ Ky Mus, 86. *Mem:* Jimmy Ernst Artists Alliance, East Hampton, NY; Nat Arts Club, NY. *Media:* All Media. *Publ:* Illusr, Sci Am Mag, 50-75; Bantam Books, 60-77; Simon & Schuster, 65-77; Forbes Mag, 67-77; Woman's Day, 67-77. *Dealer:* Mary Ryan Gallery 452 Columbus Ave New York NY 10024. *Mailing Add:* 281 Old Stone Hwy East Hampton NY 11937

WELLING, JAMES
PHOTOGRAPHER
b Hartford, Conn, Apr 19, 51. *Study:* Carnegie-Mellon Univ, studied studio art, 69-71; Calif Inst Arts, Valencia, BFA, 72, MFA, 74. *Work:* Mus Mod Art, Vienna. *Exhib:* One-person exhibs, Jay Goreny Modern Art, NY, 88, 91, 93 & 95, Waco Works of Art, Tokyo, 93 & 95, Arts Club Chicago, 94, Kunstmuseum Wolfsburg, Ger, 94, Am Fine Arts Co, NY, 95; Expiramental Vision, Denver Art Mus, Colo, 94; The Abstract Urge, Ansel Adams Ctr Photog, San Francisco, 94; Werkstattquartier, Inst for Gegenwartskunst, Vienna, 94; L'Amour Toujours, Le Carré/Museé Bonnat, Bayonne, France, 94; Transport, Maier Mus Art, Randolph-Macon Women's Col, Lynchburg, Va, 94. *Awards:* NY Found Arts Fel, 86; Artist-in-residence, Lightworks, Syracuse, NY, 86; NEA 87. *Bibliog:* Alain Ceuff (auth), Et Welling Aussi, Beaux Arts Mag, Paris, 89; Reagan Upshaw (auth), James Wellington at Jay Gorney, Art in Am, 12/93; Janet Abrams (auth), The Solid Geometry of Sight, James Welling, Arts Club of Chicago, 94

WELLS, BETTY CHILDS
PAINTER, ILLUSTRATOR
b Baltimore, Md, Dec 7, 26. *Study:* Johns Hopkins Univ, 46; Md Inst Art, grad, 48, scholar, 49, Hon BFA, Md Inst, Col Art. *Hon Degrees:* Md Inst Col Art, Hon BFA, 96. *Work:* Peale Mus, Baltimore; White House & Supreme Court, Washington; NZ Nat Gallery Art; Ariz State Univ Art Mus, Ariz, 2005. *Comn:* Interior murals (plaster & mosaic), Taylor Manor Psychiat Ctr, Ellicott City, Md, 69; interior murals (mosaic), Lake Clifton Sch, Baltimore, 71; exterior mural (mosaic), Templeton Sch, Baltimore, 73; Chief Justice Warren E Burger (portrait sketch), 76; Mrs Warren E Burger (portrait), Col William & Mary, 83. *Exhib:* Audubon Artist Ann, Nat Acad Art, NY; An Am Album: Images from women artists, Nairobi, Kenya, 85; and others; one-woman shows, Betty Wells, Pen & Inks & Collages, Int Gallery, Baltimore, 66, Baltimore Mus Art, 74, US Supreme Ct, WAshington, 78-79, Fla State Univ, 80, Supreme Court Odyssey, Grinter Galleries, Univ Fla, 80, Art of Betty Wells, Va Beach Arts Ctr, 87, Watergate Drawings by Betty Wells, Newseum, Arlington, Va, 97. *Collection Arranged:* Ariz State Univ Art Mus, 2005; Harry Ransom Ctr, Univ Tex, 2005. *Pos:* Freelance courtroom illusr, Washington Post, 72-77 & WTOP, Washington, 73-74; courtroom illusr, NBC, 74-; Comnr, Va Beach Resort Area Adv Comn, 84-88 & 94-; juror, Chesapeake Bay Watercolorists, 2003 & Chesapeake Bay Art Asn, 2003. *Teaching:* Instr basic drawing, Md Inst Art, 46-48. *Awards:* Best in Show, Easton Acad Arts, Md, 66; Two Emmies, 78; Distinguished Alumni Award, Md Inst, Col Art, 96. *Bibliog:* Robert Leslie (auth), Walls designed by Betty Wells, Idea, Japan, Vol 23, No 130; cover story, Am Bar Asn J, 7/79; Patricia Paul Newsom (auth), Betty Wells: Veteran Washington Reporter, Am Artist, 11/84. *Mem:* Artists Equity Asn (pres, Md Chap, 66-68); Arts and Humanities Comn, Virginia Beach, Va; Nat Acad TV Arts & Sci. *Media:* Multimedia, Oil. *Res:* Nature. *Specialty:* Fine Art; Story telling art. *Interests:* Swimming; Ballroom dancing; Biking; the news. *Collection:* tropical scenes & semi-abstracts. *Publ:* Contribr, Designing and Making Mosaics, Davis, 71; Arts for Architecture, Dept Housing & Urban Develop, 73; illusr, Supreme Court on Nixon

Tapes, New York Times, US News & World Report, 74 & Newsweek, 10/77 & 12/77; cover, Am Bar Asn J, 3/77; cover design & illusr, Bryson B Rash's Footnote Washington, EPM Publ Inc, 83. *Dealer:* Mickey and Arlene Sego The Art-Cade Gallery 1321 Jamestown Rd 204 Williamsburg Va 23185. *Mailing Add:* 2180 Rosewell Dr Virginia Beach VA 23454

WELLS, CHARLES
SCULPTOR, PRINTMAKER
b New York, NY, Dec 24, 35. *Study:* Student, George Sch, Newton, Pa; Student, Amherst Col; Apprentice, Leonard Baskin, 61—64. *Work:* Represented in permanent collections Nat Mus Am Art, Wash, Whitney Mus, New York City, James A Michener Art Mus, La Salle Univ Art Mus, 2004. *Exhib:* Represented in permanent collections, Nat Portrait Gallery, Libr Congress, Mass Inst of Technol, Nat Acad of Design, New York City; group shows, at Brooklyn Mus Art, Whitney Mus, Spoleto Festival, Italy, Macedonian Mus of Modern Art, Thessaloniki, Greece, Amsterdam Concertgebouw, Corcoran Gallery. *Teaching:* With Am Sch, Rome, 1964-1965. *Awards:* Recipient Prix de Rome, 64, 3 gold medals, Nat Acad of Design Annual. *Mem:* Fel Am Acad, Rome; Nat Acad (assoc, 88, acad 94-). *Mailing Add:* PO Box 22 Washington Crossing PA 18977

WELLS, LYNTON
PAINTER
b Baltimore, Md, Oct 21, 40. *Study:* RI Sch Design, Providence, BFA, 62; Cranbrook Acad Art, Bloomfield Hills, Mich, MFA, 65. *Work:* Mus Mod Art, NY; Dallas Mus Fine Art, Tex; Henry Gallery, Washington; Walker Art Ctr, Minneapolis; Indianapolis Mus Art. *Exhib:* One-man shows, Andre Emmerich Gallery, NY, 75, Clair Copley, Los Angeles, 76, Droll/Kolbert Gallery, 78, Univ Wis-Eau Claire, 79, Sable-Castelli, Can, 85 & Mary Delahoyd Gallery, NY, 94, Post Gallery, Los Angeles, 2001; retrospective, Princeton Univ Art Mus, 79; Baron/Boisanté, NY, 92; Univ Nev, Las Vegas, 95; 109 Crosby St, NY, 2005; Jonathan Shorr Gallery, 2006. *Awards:* NY State Coun Arts, 73 & 77; Nat Endowment Arts Grant, 75. *Bibliog:* Bruce Boice (auth), article, Artforum, 5/73; Peter Bunnell (auth), catalogue, Princeton Univ, 79; Dave Hickey (auth), catalogue, Univ Nev, Las Vegas, 95; Dave Hickey (auth), catalog, Post Gallery, Los Angles, 2001. *Dealer:* Jonathon Shor 109 Crosby St NY NY 10013; Rebecca 1Bel Gallery North High St Columbus OH. *Mailing Add:* 307 W Broadway New York NY 10013

WELLS, MAC
PAINTER, EDUCATOR
b Cleveland, Ohio, Feb 3, 25. *Study:* Oberlin Col, BA, 48; Cooper Union, 48-49; also with Nahum Tschacbasov & Yasuo Kuniyoshi. *Work:* Denver Mus Art, Colo; Herron Mus Art, Indianapolis, Ind; Guggenheim Mus; Wadsworth Athenaeum, Hartford, Conn; Tides Inst, Eastport, Maine; and others. *Comn:* Three-dimensional card, Mus Mod Art, NY, 65. *Exhib:* One-man shows, Aegis Gallery, NY, 63, A M Sachs Gallery, NY, 65 & 67, Max Hutchinson Gallery, NY, 70 & 72, Susan Caldwell Gallery, NY, 75, Landmark Gallery, 79, 55 Mercer Gallery, NY, 81, Dwight Frederic Boyden Gallery, St Marys Col Md, 92, Rothko Found Award Exhib, Artist's Space, NY, 93; Hunter Col Times Square Gallery, 96; Art Sites Gallery, Greenport, NY, 2000, 2002; Mitchell Algus Gallery, NY, 2000; Ann Kolb Gallery, Easthampton, NY, 2000, 2002; Art Sites Gallery, Riverhead, NY, 2006. *Teaching:* Asst prof, gen studio, Hunter Col, 66-81, assoc prof, 81-90, prof, 90-95, ret; vis instr art, Purdue Univ, West Lafayette, Ind, spring 66; instr painting & design, Moore Col Art, Philadelphia, 66-72; instr painting, Skowhegan Sch Painting & Sculpture, Maine, 69. *Awards:* Yaddo fel, 64 & 65; Rothko Found Award, Exhibit Artists Space, NY, 93. *Bibliog:* New Talent, Art in Am, 7-8/65; Lucy Lippard (auth), New York letter, Art Int, 11/20/65; Laurie Anderson (auth), article, Art News, 1/71. *Mem:* Am Abstract Artists. *Media:* Multimedia. *Publ:* Mac Wells - Light into Being, Lucy Lippard, Et Al, the Art Gallery, Hunter Col, 96. *Dealer:* Mitchell Algus Gallery 511 W 25th St New York NY 10001; Art Sites Gallery East Main St Riverhead NY. *Mailing Add:* 500 Soundview Rd Orient NY 11957-1337

WELLS, MENTHE
PAINTER, SCULPTOR
b New York, NY, July 3, 42. *Study:* Univ Bridgeport, with Jennett Lam, BS, 63; Rutgers Univ, MA, 64; Univ Conn, DPED, 81, PhD(synaesthetics), 84; study with Michael Andrews, PhD(art/psychology). *Work:* Jane Voorhees Zimmerli Art Mus, New Brunswick, NJ; Eastern Conn State Univ; Univ Calif, Riverside; Univ Conn; Univ Bridgeport, Conn; and others. *Comn:* Thirty-two ft mural, Windsor Bd of Educ, Conn; Impressions (sight-sound intermedia), Enfield Bd of Educ & Wadsworth Atheneum Art Mus. *Exhib:* One-man show, Animated sculpture, Lutz Mus, Manchester, Conn, 79; Winter juried exhib, Bushnell Gallery, 80; invitational show, Bosham Gallery, Sussex, Eng, 84 & 85; Carlson Gallery, Arnold Bernhard Arts & Humanities Ctr, 88; Zimmerli Art Mus; Wadsworth Atheneum Art Mus; Fac Gallery; Sculpture, (ECOARTS) EcoArts Mus, 2002-2006. *Pos:* Dir, Acad Assoc, Beverly Hills. *Teaching:* Instr, synaesthetics, Wadsworth Atheneum, Art Mus, 69-76; instr sculpture, drawing & art hist, Manchester, Greater Hartford & Tunxis Col, 77-79; instr animated sculpture, Trinity Col & Skidmore Col. *Bibliog:* L Guica (auth), Animated sculpture-puppets lead the class, Hartford Courant, 8/14/77; L Margolies (auth), Carol Menthe soft sculpturist extraordinaire, Farmington Valley Herald, 3/39/79; and others. *Media:* Oil, Enamels; Granite Installation; Mixed. *Res:* Synaesthesia. *Publ:* Impressions Workshop, Sight Sound Intermedia, Arts in Soc. *Dealer:* Academic Assoc PO Box 325, Silver Springs, NV, 89429. *Mailing Add:* PO Box 3854 Fullerton CA 92634

WELPOTT, JACK WARREN
PHOTOGRAPHER, EDUCATOR
b Kansas City, Kans, Apr 27, 23. *Study:* Ind Univ, BS, 49, MS, 55, MFA, 59. *Work:* Mus Mod Art, NY; Bibliot Nat, Paris; Eastman House, Rochester, NY; Ctr Creative Photog, Tucson, Ariz; San Francisco Mus Art. *Exhib:* One-man shows, Eastman House, 66, Art Inst Chicago, 72, San Francisco Mus Art, 76, Univ Southern Calif, Los Angeles, 77, Univ Ore, 79 & Ctr Creative Photog, 79; Metrop Mus Art, NY. *Collection Arranged:* Artist as Teacher-Teacher as Artist, San Francisco Mus Art, 76. *Teaching:* Prof photog, San Francisco State Univ, 59-; vis prof, Univ Ariz, Tucson, 77; prof emer, San Francisco State Univ, 94-. *Awards:* Nat Endowment for Arts Fel, 79. *Bibliog:* Arthur Öllman (auth), Jack Welpott: Photographer, Vidio, 75. *Mem:* Friends Photog. *Publ:* Co-auth, Women and Other Visions, Morgan & Morgan, 75. *Dealer:* Barry Singer Gallery 11 Petaluma Blvd N Petaluma CA 94952. *Mailing Add:* PO Box 496 Inverness CA 94937

WELTER, COLE H
PAINTER, EDUCATOR
b Watertown, SDak, July 26, 52. *Study:* Univ Tex, Austin, with Bob Levers & Everett Spruce, BFA, 74, MFA, 76; Tex Tech Univ, with Gene Mittler & Bill Lockhart, PhD,89. *Work:* Huntington Gallery, Univ Tex, Austin; Anchorage Mus Hist Art, Alaska; San Antonio Mus Mod Art, Tex; Abilene Fine Arts Mus, Tex; Univ Alaska Anchorage Permanent Collection. *Comn:* Windows, First Christian Church, Anchorage, Alaska, 92. *Exhib:* 39th Ann Midyear Show, Butler Inst Am Art, Youngstown, Ohio, 75; 69th Ann Am Exhib, Newport Fine Arts Asn, RI, 76; 34th Ann Competition, Abilene Fine Arts Mus, Abilene, Tex, 76; 43rd Ann Competition, Abilene Fine Arts Mus, Tex, 87; 10th Ann Regional Exhib, McCormick Gallery, Midland Col, Tex, 87; Alaska '92, Alaska Visual Arts Ctr, 92; and others. *Pos:* Exec bd dir, Anchorage Mus Asn, 88-92; ed, Alaska J Art, 88-95; mem, NASAD comn on accreditation, 2001-2006. *Teaching:* Instr, design, Univ Tex, Austin, 75-76, Tex Tech Univ, 86-88; Chmn, Dept Art, painting, Univ Alaska Anchorage, 88-95; prof & dir, James Madison Univ, Sch Art & Art Hist, 95-2004, prof Art, James Madison Univ, 2004-. *Awards:* Fel, Ford Found, 75 & 76; Reston Prize, Nat Asn Schs Art & Design, 87; Distinguished Art Alumni Award, Tex Tech, 91 & 2004. *Bibliog:* Jan Ingram (auth), Exhibits make happy partners, 9/10/89 & Alaska 92 offers a fresh, bold view of state arts scene, 7/26/92, Anchorage Daily News. *Mem:* Col Art Asn. *Media:* Mixed-Media. *Publ:* Auth, Discipline based art education: not if, but where?, Design Arts Educ, 87; Art and Computers: is there room in the studio for both?, Design Arts Educ, 89; ed, Technological segregation: A peek through the looking glass at the rich and poor in an information age, Arts Educ Policy Review, 97. *Mailing Add:* James Madison Univ Sch Art & Art History Duke Hall MSC7101 Harrisonburg VA 22807

WELTZHEIMER, MARIE KASH See Kash, Marie (Marie Kash Weltzhemer)

WELU, JAMES A
MUSEUM DIRECTOR
b Dubuque, IA, Dec 15, 43. *Study:* Loras Col, BA, 1966; Univ Notre Dame, MA, 1967; Univ Notre Dame, MFA, 1968; Boston Univ, PhD, 1977. *Pos:* asst cur, Worcester Art Mu, Mass, 1974-76; assoc cur, 1976-80, instr, 1977-78, 80-81, chief cur, 1980-86, dir, 1986-. *Teaching:* Instr, St Mary-of-the-Woods (Ind) Col, 1968-70; Instr, Clark Univ, Worcester, 1980. *Awards:* Boston Univ grantee, 1973, Nat Educ Asn Mus' Prof grantee, 1976-81; Samuel H Kress Found fel, 1973; recipient Netherland-Am Found award Nether Found, 1973, Distinguished Alumni award Boston Univ Grad Sch, 1986. *Mem:* Historians Netherlandish Art, Northeast Mus Assoc, Am Asn Mus (accreditation comnr 2000-), Col Art Asn Am, Am Fedn Arts (trustee), Asn Art Mus Dirs (pres, 1999-2000, trustee). *Mailing Add:* Worcester Art Mus 55 Salisbury St Worcester MA 01609

WENDORF, RICHARD HAROLD
DIRECTOR
b Cedar Rapids, IA, Mar 17, 48. *Study:* Williams Col, BA, 70; Univ Oxford, Eng, PhB, 72; Princeton Univ, MA, 74; Princeton Univ, PhD, 76; Phi Beta Kappa. *Awards:* Res grantee Folger Shakespeare Libr, Wash, 1976; Nat Endowment of the Humanities res fel Newberry Libr, Chicago, 1988-89; Brit Accad, 2003. *Mem:* Am Soc 18th Century Studies (pres, Midwest reg soc 86); Mass Hist Soc, The Johnsonians (chmn, 94-95, 97-98); Nat Comt on Standards in Arts; Colonial Soc Mass; Am Antiquarian Soc. *Publ:* Auth: William Collins and Eighteenth-Century Eng Poetry 1981, The Elements of Life: Biog and Portrait Painting in Stuart and Georgian Eng, 1990, paperback edition, 1991, Sir Joshua Reynolds: The Painter in Society, 1996; editor: Articulate Images: The Sister Arts from Hogarth to Tennyson, 1983, Rare Book and Manuscript Libraries in the Twenty-First Century, 1993, (with Charles Ryskamp) The Works of William Collins, 1979; contribr essays in field; mem ed board Studies in 18th Century Culture, 1985-89, Word and Image, 1992-2000, Yale edition Writings of Samuel Johnson, Old-Time NE, 1996-99. *Mailing Add:* Boston Athenaeum 10 1/2 Beacon St Boston MA 02108-3777

WENGER, BRUCE EDWARD
PRINTMAKER, GRAPHIC ARTIST
b Grand Rapids, Mich, Mar 10, 1948. *Study:* Western Mich Univ, BA, 70; Ohio Univ, MFA, 73. *Work:* Grand Rapids Art Mus, Mich; US Info Agency, Washington, DC; Western Mich Univ Print Collection, Kalamazoo; Chicago Gallery, Univ Ill; Ohio Univ Print Collection, Athens. *Exhib:* 6th Biennial Paper & Clay Exhib, Memphis State Univ, Tenn, 87; LaGrange Nat XII, Chattahooche Valley Art Asn, Ga, 87; 7th Ann Faber Birren Color Award Show, Stamford, Conn, 87; 2nd Nat Juried Exhib, Viridian Gallery, NY, 88; 20th Nat Works on Paper Exhib, Minot State Col, NDak, 90; LaGrange Nat XVII, Chattahooche Valley Art Asn, Ga, 92; 10th Ann Maine/Maritime Flatworks Exhib, Univ Maine, Presque Isle, 92. *Teaching:* Asst prof studio art & art hist, Houghton Col, NY, 78-86, head dept art, 82-86; lectr in drawing & printmaking, Rochester Inst Technol, NY, 86-92 & asst prof 2D design, 92-2003. *Awards:* Purchase Award, Fourth Ann Maine Maritime Flat Work Exhib, Univ Presque Isle Maine, 86. *Mem:* Col Art Asn; The Print Club. *Media:* Computer Graphics. *Publ:* coauth, Design Dynamics: Integrating Design and Technology, Prentice-Hall, 2003. *Mailing Add:* PO Box 21 Fillmore NY 14735-0021

WENGER, JANE (B)
PHOTOGRAPHER, CONCEPTUAL ARTIST
b New York, NY, Jan 24, 44. *Study:* Alfred Univ, NY, BFA, 66; Ill Inst Technol, Chicago, 69; Univ Ill, Chicago, MFA, 80. *Work:* Mus Mod Art, NY; Mus Contemp Art, Chicago, Ill; Milwaukee Art Mus, Wis; Lehigh Univ, Bethlehem, Pa; Southern Ill Univ, Edwardsville. *Exhib:* One-person shows, Artemisia Gallery, Chicago, Ill, 76, Foto Gallery, NY, 78 & 80, Allen Frumkin Photographs, Chicago, Ill, 80, Mus Contemp Art, Chicago, Ill, 81, Milwaukee Art Mus, Wis, 82 & PS 1, NY, 82; Art in Chicago, 1945-1995, Mus Contemp Art, Chicago. *Teaching:* Instr photog, Univ Ill at Chicago, 75-90. *Awards:* Project Completion Grants, Ill Arts Coun, 79-83. *Bibliog:* Carole Harmel (auth), The dialectics of sexuality, New Art Examiner, 79; Lynne Warren (auth), Jane Wenger, Arts Mag, 3/81; Mary Jane Jacob (auth), Options 7, Jane Wenger: An Environmental Installation, Mus Contemp Art, 81. *Mem:* Soc Photog Educ. *Mailing Add:* 1509 N Wicker Park Chicago IL 60622

WENGROVITZ, JUDITH
PAINTER, INSTRUCTOR
b Brooklyn, NY, Jan 3, 31. *Study:* Hunter Col, New York, NY, with Dong Kingman, BA(art educ), 52; workshops with Frank Webb, Millard Sheets and Carlton Plummer. *Work:* Pen Arts Bldg, Washington; NIH, Bethesda, Md. *Comn:* Series of paintings of country musicians, Quality Inn, Nashville, Tenn, 80; Nat Bus Educator's Asn, Reston, Va, 82; IBM, Washington, 83; painting, comm by Judge Stanley Sporkin, Washington, 87 & 88; NIH Children's Inn, Bethesda, Md, 92 & 98. *Exhib:* Solo exhibs, Torpedo Factory, Alexandria, 88 & 97, 20th Century Gallery, Williamsburg, Va, 91 & Nat Inst Health Bethesda, Md, 94; Allied Artists Am 76 exhib, Nat Arts Club Galleries, NY, 89; traveling exhib, Southern Watercolor Soc, Japan, 89, Tex, 99; Int Exhib of Miniature Painters, Sculptors & Gravers Soc, Wash, 1996-2006; Va Watercolor Soc, 1980-2006. *Pos:* Layout artist, Woodward & Lothrop, Washington, 52-54; judge, Arts on the Lawn at Bellgrade, Richmond, Va, 96. *Teaching:* Instr drawing, design & painting, Judy Wengrovitz Sch Art, 62-2006; guest lectr painting, George Mason Univ, 94, Vienna Arts Soc, MeLean Arts Soc, Manassas Art Guild & Springfield Art Guild, 96-2003 & Brush & Pallete Club, Sanford, NC, 2003. *Awards:* Equal Merit award, Art League 2004; Excellence award, NLPW, Washington, DC, 2004; Mid Atlantic Watercolor Exhib, 2006. *Bibliog:* Kathryn Evans (auth), Springfield artist details in watercolor, Springfield Connection, 87; Daniel Seligson (auth), Wengrovitz: Matron of the Arts, The Connection, 4/98; Alice Ross (auth), Elan Mag, 4/03. *Mem:* Nat League Am Pen Women (NLAPW) (prog chmn, 2004-05, pres, 74-76); Va Watercolor Soc (pres, 88-); Washington Watercolor Soc; Southern Watercolor Soc; Springfield Art Guild (pres, 97-98). *Media:* Watercolor, Mixed Media. *Publ:* Best of Watercolor Places, 97, Best of Watercolor Textures, 98, Rockport Publ; The Artists Mag, 9/98; illusr book cover design Vital Signs of Poetry, NIH, Bethesda, Md, 99; Int Artist Mag, 4-5/2000; The Collected Best of Watercolor selected by Betty Lou Schlemm, 2002. *Dealer:* The Art League 105 N Union St Alexandria VA 22314. *Mailing Add:* 5220 Cather Rd Springfield VA 22151

WENTWORTH, ELAINE
PAINTER, ILLUSTRATOR
b Boston, Mass, June 16, 24. *Study:* Colorado Springs Fine Arts Ctr, painting with Boardman Robinson, 46; Sch Mus Fine Arts, Boston, printmaking with Ture Bentz & painting with Karl Zerbe, dipl, 50. *Work:* Farnsworth Mus Art, Rockland, Maine; Chase Fine Arts Mus, Utah State Univ, Logan; Ill State Univ Mus, Bloomington; Nat Shawmut Bank, Boston; Bk Illus, Mazza Collection of Children's Univ Findlay, Ohio; Mazza Mus, International Art from Picture Books, Univ Findlay, Ohio. *Exhib:* Rocky Mountain Nat Watermedia, Rocky Mountain Art Ctr, Golden, Colo, 80-82 & 85; New Eng Watercolors, Fitchburg Mus, Mass, 82; Allied Artists Am, Nat Arts Club, NY, 83 & 86; 12th Ann Watercolor West, Frye Mus, Seattle, 88; Brave Little Girls (traveling), Nat Mus Women Arts, Washington, DC, 95-98, Los Angeles Pub Libr Gallery, San Francisco Pub Libr Civic Ctr, Denver Pub Libr Gallery & Chicago Children's Mus, 95-98; and others. *Teaching:* Art instr design, painting, Art Inst Boston, 67-71; instr watercolor, private classes and workshops. *Awards:* Nat League Am Pen Women Best Show Gold Medal, Washington, 80; Gold Medal of Hon, New Eng Watercolor Soc, 86; CC Lowell Award, Nat Open Show, New Eng Watercolor Soc, Boston, 98; Acad Artists Asn National, Springfield, MA, 2002; Artists Profl League Award for watercolor, 2002. *Mem:* Artist mem Am Watercolor Soc; New England Watercolor Soc; Guild Boston Artists; Int Soc Marine Painters Inc; Oil Painters of Am. *Media:* Watercolor, Acrylic, Oil. *Publ:* Auth & illusr, Mission to Metlakatla, Houghton Mifflin, 68; coauth & illusr, Watercolor for All Seasons, North Light, 84; illusr, The Lighthouse Keeper's Daughter, Little Brown & Co, 87. *Dealer:* Peel Gallery of Art Box One Gallery Rd Danby VT 05739; llery PO Box 361 Kennebunkport ME; Alison Senning Dealer

WENTWORTH, JANET
PAINTER
b Norwell, Mass, May 5, 57. *Study:* Parsons Sch Design, New York, BFA, 80; Nat Acad Sch Fine Arts, New York, with Harvy Dinnerstein, 81-82; Art Students League, New York, with Harvy Dinnerstein, Ted Seth Jacobs & Frank Mason, 83-87; La Napoule Arts Found, France & Durham, NH, with Jack Beal, 85-86; Brooklyn Col, New York, with Philip Pearlstein & Lennert Anderson, MFA, 91; Sch Visual Arts, New York, cert(art educ), 92. *Work:* Art Students League Permanent Collection, NY. *Exhib:* Am Watercolor Soc Ann Exhib, Nat Acad Fine Arts, NY, 76; Pastel Soc Am Ann Exhib, Nat Arts Club, NY, 85; League Am Pen Women Ann Exhib, Copley Soc, Boston, 87; Choice, AIR Gallery, NY, 91; Nat Acad Design 167th Ann, Nat Acad Fine Arts, NY, 92. *Awards:* Bd Dirs Award, Pastel Soc Am, 84; Gold Medal Honor, Knickerbocker Artists, NY, 85; Cert Merit, Nat Acad Design 167th Ann, 92. *Mem:* Nat Asn Women Artists; Pastel Soc Am; NY Arts Group; Col Art Asn. *Media:* Pastel, Oil. *Dealer:* Harris Peel Box 1 Peel Gallery Rd Danby VT 05739. *Mailing Add:* 665 Kortwright Church Rd East Meredith NY 13757-1055

WENTWORTH, MURRAY JACKSON
PAINTER, INSTRUCTOR
b Boston, Mass, Jan 18, 27. *Study:* Art Inst Boston. *Work:* Farnsworth Mus Art, Rockland, Maine; Springfield Mus Art, Mo; First Nat Bank, Boston; DeCordova Mus, Lincoln, Mass; Utah State Univ, Logan. *Exhib:* Metrop Mus Art, NY, 66; Butler Inst Am Art, Youngstown, Ohio, 69; Brockton Fuller Mem Mus, Mass, 70; DeCordova Mus, Mass, 77; one-man shows, Farnsworth Mus, 72 & Guild of Boston Artists, 77 & 80; Rocky Mountain Nat Watercolor Exhib, 82; Nat Acad Design, NY. *Teaching:* Instr watercolor, pvt & watercolor workshops, 77-. *Awards:* Ranger Fund Purchase Prize, Nat Acad Design, 65; Nat Arts Club Bronze Medal Hon, 68; Am Watercolor Soc Bronze Medal Hon, 69. *Mem:* Allied Artists Am; New Eng Watercolor Soc (vpres, 71-); Guild Boston Artists; Nat Acad (assoc, 72, acad, 94-); Hudson Valley Art Asn. *Media:* Watercolor. *Publ:* Contribr, watercolor page, Am Artist Mag, 70; Watercolor for All Seasons, Northlight, Writers Digest Books. *Dealer:* Peel Gallery Danby VT; Guild Boston Artists 162 Newbury St Boston MA

WENZEL, JOAN ELLEN
ASSEMBLAGE ARTIST, SCULPTOR
Study: Syracuse Univ, 62-64; NY Univ, BS(painting), 66 & MA(painting), 76; Harvard Univ 66-67. *Work:* Skirball Mus Jewish Art, Los Angeles; Aldrich Mus Contemp Art, Ridgefield, Conn; City of Orlando, Fla. *Comn:* Multi-section wall structures, Prudential Life, Newark, NJ, 89, Citibank, NY, 87, Peerless Corp, Greenpoint, NY, 87, Nevele Hotel, Ellenville, NY, 88 & IBM Corp, NY, 90. *Exhib:* Approach, Avoidance Art in the Obsessive Idiom (with catalog), 81 & Off the Wall (with catalog), 85, Queens Mus, NY; solo exhibs, Gallery Yves Arman, NY, 82 & Helander Gallery, Palm Beach, Fla, 89 & 94; Kisch & Wenzel, SoHo Crt Visual Art, NY, 86; 10 Yrs of Collecting, Aldrich Mus Contemp Art, 86; Solo exhib, Albertson Peterson, Orlando, Fla, 92, Univ Jacksonville Art Mus, Fla, 93 & Admar Fine Art; and others. *Media:* Wood and Metal. *Dealer:* Albertson Peterson Gallery 329 Park Ave S Winter Park FL 32789; Helander Gallery 350 S County Rd Palm Beach FL 33480. *Mailing Add:* 2275 Ibis Isles Dr E Palm Beach FL 33480-5367

WERFEL, GINA S
PAINTER, EDUCATOR
b Brooklyn, NY, July 1, 51. *Study:* Kirkland Col, NY, with Elias Friedensohn, BA, 74; New York Studio Sch, with Mercedes Matter, Leland Bell & Andrew Forge, cert, 76; Columbia Univ, with David Lund, Leon Goldin & Jane Wilson, MFA, 79. *Exhib:* One-woman shows, Prince Street Gallery, NY, 80, 82, 85, 86, 89, 92, 94 & 98, Col Mus Art, Waterville, Maine, 89 & Maier Mus Art, Randolph-Macon Woman's Col, Lynchburg, Va, 92 & Monty Stabler Gallery, Birmingham, Ala, 93; two-person shows, Cong Sq Gallery, Portland, Maine & Colby Col Mus Art, Waterville, Maine, 81, 83 & 84 & Second St Gallery, Charlotteville, Va, 94 & Monty Stabler Gallery, Birmingham, Ala, 95; Drawings from Nature, Joan Whitney Payson Mus, Portland, Maine, 82; Maine Coast Artists Gallery, Rockport, 83, 87, & 90; Jersey City Mus, NJ, 86; Personal Views: Four Painters & Landscape, Plymouth State Col, NH; 30 Years of Drawing, NY Studio Sch; Contemp Landscape, Art Inst Boston, Mass; 3 Landscape Painters: Armstrong, Lewis & Werfel, Washington Art Asn, Conn, 99. *Pos:* Co-dir, NY Studio Sch, Paris, France, summers, 74 & 75; artist-in-residence, Va Ctr Creative Arts, Sweetbriar, 81, Rockefeller Found Ctr, Bellagio, Italy, 84 & Djerassi Found, Woodside, Calif, 86; vis artist, Washington & Lee Univ, Lexington, Va, 94 & Fairbanks Art Asn, Alaska, 94. *Teaching:* Assoc prof art, Colby Col, Waterville, Maine, 80-91; chair & prof, Randolph-Macon Woman's Col, Lynchburg, Va, 91-97; head & prof, Dept Art & Art Hist, Univ Conn, Storrs. *Bibliog:* Carl Little (auth), Gina Werfel at the Colby Mus, Art in Am, 10/89; David Little & Arnold Skolnick (auth), Paintings of Maine, NY, 91; John Driscoll & Arnold Skolnick (auth), The Artist & the American Landscape, First Glance Bks, 98. *Mem:* Col Art Asn. *Media:* Oil. *Dealer:* Prince Street Gallery 121 Wooster St New York NY 10012. *Mailing Add:* 2855 Mallorca Ln Davis CA 95616-6579

WERGER, ART(HUR) LAWRENCE
PRINTMAKER, EDUCATOR
b Ridgewood, NJ, Dec, 4, 55. *Study:* RI Sch Design, BFA, 78; Univ Wis, Madison, with Warrington Colescott, MFA, 82. *Work:* High Mus Art, Atlanta, Ga; Boston Pub Libr; Brooklyn Mus, NY; Philadelphia Mus Art, Pa; Mus Fine Arts, Boston. *Exhib:* Southeast Seven 9, Southeastern Ctr Contemp Art, Winston-Salem, NC, 86; Georgia Printmakers (with catalog), High Mus Art, Atlanta, 86; 10 Yrs of Southeast Seven, Southeastern Ctr Contemp Art, 87-88; Fact/Fiction/Fantasy: Recent Narrative Art in the Southeast, Univ Tenn, Knoxville, 87-88; Colorprint USA Update 88, Mus of Tex Tech Univ, 88; Art Werger: In Print, Macon Mus Arts & Sci, 88; Technique is not always cheap: Extraordinary Printmaking, Art & Sci Ctr, Statesville, NC, 89; solo exhibs, Peterson Hall Gallery, SGa Col, Douglas, 90, Overview, Gertrude Herbert Inst Art, Augusta, Ga, 91, The Graphic Narrative, Alexander Best Gallery, Jacksonville State Univ, Fla, 92, Chattahoochee Valley Art Mus, La Grange, Ga, 92, Middle Tenn State Univ, Murfreesboro, 92 & Prints, The Theater Arts Gallery, Greenville, NC, 97; Southern Printmakers 90, Southern Graphic Coun, Traveling Exhib, 90-91; The Graphic Narrative, Shelton State Community Col, Tuscaloosa, Ala, 90; Overview, NGa Col, Dahlonega, 91, Carriage Wks Gallery, Ga Coun Arts, Atlanta, 93 & Davidson Gallery, Seattle, Wash, 96; Man/Woman: Different Perspectives, N Arts Ctr, Atlanta, Ga, 91; Images 1990: A Portfolio of Thirty Six Prints, Davis Gallery, Idaho State Univ, Pocatello, 91, Merwin Gallery, Ill & Wesleyan Univ, 92; Temporary Positions, E Gallery, Porter Auditorium, Wesleyan Col, Macon, Ga, 92; Combined Talents, Fla Nat Exhib, Fla State Univ, Tallahassee, 92; Consumenta '91, Nuremberg, Ger, 92; Casual Observations, John Marlor Arts Ctr, Milledgeville, Ga, 93, Madison/Morgan Cult Ctr, Ga, 94 & Stephen F Austin Univ, Nacoqdoches, Tex, 96; Recent Works, S Vt Art Ctr, Manchester, Vermont, 94, Halsey Gallery, Col Charleston, SC, 94, Stone & Press Gallery, New Orleans, La, 94 & Columbia Col, SC, 94; Recent

Works on Paper, Fanny Garver Gallery, Madison, Wis, 95 & 96; Printmaking Invitational, Ball State Mus Art, Ball State Univ, Muncie, Ind, 98-99; Beneath the Surface, Five Am Printmakers, St Mary's Univ, Winona, Minn, 98; Common Ground, Am Print Alliance, Roanoke Col, Salem, Va, Univ SColo, Pueblo, Lankershim Arts Ctr, Gallery N Hollywood, Calif & Iowa Wesleyan Col, Mt Pleasant, 99; 12th Norwegian Int Print Trienale, Fredrikstad, Norway, 99; Recent Impressions, Wesleyan Col, Macon, Ga, 96. *Teaching:* Assoc prof graphics & print, Wesleyan Col, 82-, chmn, Visual Art Area, 85-, Fine Art Dept, 82- & prof art, 82-. *Awards:* Southern Arts Fed/Nat Endowment Arts Regional Fel, 92; Grant, State of Ga, 93; 2nd Place Award, 17th Ann Hoyt Nat Art Show, Hoyt Inst Fine Arts, New Castle, Pa, 98. *Bibliog:* Patrick E White (auth), Passionate Attention, Southeast Seven 9, 86. *Mem:* Col Art Asn; Southern Graphics Coun; Los Angeles Printmaking Soc; Philadelphia Print Club. *Media:* Etching. *Dealer:* Eve Mannes Gallery Atlanta GA; Wenninger Graphics Boston MA. *Mailing Add:* 8245 Rock Riffle Rd Athens OH 45701-8823

WERNER, DONALD (LEWIS)
COLLAGE ARTIST, PAINTER
b Fresno, Calif, Feb 2, 29. *Study:* Fresno State Col, BA, 52, with Adolf & Ella Odorfer & Jane Gale; Chouinard Art Inst, Los Angeles; costuming with Majorie Best. *Work:* Fresno Art Mus, Calif; Hudson River Mus, Yonkers, NY; Mus Am Indian, Nat Mus Am Indian, Smithsonian Inst. *Comn:* Collage murals, NY World's Fair; The Ancestors: Native Artisans of the Americas (exhib & graphic design), US Custom House, New York, 79. *Exhib:* Solo exhibs, Gallery 84, NY, 59-75, 79, 82 & 84-96, Fresno Art Mus, 67 & 79, Focus Gallery, San Francisco, 68, Hudson River Mus, 69 & 72 & St Paul Civic Ctr, Minn, 70; Through the Lens: Time, Space, Matter, Rye Art Ctr, NY, 98. *Collection Arranged:* Mus of Am Indian, New York, 78; Echoes of the Drums, US Custom House, New York, 78; The Ancestors, Peking, China, 81-82; Star Gods, Am Mus Natural Hist, New York, 82-83; Nat Mus Am Indian, Smithsonian Inst; Fresno Art Mus, Calif. *Pos:* Display designer, Seventeen Mag, 11 yrs; mus artist & designer, Hudson River Mus, 68-75, Mus of Am Indian, New York, 78-90 & Nat Mus Am Indian, Smithsonian Inst, New York, 90-94. *Awards:* First Prize for Watercolor, Fresno Art Ctr, 60; artist-in-residence, Fresno Art Mus, 67, 74, 94. *Bibliog:* Robert Beeching (dir), Theatrical Displays and Display Techniques (film), 69 & A China Diary (film), 85, Scope Prod, Calif; Bicycles and Dragons (exhib catalog), Am Mus Natural Hist, 85 & Great Neck Libr, 86, NY. *Mem:* Am Mus Asn; Photog Adminrs Inc. *Media:* Watercolor; Photography. *Publ:* Auth, photogr & designer, Reflections of Winter: Holt, Rhinehart & Winston, 78; bk designer, The Peaceable Kingdom, Macmillan, 79; designer (with Eagle Glance), Mus Am Indian, 82; Americans in Venice, Coe Kerr, 83; The Stuff of Dreams, Mus Am Indian, New York, 86. *Mailing Add:* 156 President St Apt 1 Brooklyn NY 11231

WERNER, FRANK ROBERT
ENVIRONMENTAL ARTIST, WRITER
b New York, NY, Sept 16, 36; US citizen. *Study:* Univ Idaho, BGS, 84. *Work:* Latah Co His Mu; Hospicio Cabanas Cult Inst, Guadalahara, Jalisco, Mex; St Joseph Regional Med Ctr, Lewiston, Idaho. *Exhib:* solo exhibs, Nicholaysen Art Mus, Casper,Wyo, 93, Port Angeles Fine Arts Ctr, Port Angeles, Wash, 93, Beall Park Art Ctr, Bozeman, Vt, 94, San Juan Col Art Gallery, Farmington, NMex, 94, Maryhill Mus Art, Goldendale, Wash, 94, Central Utah Art Ctr, 95 & Cooper Village Mus & Arts Ctr, Mont, 96; Please Touch the Art, Missoula Art Mus, Mont, 93; Idaho Triennial Exhib, Boise Art Mus, 95; Pendelton Art Ctr, Ore, 98; Corvallis Arts Ctr, Oreg, 99; Hecho Em Idaho, Hospicio Cabanas Cult Inst, Guadalajara, Jalisco, Mex, 99; Lewis-Clark Ctr for Arts & History, Lewiston, Idaho, 2000. *Pos:* Auth, Art Matters, Quaterly Column, Wildfowl Carving & Collecting Mag, 90-96; mem, Idaho migratory Waterfowl Art Comn, 95. *Awards:* Award, Idaho Comn Arts Fel, 87 & 92; Mayor's Award for Individual Excellence in the Arts, City of Moscow. *Bibliog:* Spokane Chronicle/Rev, 5/27/81 & 8/6/89; ICA Folk Art Exhib (catalog), 84 (in Arabic, 86); Casper Star-Tribune, Casper, Wyo, 1/93. *Media:* Idaho White Pine, Polychrome Sculpture. *Res:* Re-defining traditional art in post modern culture. *Publ:* Idaho Wildlife Mag, 9/85 & 10/85

WERNER, HOWARD
SCULPTOR
b Deal, NJ, July 27, 51. *Study:* Rochester Inst Technol, BFA, 77; Sch Am Craftsmen. *Work:* Sch Am Craftsmen, Rochester, NY; Ariz State Univ Mus Fine Art, Tempe; Am Craft Mus, NY. *Exhib:* Okun Gallery, Santate, 92; Sybarus Gallery, Royal Oak, Mich, 92; Joann Rapp Gallery, Scottsdale, 93; Snyderman Gallery, 93; solo shows, Sneiderman Gallery, Philadelphia, 96 & Rapp Gallery, Scottsdale, Ariz, 96-97; Expressions in Wood, Oakland Mus, Calif, 97; Oakland Mus Art, Calif, 97; Expressions in Wood: The Wornick Collection, Am Craft Mus, NY, 98. *Pos:* Resident, Art Park, Lewiston, NY, 75-77; traveling residency, NY State Parks & Recreation Cult Program, 76; vis artist, Nat Endowment Arts Omni Int, Atlanta, Ga, 77; resident, Peters Valley, Layton, NJ, 77-78. *Teaching:* Instr sculpture & furniture design, Peters Valley, Layton, NJ, 77-82; instr sculpture, Haywood Tech Inst, NC, 78; instr sculpture, Keane Col, NJ, 81; instr workshop, State Univ NY, New Paltz, 83; adj prof, Ariz State Univ, Tempe, 86-88. *Awards:* NY State Fel Grant, 87 & 93; Nat Endowment Arts, 88; Fel for the Arts, NY State, 92. *Bibliog:* Review, Craft Horizons, 78; John Kelsey (auth), New Handmade Furniture, Fine Woodworking, 79; Michael Stone (auth), review, New York Times, 10/81. *Mem:* Am Craft Coun; Peters Valley. *Media:* Wood. *Publ:* Coauth, Carving, Fine Woodworking, 77. *Dealer:* Sneiderman Gallery 303 Cherry St Philadelphia PA; Rapp Gallery Marshall Way Scottsdale AZ. *Mailing Add:* PO Box 430 Shokan NY 12481

WERNER VAUGHN, SALLE
PAINTER, ILLUMINATOR
Work: San Francisco Mus Mod Art, Calif; Akron Art Inst, Ohio; Bridwell Libr, Southern Methodist Univ, Dallas; Mus Fine Art, Boston; Mus Fine Art, Houston; Metrop Mus Art, NY; Mus Modern Art, Moscow; and others. *Exhib:* Biennial Exhib Painting & Sculpture Show, Whitney Mus, NY, 73; one-man show, Tyler Mus Art, Tex, 73; Contemp Watercolors, Akron Art Inst, Ohio, Indianapolis, Ind & Rochester, NY, 76; Helen Serger, La Boetie Inc, NY, 77; Carus Gallery, NY, 79. *Teaching:* Founder experimental art, Art Involvement & Motivation, 70-; founder, Crystal Press, 79. *Bibliog:* Patsy Swank (auth), Salle Werner (film), Dallas Educ TV, 72; Arch Am Art, Smithsonian Inst. *Media:* Watercolor, Oil; Tempera. *Mailing Add:* 4618 Blossom St Houston TX 77007

WERNESS, HOPE B
HISTORIAN
b Del Rio, Tex, Feb 10, 43. *Pos:* Dir, Univ Gallery, 82-87. *Teaching:* Vis lectr art hist, San Jose State Univ, Calif, 76-77; asst prof art hist, Calif State Col, Stanislaus, Turlock, Calif, 77-81, assoc prof & chair, 81-86, prof, 86-. *Awards:* Nat Endowment Humanities Summer Seminar, 80. *Mem:* Col Art Asn. *Res:* Nineteenth century art history, specializing in Van Gogh, twentieth century art history; pre-Columbian and primitive art. *Mailing Add:* 913 Dianne Dr Turlock CA 95380

WERT, NED OLIVER
EDUCATOR, PAINTER - ACRYLIC, OIL
b Millersburg, Pa, May 26, 36. *Study:* Indiana Univ of Pa, BA(art educ), 58; Pa State Univ, MEd(art), 64; Kent State Univ, with Alex Katz, Jim Melchert & Jack Tworkov, 70. *Work:* Southern Alleghenies Mus Art, Loretto, Pa; Pittsburgh Plate Glass Corp, Alcoa Corp, Pittsburgh, Pa; Am Int Sch, Dusseldorf, Ger; Pa State Mus, Harrisburg, Pa; Blue Cross, Blue Shield. *Exhib:* Assoc Artists Pittsburgh, Carnegie Mus Art; Butler Inst Art; Three Rivers Festival, Pittsburgh, Pa; La Mostra CAS, Lucca, Italy; Triennial Invitational, Southern Alleghenies Mus Art, Loretto, Pa; Noho Gallery, NY; Six Am Painters, Nancy, France; Lynden Gallery, Elizabethtown, Pa. *Collection Arranged:* 25 Exhibs, Univ Mus, Indiana, Pa. *Pos:* Dir, Univ Mus, Indiana, Pa, 88-96, retired; Eastern vpres, Nat Art Educ Asn; pres, Pa Art Educ Asn. *Teaching:* Art, Elizabethtown Area Sch Dist, Pa, 58 70; prof emer painting, Ind Univ Pa, 70-88. *Awards:* Best of Show, Fourth Ann Exhib, Westmoreland Mus, 82; Jurors Award, Assoc Artists Pittsburgh, Carnegie Mus Art, Pittsburgh, Pa, 82 & 97; Outstanding Educator, Nat Art Educ Asn, 86; Distinguished Alumnus, Indiana Univ of Pa, 88. *Mem:* Asn Artists Pittsburgh; Found IUP Presidents Coun; Allied Artists Johnstown; Millersburg Hist Soc. *Media:* Acrylic, oil pastel. *Collection:* Contemporary artists in Western Pennsylvania; Folk Art, American Mexican origins, circa 1850 to present; Latin America & South Africian Folk Art. *Publ:* Coauth, Multiple image and sound: Motivation for creative activity, Art Teacher Mag, fall 74; Colored light and shadow: A stimulus for creative movement, Pa J Physical Educ, winter 74; Multi-media: Motivation for the arts and basic education, Learning Resources Mag, 4/75; Readings: Developing arts programs for handicapped students, Pa Dept Educ, 82. *Dealer:* Lynden Gallery Elizabethtown PA. *Mailing Add:* PO Box 1 Brush Valley PA 15720

WERTHEIMER, ALAIN
COLLECTOR
Pos: Chmn, Chanel Inc, 1974-; co-owner, Chateau Canon, Margaux, 1994-, Chateau Rausan Segla. *Awards:* Named one of World's Richest People, Forbes Mag, 1999 2004; named Top 200 Collectors, ARTnews Mag, 2004. *Collection:* Modern Art. *Mailing Add:* Chanel SA 135 Ave Charles de Gaulle 92521 Neuilly-sur-Seine France

WESCHLER, ANITA
SCULPTOR, PAINTER
b New York, NY. *Study:* Horace Mann Sch, grad, Le Grand Verger, Lausanne, Switz; Parsons Sch Design, grad; Nat Acad Design; Pa Acad Fine Arts, with Albert Laessle; Art Students League, with William Zorach; Columbia Univ; Barnes Found. *Work:* Whitney Mus Am Art, Amherst Univ; Brandeis Univ; Metrop Mus Art; Yale Univ; Pa Acad Fine Arts & Univ Pa; Michael Wolfson Found, Miami, Fla; plus other pvt collections. *Comn:* Sculpture, US Treas Dept, US Post Off, Elkin, NC; seven life-size portrait heads (bronze), Inst for Achievement of Human Potential, Philadelphia; seven bronze replicas Inst Achievement of Human Potential, Italy & Brazil, 90. *Exhib:* Whitney Mus Am Art; Nat Inst Arts & Lett; Metrop Mus Art; Philadelphia Mus Art; Mus Mod Art; Jewish Mus; Storm King Ctr; over 40 solo shows nationwide; Los Angeles Co Mus Art; Lehigh Univ; and others. *Pos:* Deleg to US Comt Int Asn Art; deleg, Fine Arts Fedn New York. *Teaching:* Var lect-demonstrations, 89;. *Awards:* Prizes, Corcoran Gallery Art, Montclair Art Mus & San Francisco Mus Art; Audubon Artists Medal of Honor; MacDowell Colony & Yaddo Fels. *Bibliog:* Var critical reviews in newspapers & art press. *Mem:* Fedn Mod Painters & Sculptors; Nat Asn Women Artists; Artist Craftsmen NY; Sculptors Guild; Nat Mus Women Arts. *Media:* Multimedia; Synthetic Gazes, Plastic Resins. *Publ:* Auth, Nightshade, Colony Press; A Sculptor's Summary, Mag of Art. *Dealer:* Berman/Daferner 568 Broadway New York NY 10012; Portraits Inc 945 Park Ave New York NY 10028

WESLEY, ERIC
SCULPTOR
Study: UCLA, BA. *Work:* Snapshot: New Art From Los Angeles, UCLA Hammer Mus, 2001; Mus Contemp Art, Miami, 2001; Santa Monica Mus Art, 2001; Freestyle, Studio Mus, Harlem, NY, 2001; Craft & Folk Art Mus, Luckman Gallery, Los Angeles, 2004; Whitney Biennial, Whitney Mus Am Art, 2004. *Exhib:* One-man shows, Camper, China Art Objects Galleries, Los Angeles, 99, 2000 & 2004, Two Story Clocktower, CalTech, Pasadena, Calif, 2001, Meyer Riegger Galerie, Karlsruhe, 2002, Metro Pictures, NY, 2002, Galleria Franco Noero, Turin, 2002, Art Basel, 2003,

Pico Youth Ctr; group shows, Brent Petersen Gallery, Los Angeles, 98, I-Candy, Rosamund Felsen Gallery, Santa Monica, Calif, 98, LA Edge Festival, 99, Young & Dumb, ACME, Los Angeles, 2000, Drive: Power, Progress, Desire, Govett Brewster Art Gallery, New Plymouth, New Zealand, 2001, Circles 3: Silver Lake Crossings, Zentrum Fur Kunst und Mediatechnologie, Karlsruhe, Ger, 2001, Purloined, Artists Space, NY, 2001, Drive By: Nine Artists from Los Angeles, Reynolds Gallery, Va, 2002, Adios Pendejos, Oficina Para Proyectos de Arte, Guadelajara, Mex, 2003, New Space! New Show!, Galeria Franco Noero, Italy, 2003, More Boots = Many Routes, Transmisson Gallery, Glasgow, Scotland, 2003, Fade (1990-2003), Luckman Gallery, Los Angeles, 2004, Whitney Biennial, Whitney Mus Am Art, 2004. *Mailing Add:* c/o MOCA Pacific Design Ctr 8687 Melrose Ave West Hollywood CA 90069

WESLEY, JOHN
PAINTER
b Los Angeles, Calif, Nov 25, 28. *Work:* Albright-Knox Art Gallery, Buffalo, NY; Mus Mod Art, Whitney Mus Am Art, NY; Portland Art Mus, Ore; Univ Ky, Lexington; Chinati Found, Marfa, Tex; Speed Mus, Louisville, Ky; Detroit Inst Arts; Fogg Art Mus, Cambridge, Mass; Hirshhorn Mus and Sculpture Garden, Washington; and others. *Exhib:* one-man shows, (13) Robert Elkon Gallery, NY, 63-83, Univ Rochester, 74, Carl Solway, Cincinnati, 74, 84 & 89, Reinhard Onnasch Galerie, West Berlin, 82, 101 Spring Street Gallery, 87 & 93, Chinati Found, Marfa, Tex, 90 & 98, Drew Gallery, Canterbury, eng, 90, fiction/nonfiction (catalogue), NY, 91, Galerie Marc Jancou, Zurch, 93, Jose Freire Fine Art, NY, 94, Galerie Haus Schneider, Karlsruhe, Ger, 96, Jessica Fredericks Gallery, NY, 96, 98 & 99, Danese Gallery, NY, 98, Daniel Weinberg Gallery, Los Angeles, 2000, Tex Gallery, Houston, 2000, PSI Contemp Art Ctr, Long Island City, 2000 & Fogg Art Mus, Harvard Univ, Cambridge, Mass, 2001 & many others; Kunstverein, Ludwisburg, Ger, 93; Mus Am Art Pa Acad Fine Arts, Philadelphia, 98; Galerie Nacht St Stephen, Vienna, 99; Newhouse Ctr Contemp Art, NY, 2000; Ludwig Gallery, Houston, 2001; the Menil Collection, Houston, 2001. *Teaching:* Instr, Sch Visual Arts, New York, 70-73. *Awards:* Guggenheim Fel, 76; Nat Endowment Arts, 89. *Bibliog:* Hannah Green (auth), A journal in praise of the art of John Wesley, In: The Unmuzzled Ox, spring 74; Ken Johnson (auth), Troubled toons, Art in Am, 2/93; Martin Hentschel, John Yau & Hannah Green (auths), John Wesley Paintings 1963-1992 (catalog esseys), Daad Galerie, 93; Wayne Koestenbaum, Best of 2000, Artforum, 12/2000; Michael Kimmelman (auth), Comforting funny outlandishness that sticks to its own logic, The New York Times, 12/2000

WESSEL, FRED W
PAINTER, PRINTMAKER
b Amityville, NY, June 14, 46. *Study:* Syracuse Univ, BFA, 68; Univ Mass, MFA, 76. *Work:* Mus Mod Art, NY; Brooklyn Mus, NY; Philadelphia Mus Art, Pa; Libr Cong, Washington; De Cordova Mus Art, Lincoln, Mass. *Comn:* Watercolor with tempera painting, Marriott Hotels, Washington, 86; gold leaf prints, Cutter Financial Ctr, Hartford, Conn, 87; watercolor with tempera painting, Univ Mass Fine Arts Ctr Theater, 90; portrait, Pres Univ Hartford, 98. *Exhib:* Hanga Print Ann, Tokyo Metrop Mus Art, Tokyo, Japan, 86; Int Prints, Fine Arts Ctr, Seoul, Korea, 87; Philadelphia Col Art, 87; Schneider Mus Art, Ashland, Ore, 87; one-person show, Printworks Gallery, Chicago, Ill, 88, Stonepress Gallery, Seattle, Wash, 88, Arden Gallery, Boston, Mass, 93, 95, 97 & 98 Springfield Mus Fine Arts, 94; Sherry French Gallery, 97 & 98. *Pos:* Artist advisory bd, Offset Inst, 85-. *Teaching:* Instr printmaking, Univ Mass, 76-77; prof printmaking, Hartford Art Sch, Univ Hartford, 77-. *Awards:* Purchase Award, Gallery Tolbuchin, Bulgaria, 85; Juror's Award, Boston Printmaking 39th Ann, Strathmore Paper, 86; Color Print USA, Tex Tech Univ, 86. *Bibliog:* Feature article, Am Artist Mag, 4/95. *Mem:* Philadelphia Print Club. *Media:* Tempera; Lithography. *Publ:* Auth, Hartford print workshop, Print News, 80; illusr, Motherlode of gamefish, Country J, 86; North America's Freshwater Fishing Book, Charles Scribners & Sons, 88. *Dealer:* Arden Gallery Newbury St Boston MA 02115; Sherry French Gallery 57th St New York NY. *Mailing Add:* 4 Edgewood Terr Northampton MA 01060

WESSEL, HENRY
PHOTOGRAPHER
b Teaneck, NJ, July 28, 42. *Study:* Pa State Univ, BA, 66; State Univ NY, Buffalo, Visual Studies Workshop, MFA, 72. *Work:* Mus Mod Art, Metrop Mus Art, NY; Nat Gallery Can, Ottawa; Int Mus Photog, George Eastman House, Rochester, NY; Philadelphia Mus Art; Los Angeles Co Mus Art, Mus Contemp Art, Los Angeles. *Exhib:* Mus Mod Art, NY; Nat Gallery Can, Ottawa; Contemp Photog V, 70 & New Topographics, 75, George Eastman House Traveling Exhibs; one-man shows, Mus Mod Art, NY, 73, Pa State Univ, 74, Fraenkel Gallery, San Francisco, 81, Charles Cowles Gallery, NY, 81 & Mus Contemp Art, Los Angeles, Calif, 98; and many others. *Teaching:* Instr, Pa State Univ, 67-69, Ctr Eye, Aspen, Colo, 73, Univ Calif, Berkeley, 73 & San Francisco Art Inst, 73-; asst prof, San Francisco State Univ, Calif, 74; vis artist, Univ Calif, Davis, 77; vis lectr, Calif Col Arts & Crafts, 77. *Awards:* Guggenheim Fel, 71 & 78; Nat Endowment Arts Grant, 75, 77 & 78. *Bibliog:* Articles, Art News, 9/73, Camera, Lucerne, Switz, 5/74 & Art in Am, 1/76; Artforum, 2/90; Art News, 5/92. *Publ:* Contribr, Looking at Photographs, 73 & Mirrors and windows, 79, Mus Mod Art, New York, 79; Nude, Harper & Row, 80; Pleasures & Terrors of Domestic Comfort, Moma, NY. *Dealer:* Rena Bransten Gallery 77 Geary St San Francisco CA 94108; Luisotti Gallery 2525 Michigan Ave Bergamot Station Santa Monica CA 94108. *Mailing Add:* PO Box 475 Richmond CA 94807

WESSER, YVONNE D
PAINTER, CONCEPTUAL ARTIST
b London, Eng, Jan 28, 35. *Study:* Art Students League, 71-81; Hunter Col; studied anatomy with Robert Beverly Hale & modern painting with Theodoros Stamos. *Work:* Barsky Hosp, Saigon, Vietnam; Art Students League, NY; Nat Art Mus, West Haven, Conn; Univ New Haven; Smithsonian Instn; Mr & Mrs Greene of Greene Art Gallery, guilford, Conn; many others. *Comn:* Portrait, State Dept, Saigon, Vietnam. *Exhib:* Preconception figure, Col Design, Ames, Iowa, 88; Award Exhib, Stuhr Mus, Grand Island, Nebr, 90 & Govt Mansion, Lincoln, Nebr, 90; Third Nat Juried Competition, Viridian Gallery, NY, 90; group shows, Corner Gallery, World Trade Ctr, NY, 91, Multi Media Gallery W B'Way, Soho, NY, 91, Columbus Art Gallery, Columbus, Neb, 91, Cork Gallery, Lincoln Ctr, NY, 92, Small Works Exhib, Scoharie Co Arts Coun, Cobbleskill, NY, 92, Hall of Fame from NY-France in Contemp Art Scene, Cannon House Rotunda, Washington, DC, 92 & Environmental Perspectives, Erb Mem Union, Univ Ore, Eugene, 92; solo exhibs, Pleiades Gallery, 92 & Space Lab Gallery, Huntington, NY, 92, Stehle Reed Gallery, Tex, Greene Art Gallery, Guilford, Conn, Plaza Gallery, Binghampton, NY, Discovery Art Gallery, Glen Cover, NY, 84, 85, Gallery 84, NY, Lida Gallery, NY, 82, 34th St Theater Gallery, NY, 80, Little Carnegie Art Gallery, NY, Main St Gallery, Brewster, NY, 75; and others. *Awards:* Elmer Perkin Award, Linda Shearer Mus Mod Art, 86; Second Prize, Greater Midwest Int Exhib IV, Richard Koshalek Mus Contemp Art, Los Angeles, 90; Prize F, Int Competition, Agora Gallery, NY, 92; Stuhr Mus, Grand Island; Mus Modern Art, San Francisco, Calif; 1st Prize, Whitney Mus Contemp Art, NY; Mus Contemp Art, Los Angeles, Calif; Mus Modern Art, NY; Heckscher Mus, Huntington, NY; Juror's Merit Award, Alexandria Mus, 86; 2d prize, Mus Contemp Art, Los Angeles, 86. *Mem:* Burr Artists; Nat League Pen Women; Am Registry of Outstanding Profls. *Media:* Oil. *Dealer:* Greene Art Gallery Guilford CT; Dealers Choice

WEST, ALICE CLARE
PAINTER
b Detroit, Mich, Oct 5, 51. *Study:* San Francisco State Univ, with Robert Bechtle & Richard Mclean, BA, 75; Univ Calif, Berkeley, with Joan Brown, Chris Brown, Elmer Bischoff, David Simpson & Anne Healy, MFA, 86. *Work:* Levinson Brothers Inc, San Francisco; SAP Am, San Jose, Calif; Del Mondo LLC, San Francisco. *Exhib:* Recipients of MFA Show, Univ Art Mus, Berkeley, Calif, 87; 5th Int Exhibition, Rolando Castellon Contemp Art Gallery, San Francisco, 87; Art & the Woman Artist, Clary-Miner Gallery, Buffal, NY, 89; Registered, Installed & Nailed, Calif Mus Art, Santa Rose, Calif, 91; Sixty-Eighth Crocker Kingsley Ann, Crocker Art Mus, Sacramento, 94; Print & Draw: Biennial, Triton Mus Art, Santa Clara, Calif, 95; California Small Works, Calif Mus Art, Santa Rosa, Calif, 96. *Pos:* libr asst, UC Berkeley, 84-86; libr asst, Acad Art Col Libr, 89-90. *Teaching:* tchr, Art Sch, 88-89; artist-in-residence, Exploratorium, 76-78; teaching asst, UC Berkeley, 85. *Awards:* Richmond Art Ctr for Juror's Prize, 83; John Michael Welcome Prize, Univ Calif, Berkeley, 85; Calif Small Works Exhib for Juror's Prize, 96. *Bibliog:* Mark Van Proyen (auth), Drama of Space and Surface, Artweek, 4/2/88; Mary Hull-Webster (auth), Primarily Paint, Artweek, 3/4/93; Michael Schwager (auth), Registered, Installed and Nailed, Art Muse, summer 97. *Media:* Acrylic; Drawing. *Publ:* Contribr Univ Art Mus Calendar, Univ Calif Berkeley, 87; contribr Contemporary Women Artists, Bo-Tree Press, 87; contribr Five Fingers Review, McNaughton & Gunn, spring 98. *Dealer:* San Francisco Mus Modern Art Artists Gallery Bldg Fort Mason Center San Francisco Calif 94123. *Mailing Add:* 4047 Cesar Chavez St San Francisco CA 94131

WEST, ANNIE
SCULPTOR, PHOTOGRAPHER
Study: DEUG,1ére, Univ Provence, Aix-Marseilles, France, 84; Univ Mich, Ann Arbor, BA, 86; Art Inst Chicago, grad travel grant, 90, univ fac award, 90, merit scholar, 91, Isabella A Brown award, 90, merit scholar, 91, Isabella A Brown traveling fel, 92, MFA(interdisciplinary media), 92; Whitney Mus Am Art independent study prog, Van Lier Fel, 93. *Work:* San Francisco Mus Mod Art; Visual Studies Workshop, Rochester, NY; Mus Fine Arts Houston; Photog Collection & Joan Flasch Artists' Bk Collection, Art Inst Chicago; Franklin Furnace Arch, Mus Mod Art, NY. *Exhib:* Whitney Mus Am Art, 93; Aldrich Mus Contemp Art, Ridgefield, Conn, 95; Show & Tell, Soho Biennial, Gallery 450, NY, 95; Bank Job, Washington Proj Arts, 95; Multiple Mediations, Colgate Univ Art Gallery, NY, 95; Longwood Arts Proj Benefit, PPOW Gallery, NY, 95; The Cult of Terror, ATA Gallery, San Francisco, 96. *Pos:* Studio residency, Banff Ctr Arts, Alta, 94, Sculpture Space, Utica, NY, 95, Ucross Found, Wyo, 96 & Kala Inst, Calif, 97. *Teaching:* Vis artist, Temistocles 44, Mexico City, 94. *Awards:* Art Matters Grant, NY, 94; Ernst Haas Photog Fel, Anderson Ranch, 95; Artist Fel, Nat Endowment Arts, 95-96. *Bibliog:* William Zimmer (auth), Adventurous homeowners, modern look, NY Times, 95; Molly Hankwitz (auth), Renew: Moving the message, Art Papers, 95; Lori Gray (auth), Girl Germ's exhib works to keep it clean, Chicago Tribune, 95. *Dealer:* Sculpture Space 12 Gates St Utica NY 13502

WEST, E GORDON
PAINTER
b Salt Lake City, Utah, June 1, 33. *Study:* Art Inst Chicago; Univ Louisville, BS, 55. *Work:* McNay Art Mus, San Antonio, Univ Louisville, Ky; Tex A&M Univ, College Station, Tex. *Exhib:* Watercolor USA; Tex Watercolor Soc; Am Watercolor Soc; Nat Watercolor Soc; and many others. *Awards:* Artist of Year, San Antonio Art League, 85; and many others. *Mem:* Signature mem Am Watercolor Soc; signature mem Tex Watercolor Soc; San Antonio Watercolor Group; signature mem Nat Watercolor Soc; signature mem Western Fedn Watercolor. *Media:* Watercolor. *Publ:* Tex Hill Country, 81, Pecos to Rio Grande, 83, Tex A & M Press; Watercolor Magic, 3/95 & 10/95; The Artists' Mag, 4/95 & 6/96; The Best of Watercolor, 95 & No 2, 97. *Mailing Add:* 2910 Briarcroft St San Antonio TX 78217-3801

WEST, PETER
PAINTER, PRINTMAKER
b Washington, Pa, July 14, 53. *Study:* Tyler Sch Art, Temple Univ, Philadelphia, Pa, BFA, 75; Ohio Univ, Athens, MFA, 77. *Work:* Lyndon Baines Johnson Presidential Libr, Austin, Tex; War Memorial Mus Va, Newport News; Penn State Univ, McKeesport; Westinghouse Corp, Pittsburgh, Pa; Jessop Steel Corp, Washington, Pa.

Comn: Sculpture (stainless steel), City of Washington, Pa, 80; sculpture (stainless steel), Jessop Steel Corp, Washington, Pa, 82; wall installation, Westinghouse Corp, Pittsburgh, Pa, 83; mural, War Memorial Mus Va, Newport News, 91. *Exhib:* Alternative Mus, NY, 90; War Mem Mus Va, Newport News, 90; Winterfest Invitational, Westmoreland Mus Art, Greensburg, Pa, 90; Foster Goldstrom Gallery, NY, 91; Foster Goldstrom Gallery, NY, 92; Lyndon Baines Johnson Presidential Libr, Austin, Tex, 92-93; Pa Coun Arts Visual Arts Fels traveling Exhib, 93-94; Illumination Show, Pittsburgh, Pa, 93; Gallery G, Pittsburgh, Pa, 93; Pittsburgh Ctr Arts, Assoc Gallery, Pa, 94; Washington & Jefferson Col, Washington, Pa, 94. *Teaching:* Assoc prof studio arts, Bethany Col, WVa, 81-84; consult/lectr, Badger Air-Brush Co, 82- & Learn Shops, Intensified Educ Workshop, 84-. *Awards:* Visual Artists Fel Grant/Painting, Pa Coun Arts, 91; Achievement Award/Acrylics, Am Artist Mag, 92; Buncher Family Found Award, Asn Artists of Pittsburgh Ann Exhib. *Bibliog:* Hedy O'Beil (auth), article, Arts Magazine, 76; Robert Paschal, Robert Anderson (coauth), Art of the Dot, Van Nostrand Reinhold, 85; Am Artist Mag, 92. *Mem:* Assoc Artists Pittsburgh; Group A-Pittsburgh; Pittsburgh Ctr Arts. *Media:* Acrylic, Silkscreen. *Publ:* Auth, Step by Step Airbrushing, Techniques, Tools, Materials, Foster Art Series, 86. *Dealer:* Gallery G 211 9th St Pittsburgh PA

WEST, RICHARD VINCENT
MUSEUM DIRECTOR, HISTORIAN
b Prague, Czech, Nov 26, 34; US citizen. *Study:* Univ Calif, Santa Barbara, BA(with highest honors), 61; Akad Bildenden Kuenste, Vienna, with Wotruba, 61-62; Univ Calif, Berkeley, MA(art hist), 65; Mus Mgt Inst, 81. *Collection Arranged:* Section d'Or (auth, catalog), 67-68; Language of the Print (auth, catalog), 68-69; Rockwell Kent: The Early Years (auth, catalog), 69; Howard Warshaw: A Decade of Murals (auth, catalog), 72; Pre-Rembrandtists (auth, catalog), 74; Munich & Am Realism (auth, catalog), 78; An Enkindled Eye: The Paintings of Rockwell Kent (auth, catalog), 85; Orbis Pictus: The Prints of Oskar Kokoschka (ed catalog) 87; Standing in the Tempest: Painters of the Hungarian Avant-Garde, 1908-1930 (auth, catalog), 91; America in Art (auth, catalog), 91; A Significant Story: American Painting and Decorative Arts from the MXM Karolik Collections, 93; A Bounty of Flowers: Masterpieces of American Floral Painting, 94; Rounding the Mark: 150 Years of Treasures from the New York Yacht Club, 1844-1994, Newport Art Mus, RI, 94; Old Master Existentialism: Recent Paintings by Odd Nerdrum, Frye Art Mus, Seattle, 97; Contemporary American Marine Art: American Society of Marine Artists, Frye Art Mus & Cummer Mus Art & Gardens, 97; Circle of Lyon: 7 French Painters of Reality, Frye Art Mus, 98; Children of the Yellow Kid: The Evolution of the American Comic Strip, Frye Art Mus & San Francisco Cartoon Art Mus, 98-99; Representing LA: Contemporary Pictorial Art from Southern California, Frye Art Mus & Art Mus of S Tex, 2000-2001. *Pos:* Cur, Cleveland Art Mus, 65-66; Albright-Knox Art Gallery, 66-67; dir, Bowdoin Col Mus Art, 67-72, Crocker Art Mus, 73-83, Santa Barbara Mus Art, 83-91, Newport Art Mus, 92-94, Frye Art Mus, 95-. *Teaching:* Lectr, Bowdoin Col, Univ Calif, Davis & Calif State Univ, Sacramento. *Awards:* Ford Fel, 65-67; Smithsonian Fel, 71. *Mem:* Am Asn Mus; Western Asn Art Mus (pres, 75-77); Calif Asn Mus (vpres, 86-91); Col Art Asn; Int Coun Mus. *Publ:* Coauth, Language of the Print, Random House, 68; Walker Art Building Murals, 72; Rockwell Kent Reconsidered, Am Art Rev, 12/77; An enkindled eye: Paintings of Rockwell Kent, 85; auth, Rockwell Kent (monograph), Abrams (in prep). *Mailing Add:* c/o Frye Art Mus 704 Terry Ave Seattle WA 98104

WEST, VIRGINIA M
FIBER ARTIST, WRITER
b Boston, Mass. *Study:* Goucher Col; Philadelphia Col Textiles; Md Inst Col Art. *Work:* Baltimore Mus Art; Del Art Mus; Hilton Hotel, Baltimore, Md; Goucher Col Kraushaar Gallery, Baltimore; Peterson Howell & Heather, Hunt Valley, Md. *Comn:* Ark curtain, Shaarei Zion Synagogue, Baltimore, Md, 68; tapestry, The Center Club, Baltimore, 80; fiber artwork, Community Ctr, Baltimore, 80; fiber murals, Lucayan Beach Hotel, Freeport, The Bahamas, 82; other commns for pvt collections. *Exhib:* Contemp Crafts Exhib, Del Art Mus, Wilmington, 70-75; Md Artists Exhib, Baltimore Mus Art, 70 & 75; Fibre Art Am Artists, Ball State Univ, 72; Mus Contemp Crafts, NY, 72; Galleria d'Assisi, Italy, 79. *Pos:* Conference keynote speaker; writer, Shuttle, Spindle & Dyepot, 72-, Fiber Arts, 78-81, Handwoven, 80- & Weavers, 85-. *Teaching:* Instr weaving, fiber sculpture & textile design, Md Inst Col Art, 69-; instr sem & workshops, US, Can, New Zealand & Australia. *Awards:* First Award, Creative Crafts Biennial, 68; Purchase Award, Baltimore Mus Art, 70; Purchase Award, Del Art Mus, 75; and others. *Mem:* Baltimore Weavers Guild (pre, 59-61); Md Crafts Coun (pres, 62-64); Am Crafts Coun (secy, 69-72). *Media:* Fiber. *Res:* Basketry styles & techniques, original designs for handwoven clothing. *Publ:* Auth, The Virginia West Swatch Book, 85-86; Finishing Touches for the Handweaver (rev ed), 87; Designer Diagonals, A Portfolio of Patterns for Bias Clothing, 88; A Cut Above, 92

WESTERVELT, ROBERT F
HISTORIAN, CERAMIST
b New York, NY, Apr 6, 28. *Study:* Williams Col, AB; Claremont Grad Sch, MFA; Emory Univ, PhD. *Work:* Delgado Mus, New Orleans; High Mus of Atlanta, Ga; Frank Wingate Collection of Contemp Am Ceramics, Syracuse Univ; Scripps Col Collection, Claremont, Calif. *Comn:* Ceramic decoration (with Joseph Amisano, archit), Visual Arts Bldg, Univ Ga, 59. *Exhib:* Georgia Artists, Smithsonian Inst, Washington, DC, 64; Scripps Col Invitational, Claremont, 69. *Pos:* Consult, Ctr Study Southern Cult, Univ Miss, 81-85. *Teaching:* Assoc prof hist Am art, Agnes Scott Col, Decatur, Ga, 57-81; prof art, Gainesville Col, Ga, 83-96. *Awards:* Cash grant, Atlanta Arts Festival, 64; Purchase Awards, Delgado Mus & Arts Festival of Atlanta; Ga Coun Arts Grant, 81-82. *Mem:* Ga Designer Craftsman; Southeastern Col Art Asn; Ga Mountain Crafts. *Media:* Stoneware, Porcelain. *Res:* 19th century American painting and demotic culture. *Interests:* In process; illustrated computer book-An Insiders View of Art. *Publ:* Auth, The Whig painter of Missouri, Am Art J, Kennedy Gallery, 70

WESTFALL, CAROL D
ARTIST, EDUCATOR
b Everett, Pa, Sept 7, 38. *Study:* RI Sch of Design, BFA; Maryland Inst, Col of Art, MFA. *Work:* Del Mus of Art, Wilmington; NJ State Mus, Trenton; Michael Carson Productions, NY; PD 100, Architects, Mexico City; Zimmerli Mus, Newark Pub Libr; and others. *Comn:* Nine batiks, R F Kennedy Family Collection, 70 & three batiks, L B Johnson Family Collection, 70, Washington Gallery of Art, DC. *Exhib:* Washington Co Mus, Hagerstown, Md, 72; Del Mus of Art, Wilmington, 73; Baltimore Mus of Art, Md, 74; 7th Biennial of Tapestry, Mus Contonal des Beaux Arts, Lausanne, Switz, 76; Auditorium Gallery, NJ State Mus, Trenton, 75; Mus of Art, Carnegie Inst Int, Pittsburgh, Pa, 76; Mus of Contemp Crafts, NY, 76 & 87; Textile Mus, Wash, DC, 86; Bermuda Arts Centre, 87; Gryphon Gallery, Melbourne, Australia, 88; one-woman shows, Conde Gallery, Inst Allende, Mex, 75, NJ State Mus, 76, Florence Duhl Gallery, NY, 76, Am Ctr, New Delhi, India, 8a, Ruth Kaufman Gallery, NY, 81; Gallery/Gallery, Kyoto, Japan, 92. *Teaching:* Instr fibers & fabrics, Md Inst, Baltimore, 68-73; asst prof fibres & fabrics, Montclair State Col, NJ, 73-79, assoc prof, 79-88, prof, 88-; guest assoc prof, Teachers Col, Columbia Univ, NY, 77-87 & Sch Am Craftsmen, Rochester Inst Technol, 77 & 86. *Awards:* Morton & Sophie Macht Found Award, Baltimore Mus of Art, 72; Levi Sculpture Award, Baltimore Mus of Art, 74; Governor's Purchase Award, NJ Biennial, State of NJ, 75; Indo-Am Fel, 80-81; Master Print Award, Rutgers Ctr Innovative Printmaking, 88; and others. *Bibliog:* Articles in Crafts Horizons, 69-77; Shuttle, Spindle & Dyepot, 77-85; Ars Textrina, 86-96. *Mem:* Handweavers Guild of Am; Am Crafts Coun; NJ State Coun on the Arts, Artists in Schs Prog; NY Rug Soc; Ars Textrina (bd mem). *Media:* Mixed. *Publ:* Coauth, Plaiting Step by Step, Watson-Guptill, 76. *Mailing Add:* Montclair State Univ Dept Fine Arts Upper Montclair NJ 07043

WESTFALL, STEPHEN V R
PAINTER, CRITIC
b Schenectady, NY, 1953. *Study:* Univ Calif, Santa Barbara, MFA, 78. *Work:* Art Mus, Univ Calif, Santa Barbara; Baltimore Mus Art, Md; Munson Procter-Williams Inst, Utica, NY; Albertina Mus, Vienna. *Exhib:* One-man exhibs, Galerie Zurcher, Paris, 97, 98, Belk Gallery at Western Carolina Univ, 99, Galerie Paal, Munich, Ger, 99, Lennon Weinberg, NY, 99, 00, 01, Colgate Univ, Hamilton, NY, 00, St Gallen, Switz, 02; Compliments, Educ Alliance, Ernest Rubenstein Gallery, NY, 99; OM, Dorsky Gallery, NY, 99; The Aldrich Mus Contemp Art, Ridgefield, Conn, 99; Abstraction and Immanence, Hunter Col/Times Square Gallery, NY, 01; Beauty Without Regret, Bellas Artes Gallery, Santa Fe NMex, 01; Nat Acad Design Mus, New York City, 02; The Richard A and Rissa W Grossman Gallery, Lafayette Col, Easton, Pa, 02; and others. *Collection Arranged:* Albertina Mus, Vienna; Baltimore Mus Art; Munson Proctor-Williams Inst, Utica; Univ Art Mus, Univ Calif at Santa Barbara; La Mus Mod Art, Humlebaek, Denmark. *Pos:* Contribr, Artweek, 76-79 & Art in Am, Arts & Flash Art mags, currently. *Teaching:* Vis artist, Ohio State Univ, 81; teacher painting, Sch Visual Arts & Cooper Union, New York, 88. *Awards:* NY State Coun Arts, 86 & 88; Fel, Nat Endowment Arts, 87, 89 & 93. *Bibliog:* Meghan Dailey (auth), Stephen Westfall, TimeOut, 5/01; Mario Naves (auth), Stephen Westfall, Still Kicking Ass, The New York Observer, 5/01; Edith Newhall (auth), All the Right Moves, New York Mag, 5/01; Michaël Amy, Stephen Westfall at Lennon, Weinberg, Art in Am, 11/01; Kim Levin (auth), Voice Choices: Stephen Westfall, The Village Voice, 3/30/99; and others. *Media:* Acrylic, Oil. *Dealer:* Lennon Weinberg 560 Broadway New York NY 10012-3945

WESTHEIMER , ESTHER
SCULPTOR
b Poland. *Study:* studies, Montreal Mus Fine Arts, Quebec, Can, 1958-63; studies, Int Acad, Austria; studies, Acad Belle Arte, Florence; Loyola Montreal, BA, 1973; Goddard Col, MA, 1975. *Work:* Reaching & Melee/Football (bronze), Douglas Hosp, Verdun, Can; Airborn & Family, City Place, West Palm Beach, Fla; Airborn (bronze), Civic Ctr Lib, Livermore, Calif; Water Babies, Royal Palm Plaza; Democracy/Primavera (bronze), city hall, Fukuoka, Japan; Hakone Open Air Mus, Tokyo. *Comn:* Merle with Ribbon II (bronze), comn by Govt of Quebec, Montreal Casino; monumental sculpture of Count & Countess de Hoernle (corten steel, in progress), comn by Countess Henrietta de Hoernle, Mizner Park, Boca Raton, Fla; bust of Rita Hobbs (bronze). *Exhib:* Boca Pointe Country Club, Boca Raton, Fla, 1997, 98, 99, 2000 & 2001; J & W Gallery, New Hope, Pa, 1998 & 99; Yvan Methot Gallery, Sydney, Australia; one-woman show, Ritz-Carlton Hotel, Sydney, Australia, 2000; D'Adamo/Hill Gallery, Seattle, 2001. *Teaching:* prof drawing, painting & sculpture, Loyola Col, Montreal, 70-74. *Awards:* Govt of Can grant for exhib, Singapore, 1994; B'nai B'rith Int Arts award, 1997; best sculpture for Expressions 4, Mountain Lake PBS show, 1999; numerous others. *Bibliog:* Sandra Giannahasio (auth), Forma e crescita nella scultura di Wertheimer, Trevi Editori, 76; film, Achievers, CBC, 90; Roberta Sandler (auth), Sculpting life's energy, Simply the Best, 12/2000. *Mem:* Int Sculpture Ctr; Canadian Sculpture Soc; Mus Art (Fort Lauderdale); Norton Mus (West Palm Beach); Boca Raton Mus Art; Nat Soc Arts & Letters. *Media:* Bronze, Steel, Metal, Cast. *Res:* Research with epoxy and bronze powder; Thixatropic application on wine armature; Larger than life size. *Publ:* contribr articles to, Peak Mag, 95, "B" Mag, 5/2002, Simply Best Mag, 12/2002, Boca Life Mag, 2003. *Dealer:* Bal Harbor Art Gallery Bal Harbor Fla; Sher Gallery, Miami, Fla; Joy Gallery, Key West Fla; CIMA Gallery, West Palm Beach, Fla; West End Gallery, Montreal, Can; Charles Hecht Galleries, Tarzana and La Jolla, Calif. *Mailing Add:* 6507 Brava Way Boca Raton FL 33433

WESTIN, ROBERT H
HISTORIAN
b St Paul, Minn, Jan 11, 46. *Study:* Univ Minn, BA, 68; Pa State Univ, MA, 70, PhD, 78; Birbeck Col, Univ London, with Sir Nikolas Pevsner & Sir John Summerson. *Collection Arranged:* Figurative Drawings from Windsor Castle of the Roman Baroque; Collection of Her Majesty the Queen; Carlo Maratti and His Contemporaries

(coauth, catalog), Mus Art, Pa State Univ, 75. *Teaching:* Asst prof Renaissance-Baroque art hist, Ariz State Univ, Tempe, 73-78; assoc prof art, Univ Fla, Gainesville, 78-. *Awards:* Nat Defense Educ Art Title IV, US Govt, 71-72; Ariz State Univ Fac Fel, 74. *Mem:* Col Art Asn; Mid-Am Col Art; Nat Coun Art Adminr; SE Col Art Conf; Southeastern Am Soc Eighteenth Century Studies. *Res:* Collections of Metropolitan Museum of New York, Philadelphia Museum of Art and the collection of Janos Scholz, Cooper-Hewitt Union; Roman Baroque sculpture and Michelangelo. *Publ:* Auth, Antonio Raggi's Death of St Cecilia, Art Bull 74; co auth, Contributions to the late chronology of Giuseppe Mazzuoli, Burlington Mag, 74; auth, Ars Mohendi tradition and the visualization of death in Seventeenth Century Roman Baroque sculpture, Int J Death Educ, 80; coauth, Carlo Maratti and Camillo Rusconi: Two new portrait medallions, Burlington Mag, 80. *Mailing Add:* Univ Fla Dept Art 302 FAC Gainesville FL 32611

WESTLAKE, MERLE T, JR
ARCHITECT
Study: Carnegie Inst Tech, BArch; Cranbrook Acad of Art, MArch and Urban Design. *Mem:* Fel, Am Inst of Archits; Nat Acad (assoc, 90, acad, 94-). *Publ:* Auth: Josiah Fox (1763-1847), 2001; contribr, articles to Pa Mag of Hist and Biography, to Am. Neptune, numerous archit jous

WESTLUND, HARRY E
PUBLISHER, DEALER
b Chicago, Ill, Nov 20, 41. *Study:* Calif State Col, Long Beach, BA, 67; Tamarind Inst, Albuquerque, Master Printer cert, 70. *Work:* Pasadena Mus, Calif; Gruenwald Found, Univ Calif, Los Angeles; Mus Mod Art, NY, Los Angeles Co Mus Art, Los Angeles; Tamarind Inst Collection, Univ NMex. *Exhib:* Eight Tamarind Printers, Motel Gallery, Albuquerque, Nmex; New Multiples, San Diego; Art of the Master Printer, Robinson Galleries, Houston, Tex; Collectors Exhib, Starline Gallery, Albuquerque, 78; Bramante Gallery, Walla Walla, Wash, 80. *Pos:* Shop mgr, Lakeside Studios, Mich, 71; mgr, Tamarind Publ, Tamarind Inst, 72-75; litho/silkscreen staff printer, Cirrue Ed, Hollywood, Calif, 75-76; dir, Serigraphics Custom Silkscreen Workshop, Albuquerque, 76-84; gallery mgr, Rie Munoz Ltd, Juneau, Alaska, 84-85; owner, Halibut Fine Arts, Juneau, Alaska, 85-87; picture framer, Legacy Framing, Albuquerque, NMex, 87-88; owner, Centipede Custom Serigraph, Albuquerque, NMex, 88-91, Westlund Arts, 93-. *Teaching:* Instr silkscreen, Univ NMex, 78; numerous workshops at many univ from 74-87. *Specialty:* Publishing, custom printing, silkscreen process. *Collection:* Contemporary; Old Master. *Publ:* Auth, Polymer Reversal Technique as Applied to Zinc Plates, Tamarind, 71

WESTMORELAND, TERESA D
DESIGNER
b Comanche, Tex, Feb 1, 70. *Study:* Tarlton State Univ, BS, 96. *Exhib:* Solo show, Colletiva Works, Tarlton State Univ Longdon Cult & Educ Ctr, Grandbury, Tex, 98. *Pos:* Dir & cur, Bernards Mill Art Mus, 93-96. *Media:* Jewelry. *Collection:* Western art & bronzes; works by Amy Miers Jackson, Robert Summers & Jack Bryant. *Publ:* Anthologies, Vol I, 95. *Mailing Add:* c/o Shimmer Jewelry 1313 Paluxy Rd Granbury TX 76048-5663

WESTPHALEN, OLAV
SCULPTOR
b Hamburg, Ger, 1963. *Study:* Fachhochschule fur Gestaltung, Hamburg, Ger, MA, 90; Univ Calif San Diego, MFA, 93. *Work:* End Papers, Neuberger Mus Art, NY, 2000; Whitney Biennial, Whitney Mus Am Art, NY, 2004. *Exhib:* group shows, ACME Gallery, Santa Monica, Calif, 96, Kunstverein Kassel, Ger, 97, Yerba Buena Ctr Arts, 97, Apex Art, NY, 99, Fido, Hunter Col Gallery, NY, 2000, Greater NY; New Art in NY Now, PS 1 Contemp Art Ctr, Long Island City, NY, 2000; one-man shows, Swiss Inst, NY, 2001, Mus Liljewalchs, IASPIS, Stockholm, 2001, Michael Neff Gallery, Frankfurt, 2002, Maccarone Inc, NY, 2002, Sculpture Ctr, NY, 2003, Galerie Georges-Philippe & Nathalie Vallois, Paris, 2004; Out of Bounds, Luckman Gallery, Calif State Univ, Los Angeles, 2001; Televisions, Kunsthalle Wien, Austria, 2001; After Effect, Centre d'Art Neuchatel, Switz, 2001. *Mailing Add:* c/o Maccarone Inc 45 Canal St New York NY 10002

WESTWATER, ANGELA KING
ART DEALER, EDITOR
b Columbus, Ohio, July 6, 42. *Study:* Smith Col, BA; NY Univ, MA. *Pos:* Asst dir, Ctr Int Studies, NY Univ, 67-69; res assoc, Inst Govt & ed, Ga Govt Rev, Univ Ga, 69-71; managing ed, Artforum, 72-75; trustee, Louis Comfort Tiffany Found, pres, 80-; vis comt, Smith Col, Mus Art; partner, Sperone Westwater Inc, NY, 75-. *Mem:* Art Dealers Asn Am (vp 2000-). *Specialty:* Contemporary painting and sculpture. *Mailing Add:* Sperone Westwater Inc 415 W 13 St New York NY 10014

WETENHALL, JOHN
MUSEUM DIRECTOR
b Jun 1, 57. *Study:* cum laude, Dartmouth Col, AB, 1979; Williams Col, Williamstown, Mass, MA, 1982; Stanford Univ, MA, 1985, PhD, 1988; Vanderbilt Univ, MBA, 1999. *Pos:* Cur, painting and sculpture Birmingham (Alabama) Mus Art, 1989-95; dir, Checkwood Mus Art, Nashville, 1995-2001; exec dir, John and Mable Ringling Mus Art, Sarasota, Fla, 2001-; founder, Thomas Art Projects, Birmingham, 1992-95; Carell Woodland Sculpture Trail, Nashville, 1996-99; consult, Vietnam Women's Mem Proj, Wash, 1988-89. *Teaching:* Lectr, Santa Clara (Calif) Univ, 1985; fel, Smithsonian Inst, Wash, 1986-87, 88-89; Univ Minn, Minneapolis, 1988; Univ, Southern Calif Pub. Art Prog, 1991; dean, Fla State Univ, 2001-. *Awards:* Lyndon Baines Johnson Found Moody Travel grantee, 1986; John F Kennedy Libr Found grantee, 1986, Inst Mus and Libr Servs grantee; B Gerald Cantor fel, 1986; Nat Endowment for the Arts grantee, 1991; Recipient Award of Excellence Tenn Asn Mus, 1996, 2001; Gold and Silver medals for educ prog Southeastern Mus Conf. *Mem:* Am Teachers Asn of the Martial Arts (sensei), Rotary (Paul Harris fel), Kiwanis, Beta Gamma Sigma, Asn Art Mus Dir; Sarasota Chamber Commerce (bd); Sarasota Convention & Vistors Bureau (bd). *Publ:* Auth: (with Karal Ann Marling) Iwo Jima: Monuments, Memories and the Am Hero, 1991, (with David Cass) (catalogue) Italian Paintings, 1850-1910, 1982; editor: (catalogue) Splendors of the Am West, 1990; contribr articles to prof jours.; appearance in Am. Masters: Alexander Calder, PBS, 1998. *Mailing Add:* Ringling Mus Art 5401 Bay Shore Dr Sarasota FL 34243

WETHINGTON, WILMA
PAINTER, INSTRUCTOR
b Clinton, Iowa, Apr 15, 18. *Study:* Marshall Univ, Huntington, WVa; Wichita State Univ; also with Mario Cooper, John Pike, Dale Meyers, Charles R Kinghan, Tom Hill, Clayton Henri Staples, Robert E Wood, Robert Wade, Joe Bohler, Jim Wilcox & others. *Work:* Wichita State Univ, Kans; Episcopal Diocese Kans, Topeka; Smithsonian Inst, Washington; US Fed Bldg, Wichita, Kans; Off Secy Transportation, Washington; Off Sen Nancy Kassebaum, Washington; US Fed Bldg, Kans City. *Comn:* Portrait, Hon Richard Rogers, 90; portrait, Hon Dale Saffels, 91; portrait, Hon Earl E O'Conner, 92; portrait, Miss Am (Debbie Bryant), Gov Kans; portrait, Miss USA (Kelly McCarthy), City Wichita, 92; Hon John Pearson, 99, and others. *Exhib:* Salmagundi Club, NY, 85, 86, 2000; Air & Space Mus, Washington; Southern Watercolor Soc; Am Watercolor Soc; Pastel Soc West Coast; Nat Watercolor Soc, Okla; Wichita Ctr for Arts. *Pos:* Owner, Accent Frames & Gallery, 74-79; com artist & illustr, Boeing Airplane Co & McCormick-Armstrong Printing Co, Wichita. *Teaching:* Pvt art instr, Wichita, Kans, 50-; instr painting, McConnell Air Base, Wichita, spring 73; instr painting, portraiture & drawing, Wichita Art Asn, 81-; painting workshops, Kans, Colo & NMex. *Awards:* First Award in Watercolor, Okla Mus Art, 75; Best of Show, 2nd Scottsdale Artist Ann Show, Scottsdale Artist League, 93; Best Show, Kingman, Kans, 93; and 75 other awards; Best of Show, NLAPW, Fayetteville, Ark, 98. *Mem:* Am Watercolor Soc (assoc mem); Pastel Soc Kans; Kans Watercolor Soc (sig mem); Southern Watercolor Soc; Nat Asn Am Pen Women; Pastel Soc Am (sig mem); Oil Painters Am; Kans Acad Oil Painters. *Media:* Pastel, Watercolor. *Publ:* Wichita pizzazz, 84: Smithsonian Book of Flight & The Best of Oil Paintings, Rockport Press. *Mailing Add:* 2 Linden Dr Wichita KS 67206

WETHINGTON-HADLEY, WILMA ZELLA See Wethington, Wilma

WETHLI, MARK
PAINTER, EDUCATOR
b Westfield, NY, Nov 9, 49. *Study:* Univ Miami, Fla, BFA, 71, MFA, 73. *Work:* Metrop Mus Art, NY; Portland Mus Art, Maine; Ark Arts Ctr, Little Rock; DeCordova Mus Art, Lincoln, Mass; Farnsworth Mus Art, Rockland, Maine. *Exhib:* Biennial, Whitney Mus Am Art, NY, 75; Am Drawings in Black & White, Brooklyn Mus Art, NY, 80; solo exhibs, Koplin Gallery, Los Angeles, 85 & 87; DeCordova Mus Art, 89; Portland Mus Art, Maine, 89, Tatistcheff & Co, NY, 92, 95 & 97 & Icon Contemp Art, Brunswick, Maine, 96; Reinventing Realism, Everhart Mus, Scranton, Pa, 96; Md Inst Col Art, 96; ICON Contemp Art, Brunswick, Maine, 96; Farnsworth Art Mus, Rockland, Maine, 96; Re-Presenting Representation, Arnot Art Mus, Elmira, 97; Drawings IV, Koplin Gallery, Los Angeles, 98; Drawing from Perception II, Wright State Univ Art Galleries, Dayton, 98; After Dark, Maine Coast Artists, Rockport, 98; Portland Mus Art Biennial, Maine, 98; and others. *Teaching:* Instr, Barry Col, Fla, 74; asst prof art, Univ Northern Iowa, Cedar Falls, 76-78 & Calif State Univ, Long Beach, 78-85; assoc prof art, Calif State Univ, Long Beach, 84-85; prof, chair, Bowdoin Col, Brunswick, Maine, 85-. *Awards:* Fels, Nat Endowment Arts, 74, MacDowell Colony, 83 & Rockefeller Found, 88. *Bibliog:* Haines Sprunt Tate (auth), New Farnesworth show explores harmony & dissonance, Maine Times, 4/11/96; Bernie Monegain (auth), Abstract or real, two Brunswick artists challenge a couple of isms, Times Rec, 5/2/96; Ken Greenleaf (auth), Degrees of light, paintings by Katherine Bradford & Mark Wethli, Art New Eng, 10-11/96. *Media:* Oil

WETMORE, GORDON (STANLEY GORDON)
PAINTER, WRITER
b Memphis, Tenn, July 9, 38. *Study:* Univ Tenn, Chattanooga, BS(art), 65; Art Students League, New York, 71-73. *Work:* Duke Univ, Durham, NC; Emory Univ, Atlanta, Ga; Harvard Univ Med Ctr, Boston, Mass; White House, Washington, DC; Royal Palace, Monaco; and others. *Comn:* Comn by Richard Nixon, Princess Grace, Prince Rainier, Norman Vincent Peale, Leon Uris & Jack Nicklaus. *Exhib:* Hunter Mus Am Art, 89 & 96. *Teaching:* Fac mem Nat Portrait Seminar, 78-93; portrait forum, Carnegie Hall, 92; seminars, The Art of the Portrait, 1999-2006. *Bibliog:* Wendon Blake (auth), Learning from the Pros, Watson-Guptill Publ, 84; M Stephen Doherty (auth) Portrait painting today, Am Artist, 4/99, People and places, Am Artist, 6/2000; Gordon Wetmore (auth) Four color bands-any face, Pastel Artist Int, 2/2000, The Art of the portrait, Int Artist, 2000-06. *Mem:* Nat Portrait Inst; Portrait Soc Am (chmn, 98-2006); The Artist's Fellowship of New York; Bd Oil Painters; Overseers of Opera Boston of America. *Media:* Oil, Watercolor, Pastel. *Publ:* Illusr, Promised Land, Rev ed, 98 & illusr & auth, Ireland: Portrayed by Gordon Wetmore, 80, Thomas Nelson Co; Gordon Wetmore's Prayers for Boys and Girls, Ideals Pub, 87; auth, Vanishing Kingdoms - The Irish Chiefs and their Families, Lilliput Press, Dublin, Ireland, 2004. *Dealer:* Portraits Inc New York; Portraits South Raleigh NC; Portrait Brokers of America Birmingham AL; The Portrait Source Hendersonville NC; Portraits International Boston MA; Beverly McNeil Gallery Destin FL. *Mailing Add:* Chattanooga Bank Bldg/Penthouse West 737 Market St Chattanooga TN 37402

WEXLER , ALLAN
DESIGNER
Study: RI Sch Design, BFA, 71, BA(archit), 72; Pratt Inst, MA(archit), 76. *Comn:* Park and plaza entrance, New York City Bd of Educ, NY, 99; Tool shed/sukkah, Aldrich Mus Contemp Art, 2000; Walking paths, pavillions, study classrooms for park, Chastain Park, Atlanta, Ga, 2000; Picnic tables Douglas Park, Santa Monica Dept Cult Affairs, Calif, 2000; Permanent picnic park, Expo 2000, Hanover, Ger, 2000, many others. *Exhib:* Too Jewish?, Jewish Mus, NY, 96; Subversive Domesticity, Edwin A Ulrich Mus Art, Wichita State Univ, 96; Art Auction at MCA in La Jolla, Mus Contemp Art, San Diego, 96; Home Show II (with catalog), Santa Barbara Contemp Arts Forum, 96; People in Glass Houses, Robert Lehman Gallery Urban Glass, NY, 96; Inside (with catalog), Calif Ctr Arts Mus, Escondido, 96; Sit On This: The Chair as Art, Palm Beach Community Col Mus Art, Lake Worth, Fla, 97; Gallery Joe, Chicago Art Fair, 97; Pub Pvt Landscapes, Union Brauerei/Dortmunder Univ, Dortmund, Ger, 98; and many others; one-man shows, Custom Built: A Twenty-Year Survey of Work by Allan Wexler, Atlanta Col of Art Gallery, City Gallery at Chastain, Atlanta, Ga, 3/19-4/25/99, Travel to Contemp Arts Ctr, Cincinnati, Ohio, 11/99-1/2000, Forum for Contemp Art, St Louis, Mo, 3/2000 5/2000, Custom Built: A Twenty-Year Survey of Work, San Francisco Mus Art, Calif, 3/30-6/24/2001, Travel to Space One Eleven and Visual Art Gallery, Univ Ala at Birmingham, Ala, 10/12-1/2002, WORKS, Ronald Feldman Fine Arts, NY, 3/23-4/20/2002 & Allan Wexler: Recent Works, Parrish Art Mus, Southampton, NY, 10/20-1/5/2003, many others; group shows, Unquiet Urbanism, White Box, NY, 4/99-5/99, Faith: The Impact of Judeo Christian Religion on Art at the millennium, Aldrich Mus Contemp Art, Ridgefield, Ct, 1/2000-5/2000, Wave Hill Glyndor Gallery, Bronx, NY, 5/2000-8/2000, Multiformity: Multiples from the MCA Collection, Mus Contemp Art, Chicago, Ill, 7/5/2002-7/28/2002, Neuberger Mus Biennial Mus Pub Art, Neuberger Mus, 6/22/2003-10/19/2003 & many others; Investigations 30, Inst Contemp Art, 89; Dining Rooms and Furniture for the Typical House, Univ of Mass, Amherst, Mass, 89. *Teaching:* Asst prof, NJ Inst Technol, Sch Archit, 74-83; fac, Brown Univ Sch Art, 86, Environ Design, Parsons Sch Design, 83-94, sculpture, Tyler Col Art, Temple Univ, 89 & Cooper Union Sch Fine Arts, 89; vis prof, Sch Archit, RI Sch Design, 92 & Hochschule der Kunste, Berlin, Ger, 94; vis critic sculpture, State Univ NY, Purchase, 93; assoc adj prof, Sch Archit, Pratt Inst, 94-; workshop leader, Bauhaus Sch Architecture, Weimar, Ger, 99. *Awards:* Chrysler Award for Design Innovation, 97; Expo 2000, Hannover, Ger, 98; George Nelson Design Award, 99; Sponsored Project Award, NY State Coun on the Arts, 89; Fel Award, NY Found for the Arts, 90. *Bibliog:* Willaim Zimmer (auth), Pieces of Domesticity And Links to Nature, The NY Times, 6/11/2000; Grace Glueck (auth), Creative Souls Who Keep the Faith or Challenge its Influence, NY Times, 4/21/2000; Sonnenwende wird am Windrad groB gefeiert, Calenberger Zeitung, Germany, 5/19/2000; Allan Wexler: custom built, The Art Newspaper, 5/2001; The Aldrich Museum, Tema Celeste 92, 7/8/2002. *Mailing Add:* c/o Ronald Feldman Fine Arts 31 Mercer St New York NY 10013

WEXLER, GEORGE
PAINTER
b Brooklyn, NY, Jan 18, 25. *Study:* Cooper Union Sch Art; NY Univ, BA; Mich State Univ, MA. *Work:* Mitsubishi Corp; Kemper Collection; Chemical Bank NY; Manufacturers Hanover; Commerce Bancshares; and others. *Exhib:* Landscape in Am, New Sch Social Res, 63; one-man shows, Angeleski Gallery, NY, 61, Albany Inst Art, NY, 66, First St Gallery, NY, 72, 75 & 78 & Schenectady Mus Art, NY, 72; Fischbach Gallery, NY, 84, 86, 89 & 92; Contemp Painters of the Hudson River, Albany, Poughkeepsie, NY, 85-86; Landscape, Cityscape, Seascape, New Orleans, La & NY, 86; Contemp Landscapes, Tortue Gallery, Santa Monica, Calif. *Teaching:* Asst prof design, Mich State Univ, 50-57; prof painting, State Univ NY Col New Paltz, 57-87. *Awards:* Grumbacher Award, Nat Acad, 88; New York Found Arts Fel, 88. *Bibliog:* Gussow (auth), Sense of Place, Sat Rev, 72; Agar (auth), American Artist Mag, 5/81; Hubbard (auth), article Modern Maturity Mag, 6/85. *Media:* Oil

WEXLER, JEROME LEROY
PHOTOGRAPHER, ILLUSTRATOR
b New York, NY, Feb 6, 23. *Study:* Self-taught; student, Univ of Conn, Pratt Inst Bklyn. *Awards:* Twelve Outstanding Sci Books Children awards, Nat Sci Teachers Asn & Childrens Book Coun, Joint Comt. *Publ:* 50 bks publ to date. *Mailing Add:* 13 Langshire Dr Madison CT 06443

WEXLER, PETER J
DESIGNER, PHOTOGRAPHER
b New York, NY, Oct 31, 36. *Study:* Art Students League, New York, NY; Univ Mich, BS (design), 1958; Yale Sch Drama, 1958. *Work:* Univ Libr, Univ Ariz, Tucson, Ariz; The Tobin Collection, McNay Art Mus, San Antonio, Tex; Harvard Theatre Collection, Harvard Univ, Mass; Smithsonian Inst, Cooper Hewitt, Nat Design Mus, New York, NY; NY Pub Libr Performing Arts, Lincoln Center, Billy Rose Theatre Collection, New York, NY. *Comn:* Sculpture, NY City Opera, New York, NY, 1991. *Exhib:* Kennedy Center Exib Gallery, Wash DC, 1970's; Libr Mus Performing Arts, New York, NY, 1975; The Look of Music, Avery Fisher Hall, New York, NY, 1978; Reflections, Photography of Venice, Cult Center, Chicago, Ill, 2007. *Awards:* Maharam Award, Maharam Corp, 1967; LA Drama Critics Circle, LA Drama Critcs, 1970's; Bard Award, City Club NY, 1996. *Bibliog:* Dorle Soria (auth), Artist Life, Musical Am, 11/1973; Laurie Shulman (auth), The Meyerson Symphony Center, Univ N Tex Press, 2000; Ari Teplitz (auth), Profile: Peter Wexler, Yale Sch Drama Alumni Mag, 2003. *Media:* Large Scale, Site Spec, Multi Media. *Publ:* Illusr, White House Stage, NY Times, 10/5/61; illusr, Peter Wexler's War & Peace, Theatre Design & Technol, 1968; illusr, A Win for The Trojans, Time Mag, 3/25/74; illusr, Theatre in the Raw, Progressive Archit, 1975; auth, Photos, Reflections, US Equities Chicago, 2006. *Mailing Add:* 277 West End Ave New York NY 10023

WEXNER, ABIGAIL
COLLECTOR
Pos: Dir, Ltd Brands, Inc, Columbus, Ohio, 97—; founder, chmn, Columbus Coalition Against Family Violence; chmn, Ctr for Child & Family Advocacy, currently. *Awards:* Named one of Top 200 Collectors, ARTnews Mag, 2004. *Mem:* Columbus Found (chmn, formerly, governing comt); Children's Hospital, Inc, The Columbus Acad, The Wexner Ctr Found (mem bd trustees, currently). *Collection:* Modern & Contemporary Art; British Sporting pictures. *Mailing Add:* LTD Brands Inc Three Limited Pkwy Columbus OH 43216

WEXNER, LESLIE HERBERT
COLLECTOR
b Dayton, Ohio, 37. *Study:* Ohio State Univ, BSBA, 59, HHD, 86; Jewish Theological Seminary, PhD. *Hon Degrees:* Hofstra Univ, LLD, 87; Brandeis Univ, LHD, 90. *Pos:* trustee, Columbus Mus Art, Columbus Symphony Orchestra, Whitney Mus Am Art, Capitol S Community Urban Redevel Corp, formerly; memr Gov Comt, Columbus Found, formerly; Founder, pres, chmn bd, The Limited, Inc, fashion chain, Columbus, 63-; trustee, Columbus Jewish Fedn, 72, Columbus Jewish Found, Aspen Inst, Ohio State Univ, Columbus Capital Corp for Civic Improvement; bd dir, Columbus Urban League, 82-84, Hebrew Immigrant Aid Soc, New York City, 82-; mem bus admin adv, coun Ohio State Univ; co-chmn, International United Jewish Appeal Comt; nat vchmn, treas, United Jewish Appeal; chmn, Retail Industry Trade Action Coalition; Dir, mem exec comt, Banc One Corp, Sotheby's Holdings Inc, vis comt Grad Sch Design Harvard Univ; bd dir, mem exec comt Am Jewish Joint Distrib Comt, Inc; founding mem, first chmn, The Ohio State Univ Found; exec comt, Am Israel Pub Affairs Comt. *Awards:* Decorated cavaliere Republic of Italy; Named Man of Yr, Am Marketing Asn, 74; named one of Top 200 Collectors, ARTnews Mag, 2004. *Mem:* Young Pres's Orgn & Sigma Alpha Mus Clubs. *Collection:* Modern & Contemporary art; British sporting pictures. *Mailing Add:* Limited Inc PO Box 16000 3 Limited Pkwy Columbus OH 43230-1450

WEYHE, ARTHUR
SCULPTOR
b New York, NY. *Work:* Everson Mus Art, Syracuse, NY; Herbert F Johnson Mus Art, Cornell Univ; Neuberger Mus, Purchase, NY; William Benton Mus of Art, Storrs, Conn; Storm King Art Ctr, Mountainville, NY. *Exhib:* NY Sculpture Selected by Ivan Karp, William Paterson Col, Wayne, NJ, 74; 55 Mercer Gallery, NY, 75 & 77; O K Harris Gallery, NY, 76; Waterside Plaza, NY, 78; PS1, Long Island City, 79; and others. *Mailing Add:* 140 Sullivan St New York NY 10012-3058

WEYMAN, TODD D
APPRAISER
Study: Conn Col, BA; Williams Col, MA(art hist). *Pos:* Cur asst, British Arts Ctr, Yale Univ, New Haven; head, acquisitions. Johnson Art Mus, Cornell Univ, Ithaca, NY; vpres, dir, print, drawings dept, Swann Gallery, New York City; Appraiser Antiques Roadshow, WGBH-PBS, 1997-. *Mailing Add:* Swann Galleries 104 E 25th St New York NY 10010

WHARTON, ANNABEL JANE
HISTORIAN
b New Rochelle, NY. *Study:* Univ Wis, Madison, BSc, 66; Univ Chicago, MA, 69; Courtauld Inst, London Univ, PhD, 75. *Teaching:* Res fel Byzantine art, Barber Inst, Univ Birmingham, Eng, 71-75; asst prof Medieval art, Oberlin Col, 75-78; asst prof Medieval art, Duke Univ, 79-86, assoc prof, 86-95, prof, 95-; prof (William B Hamilton), Art Hist, 2002. *Awards:* Dumbarton Oaks Fel, 78-79; ACLS Fel, 81-84; Nat Humanities Ctr Fel, 85-86; Fel CASVA, Nat Gallery, Washington, DC, 91-92; Nat Humanities Ctr Fel, 2002-03. *Mem:* Byzantine Studies Conf (bd pres); Art Bulletin (ed bd mem); Int Ctr Medieval Art (bd mem). *Res:* art and architecture of the Late Ancient and Byzantine periods; modern architecture. *Publ:* Tokali Kilise, Dumbarton Oaks Ctr of Byzantine Studies Press, 87; Art of Empire, Penn State Univ Press, 88; Change in Byzantine culture in the 11th and 12th century, Univ Calif Press, 84; Refiguring the Post Classical City, Cambridge Univ Press, 95; Building the Cold War: Hilton International Holds and Modern Architecture, Univ Chicago Press, 2001; Selling Jerusalem: Relics Replicas, Theme Parks, Univ of Chicago Press, 2006. *Mailing Add:* 3624 Carlisle Dr Durham NC 27707

WHARTON, DAVID W
PRINTMAKER, PAINTER
b Wichita Falls, Tex, Nov 19, 51. *Study:* Univ Okla, BFA, 74; Cranbrook Acad Art, MFA, 77. *Work:* Pacific Nat Bank, Guadelope, WI; Levi Strauss Corp, San Francisco, Calif; Cranbrook Acad Art, Bloomfield Hills, Mich; Col Southern Idaho, Caldwell; Univ Lethbridge, Alta; Inst N Am West; Boise Gallery Art. *Comn:* Rocky Mountain Mag, comn by Leslie Sielko, Boulder, Colo, 79; Seattle Art Comn; First Security Bank, Idaho. *Exhib:* Los Angeles Printmaking Soc, Los Angeles Co Mus, Calif, 80; Regional Printmakers, Blue Door Too, Denver, Colo, 80; Cranbrook Printmakers, St Mary's Col, Notre Dame, 81; Denver Art Mus, Colo, 81; Northwest Printmakers, Mont State Univ, Bozevian, 81; Recent Decents, Colo Mountain Co, Breckenridge, 81; Mint Mus, Charlotte, NC; Schneider Mus, Ashland, Ore; Kunstsammlungen Der Veste Coburg, Fed Repub Ger; Pilchuck Glass Sch; Lorinda Knight Gallery, Spokane, Wash; Pendleton Ctr for the Arts; Univ Colo Gallery Contemp Art. *Collection Arranged:* Boise Art Mus, Mint Mus, Windsor Art Mus; Rockwell Mus. *Pos:* Dir printmaking, Sun Valley Ctr Art, 77-86; exec dir, Mus AK Transportation & Industry, currently. *Teaching:* Prof printmaking, Univ Wash & Humboldt State Univ, 81; Pilchuck Glass Sch, Wash, formerly; Univ Windsor, Ont, Can, formerly; asst prof, Whitman Col, Walla Walla, Wash; vis asst prof book arts, Colo Col. *Awards:* Ford Found Fel, 76; Western States Arts Found Fel, 79; Art Pub Places Award, Wash State,

83. *Bibliog:* Leslie Silka (auth), Storyteller, Rocky Mountain Mag, 79; James Mills (auth), Printmakers, Denver Post, 80; What's western about western art, Milkweed Chronicle, 80; Luminous Impressions, Mint Mus; The Primal Plastic Pool, Missoula Mus Art, Mont; Northern Lights, Missoula, Mont; Peter Hasspick (auth), Drawn to Yellowstone, An Accidental Assemblage, Sun Valley Mag. *Mem:* Col Art Asn. *Media:* Printmaking, Digital Media; Watercolor. *Interests:* Digital media. *Publ:* Auth, Suite Southern Prints, Cranbrook Acad Art, Bloomfield Hills, Mich, 77; The Rain Baby, Univ Wash Press, 81; Indian Self Rule, Inst Am West, 82; Potters and Prints, Sun Valley Ctr Publ, 83. *Dealer:* Lorinda Knight Spokane Wash. *Mailing Add:* Whitman Coll Art Dept 345 Boyer Ave Walla Walla WA 99362

WHARTON, MARGARET AGNES
SCULPTOR
b Portsmouth, Va, Aug 4, 43. *Study:* Univ Md, BS, 65; Sch Art Inst Chicago (Anna Louise Raymond Fel), MFA, 75. *Work:* Whitney Mus Am Art, NY; Mus Contemp Art, Chicago; Corcoran Gallery Art, Washington; Seattle Art Mus; Art Inst, Chicago; Dallas Art Mus, Tex. *Comn:* Multiple commission, Mus Contemp Art, Chicago, 85; Rehearsal, Chicago Pub Libr, W Lawn Br, Chicago, 86. *Exhib:* Solo exhibs (with catalog), Mus Contemp Art, Chicago & traveling nationally, 81-82, Phyllis Kind Gallery, NY, 83, 87 & 90, Chicago, 85, 88 & 91, Slicing it Thin, Zolla/Lieberman Gallery, Inc, Chicago, 92, 94, Evanston Art Ctr, IL, 95, Western Mich Univ, Kalamazoo, 96, Jean Albano Gallery, Chicago, Ill, 96, 97, 00, Rockford Col, Ill, 2000; Improbable Furniture (with catalog), Inst Contemp Art, Univ Pa, Philadelphia, 76; Drawing in Air, Frith Gallery, Sunderland Art Ctr, Eng, 83-84; Awards Show, San Antonio Mus Art, 84; Contemp Wood Sculpture, Crocker Art Mus, Sacramento, Calif, 84-85; Making Their Mark, 89-90 & Diamonds are Forever, 87-90, Mitchell Mus, Mt Vernon, Ill; Assemblage, Southeastern Ctr Contemp Art, Winston-Salem, NC, 92; Reflections: 15th Anniversary Show, Jean Albano Gallery, Chicago, Ill, 2001; Art Chicago 2001, Navy Pier, Chicago, Ill, 2001. *Teaching:* Vis artist, Art Inst Chicago, 89-90. *Awards:* Nat Endowments Arts Fel, 79, 88 & 93; Award Visual Arts Grant, 84; IL Arts Coun Grant, 99. *Bibliog:* Jeffrey Hoffeld (auth), Chairperson Margaret Wharton, Art Mag, 11/78; Alan Artner (auth), MCA unfolds a top notch show of chair sculpture, Chicago Tribune, 9/13/81; Judith Ross-Kirshner (auth), Margaret Wharton, Artforum, 1/82; Chicago Mg, 9/88; Alan Arther (auth) article, Chicago Tribune, 88. *Media:* Wood. *Publ:* Auth, Breaking Boundaries, Prentice-Hall, 83; Standing Ground, Cincinnati, 87. *Dealer:* Jean Albano Gallery Inc 215 West Superior Chicago IL 60610. *Mailing Add:* 5520 N Pauline St Chicago IL 60640-1183

WHEELER, JANET B
COLLAGE ARTIST, PAINTER
b Poughkeepsie, NY, Feb 12, 36. *Study:* Antioch Col, 54-57; Stanford Univ, BA, 57-59; Corcoran Sch Art, with James Twitty, 64-66. *Work:* Stanford Univ, Calif; Johns Hopkins Univ, Baltimore; Gettysburg Col, Pa. *Comn:* Paper collage (3' x 5'), Standard Oil of Ohio, Washington, 83; paper collage, triptych (each 3' x 4'), Marriott Hotel, Oklahoma City, 84; paper collage (3' x 5'), Georgetown Univ Fac Club, Washington, 85; paper collage (3' x 5'), TIAA, NY, 85. *Exhib:* New Acquisitions, Rosenfeld Gallery, 91; 2nd Ann Invitational Show, Perry House Galleries, Alexandria, Va, 93; Art on Paper, Md Fedn Art, Annapolis, 96; Greater Reston Arts Ctr, Va, 2000; Contemp Md Artists, Govt House, Annapolis, Md, 2000; Touchstone Gallery, Wash, DC, 03 & 05; Montpelier Cult Arts Ctr, Laurel, MD, 05. *Pos:* Bd dir, Artists Equity Asn, 85-. *Awards:* Best in Show, Perry House Galleries, 93; Individual Artist Award in Visual Arts, Md State Arts Coun, 96; Best in Show, Artists Equity Asn, 2000; Best in Show Award, Greater Reston Art Ctr, 02. *Bibliog:* Lenore D Miller (auth), Mythric worlds, parallel pathways, Washington Rev, 90; Hobart Rowland (auth), A jury's search for the best, Gazette Packet, 93; Rima Schulleind (auth), Critics Roundtable-Must See, KOAN, 98. *Mem:* Touchstone Gallery (pres, 76-77, treas, 78); Artists Equity Asn (vpres, 85-); Nat Asn Women Artists. *Media:* Collage. *Dealer:* Touchstone Gallery 406 Seventh St NW Washington DC 20004. *Mailing Add:* 10019 Reddick Dr Silver Spring MD 20901

WHEELOCK, ARTHUR KINGSLAND, JR
CURATOR, EDUCATOR
b Worcester, Mass, May 13, 43. *Study:* Williams Col, BA, 65; Harvard Univ, PhD, 73. *Pos:* Cur Northern Baroque painting, Nat Gallery Art, Washington, DC, 76-. *Teaching:* Prof Northern Baroque art, Univ Md, College Park, 74-. *Awards:* Johannes Vermeer Prize for outstanding achievement in Dutch art, The Hague, 96; Bicentennial Medal, Williams Col, 96; Dutch Am Achievement Award, Neth-Am Amity Trust, 96. *Mem:* Col Art Asn. *Res:* Dutch and Flemish art of the seventeenth century, primarily Vermeer and Rembrandt; artists' techniques; problems of optics and perspective. *Publ:* Co-ed, Van Dyck 350, Nat Gallery Art, 94; Dutch Paintings of the 17th Century, Nat Gallery Art & Oxford, 95; Vermeer & the Art of Painting, Yale, 95; ed & coauth, Johannes Vermeer, (exhib, catalog), Yale, 95; coauth, Jan Steen, Painter & Storyteller, Yale, 96; Saint Praxedis: New light on the early career of Vermeer, Artibus et Historiae, 86; Masterworks from Munich: 16th to 18th Century Paintings from the Alte Pinakothek, (exhib, catalog), Nat Gallery Art, 88; and others. *Mailing Add:* 3418 Rodman St NW Washington DC 20008

WHEELWRIGHT, JOSEPH STORER
SCULPTOR
Study: Yale Univ, BA, 70; RI Sch Design, MFA, 75. *Work:* Charlestown Navy Yard; DeCordova Sculpture Park; St Paul's Sch, Concord, NH. *Comn:* Large works in stone, bronze & wood. *Exhib:* Allan Stone Galleries, NY, 78, 81, 83, 86 & 96; Hall Gallery, Wash, 85; Zoe Gallery, Boston, 87, 88; Boston Sculptors Gallery, 92, 94, 96, 98 & 00; De Cordova Mus & Sculpture Park, Lincoln, WA, 2003-2004. *Pos:* Asst prof, Wellesley Col. *Teaching:* Pvt lessons wood & stone carving in own studio, 75-; De Cordova Mus Sch. *Awards:* Nat Endowment Arts Grant, 81; Fund for Arts Award, WBZ Radio Station, Boston, 84. *Bibliog:* Numerous articles in Boston Globe, Boston Herald, ArtSpeaks & New Art Examiner. *Mem:* Founding mem Boston Sculptors Gallery. *Media:* Stone, Wood. *Dealer:* Allan Stone Galleries 48 E 86th St New York NY 10028; Boston Sculptors at Chapel Gallery Newton MA. *Mailing Add:* 1 Waldorf St Boston MA 02124

WHIPPLE, ENEZ MARY
ADMINISTRATOR
b Syracuse, NY. *Study:* Syracuse Univ, BS; Southampton Col Long Island Univ, Hon DFA, 81. *Pos:* Exec dir, Guild Hall East Hampton Inc, NY, 48-82, bd trustees & pres, 84-, retired currently life hon trustee. *Teaching:* Adj prof humanities, Southampton Col, Long Island Univ, 71, retired. *Awards:* Dir Emer Guild Hall E Hampton Inc, NY, 82; Suffolk Co Arts Achievement Award, 82. *Mem:* Archives Am Arts; E Hampton Hist Soc (hon trustee). *Publ:* Auth, Guild Hall of East Hampton: An Adventure in the Arts, Harry N Abrams Inc, New York, 94; contribr, East Hampton Invents the culture of summer, East Hampton Hist Soc, 6/94

WHITAKER, WILLIAM
PAINTER, ILLUSTRATOR
b Chicago, Ill, Mar 5, 43. *Study:* Univ Utah, BA; Otis Art Inst. *Work:* Brigham Young Univ; Weber State Univ; Nat Cowboy Hall of Fame; Utah State Univ, Logan; Springville Mus Art, Utah. *Comn:* Many portraits, 67-2001. *Exhib:* Utah Inst Arts, 72-73 & 76; Nat Acad Western Art, Oklahoma City, 75-2000; Am Western Art Exhib, Beijing, China, 81; Artists Am, Denver, 80-2000; Am Embassy, Australia, 94-2000. *Pos:* Advert mgr, Capital Records Inc, Hollywood, Calif, 68-69. *Teaching:* Assoc prof art & design, Brigham Young Univ, 69-81. *Awards:* Gold Medal, 76 & Silver Medal, 77, Nat Acad Western Art; Press Award, Western Rendezvous Art, 82. *Bibliog:* Articles, Ariz Hwy, 4/74 & 7/75; article, SW Art, 3/82; Stratos, 6/97. *Mem:* Nat Acad Western Art; Prix de West Soc; AOA master; Oil Painters Am (master signiture mem). *Media:* Oil, Pastel. *Dealer:* Nedra Matteucci Gallery 1075 Paseo de Peralta Santa Fe NM 87501. *Mailing Add:* 4325 Ivy Lane Provo UT 84604

WHITCHURCH, CHARLES A
ART DEALER, EDUCATOR
b Long Beach, Calif, Sept 29, 40. *Study:* Studies with Ben Messick, 57; Santa Clara Univ, BA, 62; Univ Calif, Irvine, MA, 70. *Collection Arranged:* Prints '85, Golden West Col, 85; Rufino Tamayo (auth, catalog), Mod Mus Art, Santa Ana, 87; Rufino Tamayo, Riverside Mus, 89; Rauschenberg (auth, catalog), Pyo Gallery, Seoul, 90; Peter Alexander, Charles Whitchurch Gallery, 92. *Pos:* Owner, Charles Whitchurch Fine Arts, 79-. *Teaching:* Teaching assoc/fel, Univ Calif, Irvine, 68-70; prof humanities, Golden West Col, Huntington Beach, Calif, 72-, prof appreciating fine art, 82-85. *Bibliog:* Charles Whitchurch, Mizue, Tokyo; Whos Who in the World, 96; Whos Who in Am, 97; Who's Who in American Art, 1998-. *Mem:* Art Dealers Asn Calif (secy, 88-89, pres, 90-92, bd dir, currently); founding mem Huntington Beach Art Asn; Found Creative Arts (bd dir, 96-); Robert Gumbiner Found (bd dir, 94-95). *Media:* Original Prints, Paintings. *Specialty:* Modern and contemporary art. *Interests:* US and Latin Am Art. *Publ:* Contribr, Art is hot, but buy it cautiously (interview), USA Today, 88; auth, Meaning in the Art of Tamayo, Mizue, Tokyo, 89; Discontinuities: Nam June Paik and Ku-Lim Kim, Charles Whitchurch Gallery, 92. *Mailing Add:* 16172 Brent Cir Huntington Beach CA 92647

WHITCOMB, KAY
ENAMELIST, MURALIST
b Arlington, Mass, May 20, 21. *Study:* RI Sch Design, 39-42, Hon BFA, 90; Cambridge Sch Art, 40-41; apprentice in enameling to Doris Hall, 46-47, studied with Aldro Hibbard & Fred Hocks. *Comn:* Creche (needlepoint), Better Homes & Gardens, Des Moines, 75; Infinite Wisdom (enamel on steel), Univ Hosp, San Diego, 76; Arab Transportation, Int Airport, Dubai, United Arab Emirates, 81; Baranof, Russian Alaska Kodiak, Alaska High Sch, 86; Niles Col, Chicago, 92; and many other pvt comns. *Exhib:* Solo show, San Diego Mus Art, 65, 80, 84 & 87; Int Biennale, Art Enamel, Limoges, France, 75-84; Int Festival Enamel, Laguna Beach Mus Art, Calif, 86; Int Shippo, Cent Mus, Tokyo, 81, 85 & 96; Enamels 50-80, New Eng, 81; Int Enamel II & III, Coburg, Ger, 87 & 95; Boston Publ Libr, Mass; and many others. *Pos:* Cur & dir, Int Festival of Enamel, Laguna Beach Mus, Calif, 76; ed, Cloison, 80-, prof, 89. *Teaching:* Instr design & enameling, San Diego Community Col, 74-81; workshop dir enameling, 91-96. *Awards:* Prix Syndicat d'Initiative, Int Biennale, Art Enamel, Limoges, France, 78; Int Shippo Prize, Tokyo, 81 & 85; Grand Prize, Int Cloisonné, Tokyo, 94. *Bibliog:* Wayne Endicott (auth), Artist turns enameling paste into art, Ceramic Industry, 10/81; Susan Vreeland (auth), Enamelles of Kay Whitcomb, Hill Courier, 5/84; Calif Art Rev, 89; Shippo Mag, 89; Archit Design Collaborators, 92; and others. *Mem:* founder Enamel Guild West (pres, 76-78); Allied Craftsmen San Diego (vpres, 72-73); San Diego Art Guild (chmn, 68-69); USA-Int Comt Enamel Creators, Limoges, France (vpres, 85-89); Cloisonné Collectors Club (ed, 80-, vpres, 85, pres, 89); Enamel Guild NE (bd, 94). *Media:* Enamel. *Res:* Byzantine to turn of century golden era enameling; American enameling 1940 to 1970; Japanese Meiji Cloisonné; liturgical enamels. *Publ:* Auth, Germany Stuttgart: International handcraft, Craft Horizons, 71; Shippo Yaki excursion--enamel tour of Japan, 78, First international Shippo exhibition May 1978, Tokyo, Japan, 78 & Multi techniques of enamel, 78, Goldsmith J. *Mailing Add:* 115 South St Box 96 Rockport MA 01966

WHITCOMB, MILO W SKIP
PAINTER, PRINTMAKER
b Sterling, Colo, 46. *Study:* Art Ctr Col Design, Los Angeles, Calif, BFA, 71; studied with Ned Jacob, 73, Colo State Univ, Fort Collins, 64-67. *Work:* Fine Arts Col, Cambell Co Libr, Gillette, Wyo; Bank One Collection; Merrill Lynch, New York, NY; Solomon Smith Barney, Lasper, Wyo; Sen & Mrs Alan K Simpson; Sen John Warner.

Exhib: Allied Artists Am, Nat Acad Art, NY, 74 & 76; Am Watercolor Soc, Nat Acad Gallery, NY, 75; Western Visions, Wildlife of Am West Mus, Jackson, Wyo, 88-2005; Govs Invitational, Colo 94-2002; Am Art Invitational, Gilcrease Mus, Tulsa, Okla, 92-94, 96-98; Coors Western Art Exhib (Ann Invitational), Nat Western Exhib Ctr, Denver, Colo, 99-2006; From Sea to Shining Sea (with catalog), Traveling Mus Exhib, Haggin Mus, Stockton, Calif, 2004-; Variations on a Theme (with catalog), Gerald Peters Gallery, Santa Fe, NMex, 2005. *Awards:* Best of Show, Western Visions, Nat Wildlife Mus, 91 & 2000; Best of Show, Buffalo Bill Hist Ctr Mus, Cody, Wyo, 98-2000; Grand Award, Pastel Journal Int Juried Exhib, 2000; Elliot Award for Excellence in Landscape Art, Colo Mountain Club, Golden, Colo, 2003. *Bibliog:* Elizabeth Clair Flood (auth), feature, SW Art Mag, 9/94; Ken Schuster (auth), feature, SW Art Mag, 8/96; Karen Frankel (auth), feature, Am Artist Mag, 96; Jennifer King (auth), feature, Fine Art Connoisseur Mag, 9/2005; Todd Wilkenson (auth), feature, Swart Mag, 8/2005; Jean stein, Roy C Rose & Molly Siple (auths), Enchanted Isle, A History of Plein Air Painting in Santa Catalina Island, Soc for Advancement of Plein Air Painting, Avalon, Calif, 2003. *Mem:* Plein Air Painters Am, 2003. *Media:* Oil, Pastel; Etching, Watercolor. *Publ:* Auth, Figures in Watercolor, Am Artist Mag, 76. *Dealer:* Simpson-Gallagher Gallery 1161 Sheridan Ave Cody Wyo 81414; Gerald Peters Galleries 1011 Paseo De Peralta Santa Fe NMex 87501. *Mailing Add:* PO Box 271940 Fort Collins CO 80527-1940

WHITCOMB, THERESE TRUITT
CURATOR, DESIGNER
b Evanston, Ill, Sept 19, 30. *Study:* Rosemont Col; San Diego Col for Women, BA, 53; San Diego State Univ, MA, 69. *Work:* Mission San Diego de Alcala; Mission San Luis Rey. *Comn:* Interior: San Diego Mission, Diocese of San Diego, 71; Mission San Luis Rey Mus (designed & executed), Franciscan Friars, 79; Sacred Heart Church (Irving Gill), Coronado, Calif, 82; St Agnes Church, San Diego, 83; Univ San Diego, 84-. *Collection Arranged:* Contemporary Primitives, 76, Founder's Gallery Univ San Diego, Carousel Animals as Sculpture, 77, California Chair, 79 & The Naive Eye Now, 79; San Luis Rey Museum, 79; Univ San Diego. *Pos:* Dir, Founder's Gallery, Univ San Diego, 71-93; trustee, San Diego Mus Art, 75-82; pres, bd trustees, Decorative Arts Study Ctr, San Juan Capistrano, 90-92. *Teaching:* Prof art hist, Univ San Diego, 68-, coordr exhib, 70-, cur, univ collection & dir design, currently. *Awards:* Outstanding Teacher, 77, Bishop Buddy Award, Univ San Diego; Lowell Davies Fac Achievement Award, Davies Found, 85; Women of Achievement, President's Coun Prof Women. *Bibliog:* Elise Miller (auth), San Diego art, Los Angeles Times; George Maher (auth), Twilight of Splendor, Little Brown & Co, 76; Zenia Cleigh (auth), Mission as art, San Diego Mag, 79. *Mem:* Asn Archit Historians; Southern Calif Art Historians; Western Asn Art Mus; Col Art Asn. *Res:* California missions, 19th and 20th century California Architecture, American primitive art and contemporary American art; 16th century Spanish Renaissance decorative arts. *Publ:* Sword and the Cross, San Diego Mus, 76; contribr, California's Catholic Heritage, Penguin Press, 76; Impressionist as Printmaker & Arbol de la Vida, Founders Press

WHITE, AMOS, IV
CERAMIST, PHOTOGRAPHER
b Montgomery, Ala. *Study:* Ala State Univ, BS, 58; Sculpture Studio, with Isaac S Hathaway, 58; Univ Southern Calif, MFA, 61; Long Island Univ, 66; Univ Md, PhD, 82. *Work:* Quinn Gallery, Univ Southern Calif; Lemoyne Art Found, Tallahassee, Fla. *Exhib:* Designer-Craftsmen USA, 60 & Young Americans, 62, Mus Contemp Crafts, NY; Am Fedn Arts Traveling Exhib, 63; 18th Nat Decorative Arts & Ceramics Exhib, Wichita, 64; Outstanding Atlantic Seaboard Artists, Jacksonville, Fla, 73; Black Artists South, Huntsville Mus Art, 79; plus many others. *Pos:* Md Conf pres, Am Asn Univ Prof, 78-79. *Teaching:* Assoc prof ceramics, Fla A&M Univ, Tallahassee, 61-69; prof & chmn art dept, Bowie State Col, Bowie, Md, 69-77, prof photog, 70-, chmn dept fine & performing arts, 83-86, chmn dept humanities & fine arts, 86-. *Awards:* Design West, Los Angeles Mus Sci & Indust, 60; Merit Award, Am Craftsmen's Coun, 61; Ceramic Award, Fla State Fair Fine Arts Comn, 65; Outstanding Alumnus, Univ Southern Calif, 82. *Bibliog:* Lewis & Waddy (auths), Black artists-art, Contemp Crafts, 69; J W Chase (auth), Afro-American Art & Crafts, Von Nostrand-Reinhold, 71. *Mem:* Am Craftsmen's Coun NY (Fla state councilman, 68-69); Fla Craftsmen (pres, 69); Md Fedn Art; Nat Coun Art Adminr; Col Art Asn Am. *Media:* Clay. *Mailing Add:* Fine & Performing Arts Dept Bowie State Univ 14000 Jericho Park Rd Bowie MD 20715

WHITE, B J (BEVERLY)
PAINTER, INSTRUCTOR
b Hobart, Okla. *Study:* Oklahoma City Univ, BS, 69; Phillips Univ, 74-76; La Tech Univ, 80, 82, 84 & 85; Univ Okla MFA, 96. *Work:* Arts Coun Okla City, Okla Health Care Corp, Fred Jones Jr Mus Art, State Collection of OK Kirkpatrick Ctr Museum Complex & Okla Christian Col; Tex Educ Corp, CESSNA Inc. *Comn:* Painting, Arts Coun Okla City, 93; paintings and sculpture, City of Edmond, Okla, 2005. *Exhib:* Goddard Ctr for Visual Arts, Ardmore, Okla, 91; Nat WC Muckenthaler Cult Ctr, Fullerton, Calif, 92; Kirkpatrick Ctr Mus Complex, Oklahoma City, 99; Fred Jones Mus Art, Norman, Okla, 96; Norick Art Ctr, Okla City Univ, 98; Untitled Gallery, Oklahoma City, Okla, 2000; plus others; Spiva Ctr for the Arts, Joplin, Mo, 2001. *Teaching:* Instr drawing & painting, City Arts Ctr, 98; studio class, Fine Arts Inst, Edmond, Okla, 98, 99; instr mixed media and collage workshop, 2000. *Awards:* Grumbacher Gold Medallion/Cash Award, Kans Watercolor Soc Five-State Competition, 89; Hederman Brothers Printers Award, Southern Watercolor Soc, 85; Third, Nat Watercolor Okla Exhib, 89. *Bibliog:* Marcia Lionberger (auth), The nature of her art, Art Gallery, 5-6/83; Lynne Jones (producer), BJ White, Artist in Okla, Okla Educ Television Authority Inc, 93; George Lange (auth) BJ White, Hist Living, Vol 1, 7/2000. *Mem:* Okla Visual Arts Coalition; Nat Watercolor Soc; Individual Artists of Okla; Okla Watercolor Asn. *Media:* All Media. *Dealer:* JRB Art 2810 N Walker Oklahoma City Okla 73103-1329, 405-528-6336, PO Box 18446, Oklahoma City, 73154. *Mailing Add:* 7874 Pleasant Oaks Dr Edmond OK 73034

WHITE, BROOK FORREST, JR
GLASS BLOWER
b Columbus, Ga, June 25, 69. *Study:* Centre Col, BA, 91, with Lino Tagliapietra & Marvin Lipofsky, 2000; Appalachian Center Crafts, with Curtiss Brock, 93. *Work:* Owensboro Mus Fine Art, Ky; Ky History Ctr, Frankfort; Centre Col, Danville, Ky; CINergy, Cincinnati, Ohio; Trans Financial Bank, Bowling Green, Ky. *Comn:* Recognition Awards, Cent Ky Cancer Prog, Danville, Ky, 99; Real Hero Awards, Am Red Cross, Owensboro, Ky, 2000; Vice-Presidential Debate Paperweight, Centre Coll, Danville, Ky 2000. *Exhib:* A Kentucky Cycle, Kennedy Ctr, Washington, DC, 93; Southeast Glass, Asheville Art Mus, NC, 95; Exhibition 280, Huntington Mus Art, WVa, 97; 36th Mid-State Exhibition, Evansville Mus Arts & Sci, Ind, 99; One-man show, Owensboro Mus Fine Art, Ky, 2000; Am Craft Council Spotlight 2000, Kennesaw State Univ, Ga, 2000. *Pos:* grad fel art, Centre Col, Danville, Ky, 91-92. *Bibliog:* Keith Lawrence (auth), Glass work, Owensboro Messenger-Inquirer, 4/98; Susan Gosselin (auth), Through glass, brightly, Louisville Mag, 10/1998; Jennifer King (auth), Over the moon, Cincinnati City Beat, 4/99. *Mem:* Glass Art Soc; Am Craft Coun; Ky Guild Artists & Craftsmen. *Dealer:* Marta Hewett Gallery 815 W Market St Louisville KY 40202

WHITE, BRUCE HILDING
SCULPTOR, EDUCATOR
b Bay Shore, NY, July 11, 33. *Study:* Univ Md, BA; Columbia Univ, MA & EdD. *Work:* Revenue Bldg, Springfield, Ill; Ill State Mus, Springfield; Indianapolis Mus Art, Ind; Rogers Libr & Mus Art, Laurel, Miss; Ill Ctr, Chicago. *Comn:* Mellerud, Sweden, 92; Ill Acad Math & Sci, 92; Fla Solar Energy Ctr, Cocoa, Fla, 96; Appalachian State Univ, NC, 97; Millennium sculpture, City of Woodlands, Tex, 2000; Peter Melendy Park, Cedar Falls, Iowa, 2000; The Farallon, Chicago, 2001; Jacksonville, Fla, 2002; Wilmette, Ill, 2003; Harper Col, Palatine, Ill, 2004; Wiley Post Skate Park, Oklahoma City, 2006. *Exhib:* Solo exhibs, Boyd Gallery, Chicago, Ill, 81, 82, 85 & 90; Festival of Arts, Oklahoma City, 85; Outdoor Sculpture Invitational, Appalachian Summer Festival, NC, 87-88; Sculpture in the Landscape, Paine Art Ctr & Arboretum, Oskosh, Wis, 88; Pierwalk '96, 97, 98, 99, 2001; Pub Sculpture Proj Univ Notre Dame, 96; Sarasota Seasons of Sculpture, 2001, 2003, 2005; 7th Odyssey Conf Sculpture, Purdue Univ, 2005; Art Connects, Chicago River Show, 2005 & 06. *Teaching:* Distinguished res prof, emer sculpture, Northern Ill Univ, 68-. *Awards:* Percent for Art, Ill, 81, 83, 92 & 98, Iowa 86 & 91, Wis, 94, Fla, 96, Minn, 96; First Prize, sculpture, Appalachian Summer Festival, Boone, NC, 87. *Media:* Sheet Metal, Cast Metal. *Mailing Add:* 521 E Locust St De Kalb IL 60115

WHITE, DEBORAH
DEALER
b Toronto, Ont. *Study:* Univ Toronto, BA; Univ Florence, spec cert. *Pos:* Dir, Albert White Gallery, currently. *Mem:* Can Prof Art Dealers Asn. *Specialty:* Modern art, international artists, Moore, Chagall, Picasso, Leger, Miro, Lichtenstein, and others; primitive and pre-Columbian art. *Mailing Add:* c/o Albert White Gallery 80 Spadina Ave Toronto ON M5V 2J4 Canada

WHITE, E ALAN
ADMINISTRATOR, PAINTER
b Rutherglen, Lanarkshire, Scotland, Sept 13, 46. *Study:* La State Univ, New Orleans, BA(art), 70; Univ Cincinnati, MFA, 72. *Work:* Hunter Mus Art, Chattanooga, Tenn; Univ Cincinnati. *Exhib:* Tennessee Painting, Cheekwood Gallery, Nashville, 73; Nat Drawing Exhib, Southern Ill Univ, Carbondale, 74; Two by Two in Wuxi, At Mus, China, 83; A White Still Life: An Installation, George Cress Gallery, Chattanooga, Tenn, 91; White Houses: An Installation, George Cress Gallery, Univ Tenn, Chattanooga, 92. *Teaching:* Prof painting & dept head, Univ Tenn, Chattanooga, 72-. *Awards:* Outstanding Teacher Award, 86 & 88 & Distinguished Service Award, Univ Tenn, Chattanooga, 93; Outstanding Prof, Univ Tenn Alumni Asn, 95. *Mem:* Nat Asn Schs Art & Design; Col Art Asn; Charles Rennie Mackintosh Soc, Glasglow, Scotland; Found Art: Theory & Educ; Southeastern Col Art Conf. *Publ:* Auth, Hilda Gilkeson: A Critical Review, 86, Genuflections at Misogynist Altars, 91, Art Papers; 15th Ann Tenn Watercolor Soc Exhib, Chattanooga Times, 87; George Cress: 50 Yrs Painting, Hunter Mus Art, 90. *Mailing Add:* Dept Art Univ Tenn 615 McCallie Ave No 1301 Chattanooga TN 37403

WHITE, FRANKLIN
PAINTER, DRAFTSMAN
b Richmond, Va, 1943. *Study:* Skowhegan Sch Painting & Sculpture, Maine, 66; Brooklyn Mus Art Sch, 67-68; Nat Collection Fine Arts Internship, 69-70; Howard Univ, BFA, 69, MFA, 71. *Work:* Woodward Found, Washington, DC; Am Fedn Arts; Stern Found, Washington, DC; Washington Post; Corcoran Gallery Art. *Comn:* Three multi-color serigraphs, The Workshop, Washington, DC, 72 & 78. *Exhib:* Contemp Black Artists in Am, Whitney Mus Am Art, NY, 71; 2nd Ann Exhib Washington Artists, Phillips Collection, 72; Corcoran Mus Art, 72 & 75; Directions in Afro-Am Art, Johnson Mus, Cornell Univ, Ithaca, NY, 74; 77 Artists, Wash Project for the Arts, 77; one-man shows, Corcoran Gallery, Washington, DC, 72, Jefferson Pl Gallery, 72 & 74 & Gallery Rebecca Cooper, Washington, DC, 75 & 77; and others. *Pos:* Info guide intern, Nat Collection Fine Arts, 69-70. *Teaching:* Instr painting & drawing, Georgetown Univ & Md Sch of Arts & Design; artist-in-residence, DC Pub Sch & DC Comn on the Arts, 70-71; instr, Corcoran Gallery Art Sch, 75-. *Awards:* Painting Award, Skowhegan Sch Arts & Design; Nat Endowment Arts Grant, 70-71. *Bibliog:* Roberta Smith (auth), Directions in Afro American art, Artforum, 75; Henri Ghent (auth), article, Art in Am, 1-2/75; Benjamin Forgery (auth), Washington DC round-up, Artnews, 2/75. *Mailing Add:* 1415 Swann St NW Washington DC 20009

WHITE, JACK
PAINTER
b Raleigh, NC, July 23, 31. *Study:* Morgan State Univ, Baltimore, with James Lewis & Albert Sangiamo BS, 58; Syracuse Univ, mus studies with Richard Porter, 86-87. *Work:* Schomberg Cult Ctr, NY; Ark Arts Ctr, Little Rock; Munson-Williams-Proctor Inst, Utica, NY; Everson Mus, Syracuse, NY; James E Lewis Mus Art, Baltimore. *Comn:* John Mulroy Civic Ctr, Syracuse, NY, 76; Urban League, Niagara Mohawk Power, Syracuse, NY, 89. *Exhib:* One-man shows, Asheville Art Mus, NC, 77, Whittaker Gallery, SC State Col, Orangeburg, 77, NC Mus Art, Raleigh, 80, Colgate Univ, Hamilton, NY, 80, Ark Arts Ctr, Little Rock, 82, Danville Mus Art, Va, 87 & NC State Univ, Greensboro, 90, Beach Inst, Savannah, Ga, 2000, Galerie Zygos, Athens, Greece, 2005 & 06, Onondaga Com Col, Onondagahill, NY, 2005; Collage/Assemblage Nat Traveling Exhib, 81-83; The Side Show, Chapman Cult Ctr, Cazenovia, NY, 88; Dedicated Exhib, James E Lewis Mus Art, Morgan State Univ, Baltimore, 90; In Our Own Voices, Bevier Gallery, Rochester Inst Technol, 91; Group shows, Pantazidis Art Ctr, Athens, Greece, 2003. *Awards:* Artist of the Year, Cayuga Coun Arts, Auburn, NY, 93. *Bibliog:* Mary Schmidt Campbell (auth), American art with African roots, Syracuse New Times, 9/29/74; Ruth Ann Appelhof (auth), The Flight Genesis, Cat Essay, 77; John Dorsey (auth), Artist uses computer cards to create collage, Evening Sun, Baltimore, 5/18/90; Katherine Rushworth (auth), Tapping into Ancestry, The Post Standard, Syracuse, NY, 10/30/2005. *Mem:* Nat Conf Artists. *Media:* Mixed Media, Acrylics. *Dealer:* Julia Hotton 7C Lakeshore Village Port Ewen NY 12466. *Mailing Add:* 106 Franklin St Auburn NY 13021

WHITE, JAMES RICHARD
SCULPTOR, EDUCATOR
b Dayton, Ohio, Jan 14, 50. *Study:* Ohio Univ, BFA(painting), 72, MFA(sculpture), 74. *Work:* USAF, Dayton, Ohio. *Comn:* Murray State Univ, Ky. *Exhib:* One-man shows, Wright State Univ, Dayton, Ohio, 79 & SE Mo State Univ, Cape Girardeau, 79; Evansville Mus Arts & Sci, Ind, 79 & 80. *Teaching:* Asst prof, Murray State Univ, Ky, 74-81; assoc prof, Ariz State Univ, Tempe, 81-. *Awards:* Ind Found Arts & Sci Award, 80. *Bibliog:* Jerry Speight (auth), Shelter skelter, Ky Art Educ J, 12/79, Air city, free air, air fair affair, School Arts/Davis, 9/80 & James R White, sculptor, Art Voices S/Davis, 7/80. *Mem:* Col Art Asn. *Media:* Metal, Wood. *Mailing Add:* 5504 S Heather Dr Tempe AZ 85283

WHITE, JOHN M
PAINTER, CONCEPTUAL ARTIST
b San Francisco, Calif, May 10, 37. *Study:* Patri Sch Art Fundamentals, San Francisco, 62-65; Otis Art Inst, Los Angeles, MFA, 69. *Work:* Los Angeles Co Art Mus, Los Angeles; Smithsonian Arch Am Art; Newport-Harbor Art Mus, Newport Beach, Calif; Solomon R Guggenheim Mus, NY; St Louis Art Mus, Mo; and others. *Exhib:* New Work, New Talent, Los Angeles Co Art Mus, 74; Drawing Show, Newport Harbor Art Mus, 75; one-man shows, Barbara Okun Gallery, St Louis, 77, Baum-Silverman Gallery, Los Angeles, 78 & 81 & Roy Boyd Gallery, Chicago, 81; performances, Vancouver Art Gallery, BC, 74, Miami-Dade Community Col, Fla, 75, St Louis Mus Contemp Art, 77 & Chicago Art Inst, 78; Solomon R Guggenheim Mus, 81; Dorothy Goldeen Gallery, Santa Monica, 88; retrospective, Los Angeles Munic Art Gallery, Barnsdall Park, 83; and many others. *Pos:* Panelist, Nat Endowment Arts, 86. *Teaching:* Vis artist performance workshop, Claremont Grad Sch, 77- & Otis Art Inst, 77-79; Univ Calif, Irvine, 84-. *Awards:* New Talent Award, Los Angeles Co Art Mus, 72; Nat Endowment Arts Grants, 76-77, 78-79, 84 & 85; CETA Grant Artist in Residence, 78-79. *Media:* Mixed. *Dealer:* Contemporary Artists 1001 A Colorado Santa Monica CA 90401

WHITE, KAREN J
SCULPTOR, CRAFTSMAN
b Coshocton, Ohio, Jan, 43. *Study:* Ohio State Univ, BFA, 69; Metrop State Col 74-75; Univ Colo, 85. *Work:* Mus du pays et Val de Charmey, Switz; Imadate Art Hall, Japan. *Exhib:* Nat Assoc Women Artists, NY, 2000; Gallery Cont Art, Univ Colo, Colorado Springs, 2001; Mus Outdoor Art, Littleton, Colo, 2002; Triennale Int Du Papier, Switz, 93; Int Exhib Contemp Paper Imadate, Fukai, Japan, 95; and others. *Collection Arranged:* Musee Du Pays Charmey, Switzerland; Imadate Art Fukui, Japan; Comty Col, Denver. *Pos:* co-founder Womens Art Ctr & Gallery, Denver, Colo, 1997, Bus Corridor Arts Alliance, Denver, 96; nat juror NEA Pres Com on Arts, 99, NEA for Youth, 2001. *Teaching:* Workshop handmade paper, Univ Northern Colo, 88, Arvado Ctr Arts, Colo, 90, Colo Inst Art, 91- & Front Range Community Col, 96. *Awards:* Colo Coun on Arts Grant, 2000; Juror's Choice Award, Colo, 93; Neighborhod Cult of Denoer Pub Art Grant, 95. *Bibliog:* Nancy Clegg (auth), Pulp novel, Westword, 9/89; Renelda Muse (dir), Art Around Town (film), KCNC-TV, Colo, 2/90; Nancy Orban (ed), Fiber Arts Design Book Four, Lark Bks, 91. *Mem:* Nat Asn Women Artists Inc; Int Asn Hand Papermakers & Paper Artist. *Media:* Miscellaneous Media; Handmade Paper. *Specialty:* Contemporary mixed media dimensional art. *Interests:* creating, politics. *Dealer:* KW Studio/Galleries 280 Delaware Denver CO 80223. *Mailing Add:* 282 Delaware St Denver CO 80223

WHITE, NORMAN TRIPLETT
SCULPTOR, KINETIC ARTIST
b San Antonio, Tex, Jan 7, 38. *Study:* Harvard Col, with T Lux Feininger, 55-59, BA(biol), 59. *Work:* Nat Gallery Can & Art Bank, Ottawa; Vancouver Art Gallery. *Comn:* Light mural, CBC Bldg, Vancouver, BC, 75. *Exhib:* Some More Beginnings, Exp in Art & Technol Show, Brooklyn Mus, NY, 68; Norm White at the Electric Gallery, Toronto, 71; retrospective, Vancouver Art Gallery, BC, 75; New Directions, Nat Gallery of Can, 77; Hearsay, Global Telecommun Event, 85; Ubiqua, Venice Biennale, 86; Like Life, Europ Conf Artificial Life, 97. *Teaching:* Instr, Ont Col Art, Toronto, 78-99. *Awards:* La Villette, Paris, 85; Prix Ars Electronica-Interactive Sculpture, 90; Petro Can Award, 95. *Bibliog:* John Turnbull (auth), article, Vanguard, 9/75; Joe Bodolai (auth), article, Artscanada, 5/76; Brian Reffin Smith (auth), Soft Computing, Addison-Wesley, 84. *Mem:* Artex-IPSA Telecommun Group; Inter-Access. *Media:* Multi. *Mailing Add:* PO Box 1032 Durham ON N0G 1R0 Canada

WHITE, PHILIP BUTLER
PAINTER, COLLECTOR
b Chicago, Ill, Jan 23, 35. *Study:* Univ Southern Calif, BFA (painting). *Work:* River Forest Centennial Comn. *Exhib:* Butler Inst Am Art, Youngstown, Ohio, 62-64; Ill State Fair, Springfield, 63, 65, 67, 69 & 70; Nat Acad Design, NY, 63-65, 67-70 & 74-76; Am Watercolor Soc, NY, 70-71. *Awards:* First Prizes, Ill State Fair, 60 & 65; Thomas B Clark Awards, Nat Acad Design, 65, 68 & 70; Munic Art League Award of Execellence, 95. *Bibliog:* Cover story, Am Artist, 8/78; Les Krantz (ed), Am Artists, 85. *Media:* Oil, Egg Tempera. *Collection:* Contemporary realistic art. *Publ:* Contribr, 20 Figure Painters and How They Work, Watson-Guptill, 79. *Mailing Add:* 710 Clinton Pl River Forest IL 60305

WHITE, ROBERT RANKIN
HISTORIAN, WRITER
b Houston, Tex, Feb 8, 42. *Study:* Univ Tex, Austin, BA, 64; Univ Ariz, MS, 71; Univ NMex, PhD, 93. *Res:* Nineteenth and early twentieth century New Mexico art. *Publ:* Auth, The Taos Society of Artists, Univ NMex Press, 83 & 98; coauth, Pioneer Artists of Taos, Old West Publ Co, 83; coauth, The New Mexico Painters, Gerald Peters Gallery, 99; coauth, Bert Geer Phillips and the Taos art colony, Univ NMex Press, 94; auth, The Southwestern Etchings of Peter Moran, Imprint, 94. *Mailing Add:* 1409 Las Lomas Rd NE Albuquerque NM 87106

WHITE, SAMUEL GILTINAN
ARCHITECT
b Chicago, Il, Nov 1, 46. *Study:* Harvard Col, BA, 68; Univ Pa, MArch, 75. *Pos:* Regist archit, NY, Pa; NJ Partner, Maxwell & White, Philadelphia, 77-78; Assoc, Harold Buttrick & Assocs, New York City, 78-83; Buttrick White & Burtis, New York City, 84-. *Teaching:* Adj prof, fine art, NYU, currently. *Awards:* Fel Am Inst of Archits; Nat Acad of Design (acad, 97 -). *Publ:* auth, Houses of McKim, 1998; McKim, Mead & White Masterworks, 2003. *Mailing Add:* NYU Dept Fine Arts 303 Silver Ctr 100 Washington Square East New York NY 10003

WHITE, SELBY

WHITE, SHELBY
COLLECTOR
Study: Mt Holyoke Col, BA; Columbia Univ, MA. *Awards:* Named one of Top 200 Collectors, ARTnews Magazine, 2004, 2006. *Publ:* Chairman Shelby White-Leon Levy Progressive for Archaeol. Publications, 97—. *Mailing Add:* Semitic Mus Harvard Univ 6 Divinity Ave Cambridge MA 02138

WHITE, STEPHEN LEON
COLLECTOR, ART DEALER
b Jacksonville Fla, May 4, 38. *Study:* San Francisco State Col, BA(hist), 62; Univ Calif Los Angeles, MFA(motion pictures), 68. *Collection Arranged:* A Window to the Orient, GEH Photographs, John Thomson, 85; Parallels and Contrasts (auth catalog), New Orleans Mus Art, 88; Industry in California, Laguna Art Mus, 94; The Photograph and The Am Dream, Van Gogh Mus, Amsterdam (catalog), 2001. *Pos:* Founding pres, Asn Int Photog Art Dealers, 79-80; vpres photog coun, Mus Contemp Art, Los Angeles, 90-91; bd mem, Mus Photog Arts, San Diego, 92-94; adv bd & chair photog comt, Ransom Humanities Res Ctr, Univ Tex, 93-99. *Teaching:* tchr history of photog Orange Coast Col, 76. *Mem:* Getty Photography Council; Lacma Photo Art Council. *Specialty:* 19th & 20th Century photography. *Collection:* Collection of over 10,000 photographs, subjects: Alaska, American West, 20th century Russia, industrial history, aviation & others. *Publ:* Auth & ed, Harry Smith: Magic Moments, pvt publ, 82; auth, John Thomson, Life and Times, Thames & Hudson, 85; auth, The far east, Image Mad, 91; Author The Photograph & The American Dream, Van Gosh Mus, 2001; ed Stephen White Editions, 2006. *Mailing Add:* c/o Stephen White Assocs PO Box 1664 Studio City CA 91614

WHITE, STUART JAMES
SCULPTOR, ASSEMBLAGE ARTIST
b Salisbury, Md, May 31, 44. *Study:* Carnegie-Mellon Univ, BFA, 68, MFA, 70, DA, 78. *Work:* Newark Mus, NJ; NJ State Mus, Trenton; Crawford Art Gallery, Cork, Eire; Univ Salisburg & Peninsula Gen Hosp, Salisbury, Md; pvt collections of Peter Homitzky, Hoboken, NJ, Bruce Arnold, critic, Dublin, Eire & Deirdre Carroll, dealer, Dublin, Eire, Paddy McEntee, collector, Daniel Whealton, Salisbury, Md. *Comn:* Construction (wallpiece), Tanners Coun Am, Washington, DC, 79. *Exhib:* solo exhib, NJ Biennial, Newark Mus, 82, figurative work, NJ State Mus, Trenton, 83, Crawford Art Gallery, Cork, Ireland, 89, Proj Art Ctr, Dublin, 89 & Wyvern Gallery, Dublin, 91 & 93; Scottish Sculpture Open, Kildrummie Castle, Scotland, 85; Sculpture Biennale Int, Invitational Ctr d'Arts du Normandie, Jouy sur Eure, France, 86; Wyvern Gallery, 95, 96; Bridge Gallery, 99, 2000; and others. *Pos:* Dir, Robeson Gallery, Rutgers Univ, Newark, 79-; Head fine art & ceramic design, Crawford Col Art & Design, Cork, Ireland, 87-. *Teaching:* Intern drawing, Carnegie-Mellon Univ, 72-73; asst prof art hist, Mt Union Col, 74-78; dept head resins, Johnson Atelier, Princeton, 78-79; vis specialist, Montclair State Col, 79-; asst prof sculpture, Rutgers Univ, Newark, 79-. *Awards:* Grant, Newark: Genesis of a City, NJ Comt Humanities, 80; Sculpture Fel, NJ State Coun Arts, 83 & 87; Res Fel, Scottish Sculpture Workshop, Rutgers Univ, Lumsden, Scotland, 84. *Bibliog:* Hildreth York (auth), Stuart White: The Figurative

Work, NJ State Mus, 83; Peter Murray (auth), Stuart White: Corpus, Crawford Art Gallery, Cork, Ireland. *Mem:* Col Art Asn Am; Assoc Irish Artists. *Media:* Miscellaneous Media, Wood. *Collection:* Coll of Paddy McEntee; Coll of Bruce Arnold, Art Critic; Coll of Daniel Whealton, Salisbury, MD. *Publ:* Auth, Calvin Albert, 78 & Dennis Oppenheim, 79, Sculpture News Exchange; coauth, Stalking the post office mural: An artful odyssey, New York Sunday Times, 80; foreward, catalog, Talk Less, 2005. *Dealer:* Deirdre Carroll Bridge Gallery Dublin Ireland

WHITE, SUSAN CHRYSLER
PAINTER
b Chico, Calif, June 12, 54. *Study:* Univ Calif, Berkeley, BA, 77; Univ Calif, Davis, with Wayne Thiebaud, Roy DeForest, Robert Arneson, Ellen Lanyon & Manuel Neri, MFA, 80. *Work:* Worcester Art Mus, Mass; Prudential Insurance Co, Newark, NJ; Rutgers Univ; Meniscus Med Communications, Philadelphia. *Exhib:* One-man shows, Janet Fleisher Gallery, Philadelphia, 85, 89 & 92 Cavin Morris Inc, NY, 87, Paintings & Proposals, Alverno Col, Milwaukee, 88, Weatherspoon Art Gallery, Univ NC, 91, Curt Marcus Gallery, NY, 92, Kim Foster Gallery, NY, 95; Philadelphia Artists, Philadelphia Mus Art, 82-83; Contemp Philadelphia Artists, Philadelphia Mus Art, 90; Contemp Concerns in Drawing, High Mus, Atlanta, 90; Works on Paper, Mollica Guidarte, NY; The Politics of Cloth-Selections from the Fabric Workshop, Decordova Mus & Sculpture Park, Mass, 92; Introductions, Stephen Wertz Gallery, San Francisco, 92; Painting Faculty, The Cooper Union Sch Art, NY, 95; and others. *Teaching:* Instr & vis artist, La State Univ, 80; vis lectr, Tyler Sch Art, 81 & Rutgers Univ, 82. *Awards:* Ann Bremmar Award, Berkeley Mus, 77; Purchase Award, Rutgers Univ Nat, 82; Philadelphia Mus Art Purchase Award, Cheltenham Art Ctr 41st Ann Painting Exhib, 82. *Media:* Oil, Oil Pastels. *Dealer:* Peter Miller Gallery Huron St Chicago IL

WHITEHEAD, FRANCES
SCULPTOR, EDUCATOR
b Richmond, Va, Oct 20, 53. *Study:* East Carolina Univ, Greenville, NC, BFA, 75; Northern Ill Univ, DeKalb, MFA, 78. *Work:* Mus Contemp Art, Chicago; Ariz State Mus, Tucson; Lakeview Mus, Peoria, Ill; Arthur Anderson, Chicago, Detroit, NY; State Ill. *Comn:* Sculpture, Chicago; Sette & Segura Pub, Tempe; sculpture, South Bend, Ind; National Site Works, Atlanta; Laumeier Sculpture Park, St Louis, Mo. *Exhib:* Kansas City Art Inst, 92; Neuberger Mus, State Univ NY, Purchase, 93; Chicago Cult Ctr, 93; Am Acad Arts & Letters, NY, 96; Mus Contemp Art, Chicago, 96; and many others. *Teaching:* Vis asst prof/2D & 3D, Tex Tech Univ, Lubbock, 79-80; vis asst prof painting, Ill State Univ, Normal, 80-81; asst prof/sculpture, Ind Univ, Bloomington, 81-84; prof sculpture, Sch Art Inst Chicago, 84-. *Awards:* Ill Arts Coun, 85 & 87; Nat Endowment Arts, 86; Tiffany Found Award, 91. *Bibliog:* James Yood (auth), Frances Whitehead, Artforum, 12/89; Art in Chicago 1945-present (catalog), Mus Contemp Art Chicago, 96. *Media:* Miscellaneous Media. *Dealer:* Tough Gallery 415 N Sangamon St Chicago IL 60622; Lisa Sette Gallery 4142 N Marshall Way Scottsdale AZ. *Mailing Add:* 1858 W Huron Chicago IL 60622

WHITEHOUSE, DAVID BRYN
MUSEUM DIRECTOR, HISTORIAN
b Worksop Nottinghampshire, Eng, Oct 15, 41. *Study:* St John's Col, Cambridge, Eng, BA, 63, MA, 65, PhD, 67. *Collection Arranged:* Glass of the Caesars (co-auth, catalog), Corning Mus Glass, 87; The Art of Glass, IBM Gallery, NY, 89 & Nat Gallery, Wash, DC, 90; Nature's Wonders in Glass, Corning Mus Glass, 91; Glass of the Sultans (coauth, catalog), Corning Mus Glass, 2001; Beyond Venice, Corning Mus Glass, 2004. *Pos:* Dir, Brit Inst Afghan Studies, Kabul, Afghanistan, 73-74, Brit Sch Rome, Italy, 74-84 & Corning Mus Glass, NY, 92-. *Mem:* Acad Fiorentina Delle Arti del Disegno; Soc Antiquaries London; Royal Geographical Soc; Pontificia Acad Roman Archelogia. *Res:* Archaeology of the Mediterranean region and western Asia AD 500-1500; Roman, Medieval European and Medieval Islamic glass. *Publ:* Co-auth, Mohammed, Charlemagne and the Origins of Europe, Duckworth, 83; Glass of the Caesars, Olivetti, 87; auth, Glass: A Pocket Dictionary, 93, English Cameo Glass, 94 & Roman Glass in the Corning Museum of Glass, Vol 1, 97, Corning Mus Glass; Excavations at ed-Dur, Vol 1, The Glass Vessels, Peeters, 98; Roman Glass in The Corning Museum of Glass, Vol 2, 2000, Vol 3, 2003; Sasanian and Post-Sasanian Glass in the Corning Musuem of Glass, 2005. *Mailing Add:* 81 E Third Corning NY 14830

WHITEHOUSE, DEBORAH WIAN
PHOTOGRAPHER, MURALIST
b Lewistown, Pa, Oct 5, 51. *Study:* Internat Ctr Photography, 88; Univ Md, BA, 75. *Work:* Brooklyn Mus Art, NY; Bibliotheque nat France, Paris; High Mus Art, Atlanta, Ga; New Orleans Mus Art, La; Denver Art Mus, Colo; Harry Ransom Ctr, Univ Tex. *Comn:* photo mural, Water Spirits, City of Atlanta, Ga, 98; photo mural, Spirit of Atlanta, Atlanta Airport, Ga, 2000; photo mural, Transparent Day, Fueton Co, Ga, 02. *Exhib:* Look Back Get Down, Nexus Contemp Art Ctr, Atlanta, Ga, 97; Fountains: Splash and Spetacle, Cooper Hewitt Nat Design Mus, NY, 98; New Orleans Triennial, New Orleans Mus Art, La, 98; New Acquisitions, The Brooklyn Mus Art, NY, 99; solo show Lamar Dodd Art Ctr, La Grange Col, Ga, 99; New Acquisitions, The High Mus Art, Atlanta, Ga, 2000; To See a World, Ga Mus Art, Athens. *Pos:* still photogr for My Dinner with Abbey, Documentary Film, 92; photog juror, 4th Ann Photo Competition, Kennesaw State Univ, Ga, 97; pub art panelist, Hartsfield Atlanta Internat Airport, 2001. *Teaching:* instr color night photog, Int Ctr Photog, NY, 92-94; instr photog, color printing, The Creative Circus, Atlanta, 96-; instr, basic photog Georgia Perimeter Col, 96-98; instr Polaroid transfer printing, Atlanta Col Art, Ga, 96-97; instr color photog, photojournalism, stock photog, Am Intercontinental Univ, Atlanta, 97-98; instr color photog, Maine Photog Workshops, 99. *Awards:* grantee Nat Endowmwnt for Arts, Media Programs, 76-77; grantee City of Atlanta, Bur Cult Affairs, 97; City of Atlanta Urban Design Commn Award Excellence, 99. *Bibliog:* Manfred Zollner (auth) Buhren der Nacht, FotoMagazin, 8/2000; Michael Plante (auth) Art in Am, 99. *Mem:* Am Soc Media Photographers. *Media:* Photo Murals

WHITELEY, ELIZABETH
PAINTER, SCULPTOR
b Erie, Pa, Sept 6, 45. *Study:* Carnegie-Mellon Univ, BA, 68; Case Western Reserve Univ, MS, 69; Sch of Art Inst Chicago, BFA, 76; Am Univ, studied with Luciano Penay, 2001-03. *Work:* Carengie Mus of Art, Pittsburgh, PA; Mus of Modern Art, NY; Natl Mus of Women in the Arts, Washington, DC; Smithsonian Mus of Am Art, Washington, DC; Victoria & Albert Mus, London, England. *Comn:* Painting, Linowes & Blocher, Washington, 88; painting, Montgomery Co exec off, Md, 2001; painting, Sch of Art Inst Chicago, 2001; painting, The Connecticut, 2003, Embassy suites, 2005. *Exhib:* Founding: The Pouring of Hot Metal, Art Inst Chicago, 75; solo exhib, Arnold & Porter, Washington, 93; 10,000 Plus Alumni Show, Sch of Art Inst Chicago, 94; Organization of American States, Mus of Americas, Washington, 94; Am Ctr Physics, College Park, Md, 96 & 2003; The Ralls Collection, Washington, 2002; London Univ Inst Educ, London, 2006. *Pos:* Ed, Eye Wash Peer Reviews, 89-93; moderator & speaker, Smithsonian Inst sem, 96; presenter, Art & Mathematics, State Univ, NY, Albany, 94-2000; presenter, ISAMA/CTI, Chicago, IL, 2004; editor bd, Journal Mathematics & Arts. *Teaching:* Instr drawing & etching, Ivy Sch Prof Art, Pa, 78-79. *Awards:* Asn Artists Painting Purchase Award, Carnegie Inst Mus Art, 80; Berthe vonMoschzisker Cash Award, Philadelphia Print Ctr Int Competition, 81; Gallery West Juror's Award, Alexandria, Va, 2003. *Bibliog:* Mary McCoy (auth), Earth views at RAP, Wash Post, 1/16/93; Margaret Paris (auth), Valued Women, 94; Johanna Drucker (auth), The Century of Artists Books, 95; Nicole Miller (auth), WPA/Corcoran Open Studios, Wash Post 10/27/2002. *Mem:* Coalition Wash Artists (steering comt, 87-88 & 90-91, rec secy, 88); Intl Soc of the Arts, Mathematics and Architecture (ISAMA); WPA/Corcoran; Int Sculpture Ctr; Washington Sculptors Group. *Media:* Acrylic; Wood; Metal-point Drawing. *Publ:* Coauth, The Fine Art Print: An Introduction, Pittsburgh Print Group, 83; illusr, Deck of Cards Pyramid Atlantic Press, (Peter Beaman, auth), 89; Visually transforming square root rectangles, In: Symmetry: Culture and Science, Vol 6, No 3, 95; Art and Mathematics: Symmetry, Series and Systems, in: YLEM, Vol 17, No 2, 97; Lines and Spaces: Dynamic Symmetry in 2-D Art, Proceedings; ISAMA/CTI 2004. *Mailing Add:* 3001 Veazey Terr NW No 803 Washington DC 20008-5404

WHITEMAN, EDWARD RUSSELL
PAINTER
b Buffalo, NY, Dec 16, 38. *Study:* Univ Buffalo Albright Art Sch, AD. *Work:* Nat Collection Fine Arts, Washington, DC; Albright-Knox Art Gallery, Buffalo; New Orleans Mus Art, La; Montgomery Mus Fine Arts, Ala; Crysler Mus Art, Mass. *Exhib:* Whitney Biennial Contemp Am Art, NY, 75; Eight State Exhib Paintings & Sculpture, Okla Art Ctr, 75; Pratt Graphic Ctr, 75; La Jolla Mus Contemp Art, Calif, 79; Columbia Mus Art, SC; Paper Making & Paper Using, Southeastern Ctr Contemp Art, Winston-Salem, NC; Edward Whiteman: Works on Treated Paper, 1975-1982, Mus Art, Carnegie Inst, 82; Corcoran Biennial, Corcoran Gallery Art, Washington, DC, 88. *Awards:* Artist Fels, Nat Endowment for the Arts & Southeastern Ctr Contemp Art, 78-79; Ford Found Grant, 80; Grant, Penny McCall Found, 90. *Bibliog:* Jean Nathan (auth), Newswatch Art, Channel 6 News, 75; Calas & Terrington (coauths), Edward Whiteman and the unlovely metaphor, Arts Quarterly New Orleans, Vol 4, No 3, 82. *Media:* Liquitex, Pastel. *Dealer:* Arthur Roger Gallery. *Mailing Add:* c/o Arthur Roger Gallery 432 Julia St New Orleans LA 70130

WHITEN, COLETTE
SCULPTOR, INSTRUCTOR
b Birmingham, Eng, Feb 7, 45; Can citizen. *Study:* Ont Col of Art, AOCA. *Work:* Nat Gallery of Can, Ottawa; Art Gallery of Ont, Toronto; Art Bank, Ottawa; Oakville Galleries, Ont, Can; Art Gallery Hamilton, Ont, Can. *Comn:* sculpture, Mental Health Ctr, Toronto, 78; Manufacturer's Life Insurance Bldg, Toronto, 85-86; sculpture, Bankers Hall, Calgary, Alberta, Can. *Exhib:* En Scene, Amsterdam; The Power Plant, Toronto, Ont, Can, 92; Susan Hobbs Gallery, Toronto, 94, 96, 98, 2000; Trayecto Galeria, Vitoria, Spain, 97; Museu d'Art de Girona, Spain, 97. *Teaching:* Instr concept develop, Ont Col of Art, Toronto, 74-; resident artist, Univ Western Ont, London, 78-79. *Awards:* Toronto Arts Award, 90; Can Coun Sr Grant, 93, 94, 96; Ont Arts Coun Sr Grant, 97. *Bibliog:* David Burnett & Marilyn Schiff, Contemporary Canadian Art, Hurtig Publ, Edmonton, 83; Elke Town (auth), Prince Charming and the Associated Press: The Needlepoint Work of Colette Whiten, Descant, 80-98, winter 87; Carol Laing (auth), Colette Whiten, Parachute, 42-43, 6-8/87. *Media:* Plaster, Wood; Mixed Media. *Publ:* Contribr, Carmen Lamanna Gallery at Owens Art Gallery, Owens Art Gallery, Sackville, NB, 75; auth, Photographiclnscription: Kunst Aus Toronto (exhib catalog), 90, Denonication (exhib Catalog), 91, Power Plant Catalogue, 92, Seducing the Receiver (exhib catalog), 96. *Dealer:* Susan Hobbs Gallery, Toronto, Ont, Can. *Mailing Add:* Dept Studio Art Ont Col Art & Design Dept Sculpture Installation Ont Col Art Toronto ON M5T 1W1 Canada

WHITEN, TIM (TIMOTHY) GROVER
SCULPTOR, ENVIRONMENTAL ARTIST
b Inkster, Mich, Aug 13, 41. *Study:* Cent Mich Univ, BS, 64; Univ Ore, creative arts grant, 65, MFA, 66. *Work:* Nat Gallery Can, Can Coun Art Bank & Ministry External Affairs, Ottawa, Ont, Can; Art Gallery Ont, Toronto; Ingalls Stone Co, Bedford, Ind. *Comn:* Cast concrete walls, Dept Parks & Recreation, Jasper, Ore, 64; monumental sculpture, Lane Co Parks Comn, Orchard Lake, Eugene, Ore, 66; Earth Work Ritual Installation, Art Park, Lewiston, NY, 77; Ritual Installation, Cent Park, Art Across the Park, NY, 82. *Exhib:* Solo exhibs, Art Gallery York Univ, North York, Ont, 72, Morris

Gallery, Toronto, Ont, 72 & 74: York Univ, Zacks Gallery, Stong Col, North York, Ont, 74, St Lawrence Col Appl Arts & Technol, Kingston, Ont, 74 & 79, Univ Waterloo, Ont, 76, Bau-Xi Gallery, Toronto, Ont, 76, 77, 78, 79, 81, 82, 83 & 85 & Olga Korper Gallery, Toronto, Ont, 86, 90 & 93; Maquette Auction, Harbourfront Art Gallery, Toronto, 85; Cult Exchange Exhib, Zhejlang Acad, Hangzhou, People's Repub China, 86; York Work I, Art Gallery York Univ, NY, 86; Membership Sales, Art Gallery Ont, Toronto, 87 & 88; Int Art Fair, Chicago, 87; Int Art Fair, Cologne, Ger, 88; Day of the Dead, York Quay Gallery, Harbourfront, Toronto, 88. *Teaching:* Assoc prof fine arts, York Univ, Downsview, Ont, 68-; vis lectr, univs & arts schs, Can, 70-; chmn, Fine Arts Coun; chmn visual arts dept, York Univ, 84-87 & assoc prof, 87-; instr, Atlin Ctr Arts, BC, 86. *Awards:* O'Connell Purchase Award, 63. *Bibliog:* Numerous articles in periodicals & newspapers including, Artpost 24, Harpers, Artscanada, Arts Mag & Village Voice. *Media:* Human Skulls, Mud; Found Objects, Paper. *Res:* Investigation of consciousness as it manifests in a variety of cultures, historically and contemporarily. *Mailing Add:* c/o Olga Korper Gallery 17 Morrow Ave Toronto ON M6R 2H9 Canada

WHITESELL, JOHN D
PRINTMAKER
b Hamilton, Ohio, Dec 1, 42. *Study:* Earlham Col, Richmond, Ind, BA; Miami Univ, Ohio, with Robert Wolfe, Jr; Ind Univ with Rudy Pozzatti & Marvin Lowe, MFA. *Work:* Bradford City Art Gallery, Yorkshire, Eng; Libr Cong, Washington, DC; Miami Art Ctr, Fla; US Info Agency, Prints in Embassies Prog. *Comn:* Vermillion Seven (suite of prints), comn & publ by Univ SDak, 75. *Exhib:* Nat Print, Libr Cong, 71 & 73; 5th Ann Nat Exhib Prints, San Diego, Calif, 72; 1st Int Graphics Biennial, Miami, Fla, 73; Nat Print Los Angeles, 73; Bradley Nat Print Show, Peoria, Ill, 75. *Teaching:* Assoc prof printmaking, Univ Louisville, Ky, 73-. *Awards:* Third Award, Miami Print Int, 73; Purchase Awards, Libr Cong, 73 & Bradley Univ, 75. *Media:* Silkscreen, Lithographs. *Mailing Add:* Dept of Art Rm 104 Univ of Louisville Schnider Hall Louisville KY 40292

WHITESIDE, WILLIAM ALBERT, II
PAINTER, INSTRUCTOR
b Bradenton, Fla, Aug 1, 25. *Study:* Ringling Sch Art, 48-51; Fla State Univ, Tallahassee, with Karl Zerbe & Arthur Deshaies, BS(art educ), 58, MFA(painting), 66. *Work:* Marine Corps Mus, Washington, DC; New Eng Air Mus, Windsor Locks, Conn; Marine Corps Mus, Quantico, Va; Marine Corps Air Mus, MCAS, El Toro, Calif; Marine Corp Mus, Washington, DC; New Englad Air Mus, Windsor Locks, CT; Marine Corps Air Mus, MCAS, El Toro, CA; North Carolina Aviation Mu, Ashboro, NC; Burt Reynolds Mus, Jupiter, FL; Marine Corps Mus, San Diego, CA; Nat Mus Naval Aviation, Pensacola, Fla; Military Mus, Palmetto, Fla; Heard Mus, McKinney, Tex. *Comn:* Portrait-riverscape, Burt Reynolds, 81; Portrait, Charles Coody, Augusta Masters. *Exhib:* Third Monroe Ann, Masur Mus Art, La, 66; Midyear Show, Butler Inst Am Art, 66 & 67; Seventh Ann Nat Western Art Show, San Antonio, Tex, 69; solo exhib, Asheville Mus Art, NC, 72, 2002; 30th Ann Painting Exhib, Abilene Fine Arts Mus, Tex, 73; NC Watercolor Soc, Asheville Art Mus, NC, 76; and others. *Teaching:* Instr art, Fla State Univ, 64-65; instr painting, NTex State Univ, 66-68 & Western Carolina Univ, 73-75; artist in residence, High Hampton Inn & Country Club, 69-74. *Awards:* Transparent Watercolor Award, 73 & Purchase Award, 74, Tex Watercolor Soc; NC Watercolor Soc Purchase Award, 76; Acrylic Best of Show, Anderson Artists Guild, 2005 & 2006; Best of Show, Anderson Co Fair, 2005. *Mem:* NC Watercolor Soc. *Media:* Acrylic, Watercolor, Egg Tempura. *Mailing Add:* PO Box 522 Cashiers NC 28717

WHITLOCK, JOHN JOSEPH
MUSEUM DIRECTOR, EDUCATOR
b South Bend, Ind, Jan 7, 35. *Study:* Ball State Univ, BS, 57, MA, 63; Ind Univ, EdD, 71. *Work:* Ball State Univ, Muncie, Ind; Hanover Col, Ind. *Exhib:* One-man shows, Franklin Col, Ind, 69, Westminster Presby Church Gallery, 71, Unitarian Church Gallery, 71, Rockford, Ill, Grace St Luke's Festival Arts in Relig, 76 & Unitarian Fel, 83; John A Logan Col, 86; Tupelo Art Gallery, 87. *Collection Arranged:* Warrington Colescott: Fifty Years of Printmaking, 90; Mr Imagination, Dawson, Philpot and Sparrow: Black Chicago Artists, 91; Dale Leys: Drawings, 91; Melanesian Artifacts from the Southern Illinois University Collections, 92; Brent Kington: An Artist Looking Forward, 93; Robert Paulson: Retrospective Exhibition, 93; Harlan W Butt: Metalsmith, 94; Allen Moore Paintings, 95; US/Mexico Prints, 95; Arch Connelly Paintings and Mixed Media, 96; Polly and Marion Mitchell: Scherensncitte & Collage and Traditional Bentwood Containers, 96; Bruce Richmond Paintings and Wood Carvings, 96; American Tapestry Alliance Biennial-I, 96; Richard Nickel Photographs and Louis Sullivan Architectural Ornaments, 96; C & P 20th Anniversary Exhib, 97; Leendert Van Der Pool & Eleanor Winters Paintings, Drawings & Collage, 97; Pierre Neveu Paintings, France, 97; S Ill Metalsmiths, 97; Todd Wolf Paintings, 97; Loetitia Lilot Paintings & Books, Sch Paris, 98; Contemporary Stitch: Japan Style, 98. *Pos:* Dir & cur, Burpee Art Mus, Rockford, Ill, 70-72; dir, Brooks Mem Art Gallery, Memphis, Tenn, 72-78; dir, Univ Mus & Mus Studies Prog, Southern Ill Univ, Carbondale, 78-, actg cur art, 89-. *Teaching:* Instr educ, Hanover Col, 64-66, asst prof art, 66-69; teaching assoc art educ, Ind Univ, Bloomington, 69-70; prof arts & humanities, Elgin Community Col, 70-72; prof mus studies prog, Southwestern at Memphis, 73-78; prof museology, Memphis State Univ, 76-78; prof mus studies, Southern Ill Univ, Carbondale, 78-; mem grad fac. *Awards:* Ball State Univ Fine Arts Purchase Award, 57. *Mem:* Am Asn Mus; Midwest Asn Mus; Int Coul of Mus; Asn Art Mus Dirs. *Media:* Painting; Printmaking. *Publ:* Auth, Return to Alexandria, Viewpoints, Vol 54, No 3, Ind Univ, 5/76; Museum Studies, Mus Scope, 76; Relativistic Thought: Charting the Future of Museums, ICOFOM Study Series, No 10, ICOM, 10/86; Museology and Museums, ICOFOM Study Series, ICOM, 9/87; Museology: Preserving the National Patrimony, No 14, ICOFOM Study Series, 11/88; auth, The Creative Use of Reproductions in Museum Exhibits, ICOFOM Study Series, No 8, ICOM Conf on Museology, Zagreb, Yugoslavia, 85

WHITMAN, KAREN
PRINTMAKER
b Bronx, NY, Feb 22, 53. *Study:* State Univ NY, Buffalo, with Harvey Breverman, BFA, 75; Parsons Sch Design, cert graphic design, 90; studied at Woodstock Sch Art, 91, Art Students League NY, with Peter Homitzky, 92-94. *Work:* NY Pub Libr; Mus of the City of New York; NY Transit Mus; NY Historical Soc; The British Mus, London; Taiwan Univ Inst of Fine Arts, Taipei, Taiwan; Jane Voorhees Zimmerli Art Mus, New Brunswick, NJ; Hofstra Mus, Hofstra Univ, Hemstead, NY; Samuel Dorsky Mus Art, New Paltz, NY. *Exhib:* Soc of Am Graphic Artists Exhib, 94-present; Schenectady Mus, NY, 95 & 98; NY by New Yorkers: Artist Views in Prints, Mus of the City of NY, 02; A Century on Paper; Prints by Art Students League Artists, UBS/Paine Webber Gallery, 2002; Zimmerti Art Mus, New Acquistitions, 2002; Hofstra Mus at 40, Works on Paper, 2003; Trans Views, Ny Transit Mus, 2003; Allied Artists of Am Ann Exhib, 2003-2004; Solo Exhib: The Old Print Shop, NY, 2002, The Pen & Brush, Inc, 2004; St Thomas Aquinas Col, 2004, Woodstock Artists Asn, Woodstock, NY, 2005-2006. *Pos:* Coun mem, Soc Am Graphic Artists, 94; Artists Council, Nat Asn Women Artists, 2003-2005. *Teaching:* guest lectr, Woodstock Sch Art, 99, instr, 03. *Awards:* Medal of Honor for Graphics Award, Catharine Lorillard Wolfe Art Club, 99, Nat Asn Women Artists, 02; Elizabeth Morse Genius Found Award, 02. *Bibliog:* Antiques and the Arts Weekly, 12/7/2001; Journal of the Print World, fall 2002; Am Artist Mag, 12/2002; Impressions of NY-Prints from the NY Historical Soc by Maryilyn Symmes, Illus, 2004; Ray Steiner (auth), Art Times, 12/05-1/06. *Mem:* Soc Am Graphic Artists; Allied Artists Am; Catharine Lorillard Wolfe Art Club; Nat Asn Women Artist; Audubon Artists. *Media:* Linoleum Cut, Etching. *Dealer:* Old Print Shop 150 Lexington Ave New York NY 10016. *Mailing Add:* PO Box 550 Bearsville NY 12409

WHITMAN, ROBERT
ARTIST
b New York City, NY 35. *Study:* Studied literature, Rutgers Univ, 53—57; Studied art history, Columbia Univ, 58. *Comn:* Co-founder (with artist Robert Rauschenberg and engineers Fred Waldhauer and Billy Klüver) Experiments in Art and Technology (EAT), 66. *Pos:* Performance artist, Am Moon, 60, Prune Flat, 65, A Walk in the Park, 81, Raincover, 82, Eclipse, 83-84, Black Dirt, List Visual Arts Ctr, Mass Inst of Technology, Cambridge, 90, Ghost, PaceWildenstein Galleries, 2002, solo exhibs, Jewish Mus, 68, Robert Whitman: 4 Cinema Pieces, Mus Contemp Art, Chicago, 68, Mus Modern Art, New York City, 73, Palisade, Hudson River Mus, 79, Playback, Dia: Chelsea, New York City, 2003-2004, Museo Serralves, Porto, Portugal, 2004, Robert Whitman: Shading, Pace Wildenstein Gallery, New York City, 2004, Playback, Museo Arte Contemporanea Barcelona, 2005, Les années Pop, Centre Georges Pompidou, Paris, 2001, Into the Light: The Projected Image in Am Art 64-77, Whitney Mus Am Art, 2001-2002. *Mailing Add:* PaceWildenstein Gallery 32 E 57th St 2nd Fl New York NY 10022

WHITMAN-ARSENAULT, KATE
PAINTER
b Camden, NJ, Oct 25, 22. *Study:* Wellesley Col, BA, 44; Univ Bridgeport, MS, 77; Silvermine Sch Art, Conn, studied with Don Stone, Charles Reid, Herb Olsen & Ed Whitney, MA in Art Therapy. *Work:* Union Trust Co, Darien, Conn; Darien Libr, Conn. *Comn:* Long Island Sound House, comn by Eliz Lucas, Darien, Conn, 78; Vt pitcher & bowl, St Lukes Church, Darien Conn, 79; Cape Cod House, comn by Barbara Moyes, Vero Beach, Fla, 81; Wellfleet House, comn by Stephen Ambler, Peterborough, Ont, 83; shells, comn by Jeanne Rich, Dallas, Tex, 87. *Exhib:* Wellesley Col-Jewett M Wellesley, Mass, 70; one-woman shows, Salmagundi Club, NY, 80, Copley Soc, Boston, Mass, 85-86, New Eng Gallery Art & Cape Cod Art Asn, Heritage Plantation, Sandwich, 94 & Cataumet Art Ctr, Mass, 94; Boston Univ Art Gallery, Mass, 80; Cape Cod Conserv, Barnstable, Mass, 87; Monotype Guild New Eng Inc, Clyde Gallery, Mosman Park, Boston, Mass, 88; two-woman show, Creations of Cap Artists, Osterville, Mass, 90; Cahoon Mus Am Art, Cutuit, Mass; Gallery of Creations, Nokomis, Fla. *Pos:* News ed, Darien News, 70-80. *Teaching:* Instr, Darien Art Gallery, Conn, 74-76; instr, Darien Adult Educ, 76-77; art therapist, Darien Convalescent Ctr, 77-80; art therapist, Pocasset Mental Health Ctr, 87-; instr, Catamet Art Ctr, Mass, formerly. *Awards:* Award Falmouth Aritst Guild-Cape Cod Art Asn. *Bibliog:* Peter Konig (auth), Dir Duxbury, Mass Art Asn, 87. *Mem:* Salmagundi Club; Am Watercolor Soc; Copley Soc; Guild of Boston Artists; Cape Cod Art Asn; assoc mem New Eng Watercolor Soc; fel Roy Soc Arts, London, Eng. *Media:* Watercolor, Oil. *Publ:* Illusr, Print-Nantucket, Globe Press, 87; L and Art, Cape Cod Life, Nantucket, Cape Cod Life, 88. *Dealer:* Arlene Hecht Gallery 333 North Falmouth, MA. *Mailing Add:* 9 Red Brook Pond Dr PO Box 710 Cataumet MA 02534

WHITNEY, MAYNARD MERLE
SCULPTOR, EDUCATOR
b Cedar Rapids, Iowa, Dec 18, 31. *Study:* Iowa Wesleyan Col, BA, 58; Univ Calif, Los Angeles, 60; Univ Iowa, 61; Univ Ore, MFA (sculptor), 65. *Work:* Joslyn Art Mus, Omaha, Nebr; Sheldon Art Gallery, Lincoln, Nebr; Denver Art Mus, Colo; Elder Art Gallery, Nebr Wesleyan Univ, Lincoln; Omaha Nat Bank, Nebr. *Comn:* Hanging Plexiglas sculpture, Ford-Warren Libr, Denver Pub Libr, 75. *Exhib:* Artrain (toured nine western states), 73; 13th Midwest Biennial, Joslyn Art Mus, Omaha, 74; 14th Ann Own Your Own Show, Pueblo Art Ctr, Colo, 74; one-man shows, Sheldon Art Gallery, Lincoln, 70 & Kans State Univ, Manhattan, 71; and others. *Teaching:* Chmn dept art, Nebr Wesleyan Univ, Lincoln, 65-72 & Colo Women's Col, Denver, 72-81; Aurora Pub Sch, 84-88. *Awards:* Creative Teaching Award, Nebr Wesleyan Univ, 67; Mus Purchase, 11th Midwest Biennial, Joslyn Art Mus, Omaha, 70; Purchase Award, 6th Ann Midland Exhib, Omaha Nat Bank, 70. *Media:* Multimedia, Stone. *Mailing Add:* 20137 Summit Hwy Blodgett OR 97326

WHITNEY, RICHARD WHEELER
PAINTER, INSTRUCTOR
b Burlington, Vt, Jan 22, 46. *Study:* Univ NH, Durham, BA, 68; with Sidney F Willis, Bennington, NH, 65; with R H Ives Gammell, Boston, 66-71. *Work:* Harvard Univ; Univ Chicago; Anchorage Hist & Fine Arts Mus; Newark Mus Art, NJ; Anderson House Mus, Washington, DC; Mass State Capital; NH State Capital; Ohio State Univ Sch of Law; Northeastern Univ; Mt Sinai Hosp; Stanford Univ, MIT; and others. *Comn:* portrait of Cardinal Humberto Medeiros, Cath Univ Portugal, 88; portrait of James H Webb, Jr, Secy of Navy, Pentagon, Washington, DC, 89; mural, comn by Frederick Hart Family, Hume, Va, 91-93; portrait of Lane Kirkland, president AFL-CIO, Washington, DC, 93; Robert Reich, Sec of Labor, Washington, DC, 98. *Exhib:* Allied Artists Am Nat Exhibs, NY, 76-77, 80-81 & 83; solo exhibs, Guild Boston Artists, 80 & 82; Maryhill Mus, Wash; Springfield Mus, Utah; Amarillo Art Ctr, Tex, 83; and others. *Collection Arranged:* Allied Artists Am, New Eng Exhib, 82. *Pos:* Bd mem Am Renaissance of the Twenty First Century, NY, Art Renewal Ctr, NYC; bd chmn Am Soc Portrait Artists Found. *Teaching:* Instr painting, Sharon Arts Ctr, NH, 71-77; instr art, Cushing Acad, Ashburnham, 71-80; pvt instr & workshops, 81-. *Awards:* 3 Greats Award, Elizabeth T Greenshields Found, Montreal, Can, 70-72; Gold Medal, Guild Boston Artists Competition, 83 & 87; Medal Hon, Am Artist Prof League, 84 & 91; Silver Medal, Soc Illusr, New York, 87. *Bibliog:* Charles Movalli (auth), A conversation with Richard Whitney, Am Artist Mag, 82; Alexandra York (auth), Richard Whitney, neoclassical impressionist, Am Arts Quart, winter 92; Colin Berry (auth), A Sensitive Eye, Am Artist Mag, 2000. *Mem:* Portraits Inc; Guild Boston Artists; Portraits South, Raleigh, NC; and others. *Media:* Oil, Pastel. *Interests:* Boating, Hiking; Classical Pianist, specializing in the works of Scriabin. *Publ:* Auth, Return to Excellence, Profile, fall 83; coauth, Realism in Revolution: The Art of the Boston School, Taylor Publ Co, 86; auth, Painting the Visual Impression, Minn River Sch Fine Art, 93. *Dealer:* Studios at Crescent Pond 100 Chalet Dr Stoddard NH 03464. *Mailing Add:* 100 Chalet Dr Stoddard NH 03464

WHITNEY (STEVENS), CHARLOTTE ARMIDE
PAINTER, JEWELER
b New York, NY, Dec 13, 23. *Study:* Corcoran Sch Art, George Washington Univ, with Eugen Weiscz & Peggy Bacon, BFA, 45; Cranbrook Acad Art, with Zoltan Sepeshy, MFA, 46. *Work:* Series of 24 wild plant watercolors & series of 32 tree flower watercolors Kingman Mus, Battle Creek, Mich. *Exhib:* one-person shows, Pasghetti's, Kalamazoo, 88, Triola Gallery, Lansing, Mich, 92, Olivet Col Art Gallery, Saginaw Art Mus, Mich, 95 & Northwood Univ, Midland, Mich, 97, The Gallery, Battle Creek, Mich, 00, Surveying Mus, Lansing, Mich, 00, Milbridge Hist Mus, Maine, 00, Charlotte Community Libr, Mich, 01, New Scenes of Maine, Milbridge Hist Soc, Maine, 03, East Lansing, Mich Pub Art Gallery, 2005; Paintings of Miami and Mich Art Deco Archit, CompuServe's Fine Art Forum, 93; two-person retrospective 1939-1993, Battle Creek Art Ctr, 94; Mich Art Deco Archit Exhib, Mich Touring Arts Directory, Mich Coun Arts & Cult Affairs, 96-98; group shows, Barn Again, Eaton Co Hist Comn Courthouse Sq Asn, Charlotte, Mich, 99, The Eclectic Gallery, Battle Creek, Mich, 2000; and others. *Collection Arranged:* Battle Creek Art Ctr, Mich. *Pos:* Co-dir, Whitney Galleries, Birmingham, Mich, 50-59; dir traveling exhib Olivet Restoration Drawings, Mich Coun Arts & Olivet, Mich City Hall, 74-75. *Teaching:* Art, Roeper City & Country Sch, Bloomfield Hills, Mich, 50-59, Olivet Col, Mich, 65-70, 87 & 90 & Olivet Schs, Mich, 72-89. *Awards:* Olivet Downtown Storefronts Restoration Award, Keep Mich Beautiful, 73; Graham Found Grant, 93. *Bibliog:* Virginia Gust (auth), Olivet woman sketches youth into old buildings, Enquirer & News, Battle Creek, Mich, 2/4/73; Linda Scott (auth), A Most Retiring Journey, Battle Creek Enquirer, 3/21/95; Patty Maher (auth), for the Love of Art and Architecture, Battle Creek Enquirer, 2/6/2000. *Mem:* Southwest Michigan Watercolor Soc; Eaton Art League. *Media:* Watercolor, Acrylic; Metalcraft. *Specialty:* watercolors. *Publ:* Auth, Children's Art, Olivet Col Press, 65. *Dealer:* Woodwind Gallery Machias ME. *Mailing Add:* PO Box 305 Olivet MI 49076

WHITSON, ANGIE
SCULPTOR, PAINTER
b San Jose, Calif. *Study:* Pasadena Mus Art, 74; Art League, Los Angeles, Calif, 74-78; Northridge Univ, Calif. *Work:* Ore Hist Soc; Xerox Corp; Virginia City CofC; Paper Source Mus, Los Angeles, Calif; Television Acad Arts & Scis; and others. *Comn:* Sculptures, Golden Nugget, Atlantic City, NJ, McDonald's, Greenville, NC, Lozano, Mexico City & Sterns, Nevada; Television Acad Arts & Sci, Joyce Hall of Hallmark Cards; Leonard Goldenson, Exec Paramount Films & ABC TV; Ernie Kovacs, Comedian. *Exhib:* Art Festival Laguna, Laguna Beach, Calif, 77-95; Miniature Soc NJ, Nutley Gallery, NJ, 79; Miniature Soc Washington, Archit Inst, 79; Cody Mus Art, Wyo, 79; La Luz, NMex, 83; Paramont Invitational, 86-91. *Pos:* Founder, Ume Publ, 86. *Teaching:* Instr sculpture, Pierce Col, Woodland Hills, Calif, 78-80 & Univ Judism, Belair, Calif, 95-96. *Awards:* Gold Medals, San Gabriel Fine Art Asn, 79-81; Miniature Soc Washington; two Gold Medals, Paramont Invitational, 87, 90 & 91. *Bibliog:* Article, Nevada Sun, Las Vegas, 82; This Week in Laguna, 84-86. *Mem:* Women Artists Am West; Golden State Sculpture Soc. *Media:* Etching, Sculpting. *Publ:* The Sophistiguins, Cartoon Serial Penguins, Warner Ctr News. *Mailing Add:* 5105 Tendilla Ave Woodland Hills CA 91364

WHITSON, PETER WHITSON WARREN
COLLAGE ARTIST, EDUCATOR
b Concord, Mass, Sept 7, 41. *Study:* Univ NH, BA, 63; Univ Iowa, MA & MFA, 67; Eastern Montana Col, 83-84. *Work:* Univ NH; Univ Iowa; Kansas City Art Inst; Mod Museet, Stockholm, Sweden; Galeria Teatru Studio, Warsaw, Poland. *Exhib:* One-man shows, Univ Iowa, 65 & 67, Univ Buffalo, NY, 70, Scalping Gallery, Regina, Sask, 75, Eastern Mont Col, 79, Yellow Art Ctr, Billings, Mont, 80; Nat Art Gallery, Wellington, NZ, 76; San Francisco Art Inst, 84; Idaho State Univ, Pocatello, 86; Eastern Mont Col, 92; The Dead School Show, 96; Kaleidoscope, Billings, Mont, 96; Anderson Gallery, Billings, Mont, 98; Faculty Show, Mont State Univ, Billings, 2005; plus many others. *Pos:* Pres, founder, Western Dakota Junk Co, Billings, Mont, 69-; founder & pres, Acad Neodada, 74-79; pres, Nat Acad Conceptualists, 79-80; ed & publr, SLUJ Press, 75-; gallery dir, Eastern Mont Col, 78-79, slide librn, 79-80; art ed, Alkali Flats Mag, 81-; bd dir, Photog Inst Billings, 84-86; publ & ed, The Dead School Epitaph, currently. *Teaching:* Asst drawing, Univ Iowa, 65-67; from instr to prof drawing, design, photog & art hist, Eastern Mont Col, formerly; chmn art dept, 86, 87 & 92-96; prof, Mont State Univ, Billings, currently. *Awards:* Third Place Black & White Print, Photog Inst Billings 9th Ann Competition, Yellowstone Art Ctr, Mont, 85; Two Honorable Mentions, Artists Valentines, HG Merriam Gallery, Billings, 86; Cash Award, Big Sky Biennal IV, Idaho State Univ, 86. *Bibliog:* Ronny Cohen (auth), Please Mr Postman look & see-Is there a work of art in your bag for me?, Art News, 12/81; Michael Crane & May Stofflet (auths), Correspondence art, Contemp Arts Press, San Francisco, 84. *Mem:* Yellowstone Art Mus; Photographic Hist Soc, New Eng; MNO; AANR. *Media:* Oil Stick, Pencil & Oil; Photomontage, Gelatin Silver Prints. *Res:* Photographic documentation. *Interests:* Figure photography, The Dead School, Postcards. *Publ:* Auth, Al's Ham 'n' Egger & Body Shop Again, Basilisk Press, 74; The SLUJ Book, 76, SLUJ Press; ed, The Dead School Epitaph, The Jour of the Dead Sch, 1996-2006. *Mailing Add:* Mont State Univ Art Dept 1500 University Dr Billings MT 59101-0298

WHITTINGTON, JON HAMMON
EDUCATOR, PAINTER
b Jackson, Miss, Oct 20, 38. *Study:* Belhaven Col, BA(art), 64; Miss Col, MEd, 66; Univ Miss, MA(art), 73. *Work:* Belhaven Col Permanent Collection, Jackson, Miss. *Exhib:* Ark Art Ctr, Little Rock, 73 & 74; Miss Art Asn Gallery, Jackson, 73 & 74; Images on Paper, Jackson, 74; solo exhibs, Meridian Mus, Miss, 74 & 75, Belhaven Col, 83 & 84 & Miss Art Asn Gallery, Jackson, 73 & 74; Miss Arts Festival, Jackson, 81. *Pos:* Mem, Governor's Comt Arts, Miss & Bd Regents, Miss Mus Art. *Teaching:* Chmn, art dept, East Miss Jr Col, 66-76; prof & chmn art dept, Belhaven Col, 76-86. *Awards:* First Place Award, Miss Medal Design for 1976 US Bicentennial, Franklin Mint, 76; Phil Hardin Found Grant; Inducted into Legacy of Learning, Belhaven Col, Jackson, Miss. *Mem:* Southeastern Col Art Conf; Nat Asn Schs Art & Design. *Media:* Watercolor. *Res:* Silver point drawing. *Mailing Add:* 1815 Howard St Jackson MS 39202

WHITTLESEY, STEPHEN
PAINTER, SCULPTOR
b Norwood, Mass, Dec 28, 38. *Study:* Columbia Univ, BA, 62, MFA, 65. *Exhib:* Solo shows, Snyderman Gallery, Philadelphia, 90, 92 & 94 & Naga/Clark Galleries, Boston, 92, Fuller Mus, Brockton, Mass, 97 & John Elder Gallery, NY, 98; Franklin Parrasch Gallery, NY, 94; Snyderman Gallery, 96; Nancy Margolis Gallery, Portland, Maine, 96; Peter Joseph Gallery, NY, 96; group exhib, Boston Mus of Fine Arts, 2003, Fuller Craft Mus, 2004 & 05. *Teaching:* Assoc prof, Fine Arts/Design Dept, dir, grad wood & furniture design prog, Univ Mass, Dartmouth, 92-. *Awards:* Fulbright Grant in Painting & Sculpture, Spain, 67-68; Nat Endowment Arts Grant, 92; Nat Endowment Arts Residence, France, 93. *Bibliog:* Yankee Mystique, Cape Cod Life, 7/95; Fuller Mus Installation Review, Sculpture Mag, 98; Show Review, John Elder Gallery, Am Craft Mag, 98. *Mem:* Furniture Soc. *Media:* Oil; Wood. *Dealer:* Galleries Clark/Naga Gallery 67 Newbury St Boston MA. *Mailing Add:* 1560 Main St West Barnstable MA 02668

WHITTOME, IRENE F
SCULPTOR, PAINTER
b Vancouver, BC, Mar 4, 42; Can citizen. *Study:* Vancouver Sch Art, BFA, 63. *Work:* Nat Gallery Can; Montreal Mus Fine Arts; Bibliot Nat, Paris; Mus Art Mod, Buenos Aires; Munic Mus, Birmingham, England. *Comn:* Print, Art Bank Can, 78; installation, Can Coun, NY, 79; sculpture, Hakone Open-Air Mus, Tokyo, 84. *Exhib:* Int Grafik-Bienale, Frenchen, Ger, 72; Paperworks, Nat Gallery Can, 78; solo exhibs, Montreal Mus Fine Arts, 80, Vancouver Art Gallery, 81, Winnnipeg Art Gallery, 81 & Hamilton Art Gallery, 81, Galerie Yajima, Montreal, Que, 82, Alberta Col Art Gallery, 83, Galerie du Mus du Que, 84, Walter Philips Gallery, Alberta, 86, Galerie Christiane Chassay, Montreal, 87, Musée des Traces, Montreal, Que, 89, Galerie Samuel Lallouz, Montreal, Que, 90 & Musée des Traces, Art Gallery Ont, Toronto, 90-91; Mus des beaux-arts du Can, Ottawa, 84; Mus d'Art Contemp de Montreal, Que, 85; Art Gallery Acadia Univ, Welpville, 85; Ctr Saidye Bronfman, Montreal, 86; Galerie 13, Montreal, 87; Mus d'Art Contemp de Montreal, Que, 87; Centre int d'art contemporain (CIAC), Montreal, Que, 89; and others. *Collection Arranged:* The Second Dalhousie Drawing Exhibition (auth, catalog), Dalhousie Art Gallery, Halifax, NS, 77. *Teaching:* Assoc prof art, Concordia Univ, Montreal, 68-. *Awards:* Medal Hon, Int Grafik-Biennale, Frechen, Ger, 72. *Bibliog:* Monique Brunet Weinmann (auth), L'Eternité transitoire d'Irene Whittome, Vie des Arts, Montreal, 3/91; Linda Genereux (auth), Irene F Whittome, Artforum, New York 3/91; John K Grande (auth), Vice Versa, Montreal, No 32, 2/91. *Mem:* Royal Can Acad Arts; Jack Chambers Found. *Publ:* Auth, Book of Insects, Vancouver Art Gallery, 63; Reproduction de quatre oeuvres, Rebirth 1987, dans C Mag, No 13, 87; and many others. *Mailing Add:* 18 Rue Laurier Ouest Montreal PQ H2T 2N3 Canada

WHYTE, BRUCE LINCOLN
CONSULTANT, ADMINISTRATOR
b New York, NY, Mar 13, 41. *Study:* Fordham Univ, BS, 62; NY Univ, MS, 63; San Francisco Univ, PhD, 2005. *Pos:* Founder & chmn, Original Print Collectors Group, Ltd, 72-84; gov, Nat Arts Club, 73-76 & 86-, chmn graphic arts, 73-, treas, 86-; expert art witness, US Treas Dept, 83-; founder & pres, Bruce Whyte Art Bus Develop Enterprises, Inc, 84-; managing consult, Knoedler-Modarco Galleries, 84-88; Am art

liason, Found Mitterand, Declaration of Human Rights on behalf of United Nations, UNESCO, Heads of State, Nat Mus, 89; consult, Mystic Seaport Mus Stores, 91; am art liaison, Doctors of the World, Paris, 92; chmn, Mus Arts & Technol, 93-94; pres, Ulster Arts Alliance, 93-95; tech assistance prog consult, NY State Coun Arts, 96-; marketing consult, Evercolor Fine Art, 98-; to Chief Exec Officer of Conceptual Art and Beyond, 2003-. *Teaching:* Lectr advan OMNA, NY Univ, 82. *Awards:* Best in Art Catalogs USA, Maxwell Sroge Publ; Nat Arts Club Award, 86; Fel of the Int Biographical Centre, Cambridge, Eng, 2002-; Int Order of Merit, Univ England, Cambridge, 2003; Deputy Dir Gen of the Americas, Cabridge, 2003. *Bibliog:* Leo Lloyd (auth), Graphic art by mail, United Press Int, 6/4/79; Sandra Salmans (auth), Good buys in fine art, New York Times, 1/25/81; Maxwell Sroge (auth & publ), Inside the 250 US Leading Mail Order Houses, 88. *Mem:* Soc Am Graphic Artists; Fine Arts Publ Asn (dir); Artist Fel; Greenwich Village Soc Hist Preserv (trustee); Nat Arts Club. *Specialty:* Contemporary original prints and fine old master prints. *Interests:* photography and study of cultures. *Publ:* publ, The Multiple Image: A Guide to Collecting Original Prints, 83; auth, The Original Print Collectors Newsletter (bi-monthly), 72-90. *Mailing Add:* 331 Stratfield Rd Fairfield CT 06825

WIBLE, MARY GRACE
PAINTER, EDUCATOR
b Three Springs, Pa, Apr 27, 11. *Study:* Pa State, BS, 38 & MEd, 42; Denver Univ, 54; Tyler Sch Art, Temple Univ, 67-68. *Work:* Kutztown Univ Gallery, Pa; Brandlywine Sch, Topton, Pa; Reading Community Col, Pa; Kutztown Univ, Pa. *Exhib:* Ann Exhib, Reading Pub Mus, 58, 61-63, 74 & 88; Harrisburg State Juried, William Penn Mem Mus, 74; Juried Ann Regional, Reading Pub Mus, 82, 84 & 88; 50th Ann Exhib, Muhlenberg Col Art Ctr, Allentown, 85. *Teaching:* Art supervisor, State Col Pa & Bradford, 38-46; asst prof art, Lock Haven Univ, 46-54; assoc prof art, Kutztown Univ, 54-68, prof emeritus, 68-. *Awards:* Lehigh Art Alliance, 50th Anniversary Exhib, 85; 1st Place Watercolor, Allentown Col St Frances, 86; Award Excellence, Pa Watercolor Show, 93. *Mem:* Pastel Soc. *Media:* Watercolor. *Publ:* Contribr, several articles, Design Mag, 46; illusr, Lock Haven Express Newspaper, 10/24/53. *Mailing Add:* 315 Wenz St Kutztown PA 19530

WICKLANDER, EDWARD A
SCULPTOR
b Puyallup, Wash, 52. *Study:* Cent Wash Univ, BA, 75, MA, 77; Univ Ill, MFA, 80. *Work:* Sage Co, Minneapolis; Wash State Arts Comn; Seattle Arts Comn; Univ Georgia, Athens; Frederick R Weisman Found of Art, Los Angeles. *Exhib:* One-man shows, Louisville Sch Art, 79, Northlight Gallery, Everett Community Col, 81, Sarah Spurgeon Gallery, 82, Glass Eye Gallery, Seattle, 84, Window Installation & Nine One One, Seattle, 85, Greg Kucera Gallery, Seattle, 85, 87, 88, 92 & 94 & Greg Kucera Gallery, Seattle, Wash, 96; Wunderkammer, Rena Bransten Gallery, San Francisco, Calif, 94; Musical Variations: Contemp Sound and Vision, Port Angeles Fine Art Ctr, Wash, 94; Fallen Timber, Tacoma Art Mus, Wash, 94; Off the Wall, Phyllis Kind Gallery, Chicago, 95. *Pos:* Instr sculpture, Cornish Col Arts, Seattle. *Awards:* Nat Endowment Arts, 88; Artist Trust Fel Award, Seattle, 90; Art Matters Grant, 94; and others. *Mailing Add:* 212 Third Ave S Seattle WA 98104

WIDING, ERIC P
COLLECTOR, ART DEALER
Study: Williams Col, BA (art hist and Am studies); Phi Beta Kappa. *Pos:* Head, Am Paintings Dept, Christie's, New York City, sr vpres, currently. *Mem:* Light House Int (bd dir, currently). *Publ:* Contribr, articles to art journals. *Mailing Add:* Christie's NY 20 Rockefeller Plaza New York NY 10020

WIDMER, GWEN ELLEN
PHOTOGRAPHER, EDUCATOR
b Chicago, Ill, Mar 10, 1945. *Study:* Goshen Col, Ind, BA, 67; Art Inst Chicago, MFA, 73. *Work:* J B Speed Art Mus, Louisville, Ky; Madison Art Ctr, Wis; Kalamazoo Inst Arts, Mich. *Exhib:* Photogr Midwest, Walker Art Ctr, Minneapolis, 73; The Invented Landscape, New Mus, NY, 79; The Hand Colored Photograph, Philadelphia Col Art, Pa, 79; Attitudes: Photog in the 1970's, Santa Barbara Mus Art, Calif, 79; one-person show, Camerawork Gallery, San Francisco, Calif, 80, & Ctr Contemp Arts, Santa Fe, NMex, 82; Playing It Again: Strategies of Appropriation, traveling 85-86, Santa Fe, NMex, Boulder, Colo, Los Angeles Ctr Photo Studies, Camerawork, San Francisco, Diverse Works, Houston, Photo Resource Ctr, Boston, Univ RI, Kinston; Am Photog today, Univ Denver, 82 & 84; Sights Unseen, AIR Gallery NY, traveling to Bard Col. *Teaching:* Instr photog, Univ Ill, Urbana/Champaign, 72-74; instr photog, Univ Northern Iowa, Cedar Falls, 76-; Univ NMex, Albuquerque, 80-86; Kansas City Art Inst, Kansas, 87-. *Awards:* Photog Fel, Nat Endowment Arts, 75 & 80; Third Prize, Bicentennial Exhib of Photog, Andromeda Gallery, Buffalo, NY, 77; Purchase Award, Light II, Humboldt State Univ, 77. *Mem:* Soc for Photog Educ. *Publ:* Contribr, Popular Photography, Vol 75 (2), Ziff-Davis, 74; Self--Portrayal, Friends of Photog, Carmel, Calif, 78; Darkroom Dynamics, Curtin & London, Marblehead, Mass, 79; Color, Life Libr of Photography, Time-Life Bks, 80; and others. *Mailing Add:* 6 E 62nd Terr Kansas City MO 64113

WIEBE, CHARLES M
DEALER, HISTORIAN
b Morgantown, WVa, Oct 8, 49. *Study:* Carnegie Mellon Univ, with Robert Lepper, 66; W Va Univ, Morgantown, BA (painting), 72; Univ Florence, Italy, with Eugenio Battisti, 74-75; Pa State Univ, MA (art hist), 79. *Collection Arranged:* Bijutsu, The Fine Arts Japan (co-cur), Southern Alleghenies Mus Art, Hollidaysburg, Pa, 87; Changing Lives, Ill Col, Jacksonville, 98. *Pos:* Gallery rep, Marson Ltd, Baltimore, 78-80; owner & dir, Wiebe Gallery, Pittsburgh, 80-87; dir exhibs, Int Images Gallery, Sewickley, Pa, 87-2002; Development Office, Carnegie Mus, of Pittsburgh. *Teaching:* Lectr, Vatican Mus, Rome, 75; lectr Japanese prints, Univ Pittsburgh, 84-; lectr, Point Park Col, Pittsburgh, 85-87, 2005; faculty mem humanities & film studies, Univ Phoenix, Pittsburgh. *Mem:* Col Art Asn Am; Am Mus Asn; Am Film Inst. *Res:* Italian Renaissance Art; Early American. *Specialty:* Japanese woodblock prints; old master prints; contemporary paintings and sculpture, Eastern European Art. *Publ:* Auth, Meaning in Hokusai's art, J Print World, winter 88; The New Soviet Avant-Garde, Int House, New York, 89; Women Between Times (catalogue), 93; Ed, The Mezzotint: Joop Vegter, Antwerp, Belgium, 98. *Mailing Add:* 315 Joseph's Ln Pittsburgh PA 15237

WIEGARDT, ERIC THOMAS
PAINTER, INSTRUCTOR
b Ilwack, WA. *Study:* Univ Wash, Seattle, Wash, BS, 1980; Am Acad of Art, Chicago, Ill, BFA, 1985. *Work:* Ilwaco Heritage Mus, Ilwaco, Wash; Fred Hutchinson Cancer Center, Seattle, Wash; Standard Oil, Bartlesville, Okla. *Exhib:* Transparent Watercolor Soc, Int Show, Wis, 1985-2006; Northwest Watercolor Soc, Int Show, Wash, 1988-2006; Allied Artists of Am, Int Show, NY, 1990-2006; Nat Watercolor Soc, Int Show, Calif, 1995-2006; Am Watercolor Soc, Traveling Show (throughout US), NY, 2000-2006. *Teaching:* Instr watercolor, workshop (nat & int), 1985-2006. *Awards:* Mary S Litt Medal, Am Water Soc, 2001; President's Awart, Nat Watercolor Soc, 2004; Watercolor Magic (Artists Mag), Am Watercolor Soc, 2005. *Bibliog:* Kelly Kane (auth), Let Loose!, Watercolor Magis, 2005; Michael Kinch (auth), The Power of Suggestion, Watercolor. *Mem:* Am Watercolor Soc (AWS), (signature mem); Nat Watercolor Soc (NWS), (signature mem); Transparent Watercolor Soc (TWS), (signature mem); Northwest Watercolor Soc (NWS), (signature mem); Allied Artists of Am. *Media:* Watercolor. *Specialty:* Watercolors. *Interests:* Watercolor, especially on damp paper to get as direct a statement as possible. *Publ:* Auth (bk), Watercolor Free & Easy, Northlight/Wiegardt, 1996-2004; auth (art), Workshop (4 part series), Int Artists Mag, 2001; auth (art), New Horizons, Artists Mag, 2002; auth (art), Brushing Up, Artists Mag, 2004. *Dealer:* Wiegardt Studio Gallery Box 1114 Ocean Park, WA 98640

WIENER, DANIEL
SCULPTOR
b Cambridge, Mass, Dec 30, 54. *Study:* Univ Calif, Berkeley, AB, 77. *Work:* Int Paper Co, NY; Atlantic Richfield Co, Los Angeles; La Jolla Mus Contemp Art, Calif. *Exhib:* Santa Barbara Mus, Calif, 79; Mus Mod Art, Kyoto & Tokyo, Japan, 81; Exhib Ctr MRO, Kanazawa, Japan, 82; Visual Arts Ctr Anchorage, 82; Oakland Mus, Calif, 82; Brown Univ Art Gallery, 83; and others. *Awards:* Exhib Award, Nat Small Format Show, Newspace Gallery, Corvallis, Ore, 79. *Bibliog:* Kyoto Mus, Glass in the Modern World, Tankosha Publ, 81; Suzaan Boettger (auth), From the sunny side..., Artforum, 1/83; Kenneth Baker (auth), Space invaders, Boston Phoenix, 1/18/83; and others. *Media:* Glass, Wood

WIENER, PHYLLIS
PAINTER, SCULPTOR
b Iowa City, Iowa, Sept 17, 21. *Study:* Univ Minn, 52, 54 & 56, with Cameron Booth. *Work:* Minneapolis Art Inst, Walker Art Ctr, Frederick Weisman Art Mus & Pillsbury Collection, Minneapolis; MacAlester Col, Minn Mus Art & 3M Co, St Paul; Downers Grove Pub Libr, Ill; Minn State Historical Society, St Paul, Minn; Mayo Clinic, Scottsdale, Ariz, 89; Total Petroleum Co, Denver, Colo, 88; Coll St Catherine, Murphy Gallery, St Paul, Minn, 2001. *Comn:* diptych, Cathedral St Mark, Minneapolis, 83; three dimensional paintings, Cardiac Surgical Asn Clinic, San Antonio, Tex, 85; Lutheran Brotherhood, 86, Minneapolis; Temple Aaron St Paul, Minn, 94; Hutchinson Technol, Minn. *Exhib:* Walker Biennial, 52-64; Pa Acad Fine Arts, Philadelphia, 64; solo show, Minneapolis Art Inst, 67; retrospective (with catalog), Tweed Mus, Univ Minn, Duluth, 81; Pindar Gallery, NY, 84, 86 & 88; Minn Mus Art, St Paul, Minn, 88; AIR Gallery, NY, 90; Univ Wis, LaCrosse, 92; Retrospective with catalog, Macalester Col Janet Wallace Gallery, St Paul, Minn, 93; Phipps Art Ctr, Hudson, Wis, 95 and 2004; Minnesota Mus of Am Art St Paul Minn 2005; and others. *Pos:* Mem adv panel, Minn artists prog, Minneapolis Art Inst, 85-88; mem art exhib panel, Warm Gallery, 88-90; bd dir, Women's Art Registry, Minn, 92-94. *Teaching:* Instr oil painting, Walker Art Ctr, 60-66; instr composition, Univ Minn Exten Div, 62-74; instr, Art Ctr Minn, 60-85. *Awards:* Individual Artist's grant, Minn State Arts Bd, 80; Humanitarian Award Artist, St Paul YWCA, 87; Women's Press Newsmaker, 91. *Bibliog:* Nancy Roth (auth), Maps of the Mind, 12/85 & speculations St Paul-Minneapolis Mag; Rob Silberman (auth), review, Art Paper, 1/86; A Shared Legacy, St Catherine's Col, St Paul, Minn 2001; Catalog Essay by Rob Silberman Excitement of Vision 1993; Catalog Essay by Thom Barry Abstract PTG in MI 2005. *Mem:* Women's Art Registry Minn. *Media:* Acrylic, Three-D Constructions. *Publ:* The Excitement of Vision, MacAlester Col, St Paul, Minn, 93. *Dealer:* Pangaia Gallery Fish Creek Wis. *Mailing Add:* 1225 La Salle Apt 801 Minneapolis MN 55403

WIENER, SAM EVANGELINE TABASCO
SCULPTOR, CONCEPTUAL ARTIST
b Shreveport, La, Mar 24, 28. *Study:* Yale Sch Fine Arts, BFA, 51; Univ Mich. *Work:* Va Mus Fine Arts, Richmond; NY Univ; Mus Fine Arts, Columbia, SC. *Comn:* Glazed tile murals, Am Airlines Terminal, Kennedy Airport, NY, 60; stained glass windows, Agudath Sholom Congregation, Stamford, Conn, 67; glazed tile murals, Abraham and Straus, Smithtown, NY, 68. *Exhib:* Objects USA, Smithsonian Inst & traveling, 69-71; NY Correspondence Sch, Whitney Mus Am Art, 70; Am Painting & Sculpture Today, Indianapolis Mus, 77; solo exhibs, Anderson Gallery, Va Commonwealth Univ, 81, Herbert Johnson Mus, 81, Aspen Ctr Fine Arts, Lowe Mus, Miami, Fla & seven others, 82-83; Vietnam: A Different War, Whatcom Mus, Bellingham, Wash & traveling, 90-92; Alternative Mus, NY, 94; retrospective, Creative Arts Workshop, New Haven, Conn, 94; Mus Am Art, New Britian, Conn, 98; Brattleboro VT Mus, 99.

Teaching: Adj asst prof design & drawing, Columbia Univ Archit Sch, 60; instr visual commun, Cooper Union Art Sch, 67-68; instr drawing & compos, Parsons Sch Art, 82-86 & Hampshire Col, 91. *Awards:* MacDowell Fel, 90. *Bibliog:* Vivian Raynor (auth), article, NY Times; Peter Frank (auth), article, Village Voice, 4/78; Mark Stevens (auth), The splendors of ancient Soho, Newsweek, 10/6/80. *Mem:* Century Asn. *Media:* All

WIENS, ANN
WRITER, EDITOR, CRITIC
Exhib: exhib paintings in numerous group and solo shows throughout the Midwest and East Coast, represented by Byron Roche Gallery, Chicago. *Mem:* Chicago Art Critics asn. *Publ:* East Coasr editor, senior editor, editor New Art Examiner, 1991-98; art critic New City, 1998-2000. *Mailing Add:* 2010 W Eastwood Ave Chicago IL 60625

WIGGINS, BILL
PAINTER
b Roswell, NMex, Sept 24, 17. *Study:* NMex Mil Inst, Roswell; Abilene Christian Univ; Am Shrivenham Univ, Eng, with Francis Speight; Fed Art Proj, Work Proj Admin, Roswell. *Work:* Roswell Mus & Art Ctr. *Exhib:* 5th Arts Nat, Tyler, Tex, 68; Mainstreams 68, Marietta Col, Ohio; Ark State Univ Nat, Jonesboro, 70; Art Inst for the Permian Basin, Odessa, Tex, 91; Fifty yr retrospective, Roswell Mus Art Ctr, NMex, 95; Macular Degeneration Series, Peter Eller Gallery, Albuquerque, NMex, 2002. *Teaching:* Instr art, Roswell Mus & Art Ctr, 55-63. *Bibliog:* Elena Montes (auth), Bill Wiggins of Roswell, NMex Mag, 10/65; United States art, La Rev Mod, Paris, 12/65; Walt Wiggins (auth), Wiggins: A Thirty-Year Retrospective, 82. *Media:* Oil, Watercolor. *Publ:* Contribr, Am Psychologist (cover), 10/95; Savoring the Southwest Again (painting reproduction), Roswell Symphony Guild Publ, 98. *Mailing Add:* 711 W Eighth St Roswell NM 88201

WIGGINS, GUY A
PAINTER, LECTURER
b New London, Conn, Aug 23, 20. *Study:* Univ Calif, Los Angeles, BA, 50; Harvard Univ, MA, 51; London Univ, Msc, 56; Corcoran Mus Sch, 68-69; Art Students League & Nat Acad Sch, 75-78. *Work:* Trenton Mus Art, NJ; Florence Griswold Mus, Old Lyme, Conn; City Hall, New York, NY; New Britain Mus Am Art, Conn; US Embassy, London. *Comn:* Cartier (painting), Caspari, Inc, 2005. *Exhib:* Three Generations of Wiggins, New Britain Mus Am Art, 79; Winter Exhibs, Salmagundi Club, NY, 87-88 & 94-96; Landscape Painters of the Delaware Valley, Trenton Mus Art, NJ, 88; Paintings of Food, Grand Central Galleries, NY, 89; 150 Yrs of Painting: The Wiggins Tradition, Lyme Acad Gallery, Old Lyme, Conn, 96; one-man shows, Marbella Gallery, NY, 81, Reyn Gallery, NY, 84, Optique Gallery, Lambertville, NJ, 87, Lyme Acad Gallery, Old Lyme, Conn, 88, Caroline Hill Gallery, New York, 91 & Elizabeth Bartholet Gallery, NY, 92; Wiggins, Wiggins & Wiggins, Joan Whalen Fine Art, NY, 98; Joan Whalen Fine Art, 02, Salmagundi Club, 04, 05. *Bibliog:* Richard T Boyle (auth), Guy A Wiggins--painter (catalog), 87; Alexander Cokos (auth), Guy A Wiggins (catalog), 88; Shirley C Lally (auth), Guy A Wiggins-The third generation, Fine Arts Trader, Oct 96. *Mem:* Art Students League; Salmagundi Club; Nat Arts Club. *Media:* Oil. *Dealer:* Joan Whalen Fine Art 954 Third Ave New York NY 20022; Lambertville Gallery of Fine Art 20 N Union St Lambertville NJ 08530. *Mailing Add:* 258 W Fourth St New York NY 10014

WIGGINS, K DOUGLAS
PAINTER, ART DEALER
b Roswell, NMex, Apr 8, 59. *Study:* San Antonio Col, Tex, 78-79; Independent Baptist Col, Dallas, Tex, 82-83; Eastern NMex Univ, Roswell, 83-85; Santa Fe Inst Fine Arts, 89. *Work:* Jon R Stuart Collection, Tulsa, Okla; Charles Geneux Collection, Epalingers, Switz; Mus Fine Arts; Mus NMex, Santa Fe; and many others. *Comn:* Painting, Powell Adams Co, Kansas City; painting, Park 39 Consult, NY; paintings, Hilbert Partnership, Newport Beach, Calif; paintings, Four Sixes Ranch, Guthrie, Tex; painting, Anschutz Collection, Denver, Colo. *Exhib:* One-man shows, Johnson-Kraynick Galleries, Dallas, Tex, 84, Geoffery Cline Gallery, Santa Fe, NMex, 86-96 & Altermann & Morris, Houston, Tex, 92, 93, 94 & 95; Gov Gallery Exhib, Santa Fe NMex, 88, 89 & 90; RD Hubbard Mus, Ruidoso, NMex, 92, 93 & 94; Pa Acad Fine Art, Philadelphia, 92-96; MH DeYoung Mem Mus, San Francisco, 93-96; Mus NMex, Santa Fe, 94-95; and others. *Pos:* Mgr, Wiggins Galleries, Santa Fe, NMex, 83-; owner, Print & Promise, Roswell, NMex, 96. *Bibliog:* Les Krantz (auth), American Artists, Am Ref Publ Corp; Peggy & Harold Samuels (coauths), The New American Impressionism, Castle; Sandra D'Emilio (auth), Douglas Wiggins-A Sense of Spirit. *Mem:* Soc Am Impressionists; Int Platform Asn. *Media:* Oil. *Specialty:* 19th century American and European, Hudson River, Taos founders and regional masters. *Publ:* Southwest Art, 3/91; Int Fine Art Col, 5/91; Archit Dig, 6/92. *Mailing Add:* Altermann Galleries 225 Canyon Rd Santa Fe NM 87501

WIITASALO, SHIRLEY
PAINTER
b Toronto, Ont, 1949. *Study:* Ont Col Art, Toronto, 67-78. *Work:* Can Coun Art Bank & Nat Gallery Can, Ottawa; Owens Art Gallery, Mt Allison Univ, Sackville, NB; Mem Univ Art Gallery, St John's, Nfld; Art Gallery Ont, Toronto. *Exhib:* Solo exhibs, Carmen Lamanna Gallery, 74, 76, 78, 80-82, 87, 89 & 90, Art Gallery Ont, traveling, London Regional Gallery, London, Can, Thunder Bay Art Gallery, Can, Winnipeg Art Gallery, Can, 87; Contemp Ont Art, Art Gallery Ont, Toronto, 74; Carmen Lamanna at Owens Art Gallery, Mt Allison Univ, Sackville, NB, 75; Some Canadian Women Artists, Nat Gallery Can, Ottawa, 75; Ont Now-A Survey of Contemp Art, Kitchener-Waterloo Gallery, Art Gallery of Hamilton, Ont, 76; 17 Canadian Artists-A Protean View, Vancouver Art Gallery, BC, 76; Kanadische Künstler Kunsthalle, Basel, Switz, 78; 20th Century Can Painting, Nat Gallery Can, 81; Canadian Horizon, Can Coun, 82; Fiction (with catalog), Art Gallery Ont, 82; Toronto Painting (with catalog), traveling exhib, 84; Six Toronto Artists in Amsterdam, Fodor Mus, Amsterdam, 84; Late Capitalism, Art Gallery at Harbourfront, 85; Canadian-Swiss Art Connection, Toronto, 85; Canadian Biennial Contemp Art, Nat Gallery Can, 89; and many others. *Awards:* Can Coun Grants, 69, 70, 72 & 73, Sr Grant, 82; Ont Arts Coun Grant, 75-76. *Media:* Oil on Canvas. *Mailing Add:* 57 Pemberton Ave Willowdale ON M2M 1Y2 Canada

WILBERT, ROBERT JOHN
PAINTER, EDUCATOR
b Chicago, Ill, Oct 9, 29. *Study:* Univ Ill, BFA, 51, MFA, 54. *Work:* Saginaw Mus, Mich; South Bend Art Ctr, Ind; Kresge Art Ctr, Mich State Univ; Detroit Inst Arts; Wayne State Univ, Detroit. *Comn:* Design, Mich Statehood Stamp, US Postal Serv, 87. *Exhib:* Am Watercolors, Drawings & Prints, Metrop Mus Art, 52; Butler Inst Am Art Midyear Ann, 60, 62, 63 & 68; Pa Acad Fine Arts Ann, 61 & 63; J B Speed Art Mus, Louisville, Ky, 65 & 75; Kalamazoo Art Ctr, Mich, 73; Slusser Art Ctr, Univ Mich, Ann Arbor, 74 & 76; Detroit Inst Arts, 76 & 82; Muskegon Mus Art, 82. *Teaching:* Instr painting, Flint Inst Arts, Mich, 54-56; prof painting, Wayne State Univ, 56-. *Awards:* 57th Exhib Mich Artists Werbe Award, Detroit Inst Arts, 69; Nat Endowment Arts Fel, 77; Mich Found Arts Award, 80. *Mem:* Detroit Artists Market; Detroit Focus. *Media:* Oil, Watercolor. *Mailing Add:* c/o Donald Morris Gallery PO Box 1508 Birmingham MI 48012-1508

WILCOX, T J
PHOTOGRAPHER
b Seattle, Wash, Oct 10, 65. *Study:* Sch Visual Arts, BFA, 89; Art Ctr Col Design, MFA, 95. *Exhib:* Whitney Mus Am Art Biennial, NY, 97; Sunshine & Noir Art in Los Angeles, La Mus Art, Kunstmuseum Wolfsburg, Ger, Castello di Rivoli, Ital & Armand Hammer Mus Art, Los Angeles, 97; Dialogues (with catalog), Walker Art Ctr, Minneapolis, 98; one-man shows Gavin Brown's Enterprise, NY, 96, 99, 2000, Galerie Daniel Bucholz, Cologne, 97, 99, 2001, Inst Contemp Arts, London, 98, Neu, Berlin, 99, Sadie Coles HQ, London, 99, 01, Kunsthaus, Glarus, Switz, 2000, Metro Pictures, NY, 2002, Garlands, Sadie Coles HQ, London, 2003; Mus Abteiberg, Moenchengladbach, Ger, 98, Ctr for Curatorial Studies, Bard Col, Annandale on Hudson, NY, 99; Whitney Mus Am Art, NY, 2000; Rapture, Barbican Gallery, London, 2002; Drawings, Metro Pictures, NY, 2003. *Bibliog:* Sarah Kent (auth) Time Out/London, 98, 99; Holland Cotter (auth) T.J. Wilcox at Sadie Coles HQ, Artforum, 2000; Charles Russ (auth) T.J. Wilcox at Gavin Brown's Enterprise, Art in America, 2001. *Media:* Film. *Mailing Add:* c/o Metro Pictures Gallery 519 W 24th St New York NY 10011

WILDE, STEPHANIE
CONCEPTUAL ARTIST, PRINTMAKER
b Coalville, Utah, July 1, 52. *Work:* Harris Fine Art Mus, Provo, Utah; Boise Art Mus, Idaho; Marriott Libr, Univ Utah. *Comn:* Pen & ink drawing, Springville Mus, Utah, 87 & Boise State Univ, Idaho, 88. *Exhib:* 3rd Biennial Juried Show, Boise Art Mus, 83; one-woman show, Harris Fine Art Mus, Provo, 86 & Herrett Art Mus, Twin Falls, 86; Critic Collects, Art Attack Gallery, Boise, 86; 2nd Biennial, Maryhill Mus, Glendale, Wash, 87; 64th Nat Spring Salon, Springville Mus, 87-88; Works on Paper, Springville Mus Art, 88; Stewart Gallery, Boise, Idaho, 89; Aids, Mus Fine Art, Montana, 89; Long Beach Art Mus, 93; Boise Art Mus, 98; Salt Lake Art Ctr, 99; Evolving Space, 98; and others. *Awards:* Visual Arts, Fel Idaho Art Asn, 88. *Bibliog:* Jeanette Ross (auth), Women of visible power, Boise Mag, 88. *Media:* Ink. *Publ:* Coauth, The Wilde Birds, private publ, 86. *Dealer:* Lane Stewart Bune 426 North 8th St Boise ID 83702; Evolving Space San Francisco CA. *Mailing Add:* 406 E Crestline Dr Boise ID 83702

WILEY, LOIS JEAN
PAINTER, WRITER
b West Mifflin, Pa, Sept 17, 28. *Study:* Allegheny Col, BA, 50; studies with Andrew Sanders, Art Sch, Erie, Pa, 64-74; Edinboro Univ Pa, MFA, 79. *Comn:* portraits of individuals and pets for pvt collections. *Exhib:* Audubon Artists Ann, Nat Acad Galleries, NY, 73; Butler Midyear Show, Butler Inst Am Art, 76, 77, 78 & 80; Silvermine Guild of Artists, New Canaan, Conn, 78; Salmagundi Club 1st Open Exhib, Salmagundi Club Galleries, NY, 78; Allied Artists 61st Ann, Nat Acad Galleries, NY, 80; Grand Exhib, Akron Soc Artists Juried Exhib, Ohio, 96; 23rd Ann October Evenings Exhib, Meadville, Pa, 97, 00, 01; Erik Art Mus Spring Show, 02; Nat Asn of Women Artists Ann, 02; solo exhibition, Homage to the Orange, Kada Gallery, Erie, PA, 2004; Regional Invitational, Meadville Council on the Arts, 2004; Watrerfor Artsists, Biannual 2004. *Pos:* Dir publicity, Cur Exhib Series, 75-77; publicity chairperson, Northwestern Pa Artists Asn, 81-82; freelance writer-art rev, Times Publ-Showcase, 88-; asst producer, Heart of the Arts of Series, PBS, 95; mem, Collections Comt, Erie Art Mus, 95-02. *Teaching:* pub sch tchr, 59-89. *Awards:* Berta N Briggs Mem Award, 77 & Elizabeth Stanton, Blake Prize for Portrait in Oil, 81, Nat Asn Women Artists; Muriel Ritchie Mem, Acad Artists Asn, 78; Jurors Choice Award, Panorama Erie Arts Festival, 96; second prize, Campbell Pottery Lily Ann, 01. *Mem:* Nat Asn Women Artists; Northwestern Pa Artists Asn; Presque Isle Artists Asn. *Media:* Oil, Colored Pencil. *Interests:* Conservation, Animal Rights. *Publ:* Auth, Shuttle spindle and dyepot, Handweavers Guild Am Inc, fall 78; Fiberarts, Fiberarts Mag, 1-2/79. *Dealer:* Kada Gallery Erie PA; Glass Growers Gallery Erie PA. *Mailing Add:* 917 High St PO Box 816 Waterford PA 16441-0816

WILEY, WILLIAM T
PAINTER
b Bedford, Ind, Oct 21, 1937. *Study:* San Francisco Art Inst, BFA, 61, MFA, 62. *Work:* Philadelphia Mus Art, Pa Acad Fine Arts, Philadelphia, Pa; Seattle Art Mus, Wash; Mus Mod Art, Whitney Mus Am Art, NY; Art Inst Chicago; San Francisco Mus Mod Art, City of San Francisco, San Francisco Art Inst; Los Angeles Co Mus Art; Nat Mus

Am Art, Hirshhorn Mus & Sculpture Garden, Corcoran Gallery Art, Washington, DC; Brooklyn Mus, NY. *Exhib:* Solo exhibs, LA Louver, Venice, Calif, 84, 87, 91 & 92, Max Protetch Gallery, NY, 91 & 94, Marsha Mateyka Glalery, Washington, DC, 91 & 93, Corcoran Gallery Art traveling show, Washington, DC, 91, Marian Locks Gallery, Philadephia, Pa, 92 & 94, Ind State Univ, Bloomington, 93 & Rena Bransten Gallery, San Francisco, 93; The Making of a Legend: Chief Seattle's Reply, Hatley Martin Gallery, San Francisco, 90; Rain of Talent: Umbrella Art,The Fabric Workshop, Philadelphia, Pa, Traveling, 89-94; Selections from the Anderson Collection, San Jose Mus Art, Calif, 92; Directions in Bay Area Printmaking: Three Decades, Palo Alto Cult Ctr, Calif, 92-93; Clearly Art, Whatcom Mus Hist & Art, Bellingham, Wash, traveling, 92-95; Here and Now: Bay Area Masterworks from the di Rosa Collections (with catalog), Oakland Mus, Calif, 94; Advice and Dissent: Collaborative Work, William Allan, Robert Hudson, William T Wiley, John Berggruen Gallery, San Francisco, Calif, 94; plus many others. *Teaching:* Assoc prof art, Univ Calif, Davis, 62-73; instr, San Francisco Art Inst, 63, 66-67, Univ Nev, Reno, 67, Wash State Col, Pullman, 67, Univ Calif, Berkeley, 67, Sch Visual Art, New York, 68, Univ Colo, Boulder, 68. *Awards:* Purchase Prize, Whitney Mus Am Art, 68; Nealie Sullivan Award, San Francisco Art Inst, 68; Bartels Prize, 72nd Am Exhib, Art Inst Chicago, 76; Traveling Grant, Australian Arts Coun, 80; and others. *Bibliog:* Lee Fleming (auth), Talents that brush into each other, The Washington Post, 5/15/93 & San Francisco Examiner, 3/23/93; Three Artists Collaborative Riddles, San Francisco Chronicle, 1/15/94; Holland Cotter (auth), William T Wiley, New York Times, 2/4/94. *Mem:* Nat Acad. *Publ:* Contribr, Over Evident Falls (theater event), Sacramento State Col, 68; auth, Man's Nature (film), shown Hansen Fuller Gallery, 71; Wiley Mind, tricycle, The Buddhist Review, fall 91. *Mailing Add:* c/o Wanda Hansen 615 Main St Sausalito CA 94965-1317

WILHELMI, WILLIAM MERLE
CERAMIST, SCULPTOR

b Garwin, Iowa, Feb 4, 39. *Study:* San Diego State Col, BA, 60; Univ Calif, Los Angeles, MFA, 69. *Work:* Long Beach Mus Art, Calif; Everson Art Mus, Syracuse, NY; Tweed Mus Art, Duluth, Minn; Libr Cong; Renwick Gallery, Smithsonian Inst, Washington; Gene Autry Western Heritage Mus, Los Angeles, Calif. *Comn:* Tile mural, Whataburger Nat Hq, Corpus Christi, 79; planters & tile murals, Corpus Christi State Univ, 79; Corpus Christi Nat Bank, 82; tile floor mosaic, Corpus Christi City Hall rotunda, 88; mosaic design, Six-Points Station (RTA-CC), 92. *Exhib:* Renwick Gallery, Washington, 76, 80 & 82; 20th Century Ornament, Cooper-Hewitt Mus, NY, 78; Contemp Am, STex Art Mobile, Corpus Christi, 79; Hill's Gallery, Santa Fe, 81; Marilyn Butler Gallery, Scottsdale, Ariz, 81; Libr Cong, 83; Emily Edwards Gallery, Southwest Craft Ctr, San Antonio, Tex, 89; Twenty-five Yr Survey Show, Art Mus STex, 96. *Pos:* Resident potter, Richard Colley, architect, Corpus Christi, 69-76, Kaffie Gallery, Corpus Christi, 76-83 & Carancahua Gallery, 83-86; bd trustees, Art Mus STex, 80-87; Wilhelm/Holland Gallery, Corpus Christi, 86-. *Awards:* Two Purchase Awards, San Mateo Col, 69; First Place & One-Man Show Art Found Award, Art Mus STex, 73; Tex Arts Comn, 81; Dirs Award, CC Carts Coun, 92. *Mem:* Am Crafts Coun; Tex Designer Craftsmen; Tex Potters Guild; Art Found. *Publ:* contribr, Studio Potter, Daniel Clark Found, 78; Tex Monthly, 12/80; New York Art Rev, 88-89; Chicago Art Rev, 90; American Ceramics, Rizzoli, New York, 92; ARTODAY, Phaidon, 96. *Mailing Add:* 402 Palmero St Corpus Christi TX 78404-1939

WILKIN, KAREN
CURATOR, CRITIC

b New York, NY. *Study:* Barnard Col, BA(cum laude); Columbia Univ, MFA. *Collection Arranged:* Sculpture in Steel: Gonzalez, Caro, Steiner & Scott (with catalog), 74; The Collective Unconscious: US/Canada 1940s (with catalog), 75; Adolph Gottlieb: The Pictographs Touring Exhib (with catalog), 77-78; David Smith: The Formative Years Touring Exhib (with catalog), 81-82; Frankenthaler: Works on Paper 1949-1984 Touring Exhib (with catalog), 85-86; Stuart Davis Drawing Retrospective, touring exhib (with catalog), 92-93; Judith Rothschild (with catalog), 2002; Hans Hofmann Retrospective (with catolog), 2004; Jules Olitski: Six Decades (with catolog), 2005. *Pos:* Chief cur, Edmonton Art Gallery, Alta, 71-78. *Teaching:* Lectr art hist, Univ Alta, Edmonton, 67-70; adj prof, Trent Univ, Peterborough, Ont, 79-85, SUNY, Purchase, NY, 86; vis prof, Univ Toronto, 91-97; New York Studio Sch, 97-. *Awards:* Woodrow Wilson Fel; Fulbright Fel, Rome, 64-65; Can Coun Sr Arts Grant, 81. *Mem:* Int Asn Art Critics; PEN. *Res:* 20th Century Art. *Publ:* Stuart Davis, Abbeville Press, 87; Kenneth Noland, Rizzoli, 90; Anthony Caro, Prestel, 91; Georges Braque, 92 & Cézanne, 96, Abbeville, 92. *Mailing Add:* 28 W 38th St New York NY 10018

WILKINS, DAVID GEORGE
HISTORIAN

b Battle Creek, Mich, Sept 12, 39. *Study:* Oberlin Col, BA, 61; Univ Mich, MA, 63 & PhD, 69. *Pos:* Dir, Univ Art Gallery, Univ Pittsburgh, 76-92. *Teaching:* Prof art hist, Dept Hist Art & Archit, Univ Pittsburgh, 67-2004, chmn, 89-92, & 98, 2004. *Awards:* Chancellor's Distinguished Teaching Award, 87; Col Art Asn Award for Distinguished Teaching of Art Hist, 2005. *Mem:* Col Art Asn; Renaissance Soc Am; Italian Art Soc. *Res:* Florentine painting and sculpture; American painting; World art. *Publ:* Coauth, Illustrated Bartsch, Vol 53, 85; Paintings & Sculpture of Duquesne Club, 86; coauth, Hartt, History of Italian Renaissance Art, 4th ed, 94, 5th ed, 2004; coed, The Search for a Patron in the Middle Ages and the Renaissance, 96; coauth, Art Past/Art Present, 5th edit, 2003. *Mailing Add:* 1217 Shady Ave Pittsburgh PA 15232-2811

WILL, JOHN A
PAINTER, VIDEO ARTIST

b Waterloo, Iowa, June 30, 39. *Study:* Univ Iowa, MFA, 64; Rijsacadamie von Beeldende Kunston, Amsterdam, 64-65; Tamarind, Albuquerque, NMex, 70-71. *Work:* NY Pub Libr; Art Inst Chicago; Libr Cong; Art Gallery Nova Scotia; Glenbow Mus; Univ Lethbridge; Art Gallery Ontario. *Exhib:* Brit Int Print Biennial, Bradford, Yorkshire, 74; 11th Int Biennial Graphic Art, Ljubljana, Yugoslavia, 75; Glenbow Mus, Calgary, 80; 49th Parallel Gallery, NY, 88; Dunlop Art Gallery, Regina, 88; The Miracle of OJ as Revealed By the Man they once called Prince, OWW, Calgary; Ain't Paralysed Yet, Nichle Arts Mus, 91; Mendal Art Gallery, Saskatoon, 91; Kitchener Waterloo Art Gallery, 91; Walter Phillips Gallery, Banff, 91. *Teaching:* Asst prof drawing, Univ Wis-Stout, 65-70; resident artist, Yale Univ, summer 66 & Peninsula Sch Art, Fish Creek, Wis, summer 68; prof lithography, Univ Calgary, 71-97; instr, Nova Scotia Col Art & Design, summers 73-75, 77, 79 & 84, Baniff Ctr, summers 80 & 81 & Emily Carr Sch Design, 85. *Awards:* Fulbright Fel, Holland, 64-65; Ford Found Grant, 70-71; Can Coun Grant. *Bibliog:* John Will-Triple Threat Artist (exhib catalog), Dunlop Art Gallery, 88; Atomic Haiku (exhib catalog), Truck Gallery, 95; John & Lou's 1923 Voyage (exhib catalog), Banff Ctr, 2000; Willagio, (exhib catalog), Art Gallery of Calgary, 2001; Ain't Paralysed Yet (exhib catalog), Nickle Art Mus, 2001. *Media:* Painting; Video. *Mailing Add:* 1818 18A St SW Calgary AB T2T 4V9 Canada

WILLARD, CHRISTOPHER A
PAINTER, EDUCATOR

b Bangor, Maine, Sept 15, 60. *Study:* Portland Sch Art, Maine Col Art, BFA, 82; State Univ NY, Hunter Col, MFA (Hunter Alumni Scholar), 92. *Work:* Metrop Mus Art, NY; Reader's Digest Corp, Pleasantville, NY; Univ Art & Design, Helsinki, Finland. *Comn:* Poster, RAPP Arts Ctr, NY, 91; poster, Erroll Simpson Dance Co, NY, 91; New York Philharmonic Symphony Soc, 93. *Exhib:* Salon du Printemps, Soc Lyonnaise des Beaux Arts, Lyon, France, 90; ART/Umjepnost, Obala Theatre, Sarajevo, Bosnia, 93; Presentational Painting, Hunter Col, NY, 93; Repetitions, Marymount Col, NY, 94; one-man show, Centreville Mus Art, Ohio, 95, Art Vivant Gallery, Charlotte, 96, John Jay Col Gallery, NY, 96 & Empire State Bldg, NY, 97; Abstraction Index, Condeso Lawler Gallery, NY, 97. *Pos:* Column writer, Methods & Materials, Am Artist Mag, 96-; vis artist, Alta Col Art & Design, Calgary, Can, 96. *Teaching:* Instr painting, Univ Vt, Burlington, 84-85; painting/drawing, Westchester Community Col, White Plains, NY, 93-; color theory/visual experience, Hunter Col, New York, 94-. *Awards:* Veritas Award for Outstanding Creativity, Veritas Soc, 78-82; Artists Housing Award, Dept Cult Affairs, New York, 89; E D Found Grant, 96. *Bibliog:* Rob Daniels (auth), Blurred Systems: Christopher Willard, Canvas Imaging, 96; J Boyer Bell (auth), Review of "Slow Colors", New York, 2/1/97; Lawrence Toppman (auth), Painter Opts for Op Art: Many-Layered Works Fool the Eye Into Seeing Colors that Aren't There, The Charlotte Observer, 5/16/97. *Mem:* Col Art Asn; Inter-Soc Color Coun, 94-. *Media:* Acrylic, Oil. *Publ:* Coauth (with L Hurwitz), Painting with a palette knife, Am Artist, 93; auth, Surface Film Colour-Perception and Painting, in Aspects of Colour, 95; Color Mixing Made Simple, Am Artist, 96; Constructs of Color Evidence: The Psychological Ordering of Color Relationships in the Teaching of Color Theory, Color and Psychology, AIC: Goteborg, Sweden, 97; Experimenting with Acrylic, Am Artist, 9/98

WILLARD, GARCIA LOU
GRAPHIC ARTIST, PAINTER

b Apr 15, 44. *Study:* Marshall Univ, with George Bobby Jones, 78-83; studied with Ben Konis, 89; WVa Univ, 93; Univ NDak, 94. *Comn:* The honorable Russell Daughtery (oil portrait), Cabell Co Bar Asn, Huntington, WVa, 78; Figurative (fresco mural), Vanco Park, Loganville, Ga, 78; fresco mural, Western Savings & Loan, Phoenix, 91; fresco mural, Silverton & Williams, Durango, Colo, 93; oil mural, Franklin Enterprises, Phoenix, 93. *Exhib:* Am Artist Prof League, 60th Grand Nat Exhib, Salmagundi Club, NY, 88; Catharine Lorillard Wolfe Art Club 92nd Grand Nat Exhib, Gramercy Park, NY, 88; Eighth Ann Exhib Pastel Soc Southwest, D'Art Visual Art Ctr, Dallas, 88; Hermitage Found Mus, Va, 88; 20th W & J Nat Painting Show, Olin Fine Arts Ctr, Washington, Pa, 88; 2nd Biennial Nat Exhib, Degas Pastel Soc, New Orleans, 88; Sonoran Gallery, 88; Two Flags Int Exhib, Little Gallery, Ariz, 89; and others; Ariel Gallery, New York City, 88; Pen & Brush Club, New York City, 88. *Pos:* Exhib juror for numerous art orgns, 87; lectr for numerous art orgns, 88. *Teaching:* Instr figure drawing, pastel & portraitures, Stifel Fine Art Ctr, Oglebay Inst, 84-87; instr portraiture in pastel & graphics, Ohio Univ, 87. *Awards:* Grumbacher Silver Award for Pastel Excellence, Degas Pastel Soc, 88; Molly Guion Mem Graphic Award, Catharine Lorillard Wolfe Art Club, 88; Pastel Award, Am Artists Prof League, 88. *Bibliog:* Jack Hardin (auth), Huntington artist, Herald-Dispatch, 85; Kitty Doepken (auth), Nationally recognized artist, Family-News, 86; Gladys Van Horne (auth), Museum reception, News Register, 87. *Mem:* Fel Am Artists Prof League; signature mem Pastel Soc Am; Catharine Lorillard Wolfe Art Club; Nat Drawing Asn; Acad Artists Asn. *Media:* Pastel, Oil; Silverpoint. *Publ:* Illusr, Dr Horton on African Art, Carnegie-Mellon, 85; contribr, The California Art Review, Am References, 89. *Dealer:* Sonoran Gallery; Roger Willard. *Mailing Add:* 8819 W Corrine Dr Peoria AZ 85381-8166

WILLENBECHER, JOHN
SCULPTOR, PAINTER

b Macungie, Pa, May 5, 36. *Study:* Brown Univ, BA, 58; NY Univ Inst Fine Arts, 58-61. *Work:* Whitney Mus Am Art, NY; Albright-Knox Art Gallery, Buffalo, NY; James A Michener Found Collection, Univ Tex, Austin; Hirshhorn Mus & Sculpture Garden, Washington, DC; Solomon R Guggenheim Mus, NY. *Comn:* US Fed Bldg & Court House, Providence, RI, 82; Republicbank, Houston, 83; Minneapolis Inst Arts, Minn, 93. *Exhib:* Mixed Media & Pop Art, Albright-Knox Art Gallery, Buffalo, 63; Young Americans, Whitney Mus Am Art, NY, 65; Arts Club, Chicago, 76; Allentown Art Mus, Pa, 79; Neuberger Mus, Purchase, NY, 79; Minneapolis Inst Art, Minn, 93; Univ NMex Mus Art, Albuquerque, NMex, 96. *Teaching:* Lectr painting, Philadelphia Col Art, 72-73; artist in residence, Dartmouth Col, 77 & Univ Wis, Milwaukee, 83. *Awards:* Nat Endowment Arts Fel, 76; Esther & Adolph Gottlieb Found Grant, 94.

Bibliog: Joseph McElroy (auth), Through the labyrinth: The art of John Willenbecher, Art Int, 3/75; William Wilson (auth), John Willenbecher: Pyramids, spheres & labyrinths, 3/75; Daniel Cameron (auth), John Willenbecher & the riddle of Grandeur, Arts Mag, 9/83. *Mem:* Art Comn New York. *Media:* Acrylic. *Mailing Add:* 145 W Broadway New York NY 10013

WILLIAMS, BENJAMIN FORREST
CURATOR, HISTORIAN
b Lumberton, NC, Dec 24, 25. *Study:* Corcoran Sch Art, with Eugene Weisz; George Washington Univ, AA; Univ NC, AB; Columbia Univ, Paris Exten, Ecole du Louvre; Netherlands Inst Art Hist; Art Students League New York. *Exhib:* Va Intermont, Bristol; Weatherspoon Gallery, Greensboro; Person Hall Gallery, Chapel Hill, NC; Asheville Art Mus; Traveling Exhib, Am Fedn Arts; and others. *Collection Arranged:* Retrospectives for Josef Albers, Hobson Pittman, Jacob Marling, Victor Hammer, Fedor Zakharcv, Henry Pearson & the collections of the NC Mus Art; Atlanta Art Asn; NC Mus Art; Duke Univ; Greenville Civic Art Gallery, NC; Knoll Assoc, New York. *Pos:* Retired curator, art. *Teaching:* Lectr, art criticism, City of Raleigh, NC. *Awards:* Ronsheim Mem Award, Corcoran Sch Art, 46; Washington Soc Arts, 47; Prizes, Southeastern Ann, 47. *Mem:* Am Asn Mus; Southeastern Mus Conf; Col Art Asn Am. *Res:* 19th Century Art. *Publ:* Contribr articles on 19th century American painting & sculpture to NC Mus Art Bull & NC Hist Rev. *Mailing Add:* 2813 Mayview Rd Raleigh NC 27607

WILLIAMS, CHESTER LEE
SCULPTOR
b Durham, NC, July 24, 44. *Study:* NC Cent Univ, BA, 68; Univ Mich, MFA, 71. *Work:* Student Union Gallery, NC Cent Univ, Durham; Art Dept Gallery, Univ Mich, Ann Arbor; Univ Gallery, Appalachian State Univ, Boone, NC; Black Arch Mus & Res Ctr, Fla A&M Univ, Tallahassee; Voorhees Col Libr, Denmark, SC. *Comn:* Sculpture, bronze casting, comn by Dr Oscar Cole, NY, 71 & Dr & Mrs Robert Zakarin, Tallahassee, 77; painting & sculpture, Fla A&M Univ, 77-78; bronze bust of Johnathan Gibbs, Fine Arts Coun of Fla, Div Cult Affairs, State of Fla, Tallahassee, 77-78; and others. *Exhib:* One-man exhibs, Spec Exhib, Div Dult Affairs, State Fla, 77, Fla House Rep, Ms Gwendolyn S Cherry, 106th Dist, 77, Fla Dept Com, Tallahassee, Fla, 77, Bainbridge Jr Col, Ga, 80, Winston-Salem State Univ, NC, 82, Elizabeth City State Univ, NC, 84, OMNI Gallery, Greenville, NC, 90; Fla A&M Univ, 75, 78, 84 & 91, LeMoyne Art Found, 77, 79 & 83 & Fla Ctr Prof Develop, Fla State Univ, Tallahassee, Fla, 84; Smith-Mason Gallery, 80, Power Objects: Ancient and to the Future, Howard Univ, Washington, DC, 80; Dimensions and Directions: Black Artists of the South, Miss Mus Art, Jackson, Miss, 80; The Harmon Gallery, 80, Fine Arts Exhib, Naples, Fla, 80; Atlanta Life Ins Co, Ann Afro-Am Nat Art Competition & Exhib, 80, 87, 89, 90 & 91; NC Cent Univ, Durham, 85, Waterways Visual Arts Ctr, Salisbury, 88, Greensboro Artists' League, Greensboro, 89, Rocky Mt Arts Ctr, NC, 89; Beaufort Co Arts Ctr, 89 & 90, African-Am Art Extravaganza, 89, Greenville Mus Art, 91, Ubiquitous Gallery, Charlotte, 90, Onslow Co Coun Arts, Jacksonville, NC, 90; ABC Art Buyers Caravan, Orlando, Fla, 90; Third World Art Gallery, Cincinnati, Ohio, 92; Phillip Cult Ctr Gallery, Albany, Ga, 92. *Pos:* Illusr, Nat Air Pollution Control Ctr, Durham, NC, 69-70; mem, Arts Selection Comt, Tallahassee City Comn, 77-79; mem bd, LeMoyne Art Found, Tallahassee, 79-84; pres, Williams Foundry, Tallahassee & Durham, NC, 79-; dir, Fla A&M Univ Art Gallery, Tallahassee, Fla, 74-78, 83-84 & 92-. *Teaching:* Instr creative woodwork, Sch Design, Durham, NC, 68-69; asst prof sculpture & art appreciation, Voorhess Col, Denmark, SC, 71-74; assoc prof sculpture & painting, Fla A&M Univ, 74-84; assoc prof sculpture & design drawing, NC Cent Univ, Durham, 84-; vis artist at numerous universities and institutions since 69. *Awards:* Sculpture Award, Harmon Gallery, Naples, Fla, 80; Purchase Award, Summer of 80 Fine Art Exhib, Naples, Fla, 80; Prince Hall Grand Lodge Econ Grant Prog, Durham, NC, 91. *Bibliog:* Joy McIlwain (auth), Sculptor with a message of hope, Tallahassee Mag, fall 84; Chris Redd (auth), Four Artists at Waterworks, Contemp Southeastern Vis Arts, Vol 2, 88; Kathy McQuaid (auth), Area exhibit shows black artists' work, The Daily News, 2/8/90. *Mem:* Col Art Asn Am; Nat Conf Artists; LeMoyne Art Found; Tri-State Sculptors. *Media:* Bronze Casting. *Dealer:* LeMoyne Art Found Tallahassee FL; Gallery of Art Panama City FL

WILLIAMS, CHRISTOPHER
PHOTOGRAPHER
b Los Angeles, 65. *Work:* Carnegie Mus, Pittsburgh, Pa; Mus Boijmans Van Beuningen, Rotterdam; Lenbachhaus, Munich; Mus Contemp Art, Los Angeles; The UBS Corp Art Collection. *Exhib:* Whitney Biennial, Whitney Mus Art, NY, 2006; David Zwirner Gallery, NY. *Mailing Add:* c/o David Zwirner Gallery 525 W 19th St New York NY 10002

WILLIAMS, CLARA A
SCULPTOR
b Nashville, Sept 16, 72. *Study:* Attended, School Visual Arts; Yale Univ, MFA. *Exhib:* Exhibited in group shows at PS 1 Some Young New Yorkers, 97, PPOW Gallery, 99, Richard Tells Gallery, 99, Friedrich Petzel Gallery, 99, Mus Contemp Art, San Diego, 2000, Zobeide & Man With Bags, Nicole Klagsbrun Gallery, 2000, The Price, Pub Art Fund, 2003, Man with Luggage, Pierogi Gallery, 2000. *Awards:* Fel Conn Comn on Arts, 2001, Guggenheim Mem Found, 2004

WILLIAMS, DAVE HARRELL
COLLECTOR, PATRON
b Beaumont, Tex, Oct 5, 32. *Study:* Univ Tex, BS(chemical eng), 56; Harvard Univ, MBA, 61. *Pos:* trustee, USS Intrepid Mus Found Serv with US Naval Res, 56-59; financial anal, chemical eng, Exxon Corp, Baton Rouge, 59; security analyst, deVegh & Co, New York City, 61-64; dir res, Waddell & Reed, Kansas City, Mo, 64-67; exec vpres, Mitchell Hutchins, Inc, New York City, 67-77; chmn bd, Alliance Capital Mgt Corp, 77-2001, chmn emer, 2001-2004; trustee, Skyscraper Mus, currently; trustee, USS Intrepid Mus Found, currently. *Awards:* Named one of Top 200 Collectors, ARTnews Mag, 2004, 2006. *Mem:* NY Soc Security Analysts (pres, formerly); Financial Analysts Fedn (off, dir, formerly); Chartered financial analyst; Bond Club NY, Econ Club NY, Knickerbocker Club, Grolier Club. *Specialty:* study ctr and exhib space for scholars, mus profls, and groups interested in prints by Am artists. *Collection:* American prints mid 19th century up to and including contemporary artists, emphasis 1910-1940. *Publ:* Articles in Print Quart. *Mailing Add:* The Print Research Found 258 Atlantic St Stamford CT 06901

WILLIAMS, DAVID JON
MEDICAL ILLUSTRATOR, HISTORIAN
b Muskegon, Mich, June 21, 44. *Study:* Muskegon Community Col, AA, 64; Mich State Univ, BA, 66, MA, 73; studied medical illus with Prof Mary Maciel, Univ Cincinnati Sch Med, 68-70; anatomical art with Franz Batke, Innsbruck, Austria, 80. *Pos:* Med illusr, Mich State Univ, East Lansing, Mich, 70-73. *Teaching:* From asst prof to prof med art, Purdue Univ, West Lafayette, Ind, 73-. *Awards:* First Award, 11th Eaton-Student Am Med Asn Competition, 69, Third Award, 17th Competition, 75 & Third Award, 18th Competition, 76; First Place, Med Illus, Cent Ind Chap, Biol Photog Asn, 84; Literary Award, Asn Med Illustrators, 89, 94 & 2005; 23rd Charles H Hackley Distinguished Lecture in The Humanities Award, 2004. *Mem:* Asn Med Illusr (archivist, parlimentarian & mem, bd dir); Guild Natural Sci Illusr; Am Asn Hist Med; World Asn Hist Vet Med; Am Vet Med Hist Soc; Med Artists Asn of Gt Britain. *Media:* Carbon Dust on Media Paper, Transparent Watercolor. *Res:* History of Wilhelm Ellenberger's Handbuch der Anatomie der Tiere fur Kunstler, pub in Leipzig 1898, others. *Publ:* Coauth, Fundamental Techniques in Veterinary Surgery, W B Saunders Co, 75, rev ed, 81 & 87; contribr, Anatomy of the Rat, Williams & Wilkins, 76; Atlas of Human Anatomy, Urban & Schwarzenberg, 81; illusr, Intervertebral Disk Diseases, J B Lippincott Co, 85; Natural Voltage Gradients in Limb Regneration and Development, Oxford Univ Press, 85; The History of Eduard Pernkoof's 'Topographische Anatomie des Menschen,' J Biocommunication, spring 88; Art Anatomy and Medi; The Evolution of Medical Illustration, Helix, 92; The History of Werner Spalteholz's Handatalas der Anatomie des Menschen J Biocommunication 2003; Vet Med An Illustrated History, 96. *Mailing Add:* 824 Carrolton Blvd West Lafayette IN 47906

WILLIAMS, FRANKLIN JOHN
PAINTER
b Ogden, Utah, Feb 5, 1940. *Study:* Carbon Col, 58-60; Calif Col Arts & Crafts, BFA, 60-64, MFA(Spencer Mackey Scholarship), 64-66. *Work:* Oakland Art Mus, Calif; Univ Calif, Berkeley Mus; Corcoran Mus, Washington, DC; San Francisco Mus Mod Art; Sheldon Mem Mus, Lincoln, Nebr; San Jose Mus Art; Noru Eccles Harrison Mus Art; DeRosa Preserve, Napa, Calif; Crocker Art Mus, Sacramento, Calif. *Comn:* Painting, comn by Marc Moyens, Washington, DC, 83; Lizabeth Oliveria Gallery, Oakland, Calif. *Exhib:* Seattle Art Mus, Washington, 66; 1967 Painting Ann, 1968 Sculpture Ann, Whitney Mus Am Art, NY; New Zealand Mus, Auckland, 71; Nat Mus, Washington, DC, 72; On and Off the Wall, Oakland Mus, Calif, 83; solo exhib: San Jose Mus Art, Calif, 83 & Utah Mus Fine Art, Salt Lake City, 84; San Francisco Bay Area Painting, Calif, 84; Formative Acts, San Francisco, 98. *Collection Arranged:* DeRosa Preserve, Napa, Calif. *Teaching:* Prof painting & drawing, San Francisco Art Inst, 66-; Calif Col Arts & Crafts, 69-; Tutor painting & drawing, Ruskin Sch, Oxford, England, 90. *Awards:* Grant Ford Found, 66; Nat Endowment Arts, 68; Conference on World Affairs, 98, 99 & 2000. *Bibliog:* Fred Martin (auth), article, Art Int, 63 & 76; Thomas Albright (auth), Art in the San Francisco Bay Area 1945-1980, 85, The American Painting Collection Sheldon Memorial Art Gallery, The Painting & Sculpture Collection, San Francisco Mus Art. *Media:* Oil, Acrylic. *Publ:* Contribr, Soft as Cotton, Centered and Hard, 97. *Dealer:* Lizabeth Oliveria Gallery 2712 S La Cienega Blvd Los Angelees CA 90034; 49 Geary St #411 San Francisco CA 94108. *Mailing Add:* 713 Elm Dr Petaluma CA 94952

WILLIAMS, IDAHERMA
PRINTMAKER, PAINTER
b Bronx, NY. *Study:* Philadelphia Col Art, BFA(scholar) 1959; Pa Acad Fine Art, 1959-63; Univ Pa, MFA, 1963. *Work:* Bristol-Myers Squibb Co, NJ; Zimmerli Art Mus, Rutgers Univ, NJ, 66; Kyoto Int Woodblock Asn; Graphic Arts Libr, Princeton Univ; Print Consortium, Kansas City, Mo; Newark Public Library, Special Col, Newark, NJ; Kendall at Hanover, NH; Zimmerli Art Mus, NJ. *Exhib:* Solo exhibs NJ State Mus, Trenton, 1975, Ursinus Col, Collegeville, Pa, 1983, Johnson & Johnson Corp World Hq, New Brunswick, NJ, 1992, Gloucester Co Col, Sewell, NJ, 1998, Café Gallery, NJ State Mus, Trenton, 2002, others; TAWA in the USSR, the Soviet Union, 90; 3rd Biennial Int Print Exhib, Somerstown Gallery, Somers, NY, 90; FRRIC Int, Salon de Peinture et d'Estampe de Montreal, Montreal, Quebec, 90; The Francis Witherspoon Ann Printmakers Award Exhib, An Int Juried Exhib, Dome Gallery, NY, 91; Philadelphia Int Contemp Art Competition of Old City, 479 Gallery, Inc, Rodger LaPelle Galleries, Pentimenti Gallery, Convergence Ctr, Philadelphia, Pa, 94; Mangum Opus VIII, 8th Int Open Exhib, Sacramento Fine Arts Ctr, Carmichael, Calif, 95; The May Exhibitions, Kyoto Int Woodprint Asn, Kyoto, Japan, 98; World Artists for Tibet, 1860 House Montgomery, Skillman, NJ, 98; 102nd Ann Exhib, Catherine Lorillard Wolfe Art Club, Nat Arts Club, NY, 98; Members' Exhib, Catherine Lorillard Wolfe Art Club, Broome St Gallery, NY, 98; Ann Fleisher Fac Exhib, Philadelphia, Pa, 98; SAGA at Krasdal Foods, Inc, Corp Hq, White Plains, NY, 98; Realism 98, Parkersburg Art Ctr 10th Ann Nat Exhib, Parkersburg, WVa, 98; Digital Print Exhib, AIR Gallery, NY, 98; TAWA Invitational, NJ; In the Tracks of Hercules (Lucis Trust), Lennox Gallery (Fulham), London, United Kingdom, 2005; S A G A Prague, Hallar Soc Gallery, Ceska Republica, 2006. *Pos:* Bd trustees, Catherine

Lorillard Wolfe Art Club, NY, 98; Pres, Am Color Print Soc, Bd Soc Am Graphic Artists, 2001-. *Awards:* 1st prize, Kyoto Int Wood Block Asn exhib, 2003; Antonio Frasconi award for woodblock print, Soc Am Graphic Artists, New York, 2002; Stella Drabkin Memorial Award, 2d prize, Am Color Print Soc, Am Col Bryn Mawr, Pa, 2001; 18 Nat Gallery '76, Wenatchee Valley Col, Wenatchee, Wash, 2001; Frank B & Mary Anderson Cassidy Memorial Award, 100th Annual Catherine Lorillard Wolfe Art Club, New York, 1996; May Audubon Post Award Fel, Philadelphia, Pa, 2005. *Bibliog:* All the Plants that are Fit to Print, Patrick Mongahan, Time Off Princeton, Packet, 93; G Suriano (auth), Printmaking - the state of the art, NJ Goodlife Mag, 3/90. *Mem:* Printmaking Coun NJ; Audubon Artists Inc, NY; Am Color Print Soc (vpres, 88-95 & 2000, bd trustees, 96, pres 2003); Philadelphia Watercolor Club; Soc Am Graphic Artists, NY; The Print Consortium, St Joseph, Mo; Los Angeles Printmaking Soc; Cultural Heritage Comn Somerset Co NJ (adv bd); Franklin Twp (NJ) Coun Chambers; Hist Comn, Franklin Twp, NJ. *Media:* Woodblock Prints; Watercolor, Acrylics. *Specialty:* Old Print Shop, NYC; Graphic Arts Libr, Princeton, Univ. *Publ:* Listening to the Wood, Princeton Packet, S Van Dougen, 4/19/02; interview, Kyoto Int Woodprint Asn, 2001; Going with the Grain, Laurie Gronieri, On the Go, 2000; Newark Pub Libr, Print Collection. *Dealer:* Zimmerli Art Mus New Brunswick NJ; Old Print Shop NYC. *Mailing Add:* 61 Coppermine Rd Princeton NJ 08540

WILLIAMS, JANICE E
PAINTER, SCULPTOR

b Augusta, Ga, Dec 12, 54. *Study:* Univ Ga, BFA (cum laude), 77; Ind State Univ, MFA (drawing & painting), 79; Ohio State Univ; Western Carolina Univ. *Work:* Morris Mus Art. *Exhib:* Solo exhibs, Lander Col, SC, 86, Etherridge Ctr Gallery, Univ SC, Aiken, 87, Quinlan Art Ctr, Augusta Col, Ga, 89, NGa Col Gallery, Dahlonega, 89; Southdown Fine Arts Exhib, Houma, La, 88; La Grange Nat XIV, Ga, 89; Augusta Col Fac Exhib, Istituto D'Arte Dosso Dossi, Ferrara, Italy, 90; two-person exhib, Vanderbilt Univ, Sarratt Gallery, 92; three-person exhib, Univ Dayton, 92; Elvis & Marilyn: 2 X Immortal Traveling Exhib, 95-97. *Teaching:* Instr art, Augusta State Univ, 81-85, asst prof, 87-90, assoc prof, 91-. *Awards:* Fel, Soc Art Religion & Contemp Cult; Asian Studies Bd Grant, Madras Christian Col, India, 96. *Media:* Oil. *Publ:* Auth, Icon Series: Graces Under Fire in Elvis and Marilyn 2 X Immortal (ed by Geri DePaoli), Rizzoli Int, New York, 94. *Mailing Add:* 960 Hickman Rd Augusta GA 30904

WILLIAMS, JOHN ALDEN
HISTORIAN

b Ft Smith, Ark, Sept 6, 28. *Study:* Am Univ Beirut, 50-51; Univ Munich, with Hans Sedlmayer, 51-52; Univ Ark, BA(hist & philos), 53; Princeton Univ, MA & PhD, 53-57; further work under Sir K A C Creswell in Cairo on hist of Islamic art & archit, 57-59. *Pos:* Asst field dir, Am Ctr for Res in Egypt, 57-59; sr res fel, Ctr Middle East Studies, Harvard Univ, 71-72. *Teaching:* Asst & assoc prof Islamic studies, McGill Univ, Montreal, Que, Can, 59-66; dir & prof, Ctr for Arabic Studies, Am Univ Cairo, 66/69; prof art hist & Middle East studies, Prof Ctr for Arabic Studies, Univ Cairo, 69-72; prof art hist & Islamic study, Univ Tex, Austin & Univ Cairo, alternate yrs, 72-88; Wm R Kenan Jr prof humanities, Col William & Mary, Williamsburg, Va, 88-. *Mem:* Col Art Asn Am. *Res:* History of Islamic art and architecture, Islamic inst(s). *Publ:* Coauth, Architecture of Muslim India (400 slides with commentary), Art and Architecture of Ancient Egypt (400 slides with commentary) & Timurid Monuments of Central Asia (40 slides with commentary), Visual Educ Inc, 77; auth, The Khanqah of Siryaqus, In: Towards an Islamic Humanism, Cairo, 83; Urbanization and Monument Construction in Mamluk Cairo, In: Muqarnas II, 84; and others. *Mailing Add:* 6 Coventry Rd Williamsburg VA 23188

WILLIAMS, JOHN WESLEY
HISTORIAN, EDUCATOR

b Memphis, Tenn, Feb 25, 28. *Study:* Duke Univ; Yale Univ, BA; Univ Mich, PhD. *Teaching:* From instr to assoc prof Medieval art, Swarthmore Col, Pa, 60-72, chmn fine arts dept, 71-72; prof, Univ Pittsburgh, retired, chmn fine arts dept, 79-84, retired. *Awards:* Fulbright-Hays Res Grant, Spain, 64 & 69; Nat Endowment Humanities Project Grant, 71-73; Guggenheim Fel, 84-85. *Mem:* Medieval Acad Am; Int Ctr Medieval Art. *Res:* Spanish Medieval art. *Publ:* Auth, Romanesque Bible of San Millan, JWCI, 65; auth, Valeranica and the Scribe Florentus, Madrider Mitteilungen, 70; auth, San Isidoro: Evidence for a new history, Art Bulletin, 73; auth, Early Spanish Manuscript Illumination, George Braziller, 77; ed, Actas del Simposio sobre Beato de Liebana, Vol II, Madrid, 80; and others. *Mailing Add:* 749 Linden Ave S Pittsburgh PA 15208

WILLIAMS, KATHERINE
COLLECTOR, PAINTER

b Trinidad, W Indies, Sept 7, 41; US citizen. *Study:* Harvard Univ, EdM, 84, EdD, 87. *Exhib:* Solo exhib, (photographs) Mus Mod Art Latin Am, Washington, 81, (paintings) Another Look, Touchstone Gallery, Washington, 98, In the Cosmos II, Gutman Libr, Harvard Univ, 98 & In the Cosmos, Summer Sch Mus & Archives, Washington, 98, Space Telescope Sci Inst, Johns Hopkins Univ and Nat Ctr Gallery, US Geol Survey, 99, Another Lock, Gutman Libr, 99, Fitting Them Together, Gutman Libr, Harvard Univ, 2000; (photographs), Give Me Your Tired, Your Poor, Schomberg Ctr, NY, 86; In The Cosmos, NASA, Greenbelt, Md, 2001; Group shows, Trinidad and Tobago Week at the Orgn of Am States, Wash, DC, 98 & 2002; Art Soc Int Monetary Fund, Washington, DC, 98; Exhibicion de Pinturas: Mujer Y Arte en las Americas, OAS, Washington, DC, 98; Art for Life - Hope for Our Children, Mus Americas, Washington, DC, 98; Women of the World: A GlobalCollection of Art, Tuscon Mus Art, Ariz, 2001; White Columns Gallery, New York City, 2000; Univ of New Eng, Portland, Maine, 2001; Womens Art Gallery, Ohio, 2002. *Media:* Watercolor, Acrylic. *Collection:* Nineteenth century American and European oils and watercolors, twentieth century European prings. *Publ:* Auth, Where Else But America?, Fishergate Pub, Annapolis, MD, 77; Computers: Our Road to the Future, DC Pub Sch System, Washington, 82; Fitting Them Together, DC ABC, Inc Washington, 2000. *Mailing Add:* 1440 N Street NW No 616 Washington DC 20005

WILLIAMS, MELISSA
ART DEALER

b Kansas City, Mo, June 1, 51. *Study:* Univ Mo, BA & MA(summa cum laude), 78; Phi Beta Kappa, 73. *Pos:* Owner, Antiques at Greenwood, 73-86, Williams & McCormick, 83-89, & Melissa Williams, Am Arts, 89-. *Mem:* Univ of Mo, Mus Art & Archaeology, (bd mem assoc). *Specialty:* American paintings 1840-1940. *Publ:* Auth, Portrait of a Lady, Muse, 72. *Mailing Add:* 11 S 9th St Columbia MO 65203-2863

WILLIAMS, PAT WARD
PHOTOGRAPHER

b Mar 19, 48, US citizen. *Study:* Moore Col Art, BFA, 82; Md Inst Col Art, MFA, 87. *Exhib:* New Photo Artists, Fox Gallery, Md Inst Col Art, Baltimore, 85; Humor, Wit & Whimsey, Artists Today Touring Exhib, Montpelier Cult Arts Ctr, Laurel, Md, 86; Baltimore Artists Exchange Exhib, Painted Bride Art Ctr, Philadelphia, 86; Invitational Black Artists Exhib, Life Md Gallery, Baltimore, 86; Seventh Ann Nat Art Exhib, Atlanta, Ga, 86; Eighth Ann Nat Exhib, JB Speed Mus, Louisville, Ky, 87; Artquest 88, Los Angeles, 88; Autobiography: In Her Own Image, INTAR Gallery, New York, 88; solo exhibs, Social/Sexual/Personal: Politics, Getehouse Gallery, Washington, DC, 87 & Political Variations, INTAR Gallery, NY, 88. *Teaching:* Baltimore Sch Arts, Md, 84-87; Md Arts Coun, Artist-in-Residence Prog, Snow Hill Middle Sch, Snow Hill, Md, Easton High Sch, Easton, Md & Lake Clifton High Sch, Baltimore, 87; instr, Col Notre Dame Md, Baltimore, 87-. *Awards:* Ford Found Grant, 85-87; Nat Newpaper Publ Asn Award, Best News Photog 1985, 86; City Arts Individual Artist's Grant, Mayor's Adv Comt Arts & Cult, Baltimore, Md; NEA/Mid-Atlantic Regional Visual Arts Fel for Works on Paper, 88. *Bibliog:* Dakai Asim (auth), St Louis Am, 11/10/88. *Mem:* (Bd Trustees) Artist Advisory Bd, Md Art Place Gallery, Baltimore, Md; Col Art Asn, Soc Photog Educ. *Mailing Add:* FSU 220-B Fine Arts Bldg Tallahassee FL 32306-1150

WILLIAMS, PAUL ALAN
PAINTER, ILLUSTRATOR

b Detroit, Mich, Sept 10, 34. *Study:* Chadsey Art Sch, Detroit, 48-49; Meinzinger Arts, 50-51; Art Ctr Sch, Los Angeles, BPA, 59. *Work:* Jack McCormack & Co Inc, NY; Radio City Music Hall Mus; Readers' Digest Col; La Maison du Temps, Conn; Stadtisches Mus Leipzig. *Comn:* production & prom, ABC & NBC TV, NY, 80's; space illus, United Tech-Norden, 80's; St Mary's, 98. *Exhib:* Connolly & Alterman Gallery, Tex, 85; Eagles Lair Gallery, Conn, 86; Int Show, Waveny Park Mus, Conn, 86-88; Cath Charity Show, Bruce Mus, Greenwich, Conn, 87; Doyle Gallery, NY, 87 & 88; Litchfield Auction Gallery, Conn, 87, 88, 89, 90, 91 & 92; Wilton Historical, Soc Am Craftsmanship Show, Conn, 91 & 92; Westport Merchants Show, Conn, 92-98; Gracie Mansion Park Show, NY, 92; Westpoint Art Show, 92-2001. *Teaching:* Oliver & Williams Studio, 98 & 2004. *Awards:* Best in Show, Casa D'Oliver Garden Show, Conn, 91 & 2004. *Bibliog:* Vision of flowers (article), Your Family, 3/90; Sandi Oliver (auth), American Impressionist Paul Alan Williams: His Garden & His Oil Paintings, (catalog raissone), 91, 92 & 93. *Mem:* Soc Am Impressionists; Soc Illus (special honors). *Media:* Oil. *Interests:* Collecting Antiques, rasing dogs, walking. *Publ:* Paul A Williams' His Garden & His Oil Paintings, Am Impressionist, 91, 92, 93-98. *Dealer:* Sandi Oliver. *Mailing Add:* c/o Sandi Oliver Fine Art PO Box 1203 Weston CT 06883-0203

WILLIAMS, RAYMOND LESTER
PAINTER, INSTRUCTOR

b Lenoir City, Tenn, Nov 10, 26. *Study:* Chicago Acad Fine Arts, study with Edgar Whitney, John Pellew, Edmound Fitzgerald & Zolton Zabo, cert. *Work:* United Tel Co, Bristol, Tenn; Dobyns-Bennett High Sch & Tenn Eastman Co, Kingsport; Carrol Reese Mus & Tipton-Haynes Mus, Johnson City, Tenn. *Comn:* Highlands of Roan, Southern Appalachian Highlands Conservancy, 77; Church Circle, City of Kingsport, Tenn, 79; Four Homecoming '86 Print-Tri Cities Radio, 86; Directory Covers, United Tel System, 86; and others. *Exhib:* Tenn State Mus, Nashville, 73; Emory & Henry Univ, Emory, Va, 86; Mount Dora Art Festival, Mount Dora, Fla, 88; Lenox Square Fine Art, Atlanta, 87; Wilkes Art Gallery, North Wilkesboro, NC, 88; and many others. *Pos:* Graphic artist, Tenn Eastman Co, 50-74; painter & gallery owner, 74-. *Awards:* Best of Show, Jonesboro Days, Jonesboro, Tenn, 75 & 81; Award, Tenn Watercolor Soc, 79; Best of Show, Dunwoody Fine Arts Asn, Atlanta, Ga, 87; and others. *Mem:* Tenn Watercolor Soc (dist dir, 74-75); Tenn Artists; Kingsport Art Guild (pres, 75-76). *Media:* Watercolor, Oils. *Dealer:* Gallery 81 PO Box 5538 Kingsport TN. *Mailing Add:* 3322 Roller Dr Kingsport TN 37663

WILLIAMS, REBA WHITE
COLLECTOR, WRITER

b Gulfport, Miss, May 21, 36. *Study:* Duke Univ, BA; Harvard Grad Sch Bus Admin, MBA, 70; Hunter Col, MA(art hist), 88; Grad Ctr, CUNY, PhD(art hist), 96. *Exhib:* Am Screenprints Traveling Exhib (with catalog), Nat Acad Design, NY, 87, Reynolda House, Winston-Salem, NC, 88, Fed Reserve Bd, Washington, DC, 88, Butler Inst Am Art, Youngstown, Ohio, 88, Addison Gallery Am Art, Andover, Mass, 89, Guild Hall, E Hampton, NY, 89, Mary & Leigh Block Gallery, Northwestern Univ, Evanston, Ill, 89, Columbia Mus Art, SC, 90, Japan US Embassy in Tokyo & Sogetsu Found, 90, Mus Mod Art in Sapporo, Japan, 90, State St Bank, Boston, 91, Acad Art, Vienna, Austria, 91-92, Fitzwilliam Mus, Cambridge, Eng, 92, Parpallo Mus, Valencia, Spain, 90, Instituto de Estudios Northeamericanos, Barcelona, Spain, 92, Calcografia Nat

Real Academia de Bellas Artes de San Fernando, Madrid, Spain, 92, Nat Mus Wales, Glasgow, Scotland, 93, Mona Bismarck Found, Paris, France, 93, Kuntshalle Breman, Ger, 93; Black & White Since 1960 (with catalog), City Gallery Contemp Art, Raleigh, NC, 89, Aldrich Mus Contemp Art, Ridgefield, Conn, 90; The Mexican Muralists & Prints (with catalog), Span Inst, NY, 90, Franz Mayer Mus, Mex City, 91, Bard Col, Annandale-on-Hudson, NY, 92, Herbert F Johnson Mus Art, Cornell Univ, Ithaca, NY, 94; Blossoms in Black & White, The Equitable, NY, 91; Alone in a Crowd (with catalog), Newark Mus, NJ, 92-93, The Equitable Gallery, NY, 92-93, Long Beach Mus Art, Calif, 93, Fitzwilliam Mus, Cambridge, Eng, 93, NY State Mus, Albany, NY, 94, Yale Univ Art Gallery, New Haven, Conn, 94, JB Speed Art Mus, Louisville, Ky, 94, Philadelphia Mus Art, Pa, 94; NY Exhib, Fitzwillim Mus, Cambridge, Eng, 94. *Pos:* Res, McKinsey & Co, Inc, formerly; Art Comn, New York City, 95-98, pres, 97-98; mem, NY State Coun, on the Arts, 96-99, vchmn, 99; mem, Manhattan Community Board 8, 99-2000; vchmn, White Williams Holdings, Ltd, 2001-; hon keeper, of Am prints The Fitzwilliam Mus, Cambridge, Eng; dir, spec projects, mem bd dir, Alliance Capital Mgt; securities analyst, Mitchell Hutchins, Inc. *Awards:* Polish Order Merit, Cavalier Grand Cross Poland, 97; recipient Pacesetter award, New York City Coun, 99; Distinguished Cult Leadership award, NY Rep Co Cot, 99; Woman of Distinction award, NY State Senate, 2000; named one of Top 200 Collectors, ARTnews Mag, 2004, 2006; The Augustus Medal, Brooklyn Mus Art. *Mem:* Art Comm City of NY (pres, 97-98); mem, NY State Coun Arts (vchmn, 2000-); Munic Art Soc. *Collection:* American prints. *Publ:* and many others. *Mailing Add:* White Williams Holdings 41 W 57th St 4th fl New York NY 10019

WILLIAMS, SUE
PAINTER, SCULPTOR
b Chicago Heights, Ill, 54. *Study:* Calif Inst Arts, BFA, 76. *Exhib:* Connections, Contradictions, Emory Univ, 98; Pop Surrealism (with catalog), Aldrich Mus Contemp Art, Conn, 98; Submit, Bricks & Kicks, Austria, 98; Skulptur Figur Weiblich, Landesgalerie, Oberosterreich, Austria, 98; Unbearable Laughter, Ctr Curatorial Studies, Bard Col, NY, 98; Whitney Biennial, Whitney Mus Am Art, NY, 97. *Bibliog:* Roberta smith (auth), rev, NY Times, 10/30/98; rev, New Yorker, 10/26/98-11/2/98; Under the influence, New Yorker, 11/2/98. *Mailing Add:* 330 Gallery 525 W 23rd St New York NY 10011

WILLIAMS, WAYNE FRANCIS
SCULPTOR
b Newark, NY, July 22, 37. *Study:* Syracuse Univ, BFA, 58, MFA, 62; Chaloner Found Fel, 58 & 59; Europe-Ghent Belgium, 58-60. *Work:* Ministry Pub Educ Collections, Brussels, Belg; Murdock Collection, Wichita Mus, Kans; Whitney Found Collection, Cornell Univ; Nebr Art Asn, Univ Nebr-Lincoln; NY State Univ Col Albany; Univ of Rochester; Katonah Mus, NY. *Comn:* Life size welded sculpture, North Rose Wolcott Sch, NY, 72; Life size bronze figure of Wm Simon, Univ Rochester, NY, 88; life size bronze, Vietnam Mem, Rochester, NY, 96; Mem bronze, Woodcliff Inn, Rochester, NY, 98. *Exhib:* Belg Salon des Beaux Arts, Mus voor Schone Kunsten, Ghent, Belg, 60; one-man shows, Maynard Walker Gallery, 61 & 64 & Frank Rehn Gallery, NY, 74; NY Art Dealers Exhib, Park Bernet Gallery, NY, 64; Oxford Gallery, Rochester, NY, 95, 99, two-man show, Metaphysical, 2001-2005; Fingerlakes Art Ctr, 2000; Saratoga Arts Ctr, NY, 2000; Arnot Mus, Elmira, NY, 2000 & 2003; Face to Face, Keuka College, Keuka Park, NY, 2005; Wayne Arts Members Show, Newark, NY, 2004-2006; 15 at 1570 Rochester, NY, 2005; Oswego Arts Coun Int, Oswego, NY, 2005. *Pos:* Prof Emer-Sculpture, 68-2003. *Teaching:* Instr drawing, Syracuse Univ, 60-63; prof drawing & sculpture, Community Col Finger Lakes, 68-2003. *Awards:* Louis Comfort Tiffany Found Award for Sculpture, 64. *Bibliog:* John Canaday (auth), Wayne Williams-Maynard-Walker, NY Times, 10/64; Dorothy Hall (auth), Williams at Rehn, Park East, NY, 4/74; Roberta Olson (auth), Wayne Williams-Rehn, Arts Mag, 6/74. *Mem:* Ontario Co Arts Coun; Wayne Co Arts Coun; State Univ Gallery & Mus Asn. *Media:* Metals, Copper, Steel, Bronze. *Specialty:* Painting & Sculpture. *Interests:* Sailing, Horsebacking Riding, Visiting Mus. *Publ:* Auth, The art program at Community College of Finger Lakes, NY State Art Teachers Mag, 5/74. *Dealer:* Oxford Gallery Rochester NY. *Mailing Add:* 1954 Gardner Rd Newark NY 14513

WILLIAMS, WILLIAM EARLE
PHOTOGRAPHER, CURATOR
b Vicksburg, Miss, Apr 19, 50. *Study:* Hamilton Col, BA, 73; Yale Univ, MFA, 78. *Work:* Philadelphia Mus Art; Lehigh Univ, Bethlehem, Pa; Metrop Mus & Brooklyn Mus, NY; Univ Md & Baltimore Mus Art, Baltimore; Allentown Art Mus; Princeton Univ Mus, Princeton, NJ. *Comn:* Philadelphia Conv Ctr, Pa, 93; Chester Springs Art Ctr, Pa, 97; Philadelphia Print Collaborative, 2002. *Exhib:* Solo exhibs, Butler Inst Am Arts, Youngstown, Ohio, 80, Party Photographs, Univ Md, Baltimore, 86, Trumbull Art Gallery, Warren, Ohio, 90, Sol Mednick Gallery, Univ Arts, Philadelphia, Pa, 94, Smith Col, Northampton, Mass, 95, W Moreland Mus, Greensburg, Pa, 96 & Esther Klein Art Gallery, Philadelphia, Pa, 97; Am Photog, 1910-1983 (with catalog), Tampa Mus, Fla, 83; Contemp Photogrs, Pa Acad Fine Arts, Philadelphia, 84; Pa Photographers IV, Allentown Art Mus, Pa, 85; 61st Int Print Club Competition, Philadelphia, 85; Contemp Philadelphia Artists (catalog), Philadelphia Mus Art, 90; Baltimore Mus Art, Md, 90; Allentown Art Mus, Pa, 95; Chrysler Mus Art, Norfolk, Va, 98; S Eastern Mus Photog, Daytona Beach Community Col, Fla, 98; Canady Libr, Bryn Mawr Col, 2002; Princeton Univ Mus Art, African Am Mus Ar, Phildelphia, 2005. *Collection Arranged:* Lewis Hine: Child Labor Photographs, 79, Muybridge and Eakins, Photographers of Motion, 80, Walker Evans: A Retrospective, 81, Arbus, Weegee and Model Photographers, 82, Masterpieces of Photography from the Collection, 84, & Adolphe Brown, Walker Evans, Andre Kertesz: Photographers of Sculpture, 88, Comfort Gallery, Haverford Col, Pa, Paul Sttrand Prints in Ink, 2000, Remembering September 11, 2001, Cantor-Fitzgerald Gallery, Haverford Col; Sol Mednick Remembered, Mcgill Libr, Haverford Col, 2005; W Eugene Smith, Mcgill Libr, Haverford Col, 2006. *Pos:* Cur photog, Haverford Col, 79- & gallery dir, 81-93. *Teaching:* Prof fine arts photog, Haverford Col, Pa, 78-. *Awards:* Purchase Award, 61st Ann Int Competition, The Print Club, Philadelphia, 85; Pa Individual Arts fel, 85 & 87; Pew Charitable Trusts Individual Artist Fel Award, 97; Pa Individual Artists fel, 85, 97, 2003; Guggenheim fel, 2003. *Bibliog:* Porter Aichele (auth), William Earle Williams, Party Photographs, Comfort Gallery, Haverford Col, Pa, 85; William Southwell (auth), Documentary revival, Lens on Campus, Hearst, New York, 86; Deborah Willis-Thomas (auth), Black Photographers, 1940-1988: An Illustrated Bio-Bibliography, Garland Press, NY, NY, 88. *Mem:* Col Art Asn; Soc Photog Educ; Am Studies Asn; Soc Photographic Educ (Nat bd dir, 96-03); Civil War Preservation Trust (Nat bd dir, 97-00). *Media:* Medium & large format photog. *Res:* Walker Evans, Robert Frank, Paul Strand, 19th century landscape photog. *Publ:* Illusr, William Williams Portfolio, Philadelphia Photo Rev, Perloff, 82; Party Pictures, Aronis Press, 85; auth Gettysburg a Journey in Time, Klein Gallery, Philadelphia, 97; Deborah Willis Reflections in Black: A History of Black Photographers 1840 to the Present, Norton, NY, 2000. *Mailing Add:* Dept Fine Arts Haverford Col Haverford PA 19041

WILLIAMS, WILLIAM THOMAS
PAINTER, EDUCATOR
b Cross Creek, NC, July 17, 42. *Study:* Skowhegan Sch Painting & Sculpture, summer 65; Pratt Inst, BFA, 66; Yale Univ, MFA, 68. *Work:* Mus Mod Art & Whitney Mus Am Art, NY; Yale Univ, New Haven, Conn; Wadsworth Atheneum, Hartford, Conn; Johnson Mus, Cornell Univ, Ithaca, NY. *Comn:* Print, Jewish Mus, NY, 70; environ sculpture, Menil Found, Houston, 70; environ murals, Gottesmans Plaza, NY, 70; print portfolio, HKL Ltd Publ, NY, 71; print, LD Group Int, NY, 78. *Exhib:* Whitney Ann, Whitney Mus Am Art, 69 & Struct of Color, 71; L'Art Vivant Aux Estats-Unis, Found Maeght, St Paul, France, 70; DeLuxe Show, Menil Found, Houston, 71; Acquisitions, Mus Mod Art, NY, 72; Contemp Visual Expressions, Anacostia Mus/Smithsonian Inst, Wash, DC, 87; The Art Black Am in Japan, Tokyo, Japan, 87; 40th Ann Acad-Inst Purchase Exhib, Am Acad & Inst Art & Letters, NY, 88. *Teaching:* Prof art, City Univ New York, Brooklyn Col, 70-. *Awards:* Nat Endowment for Arts & Humanities traveling grant, 65 & artist fels, 70; John Simon Guggenheim Fel, 87; Grant, Joan Mitchell Found, 96. *Bibliog:* H W Janson (auth), The History of Art, Harry Abrams, 86. *Mailing Add:* 654 Broadway New York NY 10012

WILLIAMSON, JASON H
PAINTER
b Bristol, Va, Mar 20, 26. *Study:* Emory & Henry Col, Va; Vesper George Sch Art, Boston, Mass, cert. *Work:* Time Life; Emory & Henry Col. *Comn:* Signed and numbered reproduction color prints, comn by Grey Stone Press, Nashville, Tenn; Union Planters Bank, Memphis, Tenn. *Exhib:* Am Watercolor Soc, 65, 74-77 & 80; Watercolor USA, Springfield, Mo, 63, 72 & 74; one-man shows, East Tenn State Univ, Johnson City, 54, Memphis Acad Arts, Tenn, 60, 67, Emory and Henry Col, Va, 67, Tenn Tech Univ, 73 & Ark Arts Ctr, Pine Bluff, 74; and others. *Pos:* Art dir, SE Massengill Co, Bristol, Tenn, 49-56 & Plough Inc, Memphis, 56-58; free lance advert art, Memphis, 58-62; advert art studio head, Williamson--Parker, 62-75; gallery owner, Golden Fleece Art Gallery, Memphis, 70-75 & Carefree, Ariz, 76-87. *Teaching:* Dept head advert art, The Memphis Acad Art, Tenn, 60-69; nat competition judge, pvt classes & workshops, artist watercolor & oil. *Awards:* John Young Hunter, Am Watercolor Soc, 74; Annenberg Fund Award, Nat Watercolor Soc, 76; Colo Watermedia Award, Rocky Mountain Nat, 77. *Bibliog:* Watercolor Page, Am Artist Mag, 6/78, Southwest Art, 10/79. *Mem:* Am Watercolor Soc (Signature mem); Nat Watercolor Soc (signature mem); 22 x 30 Watercolor Group Ariz; Tenn Watercolor Soc (hon lifetime); Memphis Watercolor Group (hon lifetime). *Media:* Watercolor, Oil. *Specialty:* Watercolor and oil. *Interests:* Support many worthwhile art organizations. *Publ:* Producer & dir, Video Ins, Master Watercolor Video, 79 & 89. *Mailing Add:* PO Box 1943 Cave Creek AZ 85331

WILLIAMSON, PHILEMONA
PAINTER
b New York, NY. *Study:* Bennington Col, Vt, BA, 73; NY Univ, MA, 79. *Work:* Mint Mus Art, Charlotte, SC; AT&T, NJ; Reader's Digest, Pleasantville, NY. *Exhib:* ArtSounds, Nohra Haime Gallery, NY, 86; Artist in the Marketplace, Bronx Mus Arts, NY, 88 & 90; Alice and Look Who Else Through the Looking-Glass, Bernice Steinbaum Gallery, NY, 88; Introductions, June Kelly Gallery, NY, 89; Five from Bennington, Krasdale Foods Art Gallery, Bronx, NY, 90; solo shows, June Kelly Gallery, NY, 90, 92, 95 & 98, African Am Mus, Hempstead, NY, 91, Powers Art Gallery, E Stroudsburg Univ, Pa, 92, Pa State Univ, Univ Park, 93, Flushing Coun Cult & Arts, NY, 93, Hypo-Bank, NY, 94 & John Michael Kohler Arts Ctr, Sheboygan, Wis, 99, June Kelly Gallery, NY, 00, Amelie A Wallace Gallery, SUNY Coll, Old Westbury, NY, 01; Visions of Life, Nat Conference Women's Caucus Art, Islip Art Mus, E Islip, NY, 91; The Children Among Us, Krasdale Foods Gallery, White Plains, NY, 91; Selections from Artists in the Marketplace, PepsiCo Gallery, Purchase, NY, 91; In the Looking Glass: Contemp Narrative Painting (with catalog), Mint Mus Art, Charlotte, NC, 91; Present Tense, Univ Wis Fine Arts Gallery, Milwaukee, 92; Child's Play, Art in General, NY, 93; Empowerment: The Art of African-Am Artists, Col Art Gallery & Krasdale Foods Art Gallery, Bronx, NY, 94; June Kelly: A Particular Vision, Anderson Gallery, Buffalo, NY, 94; Current Identities: Recent Painting in the United States (with catalog), IV Int de Pintura, Cuenca, Ecuador & Ctr Ctontemp Art, Newark, NJ, 94; Other Agendas, Kingsborough Community Col Art Gallery, City Univ NY, Brooklyn, 96; The Boat, Object and Metaphor, Pratt Manhattan Gallery, NY & Rubelle & Norman Schafler Gallery, Pratt Inst, Brooklyn, NY, 96; Real: Figurative Narratives in Contemp African-Am Art, Bass Mus Art, Miami Beach, Fla, 96; Bearing Witness: Contemp Works by African Am Women Artists, Spelman Col Mus Fine Art, Atlanta, Ga, Fort Wayne Mus Art, Ind, Polk Mus Art, Lakeland, Fla, Columbus Mus, Ga, African Am Mus, Dallas, Tex, Minn

Mus Am Art, St Paul & Ulrich Mus Art, Wichita, Kans, 96; Women in Full Effect, RUSH Philanthropic Art Found, NY, 97; Walk the Walk, Forum Contemp Art, St Louis, Mo, 98; Postcards from Black Am (with catalog), Ctr Contemp Art, Breda, The Neth & Frans Hals Mus, Haarlem, The Neth, 98. *Pos:* Vis artist, Norfolk State Univ, Va, 82, Ctr d'Art, Port-Au-Prince, Haiti, 87, Univ NC, Chapel Hill, 92 & Parsons Sch Design, 94. *Teaching:* Instr, Harlem Sch Arts, 78-83, Metrop Mus Art, 83; adj fac, RI Sch Design, 89-90, Parsons Sch Design, 91-92 & Cooper Union, 91-92; fac painting, Milton Avery Grad Sch Arts, Bard Col, 91. *Awards:* Nat Endowment Arts Fel Painting, 87-88; Ludwig Vogelstein Grant, New York, 93-94; Joan Mitchell Found Award Painting, 97. *Bibliog:* Grady T Turner (auth), article, ARTnews, 9/98; Halima Taha (auth), Collecting African American Art: Works on Paper and Canvas, Crown Publ, New York, 98; Susan Osmond (auth), Philemona Williamson: half-remembered dreams, World & I Mag, Washington, DC, 2/99. *Dealer:* Kelly Gallery New York NY. *Mailing Add:* 11 LaSalle Rd Upper Montclair NJ 07043

WILLIFORD, HOLLIS R
PAINTER, SCULPTOR
b Hill Co, Tex, Oct 31, 40. *Study:* Univ Tex, Arlington, 59-63; N Tex State, 63-64; Art Ctr Col Design, BA, 71. *Work:* Denver Art Mus, Colo; Nat Cowboy and Western Heritage Mus, Oklahoma City; Lacrosse Hall of Fame, John Hopkins Univ; Buffalo Bill Hist Center, Cody, Wyo; Gunesse Contry Mus, Rochester, NY; Thomas Gilcrease Mus, Tulsa. *Exhib:* Nat Acad Western Art, Nat Cowboy Hall Fame, Oklahoma City, Okla, 80-88; Nabisco Invitational, Nabisco Brands World Hq, E Hanover, NJ, 84; Gilcrease Rendezvous, Thomas Gilcrease Mus, Tulsa, Okla, 88; Prix de West Collection, Wildlife Am W Mus, Jackson, Wyo, 88. *Teaching:* Drawing, Art Ctr Col Design, Los Angeles, 69 & 70; drawing & illus, Rocky Mountain Sch Art, Denver, 71-72; sculpture, Fechin Inst, Taos, NMex, 97; drawing, Loveland Acad Fine Art, Colo. *Awards:* Prix de West, Nat Acad Western Art, Cowboy Hall Fame, 80 & 88 & Gold Medals, 80 & 86. *Bibliog:* John Jellico (auth), Hollis Williford, Artist Rockies & Golden West, 80; Carol Dickinson (auth), Facing the Challenge of Nature, SW Art, 87; Fred Myers (auth), Hollis Williford, Gilcrease Mag, 88. *Media:* Bronze, Oil. *Dealer:* Williford Arts Ltd Loveland CO; Simpson Gallagher Gallery Cody WY; Ernest Fuller Fine Art, Denver. *Mailing Add:* 813 S St Louis Ave Loveland CO 80537

WILLIS, BARBARA FLORENCE
PAINTER
b Bronx, NY, Dec 17, 32. *Study:* Vesper George Sch Art, with Robert Douglas Hunter & Robert Cummings. *Exhib:* Solo exhibs, Peel Gallery, Danby, Vt, 88 & Cumeo Mus, Vernon Hills, Ill, 92; Pastel Soc Am 20th Nat Show, 92; joint show, Peel Gallery, Danby, Vt; Ringmaster, Pastel Soc Am, 94; Grandmother's Doll, Am Artists Prof League, 94; 23rd Nat Pastel Soc Am Show, 95 (Catherine Lorillard Wolf Art Club Award & Master Pastelist Designation); 46th Nat Show Acad Artists Asn, 96 (Gulluip Watson Award); 68th Grand Nat Exhib of Am Artists Prof League, 97 (Michael Werwolf Mem Award); Peel Gallery, Danby, 2002; 3-person show of pastels, Love Gallery, Chicago; and many others. *Awards:* First Prize, Conn Pastel Soc, 92; Nat Arts Club Award, 94; Master Pastelist, Pastel Soc Am, 95. *Bibliog:* Hazel Harrison (auth), Pastel School, Readers Digest. *Mem:* Charter mem Conn Pastel Soc; Am Artists Prof League; Pastel Soc Am; Copley Soc, formerly; Guild Boston Artists. *Media:* Oils, Pastels. *Publ:* Encyclopedia of Oil Painting Techniques, Quartro Pub Co, London, Eng. *Dealer:* Guild of Boston Artists 162 Newbury St Boston MA 02116; Quidley and Co 466 Main St Chatham MA 02633. *Mailing Add:* 64 State Rte 202 Bennington NH 03442

WILLIS, DEBORAH
CURATOR, PHOTOGRAPHER
b Philadelphia, Pa, 48. *Study:* Temple Univ, 72; Philadelphia Col Art, BFA, 75; Pratt Inst, MFA, 79; City Univ NY, MA, 86. *Work:* Los Angeles Co Mus Art, Calif; Ctr Creative Photog, Tucson, Ariz. *Exhib:* Conceptual Textiles, John Michael Kohler Arts Ctr, Wis, 95-96; Family Matters, Steinbaum Krauss Gallery, NY, 95 & 96; Photo/Quilt Stories, Tex Woman's Univ, Denton, 96; Aspects of African Am Art, Walsh Libr Gallery, Seton Hall Univ, South Orange, NJ & Chubb Group Ins Co, Warren NJ, 96; Visual Griots, Univ Md, 96; Artists at Work, Smithsonian Inst, Washington, DC, 96; Love's Labor Lost, City Gallery Chastain, Atlanta, Ga, 96; Mirror My Presence, Univ Conn, 96; Tragic Wake: Legacy of Slavery & African Diaspora in Contemp Am Art, Middleton McMillan Gallery, NC, 96-97; Family Stories, Hartwick Col, Onconta, NY, 97; Memorable Histories and Historic Memories, Bowdoin Col, Maine, 98; Selections from Soho-Steinbaum Krauss Gallery Artists, Ft Lewis Col, Colo, 98. *Collection Arranged:* VanDerZee, Smithsonian Inst, Washington, DC, 93, Imagining Families: Image & Voices, 94-95 & Resonant Forms; Contemporary African, American Women Sculptors, 98; Techno Seduction, Cooper Union Sch Art, NY, 97. *Pos:* Cur, The NY Libr, 80-92; exhib cur, Smithsonian Inst, 92-. *Teaching:* Adj prof, City Univ NY, 89-90; vis artist, Columbia Univ, NY & Art Inst Boston, 96. *Awards:* Alumni Achievement Award Educ, Pratt Inst, 93; Infinity Award for Writing in Photog, Int Ctr Photog, 95; Alumni of the Year, Univ Arts, Philadelphia, Pa, 95. *Mem:* Women Caucus Arts; Soc Photog Educ (bd mem, 86-96 & chair, 94-96); Col Art Asn (bd mem, 94-97). *Publ:* Auth, Van Der Zee: The Portraits of James Van Der Zee, Harry Abrams Publ, NY, 93; Picturing Us: African American Identity in Photography, New Press, NY, 93; Visual Journal: Photography in Harlem and DC in the 30's and 40's, Smithsonian Inst Press, 96; coauth, The Family of Black America, Crown Publ, 96

WILLIS, JANE B(ROOME)
GRAPHIC ARTIST, PAINTER
b New Orleans, La, July 25, 37. *Study:* Louisiana State Univ, BS, 59; Burlington Co Col, NJ, with Merton Howe, 78; Camden Co Col, NJ, with Bill Marlin, 80-82; Univ New Orleans, 83; New Orleans Acad Fine Arts, with Auseklis Ozols, 92. *Work:* World Trade Ctr, New Orleans; Curray & Co, Monroe, La; Wood Treating Inc, Picayune, Miss. *Exhib:* New Orleans Art Asn Fine Arts Fest, World Trade Ctr, New Orleans, 92-93; A Shared Element - Artists Work on Paper, Slidell Cult Ctr, La, 92; Southeastern Exhib, Fine Arts Mus South, Mobile, Ala, 93; Salon Int, Jackson, Miss, 94; Catharine Lorillard Wolfe's 100 Yr Traveling Exhib, 96 & 97. *Pos:* Mem oper comt, Slidell Cult Ctr, 89-95. *Awards:* Nellie Evans Mem Award, Artwave's 7th Ann 93; Artists Mag Award Merit, Westbank Art Guilds Nat, 94; Second Place, New Orleans Art Asn, 94. *Mem:* Nat League Am Pen Women; Artwave; Catharine Lorilland Wolfe Art Club; New Orleans Art Asn; Slidell Art League Inc. *Media:* Graphite, Oil. *Publ:* Contribr, The Best of Colored Pencil 2, Rockport Publ, 93; illusr, cover, Art Calendar Mag, 9/96. *Mailing Add:* 859 Cross Gates Blvd Slidell LA 70461

WILLIS, JAY STEWART
SCULPTOR, EDUCATOR
b Fort Wayne, Ind, Oct 22, 40. *Study:* Univ Ill, Urbana, BFA(sculpture), 63; Univ Calif, Berkeley, MA(sculpture), 66. *Work:* Hirshhorn Mus, Washington; Del Mar Col, Corpus Christi, Tex; Am Tel & Tel, Chicago; Metrop Mus Art, NY; Calif State Univ, Fullerton; Walker Hill Art Mus, Seoul, Korea. *Comn:* Multiple Structures, Cirus Ed, 73; ALCOA, Univ Southern Calif sculpture garden, Los Angeles, 78; sculpture, comn by Ernesto W Hahn & Charles Kober Assocs, Pasadena, Calif, 80; Bankers Trust, Los Angeles; Pac Enterprises, Los Angeles. *Exhib:* One-person exhibs, Cirrus Gallery, Los Angeles, 81, 83, 85, 86, 88 & 91; A Broad Spectrum: Contemp Los Angeles Painters, Design Ctr Los Angeles, 84; Olympic Project, Los Angeles Co Mus Art, Calif, 84; Sculpture Installation, Fisher Art Gallery, Univ Southern Calif, Los Angeles, 85; Los Angeles Int Art Fair, 86-89; Beverly Hills Sculpture Garden, Calif, 87; Calif Artist in Educ, San Francisco, 89; Monumental Sculpture, Calif State Univ, San Bernardino, 89; Made in LA: The Prints of Cirrus Editions, Los Angeles Co Mus Art, 95; Blessings and Beginnings, Skinball Cult Ctr, Hebrew Union Col, Los Angeles, 96; plus many others. *Teaching:* Instr sculpture, Univ Ariz, Tucson, 66-69; asst prof fine arts, Univ Southern Calif, Los Angeles, 69-73, prof fine arts (sculpture), 74-, chmn studio arts, 88-89, dir pub art studies, 92-. *Awards:* Purchase Award, Los Angeles Art Ann, Barnsdall Park, Calif, 76; Runner-Up, Los Angeles Int Airport Sculpture, Calif, 76; Univ Southern Calif Fac Innovation & Res Grant, Color & Structure, 85-86; Art in Pub Places Award, Calif Arts Coun, 90; and others. *Bibliog:* Suzanne Muchnic (auth), Los Angeles Time, 5/5/81 & 3/1/85; Kathy Zimmer-McKelvie, Images & Issues, spring 82; Betty Brown (auth), Artweek, 11/12/83; Sandy Nelson (auth), Images & Issues, 7-8/84; Stephen Grossman (auth), Artweek, 3/23/85; Colin Gardner (auth), Los Angeles Times, 10/10/86; Marlene Donahue (auth), Los Angeles Times, 5/13/88; and many others. *Mailing Add:* c/o School of Fine Arts USC Watt Hall Rm 103 Los Angeles CA 90089-0292

WILLIS, SIDNEY F
PAINTER
b Newark, NJ, Dec 14, 30. *Study:* Vesper George Sch Art, grad, continued study with Robert D Hunter. *Work:* over 1,000 works sold to various collectors. *Exhib:* Southern Vt Artists, 72; Jordan Show, Boston, Mass, 73; Ogunquit Art Ctr, Maine, 74; Am Artists Prof League, NY, 74; Coun Am Artists Show, NY. *Teaching:* Instr painting & drawing, Vesper George Art Sch, Boston, Mass, 67-69 & Sharon Art Ctr, Peterborough, NH, 65-75. *Awards:* Grand Prize, Jordan Show, Boston, 58 & 62; First Prize, Ogunquit Art Ctr, Maine, 61; Gold Medal, Heritage Salon, 88; and many others. *Bibliog:* Classical Realism (video). *Mem:* Guild Boston Artists; NH Art Asn; Am Artists Prof League; Paste Soc Am. *Media:* Oil, Pastel. *Publ:* Contribr, New York Graphic Soc, Yankee Mag; Techniques in Oil Painting, Quartro Pub, London, Eng. *Mailing Add:* 64 Rte 202 Bennington NH 03442

WILLIS, THORNTON
PAINTER
b Pensacola, Fla, May 25, 36. *Study:* Auburn Univ, Ala; Univ Southern Miss, Hattiesburg, BS; Univ Ala, MA. *Exhib:* Lyrical Abstraction, Aldrich Mus, 69 & Whitney Mus, 71; one-man shows, Sydney Janis Gallery, 80, Oscarsson-Hood Gallery, NY, 80-81 & 84, Marianne Deson Gallery, Chicago, 81, Galerie Nordenhake, Stockholm & Pensacola Mus, Fla, 88; Mus Mod Art, NY, 81 & 84; Galerie Gonet, Lausanne, Switz, 82; Art Mus Ateneum, Helsinki, Finland, 83; Gloria Luria, Miami, Fla, 85; Univ Southern Miss, Hattiesburg, 85; Twining Gallery, NY, 88, 89, 90 & 91; Andre Emmerich Gallery, NY, 92; Andre Zarre Gallery, NY 92; Abstraction and Immanence, Hunter Col, 2001; NY Artists, Emily Lowe Gallery, Hofstra Mus, 2001; Musee Cantonal Des Beaux-Arts De Lausanne, Switz, 2000; Am Abstract Artists, 1930-2000, Hillwood Art Mus, 2000. *Collection Arranged:* Mus Modern Art, NYC; Solomon Guggenheim Mus, NYC; Whitney Mus Am Art, NYC; Mus Art, Carnegie Mellon; Albright-Knox Gallery; New Orleans Mus Fine Art; Power Institute Fine Arts, Sydney, Australia; Phillips Collection, Washington DC; Rose Art Mus, Brandeis Univ; Denver Mus Fine Art. *Teaching:* Wagner Col & La State Univ; grad lectr, Pratt Inst, 74, 77 & 80; lectr, Art Inst Chicago, Ill, 81; assoc prof art, Univ La, Baton Rouge, 83 & State Univ NY, Purchase, 86. *Awards:* Fel Award, John Simon Guggenheim Found, 78-79; Nat Endowment Arts Painting Fel, 80; Adolph & Esther Gottlieb Found, 91; Fel, The Pollock-Krasner Foundation, 2001. *Bibliog:* Peter Bellamy (auth), The Artist Project: Portraits of the Real Art World, New York Artists, 91; Reviews in Art in Am, Arts Mag, ArtForum Mag & Art News, 79-94, New Criterion, 93, New Republic, 2003, NY Times, 2003. *Mem:* Am Abstract Artists Asn, NY. *Media:* Oil, Acrylic. *Publ:* Joseph Masheck (auth), Historical Present: Essays of the 1970's, Contemporary Am Art Critics, Univ Mich Press, 1984. *Dealer:* Elizabeth Harris Gallery 529 W 20th St New York NY 10011; Claes Nordenhake Stockholm Sweden. *Mailing Add:* 85-87 Mercer St New York NY 10012

WILLMOTT, ELIZABETH ANN
SCULPTOR, PHOTOGRAPHER
b Indianapolis, Ind, June 18, 28. *Study:* Oberlin Col, Ohio, BA, 50; Univ Mich, Ann Arbor, MA, 52; Univ Saskatchewan with Eli Bornstein, 59-62. *Work:* Erindale Col, Univ Toronto; Glendon Col, York Univ, Toronto, Ont; Kenderdine Gallery, Univ Saskatchewan, Saskatoon, Sask, CA; Mondriaanhuis, Amersfort, Neth; Gallery One One One, Univ Manitoba, Winnipag, Manitoba, Ca. *Exhib:* Solo shows: Dunkleman Gallery, Toronto, Ont, 1970; Lattice, Light, and Landscape, Durham Art Gallery, Durham, Ont, 1998; The Scanner as a Camera, The Gallery Rm, Collingwood Pub Libr, Collingwood, Ont, 2002; Jewellery 71, Art Gallery of Ont, Toronto, 1971; Structurist Reliefs with Dave Barr, Marianne Friedland Gallery, Toronto, 1975; The Constructivist Heritage, Harbourfront Gallery, Toronto, 1981; Global Echoes, Mondriaanhuis, Amersfort, Neth, 2000, 2001. *Awards:* Second Prize, Newfoundland Provincial Exhib, 58; Exhib Grant, Durham Art Gallery, Ont Arts Coun, 98. *Bibliog:* Harold Hayden (auth), Structurist Movement, Chicago Omnibus, 5/67; Jim Purdie (auth), The Structurists, Globe & Mail, 7/75; Michael Greenwood (auth), Relief Structures: Elizabeth Willmott & Dave Barr, Arts Can, 75-76. *Mem:* Visual Arts Ont; Owen Sound Art Town Collective. *Media:* Relief Constructions; Photography. *Publ:* Auth & illustr, the Structurist Art Ann, Univ Saskatchewan, 65-; Lattice, Light and Landscape, New Circle Publ, 1/95; contribr, Blank Page 3, B4 Publ, London, 90. *Dealer:* Gallery de Boer 970 2nd Ave E Owen Sound ON Canada N4K 2H6. *Mailing Add:* 450 Sixth Ave W Owen Sound ON N4K 6K2 Canada

WILLOUGHBY, JANE BAKER
COLLAGE ARTIST, PAINTER
b Toledo, Ohio. *Study:* Smith Col, Mass, BA, 43; Art Students League with George Grosz, 45-49; New Sch Social Res, New York, 50-51. *Work:* Lyman Allyn Mus, New London, Conn; Discovery Mus, Bridgeport, Conn; The Robert Benjamin Collection, NY; Conn Bank & Trust Co, New Haven; Sen & Mrs George McGovern, Washington, DC; Pres & Mrs Ronald Reagan, Washington, DC. *Exhib:* One-man shows, Silvermine Guild Artists, New Canaan, Conn, 63 & 76, Slater Mem Mus, Norwich, Conn, 76, Lyman Allyn Mus, New London, Conn, 80, Bridgeport Mus Art, Sci, Conn, 80 & Whitney Mus Am Art, New Haven, Conn, 81; The Benjamin Collection, Yale Univ Art Gallery; Viridian Gallery, NY, 83 & 86; Albertus Magnus Col, 90; Fairfield Univ, 85. *Teaching:* Instr, Silvermine Guild Artists. *Awards:* Munson Award & Purchase Prize, New Haven Paint-Clay Club, 75; Arches Paper, Nat Asn Painters in Casein & Acrylic, 78; Audubon Medal Honor, Audubon Artists Am, 78; Conn Women Artists, 90; Best in Show, Conn Women Artists, New Brit Mus Am Art, 92. *Bibliog:* Shirley Gonzales (auth), New Haven Register, 9/16/83; Shirley Sandler (auth), Manhattan Arts, 11/16/83; Amy Friedman (auth), Artspeak, 11/16/83; and others. *Mem:* Silvermine Guild Artists; Conn Acad Fine Arts; Conn Watercolor Soc; Audubon Artists Inc; Conn Women Artists Asn. *Media:* Monotype. *Mailing Add:* 1150 Ridge Rd North Haven CT 06473

WILLUMSON, GLENN GARDNER
EDUCATOR, CURATOR
b Glendale, Calif, June 22, 49. *Study:* St Mary's Col, BA, 71; Univ Calif, Davis, MA, 84; Univ Calif, Santa Barbara, PhD, 88. *Collection Arranged:* Masterpieces of the Rubel Collection, Crocker Mus Art, 82; Collecting with a Passion (auth, catalog), Palmer Mus Art, 93; Double Plots, Palmer Mus Art, 94; Wayne Miller: Tokyo, Hiroshima, Palmer Mus Art, 95; Capturing the Light, Palmer Mus Art, 96; History Past, History Present: Am Daguerreotypes, 00. *Pos:* Collection development, Getty Inst, Santa Monica, Calif, 88-92; cur, Palmer Mus Art, State College, Pa, 92-2000, sr cur 2000-. *Teaching:* Adj prof, Univ Calif, Santa Barbara, 86-87; vis prof mod art, Univ Calif, Irvine, 89-90; affil prof contemp art & theory, history of photography, Pa State Univ, 94-2000; Assoc Prof Art history of photography, Univ Fla, 01-; dir grad program in Mus Studies. *Awards:* Getty Publ Grant, Getty Found, 91; John Randolph & Dora Hayes Fel, Huntington Libr, 95; Univ Teacher's Fel, Nat Endowment Humanities, 97-98; NEH Summer Fel, 2005; Fla Humanities Grant, 2005-2006. *Bibliog:* P Palmquist (auth), Thesis review, Stereo World, 85; J Carson (auth), review, Winterthur Portfolio, 92; A Ellenzweig (auth), Life and Eugene Smith, Times Lit Suppl (London), 93. *Mem:* Soc Photog Educ (regional bd, 92-97); Col Art Asn; Am Studies Asn; Asn Historians Am Art; Am Asn Mus; (compt bd, 2004-). *Publ:* Auth, AA Hart: Photographer of the transcontinental railroad, Hist Photo Mag, 88; contribr, Anthony Van Dyck's Antwerp, Sedelijk Prenteenkab, 91; auth, W Eugene Smith and the Photographic Essay, Cambridge Univ Press, 92; The Getty Research Inst; Materials for a New Photo-History, Hist Photo, Mag 98; The Shifting Audience of the Univ Mus, Mus International, 2000; contribr, Photos Objects Histories, Rutledge, 04. *Mailing Add:* Univ Fla PO Box 115801 Gainesville FL 32611-5801

WILMERDING, JOHN
EDUCATOR, HISTORIAN
b Boston, Mass, Apr 28, 38. *Study:* Harvard Col, AB, 60; Harvard Univ, AM, 61 & PhD, 65; also Am art with Benjamin Rowland. *Hon Degrees:* Univ Vt, DLitt, 90. *Collection Arranged:* Fitz Hugh Lane, De Cordova Mus, Lincoln, Nebr, 66 & Robert Salmon, 67; American Marine Painting, Va Mus Fine Arts, Richmond, 76; 100 American Drawings from the JD Hatch Collection, Nat Gallery Ireland, 76; American Light: The Luminist Movement (auth, catalog), Nat Gallery Art, Washington, DC, 80, An American Perspective: The Ganz Collection, 81, Important Information Inside: The Art of John F Peto (auth, catalog), 83 & The Paintings of Fitz Hugh Lane (coauth, catalog), 88; Winslow Homer in the 1870s (coauth, catalog), Art Mus, Princeton Univ, 90; Thomas Eakins (coauth, catalog), Nat Portrait Gallery, London, 93. *Pos:* Cur Am art & sr cur, Nat Gallery Art, Wash, 77-82, deputy dir, 83-88; trustee, Solomon R Guggenheim Mus, New York City, currently; sr cur, Am Art Nat Gallery Art, 77-83, dept dir, 83-88; vis cur, Metrop Mus, 98-; hon cur, painting Peabody Mus, Salem, Mass. *Teaching:* prof, Am art, Leon E Williams, Dartmouth Col, 65-77; vis lectr art, Yale Univ, 72; vis prof fine arts, Harvard Univ, 76, Univ Md, 79 & Univ Del, 82; Sarofim prof Am art, Princeton Univ, 88-, chmn dept art & archeol, 92-99; asst prof art, Dartmouth Col, 65-68, assoc prof, 68-73, Leon E Williams prof, 73-77, chmn dept art, 68-72, chmn humanities div, 71-72. *Awards:* Guggenheim Found Fel, 73-74; Comt for Preservation of White House (Presidential app); Fleischman Award for Scholarly Excellence in Am Art Hist, Archives Am Art, 98. *Mem:* Col Art Asn; Am Studies Asn. *Res:* American 19th century art and culture. *Publ:* American Art, Pelican-Penguin, 76; Important Information Inside, Harper & Row, 83; American Marine Painting, Abrams, 87; American Views: Essays on American Art, Princeton, 91; The Artist's Mount Desert: American Painters on the Maine Coast, Princeton, 94; Compass & Clock: Defining Moments in Am Cult, 99; Signs of the Artist, Signatures and Self Expression in American Paintings, 2003; auth, West to Wesselmann: American Drawings and Watercolors in the Princeton Univ & Mus, 2004 (catalog) Princeton Univ.; auth, Richard Estes, Rizzoli, 2006. *Mailing Add:* Dept Art & Archaeol Princeton Univ 105 McCormick Hall Princeton NJ 08544-1018

WILMETH, ERNEST, II
COLLAGE ARTIST, POTTER
b Perryton, Tex, Dec 21, 52. *Study:* Northern Ariz Univ, BFA, 76. *Work:* Bowne Corp, Nashville; Brownstein, Hyatt, and farber, Albuquerque, NMex; Delancy Street Found, San Francisco; First State Bank & First Nat Bank, Spearman, Tex; pvt collection of Gov and Mrs Bruce King; UNM Health Sci Ctr. *Exhib:* two person shows, Coupland/Jackson Fine Art, Taos, NMex, 91, Cone 10 Gallery, Albuquerque, 92 & First State Bank, Spearman, Tex, 92; Sixteen Squared, Nina Bean Gallery, 96, Impressions: Works on Paper, 2000, NMex Clay, 2000, Contemp Clay, Dearing Gallery, Taos, 2000; Abstract Art, Anderson Contemp Gallery, Santa Fe, NMex, 2003; Less is More, A Prespective, Harwood Art Ctr, Albuquerque, NMex, 2004; From the Ground Up, Mus of Fine Arts, Las Cruces, NMex, 2004; Paper in Particular, Columbia Col, Columbia, MO, 2004; Fusion Form Function, Union St Gallery, Chicago, Ill, 2004; 8th National Juried Show, Gallery West, Alexandria, Va; 33rd Annual Juried Competition, Masur Mus Art, Monroe, La. *Awards:* Juror's Award, Impressions: Works on Paper, 2000; Best of Show, Arts Int, El Paso, 2004; Award of Achievement, From the Ground Up, LAs Cruces, 2004; VNU Business Publications Award, 37th Annual Visual Arts Exhib, 2005. *Bibliog:* Mary Alice Hines (auth), article, in: Accent W, 7/78; articles in Albuquerque Monthly, 96, Albuquerque Jour, 96, Phoenix Gazette, 91, Ceramics Monthly, 89. *Mem:* Fel Royal Soc Arts; life mem Royal Soc Encouragement Arts Manufactures & Com; Southwest Arts and Crafts Festival (bd mem, 90, 91 & 97); MAGNIFICO The Art Albuquerque (visual comt mem, 92-96, chair & bd mem, 95-97). *Media:* Collage; Clay. *Publ:* Stuart Ashman & Suzanne Deats (auth), Abstract Art, 7/03; Albuquerque J, Art Review, Wesley Pulka, 9/04. *Mailing Add:* PO Box 3104 Albuquerque NM 87190

WILSON, ANNE GAWTHROP
SCULPTOR, EDUCATOR
b Detroit, Mich, Apr 16, 49. *Study:* Cranbrook Acad Art, Bloomfield Hills, Mich, BFA, 72; Calif Col Arts & Crafts, Oakland, MFA, 76. *Work:* M H DeYoung Mem Mus, San Francisco, Calif; State of Ill Ctr, Chicago; The Art Inst Chicago; Smith Hinchman and Grylls Architects, Detroit, Mich; Cranbrook Acad Art Mus, Bloomfield Hills, Mich; Mus Contemp Art, Chicago; Art Inst Chicago; Met Mus Art, NY; plus others. *Exhib:* Tangents, Md Inst, Oakland Mus, Calif & Cleveland Inst Art, Ohio, 87-88; Biennial of Tapestry, Musee Cantonal des Beaux-Arts, Palais de Rumine, Lausanne, Switz, 89; Anne Wilson: Recent Work, Roy Boyd Gallery, Chicago, 91; Domestic Ontogeny: New Textile Forms, Oliver Art Ctr, Calif Col Arts & Crafts, Oakland, 92; The Furs (1985-1991), Halsey Gallery, Sch Arts, Col Charleston, SC, 92; Hair, John Michael Kohler Arts Ctr, Sheboygan, Wis, 92-93; Body into Cult, Madison Art Ctr, Wis, 93-94; Recent Work, Roy Boyd Gallery, Chicago, 94; Mendings, Roy Boyd Gallery, Chicago, Ill, 96; Canberra Sch Art, Australian Nat Univ, Australia, 96; Revolution Gallery, Detroit, Mich, 98; Defining Fiber, Braustein Quay Gallery, San Francisco, Calif, 98; Solo shows incl Anne Wilson: Mendings, Roy Boyd Gallery, Chicago, Ill, 96, Anne Wilson: Voices, Revolution, Detroit, Mich, 98, NY, 98, Told & Retold sound installation, The Mus for Textiles Contemp Gallery, Toronto, Can (catalog), 99, Anne Wilson: Anatomy of Wear, Mus Contemp Art, Chicago, 2000, Revolution, Detroit, 01; Colorado 2000, Boulder Mus Contemp Art, Boulder, Colo, 2000; Blemish, Tobey Gallery, Memphis Col Art, Tenn, 2001; Obsession, Univ Calif San Diego, La Jolla, 2001; Univ Art Gallery, San Diego State Univ, 03; Whitney Mus Am Art, New York City, 02; Union League Club Chicago, 03; and many others. *Collection Arranged:* Metrop Mus Art; Art Inst Chicago; Mus Contemp Art, Chicago. *Teaching:* Prof, Fiber Dept, Art Inst Chicago, 79-. *Awards:* Nat Endowment Arts Visual Artists Fel Grant, 82; Louis Comfort Tiffany Found Award, 89; Chicago Artists Int Prog Grant, artist-in-residence, Australia, 96; Arts Coun Individual Artist's Grant, 01; Ill Arts Coun, Individual Artist's Grant, 83, 84, 87, 93, 96, 99, 01. *Bibliog:* Nathan Budoff (auth), New Art Examiner, 2/92; James Yood (auth), Art Forum, 5/94; Laurie Palmer (auth), New Art Examiner, summer 94; Elearno Heartney (auth), Art in Am, Revolution, 3/99; Jenni Sorkin (auth), Make, London, MCA Chicago, 2000; plus others. *Media:* Fiber. *Dealer:* Roy Boyd Gallery 739 N Wells St Chicago IL. *Mailing Add:* 1302 Davis St Evanston IL 60201

WILSON, BLENDA JACQUELINE
PATRON
b Woodbridge, NJ, Jan 28, 41. *Study:* Cedar Crest Col, AB, 62; Seton Hall Univ, AM, 65; Boston Col, PhD, 79. *Hon Degrees:* Numerous US cols & univs, 87-2003. *Pos:* sr assoc, dean Grad Sch Educ Harvard Univ, Cambridge, Mass, 72-82; vpres, effective sector mgt Ind Sector, Wash, 82-84; exec dir, Colo Comn Higher Educ, Denver, 84-88; chancellor and prof, pub admin & educ Univ Mich, Dearborn, 88-92; pres, Calif State Univ, Northridge, 92-99; Northridge Hosp Med Ctr, 93-99; James Irvine Found, 96-99; mem bd trustees, J Paul Getty Trust, currently; dir, Univ Detroit Jesuit High

Sch; Arab Community Ctr for Econ & Social Serv's; Int Found Educ & Self-Help, Achievement Coun, LA; dir, vchmn, Metrop Affairs Corp; exec bd, Detroit area coun Boy Scouts Am; bd dir, Commonwealth Fund, Henry Ford Hosp-Fairlane Ctr, Henry Ford Health System, Metrop Ctr for High Tech, United Way Southeastern Mich; mem Nat Coalition 100 Black Women, Detroit, Race Relations Coun Metrop Detroit, Women & Found, Greater Detroit Interfaith Round Table Nat Conf of Christians & Jews, Adv. Bd Valley Cult Ctr, Woodland Hills; trustee assoc, Boston Col; trustee emer, bd dir, Found Ctr; trustee emer, Cambridge Col; trustee, Henry Ford Mus & Greenfield Village; Sammy Davis Jr Nat Liver Inst. *Teaching:* Teacher, Woodbridge Township Pub Sch, 62-66. *Mem:* Am Asn of Univ Women; Asn Gov Boards (adv coun of pres, currently); Asn Black Women in Higher Educ; Am Asn State Cols & Univ (comt, on policies & purposes, acad leadership fel selection comt). *Mailing Add:* Nellie Mae Educ Found 1250 Hancock St 205N Quincy MA 02169-4331

WILSON, CARRIE LOIS
LECTURER
b Philadelphia, Pa, Sept 15, 1944. *Study:* Barnard Col, Columbia Univ, BA(art hist), 66; Neighborhood Playhouse School of the Theatre, Sanford Meisner, 68; philosophy of Aesthetic Realism with its founder, Eli Siegel, 69-78, with class chmn, Ellen Reiss, 78-. *Pos:* Co-dir, Terrain Gallery, 72-84, dir, 84-88, Co-Dir 88-; lectr, 84-. *Teaching:* Consult & instr, Aesthetic Realism Found, 72-. *Mem:* The Kindest Art; Int Soc Educ Through Art; Aesthetic Realism Theatre Co; Actor's Equity. *Specialty:* contemporary American & European Art. *Publ:* Auth, Popular Mistakes in Love, 12/20/00; Aesthetic Realism Shows How Art Anwers the Questions of Your Life, Columbia Univ, 2003; Surprising and Abiding Opposites, Jour Print World, Winter/2002; A Brief History of the Terrain Gallery, 2005; Terrain Gallery Celebrates 50th Anniversary, Printmaking Today, 2006. *Mailing Add:* Aesthetic Realism Found 141 Greene St New York NY 10012

WILSON, CHARLES BANKS
PAINTER, PRINTMAKER
b Springdale, Ark, Aug 6, 18. *Study:* Art Inst Chicago, lithography with Francis Chapin, painting with Louis Ritman & Boris Anisfeld & watercolor with Hubert Ropp; Univ Okla, DSc, 76. *Work:* Metrop Mus Art, NY; Corcoran Gallery Art, Washington; Gilcrease Inst Am Hist & Art, Tulsa, Okla; US Capitol Speaker's Gallery; Smithsonian Inst, Washington; mural, Roots of Oklahoma, State Capital Bldg Rotunda; Will Rogers Mem Mus; and numerous others. *Comn:* oil mural, comn by J D Rockefeller, Jr, Jackson Lake Lodge, Wyo, 55; portraits of Thomas Gilcrease, Gilcrease Inst Am Hist & Art, 57, Will Rogers, Okla Press Asn, Oklahoma City, 61, Sen Robert Kerr & Jim Thorpe; rotunda murals, Okla State Legis, 63 & Okla Capitol, 76; US Speaker Carl Albert (portraits), US Capitol & Okla Capitol Bldg, 83; Sequoyah. *Exhib:* Int Watercolor Exhib, Art Inst Chicago, 39; Am Watercolor Exhib, Springfield, Mo, 70; some 200 nat & regional exhibs. *Collection Arranged:* Gilcrease Mus, Tulsa, Okla. *Teaching:* Head art, Northeastern Okla Agr & Mech Col, 47-60; adj prof, Am Univ, Washington, DC; vis lectr, Univ Mass, Amherst; artist in residence, Bryn Mawr Col, Pa. *Awards:* Gov's Art Award, 76, 2002 & 06; Okla Hall of Fame, 77; Nat Cowboy Hall Fame, 79; Hist Hall of Fame, 2002; Lifetime Achievement Award, Ark Arts Coun, 2006. *Bibliog:* An Oklahoma Portrait, Gilcrease Mus, 89; Search for the Purebloods, Univ Okla, Norman, 89; The lithographs Charles Banks Wilson, Univ Okla, Norman, 89; Before death do us part, Wash Post Mag, 81; NBC - Names We Never Knew. *Media:* Lithography, Oil. *Interests:* Am Indians. *Publ:* Illusr, Treasure Island, 48, Company of Adventures, 49, Mustangs, 52 & Geronimo, 58; auth, Search For the Purebloods, 83; The Lithographs of Charles Banks Wilson, Univ Okla Press, 89; Oklahoma Portrait Gilcrease Mus, 89; and many others; Search for the Native American Purebloods, 2001. *Dealer:* Gables Gallery Joplin Mo; Palmer Gallery Hot Springs Ark; Boston Art Gallery, Tulsa Okla. *Mailing Add:* 1611 Mission Blvd Fayetteville AR 72701

WILSON, CLARENCE S, JR
CONSULTANT, PATRON
b Brooklyn, NY, Oct 22, 45. *Study:* Williams Col, Williamstown, Mass, BA, 67; Northwestern Univ Sch Law, Chicago, JD, 74. *Pos:* Trustee, Chicago Symphony Orchestra, 87-96, Art Inst Chicago, 90- & MERIT Music Prog, 91-96; pres, Lawyers for Creative Arts, 87 & 88; outside gen coun, DuSable Mus African Am Hist, Chicago, Ill, 88-95 & 98-; gov, Sch Art Inst Chicago, 94-; vchmn, Jazz Mus Chicago, 94-97; vis comt on visual arts & dept of music, Univ Chicago, 95-. *Teaching:* Adj prof Law, Chicago-Kent Col Law, 81-94; lectr, Columbia Col Chicago, 95-97 & 99-. *Mem:* Ill Arts Coun, 83-89; Arts Midwest, 83-89. *Interests:* Masterworks by Americans of African Descent, Latin America, Chicago. *Publ:* Contribr, Visual Arts & the Law, in the book, Law & the Arts-Art & the Law, 79

WILSON, CYNTHIA LINDSAY
PAINTER
b Washington, DC, May 3, 45. *Study:* Auburn Univ, BFA, 67; Conn Graphic Art Ctr, 97; Penland School, 2002. *Work:* Housatonic Mus Art; Ga Tech Coll, Atlanta; US Tobacco Co, Conn; Fairfield Univ, Conn; Westport Sch Permanent Art Collection; and many others. *Comn:* Kitchen Interiors, 2002. *Exhib:* Pa Watercolor Soc Ann Exhib, Mechanicsburg, 89, 90 & 92; Adirondack's Nat Exhib Am Watercolors, Old Forge, NY, 89; Am Artists Prof League Exhib, Salmagundi Club, NY, 89, 90 & 94; 1990 Am Realism Competition, Parkersburg Art Ctr, WVa, 90; Salmagundi Non Member Exhib, Salmagundi Club, NY, 90, 91, & 93; New Eng Watercolor Soc NAm Open Exhib, Boston, 90, 94 & 95; Springfield Art League Nat Exhib, Springfield Mus Fine Arts, Mass, 92; Nat Acad Design Ann Exhib, NY, 92; Nat Soc Painters in Casein & Acrylic, 91, 93-96, 98-2006; Am Watercolor Soc Ann Exhib, Salmagundi Club, NY, 96; Spartanburg Mus Biennial Juried Art exhib, SC, 2003; South Carolina Watercolor Soc, 2004-2006; New Eng Watercolor Soc, Masters of Watercolor, New Bedford Art Mus, 2006. *Teaching:* Watermedia painting, Ridgefield Guild Artists, Conn, 95-96 & Mooresville Art Guild, Mooresville, NC, 97-98; tchr Process & Possibilities Workshops, NC, 98-2006. *Awards:* Margaret Hamlin Mem Award, Acad Artists, 92; Joseph Cain Award, nat Soc Painters in Casein & Acrylic, 98; Elsie Ject Key award, Nat Soc Painters in Casin & Acrylic, 2001, Liquitex award, 2002; Regional Projects grant, 2001; Nat'l soc Painters in Casein & Acrylic Glenn Bradshaw Award, 2004; Best in Show Award, Wickwire Gallery City of Four Seasons, 2004; M Graham & Co Award, SC Watercolor Soc, 2005; Arches Paper Co Award, SC Watercolor Soc, 2006. *Mem:* New Eng Watercolor Soc; Pa Watercolor Soc; Am Artists Prof League; Nat Soc Painters in Casein & Acrylic; SC Watercolor Soc. *Media:* Acrylic, Watercolor. *Publ:* Auth, Steps to painterly acrylics, Artist's Mag, 3/93; The Best of Watercolor, Flowers in Watercolor & Floral Inspirations, Rockport Publ. *Dealer:* Maralyn Wilson Gallery Birmingham Ala; Wickwire Gallery Hendersonville NC. *Mailing Add:* 521 Orchard Circle Hendersonville NC 28739

WILSON, DOUGLAS FENN
PAINTER, SCULPTOR
b Orinda, Calif, July, 18, 1953. *Study:* Dartmouth Col, Hanover, NH, BA, 75. *Work:* Fine Arts Mus San Francisco, Calif; Worcester Art Mus, Mass; Minneapolis Mus Art, Minn; Tucson Mus Art; Hood Mus Art, Dartmouth Col. *Comn:* Constructed paintings, The Hibernia Bank, 79, Dean Witter Reynolds, 83 & Bay West Development Co, 85, San Francisco, Calif; constructed painting, Deloitte, Haskins & Sells, New York, NY, 86. *Exhib:* 30 Watercolors & Pastels, Worcester Art Mus, Mass, 76; 20 Watercolors & Pastels, Dartmouth Col, Hanover, NH, 76; Recent Acquistions, Fine Arts Mus San Francisco, 77; Fishabach Gallery, NY, 82; Contemp Images, Univ Wis, Oshkosh, 83; John Pence Gallery, San Francisco, 84; Jan Cicero Gallery, Chicago, Ill, 85. *Awards:* Marcus Hieman Achievement Award, Dartmouth Col, 75, Marcus Hieman Proj Grant, 75 & Dartmouth Gen Fel, 79. *Media:* Watercolor, Acrylic. *Mailing Add:* PO Box 848 Glen Ellen CA 95442

WILSON, ELIZABETH (JANE)
PAINTER, EDUCATOR
b Philadelphia, Pa, June 24, 59. *Study:* Corcoran Sch Art, Wash, 78-79; Pa Acad Fine Arts, Philadelphia, 80-84; Univ Pa, Philadelphia, 85. *Work:* Bryn Mawr Col, Pa; E I DuPont de Nemours Co, Wilmington, Del; Robert Half Assoc, Pa; Johnson & Johnson, NJ; Price Waterhouse, Pa. *Comn:* Portrait, Joseph Paradise, Pennsauken, NJ, 83; Portrait, Lee & Rosie Hymerling, Haddonfield, NJ, 90; Portrait, Michael & Betina Bernstein, Bala Cynwd, NJ, 90. *Exhib:* One-woman shows, Pa State Univ, Middletown, 88, Gross McCleaf Gallery, Philadelphia, 90, 92 & FAN Gallery, Philadelphia, 94, 96 & 98; Contemp Philadelphia Artists, Philadelphia Mus Art, 90; Award Winners - Fel Exhib, Mus Am Art Pa Acad Fine Arts, Philadelphia, 94; Women: Object/Subject, Rosemont Col, Pa, 96; 171st Nat Acad Design, NY, 96. *Teaching:* Adj assoc prof, drawing & design, Temple Univ, Philadelphia, 88-95; adj asst prof, drawing, Univ Arts, Philadelphia, Pa, 94-97; adj prof 2D-3D design & drawing, Philadelphia Col Textiles & Sci, 96-. *Awards:* First Prize, Rutgers Univ, 88; Catherine Gibbons Granger, Pa Acad Fine Arts, 93; First Prize, Am Col, 98. *Bibliog:* Karen Heller (auth), Contemporary Philadelphia Artists, Philadelphia Inquirer Mag, 5/90; Victoria Donohoe (auth), Philadelphia Inquirer, 4/96; Edward Suzanski (auth), Philadelphia Inquirer, 5/96. *Mem:* Fel Pa Acad Fine Arts, 82-. *Media:* Oil. *Dealer:* FAN Gallery 311 Cherry St Philadelphia PA 19106; Mulligan Shanoski Gallery 747 Post St San Francisco CA 94109. *Mailing Add:* 340 Oxford Rd Havertown PA 19083

WILSON, EVAN CARTER
PAINTER
b Tuscaloosa, Ala, Oct 31, 1953. *Study:* NC Sch Arts, 70-73; Md Inst, Col Art, with Joseph Sheppard, 72-75; Schuler Sch Fine Art, 75-76. *Work:* Altos de Chavon, La Romana, Dominican Republic; Gulf States Paper Corp, Tuscaloosa, Ala; Greenville Co Mus Art, SC. *Comn:* Oil portraits, Congressman Walter Flowers, Ala, 75, George A LeMaistre (chmn, FDIC), 84 & Vahakn Hovnanian, Red Bank, NJ, 84; interior paintings, Mildred Warner House, Tuscaloosa, Ala, 91; landscape paintings, comn by Jack Warner, Tuscaloosa, Ala, 92; oil portraits, comn by Arthur & Holly MaGill, Greenville, SC. *Exhib:* Mid-Year Show, Butler Mus Art, Youngstown, Ohio, 74 & 90; Impressions of Am: The Warner Collection, Montgomery Mus Fine Art, Ala, 91; Robert M Hicklin Jr Inc Fine Arts of the Am South, 94 & 95; Southern Vt Arts Ctr, Manchester, 94; Alabama Impact: Contemp Artists with Ala Ties, Fine Arts Mus South, Huntsville Mus Art, 95; Gracious Plenty: Still Life Paintings from Southern Collections, 95-96; Morris Mus Art, Augusta, Ga; Hunter Mus Art, Chattanooga, Tenn; Telfair Acad, Savannah, Ga, 96; Parson's Sch Design, NY, 97; Solo shows incl JR Leigh Gallery, Tuscaloosa, Ala, 80-87, 92-98, 2000, Il Punto Gallery, Florence, Italy, 79, Huntsville Mus Art, Huntsville, Ala, 2001, plus others; John Pence Gallery, San Francisco, Calif, 1988-2000; plus others. *Awards:* Gold Medal, Knickerbocker Artists, 86; Macowin Tuttle Award, Ann Mem Exhib, Salmagundi Club, 87; Ala Arts Award, Soc Fine Arts/Univ Ala, 99; plus others. *Bibliog:* Ben Windham (auth), Ransom and Evan Wilson, Arts Review, Univ Ala, summer 84; Sonny Tiedeman (auth), Festival Brushstrokes, Horizon Mag, 1-2/86; Martha R Severens (auth), Greenville County Museum of Art: The Southern Collection, 95; Ben Windham (auth) Local man's painting takes viewers "down to the river", The Tuscaloose News, 2/13/2000; plus others. *Mem:* Salmagundi Club; Southern Vt Art Ctr, Manchester; Portraits, Inc, NY. *Media:* Oil, Watercolor. *Publ:* Auth, Sizing up a portrait, 86 & The Italian lesson, 86, Artists Mag; Create a World Inside a Painting, Am Artist, 11/90. *Dealer:* Robert M Hicklin Jr Inc Spartanburg SC; Robert Wilson Galleries Nantucket MA. *Mailing Add:* 601 South St PO Box 159 Hoosick NY 12089

WILSON, FRED
SCULPTOR
b Bronx, NY, 54. *Study:* State Univ NY, Col Purchase, BFA, 76. *Work:* New Sch Social Res, NY; Baltimore Mus Art; Denver Art Mus; Kresge Art Mus; Seattle Art Mus. *Exhib:* Solo exhibitions at Seattle Art Mus, 93, Beaver Col Art Gallery, 93 & 96, Capp Street Proj, 93, Mus Contemp Art, Chicago, 94, South Eastern Ctr Contemp Art, Winston-Salem, NC, 94 & Metro Pictures, 95; group shows include SITEseeing: Travel and Tourism in Contemp Art, Whitney Mus Am Art, 91; 1993 Biennial Exhib, Whitney Mus Am Art, 93; Readymade Identities, Mus Mod Art, NY, 93; Crash: Nostalgia for the Absence of Cyberspace (with catalog), Thread Waxing Space, NY, 94; Notational Photographs, Metro Pictures, 94; Transformers: The Art of Multiphrenia, Bard Ctr Curatorial Studies, Bard Col, NY, 94; Heroes & Heroines: From Myth to Reality, NJ Ctr Visual Arts, 95; Cult Economies: Histories from the Alternative, Drawing Ctr, NY, 96; Is this Now Just Beginning, Fosdick-Nelson Gallery, Alfred Univ, NY, 2002; Drawings, Metro Pictures, NY, 2003; Fred Wilson: Objects and Installations 1979-2000, Univ of Md, Baltimore Co, 2002, Tang Mus, Skidmore Coll, NY, Berkeley Art Mus, Blaffer Gallery, Univ of Houston, Addison Gallery of Am Art, Andover, Santa Monica Mus of Art, PaceWildenstein Gallery, New York City, 2004, Sidney R Yates Gallery, 2004. *Pos:* Bd dir, Artists Space, 88- & Nat Asn Artists Orgns, 88-; panelist, Nat Endowment Arts, Inter-Art Prog, 89-; cur, Bronx Coun Arts, 90; lectr, Hirshhorn Mus, 91, Whitney Mus, 91, Bard Col, 92 & New Mus, NY, 92. *Awards:* Nat Endowment Arts, Inter-Arts/Artist Proj, 90; Riverside South Pub Art Comn, Pub Park Proj, NY, 92; Fel Sculpture, Nat Endowment Arts, 94; The Aldrich Mus of Contemp Art, Ridgefield, Conn, 2002; Am Rep at the US Pavilion, 50th Venice Biennale, Ital Col art Assoc, Distinguished Body of Work Award, 2003. *Bibliog:* M Franklin Sirmans (auth), rev, Artnews, 3/96; Jennifer Gonzalez (auth), rev, Frieze, 5/96; David Colman (auth), Pretty on the outside, George, 6-7/96; and others. *Mem:* Artists Space; Nat Asn Artists Orgns; Nat Endowment Arts, Inter-Arts Progs, 90; and others. *Mailing Add:* c/o PaceWildenstein Gallery 32 E 57th St 2nd Fl New York NY 10022

WILSON, HELENA CHAPELLIN WILSON
PHOTOGRAPHER
b Caracas, Venezuela. *Study:* Inst de Dibujo Tecnico y Arquitectura; Columbia Col, Chicago, BA, 76. *Work:* New Orleans Mus Art, La; Ill State Mus, Springfield; Art Inst Chicago, Mus Contemp Photog, Chicago, Ill; Galeria de Arte Nacional & Museo de Bellas Arts, Caracas, Venezuela. *Exhib:* Hecho en Venezuela, Mus Arte Contemp, Caracas, 78; solo exhibs, Marianne Deson Gallery, Chicago, Ill, 81, Hewlitt Gallery, Carnegie-Melon Univ, 83, Galeria de Art Nacional, Caracas, Venezuela, 90; Illinois Photographers 1985, Ill State Mus, Springfield, 85; Clarence John Laughlin Collection, New Orleans Mus Art, La, 89; Under the Spell of Dreams, Rachel Adler Gallery, NY, 93-94; Aldo Castillo Gallery, Chicago, 99 & 2001. *Pos:* Artist and designer, 60-; mem, comt on photog, Art Inst Chicago, currently; trustee, Columbia Col, Chicago, currently; mem, comt on acquisitions, Mus Contemp Photog, currently. *Awards:* Photography Award, Univ Iowa, 75. *Bibliog:* Hans Neumann (auth), Fotografias, El Nacional, Caracas, Venezuela, 7/29/90; rev, Art in Am, 7/94. *Publ:* Contribr, Women Photograph Men, William Morrow, 77; auth, Basic gum bichromate printing, Darkroom Techniques, 6/81; Out of the Darkroom (didactic mats), Art Inst Chicago, 95. *Dealer:* Rachel Adler Fine Art 1200 Broadway New York NY 10001; Castillo Gallery 233 Witturon Chicago IL 60610

WILSON, JANE
PAINTER
b Seymour, Iowa, Apr 29, 24. *Study:* Univ Iowa, BA & MA. *Work:* Mus Mod Art, Metrop Mus Art, Whitney Mus Am Art, NY; Wadsworth Atheneum, Hartford, Conn; Hirshhorn Mus, Washington, DC; and many others. *Exhib:* Whitney Mus Am Art, NY, 61, 63 & 68; Am Women of the 20th Century, Lakeview Ctr Arts & Sci, 72; Painterly Realism in Am, A J Wood Gallery, Philadelphia, Pa, 79; The Fifties: Hirshhorn Mus, 80; plus many others. *Teaching:* Instr art hist, Pratt Inst, 67-69; instr painting and drawing, Fine Arts Division, Parsons Sch Design, 73-; prof, Dept Painting & Sculpture, Sch Arts, Columbia Univ, 75-88, acting chmn, 86-88. *Awards:* Tiffany Grant, 67; Ranger Fund Purchase Prize, 78; Award in Art, Acad Arts & Letters, 81. *Mem:* Nat Acad (assoc, 74, acad, 77); Skowhegan Sch, Bd Gov Coun

WILSON, JEAN S
MUSEUM DIRECTOR, HISTORIAN
b Lakeland, Fla. *Study:* Metrop State Col, Denver, Colo, BA, 79; Univ Denver, Colo, MA, 82. *Collection Arranged:* Personal Landscapes; Art Quilts and Wearable Art, FACET, 90; Third Wyoming Biennial, 89; Paper Innovations, Am Mus Asn, 87. *Pos:* Educ dept, Denver Art Mus, 81-82; asst cur, Colo Gallery Arts, 83-85, dir/cur, 85-92; exhib & educ dir, Foothills Art Ctr, Golden, Colo, 92-. *Mem:* Colo Art Educ Asn (currently, state bd); Am Asn Mus; Small Mus Asn. *Res:* Renaissance and early modern art

WILSON, JOHN
SCULPTOR, PRINTMAKER
b Boston, Mass, Apr 14, 22. *Study:* Sch Mus Fine Arts, Boston, dipl; Tufts Univ, BS(educ); Fernand Leger's Sch, Paris; Inst Politecnico, Esmeralda Sch Art & Escuela Artes del Libro, Mexico City. *Hon Degrees:* Art Inst Boston, Hon DFA. *Work:* Mus Fine Arts, Boston; Smith Col Mus Art, Northampton, Mass; Mus Mod Art, NY; Atlanta Univ, Ga; Dept Fine Arts, Govt France. *Comn:* Monument to Dr Martin Luther King, Jr (bronze), Buffalo Arts Comn, NY, 83; Memorial to Dr Martin Luther King, Jr (bronze statue), US Capitol, Washington, 86; Father & Child (bronze monument), Roxbury Community Col, Boston; External Presence (bronze monument), Mus Nat Ctr, Afro-Am Artists, Boston, Mass. *Exhib:* 47th Ann Am Acad Purchase Exhib, Am Acad Arts & Letts, NY; Dialogue: John Wilson/Joseph Norman, Mus Fine Arts, Boston, Mass; Master Prints from the Mus Collections, Mus Mod Art, NY, 49; Young Am Painters, Metrop Mus Art, NY, 50; Mus Int Biennial Color Lithography, Cincinnati, Ohio, 53; Afro-Am Artists, Mus Fine Arts, NY & Boston, 70; Highlights from Univ Collection, High Mus Art, Atlanta, Ga, 73. *Teaching:* Illusr art, New York Bd Educ, 59-64; prof art, Boston Univ, 64-86, prof emer, 86-. *Awards:* John Hay Whitney Fel for study in Mex, 50; Best Cover Design, Int Fedn Periodicals Press, Paris, 71; Sculpture Fel, Mass Arts & Humanities FoundInc, 76. *Bibliog:* Edward Strickland (auth), John Wilson, Art New Eng, 2/88 & 8/98; Dialogue: Joseph Norman (co-auth), Mus Nat Ctr, Afro-Am Artists, Boston Mass, 95; Lois Tarlow (auth), Profile: John Wilson, Art New Eng, 8-9/98. *Mem:* Nat Acad (acad, 03-). *Media:* Mixed. *Publ:* Co-illusr, New Worlds of Reading, Harcourt, 59, American Negro Art, Graphic Soc, NY, 60, Who Look at Me, Crowell, NY, 69, 17 Black Artists, Dodd Mead Co, New York, 71 & Land of Progress, Ginn, 75; co-illusr, Martin Luther King Jr Sculpture, Nat Endowment Arts Rev, Vol 3, No 3, spring 86; Public Art & the Public Image, Art New Eng, 7-8/89. *Mailing Add:* 44 Harris St Brookline MA 02146

WILSON, JOHN DAVID
ADMINISTRATOR, ART DEALER
b Flint, Mich, Aug 30, 34. *Study:* Mich State Univ, BA, 60; Univ Notre Dame, MA, 67. *Pos:* Dir, Lakeside Studio, formerly; pres, Chicago Int Art Exposition, currently; pres, Lakeside Group, Shanghai Int Art and Antique Exposition; Consultant, Art Caucasus, 2004. *Awards:* Chevalier De L'Ordre Des Arts et Des Lettres, City Milan, Milan CofC; Moscow Arts Award. *Bibliog:* David & Cecile Shapiro (coauth), Lakeside Studio: conserving the printmaking tradition, Art News, 3/77; Charlotte Moser (auth), John Wilson brings art world to Chicago, Chicago Sun-Times, 9-11/83; 20 people who changed Chicago, Chicago Mag (20th anniversary issue). *Mem:* Artist Union Republic of Ga (bd dir); The Cliff Dwellers Club; The Tavern Club. *Specialty:* Original graphics, old masters, modern and contemporary; ceramics. *Mailing Add:* Lakeside Group Red Arrow Hwy PO Box 299 Lakeside MI 49116

WILSON, JUNE
PAINTER, EDUCATOR
b Somerville, NJ, July 12, 46. *Study:* Ithaca Col, NY, 64-65; Monmouth Col, West Long Branch, NJ, BA(hons), 68; Pratt Inst, Brooklyn, NY, MFA, 72. *Work:* The Newark Mus, NJ; Aldrich Mus Contemp Art, Ridgefield, Conn; Franklin Furnace, & Jewish Mus, NY; Art & Cult Ctr, Hollywood, Fla; Michael Grainger Collection, Tyler Mus, Tex; Jewish Mus, NY; Tyler Mus, Tex; Prudential Ins Co, Newark, NJ; Johnson & Johnson, New Brunswick, NJ. *Comn:* Lobby painting, Sheraton Meadowlands Hotel, NJ, 86; Weather Vanes, NJ Transit, Exchange Place Station, Jersey City, NJ, 99. *Exhib:* One-woman shows, Newark Mus, NJ, 90, Johnson & Johnson Hq, New Brunswick, NJ, 93, Seton Hall Univ Sch Law, Newark, 94, Mercer Co Col, W Windsor, NJ, 95, Georgian Court Col, Lakewood, NJ, 97 & Aljira at the Academy, Montclair, NJ, 2000; Drawing into the 90's (catalog & tour), Laguna Gloria Mus, Austin, Tex, 93; Made to Order, The Alternative Mus, NY, 95; Colors, Contrasts, Cultures, Discovery Mus, Conn, 97; Paintings with an Edge, Hunterdon Mus, Clinton, NJ, 98; New Am Talent 13, Ctr Space, Austin, Tex, 98; Simon Gallery, Morristown, NJ, 2000; Tyler Mus, Tex, 2002. *Collection Arranged:* The Punch Line: Humor in Art, Tweed Arts Group, Plainfield, NJ, 83; Urban Spirit, City Without Walls (co-cur with G Graupe-Pillard), Newark, NJ, 85. *Teaching:* Adj asst prof, painting & drawing, Ocean Co Col, Toms River, NJ, 76-; spec projs, NJ Sch Arts, Trenton, 98-2002. *Awards:* NJ State Coun Arts Fel, 81 & 85; Fel, Rutger's Ctr for Innovative Print & Paper, 2003; Fel (painting), NJ State Coun Arts, 2004. *Bibliog:* Robert Mahoney (auth), New York in Review, Arts Mag, 3/91; Judith Friedman (auth), Suburban Landscape, Views of NJ Artists, Visual Sociolgy, Univ SFla, Tampa, Fall, 93; Barry Schwabsky (auth), Borrowing from Nature, New York Times, 1/18/98. *Media:* Oil and Acrylic on Canvas, Wood, & Paper. *Dealer:* Simon Gallery, Morristown, NJ. *Mailing Add:* 47 Brandywine Way Middletown NJ 07748

WILSON, KAREN LEE
MUSEUM DIRECTOR
b Somerville, NJ, Apr 2, 49. *Study:* Harvard Univ, AB, 71; Inst Fine Arts, NY Univ, MA, 73, PhD, 85. *Exhib:* Vanished Kingdoms of the Nile: The Rediscovery of Ancient Nubia, 92; Faces of Ancient Egypt, Smart Mus Art, 96-97; In the Presence of the Gods: Art from Ancient Sumer, Smart Mus Art, 97-98; Mary and Joseph Grimshaw Egyptian Gallery, 99; Persian Gallery, 2000; Treasures from the Royal Tombs of Ur, 2000-01; Edgar & Deborah Janotta Mus Gallery, 2003. *Pos:* Cur/dir, Oriental Inst Mus, 88-96, dir, 96-2003; adminr cataloguer, 82-83, Jewish Mus, NY & coordr curatorial affairs, 84-86; res assoc, Oriental Inst, 1988-; proj coordr, Kish Field Mus, 2004-. *Teaching:* Instr various courses, 90-2001. *Mem:* AAM; Am Oriental Soc; Archeol Inst Am; Col Art Asn. *Publ:* Auth & ed, Mendes, ARCE, 82; Preliminary Report Excavations at Tell Genj, Sumer, 85; auth, Definition & Relative Chronology of the Jamdat Nasr Period, NY Univ, 85; Nippur: The Definition of a Mesopotamian Jamdat Nasr Assemblage, AVO, 86; Oriental Institute Discoveries at Khorsabad, 95; and others. *Mailing Add:* Oriental Institute Museum 1155 E 58th St Chicago IL 60637

WILSON, KAY E
CURATOR, DIRECTOR
b Rockford, Ill. *Study:* Rockford Col, BA, 72; Art Inst Chicago, Collection Mgt, Cert, 88. *Exhib:* Art in Exile; Contemp Iraqui Art; Contemp Estonian Art. *Collection Arranged:* Jiri Anderle: The Grant Lawrence Collection, Grinnell Col Print & Drawing Study Room, 97. *Pos:* Dir, Print & Drawing Study Room, Grinnell Col, 86-, Cur Art Collection. *Media:* Paper. *Publ:* Coauth, Jan Krejci: The Werksman Collection, Grinnell Col, 87. *Mailing Add:* Grinnell College Print and Drawing Study Room Grinnell IA 50112-0811

WILSON, MARC FRASER
MUSEUM DIRECTOR
b Akron, Ohio, Sept 12, 41. *Study:* Yale Col, BA, 63; Case Western Univ, Cleveland Mus Art, 63-64; Yale Univ, MA, 67; Fel, Ford Found Mus Training Prog, Nelson Gallery-Atkins Mus, Kansas City, 67-69; Study Grant, Ford Found, Japan, Taiwan, Hong Kong, 69-71; Univ Kans, 68. *Pos:* Dept asst prints & drawings, Cleveland Mus Art, 64; translr & project consult, Nat Palace Mus, Taipei, Taiwan, 68-71; assoc cur Chinese Art, dept Oriental art, Nelson Gallery-Atkins Mus, 71-73, cur Oriental art, 73-, interim dir, 82-, dir, 82-; mus dir, Nelson-Atkins Mus Art, Kansas City, Mo, 82-; mem ad hoc committee, Munic Art Comn Urban Sculpture, 84-; mem, China Inst Am Adv Comt, 85-; mem, Asia Soc Galleries Adv Comt, 85-; mem, K C Planning Comt Sister City, Xian, China 86-; chmn works of art comt, Asn Art Mus Dirs, 86-88, arts & artifacts indemnity advisory panel, Fedn Coun Arts & Humanities 86-89 & Am subcomt Mus Exchanges of CULCON, 86-88; Am panel, Joint Comt Japan-US Cult & Educ Coop, 86-88; trustee & treas, Asn Art Mus dirs, 88-89; indemnity panel, Washington, 93-; cur, Oriental Art Nelson-Atkins Mus Art, 1982-99, dir/Chief Exec Officer, 1999-. *Teaching:* Grad teaching asst, Dept Hist Art, Yale Univ, 65-66. *Mem:* Assoc Art Mus Dir (treas, trustee 1988-90, chmn works of art comt 1986-90), Missouri China Coun, Fed Coun Arts and Humanities (chmn arts and artifacts indemnity adv panel 1986-89, 1995-98). *Publ:* Auth, The Chinese painter and his vision, Apollo, No 97, 3/73; coauth, Friends of Wen Cheng-ming, 74; auth, Potter's choice, Am Craft, Vol 40, No 4, 8-9/80; coauth, Eight Dynasties of Chinese Painting, Ind Univ Press, 80; auth, Indentification of the subject of an important scroll painting by Ma Yuan, Museum, 11/82. *Mailing Add:* Nelson-Atkins Mus Art 4525 Oak St Kansas City MO 64111

WILSON, MELISSA ANNE
SCULPTOR
b New Rochelle, NY, July 9, 68. *Study:* Silvermine Sch Art, 86-89; Wooster Art Ctr, 87-90. *Hon Degrees:* Stanley Bleifield sculpture degree, 89-2000. *Work:* Lever House, New York, NY; New Britain Mus, Conn; Hillsberg Mus Collection, Indian Wells, Calif; Lever House Collection; Bleifield Collection. *Comn:* Georgetown Saloon Gallery, 98. *Exhib:* Waveny Barn Mus, New Canaan, Conn, 87, 88 & 89; All New Eng Show, 89 & 90; Pietrasanta, Italy, 89 & 90; Int Sculpture Show, Roxensteins, Helsingborg, Sweden, 90; Chicago Int Art Show, 90; Stanley Bleifield Asn of Fairfield, Lever House, NY, 90; Bliefield Sculpture Asn, 92; group show, Waveny Park Carriage Barn Mus, New Canaan, Conn, 92. *Teaching:* various galleries. *Awards:* First in Show, Sandi Oliver Fine Art, Weston, Conn; Best Sculpture, Casa D'Oliver, Conn, 91 & 98 & 2004. *Mem:* Int Sculpture Asn; Bleifield Sculpture Asn. *Media:* Bronze, Clay & Oil Painting. *Interests:* Running, Writing. *Publ:* Bleifield Sculpture Group Catalog Raissone, Bleifield, 92; Casa D' Oliver, CT, 2004. *Dealer:* Sandi Oliver Box 1203 Weston CT 06883. *Mailing Add:* c/o Sandi Oliver Fine Art PO Box 1203 Weston CT 06883

WILSON, MILLIE
CONCEPTUAL ARTIST
b Hot Springs, Ark, Nov 26, 48. *Study:* Yale Summer Sch Music & Art; Univ Tex, Austin, BFA, 71; Univ Houston, MFA, 83. *Work:* San Francisco Mus Mod Art; Newport Harbor Art Mus. *Comn:* Thresholds, Servales Found, Oporto, Port, 95. *Exhib:* Solo exhibs, Fauve Semblant: Peter (A Young Eng Girl), San Francisco Camerawork, 90, Sweet Thursday, Meyers, Bloom Gallery, Santa Monica, 91, Living in Someone Else's Paradise, New Langton Arts, San Francisco, 92, A Disturbing Emotional Coloring, White Columns, NY, 92, Wolf in the Garden, Ruth Bloom Gallery, Santa Monica, Calif, 93, Not a Serial Killer, Jose Freire Fine Art, NY, 94 & Monster Girls, Ruth Bloom Gallery, 95; Something Borrowed, Mus Fine Arts, Santa Fe, NMex, 95; Addressing the Century: 100 Yrs Art & Fashion, Hayward Gallery, London, 98; Cola, Hammer Mus, 2000; Laguna Art Mus, 2004; Univ of Va Mus, 2005; Threshold/Recent Am Sculpture, Serrabes Found, Oporto, Port. *Pos:* Reg fac, program art, Calif Inst Arts, 90-95. *Teaching:* Fel drawing, Univ Houston, 81-83; asst prof painting, Univ Ill, Urbana-Champaign, 83-85; fac, Calif Inst Arts, 85-. *Awards:* Nat Endowment Arts Fel, 93; Pollock-Drasner Found Grant, 96; Individual Artist Fel, Los Angeles Cult Affairs, 98. *Bibliog:* Tania Guha (auth), Disrupted borders, Time Out, London, 7/20/94-7/27/94; David A Greene (auth), A feast for the eyes, Los Angeles Reader, 7/29/94; PC Smith (auth), Millie Wilson at Jose Freire, Art in Am, 9/94. *Mem:* Col Art Asn. *Media:* New Genres, Conceptual. *Publ:* Facing the Finish (exhibition catalog), San Francisco Mus Mod Art, 91-92; Errors of Nature, 92; Longing & Belonging, Site Santa Fe, 95. *Mailing Add:* Art Dept Calif Inst Arts 24700 McBean Valencia CA 91355

WILSON, PAMELA
PAINTER
b Salt Lake City, Utah, Sept, 62. *Study:* Brigham Young Univ, FA, 80; San Diego State Univ, BA(art), 90; Univ Calif, Santa Barbara, MFA(painting, Abrams Grant Proj & Univ Calif Regents Fel), 92. *Work:* Nat Mus Women Arts, Washington, DC; Ft Lauderdale Mus Art; Gallery 1434, Univ Calif, Santa Barbara; S Bay Mus, Long Beach, Calif; Laguna Mus Art, Calif. *Exhib:* Inquiry into Nothing, Gallery 1434, Univ Calif, 91; Artist Choose Artists, Contemp Art Forum, Santa Barbara, 92; Addiction to a Nuisance, Norton Gallery, Santa Barbara, 94; Imagase without Words, Ft Lauderdale Mus Art, 98; Artists on the Road, Nat Mus Women Arts, Washington, DC, 98. *Bibliog:* Douglas Deaver (auth), Pamela Wilson, Paintings & Etchings, Stuart Katz, 94; Patty Au (auth), Figurative paintings, Art Week, 94; Gabriel Weisberg (auth), The Realist Narritive, Poloma Publs, 96. *Media:* Oil on Canvas

WILSON, RICHARD BRIAN
PAINTER
b Wichita, Kans, June 12, 44. *Study:* Calif State Univ, San Jose, BA & MA. *Work:* Downey Art Mus, Calif; IBM Corp, San Jose, Calif; Mobil Oil Co, San Francisco; Am Tel & Tel Co, Chicago; Fort Steilicom Col; and others. *Exhib:* Looking West 1970, Joslin Art Mus, 70; Drawings 70: First Ann Drawing Show, St John's Univ, NY, 70; Boxtop Painting Exhib, Ill State Univ, 71; Ariz Nat Painting Competition, Scottsdale Ctr Arts, 77 & 78; Int Art Fairs, Basil & Cologne, 78; The Plannar Dimension, Civic Arts Gallery, Walnut Creek, Calif, 83; Ten California Colorists, Pomona Col, Univ NMex & Palm Desert Mus, 85-86; and others. *Pos:* Gallery dir, Shasta Col & Art Gallery, Redding, Calif, 70-; bd mem, Redding Mus, 77-79. *Teaching:* Instr art, Shasta Col, Redding, Calif, 68-. *Awards:* Third Prize (painting), 1st Ann Grand Galleria Nat Art Show, 72; Purchase Prize, 15th Printing Ann, Downey Mus, 72; First Prize (painting), 5th Ann North Valley Art Show, Redding, 73. *Bibliog:* Alfred Frankenstein (auth), Serene and mystic art works, San Francisco Chronicle, 11/17/72; William Wilson (auth), Art walk, Los Angeles Times, 3/5/76; Thomas Albright (auth), Art in the San Francisco Bay Area 1945-1980, Univ Calif Press, 85; and others. *Media:* Acrylic. *Dealer:* Triangle Gallery 165 Post St San Francisco CA 94108; Frederick and Spratt Galleries 920 S 1st St San Jose CA 95113

WILSON, ROBERT
GRAPHIC ARTIST, DESIGNER
b Waco, Tex, 1941. *Study:* Univ Tex, Austin, 59-62; Painting with George McNeil, Paris, France, 62; Pratt Inst, New York, BFA, 65; apprenticed to Paolo Soleri, Phoenix, Ariz, 66; Calif Col Arts & Crafts, Hon Dr, 94. *Work:* Mus Mod Art, NY; Mus Mod Art, Paris, France; Australian Nat Gallery, Canberra; Stedelijk Mus, Amsterdam; Menil Collection, Houston; and others. *Exhib:* Whitney Biennial, Whitney Mus Am Art, 80 & 97; An Int Survey of Contemp Painting & Sculpture Mus Mod Art, NY, 84; New Works on Paper 3, Mus Mod Art, NY, 85; Special Relationships in Video, Mus Mod Art, NY, 85; The New Figure, Birmingham Mus Art, 85; High Style, Whitney Mus Am Art, 85; Big Drawings, Mus Mod Art, NY, 85; one-person exhibs, Inst Contemp Art, Boston, 85, Paula Cooper Gallery, NY, 93, 94 & 96, Galerie Biedermann, Munchen, Ger, 94, Galerie Lehmann, Lausanne, Switz, 96, Modernism, San Francisco, 96, Fotouhi Cramer Gallery, East Hampton, NY, 96, Robert Wilson, Mus Villa Stuck, Munich, 97 & Robert Wilson, Installation Galeria Luis Serpe, Lisboarte Contemporanea, Lisbon, Portugal, 98; Passge de L'image Traveling Exhib, Mus Nat d'Art Mod, Paris, 91; Die Muse?, Galerie Thaddaeus Ropac, 95; Alice, Brooklyn Acad Music, 95; Breaking the Frame, The Drawing Legion, Cedar Rapids, Iowa, 95; Prints: To Benefit the Found for Contemp Performance Arts, Brooke Alexander, NY, 95; Link, Gerald Peters Gallery, Dallas, Tex, 96; Graphit Auf Papier, Galerie Thomas Von Lintel, Munich, 97; Tableaux Contemp Art Mus, Houston, Tex, 97; and many others. *Pos:* Artistic dir, Byrd Hoffman Found, 70-. *Awards:* Tadeusz Kantor Prize, Crakow, Poland, 97; First Prize, Venice Biennale 45th Int Art Exhib, 93; Harvard Excellence in Design, Harvard Design Sch, Cambridge, Mass, 98. *Bibliog:* Howard Brookner (dir), A Minute with Bob Wilson (film), BBC, London, 85; Bice Curiger (ed), Collaboration Robert Wilson Parkett, 88; Mel Gussow (auth), Conjuring works of art that live mostly in memory, NY Times, 10/22/98. *Mem:* Hon mem Am Repertory Theater; PEN Am Ctr; Dramatist Guild; trustee Nat Int Music Theater; Soc des Auteurs et Compositeurs Dramatiques. *Publ:* Contribr, Swan Song (play), Kammerspiele Theater, Munich, 90; Konig Lear (play), Schauspiel, Frankfurt, 90; The Black Rider: The Casting of the Magic Bullets (play), Theatre Musical de Paris, Le Chatelet; When We Dead Awake (play), Am Repertory Theatre, Boston, 91. *Mailing Add:* c/o Paula Cooper Gallery 534 W 21st St New York NY 10011

WILSON, ROBERT ALAN
GALLERY DIRECTOR, MURALIST
b Windsor, Ont, Feb 6, 49; US citizen. *Study:* Col San Mateo, AA, 69; Calif State Univ, Chico, BA, 72, MA, 76. *Work:* Erie Pub Mus, Pa. *Comn:* Celebration (mural), J F Kennedy Community Ctr, Erie, Pa, 80; Chapmantown (mural), Chico Area Recreation & Park Dist, Calif, 81; Recreation (mural), Calif Arts Coun, Chico, 82; mural, Murdock Elementary Sch, Williams, Calif, 82. *Exhib:* Downtown Dog Show, Fine Arts Show, Fine Arts Mus, San Francisco, Calif, 78; Washington & Jefferson Col Nat Painting Show, Washington, Pa, 79; California Works, Calif State Fair, Sacramento, 82; Western Figurative Realism, Cypress Col Gallery, Calif, 83; Calgene Fine Arts Competition, Natsoulos/Novelozo Gallery, Davis, Calif, 88. *Pos:* Coordr, Multicultural Arts Coun, 76-; exec dir, Chico Arts Ctr, Calif, 83-87; art cur, Redding Mus & Art Ctr, Calif, 87-. *Teaching:* Instr art hist & painting, Am Col, Leysin, Switz, 76-77; instr art hist, Butte Community Col, 86-87; instr art hist (ethnic), Shasta Community Col, 90-. *Dealer:* Candy Store Gallery 605 Sutter St Folsom CA 95630

WILSON, ROBERT WARNE
PATRON
b Detroit, Mich, Nov 3, 26. *Study:* Amherst Col, Mass, BA(econ)(magna cum laude), 46; Univ Mich, MA(econ), 47; Mich Law Sch, postgrad, 49; Phi Beta Kappa. *Pos:* Trainee, First Boston Corp, New York City, 49-50, 52-53; securities analyst, Nat Bank Detroit, 53-58; securities analyst to vpres, Gen Am Inv, New York City, 58-62; securities analyst, AG Becker & Co, 62-68; investor, 68; bd dir, Brooklyn Mus, 74-88, Brooklyn Botanic Garden, 74-88, New York City Opera, 77-98, chmn 81-93; Whitney Mus of Am Art, 78-; adv bd Metrop Opera, 79-81; Manhattan Inst, 86-2002; trustee Environ Defense, 86-; vpres, World Monuments Fund, 90-; Lyric Opera of Chicago Nat Bd, 95-2001; vchmn, Deafness Res Found, 98-2001; financier, NY Pub Libr. *Interests:* Opera, museums, theater, movies & sightseeing. *Mailing Add:* 520 83rd St Brooklyn NY 11209-4520

WILSON, STEVE
MUSEUM DIRECTOR
Study: Univ Southern Calif, BFA; Nat Theatre Conservatory, Denver, MFA in acting. *Pos:* artist-in-residence Cherry Creek and Denver Pub Sch Dists; Denver Sch Arts; exec artistic dir, acting dir, Mizel Ctr for Arts and Cult; dir, Wolf Theatre Acad. *Teaching:* Teacher, performing arts chrmn St. Mary's Acad, Colo; fac mem, Wolf Theatre Acad and Stage Eleven. *Mailing Add:* Mizel Ctr Arts and Cult 350 S Dahlia St Denver CO 80246

WILSON, TOM
CARTOONIST
b Grant Town, WVa, Aug 1, 31. *Study:* Art Inst Pittsburgh, dipl. *Pos:* Designer, Am Greetings Corp, Cleveland, 55-56, vpres creative div, 57-78, vpres creative develop, 78-81, vpres, ideas dept, formerly; pres, Those Characters from Cleveland, formerly; cartoonist, Ziggy, currently; pres, Ziggy & Friends Inc, 87-. *Teaching:* Mem fac, Cooper Sch Art, formerly. *Awards:* Butler Mus Nat Painting Competition Purchase Award. *Mailing Add:* c/o Universal Press Syndicate 4520 Main St Kansas City MO 64111

WILSON, TOM MUIR
DESIGNER
b Bellaire, Ohio, Dec 6, 30. *Study:* WVa Inst Technol; Cranbrook Acad Art, BFA; Rochester Inst Technol, MFA. *Exhib:* One-man shows, Rochester, NY & Wheeling, WVa, 57, 59 & 61; Boston Art Festival, 61; Photog Exhib, George Eastman House, Rochester, 63; Western NY Ann, Buffalo, 63 & 64; Art of Two Cities, Minneapolis, 65; and others. *Pos:* Designer exhib galleries, George Eastman House Mus Photog, 61-62; freelance photogr & graphic designer, New York, Rochester & Minneapolis, 61-. *Teaching:* Prof art & instr photog & graphic design, Minneapolis Sch Art, formerly; instr photog, Rochester Inst Technol, assoc prof photog arts, 77-; instr sculpture & design, Nazareth Col, Rochester. *Awards:* Award for Sculpture, Art Inst Am Inst Architects, 56; Prize, Philadelphia Print Club, 61. *Media:* Graphic. *Mailing Add:* 6776 Warboys Rd Byron NY 14422

WILSON, WALLACE
PHOTOGRAPHER, EDUCATOR
b Dallas, Tex, June 10, 47. *Study:* Univ Tex, Austin, BA, 70; pvt study with Ralph Eugene Meatyeard, Lexington, Ky, 71-72; Art Inst Chicago, MFA, 75. *Work:* Mus Mod Art, NY; Art Inst Chicago; Baltimore Mus Art, Md; Bibliotheque Nationale, Paris; Brooklyn Mus, NY. *Exhib:* One-man shows, Baltimore Mus Art, 76, OK Harris, NY, 77 & 87, Photogalerie Lange-Irschl, Munich, WGer, 79, Marcuse Pfeifer Gallery, NY, 87 & 89, The Tartt Gallery, Washington, DC, 87, 90 & 92, The Photographers Gallery, London, 89, Robert Klein Gallery, Boston, 91, Southeast Mus Photog, Daytona Beach, Fla, 93. *Teaching:* Asst prof photog & design, Univ Del, 75-79; prof art & contemp criticism, Univ Fla, 79-94; prof & chair art dept, Univ SFla, Tampa, 94-. *Awards:* Individual Artists Fel, State Fla, 82 & 88. *Bibliog:* Fred McDarrah (auth), Voice Choices, Village Voice, 10/10/77; Vince Aletti (auth), Voice Choices, Village Voice, 11/10/87 & 12/12/89; Pamela Kessler (auth), The Washington Post, 9/19/89. *Mem:* Soc Photog Educ. *Publ:* Contribr, Camera, Bucher Press, Zurich, Switz, 73; Fifteen Photographs in Color, Mancini Gallery, 78; Artwords and Bookworks, Los Angeles Inst Contemp Art, 78; Victims of Paradox, by Alison Nordstrom, Southeast Mus Photog, 92. *Dealer:* The Tartt Gallery Washington DC. *Mailing Add:* 1725 Ryan Dr Lutz FL 33549

WILSON, WILLIAM S
CRITIC
b Baltimore, Md, Apr 7, 32. *Study:* Univ Va, BA, 53; Yale Univ, MA, 56, PhD, 61. *Teaching:* Prof, Queens Col, 61-90. *Res:* Color and language. *Publ:* Auth, Robert Morris: Hard questions and soft answers, 69 & Dan Flavin: Fiat lux, 70, Art News; John Willenbecher: Pyramids and labyrinths, Arts, 75; Ralph Humphrey: An apology for painting, Artforum, 77; Cezanne's Rapport, Antaeus, 54, 85. *Mailing Add:* 458 W 25th St New York NY 10001

WILSON-HAMMOND, CHARLOTTE EMILY
VISUAL ARTIST, PAINTER
b Montreal, Que, Nov 19, 41. *Study:* Ind Univ, 62; 3 schs, Toronto, 66-68. *Work:* Art Gallery NS & Royal Trust Corp, Halifax; Confederation Ctr Arts, Charlottetown, PEI; Shell Energy Sources Can, Calgary, Alta; Norcen Energy Corp, Toronto. *Comn:* Drawings for feature film, Life Classes, William MacGillivrey, producer, 87. *Exhib:* Osaka World's Fair, Japan, 79; Confederation Ctr Arts, Charlottetown, PEI, 80-81; Centre Art Tapes, Halifax, 88; Naked/Nude, A Twenty Yr Survey, Art Gallery NS, 90; Intimate Communion, St Marys Art Gallery, 94. *Pos:* Bd mem, NS Col Arts & Design, Halifax, 87-; bd dir, Vis Art Copyright Inc; bd govs, Nova Scotia College of Art & Design, currently. *Teaching:* Artist-in-residence, Holland Col, PEI, 80. *Awards:* Can Coun Explorations Grant, 85; NS Dept Cult Grant, 85, 90, 94 & 98. *Bibliog:* Maria Tippett (auth), Three Centuries of Canadian Women Artists, Pengiun, 10/92; The Creators, WTN Television, 94; review, Arts Atlantic, 95. *Mem:* Can Artists Representation; Visual Arts NS (chmn, 78-79); Women Arts (organizer, 80-); Can Conf Arts-Coun of Candians; NS Col Art & Design. *Media:* Oil, Conte; Multimedia. *Dealer:* Gallery at Clam HBR 33 Beach Road Clam HBR NS BOJ 1YO

WILTRAUT, DOUGLAS SCOTT
PAINTER
b Allentown, Pa, July 12, 51. *Study:* Kutztown Univ, Pa, BFA(painting), 73. *Work:* Philip & Muriel Berman Mus Art, Collegeville, Pa; Yale Law Sch Libr, New Haven, Conn; Binney & Smith Corp, Easton, Pa; Pentamation Corp, Bethlehem, Pa; Pa Dept Educ, Harrisburg. *Comn:* Portrait, Myres McDougal, Yale Law Sch, New Haven, Conn, 76; portrait, Philip I Berman, chmn bd trustees, Philadelphia Mus Art, 80; Still Life, Lehigh Valley Hospital, 01-. *Exhib:* Inaugural Exhib, Philip & Muriel Berman Mus Art, Collegeville, Pa, 90; Am Watercolor Soc, 93, 04 & 05; The Face of Am: Contemp Portraits in Watercolor, Arts Guild Old Forge, NY, 94; Aim for Arts Int Exhib, Vancouver, Can, 2000; Butler Am Art, 01, 03 & 04; plus others. *Collection Arranged:* Philip & Muriel Berman Collection, Raymon Holland Collection, Jack Richeson Collection. *Awards:* Ralph Fabri Medal, 72nd & 74 Ann Exhibs, Allied Artists Am, 85-87; Butler Inst Am Art Award, 50th Anniversary Midyr, 86; Gold Medal Hon, 38th Ann Knickerbocker Artists, 88; Rouse Gold Medallion, Adirondacks Nat Exch of Am Watercolors, 99; Crest Medal, Philadelphia Watercolor Soc, 99; Trails & Streams Medal, Adirondacks, Nat Exhib Am Watercolors, 2000; Keystone Medallion, Pa Watercolor Soc 25th Ann Ex, 04; Sylan Grouse Guild Medal, Pa Watercolor Soc, 02; Rothermal Award, Kutztown Univ Alumni Assoc; Gerry Lenfest Award for Am Art, NSPC & A, 04. *Bibliog:* Ralph Fabri (auth), Youngest medal winner, Today's Art Mag, 75; Valerie R Rivers (auth), Douglas Wiltraut, Am Artist Mag, 88; Walter Garver (auth), Enrich the familiar with egg tempera, Artist's Mag, 91; Marilyn Fox (auth) Douglas Wiltraut, Lehigh Valley Mag, 98; Cathy Bennett (auth), A Most Versatile Paint, Artist Mag, 04; plus others. *Mem:* Nat Soc Painters Casein & Acrylic (dir, 77-86 exhib chmn, 87-90 & pres, 89-); Allied Artists Am; Audubon Artists Inc (exhib chmn, 88-90 & sr vpres, 89-92); Knickerbocker Artists; Pa Watercolor Soc; Philadelphia Watercolor Soc; Salmagundi Club (honorary); American Watercolor Soc. *Media:* Egg Tempera, Watercolor. *Res:* Shedding Light on a Marvelous Medium That Has Been Kept in the Shadows, Artist Mag, 05. *Publ:* Contribr & illusr, How to Discover Your Personal Painting Style, David P Richards (auth), N Light Bks; Best of Acrylic Paintings, Alfred M Duca & Lynn Loscutoff (eds), Rockport Publ; auth, article, Ultra realism in the unorthodox way, Palette Talk, 79; illustr, cover, Prevention Mag, Rodale Press, 83; contribr & illusr, The Artist Illustrated Encyl, Phil Metzger (auth), Northern Light Books. *Mailing Add:* 969 Catasauqua Rd Whitehall PA 18052

WIMAN, BILL
PAINTER, EDUCATOR
b Roscoe, Tex, Nov 12, 40. *Study:* E Tex State Univ, BS, 1962; Univ Fla, MFA, 1964. *Work:* Butler Inst of Am Art, Youngstown, Ohio; Okla Art Ctr, Oklahoma City; San Antonio Mus Art; Am Tel & Tel, NY; Mus of Arts & Sci, Evansville, Ind. *Exhib:* Real, Really Real, Super Real, San Antonio Mus Art, 81; New Works, Laguna Gloria Art Mus, Austin, 85; one person exhib, Adams-Middleton Gallery, Dallas, 85, 90; Five Figurative Painters, Abilene Fine Arts Mus, 86; Accurate Depictions? Figurative Realist Paintings, Bowling Green State Univ, 86. *Teaching:* Tchr, Frank Phillips Col, 64-66; asst prof painting, E Tex State Univ, 66-71; guest prof, Central Washington State Univ, fall 70; prof, Murray State Univ, 71-72; prof painting, Univ Tex, Austin, 72-. *Awards:* Ford Found Grant, 79; Teaching Excellence Award, Univ Texas, 87; Univ Res Inst Grant, Univ Texas, 89. *Bibliog:* 50 Texas Artists: A Critical Selection, Chronical Books, 86; articles, Arts Mag, 10/85 & ArtNews, 5/86. *Media:* Oil. *Dealer:* Adams-Middleton Gallery 3000 Maple Dallas TX 75201

WIMBERLEY, FRANK WALDEN
PAINTER, COLLAGE ARTIST
b Pleasantville, NJ, Aug 31, 26. *Study:* Howard Univ, with Lois M Jones, James Wells & James Porter. *Work:* Mus Mod Art, Metrop Mus, NY; Art Inst Chicago; Pitney Bowes, Stamford, Conn; Islip Art Mus, East Islip, NY; Brooklyn Union Community Gallery, Brooklyn, NY. *Comn:* Clearly, Gottlieb, Steen & Hamilton, NY, 86; Crown Plaza Hotel, E Elmhurst, NY, 89; Bruce Llewellyn, Coca Cola Bottling, Philadelphia, 91; Don Anderson, Time Warner, NY, 92. *Exhib:* Albright-Knox, Buffalo, NY, 86; Jamaica Arts Ctr, Jamaica, NY, 92; Brooklyn Union Community Gallery, NY, 92; Russel Sage Col, Albany, NY, 93; Adelphi Univ, Garden City, NY, 94; Gallery Authentique, Roslyn, NY, 94; Cinque Gallery, NY, 94; Arlene Bujese Gallery, East Hampton, NY, 94; and others. *Awards:* Best Work on Paper, 79, Best Abstract, 83, Best Mixed Media, 87, The Guild, NY. *Mem:* Guild Hall, East Hampton, NY. *Media:* Collage. *Dealer:* Arlene Bujese Gallery East Hampton, NY; June Kelly Gallery 591 Broadway New York NY. *Mailing Add:* 99-11 35th Ave Flushing NY 11368-1834

WIMMER, GAYLE
SCULPTOR, EDUCATOR
b Pittsburgh, Pa, Oct 2, 43. *Study:* Pratt Inst, Brooklyn, NY, BFA, 67; Tyler Sch Art, Philadelphia, Pa, MFA, 70; Acad Fine Art, Warsaw, Poland, with Wojclech Sadley, 71. *Work:* Cent Mus Textiles, Lodz, Poland; Stedman Gallery, Rutgers Univ, Camden, NJ; Nat Mus Mod Art, Sofia, Bulgaria; Nelson Ctr Mus Art, Tempe, Ariz; Arrowmont Sch, Gatlinburg, Tenn. *Comn:* US Nat Park Serv, Harper's Ferry, WVa, 77; Nat Steel Corp Serv Ctr, Wayne, NJ, 77; Pittsburgh Glove Mfg Co, Pa, 82; Roda Machine S A, Ticino, Switz, 86; Ctr for English as a Second Language, Tucson, Ariz, 89. *Exhib:* Solo exhibs, Annenberg Ctr, Philadelphia, 82, Mandell Theatre, Philadelphia, 83, Galerie Rzezby, Warsaw, Poland, 86, Galerie Faust, Geneva, Switz, 86 Am Cult Ctrs, Jerusalem & Tel Aviv, Israel, 88, Univ Mus Art, Tucson, Ariz, 89, Allersnaweg Castle, The Neth, 94, Women of the Book, The Finegood Gallery, Los Angeles, 97 & Int Biennial of Textile Art, Cite des Arts, Paris, France, 98; Ariz Biennial, Tucson Mus Art, Ariz, 88, 92 & 97; Contemp Ariz Textiles, Ariz State Univ Mus Art, Tempe, 91; Black & White, Ariz Mus Youth, Mesa, 92; 2eme Biennale Int Tapisserie Contemp, Beauvais, France, 96. *Collection Arranged:* Head curator, Contemporary Polish Fiber Art, Mus Ein Harod, Israel, 91; curator, contemporary Israeli Textile Art, Lodz, poland, 93. *Teaching:* Lectr textile art, Hunter Col, NY, 72-77; instr fiber sculpture, The New Sch, NY, 73-77; prof art & initiator Fiber Prog, Sch Art, Univ Ariz, Tucson, 77-. *Awards:* Individual Artist's Grant, Nat Endowment Arts, 73; Grant Research in Poland, Int Research & Exchanges Bd, New York, 82, 82-83, 99; Fulbright Fel, Artist-in-Residence, Israel, 87-88; Visual Artists' Fel, Tucson/Pima Arts Coun, Ariz, 90, 99. *Bibliog:* Irena Huml (auth), The Sphere of Time-Memory Transience: Gayle

Wimmer, Projekt Mag, 2/91; Suzanne McCormick (auth), The Woven Word, Ariz Daily Star, 5/11/92. *Mem:* Textile Soc Am; Fulbright Asn. *Media:* Mixed Media, Fiber. *Publ:* Auth, Seasonal Marks, 10-11/84 & Polish Textile Art: Photorealism in the second generation, 2-3/86, Am Craft Mag; Contemporary Polish fiber (essay), Modan Publ House Ltd, Tel Aviv, Israel, 91; Contemporary Israeli fiber art (essay), Cent Mus Textiles, Lodz, Poland, 93. *Mailing Add:* Schenley Gardens #516 3890 Bigelow Blvd Pittsburgh PA 15213

WIND, DINA
SCULPTOR
b Haifa, Israel, Jan 15, 38; US citizen. *Study:* Hebrew Univ, Jerusalem, BA, 61; Barnes Found, Merion, Pa, cert art appreciation, 72; Univ Pa, MA, 74. *Work:* Field Assocs, Tokyo, Japan; Hechinger Collection, Landover, Md; Interdisciplinary Ctr, Herzlia, Israel; Morgan Lewis & Bockius & Venturi Scott Brown & Assocs, Philadelphia. *Exhib:* Scatterpins (sculpture), Nexus Gallery, Philadelphia, 96; Chain Reactions, Viridian Gallery, NY, 97; Art of the State: Penn '97, State Mus Pa, Harrisburg, 97; Sculptors' Terrain, Philadelphia Sculptors Washington Square, Washington, DC, 98; Philadelphia Sculptors: a Group Exhibition, Grounds for Sculptor, Hamilton, NJ, 98. *Pos:* Bd mem & comn chmn, Fleisher Art Mem, 91-; assocs adv bd, Philadelphia Mus Art, 95-; bd mem, treas, Nexus-Found Today's Art, 96-. *Awards:* Merit Award Sculpture, Visual Arts Exhib, Three Rivers Art Festival, 98. *Bibliog:* Alexandra Shaw (auth), Dina Wind - Viridian Gallery, Manhattan Arts, 1/89; Diana Roberts (auth), Dina Wind breaking new ground, Manhattan Arts, 3-4/92; Ann Sargent Wooster (auth), Dina Wind - metal sculpture, Mid-Career Catalogue, 97. *Media:* Metal. *Dealer:* Contemp Artists Services 560 Broadway No 206 New York NY 10012. *Mailing Add:* 1041 Waverly Rd Gladwyne PA 19035

WINDEKNECHT, MARGARET BLAKE
FIBER ARTIST, WRITER
b Alma, Mich, June 27, 36. *Study:* Univ Mich, BS(design); Memphis State Univ, MEd. *Work:* Carroll B Reese Mus, Johnson City, Tenn; Tenn State Mus, Com Union Bank & Northern Telecom, Nashville; Cook Industs Collection, Memphis; Botsford Hospital, Detroit, Mch. *Comn:* Cardweaving, Unitarian Church Elliot Mem, Memphis, 77; loom-controlled, St John's United Methodist Church, Memphis, 78. *Exhib:* Miss River Craft Show, Brooks Mem Art Gallery, Memphis, 73, 75, 77 & 79; Fiber Structures, Heinz Gallery Mus Art, Carnegie Inst, Pittsburgh, Pa, 76; Superior, Tweed Mus of Art, Duluth, Minn, 77 & 81; Intent 78--Fabrics, Bruce Gallery, Edinboro, Pa 78; Fiber as Art, Metrop Mus Manila, Philippines, 80; Artist-Artisan, Bass Mus, Miami, Fla, 80-81; Premonitions Exhib, Cheekwood, Nashville, Tenn, 85; Woven Struct Computer Age, Tex Woman's Univ, Denton, Tex. *Awards:* Purchase Award, 6th Biennial, Tenn Artist-Craftsmen, 76; Purchase Awards, 9th & 10th Prints, Drawings & Craft Shows, Ark Art Ctr, 76 & 77; Best of Show, Mich League Handweavers Biennial Exhib, 97. *Bibliog:* Burry & Calonius (auths), Weaving, City of Memphis Mag, 78; M E Riccardi (auth), Creative Overshot rev, Shuttle Spindle & Dyepot, summer 79; A Xemakis (auth), A time to revitalize, Prairie Wool Companion, winter 85. *Mem:* Handweavers Guild Am; Am Crafts Coun. *Media:* Fiber. *Publ:* Coauth, Color and Weave, Van Nostrand Reinhold, 81; The two-tie unit weave, Shuttle Spindle & Dyepot, winter & spring 85; auth, The Rosepath Motif & Point Twill with Color-and-Weave, TGW Publ, 89; The Pinwheel: An Exploration in Color-and-Weave Design, TG Windeknecht, 92; Color-and Weave, II, TG Windeknecht, 94; Color-and-Weave (CD Rom), TG Windeknecht, 200; plus others. *Mailing Add:* 7676 Park Ridge Dr SW Jenison MI 49428

WINER, HELENE
DIRECTOR
b Chicago, Ill, Mar 27, 46. *Study:* Univ Southern Calif, BA, 68. *Pos:* Co-owner, Metrop Pictures, NY, currently. *Mailing Add:* Metro Pictures 519 W 24th St New York NY 10011

WINES, JAMES N
ARCHITECT
b Oak Park, Ill, June 27, 32. *Study:* Syracuse Univ Sch Art, BA(summa cum laude), 56. *Work:* Albright-Knox Art Gallery, Buffalo; Stedelijk Mus, Amsterdam, Holland; Whitney Mus Am Art, NY; Tate Gallery, London, Eng; Walker Art Ctr, Minneapolis. *Comn:* Allsteel Showroom, Allsteel Corp, NY, 88; Four Continents Bridge, World Fair Bridge, Expos 89, Hiroshima, Japan, 89; Isuzu Space Station, Yokohama, Japan, 89; Theater for the New City, Ctr Performing Arts, NY, 90; Shinwa Resort, Kisokoma-Kogen, Japan, 90. *Exhib:* Centre Pompidou, Paris, France, 75; Am Now, US Govt Traveling Show, Yugoslavia & Hungary, 79; SITE: Bldgs & Spaces Traveling Exhib, 81-82; Boston Archit Ctr, 82; Deutsches Architektur Mus, Frankfurt, Ger, 84; Triennale di Milano, Milan, Italy, 85-86; Archit Asn, London, Eng, 86; Nat Bldg Mus, Washington, 86. *Pos:* Dir, Site, Inc, NY, 69-; mem, Fed Design Assembly, Washington, 72; mem arts adv coun, Bicentennial Celebration, Washington, 72. *Teaching:* Instr environ art, Sch Visual Art, 65-; instr environ workshop, NY Univ, 65-; instr, NJ Sch Archit, 75-; Mellon prof, Cooper Union, NY, 77-; chmn dept environmental design, Parsons Sch Design, NY, currently. *Awards:* Sr Sabbatical Grant, 82 & Distinguished Designer Award, 83, Nat Endowment Arts; Winning Entry, Highway 86, World's Fair Transportation Pavilion & Plaza, Expo 86, Vancouver, Can, 85; and many others. *Bibliog:* Article, L'Archit d'Aujourd'hui, France, 2/85; Connoisseur, 7/86; and more than 2,000 other major features & cover stories in 22 countries. *Publ:* Auth, Architexture as Art (monogr), SITE Acad Ed Eng, 80; The Highrise of Homes, Rizzoli Int, 82; The Pratt J & Archit Now, 85; Japan Architect, SITE, Japan, 86 & 90; and many others. *Mailing Add:* SITE 25 Maiden Ln New York NY 10038

WINFIELD, RODNEY M
PAINTER, DESIGNER
b New York, NY, Feb 6, 25. *Study:* Univ Miami, 43; Cooper Union, 44-45; Atlier 17, 45-46; Wash Unvi, 70-71; Maryville Univ, St Louis, Mo, 92-93. *Work:* City Art Mus Tampa, Fla; Maryville Univ, St Louis; Smithsonian Inst Nat Design, NYC; Boston Fine Arts Mus; and pvt collections. *Comn:* doors, interior artifacts, Good Samaritan Hosp, Chapel, Mt Vernon, Ill, 68; space window, Washington Cathedral, 73; shrine, Our Lady of Perpetual Help Chapel of Christ the Crucified King, St Louis Univ Hospitals; stained glass, United Hebrew Temple, St Louis, 83-84; St Louis Univ Marquette Rm, 95-96; Sheldon Concert Hall, 01-05; rosewood plaque, Grace Cathedral, San Francisco, 02006; and others. *Exhib:* One-man shows, Galerie Creuze, Paris, 50, Martin Schweig Gallery, St Louis, Craft Alliance, St Louis, Mo, 80, Soroban Gallery, Wellfleet, Mass, 86 & Matrix Gallery, Provincetown, Mass, 94; Pope Pius Libr, St Louis Univ; Pallette Bleau, Paris; City Art Mus, St Louis. *Pos:* Stained glass designer, Emil Frei Assocs, St Louis, 53-; designer, Winfield Jewelry, St Louis, 70-. *Teaching:* Prof emer, Maryville Univ, St Louis, 64-90. *Awards:* Outstanding Tchr Award, Marysville Univ, 90. *Media:* Acrylic; Stained Glass, Silver. *Dealer:* Chris Winfield Gallery Carmel CA 93923. *Mailing Add:* 3483 Ocean Ave Carmel CA 93923

WINGATE, ARLINE (HOLLANDER)
SCULPTOR
b New York, NY. *Work:* Syracuse Univ Mus, NY; Nat Mus Stockholm, Sweden; Ghent Mus Belg; Joseph H Hirshhorn Collection; Guild Hall Mus, East Hampton, NY; plus many others. *Exhib:* Metrop Mus Art & Whitney Mus Am Art, NY; Wadsworth Atheneum Mus; San Francisco Mus Mod Art, Calif; Baltimore Mus, Md; plus many others in Paris, France, Belg, Buenos Aires, Arg, London, Eng & US incl five one-man shows. *Teaching:* Instr, Young Men's Hebrew Asn, Southhampton Col. *Mem:* Sculptors Guild; Nat Asn Women Artists. *Media:* All

WINGATE, GEORGE B
PAINTER
b Mt Holly, NJ, Oct 13, 41. *Study:* Univ Rochester, BA, 63; Syracuse Univ Sch Archit, 65; New Sch, with Henry Pearson, 72-76; Art Students League, with Frank Mason, 73-78; Vt Col, MFA, 93 with Will Barnet. *Work:* Everson Mus; Mus City New York. *Exhib:* Butler Art Inst Ann, 80 & 83; Foxhall Gallery, Washington, DC, 82-; solo exhibs, Everson Mus, 82, Katonah Gallery, NY, 83 & John Pence Gallery, San Francisco, 83; Painting NY, Mus City NY, 83; New York City Anthology, Grace Borgenicht Gallery, 88; Century Asn, NY, 90; Cooley Gallery, Old Lyme, Conn, 90-95; Nat Acad, 94. *Teaching:* Instr drawing, Parsons Sch Design, NY, 85-88; instr printmaking & drawing, Gordon Col, 89-2001. *Awards:* Emil Carlsen Prize for Best Still Life, 173rd Ann Exhib, Nat Acad; Emil Carlsen Prize 179th Annual Exhib, Nat Acad, 2004. *Bibliog:* Gordon Muck (auth), Wingate's Cazenovia, Syracuse Post Standard, 9/15/80; Vivien Raynor (auth), article, NY Times, 10/16/83; Stephen Doherty (auth), article, Am Artist Mag, 10/83; Bruce Herman Image Mag Looking again, The Art of George Wingate, Fall 2004. *Mem:* Art Students League; CIVA. *Media:* Oil, Sculpture. *Publ:* The World Below the Window A Poem by William Jay Smith; Stone House Press, Morris Gelfand (pub), 98; Broadside Illustrated by George Wingate; Paintings by George Wingate poems by Mark Stevick: The language of Objects, Gordon College, 99. *Mailing Add:* 72 Dodges Row Wenham MA 01984

WINGERTER, JOHN PARKER
PAINTER
b New York, NY, July 27, 1940. *Study:* Columbia Univ, 66; LaSalle Univ, LLB, 64-66; Art Students League, New York, 68-70. *Work:* Jouvet Ctr & Customs House, Asn Artist-Run Galleries, World Trade Ctr, NY; The Artists Forum, Long Island, NY. *Comn:* Acrylic canvas, comn by Dr & Mrs Ravitz, Long Island, 83; two large panels, Continental Grain Corp, NY, 84; Gestalt Learning Ctr, comn by Mr Levy, Long Island, 86. *Exhib:* Small Works Competition, Gallery East, NY Univ, 80; Survey of Geometric Expressionism, NY State Arts Coun & Mobil Oil, Borough Hall, NY, 82; Reflections, Adelphi Univ, Long Island, NY, 83; Le Salon Des Nations, Int Ctr Contemp Arts, Paris, France, 84. *Bibliog:* E Buonagurio (auth), artic le, Arts Mag, 10/77; Helen Harrison (auth), Truth redefined, 3/1/80 & Five artists works, 5/13/84, New York Times. *Media:* Acrylic, Oil. *Dealer:* Noho Gallery 168 Mercer St New York NY 10012. *Mailing Add:* 58 Meadow Glen Rd Northport NY 11768

WINGO, MICHAEL B
PAINTER, DRAFTSMAN
b Los Angeles, Calif, Nov 21, 44. *Study:* Art Ctr Col Design, 60-62; Claremont McKenna Col, BA, 64; Otis Art Inst(scholar), BFA, 65, MFA, 67. *Work:* Santa Barbara Mus Art, Calif; Oakland Mus, Calif; Manatt, Phelps, Rothenberg & Phillips, Los Angeles; Security Pac Nat Bank, Los Angeles; IBM, Crocker Ctr, Los Angeles; and others including private collections. *Exhib:* One-man shows, Santa Barbara Mus Art, 70, Newport Harbor Art Mus, Newport Beach, 76, Turnbull Lutjeans Kogan Gallery, Costa Mesa, 83, Janet Steinberg Gallery, San Francisco, 83 & Terry DeLapp Gallery, Los Angeles, 84; Art & Archit Tour, Los Angeles Co Mus Art, 85; New Art: Paintings from NY, Tex, Calif, Laguna Gloria Art Mus, Austin, Tex, 89; Feitelson, Artist & Teacher, Long Beach City Col, 89; Contemp Abstractions, Weingart Ctr, Occidental Col, 90; LA Current: Armand Hammer Mus Rental & Sales Gallery, Los Angeles; The New Minimalism, Gensler, Santa Monica, Calif, 2000; solo exhib, Resende Ctr, Porto Portugal, 2001. *Pos:* vis artist, School Fine Arts, Porto, Portugal, 2001. *Teaching:* Instr painting & drawing, Pasadena Art Mus, 68-72; guest lectr, San Francisco Art Inst, 84 & vis artist, 87; instr drawing & painting, Otis Art Inst, Parsons Sch Design, Los Angeles, 85-95; inaugural fac, Calif State Summer Sch Arts, 87; vis lectr, Royal Academy Art, London, 2001. *Awards:* Visual Artists Fel Grant in Painting, Nat Endowment Art, 89-90; Who's Who in the West, 23rd ed, Marquis Who's Who, 91; Individual Support Grant in Painting, Adolph & Esther Gottlieb Found, 92.

Bibliog: (Monogr), Los Angeles Valley Col Art Gallery, 85; Joseph Mugnaini (auth), Expressive Drawing Through the Schematic Approach, Davis, 88; Les Krantz (ed), The California Art Review, Am References Inc, 88; Mark Van Proyen (auth), Dissonant Abstractions Catalogue, San Jose Inst of Contemp Art, 86; Henry T Hopkins (auth), California Painters: New Work, Chronicle Bks, San Francisco, page 7, 89; Michael WIngo Catalogue Essay, Resende Center, 2001. *Media:* Oil. *Publ:* Mark Van Proyen (auth), Artweek; Review, Vol 15 No 36, 10/27/84; Debra Koppman (auth), Artweek: Previews, Vol 35 No 6, 7/2004-8/2004; Mark Van Proyen (auth), Art in America Reviews, 11/2005. *Dealer:* Robin Ficara Fine Arts Los Angeles Calif. *Mailing Add:* 7051 N Figueroa St Los Angeles CA 90042

WINIARSKI, DEBORAH
PAINTER
b Ft Meade, Md, Dece 22, 59. *Study:* Queens Col, Flushing, NY, MS, 95; Arte Sch Art & Photography, Florence, Italy, 2001; Art Students League of NY, studied with Bruce Dorfman, 2003-2004. *Exhib:* Small Works, 27th Ann, 80 Wash Sq E Galleries, NY, 2004; Ann Concours, Art Students League of NY, 2004-2005, Invitational Exhib, 2004-2005; Sources, Int Group Exhib, Roseline Koener Atelier, Westhampton, NY, 2005; Monmouth Festival Arts, NJ, 2006; Summer Invitational, Denise Bibro Fine Art, NY, 2006. *Teaching:* Asst Instr, combined media, Art Students League NY, 2003-2004, guest instr, 2005-. *Awards:* Painting Award, Annual Concours, ASL of NY, 2004; First Prize Award, Annual Concours, ASL of NY, 2005. *Mem:* Art Students League of NY; NY Artists Equity Asn Inc. *Media:* Combined media painting. *Publ:* Contribr, Broadhurst Gallery Artists, 2005; contribr, Linea, Vol 9, No 2, fall/winter 2005, 21. *Dealer:* Broadhurst Gallery 2212 Midland Rd Pinehurst NC 28374; Kouros Gallery 23 E 73rd St New York NY 10021. *Mailing Add:* 355 W 85th St New York NY 10024

WINICK, BERNYCE ALPERT
PAINTER, PHOTOGRAPHER
b Brooklyn, NY, Oct 20, 22. *Study:* NY Univ, BA (fine arts & music), 43; Art Students League with Mario Cooper, 61-64; Nat Acad Sch Fine Arts, 68-72 & additional studies at Brooklyn Mus Art Sch, Traphagen Sch Fashion & Nat Acad Design Sch. *Comn:* Large watercolor, comn by Dr & Mrs Marcel Weinberger, Woodmere, NY, 84; 2 large watercolors, comn by Pittway Corp, Syosset, NY, 89. *Exhib:* Am Watercolor Soc, Salmagundi Club, NY, 92; Nat Asn Women Artists, Jacob Javits Fgd Bldg, NY, 92; Nat Asn Women Artists, Washington & Lee Univ, Lexington, Va, 93; Discovery Gallery, Glen Cove, NY, 93 & 94; Soho, Z Gallery, NY, 94; Fine Arts Mus Long Island, 97; Discovery Art Gallery, Sea Cliff, NY, 98; Town Hall, Town of Hempsead, NY, 2000; NY Inst Tech, 2003; Mem Libr, 2003-04; Carnegie Hall, 2006; Julliard, 2006; Solo exhibs, Salmagundi Club, NY, 1982, Discovery Art Gallery, Sea Cliff, NY, 1989, 96, 98, Glen Cove, NY, 1991, Chelsea Ctr, East Norwich, NY, 1993, 96, 98 & 2000, Z Gallery, Soho, NY, 1994, Fine Arts Mus Long Island, NY, 1997, NY Inst Technol, Wisser Mem Libr, 2001 & 2006, Nat Arts Club, NY, 2002. *Awards:* First Prize, Nat Arts Club-86th Ann, 85; First Prize, Salmagundi Club, 90, Salmagundi Club Award, 2004; Doris Kreindler Mem Award, Nat Asn Women Artists, 92; Best in Show Photography Rockville Ctr Guild for the Arts, NY, 97; First Prize in Black and White Photography, Long Island Arts Coun, Freeport, NY, 99; Showcase Award Chelsea Ctr, NY, 2000; First Prize Photog, Nat Arts Club, NY, 2001; Thomas Moran Mem Award for Watercolor, First Prize, Salmagundi Club, NY, 2002; Salmagundi Club Award, 2004; First Prize, Mills Pond House, St. James, NY, 2005; Farian Adler Mem Award, Long Island Council, Freeport, NY, 2006. *Bibliog:* Robin Earl (auth), Artist with an everchanging palate, Nassau Herald, 12/85; Roberta Graff (auth), A symphony of paintings by Bernyce Winick, South-Shore Record, 5/89; Chris Jonny (auth), A Stroke of Genius, Nassua Herald, 10/94; Helen Harrison (auth), 19th ann juried photography in show, NY Times, 4/25/99; Herbert Keppler (auth), Me and my shadows, Popular Photography, 2/99, Keep it simple, 5/2000; Chris Unwin (auth), The Artistic Touch 3, West Bloomfield, Michigan: Creative Art Press, 99. *Mem:* Am Watercolor Soc; Nat Asn Women Artists; Fel Royal Soc Artists, London; Hempstead Harbor Artists Asn (Discovery Gallery); Nat Arts Club NY; Harvard Club Arts Group. *Media:* Aquamedia. *Interests:* classical piano. *Publ:* Auth, The Encyclopedia of Watercolour Landscape Techniques, Headline Publ Ltd, Gt Brit, 96; Curated Collection III (CD-Rom), ACI Art Communication Int, 96; Abstracts in Watercolor, Rockport Publ, 96; plus others. *Mailing Add:* 923 Beth Lane Woodmere NY 11598-1507

WINK, CHRIS
CONCEPTUAL ARTIST, KINETIC ARTIST
b New York, NY, Jan 24, 61. *Study:* Weslean, Am Studies, 84. *Work:* New Mus Contemp Art (performance), NY; Milwaukee Art Mus (performance), Wis; Contemp Art Ctr New Orleans (performance), Fla. *Awards:* Obie, Tubes, Village Voice, 91; Drama Desk, Tubes, 92; Lucille Lortel Found Award, Tubes, 92. *Bibliog:* Alisa Soloman (auth), Pissing on propriety, Village Voice, 1/15/91; Vicki Goldberg (auth), Hi tech meets God with Blue Man Group, NY Times, 1/17/91; Thomas M Disch (auth), Blue Man Group: Tubes, Nation, 1/20/92. *Media:* Performance. *Mailing Add:* c/o The Astor Place Theater 434 Lafayette St New York NY 10003

WINK, DON (JON DONNEL)
PAINTER, EDUCATOR
b San Angelo, Tex, July 13, 38. *Study:* Univ Tex, BFA, 60; Ohio Univ, 61-62; Univ Wash, MFA, 63. *Exhib:* The Texas General, Dallas Mus Fine Arts, 61; two-man exhib, Witte Mus, San Antonio, 66; Texas Painting & Sculpture, Dallas Mus Fine Arts, 68; Associated Artist, Carnegie Mus, Pittsburgh, 71-75; Westmoreland Co Mus, Greensburg, Pa, 72-75; Mus STex Ann, Corpus Christi, 82; Recent Works from East Texas, Tyler Mus Art, 82. *Teaching:* Instr painting & drawing, Southwestern Univ, Tex, 65-69; prof & chmn dept art, Slippery Rock State Col, 69-76 & Stephen F Austin State Univ, 76-. *Awards:* First Prize, 13th Ann 180, Huntington Galleries, WVa, 65 & 30th Ann Allied Artist, 65; Jury Award, Asn Artist, 72. *Mem:* Nat Coun Art Adminr; Tex Asn Schs Art (secy, 79-80). *Media:* Acrylic, Oil. *Mailing Add:* Box 13001 Stephen F Austin State Univ Nacogdoches TX 75962

WINKLER, MARIA PAULA
PAINTER, EDUCATOR
b Krakow, Poland, Oct 24, 45; US citizen. *Study:* Univ Pa, study with Karl Umlauf, BA(art & art hist); Pa State Univ, study with Enrigue Montenegro, MFA(painting & drawing) & study with Kenneth Beittel, PhD(art educ). *Work:* Pa State Univ, State Col; Boise Art Mus, Idaho; Univ Calif Med Ctr, Sacramento; Sutter Mem Hosp, Sacramento; Kaiser Permanente, N Calif. *Comn:* Two paintings, Raley's Corporate Offices, Sacramento, Calif; two paintings, Kronick, Moskovitz, Tiedemann and Girard, Prof Corporation, Sacramento, Calif; two paintings, TCSI Commun Corp, San Francisco, Calif; painting, El Dorado Hills Develop Co. *Exhib:* Nat Drawing & Small Sculpture Exhib, Ball State Univ, Muncie, Ind, 70; NY Exhib of Paintings, Sculpture & Graphics, Avanti Galleries, NY, 71; New Generation Drawing, Cheney-Cowles Mem State Mus, Spokane, Wash, 73; Contemp Watercolor Paintings, Pence Gallery, Davis, Calif, 88; Contemp Realists, Gump's Gallery, San Francisco, 91; 69th Ann Crocker-Kingsley Open Exhib, Crocker Art Mus, Sacramento, Calif, 94. *Pos:* Tech illusr, Aerojet Gen Corp, Sacramento, 63. *Teaching:* Asst prof art & art educ, Boise State Univ, Idaho, 73-75; asst prof art educ, Univ BC, Vancouver, 75-77; prof art, Calif State Univ, Sacramento, 77-. *Awards:* First Place & William Harrington Mem Award, Northern Calif Arts 26th Ann Open Show, Sacramento, 80; Mixed Media, Second Place, Northern Calif Arts 36th Ann Open Exhib, Carmichael, 91; Gold Discovery Award, Works on Paper, Art Calif Mag, 93 & 94. *Bibliog:* A Survey of Contemporary Art of the Figure, Am Artist, 2/85. *Mem:* Nat Art Educ Asn. *Media:* Watercolor, Pastels. *Res:* Research and writings on techniques of teaching art appreciation to teachers and museum volunteers; curriculum development in art. *Publ:* Illusr, Art: Magic, Impulse and Control, A Guide to Viewing, Prentice-Hall, 73; Eight Posters, Editions Limited, San Francisco, 90-91; Two Artists Cards, Allport Editions Artist Cards, Portland, 90; Four Mini-Prints, Portal Publications, Corte Madera, 91. *Dealer:* Susan Willoughby Art Consult 73 Starlit Cir Sacramento CA 95831. *Mailing Add:* c/o Art Dept Calif State Univ Sacramento CA 95819

WINKLER, MAX-KARL
EDUCATOR, ILLUSTRATOR
b New Braunfels, Tex, May 14, 38. *Study:* Univ Tex, Austin, BA, 59, BFA, 63, MFA, 68. *Pos:* Illusr & graphic designer, Washington, DC, 84-88; illusr, Nat Sci Resources Ctr, Washington, DC, 88-94. *Teaching:* Instr studio art & art hist, Col Mainland, Texas City, Tex, 68-73; asst prof, Colo Mountain Col, Glenwood Springs, Colo, 73-76; instr studio art, Smithsonian Resident Assoc Prog, Washington, DC, 86-. *Mem:* Guild Natural Sci Illustrators. *Media:* Pen, Ink. *Publ:* Illusr, Science & Technology for Children: Teachers' Guides & Student Activity Books, Nat Sci Resources Ctr, 88-; Almanac Edition, Chronicle of Higher Education, 89-. *Mailing Add:* 10309 Drumm Ave Kensington MD 20895

WINKLER, MICHAEL
CONCEPTUAL ARTIST
b Lima, Ohio, Feb 28, 52. *Work:* Mus Mod Art, NY; Stanford Univ, Calif; Staatsgalerie, Stuttgart, WGer; King Stephen Mus, Szekesfehervar; Sackner Archive, Miami Beach, Fla. *Comn:* Spoke of the Wheel, Intermedia Dance Proj, Portland Ballet Co, 2006. *Exhib:* Solo exhibs, Kunstraum Kunoldstrasse 34, Kassel, WGer, 84, Univ Md, Baltimore, 85, Kansas City Art Inst, 88 & Univ Mass, Lowell, 94; Text Out of Context, Soho Ctr, NY, 91; Univ of Penn, 2004; Poetic Positions, Kasseler Kunstverein, 2004. *Pos:* NY Correspondent, Rampike Mag, Toronto, 85-93. *Awards:* Spec Proj Fel, Pa Coun Arts, 84; Visual Artists Fel, Nat Endowment Arts, 85; LINE Grant, Line II Asn, NY, 85. *Bibliog:* Sue Scott (auth), Alphastructures, Art Res Ctr, 84; Skuta Helgason (auth), Regular words, Afterimage, 84; Rasula & McCaffery (auth), Imagining Language, MIT Press, 98. *Media:* Mixed Media. *Publ:* Auth, Word Art/Art Words, 85, An Artist's Statement, 86 & Equivalents, 87, Extreme Measures, 89, Printed Matter. *Mailing Add:* 1392 W 2nd Ave Grandview Heights OH 43212-3406

WINOKUR, JAMES L
COLLECTOR, CRITIC
b Philadelphia, Pa, Sept 12, 22. *Study:* Univ Pa, BS(econ), 43. *Pos:* Exec comt & mem, other comts, Carnegie Inst, 67-, founder fel fund & life trustee, Mus Art, 67-; vpres & gov, Pittsburgh Plan for Art, 67-84; trustees comt mem, AAM, 72-; trustee & vchmn, Sarah Scaife Found, 72-87; art critic, Greensburg Tribune-Rev, 72-87; trustee, St Edmunds Acad & Landmarks Soc, 75-94; art adv comt, Trust for Cult Resources, Pittsburgh, Pa; mem, Arch Am Art, 75-; dir & mem exec comt, 100 Friends of Pittsburgh Art, 75-. *Teaching:* Instr art, Duquesne Univ, 80. *Bibliog:* Harry Schwalb (auth), Living with Art, Pittsburgh Mag; Donald Miller (auth), Rebirth in Strip, Pittsburgh Post-Gazette. *Mem:* Hon mem Asn Artists Pittsburgh; Carnegie Mus Art; Andy Warhole Mus; Pittsburgh Ctr Arts. *Interests:* Joseph Goto, American sculptor in welded steel. *Collection:* Cobra paintings, drawings and sculpture including Carl-Henning Pedersen, Jorn, Corneille, Alechinsky, Ubac, Reinhoud and others; 20th century American paintings, drawings and sculpture including Varujan Boghosian, Sam Francis, Joseph Goto and others; prints from Old Masters to the 20th century; Australian Aboriginal art; Southwest American Indian pottery and weavings; art deco furniture and objects. *Publ:* Numerous articles & rev for Tribune. *Mailing Add:* 5625 Darlington Rd Pittsburgh PA 15217

WINOKUR, NEIL
PHOTOGRAPHER
b New York, NY, June 28, 45. *Study:* Hunter Col, City Univ NY, BA, 67. *Work:* Mus Mod Art, Metrop Mus Art, Jewish Mus & Chase Manhattan Bank, NY; Los Angeles Co Mus Art; Centro Cult Arte Contemporaneo, Mex City, Mex; Philadelphia Mus Art, Pa; Denver Mus Art, Colo. *Comn:* New York Food, Columbia Univ Sch Arts, Metrop

Transp Authority, Arts for Transit, LIRR Pa Station, NY; Movie Portraits, 42nd St Art proj, NY; Progressive People (10 multiple portraits), Progressive Ins Co, Cleveland, Ohio, 93; Dynamics of an Insurance Giant, Caroon/Black Plaza, Nashville, Tenn; Transit Art: LIRR Worksers and Objects, Pub Art Fund, Pa Station, NY. *Exhib:* Commission a Portrait, PS 122 Gallery, NY, 91; Artist's Choice: Chuck Close, Head-On The Modern Portrait, Mus Mod Art, NY, 91 & The Pleasures and Terrors of Domestic Comfort (auth, catalog), 91; Special Collections, The Photog Order from Pop to Now, Int Ctr Photog Midtown, NY, 92; Persona, Mus Photogr Arts, San Diego, Calif, 92; Solo exhibs, Portraits, Barbara Toll Fine Arts, NY, 92, Progressive People: Photographs by Neil Winokor, Cleveland Contemp, Ohio, 93, Neil Winokur: Photographs, Denver Mus Art, Colo, 93, For Bill, A Memorial, Janet Borden Inc, NY, 93, Galerie du jour Agnes b, Paris, France, 95, Daily Life, Janet Borden Inc, NY, 97 & NY Food, LIRR Pa Station Lightboxes, NY, 98; Multiple Images: Photographs Since 1965 from the Collection, Mus Mod Art, NY, 93; Autour de Rogier Vivier (auth, catalog), Galerie Enrico Navarra, Paris, France, 95; The Dead (auth, catalog), Nat Mus Photog, Film & TV, Bradford, Eng, 95; New in the Nineties, Katonah Mus Art, NY, 96; Portrait Paintings, Bernard Toale Gallery, Boston, Mass, 96; New Art on Paper (auth, catalog), Philadelphia Mus Art, Pa, 96; Bathrooms, Thomas Healy Gallery, NY, 98; Food, SF Camerawork, San Francisco, Calif, 98; NY Photographs, Janet Borden Inc, 2000; Double Vision, Univ Art Mus, Calif State Univ, Santa Barbara, 2001; Monochromes, Janet Borden Inc, 2002; Great Investions, Thief Burden, 2005. *Awards:* Fel in Photography from Art Matters Mc, 84, Nat Endowment Arts, 84 & Guggenheim Found, 87; Grant, Art Matters Inc, 86 & 88. *Bibliog:* Pepe Karmel (auth), Out of the Ghetto?, ARTnews, 4/94; Charles Hagen (auth), Review-Neil Winokou, 7/1/94 & 2/2/96, NY Times; Edith Newhall (auth), Portrait Parts-Neil Winokur, NY Mag, 1/15/96; Charles Hogen (auth), Neil Winokar-Barbara Tull Fine Arts, Vol XXVI, Arttorum, 88; Vince Aletti (auth), Choices-Neil Winnkur, Village Voice, 1/3/89; Carter Radcliff (auth), Elle, 11/89; Max Kozloff, Hapless Figures in an Artificial Storm, Artforum, 11/89. *Media:* Photography. *Specialty:* Photography-Contemporary. *Interests:* Cooking, gardening. *Publ:* The Dog in Art from Rococo to Post-Modernism, Robert Rosenblum & Harry N Abrams, New York, 88; New Art, Phyllis Freeman, Mark Greenberg, Eric Himmel, Andreas Landshoff, Charles Miers & Harry N Abrams, New York, 90; How to Look at Modern Art, Philip Yenawine & Harry N Abrams, 91; Everyday Things, Smithsonian Press, Washington, DC, 5/94; Album, Gabriel Bauret, L'Ecole des loisirs, Paris, France, 95. *Dealer:* Janet Borden 560 Broadway New York NY 10012. *Mailing Add:* 16 Hudson St No 2A New York NY 10013

WINOKUR, PAULA COLTON
CERAMIST, CRAFTSMAN
b Philadelphia, Pa, 35. *Study:* Temple Univ, BFA, BSEd, 58, with Rudolf Staffel; Alfred Univ, New York, summer 58. *Work:* Montreal Mus Decorative Arts; Philadelphia Mus of Art; Nat Mus Am Art, Washington, DC; Mint Mus Crafts/Design, Charlotte, NC; Los Angeles Co Mus Art. *Comn:* Ed patrons plates (60), Nat Mus Am Jewish Hist, 83; fireplace installations, pvt residences, Philadelphia, 84, 85 & 86; lintel (A view of Diamond Head), Hawaii Sch for Girls, Honolulu, 88; fireplaces, comn by Mr & Mrs Robert Coon, Montclair, NJ, 89 & Mr & Mrs William Harris, Lynchburg, Va, 90; large wall installation, Pa Convention Ctr, 93. *Exhib:* 100 Artists Celebrate 100 Yrs, Fairtree Gallery & Xerox Gallery, 76; Inaugural Exhib, Am Crafts Mus, 86; Solo show, Helen Drutt Gallery, NY, 90, Helsinki, Finland, 2005; First Yixing Ceramic Invitational, Yixing & Jingdezen, China; Int Biennial, Khon, Korea; Color & Fire: Defining Moments in Studio Ceramics, Los Angeles Co Mus, Calif; Contemp Mus, Honalulu, 2004. *Teaching:* Asst prof ceramics, Philadelphia Col Art, 67; prof, Arcadia Univ, Glenside, Pa, 73- & Tyler Sch Art, 83; prof emer, Arcadia Univ, 2003. *Awards:* Merit Award, Craftsmen USA, Am Crafts Coun, 66; Prize, Ceramics Int 73, Calgary, Alta, 73; Nat Endowment for the Arts Craftsmen's Fel, 76 & 88; PA Coun Craftmen's Fel, 86 & 2005. *Bibliog:* Robin Rice (auth) American Craft Mag, 2000; Ed Sozanski (auth) The Philadelphia Inquirer, 2000; Ivy Barsky (auth), Art & Perception #13, Winokur Landamarks; Paula Winokur, Gerald Brown (coauths), Ceramic Art & Perception (Poetic Earth) #59. *Mem:* Fel Am Crafts Coun; Fel Nat Coun Educ Ceramic Arts (bd dir, 79-82); Int Acad Ceramics. *Media:* Porcelain. *Specialty:* Fine arts. *Interests:* Geology, The landscape. *Collection:* Montreal Mus of Decorative Arts; Mus Art & Design, NY; Philadelphia Mus Art; L.A. Co Mus; Mus Design, Helsinki, Finland. *Publ:* Coauth, The light of Rudolph Staffel, Craft Horizons, 77. *Dealer:* Helen Drutt: Philadelphia 2220 Rittenhouse St Philadelphia PA 19103. *Mailing Add:* 435 Norristown Rd Horsham PA 19044

WINOKUR, ROBERT
CERAMIST, EDUCATOR
b Brooklyn, NY, Dec 24, 33. *Study:* Tyler Sch Art, Temple Univ, with Rudolph Staffel, BFA, 56; NY State Col Ceramics, Alfred, MFA, 58. *Hon Degrees:* Am Craft Council Col Fel, Fel Nat Council Educ Ceramic Arts; hon mem, Int Acad Ceramics, Geneva, Switz, 2005. *Work:* Houston Mus Fine Arts, Tex; Contemp Mus, Honolulu, HI; Los Angeles County Mus Art, Calif; Mus Boymans can Beuningen, Rotterdam, Neth; Philadelphia Mus Art, Pa. *Comn:* pvt comn by Helen Drutt; Trammel-Crowe corp; Ford & Earl Architectural, First Nat Bank Chicago. *Exhib:* 300 Yrs of Am Art, Philadelphia Mus Art, 76; Philadelphia Contemp Artists, Philadelphia Mus Art, 90; Haldane Connections Exhib, Int Acad Ceramics with Glasgow Sch Art, Edinburgh, Scotland, 90; Furniture Philadelphia, Morris Gallery Pa, Acad Fine Art, Philadelphia, 91; Three In Clay-Three Points of View, Nat Mus Ceramic Art, Baltimore, Md, 92; From the Ground Up, Ten Philadelphia Artists Invitational, Levy Gallery, Moore Col Art & Design, 92; Retrospective, The Philadelphia Yrs, 62 to 92, Helen Drutt Gallery, Philadelphia, Pa, 92; solo-exhib, Dorothy McRae Gallery, Atlanta, Ga, Helen Drutt Gallery, Philadelphia, 2001, Ceramics 1950-1990: A Survey of Contemp Am Ceramics, Nat Mus Modern Art, Kyoto, 2002, Setaquya Art Mus, Tokyo, 2002, Poetics of Clay: An Int Perspective, Philadelphia Art Alliance, Mus Art & Design, Helsinki, Finland, 2002, Houston Ctr for Contemp Crafts, 2003, The Aileon Osborn Webb Awards Exhib, Contemp Crafts Gallery, Portland, Ore, 2003, The Schein-Joseph Int Mus Ceramic Art, NY State Col Ceramics, Alfred, NY; Chinese & Foreign Ceramic Artists Works Invitational Show, Yixing Int Ceramics Symposium, Yixing, China; Color and Fire: Defining Moments in Studio Ceramics 1950-2000, Los Angeles Co Mus Art, Calif; 21st Century Ceramics, Cahzahi Ctr Gallery, Columbus Col Art & Design, Columbus, Ohio; In Our Own Backyard, Pa Council on Arts, Fel Traveling Exhib, 2004-2006; Standing Room Only, Invitational, 60th Scripps Ann, Scripps Col, Claremont, Calif, 2004. *Pos:* Proj dir, Philadelphia Ceramic Consortium, currently; on site prog chmn, Nat Coun Educ Ceramic Arts, 75 & 92; adv bd, Clay Studio, Philadelphia, currently; vis artist/exchange lectr, Glasgow Sch Art, Scotland, 87; invited participant, Symp Contemp Ceramics, Int Ceramic Studio, Kecskemet, Hungary, 93. *Teaching:* Coordr two-dimensional visual design dept, NTex State Univ, Denton, 58-63; area chmn ceramics, Tyler Sch Art, Temple Univ, 66-, chmn craft dept, 79-82 & 88-91; vis artist & guest lectr, Glasgow Sch Art, Scotland, 87. *Awards:* Nat Endowment Arts Fel, 79, Nat Coun Educ Ceramic Arts, Fel, 83; Pa Coun Arts Fel, 88; Fel in crafts, Pa Coun on Arts, 2003. *Bibliog:* Elaine Levin (auth), American Ceramics, Abrams; Jack Troy (auth), Salt Glazed Ceramics, Watson-Guptill; Susan Peterson (auth), The Craft & Art of Clay, Prentice Hall; Richard Polsky (auth), the Columbia University Oral History Collection, Columbia Univ Archives; Susan Peterson (auth) Contemporary Cermaics, Wetson-Guptill; Daniel Rhodes (auth), Clay and Glaze for the Potter, Krouse Pub; Emanuel Cooper (auth) Ten Thousand Years of Pottery, 4th ed, U Pa Press; Suzanne Ramljak (auth), Crafting: A Legacy of Contemporary American Crafts for the Philadelphia Mus of Art, Philadelphia Mus Art Publ; Janet Kaplos (auth), At Helen Drutt, Art in Am, 10/2001; Bai Ming (auth), Oversea Contemporary Ceramic Art Classics, Hubei Fine Art Publishing House, China; Robin Hopper (auth), Making Marks, Kraus Pub. *Mem:* Am Crafts Coun; Nat Coun Educ Ceramic Arts (br dir, 69-70, vpres, 72-73); Philadelphia Coun Professional Craftsmen; adv bd, The Clay Studio, Philadelphia, Pa, 85; Int Acad Ceramics. *Media:* Salt Glazed Stoneware. *Publ:* Auth, The Tyler School of Art of Temple University, Ceramics Mo, 75; coauth, The light of Rudolph Staffel, Craft Horizions, 77. *Dealer:* Helen Drutt Philadelphia PA 19103. *Mailing Add:* 435 Norristown Rd Horsham PA 19044

WINSLOW, HELEN
PAINTER
b New Salem, NC, Mar 24, 16. *Study:* Fla Southern Col, BA; Art Students League, NY; Otis Art Inst, Los Angeles. *Work:* La Mirada Mus, Monterey, Calif. *Exhib:* Frye Art Mus, Seattle, Wash, 60, 62 & 68; De Young Art Mus, San Francisco, 69 & 70-71; San Bernardino Art Mus, Calif, 79 & 81-83; many other group and solo shows. *Teaching:* Pvt 54-, painting workshops, Colo, 71-80. *Awards:* Special Award, San Bernadino Mus, 78. *Bibliog:* Articles in Southwest Art Mag, 11/77; article, US Art Mag, 11/88. *Mem:* Royal Soc Arts, Great Britain. *Media:* Oil. *Dealer:* Cottage Gallery PO Box 335 Carmel CA 93921; Dassin Gallery 8687 Melrose Los Angeles CA 90069. *Mailing Add:* 4000 Rio Rd No 39 Carmel CA 93923

WINSOR, JACKIE
SCULPTOR
b St John's, Nfld, Oct 20, 41; US citizen. *Study:* Yale Summer Sch Art & Music, 64; Mass Col Art, BFA, 65; Rutgers Univ, MFA, 67; Univ Nfld, LHD, 94. *Work:* Mus Mod Art, NY; Whitney Mus Am Art, NY; Australia Nat Gallery, Canberra; Detroit Inst Arts, Mich; Mus d'Arte Mod, Paris, France; Tehran Mus Contemp Art, Iran; Albright-Knox Art Gallery, Buffalo. *Exhib:* Whitney Mus Am Art, NY, 70, 73, 74, 77, 78, 79, 82, 83, 84, 85, 88, 89 & 94; Aldrich Mus Contemp Art, Ridgefield, Conn, 71, 79, 82, 88 & 94; Mus Mod Art, NY, 73, 74, 79, 84, & 86; 8th Biennial of Paris, Mus Mod Art, Paris, 73; solo exhibs, Paula Cooper Gallery, NY, 73, 76, 82, 83, 86, 89, 92 & 95, Mus Mod Art, NY, traveling, 79, Va Mus, Richmond, 81, Margarete Roeder Fine Arts, NY, 85, Margo Leavin Gallery, Los Angeles, Calif, 87, Ctr d'Art du Domaine de Kerguehennec Bignan, Locmine, France, 88 & Milwaukee Art Mus, Wis, traveling, 91-92; 71st Am Exhib, Art Inst Chicago, Ill, 74; Four for the Fourth, Albright-Knox Art Gallery, Buffalo, NY, 76; Art in Our Time: HHK Found, Va Mus, Richmond, 81; Mus Fine Arts, Boston, 85; San Francisco Mus Mod Art, Calif, 85; Transformations in Sculpture, Solomon R Guggenheim Mus, NY, 85; 1988: The World of Art Today, Milwaukee Art Mus, Wis, 88; In Three Dimensions: Women Sculptors of the 90's, Newhouse Ctr Contemp Art, Harbor Cult Ctr, Staten Island, 95; The Material Imaginations, Solomon R Guggenheim Mus, 95; 25 Yrs: An Exhibition of Selected Works, Margo Leavin Gallery, Los Angeles, 95; 15 Degrees from Rutgers, Mason Gross Sch Arts, Rutgers, State Univ NJ, 96; More Than Minimal: Feminism & Abstraction in the 70's, Rose Art Mus, Brandeis Univ, 96; Masters of the Masters, Butler Inst Am Art, NY, 98; Sculpture: Donald Judd, Sherrie Levine, Sol Lewitt, Tony Smith, Jackie Winsor, Paula Cooper Gallery, NY, 98; Crossroad, Groninger Mus, The Neth, 98. *Teaching:* Instr art introd & ceramics, Douglass Col, 67; instr art introd, Middlesex Co Col & Newark State Teachers' Col, 68 & 69; instr ceramics, Mills Col Educ, 68 & 71 & Greenwich House Pottery Sch, NY, 69-72; instr graphics, Loyola Univ, New Orleans, summer 69; instr sculpture, Sch Visual Arts, NY, 71 & 75; instr art introd, Hunter Col, 72-75; lectr, NY Studio Sch Drawing, Painting & Sculpture, fall 87. *Awards:* Nat Endowment Arts Grant, 74, 77 & 84; Guggenheim Fel, 78; Creative Artist Award, Brandeis Univ, 79; and others. *Bibliog:* Robert Pincus-Written (auth), Entries maximalism, Out of London Press, 83; Craig Gholson (auth), Jackie Winsor, Bomb, winter 86; Tobine Siebers (auth), The subject and other subjects: On ethical, aesthetic and political indentity, Univ Mich Press, 98. *Media:* All. *Mailing Add:* c/o Paula Cooper Gallery 534 W 21st St New York NY 10011

WINT, FLORENCE EDYTHE
PRINTMAKER, SCULPTOR
b Newark, NJ, 28. *Study:* NY Univ, BS, 51; Teachers Col, Columbia Univ, MEA, 68; Art Students League, 69-71; Pratt Graphic Ctr, 72-77. *Work:* Exxon NJ, Linden; Johnson & Johnson, New Brunswick, NJ; The Collective Portfolio II, Somerville, NJ; Rabbet Gallery, New Brunswick, NJ; Noyes Mus, Oceanville, NJ. *Exhib:* Flower

Show, Gallery at Squib, Princeton, NJ, 94; one-person show, Fantasy Mania, Woodouts and Sculptures, Kent Place Sch, 2000; Grounds for Sculpture, NAWA, 2001; Northeast Prints, Ben Shahn Gallery, William Patterson Univ, 2002; Women in the New Millenium, Seton Hall Univ, 2003; Point of View, Poukeepsie Art Mus, Bernardsville, NJ, 2004; Pfeiser, Morris Plains, NJ, 2005; Montclair Stat Univ, NJ. *Collection Arranged:* Exxon; Johnson & Johnson; Bristle Meyers; Law Offices of Neal Brickan, NY City. *Teaching:* Teacher ceramic sculpture, Greenwich House Pottery, 79-2003. *Awards:* V Johnson Graphic Prize, NJ Show, Ctr Visual Arts, 87; First Prize, Printmaking Coun, NJ, 91; First Prize, Sculpture's Affiliates Show, 98; Merit Award, Heart of The Artist; Fel, NJ Coun Arts, 2002. *Bibliog:* Gene Kleinsmith (auth), Twenty Americans in Clay, Multi-Visual Sound Prod, 84. *Mem:* Printmaking Coun NJ; Salute to Women in the Arts; Nat Asn Women Artists Inc; Contemp Artists Guild; Sculpture Affil NJ. *Media:* All Media. *Publ:* Illusr, Cowboy Ed, Harper Collins, 93. *Mailing Add:* 93 Hillcrest Rd Maplewood NJ 07040

WINTER, AMY H
DIRECTOR

b Bridgeport, Conn., Oct 13, 48. *Study:* Univ Iowa, BA, 74; Univ Iowa, MA, 78; CUNY, PhD, 95. *Work:* The Godwin-Ternbach Mus, CUNY, Flushing, NY; Broc Art Galley, Northwertern Univ, Evanston, Ill; Whitney Mus of Am Art, NY; The Jewish Mus, NY; Metropolitan Mus Art, NY. *Collection Arranged:* Narrative and Abstraction in 20th Century Photography, Block Art Gallery, Northwestern Univ, 97; Clinton Hill Retrospective, 80-2002, 2003; Ilya Bolotowsky Harmony & Equilibrium, Col of Staten Islany, 2001; Traditional Society-19th Cent Photog, CUNY, 2001; Renaissance to Modern Art, Highlights of the Godwin Ternbach Col, Queens Col, 2002; Ancient to Renaissance Art, Highlights of the Godwin-Ternbach Col, Queens Col, 2002; The Light of Infinate Wisdom: Asian Art from the Godwin-Ternbach Mus and other collections, 2003. *Pos:* dir and cur. *Teaching:* lectr, Parsons Sch of Design, NY, 85-87; Vis Ast Prof, Col New Paltz, CUNY, 89-90; Ast Prof, Col Staten Island, 99-2001. *Awards:* Henry Luce Found Scholar in Am Art 1990-91; Kress Found Rsch Fel, Samuel H Kress Found, 1990-91; Smithsonian Inst Fel, Hirshhorn Mus, 1993-94; Pollock-Krasner Study Ctr Residency, 1994; Camargo Found Residency Fel, 1995. *Bibliog:* Mary Ann Caws (auth) Amy Winter (review), Art Jour, 2003; Wolfgang Paalen (auth), Artist and Theorist of the Avant-Garde, Art Jour, 2003; Terence Diggory (auth), Amy Winter (review), American Book Review, 2003; Wolfgang Paalen Artist and Theorist of the Avant-Garde, Praeger, 02. *Mem:* CAA; AICA; AAM. *Res:* Surrealism; Non-Western Art; History of the Avant Garde. *Publ:* Wolfgang Paalen, DYN and the Origins of Abstract Expressionism, Vienna Mus Mod Art and Museo Carillo Gil, Inst Nac de Bellas Artes, Mexico City, 93-94; Surrealism, Lacan, and the Metaphor of the Headless Women, REAL TEXT, Vienna, 93; The Germanic Reception of Native American Art, European Review of Native American Studies, 92-93; Wolfgang Paalen, Pacific Dreams, UCLA Wight Gallery, 1995; Surrealism Revisited, Art Jour, 97; Sur les Paysages totemiques de Wolfgang Paalen, Melosine, 97; Millard Meiss, Am Nat Biog, 98; Peggy Guggenheims The Women and Women and Abstract Expressionism, Art Jour, 99; L'aventure Mexicain de Wolfgang Paalen, Mulusine, 99. *Mailing Add:* Queens Coll/CUNY Godwin-Ternbach Mus 65-30 Kissena Blvd Flushing NY 11367-1597

WINTER, GERALD GLEN
PAINTER, EDUCATOR

b Milwaukee, Wis, Sept 1, 36. *Study:* Univ Wis-Milwaukee, BFA, Madison, MS & MFA. *Work:* Milwaukee Art Ctr; Lowe Mus, Univ Miami, Coral Gables, Fla; Ringling Mus, Sarasota, Fla; Dade Co Pub Libr, Miami. *Exhib:* 39th, 40th, 43rd, 44th & 53rd Exhib Contemp Am Painting, Palm Beach; one-man shows, Miami-Dade Community Col, 75, Lowe Mus, Univ Miami, 75 & 87 Univ Miami Art Dept Gallery, 79; Metrop Mus & Art Ctr, Coral Gables, Fla, 83; Galerie Helene Grubair, Miami, Fla, 90; Lowe Mus, Univ Miami, 94; Sarasota Biennial 2000, Ringling Mus Art, 2000; Miami Pub Libr, 2006; and others. *Teaching:* Prof art, Univ Miami, 65-99, prof emeritus, 99, chmn dept, 75-79. *Awards:* Ford Found Purchase Award, 62; Third Prize, Corcoran Gallery of Art Biennial, 62; Honorable Mentions, Hortt Mem Exhib, 69, 80 & 81. *Media:* Oil, Beadwork. *Mailing Add:* 6629 SW 62nd Terr Miami FL 33143

WINTER, HOPE MELAMED
COLLECTORS, PATRONS

Study: Univ Wis, Madison, 38-40; Goodman School, Art Inst Chicago, 40-42. *Pos:* Trustee, Milwaukee Art Mus, Wis, 74-83 & 92-; coun, Elvehjem Art Mus, Univ Wis, Madison. *Bibliog:* Cubist Prints in Collection of Dr and Mrs Abraham Melamed, Univ Wis, 72; Selections from Collection of Hope and Abraham Melamed, Milwaukee Art Mus, 83. *Mem:* Art Inst Chicago; Am Asn Mus; Arch Am Art. *Collection:* Principally cubist prints, drawings & paintings; Cubism, primarily French between 1909-1914, including Picasso, Braque, Gleizes, Metzinger, Jacques Villon, Duchamp, Marcoussis, Gris, Severini, Chagall and others. *Mailing Add:* 1107 E Lilac Ln Milwaukee WI 53217

WINTER, ROGER
PAINTER

b Denison, Tex, Aug 17, 34. *Study:* Univ Tex, BFA, 56; Univ Iowa, MFA, 60; Brooklyn Mus Sch, Beckmann scholar, 60. *Work:* Mus Art, Univ Okla, Norman; Southern Methodist Univ & Dallas Mus Fine Arts, Dallas; Longview Mus & Art Ctr, Tex; El Paso Mus Art, Tex; Portland Mus Art, Maine; Dallas Mus Art, Tex; many others. *Comn:* Fed Reserve Bank of Dallas, 83. *Exhib:* Tex Painting & Sculpture, 20th Century Dallas, 71-62; two-man show, Whitte Mus, San Antonio, Tex, 67; one-man shows, Pollock Gallery, 68 & 79, One i at a Time, 71, Southern Methodist Univ, Dallas, Delgado Mus, New Orleans, La, 68 & Fischbach Gallery, NY, 84, 86, 88 & 89, Eugene Binder Gallery, Dallas, Tex, 92, Maine Col Art, Baxter Gallery, Portland, Maine, 96, Maine Coast Artists, Rockport, Maine, 96, Greenville Co Mus Art, SC, 96, El Paso Mus Art, Tex, 96, The McKinney Ave Contemp, Dallas, Tex, 96, Art Gallery, Univ Tex, San Antonio, Tex, 97, Edith Baker Gallery, Dallas, Tex, 98, 2000, Fishbach Gallery, New York City, 98, Artist's Gallery, San Antonio, Tex, 2000; group shows, Behold, Narrative Visions, 55 Mercer Gallery, New York City, 99, Outward Bound, Meridian Corp, Washington, DC, 99, Y2$, fishbach Gallery, NY, 2000, Animals in Art, Bates Mus, Henkley, Maine, 2000, many others. *Pos:* Installation asst, Dallas Mus Contemp Arts, 62-63; gallery tours & lectr, Dallas Mus Fine Arts, 63-76; guest critic, many various orgs, 89-2000. *Teaching:* Instr painting, Ft Worth Art Ctr, 61 & Dallas Mus Fine Arts, 62-68; prof painting, Southern Methodist Univ, 65-89; instr painting, Washington Univ, St Louis, 89, Univ Pa, Philadelphia, 90, Brooklyn Col, NY, 91 & Vermont Studio Ctr, 90 & 92, 95, 2000. *Awards:* Top Award, Dallas Ann, Dallas Mus Fine Arts, 64; Nat Endowment Arts Grant, 88; Painting Fel Award Mid-Am Arts Aliance/NEA, 88. *Bibliog:* Film on work produced on KERA-TV, Dallas, 71; Maine Light: The Ambassador's Residence, US State Dept Santiago, Chile, 99; Outward Bound: American Art at the Brink of the 20th Century (catalogue), Meridian Int Ctr, 99. *Media:* Oil. *Publ:* Auth, Introduction to Drawing, Prentice Hall, 83; On Drawing, Collegiate Books, 91, 2d edition, 97. *Mailing Add:* 35 W 92nd Apt 9D New York NY 10025

WINTER, RUTH
PAINTER

b New York, NY, Jan 17, 13. *Study:* NY Univ, BS, 31, MA, 32; Art Students League, with Corbino, Bosa & Morris Kantor, 57-61. *Work:* In collections of Reginald Cabral, Provincetown, Mass, Marlo Lewis, Scarsdale, Mr Frantz, Great Neck, Lawrence Koenisberg, South Lawrence, & Semour S Alter, West Hempstead, NY. *Exhib:* Silvermine, Conn, 57-61; Nat Asn Women Artists, 57-68 & 74; Gallery 15, NY, 59; Brooklyn Mus, 60; Nat Acad Design, 60; Lever House, NY, 63 & 67; Pepsi Cola Exhib, 64. *Awards:* Marcia Brady Tucker Prize, Nat Asn Women Artists, 57; Max Low Award, 59; Mr & Mrs Gomes Award, Mahopac Art League, 59. *Bibliog:* Robert M Coates (auth), Art galleries, New Yorker, 5/57; Stuart Preston (auth), Art: a game of styles, N Y Times, 5/57; Painting televised, Boston, 7/58. *Mem:* Nat Asn Women Artists; life mem Art Students League New York; Mahopac Art League. *Media:* Oil. *Mailing Add:* 357 Malin Rd Newtown Square PA 19073-4318

WINTERBERGER, SUZANNE
PHOTOGRAPHER, ASSEMBLAGE ARTIST

b Binghamton, NY, June 23, 52. *Study:* Rochester Inst Technol, NY, BFA, 75; Cranbrook Acad Art Bloomfield Hills, Mich, MFA, 78. *Work:* Visual Studies Workshop, Rochester, NY; Franklin Furnace Archives, NY; Cranbrook Acad Art, Bloomfield Hills, Mich; Erie Art Mus, Pa; WGBH-TV, Boston, Mass. *Exhib:* Solo exhibs, Ideas About Life, Color Servs, Santa Barbara, Calif, 81, Maxims, Rutger Gallery, Utica, NY, 82, Aging Barbies, New Art Ctr, Washinton, DC, 87 & Prisoner of the Pedestal, Bayfront Gallery, Erie, Pa, 90; Bookworks Invitational, Erie Art Mus, Erie, Pa, 86; NoNeo, Zoller Gallery Invitational, State Col, Pa, 89; Pennsylvania Photo Educators Invitational, Pittsburgh, Pa, 91; 20 Yrs of Cranbrook Photog, Juried Invitational, Cranbrook Art Mus, Bloomfield Hills, Mich, 92; Everyday Gothic, Sandford Gallery, Clarion, Pa, 94; and others. *Collection Arranged:* Photo Collaborations, Bruce Gallery, Edinboro, Pa, 86; Neighboring Novellas, Sandford Gallery, Clarion, Pa, 94. *Pos:* Collabr, Aunt Marion & Cousin Mimi photog postcards series, Enthusiastic Enterprises, Edinboro, Pa, 82-86, Edinboro Bookarts Collective, 86-. *Teaching:* Asst prof photog, Edinboro Univ, 82-. *Awards:* Nat Endowment Arts Fel, 85; Pa Coun Arts Fel, 86. *Bibliog:* Julie Moran (auth), Women artists on women, Pulse, 10/13/87; Gary Wykoff (auth), Heart of a humanist, Erie, Pa Times-News, 4/90; Richard Briggs (filmmaker), Suzanne Winterberger A Portrait, PBS Documentary, WVIA-TV, Pittston, Pa, 90; PhotoPaper, Blatent Image/Silver Eye Quarterly, Pittsburgh, Pa, 91. *Mem:* Soc Photog Educ. *Publ:* Contribr, In-Sights, Godine, 79; How To Spot a Patriarch, 90; Go Ask Elvis, 91; Fat Girl Meditations, 93. *Mailing Add:* Art Dept Edinboro Univ Edinboro PA 16444

WINTERS, SANDY L
PAINTER

b Arcadia, Calif, Feb 10, 49. *Study:* Univ Kans, Lawrence, 67; Univ NH, Durham, BSc(art educ), 71; Cornell Univ, MFA, 77. *Work:* Prudential Insurance Co Am & Manufacturers Hanover Trust Co, NY; Bank of Boston, Mass; Southeast Banking Corp, Miami, Fla; Arnot Art Mus, Elmira, NY; Metro-Dade Art in Public Places, NY. *Comn:* 50 prints for Graymoore, Comn by Rollins Found Tex, Garrison, NY. *Exhib:* Selections 14, Drawing Ctr, NY, 81 & 82; Everson Mus Art, Syracuse, NY, 82; Soc Four Arts, Palm Beach, Fla, 84; The Art of Miami, Southeastern Ctr Contemp Art, Winston-Salem, NC, 86; Pensacola Mus Art, 88; Jacksonville Mus Art, Fla, 89; Fresh Cuts: Large Scale Installation, George Adams Gallery, NY, 98; Ann Collector's Show, Ark Arts Ctr, Little Rock, 98; Sandy Winters: Recent Works, Frederic Snitzer Gallery, Miami, Fl, 99; Sarasota Biennial 2000, The John and Mable Ringling Mus, 2000; Move, Barbara Gillman Gallery, Miami, Fla, 2002; Collector's Show, Ark Art Ctr, Little Rock, 2003; Under the Influence of, George Adams Gallery, NY, 2004; The Body and Its Dangers, Painting Ctr, NY, 2005. *Teaching:* Asst prof printmaking & drawing, Univ Tulsa, Okla, 78-80; vis asst prof drawing, printmaking & painting, Cornell Univ, Ithaca, NY, 82-86; assoc prof painting & drawing, Fla Int Univ, Miami, 84-97; prof painting, Mus Fine Arts, 97-. *Awards:* Fla State Visual Art Fel; SAF/Nat Endowment Arts Fel; Fac Res Develop Grant, Fla Int Univ, Miami. *Bibliog:* Vivien Raynor (auth), Selections 14, NY Times, 7/17/81; Helen Kohen (auth), Gallery salutes, Miami Herald, 7/5/85; Ronny Cohen (auth), Sandy Winters, (exhib catalog), Frances Wolfson Gallery, 11/86; Stephen Westfall (auth), The Art Mus at Fla Int Univ, Miami. *Mem:* Col Art Asn; Women's Caucus Arts. *Media:* All. *Publ:* Auth, Human Ecology Forum (cover), Vol 9, No 2, Cornell Univ, fall 78; New Directions in American Drawing, Catalog Drawing Ctr, 82; contribr, Art in Bloom, Jacksonville Mus Art Catalog; The Art of Miami, (exhib catalog), Southeastern Ctr Contemp Art, Winston, Salem, 86. *Dealer:* George Adams Gallery 41 W 57th St New York NY 10019

WINTERS, TERRY
PAINTER
b Brooklyn, NY, 49. *Study:* Pratt Inst, Brooklyn, NY, BFA, 71. *Exhib:* Solo shows include Whitney Mus Am Art, NY, 92, Galerie Lawrence Rubin, Zurich, 96, Akira Ikeda Gallery, Tokyo, 97, Galerie Samia Saouma, Paris, 97, Sch Mus Fine Arts, Boston, 97, Matthew Marks Gallery, NY, 97, 99 & 2001, IVAM Ctr Julio Gonzales, Valencia, 98, Detroit Inst of Art, 99, Centre Julio Gonzales, Valencia, 99, Galerie Fred Jahn, Munich, 99 & Lehmann Maupin Gallery, NY, 2001, White Cube 2, London, 2002, Margo Leavin Gallery, Los Angeles, 2002, Mixographia, 2006; groups shows include Thinking Print, Mus Mod Art, NY, 96; Monika Spruth Galerie, Cologne, Ger, 96; Galerie Brigitte Ihsen, Cologne, Ger, 96; The Robert and Jane Meyerhoff Collection, Nat Gallery Art, Washington, DC, 96; Works in Progress: Recent Graphics, Susan Sheehan Gallery, NY, 96; Nuevas Abstracciones, Museo Nacional Centro de Arte Reina Sofia, Madrid, 96; Sonnabend Collection, Deichtorhallen, Hamburg, Ger, 96; Natural Process, Gallery Williams Ctr Arts, Lafayette Col, Easton, Pa & Ctr Gallery, Bucknell Univ, Lewisburg, Pa, 96; (Ap)praising Abstraction, Art Initiatives at Tribeca 148 Gallery, NY, 96; On Paper, Marlborough Chelsea, NY, 96 & icon/iconoclast, 97; Spiders and Webs, Barbara Krakow Gallery, Boston, Mass, 97; New Editions, Pace Prints, NY, 97; The View from Denver: Contemp Am Art from the Denver Art Mus, Mus Mod Kunst Stiftung Ludwig Wien, Vienna, Austria, 97; Views from Abroad: European Perspectives on Am Art3/Am Realities, Whitney Mus Am Art, NY, 97; Proof Positive: ULAE 1957-1997, Corcoran Gallery Art, Washington, DC, 97; 8 Paintings, Luhring Augustine Gallery, NY, 97; Now and Forever: Part I, Matthew Marks Gallery & Pat Hearn Gallery, NY, 98; Printfest Chicago: Contemp Prints at the Drake Hotel, Chicago, Ill, 98; Elements of the Natural: 1950-1992, Mus Mod Art, NY, 98; Am Drawings 1969-1996, Galerie Tony Wuethrich, Basel, 98; Master Drawings of the Twentieth Century, Mitchell-Innes & Nash, NY, 98; Paper plus: Works on Dieu Donne Paper, Gallery at Dieu Donne Papermill, NY, 98; Mukai Gallery, Tokyo, 98; Prints in the 90's from the ULAE, Marlborough Chelsea, NY, 98; Am Acad Invitational Exhib Painting & Sculpture, Am Acad Arts & Letts, NY, 98; Proof Positive: 40 Yrs of Contemp Am Printmaking at ULAE 1957-1997, Sezon Mus Art, Tokyo, 98; Young Americans 2: New Am Art, Saatchi Gallery, London, 98; plus many others. *Awards:* Artists Award, Am Acad Arts & Letts, 98. *Mailing Add:* c/o Matthew Marks Gallery 523 W 24th St New York NY 10011

WINTROB, JAY S
PATRON
Study: Univ Calif, grad (summa cum laude), 1979, JD, 1982. *Pos:* With, O'Melveny & Myers; asst to chmn, AIG Sun Am, 1987, corp vpres, 1987-89, sr vpres, 1989-91, exec vpres, 1991-95, vchmn, 1995-98, pres, 2000-, chief exec officer, 2001-; exec vpres, Am Int Group, 2002-; bd trustees, J Paul Getty Trust, 2004-. *Awards:* Ecumenical Coun Leadership award, Archdiocese Los Angeles, 2001; Luis Lainer Founder's award, Bet Tzedel Legal Servs, 2002. *Mem:* Order of Coif. *Mailing Add:* Am Internat Group 70 Pine St New York NY 10270

WIRSUM, KARL
PAINTER, SCULPTOR
b Chicago, Ill, Sept 27, 39. *Study:* Sch Art Inst, Chicago, BFA, 61. *Work:* AT&T, Chase Manhattan, Citibank & Whitney Mus Am Art, NY; Art Inst Chicago, First Nat Bank, Smart Gallery/Univ Chicago & Mus Contemp Art, Chicago; Nat Mus Am Art, Smithsonian Inst, Washington, DC; Mus des 20, Jahrhunderts, Vienna; Weatherspoon Art Gallery, Univ NC, Greensboro. *Comn:* First Nat Bank, Chicago, Ill; Harold Washington Libr, Chicago, Ill. *Exhib:* Solo exhibs, Hare Toddy Kong Tamari, Mus Contemp Art, Chicago, 81, Southeastern Ctr Contemp Art, Winston-Salem, NC, 82, Du Page Col, Glen Ellyn, Ill, 88, and many others; Made in USA: An Americanization in Mod Art, the 50's & 60's Traveling Show, 87; Friday Diego: Una Pareja, Prairie Ave Gallery, Chicago, 87; Contemp Cutouts: Figurative Sculpture in Two Dimensions, Whitney Mus Am Art, NY, 87-88; Diamonds are Forever: Artists & Writers on Baseball, Traveling Show, 87-90; Seymour Rosofsky & the Chicago Imagist Tradition, Milwaukee Art Mus, Univ Wis, 88; Birthday Cake, Hyde Park Art Ctr, Chicago, 89; Chicago Painters in Print, Landfall Press, 89-90; and many others. *Teaching:* Part-time instr painting & drawing, Sch Art Inst, Chicago, 74-. *Awards:* Logan Medal, Chicago and Vicinity Show, Chicago Art Inst, 69; Nat Endowment Arts Fel, 71, 77 & 83; Ill Arts Coun Fel, 86. *Bibliog:* Comic Iconoclasm, Inst Contemp Arts, London, Eng, 87; A broad brush colors Terra's exhib of Chicago Art, Chicago Tribune, 9/11/87; The Import of Imagism, Dialogue Mag, 5/6/88. *Media:* Acrylic; Wood. *Dealer:* Phyllis Kind Gallery 313 W Superior Chicago IL 60610 & 136 Greene St New York NY 10012. *Mailing Add:* Jean Albano Gallery 215 W Superior St Chicago IL 60610

WIRTZ, STEPHEN CARL
GALLERY DIRECTOR
b Peoria, Ill, Apr 9, 45. *Study:* Occidental Col, 63; Univ Calif, Berkeley, BA, 67; Antioch Col, Ohio, MA, 68. *Specialty:* Contemporary American and European sculpture & photography. *Mailing Add:* c/o Stephen Wirtz Gallery 49 Geary St San Francisco CA 94108

WISDOM, JOYCE
PAINTER
b Los Angeles, Calif, 40. *Study:* Pasadena City Col, 58-59; Univ Calif, Los Angeles, 59-61; Univ Southern Calif, BFA, 62. *Work:* Los Angeles Inst Contemp Art. *Exhib:* solo show, Municipal Art Gallery, 1978 & Barnsdall Art Center Gallery, 1990, Los Angeles, Calif,; Directions, Mt San Antonio Col Art Gallery, Calif, 95; Korean Cult Ctr, Los Angeles, 98; Shock of the New, Gallery 825, Los Angeles, 2000; Los Angeles Nat Juried Art Exhibit, Ruth Bachotner Gallery, 2000; Black & White, BGH Gallery, Los Angeles, Calif, 2003; Group show, I 5 Gallery, Bewery Art colony, Los Angeles, 2006. *Teaching:* Instr drawing & design, Calif State Univ, Northridge, 78-80; instr, Junior Art Ctr, Los Angeles, 78-95; instr, Life drawing & painting, Barnsdall Art Ctr, 81-97; instr, landscape painting, Univ Calif, Los Angeles, 91-97. *Awards:* Silver Mat Award, Oil Pastel Asn, 88; Lucille Julia Award, Oil Pastel Asn, 90; First Prize Juried Exhib, Long Beach Art Asn, 90. *Bibliog:* Louise Lewis (auth), Desert moods & sensuality, Artweek, 6/1/78; Suzanne Muchnic (auth), Wisdom's world in landscape, Los Angeles Times, 6/8/78; S Muchnic (auth), The Galleries, Los Angeles Times, 83. *Mem:* Gallery 825, Los Angeles, Calif. *Media:* Oil, Watercolor. *Collection:* Peter Plagens, NY; Brooke Alderson & Peter Scheldahl. *Mailing Add:* 21144 Hillside Dr W Topanga CA 90290

WISE, GERALD LEE
GRAPHIC ARTIST, PRINTMAKER
b Pittsburgh, Pa, Dec 15, 41. *Study:* Wheaton Col, Ill, BA, 63; Northern Ill Univ, MA(design), 67, MFA(printmaking), 69. *Work:* Mankato State Univ; Ball State Univ; St Lawrence Col. *Exhib:* Drawings USA, Minn Mus Art, 73; Ball State Drawing & Sculpture, 73 & 82; 24th Nat Prints & Drawing Exhib, Okla Art Ctr, 82; Springfield Nat Exhib, Mus Fine Arts, Mass, 82 & 83; West 82--Art and the Law Traveling Exhib, 82 & 83; Tex Fine Arts Nat, Laguna Gloria Mus, Austin, 83; 17th Nat Drawing & Sculpture Exhib, Del Mar Col Gallery, Tex, 83. *Teaching:* Asst prof art, Mankato State Univ, 69-74 & Westfield State Col, 82-; instr, G Walter V Smith Art Mus, Springfield, Mass, 80-82. *Awards:* Purchase Awards, 24th Nat Drawing & Print Exhib, Okla Art Ctr, 82, 63rd & 64th Springfield Nat Exhib, Holyoke Community Savings Bank, Mass, 82 & 83 & Mattoon Art Festival, Bank Boston, 83. *Bibliog:* Robert Girouard (auth), Wiser yet, Mankato Free Press, 4/4/74; Mary Kronholm (auth), Wise makes living an art, Country J, 6/82; Sally Robinson (auth), A profile: Gerald Wise, Westfield Sunday News, 9/82. *Mem:* Col Art Asn; Springfield Artists League. *Media:* Ink, Pen and Brush. *Dealer:* Hill Gallery Worthington MA 01098. *Mailing Add:* Dept Art Westfield State Col Western Ave Westfield MA 01086

WISE, JOSEPH STEPHEN
PAINTER
b Seattle, Wash, 39. *Study:* Purdue Univ, 57-58, Univ Puget Sound, 59-60, San Jose State Univ, Ma, 66; Indiana Univ, BS, 63; San Jose State Univ, MA, 66. *Work:* San Jose Art Mus, Calif; De Saisset Art Mus, Santa Clara, Calif; IBM Corp, Westview Gallery, 87-88, San Jose, Calif. *Comn:* Abstract, Owens/Corning Fiberglass Corp, Sunnyvale, Calif, 70; abstract mural, comn by Mr & Mrs Domingo Escamilla, Milpetas, Calif, 78; five paintings (abstract), Amdahl Corp, Sunnyvale, Calif, 79; abstract, IBM Corp, San Jose, Calif, 82; abstract, San Jose Pub Libr, Calif. *Exhib:* One-man shows, Old Triton Art Mus, San Jose, Calif, 67, Idaho State Col, Moscow, Idaho, 69, Wash State Col, Pullman, 69, Cabrillo Jr Col Art Gallery, Aptos, Calif, 74, Dunn Instruments, San Francisco, Calif, 77; Bingham Gallery, 87 & Toll House, Los Gatos, 92, Ast Gallery Moragn Hill, 2006; 85th Ann Nat Exhib, Mus Art, San Francisco, 67; Discovery Gallery, San Jose, Calif, 77; Agnes Fine Arts Gallery, San Jose, Calif, 80; Greenleaf Gallery, Saratoga, Calif, 81; James Bond Gallery, Los Gatos, 2003-. *Pos:* Judge, Los Gatos Cats Art Exhib, 88; Pulicity dir, Art Mus Los Gatos, 2001-2004. *Teaching:* Instr art, W Valley Jr Col, 64-67 & San Jose Pub Schs, 68-2000. *Awards:* Award for Oil Painting, San Jose Art League, 71; Award for Oil Painting, Los Gatos Art Asn, 94, 96, 99 & 2003; Plein Air painting, Hidden Villa, Los Rltos, Calif, 2005. *Mem:* Nat Educ Asn; Calif Teachers Asn; Life mem West Point Alumni Asn; Calif Art Educ Asn; Los Gatos Art Asn; Valle del Sur PleinAir Painters, Morgan Hill, Calif (pres). *Media:* Oil, Canvas. *Specialty:* Truthfully interpreting the Am landscape. *Interests:* writing; poetry; reading; hiking; golf. *Collection:* Original artwork By Goya, Boucher, Miro, P Jenkins & more. *Dealer:* The Affordable Masterworks Gallery 4383 Glenmont Dr San Jose Calif 95136. *Mailing Add:* 4383 Glenmount Dr San Jose CA 95136

WISE, KELLY
PHOTOGRAPHER, CRITIC
b New Castle, Ind, 1932. *Study:* Purdue Univ, BS, 55; Columbia Univ, MA, 59. *Work:* Int Mus Photog; Nat Portrait Gallery; Mus Fine Arts, Houston; Library of Congress, Washington, DC; Baltimore Art Mus; Biblioteque Nationale, Paris. *Exhib:* Solo exhib, Fogg Art Mus, 73, Addison Gallery Am Art, Andover, Mass, 85, Art Ctr, Delaware Univ, 86, Art Gallery, Con Col, 86, Yuen Lui Gallery, Seattle, 86, Kresge Art Mus, Mich State Univ, 87, Brockton Art Mus, 87; Private Realities, Mus Fine Arts, Boston, 74; Recent Photographs, Il Diaframma, Milan, Italy, 77; Warm Truths & Cool Deceits, Sidney Janis Gallery, NY, 78; Color Photographs, Snite Art Mus, Univ Notre Dame, 81; Still Points, Rose Art Mus, Brandeis Univ, 81; Portraits: Men & Women of Letters, Vision Gallery, Boston, 83; Iisalmon Kamera, Helsinki, Finland, 84; Archive Gallery, NY, 87. *Collection Arranged:* Libr Cong; Bibliotheque Nat, Paris; George Eastman House, Int Mus Photog, Rochester, NY; Mus Fine Arts, Boston; Mus Fine Arts, Houston; Baltimore Art Mus; Polaroid International; Fogg Art Mus. *Pos:* Photog consult, Nat Humanities Fac, Concord, Mass, 70-74 & Polaroid Corp, Cambridge, Mass, 74-77; photog critic, Boston Globe, 82-93; art commentator, Nat Pub Radio 87-89. *Teaching:* Phillips Academy, Andover, Mass, 1966-2000. *Awards:* City Limits Proj Grant, Polaroid Corp, 85-87; Distinguished Alumnus Award, Purdue Univ, 96. *Bibliog:* Max Kozloff (auth), Photography & Fascination, Addison House Publ, 79. *Mem:* Soc Photog Educ; Photog Resource Ctr, Boston. *Publ:* Ed, The Photographers Choice, 75, auth, Still Points, 77 & ed, Lotte Jacobi, 78, Addison House; assoc ed, Views Jour Photog, 80-81; ed, Portrait: Theory, Lustrum Press, 81; ed, Photo Facts and Opinions, Addison Gallery Am Art, 81; ed & auth, Photog, City Limits, 87. *Mailing Add:* 427 B Pond St Jamaica Plain MA 02130

WISE, SUE
PAINTER
b Bronx, NY, Mar 22, 21. *Study:* Univ Colo with Gene Mathews & Frank Sampson; special study with Thomas Currey & William Schimmel. *Work:* Colo Council Arts & Humanities, First Nat Bank, United Bank, Denver, Colo; Nat State Bank, Boulder, Colo; Midland Federal Savings, Longmont, Colo; Coot Lake Interpretive Trail, City Boulder Parks. *Exhib:* Own Your Own Exhib, Denver Art Mus, Colo, 68; Watercolor USA, Springfield Art Mus, Mo, 71; 60th Ann Exhib, Nat Watercolor Soc, Laguna Beach, Calif, 80; Fine Arts Exhib, State Fair, Pueblo, Colo, 81; Rocky Mountain Nat, Foothills Art Ctr, Colo, 81; 114th Ann Exhib, Am Watercolor Soc, Nat Acad Galleries, NY, 81; and others. *Awards:* Bronze Medal of Honor, Am Watercolor Soc, 74; Foothills Art Ctr Award, 78; Mary Pleissner Mem Award, Am Watercolor Soc, 82. *Mem:* Am Watercolor Soc; Nat Watercolor Soc; Dolphin Fel; Muse Gallery, Longmont; Red Canyon Art Company, Lyons, CO. *Media:* Mixed Watermedia, Collage. *Publ:* Auth, The watercolor page, Am Artist Mag, 2/77; contribr, Easy Living Mag, The Webb Co, 78; Creative Seascape Painting, Watson-Guptill; Exploring Painting, Davis Publ Inc; Collage Techniques, Watson Guptill. *Mailing Add:* 2424 9th Ave Apt 2110 Longmont CO 80503

WISE, SUZANNE TANDERUP
ADMINISTRATOR, HISTORIAN
b Great Lakes, Ill, Jan 31, 52. *Study:* Univ Nebr, Lincoln, BA, 74; Univ Kans, MA, 80. *Pos:* Cur, Mary & Leigh Block Gallery, Northwestern Univ, 82-84; educ specialist, Sheldon Art Gallery, Univ Nebr, Lincoln, 84-; visual arts mgr, Nebr Arts Coun, 88-. *Teaching:* Instr art hist, Univ Nebr, 79 82 & 85 & Creighton Univ, 80. *Mem:* Col Art Asn; Am Asn Mus; Midwest Art Hist Soc; Nat Art Educ Asn. *Res:* Nineteenth and twentieth century American painting and photography. *Publ:* Contribr, Jules Breton and the French Rural Tradition, 82 & Joslyn Art Museum Handbook of the Permanent Collection, 83, Joslyn Art Mus; Alice Aycock: The Machine That Makes the World, Nouveau and Deco Art Glass, 85; American Impressionism from the Sheldon Collection, Sheldon Art Gallery, 86. *Mailing Add:* Nebr Arts Coun 3838 Davenport Omaha NE 68131-2329

WISE, TAKOUHY
GALLERY DIRECTOR, ART DEALER
b Teheran, Iran; US citizen. *Study:* Univ Lausanne, Switz, 61-63; Int Ctr Photog, 77-80. *Collection Arranged:* Hollywood Fashion, 83, Nudes by Fashion Photographers, 83, Portraits of Artists, 84, Louise Dahl Wolfe, 84 & Horst: His Work and World, 85, Staley-Wise Gallery, NY. *Pos:* Fashion & photog ed, Seventeen Mag, 67-70; co-dir, Staley-Wise Gallery, New York, currently. *Specialty:* 20th century photography. *Mailing Add:* Staley-Wise Gallery 560 Broadway New York NY 10012

WISNESKI, KURT
PRINTMAKER
Study: Syracuse Univ, NY, MFA, 1974; Univ of Mass, Amhurst, BFA, 1972. *Exhib:* Miami Int Print Biennial Exhib, Metrop Mus, Miami Fla, 1982; Int Exhib of Smaller Prints, Taller Galeria, Barcelona, Spain, 1985-1987; Works on Paper, Fine Arts Acad, Warsaw, Poland, 1988. *Pos:* Printmaking Lab Demonstrator, Univ of Mich, Ann Arbor, 1975-76; printmaking staff asst, Univ of Mass, Amherst, 1976-80. *Teaching:* Vis Lectr, Univ of Mass, Dartmouth, 1980-86; asst prof, Univ of Mass, Dartmouth, 1986-91; prof, Univ of Mass Dartmouth, 1996-. *Awards:* Group Exhib at Art Adv/Boston, 2000; One person Exhib at Brown Univ Art Gallery, 2000; NH Inst of Art Print Exhib, 2001; Photo Into Art, Bridgewater State Univ, 2001; South Coast New Eng Printmaking, Univ of Mass Dartmouth Art Gallery, 2003. *Publ:* Auth: Monotype/Monoprint, Hist and Tecn, Bullbrier Press, Ithaca, NY, 1995. *Mailing Add:* Univ of Mass Dartmouth 285 Old Westport Rd Dartmouth MA 02747-2300

WISNOSKY, JOHN G
PAINTER, EDUCATOR
b Springfield, Ill, Mar 21, 40. *Study:* Yale Univ Summer Sch Art, 61; Univ Ill, Urbana, BFA, 62, MFA, 64. *Work:* Honolulu Acad Arts, Hawaii; Southern Ill Univ, Carbondale; Contemp Arts Ctr, Hawaii, Honolulu; State Hawaii Found Cult & Arts; Mint Mus, Charlotte, NC; Rose Art Mus, Brandeis Univ. *Comn:* Flora Pacifica design, Ethnobotanical Expos, 71 & 82; Inst Astronomy, Mauna Kea, Hawaii, 85; Hilo Hosp, Hawaii, 85; Mandarin Oriental Hotel, 95; Hawaii Conv Ctr, 96; Honolulu Int Airport, 2002; Four Seasons Hotel, Kobe, Japan, Central Aquatic Ctr, 2004. *Exhib:* Presentation Artist Show, Boston Printmakers, Boston Mus Fine Art, 66; Drawings-USA, St Paul Art Ctr, Minn, 67; Am Printmakers Exhib, Otis Art Inst, 68; Pan Pac Exhib, Seoul, S Korea, 85; Cityscape/Landscape, Franz Bader Gallery, Washington, 88; The Contemp Mus at First Hawaiian Ctr, 2000; Univ of HI Faculty, 78-2005. *Teaching:* Instr painting & design, Va Polytech Inst, 64-66; prof & chmn, Univ Hawaii, 66-75; Acting Chmn George Mason Univ, 87-88; prof & grad chmn, Univ of Hawaii, 90-92, chmn, 98-2004, chmn, art dept. *Awards:* Henry B Shope Prize, Soc Am Graphic Artists, 65; Purchase Award, Honolulu Acad Arts, 70. *Bibliog:* Neogy & Turnbull (ed), Artists of Hawaii, Vol II; G & W Radford (auth), Sculpture in the Sun, 78, visions. *Mem:* Fel, Hand Hollow Found, 83. *Media:* Acrylic, Watercolor. *Res:* Large scale Acrylic painting for pub places. *Specialty:* Mixed media, contemp. *Dealer:* Fine Arts Assocs Honolulu HI. *Mailing Add:* Univ Hawaii Manoa 2535 McCarthy Mall Honolulu HI 96816

WISSEMANN-WIDRIG, NANCY
PAINTER
b Jamestown, NY. *Study:* Syracuse Univ, NY, BFA; Ohio Univ, Athens, MFA. *Work:* Canton Art Inst, Ohio; Univ Kans Mus Fine Arts; Port Authority of NY; Univ Tulsa, Okla; Farnsworth Mus Art, Rockland, Maine; American Telephone & Telegraph Co; Amerada Hess Corp; Bank of Boston, MA; CondeNast Publications; DeLoitte and Touche; ICI Americas; Mony Corp, NY; Port Authority, NY. *Exhib:* Farnsworth Art Mus, Maine, 96; Flowers, Heckscher Mus, Huntington, NY, 96; solo show, Gleason Fine Arts, Boothbay Harbor, Maine, 96; Roundtop Ctr Arts, Damariscotta, Maine, 96; G Watson Gallery, Stonington, Maine; New O'Farrell Gallery, Brunswick, Maine, 2001; Caldbeck Gallery, Rockland, Maine, 2003; Whitney Artworks, Portland, ME, 2004; Water Paintings, Caldbeck Gallery, Rockland, ME, 2005; The Sea Garden, Gallery North,Satauleet, NY, 2006. *Teaching:* Oysterponds Sch, 69-85 & Laurel Sch, 77-85. *Awards:* Outstanding Realist, Western New York Artists, Albright-Knox Art Gallery, 64; Purchase Award, Am Acad of Arts & Lett, Childe Hassam Fund, 69. *Bibliog:* Carl Little & Arnold Skolnick (coauths), Painting of Maine, Potter, 91; Bernice Steinbaum (auth), The Rocking Chair, Rizzoli, 92; Theodore Wolfe (auth), On The Edge 40 Years of Maine Painting, 92; C. Little & A. Akolnick (coauths), The Art of Maine in Winter; Stephen May (auth), Painting the Sea, Maine's Moving Target, Portland Magazine; Philip Isaacson (auth), Visit to the Peaks, Three Artists Currently Residing There, Maine Sunday Telegram, 2001; Liz Wood (auth), A Moveable Feast, Liz Wood, The Suffolk Times. *Mem:* E End Arts & Humanities Long Island. *Media:* Acrylic, Oil. *Dealer:* Calbeck Gallery 12 Elm St Rockland ME. *Mailing Add:* 87 Bird Pt Rd Cushing ME 04563-9508

WITHAM, VERNON CLINT
PAINTER, PRINTMAKER
b Eugene, Ore, Dec 6, 25. *Study:* Univ Ore; Calif Sch Fine Arts, San Francisco. *Work:* Univ Ore Mus Art, Eugene; Univ Wyo Mus Art, Laramie. *Comn:* Murals, Multnoma Athletic Club, Portland, Ore. *Exhib:* Under 25, Seligmann Gallery, NY, 49; Artists of Oregon, Portland Art Mus, 53; one-man shows, Calif Palace Legion of Honor, San Francisco, 60 & Univ Ore Mus Art, 80; Maxwell Gallery, San Francisco, 61; Am Landscape, Peridot Gallery, NY, 68. *Teaching:* Resident artist, Univ Wyo, 71-. *Awards:* Purchase Award, Northwest Painting Ann, 72. *Media:* Oil; All. *Collection:* Antique primitive art from around the world. *Publ:* Coauth, 12 new painters (serigraph folio), 53; contribr, insert 4, Written Palette, 62. *Dealer:* Tiqua Gallery 812 Canyon Rd Santa Fe NM 87501. *Mailing Add:* 901 Paseo de la Cuma Santa Fe NM 87501

WITHERS, JOSEPHINE
HISTORIAN, WRITER
b Cambridge, Mass, July 3, 38. *Study:* Oberlin Col, BA(art hist), 60; Columbia Univ, MA, 65, PhD, 71. *Collection Arranged:* Julio Gonzalez, Sculpture and Drawings, Mus Mod Art, New York, 68; 350 Years of Art in Maryland, 20th Century Section (auth, catalog), Univ Md Art; Women Artists in Washington Collections (auth, catalog), Univ Md Art Gallery, 79. *Pos:* Assoc dir, Univ Md Art Gallery, 70-73; chief reader art hist, Advan Placement Educ Testing Serv, 79-83; art consult, Feminist Studies, 78-. *Teaching:* Asst prof art hist, Temple Univ, Philadelphia, Pa, 68-69; assoc dir, Art Gallery, Univ Md, 70-73, asst prof art hist, 71-78, actg dir women's studies prog, 82-84, assoc prof art hist, 78-. *Awards:* Aelioian Fel, Oberlin Col, 64; Gen Res Bd, Univ Md, 72, 77 & 85; fel, Nat Endowment Arts, 72 & 78. *Mem:* Col Art Asn; Women's Caucus Art (nat bd dir, 80-83); Washington Women's Art Ctr (bd dir, 76-77); Conf of Women in the Visual Arts (steering comt, 72); Wash New Art Asn (bd mem, 87-91). *Res:* Twentieth century art; American women artists of the nineteenth and twentieth centuries. *Publ:* Auth, Artistic women and women artists, summer 76 & The artistic collaboration of Picasso and Gonzales, winter 76, Art J; auth, The Famous Fur-Lined Teacup and The Anonymous Meret Oppenheim, Arts Mag, 11/77; Julio Gonzalez, Sculpture in Iron, New York Univ Press, 77; In search of the magic kingdom, New Art Examiner, 10/81; Musing about the muse, Feminist Studies, spring 83. *Mailing Add:* Art History Dept-Art/Sociology Bldg Univ Maryland Rm 4212 College Park MD 20742

WITHROW, WILLIAM J
ADMINISTRATOR
b Toronto, Ont, Sept 30, 26. *Study:* Univ Toronto, BA, 50, BEd, 55 & MEd, 58, MA, 60. *Pos:* Dir, Art Gallery Ont, Toronto, 60-91, emer dir, currently. *Teaching:* Head art dept, Earl Haig Col, 51-59. *Awards:* Can Centennial Medal, 67; Order Can. *Mem:* Fel Can Mus Asn; Asn Art Mus Dirs; Can Art Mus Dirs Orgn; fel Ont Col Art. *Publ:* Auth, Sorel Etrog sculpture, 67 & Contemporary Canadian painting, 72. *Mailing Add:* 7 Malabar Pl Don Mills ON M3B 1A4 Canada

WITKIN, JEROME
PAINTER, DRAFTSMAN
b Brooklyn, NY, Sept 13, 39. *Study:* Cooper Union Art Sch, 57-60; Skowhegan Sch Painting & Sculpture; Berlin Acad, WGer, Pulitzer traveling fel, 60; Univ Pa, MFA, 70. *Work:* Hirshhorn Mus; Uffizi Gallery, Florence, Italy; Butler Inst Am Art, Youngstown, Ohio; Am Acad Arts & Letters; Everson Mus Art, Syracuse; Nat Acad Design; Metrop Mus Art, NY; Minn Mus, St Paul, Minn; Nat Acad Design, NY; Ark Art Ctr, Little Rock, Ark; Achenback Found Graphic Arts, San Francisco, Calif; numerous others. *Comn:* Portraits, Flower Veterinary Library, NY State Col Veterinary Medicine. *Exhib:* Drawings USA, Minn Mus Art, 71; Sherry French Gallery, NY; Drawings, Kraushaar Gallery, NY, 71; Pa State Mus, 78; Religion into Art, nat traveling exhib, 81; Real, Really Real, Super Real, San Antonio Mus, 81-82; traveling show, West '85 Art & the Law; Morality Tales: Hist Painting in the 80's, Independent Curators Inc, NY, 87-88; Noctures & Nightmares, Fla State Univ Gallery & Mus, 87; Life Stories, Henry Art Gallery, Univ Wash, Seattle, 88. *Teaching:* Instr drawing, Md Inst Art, Baltimore, 63-65; lectr painting, Manchester Col Art, Eng, 65-67; vis prof design, drawing & painting, Moore Col, 68-71; assoc prof art, Syracuse Univ, 71-81, prof, 82-; lectr, Columbia Mus Art, SC, 83, Ark Art Ctr, Little Rock, 83; vis artist, Univ Utah, 86, Univ Wis, 88 & Univ Wash, 88. *Awards:* Guggenheim Found Fel Painting, 63-64; Paul Puzinas Award, Nat Acad Design, 80; Fund Purchase Prize, Am Acad Arts & Letters, 81; Chancellor's Citation for Excellence in Teaching, Syracuse Univ, 83. *Bibliog:* Theodore F Wolff (auth), The excellence of the work of Jerome

Witkin, 4/28/83 & A master storyteller on the threshold of great art, 11/6/85, Christian Sci Monitor; Kenneth Baker (auth), Paintings not to miss: Jerome Witkin in Santa Clara, San Francisco Chronicle, 87; W S Di Piero (auth), Force & witness: on Jerome Witkin, Arts Mag, 11/87. *Mem:* Nat Acad Design; Nat Acad (assoc, 83, acad, 90-). *Media:* Oil on Linen. *Publ:* Life Lessons: The Art of Jerome Witkin, SU Press, 94. *Dealer:* Jack Rutberg Fine Arts, 357 N La Brea Ave, Los Angeles, Calif. *Mailing Add:* 201 Whitestone Dr Syracuse NY 13215

WITKIN, JOEL-PETER
PHOTOGRAPHER
b Brooklyn, NY, Sept 13, 39. *Study:* Cooper Union, New York, BFA, 75; Univ NMex, MA, 77, MFA, 86. *Work:* Metrop Mus Art & Mus Mod Art, NY; Nat Gallery Art & Nat Mus Am Art, Smithsonian Inst, Washington; San Francisco Mus Mod Art, Calif; Boston Mus Fine Arts, Mass; Victoria & Albert Mus, London, Eng; Walker Art Ctr, Minneapolis, Minn. *Exhib:* Great Photographs from the Museum Collection, 59 & Paintings from City Walls, 69, Mus Mod Art, NY; Contemp Photogrs of NMex, Art Inst Chicago, Ill, 80; Form, Freud & Feeling, 82, Biennial Exhib, 84 & Signs of the Times (with catalog), 86, San Francisco Mus Mod Art, Calif; Mois de la Photo, Mus Mod Art, Paris, France, 82; Personal Choice, Victoria & Albert Mus, London, Eng, 83; Whitney Biennial, 85 & Sacred Images in Secular Art, 86, Whitney Mus Am Art, NY; solo exhibs, Forty Photographs (with catalog), San Francisco Mus Mod Art, traveling, 85, Brooklyn Mus Art, NY, 86, Pace/MacGill Gallery, NY, 87, 89, 91, 93 & 95, Fraenkel Gallery, San Francisco, 91, 93 & 95, Mus de Cahors, France, 93, Galerie Mokka, Rayjkavik, Ireland, 94, Solomon Guggenheim Mus, 95 & Castello Di Rivoli, Mus d'Arte Contemp, Torino, Italy, 95, Mus of Fine Arts, Mus of NM, 98; Crosscurrents, Forty Yrs of Photog Art (with catalog), Los Angeles Co Mus Art, Calif, 87; The Photog of Invention, Nat Mus Am Art, Washington, 89; Ojects O Trouves d'Artiste, Galerie Urbi et Orbi, Paris, France, 92; Magicians of Light, Nat Gallery Can, 93; Mexico Through Foreign Eyes, Mus Art Contemp, Mexico City, 93; Photo Dessin/Dessin Photo, Espace Van Gogh, Arles, France, 94; Still Pictures/Still Life, Univ RI, 94; Interkamera Photo Festival, Prague, 95; The Mythic Image, David Adamson Gallery, Washington, 97; Presence of Greek Myth, Univ di Palermo, Sicily, 98; and many others. *Awards:* Nat Endowment Arts Fel Photog, 80, 81, 86 & 92; Int Ctr Photog Award in Art Photog, 88; Cooper Union Distinguished Alumni Citation, 88; Decorated Chevalier Des Arts et de Lettres, France, 90; Augustus Saint Gaudens Medal, Cooper Union Sch Art, 96. *Bibliog:* Hofman (auth), Physical prodigies of all kinds, The Times Literary Supplement, London, 3/1/96; William Messer (auth), A tale of two festivals, World Art, 97; Hubert Filser (auth), Spiel mit der asthetik des schrecklichen, Munchner Kultur, 6/97. *Media:* Photography. *Publ:* Auth, Forty Photographs, San Francisco Mus Mod Art, 85; Photovision, Madrid, Spain, 88; Gods of Earth & Heaven, Twelvetrees Press, 91; Joel-Peter Witkin, Twelve Photographs in Gravure, Kevin Begos, 94; ed, Harms Way, Twelvetrees Press, Santa Fe, NMex, 94. *Mailing Add:* c/o Pace MacGill 32 E 57th St New York NY 10022

WITMEYER, STANLEY HERBERT
PAINTER, CONSULTANT
b Palmyra, Pa, Feb 14, 1913. *Study:* Sch Art & Design, Rochester Inst Technol, dipl; State Univ NY Col Buffalo, BS; Syracuse Univ, MFA; Univ Hawaii, with Ben Norris. *Exhib:* Rochester Mem Art Gallery; Albright-Knox Gallery, Buffalo; Honolulu Acad Fine Arts; Everson Mus, Syracuse. *Pos:* Dir sch art & design, Rochester Inst Technol, 52-68, assoc dean Col Fine & Appl Arts, 68-82. *Teaching:* Instr art, Cuba Pub Schs, NY, 39-44; prof painting & design, Sch Art Design, Rochester Inst Technol, 46-52. *Awards:* Distinguished Alumni Award, Rochester Inst Technol, 72; Distinguished State Art Teachers Award, NY, 78; Distinguished Alumni Award, State Univ NY, Buffalo, 80. *Mem:* Rochester Torch Club (pres, 52); Nat Art Educ Asn; Rochester Art Club (pres, 56); NY State Art Teachers Asn. *Media:* Mixed. *Collection:* American printmakers and painters. *Publ:* Auth, articles in, Everyday Art, Design Mag, Sch Arts, Nat Art Educ J & NY Art Teachers Bulletin. *Mailing Add:* 1570 East Ave Apt 102 Rochester NY 14610-1635

WITOLD , KACZANOWSKI
PAINTER, SCULPTOR
b Warsaw, Poland, May 15, 32; US citizen. *Study:* Acad Fine Arts, Warsaw, with W Fangor & H Tomaszerski, dipl, 56. *Work:* Mus NMex, Santa Fe; Phoenix Art Mus, Ariz; Nat Libr, Paris, France; Conoco Oil Co, Houston, Tex; United Calif Bank. *Comn:* Mural, Polish Exhib, Moscow, USSR, 60; Auschwitz (mural), Govt Poland, 61; painting, United Bank Calif, Beverly Hills, 71; painting, Conoco Oil Co, Houston, Tex, 74; mural, Mainstreet Art Festival, Houston, 75. *Exhib:* Solo exhibs, Keystone Ctr, Colo, 77, Anneke Whatley Gallery, Keystone, Colo, 78, Gallery 400, Aspen, Colo, 79, J Houston Gallery, Vail, Colo, 81 & Richtofen Castle, Denver, 81; Gallery Arte, Denver, Colo, 86; Classic Century Sq Gallery, NMex, 87. *Teaching:* Lectr, Seton Hall Univ, 71, Cranbrook Acad Art, 78, Univ Detroit, 78, Wedgewood Soc, Chicago, 79 & Alliance Francaise Soc, Calif, 87. *Bibliog:* Michel Casse (ed), Le Crevasses du Ciel, Paris, 67. *Media:* Oil, Acrylic; Metal. *Mailing Add:* 329 Detroit St Denver CO 80206

WITT, DAVID L
WRITER, CURATOR
b Kansas City, Mo, Nov 3, 51. *Study:* Kans State Univ, BS, 74; Univ Okla, MA, 2000. *Collection Arranged:* Emil Bisttram, 83; True Fresco: The Artistic Descendants of Diego Rivers, 86; Larry Calcagno, 87; Joe Waldrum, 88; Earl Stroh, Paintings 1953-1990, 90-91; Ken Price, Ceramic Sculpture and Drawings, 94; Agnes Martin, Recent Paintings, 94; Linda Benglis, Ceramic Sculpture, 94; Patroriño Barela, 96; Michio Takayama, 99; Three Taos Puelbo Painters, 2003; and numerous others. *Pos:* Curatorial asst, Seton Mus, Cimarron, NMex, 72-74; cur, Gaspard House Mus, Taos, NMex, 78-79; cur, Harwood Found Mus, Taos, NMex, 79-2005. *Awards:* SW Bk Award, Border Reg Libr Asn, 93, 98 & 2003; Ralph Emerson Twitchell Award, Hist Soc NMex, 2003. *Mem:* NMex Asn Mus (pres, 86-88); NMex Art Hist Conf (founder, 86). *Res:* Specializes in the artists and art history of twentieth century New Mexico; contemporary art. *Publ:* auth, The Taos Artists - A Historical Narrative and Biographical Dictionary, Ewell Publ, 84; contribr, The Transcendental Art of Emil Bisttram, Pintores Press, 88; Taos Moderns: Art of the New, Red Crane Bks, 92; The Harwood Foundation of the University of New Mexico, Taos 1923-1993, History and Collection, Harwood Found, 93; co-auth, Spirit Ascendant, The Art and Life of Patrocino Barela, Red Crane Books, 96; publ & contribr, New Mexico Art History Conference Abstracts, SWAHC, 96; contribr, Taos Artists and their Patrons, UNM Press, 99, The New Mexico Millennium Collection, NMMC, Ltd. *Mailing Add:* PO Box 317 Taos NM 87571

WITT, JOHN
PAINTER, PRINTMAKER
b Wilmington, Del, Jan 30, 40. *Study:* Philadelphia Col Art, BFA, 62; Univ Md Grad Sch; Brooklyn Mus Sch Art. *Work:* New Britain Mus Am Art; Smithsonian Inst, USMC Combat Art Collections, US Navy Combat Art Collection, Pentagon & US Army, Off Chief Mil Hist, Washington, DC; USAF Art Program. *Comn:* Oil Painting, Ida Lewis Rescue 1869, US Coast Guard 200th Anniversary Moments in History Collection; oil painting, CMSGT Etchberger, Air Force Cross, A1C Pitsenbarger; Medal of Honor, USAF Heritage Hall, 2000; Ssgt Henry Erwin Medal of Honor; USAF Res Libr, Ala, 03; USAF Documentation of "Enduring Freedom" Pacific Theater, 01; Iraqi Freedom, 2003; Tsunami Relief, 2005. *Exhib:* Smithsonian Inst Vietnam Exhib, Wash, DC, 69; Nat Arts Club, NY, 72; Hudson Valley Art Asn Ann, White Plains, NY, 72; Audubon Artists Ann, NY, 73; Am Artists Prof League Ann, NY, 73; Iraq War, 2003; Tsunami Relief, 2005. *Pos:* Combat artist, USMC Civilian Comn, 68 & 69; combat artist, US Navy, 73 & 76; courtroom trial artist, ABC News, 74; chmn, Soc Illusrs Mus Am Illus, 88-. *Teaching:* Instr illus, State Univ NY, 84-. *Awards:* Gold Medal, Hudson Valley Art Asn, 72; Best in Show, Nat Arts Club, New York, 72; Gold Medal, Louis E Seley NACAL Award, 78; Dean Cornwell Award, Soc of Illustr, 90. *Bibliog:* US Army, Executive Corridor Section of the Army, USGPO, 66; Mark Goodman (auth), Trial of art, New Times Mag, 5/17/74; Col Raymond Henri (auth), Combat art since 1775, Marine Corps Gazette, 74; US Coast Guard Moments in History, 90. *Mem:* Soc Illusr (pres, 80-83). *Media:* Multimedia. *Publ:* Auth & illusr, Vietnam, Sterling, 72; illusr, Mitchell-Stans Trial, Newsweek Mag, & Mitchell-Stans Trial Courtroom Drawings, ABC News, 74; illusr, Marine Corps Gazette, 74; illusr, Portraits of Valor, USMC, 74. *Mailing Add:* 1450 Baptist Church Rd Yorktown Heights NY 10598

WITT, NANCY CAMDEN
PAINTER, SCULPTOR
b Richmond, Va, Oct 24, 30. *Study:* Randolph-Macon Woman's Col; Old Dominion Univ, BA, 65; Va Commonwealth Univ, MFA, 67. *Work:* Miss Mus Art; Mint Mus Art, Charlotte, NC; Randolph-Macon Woman's Col, Lynchburg; Chase Manhattan Bank, NY; Chrysler Mus, Norfolk, Va; CSX Corp, Richmond, Va; and others. *Comn:* Mobile construct, Philip Morris Tobacco Co, Richmond, 69-70; mural, Security Fed Savings & Loan Co, Richmond, 71; portrait, Randolph-Macon Col, Ashland, Va, 79; portrait, Richmond Symphony, 79; portrait, Crowder United, 81; and others. *Exhib:* Mint Mus Art, 71, 75, 77 & 79; Mainstreams, Marietta, Ohio, 75-77; Int Woman Artists Exhib, 76; Realist Invitational, Southeastern Ctr for Contemp Art, Winston-Salem NC, 78 & 80; retrospective, Roanoke Col, Salem, Va, 79; Miss Mus Art, 79; Va Mus, Richmond, 79-80; solo exhib, Southeastern Ctr Contemp Art, Winston-Salem, NC, 80; Portsmouth Mus, Va, 85; Touchstone Gallery, NY, 86; Cudahy's, Richmond & NY, 90; and others. *Teaching:* Actg chmn dept art, Richard Bland Col, Col William & Mary, 61-63 & 64-65. *Awards:* Purchase Prize, Exec Towers Sculpture, Va Comn on Arts & Humanities, 75; Award, Int Woman Artists Exhib, 76; Purchase Prize, Henrico Libr, Richmond, Va, 80. *Bibliog:* Subject of Vanishing Point (film), 78. *Media:* Oil; Constructions

WITTE, JUSTIN
PAINTER
Study: Student, Lacoste Sch Fine Art, France, 97; Student, NY Studio Prog 98; Milwaukee Inst Art and Design, BA, 99. *Work:* Contemp Mus, Baltimore, 2000. *Exhib:* Solo exhibs, Ontploffing, Vox Populi, Philadelphia, 2002, Lurk, 2004, work has also been exhib at, NY Studio Prog, 1998, Vox Populi, 2001, 2002, Nexus Found for Today's Art, Philadelphia, 2003, Abington Art Ctr, Jenkintown, Pa, 2003, Space 1026, Philadelphia, 2003, Basekamp, Philadelphia, 2004, Cheltenham Ctr for the Arts, Beaver Col Art Gallery, Artists Space, New York City. *Awards:* Pew Fel in the Arts, 2004; Independence Found Fel in the Arts, 2004

WIXOM, WILLIAM D
CURATOR, ART HISTORIAN
b Philadelphia, Pa, July 17, 29. *Study:* Haverford Col, BA, 51; NY Univ Inst Fine Arts, MA, 63. *Collection Arranged:* Treasures from Medieval France (auth, catalog), loan exhib, 66-67, Early Christian, Byzantine, Medieval & Renaissance Galleries Permanent Collection, 73-77 & Renaissance Bronzes from Ohio Collections (auth, catalog), loan exhib, 75, Cleveland Mus Art; The Glory of Byzantium, Metrop Mus Art, New York, 97. *Pos:* From asst cur to cur, Medieval & Renaissance Decorative Arts, Cleveland Mus Art, 58-78, chief cur, Early Western Art, 79; chmn, Dept Medieval Art & The Cloisters, Metrop Mus Art, New York, 79-98 & cur, 98-. *Teaching:* Instr, Barnes Found, Merion, Pa, 51-52 & Grad Sem Medieval Art, Case Western Reserve Univ, Cleveland, Ohio, 64-74, adj assoc prof, 67-78, adj prof, 78-79; adj prof fine arts, New York Univ, 81-82; The Glory of Byzantium, Metrop Mus Art, New York, 97. *Awards:* Belg-Am Educ Found fel, 62; Nat Endowment Arts Mus Prof Fel Grant, 73; J Paul Getty Mus, Guest Scholar, 96. *Mem:* Col Art Asn (bd dir, 79-82); Int Ctr Medieval Art (pres, 71-74, bd mem, 71-82); Medieval Acad Am; Fel Pierpoint

Morgan Libr, NY; Fel Soc Antiquaries, London; Snite Art Gallery, Notre Dame Univ (adv coun). *Res:* Early Christian, Byzantine, medieval and renaissance art. *Publ:* Auth, 45 articles in African Arts, Art Quart, Art Bull, Bull of Detroit Inst Arts, Burlington Mag, Cleveland Mus Art Bull, Gesta, Metropolitan Mus Art Bull, Zeitschrift für Kunstgeschichte, 59-88; contribr, Age of Spirituality, Year 1200 II, Metrop Mus Art Notable Acquisitions and Recent Acquisitions & Radiance and Reflection, Abbot Suger and Saint-Denis, A Symposium, 86, Homageá Hubert Landais, Festschrift Gerhard Bott, Festschrift Gerhand Schmidt, 70-94; contribr exhib catalogs, sculpture from Notre Dame, Paris, 79, Royal Abbey of Saint-Denis, 81, The Treasury of San Marco, 85, Gothic and Renaissance Art, Nuremburg, 86, Enamels of Limoges, 96. *Mailing Add:* Metrop Mus Art Fifth Ave at 82nd St New York NY 10028

WIZON, TOD
PAINTER
b Newark, NJ, June 1, 52. *Study:* Sch Visual Arts, New York, BFA, 74-76. *Work:* Metrop Mus Art, NY; Mus Contemp Art, Los Angeles; Minneapolis Mus Art. *Exhib:* one-man exhibs, PPOW Gallery,NY & Willard Gallery, NY, 84, Phyllis Kind Gallery, Chicago, 85 & Annina Nosei Gallery, NY, 87; A Contemp View of Nature, Aldrich Mus Contemp Art, 86 & State of the Artists, 87; Bischofberger, Switz, 91 & 96; Galeria Ramis Barquet, Mex, 93; Galerie Daniel Templon, Paris, 94; Earl McGrath Gallery, NY, 95; Briggs Robinson, NY City, 2004. *Bibliog:* Michael Krugman (auth), Tod Wizon at Willard, Art in Am, 3/81; Ronnie Cohen (auth), article, Art News, 9/84; Laura DeCoppet &Alan Jones (auths), The Art Dealers, Clarkson Potter, New York, 84; Theodore Wolff (auth), Many masks of modern art, Christian Sci Monitor, 11/84. *Media:* Acrylic, All. *Publ:* Contribr, Appearance Mag, 77. *Dealer:* Briggs Robinson New York City; Luca Marenzi London England. *Mailing Add:* 25 Monroe Pl Apt 10F Brooklyn NY 11201

WODICZKO, KRZYSZTOF
EDUCATOR
b Warsaw, Poland, 43. *Study:* Acad Fine Arts, Warsaw, Poland, MFA, 68. *Work:* Personal Instruments, Warsaw, Poland; First Vehicle; Homeless Vehicle; plus more than 70 public projs in Australia, Austria, Can, Eng, Ger, Holland, Ireland, Israel, Italy, Mex, Poland, Spain, Switz, United States & Poland, 81-92. *Exhib:* Life-Size, A Sense of the Real in Recent Art, Israel Mus, Jerusalem, 90; The Projected Image, Mus Mod Art, San Francisco, 91; Pour la suite du Monde, Mus d'Art Contemporain, Montreal, 92; In and Out of Place: Contemp Art and the Am Social Landscape, Mus Fine Arts, Boston, 93-94; The Decade Show, Rhetorical Image, New Mus Contemp Art, NY, 93; Europa-Europa, Kunstmuseum, Bonn, 94; Contemp Canadian Art: Beyond (National) Identities, Setagaya Mus Art, Tokyo, 95; Retrospective, De Appel Found, Amsterdam, 95 & Centrum Sztuki, Warsaw, 95; Horizons, 14 Polish Artists, Sonje Mus Contemp Art, Seoul, Korea, 96; NowHere, Walking and Thinking, La Mus, Denmark, 96; Project for Survival, Nat Mus Mod Art, Kyoto, Japan, 96; Face a l'histoire, Ctr Georges Pompidou, Paris, France, 96-97; plus many others. *Pos:* Dir, Ctr Advan Visual Studies, Mass Inst Technol, 94-96 & Interrogative Design Work Group, 94-; dir, Ctr Advanced Visual Studies (CAVS), 1994-1996, 2003-. *Teaching:* Adj prof, Warsaw Polytech Inst, 70-75 & Indus Design, Ont Col Art, 79; vis prof, Nova Scotia Col Art & Design, 77-79 & Calif Inst Arts, 88; asst prof, Nova Scotia Col Art & Design, 80-81, Univ Hartford, 88-89 & Calif Inst Technol, 91; guest prof sculpture, Cooper Union Sch Art, 87 & 89; prof, Ecole Nat Sup rieure des Beaux Arts, 91-95; prof visual arts Mass Inst Tech, 97-. *Awards:* Recipient Hiroshima Art Prize, 1998; Kepes Art Prize, Coun for Arts, Mass Inst of Technol, 2004; Artist Award for Distinguished Body of Work, Col Art Asn, 2004. *Publ:* Auth, Art Public, Art Critique: The Collected Writings of Krzysztof Wodiczko, Ecole Nat Superieure des Beaux Arts, 95; Assemblage, Ctr Advan Visual Studies, Mass Inst Technol, No 23, 95. *Mailing Add:* Mass Inst of Technol Ctr Advanced Visual Studies 265 Massachussetts Ave N51-315H Cambridge MA 02139

WOFFORD, PHILIP
PAINTER, WRITER
b Van Buren, Ark, Aug 14, 35. *Study:* Univ Ark, BA, 57; Univ Calif, Berkeley, 57-58. *Work:* Whitney Mus Am Art, Brooklyn Mus, NY; Corcoran Gallery Art, Washington; Mus Art, RI Sch Design, Providence; Aldrich Mus Contemp Art, Conn; Seattle Mus Art, Wash; Brooklyn Mus, NY; and others. *Exhib:* San Francisco Mus Mod Art, 58; Oakland Mus, 58; Contemp Arts Mus, Houston, 65; Whitney Mus Am Art Biennials, 69, 71 & 73 (with catalog); Fogg Art Mus, Harvard Univ, Cambridge, Mass, 71; Whitney Mus Am Art, 71 (with catalog) & 72 (with catalog); solo exhibs, Corcoran Gallery Art, 72, Frumkin/Adams Gallery, NY, 88 (with catalog), 89, 90, 91, 92, & 94, Arthur Roger Gallery, New Orleans, 89, Howard Yezerski Gallery, Boston, 95 & 97 & George Adams Gallery, NY, 96; Baltimore Mus Art, 72; Corcoran Gallery Art, 73 & 74 (with catalog); Brooklyn Mus, 78; Mus Mod Art, NY, 81; Mint Mus Art, 82; Cranbrook Acad Art Mus, 86-87 (with catalog); Inst Contemp Art, Boston, 93; NY Painters: Works on Paper, Ctr Gallery, Adelphi, Univ, Garden City, 93; Around the House, Frumkin/Adams Gallery, NY, 94; Am Abstraction: A New Decade (with catalog), Southern Alleghenies Mus Art, Loretto, Pa, 94; Mixing Business with Pleasure, Sawhill Gallery, James Madison Univ, Va, 97; and others. *Teaching:* Instr art, NY Univ Exten, 64-68, Bennington Col, Vt, 69-. *Awards:* Woodrow Wilson Fel; Nat Endowment Arts Fel. *Bibliog:* David Hornung (auth), Philip Wofford, ARTnews, 12/89; Philip Wofford, NY Times, 2/8/91; Philip Wofford, Artforum, 5/91. *Publ:* Auth, article, Art Now: New York, 70; Grand Canyon Search Ceremony, Barlenmir House, 72; In the Belly of the Shark, Random House, 72; work in, Poetry Rev, 4/75. *Dealer:* George Adams Gallery 41 W 57th St New York NY 10019. *Mailing Add:* c/o George Adams Gallery 41 W 57th St 7th Fl New York NY 10019

WOGSTAD, JAMES EVERET
EDUCATOR, ILLUSTRATOR
b Lordsburg, NMex, Sept 24, 39. *Study:* San Antonio Col, cert, 59; Univ Tex, Austin, BFA, 61, MFA, 68. *Comn:* Original graphics prog, Univ Tex Med Sch, San Antonio, 68-69; dioramic backgrounds & natural hist graphic displays, Witte Mus, San Antonio, 70-74. *Pos:* Lead illusr, Creative Commun, Houston, 62-63; chief illusr, Finger Contract Supply, Houston, 63-65; preparator-cur, Witte Mus, 70-74; ed-illusr, Replica in Scale, 72-76 & Aerophile, 76-. *Teaching:* Prof art, San Antonio Col, 68-, chmn dept, 73-77, graphic arts prog coordr, 73-95. *Mem:* Col Art Asn Am; Tex Asn Schs Art (bd dir, 94-); Tex Jr Col Teachers Asn. *Media:* Acrylic on Canvas; Black Ink on Paper. *Publ:* Illusr, Any Time is Party Time, 67, Auschuitz, 67 & Belsen, 67, Naylor; auth/illusr, AV-8 Harrier, Aerophile, 82; EA-6 Prowler/Intruder, Aerophile, 85. *Mailing Add:* 4014 Belle Grove St San Antonio TX 78230-1602

WOHLENHAUS, GRACE FORCIER
PAINTER
b Stewart, Minn, Sept 5, 19. *Study:* Famous Artist Schools, Cert, 61. *Work:* Traverse Co Historical Mus, Wheaton, Minn; Romer Gallery, Casa Erande, Ariz. *Comn:* Mallard duck, City Hall, Wheaton, Minn, 87; wild life mural, Travers Co Sportsmen Club, Wheaton, Minn, 90. *Exhib:* Art of the Prairie, Mus Art, Fargo, NDak, 83 & 84; Regional Ajo Alliance of Art, Greenway Mansion, Ajo Ariz, 89-90. *Teaching:* Art, Wheaton Pierson Sch, 81-83. *Awards:* Acceptance Award, Univ Minn, 67; Best of Show, Graceville, Minn, 70; and others. *Mem:* Minn Rural Artists Asn (slide chmn 3 yrs); Ajo Alliance Art. *Media:* Oil, Watercolor. *Mailing Add:* 2225 Ferguson Rd Winterhaven CA 92283 9700

WOIDE, ROBERT E
PAINTER, PHOTOGRAPHER
b Cleveland, Ohio, Jan 27, 27. *Study:* Cleveland Inst Art, with Carl Gaertner, Louis Bosa, Henry Wilcox & Paul Travis, cert, 50; Kent State Univ, with Elmer Novotney, BSE, 51, ME, 62. *Work:* Homerton Gallery, Cambridge, England; Int Inst Gallery, Glion, Switz; Butler Art Inst, Youngstown, Ohio. *Comn:* several murals, Medina, Ohio. *Exhib:* Cleveland May Shows, Cleveland Mus Art, 49, 52, 66, 67 & 69; Butler Int, 51 & Mid-Year Exhib, 79, Butler Art Inst; two-person exhib, Int Inst Gallery, Glion, Switz, 79, Massillon Mus, Ohio, 80, Womens City Club, Cleveland, 80 & Garden Ctr, Cleveland, 82, Intown Gallery, Cleveland, 89, Palace Gallery, Graz Austria, 89 & Natural Hist Mus, Cleveland, 90; Univ Circle Gallery, 90-. *Pos:* Asst dir, Canton Art Inst, Ohio, 51-52; vpres, Univ Circle In, 85-97; trustee, Altahouse, 90- & Abgington Arms, 90-. *Teaching:* Instr, lectr & supervisor, Cleveland Mus Art, 52-66; visual arts educ, Case Western Reserve Univ, 54-57 & 61-67, adj prof 85-97; art educ instr, Kent State Univ, 61-63; supervisor & dir fine arts educ, Cleveland pub schs, 63-85. *Awards:* Sr Exhib Award, Cleveland Inst Art, 50; Purchase Prizes, Mid-Year Exhib, Butler Art Inst, 51 & Canton Art Inst, 52; special citation, Contrib to Arts, Cleveland Women's City Club, 86. *Mem:* Ohio Art Educ Asn (vpres, 74-75); Cleveland Inst Art Alumni Asn (pres, 83-89); Alliance Arts Educ; Cleveland Inst Art (trustee, 84-); Cleveland Artists' Found (adv bd, 90-); River Bend Asn (trustee 96-). *Media:* Watercolor; Slide Film. *Specialty:* Art in Walking Sticks, Photography. *Publ:* Contribr, Art Teachers Guides, 63-73, contribr, Proxemics, Edges and Nodes--Artistic Judgement and the Environment, 73, ed, A Guide to the Development of Afro American Art in the United States, 74 & auth, Graded Course of Study for the Arts, 83, Cleveland Pub Schs; ed & contribr, The World of Creative Expression, Coun Human Relations, 84. *Dealer:* NOVA 4614 Prospect Park Bldg Cleveland Ohio 44103; Imagine Friends 2003 St Claire Ave Cleveland Ohio. *Mailing Add:* c/o R & VW Inc 4931 Nettleton Rd Medina OH 44256

WOIT, BONNIE FORD
PAINTER
b New York, NY, Jan 19, 31. *Study:* Allegheny Col, BA(cum laude), 53; Harvard Univ exten, 54-55; Westchester Workshop, 60-61; Silvermine Sch Art, 70-73; photog graphics workshop, 75. *Work:* Bankers Trust Co, NY; Sapolin Co, Danbury, Conn; IBM, Green Castle, Ind; Sea Containers, NY. *Exhib:* Silvermine Guild Artists, New Canaan, Conn, 74; Munson Gallery, 90; Kohn Pederson & Fox Gallery, NY, 94; Hastings Art Gallery, 94; Hammond Mus, North Salem, NY, 94; Stamford Mus, 97; Gallery BAI, NY, 99 & Barcelona, 2000; solo exhib Bowman Gallery, Allegheny Col, 2002. *Pos:* Chmn & founder, Inst Visual Artists, 85-88; bd trustees, Silvermine Guild Artists, 94. *Awards:* William Lowman Award, 78 & New Eng Award, 79, New Eng Exhib. *Bibliog:* rev, Profile Mag, 3/89; Abstract Expressionism (rev), NY Times, 11/27/94; Zimmer (auth), rev, NY Times, 4/14/96. *Mem:* Silvermine Guild Artists (secy, 74-75, vpres, 75-80 & 83-84). *Media:* Acrylic on Canvas, Paper and Wood. *Mailing Add:* 55 W 16th St 5th Floor New York NY 10011

WOITENA, BEN S
SCULPTOR, EDUCATOR
b San Antonio, Tex, Mar 24, 42. *Study:* Univ Tex, Austin, BFA, 64; Univ Southern Calif, MFA, 70. *Work:* Houston Mus Fine Arts, Tex; City of Houston, Tex; Trammell Crow Co, Tex; San Antonio Mus Art, Tex; Jack Kerouac Commemorative Park. *Comn:* Sculpture, Jack Kerouac Commemorative Park, Lowell, Mass, 88; sculpture, Mayor Emmett F Lowry Commemorative, Texas City, Tex, 90; sculpture, Alley Theatre, Danton's Death, Robert Wilson, Dir, Houston, Tex, 92; sculpture, Amarillo Mus Art Archway Amarillo, Tex, 94. *Exhib:* Collector's Exhib, Houston Mus Fine Arts, 75; A Century of Sculpture in Tex, 1989-1990, Archer M Huntington Art Gallery, Austin, Tex, 89; 64 Beds, Blue Star Art Gallery, San Antonio, Tex, 91; Politics as usual, Lawndale Art and Performance Ctr, Houston, Tex, 92; Artistic Views on Cult Diversity, Tex A&M Univ Art Galleries, Col Station, Tex, 93; Afterimages, The Omni Houston, Solo Exhib, Houston, Tex, 94; Amarillo Mus of Art, Ben Woitena: Realted Works, Amarillo, Tex, 94; Dana Campbell/Paul McCoy/Ben Woitena, Waco Crative

Art Ctr, Waco, Tex, 94; and others. *Teaching:* Instr sculpture, Glassell Sch Art, 71-. *Bibliog:* George F Will (auth), Daddy who was Kerouac, Newsweek, 88; staff writer (auth), The talk of the town, The New Yorker, 88; Sculpture on the Green (film), The Omni Houston, 94. *Mem:* Nat Arts Club, NY. *Media:* Welded Steel, Cast Bronze. *Dealer:* Ben S Woitena, 1547 Waverly Houston TX 77008. *Mailing Add:* 1547 Waverly Houston TX 77008

WOJTYLA, HAASE (WALTER) JOSEPH
PAINTER, DRAFTSMAN
b Chicago, Ill, Feb 10, 33. *Study:* Art Inst of Chicago; Univ of Ill, BFA(painting); Univ Cincinnati, MFA; Brooklyn Mus Art Sch. *Work:* Scripps Mem Hosp, Mus Contemp Art, San Diego, Calif. *Exhib:* Int Drawing Competition, State Univ of Educ, Potsdam, NY, 60; Tenth Ann Nat Exhib of Painting & Sculpture, Ringling Mus Art, Sarasota, Fla, 60; Brooklyn & Long Island Artists Biennial Exhib, Brooklyn Mus Art, 60; Art in Am Exhib, NY, 62; All Ohio Painting & Sculpture Exhib, Dayton Art Inst, 66; Calif-Hawaii Biennial, Fine Arts Gallery San Diego, 76 & 78; one-man show, Recent Paintings, Fine Arts Gallery San Diego, 75. *Teaching:* Instr, San Diego State Univ, Calif, 76 & 80. *Awards:* Singer & Sons Prize, Artists of Chicago & Vicinity, Art Inst Chicago, 56; Painting Award, All Calif Juried Exhib, Laguna Beach Mus Art, 76; Painting Award, Calif Ann Award Show, Jewish Community Ctr, San Diego, 77. *Bibliog:* Artist-in-Residence, KPBS-TV, San Diego, 82; The black comic art of Walter Wojtyla, Hill Courier, 9/83. *Mem:* San Diego Art Inst; Art Guild, San Diego Mus Art. *Media:* Oil, Mixed Media; Ink, Charcoal. *Publ:* Auth, San Diego Artists, Atra Publ Inc, 88. *Dealer:* Oneiros Gallery 711 Eight Ave Studio A San Diego CA 92101. *Mailing Add:* 2102 C St San Diego CA 92101

WOLANIC, SUSAN SESESKE
PAINTER, GRAPHIC ARTIST
b Hartford, Conn, Mar 25, 47. *Study:* Paier Sch Art, 69; Univ Hartford. *Work:* Yale New Haven Hosp, Conn; Constitution Nat Bank, Hartford, Conn; Storer Cable, New Haven, Conn; Carriage House, Guilford, Conn. *Comn:* Family portrait-impressionism, Expressions Furniture, Milford/Cheshire, Conn, 89; illus of house for mag, comn by Lois & Vicent La Bonia, Palm Springs, Calif, 90; logo & stationery, Bethany Community sch, 92; Watercolor, Assumption Church, Woodbridge, Conn, 94; pewter Christmas Ornaments, Bethany Volunteer Fire Dept Womens Auxilliary, 93, 94, & 95; Picnic in the Park (poster), 94. *Exhib:* St Raphaels Hosp, art corridor, 92. *Pos:* Archit secy (draftsperson), off of John Damico, AIA, Waterbury, Conn, 76-; art dir, Marketing Serv Corp, Waterbury, Conn. *Teaching:* Instr, lectr, demonstrator, watercolor, various art organizations, Conn & adult educ prog, Watertown, 75-; instr watercolor, Arts Alive Studio, Cheshire, Conn & Thomaston Adult Ed, Prospect, Conn; instr adult ed, orange arts & crafts. *Awards:* Picador, Ligoa Duncan Gallery, New York & Paris, 79. *Bibliog:* Vincent & Lois La Bonia (auths), Illustrations of California house, Palm Springs Life Mag, 90; Yale Art Gallery & Hosp, American Artists Publication, Yale Art Library, 90; Joyce Zimmerman (auth), Easy Line II, (article). *Mem:* Conn Watercolor Soc; Cheshire Art League (vpres, pres, 80's); Conn Classic Artists; Watertown Art League; Mt Carmel Art Asn. *Media:* Watercolor. *Publ:* Auth, 5 cookbooks: Vegetables, Ethic Artistry, Cookies, HorDoevres, Seafood, Private Publ, 89; illusr, 2 Views of a Palm Springs California Home (watercolors), Palm Springs Life Mag, 90 (in prep); The Day of the Fish, 90; ann report cover, Meridan-Wallingford Hosp, 92; cover & illus, Bethany Cookbook. *Mailing Add:* 66 Sperry Rd Bethany CT 06524-3530

WOLANIN, BARBARA A
HISTORIAN, CURATOR
b Dayton, Ohio, Dec 12, 43. *Study:* Oberlin Col, BA, 66, MA(art hist, Woodrow Wilson Fel), 69; Harvard Univ Grad Sch Educ, MAT(fine arts), 67; Univ Wis, Madison, PhD(art hist), 81. *Collection Arranged:* Arthur B Carles Collection (auth, catalog), Hirshhorn Mus, 77; Arthur B Carles, Painting with Color (auth, catalog), Pa Acad Fine Arts, Corcoran Gallery Art & Nat Acad Design, 83-84; Jane Piper Retrospective: Paintings 1940-1985 (auth, catalog), James Madison Univ, Pa Acad Fine Arts & State Univ NY, Oswego, 86-87; Arthur B Carles Prints (auth, catalog), Print Club, Philadelphia, 89. *Pos:* Cur for arch of US Capitol, 85. *Teaching:* Asst prof art hist, Trinity Col, Washington, 78-83 & James Madison Univ, 83-85; pub lectures, Jurying Art Exhib. *Awards:* Kress Fel, 74; Smithsonian Fel, 76; James Madison Univ Fac Develop Award, 85; Woodrow Wilson Fel, 1966; Architect of the Capitol Spl Contribution, 1998. *Mem:* Col Art Asn; Asn Historians Am Art; Women's Caucus Art; Am Asn Mus; Phi Beta Kappa; Am Inst Conservation: Art Table. *Res:* Arthur B Carles, pioneer American modernist, Constantino Brumidi. *Publ:* Auth, The Advent of Modernism, 86; revs, Art Am, 92, 93 & 96; Constantino Brumidi: Artist of the Capitol, 98; The Orchestration of Color: The Paintings of Arthur B Carles, 2000. *Mailing Add:* 7807 Hamilton Spring Rd Bethesda MD 20817

WOLBER, PAUL J
PAINTER, EDUCATOR
b Deer Creek, Ill, June 23, 35. *Study:* Ill State Univ; Southern Ill Univ, Edwardsville; Bob Jones Univ, BS & MA. *Work:* Evansville Mus Art, Ind; Franklin Life Ins Co, Springfield, Ill; Mitchell Mus Art, Mt Vernon, Ill; Calumet Nat Bank, Ill; Ill State Mus, Springfield. *Comn:* Mural, Spring Arbor Free Methodist Church, 80; mural, Ingham Co Correctional Ctr, Ingham Co Arts Comn, 81. *Exhib:* Ill State Mus, Springfield, 74; Grand Galleria Nat Ann, Seattle, 74; Gov Exhib, 30 Ill Artists, Springfield, 75; Marietta Nat, Ohio, 78. *Pos:* Art educ consult, State Off Pub Instr, Springfield, Ill, 74-75. *Teaching:* Assoc prof art, Spring Arbor Col, Mich, 76-81, prof, 81-. *Awards:* Nat Small Painting Award, NMex Art League, Albuquerque, 74 & 75; Illinois-Indiana Bicentennial Purchase Award, Hammond, Ind, 77. *Bibliog:* Glen P Ives (auth), Museum object of the week, Sunday Courier, Evansville, Ind, 10/6/74; Abner Hershberger (ed), Monnonite Artists Contemporary, Goshen Col Art Gallery, 75; Howard Derrickson (auth), article, The Advocate, Greenville, 1/28/75. *Mem:* Mid Am Col Art Asn; Nat Art Educ Asn; Bond Co Art & Cult Asn (vpres, 73-74). *Media:* Oil, Acrylic. *Mailing Add:* 1660 Chapel Rd Parma MI 49269

WOLF, PATRICIA B
MUSEUM DIRECTOR
Pos: Dir, exec dir, Anchorage Mus Hist and Art, 1989—. *Mem:* Arctic Studies Ctr (steering comt, currently). *Mailing Add:* Anchorage Mus History and Art 121 W Seventh Ave Anchorage AK 99501

WOLF, SHERRIE J
PAINTER, PRINTMAKER
b Portland, Ore, July 4, 52. *Study:* PNCA formerly Mus Art Sch, Portland, BFA, 74; Chelsea Col Art, MA, London, 75. *Work:* Ore Arts Comn; Gordon Gilkey Print Collection, Portland Art Mus; Portable Works Collection, City of Seattle; State of Wash. *Comn:* drawing & etching of Pittock Mansion, Chronicle of Portland Collection, Regional Arts Comn, Portland, 85; painting of Portland, Portland Develop Comn, 91; Absolut Oregon (illustration), Absolut Vodka, Teaneck, NJ, 92; suite of lithographs, Claremont Hotel, Oakland, Calif, 96; painting, 1% for Art Ore State Univ, 97. *Exhib:* Ore Biennial, Portland Art Mus, 91; Biennial Exhib Prints, Mus Mod Art, Wakayama, Japan, 97; Am Print Exhib, China Nat Acad, Hangzhou, China, 98; Interior Pauses: Contemp Northwest Realism, Mary Hill (Wash) Mus, 98; Ana 29 Show, Holter Mus Art, Helena, Mont, 2000; Degrees of Realsim, Megahan Gallery, Allegeny Col, Meadville, Pa, 99. *Collection Arranged:* Westin Hotel, Porltand, Oreg, Harsh Investments, Portland, State of Oregon 1% for Art Collection, State of Washington, Gordon Gilkey for Graphic Arts, Portland Art Mus. *Teaching:* instr drawing, design, painting & printmaking, Pacific Northwest Col Art, Portland, 77-85. *Awards:* Artist fel, Ore Arts Comn, 99-2000. *Bibliog:* Joel Wienstien (auth), Wolf still lives, Oregonian, 6/11/93; Lois Allan (auth), Sherrie Wolf at Jacobsen, Artweek, 7/98; Ted Lindberg (auth), Sherrie wolf: New works preview, The Gallery Guide, 4/2000. *Mem:* Northwest Print Coun (mem bd 83-86). *Media:* oil on canvas, etching, printmaking, ceramic tile. *Publ:* auth, Third Annual Realism Invitational catalog. *Dealer:* Margo Jacobsen 1039 NW Glisan Portland OR 97210; Jenkins Johnson Gallery 464 Sutter St San Francisco CA; Lindattodges Gallery Seattle WA. *Mailing Add:* 2334 NW Northrup St Portland OR 97210

WOLFE, JAMES
SCULPTOR
b New York, NY, Apr 28, 44. *Work:* Mus Fine Arts, Houston; Whitney Mus, NY; Mus Fine Arts, Boston; Kresge Art Ctr, Mich State Univ; Storm King Art Ctr; Hirshhorn Mus & Sculpture Garden, Washington, DC; Ft Worth Art Mus, Tex; Portland Mus Art, Portland, OR; Ackland Art Mus, Chapel Hill, NC; Huntington Mus Art, Huntington, WV; Art Mus Western Va, Roanoke, VA. *Comn:* Ten painted steel sculptures, comn by Johnstown Flood Mus, Centennial Comt & Bethlehem Steel for James Wolfe Sculpture Trail, Johnstown, Pa, 89; steel sculpture, comn by Harold Kant, Reno, NV. *Exhib:* One-man shows, Don Stewart Gallery, Montreal, Can, 88, Andre Gmmerich Gallery, NY, 88, Huntington Mus Art, Huntington, WVa, Galarie Am Tiergarten 62, Ger, 89, & Lucy Berman Gallery, Palo Alto, Calif, 90; Andre Emmerich Gallery, NY, NY, 73, 74, 75, 76, 77, 85, 86, 88; Monumenta, Newport, RI, 74; one-man shows, Meredith Long Contemp, 78 & 79, Osuna Gallery, 80, Wentzel Gallery, Cologne, WGer, 87, Baumgartner Galleries, Washington, DC, 88, Innenhof des Historischen Rathauses, Koln, WGer, 88, Huntington Mus Art, WVa, 89 & Lucy Berman Gallery, Palo Alto, CA, 90; Clayworks Studio Workshop, NY, 81; Stephen Roseberg Gallery, 83 & 84; Lucy Berman Gallery, Palo Alto, Calif, 93; Marion Meyer Gallery, Laguna Beach, Calif, 99, 2002; and others. *Pos:* Tech dir, Theater Dept & tech asst, Sculpture Dept, Bennington Col; fac mem, Va Polytechnic & State Univ, 78, Sch Visual Arts, 79 & Boston Mus Sch, 80. *Awards:* Nat Endowment Arts, 74; Saint Gaudens Found Prize, 84. *Bibliog:* Karen Wilkin (article), James Wolfe Sculpture Trail, Sculpture Mag, 5-6/90; Karen Wilkin (auth), James Wolfe's New Sculpture, Arts, 4/85; Karen Wilkin (auth), James Wolfe Sculpture Trail, 5-6/90; and others. *Dealer:* Andre Emmerich 41 E 57 St New York NY 10022; Marion Meyer Contemporary Art 354 N Coast Hwy Laguna Beach CA 92651. *Mailing Add:* 736 Broadway New York NY 10003

WOLFE, LYNN ROBERT
PAINTER, EDUCATOR
b Red Cloud, Nebr, Sept 11, 17. *Study:* Univ Nebr, BFA; Univ Colo, with Max Beckman, MFA; Paris Atelier with Ossip Zadkine. *Work:* Univ Nebr State Mus, Lincoln; Univ Colo, Boulder. *Comn:* Copper doors, Danforth Chapel, Colo State Univ, Ft Collins, 54; mosaic (stained glass), McPherson Chapel, Durango, Colo, 60; stained glass window, Norgren Chapel, Denver, 65; stained glass windows, St Aidans Episcopal Church, Boulder, 70; bronze sculpture, Yampa River Botanic Park, Steamboat Springs, Colo, 99; sculpture, St Johns Episcopal Church, Boulder, 93. *Exhib:* Nat Watercolor & Drawing, Metrop Mus, NY, 52; Nat Drawing & Small Sculpture, Muncie, Ind, 58; Mus Contemp Crafts, NY, 59; Western Artists, Denver Art Mus, 72. *Pos:* Cur collections, Univ Colo, Boulder, 64-74. *Teaching:* Instr sculpture, Univ Nebr, Lincoln, 45-46; vis artist watercolor, Univ Alaska, summer 46; prof painting, Univ Colo, Boulder, 47-, chmn dept fine arts, 72-74; vis artist, Univ Hawaii, 82. *Awards:* Sculpture Award, Ball State Teachers Col, 58; Univ Colo Fac Fel, 67; Award, Outstanding Educators Am, 75. *Media:* Acrylic, Canvas; Stained Glass, Faceted Dalles. *Mailing Add:* 701 Euclid Boulder CO 80302

WOLFE, MAURICE RAYMOND
CONSULTANT
b Paris, France, Oct 13, 24; US citizen. *Study:* Univ Calif, Berkeley, BA, 48, MA, 52, grad study; Fr Govt fel to Univ Paris at Sorbonne. *Collection Arranged:* Art from Mobilier of the Djukas of Surinam, Pacific Northwest & Eskimo Material Culture, Meso-American Prehistory, Mohave Desert Culture, African Musical Instruments &

Domestic Objects & The Art of New Guinea, 74-75, The Cuna of Panama--Arts & Crafts, West Africa, Aboriginal Australian Art from Expo 74 & California Gatherers & Hunters, Circa 1776 (Bicentennial celebration), 75-76, Oceanic Cultures: Emphasis on American Trust Territories, Folk Art of Mexico & Archaeology, 77-78, Merritt Col Anthrop Mus; Carmel Valley Hist Soc Exhib, Carmel Valley Centennial Celebration, 89. *Pos:* Dir, Merritt Col Anthrop Mus, 73-87, consult, currently. *Teaching:* Instr, Merritt Col, Oakland, formerly, prof prehist art, formerly; adj prof, Golden Gate Univ, Monterey, 94-. *Awards:* Fel, French Govt, 66. *Mem:* Am Asn Mus; Western Art Asn; Calif Archaeol Soc. *Mailing Add:* 33751 Carmel Valley Rd Carmel Valley CA 93924

WOLFE, MILDRED NUNGESTER
PAINTER, DESIGNER
b Celina, Ohio, Aug 23, 1912. *Study:* Athens Col; Univ Montevallo, AB, 32; Dixie Art Colony, with J Kelly Fitzpatrick; Art Students League, with Will Barnet; Chicago Art Inst; Colorado Springs Fine Arts Ctr, with Boardman Robinson; Colo Col, MA, 44. *Work:* Miss Mus Art, Jackson; Montgomery Mus Art, Ala; Print Collection, Libr Cong, & Nat Portrait Gallery, Washington; Huntsville Mus Art, Huntsville, Ala; Georgia Mus Art, Athens, Ga. *Comn:* Orpheus (mosaic), McDowell Br Libr, Jackson, 58; Stations of the Cross, comn by Monsignor Joseia Chatham for St Richards, Jackson, 60; David (mosaic), comn by Elizabeth Kingford for St Dominic's Hosp, Jackson, 61; chapel window (stained glass), First Baptist Church, Hazelhurst, Miss, 65; symbolic windows, Independent Methodist Episcopal Church, Jackson, 71-74. *Exhib:* Nat Exhib Prints, Libr Cong, 44; Grumbacher Int Exhib, Lakeland, Fla, 52; Painters of Southeastern US, Univ SFla, 62; Bertrand Russell Peace Found Exhib, Nottingham, Eng, 73; Lauren Rogers Mus of Art, Laurel, Miss, 77; Old Capitol Mus, Jackson, Miss, 77 & 77-78; and others. *Teaching:* Instr hist art & printmaking, Millsaps Col, 58-68, ret. *Awards:* First Prize for Cotton Pickers, Southern Painter, McDowell Gallery, 38; First Prize for Watercolor, Miss Art Asn, 46; Award of Merit for Still Life, Grumbacher Int Exhib, 52. *Mem:* Miss Art Asn. *Media:* All. *Dealer:* Wolfe Gallery. *Mailing Add:* c/o Wolfe Gallery 4308 Old Canton Rd Jackson MS 39211

WOLFE, ROBERT, JR
PRINTMAKER, PAINTER
b Oxford, Ohio, May 15, 30. *Study:* Miami Univ, BFA, 52; Cincinnati Art Acad, 55; Univ Iowa, scholar, 59, with M Lasansky, MFA(printmaking), 60; Tamarind Inst Workshops, 75 & 79. *Work:* Ohio State Univ; Univ Wis-Madison; Sheldon Mem Art Gallery, Univ Nebr, Lincoln; Casa da Gravura, State Collection, Curitiba, Parana, Brazil; Rajasthan Sch Art, Jaipur, India; and others; Cincinnati Art Mus; The Dayton Art Inst, Ohio; Ball State Univ. *Comn:* Five color intaglios, Miami Univ, 71. *Exhib:* Nine Midwest Printmakers, Mt St Joseph Col, Cincinnati, Ohio, 77; Rutger's Drawing, Camden, 79; Honolulu Acad Arts 5th Nat, Hawaii, 80; Intaglio Printmakers 81, Univ Louisville, Ky; Rajasthan Sch Art, Jaipur, India, 88; and many others. *Pos:* Artist-illusr, US Army, 52-54. *Teaching:* Instr design, Clarion Col, Pa, 61-62; prof printmaking, Miami Univ, 62-93, emer prof, 94-; vis artist, Univ Nebr, Grinnell Col, Ohio State Univ, Fed Univ Parana, Brazil & Western Kentucky Univ. *Awards:* Purchase Award, Intaglio Printmakers 81, Univ Louisville, Ky, 81, Ball State Univ, Ind, 2006; Alumni Award for Painting, Miami Univ, 82; and others; Effective Educator Award, Miami Univ, 91; and others. *Media:* Mixed, Oil. *Publ:* Contribr, Voiles Before Regatta, Finial Press, 84. *Mailing Add:* 418 Bouden Ln Oxford OH 45056

WOLFE, TOWNSEND, III
DIRECTOR, CHIEF CURATOR
b Hartsville, SC, Aug 15, 35. *Study:* Ga Inst Technol; Atlanta Art Inst, BFA; Cranbrook Acad Art, MFA; Inst Art Admin, Harvard Univ, cert. *Work:* Ark Arts Ctr, Little Rock; Mint Mus Art, Charlotte, NC; Okla Arts Ctr, Oklahoma City; Miss Art Asn, Jackson; Carroll Reece Mem Mus, E Tenn State Univ. *Exhib:* Ball State Teacher's Col Drawing Nat, Muncie, Ind, four shows, 59-67; Mead Painting of Yr Exhib, Atlanta, 62; Watercolors USA, Springfield, Mo, 63-64; Alice Bingham Gallery, Memphis, Tenn, 80; First Nat Bank, Little Rock, Ark, 81; and others. *Pos:* Dir, Wooster Community Art Ctr, Danbury, Conn, 65-68; art dir, Upward Bound Proj, Danbury, summers 66-68; dir & chief cur, Ark Arts Ctr, 68-. *Teaching:* Instr painting & drawing, Memphis Acad Arts, Tenn, 59-64; instr painting & drawing, Scarsdale Studio Workshop, NY, 64-65. *Awards:* N Hodson Wheeler Award, 56; Winthrop Rockefeller Mem Award, 73; Award Merit & Purchase Prize, 57th Nat Painting Exhib, Miss Art Asn, 67; James R Short Award, Southeastern Mus Conf, 81; Individual Achievement Award, Ark Mus Asn, 84; Ark Art Educ Advocacy Award, 85; Promethean Award for Excellence in the Arts, March of Dimes, 86. *Mem:* Am Asn Mus; Am Fedn Arts; Southeastern Asn Mus; Asn Art Mus Dirs. *Media:* Oil, Gouache. *Publ:* Auth, National Drawing Invitational (catalog), 86, 88, 90, 91, 92; National Objects Invitational (catalog), 87, 88, 89, 91; The Figure (catalog), 90; Will Barnet Drawings 1930-1990 (catalog), 91; Silverpoint Etcetera (catalog), 92; and others

WOLFF, DEE I
PAINTER
b Springfield, Minn, 48. *Study:* Univ Houston, BA, 71; Glassell Sch Art, cert art, 76; Oomoto Sch Traditional Art, Oomoto, Japan, 84. *Work:* Mus Fine Arts, Houston; Mus of Southeast Tex, Beaumont, Tex; Art Mus S Tex, Corpus Christi, Tex; Archer M Huntington Mus, Austin, Tex; Gihon Found Collection, Dallas; Concordia Univ, Austin, Tex. *Comn:* Twenty three stained glass windows, St Theresea of Lisieux, Sugarland, Tex; Corpus Christi Pub Libr, Tex; St Philip Church, Houston; stage-work design for Kabbalah. *Exhib:* one-woman shows, Watson Gallery, Houston, 78, 81, 85, Mus Southeast Tex, Beaumont, Tex, 89, Diverseworks Artspace, Houston, 89, D'Art Artspace, Dallas, 90 & Mus Fine Arts, Houston, 90; Galveston Art Ctr, Tex, 2000. *Awards:* Nat Endowment Arts Visual Arts Grant, 89; NY State Coun on the Arts Grant, 89; Spirit of S Award, Univ Mobile, Ala, 99; others. *Bibliog:* Joan Robinson (auth), Dee Wolff-Diverseworks Artspace, Art Forum Int, 4/89; Ten souls act out the mysticism of kabbalah, New York Times, 11/20/89; Selah: Stations of the Cross, Diverseworks Artspace, Houston, 89; Janet Cutner (auth), Following Christ's Journey: An Artist's Life, Growth and Change, Dallas Morning News, 90. *Mem:* Diverseworks Artspace, (bd dir & artists adv bd 89-91); Lawndale Art and Performance Space; Art League of Houston. *Media:* Gouache, Acrylic Paint. *Publ:* No Bluebonnets, No Yellow Roses, Essays on Texas Women in the Arts, Midmarch Arts Press, New York, 88; Exposures, Women and Their Art, Newsage Press, 89; Texas 150 Works from the Museum of Fine Arts, Houston, Alison de Lima Greene & Harry N Abrams, publs, 2000. *Mailing Add:* 421 Arlington Houston TX 77007

WOLFF, ROBERT W, JR
DEALER
b Monroe, La, Feb 18, 47. *Study:* Troy State Univ, Ala, BS, 74. *Pos:* Art dealer, Ashland Gallery, Mobile, Ala, currently. *Mailing Add:* 32 S Section St Fairhope AL 36532-2212

WOLFSON, JORDAN
ARTIST
b New York, NY, 80. *Study:* RI Sch Design, BFA, 2003; Studies at Konfstack Col Arts & Krafts, Stockholm, Sweden, 2003. *Exhib:* solo shows, Radar, Galleri Brandstrom & Stene, Stockholm, 2002, Nostalgia is Fear, Irma Vep Lap, Champagne, France, 2004, Jordan Wolfson, Kunsthalle, Zurich, 2004, Neverland, Jordan Wolfson, Yvon Lambert, Paris, 2005, Jiem-no-Pedli, t293, Naples, 2005, Wako Works of Art, Tokyo, 2006; group exhibs, Fort Thuder, Providence, RI, 2000; Nada Art Fair, Miami, 2003; Palm D'Or Social Club, Berlin Art Fair, 2004; Festival of Dreams, Lombard-Freid Gallery, NY, 2004; None of the Above, Swiss Inst, NY, 2004; There Is No Such Thing As The Real World, Galleri MGM, Oslo, 2005; BUIA Gallery, 2005; Post note, Midway Contemp Art Mus, Minn, 2005; U-Move, Utopia & Image on the Move, Gallery Contemp Art, Monfalcone, Italy, 2005; Sold Out, Spazio, More Fools IN Town, Turin, Italy, 2005; Hudson Valley Ctr Contemp Art, 2006; Uncertain States of Am, 2006; Whitney Biennial, Whitney Mus Art, 2006. *Mailing Add:* c/o Whitney Museum 945 Madison Ave New York NY 10021

WOLIN, JEFFREY ALAN
PHOTOGRAPHER
b New York, NY, Feb 25, 51. *Study:* Kenyon Col, AB, 72; Rochester Inst Tech, MFA, 77. *Work:* Israel Mus, Jerusalem; Mus Mod Art, NY; San Francisco Mus of Mod Art, Calif; Los Angeles Co Mus Art; Mus Fine Arts, Houston, Tex; Art Inst, Chicago; Mus Contemp Photography, Chicago. *Exhib:* Recent Acquisitions, Seattle Art Mus, Wash, 86; Selections, Mus Mod Art, NY, 92; New Work/New Directions, Los Angeles Mus Art, 92; Recent Acquisitions, Mus Fine Arts, Houston, Tex; Portraits of the Holocaust (traveling), 94; Portraits of the Holocaust, Catherine Edelman Gallery, Chicago, 94; The New Face of the Portrait, Fuller Mus Art, Brockton, 94; An Am Century of Photog from Dry-Plate to Digital (traveling), Nelson-Atkins Mus Art, Kansas City, Mo, 94; The Photog Body (catalog), Contemp Arts Ctr, New Orleans, La, 94; Witness and Legacy: Contemp Art about the Holocaust (with catalog), Minneapolis Mus Am Art, St Paul, Minn & Columbus Mus Art, Ohio, 95; Written in Memory, Art Inst Chicago, 96 & 97; The Holocaust: Vaoices, Portraits, Places, Gallery 312, Chicago, 97; Shattered Visions, Suburban Fine Arts Ctr, Highland Park, Ill, 97; Portraits of the Holocaust, Rochester Inst Technol, NY, 97; Backyard, Robert Mann Gallery, NY, 97; Gallery Artists, Catherine Edelman Gallery, Chicago, 97; Portraits From the Collection, Art Inst Chicago, 97; Family and Friends, Mus Contemp Photog, Chicago, 97; Selections From Written in Memory, Snite Mus, South Bend, Ind, 98; Celebrating 10 Yrs: A Chronological History of Exhibition, Catherine Edelman Gallery, Chicago, 98; Waterproof, 98 World's Fair, Belem Cult Ctr, Lisbon, Portugal, 98; Catherine Edelman Gallery, Chicago, 2000. *Teaching:* From asst prof to assoc prof photog, Ind Univ, Bloomington, 80-92, prof, 93-, dir, Sch Fine Arts, 94-. *Awards:* Vis Artist Fel, Nat Endowment Arts, 88 & Photog Fel, 92; John Simon Guggenheim Meml fel, 91; US/France Fel for Res in Paris, 94; and others. *Bibliog:* Article, San Diego Reader, 3/5/92; article, Indianapolis Star, 1/27/93; article, Chicago Tribune, 4/30/93. *Mem:* Soc Photog Educ. *Publ:* Co-auth & illusr, Stone Country, Indiana Univ Press, 85; illusr, Swimmers, Aperture, 88; The Archive No 29, Ctr Creative Photog, 91; An American Century of Photography, New York, 94; Written in Memory: Portraits of the Holocaust, Chronicle Bks, 97. *Dealer:* Catherine Edelman Gallery 300 W Superior Chicago Ill 60610. *Mailing Add:* Sch Fine Arts Indiana Univ Bloomington IN 47405

WOLPERT, ETTA
PAINTER, PRINTMAKER
b Dec 6, 30. *Study:* Univ Minn, BA MA(magna cum laude), 54; Columbia Grad Sch, 53; DeCordova Mod Art Sch, 68. *Exhib:* Walker Art Ctr, Minneapolis, 47; one-women shows, Cary Libr, Lexington, Mass, 62, Int Student Center, Cambridge, Mass, 62, Lexington Theatre, 72 & Lexington Trust Co, 74; Fourth Ann Int Exhib Miniature Art, Toronto, Can, 89; Cambridge Pub Libr, North Branch, 92. *Teaching:* Asst prof, Northern Essex Community Col, Mass, 65. *Awards:* First & Third Prize, drawing, Minn State Fair, 49. *Media:* Acrylic, Oil; Silkscreen. *Publ:* Contribr, Harvard Advocate, 64; auth, Selections from her writings, 73. *Mailing Add:* 4 Revere St Lexington MA 02173-6876

WOLSKY, JACK
PAINTER, EDUCATOR
b Rochester, NY, Aug 5, 30. *Study:* Rochester Inst Technol, AS, 51; State Univ NY Col, Buffalo, BS, 55, MS, 57. *Work:* Rochester Mem Art Gallery, NY; New Britain Mus Am Art, Conn; Munson-Williams-Proctor Inst, Utica, NY; Rochester Inst Technol; State Univ NY Col, Brockport. *Exhib:* Am Fedn Arts Exhib, Turkey, Iran & Pakistan; 154th Exhib, Pa Acad Fine Arts; State Univ NY Arts Convocation Exhib,

Albright-Knox Gallery; Chautauqua Exhib Am Art; Univ Omaha Nat Exhib; State Capital Bldg, Albany, NY; NY Ten Exhib, Ithaca Col; Bellair Gallery Int Art, Toronto, Can; Corning Glass Center; Pioneer Gallery, Cooperstown, NY; DE Kendall Galleries, Wellfleet, Mass; Rochester Inst Technol, NY; solo shows, Zenith Gallery, Washington, DC, Galerie Int, New York, NY & Mem Art Gallery, Rochester, NY. *Teaching:* Prof studio art, State Univ NY Col, Brockport, 59-85, prof emeritus, 85-. *Awards:* Fac Exchange Scholar, State Univ NY, 74; Civic Award in Culture & Arts, Rochester Chamber of Commerce, 1999; Visual Artist award, Arts & Cult Coun Greater Rochester, 2002. *Bibliog:* Talis Bergmanis (auth), Exuberant art of Jack Wolsky, Dem & Chronicle Publ, 12/13/70; Karen Ibrahim (auth), Abstract art of Jack Wolsky, News & Rev, Rochester Inst Technol, 71; Evolution of a moment, Channel 21 TV, Rochester, NY, 74; Robert Henkes (auth), Themes in American Painting: A Reference Work to Common Styles & Genres, McFarland & Co Publ, 92. *Media:* Acrylic, Encaustics. *Publ:* Memory and Mastery: Primo Levi as Writer & Witness ed by Roberta S. Kremer, Pub, by State Univ of NY Press. *Dealer:* Oxford Gallery 267 Oxford St Rochester NY 14607. *Mailing Add:* 295 Washington St Spencerport NY 14559

WOMACK, ROB (ROBERT) ROBINSON
PAINTER
b Norfolk, Va, July 3, 57. *Study:* Va Commonwealth Univ, BFA(painting), 80. *Work:* Renwick Gallery, Smithsonian Am Art Mus. *Comn:* The Woman's Place (mural), Univ Va Hosp, Charlottesville, 93; Landmark Theatre (mural), City of Richmond Percent for Art, 95. *Exhib:* Bravura Coloratura, Anderson Gallery, Va Commonwealth Univ, 85; Furniture as Art/Room as Allusion, Md Art Place, Baltimore, 86; Dream House, Peninsula Fine Arts Ctr, Newport News, Va, 92; Coloratura: Sories & Scenarios (with catalog), Hand Workshop Art Ctr, Richmond, Va, 92; Coloratura, Spirit Square Ctr Arts, Charlotte, NC, 93; By Heart and Hand - Collecting Southern Decorative Art, Art Mus W Va, Roanoke, Va, 98; Commonwealth Collects - 1998, Contemp Art Ctr, Va Beach, Va, 98; Residency Va Ctr Creative Arts, 2001, 2002, 2004; group shows, Cudahy Gallery, 2001; Sleight of Hand, McDonough Mus Art, Youngtown, Ohio, 2004; Right at Home: Am Studio Furniture, Renwick Galler, Smithsonian Am Art MusWashinton, DC, 2004. *Pos:* Mem bd dir, Folk Art Soc Am, 86-90. *Awards:* Visual Artist Fel, Nat Endowment Arts, 94; Individual Artist Fel, Va Comn Arts, 94 & 2000. *Bibliog:* Akiko Busch (auth), Unusual comforts, Metropolis, 89; Liz Seymour (auth), Furniture with something to say, Elle Decor, 90; Dan Tranberg (auth), Sleight of Hand (catalog), McDonough Mus, Youngstown Stae Univ, Youngstown, OH, 2004. *Mem:* Fok Art Soc Am. *Media:* Mixed. *Publ:* Illusr of article, J Am Planning Asn, 94. *Mailing Add:* 3810 Thimble Lane Richmond VA 23222

WONG, ALBERT Y
PAINTER
Study: Columbus Col Art & Design, BFA, 70; Kent State Univ, MFA, 74. *Exhib:* 38th Ann Mid-Yr Exhib, Butler Inst Am Art, Youngstown, Ohio, 74; Springfield and Vicinities, Ill State Mus, 81; solo exhibs, Millikin Univ, Decatur, Ill, 81, Quincy Col, Ill, 82, Evansville Mus, Ind, 86, Auburn Univ, Ala, 91, Dept Art Resources, City of El Paso, Tex, 92, Deming Art Ctr, NMex, 93 & Gallery V, Columbus, Ohio, 96 & 98. *Awards:* Visual Artists Award, Flintridge Found, 98. *Mailing Add:* c/o Gallery V 694 N High St Columbus OH 43215

WONG, AUDREY E(LIZABETH)
PAINTER, GRAPHIC ARTIST
b Kingston, Jamaica, Sept 2, 50. *Study:* Jamaica Sch Art, BFA, 72: Sch Visual Arts, painting with George Rodney, graphic design with Werner Starzman & painting with Colin Garland. *Work:* Cult Ctr Collection, Univ West Indies, Creative Arts Ctr, Kingston, Jamaica. *Comn:* Urban Pollution (no I ecology series), comn by Dr Allison Charles, Kingston, Jamaica, 77; Solitude, Yan Yan Restaurant, Kingston, 78; When the Tide Comes In, comn by G Woon Choy, Kingston, 78; Target, comn by Louis Marriott, Kingston, 78; Writings on the Wall, comn by Audley St John Vaughan, London, 79. *Exhib:* Inst Jamaica Ann, Kingston, 72-74; 2nd Caribbean Festival of the Arts, Nat Gallery Jamaica, Kingston, 76; solo exhib, John Peartree Gallery, Kingston, 77, Mutual Life Gallery, Kingston, 78 & Bolivar Gallery, Kingston, 80; 3rd Caribbean Festival of the Arts, Havana, Cuba, 78; Artist in the Market Place XIV, Bronx Mus Arts, NY, 94. *Collection Arranged:* The Jamaican Artist & Craftsmen Guild (with catalog), Mutual Life Inaugural, 77; Three Women Artists (with catalog), Mutual Life Gallery, 77; Protest '78, Mutual Life Gallery, 78; Seven Plus One, Mutual Life Gallery; International Year of the Child, Mutual Life Gallery, 79. *Pos:* Graphic designer, New York Urban Coalition, 81-86 & Matthew-Lawrence-Pelletier Inc, 83-86; creative dir/artistic dir, Caribbean-Am Enterprises, 86-89. *Teaching:* Art instr book & art/creative writing, Pub Sch 198, Bronx, NY, 93-; art instr interpretive day sch, Bronx Mus Art, 94-. *Awards:* Honorable Mention, Govt of Jamaica, 73. *Bibliog:* Andrew Hope (auth), Images of protest, Jamaican Daily Gleaner, 5/14/78; Sandy McIntosh (auth), An angry artist, Jamaican Daily News, 5/19/78; William Doyle-Marshall, From the heart of Jamaica, Jamaican Daily Gleaner, 11/18/80. *Mem:* Artist Marketplace XIV Group. *Media:* Acrylic Polymer Paint, Watercolor; Collage, Assemblage. *Publ:* Illusr, Through A Child's Eye, Pat Persaud, Roman Catholic Church, 79. *Dealer:* Loris Crawford 249 E 13th St New York NY 10003. *Mailing Add:* c/o Bronx Mus Arts 1040 Grand Concourse Bronx NY 10456

WONG, FREDERICK
PAINTER, GRAPHIC ARTIST
b Buffalo, NY, May 31, 29. *Study:* Univ NMex, BFA & MA. *Work:* Butler Inst Am Art, Youngstown, Ohio; Reading Mus Art, Pa; Philbrook Art Ctr, Tulsa, Okla; Neuberger Collection, Purchase, NY; Smithsonian Inst, Washington, DC. *Exhib:* Los Angeles Co Mus Art, 59; Butler Inst Am Art, Youngstown, 60; Am Watercolor Soc, NY, 60-69; Watercolor USA, Springfield, Mo, 63; Mainstreams '69, Marietta, Ohio, 69. *Teaching:* Instr form & structure, Pratt Inst, 66-69; instr painting, drawing, calligraphy & design, Hofstra Univ; Watercolor, Art Students League. *Awards:* Butler Midyear Ann Bronze Medal, Butler Inst Am Art, 60; Gold Medal, Nat Arts Club, 61; Mainstreams '69 Award of Excellence, Marietta Col, 69. *Mem:* Am Watercolor Soc; Allied Artists Am; Audubon Artists Inc. *Media:* Watercolor. *Publ:* Auth, Oriental Watercolor Techniques, 77 & The Complete Calligrapher, 80, Watson-Guptill; The Zen of Watercolor, Watercolor '90, Am Artist Publ. *Dealer:* Self 77 Chambers St New York NY 10007. *Mailing Add:* 315 Riverside Dr New York NY 10025

WONG, LUCILLE (LUCILA) GUERRA WONG
PAINTER, PRINTMAKER
b Mex City, Mex, Oct 20, 49. *Study:* Univ Nac Autonoma Mex, BA, 74; Univ Kent, Eng, MA, 76; studied art with Robin Bond, ARCA, London, 79. *Work:* Mus Escuela Nac Preparatoria, Inst Nat Nutricion, Facultad Veterinaria Univ Nac, Acervo Patrimonial y Bibliotecas, Mex City; Mus Art Mod, Toluca, Mex. *Comn:* Caballos, Univ Nac, Mex, 89. *Exhib:* LaMujer en la Plastica, Mus Acuarela, Mex, 89; Grabadores Mexicanos, Mus Metrop, Tokyo, 91; Primera Bienal Monterrey, Mus Monterrey, Mex, 92; Arte Mexicano Hoy, Maison Am Latine, Monaco, 94; Ofrendo de Muertos, Mus Casas Aguila, Santillana, Spain, 94; Presencio de Arte Mexicano, Univ Cantabria, Spain, 94; Romances del Viento y la Har, Museo de Yucatan, 97, Corceles que cabalca elalma, Museo de pueretaro, 2000. *Bibliog:* Daniel Higuera (auth), Lucille Wong, Fomento Cultural; Daniel Higuera (auth), La Magia de Lucille Wong, Estudio, San Angel, Mex, 95; Daniel Higuera (auth), Corceles de Viento, Estudio, San Angel, Mex, 96; El Silevcio y la Luz, Leomosa Hastin del Campo (auth), DAP, 98; Corceles que cabalga el alma, Leonora Hastin del Campo (author), DAP, 2000. *Mem:* Ideas Artisticas (pres, 91-94); Consejo Mundial Artistas Visuales, 92; Asn Int Artistes Plastiques, Unesco, 92; Asn Ex-Alumnos Col Aleman Comn Cult (dir, 95). *Publ:* coauth, Presencia de Arte Mexicano, Fomento Cultural, 90; auth, Carpeta Serigrafica, Universidad Nac, 91; coauth, Ayer, Hoy y Mañano, 91 & Arte Mexicano en Europa, 93, Fomento Cultural; Lucille Wong, 37 Formas de describir la Luz, poesia, 2000; E R Blackaller (auth), 24 Invenciones y Preludior Según imágeres de Lucille Wong, 2000. *Mailing Add:* Calle de la Otra Banda 80-14 San Angel DF CP 01090 Mexico DF Mexico

WONG, PAUL KAN
PAINTER, SCULPTOR
b Fargo, NDak, Oct 30, 51. *Study:* Moorhead State Univ, BA, 73; Univ Wis, Madison, MFA, 76. *Work:* Madison Art Ctr; New York Pub Libr. *Comn:* Suspended sculpture installation, Hudson River Mus, Yonkers, NY, 83. *Exhib:* 21st Ann Print Exhib, Brooklyn Mus, 78; 77th Vicinity Exhib, Chicago Art Inst, 78; Shaped Field, Eccentric Formats, PS1, Long Island City, 81; Making Paper, Am Craft Mus, 82; Paper as Image Traveling Exhib, Brit Art Coun, UK, 82; one-man show, Air Space: Projection, Hudson River Mus, Yonkers, NY, 83 & Condeso-Lawler Gallery, NY, 83 & 85. *Pos:* Dir, Dieu Donne Press & Paper, NY; cur, Paper as Paint, Fashion Inst Technol, NY. *Teaching:* Instr hand papermaking, The New Sch, NY, 80-86. *Awards:* Apprenticeship Grants, Louis Comfort Tiffany Found, 78 & Nat Endowment Arts, 80; Graphics Grant, Creative Artists Pub Serv, 83. *Bibliog:* Judd Tully (auth), Paper chase, Portfolio Mag, 83; Ronny Cohen (auth), Paper routes, 83 & rev, 84, Art News; rev, Artforum, 85. *Publ:* Illusr, Our Lady of the Three Pronged Devil, Red Ozier Press, 81. *Dealer:* Condeso-Lawler Gallery 76 Greene St New York NY 10013. *Mailing Add:* 40 N Moore St 2W New York NY 10013

WONNER, PAUL JOHN
PAINTER
b Tucson, Ariz, Apr 24, 20. *Study:* Calif Col Arts & Crafts, Oakland, BA, 41; Univ Calif, Berkeley, BA, 52, Anne Bremmer Scholar, MA, 53, MLS, 55. *Work:* Guggenheim Mus, Mus Mod Art, Metrop Mus Art, NY; San Francisco Mus Art; Nat Collection Fine Arts, Smithsonian Inst, Washington, DC; Oakland Mus, Calif; Joseph H Hirshhorn Found; Boston Mus Fine Arts; Charles A Worst Mus Fine Arts, Racine, Wis; Minneapolis Inst Art, Minn. *Exhib:* Young Am Painters, Solomon R Guggenheim Mus, NY, 54; Vanguard 1955, Walker Art Ctr, Minneapolis, 55; Ann Exhib Contemp Am Painting, Whitney Mus Am Art, 59 & 67; Recent Painting USA: The Figure, Mus Mod Art, NY, 62; Am Painting 1962, Va Mus Fine Arts, Richmond, 62; 73rd Ann, Denver Art Mus, 71, solo exhibs, Charles Campbell Gallery, San Francisco, 74, Art Mus Galleries, Calif State Univ, Long Beach, 75 & 81, James Corcoran Gallery, Los Angeles, 79 & 81, Marion Koogler McNay Art Inst, San Antonio, 81, San Francisco Mus Mod Art, 81, Los Angeles Municipal Art Gallery, 82, Hirschl & Adler Modern, NY, 83 & Coe Kerr Gallery, NY, 92; Painting & Sculpture in California: The Modern Era, San Francisco Mus Mod Art, 76; Am Still Life 1945-1983, Contemp Art Mus, Houston, 83; The Figurative Model: Bay Area Painting, 1956-1966, Grey Art Gallery, NY Univ, 84; New Narrative Painting, Mus Art, Ft Lauderdale, 85; Am Realism: The Precise Image, Iceman Mus Art, Tokyo, Daimanu Mus, Osaka, Yokohama Takashimaya, Yokohama, Japan, 85; Am Realism from the Glenn C Janss Collection, San Francisco Mus Mod Art, Calif, 86; Painting from the San Francisco Bay Area (with catalog), Paine Art Ctr & Arboretum, Oshkosh, Wis, 88; Bay Area Figurative Art, 1950-1965, San Francisco Mus Mod Art, 89; plus many others. *Teaching:* Instr painting, Univ Calif, Los Angeles, 63-64 & Otis Art Inst, 66-68; instr, Col Creative Studies, Santa Barbara, 68-71, Univ Calif, Davis, 75-76 & Univ Calif, Long Beach, 81. *Mem:* Nat Acad (assoc, 92, acad, 94-)

WOOBY, WILLIAM JOSEPH
ART DEALER, CURATOR
b Kearny, NJ, Sept 25, 47. *Exhib:* official presidential inaugural exhibs, 93,97,2001. *Collection Arranged:* Official Arkansas Inaugural Exhib, 93; Freedom Quilt Exhib for 1996 Olympics, Afro-American History in Quilts, 96. *Pos:* Mus Dir, Millennium Arts Ctr. *Awards:* Washington Art Coalition Award, 89; Nominated DC Mayor's Arts

Award, 92 & 94; Ark Traveler Award, 94; Vision Award, Committee of 100 on the Federal City, 2002. *Mem:* Life Skills Ctr, Friends of Alice Pike Barney; Kearny NJ Hist Soc. *Specialty:* Nat and Internat artists, performing and visual. *Mailing Add:* 1327 Corcoran St Washington DC 20009-4310

WOOD, ALAN
PAINTER
b Widnes, Lancashire, Eng, Aug 3, 35; Can citizen. *Study:* Liverpool Col Art, Eng, Nat Dipl Design, 58; Liverpool Univ, Inst Educ, Eng, Art Teachers Dipl, 59. *Work:* Seattle Art Mus, Wash; Art Gallery Greater Victoria, BC; Art Gallery South Australia, Adelaide; Tate Gallery, London; Nat Mus Wales, Cardiff; Vancouver Art Gallery, BC; and others. *Comn:* Mural, Leeds Univ, Yorks, 65; mural, BC Govt, Victoria, 77; mural, Fed Govt Can, Calgary, Alta, 81; Cineplex, Vancouver, BC, 85. *Exhib:* New Abstract Art, Edmonton Art Gallery, 86; Land/Scape, Vancouver Art Gallery, 86; solo exhibs, Galerie Franklin Silverstone, Montreal, 88, Kelowna Art Gallery, 89, Heffel Gallery, Vancouver, 89 & 93, Franklin Silverstone Gallery at Olga Korper, Toronto, 90, Gillian Jason Gallery, London, Eng, 90, John Ramsay Contemp Art, Vancouver, 92 & Project Gallery, Vancouver, 93; Recent Acquisitions, Vancouver Art Gallery, 90, 91 & 92; The First Five Yrs, Art Gallery of Southern Alta, Lethbridge, 93; Contemp Landscape, Project Gallery, Vancouver, 94; and others. *Awards:* Sr Can Coun Grant, 78; Can Coun Proj Cost Grant, 81; Can Coun A Grant, 82 & 85-86; and others. *Bibliog:* John Beardsley (auth), Earthworks and Beyond, Abbeville Modern Art Movements, New York, 84; Steven Denure & Christopher Lowry (dirs), Ranch: The Alan Wood Ranch Proj (film), 86; The Octagon Expedition (film), Pacific Report, CBC, 88. *Media:* Acrylic; Wood Constructions. *Mailing Add:* c/o Jenkins Showler Gallery 1539 Johnston Rd White Rock BC V4B 3Z6 Canada

WOOD, JAMES ARTHUR (ART)
CARTOONIST, LECTURER
b Miami, Fla, June 6, 27. *Study:* Washington & Lee Univ, BA; Mich State Univ. *Work:* Libr Cong, Washington, DC; Permanent Libr Collection, Univ Va, Charlottesville; Univ Akron Collection, Ohio; William Allen White Collection, Univ Kans; Truman Libr Collection, Kennedy Libr, Johnson Libr, Nixon Libr & Ford Libr; Annenberg Collection, Syracuse Univ. *Exhib:* Brussels World's Fair, 58; one-man show, Pittsburgh Press, 59; Great Challenge, Int Cartoon Exhib, 59-60; Cartoon Show, Nat Portrait Gallery, 72; Draw, Nat Arch, 95. *Pos:* Ed cartoonist, Richmond Newsleader, 50-56; chief political cartoonist, Pittsburgh Press, 56-63; cartoonist, US Tel Asn, 63-80 & Farm Bureau News, 782001; partner, Stam-Wood Productions, 80-94; cur, Nat Gallery Caricature & Cartoon Art, 9597; cartoonist, Washington Star, 48-50. *Awards:* Freedoms Found Awards, 53, 54, 58-60, 78-79, 82 & 89; Christopher Award, 54; Golden Quill Award, 60 & 62; Huevos de Onox, Mexico City, 77. *Mem:* Asn Am Ed Cartoonist (bd mem, 59-63, pres, 75-); Nat Cartoonists Soc; Nat Press Club; Phi Gamma Delta; Sigma Delta Chi. *Media:* Pen & Ink, Crayon. *Publ:* Great Cartoonists and Their Art, 86

WOOD, JAMES NOWELL
HISTORIAN, ADMINISTRATOR
b Boston, Mass, Mar 20, 41. *Study:* Williams Col, BA; Inst Fine Arts, NY Univ, MA. *Pos:* Asst to dir, Metrop Mus Art, New York, 67-68, asst cur, dept 20th century art, 68-70; cur, Albright-Knox Art Gallery, Buffalo, NY, 70-73, assoc, 73-75; dir, St Louis Art Mus, 75-80, dir and pres; dir & pres, Art Inst Chicago, 80-. *Res:* Nineteenth and twentieth century American and European painting, sculpture and photography. *Publ:* Auth, Rockne Krebs, 71; Six Painters, 71; Max Bill: Painting, Sculpture, Graphics, 74; Era of Exploration, 75. *Mailing Add:* Art Inst Chicago 111 S Michigan Ave Chicago IL 60603-6110

WOOD, JOHN AUGUST
WRITER, HISTORIAN
b Jan 2, 47; US citizen. *Study:* Univ Ark, MFA, 72, PhD, 77. *Collection Arranged:* Secrets of the Dark Chamber: The Art of the American Daguerrotype, Nat Mus Am Art, 95. *Pos:* Ed, Journal of Contemp Photography, currently. *Teaching:* Prof photog hist, McNeese Univ, 76-. *Awards:* Outstanding Book of Yr, Am Photog Hist Soc, 89; Choice Outstanding Academic Book, Am Libr Asn, 92; Best Photobook of Yr, New York Times, 95. *Res:* All aspects of photographic history from 1839 to the present. *Publ:* Auth, The Art of the Autochrome, Univ Iowa Press, 92, In Primary Light, 94, The Scenic Daguerrotype: Romanticism & Early Photography, 95; Secrets of the Dark Chamber, Smithsonian Inst Press, 95; The Photographic Arts, Univ Iowa Press, 97; Songs of Innocence and Experience, Joel-Peter Witkin, 2003. *Mailing Add:* 911 7th St Lake Charles LA 70601

WOOD, JOSEPH A
DESIGNER
b Queens, NY, May 16, 54. *Study:* State Univ NY Col, Buffalo, BS(art educ & design), 77; Kent State Univ, MFA, 84. *Work:* Pvt collections of Ivy Ross, Claire Sanford, Robert Lee Morris & Daphne Farago. *Exhib:* Artists Found Gallery, Boston, Mass, 90; Int Handwerksmesse, Munich, traveling, Ger, Dublin, Ireland, 91; Int Exhib Contemp Jewelry, Prague, Czech, 91; Artwear Gallery, NY, 92; 2nd Australian Int Crafts Triennial, Art Gallery, Western Australia, 92. *Teaching:* Grad Teaching Assistantship jewelry/metals prog, Kent State Univ, 81-84; asst prof jewelry/metalsmithing, Mass Col Art, Boston, 85-; design consult, Verne Q Powell Flutes, 91-92. *Awards:* Jurors Award, US Metal, San Francisco State Univ, 89; Fel, Nat Endowment Arts, 90; Fel, Mass Arts Coun, 91. *Bibliog:* Jill Slosburg (auth), Art Jewelry (feature), Art NEng, 5/87; Daniel Jocz (auth), exhib rev, Ornament, Vol 13, No 4, summer 92; Cynthia Cuadra (Auth), article on brooches, Ornament, Vol 15, No 3, spring 92. *Mem:* Distinguished mem Soc NAm Goldsmiths, 82; Top Dog Coop Metal Group, Waltham, Mass, 88-92; Boston Computer Soc, 91. *Mailing Add:* 202 Charles St Cambridge MA 02141

WOOD, MCCRYSTLE
EDUCATOR, ADMINISTRATOR
b Cincinnati, Ohio, Sept 20, 47. *Study:* Kansas City Art Inst, with Ron Slowinski, BFA, 73; Ind Univ, with Rudy Pozzatti, MFA, 76. *Work:* Cincinnati Art Mus; Atlantic Richfield Corp, Columbus, Ohio; Hyatt Hotels, Washington; AT&T, Cincinnati; Proctor & Gamble Co, Cincinnati. *Comn:* Litton Ind. *Exhib:* Centennial Invitational, Cincinnati Art Mus, 81; Gifts, Contemp Art Ctr, Cincinnati, 88; Prevailing Light, Portsmouth Mus, Ohio, 90; Siggraph, 95. *Pos:* Dir, sch design, Univ Cincinnati, 89-90; assoc dean, Col DAAP, Univ Cincinnati, 96-. *Teaching:* Prof design/art, Univ Cincinnati, 82-. *Awards:* Individual Artist Fel, Ohio Arts Coun, 86; Grant, Ky Found Women, 87. *Mem:* Col Art Asn; Siggraph; Am Asn Univ Prof. *Media:* Electronic Media. *Dealer:* Toni Birckhead Gallery W 4th St Cincinnati OH 45202. *Mailing Add:* 3662 Grandin Rd Cincinnati OH 45226-1117

WOOD, MELISSA
PAINTER, COLLAGE ARTIST
b Little Rock, Ark, Dec 7, 57. *Study:* Sch Fine Art, Washington Univ, St Louis, Mo, BFA, 80; Visual Art Access, San Francisco, Calif, cert, 92; studied with Edward Stanton & Carol Levy, Col Marin, Kentfield, Calif, 98; studied with Raymond Saunders, Kala Inst, Oakland, Calif, 98; L'Atelier, L'Ecole d'Art, Aix-en-Provence, France, 99. *Comn:* Set design, Luther Col, Decorah, Iowa, 89. *Exhib:* 3rd Ann Warehouse Sale, San Francisco Mus Mod Art Rental Gallery, San Francisco, Calif, 96; Carving the Forces of Change, Women's Caucus Art, Artemisia Gallery, Chicago, Ill, 97; Alternative Interpretations, Cox Gallery, Drury Col, Springfield, Mo, 98; Animals in Art, Anchorage Mus His & Art, Alaska, 2000; Hang Gallery, San Francisco, 2002; Melissa Wood Liquid What it is, What you do with it & Why Artist Studio Residency, Exhib/Demonstrations, de Young Art Ctr and Legion of Honor, San Francisco Fine Arts, Mus, San Francisco CA, 2003; ICA Ann Fall Art Auction San Jose Inst of Contemp Art, San Jose, Calif, 2004; The Crocker-Kingsley Biennial Crocker Art Mus, Sacamento, Calif, 2005. *Teaching:* Extended educ instr, Col Marin, Kentfield, Calif, 92-95, Univ Calif, Berkeley, 93 & Tamalpais Union High Sch Dist, 93; Artreach Grant, SADVC, Yolo Co, Calif, 2000; Art Workshops de Young Art Ctr, Fine Arts Mus of San Francisco, 2003 & 2004. *Awards:* Fel, Women Studio Workshop, NY, 93; Third Place Award, North Coast Collage Soc 9th Ann Exhib, 93; Artreach grant, Nelson Art Friends, Davis, Calif, 2000; Artist Studio Residency, de Young Art Ctr and Legion of Honor, San Francisco Fine Arts Mus, 2003. *Bibliog:* Melissa Wood (auth), Gallery Town Meeting, Art Calendar, Vol 10, No 4, 2/96; Ryan Kim (auth), National Show Exhibits at Gallery in Concord, Ledger Dispatch, 7/11/96; Anita Creamer (auth), The Sacramento Bee, Art Showcases Mending Lives, 8/7/2000; Alix Williams (auth), Healing Power of Art, The Davis Enterprise, 4/11/2000; Dewitt Cheng Artweek, Introductions South at the San Jose Institute of Contemporary Art, Oct, 2003, page 17; Brown Turtle Series #2, with Aries Corridor, 2003 Spring Newletter, San Jose Inst. of Contemporary Art; Here's Series #3 Gate, Jardins a Versailes, France with Rain and France, The Greater Sacramento Arts Reporter, July-August, 2003, pg 6. *Mem:* Nat Women's Caucus Art; Calif Lawyers Arts; Pac Rim Sculptors Group. *Media:* Mixed Media. *Publ:* Palace Chain, 1996 Contemp Women Artists Datebook, Cedco Publ, San Rafael, Calif, 96; House of Apples, Women Artists Wall Calendar, Cedco Publ, 97, House Of Rain, 99.; ed, People in the News, Mill Valley Herald, 11/3-10/97; House of Rain, Women Artists Datebook, Cedro Publ, 99 & Arched Door, Fallow Deer, 2001. *Dealer:* San Francisco Mus Mod Art Rental Gallery Ft Mason Bldg A San Francisco CA 94123; Oakland Mus Collector's Gallery Oakland CA 94601. *Mailing Add:* PO Box 567 Davis CA 95616

WOOD, NICHOLAS WHEELER
SCULPTOR, PAINTER
b San Francisco, Calif, Sept 21, 46. *Study:* San Francisco State Univ, BA, 72; Alfred Univ, NY, MFA, 77. *Work:* Lannan Found, Palm Beach, Fla; Arts Comn, San Francisco; Atlantic Richfield Co, Dallas, Tex; Southwestern Bell Telephone, Dallas; NY State Col Ceramics, Alfred; Veronica & Rene di Rosa Found, Napa, Calif; Palm Beach Col Found, Mus Contemp Art, Palm Beach, Fla; Nora Eccles Mus Art, Utah State Univ, Logan, UT. *Comn:* Sculpture, Criswell Develop Corp, 84; St Paul's Med Ctr, Dallas. *Exhib:* Oakland Mus Art, Calif, 74; Group Invitational, Dallas Mus Fine Arts, 79; solo shows, Ft Worth Art Mus, 79, Delahunty Gallery, Dallas, 81 & 500X Gallery, Dallas, Tex, 84; Janus Gallery, Los Angeles, 81; Showdown, Alternative Mus, NY, and traveling, 83; Sculpture on the Wall, San Antonio Art Inst, Tex, 83; American Ceramics Now, Everson Mus Art, 87; At the Edge, Laguna Gloria Art Mus, Austin, Tex, 90; Within Sight, Arlington Mus Art, Tex, 2001; Holga in Germany, Vorgeschicts/Archaologischen Mus, Bad Konigshofen, Ger, 2002. *Collection Arranged:* Drawing by Sculptors, 500X Gallery, Dallas, 85; Presence (with catalog), Center for Research in Contemp Art, Arlington, Tex, 92; OBJECTification (with catalog), The Gallery at Univ Tex, Arlington, 04; Layered, Stacked, Assembled (with catalog), Arlington Mus Art, Tex, 2005. *Teaching:* Assoc prof, Univ Tex, Arlington, 77-. *Awards:* Individual Res Grant, Univ Tex, Arlington, 81; Fel, Nat Endowment Arts, 81-82; Honorable Mention, Art Gallery, Tex Christian Univ, 84; Grumbacher Gold Medallion Award, Drawing, 90; Artist Grant Sculptue, Connemara Conservancy Found, 92; Millenium Award Art, Hawn Mem Found, 2000. *Bibliog:* Ned Rifkin (auth), Tablets and grids: Clay by Wood, 6/2/79 & Robert Raczka (auth), Nicholas Wood: Evolution of a theme, 3/21/81, Artweek; Spencer L Davis (ed), Tablet series: Nicholas Wood, Ceramics Monthly, 2/80. *Mem:* Int Sculpture Ctr; Nat Coun Educ Ceramic Arts; Mod Art Mus, Fort Worth, Tex; Dallas Mus Art; Arlington Mus Art, Tex; Dallas Ctr Contemp Art; McKinney Ave Contemp, Dallas. *Media:* Wood, Paint, Clay, Mixed Media. *Interests:* Curating Exhibitions & Photography. *Mailing Add:* 510 Lynda Ln Arlington TX 76010

WOOD, ROBERT L
SCULPTOR, CERAMIST
b Racine, Wis, May 27, 60. *Study:* St Joseph Univ; Univ Dallas, BA, 83; Ind State Univ, MFA, 87. *Work:* Burchfield-Penny Art Ctr & M&T Bank Permanent Collection, Buffalo, NY; Univ Indianapolis, Ind. *Exhib:* 1995 Ceramics USA Exhib, Meadows Gallery, Denton, Tex, 95 & 03; 10th Rosen Nat Outdoor Sculpture Exhib, Appalachian State Univ, Boone, NC, 96; Contemp NY State Crafts, NY State Mus, 97; Sculpture in Clay, Rockefeller Arts Ctr Gallery, Fredonia, NY, 2000; Rendezvous 2001, Mus of Nebr Art, Kearney, 2001; ESP Writing on the Wall Exhib, Castellani Art Mus, Lewistown, NY, 2002; 14th San Angelo Nat, San Angelo Mus Fine Arts, San Angelo, Tex, 2002; Creating Old & New Ceramics, Ind Hist Soc, Indianapolis, 2004; Materials: Hard & Soft, Center for Visual Arts, Denton, Tex, 2005, 2006. *Teaching:* Assoc prof ceramics, Buffalo State Col, 87-, prof, 96-, chair design, 97-99, asst to dean of arts & humanities, 2000. *Awards:* Sylvia Rosen Purchase Award, Craft Art, 96; Nat Award Excellence & Best of Both Exhibs, Westmoreland Art Nat, 98; First Place Award, ceramics, Guildford Handcraft Ctr, 2003. *Bibliog:* Robert A Ellison Jr (auth), Judgement call: the 29th Ceramics National, Am Craft Mag, 10 & 11/93; Gerry Williams (auth), Rollerblading along the Erie Canal, Studio Potter Mag, 12/95; Susan Peterson (auth), Ceramics 2003, Ceramics Monthly, 10/03. *Mem:* Nat Coun Educ Ceramic Arts; Am Craft Coun; Burchfield-Penney Art Ctr. *Media:* Clay. *Publ:* The Ceramic Design Book, Lark Bks, 98; The Best of Pottery 2, Rockport Publ, 98; Making Ceramic Sculpture, Lark Books, 2000; Contribr, Ceramics: Mastering the Craft, Chilton Bk Co, 2001; The Ceramic Glaze Handbook, Lark Books, 2001. *Mailing Add:* 135 Stillwell Ave Kenmore NY 14217

WOOD, RON
GLASS ARTIST, SCULPTOR
b Miami, Fla, Sept 16, 39. *Study:* Long Beach State Col, BA (rhetorical theory & sociology), 66, postgrad (fine arts, studio), 70-72. *Work:* Laguna Beach Mus Fine Art, Calif; Four Seasons Hotel, San Francisco. *Comn:* dome, Boyd Jeffires, Laguna Beach, Calif, 72; glass piece, Steigenberger Hotel, Berlin, Ger, 83; bent glass doors, comn by Joan Borinstine, Beverly Hills, Calif, 89; sculptures, Sheaton Waikiki Hotel, Honolulu, 96; glass pieces, St Vincent de Paul Catholic Church, Houston, 2000. *Exhib:* Festival Fine Arts, Festival Arts Pagent Masters, Laguna Beach, Calif, 72-75; Calif Artist Exhibit, Laguna Beach Mus Fine Art, Calif, 75; one-man show, Nat Galerie Mus, Berlin, 83-84. *Teaching:* instr multimedia, Mt San Jacinto Coll, Meniffe, Calif, 97-99. *Awards:* Pacific Northwest Photo Exhibition for Best Still Life Blue Ribbon, Ocean Shores, Wash, 89. *Bibliog:* Horst Hartman (auth), Galleriest, Kunstler/Art in Berlin, 83; Beverly Inskeep (auth), Fine Arts Commissioner, Orange Co Mag, 85; Angela Geiser (auth), Editor, The Californian, 99/2000. *Mem:* Sigraph. *Mailing Add:* 25801 Roanoke Rd Sun City CA 92586

WOODARD, CATHERINE
PATRON
Study: History magna cum laude, Wake Forest Univ, BA, 81; Journalism, Columbia Univ, MS, 82. *Pos:* Reporter, Ft Worth Star-Telegram, Tex, 82-84, NY Newsday, 84-94; deputy ed, Newsday Direct, 94-95; news ed, iGuide News Corp, New York City, 95-96. *Awards:* Named one of Top 200 Collectors, ARTnews Mag, 2004; recipient James Wright Brown Pub Serv award, Deadline Club, NY Newspaper Pub award, Society of Silurians award. *Mem:* Mus Modern Art Print Assoc, Artists Space (board dir, coordinator new media), Phi Beta Kappa. *Collection:* Viennese furniture, prints and works on paper, especially Much, Picasso, Kirchner and Johns

WOODFORD, DON (DONALD) PAUL
PAINTER, EDUCATOR
b Kansas City, Kans, June 16, 41. *Study:* Cornell Col, BA, 63; Ill State Univ, MA, 64; Univ Wis, MFA, 65. *Work:* Cedar Rapids Art Ctr Mus, Coe Col Gallery, Iowa; Davenport Munic Mus, Iowa; Wright State Univ Mus, Dayton, Ohio; Western Ill Univ Gallery, Macomb. *Exhib:* Sixty-ninth Ann Exhib Chicago & Vicinity, Art Inst Chicago, 66; 6th Nat Drawing Exhib, Erie Art Ctr, Pa, 66; Northwest Ann, Seattle Mus, 70; one-man show, Tacoma Art Mus, Wash, 71 & Univ Redlands, Calif, 80; Calif Artist-Works on Paper, Int Art Fair, Basel, Switz, 77. *Teaching:* Asst prof art-painting, Cornell Col, Mt Vernon, Iowa, 65-68; asst prof art-painting, Reed Col, Portland, Ore, 68-72; prof art-painting, Calif State Univ, San Bernardino, 72-. *Awards:* Arts & Riverwoods Prize, Riverside Art Ctr, 74. *Bibliog:* Thomas Albright (auth), Paintings on paper, San Francisco Chronicle, 6/7/75; Louis Fox (auth), Roplex and assemblage in relief, Artweek, 4/15/78; Julous Kaplin (auth), Don Woodford's Recent Constructions, Univ Redlands, 80. *Mem:* Col Art Asn Am. *Dealer:* Hank Baum Gallery 2140 Bush San Francisco CA 94115; Getler/Paul Gallery 50 W 57th St New York NY 10019. *Mailing Add:* 3334 N Arrowhead Ave San Bernardino CA 92405

WOODHAM, DERRICK JAMES
SCULPTOR
b Blackburn, Eng, Nov 5, 40. *Study:* SE Essex Tech Col Sch Art, intermediate dipl design; Hornsey Col Arts & Crafts, nat dipl design; Royal Col Art, dipl. *Work:* Tate Gallery, London, Eng; Mus Contemp Art, Nagaoka, Japan. *Comn:* Sculpture, Gates, comn by North Jersey Cult Coun, Paramus, NJ, 74; C G and E Atrium Sculptures, Moire Screen, 88 & Emerging Cube, Cincinnati, Ohio, 89. *Exhib:* Paris Biennale, Mus Art Mod, 65; Der Geist Surrealismus, Baukunst Galerie, Koln, WGer, 71; Sculpture in the Park, Paramus, NJ, 71 & 74; Wright State Univ Gallery, 76; Nat Sculpture Exhib traveling exhib, 76-77; Artists Choose Artists, Tweed Mus, Duluth, 77; one-man show, Jewish Mus, 69. *Teaching:* Instr sculpture, Philadelphia Col Art, 68-70; asst prof art forms found, Univ Iowa Sch Art, 70-73; assoc prof, Dept Art, Univ Ky, Lexington, 73-80; prof & dir, Sch Art, Univ Cincinnati, 80. *Awards:* Stuyvesant Found Bursary, 65; Prix de la Ville, Sculpture, Paris Biennale, 65. *Bibliog:* Otto Kulturman (auth), The New Sculpture, Praeger, 69; Teruo Fujieda (auth), Form and Structure, Kodansha Ltd, 72; Michael Findlay (auth), Contemporary Artists, St James Press, 77, 88 & 96; plus others. *Mem:* Mid-Am Col Art Asn; Col Art Asn. *Mailing Add:* 1910 Bluebell Dr Cincinnati OH 45224

WOODHAM, JEAN
SCULPTOR
b Midland City, Ala, Aug 16, 1925. *Study:* Auburn Univ, BA; Sculpture Ctr, New York; Univ Ill, Kate Neal Kinley Mem fel. *Work:* Massillon Mus Permanent Collection, Ohio; US Merchant Marine Mus, NY; Telfair Acad Arts & Sci, Savannah, Ga; Alfred Khouri Mem Collection, Norfolk Mus Arts & Sci, Va; Westport Permanent Collection, Conn; 20th Century American Painting & Sculpture, Foreign Mus, Sophia, Bulgaria; Spinoff acquired by The Jule Collins Smith Mus Art, Auburn Univ, Ala. *Comn:* Fountain pieces, Gen Elec Credit Corp, Stamford, Conn, 71-72; Scholars' Sphere (four and one-half ton sculpture), Harry S Truman High Sch, NY, 77; Monody (welded bronze sculpture), Goodwin Hall, Archit & Fine Arts Ctr, Auburn Univ, Ala, 79; Cent Conn State Univ, New Britain, Conn, 87; Conn State Comn Arts, Comn Med Examiner's Off, Farmington, Conn, 89. *Exhib:* Master Sculptors of Conn, Conn State Comn Arts Showcase, Bradley Int Airport, Conn, 90, within 12" x 12", Cast Iron Gallery, NY, 91; The Coming of Age of Am Sculpture: The First Decades of the Sculptors Guild, 1930s-1950s, Hofstra Mus, Hofstra Univ, Hempstead, NY, 90, traveling, 92zx; one-woman shows, Conn State Comn Arts Showcase, Bradley Int Airport, Conn, 91, Jean Woodham Fifty Years of Sculpture, Foy Union Gallery, Auburn Univ, Ala & Jean Woodham Fifty Yrs of Sculpture (with catalog), Stamford Mus, Conn, 98, Borglum Gallery, Silvermine Guild Galleries, New Caanan, Conn 2000, PMW Gallery, Stamford, Conn, 2001, Art/Place, Southport, Conn Art/Place, 2003, plus others; Collaborative Exhib of Sculptors, Kyoto Gallery, Kyoto, Japan, 93; The Sculptors Guild at PPG Wintergarden, Three Rivers Arts Festival, Pittsburgh, Pa, 94; Chesterwood Mus, Stockbridge, Mass, 2000; Dialogues in Abstraction, Univ of Conn, Stamford Art Gallery, 2004. *Pos:* Charter mem, Fine Arts Adv Coun, Liberal Arts Col, Auburn Univ, 88-94; adv bd Julie Collins Smith Mus Art, Auburn Univ, Ala, 2000. *Teaching:* Head dept sculpture, Silvermine Guild Artists, 55-56; instr sculpture, Stamford Mus, Conn, 67-69; vis asst prof sculpture, Auburn Univ, 70, assoc prof, 74-75; vis critic, Cornell Univ, Col Archit, Art & Planning, 80. *Awards:* Franklin Lectr, John & Mary Franklin Found, Auburn Univ, 96; Audubon Artists Medal for Creative Sculpture, 62; Medals of Honor for Sculpture, Nat Asn Women Artists, 66 & 74; Djerassi Found Grant, Woodside, Calif, 83; Finch Award, Art of the Northeast USA, 85; Citation for Contribution to Arts, Conn Gen Assembly & Gov Conn, 86; Citation for Contribution to Arts, Gov Ala, 89; Malvina Hoffman Artists Fund Prize for Best Sculpture in Exhib, Nat Acad 175th Ann Exhib, New York, 2000; Lifetime Achievement Award Westport Arts, Ct, 99; Artist of the Year, Art/Place, Southport, Conn, 2003. *Bibliog:* Dolly Curtis (dir), Jean Woodham, Sculptor, Extraordinaire (film), Curtis/Cromwell Productions, 89; Phillipe Clerin (auth), La Sculpture En Acier, Dessain et Tolra, Paris, 93; Jean Woodham, Franklin Lecture Series, Auburn Television (film), 96; Monograph on the Jule Collins Smith, Mus of Finearts, Lethander Family foundation, 2003; and others. *Mem:* Sculptors Guild (treas, 60-65, exec bd, 66-68 & 77-82, secy, 72-74, vpres for mem, 82-83, pres, 90-93, bd adv, 94; Sculptor's Guild (exec bd mem, 88, 89 & 95-96); Westport-Weston Arts Coun (bd dir, 82-83); Artists Equity Asn; Sculptors Guild (pres, 90); Silvermine Guild Artists (bd mgrs, 58-60, bd trustees, 81-83, chmn admissions, 83). *Media:* Metal, Welded; All Media. *Publ:* Alabama-Bound for New York, The Guild Reporter, Vol 7 no 1. *Mailing Add:* 26 Pin Oak Ct Westport CT 06880-1022

WOODMAN, BETTY
CERAMIST
b Norwalk, Conn, May 14, 30. *Study:* Alfred Univ, Sch Am Craftsman, New York, 48-50. *Work:* Albright Col, Reading, Carnegie-Mellon Inst, Pittsburgh, Pa; Alfred Univ, Greenwich House, Metrop Mus Art, NY; Joslyn Art Mus; Boston Mus Fine Arts; Cleveland Mus Art, Ohio; and others. *Comn:* Denver Munic Airport, Colo; Inst Contemp Art, Univ Pa, Philadelphia. *Exhib:* One-persons exhibs, Stedelijk Mus, Amsterdam, The Neth, 94 & 96, Int Mus Ceramics, Faenza, Italy, 95, Denver Art Mus, Colo, 95, Max Protetch Gallery, 96, 97 & 98, Musee d' Art Contemporai, 97, NJ Ctr Visual Arts, Summit, 98 & Provincial Mus Voor Moderne Kunst, Oostende, Belg, 98, Blanden Mem Art Mus, Fort Dodge, Iowa, 99, Pots Paper Prints, Mizel Arts Ctr at JCC, Denver, 2000, Clay, Bronze, Paper, Max Protetch Gallery, NY, 2000, Betty Woodman & Robert Barni: due e casi, Centro D'Arte La Loggia Monterfiridolfi, Italy, 2000; Am Crafts '77, Philadelphia Mus Art, 77; Ceramics Echos (with catalog), Nelson-Atkins Mus Art, Kansas City, Mo, 83; Silvermine Guild Artists, New Canaan, Conn, 84; Contemp Am Clay (with catalog), Boston Mus Fine Arts, 84; High Styles: 20th Century Am Design, Whitney Mus Am Art, NY, 85; Am Potters Today (with catalog), Victoria & Albert Mus, London, 86; Clay Revisions (with catalog), Seattle Art Mus, Wash, 87; Artful Objects: Recent Am Crafts, Fort Wayne Mus Art, Ind, 89; Vessels From Use to Symbol, Am Craft Mus, NY, 90; The Painted Vessel, Oriel Gallery, Cardiff, Wales, 91; The Shigaraki Ceramic Cult Park, Shigaraki-yaki, Japan; Investigations 1992, Inst Contemp Art, Univ Philadelphia, Pa, 92; Greenberg Gallery, St Louis, Mo, 92; In Touch, Olympic Winter Games, Lillehammer, Norway, 93; Bernard Toale Gallery, Boston, Mass, 94; Wadsworth Atheneum, Hartford, Conn, 95; Tuscia Electra, Commune Di Greve in Chianti, Italy, 96; Working Proof: 20 Yrs of Prints from Shark's Inc, CU Art Galleries, Univ Colo, Boulder, 96; View From Denver, Mus Moderne Kunst Stiftung Ludwig, Vienna, Austria, 97; Image, Plate, Vessel, Andrew Lord, Ken Price, Betty Woodman, Franklin Parrasch Gallery, NY, 97; La Geste et la Couleur, Une Poetique Ceramique, Biennale Int de Ceramique Contemporaine, Museemagnelli, Vallauris, France, 98; Color and Fire: Defining Moments in Studio Ceramics, 1950-2000, Los Angeles Co Mus Art, 2000; 34th Ann Auction and Gala, Yellowstone Art Mus, Billings, Mont, 2002; Shark's Ink, 1976-2001, Gallery Contemp Art, UCCS, Colorado Springs, 2002; Prints from

Shark's Inc, Flanders Graphics, Minneapolis, 2002; and others. *Pos:* Cur, Boulder Ctr Visual Arts, Colo, 83; panelist, Nat Coun Educ Ceramics Arts Conf, St Louis, Mo, 85, NY State Coun Arts, Visual Arts Prog, 86 & 87 & Nat Endowment Arts, Visual Artist Forum, 90. *Teaching:* Vis artist, Alfred Univ, NY State Col Ceramics, 75; prof, Fine Arts Dept, Univ Colorado, Boulder, 79-98, prof emer, 98-. *Awards:* Governor's Award Arts, Colo, 87; Visionary Award, Am Craft Mus, New York, 98; Fel, Rockefeller Found, Bellagio Study Ctr, Italy, 95; The Visionary Award, Am Craft Mus, New York, 98. *Bibliog:* Garth Clark (auth), American Ceramics 1876-Present, Abbeville Press, 88; Patricia Conway (auth), Art for Everyday: The New Craft Movement, Clarkson Potter, New York, 90; Craig R Miller (auth), Modern Design 1890-1990 in the Metropolitan Museum of Art, Abrahms, NY, 90. *Mailing Add:* c/o Shark's Inc 550 Blue Mountain Rd Lyons CO 80540

WOODMAN, TIMOTHY
SCULPTOR
b Concord, NH, Mar 4, 52. *Study:* Skowhegan Sch Painting & Sculpture, 70; RI Sch of Design, 71; Cornell Univ, BFA(sculpture), 74; Yale Univ, MFA(sculpture), 76. *Work:* Hirshhorn Mus & Sculpture Garden, Washington; Australian Nat Collection, Canberra; Metrop Mus Art, NY; Newark Mus, NJ; Memphis Brooks Mus Art, TN; Nat Mus Am Art, Smithsonian Inst, Washington. *Comn:* Sculpture, WK Kellogg Found, Mill Race Park, Battle Creek, Mich, 91; Sculpture, Gen Serv Admin, Ribicoff Fed Bldg & Courthouse, Hartford, Conn, 92; Western Hist Trails Ctr, Coun Bluffs, Iowa, 97. *Exhib:* Solo shows, Robert Freidus Gallery, NY, 77 & 78, Cherry Stone Gallery, Wellfleet, Mass, 77, 81 & 84, Zabriskie Gallery, NY, 81, 83, 85, 87, 89, 91, 93 & 95, Fayerweather Gallery, Univ Va, Charlottesville, 81, Greenberg Gallery, St Louis, Mo, 83 & 87, Fuller Goldeen Gallery, San Francisco, 84 & Asher Faure Gallery, Los Angeles, 86, Cherry Stone Gallery, Wellfleet, Mass, 99, Tibor de Nagy Gallery, NY, 2000, 02, Albert Merola Gallery, Provincetown, Mass, 2001; Whitney Mus Am Art (with catalog) Stamford, Conn, 87; Metrop Mus Art, NY, 87, 88; Yankee Mystique, Cape Mus Fine Arts, Dennis, Mass, 95; Primarily Small Works, Hunsacker/Schlesinger Gallery, Santa Monica, Calif, 95; By the Sea, Fotonhi Cramer Gallery, East Hampton, NY & NY, 96; Field & Stream, Monique Knowlton Gallery, NY, 96; Tibor De Nagy Gallery, NY, 98; and others. *Teaching:* Lectr, Univ Va, Charlottesville, 81. *Awards:* RS Reynolds Mem Award for Sculpture, 83. *Bibliog:* Gerrit Henry (auth), rev, Artnews, summer 93; Robert Taplin (auth), rev, Art in Am, 9/93; Hilton Kramer (auth), Art & Antiques, 6/98. *Media:* Aluminum, Paint. *Dealer:* Tibor De Nagy Gallery 724 Fifth Ave New York NY 10019. *Mailing Add:* Tobor de Nagy Gallery 724 5th Ave NE New York NY 10017

WOODS, BURTON ARTHUR
PAINTER
b Brooklyn, NY, Sept 3, 35. *Study:* Studied painting with Charles Sovek & Dan Gilhooley, portrait painting with Bob Behrens & drawing with Dan Gilhooley. *Work:* Clayton Liberatore Gallery, Bridgehampton, NY, Suffolk Co Court Bldg, Riverhead, NY; Tuthill House, Easthampton, NY. *Comn:* Reitano House, Setauket, NY, 93; Randall House, Mt Sinai, NY, 93; Tooker House, Port Jefferson, NY, 94; Infant Jesus Church, Port Jefferson, NY, 94. *Exhib:* 41st Ann Open Juried Exhib, Heckser Mus, Huntington, NY; 24th Ann Open Juried Exhib, Pastel Soc Ann, NY; Mills Pond House, Smithtown, NY, 93; Carriage House Mus, Philadelphia, Pa, 93; 2nd Ann Pastel Show, Paul Mellon Art Inst, Wallingford, Conn, 94; Long Island Artists Show, Bald Hill Cult Ctr, Farmingville, NY, 94; Vanderbelt Mus, Centerport, NY, 94; Water Mill Mus, NY, 94; Open Juried shows, Paul Melton Art Ctr, Wallingford, Conn, 95, 97, & 98, Duck Decoy Mus, Havre de Grace, Md, 96, Nat Art League, Dougleston, NY, 96, Ridgewood Art Inst, NJ, 97, Brookhaven Arts, Conn, 97 & 98; Int Juried Exhib, NJ Ctr Visual Arts, Summit, 96. *Awards:* First Place Pastels, North Shore Art Guild, Bald Hill Cult Ctr, 94; Best in Show, First Place & Second Place, Brookhaven Art Coun. *Bibliog:* K Mandracchia (auth), Harvest Times Mag; Carol Paquette (auth), Gatehouse critique, Port Jefferson Record, 93; article in North Light, 10/95. *Mem:* Wet Paint Soc, Sayville, NY; East End Arts Coun, Riverhead, NY; Allied Artists Am, NY; Conn Pastel Soc. *Media:* Pastel, Oil. *Dealer:* Jane Fuhrer Sidewalk Alley Gallery 5507 Rte 347 Mt Sinai NY 11766; Champlain Collection Fine Art Publs Highgate Commons 223 Swanton Rd Saint Albans VT 05478. *Mailing Add:* 27 Ridgeview Pl Mt Sinai NY 11766

WOODS, DAVID G
EDUCATOR
Study: Washburn Univ, BA; Northwestern Univ MA; Northwestern Univ, PhD; Attended, Aspen Inst, Coppenhagen Conversatory Music. *Exhib:* Coauth: Jump Right In!; author: Phoebe in Her Petticoat, Congotay; coauth: Teaching Music in 21st Century; contributor chapters to books Promising Practices in Pre-Kindergarten Music Education, Handbook for Research in Music Teaching & Learning, Second Handbook for Research in Music Teaching & Learning. *Teaching:* Chmn div music educ, Iowa State Univ, Ames, 1974-84; dir, Sch Music Univ Ariz, 1985-91; Dean, Col Fine Arts Univ Okla, 1991-97; Dean, Sch Music Ind Univ, 1997-99; Dean, Sch Fine Arts Univ Conn, 2000-. *Mailing Add:* Off Dean Univ Conn Sch Fine Arts 875 Convetry Rd Rm 202 Unit 128 Srotts Mnsfield CT 06269

WOODS, ROOSEVELT (RIP)
PAINTER, PRINTMAKER
b Idabel, Okla, Aug 15, 33. *Study:* Ariz State Univ, MAE, 58. *Work:* Phoenix Art Mus, Ariz; Ariz State Univ, Tempe; Ark State Univ, Jonesboro; Yuma Fine Arts Ctr, Ariz; Philip Morris Collection. *Comn:* Too (with Jeff Donaldson), Howard Univ, Washington; Relief-assemblage mural (with Ray Fink), Nat Housing Industs, Phoenix, 70; mosaic & bas relief painting (with Ray Fink), Greyhound-Armour, Phoenix, 71; Christmas bk cover, Neiman Marcus, 90; snow globe design, Neiman Marcus, 90-93. *Exhib:* Black Art, Ancestral Legacy, Dallas, Tex; High Mus Art; Milwaukee Art Mus; Va Mus Fine Arts; Artists from the Black Community of Ariz; and others; FESTAC Visual Art Exhib, Lagos, Nigeria, 77; Phoenix Art Mus; Nev Southern Univ, Las Vegas; Univ Wyoming, Laramie; Bosie Fine Art Ctr, Idaho; Bolles Gallery, San Francisco; Ill Bell Traveling Show, Chicago; Roswell Art Ctr, NMex; and others. *Teaching:* Prof painting & drawing, Ariz State Univ, 65-; assoc prof painting, Colorado Springs Fine Art Ctr, Colo, summer 67, prof emer drawing & painting, 92. *Awards:* COBA Artist, Consortium Black Orgns & Others Arts, 95. *Bibliog:* Black Art, Ancestral Legacy, Dallas Mus Art, Harry N Abrams; Dr Eugene Grigsby & WC Brown (auths), Art & Ethnics; Wayman R Spence, MD (auth), The Healing Arts, The Best American Artist Look at Medicine. *Media:* Mixed. *Publ:* Contribr, Voices, Nat Conf Artists, Mich Chapter. *Mailing Add:* 7817 S 13th Pl Phoenix AZ 85040

WOODSIDE, GORDON WILLIAM
DEALER, COLLECTOR
b Seattle, Wash. *Study:* Univ Wash. *Pos:* Dir, Woodside-Braseth Galleries, Seattle. *Specialty:* Artists of the Pacific Northwest. *Collection:* Representative works by prominent artists of the Northwest. *Mailing Add:* Woodside/Braseth Gallery 2101 Ninth Ave Seattle WA 98121

WOODSON, DORIS
PAINTER
b Richmond, Va, Jan 13, 29. *Study:* Xavier Univ, New Orleans, BA; Commonwealth Univ, Richmond, Va, MFA. *Work:* Bank of Va, Richmond; Pa State Univ. *Exhib:* 11th Ann Piedmont Painting Show, Mint Mus, Charlotte, NC, 71; Mainstreams 71, Int Painting, Marietta, Ohio, 71; Virginia Artists, Va Mus, Richmond, 71 & 75; Artists Showcase Gallery, Virginia Beach, Va, 73; Black Artists/S, Huntsville Mus Art, Ala, 79. *Pos:* Dir gallery, Va State Univ, Petersburg, 69-81. *Teaching:* Instr painting, Richard Bland Col, Petersburg, Va, 69; asst prof painting & drawing, Va State Univ, Petersburg, 69-91; adj instr design & drawing, Commonwealth Univ, Richmond, Va, 79-82; retired, 91. *Awards:* Petersburg Art Festival, Petersburg Area Art Leagues, 68-74; Norfolk Art Festival, Tidewater Artists Asn, 73; Lynchburg Art Festival, Lynchburg Art Asn, 74. *Mem:* Petersburg Art League. *Media:* Oil, Acrylic, Photography

WOODSON, SHIRLEY ANN
PAINTER, COLLAGE ARTIST
b Pulaski, Tenn, Mar 3, 36. *Study:* Wayne State Univ, BFA, MA; Grad Study, Art Inst Chicago. *Work:* Detroit Inst Arts, Detroit, Mich; Studio Mus Harlem, NY; United Am Health Care, Detroit, Mich; Mus Nat Ctr Afro Am Artist, Boston, Mass; Mus African Am History, Detroit, Mich. *Comn:* Site installation, Chene Park, City of Detroit, 86; mural, Fairlane Town Ctr, Dearborn, Mich, 90; Detroit Rigers, Comerica Park, Mich, 2000; Cobo Convention Ctr, Detroit, Mich, 2004. *Exhib:* Share the Memories, Detroit Inst Arts, 87; Coast to Coast, Nat Women Color Bookworks (with catalog), Radford Univ, Va, 90; Ancestors Known and Unknown, Box Works, Islip Art Mus, Islip, NY, 91; solo show, Sherry Wash Gallery, Detroit, Mich, 92; I Remember--30 Yrs After March on Washington, Concoran Gallery, Washington, DC, 93; Contemp African Am Artists 1980-1994, Nat Arts Club, NY, 94; 20th Century DIA Collection of Drawings & Graphics, Detroit Inst Arts, 2001; Seasons: Paintings & Collages by Shirley Woodson, Ft Valley State Univ, Ga. *Collection Arranged:* Detroit Inst Arts Fabric Workshop & Mus, Phila, Pa; Florida A & M Univ, Tallahassee; Wayne State Univ, Detroit, Mich. *Pos:* Dir exhibs, Arts Extended Gallery, 63-71; pres, Nat Conf Artists, Mich, 96-2000. *Teaching:* Instr painting, design, drawing & art hist, Highland Park Community Col, 66-78; consult, Highland Park Schs, Mich, 78-; vis prof, Eastern Mich Univ, 87-88; adminr & supervisor fine arts, Detroit Pub Schs, 92-; adj prof, Wayne State Univ, 96-. *Awards:* Fel, MacDowell Colony, 66-67; Mich Coun Arts Grant, 83-84 & 87-88; Arts Achievement Award, Wayne State Univ, Detroit, 95; New Initiatives for Arts Exhib Grants, 1994-96. *Bibliog:* Bamidele Demerson (auth), The Nile as vivifying power: Art of Shirley Woodson, Int Quart African-Am Art, 90; Anthony Murphy(auth), Portfolio/Shirley Woodson, American Visions, 92; Robert Henkes (auth), Art of Black American Women: Works by 24 Artists of the 20th Century, MacFarland & Co Publ, 93. *Mem:* Nat Conf Artists; Col Art Asn. *Media:* Painting, Collage, Assemblage. *Publ:* Auth, African American Women Artists in Michigan (study guide), Detroit Hist Mus, 85; contribr, Walter O Evans Collection of African American Art (catalogue), King Tisdell Cottage Mus, 91. *Dealer:* Sherry Washington 1274 Library St Detroit MI 48226. *Mailing Add:* 5656 Oakman Blvd Detroit MI 48204

WOODWARD, KESLER EDWARD
PAINTER, CURATOR
b Aiken, SC, Oct 7, 51. *Study:* Davidson Col, NC, BA, 73; Idaho State Univ, Pocatello, MFA, 77. *Work:* Alaska State Mus, Juneau; Univ Alaska Mus, Fairbanks; Atlantic Richfield Co, Los Angeles; Anchorage Hist & Fine Arts Mus & Alaska Contemp Art Bank, Anchorage; Morris Mus Art, Augusta, Ga; Tacoma Art Mus, Wash; plus others. *Comn:* Pacific Rim Hospital, Fort Richardson, Alaska; Morris Communications Corp Offices, Anchorage, Alaska; Holy Family Chapel, Fairbanks, Alaska; Alaska Airlines Corp Offices, Seattle. *Exhib:* one-man shows, Univ Alaska Mus & Alaska State Mus, 85, Jerald Melberg Gallery, NC, 86, Davidson Col Art Gallery, 86, Univ Ala, Huntsville, 90, Anchorage Mus Hist & Art, 91 & Univ Alaska, Anchorage Art Gallery, 91, Univ Alaska Fine Arts Gallery, 2000, Well St Gallery, Fairbanks, 2001, Decker/Morris Gallery, Anchorage, 02, Univ Alaska Anchorage Kenai Campus Gallery, 03; Terra Borealis, Visual Art Ctr Alaska, Anchorage, 91; Contemp Art from Alaska, Magadan, Art Gallery, Russia, 92; SC Artists, Greenville Mus Art, SC, 91; True North, Achorage Mus Hist & Art, 96; Morris Mus of Art, Augusta, Ga, 2001. *Collection Arranged:* New Possibilities: Works from the Canadian Art Bank (auth, catalog), Alaska State Mus, 78; A Celebration of Tradition, Visual Arts Ctr of Alaska, 78 & National Invitational, 78-79; Canadian Horizons (with

catalog), 81-82; Sydney Laurence Retrospective (with catalog), Anchorage Mus Hist & Art, 90 & Eustace Ziegler Retrospective (with catalog), 98; Fred Machetanz Retrospective, Anchorage Mus of History & Art, 04. *Pos:* Cur temp exhib, Alaska State Mus, Juneau, 77-78, cur visual arts, 79-81; artistic dir, Visual Arts Ctr of Alaska, Anchorage, 78-79; dir, Univ Alaska Fine Arts Gallery, 82-88; dir, Fine Arts & Humanities Proj, Inst Canada, Dartmouth Col, 88-91; chair, Dept Art & Div Arts & Communications, Univ Alaska, 96-. *Teaching:* Asst prof painting, Univ Alaska, 81-88, assoc prof, 88-96, prof, 96-, prof emeritus, 2000-. *Awards:* Alaska State Coun Arts Fel, 82; Vis Res Fel, Dartmouth Col, 88-91. *Mem:* Col Art Asn. *Media:* Acrylic, Oil. *Res:* Early pictorial material pertaining to polar regions and little-known Alaskan historical artists. *Publ:* Sydney Laurence, Painter of the North, 90; Painting in the North, 93; A Sense of Wonder, Art from Alaska, 95; Spirit of the North: The Art of Eustace Paul Ziegler, 98; Painting Alaska, 00; Modernist Mind and Mystical Spirit: The Art of Oscar Gluemner, 02; exhib catalog Frank Soos, Morris Mus of Art, 01; exhib review Art News, 01; color reproduction, Harpers, 02. *Dealer:* Jerald Melberg Gallery Charlotte NC; Braarud Fine Art La Conner WA. *Mailing Add:* Dept Art Univ Alaska Fairbanks AK 99775

WOODWARD, STEVEN P
SCULPTOR
b Little Falls, Minn, 53. *Study:* St Cloud State Univ, BA, 76. *Work:* Walker Art Ctr, Minneapolis; Tweed Mus, Duluth, Minn; First Bank System, Minneapolis; Minn State Arts Bd, St Paul. *Comn:* Univ Upper Iowa, Fayette; One Percent for Arts program, Univ Minn, Duluth, 96; One Percent for Arts program, Univ Minn, Minneapolis, 96; The St Paul Cos, Inc, St Paul, 97; US Gen Svcs Administration Art and Arch Program US-Can border crossing Sta, Pembina, ND, 97; Percent for Arts Commn, Univ Wis, Madison, 97; Percent for Arts Commn Minn Dept Revenue Bldg, St Paul; Percent for Arts Commn, Kirchbak Gardens, Richfield, Minn. *Exhib:* Ann Juried Exhib, Queen's Mus, NY, 84; Bim Bam Botterham, Stokker Stikker Gallery, NY, 85; Bockley Gallery, Minneapolis, 88; Thomas Barry Fine Arts, Minneapolis, 90, 91 & 92; Kiehle Gallery, St Cloud State Univ, Minn, 91; one person shows, Recent Sculpture, Thomas Barry Gallery, Minneapolis, 88 & 90, New Sculpture, Thoms Barry Gallery, 92, Open Studio, 233 Park Avenue, Minneapolis, 96 & 2000; Forms '92, 13th Ann Invitational Sculpture show, Hennepin Avenue United Meth Ch, Minneapolis, 92; Landscape as Object, Thomas Barry Gallery, 93; The Key to the Garden (installation with David Culver and Kate Hunt), Walker Art Ctr Educ Dept, 94; Six McKnight Artists, Minneapolis Col Art and Design, 96; Cast Metal Invitation Exhib, Humanities Fine Arts Ctr, Univ Minn, Morris, 96; and others. *Awards:* Juror's Award, Small Works Show, New York Univ, 84; Nat Endowment Arts, 88; Jerome Travel and Study Grant, 94 & 98; McKnight Found Fel, 94; Minn State Arts Bd Fel, 95

WOODWARD, WILLIAM
PAINTER, MURALIST
b Washington, DC, Mar 11, 35. *Study:* Abbott Sch Art, Corcoran Sch Art, Am Univ, BA & MA, Washington, DC; Acad de Belli Arti, Florence, Italy. *Work:* Corcoran Gallery; Speed Mus, Louisville; Washington Co Mus Fine Art; Ogunquit Mus Fine Art, Ogunquit, Maine; Payson Col, Delaplans, Va; and others. *Comn:* Drawing, The White House, DC, 68; mural, Clydes Inc, Tysons Corner, Va, 80; mural, City Hall Rockville, Md, 82; mural, History of Medicine, Fairfax Hosp, Va, 97; US Army Mus, Washington, DC. *Exhib:* One-man shows, Mickelson Gallery, DC, 66-74, Hirschl & Adler Gallery, NY, 71, John State Col, Vt, 74 & Int Monetary Fund, Washington, DC, 75; Fendrick Gallery, Washington, DC, 82 & 89; Marin-Price Galleries, 2000. *Teaching:* Instr painting, Corcoran Sch Art, DC, 65-; from asst prof painting to prof & program dir, George Washington Univ, DC, 69-; dir, Summer Fine Arts Prog, Brittany, France, 76-79. *Awards:* Painting Fel in Italy, Leopold Schepp Found, 57-59; Mary Graydon Scholar, Am Univ, 53-57 & Teaching Fel, 58-61; Design Prize, Silver Dollar Cong Commemorative Coin, 89; First Prize, 49th Ann Contemp Am Painting, Soc of the Four Arts, Palm Beach, Fla, 97. *Bibliog:* Rafael Sqirru (auth), The Washington mannerists: the foresight to look backwards, Americas, Vol 19, No 1; Legrace N Benson (auth), The Washington scene, Art Int, Vol 13, No 10; Jill Weschsler (auth), William Woodward: Traditional themes, modern methods, Am Artist, 12/76; D Bowers (auth), Commemorative Coins of the US, Bowers & Merena, 91; M Shwartz (auth), The Greatest Mural on Earth, Am Artist, 3/92. *Publ:* Contribr, Art in America, 1760-1860, 69; contribr, Leonardo da Vinci, 70 & Dreamers of Decadence, 72, Washington Post. *Dealer:* Marin-Price Galleries 7022 Wisconsin Ave Chevy Chase Md 20815. *Mailing Add:* Dept Art George Washington Univ Smith Hall Art-A101 801 22nd St NW Washington DC 20052

WOODY, (THOMAS) HOWARD
SCULPTOR, ENVIRONMENTAL ARTIST
b Salisbury, Md, Sept 26, 35. *Study:* Richmond Prof Inst, BFA; ECarolina Univ, MA; Univ Iowa; Art Inst Chicago; Kalamazoo Art Ctr; Univ Ky. *Work:* SC State Art Collection, Columbia; Gibbes Art Gallery, Charleston, SC; Mus Art, Charlotte, NC; Birmingham Mus Art, Ala; Columbus Mus Arts & Crafts, Ga; and others. *Exhib:* Tenth Int Sculpture Conf, Toronto, 78; Arcosanti Conf, 78; 11th Int Sculpture Conf, Washington DC, 80; Col Art Conf, New Orleans, La, 80; Sky Art Conferences, Mass Inst Technol, Cambridge, 81 & 86, Linze, Austria, 82 & Munich, Ger, 83. *Teaching:* Instr sculpture, Roanoke Fine Art Ctr, Va, 59-61; assoc prof sculpture, Pembroke State Univ, 62-67; prof sculpture, Univ SC, 67-. *Awards:* Spec Citation Award, Atlanta Festival Sculpture, 68; SC State Art Collection Award, 71 & 74 & Fel grants, 73 & 77, SC Arts Comn. *Bibliog:* Ann Weinstein (auth), The sky's no limit, Art Voices, 7/81; L G Redstone (auth), Public Art: New Directions, McGraw-Hill, 81. *Mem:* Southern Asn Sculptors (pres, 65-70); Nat Sculpture Ctr (adv, 66-80); Guild SC Artists (mem bd, 69); SC Craftsmen (mem bd, 68); Southeastern Col Art Conf. *Media:* Plastic. *Publ:* Auth, Atmospheric sculpture: An event, not an object, Vol 7, No 1 & Atmospheric concepts, Vol 6, No 2, Southeastern Col Art Conf Rev; Workshops in environmental sky art, Design for Arts in Educ, 3-4/79; Environmental art, Sculptor's News Exchange, Princeton, NJ, 9-10-11/79; and others. *Mailing Add:* 433 Arrowwood Rd Columbia SC 29210

WOOF, MAIJA GEGERIS ZACK See Peeples-Bright, Maija Gegeris Zack Woof

WOOL, CHRISTOPHER
PAINTER
Exhib: Boymans-Van Beuningen, Rotterdam, 91; Kolnischer Kunstverein, Koln, 91; Kunsthalle Bern, Bern, 91; Galerie Max Hetzler, Koln, 93; Brandl/Oehlen/Wool, Nat Gallery, Prague, 94; The Whitney Mus, NY, 95, 97; Mus of Modern Art, NY, 96, 97, 98; Ctr d'Art Contemporain, Geneva, 99; Skarstedt Fine Art, NY, 00; Eleni Koroneou Gallery, Athens, 2000; Galerie Micheline Szwajcer, Antwerp, 2001; Luhring Augustine NY, London, 2001; Le Consortium, Dijon, 2002; group exhibs, Aspen Art Mus, 99, Angles Gallery, Santa Monica, Calif, 99, Greene Naftali, NY, 99, Mus Modern Art, 2000, New Mus Art Lucerne, Switz, 2000, Barbara Gladstone Gallery, New York City, 2000, Alexander Gallery, New York City, 2000, Whitney Mus Am Art, 2001, Sabine Knust, Munich, 2001, Mus des Beaux Arts, Dole, France, 2001, Paine Webber Art Gallery, NY, 2002, Norton Mus Art, West Palm Beach, Fla, 2002; and others. *Awards:* Fel, Nat Endowment Arts, 87. *Bibliog:* Gray Indiana (auth), Chronicle in black & white, The Village Voice, 3/31/87; Jerry Saltz (auth), This is the end, Art Mag, 9/20/88; Parkett, No 33, 92. *Mailing Add:* c/o Luhring Augustine & Hodes Gallery 531 W 24th St New York NY 10011

WOOLSCHLAGER, LAURA TOTTEN
PAINTER, PRINTMAKER
b Dallas, Tex, Sept 1, 32. *Study:* Syracuse Univ, BFA(magna cum laude), 54; Southern Ore Col, with Robert Alston, 65. *Work:* Carnegie Libr, Lewiston, Idaho; Mus Native Am Cult, Spokane, Wash; Favell Mus Western Art, Klamath Falls, Ore. *Exhib:* Southwest Rendezvous, Oro Valley Country Club, Tucson, Ariz, 79-81; C M Russell Show, Heritage Inn, Great Falls, Mont, 79-81; Western Experience, Stewart Anderson Ranch, Ellensburg, Wash, 80; Artist in Residence, Mus Native Am Cult, Spokane, Wash, 80; Ceres Western Art Show, 92-95. *Awards:* Best of Show, Artists of the Old West, 79 & Nat Western Art Show, Western Art Asn, 79. *Bibliog:* Dr Darwin Goodey (auth), An inner view, Art West Mag, 1/80; Paula Hartwig (auth), Northwest Originals, Washington Women & Their Art, Ann 90. *Mem:* Western Art Asn. *Media:* Acrylic, Watercolor; Intaglio, Monoprint; Assemblages; Mised Media. *Mailing Add:* 1221 Poe St Wenatchee WA 98801

WOOLWICH, MADLYN-ANN C
PAINTER, INSTRUCTOR
b Fall River, Mass, Sept 14, 37. *Study:* Bridgewater Col, BS(educ), 59, MEd, 61; Parsons Sch Design, with Barbara Nechis, 86; Nat Acad Design, with Wolf Kahn, 87; Vt Studio Ctr, 96. *Work:* Archival Collection, Pastel Soc Am Gallery, NY; Dow Jones Info Servs, Princeton, NJ; Mason Gross Gallery, Rutgers Univ, New Brunswick, NJ; Eastern Branch, Monmouth Co Libr, Red Bank, NJ; Georgian Court Col, Lakewood, NJ. *Comn:* Acrylic painting, Gerber Sommer Asn, Hackensack, 86; oil painting of dog, comm by parishioners for Father James, Middletown, NJ, 86; floral triptych, comm by Kimberly Crawford, Vero Beach, Fla, 87; pastel floral, comm by Evelyn Cole, Fort Pierce, Fla, 87; pastel painting, comm by Mr & Mrs Vin Scully, Pacific Palisades, Calif, 87; pastel painting, Evergreen Gallery, Cancer Soc, 90; pastel painting, Canyon Suite, Russell Thacker, Esq. *Exhib:* Pastel Soc Am Exhib, Nabisco Gallery Invitational, Hanover, NJ, 88; invitational pastel exhib, Quincy Art Mus, Ill; state show, Ocean Co Art Guild, 90; Biennial Exhib, Pastel Soc N Fla, Pensacola, 91; Ann Exhib, Pastel Soc Am, NY, 78-92; Pastel Soc West Cost/Traveling Show, Kaiser Permanente Ctr, Sacramento & Oakland, Calif, 92; Int Soc Marine Painters, 92; Newark Mus Benefit, NJ, 92; solo exhib, Educ Testing Serv, Conant Gallery, Princeton, NJ, 92; Am Embassy, Uruguay, 92-96; Swain Gallery, Plainfiled, NJ, 96; Lupine Gallery, Monheyon Island, 92-2000; Evergreen Gallery, 98-2001. *Pos:* writer, The Artists' Mag, Pastel J, & The Artist's Sketchbook; coordr, Pastel Website for 45 Pastel Artists. *Teaching:* Instr drawing & design, Guild Creative Art, Shrewsbury, NJ, 82-88, adult class pastel/oil landscape, 84-90; drawing & painting, Spring Lake Recreation Comn, 87-88; workshops, Pastel Soc Am, 86-96; judge in field, 87-96; demonstr & workshop teacher, Int Asn Pastel Soc. *Awards:* Trump Purchase Award, 88 & Duane Wakeham Award, 98, Pastel Soc Am; Best in Show, Ocean Co Artists Guild, 90; Best in Show, Guild Creative Art State Show, 96; Award of Excellence, Manhattan Arts Mag, 96; Conn Pastel Soc Award, 99; Residency Award, Carillin Art Inst. *Bibliog:* Carol Katchen (auth), Creative painting with pastel, Art Times, Rhinebeck, NY, 92; Coloring Their World, Asbury Park Press, 93; Best of Pastel, Rockport Publ, 96. *Mem:* Guild Creative Art (vpres, educ facilities, 80-); Monmouth Arts Gallery (vpres, 84-86); Pastel Soc Am (secy & pub relations, 86-95); Nat Mus Women Arts; Salmagundi Club; Knickerbocker Artists USA (vpres, 91-96). *Media:* Pastel, Oil. *Publ:* Contribr, Vitality Mag (cover), 4/92; Pastel Interpretations, Ulysses Publ Co, rev ed, 95; Roughing it in pastel, North Light Mag, 95; The Art of Pastel Portraiture, Watson-Guptill Publ, 96. *Dealer:* Evergreen Gallery 310 Morris Ave Spring Lake NJ 07762; Swain Galleries 703 Watchung Ave Plainfield NJ 07060. *Mailing Add:* 473 Marvin Dr Long Branch NJ 07740

WOOSTER, ANN-SARGENT
PAINTER
b Chicago, Ill, Jan 19, 46. *Study:* Bard Col, AB, 68; Hunter Col, with Robert Morris, MFA, 73, and Leo Steinberg, Rosalind Krauss & Ray Parker, MA(art hist), 78. *Exhib:* Anthology Film Archives; Black Maria Festival; Contemp Arts Ctr, Cincinnati; New Arts Ctr, Kutztown, 94. *Pos:* Ed educ dept, Shorewood Publ, New York, 69-72; free

lance writer, Art Am, New York, 73-; staff writer, Art Forum, 75-76, Village Voice, 79-83 & Afterimage, 81-92; contrib ed, East Village Eye, 83-86, Amtrak Express, 87-91 & High Performance, 88-. *Teaching:* Instr, Sch Visual Arts, New York, 75-, Kean Col, Union, NJ, 79-83, New York Univ, 85; New York Sch Interior Design, 89-; instr, MFA Prog, Pa Acad Fine Arts, 94-. *Awards:* Helen Rubenstein Fel, Whitney Mus Am Art, 75; Award, 82, Grant for Media Production, 85, NY State Coun Arts; Logan Grant for New Writing on Photography, 88; Video Fel, New York Found of the Arts, 88. *Bibliog:* Jean Sousa (auth), NAME events, NAME Gallery, 80; Charlene Spretnak (auth), Politics of Women's Spirituality, Anchor Doubleday, 82. *Mem:* Int Art Critics Asn; Women's Caucus; Int Art Critics Asn (secy Am Sect, 92-96). *Media:* Miscellaneous Media. *Publ:* Auth, Moving to dance, 12/80 & Yvonne Rainer: Journeys to Berlin 1971, 5/81, Drama Rev; Making Their Mark: Women Artists Move Into The Mainstream (catalog essay), 89; essay, Reach Out & Touch Someone: The Romance of Interactivity (book), Illuminating Video, New York, Aperture Press, 91; chapters in American Painting, Goodman Publ, 91; The First Generation: Women and Video (catalog essay), 93. *Mailing Add:* 170 Second Ave New York NY 10003-5754

WORDELL, EDWIN HOWLAND
PAINTER
b Philadelphia, Pa, Aug 27, 27. *Study:* San Diego State Univ, dipl(hon), 61. *Work:* San Diego Zoological Soc; NASA; Tex Instruments; Transco Energy Co, Houston, Tex; Scripps Clinic & Res Found, The Burnham Inst & Univ Calif San Diego Burn Ctr, La Jolla, Calif. *Comn:* Triptich (watercolor), Zoological Soc, San Diego; three watercolor paintings, San Diego Trust & Savings Bank; two watercolor paintings, Great Am Development Co, San Diego; US Coast Guard; Borden Chemical, N Am Terminals, Inc. *Exhib:* Butler Inst Am Art, Youngstown, Ohio, 92, 95 & 2002; Sangre de Cristo Arts Ctr, Pueblo, Colo, 99; Van Vechton-Lineberry Taos Art Mus, N Mex, 2000; Winston Churchill Meml & Lib, Fulton, Mo, 2001; Segreto Contemp Art, Santa Fe, NMex, 2002; Aesthetics, Inc, San Diego, 2003; CSG Dominquez Hills, Carson, Calif, 2005. *Pos:* Juror: Nat Watercolor Soc, 94, Carlsbad/Oceanside Art League, Calif, 96, Southbay Watercolor Soc, San Pedro, Calif, 96 & local art orgs, 2000-03; Univ Calif San Diego, Burn Ctr; Utah State Univ; San Bernardino Valley College; NASA. *Teaching:* Instr watercolor workshop, Greece, 85, NZ, Fiji & Australia, 86, Mex, 88, 89, 93, 96 & 97, Port, 90, Guatamala, 91, Turkey, 92 & Bora Bora Imauri, 99, Hendersonville, NC, 1999 & 2003 & local workshops. *Awards:* Merit award, La Watercolor Nat Exhib, 2001; Award of Merit, Internat Soc Exptl Artist, 2002 & 2003; Donor's Award Taos, Hist Mus NMex, 2004; Mem Award San Diego Watercolor Soc, Int Exhib, 2005. *Bibliog:* Jann Lawrence & Terry James Little (auths), Creative Tools for the Artist, 2001. *Mem:* Nat Watercolor Soc; Watercolor West; San Diego Art Guild (pres, 90-91); Taos Soc Watercolorists; Rocky Mountain Watermedia Soc, Boulder, Colo. *Media:* Watermedia, Mixed. *Interests:* Reading; Music. *Collection:* pvt collections, Millard Sheets, Nat Acad, George Gibson, Nat Acad, Robert E Wood, Walter W Joty & Richard E Morris. *Publ:* First issue cover, San Diego Metro Mag, 85 & 90; Creative Collage Techniques, 94, Creative Watercolor, 96 & Exploring Color (rev ed), 98, Northlight Bks; NC & Ga State Bar J, 96; Watercolor: Abstract 96, Artists Mag, 9/2000; Watercolor Mag, winter 2000. *Dealer:* Aesthetics Inc 301 Spruce St San Diego CA 92103. *Mailing Add:* 6251 Lorca Dr San Diego CA 92115

WORKMAN, ROBERT P
PAINTER, ILLUSTRATOR
b Chicago, Ill, Jan 27, 61. *Study:* Sch Art Inst Chicago; Roosevelt Univ (Belg, Europe), PhD, 86; Pac Western Univ, BA, 87, MA, 92; Ecole du Louvre, Doctorate, 97. *Hon Degrees:* First American Artist Accepted into Louvve for 21st Century. *Work:* Libr Nat Mus Am Art Portrait Gallery, Nat Arch, Washington; Ridge Hist Soc Mus, Chicago; The Vatican, Rome, Italy; Ill State Mus, Springfield; Musee de Louvre; and others. *Comn:* Portrait, Mayor Richard J Daley, Daley Branch Libr, Chicago Pub Libr, Ill, 89; Mt Greenwood Br Libr, Chicago; Walker Br Libr, Chicago. *Exhib:* Nat Vet For War Conv, Chicago, 87; Int Cartoon Festival, Europe, 87; Sch Art Inst, Nat Reunion Alumni, Chicago, 91; Ridge Hist Soc Mus, Chicago, 92; Expo 92, Seville Worlds Fair, US Pavilion, Spain, 92; Nat Exhib, sch Art Inst Chicago; Royal Acad Arts, London, 95 & 96; Expo 98, Lisbon, Portugal, US Pavilion, 98; Kennedy Park Lib/Mus; and others. *Pos:* Graphic artists/cartoonist, Village View Publs, 83-88; artist, Villager (newspaper), 91-; founder, Kennedy Park Libr, Chicago. *Teaching:* Instr art/writing, St Xavier Col, 85; artist-in-residence, Chicago Pub Libr, 91-; adj lectr, Univ Ariz, 96; Maitre de Conf, Paris, 97; prof, Mus Nat d'Histoire Naturelle France. *Awards:* Plaque, Ill Dept Conserv; Chicago, 150th cert, City of Chicago, 87; Plaque/Cert Appreciation, Vet For War, Post 5220. *Bibliog:* Stan Barker (auth), Home grown, Artists Mag, 90; Dan Rafter (auth), Seville expo, Beverly Rev, 92; Steve Metsch (auth), Artist wins spot at worlds fair, 92. *Mem:* Assoc mem Am Watercolor Soc; Ridge Art Asn; Sch Art Inst Chicago; Artists Resource Inst, Ft Wayne Mus Art; Reader, Oxford Univ, Eng. *Media:* Watercolor, Acrylic. *Res:* Egyptian hieroglyphics nd culture; Maya hieroglyphics and culture and the possible influences and similarities between the two since 1997. *Publ:* Auth & illusr, Angels of Doom; Sesqui Squirrel, Hist Mt Greenwood, Ill; Sesqui Squirrel Meets George Washington; Sesqui Squirrel presents the Wright Brothers First Flight; Sesqui Squirrel Tours the Art Inst Chicago. *Mailing Add:* 2509 W 111th St Chicago IL 60655

WORTH, KAREN
SCULPTOR
b Philadelphia, Pa, Mar 9, 24. *Study:* Tyler Art Sch, Temple Univ; Pa Acad Fine Arts; Acad Grande Chaumiere, Paris. *Work:* Smithsonian Inst; West Point Acad, NY; Am Jewish Hist Asn, Boston; Jewish Mus, NY; Israel Govt Coins & Medals Div, Jerusalem. *Comn:* Space Age (medal), Soc Medalists, 63; Hist Jews of Am, Judaic Heritage Soc, 69, Presidents USA, Whittnauer Precious Metals Guild, 74; Bicentennial Presidents (medal), Galaxies Unlimited Inc, 75. *Exhib:* Nat Acad, NY, 65; Lever House, NY, 66-; Ceramic Sculpture of Western Hemisphere. *Teaching:* Pvt sculpture classes, 72-73. *Awards:* Saltus Award, 80, Numismatics Lifetime Achievement Award; Lindsey Morris Award (for a portrait), 86. *Bibliog:* Ed Trautman (auth), Almanac, Franklin Mint, 68. *Mem:* Fel Nat Sculpture Soc (coun, 69-); Fine Arts Fedn New York. *Media:* Clay, Bronze. *Mailing Add:* 19 Henry St Orangeburg NY 10962

WORTH, PETER JOHN
SCULPTOR, HISTORIAN
b Ipswich, Eng, Mar 16, 17; US citizen. *Study:* Ipswich Sch Art, 34-37; Royal Col Art, London, with E W Tristram, Paul Nash, Edward Bawden, Douglas Cockerell & Roger Powell. *Work:* Denver Art Mus; Joslyn Art Mus; Sheldon Gallery Art, Univ Nebr. *Exhib:* San Francisco Mus Art, 50; Nelson Gallery Art, 50, 53, 54 & 57; Art Inst Chicago, 51; Walker Art Ctr, 51, 52 & 56; Denver Art Mus, 52, 53, 55-57 & 60-63. *Teaching:* Prof art hist, Univ Nebr, Lincoln, currently. *Mem:* Egypt Explor Soc, London; Col Art Asn Am. *Res:* Stylistic transformations in late antique and early medieval art, especially in iconography. *Publ:* Photogr, Life Library of Photography, 70; photogr, Bilder, Stuttgart, 70

WORTHEN, AMY NAMOWITZ
PRINTMAKER, HISTORIAN
b New York, NY, Aug 13, 46. *Study:* Smith Col, with Leonard Baskin, BA, 67; Univ Iowa, with Mauricio Lasansky, MA, 69; Sir John Cass Col, City London Polytechnic, 86- 87. *Work:* Metrop Mus Art, NY; Cooper-Hewitt Mus, NY; Des Moines Art Ctr, Iowa; Nat Mus Am Art, Washington; Mus Fine Arts, Boston. *Comn:* Two engravings, Terrace Hill Soc, Des Moines, Iowa, 79; Patron's Print, Univ Iowa, 82; Aida in Des Moines (engraving), Des Moines Metrop Opera; Centro Internazionale di Grafica, Venice, 92. *Exhib:* World Print III, San Francisco, Mus Mod Art, 80; Smithsonian Touring Exhib, II Int Mus, 80-83; solo exhibs, Brunnier Gallery, Iowa State Univ, Ames, 81, Selected Prints and Drawings, 1979-84 (with catalog), Sioux City Art Ctr, 84, State Univ NY, Binghamton, 89, Grinnell Col, Iowa, 90, Louise Noun Collection: Art by Women, Des Moines Art Ctr, Iowa, École des Beaux-Arts, Saint-Étienne, France, 92, Scuola Int di Grafica, Venice, Italy, 94 & Associazione Int Incisori, Rome, Italy, 94; Boston Printmakers 33rd, 35th, 36th & 38th Nat Exhibs, 81, 83, 84 & 86; Print Club Philadelphia, 82 & 83; Playing Cards, Cooper Hewitt Mus, NY, 86; Art Quest 88, CW Post Col, NY, Beaver Col Pa & Univ Calif, Irvine, 88; plus many others. *Collection Arranged:* The Etchings of Jacques Bellange (com auth, catalog), Des Moines Art Ctr, Mus Fine Arts, Metrop Mus, 75-76; Benton, Curry, Wood--Lithographs, Iowa Arts Coun touring exhib (auth, catalog), 78; Giorgio Morandi (auth, catalog), Des Moines Art Ctr, San Francisco Mus Mod Art, Guggenheim Mus, 81; Etchings of JN Darling (auth, catalog), Brunnier Gallery, Iowa State Univ, 84; Centro Internazionale di Grafica (Iowa Printmakers), Venice, 89; Maestri della Scuola Internazionale di Grafica di Venezia, Drake Univ, 89 & Sioux City Art Ctr, 90; Des Moines Art Center (manuscripts & early printed book pages), 91. *Teaching:* Instr printmaking hist prints, Des Moines Art Ctr, Iowa, 71-; lectr, Drake Univ, Iowa, 72-74, 81, 83, 85, 92 & 94; Instr drawing & engraving, Scuola Int di Grafica, Venice, Italy, 93-99. *Awards:* Iowa Arts Coun Touring Exhib Grant, 78; Art Quest Printmaking, 88. *Mem:* Print Coun Am; Women Caucus Art; Boston Printmakers; Mid Am Print Coun; Col Art Asn. *Media:* Engraving. *Res:* History of prints. *Dealer:* Olson-Larson Galleries 203 Fifth St W Des Moines IA 50265. *Mailing Add:* 5130 Shriver Ave Des Moines IA 50312

WORTZ, MELINDA FARRIS
GALLERY DIRECTOR, CRITIC
b Ann Arbor, Mich, Apr 30, 40. *Study:* Radcliffe Col, BA(cum laude), 62; Otis Art Inst, 62-63; Univ Calif, Los Angeles, MA, 70; also with John Altoon. *Pos:* Gallery dir, Univ Calif, Riverside, 72-74 & Univ Calif, Irvine, currently; Southern Calif ed, Artweek, currently; contrib ed, Arts Mag, Art Gallery, Art News & Archit Dig, currently. *Teaching:* Asst prof issues in art, Calif State Univ, Long Beach, 72-75 & Calif State Univ, Los Angeles, 74-75; lectr, Univ Calif, Irvine, currently. *Res:* Contemporary American art. *Publ:* Auth, Seven Southern California Artists (catalog), Cirrus Gallery, Los Angeles, 74; auth, Dewain Valentine (exhib catalog), Long Beach Mus Art, 75; auth, Ludwig Redl (catalog essay), 75. *Mailing Add:* 1725 Cedar St Santa Monica CA 90405-2723

WORTZEL, ADRIANNE
PAINTER, PRINTMAKER
b Brooklyn, NY, Oct 7, 41. *Study:* Brooklyn Mus Art Sch, NY, 57-65; Brooklyn Col, with Ad Reinhardt, Burgoyne Diller & Louise Bourgeois, BA(with honors fine art), 63; Hunter Col, New York, with Mark Rothko, MA, 69. *Work:* Moderna Museet, Stockholm Sweden; Citibank, NY; City of Lund, Sweden; pvt collection of Mr & Mrs Larry Hagman, Malibu, Calif. *Comn:* Landmark Systems, Philip Johnson Bldg, Vienna, Va. *Exhib:* Galleriet, Sweden, 79 & 82; New Acquisitions, Moderna Museet, Stockholm, Sweden, 80; one-person show, Scottsdale Ctr Arts, Ariz, 80 & Bernice Steinbaum Gallery, NY, 81 & 83; Graphic Plus, Herbert F Johnson Mus, Ithaca, NY, 81; Stamford Mus, Conn, 89. *Teaching:* Lectr contemp art, Great Neck Adult Educ Program, 70-73; guest artist, printmaking workshop, 89. *Awards:* Creative Artists Pub Serv Grant, NY State Coun Arts, 81. *Bibliog:* Patricia Ensworth, Adrianne Wortzel, Arts Mag, 3/80; Sarah Cecil (auth), article, Artnews, 3/82; Donna Harkavy (auth), Adrianne Wortzel, Arts Mag, 9/83. *Media:* Acrylic on Canvas; Etchings. *Mailing Add:* 19 E Seventh St No 5 New York NY 10003

WOSTREL, NANCY J
PAINTER, ILLUSTRATOR
b San Diego, Calif. *Study:* With John C Pellew, 70 & 71; Famous Artists Sch, cert, 72; studied with Robert E Wood, 80. *Work:* James S Copley Libr, La Jolla, Calif; Vesti Corp, Boston, Mass; Troth Corp, New Orleans, La; Scripp's Women's Ctr, La Jolla, Calif. *Comn:* Numerous portrait comns. *Exhib:* Am Watercolor Soc & AWS Traveling

Exhib, 72, 76, 80, 90, 97 & 99, 2000; one-man shows, Knowles Gallery, La Jolla, Calif, 74, 77, 79, 81, 84 & 88-96, The Artists Gallery, La Jolla, Calif; Watercolor W, Riverside Art Ctr & Mus, Calif, 75, 77, 78 & 79; Watercolor USA, Springfield Art Mus, Mo, 79; Nat Acad Ann, NY, 81; and others. *Awards:* Purchase Awards, San Diego Watercolor Soc Nat Ann, 73, 76, 79 & 80; Hon Mention, San Diego Watercolor Soc Nat, 79; Second Prize for Watercolor, Southern Calif Expo, Del Mar, 79; Barbara McDermott Mem Award, Am Pen Woman, SDWS Annual Int Exhib, 2004; WB Romeling mem award, Adirondack Exhib Am Watercolors, 2005; and others. *Bibliog:* Richard Reilly (auth), Frost poems inspire art, 77, Watercolor show a breath of sweet air, 79, Compositions of beauty & joy, 81, San Diego Union, Copley Publ. *Mem:* signature mem Watercolor W; signature mem Am Watercolor Soc. *Media:* Watercolor, Pastel, Gouache. *Publ:* Auth, North Light Mag, Fletcher Art Serv Inc, 76. *Dealer:* Newman Galleries 1625 Walnut St Philadelphia PA 19103. *Mailing Add:* 2505 Montclair St San Diego CA 92104

WRAY, DICK
PAINTER
b Houston, Tex, Dec 5, 33. *Study:* Univ Houston. *Work:* Albright-Knox Art Gallery, Buffalo; Mus Fine Arts, Houston. *Exhib:* Mus Contemp Art, Houston, 61; Southwest Painting & Sculpture, Houston, 62; Hemisfair, Houston, 68; Homage to Lithographytemp Art, Houston, 61; Response, Tyler Mus, Tex, 80; Houston Artists Exhibition, Stavanger Mus, Norway; In Our Time: Houston's Contemp Arts Mus 1948-1982, Contemp Arts Mus, Houston, 82; Fresh Paint: The Houston Sch, Mus of Fine Arts, Houston (catalog), traveling exhib, 85; Third Western States Exhib, The Brooklyn Mus, NY, (catalog), traveling exhib, 86; Line and Form: Contemp Tex Figurative Drawing, Art Mus of S Tex, Corpus Christi, 87; Texas Art: An Exhibition Selected from the Menil Collection, The Mus of the Menil Collection-Richmond Hall, Houston, 88. *Teaching:* Glassell Sch of Art, Mus Fine Arts, Houston, Tex, 68-82. *Awards:* Purchase Prize, Ford Found, 62; Purchase Prize, Mus Fine Arts, Houston, 63. *Media:* Painting, Works on Paper. *Mailing Add:* c/o Moody Gallery 2815 Colquitt Houston TX 77098

WRIGHT, BAGLEY
COLLECTOR
Study: Princeton Univ, BA, 46. *Pos:* With Daily Mirror, Newsweek; real estate developer Pentagram Corp, Harbor Properties; chmn Physio Control Corp, 68-80; Developer Space Needle, Seattle. *Awards:* Named one of Top 200 Collectors, ARTnews Magazine, 2004, 2006. *Collection:* Contemporary Art; Japanese Art. *Mailing Add:* 407 Dexter Ave Seattle WA 98109

WRIGHT, BARTON ALLEN
WRITER, GRAPHIC ARTIST
b Bisbee, Ariz, Dec 21, 20. *Study:* Univ Ariz, BA, MA (anthropology & geology). *Work:* Ariz Bank (now Bank of Am); Mus N Ariz; pvt collections. *Comn:* Wupatki Nat Monument, Ft Union Nat Monument, Babbitt Stores; Great Sand Dunes Nat Monument; Montezuma Castle Nat Monument. *Exhib:* La Jolla Art Asn, Calif, 69; The Athenaeum, La Jolla, 70; Festival of Arts, Lake Oswego, 71; one-man show, San Diego, 71-75; Thorne Gallery, Scottsdale, 74 & 75; Indian Summer Gallery, Estes Park, Colo; Blaire Gallery, Santa Fe; and others. *Collection Arranged:* M R F Colton, 58; G E Burr, 59; Indian Artists, 60; Western Artists, 62; Paul Dyck, 64; American Art, 65; Frederick Sommers, 67; Southwest Art, 68; Widforss, 69; Santa Fe Indian Art, 70; Nat Park Illustrated, 71; N Fechin, 72; and others; History of Hopi Kachinas. *Pos:* Cur arts & exhib, Mus Northern Ariz, 55-58, cur, Mus, 58-77; sci dir, Mus of Man, 77-82; res anthropologist, Heard Mus, 83; sci lect & guide, Sierra Club, Stanford Alumni, Canyonlands. *Teaching:* Vis instr, Univ Calif, Riverside, 77, Univ Calif, San Diego, spring 83, Pitzer Col, spring 83. *Awards:* Anisfield Wolf-Cleveland Found, 86; Rounce & Coffin, 86; Border Regional Libr Asn, 86. *Mem:* Am Asn Mus; Indian Arts & Crafts Asn; Ariz/Nev Acad Sci; Westerners, San Diego & Phoenix. *Media:* Acrylic, Scratchboard, carvings. *Res:* Hopi kachinas. *Interests:* Western Art; Indian Art. *Publ:* Auth, Hopi Clowns, 94, Kachinas, a Hopi Artist's Documentary, 73, Unchanging Hopi, 75, Pueblo Shields, 76, Hopi Kachinas, The Complete Guide, 77; Mythic World of the Zuni, 88; Hallmarks of the Southwest, rev 2, 2000; auth catalog, Kachinas, Flak Galerie, Paris, 2003; Spirits of the Past, Vendome Press, in press; coauth (with Andrea Portago), Classic Hopi & Zuni Figures, 2006. *Mailing Add:* 4143 Gelding Dr Phoenix AZ 85023

WRIGHT, BERNARD
PAINTER, GRAPHIC ARTIST
b Pittsburgh, Pa, Feb 23, 38. *Study:* Otis Art Inst, Los Angeles, 69-70; Los Angeles Trade Tech Col, 71-74. *Work:* NY Pub Libr; Howard Univ, Washington, DC; Libr Cong; Morehouse Col, Atlanta, Ga; Los Angeles Pub Libr; Quincy Jones Collection. *Comn:* Numerous furniture and garment exclusive designs. *Exhib:* Detroit Inst Arts, 74; Fisher Art Galleries, Univ Southern Calif, 74; Calif Mus Sci & Indust, Los Angeles, 75; Ava Dorog Galleries, Los Angeles, 82; Pittsburgh City Hall Gallery, Pa, 82; Los Angeles City Hall Main Bridge Art Gallery, 83. *Pos:* Pres & co-founder, Westly & Wright Products, Los Angeles, 72-. *Bibliog:* Frank Johnson (auth), The art of Bernard Wright, Grapevine Mag, 10/80; Ronald Moore (auth), City honors 12 Black artists, Los Angeles Sentinel, 5/7/81; Judith Grout (auth), Art to art in Black history, Los Angeles Mag, 2/82; Lewis and Waddy (auths), Black Artists on Art, Vol I, 77, 132, 1969; Cederholm (auth), Afro-American Artists, 319, 1973; Lynn Moody Igoe with James Igoe (auths), 250 Years of Afro-American Art, 1256, 1981; and others. *Mem:* Art W Asn Inc, (mem bd dir, 67-73); Artist Equity Asn. *Media:* Oil, Ink. *Dealer:* Edwward Smith & Co PO Box 76169 Los Angeles CA 90076-0169. *Mailing Add:* PO Box 76169 Los Angeles CA 90076-0169

WRIGHT, CHARLES CLIFFORD
PAINTER, COLLAGE ARTIST
b Cosmopolis, Wash, Nov 19, 19. *Study:* Cornish Sch, Seattle, with Dr W Reese, 36; with Mark Tobey, 37-43. *Work:* Ringling Brothers Mus, Sarasota, Fla; Edward James' Collection, Mex; Nordjyllands Kunstmuseum, Aalborg, Denmark; Whitney Mus & Brooklyn Mus, NY. *Comn:* Light mural for Danish Railroad, 89. *Exhib:* Seattle Art Mus, Wash, 42; Dada, Surrealism & Heritage, Mus Mod Art, 68; Retrospective, Nordjyllands Kunstmuseum, Aalborg, Denmark, 81; Helander Gallery, Stockholm, 82; Danish Railroad Six Posters, Asbaks Gallery, Copenhagen, 83 & Monumental Paintings, Nordjyllands Kunstmuseum, Aalborg, Denmark, 86. *Awards:* Mus des Beaux Arts, Brussels, Am Acad Arts & Letters, 57; Encouragement Grant, Columbia Univ, 59; State Art Found Grants, Denmark, 79 & 80; Tugran Merrittt Found Grant, 84. *Bibliog:* A painter of the grotesque, Mag Am Art, 47; L Kochnitzsky (auth), Something different, Les Beaux Arts, Belgium, 57; O Braunschwig (auth), Portrait, Danish State TV, 74. *Media:* Oil, Gouache. *Publ:* Auth, Hero in the New World, Borgen, 63; contribr, Philoctetes Wounded, State TV, Denmark, 74; coauth & illusr, Demoniac Dames, Gyldendal, 79; Insights, Mistral, Denmark, 81. *Dealer:* Decenter Marienborg 4780 Stege Denmark

WRIGHT, FRANK
PAINTER, EDUCATOR
b Washington, DC, Oct 10, 32. *Study:* Am Univ, BA, 54; Univ Ill, Urbana, MA, 60; Fogg Mus, Harvard Univ, fel, 60-61; Villa i tatti, with Bernard Berenson, Florence, Italy, 56-58; Atelier 17, Paris, 61-64. *Work:* Bibliot Nat, Paris; Nat Collections Fine Arts, Washington, DC; Univ Seattle Law Sch, Wash; Nat Gallery Art, Rosenwald Collection, Washington, DC; Tucson Mus Art, Tucson, Ariz; Am Univ & Georgetown Univ, Washington, DC; Guilford Col, Greensboro, NC; Morris Mus Art, Augusta, Ga; Sallie Mae, Washington; Deloitte and Touche, Washington. *Comn:* Deepbite etching demonstration plate & ed, Lessing J Rosenwald, Jenkintown, Pa, 68; oil painting - Cityscapes, WC Bradley Co, Columbus, Ga, 85; oil painting - Hist, Pershing Assoc, Washington, DC, 86; oil painting - Washington Scene & Washington Hist, Perpetual Am Bank, Washington, DC, 87; oil painting 18 x 7' Mural for Lobby of Rep PL, Oliver Carr Co, Washington, DC, 88; portrait - US House of Rep Speaker Thomas Foley, US Capitol; painting, Pennsylvania Ave in 1890, Chevy Chase Bank, Bethesda, Md, 2003; painting, Harpers Ferry, WVa, Capital One Bank, Tyson's Corner, Va, 2005. *Exhib:* West 83/Art & The Law, Woodruff Arts Ctr, Atlanta, 83; Allentown Art Mus, Pa, 83; Frank Wright: Painting 1968-1980, Corcoran Gallery of Art, Washington, DC, 81; Frank Wright: Washington Past & Present, Int Monetary Fund Visitors' Ctr, Washington, DC, 86; Paintings, Covington & Burling, Washington, DC, 93; Paintings, Susquehanna Art Mus, Harrisburg, Pa, 93; Remembering Times Past; Savoring Times Present, George Washington Univ, 94; Frank Wright: A Look Back, Paintings and Prints 1963-1998, Strathmore Hall Arts Ctr, North Bethesda, Md, 98, Frank Wright: Annapolis and the Bay Paintings 1989-1996, Md Hall for the Creative Arts, Annapolis, Md, 98; Pulse 2006, Hillyer Art Space, 2006. *Pos:* Prof drawing & graphics & fine arts, George Washington Univ, 70-. *Teaching:* Instr master drawings, Corcoran Sch Art, Washington, DC, 66-70; asst prof design & graphics, George Washington Univ, 70-78, assoc prof drawing & graphics, 79-83, prof, 83-. *Awards:* Schepp Found Fel, 56-58; Paul J Sachs Fel, Nat Gallery Art, 59-60; Fel, Fogg Mus Harvard, 60-61. *Bibliog:* Jill Wechsler (auth), Frank Wright an artist with a sense of history, Am Artist, 9/82; Ruth Palombo (auth), DC Artist is Historian with a Paint Brush, Chevy Chase Gazette, 12/21/89; Sandra Martin (auth), Frank Wright's Ideal America, The New Bay Times Vol II, No 15, 6/30/94-7/6/94; and others. *Mem:* Cosmos Club of Washington; Columbia Historical Soc; Omicron Delta Kappa; NAt Soc Arts & Letters (Wash chap). *Media:* Oil; Graphics (Engraving, Deep-bite Etching). *Res:* Civil War in Washington. *Publ:* Auth, Why I love to engrave, GW Forum, Vol 7, No 1 (winter 77). *Mailing Add:* Dept Art George Washington Univ 801 22nd St NW Washington DC 20052

WRIGHT, HAROLD DAVID
PAINTER
b Rosine, Ky, June 13, 42. *Study:* Harris Sch Advert Art, Nashville, Tenn; watercolor painting in Italy. *Work:* Tenn State Mus, Nashville; Northern Telecom, Nashville. *Comn:* Portraits of Civil War Generals, General's Retreat, Franklin, Tenn, 74. *Exhib:* Cent South Show, Parthenon, Nashville, 74; Sardella Art Show, Atlanta, Ga, 74; High Plains Exhib, Lubbock, Tex, 79; Western Collectors Exhib, Dallas Tex, 80-86; Miniatures, Minneapolis, 84-86. *Pos:* Art dir, Buntin & Assocs Advert, 66-69; partner, Nova Group, Nashville, 69-; vpres, Graystone Press, Nashville, 73-. *Awards:* First Award Fine Art Competition, 73. *Media:* Watercolor, Gouache, Casein. *Publ:* Illusr, Nashville Tennessean Mag, 66 & 78; Tenn Conservationist Mag, 74 & 76-79; Nashville, the faces of two centuries, Southwest Art Mag, 80; Am Rendezvous Mag, 84

WRIGHT, JESSE GRAHAM, JR
DIRECTOR
b Sidney, Ohio, July 29, 39. *Study:* Loyola Univ, Chicago, BA, 64, MA, 65; Univ Notre Dame, Ind, MFA(painting & sculpture), 69; Univ Tulsa, Olka, 84. *Pos:* Dir, South Bend Art Ctr, Michael C Rockefeller Art Ctr Gallery, Fredonia, NY, 68-71, Canton Art Inst Ohio, 74-77, Philbrook Art Ctr, Tulsa, Okla, 77-84, J B Speed Art Mus, Louisville, Ky, 84-86 & Mus of the Horse, NMex, 94-96; pres, Wright Group, 86-90; develop dir, Buffalo Bill Hist Ctr, Cody, Wyo, 91-94. *Teaching:* Fac mem, St Mary's Col, Notre Dame, Ind, 68-77; asst prof, State Univ NY, Fredonia, 68-77; dean, Col Fine Arts, Jacksonville, Fla, 96-. *Mem:* Am Asn Mus. *Mailing Add:* 7925 Merrill Rd Apt 2106 Jacksonville FL 32277-6540

WRIGHT, JIMMY
PAINTER, PRINTMAKER
b Ky, July 8, 44. *Study:* Art Inst Chicago, BFA(George D Brown Fel), 67; Southern Ill Univ, Carbondale, MFA, 71; student, Murray State Univ, Ky, 62, 63. *Work:* St Paul Art Ctr, Minn; Okla City Art Ctr; Univ Ohio, Athens; Yeiser Art Ctr, POaducah, Ky; Sch Art Inst Chicago, Ill. *Comn:* Sets & Costumes, Stan Dancers Ballet, Tokyo, Japan, 79; cover painting, Readers Digest, Pleasantville, NY, 98; four screenprint eds, AFA Press, Lakeside, Mich, 98. *Exhib:* Nat Drawing Exhib, San Francisco Art Mus, 70; one-man show, Tochigi Fine Arts Mus, Japan, 79; L Atelier de L Artiste, Maison Natale Gustave Courbet, Ornans, France, 87; An Artists Ode to Flowers, Nassau Co Mus Art, Roslyn, NY, 92; The Flower Show, Portland Mus Art, 92; Self Portrait: the changing self, NJ Ctr Visual Arts, Summit, 93; Painting After Nature (with catalog), Mus Contemp Art, N Miami, Fla, 94; In Bloom, NJ Ctr Visual Arts, Summit, NJ, 96; One-man shows, Eagle Art Gallery, Murray State Univ, Ky, 74, Tavelli Gallery, Aspen, Colo, 92, DC Moore Gallery, New York City, 97, Roger Ramsay Gallery, Chicago, 97, Wild Flosers Katonah Mus Art, Katonah, NY, 99, Fen Way Gallery, Chicago, Ill, 2001. *Awards:* Jurors Award, NY Univ, 87; Grant, Lower E Side Printshop, 90. *Bibliog:* Donna Gustafson (auth), Jimmy Wright, Arts Mag, 97. *Mem:* Pastel Soc Am. *Publ:* illusr, BOMB, Vol XVII, 84-95, winter 87, BOMB, New York, 87 & Vol XXXX, No 1, 73-79, fall 92; Kaleidoscope, Vol 6, No 1, 1-3, Cornell Univ, 8/97; Readers Digest, 98; illustr, Architectural Digest, 97. *Dealer:* DC Moore Gallery 724 Fifth Ave New York NY 10019. *Mailing Add:* Knikerbocker Station PO Box 278 New York NY 10002

WRIGHT, MICHAEL FITZHUGH
PAINTER
b New Rochelle, NY, Dec 3, 31. *Study:* Yale Music & Arts, 50; Albright Knox Art Sch, 51; Brooklyn Mus, 52. *Work:* Phoenix Art Mus, Ariz; Guild Hall, E Hampton, NY; Mus Fine Art, Santa Fe, NMex. *Exhib:* Drawing Show, New Sch Social Res, NY, 54-55 & Nat Arts Club, NY, 55; Drawing Exhib, Mus Mod Art, NY, 54; Long Island Painters Ann Show, Guild Hall, E Hampton, NY, 67; one-man show, Long Island Univ, S Hampton NY, 72; Boundless Realism, Rockwell Mus, Corning, NY, 87; NMex Traveling Show, Denver Art Mus & Mus Fine Arts, Santa Fe, 91; New Mexico Artists, Cedar Rapids Art, Iowa, 98. *Teaching:* Invitational master artist, Santa Fe Art Inst, 96. *Awards:* Rosenthall Award, Brooklyn Mus, 55; 1st Prize, Long Island Painters, Guild Hall, 67; Yaddo Fel. *Bibliog:* Articles in NY Times, E Hampton Star & Village Voice. *Media:* Paint, Mixed Media. *Dealer:* Riva Yares Gallery 3625 Bishops Lane Scottsdale AZ 85251

WRIGHT, VICKI C
MUSEUM DIRECTOR, MUSEOLOGIST
b Willard, Ohio, Apr 13, 56. *Study:* Ohio Wesleyan Univ, BFA, 77; Ariz State Univ, MA, 86. *Collection Arranged:* Proj dir, 350 Years of Art & Architecture in Md (with catalog), 84; proj co-dir, New Hampshire Folk Art (with catalog), 89; cur, Prints by Honoré Daumier, 91; co-cur & coordr, Artists & Environment: NH, 91; proj dir, Hyman Bloom: Paintings & Drawings, 92; proj dir, Realism & Invention in the Prints of Albrecht Durer (with catalog), 95; NH Traditions in Wood (with catalog), 97; Art & Architecture: The Vision of Graham Gund, 98; Against the Grain: The 2d Generation of Boston Expressionism, 2000; On Great Bay: Paintings by C Cook and A Mambro, 2001; co-cur, Art of Samuel Bak: Memory and Metaphor (catalog), 2006; proj dir, The Simple Art: Printed Images in an Age of Magnificence (catalog), 2006. *Pos:* Asst dir, 82-84 & acting dir, 84-86, Art Gallery, Univ Md, College Park; dir, Art Gallery, Univ NH, Durham, 86. *Teaching:* Adj asst prof mus studies, Univ NH, Durham, 87-. *Mem:* Am Asn Mus; NH Visual Arts Coalition (co-pres, 91-92, secy, 97-99). *Publ:* Auth, La Reunion des Plus Celebres Monuments Antiques de la France, Phoebus III, Ariz State Univ, 79; ed & contribr, Portfolios: Artists' Series from the Collection of Univ of Md, Art Gallery, Univ Md, 86; auth, The Artists Revealed, Art Gallery, Univ NH, 89. *Mailing Add:* The Art Gallery Paul Creative Arts Ctr Univ NH 30 Coll Rd Durham NH 03824-3538

WRIGHT, VIRGINIA
COLLECTOR, CURATOR
Study: Barnard Col, BA, 51. *Pos:* Asst Sidney Janis Gallery; trustee Virginia Wright Fund, Seattle Art Mus; Cur Color Field Paintings and Related Abstractions, 2005. *Awards:* Named one of Top 200 Collectors, ARTnews Magazine, 2004, 2006. *Mailing Add:* 407 Dexter Ave Seattle WA 98109

WRIGLEY, RICK
DESIGNER, CRAFTSMAN
b Arlington, Va, Dec 9, 55. *Study:* Rochester Inst Tech, Sch Am Craftsmen, BFA, 81. *Work:* Contemp Crafts Asn, Portland, Ore. *Comn:* Boardroom table (with Kohn Pedersen, Fox Conway Asn), Home Box Office Inc, NY, 84; 22 hearing room doors, Conn Comn on Arts, Hartsford, 88; mantlepiece, Babson Col Ctr Educ, Wellesley, Mass, 88; dining-conference tables, Time Inc, NY, 88. *Exhib:* Material Evidence, Renwick Gallery, Nat Mus Am Art, Washington, DC, Fine Arts Mus South, Mobile, Ala & Mus des Art Decoratifs, Montreal, Can, 84; Artist Designed Furniture, Norton Gallery Art, W Palm Beach, 86; World of Art Today, Milwaukee Art Mus, 88; Architectural Art, Am Craft Mus, NY, 88. *Pos:* Artist-in-residence, Art Park, Lewiston, NY, 79. *Awards:* Daphne Award for Residential Furniture Design, Hardwood Inst, 86. *Bibliog:* Pamela Scheinman (auth), Dialogue with architecture, Am Craft, 6/88; Robert Jensen (auth), Angels in the architecture, Metrop Home, 5/88; Clair Whitcomb (auth),article in: House Beautiful Today, 4/88. *Mem:* Am Craft Coun; Soc Arts & Crafts. *Mailing Add:* c/o Meredith Gallery 805 N Charles St Baltimore MD 21201

WRISTON, BARBARA
HISTORIAN, LECTURER
b Middletown, Conn, June 29, 17. *Study:* Oberlin Col, AB; Brown Univ, AM; hon LittD, Lawrence Univ. *Work:* Rare Doings at Bath. *Pos:* exec dir, formerly, mus ed, Art Inst Chicago, 61-78; trustee, secy & antiqn, Conn; mem adv comm, Hist Am Bldgs Survey, 72-78. *Teaching:* State Univ NY, Bronx, formerly. *Mem:* Benjamin Franklin fel Royal Soc Arts; Soc Archit Historians (pres, 60-61); Furniture Hist Soc. *Res:* Seventeeth and eighteenth century English and American architecture and furniture. *Interests:* Architectural history and decorative arts. *Publ:* Auth, Who was the architect of the Indiana Cotton Mill, 1848-1850?, J Soc Archit Historians, 5/65; Joiner's tools in The Art Institute of Chicago, 67 & The Howard Van Doren Shaw Memorial Collection in the Art Institute of Chicago, 69, Mus Studies; Visual Arts in Illinois, 68; Rare Doings at Bath, 78 & 79; Articles on architectural history in decorative arts and art museums education. *Mailing Add:* 455 E 86th St New York NY 10028

WU, WAYNE WEN-YAU
PAINTER
b Tachia, Taiwan, Oct 5, 35; US citizen. *Study:* Taiwan Normal Univ, BA(fine arts), 59; Art Students' League, New York, 75. *Work:* Nat Mus Hist, Taipei, Taiwan; Nat Taiwan Arts Ctr, Taipei; Hunter Mus Am Art, Tenn; Taiwan Mus Art; Asian Studies Ctr, St John's Univ, Jamaica, NY; Taichung Seaport Art Center,; Taichung Co Cult Center. *Comn:* Chattanooga Shines, Carter St Corp, Tenn, 85; Chattanooga-Yesterday & Today, Arthur Andersen & Co, Chattanooga, Tenn, 85; Daufuskie Island No 1 & No 2, Melrose Club, Daufuskie Island, SC, 86; The Clubhouse, Chattanooga Golf & Country Club, Tenn, 90; Baylor Sch, Chattanooga, Tenn, 92. *Exhib:* solo shows, Taiwan Mus Art, 95 & Hunter Mus Art, Chattanooga, 80 & 98; East Gallery, Taipei, Taiwan, 99; East Gallery, Taipei, Taiwan, 01; Taipei Int Art Fair, 2001, & 2004; Korea Int Art Fair, 2004; East Gallery, Taipei, 2004; Taichung Seaport Art Center, 2006. *Pos:* Supervisor, Fine Arts Ctr, Taichung Libr, Taiwan, 70-74. *Teaching:* Instr, oil painting, watercolor, Taiwan Normal Univ, 73-74, Hunter Mus Art, Chattanooga, 80-92 & Wayne Wu's Art Studio, Atlanta, Ga, 94-2000; instr, San Jose, Calif, 2000; instr, Salinas, Calif, 2000-2004; instr, Gilroy, Calif, 2004-. *Mem:* Am Watercolor Soc. *Media:* Oil, Watercolor. *Mailing Add:* 7440 Carnoustie Ct Gilroy CA 95020-3004

WUJCIK, THEO
PAINTER, PRINTMAKER
b Jan 29, 1936; US citizen. *Study:* Ctr Creative Studies, dipl, 64; Tamarind Lithography Workshop, TMP, 68. *Work:* Mus Mod Art, NY; Los Angeles Co Mus Art, Calif; Mus Fine Arts, Boston; Libr Cong, Washington; Nat Gallery Art, Washington. *Comn:* 40th anniversary poster, Univ SFla Contemp Art Mus, Tampa, 1995; First Night St Pete, Mus Fine Arts, St Petersburg, Fla, 1999; 90 X 40' bldg wrap, Ouutdoor Art Found, Tampa, Fla, 2003; official portraits, Moffitt Cancer Center, Tampa, 2003. *Exhib:* Drawings of the 70's, Art Inst Chicago, 77; Recent Acquistions, Drawings, Mus Mod Art, NY, 77; Am Drawings in Black & White, 1970-80, Brooklyn Mus, NY, 80; Richard Brown Baker Collection, Mus Art, RI, 85; Mus Mod Art, NY, 91; Artists Choice, Chuck Close, Head-On/The Mod Portrait; Silverpoint Etcetera-Contemp Am Metalpoint Drawings, Huntsville Mus Art, Farnsworth Art Mus & Philadelphia Art Alliance, 93; Omni Gallery, NY, 96; Three Levels of Abstraction, Indigo Galleries, Boca Raton, 96; 30-yr retrospective, Gulf Coast Mus Art, Largo, Fla, 2000; Fla Fel exhib, Lowe Mus Art, Miami, 2002, Gulf Coast Mus Art, Largo, 2003; Global Warming, Tampa Mus Art, Fla, 2006. *Pos:* Mgr, Graphicstudio, Tampa, Fla, 70-72. *Teaching:* Instr printmaking, Ctr Creative Studies, 64-70; assoc prof printmaking & drawing, Univ South Fla, Tampa, 72-2003. *Awards:* Louis Comfort Tiffany Found, 64; Grant Lithography, Ford Found, 67; Award Drawing, Nat Endowment Arts, 77. *Bibliog:* Marvin Sadik & Harold Pfister (coauth), American Portrait Drawings, Smithsonian Inst Press, 80; Frank H Goodyear (auth), Contemporary American Realism Since 1960, New York Graphic Soc, 80; Hilarie Faberman (auth), Modern Master Drawings (catalog), 86. *Media:* Acrylic; Lithography, Etching. *Publ:* Auth, Robert Rauschenberg Etching, Brooke Alexander Inc, New York, 77; Tatyna Grosman, Self-Portrait, Chiseled Engravings, Brooke Alexander Inc, New York, 79; Jasper Johns Etching, Graphicstudio, Tampa, Fla, 85; Ed Ruscha Etching, Graphicstudio, 96; Paradiso Etching, Graphicstudio, 2000. *Dealer:* Millenia Gallery, 4190 Mellenia Blvd, Orlando, FL 32839. *Mailing Add:* 1507 E 9th Ave Tampa FL 33605-3711

WULFERS, MONIKA A
SCULPTOR, CONCEPTUAL ARTIST
b Berlin, Ger, May 10, 42. *Study:* North Cent Col, BA, 68; Sch of Art Inst Chicago, MFA, 73. *Work:* Kemper Collection, Chicago, Ill; Wilhelar-Hack-Mus, Ger. *Exhib:* Artists Books, Mus Contemp Art, Chicago, Ill, 81; Chicago and Vicinity, Art Inst Chicago, Ill, 85; Emerging, State Ill Gallery, 85; Zufall, Spiel, Methode und System, Wilhelm-Hack-Mus, Ludwigs, Ger, 92. *Pos:* gallerist, Washington Island Gallery & Gardens, 87-; dir, curator, Reider Gallery Baint Col, 2000-. *Teaching:* vis prof, Barat Col De Paul Univ, 2000-. *Media:* Miscellaneous Media

WUNDERLICH, PAUL
PAINTER, PRINTMAKER
b Eberswalde, Brandenburg, Ger, Mar 10, 27. *Study:* Hamburg Col Art Develop, Landeskunstschule, 47-51; Hochschule fur Bildende Kunste, Hamburg, 63-68. *Exhib:* Mus Goteborg, Sweden, 70; Kunsthalle Kiel, Ger, 80; Seibu Mus, Tokyo, Japan, '80; Schleswig-Holsteinisches Landesmuseum, Ger, 87; Schleswig, Schloss Gottorf, Ger, 87. *Teaching:* Etchings & lithograph, Hamburg Col Art Develop, 51-60; lectr free graphics & painting, Col Creative Arts, 63-68. *Awards:* M S Collins Prize, Er wird alt, Philadelphia, Pa, 62; Edwin Scharff Prize, 65; Gold Medal, Florence, Italy, 70. *Bibliog:* Volker Zielke (dir), Portrait of Paul Wunderlich (film), 73; Notizen (sketches 66-74), Volker Huber, 74; Homo sum, Volker Huber, 78; and others. *Media:* Gouach, Oil; Original Lithograph

WUNDERLICH, SUSAN CLAY
ART DEALER
b Indianapolis, Ind, Jan 30, 42. *Study:* Colby Col. *Pos:* Dir, Mongerson Wunderlich Gallery, currently. *Mem:* Chicago Art Dealers Asn. *Specialty:* Nineteenth and 20th century American art, such as: Frederic Remington, C M Russell, Nicolai Fechin, Leon Gaspard, Taos Founders and the American impressionists; illustrators, N C Wyeth and Howard Pyle; sporting art; sculpture. *Mailing Add:* Mongerson-Wunderlich 704 N Wells St Chicago IL 60610-3310

WUNDERMAN, JAN (LILJAN) DARCOURT
PAINTER, PRINTMAKER
b Winnipeg, Man, Jan 22, 21; US citizen. *Study:* Otis Art Inst, Los Angeles, BFA, 42; Studied with Reuben Tam, Brooklyn Mus Art Sch, 54-56. *Work:* Alfred Khouri Collection, Norfolk Mus, Va; Ball State Univ Art Gallery, Muncie, Ind; Univ SC Art Gallery, Columbia; CW Post Col, Long Island, NY; Nat Asn Women Artists Permanent Collection, Zimmerlee Mus, Rutgers, NJ; and others. *Comn:* Painting, NY off, Bank of Am, 76; painting, NY off, The Boston Co, 77; Warner Lambert, NY; Bank One, Columbus, Ohio; Freeport Mac-Moran Corp, New Orleans, La; and others. *Exhib:* one-woman show, Pasadena Art Inst, Calif, 43, Dabney Hall, Calif Inst Tech, 43, Gastine Gallery, Los Angeles, Calif, 45, Golde Gallery, Great Neck, NY, 57-60, Angeleski Gallery, NY, 61-62, Roko Gallery, NY, 63, 66, 68, 71, 73, 76, East Hampton Guild Gallery, NY, 65, 66, Talisman Gallery, Bartelsville, Okla, 75, 77, Voltaire Gallery, New Milford, Conn, 69-83, Les Mouches, NY, 80 & Denise Bibro Fine Arts, New York, NY, 96-98, 2002; Pasadena Mus, Calif, 45; Los Angeles Co Mus Art, 45; Brooklyn Mus, NY, 56; Philadelphia Mus Art, 56-62; Pa Acad Fine Arts, Philadelphia, 59-65; Butler Inst Am Art, Youngstown, Ohio, 59-66; Va Mus Fine Arts, Richmond, 67; traveling show, 100 Yrs-100 Works, Nat Asn Women Artists; Plaides Gallery Invitational, NY, 88; Nat Acad Design, NY, 94 & 96; Sarah Lawrence Col, 2002. *Collection Arranged:* Jane Vorhees Zimmerli Mus, Rutgers Univ, NJ; Skidmore Print Collection; NYU Loeb Col, NYC; Ball State Univ; Norfolk Mus, Va; CW Post Col, Brookville, NY; Harry N Abrams Col, NYC; Daimler Chrysler Col, Germany; Northwest Airlines; Dillingham Corp, Honolulu. *Teaching:* Great Neck Art Ctr, NY, 59-63. *Awards:* Ohaski Award, Pan Pac Exhib, Tokyo & Osaka, Japan, 62; Marcia Brady Tucker Award, Nat Asn Women Artists, 65, Medal of Honor, 66, Joseph J Akstone Prize, 76, Jane C Stanley Award, 77, Canaday Mem Prize, 79, De Solo Mendes Prize, 81, Charles Hormon Mem Prize, 83, Bertha P Greenblatt Award, 86, Moore Greenblatt Award, 90, Amelia Peabody Award, 91, Grumbacher Gold Medal of Honor, 92 & Florence B Andresen Award, 94; Emily Lowe Award, NY, 65; Int Women's Year Art Festival Award, Ford Found Auditorium, 75; Bocour Award, Am Soc Contemp Artists, 80, Elizabeth Erlanger Mem Award, 89 & Kreindler Award, 92. *Mem:* Nat Asn Women Artists; Artists Equity; Am Soc Contemp Artists; Soc Am Painters and Sculptors; Soc Painters Casein and Acrylic; Contemp Artists Guild. *Media:* Oil, Acrylic; Black & White Intaglio Prints. *Interests:* travel; music. *Publ:* contribr, My background & intent as an abstract painter, Leonardo Publs, 8/81. *Dealer:* Denise Bibro Fine Arts. *Mailing Add:* 131 E 19th St New York NY 10003

WURMFELD, SANFORD
PAINTER, EDUCATOR
b New York, NY, Dec 6, 42. *Study:* Dartmouth Col, BA, 64; Independent study Rome, Italy, 64-65; Hunter Col, 66. *Exhib:* Art of the Real, Mus Mod Art, NY, 68, Grand Palais, Paris, 68, Kunsthaus, Zurich, 68 & Tate Gallery, London, 69; Contemp Painting Review, Lehigh Univ, Pa, 76; Susan Caldwell Gallery, NY, 76 & 78; Patterns Plus, Art Mus, Dayton, 79; Carnegie Int, Mus Art, Pittsburgh, Pa, 82; Labor Intensive Abstraction, Clocktower, NY, 84; Approaches to Abstraction, Shanghai, 86; A Debate on Abstraction, Hunter Col, 89; Choices, Long Beach Mus Art, Calif, 89; The Grid, Ben Shahn Galleries, William Paterson Col, NJ, 90; Red, Karl Ernst Osthaus-Mus, Ger, 99, Cyclorama, 2000-; and others. *Pos:* Dir, Hunter Galleries, Hunter Col, City Univ NY, 78-; external examiner, Acad Minerva, Groningen, Netherlands, 98, Glasgow Sch Art, 99-. *Teaching:* From lectr to prof art, Hunter Col, 67-, chmn dept, 78-; visiting artist, Calif State Col, 70; visiting instr in color theory, Cooper Union, NY, 71-72. *Awards:* Ames Award, Dartmouth Col, 64; Guggenheim Fel, 74-75; Nat Endowment Arts Individual Artist Fel, 87-88; City Univ NY Fac Res Award, 79-81, 84, 85, 87, 91, 93 & 97. *Publ:* Auth, Color documents: A presentational theory, Hunter Col Art Gallery, 4/85; Approaches to Abstraction, City Univ New York, 86; On Color Charts and Painting, Color Order and Aesthetics: The Oeuvre of Dr Amelius Muller, Hunter Col Art Gallery, NY, 87; From Surface to Luminous from Color in Abstract Painting, Wake Forest Univ, 96; Color in Abstract Painting, Elsevier Press, Amsterdam, 98; and others. *Mailing Add:* 18 Warren St No 5 New York NY 10007-1066

WÜRTH, REINHOLD
COLLECTOR
b Ohringen, Apr 20, 35. *Hon Degrees:* Univ Tubingen, Hon Dr. *Pos:* First apprentice screw trade Wurth Group, Kunzelsau, 49, head bus & mgt, 54, chmn adv bd, 1994-; Head Interfacultative, Inst Entrepreneurship Univ Karlsruhe, 99-2003; mem supervisory bd, IKB Deutsche Industriebank AG, Dusseldorf; shareholder, mem bd trustees, Robert-Bosch Found; chmn adv bd, Entrepreneurs Soc Int Cooperation Baden-Wurttemberg. *Awards:* named one of World's Richest People, Forbes Mag, 99—2004; Ludwig-Erhard Medal, Ludwig-Erhard Found, 2004; Top 200 Collectors, ARTnews Mag, 2004. *Collection:* Modern & Contemporary Art. *Mailing Add:* A Wurth GmbH & Co KG Reinhold-Wurth Str 12-17 Kunzelsau Germany

WYATT, GREG ALAN
SCULPTOR
b Nyack, NY, Oct 16, 49. *Study:* Columbia Col, BA, 71, MA, 74; Nat Acad Sch Design, 72-74; Columbia Univ, EdD, 74-76. *Work:* Brookgreen Gardens, Murrells Inlet, SC; Nat Arts Club, Gramercy Park, NY; Princeton Univ Libr, NJ; Bergen Mus Art, NJ. *Comn:* Fantasy Fountain, Gramercy Park, NY, 83; Standing portrait James Cash Penney, Tex, 92; Life Forces, Am Cynamid, 93; Soul of the Arts, Newington-Cropsey Found, 94; Olympic Woman, Avon Products, NY, 96; Victory Eagle and Hippomenes, Hofstra Univ, 98-99; Tree of Learning, Vanderbilt Univ, 99; and others. *Exhib:* Harvard Univ, Cambridge, Mass, 91; Bronze Casting Exhib (in conj with Paul Manship Retrospective), Metrop Mus Art, NY, 91; US Cong, Washington, 92; Nat Acad Design, NY, 92; US Senate, Russell Rotunda, 93; Newington-Cropsey Found, 94; Kennedy Gallery, NY, 94; US Supreme Ct, 95; NY State Govs Mansion (Red Room), 1998-2000. *Pos:* sculpture in residence, Cathedral St John the Devine. *Teaching:* Instr, NY Univ, 73-75 & Gallitin Sch, San Marino, Italy, 91-2000; Newington-Cropsey Found Acad Art, currently; Fantasy Fountain Fund, currently. *Awards:* Helen Foster Barnett Award, Nat Acad Design Nat Ann, 79; Walter Lantz Award, Nat Sculpture Soc Young Sculptors Ann, 79; Citation, US Cong, 92; Nat Arts Club Pres Award, 85. *Bibliog:* Michael Lantz (ed), Woman, the sculptor's vision, Nat Sculpture Rev, spring 79; Pam Lambert (auth), The eagle has landed off lower Broadway, Columbia Univ Mag, winter 79; Greg Wyatt & His Work, Charles Kuralt, CBS-TV, 12/90 & 94. *Mem:* Nat Arts Club; Nat Sculpture Soc. *Media:* Bronze, Marble. *Publ:* Manhattan Guide to Public Sculpture, Municipal Art Soc; Guide to Collection, Brookgreen Gardens. *Mailing Add:* 320 W 86th St Penthouse South New York NY 10024

WYCKOFF, SYLVIA SPENCER
EDUCATOR, PAINTER
b Pittsburgh, Pa, Nov 14, 15. *Study:* Col Fine Arts, Syracuse Univ, BFA, 37, MFA, 44. *Work:* Radio Sta WSYR, Syracuse, NY; R E Dietz Co, Syracuse; Marquardt Switches, Cazenovia, NY; Marine Midland Bank, Syracuse, NY; in pvt collections. *Exhib:* Mem Art Gallery, Rochester, NY; Everson Mus Art, Syracuse; Cooperstown Art Asn, NY; Nat Asn Women Artists, NY; Nat League Am Pen Women, Wash, DC; Solo shows, Nationally with Eight Syracuse Water Colorists, NY, 42-45, Coleman Hall, Cazenoviz Col, 75, Chancellor's Off, Syracuse Univ, Oneida, NY, 76, Opening of New Col Art Bldg, Cazenovia Col, 2004. *Teaching:* Prof watercolor & drawing & chmn, Freshman Core Progs Dept, Syracuse Univ, 42-81; prof, art, painter chmn, Prog in London, 71-71; retired. *Awards:* Outstanding Am Educ, 74; Spec Citation, NY State Art Teachers Asn, 81; Priscilla Hancock Award, Serv to the Arts, Cazenovia Watercolor Soc, 92. *Mem:* Cazenovia Watercolor Soc (pres & founder), 76-; Women in the Arts (charter mem); Stone Quarry Art Park, Cazenovia, NY. *Media:* Watercolor, Drawing. *Interests:* Painting, drawing, bridge and knitting. *Mailing Add:* 4 Liberty St Cazenovia NY 13035

WYETH, ANDREW NEWELL
PAINTER
b Chadds Ford, Pa, July 12, 1917. *Study:* With N C Wyeth; Harvard Univ, Hon DFA, 55; Colby Col, Hon DFA, 55; Dickinson Col, Hon DFA, 58; Swarthmore Col, Hon DFA, 58. *Work:* Metrop Mus Art, NY; Mus Fine Arts, Boston; Los Angeles Co Mus Art; Art Inst Chicago; Nat Gallery Art, Washington; Brandywine River Mus, Chadds Ford, Pa; Joslyn Art Mus, Omaha, Nebr; Nat Gallery, Oslo, Norway. *Exhib:* The Helga Pictures, Nat Gallery Art, Washington, 87; Pa Acad Fine Arts, Philadelphia; Fogg Art Mus, Mass; An Am Vision: Three Generations of Wyeth Art, Corcoran Gallery Art, Washington, 87; Mus Fine Arts, Boston, 87; Nat Mus of Mod Art, Tokyo, Japan; Metrop Mus of Art, NY; Royal Acad, London; H M De Young Mem Mus, Santa Fe, NMex; An Am Vision: Three Generations of Wyeth Art, Dallas Mus Art, Tex, 87; The Helga Pictures, Houston Mus Fine Arts, Tex, 88; Helga: Then and Now, Brandywine River Mus, Chadds Ford, Pa, 92; The Helga Pictures, Then and Now, Portland Mus Art, Maine, 93; Maine in Am, Farnsworth Art Mus, Rockland, 94; An Eye for Maine, Farnsworth Art Mus, Rockland, Maine, 94; George Washington: Am Symbol, Brandywine River Mus, 99; Wondrous Strange: Del Art Mus, 99; On Island: A Century of Continuity and Change, Maine, 2000; River Mus, Pa, 2000; Mississippi Mus of Art, 2001; From Wyeth to Welliver: Am Realism of the 20th Century, Currier Gallery of Art, NH, 2001; Andrew Wyeth's Helga Pictures: An Intimate Study, Joslyn Art Mus, Nebr, 2002. *Awards:* Pa Acad Fine Arts; Carnegie Inst; Am Watercolor Soc; Associe Etranger de l'Institut de France; Congressional Medal, President George Bush, 90; and many others. *Bibliog:* Richard Merryman (auth), Andrew Wyeth, Houghton; Wanda Corn (auth), The Art of Andrew Wyeth, New York Graphic Soc; George Plimpton & Donald Stewart (coauth), Andrew Wyeth, Horizon, 61; Margaret Graham Neeson (auth), The watcher from the shore, The Skipper, 4/63. *Mem:* Nat Acad (assoc, 44, acad, 45-); Am Watercolor Soc; Am Acad Arts & Lett. *Media:* Tempera, Watercolor. *Mailing Add:* c/o Frank E Fowler PO Box 247 Lookout Mountain TN 37350

WYETH, JAMES BROWNING
PAINTER
b Wilmington, Del, July 6, 46. *Study:* With Carolyn Wyeth; Elizabethtown Col, hon DFA. *Work:* Nat Gallery & Nat Portrait Gallery-Smithsonian Inst, Washington; Mus Mod Art, NY; Joslyn Art Mus, Omaha, Nebr; Del Art Mus, Wilmington; Brandywine River Mus, Chadds Ford, Pa; and others. *Exhib:* An Am Vision: Three Generations of Wyeth Art, Corcoran Gallery Art, Washington & Dallas Mus Art, Tex, 87; By Land and Sea: Selections from the Collection of Andrew & Betsy Wyeth, Farnsworth Art Mus, Rockland, Maine, 92; Maine in Am-Selections from the Farnsworth Collection, Farnsworth Art Mus, 94; An Eye for Maine-Paintings from a Private Collection, Farnsworth Art Mus, 94; Andrew Wyeth-Highlights from the Andrew and Betsy Wyeth & Farnsworth Collections, Farnsworth Art Mus, 94-; solo exhibs, Coe Kerr Gallery, NY, 90, James Graham & Sons, NY, 93, 95 & 96, William A Fransworth Art Mus, Maine, 92 7 95, Brandywine River Mus, Chadds Ford, Pa, 92, 95 & 95 & Butler Art Inst, Youngstown, Ohio, 99; and others. *Pos:* Bd govs, Nat Space Inst; adv comt, US Postal Serv. *Bibliog:* Joseph Roody (auth), Another Wyeth, Look Mag, 4/2/68;

Wyeth Phenomenon (film), CBS TV, 69; Richard Meryman (auth), Wyeth Christmas, Life Mag, 12/17/71. *Mem:* Nat Acad (assoc, 69, acad, 80-); Am Watercolor Soc; Nat Endowment Arts. *Media:* Oil, Watercolor. *Publ:* An American Vision: Three Generations & Wyeth Art Exhibits. *Mailing Add:* c/o James Graham & Sons 1014 Madison Ave New York NY 10021

WYLAN, BARBARA
PAINTER
b Providence, RI, Oct 23, 33. *Study:* RI Sch Design, BFA, 55. *Work:* Mobile Mus Art, Ala; Cahoon Mus Am Art, Cotuit, Mass; Cape Cod Mus Art, Dennis, MA; Springfield Art Mus, MO. *Exhib:* Rocky Mountain Nat Watermedia, Foothills Art Ctr, Golden, Colo, 81; Watercolor USA, Springfield Ar Mus, Mo, 82; Nat Soc Painters Casein & Acrylic, Nat Arts Club, New York City, 88; Dawn and Dusk, Cahoon Mus Am Art, Cotuit, Mass, 98; Twenty-One in Truro, Truro (Mass) Hist Mus, 2002; Women Creating 2002, Cape Cod Mus Fine Arts, Dennis, Mass, 2002; Springfield Mo Art Mus, Springfield, Mo; many other solo and group exhibs. *Awards:* Best Cape Cod Art, Chatham Festival Arts, 80; Dr David Soloway Mem, Nat Soc Painters Casein & Acrylic, 91. *Bibliog:* China at Cape Cod Conservatory, The Register, 1984; Carol Dumas (auth), Simple Beauty, The Cape Codder, 93; The Best Sunsets on Cape Cod, Spyglass, 1998. *Mem:* Nat Soc Painters in Casein and Acrylic; Watercolor USA Honor Soc; New England Watercolor Soc; Twenty-One in Truro; The Copley Soc Art, Boston, MA. *Media:* Watercolor, Acrylic. *Dealer:* The Spectrum of Am Artists and Craftsmen Inc 369 Old King's Hwy Brewster MA 02631; The Field Gallery Box 790 1050 State Rd West Tisbury MA 02575. *Mailing Add:* Box 548 Barnstable MA 02630

WYLAND, STEVE CREECH
ENVIRONMENTAL ARTIST, PAINTER
b Detroit, Mich, July 9, 56. *Study:* Ctr for Creative Studies, Detroit, 76-77, study with Jay Holland (sculpture), Russel Ketter (painting) & Bill Girrard (painting). *Hon Degrees:* Am Int Univ, Atlanta, Ga, LHD, 2001. *Work:* Provincial Mus, Victoria, BC; Ellis Island Mus, NY; Whaling Mus, Taiti, Japan; USA Today, Gannette, Cocoa Beach, Fla; Royal Ont Mus, Toronto. *Comn:* Whaling Wall XXII (ceiling), comn by Mr Kawada, Yamagata, Japan, 90; Planet Ocean, City Long Beach, Calif, 92; Art in Public Place (mural), Smithsonian Inst Nat Zoo, Washington, DC, 93; Whaling Wall 50, The Underground, Atlanta, 93; 91 Life-size Whaling Wall Murals, 1981-2004. *Exhib:* One-man shows, Nat Zoo, Wash, DC, 83, Nice Exhib, France, 89, Exhib, Sydney, Australia, 90 & Toyko, Japan, 91; East Coast Whaling Wall Tour, 93; West Coast Whaling Wall Tour, 94; Midwest Whaling Wall Tour, 97; Wyland Ocean Challenge of Am Tour-50 States in 50 Days, Reaching out to 120,000 pub and pvt sch and 67 million students, Fall 1998-; celebrating the United Nations "Int Year of the Oceans"; Wyland Ocean Challenge, "Clean Water for the 21st Century" Underwater Village 11-city Aquarium Tour, 2003; Wyland Ocean Challenge16-City East Coast Clean Water Tour, 2004. *Pos:* Founder, Dir, Wyland Found, a 501 c3 non-profit orgn, devoted to marine conservation & educ, currently; hon chmn, Orange Co March of Dimes, WalkAmerica, 2002; adv bd, The Cousteau Soc, Artist in Residence, Acad of Underwater Arts & Sci, 2002; developed, Wyland Ocean Challenge "Clean Water for the 21st Century and Beyond" with Scripps Inst of Oceanography and the Birch Aquarium; created, Wyland Ocean Challenge, "Clean Water for the 21st Century" 5-year Int Clean Up Tour Series. *Awards:* Congressional Tribute to Wyland-103rd Congress of the US; John M Olguin Marine Environ Award, Cabrillo Marine Aquarium, San Pedro, Calif, 2002; Hon Chief, Repub of Palau, 2003. *Bibliog:* The Art of Wyland (video), 97; Wyland's Ocean World (13 part series), Animal Planet, 98; Wyland's Ocean Planet, The Quest to Paint 100 Whaling Walls (video), 98. *Mem:* Founding mem, Wyland Found; founding artist, The Very Spec Arts. *Media:* Oil, Watercolor; Sculpture, Mural. *Publ:* Co-auth, The Art of Wyland, Wyland Studios, 92; Whale Tales, Wyland Studios, 94; Celebrating 50 Wyland Whaling Walls, Wyland Studios, 94; Undersea World of Wyland, Time Life Bks. *Mailing Add:* c/o Wyland Galleries 5 Columbia Aliso Viejo CA 92656-1460

WYNGAARD, SUSAN ELIZABETH
LIBRARIAN
Study: Univ Wis, Madison, BA & MLS; Univ Per Stranieri, Siena, Italy, cert; Taos Valley Weaving Sch, with Kristina Wilson; Univ NMex. *Pos:* Assoc librn, Univ Calif, Santa Barbara, 74-79; dir archives, Int Mus Photog, George Eastman House, 80-81; head, Fine Arts Libr, Ohio State Univ, currently. *Mem:* Art Libr Soc NAm (midwest rep exec bd, 85-87); Am Libr Asn. *Interests:* History of photography; art librarianship; library management. *Publ:* Coauth, Printed catalogues of the Art Exhibition Catalogue Collection of the Arts Library, Univ Calif, Santa Barbara, Somerset House, Cambridge, Eng & Teaneck, NJ, 77; The Humanities and the Library, Am Libr Asn, Chicago, 93. *Mailing Add:* Ohio State Univ Fine Arts Libr Wexner Ctr for the Visual Arts Columbus OH 43210

WYNN, DONALD JAMES
PAINTER, LECTURER
b Brooklyn, NY, Sept 26, 42. *Study:* Pratt Inst, BFA, 67; Ind Univ, MFA, 69. *Work:* Metrop Mus Art, NY; Adirondack Mus; Newark Mus; Ind Univ Mus Art; Okamura Collection, Kyoto. *Comn:* Portraits of Dr & Mrs Crawford Campbell, Upsata Med Ctr; portrait of State Supreme Court Justice Norman L Harvey, Plattsburgh Govt Ctr, NY. *Exhib:* Poetischer Amerikanischer Realismus: Paul Weissenfeld, Don Wynn, Gal RP Hartmann, Munich & Wiesbaden Kunst, 69; 22 Realists, Whitney Mus Am Art, 70; Michael C Rockefeller Arts Ctr, State Univ NY Cortland; one-man shows, Alpha Gallery, Boston, 75, Robert Schoelkopf Gallery, NY, 76, Adirondack Mus, 78, Nina Freudenheim Gallery, Buffalo, 93, Arnot Art Mus, Elmira, 85, Alice Simsar Gallery, Ann Arbor, 88 & Hillside Gallery (with catalog), Tokyo, 90; A Wild Sort of Beauty: Pub Places and Private Visions, Adirondack Mus, NY, 92; Cradall Pub Lib, NY, 97; Southern Vt Art Ctr, 99; Helen Day Art Ctr, Stowe, Vt, 2001; Chaffee Ctr for Visual Arts, Rutland, Vt, 2002. *Teaching:* Vis artist, Yale Univ, Art Inst Chicago, Skidmore Col, Moore Col Art, Ohio Univ, E Mich Univ, State Univ NY, 70-81. *Awards:* Elizabeth T Greenshields Mem Found Grant, Montreal, 70; Residence Grant, Fine Arts Work Ctr, Provincetown, 71; CAPS Grant, NY State Coun Arts, 75. *Bibliog:* Gerrit Henry (auth), A realist twin bill, Art News Mag, 1/73; Judith Tannenbaum (auth), article, Arts Mag, 1/77; Peter Lemon (auth), Don Wynn: Taxidermy and works of art, Am Artist, New York, 9/83. *Media:* Oil, Acrylic. *Dealer:* Motif Ltd Nerima-ku Hikawadai 3-17-9 Paumville H202 Tokyo 179 Japan; Gallery 100 445 Broadway Saratoga Springs NY 12866

WYNN, GAINES CLORE
PAINTER, CURATOR
b Lamesa, Tex, Jan 13, 46. *Study:* Tex Tech, with Hugh Gibbons, BA, 68; Ariz State Univ, with Rip Woods & Eugene Grigsby, MFA(summa cum laude), 71, PhD(art educ). *Work:* Nat Mus Women Arts, Washington; pvt collection of Queen Elizabeth the Queen Mother, Clarence House, London; Ariz State Fine Arts Collection; Ten Years of Painting Retrospective Gaines Clore Wynn, Bradley School of the Arts, York Penn, 2001. *Comn:* Portrait of A L Stamper, Calvert Co Bd Educ, Prince Frederick, Md, 81; portrait of Karen, Al Bird Assoc, Annapolis, Md, 90; Hewlett Packard, 98. *Exhib:* Four States Invitational, Phoenix Art Mus, 73; Realists of Washington, Arlington Arts Ctr, Va, 80; Mus Invitational, Nat Mus Women Arts, Washington, 88; Bright Visions: The Making of Myth, Rahr-West Mus, Manitowoc, Wis, 90, Charles Allis Art Mus, Milwaukee, Wis, 91; Ann Juried Exhib, Montpelier Arts Ctr, Laurel, Md, 95. *Collection Arranged:* Nat Hons Exhib (auth, catalog), Nat Mus Women Arts, 91; A Glimpse of Joy: Corrine Mitchell (auth, catalog), Nat Mus Women Arts, 92; Pulse Points: Transforming Tradition (auth, catalog), Harvard Univ, 96. *Pos:* Educ prog consult, Nat Mus Women Arts, 88-; Currently Adv on African Am Women Artist Collectors in US for Chair Fine Art Dept, Charles Herbert Flowers Sch, 2000-; Nat Adv Bd-NMWA. *Teaching:* Chmnn, art dept, Calvert High Sch, 75-81 & 90-. *Awards:* Presidential Award, Nat Art Educ Asn, Houston, 95; Founder for the Nat Art Honor Soc 1975 Calvert Co, MD; 1500 Chap in Secondary Sch in US 2005. *Mem:* Women's Caucus for Art (nat bd dir, 90-94); Nat Art Educ Asn; Nat Dem Spouse Org, 2001-Present; Nat Congressional Black Causus Spouse Org, 2001-Present; Md State Arts Council 2 terms 2001-Present (Appointed by Gov Md). *Media:* Oil, Pastel. *Interests:* Gardening, reading, Journal writing,. *Collection:* Hewlett-Packard. *Publ:* Coauth, Gumba Ya Ya: An Anthology of African Women Artists, Mid March Press, NY, 95; Violence Against Women: Breaking the Silence Greenbelt Art Center; Greenbelt, Maryland, wrote exhib Cataoogue as well as curated exhib, 2003; Seven Artist of St Martins VI The Influence fo Romare Bearden, Parish Gallery, Georgetown, Wash DC, 2004. *Dealer:* Soho 20 469 Broome St NY 10013; Parish Gallery Georgetown Washington DC Present; The Gaines Clore Wynn Studio/Gallery 3711 Rhode Isl Ave Mt Rainier MD. *Mailing Add:* 2410 Enterprise Rd Bowie MD 20721-2529

WYNN, STEPHEN A
COLLECTOR
b 42. *Study:* Univ Pa, BA, 63. *Pos:* Pres, Chief Exec Officer Best Brands, Inc, 69-72; chmn bd dir, pres, Chief Exec Officer, Mirage Resorts Inc (formerly Golden Nugget Inc), 73-2000; managing mem, Valvino Lamore, LLC, 2000-02; chmn, Chief Exec Officer Wynn Resorts Ltd, 2002-. *Awards:* Named one of Top 200 Collectors, ARTnews Mag, 2004, 2006. *Collection:* French Impressionism; Modern and Contemporary Art. *Mailing Add:* Wynn Resorts Ltd 3145 Las Vegas Blvd S Las Vegas NV 89109

WYNNE, ALBERT GIVENS
PAINTER, CALLIGRAPHER
b Colorado Springs, Colo, Jan 3, 22. *Study:* Univ Denver; Iowa Wesleyan Col, BA; Univ Iowa, MA; also with S Carl Fracassini, Boardman Robinson, James Lechay & others. *Work:* Univ Denver & Univ Southern Colo; Rawlins Bank, Wyo; El Pomar Found; Mus Contemp Art, Boulder, Colo; Mus Contemp Art, Denver; Vance Kirkland Art Mus, Denver. *Comn:* Stained glass windows, Black Forest Colo Community Church, 81. *Exhib:* Walker Art Ctr; Corcoran Gallery Art; Denver Art Mus; Des Moines Art Ctr; Colorado Springs Fine Arts Ctr; Roswell Arts Ctr; Sioux City Art Ctr; Butler Inst Am Art; and others. *Pos:* Art consult, Anchorage, Alaska Sch Dist; artist-in-residence, Colorado Springs Fine Arts Ctr. *Teaching:* Hon instr, Univ Colo, Colorado Springs Fine Arts Ctr; prof art, Iowa Wesleyan Col, Morningside Col & Colorado Col. *Awards:* Prizes, Des Moines Art Ctr, Roswell Art Ctr & Colorado Springs Fine Arts Ctr. *Media:* Oil, Watercolor. *Mailing Add:* 7420 Swan Rd Colorado Springs CO 80908

WYNNE, ROB
CONCEPTUAL ARTIST, PAINTER
b New York, NY, Nov 28, 48. *Study:* Pratt Inst, Brooklyn NY, BFA, 70. *Work:* Chase Manhattan Bank, NY; Arthur Anderson & Co, Chicago; Prudential Life Insurance, Newark, NJ; Guerlain Found, Les Mesnuls, France. *Comn:* Silk screen on enamel panels, Allianz, Munich, Ger, 98. *Exhib:* The Unique Print, Mus Fine Arts, Boston, 90; Slow Art, PS 1, Mus Contemp Art, Long Island City, NY; Window Shopping, Grey Art Gallery, NY Univ, 94; A Dress, Winnepeg Art Gallery, Can, 95; Le Corps du Livre, Carre d'Art, Niemes, France, 98. *Awards:* Pollack Krashner Found Award, 92. *Bibliog:* Ed Leffingwell (auth), The paintings of Rob Wynne, Arts Mag, 88; Nancy Princenthal (auth), Review, Art Am, 96; Naumann & Rimanelli (co-auths), Afterglow, Oliver Schweden, Munich, 97. *Dealer:* Holly Solomon 172 Mercer Ct New York NY 10012. *Mailing Add:* c/o Holly Solomon Gallery 222 W 23rd St Ste 425 New York NY 10011

WYRICK, CHARLES LLOYD, JR
PUBLISHER, EDITOR
b Greensboro, NC, May 5, 39. *Study:* Davidson Col, BA; Univ NC, MFA; Univ Mo. *Exhib:* Corcoran Biennial Exhib Am Painting, 67; Assoc Artists NC Ann, 68; Univ Va Print Exhib, 68; Va Mus Fine Arts; Weatherspoon Art Gallery; Carspecken-Scott Gallery. *Collection Arranged:* Art from the Ancient World, The Human Figure in Art, A Wyeth Portrait & Light as a Creative Medium, Va Mus Fine Arts, 66-68; Contemporary American Paintings from the Lewis Collection, Del Art Mus, 74; Louise Nevelson, Spoleto Festival USA, 83; and others. *Pos:* Artmobile coordr, Va Mus Fine Arts, Richmond, 66-68; exec dir, Asn Preservation Va Antiq, 68-70; pres, Fine Arts Consults, Richmond, 71-73; art critic, Richmond News Leader, 71-73; dir, Del Art Mus, 73-79; dir, Gibbes Art Gallery, 80-86; pres, Wyrick & Co, 86- & Dixie Media, Inc, 89-. *Teaching:* Instr, Stephens Col, 64-66. *Awards:* First for Column, Va Press Asn, 72. *Mem:* Am Asn Mus; Publ Asn S. *Media:* Photography. *Res:* Contemporary American painting; 18th to 20th century American architecture; 20th century American photography. *Publ:* Auth, Art & urban aesthetics (weekly column), Richmond News Leader; A Wyeth Portrait, 67 & Contemporary Art at the Virginia Mus, 72, Arts in Va; ed, Oystering: A Way of Life, 83; Nets & Doors: Shrimping in Southern Waters, 89; The A B Frost Book, 93; ed of numerous museum catalogs and books. *Mailing Add:* Wyrick & Co PO Box 89 Charleston SC 29402-0089

X

XIE, XIAOZE
PAINTER, EDUCATOR
b Guangdong, China, June 26, 66. *Study:* Tsinghua Univ, Beijing, BArch, 1988; Ctrl Acad Arts & Design, Beijing, MA, 1991; Univ North Tex, Sch Visual Arts, MFA, 1996. *Work:* Mus Fine Art, Houston; Scottsdale Mus Contemp Art; Eastfield Coll, Dallas; Univ Seattle. *Comn:* Art in Archit Prog Comn for the Fed Bldg and US Courthouse, Daveport, Iowa. *Exhib:* Building for the Millennium: Recent Acquisitions, Scottsdale (Ariz) Mus Contemp Art, 1998; One-man shows, Devin Borden Hiram Butler Gallery, Houston, 1998 & 99, The Blinding Light: Paintings and Photographs by Xiaoze Xie, Davidson Galleries, Seattle, 1999 & The Gold Paintings, 2000, Order: An Installation and Paintings by Xiaze Xie, Scottsdale Mus Contemp Art, 2000; Rosalyn Richads & Xiaoze Xie, Bucknell Univ Art Gallery, Lewisburg, Pa, 2000; Recipients of 1999 Arizona Artists Materials Fund Grants, Contemp Forum, Phoenix Art Mus, 2000; Guangdong Mus Art, Guangzhou, China, 2000; Allentown (Pa) Art Mus, 2001; Sally Packard and Xiaoze Xie, Art League Houston, 2001; One Man Shows, Charles Cowles Gallery, NY, 2002-2004; History; A Microscopic View China Art Archives and Warehouse, Beiing, 2003; Nat Forces; Earth, Air, Fire and Water, Boise Art Mus, Boise, ID, 2003-2004; The Meadows Mus, Southern Methodist Univ, Dallas, 2004; Regeneration: Contemp Chinese Art from China and the US, Samek Art Gallery, Bucknell Univ, PA, 2004-2006; One Man show, Nicholas Metivier Gallery, Toronto, Canada, 2005; The Daily News, Salt Lake Art Ctr, Salt Lake City, UT, 2005-2006; numerous others. *Teaching:* asst prof, dept arts & design, Shantou Univ, Guangdong, China, 91-92; tchg fellow, Sch Visual Arts, Univ North Tex, Denton, 94-96, adj instr, 96; vis artist, The Evergreen State Col, Olympia, Wash, 96-97; asst prof, Bucknell Univ, Lewisburg, Pa, 99-; numerous lectr positions. *Awards:* Kimborugh Fund award, Dallas Mus Art, 1996; Ariz Artists Materials Fund grant, Phoenix Art Mus, 1999; Minority Jr Faculty award, Chirstian R & mary F Lindback Found, 2001. *Bibliog:* Robin Updike (auth), Show wrestles with reality, books dominate Xie's haunting, ambiguous work, Seattle Times, Wash, 2/25/99; Ted Loos, Fish Wrap, Bird CageLiner, Still Life, The New York Times, 3/21/2004; Matthew Guy Nichols, Xiaoze Xie at Charles Cowles, Art in America, June/July 2004. *Media:* Oil. *Mailing Add:* c/o Charles Cowles Gallery 537 W 24th St New York NY 10011

XU, JINYI See Chee, Cheng-Khee (Jinyi Xu)

Y

YAGER, DAVID
PHOTOGRAPHER, PRINTMAKER
b Bronx, NY, Mar 16, 49. *Study:* Univ Conn, BA, 71; Fla State Univ, MFA, 74, DeMontfort Univ, United Kingdom, HDD, 96. *Hon Degrees:* DeMontfort Univ, Dr Design. *Work:* Mus Mod Art, NY; Art Inst Chicago & Columbia Col, Chicago; Univ S Fla, Tampa; Boston Mus Fine Arts. *Comn:* Photographic mural, Bell Tel Co, Atlanta. *Exhib:* Light, Loch Haven Mus, Orlando, Fla; New Photographers, Ellenburg, Wash, 79-81; Magic Silver Show, Washington, DC, 80; Sch Art Inst Chicago, 81; Daytona Beach Gallery, Fla, 81; Tampa Mus, Fla, 82; Silver Int, Univ S Fla, Tampa, 82; Univ S Fla, Tampa, 83 & 85. *Teaching:* Prof art & chmn dept, Univ Md, Baltimore, 86-, distinguished prof art. *Awards:* Grant, State of Fla, 82, Warhol Found & Streurr Found. *Mem:* Soc Photog Educ; Col Art Asn. *Res:* digital imagery. *Publ:* Contribr, Bomb Mag, Winter, 98. *Mailing Add:* Visual Art Dept Univ Md Baltimore Co Catonsville MD 21228

YAMASHIRO, TAD
PHOTOGRAPHER
b Calif, Nov 24, 30. *Study:* Cooper Union, 54-58. *Work:* George Eastman House Int Mus Photog, Rochester, NY; Mus Mod Art, NY. *Exhib:* Tad Yamashiro, George Eastman House, Rochester, NY, 83; Big Picture Show, Mus Mod Art, NY, 83; Photog Moma, Univ Hawaii Mus Art, Honolulu, 83; 20th Century Photog from Moma, Seibu Mus Art, Tokyo, 84; Treasure from the Collection, George Eastman House, Rochester, NY, 85. *Teaching:* Instr, seminar & thesis, Sch Visual Arts, 63-84. *Mailing Add:* 224 E 12th St New York NY 10003

YAMIN, MARTINA (SCHAAP)
CONSERVATOR
b Amsterdam, Neth, May 5, 37. *Study:* Wellesley Col, Mass, BA(art hist), 58; Fogg Art Mus, Harvard Univ Conserv Dept, Lab Asst & Study, 58-61. *Comn:* Whitney Mus Art, pvt collections & galleries. *Pos:* Conservator, pvt practice, Paper Studio, New York, 61-; vis, paper conservator, Philadelphia Mus, 64-79. *Bibliog:* D Brewer (auth), The Delicate Art Restoring Paper, New York Times, 5/4/89; T Trucco (auth), Saving Old Documents, New York Times, 9/5/91. *Mem:* Fel Int Inst Conserv; fel Am Inst Conserv; Drawing Soc, NY (bd mem, trustee); Nat Arts Club (curatorial comt mem); Wellesley Col Friends of Art, NY (comt mem); Art Table, NY. *Publ:* Auth, Report on the Inst of Paper Conserv Conf, Drawing, 92. *Mailing Add:* 206 E 30th St New York NY 10016

YAMIN, STEVEN EDWARD
PRINTMAKER
b New York, NY, Apr 5, 46. *Study:* Olivet Col, BA, 68; Pratt Inst, MFA, 71. *Work:* Victoria & Albert Mus, London, Eng; Libr Congress, DC; Mary Armstrong Print Collection, Olivet Col, Mich; NJ State Mus, Trenton; NY Pub Libr. *Exhib:* New Printmakers, Victoria & Albert Mus, London, Eng, 74, 19th Nat Print Exhib, Brooklyn Mus, 75; 5th British Int, Bradford Mus, Eng, 75; 55th Soc Am Graphic Artists Nat, AAA Gallery, NY, 77; 12th Nat Print Exhib, Silvermine Guild, New Canaan, Conn, 78; 7th Int Miniature Print, Pratt Graphics Ctr, NY, 79; Sense of Scale III, Univ Albuquerque Mus, 79; Davidson Galleries, Seattle, Wash, 2004; 5th Biennial Int Miniature Print Exhib, Norwalk, Conn, 2005; Contemp Printmakers, The Old Printshop, NY, 2005. *Collection Arranged:* Prints from Fitch-Febvrel Gallery, NY; Cantor-Lemberg, Birmingham, Mich. *Pos:* Guest instr, Pratt Graphics Ctr, NY, Feb-Mar 75 tech asst, Am Atelier, NY, 76-. *Teaching:* Lectr printmaking, Brooklyn Col, 74-76; Pratt Manhattan Ctr, 81. *Awards:* Purchase Awards, 16th Ann Nat Print Exhib, Okla Art Ctr, Oklahoma City, 74 & Potsdam '78, State Univ NY Potsdam, 78; Graphic Chemical & Ink Co Award, 7th Miniature Print Exhib, 79; Purchase Award, 5th Biennial Int Miniature Print Exhib, 2005. *Bibliog:* W A S Hatch (auth), The European Graphic Biennale; Matthew Kangas (auth), Seattle Times, 4/2/2004; Journal of the Print World, Vol 28, No 4, fall 2005. *Mem:* Print Club, Philadelphia; Exec Coun Soc Am Graphic Artists; Visual Artists & Galleries Asn. *Media:* All. *Dealer:* The Old Print Shop 150 Lexington Ave New York NY 10016. *Mailing Add:* 3903 Ave I Brooklyn NY 11210

YAMPOLSKY, PHYLLIS
CONCEPTUAL ARTIST, PAINTER
b Philadelphia, Pa, Aug 23, 32. *Study:* Philadelphia Col Art, 50-52; Inst Allende, 54-55; Hans Hoffman Sch, New York, 56-58; Ecole de Beaux Arts, Fontainbleau, France, 56. *Work:* Dallas Mus Fine Arts, Tex; Mus Erotic Art, Stockholm, Swed; Nat Archives, Washington; also pvt collections of Marcel Duchamp, Robert Graham, Sr, JP Lannin & Herbert Mayer. *Comn:* Mural, Concord Hotel, Kiamesha Lake, NY, 56; mural, Monticello Raceway, NY, 65; collective mural, Pathfinder Press, NY, 89. *Exhib:* Philadelphia Mus Art, 57; Dallas Mus Fine Arts, 76; McNay Inst, San Antonio, Tex, 77-78; one-man show, OK Harris & Susan Caldwell Galleries, NY, 78; Teilhard & Metamorphosis, Arcosanti, Ariz, 81; Women in our Midst, Peter David Galleries, Minneapolis, Minn, 85; Town Hall Wall, America's Reunion on the Mall, Clinton Inaugural Comt, Wash, 93; The March Against Cancer, Washington, DC, 97-98; The Hague Appeal Peace Conference, The Hague, The Neth, 99; Main St Millennium, Washington, DC Millennium Celebration, 99-2000; Williamsburg Art & Hist Ctr, 2000-2004; 1st Anniversary of 9/11, Union Sq, NY & Am Constitution Ctr, Philadelphia, 2002. *Pos:* New York City's 1st artist-in-residence, New York City Parks, Recreation & Cult Affairs, 66-67; consult, NY State Coun Arts, 67-70. *Teaching:* Dir, founder & instr drawing & painting, Workshop Yampolsky, NY, 56-66; instr, 92nd St YMHA, NY, 58-60; founder & dir Hall of Issues, Judson Church, NY, 60-61; dir, Portrait of Ten Towns, NY State Coun Arts, 67-70; instr, Impact, Marylerose Accad, Albany, NY, 69; instr, The New Millenium, Bennett Col, Millbrook, NY, 76; founder & officer, Northeast Windham Coun Arts, Vt, 78-79; instr, Vermont Acad, Saxton's River, 79-81; co-founder & instr, New Vt Sch Arts, Putney, 81-82. *Awards:* Walter Damrosch Award, Ecole de Beaux Arts, Fontainbleau, France, 56; NY State Coun Arts Award, 67; Ann Valentine Awards, Cue Mag, 67; Betsy Barlow Rogers Environmental Award, 95. *Bibliog:* Grace Glueck (auth), The reports were greatly exaggerated, NY Times, 7/9/67; Philip Hyde (auth), Festival Program, NY State Coun Arts Ann Report, 69; Matthew Naythons (auth), An American Reunion, The 52nd Presidential Inauguration, Warner Books, 93; Feast of Connections for the First 50 Strangers, Woodstock, NY, 67; New York, WW Norton, 98; The New Amazon, The New Mus, New York, 2000. *Mem:* founder & pres, Independent Friends of McCarren Park, The Brooklyn Accent, Greenpoint Coun Arts; co-founder, McCarren Park Conservancy (bd mem); Windham Co Coun Arts, Vt; Commun Coord Comt United Nations (adv bd). *Media:* Visual Arts, Public Event and Program Design. *Res:* design & restoration of McCarren Pool Complex, Brookly, NY. *Specialty:* Painting, sculpture, mixed media. *Interests:* The Participatory Agenda. *Publ:* Auth, Multiples, Art News 40th Ann, 67; contribr, Erotic Art, 1st ed, Bell/Grove Press, 68; auth & illusr, The American diner, Country J, 81; auth, The 10,000 things: Aesthetics as a system of morality, Breakthrough Mag, Global Educ Asn, 90; coauth & illusr, Sculpting With the Environment, Van Nostrand-Reinhold, 95. *Dealer:* Stephen Gang Gallery 529 W 20 New York NY 10111

YAMRUS, FRANK
PHOTOGRAPHER
b Kingston, Pa, Nov 23, 58. *Study:* Wilkes Univ, Pa, BA, 80; Drexel Univ, Pa, MBA, 86. *Work:* Mus Fine Arts, Houston; Victoria & Albert Mus, London. *Exhib:* Orange Co Ctr Contemp Arts, Santa Cruz, Calif, 93; Falkirk Cult Ctr, San Rafael, Calif, 93; Alexandria Mus Art, La, 95; Provincetown Art Mus, Ma, 95-97; Soc Contemp Photog,

Kansas City, Mo, 95-97; Mus Fine Arts, Houston, Tex, 97; Discoveries of the Fotoplace, Fotofest 98, Houston, 98; San Francisco Cameraworks, Calif, 98. *Awards:* Bronze, Calif Discovery Awards, 94 & 95; Purchase Award, Soc Contemp Photog, 95 & Merit Award, 97. *Bibliog:* Portfolio, Paris Rev, 97; J A Hager (auth), Ferral portraiture, Provincetown Mag, 8/96. *Publ:* Contribr, Full Exposed: The Male Nude in Photography, Routledge, 95; Whitman's Men, Universe/Rizzoli, 96; One Thousand Male Nudes, Taschen Publ, 97; articles in Paris Rev, 97 & Not Only Blue Mag, 98. *Dealer:* Sara Morthland 225 Tenth Ave New York NY 10011. *Mailing Add:* 2140 Pacific Ave No 602 San Francisco CA 94115

YANISH, ELIZABETH SHWAYDER
SCULPTOR, LECTURER
b St Louis, Mo. *Study:* Wash Univ; Denver Univ; also with Frank Varra, Wilbur Verhelst, Edgar Brittor, Marian Buchan & Angelo DiBenedetto. *Work:* Tyler Mus, Tex; Colo State Bank, Denver, Martin-Marietta Co, Denver; Colo Women's Col; Ball State Col; and numerous pvt collections. *Comn:* Carved doors, eternal light, Menorah, BMH Synagogue, Denver, 72-74; complete interior, Har Ha Shem Congregation, Boulder, 74; Relief Tree (bronze), Beth Israel Hosp, Denver, 74; mem relief, Denver Gen Hosp, 75. *Exhib:* Denver Art Mus Exhib, 61-75 & Western Ann, 65; Midwest Biennial, Joslyn Mus, Omaha, Nebr, 68; Int Exhib, Lucca, Italy, 71; one-man show, Woodstock Gallery, London, Eng, 73, Randi's Art Gallery, Denver, Colo Women's Col Honor Exhib, Denver, Northeastern Jr Col, Sterling, Colo, The Denver, Colo, Brass Cheque Gallery, Denver; Artrain, Mich Fine Arts Coun, 74; Univ No Colo, Greeley; Fine Arts Ctr, Canon City, Colo; and numerous others. *Pos:* Trustee, Denver Ctr Performing Arts, 73-75; chmn, Visual Arts Festival, Bicentennial, 74-75; bd educ, Arts in Elem Educ, 77-78; bd mem, Mizel Mus, Denver, 88; mem, Denver Cult Action Steering Comt, 88. *Teaching:* Lectr contemp sculpture, var cols & univs. *Awards:* 1st Place Award Airspace Exhib; 1st Place Award Air Force Acad; Woman of Year, Am Biographical Inst, 98. *Bibliog:* Article in Artforum, 63; Jim Mills (auth), var feature stories, Denver Post Art Ed, 64-75; John Manson (auth), Artists of the Rockies, 74. *Mem:* Artists Equity Asn (pres, 63); Rocky Mountain Liturgical Arts; Allied Sculptors Colo; Denver Coun Arts (pres, 73-75); Colo Artists Equity Asn (pres, 79-80); Mus Nat Hist; Nat Mus Women Arts; Eden Theatrical Workshop; Rose Hosp Auxilary; Nat Coun Jewsih Women; Asian Arts Asn; Denver Art Mus; Womens Art Ctr & Gallery Denver. *Media:* Welded Steel, Bronze. *Dealer:* Elizabeth Schlosser Fine Art 311 Detroit St Denver CO 80206. *Mailing Add:* 2400 Cherry Creek S Dr Unit 503 Denver CO 80209-3259

YANOFF, ARTHUR (SAMUEL)
PAINTER
b Boston, Mass, May 9, 39. *Study:* Mus Sch Fine Arts, Boston, 58-61; studied with Jason Berger, 62-65. *Work:* Mus Fine Arts, Santa Fe; Congregation Ahavath Chesed, Jacksonville, Fla; Rose Art Mus, Bradeis Univ, Waltham, MA; Mus Fine Arts, Boston, MA; Detroit Inst Am Arts, Detroit, MI; and others; Yeshiva Univ Mus, NY; Currier Mus Art, Manchester, NH. *Comn:* Portrait (Gil Williams), Bellevue Gallery, Binghamton, NY, 73; charcoal studies, NH Composition, Concord, 74 & Mrs Gereard Derepentigny, Manchester, NH, 74; portrait (Paul Metcalf), Lillabulero Press, Northwood, NH; portrait (Mrs Charles Gordon), comn by Charles Gordon, Concord, NH. *Exhib:* Collectors Show, Va Mus Fine Arts, 70; Drawings from Holst's Sculpture, Addison Gallery Am Art, 74; solo exhibs, Mus Fine Arts, Boston, 83, New Images in Watercolor, Currier Gallery Art, Manchester, NH, 85, Concordia Col, Bronxville, NY, 86, Babson Col, Wellesley, Mass, 88, New Eng Col Gallery, NH, 95, Yeshiva Univ Mus, NY, 96 & 97 & Lingo Fine Arts Gallery, West Stockbridge, Mass, 99, Steerage to Ellis Island, Gallery at Stageworks, 2006; Wade Gallery, Los Angeles, 87; Sound Shore Gallery, Stamford, Conn, 89; New Eng Col Gallery, 94; New Directions, Contemp Art from the Currier Collection, Manchester, NH, 94; The Luria Series, Cline Fine Art Gallery, 95; Koussevitzky Arts Festival, Berkshire Community Col, Pittsfield, Mass, 97; Eastern Spririt in Contemp Art, Creative Projs, Warehouse Gallery, Lee, Mass, 97; Made in the Americas, Coun Creative Projs, Warehouse Gallery, Lee, Mass, 97; Sarah Y Rentschler Gallery, Hudson, NY, 2000; Western Wall Project, Deborah Davis Fine Art, Hudson, 2002-03; Rural Artists with Urban Sensibilities, Perrala Gallery, Fulton Montgomery Community Col, Johnstow, NY, 2003; CW White Gallery, Portland, Maine, 2003; Drawings, Deborah Davis Gallery, Hudson, NY, 2005. *Pos:* Art design consult, Lillabulero Press, Northwood Narrows, NH, 67-74; art therapist, NH Hosp, 70-71 & pvt clinic, 75-. *Teaching:* Instr, pvt students, 67-, Manchester Inst Art, NH, 73-74, painting workshops, Berkshire Community Col, S Co Campus, Great Barrington, Mass, 97 & Coun Creative Proj, Lee, Mass, 98; art instr, Adult Educ Prog, Coe-Brown Acad, Northwood, NH, 72; Berkshire Comm Col, 97; workshop instr, Iterlaken Sch Art, Stockbridge, Mass, 98-; workshop instr, Hudson Opera House, 2005. *Awards:* Direct Vision Exhib Awards, Mass Coun Arts, 73 & 75; Priy Pene Richard, Symposium, 88; Grant, Max and Anna Levinson Foundation, Santa Fe, NMex, 99. *Bibliog:* Piri Halasz (auth), From the Mayor's Doorstep, Electronic Edition, no 43, 12/1/02; Richard Roth (auth), Making Memory Come Alive, The Independent, 11/29/02; The Western Wall Project, Register Star, 12/6/02; Vicky Perry (auth), Abstract Painting: Concepts & Techniques, Perry Watson-Guptil Publ, 2005. *Mem:* Boston Painters & Sculptors; NH Art Asn; Am Art Therapy Asn. *Media:* Acrylics, Watercolor. *Publ:* Illusr, Broken Syllables, 67 & Waiting to Freeze, 69, Lillabulero Press; auth, The paste-up autobiography: Collage in the treatment of disturbed adolescents, Am J Art Therapy, 73; illusr, Raw Honey, Alice James Books, 75. *Dealer:* Lascano Gallery 297 Main St Great Barrington MA 01230. *Mailing Add:* 624 S Egremont Rd Great Barrington MA 01230

YANOW, RHODA MAE
PAINTER, ILLUSTRATOR
b Newark, NJ. *Study:* Newark Arts Club; Parsons Sch Design; Newark Sch Fine & Indust Arts; Heritage Art Sch; Nat Acad Design, with Henry Gasser, Daniel Greene, Harvey Dinnerstein & John Grabach. *Work:* West Orange Home for Senior Citizens, NJ; Newark Pub Libr; Meadowlands Sport Arena; West Orange Town Hall; NJ Ballet; Prince Albert Mus; Jack Richardson; Pastel Soc Am; Pegausus Meadowlands. *Comn:* Portraits, comn by Thuryoung Family, 92-94; Nat Acad Design, 79-81; Rensselaer Univ. *Exhib:* Nat Arts Club Pastel Show,74; Muhlenberg Col Festival of Arts, 75; Am Artists Prof League Grand Nat Exhib, 75; Salmagundi Club Watercolor Show, 75; Nat Acad Design, 78-80; and others; Solo shows incl Nathan's Art Gallery, West Patterson, NJ, Swain's Art Gallery, Plainfield, NJ, Hait Gallery, Maplewood, NJ, Gallery of South Orange & Maplewood, NJ, others; Int Mus Cartoon Art, 2000. *Collection Arranged:* Butler Institute of Am Art; First Pastel Mus, China. *Pos:* costume designer, NJ Ballet. *Teaching:* Instr pastel painting & life drawing, Du Cret Sch Arts & Newark Mus, 93-94; instr figure painting in pastel, PSA Nat Arts Sch, NY; instr drawing, Newark Mus, NJ. *Awards:* Gold Medal, Nat Asn Women Artists, 89; Bronze Medal Hon, Pastel Soc Am, 90; Pen & Brush Award, Gene Alder Walker, 96; Knickerbocker Artists Silver & Gold Medal Honor, Catharine Lorillard Wolfe Art Club, 87; Ladies Auxilary Award, Columbus Club, 90; Best in Show, Conn Pastel Soc, 2003. *Bibliog:* Ruthann Williams (auth), Graven images, NJ Music & Arts, 6/74. *Mem:* Am Artists Prof League; Nat Asn Women Artists; Catharine Lorillard Wolfe Art Club; Pen & Brush; Pastel Soc Am; Am Women Artists. *Media:* Pastels, Pen & Ink; Lithography. *Res:* Observing human behavior. *Specialty:* Ballet paintings, people. *Publ:* Illusr, The Art of Pastel Portraiture, Watson-Guptil Publ; contribr, Star Ledger & other local newspapers; Am Artist Mag, 2/89; cover, NJ Goodlife, 10/89; illusr, The Best of Pastel I & II, Rockport Publ, 96; Ron Lister (auth) Drawing With Pastels. *Dealer:* Louisa Melrose Gallery, 41 Bridge St, Frenchtown, NJ, 08825. *Mailing Add:* 12 Korwell Cir West Orange NJ 07052

YARBER, ROBERT
PAINTER
b Dallas, Tex, 48. *Study:* Cooper Union Col, NY, BFA, 71; La State Univ, Baton Rouge, MFA, 74. *Comn:* Created a medal commemorating the millennium for the Vatican's Jubilee Campaign, 2001. *Exhib:* Oakland Mus, 79, (with catalog), 83 & 91 (with catalog); San Francisco Mus Mod Art (with catalog), 84; Whitney Mus Am Art (with catalog), 85-86; Mus Fine Arts, Boston (with catalog), 86; Walker Arts Ctr, 87; Pa Acad Fine Arts, 87; Baltimore Mus Art, 87; Nat Mus Mod Art, Kyoto, Japan, 88; Galleria Naz Roma, Italy, 88; Stedelijk Mus (with catalog), Amsterdam, The Neth, 89; solo exhibs, Va Mus Fine Arts, 89, Sonnabend Gallery, NY, 93 & 95, Galerie Lehmann, Lausanne, Switz, 94, Nev Inst Contemp Art, Las Vegas, 95, Patricia Faure Gallery, Los Angeles, 95 & Marella Arte Contemp, Italy, 96, Milan, Rome, Florence, and Prato; Butler Inst Am Art (with catalog), 90; Mint Mus Art, 91; The World Tomorrow, Thomas Solomon's Garage, Los Angeles, 94; In the Field, Margo Leavin Gallery, Los Angeles, 94; Go Figure, Patricia Faure Gallery, Los Angeles, 95; 16 Artists, Patricia Faure Gallery, Santa Monica, Calif, 96. *Teaching:* Vis instr painting, Univ Calif, Berkeley, 82 & vis lectr, 83; vis lectr, Univ Tex, Austin, 82 & lectr, 84; vis artist, Univ Calif, Santa Barbara, 88; asst to full prof art, Pa State Univ, 94-, named distinguished prof, 2003. *Awards:* Nat Endowment Arts Fel Grant, 83 & 85. *Bibliog:* Ivana Mulatero (auth), Robert Yarber, Juliet Art Mag, No 61, 2-3/93; The horror: Robert Yarber (artist)-All around esthetes, Artforum, Vol 32, No 8, 94; David Pagel (auth), Taking a glimpse into the world of tomorrow, Los Angeles Times, 2/24/94; and others. *Dealer:* Patricia Faure Gallery Bergamot Sta 2525 Michigan Ave B7 Santa Monica CA 90404. *Mailing Add:* 725 Unionville Pike Julian PA 16844

YARBROUGH, LEILA KEPERT
PRINTMAKER, PAINTER
b Katoomba, NSW, Australia, Mar 23, 1932; US citizen. *Study:* Univ Fla; Atlanta Col Art, Ga. *Work:* Augusta Mus Art, Ga; Agnes Scott Col, Decatur, Ga; Loch Haven Art Ctr, Orlando, Fla; Piedmont Col, Demorest, Ga; Piedmont Hosp, Atlanta, Ga; and others. *Comn:* Sen Paul Coverdell and US Senate Office; inspirational landscapes, Prayer Room, Tanner Medical Ctr, Douglasville, GA. *Exhib:* Eastern US Drawing Competition, Cummer Gallery Art, Jacksonville, Fla, 70; Contemp Am Drawing V: Norfolk, Smithsonian Inst Travel Exhib, 71-73; 34th Ann Contemp Am Painting, Soc of Four Arts, Palm Beach, Fla, 72; 1st Nat Monoprint-Monotype, Oglethorpe Univ, Atlanta, Ga, 73; 64th Ann, Conn Acad Fine Arts, Hartford, 74; Am Drawings, Portsmouth Community Art Ctr, Va, 76; 12th Nat Print Exhib, Silvermine Guild Artists, New Caanan, Conn, 77; Salute to Louis XIV, Miriam Perlman Gallery, Chicago, Ill, 91; Drawing Soc Nat Travel Exhib, Am Fedn Arts, NY; Norman Wagner and his Students -34 yrs, Chattahoochee Valley Art Mus, LaGrange, Ga, 97; Colors, Exhib, Roswell, GA, 2005. *Teaching:* Printmaking workshop, Yarbrough Graphics, 74; Demonstr viscosity etching, Southern Graphics Coun, Atlanta Col Art, 86; etchings, art workshop instr, Atlanta Artists Club, 96. *Awards:* Am Drawing Purchase Award, Norfolk Mus, 71; First Prize, The Single Impression, Oglethorpe Univ, Atlanta, 73; Great Smoky Mts Nat Park Purchase Award, US Govt Art Purchase Prog, 74. *Bibliog:* Martin Sharter (auth), Art, Atlanta Mag, 12/73; Selma Smith (ed), Printworld Directory of Contemporary Prints and Prices, Printworld, Inc, 88-2006. *Media:* Etchings, Monoprints; Watercolor, Oil, Glass Works. *Interests:* Travel; Tennis; Swimming; Writing. *Dealer:* Monty Stabler Gallery Birmingham AL. *Mailing Add:* 3342 Pebble Hill Dr Atlanta GA 30062

YARD, SALLY ELIZABETH
HISTORIAN, CURATOR
b Trenton, NJ, Sept 24, 51. *Study:* Harvard Univ, AB, 73; Princeton Univ, MFA, 75, PhD, 80. *Collection Arranged:* Christo: Oceanfront (auth, catalog), Princeton Univ, 75; John Roy, Christopher Sproat (auth, catalog), Vincent Smith Art Mus, 78; Images of the Self (auth, catalog), 79 & A Sense of Place--The American Landscape in Recent Art (auth, catalog), 80, Hampshire Col Gallery; The Shadow of the Bomb (auth, catalog) Mt Holyoke Col Art Mus, S Hadley, Mass & Univ Gallery, Univ Mass, Amherst, 84; An Architect's Eye: Selections from the Collection of Graham Gund (auth, catalog), Mt Holyoke Col Art Mus, South Hadley, Mass, 85; Place and Preference - Studies of San Diego's Art in Public Spaces Since 1980 (auth, catalog),

Univ San Diego, 91. *Pos:* Acting cur, Univ Gallery, Univ Mass, Amherst, 80; ed dir, inSITE 97, San Diego/Tijuana, 94-97 & co-cur, 96-97. *Teaching:* Instr mod art, Mt Holyoke Col, Mass, 78-79, lectr mod art, 80-81, asst prof mod art, 81-83; vis asst prof mod art, Amherst Col, Mass, 81-83; lectr mod art, vis asst prof & vis assoc prof, Univ of Calif, San Diego, 87-96; asst assoc prof art, Univ San Diego, 89-. *Mem:* Col Art Asn. *Res:* Abstract expressionism, especially Willem de Kooning; contemporary painting & sculpture; public space; popular culture. *Publ:* Auth, Deep Time, Mus Contemp Art, Los Angeles, 93; Tagged Turf in the Public Sphere (exhib catalog), inSITE 94, San Diego/Tijuana, 95; Willem de Kooning, Poligrafa, Barcelona & Rizzoli, New York, 97; coauth, Francis Baum, Abrams, New York, 99; Private Time in Public Space, Installation, San Diego, 98. *Mailing Add:* PO Box 12985 La Jolla CA 92039

YARDE, RICHARD
ARTIST
b Boston, October 29, 39. *Study:* Boston Univ, BFA in Painting cum laude, 62; Boston Univ, MFA, 64; Mass Col Arts, Boston, DFA (hon), 98. *Pos:* Asst prof art, Boston Univ, 65-71; assoc prof art Wellesley Col, 71-76; vis assoc prof Amherst Col, 76-77, Mount Holyoke Col, 80-81; vis artist, Mass Col Art, 77-80; prof art, Univ Mass, Boston, 81-90, Amherst, 90—; Visual arts panelist, Mass Council Art and Humanities, 76-78; bd overseers Inst Contemp Art, Boston, 91-2003; panelist Painting Mass Cult Council; One-man shows include Studio Mus in Harlem, San Diego Mus, Baltimore Mus, Smith Col Mus Art, Northampton, Mass, 97, Mass Col Art, 96-99, Worcester Mus Art, Mass, 2003; exhib in group shows at Newport (RI) Art Mus, Nat Acad of Design, New York City, Mass, Smithsonian Institute, Washington, 99, New Mus Contemp Art, New York City, 99, Mus Fine Arts, Boston, 99, Master Drawings from the Smith Col Art Mus, Lacaixa, Madrid, Spain, 2002, DeCordova Mus, Lincoln, Mass, 2002, Inst Contemp Art, Boston, 2003, Heckscher Mus Art, Huntington, NY, 2003, Nat Acad of Sciences, Washington, 2004, Sheldon Mem Art Gallery Univ Nebraska, Lincoln. *Awards:* Recipient Alumni award for distinguished contribution to arts Boston Univ, 87, Chancellor's award for distinguished scholarship Univ Mass, Boston, 84, Acad award in art Am Acad Arts and Letters, 95, Distinguished Teaching award Univ Mass Amherst, 97, Works on Paper award New England Found for the Arts, Boston, 98; Nat Endowment for Arts fel, 76, Samuel F Conti faculty fellow Univ Mass, 2000, When the Spirit Moves Group Exhib, Spelman Col Mus, 2000, Charles Wright Mus, 2000, Commonwealth Award, Artist Category, Mass Cult Council, 2001, William P and Gertrude Schweitzer prize Nat Acad of Design, NY, others. *Mem:* Nat Acad (assoc, 81, acad, 94-). *Mailing Add:* U Mass Amherst care Arts Dept Fine Arts Ctr Box 32150 Amherst MA 01003

YARES, RIVA
ART DEALER, PUBLISHER, WRITER
b Tel-Aviv, Aug 17, 40. *Study:* Univ Jerusalem, BA(art & Psychology). *Pos:* art dealer, Riva Yares Gallery, Scottsdale, Ariz, 64-, Santa Fe, 90-; pres, Pueblo Arts & Real Estate, Scottsdale, Ariz, 70-; Riva Yares Sculpture Park, Ariz, 85-. *Awards:* Archit award City of Scottsdale, 72. *Publ:* var books on artists. *Mailing Add:* Riva Yares Gallery 3625 N Bishop Ln Scottsdale AZ 85251-5511

YAROS, CONSTANCE G
PAINTER, SCULPTOR
b Philadelphia, Pa. *Study:* Tyler Sch Art, Temple Univ, Philadelphia, 57-60; Boris Blai Studio, 76-81; Pa Acad Fine Arts, 78, 79, 87 & 88; Schuler Sch Art, Baltimore, 90, 91. *Work:* Tyler Sch Libr, Elkins Park, Pa; Temple Univ-Paley Libr, Philadelphia; Jefferson Park Hospital, Pa Board of City Trusts Philadelphia, Pa; Fed Court House, Philadelphia, Pa. *Comn:* Portraits, comn by Mr & Mrs Herbert Pincus, Glenside, Pa, 80, Mr & Mrs Mark Hankin, Erwinna, Pa, 88, Mr & Mrs Francis Strawbridge III, Merion, Pa, 89, Mr & Mrs William Silverman, Lafayette Hill, Pa, 94 & Mr William Austin Meehan, Philadelphia, Pa, 92; many other commissions including portraits, landscapes, equines, ballet & still lifes; Fed Judge Joseph L McGlynn, 2000. *Exhib:* Old York Rd Art Guild, 75; Artists Equity Triennial, Port of History Mus, Philadelphia, 84 & 88; Sketch Club, Philadelphia, 87; Catharine Lorillard Wolfe Art Club, NY, 88; Salmagundi Art Club, NY, 88; Allied Artists Am, NY, 88; Art at Amory, Philadelphia, 90-92; one-woman shows, Tyler Alumni Gallery, Diamond Club, Temple Univ, Philadelphia, 92, Allied Artists Prof League, NY, 93 & Oil Painters of Am, Chicago, Ill, 94; Woodmere Art Mus, Philadelphia Pa. *Awards:* Len G Everett Painting Award, Allied Artists Am, 88. *Bibliog:* Denise Breslin Kachin (auth), Artist achieves recognition hoped for, Philadelphia Evening Bulletin, 81. *Mem:* Artists Equity (bd mem 76-90); Pa Acad Fine Arts; Philadelphia Art Alliance; Am Soc Portrait Artists; Plastic Art Club; Women's Mus Art Archives; Allied Artists of Am; Am Soc Classic Realism; Oil Painter Am; Portrait Soc Am. *Media:* Pastel, Oil; Metal (Bronze), Hydrocal. *Mailing Add:* c/o Portraits Philadelphia 2401 Pennsylvania Ave 4A5 Philadelphia PA 19130

YAROTSKY, LORI
ART DEALER, CURATOR
b Houston, Tex. *Study:* Haystack-Hinckley Sch Crafts, Hinckley, Maine, studied weaving, 72-73; Sam Houston State Univ, BFA(painting & drawing), 76, Tex A&M Univ, MFA(painting), 80; NY Univ, studied fine art conserve & old master paintings, 93-94. *Work:* La State Mus, New Orleans; Univ St Thomas, Houston. *Collection Arranged:* Wemco (textile-related artworks), New York, 93; Granite Capital (19th-20th century photographs), New York, 94; Rubenstein Assoc (paintings and works on paper), New York, 94-; Ramius Capital (vintage & contemp photogs), New York, 97-98; Gerard Huber (paintings & drawings) (with catalog), Grace Cult Ctr & Mus Abilene, Tex, 98. *Pos:* Consult, Grad Sem Elem Art Educ, 80; dir, Tilden-Foley Gallery, New Orleans, La, 83-88 & Lori Yarotsky Gallery, 96-; proprietor, Res Nova Gallery, New Orleans, La, 88-, dir, 91-96; adv bd, Curric Rev, Dept Fine Art, Delgado Col, New Orleans; bd dir, Red Bass Lit Mag; adv bd, Sac-O-Lait Found, Mamou, La. *Teaching:* Fel, East Tex State Univ, 77; lectr, Grad Studies Arts Admin, Univ New Orleans, 84. *Awards:* Scholar, Haystack-Hinckley Sch Crafts, Maine, 73; Fel, ETEx State Univ, 77; Scholars, Houston Northwest Art League, Tex, 77. *Bibliog:* Errol Laborde (auth), Gallery growth, Gambit, 12/15/87; Roger Green (auth), New gallery will open in warehouse district, Times-Picayune, 12/23/87; Roger Green (auth), 1987: Warehouse district renaissance, Times-Picayune, Lagniappe, 1/1/88; George Jordon (auth), Critics choice: New Orleans art community, GO: New Orleans, 5/88; John Kemp (auth), Art mecca in the warehouse district, New Orleans Mag, 9/88. *Mem:* Friends Contemp Art, New Orleans Mus Art (adv bd); La Composers Guild; Jr Comt New Orleans Opera Asn. *Res:* Louisiana Purchase; French and America Revoltions. *Specialty:* Contemporary fine art (paintings, sculpture, photographs, drawings, site-specific installations and video); 19th century American and European paintings; French Barbizon School paintings; Old Master paintings; 19th c. French Papier Peints Panoramiques; Vintage and Modern Photgraphs. *Publ:* Auth, Garden notes, Blackjack J, 79-80; Auth, îledes cartes, 99. *Mailing Add:* PO Box 2028 New York NY 10021

YASKO, CARYL A(NNE)
MURALIST, SCULPTOR
b Racine, Wis, Mar 11, 41. *Study:* Dominican Col, Wis, sculpture with Monica Gabriel & painting with Branislov Bak, grad, 63. *Work:* Fulbright Off, Tokyo, Japan; Prairie Wave, McKenzie Environ Ctr, Poynette, Wis; The Inland Sea, Prairie Wave II, Palmyra, Wis Elem Sch Libr; Wind Prairie, Evansville, Wis. *Comn:* The Stonecutters, Lemont, Ill, 75 & 93; The Wind Whistlers of Ixonia, Rise to the Sky, sculpture of 57 giant pole's with airplane beacon and flags, Wis Arts Bd, Oconomowoc Sch Dist, Wis Elec Power Co; Unity with Yasko, Catch a Turtle, contrete fresco, Municipal Pool, Monona, Wis Arts Bd, Monona City, Monona Sch Dist, 93 & 94; Cup of Light, mural, Evansville, Wis Elem Sch, Wis Arts Bd, Evansville Sch Dist; Reach, mural, Very Special Arts Wis & City of Sun Prairie, 94; Forest Mem Sculpture, McKenzie Environ Ctr, Poynette, Wis; Rainbow, mural, Madison, Wis, 2002; Pride, mural, Manitowoc City Hall, Wis, 2003; Brainstorm, rotunda mural, Manitowoc Pub Libr, 2002. *Exhib:* On Chicago Walls, Chicago State Univ, 74; Civic Sculpture, Appleton, Neenah & Menasha, Wis, 77; Levi Strauss & Co, Europ Exhib of US Murals, Mus Royal d'Art, Ancien, Brussels, 78; Chicago, The City & Its Artists, 1945-1978, Univ Mich, Ann Arbor, 78; French Ministry Foreign Affairs, traveling exhib, Caen, Normandy, 81; Working Together: Forms of Collaboration, Montgomery Ward Gallery, Univ Ill, Chicago, 81; Healing Walls, Ill Art Gallery, Chicago, 95 & Springfield, 96. *Pos:* Panelist, Chicago Art Asn, Chicago & Nat Conf Mural Artists, 76 & State Arts Conf, 78-92; guest speaker, Chicago State Univ, 76, Univ Mich, Ann Arbor, 78, Waterloo, Wis, 79, Waupan State Prison, 79, UW Parkside, 80, Kamakura, Kanazawa & Tokyo, Japan, 82 & The Community Develop Wis, 86; artist-in-residence, Wis & Midwest, 78-92; visual arts panel, Wis Arts Bd, 79; guest artist, Brigada L'Eteiller Mural Proj, Chicago, 79, Artists for Peace Proj, Chicago, 80, State of Wis, Arts World, 82-91 & Chicago Pub Art Group, 90; speaker, Community Built Asn, 95, 97 & CBA Conf, Phoenix, Ariz, 2000; keynote speaker, Line Drawing WEA Conf, Madison, Wis, 97 & Mich Asoc Community Arts Agency, E Lansing, 2001. *Teaching:* Instr, Art Inst Chicago, 75 & 76, Oakton Community Col, Morton Grove, Ill, 77 & Carthage Col, 81-; lectr murals, Loop Jr Col, Valparaiso Univ, 76; lectr, Univ Wis, River Falls, 81 & mural instr, 82; concrete fresco instr, Joseph Art Sch, Joseph, Ore, 94. *Awards:* Chicago Beautiful Award, Mayor Daley, 75 & 76; Hon Citizen, Lemont, Ill, 75 & 94; Key to the City of Manitowoc, 2003. *Bibliog:* John & Eva Corckroft, John Weber (coauth), Towards a People Art, Dutton, NY, rev ed, 97; Phyllis Berg Pagorsch (dir), The Great Wall of Waunakee (film), Yahara Films, Madison, Wis, 78; Alan Barnett (auth), Community Murals, Art Alliance Press, Philadelphia & Cornwall Books, NY, London, 83; Mary Gray (auth), A Guide to Chicago's Murals, 2000; and others. *Mem:* Chicago Pub Art Group; Community Built Asn, Ithaca, NY. *Media:* Oil, Watercolor; Reinforced Concrete, Mixed Media. *Publ:* Contribr, Art Workers News, 73, New Art Examr, 74 & 80 & Nat Murals Newsletter, 78. *Mailing Add:* 136 Whiton St Whitewater WI 53190

YASSIN, ROBERT ALAN
MUSEUM DIRECTOR, CURATOR
b Malden, Mass, May 22, 41. *Study:* Dartmouth Col, BA (Rufus Choate Scholar), 62; Boston Univ, 62-63; Univ Mich, MA (hist art, Teachingg Fel), 65, PhD (Samuel H Kress Found Fel), 70. *Collection Arranged:* American Art from Alumni Collections (auth, catalog), Yale Univ Art Gallery, 68; Art & the Excited Spirit (with catalog), Yale Univ Art Gallery, 72; Victor Higgins Retrospective (auth, catalog), Notre Dame Univ Art Gallery & Indianapolis Mus Art, 75; Eiteljorg Collection of Western American Art, 76; Leonard Baskin (auth, catalog), Indianapolis Mus Art, 76; Painting & Sculpture Today (auth, catalog), Indianapolis Mus Art, 76, 78, 80, 82, 84 & 86; Art in Business and Corporate Collections (auth, catalog), Indianapolis Mus Art, 77; Ind Artists Show, 77-79, 81, 83 & 85; Enrico Baj (auth, catalog), Indianapolis Mus Art, 78; George Carlson, Sculptures and Drawings (auth, catalog), Indianapolis Mus Art & Grand Cent Art Galleries, New York, 79; Batuz: Works in Paper (auth, catalog), Indianapolis Mus Art, 82; Sasson Soffer Sculpture (auth, catalog), Indianapolis Mus Art, 84; Masks (auth, catalog), Tucson Mus Art, 90; Fine Art for Fine Causes (auth, catalog), Tucson Mus Art, 91; American Primitive Paintings and Drawings: The Dr Paul Schiffman Collection (auth, catalog), Tucson Mus Art, 91; Women Artists and the West (auth, catalog), Tucson Mus Art, 91-96; James Cook: New Paintings (auth, catalog), Tucson Mus Art, 92; Harmony Hammond: Ghost Farms (auth, catalog), Tucson Mus Art, 93; Rebecca & Roger, Tucson Mus Art, 95; Jim Ward, Tucson Mus Art, 96; Dave Asay (with catalog), Tucson Mus Art, 99; Miriam Sckopow: Waste in Paper (with catalog), Tuscon Mus Art, 99; Joanne Kerrikard (with catalog), Tucson Mus Art, 2000. *Pos:* Asst to dir, Mus Art, Univ Mich, Ann Arbor, 65-66, instr, co-dir joint prog mus training, ed Art Bull, 70-73, from asst dir to actg dir Mus Art, 70-73; asst to dir, Yale Univ Art Gallery, 66-68, ed, Bull, 66-68; chief cur, Indianapolis Mus Art, 73-75, actg dir, 75, dir, 75-89; exec dir, Tucson Mus Art, Ariz, 90-2001 & Palos

Verdes Art Ctr, 2002-. *Teaching:* Instr graphic arts & mus practice & co-dir joint mus training prog, Univ Mich, Ann Arbor, 70-73; adj prof, Herron Sch Art, Purdue Univ, Indianapolis, 76-78. *Awards:* Ford Found Fel, Yale Univ, 66-68; Sagamore of the Wabash, State of Ind, 85. *Mem:* Col Art Asn Am; Am Asn Mus (sr accreditation examiner, 80-, co-chmn, ann meeting, 81, int coun mus, bd dir, 86-89); Asn Art Mus (dir, 75-89); Nat Trust Hist Preservation; Am Asn State and Local Hist; Ariz Hist soc; Asn Art Mus Dirs (mem prof ethics and standards comt, 75-89, mem nominating com, 78-89); Intermuseum Conserv Asn (trustee, 73-89, mem exec comt, 75-77, chmn, 77-79, mem int comt exhib exchange); Mus Asn Ariz; Midwest Col Art Asn; Tucson Arts Coalition; Tuscon Asn Mus; Calif Asn Mus. *Res:* Late 19th and 20th century American art; contemporary art. *Mailing Add:* 3900 N Calle Casita Tucson AZ 85718

YASUDA, ROBERT
PAINTER, EDUCATOR

b Lihue, Kauai, Hawaii, Nov 14, 40. *Study:* Pratt Inst, Brooklyn, NY, BFA, 62, MFA, 64. *Work:* Brooklyn Mus, NY; Libr Cong, Washington, DC; State of Hawaii Found Arts; Hillwood Mus, Long Island Univ, NY. *Exhib:* One-man exhibs, Sculpture at the Coliseum, NY Coliseum, 80, Albuquerque Sight-Line, Hoshour Gallery, NMex, 81, Koplin Gallery, Los Angeles, Calif, Marianne Deson Gallery, Chicago, Ill, 82, Betty Parsons Gallery, NY, 83 & Hanalei Gallery, Kauai, Hawaii, 84; A More Store, Jack Tilton Gallery, NY, 84; The Anchorage Exhib, Large Scale Painting Installations, Brooklyn Bridge Anchorage, NY, 85; 8x10, Washington Co Mus Fine Arts, Hagerstown, Md, 86; Opening exhib, Cutler-Schreiber Gallery, NY, 86; Koplin Gallery, Los Angeles, Calif, 87; Julian Pretto Gallery, 91, Stark Gallery, 92, The Inst for Contemp Art, PS1 Mus, NY, 92; and others. *Teaching:* Prof art, Long Island Univ, C W Post, painting & drawing, 69-92. *Awards:* J H Whitney Found Grant, 62-63; Nat Endowment for the Arts Fel Grant, Washington, DC, 81. *Bibliog:* Kathleen Shields (auth), Robert Yasuda-Albuquerque sight line, Art Space, spring 82; Alan Artner (auth), Best solo shows, art 1982, Chicago Tribune, 1/2/83; Kim Levin (auth), Art in the Anchorage, Village Voice, 5/21/85; Susan Fleminger (auth), Inside the Bridge, Art in the Depths of the Anchorage, Prospect Press, 5/30/85. *Media:* Acrylic, Oil. *Dealer:* Betty Parsons Gallery 24 W 57th St New York NY 10019; Stark Gallery 594 Broadway New York NY 10012. *Mailing Add:* 429 W Broadway No 5 New York NY 10012

YATES, MARVIN
PAINTER, INSTRUCTOR

b Jackson, Tenn, Sept 22, 43. *Study:* Memphis Acad Art, BFA, 66. *Exhib:* Am Watercolor Soc, Nat Acad Gallery, NY, 73-79; Watercolor USA, Springfield Art Mus, Mo, 75 & 76; Mainstreams, Grover Hermann Mus, Marietta, Ohio, 76; Southern Watercolor Soc, Cheekwood Gallery, Nashville, 77-79; Rocky Mountain Nat Water Media, Foothills Art Ctr, Golden, Colo, 78; Real Show, Grand Cent Art Gallery, NY, 79. *Pos:* Art dir, Memphis Publ Co, currently. *Teaching:* Instr watercolor, Memphis State Univ, 75-. *Awards:* Rechenbach Award, Rechenbach Gallery, 73 & 80; Washington Sch of Art Award, 74; Second Place Watercolor, Sterling Regal Inc, 79. *Bibliog:* Susan Meyer (auth), Watercolor Page, Am Artist Mag, 75; Ralph Fabri (auth), Watercolor Page, Today's Art, 75. *Mem:* Am Watercolor Soc; Southern Watercolor Soc; Tenn Watercolor Soc; Memphis Watercolor Group. *Media:* Watercolor, Pencil. *Publ:* Contribr, 40 Watercolorists and How They Work, Watson-Guptill, 76. *Mailing Add:* 1457 Hwy 304 Hernando MS 38632

YATES, SHARON
EDUCATOR

b Rochester, NY, 42. *Study:* Syracuse Univ, Sch Art, BFA, 1964; Tulane Univ, MFA, 1966. *Work:* exhib in group shows at Nat Acad of Design Mus, New York City, 1997, Bates Col Mus Art, Maine, 2000, LC Bates Mus, Hinkley, Maine, 2000, Bates Col Mus Univ Louisville, Oklahoma City Art Mus. *Exhib:* One-woman shows incl Fishbach Gallery, New York City, 1976, Univ Maine, Macias, 1991, 1997, Maine Coast Artists Exec Gallery, Rockport, 1993; exhib in group shows at Turtle Gallery, Deer Isle, Maine, 1997, Maine Coast Artists Gallery, Rockport, 1999, Va Hist Soc, Richmond, 2000, Rep in permanent collections Nat Acad of Design, New York City, United Technol, Conn, Lucent Technol, Univ Louisville. *Teaching:* Fac Maryland Inst Col Art, Baltimore, 1968—. *Awards:* Recipient Prix de Rome, 1972-74; grantee Ingram-Merrill Found fel, France, 1977-78, Ludwig Vogelstein Found, 1996. *Mem:* Nat Acad (acad, 95-, Shatalov award). *Mailing Add:* Md Inst Col Art 1300 Mount Royal Ave Baltimore MD 21217

YATES, STEVEN A
CURATOR, PHOTOGRAPHER

b Chicago, Ill. *Study:* Univ Nebr, BFA, 72; Univ NMex, with Beaumont Newhall & Van Deren Coke, MA, 75, MFA(doctoral degree)(Ford Found Fel), 78. *Work:* Hist Photog Mus; San Francisco Mus Mod Art; Univ NMex Art Mus; Ctr for Creative Photog, Tucson; Sheldon Mem Art Gallery; Mint Mus Art, NC; Hist Collection, Russian Union Art Photographers; Latvian Mus Photography. *Comn:* numerous pvt collections internationally. *Exhib:* The Markers (with catalog), San Francisco Mus Mod Art, 81; Extending the Perimeters of 20th Century Photog (with catalog), San Francisco Mus Mod Art, 85; 21 NMex Photogrs, Vision Gallery, San Francisco, 91; Contemp Am Photog Masters, Cinema Inst, Moscow, 91; NMex Impressions: Printmaking, 1880-1990, (traveling), 91-92; one-man shows, Cent Photog Gallery, Mensk, Belarus, 94, New Contemp Art Gallery, Mensk, Belarus, 95, Gallery A3, Moscow, 95 & Col Fine & Performing Arts, Univ Nebr, 96; The Painted Photograph: A Survey of Hand Colored Photog, 1839 to the Present (traveling), Art Mus, Univ Wyo, 96; 9 Photog Reconstructions from Moscow, Prague, St Petersburg, Nikolaevsk, Paris, River Amur, Gallery A3, Moscow, 2002; Empires, collaborative installation, Irving Arts Ctr, Irving, Tex, 98-99; Photographic Icons: Film Form and Montage, homage to Sergei Eisenstein and Gustav Klucis, Mus Photog, Riga, Latvia, 98; Experimental Gallery Up-Down, Kharkov, Ukraine, 96. *Collection Arranged:* To collect the Art of Women: The Jane Reese Williams Photography Collection, Mus Fine Arts, NMex Mus, 91; Contemporary American Masters, Cinema Inst, Moscow, 91; Proto-Modern Photography (auth, catalog), co-cur Beaumont Newhall, Mus Fine Arts, NMex Mus, 92; 4+4, Late Modern: Photography Between the Mediums (auth, catalog, essay), Mus Fine Arts, NMex Mus, 94; Early Modern Photography: Selections from the Collection of the Russian Union of Art Photographers, Union Gallery, Moscow, 94; Betty Hahn: Photography or Maybe Not (traveling), 95; Georgia O'Keeffe: From 291 to New Mexico, Mus Fine Arts, Mus NMex, 96-97; Betty Hahn: 30 Year Retrospective, Mus Fine Art, NMex Mus, 95; New Histories in Photography, Mus Fine Art, NMex Mus, 97; Joel Peter Witkin: Unpublished & Unseen, Mus Fine Art, NMex Mus, 98; Betty Hahn: Photog or Maybe Not, Mus Fine Arts, Mus NMex, 1995, State Russian Art Mus, St Petersburg, Mable Palace, Spain, 99; Theatre as Memory, Photographic Installation Works by Laurent Millet, Musee Nicephore Niepce, Chalon-sur-Saone, France and Santa Fe Ctr for Visual Arts, 99-2000; 20/20 Twentieth Century Acquisitions by Twenty Leading Patrons, Mus Fine Arts, Mus NMex, 2000; Classic Russian Photog 1900 to WWII, Russian Art Photographers Union, Press Photo 2000, Moscow; In His Native Land: Early Modern Photog John Candelario, 2000-01; Avant-Garde Document: Photogs by Aleksandras Macijauskas, Mus Fine Arts, Mus NMex2001-02; Alexander Rodchenko: Photomontage, Modern Photog and Film, Curatorial Assistance, Pasadena, Mus Fine Art, NMex Mus, 2001; Brett Weston, From the Collection: New Hists of Photog, pvt collection Erica Weston, 2002-03; Idea Photographic: After Modernism, Mus Fine Arts, San Francisco Mus MOdern Art, Princeton U Art Mus, 2002; Georgi Zelma, Documentary Photographs of Eastern Europe, 1924-1944, Modernity & Chnge. From the Collection: New Histories of Photography, Coll Mus Fine Arts; Alexander Rodchenko: Photomontage, Modern Photography and Film, Intl Touring Exhib, 2001-2004. *Pos:* Cur asst, Sheldon Mem Art Gallery, Univ Nebr, 72-73 & Univ Art Mus, Univ NMex, 73-75; cur photog prints & drawings, Mus Fine Arts, Mus NMex, 80-87, cur photog, 87-. *Teaching:* Instr part-time, Univ NMex, Albuquerque, 75-78; vis instr, Pomona Col, Claremont Col, 76-; vis instr art dept, Summer Exten Prog, Univ Calif, Los Angeles, 76; lectr, Humboldt State Univ Workshop, 86; adj prof, Art Dept, Univ NMex, 94-; pub lect in Am & Eastern Europe (former USSR); lectr hist photog and contemp courses, Santa Fe Cmty Col, 98-2002; lectr, master seminars US, eastern Europe, Russia. *Awards:* Guest Artist, Taramind Inst, Albuquerque, 88; Guest Artist, 20x24 Polaroid Camera Proj, 88; Sr Fulbright Scholars Award to USSR, 91 & Russ, 95; Outstanding Alumni Achievement Award, Col Fine & Performing Arts, Univ Nebr, Lincoln, 94. *Bibliog:* Idea Photographic: After Modernism, Santa Fe: Mus Fine Arts, Mus NMex, 2002; poeticas del espacio, Barcelona: Editorial Gustavo Gili, FotoGGrafia, Spanish edit, 2002; Poetics of Space: A Critical Photographic Anthology, Albuquerque, Univ NMex Press, 1995; The Avant-Garde Document: Photographs by Aleksandras Macijauskas, Santa Fe: Mus Fine Arts, Mus NMex, 2001; Theatre of Memory, Photographic Installation Works by Laurent Millet, Santa Fe: Mus Fine Arts, Mus NMex, 1999; 4 + 4, Late Modern: Photography Between the Mediums, Santa Fe: Mus Fine Arts, Mus NMex, 94; Threads of Culture: Pinewood Collection of Farm Security Administration Photographs in New Mexico, 1939-43, Santa Fe: Mus Fine Arts, Mus NMex, 93; expanded edit, Far from Main Street, New Mexico Farm Security Administration (FSA), 94; Beaumont Newhall: Colleagues and Friends, Santa Fe: Mus Fine Arts, Mus NMex, 93; Proto Modern Photography, Santa Fe: Mus Fine Arts, Mus NMex, 92; Betty Hahn: Photography or Maybe Not, Albuquerque: Univ NMex Press, 95; The Essential Landscape: The New Mexico Photographic Survey with Essays by JB Jackson, Albuquerque: Univ NMex Press, 85. *Media:* Photography. *Res:* The photographic contributions of the avant-garde and first modern photographers during the early Soviet era (1917-1933); early and late modern photography in the 20th century; contemporary photographic art after modernism including America and the new photographic work throughout the commonwealth of Independent States (former USSR). *Mailing Add:* c/o Mus Fine Arts PO Box 2087 Santa Fe NM 87504-2087

YAU, JOHN
WRITER, CURATOR

b Lynn, Mass, June 5, 50. *Study:* Bard Col, BA, 69-72; Brooklyn Col, MFA, 76-78. *Pos:* Freelance writer, 77-; freelance cur, 82-; dir, Poetry Reading Series, Md Inst, Col Art; Pupl, Black Square Eds, 2000-. *Teaching:* Instr, Pratt Inst, 85-90 & Sch Visual Arts, NY, 88-90; vis writer, Brown Univ, 92; instr, Univ Berkeley, Calif, 93-94; Grad Art Dept Instr, Yale, 2003-. *Awards:* Chevalier in Order of Arts and Letters by Fr Govt; Peter S Reed Found Grant, 2002; NY Found for the Arts, Grant, 2003; Found for the Performance of Contemp Art, Grant, 2002-03. *Publ:* Auth, Giant Wall, Limestone Press, 91; Flee Advice, Collectif Generation, 91; Postcards from Trakl, Universal Ltd Art Eds, 92; Edificio Sayonara, Black Sparrow Press, 92; Genghis Chan: Private Eye, Art Inst Chicago, 93; ed, Four Walls Eight Windows, 98. *Mailing Add:* 1200 Broadway Apt 3C New York NY 10001-4316

YEAGER, SYDNEY PHILEN
PAINTER, PRINTMAKER

b Lufkin, Tex, Feb 12,45. *Study:* Univ Tex, Austin, BA, 67, BFA, 87, MFA, 87. *Work:* Belo Corp Collection & Barrett Collection, Dallas; Austin Mus Art & Samsung Corp Collection, Austin. *Exhib:* Dual Intention, Amarillo Art Mus, 94. *Pos:* Artist adv coun, women & Their Work, Austin, 93-95. *Awards:* Cutural Arts Grant, City of Austin, 90; Nat Endowment Arts Fel/Mid Am Arts Alliance, 96. *Bibliog:* Sandra Goldman (auth), Review New Art Examiner, 93; Mark Smith (auth), Review Art Lies, 98. *Mem:* Tex Fine Arts Asn. *Media:* Oil. *Dealer:* McMurtrey Gallery 3508 Lake St Houston TX 78705. *Mailing Add:* 1310 Ardenwood Austin TX 78722

YEDIDSION, MEIRA
PAINTER, SCULPTOR
b Tehran, Iran; Ital citizen, Oct 29, 55; US citizen. *Study:* Univ Fine Arts, Tehran, MAF, 72-76; Acad Fine Arts, Rome, Italy, MFA, 77-81. *Work:* Israel Mus, Jerusalem; Hebrew Union Col, Skirball Mus, Los Angeles; Mus Modern Art, NY; Detroit's Mus New Art. Mich; Fuller Mus, Brockton, Mass. *Comn:* Detroit Mus New Art; Fuller Mus Art. *Exhib:* Meira Yedidsion, Palazzo Valentini, Rome, Italy, 85, Nat Mus Villa Pisani, Stra, Venice, Italy, 96 & Mus Palazzo Ducale, Isabella D'Este Apartment in Santa Croce, Mantua, Italy, 96; Arie, 34th Festival of the Two Worlds, Fonti Del Clitunno, Spoleto, Italy, 91; Selected Group Exhib, Israel Mus, Jerusalem, 92; Few Views of the Contemp Art in Italy, Art Pavilion at Seville, Spain, 92; Selected Group Exhib & Beyond Boundaries, Hebrew Union Col Skirball Mus, Los Angeles, 96-97; Baltimore Mus Art, Baltimore, MD, 2002; Music Mus, Phillipines, 2002; Smith Cols Walker Libr, Minneapolis, MN, 2002; Open 2003, Art & Cinema in Conjunction with the 60th Venice Film Festival, Venice Biennial, Italy, 2003. *Awards:* La Mimosa, Pres Regional Coun Rome & Lazio, Italy, 92; Sagra Del Mandorlo, City Province Region Agrigento, Italy, 93; Gold Medal Award, Intl Biographical Ctr, Cambridge, England, 2003. *Bibliog:* RAI, Italian Nat State Television & Radio, Meira Yedidsion, 83-98; Costanzo Costantini (auth), Meira Yedidsion, Mus Palazzo Ducale Mantova, 96; Fontanella Borghese (auth), Flash Art, 1987-2001; One Thousand Greats-Meira Yedidsion, 2003; Great Lives of the 21st Century, Intl Biographical Ctr, Cambridge, England, 2003. *Media:* Multimedia. *Publ:* Auth, Enrico Crispolti, Meira Yedidsion, Palazzo Valentini, 85; Achille Bonito Oliva, Giovanni Carandente, ARIE, 91; Laura Cherubini: Meira Yedidsion, Giancarlo Politi Editore, Flash Art, 92; Paolo Balmas, Meira Yedidsion, D'oro, 93; Meira Yedidsion (auth), Flash Art, Fontanella Borghese Cult Ctr, 92. *Mailing Add:* 411 N Palm Dr Beverly Hills CA 90210

YEGUL, FIKRET KUTLU
EDUCATOR, ARCHITECT
b Themiscyra, Turkey, Oct 27, 41. *Study:* Middle East Technical Univ, BA(archit), 64; Univ Pa, MA(archit), 66; Harvard Univ, PhD(art hist), 75. *Exhib:* Mamluk Architecture of Cairo (photographs), Fogg Art Mus, 74. *Teaching:* Asst prof art hist, Wellesley Col, 75-76; asst prof, Univ Calif, Santa Barbara, 76-82, assoc prof, 82-88, prof, 88-. *Awards:* Fulbright Fel, 64-66; Senior fel, CASVA, Nat Gallery Art, 85-86; Alice Davis Hitchock Award, 94. *Mem:* Sardis Archaeol Expedition; Am Inst Archaeol. *Res:* Roman art and architecture. *Publ:* Auth, A reconstruction study of Lucian's Baths of Hippias, Archaeol Classica, Vol 31, 79; Kaisersaal and the Imperial Cult, Art Bulletin, 3/82; Bath-Gymnasium Complex in Sardis (Report 3), Harvard Univ, 86; Gentlemen of Instinct & Breeding: Architecture at the American Academy in Rome 1894-1940, Oxford Univ, 91; Baths & Bathing in Classical Artiquity, Mass Inst Technol, 92. *Mailing Add:* Univ Calif Art Hist Dept Santa Barbara CA 93106

YEISER, CHARLES WILLIAM
PAINTER, ART DEALER
b Womelsdorf, Pa, Nov 20, 25. *Study:* Kutztown State Teachers' Col, 43; Pratt Inst Art Sch, cert, 49; New York Univ, 49-51. *Work:* Westmoreland Mus Art, Greensburg, Pa; Southern Alleghenies Mus Art, Loretto, PA; Tulpehocken Settlement Hist Soc, Womelsdorf, PA. *Comn:* The Good Shepherd (panel), Dutch Reformed Church, West Nyack, NY, 60. *Exhib:* Board of Directors Exhib, Hopper House, Nyack, NY, 76; The New Am Still Life, 80, Small Works for the Armchair Collector, 82 & Regional Artists Salute the Mus 25th Anniversary, 83, Westmoreland Mus Art, Greensburg, Pa; The Am Still Life Tradition 1955-1985, Montgomery Gallery, San Francisco, Calif; Recent Paintings, Westmoreland Mus Art, Greensburg, Pa, 86, O'Hara Gallery, NY, 93 & Owen Gallery, NY, 96. *Pos:* Asst dir, FAR Gallery, New York, 51-70, dir, 71-80. *Teaching:* Workshop, Rockland Ctr Arts, 94. *Awards:* First Prize Watercolor, Rahway Pub Libr, Rahway, NJ, 48. *Bibliog:* Martha B Scott (auth), Charles Yeiser: A painter of still life, Westmoreland Mus Art, 86; Muriel Hitzig (auth), Art works by Hopper House trustees, Rockland J News, 1/30/77; Nancy Cacioppo (auth), Realities, the Rockland Center for the Arts presents 8 area realists, Rockland J News, 3/14/93; Richard Gutwillig (auth), Artist captures the moment, Rockland J News, 1/30/96. *Mem:* Hopper House (bd dir, 75-78); Rockland Ctr Arts (bd dir), West Nyack, NY. *Media:* Oil on Canvas or Panel. *Mailing Add:* 11 Wheeler Pl West Nyack NY 10994

YEKTAI, MANOUCHER
PAINTER
b Tehran, Iran, Dec 22, 22; US citizen. *Study:* Univ Tehran; Ecole Superior Beaux Arts, Paris, 45, 46 & 47; studied with Ozenfant in New York, 45-47; Art Students League, 47-48. *Work:* Baltimore Mus Art, Md; Mus Mod Art, NY; Everson Mus, Syracuse, NY; Hirshhorn Mus, Washington, DC; and others. *Exhib:* one-man shows: Grace Borgenicht Gallery, NY, 51, 52 & 53; Robert Elkon Gallery, NY, 56; Poindexter Gallery, NY, 57, 58, 61, 62, 64; Felix Landau Gallery, Los Angeles, 59; Anderson-Meyer Gallery, Paris, 62; Feingarten Gallery, Chicago, 62; Gumps, San Francisco, 59, 64; Semiha Huber Gallery, Zurich, 65; Gertrude Kasle Gallery, Detroit, 65, 66, 67, 68 & 70; Piccadilly Gallery, London, 61, 69 & 70; USIS Teheran, Iran, 70; Benson Gallery, Bridgehampton, NY, 66, 72, 73, 75, 84, 96 & 2004; Teheran Galerie Zand, 77-78; Alex Rosenberg Gallery, NY, 81, 84 & 86; Watershed Yrs, Frumkin Gallery, NY, 74; Alex Rosenberg Gallery, NY, 86; NY Joseph Lubin Gallery, 85; Guild Hall Mus, East Hampton, NY, 88; and others. *Media:* Oil. *Publ:* Auth, Hooye Cagaxe Sfid, 94. *Mailing Add:* 225 W 86th St New York NY 10024

YENAWINE, PHILIP
EDUCATOR
b Athens, Ga, July 12, 42. *Study:* Govern State Univ, BA, 77; Goddard Col, MA, 79. *Hon Degrees:* Doctorate of Fine Arts Honoris Causa, Kansas City Art Inst, 2003. *Pos:* Dir educ, Mus Contemp Art, Chicago, Ill, 77-78; dir, Aspen Art Mus, Colo, 78-82; curatorial consult, Aspen, Colo & Santa Fe, NMex, 82-83; dir educ, Mus Mod Art, NY, 83-93; vis cur, Inst Contemp Art, Boston, 92-94; partner, Development Through Art, NY & Cambridge, Mass, 94-97; co-dir, Visual Understanding in Educ (non-profit educ research orgn), Projects in Russ, Eastern Europe, Cent Asia & four US sites, 97-. *Teaching:* Vis fac, Univ Ill, Chicago, 76-77; vis prof, Mass Col Art, 93-94; George A Miller vis scholar, Univ Ill, 96. *Awards:* Gov's Award, Prog People with Hearing Disabilities, Mus Mod Art, 84 & Visual Aids & Day Without Art, NY, 90; Mus Educ Yr, Eastern Div, 87 & Mus Educ Yr, 91, Nat Art Educ Asn; Distinguished Serv Award, Nat Art Educ Asn, 93. *Mem:* Mus Educ Consortium (chmn, 86-89). *Publ:* Auth, Looking Books: Colors; Lines; Shapes; Stories, Mus Mod Art & Abrams, 90; How to Look at Modern Art, Harry N Abrams, 90; Inheriting the theory: new voices and multiple perspectives on discipline based art education, Univ Tex, 90; Visual Thinking Strategies Starter Lessons, 98; Art Matters: How the Culture Wars Changed America, New York Univ Press, 99; plus others. *Mailing Add:* Box 677 Wellfleet MA 02667

YES, PHYLLIS A
PAINTER, SCULPTOR
b Red Wing, Minn, May 15, 41. *Study:* Luther Col, BA, 63; Univ Minn, MFA, 68; Univ Ore, PhD, 78. *Work:* Levi-Strauss, San Francisco; Microsoft Art Collection, Redmond, Wash & Seattle, Wash; Portland Art Mus; Security Pacific Nat Bank, Los Angeles; Univ Wash Med Ctr, Seattle; and others. *Exhib:* One-person shows, Recent Work, John Edward Hughes Gallery, Dallas, 84, Tables, etc, Linda Rhodes Gallery, Winterpark, Fla, 84, Paintings and Lacquered Work, Elizabeth Leach Gallery, Portland, Ore, 84 & Nishiazabu Gallery, Tokyo, Japan, 93; Lace/War, Bernice Steinbaum Gallery, 86, Northwest Biennial, Brooklyn Mus, 86, NY; mini retrospective, Seattle, Wash, 94; Tools & Flowers, Hanson-Howard Gallery, Ashland, Ore, 94; one-woman retrospective, Freed Gallery, Lincoln City, Ore, 95; Tool Show, Portland Inst for Contemp Art, Lewis-Clark, Lewiston, Idaho, 96. *Pos:* Juror of Nat, Regional Exhibs. *Teaching:* Asst prof, Ore State Univ, 76-79; prof, Lewis & Clark Col, 79-, dean arts & humanities & chair, Art Dept, currently. *Awards:* Barbara Deming Grant, 87; Distinguish Alumni Award, Luther Col, Decorah, Iowa, 88; Burlington Northern Achievement Award, 91. *Bibliog:* Focus: Phyllis Yes, NW Gallery Mag, fall 90; Paintings have grace of lace, Japan Times, 3/31/91; Phyllis Yes, Styling Mag, 7/91; and numerous other articles in national periodicals. *Mem:* Artists Equity Asn; Col Art Asn Am; Women's Caucus Arts; Contemp Arts Coun. *Media:* Acrylic, Mixed. *Publ:* Auth, History of lace, Art & Antiques Mag, 12/87. *Dealer:* Lee Freed Gallery Hwy 101 Lincoln City OR 97367; Lisa Harris Gallery, Seattle WA. *Mailing Add:* 1109 SW 62d St Lincoln City OR 97367

YODER, JANICA
PHOTOGRAPHER, EDUCATOR
b Milwaukee, Wis, June 21, 50. *Study:* Univ Wis, Madison, BS (art), 74, MA (photog), 76, MFA (photog), 77. *Work:* Corcoran Gallery, Washington, DC; J Paul Getty Mus, Malibu, Calif; Madison Art Ctr, Wis; Milwaukee Art Mus, Wis. *Exhib:* Solo exhibs, Michael H Lord Gallery, Milwaukee, 91 & 94, New Work, The Pain Mus, Oshkosh, Wis, 92-93, Honolulu Acad Art, 93, Contemp Art Mus, Honolulu, Hawaii, 95, Wis Acad Gallery, Wis Acad Arts & Scis, Madison, 97; Woman Photographers, Corcoran Gallery Art, Washington, DC, 82; Multiple Exposure: 5 Contemp Photogrs, Milwaukee Art Mus, Wis, 88; A Decade of Exhibitions, Madison Art Ctr, Wis, 90; Recent Acquisitions in Photog, Corcoran Gallery Art, Washington, DC, 83, 86 & 90; May 1992, Betsy Rosenfield Gallery, Chicago Int Art Expo, 92; Color Photog Invitational, Crossman Gallery, Univ Wis, Whitewater, 92; The Wisconsin Triennial, Madison Art Ctr, 93 & 96; Regarding Beauty, Halsey Gallery, Sch Arts, Col Charleston, SC, 93; Highlights from the Permanent Collection, Madison Art Ctr, Wis, 94; Gallery Artists, Michael Lord Gallery, Milwaukee, Wis, 98. *Teaching:* Instr photog, Int Ctr Photog, New York, 78-80; asst prof, Herron Sch Art-Ind Univ, 80-86; instr, Milwaukee Inst Art & Design, 89-; lectr, Madison Art Ctr, Wis, 96; guest lectr photog, Milwaukee, Wis, 97; vis lectr, art dept, Waukesha, Wis, 97. *Bibliog:* Popular Photog, winter 78; AfterImage, spring 79; Photography Ann, Popular Photography, 86. *Media:* Color and black & white photography. *Mailing Add:* W349 S4051 Town Hwy G Dousman WI 53118

YODER, ROBERT EDWARD
ARTIST
b Danville, Va, May 22, 62. *Study:* James Madison Univ, BFA, 84; Univ Washington, Seattle, MFA, 87. *Work:* Mus of Fine Arts, Houston; Seattle Tacoma Internat Airport, WA; Microsoft, Redmond, WA; City of Seattle Pub Art Collection. *Comn:* Four Paintings, Portland Bureau of Gen Service, 2000; Integrated Installation, Seahawks Stadium, Seattle, 2000. *Exhib:* New Am Talent, Centerspace, Austin, 2001; The End, Tacoma Art Mus, 99; Material Process and Object, Univ Idaho, 2000. *Awards:* Pollack Krasner, Pollock Krasner Found, 2001; Artists Trust Fel, Artist Trust, 2000. *Bibliog:* Rhonda Lane Howard, Holly A. Getch Clarke, (auth), Abfall (essays), Thread for Art. *Media:* Mixed Media Painting, Collage. *Publ:* Fionn Meade, Courting the Off Modern, FISURA, 2002; Joyce Korotkin, Yoder, Kurten and Greenfild, NY Arts, 2002. *Dealer:* Charles Cowles Gallery Inc 537 W 24th St NY 10011; Howard House 2017 2nd Ave Seattle WA 98121. *Mailing Add:* 1222 NE Ravenna Blvd Seattle WA 98105

YOOD, JAMES W
CRITIC, HISTORIAN, EDUCATOR, WRITER
Teaching: Asst prof, art hist Sch Art Inst Chicago, currently; vis, art prof, Northwestern Univ, Evanston, Ill, 92, prof, contemp art theory and crticism, 1995-, lect. asst, chmn, dept art theory & practice, 2003-. *Mem:* Chicago Art Critics Asn. *Publ:* co-auth: (with Refco Group, Eleanor Heartney, Anne Rorimer, Adam Brooks, and Sue Taylor) The Refco Collection, 90; co-auth: (with Patty Carroll(photog) & Debora Duez Donato) Spirited Visions: Portraits of Chicago Artists, 91; co-auth: (with Art Inst of Chicago) Feasting: A Celebration of Food in Art, 92; co-auth: (with Hollis

Sigler) Hollis Sigler's Breast Cancer Jour, 99; co-auth: (with Robert Vinnedge(photog) & Amy Herd (photog) William Morris: Animal/Artifact, 2000; co-author: (with Blake Edgar, William Morris, and Robert Vinnedge) William Morris: Man Adorned, 2002; co-author: (with Jack H. Bloom) The Rabbi as Symbolic Exemplar: By the Power Vested in Me, 2002. *Mailing Add:* School of the Art Inst of Chicago Dept of Art History Theory & Criticism 112 S Michigan St Chicago IL 60603

YORK, RICHARD TRAVIS
ART DEALER, GALLERY DIRECTOR
b Nashville, Tenn, Oct 22, 50. *Study:* Vanderbilt Univ, BA, 72. *Pos:* Dir Am art, Hammer Galleries, New York, 74-76; coordr Am dept, M Knoedler & Co, New York, 76-77; assoc, Hirschl & Adler Galleries, 77-81; pres, Richard York Gallery, New York, 81-. *Awards:* Recipient the 50th Anniversary Medal, Nat Gallery Art. *Mem:* William C Bryant Fel; Art Dealers Asn Am; Art Adv Panel Internal Revenue Serv. *Specialty:* American paintings, drawings and sculpture of 1800-1950. *Publ:* Auth, Joseph Stella: The Tropics, 88, The Italian Presence in American Art: 1860-1920, 89, An American Gallery, Vol I-VIII, 86-92, Richard York Gallery, NY; Joseph Goldyne, 93; American Paintings from the Collection of James H Ricau, 93; Modernism of the Salons of America, 1922-1936, 95; California, 96 & John Marin: The 291 Years, 98, Richard York Gallery, NY

YORK, TINA
PAINTER
b Bautzen, Ger, Feb 9, 51; US citizen. *Study:* Sch Mus Fine Arts, MA, 69; George Dergalis, MA, 67-75; Brandeis Univ BA(cum laude), 78; NY MedCol, 83; pvt studies, 83-88. *Work:* Mus Art, Las Vegas; Downey Mus Art, Calif; Mus Fine Arts, Salt Lake City; Columbia Univ, NY; Planetary Soc, Pasadena, Calif; and many others. *Comn:* Columbia Univ, NY, 86; Merck, Sharp & Dohme Int, NJ, 87; High Technol Products, NY, 87 & 88; Nat Aeronautics Space Admin, Washington, 89, 93 & 94; Nat Cancer Inst, Washington, 90; and many others. *Exhib:* Solo shows, Art 5, Nuremburg, Ger, 90, Art Expo, NY, 90, La Foire Int d'Art Contemp, Paris, France, 92, Ambiente, Frankfurt, Ger, 93, Kunstforum Int, Aachen, Ger, 93; Expos of Art, Sydney, Australia, 93; Art Cologne, Ger, 93; Toronto Trade Show, Can, 93; plus numerous others solo & group. *Awards:* First Prize, Inst Contemp Art, Boston, 79; First Prize, Southern Contemp Exhib, Los Angeles, 84; First Prize, One Fifty Three Gallery, New York, 87. *Bibliog:* Barbara Rollmann (auth), The Beauty of the Computer Chip, Regensburger Tageblatt, Ger, 90; Molly Siple (auth), The Realities We Never See, Designers West, 92; many others. *Media:* Mixed Media, Oil. *Res:* Scanning electron micrographs of the human body; virtual reality, aviation. *Publ:* art cards, Dharma Enterprises, 93; Biology and Reproduction, 93-95; Psychosocial Nursing, 94; calendar, Amber Lotus, 94; numerous others. *Dealer:* Exklusiv PO Box 17161 Fountain Hills, AZ 85269

YOSHIDA, RAY KAKUO
PAINTER, EDUCATOR
b Kapaa, Kauai, Hawaii, Oct 3, 30. *Study:* Art Inst Chicago, BA, 53; Syracuse Univ, MFA, 58; Univ Chicago; Univ Hawaii; also with A D Reinhardt. *Work:* Everson Mus, Syracuse, NY; Art Inst Chicago; Mus des 20, Jahrhunderts, Vienna; Am Tel & Tel, NY; Ball State Univ, Muncie, Ind. *Exhib:* Spirit of the Comics, Inst Contemp Art, Univ Pa, 69; Art Inst Chicago, 69, 71, 77, 79 & 82; Am Painting, Indianapolis Mus Art, 72 & 77; 12th Bienal de Sao Paulo, Brazil, 73; Chicago Currents: The Koffler Foundation, Nat Mus Am Art, 79; Who Chicago? An Exhib of Contemp Imagists, Sunderland Arts Ctr, Eng & traveling, 80-82; The Comic Art Show, Whitney Mus Am Art, 83; and others. *Teaching:* Frank Harrold Sellers Prof, Art Inst Chicago, 60-. *Awards:* Walter M Campana Prize, 60, Frank G Logan Medal & Prize, 71 & Virgine K Headberg Prize, 77, Art Inst Chicago; Nat Endow Arts Grant, 89. *Bibliog:* Franz Schulze (auth), Chicago Art, Follett, 72; articles in Art Int & Art News. *Mem:* Art Club Chicago; Am Asn Univ Profs. *Media:* Oil, Acrylic. *Dealer:* Phyllis Kind Gallery 226 E Ontario Chicago IL 60611. *Mailing Add:* 1944 N Wood St Chicago IL 60622

YOSHIHARU, HIGA
PRINTMAKER, PHOTOGRAPHER
b Okinawa, Japan, Jan 15, 38. *Study:* Tama Art Univ, Tokyo, BFA; Art Students League, NY, 64-67; Pratt Graphic Ctr, NY, 68-69; Columbia Univ, NY, MFA, 77. *Work:* Mus Mod Art, NY; Brooklyn Mus; Philadelphia Mus; Los Angeles Co Mus; and others. *Exhib:* Contemp Japanese Art Exhib, Mus Tokyo, 64; 50th Ann Exhib, Soc Am Graphic Artists, 69; New Talent Printmaker, Assoc Am Artists, NY, 70; Int Engraving Biennial, Buenos Aires, Arg, 70; Am Graphics Artists traveling show to tour the East, US Info Agency, 70. *Teaching:* Asst prof fine arts, Southampton Col, Long Island Univ, prof photography, currently. *Awards:* Best Print in Show, 50th Ann Exhib, Soc Am Graphic Artists, 69; Mus Purchase Awards, Int Print Exhib, Seattle Art Mus, Wash, 70 & Nat Print Exhib, Boston. *Bibliog:* Original art, hot off the presses, Life, 6/23/70; Famous Artist Annual, A Treasury of Contemporary Art, Famous Art Sch, 70. *Mailing Add:* Southampton College Long Island Univ 293 Montauk Highway Southampton NY 11968-4196

YOST, ERMA MARTIN
ASSEMBLAGE ARTIST, INSTRUCTOR
b Goshen, Ind, Jan 12, 47. *Study:* James Madison Univ, Harrisonburg, Va, BA(art educ), 69, MA(painting), 75. *Work:* Pace Univ Art Mus & Am Craft Mus, NY; James Madison Univ, Va; East Tenn State Univ, Johnson City; Bethel Col, North Newton, Kans; Bristol-Meyers Squibb, Princeton, NJ. *Comn:* Painting & quilt assemblage, Rockingham Mem Hosp, Harrisonburg, Va, 82 & Philhaven Hosp, Mt Gretna, Pa, 85, Chicopee, Inc, New Brunswick, NY, 90. *Exhib:* One-person shows, Noho Gallery, NY, 75-2005 & Int Embroidery Exhib, Japan (6 cities), 94; Desert Images, Jersey City Mus, NJ, 79; Invitational, Southwestern Exposure, Gayle Willson Gallery, Southampton, NY, 89; Contemp Quilts, Perimeter Gallery, Chicago, Ill, 89; New Jersey Arts Ann, NJ State Mus, Trenton, 92, 96 & 97; New Acquisitions, Am Craft Mus, NY, 94 & 9 x 3 x 9, 98; Invention & Diversity, Trenton City Mus, NJ, 98; and others. *Pos:* Illusr, Simplicity Pattern Co, NY, 72-73; Greer fine arts endowment vis artist, Bethel Col, Kans, 91; exchange teacher, Abbotsleigh Sch, NSW, Australia, 93. *Teaching:* Instr art, Eastern Mennonite Univ, 69-70; instr art, Spence Sch, 77-2000 & St Petet's Prep Sch, 2002-06. *Awards:* NJ State Coun Arts Fel, 92 & 99. *Bibliog:* Jean Ray Laury (auth), Imagery on Fabric, ed No 1, C & T Publ, 92 & ed No 2, 97; The Surface Designer's Art, Lark Books, 93; Robert Shaw (auth), The Art Quilt, Levin Assoc, 97; Object Lessons, The Guild, 2001. *Mem:* Textile Study Group of New York; Pro Arts; Ind Sch Art Instr Asn (co-pres, 96-98); Am Crafts Coun. *Media:* Fiber, Stiched Construction, Felt. *Dealer:* Noho Gallery Inc 530 W 25th St New York NY 10001. *Mailing Add:* 223 York St Jersey City NJ 07302

YOST, LEON C
PHOTOGRAPHER
b Atglen, Pa, July 7, 43. *Study:* Eastern Mennonite Univ, 63-65; Pace Univ, 72-77. *Work:* Pace Univ, NY; Cenlar Corp, NJ; E Tenn State Univ; Goshen Col, Ind; Chikapee Corp, Princeton, NJ. *Exhib:* Solo exhibs, Noho Gallery, NY, 77, 83, 85, 87, 90, 92, 95, 97, 2000, 2002 & 2006 CEU Prehistoric Mus, Price, Utah, 95 & San Diego Mus Man, 97; Fel Exhib, Monmouth Mus, NJ, 88; NJ Arts Ann, NJ State Mus, 89. *Pos:* Mem bd, Printmaking Coun NJ, 88-89; mem, Artist's Certification Bd, City of Jersey City, 96-2006; mem adv comt, Jersey City Mus, 2000. *Awards:* Fel, NJ State Coun Arts, 86. *Bibliog:* Peter Fingesten (auth), article, Arts Mag, 2/83; Vivian Raynor (auth), review, New York Times, 12/9/89; Ed McCormack (auth), Leon Yost's Stunning Images from the Outback, Artspeak, 1/95. *Mem:* Am Rock Art Res Asn; Australian Rock Art Res Asn; Utah Rock Art Res Asn. *Publ:* Contribr, The depiction of sexuality in art, from premodern awe to postmodern ennvi, The World I, 1/93 & Art and Intimacy, Univ Wash Press, 2000. *Dealer:* Noho Gallery 530 W 25th St New York NY 10001. *Mailing Add:* 223 York St Jersey City NJ 07302

YOUKELES, ANNE
PAINTER, PRINTMAKER
b Bad Ischl, Austria; US citizen. *Study:* Kunstgewerbeschule Vienna, Austria; Acad de la Grande Chaumiere, Paris; Ohio State Univ; painting with Alexander Dobkin & Rudolf Baranik; printmaking with Sidney Chafetz & Carol Summers. *Work:* Philadelphia Mus Art; Rosenwald Collection, Smithsonian Inst; Bibliotheque Nat, Paris; Lehman Collection; Atlantic Richfield Co; DeCordova Mus, Lincoln, Mass; Minneapolis Mus Art. *Comn:* Editions of prints, Int Graphic Arts Soc, 72, Jewish Mus, 73 & Print Club, Philadelphia, 75; acrylic triptych, Guaranty Bank, Milwaukee, 79. *Exhib:* Ann Print Exhibs, Brooklyn Mus, 70 & 72; Art Today USA II, Mod Art Mus, Tehran, Iran, 77; one-person shows, Marion Locks Gallery, Philadelphia, 73 & 77, Dubins Gallery, Los Angeles, 78 & 80, Posner Gallery, Milwaukee, 79, 84 & 86; Benjamin Mangel Gallery, Philadelphia, 82 & 86; and others. *Awards:* Purchase Prizes, Pratt Miniature Show, Boston Printmakers Ann & Philadelphia Print Club. *Bibliog:* Gabor Peterdi (auth), Printmaking, Macmillan Publ Co, New York, 72; Ross & Romano (auths), Techniques in Printmaking, 74. *Mem:* Soc Am Graphic Artists; Boston Printmakers; Silvermine Guild Artists; Am Colorprint Soc; Print Club, Philadelphia. *Media:* Acrylic, Work in Handmade Paper. *Mailing Add:* 81-42 193rd St Jamaica NY 11423-1047

YOUNG, AARON
CONCEPTUAL ARTIST
Study: San Francisco Art Inst, BFA, 2001; Yale Univ, MFA, 2004. *Work:* Mus Contemp Art, Kansas City, Kans; Mus Mod Art, NY. *Exhib:* solo shows, Tender Buttons, Midway Contemp Art, Minneapolis, Minn, 2004; group shows, Paladar, 7th Havana Bienal, Havana, Cuba, 2000; Strictly Ballroom, Stanford Univ Mus, Palo Alto, Calif, 2001; New Orleans Performance Festival, 2001; Circus, 8th Havana Bienal, 2002; From Here On, Guild & Greyshkul Gallery, NY, 2003; Miami Heat, Miami Pacemaker Gallery, Fla, 2004; Some Exhaust, Lehmann Maupin Gallery, NY, 2004; Curatorial Choices: Drawing, Univ Minn Mus, 2005; Mus Mod Art, NY, 2005; Absolute Summer Show, Kirkhoff Contemp Art, 2005; Day LABOR, PS 1, MOMA, Long Island City, 2005; Whitney Biennial, Whitney Mus Art, NY, 2006. *Mailing Add:* c/o PS1 Contemporary Art Center 22-25 Jackson Ave Long Island City NY 11101

YOUNG, ANDREW
PAINTER
b Mt Kisco, NY, Nov 23, 62. *Study:* Univ Calif, Berkeley, BA, 87; Sch Art Inst Chicago, MFA, 89. *Work:* Arthur Anderson & Co, Detroit, Mich; Ill State Mus, Springfield; Jones, Day, Revas & Poge, Los Angeles; Proskauer, Rose, Goetz & Mendelsohn, NY; Prudential Insurance Co, Newark, NJ. *Comn:* Harbor (triptych), McKinsey & Co Inc, NY. *Exhib:* Solo Exhibs, Betsy Rosenfield Gallery, Chicago, 90 & 92, Chicago Int Art Expo, Ill, 90, David Beitzel Gallery, NY, 91 & 92, Dorothy Goldeen Gallery, Santa Monica, Calif, 91en Gallery, Santa Monica, Calif, 91; two-person exhib, Bilder uber dem Wasser (traveled), USIS, Bonn, Ger, 91-92; four-artists show, Haines Gallery, San Francisco, Calif, 92; Paper Houses, David Beitzel Gallery, NY, 92; Betsy Rosenfield Gallery, Chicago, Ill, 92; Art Fair/Seattle, Betsy Rosenfield Gallery, 92; and others. *Awards:* Maybelle M Toombs Prize, Univ Calif, Berkeley, 86-87; Competitive Scholar, 87-89 & Fred J Forster Fel, 90, Sch Art Inst Chicago; Community Arts Assistance Grant, Chicago Office Fine Arts, 91. *Bibliog:* Justin Spring (auth), Andrew Young, ArtForum, 11/91; Eileen Myles (auth), Andrew Young at David Beitzel, Art Am, 12/91; Amerikanische Kunstler in Koln, Deutsche Welle PBS/Europ J, 12/30/91. *Media:* Egg Tempera on Panel

YOUNG, BARBARA
PHOTOGRAPHER
b Chicago, Ill, Oct 27, 20. *Study:* Knox Col, Galesburg, Ill, AB, 42; Johns Hopkins Univ Med Sch, MD, 45; Baltimore Psychoanal Inst, grad, 55. *Work:* Mus Mod Art, NY; Baltimore Mus Art; Eastman House, Rochester, NY; Santa Barbara Mus Art, Calif; Yale Univ Gallery. *Exhib:* One-woman shows, Butler Inst Am Art, Youngstown,

Ohio, 74, Santa Barbara Mus Art, Calif, 78; 2nd Generation Pioneers: Blance DeBra & Harvey Young, Baltimore Mus Art, 76 & Timberlane, A Sculpture Garden, 77; Am Vision, Nat Artists Alliance, NY Univ Galleries, 79; Maryland Artscape, 86; one person retrospective, The Passage of Time, Univ Md, Baltimore Co, 87 & Col Notre Dame, Baltimore, 96; Francoise Gallery, Baltimore, 94; A Photographer's Vision: Gifts to the Collection from Barbara Young, Baltimore Mus Art, 96. *Awards:* First Prize, Nat Artists Alliance, 79; First Prize, Md Mag, 12/82. *Publ:* Auth, Our garden in the city, Horticulture, 70; Hunting for the ostrich, Hasselblad, Mag, 71; Getting acquainted with Maine, Am Forests Mag, 72; The Coleman's vegetable garden at Cape Rosier, Downeast Mag, 75; The Plop-A-Lop Tree, photographic study of a Bahama Community, 93; Tales of Courage: Recovering Life After Catastrophe Articles, 2003; Mamma and Me, The Awakenings Review, an Outreach Program for People with Psychiatric Disabilities, Univ Chicago, 2003; Yale Journal of the Humanities in Medicine; GVirginia Woolf: Her Cries of Joy and Longing, 2003; Perspectives in Biology and Medicine, 2004. *Mailing Add:* 5307 Herring Run Dr Baltimore MD 21214

YOUNG, BARBARA NEIL
LIBRARIAN, CURATOR

b Bristol, Va, July 18, 43. *Study:* Fla State Univ, Tallahassee, BA, 65; Drexel Univ, Philadelphia, MLS, 75. *Collection Arranged:* Books & Pages, South Florida Artists Books, 87; Purvis Young, Me and My People, (with Cesar Trasobares), 89; Miami Thriving in Change/Fifty Years of Photography, 90; Miami Thriving in Change 1940-1990/Fifty Years of Collecting, 90; Narratives from the Diaspora, Willie Birch, Kabuya Pamela Bowens, Gary Moore, 90; Flora and Fauna in Illustration, 91; Miami/Clay/5, 92; Something About Libraries (3″ x 5″), 94; Becalmed in Miami, South Florida Artists Made Boats, 95; Drums of Steel, 96; 100 Years of Architecture, 96; The Artful Book, 98; Touched by AIDS (with Helen Kohen & Margarita Cano), 98; A Declaration of Place African Influences in Vernacular Architecture of South FL, 2002; Young at Sixty: Paintings Drawings and Artist's books by Purvis Young, 2003. *Pos:* Artmobile librn, Miami-Dade Pub Libr, Fla, 76-81, art & music reference librn, 81-85 & art serv coordr, 85-2005; Vasari Project Coord 2000-2005. *Mem:* Art Librn Soc NAm; Am Libr Asn; Soc Fla Archs; Art Table. *Res:* Afro-American, Hispanic and South Florida artists Library System, Fla Assoc Newslett, 77. *Mailing Add:* 7231 SW 61st St Miami FL 33143

YOUNG, CHARLES ALEXANDER
PAINTER; EDUCATOR

b New York, NY, Nov 17, 30. *Study:* Hampton Inst, BS; NY Univ, with Hale Woodruff, MA; Cath Univ Am. *Work:* Phelps Stokes Found, DC; Le Centre D'Art Haitien & Le Musee d'art Haitien, Port au Prince, Haiti; Univ DC Art Collection; Fisk Univ, Nashville, TN; Hampton Mus, VA & VA Ctr Creative Arts, Sweet Briar, VA; and others. *Exhib:* One-man show, Smith-Mason Gallery, 69, Agra Gallery, Washington, DC, 72 & Hampton Mus, Va, 89; Ten & Ten & Ten Washington Painting, Corcoran Gallery, Washington, DC, 82; Martin Luther King Libr, Washington, DC, 87; African American Contemp Art Mus of Contemp Art - Gibellina, Italy, 90; Mus Sci Indust, Chicago, Ill, 91; New Eng Fine Arts Inst Nat Exhib, Woburn, Mass, 93; State Fine Arts Mus of Alma-Ata, Kazakhstan, Russia, 93; Fannie Mae Exhib, 96; Univ DC Exhib, 97; Hampton Mus, Va, 99. *Collection Arranged:* Hampton Univ, Va; Univ of the District of Columbia; Fisk Univ, Nashville; Freddie Mae, Vienna, Va. *Teaching:* Instr art, Fayetteville State Univ, 60-63; asst prof, Tenn A&I Univ, 63-68; chmn dept art, Univ DC, 68-84 & prof art & chair person, 91-94; prof, Emer UDC, 2004-. *Awards:* First & Second Prizes, First Open Exhib, Fayetteville, 62; Phelps-Stokes Grant to travel in Africa, 75; Fel Virginia Ctr Creative Arts, 89. *Bibliog:* Theresa Cederholm (auth), Afro-American Artists, Trustees Boston Libr, 73; Samella Lewis (auth), Art: African American, Harcourt Brace Jovanovich, 78; Lynn M & James Igor (auths), 250 Years of Afro-American Art, 81; Edward Atkins (auth), Black Dimensions in Contemporary Art, 68; Lewis and Waddy (auths), Black Artists on Art, 71; and others. *Mem:* Col Art Asn; Nat Art Educ Asn; Nat Conf Artists; Am Asn Univ Prof. *Media:* Oil, Acrylic, Watercolors. *Publ:* Auth, African odyssey, Haitain Art Newsletter, Vol 6, 78; Mainstream: A place for Afro-American artists, Metro-Washington Mag, 3/84. *Mailing Add:* 8104 W Beach Dr NW Washington DC 20012

YOUNG, CYNTHIA M
PAINTER

b Ravenna, Ohio, May 20, 33. *Study:* RI Sch Design, 54; Corcoran Sch Art, with G Davis & Leon Berkowitz, 78-79; Conn Col Women, BA, 55; Univ Hawaii, 75; George Washington Univ, MFA, 79. *Work:* Gibbes Art Mus, Charleston, SC; Gettysburg Col, Gettysburg, Pa; Nat Park Serv, DC Superior Court, George Washington Univ, Washington, DC. *Comn:* Abstr & oil painting, Overseas Priv Investment Corp, Washington, DC, 89; watercolor renderings (of proposed structure), Northern Va Sci Ctr, 95. *Exhib:* At the Crosshairs, Westbeth Gallery, NY, 91; Water: A Group Show of Five Washington Artists, Mahler Gallery, Washington, DC, 92; National Works on Paper, Marsh Gallery, Richmond, Va, 93; For the Love of Children, Mus Americas, OAS, Washington, DC, 94; Global Focus 4th Ann World Conf, Women in Art & Cult, Beijing, China & Nat Mus Women Arts, Washington, 95. *Pos:* Bd, Artist Equity, DC Chap, 89-91; Vpres, Touchtone Gallery, 93, bd, 93-96. *Teaching:* Adj fac drawing & watercolor, Northern Va Community Col, 79-94. *Awards:* Award of Merit, Ninth Ann Artist Equity Exhib; David Lloyd Kreeger First Prize for Painting, Grad Awards Show, 79; Fel, Va Ctr Creative Arts, 81. *Bibliog:* Linda Joyce (auth), Memories of La Napoule, Freelance Star, 91; Michael Welzenbach (auth), Water paintings at Mahler, Washington Post, 92; Bill Dunlop (auth), Around Town, WETA CPBS, 2/5/95. *Mem:* Artists Equity, Washington, DC; Col Art Asn. *Media:* Oil, Mixed Media. *Publ:* A French connection, Washington Artist News, 90. *Dealer:* Touchstone Gallery 406 7th St NW Washington DC 20009. *Mailing Add:* 6903 Southridge Dr McLean VA 22101

YOUNG, JANIE CHESTER
MUSEUM DIRECTOR, EDUCATOR

b Port Huron, Mich, Apr 19, 49. *Study:* Univ Mich, BA(Eng lit & art hist), 71, MA(mus practice), 75; Toledo Mus Art, Nettie Poe Ketcham Fel Mus Educ, 72-73. *Collection Arranged:* Art, Ann Arbor, 71; Decorative Arts of New Brunswick, 76 & What's It To You? (auth, catalog for children), 77, Rutgers Univ Art Gallery; Patrick Thibert: Young Canadian Sculpture, 77, Young New York Painting, 79 & Helen Frankenthaler: The Artist in three Media, Saginaw Art Mus; The Queen's Choice: Burmese, 1885-1985, (auth, catalog) New Bedford Glass Mus. *Pos:* Fel coordr, Toledo Mus Art, Ohio, 73-75; cur educ, Rutgers Univ Art Gallery, 75-77; dir, Saginaw Art Mus, Mich, 77- & New Bedford Glass Mus, Mass, 82-. *Teaching:* Instr mus arts & educ, Grad Sch Educ, Rutgers Univ, New Brunswick, NJ, 76; Paipoint Cup Plate Collector's Am, 85; Nat Early Am Glass Club, 86. *Mem:* Nat Early Am Glass Club, 82-; Glass Asn (G B), 88-. *Res:* First interdisciplinary, professional bibliography of museum education; 19th century American and English art glass. *Publ:* Auth, An Annotated Bibliography of Museum Education, Univ Mich Mis Pract Prog, 75; Evolution of Burnage Glass, Bull, Nat Early Am Glass Club, spring 89. *Mailing Add:* 134 Quaker St Weare NH 03281

YOUNG, JOSEPH LOUIS
SCULPTOR, MURALIST

b Pittsburgh, Pa, Nov 27, 19. *Study:* Westminster Col, AB, 41, Hon LLD, 60; Boston Mus Sch Fine Art, hon grad, 51; Carnegie Inst Technol; Mass Inst Technol; Cranbrook Acad Art; Art Students League; also with Karl Zerbe, David Aronson, Mitchell Siporin, Oskar Kockoshka & Gyorgy Kepes. *Comn:* West apse, Nat Shrine Immaculate Conception, Washington, DC, 67; History of Math (mosaic murals), Math Sci Bldg, Univ Calif, Los Angeles, 70; The Triforium (multi-media tower), Los Angeles Mall, 70-75; 30ft theme sculpture, City of La Mirada Civic Theatre, 78; stained glass windows, Temple Ahavat Shalom, Northridge, 83 & Temple Tifereth Israel, Los Angeles, 83. *Exhib:* Ten Yr Retrospective, Art in Architecture, Palm Springs Desert Mus, 63; Int Exhib Muralists, Brussels, Belg, 65; VII Triennale, UNESCO, Varna, Bulgaria, 73; traveling retrospective, NY, Los Angeles, San Francisco, Chicago & Jerusalem, Israel, 86-. *Pos:* Owner, Art in Architecture, 53-; dir, Mosaic Workshop, 55-; mem, Fine Arts Adv Bds, W Hollywood City Coun & Platt Art Gallery, Univ Judiasm, Los Angeles, 88-. *Teaching:* Instr art hist, Tufts Col, Medford, Mass, 50; instr painting, Boston Mus Sch Fine Arts, 50; artist-in-residence, Brandeis Inst, 62-72; chmn dept archit arts, Santa Barbara Art Inst, 70-75. *Awards:* Am Acad Rome, Italy, 51; Huntington Hartford Found Fel, 52; Nat competition to create Los Angeles Holocaust Monument, Pan-Pacific Park, 85-91; and others. *Mem:* Fel Int Inst Arts & Lett; Nat Sculpture Ctr, Lawrence, Kans; Nat Soc Mural Painters; Artists Equity Asn. *Media:* Multi-Media. *Publ:* Auth, The World of Mosaic (film), Univ Calif, Los Angeles, 57; Arts & crafts in architecture, Creative Crafts, Vol 2, No 1; Mosaics: Principles & Practice, Reinhold, 63; Dialogues in Art, KNBC-TV Series, 67. *Mailing Add:* 7917 1/2 Norton Ave Los Angeles CA 90046-5204

YOUNG, KENNETH VICTOR
PAINTER, DESIGNER

b Louisville, Ky, Dec 12, 33. *Study:* Ind Univ; Univ Louisville, BS(design, painting & humanities), 62; Art Workshop, Assis, Italy 2000. *Work:* Corcoran Gallery Art, Washington, DC; Va Nat Bank, Alexandria; Johnson Publ Co, Chicago; Am Tel & Tel, NY; Fisk Univ, Nashville; Univ of Louisville, KY; Univ District of Columbia, Washington. *Comn:* DC Com of Art & Humanity. *Exhib:* Inst Contemp Arts, Washington, DC, 67; Baltimore Mus, 69; Indianapolis Mus, 72; Corcoran Gallery Art, 74; Black Artist from the South, Huntsville Mus, Ala, 79; Gallery K Washington, DC, 79-89, 99 & 2001; Owensboro Mus, Kent, 84; African Am Exhib, Gibellina Museo Civico D'Arte Contemporanea, Italy, Washington, DC, 90; one-man shows, Univ of Louisville, Ky, 60-63, 85, Bellarmine Col, Louisville, Ky, 63, Frame House Gallery, Louisville, 63, Franz Bader Gallery, Washington, DC, 68-71, 75, AM Saks Gallery, New York City, 72, Studio Gallery, Washington, Ed, 72-74, Fisk Univ, Nashville, Tenn, 73, Corcoran Gallery Art, Washington, DC, 74, St Mary's Col, Md, 76, Gallery K, DC, 78, 79, 84, 88 & 91, Grimaldis Gallery, Balt, 78, C Grimaldis Gallery, Baltimore, 80, Owensboro Mus, Ky, 83, & Howard Univ, Washington, DC, 86; Gallery K, 92, 94, 95; Roads to Liberty: Bicentennial on Constutition, Africans-Am Mus Asn. *Collection Arranged:* Music Machines, Hall of Graphic Arts, Women & Politics, Gandhi Centennial Exhib, Explorers NZ, Black Wings traveling exhib & Egyptian Antiquities; Mel Fisher Heritage Society; Henrictta Marie Exhib.; Arts America Program to Enitrea; Mus of Beni-Senf Cairo Egypt. *Pos:* Designer, Smithsonian Inst, 64-94; Washington artist, Health, Educ & Welfare Dept, DC, 79; acad specialist, Egyptian Mus, Cairo, currently; mus consult, currently. *Teaching:* Instr painting, Louisville Pub Sch, 62-63; instr design & painting, Corcoran Sch Art, 70-, Duke Ellington Sch Art, studies prog. *Awards:* Arts Am Grant, 97 & 98. *Bibliog:* B Rose (auth), Black artist in America, Art in Am, 70. *Mem:* AMA. *Media:* Watercolor, Acrylic. *Mailing Add:* 1930 Columbia Rd NW No 03 Washington DC 20009

YOUNG, LEEMEI
PAINTER

b Taiwan, Mar 28, 51. *Study:* School for Pastel Only Nat Arts Club, with Jason Cheng,1999; The Ridgewood Art Inst, with Betty Kaytes, 2001; The Art Students League of NY, with Barbara Adrian, 2002. *Hon Degrees:* Unv Chia-Nan School of Pharmacy, BS, 1973; Univ North Carolina at Charlotte, 1983. *Work:* Yi-Yeh Art Gallery, Chiba, Japan; Gallery of First Am Int Bank, Flushing, NY; Gallery of Taipei Economic & Cul Ctr, New York City; DSA Gallery, Tainan, Taiwan; Feng Ming Art Gallery, Chung Shan, China. *Comn:* Still Life with Fruits, Pastel Soc of Am, New York City, 2000; Spring, Sou Clinic, Chiba, Japan, 2003; Forever Love, Gallery of Amerasia Bank, Tom & Liz Mao, Flushing, NY, 2004; Autumn, Taiwanese Women Asn, Irene & Mike Lee, Flushing, NY, 2005; Sunflowers, Taiwanese Women Asn,

Tom & Liz Mao, Flushing, NY, 2005. *Exhib:* CPS Renaisance in Pastel, Slater Mem Mus Converse, Norwich, Conn, 2000-02; Pastel Soc of Am Ann, Natiional Arts Club, New York City, 2001; Hawaii Pastel Soc, Hawaii Art Ctr, Honolulu, Hawaii, 2002; Audubon Artists Inc Ann, Salmagudi Club, New York City, 2002-05; Am Artists Prof League, Salmagudi Club, New York City, 2001-03 & 2005; Taiwanese Am Pastel Artists Asn, Gallery of Taipai Cultural Ctr, New York City, 2005; Taiwan Ctr 1st Int Open Juried Exhib, Taiwan Ctr Gallery, Flushing, NY, 2005; Taiwan Ctr 2nd Int Open Juried Exhib, Taiwan Ctr Gallery, Flushing, NY, 2006. *Pos:* vpres, North Am Pastel Artists Asn, 2004-; exhib chair, Taiwan Ctr Int Open Juried Exhib, 2005-. *Teaching:* pastel inst, Tzu-Chi Cultural Dev Ctr, 2002. *Awards:* Pastel Painter Cape Cod, Conn Pastel Soc 7th Ann, 2000; Myra Biggerstaff, Pastel Soc of Am 29th Ann, 2001; Paul Bransom, Am Artists Prof League 77th Grand Nat, 2005. *Bibliog:* Kevin Shih (auth), Lee Mei Young's Pastel World, NY Community Time, 12/2004; Sonia Shi (auth), Donation to Tsunami, The Epoch Time, 2/2005; Shirly Chiu (auth), Nat Competition Winner, World Journal, 11/2005. *Mem:* North Am Pastel Artists Asn, 1999; Chinese Calligraphy Arts Soc, 2000; The Am Artists Prof League, 2002; signature mem, Pastel Soc of Am, 2004; Audubon Artists Inc, 2005. *Media:* Pastel. *Publ:* auth, Pastel World of Jason Chang, G&P Co/Marshall Wei, 1999; auth, Chinese Artists, Chinese Calligraphy Arts/City King, 2003 & 2005; auth, L'Art du Pastel, Art Du Pastel En France/Sylvie Cabal, 2005. *Dealer:* Sone Co Ltd 738-2 Dainichi Yotsukaido Chiba Japan 284-0001. *Mailing Add:* 136-24 Maple Ave #9D Flushing NY 11355

YOUNG, LESLIE (MCCLURE)
PAINTER, MURALIST
b Greensboro, NC, 54. *Study:* Univ NC, Greensboro, BFA(studio painting), 76, MFA(studio painting), 79. *Work:* Flower Mound CofC, Tex. *Comn:* portrait, comn by Dr Matthew Harden, Highland Village, Tex, 96; portrait, comn by Mr & Mrs Allen Hoggatt, Double Oak, Tex, 96; portrait, comn by Dr Rita Sherbenou, Denton, Tex, 96; interior with figures, comn by Dr Jane Chihal, Carrollton, Tex, 96; murals, comn by developer Ken Hodge, Flower Mound, Tex, 98. *Exhib:* Arlington Art Asn Regional, Arlington Mus Art, Tex, 90; Members Exhib, Arlington Mus Art, Tex, 93; 27th Ann Regional Painting Exhib, Richardson Civic Arts Ctr, Richardson, Tex, 93; The Kempinski, Dallas, Tex, 95; Silver Gala, Lewisville, Tex, 96; Women's Asn, Denton, Tex, 96; Univ NTex, Dept Cognition & Technol, Denton, 98. *Awards:* Gold Ltd & Merrill Award, Arlington Art Asn Regional, 90; Oil Painting Honary, Richardson 27th Ann Regional, Grumbacher Co, 93. *Bibliog:* Greensboro Daily News, 72 & 79; Liberty News, 79; Denton Record-Chronicle, 96. *Mem:* Women in Arts, Washington. *Media:* Alkyd Oil. *Res:* Development of teaching program for very young children - piano performance and signt-reading. *Publ:* Auth & illusr, Progressive Piano, 90; Garden Gate, Garden Pond, Iris and Water Lilies I & II, pvt publ, 3/96. *Dealer:* O'Delle Abney Abney Galleries 591 Broadway 3rd Flr New York NY 10012; Margie Art 5111 Winewood Lane Milford MI 48382-1543. *Mailing Add:* 211 Valley View Double Oak TX 75077-8432

YOUNG, MARJORIE WARD
PAINTER, DRAFTSMAN
b Chicago, Ill, June 25, 1910. *Study:* Art Inst Chicago, 25-35; with Jossey Bilan, 58-62, Edgar A Whitney, 69, 71 & 75, Richmond Yip, 70, J Dougles Greenbowe & Milford Zornes, 72, Robert Wood, 77 & 81, Charles Reid, 80 & Frank Webb, 84. *Work:* Ariz Bank, First Nat Bank Ariz & Valley Nat Bank, Phoenix; Thunderbird Bank; Glendale Community Col, Ariz. *Exhib:* Ariz Watercolor Asn Show In Taiwan, 74; Watercolor SW One, Albuquerque, 76; Watercolor SW Two, Tucson, 76; Watercolor SW Four, San Antonio; 110th Ann Am Watercolor Soc, NY, 77; Watercolors '78, O'Briens Art Emporium, Scottsdale; Glendale Community Col, 85; 77th Ann Catherine Lorillard Wolfe exhib. *Pos:* Background artist, Fleischer, Famous & Paramount Studios, Miami, Fla, 38-42; gallery dir, Phoenix YWCA, 70-79. *Teaching:* Instr drawing & watercolor, Phoenix Art Mus, 70-72, 77 & 79 & pvt students, 97; conservator old animated cartoon cells, 85-94. *Awards:* Second Watercolor, Low Ruins Spring Nat, Tubac, Ariz, 65; First Watercolor & Best Show Pencil Sketch, Nat League Am Pen Women, 75. *Mem:* Ariz Artists Guild (pres, 61-62); life mem Ariz Watercolor Asn (pres, 68-83); Nat League Am Pen Women (br art chmn, 72); Phoenix Art Mus Fine Arts Asn; hon mem Contemp Watercolorists Ariz. *Media:* Watercolor; Felt Tip Pen. *Publ:* Illusr, Many Lives of the Lynx, 64, Functional Spanish, 68 & Simply Messin, 82; illusr, Functional Spanish, 68, Homestead on the San Juan, 87. *Mailing Add:* HC 31 Box 178 Prescott AZ 86303

YOUNG, PURVIS
PAINTER
b Miami, Fla, 43. *Work:* New Orleans Art Mus, La; Nat Mus Am Art, Washington; Philadelphia Mus Art, Pa. *Comn:* Visions of the Street, Miami Dade Pub Libr, Fla, 83; Culmer/Overtown Br Libr, City Miami/Miami Dade Pub Libr, Fla, 84; Northside Metrorail Sta, Metro Dade Art Pub Places Trust, Fla, 85. *Media:* Mixed Media

YOUNG, ROBERT JOHN
PAINTER
b Vancouver, BC, Aug 8, 38. *Study:* Univ BC, BA(art hist); City & Guilds London Sch Art, Eng; Vancouver Sch Art, dipl(graphics). *Work:* Can Coun Art Bank, Ottawa; Govt BC Prov Collection; deBeers Consolidated Mines; Art Gallery Ont; Montreal Mus Fine Arts; and others. *Comn:* Christmas card Clothworkers Guild, London, 63; portrait, comn by Paul William White, London, 73; portrait, comn by Donna MacDonald, London, 76. *Exhib:* One-man shows, Redfern Gallery, London, 71, 73, 75, 79 & 82 & Vancouver Art Gallery, 74; Realismus und Realitat, Darmstadt, WGer, 75; Time Mag, Can Canvas, Across Can, 75-76; Can Cult Ctr, Embassy, Paris, 76; Vancouver Art Gallery, BC, 76 77; Marlborough-Godard, Toronto & Montreal, 76-77, 80 & 82; 10-Year Retrospective, Charles M Scott Gallery, Vancouver, 84; Vancouver Art Gallery, 88. *Teaching:* Instr painting, Banff Sch Fine Arts, Alta, 75 & 81; vis artist, Royal Col Art, London, 76, Vancouver Sch Art, 77 & 81 & Alta Col Art, 78; assoc prof, Univ BC, 82-. *Bibliog:* Doris Shadbolt (auth), Robert Young, The Implacable Image, Vanguard, Vancouver Art Gallery, 77; Fenella Crichton (auth), A juggler of styles, Art & Artists, 4/79. *Media:* Oil; Intaglio Printmaking. *Dealer:* Atelier Gallery Vancouver; Redfern Gallery 20 Cork St London ON Can. *Mailing Add:* 3940 Quebec St Vancouver BC V5V 3K8 Canada

YOUNG, ROBERT S W
SCULPTOR
b Honolulu, Hawaii, Nov 24, 48. *Study:* Univ Hawaii, BFA, 76, MFA, 80. *Work:* Honolulu Acad Art; Contemp Arts Ctr, Honolulu; Hawaii State Found Culture & Arts. *Exhib:* Artist of Hawaii, 77-80 & 82 & Art Flora, 84, Honolulu Acad Art; Clay-Form, Function & Fantasy, Long Beach Gallery, 79; We're Talking About 3 Artists, 81 & Sculpture Syntaxis: Best Shot, 84, Contemp Arts Ctr; 30th Ann Drawing & Sculpture Exhib, Ball State Univ, Muncie, Ind, 84. *Pos:* Chmn, Raku Ho'olaulea, Hawaii Craftmen, Honolulu, 80-82. *Teaching:* Instr pottery, Hickam Air Force Base, Honolulu, 76-82; instr ceramics, Univ Hawaii, Honolulu, 80-81. *Awards:* Col Art Award, Col Art Comt, 79 & 80; Crafts Excellence Award, Hawaii Craftsmen, 81; First Place Sculpture, Art Flora '84, Honolulu Garden Club, 84. *Mem:* Hawaii Artist League. *Media:* Clay. *Mailing Add:* 1056 Brandon Ave Norfolk VA 23507

YOUNG, TOM (THOMAS) WILLIAM
PAINTER, PHOTOGRAPHER
b Huntington, WVa, Oct, 7, 1924. *Study:* John Herron Art Inst; Cincinnati Art Acad, Univ Cincinnati; Univ Ala, BFA & MA(fine arts); Ohio State Univ; Chouinard Art Inst; Univ Southern Calif; Columbia Univ, EdD; also with Hans Hofmann, New York. *Work:* Mus Mod Art; Univ Southern Ill; Victoria & Albert Mus; New Orleans Mus Art; Pan American Life Insurance Bldg, New Orleans. *Comn:* Mural, US Air Base, Altus, Okla, 43. *Exhib:* After Twenty Yrs, Birmingham Mus Art, 71; Ft Wayne Ind Art Mus, 84; Independent Curators 10th Anniversary Exhibition, Puck Bldg, NY, 85; solo exhib, Malton Gallery, Cincinnati, Ohio, 86-88; Still-Zinsell Gallery, New Orleans, 88; Mus Folkwang Essen, Ger, 92; John Stinson Fine Arts and Ogden Mus of Southern Art, New Orleans, La, 2004; and others. *Pos:* Illusr exp aircraft, Douglas Aircraft Corp, Los Angeles, 52-53; art dir, Good Health Mag, New York, 53-57; cover designer, Electronic Design Mag, New York, 55-56; design & color consult, Royal Metal Mfg Co, 56-57; color consult, New Orleans Dock Bd, 71-72. *Teaching:* Prof fine arts & chmn dept, Wagner Col, 53-69; head prof art, Auburn Univ, 69-70; prof fine arts & mem grad fac, Univ New Orleans, 70-, chmn dept, 70-78, prof emer, 92. *Awards:* Weissglass Award, Staten Island Mus,1955; Hon Mention, New York City Ctr Gallery, 1956; Winner, Nat Exhib, Contemp Arts Ctr, New Orleans, 1982. *Mem:* New Orleans Mus Art (bd trustees, 73-); Col Art Asn Am. *Media:* All Media; Color Film. *Mailing Add:* 5605 W Esplanade Ave Metairie LA 70003

YOUNGBLOOD, DAISY
SCULPTOR
b Asheville, NC, Sept 14, 45. *Study:* Va Commonwealth Univ, 66; Am Acad Arts and Letters, Hon Degree, 1989. *Exhib:* Sculpture Now, Va Mus Fine Arts, Richmond, 83; Modern Masks, Whitney Mus Am Art, NY, 84; Standing Ground: Sculpture by Am Women, Contemp Arts Ctr, Cincinnati, Ohio, 87; One-woman shows, Beaver Col Art Gallery, Glenside, Pa, 92; Next of Kin, List Visual Arts Ctr, Mass Inst Technol, Cambridge, 95; A Labor of Love, New Mus Contemp Art, NY, 96; Mint Mus Craft & Design, Charlotte, NC, 2000. *Awards:* grantee fellow, MacArthur Foundation, 2003. *Bibliog:* Regina Coppola (auth), Daisy Youngblood, Univ Mass, 96; Eleanor Heartney (auth), Daisy Youngblood at David McKee, Art Am, 11/99. *Media:* Clay. *Mailing Add:* McKee Gallery 745 Fifth Ave New York NY 10151

YOUNGBLOOD, JUDY
PRINTMAKER, PAINTER
b El Paso, Tex. *Study:* Univ Wis, Madison, BS, 71, MFA, 74; Hayter's Atelier 17, Paris, Fulbright Scholar, 79. *Work:* DeCordova Mus, Boston; Boston Mus Fine Arts, Mass; Ark Art Ctr, Little Rock; Mus Fine Arts, Houston, Tex; Mus Mod Art, Ft Worth, Tex; Elvejhem Mus Art, Madison, Wis. *Comn:* Presentation print, Madison Print Club, 83; Centennial Print, Univ N Tex, 90. *Exhib:* Mini Print Int, Galeria Taller Fort, 88, 90 & 92; William Campbell Fine Art, Ft Worth, Tex, 90-92; Edith Baker Gallery, Dallas, Tex, 90-92; Printmaking in Texas: The 1980's, Mod Art Mus Ft Worth, 91; Flatbed Press, Austin, Tex, 96; solo exhibs, Transitions, Art Mus SE Tex, Beaumont, 97, Human Presence, William Campbell Contemp Art, Ft Worth, Tex, 98, Recent Works, Edith Baker Gallery, Dallas, Tex, 98, Univ Tex Tyler, 99; Accross the Grain, Am Woodcut Portfolio, Univ Del, Newark & Univ Tex, Tyler, 98; Texas Roots, Ctr Visual Arts, Denton, 98; In Relief: Contemp Am Relief Prints, Neb Art Asn, Lincoln & Hastings Col, Nebr, 98; Ashland Univ Printmaking Invitational Exhib, Ohio, 99; 27th Ann Bradley Univ Print & Drawing Exhib, Peoria, Ill, 99; The Boston Printmakers Biennial 1999, Boston Univ, Mass, 99. *Pos:* Fel residency, MacDowell Colony, Peterborough, NH, 82 & 85. *Teaching:* Prof printmaking, Univ N Tex, 76-98, prof emer, 98-. *Awards:* Artistic Achievement Award, Okla State Univ, 82; Award, 22nd Bradley Nat Print & Drawing Exhib, 89; Award, 42nd North Am Print Exhib, 90; Award, Am Miniature Printmakers Exhib, 88. *Bibliog:* Scott Gordon (auth), Judy Youngblood: New Work, New Art Examiner, 11/81; Andrew Stasik (auth), Toward a broader view, 81 & Betti & Sale (auths), Print Rev, 81, Drawing: A contemporary approach, 91; Lynne Allen & Phyllis McGibbon (auths), The Best of Printmaking: An International Collection, Rockport Publ, Gloucester, Mass, 97. *Mem:* Philadelphia Print Club; Women's Caucus Art; Southern Graphics Coun. *Media:* Miscellaneous Media. *Publ:* Auths, Lynne Allen & Phyllis McGibbon, The Best of Printmaking: An International Collection, Rockport Publ, Gloucester, Mass, 97; Hayden's Ferry Review, Ariz State Univ, Tempe, Ariz, 99. *Mailing Add:* Univ NTex Sch Visual Arts PO Box 5098 Denton TX 76203

YOUNGBLOOD, NAT
PAINTER, ILLUSTRATOR
b Evansville, Ind, Dec 28, 16. *Study:* Univ NMex, Albuquerque, with Millard Sheets; Am Acad Art, Chicago; also with Barse Miller, Raymond Joahnson, Ralph Douglass & Howard Mosby. *Hon Degrees:* Washington and Jefferson Col, Hon DFA, 1999. *Work:* Indiana Univ Pa; Calif State Col, Pa; Rockwell Int Col, Ft Pitt Mus, Pa. *Comn:* Oil portraits (indust leaders), Pittsburgh Press, Pa, 56; portrait President Kennedy, Metro News Service, 61; ten hist paintings (pioneer life), Ft Pitt Mus, Pittsburgh, Pa; Duquesne Club, Pittsburgh, Pa; numerous works in pvt collections. *Exhib:* Artist of the Yr, Pittsburgh Ctr Arts, 76; Am Painters in Paris, 76; one-man shows, Atheneum, New Harmony, Ind, 84 & Main Trail Galleries, Scottsdale, Ariz, 85, Dewey Galleries, Santa Fe, 91, Albuquerque Mus Art, 91, 92 & 95, Wash & Jefferson Col, 95; Four-man show, Dewey Galleries, Santa Fe, NMex, 85; Pioneer Mus, Colorado Springs, Colo, 85 & 86; Artists of Am, 86-2000; Arts for the Parks Top 100, 98. *Pos:* Art dir, cartoonist, illusr & painter, Pittsburgh Press, 46-79. *Teaching:* Instr painting & design, LaRoche Col & Art Inst Pittsburgh, 74. *Awards:* First Place, Pennational Exhib, 66; First Prize Alcoa Award, Aqueous Open, 86; Best Show, Art in the Mountains, 96. *Bibliog:* Nancy Ellis (auth), Nat Youngblood, Focus, Santa Fe, NMex, 1-2/89; Rita Simmons (auth), Nat Youngblood, Southwest Art, 8/90; Santa Fe Focus, 8/9/94. *Mem:* Pittsburgh Experiment; Fortnightly Wash Jefferson Univ. *Media:* Watercolor, Oil. *Publ:* Ed, 101st Airborne Division Picture History, 45; auth, Watercolor page, Am Artist Mag, 59; Western Art Digest, 85. *Dealer:* Dewey Galleries Ltd 74 E San Francisco St Santa Fe NM 87501. *Mailing Add:* PO Box 73 West Middletown PA 15379

YOUNGER, DAN FORREST
PAINTER, PRINTMAKER
b Denver, Colo, Sept 14, 54. *Study:* Kansas City Art Inst, BFA, 76. *Work:* Am Express, Salt Lake City; Nat Mus, Brazil; Continental Insurance Co, NY; AT&T, Kansas City, Mo; Dean Witter Reynolds, Kansas City; and others. *Comn:* Mural, Dixons Inc, Independence, Mo, 78. *Exhib:* Atkins Mus Fine Arts, Kansas City, Mo, 76-81; Univ Dallas, Irving, 77; Sheldon Mus, Lincoln, Nebr, 81; Univ Mo, Kansas City, 81; and others. *Pos:* Originator & dir, Squadron Press Fine Art Printing, 79-84. *Teaching:* Print technician, Kansas City Art Inst, Mo, 76-83. *Awards:* Best Show, Dixie Ann, Montgomery Mus, Ala, 78; Purchase Prize, Mid Four Ann, 79 & 81; 2nd Place, William Rockhill Nelson Gallery Art, 80. *Bibliog:* Elizabeth Kirsch (auth), Squadron Press, Kansas City, 2/80; Vicki Melcher (auth), Kansas City, Art News, 10/80; Barbara Westerfield (auth), Dan Younger, New Art Examiner Vol 13 No 3, 11/85. *Mem:* Print Soc Kansas City; Friends Art, Kansas City. *Mailing Add:* 5911 McGee Kansas City MO 64113

YOUNGER, ROBERT M
SCULPTOR
b Philadelphia, Pa, 47. *Study:* Philadelphia Col Art, BFA, 69; Fulbright-Hayes Grant, Italy, 69-70; Yale Univ Grad Sch Fine Arts, 71-72. *Exhib:* Solo exhibs, Pa Acad Fine Arts, 80, Craig Cornelius Gallery, NY, 89, Drexel Univ, Philadelphia, 90, Kees Schouten Gallery, Haarlem, The Neth, 93, Univ Arts, Philadelphia, 94, InterArt Gallery, NY, 94 & De Etalage, Haarlem, The Neth, 95; The Gift Show, Dooley Le Cappellaine, NY, 92; Brides and Topiaries, Flamingos East, NY, 92; The Return of the Cadavre Exquis, Drawing Ctr, NY, 93; Souvenirs, Rosenwald/Wolf Gallery, Univ of Arts, Philadelphia, 94; Drexel Univ Gallery, Phildelphia, 99; and others. *Awards:* Nat Endowment Arts Grant, 82 & 90; NY State Coun Arts Sponsored Proj Award, 86. *Mailing Add:* 274 Water St New York NY 10038

YOUNGERMAN, JACK
PAINTER, SCULPTOR
b St Louis, Mo, Mar 25, 26. *Study:* Univ NC, Chapel Hill, 44-46; Univ Mo, Columbia, BA, 47; Sch Fine Arts, Paris, 47-49. *Work:* Whitney Mus Am Art, Mus Mod Art & Solomon R Guggenheim Mus, NY; Corcoran Gallery Art, Hirshhorn Mus & Sculpture Garden, Nat Mus Am Art, Smithsonian Inst, Washington, DC; Art Inst Chicago; Albright-Knox Art Gallery, Buffalo, NY; Baltimore Mus Art, Md; Yale Univ Art Gallery, New Haven, Conn; Carnegie Inst, Mus Art, Pittsburgh, Pa; Walker Art Ctr, Minneapolis, Minn. *Comn:* First Pa Bank, Philadelphia, 69; painted wall reliefs, First Wis Bank, Milwaukee, 71; Rumi's Dance (tapestry), Fed Court Bldg, Portland, Ore, 76; The Ohio (fiberglass), Pittsburgh, 77; Dryad (wood & resin), Neiman-Marcus, Chicago, 83. *Exhib:* Corcoran Biennial, Washington, DC, 59, 61 & 63; Art Inst Chicago, 62; Decade of Am Drawings 1955-65, Whitney Mus Am Art, 65; Systemic Painting, Guggenheim Mus, 66; Fall Exhib, Aldrich Mus Contemp Art, 73; 9 Artists/Coenties Slip, Whitney Mus Am Art, 74; Thirty Yrs of Am Art: 1945-75, Selections from the Permanent Collection, Whitney Mus Am Art, 77; Private Images: Photog by Painters, Los Angeles Co Mus Art, 77; Art, Inc: Am Painting from Corporate Collections, Corcoran Gallery Art, 79; Art in Am after World War II, Guggenheim Mus, 79; NY Sch: Four Decades, Guggenheim Mus, 79; solo exhibs, Fine Arts Ctr, State Univ NY, Stony Brook, 82, Heath Gallery, Atlanta, 84, Guggenheim Mus, New York, 86, Washburn Gallery, NY, 86, 87 & 91, Heland Wetterling Gallery, Stockholm, 89-90, Glenn Horowitz Booksellers, East Hampton, NY, 96 & Washburn Gallery, New York, 97; Contemp Prints & Drawings, Nat Gallery Art, 81 & 83; Intermedia, Aldrich Mus, 84; The Folding Image, Nat Gallery Art, 84; Transformations in Sculpture, Guggenheim Mus, 86; Fifty Years of Collecting, Guggenheim Mus, NY, 88; Vital Signs: Organic Abstraction from the Permanent Collection, Whitney Mus Am Art, NY, 88; The Gestural Impulse 1945-1960, Whitney Mus, NY, 89; Twentieth Century Art, Nat Gallery Art, Washington, DC, 89; Table Sculpture, Andre Emmerich Gallery, NY, 92 & 93; Coenties Slip, Pace Gallery, NY, 93; They Quoted Matisse, Calerie de France, Paris, 93; Drawings, 30th Anniv, Found Contemp Performance Arts, Leo Castelli Gallery, NY, 93; Les Americains, Fecamp, Joinville, Paris, 94. *Teaching:* Instr, Yale Univ, 74-75, Hunter Col, 81-82, Sch Visual Arts, New York, 78-95. *Awards:* Nat Endowment Arts Award, 72 & 84; US/Japan (Kyoto) Exchange fel, 87; Nat Acad Design, 92; Am Acad Award, Rome, 995. *Bibliog:* Adam McGovern (auth), Jack Youngerman, Washburn Gallery, Cover Mag, 5/91; Holland Cotter (auth), Where city history was made, a 50's group made art history, The Arts, NY Times, 1/5/93; Roberta Smith (auth), Coenties Slip, Art in Review, NY Times, 2/12/93. *Dealer:* Washburn Gallery 20 W 57th St New York NY 10019. *Mailing Add:* PO Box 508 Bridgehampton NY 11932

YOURITZIN, VICTOR KOSHKIN
HISTORIAN, EDUCATOR
b New York, NY, Dec 20, 42. *Study:* Williams Col, BA(cum laude with honors), 64; Sch of Archit, Int Fels Prog, Columbia Univ, 64-65; Inst Fine Arts, NY Univ, MA, 67; Cert Mus Training, Inst of Fine Arts & Metrop Mus Art, New York, 69. *Work:* Bibliothèque nationale de France, Paris; NY Pub Libr; Bienecke Libr, Yale Univ; Wadsworth Atheneum Mus Art, Hartford; Mus of NMex, Santa Fe. *Exhib:* 27th Ann La State Art Exhib for Prof Artists, 1971; and others. *Pos:* Mem bd trustees, Okla Mus Art, Oklahoma City, 78-84; regional corresp, Art Voices-South, 78-79, contrib ed, 79-82; mem exhibs & collections comt, Philbrook Art Ctr, Tulsa, Okla, 83-85; mem exhib comt, Okla Art Ctr, 84-87; panelist, Nat Endowment Humanities, 84; panelist, Prog for Art on Film, Getty Trust, Metrop Mus of Art, 87; co-cur, Am Watercolors, Metrop Mus Art, 91-92; mem, Collections Mgt Comt, Oklahoma City Art Mus, 92-96; coun adv mem, Ogden Mus Southern Art, Univ New Orleans, 95-; chmn bd trustees, Mabee-Gerrer Mus Art, Shawnee, 96-99. *Teaching:* Instr art hist, Vanderbilt Univ, Nashville, Tenn, 68-69 & Newcomb Col, Tulane Univ, New Orleans, 69-72; asst prof art hist, Univ Okla, Norman, 72-80, assoc prof, 80-94, prof, 94-97 & David Ross Boyd distinguished prof, 97-. *Awards:* Ford Found Fel, Dept of Am Painting & Sculpture, Metrop Mus of Art, New York, 67-68; Gov's Arts & Educ Award, State Okla, 92; Honorable Citation, House Reps, State Okla, 93; Award Winning Author, Book-of-the-Month Club, Am Watercolors from the Metropolitan Mus of Art, Abrams, 91. *Mem:* Koussevitzky Recordings Soc Inc (vpres, 92-). *Res:* Nineteenth and twentieth century art; museology. *Publ:* Auth, The Irony of Degas, Gazette des Beaux-Arts, 1/76; Oklahoma City: Getting rid of Bambi, Artnews, 9/78; Thomas Hart Benton: Bathers rediscovered, Arts Mag, 5/80; coauth, Am Watercolors from the Metrop Mus of Art, Abrams, 91; auth, Pavel Tchelitchew, Fred Jones Jr Mus of Art, Univ of Okla, 2002; and others. *Mailing Add:* 1721 Oakwood Dr Norman OK 73069

YU, SHAN
ARTIST
b Fuzhou, China, Oct 24, 49. *Study:* Fujian Art Sch, China, BA, 80; Shanghai Theater Acad, grad study, 85-86; Boston Univ, MFA, 89. *Work:* National Great River Mus, Indiana State Mus, Angel Mounds Historic Site, Evansville, Ind, Mus Sci, Boston. *Comn:* Murals, Ind State Mus, Indianapolis; Murals, Mus Ctr, Cincinati, OH; Mural, Mus of Sci, Boston; Mural, Childrens Mus, Boston; panoramic mural, Nat Great River, Mus, Alton Ill; 2 murals, Seacoast Sci Ctr, Rye, NH, 2004; 3 murals, exhib Sci Mus Minn, St. Paul, 2005; and others. *Exhib:* one-man shows, Hong Kong Arts Ctr, 89, CCI Gallery, Boston, 98, Hong Kong Art & Design Gallery, 03; Creative Arts Workshop Gallery, New Haven, Conn, 92; Hewlett Packard HQ, Mass, 94; Kane Gallery, Boston, 95; Juried Ann Exhib, Am Watercolor Soc, NY, 99; Salmagundi Club Gallery, New York City, 99; Shanghai Theater Acad Gallery, China, 01; murals, Ind State Mus, 01, 02, Royal BC Mus, Victoria, Can, 03. *Pos:* sr set designer, VDA Inc, 89-99; pres, Eastern Decor & Art Co, 98-. *Teaching:* Teacher, Fujian Art Sch, 80-85; Vis Prof, Shanghai Theater Acad, 2001. *Awards:* Fel, Asian Cult Coun, 86; Outstanding Int Scholar, Boston U, 89; Am Citizenship, 98. *Bibliog:* Christine Temin(auth), Watercolors on a Pleasing Scale, The Boston Globe, 93; Zhu Weiyi (auth), Yushans Mural in Mus, World Jour, No. 872, 00. *Mem:* Nat Mural Painters Soc. *Media:* Acrylic, Watercolor, Oil. *Publ:* Watercolor Painting, Silent Night, The Boston Globe, 93; Landscape Painting by Yu Shan, Kiaoning Art Press, 97; Painting with Article, Am Artist Mag, 7/92. *Mailing Add:* 45 Robinson St Somerville MA 02145

YU-HO, TSENG
PAINTER, HISTORIAN
b Peking, China, Nov 29, 24; US citizen. *Study:* Fu-jen Univ, Peking, BA, 42; Univ Hawaii, MA, 66; Inst Fine Arts, NY Univ, PhD, 72. *Work:* Honolulu Acad Arts, Hawaii; Walker Art Ctr, Minneapolis; Nat Mus Mod Art, Stockholm, Sweden; Mus Cernuschi, Paris, France; Stanford Art Gallery, Calif. *Comn:* Mural, St Katherine's Church, Kaui, Hawaii, 57; mural, Manoa Chinese Pavilion, Honolulu, 68; mural, Golden West Savings & Loan, San Francisco, Calif, 64; wall painting, Castle & Cooke Co, Ltd, Honolulu, 68; wall painting, Honolulu Int Airport, 72. *Exhib:* Contemp Am Painting & Sculpture, Univ Ill, Urbana, 58, 61 & 65; Carnegie Inst Painting & Sculpture Int, Pittsburgh, Pa, 61 & 65; Kunstverein, Munich & Frankfurt, Ger; Walker Art Ctr; San Francisco Mus Art, Calif; and others. *Teaching:* Instr studio art, Honolulu Acad Art, 50-63, consult Chinese art, 53-; assoc prof Chinese art hist, Univ Hawaii, 63-66; prog chmn art hist, Univ Hawaii, 71-, prof art, 73-. *Awards:* Am Artists of the Western States Award, Stanford Art Gallery; NY Univ Founders Day Award for Outstanding Scholarship, 72. *Bibliog:* Article, Time Mag, 1/19/62; Seldis (auth), Pacific heritage, Art in Am, 65. *Mem:* Am Col Art Asn; Asian Soc; Asian & Pacific Art Asn Hawaii (organizer, 72). *Media:* Watercolor, Collage. *Res:* Chinese art; the Art of Chinese folding fan; folk art. *Publ:* Contribr, four articles, Studies of 16th Century Chinese Artists, 54-63; contribr, Encyclopedia World Art, Rome, 64; auth, Some Contemporary Elements on Chinese Classic Pictorial Art, 65 & 71; illusr, The Analects of Confucious, 70. *Mailing Add:* 1024 Kamehame Dr Honolulu HI 96825

YUEN, KEE-HO
SILVERSMITH, SCULPTOR
b Hong Kong, China, Aug 7, 56; US citizen. *Study:* Chinese Univ Hong Kong, BA (fine arts), 83; Sch Art & Art Hist, Univ Iowa, MA (metalsmithing & jewelry), 88, MFA, 89. *Work:* Am Craft Mus, NY; Univ Iowa Mus Art, Iowa City; Univ Mus, Chinese Univ Hong Kong; Waterloo Mus, Iowa. *Comn:* flatware, comn by BS Rabinovitch, Seattle, Wash, 96; sculpture, comn by Todd & Jennifer Duncan, St Louis, Mo, 2000; sculpture, comn by Ivan Jacklin & Alison Weianstein, Richmond, Va, 2000; flatware & sculpture, comn by Lois Jecklin, Davenport, Iowa, 2001. *Exhib:* Nat Fortunoff's Silver Design Competition, NY, 92; Born with a Silver Spoon, Nat Ornamental Metal Mus, Memphis, Tenn; one-man show, Pivoine Gallery, Taipei, Taiwan, 95 & Waterloo Mus Art, Iowa, 98; British and Am Contemp Server, Goldsmith Hall of Worshipfull Co of Goldsmith, London, Eng, 96; Guests of USA, Mus fur Kunst und Gewerbe, Hamburg, Ger, 97; Contemp Silver Servers, Seattle Art Mus, 98; The Teapot Redefined, Mobilia Gallery, Cambridge, Mass, 2001. *Teaching:* head art area, Hong Kong Salesian Sec Sch, 83-86; prof metalsmithing & jewelry, Univ Northern Iowa, Cedar Falls, 89-2000; assoc prof metalsmithing & jewelry, Univ Iowa, Iowa City, 2000-. *Awards:* First Place, Nat Crafts Competition, Pa, 87; Third Place, Fortunoff's, 89; Certificate of Excellence & Outstanding Achievement in Metalwork, Artitude Int, 89. *Bibliog:* Helen Clifford & Seymour Rabinovitch (auths), Slices of Silver, American Craft, 97 & Contemporary Silver: Commissioning, Designing Creating, Merrell Halberton Publ, 2000; Jean Sampel, Forging Ahead: Contemporary Metalwork in Iowa, Metalsmith, 97; CJ Hines, Exhibit a study in Contrast, Waterloo Courier, 5/7/98. *Mem:* SNAG; Soc Am Silversmiths. *Media:* Metal, All Media. *Publ:* contrib, The Metalsmith's Books of Boxes and Lockets, 99; auth, Seen and Unseen, 99. *Dealer:* 167 E 61st St New York NY 10021. *Mailing Add:* 2106 13th St Coralville IA 52241

YUNICH, BEVERLY B
COLLAGE ARTIST, JEWELER
b New York, NY, Nov 11, 20. *Study:* Studied at Parsons Sch Design; Skidmore Col, BA, 42; studied with Moses Soyer & Robert Kulicke. *Work:* Albany Inst Hist & Art, Albany, NY; Meade Collection, Amherst Col, Mass; Hudson River Mus, Yonkers, NY; Ringling Mus, Sarasota, Fla; Skidmore Col Art Gallery, Saratoga Springs, NY. *Exhib:* Solo show, Albany Inst Hist & Art, NY, 72-80; Paper Works, Hudson River Mus, NY, 80; Jewelry-original, Rochester Mem Art Gallery, NY, 80-94; Skidmore Alumni Invitational, Skidmore Art Col & Gallery, 92; Painters & Sculptors Soc NJ, Newark Mus; Selected Artists Gallery, Ringling Mus, Sarasota, Fla. *Teaching:* Instr collage-mixed media, Westchester Art Workshop, 78-84. *Awards:* Purchase Award, Yonkers & Hudson River Mus, 88; Pen & Brush Club Solo Awards for Oil & Pastel Mixed Media; Best in Show, Mamaroneck Artists Guild. *Mem:* Nat Asn Women Artists; Audubon Artists Nat Acad; Scarsdale Art Asn. *Media:* Collage, Mixed Media; Gold on Silver. *Specialty:* Well known Contemp Artist, Lee Weber Gallery, Westchester, Greenwich. *Publ:* Jewelrey Designs, jewelers cir Voque Maqazine, NY Times. *Dealer:* Lee Weber Fine Arts. *Mailing Add:* 26 Cooper Rd Scarsdale NY 10583

YUST, DAVID E
PAINTER, EDUCATOR
b Wichita, Kans, Apr 3, 39. *Study:* Birger Sandzen; Wichita State Univ; Kans State Univ; Univ Kans, BFA, 63; Univ Ore, MFA, 69. *Work:* Denver Art Mus; Indianapolis Mus Art; Rockford Art Mus, Ill; Minnesota Mus Art, St Paul; Butler Inst Art, Youngstown, Ohio; Kirkland Mus Fine and Decorative Arts, Denver; and others. *Exhib:* One-man shows, Purdue Univ, West Lafayette, 99, Colo State Univ, Fort Collins, 99, Rourke Art Mus, Moorhead, Minn, 2003, Ft Collins Mus Contemp Art, Colo, 2003, Regis Univ, Denver, 2004, Gallery 72, Omaha, 2005, Plus Gallery, Denver, 2006. *Teaching:* Prof painting, drawing & grad painting coord, Colo State Univ, 65-. *Awards:* Purchase Awards, 11th Biennial, Kans State Univ, 70, Colo State Univ, 70, Okla Art Ctr, 73, Rourke Gallery, Moorhead, Minn, 89, Binney and Smith, Easton, Pa, 90; Arkey Award, Alliance for Contemp Art/Denver Art Mus, 2000; First Place Award, Foothills Art Ctr, Golden, 2001. *Bibliog:* Charles Parson (videotape), 90 & 2004. *Mem:* Denver Art Mus. *Media:* Acrylic, Oil, Lithography. *Dealer:* James O'Rourke 521 Main St Moorhead, MN 56560; Ivar Zeile + Gallery 2350 Lawrence St Denver CO 80205. *Mailing Add:* 1301 Patton St Fort Collins CO 80524-4231

YVON, JOSEPH See Fafard, Joe (Joseph) Yvon

Z

ZAAGE, HERMAN H
PRINTMAKER, EDUCATOR
b Jersey City, NJ, 27. *Study:* WPA Art Workshops; New Sch Univ, New York, 62-64; studied printmaking with John Ross. *Work:* Univ Ariz Art Mus, Tucson; Portland Mus Art, Ore; Queensborough Community Col, NY; Housatonic Mus Art, Bridgeport, Conn; Noble Maritime Mus, Staten Island, NY. *Comn:* 3 mezzotint prints, Soc Am Graphic Artists, NY, 93-2003; mezzoting print, Albany Print Club, NY, 99; mezzotint print, Protectors of Pine Oak Woods, 2001. *Exhib:* Lynd Ward Mem, Portland Art Mus, Ore, 90; Mezzotints, Wagner Col Art Gallery, Staten Island, NY, 91; Rockin & Rollin: 300 Yrs Mezzoprints Traveling Exhib, 96; Art of Darkness, New Orleans Mus, La, 96; Chronicles of Nature, Staten Island Inst Art Sci, NY, 99; 175th Ann, Nat Acad Design, NY, 2000; Print Retrospective, Noble Maritime Collection, 2001. *Teaching:* instr printmaking, New Sch Univ, NY, 64-; instr, The Art Lab, Art Sch Snug Harbor, Staten Island, NY, 75-. *Awards:* Audubon Artists Gold Medal, 97; Richard Reccia Mem Award, Nat Acad Design, 98, Orville Lance Prize, 2000. *Bibliog:* Rubenstein/Miller (dir), Master of the Mezzotint (film), CTV Staten Island/Rubenstein, 90; Carol Wax (auth), History & Technique of the Mezzotint, Harry Abrams, 90; Ross/Romano (auth), The Complete Printmaker, The Free Press, 72-90. *Mem:* Soc Am Graphic Artists; Boston Printmakers; Fla Printmakers; Audubon Artists; Printmaking Coun NJ. *Media:* Mezzotint, Etching, Woodcut. *Publ:* Stanley Berne (auth), Illusr, Multiple Modern Gods, 64, Abraxas, 64, Unconcious Victorious, 69, Arleen Zekowski (auth), Seasons of the Mind, 69, Wittenborn; auth, Erin Urban (ed), Bon A Tirer (catalog), Noble Maritime collection, 2005. *Dealer:* Earl Retif Stone & Press 238 Chartres St New Orleans La; Vlepo Gallery 36 Richmond Terrace Staten Island NY 10301. *Mailing Add:* 160 Simonson Ave Staten Island NY 10303

ZABARSKY, MELVIN JOEL
PAINTER, EDUCATOR
b Worcester, Mass, Aug 21, 32. *Study:* Sch Worcester Art Mus; Ruskin Sch Drawing & Fine Arts, Univ Oxford; Sch Fine & Appl Arts, Boston Univ, BFA; Univ Cincinnati, MFA. *Work:* Mus Mod Art, NY; De Cordova Mus, Lincoln, Mass; Addison Gallery Am Art, Andover, Mass; Wiggins Collection, Boston Pub Libr; Currier Gallery Art, Manchester, NH. *Exhib:* One-man exhibs, Boris Mirski Gallery, Boston, 62, Tragos Gallery, Boston, 66, De Cordova Mus, 70, Circulo Bellas Artes, 82 & Salones Berkowitoch, 83, Madrid; Surreal Images, De Cordova Mus, 68; New Eng Painters Traveling Exhib, Ringling Mus, Sarasota, Fla, 69. *Teaching:* Instr painting, Swain Sch Design, New Bedford, Mass, 60-64; asst prof painting, Wheaton Col, 64-69; prof painting, Univ NH, 69-. *Awards:* Painting Prize, Boston Arts Festival, 62; Ford Found Grant in humanities, 68. *Bibliog:* B Schwartz (auth), Humanism in 20th Century Art, Praeger, 73. *Media:* Oil. *Mailing Add:* Dept of Art Univ NH Durham NH 03824

ZABOROWSKI, DENNIS J
PAINTER, EDUCATOR
b Cleveland, Ohio, Jan 31, 43. *Study:* Cleveland Inst Art, cert, 61-65; Yale Univ, BFA, 65 & MFA, 68 with Jack Tworkov & Bernard Chaet. *Work:* Mint Mus of Art, Charlotte, NC; NC Nat Bank, NC Collection; Rauch Indust Inc, Gastonia, NC; Ackland Art Mus, Chapel Hill, NC; NC Mus Art, Raleigh. *Comn:* Youth Ctr mural, New Haven Redevlop Agency, 68. *Exhib:* Arts Festival of Atlanta, Ga, 69; 4th Ann James River Art Exhib, Mariners Mus, Newport News, Va, 70; 3rd Am Exhib, Washington & Lee Univ Mus, Lexington, Va, 71; solo exhibs, Gallery Contemp Art, Winston-Salem, NC, 72, NC Mus Art, Raleigh, 86 & Mint Mus, Charlotte, NC, 90; 39th Triannual NC Artists Exhib, NC Mus of Art, Raleigh, 90; and others. *Collection Arranged:* Fac Choice Exhib, Va Polytech Inst, Blacksburg, Va, 71; New Talent Show, Allan Stone Gallery, New York, 75; 200 Yrs of the Visual Arts in NC, NC Mus of Art, Raleigh, 76. *Teaching:* Prof painting, drawing & design, Univ of NC, Chapel Hill, 68-; asst prof design, Duke Univ, Durham, NC, 72. *Awards:* Purchase Awards, NC Artists Exhib, Rauch Indust, 73 & Realism in NC, Mint Mus of Art, Charlotte, 74; Best Oil Painting, Spring Mills Exhib, Spring Mills Corp, 75; Honor Award, Durham Art Guild Exhib, 87. *Mem:* Nat Asn Schs Art. *Media:* Mixed Media. *Mailing Add:* 100 Birchcrest Pl Chapel Hill NC 27516

ZACHARIAS, ATHOS
PAINTER
b Marlborough, Mass, June 17, 27. *Study:* Art Students League, summer 52; RI Sch Design, BFA, 52; Cranbrook Acad Art, MFA, 53. *Work:* Mus Art, Providence, RI; Inst Contemp Art, Boston; Kalamazoo Inst Art, Mich; Phoenix Art Mus, Ariz; Westinghouse Corp, Pittsburgh; Corcoran Gallery Art, Washington, DC. *Comn:* Decor for Manhattan Festival Dancers, comn by Robert Ossorio, NY, 63; designed & executed opaque Projections for Edith Stephan Dance Co. *Exhib:* Joachim Gallery, Chicago, Ill, 61; one-man shows, Gallery Mayer, 61, Louis Alexander Gallery, 63, Landmark Gallery, 73 & James Yu Gallery, NY, 77, Owl 57, Woodmere, NY, 88-93, Ann Harper Gallery, Amagansett, NY, 95, Nabi Gallery, Sag Harbour, NY, 99 and many others; Bologna Landi Gallery, East Hampton, NY, 86; Benton Gallery, Benton Plaza, Southampton, NY, 86; Galerie Kwartijin Amsterdam, The Neth, 86; Nat Acad Design, NY, 86; mus exhibs, NC Mus Art, Raleigh, NC, 59, Riverside Mus, NY, 62, Guild Hall Mus, East Hampton, NY, 79, Hempstead Mus, Hempstead, NY, 86 & Laforet Mus, Tokyo, Japan, 87; group exhibs, Boston Arts Festival, 54, Image Gallery, Stockbridge, Mass, 71, Lehigh Univ, Bethlehem, PA, 74, Object of Artists, Guild Hall, East Hampton, NY, 84, Jaski Art Gallery, Amsterdam, The Neth, 96, Fed Reserve Bank, NY, 97 and many others. *Teaching:* Instr painting, Brown Univ, 53-55 & Parsons Sch Design, 63-66; assoc prof painting, Wagner Col, 67-88; instr, SUNY New Paltz, NY, 71. *Awards:* Best in Show Award, Guild Hall, 61; Longview Found Grant, 62; Festival Arts Purchase Award, Southampton Col, 68; Best Show Award, Guild Hall, East Hampton, NY, 79; First Prize, Am Inst for Creative Living, Staten Island, NY, 87. *Bibliog:* reviews, Nancy Reynolds (auth), Pembroke Record, 1955, Gordon Brown (auth), Arts Mag, 1973, Phyllis Braff (auth), The E.H. Star, 1983, Rose C.S. Slivka (auth), The E.H. Star, 1986-1988, 1994-1995, 1998 & 1999 and many others. *Media:* Oil. *Publ:* Illusr cover, Sci & Technol, 63. *Dealer:* Owl 57 Galleries 1074 Broadway Woodmere Long Island 11598. *Mailing Add:* 141 Copeces Lane East Hampton NY 11937-1707

ZACK, BADANNA BERNICE
SCULPTOR, WRITER
b Montreal, Que, Can. *Study:* Concordia Univ, Montreal, BA, 64; Rutgers Univ, MFA, 67. *Work:* Concordia Univ, Montreal; Rutgers Univ, Douglass Col, New Brunswick, NJ; Art Gallery Hamilton, Ont; and pvt collections. *Comn:* Cambridge Gallery & Libr, Ont, 94. *Exhib:* Reflecting a Rural Consciousness, traveling in US, Can & France, 78-80; Home Sweet Home, Toronto, Ont, 85; Eighteenth Sculpture Biennial, Antwerp, Belg, 86; Twelfth Int Biennial of Tapestry, Lausanne, Switz, 86; solo exhibs, Tom Thompson Gallery, Owen Sound, Ont, 87, Lynnwood Arts Ctr Simcoe, Ont, 90, Homage to My Grandfather Sculpture Installation Exhib, Justina Barnicke Gallery,

Hart House, Univ Toronto, Ont, 91, Art Gallery Algoma, Sault Ste Marie, Ont, 91, Cambridge Libr & Art Gallery, Ont, 94, Cast Offs, Art Gallery of Mississauga, Ont, 99 & The Pool Room, Justina Barnicke Gallery, Hart House, Univ Toronto, Ont, 99; Perfect Fit, Oakville, Ont, 88; Wild Life Exhib, Koffler Gallery, Toronto, Ont, 96; The Tree Mus, Gravenhurst, Ont, 98; and many others. *Awards:* Arts Grants, Can Coun, 68-69, 74-75 & 78 & Ont Arts Coun, 75-83; Gottlieb Found Grant, 96. *Bibliog:* William Fabrycki (auth), Badanna Zack: L'Enfant terrible, Artmag, 81; Jim Tiley (auth), Badanna Zack at Studio Gallery Nine, Artmag, 83; John Bentley Mays (auth), Hand stiched visions cut from fabric of life, Globe & Mail, 86. *Mem:* Royal Can Acad. *Media:* Miscellaneous. *Publ:* Auth, Toronto: A look back at sculpture during the sculpture conference, 78, Paul Dempsey at the art gallery of Hamilton, 79, Deiter Hastenteufel at Factory 77, 81-82 & The dinner party by Judy Chicago, 82, Artmag; co-producer, Horse to Horsepower (videotape), 83. *Mailing Add:* 83 Elm Grove Ave No 6 Toronto ON M6K 2J2 Canada

ZAFRAN, ERIC MYLES
CURATOR, HISTORIAN
b Malden, Mass, Apr 19, 46. *Study:* Tilton Sch, NH, 63; Brandeis Univ, BA, 67; Inst Fine Arts, NY Univ, MA, 70, PhD, 73. *Collection Arranged:* Master Paintings from the Hermitage (coauth & ed, catalog), Nat Gallery, 75; One Hundred Drawings in the Chrysler Museum (auth catalog), 79; French Salon Paintings from Southern Collections (auth, catalog), High Mus, 82; The Rococo Age (auth, catalog), High Mus, 83; Master Drawings from Titian to Picasso in The Curtis O Baer Collection (auth, catalog), Nat Gallery, 85; Cavaliers and Cardinals: Nineteenth-Century French Anecdotal Paintings (auth, catalog), Taft Mus, 92. *Pos:* Curatorial asst, Rose Art Mus, Waltham, Mass, 65-67; print cataloguer, Parke-Bernet Galleries, New York, 68-71; res asst, Metrop Mus Art, New York, 72-75; chief cur, Chrysler Mus at Norfolk, 76-79; cur Europ art, High Mus, Atlanta, 79-84; cur, Renaissance & Baroque Art, Walters Art Gallery, Baltimore, Md, 84-89; cur, Europ Painting, Mus Fine Art, Boston, formerly; dep dir curatorial affairs, Jewish Mus, New York, 95-97; cur, European Painting, Wadsworth Atheneum, Hartford. *Teaching:* Assoc prof Rembrandt, City Col New York, 75-76; assoc adj, Northern Paintings, Old Dominion Univ, 77-78; assoc prof, French 19th Century Acad Art, Emory Univ, 81 & 83; adj prof, Rennaissance & Baroque Art, Johns Hopkins SCE, 86 & 87; sem, French 18th Century Painting, Mus Fine Arts, Boston, 90. *Mem:* Col Art Asn; Am Asn Mus. *Publ:* European Art in the High Museum, Atlanta, 84; Fifty Old Master Paintings in the Walters Art Gallery, 88; The Forsyth Wickes Collection of Paintings and Drawings in the Museum of Fine Arts, 92; Collecting Italian Baroque Painting in America, 94; French Paintings in the MFA, Boston, 98. *Mailing Add:* 600 Main St Hartford CT 06103

ZAGO, TINO (AGOSTINO) C
PAINTER
b Crespano del Grappa, Italy, 1937; US citizen. *Study:* Lawrence Inst Technol, Mich, BS(archit), 60; Cranbrook Acad Art, MFA(painting), 66; Yale Univ, 69. *Work:* Cranbrook Acad Art, Bloomfield Hills, Mich; State Univ New York at Buffalo; TRW Corp, Cleveland, Ohio; AT&T, Long Lines, Va; and others; TRW Corp, Cleveland, Ohio. *Comn:* Painting, comn by Hyatt Regency Hotel, Aruba, 90; painting, comn by New York Hilton Hotels, 92; painting, comn by Benesch Friedlander Coplan & Aranoff, Cleveland, Ohio, 95. *Exhib:* OK Harris Gallery, NY, 81-98; McIntosh Gallery, Atlanta, Ga, 86 & 89; Tortue Gallery, Santa Monica, Calif, 88; Jaffe Baker Gallery, Boca Raton, Fla, 92; Robert Kidd Gallery, Birmingham, Mich, 96. *Teaching:* Vis artist, Mich State Univ, East Lansing, Yale Univ, New Haven, Conn & Summit Art Ctr, Summit, NJ. *Awards:* Emerging Artist Grant, Nat Endowment Arts, 82; Nat Endowment Arts Grant, 85. *Bibliog:* M H Stolback (auth), Tino Zago, Arts Mag, 81; Theodore F Wolff (auth), Zago's American Vision, The Christian Sci Monitor, 83; Suzanne Muchnic (auth), At the Galleries--Tino Zago, Los Angeles Times, 88. *Media:* Acrylic. *Dealer:* OK Harris Gallery 383 W Broadway New York NY 10012. *Mailing Add:* 376 Broome St 2nd Flr No 3 New York NY 10013

ZAHEDI, CAVEH
FILMMAKER, VIDEO ARTIST
b Washington, DC, Apr 29, 60. *Study:* Yale Univ, BA(philos), 81; Sch Film & Television, Univ Calif, Los Angeles, MFA(film production), 91. *Work:* I Was Possessed by God (film); I Don't Hate Las Vegas Anymore (film); A Little Stiff (with Greg Watkins). *Comn:* Worm (with Jay Rosenblatt), comn by Con Works, Seattle. *Exhib:* Sundance Film Festival, Sundance Inst, Park City, Utah, 91; New Directors/New Films, Mus Mod Art, NY, 91; Pesaro Film Festival, Lincoln Ctr, Pesaro, Italy, 91; Am Independents Ser, WDR Television, Koln, Ger, 92; Towards a New Narrator, Centro Galego Arte Contemporanea, Santiago, Spain, 96. *Teaching:* San Francisco State Univ, 99-2000; Acad Art Col, San Francisco, 99; City Col, San Francisco, 2000. *Awards:* Rotterdam Film Festival Critics Award, Asn Dutch Critics, 94; Atlanta Film Festival Best Feature, Image Film & Video Ctr, 97; Guggenheim Fel, 97. *Bibliog:* Elizabeth Royle (auth), The Sundance Kids, Details Mag, 91; Jonathan Rosenbaum (auth), A few things well, Chicago Reader, 91; Janet Maslin (auth), The awkward appeal of a young man's chase, NY Times, 91. *Mem:* Independent Feature Project; Film Arts Found. *Media:* Film. *Publ:* Contribr, Treize Facons De Regarder un Merle, Babylone, 84; On Recent Cinema, Passion, 86; Wanting to say thank you, thank you, thank you, The Voyeur, 89; I Love Kath Bloom With Platonic Love, Dear CMJ, 96. *Mailing Add:* 1236 3rd Ave No 3 San Francisco CA 94122

ZAHOUREK, JON GAIL
PAINTER, SCULPTOR
b Oklahoma City, Okla, Jan 5, 40. *Study:* Univ Northern Colo, 58-59; Colo Inst Art, with Charles Dye & John Jellico, cert, 61; New Sch Social Res, 79-81. *Work:* Ariz State Univ Matthews Ctr; City & Co Denver; Oklahoma City Chamber Commerce. *Exhib:* Missouri Valley Drawing, Mulvane Art Ctr, Topeka, Kans, 67; Changing Image of the Indian, Mus NMex, Santa Fe, 70; Colo Biennial, Denver Art Mus, 75; Mainstreams of Am Art, Marietta Col, 76; Am Bronzes, Ariz State Univ, 81; Drawing Defined, Nat Arts Club, NY, 82; solo exhib, Newhouse Gallery, NY, 84. *Teaching:* Instr graphics, Univ Denver, 67; Instr drawing & anatomy, Parsons Sch Design, 78-; instr anatomy, New York Acad, 82- & Art Students League, 84. *Awards:* Second Prize, Black & White on Paper, Nat Arts Club, 82. *Bibliog:* John Jellico (auth), Jon Zahourek--draughtsman, Am Artist, 67. *Mem:* Soc Artists & Anatomists (chmn, 82-84). *Media:* Oil. *Publ:* Auth, Drawings I, pvt publ, 75; Maniken--A Comprehensive Educational System for the Study of Human & Comparative Gross Anatomy, Zahourek Systems Inc, 82. *Mailing Add:* 2198 W 15th St Loveland CO 80538

ZAIKINE, VICTOR (ZAK) EUGENE
SCULPTOR, PAINTER
b Queens, NY, Sept 7, 41. *Study:* Pratt Inst, NY, 59-64, sculpture with Charles Ginnever, 63, also painting with Nicholas Buhalis, 81-83. *Work:* Wright State Univ Mus, Dayton, Ohio; Brooklyn Automotive High Sch, NY. *Comn:* Sculpture, Midwood High Sch, Brooklyn. *Exhib:* Solo exhibs, The Woodstock Yrs and Beyond, 93, Sebastopol Ctr Arts 20 X 1, Calif, 95, New Works, Franki Waters Gallery, Bodega Bay, Calif, 96, Tribute to Landscape, Impressions Gallery, Healdsburg, Calif, 97, The Joyful Feeling Again, Santa Rosa, Calif, 98, A Survey of Studio Ceramics: 1998-2002, C Street Gallery, Davis, Calif & And the River Flows Etcetera, Etcetera, Guerneville, Calif; Big Fruit and Big Flowers, State of Calif Bldg, Santa Rosa, Calif, 96; The Joyful Feeling Again, Mendocino, Calif, 97; Raining Cats and Dogs, Studio Gallery, Alameda, Calif, 98; Magical Lillies, New Ceramics Wimberly, Sable V Fine Art Gallery, Tex, 98; Art Full Living at Home and with Art, Sebastopol, Calif, 98; Getting the Pearls and New Sprit, Bodega, Calif, 98; Laguna Gloria Art Mus, Austin, Tex; Heckscher Mus, Huntington, NY; Woodstock Mus and Hist Soc, NY; and others. *Pos:* 1st Ann Woodstock Guild-Members Show, Kleinert Art Ctr, 85; Adjudicator, State Grants, Mich Coun Arts, 88; exhib Form & Line, Woodstock Artist Asn, Woodstock, NY, 88; cur, Working in Woodstock, Six contemp artists, Pittsfield Arts Ctr, Pittsfield, Mass. *Awards:* First Place, Fiesta de Artes, Los Gatos, Calif, 76; Distinction Award, State Univ NY, Albany, 85; Best of Show, Laquinta Arts Found, 86. *Bibliog:* Tram Combs (auth), Zak Zaikine's drypoints, 12/23/82 & Zaikine's tribute to the landscape, 6/1/83, Woodstock Times; Bernard Bovasso (auth), Zaikine's works defy morality, Daily Freeman, 5/31/83; Rebecca Daniels (auth), Zak Zaikine, Woodstock Times, Vol 14, No 25, NY, 85; Olivia Casey (auth), Zak's magic, Sonoma Index-Tribune, Calif, 2/21/86. *Mem:* Sonoma Co Arts Coun; Woodstock Arts Asn Inc; Cooperstown Art Asn Inc; Woodstock Guild Craftsmen Inc; Sebastopol Ctr for Arts; Asn Clay and Glass. *Media:* Steel, Mixed; Bronze. *Dealer:* Landmark Gallery Bodega CA. *Mailing Add:* 8885 Oak Grove Ave Sebastopol CA 95472

ZAIMA, STEPHEN GYO
PAINTER, SCULPTOR
b San Jose, Calif, Jan 3, 47. *Study:* Pratt Inst, 68; Sch Visual Arts, New York, 68; Calif State Univ, San Jose, BA, 69; Univ Calif, Davis, MFA, 71. *Work:* Univ Calif, Davis & Veterans Mem Bldg, Long Beach. *Comn:* Long Beach Mural, Calif Arts Coun, 83. *Exhib:* Gallery Tamura, Tokyo, Japan, 74; Queens Mus, NY, 85; Everson Mus Art, Syracuse, NY, 85; City Univ NY Grad Ctr, 86; Stephen Rosenberg Gallery, 86; McNay Found, 87; One Penn Plaza, NY, 87. *Teaching:* Syracuse Univ, 80-. *Awards:* Fel, Nat Endowment Arts, 74; Grant, Ford Found, 80 & 81; Fel, Edward Albee Found, 81. *Bibliog:* Peter Morrin (auth), article, Atlanta Art Papers, 3/80; Vered Lieb (auth), A study of scale, Arts Mag, 2/87; Kenneth Baker (auth), catalog essay, Everson Mus Art, 85. *Media:* Oil; Mixed. *Publ:* Contribr, Contesting the Boundaries Between Liberal & Professional Educ, Syracuse Univ Press, 88. *Mailing Add:* One Schneiders Ln Ruby NY 12475

ZAJAC, JACK
SCULPTOR
b Youngstown, Ohio, Dec 13, 29. *Study:* Scripps Col, 49-53; also with Millard Sheets, Henry McFee & Sueo Serisawa; Am Acad in Rome. *Work:* Whitney Mus Am Art, Mus Mod Art, NY; Los Angeles Mus Art; Pa Acad Fine Arts, Philadelphia; Israel Mus, Jerusalem; Hirshhorn Mus & Sculpture Garden, Washington; plus others. *Comn:* Reynolds Metals Co, 68; Wells Fargo Bank Plaza, Beverly Hills, Calif; Univ Calif, Santa Cruz; Civic Ctr Mall, Inglewood, Calif; Civic Ctr Plaza, Huntington Beach, Calif. *Exhib:* Whitney Mus Ann, 59; Recent Sculpture USA, Mus Mod Art, 59; Am Painting, Va Mus Fine Arts, Richmond, 62; Fifty California Artists, Whitney Mus Mod Art, NY, 62-63; Pittsburgh Int, Carnegie Inst, 65; retrospectives, Newport Harbor Art Mus, Balboa, Calif, 65, Temple Univ, Rome, 69, Santa Barbara Mus, 75 & Fine Arts Gallery San Diego, 75; Stephen Wirtz Gallery, San Francisco, Calif, 84 & 87; Monterey Penninsula Mus Art, Calif, 88; Palo Alto Cult Ctr, Calif, 88; Jack Zajac Sculpture: 1954-1987, Art Special Gallery, Oakland Mus, Calif, 90; Art Mus Santa Cruz Coun, Calif, 93; solo exhibs, Art Mus Santa Cruz Co, Calif, 93, Acad Art Col, San Francisco, 96 & Meditations on Falling Water & Other Works, Frederick Spratt, Calif, 97; Sculptor Exhib, Acad Art Col, San Francisco, 94; Still Working, Former IBM Gallery, NY, 95; Lost Wax Foundry Friends III, Conley Art Gallery, Calif State Univ, Fresno, 96. *Teaching:* Instr, Pomona Col, 59; prof, Univ Calif, Santa Cruz, retired. *Awards:* Artist-in-residence, Am Acad in Rome, 68; artist-in-residence, Dartmouth Col, 70; artist in residence, Univ Calif, Santa Cruz, 69-70. *Bibliog:* Kenneth Baker (auth), San Francisco Chronicle, 3/31/88; Mary Ann Toal (auth), Jack Zajac, Art Calif, 10-11/89; Susan Greer (auth), Un-Sitely specific, Artweek, 11/30/89. *Mem:* Nat Acad (assoc, 81, acad, 02-). *Media:* Bronze, Marble. *Mailing Add:* c/o Stephen Wirtz Gallery 49 Geary St 3rd Flr San Francisco CA 94108

ZAKANITCH, ROBERT RAHWAY
PAINTER
b Elizabeth, NJ. *Study:* Newark Sch Fine & Indust Art. *Work:* Whitney Mus Am Art, NY; Munich Mus Mod Art, WGer; Philadelphia Mus, Pa; Wadsworth Atheneum, Hartford, Conn; Phoenix Mus, Ariz; Hirshhorn Mus & Sculpture Garden, Washington; Rothschild Bank, Zurich, Switz; AT&T, NY; High Mus, Atlanta, Ga. *Exhib:* The Expressionist Image: Am Art from Pollock to Today, Sidney Janis Gallery, NY, 82; The Restoration of Painterly Figuration, Kitakyushu Munic Mus Art, Japan, 84; Works on Paper, Robert Miller Gallery, NY, 85; An Am Renaissance: Painting and Sculpture Since 1940 (with catalog), Mus Art, Ft Lauderdale, Fla, 86; one-man show, Sidney Janis Gallery, NY, 90, Jason McCoy Gallery, NY, 94, Hirschl/Adler Modern, NY, 97, Spike Gallery, NY, 03; Patricia Faure Gallery, Los Angeles, 97 & 2003; Spike Gallery, 2005. *Teaching:* Painting, Univ Calif, San Diego, 73; vis artist, Chicago Art Inst, 78; instr drawing & painting, Ok Summer Arts Inst, 89, 90 & 91-. *Awards:* Guggenheim Fel, 95. *Bibliog:* Cover review, Art in Am, 10/94; Arthur Danto (auth), Colossal canvases, Nation, 3/94; John Perreault (auth), Patterning, Artforum, 11/78; John Ashbery (auth), Climbing the wallpaper, NY Mag, 1/29/79; Carter Ratcliff (auth), Art in Am, The Politics of Ornamentation, 4/98. *Mailing Add:* 119 N 11th St Brooklyn NY 11211

ZAKIAN, MICHAEL
MUSEUM DIRECTOR, CURATOR
b New York, NY, April 7, 57. *Study:* Columbia Univ, BA, 79; Rutgers Univ, MA, 84, PhD, 94. *Collection Arranged:* Agnes Pelton: Poet of Nature, 95; Nathan Oliveira: The Wind Hover, 96; Sam Francis: The Archetypes Image, 97; Historical Landscapes of Malibu, 98; Sanoro Chia: New Paintings, 99; Peter Lodato: From Installation to Painting, 2000. *Pos:* assoc cur, Palm Springs Desert Mus, 86-95; dir, Pepperdine Univ Federick Weisman Mus of Art, 95-. *Teaching:* instr modern art Rutgers Univ, NJ, 85; instr American art Calif State Univ, San Bernardino, 89; instr modern art, Univ of the Redlands, Calif. *Mem:* Art Historians of Southern Calif (vp 2000, pres 2001). *Interests:* abstract expressionism, modern American art. *Publ:* Auth, Barnett Newmon and the Sublime, Arts Mag, 2/88; Barnett Newmon: Paintings and a Sense of Place, Arts Mag, 3/88. *Mailing Add:* Pepperdine Univ Frederick R Weisman Mus of Art 24255 Pacific Coast Hwy Malibu CA 90263

ZAKIN, MIKHAIL
SCULPTOR, EDUCATOR
b Brooklyn, NY, June 23, 20. *Study:* Sch Mus Fine Arts, Boston, Mass; Art Students League, sculpture with William Zorach & Albino Manca; also ceramics with Karen Karnes & David Weinrib. *Work:* Peat Marwick Art Collection, Montvale, NJ; Brooklyn Mus; Nagamatso Collection, Japan; Mobach Potten Bakker, Holland; Epstein Collection, Paris, France. *Exhib:* Am Potters, Mus Arts & Sci, Salt Lake City, 75; Four US Potters, Fair Tree Gallery, 75; Pratt Grad Sch, NY, 75-77; Brooklyn Col, 75-77; Baruch Col, NY, 75-77; Retrospective, Sarah Lawrence Col, 91; Retrospective, Worcester Ctr Craft, 2002. *Pos:* Founder & dir, Old Church Cult Ctr & Sch Art, Demarest, NJ, 74-; potters sem leader, England, 76, Japan, 77, Mexico, 78, Italy, 79, China, 81, Holland, 82 & Korea, 83; co-founder, Scotland-North Coast Continuum, 78-; co-founder, East-West Inst ARts & Sch Art, Old Church Cult Ctr, Demarest, NJ. *Teaching:* Advan ceramics instr, Greenwich House Pottery, 71-75; head ceramics dept, Brooklyn Mus Art Sch, 72-75 & Sarah Lawrence Col, 76-90; instr, Castle Hill Ctr Arts, Mass, 76-. *Awards:* Lebensburger Found Grant, 74; Craftsmen's Fel, NJ Coun Arts, 75 & Nat Endowment Arts, 76; NJ State Coun, 89. *Bibliog:* Elsbeth Woody (auth), Hand Building Ceramics, Farrar Strauss Giroux, 79; Anthony Padovano (auth), Sculpture Practice, Doubleday, 81; Nino Caruso (auth), Ceramica Raku, Hoepli-Milano, 82. *Mem:* Am Crafts Coun; World Crafts Coun; Nat Conf Ceramic Educators; NY Artist Craftsman; Korea Cult Coun (video documentation grant, project dir Korean pottery making 82, 83, 84). *Media:* Clay. *Interests:* Visual commun in the arts. *Publ:* Contribr, Poletechnic Design, Korea, 84, Keranos-Madrid, 86; Jack Troy & Watson Guptil (auth), Salt Glaze Ceramics, 77; Padouado (auth), Process of Sculpture, Double Day, 81; Hand Built Ceramics, Lark Book Tripplet. *Mailing Add:* 37 County Rd Closter NJ 07624

ZALESCH, SAUL E
EDUCATOR
b Baltimore, Md, Jan 7, 52. *Study:* Johns Hospkins, BA, 73; Univ Del, MA, 84, PhD, 92. *Teaching:* Ast Prof, La Tech Univ, 94-2000, assoc prof, 2000-. *Mem:* N Central La Arts Coun; CAA; Popular Culture Asn; Am Studies Asn. *Mailing Add:* 212 E Louisiana Ave Ruston LA 71270

ZALESKI, JEAN
PAINTER, LECTURER
b Malta; US citizen. *Study:* Art Students League; New Sch, New York; Pratt Inst, New York; Parsons Sch Design, New York; Moore Col Art, Philadelphia. *Work:* Mus City NY; Va Ctr Creative Arts; Metrop Mus Art; NY Pub Libr; Nat Mus Fine Arts, Malta. *Exhib:* Faces, Philadelphia Mus Art, 71; Works on Paper--Women Artists, Brooklyn Mus, NY, 75; one-person shows, Va Ctr Creative Arts, 81 & Elaine Starkman Gallery, NY, 86, Citicorp Ctr, NY, 88-89, "Z" Gallery, NY, 91, Sweet Briar Col, Va, 93, Trinity Col, Hartford Conn, 96, A/E Gallery, NY, 96 & Myung Sook Lee Gallery, NY, 97-98, Retrospective: Four Decades of Painting, Westbeth Gallery, NY, 2000, St James Cavalier Ctr for Creativity, Malta, Europe, 2002; group shows, Bayly Mus, Charlottesville, Va, 86 & Albright-Knox Art Gallery, Buffalo, NY, 86; New Acquisitions, Mus City NY, 94. *Collection Arranged:* Pfizer, Inc.; Cargill, Ltd. *Pos:* Exec coordr, Women in the Arts Found, 75-77; spec appt 5-mem adv comt, White House, Washington, DC, 3/77. *Teaching:* Instr drawing & painting & art dir, Studio 733 Art Sch, Great Neck, NY, 63-67; instr life drawing, Hussian Col Art, Philadelphia, 70-71; instr drawing & painting, Am Studies Ctr, Naples, Italy, 72-73 & Northern Atlantic Treaty Orgn Hq, Naples, 72-73; adj lectr painting, Brooklyn Col, 74-76 & Hofstra Univ, Hempstead, NY, 77; instr, Cooper Union, NY, 86-. *Awards:* Va Ctr Creative Arts Fel, 75-2005; Susan B Anthony Award, Nat Orgn Women, NY, 86; Ragdale Found Fel, 86-2005; MacDowell fel, 1970-2005; Gold medal Int Women's Art Festival, Cannes, France, 1970. *Bibliog:* Joan Marter (auth), Pasture forms, 2/79 & exhib rev, 5/79, Arts Mag; Shiela Elliot (auth), The Allure of Shifting Light, Artists' Mag, 9/87; book/catalog, Malta: Memories and Explorations, 89-2001; Tracy Cochran (auth), profile, Ms Mag; catalog, A Retrospective, Four Decades of Painting, 2000. *Mem:* Women in the Arts; Artists Equity. *Media:* Acrylic, Oil. *Interests:* music; writing. *Collection:* Pfizer Inc, Cargill Ltd. *Publ:* Isolation as Inspiration, Women Artist' News, 81; coauth (with Edwin Honig), Cow-Lines, Copper Beech Press, 82; auth, Day in the life, Artists Mag, 9/85; Catalog 2000 Four Decades of Painting - A Retrospective Exhibit, 00; auth, Winged Spirits, Bayeux Arts Publ, 95; book/catalog, Malta, Memories and Explorations, 2002. *Dealer:* Dir Jack Dowling Westbeth Gallery 155 Bank St NYC 10014. *Mailing Add:* 55 Bethune St 807A New York NY 10014

ZALLINGER, JEAN DAY
ILLUSTRATOR, EDUCATOR
b Boston, Mass, Feb 15, 1918. *Study:* Mass Col of Art, cert (drawing & painting), 35-39; Yale Sch Fine Arts, BFA, 42. *Work:* Kerlan Found; Univ Minn; Rutgers Univ; Univ Southern Miss; De Grummond, permanent collection, Paint & Clay Club, NH; Univ Conn Collection. *Exhib:* Dinosaurs Past & Present, Los Angeles Co Mus Natural Hist (travel US & Europe), 86-90; Aetna Gallery, Hartford; Mass Col Art, 92; Mellon Gallery, Cheshire, Conn, 94. *Pos:* Tech illus draftsman, Applied Physics Lab, Univ Wash, Seattle, 51-53. *Teaching:* Prof drawing & illusr, Paier Col Art, Hamden, Conn. *Awards:* Nat Sci Teachers Awards for Biography of a Fish Hawk & I Watch Flies, 77; Alumna of the Year, 92; Mass Col Art, 92. *Bibliog:* NH Register, 1/83; Rocks & Minerals, Heldref Publ, 3-4/92. *Mem:* Paint & Clay Club, New Haven, Conn; Arts Coun New Haven; Artspace, New Haven; Soc Children's Book Writers. *Publ:* Biography of a Fish Hawk, Putnam Bk, 77; Nature's Champions, 80, Dinosaurs, Asteroids & Super Stars, 82, Baby Dinosaurs, 84, Sharks, 86, Whales, 87 & Eagles, 88, Lothrop Lee Shepard; Sesame St Q & A Book About Animals, 83; Monsters of the Sea, Little Brown, 90-; The Earliest Americans, Clarion, 93. *Mailing Add:* c/o Paier Col 20 Gorham Ave Hamden CT 06514

ZALOUDEK, DUANE
PAINTER
b Enid, Okla, Jan 15, 31. *Study:* Portland Mus Art Sch, Ore, cert, 56. *Work:* Portland Art Mus, Ore; Dallas Mus Fine Arts, Tex; Aargauer Kunsthaus, Aarau, Switz; Schweizerische Landesbibliothek, Bern, Switz. *Exhib:* Various exhib, Portland Art Mus, 49-86; Northwest Ann, Seattle Art Mus, 59-68; W Coast Ann, San Francisco Art Mus, 60-61; W Coast Now, Los Angeles City Mus, 68; Watercolors, Akron Art Inst, Ohio, 76; Radikal Auf Papier, Aargauer Kunsthaus, Aarau, Switz, 90; 3Ness, Mus Dhondt-Dhaenes, Deurle, Belgium, 2000; Das Gedachtnis Der Malerei, Aargauer Kunsthaus, Aarau, Switz, 2000; 26 solo exhibs, 55-2005. *Teaching:* Artist-in-residence, Portland Univ, 62-65; vis artist, Univ Calif, Davis, 70-73. *Awards:* Adolph Gottlieb Found Award, 78; Mark Rothko Found Award, 86; Nat Endowment Arts, 87. *Bibliog:* Charlotte Hughes (auth), A profile, Univ Portland Rev, 65; Tiffany Bell (auth), article, Arts Mag, 4/78. *Media:* Acrylic, Oil, Watercolor. *Specialty:* Contemp Art. *Dealer:* Galerie Mark Muller Gessnerallee 36 CH8001 Zurich Switz; Akira Ikeda Gallery Nagoya Japan & New York NY. *Mailing Add:* 431 E 12th St New York NY 10009

ZALUCHA, PEGGY FLORA
PAINTER
b Peoria, Ill, Sept 18, 48. *Work:* Lakeview Mus Arts & Scis, Peoria, Ill; Hoyt Inst Fine Art, New Castle, Pa; Brea Mus Fine Art, Calif; Paine Mus Art, Oshkosh, Wis; Charles A Wustum Mus Fine Art, Racine, Wis. *Comn:* Seventeen paintings, Wis Chamber Orchestra, Madison, 83-2000; six paintings, 84 & two mem paintings, 88 & 93, Dane Co, Madison, Wis, 88; painting, Madison Civic Ctr, Wis, 87. *Exhib:* Nat Watercolor Soc Exhibs, Brea Cult Ctr, Calif, 82, 83, 87, 89-92; Nat Soc Painters Casein & Acrylic Exhib, Nat Arts Club, NY, 83, 84, 89, 92; Rocky Mountain Nat Watermedia Exhib, Foothills Art Ctr, Golden, Colo, 85, 88, 89, 92, 93 & 94; solo exhibs, West Bend Gallery Fine Art, Wis, 86, Lakeview Mus (exhib catalog), Peoria, Ill, 90, Neville Mus, Green Bay, Wis, 91 & Wis Acad Fine Arts, Madison, 91. *Awards:* Best of Show, Nat Watercolor Soc Exhib, 87; Century Merit Award, Rocky Mountain Nat Watermedia Exhib, Foothills Art Ctr, 88 & 92; Nat Galleries Award, Nati Watercolor Soc Exhib, Nat Galleries, 91. *Bibliog:* Bebe Raupe (auth), Award winning watercolorists, Artists Mag, 7/88; William C Landwehr (auth), Defining light with tight control, Am Artist Mag, 9/90; Gerald Brommer (auth), Understanding Transparent Watercolor, Davis Publ Inc, 93. *Mem:* Am Watercolor Soc; Nat Watercolor Soc; Nat Soc Painters Casein & Acrylic; Midwest Watercolor Soc; Wis Painters & Sculptors/Artists All Media, (chap bd 88-). *Media:* Transparent Watercolor, Acrylic on Paper. *Mailing Add:* 109 Sunset Lane Mount Horeb WI 53572-1865

ZAMMITT, NORMAN
PAINTER, SCULPTOR
b Toronto, Ont, Feb 3, 31; US citizen. *Study:* Pasadena City Col, AA, 57; Otis Art Inst, MFA, 61. *Work:* Mus Mod Art, NY; Hirshhorn Mus, NY; Libr Cong, Washington, DC; Otis Art Gallery, Los Angeles; Larry Aldrich Mus, Conn. *Exhib:* Mus Mod Art, NY, 65 & Show of New Acquisitions, 67; Am Sculpture of the Sixties, Los Angeles Co Mus Art & Philadelphia Mus Art, 67; Metromedia, Los Angeles; one-man shows, Los Angeles Co Mus Art, 77 & Corcoran Gallery, 78. *Awards:* Tamarind Fel, 67; Guggenheim Mem Found Fel, 68. *Bibliog:* Various articles in Art Int, Artforum, Art in Am & Los Angeles Times. *Mailing Add:* 233 N Wilson Ave Pasadena CA 91106

ZAMOISKI SEGAL, CLAIR
CURATOR, ARTS ADMINISTRATOR
b Baltimore, Md, Dec 2, 53. *Study:* Univ Pa, BA & MA, 75. *Collection Arranged:* Images of the 70's: 9 Washington Artists (auth, catalog), Corcoran Gallery Art, 80 & John Dickson-Ed Mayo (auth, catalog), 80; 22nd Area Exhib: Works on Paper, 80; Personal Narratives: Will Brunner-John Ryan, 80; Collage on Paper, 81; Corcoran After Hours, 81; Narrative Wood, 81; On-going Dialogue: Andrew Hudson-Blaine Larson, 81; Video, 82, 38th Corcoran Biennial Exhibition of American Painting, (with catalog), 83 & Watercolors Washington (with catalog), 84, Corcoran Gallery Art. *Pos:* Curatorial asst, Solomon R Guggenheim Mus, New York, 76-78, curatorial coordr, 78; assoc cur contemp art, Washington Region, Corcoran Gallery Art, DC, 79-84; dir, Mayors Adv Comm Art Culture, Baltimore, Md, 87-. *Mem:* Col Art Asn

ZANSKY, MICHAEL
PAINTER, SCULPTOR, PHOTOGRAPHER
b New York City, 47. *Study:* Boston Univ, Sch Fine Arts, BFA, 69. *Work:* Brooklyn Mus, NY; De Cordova Mus, Lincoln, Mass; Neuberger Mus, Purchase, NY; Prudential Life, NY; Whitney Mus, NY; Berkeley Art Mus, Berkeley, Calif. *Exhib:* Solo Exhib, Cavin-Morris Gallery, NY, Veem Gallery, Philadelphia, Pa, Gallery Camino Real, Boca Raton, Fla, Universal Concepts Unlimited, NY, 2000; John Michael Kohler Art Ctr, Sheboygan, Wis, 2000; Norton Mus, West Palm Beach, Fla, 2001; Briggs Robinson Gallery, NY, 2003; Slought Found, Philadelphia, Pa, 2003; Am Panopticon, Gigantic Art Space (GAS), 2005; Aldrich Mus Contemp Art, Ridgefield, Conn, 2006. *Pos:* Production designer, master set painter. *Awards:* Fulbright-Hayes Fel, Peru; Louis Comfort Tiffany Found Award, 78; Fel, Creative Artists Pub Serv. *Bibliog:* Christopher Chambers (auth), Sculpture Mag, 2003; Raymond Jon (auth), Artforum, 2004. *Mem:* Sculpture Guild, NY; United Scenic Artists, NY. *Media:* Painting, optics, sculpture, photog. *Specialty:* Comtemp Art. *Publ:* Gerrit Henry (auth), Art in Am, 2000. *Dealer:* Berry Hill Gallery 11 E 70th St NY; Briggs Robinson Gallery 527 W 29th St NY; Gigantic Art Space 59 Franklin St NY. *Mailing Add:* PO Box 42 West Nyack NY 10994

ZAPEL, ARTHUR LEWIS
ILLUSTRATOR BOOKS, PAINTER
b Chicago, Ill, Nov 17, 21. *Study:* Columbia Col Radio & Theatrical Arts, 40; Univ Wis, BA, 46. *Work:* Pikes Peak Ctr, Colorado Springs, Colo; Koshare Indian Mus, La Junta, Colo. *Comn:* Off mural, Meriwether Pub Ltd, Colorado Springs, 84. *Exhib:* Artists of the West, Pioneer Mus, Colorado Springs, 92; Rotary Art Show, Pioneer Mus, Colorado Springs, 93; Colorado Springs Opera Festival Exhib, Pikes Peak Ctr, 94, 95, 96 & 97; Arts Students League Exhib, Smoke Brush Ctr Arts, Colorado Springs, 94; Country Club Colo, 2000; Colorado Springs Open Festival, 94-2000. *Pos:* Creative dir, Kling Studios, Chicago, 52-54; writer & producer, J Walter Thompson Advert, Chicago, 54-70; pres, Arthur Meriwether Inc, 70-83, chmn, exec; chmn, exec ed, Meriwether Publ Ltd. *Awards:* DuKane Gold Camera Award, US Indust Film Festival, 83; Gold Award, Houston Int Film Festival, 84. *Mem:* Arts Students League (pres, 92-93). *Media:* Oil, Alkyds. *Publ:* Illusr, 'Twas the Night Before, Meriwether Publ, 93; ed, Theatre Alive, Meriwether Publ, 93; illusr, The Jabberwocky, Meriwether Publ, 94; auth, Sweet Uncertainty (novel). *Dealer:* Ravens Gallery, Westcliffe, CO. *Mailing Add:* 228 Cobblestone Dr Colorado Springs CO 80906-4803

ZAPKUS, KES (KESTUTIS) EDWARD
PAINTER
b Dabikine, Lithuania, Apr 22, 38; US citizen. *Study:* Art Inst Chicago, BFA, 60; Syracuse Univ, Ryerson fel, 60, MFA, 62. *Work:* Stedelijk Mus, Amsterdam, Holland; Hirshhorn Mus, Washington, DC; Va Mus Fine Arts, Richmond; Art Inst Chicago; Carnegie-Mellon Inst; and others. *Exhib:* Solo exhibs, Paula Cooper Gallery, 71, 73, 75, 77 & 79, Galerie Darthea Speyer, Paris, 78, John Weber Gallery, NY, 81, 82 & 74 & Hecksher Mus, Huntington, NY, 82; Inst Contemp Art, Boston, 75; Butler Inst Am Art, Youngstown, Ohio, 76; Comino a Cuba, Museo Universitario Chopo, Mex City, 86; Mus Fine Arts, Budapest, Hungary, 89; Retrospective, Vilnius Mus Fine Arts, 89; A Zarre Gallery, 95; and others. *Teaching:* Princeton, Parsons Sch Design, Univ Pa & State Univ NY. *Awards:* Invitational First Prize, Chicago Arts Festival, 64; Creative Artists Pub Serv Grant, 78; Nat Endowment Arts Grant, 79. *Bibliog:* Lucy Lippard (auth), Battle cries, Village Voice, 12/4/84; Ron Warren (auth), Kes Zapkus at John Weber, Arts, 1/85; Kenneth Baker (auth), Kes Zapkus at John Weber, Art Am, 3/85. *Media:* Oil. *Dealer:* John Weber Gallery 142 Greene New York NY 10012. *Mailing Add:* 35 Bond St New York NY 10012

ZARAND, JULIUS JOHN
PAINTER, RESTORER
b Nagyvarad, Hungary, June 27, 13; Can citizen. *Study:* Royal Acad, dipl & dipl(educ); also with Oskar Kokoschka, Salzburg, Austria; Acad Ital, Dipl Hon Causa Maestro Pittura, 83. *Work:* City Hall, Halifax, NS; Yokahama Univ Gallery, Japan; Art Bank Nova Scotia; Govt House, PEI. *Comn:* Portrait of Pope Pius XII, comn by Prime Cardinal of Hungary, 38; portrait, comn by Lord Thompson, Toronto, 54; murals, St Bridgid Church, Toronto, 55; portrait of Sir John Thompson, City of Halifax, NS, 68; portraits of all presidents of the co, Maritime Telegraph & Telephone Co, Halifax, NS; murals, Veterans Mem Hosp, Halifax, 88; and others. *Exhib:* One-man shows, Halifax Libr, 64, Lafayette Art Ctr, Ind, 69, Purdue Univ Gallery, 69, Zwicker's Gallery, Halifax, 70, Lunenburg Art Gallery, Lunenburg, NS, 89 & Annapolis Valley MacDonald Mus, Middleton, NS, 94. *Teaching:* Asst prof fine arts, St Mary's Univ, Halifax, 56-65. *Awards:* Goid Medal, Acad Italy, 81; Primo Oscar D'italia, 85; Centauro d'Oro, Acad Italy, 88. *Mem:* Acad Ital; Lunenburg Co, Art Coun; Art Gallery NS; Art Gallery, Lunenburg. *Media:* Oil, Egg Tempera. *Mailing Add:* Chester Basin NS B0J 1K0 Canada

ZAUSNER, TOBI
PAINTER
b New York, NY, Oct 8, 42. *Study:* Hunter Col, BFA (studio art & art hist), 63; NY Univ, MA (studio art & art theory), 83, Icasa Fel, Int Art Symp, 83, PhD (art & psychology), 93. *Work:* Mus Stony Brook, NY; Williams Ctr Arts, Rutherford, NJ; Art Students League, Mus City New York, NY; Bellevue Hosp, NY; Armenian Archdioces, Venice, Italy; Mus City of New York; Am Mus Natural Hist; NY Pub Libr Print Collection; Bancroft Pub Libr, Univ Calif, Berkeley; numerous private collections. *Comn:* commn by Lena Albert, Santa Fe, Iris and Stanley Ashkinoz, NY, Leslie Bauman, NY, Charles Biderman, Los Angeles. *Exhib:* In Her Own Image, Philadelphia Mus Art, Fleischer Mem, 73; Heresies Show, Grey Art Gallery, NY, 81; Figure in Landscape, Artists' Choice Mus, NY, 85; solo-show, Vision Quest, William Carlos Williams Ctr Arts, 93, Adobe Gallery, NJ, 95, Nat Asn Women Ann Exhib, NY, 96, Small Works Show, Gallery Art 54, NY, 1997, Johnson Gallery, Bedminster, NJ, 1998, Nat Asn Women Artists, NY, 1999, Fragments: Collage and Assemblage, ISE Art Found, NY, 2000, Small Things Considered: A Large Show of Small Works, Elizabeth Found, NY, 2001; The Big Picture, Javits Fed Bldg, NY, 94; Nat Asn Women Ann Exhib, NY, 96; Small Works Show, Gallery Art 54, NY, 97; Continuity and Change, New World Art Ctr, NY, 98; Johnson Gallery, Bedminster, NJ, 98; Nati Asn of Women Artists, New York City, 99; Fragments: Collage and Assemblage, ISE Art Found, New York City, 2000; Small Things Considered: A Large Show of Small Works, Elizabeth Found, New York City, 2001; Ann Exhib, Nat Assoc of Women Artists, New York City, 2002-2003; Meditations on War, NAWA, New York City, 2004, Small Works Exhib, NAWA Gallery, NY, 2005, Women & Spirituality, Interchurch Center, NY, 2006. *Collection Arranged:* The Mus of the City of New York; The American Mus of Natural History; The New York Public Library Print Collection; The Bancroft Library, Univ of California, Berkeley; Williams Cente for the Arts, Rutherford, NJ; The Long Island Mus, Stony Brook, NY. *Pos:* Chair art/art hist, Soc for Chaos Theory in Psychology & the Life Sci, 93-; moderator/chair, Symp on Chaos Theory & the Creative Process, Johns Hopkins Univ, 94. *Teaching:* Guest lectr psychology art, NY Univ, 85, 90, 91 & 93; instr psychology art/art theory, New Sch Social Res, NY Col, 94-; CG Jung Ctr, NY, 96-98; Saybrook Grad Sch, 98-2000; lectr, participant symposia in field. *Awards:* Gottlieb Award, A & E Gottlieb Found, 90; Susan Kahn Award, Nat Asn Women Artists, 92; Drawing reproduced in Parabola, 2002-2003; chair, Symp Challenges and Creativity, 113th ann Conv of the Am Psychological Assoc in Wash, DC. *Bibliog:* Peter Frank (auth), Where is New York, Art News, 11/79; Art centers around Native Americans, Twin-Boro News, NJ, 7/23/93; Eileen Watkins (auth), Art, Sunday Star Ledger, NJ, 7/25/93. *Mem:* Nat Asn Women Artists; Soc Chaos Theory Psychology & Life Sci; Archive Res Archetypal Symbolism; Am Psychological Asn, Div Psychology & Arts & Div Humanistic Psychology (chmn symposium film on art & disabilities). *Media:* Oil, Acrylic. *Res:* Psychology of art; research in creativity; non-linear dynamics; psychology of art in the Renaissance. *Interests:* physics. *Publ:* Georgia O'Keefe, Encyl Creativity, Acad Press, San Diego, Calif, 98; Chaos, Dict Symbols, Arch Res Archetypal Symbolism, 98; When Walls Become Doorways: Creativity, Chaos, Theory and Physical Illness, Creativity Res J, Vol II, 1, 98; Utke's Rainbow: Phenomenology, Mythology, and Physical Science in Dialogues, summer 99; contribr, Trembling-Trembling Patients in Panic-Patients in Awe, 99; Psychological revelations: the outsider artists of hospital audiences, inc, Bull Div 10 Psychology & Arts, Am Psychol Asn, 2000; Trembling and nscendance: chaos theory, panic attacks, and awe, Psychotherapy Patient vol 11, no 1-2, 1999, & chpt in Trembling-Trembling, Patients in Panic-Patients in Awe, 2000; The Transcendent profane: recognizing the hidden self, in Psychotherapy Patient, 2002; The Mind's mirror: visual art, in Bull Psychology and Arts Div 10, Am Psychol Asn, 2002; When Walls Become Doorways: Creativity and the Transforming Illness, Harmony, 2006. *Mailing Add:* 137 E 38th St No 6J New York NY 10016

ZED, AGGIE
SCULPTOR
b Charleston, SC, Nov 13, 52. *Study:* Univ SC, BFA, 74. *Work:* Fed Reserve Bank, Richmond, Va. *Exhib:* Southern Comfort Discomfort, Mint Mus, Charlotte, NC, 86; Rock Holders, Med Col Va, Richmond, Va, 88; Sally Brown Interiors (drawings), Richmond, 4-6/92; one-person shows, Nina Liu & Friends (sculptures & drawings), Charleston, SC, 5/93, Corp Mus Frame (drawings), Richmond, Va, 93, Paintings, Sweetbriar Coll, Va, 2000, Scrap Floats and Jetsam, Astra Design, Va, 2001; Va Women in clay (sculpture), Sweetbriar Col, Va, 93; Nina Liu Sculpture & Drawings, Charleston, SC, 94; Astra Design, Nina Liu, Charleston, SC, 95; and others. *Awards:* Prof Fel, Va Comn Arts, 83; Prof Fel Sculpture, Nat Endowment Arts, 86. *Media:* Clay, Mixed Media. *Dealer:* Nina Liu 24 State St Charleston SC 29401; Somerhill Gallery 3 Eastgate E Franklin St Chapel Hill NC 27514. *Mailing Add:* 2971 Valentine Mill Rd Gordonsville VA 22942

ZEGART , MAR(GARET) JEAN KETTUNEN
ARTIST, EDUCATOR
b Lansing, Mich, Aug 19, 26. *Study:* Univ Calif, Berkeley, MA, 54; Mich State Univ, BA (cum laude). *Exhib:* Ann Juried Exhib, Pasadena Art Mus, 80; Marinscapes, Escalle, Greenbrae, Calif, 1995-98; Works on Paper, Met Mus, 48; Pastel Drawing, Metrop Mus, 48; Invitational Painting Shows, Palace of the legion of Honor, San Francisco, 55-60; solo shows, Wittenborne Schultz Inc, NY; Mus of Modern Art, San Francisco; Marin Co Civic Ctr; Kings Gallery; many others. *Collection Arranged:* Usher Gallery, Lincoln, The Brit Mus, London, Whitney Mus, Mus of Modern Art, NY Pub Libr, Guggenheim Mus, NYC, The Achenbach Graphic Arts Collection, Palace of the Legion of Honor, San Francisco; Museo de Arte Moderna, Sao Paolo, Brazil. *Pos:* Ast to Art Editor, Glamour Mag, New York City, 47-53. *Teaching:* Art Instr, Tamalpais Union High Sch Dist, 61-91; Instr, Fulbright Exchange Teacher, 79-80, Testwood, Winchester Dist; Laserna High Sch, East Whittier, 60-61; Col of Marin, 60. *Awards:* Rockefeller Purchase Award, Brooklyn Mus Print Juried & Invitational Ann, Brazil, 50; Smith Col Purchase Award; Stanford Univ Global Educ

Project; Korea and Hong Kong Arts Instruction and Visual Arts Consultant. *Mem:* Calif Teachers' Asn (life mem); Nat Educator's Asn (life mem); Fine Arts Mus, San Francisco, Calif. *Media:* Copper Engraving; Painitng Oil and Acrylic. *Specialty:* Susan Teller, graphic fine arts, focused on mid 20th century. *Interests:* Poetry and graphics to accompany text folios; Community Planning; Development Advocacy. *Dealer:* Susan Teller Gallery, 568 Broadway, New York, 10012. *Mailing Add:* 118 Highland Lane Mill Valley CA 94941

ZEHR, CONNIE
ART EDUCATOR, SCULPTOR
b Ohio, 38. *Study:* Ohio State Univ, BFA. *Exhib:* Connie Zehr, Taipei Fine Arts Mus, Taiwan, 87; Influence III, West Gallery, Claremont Col Grad Sch, 88; A Woods in the Clearing, Santa Monica Coll Art Gallery, 89; Complementary, Weingart Gallery, Occidental Col, 91; Connie Zehr, Harris Art Gallery, Univ LaVerne, Calif, 98; One-woman shows incl Episodes, Newspace, Los Angeles, 2002. *Teaching:* Vis, artist Calif State Univ Fullerton, 78-80; Claremont Grad Sch, 81; UCLA, 81; Univ Calif Irvine, 81-82; prof, Claremont Grad Sch, 82-, chmn, depart art. *Awards:* Artist Grant, Nat Endowment Arts, 75; Landmark Projects, Art Collaboration, 84; Artist Grant, 86; Mentor Grant, Lorser Feitelson & Helen Lundeberg-Feitelson arts Found, 87. *Mailing Add:* Claremont Grad Art Dept U 251 East 10th St Claremont CA 91711

ZEIDENBERGS, OLAFS
SCULPTOR
b Latvia, Mar 17, 36; US citizen. *Study:* Univ Hartford, BFA, 61; Yale Univ, MFA, 63. *Work:* Morse Col, Yale Univ; Valley Bank & Trust Co, Springfield, Mass; Avon Corp, Rye, NY; McGraw-Hill Corp, NY; Unitarian Soc New Haven, Hamden, Conn. *Exhib:* Outdoor Sculpture, DeCordova Mus, Lincoln, Mass; Four Sculptors & Small Packages, Univ Conn; Mainstreams, Marietta Col; Tex Fine Arts Asn Ann, Austin. *Teaching:* Prof sculpture, Southern Conn State Univ, 66-. *Awards:* Silvermine Guild Artists Award; New Haven Festival Arts Award; Conn Acad Fine Arts Award. *Mem:* Conn Acad Fine Arts. *Media:* Metal, Plastics. *Mailing Add:* 66 N Lake Dr No A1 Hamden CT 06517

ZEIDLER, EBERHARD HEINRICH
ARCHITECT, DESIGNER
b Braunsdorf, Ger, Jan 11, 26; Can citizen. *Study:* Bauhaus Weimar, Cand Arch, 45-48; Karlsruhe Univ, Dipl Ing, 49; McMaster Univ, LLD, 82; Tech Univ NS, DEng 87; Univ Toronto, DArch, 89; York Univ, LLD, 92. *Hon Degrees:* Hon FAIA. *Comn:* Designer, Eaton Ctr, Toronto, 73-79, Can Place, Vancouver, 86; MediaPark, Cologne, 88; Raymond F Kravis Ctr Performing Arts, W Palm Beach, 92-96; Hosp for Sick Children, Toronto, 93. *Pos:* Guest speaker, var world confs; sr partner, Zeidler Partnership/Architects, 80-. *Teaching:* Lectr archit design, Univ Toronto, 53-55; adj prof, Univ Toronto, 83-. *Awards:* Order of Can, 84; 75 national and international design awards; Gold Medal, Royal Archit Inst Can, 86. *Bibliog:* Robert Fulford (auth), The rise and fall of modern architecture, Saturday Night Mag, 80; Geoffrey Simmons (auth), Eberhard Zeidler, City & Country Home, spring 83; Christian W Thomsen (auth), Eberhard Zeidler: In Search of Human Space, Ernst & Sohn, 92. *Mem:* Academician Royal Can Acad Arts; fel Royal Archit Inst Can; Ont Asn Architects; hon fel Am Inst Archits; Archit Inst BC; and others. *Publ:* Auth, Healing the Hospital-McMaster Health Science Centre: Its Conception & Evolution, 74; Multi-Use Architecture in the Urban Contex, Karl Kramer Verlag, 83; and many articles in leading prof mags. *Mailing Add:* 315 Queen St W Toronto ON M5V 2X2 Canada

ZEIGLER, GEORGE GAVIN
PAINTER,SCULPTOR
b Nashville, Tenn, 1962. *Study:* Atlanta Col Art; Pratt Inst, Cert Prog Graphic Arts, NY, 88; Fordham Univ, NY, BA(art hist), 94. *Work:* Peat, Marwick & Mitchell, Loews Vanderbilt Plaza, Nashville, Tenn; Cramer Berkowitz & Co, Freedom Mgt Asn, Inc, NY; Victory Systems Inc, Southport, Conn; Southern Energy Corp Hdqtrs, Atlanta, Ga; Honorable Michael R. Bloomberg, New York City; Judge Phyllis Kravitch, Ark, Ga; The Ritz Carlton, South Beach, Fla; Mr & Mrs William Scharf. *Exhib:* one-man shows, Kenneth Winslow Gallery, 97 & Chuck Levitan Gallery, NY, 97; The Altered Image, Islip Art Mus, East Islip, NY, 97; 11th Ann Art Exhib, Hunter Mus Am Art, Chattanooga, Tenn, 98; Savannah Col Art & Design, Savannah, Ga, 99; Lizan Tops Gallery, NY, 2002; Anita Shapolsky Gallery, New York City, 2003; Springfield Art Mus Springfield Mo, 2004; Red Dot Fine Art, Santa Fe, 2005; World's Exhibition Aichi, Japan, 2005. *Pos:* Admin asst, Hilde Gerst Gallery Inc, NY, 94-95. *Awards:* Exhib Award for Donald Kuspit, 98; First Place Ivan Karp of Okla Harris Gallery, 95; Artist of Month, Liquitex, 2002. *Bibliog:* Erica Weitzman (auth), Illustrations, William & Mary Rev, 97; H I Gliick (auth), Illustrations, New Am Paintings, 97; Phyllis Braff (auth), Subjective & abstract flow in many directions, NY Times, 98; Emerging artist, Art & Antiques Mag, 4/2003. *Mem:* Soc Illustrators; Int Sculpture Ctr. *Media:* Acrylic, Metal,Wood. *Specialty:* Contemporary. *Collection:* E. Vicente; W. Scharf; Y Thomas; H Newman. *Publ:* New American Paintings, H I Glick, Book # 10, 97; Living Artists, Constance Smith, ed. 13th Ed, 2003. *Dealer:* www.GavinZeigler.com. *Mailing Add:* PO Box 137 Shelter Island Heights NY 11965

ZEITLIN, HARRIET
PAINTER, SCULPTOR
b Philadelphia, Pa, Feb 12, 29. *Study:* Pa Acad Fine Arts, Univ Pa, BFA, 46-50; Barnes Found, 49 & 50; Univ Calif, Los Angeles, 63-69. *Work:* Libr Cong; Am Embassy, New Delhi, India; Los Angeles Co Mus Art, Los Angeles Athletic Asn & Grunwald Ctr Graphic Arts, Univ Calif, Los Angeles; Penna Acad Fine Arts. *Comn:* Mixed media painting, comn by City Los Angeles Cult Affairs Dept, 91. *Exhib:* Los Angeles Co Mus Art; Weyhe Gallery, NY; Bernice Steinbaum Gallery, NY; Lobby Gallery/Am Craft Mus, NY; Biblioteque Formey, Paris. *Pos:* Exec bd mem, Los Angeles Printmaking Soc, 64-69; artist/community relations & exec bd mem, Graphic Arts Coun Los Angeles Co Mus Art, 73-75; corresp secy, Artists for Economic Action, 73-74, vpres, 75-76, pres, 77-78 & exec dir CETA Title VI, Art in Pub Places, 77-78. *Teaching:* Mirman Sch Gifted Children, Los Angeles, 80-82; UCLA Exten Artsreach, Univ Calif, Los Angeles, 86; Los Angeles High Sch Music & Art, 88. *Awards:* Calif Arts Coun Grant, 77; Los Angeles City Cult Grant, 90-91. *Bibliog:* Barbara Wilson (auth), Interview, Currant Art Mag, 75; Kathy Zimmerer-McKelvie (auth), Three from Los Angeles, Art Scene, 85; Eleanor Tufts (auth), Am Women Artists, Vol II, 89. *Mem:* Int Sculpture Ctr; Arelis Fiber Soc, Paris, France; Pen Ctr West. *Media:* Fiber, Sculpture, Mixed Media. *Publ:* Auth, A community of artists, Graphic Arts Coun Newsletter, Vol IX, No 4, Los Angeles Co Mus, 74; President's report, Artists for Econ Action Newslett, 77-78; Calif Art Rev, Am References, 89; Los Angeles Times, 2000; Art of the Fiber, Biblioteque Forney, Paris, 2004. *Mailing Add:* 202 S Saltair Ave Los Angeles CA 90049

ZEITLIN, HARRY LEON
PHOTOGRAPHER
b Denver, Colo, 1952. *Study:* Yale Univ, BA, 74; pvt studies with Hisashi Ohta, Los Angeles, 80-82; Univ Calif, Los Angeles, with Robert Heinecken & Edmund Teske, 77-79. *Hon Degrees:* Rabbinic Ordination, 1998. *Work:* Israel Mus, Jerusalem; Fogg Art Mus Harvard Univ; Bibliotheque Nationalé, Paris, France; Denver Art Mus, Colo; Yale Univ Art Gallery. *Comn:* Aaron Copland (portrait), comn by Aaron Copland, NY, 78; Elliot Carter (portrait), comn by Elliot Carter, NY, 78; Eugene Ionesco (portrait), comn by Eugene Ionesco, Los Angeles, 79; Bob Marley (portrait), comn by Bob Marley, Los Angeles, 80; Hisashi Ohta (portrait), comn by Hisashi Ohta, Los Angeles, 82. *Exhib:* One-man shows, Am Cult Ctr, Jerusalem, 86, Bezalel Acad Art, Jerusalem, 86, Bertha Urdang Gallery, NY, 88 & 91, Henry Art Gallery, Univ Wash, Seattle, 91, Silver Image Gallery, Seattle, 91 & 93, CG Jung Soc Chicago, Evanston, Ill, 93, Anigrafix, Jersualem & Goldwasser & Wilkinson, San Francisco, 96; Skyline, Tel Aviv Mus, Israel, 88; Art-Cubic, Barcelona, Spain, 2003; La State Univ, Baton Rouge, La, 2005; Cafe Flora, Seattle, Wash, 2006; Hadash, Jerusalem, Israel, 2006; and others. *Teaching:* Photog, Art is the Spiritual, Seattle, Wash, 92- & The Evergreen Sch, Seattle, 96. *Awards:* Jerusalem Found Artist Studio Award, 88. *Mem:* Seattle Art Mus Photog Coun. *Media:* Black and White Photography, Digital color photography. *Interests:* interconnectedness of reality, transcendence via visual. *Publ:* Houston Photofest Laser Disc, 92; cover photo, Musica de Sobrevivencia, Egberto Gismonti Group, ECM Records, 93; cover photo, Reflections, Bobo Stenson Trio, ECM Records, 96; Harvester, Geffen Records, 96; Pathways, Richard Greenberg, Jason Aronson Books, 96; Songs to an Invisible God, Ruth Weider Magan, Sounds True Records. *Dealer:* Art is the Spiritual 5508 35th Ave NE Seattle WA 98105; Silver Image Gallery 300 Queen Anne Ave N No 701 Seattle WA 98109. *Mailing Add:* 5508 35th Ave NE Seattle WA 98105

ZEITLIN, MARILYN A
CURATOR, WRITER, MUSEUM DIRECTOR
b Newark, NJ, July 14, 41. *Study:* Harvard Univ, AB, 66 MAT, 67; Cornell Univ, 74. *Collection Arranged:* Messages: Words & Images (auth, catalog), 79 & 80, Freedman Gallery, Reading, Pa; Masters of Contemporary Drawing (auth, catalog), 83-85 & As if the Universe were an object: Larry Miller Retrospective (coauth, catalog), Anderson Gallery, Richmond, Va, 86; Happy Families: Works by Ida Applebroog (coauth, catalog), 89, S Bronx Hall of Fame: Sculpture by John Ahearn & Rigoberto Torres (coauth, catalog), Houston, 90; Too Late for Goya: Works by Francese Torres (auth, catalog), Tempe, Ariz, 94; Art Under Duress: El Salvador 1980-Present (auth, catalog), Tempe, Ariz, 94; Contemporary Art from Cuba: Irony and Survival on the Utopian Island, 98. *Pos:* Dir, Ctr Gallery, Bucknell Univ, Lewisburg, 76-79, Freedman Gallery, Albright Col, Reading, 79-82, Anderson Gallery, Va Commonwealth Univ, Richmond, 82-87, Contemp Arts Mus, Houston, 87-90, WPA, Washington, DC, 90-92 & Univ Art Mus, Ariz State Univ, 92-; comnr, US to Venice Biennale, 95. *Teaching:* Instr, Bucknell Univ, Albright Col & Va Commonwealth Univ, formerly. *Awards:* Samuel H Kress Fel, 71-72. *Mem:* Am Asn Mus; Asn Col & Univ Mus & Galleries (vpres, 84-86). *Res:* Contemporary art, chiefly video, painting & sculpture; political art. *Publ:* Auth, Magic & Medicine: Chinese Ceramics in Southeast Asia, Pac Press, 78; Small is Beautiful, Bucknell Univ, 79; Jo Sandman: Work in process, Anyart, 80; Attemped, Not Known, Paintings by Benito Huerta, Artspace, 89. *Mailing Add:* Ariz State Univ Art Mus PO Box 872911 Tempe AZ 85287-2911

ZELANSKI, PAUL JOHN
PAINTER
b Hartford, Conn, Apr 13, 31. *Study:* Cooper Union, cert, 55; Yale Univ, BFA, 57; Bowling Green State Univ, MFA, 58. *Work:* Univ Mass, Amherst; Slater Mus, Norwich, Conn; The Leonard Bacour Collection, NY; Hampshire Col, Northampton, Mass; Yale Univ Print Collection. *Exhib:* New Eng in Five Parts, De Cordova Mus, Lincoln, Mass; Harvard Univ Carpenter Ctr, Boston; New Directions in Painting, Univ Mass, Amherst; The Peterdi Yrs, Yale Univ, New Haven; Acad Fine Arts, Krakow, Poland; Amel Gallery, New York City; Amon Carter Mus, Fort Worth, Tex; Benton Mus, Storrs, Conn; Boston Mus Contemp Art; Bowling Green State Univ, Ohio; Dallas Mus Fine Art; ETC Collection, Hartford, Conn; Grand Street Gallery, New York City; Hampshire Col, Mass; Maastricht Academy,The Neth; Nexus Gallery, Boston; North Tex State Univ, Denton; Shippensburg Univ, Pa; Slater Memorial Mus, Norwich; Smith Col, Northampton, Mass; Cooper Union, New York City; The Gallery, Provincetown, Mass; Trinity Col, Hartford; Wadsworth Mus, Hartford. *Collection Arranged:* Academy Fine Arts, Krakow; Calmann & King Collection, London; John Slade Ely House Collection, New Haven; Forth Worth Art Ctr, Ft. Worth; Hampshire Col Collection, Mass; Harcourt Brace Collection, Tex; Housatonic Mus, Norwalk, Conn; IBM Collection; Kearns Collection, Guilford, Conn; La Corrie

Collection, NY; Univ Mass Drawing Collection, Amherst; Univ North Tex, Denton; Leonard Bocour Collection, NYC; Cooper Union Collection, NYC; Dodd Ctr, Storrs, Conn; Slater Memorial Mus, Norwich, Conn; Takenaga Collection, Japan; Verda Am, Japan; Yale Univ Art Mus, New Haven. *Pos:* Vis Art, Acad Fine Arts, Kraskow, Poland, 90 & Acad Visual Arts, Maastsricht, Holland, 94. *Teaching:* Instr painting, drawing & design, N Tex State Univ, 58-61; instr painting, Ft Worth, Tex, 61-62; assoc prof art, Univ Conn, 62-76, prof, 76-95, prof emeritus, 95-. *Awards:* Painting Prize, New Haven Art Asn, 94, 95 & 96; Painting Prize, Guliford Art Asn, 94, 95 & 96; Painting Prize, Mystic Art Asn, 95 & 96; Painting Prize, Essex Art Asn, 2005, 2006. *Bibliog:* Alan Graham Collier (auth), Form, Space and Vision, Prentice-Hall; Barnard Chaet (auth), Artists at work, Webb, Studio Talk; B. Chate (auth), Studio Talk, Prentice Hall; B. Chate (auth), Drawing, Prentice Hall; Albers (auth), Interaction of Color, Yale Press. *Mem:* Silvermine Guild Artists; Conn Acad Fine Arts; Berkshire Art League; Munsell Group; Comput Art & Design Educ; Essex Art Asn Gallery. *Media:* Acrylic, Collage. *Publ:* Auth, Design Principles and Problems, 2 edits, Harcourt Brace; The Art of Seeing, 7 edits, Prentice Hall; Auth, Shaping Space, 3 edits, Harcourt Brace; Color, 6 edits, Prentice Hall. *Mailing Add:* Cowles Rd West Willington CT 06279

ZELENAK, EDWARD J
SCULPTOR

b St Thomas, Ont, Nov 9, 40. *Study:* Meinszinger Sch Art, Detroit, Mich; Ft Worth Art Ctr, Tex; Ont Col Art, Toronto. *Work:* Cantonal Mus, Lausanne, Switz; Nat Gallery Can, Ottawa; Ont Art Gallery, Toronto; Rothman's Ltd, Stratford, Ont; Dept Pub Works, Toronto. *Comn:* Major outdoor sculpture, Nat Gallery Can, 72, Dept Pub Works, Toronto, 73 & North York, 76, Rothman's Art Gallery, 73 & Northfield Minn, Carleton Col, 73; major sculpture, Prov Dept Pub Works, Kitchener, Ont, 77; Forest City Gallery, London, Ont, 85-86. *Exhib:* One-man exhib, Maj Outdoor Sculpture, Nat Art Ctr, Ottawa, 69, Carleton Col, 72, Christopher Cutts Gallery, Toronto, 97 & Two Sculptors Inc, NY, 98; Tendence Actuelles, Galerie de France, Paris, 69; 3rd Int Pioneer Galleries Exhib, Cantonnal Mus, Lausanne & Mus Mod Art, Paris, 70; 49th Parallels, Ringling Mus, Sarasota, Fla & Mus Contemp Art, Chicago, 71; Washington, Northfield, Milwaukee major touring sculpture, Minn State Art Coun & Henry Gallery, 73-74; Mt Allison Univ, 75; Art Fiera, Bologna, Italy, 77; Chicago Atheneum, Chicago, 98; Art Forum, Berlin, 98. *Teaching:* Instr, Univ Western Ont, 79-88. *Awards:* Can Coun Jr Arts Grant, 68-71, Sr Arts Grant, 73-75; Prov Ont Coun Arts Grant in Aid, 74. *Bibliog:* Jean Noel Chandler (auth), article in Artscanada, 4/69; Barry Lord (auth), articles in Art in Am, 1-2/69; R Naasgard (auth), article in Artscanada, 6/73. *Mem:* Royal Can Acad Acad Arts. *Media:* Metal, Fiberglas. *Specialty:* Contemporary painting and sculpture. *Dealer:* Christopher Cutts Gallery 21 Morrow Ave Toronto Ont Canada MGR 2H9. *Mailing Add:* RR 1 West Lorne ON N0L 2P0 Canada

ZELEVANSKY, LYNN
CURATOR

Study: Student in art history, NYU. *Work:* Cur (exhibs) Sense and Sensibility: Women Artists and Minimalism in the 90s, 1994, Love Forever: Yayoi Kusama 1958-68, 1998-99, Robert Therrian retrospective, 2000, Jasper Johns to Jeff Koons: Four Decades of Art from the Broad Collections, 2001, Keith Edmier and Farah Fawcett, 2002, Beyond Geometry: Experiments in Form, 1940s-70s, 2004 (Award for Best Thematic Mus Show Nationally, Inter Asn Art Critics/USA, 2005), many others. *Pos:* Cur, Mus Modern Art, New York City, 1987-1995; named assoc cur, dept 20th century painting Los Angeles Co Mus Art, 1995, assoc cur modern and contemp art, cur, dept head modern and contemp art. *Mailing Add:* LACMA 5905 Wilshire Blvd Los Angeles CA 90036

ZELIN, ELAINE
SCULPTOR

b New York, NY, Dec 13, 31. *Study:* Stephens Col, AA, 51; Fairleigh Dickinson Univ, BA, 80; Art Students League; New School; studied with J Hovannes, Tony Paderano & Minouri Niizuma. *Work:* New England Ctr Contemp Art, Brookline, Conn. *Comn:* Marble seal, Dart Indust, Paramus, NJ, 81; Windswept (marble sculpture), Accurate Box Co, Newark, NJ, 82; Pinnacle, Ft Lee Marketing Co, NY, 84; Citiscape, Cosmetic Scenting Co, NY, 85. *Exhib:* Stone Sculpture Soc NY, Lever House, 81, 86, 90; Nat Asn Women Artists, Jacob Javits Plaza, NY, 82, 83, 85; Tri Co, Bergen Co Mus, Paramus, NJ, 84; Norton Artists Guild, Norton Mus, West Palm Beach, 92; NAWA Cornell Mus, Delray Beach, Fla, 2001-02; Boca Mus Artists Guild, Boca Raton, Fla, 2002, 03; Rosetta Stone Fine Art Gallery, Juno Beach, Fla. *Awards:* Anonymous Members Prize, Nat Asn Women Artists, 82 & 83. *Bibliog:* NY Art Yearbook, 76. *Mem:* NY Artists Equity; Nat Asn Women Artists; Norton Artists Guild; Boca Raton Mus Artists Guild; Alabaster. *Media:* Marble. *Mailing Add:* 25 D Southport Ln Apt D Boynton Beach FL 33436

ZELLEN, JODY
PHOTOGRAPHER, WRITER

b Boston, Mar 18, 61. *Study:* Wesleyan Univ, BA, 83; Calif Inst Arts, MFA, 89. *Work:* Los Angeles Co Mus Art, Los Angeles; San Francisco Mus Art; Laguna Art Mus, Laguna Beach, Calif; Orange Co (Calif) Mus Art; Ruth and Marvin Sackner Archives Concrete and Visual Poetry, Miami Beach. *Comn:* Hollywood (Calif) Fence Project, Los Angeles MTA, 94-97; Windows on Wilshire, Los Angeles Co Mus Art, 98; Pan Pacific Recreation Ctr, Los Angeles Cult Affairs Dept, 99. *Exhib:* Photog and the Photog: Theories, Practices, Histories, Calif Mus Photog, Riverside, 94; PLAN - Photog Los Angeles Now, Los Angeles Co Mus Art, 95; Documenta, Huntington Beach (Calif) Art Ctr, 96; The Space Between, The Other Gallery, Banff Ctr Arts, Alta, Can, 96; The Far Bazaar, Los Angeles Zoo, 97; Recycling Art Hist (catalog), Pittsburgh Ctr Arts, 98; Los Angeles Art in the 90s Recharge: The Gift of Eileen and Peter Norton, Laguna Art Mus, 2000; Selections from the Norton Collection, Los Angeles Co Mus Art, 2000; Mirades Impudiques, Fundaciio La Caixa, Barcelona, 2000; Experiments: Recent Acquisitions of the Permanent Collection of Architecture & Design, San Fracisco Mus Mod Art, 2000; Made in Calif, Los Angeles Co Mus Art, 2000; Gallery 2211, 2001; Fullerton Art Mus, 2001; Of Nearby Stars and Distant Suns, Terrain, San Francisco, 2001; Transpolyblu: A Digital Exposition, Elliot Smith Contemp Art, St Louis, 2001; City Rhythms, Pelham Art Ctr, NY, 2001; Cyborg Manifesto or the Joy of Artifice, Laguna Art Mus, Calif, 2001; Telling Stories, Eye Five Gallery, Los Angeles, 2001; Silent Motion, Stanley Picker Gallery, Kingston upon Thames, Eng, 2001; Barnsdall Art Park Targets: Art Crawl 4, Los Angeles, 2001; LA-NY Benefit, Yamagata Studio, Los Angeles, 2001; Human Interaction in an Interaction Age, Pittsburgh Ctr for Arts, 2002; Reactions, Exit Art, New York City, 2002; Metrop Iconographies, XXV, Bienal De Sao Paulo, Brazil, 2002; Glass Membrane: Scanner to Screen, CMP, Riverside, Calif, 2002; Aim IV: Interference Patternsn, Armory Northwest, Pasadena, Calif, 2003; Americana, Sch Visual Arts West Side Gallery, New York City, 2003; solo shows, Metropolis Captured, The Lab, San Francisco, Calif, 89, What is Legitimate Art? Beyond Baroque, Venice, Calif, 90, Dorothy Golden Gallery, Santa Monica, Calif, 93, Robert Berman Gallery, Santa Monica, 94, SF Camerawork, San Francisco, 95, Site-Seeing Ctr for Contemp Photog, Melbourne, Australia, 95, Parts, Amanda Obering Gallery, Los Angeles, 96, Richard Heller Gallery, Santa Monica, 96, Mesa Col Art Gallery, San Diego, 97, Post, Los Angeles, 97, Jan Kesner Gallery, Los Angeles, 98, Post, Elevator Project, LA, 98, Grid City, Nexus, Atlanta, 99, Still, Art Resources Transfer, NYC, 2000, Path Grides, Montgomery Gallery, Pomona Col, Claremont, Calif, 2000, City Views, Robert V Fullerton Art Mus, Calif State Univ, San Bernardino, 2001, The Life and Death of Building, Deep River, LA, 2001, Urban Evidence, Sesnon Gallery, Univ Calif Santa Cruz, 2002, Susanne Vielmetter Projects, LA, 2002, Artport Whitney, Gatepage, 2002, Art Over Your Head, One Colorado, Pasadena, Calif, 2003; Cola, Los Angeles, Calif, 2004; Laguna Art Mus, 2005. *Collection Arranged:* Inheritance (auth, catalog), Los Angeles Contemporary Exhibs, 92. *Teaching:* lectr, Calif State Univ, Long Beach, 96, 97, 2000; lectr, Otis Col Art and Design, Los Angeles, 98; lectr, Soc Photographic Educ Conf, San Francisco, 98; lectr, The Art Inst Chicago, 98; lectr, Art Ctr Coll Design, 99; lectr, Pomona Col, 2000; lectr, Scripps Col, 2000; vis lectr, Univ Calif, LA, 2001 & 2002; asst prof, Cal Poly, Pomona, Calif, 2002. *Awards:* Aaron Siskind Fel, 97; Individual Fel, Calif Arts Coun, 98; Grant, Durfee ARC, 2002. *Bibliog:* Michal Reed (auth), Jody Zellen - City of Dreams, Artpress, 11/97; Leah Ollman (auth), Art rev, LA Times, 5/15/98; Christopher Mount (auth), Lost travelers in a digital city, Print LIV:I, 1-2/2000. *Media:* photographic installations. *Publ:* co-ed, designer, Censorship, Frame-Work, Vol 3, issue 2/3, 90, Misinformation, Vol 4, issue 1, 90, Fashion, Vol 4, issue 3, 91, Violence, Vol 5, issue 2/3, 92, Impolitcs, Vol 6, issue 1, 93, Gossip, Vol 6, issue 3, 94, Home, Vol 7, issue 1, 94, Love, Vol 7, issue 2, 95, Nature, Vol 7, issue 3, 95; auth, Children, Youth & City, Lure Art Books, 93; auth, Beneath the Ruins, 96; co-ed, designer, inaugural issue, Site Street, fall, 97, Memory, winter, 98, Spectacle, summer, 98, Truth, winter, 99, Travel, summer, 2000; auth, The Architecture of Fear, Princeton Archit Press, 97; auth, Blur, 97; auth, Pinspot # 2, 98; auth, Standing Still: Still Standing, 2000. *Mailing Add:* 843 Bay St Apt 11 Santa Monica CA 90405

ZELLER, FREDERIC
SCULPTOR

b Ger, May 20, 24. *Study:* Univ London, BA, 55; Art Students League, NY, studied with Stephen Green, 59-61; The Greenwich House, studied with Paul Frazier, 61-64; Educ Alliance Art Sch, studied with Licio Isolani, 65-70. *Exhib:* Vorpal Gallery, NY, 82; Centre Articule, Montreal, Quebec, 83; Sarah Y Rentschler Gallery, Bridgehampton, NY, 85; Clark Whitney Gallery, Lenox, Mass, 85; Elaine Benson Gallery, Bridgehampton, 86; Benton Gallery, Southampton, NY, 86, 87 & 88; solo shows, Pace Univ Art Gallery, NY, 80, Vorpal Gallery, 82 & 83, Studio 99, Westhampton Beach, 82, Benton Hallery, 88. *Mailing Add:* 775 Ave of the Americas No 5 New York NY 10001

ZELLER, JOSEPH R
EDUCATOR, CERAMIST

b Chicago, IL, Aug 8, 45. *Study:* Univ Ill, Urbana, BFA, 68; State Univ NY, Alfred, MFA, 70. *Pos:* Trustee design div, Am Ceramic Soc, 92-96. *Teaching:* Instr art, Cleveland Inst Art, 70-77; assoc prof art, Ohio Univ, 77-88; prof & chmn design, Univ Kans, 88-. *Mem:* Am Ceramic Soc; Nat Coun Educ Ceramic Arts; Tile Heritage Found; Am Craft Coun; Ohio Designer Craftsman. *Media:* Ceramics. *Mailing Add:* Univ Kans 300 Art & Design Lawrence KS 66045

ZELT, MARTIE
PRINTMAKER, MURALIST

b Washington, Pa, Nov 16, 30. *Study:* Conn Col; Pa Acad Fine Arts; New Sch Social Res, with Antonio Frasconi; Mus Arte Mod, Brazil, with John Friedlaender; Univ NMex, with Garo Antreasian; Temple Univ, BA. *Work:* Carnegie Inst, Mus Art; Pa Acad Fine Arts; Princeton Univ; Philadelphia Mus Art; Brooklyn Mus; and others. *Comn:* Tile mural, City Roswell, NMex, 96, Bitter Lake Nat Wildlife Refuge, 2000. *Exhib:* Int Bienale, Sao Paulo, Brazil, 61; Pa Acad Fine Arts Nat Ann, 61-70; one-man shows, Pa Acad Peale Galleries, 72, Print Club, 75, Brooklyn Mus, 80 & Carnegie Inst, Mus Art, 81; group shows, 30 Yrs Am Printmaking, Brooklyn Mus, 76; New Ways With Paper, Nat Collection of Fine Arts, Washington, DC; Brandywine Graphic Workshop, 80; Tamarind Inst, 83 & 86; Pyramid Print & Paperworks, Dolan/Maxwell, 85; Morris Gallery, Pa Acad Fine Arts; retrospective, Roswell Mus Art Ctr, 98. *Pos:* Dir graphic workshop prof artists, Pa Acad Fine Arts, 63-65; demonstrating artist & printmaker, Prints in Progress, Philadelphia, 63-71. *Teaching:* Instr printmaking, Pa Acad Fine Arts, 68-82, Philadelphia Col Art, 69-82; Univ NC, Chapel Hill, 81; chmn, Art Dept, Va Intermont Col, 85-89; distinguished vis prof, Univ Del, 88-89. *Awards:*

Cresson Traveling Award, 54 & Scheidt Mem Traveling Award, Pa Acad Fine Arts; Print Club Fel, 65; Artist in Residency, Roswell Mus, 82, 89. *Bibliog:* Prints--History of an Art, Beguin, Field, Griffes, Skira-Rissoli, 81; The Complete Printmaker, Ross/Romano, MacMillan, 90; Clinton Adams (auth), Printmaking in New Mexico, 1880-1990, Univ NMex Press, 91. *Media:* All. *Publ:* Whole Cloth, Constantine/Reuter, Monacelli Press, 97; Tamarind: 40 Years, UNM Press, 2000. *Dealer:* Hodges-Taylor Gallery 401 N Tryon Charlotte NC; Nason-Williams 246 A Ledoux St Taos NMex; Sharon Campbell Greenville Sc

ZEMANS, JOYCE L
EDUCATOR, ART HISTORIAN
b Toronto, Can, Apr 21, 40. *Study:* Univ Toronto, BA, 62, MA, 66. *Pos:* Dir grad prog art hist, York Univ, 94-95, co-dir prog MBA arts & media admin, Schulich Sch Bus, York Univ, 94-, acting dir MBA prog in non-profit mgt and leadership, 00-01. *Teaching:* Art historian, Ont Col Art, Toronto, 66-75, chmn, Art Hist Dept, 69-71, chmn, Liberal Arts Studies, 72-75; assoc prof art hist, York Univ, Toronto, 75-95, chmn, Dept Visual Arts, 75-81, dean, fac fine arts, 85-88; dir, Can Coun, 89-92; prof, York Univ, 95-. *Mem:* Int Asn Art Critics; Nat Coun Arts Admins; Can Asn Fine Arts Deans (bd mem); Int Coun Fine Arts Deans (bd mem). *Res:* art history (20th century, North American); cultural policy. *Publ:* Contribr, Bertram Brooker & Emergent Modernism, Vol 7, 89; Free Expression, Public Support & Censorship: Examining Government's Role in the Arts in Canada and the United States, Univ Press Am, Lanham, Md, 94; Beyond Quebec: Taking Stock of Canada, McGill-Queen's Press, 95; auth, Establishing the canon: The early history of reproductions at the National Gallery of Canada, J Can Art Hist, spring 95, Where is Here? Canadian Cultural Policy in a Globalized World, 96, Comparing Cultural Policy: A Study of Japan & the United States, 99; And the lion shall lie down with the lamb: US-Canada cultural relations in a free trade environment, Am Rev Can Studies, Vol 24, No 4, 95. *Mailing Add:* York Univ 265A CFA 4700 Keel St Toronto ON M3J 1P3 Canada

ZENTZ, PATRICK J
SCULPTOR
b Cando, NDak, Jan 22, 47. *Study:* Westmont Col, Santa Barbara, Calif, BA, 65-69; Univ Mont, MFA(sculpture), 70-74. *Work:* Yellowstone Art Mus, Billings, Mont; Cheney Cowles Mus, Spokane, Wash; Hockaday Ctr Arts, Kallispell, Mont; Oates Park Art Ctr, Fallon, Nev, 96; Miami Univ, Oxford, Ohio; Montana Mus Art Culture, Missoula, Mont; Paris Gibson Square Mus, Great Falls, Mich. *Comn:* Western State Hosp, Wash State Arts Comn, Ft Steilecom, 91; Richard Tam Alumni Ctr, Univ Nev, Las Vegas, 91; Snake River Correctional Inst, Ontario, Ore, 93; Salt Palace, Salt Lake City, Utah, 96; Tri-Met, Westside Light Rail, Hawthorn Farm Sta, Portland, Ore, 97; Food & Drug Admin, Col Park, Md, 98; Yellowstone Art Mus, Billings, Mont, 99; Sanderegger Science Ctr, Edgewood Col, Madison, Wis, 99; Boise City Arts Comn, Idaho, 2000; Washington State Arts Comn, Riverpoint Campus, Spokane, 2001; Reno, Sparks Convention Ctr, Nevada, 2001; 4Culture, Harborview Hosp, Seattle, Wash, 2003; Olympic Col, State Art Comn, Wash, 2004. *Exhib:* St John's Nfld, Can, 92; Beam Art Gallery, Univ Nev, Las Vegas, 92; solo exhibs, Cheney Cowles Mus, Spokane, Wash, 94 & Boise Art Mus, Idaho, 94; San Antonio Art Mus, Tex, 94; Neuberger Mus Art Biennial Exhib Pub Art, State Univ NY, Purchase, 97; Curatorial Choice: A Northwest Survey, Holter Mus Art, Helena, Mont, 97; Unfettered Spirit: Art and History on the Open Plains, Paris Gibson Sq Mus Art, Great Falls, Mont, 98; Inaugural Exhib, New Yellowstone Art Mus, Billings, Mont, 98; Anne Appleby, Mario Reis, and Patrick Zentz, Yellowstone Art Mus, Billings, Mont, 99; Action/Reaction, McAllen Int Mus, Tex, 99; Wind (with catalog), Suyama Space, Seattle, 99; Custer Co Arts Ctr, Miles City, Mont, 2000; Missoula Mus of Arts, Mont, 2000; Mont State Univ Sch of Archit, Bozeman, 2000; Emerson Cult Ctr at Beall Park, Bozeman, Mont; Churchill Arts Coun, Fallon, Nev; and others. *Pos:* Panelist, var comns, asns & mus, 86-91; artist adv task force, Western States Arts Fedn, Portland, Ore, 91. *Teaching:* Lectr, many mus, cols & univs, 77-94; keynote speaker, Am Inst Architects Comt Design Ann Conf, Big Sky, Mont, 92; lectr, Sch of Archit, Mont State Univ, 2000 & Nev Mus Art, Reno, 2001. *Awards:* Grant, Art Matters, Inc, 88; Nat Endowment Arts Fel, 90; Grant, LEF Found, 92. *Bibliog:* Beth Sellars (ed), Patrick Zentz/Flow: A Transcontinental Soundwork (exhib catalog); Don Wherry (ed), Sound symposium 6 (catalog), p 85-86, 92; Baile Oakes (auth), Sculpting with the Environment/A Natural Dialogue, Van Nostrand Reinhold, 94; Christopher Hallowell (auth), Profile: The environmental artist, Audubon Mag, Vol 101, No 2, 20, 3-4/99; William Fox (auth), Mapping the Empty, Univ of Nev Press, 99; Regina Hackett (auth), Sculptures Harness the Wind, Seattle Post-Intelligencer, 5/28/99, Robin Updike (auth), Poetic Sounds that are here with the Wind, Seattle Times, 5/28/99; Sherri Jones (auth), Inspired by Their Land, Missoulian, Mont, 2000; Brandon Griggs (auth), Eyes of the Beholder, Salt Lake Tribune, Utah, 10/8/2000; and others. *Mailing Add:* 10152 Duck Creek Rd Laurel MT 59044

ZERNER, HENRI THOMAS
HISTORIAN, CURATOR
b Suresnes, France, May 15, 39. *Study:* Univ Paris, Lic es Lett, 61, Dr(fine arts), 69; Ecole Pratique des Hautes Etudes, Paris, dipl(fine arts), 63. *Collection Arranged:* Venice in the Eighteenth Century (cataloged), Mus Art, RI Sch Design, 67 & J J J Tissot (cataloged), 67; The School of Fontainebleau (cataloged), Grand Palais, Paris, 72-73. *Pos:* Cur, Painting & Graphic Arts Mus, RI Sch Design, 65-66 & Prints & Drawing Mus, 66-72; cur prints, Fogg Mus, Harvard Univ, presently. *Teaching:* From asst prof to assoc prof fine arts, Brown Univ, Providence, RI, 66-72; prof fine arts, Harvard Univ, Cambridge, Mass, 72-. *Awards:* Guggenheim Fel, Paris, 71; Prix Achille Fould, Acad des Inscriptions et Belles Lett, 71; and others. *Publ:* auth, Tout l'oeuvre peint de Raphael, Flammarion, 69; auth, L'Ecole de Fontainebleau-Gravures, Abrams, 70; auth, Illustrated Bartsch, Vol XVI, In: Sixteenth Century Italian Etchings, 79; coauth (with Charles Rosen), Romanticism and Realism: The Mythology of 19th Century Art, Viking, 84; L'Art de Le Renaissance in France, L'invention du classicisure, Paris, Flammarion, 96. *Mailing Add:* Fogg Art Mus 32 Quincy St Cambridge MA 02138

ZGODA, LARRY
STAINED GLASS ARTIST, DESIGNER
b Chicago, Ill, Oct 27, 50. *Study:* Columbia Col, Ill, BA, 75. *Work:* City Chicago Public Art Collection. *Comn:* Clerestory panels, Wesley-Jesson Co, Chicago, Ill, 88; archit stained glass, 90, stained glass entry, 95, City of Chicago, Chicago Pub Libr, Ill; archit stained glass, Asn Retired Persons, Washington, DC, 91; clerestory panels, American Family Insurance Int Hq, Madison, Wis, 93; Wall of Glass, TCF Tower, Minneapolis, Minn, 97; ten windows, Our Lady of Angels Chapel, Marian Village, Homer, Ill, 2000; lighted wall of glass, Woodsin Suites, Emeryville, Calif, 2000; stained glass for partitioning wall, Huron Pub Libr, Huron, Ohio, 2002; 5 stained glass entries, Sacred Heart of Jesus Chapel, Our Lady of Victory Convent, Lemont, Ill, 2002; Windows & decorative inserts, Craig Hall, Grad School Social Work, Univ Denver, 2005. *Exhib:* 1st Int Stained Glass Exhib, Corning Mus Glass, NY, 87. *Awards:* Guild Am Craft Awards, Guild, 87; Graham Found grant. *Bibliog:* article, Contemporary Crafts for the Home, Klaus Sikes Inc, 90; Chris Peterson (auth), The Art Stained Glass, Quarry Bks, 98; Beautiful Things, Guild.com, 2000; Object Lesson, Guild.com, 2001. *Mem:* Friends of Kebyar. *Media:* Stained Glass, Wood, Tile, Mosaic, Metals. *Res:* Art and life of Edgar Miller (1899-1993). *Interests:* Architectural Ornament, history of crafts in architecture. *Publ:* Auth, Beauty of stainless glass, Professional Stained Glass, 5/90; article, Am Craft, 8-9/90; Lines of Poetry, Prof Stained Glass, 8/91. *Dealer:* Aesthetic Eye Gallery 1520 W Chicago Chicago Ill 60622. *Mailing Add:* 3932 N Oakley Chicago IL 60618-3923

ZHEUTLIN, DALE R
SCULPTOR, EDUCATOR
b Newark, NJ, July 27, 48. *Study:* RI Sch Design, BFA, 70; Columbia Univ, MFA, 72. *Work:* The Robert Martin Co, White Plains, NY; Wang Laboratories Inc, NY; IBM Collection, NY; Chase Manhattan Bank, NY; Pfizer Corp, NY; and others. *Comn:* Kramer, Levin, Nessen, Kamin & Frankel, 86; Peat, Marwick & Main, Indianapolis, Ind, 88; Citibank Tower, Phoenix, Ariz, 90; Am Int Group, NY, 90; Aetna, Hartford, Conn, 90; and others. *Exhib:* Aldrich Mus, Trustees Choice, Ridgefield, Conn, 83; 46th Concorso Int della Ceramica a'arte, Faenza, Italy, 89; Katonah Mus Art, NY, 90; 2nd Int Ceramics Competition, Mino, Japan, 90; San Angelo Mus Art, Tex, 90; Wheeler Seidel Gallery, NY, 92; and others. *Teaching:* Art fac, New Rochelle High Sch, NY, 74-84, Mamaroneck High Sch, 84-; adj prof ceramics, Col New Rochelle, NY, 77-; guest lectr, NY Univ, 86. *Awards:* Award Merit, Mamaroneck Artists Guild, 79; Pauline Law Prize, Nat Asn Women Artists, NY, 80; Sculpture Award, Hudson River Mus, NY, 81. *Bibliog:* Jennifer Dunning (auth), A chance to find if the art of women in special, 86, Vivian Raynor (auth), Four artists at gallery shows, 1/89, NY Times; Bill Kraus (auth), Contemporary Crafts for the Home, Kraus Sikes Inc, 90; Leon Nigrosh (auth), Sculpting Clay, Davis Publ Inc, 91; and others. *Mem:* Nat Asn Women Artists Inc; Artists Equity Asn; Empire State Crafts Alliance (bd dir). *Media:* Clay; All Media. *Publ:* Contribr, Apprenticeship in Craft, Daniel Clark Bks, 81. *Dealer:* Wheeler Seidel Gallery New York NY. *Mailing Add:* 71 Glenwood Ave New Rochelle NY 10801-3126

ZIB, TOM (THOMAS) A ZIBELLI
CARTOONIST
b Mt Vernon, NY. *Study:* Grand Cent Sch Art; Com Illus Studios. *Publ:* Contribr, Saturday Rev & Weight Watchers, 1972, Saturday Evening Post, Nat Enquirer, Reader's Digest, 1973-81, Wall Street J, 1981, Good Housekeeping & Woman's World, Cosmopolitan, Better Homes & Gardens. *Mailing Add:* 167 E Devonia Ave Mt Vernon NY 10552

ZIBELLI, THOMAS A See Zib, Tom (Thomas) A Zibelli

ZIEGLER, DOLORES ANN
PAINTER, CONCEPTUAL ARTIST
b Northampton, MA, Sept 6, 30. *Study:* Dean Jr Col, AA, 1949; Northampton Com Col, 1950. *Work:* St Clair Hosp, Denville, NJ; Norton Hosp, Louisville, Ky; Ryder Trucking, Harrisburg, Pa; Dominion Bank, Montreal, Can. *Comn:* Holiday Inn, Penns Grove, NJ, 1989; St Claire Hosp, Denville, NJ, 1990. *Exhib:* Blue Heaven, Huntsville Mus Art, Huntsville, Ala, 1999; Traveling show, Nat Watercolor Soc, 2005; Northeast Watercolor Int Exhib, Conn, 2002; Am Watercolor Soc, Salamagundi Club, NY, 2004-2006; Am Watercolor Soc, Traveling Show, 2005-2006; Lincroft Monmouth Mus, Lincroft Mus, Monmouth, NY, 2006. *Collection Arranged:* Atrium Art Gallery, Morris Records Bldg, 1991; Morris Co Art Asn, Morris Co Libr, 2002. *Pos:* Jury of selection, NJ Watercolor Soc, Guild Creative Art, Shrewsbury, NJ, 2005; Judge, Pasacat Show Outdoor, 2006. *Teaching:* Instr, Morris Co Art Asn, 85-2004; instr, Guild Creative Arts, Shrewsbury, NJ, 2004-05; instr acrylic collage, Somerset Art Asn, Somerset, NJ, Lakeland Arts, Denville, NJ, 2005-2006; instr, Markham Art Ctr, Haddonfield, NJ, 2006; instr, Ctr Visual Arts, Summit, NJ, 2006. *Awards:* Endico Award Excellence, North East Watercolor Soc, 2002; Art Competition, Artist Magazine, 2003; Hardie Gramatky (AWS), Daughter, 2005; and others. *Bibliog:* Greg Schaber (auth), Take Command College, Artist Mag, 1998; Joanne Moore (auth), Starting Points, Artist Sketch Book, 2003; Rachel Hunter (auth), Holiday Windows, Splash 6, 2003. *Mem:* Int Soc of Acrylic Painters,; NJ Watercolor Soc (juror, workshop organizer); Baltimore Watercolor Soc; North East Watercolor Soc (juror); Am Watercolor Soc; Nat Watercolor Soc. *Media:* Acrylic/Collage. *Mailing Add:* 41B Molly Pitcher Blvd Whiting NJ 08759

ZIEMANN, RICHARD CLAUDE
PRINTMAKER, EDUCATOR
b Buffalo, NY, July 3, 32. *Study:* Albright Art Sch; Yale Univ, BFA & MFA; painting with Albers & Brooks; printmaking with Peterdi; drawings with Chaet. *Work:* Brooklyn Mus, NY; Silvermine Guild Art; Seattle Art Mus, Wash; De Cordova & Dana Mus; Libr Cong & Nat Gallery Art, Washington, DC; and others. *Comn:* Print Editions for Int Graphic Arts Soc, 58 & 60, Yale Univ Alumni Asn, 60 & Pan-Am Airlines, 62. *Exhib:* Am Prints Today Touring Exhib, most maj print exhibs, 58-65, 24 mus, 62-63 & Paris Biennale, 63; one-man shows, Allen R Hite Art Inst, Univ Louisville, 67, Alpha Gallery, Boston, 67, Univ Conn Art Gallery, 68, Jane Haslem Gallery, Washington, DC, 71, 72, 80 & 89, Bowden Col Mus Art, Maine, 72, Brooklyn Mus, NY, 79 & Francis Kyle Gallery, London, Eng, 82; Oversize Prints, Whitney Mus Am Art, Jane Haslem Gallery, Washington, DC, 71, 72, 80 & 89; Arte Norte Americano, US Embassy, Madrid, Spain, 87; Nat Acad Design, 163rd Ann Exhib, NY, 88. *Pos:* Supvr, Graphic Workshop in Graphic Arts USA Touring Exhib, Soviet Union, 63-64; artist in residence, Dartmouth Col, summer 71. *Teaching:* Asst prof art, Hunter Col, 66; instr printmaking, Yale Univ Summer Sch, 66-67; from assoc prof to prof art, Lehman Col, 78-. *Awards:* Fulbright Grant to Netherlands, 58-59; Nat Inst Arts & Lett Grant, 66; Tiffany Found Grant, 60-61; Louis Comfort Tiffany Found Biennial, 97. *Mem:* Soc Am Graphic Artists; Nat Acad (acad, 04-). *Dealer:* Jane Haslem Gallery 2121 P St NW Washington DC 20037; Alpha Galleries 121 Newbury St Boston MA 02116. *Mailing Add:* c/o Jane Haslem 2025 Hillyer Pl NW Washington DC 20009

ZIFF, JERROLD
HISTORIAN, COLLECTOR
b Los Angeles, Calif, Dec 20, 28. *Study:* Occidental Col, BA, 51; Univ Southern Calif, MA, 54; Harvard Univ, PhD, 59. *Collection Arranged:* French Masters: Rocco to Romanticism (coauth, catalog), Univ Calif, Los Angeles, 60-61; George F Mc Murray Collection of 19th century American Paintings, Trinity Col, Hartford, Conn, 68; Drawings from Four Collections (co-auth, catalog), 73 & II (auth, catalog), Univ Ill. *Pos:* Asst prof 19th century art, Univ Calif, Los Angeles, 58-66; prof 18th & 19th century art, Trinity Col, Hartford, 66-69; prof 18th & 19th century art & drawings, Univ Ill, Champaign, 69-94. *Mem:* Col Art Asn; Midwest Art Hist Soc; Turner Soc. *Res:* Art of J M W Turner; old master drawings. *Collection:* Old master and 19th century drawings. *Mailing Add:* 104 W Holmes St Urbana IL 61801

ZILCZER, JUDITH KATY
CURATOR, HISTORIAN
b Waterbury, Conn, Nov 6, 48. *Study:* George Washington Univ, BA, 69 & MA, 71; Univ Del, PhD, 75. *Collection Arranged:* Willem de Kooning: Hirshhorn Mus Collection (auth, catalog), 93; The Noble Buyer: John Quinn, Patron of the Avant-Garde (auth, Catalog), Hirshhorn Mus & Sculpture Garden, 78; Joseph Stella: The Hirshhorn Museum Collection (auth, catalog), 83; The Advent of Modernism: Post-Impressionism and North American Art 1900-1918 (coauth, catalog), High Mus Art, Atlanta, Ga, 86; Keith Sonnier: Neon (auth, catalog), Hirshhorn Mus, 89; Richard Lindner: Paintings and Watercolors, 1948-1977 (auth, catalog), Hirshhorn Mus, 96; Directions: Cecily Brown, 02; Visual Music, Mus Contemp Art & Hirshhorn Mus (auth, catalog), 05. *Pos:* Historian, Hirshhorn Mus & Sculpture Garden, 74-88; assoc cur painting, 88-92, cur paintings, 92; cur Emeritas, 2003-. *Teaching:* Asst professorial lectr Am studies & art hist, George Washington Univ, 75-76, assoc professorial lectr, 80-86 & 91. *Awards:* Smithsonian Fel, Nat Collection of Fine Arts, 73-74; Penrose Fund res grant, Am Philos Soc, 76-77; Award Exceptional Serv, Smithsonian Inst, 86, 92, 93, 94-98; Smithsonian Scholary Studies Grant, 2003-04; Best Time Based Exhib, Int Asn Art Critics, 2006; George Wittenborn Mem Book Award, 2006. *Mem:* Women's Caucus for Art; Asn of Historians Am Art; Am Asn Mus; Archives Am Art; Catalogue Raisonne Scholors Asn. *Res:* Nineteenth and twentieth century art; history of patronage. *Publ:* The Face of War: The Last Works of Raymond Duchamp-Villon, Art Bulletin, 3/83; Synaesthesia and popular culture: Arthur Dove, George Gershwin and the rhapsody in blue, Art J, winter 84; Color Music: Synaesthesia and Nineteenth-century sources for Abstract Art, Artibus et historiae 16, 87; De-coding John Covert's Time, 1919, Art Bull, 12/93; A Not So Peaceable Kindon, Horace Pippin's Holy Mountain, Archives Am, Art Jou, 01. *Mailing Add:* 2351 N Quantico St Arlington VA 22205-2045

ZILIUS, VLADAS
PAINTER
b Silale, Lithuania, May 13, 39; US citizen. *Study:* Vilnius Art Acad, DFA, 59-65. *Work:* Vilnius State Mus & Vilnius State Gallery, Lithuania. *Exhib:* Int Biennial, Cracow, Poland, 68; Barcelona Mus, Spain, 70; Graphic Arts from USSR, State Mus, Sophia, Bulgaria, 72; solo exhib, Drawing Center, Queens Col, NY, 84. *Teaching:* Instr drawing, Archit Inst, Vilnius, Lithuania, 74-75. *Media:* Miscellaneous Media. *Dealer:* Galerie Aldonna 215 E 79th St New York NY 10021

ZIMILES, MURRAY
PAINTER, EDUCATOR
b New York, NY, Nov 30, 41. *Study:* Univ Ill, BFA, 63; Cornell Univ, MFA, 65; Ecole Nat Superieure Beaux-Arts, Paris, 66-67. *Work:* Brooklyn Mus, NY; Neuberger Mus, NY; Mus Mod Art, NY; Nat Collection Fine Arts; NY Pub Libr. *Comn:* Civic Ctr, Dutchess Co Arts Coun, Poughkeepsie, NY, 81. *Exhib:* Prints from Portfolios, Brooklyn Mus, 70; one-man shows, Kunstnerforbundet Gallery, Oslo, Norway, 72, Vassar Col Gallery, 77, Neuberger Mus, NY, 80-81 & Johnson Mus, Cornell Univ, Ithaca, NY, 81; Cathedral St John the Divine, NY, 92; Suffolk Co Community Col, Selden, NY, 93; Holocaust Mem Mus, Madeira Beach, Fla, 94; Sydney Jewish Mus, Australia, 96; BMG Gallery, Adelaide, Australia, 98; DFN Gallery. *Pos:* Guest cur, Mus Am Folk Art, NY. *Teaching:* Instr printmaking, Pratt Graphics Ctr, NY, 68-71; asst prof drawing & printmaking, Silvermine Col Art, New Canaan, Conn, 68-71; asst prof drawing & printmaking, State Univ NY, New Paltz, 72-77; prof drawing & printmaking, State Univ NY, Purchase, 77-; Kempner Disting prof, State Univ NY, Purchase, 98-. *Awards:* Dorot Found Grant, 93-94; NY State Coun Arts Grant, Artists' Books Fel, 95-96; Smart Found Grant, 95 & 96. *Bibliog:* Review, NY Times, 1/4/81; Article, Art News, 4/92; Article, NY Newsday, 2/93. *Mem:* Soc Am Graphic Artists. *Media:* Oil, Lithography, digital prints. *Specialty:* New arts gallery, Litchfield, Conn. *Collection:* Brooklyn Mus; Jewish Mus; Mus Modern Art; NY Pub Libr; Neuberger Mus; Purchase, Johnson Mus, Ithaca; Portland Mus. Ore. *Publ:* Coauth, The Technique of Fine Art Lithography, Van Nostrand Reinhold, 70; Early American Mills, Clarkson Potter, 73; The Lithographic Workshop Around the World, Van Nostrand Reinhold, 74; Boris Margo, A Retrospective (exhib catalog), Provincetown Art Asn; review, The book of Fire at the Sydeny Jewish Mus, Australian Mag, 3/96. *Dealer:* BMG Gallery 94-98 Melbourne St North Adelaide S Australia 5006. *Mailing Add:* Visual Arts Dept SUNY Col Purchase Purchase NY 10577

ZIMMER, WILLIAM
CRITIC
Study: Columbia Univ, Undergraduate work; Univ Tex, Art Hist Degree. *Pos:* The Soho News, 77; Art Critic New York Times, 81; Lectr in field; juried art exhib. *Mailing Add:* NY Times 229 W 43rd St New York NY 10036

ZIMMERMAN, ALICE A
COLLECTOR, ART DEALER
b Chicago, Ill, June 6, 39. *Study:* Univ Wis, Madison, 57-58; Emory Univ, BA, 77; Vanderbilt Univ, MA, 79. *Pos:* Mem, adv comt, Southeastern Ctr Contemp Art, Winston-Salem, NC, 78-; exec dir, Metrop Nashville Arts Comn, 81-83; trustee, Am Craft Coun, NY, 83-; dir, Zimmerman-Saturn Gallery, Nashville, Tenn, formerly. *Specialty:* Emerging artists; fine crafts; contemporary art. *Collection:* Photo-realists; painters and sculptors; contemporary Europeans; handmade furniture and crafts. *Mailing Add:* 6004 Dunham Springs Rd Nashville TN 37205

ZIMMERMAN, ELYN
SCULPTOR, ENVIRONMENTAL ARTIST
b Philadelphia, Pa, Dec 16, 45. *Study:* Univ Calif, Los Angeles, BA, 68, MFA, 72. *Work:* Los Angeles Co Mus Art; Whitney Mus Am Art & Chase Manhattan Bank, NY; Mus Mod Art, NY; General Mills Corp, Minne, Minn; Birmingham Mus Art. *Comn:* Keystone Island, Dade Co Art Pub Places, Miami, Fla, 89; Two waterwalls & pools, CRA Art Prog, Los Angeles, 90; Plaza Design, pvt comn, 525 Market St, San Francisco, 90; Sanctuary, Univ SFla, Tampa, 90; World Trade Ctr Mem, NY, 95; Comn Arts, 98. *Exhib:* Palisades Project, Hudson River Mus, Yonkers, NY, 82; Directions 1983, Hirshhorn Mus, Washington, DC, 83; Art & Archit & Landscape, San Francisco Mus Mod Art, 85; Artist As Social Designer, Los Angeles Co Mus Art, 85; solo exhib, Projects Wave Hill, Riverdale, NY, 88; Art Mus Univ SFla, Tampa, 91; Hoffman Gallery, Los Angeles, Calif, 92; 65 Thompson Gallery, NY, 92; Gagosian Gallery, NY, 93, 96 & 98; and others. *Pos:* Appointed memb, Comn Fine Arts, 2003. *Awards:* New Talent Award, Los Angeles Co Art Mus, 76; Artist Fel Grant, Nat Endowment Arts, 76, 80 & 82; CAPS Grant, NY State, 80. *Bibliog:* Marc Treib (auth), Elyn Zimmerman: A decade of projects (exhib catalog), Wavehill, Riverdale, NY, 88; John Beardsley (auth), Earth works & beyond, Abbeville Press, 89; John Beardsley (auth), Elyn Zimmerman (exhib catalog), Art Mus Univ SFla, 91; Robert Pincus Witten (auth), Elyn Zimmerman (exhib catalog), Gagosian Gallery; Pepe Karnel (auth), New Drawings (exhib catalogue), 01. *Mem:* Creative Time Inc (bd dir, 85-92); Int Sculpture Ctr (bd dir, 89-95); Columbia Land Conserv (bd dir, 93-). *Media:* Mixed Media. *Dealer:* Gagosian Galery 980 Madison Ave New York NY 10021. *Mailing Add:* 140 Greene St New York NY 10012

ZIMMERMAN, KATHLEEN MARIE
COLLAGE ARTIST, PAINTER
b Floral Park, NY, Apr 24, 23. *Study:* Art Students League; Nat Acad Sch Fine Arts, NY. *Work:* Butler Inst Am Art, Youngstown, Ohio; NC Mus Art, Raleigh; Nat Acad Design, NY; Zimmerli Mus, Rutgers Univ, New Brunswick, NJ; Nat Mus Women in the Arts, Washington, DC. *Exhib:* Art USA, 58; Silvermine Guild, Conn, 62; Nat Acad Design, 69, 75-78, 80, 82, 84, 86, 88, 90, 91, 93-95, 97, 99, 2001; solo shows, Westbeth Gallery, 73 & 74 & St Mary's Col, Md, 90; Am Watercolor Soc, NY, 75-78 & 80; Butler Inst of Am Art, Ohio, 78 & 2000; and many others. *Teaching:* Instr drawing & painting, Midtown Sch Art, NY, 47-52. *Awards:* Scholar, John F & Anna Lee Stacey Found, 54; Fourteen prizes, Nat Asn Women Artists, 57-96; Henry Ward Ranger Fund Purchases, 76 & 82, Awards, Nat Acad Design, 88, 91, 93, 97, 2001; and others. *Bibliog:* James Mellow (auth), review, NY Times, 2/17/73; Hilton Kramer (auth), review, NY Times, 6/10/77; Gerald F Brommer (auth), The Art of Collage, Davis Publ, 78; John & Joan Digby (auth), The Collage Handbook, Thames & Hudson Publ 85; and others. *Mem:* NY Artists Equity; Am Watercolor Soc; Audubon Artists; Allied Artists Am; Nat Acad (assoc, 91, acad, 94-). *Media:* Acrylic; Paper. *Publ:* Co-illusr, Diet for a Small Planet, Ballantine Bks, Publ, 71. *Mailing Add:* 463 West St A1110 New York NY 10014

ZIMMERMAN, PAUL WARREN
PAINTER, INSTRUCTOR
b Toledo, Ohio, Apr 29, 21. *Study:* John Herron Art Sch, BFA. *Work:* Pa Acad Fine Arts, Philadelphia; Houston Mus Fine Art; Butler Inst Am Art, Youngstown, Ohio; Springfield Mus Fine Art, Mass; Wadsworth Atheneum, Hartford, Conn. *Comn:* Mural, First New Haven Nat Bank, Conn, 65. *Exhib:* Indiana Artists Exhibition, John Herron Art Mus, Indianapolis, 57; Am Painting & Sculpture, Univ Ill, 61; Pa Acad Fine Arts, Philadelphia, 62; 144th Ann Exhib, Nat Acad Design,NY, 69; Midyear Show, Butler Inst Am Art, Youngstown, 70. *Teaching:* Prof painting & design, Univ

Hartford Art Sch, 47-. *Awards:* First Prize, Conn Watercolor Soc, 64; Altman Landscape Prize for Second Place, 67 & First Place, 69, Nat Acad Design. *Bibliog:* Henry Pitz (auth), Paintings of Paul Zimmerman, Am Artist Mag, 1/60. *Mem:* Nat Acad (assoc, 70, acad, 72-); Conn Acad Fine Arts; Conn Watercolor Soc (pres, 52-53). *Media:* Oil. *Dealer:* Munson Gallery New Haven CT; Korn Bluth Gallery Fair Lawn NJ. *Mailing Add:* 257 Victoria Rd Hartford CT 06114-2800

ZIMMERMANN, PHILIP
PUBLISHER, PAINTER
b Bangkok, Thailand, Jan 24, 51. *Study:* Cornell Univ, Ithaca, NY, BFA(hons), 73; State Univ NY, Buffalo, visual studies workshop, 77-80, MFA, 80. *Work:* J Paul Getty Mus; Victoria & Albert Mus; Art Inst Chicago; Walker Art Ctr; numerous other pvt & pub collections. *Exhib:* Multiple World (with catalog), Atlanta Col Art Gallery, 94; Letterforms from Hand to Digital, Pratt Manhattan Gallery, NY, 95; Science and the Artists' Book (with catalog), Mus Am Hist, Smithsonian Inst, 95-96; Beyond the Book (with catalog), Forum Contemp Art, St Louis, Mo, 95; Transformation of the Work in Art (with catalog), Fosdick-Nelson Gallery, Alfred Univ, NY, 96. *Pos:* Founder, Space Heater Editions (artist's press), Chicago, 79; grants panelist, NY Found Arts, 89 & bd govs, 90-94; bd trustees, Printed Matter Inc, NY, 93-. *Teaching:* Fac, Visual Studies Workshop Summer Inst, Rochester, NY, 80-87 & Nat Endowment Arts residence, 84; artist-in-residence, Nexus Press, Atlanta, 82; assoc prof design/bk arts, State Univ NY, Purchase, 84- & prof, 87-; vis artist, Univ Arts, Philadelphia, spring 91. *Awards:* Nat Endowment Arts Line II Grant, 83; Regional Fel, Nat Endowment Arts, Works on Paper, Mid Atlantic Arts Found, 94; Nat Endowment Arts Fel, Works on Paper, 95. *Mailing Add:* PO Box 325 Rhinecliff NY 12574-0325

ZIMON, KATHY ELIZABETH
LIBRARIAN
b Szeged, Hungary, Feb 20, 41; Can citizen. *Study:* Univ BC, BA(art hist), 66, BLS, 69, MA(art hist), 70. *Pos:* Fine arts librn, Univ Calgary Libr, Alta, 69-; cur, Can Archit Arch. *Mem:* Can Libr Asn; Can Asn of Spec Libr & Info Serv (newsletter ed, 75-78, chmn art sect, 79-80); Art Libr Soc North Am. *Res:* Alberta artists: currently working on an index. *Mailing Add:* Fine Arts Libr 9LT Univ Calgary 2500 University Dr NW Calgary AB T2N 1N4 Canada

ZINC, RUTA See Dean, Nat

ZINGALE, LAWRENCE
PAINTER
b Florida, NY, Aug 12, 38. *Work:* Int Mus Folk Art, Santa Fe, NMex; Chase Manhattan Bank, NY; Silvermine Guild Ctr Arts, New Caanan, Conn. *Exhib:* Int Mus of Folk Art, Santa Fe, 76; The All-Am Dog, Mus of Folk Art, NY, 77-78; The Am Game, Wilson Art Ctr, Rochester, NY, 78; one-man shows, Am Hurrah Antiques, NY, 78, Jay Johnson Gallery, NY, 81 & 88 & Frank Miele Gallery, 93; Jay Johnson Gallery, NY, 88-91; Frank Miele Gallery, NY, 93; Fenimore House, Cooperstown, NY, 92. *Bibliog:* Robert Bishop (auth), The All-American Dog, Avon Publ, New York, 77; Ellen Stern (auth), article, New York Mag, 10/78; article, Attenzione Mag, 12/81; Jay Johnson & William Ketchum (auths), American Folk Art of the Twentieth Century, Rizzoli Publ; and others. *Media:* Oil, Acrylic. *Mailing Add:* c/o Frank Miole Gallery 1086 Madison Ave New York NY 10128

ZIRKER, JOSEPH
PRINTMAKER, LECTURER
b Los Angeles, Calif, Aug 13, 24. *Study:* Univ Calif, Los Angeles, 43-44, 46-47; Univ Denver, BFA, 49; with Jules Heller & Francis de Erdely, Univ Southern Calif, MFA, 51; Tamarind Lithography Workshop, printer fel, 62-63 & res fel, 64. *Work:* Achenbach Found, Calif Palace Legion Honor, San Francisco; Portland Art Mus, Ore; La Art Mus, Denmark; Koninklijk Mus voor Schone Kunsten, Antwerp, Belgium; and others. *Exhib:* Solo exhibs, Calif Palace Legion of Honor, San Francisco, 74, De Saisset Art Gallery & Mus, Univ Santa Clara, Calif, 75, Univ Art Collection, Ariz State Univ, Tempe, 83, Portland State Univ, Ore, 84, Espace Latino Americain, Paris, France, 87, Centrum Frans Masereel, Kasterlee, Belg, 89, Galerie Witteveen, Amsterdam, The Neth, 90, Smith Andersen Gallery, Palo Alto, 91, 93, 95, 97, 99, 2001 & 2003, de Saisset Mus, Univ of Santa Clara, 2005, Nev Mus Art, Reno, 2005-06; New Ways With Paper, Nat Collection of Fine Arts, Smithsonian Inst, Wash, DC, 77-78; New Am Monotypes & Paper as Medium, Smithsonian Traveling Exhib, 78-80; Paper-Art, Crocker Art Mus, Sacramento, Calif, 81; New Am Paperworks, Orient & United States, 82-86; Calif Palace of Legion of Honor, San Francisco, 2000; Nat Acad Design, NY, 92, 93, 95, 97, 99, 2001. *Pos:* Dir, Joseph Press, Venice, Calif, 63-64. *Teaching:* Lectr printmaking, Univ Southern Calif, 63; instr drawing, San Jose City Col, 66-82; lectr, Stanford Univ, Calif. *Awards:* Nat Acad Design, 92; Pollock-Krasner Grant, 2003-04. *Bibliog:* Jules Heller (auth), Papermaking, Watson-Guptill Publ, NY, 78. *Mem:* Nat Acad (assoc, 92, acad, 94-). *Media:* Monotype, Paper Art, Sculpture. *Specialty:* Prints. *Interests:* Achenback Foundation for the Graphic Arts, Stanford University Art Museum, The de Saisset Museum. *Publ:* auth, Survey Exhibition 1962-82 (exhib catalog), Smith-Andersen Gallery, Palo Alto, 82; Innovations in monotype and paper art, Arte Grafika, Antwerp, Belg, spring 90; The Cast Acrylic Print, (manual), Joseph Zirker, 2002; Translucent Transformations (catalog), de Saisset Mus, 2005; The Cast Acrylic Print, 2005. *Dealer:* Smith Andersen Editions 440 Pepper Ave Palo Alto CA 94306; Smith Andersen North 2240 Fourth St San Rafoal CA 94901. *Mailing Add:* 451 O'Connor St Menlo Park CA 94025

ZISLA, HAROLD
PAINTER, GRAPHIC ARTIST
b Cleveland, Ohio, June 28, 25. *Study:* Cleveland Inst Art; Western Reserve Univ, BS(cduc) & AM. *Work:* South Bend Regional Mus Art; Midwest Mus Am Art; Snite Mus Art, Notre Dame. *Exhib:* Cleveland Mus Art; South Bend Michiana; John Herron Art Mus; Ft Wayne Art Mus; Kalamazoo Art Inst; and others. *Pos:* Dir & bd mem, South Bend Art Ctr, 57-. *Teaching:* instr, South Bend Art Ctr, 53-89; prof emer fine arts, Ind Univ, South Bend. *Awards:* Amoco Found Award; All Univ Teaching Award, 79; First Eldon Lundquist Fac Fel, Ind Univ South Bend, 85; Arts Midwest Fel Award, 86. *Dealer:* Blue Gallery Three Oaks Mich. *Mailing Add:* 1230 Dennis Dr South Bend IN 46614

ZITO, JOSEPH (PHILLIP)
SCULPTOR, CONCEPTUAL ARTIST
b Brooklyn, NY, June 6, 57. *Study:* Sch Visul Arts, BFA, 79. *Work:* Harvard Univ Art Mus. *Exhib:* One-man shows, Il Ponte Gallery, Rome, Italy, 88 & 91, Greenberg Gallery, St Louis, Mo, 89, Resa Esman Gallery, NY, 88, 89 & 91; Oltreluce, Claudio Bottello Arte, Turin, Italy, 90; Joseph Zito & Gerald Giamportone, Blumhelman Gallery, Los Angeles, Calif, 90. *Bibliog:* Walter Thompson (auth), Joseph Zito, Art in America, 10/88; William Zimmer (auth), 7 Days Mag, 4/6/88; Michael Welzenbach (auth), Washington Post, 2/17/90. *Mailing Add:* 57 Cheever Pl Brooklyn NY 11231

ZITTEL, ANDREA
ARTIST
b Escondido, Calif, 65. *Study:* San Diego State Univ, BFA in Painting & Sculpture, 1988; RI Sch Design, MFA in Sculpture, 1990. *Work:* Carnegie Mus Art, Pittsburgh, 1994, New Work, San Francisco Mus Modern Art, 1995, Sch Mus Fine Arts, Boston, 1996, New Art 6, Cincinnati Art Mus, 1996, Mus Modern Art, Humlebaek, Denmark, 1996, Mus Modern Art, NY, 1994, Whitney Biennial, Whitney Mus Am Art, NY, 1995, 2004, Just Past, Mus Contemp Art, Los Angeles, 1996, Mus Contemp Art, San Diego, Calif, 2001, Tempo, Mus Modern Art, NY, 2002, Just Love Me, Bergen Art Mus, 2003. *Exhib:* One-person shows incl A-Z Living Units, Jack Hanley Gallery, San Francisco, 1993, A-Z Carpet Furniture, Christopher Grimes Gallery, Santa Monica, Calif, 1993; One-woman shows incl Purity, Andrea Rosen Gallery, NY, 1993, Comfort, Anthony d'Offay Gallery, London, 1994, Three Living Systems, A Series of Rotating Installations, Andrea Rosen Gallery, NY, 1994, 1995, New Work, Social Fictions, Barbara & Steven Grossman Gallery, A-Z Escape Vehicles, Andrea Rosen Gallery, NY, 1996, RAUGH, 1998, A-Z Personal Panels, Saide Coles Hq, London, 1999, Point of Interest, Pub Art Fund, Central Park, NY, 1999, A-Z Time Trials: Free Running Rhythms, Regen Projects, Los Angeles, 2002, Philomene Magers Projekte, Munich, Ger, 2003, Sammlung Goetz, Munich, Ger, 2003, Small Liberties, Whitney Mus Am Art, 2006; Exhib in group shows at Ornament: Ho Hum All Ye Faithfull, John Post Lee Gallery, NY, 1991, One Leading to Another, 303 Gallery, NY, 1992, Writing on the Wall, 1992, Radio Show, Artist's Space, NY, 1992, Add Hot Water, Sandra Gering Gallery, NY, 1993, Don't Look Now, Thread Waxing Space, NY, 1994, Sense & Sensibility, Light for the Dark Days of Winter, A/D Gallery, NY, 1995, About Place: Recent Art of Am, Art Inst Chicago, 1995, Staging Realism, Wexner Ctr Arts, Ohio, 1997, Patrick Painter Editions, Lehmann-Maupin Gallery, NY, 1997, Travel & Leisure, Paula Cooper Gallery, NY, 1998, Inglenook, Feigen Contemp, NY, 1998, Art in Pub Places at Miami Design District, Dacra Companies, Miami Beach, 1999, Elysian Fields, Ctr Georges Pompidou, Paris, 2000, Threshold: Invoking Domestic in Contemp Art, Contemp Art Ctr, Va, 2000, Drawings, Regen Projects, LA, 2001, Everything Can Be Different, Calif Ctr Arts, 2002, Living Units, Triple Candie, Harlem, NY, 2003. *Awards:* Recipient Distinction Art, San Diego State Univ, 1988, Award Excellence, RI Sch Design, 1989, 1990, catalogue support prize, Alfried Krupp Von Bohlen und Halbach Found, 1999; Deutschen Akademischen Austauschdienst Grant, Berlin, Ger, 1995, Coutts Contemp Arts Found, Zurich, Switz, 1996. *Mailing Add:* c/o MOCA Grand Ave 250 S Grand Ave Los Angeles CA 90012

ZIVIC, WILLIAM THOMAS
PAINTER, SCULPTOR
b Ironwood, Mich, Aug 31, 30. *Work:* City of Tucson; Univ Ariz; Pima Col; Lockheed Aircraft, Los Angeles; Grissmer Corp, Indianapolis, Ind; Toyota Corp, Tokyo, Japan; plus over 1,000 pvt collections, US, Europe, Africa & Asia. *Comn:* Paintings, Great Western Bank, Phoenix, 73; painting, Ariz Bank, Tucson, 75; painting, US Postal Serv, 75. *Exhib:* Tucson Art Ctr Ann, 74; Alamo Kiwanis Art Show, San Antonio, 74; Casa Grande Art Fiesta, Ariz, 75; Tubac Art Festival, Ariz, 75. *Awards:* Best of Show, Int Fine Arts; 1st place sculpture, Palm Springs, Calif. *Mem:* Tucson Art Ctr; Casa Grande Art Asn; Santa Cruz Valley Art Asn; SW League Fine Arts. *Media:* Bronze; Multimedia. *Publ:* Illusr, Tucson Bi-Centennial Mag, 75; Southwest Memories, 75. *Dealer:* Sonoita Creek Gallery Box 159 Sonoita AZ 85637. *Mailing Add:* 1778 E Bishop Pl Casa Grande AZ 85222-6324

ZLATKOFF, CHARLES
PAINTER, SCULPTOR
b Chicago, Ill, Feb 24, 35. *Study:* Unv Ill, Champaign-Urbana, BFA, 1957; Art Inst Chicago, student; Royal Col Art, London, student. *Work:* Art Inst Archit Chicago; Mus New Mex, Santa Fe; The Albuquerque Mus; Crocker Art Mus, Sacramento; New Mex Capitol Art Found, Santa Fe. *Exhib:* Munic Art Gallery, Los Angeles, 63-66; Long Beach Mus Art, Calif, 64; Fine Arts Mus, San Diego, 65; 161st Ann, Pa Acad Fine Arts, Philadelphia, 66; Am Now-A Look at 70's, Belgrade & Zagreb, Yugoslavia, Budapest, Hungary, 80-81; Alternative Media, Downey Art Mus, Downey, Calif, 82; The Joyful Vision, Craft & Folk Art Mus, Los Angeles, 86; Skirball Mus, Bellair, Calif, 92; Capitol Art Collection, NMex Capitol Art Found, Santa Fe, 03; Pasadena Mus of Calif Art, Pasadena, Calif, 2003; Weisman Art Mus, Malibu, Calif, 2003, 2006. *Teaching:* lectr art & design, UCLA, 67-70; lectr art & design, Univ Calif, ext, LA, 67-90; instr art,Santa Barbara Arts Inst, Santa Barbara, Calif, 71-72. *Bibliog:* William Wilson (auth), Potpourri of work - Art Festival Calendar, Los Angeles Times, 7/18/65; Jason Silverman (auth), Zlatkoff's paintings embrace spirit - Pasatiempo, Santa Fe New Mexican, 94. *Mem:* Calif Art Club. *Media:* Watercolor; All Media. *Dealer:* Canfield Gallery 414 Canyon Rd Santa Fe NM 87501. *Mailing Add:* c/o California Art Club PO Box 92555 Pasadena CA 91109-2555

ZLOWE, FLORENCE M
PAINTER, DRAFTSMAN
b Allentown, Pa. *Study:* Philadelphia Col Art, cert, 33; New York Univ, with Samuel M Adler, 51-54. *Work:* Philadelphia Mus Art; Butler Inst Am Art, Youngstown, Ohio; Smithsonian Inst; Minn Mus Art, St Paul; Cooper-Hewitt Mus, NY; and seven others. *Exhib:* Nat Acad Design, NY, 58 & 65; Chrysler Mus, Norfolk, Va, 64; Chateau de la Napoule, Alpes Maritime, France, 65; Jersey City Mus, NJ, 70; Minn Mus Art, St Paul, 75. *Awards:* Medal Hon First Prize, Nat Asn Women Artists, 58 & Ann Award, 65-80; Oil Award, NJ Soc Painters & Sculptors, 58, 61 & 83; Am Soc Contemp Artists, 59, 64, 75 & 84; and others. *Mem:* Am Soc Contemp Artists (treas, 76-80); Nat Asn Women Artists; NJ Soc Painters & Sculptors; Artists Equity Asn New York. *Media:* Oil, Watercolor; Pen & Ink. *Dealer:* 41 Union Sq New York NY 10003

ZOKOSKY, PETER L
PAINTER
b Long Beach, Calif, 57. *Study:* Univ Calif, Riverside, BA, 79, Otis Art Inst, Los Angeles, MFA, 81. *Work:* Chemical Bank, NY; Kaufman & Broad, Paris, France; Security Pacific Bank & Union Bank, Los Angeles, Calif; Union Bank, Los Angeles; Pacific Bell, San Ramone, Calif; and many others. *Exhib:* Solo exhibs, Inland Empire Gallery, Riverside, 79, Otis Art Inst, Los Angeles, 81, Rio Hondo Col, Whittier, Calif, 84, Newspace, Los Angeles, 86, 88, 89, 91 & 93, Mt San Jacinto Col Art Gallery, 88, Hsiung Shih Gallery, Taipei, Taiwan, 88 & Felicita Found, Escondido, 90; Beyond Appearance, Armory Ctr Arts, Pasadena, Calif, 94; September, Jerrold Burchman Contemp Art, Santa Barbara, 94; The Way of the Flesh, Mt San Antonio Col Gallery, Walnut, Calif, 94; Observance, Warner/Higuera Gallery, Culver City, Calif, 94; Beyond Appearance, Calif Col Arts & Crafts, Oakland, Calif, 95; The Changing Face of Portraiture, Guggenheim Gallery, Chapman Univ, Orange, Calif, 2000; Representing LA, Frye Art Mus, Seattle, Wash, 2000 & Art Mus S Tex, Corpus Christi, 2001; and others. *Awards:* Fel, Nat Endowment Arts, 87; Artist in Residence Grant, Roswell Mus & Art Ctr, NMex, 91. *Bibliog:* Peter Zokosky (auth), Duality a perceptual problem, Psychological Perspectives, spring-summer 94; Artscene, 7-8/94; Peter Frank (auth), Pick of the week, LA Weekly, 7/1/94; Mark Johnstone (auth), Contemporary Art in Southern California, Craftsman House, Sydney, Australia; Edward Lucie-Smith (auth), Zoo: Animals in Art, Watson-Guptill Publ, NY; John Gunnin (auth), Juxtapoz, 1-2/2000. *Mailing Add:* 2020 Raymond Long Beach CA 90806

ZOLLWEG, AILEEN BOULES
PAINTER, SCULPTOR
b East St Louis, Ill. *Study:* Sch Art Inst, Chicago, Ill; Carnegie Mellon Univ, Pittsburgh, Pa. *Work:* 100 Friends of Carnegie Mus Art, Corning Glass Corp & Mellon Bank Collections, Pittsburgh; Dresser Ctr Arts; Southern Alleghenies Mus of Art. *Comn:* Moat tracing, Three Rivers Arts Festival, Pittsburgh, 83; Swimming Pool Mural, San Diego, Calif, 88; Greater Pittsburgh Comn for Women. *Exhib:* One-person exhib, Washington & Jefferson Univ, Washington, Pa, 84, Pittsburgh Ctr Arts, 90, 02-03, 05-06, Laurel Arts, Somerset, Pa, 92 & Gallery 937, Pittsburgh, 96, Southern Alleghenies Mus Art, 99, AAP Ann, Carnegie Mus Art, 01, Westmoreland Mus Art Southwestern Artists Exhibit, 01, Butler Mus Am Art, 01, Southern Allegheny Mus Arts Biennial, 02, 05, Gallery Chiz, 02, 05, AAP Ann, Warhol Mus, 02; Westmoreland Art Mus, Greensburg, Pa, 85 & 2003; New Technol Invitational, Carnegie Mellon Univ Gallery, 85; Butler Inst Am Art, Youngstown, Ohio, 88; Univ Pittsburgh Gallery, 2003; Carnegie Mus Art, Pittsburgh, Pa; Seton Hill Col, 2003. *Awards:* Purchase Award, 83 & 84, Juror's Award, 84 & 91, Asn Artists Carnegie Mus; Jurors Award, Pittsburgh Soc Artist, 97 & 98; Purchase Award, Asn Artists, Warhol Mus, 02. *Bibliog:* TV prog, Women in Art, Monroeville Cable, 83; TV prog, Pittsburgh Women Artists, 92, (no publ & no date); article, Successful-Women-96. *Mem:* Asn Artists Pittsburgh; Pittsburgh Soc Artist; Nat League of Am Pen Women. *Media:* Acrylic; Miscellaneous Media. *Dealer:* Azalea Gallery. *Mailing Add:* 4560 Bulltown Rd Murrysville PA 15668

ZONA, LOUIS A
MUSEUM DIRECTOR, EDUCATOR
b New Castle, Pa, June 28, 44. *Study:* Youngstown State Univ, BS(art educ), 66; Univ Pittsburgh, MS(art educ), 69; Carnegie-Mellon Univ, doctorate, 73. *Collection Arranged:* Patrick Ireland, Blue Room Exhib, 83; Alfred Leslie, 100 Views Along the Road, 85; George Segal: The Drawings, 85; Fireworks: Americans Celebrate the Eighth Art, 86; Ray Parker: A Retrospective Exhibition, 86; Anatomy of a Cloud: The Collage Paintings of Paul Jenkins, Butler Inst Am Art, 86; Leo Castelli: A Tribute (auth, catalog), 87; Jasper Johns: Drawings and Prints from the collection of Leo Castelli, 89; Gregory Arnenoff: Monotypes/Prints, 89; Michael Hardesty: Polar Event & Vigil II, 89; Chuck Close: Editions, 89; Philip Pearlstein: The Abstract Landscapes, 92; The Artist at Ringside, 92; Nassas Daphnis: Color & Form: A Retrospective, 93; Patrick Ireland: Gestures, 94; Robert Motherwell: The Elegy Series, 94; The Comple Prints of Alfred Leslie, 94; Norman Bluhm: A Tribute Exhibition (auth, catalog), 99; Robert Passchenberg & Darryl Pottorf, 99; Chuck Close: The Photographic Work, 2000. *Pos:* Asst to dir, Butler Inst Am Art, Youngstown, Ohio, 80-81 & exec dir, 81-. *Teaching:* Adj prof art & museum studies, Westminster Col, Pa, 76-80; prof art hist & museology, Youngstown State Univ, 70-; chmn, Dept Art, Youngstown State Univ, 78-82. *Awards:* Distinguised Prof Award, Youngstown State Univ, 78; Gov Award Arts (Admin Category), Ohio, 90; Gary Melcher Mem Award for Contribution to Am Fine Arts, Nat Arts Club, 96; Patron of the Yr Am Inst Architects Ohio chap, 98. *Mem:* Hoyt Inst Fine Arts, Pa (trustee); Intermuseum Conserv Asn, Ohio (trustee); Youngstown Area Arts Coun (trustee); Ohio Mus Asn (chmn ann meeting, 89); Asn Art Mus Dir; Portrait Soc Am. *Publ:* Auth, Anatomy of a cloud: the collages of Paul Jenkins, Dialogue Mag, 86; Leo Castelli, interview, Dialogue Mag, 87; Jasper Johns: Drawings & Prints from the Collection of Leo Castelli, 89; Nassos Daphis, Color and Form: A Retrospective (catalog) monograph), 93; Aaron Bohrod, Am Art Rev. *Mailing Add:* Butler Inst Am Art 524 Wick Ave Youngstown OH 44502

ZONIA, DHIMITRI
PAINTER, GRAPHIC ARTIST, SCULPTOR
b St Louis, Mo, June 12, 21. *Study:* Independent study in Italy, Eng & Albania. *Work:* I Gallerise Kombetare Te Arteva, Tirana, Albania; Ark Art Ctr; Albrecht Mus, St Joseph, Mo; Planetarium Prague, Czech Republic; Jewish Community Ctr, St Louis; and others. *Comn:* poster, McDonnell Planetarium, St Louis; murals, St Cyril and Methody Ch, Granite City, Ill; Political Cartoons, The Scene, Forest Park Comnunity Col; St Bernadette Inst Art, Albuquerque; Arber Restaurant, St Louis; and others. *Exhib:* Midyear Show, Butler Inst Am Art, Youngstown, Ohio, 74; Western Ill Univ, 79; Nat Traveling Exhib, Minn Mus Art, 80; Ariz State Univ, 80; Univ Mo, Cape Girardeau, 85. *Teaching:* Instr painting & drawing, Crestwood Community Ctr & Parkway Unitarian Church, Educ Ctr, currently; lectr and demonstration, computer graphics, St Louis Community Col; staff, Louis Community Col. *Awards:* Second Prize Painting, Spiva Art Ctr, Joplin, Mo, 85; Popular Choice Award, Dakota Art Ctr, Rapid City, SDak, 85; 1st Prize Painting, Aesthetics 2000, Linsborg, Kansas; Best of Show, Arcon, Collinville, Ill. *Mem:* St Louis Artists Guild (bd gov, 79-81); Albanian Asn Fine Art; Soc Independent Artists; Catholic Fine Arts Soc. *Media:* Animation, Painting, Computer Art. *Res:* Church Fresco Restoration, Albania; Art Restoration. *Specialty:* Phoenix Pottery, Ceramics. *Interests:* Digital animation, three dimensional modeling. *Collection:* Institute of Sacred Art, New Mexico, Meramec Community College. *Publ:* Air and Space Mag; Step by Step; Am Artist Mag; Song of Solomon; The Scene; and others. *Dealer:* Phoenix Potteries St Louis MO; Mus Sacred Art Albuerquerqe NMex. *Mailing Add:* 4680 Karamar Dr St Louis MO 63128

ZOOK, MAURINE JOYCE
PAINTER; ILLUSTRATOR
b July 17, 1929. *Study:* Univ Kans, 47-50; studies with William F Reese, 85-87; El Camino Col, studies with Willy Suzuki, 87-88; Calif State Univ, Long Beach, studies with Steven Warlick, 89-90, Charles Reid, 2000. *Comn:* Red Lilies at Sunset (painting), Clayton Morgan. *Exhib:* Sol Del Rio Gallery, San Antonio, Tex, 77-98; Los Angeles Int Art Fair 1989, Calif, 89; Feingarten Gallery, 89-98; Chain Reaction (with catalog), Franklin Plaza, Austin, Tex, 91; Watercolor USA 1994, Springfield Art Mus, Mo, 94; Western Fedn Watercolor Soc Ann Exhib, Sun City Art Mus, Ariz, 94 & Lubbock, Tex, 98; Watercolor USA, Springfield, Mo, 2006. *Teaching:* Drawing with children, Dougherty Arts Ctr, 87-88; drawing & watercolor & children at risk, Austin Schs, Tex, 91-94. *Awards:* Best of Show, KLRU 96 Auction; Art Patron Award, Waterloo Watercolor Show, 97. *Bibliog:* John Hay (auth), Book displays artist talents, Pittsburgh Sun, 80; Pete Szilagyi (auth), Review show, Austin Statesman, 91; Dian Covey Birdwell (auth), Austin watercolor artist, Austin Mag, 2000. *Mem:* Nat Watercolor Soc. *Media:* Watercolor, Oil. *Res:* Large watercolor collage-Landscapes and waterscapes. *Interests:* Gardening; Reading; Tai Chi. *Publ:* Illusr, Gabbys Christmas Wish, Shoal Creek Publ, 80. *Dealer:* Art Inc 9401 San Pedro San Antonio Tex 78216

ZOPP, DUDLEY
PAINTER, INSTALLATION ARTIST
b Lexington, Ky, Apr 12, 41. *Study:* Univ Ky, BA, 1963, MA, 1964; postgraduate studies, Allen R Hite Art Inst, Univ Louisville, 1986-91. *Work:* Farnsworth Art Mus, Rockland, Maine; Portland Mus Art, Maine; Boston Athenaem, Boston; Univ Chicago Libr; Univ Ky, Lexington; Univ Maine, Presque Isle, Maine. *Exhib:* Exhibition 280, Huntington Mus Art, Huntington, 1992; Am Drawing Biennial,Muscarelle Mus Art, Williamsburg, Va, 1992; one-person shows, Erratics, Maine Coast Artists, Rockport, Maine, 1997, Reading the Landscape, Univ Maine at Farmington, 1998; Ctr for Maine Contemp Art, 2004; Univ Maine, Presque Isle, Maine, 2004; group shows, Portland Mus Art, Portland, Maine, 1998; Art of Northeast USA, Silvermine Guild Arts Ctr, New Canaan, Conn, 1999; Maine in Am, Farnsworth Art Mus, Rockland, Maine, 2000-02; Univ Southern Maine/Lewiston-Auburn, 2006. *Pos:* studio resident, Pouch Cove Found, Saint Johns, Newfoundland, Can, 97; resident, Art in Nature, Arts Ctr Kingdom Falls, 2001. *Teaching:* instr drawing, Arts Ctr Kingdom Falls, Montville, Maine, 2000-; painting instr, Vt Col, Montpelier, Vt, 2002-. *Awards:* fel, Eleven Artists, Maine Arts Comn, 2002; GIE Grant, Maine Arts Comm, 2003. *Bibliog:* Sarh R Maline (auth), Eleven Artists, Univ Maine, 2002; Jeremy Antworth (auth), Dudley Zopp, Installation Artist, Univ So Maine (video), 2001. *Media:* Oil, Acrylic. *Publ:* CoAuth, A Butterfly Careless, Stinehour Press, 2002. *Dealer:* June Fitzpatrick Gallery, 112 High St, Portland, ME 04101. *Mailing Add:* 68 Main St Belfast ME 04915

ZOX, LARRY
PAINTER
b Des Moines, Iowa, May 31, 37. *Study:* Univ Okla; Drake Univ; Des Moines Art Ctr, with George Grosz. *Work:* Mus Fine Arts, Houston, Tex; Hirchhorn Mus; Whitney Mus Am Art, Metrop Mus Art, Mus Mod Art, NY; Guggenheim Mus; Palm Springs Desert Mus, Calif; Art Inst Chicago. *Exhib:* Whitney Mus Am Art Ann, NY, 69-70 & 72; Indianapolis Mus Art, Ind, 72; one-man retrospective, Whitney Mus Art, 73; Palm Springs Desert Mus, Calif, 73; one-man shows, Daniel Templon Gallery, Paris, France, 75, Alan Rubiner Gallery, Royal Oak, Mich, 79, Carolyn Schneebeck Gallery, Cincinnati, 79, Rubiner Gallery, W Bloomfield, Mich, 85 & 90, Images, Gallery, Toledo, Ohio, 86, 90 & 91, Percival Gallery, Des Moines, 87, 89 & 91, Gallery One, Toronto, Can, 91 & Stein Gallery, St Louis, Mo, 92; Works on Paper: Allen Rubiner Gallery, Royal Oaks, Mich & Meredith Long Gallery, NY, 80; Inaugural Installation, Mus Fine Arts, Boston, 81; Recent Acquisitions, Guggenheim, 81; Images Gallery, Toledo, 86; Rubiner Gallery, West Bloomfield, Mich, 85 & 86; Percival Gallery, Des Moines, 87 & 89; C S Shulte Gallery, NY & NJ, 91; Ann Jaffe Gallery, Bay Harbor, Fla, 92; The Marsh Gallery, Richmond, Va, 93; C S Shulte, Milburn, NJ, 94. *Teaching:* Artist-in-residence, Juniata Col, 64; guest critic, Cornell Univ, 67; artist in resident, Univ NC, Greensboro, 67, Des Moines Art Mus, 74; instr art, Sch Visual Arts, 67-70;

instr art, Dartmouth Col, winter 69; guest speaker & critic, Univ Syracuse, NY, 85. *Awards:* Guggenheim Fel, 67; Nat Coun Arts Award, 69; Ester & Adolph Gottlieb Found, 85. *Dealer:* John Szoke 164 Mercer St New York NY 10012; C S Shulte Gallery 565 Broadway New York NY 10012

ZUCCARELLI, FRANK EDWARD
PAINTER, INSTRUCTOR
b Pa, Oct 23, 21. *Study:* Newark Sch Fine & Indust Art, with William J Aylward & John Grabach; Art Students League, with Robert Philip; Kean Univ, NJ, BA, 75. *Work:* Marine Corps Base, Barstow, Calif; Egan Corp, Bridgewater, NJ; Malcolm Forbes Collection, NY; US Navy Mus, Washington, DC; MCC Corp, Murray Hill, NJ. *Comn:* Paintings for US Navy, Newport RI, 71 & US Coast Guard, Washington, DC, 75; Dahlgren Weapons Lab, Va, 71 & Mediterranean Sixth Fleet, 72; Recovery of Astronauts in Pacific, Apollo-Soyuz Test Proj, 75; Carrier Flight Qualifications, USS Kennedy, 82. *Exhib:* Combat Art Collection, Washington, DC; Essex Fine Arts, Montclair, NJ; Miller Gallery, Cincinnati, Ohio; Palais Rameau, Lille, France; and others. *Teaching:* Pvt instr oils, pastels & watercolor. *Awards:* Hall of Fame, Pastel Soc, 96; Grand Nat Award, Am Artist Prof League, 2000-02; Liskin Mem Award Salmagundi Club, Salmagundi Prize, 2003-2005; and many others. *Bibliog:* Somerset Artist, Painter of all Seasons, 88; Magic of Pastel (video), Pastel Soc New York; Dedication & hard work, Courier News, 93. *Mem:* Pastel Soc Am, NY; Salmagundi Club, NY; Am Artist Prof League; Hudson Valley Art Asn; Allied Artists, NY; and others. *Media:* Oil, Pastel. *Interests:* Photography & Gardening. *Publ:* Am Artist Mag, 11/96; Best of Pastel-Best of Oils, Rockport Publ, 96; Art with Element of Mystery, Pastel Jous, 5-6/2002; Pastelagram, winter 2003; Pastel Artists of the World, Int Artist, 12/2003. *Dealer:* Swain Gallery Plainfield NJ; Swerdlow Gallery Bound Brook NJ; Miller Gallery Cincinnati OH; Louise Melrose Gallery Frenchtown NJ. *Mailing Add:* 61 Appleman Rd Somerset NJ 08873

ZUCCARINI, DAVID ANTHONY
PAINTER, INSTRUCTOR
b Baltimore, Md, 53. *Study:* Corcoran Sch Art, 69-71; Md Inst, BFA(painting), 71-76. *Work:* Univ Md, Md Artists Col, College Park; Howard Community Col; Nat Inst Health Libr. *Exhib:* Mid-Year, Butler Inst, Youngstown, Ohio, 76-82 & 85-90; Int Pastels, Soc Des Pastellistes, Paris, France, 87; Nat Works on Paper, Univ Tex, Tyler, 88; African Influences, Md Mus African Art, Columbia, 90; Drawing 1990, Brigham Young Univ, Provo, Utah; Contemp Self Portraits from the James Goode Collection (with catalog), Nat Portrait Gallery, 93; Legacy, Univ Md. *Teaching:* Instr drawing & painting, pvt studio, 76-. *Awards:* Artists Fel, Md State Arts Coun, 85; Distinguished Teacher, White House, 87; Juror Award, Drawing 1990, Brigham Young Univ. *Bibliog:* Pearl Oxorn (auth), Narrow world/wide vision, Baltimore Sun, 81; Pamela Kessler (auth), Zuccarini's curious studio, Washington Post, 87; Fran Fanshel (auth), Columbia's realist, Columbia Flier, 87; Wayward Passions, Art News, summer 96; E Lynne Moss (auth), Self Portraits Pubic and Private Collections, Am Artist, 9/97. *Mem:* Pastel Soc Am, 78-; Acad Artists Asn, 78-. *Media:* Oil, Charcoal. *Publ:* Auth, Painting figure compositions, Am Artist, 84. *Dealer:* Foxhall Gallery 3301 New Mexico Ave NW Washington DC 20016. *Mailing Add:* 9402 Mellenbrook Rd Columbia MD 21045

ZUCKER, BARBARA
SCULPTOR
b Philadelphia, Pa, Aug 2, 40. *Study:* Univ Mich, BS(design), 62; Cranbrook Acad Art, Bloomfield Hills, Mich; Kokoschka Sch Vision, Salzburg, Austria, 61; Hunter Col, MA, 77. *Work:* Whitney Mus Am Art, NY; Fine Arts Ctr, Univ Mass, Amherst; Indianapolis Mus; Chase Manhattan Bank; Am Can Co; Brooklyn Mus, NY. *Comn:* Greenwich Libr sculpture, Conn, 84. *Exhib:* 26 Contemp Women Artists, Aldrich Mus Art, 71; one-woman shows, Joslyn Art Mus, 81, Queens Mus, 87, Sculpture Ctr, NY, 89, Haneh Kent, NY, 90, Artists Space, NY, 94 & Paley Gallery, Moore Col Art, 96. *Pos:* Co-founder, AIR Gallery, New York, NY, 72; ed assoc, Art News Mag, 74-81. *Teaching:* Instr art, La Guardia Community Col, Queens, NY, 74-77; instr, Fordham Univ, Lincoln Ctr, New York, 74-79; artist-in-residence, Princeton Univ, fall 75 & Fine Arts Work Ctr, Provincetown, winter 75; artist-in-residence, Fla State Univ, 76; instr, Philadelphia Col of Art, 77-79; prof & chairperson art dept, Univ Vt, 79-84; prof art, Univ Vt, 79-2000, prof emer, 2000-; vis prof sculpture, Yale Univ, 87-88. *Awards:* Nat Endowment Arts Fel Grant, 75; Artpark, 78; Yaddo, 85, 89 & 94; Reader's Dig Fel Award, Giverny, France, 90; Ucross Found, 94. *Bibliog:* Richard Martin (auth), Barbara Zucker, Arts Mag, 83; Nancy Princenthal (auth), review, Art in Am, 94; review, Sculpture Mag, 96. *Mem:* Col Art Asn; Women's Caucus for Art (mem adv bd, 78, bd dir, 83-86). *Publ:* Contribr, Art News, 74-79; contribr, Village Voice (centerfold), 7/2/75 & 7/9/75 & article on Red Grooms, 76; auth, article on Florine Stettheimer (American painter), Art News, 2/76 & Women's Studies, 79; Unusual materials, Art J, 80, Heresies, Making Air, 80 & Sculpture New Hampshire, 82. *Mailing Add:* Univ Vt Art Dept 304 Williams Hall Burlington VT 05405

ZUCKER, BOB
ARCHITECTIVRAL PHOTOGRAPHOR, PORTRAIT
b New York, NY, Dec 10, 46. *Study:* Hunter Col, BA; and with Philippe Halsman, NY. *Work:* Libr of Cong; J P Morgan libr; Soc Preservation Long Island Antiquities; Nat Trust Hist Preservation; Sotheby's Int Realty. *Comn:* Photos, 19th Century Pub Sculpture, Metrop Mus, 73; Sculpture of Isodor Konti, Hudson River Mus, 74; Historic Architectural Documentation of Old Westchester Co Courthouse Complex, Co of Westchester, 74; Bicentennial Exhib, Venturi & Rauch AIA & Whitney Mus, 75; Am Bicentennial: Signs of Life in the City, Renwick Gallery, Smithsonian Inst, 75; and others. *Exhib:* 19th Century Pub Sculpture in NY Parks, 73; Life in Am in the 18th Century, Nat Mus Am Hist, 85. *Teaching:* Long Island Univ, CW Post Col. *Publ:* Auth, American Architecture: Westchester Co, 77; Architectural Guide to Nassau & Suffolk Counties, Am Inst Architects, Long Island. *Mailing Add:* 3 Burbank Ct Greenlawn NY 11740

ZUCKER, JOSEPH I
PAINTER
b Chicago, Ill, May 21, 41. *Study:* Miami Univ, 59-60; Art Inst Chicago, BFA & MFA. *Work:* Walker Art Ctr, Minneapolis; Whitney Mus Am Art; Albright-Knox Gallery, Buffalo; Metrop Mus, NY; Philadelphia Mus Art; and others. *Exhib:* Art Inst Chicago, 64 & 81; Walker Art Ctr, 68; New Am Abstract Painting, Madison Art Ctr, 72; Prospect, Dusseldorf, Ger, 73; Bykert Gallery, NY, 74; Whitney Biennial, Whitney Mus, 79, 92 & 83; Venice Biennale, 80; Surfacing Images, The Paintings of Joe Zucker 1969-82, Albright-Knox Gallery, Buffalo, 82; Queens Mus Traveling Exhib, 85-86; Arts Club Chicago, 88; Guild Hall, East Hamptin, NY, 99. *Teaching:* Instr painting, Minneapolis Sch Art, 66-68, Sch Visual Arts, NY, 68-71 & NY Univ, 71-74. *Bibliog:* Edward Lucie-Smith (auth), Art in the Seventies, Cornell Univ Press, 81;. *Mem:* Nat Acad (acad, 95-). *Dealer:* Hirschl & Adler Mod 851 Madison Ave New York NY 10021. *Mailing Add:* PO Box 553 Wainscott NY 11975-0553

ZUCKER, MURRAY HARVEY
SCULPTOR, COLLAGE ARTIST
b New York, NY, Dec 14, 20. *Work:* AFL-CIO Hq, Washington; Community Blood Coun, NY; Omaha Nat Bank, Nebr; Slater Mem Mus, Norwich, Conn; Butler Inst Am Art, Ohio. *Comn:* Paintings, Atlantic Richfield Co, NY, 68, Technicon Corp, Ardsley, NY, 69 & Police Benevolent Asn, NY, 70. *Exhib:* Gallery Carron, NY, 79; Lever House, NY, 80; Salmagundi Club, NY, 81; Springs Invitational, 96; Seven Sculptors, 96; and others. *Awards:* First Prize Graphics, Am Soc Contemp Artists, 76; Kulicke Award for Graphics, 78; Feigin Award Graphics, 81; and others. *Bibliog:* C Crane (auth), Contemporary collages, Interiors, 5/70; Gerald F Brommer (auth), The Art of Collage, Davis Publ, Inc, 78; and others; Gerald F Brommer (auth), Collage Techniques, Watson-Guptill Publ, 94. *Mem:* Artists Equity Asn; Am Soc Contemp Artists; Metrop Painters & Sculptors; Jimmy Ernst Artists Alliance; and others. *Media:* Wax for Bronze; Paper on Paper. *Mailing Add:* 54 Cosdrew Ln East Hampton NY 11937

ZUGOR, SANDOR
PAINTER, PRINTMAKER
b Brod, Repub of Bosnia (formerly Yugoslavia), Feb 7, 23; US citizen. *Study:* Acad Fine Art, Budapest, 41-45, with Istvan Szonyi; graphics with Varga Nandor Lajos. *Work:* Mus Fine Art Budapest; Gallery of Mod Art, Taipei, Taiwan; Butler Inst of Am Art, Youngstown, Ohio; Georgia Univ Mus Fine Art, Athens; Hungarian Nat Gallery; Fairleigh Dickinson Univ Art Col, NJ. *Exhib:* Nat Mus Hist, Taipei, Taiwan; Young Americans, Mus Contemp Crafts, NY, 62; Brooklyn Mus, 69; Palacio Bellas Artes, Mexico City, 72; Hungarian Nat Gallery, 88; Westbeth Galleries, NY; Retrospective exhib, Szekesfehervar, Hungary, 88; Budapest Gallery, Hungary, 89. *Teaching:* Lectr drawing, Brooklyn Col Adult Educ, 66-71. *Awards:* Prix du Rome, Hungarian Acad Rome fel, 46-48; First Prize for Drawing Competition, Peace & War, Fedn Hungarian Artists, 54. *Media:* Acrylics, Oil; Etching

ZUHN-MOULDER, CHERYL
EDUCATOR, DESIGNER
b Chicago, Ill, June 7, 59. *Study:* Ray-Vogue Col Design (visual merchandising), 78; Thornton Community Col (Europ art hist study tour), dipl, 84. *Pos:* Designer & fashion coordr, Dept Visual Merchandising, Chicago, Ill, 78-81; fashion show stage set designer, Chicago Apparel Ctr, Ill, 82-; merchandise presentation designer, Abercrombie & Fitch, Chicago, Ill, 85-89; interior designer, Woodfield Summer Showcase House, Ill, 86, 87 & 88; principal designer, Zular Designs, 84-. *Teaching:* Instr visual merchandising, chmn dept & dir mannequins, fixtures & props, Ray-Col Design, Ill, 81-96; merchandising mgt instr, Int Acad Merchandising & Design, 96-. *Awards:* Best Store Visual Presentation, Woodfield Mall, Schaumberg, Ill, 85. *Mem:* Art Inst Chicago. *Res:* European art history. *Mailing Add:* 9422 Presidio Rd Scottsdale AZ 85260-4389

ZUPAN, BRUNO
PAINTER, PRINTMAKER
b Yugoslavia, June 21, 39; US citizen. *Study:* Zagreb Art Inst, Yugoslavia, 59. *Comn:* Lithograph (with Annabelle Wiener), World Fedn UN Asn, NY, 81. *Exhib:* Boston Col Student Ctr, Mass, 64; Columbia Mus Arts, Columbus, SC, 65; Salon des Artists Francais, Paris, 73 & 76; Nat Acad, NY, 74; Butler Inst Am Art, Youngstown, Ohio, 74. *Bibliog:* Mary Carroll Nelson (auth), Through a Sunny Window, Am Artist Mag, 3/79. *Media:* Oil, Watercolor; Serigraph, Lithograph

ZURIER, REBECCA F
CURATOR, EDUCATOR
b San Francisco, Calif, Sept 9, 56. *Study:* Harvard U, AB, Yale U, PhD, 88. *Collection Arranged:* Nat Mus Am Art, Smithsonian Inst, 93; Art for The Masses: A Radical Magazine and Its Graphics, Yale U Art Gallery, 85; Metropolitan Lives: The Ashh Artists and Their New York, Nat Mus Am Art, 95. *Teaching:* Asst prof art hist & dir undergrad studies, Univ Mich, Ann Arbor, 92-99, assoc prof art hist & fac assoc, prog in Am cult, 99-. *Awards:* Barr Award, Col Art Asn; Charles Warren Ctr for Studies in Am Hist Fel, Harvard Univ, 99-2000. *Publ:* Auth, The American Firehouse: An Architectural and Social History, 82; Art for the Masses (1911-1917): A Radical Magazine and its Graphics, 88; Classy Comics, 91; Metropolitan Lives: The Ashcan Artists and Their New York, 95. *Mailing Add:* Univ of Mich Dept of History of Art Tappan Hall Ann Arbor MI 48109-1357

ZURIK, JESSELYN BENSON
PAINTER, SCULPTOR
b New Orleans, La, Dec 26, 19. *Study:* Newcomb Col Art Sch, Tulane Univ, BD, 38; Univ Col Sch Art, Tulane Univ, 58-61; with Xavier Gonzales, Angela Gregory, Caroline W Durieux, Harold Carney, Will Stevens & Harold Thurman. *Work:* New Orleans Pub Libr, New Orleans Mus Art; Rose Art Mus, Brandeis Univ; Light &

Power Co, Birmingham, Ala; Nat Mus Women Arts, Washington, DC. *Comn:* Mosaic stairwell, comn by Mr & Mrs M Fishman, New Orleans, 58; design for Hearing & Speech Ctr, New Orleans, 65; design for Touro Infirmary, New Orleans, 65; assemblage coppery printing blocks, Lubat Co, New Orleans, 78; beaded entire 1970 Gremlin, Contemp Arts Ctr, New Orleans, 82-83. *Exhib:* Artists of the Gulf States, New Orleans Mus Art, 64; Southeastern Ann, High Mus, Atlanta, 65; Southern Asn Sculptors, Ark Art Ctr, Little Rock, 66 & Mint Mus Art, Charlotte, NC, 66; Selected Artists: Glade Gallery Invitational, Lauren Rogers Mus Art, Laurel, Miss, 70; Tiennial Nat (art about ties), Contemp Arts Ctr, New Orleans, 79; Int Women's Postcard Exhib, Glyptoteck Mus, Copenhagen, Denmark, 80; Second Louisiana Sculptors Biennial, Contemp Arts Ctr, New Orleans, 82; Art Cars, PS 1, NY, 82 & Focus Int, Nairobi, Kenya, 85; Contemp Arts Ctr, New Orleans, La, 91; and 255 invitational and group shows and 31 solo shows; Wild Wheels # II, New Orleans Mus Art, New Orleans, La, 2002. *Pos:* Illusr, Katz & Besthoff Co & Adler's Jewelry, New Orleans, 38-40; marine drafting, Higgins Co, New Orleans, 43. *Teaching:* Instr assemblage art, var groups & orgn, New Orleans, 62-75 & 80. *Awards:* Purchase Prize, Brandeis Univ Invitational, 63; Honorable Mention, 2nd Ann New Orleans Art Asn, 72; Third Place, Nat Triennial, Wembley Indust, Contemp Arts Ctr, New Orleans, 79. *Bibliog:* Luba Glade (auth), Dazzling superspectacle, States/Item, 74; Dana Standish (auth), Getting down to brass tacks, Gambit, 81; Geoff O'Connell (auth), Book inspires wheel-life art, Dallas Morning News, 82. *Mem:* Nat Mus Women Arts; Southeastern Women's Caucus Art; Contemp Arts Ctr New Orleans; New Orleans Mus Art; Arts Coun New Orleans. *Media:* Wood, Oil. *Dealer:* Wendy Morehead Gallery 603 Julia St New Orleans LA 70130. *Mailing Add:* 7740 Belfast St New Orleans LA 70125-3402

ZWACK, MICHAEL
PAINTER, SCULPTOR
b Buffalo, NY, Oct 25, 49. *Study:* Buffalo State Col, BA, 70. *Work:* Metrop Mus Art, NY; Albright-Knox Art Gallery, Buffalo; Weatherspoon Art Gallery, Greensboro, NC; Ft Worth Mus, Tex; Burchfield Art Ctr, Buffalo. *Exhib:* Solo exhibs, Tough Bridge to Cross, Essex Art Ctr, Buffalo, NY, 77, The Levitation of Anna, Atrists Space, NY, 79, Studio D'Arte Cannaviello, Milan, Italy, 80, Weatherspoon Art Gallery, Univ NC, Greensboro, 86, Curt Marcus Gallery, NY, 87-90, 93, 94, Thomas Solomon's Garage, Los Angeles, 90, 95, Paul Kasmin Gallery, NY, 98, 99, David Floria Gallery, Aspen, 01; Great Big Drawings: Contemp Works on Paper, Hayden Gallery MIT, Cambridge, Mass, 82; Painting & Sculpture Today 1984, Indianapolis Mus Art, Ind, 84; Nature Genre, Fine Arts Ctr, Fla State Univ, Tallahassee, 84; Monumental Drawing: Works by Twenty Am Artists, Brooklyn Mus, NY, 87; New Visions of the Apocalypse, Mus Art, RI Sch Design, Providence, 88; Moscow-Vienna-NY, Messelpalast, Vienna, Austria, 89; Romance and Irony, Art Gallery W Australia, Perth, 89; Elizabeth Leach Gallery, Portland, Ore, 94; Paul Kasmin Gallery, NY, 96; David Floria Gallery, Aspen, Colo, 98. *Collection Arranged:* Albright-Knox Art Gallery, Buffalo, NY; Brooklyn Mus, NY; Chase Manhattan Bank Art Prog Collection, NY; Memorial Art Gallery, Univ Rochester, NY; Metrop Mus Art; Modern Art Mus Fort Worth, Tex; Readers Digest Collection, NY. *Awards:* Nat Endowment Arts Award, 78; Grantee: Pollock-Krasner Found, 97, Adolph and Esther Gottlieb Found, 98. *Bibliog:* Richard Amstrong (auth), Otherviews, Artforum, 12/83; Album: Michael Zwack, Arts Mag, 4/87; Douglas Blau (auth), Michael Zwack, Thaddeus Ropac & Curt Marcus, 91; Brooks, Rosetta (auth.) Michael Zwack, Thomas solomon's Garage, Artforum, 95; Medwick, Cathleen, (auth) Solitary Splendor, House & Garden Mag., 99; Grace Glueck (auth), NY Times, 6/18/1999. *Media:* Oil. *Dealer:* Paul Kasmin Gallery 293 10th Ave New York NY 10013. *Mailing Add:* 10 Kenmare St Apt 2 New York NY 10012-4605

ZWEERTS, ARNOLD
PAINTER, MOSAIC ARTIST
b Bussum, Neth, 18; US citizen. *Study:* Sch for Arts & Crafts & Sch for Art Teacher Training, Royal Acad Art, Amsterdam; Royal Acad Art, Copenhagen, Denmark; Acad Belli Arti, Ravenna, Italy; Inst Allende, Univ Guanajunto, Mex, MFA; also study with Jos Rovers, Riseby, Orselli, Signoriny & Kortlang. *Work:* Stedelijk Mus, Amsterdam; Collection of the State, The Hague, Neth; and others. *Comn:* Mosaics, Hengelo, Neth, 54, Lockhorst, Koldewyn, Van Eyck, Rotterdam Architects, 55-56, Chicago Process Gear Co, 61, Boulder Med Arts Bldg, Colo, 63-64, Lombard Dental Med Bldg, 72, 73 & 74 & Postville Sch House, Wis, 76-77; 220' mosaic, comn by US Dept Agr, Multnomah Falls Pedestrian Tunnel, Ore, 84; First Hood River Mosaic Wall, 88; Second Hood River Mosaic Wall, 89; Third Hood River Mosaic Wall, 92. *Exhib:* Art Inst Chicago, 66; Gallery Margaret Huisman, The Neth, 80; Mosaic Proposals, Mt Hood Col, Gresham, Ore, 86; Giverny Gallery, Gresham, Ore, 87; The Dalles Art Gallery, The Dalles, Ore, 88; two-man show, Columbia Gorge Arts Asn & Gallery, Hood River, 91; and others. *Teaching:* Instr mosaic & color, Kingston Upon Thames, Surrey, Eng, 51-53; instr appreciation of art, Stedelijk Mus, Rijksmus, Amsterdam, 54-57; asst prof drawing & painting, Art Inst Chicago, 57-73; lectr, dept fine arts, Loyola Univ Chicago, 68-78. *Awards:* First Prize-Printmaking, Civic Fine Arts Asn, Sioux Falls, 76; Award of Hon, 63 Salon, Madison Art Mus, 77. *Bibliog:* Pieter Scheen (auth), Lexicon Nederlandse Beeldende Kunstenaars 1750-1950, Part II, Kunsthandel P Scheen N V, The Hague, 70. *Mem:* Columbia Gorge Creative Arts League. *Media:* Oil; Mosaic Glass. *Publ:* Delphian Quart, Vol 43, No 4, A Renaissance in Architectural Art. *Dealer:* Ricciardi Gallery 108 Tenth St Astoria OR 97103. *Mailing Add:* 817 Sherman Ave Hood River OR 97031

ZWIETNIG-ROTTERDAM, PAUL See Rotterdam, Paul Zwietnig-Rotterdam

ZYNSKY, TOOTS
SCULPTOR
b Boston, Mass, 51. *Study:* RI Sch Design, Providence, BFA, 73. *Work:* Mus Mod Art, Cooper-Hewitt Mus, NY; Corning Mus Glass, Corning, NY; High Mus Art, Atlanta, Ga; Hokkaido Mus Mod Art, Sapporo, Japan; Musee des Arts Decoratifs, Paris, France; Philadelphia Mus Art; and many others. *Exhib:* Glass Now '89, Yamaha Corp, Tokyo, Japan, 89; Stedelijk Mus, Amsterdam, The Neth, 89; Clara Scremini Gallery, Paris, France, 90; Masterpieces of Glass from the Corning Collection, Nat Gallery Art, Washington, DC, 90; Gaste aus Frankreich, Kunstmuseum, Hamburg, Ger, 90; Snyderman Gallery, Philadelphia, Pa, 91 & 92. *Pos:* Asst dir, NY Experimental Glass Workshop, 80-81 & dept head, 81-82. *Teaching:* Instr, RI Sch Design. *Awards:* Visual Arts Fel, Nat Endowment Arts, 82 & 86; Grant, Stiching Klanschap, Amsterdam, 84. *Media:* Glass. *Publ:* Auth, International Crafts, Am Craft Mag, 91; auth, (article), Thames & Hudson, London & New York Times, 12/93. *Mailing Add:* c/o Snyderman Gallery 303 Cherry St Philadelphia PA 19106

Geographic Index

ALABAMA

Auburn

Furr, Jim   Painter, Printmaker
Gluhman, Margaret A   Graphic Artist, Photographer
Hatfield, Donald Gene   Painter, Educator
Olson, Douglas John   Educator, Photographer
Ross, Conrad H   Painter, Printmaker
Ross, Janice Koenig   Painter

Birmingham

Chapman, Gary Howard   Painter
Finley, Donny Lamenda   Painter
Fleming, Frank   Sculptor
Lewis, Ronald Walter   Painter, Educator
Livingston, Margaret Gresham   Administrator, Patron
Medenica, Branko   Sculptor
Nordan, Antoinette Spanos Johnson   Curator, Historian
Rankin, Don   Painter, Instructor
Rembert, Virginia Pitts   Educator, Art Historian
Shelton, Robert Lee   Designer, Educator
Trechsel, Gail Andrews   Director

Dothan

Rutland, Lilli Ida   Painter, Illustrator

Fairhope

Wolff, Robert W, Jr   Dealer

Hartselle

Howell-Coon, Elizabeth (Mitch)   Painter

Huntsville

Baldaia, Peter Joseph   Curator, Director
Boyd, Lakin   Educator, Printmaker
Crouse, Michael Glenn   Educator, Printmaker
Parrish, David Buchanan   Painter
Parsons, Cynthia Massey   Painter, Writer
Pope, Mary Ann Irwin   Painter
Reeves, James Franklin   Historian, Collector
Robb, David Metheny, Jr   Historian, Museum Director
Rubin, Donald Vincent   Sculptor
Savas, Jo-Ann   Painter, Instructor

Mobile

Conlon, James Edward   Sculptor, Historian
Kennedy, James Edward   Painter, Sculptor
Rathle, Henri (Amin)   Painter
Thomason, Michael Vincent   Photographer, Curator

Montgomery

Johnson, Mark M   Museum Director
Tolliver, Mose   Painter

Ozark

Deloney, Jack Clouse   Painter, Illustrator

Tuscaloosa

Kakas, Christopher A   Printmaker, Painter
Musgrave, Shirley H   Educator, Photographer
Sella, Alvin Conrad   Painter, Educator
Warner, JacK   Collector

Tuskegee

Thomas, Elaine Freeman   Educator, Administrator

ALASKA

Anchorage

Appel, Keith Kenneth   Sculptor, Muralist
Ard, Saradell   Educator, Painter
Birdsall, Byron   Painter
Conaway, Gerald   Sculptor, Painter
Erikson, Christine   Educator
Hedman, Teri Jo   Printmaker, Painter
Jaeger, Brenda Kay   Painter, Craftsman
Kaulitz, Garry Charles   Printmaker, Painter
Owens, Tennys Bowers   Dealer
Redmond, Rosemary   Painter
Regat, Jean-Jacques Albert   Sculptor, Muralist
Regat, Mary E   Sculptor, Muralist
Shadrach, Jean H   Painter, Educator
Vallee, William Oscar   Painter, Graphic Artist
Wolf, Patricia B   Museum Director

Cooper Landing

Downer, Spelman Evans   Painter, Photographer

Cordova

Bugbee-Jackson, Joan (Mrs John M Jackson)   Sculptor, Educator

Fairbanks

Amason, Alvin Eli   Painter
Brody, Arthur William   Printmaker, Painter
Freer, Fred-Christian   Painter, Sculptor
Jonaitis, Aldona   Historian, Administrator
Nakoneczny, Michael   Painter
Woodward, Kesler Edward   Painter, Curator

Juneau

DeRoux, Daniel Edward   Painter, Sculptor
Munoz, Rie   Painter, Printmaker

Sitka

De Armond, Dale B   Printmaker, Illustrator

ARIZONA

Apache Junction

Coe, Anne Elizabeth   Painter

Bowie

Stutesman, Cezanne Slough   Painter

Carefree

Harris, Robert George   Painter, Illustrator
Swanson, Ray V   Painter

Casa Grande

Zivic, William Thomas   Painter, Sculptor

Cave Creek

Williamson, Jason H   Painter

Chandler

Missal, Joshua M & Pegge   Art Dealers, Consultants

Cornville

Waddell, John Henry   Sculptor, Painter

Douglas

Dusard, Jay   Photographer, Writer

Flagstaff

Edgerton, Debra   Painter, Educator
Horn, Bruce   Painter, Educator

Glendale

Manhold, John Henry   Sculptor

Globe

Kilb, Jenny   Painter, Muralist

Gold Canyon

Braig, Betty Lou   Painter, Educator

Green Valley

Allen, Constance Olleen Webb   Painter, Jewelry Designer

Marana

Tobias, Robert Paul   Painter, Sculptor

Mesa

Dawson, John Allan   Painter, Sculptor
Hulick, Diana Emery   Sculptor, Photographer
O'Dell, Erin (Anne)   Painter, Designer
Pile, James   Painter
Schultz, Marilou   Weaver, Instructor
Slater, Gary Lee   Sculptor
Tyser, Patricia Ellen   Stained Glass Artist, Assemblage Artist

Munds Park

Carpenter, Earl L   Painter

Oracle

Davis, James Granberry   Painter
McGrew, Bruce Elwin   Painter
Rush, Andrew   Printmaker, Sculptor

Paradise Valley

Gale, Nessa   Sculptor, Painter
Harnett, Lila   Collector
Keane, Bill   Cartoonist
Kipp, Lyman   Sculptor
McCall, Robert Theodore   Illustrator, Painter
Quinn, Brian Grant   Sculptor, Painter
Rothschild, John D   Dealer

ARIZONA (cont)
Soleri, Paolo Architect, Sculptor

Peoria
Charles, Larry Painter, Lecturer
Hillis, Richard K Painter, Printmaker
Toschik, Larry Painter, Writer
Willard, Garcia Lou Graphic Artist, Painter

Phoenix
Ballinger, James K Museum Director, Historian
Dignac, Geny (Eugenia) M Bermudez Sculptor, Environmental Artist
Frerichs, Ruth Colcord Painter, Lithographer
Grigsby, Jefferson Eugene, Jr Educator, Painter
Haozous, Bob Sculptor
Kniffin, Ralph Gus Graphic Artist
McGuire, Maureen Designer, Stained Glass Artist
Moore, Ina May Painter, Instructor
Nisula, Larry Painter, Sculptor
Oliver, Robert S Painter, Architect
Richter, Hank Painter, Sculptor
Rider Berry, Tarah J Photographer, Instructor
Sansone, Joseph F Craftsman
Ullman, (Mrs) George W Collector
Woods, Roosevelt (Rip) Painter, Printmaker
Wright, Barton Allen Writer, Graphic Artist

Prescott
Dutton, Allen A Photographer, Painter
Stasack, Edward Armen Painter, Printmaker
Young, Marjorie Ward Painter, Draftsman

Prescott Valley
Decil, Stella (Del) W Painter, Instructor

Scottsdale
Afsary, Cyrus Painter
Cawley, Joan Mae Art Dealer, Publisher
Clymer, Albert Anderson Painter
Collins, Dan (Daniel) McClellan Painter
DeLoyht-Arendt, Mary Arendt Painter
Doyle, John Lawrence Printmaker, Painter
Gentry, Warren Miller Painter
Gillingwater, Denis Claude Sculptor, Educator
Hack, Phillip S & Patricia Y Collectors
Haverty, Grace Painter
Hill, John Conner Art Dealer, Designer
Jacobson, Frank Administrator
Krane, Susan Curator, Museum Director
Kroll, David Painter
Magenta, Muriel Sculptor, Video Artist
May, Daniel Striger Dealer
Mayer, Robert Anthony Administrator, Photographer, Writer
Missal, Stephen J Painter, Instructor
Norton, Mary Joyce Painter, Jeweler
Phillips, Dick (Richard) Cortez Painter, Instructor
Pritzlaff, (Mr & Mrs) John, Jr Collectors
Reynolds, James Elwood Painter
Schmidt, Randall Bernard Sculptor, Educator
Simmons, Julie Lutz Painter, Sculptor
Stuart, Sherry Blanchard Painter
Swartz, Beth Ames Painter
Taylor, Ann Painter
Waid, Jim (James) E Painter
Yares, Riva Art dealer, Publisher, Writer
Zuhn-Moulder, Cheryl Educator, Designer

Sedona
Coleman, M L (Michael Lee) Painter, Instructor
De Mille, Leslie Benjamin Painter, Sculptor
Garrison, Gene K Photographer, Painter, Writer
Hull, Gregory Stewart Painter
Jennerjahn, W P Educator, Painter
Juharos, Stephen Painter
Mahoney, Joella Jean Educator, Painter

Sonoita
Copenhaver-Fellows, Deborah Lynne Fellows Sculptor, Painter
Hampton, John Wade Sculptor, Painter
Irving, Donald J Administrator, Writer

Sun City
Moses, Bette J Painter

Tempe
Britton, Daniel Robert Printmaker, Educator
Codell, Julie Francia Historian, Administrator
DeMatties, Nick Painter
Eder, James Alvin Printmaker, Painter
Fahlman, Betsy Lee Historian
Gully, Anthony Lacy Historian, Administrator
Jay, Bill Photographic Historian, Critic
Klett, Mark Photographer
Lewis, William R Instructor, Painter
Sol'Sax Painter, Educator
Stuler, Jack Photographer, Educator
Sweeney, J Gray Historian, Curator
Taylor, Janet R Tapestry Artist, Weaver
Turk, Rudy H Museum Director, Painter
Weiser, Kurt D Ceramist
White, James Richard Sculptor, Educator
Zeitlin, Marilyn A Curator, Writer, Museum Director

Tubac
Cabot, Hugh Painter

Tucson
Anderson, Warren Harold Graphic Artist, Painter
Balaban, Diane Painter
Bautzmann, CA-OPA (Nancy Annette) Painter
Birdsall, Stephanie Artist
Bishop, Jerold Educator, Painter
Bloomfield, Suzanne Painter, Printmaker
Borgia-Aberle, Nina Ceramist, Instructor, Public Artist
Bredlow, Tom Designer, Blacksmith
Cajero, Michael Ray Environmental Artist, Sculptor
Chabot, Aurore (Martha) Sculptor
Cole, Julie Kramer Painter
Doogan, Bailey Painter, Instructor
Doren, Henry J T Painter, Educator
Garzon-Blanco, Armando Designer, Painter
Gilbert, Herb Painter
Greer, Wesley Dwaine Educator, Craftsman
Grossman, Maurice Kenneth Educator, Ceramic Artist
Grygutis, Barbara Sculptor, Environmental Artist
Heldt, Carl Randall Educator, Painter
Heric, John F Sculptor
Hitner, Chuck Painter, Educator
Hupp, Frederick Duis Painter, Educator
Josten, Katherine Ann Conceptual Artist, Director
Kuhn, Bob Draftsman, Painter
Lowe, Marvin Painter, Printmaker
Martin, Lucille Caiar Painter, Muralist
Murray, Frances Photographer
Paravano, Dino Painter
Parry, Ellwood Comly, III Historian
Parry, Pamela Jeffcott Librarian, Administrator
Quiroz, Alfred James Painter, Educator
Rogers, Barbara Painter, Educator
Rufe, Laurie J Museum Director
Sevigny, Maurice Joseph, II Educator, Administrator
Stefan, Ross Painter
Stonebarger, Virginia Painter, Instructor
Yassin, Robert Alan Museum Director, Curator

Tuscon
Caldwell, Eleanor Jeweler, Educator
Denzler, Nancy J Sculptor, Painter

Wickenburg
Harrison, Myrna J Painter, Instructor

Williams
Seaman, Drake F Painter

ARKANSAS

Arkadelphia
Linn, John William Administrator, Writer

Benton
Criswell, Warren Painter, Printmaker

Conway
Burchett, Kenneth Eugene Educator, Consultant
Jenkens, Garlan F Curator, Painter
Larsen, Patrick Heffner Painter, Sculptor

Fayetteville
Brody, Myron Roy Sculptor, Photographer
Cockrill, Sherna Painter, Instructor
Musgnug, Kristin A Artist
Peven, Michael David Photographer, Educator
Sandol, Maynard Painter
Wilson, Charles Banks Painter, Printmaker

Fort Smith
Farris, Greer Sculptor

Glenwood
Klopfenstein, Philip Arthur Administrator, Historian

Harrison
Langford-Stansbery, Sherry K Environmental Artist, Painter

Hot Springs
Katchen, Carole Lee Painter, Writer

Jonesboro
Allen, William J Historian, Educator
Lindquist, Evan Printmaker, Educator
Salvest, John Sculptor, Educator

Little Rock
Bailin, David Painter, Educator
Cawood, Gary Kenneth Photographer - Gelatin Silver
DuBois, Alan Beekman Curator, Administrator
Mapes, Doris Williamson Painter
Martin, Floyd W Historian, Editor
Mitchell, Shannon Dillard Curator, Administrator
Pasquine, Ruth Curator, Lecturer
Smith, AJ Printmaker

Newport
Hembrey, Shea Painter

ARKANSAS (cont)

Pettigrew

McNamara, William Patrick, Jr Painter, Printmaker

Pine Bluff

Detmers, William Raymond Printmaker, Educator
Murray, Reuben Administrator
Shaw, Donald Edward Sculptor, Painter

Siloam Springs

Anderson, Troy Painter, Sculptor

State University

Hickman, Paul Addison Educator, Slide Curator
Keech, John H Painter

CALIFORNIA

Acampo

Eger, Marilyn Rae Painter, Educator

Alameda

Argue, Douglas Painter
Davis, James Wesley Painter, Writer
Unterseher, Chris Christian Sculptor
Valesco, Frances Muralist, Printmaker

Alamo

Pochmann, Virginia Painter, Draftsman

Albion

Martin, Bill Painter, Sculptor

Aliso Viejo

Wyland, Steve Creech Environmental Artist, Painter

Alta Loma

Maloof, Sam Sculptor

Altadena

Green, David Oliver Sculptor, Educator
Sterritt, Coleen Sculptor, Educator

Antioch

Paskewitz, Bill, Jr Painter, Educator

Aptos

Brown, Lawrie Photographer, Educator

Arcadia

Hawkins, Thomas Wilson, Jr Painter, Instructor

Arcata

Anderson, William Thomas Painter, Printmaker
Johnson, Ronald W Historian, Educator
Land-Weber, Ellen E Photographer, Educator
La Plant, Mimi Painter, Educator
Price, Leslie Kenneth Painter, Educator

Aromas

Nutzle, Futzie (Bruce) John Kleinsmith Cartoonist, Painter

Atascadero

Davis, Robert Painter

Atherton

Anderson, Harry W Collector

Auburn

Schulzke, Margot Seymour Painter, Writer

Bakersfield

Kerzie, Ted L Painter, Educator
Reep, Edward Arnold Painter, Writer

Barstow

Lorelli, Elvira Mae Sculptor, Painter

Bellflower

Theroux, Carol Painter

Belvedere

Knepper-Doyle, Virginia Painter, Environmental Artist

Benicia

Shannonhouse, Sandra Sculptor
Stern, Arthur I Stained Glass Artist, Sculptor

Berkeley

Abel, Ray Illustrator, Printmaker
Akawie, Thomas Frank Educator, Painter
Antokal, Gale Painter
Babior, Daniel Photographer
Burch, Claire R Painter, Writer, filmaker
Bussche, Wolf von dem Photographer, Painter
Cahill, James Francis Historian, Educator
Candau, Eugenie Librarian
Carson, G B Consultant, Art Dealer
Casida, Kati Printmaker, Sculptor
Church, Maude Painter, Assemblage Artist
Consey, Kevin E Museum Director, Administrator
Cook, Lia Tapestry Artist, Educator
Cope, Louise Todd Collage Artist
Crumpler, Dewey Painter, Muralist
Dater, Judy Photographer, Writer
Davis, Jerrold Painter
Delaney, Janet Clare Photographer
DeStabler, Stephen Sculptor
Elliott, Lillian Weaver, Tapestry Artist
Feldman, Bella Sculptor, Educator
Felter, June Marie Painter, Printmaker
Genn, Nancy Painter, Sculptor
Grossman, Bonnie Gallery Director
Healy, Anne Laura Sculptor, Educator
Henderson, Robbin Legere Painter, Curator
Hoare, Tyler James Sculptor, Printmaker
Holland, Tom Painter
Isaacs, Claire Naomi Administrator
Kasten, Karl Albert Painter, Printmaker
Kehlmann, Robert Critic, Artist, Curator
Lipofsky, Marvin B Sculptor, Glass Artist
Lovell, Margaretta Markle Historian, Curator
Mitchell, Margaretta K Photographer, Writer
Partridge, Loren Wayne Educator, Historian
Rapoport, Sonya Conceptual Artist
Reid, Laurie Frances Painter
Rokeach, Barrie Photographer, Writer
Sargent, Richard Painter, Photographer
Selvin, Nancy Ceramist, Sculptor
Selz, Peter H Historian, Curator
Shaw, Richard Blake Sculptor
Sher, Elizabeth Video Artist, Printmaker
Simpson, David Painter
Skoff, Gail Lynn Photographer
Slusky, Joseph Sculptor, Educator
Snow, Maryly A Librarian, Printmaker
Washburn, Stan Printmaker, Painter

Beverly Hills

Barnes, Molly Art Dealer, Writer
Cross, Yvonne Sculptor, Painter
Demissie, Yemane I Filmmaker
Drohojowska-Philp, Hunter Writer, Art Critic, Journalist
Elliot, Catherine J Painter, Graphic Artist
Holland, Diane Lee Collage Artist, Conceptual Artist
Hopper, Dennis Photographer
Katselas, Milton George Painter, Art Dealer
Marton, Pier Video Artist, Educator
Morales, Armando Painter, Printmaker
Okun, Jenny Photographer
Swofford, Beth Collector
Velick & Shishim, Paul & Bob Performance Artists
Yedidsion, Meira Painter, Sculptor

Bishop

Wagoner, Robert B Painter, Sculptor

Bodega

Bloom, Alan David Painter, Sculptor

Bolinas

Brooke, Pegan Painter
Harris, Paul Sculptor
Okamura, Arthur Painter

Boonville

Rubin, Sandra Mendelsohn Painter

Brea

Hashimoto, Kelly Ann Conceptual Artist, Video Artist

Burbank

Asmar, Alice Painter, Printmaker
Charlot, Martin Day Painter, Muralist
Horn, Alan F. Collector

Burlingame

Pollard, Jann Lawrence Fine Artist, Instructor
Voelker, Elizabeth Painter, Collage Artist

Calistoga

Nechis, Barbara Painter, Lecturer
Thollander, Earl Illustrator, Graphic Artist

Camarillo

Fumagalli, Barbara Merrill Printmaker

Cambria

Harden, Marvin Painter, Educator
Tress, Arthur Photographer

Cameron Park

Coover, Doris Gwendolyn Painter, Printmaker

Canoga Park

Rosenfeld, Sarena Painter

Capistrano Beach

Cederquist, John Furniture Maker, Sculptor
Clark, Timothy John Painter, Educator

Capitola

Reding, Barbara Endicott Artist

Carlsbad

Asaro, John Painter, Illustrator
Capps, Kenneth P Sculptor

Carmel

Clark, Robert Charles Painter, Lecturer
Cook, Joseph Stewart Painter
Crispo, Dick Painter, Printmaker
Jacobs, Ralph, Jr Painter
Johnson, Barbara Louise Painter, Printmaker
Kenna, Michael Photographer
Millea, Tom (Thomas) Francis Photographer
Winfield, Rodney M Painter, Designer
Winslow, Helen Painter

Carmel Valley

Pomeroy, Frederick George Painter, Restorer
Pomeroy, Mary Barnas (Mrs F G Pomeroy) Painter, Illustrator
Sexton, John (William) Photographer
Swanson, J N Painter, Sculptor
Wolfe, Maurice Raymond Consultant

CALIFORNIA (cont)

Carpinteria

Hansen, Robert Painter, Sculptor

Carson

Hirsch, Gilah Yelin Painter, Writer
Ivers, Louise H Historian, Administrator

Castro Valley

Erwin, Fran (Frances) Suzanne Painter, Sculptor

Cathedral City

Lupper, Edward Painter

Cazadero

Beall, Dennis Ray Printmaker, Educator

Cerritos

Sun, May Sculptor

Chico

Epting, Marion Austin Printmaker, Educator
Feldhaus, Paul A Educator, Printmaker
Hornaday, Richard Hoyt Painter, Educator
Latour, Ira Hinsdale, Jr Photographer, Historian
Pierce, Ann Trucksess Painter, Educator
VanDerpool, Karen Weaver, Educator

Chowchilla

Barton, Billie Jo Instructor, Painter

Claremont

Ackerman, Gerald Martin Historian, Educator
Benjamin, Karl Stanley Painter, Educator
Blizzard, Alan Painter, Educator
Casanova, Aldo John Sculptor, Educator
Furman, David Stephen Sculptor, Educator
Hueter, James Warren Sculptor, Painter
Medrich, Libby E Sculptor
Rankaitis, Susan Painter, Photographer
Reiss, Roland Sculptor, Painter
Simon, Leonard Ronald Administrator, Writer
Zehr, Connie Art Educator, Sculptor

Coarsegold

Solem, (Elmo) John Painter, Sculptor

Coleville

Petterson, Margo Painter

Corona Del Mar

DeLap, Tony Sculptor, Painter

Costa Mesa

Muller, Jerome Kenneth Art Director, Photographer
Romans, Van Anthony Sculptor, Designer

Cotati

Hudson, Robert H Painter, Sculptor

Cruz

Anderson, David Kimball Sculptor

Culver City

De Larios, Dora Sculptor

Cupertino

Rindfleisch, Jan Director, Curator

Cypress

George, Patricia Painter
Hardy, Robert Educator, Ceramist

Dana Point

Strand, Sally Ellis Painter, Instructor

Davenport

Deutsch, Richard Sculptor

Davis

Gefter, Judith Michelman Photographer
Pardee, William Hearne Painter, Educator
Reinertson, Lisa Sculptor
Rosen, Annabeth Ceramist, Sculptor
Suzuki, James Hiroshi Painter
Vanden Berge, Peter Willem Sculptor, Muralist
Werfel, Gina S Painter, Educator
Wood, Melissa Painter, Collage Artist

Del Mar

Antin, David A Art Critic, Writer
Antin, Eleanor Conceptual Artist, Photographer
Kittredge, Nancy (Elizabeth) Painter
Turner, Herbert B Painter

Eagle Rock

Andrews, Charleen Kohl Sculptor

El Cajon

House, Suda Kay Photographer, Video Artist
Lawrence, Jaye A Sculptor, Craftsman
Lawrence, Les Ceramist, Sculptor
Markarian, Alexia (Mitrus) Painter, Sculptor, Designer
Tatro, Ronald Edward Sculptor, Instructor

Elk Grove

Kaiser, Benjamin Sculptor, Designer

Elmira

Montoya, Malaquias art educator, artist

Emeryville

Grafton, Rick (Frederick) Wellington Painter
Jensen, Clay Easton Sculptor, Educator
Jones, David Lee Sculptor, Assemblage Artist
Lang, Cay Photographer
Misrach, Richard Laurence Photographer
Stanley, M Louise Painter

Encinitas

Breslaw, Cathy L Painter, Educator
Provder, Carl Painter, Instructor

Encino

LaCom, Wayne Carl Painter, Graphic Artist

Escondido

Bonilla-Martinez, Natasha Director
Ecker, Robert Rodgers Painter, Printmaker
Jones, Doug Douglas McKee Painter, Sculptor

Eureka

Marak, Louis Bernard Ceramic Sculptor, Educator

Fair Oaks

Barrios, Benny Perez Painter, Art Dealer
Potter, (George) Kenneth Painter, Printmaker

Fairfax

Dern, F Carl Sculptor

Fallbrook

Perhacs, Les Sculptor, Industrial Designer

Fallsbrook

Ragland, Jack Whitney Painter, Printmaker

Forestville

Meyer, El(mer) Frederick Painter, Writer

Fort Bragg

Downie, Romana Anzi Sculptor

Fresno

Curreri-Ermatinger, Dyana M Director, Curator
Maughelli, Mary L Printmaker, Painter
Monaghan, Kathleen Mary Director
Pickford, Rollin, Jr Painter
Walker, Sharyne Elaine Painter, Sculptor

Fullerton

Macaray, Lawrence Richard Painter, Educator
Wells, Menthe Painter, Sculptor

Gardena

Valentine, DeWain Sculptor

Gilroy

Wu, Wayne Wen-Yau Painter

Glen Ellen

Wilson, Douglas Fenn Painter, Sculptor

Glendale

Burchett, Debra Administrator, Curator
Geffen, David Lawrence Collector
McGinley, Maribeth Wilson Graphic Artist, Educator, Director
Pekar, Ronald Walter Painter, Sculptor

Goleta

Gabrielson, Walter Oscar Painter

Graeagle

Halbach, David Allen Painter, Historian

Gualala

Alinder, James Gilbert Gallery Owner, Photographer
Alinder, Mary Street Writer, Curator
Romeu, Joost A Conceptual Artist, Designer

Half Moon Bay

Harris, David Jack Painter, Muralist

Harbor City

Kwak, Hoon Painter

Hayward

McLean, Richard Painter

Hemet

Trejos, Charlotte (Carlota) Marie Painter

Hillsborough

Siberell, Anne Hicks Painter, Sculptor

Huntington Beach

Anderson, Bill (William) Maxwell Painter, Printmaker
Hitchcock, Howard Gilbert Educator, Sculptor
Keena, Janet Laybourn Painter, Designer
Pergola, Linnea Painter, Printmaker
Tornheim, Norman Sculptor
Whitchurch, Charles A Art Dealer, Educator

Inglewood

Antrim, Craig Keith Painter, Draftsman
Jenkins, Ulysses Samuel, Jr Video Artist, Muralist
Lebejoara, Ovidiu Painter, Sculptor

Inverness

Krebs, Patsy Painter
Smith, Gary Douglas Draftsman, Painter
Welpott, Jack Warren Photographer, Educator

Irvine

Bolen, John E Art Dealer, Collector
Bolen, Lynne N Art Dealer, Collector

CALIFORNIA (cont)
Burchfield, Jerry Lee Photographer, Educator, Author
Silverman, Ronald H Educator, Writer
Varo, Marton Geza Sculptor

Kelseyville
Fletcher, Leland Vernon Painter, Sculptor

Kentfield
Galli, Stanley Walter Painter

Kingsburg
Olson, Maxine Painter, Instructor

La Conchita
Kelm, Bonnie G Museum Director, Administrator, Consultant

La Crescenta
Injeyan, Seta L Painter

La Jolla
Adams, Robert McCormick Administrator, Writer
Beebe, Mary Livingstone Art Administrator
Cohen, Harold Artist-Theorist, Educator
Cuevas, Jose Luis Draftsman
Davies, Hugh Marlais Historian, Museum Director
Forester, Russell Painter, Sculptor
Fredman, Faiya R Sculptor, Painter
Hawkinson, Tim Sculptor
Imana, Jorge Garron Painter, Muralist
Karlen, Peter H Educator, Writer
Lonidier, Fred Spencer Photographer, Educator
Marcus, Angelo P Dealer, Collector
McGilvery, Laurence Book Dealer, Publisher
McReynolds, (Joe) Cliff Painter, Instructor
Morcos, Maher N Sculptor, Painter
Reilly, Richard Director, Historian
Seslar, Patrick George Writer, Painter
Shaw, Reesey Painter, Sculptor
Tasende, Jose Maria Gallery Director, Dealer
Trakas, George Sculptor
Yard, Sally Elizabeth Historian, Curator

La Mesa
Blackmun, Barbara Winston Educator, Curator
Lebeck, Carol E Ceramist, Painter, Educator
Phillips, Ellen T Sculptor, Assemblage Artist

Lafayette
Alexander, Kenneth Lewis Cartoonist
Kapp, E Jeanne Painter, Photographer

Laguna Beach
Challis, Richard Bracebridge Dealer, Lecturer
Darrow, Paul Gardner Painter, Educator
Galles, Arie Alexander Painter, Educator
Moore, Scott Martin Painter, Instructor

Laguna Hills
Armstrong, Roger Joseph Painter, Cartoonist
Garbutt, Janice Lovoos Painter, Writer
MacBird, Rosemary (Simpson) Painter

Laguna Woods
Upton, John David Educator, Curator

Lagunitas
Holman, Arthur (Stearns) Painter

Lake Forest
LeMieux, Bonne A Painter

Larkspur
Frances, (Sherana) Harriette Printmaker, Painter

Levcadia
Patterson, Patricia Film Critic, Painter

Livermore
Lord, Carolyn Marie Painter, Instructor

Long Beach
Aldana, Carl Painter
Braunstein, Terry (Malikin) Photographer, Educator
Colmer, Roy David Photographer
Cretara, Domenic Anthony Painter, Educator
Ferreira, Armando Thomas Educator, Sculptor
Glenn, Constance White Museum Director, Writer
Kaplan, Ilee Printmaker, Administrator
Klonarides, Carole Ann Video Artist, Curator
Lane, William Painter
Lewis, Marcia Jeweler-Metalsmith, Instructor
Luke , Gregorio Museum Director
Nelson, Harold B Director
Osborne, Cynthia A Printmaker, Educator
Viola, Bill Video Artist
Zokosky, Peter L Painter

Los Angeles
Abeles, Kim Victoria Sculptor
Adamson, Jerome D Art Dealer, Consultant
Aldrich, Lynn (Barron) Sculptor, Conceptual Artist
Alf, Martha Joanne Painter, Writer
Alhilali, Neda Environmental Artist, Painter
Amico, David Michael Painter, Instructor
Anderson, Ross Cornelius Museum Director, Historian
Ankrum, Joan Art Dealer
Apple, Jacki (Jacqueline) B Visual, Media and Performance Artist, Writer, Producer
Apt, Charles Painter, Designer
Arnold, Skip Video Artist, Performance Artist
Asher, Michael Conceptual Artist
Baden, Mowry T Sculptor
Baer, Rod Conceptual Artist, Sculptor
Baldwin, Gordon C Curator
Barkus, Mariona Graphic Artist, Painter
Barron, Stephanie Curator
Bas, Hernan Artist
Bedrick, Jeffrey K Painter, Illustrator
Bell, William J, Jr. Collector
Berger, Pat (Patricia) Eve Painter, Educator
Bermudez, Luis A Sculptor, Educator
Bierman, Irene A Educator
Bloomfield, Lisa Diane Photographer, Conceptual Artist
Bowlt, John Art Historian, Educator
Braudy, Dorothy Painter, Photographer
Brendel, Bettina Painter, Lecturer
Broad, Eli Collector, Patron
Burkle, Ronald W Patron
Butler, Eugenia P Conceptual Artist
Byrnes, James Bernard Art Historian, Museum Director
Caroompas, Carole J Painter, Instructor
Ciccone, Amy Navratil Librarian
Clayberger, Samuel Robert Painter, Educator
Clothier, Peter Dean Writer, Critic
Collier, Anna photographer
Cortines, Ramon C Patron
Cotsen, Lloyd E Patron
Couturier, Marion B Dealer, Collector
Curran, Darryl Joseph Photographer, Printmaker
Currin, John Artist
Dailey, Victoria Keilus Writer, Art Dealer
Decter, Betty Eva Painter, Sculptor, Writer
Devereux, Mara Painter
Drezner, A L Sculptor, Architect
Duke, Leilani Lattin Administrator
Edge, Douglas Benjamin Sculptor, Painter
Edwards, Jonmarc Painter, Conceptual Artist
Ela, Patrick H Director
Feher, Tony artist
Finkelstein, Max Sculptor, Painter
Firstenberg, Jean Picker Director
Frame, John Sculptor
Frank, Peter Solomon Critic, Curator
Fredericks, Beverly Magnuson Painter, Restorer
Fuglie, Gordon Louis Gallery Director, Historian
Ganz, Julian, Jr Patron
Gehry, Frank O(wen) Architect
Goodman, Calvin Jerome Consultant, Collector
Gordon, John S Sculptor, Educator
Govan, Michael Museum Director
Grimmer, Mineko Sculptor
Grinnan, Katie Painter, Sculptor
Griswold, William M Museum Director, Curator
Grotjahn, Mark Painter
Hamilton, Patricia Rose Dealer
Hart, John Lewis Cartoonist
Henderson, Victor Painter, Muralist
Herman, Roger Painter, Printmaker
Hernandez, Anthony Louis Photographer
Hess, F Scott Painter, Instructor
Higgins, Larkin Maureen Conceptual Artist, Educator
Hockney, David Designer, Photographer
Hoffman, Neil James Administrator, Educator
Hoi, Samuel Chuen-Tsung Educator, Administrator
Holo, Selma R Museologist, Museum Director
Hopkins, Henry Tyler Museum Director, Educator
Horn, Cindy Harrell Collector
Horwitz, Channa Conceptual Artist, Painter
Hugo, Joan (Dowey) Critic, Administrator
Ida, Shoichi Painter, Printmaker
Isermann, Jim Sculptor
Johnston, Ynez Painter, Printmaker
Jones, Patty Sue Painter, Curator
Kadlec, Kristine Collage Artist, Writer
Kazor, Virginia Ernst Curator
Ketchum, Robert Glenn Photographer, Curator
Kienholz, Lyn Patron, Administrator
Kiley, Katie printmaker, painter
Klein, Cecelia F Historian, Educator
Komaroff, Linda Curator
Kovinick, Philip Peter Writer, Historian
Krasnyansky, Anatole Lvovich Painter, Architect
Kuwayama, George Curator, Historian
Lang, Wendy F Administrator, Photographer
Larner, Liz Sculptor
Lawson, Thomas Painter, Writer
Leatherdale, Marcus Andrew Photographer
Leavitt, William Painter, Photographer
Leeson, Tom Painter, Sculptor
LeMay, Harry Adrian Painter & Instructor
LeMay, Nancy Painter
Lewis, Samella Sanders Painter, Historian
Longval, Gloria Painter
Lopez, Eugenio Alonso collector

CALIFORNIA (cont)
Lyons, Lisa   Historian, Consultant
Malpede, John   Performance Artist, Director
Manolakas, Stanton Peter   Painter
Mason, John   Sculptor
Mayhew, Richard   Painter
McCarthy, Paul   Artist
Milant, Jean Robert   Dealer
Min, Yong Soon   Sculptor, Educator
Morphesis , Jim (James) George   Painter
Moss, Tobey C   Art Dealer, Historian
Muchnic, Suzanne   Critic, Instructor
Mudford, Grant Leighton   Photographer
Munitz, Barry   Administrator, Educator, Patron
Munro, JP   Artist
Myers, Terry R   Critic, Curator
Natzler, Otto   Ceramist, Sculptor
Nelson, Steven D   Educator
Nogales, Luis Guerrero   Patron
Norris, Merry   Consultant, Collector
Norris, William A   Collector
Oda, Masayuki   Sculptor
Omar, Margit   Painter, Educator
Orenstein, Gloria Feman   Educator, Historian
Outterbridge, John Wilfred   Sculptor, Administrator
Owens, Laura   Painter
Pal, Pratapaditya   Curator, Historian
Palmer, Herbert Bearl   Dealer, Collector
Park, Lee   Painter
Pastor, Jennifer   Sculptor
Perlman, Hirsch   Painter
Peyton, Elizabeth Joy   Writer, Painter
Philbin, Ann   Museum Director
Piasecki, Jane B   Administrator
Picot, Pierre   Painter
Pinkel, Sheila Mae   Photographer, Computer Graphics
Pletscher, Josephine Marie   Librarian, Printmaker
Poledna, Mathias   Video Artist
Prieto, Monique N   Painter
Prina, Stephen James   Artist, Educator
Ransom, Brian   Ceramist
Ray, Charles   Sculptor
Reagan, Rourk C   Painter, Photographer
Rezac, Richard   Conceptual Artist, Sculptor
Robleto, Dario   Artist
Rophar   Painter
Rosenberg, Jane   Illustrator, Painter
Rosenthal, Rachel   Performance Artist
Sample, Steven Browning   Patron
Sargent, Margaret Holland   Painter
Saxe, Adrian A   Ceramist
Shap, Sylvia   Painter
Shire, Peter   Sculptor, Designer
Shlien, Helen S   Curator
Siedman, Scott   Painter, Illustrator
Sinner, Steve   sculptor
Snyder, Ruth (Cozen)   Sculptor, Painter
Sobol, Judith Ellen   Foundation Director, Curator
Stark, Linda   Painter
Stern, Louis   Dealer, Consultant
Stone, George H   Sculptor
Suggs, Don   Painter, Photographer
Syrop, Mitchell   Conceptual Artist
Takemoto, Henry Tadaaki   Craftsman, Sculptor
Thornycroft, Ann   Painter
Todd, Michael Cullen   Sculptor, Painter
Tonelli, Edith Ann   Museum Director, Historian
Trenton, Patricia Jean   Historian
Troy, Nancy J   Historian
Tuchman, Maurice   Museum Curator
Valentine, Dean   Collector
Vallance, Jeffrey K R   Sculptor, Painter
Vasa   Sculptor, Educator
Vasell, Chris   Artist, Filmmaker
Wayne, June   Painter, Printmaker
Weisberg, Ruth Ellen   Painter, Educator
Willis, Jay Stewart   Sculptor, Educator
Wingo, Michael B   Painter, Draftsman
Wright, Bernard   Painter, Graphic Artist
Young, Joseph Louis   Sculptor, Muralist
Zeitlin, Harriet   Painter, Sculptor
Zelevansky, Lynn   Curator
Zittel, Andrea   Artist

Los Gatos
Carson, Sol Kent   Painter, Printmaker, Sculptor, Administrator
Middlebrook, David A   Sculptor, Educator

Los Osos
Hampton, Anita   Painter, Educator
Kreitzer, David Martin   Painter
Pike, Joyce Lee   Painter, Writer

Malibu
Almond, Joan   Photographer
Almond, Paul   Filmmaker, Writer
Altfeld, Merwin Richard   Painter, Educator, Art Juror
Bowman, Bruce   Painter, Art Writer
Dunitz, Jay   Photographer
Sturman, Eugene   Sculptor, Painter
Zakian, Michael   Museum Director, Curator

Manhattan Beach
Lazzari, Margaret R   Painter, Educator

Marina Del Rey
Coleman, Judy   Photographer
Lacy, Suzanne   Conceptual Artist, Writer
Posner, Judith L   Dealer, Publisher

Mariposa
Rogers, Earl Leslie   Painter, Educator

Martinez
Keary, Geraldine   Painter

McKinleyville
Berry, Glenn   Painter, Educator

Menlo Park
Mozley, Anita Ventura   Curator, Critic
Smith, Albert E   Painter
Zirker, Joseph   Printmaker, Lecturer

Merced
Barnett, Cheryl L   Sculptor

Mill Valley
Baum, Marilyn Ruth   Painter, Printmaker
Diehl, Guy   Painter, Instructor
Jones, Pirkle   Photographer
Mayeri, Beverly   Sculptor
Meader, Jonathan (Ascian)   Printmaker, Painter
Nadel, Ann Honig   Sculptor, Ceramist
Padula, Fred David   Filmmaker, Photographer
Schreyer, Chara   Collector
Zegart , Mar(garet) Jean Kettunen   Artist, Educator

Mission Viejo
Ames, Lee Judah   Illustrator, Writer

Modesto
Hunter, John H   Painter, Printmaker
Remsing, Joseph Gary   Painter, Sculptor

Monrovia
Emerick, Judson J   Historian

Montague
Stone, Gwen   Painter, Collage Artist

Monte Sereno
Taylor, Brian David   Photographer, Educator

Montebello
Shubin, Morris Jack   Painter, Lecturer

Montecito
Fenton, Howard Carter   Painter, Educator
Wallin, Lawrence Bier   Sculptor, Painter

Monterey
Bradford, Howard   Printmaker, Painter
Gilpin, Henry Edmund   Photographer, Educator

Moorpark
Hayward, James   Painter
Le, Dinh   Photographer

Moraga
Harlow, Ann   Museum Director, Curator
Marable, Darwin William   Historian, Critic
Poupeney, Mollie   Ceramist, Writer

Morgan Hill
Freimark, Bob (Robert)   Printmaker, Painter

Napa
Chase-Bien, Gail   Painter & Pastel
Garnett, William Ashford   Photographer, Educator

Nevada City
McCauley, Gardiner Rae   Administrator, Painter

Newport Beach
Armstrong, Elizabeth Neilson   Curator
Bren, Donald L   Collector
Spitz, Barbara S   Printmaker, Photographer
Turnbull, Betty   Curator

North Hills
Squires, Norma Jean   Painter, Sculptor

North Hollywood
Easterson, Sam Peter   Video Artist, Conceptual Artist
Price, Joe (Allen)   Serigrapher, Instructor

North San Juan
Acton, Arlo C   Sculptor

Northridge
Brown, Betty Ann   Educator, Critic
Elder, David Morton   Sculptor
Fricano, Tom S   Painter, Printmaker
Lewis, Louise Miller   Gallery Director, Educator
Smith, Robert Lewis   Designer, Educator

Oakland
Andrews, Lawrence   Video Artist, Sculptor
Baczek, Peter Gerard   Painter, Printmaker
Beasley, Bruce   Sculptor
Beldner, Lynn Karen   Sculptor
Bowen-Forbes, Jorge C   Painter
Brewster, Andrea B   Photographer, Conceptual Artist
Brill, Glenn   Painter, Printmaker
Byrne, Charles Joseph   Designer
Carnwath, Squeak   Painter
Ciriclio, S(usan) E (Fay)   Photographer, Educator
Clark, Claude   Instructor, Painter
Crum, David   Painter
Crum, Katherine B   Museum Director, Educator

CALIFORNIA (cont)
Doyle, Joe Painter, Educator
Estabrook, Reed Photographer, Instructor
Gonzalez, Arthur Padilla Sculptor
Hardy, David Whittaker, III Painter, Instructor
Hartman, Robert Leroy Photographer, Educator
Hendon, Cham Painter
Kagemoto, Haro Filmmaker, Photographer
Kagemoto, Patricia Jow Printmaker, Painter
Kelso, David William Printmaker, Art Dealer
Kirk, Jerome Sculptor, Kinetic Artist
Kraft, Steve Designer
Leon, Dennis Sculptor, Educator
Levy, Mark Writer, Historian
Linhares, Philip E Curator
MacGregor, Gregory Allen Photographer
Martin, Fred Thomas Painter
Melchert, James Frederick Sculptor, Educator
Miyasaki, George Joji Printmaker, Painter
O'Banion, Nance Assemblage Artist
Perez, Vincent Painter, Illustrator
Porges, Maria Franziska Sculptor, Printmaker
Priola, J John Photographer, Instructor
Ramos, (Mel) Melvin John Painter, Educator
Rath, Alan T Sculptor
Ritchey, Rik Painter, Sculptor
Roloff, John (Scott) Sculptor, Environmental Artist
Roth, Moira Educator, Historian
St John, Terry N Painter, Curator
Saunders, Raymond Jennings Painter, Educator
Snyder, William B Painter, Educator
Southey, Trevor J T Painter, Sculptor
Stewart, John Lincoln Educator, Writer
Sussman, Wendy Painter
Tunis, Roslyn Curator, Gallery Director
Walsh, Patricia Ruth Painter
Walters, Sylvia Solochek Printmaker, Educator

Oceanside
Solberg, Morten Edward Painter

Ojai
Martin, Lys Photographer, Curator
McIntosh, Gregory Stephen Painter
Pastine, Ruth Painter, Lecturer
Stinsmuehlen-Amend, Susan Collage Artist, Painter

Ontario
Hanner, Jean Patricia Painter, Muralist

Orange
Felisky, Barbara Rosbe Painter, Printmaker
Schusterman, Gerrie Marva Art Dealer, Gallery Director
Vasquez, Emigdio Chavez Painter, Muralist

Orangevale
Walker, Ronald C Artist

Orinda
Brody, Blanche Painter, Printmaker
Light, Ken Photographer, Educator
Samimi, Mehrdad Illustrator, Painter
Thompson, Mark L Sculptor

Oro Grande
Bender, Bill Painter

Pacific Grove
Berry, Carolyn Painter, Illustrator
Downs, Douglas Walker Sculptor

Pacific Palisades
Blumberg, Ron Painter
Campbell, Richard Horton Painter, Printmaker
Chesney, Lee R, Jr Painter, Printmaker
Hannah, John Junior Printmaker, Educator
Laskin, Myron, Jr Curator, Historian
Naef, Weston John Curator, Historian
Perloff, Marjorie G Critic, Historian
Sherman, Z Charlotte Painter

Pacifica
Petersen, Roland Conrad Painter, Printmaker
Torlakson, James Daniel Painter, Filmmaker

Palm Desert
Jacques, Russell Kenneth Sculptor, Painter
Kilian, Austin Farland Painter, Educator

Palm Springs
Debonne, Jeannette Painter, Printmaker
Lewin, Bernard Dealer, Collector
Lyle, Janice S Museum Director
Maree, Wendy P Painter, Sculptor
Pollack, Reginald Murray Painter, Sculptor

Palo Alto
Bergstrom, Edith Harrod Painter
Conner, Bruce Graphic Artist, Collage Artist, Filmmaker
Eisenstat, Jane Sperry Painter
Ford, Rochelle Sculptor
Hero, Peter deCourcy Administrator, Historian
Mayfield, Signe S Curator

Palos Verdes Estates
Aitken, Doug Video Artist
Cox, Pat Assemblage Artist, Sculptor

Paradise
McManus, James William Sculptor, Gallery Director

Pasadena
Adams, Peter Painter
Dreiband, Laurence Painter, Lecturer
Dunye, Cheryl Lynn Filmmaker, Video Artist
Gill, Gene Painter, Craftsman
Grunwaldt, Carmela C Painter
Herman, Alan David Designer, Graphic Artist
Hertz, Richard A Educator, Critic
Jones, Ronald Warren Artist, Critic
Kieffer, Mary Jane Painter
Koshalek, Richard Museum Director
McOwen, C Lynn Art Dealer, Collector
McOwen, Carol M Collector
Monk, Nancy Sculptor, Photographer
Murdoch, John Museum Director
Pashgian, M Helen Painter, Sculptor
Sakoguchi, Ben Painter
Zammitt, Norman Painter, Sculptor
Zlatkoff, Charles Painter, Sculptor

Pebble Beach
Mortensen, Gordon Louis Printmaker, Painter

Penngrove
Ellison, Robert W Sculptor

Petaluma
Camhi, Morrie Photographer, Educator
Fuller, Mary (Mary Fuller McChesney) Sculptor, Publisher
McChesney, Robert Pearson Painter, Muralist

McMillan, Stephen Walker Printmaker, Photographer
Rippey, Clayton Painter, Muralist
Saturen, Ben Painter, Educator
Skalagard, Hans Painter, Lecturer
Williams, Franklin John Painter

Piedmont
Dhaemers, Robert August Sculptor, Educator, Printmaker
Gunn, Ellen Painter, Printmaker
Mendenhall, Jack Painter, Instructor
Murray, Joan Critic, Photographer
Tavenner, Patricia Video Artist

Pinole
Gerbracht, Bob (Robert) Thomas Painter, Instructor

Pismo Beach
Mitchell, Dianne Painter

Placerville
Davis, Thelma Ellen Painter
Gruver, Mary Emmett Painter, Instructor

Point Arena
Miles, Sheila Lee Painter, Consultant

Point Reyes Station
Hall, Susan Painter, Ceramist
Quinn, Thomas Patrick, Jr Painter
Rogers, Art Photographer

Pollock Pines
Tarbet, Urania Christy Painter, Writer

Pomona
Hannibal, Joseph Harry Educator, Painter
Jacobsen, Michael A Historian, Educator, Painter

Port Costa
Bailey, Clayton George Sculptor, Ceramist
De Forest, Roy Dean Painter, Sculptor

Portola Valley
Jackson, Oliver Lee Painter, Sculptor
Neri, Manuel Sculptor

Ramona
Dani Sculptor, Painter

Rancho Palos Verdes
Palko Kolosvary, Paul Collage Artist, Printmaker
Parkhurst, Violet Kinney Painter, Writer

Rancho Santa Fe
Jacobs, Scott E Painter, Illustrator

Redding
Peterson, Robyn G Curator

Redlands
Johnston, Richard M Sculptor, Educator
Slatkin, Wendy Historian

Redway
Holbrook, Peter Greene Painter, Printmaker

Redwood City
Shukman, Solomon Painter, Printmaker

Richmond
Wessel, Henry Photographer

Rimforest
Jolley, Donal Clark Painter

Riverside
Earle, Edward W Curator, Historian

CALIFORNIA (cont)

Green, Jonathan (William) Museum Director, Photographer, Filmmaker
Reeves, Esther May Painter

Rodeo

Sherwood, Katherine Painter

Rohnert Park

Moulton, Susan Gene Historian, Painter
Schwager, Michael R Educator, Curator

Rolling Hills

Agid, Lucy Bradanovic Sculptor

Sacramento

Adan, Suzanne Painter
Drachnik (Cay), Catherine Meldyn Painter, Educator
Euren, Barry A Painter
Foosaner, Judith Educator, Painter
Jones, Lial A Museum Director
Kondos, Gregory Painter, Educator
Marcus, Irving E Painter, Educator
Moment, Joan Instructor, Painter
Parker, Olivia Photographer
Piskoti, James Printmaker, Painter
Rippon, Ruth Margaret Sculptor, Ceramist
Stevens, Michael Keith Sculptor
Walburg, Gerald Sculptor, Educator
Waterstreet, Ken (James Kent) Painter, Instructor
Winkler, Maria Paula Painter, Educator

Saint Helena

Frederick, Robilee Painter, Sculptor
Hussong, Randy Sculptor, Printmaker

Salinas

Puckett, Richard Edward Painter
Smith, Gary Sculptor, Gallery Director

San Anselmo

Connor, Linda Stevens Photographer, Instructor

San Bernardino

Civitello, John Patrick Painter
De Soto, Lewis D Sculptor, Educator
Kaplan, Julius David Historian
Lintault, Roger Paul Administrator, Educator
Warehall, William Donald Glass Blower, Ceramist
Woodford, Don (Donald) Paul Painter, Educator

San Clemente

Lopina, Louise Carol Painter, Printmaker

San Diego

Alexander, Wick Painter
Angelo, Sandra McFall Writer, Instructor
Beaumont, Mona Painter, Graphic Artist
Cartwright, Derrick Museum Director
Cordy-Collins, Alana (Kathleen) Curator, Educator
Cottone-Kolthoff, Carol Painter, Illustrator
Criss, Cheryl Lynn Painter
Cutler-Shaw, Joyce Conceptual Artist, Sculptor
D'Agostino , Claudio A Sculptor
Esser, Janet Brody Historian
Farber, Amanda Painter, Sculptor
Fisch, Arline Marie Jeweler, Educator
Gabriel, Jeanette Hanisee Curator, Historian, Consultant
Gregoire, Mathieu A Sculptor
Guerrero, Raul Painter, Sculptor
Hiller, Betty R Consultant, Appraiser
Jennings, Jan Writer
Jung, Yee Wah Painter
Kosta, Angela Assemblage Artist, Writer
Levinson, Mimi W Painter, Lecturer
Madsen, Roy Sculptor, Writer
Mansfield, Robert Adams Sculptor, Educator
Maruyama, Wendy Designer
McAllister, Geraldine E Gallery Director
Ollman, Arthur L Photographer, Museum Director
Quigley, Robert Wellington Architect
Rigby, Ida Katherine Critic, Historian
Rubinstein, Charlotte Streifer Writer, Curator
Schultz, Caroline Reel Painter, Lecturer
Shirk, Helen Z Craftsman
Sisco, Elizabeth Conceptual Artist, Photographer
Sowinski, Stanislaus Joseph Painter, Iconographer
Weldon, Barbara Maltby Painter
Wojtyla, Haase (Walter) Joseph Painter, Draftsman
Wordell, Edwin Howland Painter
Wostrel, Nancy J Painter, Illustrator

San Francisco

Acebo, Davis Terry printmaker
Aiken, William A Painter
Allrich, M Louise Barco Art Dealer, Art Consultant
Alpert, Richard Henry Video Artist
Arnitz, Rick Painter
Asawa, Ruth (Asawa Lanier) Sculptor, Painter
Babcock, Jo (Joseph) Warren Photographer, Sculptor
Baker, Kenneth Critic, Writer
Barrett, William O Administrator
Benezra, Neal Museum Director, Curator
Benton, Fletcher Sculptor
Berggruen, John Henry Art Dealer
Berk, Amy Lynne artist
Berkson, Bill Critic, Poet
Bernhard, Ruth Photographer
Brady, Robert D Sculptor
Bratton, Christopher Alan Sculptor, Video Artist
Braunstein, Ruth Art Dealer
Breschi, Karen Lee Sculptor
Brown, Christopher Painter
Bruno, Ellen Filmmaker
Buchanan, John Edward, Jr Museum Director, Administrator
Bukovnik, Gary Painter, Printmaker
Cameron, Elsa S Curator, Consultant
Chadwick, Whitney Critic, Historian
Chagoya, Enrique Printmaker
Chamberlain, Ann Photographer
Cook-Contreras, Shelley Conceptual Artist, Sculptor
Dawdy, Doris Ostrander Writer, Historian
Dawson, Robert H Photographer
De Fazio, John Sculptor
DeGiulio, Lucas Artist
Dickinson, Eleanor Creekmore Painter, Graphic Artist
Donnelly, Trisha Artist
Dorsky, Nathaniel Filmmaker
Doyon, Aurora S Painter
Earls-Solari, Bonnie Curator
Erman, Bruce Painter, Educator
Eurich, Judith Appraiser
Featherstone, David Byrum Critic, Curator
Finley, Karen Writer
Fischer, Hal (Harold) Alan Writer, Consultant
Fisher, Donald G & Doris Collector
Fraenkel, Jeffrey Andrew Art Dealer
Fuller, Diana Curator, Editor
Garcia, Rupert (Marshall) R Painter, Educator
Goetzl, Thomas Maxwell Lecturer, Educator
Goldstein, Daniel Joshua Kinetic Artist, Sculptor
Gutkin, Peter Sculptor, Designer
Hall, Douglas E Video Artist, Photographer
Halprin, Lawrence Architect
Hanley, Jack Painter, Gallery Director
Hanson, Jo Sculptor, Environmental Artist
Heckert, Matthew Sculptor
Held, (John) Jonathan, Jr Mail Artist, Writer
Helder, David Ernest Painter, Sculptor
Henderson, Mike Painter, Filmmaker
Henry, Jean Painter, Instructor
Hollis, Douglas Sculptor
Horowitz, Diana Painter
Hourian, Mohammad Painter, Art Dealer
Howard, David Photographer, Filmmaker
Hunter, Leonard LeGrande, III Sculptor, Educator
Huntington, Jim Sculptor
Hyson, Jean Painter
Iannetti, Pasquale Francesco Paolo Art Dealer, Collector
Ireland, David Printmaker
Johnson, Robert Flynn Curator, Historian
Karlstrom, Paul Johnson Historian, Administrator
Katano, Marc Painter
Kikuchi-Yngojo, Alan Photographer, Collage Artist
Klausner, Betty Writer, Curator
Kos, Paul Joseph Sculptor, Educator
Kramlich, Richard & Pamela Collector
Krempel, Ralf Painter, Assemblage Artist
Kusama, Yayoi Sculptor, Painter
Labat, Tony Conceptual Artist, Sculptor
Levin, Morton D Printmaker, Painter
Lew, Weyman Painter, Printmaker
Lieber, Thomas Alan Painter
Light, Michael Rudolph Photographer
Linder, Charles Keating Sculptor
Liu, Hung Painter
Lobdell, Frank Painter
Lucero, Manuel F Ceramist
Majdrakoff, Ivan Painter, Assemblage Artist
Manera, Enrico Orlando Sculptor, Painter
Marcheschi, (Louis) Cork Sculptor, Educator
Marioni, Tom Sculptor
Maxim, David Nicholas Painter, Graphic Artist
McGee, Barry painter and graffiti artist
McNamara, John Painter
Meissner, Anne Marie Administrator
Mesa-Bains, Amalia Sculptor
Modi-Vitale, Lydia Museum Director, Curator
Morales, Rodolfo Painter
Muranaka, Hideo Painter, Printmaker
Murch, Anna Valentina Conceptual Artist, Environmental Artist
Nash, Steven Alan Historian, Curator
Nelson, Jane Gray Curator
Nickel, Douglas Robert Curator, Critic
Oliveira, Nathan Painter
Oropallo, Deborah Painter
Parker, Wilma Painter
Pence, John Gerald Dealer, Patron
Pennington, Juliana Designer, Graphic Artist
Piccolo, Richard Painter
Pijoan, Irene Maria Elizabeth Painter, Instructor
Pritzker, John A. Collector
Provisor, Janis Architect
Raciti, Cherie Painter
Rafferty, Andrew Painter, Printmaker
Rascon, Armando Conceptual Artist, Curator

CALIFORNIA (cont)

Rasmussen, Robert (Redd Ekks) Norman Sculptor, Ceramist
Renk, Merry Goldsmith, Painter
Rinder, Lawrence R Curator, Writer
Robbins, Trina Cartoonist, Illustrator
Rosenblatt, Jay Howard Filmmaker, Video Artist
Ross, David Anthony Museum Director
Roth, Michael S Administrator, Educator
Royce-Silk, Suzanne Consultant, Curator
Saito, Yoshitomo Sculptor
Samuels (Joesam), Joe Sculptor
Santos, Adele Naude Architect, Urban Designer
Sapien, Darryl Rudolph Painter
Schwab, Charles R Collector
Sencial, Gabriel Jaime Printmaker, Painter
Shepp, Alan Graphic Artist, Digital Photographer
Smith, J Weldon Museum Director, Historian
Smith, Jennie Artist
Solinas, Rico Painter
Staprans, Raimonds Painter, Sculptor
Stephens, Elisa Educator
Stermer, Dugald Robert Illustrator, Writer
Stofflet, Mary Curator, Critic
Stone, Jeremy Patricia Consultant, Appraiser, Curator
Stover, Donald Lewis Curator
Sultan, Larry A Photographer, Educator
Tait, Will(iam) H Painter
Tarshis, Jerome Writer
Taylor, Sandra Ortiz Assemblage Artist, Sculptor
Thomas, Larry W Painter, Printmaker
Tompkins, Michael Painter
Toney, Anita Karen Printmaker
Torrey, Ella King Administrator
Varnay Jones, Theodora Printmaker, Painter
Villa, Carlos Painter
Wada, Yoshi Sculptor
Wagner, Catherine Photographer
Wakeham, Duane Allen Painter, Writer
Wall, Brian Sculptor
Warnecke, John Carl Architect
Weinbaum, Jean Painter, Sculptor
Weisel, Thomas W Patron
West, Alice Clare Painter
Wirtz, Stephen Carl Gallery Director
Yamrus, Frank Photographer
Zahedi, Caveh Filmmaker, Video Artist
Zajac, Jack Sculptor

San Francisco

Sherratt, Holly

San Gabriel

Peregrin, Magda Elizabeth Painter, Instructor

San Geronimo

North, Judy K Rafael Painter

San Jose

Chapman, Robert Gordon Jeweler, Painter
French, Stephen Warren Painter, Sculptor
Goreniuc, Mircea C Paul Sculptor
Hoffman, Eric Painter, Printmaker
Keegan, Daniel T Director
Quick, Edward Raymond Museum Director
Richardson, Sam Sculptor, Educator
Spratt, Frederick R Gallery Director, Painter
Stone, M Lee Art Dealer
Suggs, Pat(ricia) Ann Painter, Conceptual Artist
Thompson, Donald Roy Painter, Educator
Thurston, Jacqueline Beverly Educator, Artist, Writer
Wise, Joseph Stephen Painter

San Juan Bautista

Masteller, Barry Painter, Craftsman

San Juan Capistrano

Aspell, Amy Suzanne Director, Weaver
Burr, Ruth Basler Painter

San Luis Obispo

McFee, June King Educator
Peluso, Marta E Photographer, Art Instructor
Robbins, Patricia Painter
Ruggles, Joanne Beaule Painter, Educator

San Marcos

Dawson, Robert E Sculptor
Small, Deborah Painter

San Marino

Wark, Robert Rodger Administrator, Historian

San Mateo

Mancini, John Painter

San Pedro

McCafferty, Jay David Video Artist, Painter
Strasen, Barbara Elaine Painter, Conceptual Artist

San Rafael

Allan, William George Painter, Educator
Dixon, Willard Painter
Fulton, Jack E Photographer, Instructor
Larsen, D Dane Ceramist, Sculptor
Lucey, Jack Painter, Educator
Rowland, Adele Photographer

San Ramon

Chen, Anna Chaihue Painter

Santa Barbara

Arnold, Nancy Ann Curator, Educator
Ayres, Larry Marshall Historian
Braiden, Rose Margaret J Painter, Illustrator
Brown, Gary Hugh Painter, Educator
Calamar, Gloria Painter
Cavat, Irma Painter, Educator
Cole, Herbert Milton Historian, Photographer
D'Andrea, Jeanne Editor, Designer
DeGuzman, Nicole Director
Del Chiaro, Mario A Historian
Eguchi, Yasu Painter
Farwell, Beatrice Historian, Educator
Freudenstein, Ellie (Eleanor) T(erenyi) Painter, Environmental Artist
Herschler, David Elijah Sculptor, Painter
Hochhauser, Marilyn Helsenrott Painter, Educator
Kenney, Douglas Ceramist, Clay Sculptor
Korenic, Lynette Marie Librarian
Legrady, George Photographer
Moir, Alfred Curator, Collector
Noble, Helen (Harper) Printmaker, Painter
Pincus, Laurie Jane Painter, Sculptor
Robertson, E Bruce Historian, Curator
Rosenthal, Earl Edgar Educator, Historian
Rossman, Ruth Scharff Painter, Instructor
Sanchez, John Painter, Photographer
Sattler, Jill Photographer, Painter
Snow, Lee Erlin Painter, Instructor
Sudbrack, Eli Artist
Venable, Susan C Sculptor, Painter
Villa, Theodore B Painter
Yegul, Fikret Kutlu Educator, Architect

Santa Clara

Fogg, Rebecca Snider Printmaker, Painter
Hawkins, Myrtle H Painter, Writer
Rivera, George Museum Director, Painter

Santa Clarita

Lavine, Steven David Educator, Writer, Administrator

Santa Cruz

Alford, Gloria K Painter, Sculptor
Alquilar, Maria Painter, Ceramist
Harrison, Helen Mayer (Mrs Newton Harrison) Environmental Artist, Conceptual Artist
Harrison, Newton A Environmental Artist, Conceptual Artist
Leites, Ara (Barbara) L Painter; Educator
Loftus, Peter M Painter
Massaro, Karen Thuesen Ceramist, Lecturer
Orland, Ted N Photographer, Writer
Summers, Carol Printmaker
Sward, Robert S Writer, Editor
Teachout, David Delano Painter

Santa Maria

Reeser, Robert D Educator, Administrator

Santa Monica

Alexander, Peter Sculptor
Alpert, Herb Painter, Sculptor
Bachardy, Don Painter, Draftsman
Baldessari, John Anthony Conceptual Artist
Blum, Helaine Dorothy Sculptor, Painter
Bordeaux, Jean Luc Art Historian, Curator, Art Expert
Bosman, Richard Painter, Printmaker
Callis, Jo Ann Photographer
Caswell, Jim (James) Daniel Caswell-Davis Sculptor, Ceramist
Cheng, Carl FK Environmental Artist, Sculptor
Chu, Julia Nee Painter
Cohen, Bruce Joel Painter
Conal, Robbie Painter
Erenberg, Samuel Joseph Painter, Printmaker
Fellows, Alice Painter
Felsen, Rosamund Art Dealer, Gallery Director
Finkel, Bruria Designer, Sculptor
Flick, Robbert Photographer, Educator
Frankel, Dextra Educator, Designer
Fukuhara, Henry Painter, Instructor
Galloway, Steve Conceptual Artist
Gilbert-Rolfe, Jeremy Painter
Greaves, James L Conservator, Restorer
Hoffberg, Judith A Publisher, Curator
Kaino, Glenn Sculptor
Kepalas Sculptor, Painter
Klarin, Karla S Painter
Martinez, Daniel J Conceptual Artist
Mayne, Thom Architect
Mitchell, Robin Painter, Educator
Moskowitz, Shirley Painter, Collage Artist
Murrill, Gwynn Sculptor
Norton, Peter K Collector & Patron
Ocampo, Manuel Painter
O'Shea, Terrence Patrick Painter, Sculptor
Ovitz, Michael S Collector, Patron
Peeps, Claire Curator, Photographer
Reilly, Jack Painter, Video Artist
Smith, Anna Deavere Patron
Soloff, Laura J Administrator
Trieff, Selina Painter, Instructor
Van Sant, Tom R Sculptor, Painter
Wortz, Melinda Farris Gallery Director, Critic
Zellen, Jody Photographer, Writer

Santa Rosa

Hein, Max Graphic Artist, Educator
Lancaster, Virginia (Ginny) Jane Educator, Painter

CALIFORNIA (cont)
Nugent, Bob L Painter, Printmaker
Weare, Shane Printmaker

Sausalito
Kuhlman, Walter Egel Painter, Educator
Maišel, David Photographer, Environmental Artist
Oda, Mayumi Painter, Printmaker
Rector, Marge (Lee) Painter, Sculptor
Wiley, William T Painter

Seaside
Erickson, Mark D Painter

Sebastopol
Caswell, Helen Rayburn Painter, Writer
Hasegawa, Noriko Painter
Kahn, Ned M Environmental Artist, Sculptor
Lipzin, Janis Crystal Filmmaker, Photographer
Stanford, Ginny C Painter
Zaikine, Victor (Zak) Eugene Sculptor, Painter

Sherman Oaks
Burg, Patricia Jean Painter, Printmaker
Carl, Joan Sculptor, Painter

Sierra Madre
Converse, Elizabeth Painter, Writer
De Kansky, Igor Painter, Sculptor

Silverado
Holste, Thomas James Painter, Educator

Solana Beach
Gronborg, Erik Sculptor, Ceramist

Sonoma
Anderson, Gunnar Donald Painter, Illustrator
Moquin, Richard Attilio Painter, Sculptor
Nottebohm, Andreas Painter

Sonora
Popovac, Gwynn Painter, Sculptor

Soquel
McClellan, Douglas Eugene Painter

Soulsbyville
Hartwig, Heinie Painter - Acrylic, Oil, Instructor

South Pasadena
Askin, Walter Miller Painter, Printmaker
Sverdlove, Zolita Painter, Printmaker

Stanford
Bryan, Sukey Painter
Corn, Wanda M Historian, Educator
Eisner, Elliot Wayne Educator
Eitner, Lorenz E A Historian, Museum Director
Fryberger, Betsy G Curator
Seligman, Thomas Knowles Director

Stinson Beach
Chapline, Claudia Beechum Painter, Art Dealer, Assemblage Artist
Schwarm, Harold Chambers Painter, Instructor

Stockton
Dennison, Keith Elkins Consultant, Curator
Gyermek, Stephen A Educator
Pecchenino, J Ronald Painter, Educator

Studio City
Brommer, Gerald F Painter, Writer
Vaccarino, Robin Sculptor
White, Stephen Leon Collector, Art Dealer

Suisun City
Irvin, Marianne Fanelli Painter, Collage Artist
Schmaltz, Roy Edgar Painter, Educator

Sun City
Guest, Richard G Painter, Consultant
Wood, Ron Glass Artist, Sculptor

Sunland
Porter, Albert Wright Educator, Painter

Sunnyvale
Semel, Terry S Patron

Templeton
Mitchell, N Donald Administrator, Dealer

Tiburon
Parker, Gertrud Valerie Sculptor

Toluca Lake
de Musée, Moran Sculptor

Tomales
Foote, Howard Reed Artist, Painter

Topanga
Oginz, Richard Sculptor, Draftsman
Wisdom, Joyce Painter

Turlock
Camarata, Martin L Artist, Educator
McGee, Winston Eugene Painter, Educator
Werness, Hope B Historian

Upland
Svenson, John Edward Sculptor, Medalist

Valencia
Buchanan, Nancy Video Artist, Conceptual Artist
Durant, Sam Educator
Fiskin, Judy Photographer, Video Artist
Hatch, Connie Photographer, Educator
Mandel, John Painter
Preston, Ann L Sculptor
Wilson, Millie Conceptual Artist

Vallejo
Bullock, James Benbow Sculptor
Fried, Howard Lee Sculptor
Livingstone, Biganess Painter
Salmon, Raymond Merle Cartoonist, Educator

Valley Glen
Reed, Dennis James Curator, Designer

Van Nuys
Davis, L Clarice Book Dealer, Art Librarian
Irmas, Audrey Menein Collector

Venice
Adams, Lisa Kay Painter
Allyn, Jerri Conceptual Artist, Educator
Bengston, Billy Al Painter
Blair, Philippa Mary Painter, Educator
Brewster, Michael Sculptor, Educator
Byrd, Jerry Painter
Campbell, Rebecca Artist, Instructor
Cheng, Fu-Ding Filmmaker, Painter
Colson, Greg J Sculpture, Conceptual Artist
Davis, Kimberly Brooke Gallery Director, Art Dealer
Davy, Woods Sculptor
Dill, Guy Sculptor, Educator
Dill, Laddie John Painter, Sculptor
Divola, John Manford, Jr Photographer
Fine, Jud Sculptor, Educator
Garabedian, Charles Painter
Hill, Charles Christopher Collage Artist, Painter
Kossoff, Leon Painter
Kraal, Lies Painter
Leaf, Ruth Printmaker, Instructor
McMillen, Michael C(halmers) Environmental Artist, Sculptor
Moses, Ed Painter
Price, Kenneth Printmaker, Sculptor
Richards, Bruce Michael Painter, Printmaker
Scheer, Sherie (Hood) Photographer, Painter
Shaffer, Richard Painter, Printmaker
Shelton, Peter T Sculptor
Smith, Alexis (Patricia Anne) Collage Artist, Conceptual Artist
Smith, Barbara Turner Video & Performance Artist, Educator

Ventura
Adkison, Kathleen (Gemberling) Painter
Koch, Gerd Herman Painter, Educator
Taback, Simms Illustrator, Designer

Verdugo City
Clayton, Christian Painter
Clayton, Robert Painter

Vista
Simmons, Cleda-Marie Painter, Muralist

Walnut Creek
Esaki, Yasuhiro Painter, Printmaker
Parton, Ralf Sculptor, Educator
Reimann, Arline Lynn Printmaker, Painter

Warner Springs
Gauvreau, Robert George Photographer, Educator

Watsonville
Hernandez, Jo Farb Museum Director, Curator
Hernandez, Sam (Samuel) Rudolph Sculptor, Educator

West Hills
Duzy, Merrilyn Jeanne Painter, Lecturer

West Hollywood
Birk, Sandow Painter, Sculptor
Gronk Painter
Valadez, John Painter
Wesley, Eric Sculptor

Westchester
Glover, Robert Sculptor, Ceramist

Westhills
Steynovitz, Zamy Painter

Westlake Village
Liu, Katherine Chang Painter, Curator

Winterhaven
Wohlenhaus, Grace Forcier Painter

Woodacre
Uzilevsky, Marcus Painter, Printmaker

Woodland Hills
Pinsker, Essie Sculptor
Stecyk, Craig R Sculptor, Curator
Turner, Bonese Collins Painter, Designer
Whitson, Angie Sculptor, Painter

Woodside
Concannon, George Robert Painter
Hogle, Ann Meilstrup Painter

Yorba Linda
Holm, Milton W Painter

CALIFORNIA (cont)
Yountville
Gillen, John Sculptor, Painter

COLORADO

Arvada
Ball, Ken Weston Artist
Jones, Jane Painter
Pech, Arleta Painter, Instructor

Aspen
Bucksbaum, Melva & Raymond Learsy Collector
Chesley, Paul Alexander Photographer
Farver, Suzanne Administrator, Collector
Guralnick, Jody Painter, Collage Artist
Hough, Jennine Painter
Lord, Andrew Sculptor
Sobel, Dean Museum Director, Curator
Soldner, Paul Edmund Sculptor, Ceramist

Aspen
Llearsy, Raymond & Melva Bucksbanm Collector

Aurora
Faris, Peter Kinzie Writer, Historian
Hughes, Paul Lucien Dealer, Consultant

Berthold
Balas, Jack J Painter, Photographer

Boulder
Barnes, Carole D Painter
Bolomey, Roger Henry Sculptor
Dowden, Anne Ophelia Todd Painter, Writer
Eades, Luis Eric Painter, Educator
Fernie, John Chipman Sculptor
Foley, David E Painter
Forsman, Chuck (Charles) Stanley Painter, Educator
Gibson, James D Video Artist, Painter
Iwamasa, Ken Educator, Printmaker
Johnson, James Alan Painter, Educator
Kuczun, Ann-Marie Painter, Illustrator
Markowitz, Marilyn Painter, Printmaker
Parker, Joni Y Painter, Instructor
Sampson, Frank Painter, Printmaker
Schleiner, Ann-Marie Graphic Artist
Valdovino, Luis Hector Video Artist, Educator
Vandersall, Amy L Historian, Educator
Walker, Melanie Photographer
Wolfe, Lynn Robert Painter, Educator

Brighton
Shaklee, Kim Sculptor

Broomfield
Vielehr, William Ralph Sculptor

Buena Vista
McCoy, Katherine Braden Designer, Educator
McCoy, Michael Dale Designer, Educator
Silva, Jude Hutton Artist

Carbondale
Powers, John & Kimiko Collector

Centennial
Herzog, Priscilla Jenne Painter, Instructor
Trumble, Beverly (Jane) Painter

Colorado Springs
Bransby, Eric James Muralist, Educator
Broome, Rick (Richard) Raymond Painter
Hoge, Robert Wilson Curator, Educator
Kinnee, Sandy Painter, Printmaker
Riggs, Gerry Museum Director, Educator
Turner, David Museum Director, Educator
Wynne, Albert Givens Painter, Calligrapher
Zapel, Arthur Lewis Illustrator Books, Painter

Creede
Quiller, Stephen Frederick Painter, Printmaker

Crestone
Marston, JD Photographer

Denver
Anschutz, Philip F Collector
Bowman, Ken Painter
Brauer Ferns, Connie Ann Designer, Goldsmith
Cline, Clinton C Printmaker, Educator
Cole, Jean (Dahl) Painter
Cunningham, E C (Eldon) Lloyd Printmaker, Educator
DeLaCruz, Jerry J Painter, Collage Artist
Dickson, Mark Amos Painter, Printmaker
Encinias, John Orlando Painter
Gerlovina & Gerlovin, Rimma & Valeriy Conceptual Artist, Photographer
Graese, Judy (Judith) Ann Painter, Illustrator
Herbert Constransitch, Phyllis Sculptor, Educator
Hersch, Jeff Photographer
Hoover, George Schweke Architect
Kremers, David Conceptual Artist
Loewy, Raymond Designer, Graphic Artist
Matthews, William (Cary) Painter
Mayer, Frederick & Jan Collector
Maytham, Thomas Northrup Consultant
Michael, Gary Painter, Writer
Miller, Nancy Tokar Painter
Morper, Daniel Painter, Printmaker
O'Hagan, Desmond Brian Painter
Ortega, Tony (Anthony) David Painter, Printmaker
Payton, Cydney M Museum Director, Curator
Ragland, Bob Painter, Instructor
Robinson, Cleo Director
Saylors, Jo An Sculptor, Instructor
Schiff, E Jean Educator
Scott, Sandy (Sandra) Lynn Sculptor
Sharp, Lewis Inman Director
Strawn, Bernice I Sculptor
Sumner, Stephen Charles Administrator, Educator
Temple, Leslie Alcott (Leslie Jane Atkinson) Sculpture, Writer
Thompson, Richard Craig Painter
Vanderlip, Dianne Perry Gallery Director, Educator
Watt, Robb Artist
White, Karen J Sculptor, Craftsman
Wilson, Steve Museum Director
Witold , Kaczanowski Painter, Sculptor
Yanish, Elizabeth Shwayder Sculptor, Lecturer

Divide
Mayes, Steven Lee Educator, Printmaker

Elizabeth
Kaplinski, Buffalo Painter, Watercolorist

Englewood
Cooper, Susan Sculptor, Painter
Hull, John Painter
Kaplan, Sandra Painter, Printmaker
Lamb, Darlis Carol Sculptor, Painter

Estes Park
Sullivan, Patrice Maureen Artist

Evergreen
Kastner, Barbara H Painter

Florissant
Elkins, Lane Educator, Ceramist

Fort Collins
De Vore, Richard E Ceramist
Getty, Nilda Fernandez Educator, Silversmith
Jacobs, Peter Alan Sculptor, Educator
Lesh, Richard D Painter, Instructor
Lundberg, Thomas Roy Fiber Artist
Marander, Carol Jean Painter, Graphic Artist
Risbeck, Philip Edward Graphic Artist, Educator
Whitcomb, Milo W Skip Painter, Printmaker
Yust, David E Painter, Educator

Glenwood Springs
Sprick, Daniel Painter

Greeley
Ruyle, Lydia Miller Printmaker, Educator

Gunnison
Johnson, Lee Painter, Educator
Julio, Pat T Educator, Craftsman

Hotchkiss
Blackstock, Virginia Harriett Painter

La Veta
Schneider, Kenny Sculptor, Painter

Lakewood
Cadillac, Louise Roman Painter, Instructor
Denton, Patry Painter, Instructor
Lang, Rodger Alan Sculptor, Educator

Littleton
Duesberry, Joellyn Painter
Meyer, Milton E, Jr Painter
Poduska, T F Lecturer, Painter

Longmont
Roots, Garrison Sculptor, Educator
Thompson, Tamara Assemblage Artist, Painter
Wise, Sue Painter

Loveland
Lundeen, George Wayne Sculptor
Maior, Philip Sculptor
Ostermiller, Dan Sculptor
Svedlow, Andrew Jay Administrator, Painter
Weimer, Dawn Sculptor
Williford, Hollis R Painter, Sculptor
Zahourek, Jon Gail Painter, Sculptor

Lyons
Woodman, Betty Ceramist

Manitou Springs
Modica, Andrea Photographer
Wallace, Gael Lynn Painter

Mesa
Fritzler, Gerald J Painter, Watercolor

Monument
Bohler, Joseph Stephen Painter

Nathrop
Schmidt, Frederick Lee Painter

Nederland
Reuman, Scott Campbell Sculptor, Writer

Ouray
Carlile, Janet (Hildebrand) Painter, Educator

COLORADO (cont)

Pagosa Springs
Mion, Pierre Riccardo Illustrator, Painter

Parker
Balciar, Gerald George Sculptor
Thies, Charles Herman Painter, Printmaker

Pueblo West
Fisher, Philip C Painter, Art Dealer

Salida
Strawn, Melvin Nicholas Painter, Sculptor

Shawnee
Tolpo, Carolyn Lee Painter, Tapestry
Tolpo, Vincent Carl Painter, Sculptor

Vail
Cotter, James Edward Sculptor, Designer
Logan, Kent Collector
Logan, Vicki Collector
Milhoan, Randall Bell Painter, Designer

Westcliffe
Merfeld, Gerald Lydon Painter, Sculptor

Wheat Ridge
Dawson, Doug Painter, Instructor

Woody Creek
Miller, Brad Craftsman, Ceramist

CONNECTICUT

Ashford
Spencer, Harold Edwin Historian, Painter

Avon
Atkinson, Tracy Consultant, Museologist

Barkhamsted
Wallace, Carol Ann (Brucker) Painter, Illustrator

Bethany
Bills, Mitchell Designer, Video Artist
Hauer, Erwin Franz Sculptor, Educator
Wolanic, Susan Seseske Painter, Graphic Artist

Bethlehem
Vestal, David Photographer, Writer

Bloomfield
Eshoo, Robert Painter
Tompkins, Alan Painter; Educator

Branford
Blake, Peter Jost Architect, Critic
Kurzen, Aaron Painter, Sculptor, Assemblage Artist
Sheard, Wendy Stedman Historian, Educator

Bridgeport
Jordan, George Edwin Historian, Consultant

Bridgewater
Abbett, Robert Kennedy Painter, Writer
Gilbert, Albert Earl Painter, Illustrator

Brookfield Center
Sottung, George (K) Painter, Sculptor

Brooklyn
McIlvane, Edward James Stained Glass Artist, Glassblower

Chester
Nilsson, Katherine Ellen Painter
Weiss, Jerome Nathan Painter, Instructor

Clinton
Mays, Victor Painter, Illustrator

Colchester
Liverant, Gigi Horr Painter

Cos Cob
Kane, Margaret Brassler Sculptor
Ubogy, Jo Sculptor

Coventry
Doudera, Gerard Painter, Educator
Hayes, David Vincent Sculptor

Danbury
Kan, Michael Historian, Administrator
Renee, Paula Tapestry Artist, Painter

Darien
Anderson, Robert Alexander Painter, Illustrator
Gibb, Ann W Painter

East Haddam
Conant, Jan Royce Representational Painter

Easton
Bogart, Richard Jerome Painter
Curtis, Dolly Powers Sculptor, Weaver
Sharp, Susan S Painter

Enfield
Gerich, Betty A Juliette Sculptor, Ceramist

Fairfield
Eliasoph, Philip Historian, Critic, Consultant
Glaser, Bruce Historian, Educator
Khachian, Elisa A Painter
Whyte, Bruce Lincoln Consultant, Administrator

Fairfield
Brier, Helene Painter, Printmaker

Falls Village
Cronin, Robert (Lawrence) Painter

Farmington
Ferguson, Charles B Museum Director, Painter
Smith, Cary Painter

Glastonbury
Bailey, Marcia Mead Painter

Goshen
Federico, Frank Painter, Pastel

Greens Farms
Weiss, Harvey Sculptor, Writer

Greenwich
Arguimbau, Peter L Painter, Lecturer
Brant, Peter M Patron
Ganek, David Kent Collector
Johnson, Lester F Painter, Educator
Landau, Jon & Barbara Collector
Moonie, Liana Painter, Lecturer
Parker, Robert Andrew Painter
Perless, Robert Sculptor
Sturges, Hollister Curator, Historian

Guilford
Pease, David G Administrator, Painter

Hamden
Cain, David Paul Painter, Instructor
Chambers, Bruce William Historian, Consultant
de Bretteville, Sheila Levrant Designer, Educator
MacClintock, Dorcas Sculptor, Writer
Zallinger, Jean Day Illustrator, Educator
Zeidenbergs, Olafs Sculptor

Hartford
Banks, Anne Johnson Painter, Educator
Boothe, Power Painter, Administrator
Hammer, Alfred Emil Painter, Educator
Holmes, Willard Museum Director
Kornhauser, Elizabeth Mankin Museum Director, Curator
Mahoney, Michael R T Historian, Educator
Soppelsa, George Painter, Collage Artist
Sutton, Peter C Curator, Historian
Zafran, Eric Myles Curator, Historian
Zimmerman, Paul Warren Painter, Instructor

Ivoryton
Jensen, Leo Sculptor, Painter
Ramanauskas, Dalia Irena Painter, Draftsman

Killingworth
Harris, William Wadsworth, II Painter, Collage Artist

Lakeville
Blagden, Thomas P Painter
Close, Mary Painter, Pastelist
Cramer, Douglas S Collector, Patron

Litchfield
McKnight, Thomas Frederick Painter, Printmaker

Madison
Davies, Kenneth Southworth Painter, Instructor
Wexler, Jerome LeRoy Photographer, Illustrator

Manchester
Chaplin, George Edwin Painter, Educator

Meriden
Bertolli, Eugene Emil Sculptor, Designer
Scalise, Nicholas Peter Painter
Tamburine, Jean Helen Painter, Sculptor

Middletown
D'Oench, Ellen Gates Curator, Educator
Frazer, John Thatcher Filmmaker, Painter
Imlah, Rachel Crawford Painter, Photographer
Ottmann, Klaus Curator, Critic
Risley, John Hollister Sculptor

Milford
Fagan, Alanna Painter, Printmaker

Mystic
De Vore, Sadie Davidson Printmaker, Painter

New Britain
Cipriano, Michael R Painter, Educator

New Canaan
Rendl, M(ildred) Marcus Painter, Writer
Richards, Glenora Painter
Seymour, Claudia Painter
Tomchuk, Marjorie Printmaker, Painter
Townsend, Teryl Painter, Educator

New Fairfield
Carlson, Jane C Painter
Mann, Jean (Adah) Ceramist, Sculptor

New Haven
Audette, Anna Held Painter
Carter, David Giles Historian, Museologist
Chaet, Bernard Robert Painter, Educator
Fussiner, Howard Painter, Educator

CONNECTICUT (cont)
Gardner, Joan A Painter, Book Artist
Hersey, George Leonard Historian
LaPalombara, Constance Painter
Lindroth, Linda Photographic Artist, Curator
Newick, Craig D Architect
Papageorge, Tod Photographer
Pelli, Cesar Architect
Pollitt, Jerome Jordan Historian, Educator
Pronin , Anatoly Photographer
Prown, Jules David Art Historian
Reed, Robert James, Jr Painter, Educator
Reynolds, John (Jock) M Director, Writer
Roche, (Eamonn) Kevin Architect
Rolland , Peter George Architect
Scully, Vincent Joseph, Jr Architecture, Educator, Writer
Smith, Raymond Walter Photographer, Book Dealer
Sorkin, Jenni Curator, Critic
Storr, Robert Curator, Painter
Weinberg, Jonathan Edman Painter, Historian

New London
Hendricks, Barkley Leonnard Painter
Leibert, Peter R Ceramist, Sculptor
Patnode, Mark William Painter, Designer

New Milford
Crawford, Rainie Painter
Kepets, Hugh Michael Painter, Printmaker
Shawna, Montepaulo Collector

Newton
Bermingham, John C Painter

Newtown
Christensen, Betty (Elizabeth) Illustrator, Painter
Cottingham, Robert Painter, Printmaker
Purdy, Donald R Painter

Norfolk
Sloan, Ronald J Painter

North Grosvenordale
Kornbluth, Frances Painter, Assemblage Artist

North Haven
Field, Richard Sampson Curator, Historian
Willoughby, Jane Baker Collage Artist, Painter

Norwalk
Black, Lisa Painter, Photographer
Frasconi, Antonio Graphic Artist, Painter
Gevas, Sophia Director, Painter
Meagher, Sandra Krebs Painter

Norwalk
Bohnen, Blythe Conceptual Artist, Photographer

Norwich
Gualtieri, Joseph P Museum Director, Painter
Topalis, Daniel P Painter

Old Greenwich
Smith, Clyde Painter

Old Lyme
Chandler, Elisabeth Gordon Sculptor, Instructor
Dirks, John Sculptor, Cartoonist
Greenleaf, Virginia Painter

Old Saybrook
Neal, Irene Painter, Sculptor, Jewelry designer

Oxford
Baldassano, Vincent Painter

Plainville
Brzozowski, Richard Joseph Painter

Poquonock
Van Winkelen, Barbara Painter, Illustrator

Quaker Hill
Braunstein, Mark Mathew Curator, Photographer
McCabe, Maureen M Collage Artist

Redding
Bloch, Babette Artist, Sculptor
Mellon, Marc Richard Sculptor, Medalist
Morton, Robert Alan Publisher, Writer, Editor, Curator

Ridgefield
Benton, Suzanne E Sculptor, Art Writer
Busino, Orlando Francis Cartoonist
Giordano, Greg Joe Painter, Photographer
Grasso, Jack Painter
Perlin, Bernard Painter, Illustrator
Sanden, John Howard Painter, Instructor
Sendak, Maurice Bernard Writer, Illustrator
Taubes, Timothy Evan Critic, Curator

Salisbury
Blagden, Allen Painter, Printmaker
Boyle, Richard J Art Historian, Writer

Sharon
Griesedieck, Ellen Muralist
Heller, Ben Dealer, Collector
Johns, Jasper Painter

Simsbury
Ford, John Painter, Sculptor

South Kent
Kaplan, Jacques Collector, Dealer

South Norwalk
Kavanagh, Cornelia Kubler Sculptor, Designer

South Windsor
Patterson, Shirley Abbott Painter, Instructor

Southbury
Jones, Franklin Reed Painter, Writer

Southbury
Rorick, William Calvin Painter, Instructor

Southington
Deckert, Clinton A Painter

Southport
Anderson, Margaret Pomeroy Appraiser, Collection Manager
Sill, Gertrude Grace Writer, Curator

Srotts Mnsfield
Woods, David G Educator

Stamford
Bechtle, C Ronald Painter, Draftsman
Burt, David Sill Sculptor
Calle, Paul Painter, Writer
Cohen, Steven A Collector
Graham, Robert C, Jr Art Dealer
Hausman, Fred S Sculptor, Designer
Heston, Joan Painter, Instructor
Hollinger, Morton Painter
Rudman, Joan (Combs) Painter, Instructor
Walker, Mort Cartoonist
Williams, Dave Harrell Collector, Patron

Stonington
Bareford, David Painter
Fix, John Robert Sculptor, Silversmith

Storrs
Crossgrove, Roger Lynn Printmaker, Educator
Gregoropoulos, John Painter
Thornton, Richard Samuel Educator, Writer

Stratford
Eisinger, Harry Painter
Passantino, George Christopher Painter, Instructor

Tariffville
Brody, Ruth Painter, Graphic Artist

Trumbull
Kozlowski, Edward C Painter, Designer
Morrison, Edith Borax Artist, Painter

Unionville
Dublac, Robert Revak Painter

Vernon
Groff, Barbara S Painter, Graphic Artist

Voluntown
Caddell, Foster Painter, Instructor

Wallingford
Lauttenbach, Carol L Painter
Neff, John A Painter, Designer

Washington
Grimes, Margaret W Painter, Educator
Phillips, Laughlin Museum Chairman, Director
Poskas, Peter Edward Painter

Washington Depot
Forge, Andrew Murray Writer, Painter
Wallace, John Painter

Waterbury
Smith, Ann Y Museum Director, Curator

Watertown
Cajori, Charles F Painter
Grossman, Barbara Painter, Educator

West Hartford
Dente, Robert Sculptor, Painter
Faude, Wilson Hinsdale Director, Curator
Levitz, Ilona S Painter, Educator
Sorokin, Janet Artist, Painter

West Redding
Grashow, James Bruce Sculptor, Printmaker
Natkin, Robert Painter

West Willington
Zelanski, Paul John Painter

Weston
Bleifeld, Stanley Sculptor, Medalist
Gropper, Cathy Painter, Sculptor
Oliver, Sandra (Sandi) Art Dealer, Painter
Reinker, Nancy Clayton Cooke Painter, Sculptor
Williams, Paul Alan Painter, Illustrator
Wilson, Melissa Anne Sculptor

Westport
Baxter, Robert Charles Painter, Educator
Bloom, Martha Collage Artist, Photographer, Educator

CONNECTICUT (cont)
Chernow, Ann Painter, Printmaker
Cifolelli, Alberta Painter, Printmaker
Fisher, Leonard Everett Painter, Illustrator
Heyman, Ronnie Feuerstein Collector
Kovatch, Jak Painter, Printmaker
Levin, Hugh Lauter Publisher
Madan-Shotkin, Rhoda Painter
Minkowitz, Norma Sculptor
Neilson, Mary Ann Painter
Reed, Walt Arnold Historian, Dealer
Reilly, Nancy Painter
Rothenberg, Barbara Painter, Educator
Sallick, Lucy Ellen Painter, Instructor
Von Schmidt, Eric Painter, Historian
Woodham, Jean Sculptor

Wilton
Thompson, Malcolm Barton Painter, Film Maker

Winchester
Jenney, Neil Painter, Sculptor

Woodbridge
Lytle, Richard Painter, Educator

Woodbury
Odate, Toshio Conceptual Artist, Educator
Seltzer, Peter Lawrence Painter

DELAWARE

Bear
Lane, Rosemary Louise Printmaker, Sculptor

Camden Wyoming
Stockman, Jennifer Blei Patron

Laurel
Blaine, Frederick Matthew Sculptor, Educator

Lewes
Costigan, Constance Frances Painter, Educator

Millsboro
Davis Price, Doris C Painter, Printmaker

Newark
Breslin, Nancy Photographer
Breslin, Wynn Painter, Sculptor
Chapman, H Perry Educator
Craven, Wayne Art Historian, Writer
Gibson, Ann Historian, Educator
Matsumoto, Roger Photographer
Morris, Gregg Painter, acrylic
Moss, Joe (Francis) Sculptor, Painter
Nees, Lawrence Educator, Historian
Rowe, Charles Alfred Painter, Illustrator
Spinski, Victor Sculptor, Educator
Stillman, Damie Historian, Educator
Stoner, (Dr) Joyce Hill Conservator, Educator
Weiss, John Joseph Photographer, Editor

Prime Hook Beach
Baxendell, Julie Painter

Rockland
Harvey, Andre Sculptor
Sculthorpe, Peter Painter, Printmaker

Seaford
Jurney, Donald (Benson) Painter

Smyrna
Bailey, Richard H Sculptor

Wilmington
Allmond, Charles Sculptor
Brown, Hilton Painter, Educator
Bruni, Stephen Thomas Museum Director
Colombo, Charles Painter
Fish, Alida Photographer
Gore, David Alan Painter, Photographer
Hatch, W A S Painter, Educator
Hayes, Tua Painter
Homer, William Innes Historian, Educator
Hummel, Charles Frederick Administrator
McFarren, Grace Painter
Messina, Charles artist
Straight, Robert L Painter
Sundin, Adelaide Toombs Ceramist, Sculptor
Tolles, Bryant Franklin, Jr Educator, Historian

DISTRICT OF COLUMBIA

Northwest Washington
Fujimara, Makota Painter
Ishaq, Ashfaq Administrator

Washington
Abbott, Rebecca Phillips Curator, Photographer
Allen, Henry Southworth Critic
Bolton-Smith, Robin Lee Curator, Historian
Bookatz, Samuel Painter, Sculptor
Broude, Norma Freedman Historian, Educator
Broun, Elizabeth Gibson Administrator, Historian
Brown, David Alan Historian, Curator
Brown, Pamela Wedd Painter, Printmaker
Buster, Kendall J Instructor
Carr, Carolyn K Curator, Historian
Carter, Yvonne Pickering Painter, Educator
Christenberry, William Painter, Sculptor, Photographer
Cikovsky, Nicolai, Jr Curator, Historian
Clark, Michael Museum Director
Cogswell, Margaret Price Instructor
Cooper, Theodore A Dealer
Cowart, Jack Museum Director, Curator
Cropper, M Elizabeth Historian, Lecturer
Cushner, Steven J Painter
Cusick, Nancy Taylor Collage Artist, Asssemblage Artist
Danziger, Joan Sculptor
Dawson, Jessica Critic
De Andino, Jean-Pierre M Dealer, Collector
Demetrion, James Thomas Museum Director
Desmidt, Thomas H Painter, Educator
Dixon, Glenn Critic
Doumato, Lamia Librarian, Historian
Downs, Linda Anne Curator, Historian
Edwards, Gary Maxwell Art Dealer, Writer
Eisenstein, (Mr & Mrs) Julian Collectors
Escallon, Ana Maria Museum Director, Curator, Writer
Faubion, S Michael Administrator
Fetting, Rainer Painter
Fine, Ruth E Curator, Printmaker
Fink, Lois Marie Historian, Curator
Fisher, Sarah Lisbeth Conservator
Fleischman, Aaron I Collector
Fletcher, Valerie J Curator, Historian
Foresta, Merry A Curator
Forgey, Benjamin Franklin Architect, Critic
Forrester, Patricia Tobacco Painter, Printmaker
Freeman, Roland L Photographer
Garrard, Mary DuBose Historian, Educator
Gates, Harry Irving Sculptor, Educator
Gates, Jay Rodney Museum Director
Gelernter, David H Critic, Painter, Educator
Gilliam, Sam Painter
Gioia, Dana (Michael) Critic
Goodman, Janis G Painter, Draftsman
Gopnik, Blake Critic
Gossage, John Ralph Photographer
Green, Tom Instructor, Sculptor
Greenhalgh, Paul
Greenwald, Alice (Alice) Marian Greenwald-Ward Consultant, Museologist
Grier, Margot Edmands Librarian, Administrator
Grossman, Sheldon Museum Curator, Historian
Grundberg, Andy (Andrew) John Critic, Curator
Gumpert, Gunther Painter
Guzy, Carol Photographer
Halegua, Alfredo Sculptor
Hall, Robert L Museologist, Painter
Hansen, Sarah Eveleth Campbell Art Dealer, Gallery Director
Hartigan, Lynda Roscoe Curator, Historian
Haslem, Jane N Dealer
Hay, (George) Austin Painter, Filmmaker
Haynie, Ron Painter, Euducator
Hilton, Alison Historian, Educator
Hogan, Felicity Museum Director
Holladay, Wilhelmina Cole Collector, Patron
Howland, Richard Hubbard Architectural Historian
Jacobsen, Hugh Newell Architect
Jacobson, Louis Critic
Jashinsky, Judy Painter, Curator
Johnson-Ross, Robyn Painter, Writer
Joost-Gaugier, Christiane L Administrator, Historian
Jurovics, Toby Curator
Kahn, Deborah Painter, Educator
Kaskey, Raymond John Sculptor, Architect
Kijek, Manon Catherine (Manon Catherine Cleary) Painter, Draftsman
Kloss, William Historian, Writer
Kraft, Craig Allan Sculptor, Curator
Kravitz, Walter Sculptor, Painter
Krebs, Rockne Sculptor
Lader, Melvin Paul Historian, Educator
Laiou, Angeliki E Educator
Langston, Mary Virginia Sculptor, Painter
Larson, Judy L Director
Laub-Novak, Karen Sculptor, Painter, Printmaker, Writer
Lawrence, Sidney S Painter, Writer
Lawton, Thomas Historian, Editor
Learsy, Raymond Collector, Patron
Leithauser, Mark Alan Painter, Designer
Leven, Ann R Administrator
Lewton, Val Edwin Painter, Designer
Lindemann, Adam Collector
Longaker, Mark Critic, Writer
Lowe, Harry Administrator, Designer
MacDonald, William L Historian, Writer
Markowski, Eugene David Painter, Sculptor
Maxwell, David Ogden Patron
McCarthy, Maura Critic, Editor
McCoubrey, Sarah Painter
McDuff, Fredrick H Painter, Printmaker
Miller, Nicole Art Columnist
Millie, Elena Gonzalez Curator
Oxman, Mark Sculptor, Educator
Pachter, Marc gallery director
Page, Jean Jepson Collector, Historian
Parish, Norman Gallery Director
Patton, Sharon Frances Art Historian, Museum Director
Perlin, Ruth Rudolph Educator, Art Historian

DISTRICT OF COLUMBIA (cont)
Polan, Annette Painter, Draftsman
Pressly, Nancy Lee Curator, Administrator
Pressly, William Laurens Historian, Educator
Raby , Julian Gallery Director
Rales, Mitchell P Collector
Rales, Steven M Collector
Rathbone, Eliza Euretta Curator
Revri, Anil Painter, Graphic Artist
Richard, Paul Critic
Rifkin, Ned Curator, Museum Director
Rivera, Elias J Painter
Robbins, Warren M Museum Director, Educator
Roberts, Steven K Sculptor, Printmaker
Robertson, Charles J Administrator
Robinson, Lilien Filipovitch Historian, Educator
Robison, Andrew Museum Curator, Writer
Rockefeller, John (Jay) D, IV Collector
Rode, Meredith Eagon Printmaker, Educator
Rose, Robin Carlise Painter, Sculptor
Rosenzweig, Phyllis D Curator
Rust, David E Curator, Collector
Sanborn, Jim (James) Sculptor
Sant, Victoria P Museum Director
Schneider, Julie Saecker Painter, Draftsman
Schottland, M Illustrator, Painter
Scott, David Winfield Painter, Consultant
Shaw-Eagle, Joanna Critic
Sherman, Claire Richter Historian, Educator
Smith, John W director
Stovall, Luther McKinley Printmaker
Swick, Linda Ann Sculptor
Szabo, Stephen Lee Photographer
Tacha, Athena Sculptor, Educator
Tepfer, Diane Curator, Historian
Tischler, Gary Critic
Viso, Olga museum director
Von Barghan, Barbara Educator, Writer
Wallach, Alan Critic, Historian
Wax, John M Painter, Collage Artist, Mixed Media Artist
Wheelock, Arthur Kingsland, Jr Curator, Educator
White, Franklin Painter, Draftsman
Whiteley, Elizabeth Painter, Sculptor
Williams, Katherine Collector, Painter
Wooby, William Joseph Art Dealer, Curator
Woodward, William Painter, Muralist
Wright, Frank Painter, Educator
Young, Charles Alexander Painter; Educator
Young, Kenneth Victor Painter, Designer
Ziemann, Richard Claude Printmaker, Educator

FLORIDA

Alachua
Tilton, John Ellsworth Ceramist

Altamonte Springs
Price, Morgan Samuel Painter, Instructor

Aventura
Weinberg, Ephraim Administrator, Painter

Beverly Hills
Larsen, Erik Consultant, Educator

Big Pine Key
Fleischer, Roland Edward Historian, Educator

Boca Raton
Amen, Irving Painter, Printmaker
Bolge, George S Museum Director
Coleman, Gayle Lecturer, Conservator
Dorst, Claire V Painter, Printmaker
Dorst, Mary Crowe Graphic Artist, Craftsman
Gartel, Laurence M Computer Artist, Photographer
Kaufman, Stuart Martin Painter, Illustrator
Keeler, David Boughton Painter
Lampasona, Eydi Artist
Lew, Fran Painter
Orze, Joseph John Administrator, Sculptor
Perrone, Jeff Ceramist
Price, Rita F Painter, Printmaker
Rebhun, Pearl G Painter, Printmaker
Westheimer , Esther Sculptor

Boynton Beach
Baumel-Harwood, Bernice Painter, Printmaker, Sculptor
Faulds, W Rod Administrator, Designer
Ludman, Joan Hurwitz Writer, Researcher
Zelin, Elaine Sculptor

Bradenton
Benjamin, Alice Benjamin Boudreau Painter, Educator
Flackman, David J Painter
Hodgell, Robert Overman Printmaker, Sculptor
Howard, Linda Sculptor
Spann, Susanna Evonne Painter, Educator

Brooksville
Watkins, Lewis Sculptor, Painter

Cape Coral
Read, Dave (David) Dolloff Photographer, Educator

Casselberry
Berkowitz, Henry Painter, Designer
Renee, Lisabeth Sculptor, Assemblage Artist

Cedar Key
Gernhardt, Henry Kendall Sculptor, Ceramist

Clearwater
Bansemer, Roger L Painter, Writer
Colman, Virginia O'Connell Sculptor, Graphic Artist

Cocoa Beach
Blum, June Painter, Sculptor

Coconut Creek
Marshak, Arthur Sculptor, Ceramist

Coral Gables
Algaze, Mario A Photographer
Bannard, Walter Darby Painter, Art Writer
Cher-Killigan, Beatrice Michelle Painter, Printmaker
Chian-Chiu, Chow Painter, Historian
Federighi, Christine M Ceramist, Sculptor
Friedman, Marvin Ross Dealer
Gerlach, Christopher S Painter
Larraz, Julio F Painter
Lloveras, Connie Artist
Staller, Eric P Photographer, Sculptor

Coral Springs
Kroll, Lynne Francine Painter, Collage Artist
Mason, Lauris Lapidos Art Dealer, Writer

Crawfordville
Siamis, Janet Neal Painter

Dania
Satin, Claire Jeanine Sculptor, Illustrator

Daytona Beach
Libby, Gary Russell Museum Director, Educator
Nordstrom, Alison Devine Administrator, Curator

Deland
Biferie, Dan (Daniel) Anthony, Jr Photographer, Educator
Bolding, Gary Wilson Painter, Curator
Messersmith, Fred Lawrence Painter, Educator
Messersmith, Harry Lee Sculptor, Museum Director

Delray Beach
Greenspan, Gladys Painter
Mills, Agnes Printmaker, Sculptor

Doral
Oyuela, Raul M Museum Director, Curator

Dunnellon
McKinney, Tatiana Ladygina Painter, Instructor

Edgewater
Michajlow, Eustachy Painter

Englewood
Carmichael, Donald Ray Painter
Jerdon, William Harlan Painter, Instructor

Enterprise
Abernethy-Baldwin, Judith Ann Painter

Fort Lauderdale
Barra, Robert Painter
Batt, Miles Girard Painter, Instructor
Bulkin Siegel, Wilma Painter
Liebowitz, Janet Painter, Sculptor

Fort Myers
Biolchini, Gregory Phillip Painter
Clemente, Joann P Painter
Picciano, Lana Patricia Picciano Oil Painter, Glicee's

Fort Pierce
Martin, Mary Finch Painter, Gallery Director

Ft Lauderdale
Gianguzzi, Joseph Custode Sculptor, Painter - Oil Painting

Gainesville
Grissom, Eugene Edward Historian, Writer
Heipp, Richard Christian Painter, Instructor
Isaacson, Marcia Jean Artist, Educator
Janowich, Ronald Painter
Kerslake, Kenneth Alvin Printmaker, Educator
Mesches, Arnold Painter, Educator
O'Connor, John Arthur Painter, Educator
Scott, John Fredrik Historian, Educator
Skelley, Robert Charles Educator, Printmaker
Smith, Nan S(helley) Sculptor, Ceramist
Uelsmann, Jerry Photographer
Ward, John Lawrence Historian, Painter
Westin, Robert H Historian
Willumson, Glenn Gardner Educator, Curator

Hallandale
Geller, Bunny Zelda Writer, Sculptor

Highland Beach
Ortlip, Paul Daniel Painter

FLORIDA (cont)

Palm City

Sloan, Richard Painter, Illustrator

Palm Harbor

Schlageter, Robert William Consultant, Museum Director
Stecher, Ruth (Rusty) L Painter, Instructor

Pensacola

Burke-Fanning, Madeleine Painter, Instructor
Maki, Countess Hope Marie Painter, Instructor
Stewart, Duncan E Collage Artist

Poiniana

Mastrangelo, Bobbi Sculptor; Environmental Artist

Pompano Beach

Lis, Janet Painter

Ponte Vedra Beach

Draper, Josiah Everett Painter, Writer

Port Charlotte

Leslie, John Painter, Fine Art Photographer, Sculptor, Designer

Port St Lucie

Castile, Rand Museum Director

Punta Gorda

Pollard, Herschel Newton Painter, Instructor

Quincy

Lindquist, Mark Sculptor

Rockledge

Samuelson, Fred Binder Painter, Educator

Roseland

Segal, Mary Graphic Artist, Printmaker

Rotonda West

Moldroski, Al R Painter, Educator

Royal Palm Beach

Vo-Dinh, Mai Painter, Printmaker

Safety Harbor

Banks, Allan R Painter
Banks, Holly Hope Painter

Saint Augustine

Crisp-Ellert, JoAnn Painter, Writer
Torcoletti, Enzo Sculptor

Saint Cloud

Bernard, David Edwin Printmaker, Educator

Saint Lucie West

Kamm, Dorothy Lila Painter, Writer

Saint Petersburg

Crane, Jim (James) G Painter, Cartoonist
Grastorf, Jean H Painter, Instructor
Harte, John Painter, Misc Media
Nyren, Edward A Painter
Rigg, Margaret R Assemblage Artist, Calligrapher
Schloder, John E Director
Scott, Bill Earl Painter

Sarasota

Bilodeau, Daniel Alain Painter, Draftsman
Capes, Richard Edward Graphic Artist, Instructor
Cave, Leonard Edward Sculptor, Educator
Chase, Jeanne Norman Painter, Printmaker
Christ-Janer, Arland F Painter, Printmaker
Clement, Shirley Painter
Corbino, Marcia Norcross Critic, Writer
Dabbert, Patricia Ann Ceramist, Sculptor
Dean, Kevin Lee Gallery Director, Educator
DeCaprio, Alice Painter, Photographer
Dowd, Jack Sculptor
Ebitz, David MacKinnon Museum Director, Historian
Elliott, Dorothy Baden Conservator
Erickson, Joy M Painter, Graphic Artist, Photographer
Farnsworth, Helen Sawyer Painter, Writer
Fulton Ross, Gale Artist
Gelinas, Robert William Painter, Educator
Gerstein, David Steven Filmmaker
Goodacre, Glenna Sculptor
Harmon, Foster Art Consultant
Jeswald, Joseph Painter
Kessler, Leonard H Illustrator
Kowal, Dennis J Sculptor, Writer
Krate, Nat Painter
Lengyel, Alfonz Historian, Writer, Museologist
Lerner, Leslie Allen Painter
Maier, Maryanne E Painter
Masterfield, Maxine Painter
Meserole, Vera (Vessa) Stromsted Painter, Photographer
Pappas, George Painter
Parton, Nike Painter, Environmental Artist
Petersen, Franklin G Painter
Rice, Anthony Hopkins Historian, Artist
Rosenzweig, Daphne Lange Historian, Museum Consultant
Sadek, George Educator, Designer
Savenor, Betty Carmell Painter, Printmaker
Silver, Rawley A Educator, Painter
Stevens, Elisabeth Goss Writer, Printmaker
Straight, Elsie H Librarian, Sculptor
Wetenhall, John Museum Director

Seminole

Scalzo, Joyce Ann Ceramist, Curator

St Petersburg

Kropf, Joan R Curator, Lecturer

Stuart

Hutchinson, Janet L Collector, Curator

Summerfield

Shaw, Nancy (Rivard) Curator, Historian

Summerland Key

Anthony, Lawrence Kenneth Sculptor, Painter

Tallahassee

Bell, Trevor Painter
Blakely, George C Photography, Sculptor
Bucher, Francois Historian, Educator
Burggraf, Ray Lowell Painter, Educator
Edwards-Tucker, Yvonne Leatrice Ceramist, Educator
Fichter, Robert W Educator
Nasgaard, Roald Curator, Historian
Palladino-Craig, Allys Director, Curator
Teilhet-Fisk, Jehanne Hildegarde Historian, Educator
Weale, Mary Jo Painter, Educator
Williams, Pat Ward Photographer

Tamarac

Goldszer, Bath-Sheba Painter, Graphic Artist
Jackson, Charlotte Painter, Instructor
Kaplan, Leo Assemblage Artist, Collage Artist
Pravda, Muriel Instructor, Restorer
Smith, Rowena Marcus Painter, Collage Artist

Tampa

Beck, Theresa Painter
Cardoso, Anthony Painter, Sculptor
Covington, Harrison Wall Painter, Sculptor
de Lama, Alberto Painter, Printmaker
Gurbacs, John Joseph Painter, Restorer
Jones, Ronald Lee, Jr Educator, Writer
Kratz, Mildred Sands Painter
Mitchell, Dean Lamont Painter
Nazarenko, Bonnie Coe Painter
Pachner, William Painter
Santiago, Richard E Sculptor, Educator
Schofield, Roberta Painter
Wujcik, Theo Painter, Printmaker

Tarpon Springs

Scarpa, Dorothea Painter, Educator

Temple Terrace

Kashdin, Gladys Shafran Painter, Educator

Tierra Verde

Tuegel, Michele Beckman Craftsman, Administrator

University Park

Scalera, Michelle Ann Conservator

Venice

Bateman, Robert McLellan Painter
Callari, Emily Dolores Painter, Restorer
Fronckowiak, Arthur Painter
Turconi, Sue (Susan) Kinder Painter, Photographer

Venice Park

Lacktman, Michael Craftsman, Jeweler

Vero Beach

Billeci, Andre George Sculptor, Educator
Christman, Reid August Painter
Ferrell, Catherine (Klemann) Sculptor
Hoffman, Martin Painter, Illustrator
Koller-Davies, Eva Assemblage Artist, Painter
Krupp, Barbara D Painter
Sprout, Francis Artist, Educator

Wellington

Brody, Carol Z Painter, Collage Artist

West Palm Beach

Aho, Paul Richard Painter
Antic, Miroslav Painter, Illustrator
Cowan, Ralph Wolfe Painter
Orr-Cahall, Anona Christina Curator, Historian
Schwartz, Ruth Painter, Instructor
Weiss, Madeline Painter

Weston

Gross, Elissa Frances Administrator, Educator

Windermere

Hubert, Anne M Curator, Collector

Winter Haven

Schepis, Anthony Joseph Instructor, Painter
Treister, Kenneth Painter, Sculptor

Winter Park

Blumenthal, Arthur R Museum Director, Historian
Booth, Dot Painter, Printmaker
Fager, Charles J Ceramist, Sculptor
Haxton, David Photographer, Filmmaker
Lemon, Robert S, Jr Educator, Historian
Ruggiero, Laurence J Museum Director

FLORIDA (cont)

GEORGIA

Alpharetta

Pond, Clayton Painter, Printmaker
Sirlin, Deanna Louise Painter, Environmental Artist

Athens

Arnholm, Ronald Fisher Designer, Educator
Barsness, Jim Painter, Cartoonist
Belville, Scott Robert Painter, Educator
Clements, Robert Donald Sculptor, Educator
Colangelo, Carmon Administrator, Printmaker
Edmonston, Paul Educator, Editor
Feldman, Edmund Burke Educator, Critic
Firestone, Evan R Administrator, Historian
Goldsleger, Cheryl Painter, Draftsman
Hammond, Gale Thomas Printmaker, Educator
Hammond, Mary Sayer Educator, Photographer
Herbert, James Arthur Painter, Filmmaker
Jones, Judy Voss Printmaker, Painter
Kaufman, Glen Printmaker, Educator
Lukasiewicz, Nancy Bechtold Administrator, Tapestry Artist
Lukasiewicz, Ronald Joseph Printmaker, Administrator
Marriott, William Allen Painter, Educator
Meyers, Ronald G Educator, Ceramist
Nasisse, Andy S Sculptor, Writer
Paul, William D, Jr Painter, Photographer
Sapp, William Rothwell Sculptor, Educator

Atlanta

Amisano, Joseph architect
Artemis, Maria Artemis Papageorge Sculptor, Educator
Borochoff, (Ida) Sloan Painter, Printmaker
Bunnen, Lucinda Weil Photographer, Collector
Carlstrom, Lucinda Painter, Printmaker
Chandler, Angelyn Sanders Museum Director
Chase, Allan (Seamans) Sculptor, Muralist
Colarusso, Corrine Camille Painter, Instructor
Creecy, Herbert Lee Painter, Sculptor
Day, Janet S Administrator
Frabel, Hans Godo Sculptor
Francis, Tom Painter
Gibson, Michael Painter
Gromala, Diane Video Artist, Critic
Guberman, Sidney Painter, Sculptor
Harkins, Dennis Richter Administrator, Photographer
Heath, David C Dealer
Henry, David Eugene Painter, Sculptor
Holland, Hillman Randall Art Dealer
Howell, George Critic
Howett, John Historian, Critic
Ketcham, Ray Winfred, Jr Dealer, Designer
Laxson, Ruth Conceptual Artist
LeBey, Barbara Painter, Printmaker, Writer
Lieberman, Laura Crowell Administrator, Critic
Longobardi, Pam Painter, Printmaker
Malone, James Hiram Painter, Writer
Mari, M Painter, Printmaker
McLean, James Albert Educator, Printmaker
McPhee, Sarah Collyer Historian, Educator
Meyer, James Sampson Writer, Historian
Mills, Lev Timothy Printmaker, Designer
Mitchell, Katherine Painter
Nick, Lloyd Museum Director, Painter
Paschall, Jo Anne Printmaker, Librarian
Patterson, Curtis Ray Sculptor, Instructor
Poling, Clark V Historian
Portman, John C, Jr Architect
Riddle, John Thomas, Jr Sculptor, Painter
Rodriguez, Rocio A Painter
Rothwell, Junko Ono Pastel
Sandman, Alan Sculptor, Publisher
Scogin, Mack Architect, Educator
Seaberg, Steve (Stevens) Assemblage Artist, Performance Artist
Shapiro, Michael Edward Administrator, Curator
Stent, Terry & Margaret Collector
Tiegreen, Alan F Painter, Illustrator
Tuttle, Lisa Conceptual Artist, Curator
Vigtel, Gudmund Director
Walker, Larry Painter, Educator
Yarbrough, Leila Kepert Printmaker, Painter

Augusta

Engler, Kathleen Girdler Sculptor
Grogan, Kevin Museum Director
Gruber, J Richard Administrator, Historian
Pennington, Estill Curtis Historian, Curator
Swanson, Caroline Painter
Williams, Janice E Painter, Sculptor

Ball Ground

Tustian, Brenda Harris Painter, Publisher

Blairsville

Sterling, Colleen Painter

Carrollton

Bobick, J Bruce Educator, Painter
Santini, Debrah A Painter, Printmaker

Colbert

Simon, Michael J Ceramist

Columbus

Butler, Charles Thomas Museum Director, Curator
James, Alfred Everett Painter, Photographer

Decatur

Bleser, Katherine Alice Painter
Greco, Anthony Joseph Painter, Administrator
Lindsay, Arturo Sculptor, Painter
Loehle, Betty Barnes Painter
Loehle, Richard E Painter, Illustrator
Moore, Wayland D Painter, Printmaker
Shaw, Louise E Director

Douglasville

Deremer, Susan René Painter, Illustrator

East Point

Asihene, Emmanuel V Educator, Painter

Farmington

Noffke, Gary L Goldsmith

Gainsville

Shead, S Ray Painter, Printmaker

Hahira

Penny, Donald Charles Craftsman, Sculptor

Lakeland

Ashton, Paul Photographer

Lawrenceville

Benjamin, Lloyd William, III Historian, Administrator

Lookout Mountain

Lynch, Mary Britten Painter, Collage Artist, Instructor

Macon

Gray, Elise Norris Sculptor
Liles, Catharine (Burns) Painter, Patron

Marietta

Eden, Glenn Draftsman, Painter
Lahtinen, Silja (Liisa) Talikka Painter, Printmaker
McAdoo, Carol Westbrook Ceramist, Painter

Martinez

Evins, Patsy Jean Painter

Mount Berry

Mew, Tommy Painter, Conceptual Artist

Mountain City

Kronsnoble, Jeffrey Michael Painter, Educator

Newnan

Harless, Carol P Sculptor

Parrott

Tilley, Lewis Lee Painter, Video Artist

Rome

Staven, Leland Carroll Painter

Roswell

Booth Cabot, M(ary Ann) Painter, Printmaker
Rayburn, Boyd (Dale) Painter, Printmaker

Saint Simons Island

Rensch, Roslyn Historian, Collector

Savannah

Ellis, Ray Painter, Lecturer
Fischer, Thomas Jeffrey Photographer, Educator
Gabeler, Jo Painter - watercolor
Hung, Chin-Cheng Calligrapher, Painter
Jackson, Suzanne Fitzallen Painter
Joseph, Stefani A Painter, Educator
Lesko, Diane Museum Director, Curator
Miller, Kathryn Painter, Printmaker
Wallace, Paula S Administrator

Snellville

Fenton, Julia Ann Curator, Conceptual Artist

Statesboro

Hines, Jessica Photographer
Tichich, Richard Educator, Administrator

Stone Mountain

Mickish, Verle L Educator, Painter

Thomasville

Powers, Donald T Painter

Tybee Island

Burr, Tricia Painter

Valdosta

Dodd, M(ary) Irene Painter, Educator
Lahr, J(ohn) Stephen Painter, Educator

Waleska

Mathis, Billie Fritz Painter, Conceptual Artist

Watkinsville

Chappelle, Jerry Leon Ceramist, Sculptor

HAWAII

Hilo

Miyamoto, Wayne Akira Painter, Printmaker

HAWAII (cont)

Honolulu

Atwell, Allen Educator, Painter
Bushnell, Kenneth Wayne Painter, Educator
De la Torre, David Joseph Museum Director
Ellis, George Richard Museum Director
Haar, Tom Photographer, Filmaker
Johnson, Bruce (James) Painter
Klobe, Tom Gallery Director Emer, Educator
Morita, John Takami Printmaker, Photographer
Morse, Marcia Roberts Printmaker, Writer
Preiss, Alexandru Petre Designer, Illusr
Roster, Fred Howard Sculptor, Educator
Ruby, Laura Sculptor, Printmaker
Sowers, Russell Frederic Gallery Director, Museum Director
Taira, Masa Morioka Gallery Director, Consultant
Wisnosky, John G Painter, Educator
Yu-ho, Tseng Painter, Historian

Kailua

Hickman, Patricia Craftsman
Kowalke, Ronald Leroy Painter, Printmaker

Kaneohe

Lagoria, Georgianna Marie M Museum Director, Curator

Kapaau

Jankowski, Theodore Andrew Painter, Muralist

Lahaina

Smith, Andrea B Painter

Lihue

Lai, Waihang Painter, Educator

Makawao

Ulrich, David Alan Photographer, Educator

Volcano

Morrison, Boone M Architect, Photographer

Waialua

Goodwill, Margaret Painter, Designer

IDAHO

Boise

Close, Timothy Museum Director
Kober, Alfred John Educator, Sculptor
Neil, J M Writer
Watia, Tarmo Painter, Printmaker
Wilde, Stephanie Conceptual Artist, Printmaker

Hailey

Johnstone, Mark Conceptual Artist, Curator

Middleton

Killmaster, John H Enamelist, Painter

Pocatello

Dial, Gail Metalsmith, Educator

Sandpoint

Schultz, Stephen Warren Painter, Educator

Sun Valley

Bennett, Don Bemco Painter, Printmaker

Yellow Pine

Auth, Robert R Printmaker, Painter

ILLINOIS

Arlington Heights

Chambers, William Thomas Painter

Belleville

Threlkeld, Dale Painter

Bloomington

Blinderman, Barry Robert Curator, Director
Butler, James D Printmaker, Painter
Finch, Richard Dean Printmaker, Educator
George, Raymond Ellis Printmaker, Educator
Gregor, Harold Laurence Painter, Educator
Hobbs, Jack Arthur Educator, Writer
Stroud, Billy Painter, Collector

Buncombe

Edgren, Gary Robert Painter, Craftsman

Carbondale

Deller, Harris Administrator, Ceramist
Kington, Louis Brent Sculptor, Craftsman
Logan, Fern H Photographer, Graphic Artist
Plochmann, Carolyn Gassan Painter, Graphic Artist
Scott, Shirley Clay Administrator
Shay, Ed Painter

Carterville

Mavigliano, George Jerome Administrator, Educator
Mawdsley, Richard Silversmith, Goldsmith

Cary

Duffy, Michael John Painter, Printmaker

Champaign

Bohen, Barbara E Historian, Museologist
Breen, Harry Frederick, Jr Painter, Sculptor
Bushman, David Franklin Painter, Educator
Gammon, Juanita L Educator, Graphic Artist
Grucza, Leo (Victor) Painter, Educator
Kotoske, Roger Allen Painter, Sculptor
Smith, Ralph Alexander Writer, Educator
Stephens, Curtis Educator, Designer
Van Laar, Timothy Painter, Writer

Charleston

Hubschmitt, William E Educator, Administrator
Sorge, Walter Painter, Printmaker
Watts, R Michael Museum Director

Chicago

Albano, Patrick Louis Art Dealer
Alexander, Karen Patron
Altman, Edith Sculptor, Conceptual Artist
Alvarez, Candida Painter, Educator
Amft, Robert Painter, Photographer
Arnold, Ralph Moffett Painter, Educator
Artner, Alan Gustav Critic
Aubin, Barbara Painter, Collage artist
Badgett, Steven Artist
Balzekas, Stanley, Jr Museum Director, Collector
Barazani, Morris Educator, Painter
Barter, Judith A Curator, Historian
Baruch, Anne Art Dealer, Lecturer
Baum, Don Sculptor, Curator
Bell, Mary Catherine Art Dealer
Berns, Pamela Kari Painter, Administrator
Blackman, Thomas Patrick Director, Printmaker
Bluhm, Neil Gary Patron
Boardman, Deborah Painter, Conceptual Artist
Bobins, Norman R Patron
Bramson, Phyllis Halperin Painter, Educator
Bryan, John Henry Patron
Bulka, Michael Critic
Burroughs, Margaret T G Lecturer, Painter
Camper, Fred Educator
Campos-Pons, Maria Magdalena Photographer, Video Artist
Caporael, Suzanne Painter
Castillo, Mario Enrique Painter, Muralist, Educator
Chambers, Park A, Jr Educator, Photographer
Christiansen, Diane Painter, Cartoonist
Coffey, Susanna Jean Painter
Cohen, Alan Barry Photographer, Educator
Cohen, Charles E Historian, Educator
Cole, Grace V Painter, Draftsman
Condren, Stephen F Painter
Conger, William Painter, Educator
Crane, Arnold H Photographer
Crane, Barbara Bachmann Photographer, Educator
Cuno, James Museum Director
Czarnopys, Thomas J Sculptor
Danhausen, Eldon Sculptor, Educator
DeGenevieve, Barbara Photographer, Educator
Dittmer, Frances R Collector
Donley, Robert Morris Painter, Educator
Donmez, Yucel Painter, Sculptor
Doremus, Susanne Educator
Dunning, Jeanne Photographer, Video Artist
Edelstein, Teri J Museum Director, Historian
Edlis, Stefan T & H Gael Neeson Collector
Facey, Martin Kerr Painter, Educator
Fairweather, Sally H Art Dealer, Consultant
Ferrara , Annette Editor, Educator
Ferrari, Virginio Luigi Sculptor, Educator
Field, Marshall Patron
Fish, Julia A Painter
Fitzpatrick, Robert John Museum Director
Fotopoulos, James Filmmaker
Gerber, Gaylen Conceptual Artist, Painter
Giuffre, Hector Painter, Graphic Artist
Godfrey, Winnie (Winifred) M Painter, Instructor
Gonzalez, Jose Gamaliel Administrator, Designer
Gray, Richard Dealer
Griffin, Kenneth C & Ann Dias Collector
Gunning, Tom Historian, Educator
Hannum, Terence J Critic, Director
Hansen, James Lee Sculptor
Hanson, Philip Holton Painter
Herzberg, Thomas Illustrator
Heyman, Steven Painter
Hild, Nancy Painter
Hill, Gary Video Artist
Himmelfarb, John David Painter, Graphic Artist
Hoffman, William A Ceramist, Sculptor
Hormuth, Jo Sculptor, Printmaker
Ischar, Doug Photographer
Jacob, Mary Jane Curator, Historian
Jaidinger, Judith C Clarann Szesko Printmaker, Painter
Jones, Tony Educator
Kahn, Katie (Kathryn) Anna Painter
Kapsalis, Thomas Harry Painter, Sculptor
Kearney, John (W) Sculptor
Kearney, Lynn Haigh Administrator, Curator
Kenney, Estelle Koval Art Therapist, Painter
Kirshner, Judith Russi Curator, Critic
Klamen, David Painter
Klement, Vera Painter
Kochman, Alexandra D Sculptor-Clay, Painter

ILLINOIS (cont)
Kolisnyk, Peter Painter, Sculptor
Kowalski, Dennis Allen Conceptual Artist
Krantz, Claire Wolf Critic, Curator
Lamantia, Paul W Zombek Painter
Lamb, Matt Painter, Sculptor
Lapkus, Danas Curator, Critic
Lee, Li Lin Painter
Lehrer, Leonard Painter, Printmaker
Lennon, Timothy Painting Conservator
Leopold, Susan Sculptor, Muralist
Livingstone, Joan Sculptor, Educator
Loving, Richard Maris Painter, Printmaker
Luecking, Stephen Joseph Sculptor, Educator
Machin, Roger Sculptor
Maldre, Mati Photographer, Educator
Marshall, Kerry James Designer, Painter
McElheny, Josiah G sculptor
Meyers, Michael K Performance Artist, Painter
Michod, Susan A Painter
Miller, Denise Museum Director, Educator
Morishita, Joyce Chizuko Historian, Painter
Neimanas, Joyce Photographer
Nordland, Gerald John Gallery Director, Critic
Parfenoff, Michael S Educator, Lithographer
Patner, Andrew Critic, Writer
Paul, Art(hur) Designer, Painter
Peart, Jerry Linn Sculptor
Phillips, Bertrand D Painter, Photographer
Phillips, Tony Painter, Draftsman
Piatek, Francis John Painter, Educator
Plotnick, Harvey Barry Collector
Postiglione, Corey M Painter, Educator, Critic
Pritzker, Thomas Jay Patron
Puryear, Martin Sculptor
Rabb, Madeline M Consultant
Reddington, Charles Leonard Painter, Educator
Reilly, Bernard Francis Historian, Curator
Restivo, Charles L Administrator
Rojek, Christine Sculptor
Rosenfield, Andrew M Patron
Rossen, Susan F Historian, Editor
Rupprecht, Elizabeth Instructor, Painter
Salomon, Lawrence Sculptor, Educator
Schnackenberg, Roy Painter, Sculptor
Seed, Suzanne Liddell Photographer, Writer
Sensemann, Susan Painter, Educator
Shaddle, Alice Sculptor, Collage Artist
Shaffer, Fern Painter, Lecturer
Silverman, Lanny Harris Director, Curator
Slemmons, Rod Museum Director, Educator, Curator
Smith, Elizabeth Angele Curator
Sorell, Victor Alexander Historian, Administrator
Spiess-Ferris, Eleanor Painter
Stack, Michael T Painter, Sculptor
Steinberg, Rubin Collage Artist, Painter
Stevens, Jane M Photographer, Administrator
Stewart, Lorelei Curator, Administrator
Stoppert, Mary Kay Administrator, Gallery Director
Stratman, Deborah Filmmaker
Stuckey, Charles F Historian, Curator
Szesko, Lenore Rundle Painter, Printmaker
Terrassa, Jacqueline Museum Director
Thall, Bob Photographer
Tigerman, Stanley Painter, Architect
Tinsley, Barry Sculptor
Trainor, Jim Filmmaker
Travis, David B Curator, Historian
Ullrich, Polly Critic
Walter, Mark R Patron
Warren, Lynne Curator, Writer
Weiss, Rachel Curator
Wenger, Jane (B) Photographer, Conceptual Artist
Wharton, Margaret Agnes Sculptor
Whitehead, Frances Sculptor, Educator
Wiens, Ann Writer, Editor, Critic
Wilson, Karen Lee Museum Director
Wirsum, Karl Painter, Sculptor
Wood, James Nowell Historian, Administrator
Workman, Robert P Painter, Illustrator
Wunderlich, Susan Clay Art Dealer
Yood, James W Critic, Historian, Educator, Writer
Yoshida, Ray Kakuo Painter, Educator
Zgoda, Larry Stained Glass Artist, Designer

Cicero
Mehn, Jan (Jan Von der Golz) Printmaker

Cissna Park
McCullough, Edward L Sculptor; Instructor

Columbia
Fondaw, Ron Sculptor

De Kalb
Bilder, Dorothea A Printmaker, Painter
Carp, Richard M Administrator, Educator
Doherty, Peggy M Museum Director, Curator
Even, Robert Lawrence Educator
Maxfield, Roberta Masur Silversmith
Meyer, Jerry Don Historian, Educator
White, Bruce Hilding Sculptor, Educator

Decatur
Cunningham, Sue Painter, Illustrator
Klaven, Marvin L Painter, Educator

Deerfield
Pounian, Albert Kachouni Painter, Curator
Trupp, Barbara Lee Painter, Designer

Des Plaines
Schildknecht, Dorothy E Painter
Smuskiewicz, Ted Painter, Educator

Downers Grove
Kind, Joshua B Educator, Critic

Edwardsville
Anderson, Daniel J Ceramist, Educator
Hampton, Phillip Jewel Painter, Educator
Harroff, William Charles Brent Conceptual Artist, Illustrator
Malone, Robert R Painter, Printmaker

Elmhurst
Weber, John Pitman Muralist, Printmaker

Elmwood Park
Hofmann, Kay Sculptor

Elwood
Bartels, Phyllis Elaine Painter

Evanston
Archer, Cynthia Printmaker, Painter
Belting, Hans Educator, Writer
Clayson, S Hollis Art Historian
Groot, Candice Beth Ceramist
Hausman, Jerome Joseph Educator
Hirshfield, Pearl Painter, Sculptor
Hixson, Kathryn Critic
Hurtig, Martin Russell Painter, Sculptor
Robertson, David Alan Museum Director, Educator
Wilson, Anne Gawthrop Sculptor, Educator

Forest Park
Poplawska, Anna Educator, Critic
Rogovin, Mark Muralist, Museum Director
Rogovin, Milton Photographer

Galena
Geisert, Arthur Frederick Printmaker, Illustrator
Narkiewicz-Laine, Christian K Museum Director, Writer
Sewell, Jack Vincent Museum Curator

Galesburg
Thenhaus, Paulette Ann Painter, Writer

Geneva
Buitron, Robert C Photographer, Video Artist

Glenview
Halliday, Nancy R Illustrator, Instructor
Hough, Winston Painter, Draftsman

Harvard
Cass, Bill Painter

Heyworth
Rush, Jean C Educator, Painter

Highland Park
Dirsmith, Ronald Architect
Feldman, Arthur Mitchell Museum Director, Art and Antiques Dealer
Hawkins, Margaret Critic, Educator. Writer

Homewood
Heller, Reinhold August Historian

Hudson
Mills, Frederick Van Fleet Designer, Educator

Indian Creek
Edwardson, John Albert Patron

Jacksonville
Calhoun, Larry Darryl Painter, Ceramist

Joliet
Brulc, Lillian G Painter, Sculptor

Kildeer
Hooper, Robert T Painter, Instructor

Lake Bluff
Booth, Laurence Ogden Sculptor, Architect

Lake Forest
Brewer, Paul Painter
Schulze, Franz Historian, Critic

Lawrenceville
Dooley, David I Painter, Educator

Lombard
Ahlstrom, Ronald Gustin Collage Artist, Painter

Long Grove
Robertson, Joan Elizabeth Mitchell Graphic Artist

Macomb
Jones, Frederick Printmaker
Parker, Samuel Murray Painter

Metamora
Hedden-Sellman, Zelda Painter, Instructor

Morris
Davidson, Herbert Laurence Painter, Printmaker

ILLINOIS (cont)

Mount Auburn

Schietinger, James Frederick Sculptor, Educator

Mount Prospect

Eliason, Birdell Painter, Illustrator

Murphysboro

Feldman, Joel Benet Printmaker, Educator
Kim, Cheonae Painter, Printmaker

Naperville

Skurkis, Barry A Painter, Sculptor

Normal

Justis, Gary Sculptor, Kinetic Artist
Mai, James L Painter, Educator
Mottram, Ronald Administrator, Historian

Northbrook

Davidson, David Isaac Painter
Perelman, Jeffrey E Collector

Oak Lawn

Jachna, Joseph David Photographer, Educator

Oak Park

Hugunin, James Richard Critic
Ledgerwood, Judy C Painter
Miller, Michael Stephen Printmaker, Painter
Sokol, David Martin Historian, Museologist

Oakbrook Terrace

McGrail, Jeane Kathryn Painter, Photographer

Palatine

Fortunato , Nancy Painter, Illustrator

Park Ridge

Fornelli, Joseph Sculptor, Painter

Payson

St Maur, Kirk Sculptor, Painter

Peoria

Ayres, Pamela Gene Director
Gillespie, Oscar Jay Printmaker
Kottemann, George & Norma Collectors
Moehl, Karl J Painter, Writer

Petersburg

Hallmark, Donald Museum Director, Lecturer

Quincy

Irwin, George M Patron, Collector
Mejer, Robert Lee Painter, Educator
Morrison, Fritzi Mohrenstecher Painter, Lecturer

Ringwood

Pearson, James Eugene Instructor, Sculptor

River Forest

Ciezadlo, Janina A Critic, Educator
Powell, Gordon Sculptor
White, Philip Butler Painter, Collector

Rock Falls

Shedosky, Suzanne Painter

Rockford

Apgar, Jean E Painter, Printmaker
Heflin, Tom Pat Painter, Designer
Pinzarrone, Paul Painter
Sneed, Patricia M Collector, Consultant
Stromsdorfer, Deborah Ann Painter, Graphic Artist

Rolling Meadows

Rebbeck, Lester James, Jr Gallery Director, Painter

Saint Charles

Darling, Sharon Sandling Museum Director, Historian

Schaumburg

Schweig Langsdorf, Martyl Painter, Muralist

Sidney

Rowan, Dennis Michael Printmaker, Educator
Savage, Jerry Painter

Skokie

Sahagian, Arthur H Painter, Instructor

Springfield

Dunbar, Michael Austin Sculptor, Administrator
Hodge, R Garey Painter
Madura, Jack Joseph Painter, Instructor

Sycamore

Peck, Lee Barnes Jeweler, Educator
Rollman, Charlotte Painter

Urbana

Bodnar, Peter Painter, Educator
Kovatch, Ronald R Ceramist
Replinger, Dot (Dorothy Thiele) Weaver, Designer
Ziff, Jerrold Historian, Collector

Washington

Sunderland, Nita Kathleen Educator, Sculptor

Wauconda

Czach, Marie Historian, Curator

Waukegan

Drapalik, Betty R Painter, Consultant

Wheaton

Das, Ratindra Painter, Instructor
Driesbach, David Fraiser Printmaker
Walford, E John Historian, Educator

Wilmette

Drower, Sara Ruth Painter, Craftsman
Nutt, Jim Painter, Draftsman
Valerio, James Robert Painter, Educator

Winnetka

Bieltvedt, Arnor G Painter, Instructor
Kramer, Linda Lewis Painter, Collector
Plowden, David Photographer, Writer

Woodstock

Trausch, Thomas V Painter, Educator

INDIANA

Albany

Davis, James Robert Cartoonist
Patrick, Alan K Ceramist, Painter

Anderson

Ryden, Kenneth Glenn Sculptor

Avon

Lucas, Georgetta Snell Painter

Bloomington

Brubaker, Jack Sculptor, Blacksmith, Designer, Painter
Calman, W(endy) L Printmaker, Photographer
Cole, Bruce Historian, Educator
Darriau, Jean-Paul Educator, Sculptor
Gealt, Adelheid Medicus Museum Director, Historian
Irvine, Betty Jo Librarian, Instructor
Jacquard, Jerald (Wayne) Sculptor
Kleinbauer, W Eugene Historian
Pozzatti, Rudy O Printmaker, Painter
Sieber, Roy Educator, Historian
Stirratt, Betsy (Elizabeth) Anne Painter, Gallery Director
Wolin, Jeffrey Alan Photographer

Brazil

Hay, Dick Sculptor, Educator

Evansville

Blevins, James Richard Art Administrator, Educator
McNaughton, John W Sculptor
Miley, Les Ceramist, Educator
Spurgin, John Edwin Administrator, Painter
Streetman, John William, III Administrator

Fishers

Sougstad, Mike Graphic Artist, Educator

Fort Wayne

De Santo, Stephen C Painter
Papier, Maurice Anthony Educator, Painter
Watkinson, Patricia Grieve Museum Director, Curator

Gary

Rosen, Kay Painter

Granger

Droege, Anthony Joseph, II Painter, Draftsman
Langland, Tuck Sculptor, Educator

Greencastle

Johnson, Kaytie Curator

Greenwood

Voos, William John Administrator, Painter

Indianapolis

Anderson, Maxwell L Museum Director, Educator
Day, Holliday T Curator, Critic
Devlin, Lucinda Alice Photographer, Educator
Dooley Waller, M L Painter
Eagerton, Robert Pierce Painter
Faust, James Wille Painter, Sculptor
Goodine, Linda Adele Photographer, Sculptor
Lee, Ellen Wardwell Curator
Orr, Leah Sculptor
Radecki, Martin John Administrator, Conservator
Roberson, Samuel Arndt Architectural Historian, Educator
Schaad, Dee Educator, Ceramist
Waller, Aaron Bret Museum Director, Art Historian

Kouts

Cooper, Wayne Painter, Sculptor

Lanesville

Delisle, Thomas Charles Filmmaker, Photographer

Logansport

Weida, Donna Lee Painter, Photographer

Madison

Gunter, Frank Elliott Painter, Educator

INDIANA (cont)

Mishawaka

Harmon, David Edward Painter, Educator

Muncie

Blume, Peter F Museum Director
Griner, Ned H Educator, Craftsman

Munster

Berrier, Wesley Dorwin Painter, Conservator
Meeker, Barbara Miller Educator, Painter

Nashville

Brown, Peggy Ann Painter, Instructor
Marsh, Charlene Marie Fiber Artist, Oil Painter
Rigley, Frederick Wildermuth Painter, Instructor

New Albany

Wegner, Nadene R Goldsmith, Consultant

New Harmony

Weinzapfel, Connie A Gallery Director, Curator

Notre Dame

Loving, Charles R Museum Director, Curator
Sandusky, Billy Ray Painter, Printmaker

Purdue University

Paul, Rick W Sculptor

South Bend

Rosenberg, Charles Michael Historian, Educator
Zisla, Harold Painter, Graphic Artist

Terre Haute

Engeran, Whitney John, Jr Painter, Educator
Evans, Robert Graves Educator, Sculptor
Lattanzio, Frances Photographer, Educator
McDaniel, Craig Milton Educator, Painter
Vollmer, David L Museum Director

Valparaiso

Hertzlieb, Gregg Director

Vincennes

Jendrzejewski, Andrew John Sculptor, Administrator

West Lafayette

Berg, Mona Lea Museum Director
Smith-Theobald, Sharon A Consultant
Williams, David Jon Medical Illustrator, Historian

IOWA

Ames

Benson, Martha J Jeweler, Assemblage Artist
Pohlman, Lynette Museum Director, Curator

Burlington

Garrison, David Earl Painter, Muralist
Middaugh, Robert Burton Painter
Torn, Jerry (Gerald J) Draftsman, Photographer

Cedar Falls

Behrens, Roy R Editor, Designer, Curator

Cedar Rapids

Barth, Charles John Educator, Printmaker
Gilmor, Jane E Sculptor, Educator
Kocher, Robert Lee Painter, Educator
Pitts, Terence Randolph Director, Curator

Coralville

Yuen, Kee-ho Silversmith, Sculptor

Decorah

Kamm, David Robert Printmaker, Educator
Kemp, Jane Librarian, Educator

Des Moines

Beam, Patrice K Administrator, Museum Director
Reece, Maynard Painter, Illustrator
Talbott, Susan Lubowsky Director
Worthen, Amy Namowitz Printmaker, Historian

Dubuque

Gibbs, Tom Sculptor

Dysart

Behrens, Mary Snyder Painter, Assemblage Artist

Fort Dodge

Helsell, Charles Paul Curator

Grinnell

Wilson, Kay E Curator, Director

Indianola

Heinicke, Janet L Hart Painter, Educator

Iowa City

Achepohl, Keith Anden Printmaker, Painter
Breder, Hans Dieter Sculptor, Video Artist
Burford, Byron Leslie Painter, Printmaker
Choo, Chunghi Silversmith, Fiber Artist, Educator
Cuttler, Charles David Historian, Lecturer
De Puma, Richard Daniel Historian, Editor
Foster, Stephen C Historian, Writer
Hindes, Chuck (Charles) Austin Ceramist, Educator
Lasansky, Mauricio L Printmaker, Draftsman
Monroe, Betty Iverson Educator
Patrick, Genie Hudson Painter, Instructor
Patrick, Joseph Alexander Painter, Educator
Rorex, Robert Albright Educator, Historian
Schmidt, Julius Sculptor
Scott, John Beldon Historian, Educator, Writer
Stratton, Margaret Mary Photographer, Educator
Tomasini, Wallace J Administrator, Historian

Marion

Prall, Barbara Jones Painter; Instructor

Mason City

Leet, Richard (Eugene) Museum Dir (Retired), Painter

Mount Vernon

Lifson, Hugh Anthony Painter, Educator

Orange City

Kaericher, John Conrad Printmaker, Educator

Solon

Myers, Virginia Anne Printmaker; Educator

Waterloo

Alling, Clarence (Edgar) Museum Director, Ceramist

KANSAS

Atchison

McCarthy, Dennis Sculptor, Educator

Baldwin City

Graber, Steven Brian Graphic Artist, Painter

Emporia

Perry, Donald Dean Painter, Educator

Hays

Jilg, Michael Florian Painter, Printmaker
Nichols, Francis N, II Printmaker, Educator
Stevanov, Zoran Painter, Sculptor
Thorns, John Cyril, Jr Designer, Painter

Lawrence

Bangert, Colette Stuebe Painter
Brawley, Robert Julius Painter, Educator
Brejcha, Vernon Lee Glass Blower, Craftsman
Craig, Susan V Librarian
Eldredge, Charles C, III Historian
Hardy, Saralyn Reece Museum Director
Iversen, Earl Harvey Photographer, Educator
Li, Chu-Tsing Historian
Norris, Andrea Spaulding Historian, Museum Director
Satz, Janet Painter, Educator
Shimomura, Roger Painter, Performance Artist
Stokstad, Marilyn Historian, Educator
Sudlow, Robert N Painter, Printmaker, Sculptor
Tefft, Elden Cecil Sculptor, Educator
Vaccaro, Luella Grace Ceramist, Painter
Zeller, Joseph R Educator, Ceramist

Leavenworth

Melby, David A Painter, Photographer

Leawood

Wahlman, Maude Southwell Administrator, Historian

Lecompton

Copt, Louis J Painter

Manhattan

Calluori Holcombe, Anna Ceramist
Garzio, Angelo C Potter, Craftsman
Ikeda, Yoshiro Ceramist, Educator
Kren, Margo Painter, Educator
Larmer, Oscar Vance Painter, Educator
Munce, James Charles Printmaker, Draftsman
Ohno, Mitsugi Glassblower
Pujol, Elliott Educator, Medalist
Schmidt, Teresa Tempero Printmaker, Draftsman

McPherson

Robinson, Mary Ann Painter, Educator

Pittsburg

Krug, Harry Elno Printmaker, Educator

Shawnee Mission

Goheen, Ellen Rozanne Historian, Curator
Kuemmerlein, Janet Fiber Artist
Stephens, Thomas Michael Kinetic Artist, Designer

Topeka

Merrill, Hugh Jordan Printmaker, Painter, Pub & Community Arts
Peters, Larry Dean Director, Painter

Wichita

Beren, Stanley O Patron
Boyd, John David Educator, Printmaker
Lincoln, Diane Thomas Painter, Curator
Plott, Paula Plott Amos Painter, Sculptor
Reese, William Foster Painter
Riegle, Robert Mack Art Dealer, Collector

KANSAS (cont)
Sanderson, Charles Howard Painter, Educator
Scott, B Nibbelink (Barbara Gae Scott) Painter, Sculptor
Steiner, Charles K Museum Director, Painter
Wethington, Wilma Painter, Instructor

KENTUCKY

Alexandria
Douthat, Anita S Photographer

Ashland
Richmond, Rebekah Printmaker, Painter

Bardstown
Cantrell, Jim Painter

Berea
Pross, Lester Fred Painter
Tredennick, Dorothy W Educator, Lecturer

Bowling Green
Klein, Michael Eugene Historian, Writer
Oakes, John Warren Educator, Painter
Schieferdecker, Ivan E Printmaker, Painter
Stomps, Walter E, Jr Educator, Painter
Trutty-Coohill, Patricia Educator, Historian

Burlington
Enstice, Wayne Assemblage Artist, Writer

Corbin
Weedman, Kenneth Russell Painter, Sculptor

Farmington
Merida, Frederick A Art Dealer, Printmaker

Florence
Goodridge, Lawrence Wayne Painter, Sculptor

Highland Heights
Houghton, Barbara Jean Photographer, Video Artist
Knight, David J Gallery Director, Educator

Lexington
Carpenter, Dennis (Bones) Wilkinson Photographer, Educator
Girard, (Charles) Jack Painter, Educator
Hamann, Marilyn D Educator, Painter
Petro, Joe, III Printmaker, Painter
Petro, Joseph (Victor), Jr Painter, Illustrator
Piwinski, Carl B Artist
Sandoval, Arturo Alonzo Educator, Weaver
Shannon, R Michael Painter
Singh, Carolyn Painter, Ceramist
Walsh-Piper, Kathy A Museum Director, Educator

Louisville
Begley, J (John) Phillip Museum Director
Blake, Jane Salley Publisher, Editor
Bratcher, Dale Painter
Chodkowski, Henry, Jr Painter, Educator
Cloudman, Ruth Howard Curator
Coates, Ann S Curator, Photographer
Covi, Dario A Historian
Hackett, Mickey Painter, Educator
Henry, John Raymond Sculptor
Hower, Robert K Photographer
Kirstein, Janis Adrian Painter, Instructor
Morrin, Peter Patrick Museum Director
Rapp, M Yvonne Art Dealer, Lecturer
Whitesell, John D Printmaker

Marion
Morris, Roger Dale Painter

Murray
Head, Robert William Painter, Educator
Leys, Dale Daniel Educator, Draftsman
Speight, Jerry Brooks Educator, Writer
Sperath, Albert Frank Museum Director, Sculptor

Newport
Storm, Howard Painter, Sculptor

Owensboro
Hood, Mary Bryan Museum Director, Administrator, Painter

Princeton
Granstaff, William Boyd Painter, Illustrator

Prospect
Garner, Joyce (Craig) Painter

Richmond
Halbrooks, Darryl Wayne Painter, Printmaker
Isaacs, Ron Painter, Sculptor
Smith, Gil R Administrator, Historian

Shelbyville
McCardwell, Michael Thomas Graphic Artist, Painter

Union
Akers, Gary Painter, Writer

Wickliffe
Frueh, Deborah K A (Debi) Painter, Sculptor

LOUISIANA

Alexandria
Tullos, Mark A, Jr Administrator, Curator

Baton Rouge
Andry, Keith Anthony Painter, Instructor
Betts, Judi Polivka Painter, Instructor
Corso, Samuel (Joseph) Stained Glass Artist, Painter
Cox, Richard William Historian, Writer
Crespo, Michael Lowe Writer, Painter
Daugherty, Michael F Educator, Sculptor
Goodell, Rosemary W Painter
Hamblen, Dr Karen A Educator, Writer
Hausey, Robert Michael Painter
Johns, Christopher K(alman) Painter, Educator
Lewis, Douglas Historian, Consultant
Pramuk, Edward Richard Painter
Price, Anne Kirkendall Critic

Breaux Bridge
Caffery, Debbie Fleming Photographer

Cecilia
Girouard, Tina Sculptor, Painter

Covington
Dautreuil, Linda Trappey Painter
Dufour, Paul Arthur Painter, Designer
Flattmann, Alan Raymond Painter, Instructor

Lafayette
Lafaye, Bryan F Museum Director, Educator
Love, Frances Taylor Writer, Publisher
Mhire, Herman P Museum Director, Curator
Miller, Joan Vita Museum Director, Administrator

Lake Charles
Dentler, Ann Lillian Painter
Fourcard, Inez Garey Painter
Kelley, Heather Ryan Painter, Draftsman
Wood, John August Writer, Historian

Mandeville
Clark, Emery Ann Painter, Environmental Artist

Metairie
Casselli, Henry Calvin, Jr Painter
Tahir, Abe M, Jr Consultant
Young, Tom (Thomas) William Painter, Photographer

New Orleans
Allen, Jere Hardy Painter, Educator
Amoss, Berthe Illustrator, Painter
Bailey, Barry Stone Sculptor, Painter
Birch, Willie M Sculptor, Painter
Bishop, Jacqueline K Painter
Bourgeois, Douglas Painter
Brumfield, William Craft Photographer
Bullard, Edgar John, III Museum Director
Casellas, Joachim Painter
Derby, Mark Ceramist, Instructor
Drummer, William Richard Gallery Director
Emery, Lin Emery Braselman Kinetic Artist, Sculptor
Fagaly, William Arthur Curator, Historian
Farrens, Juanita G Painter, Sculptor
Foley, Timothy Albert Art Dealer
Frank, Charles William, Jr Wood Carver, Writer
Gertjejansen, Doyle Painter
Glasgow, Vaughn Leslie Curator, Historian
Gunning, Simon Ben Painter, Draftsman
Harris, Ronna S Painter, Educator
Kern, Arthur (Edward) Educator, Sculptor
Lamantia, James Architect, Painter
Lucas, Charlie Painter, Sculptor
Maklansky, Steven V Curator
Muniot, Barbara King Collector
Nesbitt, Jackson Lee Printmaker
Reddix, Roscoe Chester Painter, Educator
Reese, Thomas Ford Historian, Administrator
Scott, John Tarrell Printmaker, Sculptor
Sweet, Steve (Steven) Mark Collage Artist, Graphic Artist
Trivigno, Pat Painter, Educator
Wegmann, M (Mary) K (Katherine) Consultant, Administrator
Whiteman, Edward Russell Painter
Zurik, Jesselyn Benson Painter, Sculptor

Ruston
Berguson, Robert Jenkins Painter, Educator
Dablow, Dean Clint Photographer, Educator
Walton, M Douglas Painter, Instructor
Zalesch, Saul E Educator

Shreveport
Allen, Bruce Wayne Educator, Sculptor
Morgan, Arthur C Sculptor

Slidell
Willis, Jane B(roome) Graphic Artist, Painter

Youngsville
Savoy, Chyrl Lenore Sculptor, Educator

MAINE

Acton
Lazenby, Dexter Conceptual Artist

Bangor
Richardson, John Adkins Historian, Educator

MAINE (cont)

Bar Harbor
Plummer, Carlton B   Painter, Instructor

Belfast
Zopp, Dudley   Painter, Installation Artist

Boothbay
Davies, Harry Clayton   Painter, Photographer

Boothbay Harbor
Mellor, Mark Adams   Painter, Gallery Director

Brooks
Squadra, John   Painter, Restorer

Brunswick
Bearce, Jeana Dale   Painter, Printmaker
Kline, Katy   Director
Rakovan, Lawrence Francis   Printmaker, Painter
Watson, Katharine Johnson   Historian, Consultant

Camden
Gumpel, Hugh   Painter, Instructor
Smith, Harry William   Illustrator, Jeweler

Cape Elizabeth
Campbell, David Paul   Painter, Instructor

Castine
Barrett, Thomas R   Painter, Instructor
Mancuso, Leni Mancuso Barrett   Painter, Instructor
Ortman, George Earl   Painter, Sculptor

Cumberland Foreside
Thompson, Lynn P   Painter, Photographer

Cushing
Caponigro, Paul   Photographer
Magee, Alan   Painter, Sculptor
Wissemann-Widrig, Nancy   Painter

Damariscotta
Knox, Elizabeth   Painter
Thompson, Ernest Thorne, Jr   Silversmith, Painter
Vesery, Jacques   Sculptor, Instructor

Deer Isle
Gilchrist, Elizabeth Brenda   Editor

Falmouth
Kellar, Jeff   Sculptor

Friendship
Cady, Samuel Lincoln   Painter, Instructor

Georgetown
Palazzolo, Carl   Painter

Gorham
Franklin, Patt   Painter, Sculptor

Gray
Cenci, Silvana   Sculptor

Hollis Center
Hewitt, Duncan Adams   Sculptor, Educator

Kennebunk
Betts, Edward Howard   Painter
Escalet, Frank Diaz   Painter, Sculptor
Schmalz, Carl (Nelson), Jr   Painter, Educator

Kittery
Sauter, Gail E   Painter

Lewiston
Bessire, Mark HC   Museum Director
Isaacson, Philip Marshal   Critic, Writer

Mount Desert
Pollien, Robert L   Painter, Printmaker

Mt Desert
Fuerst, Shirley Miller   Sculptor, Printmaker

New Harbor
Lyford , Cabot   Sculptor, Painter

Ogunquit
Carpenter, George Robert   Painter
Culver, Michael L   Painter, Curator

Orono
Ambley, Paul   Painter - Watercolor
Lewis, Michael H   Painter, Educator

Port Clyde
Lewis, Nat Brush   Painter, Instructor
Noland, Kenneth   Painter, Printmaker
Sublett, Carl Cecil   Painter

Portland
Buch, Gary   Painter
Douglas, Edwin Perry   Painter, Instructor
DuBack, Charles S   Painter, Printmaker
Elowitch, Annette   Dealer
Elowitch, Robert Jason   Dealer, Patron
Gilmore, Roger   Administrator, Consultant
Holverson, John   Curator, Museum Director, Art Dealer
Huntoon, Abby E   Sculptor, Craftsman
Mokeme, Oscar O   Director
O'Leary, Daniel   Museum Director
Ubans, Juris K   Painter, Educator
Ventimiglia, John Thomas   Sculptor, Educator
Vincent, Christine   Administrator

Readfield
Peladeau, Marius Beaudoin   Writer, Museum Director

Rockland
Crosman, Christopher Byron   Museum Director, Writer
Fasoldt, Sarah Lowry   Administrator, Curator
Goldsmith, Benedict Isaac   Gallery Director, Educator
Larsen, Susan C   Curator, Historian

Rockport
Fink, Herbert Lewis   Painter, Educator

Round Pond
MacDougall, Peter Steven   Ceramic Artist, Sculptor

Saint George
Pearlman, George L   Ceramist

Scarborough
Sadik, Marvin Sherwood   Dealer

Seal Harbor
Andrews, Nancy Evelyn   Artist

Searsport
Barnes, Robert M   Painter, Educator

Sebec
Cutler, Bess   Art Dealer

Solon
Shahn, Abby   Painter

South Berwick
Hardy, (Clarion) Dewitt   Painter, Instructor, Printmakers

South Freeport
Makanowitzky, Barbara   Pastel

Steuben
Haroutunian, Joseph Halsey   Painter

Stonington
Muir, Emily Lansingh   Painter, Sculptor
Pace, Stephen S   Painter, Printmaker

Trevett
Bettinson, Brenda   Painter, Printmaker

Veazie
Manter, Margaret C   Painter

Waterville
Matthews, Harriett   Sculptor, Educator
Simon, David L   Historian, Educator

Windham
O'Gorman, James Francis   Educator, Writer

Wiscasset
Leslie, Seaver   Painter

York
Hallam, Beverly (Linney)   Painter, Photographer
Roché, Robert (Richard)   Painter
Smart, Mary-Leigh   Consultant, Patron

York Beach
Davison, Nancy R   Printmaker

MARYLAND

Annapolis
Alderdice, Cynthia Lou   Painter, Printmaker
Gurlik, Philip John   Painter, Printmaker
Markman, Ronald   Painter

Baltimore
Bills, Linda   Sculptor
Bolger, Doreen   Museum Director, Curator
Caplan, Constance Rose   Collector
Carlberg, Norman Kenneth   Sculptor, Photographer
Ciscle, George   Curator
Cleaver, Richard Bruce   Sculptor
Coe, Henry   Painter
Cohen, Jean R   Ceramist, Collector
Crosby, Ranice W   Medical Illustrator, Educator
Economos, Michael E   Educator, Painter
Gilmore Ford, John   Collector
Goldstein, Gladys   Painter, Collage Artist
Hammond, Leslie King   Historian, Writer
Hanson, JB   Sculptor, Weaver
Hassinger, Maren J   Sculptor
Hofmann, Douglas William   Painter, Printmaker
Johnston, William Ralph   Administrator, Curator
Jones, James Edward   Painter, Printmaker
Katzenberg, Dena S   Consultant, Curator
Kelbaugh, Ross J   Collector, Historian
Kessler, Herbert Leon   Educator
Klitzke, Theodore Elmer   Educator, Historian
Koch, Philip   Painter, Draftsman
Kornblatt, Barbara Rodbell   Dealer
Lazarus, Fred, IV   Administrator
Lippman, Judith   Gallery Director, Educator
Maher, Janet Lynn   Printmaker, Collage Artist
Middleman, Raoul Fink   Painter

MARYLAND (cont)
Miller, Melvin Orville, Jr Painter
Moscatt, Paul N Painter, Instructor
Perlman, Bennard Bloch Painter, Writer
Printz, Bonnie Allen Painter, Photographer
Randall, Lilian M C Curator
Richardson, Frank, Jr Muralist
Sangiamo, Albert Educator, Painter
Segal, Thomas H Art Dealer
Shannon, Joe Educator, painter
Sheppard, Joseph Sherly Painter, Sculptor
Siegesmund, Richard Museum Director, Educator
Somerville, Romaine Stec Administrator
Sparks, John Edwin Printmaker, Instructor
Streett, Tylden Westcott Sculptor, Instructor
Sturgeon, John Floyd Video Artist
Vikan, Gary Kent Museum Director
Wasko-Flood, Sandra Jean Printmaker, Sculptor
Wayne, Cynthia M Curator, Historian
Wrigley, Rick Designer, Craftsman
Yates, Sharon Educator
Young, Barbara Photographer

Bethesda
Cable, Maxine Roth Sculptor
Fraser, Catriona Trafford Gallery Director, Photographer
Kan, Kit-Keung Painter
King, Elaine A Curator, Historian
Kocnig, Elizabcth Sculptor
Larson, Jane (Warren) Ceramist, Writer
Lee, Dora Fugh Painter, Sculptor
Levy, Phyllis Painter
Maddox, Jerald Curtis Curator, Historian
Miles, Ellen Gross Historian, Curator
Moser, Joann Curator, Historian
Plattner, Phyllis Painter
Siegel, Barbara Painter; Architect
Wolanin, Barbara A Historian, Curator

Bowie
Dasenbrock, Doris (Nancy) Voss Designer, Painter
Plaster, Alice Marie Painter, Instructor
Sweet, Francis Edward Painter
White, Amos, IV Ceramist, Photographer
Wynn, Gaines Clore Painter, Curator

Bozman
Cox, Ernest Lee Sculptor, Educator
Krestensen, Ann M Ceramist, Sculptor

Catonsville
Eglitis, Laimons Painter, Educator
Yager, David Photographer, Printmaker

Chevy Chase
Asher, Lila Oliver Printmaker, Painter
Buitron-Oliver, Diana Curator
Chase, W(illiam) Thomas Conservator
Curtis, Robert D Sculptor
Curtis, Verna P Curator
Fern, Alan Maxwell Museum Director
Freeman, Kathryn Painter, Instructor, Illustrator
Friend, Patricia M Painter
Ginzburg, Yankel (Jacob) Painter, Sculptor
Gorelick, Shirley Painter, Printmaker
Greene, Louise Weaver Tapestry Artist, Librarian
Kainen, Jacob Painter, Printmaker
Kranking, Margaret Graham Painter, Lecturer
Ostrow, Stephen Edward Administrator, Curator
Rand, Harry Historian, Educator
Shuler, Thomas H, Jr Photographer, Educator
Truettner, William H Curator

Cockeysville
Bartlett, Christopher E Gallery Director, Illustrator

College Park
Carrico, Anita Librarian
Richardson, WC Painter
Thorpe, James George Designer, Illustrator
Withers, Josephine Historian, Writer

Columbia
Feldman, Aline M Printmaker, Painter
Kurlander, Honey W Painter, Instructor
Lok, Joan M Painter
Morgan, Roberta Marie Painter, Writer
Zuccarini, David Anthony Painter, Instructor

Crownsville
Keck, Jeanne Gentry Painter

Cumberland
Llewellyn, Robert Printmaker, Educator

Davidsonville
Conklin, Eric Artist

Drayden
Egeli, Peter Even Painter, Illustrator

Easton
Plumb, James Douglas Painter, Educator

Edgewater
Egeli, Cedric Baldwin Painter, Instructor

Ellicott City
Baney, Ralph Ramoutar Sculptor

Fort Washington
Grady, Ruby McLain Painter, Sculptor

Gaithersburg
Balance, Jerrald Clark Painter
Gigliotti, Joanne Marie Administrator, Painter
Huff, Laura Weaver Printmaker, Instructor

Glen Echo
Stevenson, A Brockie Painter, Educator

Glenelg
Niese, Henry Ernst Environmental Artist, Painter

Gwynn Oak
Johnston, Barry Woods Sculptor

Hagerstown
Roberts, Clyde Harry Painter, Instructor

Hyattsville
Driskell, David Clyde Painter, Educator
Luchs, Alison Curator, Historian
Powell, Earl Alexander, III Director, Historian
Shestack, Alan Museum Administrator, Art Historian

Joppa
Walters, Ernest Painter

Kensington
Murray, Richard Newton Museum Director, Curator
Winkler, Max-Karl Educator, Illustrator

Landover
Hand, John Oliver Historian, Curator
Kelly, Franklin Wood Curator, Historian
Nevia, Joseph Shepperd Rogers Painter
Vogel, (Mr & Mrs) Herbert Collectors

Lanham Seabrook
Chapin, Deborah Jane Painter, Instructor

Lutherville Timonium
Wagner, Charles H Administrator, Instructor

Mount Airy
Swetcharnik, Sara Morris Painter, Sculptor
Swetcharnik, William Norton Painter, Sculptor

Phoenix
Meyerhoff, Robert E Collector

Rockville
Goldstein, Charles Barry Art Dealer, Appraiser
Hoffman, Mandy Lippman Consultant, Writer
Porter, Shirley Painter

Royal Oak
McNamara-Ringewald, Mary Ann Therese Painter, Illustrator
Saff, Donald Jay Painter, Educator

Salisbury
Richards, David Patrick Painter, Writer

Sandy Spring
Murphy, Susan Avis Murphy Colombini Painter

Savage
George, Sylvia James Painter, Illustrator

Severna Park
Stephany, Jaromir Photographer, Educator

Shady Side
Nadolski, Stephanie Lucille Painter, Printmaker

Silver Spring
Carter, Jerry Williams Video Artist, Mosaic Artist
Coleman, Floyd Willis Educator, Painter
Daniels, David Robert Painter, Educator
Edelman, Ann Painter, Lecturer
Fitzgerald, Joe Painter, Printmaker
Folsom, Rose Calligrapher, Writer
Frederick, Helen C Printmaker, Conceptual Artist
Gates, Jeff S Photographer, Designer
Gips, C L Terry Photographer, Educator
Gresser, Seymour Gerald Sculptor, Writer
Lapinski, Tadeusz (A) Printmaker, Educator
Oxman, Katja Printmaker
Peiperl, Adam Video Artist, Kinetic Artist
Pruitt, Lynn Sculptor, Assemblage Artist
Ritchie, Charles Morton, Jr Painter, Printmaker
Slate, Joseph Frank Writer, Conceptual Artist
Warren, Win (Winton) W Painter, Lecturer
Wheeler, Janet B Collage Artist, Painter

Takoma Park
Jewell, Joyce Painter, Printmaker

University Park
Kehoe, Patrice Painter
Richardson, W C Painter, Educator

Wheaton
Folsom, Fred Gorham, III Painter, Conservator

MARYLAND (cont)

MASSACHUSETTS

Amherst

Campbell, Nancy B Printmaker
Clark, Carol Art Historian, Curator
Danly, Susan Curator, Historian
De Groat, Diane Illustrator, Designer, Writer
Grant, Daniel Howard Writer, Critic
Hendricks, James (Powell) Sculptor, Painter
Liebling, Jerome Photographer, Filmmaker
Norton, Paul Foote Historian, Educator
Parkhurst, Charles Educator, Curator
Richardson, Trevor J Gallery Director, Curator
Ritz, Lorna J Painter, Sculptor
Roskill, Mark Wentworth Historian, Critic
Sandweiss, Martha Ann Museum Director
Townsend, John F Sculptor, Painter
Wardlaw, George Melvin Painter, Sculptor

Amherst

Yarde, Richard Artist

Andover

Sullivan, David Francis Painter, Printmaker

Arlington

Dahill, Thomas Henry, Jr Painter, Educator

Ashfield

Lund, Jane Painter

Ashland

Jorgensen, Bob (Robert) A Painter, Instructor

Barnstable

Lummus, Carol Travers Printmaker
Wylan, Barbara Painter

Belchertown

Claro, Paul Sculptor

Belmont

Dow, Jim D Photographer

Beverly

Bartnick, Harry William Painter, Photographer, Educator
Bauer, Ruth Kruse Painter
Bodin, Kate Educator
Broudo, Joseph David Educator, Painter
Towner, Mark Andrew Administrator, Photographer

Boston

Amalfitano, Lelia Curator, Gallery Director
Amenoff, Gregory Painter
Andrews, Edwin C Sculptor
Axelrod, John P Art Dealer, Collector
Bai, Qianshen Historian, Educator
Black, Scott M Collector
Bourque, Louise Filmmaker
Carlhian, Jean Paul architect
Cassidy, Margaret Carol (Mrs John Manship) Sculptor
Chamberlain, David (Allen) Sculptor, Painter
Cheney, Liana De Girolami Historian, Curator
Cormier, Robert John Painter, Lecturer
Crite, Allan Rohan Painter, Illustrator
Crump, Walter Moore, Jr Printmaker, Painter
Dluhy, Deborah Haigh Educator, Administrator
Driscoll, Edgar Joseph, Jr Critic
Fairbanks, Jonathan Leo Curator
Faulkner, Frank Painter
Fertitta, Angela Educator, Adminstrator
Fink, Alan Art Dealer
Fink, Joanna Elizabeth Art Dealer, Gallery Director
Flansburgh, Earl Robert Architect
Fletcher, Stephen L Appraiser
Folman, Liza Prtintmaker, Painter
Fox, Judith Hoos Curator
Freeman, Robert Painter
Fresko, Colleene Appraiser
Gaither, Edmund B Museum Director, Historian
Ghikas, Panos George Painter, Educator
Gibran, Kahlil George Sculptor
Goldstein, Nathan Painter, Writer
Grassl, Anton M Painter, Photographer
Grippe, Florence (Berg) Painter, Instructor
Gustafson, Pier Assemblage Artist
Harcus, Portia Gwen Dealer, Consultant
Harkness, John Cheesman Architect
Harle, Matt Sculptor
Harris, Conley Painter, Printmaker
Hawley, Anne Museum Director
Headley, David Allen Painter
Hemmerdinger, William John, III Painter, Critic
Herrmann, John J, Jr Curator
Hills, Patricia Historian, Curator
Horne, Ralph Albert Painter, Writer
Howard, Mildred Sculptor
Howlett, D(onald) Roger Art Dealer, Historian
Imber, Jonathan Painter, Printmaker
Isabel, Mcilvain Sculptor, Educator
James, Christopher P Photographer, Painter
Kanegis, Sidney S Dealer
Karsh, Yousuf Photographer
Keough, Jeffrey Director
Krakow, Barbara L Dealer
Laffoley, Paul (George), Jr Painter, Architect
Liotta, Jeanne Film Director
Malo, Teri (A) Painter, Printmaker
McCauley, Elizabeth Anne Historian, Writer
Medvedow, Jill Director
Meissner, Walt Administrator
Meister, Mark J Institute Director, Art Historian
Michaux, Ronald Robert Art Dealer
Montford, James Webster, Jr Educator
Nagano, Paul Tatsumi Painter, Designer
Nielsen, Nina I M Dealer
Pinckney, Stanley Painter, Tapestry Artist
Rogers, Malcolm Austin Museum Director
Rolly, Ronald Joseph Dealer
Rotenberg, Judi Painter, Art Dealer
St George, William (M) Painter, Instructor
Serenyi, Peter Historian, Administrator
Shibata, Toshio Photographer
Simpson, Bennett Curator, Critic
Sloan (Kay Sloan), Kay Educator
Smedstad, Deborah Barlow Librarian
Solman, Joseph Painter
Sonnabend, Joan Art Dealer, Collector
Sugimoto, Hiroshi photographer
Takayama, Martha Tepper Gallery Director, Publisher
Thomas, C David Printmaker
Tovish, Harold Sculptor
Trecker, Stanley Matthew Matthew Art College President
Warburg, Stephanie Wenner Painter, Instructor
Wendorf, Richard Harold Director
Wheelwright, Joseph Storer Sculptor

Boston

Kotting, Joey Artist

Bradford

Newman, Richard Charles Sculptor, Photographer

Brewster

Stoltenberg, Donald Hugo Painter, Printmaker

Bridgewater

Hausrath, Joan W Printmaker, Weaver
Smalley, Stephen Francis Educator, Painter

Brookline

Ablow, Joseph Painter, Writer
Ablow, Roselyn Karol (Roz Koyol Ablow) Painter, Instructor
Barron, Thomas Painter
Casdin-Silver, Hariet Artist
Kay, Reed Painter, Writer
Moss, Karen Canner Painter, Educator
Nixon, Nicholas Photographer
Papo, Iso Painter
Sina, Alejandro Kinetic Artist, Sculptor
Stapen, Nancy Critic, Writer
Swan, Barbara Painter
Wilson, John Sculptor, Printmaker

Brookline Village

Barron, Ros Painter, Video Artist

Cambridge

Ackerman, James S Historian, Educator
Arning, Bill A Curator, Administrator
Baden, Karl Photographer, Instructor
Bapst, Sarah Conceptual Artist
Callahan, Aileen Loughlin Callahan Painter, Muralist
Cohn, Marjorie B Curator, Historian
Denker, Susan A Historian, Critic
Dorfman, Elsa Photographer, Writer
Driscoll, Ellen Sculptor, Instructor
Farver, Jane Curator, Museum Director
Fleming, Ronald Lee Designer, Administrator
Gates, Henry Louis, Jr Patron
Gibbons, Joe Filmmaker
Goldring, Elizabeth Writer, Environmental Artist
Gund, Graham architectual firm executive
Harries, Mags (Margaret) L Sculptor, Educator
Jacob, Wendy Educator
Jonas, Joan Video Artist, Conceptual Artist
Katayama, Toshihiro Painter, Designer
Kelsey, Robin E Educator
Lee, Barbara Collector
Lent, Blair Illustrator, Writer
Lentz, Thomas W Museum Director, Curator
Magdanz, Andrew R Glass Blower
Mancusi-Ungaro, Carol Conservator, Educator
Manuel, K(athryn) Lee Craftsman
Mazur, Michael Painter, Printmaker
McKie, Todd Stoddard Painter
Moneo, Jose Rafael Architect
Parry, Marian Illustrator, Printmaker
Ranalli, Daniel Artist, Educator
Reimann, William P Sculptor, Educator
Rosenfield, John M Educator, Curator
Rosenthal, Donald A Historian, Critic
Ryerson, Mitch Craftsman
Saywell, Edward Curator
Selvig, Forrest Hall Historian, Writer
Sigel, Anthony B Conservator
Slive, Seymour Historian, Museum Director
Trachtman, Arnold S Painter
Vevers, Tabitha Painter
Welch, Stuart Cary Curator, Historian
White, Shelby Collector
Wodiczko, Krzysztof Educator
Wood, Joseph A Designer
Zerner, Henri Thomas Historian, Curator

MASSACHUSETTS (cont)

Canton

Kaiser, Diane Sculptor, Educator

Cataumet

Whitman-Arsenault, Kate Painter

Charlestown

Kelley, Donald Castell Gallery Director

Chatham

Falconer, Marguerite Elizabeth Painter, Instructor
O'Connell, Ann Brown Printmaker, Collector, printmaker - misc media
Reid, Charles Clark Writer, Painter

Chester

Pettibon, Raymond Video Artist

Chestnut Hill

Netzer, Nancy Museum Director
Ryan, Elizabeth Painter
Steczynski, John Myron Draftsman, Educator

Concord

Awalt, Elizabeth Grace Painter
Ihara, Michio Sculptor
MacNeill, Frederick Douglas Painter
Nick, George Painter, Educator

Dartmouth

McCoy, T Frank Painter, Educator
Miraglia, Anthony J Educator, Painter
Wisneski, Kurt Printmaker

Dennisport

Kochka, Al Museum Director, Administrator

Duxbury

Sloan, Robert Smullyan Painter

East Falmouth

Lincoln, Jane Lockwood Painter, Printmaker

Eastham

Pratt, Elizabeth Hayes Painter, Instructor

Fitchburg

Timms, Peter Rowland Museum Director

Florence

Houser, Caroline Mae Historian
Ravett, Abraham Filmmaker, Photographer

Framingham

Evans, Bob James Painter, Educator
Lipton, Leah Historian, Curator

Gloucester

Coburn, Ralph (M H) Painter
Collins, Pat Lowery Painter, Illustrator
Crowley, Charles A Craftsman
Manship, John Paul Painter, Sculptor
Movalli, Charles Joseph Painter, Writer
Pettibone, John Wolcott Curator, Administrator
Swigart, Lynn S Photographer

Granville

Brown, Stephen Pat Painter, Sculptor

Great Barrington

Agar, Eunice Jane Painter, Writer
Dowley, Jennifer Director
Filmus, Michael Roy Painter
Filmus, Stephen I Painter
McCurdy, Michael Charles Illustrator, Writer
Yanoff, Arthur (Samuel) Painter

Greenfield

Anthony, Amy Ellen Craftsman, Jeweler

Groton

Piene, Otto Sculptor, Painter

Hadley

Edelman, Rita Painter

Harwich

Steward, Aleta Rossi Painter, Graphic Artist

Harwich Port

Gilbertson, Charlotte Painter, Lecturer

Hingham

Dunn, Roger Terry Historian
Giovanni Painter, Printmaker
Pierce, Patricia Jobe Art Dealer, Historian
Rose, Samuel Painter, Muralist

Holliston

Harrington, William Charles Sculptor

Housatonic

Steiner, Sherry L Painter, Writer, Instructor, Gallery Director

Hyannis

Devine, Nancy Painter

Hyde Park

Pinardi, Enrico Vittorio Sculptor, Painter

Jamaica Plain

Apesos, Anthony Painter, Critic
Cantor, Mira Painter, Draftsman
Wise, Kelly Photographer, Critic

Lanesborough

Hoadley, Thomas A Ceramist

Lee

Arnold, Gloria Malcolm Painter
Patina, Rey Collage Artist, Sculpture, Lecturer

Lenox

Ginzel, Roland Painter, Printmaker

Leverett

Fornas, Leander Printmaker, Instructor

Lexington

Berman, Vivian Printmaker
Coleman, Loring W Artist
Filipowski, Richard E Sculptor, Educator
Havelock, Christine Mitchell Historian, Educator
Janney, Christopher Draper Environmental Artist, Designer
Wolpert, Etta Painter, Printmaker

Lincoln

Kumler, Kipton (Cornelius) Photographer, Lecturer
Master-Karnik, Paul Museum Director, Critic

Lowell

Edmonds, Tom Museum Director, Painter
Faudie, Fred Painter, Illustrator
Sullivan, Anne Dorothy Hevner Painter, Printmaker

Lynn

Fioravanti, Jeffrey Paul artist

Manchester-by-the-Sea

Crane, Bonnie Loyd Art Dealer, Gallery Director

Marblehead

Seamans, Beverly Benson Sculptor
Taylor, Robert Critic, Writer

Marion

Anderson, Laura (Grant) Painter
Bidstrup, Wendy administrator

Marshfield

Greenamyer, George Mossman Sculptor, Educator

Marshfield Hills

Krause, Dorothy Simpson Painter, Collage Artist

Mashpee

Searle, William Ross Painter

Mattapoisett

Mazer, Mike Painter, Artist

Medford

Raguin, Virginia C Historian, Consultant
Wechsler, Judith Glatzer Historian, Filmmaker

Medway

Burnett, Calvin Painter, Printmaker

Melrose

Hahn, Charles Sculptor

MIllls

D'Onofrio, Bernard Michael Glass Blower, Sculptor

Milton

Jans, Candace Painter, Printmaker

Montague

Coughlin, Jack Printmaker, Sculptor

Nantucket

Harris, Lily Marjorie Art Dealer, Administrator
Kemble, Richard Printmaker, Sculptor

Natick

Abany, Albert Charles Painter, Printmaker
Geller, Esther Geller Shapero Painter, Printmaker
Law, Jan Painter

Needham

Branfman, Steven Ceramist, Instr
Celli, Paul Painter, Educator
Rueppel, Merrill C Museum Director

New Bedford

Hamlet, Susan H Educator, Jeweler
Smith, David Loeffler Painter, Educator

Newton

Baratz, Robin Painter
Cobb, Ruth Painter
Hurwitz, Sidney J Painter, Printmaker
Korzenik, Diana Writer, Painter
MacDonald, Bruce K Educator, Historian, Artist
Raiselis, Richard Painter, Educator
Schon, Nancy Quint Sculptor
Schwartz, Henry Painter, Instructor

Newtonville

Polonsky, Arthur Painter, Educator

North Adams

Demartis, James J Painter

North Brookfield

Neal, (Minor) Avon Writer, Publisher

MASSACHUSETTS (cont)
Parker, Ann (Ann Parker Neal) Photographer, Writer

North Dartmouth
Lindenberg, Mary K Painter, Instructor
Taylor, Michael D Historian

North Hampton
Kopf, Silas Craftsman

Northampton
Fabing, Suzannah J Director
Gibson, John Stuart Painter, Printmaker
Gloman, David I Painter
Nettler, Lydia K Painter
Offner, Elliot Sculptor, Printmaker
Rupp, Sheron Adeline Photographer, Educator
Stubbs, Lu Sculptor
Teichman, Mary Melinda Printmaker, Calligrapher
Wessel, Fred W Painter, Printmaker

Northampton
Schneider, Katy Painter

Orleans
Minear, Beth Weaver, Tapestry Artist

Pelham
Cohen, Michael S Ceramist, Photographer
Kindahl, Connie Weaver, Craftsman

Pittsfield
Adams, Shelby Lee Photography
O'Connell, Daniel Moylan Muralist, Administrator
Patti, Tom Sculptor

Plainville
Dverin, Anatoly Painter

Provincetown
Collins, Larry Richard Painter, Photographer
Fabbris, Vico Painter, Environmental Artist
Hartley, Katherine Ann Painter, Instructor
Henry, Robert Painter, Educator
Hutchinson, Peter Arthur Conceptual Artist, Environmental Artist
Kent, H Latham Painter
Maynard, William Painter, Educator
McCarthy, Christine M Director
Roth, Marian Photographer
Vevers, Tony Assemblage Artist, Educator
Walker, Berta Art Dealer

Quincy
Wilson, Blenda Jacqueline Patron

Rehoboth
Carpenter, Joseph Allan Graphic Artist, Cartoonist
Glancy, Michael Sculptor

Rockport
Bissell, Phil Cartoonist, Illustrator
Colao, Rudolph Painter
DiStefano, Domenic Painter, Instructor
Martin, Roger Painter, Writer
Morrell, Wayne (Beam) Painter
Nicholas, Thomas Andrew Painter
Ruben, Albert Painter
Schlemm, Betty Lou Painter, Instructor
Turner, Bruce Backman Painter
Whitcomb, Kay Enamelist, Muralist

Scituate
Beale, Arthur C Filmmaker, Consultant

Seekonk
Backes, Joan Painter, Artist

Sharon
Avakian, John Printmaker, Instructor
Edmonds, Nick Sculptor

Sheffield
Friedman, Benno Photographer

Shelburne Falls
Simpson, Josh (Josiah) J L Simpson Glass Blower

Sherborn
Delaney, Roberta Printmaker

Somerville
Cooper, Mark F Sculptor, Collage Artist
Gabin, George Joseph Painter, Instructor
Goldman, Jane E Painter, Printmaker
Halevi, Marcus Photographer
Sandman, Jo Photographer, Environmental Artist
Scher, Julia Conceptual Artist, Video Artist
Slosburg-Ackerman, Jill Sculptor, Jeweler
Tourlentes, Stephen C Photographer, Sculptor
Valincius, Irene Painter, Printmaker
Yu, Shan Artist

South Chatham
Quidley, Peter Taylor Painter

South Dartmouth
Gustin, Christopher Ceramist
Swanson, Charles Craftsman, Educator

South Egremont
Parker, June Painter

South Hadley
Doezema, Marianne Museum Director, Historian
Hall, Lee Writer, Painter
Herbert, Robert L Historian, Educator
Hutt, Lee Sculptor, Photographer

Southborough
Gohlke, Frank William Photographer

Southfield
Ford, Walton Painter, Printmaker
Melvin, Ronald McKnight Museum Director

Southwick
Brodeur, Catherine R Painter

Springfield
Muhlberger, Richard Charles Writer, Educator

Sudbury
Aronson, David Painter, Sculptor
Nyman , Georgianna Beatrice Aronson Painter

Sunderland
Kamys, Walter Painter, Educator

Swampscott
Hayes, Gerald Painter, Photographer

Swansea
Caswell-Linhares, Sally Painter, Printmaker

Tewksbury
Kaufman, Mico Sculptor

Truro
Dunigan, Breon Nina Sculptor
Evaul, William H, Jr Painter, Printmaker

Johnson, Joyce Writer, Sculptor
Peters, Jim (James) Stephen Painter, Sculptor
Preston, Malcolm H Critic, Painter

Vinyard Haven
Bramhall, Kib Painter

Walpole
Hunter, Robert Douglas Painter, Instructor

Waltham
Allara, Pamela Edwards Educator
Bohlen, Nina (Celestine Eustis Bohlen) Painter, Draftsman,Prints
Campbell, Graham B Painter
Edminston, Scott Director, Educator
Hodes, Suzanne Painter, Printmaker
Ketner, Joseph Dale Museum Director, Curator

Watertown
Janowitz, Joel Painter
Mandel, Mike Photographer, Mosaic Artist
Schwalb, Susan Painter, Instructor
Weiler, Joseph Flack Photographer, Writer

Wayland
Dergalis, George Painter, Sculptor

Wellesley
Dorrien, Carlos Guillermo Sculptor
Fineberg, Gerald S Collector
McGibbon, Phyllis Printmaker, Educator
Mickenberg, David Museum Director, Historian
Moser, Barry Graphic Artist, Printmaker
Perkinson, Roy L Conservator, Historian
Rayen, James Wilson Painter, Educator
Wallace, Richard William Educator, Historian

Wellfleet
Grillo, John Painter, Printmaker
Yenawine, Philip Educator

Wenham
Wingate, George B Painter

West Barnstable
Bowman, George Leo Painter
Whittlesey, Stephen Painter, Sculptor

West Boylston
Italiano, Joan Sculptor, Liturgical Artist

West Brookfield
Higgins, Brian Alton Painter

West Hyannisport
Lynch Nakache, Margaret Painter, Sculptor

West Roxbury
Altmann, Henry S Painter, Educator
Sorokin, Maxine Ann Painter, Educator

Westfield
Wise, Gerald Lee Graphic Artist, Printmaker

Weston
Alfond, Barbara Lawrence Collector
Alfond, Ted B Collector
Torf, Lois Beurman Collector, Publisher

Westport
Sexton, Janice Louise Painter, Sculptor

Whately
Cumming, Robert H Artist, Photographer

Williamsburg
Superior, Mara R Ceramist

MASSACHUSETTS (cont)

Williamstown

Brooke, David Stopford Museum Director
Brooks, John H Museum Director, Educator
Burger, Gary C Museum Director
Conforti, Michael Peter Historian, Museum Director
Faison, Samson Lane, Jr Historian, Museum Director
Glier, Mike Draftsman, Painter
Johnson, Eugene Joseph Historian
Mathews, Nancy Mowll Historian, Curator

Wilmington

McLeod, Cheryl O'Halloran Painter, Instructor

Winchester

Fitch, Blake Museum Director, Photographer, Curator
Lee, Mack Art Dealer
Neuman, Robert S Painter

Winthrop

Garchik, Morton Lloyd Painter, Printmaker

Worcester

Barnhill, Georgia Brady Curator, Historian
Hovsepian, Leon Painter, Designer
McCorison, Marcus Allen Librarian
Nigrosh, Leon Isaac Ceramist, Writer
O'Reilly, John B Photographer, Collage Artist
Priest, Terri Khoury Struckus Painter
Shepard, Lewis Albert Dealer, Historian
Welu, James A Museum Director

Yarmouth Port

Hitch, Jean Leason Painter

MICHIGAN

Allen Park

Mandziuk, Michael Dennis Computer Artist

Allendale

McGee, J David Director, Educator

Alma

Rozier, Robert L Painter

Alpena

Bodem, Dennis Richard Consultant

Ann Arbor

Arnheim, Rudolf Educator, Writer
Busard, Roberta Ann Painter, Sculptor
Cassara, Frank Painter, Printmaker
Cervenka, Barbara Educator, Painter
Eisenberg, Marvin Educator, Historian
Forsyth, Ilene H(aering) Educator, Historian
Glasser, Norma Penchansky Sculptor
Guastella, C Dennis Painter, Instructor
Kirkpatrick, Diane Historian
Kumao, Heidi Elizabeth Photographer, Kinetic Artist
Kusnerz, Peggy Ann F Editor, Historian
Leonard, Joanne Photographer, Educator
Lewis, William Arthur Painter, Educator
McMillan, Constance Painter, Illustrator
Olynyk, Patricia J Printmaker, Educator
Pijanowski, Eugene M Educator, Craftsman
Rogers, Bryan Leigh Sculptor, Educator
Smith, Sherri Weaver, Educator
Spencer, Deirdre Diane Librarian
Spink, Walter M Educator, Administrator
Spitler, Clarc Blackford Art Dealer
Stephenson, John H Sculptor, Ceramist
Stephenson, Susanne G Ceramist, Educator
Steward, James Museum Director, Educator
Stewart, Paul LeRoy Printmaker, Educator
Zurier, Rebecca F Curator, Educator

Belmont

Powers, Linda S

Berrien Center

Constantine, Greg John Painter, Educator

Beverly Hills

Nawara, Jim Painter, Educator
Nawara, Lucille Procter Painter

Bingham Farms

Bostick, William Allison Painter - watercolor, Calligrapher, designer, Illustrator, Printmaker
Silverman, Gilbert B Collector

Birmingham

Berti, Mary Vitelli Painter
Kozlow, Richard Painter, Sculptor
Tay, Eng Painter
Wilbert, Robert John Painter, Educator

Bloomfield Hills

Jacobowitz, Ellen Sue Curator, Director
Robinson, Aviva Painter
Schwartz, Alan E Collector
Stewart, Norman Printmaker, Publisher

Brighton

Enright, Judy A Painter, Printmaker
Nestor, Lula B Painter, Administrator

Caledonia

Duren, Stephen D Painter

Canton

Beginin, Igor Painter, Educator

Detroit

Beal, Graham William John Director, Curator
Bulka, Douglas Painter, Educator
Colby, Joy Hakanson Critic
Darr, Alan Phipps Curator, Historian
Dumouchelle, Ernest J Appraiser
Dumouchelle, Lawrence F Appraiser
Hill, Draper Editorial Cartoonist, Historian
Jackson, Marion Elizabeth Historian, Educator
Jaquet, Louis Conceptual Artist, Painter - All media
Johnson, Lester L Painter, Educator
Muccioli, Anna Maria Painter, Sculptor
Nawrocki, Dennis Alan Educator, Curator
Peck, William Henry Historian, Consultant
Peters, John D Painter
Rogers, Richard L Educator, Administrator
Snowden, Gilda Painter, Writer
Woodson, Shirley Ann Painter, Collage Artist

Dexter

Rush, Jon N Sculptor, Educator

East Lansing

Berding, Thomas G Painter
Glendinning, Peter Photographer
Kingsley, April Curator, Critic, Lecturer
Stanford, Linda Oliphant Administrator, Historian

Farmington

Eisner, Gail Leon Painter, Sculptor
MacGaw, Wendy Sculptor

Farmington Hills

Glick, John P Ceramist

Flint

Davidek, Stefan Painter, Printmaker
Sharbaugh, Kathryn K Ceramist, Designer
Warner, Douglas Warfield Painter, Collage Artist

Flushing

Bohnert, Thom (Thomas) Robert Ceramist, Educator

Glenn

Rizzolo, Louis (Lou) B M Environmental Artist, Painter

Grand Rapids

Adams, Celeste Marie Museum Director, Curator
Blovits, Larry John Painter, Educator
Collins, Paul Painter
Gillie, Phyllis I Danielson Administrator, Tapestry Artist
Koster, Marjory Jean Printmaker

Grosse Ile

Stump, M Pamela Sculptor

Grosse Pointe

Miller, John Franklin Administrator

Grosse Pointe Farms

Krentzin, Earl Sculptor, Silversmith

Hamtramck

Hall, Michael David Sculptor, Educator

Harbor Springs

Kooyman, Richard E Craftsman

Harrisville

Welch, James Edward Painter

Hillsdale

Frudakis, Anthony P Sculptor

Holland

Mayer, Billy (William) Robert Mayer Sculptor

Holly

Stolpin, William Roger Printmaker

Huntington Woods

Abt, Jeffreyy Painter, Writer
Marck, Jan van der Historian, Critic
Morris, Florence Marie Dealer

Interlochen

Kimpton, Jeffrey S Administrator

Jenison

Windeknecht, Margaret Blake Fiber Artist, Writer

Kalamazoo

Bridenstine, James A Museum Director, Collector
Harrison, Carole Sculptor
Hatch, Mary Painter
Hefner, Harry Simon Painter, Educator
Kayser, Thomas Arthur Consultant, Designer
Link, Lawrence John Painter, Writer
Rhodes, Curtis A Painter, Printmaker
Ruttinger, Jacquelyn Painter, Gallery Director
Sheridan, Helen Adler Curator
Stroh, Charles Printmaker, Painter
Tye, William Roy Sculptor
VanderWeg, Phillip Dale Administrator, Sculptor

Kalkaska

Lawrence, Rodney Steven Painter

MICHIGAN (cont)

Lake Ann
Monteith, Clifton J Craftsman, Sculptor

Lakeside
Wilson, John David Administrator, Art Dealer

Lansing
Green, Roger J Critic, Historian
Nold, Carl R Museum Director, Historian

Lawton
Bowman, Jerry W Painter

Leland
Simper, Frederick Painter

Livonia
Culling, Richard Edward Painter, Collage Artist
Stamelos, Electra Georgia Mousmoules Painter, Educator

Lowell
Reid Jenkins, Debra L Painter, Illustrator

Marquette
Gorski, Richard Kenny Educator, Graphic Artist

Midland
Breed, Charles Ayars Sculptor, Designer

Montague
Bujnowski, Joel A Printmaker, Painter

Mount Pleasant
Morrisroe, Julia Marie Museum Director, Painter
Traines, Rose Wunderbaum Sculptor, Lecturer

New Buffalo
Volid, Ruth Dealer, Consultant

Novi
Barr, David John Sculptor, Conceptual Artist
DeLauro, Joseph Nicola Sculptor, Educator

Olivet
Whitney (Stevens), Charlotte Armide Painter, Jeweler

Parma
Wolber, Paul J Painter, Educator

Plainwell
Kendall, Thomas Lyle Ceramist, Administrator

Ray
Rubello, David Jerome Painter, Photographer

Riverdale
Parks, Carrie Anne Ceramist, Educator

Royal Oak
Carducci, Vincent Critic, Conceptual Artist
Levine, Edward Painter
McCarty, Lorraine Chambers Painter, Instuctor

Saginaw
Ondish, Andrea Printmaker, Educator

Saint Clair Shores
Burns, Sheila Painter, Lecturer
Burns, Stan Painter, Sculptor
Cartmell, Helen Painter, Designer

Saint Joseph
Davis, Darwin R Museum Director, Administrator

Saline
Natzmer Valentine, Cheryl Lynn Dealer, Historian

Southfield
Piet, John Frances Sculptor, Instructor

Taylor
Manoogian, Richard Alexander collector

Traverse City
De Luca, Joseph Victor Educator, Painter
Madden-Work, Betty I Painter, Historian

Troy
Belian, Garabed Dealer, Historian
Belian, Isabelle Administrator
Gallo, Frank Sculptor, Educator
Michaels, Glen Assemblage Artist, Painter
Richards, Bill Painter

W Bloomfield
Kuopus, Clinton Painter, Educator

Watersmeet
Freund, Will Frederick Painter, Educator, Writer

West Bloomfield
Hampson, Ferdinand Charles Art Dealer, Curator

Whitmore Lake
Davis, Philip Charles Photographer, Writer

Williamston
Chatterley, Mark D Sculptor
Lawton, James L Sculptor, Educator
McChesney, Clifton Painter, Educator

Ypsilanti
Avedon, Barry Painter, Educator
Fairfield, Richard Thomas Printmaker, Educator
McClure, Thomas F Sculptor, Educator

MINNESOTA

Afton
Fogg, Monica Painter, Educator

Bemidji
Nerburn, Kent Michael Sculptor, Critic

Dalton
Olson, Rick Painter

Duluth
Brush, Gloria (Elizabeth) DeFilipps Photographer, Educator
Brush, Leif Sound Sculptor, Instructor
Chee, Cheng-Khee (Jinyi Xu) Painter, Educator
Lettenstrom, Dean Roger Painter, Educator
Salminen, John Theodore Painter, Instructor

Eagan
Caponi, Anthony Sculptor, Educator

Eden Prairie
Kelly, Robert James Painter, Graphic Artist

Edina
Hallman, Gary Lee Photographer
Kunin, Myron Collector

Elk River
Olson, Gene Russell Sculptor, Tapestry Artist

Golden Valley
Raimondi, John Sculptor
Sussman, Bonnie Kaufman Dealer, Consultant

Janesville
Tanner, James L Craftsman

Lindstrom
Christianson, Linda Ann Ceramist, Sculptor

Mendota Heights
Starkweather-Nelson, Cynthia Louise Painter

Minneapolis
Asher, Frederick M Historian, Educator
Barber, Philip Judd Painter, Printmaker
Belgum, Rolf Henrik Filmmaker
Bjorklund, Lee Painter, Educator
Boler, John Alfred Art Dealer, Collector
Burpee, James Stanley Painter, Instructor
Conaway, James D Painter, Educator
Fisher, Carole Gorney Painter, Sculptor
Fiterman, Dolly Gallery Director, Collector
Flick, Paul John Collector, Painter
Gjertson, Stephen Arthur Painter, Writer
Halbreich, Kathy Museum Director
Hankey, Robert E Educator, Administrator
Holen, Norman Dean Sculptor, Educator
Hooper, Jack Meredith Sculptor
Hui, Pat Painter
Judge, Mary Frances Painter
Kareken, Michael Raymond Printmaker, Painter
King, Lyndel Irene Saunders Museum Director
Klipper, Stuart David Photographer
Larson, Philip Seely Sculptor, Educator
Lupori, Peter John Sculptor
Maurer, Evan Maclyn Museum Director
McCannel, Louise Walker Collector
McNally, Sheila John Educator, Historian
McRoberts, Sheryl Ann Sculptor
Mojsilov, Ilene Krug Painter
Mondale, Joan Adams Craftsperson, Ceramist
Munzner, Aribert Painter, Educator
Newman, Mari Alice Mae Painter, Sculptor
O'Keefe , Michael Administrator
Peterson, Harold Patrick Librarian
Pharis, Mark Ceramist
Pickett, Keri L Photographer
Poor, Robert John Historian
Preuss, Roger Painter, Writer
Rose, Thomas Albert Sculptor
Rowan, Herman Painter, Educator
Ryan, David Michael Curator
Scherer, Herbert Grover Educator
Shambroom, Paul D Photographer
Slade, George G Historian, Administrator
Slettehaugh, Thomas Chester Printmaker, Photographer
Somberg, Emilija O K Painter
Steglich, David M. Museum Administrator
Torbert, Stephanie Birch Photographer, Illustrator
Vergne, Philippe curator
Verostko, Roman Joseph Painter, Historian
Weisberg, Gabriel P Historian, Educator
Wiener, Phyllis Painter, Sculptor

Minnetonka
Lack, Richard Frederick Painter, Instructor
Morin, Thomas Edward Sculptor, Educator

MINNESOTA (cont)

Moorhead

Ray, Timothy L   Painter, Educator
Szeitz, P Richard   Educator, Sculptor

Morris

Nellis, Jennifred Gene   Sculptor

Nevis

Laske, Lyle F   Sculptor, Educator

Northfield

Arneson, Wendell H   Painter
Somers, Frederick D(uane)   Painter, Instructor

Park Rapids

Shilson, Wayne Stuart   Painter, Illustrator

Plymouth

Jardine, Donald Leroy   Administrator, Graphic Artist, Editor
Kiland, Lance Edward   Painter, Printmaker

Rochester

Gagnon, Charles Eugene   Sculptor, Consultant

Rushford

Curmano, Billy X   Conceptual Artist, Sculptor

Saint Cloud

Hendershot, J L   Printmaker, Educator
Petheo, Bela Francis   Painter, Printmaker

Saint Joseph

Becker, Johanna Lucille   Historian, Ceramist
Gordin, Misha   Photographer, Video Artist

Saint Paul

Burke, Mary Griggs   Collector
Cummings, Mary T   Administrator, Consultant
Czarniecki, M J, III   Museum Director, Consultant
Harding, Tim   Designer
Kielkopf, James Robert   Painter
Lasansky, Leonardo   Draftsman, Printmaker
Michels, Eileen Manning   Educator, Art Historian
Olson, Bettye Johnson   Painter, Instructor, Lectr
Price, Michael Benjamin   Sculptor, Educator
Rahja, Virginia Helga   Painter, Administrator
Rich, David   Painter, Educator
Rudquist, Jerry Jacob   Painter, Educator
Sears, Stanton Gray   Painter, Sculptor
Soth, Alec   Photographer

Saint Peter

Basset, Gene   Political Cartoonist
Palmgren, Donald Gene   Painter, Photographer

Silver Bay

Koestner, Don   Painter

Stillwater

Berge, Dorothy Alphena   Sculptor, Instructor
Steinworth, Skip (William) Eugene, Jr   Graphic Artist

Taylors Falls

Oestreich, Jeffrey   Ceramist

White Bear Lake

Larkin, (Dr) John E, Jr MD   Collector, Patron

Zumbrota

Lee, Margaret F   Painter

MISSISSIPPI

Belzoni

Halbrook, Rita Robertshaw   Papermaker, Painter

Carriere

Stanton, Sylvia Doucett   Painter

Clarksdale

Bouldin, Marshall Jones, III   Painter

Cleveland

Britt, Sam Glenn   Educator, Painter
Koehler, Ronald Gene   Sculptor
Norwood, Malcolm Mark   Painter, Educator

Clinton

Gore, Samuel Marshall   Painter, Sculptor

Columbia

Stringer, Mary Evelyn   Educator, Art Historian

Columbus

Ambrose, Charles Edward   Painter, Educator
Dice, Elizabeth Jane   Craftsman, Illustrator, Weaver
Imes, Birney   Photographer
Nawrocki, Thomas Dennis   Printmaker, Educator
Summer, (Emily) Eugenia   Painter

Courtland

Lindgren, Carl Edwin   Photographer, Historian

Diamondhead

Bannister, Pati (Patricia) Brown Bannister   Painter, Sculptor

Fulton

Douglas, Tom Howard   Painter, Sculptor

Gautier

Shepard, Steven L   Painter

Hattiesburg

Bagget, William (Carter), Jr   Printmaker, Muralist

Hernando

Yates, Marvin   Painter, Instructor

Jackson

Bradley, Betsy   Museum Director
Cook, Stephen D   Printmaker, Draftsman
Whittington, Jon Hammon   Educator, Painter
Wolfe, Mildred Nungester   Painter, Designer

Meridian

O'Neal, Roland Lenard   Illustrator, Graphic Artist

Natchez

Golden, Rolland Harve   Painter, Printmaker

Oxford

Dale, Ron G   Ceramist, Sculptor
Gross, Charles Merrill   Sculptor, Painter
Tettleton, Robert Lynn   Painter, Educator
Turnbull, Lucy   Museum Director, Educator

Starkville

Scucchi, Robie (Peter), Jr   Educator, Painter

Tupelo

Francis, Jean Thickens   Assemblage Artist, Painter

MISSOURI

Bonnots Mill

Schmitz, Barbara   Painter, Historian

Cape Girardeau

Grand, Stanley I   Curator, Historian
Holladay, Harlan H   Historian, Painter
Parker, James Varner   Designer
Riley, Sarah A   Painter, Educator

Charleston

Robbins, Joan Nash   Painter, Collage Artist

Chesterfield

Beckner, Joy Kroeger   Sculptor
Kagan, Andrew Aaron   Historian, Consultant

Columbia

Berneche, Jerry Douglas   Educator, Painter
Berry, William Augustus   Educator, Graphic Artist
Bussabarger, Robert Franklin   Sculptor, Painter
Cameron, Brooke Bulovsky   Educator, Printmaker
Crown, Keith Allen   Painter
Goodrich, James W   Administrator, Collector
Jackson, Paul C   Painter
Larson, Sidney   Educator, Muralist
Lenhardt, Shirley M   Painter
Peckham, Nicholas   Architect, Educator
Revington Burdick, Betty   Collector
Rugolo, Lawrence   Printmaker, Educator
Stack, Frank Huntington   Painter, Printmaker
Williams, Melissa   Art Dealer

Joplin

Christensen, Val Alan   Printmaker, Gallery Director

Kansas City

Bennett, Philomene Dosek   Painter, Ceramist
Bloch, Henry Wollman   Collector
Cadieux, Michael Eugene   Educator, Painter
Clancy, Patrick   Photographer, Conceptual Artist
Collins, Kathleen   Educator
Cozad, Rachael Blackburn   Museum Director
Crist, William Gary   Visual Artist, Educator
Davis, Keith F   Curator, Historian
Eaton, Tom   Cartoonist, Writer
Ehrlich, George   Historian
Eickhorst, William Sigurd   Educator, Curator
Fowle, Geraldine Elizabeth   Historian
Goldberg, Glenn   Painter
Goldman, Lester   Painter
Kemper, Rufus Crosby & Mary Barton Stripp   Collector
Lawrence, Susan   Art Dealer, Consultant
Lighton, Linda   Sculptor, Instructor
Marshall, James Duard   Painter, Printmaker
McKenna, George LaVerne   Curator
Scott, Deborah Emont   Curator
Self, Dana Rae   Curator, Writer
Sipho, Ella   Painter
Smith, Raechell M   Director
Thorson, Alice R   Editor, Critic
Trudeau, Garry B   Cartoonist
Van Harlingen, Jean (Ann)   Environmental Artist, Painter
Weidman, Jeffrey   Librarian, Historian
Widmer, Gwen Ellen   Photographer, Educator
Wilson, Marc Fraser   Museum Director
Wilson, Tom   Cartoonist
Younger, Dan Forrest   Painter, Printmaker

MISSOURI (cont)

Kirksville

Jorgenson, Dale Alfred Educator, Administrator

Labadie

Haynes, R (Richard) Thomas Painter, Illustrator

Lake Lotawana

Leedy, Jim (James A Leedy) Sculptor, Painter

Lamar

Bowling, Gary Robert Painter

Lees Summit

Usher, Elizabeth Reuter (Mrs William Arthur Scar) Librarian, Lecturer

Maryville

Hageman, Charles Lee Educator, Jeweler

Osage Beach

Orr, Joseph Charles Painter

Saint Joseph

Niewald, Wilbur Artist
Oldman, Terry L Museum Director
Spencer, Mark J Museum Director, Curator

Saint Louis

Bohan, Ruth L Educator, Historian
Bryant, Donald Collector
Burke, James Donald Museum Director, Administrator
Carter, Carol Painter
Childs, Elizabeth Catharine Historian, Educator
Eyerman, Charlotte curator, art historian
Greenberg, Ronald K Dealer, Collector
Sigala, Stephanie Childs Librarian, Educator
Smith, James Michael Painter, Assemblage Artist
Suhre, Terry L Director
Trova, Ernest Tino Sculptor, Painter

Sedalia

Freed, Douglass Lynn Painter, Educator, Curator, Museum Director

Springfield

Adams, Jay H Jeweler, Medalist
Armstrong, Bill Howard Painter, Educator
Berger, Jerry Allen Director, Curator
Kieferndorf, Frederick George Painter, Educator
Murphy, Dudley C Educator, Graphic Designer
Simmons, John Herbert Educator, Historian
Thompson, Wade S Painter, Educator
Warren, Jacqueline Louise Painter, Educator

St Louis

Byron, Michael Painter
Crane, Michael Patrick Museum Director, Curator
Engelhardt, Thomas Alexander Editorial Cartoonist
Goldstein, Sheldon (Shelly) Painter
Hansman, Bob Painter, Instructor
Kennon, Arthur Bruce Educator, Editor
Kodner, Martin Art Dealer, Consultant
Kornblum, Myrtle Painter, Printmaker
Krukowski, Lucian Painter, Educator
Magel, Catharine Anne Sculptor, Painter
Osver, Arthur Painter
Patton, Tom Photographer, Curator
Schactman, Barry Robert Painter, Educator
Schultz, Saunders Sculptor
Schweiss, Ruth Keller Sculptor, Designer
Severson, William Conrad Sculptor
Smith, Robert Charles Designer, Painter
Teczar, Steven W Educator, Painter
Ward-Brown, Denise D Sculptor
Zonia, Dhimitri Painter, Graphic Artist, Sculptor

Webster Groves

Boccia, Edward Eugene Painter, Writer

Wildwood

Addison, Byron Kent Painter, Educator

MONTANA

Bigfork

Fellows, Fred Painter, Sculptor
Shaner, (George) David Ceramist, Craftsman

Billings

Forbes, Donna Marie Museum Director
Fritz, Charles John Painter
Haughey, James M Painter, Calligrapher
Morrison, Robert Clifton Painter, Calligrapher
Pomeroy, Lyndon Fayne Sculptor
Selsor, Marcia Lorraine Educator, Ceramist
Steele, Benjamin Charles Painter, Educator
Whitson, Peter Whitson Warren Collage Artist, Educator

Bozeman

Anacker, John William Gallery Director, Painter
Bashor, John W Educator, Painter
Buck, John Sculptor
Butterfield, Deborah Kay Sculptor
Dreyer, Clarice A Sculptor
Helzer, Richard Brian Metalsmith, Sculptor
Volkersz, Willem Sculptor, Painter

Dillon

Corr, James D Painter, College Educator
Foolery, Tom Assemblage Artist

Great Falls

Laing-Malcolmson, Bonnie Museum Director, Painter

Hamilton

Crandall, Jerry C Painter, Historian
Crandall, Judith Ann Gallery Director, Writer

Helena

Appleby, Anne L Painter, Printmaker
Cleary, Shirley Cleary Cooper Painter, Writer
Dal Poggetto, Sandra Hope Painter
Notkin, Richard T Sculptor, Ceramist

Kalispell

Atwood Pinardi, Brenda Painter, Instructor
Sander, Sherry Salari Sculptor

Laurel

Zentz, Patrick J Sculptor

Missoula

Lo, Beth (Elizabeth) Ceramist, Educator
Rippon, Thomas Micheal Sculptor, Collector

Polson

Kerswill, J W Roy Painter

Roberts

Red Star, Kevin (Running Rabbit) Painter, Printmaker

West Yellowstone

Carter, Gary Painter, Sculptor

NEBRASKA

Amelia

Jellico, Nancy R Painter, Sculptor

Ashland

Majeski, Thomas H Printmaker, Educator

Avoca

Kunc, Karen Printmaker, Educator

Bellevue

Holoun, Harold Dean Painter, Sculptor

Culbertson

Dernovich, Donald Frederick Painter, Educator

Kearney

Dinsmore, John Norman Educator, Administrator
Peterson, Larry D Painter, Educator

Lincoln

Christensen, Neil C Painter
Collins, Howard F Historian
Dinsmore, Stephen Paul Painter
Eisentrager, James A Painter
Geske, Norman Albert Museum Director, Educator
Horvay, Martha J Painter, Environmental artist
Howard, Dan F Painter, Educator
Howlett, Ray Painter
Jacobshagen, N Keith, II Painter, Photographer
Nelson, Jon Allen Curator, Historian
Ross, Douglas Allan Sculptor, Instructor
Routon, David F Painter, Draftsman
Ruffo, Joseph Martin Printmaker, Administrator
Schorr, Paul C, III Patron
Schwieger, C Robert Educator, Printmaker

Omaha

Bartek, Tom Sculptor, Printmaker
Bradshaw, Laurence James Educator, Painter
Buchanan, Sidney Arnold Educator, Sculptor
Day, Gary Lewis Printmaker, Painter
Doll, Donald Arthur Educator, Photographer
Ferguson, Larry Scott Photographer, Curator
Hill, Peter Painter, Educator
Spencer, Jeffrey Paul Painter
Wise, Suzanne Tanderup Administrator, Historian

NEVADA

Boulder City

Burk, A Darlene Dealer, Collector

Gardnerville

Lawrence, James A Painter, Photographer

Henderson

Holder, Tom Painter
La Porta, Elayne B Painter, Printmaker

Las Vegas

Burns, Mark A Ceramist
Catterall, John Edward Painter, Educator
Herridge, Elizabeth Director
Huemer, Christina Gertrude Librarian
Lesnick, Stephen William Painter, Instructor
Tracy, Robert H Educator, Curator
Wynn, Stephen A Collector

NEVADA (cont)

Pahrump

Sullivan, Barbara Jean Painter, Instructor

Reno

Frueh, Joanna Critic
Goin, Peter Photographer, Video Artist
Growdon , Marcia Cohn Administrator, Historian
High, Steven S Museum Director, Curator
Waddell, Theodore Painter

Spring Creek

Gardner, Sheila Painter

NEW HAMPSHIRE

Bennington

Willis, Barbara Florence Painter
Willis, Sidney F Painter

Dover

Casey, Kim L Painter, Educator

Dublin

Bakanowsky, Louis J Sculptor, Architect
Tuckerman, Jane Bayard Photographer, Educator

Durham

Mugar, Martin Gienandt Painter
Wright, Vicki C Museum Director, Museologist
Zabarsky, Melvin Joel Painter, Educator

Exeter

Heath, Samuel K Museum Director
Stone, Don Painter

Hampton

Oakes, William Larry Painter, Sculptor

Hancock

Pollaro, Paul Painter
Welch, Charles D Painter, Sculptor

Hanover

Auten, Gerald painter, educator
Boghosian, Varujan Sculptor, Educator
Brooks, H(arold) Allen Historian, Lecturer
Hamlin, Louise Painter, Printmaker
Jacobus, John M Educator, Historian
Roberts, Helene Emylou Historian, Editor
Sheridan, Sonia Landy Media Artist

Holderness

Butler, George Tyssen Photographer, Filmmaker

Hooksett

Lafleur, Laurette Carignan Painter

Jackson

Beal, Mack Sculptor

Keene

Ahern, Maureen J Museum Director, Curator

Kensington

Dailey, Dan (Daniel) Owen Sculptor, Educator

Lebanon

Miller, Dolly (Ethel) B Painter, Collage Artist

Londonderry

Hoffman, Marilyn Friedman Director

Manchester

Beall, Joanna Painter, Sculptor
Keegan, Kim E Administrator, Sculptor
Strickler, Susan Elizabeth Curator, Historian

Nashua

Bloom, Hyman Painter

New Hampshire

Walp, Susan Jane

New Ipswich

Stirnweis, Shannon Painter, Illustrator

New London

Bott, John Painter, Critic

Newmarket

Essley, Roger Holmer Painter, Graphic Artist

Portsmouth

Balderacchi, Arthur Eugene Sculptor, Administrator
Bourgeault, Ronald Appraiser

Raymond

Beardsley, Barbara H Conservator

Rye Beach

Labrie, Christy Stained Glass Artist, Painter

Stoddard

Whitney, Richard Wheeler Painter, Instructor

Stratham

Fein, B(arbara) R Educator, Painter

Weare

Young, Janie Chester Museum Director, Educator

West Swanzey

Traynor, John C Painter

Wilton

Osgood, Jere Craftsman

NEW JERSEY

Allenhurst

O'Connor-Myer, Rose Ann Art Dealer, Lecturer

Allentown

Anderson, Susan Mary Painter

Alpine

Koopalethes, Olivia Koopalethes Alberts Painter, Printmaker

Asbury

Anderson, John S Sculptor

Asbury Park

Myers, Dorothy Roatz Painter, Critic
Nickerson, Scott A Painter

Atlantic City

Robbins, Hulda D Painter, Printmaker

Atlantic Highlands

Voorhees, Donald Edward Painter, Printmaker

Avon By The Sea

Mataranglo, Robert Patrick Video Artist, Muralist

Basking Ridge

Denman, Patricia (Pat Denman) Price Painter

Bay Head

Amelchenko, Alison M Painter, Instructor
Labonte, Dick Painter
Maisner, Bernard Lewis Painter

Bayonne

Gary, Jan (Mrs William D Gorman) Painter, Printmaker

Bedminster

Machiorlete, Patricia Anne Painter, Craftsman
Tromeur, Robyn Lori Curator, Director

Belvidere

Walton, Guy E Writer, Educator

Berkeley Heights

Faillace, Rachael Artist
Lorentz, Pauline Painter, Instructor

Berlin

Ascalon, David Sculptor, Stained Glass Artist
Ascalon, Eric J Director, Administrator
Feld, Augusta Painter, Printmaker

Bernardsville

Coheleach, Guy Joseph Painter, Sculptor
Folk, Tom C Art Dealer, Historian
Spofford, Sally Painter, Sculptor

Blairstown

Ayers, Carol Lee Painter, Gallery Director
Hourihan, Dorothy Dierks Painter, Educator

Bloomfield

Hughes, Siochan I Sculptor, Photographer

Boonton

Barnwell, John L Painter
Hanna, Annette Adrian Painter, Instructor

Bordentown

Barker, Al C Painter, Printmaker

Brick

Jannicelli, Matteo Painter, Photographer

Bridgewater

Glesmann, Sylvia Maria Painter
Malamed, Lyanne Painter

Brielle

Punia, Constance Edith Painter

Browns Mills

DeWitt, Edward Painter - Acyrlic, Oil, Sculptor

Burlington

Knight, William Painter, Printmaker

Caldwell

Mueller, OP, (Sister) Gerardine Calligrapher, Stained Glass Artist
Palombo, Lisa Painter

Califon

Burger, W Carl Educator, Painter
Reilly, John Joseph Painter, Instructor
Rosen, Carol M Sculptor, Collage Artist

Camden

Steel, Virginia Oberlin Gallery Director, Curator

Cape May

Turner, A Richard Historian, Educator

Cedar Grove

Lenker, Marlene N Painter, Collage Artist

NEW JERSEY (cont)

Cherry Hill
Appelson, Herbert J Educator, Printmaker
Sharrow, Sheba Painter
Tan, LiQin Educator
Toogood, James S Painter, Instructor

Chester
Duerwald, Carol Painter, Illustrator

Cliffside Park
LaMarca, Howard J Designer, Educator

Clifton
Dinc, Alev Necile Painter, Designer
Kanter, Lorna J Painter, Printmaker
Kostecka, Gloria Painter

Closter
Zakin, Mikhail Sculptor, Educator

Colts Neck
Rogers, Muriel I Painter

Cranford
Gatto, Rose Marie Painter
Lowe, Joe Hing Painter, Pastel

Cresskill
Radoczy, Albert Painter

Denville
Rafferty, Joanne Miller Painter, Collage Artist

Dover
Kearns, James Joseph Sculptor, Painter

East Brunswick
Bender, May Painter
Bloom, Donald S Painter, Illustrator

Eatontown
Preede, Nydia Painter, Illustrator

Edison
Phillips, Robert J Filmmaker, Photographer

Egg Harbor City
Ahlsted, David R Painter, Educator
Smith, Rae Painter

Emerson
Salomon, Johanna Painter, Instructor

Englewood
Anuszkiewicz, Richard Joseph Painter, Sculptor
Beltran, Elio (Francisco) Painter
Bremer, Marlene S Painter, Sculptor
Dallas, Dorothy B Painter, Printmaker
Grom, Bogdan Sculptor, Painter
Hammons, David Museum Director, Sculptor
Ringgold, Faith Painter, Sculptor

Englewood Cliffs
Liao, Shiou-Ping Painter, Printmaker

Ewing
Brooks, Wendell T Printmaker, Educator

Fair Lawn
Hurewitz, Florence K Painter, Educator

Fairfield
de Smet, Lorraine Painter
Singer, Esther Forman Painter, Critic

Fanwood
Schaeffer, S(tanley) Allyn Painter, Instructor, Aurhor

Farmingdale
Anastasia, Susanna Painter, Instructor

Flanders
Komarin, Gary Painter

Flemington
Rosenquist, Marc H Sculptor
Viera, Charles David Educator, Painter
Waksberg, Nomi Painter

Florham Park
Debarry, Christina Painter

Fort Lee
Docktor, Irv Painter, Illustrator, Printmaker
Morenon, Elise Painter, Instructor

Franklin Lakes
Baker, Cornelia Draves Printmaker, Painter
Ghahary, Zia Edin Consultant, Art Historian
Janjigian, Lucy Elizabeth Painter, Muralist
Reinkraut, Ellen Susan Painter

Freehold
Kunz, Sandra Thurber Painter

Gillette
Merkl, Elissa Frances Printmaker, Painter

Glassboro
Wasserman, Burton Painter, Educator

Glen Ridge
Kato, Kay Cartoonist, Illustrator
Konopka, Joseph Painter
Solon, Lisa H Photographer

Hackensack
Sznajderman, Marius S Printmaker, Painter

Haddon Township
Puri, Antonio Painter

Haworth
Bernstein, Saralinda Art Dealer, Historian

Highland Lakes
O'Dougherty, Winnie Painter
Ross, Joan M Painter, Instructor

Highland Park
Puniello, Francoise Sara Librarian

Highlands
Egan, Laury Agnes Photographer, Instructor
Morgan, Susan Painter, Instructor

Hightstown
Rivera, Frank Painter

Hoboken
Erbe, Gary Thomas Painter
Homitzky, Peter Painter
Rose, Roslyn Collage Artist, Photographer

Hopewell
Hein, John Craftsman

Howell
Culver, Margaret Victoria Director, Artist

Island Heights
Thorston, Ludlow Painter

Jersey City
Barrell, Bill Painter, Collector
Ching-Bor, Paul Painter
Cummings, David William Painter
Garcia, Ofelia Administrator, Printmaker
Gluck, Heidi Painter, Educator
Gurevich, Grigory Sculptor, Painter, Graphic artist, Printmaker, Inventor
Harrison, Tony Painter, Educator
Jones, Ben Painter, Sculptor
Lay, Patricia Anne Sculptor
Mady, Beatrice M Painter, Digital Artist
Magnan, Oscar Gustav Painter, Sculptor
Mount, Marshall Ward Historian, Administrator
Palaia, Franc (Dominic) Photographer, Muralist
Rodeiro, Jose Manuel Painter, Muralist
Rosenberg, Herb Sculptor, Designer
Russell, Robert S Sculptor
Yost, Erma Martin Assemblage Artist, Instructor
Yost, Leon C Photographer

Keyport
Graupe-Pillard, Grace Painter, Instructor

Lambertville
Ceglia, Vincent Painter
Cusworth, Christyl Painter, Conservator
Goodyear, John L Sculptor, Painter
Gordon, Harry H Sculptor

Lawrenceville
Naar, Harry I Painter, Educator
Saretzky, Gary Daniel Photographer, Historian

Leonia
Dickerson, Daniel Jay Painter, Instructor
Thibault, Andre (Teabo) Painter

Lincroft
Regan, Betsey Painter

Little Silver
Clark, Roberta Carter Painter, Illustrator
Stach, Judy Painter, Instructor

Livingston
Bodner, Rita R Painter
Price, Diane Miller Assemblage Artist, Collage Artist

Long Branch
Ferrari, Douglas Artist
Migliaccio, Anthony J Painter, Educator
Stamaty, Clara Gee Kastner Painter
Woolwich, Madlyn-Ann C Painter, Instructor

Madison
Henry, Sara Corrington Historian, Critic

Magnolia
Killeen, Melissa Helen Dealer, Gallery Director

Mahwah
Genute, Christine Termini Painter, Sculptor
Peck, Judith Sculptor, Writer

Manasquan
Collinson, Janice Painter, Gallery Director
Nardone, Vincent Joseph Painter, Collage Artist

Maplewood
Joffe, Bertha Designer
McNany, Tim Photographer
Wint, Florence Edythe Printmaker, Sculptor

Metuchen
Stoianovich, Marcelle Painter, Printmaker

Middletown
Wilson, June Painter, Educator

Milford
Ciardiello, Joseph G Illustrator

NEW JERSEY (cont)

Montclair

Beerman, Miriam Beerman-Jaffe Painter
Culbreth, Carl R Sculptor
Gallagher, Cynthia Painter, Educator
Harris, Ellen Schwartz Administrator, Museologist
Kawecki, Jean Mary Sculptor, Gallery Director
Kinkade, Catherine Painter, Praintmaker
Pare, Richard Photographer, Curator
Pickett, Janet Taylor Artist
Pitts, Sharon Painter
Roth, Jack (Rodney) Painter
Sims, Patterson Curator

Morris Plains

Ferris, (Carlisle) Keith Illustrator, Painter

Morristown

Klindt, Steven Administrator
Prystauk, Elissa Painter

Neptune

Ventura, Anthony Painter

Neshanic Station

Allen, E Douglas Painter, Writer, Sculptor

New Brunswick

Brodsky, Judith Kapstein Printmaker, Educator
Dodge, Robert G Painter, Sculptor
Edwards, Melvin Sculptor, Educator
Kolodzei, Natalia Administrator, Curator
Marder, Tod Historian
McHam, Sarah Blake Wilk Historian, Educator
Ortiz, Raphael Montanez Conceptual Artist, Educator
Perry, Gregory J Museum Director
Rusak, Halina R Librarian, Painter

New Milford

Leibowitz, Bernice Painter, Educator

New Providence

Rivo, Shirley Winthrope Painter

New Vernon

Bross, Albert L, Jr Painter

Newark

Auth, Susan Handler Curator, Educator
Dane, William Jerald Librarian
Grauer, Gladys Barker Painter
Mack, William L Patron
Price , Mary Sue Museum Director
Reynolds, Valrae Curator
Thomasos, Denyse Painter, Sculptor
Watkins, Eileen Frances Critic

Newton

Grodsky, Sheila Taylor Painter, Collage Artist
Hollander, Roz Painting

North Bergen

Valencia, Cesar Painter, Muralist

North Brunswick

Continos, Anna Painter, Designer

North Haledon

Heusser, Eleanore Elizabeth Heusser Ferholt Painter

North Plainfield

Delgyer, Leslie Environmental Artist, Painter
Stroppel, Betty MacNair Painter, Instructor

Nutley

Piccirillo, Alexander C Painter, Instructor

Ocean

Weber, Suzanne Osterweil Painter, Printmaker

Ocean Grove

Chesley, Jacqueline Painter, Mosaic Artist

Oceanville

Weaver, AM Administrator, Historian

Oradell

Schaefer, Gail Sculptor
Struck, Norma Johansen Painter

Paramus

Brodkin, Ed Painter, Conceptual Artist
Jacobs, Helen Nichols Painter
Menthe, Melissa Librarian, Photographer
Messer, David James Director, Museum Director

Park Ridge

Daniel, Kendra Cliver Krienke Dealer, Painter, Collector

Parsippany

LePore, Joan Artist

Passaic

Sebek, Miklos Laszlo Sculptor, Instructor

Paterson

Macarol, Victor Multimedia Artist, Photographer

Perth Amboy

Hari, Kenneth Painter, Sculptor

Plainfield

Langdo, Bryan Richard Illustrator, Writer

Point Pleasant Beach

Riccio, Louis Nicholas Painter, Curator

Pompton Plains

Kettlewood, Bea Card Painter, Stained Glass Artist

Pottersville

Lynch, Thom Painter, Muralist

Princeton

Bunnell, Peter Curtis Educator, Curator
Fong, Wen C Educator
Graves, Michael Architect, Educator
Ingalls, Eve Sculptor, Painter
Johnson, Barbara Piasecka Collector, Patron
Lavin, Irving Historian
Lavin, Marilyn Aronberg Educator, Historian
Lindenfeld, Lore Craftsman
Marrow, James Henry Historian, Educator
McVicker, Charles Taggart Painter, Instructor
Olin, Ferris Historian, Curator
Savage, Naomi Photographer
Schmidt, Mary Morris Librarian
Shimizu, Yoshiaki Historian, Curator
Stroud, Peter Anthony Painter, Educator
Taylor, Susan M Museum Director
Williams, Idaherma Printmaker, Painter
Wilmerding, John Educator, Historian

Princeton

bois, Yve-Alain Educator, Curator

Princeton Junction

Rose, Peggy Jane Painter, Instructor

Red Bank

Pezzutti, Santo C Painter
Walsh, Nan Painter - Miscellaneous Media, Sculpture

Ridgefield Park

Heidel, Theresa Troise Painter, Instructor

Ridgewood

Rudy, Helen Painter, Instructor

Ringwood

Barbour, Arthur J Painter, Writer
Osborne, John Phillip Painter, Instructor

Rumson

Cocker, Barbara Joan Painter, Gallery Director

Rutherford

Petrie, Ferdinand Ralph Painter, Illustrator

Saddle Brook

Kaye, Mildred Elaine Instructor, Printmaker

Seaside Park

Golembeski, Beverly L Painter, Instructor

Secaucus

Staloff, Fred Painter

Short Hills

Michels, Ann Harrison Painter, Conceptual Artist
Saari, Peter H Painter, Sculptor

Shrewsbury

Leslie, Jimmy Painter, Instructor

Skillman

Hunter, Sam Historian

Somerset

Spector, Jack J Historian, Educator
Ten Painter
Zuccarelli, Frank Edward Painter, Instructor

Somerville

Behr, Marion Ray Printmaker, Writer

South Orange

Ford Nussbaum Drill, Sheila Art Dealer, Consultant
Ganek, Dorothy Skeados Painter, Silversmith
Lipton, Barbara B Educator, Curator
Targan, Judy Printmaker, Painter
Walker, Larry Painter, Educator

Sparta

Einreinhofer, Nancy Anne Gallery Director, Curator

Spotswood

Espenschied, Clyde Painter

Spring Lake

Pyle, Melissa Bronwen Painter, Sculptor

Springfield

Frank, Helen Goodzeit Painter, Printmaker
Koldorf, Irene Janet Sculptor

Stockton

Farnham, Alexander Painter, Writer
Leeds, Valerie Ann Curator, Writer
Mahon, Robert Photographer
Schoenherr, John (Carl) Painter, Illustrator
Taylor, Rosemary Ceramist, Sculptor

NEW JERSEY (cont)

Summit

Baker, Alden Painter
Butera, Virginia Fabbri Curator, Historian
Rousseau, Irene Victoria Sculptor, Writer

Sussex

Dubiel, Carolyn McPeek Collage Artist

Teaneck

Glickman, Arthur Sculptor
Indick, Janet Sculptor
Karp, Richard Gordon Painter, Lecturer
Rieber, Ruth B Printmaker, Painter
Schrero, Ruth Lieberman Sculptor, Printmaker

Tenafly

Adelman, Bunny Sculptor
Koenig, Robert J Museum Director, Educator
Miccoli, Arnaldo Painter, Collage Artist

Tinton Falls

McIlvain, Frances H Painter; Instructor
St Tamara, Kolba Tamara Stahanovich Painter, Printmaker

Toms River

Matteo, Dorothy Painter
Perle, Virginia Painter
San Chirico, Joanie Artist

Township of Washington

Ade, Irene M Painter

Trenton

Bimpong, Bright Sculptor
Chavooshian, Marge Painter, Educator
Doernbach, Marguerite Painter
Dorfman, Geoffrey painter, writer, musician
Elliott, Anne Sculptor, Painter
Fowler, Eric Nicholas Illustrator, Painter
Fox, Carson Sculptor - Miscellaneous Media
Goldstein, Howard Painter, Educator
Leipzig, Melvin Donald Painter
Sakson, Robert (G) Painter
Sloshberg, Leah Phyfer Museum Director

Tuckerton

Sullivan, JuneAnn Margaret Painter, Gallery Director

Turnersville

Mauro, Robert F Educator, Printmaker

Upper Montclair

Block, Virginia Schaffer Painter, Assemblage Artist
Schnitzer, Klaus A Photographer
Shah, Ela Painter, Sculptor
Stavitsky, Gail Beth Curator, Writer
Westfall, Carol D Artist, Educator
Williamson, Philemona Painter

Verona

Ayaso, Manuel Painter, Sculptor

Vincentown

Forrest, Christopher Patrick Printmaker, Painter

Wallington

Lynds, Clyde Sculptor, Painter

Washington Township

Valenti, Thomas Painter, Instructor

Washington Twp

Lee, David (Tzeh-Hsian) Painter

Watchung

Schwartz, Lillian (Feldman) Filmmaker
Shapiro, Lois M Collage Artist, Instructor

Wayne

Fay, Ming G Sculptor, Educator
Heyman, Samuel J Collector
Lalin, Nina Painter

Weehawken

Fuhrman, Esther Sculptor, Jeweler
Goldman, Ben Painter
Samburg, Grace (Blanche) Painter, Lithographer

West Cape May

Innerst, Mark Painter

West New York

Dellosso, Gabriela Painter

West Orange

Chusid, Evette Painter
Kahan, Leonard Dealer, Painter, Art Appraiser, Consultant
Krieger, Ruth M Painter, Printmaker
Yanow, Rhoda Mae Painter, Illustrator

Westfield

Becker, Natalie Rose Painter, Instructor
Godbee, Gary Painter
Reimers, Gladys Esther Sculptor, Instructor

Whiting

ZiegLer, Dolores Ann Painter, Conceptual Artist

Williamstown

Murashima, Kumiko Educator, Tapestry Artist
Phillips, James M Museum Director, Collector

NEW MEXICO

Abiquiu

Hamilton, Juan Sculptor
Moore, Sabra Artist, Curator

Alamogordo

Stevens, William Ansel, Sr Painter, Cartoonist

Albuquerque

Abrams, Jane Eldora Painter
Anderson, Sally J Painter, Printmaker
Antreasian, Garo Zareh Painter, Educator
Barber, Cynthia Sculptor, Printmaker
Chavez, Joseph Arnold Sculptor, Instructor
Cook, Michael David Painter, Video Artist
Devon, Marjorie Lynn Administrator
Feinberg, Elen Painter
Girard, Bill Sculptor
Hahn, Betty Photographer, Educator
Hammersley, Frederick Painter
Hanks, Steve Painter
Hobbs, Robert Dean Printmaker, Consultant
Hurley, Wilson Painter
Jaffe, Ira S Educator, Critic
Jones, Norma L Painter
Karp, Aaron S Painter
King, Brian Jeffrey Environmental Artist, Publisher
King, Victoria Vranich Killough Publisher, Painter
Landis, Ellen Jamie Curator, Historian
McCulloch, Frank E Painter, Printmaker
Moyers, William Painter, Sculptor
Multhaup, Merrel Keyes Painter, Sculptor
Nelson, Mary Carroll Writer, Painter
Paulos, Daniel Thomas Printmaker, Writer
Peterson, Gwen Entz Printmaker, Graphic Artist
Pirkl, James Joseph Educator, Designer, Painter
Pruneda, Max Sculptor
Ramirez, Joel Tito Painter, Calligrapher
Rippel, M (Morris) Conrad Painter
Rise, John Ernest Painter
Robb, Peggy Hight Painter, Instructor
Sabo, Betty Jean Painter, Sculptor
Saville, Ken Sculptor, Craftsman
Sisson, Laurence P Painter
Stone, Jim (James) J Photographer, Writer
Sussman, Arthur Painter
Truby, Betsy Kirby Painter, Illustrator
Vega, Edward Sculptor, Educator
Volkin, Hilda Appel Sculptor
Walters, Billie Ceramist
Wellborn, J(eanette) D(arleen) Painter
White, Robert Rankin Historian, Writer
Wilmeth, Ernest, II Collage Artist, Potter

Albuquerque

Ré, Paul Bartlett Graphic Artist, Sculptor

Anthony

Grissom, Freda Gill Painter, Goldsmith

Arroyo Hondo

Barsano, Ron (Ronald) James Painter, Sculptor
Davis, Ronald Painter, Printmaker

Belen

Chicago, Judy Painter, Sculptor

Bosque Farms

Stouffer, Daniel Henry, Jr Painter, Designer

Carlsbad

Johanningmeier, Robert Alan Painter, Writer

Carson

Ross, Jaime Graphic Artist, Painter

Cerrillos

Pedersen, Carolyn H Painter

Corrales

Barry, Steve Sculptor
Leis, Marietta Patricia Painter
Monthan, Guy Photographer, Educator
Roberts, Holly L Painter, Photographer
Townsend, Storm D Sculptor, Instructor

Coyote

Johnson, Douglas Walter Painter, Ceramist, Publisher
Olsen Bergman, Ciel (Cheryl) Bowers Painter, Environmental Artist

Dona Ana

Smith, Jo-an Painter, Designer

El Prado

Egri, Ted Sculptor, Painter

Farmington

Cogan, John D(ennis) Painter
Farm, Gerald E Painter, Sculptor

Galisteo

Lippard, Lucy Rowland Writer

Gallup

Cattaneo, (Jacquelyn A) Kammerer Painter, Instructor

Grants

Lowney, Bruce Stark Painter, Printmaker

NEW MEXICO (cont)

Hanover

Renner, Eric   Painter, Photographer

Hobbs

Garey, Patricia Martin   Ceramist, Painter

Jemez Springs

Sweet, Roger   Sculptor, Ceramist

La Luz

Kellar, Martha Robbins   Painter, Instructor

Las Cruces

Chilton, Fred   Painter
Coker, Carl David   Painter, Educator
Fidler, Spencer D   Printmaker
Guzevich-Sommers, Kreszenz (Cynthia)   Painter, Instructor
Hutchins, Robin   Art Dealer, Gallery Director
Moffitt, John Francis   Historian, Painter
Ocepek, Lou (Louis) David   Printmaker, Painter
Oliver, Julie Ford   Painter, Instructor

Lincoln

Waterhouse, Russell Rutledge   Painter, Illustrator

Pena Blanca

Fitch, Steve (Steven) Ralph   Photographer, Instructor
Hotvedt, Kris J   Printmaker, Painter

Portales

Hamlett, Dale Edward   Painter, Educator

Ranchos De Taos

Lerner, Alexandria Sandra   Painter

Roswell

Du Jardin, Gussie   Painter, Printmaker
Fleming, Stephen   Painter, Ceramist
Peterson, Dorothy (Hawkins)   Painter, Educator
Schooley, Elmer Wayne   Painter, Educator
Wiggins, Bill   Painter

Ruidoso

Snidow, Gordon E   Painter, Sculptor

San Patricio

Rogers, Peter Wilfrid   Painter, Writer

Sandia Park

Brody, J(acob) J(erome)   Historian, Museologist
Guilloume, (Guilloume Perez-Zapata)   Painter, Publisher

Santa Fe

Adams, Phoebe   Sculptor
Allen, Terry   Multi-Media Artist
Anderson, Craig   Painter, Sculptor
Arnett, Joe Anna   Painter, Sculptor
Bacigalupa, Andrea   Sculptor, Painter
Barger, M Susan   Consultant, Conservator
Bass, David Loren   Painter, Gallery director
Batkin, Jonathan   Director
Bauer, Betsy (Elizabeth)   Painter, Printmaker
Beall, Karen Friedmann   Curator
Bendell, Marilyn   Painter, Instructor
Berg, Tom   Painter
Bol, Marsha C   Museum Director, Historian
Boylan, John Lewis   Painter, Printmaker
Bradbury-Reid, Ellen A   Administrator, Educator
Brooks, Jan   Sculptor, Lecturer
Brycelea, Clifford   Painter, Illustrator
Burgess, Joseph James, Jr   Painter, Educator
Carlson, George Arthur   Sculptor, Painter
Clift, William Brooks   Photographer
Coe, Ralph Tracy   Consultant, Historian
Coffin, J Douglas   Sculptor, Painter
Cook, Richard L   Administrator, Sculptor
Coulter, Lane   Silversmith, Historian
Dailey, Chuck (Charles) Andrew   Museologist, Painter
Deaderick, Joseph   Painter, Educator
De Amaral, Olga   Tapestry Artist
Dean, Nat   Painter, Educator
Dodds, Robert J, III   Collector
Dominguez, Eddie   Ceramist
Enyeart, James Lyle   Historian, Director
Ettenberg, Franklin Joseph   Painter, Printmaker
Evans, Dick   Painter, Sculptor
Fangor, Voy   Painter
Fincher, John H   Painter, Assemblage Artist
Gandert, Miguel Adrian   Photographer, Lecturer
Gildzen, Alex   Writer, Collector
Gorski, Daniel Alexander   Painter, Sculptor
Hackett, Dwight Vernon   Publisher, Director
Handell, Albert George   Painter
Harrison, Jimmie   Jeweler, Craftsman
Harroun, Dorothy Sumner   Painter, Graphic Artist
Hartford, Jane Davis   Textile Artist, Craftsman
Hebald, Milton Elting   Sculptor, Printmaker
Housewright, Artemis Skevakis Jegart   Painter, Sculptor
Hulings, Clark   Painter, Illustrator
Igo, Peter Alexander   Printmaker, Painter
Jean, Beverly (Beverly) Jean Strong   Painter, Art Dealer
Karp, Diane R   Educator
Kelley, Ramon   Painter
Kessler, Alan   Painter, Sculptor
King, George G   Director
Lamuniere, Carolyn Parker   Painter - Acrylic, Oil
Laurence, Geoffrey F   Painter
Lippincott, Janet   Painter, Printmaker
Lomahaftewa, Linda Joyce   Painter, Instructor
Lutz, Marjorie Brunhoff   Painter - Watercolor, Sculptor - wood, stone
Mahaffey, Merrill Dean   Painter, Instructor
Marca-Relli, Conrad   Painter, Collage Artist
Mathias, Thelma   Conceptual Artist, Sculptor
Moses, Forrest (Lee), Jr   Painter, Printmaker
Naranjo, Michael Alfred   Sculptor
Nelson, Signe   Painter
New, Lloyd H Kiva   Educator
Newberg, Deborah   Painter, Printmaker
Niblett, Gary Lawrence   Painter
Nieto, John W   Painter, Sculptor
Nuss, Joanne Ruth   Sculptor, Painter
Orduno, Robert Daniel   Painter, Sculptor
Palmer, Kate (Katharine) A   Painter
Pardington, Ralph Arthur   Ceramist, Sculptor
Parry, Eugenia   Writer
Pena, Amado Maurilio, Jr   Painter, Illustrator
Phillips, Gifford   Collector, Writer
Pletka, Paul   Painter, Printmaker
Romero, Megan H   Painter, Dealer
Roybal, James Richard   Pastel, Painter
Ruthling, Ford   Painter, Sculptor
Sarkisian, Paul   Painter
Sauer, Jane Gottlieb   Sculptor, Curator
Schenck, William Clinton   Painter, Printmaker
Scott, Sam   Painter
Shepherd, William Fritz   Painter
Sky, Carol Veth   Painter, Photographer
Sloan, Jeanette Pasin   Painter, Printmaker
Smith, Linda Kyser   Painter, Instructor
Sonnenberg, Frances   Sculptor
Stark, Ron   Painter, Photographer
Steinhoff, Monika   Painter, Printmaker
Stuart, Joseph Martin   Painter, Museum Director
Warrior, Della C   Administrator
Wiggins, K Douglas   Painter, Art Dealer
Witham, Vernon Clint   Painter, Printmaker
Yates, Steven A   Curator, Photographer

Santa Teresa

Mitchell, Ann   Printmaker, Painter

Silver City

McCray, Dorothy Westaby   Painter, Printmaker

Taos

Beck, Ursula   Educator
Bell, Larry Stuart   Sculptor
Coke, Van Deren   Photographer, Historian
Crespin, Leslie A   Painter, Assemblage Artist
Harmon, Barbara Sayre   Painter, Book Artist
Harmon, Cliff Franklin   Painter
Hensley, Jackson Morey   Painter
Macpherson, Kevin   Painter
Nes, Margaret Isabel   Painter
Reis, Mario   Painter
Richards, Tally   Dealer, Writer
Smith, Jack Richard   Painter, Printmaker
Stewart, William   Painter, Educator
Vinella, Ray (Raimondo) John   Painter, Sculptor
Witt, David L   Writer, Curator

Tesuque

Okun, Barbara-Rose   Art Dealer, Gallery Director

Tijeras

Sweet, Mary (French)   Painter, Printmaker

Truth or Consequences

Mateo, Julio   Painter, Printmaker

NEW YORK

Accord

Arum, Barbara   Sculptor
Massie, Lorna   Printmaker

Afton

Schwartz, Aubrey E   Printmaker, Sculptor

Albany

Adams, Hank M   Craftsman
Carson, Joanne   Educator
Lawton, Nancy   Painter, Graphic Artist
Marlowe, Willie   Painter
Mayer, Edward Albert   Sculptor, Educator
Miles, Christine M   Museum Director, Administrator
Mooney, Michael J   Painter, Assemblage Artist
Shankman, Gary Charles   Painter

Alfred Station

Gill, John P   Sculptor
Higby, (Donald) Wayne   Painter, Sculptor

Altamont

Cowley, Edward P   Painter, Educator
Frinta, Mojmir Svatopluk   Historian, Educator

Amagansett

Durham, William   Painter, Sculptor
Gussow, Sue Ferguson   Painter, Educator
Seelbach, Anne Elizabeth   Painter, Instructor

NEW YORK (cont)
Strong-Cuevas Sculptor, Kinetic Artist

Amenia
Hale, Nathan Cabot Sculptor, Writer, Painter

Amherst
Beman, Lynn Susan Museum Director, Historian

Ancram
Schweninger, Ann Rozzelle Illustrator
Sorman, Steven Painter, Printmaker

Ancramdale
Weinstein, Joyce Painter

Annandale On Hudson
Pfaff, Judy Sculptor, Educator
Taylor, Davis Educator

Annandale-on-Hudson
Dobkin, John Howard Administrator, Consultant
Shore, Stephen Photographer

Ardsley
Lysun, Gregory Painter, Restorer

Ardsley On Hudson
Kipniss, Robert Painter, Printmaker
Lyons, Carol Painter, Printmaker

Armonk
Gay, Betsy (Elizabeth) Dershuck Gay Painter, Instructor
Perls, Klaus G Dealer
Schaffer, Debra S Collage Artist, Sculptor

Astoria
Slovin, Rochelle Director

Athol Springs
Fitzgerald, Joan V Painter, Collage Artist

Atlantic Beach
Seckel, Paul Bernhard Painter, Designer

Auburn
White, Jack Painter

Aurora
Roberts, William Edward Painter, Educator

Babylon
Haley, Priscilla J Painter, Printmaker

Baldwinsville
Peden Wesley, Donalee Painter

Batavia
Grieger, Donald L Painter
Schirm, David Painter, Educator

Bayville
Rettegi, Steven Painter

Bearsville
Hera Sculptor, Environmental Artist
Pantell, Richard Keith Painter, Printmaker
Whitman, Karen Printmaker

Bellerose
Stecher, Pauline Painter, Instructor

Belmont
Rush, Deborah Painter, Sculptor

Binghamton
Ippolito, Angelo Painter, Educator
Lindsay, Kenneth C Historian, Writer
Sokolowski, Linda Robinson Printmaker, Painter

Brainard
Johnsen, May Anne Painter

Brewster
Rosenberg, Bernard Publisher, Book Dealer

Briarcliff Manor
Adler, Myril Painter, Printmaker

Briarwood
Klein, Ellen Lee Painter, Educator

Bridgehampton
Gribin, Liz Painter, Printmaker
Jacobson, Arthur Painter, Printmaker
Tetherow, Michael Painter
Youngerman, Jack Painter, Sculptor

Bronx
Adams, Alice Sculptor
Bacarella, Flavia Painter
Baker, Blanche Sculptor, Instructor
Behnken, William Joseph Printmaker, Educator
Blayton, Betty Blayton-Taylor Painter, Administrator
Buonagurio, Edgar R Painter, Muralist
Buonagurio, Toby Lee Sculptor
Corbin, George Allen Historian, Writer
Finnegan, Sharyn Marie Painter
Kassoy, Bernard Painter, Printmaker
Kassoy, Hortense Sculptor, Painter
Keveson, Florence Painter, Illustrator
Leetaru, Ilse Printmaker
Lewis, Carole Sculptor
Shapiro, David Joel Critic, Educator
Spinka, William J Educator, Sculptor
Waletzky, Tsirl (Cecelia) Grobla Assemblage Artist, Stained Glass Artist
Wechter, Vivienne Thaul Educator, Painter
Wong, Audrey E(lizabeth) Painter, Graphic Artist

Bronxville
Cuningham, Elizabeth Bayard (Mrs E W R Templeton) Art Dealer
D'Amato, Janet Potter Illustrator, Craftsman
Markel, Kathryn E Dealer
Prakapas, Dorothy Director
Prakapas, Eugene Joseph Art Dealer, Editor
Schneider, Ursula Painter, Sculptor
Szold, Lauren G Painter, Sculptor

Brooklyn
Abrams, Edith Lillian Instructor, Sculptor
Acconci, Vito Sculptor
Adkins, Terry R Sculptor
Agee, Ann G Sculptor, Painter
Allain, Rene Pierre Painter, Sculptor
Alpern, Merry B Photographer
Antezzo, Matthew J Painter
Anzil, Doris Painter, Sculptor
Ausby, Ellsworth Augustus Painter, Instructor
Banks, Ellen Painter
Baroff, Jill (Emily) Painter, Sculptor
Barron, Susan Collage Artist, Printmaker
Barrow, Amanda McLaughlin Printmaker, Collage Artist
Bates, Leo James Painter, Filmmaker
Beecroft, Vanessa Fiona Painter
Berman, Aaron Art Dealer, Collector
Biondi, Florence Gloria Painter, Pastel
Bishop, Jeffrey Britton Painter, Educator
Botts, Gregory Artist
Brooks, Bruce W Painter, Sculptor
Brothers, Barry A Painter, Muralist
Bruno, Vincent J Historian, Administrator
Bui, Phong painter
Burkhart, Kathe K Conceptual Artist, Writer
Burns, Josephine Painter
Busto, Ana Marie Photographer, Sculptor
Campbell, Naomi Painter, Pub Artist
Carlson, Mary Sculptor
Casey, Tim (Timothy) William Painter
Coppedge, Arthur L Painter, Educator
Crewdson, Gregory Photographer
Currie, Steve Sculptor
Cusack, Margaret Weaver Illustrator
Dantzic, Cynthia Maris Educator, Painter
De Boschnek, Chris (Christian) Charles Painter, Printmaker
DeCarava, Roy Rudolph Photographer, Educator
De Champlain, Vera Chopak Painter, Printmaker
Dechar, Peter Painter
Diamond, Jessica Graphic Artist
Dinnerstein, Harvey Painter
Dinnerstein, Lois Historian, Lecturer
Dinnerstein, Simon A Painter
Dixon, Jenny (Jane) Hodley Administrator
Dubnau, Jenny Painter
Eckart, Christian Painter
Erman, Geraldine Sculptor
Estern, Neil Sculptor
Evans, Judith Futral Painter
Fein, Stanley Painter, Designer
Ferber, Linda S Curator, Historian
Fine, Jane Painter
Fischer, R M Sculptor
Flanery, Gail Painter, Printmaker
Fleminger, Susan N Administrator, Educator
Flynn, John (Kevin) Painter, Restorer
Gardner, Susan Ross Painter
Garfield, Peter Painter, Photographer
Gatten, David Filmmaker
Gianlorenzi, Nona Elena Painter, Sculptor
Gilbert, Sharon Collage Artist, Conceptual Artist
Giro, R(alph) Victor Gironda Sculptor, Painter
Gonzalez, Maria Elena Sculptor
Gorchov, Ron Painter
Grado, Angelo John Painter, Instructor
Gradus, Ari Painter, Printmaker
Gray, Luke Painter
Greenbaum, Marty Painter, Sculptor
Greenstone, Marion Painter
Grey, Alex V Painter, Sculptor
Haber, Ira Joel Sculptor, Writer
Hafftka, Michael D Painter
Hartshorn, Willis E Director, Photographer
Hazlewood, Carl E Curator, Painter
Heller, Susanna Painter, Instructor
Henes, Donna Environmental Artist, Sculptor
Herritt, Linda S Sculptor
High, Kathryn Painter, Writer
Homma, Kazufumi Painter
Howe, Nelson S Designer, Assemblage Artist
Howes, Royce Bucknam Painter
Hoyt, Ellen Assemblage Artist, Lecturer
Kalish, Howard sculptor
Kaminsky, Jack Allan Photographer, Printmaker
Kaprov, Susan Painter, Muralist
Kariya, Hiroshi Conceptual Artist
Katzive, David H Administrator
Keltner, Stephen (Lee) Sculptor, Educator
Kessler, Linda Painter, Photographer
Kinigstein, Jonah Painter, Designer
Kjok, Sol Painter
Knutsson, Anders Painter, Curator
Kord, Victor George Painter, Instructor
Kotik, Charlotta Curator, Historian
Krieger, Florence Sculptor, Painter

NEW YORK (cont)
Kunce, Samm Conceptual Artist, Sculptor
Lambrechts, Marc Painter, Printmaker
Laramee, Eve Andree Sculptor, Conceptual Artist
Lea, Laurie Jane Sculptor, Assemblage Artist
Lehman, Arnold L Museum Director, Curator
Lerner-Levine, Marion Painter, Printmaker
Levine, David Cartoonist, Painter
Lewczuk, Margrit Painter
Lieber, Lofa Painter & Gallery Director
Lima, Jacqueline (Dutton) Painter, Draftsman
Lin, Sara Painter, Callingrapher
Lowe, Sarah Curator, Writer
Mackenzie, David, IV Painter
Main, Tim Painter
Mainardi, Patricia M Historian, Critic
Malone, Peter Painter
Malta, Vincent Instructor, Painter
Marlor, Clark Strang Historian, Collector
Martin, Chris Painter
McTwigan, Michael Critic, Editor
Miller, Marc H Curator, Writer
Mitchel, Julio Photographer
Moore, Anne F Museum Director, Educator, Fine and Decorative Art Appraiser, Art Dealer
Morgan, Robert Coolidge Artist, Critic, Writer
Morgenlander, Ella Kramer Painter, Instructor
Muniz, Vik Photographer
Munk, Loren James Painter, Collage Artist
Myers, Forrest Warden Sculptor
Myers, Martin Sculptor, Painter
Neal, Florence Arthur Sculptor, Painter
Neals, Otto Sculptor, Painter
Nemser, Cindy Critic, Writer
Olenick, David Charles Administrator, Dealer
Ornstein, Judith Painter
Peyser, Jonathan Sculptor
Pfaffman, William Scott Sculptor, Draftsman
Pitynski, Andrzej P Sculptor
Provan, David Sculptor
Pujol, Ernesto Painter
Purcell, Ann Painter
Rand, Archie Painter, Muralist
Reich, Olive B Painter
Richards, Eugene Photographer, Lecturer
Robinson, Margot Steigman Painter, Sculptor
Rochette, Anne Monique Sculptor
Rosler, Martha (Rose) Artist, Writer
Saito, Seiji Sculptor
Sakuyama, Shunji Printmaker, Painter
Saret, Alan Daniel Sculptor, Painter
Saunders, Wade Sculptor, Critic
Schutte, Thomas Frederick Administrator
Seaberg, Libby W Painter, Historian
Seller, Linda Artist
Senie, Harriet F Historian, Critic
Shaw, Kendall (George) Painter
Shechter, Ben-Zion Painter, Illustrator
Shechter, Laura J Painter, Draftsman
Sillman, Amy (Denison) Painter
Sonday, Milton Franklin, Jr Curator
Starr, Sydney Librarian, Educator
Stegman, Patricia Painter, Printmaker
Steinbach, Haim Sculptor, Conceptual Artist
Stelzer, Michael Norman Sculptor, Instructor
Subrin, Elisabeth A Video Artist, Filmmaker
Tate, Blair Tapestry Artist, Educator
Therrien, Robert Sculptor, Painter
Trakis, Louis Sculptor, Educator
Tsarikovsky, Valery (Tsar) Painter, Muralist
Uram, Lauren Michelle Conceptual Artist, Illustrator
Vaadia, Boaz Sculptor
Van Riper, Peter Printmaker, Conceptual Artist
Vena, Dante Educator, Printmaker
Verene, Chris Multimedia artist
Vizner, Nikola Art Dealer, Gallery Director, PhD
Wachtel, Julie Painter
Webb, Alex(ander) (Dwight) Photographer
Weitzman, Eileen Painter, Sculptor
Werner, Donald (Lewis) Collage Artist, Painter
Wilson, Robert Warne Patron
Wizon, Tod Painter
Yamin, Steven Edward Printmaker
Zakanitch, Robert Rahway Painter
Zito, Joseph (Phillip) Sculptor, Conceptual Artist

Brooklyn
Ripps, Rodney Painter

Brookville
Brown, Edith Rae Sculptor, Medalist
Haleman, Laura Rand Sculptor, Craftsman

Brookyn
Holden, Michael B Painter, Sculptor

Buffalo
Anderson, David Art Dealer, Collector
Auerbach, Rita Argen Painter, Instructor
Baker, Dianne Angela Assemblage Artists, Sculptor
Breverman, Harvey Painter, Printmaker
Brock, Robert W Sculptor, Educator
Cohen, Harold Larry Designer, Educator
Freudenheim, Nina Dealer, Collector
Glass, Dorothy F Historian
Hatchett, Duayne Sculptor, Painter
Krims, Les Photographer, Conceptual Artist
Martin, Margaret M Painter, Educator
Mead, Gerald C, Jr Collage Artist, Educator
Naylon, Betsy Zimmermann Painter, Muralist
Paterson, Anthony R Sculptor, Educator
Penney, Charles Rand Collector, Patron
Piccillo, Joseph Painter
Prochownik, Walter A Educator, Painter
Reedy, Susan Painter
Schroeck, R D Painter, Conceptual Artist
Schultz, Douglas George Director

Buskirk
Johanson, Patricia Sculptor, Environmental Artist
Kheel, Constance Painter

Byron
Wilson, Tom Muir Designer

Callicoon
Bastian, Linda Painter, Educator

Callicoon Center
Kreznar, Richard J Painter, Sculptor

Cambria Heights
Brown, James Painter, Graphic Artist

Campbell Hall
Greenly, Colin Environmental Artist, Conceptual Artist

Canaan
Walker, William Bond Painter, Librarian

Canastota
Hughto, Darryl Leo Painter

Carmel
Alexander, Jane Administrator
Bloes, Richard K Video Artist

Cazenovia
Ridlon, James A Sculptor, Assemblage Artist
Wyckoff, Sylvia Spencer Educator, Painter

Chappaqua
Asoma, Tadashi Painter

Charlotteville
Goings, Ralph Painter
Pettibone, Richard H Painter, Sculptor

Chatham
Andell, Nancy Painter
Noyes, Sandy Photographer

Chautauqua
Kimes, Don Painter, Educator

Chelsea
Lyle, Charles Thomas Administrator

Chestertown
Longhurst, Robert E Sculptor

Chestnut Ridge
Mesibov, Hugh Painter, Printmaker

Chichester
Honjo, Masako Painter

Climax
Adler, Lee Painter, Printmaker

Clinton
Loy, John Sheridan Painter

Cold Spring
Marzollo, Claudio Sculptor
Murphy, Hass Sculptor, Draftsman

Cooperstown
Gialanella, Donald G Sculptor, Graphic Artist

Corning
Buechner, Thomas Scharman Painter, Writer
Dowler, David P Sculptor, Designer
Whitehouse, David Bryn Museum Director, Historian

Corona
Finkelpearl, Tom Museum Director

Cortland Manor
Rosenberg, Marilyn R Painter, Printmaker

Cortlandt Manor
Obrant, Susan Elizabeth Painter, Illustrator

Cragsmoor
Tupitsyn, Margarita Critic, Curator

Croton On Hudson
Genkin, Jonathan Painter
Pinkney, Jerry Illustrator
Wandel, Sharon Lee Sculptor, Painter

Cutchogue
Dank, Leonard D Illustrator, Consultant
Penney, Jacqueline Painter, Instructor

Dix Hills
Fouladvand, Hengameh Painter, Critic

Dobbs Ferry
Hart, Allen M Painter, Administrator

Douglaston
Eisenberg, Marc S Painter, Sculptor

NEW YORK (cont)

East Amherst
Garver, Walter Raymond Painter, Writer
Stoddard, Elizabeth Jane Painter

East Chatham
Egleston, Truman G Painter

East Hampton
Barons, Richard Irwin Educator, Historian
Boterf, Check (Chester) Arthur Painter, Lecturer
Brown, David Lee Sculptor
Bujese, Arlene Curator, Printmaker
Christensen, Dan Painter
Damaz, Paul F Writer, Architect
Daskaloff, Gyorgy Painter
Gordon, Joy L Curator, Educator
Hammond, Phyllis Baker Sculptor
Hoie, Claus Painter
King, William Sculptor
Leiber, Gerson August Printmaker
Li-lan Painter
Mim, Adrienne Claire Schwartz Sculptor, Painter
Phillips, Arthur Byron Painter, Sculptor
Richenburg, Robert Bartlett Painter, Sculptor
Roth, Frank Painter
Schlesinger, Christina Painter, Muralist
Weller, Paul Photographer, Painter
Zacharias, Athos Painter
Zucker, Murray Harvey Sculptor, Collage Artist

East Hills
Newmark, Marilyn Newmark Meiselman Sculptor, Instructor

East Meadow
Herman, David H Painter
Simon, Netty D Painter

East Meredith
Wentworth, Janet Painter

East Northport
Cohen, George Michael Educator

East Quogue
Setlow, Neva C (Delihas) Sculptor, Painter

East Rockaway
Nodiff, Jack Painter

East Setauket
Remsen, John Painter, Consultant

Eastchester
Alfano, Angel Painter
Stern, Louise G Printmaker, Painter

Eddyville
Raymond, Lilo Photographer

Ellenville
Berhang, Mattie Sculptor, Lecturer

Elmhurst
Freedman, Jacqueline Painter

Elmira
Macdonell, Cameron Painter, Muralist

Endicott
Kotasek, P Michael Painter, Lecturer

Far Rockaway
Grillo, Esther Angela Sculptor, Printmaker

Farmingdale
Gatto, Paul Anthony Painter, Instructor

Fillmore
Wenger, Bruce Edward Printmaker, Graphic Artist

Fishers Island
Menil, Georges & Lois de Patron, Collector

Flushing
Chang, Jason Painter
Clark, William W Historian
de Luise, Alexandra Curator, Librarian
Feng, Ying Painter, Photographer
Hammerman, Pat Jo Painter, Printmaker
Kam, Mei K Painter, Instructor
Kochta, Ruth Martha Art Dealer, Painter
Kunsch, Louis Painter, Collage Artist
Langer, Sandra Lois (Cassandra) Art Appraiser, Historian
Ludwig, Eva Sculptor
Nicotra, Joseph Charles Painter, Muralist
Paisner, Claire Painter
Petrulis, Alan Joseph Printmaker, Photographer
Schneider, Janet M Museum Director, Painter
Smith, Valerie Curator
Vidal, Francisco Painter, Printmaker
Wimberley, Frank Walden Painter, Collage Artist
Winter, Amy H Director
Young, LeeMei Painter

Fly Creek
Dusenbery, Walter Sculptor

Forest Hills
Ashvil-Bibi, Sigalit Painter
Baer, Norbert S Educator
Balka, Sigmund Ronell Gallery Director, Curator
Pearlstein, Seymour Painter, Educator
Sax, (Steve G Sacks) Painter, Cartoonist

Franklin Square
Indiviglia, Salvatore Joseph Painter, Instructor

Fredonia
Booth, Robert Alan Sculptor

Freehold
Maltzman, Stanley Painter, Printmaker

Freeport
Abrams, Vivien (Joy) Painter
Golici, Nicolae sculptor
Terris, Albert Sculptor, Educator

Garden City
Fleming, Margaret Nielsen Graphic Artist, Illustrator
Jessen, Shirley Agnes Painter
Myron, Robert Historian

Gardiner
Oshita, Kazuma Sculptor

Garnerville
Harvey, Dermot Kinetic Artist, Sculptor

Garrison
Clifton, Michelle Gamm Sculptor, Filmmaker

Germantown
Drummond, Sally Hazelet Painter
Gladstone, M J Publisher
Shahly, Jehan Painter

Glean Cove
Watson, Clarissa H Dealer, Writer

Glen Cove
Beckhard, Ellie (Eleanor) Painter, Photographer
Paris, Jeanne C Critic, Consultant

Glen Head
Cohen, Reina Joyce Graphic Artist, Printmaker

Glenfield
Carter, (Charles) Bruce Printmaker, Educator

Glens Falls
Blackburn, Loren Hayner Painter, Illustrator
Lyons, Francis E, Jr Art Dealer, Lecturer
Suffolk, Randall Museum Director, Curator

Goshen
Bleach, Bruce R Printmaker, Painter, Sculptor
Digby, Lynne Painter, Writer

Grandview
Price, Helen Burdon Painter, Printmaker

Great Neck
Brown, Anita Painter
Dellis, Arlene B Museologist, Craftsman
Dennett, Lissy W Sculptor
Gorbaty, Norman Painter, Sculptor
Harnick, Sylvia Painter
Krieger, Suzanne Baruc Painter, Lecturer
Lytton, Constance B Printmaker, Painter
Mayer, Sondra Elster Art Dealer
Meyer, Seymour W Sculptor
Obler, Geri Printmaker, Collage Artist
Seidler, Doris Painter, Printmaker
Tanksley, Ann Painter, Printmaker

Greenlawn
Fludd, Reginald Joseph Painter, Craftsman
Zucker, Bob Architectivral Photographor, Portrait

Greenport
Rabinowitch, David Sculptor

Greenwich
Lorber, Stephen Neil Painter, Photographer
Nunnelley, Robert B Painter

Groton
Colby, Victor E Sculptor, Educator

Hadley
LaVerdiere, Bruno E Sculptor

Hamburg
Johnson, Anita Louise Painter, Graphic Artist

Hamilton
Knecht, John Filmmaker, Video Artist
Mosby, Dewey Franklin Museum Director, Historian
Van Schaack, Eric Historian, Educator

Hampton Bays
Ciancio, June (Kirkpatrick) Painter, Instructor

Hartsdale
Glanz, Andrea E Administrator, Curator
McMann, Edith Brozak Painter - All Media

Hastings On Hudson
Nikkal, Nancy Egol Collage Artist

Hastings-on-Hudson
Goldstein, Eleanor Painter
Hollingsworth, Alvin Carl Painter, Instructor
James, Catti Sculptor, Consultant

NEW YORK (cont)
Nardin, Mario Collector, Sculptor
Otani, June Illustrator, Printmaker
Sklar-Weinstein, Arlene (Arle) Graphics Artist

Hewlett
Flomenhaft, Eleanor Curator, Consultant

Hicksville
Di Cosola, Lois Bock Painter, Printmaker

High Falls
Flynn, Pat L Jeweler, Goldsmith
Sawka, Jan A Painter, Printmaker

Highland
Derrickson, Steve Bruce Painter

Hillsdale
Friedman, Alan Sculptor, Designer

Holland
Blair, Robert Noel Painter, Sculptor

Honeoye Falls
Revitzky, Dennis L Printmaker, Painter
Richards, Sabra Printmaker, Painter

Hoosick
Wilson, Evan Carter Painter

Hoosick Falls
Hatfield, David Underhill Painter
Holzer, Jenny Conceptual Artist
Sussman, Barbara J Art Appraiser, Consultant,
Sussman, Gary Lawrence Sculptor, Director
Trimm, H Wayne Illustrator, Painter

Hudson
Artschwager, Richard Ernst Sculptor, Painter
Avedisian, Edward Painter, Sculptor
Minsky, Richard Bookbinder, Conceptual Artist
Schmit, Randall Painter, Collage Artist
Schoener, Allon Designer, Consultant
Sullivan, Bill Painter, Printmaker

Huntington
Brodsky, Stan Painter, Educator
Coraor, John E Museum Director, Administrator
DeSantis, Diana Painter
Emmert, Pauline Gore Painter, Educator
Roux, Barbara Agnes Environmental Artist, Sculptor
Twardowicz, Stanley Jan Painter, Photographer
Vaux, Richard Painter, Printmaker
Walker, Marie Sheehy Painter

Huntington Station
Nagin, Mary D Painter, Educator
Webb, Jeffrey R Painter, Educator

Irvington
Schneider, Rosalind L Video Artist, Painter

Ithaca
Calkins, Robert G Historian, Educator
Daly, Norman Painter, Sculptor
Green, Nancy Elizabeth Curator, Writer
Grippi, Salvatore William Painter, Sculptor
Lowe, J Michael Sculptor, Educator
O'Connor, Stanley James Historian, Educator
Poleskie, Stephen Francis Artist, Printmaker
Robinson, Franklin W Museum Director, Historian

Spector, Buzz (Franklin Mac Spector) Conceptual Artist, Critic

Jackson Heights
Dacey, Paul Painter
Farian, Babette S Painter, Graphic Artist
Freund, Tibor Painter, Muralist
Goodwin, Guy Painter
Kanidinc, Salahattin Calligrapher, Designer
Moore, John L Painter, Curator
Schiavina, Laura M Painter
Wasserman, Albert Painter, Designer

Jackson Hts
Vos, Claudia Painter, Photographer

Jamaica
Borstein, Elena Painter, Educator
Cade, Walter, III Painter, Collage Artist
Cocchiarelli, Maria Giovanna Painter, Muralist
Eberly, Vickie Painter
Feder, Penny Joy Printmaker, Illustrator
Lovejoy, Margot R Multi-media, Educator
Simor, Suzanna B Librarian, Gallery Director
Youkeles, Anne Painter, Printmaker

Jamesville
Hughto, Margie A Ceramist, Curator
Vargo, John Educator, Painter

Jeffersonville
Craft, Douglas D Painter, Educator

Jericho
Honig, Eleanor D Painter, Printmaker
Kelmenson, Lita Sculptor, Educator
Ritter, Renee Gaylinn Painter

Jordanville
Durham, Jeanette R Painter

Katonah
Giobbi, Edward Gioachino Painter, Sculptor
Simpson, William Kelly Historian, Educator

Kendall
Markusen, Thomas Roy Craftsman, Sculptor

Kenmore
Wood, Robert L Sculptor, Ceramist

Kerhonkson
Jagger, Gillian Painter, Sculptor

Kew Gardens
Vargas, Josephine Illustrator, Painter

Kings Park
Barooshian, Martin Painter, Printmaker

Kings Point
Spiegel, Emily Joy Collector
Spiegel, Jerry Collector

Kingston
Bloodgood-Abrams, Jane Marie Painter
Friedman, Lynne Pianter, Instructor
Harrison, Jan Painter, Sculptor
Kellner, Tatana Photographer, Printmaker
McPherson, Bruce Rice Editor, Publisher
Montano, Linda (Mary) Conceptual Artist, Video Artist

Lagrangeville
Liccione, Alexander Painter, Graphic Artist

Lake Peekskill
Cutrone, Ronnie Blaise Painter
Sanders, Joop A Painter

Lake Success
Lichaw, Pessia Printmaker, Architect

Lancaster
Litz, James C Painter

Larchmont
Bogosian, Eric Conceptual Artist, Writer
Buchman, Arles (Arlette) Buchman Painter, Assemblage Artist
Demsky, Hilda Green Painter
Ingber, Barbara Dealer, Collector
Wadler, Ronni Painter, Illustrator

Laurens
Mahlke, Ernest D Sculptor, Educator

Levittown
Kaplan, Stanley Printmaker, Muralist
Schachter, Justine Ranson Graphic Artist, Illustrator

Lisle
Underhill, Linn B Photographer

Lloyd Harbor
Seiden, Arthur Painter, Illustrator

Locust Valley
Rogalski, Walter Printmaker, Lecturer

Lodi
McCue, Harry Painter, Printmaker

Long Island City
Averbuch, Ilan Sculptor
Bechtle, Robert Alan Painter
Donneson, Seena Sculptor, Graphics Artist
Gussow, Roy Sculptor, Environmental Artist
Kaufman, George S Patron
Lable, Eliot Sculptor
Leggett, Ann Vaughan Painter, Printmaker
Lobello, Peter Sculptor, Graphic Artist
Mandelbaum, Ellen Stained Glass Artist, Painter
Martin, Dianne L Painter, Printmaker
Schnurr, Elinore Painter
Tardo, Rodulfo Sculptor
Villinski, Paul S Sculptor, Painter
Von Ringelheim, Paul Helmut Sculptor
Walker, Steven Edmund Printmaker, Painter
Young, Aaron Conceptual Artist

Long Island City
Kahn, Tobi Aaron Painter, Sculptor

Mahopac
Gonzalez-Tornero, Sergio Painter, Printmaker

Mahopac Falls
Karimi, Reza Painter

Malverne
Stanton, Harriet L Painter

Mamaroneck
Arike, Michael Whitaker Printmaker, Painter
Bisgyer, Barbara G (Cohn) Sculptor, Designer
Pugh, Grace Huntley Painter, Art Historian
Topol, Robert Martin Collector

Manhasset
Catchi Painter, Printmaker
Reese, Marcia Mitchell Sculptor
Stein, Claire A Administrator

Manlius
Aistars, John Painter, Educator
Cortese, Don F Printmaker, Instructor
Groat, Hall Pierce Painter, Muralist

NEW YORK (cont)

Maryland

Johnson, Richard Walter Sculptor, Instructor

Maspeth

Blitz, Nelson, Jr Collector

Merrick

Cariola, Robert J Painter, Sculptor
Warshaw, Elaine N Sculptor, Director

Middle Grove

Ostrom, Gladys Snell Writer, Educator

Middletown

Blumenthal, Fritz Painter, Printmaker
Seawright, James L, Jr Sculptor, Educator

Millbrook

Della-Volpe, Ralph Eugene Painter, Educator

Monsey

Kruger, Barbara Conceptual Artist, Film Critic

Montauk

Lau, Rex Painter, Printmaker

Mount Vernon

Sherrill, Milton Lewis Sculptor, Painter

Mountainville

Collens, David R Director, Curator
Stern, H Peter Collector

Mt Kisco

Galen, Elaine Painter
Rubin, Irwin Painter, Designer

Mt Marion

Seckel, Cornelia Publisher, Writer
Steiner, Raymond John Critic, Writer

Mt Sinai

Woods, Burton Arthur Painter

Mt Vernon

Propersi, August J Administrator, Painter
Seliger, Charles Painter
Singletary, Michael James Painter
Zib, Tom (Thomas) A Zibelli Cartoonist

Neponsit

Rothafel, Sydell Painter

New Berlin

Huot, Robert Painter, Filmmaker

New Hampton

Sinnard, Elaine (Janice) Painter, Sculptor

New Hartford

MacDonald, Scott Critic, Educator

New Hyde Park

London, Anna Graphic Artist, Sculptor

New Kingston

Blackwell, Tom (Thomas) Leo Painter

New Paltz

Azank, Roberto Painter
Bender, Leslie Marilyn Painter, Muralist
Bull, Fran Painter, Educator
Deschamps, Francois Photographer
Martin, Alexander Toedt Educator, Painter
Masih, Lalit K Painter - Watercolor
Miller, (Richard) Guy Sculptor
Raleigh, Henry Patrick Painter, Writer
Shaw, Ernest Carl Sculptor
Stanich, Nancy Jean Photographer, Printmaker
Trager, Neil C Museum Director, Photographer
Turner, Norman Huntington Painter, Writer

New Rochelle

Adato, Linda Joy Printmaker, Instructor
Canning, Susan M Historian, Critic
Fazzino, Charles Painter, Publisher
Goldfinger, Eliot Sculptor
Liebman, Dr Sarah Educator, Painter
Livingston, Constance Kellner Collage Artist, Sculptor
Montlack, Edith Painter
Perlmutter, Merle Printmaker
Schlanger, Jeff Sculptor
Slotnick, Mortimer H Painter, Educator
Zheutlin, Dale R Sculptor, Educator

New Suffolk

Schulze, Paul Designer

New Woodstock

Scala, Joseph A Sculptor, Painter

New Yor

Vine, Richard Editor

New York

Abish, Cecile Environmental Artist, Photographer
Abram, Ruth J Writer
Abramovic, Marina Artist
Abramowicz, Janet Painter, Printmaker
Abrams, Joyce Diana Painter, Sculptor
Abularach, Rodolfo Marco Painter, Printmaker
Adams, Dennis Paul Sculptor, Conceptual Artist
Adams, Laurie Schneider Historian, Editor
Adler, Tracy L Curator, Educator
Adrian, Barbara Tramutola Painter, Collector
Aebi, Ernst Walter Illustrator, Painter
Ahearn, John Sculptor
Ahrens, Hanno D Sculptor
Akin, Gwen Photographer
Akutsu, Shoichi Painter, Instructor
Albenda, Ricci Sculptor, Painter
Alberti, Donald Wesley Painter
Alden, Todd Critic, Conceptual Artist
Alexander, Edmund Brooke Art Dealer, Publisher
Alexander-Greene, Grace George Educator, Museum Director
Ali, Laylah Painter
Allentuck, Marcia Epstein Historian, Educator
Alpert, Bill (William) H Painter, Sculptor
Altmejd, David Painter, Artist
Altshuler, Bruce J Educator, Writer
Alvarado-Juarez, Francisco Painter
Amano, Taka Painter
Amoros, Grimanesa Painter
Amos, Emma Painter, Printmaker
Anastasi, William (Joseph) Painter, Sculptor
Andersen, Leif (Werner) Painter
Anderson, Laurie Conceptual Artist
Andre, Carl Sculptor
Anker, Suzanne C Sculptor, Painter
Anthony, William Graham Painter, Draftsman
Antonakos, Stephen Sculptor
Antoni, Janine Sculptor
Aoki, Carole I Ceramist
Appel, Eric A Sculptor, Painter
Applebroog, Ida Painter
Aptekar, Ken Painter
Arai, Tomie Printmaker, Muralist
Arakawa, (Shusaku) Painter
Arcangel , Cory Graphic Artist
Arcilesi, Vincent J Painter, Draftsman
Arcomano, Cathryn Painter
Arias, Soledad M Curator
Armajani, Siah Sculptor
Armstrong, L C Painter
Armstrong, Martha (Allen) Painter, Photographer
Armstrong, Thomas Newton, III Museum Director Emer
Arnold, Ann Illustrator
Arnold, Jack Art Dealer, Publisher
Arnoldi, Charles Arthur Sculptor, Painter
Aronson, Sanda Assemblage Artist, Sculptor
Ashbaugh, Dennis John Painter
Ashbery, John Lawrence Critic
Ashcraft, Eve Painter
Ashkin, Michael Sculptor
Ashton, Dore Art Critic, Writer, Educator
Atkinson, Conrad Sculptor, Painter
Atlas, Charles Filmmaker
Attie, Dotty Painter
Audean Painter, Illustrator
Avery, Frances Painter, Photographer
Avlon-Daphnis, Helen Basilea Painter, Sculptor
Ayhens, Olive Madora Painter
Aylon, Helene Painter, Conceptual Artist
Azaceta, Luis Cruz Painter
Azara, Nancy J Sculptor, Painter
Azua, Jon Imanol Patron
Bachner, Barbara L Painter, Installation Sculpture
Bakaty, Mike Painter, Sculptor
Baker, Elizabeth C Art Editor, Critic
Bakoian, Lauren
Ball, Lillian Sculptor
Ball, Susan L Administrator, Historian
Ballard, James A Painter, Architect
Balmori, Diana Landscape Architect
Bandy, Gary Painter, Educator
Bandy, Mary Lea Editor, Administrator
Banerjee, Bimal Painter, Sculptor
Baran, Tracey photographer
Bardazzi, Peter Painter
Barnes, Curt (Curtis) Edward Painter, Instructor
Barnes, Kitt Painter
Barnes, Margo Painter
Barnet, Will Painter, Printmaker
Barnett, Emily Painter, Printmaker
Barnett, Vivian Endicott Curator, Historian
Barney, Matthew Sculptor, Filmmaker
Barowitz, Elliott Painter
Barr, Burt Video Artist, Photographer
Barr-Sharrar, Beryl Art Historian, Painter
Barrett, Bill Sculptor
Barth, Frances Painter
Barth, Jack Alexander Painter
Bartlett, Barry Thomas Sculptor
Bartlett, Jennifer Losch Painter, Writer
Barton, John Murray Painter, Printmaker
Bartscherer, Joseph Conceptual Artist, Photographer
Basquin, Kit (Mary Smyth) Curator, Educator
Bass, Ruth Educator, Critic
Bates, David Painter
Battenfield, Jackie Painter
Baum, Jayne H Art Dealer
Baxter, Douglas W Art Dealer
Baxter, Paula Adell Librarian, Writer
Baxter, Violet Painter, Calligrapher
Bayer, Arlyne Painter, Printmaker
Beal, Jack Painter
Beallor, Fran Painter, Printmaker
Beatty, Frances Fielding Lewis Art Dealer, Critic, Collector
Beck, Doreen Writer, Producer

NEW YORK (cont)
Beck, Martha Ann Museum Director, Curator
Beck, Robert Sculptor, Video Artist
Beckley, Bill Post-Conceptual Artist
Beckman, Ericka Filmmaker, Photographer
Bedia, Jose Painter, Sculptor
Beenen, Richard Photographer
Behnke, Leigh Painter
Beilin, Howard Art Dealer
Beirne, Bill Video Artist, Conceptual Artist
Belag, Andrea Painter, Graphic Artist
Bell, Byron architect
Beloff, Zoe Video Artist
Ben-Haim , Tsipi Critic, Exec Dir
Ben-Haim, Zigi Sculptor, Painter
Benes, Barton Lidice Collage Artist, Sculptor
Bennett, Tony Painter
Benton, Daniel C Patron
Ben Tre, Howard B Sculptor, Draftsman
Berg, Siri Collage Artist, Painter
Bergdoll, Barry historian, educator
Bergen, Jeffrey B Art Dealer, Director
Berger, Maurice Cult Historian & Critic
Berghash, Mark W Photographer, Painter
Berkowitz, Terry Installation Artist
Berlind, Robert Painter, Educator
Berman, Ariane R Painter, Printmaker
Bernheim, Stephanie Hammerschlag Painter, Sculptor
Bernheimer, G Max Appraiser
Bernstein, Judith Painter, Printmaker
Berthot, Jake Painter
Bethel, Denise Appraiser, Collector
Beuzenburg, Ron Sculptor
Bhavsar, Natvar Prahladji Painter
Bialler, Nancy
Bialobroda, Anna Painter
Bidlo, Mike Painter, Conceptual Artist
Billian, Cathey R Environmental Artist, Educator
Birchler, Alexander Filmmaker
Birmelin, Robert Painter, Draftsman
Birnbaum, Dara Video Artist
Blair, Dike Painter, Sculptor
Blake, Jeremy Artist
Blasco, Isidro M Sculptor, Architect
Blau, Douglas Assemblage Artist
Blaugrund, Annette Museum Director
Bleckner, Ross Painter
Blodgett, Anne Washington Painter
Bloom, Barbara Photographer
Blum, Andrea Sculptor
Boardman, Seymour Painter
Bocanegra, Suzanne H Sculptor
Bohary, James Artist
Bonino, Fernanda Art Dealer
Booker, Chakaia Sculptor, Painter
Boone, Mary Art Dealer
Bootz, Antoine H Photographer
Bordes, Adrienne Painter, Instructor
Borgatta, Isabel Case Sculptor, Educator
Borgatta, Robert Edward Painter, Sculptor
Borofsky, Jon Painter
Botero, Fernando Sculptor
Bouckaert, Harm J G Art Dealer
Bourgeois, Louise Sculptor
Boutis, Tom Painter, Printmaker
Bowers, Andrea Video and Installation Artist
Bowman, John Painter
Bowman, Ruth Art Historian, Educator
Boyd, (David) Michael Painter, Graphic Artist
Bradford, Mark painter
Bradley, Slater Photographer
Bradshaw, Dove Painter, Sculptor
Bradshaw, Ellen Painter
Braff, Phyllis Critic, Curator
Brandt, Kathleen Weil-Garris Educator, Art Historian
Breer, Robert C Sculptor, Filmmaker
Brett, Nancy Artist
Brine, Kevin R Patron
Broderick, Herbert Reginald, III Educator
Brodsky, Alexander Ilya Utkin Architect, Sculptor
Brodsky, Beverly Painter, Illustrator
Brodsky, Eugene V Painter
Brody-Lederman, Stephanie Painter, Drawings
Brookner, Jackie Sculptor, Environmental Artist
Brooks, Ellen Photographer
Brooks, Harry A Gallery Director, Art Dealer
Brosk, Jeffrey Sculptor
Brown, Cecily Artist
Brown, Diane Dealer
Brown, Jonathan Historian
Brown, Julia Director
Brown, Larry Painter
Brown, Petey Painter
Brown, Robert K Dealer
Browning, Colleen Painter
Brumer, Miriam Painter
Brumer, Shulamith Sculptor, Instructor
Brumley, Tom Museum Director
Brundage, Susan Lounsbury Dealer
Bruno, Phillip A Director, Lecturer
Brunswick, Cecile R Painter
Brus, Gunter Conceptual Artist, Printmaker
Bruskin, Grisha Painter, Sculptor
Bryant, Linda Goode Art Dealer, Gallery Director
Bryson, Louise Henry Patron
Buchwald, Howard Painter
Buckhardt, Tom artist
Budny, Virginia Sculptor, Writer
Buecker, Robert Gallery Director, Painter
Buist, Kathy Painter
Bunts, Frank Painter, Educator
Burden, Chris Conceptual Artist, Sculptor
Burdock, Harriet Historian, Printmaker
Burns, Marsha Photographer
Burson, Nancy Photographer, Conceptual Artist
Bush, Martin H Museum Director, Historian
Buszko, Irene J Painter
Butchkes, Sydney Painter, Sculptor
Butterly, Kathy sculptor
Buvoli, Luca Sculptor
Buxbaum, Robert Sculptor
Byron, Charles Anthony Dealer
Cai, Guo-Qiang Conceptual Artist, Sculptor
Caivano, Ernesto Artist
Canniff, Bryan Gregory Designer, Director
Canright, Sarah Anne Painter
Cantor, Fredrich Painter, Photographer
Cantwell, William Richard Painter, Printmaker
Caplan Ciarrocchi, Sandra Painter, Instructor
Capobianco, Domenick Painter, Sculptor
Cappellazzo, Amy Appraiser, Writer
Carbone, David Painter, Critic
Carboni, Stefano Curator
Cardillo, Rimer Angel Printmaker, Sculptor
Carey, Ellen Photographer
Carlson, Cynthia J Painter, Educator
Carrino, David Painter
Carter, Mary Painter, Printmaker
Carter, Nanette Carolyn Painter, Printmaker
Cartwright, Constance B & Carroll L Collectors
Carvalho, Josely Printmaker, Painter
Casebere, James E Photographer, Sculptor
Cassullo, Joanne Leonhardt Patron
Castanis, Muriel (Julia Brunner) Sculptor
Castoro, Rosemarie Sculptor
Castrucci, Andrew Painter, Sculptor
Cattelan, Maurizio Artist
Cavaliere, Barbara Critic, Historian
Cecula, Marek Sculptor
Celant, Germano Curator
Celis, Perez Painter, Sculptor
Celmins, Vija Painter
Cembalest, Robin Editor
Censor, Therese Sculptor
Cernuschi, Alberto C Dealer, Critic
Chamberlain, John Angus Sculptor
Chambers, William McWillie Painter, Art Dealer
Chandler, Michael Robert Painter
Charlesworth, Sarah E Photographer, Conceptual Artist
Chase, Louisa L Painter
Chase-Riboud, Barbara Sculptor, Writer
Cheang, Shu Lea Filmmaker
Chemeche, George Painter, Sculptor
Chen, Hilo Painter
Cheng, Emily Painter
Chermayeff, Ivan Designer, Painter
Chernick, Myrel Multimedia Artist
Chevins, Christopher M Painter, Draftsman
Child, Abigail Filmmaker, Video Artist
Childs, David Architect, Patron
Chin, Mel Sculptor
Cho, Y(eou) J(ui) Painter
Chong, Ping Director, Video Artist, Choreographer, Vis Artist
Christensen, Don B Painter, Collector
Chunn, Nancy Painter
Ciarrocchi, Ray Painter, Educator
Citron, Harvey Lewis Sculptor
Clark, Edward Painter
Clark, Garth Reginald Dealer, Historian
Clark, Michael Vinson Painter, Printmaker
Clarke, John Clem Painter
Clarke, Kevin Photographer, Conceptual Artist
Clemente, Francesco Painter
Close, Chuck Painter
Close, Frank Stained Glass Artist, Sculptor
Clough, Charles Sidney Painter
Clutz, William Painter
Cobb, Henry N architect
Cochran, Dorothy Parcells Printmaker, Gallery Director
Codding, Mitchell Allan Museum Director, Administrator
Code, Audrey Painter
Coe, Sue Painter
Coffin, Anne Gagnebin Patron
Cogger, Cassia Zamecki painter
Cohan, James Gallery Director
Cohen, Arthur Morris Painter, Graphic Artist
Cohen, Cora Painter
Cohen, David Critic, Gallery Director, Editor
Cohen, Elaine Lustig Painter, Designer
Cohen, Joan Lebold Historian, Photographer
Cohen, Mildred Thaler Art Dealer, Gallery Director
Cohen, Ronny Critic, Dealer
Cohn, Richard A Dealer
Cole, Max Painter
Cole, Willie Sculptor
Colen, Dan Artist
Colette, S Conceptual Artist, Sculptor
Colker, Edward Painter, Graphic Artist
Collery, Paula Painter
Collischan Van Wagner, Judy K Critic, Curator
Colnurn, Martha Filmmaker, Animator

NEW YORK (cont)
Colp, Norman B Photographer, Curator
Colquhoun, Peter Lloyd Painter, Instructor
Condeso, Orlando Printmaker
Cone, Michele C Critic, Historian, Curator
Conelli, Maria Ann Administrator, Educator, Historian
Conlon, William Painter, Printmaker
Connelly, Joan Breton Historian, Educator
Conner, Lois Photographer
Connor, Maureen Sculptor, Educator
Consagra, Pier Painter, Sculptor
Cook, R Scott & Soussan A E Art Dealer, Critic
Cooper, Paula Dealer
Coover, Christopher R Appraiser
Cornell, Henry Patron
Cortor, Eldzier Painter, Printmaker
Costan, Chris Painter, Collage Artist
Cotter, Holland Critic, Historian
Cottingham, Laura Josephine Critic, Writer
Courtney, Suzan Painter, Printmaker
Courtright, Robert Collage Artist, Painter
Cowles, Charles Art Dealer, Collector
Cox, Peter Artist
Coyle, Terence Painter
Coyne, Petah E Sculptor, Photographer
Craft, Liz Artist
Crary, Jonathan Knight Art Historian
Craven, David James Painter, Collage Artist
Crean, Hugh R Administrator, Lecturer
Creevy, Bill Painter, Writer
Crile, Susan Painter
Crimp, Douglas Critic, Educator
Crown, Roberta Lila Painter, Conceptual Artist
Cucullu, Santiago Painter
Cunningham, Francis Painter, Instructor
Cunningham, Merce Conceptual Artist
Cuppaidge, Virginia Painter, Educator
Cutler, Amy Painter, Sculptor
Cutler, Ethel Rose Painter, Designer, Educator
Cutler, Ronnie Painter
Cyphers, Peggy K Painter, Printmaker
Dalglish, Jamie Painter, Video Artist
Danoff, I Michael Museum Director, Writer
Danto, Arthur Coleman Critic
Daou, Annabel Conceptual Artist, Draftsman
Daphnis, Nassos Painter, Sculptor
Darton, Christopher Painter
David-Weill, Michel Alexandre & Helene Collector
Davidovich, Jaime Painter, Video Artist
Davidson, Maxwell, III Dealer
Davidson, Nancy Sculptor, Photographer
Davis, Douglas Matthew Artist, Critic
Davis, Ellen N Historian
Davis, Lisa Corinne Painter, Educator
Davis, Stephen A Painter
Debeers, Sue Photographer
DeBellevue, Lucky Sculptor
De Blasi, Anthony Armando Painter, Educator
de Campos, Nuno Painter, Instructor
De Donato, Louis Painter, Instructor
Deem, George Painter
Degn, Katherine Kaplan Art Dealer
De La Verriere, J J Goldsmith, Sculptor
De Lisio, Michael Sculptor
De Maria, Walter Sculptor
De Monte, Claudia Sculptor, Cur
De Montebello, Philippe Lannes Administrator, Museum Director
Denes, Agnes Environmental Artist, Conceptual Artist
Dennis, Donna Frances Sculptor, Printmaker
Dennison, Lisa Museum Director
Denson, G Roger Critic, Writer
dePaola, Tomie Designer, Illustrator
Desiderio, Vincent Painter
des Rioux (de Messimy), Deena Victoria (Coty) Graphic Artist, Photographer
Deutschman, Louise Tolliver Dealer, Curator
DeWoody, Beth Rudin Patron
Diamond, Stuart Painter
Diamonstein-Spielvogel, Barbaralee Writertelevision interviewer, producer
Diao, David Painter, Conceptual Artist
Dias-Jorgensen, Aurora Abdias Painter
Dias Griffin, Anne Patron
Di Cerbo, Michael Painter, Printmaker
Dickson, Jane Leone Painter
DiCorcia, Philip Lorca Photographer
DiDomenico, Nikki Conceptual Artist, Assemblage Artist
Diehl, Hans-Jurgen Painter
Dill, Lesley Sculptor
Di Meo, Dominick Painter, Sculptor
Dine, Jim Painter, Sculptor, Photographer
DiTommaso, Francis Director
Do, Kim V Painter, Educator
Dobbs, John Barnes Painter
Dodd, Lois Painter, Educator
Doe, Willo Critic, Writer
Dogancay, Burhan Painter, Sculptor
Doherty, Michael Stephen Editor, Printmaker
Doig, Peter Artist
Dole-Recio, Lecia Artist
Donati, Enrico Painter, Sculptor
Doner, Michele Oka Sculptor
Doo Da Post, Edward Ferdinand Higgins III Painter, Mail Artist
Dorfman, Bruce Painter, Assemblage Artist, Instr (Studio/Art Sch)
Dorfman, Elissa Painter, Printmaker, Sculptor
Dorfman, Fred Art Dealer, Gallery Director
Dorsey, Deborah Worthington Painter
Dove, Toni Video Artist
Dowell, James Thomas Painter, Filmmaker
Downes, Rackstraw Painter, Critic
Doyle, Mary Ellen Painter
Drake, Peter Painter, Draftsman
Drasler, Gregory J Painter
Driscoll, John Paul Dealer, Art Historian
Drum, Sydney Maria Painter, Printmaker
Dubasky, Valentina Painter
Dubrow, John Artist
Duff, John Ewing Sculptor
Dunkelman, Loretta Painter
Dunn, Fontaine Painter
Dunow, Esti Painter, Historian
Dupuis, David
Dwyer, Nancy Sculptor, Painter
Dyyon, Mario Painter, Sculptor
Eardley, Cynthia Sculptor
Ebony, David Editor
Eccles, Tom Administrator
Eddy, Don Painter
Edelson, Mary Beth Conceptual Artist, Painter
Edison, Diane Painter, Educator
Ehrenkranz, Joel S & Ann Collector
Eichel, Edward W Painter, Draftsman
Eins , Stefan Conceptual Artist, Painter
Eisenberg, Jerome Martin Dealer, Collector
Eisenberg, Sonja Miriam Painter
Eisner, Carole Swid Painter, Sculptor
Ekdahl, Janis Kay Librarian
Elderfield, John Historian, Curator
El Hanani, Jacob Painter
Eliot, Lucy Carter Painter
Ellenzweig, Allen Bruce Writer, Critic
Eller, Evelyn Eller Rosenbaum Collage and Book Artist, Painter
Ellis, Loren Elizabeth Painter, Photographer
Ellis, Richard Painter, Illustrator
Ellis, Stephen Painter
Ellis-Tracy, Jo Painter, Dealer
Elozua, Raymon Sculptor
Emil, Arthur D Collector
Emmerich, Andre Art Dealer, Writer
Enders, Elizabeth Painter
Engelberg, Gail May Patron
Engelson, Carol Painter
Ensrud, Wayne Painter, Printmaker
Epstein, Mitch (Mitchell) D Photographer
Erburu, Robert F Patron
Ess, Barbara Photographer
Esterow, Milton Editor, Publisher
Evans, Garth artist and educator
Evans, John Collage Artist, Painter
Evans, Tom R Painter
Evergon Photographer
Ewald, Elin Lake Fine Art Specialist Appraiser
Ewing, Lauren Sculptor
Faden, Lawrence Steven Painter, Printmaker
Fanara, Sirena Painter, Lecturer
Fane, Lawrence Sculptor
Faragasso , Jack Painter, Instructor
Farber, Maya M Painter
Fares, William O Painter
Farhi, Jean Claude Sculptor
Fasnacht, Heide Ann Sculptor
Faulconer, Mary (Fullerton) Painter, Designer
Fausel, Alan Appraiser
FeBland, Harriet Sculptor, Painter
Feder, Ben Designer, Painter
Feigen, Richard L Dealer, Collector
Feigenbaum, Harriet Sculptor, Environmental Artist
Feinberg, Jean Painter
Feingold, Ken Artist
Feininger, T Lux Painter, Writer
Feinstein, Rochelle H Painter, Printmaker
Feld, Stuart P Dealer
Feldman, Franklin Printmaker, Writer
Feldman, Ronald Dealer
Fernandez, (Jules) Jake Painter; Photographer
Ferrara, Jackie Sculptor
Ferris, Daniel B Gallery Director, Curator
Filipacchi, Daniel Patron
Finch, Spencer Painter, Sculptor
Findlay, David B, Jr Dealer
Finkelstein, Henry D Painter, Educator
Finn, David Photographer
Firestein, Cecily Barth Painter, Author
Fischer, John Painter, Sculptor
Fischer, Robert A Sculptor
Fischl, Eric Painter
Fischman, Barbara J Painter
Fish, Janet I Painter
Fisher, Kim Painter
Fisher, Vernon Conceptual Artist
Fishman, Louise Painter
Fitzgerald, Astrid Painter, Printmaker, Writer
Flack, Audrey L Painter, Sculptor
Flam, Jack D Historian, Educator
Flanagan, Barry Sculptor
Flattau, John W Photographer
Fleischer, Arthur, Jr Patron
Fleischman, Barbara Greenberg Patron
Flescher, Sharon Historian, Admin
Flood, Richard Sidney Writer, Curator
Floret, Evelyn Sculptor
Florin, Sharon June Painter
Fohr, Jenny Painter, Printmaker
Fontaine, John C Administrator

NEW YORK (cont)
Foreman, Laura Conceptual Artist, Sculptor
Forman, Alice Painter
Foulkes, Llyn Painter
Fowle, Bruce S Architect
Fox, Flo Photographer, Lecturer
Fox, Judy (Judith) C Sculptor, Ceramist
Fox, Terry Alan Conceptual Artist, Sculptor
Frailey, Stephen A Photographer
Frank, Mary Sculptor, Painter
Frankfurter, Jack Painter, Designer
Fraser, Andrea R Conceptual Artist, Museologist
Fraser, Pamela Painter, Sculptor
Fratkin, Leslie Photographer
Frecon, Suzan Painter
Fredenthal, Ruth Ann Painter
Freedman, Deborah S Painter, Printmaker
Freilicher, Jane Painter, Printmaker
Friedberg, Richard S Sculptor, Educator
Friedlander, Lee Photographer
Friedman, B H Writer
Friedman, Martin Museum Director
Friedman, Sabra Painter
Friedman, Sally Painter
Frinta, Irena Altmanova Painter
Fromboluti, Sideo Painter
Fromentin, Christine Anne Painter, Graphic Artist
Fukui, Nobu Painter
Fuller, Emily Painter
Furnas, Barnaby Painter
Furth, Karen J Photographer
Gage, Beau Sculptor; Photographer
Gallagher, Carole Photographer, Writer
Gallagher, Ellen Painter
Gallander, Cathleen S Art Dealer, Representative
Gallo, Ruben A Critic, Curator
Gamwell, Lynn Curator, Historian
Ganahl, Rainer Conceptual Artist
Ganzi, Victor Frederick Patron
Gaon, Simon Painter, Sculptor
Garrison, Barbara Printmaker, Illustrator
Garwood, Deborah A Conceptual Artist, Writer
Gebhardt, Roland Sculptor, Designer
Gechtoff, Sonia Painter, Draftsperseon
Geier, Philip Henry, Jr Patron
Gekiere, Madeleine Painter - Acrylic, oil & watercolor, Filmmaker
Gelber, Samuel Painter, Educator
Geller, Matthew Sculptor
Gellis, Sandy L Sculptor, Environmental Artist
Geltner, Danita Sue Sculptor, Painter
Gentile, Gloria Irene Designer, Sculptor, Painter
Georges, Paul G Painter
Gerbarg, Darcy Painter
Gerdts, Abigail Booth Historian, Curator
Gerdts, William H Historian, Educator
Gerst, Hilde W Dealer
Getler, Helen Art Dealer, Consultant
Ghent, Henri Critic, Writer
Giacalone, Vito Painter, Historian
Giampietro, Isabel Antonia Sculptor, Designer
Gianakos, Cris Sculptor, Environmental Artist
Gibson, Ralph H Photographer
Gibson, Sandra Painter, Filmmaker
Giffuni, Flora Baldini Painter, Lecturer
Gilden, Bruce Photographer
Gimblett, Max(well) Painter, Sculptor
Ginsburg, Max Painter, Illustrator
Giorno, John Conceptual Artist, Printmaker
Giovanopoulos, Paul Painter
Gitlin, Michael Sculptor, Draftsman
Gittler, Wendy Painter, Historian
Giurgola, Romaldo Architect
Giusti, Karin F Sculptor
Gladstone, Barbara Dealer, Historian
Glaser, Milton Designer, Illustrator
Glasson, Lloyd Sculptor, Educator
Glimcher, Arnold B Dealer, Writer
Gluska, Aharon Painter
Gobuzas, Aldona M Art Dealer, Consultant
Goddard, Donald Editor, Writer
Godwin, Judith Painter
Goell, Abby Jane Painter, Assemblage Artist, Printmaker
Goertz, Augustus Frederick, III Painter, Photographer
Goffman, Judy Goffman Cutler Art Dealer, Gallery Owner
Gold, Lois M Painter
Gold, Martha B Sculptor, Painter
Gold, Sharon Cecile Painter, Educator
Goldberg, Ira A Artist
Goldberg, Jim Photographer
Goldberg, Judith Art Dealer
Goldberg, Michael Painter
Goldberg, RoseLee Historian, Curator
Goldberger, Paul Jesse Critic, Writer, Educator, Editor
Golden, Eunice Painter, Filmmaker
Goldin, Leon Painter
Goldin, Nan Photographer
Goldman, Matt Conceptual Artist, Kinetic Artist
Goldner, Janet Sculptor
Goldring, Nancy Deborah Visual Artist, Educator
Goldsmith, Barbara Writer, Historian
Golici, Ana artist
Gomez-Quiroz, Juan Manuel Painter, Printmaker
Gonzalez-Falla, Sondra Gilman Patron
Goodman, Helen Historian, Critic
Goodman, James Neil Dealer, Collector
Goodman, Marian Dealer, Publisher
Goodnough, Robert Painter
Gordon, Coco Environmental Artist, Writer
Gordon, Douglas Sculptor
Gordon, James A Patron
Gorewitz, Shalom Video Artist
Gorney, Jay Philip Gallerist
Gornik, April Painter, Printmaker
Goss, Jared Curator
Gould, Nadia D Painter, Writer
Gould, Philip Curator, Collector
Gourevitch, Jacqueline Painter
Graham, Daniel H Conceptual Artist, Environmental Artist
Graham, Robert Sculptor
Grandpré, Mary Illustrator
Grannon, Katy Photographer
Grassi, Marco Conservator, Restorer
Grazda, Edward Photographer
Greely, Hannah Artist
Green, Denise G Painter
Green, George D Painter
Green, Wilder Administrator, Architect
Greenberg, Irwin Painter, Instructor
Greenblat, Rodney Alan Painter, Designer
Greenfield-Sanders, Timothy Photographer
Greer, Jane Ruth Sculptor
Gregorian, Vartan Patron
Griefen, John Adams Painter, Printmaker
Griffin, Chris A Sculptor
Grigoriadis, Mary Painter
Groover, Jan Photographer
Gross, Julie Painter
Gross, Rainer Painter
Grosvenor, Robert Sculptor
Gruen, John Critic, Writer
Gruss, Martin David Patron
Guccione, Juanita Painter
Guida, Dominick Painter
Gund, Agnes & Daniel Shapiro Collector, Administrator, Patron
Gunderson, Karen Painter
Gursky, Andreas Photographer
Gutzeit, Fred Painter, Educator
Guyton, Wade Painter
Gwathmey, Charles architect
GXI Painter, Writer
Haacke, Hans Christoph Sculptor, Conceptual Artist
Haas, Richard John Printmaker, Muralist
Hacklin, Allan Dave Painter, Sculptor
Haessle, Jean-Marie Georges Painter
Hafif, Marcia Painter, Educator
Hagin, Nancy Painter
Hai Chang, Willow Hai Director
Halaby, Samia A Painter, Writer
Halahmy, Oded Sculptor
Halasz, Piri Critic, Historian
Hall, William A architect
Halley, Peter Painter
Hamer, Charles James Painter
Hammond, Jane Printmaker, Painter
Handler, Janet Sculptor, Painter
Hannah, Duncan Rathbun Painter
Hapgood, Susan T Curator, Critic
Harbutt, Charles Photographer
Harder, Rodney Painter
Hardy, Hugh Architect
Hardy, John Painter
Harkins, George C, Jr Painter
Harris, Carolyn Painter
Harrison, Rachel Artist
Hartman, Joanne A Painter, Educator
Hartman, Rose Photographer, Editor
Harvest, Judith R Conceptual Artist, Painter
Harvey, Peter Francis Painter, Designer
Haskell, Barbara Curator
Hatton, Julian Burroughs, III Painter
Hauptman, Susan Illustrator
Hay, A John Historian, Educator
Hay, Alex Painter, Sculptor
Healy, Julia Schmitt Painter, Educator
Heartney, Eleanor Critic, Curator
Hecht, Irene Painter
Hedberg, Gregory Scott Art Dealer, Gallery Director
Hedstrom, Ana Lisa Craftsman
Heffernan, Julie Painter
Heiferman, Marvin Curator, Writer, Publisher
Heinemann, Peter Painter, Instructor, Educator
Heintz, Florent Appraiser
Heinz, Susan Administrator
Heizer, Michael Environmental Artist, Sculptor
Heller, Dorothy Painter
Hendricks, David Charles Painter, Visual Artist
Hendricks, Geoffrey Painter, Environmental Artist
Henry, Fredrick B Patron
Henselmann, Caspar Sculptor, Illustrator
Hepper, Carol Sculptor
Herfield, Phyllis Painter
Herrera, Arturo Collage Artist
Herrera, Carmen Painter
Herring, Oliver Painter
Hibbs, Barbara J E Painter, Instructor
Highstein, Jene Sculptor
Hildebrand, June Marianne Printmaker, Illustrator
Hill, Daniel G Painter

NEW YORK (cont)

Hill, James Berry Dealer
Hill, J(ames) Tomilson Collector
Hill, Janine collector
Hilson, Douglas Painter, Educator
Hinman, Charles B Painter, Educator
Hirsch, Faye Editor
Hobbs, Gerald S Dealer, Publisher
Hochfield, Sylvia Editor
Hodes, Barney Sculptor
Hodges, Jim Painter
Hofer, Evelyn Photographer
Hoff, Margo Painter, Collage Artist
Hoffman, Nancy Dealer
Holabird, Jean Painter, Printmaker
Holdeman, Joshua Collector, Appraiser
Holl, Steven Myron architect
Holland, Juliet Painter
Hollerbach, Serge Painter, Instructor
Holstad, Christian Artist
Holtz, Itshak Jack Painter, Printmaker
Holzman, Eric Painter
Hopkins, Budd Painter, Sculptor
Horn, Roni Sculptor
Horowitz, (Mr & Mrs) Raymond J Collectors
Horsfield, Craigie Artist
Hort, Michael Collector
Hort, Susan Collector
Horvat, Olga Painter, Collage Artist
Hotchner, Holly Museum Director, Conservator, Curator
Hoving, Thomas Consultant
Howat, John Keith Curator, Historian
Howell, James Painter, Architect
Hubbard, Teresa Filmmaker
Huffington, Anita Sculptor, Draftsman
Hughes, Robert S F Critic, Lecturer
Hull, Cathy Illustrator, Conceptual Artist
Humphrey, Nene Sculptor, Instructor
Hunt, Bryan Sculptor, Painter
Hunt, Richard Howard Sculptor
Hunter, Paul Painter, Sculptor
Hunter-Stiebel, Penelope Hunter Stiebel Curator
Hurson, Michael Draftsman, Painter
Hurst, Robert Jay Patron
Hurt, Susanne M Painter
Hurwitz, Adam
Huxtable, Ada Louise Critic, Historian
Hyman, Isabelle Historian, Educator
Icahn, Carl Celian Collector
Iimura, Takahiko Filmmaker, Video Artist
Iles, Chrissie curator
Impiglia, Giancarlo Painter, Sculptor
Incandela, Gerald Jean-Marie Photographer, Muralist
Insley, Will Painter, Draftsman
Ireland, Patrick Conceptual Artist
Irwin, Robert Environmental Artist
Isaacson, Lynn Judith Painter, Sculptor
Itchkawich, David Michael Printmaker, Illustrator
Ives, Colta Feller Curator, Educator
Iwamoto, Ralph Shigeto Painter
Jaar, Alfredo Sculptor
Jacir, Emily Photographer
Jacobs, Jim Painter, Printmaker
Jacquemon, Pierre Painter
Jacquette, Julia L Painter
Jacquette, Yvonne Helene Painter, Printmaker
Jae Sculptor, Jewelry Designer
Jaffe, Irma B Historian, Educator
Jannetti, Tony Printmaker, Designer
Jansen, Angela Bing Painter, Printmaker
Jaramillo, Virginia Painter
Jaudon, Valerie Painter
Jeff Painter, Photographer
Jeffers, Wendy Jane Curator, Artist
Jencks, Penelope Sculptor
Jennifer, Todd Filmmaker
Jensen, Bill Painter
Jerins, Edgar Painter
Jeynes, Paul Sculptor, Painter
Joelson, Suzanne Painter
Johnson, Cecile Ryden Painter, Publisher
Johnson, Guy Painter
Johnson, J Stewart Curator, Consultant
Johnson, Miani (Marianne) Guthrie Dealer, Consultant
Jones, Carter R(uthven), Jr Sculptor
Jones & Ginzel Sculptors
Juarez, Roberto Painter
Judson, Jeannette Alexander Painter, Collage Artist
Jurinko, Andy (Andrew) Floyd Painter
Kabakov, Ilya Conceptual Artist, Painter
Kahan, Alexander Dealer, Consultant
Kahn, Robin Conceptual Artist, Collage Artist
Kahn, Susan B Painter
Kaish, Luise Sculptor, Painter
Kaish, Morton Painter, Educator
Kalina, Richard Painter, Printmaker
Kalisher, Simpson Photographer
Kallir, Jane Katherine Art Dealer, Writer
Kampf, Avram S Educator, Curator
Kan, Diana Painter, Lecturer
Kane, Bob Paul Painter
Kang, Ik-Joong Painter, Sculptor
Kaplan, Flora Edouwaye S Educator, Curator
Kapp, David Painter
Karafel, Lorraine Writer, Critic
Kardon, Dennis Printmaker
Kardon, Janet Museum Director, Curator
Karlen, Mark Educator
Katz, Alex Painter
Katz, Leandro Assemblage Artist, Filmmaker
Katz, Morris Painter
Katzen, Hal Zachery Dealer
Katzman, Lawrence (Kaz) Designer, Cartoonist
Kaufman, Henry Patron
Kaufman, Irving Painter, Educator
Kaufman, Jane Painter, Sculptor
Kaufman, Jason Edward Critic, Editor
Kaufman, Nancy Art Advisor, Writer
Kaufmann, Robert Carl Art Librarian
Kavleski, Charleen Verena Conceptual Artist, Sculptor
Kawashima, Takeshi Painter, Sculptor
Kaz, Nathaniel Sculptor, Instructor
Keeley, Shelagh Historian, Painter
Keerl, Beat Painter, Photographer
Keever, Kim Photographer, Painter
Keller, Frank S Painter
Keller, Marthe Painter
Kelley, Mike Painter
Kelly, Ellsworth Painter, Sculptor
Kelly, Mary Conceptual Artist, Sculptor
Kelsey, John Director, Writer
Kersels, Martin Conceptual Artist, Illustrator
Kessler, Jon A Sculptor
Khalil, Claire Anne Painter
Khalil, Mohammad O Graphic Artist, Printmaker
Kidwell, Michele Falik Historian, Writer
Kihlstedt, Maja Painter, Printmaker
Kim, Po (Hyun) Painter
Kimmel-Cohn, Roberta Dealer, Writer
Kimmelman, Michael Critic
Kimura, Riisaburo Painter, Printmaker
Kind, Phyllis Art Dealer
Kinney, Gilbert Hart Collector, Administrator
Kinstler, Everett Raymond Painter, Instructor
Kirschenbaum, Bernard Edwin Sculptor
Klauber, Rick Painter
Kleckner, Susan Photographer, Filmmaker
Kleeblatt, Norman L Curator, Critic
Kleemann, Ron Painter
Kleiman, Alan Painter, Sculptor
Klein, Cynthia Appraiser
Klein, Doris Printmaker, Sculptor
Kleinberg, Susan Artist
Knowles, Alison Performance Artist, Printmaker
Kobayashi, Hisako Painter
Koch, David Hamilton Patron
Kogod, Robert & Arlene Collector
Kolbowski, Silvia Conceptual Artist
Koltun, Frances Lang Collector, Lecturer
Koob, Pamela Nabseth Curator
Koons, Jeff Painter, Sculptor
Koplos, Janet Collector, Editor
Koppelman, Chaim Printmaker, Educator
Koppelman, Dorothy Painter, Consultant
Kopystiansky, Igor Conceptual Artist, Painter
Kopystiansky, Svetlana Conceptual Artist, Photographer
Korshak, Yvonne Historian, Educator
Kostelanetz, Richard Media Artist, Writer
Kouns, Marjorie K Painter, Photographer
Kowalski, Libby R Fiber Artist, Educator
Kozloff, Joyce Painter, Mosaic Artist
Kozloff, Max Photographer, Writer
Kramarsky, Werner & Sarah-Ann Collector
Kramer, Harry Painter
Kramer, Louise Muralist, Sculptor
Krashes, Barbara Painter
Kraus, Peter Steven Collector
Krauss, Rosalind E Historian, Critic
Kravis, Henry R Collector
Krens, Thomas Museum Director, Educator
Kriemelman, Sheila M Painter, Educator
Kriesberg, Irving Painter
Kronzon, Ziva Printmaker, Sculptor
Kuchta, Ronald Andrew Museum Director, Editor
Kuehn, Frances Painter
Kuehn, Gary Sculptor, Graphic Artist
Kulicke, Robert M Craftsman, Painter
Kultermann, Udo Art Historian, Architectural Historian
Kurahara, Ted N Painter, Educator
Kurtz, Elaine Painter
Kuryluk, Ewa Painter, Sculptor
Kurz, Diana Painter, Educator
Kuwayama, Tadaaki Painter, Sculptor
LaChapelle, David Photographer
Laderman, Gabriel Painter, Educator
Lally, James Joseph Dealer, Consultant
Lamagna, Carlo Educator
Lamarre, Paul Conceptual Artist, Sculptor
Lamm, Leonid Izrail Conceptual Artist, Painter
Lamonte, Angela Mae Painter
Landfield, Ronnie (Ronald) T Painter
Lane, Alvin S Collector
Lane, Marion Arrons Painter, Sculptor
Lanigan-Schmidt, Thomas Assemblage Artist, Instructor
Lansner, Fay Painter
Lanyon, Ellen Painter, Printmaker
LaRico, Benje Painter
Larsen, Jack Lenor Designer, Writer
Lasker, Joe (Joseph) L Painter, Illustrator-Childrens Books
Lasker, Jonathan Painter

NEW YORK (cont)
Laster, Paul Conceptual Artist
Laub, Stephen Sculpture
Lauder, Eveyln H Collector
Lauder, Jo Carole Collector
Lauder, Leonard Alan Administrator, Collector
Lauder, Ronald Stephen Collector, Patron
Lauf, Cornelia Curator, Art Historian
Laufer, Susan Painter
Lauridsen, Hanne Painter, Sculptor
Lawson-Johnston, Peter Orman Patron
Lawson-Johnston, Peter, II Patron
Lazarus, Lois Painter
Le, An-My Photographer
Leaf, June Painter, Sculptor
Leavey, John Christopher Painter
LeBoff, Gail F Photographer
Lebron, Michael A Conceptual Artist, Graphic Artist
Lee, Catherine Sculptor, Painter
Lee, John Kemp Artist
Lee, Lara Producer, Filmmaker
Legrand, Yolene Painter, Muralist
Lehr, Janet Dealer
Lenaghan, Andrew Painter
Leonard, Zoe Photographer
Lerner, Marilyn Painter
Lerner, Martin Curator, Historian
Lerner, Sandra Painter, Collage Artist
Leslie, Alfred Painter, Filmmaker
Lethbridge, Julian Painter
Le Va, Barry Sculptor
Levering, Robert K Painter, Collage Artist
Levi, Josef Painter
Levin, Gail Historian, Photographer
Levin, Kim Critic, Curator
Levine, Jack Painter
Levine, Les Video Artist, Media Sculptor
Levine, Tomar Painter
Levinson, Mon Sculptor, Painter
Levinthal, David Lawrence Photographer
Levitt, Helen Photographer, Filmmaker
Levkova-Lamm, Innessa Critic, Curator
Levy, Bernard Dealer
Levy, S(tephen) Dean Dealer, Gallery Director
Levy, Tibbie Painter
Lewenz, Lisa Video Artist, Photographer
Lewis, Golda Assemblage Artist, Papermaker
Le Witt, Sol Painter
Libeskind, Daniel Architect
Liden, Hanna Photographer
Lieberman, Louis (Karl) Sculptor, Draftsman
Ligon, Glenn Painter
Liles, Raeford Bailey Painter, Sculptor
Lilyquist, Christine Egyptologist, Curator
Lin, Maya Y Sculptor
Linhares, Judith Painter
Linker, Kate Philippa Critic
Linn, Judy Photographer
Lippman, Sharon Rochelle Curator, Art Historian and Therapist
Lipsky, Pat Painter
Lipton, Sondra Painter, Sculptor
Little, James Painter, Printmaker
Livet, Anne Hodge Administrator, Critic
Liz-N-Val Sculptor, Painter
Loeb, Daniel S collector
Logemann, Jane Marie Painter
LoMonaco, Stephen Painter, Instructor
London, Alexander Collector, Publisher
Long, Charles Sculptor
Long, Rose-Carol Washton Historian, Administrator
Longo, Robert Sculptor, Painter
Longo, Vincent Painter, Printmaker
Lorber, D Martin H B Consultant, Historian
Lorber, Richard Critic, Educator
Lorenz, Nancy J Painter
Loring, John Painter, Printmaker
Losier, Marie Film Director
Lotringer, Sylvere Writer
Lovell, Whitfield M Painter
Lowry, Glenn D Museum Director
Lowry, Nicholas D Appraiser
Lucas, Bonnie Lynn Painter, Instructor
Lucas, Christopher Conceptual Artist
Lucchesi, Bruno Sculptor
Luce, C(harles) Beardsley Conceptual Artist
Lucier, Mary Video Artist, Photographer
Ludwig, Allan I Photographer, Art Historian
Luino, Bernardino Painter
Luisi, Jerry Sculptor, Instructor
Lukin, Sven Painter
Lurie, Boris Painter, Sculptor
Lusker, Ron Painter, Designer
Lutnick, Howard W Patron
Lynch, Florence Gallery Director
Lynn, Judith Painter, Illustrator, Tapestry Artist
Macadam, Barbara A Editor
Macaulay, David Alexander Designer, Illustrator
MacDonald, Robert R Director, Historian
MacDougall, Anne Art Dealer, Painter
Macklowe, Harry collector
Madsen, Loren Wakefield Sculptor
Madsen, Mette B Painter
Majore, Frank Photographer
Mallin, Judith Young Writer, Collector
Mallory, Ronald Painter, Sculptor
Mandelbaum, Lyn Painter, Printmaker
Manglano-Ovalle, Iñigo Sculptor
Mango, Robert J Painter
Mangold, Robert Peter Painter
Mangolte, Babette M Filmmaker, Photographer
Mann, Frank Painter, Graphic Artist
Mann, Katinka Sculptor, Photographer
Mann, Sally Photographer
Manville, Elsie Painter
Marais Painter
Marano, Lizbeth Sculptor, Photographer
Marcus, Gerald R Painter, Printmaker
Marcus, Gwen E. Sculptor
Marcus, Marcia Painter, Educator
Marden, Brice Painter, Printmaker
Margolis, Margo Painter
Mariani, Carlo Maria Painter
Marisol Sculptor
Mark, Phyllis Sculptor, Environmental Artist
Marketou, Jenny Video Artist
Marks, Matthew Stuart Art Dealer
Maron, Jeffrey Sculptor, Painter, Copper Alloy
Marron, Donald Baird Collector
Marshall, Richard Donald Historian, Curator
Marter, Joan Historian, Curator
Martin, Cameron Artist
Martin, Doug Painter
Martin, Knox Painter, Sculptor
Martin, Younghee Choi Painter, Draftsman, Curator
Martinez, Alfred Painter
Marton, Tutzi Painter, Sculptor
Martone, Michael Photographer
Masback, Dennis Painter, Instructor
Masheck, Joseph Daniel Cahill Historian, Critic
Masnyj, Yuri Painter, Sculptor
Mason, Francis Scarlett, Jr Administrator, Writer
Mason, Frank Herbert Painter, Instructor
Maurer, Gilbert Charles Patron
Maury, Richard Painter
Max, Peter Painter, Printmaker
Maxera, Oscar Painter, Assemblage Artist
Mayer, Rosemary Sculptor, Graphic Artist
Mazze, Irving Sculptor, Medalist
McCarron, Paul Art Dealer
McCarthy, Denis Painter
McCoy, Kevin & Jennifer Educator
McCoy, Pat A Writer, Critic
McDarrah, Fred William Photographer, Editor
McEvilley, Thomas Writer, Critic
McEwen, Adam sculptor, painter
McFadden, David Revere Curator
McFadden, Mary Collector, Designer
McGowin, Ed (William Edward) Painter, Sculptor
McGuire, Raymond J Patron
McKay, Renee Painter
McKee, David Malcolm Art Dealer
McKee, Renee Conforte Dealer
McKenzie, Mary Beth Painter
McKinley-Haas, Mary Painter, Designer
McMullan, James Burroughs Illustrator, Graphic Artist
McNeil, Dean S Sculptor, Photographer
McNeil, Wendy Lawson-Johnston Patron
McPherson, Craig Painter, Printmaker
McShine, Kynaston Leigh Curator, Critic
Meckseper, Josephine Sculptor
Mehretu, Julie Artist
Meier, Richard Alan Architect
Meisel, Louis Koenig Dealer, Historian
Meisel, Susan Pear Painter, Printmaker, Photographer
Mekas, Jonas Filmmaker
Melikian, Mary Painter
Mellman, Margery Painter
Mendelsohn, John Painter
Mendelson, Haim Painter, Printmaker
Menschel, Robert Benjamin Patron
Merkel, Jayne (Silverstein) Historian, Critic
Merrin, Edward H Dealer
Messer, Thomas M Museum Director, Historian
Metz, Frank Robert Painter, Designer
Metzger, Evelyn Borchard Painter, Sculptor
Metzker, Ray K Photographer, Educator
Meyer, Edward Henry Patron
Meyer, Susan E Editor, Writer
Meyer, Tobias Appraiser
Meyerowitz, Joel Photographer
Meyers, Dale (Mrs Mario Cooper) Painter, Instructor
Michaels, Barbara L Historian, Writer
Michals, Duane Photographer
Michelson, Eric Michael Painter
Mihaesco, Eugene Painter, Illustrator
Milbourn, Patrick D Painter, Illustrator
Miller, Harvey S Shipley Patron
Miller, Joan Painter, Collage Artist
Miller, Larry Painter, Video Artist
Miller, Richard Kidwell Painter
Miller, Robert Peter Art Dealer
Miller, Robert Warren Collector
Milonas, Minos (Herodotos Milonas) Painter, Sculptor
Mindich, Eric Patron
Mingwei, Lee Painter, Artist
Minskoff, Edward architectural firm executive
Minter, Marilyn A Painter
Miotte, Jean Painter
Mir, Aleksandra Artist
Miss, Mary Sculptor
Mitchell, Maceo Painter
Mitty, Lizbeth J Painter, Printmaker
Mnuchin, Steven T Patron

NEW YORK (cont)
Richter, Gerhard Painter
Riess, Lore Painter, Printmaker
Rifka, Judy Painter
Riggio, Leonard Book Dealer, Collector
Riley, Bridget Louise Painter
Rinehart, Michael Editor
Ritchie, Matthew painter
Rizzi, James Painter, Printmaker
Robbin, Tony Painter, Sculptor
Roberts, Russell L Painter
Robins, Joyce Sculptor, Landscape architect
Roche-Rabell, Arnaldo Painter
Rockburne, Dorothea Painter, Sculptor
Rockefeller, David Collector
Rodriguez, Geno (Eugene) Photographer, Museum Director
Rodriquez, Ernesto Angelo Painter, Designer
Roller, Marion Bender Sculptor, Painter
Rollins, Tim Painter, Instructor
Romano, Clare Painter, Printmaker
Romano, Salvatore Michael Sculptor, Kinetic Artist
Romberg, Osvaldo Architect
Rosand, David Historian, Critic
Rose, Herman Painter, Printmaker
Rose, Leatrice Painter, Instructor
Rose, Peter Henry Dealer
Rosenbaum, Allen Museum Director
Rosenbaum, Joan H Museum Director
Rosenberg, Alex Jacob Curator, Consultant, Appraiser
Rosenberg, Carole Halsband Art Dealer, Administrator
Rosenberg, Terry Painter, Sculptor
Rosenblum, Elizabeth Painter
Rosenblum, Robert Historian
Rosenfeld, Samuel L Art Dealer, Appraiser
Rosenfeld, Sharon Painter
Rosensaft, Jean Bloch Curator, Museum Director
Rosenthal, Deborah Maly Painter, Educator
Rosenthal, Howard Sculptor
Rosenthal, Mark L Curator, Historian
Rosenthal, Stephen Painter
Roser, Ce (Cecilia) Painter, Video Artist
Ross, Charles Environmental Artist, Sculptor
Ross, John T Printmaker, Educator
Ross, Rhoda Honore Painter, Instructor
Ross, Stephen M Patron
Roth, Steven Patron
Rothenberg, Susan Painter, Printmaker
Rovner, Michal Video Artist, Photographer
Row, David Painter
Rowland, Anne Photographer
Rubin, Lawrence Art Dealer, Collector
Rubinfien, Leo H Photographer, Filmmaker
Rubinstein, Raphael Critic
Ruda, Edwin Painter
Rudenstine, Angelica Zander Historian, Curator
Ruehlicke, Cornelia Iris Painter
Ruppersberg, Allen Conceptual Artist
Ruscha, Edward Joseph Painter, Filmmaker
Russotto, Paul Painter, Educator
Ruta, Peter Paul Painter
Rutzky, Ivy Sky Sculptor, Painter
Rychlak, Bonnie L Sculptor, Curator
Saar, Betye Assemblage Artist, Collage Artist
Sachs, Samuel, II Museum Director, Historian
Sackler, Mortimer DA Patrol
Sacks, Beverly Art Dealer, Consultant
Sade, Shuli Sculptor, Photographer
Sal, Jack Photographer, Painter
Salemme, Lucia Autorino Painter, Writer
Salle, David Painter
Salt, John Painter
Saltz, Jerry Critic, Curator
Samaras, Lucas Sculptor
Sandelman, Jonathan (Jon) E Patron
Sanders, Rhea Sanders Rabinovich Painter, Writer
Sandler, Barbara Painter
Sandlin, David Thomas Painter, Printmaker
Sandrow, Hope Photographer
Sanin, Fanny Painter
Santlofer, Jonathan Painter
Saphire, Lawrence M Writer, Art Dealer
Sato, Masaaki Painter
Saul, Andrew M Collector
Saulson, Harold Painter
Schab, Margo Pollins Art Dealer
Schaefer, Robert Arnold, Jr Photographer, Lecturer
Schaefer, Scott Jay Curator, Historian
Scharf, William Painter
Scheuer, Ruth Painter, Tapestry Artist
Schimansky, Donya Dobrila Librarian, Historian
Schjeldahl, Peter Critic, Editor
Schley, Reeve, III Painter
Schloss, Arleen P Painter
Schnabel, Julian Painter
Schneider, Jane Harris Sculptor
Schneider, Jo Anne Painter
Schneider, Lisa Dawn Dealer, Critic
Schneier, Donna Frances Dealer
Schoen, (Mr & Mrs) Arthur Boyer Collectors
Schonzeit, Benjamin Painter
Schorr, Collier artist
Schulman, Arlene Photographer, Writer
Schulson, Susan Painter, Silversmith
Schulte, Arthur D Collectors
Schuselka, Elfi Painter, Sculptor
Schwartz, Elliott S Photographer
Schwartz, Marvin D Historian
Schwartz, Sing-Si Photographer
Schwartz, Therese Painter, Writer
Scofidio, Ricardo & Elizabeth Diller Architect, Designer, Educator
Scribner, Charles, III Historian, Lecturer
Segall-Marx, Madeleine (Maddy Marx) Sculptor, Painter
Seide, Paul A Sculptor
Seidl, Claire Painter, Printmaker
Seltzer, Joanne Lynn Painter, Printmaker
Semmel, Joan Painter
Semmes, Beverly Sculptor
Sender, Adam D Collector
Seplowin, Charles Joseph Sculptor
Serra, Richard Sculptor
Serra, Rudy Sculptor
Shahn, Jonathan Sculptor
Shainman, Jack S Art Dealer, Gallery Director
Shapiro, Babe Painter
Shapiro, David Painter, Printmaker
Shapiro, Robert F & Anna Marie Collector
Sharp, Anne Catherine Painter, Collage Artist
Shashaty, Yolanda Victoria Painter
Shatter, Susan Louise Painter
Shaw, Paul Jefferson Calligrapher, Designer, Historian
Shechet, Arlene J Artist
Shechtman, George Henoch Dealer
Sheikh, Fazal Photographer
Sheirr, Olga (Krolik) Painter, Photographer
Shemesh, Lorraine R Painter
Sherman, Cindy Photographer
Sherman, Sarai Painter, Sculptor
Sherr, Ronald Norman Painter
Sherrod, Philip Lawrence Painter, Writer
Shibley, Gertrude Painter
Shore, Robert Painter, Illustrator
Shorr, Harriet Painter
Shostak, Ed (Edwin) Bennett Sculptor
Sibony, Gedi Sculptor
Sidawi, Raja Patron
Siegel, (Leo) Dink Illustrator, Cartoonist
Sigal-Ibsen, Rose Calligrapher, Painter
Sikander, Shahzia Painter
Siler, Todd (Lael) Painter, Sculptor
Silver, Shelly Andrea Video Artist, Filmmaker
Silverberg, June Roselyn Painter
Silverman, Burton Philip Painter
Simmons, Danny, Jr Gallery Director
Simmons, Laurie Photographer
Simon, Helene Sculptor
Simonds, Charles Frederick Sculptor, Architect
Simonian, Judith Painter, Collage Artist
Simpson, Merton D Painter, Dealer
Sims, Lowery Stokes Historian, Curator
Sirugo, Sal (Salvatore) Painter
Sischy, Ingrid B Editor, Curator
Skoglund, Sandy Photographer, Sculptor
Skupinski, Bogdan Kazimierz Printmaker, Painter
Sky, Alison Environmental Artist
Slavin, Arlene Sculptor
Slavin, Neal Photographer
Sleigh, Sylvia Painter, Educator
Sligh, Clarissa T Photographer, Painter
Slivka, David Sculptor
Sloan, Jennifer Sculptor
Sloat, Richard Joel Painter, Printmaker
Slone, Sandi Painter, Conceptual Artist
Slonem, Hunt Painter, Muralist
Smira, Shaoul Painter
Smith, Clare Appraiser
Smith, Elliot Dealer, Historian
Smith, Kiki Painter, Sculptor
Smith, Lawry Director, Curator
Smith, Mimi Sculptor, Conceptual Artist
Smith, Paul J Museum Director
Smith, Shirley Painter
Smith, Susan Painter, Collage Artist
Smith, Zak Artist
Smokler, Stanley B Sculptor, Assemblage Artist
Snelson, Kenneth D Sculptor, Painter
Snow, Dash Photographer
Snyder, Kit-Yin Sculptor, Environmental Artist
Soffer, Sasson Environmental Artist, Conceptual Artist
Sokolow, Isobel Folb Sculptor, Educator
Sokov, Leonid Sculptor, Painter
Solomon, Gerald Art Dealer, Painter
Solomon, Richard H Publisher, Art Dealer
Solomon, Rosalind Photographer
Solomon, (Mrs) Sidney L Collector
Sommer, Susan Painter, Printmaker
Sone, Yutaka Artist
Sonfist, Alan Environmental Artist
Sonnier, Keith Sculptor, Video Artist
Sono, Masayuki Architect
Sorce, Anthony John Painter
Soreff, Stephen Sculptor, Assemblage Artist
Sorkin, Emily Art Dealer, Gallery Director
Spector, Naomi Writer
Speiser, Stuart M Collector, Patron
Spelman, Jill Sullivan Painter
Spence, Andrew Painter
Sperakis, Nicholas George Painter, Printmaker
Spero, Nancy Painter, Collage Artist
Speyer, Jerry I Collector
Speyer, Nora Painter

NEW YORK (cont)
Youngblood, Daisy Sculptor
Younger, Robert M Sculptor
Zago, Tino (Agostino) C Painter
Zaleski, Jean Painter, Lecturer
Zaloudek, Duane Painter
Zapkus, Kes (Kestutis) Edward Painter
Zausner, Tobi Painter
Zeller, Frederic Sculptor
Zimmer, William Critic
Zimmerman, Elyn Sculptor, Environmental Artist
Zimmerman, Kathleen Marie Collage Artist, Painter
Zingale, Lawrence Painter
Zwack, Michael Painter, Sculptor

New York
Lynne, Michael Collector
Shaw, Jim Painter
Walgren, Frances J Appraiser

New York City
St. Lifer, Jane Consultant, Art Dealer

Newark
Williams, Wayne Francis Sculptor

Newburgh
Cady, Dennis Vern Conservator, Painter

Newfield
Weisman, Gary Michael Sculptor, Educator

Niverville
Abeles, Sigmund Printmaker, Painter

North Blenheim
Rotterdam, Paul Zwietnig-Rotterdam Painter

North Salem
Caporale-Greene, Wende Painter, Instructor
Greene, Daniel E Painter, Instructor
Savitt, Sam Painter, Illustrator

Northport
Jerviss, Joy Printmaker
Verzyl, June Carol Dealer, Collector
Wingerter, John Parker Painter

Norwood
Robbins, Michael Jed Painter, Printmaker
Strong, Leslie (Sutter) Sculptor, Ceramist
Sutter, James Stewart Sculptor, Educator

Nyack
Laemmle, Cheryl Painter
Rosen, Diane Painter, Muralist

Oakdale
Stewart, Dorothy S Painter, Printmaker

Oceanside
Bragg, E Ann Bragg Painter

Odessa
Stillman(Myers), Joyce L Painter, Lecturer

Olean
Pierce, Constance Laundon Printmaker, Painter

Olivebridge
Noble, Kevin Painter, Photographer

Oneida
Colway, James R Painter

Oneonta
Freckelton, Sondra Painter
Mullen, James Martin Educator, Printmaker

Orangeburg
Worth, Karen Sculptor

Orchard Park
English, Hal (Harold) J Painter

Orient
Weil, Marianne Sculptor
Wells, Mac Painter, Educator

Ossining
Adamy, George E Educator, Sculptor

Oswego
D'Innocenzo, Nick Sculptor, Painter, Printmaker, Designer
Fox, Michael David Sculptor, Professor,Photographer
O'Connell, George D Printmaker, Educator

Otego
Griffith, Roberta Ceramist, Painter

Otisville
Hodgkins, Rosalind Selma Painter

Oweto
Ahrens, Kent Museum Director, Historian

Oyster Bay
Bellospirito, Robyn Suzanne Painter, Writer
Kunstler, Morton Painter, Illustrator
Prey, Barbara Ernst Painter

Palisades
Galinsky, Norman Painter, Graphic Artist
Hyams, Harriet Stained Glass Artist, Sculptor
Knowlton, Grace Farrar Sculptor, Photographer
Porta, Siena Gillann Sculptor

Peekskill
Adelman, Dorothy (Lee) McClintock Printmaker, Instructor
Brown, Alice Dalton Painter
Osyczka, Bohdan Danny Painter
Straus, Marc Joshua Educator

Pelham
Gallagher, Kathleen Ellen Printmaker, Painter

Penn Yan
Berlyn, Sheldon Painter, Printmaker

Piermont
Berkon, Martin Painter
Schmidt, Edward William Painter

Pine Plains
Hoffman, Michael E Editor, Curator

Pittsford
Bliss, Harry James Painter, Illuminator

Plainview
Margulies, Isidore Sculptor, Kinetic Artist

Pleasantville
Barkley, James Painter, Designer

Port Chester
Sayles, Eva Painter

Port Ewen
Cote, Alan Painter

Port Jefferson
Flecker, Maurice Nathan Painter, Educator
Mason, Molly Ann Sculptor, Environmental Artist

Port Washington
Betensky, Rose Hart Painter, Art Administrator
Cunnick, Gloria Helen Painter
Fishman, Barbara (Ellen) Schwartz Painter, Printmaker
Schneider, Shellie Collage Artist, Painter

Potsdam
Hildreth, Joseph Alan Printmaker, Painter
McNamara, Mary Jo Historian, Educator

Poughkeepsie
Atlas, Nava Writer, Designer
Mundy, E James Museum Director, Educator
Reynard, Carolyn Cole Painter, Instructor
Tabak, Chaim Painter, Sculptor

Pound Ridge
Beckerman, Nancy Greyson Painter, Craftsman, Studio Art Quilter
Herbert, April H Sculptor
Korot, Beryl Video Artist, Painter
Manspeizer, Susan R Sculptor
Schwebel, Renata Manasse Sculptor

Purchase
Black, Leon David Collector
Gedeon, Lucinda Heyel Museum Director, Administrator
Hannum, Gillian Greenhill Educator, Historian
Parrino, George Painter, Educator
Sandler, Irving Harry Critic, Historian
Torlen, Michael Arnold Painter, Educator
Wachenheim, Edgar, III Patron
Zimiles, Murray Painter, Educator

Putnam Valley
Toulis, Vasilios (Apostolos) Printmaker, Educator

Queens Village
Ponsot, Claude F Educator, Painter

Quogue
Burkhardt, Ronald Robert Conceptual Artist, Painter
Kuehnl, Claudia Ann Goldsmith

Red Hook
Flynt, Robert Photographer

Rego Park
Maas, Marion Elizabeth Painter

Rensselaer
Semowich, Charles John Historian, Painter

Rhinebeck
Ewald, Wendy T Conceptual Artist, Educator
Froman, Ann Sculptor, Designer
Mavros, Donald Odysseus Ceramist, Sculptor
Rabinovich, Raquel Painter, Sculptor

Rhinecliff
Zimmermann, Philip Publisher, Painter

Richmond Hill
Eres, Eugenia Painter

Riverdale
Link, Phyllida K Painter, Educator
Putterman, Susan Lynn Curator, Administrator
Schaeffer, Martha J Art Dealer
Silberstein-Storfer, Muriel Rosoff Art Educator, Instructor

NEW YORK (cont)

Riverhead

Gilhooley, Dan Painter

Rochester

Chiarenza, Carl Photographer, Historian
Feuerherm, Kurt K Painter
Franklin, Don Painter, Photographer, Sculptor
Goodspeed, Barbara Painter
Holcomb, Grant Museum Director, Educator
Lyons, Joan Photographer
Margolis, Richard M Photographer, Artist
Marx, Robert Ernst Printmaker, Painter
Mertin, Roger Photographer
Paley, Albert Raymond Goldsmith, Designer
Sellers, William Freeman Sculptor, Painter
Sheller, G A Painter, Instructor
Singer, Alan Daniel Painter, Printmaker
Smith, Keith A Photographer, Printmaker
Taylor, Michael (Estes) Instructor, Sculptor
Witmeyer, Stanley Herbert Painter, Consultant

Rockville Centre

Resnick, Don Painter

Rocky Point

Aunio, Irene Painter

Romulus

Bermingham, Debra Pandell Painter

Ronkonkoma

Barbera, Ross William Painter

Roscoe

De Palma, Brett Painter, Sculptor

Roslyn

Finke, Leonda Froelich Sculptor, Draftsman, Educator
Treitler, Rhoda Chaprack Painter

Roslyn Heights

Faegenburg, Bernice K Painter, Printmaker
Hermann, Mildred L Collage Artist, Painter
Rotholz, Rina Printmaker

Ruby

Zaima, Stephen Gyo Painter, Sculptor

Rye Brook

Kline, Harriet Painter, Printmaker, Papermaker, Sculptor

Sag Harbor

Blanc, (William) Peter Sculptor, Painter
David, Cyril Frank Drawings, Painter
Diamond, Mary E B Painter
Harrison, Helen Amy Museum Director, Critic
Nicholson, Roy William Painter, Educator
Rizzie, Dan Collage Artist, Painter

Sagaponack

Dash, Robert Painter
Dunlap, Loren Edward Painter, Instructor

Saint Albans

Jones, Cynthia Clarke Collage Artist, Graphic Artist

Salem

Orlyk, Harry V Painter

Sands Point

Hanchey, Janet L Painter, Gilder
Stevens, Thelma K Educator, Dealer

Saratoga Springs

Bouchard, Paul E Painter
Brodie, Regis Conrad Ceramist, Painter
Cunningham, J Sculptor
Myers, Philip Henry Painter
Stake, Peter Educator
Upton, Richard Thomas Painter, Printmaker

Saugerties

Strider, Marjorie Virginia Sculptor, Painter

Scarsdale

Brilliant, Richard Educator, Writer
Frackman, Noel Critic, Historian
Mannor, Margalit Photographer, Conceptual Artist
Melnick, Myron J Sculptor, Collage Artist
Ries, Martin Painter, Printmaker
Roda, Rhoda Lillian Sablow Painter, Tapestry Artist
Yunich, Beverly B Collage Artist, Jeweler

Schenectady

Gilson, Giles Sculptor, Designer
Hatke, Walter Joseph Painter, Educator
Shaheen, Gary Edward Administrator, Collage Artist

Scottsville

Castle, Wendell Keith Sculptor
Urso, Leonard A Sculptor, Painter

Sea Cliff

Germano, Thomas Painter, Educator
Jacobs, David (Theodore) Sculptor, Kinetic Artist
Leipzig, Arthur Photographer, Educator
Seiden, Katie Sculptor, Assemblage Artist

Searingtown

Chichura, Diane B Administrator, Art Dealer

Setauket

Badalamenti, Fred L Painter, Educator
Guilmain, Jacques Historian, Painter
Kemp, Flo Printmaking

Shelter Island Heights

Culbertson, Janet Lynn (Mrs Douglas Kaften) Painter, Environmental Artist
Zeigler, George Gavin Painter,Sculptor

Shirley

Cohen, Jean Painter
Lieber, Edvard Painter, Filmmaker

Shokan

Werner, Howard Sculptor

Skaneateles

Crawford, Thom Cooney Painter, Sculptor

Sleepy Hollow

Perlmutter, Linda M Painter, Instructor

South Nyack

Beerman, John Thorne Painter
Churchill, Diane Painter

Southampton

Kanovitz, Howard Painter
Koehler, Henry Painter
Lerner, Abram Museum Director, Painter
Yoshiharu, Higa Printmaker, Photographer

Spencer

Grunberg, Slawomir Filmmaker

Spencerport

Stewart, Bill Sculptor, Ceramist
Wolsky, Jack Painter, Educator

Staatsburg

Fujita, Kenji Sculptor

Stamford

Powley, Donald Painter

Stanfordville

Anderson, Bruce A Goldsmith, Sculptor

Staten Island

Butti, Linda Painter, Educator
Coleman, A(llan) D(ouglass) Critic, Lecturer
Egbert, Elizabeth Frances Sculptor, Educator
Grabel, Susan Sculptor, printmaker - Misc. Media
Greenfield, Amy Filmmaker, Video Artist
Mailman, Cynthia Painter, Educator
Moore, Alan Willard Art Critic, Historian
Newhouse, Samuel I & Victoria, Jr Collector
Zaage, Herman H Printmaker, Educator

Stephentown

Gordon, Albert F Art Dealer

Stone Ridge

Bennett, Jamie Enamelist, Sculptor

Stony Brook

Bogart, Michele Helene Historian, Curator
Cooper, Rhonda H Gallery Director, Curator
Ellinger, Ilona E Painter, Educator
Kuspit, Donald Burton Historian, Critic
Levine, Martin Printmaker, Educator
Pekarsky, Mel(vin) Hirsch Painter, Educator
Pindell, Howardena Doreen Painter, Educator

Stuyvesant

Tripp, Susan Gerwe Museum Director

Suffern

Leigh, Harry E Sculptor, Painter

Syosset

Greene, Chris (Christine) E Cartoonist, Painter

Syracuse

Bakke, Karen Lee Assemblage Artist, Calligrapher
Belfort-Chalat, Jacqueline Sculptor, Painter
De Wan-Carlson, Anna Printmaker, Painter
Dwyer, James Painter, Educator
Harootunian, Claire M Sculptor, Educator
Jerry, Michael John Educator, Craftsman
Lantzy, Donald Michael Administrator, Printmaker
Orentlicher, John Video Artist, Sculptor
Reed, Cleota Historian, Lecturer
Sadle, Amy Ann Brandon Printmaker, Publisher
Sellers, John Lewis Educator, Designer
Sickler, Michael Allan Painter, Educator
Skoler, Celia Rebecca Consultant, Gallery Director
Smith, Lawson Wentworth Sculptor, Educator
Spencer, Susan Elizabeth Painter, Instructor
Tatham, David Frederic Historian
Trop, Sandra Director
Waddy, Patricia Historian
Witkin, Jerome Painter, Draftsman

Tappan

Dell, Robert Christopher Environmental Artist, Educator
Golbert, Sandra Artist, Craftsman

Tarrytown

Butler, Joseph Thomas Curator, Writer
Gursoy, Ahmet Painter

NEW YORK (cont)
Holt, David John Painter, Educator

Tillson
Debrosky, Christine A Painter

Tivoli
Sillman, Amy Painter, Educator

Treadwell
Macek, M D (Mila D) Painter

Trumansburg
Vann, Samuel LeRoy Painter

Tuxedo Park
Domjan, Evelyn Painter, Printmaker
Simon, Robert Barry Art Dealer, Historian

Ulster Park
Clarke, Bud (Warren) F Designer, Painter

Upper Nyack
Elliot, John Theodore Painter, Writer,Teacher
Elliot, Sheila Arts, Writer, Administrator

Utica
Baber, Bob Administrator
Bloch, Milton Joseph Art Administrator, Museum Director
Cimbalo, Robert W Painter, Printmaker
Schweizer, Paul Douglas Art Historian, Museum Director

Valhalla
Lombardi, Don Dominick Artist

Valley Cottage
Heinzen, MaryAnn Painter, Assemblage Artist
Longo-Muth, Linda L Painter, Instructor

Valley Stream
Borg, Joseph Printmaker
Fusco, Yolanda Painter, Printmaker
Wasserman, Muriel Painter

Verbank
Streeter, Tal Sculptor, Writer

Victor
Keyser, William Alphonse, Jr Craftsman, Painter, Sculptor

Voorheesville
O'Connor, Thom Printmaker

Wading River
Marlow, Audrey Swanson Painter, Designer

Wainscott
Brach, Paul Henry Painter
Knigin, Michael Jay Painter, Printmaker
Russo, Alexander Peter Painter, Educator
Zucker, Joseph I Painter

Wallkill
Koch, Edwin E Sculptor, Painter

Wantagh
Glaser, David Painter, Sculptor

Wappingers Falls
Di Fate, Vincent Illustrator, Painter

Warrensburg
Collado, Lisa Collage Artist, Assemblage Artist

Warwick
Lane, Lois Painter, Printmaker
Mack, Daniel R Designer, Craftsman
Talbot, Jonathan Painter, Collage Artist

Wang, Gar Painter

Washingtonville
Mangold, Sylvia Plimack Painter

Water Mill
Chalif, Ronnie Sculptor
Mac Whinnie, John Vincent Painter, Sculptor

Webster
Mann, Ward Palmer Painter

Wells
Van Alstine, John Richard Sculptor

Wellsville
Underhill, William Sculptor

West Falls
Lindemann, Edna M Museum Director, Educator

West Nyack
Ramos, Julianne Administrator, Consultant
Yeiser, Charles William Painter, Art Dealer
Zansky, Michael Painter, Sculptor, Photographer

West Point
Reel, David Mark Museum Director, Curator

Westburg
Barboza, Anthony Photographer, Painter

Westbury
Sherbell, Rhoda Sculptor, Consultant
Slapo, Daniel E Painter

Westport
Owen, Frank (Franklin) Charles Painter
Schira, Cynthia Tapestry Artist

White Plains
Cove, Rosemary Sculptor, Painter
Manes, Belle Painter

White Plains
Fisher, Jerome & Anne Collector

Whitestone
Andrews, Marion Painter
Rahr, Stewart & Carol

Willow
Goetz, Mary Anna Painter, Instructor

Willsboro
Reynolds, Patricia Ellen Painter

Wilmington
Leary, Daniel Draftsman, Printmaker

Woodmere
Ginsburg, Estelle Painter, Sculptor
Greenfield, Joan Beatrice Painter, Enamelist
Winick, Bernyce Alpert Painter, Photographer

Woodside
Fluek, Toby Painter, Graphic Artist
Katz, Don Sculptor, Stained Glass Artist
Salgian, Mitzura Artist
Warren, Tom Photographer, Conceptual Artist

Woodstock
Allen, Roberta Conceptual Artist, Photographer, Collage Artist
Angeloch, Robert Painter, Printmaker
Currie, Bruce Painter, Printmaker
Epstein, Yale Painter, Printmaker
Jordan, John L Sculptor, Video Artist

Lieberman, Meyer Frank Painter, Printmaker
Mackintosh, Sandra Sculpture, Collage Artist
McGloughlin, Kate Printmaker, Painter
Morse, Mitchell Ian Dealer, Consultant

Worcester
Habenicht, Wenda Sculptor
Parisi, Martha Graphic Artist, Printmaker

Yaphank
Freund, Pepsi Painter, Collage Artist

Yonkers
Agee, William C Educator, Historian
Botwinick, Michael Museum Director
Byars, Donna Sculptor, Collage Artist
Civale, Biagio A Printmaker, Painter
Gallo, William Victor Cartoonist, Illustrator
Gioello, Debbie Painter, Designer
Segal, Barbara Jeanne Sculptor, Instructor

Yorktown Heights
Kaupelis, Robert John Painter, Educator
Naumann, Francis M Historian, Curator
Witt, John Painter, Printmaker
McCall, Anthony Filmmaker

NORTH CAROLINA

Conley, Zeb Bristol, Jr Collector, Gallery Director

Asheboro
Halligan, Roger Phillip Sculptor, Designer

Asheville
Blunk, Joyce Elaine Assemblage Artist, Sculptor
Bora (Borayer), Vadim Makharbekovich Sculptor, Painter
Cooke, Samuel Tucker Painter, Educator
Godfrey, Robert Painter, Critic
Gray, Robert Ward Administrator
Krause, Bonnie Jean Museum Consultant
Loewer, Henry Peter Writer, Illustrator
Martin, Doris-Marie Constable Designer, Sculptor
McDaniel, William Harrison (Harry) Sculptor
Outland, Wendy Helen Consultant, Lecturer

Belmont
Mintich, Mary Ringelberg Sculptor, Craftsman

Black Mountain
Buck, Porge Printmaker

Blowing Rock
Haley, Gail E Illustrator, Collector

Boone
Humphrey, Judy Lucille Graphic Artist, Printmaker
Hutchens, James William Administrator, Educator

Brevard
De Nike, Michael Nicholas Sculptor, Writer

Burnsville
Bernstein, William Joseph Designer, Glassblower
Levin, Robert Alan Glass Blower, Sculptor

Cary
Baker, Nancy Schwartz Painter, Printmaker
Daniels, Astar Charlotte Louise Daniels Stained Glass Artist, Painter

NORTH CAROLINA (cont)

Casar

Trotman, Bob Sculptor

Cashiers

Whiteside, William Albert, II Painter, Instructor

Chapel Hill

Bolas, Gerald Douglas Museum Director, Educator
Dougherty, Patrick T Sculptor
Folda, Jaroslav (Thayer), III Historian
Hirschfield, Jim Sculptor
Huggins, Victor, Jr Painter, Printmaker
James, A Everette, Jr Patron, Writer
Kinnaird, Richard William Painter, Educator
Millard, Charles Warren, III Director, Writer
Noe, Jerry Lee Sculptor, Educator
Phoenix, Kaola Allen Collage Artist, Painter
Prange, Sally Bowen Ceramist, Sculptor
Rogers, John H Sculptor, Consultant
Saltzman, Marvin Painter
Sturgeon, Mary C Educator, Historian
Zaborowski, Dennis J Painter, Educator

Charlotte

Byrum, Donald Roy Educator, Printmaker
Haack, Cynthia R Painter, Printmaker
Hobbs, Frank I, Jr Painter, Instructor
MacKillop, Rod Painter, Educator
Melberg, Jerald Leigh Art Dealer, Collector
Segal, Tama & David Dealer, Curator
Shaw, Mary Todd Sculptor, Painter
Sires, Jonathan Paul Sculptor
Stout, Donna Phipps Painter
Strassberg, Roy I Ceramist, Sculptor
Walker, John Seibels painter

Columbus

Kornmayer, J Gary Painter, Photographer

Davidson

Grosch, Laura Painter, Printmaker
Jackson, Herb Painter, Printmaker
Strawn, Martha (A) Photographer, Educator
Warren, Russ Painter

Durham

Bruzelius, Caroline Astrid Director, Historian
Markman, Sidney David Administrator, Historian
Mezzatesta, Michael Historian, Museum Director
Noland, William Sculptor, Photographer
Pendergraft, Norman Elveis Museum Director, Historian
Rorschach, Kimerly Museum Director
Skoler, Celia Rebecca Librarian, Writer
Tempest, Gerard Francis Painter, Sculptor
Wharton, Annabel Jane Historian

Elizabeth City

McIntosh, Jerry C Educator, Administrator

Fayetteville

Prewitt, Merle R(ainey) Painter

Four Oaks

Creech, Franklin Underwood Sculptor, Graphic Artist

Garner

Sweitzer, Charles Leroy Muralist, Painter

Gastonia

Waufle, Alan Duane Museum Director

Goldsboro

Turlington, Patricia R Painter, Sculptor

Greensboro

Barker, Walter William, Jr Painter, Writer
Doll, Nancy Director
Goldstein, Carl Historian
Gregory, Joan Educator, Painter
Janschka, Fritz Painter, Graphic Artist
Mason, Novem M Sculptor, Educator
Tucker, James Ewing Curator, Painter

Greenville

Chamberlain, Charles Ceramist, Educator
Dorsey, Michael A Painter, Administrator
Edmiston, Sara Joanne Educator, Designer
Hartley, Paul Jerome Painter, Educator
Laing, Richard Harlow Administrator, Artist
Ritzer, Gail L Collage Artist, Ceramist
Sexauer, Donald Richard Instructor, Printmaker
Stanforth, Melvin Sidney Educator, Painter
Wallin, Leland Dean Painter, Educator

Hendersonville

Wilson, Cynthia Lindsay Painter

High Point

Fick, William George Printmaker

Hillsborough

DeGette, Andrea M Filmaker, Director
Fantazos, Henryk Michael Painter, Printmaker

Jacksonville

De La Vega, Antonio Painter, Designer

Kinston

Dance, Robert Bartlett Painter, Printmaker

Lenoir

Michaux, Henry Gaston Educator, Sculptor

Lexington

Frontz, Leslie Painter
Moon, Jim (James) Monroe Painter, Printmaker

Marshville

Griffin, Sallie Thompson Painter, Photographer

Mc Leansville

Lindahl, Toni Painter

Mebane

Troutman, Jill Painter

Mount Pleasant

Kessler, Jane Q Curator, Writer

New Hill

Bane, McDonald (Mackey) Painter, Curator

Oak Ridge

Nydorf, Roy Herman Painter, Printmaker

Penland

Fero, Shane Glass Blower, Collage Artist
McLaughlin, Jean Wallace Administrator, Consultant

Pittsboro

Higgins, Edward Koelling Ceramist, Jeweler
Higgins, MaryLou Ceramist, Painter
Schabacker, Betty Barchet Painter

Pleasant Garden

Chin, Ric Lecturer, Painter, Calligrapher

Raleigh

Banker, Maureen Director, Printmaker
Brown, Charlotte Vestal Museum Director, Historian
Chianese, Carol Burnard Painter
Coffey, John William, II Curator, Museum Director
Davis, Meredith J Graphic Artist, Educator
Diaz, Lope (Max) Painter, Educator
Hansley, Lee Art Dealer, Curator
Harrell, Margaret Ann Photographer
Hertzman, Gay Mahaffy Administrator, Historian
Jenkins, Mary Anne Keel Painter, Instructor
Jones, W Louis Painter, Sculptor
McKim, George Edward Painter, Graphic Artist
Morgan, Clarence (Edward) Painter, Educator
Shields, Anne Kesler Painter, Assemblage Artist
Williams, Benjamin Forrest Curator, Historian

Salisbury

Hood, Walter Kelly Historian, Painter
Shalkop, Robert Leroy Consultant
Waller, Susan Gallery Director, Writer

Sanford

Higgins, (George) Edward Sculptor

Southport

Brown, June Gottlieb Painter, Instructor

Spruce Pine

Littleton, Harvey K Educator, Glass Blower

Washington

Jakub, Jeffrey Andrew Painter, Illustrator

Waynesville

Conneen, Jane W Printmaker, Book Artist
Conneen, Mari M Painter

Wilkesboro

Nichols, Ward H Painter

Wilmington

Conner, Ann Printmaker, Painter

Wilson

Marshall, Thomas E Educator, Printmaker

Winston Salem

Potter, Ted Painter, Administrator

Winston-Salem

Browning, Dixie Burrus Painter, Writer
Faccinto, Victor Paul Painter, Filmmaker
Finn, David Sculpture
Funderburk, Amy Elizabeth Painter, Photographer
Gray, Thomas Alexander Collector
Oubre, Hayward Louis Sculptor, Painter
Saunders, Edith Dariel Chase Painter, Instructor

NORTH DAKOTA

Fargo

Pauley, Edward E Administrator

Grand Forks

Krueger, Lothar David Painter, Educator
Paulsen, Brian Oliver Painter, Printmaker
Reuter, Laurel J Museum Director, Writer

Minot

Olson, Linda A Sculptor, Educator
Piehl, Walter Jason, Jr Painter, Educator

New Rockford

Schaefer, Ronald H Printmaker, Educator

NORTH DAKOTA (cont)

Thompson

McElroy, Jacquelyn Ann Printmaker, Educator

OHIO

Akron

Bierbaum, Gretchen Ann Collage Artist, Educator
Borowiec, Andrew Photographer, Educator
Drumm, Don Sculptor, Craftsman
Kahan, Mitchell Douglas Museum Director, Historian
Keener, Polly Leonard Illustrator, Writer
Kleidon, Dennis Arthur Educator, Designer
Korow-Bieber, Elinore Maria Vigh Painter, Educator
Moon, Marc Painter, Instructor
Rogers, P J Printmaker, Collage
Rohrbacher, Patricia Painter, Instructor
Tannenbaum, Barbara Lee Curator, Historian

Ashtabula

Morisue, Glenn Takanori Painter, Instructor

Athens

Hostetler, David L Sculptor
Kortlander, William Painter, Historian
Lazuka, Robert Artist
Roberts, Donald Educator, Printmaker
Werger, Art(hur) Lawrence Printmaker, Educator

Aurora

Lawton, Florian Kenneth Painter, Lecturer

Bay Village

Kocar, George Frederick Painter, Illustrator
St Denis, Paul Andre Painter, Instructor

Berea

Cole, Harold David Historian, Educator

Bluffton

Velasquez, Oscar Painter, Illustrator

Bowling Green

Bandy, Ron F Painter, Educator
Hilty, Thomas R Graphic Artist, Painter
Lee, Briant Hamor Historian, Educator
Ocvirk, Otto G Sculptor, Printmaker

Brecksville

Miller, John Paul Jeweler

Chagrin Falls

Toole, Lois Salmon Painter, Watercolor

Chillicothe

Gough, Robert Alan Painter

Cincinnati

Betsky, Aaron Museum director
Brod, Stanford Designer, Educator
Brown, Daniel Critic, Collector
Burleigh, Kimberly Printmaker, Educator
Cartwright, Roy R Ceramist
Chatterjee, Jay (Jayanta) Administrator, Educator
Coleman, Constance Depler Painter
Dewitt, Katharine Cramer Museum Director
Driesbach, Walter Clark, Jr Sculptor, Instructor
Foster, April Printmaker, Educator
Harper, Gregory Franklin Director, Curator
Helgeson, Phillip Lawrence Painter, Illustrator, Graphic Artist
Kelley, Donald William Printmaker, Sculptor
Kowal, Cal (Lee) Curator, Photographer
Lohre, Thomas George, Jr Painter, Sculptor
Lynch, Matthew Artist
Reichert, Marilyn F Museum Director
Rub, Timothy F Museum Director
Samson, Carl Joseph Painter, Instructor
Schrohenloher, Sally A Painter
Shearer, Linda Museum Director
Smith, Gregory Allgire Educator, Administrator
Solway, Carl E Dealer
Spangenberg, Kristin L Curator, Historian
Stevens, Jane Alden Photographer, educator
Stewart, John P Painter, Printmaker
Timpano, Anne Museum Director, Historian
Warren, Julianne Bussert Baker Photographer, Historian
Wood, McCrystle Educator, Administrator
Woodham, Derrick James Sculptor

Cleveland

Abid, Ann B Librarian
Barrie, Dennis Ray Museum Director, Historian
Bates, Kenneth Francis Enamelist, Craftsman
Cassill, Herbert Carroll Printmaker, Educator
Channing, Susan Rose Administrator, Photographer
Checefsky, Bruce E Photographer
Cintron, Joseph M Painter, Educator
Curnow, Kathy Educator
Czuma, Stanislaw J Historian, Curator
Deming, David Lawson Sculptor, Educator
Dingwall, Kenneth Painter, Instructor
Fechter, Claudia Zieser Curator, Writer
Ferbert, Mary Lou Painter
Floyd, Carl Leo Sculptor, Environmental Artist
Hinson, Tom Everett Curator, Historian
Jergens, Robert Joseph Painter, Educator
Kangas, Gene Sculptor, Author
Kowalski, Raymond Alois Painter
Landau, Ellen Gross Historian, Critic
Lewis, Peter Benjamin Collector
Pearman, Sara Jane Historian, Librarian
Plevin, Gloria Joy Painter, Printmaker
Reid, Katharine Lee Museum Director, Curator
Schreckengost, Viktor Designer, Sculptor
Snyder, Jill Museum Director
Sweet, Marsha (Marsha) Sweet Welch Printmaker, Painter
Taft, Frances Prindle Educator, Painter - Watercolor
Thurmer, Robert Sculptor, Gallery Director

Cleveland Heights

Schneider, Richard Durbin Ceramist, Instructor

Columbus

Accetta, Suzanne Rusconi Painter, Instructor
Barrett, Terry M Writer, Educator
Bell, Karen A Educator
Bennett, John M Writer, Graphic Artist
Black, David Evans Sculptor
Chafetz, Sidney Printmaker, Educator
Dodrill, Donald Lawrence Painter, Illustrator
Griffith, Dennison W Educator, Adminstrator, Artist
Hamilton, Ann Katherine Sculptor
Kuehn, Edmund Karl Painter, Lecturer
Massey, Charles Wesley, Jr Printmaker, Educator
Miller, Tracy A Video Artist
Morganstern, Anne McGee Historian, Educator
Morganstern, James Historian, Educator
Payne Goodwin, Louis (Doc) Cartoonist, Painter
Robinson, Aminah Brenda Lynn sculpture, painter
Rogers, Sarah Curator
Sakaoka, Yasue Sculptor
Simson, Bevlyn A Painter, Printmaker
Stearns, Robert Curator, Administrator
Sullivan, Billy Artist
Tellier, Cassandra Lee Museum Director, Educator
Verzar, Christine B Educator
Wahling, Jon B Sculptor, Weaver
Wexner, Abigail Collector
Wexner, Leslie Herbert Collector
Wong, Albert Y Painter
Wyngaard, Susan Elizabeth Librarian

Cuyahoga Falls

Richard, Jack Painter, Restorer

Dayton

Houk, Pamela P Curator
Ostendorf, (Arthur) Lloyd, Jr Painter, Instructor
Sayre, Roger L Sculptor, Painter

Delaware

Kalb, Marty Joel Painter, Educator

Dublin

Arnold, Robert Lloyd Painter, Educator
Meyer, Morris Albert Painter

Euclid

Hill, Robyn Lesley Painter, Designer

Gambier

Dwyer, Eugene Joseph Historian
Garhart, Martin J Painter
Gunderson, Barry L Sculptor

Gates Mills

Kozmon, George Painter

Georgetown

Ruthven, John Aldrich Painter, Lecturer

Grandview Heights

Winkler, Michael Conceptual Artist

Hilliard

Benzle, Curtis Munhall Ceramist, Educator

Hudson

Carducci, Judith Painter

Johnstown

Harvey, Donald Gene Sculptor, Instructor

Kent

O'Sickey, Joseph Benjamin Painter, Educator
Sullivan, Scott A Historian, Educator

Lakeview

Earl, Jack Eugene Ceramist

Mansfield

Butts, H Daniel, III Gallery Director
Kraus, (Ersilia) Zili Sculptor, Jeweler

Marietta

Tasse, M Jeanne Historian, Calligrapher

Marion

Beery, Arthur O Painter

Medina

Basham, Charles Painter
Graff, Frederick C Painter, Instructor
Woide, Robert E Painter, Photographer

OHIO (cont)

New Carlisle

Macaulay, Thomas S Environmental Artist, Sculptor

North Canton

Elliott, Bette G Painter, Instructor

North Lima

Mohn, Cheri (Ann) Painter, Instructor

Oberlin

Arnold, Paul Beaver Educator, Printmaker
Coleman, Donna Leslie Painter, Instructor
Pearson, John Painter, Educator
Spear, Richard Edmund Educator

Olmsted Township

Laessig, Robert Painter, Illustrator

Oxford

Dietrich, Linnea S Historian, Educator
Ewing, Susan R Educator
Johnston, Roy Painter, Historian
Taulbee, Ann Director
Wolfe, Robert, Jr Printmaker, Painter

Parma

Kiousis, Linda Weber Painter, Illustrator

Peebles

Rauf, Barbara Claire Instructor, Painter

Perrysburg

Autry, Carolyn Printmaker, Educator
Elloian, Peter Graphic Artist
Hurlstone, Robert William Glass Artist, Educator

Poland

Vaccaro, Patrick Frank Printmaker, Painter

Ravenna

Tyrrell, Lilian Craftsman, Tapestry Artist

Rocky River

Erdelac, Joseph Mark Collector, Patron
Levine, Phyllis Jean Painter

Seven Hills

Stanczak, Julian Painter, Educator

Shaker Heights

McCullough, Joseph Administrator, Painter

Springboro

Sousa, John Philip Photographer, Collage Artist

Springfield

Chepp, Mark Museum Director, Administrator

Strongsville

Myers, Jack Fredrick Painter,

Sylvania

Chapman, Walter Howard Painter, Illustrator

Tallmadge

Ertman, Earl Leslie Historian, Educator

Toledo

Bacigalupi, Don Museum Director, Curator
Cohn, Frederick Donald Dealer, Appraiser
Gonzalez, Mauricio Martinez Administrator, Gallery Director
Luckner, Kurt T Curator
McGlauchlin, Tom Sculptor
Nordin, Phyllis E Sculptor, Painter
Steadman, David Wilton Museum Director

University Heights

Toth, Georgina Gy Art Librarian

Upper Arlington

Collings, Betty Sculptor, Writer

Van Wert

Liljegren, Frank Painter, Instructor

Washington Court House

Ahysen, Harry Joseph Painter, Educator

Wooster

Shie & Acord, Susan & James Craftsman, Painter

Worthington

Pentak, Stephen Painter, Educator

Yellow Springs

Hudson, Jon Barlow Sculptor, Environmental Artist
Jones, Michael Butler Sculptor, Freelance Curator

Youngstown

Zona, Louis A Museum Director, Educator

Zanesville

LaDouceur, Philip Alan Administrator, Director

OKLAHOMA

Anadarko

Little Chief, Barthell Painter, Sculptor

Bartlesville

Price, Joe D & Etsuko Collector
Schmid, Richard Alan Painter

Carney

Bales, J (Jean) Elaine Painter, Sculptor

Chouteau

Ayres, Julia Spencer Painter, Printmaker

Clinton

Lee, Mary Virginia Muralist, Painter

Edmond

Kash, Marie (Marie Kash Weltzhemer) Painter, Graphic Artist
Muno, Richard Carl Sculptor, Director
White, B J (Beverly) Painter, Instructor

Guthrie

Owens, Wallace, Jr Administrator, Painter

Lawton

Bryan, Jack L Painter, Sculptor

Norman

Armstrong, Carol Painter
Bavinger, Eugene Allen Painter, Educator
Bogart, George A Painter
Henkle, James Lee Sculptor, Designer
Lafon, Dee J Painter, Sculptor
Phelan, Andrew L Educator, Writer
Reedy, Mitsuno Ishii Painter
Youritzin, Victor Koshkin Historian, Educator

Oklahoma City

Bell Zahn, Coca (Mary) Catlett Painter
Busch, Rita Mary Painter, Sculptor
Davis, Jack R Painter, Educator
Harjo, Benjamin, Jr Painter, Printmaker
Johnson, Brent Painter
Jones, Donald Glynn Painter, Illustrator
Jordan, Beth McAninch Painter
Littrell, Doris Marie Dealer
Richardson, Jean Painter, Sculptor
Seabourn, Bert Dail Painter, Printmaker
Seabourn, Connie Painter, Printmaker
Warriner, Laura B Assemblage Artist, Collage Artist

Okmulgee

Jones, Ruthe Blalock Painter, Educator

Porum

Frederick, Deloras Ann Painter, Instructor

Stillwater

Smith, B J Museum Director, Instructor

Stonewall

Sieg, Robert Lawrence Sculptor, Educator

Tulsa

Anderson, David C Sculptor, Photographer
Bryce, Eileen Ann Painter
Echohawk, Brummett Painter, Illustrator
Godsey, Glenn Educator, Painter
Goree, Gary Paul Instructor, Painter
Joyner, John Brooks Historian, Museum Director
Kallenberger, Kreg Sculptor
Malone, Patricia Lynn Painter
Manhart, Marcia Y Administrator, Curator
Manhart, Thomas Arthur Educator, Ceramist
Place, Bradley Eugene Educator, Graphic Artist
Snodgrass-King, Jeanne Owen (Mrs M Eugene King) Consultant, Writer
Valero, Maria Teresa Photographer, Educator

OREGON

Amity

Van Leunen, Alice Louise Sculptor,Texture & Paper Artist

Ashland

Engle, Steve Sculptor, Painter
La Duke, Betty Artist
Markle, Greer (Walter Greer Markle) Museum Director, Historian

Beaverton

Cheshire, Craig Gifford Painter, Educator

Blodgett

Whitney, Maynard Merle Sculptor, Educator

Brookings

Mayes, Elaine Photographer, Video Artist

Cannon Beach

Greaver, Hanne Printmaker, Painter
Greaver, Harry Painter, Printmaker

Cheshire

Pendergrass, Christine C Ceramist, Sculptor

Clackamas

San Soucie, Patricia Molm Painter, Instructor

Corvallis

Chappell, Berkley Warner Painter, Printmaker
Gunn, Paul James Painter, Educator
Levine, Shepard Painter, Educator

Dallas

Mattingly, James Thomas Printmaker, Painter

OREGON (cont)

Eugene

Buckner, Kay Lamoreux Painter, Draftsman
Buckner, Paul Eugene Sculptor, Educator
Donnelly, Marian Card Historian, Educator
Ettinger, Susi Steinitz Painter, Lecturer
Fry, Judy Arline Painter, Jeweler
Gurdjian, Annette Painter, Photographer
Hoy, Harold H Sculptor
Joyce, J David Photographer, Sculptor
McKenzie, Allan Dean Educator, Historian
O'Connell, Kenneth Robert Filmmaker, Administrator
Paul, Ken (Hugh) Printmaker, Painter
Roth, Leland M(artin) Historian, Writer
Talaba, L (Linda) Talaba Cummens Sculptor, Printmaker

Florence

Niederer, Carl Painter

Grants Pass

Marchini, Claudia H Painter, Muralist

Hood River

Zweerts, Arnold Painter, Mosaic Artist

Lake Oswego

Hoffman, Elaine Janet Painter, Lecturer

Lincoln City

Yes, Phyllis A Painter, Sculptor

Marylhurst

Hopkins, Terri Curator, Administrator

McMinnville

Bell, Lilian A Sculptor, Conceptual Artist
Casey, John Thayer Painter, Sculptor

Newport

Gilhooly, David James, III Sculptor

Pendleton

Booth, Michael Gayle Painter, Sculptor
Lavadour, James Painter

Portland

Adamson, Linny J Curator, Weaver
Bigelow, Anita (Anne) (Edwige Lourie) Graphic Artist, Printmaker
Bonansinga, Kate Critic, Curator
Buehler, Stuart M Jeweler, Painter
Cook, Silas Baldwin Director
Fillin-Yeh, Susan Museum Director, Curator
Grenon, Gregory Painter
Grimm, Raymond Max Sculptor, Potter
Hamilton, George Earl Painter, Educator
Hardy, Thomas (Austin) Sculptor
Jenkins, Donald John Curator, Historian
Johanson, George E Painter, Printmaker
Katz, Ted Painter, Educator
Kimbrell, Leonard Buell Historian
McCready, Eric Scott Administrator, Educator
Rhyne, Charles Sylvanus Historian
Savinar, Tad Video Artist
Schiebold, Hans Painter
Schnitzer, Arlene Patron
Sheehan, Evelyn Painter
Stacy, John Russell Illustrator
Sylvester, Robert Educator
Wedding, Walter Joseph Ceramist, Educator
Wolf, Sherrie J Painter, Printmaker

Rainier

Lewis, Mary Sculptor

Salem

Melton, Terry R Administrator, Printmaker, Painter

Seal Rock

Sponenburgh, Mark Historian, Sculptor

Seaside

Navratil, Greg Allan Artist

Sheridan

Turner, Ralph James Sculptor, Painter

Talent

Cornell, David E Ceramist, Sculptor

Tillamook

Wagner, Richard Ellis Painter

PENNSYLVANIA

Allentown

Ackerman, Rudy Schlegel Painter, Educator
Berman, Bernard Collector
Moller, Hans Painter
Tenzer, (Dr & Mrs) Jonathan A Collectors
Van Horn, Dana Carl Painter

Annville

Massad, George Daniel Painter, Educator

Bala Cynwyd

Bensignor, Paulette (Mrs Philip Steinberg) Painter, Printmaker
Metcalf, Bruce B Jeweler, Writer

Bally

Bertoia, (Mr) Val Designer, Sculptor

Bangor

McInerney, Gene Joseph Painter

Bellefonte

Fisher, Rob (Robert) Norman Sculptor, Lecturer

Bethlehem

Donnangelo, David Michael Painter, Art Dealer
Ganes, Lucy Sculptor, Educator
Grainger, Nessa Posner Painter, Collage Artist
Livingston, Valerie A Educator, Museum Director
Redd, Richard James Printmaker, Educator
Reker, Les Painter, Educator
Viera, Ricardo Painter, Printmaker

Bloomsburg

Viditz-Ward, Vera Louise Photographer, Historian

Blue Bell

Gutman, Bertha Steinhardt Painter, Professor
Martino, Babette Painter
Martino, Eva E Painter, Sculptor
Martino, Nina F Painter

Boalsburg

Amato, Michele (Micaela) Painter, Sculptor
Muhlert, Christopher Layton Painter, Photographer
Schule, Donald Kenneth Sculptor, Instructor

Boyertown

Slider, Dorla Dean Painter

Bridgeville

Dzierski, Vincent Paul Painter, Designer

Bristol

Blackey, Mary Madlyn Painter, Printmaker

Brush Valley

Wert, Ned Oliver Educator, Painter - Acrylic, Oil

Bryn Mawr

Costanza, John Joseph Sculptor, Ceramist
Mangel, Benjamin Dealer
Mangel, Deborah T Art Dealer, Curator
Markson, Eileen Librarian

Camp Hill

Rowe, Michael Duane Painter

Canonsburg

Sulkowski, James M Painter, Instructor

Carversville

Crilley, Joseph James Painter

Catasauqua

Tabor, Virginia S Painter, Printmaker

Chadds Ford

Duff, James H Museum Director

Cheltenham

Spandorfer, Merle Sue Painter, Printmaker

Chester Springs

Kling, Vincent George Architect

Christiana

Miller, Daniel Dawson Printmaker, Sculptor, Painter

Coatesville

Danziger, Fred Frank Painter

Cochranville

Sazegar, Morteza Painter

Cogan Station

Shipley, Roger Douglas Sculptor, Educator

Collegeville

Larson, William G Photographer, Educator
Morin-Miller, Carmen A Author, Curator

Coopersburg

Walsh, Janet Barbara Painter

Delta

Gilchriest, Lorenzo Constructionist, Educator

Downingtown

Freeland, Bill Sculptor, Painter

Doylestown

Ferguson, Alice C Painter
Mishler, John Milton artist
Thompson, Jack Sculptor, Educator
Thompson, Rena Weaver, Painter

Easton

Harding, Ann Painter
Kerns, Ed (Johnson), Jr Painter
Smith, Jos(eph) A(nthony) Illustrator, Painter
Wall, Bruce C Painter, Instructor
Wall, Rhonda Painter, Instructor

Edinboro

Gibson, Benedict S Painter, Educator
Kemenyffy, Steven Ceramist, Educator
Nicholas, Donna Lee Ceramist, Sculptor
Winterberger, Suzanne Photographer, Assemblage Artist

Elkins Park

Clark, Jon Frederic Educator, Glass Blower
D'Agostino, Peter Video Artist, Educator
Daley, William P Ceramist
Desmett, Don Curator, Gallery Director

PENNSYLVANIA (cont)
Erlebacher, Martha Mayer Painter, Educator
Lechtzin, Stanley Goldsmith, Educator
Stinnett, Hester A Printmaker

Elysburg
Knoebel, David J Video Artist, Writer

Emmaus
Ruhe, Barnaby Sieger Painter, Critic
Smith, Greg Painter, Graphic Artist
Vitali, Julius M Photographer, Painter

Erdenheim
Murphy, Mary M Painter, Instructor

Erie
Ahlgren, Roy B Painter, Printmaker
Kaiser, Vitus J Painter
Pizzat, Joseph Educator, Collage Artist
Sundberg, Carl Gustave Enamelist, Director
Sundberg, Wilda (Regelman) Painter, Instructor
Vanco, John Leroy Administrator, Curator

Export
Hersch, Gloria Goldsmith Painter, Lecturer

Fayetteville
Etchison, Bruce Conservator, Painter

Fort Washington
Schmidt, Charles Painter, Curator

Forty Fort
Thomas, Thalia Ann Marie Painter, Educator

Gladwyne
Wind, Dina Sculptor

Glen Mills
Crawford, Bill (Wilbur) Ogden Illustrator, Administrator
Turner, Janet Sullivan Painter, Sculptor

Glenmoore
De Guatemala, Joyce Bush Vourvoulias Sculptor

Glenside
Crimmins, Jerry (Gerald) Garfield Painter, Sculptor
Frudakis, Zenos Sculptor
Medel, Rebecca Rosalie Sculptor, Environmental Artist

Grantham
Forsythe, Donald John Printmaker, Educator

Greensburg
O'Toole, Judith Hansen Museum Director, Writer

Grove City
Myford, James C Sculptor, Educator

Harrisburg
Bottini, David William Painter, Educator
Mahey, John A Museum Director

Haverford
Stegeman, Charles Painter, Educator
Williams, William Earle Photographer, Curator

Havertown
Fish, Richard G Designer, Painter
Gasparro, Frank Sculptor, Instructor
Kindermann, Helmmo Photographer, Painter
Spicer, Jean (Doris) Uhl Painter, Instructor, Writer, Author
Wilson, Elizabeth (Jane) Painter, Educator

Hazleton
Klesh-Butkovsky, Jane Graphic Artist, Painter

Horsham
Sachs, Keith L Collector
Winokur, Paula Colton Ceramist, Craftsman
Winokur, Robert Ceramist, Educator

Huntingdon Valley
Edelman, Janice Painter - Watercolor, Instructor

Huntington
Lutz, Winifred Ann Sculptor, Instructor

Indiana
Cunningham, Ben Sculptor, Jeweler
LaRoche, Lynda L Craftsman, Designer
Olson, Charles Painter, Instructor

Jenkintown
Goldfine, Beatrice Painter, Sculptor
Langman, Richard Theodore Gallery Director
Miller, Elaine Sandra Painter, Printmaker
Roediger, Janice Anne Artist

Jim Thorpe
Nagano, Shozo Painter

Julian
Yarber, Robert Painter

Kennett Square
Naeve, Milo M Curator, Historian

Kutztown
Carroll, James F L Painter, Sculptor
Malenda, James William Enamelist, Educator
Niedzialek, Terry Sculptor, Environmental Artist
Quirk, Thomas Charles, Jr Painter, Sculptor
Summer, Evan D Artist
Talley, Dan R Curator, Writer
Wible, Mary Grace Painter, Educator

Lancaster
Hay, Ike Sculptor, Educator
Kermes, Constantine John Painter, Printmaker
Musselman, Darwin B Painter

Lansdale
Dallmann, Daniel Forbes Painter, Printmaker

Laverock
Fine, Elsa Honig Historian, Editor

Lederach
Hallman, Ted, Jr Designer, Educator

Lehigh Valley
Kocsis, James Paul Painter

Lenhartsville
Daub, Matthew Forrest Painter, Graphic Artist

Lewisburg
Newman, Elizabeth H Sculptor
Richards, Rosalyn A Director
Turnure, James Harvey Educator, Historian

Ligonier
Hoffman, William McKinley, Jr Painter, Educator

Lumberville
Katsiff, Bruce Photographer, Museum Director

Mansfield
Hamwi, Richard Alexander Painter, Educator

Martins Creek
Fink, Larry (Laurence) B Educator, Photographer

McKean
Kemenyffy, Susan B Hale Artist

Mechanicsburg
Annis, Norman L Educator, Sculptor

Media
Berd, Morris Painter, Educator
Crivelli, Elaine Environmental Artist, Sculptor
Lisk, Penelope E Tsaltas Painter, Printmaker
Reichel, Myra Tapestry Artist, Weaver
Vitale, Magda Painter

Mendenhall
Boucher, Tania Kunsky Painter, Sculptor

Merion Station
Gillman, Derek A Museum Director, Administrator

Merrittstown
Kenton, Mary Jean Painter, Environmental Artist

Milford
Kaplan, Phyllis Painter, Computer Artist

Millersville
Andriulli, Robert Painter, Educator

Mohnton
Gore, Jefferson Anderson Curator

Murrysville
Zollweg, Aileen Boules Painter, Sculptor

Narberth
Alten, Jerry Director, Designer
Atlee, Emilie Des Painter, Instructor
Donohoe, Victoria Historian, Critic
McGovern, Robert F Painter, Sculptor

New Freedom
Theofiles, George Historian, Dealer

New Hope
Lachman, Al Painter
McGinniss, Jim Sculptor

New Oxford
Scarpitta, Salvatore Sculptor, Painter

Newtown
Bove, Richard Painter, Educator
Jansen, Catherine Sandra Photographer, Environmental Artist

Newtown Square
Winter, Ruth Painter

Norristown
Grimley, Oliver Fetterolf Painter, Sculptor
Markley, Doris Yocum Photographer, Writer

North Wales
Szabo, Joseph George Cartoonist, Editor

Oakdale
Mulcahy, Kathleen Glass Artist, Sculptor

Ottsville
Smith, Michael A Photographer, Publisher

Oxford
Holmes, Larry W Painter, Educator

PENNSYLVANIA (cont)

Pennsburg

Hendershot, Ray Painter

Pennsylvania Furnace

Maddox, Jerrold Warren Educator, Painter

Petersburg

Van Dommelen, David B Writer, Fiber Artist

Philadelphia

Akers, Adela Weaver, Craftsman
Asman, Robert Joseph Photographer, Printmaker
Auth, Tony (William Anthony), Jr Editorial Cartoonist
Bach, Laurence Photographer, Educator
Bantel, Linda Museum Director
Batchelor, Betsey Ann Painter, Educator
Bateman, Ronald C Painter
Bernstein, Edward I Collector
Bobrowicz, Yvonne Pacanovsky Instructor, Weaver
Bower, John Arnold, Jr Architect, Educator
Brady, Luther W Collector, Patron
Brantley, James Sherman Painter
Burke, Daniel Museum Director, Educator
Burko, Diane Painter, Educator
Camp, Donald Eugene Photographer
Campbell, William Henry Painter - Acrylic & Watercolor
Casadei, Giovanni Painter
Castagno, John Edward Art Dealer, Painter
Chimes, Thomas James Painter
Davidson, Abraham A Art Historian, Photographer
DeLong, David G Educator, Curator
Dessner, Murray Painter
D'Harnoncourt, Anne Historian, Museum Director
Dickerson, Brian S Painter
Dolan, Margo Director, Art Dealer
Dos Santos, Jonas Alves Environmental Artist, Sculptor
Douglas, Leah Gallery Director, Curator
Dowell, John E, Jr Educator, Printmaker
Drutt, Helen Williams Dealer, Lecturer
Edmunds, Allan Logan Printmaker, Administrator
Eiswerth, Barry Architect, Educator
Ellis, Andra Painter, Ceramist
Formicola, John Joseph Painter, Educator
Fuller, Jeffrey P Dealer, Gallery Director
Goodman, Sidney Painter
Gould, Claudia Museum Director
Gregory, Joseph F Director
Hahn, Maurice & Roslyn Dealers
Haller, Douglas Martin Curator, Historian
Hanes, James (Albert) Painter
Healy, Deborah Ann Illustrator, Educator
Hom, Mei-ling Sculptor
Horvitz, Suzanne Reese Painter, Sculptor
Hughes, Beverly Designer, Weaver
Hurwitz, Michael H Craftsman, Mosaic Artist
Kerrigan, Maurie Sculptor, Painter
Kettner, David Allen Artist, Educator
Kimmelman, Harold Sculptor
King, Ray Sculptor, Light Artist
Knobler, Lois Jean Sculptor, Painter
Kocot & Hatton Painter, Video Artists
Lang, J T Printmaker, Educator
La Pelle, Rodger Painter, Dealer
Lasuchin, Michael Printmaker, Painter
Le Clair, Charles Painter, Educator
Locks, Marian Art Dealer, Collector
Madigan, Martha Photographer
Maksymowicz, Virginia Ann Sculptor, Writer
Mark, Enid Epstein Printmaker, Photographer
Marzano, Albert Painter, Designer
Maxwell, Peter Designer, Art Dealer
McClenney, Cheryl Ilene Administrator
McCormick, Rod Sculptor, Craftsman
McGinnis, Christine Painter, Printmaker
Meister, Michael William Historian, Educator
Millett, Caroline Dunlop Designer, Art Dealer
Miraglia, Peter F Photographer
Moore, Susan Painter
Moss-Vreeland, Patricia Painter, Draftsman
Newman, Libby Painter, Printmaker
Newman, Walter Andrews, Jr Art Dealer, Gallery Director
Nissen, Chris (John Christian Nissen), III Painter
Olin, Laurie Dewar Architect, Educator
Osborne, Frederick S Educator, Administrator
Paone, Peter Painter, Printmaker
Percy, Ann Buchanan Curator, Historian
Pildes, Sara Painter, Collage Artist
Rishel, Joseph John, Jr Curator
Roesch, Robert Arthur Sculptor, Designer
Rosenfeld, Richard Joel Dealer
Rossman, Michael Draftsman, Painter
Rumford, Ronald Frank Printmaker, Painter
Rutstein, Rebecca Painter
Sachs, Katherine Stein historian, collector
Schaechter, Judith Stained Glass Artist, Painter
Schaff, Barbara Walley Artist
Schlesinger, John Photographer
Searles, Charles Painter, Sculptor
Sewell, Darrel L Curator, Historian
Sewell, Leo Assemblage Artist, Sculptor
Seyler, Monique G Painter
Shea, Judith Sculptor
Shih, Joan Fai Painter, Instructor
Shoemaker, Innis Howe Curator
Shores, (James) Franklin Painter
Simkin, Phillips M Sculptor
Staffel, Doris Painter, Educator
Stearns, Thomas Robert Sculptor, Educator
Stein, Judith Ellen Historian, Curator
Stitt, Susan (Margaret) Museum Director, Administrator
Strauss, Zoe Photographer
Striker, Cecil L Historian, Educator
Temple, Byron Ceramist
Tobia, Blaise Joseph Photographer, Educator
Turner, Evan Hopkins Museum Director
Tyng, Anne Griswold Architect
Venturi, Robert Architect
Visco, Anthony Salvatore Educator, Sculptor
Warner, Herbert Kelii, Jr Printmaker
Wasserman, Jack Educator
Yaros, Constance G Painter, Sculptor
Zynsky, Toots Sculptor

Phoenixville

Weidner, Marilyn Kemp Conservator, Lecturer

Pipersville

Gordley, Marilyn Classe Painter, Printmaker
Gordley, Metz Tranbarger Painter
Roseman, Susan Carol Printmaker, Painter

Pittsburgh

Armstrong, Richard Curator, Museum Director
Batista, Kenneth Painter, Educator
Benedict-Jones, Linda Photographer, Curator
Burgess, David Lowry Environmental Artist
Cantini, Virgil D Educator, Enamelist, Sculptor
Clark, Vicky A Curator, Historian
Eberle, Edward Samuel Ceramist, Draftsman
Feller, Robert L Conservation Scientist
Gruber, Aaronel deRoy Painter, Sculptor, Photographer
Harris, Ann Sutherland Historian, Administrator
Haskell, Jane Environmental Artist, Painter
Hearn, M F (Millard Fillmore), Jr Administrator, Historian
Hollen-Bolmgren, Donna Painter, Papermaker
Karn, Gloria Stoll Painter, Printmaker
La Bobgah, Robert Gordon Sculptor, Video Artist
Mannino, Joseph Samuel Sculptor
Morrill, Michael Lee Painter, Educator
Nelson, James P Painter
Prekop, Martin Dennis Painter, Sculptor
Rice, Norman Lewis Painter, Educator
Sheon, Aaron Historian, Administrator
Slavick, Susanne Mechtild Painter, Educator
Stones, Margaret Alison Educator, Historian
Toker, Franklin Historian, Educator
Webb, Frank (Francis) H Painter, Instructor
Weidner, Mary Elizabeth Painter, Educator
Wiebe, Charles M Dealer, Historian
Wilkins, David George Historian
Williams, John Wesley Historian, Educator
Wimmer, Gayle Sculptor, Educator
Winokur, James L Collector, Critic

Pleasant Mount

Sticker, Robert Edward Painter

Pottstown

Kun, Neila Photographer

Quakertown

Opie, John Mart Painter

Reading

Bentz, Harry Donald Educator, Painter
Metzger, Robert Paul Curator, Director

Richboro

Burtt, Larice Annadel Roseman Painter, Sculptor

Roaring Spring

Mock, Martha L Curator

Roscoe

O'Hara, Paul Printmaker, Sculptor

Selinsgrove

Putterman, Florence Grace Painter, Educator

Sewickley

Kornetchuk, Elena Dealer, Historian
Mayo, Pamela Elizabeth Consultant

Shamokin Dam

Connolly, Jerome Patrick Painter, Muralist

Shavertown

Simon, Herbert Bernheimer Sculptor

Solebury

Anthonisen, George Rioch Sculptor, Painter

Souderton

Bock, William Sauts-Netamux'we Illustrator, Painter

State College

Alden, Richard Painter
Frost, Stuart Homer Educator, Painter

PENNSYLVANIA (cont)

Garoian, Charles Richard   Conceptual Artist, Educator
Hager, Hellmut W   Historian
Hampton, Grace   Administrator, Craftsman
Porter, Jeanne Chenault   Educator, Historian
Stankiewicz, Mary Ann   Educator
Stanley, Christopher P   Ceramist
Sturtz-Davis, Shirley Zampelli   Painter, Educator

Susquehanna

Laughlin, Mortimer   Painter

Swarthmore

Cothren, Michael Watt   Educator
Hollister, Valerie (Dutton)   Painter
Hungerford, Constance Cain   Educator, Historian
Kitao, T Kaori   Historian, Educator

Union Dale

Stark, Robert   Painter, Photographer

University Park

Graves, Kenneth Robert   Photographer
Muhlert, Jan Keene   Museum Director, Historian
Sommese, Lanny Beal   Educator, Designer

Upper Darby

Samten, Losang   Artist

Venango

Spinosa, Gary Paul   Sculptor

Verona

Brust, Robert Gustave   Painter, Writer

Villanova

Boyer, Marietta P   Librarian
Cannuli, Richard Gerald   Painter, Gallery Director
Radan, George Tivadar   Administrator, Historian

Volant

McNickle, Thomas Glen   Painter

Walnutport

Magno, Liz   Sculptor, Conceptual Artist

Warren

Mariner, Donna M   Painter, Writer

Warrington

Keene, Paul   Painter

Washington

Pablo   Painter, Educator

Washington Crossing

Wells, Charles   Sculptor, Printmaker

Waterford

Stull, Jean Himrod   Painter
Wiley, Lois Jean   Painter, Writer

Wayne

Key, Ted   Cartoonist, Illustrator-Childrens Books
Sefarbi, Harry   Painter
Silver, Larry Arnold   Curator, Historian

Weatherly

Molnar, Michael Joseph   Painter, Instructor

West Chester

Baldwin, Richard Wood   Illustrator, Sculptor
Everhart, Don, II   Sculptor, Medalist
Hawkes, Elizabeth H   Curator, Consultant
Rufo, Caesar Rocco   Medalist, Sculptor

West Grove

Allman, Margo   Painter, Sculptor
Murray, Robert (Gray)   Sculptor, Painter

West Middletown

Youngblood, Nat   Painter, Illustrator

Westtown

Valetta   Painter

Wexford

Osby, Larissa Geiss   Painter
Schumacher, Judith Klein   Sculptor

Whitehall

Wiltraut, Douglas Scott   Painter

Wilkes Barre

Bart, Georgiana Cray   Painter, Educator

Wyncote

Bayliss, George   Painter, Educator
Watson, Howard N(oel)   Painter, Printmaker

Wyndmoor

Kogan, Deborah   Painter, Illustrator

Wynnewood

Bowes, Betty Miller   Painter, Consultant
Kardon, Carol   Painter, Instructor
Pincus, David N   Collector

Wyomissing

Dietrich, Bruce Leinbach   Museum Director, Administrator

Yardley

Harris, Charney Anita   Painter, Sculptor

RHODE ISLAND

Bristol

Knowlton, Daniel Gibson   Restorer, Conservator

Carolina

Bach, Dirk   Painter, Educator

Central Falls

Scheiner, Michael L   Craftsman

Charlestown

Rohm, Robert   Sculptor

Coventry

Beaudoin, Andre Eugene   Press Manufacturer, Photographer

Cranston

Crooks, W Spencer   Painter, Lecturer
Friese, Nancy Marlene   Painter, Printmaker

Cumberland

Kissik, Kathy Lynne   Painter; Photographer

Jamestown

Prip, Janet   Craftsman, Sculptor

Johnston

Smith, Donald C   Painter

Kingston

Onorato, Ronald Joseph   Historian, Curator

Middletown

Van Duinwyk, George Paul   Goldsmith, Silversmith

Narragansett

Bentley-Scheck, Grace Mary   Printmaker
Calabro, Richard Paul   Sculptor, Painter

Newport

Barry, Robert E   Illustrator, Educator
Cutler, Judy A Goffman   Museum Director
Cutler, Laurence S   Museum Director
Gaines, Alan Jay   Printmaker, Publisher
Goehlich, John Ronald   Educator, Administrator
Nesbitt, Ilse Buchert   Printmaker, Illustrator
Sarantos, Bettie J   Painter, Printmaker

North Kingstown

Kilguss, Elsie Schaich   Painter, Instructor

North Scituate

LaMontagne, Armand M   Sculptor, Painter

Pascoag

Bertoni, Christina   Ceramist, Painter

Peace Dale

Petrie, Sylvia Spencer   Printmaker, Painter

Portsmouth

FitzSimonds, Carol Strause   Printmaker, Gallery Director

Providence

Alling, Janet D   Painter
Bonner, Jonathan G   Sculptor
Chao, Bruce   Sculptor
Conklin, Jo-Ann   Museum Director, Curator
Corkery, Tim (Timothy) James   Painter, Educator
Deal, Joe   Photographer, Educator
Feldman, Walter (Sidney)   Painter, Printmaker
Fessler, Ann Helene   Video Artist, Writer
Fleischner, Richard Hugh   Environmental Artist, Sculptor
Geran, Joseph, Jr   Sculptor, Designer
Golden, Hal   Painter, Conservator
Grimaldi, Vince   Photographer, collage artist, painter
Heyman, Lawrence Murray   Painter, Printmaker
Holmes, Wendy (Diana) H Noyes   Photographer
Immonen, Gerald   Painter
Johnson, Diana L   Gallery Director, Curator
Johnston, Phillip M   Curator, Museum Director
Kelman, Maureen S   Sculptor, Educator
Lambrix, Todd   Sculptor
Liebermann, Philip   Photographer, Educator
Mandle, Earl Roger   Administrator
Marcoux, John W   Designer
Morgan, William   Historian, Writer
Mueller, Louis Albert   Sculptor, Craftsman
Ockerse, Thomas   Designer, Educator
Perroni, Carol   Collage Artist, Painter
Quigley, Robin L   Jeweler, Metalsmith
St Florian, Friedrich Gartler   Educator, Architect
Schulz, Anne Markham   Historian, Educator
Schulz, Juergen   Educator, Historian
Sgouros, Thomas   Painter
Sharlin, Jonathan   Photographer, Educator

Rumford

Burleson, Charles Trentman   Painter, Educator
McSheehy, Cornelia Marie   Printmaker, Painter

Saunderstown

Leavitt, Thomas Whittlesey   Museum Director

Tiverton

Moore, Todd Somers   Painter, Educator

RHODE ISLAND (cont)

Wakefield

Leete, William White Painter
Taylor, Brie (Benjamin de Brie) Educator, Painter

Warren

Udvardy, John Warren Sculptor, Educator

SOUTH CAROLINA

Beaufort

Davenport, Rebecca Read Painter, Lecturer

Bishopville

Adams, Bobbi (Barbara) Jean Austin Painter, Collage Artist

Chapin

Hampton, Ambrose Gonzales, Jr Collector
Saunders, J Boyd Printmaker, Educator

Charleston

Civitico, Bruno Painter, Educator
Fraser, Mary Edna Environmental Artist, Craftsman
Goodbred, Ray Edward Instructor, Painter
Johnson, Diane Chalmers Historian, Educator
McCallum, Corrie Parker Instrucator, Painter
Peacock, Cliffton Painter
Phillips, Michael Painter, Sculptor
Sloan, Mark Museum Director
Wyrick, Charles Lloyd, Jr Publisher, Editor

Columbia

Brosius, Karen Museum Director
Chesley, Stephen C Painter, Printmaker
Dunn, Phillip Charles Educator, Administrator
Edwards, James F Painter, Educator
Elkins, Toni Marcus Painter, Designer
Hansen, Harold (Harry) John Educator, Painter
Lyon, Robert F Sculptor, Educator
Mack, Charles Randall Educator, Historian
McWhorter, Elsie Jean Painter, Sculptor
Mullen, Philip Edward Painter
Woody, (Thomas) Howard Sculptor, Environmental Artist

Easley

Cheek, Ronald Edward Painter, Instructor
Flowers, Thomas Earl Painter, Educator

Greenville

Blair, Carl Raymond Painter, Art Dealer
Bopp, Emery Painter, Educator
Coburn, Bette Lee Painter
Dreskin, Jeanet Steckler Painter, Educator
Hodge, Dorothy (Scottie) W Gallery Director, Assemblage Artist
Koons, Darell J Educator, Painter
Ritts, Edwin Earl, Jr Administrator, Museum Director

Hilton Head Island

Bowler, Joseph, Jr Painter, Illustrator
Greer, Walter Marion Painter
Morris, Jack Austin, Jr Museum Director, Art Dealer

Honeapath

Van Osdell, Barrie (Calabrese) Smith Painter, Instructor

Irmo

Robinson, Chris (Christopher) Thomas Conceptual Artist, Educator

McCormick

Hofer, Ingrid (Ingeborg) Painter, Instructor

Myrtle Beach

Powers, W Alex Painter

North Augusta

Rice, Edward Painter

Orangeburg

Twiggs, Leo Franklin Painter, Educator

Pawleys Island

Tarbox, Gurdon Lucius, Jr Museum Director, Administrator

Rock Hill

Freeman, David L Painter, Graphic Artist

Spartanburg

Boggs, Mayo Mac Sculptor, Educator
Nodine, Jane Allen Painter, Sculptor

Sumter

Davenport, Ray Painter, Printmaker
McKoy, Victor Grainger Sculptor

West Columbia

Lipscomb, Guy Fleming, Jr Painter, Instructor

SOUTH DAKOTA

Burbank

Navrat, Den(nis) Edward Educator, Painter

Pine Ridge

Simon, C M Museum Director

Rapid City

Clark, Lynda K Museum Director, Educator

Sioux Falls

Grupp, Carl Alf Painter, Printmaker
Huseboe, Arthur Robert Writer, Collector

Spearfish

Termes, (Dick A) Painter, Sculptor

Vermillion

Freeman, Jeff(rey Vaughn) Painter, Educator
Neal, Mo Sculptor

Wilmot

Aadland, Dale Lynn Printmaker; Painter

TENNESSEE

Brentwood

Goad, Anne Laine Art Dealer, Publisher
Harmon, Paul Painter, Printmaker

Chattanooga

Craft, David Ralph Painter, Photographer
Cress, George Ayers Painter, Educator
Martin, Chester Young Painter, Medalist
Scarbrough, Cleve Knox, Jr Museum Director, Historian
Wetmore, Gordon (Stanley Gordon) Painter, Writer
White, E Alan Administrator, Painter

Clarksville

Bryant, Olen L Sculptor, Educator
Crouch, Ned Philbrick Sculptor, Curator
Hochstetler, T Max Painter, Educator

Cookeville

Lee-Sissom, E (Evelyn) Janelle Sissom Painter

Cosby

Beam, Mary Todd Painter

Erwin

Slatton, Ralph David Printmaker, Graphic Artist

Franklin

Sulkowski, Elizabeth Brandon Painter
Sulkowski, Joseph H Painter

Gallatin

Baker, Jill Withrow Collage Artist, Painter

Germantown

Purtle, Carol Jean Historian, Educator

Goodlettsville

Vatandoost, Nossi Malek Educator, Painter

Greenfield

Engler, Sherrie Lee Painter, Illustrator

Hendersonville

Jones, Theodore Joseph Sculptor, Printmaker

Hixson

Townsend, Gavin Edward Historian, Educator

Jefferson City

Cleveland, Robert Earl Administrator, Educator

Johnson City

Dyer, M Wayne Painter, Designer
Logan, David George Metalsmith, Educator
Ropp, Ann L Painter, Gallery Director

Kingsport

Cassell, Robert E, Jr Photography
Williams, Raymond Lester Painter, Instructor

Kingston Springs

Nutt, Craig Craftsman, Sculptor

Knoxville

Brakke, P(erry) Michael Painter, Educator
Gray, Jim Painter, Sculptor
Leland, Whitney Edward Painter, Educator
Lyons, Beauvais Printmaker, Educator
Magden, Norman E Filmmaker, Video Artist
Smith, Todd D Museum Director
Stewart, F Clark Draftsman, Painter

Livingston

Bishop, Budd Harris Painter, Museum Director

Lookout Mountain

Fowler, Frank Eison Art Dealer, Consultant
Wyeth, Andrew Newell Painter

Memphis

Allgood, Charles Henry Art Historian, Painter
Califf, Marilyn Iskiwitz Painter, Collage Artist
Carmean, E A, Jr Historian, Curator
Czestochowski, Joseph Stephen Museum Director
Davila, Maritza Printmaker
Feldman, Kaywin Museum Director, Curator
Herbert, Pinkney Painter, Educator
Jasud, Lawrence Edward Photographer, Educator
Knowles, Richard H Painter, Educator
McPherson, Larry E Photographer, Educator
Myatt, Greely Sculptor
Nesin, Jeffrey David Educator
Penczner, Paul Joseph Painter

TENNESSEE (cont)

Riseling, Robert Lowell Educator, Painter
Riss, Murray Photographer, Educator
Roberson, William Tapestry Artist, Collage Artist
Rust, Edwin C Sculptor, Administrator

Milligan College

Blosser, Nicholas Painter

Murfreesboro

Johnson, Erin (Stukey) Painter, Sculptor

Nashville

Aurbach, Michael Lawrence Sculptor, Educator
Baeder, John Painter
Dettwiller, Kathryn King Painter
Edwards, Susan Harris Director
Forrester, Charles Howard Sculptor
Gannon, Lanie E Sculptor
Havens, Jan Sculptor, Printmaker
Hazlehurst, Franklin Hamilton Historian, Educator
Hooks, Earl J Educator, Sculptor
Kaufman, Loretta Ana Sculptor, Painter, Instructor
King, Myron Lyzon Dealer
Knowles, Susan Williams Curator, Critic
Kreger, Philip Director
McGee, Carrie L Painter
Mode, Carol A Painter
Murphy, Marilyn L Painter, Educator
Pletcher, Gerry Painter, Printmaker
Webb, Sarah A Painter
Zimmerman, Alice A Collector, Art Dealer

Pikeville

Saftel, Andrew P Painter, Sculptor

Sewanee

Ende, Arlyn Director
Hastings, Jack Byron Sculptor

Signal Mountain

Childers, Malcolm Graeme Photographer, Printmaker
Collins, Jim Sculptor, Collage Artist

Tullahoma

Blumrich, Stephen Designer

TEXAS

Albany

Blagg, Margaret Director

Alpine

Cutforth, Roger Conceptual Artist, Painter
Fairlie, Carol Hunter Educator, Painter

Amarillo

Fraze, Denny T Collage Artist, Educator
Hyde, Scott Photographer, Printmaker
Toperzer, Thomas Raymond Museum Director, Painter

Arlington

Curry, Kevin Lee Curator, Director
Grandee, Joe Ruiz Painter, Gallery Director
Huerta, Benito Painter, Curator
Maroney, Dalton Sculptor
Munoz, Celia Alvarez Photographer
Rascoe, Stephen Thomas Painter, Educator
Spurlock, William Historian, Critic
Turner, William Eugene Painter, Educator
Wood, Nicholas Wheeler Sculptor, Painter

Austin

Albrecht, Mary Dickson Sculptor, Designer
Anderson, Robert Dale Painter, Draftsman, Printmaker
Attal, M George Art Dealer, Consultant
Barnett, Helmut Painter, Printmaker
Barnitz, Jacqueline Educator, Historian
Brauchli, Byron T Photographer, Instructor
Bucknall, Malcolm Roderick Painter
Charles, Michael Ray Artist
Chesney, Lee Roy, III Printmaker, Educator
Clarke, John R Historian, Critic
Coles, Thelma Educator
Daly, Stephen Jeffrey Sculptor, Draftsman
Donley, Ray Painter
Fearing, William Kelly Educator, Painter
Gould, Karen Keel Writer, Consultant
Grieder, Terence Historian
Guerin, John William Painter, Educator
Hatgil , Paul Educator, Painter
Henderson, Linda Dalrymple Historian, Educator
High, Timothy Griffin Printmaker, Sculptor
Hite, Jessie Otto Museum Director
Jalapeeno, Jimmy (Albert) J Bonar Painter, Photographer
Lansdon, Gay Brandt Printmaker, Jeweler
Long, Teresa Lozano Administrator, Educator
Lundberg, William Assemblage Artist, Filmmaker
Marshall, Bruce Painter, Illustrator, Writer
Mayer, Susan Martin Educator, Museologist
McFarland, Lawrence D Photographer
Miller, Melissa Wren Painter
Milliken, Gibbs Painter, Educator
Perzynski, Bogdan P Video Artist
Popinsky, Arnold Dave Sculptor, Ceramist
Sawyer, Margo Sculptor, Environmental Artist
Schmandt-Besserat, Denise Historian, Archaeologist
Schuller, Nancy Shelby Librarian, Historian
Smith, Jeffrey Chipps Historian
Stratakos, Steve John Craftsman, Tapestry Artist
Vater, Regina Vater Lundberg Conceptual Artist, Lecturer
Wade, Robert Schrope Painter, Sculptor
Waldman, Louis A Educator
Yeager, Sydney Philen Painter, Printmaker

Bastrop

Goodman, Mark Photographer

Beaumont

Meeks, Donna Marie Administrator, Painter

Bell Aire

Long-Murphy, Jenny Art Dealer, Consultant

Boerne

Broderick, James Allen Administrator, Graphic Artist

Brenham

Vernon, Karen Painter, Instructor
Vernon, Karen Painter, Printmaker

Burkburnett

Cokendolpher, Eunice Loraine Painter, Instructor

Canton

Graham, Bob Painter, Muralist

Carrollton

Judd, De Forrest Hale Painter, Educator
Mohle, Brenda Simonson Art Dealer

Cedar Hill

Tillman, Patricia Ann Sculptor

Clifton

Grelle, Martin Glen Painter

Clint

Herring, William Arthur Painter

College Station

Hammer, Elizabeth B Painter, Assemblage Artist

Commerce

Frey, Barbara Louise Ceramist, Educator
McGough, Charles E Printmaker, Educator
Seawell, Thomas Robert Printmaker, Photographer

Corpus Christi

Cain, Joseph Alexander Painter, Educator
Lambert, Ed Printmaker, Painter
Locke, Michelle Wilson Curator
Peters, Diane (Peck) Painter, Muralist
Riley, Barbra Bayne Photographer, Educator
Silvertooth, Dennis Carl Sculptor
Tsai, Hsiao Hsia Painter, Sculptor
Ullberg, Kent Sculptor
Wilhelmi, William Merle Ceramist, Sculptor

Crowley

Geffert, Harry Sculptor

DENTON

Milnes, Robert Winston Sculptor, Educator

Dallas

Allumbaugh, James Sculptor, Educator
Altermann, Tony Art Dealer
Amend, Eugene Michael Historian, Advisor
Banks, Marcia Gillman Painter, Illustrator
Banks, Robert Harris Art Dealer, Publisher
Barta, Dorothy Elaine Photographer, Writer
Bogdanovic, Bogomir Painter
Brandt, Carole Educator
Brettell, Richard Robson Educator, Consultant
Comini, Alessandra Historian, Writer, Educator
Davenport, Bill Sculptor
Davidow, Joan Carlin Director, Curator
Dezzany, Frances Jean Assemblage Artist, Sculptor
Di Giacomo, Fran Painter
Gantz, Ann Cushing Painter, Instructor
Glatt, Linnea Sculptor
Gregory-Goodrum, Ellna Kay Painter, Printmaker
Gummelt, Samuel Painter
Harris, Paul Rogers Photographer, Curator
Hoffman, Marguerite Steed Collector
Hunter, Debora Photographer, Educator
Jones, Lois Swan Writer, Historian
Jordan, William B Historian, Consultant
Koch, Arthur Robert Painter, Educator
Komodore, Bill Painter, Educator
Krause, George Photographer
Kutner, Janet Critic, Writer
Lane, John Rodger Museum Director, Historian
Lecky, Susan Painter
Leeber, Sharon Corgan Art Dealer, Consultant
Lunsford, John (Crawford) Historian, Curator
Meadows, Patricia B Curator, Consultant
Nasher, Raymond Donald Collector
Nelson, Pamela Hudson Assemblage Artist, Sculptor
Rachofsky, Howard Collector, Patron
Scholder, Laurence Printmaker, Educator
Smither, Edward Murray Dealer, Consultant
Stewart, John Stewart Houston Dealer

TEXAS (cont)
Stoffel, Paul T Collector
Tyler, Valton Printmaker, Painter
Warden, P Gregory Administrator, Writer

Denton
Bertine, Dorothy W Painter
Butt, Harlan W Silversmith, Enamelist
Davis, D Jack Educator, Administrator
Erdle, Rob Painter, Educator
Falsetta, Vincent Mario Painter, Educator
Gough, Georgia Belle Leach Craftsman, Educator
Jessup, Robert Painter
Lawrence, Annette Conceptual Artist, Educator
Washmon, Gary Brent Painter, Printmaker
Weller, Laurie June Painter
Youngblood, Judy Printmaker, Painter

Dilley
Avant, Tracy Wright Painter, Graphic Artist

Double Oak
Young, Leslie (McClure) Painter, Muralist

Dumas
Stallwitz, Carolyn Painter, Photographer

Edinburg
Field, Philip Sidney Painter, Printmaker
Manuella, Frank R Designer, Conceptual Artist

El Paso
Carter, Frederick Timmins Painter, Illustrator
Cisneros, Jose B Illustrator, Painter
Drake, James Printmaker, Sculptor
Enriquez, Gaspar Painter, Metalsmith
Fensch, Charles Everette Administrator, Educator
Garnsey, Clarke Henderson Historian, Educator
Martinez, Ernesto Pedregon Muralist, Artist
Rakocy, William (Joseph) Muralist, Museologist
Schuster, Cita Fletcher (Sarah E) Painter, Consultant
Sipiora, Leonard Paul Museum Director, Museologist
Szilvasy, Linda Markuly Painter, Writer

Elgin
Hallenbeck, Pomona Juanita Painter, Printmaker

Fort Worth
Bass, Robert Muse Patron
Bass, Sid R Patron
Breuer, Bradford R Patron, Museum Director
Durham, Jo Ann Fanning Painter
Fortson, Ben J Patron
Fortson, Kay Kimbell Carter Patron, Administrator
Hixon, Karen J Patron
Hudson, Edward Randall Patron
Moncrief, Richard W Patron
Potts, Timothy Museum Director
Price, Marla Museum Director, Curator
Stevenson, Ruth Carter Collector, Patron
Tucker, William Edward Patron
Tyler, Ron C Art Historian, Museum Director

Ft Worth
Auping, Michael Graham Curator, Historian
Blackburn, Linda Z Painter
Bush, Jill Lobdill Painter
Carlin, Electra Marshall Dealer
Conn, David Edward Printmaker
Demanche, Michel S Painter, Photographer
Huston, Perry Clark Conservator
Lincoln, Richard Mather Ceramist, Educator
McCandless, Barbara Ann Curator, Historian
McCullough, David William Painter, Sculptor
Phillips, Dutch (James) O, Jr Gallery Director, Dealer
Smith, Luther A Photographer
Sullivan, Ruth Wilkins Curator, Author
Thistlethwaite, Mark Edward Educator, Historian
Watson, Ronald G Painter, Educator

Galveston
Ryan, Joyce Ethel Illustrator, Painter
Samuels, John Stockwell, III Collector, Patron

Georgetown
Veerkamp, Patrick Burke Educator, Ceramist

Granbury
Westmoreland, Teresa D Designer

Guthrie
Marion, Anne Windfohr Patron, Administrator, Collector

Helotes
Snyder, Hills Sculptor, Writer

Henderson
Bynum, E (Esther Pearl) Anderson Curator, Printmaker

Houston
Adickes, David (Pryor) Painter, Sculptor
Andersen, David R L Painter, Curator
Anderson, Dawolu Jabari Illustrator
Ayoub, Roula Painter
Balahutrak, Lydia Bodnar Painter
Blackemore, Amy Photographer
Bott, H(arvey) J(ohn) Sculptor, Painter
Bowron, Edgar Peters Administrator, Historian
Boynton, Jack (James) W Painter, Printmaker
Broker, Karin Draftsman, Printmaker
Brown, Peter Thomson Photographer, Educator
Butler, Hiram Art Dealer
Cahana, Alice Lok Painter
Camfield, William Arnett Historian
Caslin, Jean Arts Administrator
Conrad, Nancy R Painter
Deats, Margaret (Margaret) Deats Bott Art Dealer, Writer
Dodd, H(elen) C(arolyn) Painter
Evans, Burford Elonzo Painter, Lecturer
Evans, Kenya Artist
Frace, Charles Lewis Painter
French, Christopher Charles Painter, Writer
Goldberg, Arnold Herbert Painter, Printmaker
Hamilton, Jacqueline Consultant, Lecturer
Hammett, Polly Horton Painter, Instructor
Havel, Joseph G Sculptor
Hendricks, Edward Lee Sculptor, Kinetic Artist
Hooks, Geri Dealer, Collector
Kapheim, Thom Printmaker, Painter
Kempner, Helen Hill Collector, Patron
Kopriva, Sharon Painter, Sculptor
Lee, Janie C Curator
Lhotka, Bonny Pierce Painter
Link, Val James Jeweler, Educator
Long, Meredith J Dealer
Ludtke, Lawrence Monroe Sculptor
Lyon, Giles Andrew Painter
Manual, Ed Hill & Suzanne Bloom Photographer, Video Artist
Marks, Lester Collector
Marzio, Peter Cort Historian, Museum Director
Mayo, Marti Museum Director, Curator
Metyko, Michael Joseph Consultant
Moody, Elizabeth C Dealer, Gallery Director
Murtic, Edo Painter, Enamelist
Nunn, Ancel E Painter, Printmaker
Parkerson, John E Art Dealer, Gallery Director
Pruitt, Robert A Artist
Ramirez, Mari Carmen Curator
Randolph, Lynn Moore Painter
Robinson, Thomas V Dealer, Collector
St John, Adam Craftsman
Sarofim, Fayez S Collector
Sarofim, Louisa Stude collector
Stack, Gael Z Painter, Educator
Stockholder, Jessica Sculptor and Educator
Stout, Richard Gordon Painter
Sultan, Terrie Frances Museum Director
Tennant, Donna Kay Writer, Editor
Thompson, Judith Kay Painter
Tucker, Anne Wilkes Curator, Historian
Turner, (Charles) Arthur Painter, Instructor
Twaddle, Randy Painter
Twombly, Cy Painter
Warren, David Boardman Curator
Watriss, Wendy Photographer, Curator
Werner Vaughn, Salle Painter, Illuminator
Woitena, Ben S Sculptor, Educator
Wolff, Dee I Painter
Wray, Dick Painter

Huntsville
Breitenbach, William John Sculptor, Educator
Eastman, Gene M Painter
Lea, Stanley E Painter, Printmaker
Patrick, Darryl L Historian

Hurst
Martin, Loretta Marsh Cartoonist, Calligrapher
Rippe, Dan (Christian) Painter, Instructor
Saladino, Tony Painter, Printmaker

Irving
Novinski, Lyle Frank Painter, Educator
Strunck, Juergen Printmaker

Johnson City
Benini Painter, Sculptor

Kerrville
Burt, Dan Painter, Instructor
Cook, Kathleen L Painter
Frudakis, Evangelos William Sculptor, Instructor

Kingsville
Scherpereel, Richard Charles Educator, Painter

Kingwood
Kagle, Joseph L, Jr Painter, Museum Director, Art Historian

Laredo
Harkness, Madden Painter

Longview
Herbert, Frank Leonard Painter, Educator
Statman, Jan B Painter, Sculptor

Lorena
Umlauf, Karl A Painter, Sculptor

TEXAS (cont)

Lubbock

Akins, Future Rene Printmaker, Sculptor
Briggs, Peter S Curator, Historian
Dingus, Phillip Rick Photographer
Dixon, Ken Painter
Edson, Gary F Museologist, Museum Director
Gibbons, Hugh (James) Painter, Educator
Hanna, Paul Dean, Jr Painter, Printmaker
Howze, James Dean Draftsman, Writer, Assemblage Artist
Kreneck, Lynwood Printmaker, Educator
Morrow, Terry Draftsman, Printmaker
Stephen, Francis B Jeweler, Sculptor
Weiler, Melody M Administrator, Educator

Marfa

Shaffer, Mary Sculptor

Mission

McClendon, Maxine McClendon Nichols Painter
Nichols, Edward Edson Painter, Educator

Montgomery

Herring, Jan (Janet) Mantel Painter, Writer

Nacogdoches

Beason, Donald Ray Educator, Sculptor
McCleary, Mary Fielding Collage Artist, Educator
Wink, Don (Jon Donnel) Painter, Educator

New Braunfels

Wall, Ralph Alan Painter

Odessa

Lee, Nelda S Dealer

Orange

Hunt, David Curtis Museum Director, Curator

Paris

Hancock, Trenton Doyle Painter

Refugio

Branstetter, Gwendolyn H Painter

Richardson

Kessler, Margaret Jennings Painter
McNary, Oscar L Painter, Collector
Stott, Deborah Historian

San Antonio

Amado, Jesse V Sculptor
Barzun, Jacques Martin Writer, Art Critic
Binks, Ronald C Photographer, Painter
Bristow, William Arthur Painter, Educator
Casas, Melesio (Mel) Painter, Educator
Cobb, James Painter
Colpitt, Frances Historian, Critic
Elder, Gene Wesley Collage Artist, Writer
Embrey, Carl Rice Painter, Instructor
Flume, Violet Sigoloff Dealer, Restorer
Funk, Charlotte M Tapestry Artist, Weaver
Funk, Verne J Ceramist, Sculptor
Haynes, David Historian, Consultant
Hyland, Douglas K S Museum Director
Little, Ken Dawson Sculptor
Maurer, Neil Photographer
McDougal, Ivan Ellis Painter, Instructor
Notestine, Dorothy J Instructor, Painter
Parsons, Merribell Maddux Museum Director, Curator
Prescott, Kenneth Wade Museum Director, Administrator
Quirarte, Jacinto Historian, Administrator
Relkin, Michele Weston Painter, Instr
Rowe, Reginald M Painter, Sculptor
Rubin, David S Curator, Writer
Rush, Kent Thomas Photographer, Printmaker
Tiemann, Robert E Painter, Sculptor
West, E Gordon Painter
Wogstad, James Everet Educator, Illustrator

San Ignacio

Tracy, Michael Sculptor, Painter

Seminole

Clark, Vicky Jo Painter

Sherman

Neidhardt, (Carl) Richard Painter, Sculptor

Smithville

Kohut, Lorene Painter

Southlake

Sherwood, Leona Painter, Instructor

Tyler

Gentry, Augustus Calahan, Jr Painter, Printmaker
Ott, Wendell Lorenz Museum Director, Painter
Pace, James Robert Collage Artist, Printmaker
Stephens, William Blakely Educator, Painter

Waco

Chatmas, John T Painter, Sculptor
Kemp, Paul Zane Educator, Sculptor
McClanahan, John D Painter, Educator

Wichita Falls

Band, David Moshe Painter, Art Dealer

Wylie

Pototschnik, John Michael Painter, Instructor

UTAH

Draper

Moyer, Linda Lee Painter, Educator

Lindon

Speed, (Ulysses) Grant Sculptor

Logan

Terry, Christopher T Painter, Draftsman
Van Suchtelen, Adrian Printmaker, Educator

Mendon

Morgan, James L Painter

Ogden

Brooks, Drex M Photographer, Educator

Pleasant Grove

Jarvis, John Brent Painter
Kimball, Wilford Wayne, Jr Lithographer, Draftsman

Provo

Barsch, Wulf Erich Painter, Printmaker
Bronson, Clark Everice Sculptor
Coleman, Michael B Painter
Gray, Campbell Bruce Museum Director, Museologist
Marshall, Robert Leroy Educator, Painter
Myer, Peter Livingston Kinetic Artist, Painter
Whitaker, William Painter, Illustrator

Redmond

Pierce, Diane Jean Painter, Illustrator

Saint George

Lindstrom, Gaell Painter, Educator

Salt Lake City

BrestvanKempen, Catel Pieter Painter
Christensen, Larry R Painter, Instructor
Christensen, Sharlene Painter, Instructor
De Waal, Ronald Burt Collector, Patron
Frazer, James (Nisbet), Jr Assemblage Artist, Writer
Friberg, Arnold Painter, Publisher
Lake, Randall Painter, Printmaker
Olpin, Robert Spencer Historian, Administrator
Rasmussen, Anton Jesse Painter, Administrator
Tierney, Patrick Lennox Historian, Educator, Lecturer

Sandy

Wanlass, Stanley Glen Sculptor, Painter

South Jordan

Fraughton, Edward James Sculptor

Spring City

Bennion, Joseph W Ceramist

Springville

Swanson, Vern Grosvenor Museum Director, Historian

VERMONT

Arlington

Housman, Russell F Painter, Educator

Barnard

Duckworth, Ruth Sculptor, Ceramist

Barre

Gaylord, Frank Chalfant, II Sculptor, Designer

Bennington

Adams, Pat Painter, Educator
Federhen, Deborah Anne Curator, Historian
Lum, Mary Educator

Bethel

Townley, Hugh Sculptor, Printmaker

Braintree

Robbins, Eugenia S Writer, Editor

Brattleboro

Heiskell, Diana Painter
Mason, Emily Painter

Brookfield

Koren, Edward B Cartoonist, Illustrator

Burlington

Davison, Bill Educator, Printmaker
Parris, Nina Gumpert Educator, Photographer
Stone, Judith Elise Collage Artist, Educator
Zucker, Barbara Sculptor

Castleton

Farrow, Patrick Villiers Sculptor

Dorset

Marron, Pamela Anne Painter
Pitcher, John Charles Painter

East Calais

de Gogorza, Patricia (Gahagan) Sculptor, Printmaker

VERMONT (cont)

East Dorset

Howe, Nancy   Painter

Fairlee

Walker, Herbert Brooks   Sculptor, Designer

Greensboro Bend

Roosevelt, Michael Armentrout   Printmaker, Writer

Groton

Sultan, Altoon   Painter

Jericho

Chase, Jack S(paulding)   Sculptor

Marlboro

Boylen, Michael Edward   Craftsman, Art Writer
Olitski, Jules   Painter, Sculptor
Stout, Frank J   Painter, Sculptor

Middlebury

Andres, Glenn Merle   Historian, Educator
Bumbeck, David   Printmaker, Educator
Perry, Edward (Ted) Samuel   Administrator
Saunders, Richard Henry   Museum Director, Historian

Morgan

Karnes, Karen   Ceramist, Craftsman

Newark

Van Vliet, Claire   Printmaker, Publisher

Newbury

McGarrell, James   Painter, Educator

North Hartland

Watson, Aldren A   Designer, Illustrator

North Pomfret

Semple, John Paulus   Painter

North Pownal

Lubeck, Gerald Louis   Painter, Printmaker

North Troy

Fisher, Joel   Sculptor

Pawlet

Torak, Elizabeth   Painter
Torak, Thomas   Painter

Pownal

Gibson, Walter Samuel   Educator, Writer

Putney

Sproat, Christopher Townsend   Sculptor

Ripton

Purdum, Rebecca   Painter

Saint Albans

Prent, Mark   Environmental Artist, Sculptor

Saxtons River

Aho, Eric   painter

Shaftsbury

Bubriski, Kevin E   Photographer

Shelburne

Sanderson, Warren   Art Historian, Lecturer, Archit

Springfield

Baldwin, Harold Fletcher   Sculptor, Painter
Eldredge, Mary Agnes   Sculptor

Thetford

Matteson, Ira   Sculptor, Draftsman

Weston

Kasnowski, Chester N   Collage Artist, Conceptual Artist, Painting

Williamsville

Bowen, Paul   Sculptor

Woodstock

Gyra, Francis Joseph, Jr   Instructor, Painter
Horrell, Jeffrey L   Librarian

VIRGINIA

Afton

Schneiderman, Richard S   Museum Director

Alexandria

Campello, Florencio Lennox   Critic, Painter Watercolor
Clapsaddle, Jerry   Painter, Designer
Covey, Rosemary Feit   Printmaker, Illustrator
Furman, (Dr & Mrs) Arthur F   Collectors, Patrons
Huddy, Margaret Teresa   Painter, Photographer, Illustrator, Writer
Levin, Carol Gellner   Sculptor
Merrill, Ross M   Conservator, Painter
Spagnolo, Kathleen Mary   Printmaker, Illustrator
Thompson, Jean Danforth   Photographer
Uchello, Patricia Miller   Painter, Educator

Annandale

Dean, James   Painter, curator
Spink, Frank Henry   Painter

Arlington

Anderson, Mark Robert   Stained Glass Artist, Sculptor
Burford, James E   Painter, Educator
Cash, Sarah   Museum Director, Curator
Dunlap, William   Art Educator
Fleming, Lee   Writer, Curator, Critic
Gast, Carolyn Bartlett (Lutz)   Illustrator, Illuminator
Gast, Michael Carl   Painter
Goley, Mary Anne   Historian, Director
Gurney, George   Curator, Historian
Knippers, Edward   Painter, Printmaker
Osborn, Kevin Russell   Book Artist, Printmaker
Reed, Paul Allen   Painter
Zilczer, Judith Katy   Curator, Historian

Ashburn

Glick, Paula F   Art Dealer, Writer, Art Historian

Blacksburg

Bickley, Gary Steven   Educator, Sculptor
Carter, Dean   Sculptor, Educator
Crane, David Franklin   Ceramist, Educator
Gablik, Suzi   Painter, Writer
Harman, Maryann Whittemore   Painter

Bristol

McGlothlin, James W   fine art collector

Cartersville

Henry, Dale   Painter

Charlottesville

Barbee, Robert Thomas   Painter, Graphic Artist
Crozier, Richard Lewis   Painter, Educator
Dass, Dean Allen   Printmaker, Painter
Dunnigan, Mary Catherine   Librarian
Geiger, Phillip Neil   Painter, Draftsman
Hartz, Jill   Museum Director, Curator
Lawall, David Barnard   Historian, Museum Director
Stein, Roger Breed   Historian, Educator

Christiansburg

Kass, Ray   Painter

Clifton

Hennesy, Gerald Craft   Painter

Covington

Walton, Harry A, Jr   Collector

Deltaville

Bumgardner, James Arliss   Painter, Educator

Fairfax

Hull, Margarida Kendall   Educator, Painter
Matternes, Jay Howard   Painter, Illustrator
Watson, Darliene Keeney   Painter

Falls Church

Bass, Judy   Painter
Brunsvold, Chica   Painter
Grosse, C(arolyn) Ann Gawarecki   Painter, Instructor
Jones, Lou Mary Louise Humpton   Painter, Sculptor
Robinson, Charlotte   Painter, Printmaker
Stratton, Dorothy   Painter, Printmaker

Farmville

Coopersmith, Georgia A   Museum Director
Lewis, David Dodge   painter

Flint Hill

Paige, Wayne Leo   Painter, Draftsman

Fort Belvoir

Marker, Mariska Pugsley   Painter, Writer, Lecturer, Collector

Fredericksburg

Berreth, David Scott   Museum Director
Nikolic, Jean   Painter, Graphic Artist
Schmutzhart, Berthold Josef   Sculptor, Educator
Somma, Thomas P   Historian, Museum Director

Gloucester

Mayo, Robert Bowers   Art Dealer, Collector

Gordonsville

Zed, Aggie   Sculptor

Great Falls

Ganley, Betty   Artist

Hampton

Beachum, Sharon Garrison   Photographer, Graphic Artist

Harrisonburg

Beer, Kenneth John   Educator, Sculptor
Crable, James Harbour   Multi-Media Artist, Instructor
Downs, Stuart Clifton   Administrator, Educator
Welter, Cole H   Painter, Educator

Herndon

Pisani, Joseph   Muralist, Painter
Robertson, Ruth   Art Dealer, Painter

Independence

Craig, James Hicklin   Consultant

Leesburg

Sanabria, Robert   Sculptor, Writer
Sanabria, Sherry Zvares   Painter

VIRGINIA (cont)

Lovettsville

Lake, Jerry Lee Photographer, Educator

Lynchburg

Agnew, Ellen Schall Director
Lawson, Karol Ann Museum Director, Curator
Massie, Anne Adams Robertson Painter
Muehlemann, Kathy Painter

Mc Lean

MacDonald, Betty Ann Kipniss Printmaker
Steiner, Jeffrey Josef Administrator, Collector

McLean

Harrison, Carol Love Photographer
Kamen, Rebecca Sculptor, Educator
Safer, John Designer, Environ Artist
Young, Cynthia M Painter

McLean

Scott, Concetta Ciotti Painter, Instructor

Midlothian

Baldridge, Mark S Goldsmith, Editor
McEachron, (Genevieve) Ann Painter, Instructor

Mount Vernon

Royer, Mona Lee Painter

Newport News

Alexick, David Francis Educator, Painter
Hightower, John B Administrator, Museum Director
Sheaks, Barclay Painter, Writer

Norfolk

Hennessey, William John Museum Director
Moore, Myreen Painter, Consultant
Young, Robert S W Sculptor

Onancock

Kidd, Rebecca Montgomery Painter

Orange

Marlatt, Megan Bronwen Painter
Marsh, Thomas A Sculptor

Petersburg

Joyaux, Alain Georges Museum Director

Purcellville

DiPerna, Frank Paul Photographer, Instructor

Radford

Feng, Z L Painter, Educator
Gillespie, Dorothy Muriel Painter, Sculptor

Reston

Mahlmann, John James Publisher, Administrator
Norelli, Martina Roudabush Curator

Richmond

Blank, Margot Painter, Photographer
Brand, Michael Museum Director
Cormack, Malcolm Curator, Historian
DePillars, Murry N Administrator, Illustrator
DiPasquale, Paul Albert Sculptor, Lecturer
Freed, David Printmaker, Painter
Hobbs, Robert Carleton Museum Director, Historian
Ipsen, Kent Forrest Glassworker, Craftsman
Johnson, Charles W, Jr Educator, Historian
Kevorkian, Richard Painter
Klein, Beatrice (T) Painter, Printmaker
Lee, Katharine C Director
Levit, Ginger Art Dealer, Writer
Martin, Bernard Murray Painter, Educator
Mavroudis, Demetrios Sculptor
Mayo, Margaret Ellen Curator
Newman-Rice, Nancy Painter, Critic
Nyerges, Alexander Lee Museum Director, Historian
Perry, Regenia Alfreda Historian
Ravenal, John B Curator
Roth, Richard Painter, Educator
Softic, Tanja Painter, Printmaker
Taliaferro, Nancy Ellen Taylor Painter
Thompson, Nancy Kunkle Jeweler, Educator
Toscan, Richard Eric Educator
Van Winkle, Lester G Sculptor, Educator
Welch, James Wymore Painter, Muralist
Womack, Rob (Robert) Robinson Painter

Springfield

Wengrovitz, Judith Painter, Instructor

Staunton

Desportes, Ulysse Gandvier Painter, Historian

Sterling

De Guzman, Evelyn Lopez Painter, Printmaker
Holvey, Samuel Boyer Sculptor, Designer

Syria

Altaffer, Lawrence F, III Artist

Timberville

Barnard, Rob(ert) E Ceramist, Critic

Triangle

Martell, Barbara Bentley Painter

Troutville

Dickerson, Vera Mason Painter, Instructor

Vienna

Flax, Florence P (Roselin Polinsky) Photographer, Writer
Johnson, Carol M Curator
Lorfano, Pauline Davis Painter
Sandground, Mark Bernard, Sr Collector, Painter
Von Zur Muehlen, Bernis Susan Photographer
Von zur Muehlen, Peter Photographer

Virginia Beach

Antol, Joseph (Jay) James Sculptor, Conceptual Artist
Johnson, Martin Brian Illuminator, Assemblage Artist
Lewis, Donald Sykes, Jr Painter
Wells, Betty Childs Painter, Illustrator

Washington

Purnell, Robin Barker Painter

Williamsburg

Barnes, William David Painter, Printmaker
Chappell, Miles Linwood Historian, Educator
Christison, Muriel B Educator, Museum Director, Historian
Cohen, Lewis Carroll Sculptor, Educator
Hood, Graham Stanley Museum Director, Writer
Madonia, Ann C Curator, Administrator
Robinson, Jay Painter
Williams, John Alden Historian

WASHINGTON

Anacortes

Bergner, Lanny Michael Sculptor
McCracken, Philip Sculptor

Auburn

Dingus, Marita Teresa Sculptor

Bainbridge Island

Bard, Gayle Painter, Sculptor
Carlson, Robert Michael Glass Blower, Painter
Donahue, Philip Richard Painter, Educator

Bellevue

Correa, Flora Horst Painter
Warsinske, Norman George Sculptor, Painter

Bellingham

Abraham, Carol Jeanne Assemblage Artist, Ceramist
Clark-Langager, Sarah Ann Gallery Director, Curator
Feodorov, John Artist
Langager, Craig T Painter, Sculptor
Marsh, David Foster Educator, Painter
Vassdal Ellis, Elsi M Graphic Artist, Educator

Bothell

Krieg, Carolyn Ruth Photographer, Painter

Camano Island

Watson, Donna Painter

Colfax

Ely, Timothy Clyde Book Artist

Eastsound

Bevlin, Marjorie Elliott Painter, Writer

Edmonds

D'Elaine Painter, Lecturer
Laico, Colette Collage Artist, Painter

Ellensburg

Sahlstrand, James Michael Photographer
Sahlstrand, Margaret Ahrens Printmaker, Craftsman

Friday Harbor

Bratt, Byron H Printmaker

Grapeview

Hoover, John Jay Sculptor

Issaquah

Pennington, Sally Painter

Kent

Broer, Roger L Printmaker, Painter
Gard, Suzanne E Painter
Pierce, Danny P Sculptor, Painter

Kingston

Maki, Robert Richard Sculptor, Painter

Kirkland

Ho, Francis T Photographer, Educator

Longview

Powelson, Rosemary A Painter, Printmaker

Lopez

Perry, Kathryn Powers Collage Artist, Painter

WASHINGTON (cont)

Lynnwood

Brody, David Painter, Instructor

Medina

Tse, Stephen Painter, Educator

Mercer Island

Glazer, Jay M & Marsha S Collectors, Patrons
Nix, Nelleke Langhout Writer, Publisher

Ocean Park

Wiegardt, Eric Thomas Painter, Instructor

Olympia

Fitzgerald, Betty Jo Painter, Printmaker
Haseltine, James Lewis Printmaker, Painter, Consultant
Hopkins, Kenneth R Museum Director, Restorer
Johnston, Thomas Alix Painter, Printmaker
Randlett, Mary Willis Photographer

Port Townsend

Ainsworth, Diane Painter
Austin, Pat Painter, Printmaker
Hirondelle, Anne E Ceramist
Kepner, Rita Sculptor

Pullman

Coates, Ross Alexander Historian, Painter
Siler, Patrick W Painter, Ceramist

Redmond

Gates , Bill (William Henry) & Melinda French, III Collector

Sammamish

Rushworth, Michele D Painter, Instructor

Seattle

Allen, Judith S Photographer, Educator
Andrews, Richard O Museum Director, Administrator
Angell, Tony Sculptor, Painter
Berger, Paul Eric Collage Artist, Photographer
Blomdahl, Sonja Glass Blower
Braseth, John E Art Dealer, Consultant
Bravmann, Rene A Art Historian, Educator
Brewster, Riley Painter
Celentano, Francis Michael Painter, Educator
Chihuly, Dale (Patrick) Sculptor, Glass Artist
Dailey, Michael Dennis Painter, Educator
De Lory, Peter Photographer, Instructor
Farbanish, Thomas Sculptor
Fear, Daniel E Consultant, Editor
Feldman, Roger Lawrence Sculptor
Gardiner, T Michael Painter, Instructor
Gardner, Ann Ceramist
Garvens, Ellen Photographer
Gates, Mimi Gardner Museum Director
Govedare, Philip Painter
Graham, Lois (M Gord) Painter
Gray, Marie Elise Painter
Hansen, Gaylen Capener Painter, Educator
Hatch, (Mr & Mrs) Marshall Collectors
Hayes, Randy (Randolph) Alan Painter
Hedreen, Betty Collector
Hedreen, Richard
Herard, Marvin T Sculptor, Educator
Hornschemeier, Paul graphic novelist
Hu, Mary Lee Goldsmith, Educator
Huchthausen, David Richard Sculptor, Educator
Hurley, Denzil H Painter, Printmaker
Jonsson, Ted (Wilbur) Sculptor
Kipness, Robert Painter
Kirsten-Daiensai, Richard Charles Painter, Printmaker
Koenig, John Franklin Painter, Photographer
Lundin, Norman K Painter, Educator
Marioni, Paul Sculptor, Glass Blower
Mason, Alden C Painter, Educator
McDonnell, Joseph Anthony Sculptor, Painter
Morris, William Glass Blower
Oliver, Marvin E Craftsman
Rathbun, William Jay Curator
Reiquam, Peter Sculptor
Ritchie, William (Bill) H, Jr Printmaker, Video Artist
Rood, Kay Painter, Printmaker
Ross, Joan Stuart Painter, Printmaker
Ross, Sueellen Painter, Printmaker
Royal, Richard P Craftsman
Ruffner, Ginny Martin Sculptor, Glassblower
Sato, Norie Environmental Artist, Sculptor
Seders, Francine Lavinal Dealer
Siems, Anne Painter
Simpson, Buster (Lewis Buster C) Sculptor
Spafford, Michael Charles Educator, Painter
Takamori, Akio Ceramist
Theobald, Gillian Lee Painter, Lithographer
Thompson, Cappy (Catherine) Painter
Trimpin Conceptual Artist
True, William L Collector
Warashina, M Patricia Ceramist, Educator
Washington, James W, Jr Sculptor, Painter
Weiss, Dick J Enamelist, Stained Glass Artist
West, Richard Vincent Museum Director, Historian
Wicklander, Edward A Sculptor
Woodside, Gordon William Dealer, Collector
Yoder, Robert Edward Artist
Zeitlin, Harry Leon Photographer

Seattle

Allen, Paul Collector
Chase, Doris (Totten) Video Artist, Sculptor
Wright, Bagley Collector
Wright, Virginia Collector, Curator

Sequim

Ervin, Kathey Ceramist
Guilmet, Glenda J Painter, Photographer

Shoreline

Felker, David Larry Sculptor, Gallery Director
Holm, Bill Historian, Painter

Silverdale

Hess, Stanley William Curator, Librarian

Snohomish

Guzak, Karen W Painter, Printmaker,Public Artist
Jones, Thomas William Painter

Spokane

Beattie, Elise Meredith Painter, Educator
Eldredge, Bruce B Museum Director, Administrator
Flahavin, Marian Joan Painter, Sculptor
Fyfe, Jo Suzanne (Storch) Instructor, Painter
Mobley, Karen R Painter, Administrator
Patnode, J Scott Educator, Museum Director

Steilacoom

Clinton, Paul Arthur Printmaker, Instructor

Tacoma

Hallam, John S Historian, Administrator
Rades, William L Painter, Sculptor

University Place

Marshall, John Carl Craftsman

Vancouver

Maurice, Alfred Paul Painter, Printmaker

Vashon

Cole, Donald Painter

Walla Walla

Hara, Keiko Painter, Printmaker (Installation)
Meitzler, Neil (Herbert) Painter
Sawada, Ikune Painter
Wharton, David W Printmaker, Painter

Washougal

Plous, Phyllis Curator

Wenatchee

Woolschlager, Laura Totten Painter, Printmaker

WEST VIRGINIA

Charleston

Ambrose, Richard Michael Director, Curator
Atkins, Rosalie Marks Painter
Black, Mary McCune Curator, Painter
Toth, Caryl Photographer

Elkins

Reed, Jesse Floyd Painter, Printmaker

Fairmont

Smigocki, Stephen Vincent Painter, Printmaker

Huntington

Culligan, Jenine Elizabeth Curator, Admin
Hage, Raymond Joseph Art Dealer, Lecturer

Milton

Anderson, Winslow Designer, Painter

Morgantown

Couch, Urban Consultant, Educator
Schultz, John Bernard Educator, Historian

Shepherdstown

Suttenfield, Diana Painter

Wheeling

Peace, Bernie Kinzel Printmaker, Collage Artist
Phillis, Marilyn Hughey Painter, Instructor

WISCONSIN

Arena

Weege, William Printmaker, Educator

Beloit

Boggs, Franklin Muralist, Sculptor
Olson, Richard W Painter, Educator

Cedarburg

Crane, Jean Painter
Geniusz, Robert Myles Printmaker, Filmmaker

De Pere

Noel, Donald Claude Sculptor, Mosaic Artist

Delafield

Hopkins, B(ernice) Elizabeth Painter, Sculptor

Dousman

Yoder, Janica Photographer, Educator

WISCONSIN (cont)

Elkhorn

Herr, Richard Joseph   Sculptor, Instructor

Fond du Lac

Griffiths, William Perry   Educator, Jeweler

Gleason

Raash, Kathleen Forecki   Painter

Green Bay

Barone, Mark   Painter

Hager City

Buckman, Jan K   Weaver

Hartland

Stamsta, Jean   Painter

Hollandale

Colescott, Warrington W   Printmaker, Painter

Jefferson

Norgard, Karen-Sam   Sculptor, Educator

Kaukauna

Brewster, Margaret Emilia   Painter

Kenosha

Simoneau, Daniel Robert   Painter

Madison

Anderson, Wilmer (Louis)   Painter, Writer
Applebaum, Leon   Glass Blower, Sculptor
Bero, Mary   Painter
Breckenridge, Bruce M   Ceramist, Educator
Conniff, Gregory   Photographer, Writer
Daily-Birnbaum, Elaine   Painter
Drewal, Henry John   Historian, Educator
Fleischman, Stephen   Museum Director, Curator
Garver, Fanny   Art Dealer
Garver, Thomas H   Consultant, Curator
Handler, Audrey   Glass Blower, Sculptor
Hutchison, Jane Campbell   Educator, Historian
Kreilick, Marjorie E   Mosaic Artist, Educator
Lakes, Diana Mary   Painter
Loeser, Thomas   Sculptor
Lowe, Truman T   Educator, Sculptor
Myers, Frances J   Printmaker
Nice, Don   Painter
Nicholson, Natasha   Assemblage Artist, Sculptor
Overland, Carlton Edward   Curator, Historian
Panczenko, Russell   Museum Director
Roman, Shirley   Printmaker, Painter
Sheehan, Diane   Craftsman
Stevens, Andrew Rich   Curator, Historian
Tarrell, Robert Ray   Educator, Painter
Tesfagiorgis, Freida   Printmaker, Educator
Weiss, Lee Elyse C   Painter

Marinette

La Malfa, James Thomas   Sculptor, Educator

Marshfield

Waisbrot, Ann M   Administrator, Curator

McNaughton

Bradshaw, Glenn Raymond   Painter, Educator

Mequon

Gunderman, Karen M   Ceramist
Stoeveken, Anthony Charles   Printmaker, Educator
Tucholke, Christel-Anthony   Painter

Milwaukee

Balsley, John Gerald   Painter, Sculptor
Barnett, David J   Art Dealer, Painter
Brite, Jane Fassett   Curator, Director
Carter, Curtis Lloyd   Museum Director, Educator
Dronzek, Laura Ann   Painter
Farrell, Patrick   Painter, Printmaker
Gordon, David   museum director
Hirsh, Annette Marie   Silversmith, Goldsmith
Jensen, Dean N   Dealer, Critic
Kaiser, Charles James   Painter, Graphic Artist
Kohl-Spiro, Barbara   Printmaker, Painter
Lord, Michael Harry   Dealer, Curator
Michaels-Paque, J   Painter, Sculptor
Ozonoff, Ida   Painter, Collage Artist
Poehlmann, JoAnna   Illustrator, Printmaker
Rosenblatt, Adolph   Painter, Sculptor
Rosenblatt, Suzanne Maris   Painter, Writer
Travanti, Leon Emidio   Painter, Designer
Winter, Hope Melamed   Collectors, Patrons

Mineral Point

Ross, James Matthew Akiba   Assemblage Artist, Photographer

Mount Horeb

Becker, David   Painter, Educator
Haatoum Hamady, Walter Samuel   Collage Artist
Zalucha, Peggy Flora   Painter

Neenah

Smith, Jan   Director

Onalaska

Bartz, James Ross   Painter

Oshkosh

Donhauser, Paul Stefan   Sculptor, Painter
Lipschutz, Jeff   Painter, Curator
Pontynen, Arthur   Educator, Administrator

Port Washington

Gruen, Shirley Schanen   Painter

Racine

Holmes, David Valentine   Sculptor, Painter
Mathis, Emile Henry, II   Dealer, Collector
Pepich, Bruce Walter W   Museum Director, Curator
Rozman, Joseph John   Painter, Educator

Richland Center

Penkoff, Ronald Peter   Educator, Painter

River Falls

Johnston, Randy James   Ceramist, Sculptor

Saukville

Uttech, Thomas Martin   Painter, Educator

Sheboygan

Kohler, Ruth DeYoung   Museum Director, Curator

Shorewood

Thrall, Arthur   Printmaker, Painter

Stevens Point

Dorethy, Rex E   Administrator, Educator

Stoughton

Simpson, Gail A   Sculptor, Educator

Wausau

Fleming, Thomas Michael   Sculptor, Painter

West Allis

Stonehouse, Fred A   Painter, Collage Artist

West Bend

Ulm-Mayhew, Mary Louise   Painter, Instructor

Whitefish Bay

Miotke, Anne E   Painter, Educator

Whitewater

Yasko, Caryl A(nne)   Muralist, Sculptor

WYOMING

Casper

Naegle, Montana   Painter

Cheyenne

Johnson, Dean P   Sculptor

Cody

Fillerup, Mel   Painter
Goodyear, Frank H, Jr   Administrator, Historian
Jackson, Harry Andrew   Painter, Sculptor

Cora

Nash, Mary   Painter, Lecturer

Fort Washakie

Greeves, R V (Richard Vernon)   Sculptor

Jackson

Hessel, Marieluise   Collector

Laramie

Arnold, Joseph Patterson   Painter
Evans, Richard   Painter, Educator
Flach, Victor H   Designer, Writer
Moldenhauer, Susan   Museum Director, Curator
Reif, (F) David   Sculptor, Educator, Painter
Valdez, Vincent E   Sculptor

Sheridan

Martinsen, Ivar Richard   Painter, Educator

PUERTO RICO

Anasco

Carrero, Jaime   Painter, Educator

Carolina

De Castro, Lorraine   Sculptor, Ceramist

Mayaguez

Alvarez-Cervela, Jose Maria   Educator, Historian
Robles-Galiano, Estela   Painter

Old San Juan

Alicea, Jose   Printmaker

Rio Piedras

Castrillo, Rebecca   Printmaker, Painter

San Juan

Balossi, John   Sculptor, Painter
Santiago-Ibarra, Beatrice Mayte   Editor, Critic

PUERTO RICO (cont)

Santurce

Venegas, Haydee E Consultant

CANADA

ALBERTA

Calgary

Bershad, David L Historian, Educator
Besant, Derek Michael Painter, Instructor
Cameron, Duncan F Museum Director
Cameron, Eric Painter, Educator
Chalke, John Ceramist, Sculptor
Hushlak, Gerald Computer Artist, Painter
Kostyniuk, Ronald P Sculptor, Educator
Ohe, Katie (Minna) Sculptor, Instructor
Polzer, Joseph Historian
Smith, Frances Kathleen Curator, Historian
Will, John A Painter, Video Artist
Zimon, Kathy Elizabeth Librarian

Edmonton

Bauer, Will N Conceptual Artist, Video Artist
Cantine, David Painter
Dmytruk, Ihor R Painter, Educator
Forbes, John Allison Historian, Painter
Haynes, Douglas H Painter, Educator
Hide, Peter Nicholas Sculptor, Educator
Sinclair, Robert (W) Painter, Sculptor

BRITISH COLUMBIA

Chemainus

Newton, John Neil Photographer, Printmaker

Courtenay

Varney, Edwin Conceptual Artist, Printmaker

Duncan

Hughes, Edward John Painter

Gibsons

Smedley, Geoffrey Educator, Sculptor

Hope

Weaver, John Barney Sculptor

Hornby Island

Pethick, Jerry Thomas Bern Sculptor, Assemblage Artist

Kelowna

Helfand, Fern M Photographer, Digital Artist

New Westminster

Poole, Leslie Donald Painter, Printmaker

North Saanich

Gore, Tom Photographer, Educator

North Vancouver

Curran, Douglas Edward Photographer, Writer
Mayrs, David Blair Painter, Educator
Mignosa, Santo Ceramist, Sculptor
Muirhead, Ross P Kinetic Artist, Photographer
Perry, Frank Sculptor
Peter, Friedrich Gunther Painter, Calligrapher, Graphic Designer
Shives, Arnold Edward Painter, Sculptor

Port Coquitlam

Eastcott, Robert Wayne Printmaker, Painter
Ng, Natty (Yuen Lee) Painter, Graphic Designer

Salt Spring Island

Raginsky, Nina Painter, Photographer

Vancouver

Alexander, Vikky M Conceptual Artist
Barry, Anne Meredith Printmaker, Painter
Bull, Hank Conceptual Artist, Video Artist
Carter, Sam John Painter, Sculptor
Davidson, Ian J Collector, Patron
Doray, Audrey Capel Painter
Grauer, Sherrard Painter, Sculptor
Knox, George Historian, Writer
Lum, Ken (Kenneth) Robert Conceptual Artist, Photographer
Metcalfe, Eric William Video Artist
Plear, Scott Painter
Prince, Richard Edmund Sculptor, Educator
Sawai, Noboru Printmaker
Smolarek, Waldemar Painter, Printmaker
Takashima, Shizuye Violet Illustrator, Painter
Wallace, Kenneth William Painter, Educator
Young, Robert John Painter

Victoria

Gunasinghe, Siri Educator, Historian
Harvey, Donald Painter, Printmaker
Jorgensen, Flemming Painter
Lansdowne, James Fenwick Painter
Redgrave, Felicity Painter, Printmaker
Segger, Martin Joseph Historian, Museum Director
Stanbridge, Harry Andrew Painter, Printmaker
Stephanson, Loraine Ann Painter
Travers-Smith, Brian John Painter, Instructor

White Rock

Wood, Alan Painter

MANITOBA

Winnipeg

Dukes, Caroline Painter, Printmaker
Eyre, Ivan Painter
Head, George Bruce Painter, Designer
Leathers, Winston Lyle Painter, Printmaker
Pura, William Paul Printmaker, Painter
Reichert, Donald Karl Painter, Photographer
Tascona, Antonio Tony Painter, Printmaker
Tillenius, Clarence Ingwall Painter, Writer
Topper, David R Educator, Historian
Warkov, Esther Painter

NEW BRUNSWICK

Cap-Pele

Roussel, Claude Patrice Sculptor, Educator

Jolicure

Holownia, Thaddeus J Photographer, Educator

Sackville

Hammock, Virgil Gene Critic, Painter
Murchie, Donald John Writer, Artist

NEWFOUNDLAND AND LABRADOR

Corner Brook

Coyne, John Michael Painter, Educator

Holyrood

Squires, Gerald Leopold Painter, Sculptor, Printmaker

Port Rexton

Lapointe, Frank Painter, Printmaker

Saint John's

Shepherd, Helen Parsons Painter
Shepherd, Reginald Painter, Printmaker

NOVA SCOTIA

Bear River

Couper, Charles Alexander Painter, Instructor

Cape Breton

Hurtubise, Jacques Painter

Chester

Curley, Donald Houston Painter, Lecturer

Chester Basin

Zarand, Julius John Painter, Restorer

Dartmouth

Askevold, David Conceptual Artist, Instructor
Forrestall, Thomas De Vany Sculptor, Painter

Halifax

Barber, Bruce Alistair Installation Performance & Video Art, Cult Historian,
Ferguson, Gerald Painter
Gauthier, Suzanne Anita Painter
Jackson, Sarah Sculptor, Graphic Artist
Lindgren, Charlotte Sculptor

Hubbards

Edell, Nancy Painter, Printmaker

La Have

Greer, John Sydney Sculptor

Liverpool

Savage, Roger Painter, Printmaker

Lunenburg

Pentz, Donald Robert Painter, Printmaker

Wolfville

Colville, Alexander Painter, Printmaker

ONTARIO

Baltimore

Bolt, Ron Environmental Artist, Painter

Brechin

Dimson, Theo Designer, Illustrator

Burlington

Mansaram, P Photographer, Painter
Rooke, Fay Lorraine Enamelist, Instructor
Wald, Carol Painter

Cambridge

Heine-Baux, Manfred Painter, Printmaker

Don Mills

Withrow, William J Administrator

Dundas

Lorcini, Gino Sculptor, Muralist

Durham

White, Norman Triplett Sculptor, Kinetic Artist

East Windsor

Cumming, Glen Edward Gallery Director

ONTARIO (cont)

Grand Valley
Adams, Kim Hastings Sculptor

Grimsby
Reitzenstein, Reinhard Sculptor, Environmental Artist

Guelph
Betteridge, Lois Etherington Lecturer, Goldsmith
Danby, Ken Painter, Printmaker

Hamilton
Carter, Harriet (Estelle) Manore Painter

Ingersoll
Crawford, Catherine Betty Painter

King City
Tahedl, Ernestine Stained Glass Artist, Painter

Kingston
Allen, Ralph Painter, Educator
Dorn, Peter Klaus Designer, Graphic Artist
Finley, Gerald Eric Historian
Stewart, J(ohn) Douglas Historian
Swain, Robert Francis Gallery Director

Kitchener
Goetz, Peter Henry Painter, Lecturer

Komoka
Leighton, David S R Administrator

London
Ariss, Herbert Joshua Painter, Illustrator
Ariss, Margot Joan Phillips Painter, Sculptor
Atkinson, Eric Newton Painter, Educator
Dale, William Scott Abell Historian, Educator
Favro, Murray Sculptor
Fenwick, Roly (William Roland) Painter, Educator
Livick, Stephen Photographer
Pas, Gerard Peter Painter, Sculptor
Poole, Nancy Geddes Gallery Director

Markham
Maki, Sheila Anne Printmaker, Painter

Maynooth
Miezajs, Dainis Painter, Instructor

Mississauga
La Pierre, Thomas Painter, Printmaker
Rackus, George (Keistus) Painter, Printmaker

Mount Brydges
Thibert, Patrick A Sculptor, Educator

Niagara on the Lake
Scott, Campbell Printmaker, Sculptor

North York
Bieler, Ted Andre Educator, Sculptor

Oakville
Matsubara, Naoko Printmaker, Illustrator
Shemdin, Azhar H Painter, Instructor

Ontario
Lumbers, James Richard Painter

Ottawa
Bell, Philip Michael Administrator, Historian
Borcoman, James Curator
Bourdeau, Robert Charles Photographer
Cazort, Mimi Curator, Historian
Dickson, Jennifer Joan Photographer, Lecturer
Durr, Pat (Patricia) (Beth) Painter, Printmaker
MacDonald, Colin Somerled Writer, Publisher
Reid, Leslie Painter, Photographer
Sylvestre, Guy Critic, Writer

Owen Sound
Willmott, Elizabeth Ann Sculptor, Photographer

Peterborough
Nind, Jean Painter, Printmaker

Pickering
Semak, Michael Photographer, Educator

Port Hope
Blackwood, David (Lloyd) Painter, Printmaker

Scarborough
Lampitoc, Rol Ponce Painter, Printmaker
McCarthy, Doris Jean Painter, Instructor

Shanty Bay
Bachinski, Walter Joseph Painter, Printmaker

Stratford
Green, Art Painter

Tamworth
Saxe, Henry, OC Sculptor

Thornhill
Firer, Serge Printmaker, Graphic Artist

Thunderbay
Clarke, Ann Painter, Educator

Toronto
Ames, Steven Patron
Andrews, Kim Painter
Aquino, Humberto Painter
Armstrong, Geoffrey Painter, Architect
Astman, Barbara Anne Photographer, Painter
Belanger, Ron Painter
Beveridge, Karl J Photographer
Blazeje, Zbigniew (Ziggy) Blazese Sculptor, Painter
Boigon, Brian Joseph Conceptual Artist, Writer
Bolliger, Therese Educator, Sculptor
Boszin, Andrew Painter, Sculptor
Brener, Roland Sculptor, Educator
Bronson, A A (Michael Wayne Tims) Post-Conceptual Artist, Writer
Cetin, Anton Painter, Printmaker
Cicansky, Victor Sculptor
Cliff, Denis Antony Painter, Instuctor
Cowan, Aileen Hooper Sculptor, Painter
Daley, Cathy Painter
Davies, Haydn Llewellyn Sculptor, Painter
Davis, Christine Photographer
De Heusch, Lucio Painter
De Pedery-Hunt, Dora Sculptor, Designer
Dillow, Nancy Elizabeth Robertson Administrator, Historian
Doyle, Noel Francis Painter, Sculptor
Drapell, Joseph Painter, Filmmaker
DuBois, Macy Architect, Designer
Duff, Ann MacIntosh Painter, Printmaker
Elder, R Bruce Filmmaker, Critic
Etrog, Sorel Sculptor, Painter
Feist, Harold E Painter, Sculptor
Fleisher, Pat Designer, Curator
Frick, Joan Painter, Conceptual Artist
Gale, Peggy Writer, Curator
Graham, K M Painter, Printmaker
Gurney, Janice Sigrid Conceptual Artist, Photographer
Harding, Noel Robert Sculptor, Video Artist
Heath, Dave (David) Martin Heath Photographer
Houle, Robert James Painter, Consultant
Howard, (Helen) Barbara Painter, Printmaker
Hunkler, Dennis Painter, Draftsman
Jaworska, Tamara Fiber Artist, Tapestry Artist
Kaye, David Haigh Textile Artist, Designer
Kinoshita, Gene Architect
Kramer, Burton Designer, Educator
Kravis, Janis Designer, Architect
LeRoy, Hugh Alexander Sculptor
Leshyk, Tonie Sculptor, Draftsman
Lochnan, Katharine A Curator, Writer
Luneau, Claude Sculptor
Luz, Virginia Painter
MacKenzie, Hugh Seaforth Painter
Maggs, Arnaud Cyril Benvenuti Photographer, Graphic Artist
Markle, Sam Dealer, Sculptor
Martin, Jane Painter, Draftsman
Massey, John Collage Artist, Conceptual Artist
Mongrain, Claude Sculptor
Moos, Walter A Dealer
Murdock, Greg Painter
Murray, Ian Stewart Sculptor, Conceptual Artist
Nakamura, Kazuo Painter
Newman, John (Beatty) Painter, Draftsman
Pachter, Charles Painter, Printmaker
Partridge, David Gerry Painter, Sculptor
Patton, Andy (Andrew) John Painter
Plotek, Leopold Painter
Poulin, Roland Sculptor
Rayner, Gordon Painter
Reeves, John Alexander Photographer
Schwarz, Judith Sculptor, Draftsman
Sebelius, Helen Painter
Selznick-Drutz, June Painter, Educator
Sewell, Richard George Printmaker, Painter
Shaw, Joseph Winterbotham Historian, Educator
Snow, Michael Painter, Filmmaker
Steele, Lisa Video Artist
Steinman, Barbara Conceptual Artist, Photographer
Sutton, Carol (Lorraine) Painter
Thomson, David K.R. Collector
Timmas, Osvald Painter, Lecturer
Tomcik, Andrew Michael Educator, Designer
Tuer, Dot (Dorothy) J Critic, Curator
Tulving, Ruth Painter, Printmaker
Van Ginkel, Blanche Lemco Architect, Educator
White, Deborah Dealer
Whiten, Colette Sculptor, Instructor
Whiten, Tim (Timothy) Grover Sculptor, Environmental Artist
Zack, Badanna Bernice Sculptor, Writer
Zeidler, Eberhard Heinrich Architect, Designer
Zemans, Joyce L Educator, Art Historian

Wasaga Beach
Kravjansky, Mikulas Painter, Printmaker, Designer

Waterloo
Urquhart, Tony (Anthony) Morse Sculptor, Painter

Welland
Tulumello, Peter M Consultant, Designer

ONTARIO (cont)

West Lorne

Redinger, Walter Fred Sculptor, Muralist
Zelenak, Edward J Sculptor

Wiarton

Hogbin, Stephen Sculptor
Watson, Mary Anne Printmaker, Painter

Willowdale

Collyer, Robin Sculptor, Photographer
Robb, Charles Painter
Wiitasalo, Shirley Painter

PRINCE EDWARD ISLAND

Charlottetown

Purdy, Henry Carl Painter, Educator

QUEBEC

Ayers Cliff

Beament, Tib (Thomas Harold) Painter

Beaconfield

Harder, Rolf Peter Graphic Designer, Painter

Chicoutimi

Seguin, Jean-Pierre Painter, Photographer

East Montreal

Black, Herbert Collector

Hudson

Braitstein, Marcel Sculptor, Educator

Hull

Ostiguy, Jean-Rene Painter, Art Historian

La Salle

DeAngelis, Joseph Rocco Sculptor, Painter

Laval

Bruni, Umberto Painter, Graphic Artist

Lennoxville

Ernstrom, Adele Mansfield Historian

Luskville

Hlavina, Rastislav Sculptor, Writer

Montreal

Bobak, Bruno Joseph Painter, Printmaker
Boggs, Jean Sutherland Museum Director, Art Historian
Briansky, Rita Prezament Painter, Instructor
Cardinal, Marcelin Painter, Collage Artist
Charney, Melvin Sculptor, Architect
Cohen, Sorel Conceptual Artist, Photographer
Daigneault, Gilles Curator, Critic
De Moura Sobral, Luis Historian, Critic
Dyens, Georges Maurice Sculptor
Falsetto, Mario Educator
Franklin, Hannah Sculptor, Painter
Gaucher, Yves Printmaker, Painter
Gaudard, Pierre Photographer, Graphic Artist
Gersovitz, Sarah Valerie Painter, Printmaker
Goodwin, Betty Graphic Artist, Printmaker
Goring, Trevor Painter, Writer
Hanks, David Allen Curator, Writer
Hartal, Paul Painter, Writer
Jaque, Louis Painter
Knudsen, Christian Painter, Photographer
Lambert, Phyllis Architect, Director
Lamoureux, Marie France Art Dealer, Gallery Director
Layne, Barbara J Instructor
Lerner, Loren Ruth Educator
Letendre, Rita Painter
London, Naomi Sculptor
Merola, Mario Sculptor, Painter
Molinari, Guido Painter, Sculptor
Owens, Gwendolyn Jane Administrator, Curator
Paikowsky, Sandra R Curator, Historian
Palumbo, Jacques Painter, Sculptor
Porter, Katherine Pavlis Painter, Educator
Satorsky, Cyril Painter, Printmaker
Schleeh, Hans Martin Sculptor
Schweitzer, John Andrew Collage Artist, Curator
Shaw, John Palmer Painter, Printmaker
Steinber, Blema Collector
Steinberg, H Arnold Collector
Steinhouse, Tobie (Thelma) Painter, Printmaker
Sullivan, Francoise Painter, Sculptor
Swartzman, Roslyn Printmaker, Sculptor
Tousignant, Claude Painter, Sculptor
Tousignant, Serge Photographer, Conceptual Artist
Trudeau, Yves (CM) Sculptor
Vaillancourt, Armand Sculptor, Painter
Valentin, Jean-Pierre Dealer
Walker, Laurie Ann Sculptor, Conceptual Artist
Whittome, Irene F Sculptor, Painter

Quebec

Lemieux, Irenee Painter
Martel, Richard Conceptual Artist, Editor
Schlitter, Helga Painter, Sculptor

Roberval

Dumais-Berube, Yvette Painter, Sculptor

Rosemere

Brunet-Weinmann, Monique Critic, Curator

Saint Bruno

Readman, Sylvie Photographer

Stanstead

Miller, F John Painter, Mosaic Artist

Ste Adele

Rousseau-Vermette, Mariette Tapestry Artist, Educator

Val-David

Baxter, Bonnie Jean Printmaker, Painter

West Montreal

Missakian, Berge Artin Painter

SASKATCHEWAN

Regina

Cowin, Jack Lee Printmaker, Painter
Fafard, Joe (Joseph) Yvon Sculptor
Sures, Jack Ceramist, Educator

Saskatoon

Bornstein, Eli Painter, Sculptor
Christie, Robert Duncan Painter
Hamilton, W Paul C Educator, Historian
Perehudoff, William W Painter
Ringness, Charles Obert Educator, Printmaker

Other Countries

ARGENTINA

Constantini, Eduardo Collector

AUSTRALIA

Kelly, William Joseph Draftsman, Painter
Valier, Biron (Frank) Painter, Printmaker

AUSTRIA

Essl, Karlheinz, Sr Collector
Leopold, Rudolf & Elizabeth Collector
Oscarsson, Victoria Constance Gunhild Art Dealer, Consultant

BELGIUM

Rabinowitch, Royden Leslie Sculptor

BRAZIL

Paz, Bernardo Collector

BRUNEI DARUSSALAM

Hassanal bolkiah, His Majesty Mutzzaddin Waddaulah Collector

FINLAND

Linton, Harold Painter, Administrator

FRANCE

Aminoff, Judith Gintz Editor, Writer
Arias-Misson, Alain Visual Poet, Graphic Artist
Baltz, Lewis Photographer
Barbeau, Marcel (Christian) Painter, Sculptor
Berger, John Peter Critic, Painter, Writer
Bishop, James Painter
Boltanski, Christian Painter, Photographer
Burr, Tom Artist
Crotto, Paul Painter, Sculptor
De Galbert, Antoine Art foundation Admin
De Rothschild, Eric Alain Robert David Collector
Edouard, Pierre Edward Maussion Painter, Sculptor
Gauthier, Ninon Curator, Historian
Gutierrez, Yolanda Sculptor
Jacobs, Harold Painter, Sculptor
Kurhajec, Joseph A Sculptor
Levee, John H Painter, Sculptor
Linn, Steven Allen Sculptor
Massey, Ann James Graphic Artist, Painter
Matisse, Jackie (Jacqueline) Matisse Monnier Painter, Sculptor
Noel, Jean Lambert Sculptor
Perrin, Alain-Dominique Collector
Piano, Renzo Architect
Pinault, François-Henri Collector
Plossu, Bernard Photographer
Prado-Arai, Namiko Visual Artist
Quinn, William Painter
Reid, Sheila Assemblage Artist, Writer
Renouf, Edda Painter, Printmaker
Sturtevant, E Painter, Sculptor
Wertheimer, Alain Collector

GERMANY

Anderson, Curtis Leslie Conceptual Artist, Painter
Brandhorst, Udo Collector
Durham, Jimmie Artist
Ettl, Georg Painter, Sculptor
Falckenberg, Harald Collector
Flick, Friedrich Christian Collector
Goetz, Ingvild Collector

OTHER COUNTRIES (cont)

Iannone, Dorothy   Painter, Writer
Piper, Adrian Margaret Smith   Conceptual Artist, Writer
Würth, Reinhold   Collector

GREECE

Joannou, Dakis   Collector
Martinos, Dinos   Collector

INDONESIA

Kaida, Tamarra   Photographer

IRELAND

Brady, Charles   Painter, Sculptor

ISRAEL

Shaman, Sanford Sivitz   Museum Director, Curator

ITALY

Rebaudengo, Patrizia Sandretto Re   Collector
Berlingieri, Annibale Marchese de Valle Perrotta   Collector
Cecil, Charles Harkless   Painter
Cook, Robert Howard   Sculptor, Medalist
D'Almeida, George   Painter
Hsiao, Chin   Painter, Sculptor
Irwin, Lani Helena   Painter
Maidoff, Jules   Painter, Printmaker
Shank, J William   Conservator

JAPAN

Fukutake, Soichiro   Collector

MEXICO

Aguilera, Alejandro   Sculptor
Agustin, Hernandez   Architect, Sculptor
Amaya, Armando   Sculptor
Amoroso, Nicolas Alberto Amoroso Boelcke   Painter, Filmmaker
Angulo, Chappie   Painter, Illustrator
Aquino, Edmundo   Painter, Sculptor
Autrey, Sergio   collector
Beltran, Felix   Painter, Printmaker
Biblos, Mahia   Sculptor, Designer
Birbil, Paul Gregory   Painter, Printmaker
Bragar, Philip Frank   Painter, Sculptor
Cattan, Emilia   Painter, Printmaker
Cauduro, Rafael   Painter, Muralist
Clement, Kathleen   Painter, Graphic Artist
Colina, Armando G   Gallery Director, Editor
Del la Vega, Vega Gabriela   Painter, Illustrator
Escobedo, Helen   Environmental Artist
Felguerez, Manuel   Painter, Sculptor
Fett, William F   Instructor, Painter
Flores, Carlos Marini   Architect, Historian
Garcia Guerrero, Luis   Painter
Garza Laguera, Eugenio   Collector
Goldberg, Norma   Sculptor
Guerra, Konrado Avina   Painter, Sculptor
Hayes, Carolyn Hendrick   Painter, Sculptor
Hijar, Alberto Serano   Critic, Educator
Hooper, Jack Meredith   Painter, Printmaker
Iturbide, Graciela   Photographer
Kassner, Lily   Historian, Critic
Kempe, Richard Joseph   Collector, Curator
Landau, Myra   Painter, Muralist
Leyva, Alicia   Painter
Lozoya, Agustin Portillo   Painter
Luque, Jose Antonio   Critic, Curator
Mayer, Monica P   Writer, Conceptual Artist
Mora, Francisco   Painter
Palau, Marta   Environmental Artist, Sculptor
Parra, Carmen   Painter, Printmaker
Pereznieto, Fernando   Painter, Sculptor
Ruz, Thelma   Sculptor
Stavans, Isaac   Painter
Tobler, Gisela Erna Maria   Painter, Architect
Villarreal-Castelazo, Eduardo   Architect, Painter
Wong, Lucille (Lucila) Guerra Wong   Painter, Printmaker

NETHERLANDS

Baer, Jo   Painter, Writer
Krulik, Barbara S   Director, Museologist

Rotterdam

Van Caldenborgh, Joop   Collector

NEW ZEALAND

Block, Jonathan Wolens   Educator, Writer
Dibert, Rita Jean   Painter, Photographer

NORWAY

Astrup, Hans Rasmus   Collector, Museum founder

PORTUGAL

Berardo, Jose Manuel   Collector

QATAR

Ferguson-Huntington, (Lady) Kathleen E   Sculptor, Environmental Artist

RUSSIA

Potanin, Vladimir   Patron

SERBIA

Makavejev, Dusan   Filmmaker

SPAIN

Abello , Juan   Collector
Andreason, Lee   Sculpture
Arango, Placido G, Jr   Collector
Chia, Sandro   Painter
Koplowitz, Alicia   Collector
Miller, Arthur Green   Educator, Historian
Narotzky, Norman David   Painter, Printmaker
Rocamora, Jaume   Painter

SWAZILAND

Hotz, Theo   Collector
Ringier, Michael   Collector

SWITZERLAND

Barbier-Mueller, Jean-Paul   Collector, Museum founder
Gottschalk, Fritz   Designer, Lecturer
Hess, Donald Marc   Collector
Ortiz, George   Collector
Panza , Giuseppe   Collector

TAIWAN

Huang, Frank C   Collector

TURKEY

Duben, Ipek Aksugur   Painter, Sculptor

UNITED KINGDOM

Cohen, Frank   Collector
Aliki, Liacouras Brandenberg   Illustrator, Writer
Blackburn, David   Painter
Caro, Anthony   Sculptor
Carswell, John   Museum Director, Painter
Corris, Michael   Conceptual Artist, Writer
De Rothschild, Elie Robert   Collector
Embiricos, Epaminondas George (Pandy Embiricos)   Collector
Freud, Lucian Michael   Painter
Freudenheim, Tom Lippmann   Museum Administrator
Hackenbroch, Yvonne Alix   Curator, Writer
Hiller, Susan   Conceptual Artist
Hubbard, John   Painter
Jones, Allen Christopher   Painter, Printmaker, Sculptor
Khalili, Nasser David   Collector
Kirkham, Graham   Collector
Kitaj, R B   Painter, Printmaker
Lijn, Liliane   Sculptor, Writer
Lloyd Webber, Andrew   Collector
Nash, David   Sculptor
Phillpot, Clive James   Writer, Librarian
Quentel, Holt   Painter
Ramos, Theodore   Painter, Muralist
Reeves, Daniel McDonough   Video Artist, Installation Artist
Robinson, Duncan (David)   Director, Historian
Saatchi, Charles   Collector
Said, Wafic Rida   Collector
Sherwood , James Blair   Patron
Stella, Frank   Painter
Walker, Sandra Radcliffe   Painter
Warner, Marina   Writer, Critic

VENEZUELA

Cisneros, Gustavo Alfredo & Patricia Phelps   Collector

ADDRESS NOT PUBLISHED

Abbe, Elfriede Martha   Sculptor, Printmaker
Abbott, Linda J   Stained Glass Artist, Instructor
Aber, Ita   Artist, Historian, Conservator
Abramson, Elaine Sandra   Cartoonist, Designer
Adams, Mac   Sculptor, Photographer
Ahart, Shoshanna Marie   Painter
Ahlander, Leslie Judd   Critic, Consultant
Ahrendt, Mary E   Conceptual Artist
Alexander, Anthony K   Sculptor
Alexenberg, Mel   Conceptual Artist, Educator
Allen, Edda Lynne   Painter, Art Dealer
Allen, Nancy Schuster   Librarian, Educator
Allen, Philip
Alpert, George   Photographer, Painter
Ambrose, Robin Allyson   Sculptor
Amory, Claudia   Painter
Anbinder, Paul   Art Publisher, Collector
Anderson, Bruce James   Stained Glass Artist, Video Artist
Anderson, Kenneth Edmund   Sculptor, Educator
Anderson, Lennart   Painter, Instructor
Andrade, Bruno   Painter
Andrade, Edna Wright   Painter, Educator
Andrew, David Neville   Painter, Educator

OTHER COUNTRIES (cont)
Andrews, Benny Painter, Lecturer
Anger, Kenneth Filmmaker, Director
Annus, John Augustus Painter, Photographer
Antoinetta, Greco Painter, Printmaker
App, Timothy Painter, Educator
Appel, Thelma Painter, Instructor
Archambault, Louis Sculptor
Arias-Misson, Nela Painter
Arion, Katherine Painter, Muralist
Asher, Elise Painter, Poet
Askman, Tom K Painter, Educator
Aston, Miriam Sculptor, Painter
Atkins, Gordon Lee Designer, Architect
Atkins, Robert Critic, Educator, Editor
Autio, (A) Rudy Ceramist, Educator
Aycock, Alice Sculptor
Baas, Jacquelynn Director, writer
Bachert, Hildegard Gina Art Dealer
Bacot, Henry Parrott Museum Director, Educator
Baechler, Donald Painter
Baer, Adam Photographer
Bailey, Barbara Ann Painter, Instructor
Bailey, Oscar Photographer, Educator
Bailey, William Painter
Balay, Felicie Art Dealer
Baldwin, Russell W Educator, Gallery Director
Balmaceda, Margarita S Educator, Video Artist
Banana, Anna Publisher, Conceptual Artist
Bandes, Susan Jane Museum Director, Educator
Banning, Jack, Jr Art Dealer
Barber, Sam Painter, Sculptor
Bard, Joellen Instructor, Painter
Bareiss, Walter Patron
Barnett, Earl D Painter, Portraitist
Barrow, Thomas Francis Photographer, Educator
Bartel, Todd Henry Painter, Instructor
Barth, Uta Conceptual Artist, Photographer
Bass, Joel Painter
Bassetti, Fred Forde architect
Bassin, Joan Historian, Educator
Batchelor, Anthony John Printmaker, Draftsman
Battie, David Collector
Baumgardner, Matt (Matthew) Clay Painter
Baxter, Robert James Painter
Baynard, Ed Painter, Printmaker
Beard, Richard Elliott Painter, Educator
Beck, Lonnie Lee Painter, Educator
Beckmann, Robert Owen Painter, Muralist
Bell, Dozier Painter
Benedikt, Michael Writer, Consultant
Benglis, Lynda Sculptor, Painter
Benning, James Filmmaker
Berg, Michael R Painter, Printmaker
Bergen, John Axel Sculptor, Graphic Artist
Berger-Kraemer, Nancy Painter, Sculptor
Berkenblit, Ellen Painter
Berkman, Lillian Collector
Berkowitz, Roger M Curator, Administrator
Berman, Ellen Mercil Trew Painter
Berman, Fred J Painter, Photographer
Berman, Zeke Photographer
Berridge, Mary Photographer
Bertman, Stephen Historian, Writer
Beverland, Jack E Painter
Beyer, Steven J Sculptor, Administrator
Biederman, James Mark Painter, Sculptor
Biggs, John Herron Patron
Bird, Stephanie Rose Painter, Educator
Blackburn, Ed M Painter
Blacketer, James Richard Painter, Art Dealer
Blake, Priscilla Ann Muralist, Ceramist
Blakeney, Rae Historian, Editor
Blechman, R O Illustrator, Filmmaker
Block, Amanda Roth Painter, Printmaker
Block, Gay S Photographer
Blue, Patt Photographer, Writer
Bochner, Mel Conceptual Artist, Art Writer
Bodó, Sándor Painter, Sculptor
Boepple, Willard Sculptor, Educator
Boeve, Edgar Gene Educator, Painter
Bolton, Richard Sculptor, Photographer
Bolton, Robin Jean Painter, Graphic Artist
Boodman, H Citron Painter, Printmaker
Boretz, Naomi Painter, Educator
Born, James E Sculptor
Bowen, Constance Lee Art Dealer, Consultant
Bower, Gary David Painter, Director
Bowling, Frank Painter
Bowling, Katherine Painter
Bowman, Jeff Ray Educator, Administrator
Boyd, Karen White Educator, Fiber Artist
Boyle, Keith Painter, Educator
Boyle, (James) Neil Illustrator, Painter
Brace, Hilary Painter
Bradley, Laurel E Educator, Gallery Director
Bradley, William Steven Museum Director, Curator
Bradshaw, Robert George Painter, Educator
Bramlett, Betty Jane Fine Arts Administrator, Painter, Collage Artist
Branch, Winston Painter
Brandt, Frederick Robert Curator
Brangoccio, Michael David Painter, Collage Artist
Brardo, José Manuel Collector
Brauntuch, Troy Painter, Printmaker
Breiger, Elaine Printmaker, Painter
Brickner, Alice Painter, Printmaker
Brock, Mark L Art Dealer, Consultant
Brodhead, Quita Painter, Writer
Brooker, Moe Albert Educator, Printmaker
Brookins, Jacob Boden Sculptor, Consultant
Brosen, Frederick Painter, Printmaker
Brotherton, Naomi Painter, Instructor
Brown, Bruce Robert Painter, Sculptor
Brown, Carol A Painter
Brown, Carol K Painter, Sculptor
Brown, Constance George Gallery Director, Art Dealer
Brown, Gillian Conceptual Artist, Photographer
Brown, Jeffrey Rogers Dealer, Collector
Brown, Peter C Sculptor, Painter
Brown, Sarah M Painter, Instructor
Brown, Susan LT (Haviland Slizys) Painter, Sculptor
Brownett, Thelma Denyer Painter, Restorer
Browning, Mark Daniel Painter, Sculptor
Bruder, Harold Jacob Painter, Educator
Brummel, Marilyn Reeder Collage Artist, Printmaker
Bruno, Santo M Painter
Bryans, John Armond Instructor, Painter
Bryant, Laura Militzer Weaver
Bryce, Mark Adams Painter, Printmaker
Buchman, James Wallace Sculptor, Educator
Buck, Robert Treat, Jr Art Dealer, Gallery Director
Bunn, David Photographer
Bunn, Kenneth Rodney sculptor
Burchard, Peter Duncan Writer, Illustrator, Photographer
Burford, William E Dealer, Administrator
Burke, Daniel V Painter, Educator
Burkett, Christopher G Photographer
Burks, Myrna R Printmaker, Gallery Director
Burnett, David Grant Historian, Curator
Burnett, Patricia Hill Painter, Sculptor
Burris, Bruce C Painter, Sculptor
Burshell, Sandra Eve Graphic Artist, Painter
Butter, Tom Sculptor, Instructor
Byers, Fleur Painter, Instructor
Byrd, Robert John Illustrator, Instructor
Byrn, Brian Douglas Curator, Assemblage Artist
Caiserman-Roth, Ghitta Painter, Printmaker
Calabro, Joanna Sondra Painter, Sculptor
Calderon, Eduardo T Photographer
Caldwell, Martha Belle Educator, Historian
Caldwell, Susan Havens Historian, Educator
Canier, Caren Painter, Educator
Cantone, Vic Cartoonist, Lecturer
Cantor, Rusty Painter, Sculptor
Cao, Gilda Photographer, Painter
Capa, Cornell Photographer, Museum Director
Caporaso, Pat M Art Dealer
Card, Royden Painter, Printmaker
Carone, Nicolas Artist
Carpenter, Linda Buck Sculptor, Assemblage Artist
Carswell, Rodney Painter, Educator
Casas, Fernando R Painter, Draftsman
Cassell, Beverly Painter
Cassidy, Victor Monod Editor, Writer, Critic
Cate, Phillip Dennis Historian, Director
Catlett, Elizabeth Sculptor, Graphic Artist, Printmaker
Caton, David Painter
Cava, Paul Art Dealer, Painter
Cavaglieri, Giorgio architect
Chaiklin, Amy Painter
Chalmers, Kim Educator, Administrator
Chambeaux, Jane Painter, Sculptor
Chamberlin, Scott Sculptor, Ceramist
Chambers, Karen Critic, Curator
Chambers, Timothy Jerome Painter
Chan, Lo-Yi Cheung Yuen architect
Charkow-Hollander, Natalie sculptor
Chianese, Carol Burnard
Chinn, Yuen Yuey Painter, Printmaker
Chinni, Peter Anthony Sculptor, Painter
Chmutin, Konstantin G Painter, Printmaker
Chong, Albert Valentine Photographer, Educator
Christo & Jeanne-Claude Environmental Artists
Christopherson, Howard Martin Photographer, Art Dealer
Chryssa Sculptor
Chung, Y David Painter, Printmaker
Chwast, Seymour Graphic Artist, Illustrator
Cianfoni, Emilio F Conservator, Painter
Cicero, Carmen Louis Painter
Clark, Kathryn J Conceptual Artist, Photographer
Clark, Marie Sculptor
Clark, Mark A Curator
Cleary, Barbara B Painter, Instructor
Cleary, Manon Catherine Educator
Clerk, Pierre Painter, Sculptor
Cobb, Virginia Horton Painter, Lecturer
Coffey, Douglas Robert Painter, Educator
Cogswell, Dorothy McIntosh Educator, Painter
Cohan, Zara R Gallery Director, Educator
Cohen, Adele Sculptor, Painter
Cohen, Jem Alan Filmmaker, Video Artist
Cohen, Jonathan Jacob Designer, Craftsman
Cohen, Lynne G Photographer, Educator
Coit, M B Painter, Sculptor
Colantuono, Anthony Historian
Colby, Bill Printmaker, Painter
Colescott, Robert H Painter, Educator
Collins, Harvey Arnold Muralist, Educator

OTHER COUNTRIES (cont)
Colpacci, Viorica Sculptor
Colton, Judith Educator, Historian
Colwell, Judith Kogod Ceramist
Condon, Brody Kiel Graphic Artist
Conesa, Miguel A Painter, Illustrator
Conn, Laurence Curator, Painter
Connelly, Chuck Painter
Conrad, John W Educator, Ceramist
Conrad, Paul Francis Cartoonist, Sculptor
Conte, Jeanne Larner Photographer, Enamelist
Contini, Anita Administrator, Curator
Cooke, Jody Helen Painter, Educator
Cooke, Judy Painter
Cooper, Ron Sculptor
Cornell, Thomas Browne Sculptor
Corwin, Sophia M Printmaker, Painter
Costa, Eduardo Conceptual Artist, Painter
Costello, Cynthia Ann Painter, Graphic Artist
Coupon, William Photographer, Filmmaker
Cox, Marion Averal Painter, Instructor
Cramer, Richard Charles Painter, Educator
Cranston, Meg Sculptor
Cron, Marie-Michele Curator, Critic
Crovello, William sculptor
Crystal, Boris Painter
Cyrus, Jamal Artist
Czimbalmos, Szabo Kalman Painter, Educator
Dahl, Stephen M Photographer
Dahlstrom, Nancy Gail Printmaker, Painter
D'Alessio, Natalie Marino Painter
Damianovic, Maia Critic, Curator
D'Amico, Larry Painter, Printmaker
Dana, Uriel Painter, Sculptor
Daniels, Martha K Sculptor
Davenny, Ward L Printmaker, Painter
Daves, Phillip Edward Painter, Sculptor
David, Ivo Painter, Writer
Davidson, Jean Painter
Davis, Ben H Photographer, Painter
Davis, Brad (Bradley) Darius Painter
Davis, Charles Burdis, III Art Dealer, Collector
Dawley, Joseph William Painter
Day, Burnis Calvin Painter, Instructor
DeArmond, Megan Sculptor
DeFazio, Teresa Galligan Painter, Gallery Director
De Kergommeaux, Duncan Painter, Educator
Dennis, Don W Painter, Instructor
Derryberry, Virginia Taylor Painter, Educator
DesJarlait, Robert D Muralist, Writer
Diamond, Paul Photographer
Dickinson, Norman Painter
Difronzo, Francis G Painter
Di Giacinto, Sharon Painter
Diker, Charles & Valerie Collector
Dirgo, Ray Robert Cartoonist, Illustrator - Childrens Books
Diska, (P) Sculptor
Di Suvero, Mark Painter, Sculptor
Dixson, Wendy Fay Painter, Graphic Artist
Dobard, Raymond Gerard Historian, Painter
Dodworth, Allen Stevens Consultant, Curator
Doll, Catherine Ann Painter, Designer
Doll, Linda A Painter, Instructor
Dolmatch, Blanche Painter
Donegan, Cheryl Painter
Dorosh, Daria Painter, Sculptor
Dougherty, Raymond Edward Painter, Instructor
Douglas, L(inda) J Painter, Instructor
Doyle, Tom Sculptor, Educator
Dreikausen, Margret Painter
Dubinskis, Anda Painter
Dumas, Antoine Painter
Dunham-Griggs, Margaret Painter, Sculptor
Dunn, Tom (Thomas) Charles Painter, Illustrator
Duveen, Anneta Sculptor, Designer
Ebie, William Dennis Administrator, Painter
Ebsworth, Barney A Collector
Echelman, Janet Sculptor, Painter
Eckert, William Dean Painter, Historian
Eckstein, Ruth Painter, Printmaker
Edelson, Gilbert S Administrator, Lecturer
Edmonson, Randall W Ceramist
Edwards, Ethel Visual Artist
Ehlers, Carol A Art Dealer
Eide, John Photographer, Educator
Eidelberg, Martin Historian
Eisenberg, Daniel Filmmaker, Video Artist
Ellis, Robert M Painter
Else, Robert John Painter, Educator
English, John Arbogast Painter
Enman, Tom Kenneth Painter, Museum Director
Enos, Chris Photographer, Assemblage Artist
Enterline, Sandra Jeweler
Erbe, Chantell Van Graphic Artist, Painter
Erbe, Joan Painter, Sculptor
Erickson, Marsha A Director, Administrator
Eriksen, Gary Sculptor, Medalist
Esman, Rosa Gallery Director, Dealer
Estes, Richard Painter
Evangeline, Margaret Painter, Collage Artist
Fabbri, Anne R Curator, Critic, Art Writer
Fabiano, Diane Fabian Painter - Miscellaneous Media
Fahlen, Charles C Sculptor, Educator
Farmer, John David Museum Director, Educator
Farris, Joseph Cartoonist, Painter
Faunce, Sarah Cushing Museum Curator
Feiffer, Jules Cartoonist, Writer
Feinman, Stephen E Dealer, Publisher
Fekete, Brian Painter
Felter, James Warren Painter, Printmaker
Feltus, Alan Evan Painter, Educator
Ferguson, Max Painter, Printmaker
Fetchko, Peter J Museum Director
Feuerman, Carole A Sculptor, Painter
Fiero, Gloria K Educator, Historian
Fink, Aaron Painter, Printmaker
Finkler, Robert Allan Educator, Painter
Finocchiaro, Pino Printmaker, Painter
Fiore, Joseph Albert Painter, Instructor
Fischer, Henry George Historian, Curator
Fisher, James Donald Sculptor, Museum Director
Fiss, Cinthea Photographer, Video Artist
Fitzpatrick, Tony Painter
Flanagan, Michael Painter
Fletcher, Harrell Educator, Filmmaker
Flower, Michael Lavin Art Dealer, Photographer
Folkus, Dan (Daniel) Alan Fredrickson Designer, Illustrator
Ford, Harry X Educator, Administrator
Forman, Kenneth Warner Painter
Foster, Maelee Thomson Educator, Printmaker, Collage Artist, Writer
Foster, Steven Douglas Photographer
Foulger, Richard F Painter, Printmaker
Fowler, Mary Jean Weaver
Fox, Lincoln H Sculptor
Franco, Barbara Museologist
Frank, David Administrator, Educator
Frankel, Stuart & Maxine Collector
Frankenthaler, Helen Painter, Printmaker
Frater, Hal Painter
Fredell, Gail Craftsman
Freedland, Barry Sculptor
Freeman, Tina Photographer, Consultant
Frehm, Lynne painter
Freitag, Wolfgang Martin Librarian, Lecturer
Frey, Mary E Photographer
Fried, Nancy Sculptor
Friedberg, Rachel (Ray) Painter, Director
Friedeberg, Pedro Sculptor, Painter
Frigerio, Ismael Painter
Fuente, Larry Sculptor
Fuld, Richard Severin, Jr. Collector, Patron
Fuller, Sue Sculptor, Printmaker
Fulton, Hamish Conceptual Artist
Funk, Roger L Educator, Designer
Furino, Nancy V Painter
Fusco, Laurie S Historian, Educator
Gable, John Oglesby Painter, Muralist
Gaines, William Robert Photographer, Painter
Gallo, Enzo D Sculptor
Garman, Ed Painter, Writer
Garrett, John Craftsman
Garten, Cliff Sculptor
Garwood, Audrey Painter, Printmaker
Gaucher-Thomas, Nancy A Painter, Instructor
Gauvin, Claude E Painter
Gavalas, Alexander Beary Painter
Gaydos, Tim (Timothy) John Painter,Sculptor
Gear, Josephine Writer, Curator
Geddes, Robert Architect, Educator
Gee, Helen Art Consultant, Curator
Geeslin, Lee Gaddis Painter, Educator
Genauer, Emily Critic, Writer
Geoffrey, Iqbal Conceptual Artist, Sculptor
George, Thomas Painter, Draftsman
Gerhold, William Henry Painter, Educator
Gibbs, Barbara Museum Director
Gibbs, Y Gale Painter, Sculptor
Gilbert, Creighton Eddy Historian, Writer
Gilbert, Helen Odell Painter, Printmaker
Gilboy, Margaretta Painter, Printmaker
Gilling, Lucille Printmaker
Gilman, Betty Heller Sculptor, Painter
Ginnever, Charles Sculptor
Ginzel, Andew H artist
Gipe, Lawrence Painter
Glantzman, Judy Painter
Glass, Wendy D Dealer, Collector
Glorig, Ostor Painter, Craftsman
Golbin, Andree Painter, Educator
Gold, Leah Painter, Printmaker
Goldeen, Dorothy A Dealer, Consultant
Golden, Judith Greene Photographer, Mix Media
Goldfield, Edward L Dealer, Collector
Goldman, Judith Writer, Curator
Goode, Joe Painter
Gordon, P(atrick) S(cott) Painter
Gorny, A-P (Anthony-Peter) Conceptual Artist, Illuminator
Goulds, Peter J Dealer, Designer
Goulet, Lorrie Sculptor, Painter
Grabarsky, Sheila Painter
Graeb, Don(ald) (R) Designer, Painter
Graf, Deva Artist
Gralnick, Lisa Jeweler
Granne, Regina artist, educator
Grasso, Doris Ten-Eyck Painter, Sculptor
Grasso, Salvatore Fortunato Painter, Conceptual Artist
Grausman, Philip Sculptor
Grear, J(ames) Malcolm Designer, Educator
Greeley, Charles Matthew Painter, Sculptor
Gregory, Bruce Painter, Instructor
Gregory, Stan Painter
Grooms, Red Painter, Sculptor

OTHER COUNTRIES (cont)

Grossman, Nancy Painter, Sculptor
Gruppe, Charles Painter
Gruskin, Mary Josephine Consultant, Collector
Gummer, Don Sculptor
Gund, Ann art association administrator
Gusella, Ernest Video Artist
Guthman, Leo S Collector
Hadfield, Ted Lee Sculptor
Hagan, James Garrison Sculptor, Instructor
Hagman, Jean Cassels Museum Director, Art Historian
Haley, Patience Painter, Conservator
Haley, Sally Painter
Hall, John A Painter, Educator
Halpern, Nora R Director, Curator
Hamar, Diana Kathleen Painter
Hamburger, Sydney K Sculptor, Curator
Hamill, Tim J Painter, Printmaker
Hammerbeck, Wanda Lee Photographer
Hammond, Harmony Painter, Sculptor, Curator, Writer
Hanan, Laura Molen Artist
Hannay, Janneka (Jann) Painter
Hansell, Freya Painter, Educator
Hansen, Frances Frakes Educator, Painter
Hanson, Annelies Ruth Ceramist, Craftsman
Harold-Steinhauser, Judith Photographer, Educator
Harper, Michaele Ann Painter
Harper, William Jeweler
Harrington, Chestee Marie Painter, Sculptor, Printmaker
Harrington, LaMar Curator, Director
Harris, Alfred Peter Painter, Administrator
Harris, Gloriane Painter, Educator
Harrison, Alice Painter, Collage Artist
Harshfield, Neil Alan Sculptor, Educator
Hart, Robert Gordon Administrator
Harter, John Burton Curator, Painter
Hartigan, Grace Painter
Hasen, Burt Stanley Painter, Printmaker
Haskin, Donald Marcus Educator, Sculptor
Hassrick, Peter H Museum Director, Historian
Hastenteufel, Dieter Sculptor, Painter
Hatcher, (L) Brower Sculptor
Hauft, Amy Sculptor
Haut, Claire (Joan) Painter, Graphic Artist
Hayes, Laura M Dealer, Historian
Haynes, Nancy Painter
Heaton, Janet N Painter, Gallery Director
Heeks, Willy Painter
Heginbotham, Jan Sturza Sculptor
Heimdal, Georg Painter, Instructor
Heise, Myron Robert Painter
Helioff, Anne Graile (Mrs Benjamin Hirschberg) Painter, Collage Artist
Heller, Goldie (Mrs Edward W Greenberg) Collector, Consultant
Hendrix, Connie Sandage Manus Painter, Instructor
Henrickson, Paul Robert Painter, Writer
Henry, Jean Museum Director, Curator
Herman, Lloyd Eldred Museum Director
Herms, George Sculptor, Painter
Hershey, Nona Printmaker, Painter
Heyman, Ira Michael Administrator, Educator
Highwater, Jamake Critic, Lecturer
Hillman, Arthur Stanley Graphic Artist, Educator
Hillsmith, Fannie Painter - Acylic, Oil
Hinkhouse, Forest Melick Writer, Consultant
Hobbs, Fredric Sculptor, Filmmaker
Hobgood, E Wade Administrator, Educator
Hochman, Kitty Printmaker
Hoffeld, Jeffrey M Art Dealer
Hoffman, Helen Bacon Painter
Holden, Donald Painter, Writer
Holder, Kenneth Allen Painter, Educator
Holt, Martha A Ceramist, Sculptor
Holt, Nancy Louise Sculptor, Filmmaker
Holton, William Painter, Printmaker
Hoover, Francis Louis Collector, Jeweler
Hopper, Frank J Painter, Muralist
Horman, Elizabeth Painter, Muralist
Horn, Robert Nelson Painter, Designer
Houston, Bruce Sculptor, Assemblage Artist
Howarth, Shirley Reiff Publisher, Historian
Hu, Chi Chung Painter
Hudson, Gary Painter
Hull, Richard Painter
Hull, Shayne L Instructor, Painter
Humphrey, David Aiken Painter, Printmaker
Hunter, Robert Howard Painter
Hyman, Linda Art Dealer, Historian
Ingham, Tom (Edgar) Sculptor
Ingle, John S Painter, Educator
Ingram, Michael Steven Painter
Inoue, Kazuko Painter
Ipcar, Dahlov Painter, Illustrator
Ipoustéguy, Jean Robert Sculptor, Graphic Artist
Isaacs, Avrom Art Dealer, Publisher
Isaacson, Gene Lester Collector, Historian
Isaacson, Ronald G Gallery Director, Collector
Isaak, Nicholas, Jr Painter, Conservator
Itatani, Michiko Painter
Iturralde, Teresa Art Dealer, Collector
Ivey, William J Administrator
Izuka, Kunio Sculptor, Painter
Jabbour, Mona Amal Educator, Painter
Jacklin, Bill (William) Painter, Printmaker
Jackson, Matthew Day Assemblage Artist
Jacob, Ned Painter, Lecturer
Jacobs, Ferne K Weaver
Jacques, Michael Louis Painter, Printmaker
Jamison, Philip Painter
Janis, Conrad Dealer, Collector
Jansen, Marcus Antonius Painter
Jarvis, Donald Painter, Instructor
Jay, Norma Joyce Painter
Jeck, Douglas A Sculptor
Jenkins, Paul Painter
Jenkins, Twinny Painter, Sculptor
Jenrette, Pamela Anne Painter, Costume Designer
Jezik, Enrique Sculptor, Environmental Artist
Johansen, John Maclane Architect
Johnson, Donald Ray Historian, Printmaker
Johnson, Homer Educator, Painter
Johnson, James Edwin Graphic Designer
Johnson, Lois Marlene Printmaker, Educator
Johnson, Richard A Painter, Educator
Jones, Charlott Ann Educator, Museum Director
Jones, Elizabeth A B (Mrs Ludwig Glaeser) Sculptor, Photographer
Jordan, Jack Administrator, Sculptor
Josephson, Kenneth Bradley Photographer, Assemblage Artist
Ju, I-Hsiung Educator, Painter
Judson, William D Curator, Historian
Jung, Kwan Yee Painter
Juszczyk, James Joseph Painter, Printmaker
Kahn, Cecily painter
Kahn, Wolf Painter
Kaiman, Charles Painter
Kaiser, S(haron) Burkett Painter
Kane, Bill Photographer, Assemblage Artist
Karawina, Erica (Mrs Sidney C Hsiao) Painter, Stained Glass Artist
Karwoski, Richard Charles Painter, Educator
Kass, Deborah Painter
Kawa, Florence Kathryn Painter
Keating, David Nelson Photographer, Assemblage Artist
Keister, Steve (Stephen) Lee Sculptor
Keky-Magyar, Eva Painter, Graphic Artist
Kelly, Kevin T Painter
Kendrick, Mel Sculptor
Kennedy, Gene (Eugene) Murray Photographer, Educator
Kennedy, Marla Hamburg Art Dealer, Curator
Kennington, Dale Painter
Kennon, Robert Brian Printmaker, Historian
Kenyon, Colleen Frances Photographer, Administrator
Kern, Karen R Painting
Kerne, Barbara Davis Art Dealer, Painter
Kertzer, Anita Elizabeth Painter, Sculptor
Kirsten-Honshin, Nicholas Painter
Kisch, Gloria Sculptor
Klausen, Ray Sculptor
Klein, Lynn (Ellen) Painter, Photographer
Kleinman, Sue Painter, Lecturer
Klotz, Suzanne Assemblage Artist, Educator
Knerr, Erika Tilde Painter, Muralist
Knode, Marilu Curator, Administrator
Knott, Dee D Painter, Illustrator
Knowlton, Jonathan Painter, Educator
Knox, Simmie painter
Kohn, Michael Bundy Art Dealer, Critic
Komar and Melamid Painter, Printmaker
Korman, Barbara Sculptor, Assemblage Artist
Korman, Harriet R Painter
Korn, Henry Museum Director, Writer
Kortenhaus, Lynne M Consultant, Curator
Koscianski, Leonard J Conceptual Artist
Koss, Gene H Sculptor, Educator
Kostabi, Mark Painter, Sculptor
Kozo Printmaker
Kramer, Hilton Critic, Editor
Kramer, James J Painter
Kramer, Margia Conceptual Artist, Video Artist
Kraus, Jill Gansman Collector
Kravis, Marie-Josee Collector
Kresch, Albert painter
Kretschmer, Melissa Sculptor
Krinsky, Carol Herselle Educator, Historian
Kruskamp, Janet Painter
Kuang, Ting Shao Painter
Kuchar, Kathleen Ann Painter, Educator
Kuhn, Audrey Grendahl Printmaker, Fiber Artist
Kuper, Yuri Kuperman Painter
Kurka, Donald Frank Painter,
Kustera, Carter Conceptual Artist, Sculptor
Kwiecinski, Chester Martin Educator, Painter
Kwong, Eva Sculptor, Ceramist
Lack, Stephen Painter, Filmmaker
Lackey, Jane W Fiber Artist
Ladd, Beth Painter
Lake, Shelley Photographer, Artist
La Lumia, Frank Painter
Lamis, Leroy Sculptor, Educator
Lancaster, Mark Painter
Lancel McElhinney, James Painter, Educator
Landau, Emily Fisher Collector, Administrator
Landreau, Anthony Norman Educator
Lang, Daniel S Painter
Lang, Gary Painter, Lecturer
La Noue, Terence Painter, Educator
LaPlantz, David Jeweler, Sculptor
LaPlantz, Shereen Book Artist, Writer

OTHER COUNTRIES (cont)

L'Archeveque, Andre Robert Painter, Illustrator
Larkin, Eugene Designer, Educator
Larsen, John Christian Educator, Librarian
Larsen, Mernet Ruth Painter, Educator
Larson, Kay L Critic, Writer
LaRue, Joan Marron Painter
Larzelere, Judith Ann Tapestry Artist
Lasch, Pat Sculptor
Lauck, Anthony Joseph Sculptor, Educator
Lauhakaikul, Thana Instructor, Sculptor
Lawrence, Howard Ray Designer, Educator
Lawrence, Matthew R Printmaker, Painter
Lazzarini, Robert Sculptor
Leach, Elizabeth Anne Art Dealer, Writer
Leach, Mada (Madeline) Kleiman Painter
Leandre, Juan (Joan) Graphic Artist
Le Brun, Carol Critic, Dealer
Lee, Eric McCauley Museum Director, Historian
Lee, Thomas H Collector
Leepa, Allen Painter, Educator
Leeper, Doris Marie Sculptor, Painter
Leesman, Beverly Jean Painter, Writer
Leicester, Andrew John Environmental Artist
Leighton, Patricia MacInnes Environmental Artist, Sculptor
Leiva, Nicolas Painter
Lekberg, Barbara Hult Sculptor
Leong, Lampo Painter, Educator
Leroy, Louis Painter
Levin, Golan Artist
Levine, Erik Sculptor
Levine, Tom Painter, Printmaker
Levinson, Joel D Photographer, Conceptual Artist
Levy, David Corcos Art Historian, Educator
Levy, Hilda Painter, Sculptor
Lewis, Joseph S, III Administrator, Sculptor
Lewis, Stanley Sculptor, Printmaker
Lexier, Micah Sculptor
Liebman, Norman Painter
Lillie, Lloyd Sculpture
Limont, Naomi Charles Printmaker, Painter
Linderman, Earl William Painter
Lindmark, Arne Painter, Instructor
Lineker, Bruce Museum Director, Curator
Lines, Marian B Painter
Lippmann, Janet Gurian Painter, Gallery Director
Litwin, Ruth Forbes Printmaker, Painter
Livesay, Thomas Andrew Museum Director, Administrator
Lockhart, Sharon Photographer, Filmmaker
Logan, Gene Adams Sculptor, Painter
Logothetis, Aristides Artist
Londin, Barbara Painter
London, Barbara Curator
London, Peter Painter, Educator
Long, Phillip C Museum Director
Looney, Norm Sculptor, Conceptual Artist
Losavio, Samuel R Sculptor, Painter
Loveless, Jim Painter
Lowenthal, Constance Historian
Lubell, Ellen Critic, Writer
Lucero, Michael (Lewis) Sculptor
Luebbers, Leslie Laird Museum Director, Historian
Lufkin, Martha BG Lawyer, Legal Writer, art law correspondent
Lukas, Dennis Brian Painter, Educator
Lukkas, Lynn C Video Artist
Lumsden, Ian Gordon Director
Luray, J (Schaffner) Collage Artist, Painter
Lutes, Jim (James) Painter
Lynch, Betty Painter, Instructor
Lynch, Tom (Thomas) Michael Painter, Instructor
Lynde, Stan Cartoonist, Illustrator
Magee, Alderson Graphic Artist, Printmaker
Magnuson, Eric A Conceptual Artist
Maguire, Henry Pownall Historian, Writer
Makler, Hope Welsh Art Dealer
Mallin, Joel Collector
Mallory, Nina Ayala Educator, Historian
Mandel, Saul Illustrator, Painter
Manes, Paul Painter
Mangione, Patricia Anthony Painter, Muralist
Manilow, Lewis Collector, Patron
Mann, James Robert Curator, Critic
Mansion, Gracie Art Dealer
Marasco, Rose Photographer, Educator
Margules, Gabriele Ella Illustrator, Painter
Marin, Javier Sculptor
Marinsky, Harry Sculptor, Painter
Marion, John Louis Collector
Mark, Mary Ellen Photographer
Marquis, Richard Craftsman
Marrero, Marlo R Photographer, Sculptor
Marsh, Georgia Painter
Marshall, John Painter, Instructor
Marti, Virgil Painter, Sculptor
Martin, John Rupert Historian, Lecturer
Martin, Larry Kenneth Painter, Dealer
Martone, William Robert Painter, Instructor
Massey, Ophelia Bell Painter
Masurovsky, Gregory Draftsman, Printmaker
Matthews, Gene (Eugene) Edward Painter, Educator
Matthews, Wanda Miller Printmaker
Matyas, Diane C Sculptor, Printmaker
Mazal, Ricardo Painter
McAuley, Skeet Photographer, Educator
McBride, Rita K Sculptor
McBryde, Sarah Elva Painter, Printmaker
McCall, Ann Painter, Printmaker
McClain, Robert Lee Art Dealer, Gallery Director
McClelland, Jeanne C Printmaker, Assemblage Artist
McClure, Constance Painter, Educator
McCollum, Mike L Painter, Printmaker
McConnell, Michael Patrick Sculptor
McCormick, Pam(ela) Ann Sculptor
McCoy, Ann Muralist, Draftsman
McCracken, John Harvey Sculptor, Painter
McCullough, Lee Catherine Painter
McDaniel, Richard Painter, Instructor
McDonald, Robert Herwick Writer, Critic
McDonald, Susan Strong Painter, Printmaker
McGeehan, Betty Sculptor
McGhee, John Gilmer Painter
McGinley, Ryan photographer
McIlvain, Douglas Lee Educator, Sculptor
McInerney, Sally Laird Sculptor
McKinnick, Margaret I Painter, Printmaker
McQueen, John Craftsman
Mears, Linda Shaw Painter
Meek, A J Photographer, Educator
Meek, J William, III Dealer, Consultant
Mell, Ed (Edmund) Paul, Jr Painter, Printmaker
Menses, Jan Painter, Printmaker
Merida, Margaret Braden Craftsman, Instructor
Merkin, Richard Marshall Painter, Printmaker
Merrill, David Kenneth Painter, Muralist
Merritt, David Ross Assemblage Artist, Sculptor
Metz, Matthew J Ceramist
Meyer, Melissa Painter
Meyer, Ruth Krueger Historian, Administrator
Michie, Mary Sculptor
Middlebrook, Willie Robert Photographer, Administrator
Mieczkowski, Edwin Painter
Mikus, Eleanore Painter
Milder, Jay Painter, Sculptor
Millar, Robert Conceptual Artist
Miller, Barbara Darlene Painter, Printmaker
Miller, Brenda Sculptor, Conceptual Artist
Miller, Ruth Ann Painter
Milloff, Mark David Painter, Sculptor
Milton, Peter Winslow Printmaker
Minick, Roger Photographer, Writer
Minisci, Brenda (Eileen) Sculptor, Ceramist
Mitchell, Jeffry Painter, Sculptor
Mitchell, John Blair Painter, Educator
Moeller, Robert Charles, III Consultant
Mogavero, Michael Painter
Momiyama, Nanae Painter, Educator
Mondini-Ruiz, Franco Artist
Montesinos, Vicky Painter, Printmaker
Moore, Benjamin Powell Glass Blower, Designer
Moore, John J Painter, Educator
Moore, Mark Tobin Painter, Collage Artist
Moore, Myron Neil Painter, Draftsman
Moore, Robert Eric Painter
Moores, Peter Collector
Moran, Kate Photographer, Sculptor
Morgan, Ike Edward Painter
Morris, Robert Sculptor
Morrison, Keith Anthony Painter, Educator
Morrison, Robert J Sculptor
Morrissey, Leo Conceptual Artist
Morse, Bart J Painter, Printmaker
Mosch, Deborah Cherry Educator, Painter
Moseman, M L (Mark) Painter, Collector
Moser, Kenna J Painter
Moss, Ben Frank, III painter and educator
Mowry, Elizabeth M Painter, Writer
Moya Soto, Roberto Painter, Printmaker
Muenzenmayer, Kenneth John Painter
Muller, Dave Artist
Muller, Max Paul Painter, Instructor
Murakishi, Steve Printmaking, Sculptor
Murrell, Carlton D Painter
Musgrove, Stephen Ward Administrator, Consultant
Nagatani, Patrick A Photographer
Nahas, Dominique François Museum Director, Curator
Naiman, Lee Consultant
Nardi, Dann Sculptor
Neal, Michael Shane Painter, Instructor
Neff, John Hallmark Art Historian, Museum Director
Neffson, Robert Painter
Negron, Jesus Artist
Nelson, Ruth Basha (Basha Ruth Nelson) Sculptor, Painter
Nessim, Barbara Painter, Illustrator, Educator
Netsch, Walter architect
Nevelson, Mike Sculptor
Newland, Joseph Nelson Editor, Consultant
Newsom, Barbara Ylvisaker Administrator, Writer
Newton, Richard Edward Conceptual Artist, Filmmaker
Nickard, Gary Laurence Photographer, Curator
Nierman, Leonardo M Painter, Sculptor
Norfleet, Barbara Pugh Curator, Educator
Notarbartolo, Albert Painter, Environmental Artist

OTHER COUNTRIES (cont)

Nowytski, Sviatoslav Filmmaker, Photographer
Nyambi, Obaji A Painter, Printmaker
Ocampo, Miguel Painter
O'Connell, Edward E Photographer, Printmaker
Oldenburg, Claes Thure Sculptor
Olea, Hector Curator
Oliphant, Patrick Political Cartoonist, Sculptor, Painter
Olkinetzky, Sam Collage Artist, Consultant
Ono, Yoko Conceptual Artist
Osborne, Elizabeth Painter, Critic
Oshima, Mari Sculptor
Ostendarp, Carl Painter
O'Sullivan, Judith Roberta Museum Director, Painter
Oursler, Tony Video Artist
Ox, Jack Painter, Conceptual Artist
Padovano, Anthony John Sculptor, Draftsman
Page, Casey (Vivian) Sculptor, Curator
Paik, Nam June Video Artist
Paine, Roxy Sculptor, Conceptual Artist
Palermo, Joseph Painter, Sculptor
Palmer, A Laure Sculptor, Writer
Palmer, Laura Higgins Artist
Palmer, Michael Andrew Painter, Art Dealer
Pandozy, Raffaele Martini Conceptual Artist, Lecturer
Pappajohn, John & Mary Collector, Patron
Parker, Harry S, III Museum Director
Parks, Charles Cropper Sculptor
Parsley, Jacque (Carter) Collage Artist, Gallery Director
Partin, Robert Painter, Educator
Passlof, Pat Painter, Educator
Patkin, Izhar Painter, Sculptor
Pearl, Marilyn Art Dealer
Pearlstein, Alix Video Artist
Peeples-Bright, Maija Gegeris Zack Woof Painter
Pei, I M Architect, Designer
Peppard, Jacqueline Jean Painter, Instructor
Pera, Isabella Sculptor
Perkins, A Alan Ceramist, Enamelist
Perkins, Lois Bouthillier Painter, Educator
Perret, Donna C Art Dealer, Consultant
Perry, Charles Owen Sculptor
Perry, Lincoln Frederick Painter, Sculptor
Peters, Andrea Jean Painter
Peterson, Kristin Sculptor, Assemblage Artist
Petitto, Barbara Buschell Painter, Curator
Petlin, Irving Painter
Pfeifer, Marcuse Art Dealer, Gallery Director
Phillips, Bonnie Dealer, Painter
Phillips, Harriet E Illustrator, Bookmaker, Collagist, Painter
Phillips, Richard Painter
Phillips, Sandra Curator, Historian
Piepenburg, Robert Sculptor
Pillsbury, Edmund P Museum Director
Piotrowski, Kimberly E Painter
Pipkin, Mary Margaret Artist
Pittore , Carlo Painter, Muralist
Pizzuti, Ronald A Collector
Pogany, Miklos Painter, Printmaker
Pollei, Dane F Museum Director, Curator
Pollock, Bruce Painter, Sculptor
Ponce de Leon, Michael Printmaker, Painter
Portman, Brian Printmaker
Poulos, Basilios Nicholas Painter, Educator
Powell, Dan T Photographer
Powell, Josephine photographer
Pracko, Bernard F, II Painter, Sculptor
Praczukowski, Edward Leon Painter, Educator
Preble, Michael Andrew Administrator, Photographer
Preziosi, Donald A Historian, Critic
Price, Arthur D Designer, Photographer
Price, Joan Webster Environmental Artist, Sculptor
Primm, Sylvia Marie Artist
Prohaska, Elena Anastasia Consultant, Curator
Pucker, Bernard H Art Dealer
Puett, Garnett G Sculptor
Pulitzer , Emily Rauh Collector, Consultant
Quam, Carole C Painter
Radovich, Donald Painter, Educator
Rady, Elsa Ceramist, Sculptor
Ramsauer, Joseph Francis Painter
Ramsey, Dorothy J Painter, Writer
Ransom, Henry Cleveland, Jr Painter
Ratcliff, Carter Critic, Writer
Ray, Christopher T Sculptor, Craftsman
Raydon, Alexander R Dealer, Collector
Reber, Mick Sculptor, Painter
Reger, Lawrence L Administrator
Rehm, Celeste L Painter, Educator
Rexroth, Nancy Louise Photographer
Reynolds, Jock Curator, Educator, Gallery Director
Reynolds, Robert Painter, Educator
Reynolds, Wade Painter
Rhodes, James Melvin Glass Blower, Sculptor
Richards, Jeanne Herron Printmaker, Painter
Robb, Laura Ann Painter, Instructor
Robbins, David A Conceptual Artist, Writer
Robbins, Jack C Painter, Sculptor
Roberts, Lucille (Malkia) D Painter, Educator
Robinson, Libby Painter, Sculptor
Rocco, Ron (Ronald) Anthony Sculptor, Video Artist
Rockefeller, Sharon Percy Collector
Rocklin, Raymond Sculptor, Educator
Rodan, Don Photographer, Painter
Rogers, Millard Foster, Jr Museum Director, Historian
Rogers, Otto Donald Painter, Educator
Roller, Russell Kenneth Educator, Printmaker
Romero, Rachael L Painter, Printmaker
Ronay, Matthew Sculptor
Roosen, Mia Westerlund Sculptor
Rosas, Mel Painter, Educator
Roseman, Stanley Painter, Draftsman
Rosen, Aby collector
Rosen, Hy (Hyman) Joseph Cartoonist, Sculptor
Rosenthal, John W Photographer, Publisher
Rosenthal, Seymour Painter, Lithographer
Rosenthal, Tony (Bernard) Sculptor
Ross, Wilbur Louis, Jr Collector
Rothschild, Barbara R Simon Painter
Roukes, Nicholas M Sculptor, Writer
Rowan, (C) Patrick Painter, Sculptor
Rowand, Joseph Donn Gallery Director, Art Dealer
Rubin, Ida Ely Consultant, Writer
Rudinsky, Alexander (John) Painter
Ruffing, Anne Elizabeth Painter
Russell, Robert Price Painter, Educator
Russin, Robert I Sculptor, Educator
Ryan, Richard E Painter, Printmaker
Rybczynski, Witold Marian Architect, Educator
Ryman, Robert Painter
Sabelis, Huibert Printmaker, Painter
Saccoccio, Jacqueline Artist
Sadao, Shoji Architect, Administrator
Saganic, Livio Michele Sculptor
St Clair Miller, Frances Printmaker, Painter
Salinger, Adrienne Photographer, Educator
Salloum, Jayce P Conceptual Artist, Video Artist
Sanchez, Beatrice Rivas Administrator, Printmaker
Sandel, Randye Noreen Painter, Printmaker
Sanguinetti, Eugene F Administrator, Lecturer
Santore, Joseph W Painter
Sargent, J McNeil Printmaker, Painter
Sarnoff, Arthur Saron Painter, Illustrator
Sarsony, Robert Painter, Printmaker
Sasaki, Toshio Sculptor, Environmental Artist
Sassone, Marco Painter, Printmaker
Saudek, Martha Folsom Painter
Saul, Peter Painter
Schaffer, Richard E(nos) Painter, Printmaker
Schar, Stuart Administrator, Educator
Scharf, Kenny Painter
Schenk, Joseph Bernard Director
Schiff, Lonny Printmaker, Conservator
Schlosberg, Carl Martin Art Dealer
Schmitt, Marilyn Low Historian, Administrator
Schneemann, Carolee Painter, Filmmaker
Schnorrenberg, John Martin Historian
Schreck, Michael H Painter, Sculptor
Schreiber, Eileen Sher Painter, Printmaker
Schrut, Sherry Painter, Printmaker
Schuleit, Anna artist
Schurr, Jerry M Painter, Printmaker
Schwarcz, June Theresa Craftsman, Enamelist
Schwartz, Bella Painter, Collage Artist
Schwartz, Buky Painter
Schwartz, Carl E Painter, Printmaker
Schwartz, Daniel Bennett illustrator
Scott, Arden Sculptor
Scott, Joyce T Performance Artist
Scott, Michael Painter, Printmaker
Sebastian, Jill C Environmental Artist, Sculptor
Seborovski, Carole Painter
Seeman, Helene Zucker Writer, Curator
Seerey-Lester, John Vernon Painter
Sehring, Adolf Painter, Sculptor
Selig, Manfred Collectors, Patrons
Selser, Christopher Dealer, Collector
Seltzer, Phyllis Painter, Printmaker
Semchishen, Orest M Photographer
Seppa, Heikki Markus Goldsmith, Educator
Seyle, Robert Harley Sculptor, Designer
Shapiro, Adrian Michael Lecturer, Writer
Shapiro, Joel Elias Sculptor
Sharp, Willoughby Video Artist, Consultant
Sharpe, (Norman) Blair Painter
Shaw, Isabel Sculptor, Graphic Artist
Shaw, Karen Painter, Curator
Shaw, Renata Vitzthum Administrator
Shearer, Rhonda Roland Sculptor, Writer
Sheehan, Maura A Sculptor, Painter
Sherman, Lenore Walton Painter, Writer
Sherman-Zinn, Ellen R Painter, Designer
Shikler, Aaron Painter
Shirley, Jon Anthony Collector
Shorr, Kenneth Photographer
Shuebrook, Ron (Ronald) Lee Painter, Educator
Shumaker, Rita Linder Painter, Sculptor
Shute, Roberta E Sculptor
Sichel, Kim Historian
Sideman, Carol K Painter
Siden, Franklin Dealer, Lecturer
Siegel, Fran Painter

OTHER COUNTRIES (cont)
Winters, Sandy L Painter
Witt, Nancy Camden Painter, Sculptor
Witte, Justin Painter
Wolfe, Townsend, III Director, Chief Curator
Wonner, Paul John Painter
Wood, James Arthur (Art) Cartoonist, Lecturer
Woodard, Catherine Patron
Woodson, Doris Painter
Woodward, Steven P Sculptor
Worth, Peter John Sculptor, Historian
Wright, Charles Clifford Painter, Collage Artist
Wright, Harold David Painter
Wright, Michael Fitzhugh Painter
Wulfers, Monika A Sculptor, Conceptual Artist
Wunderlich, Paul Painter, Printmaker
Wynn, Donald James Painter, Lecturer
Yampolsky, Phyllis Conceptual Artist, Painter
York, Richard Travis Art Dealer, Gallery Director
York, Tina Painter
Young, Andrew Painter
Young, Purvis Painter
Zamoiski Segal, Clair Curator, Arts Administrator
Zelt, Martie Printmaker, Muralist
Zilius, Vladas Painter
Zlowe, Florence M Painter, Draftsman
Zook, Maurine Joyce Painter; Illustrator
Zox, Larry Painter
Zugor, Sandor Painter, Printmaker
Zupan, Bruno Painter, Printmaker

Professional Classifications Index

ADMINISTRATOR

ARCHITECT

ART DEALER

CERAMIST (cont)
Hall, Susan
Hanson, Annelies Ruth
Hardy, Robert
Higgins, Edward Koelling
Higgins, MaryLou
Hindes, Chuck (Charles) Austin
Hirondelle, Anne E
Hoadley, Thomas A
Hoffman, William A
Holt, Martha A
Hughto, Margie A
Ikeda, Yoshiro
Johnson, Douglas Walter
Johnston, Randy James
Karnes, Karen
Kemenyffy, Steven
Kendall, Thomas Lyle
Kenney, Douglas
Kovatch, Ronald R
Krestensen, Ann M
Kwong, Eva
Lang, Rodger Alan
Larsen, D Dane
Larson, Jane (Warren)
Lawrence, Les
Lebeck, Carol E
Leibert, Peter R
Lincoln, Richard Mather
Lo, Beth (Elizabeth)
Lucero, Manuel F
MacDougall, Peter Steven
Manhart, Thomas Arthur
Mann, Jean (Adah)
Marak, Louis Bernard
Marshak, Arthur
Mason, John
Massaro, Karen Thuesen
Mavros, Donald Odysseus
McAdoo, Carol Westbrook
Metz, Matthew J
Meyers, Ronald G
Mignosa, Santo
Miley, Les
Miller, Brad
Mondale, Joan Adams
Moonelis, Judith C
Nadel, Ann Honig
Nagle, Ron
Natzler, Otto
Nicholas, Donna Lee
Nigrosh, Leon Isaac
Notkin, Richard T
Oestreich, Jeffrey
Orensanz, Angel L
Pardington, Ralph Arthur
Parks, Carrie Anne
Patrick, Alan K
Pearlman, George L
Pendergrass, Christine C
Perkins, A Alan
Perrone, Jeff
Pharis, Mark
Popinsky, Arnold Dave
Poupeney, Mollie
Prange, Sally Bowen
Rady, Elsa
Ransom, Brian
Rasmussen, Robert (Redd Ekks) Norman
Rippon, Ruth Margaret
Ritzer, Gail L
Rosen, Annabeth
Sadow, Harvey S, Jr
Scalzo, Joyce Ann
Schaad, Dee
Schneider, Richard Durbin
Selsor, Marcia Lorraine
Selvin, Nancy
Shaner, (George) David
Sharbaugh, Kathryn K
Siler, Patrick W
Simon, Michael J
Singh, Carolyn
Sipiorski, Dennis M
Smith, Nan S(helley)
Soldner, Paul Edmund
Spink, Frank Henry
Stanley, Christopher P
Staudinger, Bernice Marie
Stephenson, John H
Stephenson, Susanne G
Stewart, Bill
Strassberg, Roy I
Strong, Leslie (Sutter)
Sundin, Adelaide Toombs
Superior, Mara R
Sures, Jack
Sweet, Roger
Takamori, Akio
Taylor, Rosemary
Temple, Byron
Tilton, John Ellsworth
Vaccaro, Luella Grace
Veerkamp, Patrick Burke
Walters, Billie
Warashina, M Patricia
Warehall, William Donald
Wedding, Walter Joseph
Weiser, Kurt D
Westervelt, Robert F
White, Amos, IV
Wilhelmi, William Merle
Winokur, Paula Colton
Winokur, Robert
Wood, Robert L
Woodman, Betty
Zeller, Joseph R

COLLAGE ARTIST

Adams, Bobbi (Barbara) Jean Austin
Ahlstrom, Ronald Gustin
Allen, Roberta
Baker, Jill Withrow
Bardazzi, Peter
Barron, Susan
Barrow, Amanda McLaughlin
Benes, Barton Lidice
Berg, Siri
Berger, Paul Eric
Bierbaum, Gretchen Ann
Bloom, Martha
Bradford, Mark
Bramlett, Betty Jane
Brangoccio, Michael David
Brody, Carol Z
Byars, Donna
Cade, Walter, III
Cardinal, Marcelin
Collado, Lisa
Collins, Jim
Conner, Bruce
Cooper, Mark F
Cope, Louise Todd
Costan, Chris
Crable, James Harbour
Craven, David James
Culling, Richard Edward
Culver, Margaret Victoria
Cusick, Nancy Taylor
DeLaCruz, Jerry J
Dorfman, Bruce
Dubiel, Carolyn McPeek
Eden, F(lorence) Brown
Elder, Gene Wesley
Eller, Evelyn Eller Rosenbaum
Ende, Arlyn
Evans, John
Fero, Shane
Fitzgerald, Joan V
Foster, Maelee Thomson
Fraze, Denny T
Freund, Pepsi
Gilbert, Sharon
Gilchriest, Lorenzo
Goldring, Nancy Deborah
Goldstein, Gladys
Grainger, Nessa Posner
Grimaldi, Vince
Grodsky, Sheila Taylor
Guralnick, Jody
Haatoum Hamady, Walter Samuel
Harris, William Wadsworth, II
Harrison, Alice
Helioff, Anne Graile (Mrs Benjamin Hirschberg)
Hermann, Mildred L
Herrera, Arturo
Hill, Charles Christopher
Hoff, Margo
Holland, Diane Lee
Horvat, Olga
Irvin, Marianne Fanelli
Jones, Cynthia Clarke
Judson, Jeannette Alexander
Kadlec, Kristine
Kahn, Robin
Kamys, Walter
Kaplan, Leo
Kasnowski, Chester N
Kikuchi-Yngojo, Alan
Kornbluth, Frances
Krause, Dorothy Simpson
Kroll, Lynne Francine
Kuczun, Ann-Marie
Kunsch, Louis
Laico, Colette
Lenker, Marlene N
Lerner, Sandra
Levering, Robert K
Livingston, Constance Kellner
Luray, J (Schaffner)
Lynch, Mary Britten
Mackintosh, Sandra
Maher, Janet Lynn
Marca-Relli, Conrad
Marks, Roberta Barbara
Massey, John
McCabe, Maureen M
McCleary, Mary Fielding
Mead, Gerald C, Jr
Meeker, Barbara Miller
Melnick, Myron J
Miccoli, Arnaldo
Miller, Dolly (Ethel) B
Miller, Joan
Moore, Mark Tobin
Morrison, Edith Borax
Moskowitz, Shirley
Munk, Loren James
Nardone, Vincent Joseph
Newman, Louis
Nikkal, Nancy Egol
Noda, Takayo
Obler, Geri
Okoshi, E Sumiye
Olkinetzky, Sam
O'Reilly, John B
Ozonoff, Ida
Pace, James Robert
Palko Kolosvary, Paul
Parker, Wilma
Parsley, Jacque (Carter)
Patina, Rey
Peace, Bernie Kinzel
Perroni, Carol
Perry, Kathryn Powers
Peters, Diane (Peck)
Phoenix, Kaola Allen
Pildes, Sara
Pizzat, Joseph
Price, Diane Miller
Puckett, Richard Edward
Raab, Gail B
Rafferty, Joanne Miller
Ritzer, Gail L
Rizzie, Dan
Robbins, Joan Nash
Roberson, William
Rose, Roslyn
Rosen, Carol M
Saar, Betye
Schaffer, Debra S
Schiavina, Laura M
Schmit, Randall
Schneider, Shellie
Scholder, Laurence
Schwartz, Bella
Schweitzer, John Andrew
Shaddle, Alice
Shaheen, Gary Edward
Shapiro, Lois M
Sharp, Anne Catherine
Simonian, Judith
Smith, Alexis (Patricia Anne)
Smith, Rowena Marcus
Smith, Susan
Soppelsa, George
Sorokin, Janet
Sousa, John Philip
Spero, Nancy
Steckel, Anita
Steinberg, Rubin
Stewart, Duncan E
Stinsmuehlen-Amend, Susan
Stoloff, Carolyn
Stone, Gwen
Stone, Judith Elise
Stonehouse, Fred A
Sugiyama, Akiko
Sweet, Steve (Steven) Mark
Talbot, Jonathan
Tomchuk, Marjorie
Vierthaler, Bonnie
Voelker, Elizabeth
Warner, Douglas Warfield
Warriner, Laura B
Wax, John M
Weiss, Marilyn Ackerman
Werner, Donald (Lewis)
Wheeler, Janet B
Whitson, Peter Whitson Warren
Willoughby, Jane Baker
Wilmeth, Ernest, II
Wimberley, Frank Walden
Winiarski, Deborah
Wood, Melissa
Woodson, Shirley Ann
Wright, Charles Clifford
Yoder, Robert Edward
Yunich, Beverly B
Zimmerman, Kathleen Marie
Zucker, Murray Harvey

COLLECTOR

Abello, Juan
Adrian, Barbara Tramutola
Alfond, Barbara Lawrence

CONCEPTUAL ARTIST

CONCEPTUAL ARTIST (cont)

CONSERVATOR

See also **Restorer**

CONSULTANT

CRAFTSMAN

CRITIC

CURATOR

CURATOR (cont)
Martin, Lys
Mathews, Nancy Mowll
Mayfield, Signe S
Mayo, Margaret Ellen
Mayo, Marti
McCandless, Barbara Ann
McFadden, David Revere
McKenna, George LaVerne
McShine, Kynaston Leigh
Meadows, Patricia B
Metzger, Robert Paul
Mhire, Herman P
Miles, Ellen Gross
Miller, Marc H
Mitchell, Shannon Dillard
Mock, Martha L
Modi-Vitale, Lydia
Moir, Alfred
Mokeme, Oscar O
Moldenhauer, Susan
Monk, Robert Evan, Jr
Moore, John L
Morin, France
Morin-Miller, Carmen A
Morton, Robert Alan
Moser, Joann
Mozley, Anita Ventura
Muller, Priscilla Elkow
Munhall, Edgar
Murdock, Robert Mead
Murray, Richard Newton
Myers, Terry R
Naef, Weston John
Naeve, Milo M
Nahas, Dominique François
Nasgaard, Roald
Nash, Steven Alan
Naumann, Francis M
Nawrocki, Dennis Alan
Nelson, Jane Gray
Nelson, Jon Allen
Nemec, Vernita McClish N'Cognita
Nickard, Gary Laurence
Nickel, Douglas Robert
Nordan, Antoinette Spanos Johnson
Nordstrom, Alison Devine
Norelli, Martina Roudabush
Norfleet, Barbara Pugh
O'Beil, Hedy
Olea, Hector
Olin, Ferris
Olson, Roberta Jeanne Marie
Onorato, Ronald Joseph
Orr-Cahall, Anona Christina
Ostiguy, Jean-Rene
Ostrow, Stephen Edward
Ottmann, Klaus
Overland, Carlton Edward
Owens, Gwendolyn Jane
Oyuela, Raul M
Page, Casey (Vivian)
Paikowsky, Sandra R
Pal, Pratapaditya
Palladino-Craig, Allys
Pare, Richard
Parsons, Merribell Maddux
Pasquine, Ruth
Patton, Tom
Payton, Cydney M
Peeps, Claire
Pennington, Estill Curtis
Pepich, Bruce Walter W
Percy, Ann Buchanan
Perreault, John
Peterson, Robyn G
Petitto, Barbara Buschell
Pettibone, John Wolcott
Phillips, Sandra
Pitts, Terence Randolph
Platzker, David
Plous, Phyllis
Pohlman, Lynette
Pollei, Dane F
Posner, Helaine J
Pounian, Albert Kachouni
Pressly, Nancy Lee
Price, Marla
Prohaska, Elena Anastasia
Putterman, Susan Lynn
Raggio, Olga
Ramirez, Mari Carmen
Randall, Lilian M C
Rascon, Armando
Rathbone, Eliza Euretta
Rathbun, William Jay
Ravenal, John B
Raydon, Alexander R
Reed, Dennis James
Reid, Katharine Lee
Reilly, Bernard Francis
Reynolds, Jock
Reynolds, Valrae
Riccio, Louis Nicholas
Richardson, Trevor J
Rifkin, Ned
Riley, Terence
Rinder, Lawrence R
Rindfleisch, Jan
Rishel, Joseph John, Jr
Roberts, Mark Dennis
Robertson, E Bruce
Robison, Andrew
Rogers, Sarah
Rosenberg, Alex Jacob
Rosenfield, John M
Rosensaft, Jean Bloch
Rosenthal, Mark L
Rosenzweig, Phyllis D
Royce-Silk, Suzanne
Rubin, David S
Rubinstein, Charlotte Streifer
Rudenstine, Angelica Zander
Rust, David E
Ryan, David Michael
Rychlak, Bonnie L
St John, Terry N
Saltz, Jerry
San Chirico, Joanie
Sauer, Jane Gottlieb
Saywell, Edward
Scalzo, Joyce Ann
Schaefer, Scott Jay
Schmidt, Charles
Schneiderman, Richard S
Schwager, Michael R
Schweitzer, John Andrew
Scott, Deborah Emont
Seeman, Helene Zucker
Segal, Tama & David
Self, Dana Rae
Selz, Peter H
Sewell, Darrel L
Sewell, Jack Vincent
Shaman, Sanford Sivitz
Shapiro, Michael Edward
Shaw, Karen
Shaw, Louise E
Shaw, Nancy (Rivard)
Sheridan, Helen Adler
Shimizu, Yoshiaki
Shlien, Helen S
Shoemaker, Innis Howe
Sill, Gertrude Grace
Silver, Larry Arnold
Silverman, Lanny Harris
Simpson, Bennett
Simpson, Marianna Shreve
Sims, Lowery Stokes
Sims, Patterson
Sipiorski, Dennis M
Sischy, Ingrid B
Slemmons, Rod
Smith, Ann Y
Smith, Elizabeth Angele
Smith, Frances Kathleen
Smith, Jaune Quick-to-See
Smith, Lawry
Smith, Raechell M
Smith, Valerie
Sobel, Dean
Sobol, Judith Ellen
Sonday, Milton Franklin, Jr
Sorkin, Jenni
Spangenberg, Kristin L
Spencer, Mark J
Stahl, Alan M
Stavitsky, Gail Beth
Stearns, Robert
Stecyk, Craig R
Steel, Virginia Oberlin
Stein, Judith Ellen
Stetson, Daniel Everett
Stevens, Andrew Rich
Stewart, Lorelei
Stewart, Sheila L
Stofflet, Mary
Storr, Robert
Stover, Donald Lewis
Strick, Jeremy
Strueken-Bachmann, Marion
Stuckey, Charles F
Sturges, Hollister
Suffolk, Randall
Suhre, Terry L
Sujo, Clara Diament
Sullivan, Ruth Wilkins
Sultan, Terrie Frances
Sutton, Peter C
Sweeney, J Gray
Talley, Dan R
Tannenbaum, Barbara Lee
Tannenbaum, Judith E
Taubes, Timothy Evan
Tepfer, Diane
Thackston, R King
Thomason, Michael Vincent
Thurman, Christa Charlotte Mayer
Toll, Barbara Elizabeth
Tracy, Robert H
Travis, David B
Tripp, Susan Gerwe
Tromeur, Robyn Lori
Truettner, William H
Tuchman, Maurice
Tuchman, Phyllis
Tucker, Anne Wilkes
Tucker, James Ewing
Tucker, Marcia
Tuer, Dot (Dorothy) J
Tullos, Mark A, Jr
Tully, Judd
Tunis, Roslyn
Tupitsyn, Margarita
Turnbull, Betty
Tuttle, Lisa
Upton, John David
Valenstein, Suzanne Gebhart
Vanco, John Leroy
Van Haaften, Julia
Velick, Bruce
Vergne, Philippe
Vincent, Clare
Vitali, Julius M
Von Bothmer, Dietrich Felix
Vroom, Steven M
Waisbrot, Ann M
Warren, David Boardman
Warren, Lynne
Watkinson, Patricia Grieve
Watriss, Wendy
Watson, Ross
Wayne, Cynthia M
Weinberg, H Barbara
Weinzapfel, Connie A
Weiss, Rachel
Welch, Stuart Cary
Wheelock, Arthur Kingsland, Jr
Whitcomb, Therese Truitt
Wilkin, Karen
Williams, Benjamin Forrest
Williams, William Earle
Willis, Deborah
Willumson, Glenn Gardner
Wilson, Kay E
Witt, David L
Wixom, William D
Wolanin, Barbara A
Wolfe, Townsend, III
Wooby, William Joseph
Woodward, Kesler Edward
Wright, Virginia
Wynn, Gaines Clore
Yard, Sally Elizabeth
Yarotsky, Lori
Yassin, Robert Alan
Yates, Steven A
Yau, John
Young, Barbara Neil
Zafran, Eric Myles
Zakian, Michael
Zamoiski Segal, Clair
Zeitlin, Marilyn A
Zelevansky, Lynn
Zerner, Henri Thomas
Zilczer, Judith Katy
Zurier, Rebecca F

DESIGNER

Abramson, Elaine Sandra
Albrecht, Mary Dickson
Alicea, Jose
Alten, Jerry
Anderson, Winslow
Apt, Charles
Arnholm, Ronald Fisher
Atkins, Gordon Lee
Atlas, Nava
Behrens, Roy R
Berkowitz, Henry
Bernstein, William Joseph
Bertoia, (Mr) Val
Bertolli, Eugene Emil
Biblos, Mahia
Bisgyer, Barbara G (Cohn)
Blumrich, Stephen
Bostick, William Allison
Brauer Ferns, Connie Ann
Bredlow, Tom
Breed, Charles Ayars
Brod, Stanford
Brubaker, Jack
Byrne, Charles Joseph
Califf, Marilyn Iskiwitz
Canniff, Bryan Gregory
Cartmell, Helen
Chermayeff, Ivan
Choo, Chunghi

DIRECTOR

DIRECTOR (cont)
Metzger, Robert Paul
Millard, Charles Warren, III
Monaghan, Kathleen Mary
Morrisey, Marena Grant
Muno, Richard Carl
Nelson, Harold B
Palladino-Craig, Allys
Pavlova, Marina
Phillips, Laughlin
Pierce, Charles Eliot, Jr
Pitts, Terence Randolph
Powell, Earl Alexander, III
Prakapas, Dorothy
Quick, Edward Raymond
Reilly, Richard
Reynolds, John (Jock) M
Rindfleisch, Jan
Robinson, Cleo
Sadao, Shoji
Schenk, Joseph Bernard
Schloder, John E
Schultz, Douglas George
Seligman, Thomas Knowles
Sharp, Lewis Inman
Silverman, Lanny Harris
Slovin, Rochelle
Smith, Gregory Allgire
Smith, Jan
Smith, John W
Smith, Lawry
Stewart, John Lincoln
Stewart, Sheila L
Strickler, Susan Elizabeth
Stux, Stefan Victor
Suhre, Terry L
Sundberg, Carl Gustave
Sundblad, Emily
Sussman, Gary Lawrence
Talbott, Susan Lubowsky
Taulbee, Ann
Trechsel, Gail Andrews
Tromeur, Robyn Lori
Trop, Sandra
Tyler, Ron C
Valdes, Karen W
Vanier, Jerre Lynn
Vigtel, Gudmund
Warshaw, Elaine N
Wendorf, Richard Harold
White, Deborah
Wilson, Kay E
Winer, Helene
Winter, Amy H
Wolfe, Townsend, III

DRAFTSMAN

Anderson, Robert Dale
Anthony, William Graham
Antrim, Craig Keith
Arcilesi, Vincent J
Bachardy, Don
Batchelor, Anthony John
Bechtle, C Ronald
Ben Tre, Howard B
Bilodeau, Daniel Alain
Birmelin, Robert
Bohlen, Nina (Celestine Eustis Bohlen)
Broker, Karin
Brown, Gary Hugh
Buckner, Kay Lamoreux
Casas, Fernando R
Chevins, Christopher M
Cole, Grace V
Cook, Stephen D
Daou, Annabel
Drake, Peter
Droege, Anthony Joseph, II
Duncan, Richard (Hurley)
Duque, Adonay
Eberle, Edward Samuel
Eden, Glenn
Eichel, Edward W
Elloian, Peter
Fekete, Brian
Finke, Leonda Froelich
Gechtoff, Sonia
Geiger, Phillip Neil
George, Thomas
Gitlin, Michael
Glier, Mike
Goldsleger, Cheryl
Goodman, Janis G
Gunning, Simon Ben
Hough, Winston
Howze, James Dean
Huffington, Anita
Hunkler, Dennis
Hurson, Michael
Insley, Will
Isaacson, Marcia Jean
Kelley, Heather Ryan
Kelly, William Joseph
Kijek, Manon Catherine (Manon Catherine Cleary)
Kimball, Wilford Wayne, Jr
King, Clive
Kjok, Sol
Koch, Philip
Korman, Harriet R
Koscielny, Margaret
Kosta, Angela
Kuhn, Bob
Lasansky, Leonardo
Lasansky, Mauricio L
Leary, Daniel
Leshyk, Tonie
Leys, Dale Daniel
Lieberman, Louis (Karl)
Lima, Jacqueline (Dutton)
Martin, Jane
Martin, Younghee Choi
Masurovsky, Gregory
Matteson, Ira
McCoy, Ann
Moore, Myron Neil
Morrow, Terry
Moss-Vreeland, Patricia
Munce, James Charles
Murphy, Hass
Newman, John
Nutt, Jim
Oginz, Richard
Padovano, Anthony John
Paige, Wayne Leo
Pfaffman, William Scott
Phillips, Tony
Piene, Chloe
Pochmann, Virginia
Polan, Annette
Ramanauskas, Dalia Irena
Richards, Bill (William) A
Robinson, Duncan (David)
Roseman, Stanley
Ross, Janice Koenig
Rossman, Michael
Routon, David F
Schmidt, Teresa Tempero
Schneider, Julie Saecker
Schwarz, Judith
Shechter, Laura J
Smith, Gary Douglas
Steczynski, John Myron
Steinhardt, Alice
Stewart, F Clark
Terry, Christopher T
Torn, Jerry (Gerald J)
Twarogowski, Leroy Andrew
Weiss, Clemens
White, Franklin
Wingo, Michael B
Witkin, Jerome
Wojtyla, Haase (Walter) Joseph
Young, Marjorie Ward
Zlowe, Florence M

EDITOR

Adams, Laurie Schneider
Aminoff, Judith Gintz
Atkins, Robert
Baker, Elizabeth C
Baldridge, Mark S
Bandy, Mary Lea
Behrens, Roy R
Blake, Jane Salley
Blakeney, Rae
Blumrich, Stephen
Cassidy, Victor Monod
Cembalest, Robin
Chiroussot-Chambeaux, Jane
Cohen, David
Colina, Armando G
D'Andrea, Jeanne
De Puma, Richard Daniel
Doherty, Michael Stephen
Ebony, David
Edmonston, Paul
Esterow, Milton
Fear, Daniel E
Ferrara, Annette
Fine, Elsa Honig
Fuller, Diana
Gilchrist, Elizabeth Brenda
Goddard, Donald
Goldberger, Paul Jesse
Hartman, Rose
Hirsch, Faye
Hochfield, Sylvia
Hoffman, Michael E
Howarth, Shirley Reiff
Jardine, Donald Leroy
Kaufman, Jason Edward
Kennon, Arthur Bruce
Koplos, Janet
Kramer, Hilton
Kuchta, Ronald Andrew
Kusnerz, Peggy Ann F
Lawton, Thomas
Macadam, Barbara A
Martel, Richard
Martin, Floyd W
McCarthy, Maura
McDarrah, Fred William
McPherson, Bruce Rice
McTwigan, Michael
Merkel, Jayne (Silverstein)
Meyer, Susan E
Morin, James Corcoran
Morton, Robert Alan
Nemser, Cindy
Newland, Joseph Nelson
Prakapas, Eugene Joseph
Rich, David
Rinehart, Michael
Robbins, Eugenia S
Roberts, Helene Emylou
Rossen, Susan F
Santiago-Ibarra, Beatrice Mayte
Schjeldahl, Peter
Sischy, Ingrid B
Sward, Robert S
Szabo, Joseph George
Tennant, Donna Kay
Thorson, Alice R
Tobin, Nancy
Vetrocq, Marcia E
Vine, Richard
Vourvoulias-Bush, Alberto
Wechsler, Susan
Weiss, John Joseph
Westwater, Angela King
Wiens, Ann
Wyrick, Charles Lloyd, Jr

EDUCATOR (COLLEGE/UNIVERSITY)

Ackerman, Gerald Martin
Ackerman, James S
Ackerman, Rudy Schlegel
Adams, Pat
Adamy, George E
Addison, Byron Kent
Adler, Tracy L
Agee, William C
Ahlsted, David R
Ahysen, Harry Joseph
Aistars, John
Akawie, Thomas Frank
Albert, Calvin
Alexander-Greene, Grace George
Alexenberg, Mel
Alexick, David Francis
Allan, William George
Allara, Pamela Edwards
Allen, Bruce Wayne
Allen, Jere Hardy
Allen, Judith S
Allen, Nancy Schuster
Allen, Ralph
Allen, William J
Allentuck, Marcia Epstein
Allumbaugh, James
Allyn, Jerri
Altfeld, Merwin Richard
Altmann, Henry S
Altshuler, Bruce J
Alvarez, Candida
Alvarez-Cervela, Jose Maria
Ambrose, Charles Edward
Anderson, Daniel J
Anderson, Maxwell L
Andrade, Edna Wright
Andres, Glenn Merle
Andrew, David Neville
Andrews, Nancy Evelyn
Andriulli, Robert
Annis, Norman L
Antreasian, Garo Zareh
App, Timothy
Appelson, Herbert J
Arbuckle, Linda J
Ard, Saradell
Armstrong, Bill Howard
Arnheim, Rudolf
Arnholm, Ronald Fisher
Arnold, Nancy Ann
Arnold, Paul Beaver
Arnold, Ralph Moffett
Arnold, Robert Lloyd
Artemis, Maria Artemis Papageorge
Asher, Frederick M
Asihene, Emmanuel V
Askman, Tom K
Atkins, Robert
Atkinson, Eric Newton
Atwell, Allen

EDUCATOR (cont)
Crimp, Douglas
Crist, William Gary
Crosby, Ranice W
Crossgrove, Roger Lynn
Crouse, Michael Glenn
Crozier, Richard Lewis
Crum, Katherine B
Cunningham, E C (Eldon) Lloyd
Cuppaidge, Virginia
Curnow, Kathy
Cutler, Ethel Rose
Dablow, Dean Clint
D'Agostino, Peter
Dahill, Thomas Henry, Jr
Dailey, Dan (Daniel) Owen
Dale, William Scott Abell
Dalglish, Meredith Rennels
Daly, Stephen Jeffrey
Danhausen, Eldon
Daniels, David Robert
Dantzic, Cynthia Maris
Darriau, Jean-Paul
Darrow, Paul Gardner
Daugherty, Michael F
Davidson, David Isaac
Davis, D Jack
Davis, Jack R
Davis, Lisa Corinne
Davis, Meredith J
Davison, Bill
Deaderick, Joseph
Deal, Joe
Dean, Kevin Lee
Dean, Nat
De Blasi, Anthony Armando
de Bretteville, Sheila Levrant
DeCarava, Roy Rudolph
DeGenevieve, Barbara
De Kergommeaux, Duncan
DeLap, Tony
DeLauro, Joseph Nicola
Dell, Robert Christopher
Della-Volpe, Ralph Eugene
DeLong, David G
De Luca, Joseph Victor
Deming, David Lawson
Dernovich, Donald Frederick
Derryberry, Virginia Taylor
Desmidt, Thomas H
De Soto, Lewis D
Detmers, William Raymond
Devlin, Lucinda Alice
Dhaemers, Robert August
Dial, Gail
Diaz, Lope (Max)
Dickerson, Daniel Jay
Dietrich, Linnea S
Dill, Guy
Dinsmore, John Norman
Dluhy, Deborah Haigh
Dmytruk, Ihor R
Do, Kim V
Dodd, Lois
Dodd, M(ary) Irene
D'Oench, Ellen Gates
Doll, Donald Arthur
Donahue, Philip Richard
Donley, Robert Morris
Donnelly, Marian Card
Dooley, David I
Doremus, Susanne
Doren, Henry J T
Dorethy, Rex E
Doudera, Gerard
Dowell, John E, Jr
Downs, Stuart Clifton
Doyle, Joe
Doyle, Tom
Drachnik (Cay), Catherine Meldyn
Dreskin, Jeanet Steckler
Drewal, Henry John
Driskell, David Clyde
Drohojowska-Philp, Hunter
Duckworth, Ruth
Dunlap, William
Dunn, Phillip Charles
Durant, Sam
Dwyer, Eugene Joseph
Dwyer, James
Eades, Luis Eric
Economos, Michael E
Edgerton, Debra
Edison, Diane
Edminston, Scott
Edmiston, Sara Joanne
Edmonston, Paul
Edwards, James F
Edwards, Melvin
Edwards-Tucker, Yvonne Leatrice
Egbert, Elizabeth Frances
Eger, Marilyn Rae
Eglitis, Laimons
Ehrlich, George
Eickhorst, William Sigurd
Eide, John
Eisenberg, Marvin
Eisner, Elliot Wayne
Eiswerth, Barry
Elkins, Lane
Ellinger, Ilona E
Else, Robert John
Emmert, Pauline Gore
Engeran, Whitney John, Jr
Epting, Marion Austin
Erdle, Rob
Erikson, Christine
Erlebacher, Martha Mayer
Erman, Bruce
Ertman, Earl Leslie
Evans, Bob James
Evans, Garth
Evans, Richard
Evans, Robert Graves
Even, Robert Lawrence
Ewald, Wendy T
Ewing, Susan R
Facey, Martin Kerr
Fahlen, Charles C
Fairfield, Richard Thomas
Fairlie, Carol Hunter
Falsetta, Vincent Mario
Falsetto, Mario
Farmer, John David
Farwell, Beatrice
Fay, Ming G
Fearing, William Kelly
Feldhaus, Paul A
Feldman, Bella
Feldman, Edmund Burke
Feldman, Joel Benet
Feltus, Alan Evan
Feng, Z L
Fensch, Charles Everette
Fenton, Howard Carter
Fenwick, Roly (William Roland)
Ferrara, Annette
Ferreira, Armando Thomas
Fertitta, Angela
Fichter, Robert W
Fiero, Gloria K
Filipowski, Richard E
Finch, Richard Dean
Fine, Jud
Fink, Herbert Lewis
Fink, Larry (Laurence) B
Finke, Leonda Froelich
Finkelstein, Henry D
Finkler, Robert Allan
Finley, Gerald Eric
Fisch, Arline Marie
Fischer, Thomas Jeffrey
Flam, Jack D
Flecker, Maurice Nathan
Fleischer, Roland Edward
Fleminger, Susan N
Fletcher, Harrell
Flick, Robbert
Flowers, Thomas Earl
Fogg, Monica
Fong, Wen C
Foosaner, Judith
Ford, Harry X
Formicola, John Joseph
Fornas, Leander
Forsman, Chuck (Charles) Stanley
Forsyth, Ilene H(aering)
Forsythe, Donald John
Foster, April
Foster, Maelee Thomson
Frank, David
Frankel, Dextra
Fraze, Denny T
Freed, Douglass Lynn
Freeman, Jeff(rey Vaughn)
Freund, Will Frederick
Frey, Barbara Louise
Friedberg, Richard S
Frinta, Mojmir Svatopluk
Frost, Stuart Homer
Funk, Roger L
Furman, David Stephen
Fusco, Laurie S
Fussiner, Howard
Gallagher, Cynthia
Galles, Arie Alexander
Gallo, Frank
Gammon, Juanita L
Ganes, Lucy
Garcia, Rupert (Marshall) R
Garnett, William Ashford
Garnsey, Clarke Henderson
Garoian, Charles Richard
Garrard, Mary DuBose
Gates, Harry Irving
Gauvreau, Robert George
Geddes, Robert
Geeslin, Lee Gaddis
Gelber, Samuel
Gelernter, David H
Gelinas, Robert William
George, Raymond Ellis
Gerdts, William H
Gerhold, William Henry
Germano, Thomas
Geske, Norman Albert
Ghikas, Panos George
Gibbons, Hugh (James)
Gibson, Ann
Gibson, Benedict S
Gibson, Walter Samuel
Gillingwater, Denis Claude
Gilmor, Jane E
Gilpin, Henry Edmund
Gips, C L Terry
Girard, (Charles) Jack
Glaser, Bruce
Glasson, Lloyd
Gluck, Heidi
Godsey, Glenn
Goehlich, John Ronald
Goetzl, Thomas Maxwell
Golbin, Andree
Gold, Sharon Cecile
Goldberger, Paul Jesse
Goldring, Nancy Deborah
Goldsmith, Benedict Isaac
Goldstein, Howard
Gordon, John S
Gore, Tom
Gorski, Richard Kenny
Gough, Georgia Belle Leach
Gourevitch, Jacqueline
Granne, Regina
Graves, Michael
Grear, J(ames) Malcolm
Green, Art
Green, David Oliver
Greenamyer, George Mossman
Greer, Wesley Dwaine
Gregor, Harold Laurence
Gregory, Joan
Griffith, Dennison W
Griffiths, William Perry
Grigsby, Jefferson Eugene, Jr
Grimes, Margaret W
Griner, Ned H
Grippi, Salvatore William
Gross, Elissa Frances
Grossman, Barbara
Grossman, Maurice Kenneth
Grucza, Leo (Victor)
Guerin, John William
Gunasinghe, Siri
Gunn, Paul James
Gunning, Tom
Gunter, Frank Elliott
Gussow, Sue Ferguson
Gutzeit, Fred
Gyermek, Stephen A
Hackett, Mickey
Hafif, Marcia
Hageman, Charles Lee
Hahn, Betty
Hall, John A
Hall, Michael David
Hallman, Ted, Jr
Hamann, Marilyn D
Hamblen, Dr Karen A
Hamilton, George Earl
Hamilton, W Paul C
Hamlet, Susan H
Hamlett, Dale Edward
Hammer, Alfred Emil
Hammond, Gale Thomas
Hammond, Mary Sayer
Hampton, Anita
Hampton, Phillip Jewel
Hamwi, Richard Alexander
Hankey, Robert E
Hannah, John Junior
Hannibal, Joseph Harry
Hannum, Gillian Greenhill
Hansell, Freya
Hansen, Frances Frakes
Hansen, Gaylen Capener
Hansen, Harold (Harry) John
Harden, Marvin
Hardy, Robert
Harmon, David Edward
Harold-Steinhauser, Judith
Harootunian, Claire M
Harries, Mags (Margaret) L
Harris, Gloriane
Harris, Ronna S
Harrison, Tony
Harshfield, Neil Alan
Hartley, Paul Jerome
Hartman, Joanne A

EDUCATOR (cont)
Macaray, Lawrence Richard
MacDonald, Bruce K
MacDonald, Scott
Mack, Charles Randall
MacKillop, Rod
Maddox, Jerrold Warren
Mahlke, Ernest D
Mahmoud, Ben
Mahoney, Joella Jean
Mahoney, Michael R T
Mai, James L
Mailman, Cynthia
Majeski, Thomas H
Maldre, Mati
Malenda, James William
Mallory, Nina Ayala
Mancusi-Ungaro, Carol
Manhart, Thomas Arthur
Mansfield, Robert Adams
Marak, Louis Bernard
Marasco, Rose
Marcheschi, (Louis) Cork
Marcus, Irving E
Marcus, Marcia
Marriott, William Allen
Marrow, James Henry
Marsh, David Foster
Marshall, Robert Leroy
Marshall, Thomas E
Martin, Alexander Toedt
Martin, Bernard Murray
Martin, Margaret M
Martinsen, Ivar Richard
Marton, Pier
Mason, Novem M
Massad, George Daniel
Massey, Charles Wesley, Jr
Matthews, Gene (Eugene) Edward
Matthews, Harriett
Mauro, Robert F
Mavigliano, George Jerome
Mayer, Edward Albert
Mayer, Susan Martin
Mayes, Steven Lee
Maynard, William
Mayrs, David Blair
McAuley, Skeet
McCarthy, Dennis
McChesney, Clifton
McClanahan, John D
McCleary, Mary Fielding
McClure, Constance
McClure, Thomas F
McCoy, Katherine Braden
McCoy, Kevin & Jennifer
McCoy, Michael Dale
McCoy, T Frank
McCready, Eric Scott
McDaniel, Craig Milton
McElroy, Jacquelyn Ann
McFee, June King
McGarrell, James
McGee, J David
McGee, Winston Eugene
McGibbon, Phyllis
McGinley, Maribeth Wilson
McGough, Charles E
McHam, Sarah Blake Wilk
McIlvain, Douglas Lee
McIlvain, Frances H
McIlvane, Edward James
McIntosh, Jerry C
McKenzie, Allan Dean
McLean, James Albert
McNally, Sheila John
McNamara, Mary Jo
McPhee, Sarah Collyer
McPherson, Larry E
Mead, Gerald C, Jr
Meek, A J
Meeker, Barbara Miller
Meister, Michael William
Mejer, Robert Lee
Melchert, James Frederick
Mesches, Arnold
Messersmith, Fred Lawrence
Metzker, Ray K
Meyer, Jerry Don
Meyers, Ronald G
Michaux, Henry Gaston
Michels, Eileen Manning
Mickish, Verle L
Middlebrook, David A
Migliaccio, Anthony J
Mikus, Eleanore
Miley, Les
Miller, Arthur Green
Miller, Denise
Milliken, Gibbs
Mills, Frederick Van Fleet
Milnes, Robert Winston
Min, Yong Soon
Miraglia, Anthony J
Mitchell, John Blair
Mitchell, Robin
Moldroski, Al R
Momiyama, Nanae
Monroe, Betty Iverson
Monroe, Gerald
Montford, James Webster, Jr
Monthan, Guy
Monti, John
Montoya, Malaquias
Moore, Anne F
Moore, John J
Moore, Todd Somers
Morgan, Clarence (Edward)
Morgan, Dahlia
Morganstern, Anne McGee
Morganstern, James
Morin, Thomas Edward
Morrill, Michael Lee
Morrison, Keith Anthony
Mosch, Deborah Cherry
Moss, Ben Frank, III
Moss, Karen Canner
Moyer, Linda Lee
Muhlberger, Richard Charles
Mullen, James Martin
Mullen, Philip Edward
Mundy, E James
Munhall, Edgar
Munitz, Barry
Munzner, Aribert
Murashima, Kumiko
Murphy, Dudley C
Murphy, Marilyn L
Musgrave, Shirley H
Myers, Virginia Anne
Myford, James C
Naar, Harry I
Nagin, Mary D
Navrat, Den(nis) Edward
Nawara, Jim
Nawrocki, Dennis Alan
Nawrocki, Thomas Dennis
Nees, Lawrence
Nelson, Steven D
Nesin, Jeffrey David
Nessim, Barbara
Neumann, Andrew
New, Lloyd H Kiva
Nichols, Edward Edson
Nichols, Francis N, II
Nicholson, Roy William
Nick, George
Nickson, Graham G
Nochlin, Linda (Pommer)
Noe, Jerry Lee
Norfleet, Barbara Pugh
Norgard, Karen-Sam
Norwood, Malcolm Mark
Novinski, Lyle Frank
Oakes, John Warren
Ockenga, Starr
Ockerse, Thomas
O'Connell, George D
O'Connor, John Arthur
O'Connor, Stanley James
O'Connor, Thom
Odate, Toshio
O'Gorman, James Francis
Ohlson, Douglas Dean
Olin, Laurie Dewar
Olsen Bergman, Ciel (Cheryl) Bowers
Olson, Douglas John
Olson, Linda A
Olson, Richard W
Olynyk, Patricia J
Omar, Margit
Ondish, Andrea
Orenstein, Gloria Feman
Ortiz, Raphael Montanez
Osborne, Cynthia A
Osborne, Frederick S
O'Sickey, Joseph Benjamin
Ostrom, Gladys Snell
Oxman, Mark
Pablo
Papier, Maurice Anthony
Pardee, William Hearne
Parfenoff, Michael S
Parkhurst, Charles
Parks, Carrie Anne
Parrino, George
Parris, Nina Gumpert
Partin, Robert
Parton, Ralf
Partridge, Loren Wayne
Paskewitz, Bill, Jr
Passlof, Pat
Paterson, Anthony R
Patnode, J Scott
Patrick, Joseph Alexander
Patterson, Curtis Ray
Pavlova, Marina
Pearlstein, Philip
Pearlstein, Seymour
Pearson, John
Pecchenino, J Ronald
Peck, Lee Barnes
Peckham, Nicholas
Pekarsky, Mel(vin) Hirsch
Penkoff, Ronald Peter
Pentak, Stephen
Perkins, Lois Bouthillier
Perlin, Ruth Rudolph
Perlman, Joel Leonard
Perry, Donald Dean
Perry, Edward (Ted) Samuel
Perzynski, Bogdan P
Peterson, Dorothy (Hawkins)
Peterson, Larry D
Peven, Michael David
Pfaff, Judy
Phelan, Andrew L
Piatek, Francis John
Piehl, Walter Jason, Jr
Pierce, Ann Trucksess
Pijanowski, Eugene M
Pincus-Witten, Robert A
Pindell, Howardena Doreen
Pirkl, James Joseph
Pizzat, Joseph
Place, Bradley Eugene
Plagens, Peter
Plumb, James Douglas
Pokorny, Jan Hird
Pollitt, Jerome Jordan
Polonsky, Arthur
Ponsot, Claude F
Pontynen, Arthur
Poplawska, Anna
Porter, Albert Wright
Porter, Jeanne Chenault
Porter, Katherine Pavlis
Postiglione, Corey M
Poulos, Basilios Nicholas
Powell, Dan T
Praczukowski, Edward Leon
Pressly, William Laurens
Preston, George Nelson
Price, Leslie Kenneth
Price, Michael Benjamin
Prina, Stephen James
Prince, Arnold
Prince, Richard Edmund
Prochownik, Walter A
Pujol, Elliott
Purdy, Henry Carl
Purtle, Carol Jean
Putterman, Florence Grace
Quinones Keber, Eloise
Quiroz, Alfred James
Radovich, Donald
Rainer, Yvonne
Raiselis, Richard
Ramos, (Mel) Melvin John
Rand, Harry
Rascoe, Stephen Thomas
Ray, Timothy L
Rayen, James Wilson
Read, Dave (David) Dolloff
Redd, Richard James
Reddington, Charles Leonard
Reddix, Roscoe Chester
Reed, Robert James, Jr
Reeser, Robert D
Rehm, Celeste L
Reichert, Donald Karl
Reif, (F) David
Reimann, William P
Reker, Les
Rembert, Virginia Pitts
Renfro, Charles
Reynolds, Jock
Reynolds, Robert
Rhodes, David
Rice, Norman Lewis
Richardson, John Adkins
Richardson, Sam
Richardson, W C
Riggs, Gerry
Riley, Barbra Bayne
Riley, Sarah A
Ringness, Charles Obert
Risbeck, Philip Edward
Riseling, Robert Lowell
Riss, Murray
Robbins, Warren M
Roberson, Samuel Arndt
Roberts, Lucille (Malkia) D
Roberts, William Edward
Robertson, David Alan
Robinson, Chris (Christopher) Thomas
Robinson, Lilien Filipovitch
Robinson, Mary Ann
Rocklin, Raymond

EDUCATOR (cont)
Von Bothmer, Dietrich Felix
Wachs, Ethel
Walburg, Gerald
Waldman, Louis A
Walford, E John
Walker, Larry
Walker, Larry
Wallace, Kenneth William
Wallace, Richard William
Wallin, Leland Dean
Walsh-Piper, Kathy A
Waltemath, Joan
Walters, Sylvia Solochek
Walton, Guy E
Wands, Robert James
Warashina, M Patricia
Ward, Joseph Marshall
Warren, Jacqueline Louise
Wasserman, Burton
Wasserman, Jack
Watson, Ronald G
Weale, Mary Jo
Webb, Jeffrey R
Weber, Idelle Lois
Wechter, Vivienne Thaul
Wedding, Walter Joseph
Weege, William
Weidner, Mary Elizabeth
Weinberg, H Barbara
Weintraub, Annette
Weisberg, Gabriel P
Weisberg, Ruth Ellen
Weisman, Gary Michael
Wells, Mac
Welpott, Jack Warren
Welter, Cole H
Werfel, Gina S
Werger, Art(hur) Lawrence
Wert, Ned Oliver
Westfall, Carol D
Wethli, Mark
Wheelock, Arthur Kingsland, Jr
Whitchurch, Charles A
White, Bruce Hilding
White, James Richard
Whitehead, Frances
Whitlock, John Joseph
Whitney, Maynard Merle
Whitson, Peter Whitson Warren
Whittington, Jon Hammon
Wible, Mary Grace
Widmer, Gwen Ellen
Wilbert, Robert John
Wiley, William T
Willard, Christopher A
Williams, John Wesley
Williams, William Thomas
Willis, Jay Stewart
Willumson, Glenn Gardner
Wilmerding, John
Wilson, Anne Gawthrop
Wilson, Elizabeth (Jane)
Wilson, June
Wilson, Wallace
Wiman, Bill
Wimmer, Gayle
Wink, Don (Jon Donnel)
Winkler, Maria Paula
Winkler, Max-Karl
Winokur, Robert
Winter, Gerald Glen
Wisnosky, John G
Wodiczko, Krzysztof
Wogstad, James Everet
Woitena, Ben S
Wolber, Paul J
Wolfe, Lynn Robert
Wolsky, Jack
Wood, McCrystle
Woodford, Don (Donald) Paul
Woods, David G
Wright, Frank
Wurmfeld, Sanford
Wyckoff, Sylvia Spencer
Xie, Xiaoze
Yarde, Richard
Yasuda, Robert
Yates, Sharon
Yegul, Fikret Kutlu
Yenawine, Philip
Yoder, Janica
Yood, James W
Yoshida, Ray Kakuo
Young, Charles Alexander
Young, Janie Chester
Youritzin, Victor Koshkin
Yust, David E
Zaage, Herman H
Zabarsky, Melvin Joel
Zaborowski, Dennis J
Zakin, Mikhail
Zallinger, Jean Day
Zehr, Connie
Zeller, Joseph R
Zemans, Joyce L
Zheutlin, Dale R
Ziemann, Richard Claude
Zimiles, Murray
Zona, Louis A
Zuhn-Moulder, Cheryl
Zurier, Rebecca F

ENAMELIST

Bates, Kenneth Francis
Bennett, Jamie
Butt, Harlan W
Cantini, Virgil D
Conte, Jeanne Larner
Greenfield, Joan Beatrice
Killmaster, John H
Malenda, James William
Murtic, Edo
Perkins, A Alan
Rooke, Fay Lorraine
Schwarcz, June Theresa
Sundberg, Carl Gustave
Weiss, Dick J
Whitcomb, Kay

ENVIRONMENTAL ARTIST

Abish, Cecile
Alhilali, Neda
Anderson, Kenneth Edmund
Belan, Kyra
Berkowitz, Terry
Billian, Cathey R
Bolt, Ron
Brookner, Jackie
Burgess, David Lowry
Cajero, Michael Ray
Casdin-Silver, Hariet
Cheng, Carl FK
Christo & Jeanne-Claude
Clark, Emery Ann
Crist, William Gary
Crivelli, Elaine
Culbertson, Janet Lynn (Mrs Douglas Kaften)
Delgyer, Leslie
Dell, Robert Christopher
Denes, Agnes
Dignac, Geny (Eugenia) M Bermudez
Dos Santos, Jonas Alves
Escobedo, Helen
Fabbris, Vico
Feigenbaum, Harriet
Ferguson-Huntington, (Lady) Kathleen E
Fleischner, Richard Hugh
Floyd, Carl Leo
Fraser, Mary Edna
Freudenstein, Ellie (Eleanor) T(erenyi)
Gellis, Sandy L
Gianakos, Cris
Goldring, Elizabeth
Gordon, Coco
Graham, Daniel H
Greenly, Colin
Grygutis, Barbara
Gussow, Roy
Hanson, Jo
Harrison, Helen Mayer (Mrs Newton Harrison)
Harrison, Newton A
Haskell, Jane
Heizer, Michael
Hendricks, Geoffrey
Henes, Donna
Hera
Hudson, Jon Barlow
Hutchinson, Peter Arthur
Irwin, Robert
Janney, Christopher Draper
Jansen, Catherine Sandra
Jezik, Enrique
Johanson, Patricia
Kahn, Ned M
Kenton, Mary Jean
King, Brian Jeffrey
Kirschenbaum, Bernard Edwin
Knepper-Doyle, Virginia
Knowles, Alison
Langford-Stansbery, Sherry K
Leicester, Andrew John
Leighton, Patricia MacInnes
Macaulay, Thomas S
Maisel, David
Maler, M Leopoldo Mario
Mark, Phyllis
Marston, JD
Mason, Molly Ann
McMillen, Michael C(halmers)
Medei, Rebecca Rosalie
Murch, Anna Valentina
Navratil, Greg Allan
Niedzialek, Terry
Niese, Henry Ernst
Norvell, Patsy
Notarbartolo, Albert
Olsen Bergman, Ciel (Cheryl) Bowers
Palau, Marta
Parton, Nike
Pinto, Jody
Poleskie, Stephen Francis
Pondick, Rona
Prent, Mark
Price, Joan Webster
Reitzenstein, Reinhard
Rizzolo, Louis (Lou) B M
Roloff, John (Scott)
Rophar
Ross, Charles
Roux, Barbara Agnes
Safer, John
Salomon, Lawrence
Sasaki, Toshio
Sato, Norie
Sawyer, Margo
Sebastian, Jill C
Sirlin, Deanna Louise
Sky, Alison
Smith, Nelson David
Snyder, Kit-Yin
Soffer, Sasson
Sonfist, Alan
Stuhl, Michelle
Taper, Geri
Taradash, Meryl
Thacher, Anita
Tosk, Marsha
Ukeles, Mierle Laderman
Van Harlingen, Jean (Ann)
Werner, Frank Robert
Whiten, Tim (Timothy) Grover
Woody, (Thomas) Howard
Wyland, Steve Creech
Zimmerman, Elyn
Zopp, Dudley

FILMMAKER

Almond, Paul
Amoroso, Nicolas Alberto Amoroso Boelcke
Andrews, Nancy Evelyn
Anger, Kenneth
Antin, Eleanor
Atlas, Charles
Barney, Matthew
Bates, Leo James
Beckman, Ericka
Belgum, Rolf Henrik
Beloff, Zoe
Birchler, Alexander
Blechman, R O
Bourque, Louise
Breer, Robert C
Bruno, Ellen
Burch, Claire R
Cheang, Shu Lea
Cheng, Fu-Ding
Child, Abigail
Clifton, Michelle Gamm
Cohen, Jem Alan
Colnurn, Martha
Conner, Bruce
Coupon, William
DeGette, Andrea M
Delisle, Thomas Charles
Demissie, Yemane I
Dorsky, Nathaniel
Dowell, James Thomas
Drapell, Joseph
Dunye, Cheryl Lynn
Eisenberg, Daniel
Elder, R Bruce
Faccinto, Victor Paul
Fletcher, Harrell
Fotopoulos, James
Frazer, John Thatcher
Gatten, David
Gekiere, Madeleine
Geniusz, Robert Myles
Gerstein, David Steven
Gibbons, Joe
Gibson, Sandra
Golden, Eunice
Green, Jonathan (William)
Greenfield, Amy
Grunberg, Slawomir
Haar, Tom
Haxton, David
Hay, (George) Austin
Henderson, Mike

FILMMAKER (cont)
Herbert, James Arthur
Hobbs, Fredric
Holt, Nancy Louise
Howard, David
Hubbard, Teresa
Huot, Robert
Iimura, Takahiko
Kagemoto, Haro
Katz, Leandro
Kleckner, Susan
Knecht, John
Lack, Stephen
Lee, Lara
Leslie, Alfred
Levitt, Helen
Lieber, Edvard
Liebling, Jerome
Lipzin, Janis Crystal
Lockhart, Sharon
Lundberg, William
Magden, Norman E
Makavejev, Dusan
Mangolte, Babette M
McCall, Anthony
Mekas, Jonas
Newton, Richard Edward
Niblock, Phill
Noonan, Tom
Nowytski, Sviatoslav
O'Connell, Kenneth Robert
Padula, Fred David
Phillips, Robert J
Rabinovitch, William Avrum
Rainer, Yvonne
Ravett, Abraham
Rosenblatt, Jay Howard
Rubinfien, Leo H
Ruscha, Edward Joseph
Schneemann, Carolee
Schwartz, Lillian (Feldman)
Silver, Shelly Andrea
Sipho, Ella
Snow, Michael
Stratman, Deborah
Subrin, Elisabeth A
Thacher, Anita
Thompson, Malcolm Barton
Tilley, Lewis Lee
Torlakson, James Daniel
Trainor, Jim
Trecartin, Ryan
Vasell, Chris
Waters, Jack
Wechsler, Judith Glatzer
Zahedi, Caveh

GALLERY DIRECTOR

See also **Museum Director**

Alinder, James Gilbert
Amalfitano, Lelia
Ayers, Carol Lee
Baldwin, Russell W
Balka, Sigmund Ronell
Bartlett, Christopher E
Bass, David Loren
Batkin, Jonathan
Berggruen, John Henry
Brooks, Harry A
Brown, Constance George
Bryant, Linda Goode
Buck, Robert Treat, Jr
Buecker, Robert
Burks, Myrna R
Butts, H Daniel, III
Cannuli, Richard Gerald
Christensen, Val Alan
Clark-Langager, Sarah Ann
Cochran, Dorothy Parcells
Cocker, Barbara Joan
Cohan, James
Cohan, Zara R
Cohen, David
Cohen, Mildred Thaler
Colina, Armando G
Collinson, Janice
Conley, Zeb Bristol, Jr
Cooper, Rhonda H
Crandall, Judith Ann
Crane, Bonnie Loyd
Cumming, Glen Edward
Davis, Kimberly Brooke
Dean, Kevin Lee
DeFazio, Teresa Galligan
Desmett, Don
Dorfman, Fred
Douglas, Leah
Drummer, William Richard
Einreinhofer, Nancy Anne
Esman, Rosa
Feinman, Stephen E
Felker, David Larry
Felsen, Rosamund
Ferris, Daniel B
Fink, Joanna Elizabeth
Fiterman, Dolly
FitzSimonds, Carol Strause
Fraser, Catriona Trafford
Fuglie, Gordon Louis
Fuller, Jeffrey P
Goffman, Judy Goffman Cutler
Goldsmith, Benedict Isaac
Gonzalez, Mauricio Martinez
Gorney, Jay Philip
Grandee, Joe Ruiz
Grossman, Bonnie
Hanley, Jack
Hansen, Sarah Eveleth Campbell
Harmon, Foster
Heaton, Janet N
Hedberg, Gregory Scott
Hodge, Dorothy (Scottie) W
Hutchins, Robin
Isaacson, Ronald G
Johnson, Diana L
Kawecki, Jean Mary
Kelley, Donald Castell
Killeen, Melissa Helen
Klobe, Tom
Knight, David J
Lamoureux, Marie France
Langman, Richard Theodore
Levy, S(tephen) Dean
Lewis, Louise Miller
Lieber, Lofa
Lippman, Judith
Lippmann, Janet Gurian
Lotz, Steven Darryl
Lynch, Florence
Martin, Mary Finch
McAllister, Geraldine E
McClain, Robert Lee
McManus, James William
Mellor, Mark Adams
Mew, Tommy
Miller, Virginia Irene
Moody, Elizabeth C
Newman, Walter Andrews, Jr
Nordland, Gerald John
Okun, Barbara-Rose
Ostrow, Saul Lieb
Pachter, Marc
Parish, Norman
Parkerson, John E
Parsley, Jacque (Carter)
Perlow, Katharina Rich
Peters, Larry Dean
Pfeifer, Marcuse
Phillips, Dutch (James) O, Jr
Poole, Nancy Geddes
Porter, Richard James
Posner, Helaine J
Raby, Julian
Raydon, Alexander R
Rebbeck, Lester James, Jr
Reynolds, Jock
Richards, Tally
Richardson, Trevor J
Ropp, Ann L
Rowand, Joseph Donn
Ruttinger, Jacquelyn
St George, William (M)
Schusterman, Gerrie Marva
Shainman, Jack S
Simmons, Danny, Jr
Simor, Suzanna B
Sindelir, Robert John
Skoler, Celia Rebecca
Smith, B J
Smith, Gary
Sorkin, Emily
Sowers, Russell Frederic
Spratt, Frederick R
Sragow, Ellen
Steel, Virginia Oberlin
Steiner, Sherry L
Stirratt, Betsy (Elizabeth) Anne
Stoppert, Mary Kay
Sujo, Clara Diament
Sullivan, JuneAnn Margaret
Sussman, Bonnie Kaufman
Sussman, Jill
Swain, Robert Francis
Taira, Masa Morioka
Takayama, Martha Tepper
Tasende, Jose Maria
Tatistcheff, Peter Alexis
Thurmer, Robert
Tisch Sussman, Laurie
Tunis, Roslyn
Vanderlip, Dianne Perry
Vizner, Nikola
Waller, Susan
Weinzapfel, Connie A
Wilson, Carrie Lois
Wilson, Robert Alan
Wirtz, Stephen Carl
Wise, Takouhy
Wortz, Melinda Farris
York, Richard Travis

GLASS BLOWER

Applebaum, Leon
Bernstein, William Joseph
Blomdahl, Sonja
Brejcha, Vernon Lee
Carlson, Robert Michael
Chihuly, Dale (Patrick)
Clark, Jon Frederic
D'Onofrio, Bernard Michael
Fero, Shane
Handler, Audrey
Hurlstone, Robert William
Ipsen, Kent Forrest
Levin, Robert Alan
Littleton, Harvey K
Magdanz, Andrew R
Marioni, Paul
Moore, Benjamin Powell
Morris, William
Mulcahy, Kathleen
Ohno, Mitsugi
Rhodes, James Melvin
Ruffner, Ginny Martin
Simpson, Josh (Josiah) J L Simpson
Warehall, William Donald
White, Brook Forrest, Jr

GOLDSMITH

Anderson, Bruce A
Baldridge, Mark S
Betteridge, Lois Etherington
Brauer Ferns, Connie Ann
De La Verriere, J J
Enriquez, Gaspar
Floret, Evelyn
Flynn, Pat L
Getty, Nilda Fernandez
Grissom, Freda Gill
Hirsh, Annette Marie
Hu, Mary Lee
Kuehnl, Claudia Ann
Lechtzin, Stanley
Mawdsley, Richard
Noffke, Gary L
Renk, Merry
Seppa, Heikki Markus
Stuart, Donald Alexander
Van Duinwyk, George Paul
Wegner, Nadene R

GRAPHIC ARTIST

Anderson, Warren Harold
Arcangel, Cory
Arias-Misson, Alain
Avant, Tracy Wright
Barbee, Robert Thomas
Barkus, Mariona
Beachum, Sharon Garrison
Beaumont, Mona
Belag, Andrea
Bennett, John M
Bergen, John Axel
Berry, William Augustus
Bigelow, Anita (Anne) (Edwige Lourie)
Bolton, Robin Jean
Boyd, (David) Michael
Brody, Ruth
Brown, James
Bruni, Umberto
Burshell, Sandra Eve
Capes, Richard Edward
Carpenter, Joseph Allan
Catlett, Elizabeth
Church, Maude
Chwast, Seymour
Clement, Kathleen
Cohen, Arthur Morris
Cohen, Reina Joyce
Colker, Edward
Colman, Virginia O'Connell
Condon, Brody Kiel
Conner, Bruce
Costello, Cynthia Ann
Creech, Franklin Underwood
D'Almeida, George
Daub, Matthew Forrest
Davis, Meredith J
des Rioux (de Messimy), Deena Victoria (Coty)
Dickinson, Eleanor Creekmore
Dixson, Wendy Fay
Donneson, Seena
Dorn, Peter Klaus

HISTORIAN

HISTORIAN (cont)
Pierce, Patricia Jobe
Pilgrim, Dianne Hauserman
Pisano, Ronald George
Polcari, Stephen
Poling, Clark V
Pollitt, Jerome Jordan
Polzer, Joseph
Poor, Robert John
Porter, Jeanne Chenault
Powell, Earl Alexander, III
Pressly, William Laurens
Preston, George Nelson
Preziosi, Donald A
Prown, Jules David
Pugh, Grace Huntley
Purtle, Carol Jean
Quinones Keber, Eloise
Quirarte, Jacinto
Radan, George Tivadar
Raggio, Olga
Raguin, Virginia C
Ragusa, Isa
Rand, Harry
Raydon, Alexander R
Reed, Cleota
Reed, Walt Arnold
Reese, Thomas Ford
Reeves, James Franklin
Reff, Theodore
Reilly, Bernard Francis
Reilly, Richard
Rembert, Virginia Pitts
Rensch, Roslyn
Rhyne, Charles Sylvanus
Rice, Anthony Hopkins
Rice, Shelley Enid
Richardson, John Adkins
Rigby, Ida Katherine
Robb, David Metheny, Jr
Roberson, Samuel Arndt
Roberts, Helene Emylou
Robertson, E Bruce
Robinson, Duncan (David)
Robinson, Franklin W
Robinson, Lilien Filipovitch
Rogers, Millard Foster, Jr
Rorex, Robert Albright
Rosand, David
Rosenberg, Charles Michael
Rosenblum, Robert
Rosenthal, Donald A
Rosenthal, Earl Edgar
Rosenthal, Mark L
Rosenzweig, Daphne Lange
Roskill, Mark Wentworth
Rossen, Susan F
Roth, Leland M(artin)
Roth, Moira
Rudenstine, Angelica Zander
Sachs, Katherine Stein
Sachs, Samuel, II
Sanderson, Warren
Sandler, Irving Harry
Saretzky, Gary Daniel
Saunders, Richard Henry
Scarbrough, Cleve Knox, Jr
Schaefer, Scott Jay
Schimansky, Donya Dobrila
Schmandt-Besserat, Denise
Schmitt, Marilyn Low
Schmitz, Barbara
Schneiderman, Richard S
Schuller, Nancy Shelby
Schultz, John Bernard
Schulz, Anne Markham
Schulz, Juergen
Schulze, Franz
Schwartz, Marvin D
Schweizer, Paul Douglas
Scott, John Beldon
Scott, John Fredrik
Scribner, Charles, III
Seaberg, Libby W
Segger, Martin Joseph
Selvig, Forrest Hall
Selz, Peter H
Semowich, Charles John
Senie, Harriet F
Serenyi, Peter
Sewell, Darrel L
Shaw, Joseph Winterbotham
Shaw, Nancy (Rivard)
Shaw, Paul Jefferson
Sheard, Wendy Stedman
Sheon, Aaron
Shepard, Lewis Albert
Sherman, Claire Richter
Shestack, Alan
Shimizu, Yoshiaki
Sichel, Kim
Sieber, Roy
Silver, Larry Arnold
Simmons, John Herbert
Simon, David L
Simon, Robert Barry
Simpson, Marianna Shreve
Simpson, William Kelly
Sims, Lowery Stokes
Slade, George G
Slatkin, Wendy
Slive, Seymour
Smith, Elliot
Smith, Frances Kathleen
Smith, Gil R
Smith, J Weldon
Smith, James Morton
Smith, Jeffrey Chipps
Sokol, David Martin
Somma, Thomas P
Sommer, Frank H, III
Sorell, Victor Alexander
Spangenberg, Kristin L
Spector, Jack J
Spencer, Harold Edwin
Sponenburgh, Mark
Spurlock, William
Stahl, Alan M
Stanford, Linda Oliphant
Stebbins, Theodore Ellis, Jr
Stein, Judith Ellen
Stein, Roger Breed
Steinberg, Leo
Stevens, Andrew Rich
Stewart, J(ohn) Douglas
Stillman, Damie
Stokstad, Marilyn
Stones, Margaret Alison
Stott, Deborah
Strickler, Susan Elizabeth
Striker, Cecil L
Stringer, Mary Evelyn
Stuckey, Charles F
Sturgeon, Mary C
Sturges, Hollister
Sullivan, Scott A
Sutton, Peter C
Swanson, Vern Grosvenor
Sweeney, J Gray
Tannenbaum, Barbara Lee
Tasse, M Jeanne
Tatham, David Frederic
Taylor, Hugh Holloway
Taylor, Michael D
Teilhet-Fisk, Jehanne Hildegarde
Tepfer, Diane
Theofiles, George
Thistlethwaite, Mark Edward
Tierney, Patrick Lennox
Timpano, Anne
Toker, Franklin
Tolles, Bryant Franklin, Jr
Tomasini, Wallace J
Topper, David R
Townsend, Gavin Edward
Travis, David B
Trenton, Patricia Jean
Troy, Nancy J
Trutty-Coohill, Patricia
Turner, A Richard
Turnure, James Harvey
Tyler, Ron C
Vandersall, Amy L
Van Schaack, Eric
Vermeule, Cornelius Clarkson, III
Verostko, Roman Joseph
Viditz-Ward, Vera Louise
Vincent, Clare
Von Schmidt, Eric
Waddy, Patricia
Wahlman, Maude Southwell
Walford, E John
Wallace, Richard William
Wallach, Alan
Waller, Aaron Bret
Walter, Elizabeth Mitchell
Ward, John Lawrence
Wark, Robert Rodger
Warren, Julianne Bussert Baker
Wasserman, Jack
Watson, Katharine Johnson
Wattenmaker, Richard Joel
Wayne, Cynthia M
Weaver, AM
Webster, Sally (Sara) B
Wechsler, Judith Glatzer
Weidman, Jeffrey
Weinberg, Jonathan Edman
Weisberg, Gabriel P
Welch, Stuart Cary
Werness, Hope B
West, Richard Vincent
Westervelt, Robert F
Westin, Robert H
Wharton, Annabel Jane
White, Robert Rankin
Whitehouse, David Bryn
Wiebe, Charles M
Wilkins, David George
Williams, Benjamin Forrest
Williams, David Jon
Williams, John Alden
Williams, John Wesley
Wilmerding, John
Wilson, Jean S
Winter, Amy H
Wise, Suzanne Tanderup
Withers, Josephine
Wixom, William D
Wolanin, Barbara A
Wood, James Nowell
Wood, John August
Worth, Peter John
Worthen, Amy Namowitz
Wriston, Barbara
Yard, Sally Elizabeth
Yood, James W
Youritzin, Victor Koshkin
Yu-ho, Tseng
Zafran, Eric Myles
Zalesch, Saul E
Zemans, Joyce L
Zerner, Henri Thomas
Ziff, Jerrold
Zilczer, Judith Katy

ILLUMINATOR

Backes, Joan
Bliss, Harry James
Gast, Carolyn Bartlett (Lutz)
Gorny, A-P (Anthony-Peter)
Huddy, Margaret Teresa
Johnson, Martin Brian
Milbourn, Patrick D
Mueller, OP, (Sister) Gerardine
Werner Vaughn, Salle

ILLUSTRATOR

Abel, Ray
Aebi, Ernst Walter
Aliki, Liacouras Brandenberg
Anderson, Dawolu Jabari
Anderson, Robert Alexander
Angulo, Chappie
Antic, Miroslav
Ariss, Herbert Joshua
Arnold, Ann
Asaro, John
Baldwin, Richard Wood
Banks, Marcia Gillman
Barkley, James
Bartlett, Christopher E
Baxendell, Julie
Bedrick, Jeffrey K
Berry, Carolyn
Bissell, Phil
Blackburn, Loren Hayner
Blechman, R O
Bostick, William Allison
Bowler, Joseph, Jr
Boyle, (James) Neil
Braiden, Rose Margaret J
Brycelea, Clifford
Burchard, Peter Duncan
Byrd, Robert John
Carter, Frederick Timmins
Chapman, Walter Howard
Christensen, Betty (Elizabeth)
Chwast, Seymour
Ciardiello, Joseph G
Cisneros, Jose B
Cleary, Shirley Cleary Cooper
Condren, Stephen F
Covey, Rosemary Feit
Crawford, Bill (Wilbur) Ogden
Crite, Allan Rohan
Crosby, Ranice W
Cuevas, Jose Luis
Cunningham, Sue
Cusack, Margaret Weaver
D'Amato, Janet Potter
Dank, Leonard D
De Armond, Dale B
De Groat, Diane
Del la Vega, Gabriela
Deloney, Jack Clouse
DePillars, Murry N
Deremer, Susan René
Dice, Elizabeth Jane
Di Fate, Vincent
Dimson, Theo
Docktor, Irv
Duerwald, Carol
Dunn, Tom (Thomas) Charles
Echohawk, Brummett
Egeli, Peter Even
Eliason, Birdell
Eller, Evelyn Eller Rosenbaum
Ellis, Richard

ILLUSTRATOR (cont)

Ely, Timothy Clyde
Engler, Sherrie Lee
Faudie, Fred
Feder, Penny Joy
Ferris, (Carlisle) Keith
Fleming, Margaret Nielsen
Folkus, Dan (Daniel) Alan Fredrickson
Fortunato, Nancy
Fowler, Eric Nicholas
Gallo, William Victor
Gast, Carolyn Bartlett (Lutz)
Gaydos, Tim (Timothy) John
Geisert, Arthur Frederick
Gilbert, Albert Earl
Ginsburg, Max
Glaser, Milton
Golbin, Andree
Graese, Judy (Judith) Ann
Grandpré, Mary
Granstaff, William Boyd
Halliday, Nancy R
Harris, Robert George
Harroff, William Charles Brent
Hauptman, Susan
Haynes, R (Richard) Thomas
Healy, Deborah Ann
Helgeson, Phillip Lawrence
Henselmann, Caspar
Herzberg, Thomas
Hildebrand, June Marianne
Hoffman, Martin
Hulings, Clark
Itchkawich, David Michael
Jacobs, Scott E
Jakub, Jeffrey Andrew
James, Bill (William) Frederick
Jones, Donald Glynn
Kato, Kay
Kaufman, Stuart Martin
Keener, Polly Leonard
Kersels, Martin
Kessler, Leonard H
Keveson, Florence
Kiousis, Linda Weber
Knott, Dee D
Kocar, George Frederick
Kogan, Deborah
Koren, Edward B
Kunstler, Morton
Laessig, Robert
LaPlantz, Shereen
L'Archeveque, Andre Robert
Loehle, Richard E
Loewer, Henry Peter
Lynde, Stan
Lynn, Judith
Macaulay, David Alexander
Mandel, Saul
Margules, Gabriele Ella
Marshall, Bruce
Matsubara, Naoko
Matternes, Jay Howard
Mays, Victor
McCall, Robert Theodore
McMillan, Constance
McMullan, James Burroughs
McNamara-Ringewald, Mary Ann Therese
Mihaesco, Eugene
Mion, Pierre Riccardo
Nessim, Barbara
Obrant, Susan Elizabeth
Olivere, Raymond
O'Neal, Roland Lenard
Osyczka, Bohdan Danny
Pena, Amado Maurilio, Jr
Perlin, Bernard
Peter, Friedrich Gunther
Petrie, Ferdinand Ralph
Petro, Joseph (Victor), Jr
Phillips, Harriet E
Pomeroy, Mary Barnas (Mrs F G Pomeroy)
Prado-Arai, Namiko
Preede, Nydia
Rauf, Barbara Claire
Reece, Maynard
Robbins, Trina
Ross, Joan M
Rowe, Charles Alfred
Rutland, Lilli Ida
Ryan, Joyce Ethel
Samimi, Mehrdad
Sarnoff, Arthur Saron
Satin, Claire Jeanine
Schachter, Justine Ranson
Schottland, M
Schwartz, Daniel Bennett
Seiden, Arthur
Sendak, Maurice Bernard
Shechter, Ben-Zion
Shilson, Wayne Stuart
Shore, Robert
Siedman, Scott
Siegel, (Leo) Dink
Silverman, Burton Philip
Sloan, Richard
Smith, Harry William
Sorel, Edward
Spagnolo, Kathleen Mary
Spohn, Franz Frederick
Stacy, John Russell
Stanford, Ginny C
Stark, Bruce Gunsten
Stermer, Dugald Robert
Stirnweis, Shannon
Storey, David
Struck, Norma Johansen
Suba, Susanne (Mrs Bertam Bloch)
Takashima, Shizuye Violet
Thollander, Earl
Thorpe, James George
Tiegreen, Alan F
Torbert, Stephanie Birch
Trimm, H Wayne
Truby, Betsy Kirby
Uram, Lauren Michelle
Van Winkelen, Barbara
Vargas, Josephine
Velasquez, Oscar
Wadler, Ronni
Wallace, Carol Ann (Brucker)
Waterhouse, Charles Howard
Waterhouse, Russell Rutledge
Watson, Aldren A
Wells, Betty Childs
Whitaker, William
Williams, Paul Alan
Winkler, Max-Karl
Wogstad, James Everet
Wostrel, Nancy J
Yanow, Rhoda Mae
Youngblood, Nat

Children's Books

Ames, Lee Judah
Amoss, Berthe
Anderson, Gunnar Donald
Arnold, Ann
Audean
Barry, Robert E
Bock, William Sauts-Netamux'we
Brodsky, Beverly
Clark, Roberta Carter
Collins, Pat Lowery
dePaola, Tomie
Dirgo, Ray Robert
Fisher, Leonard Everett
Freeman, Kathryn
Garrison, Barbara
George, Sylvia James
Haley, Gail E
Hull, Cathy
Ipcar, Dahlov
Kessler, Leonard H
Key, Ted
Langdo, Bryan Richard
Lasker, Joe (Joseph) L
Lent, Blair
McCurdy, Michael Charles
Nesbitt, Ilse Buchert
Otani, June
Parker, Nancy Winslow
Parry, Marian
Pierce, Diane Jean
Pinkney, Jerry
Poehlmann, JoAnna
Reid Jenkins, Debra L
Rosenberg, Jane
Savitt, Sam
Schoenherr, John (Carl)
Schweninger, Ann Rozzelle
Smith, Jos(eph) A(nthony)
Swanson, Ray V
Taback, Simms
Taylor, Gage
Weihs, Erika
Weil, Lisl
Wentworth, Elaine
Wexler, Jerome LeRoy
Williams, David Jon
Workman, Robert P
Zallinger, Jean Day
Zapel, Arthur Lewis

INSTRUCTOR
(STUDIO/ART SCHOOL)

Abbott, Linda J
Ablow, Roselyn Karol (Roz Koyol Ablow)
Abrams, Edith Lillian
Accetta, Suzanne Rusconi
Adato, Linda Joy
Adelman, Dorothy (Lee) McClintock
Akutsu, Shoichi
Amelchenko, Alison M
Amico, David Michael
Anastasia, Susanna
Anderson, John S
Anderson, Lennart
Andry, Keith Anthony
Angelo, Sandra McFall
Appel, Thelma
Askevold, David
Atlee, Emilie Des
Atwood Pinardi, Brenda
Auerbach, Rita Argen
Ausby, Ellsworth Augustus
Avakian, John
Baden, Karl
Bailey, Barbara Ann
Baker, Blanche
Baldassano, Vincent
Barnes, Curt (Curtis) Edward
Barrett, Thomas R
Barta, Dorothy Elaine
Bartel, Todd Henry
Barton, Billie Jo
Batt, Miles Girard
Bendell, Marilyn
Berg, Siri
Berge, Dorothy Alphena
Besant, Derek Michael
Betts, Judi Polivka
Bieltvedt, Arnor G
Bobrowicz, Yvonne Pacanovsky
Boeve, Edgar Gene
Bordes, Adrienne
Borgia-Aberle, Nina
Brauchli, Byron T
Briansky, Rita Prezament
Brody, David
Brotherton, Naomi
Brown, June Gottlieb
Brown, Peggy Ann
Brown, Sarah M
Brumer, Shulamith
Brush, Leif
Bryans, John Armond
Burke-Fanning, Madeleine
Burpee, James Stanley
Burt, Dan
Buster, Kendall J
Butter, Tom
Byers, Fleur
Byrd, Robert John
Caddell, Foster
Cadillac, Louise Roman
Cady, Samuel Lincoln
Cain, David Paul
Campbell, David Paul
Campbell, Rebecca
Capes, Richard Edward
Caplan Ciarrocchi, Sandra
Caporale-Greene, Wende
Caroompas, Carole J
Cattaneo, (Jacquelyn A) Kammerer
Chandler, Elisabeth Gordon
Chapin, Deborah Jane
Chavez, Joseph Arnold
Cheek, Ronald Edward
Christensen, Larry R
Christensen, Sharlene
Ciancio, June (Kirkpatrick)
Clark, Claude
Cleary, Barbara B
Cliff, Denis Antony
Clinton, Paul Arthur
Clutz, William
Cockrill, Sherna
Cogswell, Margaret Price
Cokendolpher, Eunice Loraine
Colarusso, Corrine Camille
Coleman, Donna Leslie
Coleman, M L (Michael Lee)
Colquhoun, Peter Lloyd
Condren, Stephen F
Cortese, Don F
Cottone-Kolthoff, Carol
Couper, Charles Alexander
Cox, Marion Averal
Cunningham, Francis
Das, Ratindra
Davidson, David Isaac
Davies, Kenneth Southworth
Dawson, Doug
Day, Burnis Calvin
de Campos, Nuno
Decil, Stella (Del) W
De Donato, Louis
De Lory, Peter
Dennis, Don W
Denton, Patry
Derby, Mark
Dickerson, Daniel Jay

INSTRUCTOR (cont)
Dickerson, Vera Mason
Diehl, Guy
Dingwall, Kenneth
DiPerna, Frank Paul
DiStefano, Domenic
Doll, Linda A
Doogan, Bailey
Dougherty, Raymond Edward
Douglas, Edwin Perry
Douglas, L(inda) J
Draper, Josiah Everett
Driesbach, Walter Clark, Jr
Dunlap, Loren Edward
Edelman, Janice
Egan, Laury Agnes
Egeli, Cedric Baldwin
Elliott, Bette G
Embrey, Carl Rice
Estabrook, Reed
Falconer, Marguerite Elizabeth
Faragasso, Jack
Federico, Frank
Fiore, Joseph Albert
Fitch, Steve (Steven) Ralph
Flattmann, Alan Raymond
Fox, Michael David
Frederick, Deloras Ann
Freeman, Kathryn
Friedman, Lynne
Frudakis, Evangelos William
Fukuhara, Henry
Fulton, Jack E
Fyfe, Jo Suzanne (Storch)
Gabin, George Joseph
Gantz, Ann Cushing
Gardiner, T Michael
Gasparro, Frank
Gatto, Paul Anthony
Gay, Betsy (Elizabeth) Dershuck Gay
Gerbracht, Bob (Robert) Thomas
Godfrey, Winnie (Winifred) M
Goetz, Mary Anna
Golembeski, Beverly L
Goodbred, Ray Edward
Goree, Gary Paul
Grado, Angelo John
Graff, Frederick C
Grastorf, Jean H
Graupe-Pillard, Grace
Greeley, Charles Matthew
Green, Tom
Greenberg, Irwin
Greene, Daniel E
Gregory, Bruce
Grippe, Florence (Berg)
Grosse, C(arolyn) Ann Gawarecki
Gruver, Mary Emmett
Guastella, C Dennis
Gumpel, Hugh
Gunderson, Karen
Gutman, Bertha Steinhardt
Guzevich-Sommers, Kreszenz (Cynthia)
Gyra, Francis Joseph, Jr
Halliday, Nancy R
Hammett, Polly Horton
Hanna, Annette Adrian
Hansman, Bob
Hardy, David Whittaker, III
Hardy, (Clarion) Dewitt
Harrison, Myrna J
Hartley, Katherine Ann
Hartwig, Heinie
Harvey, Donald Gene
Hawkins, Thomas Wilson, Jr
Hedden-Sellman, Zelda
Heidel, Theresa Troise
Heimdal, Georg
Heinemann, Peter
Heipp, Richard Christian
Heller, Susanna
Hendrix, Connie Sandage Manus
Henry, Jean
Herr, Richard Joseph
Herzog, Priscilla Jenne
Hess, F Scott
Heston, Joan
Hibbs, Barbara J E
Hobbs, Frank I, Jr
Hofer, Ingrid (Ingeborg)
Hollerbach, Serge
Hollingsworth, Alvin Carl
Hooper, Robert T
Huff, Laura Weaver
Hull, Shayne L
Humphrey, Nene
Hunt, Courtenay
Hunter, Robert Douglas
Indiviglia, Salvatore Joseph
Irvine, Betty Jo
Jackson, Charlotte
Jarvis, Donald
Jenkins, Mary Anne Keel
Jerdon, William Harlan
Johnson, Richard Walter
Jorgensen, Bob (Robert) A
Kam, Mei K
Kardon, Carol
Kaufman, Loretta Ana
Kaye, Mildred Elaine
Kaz, Nathaniel
Kellar, Martha Robbins
Kilguss, Elsie Schaich
Kinstler, Everett Raymond
Kirstein, Janis Adrian
Kord, Victor George
Kruskamp, Janet
Kurlander, Honey W
Lack, Richard Frederick
Lampasona, Eydi
Lane, Marion Arrons
Lanigan-Schmidt, Thomas
Lauhakaikul, Thana
Layne, Barbara J
Leaf, Ruth
Leites, Ara (Barbara) L
LeMay, Harry Adrian
LeMay, Nancy
Leslie, Jimmy
Lesnick, Stephen William
Lewis, Marcia
Lewis, Nat Brush
Lewis, Ronald Walter
Lewis, William R
Lighton, Linda
Liljegren, Frank
Lindenberg, Mary K
Lindmark, Arne
Lipscomb, Guy Fleming, Jr
Lomahaftewa, Linda Joyce
LoMonaco, Stephen
Longo-Muth, Linda L
Lord, Carolyn Marie
Lorentz, Pauline
Lorfano, Pauline Davis
Lucas, Bonnie Lynn
Luisi, Jerry
Lutz, Winifred Ann
Lynch, Betty
Lynch, Mary Britten
Lynch, Tom (Thomas) Michael
Madura, Jack Joseph
Mahaffey, Merrill Dean
Maher, Janet Lynn
Maki, Countess Hope Marie
Malta, Vincent
Mancuso, Leni Mancuso Barrett
Martone, William Robert
Masback, Dennis
Mason, Alden C
Mason, Frank Herbert
McCallum, Corrie Parker
McCarthy, Christine M
McCarthy, Doris Jean
McCarty, Lorraine Chambers
McCullough, Edward L
McDaniel, Richard
McDougal, Ivan Ellis
McEachron, (Genevieve) Ann
McKinney, Tatiana Ladygina
McLeod, Cheryl O'Halloran
McReynolds, (Joe) Cliff
McVicker, Charles Taggart
Mendenhall, Jack
Merida, Margaret Braden
Meyers, Dale (Mrs Mario Cooper)
Miezajs, Dainis
Missal, Stephen J
Mohn, Cheri (Ann)
Molnar, Michael Joseph
Moment, Joan
Moon, Marc
Moore, Ina May
Moore, Scott Martin
Morenon, Elise
Morgan, Susan
Morgenlander, Ella Kramer
Morisue, Glenn Takanori
Moscatt, Paul N
Muchnic, Suzanne
Murphy, Mary M
Neal, Michael Shane
Newmark, Marilyn Newmark Meiselman
Notestine, Dorothy J
O'Beil, Hedy
Ohe, Katie (Minna)
Oliver, Julie Ford
Olson, Bettye Johnson
Olson, Charles
Olson, Maxine
Osborne, John Phillip
Ostendorf, (Arthur) Lloyd, Jr
Parker, Joni Y
Parker, June
Passantino, George Christopher
Patrick, Genie Hudson
Patterson, Shirley Abbott
Pearson, Henry C
Pearson, James Eugene
Pech, Arleta
Peluso, Marta E
Penney, Jacqueline
Peppard, Jacqueline Jean
Peregrin, Magda Elizabeth
Perez, Vincent
Perlmutter, Linda M
Perrotti, Barbara
Phillips, Dick (Richard) Cortez
Phillis, Marilyn Hughey
Piccirillo, Alexander C
Piet, John Frances
Pijoan, Irene Maria Elizabeth
Plaster, Alice Marie
Plummer, Carlton B
Pollard, Herschel Newton
Pollard, Jann Lawrence
Pototschnik, John Michael
Prall, Barbara Jones
Pratt, Elizabeth Hayes
Price, Joe (Allen)
Price, Morgan Samuel
Priola, J John
Provder, Carl
Ragland, Bob
Rankin, Don
Raskind, Philis
Reilly, John Joseph
Reimers, Gladys Esther
Relkin, Michele Weston
Reynard, Carolyn Cole
Richards, Rosalyn A
Rider Berry, Tarah J
Rigley, Frederick Wildermuth
Rippe, Dan (Christian)
Robb, Peggy Hight
Roberts, Clyde Harry
Roberts, Donald
Roediger, Janice Anne
Rohrbacher, Patricia
Rollins, Tim
Rooke, Fay Lorraine
Rorick, William Calvin
Rose, Leatrice
Rose, Peggy Jane
Ross, Douglas Allan
Ross, John T
Ross, Rhoda Honore
Rossman, Ruth Scharff
Rudman, Joan (Combs)
Rudy, Helen
Rupprecht, Elizabeth
Rushworth, Michele D
Sahagian, Arthur H
St Denis, Paul Andre
St George, William (M)
Sallick, Lucy Ellen
Salminen, John Theodore
Salomon, Johanna
Samson, Carl Joseph
Samuelson, Fred Binder
Sanden, John Howard
San Soucie, Patricia Molm
Saunders, Edith Dariel Chase
Savas, Jo-Ann
Saylors, Jo An
Schaeffer, S(tanley) Allyn
Schepis, Anthony Joseph
Schildknecht, Dorothy E
Schlemm, Betty Lou
Schneider, Richard Durbin
Schule, Donald Kenneth
Schultz, Marilou
Schwalb, Susan
Schwarm, Harold Chambers
Schwartz, Henry
Schwartz, Ruth
Sebek, Miklos Laszlo
Segal, Barbara Jeanne
Sella, Alvin Conrad
Seltzer, Peter Lawrence
Sexauer, Donald Richard
Shapiro, Lois M
Sheller, G A
Shemdin, Azhar H
Sherwood, Leona
Shih, Joan Fai
Silberstein-Storfer, Muriel Rosoff
Simpson, Marilyn Jean
Smith, Linda Kyser
Snow, Lee Erlin
Somers, Frederick D(uane)
Sorokin, Maxine Ann
Sparks, John Edwin
Spencer, Susan Elizabeth

JEWELER

KINETIC ARTIST

LECTURER

LIBRARIAN

LIBRARIAN (cont)
Rusak, Halina R
Schimansky, Donya Dobrila
Schmidt, Mary Morris
Schuller, Nancy Shelby
Simor, Suzanna B
Skoler, Celia Rebecca
Smedstad, Deborah Barlow
Snow, Maryly A
Sommer, Frank H, III
Spencer, Deirdre Diane
Starr, Sydney
Stoneham, John
Straight, Elsie H
Teague, Edward H
Toth, Georgina Gy
Usher, Elizabeth Reuter (Mrs William Arthur Scar)
Walker, William Bond
Weidman, Jeffrey
Wyngaard, Susan Elizabeth
Young, Barbara Neil
Zimon, Kathy Elizabeth

MEDALIST

Adams, Jay H
Bleifeld, Stanley
Cook, Robert Howard
Eriksen, Gary
Everhart, Don, II
Gibran, Kahlil George
Jones, Elizabeth A B (Mrs Ludwig Glaeser)
Kaufman, Mico
Martin, Chester Young
Mazze, Irving
Mellon, Marc Richard
Pujol, Elliott
Rufo, Caesar Rocco
Svenson, John Edward

MOSAIC ARTIST

Carter, Jerry Williams
Chesley, Jacqueline
Gardner, Susan Ross
Garrison, David Earl
Hurwitz, Michael H
Kozloff, Joyce
Kreilick, Marjorie E
Mandel, Mike
Miller, F John
Noel, Donald Claude
Safer, John
Zweerts, Arnold

MURALIST

Arai, Tomie
Arion, Katherine
Arnold, Joseph Patterson
Bagget, William (Carter), Jr
Beal, Jack
Beckmann, Robert Owen
Bender, Leslie Marilyn
Blake, Priscilla Ann
Boggs, Franklin
Bransby, Eric James
Brothers, Barry A
Buonagurio, Edgar R
Callahan, Aileen Loughlin Callahan
Castillo, Mario Enrique
Charlot, Martin Day
Chase, Allan (Seamans)
Cocchiarelli, Maria Giovanna
Collins, Harvey Arnold
Connolly, Jerome Patrick
Crumpler, Dewey
Czimbalmos, Szabo Kalman
DesJarlait, Robert D
Freund, Tibor
Gable, John Oglesby
Graham, Bob
Griesedieck, Ellen
Groat, Hall Pierce
Haas, Richard John
Hanner, Jean Patricia
Harris, David Jack
Healy, Julia Schmitt
Henderson, Victor
Hopper, Frank J
Horman, Elizabeth
Imana, Jorge Garron
Incandela, Gerald Jean-Marie
Janjigian, Lucy Elizabeth
Jankowski, Theodore Andrew
Jenkins, Ulysses Samuel, Jr
Kaplan, Stanley
Kaprov, Susan
Kilb, Jenny
Knerr, Erika Tilde
Kramer, Louise
Landau, Myra
Larson, Sidney
Lee, Mary Virginia
Legrand, Yolene
Leopold, Susan
Lorcini, Gino
Lynch, Thom
Macdonell, Cameron
Mangione, Patricia Anthony
Marchini, Claudia H
Martin, Lucille Caiar
Martinez, Ernesto Pedregon
Mataranglo, Robert Patrick
McChesney, Robert Pearson
McCoy, Ann
Merola, Mario
Merrill, David Kenneth
Nantandy
Naylon, Betsy Zimmermann
Nicotra, Joseph Charles
O'Connell, Daniel Moylan
Palaia, Franc (Dominic)
Peters, Diane (Peck)
Pisani, Joseph
Pittore, Carlo
Rakocy, William (Joseph)
Ramos, Theodore
Rand, Archie
Redinger, Walter Fred
Regat, Jean-Jacques Albert
Regat, Mary E
Richardson, Frank, Jr
Rippey, Clayton
Rodeiro, Jose Manuel
Rose, Samuel
Rosen, Diane
Schlesinger, Christina
Schweig Langsdorf, Martyl
Simmons, Cleda-Marie
Slonem, Hunt
Sweitzer, Charles Leroy
Tacla, Jorge
Tsarikovsky, Valery (Tsar)
Valencia, Cesar
Valesco, Frances
Vanden Berge, Peter Willem
Vasquez, Emigdio Chavez
Webb, Patrick
Weber, John Pitman
Welch, James Wymore
Whitcomb, Kay
Whitehouse, Deborah Wian
Wilson, Robert Alan
Woodward, William
Yasko, Caryl A(nne)
Young, Leslie (McClure)
Yu, Shan
Zelt, Martie

MUSEOLOGIST

Atkinson, Tracy
Bohen, Barbara E
Bol, Marsha C
Brody, J(acob) J(erome)
Carter, David Giles
Dailey, Chuck (Charles) Andrew
Dellis, Arlene B
Edson, Gary F
Franco, Barbara
Fraser, Andrea R
Gray, Campbell Bruce
Greenwald, Alice (Alice) Marian Greenwald-Ward
Hall, Robert L
Harris, Ellen Schwartz
Holo, Selma R
Krulik, Barbara S
Lengyel, Alfonz
Mayer, Susan Martin
Rakocy, William (Joseph)
Sipiora, Leonard Paul
Sokol, David Martin
Streetman, John William, III
Wright, Vicki C

MUSEUM DIRECTOR

Adams, Celeste Marie
Ahern, Maureen J
Ahrens, Kent
Alexander-Greene, Grace George
Alling, Clarence (Edgar)
Anderson, Maxwell L
Anderson, Ross Cornelius
Andrews, Richard O
Appel, Eric A
Armstrong, Richard
Armstrong, Thomas Newton, III
Bacigalupi, Don
Bacot, Henry Parrott
Bailin, David
Ballinger, James K
Balzekas, Stanley, Jr
Bandes, Susan Jane
Bantel, Linda
Barrie, Dennis Ray
Beam, Patrice K
Beck, Martha Ann
Begley, J (John) Phillip
Beman, Lynn Susan
Benezra, Neal
Berg, Mona Lea
Berreth, David Scott
Bessire, Mark HC
Betsky, Aaron
Bishop, Budd Harris
Blaugrund, Annette
Bloch, Milton Joseph
Blume, Peter F
Blumenthal, Arthur R
Boggs, Jean Sutherland
Bol, Marsha C
Bolas, Gerald Douglas
Bolge, George S
Bolger, Doreen
Botwinick, Michael
Bradley, Betsy
Bradley, William Steven
Brand, Michael
Breuer, Bradford R
Bridenstine, James A
Brooke, David Stopford
Brooks, John H
Brosius, Karen
Brown, Charlotte Vestal
Brumley, Tom
Bruni, Stephen Thomas
Buchanan, John Edward, Jr
Bullard, Edgar John, III
Burger, Gary C
Burke, Daniel
Burke, James Donald
Burnside, Madeleine Hilding
Bush, Martin H
Butler, Charles Thomas
Byrnes, James Bernard
Camber, Diane Woolfe
Cameron, Duncan F
Capa, Cornell
Carswell, John
Carter, Curtis Lloyd
Cartwright, Derrick
Cash, Sarah
Castile, Rand
Chandler, Angelyn Sanders
Chepp, Mark
Christison, Muriel B
Clark, Lynda K
Clark, Michael
Close, Timothy
Codding, Mitchell Allan
Coffey, John William, II
Conforti, Michael Peter
Conklin, Jo-Ann
Consey, Kevin E
Cook, Silas Baldwin
Coopersmith, Georgia A
Coraor, John E
Cowart, Jack
Cozad, Rachael Blackburn
Crane, Michael Patrick
Crosman, Christopher Byron
Crum, Katherine B
Culver, Michael L
Cuno, James
Cutler, Judy A Goffman
Cutler, Laurence S
Czarniecki, M J, III
Czestochowski, Joseph Stephen
Danoff, I Michael
Darling, Sharon Sandling
Davies, Hugh Marlais
Davis, Darwin R
De la Torre, David Joseph
Delehanty, Suzanne
Demetrion, James Thomas
De Montebello, Philippe Lannes
Dempsey, Bruce Harvey
Dennison, Lisa
Dewitt, Katharine Cramer
Dietrich, Bruce Leinbach
Doezema, Marianne
Doherty, Peggy M
Duff, James H
Ebitz, David MacKinnon
Edelstein, Teri J
Edmonds, Tom
Edson, Gary F
Eins, Stefan
Eitner, Lorenz E A
Eldredge, Bruce B
Ellis, George Richard
Enman, Tom Kenneth
Escallon, Ana Maria

PAINTER

PAINTER (cont)

Anderson, Robert Dale
Andrew, David Neville
Andrews, Kim
Angell, Tony
Anker, Suzanne C
Antezzo, Matthew J
Anthony, Lawrence Kenneth
Antic, Miroslav
Antokal, Gale
Apgar, Jean E
Applebroog, Ida
Arguimbau, Peter L
Arion, Katherine
Armstrong, Carol
Arnoldi, Charles Arthur
Ashvil-Bibi, Sigalit
Astman, Barbara Anne
Aston, Miriam
Attie, Dotty
Audette, Anna Held
Aunio, Irene
Auten, Gerald
Awalt, Elizabeth Grace
Ayers, Carol Lee
Ayres, Julia Spencer
Azara, Nancy J
Bachner, Barbara L
Bales, J (Jean) Elaine
Banks, Anne Johnson
Banks, Ellen
Baratz, Robin
Bard, Gayle
Barker, Al C
Barnes, Margo
Barnett, David J
Barr-Sharrar, Beryl
Barsano, Ron (Ronald) James
Barsness, Jim
Bart, Georgiana Cray
Basham, Charles
Bastian, Linda
Bavinger, Eugene Allen
Baxendell, Julie
Baxter, Robert Charles
Baxter, Violet
Bearce, Jeana Dale
Beck, Theresa
Beerman, Miriam Beerman-Jaffe
Belan, Kyra
Beltran, Elio (Francisco)
Bennett, Tony
Bensignor, Paulette (Mrs Philip Steinberg)
Berger, John Peter
Berghash, Mark W
Bergstrom, Edith Harrod
Berkenblit, Ellen
Berti, Mary Vitelli
Bertoni, Christina
Besant, Derek Michael
Bieltvedt, Arnor G
Binks, Ronald C
Biondi, Florence Gloria
Birk, Sandow
Bishop, Budd Harris
Bishop, Jerold
Blackburn, David
Blair, Philippa Mary
Blank, Margot
Blum, June
Bodó, Sándor
Boltanski, Christian
Bora (Borayer), Vadim Makharbekovich
Bornstein, Eli
Bosman, Richard
Boszin, Andrew
Bott, John
Bottini, David William
Bowling, Katherine
Brace, Hilary
Brakke, P(erry) Michael
Braudy, Dorothy
Brauntuch, Troy
Breen, Harry Frederick, Jr
Bremer, Marlene S
Brewer, Paul
Brewster, Margaret Emilia
Brewster, Riley
Brier, Helene
Brill, Glenn
Brodie, Regis Conrad
Brodsky, Beverly
Broer, Roger L
Brown, Anita
Brown, Christopher
Brown, Peter C
Brown, Petey
Brubaker, Jack
Bruno, Santo M
Brycelea, Clifford
Buchanan, Beverly
Buchwald, Howard
Buechner, Thomas Scharman
Buehler, Stuart M
Bui, Phong
Buist, Kathy
Bunts, Frank
Burtt, Larice Annadel Roseman
Busch, Rita Mary
Byron, Michael
Cabot, Hugh
Cahana, Alice Lok
Cajori, Charles F
Callari, Emily Dolores
Calle, Paul
Campbell, Graham B
Candioti, Beatriz A
Canier, Caren
Cao, Gilda
Caporael, Suzanne
Carbone, David
Carl, Joan
Carlile, Janet (Hildebrand)
Carrino, David
Carswell, John
Carter, Yvonne Pickering
Casey, Kim L
Cass, Bill
Cassell, Beverly
Castagno, John Edward
Castillo, Mario Enrique
Celmins, Vija
Chamberlain, David (Allen)
Chase-Bien, Gail
Chee, Cheng-Khee (Jinyi Xu)
Cheek, Ronald Edward
Chia, Sandro
Chianese, Carol Burnard
Christenberry, William
Chung, Y David
Chunn, Nancy
Ciancio, June (Kirkpatrick)
Clark, Timothy John
Clark, Vicky Jo
Clemente, Francesco
Cobb, James
Coffey, Susanna Jean
Cogger, Cassia Zamecki
Colby, Bill
Cole, Julie Kramer
Coleman, Floyd Willis
Colescott, Warrington W
Colquhoun, Peter Lloyd
Conal, Robbie
Conant, Jan Royce
Conesa, Miguel A
Conlon, William
Cooper, Ron
Cooper, Susan
Corkery, Tim (Timothy) James
Corr, James D
Costa, Eduardo
Cove, Rosemary
Craft, David Ralph
Crimmins, Jerry (Gerald) Garfield
Cronin, Robert (Lawrence)
Cross, Yvonne
Crumpler, Dewey
Cucullu, Santiago
Culling, Richard Edward
Cushner, Steven J
Cusworth, Christyl
Cutler, Amy
Cutler, Ethel Rose
Cutrone, Ronnie Blaise
Daily-Birnbaum, Elaine
Danby, Ken
Daniels, Astar Charlotte Louise Daniels
Dass, Dean Allen
Dautreuil, Linda Trappey
David, Cyril Frank
Davidovich, Jaime
Davies, Harry Clayton
Davies, Haydn Llewellyn
Davis, James Granberry
Davis, Lisa Corinne
Davis, Stephen A
Day, Gary Lewis
DeAngelis, Joseph Rocco
De Boschnek, Chris (Christian) Charles
De Heusch, Lucio
D'Elaine
DeLap, Tony
De Luca, Joseph Victor
Dente, Robert
Deremer, Susan René
DeRoux, Daniel Edward
Derrickson, Steve Bruce
Desiderio, Vincent
D'Harnoncourt, Anne
Diamond, Jessica
Diehl, Guy
Difronzo, Francis G
Dinc, Alev Necile
Dingwall, Kenneth
D'Innocenzo, Nick
Dinsmore, Stephen Paul
DiStefano, Domenic
Dobard, Raymond Gerard
Docktor, Irv
Donahue, Philip Richard
Donegan, Cheryl
Donhauser, Paul Stefan
Dorfman, Geoffrey
Dorsey, Michael A
Dougherty, Raymond Edward
Dowden, Anne Ophelia Todd
Dronzek, Laura Ann
Drum, Sydney Maria
Dubnau, Jenny
Duesberry, Joellyn
Dukes, Caroline
Echohawk, Brummett
Eder, James Alvin
Edmonds, Tom
Edwards, Ethel
Egri, Ted
Eichel, Edward W
Eins, Stefan
El Hanani, Jacob
Ellis, Loren Elizabeth
Ellis, Ray
Ellis, Robert M
Ellis, Stephen
Ellis-Tracy, Jo
Embrey, Carl Rice
Engle, Steve
Engler, Sherrie Lee
English, Hal (Harold) J
Ensrud, Wayne
Erickson, Joy M
Ettenberg, Franklin Joseph
Evans, Dick
Fantazos, Henryk Michael
Farrell, Patrick
FeBland, Harriet
Federico, Frank
Feinstein, Rochelle H
Feng, Z L
Ferguson, Alice C
Filmus, Stephen I
Finch, Spencer
Finkelstein, Henry D
Fischl, Eric
Fish, Julia A
Fisher, Kim
Fishman, Louise
Fitzpatrick, Tony
Fletcher, Leland Vernon
Florin, Sharon June
Fohr, Jenny
Foley, David E
Folman, Liza
Foosaner, Judith
Foote, Howard Reed
Formicola, John Joseph
Francis, Jean Thickens
Frank, Helen Goodzeit
Fraser, Pamela
Frederick, Robilee
Freedman, Jacqueline
Freud, Lucian Michael
Friedberg, Rachel (Ray)
Friedman, Sabra
Friedman, Sally
Frigerio, Ismael
Fromentin, Christine Anne
Frueh, Deborah K A (Debi)
Fujimara, Makota
Furnas, Barnaby
Gabrielson, Walter Oscar
Gale, Nessa
Gallagher, Ellen
Gammon, Juanita L
Gaon, Simon
Garabedian, Charles
Garfield, Peter
Garrison, Gene K
Gauthier, Suzanne Anita
Gelernter, David H
Genkin, Jonathan
Gertjejansen, Doyle
Gibb, Ann W
Gibson, James D
Gibson, Michael
Gibson, Sandra
Gilbert, Helen Odell
Gilbert-Rolfe, Jeremy
Gilhooley, Dan
Gillen, John
Ginsburg, Estelle
Giordano, Greg Joe
Giovanopoulos, Paul
Gipe, Lawrence
Giro, R(alph) Victor Gironda
Girouard, Tina
Glier, Mike

PAINTER (cont)
Moya Soto, Roberto
Mozley, Anita Ventura
Muehlemann, Kathy
Mueller, Stephen
Munro, Janet Andrea
Murchie, Donald John
Murdock, Greg
Murray, Judith
Musgnug, Kristin A
Myer, Peter Livingston
Nakoneczny, Michael
Nantandy
Nardone, Vincent Joseph
Nash, Mary
Navrat, Den(nis) Edward
Neal, Michael Shane
Nelson, Aida Z
Nelson, James P
Nerdrum, Odd
Neumann, Andrew
Nice, Don
Noble, Kevin
Noda, Masaaki
Nodine, Jane Allen
Nordin, Phyllis E
Nyambi, Obaji A
Nyman, Georgianna Beatrice Aronson
Oakes, John Warren
Obrant, Susan Elizabeth
O'Connor, Chuck
Oda, Mayumi
Oliphant, Patrick
Oliver, Julie Ford
Olshan, Bernard
Olson, Bettye Johnson
O'Neil, Robyn
Ortega, Tony (Anthony) David
Osborne, Elizabeth
Osorio, Pepón
Owens, Laura
Pachter, Charles
Palazzolo, Carl
Palermo, Joseph
Park, Lee
Parker, Joni Y
Parker, June
Parrino, George
Passantino, George Christopher
Passuntino, Peter Zaccaria
Patnode, Mark William
Pearson, Bruce
Pease, David G
Pech, Arleta
Pennington, Sally
Pepper, Beverly
Perlis, Donald M
Perlman, Hirsch
Peters, Larry Dean
Peyton, Elizabeth Joy
Phillips, Richard
Picot, Pierre
Pierce, Danny P
Pijoan, Irene Maria Elizabeth
Piotrowski, Kimberly E
Pirkl, James Joseph
Pittman, Lari
Plotek, Leopold
Pomeroy, Frederick George
Pomeroy, Mary Barnas (Mrs F G Pomeroy)
Poon, Hung Wah Michael
Powley, Donald
Pratt, Elizabeth Hayes
Preede, Nydia
Prekop, Martin Dennis
Prieto, Monique N
Propersi, August J
Pujol, Ernesto
Purcell, Ann
Quackenbush, Robert
Quinn, Brian Grant
Rabinovitch, William Avrum
Rafferty, Joanne Miller
Ramos, Theodore
Ramsauer, Joseph Francis
Rankin, Don
Rapoport, Sonya
Reed, Robert James, Jr
Reid Jenkins, Debra L
Reif, (F) David
Reiss, Roland
Revitzky, Dennis L
Rhodes, Curtis A
Riccio, Louis Nicholas
Rice, Edward
Richards, Bruce Michael
Richardson, WC
Richmond, Rebekah
Richter, Gerhard
Riddle, John Thomas, Jr
Rigley, Frederick Wildermuth
Rippe, Dan (Christian)
Rippel, M (Morris) Conrad
Ritz, Lorna J
Rizzie, Dan
Robbins, Patricia
Roberts, Russell L
Robertson, Ruth
Robinson, Libby
Rodan, Don
Rodriguez, Rocio A
Roediger, Janice Anne
Rogers, Barbara
Rohrbacher, Patricia
Rollins, Tim
Rollman, Charlotte
Rorick, William Calvin
Rosas, Mel
Rose, Peggy Jane
Rosen, Diane
Rosen, Kay
Rosenberg, Jane
Rosenberg, Marilyn R
Rosenberg, Terry
Rosenblum, Elizabeth
Rosenfeld, Sarena
Roser, Ce (Cecilia)
Rossman, Michael
Rothschild, Barbara R Simon
Rothwell, Junko Ono
Rowan, Frances Physioc
Roybal, James Richard
Rozier, Robert L
Rubello, David Jerome
Ruhe, Barnaby Sieger
Rush, Deborah
Rushworth, Michele D
Rutstein, Rebecca
Saccoccio, Jacqueline
Sahagian, Arthur H
Sakoguchi, Ben
Salle, David
Sanchez, John
Santini, Debrah A
Santore, Joseph W
Sapien, Darryl Rudolph
Saret, Alan Daniel
Satorsky, Cyril
Sattler, Jill
Savitt, Sam
Sayre, Roger L
Scala, Joseph A
Scarpitta, Salvatore
Scharf, Kenny
Schmit, Randall
Schmitz, Barbara
Schnabel, Julian
Schneemann, Carolee
Schneider, Katy
Schneider, Rosalind L
Schonzeit, Benjamin
Schrohenloher, Sally A
Schultz, Caroline Reel
Schuselka, Elfi
Schwartz, Buky
Scott, Concetta Ciotti
Scott, Sam
Sculthorpe, Peter
Seabourn, Bert Dail
Sears, Stanton Gray
Sebelius, Helen
Seborovski, Carole
Semple, John Paulus
Setlow, Neva C (Delihas)
Shaffer, Richard
Shannon, Joe
Shashaty, Yolanda Victoria
Shaw, Jim
Shaw, Karen
Shaw, Mary Todd
Shaw, Reesey
Shay, Ed
Shechter, Ben-Zion
Shechter, Laura J
Shepard, Steven L
Shepherd, Helen Parsons
Sherwood, Katherine
Shie & Acord, Susan & James
Shields, Anne Kesler
Shore, Robert
Shuebrook, Ron (Ronald) Lee
Shukman, Solomon
Siedman, Scott
Siegel, Fran
Siena, James
Sikander, Shahzia
Siler, Patrick W
Sillman, Amy
Simon, Netty D
Simonian, Judith
Singer, Alan Daniel
Sirlin, Deanna Louise
Smalley, Stephen Francis
Smira, Shaoul
Smith, Cary
Smith, Dennis V
Smith, Donald C
Smith, Gary Douglas
Smith, Jaune Quick-to-See
Smith, Jos(eph) A(nthony)
Smith, Kiki
Smolarek, Waldemar
Snyder, Joan
Softic, Tanja
Solberg, Morten Edward
Solinas, Rico
Solomon, Gerald
Sol'Sax
Somers, H(arry) W
Sorman, Steven
Sottung, George (K)
Spandorfer, Merle Sue
Spann, Susanna Evonne
Speyer, Nora
Staffel, Doris
Staloff, Fred
Stamsta, Jean
Stanczak, Julian
Stanford, Ginny C
Stanley, M Louise
Stark, Linda
Staven, Leland Carroll
Stecher, Pauline
Stecher, Ruth (Rusty) L
Stein, Ronald Jay
Steiner, Charles K
Steiner, Michael
Steiner, Sherry L
Stephan, Gary
Stephanson, Loraine Ann
Stewart, Regina
Stone, Jeffrey Ingram
Stonebarger, Virginia
Storr, Robert
Strand, Sally Ellis
Suggs, Don
Sugiura, Kunie
Sulkowski, Elizabeth Brandon
Sulkowski, James M
Sulkowski, Joseph H
Sullivan, Patrice Maureen
Swanson, Caroline
Sweet, Francis Edward
Swenson, Erick
Swetcharnik, William Norton
Szilvasy, Linda Markuly
Tait, Will(iam) H
Tapies, Antoni
Tarbet, Urania Christy
Tay, Eng
Taylor, Gage
Tetherow, Michael
Thiebaud, Wayne Morton
Thompson, Cappy (Catherine)
Thompson, Colin (H)
Thompson, Ernest Thorne, Jr
Thorne, Joan
Thrall, Arthur
Tinkler, Barrie Keith
Tobias, Richard
Tomchuk, Marjorie
Tompkins, Michael
Toperzer, Thomas Raymond
Tran, Tam Van
Trion, May Rolstad
Trombetta, Annamarie
True, David
Tsai, Wen-Ying
Tucker, James Ewing
Tullis, Garner H
Turner, Herbert B
Tyzack, Michael
Urquhart, Tony (Anthony) Morse
Valadez, John
Valla, Teressa Marie
Van Harlingen, Jean (Ann)
Van Horn, Dana Carl
Van Osdell, Barrie (Calabrese) Smith
Varnay Jones, Theodora
Vasquez, Emigdio Chavez
Vernon, Karen
Verostko, Roman Joseph
Violette, Banks
Vitale, Magda
Volkersz, Willem
Wachtel, Julie
Wade, Robert Schrope
Wagner, Tom
Walker, John Seibels
Walker, Kara
Walker, Kelley
Walker, Larry
Walker, William Bond
WalkingStick, Kay
Wallace, Carol Ann (Brucker)
Wallace, Gael Lynn
Wallace, Kenneth William
Wang, Gar

PAINTER (cont)

PAINTER (cont)
Plattner, Phyllis
Plotkin, Linda
Poduska, T F
Pogany, Miklos
Pollack, Reginald Murray
Pollard, Jann Lawrence
Polonsky, Arthur
Poons, Larry
Popovac, Gwynn
Potter, Ted
Powelson, Rosemary A
Prado-Arai, Namiko
Price, Morgan Samuel
Prochownik, Walter A
Pugh, Grace Huntley
Puri, Antonio
Purnell, Robin Barker
Quentel, Holt
Quiller, Stephen Frederick
Raash, Kathleen Forecki
Rackus, George (Keistus)
Ragland, Bob
Rakovan, Lawrence Francis
Ramirez, Joel Tito
Ramos, (Mel) Melvin John
Rauf, Barbara Claire
Raviv, Ilana
Rayburn, Boyd (Dale)
Reagan, Rourk C
Rebbeck, Lester James, Jr
Rebhun, Pearl G
Red Star, Kevin (Running Rabbit)
Reed, David
Reed, Jesse Floyd
Reedy, Mitsuno Ishii
Reep, Edward Arnold
Reinker, Nancy Clayton Cooke
Remsing, Joseph Gary
Renee, Paula
Resika, Paul
Reynolds, Patricia Ellen
Reynolds, Robert
Rice, Norman Lewis
Richenburg, Robert Bartlett
Ries, Martin
Ringgold, Faith
Ritchey, Rik
Ritchie, Charles Morton, Jr
Rivera, Frank
Robbins, Michael Jed
Rocamora, Jaume
Roché, Robert (Richard)
Rogovin, Mark
Romano, Clare
Romero, Rachael L
Rophar
Rose, Herman
Roseman, Susan Carol
Ross, Jaime
Ross, James Matthew Akiba
Rotterdam, Paul Zwietnig-Rotterdam
Rozman, Joseph John
Ruben, Albert
Rubin, Irwin
Rudquist, Jerry Jacob
Ruttinger, Jacquelyn
Ryman, Robert
Saff, Donald Jay
St Denis, Paul Andre
Sal, Jack
Saladino, Tony
Salemme, Lucia Autorino
Samuelson, Fred Binder
Sandler, Barbara
Sandlin, David Thomas
Sarantos, Bettie J
Saul, Peter
Saunders, Raymond Jennings
Savage, Jerry
Savage, Roger
Savas, Jo-Ann
Scarpa, Dorothea
Scharf, William
Scheer, Sherie (Hood)
Scherpereel, Richard Charles
Schieferdecker, Ivan E
Schlemm, Betty Lou
Schmid, Richard Alan
Schneider, Shellie
Schoenherr, John (Carl)
Schreiber, Eileen Sher
Schrut, Sherry
Schwartz, Therese
Scott, Michael
Seckel, Paul Bernhard
Seelbach, Anne Elizabeth
Segall-Marx, Madeleine (Maddy Marx)
Seguin, Jean-Pierre
Sehring, Adolf
Sella, Alvin Conrad
Semowich, Charles John
Seymour, Claudia
Shah, Ela
Shahn, Abby
Sharp, Susan S
Shaw, Donald Edward
Shead, S Ray
Sheaks, Barclay
Shedosky, Suzanne
Sheehan, Evelyn
Sheehan, Maura A
Sheller, G A
Shepherd, Reginald
Sheppard, Joseph Sherly
Sherrill, Milton Lewis
Shikler, Aaron
Shives, Arnold Edward
Siler, Todd (Lael)
Singh, Carolyn
Sirugo, Sal (Salvatore)
Skurkis, Barry A
Sky, Carol Veth
Slade, Roy
Sloat, Richard Joel
Slone, Sandi
Small, Deborah
Smith, Albert E
Snelson, Kenneth D
Snidow, Gordon E
Snow, Lee Erlin
Snow, Michael
Snowden, Gilda
Snyder, Ruth (Cozen)
Sokov, Leonid
Solberg, Morten Edward
Sorce, Anthony John
Sorge, Walter
Sperakis, Nicholas George
Spratt, Frederick R
Stanforth, Melvin Sidney
Stefanelli, Joseph James
Sterne, Hedda
Stevenson, A Brockie
Stewart, Dorothy S
Steynovitz, Zamy
Stillman(Myers), Joyce L
Stoltenberg, Donald Hugo
Stone, Gwen
Storm, Larue
Stout, Frank J
Stratton, Dorothy
Stronghilos, Carol
Sturman, Eugene
Sullivan, JuneAnn Margaret
Sultan, Donald K
Sussman, Arthur
Suzuki, James Hiroshi
Suzuki, Taro
Svedlow, Andrew Jay
Sverdlove, Zolita
Swan, Barbara
Sweet, Marsha (Marsha) Sweet Welch
Sznajderman, Marius S
Szold, Lauren G
Tabak, Chaim
Talbert, Richard Harrison
Targan, Judy
Tascona, Antonio Tony
Taylor, Brie (Benjamin de Brie)
Tettleton, Robert Lynn
Thackston, R King
Theroux, Carol
Thomas, Larry W
Thompson, Virginia Abbate
Thorns, John Cyril, Jr
Tillenius, Clarence Ingwall
Ting, Walasse
Tobias, Robert Paul
Tompkins, Alan
Torlen, Michael Arnold
Toscano, Dolores A
Townsend, Jean (Mrs Saul Field)
Tracy, Michael
Treister, Kenneth
Trivigno, Pat
Trova, Ernest Tino
Tsai, Hsiao Hsia
Tulving, Ruth
Turconi, Sue (Susan) Kinder
Turk, Rudy H
Turlington, Patricia R
Tuttle, Richard
Twombly, Cy
Umlauf, Karl A
Umlauf, Lynn (Charlotte)
Uzilevsky, Marcus
Vaccaro, Luella Grace
Vadia, Rafael
Valencia, Cesar
Valerio, James Robert
Vallance, Jeffrey K R
Van Laar, Timothy
Van Sant, Tom R
Vaux, Richard
Velasquez, Oscar
Vidal, Francisco
Viera, Charles David
Viera, Ricardo
Villarreal-Castelazo, Eduardo
Vinella, Ray (Raimondo) John
Violet, Ultra
Vitale, Vincent
Voelker, Elizabeth
Von Schmidt, Eric
Voos, William John
Wainwright, Robert Barry
Wald, Sylvia
Waldman, Paul
Walker, Larry
Wall, Rhonda
Wandel, Sharon Lee
Warshaw, Larry
Washington, James W, Jr
Washmon, Gary Brent
Wasserman, Albert
Watson, Darliene Keeney
Wayne, June
Webb, Jeffrey R
Weber, Idelle Lois
Wechter, Vivienne Thaul
Welden, Daniel W
Weller, Paul
Wells, Betty Childs
Wells, Mac
Welter, Cole H
Wentworth, Janet
Wesley, John
Wethington, Wilma
Wetmore, Gordon (Stanley Gordon)
Whitaker, William
White, B J (Beverly)
White, E Alan
White, John M
Whitney (Stevens), Charlotte Armide
Whittome, Irene F
Wiley, William T
Will, John A
Willard, Garcia Lou
Williams, Idaherma
Willis, Jane B(roome)
Wimberley, Frank Walden
Wingate, George B
Winiarski, Deborah
Winters, Sandy L
Wisnosky, John G
Wissemann-Widrig, Nancy
Witold, Kaczanowski
Witt, John
Wolfe, Mildred Nungester
Wong, Audrey E(lizabeth)
Wonner, Paul John
Woods, Roosevelt (Rip)
Woodson, Shirley Ann
Woolwich, Madlyn-Ann C
Wray, Dick
Wright, Michael Fitzhugh
Wyland, Steve Creech
Wynn, Gaines Clore
Wynne, Albert Givens
Wynne, Rob
Yampolsky, Phyllis
Yanow, Rhoda Mae
Yarbrough, Leila Kepert
Yasuda, Robert
Yedidsion, Meira
Young, Kenneth Victor
Youngblood, Nat
Zahourek, Jon Gail
Zaleski, Jean
Zaloudek, Duane
Zivic, William Thomas
Zonia, Dhimitri
Zopp, Dudley
Zox, Larry
Zucker, Joseph I

Egg Tempera
Akers, Gary
Baxter, Robert James
Braiden, Rose Margaret J
Coburn, Bette Lee
Dal Poggetto, Sandra Hope
Forrestall, Thomas De Vany
Freeman, Kathryn
Ghikas, Panos George
Glesmann, Sylvia Maria
Jaque, Louis
Levine, Tomar
MacKenzie, Hugh Seaforth
McBryde, Sarah Elva
Mitchell, Dianne
Moon, Jim (James) Monroe
Musselman, Darwin B
Obering, Mary M

PAINTER (cont)
Phillips, Arthur Byron
Powers, Donald T
Reding, Barbara Endicott
Rippel, M (Morris) Conrad
Rosenthal, Stephen
Sanders, Rhea Sanders Rabinovich
Schottland, M
Selznick-Drutz, June
Sherman, Sarai
Steinhoff, Monika
Stone, Don
Sussman, Arthur
Tooker, George
Van Winkelen, Barbara
Vargo, John
Vickrey, Robert Remsen
Wiltraut, Douglas Scott
Wright, Harold David
Wyeth, Andrew Newell
Young, Andrew

Miscellaneous Media
Ablow, Joseph
Ablow, Roselyn Karol (Roz Koyol Ablow)
Abrams, Joyce Diana
Abt, Jeffreyy
Adams, Lisa Kay
Alhilali, Neda
Allain, Rene Pierre
Anderson, Bill (William) Maxwell
Anderson, William Thomas
Anthonisen, George Rioch
Appel, Keith Kenneth
Arike, Michael Whitaker
Ariss, Margot Joan Phillips
Armstrong, L C
Arnold, Joseph Patterson
Aronson, David
Artschwager, Richard Ernst
Atkinson, Eric Newton
Aylon, Helene
Bailey, Barry Stone
Bakaty, Mike
Baker, Alden
Balahutrak, Lydia Bodnar
Ballard, James A
Bandy, Gary
Banerjee, Bimal
Bangert, Colette Stuebe
Barber, Philip Judd
Baroff, Jill (Emily)
Barra, Robert
Barrow, Amanda McLaughlin
Barth, Jack Alexander
Bartlett, Jennifer Losch
Bass, Joel
Bauer, Ruth Kruse
Baumel-Harwood, Bernice
Baynard, Ed
Behrens, Mary Snyder
Bender, May
Bennett, Don Bemco
Bero, Mary
Bhavsar, Natvar Prahladji
Bialobroda, Anna
Biolchini, Gregory Phillip
Bishop, Jeffrey Britton
Bjorklund, Lee
Boardman, Deborah
Booker, Chakaia
Botero, Fernando
Bouchard, Paul E
Bourgeois, Douglas
Brach, Paul Henry
Bradshaw, Ellen
Bramson, Phyllis Halperin
Brangoccio, Michael David
Briansky, Rita Prezament
Brito, Maria
Brodeur, Catherine R
Brodkin, Ed
Brown, Carol A
Brown, Pamela Wedd
Brown, Peggy Ann
Brown, Susan LT (Haviland Slizys)
Bryce, Eileen Ann
Burshell, Sandra Eve
Busard, Roberta Ann
Cadieux, Michael Eugene
Campbell, David Paul
Carducci, Judith
Carlson, Robert Michael
Carmichael, Donald Ray
Carter, Harriet (Estelle) Manore
Carter, Sam John
Carvalho, Josely
Casellas, Joachim
Cavat, Irma
Chang, Jason
Cheshire, Craig Gifford
Chicago, Judy
Christ-Janer, Arland F
Chusid, Evette
Cisneros, Jose B
Clark, Emery Ann
Clayton, Christian
Clayton, Robert
Clough, Charles Sidney
Code, Audrey
Coffin, J Douglas
Colescott, Robert H
Collins, Paul
Consagra, Pier
Cook, Michael David
Cooke, Judy
Cowan, Aileen Hooper
Cowley, Edward P
Crawford, Rainie
Crile, Susan
Cuevas, Jose Luis
Cunnick, Gloria Helen
Dahill, Thomas Henry, Jr
D'Almeida, George
Danziger, Fred Frank
Dasenbrock, Doris (Nancy) Voss
Davenny, Ward L
Davis, Brad (Bradley) Darius
Davis, Jack R
Davis, Jerrold
Dawson, Doug
Debarry, Christina
Debrosky, Christine A
Decter, Betty Eva
De Guzman, Evelyn Lopez
Deloney, Jack Clouse
Demanche, Michel S
De Mille, Leslie Benjamin
Denton, Patry
DeSantis, Diana
Dettwiller, Kathryn King
Dickinson, Eleanor Creekmore
Di Giacomo, Fran
Di Meo, Dominick
Dmytruk, Ihor R
Dooley, David I
Dooley Waller, M L
Dreikausen, Margret
Duben, Ipek Aksugur
Duerwald, Carol
Dufour, Paul Arthur
Durham, Jo Ann Fanning
Dzierski, Vincent Paul
Eckart, Christian
Edell, Nancy
Edwards, James F
Egeli, Peter Even
Eger, Marilyn Rae
Eisenstat, Jane Sperry
Elias, Sheila
Elliot, Catherine J
Ellis, Andra
Embrey, Carl Rice
Erbe, Chantell Van
Erdle, Rob
Evangeline, Margaret
Evins, Patsy Jean
Fabiano, Diane Fabian
Farber, Maya M
Faulkner, Frank
Feldman, Aline M
Fellows, Alice
Ferguson, Gerald
Fetting, Rainer
Few, James Cecil
Finkelstein, Max
Fischman, Barbara J
Fitzgerald, Astrid
Fitzgerald, Joan V
Flahavin, Marian Joan
Flick, Paul John
Forman, Alice
Forman, Kenneth Warner
Fornelli, Joseph
Foulger, Richard F
Freed, David
Freeland, Bill
Freeman, Jeff(rey Vaughn)
Frick, Joan
Friedeberg, Pedro
Frost, Stuart Homer
Fuller, Emily
Gablik, Suzi
Galen, Elaine
Galinsky, Norman
Garcia, Rupert (Marshall) R
Garcia Guerrero, Luis
Gard, Suzanne E
Garzon-Blanco, Armando
Gaucher, Yves
Gaydos, Tim (Timothy) John
Geller, Esther Geller Shapero
Genn, Nancy
Gerber, Gaylen
Gigliotti, Joanne Marie
Gillespie, Dorothy Muriel
Glantzman, Judy
Glaser, David
Gold, Leah
Goldstein, Eleanor
Goodell, Rosemary W
Grabarsky, Sheila
Graham, Lois (M Gord)
Green, Denise G
Greenberg, Irwin
Greene, Chris (Christine) E
Greene, Daniel E
Greenspan, Gladys
Greer, Walter Marion
Grimley, Oliver Fetterolf
Gualtieri, Joseph P
Halbrook, Rita Robertshaw
Hall, John A
Hall, Lee
Hamlett, Dale Edward
Handell, Albert George
Hanner, Jean Patricia
Hansen, Harold (Harry) John
Hansen, Robert
Harjo, Benjamin, Jr
Harkness, Madden
Harnick, Sylvia
Harper, Michaele Ann
Harrington, Chestee Marie
Harrison, Alice
Hartal, Paul
Hartigan, Grace
Hatgil, Paul
Haut, Claire (Joan)
Hawkins, Myrtle H
Hay, (George) Austin
Hayes, Randy (Randolph) Alan
Heimdal, Georg
Heise, Myron Robert
Herbert, James Arthur
Hermann, Mildred L
Hitner, Chuck
Hoffman, Eric
Hoffman, Helen Bacon
Hollander, Roz
Holste, Thomas James
Honig, Eleanor D
Hopkins, B(ernice) Elizabeth
Horvat, Olga
Horvay, Martha J
Horvitz, Suzanne Reese
Hotvedt, Kris J
Howell-Coon, Elizabeth (Mitch)
Howlett, Ray
Hubbard, John
Huff, Robert
Hung, Chin-Cheng
Huot, Robert
Hupp, Frederick Duis
Injeyan, Seta L
Jacobson, Arthur
Janschka, Fritz
Jarvis, Donald
Jennerjahn, W P
Jenrette, Pamela Anne
Jensen, Leo
Jerins, Edgar
Johnson, Homer
Jones, Doug Douglas McKee
Jordan, Beth McAninch
Ju, I-Hsiung
Kakas, Christopher A
Kamm, Dorothy Lila
Karawina, Erica (Mrs Sidney C Hsiao)
Karwoski, Richard Charles
Kash, Marie (Marie Kash Weltzhemer)
Kaufman, Janc
Keech, John H
Keeler, David Boughton
Keerl, Beat
Kelley, Mike
Kerns, Ed (Johnson), Jr
Kettner, David Allen
Kimura, Riisaburo
Kinnaird, Richard William
Kitaj, R B
Klarin, Karla S
Kleemann, Ron
Kleiman, Alan
Klein, Ellen Lee
Knerr, Erika Tilde
Knudsen, Christian
Knutsson, Anders
Koch, Edwin E
Kocher, Robert Lee
Kohut, Lorene
Koons, Darell J
Kornmayer, J Gary
Kravitz, Walter
Kreitzer, David Martin
Kuang, Ting Shao

PAINTER (cont)
Kuchar, Kathleen Ann
Kuehn, Edmund Karl
Kunstler, Morton
Kunz, Sandra Thurber
Kwiecinski, Chester Martin
Laderman, Gabriel
Lambrechts, Marc
Langston, Mary Virginia
Lansdowne, James Fenwick
Lawrence, Matthew R
Lawrence, Sidney S
Lawton, Nancy
Lebeck, Carol E
Le Clair, Charles
Lee, David (Tzeh-Hsian)
Lee, Margaret F
Leedy, Jim (James A Leedy)
Leeper, Doris Marie
Lehrer, Leonard
Leis, Marietta Patricia
Leland, Whitney Edward
Lerner, Alexandria Sandra
Lesh, Richard D
Levy, Phyllis
Lew, Fran
Lichacz, Sheila Enit
Lieber, Edvard
Lifson, Hugh Anthony
Lindahl, Toni
Lovejoy, Margot R
Lund, Jane
Lynch, Mary Britten
Lyon, Giles Andrew
Lytle, Richard
Lytton, Constance B
Mackenzie, David, IV
Mac Whinnie, John Vincent
Magee, Alan
Mahoney, Joella Jean
Majdrakoff, Ivan
Malone, Robert R
Mandel, Saul
Manes, Paul
Manter, Margaret C
Manville, Elsie
Marander, Carol Jean
Margules, Gabriele Ella
Marker, Mariska Pugsley
Marlowe, Willie
Marshall, Robert Leroy
Martin, Dianne L
Martin, Larry Kenneth
Massad, George Daniel
Matisse, Jackie (Jacqueline) Matisse Monnier
Matteo, Dorothy
Mazur, Michael
McCue, Harry
McGhee, John Gilmer
McNickle, Thomas Glen
Merrill, Ross M
Meyer, Milton E, Jr
Michaels-Paque, J
Mickish, Verle L
Milbourn, Patrick D
Miller, Michael Stephen
Minter, Marilyn A
Mitchell, Katherine
Moon, Marc
Moore, Fay
Moore, Mark Tobin
Morisue, Glenn Takanori
Morphesis, Jim (James) George
Morris, Roger Dale
Mosch, Deborah Cherry
Moser, Kenna J
Muenzenmayer, Kenneth John
Munk, Loren James
Munoz, Rie
Murray, John Michael
Nawara, Jim
Nelson, Joan
Nelson, Ruth Basha (Basha Ruth Nelson)
Nes, Margaret Isabel
Nickerson, Scott A
Nix, Patricia (Lea)
Nodiff, Jack
Noland, Kenneth
Nuss, Joanne Ruth
Nutzle, Futzie (Bruce) John Kleinsmith
Nyman, Georgianna Beatrice Aronson
Obering, Mary M
Oji, Helen Shizuko
Olson, Rick
Ortlip, Paul Daniel
O'Shea, Terrence Patrick
Ostendarp, Carl
Ostiguy, Jean-Rene
Osver, Arthur
Paige, Wayne Leo
Paisner, Claire
Paravano, Dino
Partridge, David Gerry
Pashgian, M Helen
Patrick, Joseph Alexander
Patterson, Shirley Abbott
Paul, Art(hur)
Paul, William D, Jr
Pearson, John
Peden Wesley, Donalee
Peeples-Bright, Maija Gegeris Zack Woof
Peppard, Blaylock A
Peruo, Marsha
Peters, Andrea Jean
Peterson, Dorothy (Hawkins)
Phoenix, Kaola Allen
Piehl, Walter Jason, Jr
Piene, Otto
Pindell, Howardena Doreen
Pitcher, John Charles
Pond, Clayton
Pope, Mary Ann Irwin
Porter, Liliana
Prewitt, Merle R(ainey)
Primm, Sylvia Marie
Promutico, Jean
Prystauk, Elissa
Quaytman, Harvey
Quirk, Thomas Charles, Jr
Radovich, Donald
Ragland, Jack Whitney
Rankaitis, Susan
Rauschenberg, Robert
Regan, Betsey
Reimann, Arline Lynn
Renner, Eric
Richards, Jeanne Herron
Richards, Sabra
Rippey, Clayton
Rise, John Ernest
Riseling, Robert Lowell
Robbins, Hulda D
Robbins, Jack C
Robinson, Aminah Brenda Lynn
Robinson, Jay
Robinson, Mary Ann
Rockburne, Dorothea
Rogers, Earl Leslie
Romero, Megan H
Rood, Kay
Rose, Robin Carlise
Rosenthal, Seymour
Ross, Joan Stuart
Ross, Sueellen
Rothenberg, Barbara
Rowan, (C) Patrick
Ruehlicke, Cornelia Iris
Ruffing, Anne Elizabeth
Ruggles, Joanne Beaule
Ruthling, Ford
Saari, Peter H
Sabelis, Huibert
Sallick, Lucy Ellen
Sangiamo, Albert
Sargent, Richard
Sarkisian, Paul
Sassone, Marco
Satz, Janet
Sauter, Gail E
Schabacker, Betty Barchet
Schaeffer, S(tanley) Allyn
Schaffer, Richard E(nos)
Scheuer, Ruth
Schlitter, Helga
Schloss, Arleen P
Schmaltz, Roy Edgar
Schneider, Julie Saecker
Schulzke, Margot Seymour
Schuster, Cita Fletcher (Sarah E)
Scucchi, Robie (Peter), Jr
Seaberg, Libby W
Sellers, William Freeman
Sencial, Gabriel Jaime
Seyler, Monique G
Shaw, Kendall (George)
Sherman, Lenore Walton
Sherwood, Leona
Shih, Joan Fai
Siegel, Barbara
Siems, Anne
Sillman, Amy (Denison)
Silva, Jude Hutton
Simmons, Cleda-Marie
Slapo, Daniel E
Smith, Greg
Smith, Nelson David
Smith, Rae
Sokolowski, Linda Robinson
Somers, Frederick D(uane)
Sorokin, Maxine Ann
Sorrin, Mary Louise
Sowers, Miriam R
Spafford, Michael Charles
Spero, Nancy
Spofford, Sally
Spurgin, John Edwin
Squires, Norma Jean
Stack, Gael Z
Stamaty, Clara Gee Kastner
Stamsta, Jean
Stark, Ron
Stavans, Isaac
Steele, Benjamin Charles
Stegman, Patricia
Stein, Ludwig
Steinberg, Rubin
Steir, Pat
Stella, Frank
Sterling, Colleen
Stevens, William Ansel, Sr
Stevenson, Harold, Jr
Stinsmuehlen-Amend, Susan
Stoianovich, Marcelle
Strasen, Barbara Elaine
Straus, Sandy
Stromsdorfer, Deborah Ann
Strucken Bachmann, Marion
Stuart, Michelle
Sullivan, Anne Dorothy Hevner
Sylvan, Rita M
Tabor, Virginia S
Tanger, Susanna
Therrien, Robert
Thibault, Andre (Teabo)
Thompson, Tamara
Tiemann, Robert E
Tolliver, Mose
Toschik, Larry
Tribush, Brenda
Trimm, H Wayne
Trupp, Barbara Lee
Turner, Bonese Collins
Twiggs, Leo Franklin
Urso, Josette
Vaccaro, Patrick Frank
Venezia, Michael
Verhoeven, Rudi
Villa, Carlos
Vo-Dinh, Mai
Wadler, Ronni
Wagner, Merrill
Wagoner, Robert B
Waid, Jim (James) E
Waitzkin, Stella
Waksberg, Nomi
Walker, Marie Sheehy
Walker, Ronald C
Walsh, Nan
Warburg, Stephanie Wenner
Wasserman, Burton
Wax, John M
Wegman, William
Weingarten, Hilde (Kevess)
Weinstein, Joyce
Welch, Charles D
Weldon, Barbara Maltby
Wells, Lynton
Weschler, Anita
White, Philip Butler
Whiteman, Edward Russell
Wilbert, Robert John
Wilson, Charles Banks
Womack, Rob (Robert) Robinson
Wong, Lucille (Lucila) Guerra Wong
Wong, Paul Kan
Wood, Melissa
Woods, Burton Arthur
Wooster, Ann-Sargent
Yoder, Robert Edward
Youkeles, Anne
Young, Charles Alexander
Young, Tom (Thomas) William
Zaima, Stephen Gyo
Zeitlin, Harriet
Zilius, Vladas
Zupan, Bruno

Sand
Aunio, Irene
Buchman, Arles (Arlette) Buchman
Chambeaux, Jane
Fredman, Faiya R
Haley, Priscilla J
Hamlin, Louise
Hansell, Freya
Hayes, Carolyn Hendrick
Kurtz, Elaine
Leroy, Louis
Pousette-Dart, Joanna
Ritter, Renee Gaylinn
Rothafel, Sydell
Ryerson, Mitch
Sandground, Mark Bernard, Sr
Smith, James Michael

PATRON

PHOTOGRAPHER

PHOTOGRAPHER (cont)
Betancourt, Carlos
Beveridge, Karl J
Biferie, Dan (Daniel) Anthony, Jr
Binks, Ronald C
Black, Lisa
Blackemore, Amy
Blakely, George C
Block, Gay S
Bloom, Barbara
Bloom, Martha
Bloomfield, Lisa Diane
Blue, Patt
Bohnen, Blythe
Boltanski, Christian
Bolton, Richard
Bootz, Antoine H
Borowiec, Andrew
Bourdeau, Robert Charles
Bradley, Slater
Brauchli, Byron T
Braudy, Dorothy
Braunstein, Mark Mathew
Braunstein, Terry (Malikin)
Breslin, Nancy
Brewster, Andrea B
Broderick, James Allen
Brody, Myron Roy
Brooks, Drex M
Brooks, Ellen
Brown, Gillian
Brown, Lawrie
Brown, Peter Thomson
Brumfield, William Craft
Brush, Gloria (Elizabeth) DeFilipps
Bubriski, Kevin E
Buitron, Robert C
Bunn, David
Bunnen, Lucinda Weil
Burchfield, Jerry Lee
Burkett, Christopher G
Burns, Marsha
Burson, Nancy
Bussche, Wolf von dem
Busto, Ana Marie
Butler, George Tyssen
Caffery, Debbie Fleming
Calderon, Eduardo T
Callis, Jo Ann
Calman, W(endy) L
Camhi, Morrie
Camp, Donald Eugene
Campos-Pons, Maria Magdalena
Cano, Margarita
Cantor, Fredrich
Cao, Gilda
Capa, Cornell
Caponigro, Paul
Carey, Ellen
Carlberg, Norman Kenneth
Carpenter, Dennis (Bones) Wilkinson
Casebere, James E
Cawood, Gary Kenneth
Chamberlain, Ann
Chambers, Park A, Jr
Channing, Susan Rose
Charlesworth, Sarah E
Checefsky, Bruce E
Chesley, Paul Alexander
Chiarenza, Carl
Childers, Malcolm Graeme
Chong, Albert Valentine
Christopherson, Howard Martin
Ciriclio, S(usan) E (Fay)
Clancy, Patrick
Clark, Kathryn J
Clarke, Kevin
Clift, William Brooks
Coates, Ann S
Cohen, Alan Barry
Cohen, Joan Lebold
Cohen, Lynne G
Cohen, Michael S
Cohen, Sorel
Cole, Herbert Milton
Coleman, Judy
Collier, Anna
Collins, Larry Richard
Collyer, Robin
Colmer, Roy David
Colp, Norman B
Conner, Lois
Conniff, Gregory
Connor, Linda Stevens
Conrad, Nancy R
Conte, Jeanne Larner
Coupon, William
Coyne, Petah E
Craft, David Ralph
Crane, Arnold H
Crane, Barbara Bachmann
Crewdson, Gregory
Cumming, Robert H
Curran, Darryl Joseph
Curran, Douglas Edward
Dablow, Dean Clint
Dahl, Stephen M
Dater, Judy
Davidson, Abraham A
Davidson, Nancy
Davies, Harry Clayton
Davis, Ben H
Davis, Christine
Davis, Philip Charles
Dawson, Robert H
Deal, Joe
Debeers, Sue
DeCaprio, Alice
DeCarava, Roy Rudolph
DeGenevieve, Barbara
Delaney, Janet Clare
Delisle, Thomas Charles
De Lory, Peter
Demanche, Michel S
Deschamps, Francois
des Rioux (de Messimy), Deena Victoria (Coty)
Devlin, Lucinda Alice
Diamond, Paul
Dibert, Rita Jean
Dickson, Jennifer Joan
DiCorcia, Philip Lorca
Dine, Jim
Dingus, Phillip Rick
DiPerna, Frank Paul
Divola, John Manford, Jr
Doll, Donald Arthur
Dorfman, Elsa
Douthat, Anita S
Dow, Jim D
Downer, Spelman Evans
DuBois, Alan Beekman
Dunitz, Jay
Dunning, Jeanne
Dusard, Jay
Dutton, Allen A
Egan, Laury Agnes
Eide, John
Ellis, Loren Elizabeth
Enos, Chris
Epstein, Mitch (Mitchell) D
Erickson, Joy M
Ess, Barbara
Estabrook, Reed
Evergon
Feng, Ying
Ferguson, Larry Scott
Fernandez, (Jules) Jake
Fink, Larry (Laurence) B
Finn, David
Fischer, Thomas Jeffrey
Fish, Alida
Fiskin, Judy
Fiss, Cinthea
Fitch, Blake
Fitch, Steve (Steven) Ralph
Flattau, John W
Flax, Florence P (Roselin Polinsky)
Flick, Robbert
Flower, Michael Lavin
Flynt, Robert
Foster, Maelee Thomson
Foster, Steven Douglas
Fox, Flo
Fox, Michael David
Frailey, Stephen A
Franklin, Don
Fraser, Catriona Trafford
Fratkin, Leslie
Freeman, Roland L
Freeman, Tina
Frey, Mary E
Friedlander, Lee
Friedman, Benno
Fulton, Jack E
Funderburk, Amy Elizabeth
Furth, Karen J
Gage, Beau
Gaines, William Robert
Gallagher, Carole
Gandert, Miguel Adrian
Garfield, Peter
Garnett, William Ashford
Garrison, Gene K
Gartel, Laurence M
Garvens, Ellen
Gates, Jeff S
Gaudard, Pierre
Gauvreau, Robert George
Gefter, Judith Michelman
Gerlovina & Gerlovin, Rimma & Valeriy
Gibson, Ralph H
Gilden, Bruce
Gilpin, Henry Edmund
Giordano, Greg Joe
Gips, C L Terry
Glendinning, Peter
Gluhman, Margaret A
Goertz, Augustus Frederick, III
Gohlke, Frank William
Goin, Peter
Goldberg, Jim
Golden, Judith Greene
Goldin, Nan
Goldring, Nancy Deborah
Gomez, Mirta & Eduardo Delvalle
Goodine, Linda Adele
Goodman, Mark
Gordin, Misha
Gore, David Alan
Gore, Tom
Gossage, John Ralph
Grannon, Katy
Grassl, Anton M
Graves, Kenneth Robert
Grazda, Edward
Green, Jonathan (William)
Greenfield-Sanders, Timothy
Greer, Jane Ruth
Griffin, Sallie Thompson
Grimaldi, Vince
Groover, Jan
Gruber, Aaronel deRoy
Guerrero, Raul
Guilmet, Glenda J
Gurdjian, Annette
Gurney, Janice Sigrid
Gursky, Andreas
Guzy, Carol
Haar, Tom
Hahn, Betty
Halevi, Marcus
Hall, Douglas E
Hallam, Beverly (Linney)
Hallman, Gary Lee
Hammerbeck, Wanda Lee
Hammond, Mary Sayer
Harbutt, Charles
Harkins, Dennis Richter
Harold-Steinhauser, Judith
Harrell, Margaret Ann
Harris, Paul Rogers
Harrison, Carol Love
Hartman, Robert Leroy
Hartman, Rose
Hatch, Connie
Haxton, David
Hayes, Gerald
Heath, Dave (David) Martin Heath
Helfand, Fern M
Hernandez, Anthony Louis
Hersch, Jeff
Hickman, Paul Addison
Hines, Jessica
Ho, Francis T
Hockney, David
Hofer, Evelyn
Holmes, Wendy (Diana) H Noyes
Holownia, Thaddeus J
Hopper, Dennis
Houghton, Barbara Jean
House, Suda Kay
Howard, David
Hower, Robert K
Huddy, Margaret Teresa
Hughes, Siochan I
Hulick, Diana Emery
Hunter, Debora
Hutt, Lee
Hyde, Scott
Imes, Birney
Imlah, Rachel Crawford
Incandela, Gerald Jean-Marie
Ischar, Doug
Iturbide, Graciela
Iversen, Earl Harvey
Jachna, Joseph David
Jacir, Emily
Jacobshagen, N Keith, II
Jalapeeno, Jimmy (Albert) J Bonar
James, Alfred Everett
James, Christopher P
Jannicelli, Matteo
Jansen, Catherine Sandra
Jasud, Lawrence Edward
Jeff
Jones, Pirkle
Josephson, Kenneth Bradley
Joyce, J David
Kagemoto, Haro
Kaida, Tamarra
Kalisher, Simpson
Kaminsky, Jack Allan

PHOTOGRAPHER (cont)
Strassheim, Angela
Stratton, Margaret Mary
Strauss, Zoe
Strawn, Martha (A)
Stuler, Jack
Sturgen, Winston
Suggs, Don
Sugimoto, Hiroshi
Sugiura, Kunie
Sullivan, Connie C
Sultan, Larry A
SuZen, Susan R Rubinstein
Swigart, Lynn S
Sylvan, Rita M
Szabo, Stephen Lee
Taylor, Brian David
Taylor, Maggie
Thall, Bob
Thomason, Michael Vincent
Thompson, Jean Danforth
Thompson, Lynn P
Thorne-Thomsen, Ruth T
Tice, George (Andrew)
Tobia, Blaise Joseph
Torbert, Stephanie Birch
Torn, Jerry (Gerald J)
Toth, Caryl
Tourlentes, Stephen C
Tousignant, Serge
Towner, Mark Andrew
Trager, Neil C
Trager, Philip
Traub, Charles H
Tress, Arthur
Tuckerman, Jane Bayard
Turconi, Sue (Susan) Kinder
Turner, Judith Estelle
Twardowicz, Stanley Jan
Uelsmann, Jerry
Uhlenbeck, Erica
Ulrich, David Alan
Underhill, Linn B
Valero, Maria Teresa
Verene, Chris
Vestal, David
Viditz-Ward, Vera Louise
Vignes, Michelle Marie
Vitali, Julius M
Von Zur Muehlen, Bernis Susan
Von zur Muehlen, Peter
Vos, Claudia
Wagner, Catherine
Waksberg, Nomi
Walker, Melanie
Wallace, Patty A
Wang, Sam
Warren, Julianne Bussert Baker
Warren, Tom
Warshaw, Larry
Wasserman, Cary (Robert)
Watriss, Wendy
Webb, Alex(ander) (Dwight)
Weems, Carrie Mae
Wegman, William
Weida, Donna Lee
Weiler, Joseph Flack
Weiss, John Joseph
Weissman, Walter
Weller, Paul
Welling, James
Welpott, Jack Warren
Wenger, Jane (B)
Wessel, Henry
West, Annie
Wexler, Jerome LeRoy
Wexler, Peter J
White, Amos, IV
Whitehouse, Deborah Wian
Widmer, Gwen Ellen
Wilcox, T J
Williams, Christopher
Williams, Pat Ward
Williams, William Earle
Willis, Deborah
Willmott, Elizabeth Ann
Wilson, Helena Chapellin Wilson
Wilson, Wallace
Winick, Bernyce Alpert
Winokur, Neil
Winterberger, Suzanne
Wise, Kelly
Witkin, Joel-Peter
Woide, Robert E
Wolin, Jeffrey Alan
Yager, David
Yamashiro, Tad
Yamrus, Frank
Yates, Steven A
Yoder, Janica
Yoshiharu, Higa
Yost, Leon C
Young, Barbara
Young, Tom (Thomas) William
Zansky, Michael
Zeitlin, Harry Leon
Zellen, Jody
Zucker, Bob

PRINTMAKER

Abramowicz, Janet
Abularach, Rodolfo Marco
Acebo, Davis Terry
Anderson, Robert Dale
Antoinetta, Greco
Asman, Robert Joseph
Avakian, John
Ayres, Julia Spencer
Bachinski, Walter Joseph
Barker, Al C
Barron, Susan
Barsch, Wulf Erich
Batchelor, Anthony John
Baynard, Ed
Bearce, Jeana Dale
Behnken, William Joseph
Bensignor, Paulette (Mrs Philip Steinberg)
Blank, Margot
Bloomfield, Suzanne
Booth, Dot
Booth Cabot, M(ary Ann)
Bosman, Richard
Bostick, William Allison
Brauntuch, Troy
Brendel, Bettina
Brill, Glenn
Britton, Daniel Robert
Brody, Blanche
Broer, Roger L
Bryan, Sukey
Bumbeck, David
Burdock, Harriet
Burleigh, Kimberly
Burnett, Calvin
Bynum, E (Esther Pearl) Anderson
Campbell, Naomi
Carter, Mary
Catlett, Elizabeth
Chagoya, Enrique
Chesney, Lee R, Jr
Chung, Y David
Cochran, Dorothy Parcells
Colangelo, Carmon
Colby, Bill
Cooper, Ron
Cortor, Eldzier
Corwin, Sophia M
Crossgrove, Roger Lynn
Davison, Bill
Day, Gary Lewis
De Boschnek, Chris (Christian) Charles
de Gogorza, Patricia (Gahagan)
Dennis, Donna Frances
De Vore, Sadie Davidson
Di Cosola, Lois Bock
D'Innocenzo, Nick
Docktor, Irv
Dowell, John E, Jr
Drum, Sydney Maria
Durr, Pat (Patricia) (Beth)
Ecker, Robert Rodgers
Eder, James Alvin
Elloian, Peter
Ensrud, Wayne
Ettenberg, Franklin Joseph
Euren, Barry A
Faden, Lawrence Steven
Fagan, Alanna
Fantazos, Henryk Michael
Farrell, Patrick
FeBland, Harriet
Feinstein, Rochelle H
Felter, James Warren
Fidler, Spencer D
Firestein, Cecily Barth
Fohr, Jenny
Folman, Liza
Foster, Maelee Thomson
Frances, (Sherana) Harriette
Frank, Helen Goodzeit
Frankenthaler, Helen
Frederick, Helen C
Friese, Nancy Marlene
Gilbert, Helen Odell
Gillespie, Oscar Jay
Goodwin, Betty
Gordley, Marilyn Classe
Grupp, Carl Alf
Haack, Cynthia R
Haley, Priscilla J
Hammond, Jane
Hara, Keiko
Harris, Conley
Haseltine, James Lewis
Hershey, Nona
Hillis, Richard K
Hochman, Kitty
Holbrook, Peter Greene
Holton, William
Hunter, John H
Hussong, Randy
Ireland, David
Jacobson, Arthur
Jacques, Michael Louis
Jacquette, Yvonne Helene
Jannetti, Tony
Jewell, Joyce
Jilg, Michael Florian
Johnston, Ynez
Jones, Allen Christopher
Jones, Frederick
Kalina, Richard
Kaplan, Ilee
Kardon, Dennis
Kassoy, Hortense
Kasten, Karl Albert
Kellner, Tatana
Kiland, Lance Edward
Kiley, Katie
Kinkade, Catherine
Kinnee, Sandy
Klein, Doris
Knight, William
Knippers, Edward
Kornblum, Myrtle
Kovatch, Jak
Krieger, Ruth M
Kronzon, Ziva
La Duke, Betty
Lane, Lois
Lane, Rosemary Louise
La Porta, Elayne B
Lau, Rex
Laub-Novak, Karen
Lazuka, Robert
Leary, Daniel
Leggett, Ann Vaughan
Liao, Shiou-Ping
Lieberman, Meyer Frank
Limont, Naomi Charles
Lippincott, Janet
Little, James
Litwin, Ruth Forbes
Longobardi, Pam
Lubeck, Gerald Louis
Luce, C(harles) Beardsley
Magee, Alderson
Mari, M
Markowitz, Marilyn
Martin, Dianne L
Marx, Robert Ernst
Mateo, Julio
McCollum, Mike L
McDonald, Susan Strong
McGibbon, Phyllis
McGinnis, Christine
McGloughlin, Kate
Mesibov, Hugh
Mitty, Lizbeth J
Morper, Daniel
Morse, Marcia Roberts
Moskowitz, Ira
Moy, Seong
Moya Soto, Roberto
Mullen, James Martin
Murakishi, Steve
Nesbitt, Jackson Lee
Nichols, Francis N, II
Noland, Kenneth
Nugent, Bob L
Nyambi, Obaji A
O'Connell, Ann Brown
Oda, Mayumi
O'Hara, Paul
Olshan, Bernard
Ortega, Tony (Anthony) David
Pachter, Charles
Paschall, Jo Anne
Piskoti, James
Pletka, Paul
Plevin, Gloria Joy
Porges, Maria Franziska
Portman, Brian
Potter, (George) Kenneth
Pyzow, Susan Victoria
Quiller, Stephen Frederick
Rackus, George (Keistus)
Raviv, Ilana
Revitzky, Dennis L
Rhodes, Curtis A
Richards, Bruce Michael
Richards, Rosalyn A
Ritchie, Charles Morton, Jr
Roosevelt, Michael Armentrout
Roseman, Susan Carol
Rugolo, Lawrence
Rush, Kent Thomas

PRINTMAKER (cont)
Vaccaro, Patrick Frank
Van Riper, Peter
Vaux, Richard
Weber, Suzanne Osterweil
West, Peter
Wong, Lucille (Lucila) Guerra Wong

Woodcut
Abany, Albert Charles
Abbe, Elfriede Martha
Arnold, Paul Beaver
Barber, Cynthia
Barton, John Murray
Bettinson, Brenda
Bigelow, Anita (Anne) (Edwige Lourie)
Bobak, Bruno Joseph
Brickner, Alice
Brody, Arthur William
Card, Royden
Carter, (Charles) Bruce
Casida, Kati
Conner, Ann
Covey, Rosemary Feit
Currie, Bruce
Dallas, Dorothy B
Dance, Robert Bartlett
Davison, Nancy R
De Armond, Dale B
Domjan, Evelyn
Enright, Judy A
Feldman, Aline M
Feldman, Joel Benet
Gary, Jan (Mrs William D Gorman)
Grashow, James Bruce
Hedman, Teri Jo
Herman, Roger
Hodgell, Robert Overman
Hotvedt, Kris J
Howard, (Helen) Barbara
Jaidinger, Judith C Clarann Szesko
Kapheim, Thom
Kemble, Richard
Kermes, Constantine John
Koster, Marjory Jean
Kunc, Karen
Lawrence, Matthew R
Lincoln, Jane Lockwood
Malo, Teri (A)
Matsubara, Naoko
McNamara, William Patrick, Jr
Mogensen, Paul
Mortensen, Gordon Louis
Mosenthal, Charlotte (Dembo)
Nesbitt, Ilse Buchert
Noble, Helen (Harper)
Offner, Elliot
Peace, Bernie Kinzel
Rowan, Frances Physioc
Sadle, Amy Ann Brandon
Sawai, Noboru
Skelley, Robert Charles
Stinnett, Hester A
Summers, Carol
Tesfagiorgis, Freida
Trueblood, Emily Herrick
Vo Dinh, Mai
Walters, Sylvia Solochek
Washmon, Gary Brent
Watia, Tarmo
Whitman, Karen
Williams, Idaherma

PUBLISHER

Alexander, Edmund Brooke
Anbinder, Paul
Arnold, Jack
Banana, Anna
Banks, Robert Harris
Blake, Jane Salley
Cawley, Joan Mae
Esterow, Milton
Fazzino, Charles
Feinman, Stephen E
Friberg, Arnold
Gaines, Alan Jay
Gladstone, M J
Goad, Anne Laine
Goodman, Marian
Guilloume, (Guilloume Perez-Zapata)
Hackett, Dwight Vernon
Heiferman, Marvin
Hobbs, Gerald S
Hoffberg, Judith A
Isaacs, Avrom
Johnson, Douglas Walter
King, Brian Jeffrey
King, Victoria Vranich Killough
Levin, Hugh Lauter
London, Alexander
Love, Frances Taylor
MacDonald, Colin Somerled
Mahlmann, John James
McGilvery, Laurence
McPherson, Bruce Rice
Morton, Robert Alan
Neal, (Minor) Avon
Nix, Nelleke Langhout
Paternosto, Cesar Pedro
Persky, Robert S
Posner, Judith L
Rosenberg, Bernard
Rosenthal, John W
Sadle, Amy Ann Brandon
Sandman, Alan
Seckel, Cornelia
Solomon, Richard H
Stewart, Norman
Szoke, John
Takayama, Martha Tepper
Torf, Lois Beurman
Tustian, Brenda Harris
Van Vliet, Claire
Westlund, Harry E
Wyrick, Charles Lloyd, Jr
Yares, Riva
Zimmermann, Philip

RESTORER
See also **Conservator**

Brownett, Thelma Denyer
Callari, Emily Dolores
Fisher, Sarah Lisbeth
Flume, Violet Sigoloff
Flynn, John (Kevin)
Fredericks, Beverly Magnuson
Grassi, Marco
Greaves, James L
Gurbacs, John Joseph
Higgins, Brian Alton
Hopkins, Kenneth R
Knowlton, Daniel Gibson
Levenson, Rustin S
Lysun, Gregory
Moore, Sabra
Pomeroy, Frederick George
Pravda, Muriel
Richard, Jack
Squadra, John
Zarand, Julius John

SCULPTOR

Adams, Phoebe
Adickes, David (Pryor)
Agee, Ann G
Ahearn, John
Ahrens, Hanno D
Alexander, Peter
Allen, Bruce Wayne
Allen, E Douglas
Amado, Jesse V
Amato, Michele (Micaela)
Anderson, Troy
Andreason, Lee
Andrews, Charleen Kohl
Andrews, Edwin C
Angell, Tony
Anker, Suzanne C
Annis, Norman L
Antoni, Janine
Anuszkiewicz, Richard Joseph
Applebaum, Leon
Aquino, Edmundo
Ariss, Margot Joan Phillips
Armajani, Siah
Ascalon, David
Ashkin, Michael
Aston, Miriam
Averbuch, Ilan
Bachner, Barbara L
Baden, Mowry T
Bailey, Clayton George
Bakanowsky, Louis J
Baker, Dianne Angela
Balciar, Gerald George
Bales, J (Jean) Elaine
Barney, Matthew
Barry, Steve
Bartek, Tom
Baum, Don
Baumel-Harwood, Bernice
Beldner, Lynn Karen
Berge, Dorothy Alphena
Berger-Kraemer, Nancy
Bernheim, Stephanie Hammerschlag
Beuzenburg, Ron
Beyer, Steven J
Biederman, James Mark
Bimpong, Bright
Birk, Sandow
Black, David Evans
Blair, Dike
Blakely, George C
Bleach, Bruce R
Blum, June
Bocanegra, Suzanne H
Bodó, Sándor
Boggs, Franklin
Bolton, Richard
Bonner, Jonathan G
Bora (Borayer), Vadim Makharbekovich
Borgatta, Isabel Case
Bornstein, Eli
Boszin, Andrew
Boucher, Tania Kunsky
Brady, Charles
Bremer, Marlene S
Brener, Roland
Brookins, Jacob Boden
Brooks, Bruce W
Brown, Stephen Pat
Brush, Leif
Bryan, Jack L
Buchanan, Beverly
Buck, John
Budny, Virginia
Bullock, James Benbow
Busch, Rita Mary
Busto, Ana Marie
Butterfield, Deborah Kay
Butterly, Kathy
Cantor, Rusty
Capobianco, Domenick
Cardoso, Anthony
Carl, Joan
Carlson, Mary
Caro, Anthony
Carter, Gary
Casebere, James E
Cassidy, Margaret Carol (Mrs John Manship)
Castanis, Muriel (Julia Brunner)
Castrucci, Andrew
Cederquist, John
Cenci, Silvana
Chabot, Aurore (Martha)
Chalif, Ronnie
Chandler, Elisabeth Gordon
Chao, Bruce
Charkow-Hollander, Natalie
Chase, Doris (Totten)
Chatmas, John T
Chicago, Judy
Chihuly, Dale (Patrick)
Chin, Mel
Christenberry, William
Claro, Paul
Close, Frank
Coheleach, Guy Joseph
Cohen, Lewis Carroll
Cole, Willie
Colette, S
Collyer, Robin
Conlon, James Edward
Connor, Maureen
Conrad, Paul Francis
Cooper, Mark F
Cooper, Ron
Cooper, Susan
Cooper, Wayne
Cotter, James Edward
Cove, Rosemary
Covington, Harrison Wall
Crawford, Thom Cooney
Crimmins, Jerry (Gerald) Garfield
Cross, Yvonne
Crovello, William
Curtis, Dolly Powers
Cutler, Amy
D'Agostino, Claudio A
Danziger, Joan
Davenport, Bill
Davidson, Nancy
Dawson, John Allan
Dawson, Robert E
DeArmond, Megan
DeBellevue, Lucky
Decter, Betty Eva
De Mille, Leslie Benjamin
De Monte, Claudia
De Nike, Michael Nicholas
Dennis, Donna Frances
Dente, Robert
DeRoux, Daniel Edward
DeStabler, Stephen
DeWitt, Edward
Dezzany, Frances Jean
Dias-Jorgensen, Aurora Abdias
Dogancay, Burhan
Doner, Michele Oka

SCULPTOR (cont)
Vielehr, William Ralph
Walburg, Gerald
Wall, Brian
Walsh, James
Warsinske, Norman George
Williams, Chester Lee
Williams, Wayne Francis
Wind, Dina
Witt, Nancy Camden
Woitena, Ben S
Wolfe, James
Woodham, Jean
Zaloudek, Duane
Zeller, Frederic

Miscellaneous Media
Abeles, Kim Victoria
Adams, Alice
Akins, Future Rene
Albenda, Ricci
Aldrich, Lynn (Barron)
Alpert, Bill (William) H
Alpert, Herb
Anderson, Kenneth Edmund
Anderson, Mark Robert
Anthonisen, George Rioch
Antonakos, Stephen
Appel, Keith Kenneth
Aronson, Sanda
Artemis, Maria Artemis Papageorge
Artschwager, Richard Ernst
Aycock, Alice
Bailey, Barry Stone
Bakaty, Mike
Baldwin, Harold Fletcher
Ball, Lillian
Banerjee, Bimal
Baroff, Jill (Emily)
Barr, David John
Bell, Larry Stuart
Benes, Barton Lidice
Ben Tre, Howard B
Berhang, Mattie
Biblos, Mahia
Bickley, Gary Steven
Bills, Linda
Bisgyer, Barbara G (Cohn)
Blum, Andrea
Blunk, Joyce Elaine
Booker, Chakaia
Booth, Robert Alan
Bowen, Paul
Brady, Robert D
Braitstein, Marcel
Breder, Hans Dieter
Brewster, Michael
Brito, Maria
Brodsky, Alexander Ilya Utkin
Brown, Susan LT (Haviland Slizys)
Buchman, James Wallace
Busard, Roberta Ann
Buvoli, Luca
Byars, Donna
Cable, Maxine Roth
Cano, Pablo D
Carpenter, Linda Buck
Carter, Sam John
Casey, John Thayer
Catlett, Elizabeth
Chase, Jack S(paulding)
Chatterley, Mark D
Christianson, Linda Ann
Cicansky, Victor
Clifton, Michelle Gamm
Cohen, Adele
Cowan, Aileen Hooper
Cox, Pat
Creecy, Herbert Lee
Cunningham, J
Curmano, Billy X
Curtis, Robert D
Dailey, Dan (Daniel) Owen
Daphnis, Nassos
Daugherty, Michael F
DeAngelis, Joseph Rocco
De La Verriere, J J
Deming, David Lawson
de Musée, Moran
De Palma, Brett
De Soto, Lewis D
Deutsch, Richard
Di Meo, Dominick
Dingus, Marita Teresa
Dodge, Robert G
Dos Santos, Jonas Alves
Douglas, Tom Howard
Dowd, Jack
Duben, Ipek Aksugur
Duff, John Ewing
Dunham-Griggs, Margaret
Dunigan, Breon Nina
Dyens, Georges Maurice
Eisenberg, Marc S
Eldredge, Mary Agnes
Elliott, Anne
Engler, Kathleen Girdler
Estern, Neil
Evans, Robert Graves
Farbanish, Thomas
FeBland, Harriet
Feuerman, Carole A
Finke, Leonda Froelich
Finn, David
Fisher, Rob (Robert) Norman
Fleming, Thomas Michael
Ford, Rochelle
Fornelli, Joseph
Forrestall, Thomas De Vany
Freer, Fred-Christian
French, Stephen Warren
Froman, Ann
Frudakis, Evangelos William
Fuller, Mary (Mary Fuller McChesney)
Gaudieri, Alexander V J
Geltner, Danita Sue
Gibbs, Y Gale
Gillingwater, Denis Claude
Giobbi, Edward Gioachino
Glaser, David
Glatt, Linnea
Golbert, Sandra
Gold, Martha B
Goldner, Janet
Goldstein, Daniel Joshua
Goodridge, Lawrence Wayne
Gordon, John S
Gorski, Daniel Alexander
Graham, Robert
Grashow, James Bruce
Grauer, Sherrard
Green, Tom
Gregoire, Mathieu A
Gunderson, Barry L
Gutkin, Peter
Habenicht, Wenda
Hacklin, Allan Dave
Hale, Nathan Cabot
Halegua, Alfredo
Halligan, Roger Phillip
Hammond, Harmony
Hanson, Jo
Hardy, Thomas (Austin)
Harrington, William Charles
Harris, Paul
Harshfield, Neil Alan
Harvey, Dermot
Harvey, Donald Gene
Hauft, Amy
Havel, Joseph G
Healy, Anne Laura
Hebald, Milton Elting
Henes, Donna
Henselmann, Caspar
Herbert Constransitch, Phyllis
Herr, Richard Joseph
High, Timothy Griffin
Hoare, Tyler James
Hooks, Earl J
Hooper, Jack Meredith
Hopkins, B(ernice) Elizabeth
Horn, Roni
Housewright, Artemis Skevakis Jegart
Howard, Linda
Huff, Robert
Indick, Janet
Ingham, Tom (Edgar)
Jacobs, Harold
James, Catti
Jendrzejewski, Andrew John
Johnson, Erin (Stukey)
Johnston, Richard M
Jones, Lou Mary Louise Humpton
Jones & Ginzel
Joyce, J David
Justis, Gary
Kalish, Howard
Kangas, Gene
Kawecki, Jean Mary
Kearney, John (W)
Kearns, James Joseph
Keegan, Kim E
Keister, Steve (Stephen) Lee
Kellar, Jeff
Kelman, Maureen S
Kemp, Paul Zane
Kipp, Lyman
Kisch, Gloria
Klausen, Ray
Kleinberg, Susan
Kline, Harriet
Knobler, Lois Jean
Kober, Alfred John
Kolisnyk, Peter
Kraft, Craig Allan
Krebs, Rockne
Krentzin, Earl
Kuehn, Gary
Lable, Eliot
La Bobgah, Robert Gordon
Lane, Rosemary Louise
Lasch, Pat
Lawrence, Jaye A
Lawrence, Les
Layne, Barbara J
Leibert, Peter R
Leon, Dennis
Leopold, Susan
Leslie, John
Lewis, Mary
Lexier, Micah
Lin, Maya Y
Livingstone, Joan
Logan, David George
Lutz, Winifred Ann
Lynds, Clyde
Macaulay, Thomas S
Mac Whinnie, John Vincent
Mahlke, Ernest D
Maksymowicz, Virginia Ann
Marzollo, Claudio
Mastrangelo, Bobbi
Mathias, Thelma
Matisse, Jackie (Jacqueline) Matisse Monnier
Mayer, Edward Albert
McClure, Thomas F
McGeehan, Betty
McMann, Edith Brozak
McMillen, Michael C(halmers)
McRoberts, Sheryl Ann
Medel, Rebecca Rosalie
Messersmith, Harry Lee
Metzger, Evelyn Borchard
Meyer, Seymour W
Michaels-Paque, J
Min, Yong Soon
Minisci, Brenda (Eileen)
Minkowitz, Norma
Mulcahy, Kathleen
Muno, Richard Carl
Myatt, Greely
Nardi, Dann
Nauman, Bruce
Neal, Irene
Nellis, Jennifred Gene
Nelson, Ruth Basha (Basha Ruth Nelson)
Newman, Richard Charles
Nicholson, Natasha
Niedzialek, Terry
Nisula, Larry
Noe, Jerry Lee
Ohe, Katie (Minna)
Okulick, John A
Oldenburg, Claes Thure
Olitski, Jules
Orentlicher, John
Orr, Leah
O'Shea, Terrence Patrick
Pardington, Ralph Arthur
Parker, Gertrud Valerie
Parks, Charles Cropper
Partridge, David Gerry
Patterson, Curtis Ray
Patti, Tom
Perless, Robert
Pfaff, Judy
Piene, Otto
Powell, Gordon
Pracko, Bernard F, II
Prent, Mark
Price, Kenneth
Prince, Arnold
Pyle, Melissa Bronwen
Rabinovich, Raquel
Rains, Baxter
Ré, Paul Bartlett
Reiback, Earl M
Reif, (F) David
Reimann, William P
Richardson, Jean
Ringgold, Faith
Robinson, Margot Steigman
Rochette, Anne Monique
Rohm, Robert
Romano, Salvatore Michael
Rose, Robin Carlise
Rose, Thomas Albert
Roukes, Nicholas M
Rousseau, Irene Victoria
Rowe, Reginald M
Ruffner, Ginny Martin
Russin, Robert I
Rychlak, Bonnie L
Ryden, Kenneth Glenn
Saari, Peter H

SILVERSMITH

STAINED GLASS ARTIST

TAPESTRY ARTIST

VIDEO ARTIST

WEAVER

WRITER

WRITER (cont)
Millard, Charles Warren, III
Miller, Marc H
Miller, Nicole
Minick, Roger
Mitchell, Margaretta K
Moehl, Karl J
Morgan, Robert Coolidge
Morgan, Roberta Marie
Morgan, William
Morin-Miller, Carmen A
Morse, Marcia Roberts
Morton, Robert Alan
Movalli, Charles Joseph
Mowry, Elizabeth M
Muhlberger, Richard Charles
Munro, Eleanor
Murchie, Donald John
Narkiewicz-Laine, Christian K
Nasisse, Andy S
Navaretta, Cynthia
Neher, Ross James
Neil, J M
Nelson, Aida Z
Nelson, Mary Carroll
Nigrosh, Leon Isaac
Nix, Nelleke Langhout
Norton, Paul Foote
O'Gorman, James Francis
Orland, Ted N
Ostrom, Gladys Snell
O'Toole, Judith Hansen
Palmer, A Laure
Parker, Ann (Ann Parker Neal)
Parker, Nancy Winslow
Parkhurst, Violet Kinney
Parry, Eugenia
Parsons, Cynthia Massey
Patner, Andrew
Paulos, Daniel Thomas
Peck, Judith
Peladeau, Marius Beaudoin
Penney, Jacqueline
Persky, Robert S
Peyton, Elizabeth Joy
Phelan, Andrew L
Phillips, Gifford
Phillpot, Clive James
Pike, Joyce Lee
Pincus-Witten, Robert A
Piper, Adrian Margaret Smith
Plowden, David
Poupeney, Mollie
Preuss, Roger
Quackenbush, Robert
Raleigh, Henry Patrick
Ramsey, Dorothy J
Ratcliff, Carter
Reep, Edward Arnold
Reid, Charles Clark
Reid, Sheila
Rendl, M(ildred) Marcus
Reuter, Laurel J
Reynolds, John (Jock) M
Richards, David Patrick
Rinder, Lawrence R
Ripstein, Jacqueline
Robbins, David A
Robbins, Eugenia S
Robison, Andrew
Rogers, Peter Wilfrid
Rokeach, Barrie
Roosevelt, Michael Armentrout
Rosenblatt, Suzanne Maris
Rosler, Martha (Rose)
Roth, Leland M(artin)
Roukes, Nicholas M
Rousseau, Irene Victoria
Rubin, David S
Rubin, Ida Ely
Rubinstein, Charlotte Streifer
Rush, Michael James
Rybczynski, Witold Marian
Salemme, Lucia Autorino
Sanabria, Robert
Sanders, Rhea Sanders Rabinovich
Sandground, Mark Bernard, Sr
Saphire, Lawrence M
Schulman, Arlene
Schulzke, Margot Seymour
Schwartz, Lillian (Feldman)
Schwartz, Therese
Scott, John Beldon
Scully, Vincent Joseph, Jr
Seckel, Cornelia
Seed, Suzanne Liddell
Seeman, Helene Zucker
Self, Dana Rae
Selvig, Forrest Hall
Sendak, Maurice Bernard
Seslar, Patrick George
Shapiro, Adrian Michael
Sheaks, Barclay
Shearer, Rhonda Roland
Sherman, Lenore Walton
Sherrod, Philip Lawrence
Sill, Gertrude Grace
Silverman, Ronald H
Simon, Leonard Ronald
Skoler, Celia Rebecca
Slate, Joseph Frank
Smith, Ralph Alexander
Snodgrass-King, Jeanne Owen (Mrs M Eugene King)
Snowden, Gilda
Snyder, Hills
Sorel, Edward
Sorrin, Mary Louise
Spector, Naomi
Speight, Jerry Brooks
Spicer, Jean (Doris) Uhl
Spivy-Anderson, C Alexandra
Squiers, Carol
Stapen, Nancy
Stavitsky, Gail Beth
Steiner, Paul
Steiner, Raymond John
Steiner, Sherry L
Stermer, Dugald Robert
Stevens, Elisabeth Goss
Stewart, John Lincoln
Stone, Jim (James) J
Streeter, Tal
Sujo, Clara Diament
Sward, Robert S
Sylvestre, Guy
Szilvasy, Linda Markuly
Talley, Dan R
Tarbet, Urania Christy
Tarshis, Jerome
Taylor, Robert
Temple, Leslie Alcott (Leslie Jane Atkinson)
Tennant, Donna Kay
Terry, Hilda
Thea, Carolee B
Thenhaus, Paulette Ann
Thornton, Richard Samuel
Thurston, Jacqueline Beverly
Tice, George (Andrew)
Tillenius, Clarence Ingwall
Tomkins, Calvin
Toschik, Larry
Tully, Judd
Turner, Norman Huntington
VanDerpool, Karen
Van Dommelen, David B
Van Haaften, Julia
Van Laar, Timothy
Vermeule, Cornelius Clarkson, III
Vestal, David
Violet, Ultra
Von Barghan, Barbara
Wakeham, Duane Allen
Waldman, Louis A
Waller, Susan
Walters, Ernest
Walton, Guy E
Warden, P Gregory
Warner, Marina
Warren, Lynne
Watson, Clarissa H
Wechsler, Susan
Weil, Lisl
Weiler, Joseph Flack
Weiss, Clemens
Weiss, Harvey
Welch, James Edward
Werner, Frank Robert
West, Virginia M
Wetmore, Gordon (Stanley Gordon)
Wexler, Jerome LeRoy
White, Robert Rankin
Wiens, Ann
Wiley, Lois Jean
Williams, Reba White
Windeknecht, Margaret Blake
Withers, Josephine
Witt, David L
Wofford, Philip
Wood, John August
Wright, Barton Allen
Yares, Riva
Yarotsky, Lori
Yau, John
Yood, James W
Zack, Badanna Bernice
Zeitlin, Marilyn A
Zellen, Jody
Zollweg, Aileen Boules

Necrology
Cumulative 1953-2006

AACH, HERB Painter, Writer (1923-1985)
AARONS, GEORGE Sculptor (1896-1980)
ABBOTE, PAUL S Sculptor (1884-1972)
ABBOTT, EDITH Painter (-1964)
ABBOTT, JOHN EVANS Library Director (-1952)
ABEELL, SAMUEL Art Patron (1925-1969)
ABEL, MYER Lithographer, Painter (1904-)
ABELL, WALTER HALSEY Educator (1897-1956)
ABRACHEFF, IVAN Painter (1903-1960)
ABRAMS, HARRY N Publisher, Collector (1905-1979)
ABRAMS, HERBERT E Lecturer, Painter (1921-2003)
ABRAMS, RUTH (DAVIDSON) Painter, Critic (-1986)
ABRIL, BEN (BENJAMIN) Painter (1923-)
ACKERMAN, FRANK EDWARD Painter, Designer (1933-)
ACKERMANN, JOHN JOSEPH Painter, Designer (1889-1950)
ADAMS, (MOULTON) LEE Painter, Illustrator (1922-1971)
ADAMS, ANSEL EASTON Photographer (1902-1984)
ADAMS, CLINTON Painter, Historian (1918-2002)
ADAMS, MARGARET BOROUGHS Painter (-1965)
ADAMS, WAYMAN Painter (1885-1959)
ADDAMS, CHARLES Cartoonist (1912-1988)
ADEN, ALONZO J Museum Director (1906-1963)
ADLER, SAMUEL (MARCUS) Painter, Educator (1898-1979)
ADLOW, DOROTHY Critic (-1964)
AGA-OGLU, MEHMET Educator, Lecturer, Writer (1896-1948)
AGOPOFF, AGOP MINASS Sculptor (-1983)
AGOSTINI, PETER Sculptor (1913-1993)
AHERN, EUGENE (GENE) Cartoonist (1896-1960)
AIDLEN, JEROME Sculptor, Instructor (1935-1986)
AIKEN, CHARLES Painter (1872-1965)
AIROLA, PAAVO Painter, Writer (-1983)
AJAY, ABE Painter, Sculptor (1919-1998)
AJOOTIAN, KHOSROV Educator (1891-1958)
AKE, JOHN Sculptor (-1998)
AKSTON, JAMES Collector, Patron
ALAN, JAY Cartoonist (1907-1965)
ALBEE, PERCY F Painter (1885-1959)
ALBERS, ANNI Textile Artist (1899-1994)
ALBERS, JOSE F Painter, Printmaker (1888-1976)
ALBERTAZZI, MARIO Painter, Art Critic (1920-1991)
ALBRIGHT, ADAM EMORY Painter (1862-1957)
ALBRIGHT, HENRY J Educator, Painter (-1951)
ALBRIGHT, IVAN LE LORRAINE Painter (1897-1983)
ALBRIGHT, THOMAS Critic, Writer (1935-)
ALCOPLEY, L Painter, Graphic Artist (1910-1992)
ALDER, MARY ANN Painter, Art Restorer (-1952)
ALDRICH, LARRY Collector (1906-2001)
ALDWINCKLE, ERIC Designer, Painter (1909-1980)
ALEXANDER, CHRISTINE Curator (1893-1975)
ALEXANDER, JUDITH Art Dealer, Collector (1932-2004)
ALEXANDER, ROBERT SEYMOUR Educator, Designer (1923-1997)
ALFSEN, JOHN MARTIN Painter (-1972)
ALLEN LORETTA B Painter, Designer (-2000)
ALLEN, (HARVEY) HAROLD Photographer, Writer (1912-)
ALLEN, ARTHUR D Painter, Lithographer (-1949)
ALLEN, CHARLES CURTIS Painter, Educator (1886-1950)
ALLEN, CLARENCE CANNING Painter, Instructor (1897-1989)
ALLEN, JANE MENGEL (MRS ARTHUR) Painter (1888-1952)
ALLEN, JUNIUS Painter (1898-1962)
ALLEN, MARGO (MRS HARRY SHAW) Sculptor, Painter (1894-1988)
ALLEN, MARY STOCKBRIDGE Painter, Sculptor (1869-1949)
ALLOWAY, LAWRENCE Art Historian, Curator (1927-1990)
ALLWELL, STEPHEN S Sculptor (1906-)
ALMY, FRANK ATWOOD Museum Director (1900-1956)
ALPS, GLEN EARL Educator, Printmaker (1914-1996)
ALQUIST, LEWIS Sculptor, Educator (1946-2005)
ALSTON, CHARLES HENRY Painter, Educator (1907-1977)
ALTMAN, HAROLD Printmaker, Educator (1924-2003)
ALTMAYER, JAY P Collector (1915-1999)
ALTSCHUL, ARTHUR G Collector, Patron (1920-2002)
ALVORD, MURIEL Painter (-1960)
AMAROTICO, JOSEPH ANTHONY Painter, Conservator (1931-)
AMATEIS, EDMOND ROMULUS Sculptor (1897-1981)
AMATNIEK, SARA Printmaker, Graphic Artist (1922-1996)
AMBERSON, GRACE D (MRS WILLIAM R) Painter (1894-1957)
AMES, ARTHUR FORBES Painter, Educator (1906-1975)
AMINO, LEO Sculptor, Instructor (1911-1989)
AMSDEN, FLOYD T Collector, Patron (1913-)
AMSTER, SALLY Painter (-1988)
ANARGYROS, SPERO, Sculptor (1915-2004)
ANDERSEN, ANDREAS STORRS Educator, Painter (1908-1974)
ANDERSON, CARL THOMAS Cartoonist, Illustrator (1865-1948)
ANDERSON, GUY IRVING Painter (1906-1998)
ANDERSON, HOWARD BENJAMIN Photographer (1903-)
ANDERSON, IVAN DELOS Painter, Printmaker (1915-1991)
ANDERSON, JEREMY RADCLIFFE Sculptor, Educator (1921-1982)
ANDERSON, KENNETH L Administrator, Architect (1939-1990)
ANDREJEVIC, MILET Painter (1925-1989)
ANDREWS, SYBIL Printmaker (1898-1992)
ANGEL, JOHN Sculptor (1881-1960)
ANGELO, DOMENICK MICHAEL Sculptor (1925-1976)
ANGELO, EMIDIO Cartoonist, Painter (1903-)
ANNENBERG, WALTER H Collector, Patron (1908-2002)
ANSBACHER, JESSIE Painter (-1964)
ANSPACH, ERNST Collector (1913-2002)
ANTONOVICI, CONSTANTIN Sculptor, Lecturer (1911-2002)
ARCHER, DOROTHY BRYANT Painter, Instructor (1919-)
ARCHIPENKO, ALEXANDER Sculptor (1887-1964)
ARDIZZONE, EDWARD Painter, Illustrator (1900-1979)
ARGALL, CHARLES G Painter
ARKUS, LEON A Museum Director, Consultant (1915-1999)
ARLT, WILLIAM H Designer, Teacher, Painter (1868-)
ARNASON, H HARVARD Art Historian, Writer (1909-1986)
ARNESON, ROBERT Sculptor (1930-)
ARNEST, BERNARD Painter, Educator (1917-1986)
ARNO, PETER Cartoonist (1904-1968)
ARONSON, BORIS Designer, Painter (1900-1980)
ARTIS, WILLIAM ELLISWORTH Educator, Ceramist (1914-1977)
ARTZ, FREDERICK B Historian, Writer (1894-1983)
ARTZYBASHEFF, BORIS Illustrator (1899-1965)
ARYE, LEONORA E Sculptor (1931-2001)
ASCHER, MARY Painter, Printmaker

ASHBY, CARL Painter, Instructor (1914-2004)
ASHTON, ETHEL V Artist (-1975)
ASHTON, MAL STANHOPE (MALONE) Artist (1878-1976)
ASKENAZY, MISCHA Painter (1888-1961)
ASKEW, PAMELA Educator, Writer
ASO, KAJI Painter, Educator (-2006)
ATHERTON, J CARLTON Craftsman (1900-1964)
ATHERTON, JOHN Painter, Illustrator (1900-1952)
ATIRNOMIS (RITA SIMON) Painter, Printmaker (1938-)
ATKINS, ALBERT H Sculptor, Painter (-1951)
AUER, JAMES MATTHEW Art Critic, Filmaker (1928-2004)
AUERBACH-LEVY, WILLIAM Etcher (1889-1964)
AULT, GEORGE Artist
AULT, GEORGE COPELAND Painter (1891-1948)
AUSTIN, DARREL Painter (1907-1994)
AUSTIN, JO-ANNE Dealer (1925-)
AUSUBEL, SHEVA Painter (1896-1957)
AUVIL, KENNETH WILLIAM Educator, Printmaker (1925-1999)
AVEDON, RICHARD Photographer (1923-2004)
AVERY, MILTON Painter (1893-1965)
AVERY, MYRTILLA Museum Director (-1959)
AVERY, RALPH HILLYER Painter, Illustrator (1906-1976)
AVINOFF, ANDREY Painter, Illustrator (1884-1948)
AVISON, DAVID Photographer (1937-2004)
AYERS, HESTER MERWIN Portrait Painter (1902-1975)
AYLWARD, WILLIAM J Painter (1875-1958)
AZUMA, NORIO Painter (1928-2004)
BABER, ALICE Painter, Printmaker (1928-1982)
BACH, OTTO KARL Museum Director, Writer (1909-1990)
BACH, RICHARD F Educator (1887-1968)
BACKUS, STANDISH, JR Painter, Muralist (1910-1989)
BACON, PEGGY Painter, Writer (1895-1987)
BADER, FRANZ Art Dealer, Bookseller (1903-1994)
BADNER, MINO Historian (1940-1978)
BAER, MORLEY Photographer (1916-)
BAILEY, CLARK T Sculptor, Educator (1932-1978)
BAILEY, WORTH Historian (1908-1980)
BAIN, LILIAN PHERNE Painter, Etcher (1873-)
BAIZERMAN, SAUL Sculptor (1889-1957)
BAKER, CHARLES EDWIN Art Historian, Writer (1902-1971)
BAKER, EUGENE AMES Painter, Serigrapher (1928-)
BAKER, GEORGE P Educator, Kinetic Artist (1931-1997)
BAKER, RALPH BERNARD Painter, Educator (1932-)
BAKER, RICHARD BROWN Collector (1912-2002)
BALA, PAUL Painter, Architect (-1998)
BALDWIN, HARRY II Painter
BALDWIN, JOHN Educator, Sculptor (1922-1987)
BALDWIN, MURIEL FRANCES Art Librarian
BALDWIN, ROGER N Critic, Curator (1950-2004)
BALL, WALTER N Painter, Educator (1930-2005)
BALLIN, HUGO Painter (1879-1956)
BALOG, MICHAEL Painter, Sculptor (1946-)
BANKS, VIRGINIA Painter (1920-1985)
BANNING, BEATRICE HARPER Etcher (1885-)
BANNISTER, EDWARD MITCHELL Painter (1828-1901)
BARANIK, RUDOLF Painter (1920-1998)
BARANOFF, MORT Printmaker, Painter (1923-1978)
BARBAROSSA, THEODORE C Sculptor (1906-1992)
BARBER MURIEL V Painter (-1971)
BARBER, JOHN Painter (1898-1965)
BARBERA, JOE Cartoonist
BARBERIS, DOROTHY WATKEYS Painter
BARINGER, RICHARD E Painter, Designer (1921-1980)
BARKER, ALBERT WINSLOW Lithographer, Teacher (1874-1947)
BARKER, VIRGIL Writer, Critic (1890-1964)
BARLQGA, VIOLA H Painter (1890-)
BARNES, EDWARD LARRABEE Architect (1915-2004)
BARNETT, EDWARD WILLIS Director, Designer (1922-1987)
BARNETT, HERBERT P Educator, Painter (1910-1972)
BARNEY, MAGINAL WRIGHT Craftsman (-1966)
BARR, ALFRED HAMILTON, JR Art Historian, Administrator (1902-1981)
BARR, ALLAN Painter (1890-1959)
BARR, ROGER Collage Artist, Sculptor (1921-1999)
BARRETT, H STANFORD Painter, Educator (1909-1970)
BARRETT, ROBERT DUMAS Painter (1903-)
BARRETT, THOMAS WEEKS Painter, Designer (1902-1947)
BARRIE, ERWIN S Painter (1886-1983)
BARSCHEL, HANS J Designer, Photographer (1912-1998)
BARTHE, RICHMOND Sculptor (1901-1989)
BARTLE, DOROTHY BUDD Curator, Lecturer (1924-2005)
BARTLETT, DANA Painter (1882-1957)
BARTLETT, FRED STEWART Administrator, Museum Director (1905-1988)
BARTLETT, ROBERT WEBSTER Painter, Designer (1922-1979)
BARTLETT, SCOTT Filmmaker (1943-1990)
BARUCH, RUTH-MARION Photographer, Writer (1922-1997)
BASKIN, LEONARD Sculptor, Graphic Artist (1922-2000)
BASQUIAT, JEAN MICHEL Painter (1961-1988)
BASS, JOHANNA (MRS JOHN) Collector, Patron (-1970)
BASS, JOHN Collector, Patron (1891-1978)
BATCHELOR, CLARENCE DANIEL Cartoonist (1888-1977)
BATE, NORMAN ARTHUR Educator, Printmaker (1916-1980)
BATES, CAROL Painter (1895-)
BATES, KENNETH Painter (1895-1973)
BATES, MAXWELL BENNETT Painter, Lithographer (1906-1980)
BATTAGLIA, PASQUALE M Painter (1905-1959)
BAUMBACH, HAROLD Painter, Printmaker (1905-2001)
BAUMGARTNER, WARREN W Illustrator (1894-1963)
BAYEFSKY, ABA Painter, Printmaker (1923-2001)
BAYER, HERBERT Painter, Architect (1900-)
BAYER, JEFFREY JOSHUA Educator, Sculptor (1942-1983)
BAYLESS, RAYMOND GORDON Painter, Writer (1920-2004)
BAYLINSON, A S Painter, Teacher (1882-1950)
BAYLOS, ZELMA U Painter, Sculptor
BAZIOTES, WILLIAM Painter (1912-1963)
BEACH, WARREN Painter, Museum Director (1914-1999)
BEAL, REYNOLDS Painter, Etcher (1867-1951)
BEALL, LESTER THOMAS Illustrator, Designer (1902-1969)
BEALMER, WILLIAM Consultant, Educator (1919-2001)
BEAMENT, HAROLD Painter (1898-)
BEAR, DONALD Museum Director (1905-1952)
BEARD, MARION L PATTERSON Lecturer, Painter
BEATTIE, GEORGE Painter, Art Administrator (1919-1997)
BECK, STEPHEN R Painter, Educator (1937-2002)
BECKER, BETTIE (BETTIE GERALDINE WATHALL) Painter, Graphic Artist (1918-1997)
BECKER, NAOMI Sculptor (-1974)
BECKWITH, JAMES Painter, Craftsperson (1907-)
BEELKE, RALPH G Educator (1917-)
BEETZ, CARL HUGO Painter, Instructor (1911-1974)
BEGG, JOHN ALFRED Designer, Sculptor (1903-1974)
BEGGS, THOMAS MONTAGUE Consultant, Painter (1899-1990)
BEL GEDDES, NORMAN Designer (1893-1958)
BELCHER, HILDA Painter (1881-1963)
BELKNAP, MORRIS B Painter (-1952)
BELL, ALISTAIR MACREADY Printmaker, Painter (1913-)
BELL, CHARLES A Sculptor (-1976)
BELL, R MURRAY Collector (-1998)
BELLAMY, RICHARD Art Dealer (1927-1998)
BELLIN, MILTON R Painter, Muralist
BELLINGER, LOUIS A Curator (-1968)
BELLMER, HANS Painter, Graphic Artist & Sculptor (1902-1975)
BELMONT, IRA JEAN Painter (1885-1964)
BEMELMANS, LUDWIG Painter (1898-1963)
BEMIS, WALDO EDMUND Designer, Illustrator (-1951)
BENDA, W T Designer, Illustrator (1891-1948)
BENESCH, OTTO Art Historian (1896-1964)
BENESON, EDWARD HARTLEY Collector, Patron (1914-2005)
BENGTZ, TURE Museum Director, Painter (1907-1973)
BENHAM, ROBERT CHARLES, Painter (1913-2002)
BENN, BEN Painter (1884-1983)
BENNETT, RUTH M Craftsman (1899-1960)
BENNEY, ROBERT Painter, Illustrator (-2001)
BENSCO, CHARLES J Painter (1894-1960)
BENSON, ELAINE KG Art Dealer, Writer (1924-1998)
BENSON, ELIZABETH POLK Historian, Writer (1924-2005)
BENSON, EMANUEL M Art Administrator, Art Dealer (1904-1971)
BENSON, FRANK W Painter, Etcher (1862-1951)
BENSON, JOHN P Painter (1865-1947)
BENTON, MARGARET PEAKE Painter (-1975)
BENTON, THOMAS HART Painter, Writer (1889-1975)
BENTON, WILLIAM Collector (1900-1973)
BENTZ, JOHN Painter (-1951)
BENY, ROLOFF Photographer, Writer (1924-)
BENZ, LEER Printmaker, Painter (-1984)
BERENSON, BERNARD Art Authority (1865-1959)
BERG, PHIL Collector, Patron (1902-)
BERGMAN, ROBERT P Museum Director, Historian (1945-1999)
BERHARD, MRS RICHARD J Collector
BERKMAN, ARRON Painter, Gallery Director (1900-1991)
BERKO, FERENC Photographer (1916-2000)
BERMAN, EUGENE Painter, Designer (1899-1972)
BERMAN, PHILIP I Collector, Patron (1915-1997)

BERMINGHAM, PETER Museum Director, Curator (1937-1999)
BERMUDEZ, JOSE YGNACIO Sculptor, Painter (1922-1998)
BERN HEIMER, RICHARD Educator (1907-1958)
BERNARDINI, ORESTES Designer (1880-1957)
BERNDT, WALTER Cartoonist (1900-1979)
BERNEY, BERTRAM S Painter (1884-)
BERNINGHAUS, OSCAR E Painter, Designer (1874-1952)
BERNSTEIN, BENJAMIN D Collector (1907-2003)
BERNSTEIN, EVA Painter (1871-1958)
BERNSTEIN, GERALD Painter, Restorer (1917-)
BERNSTEIN, SYLVIA Painter, Sculptor (1914-1990)
BERNSTEIN, THERESA Painter, Printmaker (-2002)
BERRY, WILLIAM DAVID Illustrator, Sculptor (1926-1979)
BERRYMAN, CLIFFORD KENNEDY Cartoonist, Illustrator (1869-1949)
BERTOIA HARRY Sculptor, Graphic Artist (1915-1978)
BETTISON, JAMES Painter (1957-1998)
BETTMANN, OTTO LUDWIG Historian (1903-1998)
BETTS, LOUIS Painter (1873-1961)
BIBERMAN, EDWARD Painter, Graphic Artist (1904-1986)
BICE, CLARE Administrator, Painter (1909-1976)
BIDDLE, GEORGE Painter, Sculptor (1885-1973)
BIDDLE, JAMES Administrator, Collector (1929-2005)
BIDDLE, WATSON Painter (1904-)
BIEBER, MARGARETE Art Historian (1880-1978)
BIEDEL, FRANKLIN M Museum Director (1908-1966)
BIELER, ANDRE CHARLES Painter, Muralist (1896-1989)
BIERLY, EDWARD J Painter, Illustrator (1920-2004)
BIERMAN, SAMUEL Art Advisor (1902-1978)
BIGGERS, JOHN THOMAS Educator, Printmaker (1924-2001)
BILLINGS, HENRY Painter, Illustrator (1901-1987)
BILOTTI, SALVATORE F Sculptor (1879-1953)
BIMROSE, ARTHUR SYLVANUS JR Cartoonist (1912-)
BING, ALEXANDER Painter (1878-1959)
BINNING, BERTRAM CHARLES Painter (1909-1976)
BIRCHANSKY, LEO Painter, Cartoonist (1887-1949)
BIRELINE, GEORGE LEE Painter, Educator (1923-2002)
BIRKIN, MORTON Painter (1919-)
BISCHOFF, ELMER Painter, Educator (1916-1991)
BISGARD, JAMES DEWEY Collector, Patron (1898-1975)
BISHOP, BARBARA LEE Educator, Printmaker (1938-)
BISHOP, MARJORIE CUTLER Painter (-1998)
BISHOP, RICHARD EVETT Printmaker (1897-19751)
BISHOP, ROBERT CHARLES Museum Director, Art Writer (1938-1991)
BISSETTE, SAMUEL DELK Painter, Photographer (1921-2006)
BITTLEMAN, ARNOLD I Painter, Educator (1933-)
BLACK, ELEANOR SIMMS (MRS ROBERT M) Painter (1872-1949)
BLACK, MARY CHILDS Curator, Writer (-1992)
BLACK, WENDELL H Educator (1919-1972)
BLACKBURN, MORRIS (ATKINSON) Painter, Printmaker (1902-1979)
BLACKBURN, ROBERT Printmaker, Educator (1920-2003)
BLAI, BORIS Sculptor, Educator (1898-1985)
BLAINE, NELL Painter, Printmaker (1922-1996)
BLAIR, STREETER Painter (-1966)
BLAKE, LEO B Illustrator (1887-1976)
BLANCH, ARNOLD Painter (1896-1968)
BLANCHARD, CAROL Painter, Illustrator (1918-)
BLANCHFIELD, HOWARD JAMES Painter (1896-1957)
BLANDING, DON Author (1894-1957)
BLAUSTEIN, AL Painter, Printmaker (1924-2004)
BLEIBERG, GERTRUDE TIEFENBRUN Painter, Printmaker (-2001)
BLISS, MRS ROBERT WOODS Collector (-1969)
BLISS, ROBERT WOODS Patron, Diplomat (1875-1962)
BLOCH, ALBERT Painter (1882-1961)
BLOCH, E MAURICE Art Historian, Educator (-1989)
BLOCH, JULIUS Painter (1888-1966)
BLOCK, ADOLPH Sculptor, Instructor (1906-1978)
BLODGETT, EDMUND WALTON Painter (1908-)
BLODGETT, GEORGE WINSLOW Sculptor (1888-)
BLOEDEL, LAWRENCE HOTCH KISS Collector (1902-1976)
BLOS, PETER W Painter, Instructor (1908-1986)
BLOWER, DAVID HARRISON Painter (1901-1976)
BLUMBERG, YULI Painter (1894-1964)
BLUME, PETER Painter, Sculptor (1906-1992)
BLUMENSCHEIN, ERNEST LEONARD Painter (1874-1960)
BLUMENSCHEIN, MARY GREEN Painter (1869-1958)
BLUMENTHAL, MARGARET M Designer (1905-)
BOAL, SARA METZNER Painter, Instructor (1896-1979)
BOBLETER, LOWELL STANLEY Educator, Painter (1902-1973)
BOCOUR, LEONARD Paint Manufacturer (1910-1993)
BODE, ROBERT WILLIAM Designer, Painter (1912-)
BODIN, PAUL Artist (1910-1994)
BODINE, HELEN Painter
BOE, ROY ASBJORN Historian, Educator (1919-)
BOEHLER HANS Painter (1884-1961)
BOESCHENSTEIN, BERNICE (MRS C K) Painter (1906-1951)
BOESE, ALVIN WILLIAM Collector (1910-1986)
BOHLAND, GUSTAV Sculptor (1897-1959)
BOHNENKAMP, LESLIE GEORGE Sculptor, Instructor (1943-1997)
BOHNERT HERBERT Portrait Painter (1890-1967)
BOHROD, AARON Painter, Educator (1907-1992)
BOLINSKY, JOSEPH ABRAHAM Sculptor, Educator (1917-2002)
BOLOTOWSKY, ILVA Painter, Educator (1907-1981)
BOND, ROLAND S Collector (1898-)
BONEVARDI, MARCELO Artist (1929-1994)
BONGART, SERGEI R Painter, Instructor (-1985)
BONGIORNO, LAURINE MACK Historian (1903-1988)
BONINO, ALFREDO Art Dealer (1925-1981)
BONNAR, JAMES KING Painter (1885-1961)
BONNEY, THERESE Photographer (1895-1978)
BONNYCASTLE, MURRAY C Painter
BOOGAR, WILLIAM F Sculptor (1893-1958)
BOOKBINDER, JACK Painter, Printmaker (1911-1990)
BOORAEM, HENDRIK Painter (1886-1951)
BOOTH, CAMERON Painter (1892-1980)
BOOTH, NINA MASON Painter (1884-)
BORDEN, JAMES ERWIN Painter (1921-1990)
BORDUAS, PAUL EMILE Painter (-1960)
BORGENICHT, GRACE (GRACE BORGENICHT BRANDT) Art Dealer, Collector (1915-2001)
BORGHI, GUIDO RINALDO Painter (1903-1971)
BORGLUM, JAMES LINCOLN BE LA MOTHE Sculptor, Photographer (1912-1986)
BORIS, BESSIE Painter (-1993)
BORN, WOLFGANG Historian, Writer (1893-1949)
BORNE, MORTIMER Sculptor, Painter (1902-1987)
BORSTEIN, YETTA Painter (-1968)
BOSA, LOUIS PAINTER (1905-1981)
BOSIN, BLACKBEAR Painter, Designer (1921-1980)
BOSSE, JANET C Painter, Ceramist (-2000)
BOSSERT, EDYTHE H Painter (1908-1997)
BOSWELL, PEYTON, JR Writer, Editor (1904-1950)
BOTELLO, ANGEL Painter, Sculptor (1913-1986)
BOTHMER, BERNARD V Historian, Instructor (1912-1993)
BOTKIN, HENRY Painter, Writer (1896-1983)
BOTTIS, HUGH P Printmaker (-1964)
BOUCHARD, LORNE HOLLAND Painter, Illustrator (1913-1978)
BOUCHE, LOUIS Painter (1896-1969)
BOUCHE, RENE Portrait Painter (-1963)
BOURBON, DAVID Art Critic, Writer (1934-1998)
BOURDELL, PIERRE VAN PARYS Sculptor (-1966)
BOVER, RUSS (RUSSELL WALTER) Graphic Artist, Painter (1928-)
BOWDOIN, HARRIETTE Painter (-1947)
BOWEN, GAZA Sculptor, Environmental Artist (1944-2005)
BOWER, ALEXANDER Museum Director (1875-1952)
BOWLES, JANET PAYNE Craftsman (1882-1948)
BOWLING, JACK Silversmith, Printmaker (1903-1979)
BOXER, STANLEY (ROBERT) Painter, Sculptor (1926-2000)
BOYCE, GERALD G Educator, Painter (1925-1999)
BOYCE, RICHARD Sculptor (1920-)
BOYCE, WILLIAM G Museum Director, Educator (1921-1992)
BOYD, E Art Administrator, Writer (1903-1974)
BOYD, JAMES HENDERSON Printmaker, Sculptor (1928-2002)
BOYD, RUTHERFORD Painter, Designer (-1951)
BOYER, RALPH LUDWIG Painter, Etcher (1879-1951)
BOYKO, FRED Painter, Educator (1894-1951)
BRACKMAN, ROBERT Painter, Educator (1898-1980)
BRADFORD, FRANCIS SCOTT Painter (1898-1961)
BRAIDER, DONALD Art Writer (1923-1977)
BRAINARD, JOE Graphic Artist, Designer (1942-1994)
BRAKHAGE, JAMES STANLEY Filmmaker, Lecturer (1933-2003)
BRANDON, WARREN EUGENE Painter (1916-1977)
BRANDT, REX (REXFORD ELSON) Painter, Printmaker (1914-2000)
BRANNER, ROBERT Art Historian (1927-1973)
BRANSOM, (JOHN) PAUL Painter, Illustrator (1885-1979)
BRAOLEY, MRS. HARRY LYNDE Collector
BRAXTON, WILLIAM E Painter (1878-1932)
BRAY, JOHN Cartoonist (1879-1978)
BRAZEAU, WENDELL (PHILLIPS) Painter (1910-1974)
BRECHER, SAMUEL Painter (1897-1982)
BRECKENRIDGE, JAMES D Art Historian (1926-1982)
BREESKIN, ADELYN DOHME Administrator, Consultant (1896-1986)
BREGER, DAVE (DAVID) Cartoonist (1908-1970)

BREITENBACH, EDGAR Historian (1903-1977)
BRENDEL, OTTO J Art Historian (1901-1973)
BRENNAN, FANNY (FRANCES) M Painter (-2001)
BRENNER, SHORE HODGE Weaver, Educator (1949-)
BRENSON, THEODORE Painter (1893-1959)
BREWER, BESSIE MARSH Etcher, Lithographer (1883-1952)
BREWINGTON, MARION VERNON Art Historian, Writer (1902-1974)
BRICE, WILLIAM Painter, Printmaker (1921-1997)
BRIGGS, ERNEST Painter, Instructor (1923-1984)
BRIGHTWELL, WALTER Painter (1919-2005)
BRIGOS, AUSTIN Illustrator, Collector (1808-1973)
BRIGOS, BERTA N Painter, Writer (1884-1976)
BRINLEY, DANIEL PUTNAM Painter (1879-I963)
BRISTAH, JAMES W Gallery Director (1918-)
BRITSKY, NICHOLAS Painter, Educator (1913-2005)
BRITT, NELSON CLARK Museum Director, Painter (1944-2004)
BRITTAIN, MILLER G Painter (-1968)
BRITTON, HARRY Painter (1879-1958)
BRITTON, JAMES II Critic, Illustrator (1915-1983)
BROADD, HARRY ANDREW Painter, Historian (1910-)
BROADLEY, HUGH T Historian, Administrator (1922-2005)
BROADMAN, NELL Painter (-1968)
BRODER, PATRICIA JANIS Historian, Writer (1935-2002)
BRODIE, AGNES HAHN Sculptor, Painter (1924-1992)
BRODIE, GANDY Painter, Designer (1924-1975)
BRODSKY, HARRY Printmaker, Painter (1908-)
BROMBERG, FAITH Painter (1919-1990)
BROMUND, CAL E Painter (1903-1979)
BRONER, MATHEW Painter, Printmaker (1924-2005)
BROOK, ALEXANDER Painter (1898-1980)
BROOKS, JAMES Painter (1906-1992)
BROUGH, RICHARD BURRELL Educator, Designer (1920-1996)
BROUILLETTE, AL(BERT) C Painter, Instructor (1924-2000)
BROUILLETTE, GILBERT T Art Dealer, Consultant-Research
BROUSSARD, JAY REMY Museum Director, Painter (1920-1976)
BROWN, BRIAN Director (1911-1958)
BROWN, CARLYLE Painter (-1964)
BROWN, GEORGE BYRON Painter (1907-1961)
BROWN, JAMES MONROE Museum Director (1917-1998)
BROWN, JOHN CARTER Museum Director, Administrator (1934-2002)
BROWN, JOSEPH Sculptor, Educator (1909-)
BROWN, JUDITH GWYN Illustrator, Painter (1933-1992)
BROWN, MARBURY HILL Painter, Instructor (1925-1997)
BROWN, MARGARET Writer (1910-1952)
BROWN, MILTON WOLF Historian (1911-1998)
BROWN, PAUL Illustrator (1893-1958)
BROWN, RICHARD F Museum Director (1916-1979)
BROWN, RICHARD M Portrait Painter (-1964)
BROWN, ROGER Painter (1911-1997)
BROWN, ROY Painter (1879-1956)
BROWNE, VIVIAN E Painter, Educator (1929-1993)
BROWNHILL, HAROLD Painter, Illustrator
BROWNING, G WESLEY Painter (1868-1951)
BRUN, THOMAS Sculptor, Instructor (1911-2003)
BRUNDAGE, AVERY Collector (1887-1975)
BRUNS, FREDERICK R, JR Curator (1913-1979)
BRUSCA, JACK Painter (1939-1993)
BRUSSEL-SMITH, BERNARD Printmaker (1914-1989)
BRY, EDITH Assemblage Artist, Collage Artist (1898-1992)
BRYANT, EDWARD ALBERT Writer, Consultant (1928-2003)
BUBA, JOY FLINSCH Sculptor, Illustrator (1904-)
BUCHANAN, JERRY Painter, Educator (1936-1992)
BUCK, RICHARD D Conservator (1903-1977)
BUCKLEY, JOHN MICHAEL Painter (1891-1958)
BUFF, CONRAD Printmaker, Illustrator (1886-1975)
BUKI, ZOLTAN Curator, Administrator (1929-2003)
BULLIET,CJ Art Critic (1883-1952)
BULLOCK, WYNN Photographer (1902-1975)
BULTMAN, FRITZ Sculptor, Painter (1919-1985)
BUNCE, LOUIS DEMOTT Painter (1914-1983)
BUNKER, GEORGE Painter, Educator (1923-1991)
BUNTING, BAINBRIDGE Historian, Educator (1913-1981)
BURCHFIELD, CHARLES Painter (1893-1967)
BURCK, JACOB Cartoonist, Painter (1904-1982)
BURGART, HERBERT JOSEPH Educator, Administrator (1932-2002)
BURGESS, JOSEPH E Painter (1891-1961)
BURKE, E AINSLIE Painter, Educator (1922-1991)
BURKE, WILLIAM LOZIER MUNRO Historian (1906-1961)
BURKHARDT HANS GUSTAV Painter, Printmaker (1904-1994)
BURLEY, LINA Painter (1922-2005)
BURLIN, PAUL Painter (1886-1969)
BURLUIK, DAVID Painter (1882-1967)
BURNETT, BARBARA ANN Painter (1927-2003)
BURNEY, MINNA Educator (1891-1958)
BURNS, HARRISON 0 Painter, Instructor (1946-1991)
BURNS, JEROME Painter, Printmaker (1919-2003)
BURNS, SID Sculptor, Collector (1916-1979)
BURNSHIDE, KATHERINE TALBOTT Painter
BURNSIDE, CAMERON Painter, Educator (1887-1952)
BURRISS R (RILEY) HAL Painter, Illustrator (1892-1991)
BURROWS, PEARL Painter (1903-1960)
BURROWS, SELIG S Collector, Historian (1913-1997)
BURT, CLYDE EDWIN Ceramist, Educator (-1981)
BURTON, NETTA M Painter (-1960)
BURTON, SCOTT Sculptor, Conceptual Artist (1939-1989)
BUSA, PETER Painter, Sculptor (1914-1983)
BUSBEE, JULIANA ROYSTER Craftsman (1877-1962)
BUSCH, MICHAEL Artist
BUSH, BEVERLY Painter, Sculptor (-1969)
BUSH, ELLA SHEPART Painter (1863-)
BUSH, JACK Painter (1909-1977)
BUSH, WILLIAM BROUGHTON Painter (1911-)
BUSHMILLER, ERNIE PAUL Cartoonist (1905-)
BUTLER, JOSEPH (GREEN) Administrator, Painter (1911-1981)
BUZZELLI, JOSEPH ANTHONY Painter, Sculptor (1907-)
BYARS, JAMES LEE Conceptual Artist
BYE, RANULPH Painter (1916-2003)
BYRUM, RUTHVEN HOLMES Educator (1896-)
CADGE, WILLIAM FLEMMING Designer, Photographer (1924-2003)
CADLE, RAY KENNETH Craftsman, Painter (1906-2002)
CADMUS, PAUL Painter, Printmaker (1904-1999)
CADORIN, ETTOR Sculptor (1876-1951)
CAGE, JOHN Printmaker (1912-1992)
CAHAN, SAMUEL G Artist (-1974)
CAHILL, HOLGER Art Authority (1893-1960)
CALAPAI, LETTERIO Printmaker, Painter (1902-1993)
CALAS, NICHOLAS Critic (-1989)
CALCAGNO, LAWRENCE Painter (1913-1993)
CALDER, ALEXANDER Sculptor (1898-1976)
CALDWELL, JOHN Curator (1941-1993)
CALKINS, KINGSLEY MARK Painter, Educator (1917-2004)
CALKINS, LORING GARY Designer (1887-1960)
CALLAHAN, HARRY M Photographer (1912-1999)
CALLAHAN, KENNETH Painter (1905-1986)
CALLERY, MARY Sculptor (1903-1977)
CALLICOTT, BURTON HARRY Painter, Calligrapher (1907-2003)
CALLISEN, STERLING A Historian, Lecturer (1899-1988)
CALROW, ROBERT F Instructor, Painter (1916-1998)
CALVERT, JENNIE C (MRS. FINLEY H) Painter (1878-)
CAMFFERMAN, PETER MARIENUS Painter (1890-1951)
CAMINS, JACQUES JOSEPH Painter, Printmaker (1904-1988)
CAMLIN, JAMES A Painter (1918-1982)
CAMPANELLI, PAULINE Painter, Writer (-2001)
CAMPBELL, (JAMES) LAWRENCE Painter, Writer (1914-1998)
CAMPBELL, CHARLES MALCOLM Painter, Sculptor (1908-1985)
CAMPBELL, DOROTHY BOSTWICK Painter, Sculptor (1899-2001)
CAMPBELL, EDMUND S Painter, Architect (1884-1951)
CAMPBELL, ORLAND Portrait Painter (1890-1972)
CAMPBELL, SARA WENDELL Illustrator (1886-1960)
CAMPBELL, VIVIAN (VIVIAN CAMPBELL STOLL) Collector, Writer (1919-1986)
CAMPBELL, WILLIAM PATRICK Art Historian, Curator (1914-1976)
CANADAY, JOHN EDWIN Critic (1907 1985)
CANDELL, VICTOR Painter, Educator (1903-1977)
CANFIELD, JANE (WHITE) Sculptor (1897-1984)
CANIFF, MILTON ARTHUR Cartoonist (1907-1988)
CANTEY, SAM BENTON III Collector (-1973)
CANTOR, ROBERT LLOYD Educator, Designer (1919-1986)
CAPLAN, JERRY L Sculptor, Educator (1922-2004)
CAPP, AL Cartoonist (1909-1979)
CAREWE, SYLVIA Painter, Tapestry Artist
CAREY, JOHN THOMAS Educator, Historian (1917-1990)
CARLES, ARTHUR B Painter (1882-1952)
CARMACK, PAUL R Cartoonist (1895-1977)
CARPENTER, GILBERT (BERT) FREDERICK Painter, Educator (1920-2003)
CARPENTER, JAMES MORTON Historian, Artist (1914-1992)
CARRICK, DONALD F Illustrator, Painter (1929-)
CARRILLO, LILIA Painter (1929-1974)
CARRINGTON, JOY HARRELL Painter, Illuminator (-1999)
CARRINGTON, OMAR RAYMOND Painter, Instructor (1904-1991)
CARROLL, JOHN Painter (1892-1959)
CARROLL, RICHARD S Museum Director (1929-2003)

CARRUTH, PAUL H Illustrator (1892-1961)
CARSTENSON, CECIL C Sculptor, Lecturer (1906-1991)
CARTER, DUDLEY CHRISTOPHER Sculptor (1911-1992)
CARTER, HELENE Illustrator (1887-1960)
CASARELLA, EDMOND Sculptor, Printmaker (1920-1996)
CASCIERI, ARCANGELO Sculptor, Instructor (1902-1997)
CASE, ELIZABETH Painter, Writer (1930-2006)
CASEY, ELIZABETH TEMPLE Curator (1901-1990)
CASSEL, JOHN HARMON Cartoonist
CASTANO, GIOVANNI Art Dealer, Painter (1896-)
CASTELLI, LEO Dealer (1907-1999)
CASTLE, MRS ALFRED L Art Patron (1886-1970)
CATER, AUGUSTUS D (AD) Cartoonist (1895-1957)
CATHERS, JAMES O Sculptor, Educator (1934-1982)
CATLIN, STANTON LOOMIS Musicologist, Historian (1915-1997)
CAVALLITO, ALBINO Sculptor (1905-1966)
CAVALLON, GIORGIO Painter
CAVANAUGH, JOHN W Sculptor (1921-)
CAVER, WILLIAM RALPH Sculptor, Printmaker (1932-2005)
CECERE, GAETANO Sculptor, Lecturer (1894-1985)
CELLINI, JOSEPH Illustrator (1924-)
CERNUDA, PALOMA Painter (1948-2003)
CERVENE, RICHARD Painter, Curator
CHALIAPIN, BORIS Painter (1907-1979)
CHAMBERLAIN, BETTY Art Administrator, Writer (1908-1983)
CHAMBERLAIN, SAMUEL Printmaker, Writer (1895-1975)
CHAMBERS, JOHN Painter, Filmmaker (1911-1978)
CHAMBI, MARTIN Photographer (1891-1973)
CHANDOR, DOUGLAS Portrait Painter (1897-1953)
CHANIN, ABRAHAM L Lecturer
CHAPELLIER, GEORGE Art Dealer, Collector (1890-1978)
CHAPELLIER, ROBERT Art Dealer (-1974)
CHAPIN, (M) ANNE Sculptor, Educator (1930-1986)
CHAPIN, FRANCIS Painter (1899-1965)
CHAPIN, MYRON BUTMAN Painter (1887-1958)
CHAPMAN, CHARLES SHEPARD Painter (1879-1962)
CHAPMAN, HOWARD EUGENE Director, Cartoonist (1913-1977)
CHAPPELL, WALTER (LANDON) Photographer, Curator (1925-2000)
CHARLES, CLAYTON (HENRY) Sculptor, Educator (1913-1976)
CHARLOT, JEAN Painter, Historian (1898-1979)
CHASE, EDWARD Portrait Painter (1884-1965)
CHASE, FRANK SWIFT Painter (1886-1958)
CHASE, GEORGE H Educator, Writer (1874-1952)
CHASE, JOSEPH CUMMINGS Portrait Painter (1878-1965)
CHASE, SIDNEY M Painter (1877-1957)
CHATTERTON, CLARENCE KERR Painter (1880-1973)
CHEATHAM, FRANK REAGAN Painter, Designer (1936-2002)
CHEFFETZ, ASA Engraver (1897-1965)
CHENEY, SHELDON Writer, Historian (1886-1980)
CHERNEY, MARVIN Painter (-1966)
CHERRY, BERMAN Painter (1909-1992)
CHESTERTON, DAVID Educator, Graphic Artist (1930-)
CHETHLAHE (DAVID CHETHLAHE PALADIN) Painter, Designer (1926-1984)
CHEW, HARRY Painter, Educator (1925-)
CHEW, PAUL ALBERT Historian, Educator (1925-2004)
CHIAPELLA, EDWARD EMILE Painter (1889-1951)
CHILDERS, BETTY BIVINS Collector, Patron (1913-1982)
CHILDS, BERNARD Painter, Printmaker (1910-1985)
CHILLIDA, EDUARO Sculptor (1924-)
CHOATE, NATHANIEL Sculptor (1899-1965)
CHOUINARD, MRS NELBERT Educator (-1969)
CHRISTENSEN, RALPH Painter (1897-1961)
CHRISTENSEN, RONALD JULIUS Painter, Printmaker (1923-)
CHRISTENSON, HANS-JORGEN THORVALD Designer, Silversmith (1924-1983)
CHRIST-JANER, ALBERT WILLIAM Painter, Printmaker (1910-1973)
CHRISTOPER, WILLIAM R Painter (1924-1973)
CHRISTY, HOWARD CHANDLER Painter (1872-1952)
CHUMLEY, JOHN WESLEY Painter (1928-)
CHURCH, FREDERICK E Painter (1826-1900)
CIAMPAGLIA, CARLO Muralist (1891-1975)
CIKOVSKY, NICOLAI Painter, Muralist (1894-1984)
CITRON, MINNA WRIGHT Painter, Printmaker (1896-1991)
CLAGUE, JOHN ROGERS Sculptor (1928-2004)
CLANCY, JOHN Art Dealer (-1981)
CLAPP, MAUDE CAROLINE EDE Painter (1876-1960)
CLARE, STEWART Research Artist (1913-1992)
CLARK, ALLAN Sculptor (1896-1950)
CLARK, ALSON SKINNER Painter, Lithographer (1876-1949)
CLARK, ANTHONY MORRIS Curator, Collector (1923-1976)
CLARK, ELIOT CANDEE Painter (1883-1980)
CLARK, G FLETCHER Sculptor (1899-1982)
CLARK, MABEL BEATRICE SMITH Painter (-1957)
CLARK, ROLAND Painter (1874-1957)
CLEAR, CHARLES V Museum Consultant
CLEAVER, DALE GORDON Historian, Educator (1928-2000)
CLEAVES, MURIEL MATTOCK (MRS H) Illustrator, Painter (-1947)
CLELAND, THOMAS MAITLAND Illustrator (1880-1964)
CLEVELAND, HELEN BARTH Administrator, Instructor
CLIME, WINFIELD SCOTT Painter (1881-1958)
CLINEDINST, MAY SPEAR Painter (1887-)
CLISBY, ROGER Curator, Historian (1939-1994)
CLOSE, MARJORIE (PERRY) Painter, Lecturer (1899-1978)
CLYMER, JOHN F Painter, Illustrator (1907-1989)
COATES, ROBERT M Writer, Art Critic (1897-1973)
COBER, ALAN E Illustrator, Printmaker (1935-1998)
COCHRAN, GEORGE MCKEE (REDBIRD) Painter, Writer (1908-1990)
COE, LLOYD Painter, Illustrator (1899-1977)
COE, MATCHETT HERRING Sculptor (1907-1999)
COE, ROLAND Cartoonist
COFFEY, MABEL Painter, (1874-1949)
COFFMAN HAL Cartoonist (1883-1958)
COHEN, H GEORGE Painter, Educator (1913-1980)
COHN, MAX ARTHUR Painter, Printmaker (1903-1998)
COHOE, GREY Printmaker, Painter (1944-)
COINER, CHARLES T Painter (1897-1989)
COLBORN, JANE TAYLOR Sculptor, Educator (1913-1983)
COLBURN, FRANCIS PEABODY Painter (1909-1984)
COLBY, HOMER WAYLAND Illustrator, Etcher (1874-1950)
COLEMAN, RALPH P Painter (1892-1968)
COLETTI, JOSEPH ARTHUR Sculptor, Writer (1898-1973)
COLIN, RALPH FREDERICK Collector (1900-)
COLLAZO, CARLOS ERICK Painter, Graphic Artist (1956-1990)
COLLES, GERTRUDE Painter (1869-1957)
COLLETT, FARRELL REUBEN Painter, Educator (1907-2000)
COLLEY, WILLIAM, JR Collector, Patron (1910-1984)
COLLIER, ALAN CASWELL Painter (1911-1990)
COLLIER, ALBERTA Critic, Consultant (1911-1987)
COLLIER, LEO NATHAN (NATE) Cartoonist (-1961)
COLLINS, GEORGE R, Historian, Educator (1917-1993)
COLLINS, JOHN IRELAND Painter (1926-1982)
COLLINS, KREIGH Illustrator (1908-1974)
COLLINS, LOWELL DAUNT Painter, Dealer (1924-2003)
COLLINS, ROY H Illustrator (-1949)
COLSON, CHESTER E Painter, Educator (1917-1985)
COLT, JOHN NICHOLSON Painter, Educator (1925-1998)
CONE, GERRIT CRAIG Art Administrator (1947-1997)
CONE, MARVIN Painter (1891-1964)
CONGDON, WILLIAM (GROSVENOR) Painter, Writer (1912-1998)
CONGER, CLEMENT E Curator (1912-2004)
CONKLIN, GLORIA ZAMKO Painter (1925-2000)
CONNAWAY, JAY HALL Painter (1893-1970)
CONNER, JOHN RAMSEY Painter (1869-1952)
CONOVER, ROBERT FREMONT Printmaker, Painter (1920-1998)
CONROW, WILFORD SEYMOUR Painter (1880-)
CONSTABLE, WILLIAM GEORGE Art Historian, Writer (1887-1976)
CONSTANT, GEORGE Painter (1892-1978)
COOK HOWARD NORTON Painter, Lecturer (1911-1980)
COOK, GLADYS EMERSON Illustrator, Painter (1899-)
COOK, PETER (GEOFFREY) Painter (1915-1992)
COOK, WALTER WILLIAM SPENCER Educator (1888-1962)
COOKE, HEREWARD LESTER Art Historian, Painter (1916-1973)
COOKE, KATHLEEN MCKEITH Painter, Sculptor (1908-1978)
COOLEY, DIXIE (MRS JOHN L) Painter (1896-)
COOPER, ANTHONY J Painter (1907-1992)
COOPER, FRED G Cartoonist (1883-1962)
COOPER, MARVE H Painter Curator (1939-)
COOPER, RICHARD Painter (1945-1979)
COORMARASWAMY, ANADA K Museum Curator (1877-1947)
COOTES, FRANK GRAHAM Painter (1879-1960)
COPPINI, POMPEO LUIGI Sculptor (1870-1957)
COPPOLA, ANDREW Sculptor, Draftsman (1941-1990)
CORBETT, EDWARD M Educator, Painter (1919-1971)
CORBETT, GAIL SHERMAN (MRS HARVEY WILEY CORBETT) Sculptor (1871-1951)
CORBINO, JOHN Painter (1905-1964)
CORCOS, LUCILLE Painter, Illustrator (1908-1973)
CORISH, JOSEPH RYAN Painter (1909-1988)
CORNELIUS, MARTY Painter, Illustrator (1913-1979)
CORNELL, JOSEPH Sculptor (1903-1972)
CORNETTE, MARY ELIZABETH Dealer, Painter (1909-2005)

CORNWELL, DEAN Illustrator (1892-1960)
CORPRON, CARLOTTA M Educator, Photographer (1911-1988)
CORTIGLIA, NICCOLO Painter, Restorer (1893-)
COSGROVE, J O'HARA II Illustrator (1908-1968)
COSLA, OK Collector
COST, JAMES PETER Painter (1923-)
COSTIGAN, JOHN EDWARD Painter (1888-1972)
COTSWORTH, STAATS Painter (1908-1979)
COTT, JEAN CAHAN Painter
COTTON, LILLIAN Painter (1901-1962)
COTTON, WILLIAM HENRY Painter (1880-1951)
COURT, LEE WINSLOW Painter (1903-1992)
COURTICE, RODY KENNY Painter (-1973)
COVERT, JOHN Painter (1882-1960)
COVEY, ARTHUR Painter (1878-1960)
COVEY, VICTOR CHARLES B Conservator, Consultant (1928-1989)
COWAN, WOODSON MESSICK Cartoonist, Painter (1886-1977)
COWDREY, MARY BARTLETT Art Historian, Art Critic (1910-1974)
COWLES, RUSSELL Painter (1887-1979)
COX, ALLYN Painter (1896-1982)
COX, E MORRIS Collector (1903-2003)
COX, J HALLEY Painter (1910-)
COYER, MAX R Painter (1954-1988)
COZE-DABIJA, PAUL Painter, Writer (1903-1975)
CRAMPTON, ROLLIN Painter (1886-1970)
CRANDELL, BRADSHAW Painter (-1966)
CRANE, ROY (CAMPBELL) Cartoonist, Writer (1901-1977)
CRASKE, LEONARD Sculptor, Lithographer (-1950)
CRATZ, BENJIMIN ARTHUR Painter, Cartoonist (1888-)
CRAVATH, GLENN Cartoonist (-1964)
CRAWFORD, EARL Painter (1890-1960)
CRAWFORD, RALSTON Painter, Lithographer (1906-1977)
CRAWFORD, WILLIAM H Cartoonist, Sculptor (1913-)
CRESPI, PACHITA Painter (1900-1971)
CRESSON, MARGARET Sculptor, Writer (1889-1973)
CRIQUETTE (RUTH DUBARRY MONTAGUE) Painter, Writer (-1991)
CRISS, FRANCIS H Painter (1911-1973)
CROCKETT, GIB (GIBSON M) Cartoonist, Painter (1912-2001)
CROCKWELL, DOUGLAS Commercial Artist (1904-1968)
CRONIN, TONY Gallery Director (-1979)
CROSBY, SUMNER MCKNIGHT Art Historian (1909-1982)
CROSS, WATSON JR Painter, Video Artist (1918-1997)
CROUGHTON, AMY H critic (1880-1911)
CROW, CAROL (WILSON) Sculptor, Photographer (1915-1997)
CROWELL, LUCIUS Painter, Sculptor (1911-1988)
CRUMP, KATHLEEN (WHEELER) Sculptor (1884-1977)
CRUMP, W LESLIE Painter (1894-1962)
CRUZ, EMILIO ANTONIO Painter (1938-2004)
CSOKA, STEPHEN Painter (-1989)
CULHANE, SHAMUS H Filmmaker, Writer (1908-1996)
CUMING, BEATRICE Painter (1903-1975)
CUMMINGS, FREDERICK JAMES Administrator, Historian (1933-1990)
CUMMINGS, PAUL Writer, Historian (-1997)
CUNNINGHAM, BENJAMIN FRAZIER Painter, Educator (1904-1975)
CUNNINGHAM, CHARLES CREHORE Curator, Lecturer (1910-1979)
CUNNINGHAM, IMOGEN Photographer (1883-1976)
CUNNINGHAM, MARION Serigrapher, Lithographer (1911-)
CUPRIEN, FRANK W Painter (1871-1948)
CURRIER, CYRUS BATES Painter, Designer (1868-)
CURTIS, CONSTANCE Painter (-1959)
CURTIS, DAVID Painter, Printmaker (1949-2002)
CURTIS, PHILIP Painter (1907-2000)
CURTIS, ROGER WILLIAM Painter, Dealer (1910-2000)
CUSUMANO, STEFANO Painter, Educator (1912-1975)
CUTHBERT, VIRGINIA Painter (1908-2002)
CZUFIN, RUDOLF Director (1901-1979)
D'ANDREA ALBERT PHILIP Educator, Sculptor (1897-1983)
D'AULAIRE EDGAR PARIN Illustrator, Painter (1898-1986)
DABO, LEON Painter (1868-1960)
DAGYS, JACOB Sculptor (1905-1989)
DAHL, FRANCIS W Cartoonist (1907-1973)
DAHLBERG, EDWIN LENNART Painter (1901-1984)
DAHLER, WARREN Painter (1897-1961)
DAILY, EVELYNNE MESS Painter, Etcher (1903-2003)
DAINGERFIELD, MARJORIE JAY Sculptor (-1977)
DALE, BENJAMIN MORAN Illustrator (1889-1951)
DALI, SALVADOR Designer, Painter (1904-1989)
DANIEL, LEWIS C Painter, Illustrator (1901-1952)
DANIELS, DAVID M Collector, Patron (1927-2002)
D'ARCANGELO, ALLAN M Painter (1930-1998)
DARIUS, DENYLL (DENNIS MITCHELL) Painter (1942-1976)
DARLING, JAY NORWOOD (DING) Cartoonist (1876-1962)
DARROW, WHITNEY Cartoonist (1909-1999)
DASBURG, ANDREW MICHAEL Painter (1887-1979)
DASH, HARVEY DWIGHT Administrator, Painter (1924-2002)
DATUS, JAY Painter, Art Administrator (1914-1974)
DATZ, A MARK Painter (1889-)
DAUDELIN, CHARLES Sculptor (1920-2001)
DAUGHERTY, JAMES HENRY Painter, Writer (1898-1974)
DAUGHERTY, MARSHALL HARRISON Sculptor, Medalist (1915-1991)
DAVENPORT, EDITH FAIRFAX Painter (1880-1957)
DAVEY, RANDALL Painter (1887-1964)
DAVIDSON, ALLAN ALBERT Painter, Sculptor (1913-1988)
DAVIDSON, JO Sculptor (1883-1952)
DAVIDSON, MORRIS Painter (1898-1979)
DAVIS, (MR & MRS) WALTER Collectors, Patrons (-1991)
DAVIS, DAVID E Sculptor (1920-2002)
DAVIS, DONALD ROBERT Painter, Dealer (1909-1990)
DAVIS, ESTHER M Sculptor, Painter (1893-1974)
DAVIS, GENE B Painter (1920-1985)
DAVIS, HARRY ALLEN Painter, Muralist (1914-2006)
DAVIS, JAMES Abstract Artist (1901-1974)
DAVIS, JOHN SHERWOOD Potter, Administrator (1942-2003)
DAVIS, LEW E Painter (1910-1979)
DAVIS, MARIAN B Historian, Curator (1911-)
DAVIS, PHIL Cartoonist (-1964)
DAVIS, ROBERT TYLER Administrator, Historian (1904-)
DAVIS, STUART Painter (1894-1964)
DAVIS, WAYNE LAMBERT Painter, Illustrator (1914-1988)
DAVIS, WILLIAM D Educator, Printmaker (1936-2003)
DAVIS, WILLIAM STEEPLE Painter (1884-1961)
DAVISSON, HOMERG Painter (1866-)
DAWSON, EVE Painter
DAY, CHON (CHAUNCEY ADDISON) Cartoonist (1907-2000)
DAY, HORACE TALMAGE Painter, Director (1909-)
DAY, JOHN Painter, Educator (1932-1984)
DAY, LARRY (LAWRENCE JAMES) Painter, Educator (1921-)
DAY, MABEL K Painter (1884-)
DAY, WORDEN Sculptor, Printmaker (1916-1986)
DE BORHEGYI STEPHEN Museum Director, Writer (1911-1969)
DE BOTTON, JEAN PHILIPPE Painter, Sculptor (-1978)
DE COUX, JANET Sculptor (-2002)
DE CREEFT, JOSE Sculptor, Educator (1884-1982)
DE DIEGO, JULIO Painter, Illustrator (1900-1979)
DE ERDELY, FRANCIS Painter, Educator (1904-1959)
DE FRANCISCI, ANTHONY Sculptor (1887-1964)
DE GRAZIA, ETTORE TED Painter (1909-1982)
DE JONG, GERRIT, JR Lecturer, Writer (1892-1979)
DE KOONING, ELAINE MARIE CATHERINE Painter, Writer (1920-1989)
DE LESSEPS, TAUNI Sculptor, Painter (1920-)
DE MARCO, JEAN ANTOINE Sculptor (1898-1990)
DE MARTELLY, JOHN STOCKTON Painter, Printmaker (1903-1980)
DE MARTINI, JOSEPH Painter (1896-)
DE MENIL, JOHN Collector (1904-1973)
DE MISKEY, JULIAN Sculptor, Printmaker (-1986)
DE NAGY, TIBOR J Dealer, Collector (1910-1993)
DE POL, JOHN H Printer, Designer (1913-2004)
DE PREY, JUAN Painter (-1962)
DE RIVERA, JOSE Sculptor (1904-1985)
DE RUTH, JAN Printer, Paintmaker (1922-1911)
DE TORE, JOHN E Painter (1902-1975)
DEAN, ERNEST WILFRID Painter
DEAN, NICHOLAS BRICE Printmaker, Photographer (1933-2005)
DEAN, PETER Painter (1939-1993)
DECKER, JOHN Painter (1895-)
DEDINI, ELDON LAWRENCE (1921-2000)
DEE, LEO JOSEPH Graphic Artist, Painter (1931-2004)
DEFRANCESCO, ITALO I Educator (1901-1967)
DEHN, ADOLF Graphic Artist (1895-1968)
DEHNER, DOROTHY Sculptor, Printmaker (1901-1994)
DEINES, E HUBERT Engraver (1894-1967)
DEKNATEL, FREDERICK BROACKWAY Art Historian, Educator (1905-1973)
DEL CASTILLO, MARY VIRGINIA Painter (1865-)
DELANEY, BEAUFORD Painter (1902-1979)
DELONGA, LEONARD ANTHONY Sculptor, Educator (1925-1990)
DELSON, ELIZABETH Painter, Printmaker (1932-2005)
DEMANCE, HENRI Painter (1871-1948)
DEMETROIS, GEORGE Sculptor (1896-1974)
DEMIANOFF, RENEE LOCKHART Director (1910-1962)
DEMPSEY, RICHARD W Painter, Lecturer (1909-)
DENNIS, BURT MORGAN Etcher (1892-1960)
DENNIS, CHARLES HOUSTON Cartoonist (1921-2002)

DENNIS, GERTRUDE WEYHE Art Dealer (-)
DENNISTON, DOUGLAS Painter, Educator (1921-2004)
DENSLOW, DOROTHEA HENRIETTA Sculptor (1900-1971)
DENTZEL, CARL SCHAEFER Museum Director, Writer (1913-1980)
DEO, MARJORIE NEE, Painter (1907-1996)
DEPINNA, VIVIAN Painter (1883-1978)
DERUJINSKY, GLEB W Sculptor, Craftsman (1888-1975)
DESSAR, LOUIS PAUL Painter (1867-1952)
DEVLIN, HARRY Painter, Cartoonist (1918-2001)
DEVLIN, WENDE Painter (1918-2002)
DEVREE, HOWARD Critic (1890-1966)
DIBBLE, GEORGE Painter, Writer (1904-2001)
DIBONA, ANTHONY Sculptor, Lithographer (1896-)
DICKERSON, WILLIAM JUDSON Painter (1904-)
DICKINSON, EDWIN W Painter (1891-1979)
DIEBENKORN, RICHARD Painter (1922-1993)
DIENES, SARI Assemblage Artist, Printmaker (1898-1992)
DIETSCH, C PERCIVAL Sculptor (1881-1961)
DIETZ, CHARLES LEMOYNE Museum Director, Painter (1910-2002)
DIFRANZA, AMERICO M Painter (1919-2004)
DIGIORGIO, JOSEPH J Painter (1931-2000)
DIGIUSTO, GERALD N Sculptor (1929-1987)
DILLER, BURGOYNE Painter (1906-1965)
DILLON, C DOUGLAS Patron, Collector (1909-2003)
DIMAN, HOMER Painter (1914-1974)
DIMONDSTEIN, MORTON Sculptor, Painter (1920-)
DINGER, CHARLOTTE Collector, Writer (-1996)
DIODA, ADOLPH T Sculptor, Assemblage Artist (1915-1991)
DIRK, NATHANIEL Painter (1896-1961)
DIRKS, RUDOLPH Cartoonist (-1968)
DIRUBE, ROLANBO LOPEZ Painter, Sculptor (1928-1997)
DISMUKES, MARY ETHEL Painter (-1951)
DIXON, FRANCIS S Painter (1879-1967)
DOBBS, ELLA VICTORIA Educator (1866-1952)
DOBKIN, ALEXANDER Painter (1908-1975)
DOBSON, DAVID IRVING (DIAMONOSTEIN) Painter (1883-1957)
DOCKSTADER, FREDERICK J Consultant, Historian (1912-1998)
DODGE, HAZEL (MRS WILLIAM TTURMAN) Curator (1903-1957)
DODGE, JOSEPH JEFFERS Painter, Lecturer (1917-)
DOHANOS, STEVAN Illustrator, Painter (1907-1994)
DOI, ISAMI Painter (1903-1965)
DOLE, WILLIAM Painter, Educator (1917-1983)
DOMBEK, BLANCHE M Painter, Sculptor (-1987)
DOMJAN, JOSEPH (SPIRI) Painter, Printmaker (1907-)
DONAHEY, JAMES HARRISON Cartoonist (1875-1949)
DONAHUE, BENEDICT SR Educator
DONATO, GIUSEPPE Sculptor (1881-1965)
DONNELLY, MARY E Painter (1898-1963)
DOOLIN, JAMES LAWRENCE Painter, Educator (1932-2002)
DOREN, ARNOLD T Photographer, Educator (1935-2003)
DORN, RUTH (DORNBUSH) Painter (1925-2004)
DORNER, ALEXANDER Historian (1893-)
DORR, (VIRGINIA) NELL Photographer (1893-)
DORRA, HENRI Historian, Educator (1924-2002)
DORSKY, MORRIS Historian, Educator (1918-2000)
DOUGLAS, AARON Painter (1900-1979)
DOUGLAS, FREDERIC HUNTINGTON Curator (1897-1951)
DOUGLAS, LESTER Designer (1894-1961)
DOUGLAS, ROBERT LANGTON Critic (-1951)
DOVE, ARTHUR GARFIELD Painter (1880-1946)
DOW, HELEN JEANNETTE Historian, Educator (1926-1993)
DOWLING, ROBERT W Patron (1895-1973)
DOWNEY, JUAN Video Artist, Architect (1940-1993)
DOYON, GERARD MAURICE Educator, Historian (1923-1990)
DRABKIN, STELLA Painter, Designer (1900-1976)
DRAPER, WILLIAM FRANKLIN Painter, Instructor (1912-2003)
DREIER, KATHERINE S Painter, Lecturer (1877-1952)
DREITZER, ALBERT J Collector, Patron (1902-1985)
DRESSER, LOUISA (LOUISA DRESSER CAMPBELL) Administrator, Historian (1907-1988)
DREWES, WERNER Painter, Printmaker (1899-1985)
DREWLOWE, EVE Painter, Sculptor (1924-1988)
DREXLER, ARTHUR JUSTIN Director, Curator (1925-1987)
DREXLER, LYNNE Painter (-1999)
DRIGGS, ELSIE Painter (1898-1992)
DROGKAMP, CHARLES Painter (-1958)
DRUMMOND, ARTHUR A Painter, Illustrator (1891-)
DRURY, WILLIAM H Painter (1888-1960)
DRYER, MOIRA JANE Painter, Sculptor (1957-1992)
DRYFOOS, NANCY Sculptor (1918-1991)
DRYSDALE, NANCY MCINTOSH Patron, Dealer (1931-2003)
DU BOIS, GUY PENE Painter (1884-1951)
DU MONO, FRANK V Painter (1865-1951)
DU PEN, EVERETT GEORGE Sculptor, Educator (1912-2005)
DUANE, TANYA Painter, Collage Artist
DUBANIEWICZ, PETER PAUL, Painter (1913-2003)
DUBLE, LU Sculptor (1896-1970)
DUCA, ALFRED MILTON Painter, Sculptor (1920-1997)
DUFFY, EDMUND Cartoonist (1899-1962)
DUFNER, EDWARD Painter (1871-1957)
DUHME, H RICHARD JR Sculptor, Educator (1914-2005)
DUNCAN, HARRY ALVIN Printer, Designer (1916-1997)
DUNCAN, RUTH S Painter (1908-)
DUNCANSON, ROBERT Painter (1817-1872)
DUNN, ALAN (CANTWELL) Cartoonist, Writer (1900-1974)
DUNN, CAL Painter, Filmmaker (1915-2000)
DUNN, HARVEY T Illustrator, Painter (1884-1952)
DUPONT, HENRY F Museum Curator (1880-1969)
DURLACH, MARCUS RUSSELL Painter (1911-1991)
DUVOISIN, ROGER Writer, Illustrator (1904-1980)
DWIGGINS, CLARE Cartoonist (1874-1958)
DWIGGINS, WILLIAM ADDISON Designer (1880-1956)
DWIGHT, EDWARD HAROLD Museum Director (1919-1981)
EAMES, JOHN HEAGAN Etcher, Painter (1900-2002)
EARLS, PAUL Environmental Artist (1934-1998)
EASBY, DUDLEY T JR Art Administrator, Art Historian (1905-1973)
EASTERWOOD, HENRY LEWIS Educator, Tapestry Artist (1934-2002)
EASTMAN, ALVIN CLARK Orientalist (1894-1959)
EASTMAN, WILLIAM JOSEPH Painter (1881-1950)
EASTON, FRANK LORENCE Painter (1884-)
EASTON, ROGER DAVID Painter, Jeweler (1923-2005)
EBERLE, MERAB Critic (-1959)
EBERMAN, EDWIN Administrator, Educator (1905-1988)
ECKE, GUSTAV Museum Curator (-1971)
ECKELBERRY, DON RICHARD Painter (1921-)
ED, CARL Cartoonist (1890-1959)
EDMONDSON, LEONARD Printmaker (1916-2002)
EDWARDS, EMMET Painter (1907-)
EDWARDS, GEORGE WHARTON Painter, Illustrator (1869-1950)
EDWARDS, PAUL BURGESS Painter, Educator (1935-2005)
EDWARDS, ROBERT Painter, Engraver (1879-1948)
EGAS, CAMILO Educator (1897-1962)
EGE, OTTO F Educator, Writer (1888-1911)
EGGERS, GEORGE WILLIAM Educator (1883-1958)
EGGERS, RICHARD Architect (1918-1979)
EGLESON, JIM (JAMES DOWNEY) Printmaker, Painter (1907-)
EHRMAN, FREDERICK L Collector (1906-1973)
EICHENBERG, FRITZ Graphic Artist, Illustrator (1911-1990)
EIDE, PALMER Sculptor, Designer (1906-1991)
EISENLOP, EDWARD G Painter (1873-1961)
EISENSTAT, BENJAMIN Painter, Illustrator (1915-)
EISNER, DOROTHY (DOROTHY EISNER MCDONALD) Painter, Collage Artist (1906-)
EITEL, CLIFFE DEAN Painter, Etcher (1909-)
ELDER, ARTHUR JOHN Painter, Etcher (1874-)
ELDLITZ DOROTH MEIGS Patron, Photographer (1891-1976)
ELDREDGE, STUART EDSON Painter (1902-1992)
ELIASH, ZARA Sculptor (1914-2002)
ELIASOPH, PAULA Painter, Writer (1895-)
ELISOFON, ELIOT Painter, Photographer (1911-1973)
ELKON, ROBERT Art Dealer, Collector (1928-1983)
ELLERHUSEN, FLORENCE COONEY Painter (-1950)
ELLERHUSEN, ULRIC H Sculptor (1879-1951)
ELLIOTT, JAMES HEYER Administrator, Consultant (1924-2000)
ELLIOTT, PHILIP CLARKSON Painter (1903-1985)
ELLIS, CARL EUGENE Art Administrator, Instructor (1932-1977)
ELLIS, FREMONT Painter (1897-1985)
ELLIS, JOSEPH BAILEY Educator, Sculptor (1890-)
ELLIS, ROBERT CARROLL Painter, (1923-1979)
ELLISON, SHIRLEY (SHIRLEY ELIASON HAUPT) Painter, Educator (1926-1988)
ETTLING, RUTH (DROITCOUR) Painter, Printmaker (1910-2003)
ELLSWORTH Illustrator (1885-1961)
ELOUL, KOSSO Sculptor (1920-1998)
ELSNER, LARRY EDWARD Sculptor, Educator (1930-)
ELY, FANNY G Painter (1879-1961)
EMBRY, NORRIS Painter (1921-1981)
EMERSON, ROBERTA SHINN Museum Director (1922-1998)
EMERSON, WALTER CARUTH Painter, Educator (1912-2002)
EMIL, ALLAN D Collector, Patron (1898-1976)
EMMERICH, IRENE HILLEBRAND Painter
EMMET, LYDIA FIELD Painter (1886-1952)

ENFIELD, HARRY Illustrator (1906-1958)
ENGEL, HARRY Painter (1901-1970)
ENGEL, MICHAEL M Art Publicist (1896-1969)
ENGGASS, ROBERT Historian, Educator (1921-2003)
ENO, JAMES LORNE Painter, Educator (1887-1952)
ENSER, GEORGE Designer (1890-1911)
EPSTEIN, BETTY O Sculptor, Painter (1920-1999)
EPSTEIN, ETHEL S Collector
ERICSON, BEATRICE Painter (-1997)
ERICSON, ERNEST Illustrator, Instructor (-1981)
ERLANGER, ELIZABETH N Painter, Lecturer (1901-1975)
ERNST, JIMMY Painter, Educator (1920-)
ERNST, MAX Painter, Sculptor (1911-1976)
ERSKINE, HAROLD PERRY Sculptor (1879-1951)
ESCHMANN, JEAN CHARLES Craftsman (1896-1961)
ESHERICK, W HARTON Sculptor, Designer (1887-1970)
ESLER, JOHN KENNETH Printmaker, Painter (1933-2001)
ETNER, STEPHEN MORGAN Painter (1903-)
ETON, ALLEN HENDERSHOTT Writer (1878-1962)
ETTINOHAUSEN, RICHARD Administrator (1906-1979)
EVANS, DONALD Painter (1946-1977)
EVANS, GROSE Historian, Educator (1916-2003)
EVANS, MINNIE Painter (1892-1987)
EVANS, RUDULPH Sculptor (1879-1960)
EVERETT, LEN G Painter
EVERETT, MARY O (MRS HG) Painter (1876-1948)
EVERGOOD, PHILIP Painter, Graphic Artist (1901-1973)
EVERINGHAM, MILLARD Painter, Etcher (1912-)
EVETT, KENNETH WARNOCK Painter, Critic (1913-2005)
EWEN, PATERSON Painter, Educator (1925-)
EWING, BAYARD Administrator, Collector (1916-1991)
FABE, ROBERT Painter, Educator (1917-2004)
FABRES, OSCAR Cartoonist (1895-1961)
FABRI, RALPH Painter, Writer (1894-1975)
FAHLSTROM, OYVIND Painter (1928-1976)
FAIERS, TED (EDWARD SPENCER) Painter, Printmaker (1908-1985)
FAINTER, ROBERT A Educator, Painter (1942-1978)
FAIRCHILD, MAY Painter (1872-1959)
FALKENSTEIN, CLAIRE Sculptor (-1997)
FALLS, CHARLES BUCKLES Illustrator (1874-1959)
FALTER, JOHN Illustrator (1910-1982)
FARIS, BRUNEL DE BOST Painter, Educator (1937-2005)
FARLOW, HARRY Painter (1882-1956)
FARMER, MABEL McKIBBIN Engraver (1903-)
FARNHAM, EMILY Painter, Writer (1912-2004)
FARR, FRED Sculptor (1914-1973)
FARRELL, KATHERINE L Painter, Etcher (1857-)
FASANO, CLARA Sculptor (-1990)
FASTOVE, AARON (AARON FASTOVSKY) Painter (1898-1979)
FAULKNER, BARRY Painter (1911-1966)
FAULKNER, KADY B Painter, Educator (1901-1977)
FAULKNER, RAY N Educator, Writer (1906-1975)
FAUSETT LYNN Painter (1894-1977)
FAWCETT, ROBERT Illustrator (1903-1967)
FAY, WILBUR M Designer (1904-1959)
FEDELLE, ESTELLE, Painter, Lecturer (1914-2001)
FEELEY, PAUL Painter (1913-1966)
FEHER, JOSEPH Curator, Painter (1908-1987)
FEIGIN, DOROTHY L Painter (1904-1969)
FEIGL, HUGO Art Dealer (1890-1961)
FEINBLATT, EBRIA Historian
FEININGER, ANDREAS B L Photographer, Writer (1906-1999)
FEITELSON, LORSER Painter (1898-1978)
FEJES, CLAIRE Painter, Writer (1920-)
FELS, C P Painter, Writer (1912-1991)
FENCI, RENZO Sculptor (1914-1999)
FENICAL, MARLIN E Painter, Photographer (1907-1983)
FENTON, ALAN Painter, Instructor (1927-2000)
FENTON, BEATRICE Sculptor (1887-1983)
FENTON, JOHN NATHANIEL Painter, Etcher (1912-1977)
FERBER, HERBERT Sculptor, Painter (1906-1991)
FERGUSON, BARCLAY (VISCOUNT OF LAMOND) Painter, Muralist (1924-1991)
FERNALD, HELEN ELIZABETH Educator (1891-1964)
FERRARI, FEBO Sculptor (1865-)
FERREN, JOHN Painter (1905-1970)
FICKLEN, JACK HOWELLS Cartoonist (1911-1980)
FIELD, SAUL Printmaker, Lecturer (1912-1987)
FIELDS, MITCHELL Sculptor (1901-1966)
FIENE, ALICIA W Painter (1919-1961)
FIENE, ERNEST Painter (1894-1965)
FIERO, EMILIE L Sculptor (1889-1974)
FILECKENSTEIN, OPAL R Painter, Ceramist (1911-1996)
FILMUS, TULLY Painter, Lecturer (1903-1995)
FILTZER, HYMAN Sculptor, Restorer (1911-1967)
FINCH, RUTH WOODWARD Writer, Photographer (1916-2004)
FINCK, FURMAN J Painter, Instructor (1900-)
FINDLAY, HELEN T Dealer (1909-1992)
FINDLING, SIDNEY Painter, Instructor (1922-2004)
FINE, PERLE Painter (1905-1988)
FINK, LOUIS R Painter (1925-1980)
FINK, RAY Sculptor, Educator (1922-1998)
FINKELSTEIN, LOUIS Educator, Painter (1923-2000)
FINLAYSON, DONALD LORD Educator (1897-1960)
FINLEY, DAVID EDWARD Art Administrator (1890-1977)
FINLEY, MARY L Painter (-1964)
FINTA, ALEXANDER Sculptor (1881-1951)
FISCHER, MILDRED (GERTRUDE) Designer, Craftsman (1907-2000)
FISCHETTI, JOHN Cartoonist (1916-1980)
FISH DOROTHY S Ceramist (1906-1958)
FISHER REGINALD Writer (1906-1966)
FISHER, SANDRA Painter (1947-1994)
FISKE, GERTRUDE Painter (1879-1961)
FITCH, GEORGE HOPPER Collector, Patron (1909-2004)
FITE, FIARVEY Sculptor (1903-1976)
FITZGERALD, EDMUND J Painter, Lecturer (1912-1989)
FITZGERALD, HARRIET Painter, Lecturer (1904-1984)
FITZGERALD, J EDWARD Photographer (1923-1977)
FITZSIMMONS, JAMES JOSEPH Painter, Architect (1908-)
FLAGG, JAMES MONTGOMERY Illustrator (1977-1960)
FLANAGAN, JOHN F Sculptor (1898-1952)
FLAVIN, DAN Artist, Writer (1933-1996)
FLECK, PAUL DUNCAN Director (1934-1992)
FLEISCHMANN, ADOLF R Painter (-1969)
FLEISCHMANN, JULIUS Collector
FLEISHMAN, LAWRENCE ARTHUR Art Dealer, Publisher (1925-1997)
FLEMING, ALLAN ROBB Designer, Calligrapher (1929-1977)
FLEXNER, JAMES THOMAS Writer, Historian (1908-2003)
FLIEGEL, LESLIE Painter (1912-1968)
FLINT, JANET ALTIC Curator, Historian (1935-2005)
FLOCH, JOSEPH Painter (1895-1977)
FLOETER, KENT Painter, Sculptor (1937-2004)
FLOETHE, RICHARD Illustrator, Designer (1901-1988)
FLOOD, EDWARD C Sculptor, Painter (1944-1985)
FLORSHEIM, RICHARD A Painter, Printmaker (1916-1979)
FLORY, ARTHUR L Graphic Artist, Painter (1914-1972)
FOGEL, SEYMOUR Painter, Sculptor (1911-1984)
FOLEY, DOROTHY SWARTZ Painter, Printmaker (1922-2004)
FOLLETT, JEAN FRANCES Sculptor, Painter (1917-1991)
FONDREN, HAROLD M Art Dealer (1922-1999)
FONTAINE, E JOSEPH Painter (-2004)
FONTANNINI, CLARE Educator, Sculptor (-1984)
FOOTE, JOHN JR Painter (-1968)
FOOTE, WILL HOWE Painter (1874-1965)
FORBES, EDWARD W Museum Director (1873-1969)
FORCE, JULIANA R Museum Director (-1948)
FORD, CHARLES HENRI Painter, Photographer (1913-)
FORD, ELEANOR CLAY Patron (1896-1976)
FORREST, JAMES TAYLOR Museum Director, Educator (1919-2005)
FORST, MILES Sculptor, Educator (1923-2006)
FORSYTH, CONSTANCE Painter, Printmaker (1903-1987)
FOSBURGH, JAMES WHITNEY Painter, Writer (1910-1978)
FOSOICK, SINA G Art Administrator, Collector (-1983)
FOSTER, GENEVIEVE Writer, Illustrator (1893-1979)
FOSTER, HAL Cartoonist, Painter (1892-1982)
FOSTER, JAMES W SR Museum Director
FOSTER, KENNETH E Museum Director (-1964)
FOURNIER, ALEXIS JEAN Painter (1865-1948)
FOUSEK, FRANK DANIEL Printmaker, Painter (1913-1979)
FOWLER, ALFRED Writer (1889-)
FOWLER, MEL (WALTER) Sculptor (1921-)
FOWLER, MEL Printmaker, Painter (1922-)
FOX, CHARLES HAROLD Craftsman (1905-1979)
FOX, MILTON S Painter (1904-1971)
FRALEY, DAVID K Painter (1952-)
FRAMPTON, HOLLIS Filmmaker (1936-1984)
FRANCIS, BILL DEAN Designer, Administrator (1929-)
FRANCO, ROBERT JOHN Painter, Educator (1932-)
FRANGELLA, LUIS Painter (1944)
FRANKENSTEIN, ALFRED VICTOR Art Critic, Art Historian (1906-1981)
FRANKFURTER, ALFRED Art Editor (-1965)
FRANKL, PAUL THEODORE Designer (1876-1958)

FRANKLE, PHILIP Painter (1913-1968)
FRANKLIN, CLARENCE Collector (-1967)
FRANKLIN, DOUGLAS (FERRAR) Art Historian, Educator (1929-1982)
FRANKLIN, GILBERT ALFRED Sculptor, Educator (1919-2004)
FRASER, LAURA G Sculptor (1889-1966)
FRASER, MALCOLM Painter (1869-1949)
FRAZIER, KENNETH Painter (1867-1949)
FRAZIER, RICHARD WILLIAMS Sculptor (1922-1983)
FREDENTHAL, DAVID Painter (1914-1958)
FREDERICK, EUGENE WALLACE Printmaker, Educator (1927-)
FREDERICKS, MARSHALL MAYNARD Sculptor (1908-1998)
FREED, ERNEST BRADEIELD Printmaker, Painter (1908-)
FREED, HERMINE Video Artist, Photographer (1940-1998)
FREED, WILLIAM Painter (1902-1984)
FREEDBERG, SYDNEY JOSEPH Historian, Educator (1914-1997)
FREEDMAN, DON Author, Illustrator (1909-1978)
FREEDMAN, MAURICE Painter (1904-)
FREEMAN, JANE Painter (1885-1963)
FREER, HOWARD MORTIMER Painter (1904-1960)
FREIFELD, ERIC Painter, Educator (1919-)
FREILICH, MICHAEL L Art Dealer, Collector (1912-1975)
FREIMAN, ROBERT J Painter (1917-1991)
FRENCH, RAY H Printmaker, Painter (1919-2000)
FREY, ERWIN F Sculptor (1892-1967)
FREY, VIOLA Sculptor, Painter (1933-2004)
FRICK, ROBERT OLIVER Painter, Instructor (1920-1997)
FRID, TAGE P Designer (1915-)
FRIEDENSOHN, ELIAS Painter, Sculptor (1924-1991)
FRIEDLAENDER, WALTER Art Historian (-1966)
FRIEDLANDER, ISAC Engraver (1890-1968)
FRIEND, DAVID Painter, Educator (1899-1978)
FRINK, ELISABETH Sculptor (-1993)
FRISHMUTH, HARRIET WHITNEY Sculptor (1880-1979)
FROELICH, PAUL Painter (1897-)
FROMAN, RAMON MITCHELL Painter (1908-1980)
FROMBERG, GERALD Educator, Filmmaker (1925-1977)
FROUCHTBEN, BERNARD Painter (1878-1956)
FRUHAUF, ALINE Printmaker (1907-1978)
FRUMKIN, ALLAN Dealer (1926-2002)
FRY, EDWARD F Educator, Critic (1935-1992)
FUERSTENBURO, PAUL W Commercial Artist (1875-1953)
FULLER, META VAUX WARRICK Sculptor (1877-1968)
FULLER, R BUCKMINSTER Design Scientist (1895-1983)
FULLER, RICHARD EUGENE Museum Director (1897-1976)
FULTON, CYRUS JAMES Painter (1873-1949)
FULTON, FRED FRANKLIN Painter, Historian (1920-2003)
FUMAGALLI, ORAZIO Educator, Sculptor (1921-2004)
GABO, NAUM Sculptor (1890-1977)
GAHAGAN, JAMES (EDWARD) Painter, Educator (1919-2000)
GAILIS, JANIS Painter (1909-1975)
GALE, WALTER RASIN Educator (1878-1959)
GALLATIN, ALBERT EUGENE Painter (1882-1952)
GALLI, WARREN J Painter, Writer (1923-2001)
GALOS, BEN Painter (-1963)
GALVAN, JESUS GERRERO Painter
GANNAM, JOHN Painter (1907-1965)
GARBATY, EUGENE L Collector (-1966)
GARBE, WILLIAM Painter, Editor (1948-1989)
GARBER, DANIEL Painter (1880-1958)
GARBISCH, BERNICE CHRYSLER Collector
GARBISCH, EDGAR WILLIAM Collector (1899-1979)
GARNER, ARCHIBALD Sculptor, Designer (1904-1970)
GARRETT, STUART GRAYSON Painter, Educator (1922-1996)
GARRISON, JESSE JANES Educator (1901-)
GARTH, JOHN Painter, Writer (1894-1971)
GASSER, HENRY MARTIN Painter, Writer (1909-1981)
GATCH, LEE Painter (1909-1968)
GATEWOOD, MAUD Painter (1934-2004)
GATLING, EVA INGERSOLL Consultant, Historian (1912-2000)
GATRELL, MARION THOMPSON Educator, Painter (1909-)
GATRELL, ROBERT MORRIS Educator, Painter (1906-1982)
GAUDIN, MARGUERITE Designer (1909-)
GAUGH, HARRY E Educator, Critic (-1992)
GAYNE, CLIFTON ALEXANDER, JR Educator (1912-1971)
GEARHART, MAY Etcher
GEBER, HANA Sculptor, Instructor (1910-)
GEE, YUN Painter (1906-1963)
GEESEY, TITUS CORNELIUS Collector, Patron (1893-1969)
GEHR, MARY (RAY) Printmaker, Painter (-1997)
GEIGER, EDITH R Painter (1912-2004)
GEIGER, ELIZABETH DE CHAMISSO Sculptor
GEIS, MILTON ARTHUR Painter, Designer (1926-2005)
GEISEL, THEDOR SEUSS (Dr Seuss) Illustrator, Writer (1904-1991)
GELD, JAN Painter, Printmaker (1906-1978)
GELMAN, MILTON Collector (1914-1991)
GELOZADLER, HENRY Curator, Historian (1935-1994)
GELTMAN, LILY Collage Artist, Painter (1903-2001)
GENTRY, HERBERT Painter, Graphic Artist (1919-2003)
GEPPONI, ANGELO Painter, Educator (1911-2001)
GERACI, LUCIAN ARTHUR Painter, Dealer (1923-2005)
GERARD, PAULA (RENISON) Painter, Draftsman (1907-1991)
GERARDIA, HELEN Painter, Printmaker
GERENDAY, LACI ANTHONY DE Sculptor (1911-)
GERSHOY, EUGENE Sculptor, Painter (1901-1983)
GERTH, RUTH Illustrator (-1952)
GERZSO, GUNTHER Painter, Graphic Artist (1915-2000)
GETTY, J PAUL Collector, Writer (1892-1976)
GFISSDUHLER, ARNOLD Sculptor (1897-1993)
GIAMBRUNI, TIO Sculptor (1925-1971)
GIBBERED, ERIC WATERS Painter (1897-1972)
GIBSON, ROLAND Collector, Curator (1902-)
GIBSON, SYBIL (SYBIL GIBSON DEYARMON) Painter (1908-1995)
GIESCHEN, MARTIN JOHN Educator, Painter (1918-1991)
GIKOW, RUTH (RUTH GIKOW LEVINE) Painter, Printmaker (1913-1982)
GILBERT, ARNOLD MARTIN Collector, Photographer (1921-)
GILBERT, CLYDE LINGLE Painter (1898-1986)
GILBERT, LIONEL Painter, Instructor (1912-2005)
GILCHRIST, AGNES ADDISON Art & Architectural Historian (1907-1976)
GILES, NEWELL WALTON, JR Painter (1928-2004)
GILKEY, GORDON WAVERLY Curator, Educator (1912-2000)
GILKEY, RICHARD CHARLES Painter, Sculptor (1925-1997)
GILL, FREDERICK JAMES Painter, Instructor (1906-1974)
GILLESPIE, GREGORY JOSEPH Painter (1936-2000)
GILLIES, MARY ANN Artist
GILMARTIN, F THOMAS Administrator, Consultant (1940-)
GILPIN, LAURA Photographer, Writer (1891-1979)
GILRLN, THEODORE H Painter (-1967)
GIUSTI, GEORGE Designer, Sculptor (- 1990)
GLAMAN, EUGENIE FISH Etcher (1872-1956)
GLARNER, FRITZ Painter (1899-1972)
GLASGOW, LUKMAN Ceramist Administrator (1935-1988)
GLASHAUSSER, SUELLEN Sculptor (1945-2000)
GLASSMAN, RONALD Painter, Printmaker (1940-2005)
GLEASON, JOE DUNCAN Painter (1879-1951)
GLICKMAN, MAURICE Sculptor, Writer (1906-)
GLINES, ELLEN (MRS WALTER A) Painter (-1951)
GLINSKKY, VINCENT Sculptor, Educator (1895-1975)
GLOVSKY, ALAN Sculptor, Environmental Artist (1951-2000)
GLUHMAN, JOSEPH WALTER Historian, Graphic Artist (1934-2002)
GLYDE, HENRY GEORGE Painter, Educator (1906-1998)
GODDARD, VIVIAN Painter
GODWIN, FRANCES GRAY Historian (1908-1979)
GOETZ, EDITH JEAN Painter, Instructor (1918-1986)
GOETZ, OSWALD H Lecturer (1896-1960)
GOETZ, RICHARD VERNON Painter, Instructor (1915-1991)
GOLDBERG, CHAIM Painter, Sculptor (1917-2004)
GOLDBERG, ELIAS Painter (1887-1975)
GOLDBERG, NORMAN LEWIS Writer, Lecturer (1906-1982)
GOLDIN, AMY Art Critic (1926-1978)
GOLDOWSKY NOAH Art Dealer (1909-)
GOLDSMITH, LAWRENCE CHARLES Painter, Instructor (1916-2004)
GOLDSMITH, MORTON RALPH Collector, Patron (1882-1971)
GOLDSTEIN, MILTON Printmaker, Painter (1914-2004)
GOLDWATER, ROBERT Art Historian (1907-1973)
GOLINKIN, JOSEPH WEBSTER Painter, Printmaker (1896-1977)
GOLLIN, JOSHUA A Collector, Patron (1905-)
GOLUB, LEON Painter (1922-2004)
GOLUBIC, THEODORE Sculptor, Designer (1928-1998)
GOMEZ-SICRE, JOSE Administrator, Critic (1916-1991)
GONZALEZ, JUAN J Painter (1945-1993)
GONZALEZ-TORRES FELIX Painter (1957-1996)
GOOCH, DONALD BURNETTE Painter (1907-1985)
GOODELMAN, AARON J Sculptor (1891-1978)
GOODMAN, BERTRAM Painter (1904-1988)
GOODMAN, FLORENCE JEANNE Writer, Collector (1922-2006)
GOODNOW, FRANK A Painter, Educator (1923-2004)
GOODRICH, SUSAN Painter (1933-2002)
GOOSSEN, EUGENE COONS Writer, Educator (1920-1997)
GORDER, CLAYTON J Painter, Educator (1936-1987)
GORDON, DONALD EDWARD Historian, Educator (1931-)
GORDON, JOHN Administrator, Historian (1912-1978)
GORDON, MAXWELL Painter (1910-1982)

GORDON, VIOLET Illustrator, Writer (1907-2005)
GORDY, ROBERT P Painter, Printmaker (1933-1986)
GORHAM SIDNEY Painter (1870-1947)
GORMAN, WILLIAM D Painter, Graphic Artist (1925-2005)
GORSLINE, DOUGLAS WARNER Painter, Illustrator (1913-1985)
GOSS, JOHN Illustrator (1886-)
GOTO, JOSEPH Sculptor (1920-1994)
GOTTLIEB, ADOLPH Painter (1903-1974)
GOTTLIEB, CARLA Educator, Art Historian (1912-2004)
GOTTSCHALK, MAX JULES Designer, Instructor (1909-2005)
GOUMA-PETERSON Educator, Historian (1933-2001)
GOVAN, FRANCIS HAWKS
GOVAN, FRANCIS HAWKS Educator, Painter (1916-)
GOWANS, ALAN, Historian, Lecturer (1923-2001)
GRABACH, JOHN R Painter, Instructor (1880-1981)
GRAHAM, JOHN D Painter (1881-1961)
GRAHAM, RICHARD MARTSON Sculptor, Educator (1939-)
GRAHAM, WALTER Painter, Sculptor (1903-2000)
GRAMATKY, HARDIE Painter, Writer (1907-1979)
GRANLUND, PAUL THEODORE Sculptor (1925-2003)
GRANT, ART Conceptual Artist, Educator (1927-)
GRANT, GORDON HOPE Etcher (1875-1962)
GRANT, J JEFFREY Painter (1883-1960)
GRAVES, BRADFORD Sculptor, Educator (1939-1998)
GRAVES, JOHN W Collector (-1975)
GRAVES, MAITLAND Writer, Painter (1902-)
GRAVES, MORRIS Painter (1910-2001)
GRAY, CLEVE Painter, Sculptor (1918-2004)
GRAY, DON Painter, Critic (1935-2005)
GRAY, HAROLD Cartoonist (1894-1968)
GRAY, JABEZ Painter (-1950)
GRAY, ROBERT HUGH Painter, Educator (1931-1999)
GRAY, WELLINGTON BURBANK Educator, Designer (1919-1977)
GRAYSON, CLIFFORD PREVOST Painter (1857-1951)
GRAZIANI, SANTE Painter, Educator (1920-2005)
GREACEN, EDMUND Painter (1877-1949)
GREATHOUSE, WALSER S Museum Director (-1966)
GRECO, ROBERT Painter (-1965)
GREEN, BERNARD Painter (1887-1951)
GREENBAUM, DOROTHEA SCHWARCZ Sculptor, Graphic Artist (1913-1986)
GREENBERG, ELENOR SIMINOW Painter, Printmaker (1914-2002)
GREENE, BALCOMB Painter (1904-1990)
GREENE, ELMER WESTLEY, JR Painter (1907-1964)
GREENE, ETHEL MAUD Painter (1912-)
GREENE, GERTRUDE (MRS BALCOMB GREENE) Painter (1904-1956)
GREENE, J BARRY Painter (1895-1966)
GREENE, STEPHEN Painter (1918-1999)
GREENE, VERNON VAN ATTA Cartoonist (-1965)
GREENE-MERCIER, MARIE ZOE Sculptor, Draftsman (1911-2001)
GREENES, RHODA Sculptor (1926-1979)
GREEN-FIELD, ALBERT Art Publicist
GREENLEAF, ESTHER (HARGRAVE) Painter, Printmaker (1905-1981)
GREENLEAF, RAY Illustrator (-1950)
GREENSTEIN, ILISE Painter, Conceptual Artist (1928-)
GREENWOOD, MARION Painter, Lithographer (1909-1970)
GREGG, RICHARD NELSON Museum Director (1926-1986)
GREGORY, (ELEANOR) ANNE Educator, Calligrapher (-1997)
GREGORY, ANGELA Sculptor, Educator (1903-1990)
GREGORY, JOHN Sculptor (1879-1951)
GREGORY, WAYLANDE Sculptor, Designer (1905-1971)
GREISSLE HERMANN A Printmaker, Painter (1925-1991)
GRENELL, BARBARA Tapestry Artist, Weaver (1944-2001)
GRIER, BARRY DOBSON MILLER Museum Director (1914-1972)
GRIESSLER, FRANZ ANTON Painter (1897-1974)
GRIFFIN, RACHAEL S Art Administrator, Writer (-1983)
GRIFFITH, LOUIS OSCAR Painter (1875-1956)
GRIGAUT, PAUL L Museum Curator (-1969)
GRIGGS, MAITLAND LEE Collector (1902-1989)
GRIGOR, MARGARET CHRISTIAN Sculptor (1912-1981)
GRIMES, FRANCES T Sculptor (1869-1963)
GRIMM, LUCILLE DAVIS Painter (1929-2002)
GRINAGER, ALEXANDER Painter (1865-1949)
GRODENSKY SAMUEL Painter (1894-1974)
GROOVE, MARGARET JOAN Administrator, Educator (1935-)
GROPPER, WILLIAM Painter, Lithographer (1897-1977)
GROSHANS, WERNER Painter (1913-1986)
GROSS, CHAIM SCULPTOR Instructor (1904-1991)
GROSS, ESTELLE SHANE Dealer (-1992)
GROSSMAN, MORTON Painter (1926-1998)
GROSZ, GEORGE Painter (1893-1959)
GROTELL, MAIJA Ceramist, Educator (1899-1973)
GROTENRATH, RUTH Painter, Printmaker (1912-1985)
GROTH, BRUNO Sculptor (1905-1991)
GROVES, HANNAH CUTIER Painter, Etcher (1868-1952)
GRUBAR, FRANCIS STANLEY Historian, Lecturer (1924-1991)
GRUBB, PAT PINCOMBE Painter, Writer (1922-1977)
GRUBERT, CARL ALFRED Cartoonist (1911-1979)
GRUENTHER, SUE CORY (MRS RUDOLPH) Painter (-1948)
GRUERRERO, JOSE Painter, Printmaker (1914-)
GRUGER, FREDERICK R Illustrator (1871-1953)
GRUMMANN, PAUL H Museum Director (-1950)
GRUNDY, J(OHN OWEN) Patron, Writer (1911-1985)
GRUPPE, EMIL ALBERT Painter (1896-1978)
GRUPPE, KARL HEINRICH Sculptor (1893-1982)
GRUSHKIN, PHILIP Designer, Calligrapher (1911-1998)
GUADAGNOLI, NELLO T Dealer (1929-2005)
GUENTHER, PETER W Historian, Educator (1920-2005)
GUGGENHEIM, HARRY FRANK Collector, Publisher, Writer (1890-1971)
GUGGENHEIM, PEGGY Collector, Patron (1898-1979)
GUGGENHEIMER RICHARD HENRY Painter, Writer (1906-1977)
GUGLIELMI, LOUIS O Painter (1906-1956)
GUINZBURG, FREDERICK Sculptor (1897-1978)
GUMBERTS, WILLIAM A Collector, Patron (1912-)
GUNDLACH, HELEN FUCHS Painter (1892-1959)
GUSSOW, ALAN Painter, Sculptor (1931-1997)
GUSTAVSON, LELAND Illustrator (-1966)
GUSTON, PHILIP Painter (1913-1980)
GUTMANN, JOHN Educator, Photographer (1905-1998)
GUTMANN, JOSEPH Historian, Lecturer (1923-2004)
GUY, JAMES M Painter, Educator (1910-1983)
GUZMAN-FORBES, ROBERT Painter, Illustrator (1929-2004)
GWATHMEY ROBERT Painter (1903- 1988)
HADER, ELMER (STANLEY) Illustrator, Writer (1889-1973)
HADLEY, ROLLIN VAN NOSTRAND Museum Director (1927-1992)
HADLOCK, WENDELL STANWOOD Museum Director (1911-1978)
HAERER, CAROL Painter (1933-2002)
HAGAN, FREDERICK Printmaker, Painter (1918-2003)
HAGERSTRAND, MARTIN ALLAN Museum Director, Administrator (1911-1999)
HAGGIN, BEN ALL Painter, Designer (1882-1951)
HAGUE, RAOUL Sculptor (1905-1993)
HAHN, EMANUEL OTTO Sculptor (1911-1957)
HAHN, PATIGIAN Sculptor (1876-1950)
HAINES, RICHARD Painter, Muralist (1906-1984)
HALE, LILLIAN WESTCOTT Painter (1881-1963)
HALE, ROBERT BEVERLY Administrator, Instructor (1901-)
HALEY, JOHN CHARLES Painter, Sculptor (1905-1991)
HALEY, ROBERT D Painter (1893-1959)
HALFF, ROBERT H Collector (1908-2004)
HALL, REX EARL Painter, Educator (1924-2004)
HALSEY, WILLIAM MELTON Painter, Sculptor (1915-2002)
HALSMAN, PHILIPPE Photographer (1906-1979)
HAMBLETT, THEORA Painter, Illustrator (1895-)
HAMES. CARL MARTIN Dealer (1938-2002)
HAMM, BETH CREEVY Painter (1885-1958)
HAMMER, ARMAND Collector, Dealer (1898-1990)
HAMMER, VICTOR KARL Painter (-1967)
HAMMOND, NATALIE HAYS Painter, Museum Director (1904-)
HAMPTON, BILL Painter (1925-1977)
HANCOCK, WALKER (KIRTLAND) Sculptor (1901-1998)
HAND, MOLLY WILLIAMS Teacher, Painter (1892-1951)
HANDFORTH, THOMAS S Lithographer (1897-1948)
HANFMANN, GEORGE M A Educator, Historian (1911-1986)
HANKS, NANCY Administrator (1927-1983)
HANLEN, JOHN (GARRETT) Painter, Instructor (1922-2003)
HANLEY, T EDWARD Collector (-1969)
HANNA, KATHERINE Museum Director (1913-1988)
HANNA, THOMAS KING Painter (-1951)
HANSEN, ARMIN CARL Painter (1886-1957)
HANSEN, ARNE RAE Art Dealer, Historian (1940-1992)
HANSON, ANNE COFFIN Historian (1921-2004)
HANSON, LAWRENCE Sculptor, Educator (1936-1992)
HANVILLE, ROBERT T Painter, Illustrator (1924-1993)
HAPKE, PAUL FREDERICK Painter, Educator (1922-1984)
HARARI, HANANIAH Painter (1912-2000)
HARBART, GERTRUDE FELTON Educator, Instructor (-1999)
HARDER, CHARLES MADRY Craftsman (1899-1951)
HARDIN, ADLAIS Sculptor (1901-1989)
HARDY, GEORGE Painter (-1959)
HARDY, HOWARD (COLLINS) Painter, Instructor (1900-1988)
HARE, DAVID Sculptor (1917-1992)

HARE, MICHAEL MEREDITH Scholar (1909-1968)
HARER, FREDERICK W Painter, Sculptor (1879-1949)
HARING, KEITH Painter (1958-1990)
HARLAN, ROMA CHRISTINE Painter (1912-2003)
HARLEY, RALPH LEROY, JR Photographer, Educator (1934-2005)
HARMON, LILY Painter, Writer (1912-1998)
HARPER, GEORGE COBURN Etcher (1887-1962)
HARPER, JOHN RUSSELL Art Historian (1914-1983)
HARRIS, BEN JORJ Illustrator (1904-1957)
HARRIS, HARVEY SHERMAN Painter, Educator (1915-1999)
HARRIS, JULLIAN HOKE Sculptor, Architect (1906-1987)
HARRIS, LUCILLE S Painter, Printmaker (1914-1984)
HARRIS, MARGIE COLEMAN Painter (1891-)
HARRISON, (WILLIAM) ALLEN Painter (1911-)
HARRITON, ABRAHAM Painter (1893-1986)
HARSANYL, CHARLES Painter (1905-1973)
HART MORGAN DRAKE Painter (1899-)
HART, AGNES Painter, Instructor (-1979)
HART, JOHN FRANCIS Cartoonist, Engraver (1868-)
HARTGEN, VINCENT ANDREW Educator, Painter (1914-2002)
HARTL, LEON Painter (1889-)
HARTLEY, W DOUGLAS Sculptor, Educator (1921-2006)
HARTMAN, BERTRAM Painter (1882-)
HARTMANN, GEORGE THEO Painter, Etcher (1894-1976)
HARTT, FREDERICK Historian, Educator (1914-1991)
HARTWELL, GEORGE KENNETH Lithographer (1891-1949)
HARVEY JAMES V Painter (-1965)
HARVEY, ROBERT MARTIN Painter (1924-2004)
HASELTINE MAURY (MARGARET WILSON) Painter, Consultant (1925-1998)
HASELTINE, HERBERT Sculptor (1877-1962)
HASKELL, WILLIAM H Educator (1875-1951)
HASKINS, JOHN FRANKLIN Historian, Educator (1919-1991)
HASTIE, REID Educator, Writer (1916-1997)
HASWELL, ERNEST BRUCE Sculptor (1889-1965)
HATCH EMILY NICHOLS Painter (1871-1959)
HATCH, JOHN W Painter, Lecturer (1919-1998)
HATHAWAY, CALVIN S Curator (-1974)
HATHAWAY, LOVERING Painter (1898-1949)
HATLO, JAMES Cartoonist (1898-1963)
HAUG, DONALD RAYMOND Painter (1925-1999)
HAUSCHKA, CAROL SPAETH Painter (1883-1948)
HAUSMANN, MARIANNE PISKO Painter
HAVENS, JAMES DEXTER Graphic Artist (1900-1960)
HAVENS, MURRY P Designer
HAWES, LOUIS Historian (1931-)
HAWLEY, MARARET FOOTE Portrait Painter (1880-1963)
HAWORTH, B COQUILL Painter (1904-)
HAWORTH, PETER Painter, Stained Glass Artist (1889-)
HAWTHORNE, JACK GARDNER Educator, Painter (1921-2003)
HAYDEN, PALMER C Painter (1893-1973)
HAYES, WILLIAM CHRISTOPHER Museum Curator (-1963)
HAYNES, GEORGE EDWARD Painter, Illustrator (1910-)
HAYNIE, HUGH Cartoonist (1927-1999)
HAYWARD, PETER Painter, Sculptor (1905-1994)
HAZELL, FRANK Painter (1883-)
HEALY, ARTHUR K D Painter, Lecturer (1902-1978)
HEBER, CARL A Sculptor (1885-1956)
HEBERLING, GLEN AUSTIN Painter, Illustrator (1915-2002)
HECHT, ZOLTAN Painter (1890-1968)
HECKSCHER, WILLIAM SEBASTIAN Historian, Painter (1904-1999)
HEDRICK, WALLY BILL Painter, Sculptor (1928-2003)
HEERAMANECK, NASIL M Collector, Patron, Art Dealer (1902-1971)
HEINTZELMAN, ARTHUR W Etcher (1890-1965)
HELCK, PETER Painter, Printmaker (1893-1988)
HELD, ALMA M Painter (-1988)
HELD, JOHN, JR Cartoonist (1889-1958)
HELD, JULIUS S Educator, Writer (1905-2002)
HELD, PHILIP Photographer, Painter (1920-1999)
HELIKER, JOHN EDWARD Painter, Educator (1909-2000)
HELLER, MAXWELL Painter (1881-1963)
HELM, JOHN F JR Educator, Painter (1900-1972)
HELMAN, PHOEBE Sculptor, Painter (1929-1994)
HELWIG, ARTHUR LOUIS Painter, Instructor (1899-1976)
HEMPHILL, HERBERT WAIDE JR Curator, Lecturer (1929-1998)
HENDERSON, LESTER KLERSTEAD Photographer (1906-)
HENISCH, HEINZ K Historian, Photographer (1922-2006)
HENNING, EDWARD BURK Curator, Historian (1922-1993)
HENRICKSEN, RALF CHRISTIAN Educator, Painter (1907-1975)
HENRY, GERRIT VAN KEUREN Critic (1950-2003)
HERBERT, MARIAN Painter (1899-1960)
HERING, HARRY Painter (1887-1967)
HERING, HENRY Sculptor (1874-1949)
HERMAN, VIC Painter, Writer (-1999)
HERPST, MARTHA JANE Painter (1911-)
HERRINGTON, ARTHUR W Collector, Patron (1891-1970)
HERRINGTON, NELL RAY Collector, Patron
HERSHFIELD, LEO Illustrator (1904-1979)
HERSTAND, ARNOLD Director
HERTER, ALBERT Painter (1871-1950)
HERVES, MADELINE Painter (-1969)
HERZBRUN, HELENE McKINSEY Painter, Educator (-1984)
HESKETH Sculptor (-1987)
HESS, THOMAS B Critic, Writer (1920-1978)
HESSE, EVA Sculptor (1936-1972)
HEUERMANN, MAGDA Painter (1868-)
HEWITT, FRANCIS RAY Painter, Educator (1936-1992)
HEWITT, THURMAN H Painter, Designer (1919-2001)
HEYL, BERNARD CHAPMAN Scholar (1905-1966)
HIBBARD, ALDRO THOMPSON Painter (1886-1972)
HIBBARD, HOWARD Historian, Writer (1928-1984)
HICKEN, PHILIP BURNHAM Painter, Printmaker (1910-1985)
HIGGINS, DICK Painter, Printmaker (1938-1998)
HIGGINS, EUGENE Painter (1875-1958)
HIGGINS, VICTOR Painter (1884-1949)
HILDERBRANDT, HOWARD LOGAN Painter (1874-1958)
HILER, HILAIRE Painter (1898-1966)
HILL, CLINTON J Painter, Sculptor (1922-2003)
HILL, DOROTHY KENT Museum Curator (1907-)
HILL, GEORGE SNOW Painter (1898-1969)
HILL, HAROLD WAYNE Painter, Sculptor (1933-1989)
HILL, HOMER Illustrator
HILL, (JAMES) JEROME I Painter (1905-)
HILL, JOHN HENRY Painter (1839-1922)
HILL, JOHN WILLIAM Painter (1812-1879)
HILL, POLLY KNIPP Etcher, Painter (1900-1990)
HILLIGOSS, MARTHA M Librarian (1928-I987)
HILLS, LAURA COOMBS Painter (1859-1952)
HINES, JOHN M Painter (-1982)
HINKLE, CLARENCE Painter (1890-1960)
HINTON, CHARLES LOUIS Painter (1869-1950)
HIOS, THEO Painter, Graphic Artist (1910-1999)
HIRSCH, JOSEPH Painter (1910-1981)
HIRSCH, STEFAN Educator (1899-1964)
HIRSCHFELD, ALBERT Graphic Artist (1903-2003)
HIRSCHHORN, JOSEPH H Collector (1889-1981)
HITCHCOCK, HENRY RUSSELL Historian, Critic (1903-1986)
HLLLMAN, ALEX L Collector (1900-1968)
HNIZDOVSKY, JACQUES Painter, Printmaker (1915-1985)
HOBSON, KATHERINE THAYER Sculptor (1889-1992)
HOCKADAY, HUGH Painter (1892-1968)
HOEHN, HARRY Painter, Printmaker (1819-1974)
HOFFMAN, ARNOLD JR Painter, Director (1915-1991)
HOFFMAN, ARNOLD Painter (-1966)
HOFFMAN, EDWARD FENNO III Sculptor (1916-1991)
HOFFMAN, HARRY Z Painter, Cartoonist (1908-1990)
HOFFMAN, LARRY GENE Museum Director, Consultant (1933-1991)
HOFFMAN, MALVINA Sculptor (1887-1966)
HOFFMAN, RICHARD PETER Painter, Photographer (1911-1997)
HOFMANN, HANS Painter, Educator (1880-1961)
HOFSTED, JOLYON GENE Sculptor, Educator (-2004)
HOIE, HELEN HUNT Painter, Collage Artist (-2000)
HOKANSON, HANS Sculptor, Collage Artist (1925-1997)
HOLBROOK, HOLLIS HOWARD Muralist, Painter (1909-1984)
HOLCOMB, ALICE (MCCAFFERY) Painter (1906 1977)
HOLCOMBE, BLANCHE KEATON Painter, Educator (1912-)
HOLCOMBE, R GORDON, JR Collector, Patron (1913-2005)
HOLDEN, RUTH EGRI Painter (1911-1996)
HOLGATE, EDWIN HEADLEY Painter (1882-1977)
HOLLAND, JANICE Illustrator (1913-1962)
HOLLISTER, PAUL Writer, Painter (1918-2004)
HOLLOWAY, H MAXSON Museum Director (-1966)
HOLMGREN, R JOHN Illustrator (1997-1963)
HOLT, CHARLOTTE SINCLAIR Medical Illustrator, Sculptor (1914-1990)
HOLTY, CARL ROBERT Painter, Writer (1900-1973)
HOMAR, LORENZO Painter, Printmaker (1913-2004)
HONIG, MERVIN Painter, Painting Conservator (1920-1990)
HOOD, DORTHY Painter (1919-2000)
HOOD, ETHEL Painter, Sculptor (1908-1982)
HOOD, GEORGE W Painter (1869-1949)
HOOK FRANCES A Painter (1912-1981)
HOOVER, MARIE LOUISE (ROCHON) Artist (1895-1976)

HOPKINS, KENDAL COLES Painter (1909-1991)
HOPKINS, PETER Painter, Writer (1911-1999)
HOPKINSON, CHARLES Painter (1869-1962)
HOPPER CHARLES Painter (1882-1967)
HOPPER MARIANNE SEWARD (1904-)
HOPPER, JON Painter (-1968)
HOPPES, LOWELL E Cartoonist (1913-2002)
HOPTNER, RICHARD Sculptor (1921-2002)
HORCH, LOUIS L Collector (1899-1979)
HORD, DONAL Sculptor (1902-1966)
HORNE, (ARTHUR EDWARD) CLEEVE Painter, Sculptor (1912-)
HORNUNG, CLARENCE PEARSON Designer, Writer (1899-1997)
HORNUNG, GERTRUDE SEYMOUR Lecturer, Collector (1908-2000)
HORNYANSKY NICHOLAS Etcher (1896-1965)
HOROSHAK, RICHARD J Art Dealer, Consultant (1940-)
HOROWITZ, BENJAMIN Administrator, Art Dealer (1912-2004)
HORWITT, WILL Sculptor (1934-1995)
HOUGHTON, ARTHUR A JR Administrator (1906-1990)
HOUSE JAMES CHARLES, JR Sculptor (1902-)
HOUSER, ALLAN Sculptor, Painter (1914-1994)
HOUSTON, JAMES A Designer, Painter (1921-2005)
HOVANNES, JOHN Painter (1904-1973)
HOVEY, WALTER READ Historian, Educator (1949-1992)
HOWARD, EDWARD Sculptor (1888-1956)
HOWARD, ROBERT A Sculptor, Educator (1922-1999)
HOWARD, ROBERT BOARDMAN Sculptor (1896-1983)
HOWE, KATHERINE L MALLET Painter (-1957)
HOWE, OSCAR Painter, Educator (1915-1983)
HOWELL HANNAH JOHNSON Librarian (1905-1988)
HOWITT, JOHN NEWTON Illustrator (1885-1958)
HOWLAND EDITH Sculptor (-1949)
HOWLAND GARTH Educator, Painter (1897-1950)
HOYT, FRANCES WESTON Painter (1908-2005)
HOYT, WHITNEY F Painter Collector (1910-1990)
HUBBARD, CHARLES D Painter (1876-1950)
HUBBELL, HENRY SALEM Painter (1870-1949)
HUBENTHAL, KARL SAMUEL Cartoonist, Painter (1917-1998)
HUBLER, JULIUS Printmaker, Painter (1919-2003)
HUCK, ROBERTO Educator (1923-1960)
HUDSON, JACQUELINE Painter, Graphic Artist (-2001)
HUEBLER, DOUGLAS Conceptual Artist (1924-1997)
HUEY, FLORENCE GREENE Painter (1872-1960)
HULL, MARIE (ATKINSON) Painter (-1980)
HULMER, ERIC CLAUS Curator, Conservator (1915-1988)
HULTBERG, JOHN P Painter, Printmaker (1922-2005)
HUMES, RALPH H Sculptor (1902-1981)
HUMPHROY JACK WELDON Painter (-1967)
HUNT, LYNN Fainter (1878-1960)
HUNT, WAYNE WOLF ROBE (KEWA-TSE-SHE) Silversmith, Painter (1905-1977)
HUNTER, FRANCIS TIPTON Illustrator (1896-)
HUNTER, MEL Printmaker, Painter (1927-2004)
HUNTINGTON, A MONTOOMERY Designer (-1967)
HUNTINGTON, ANNA V HYATT Sculptor (1876-1973)
HUNTINGTON, MARGARET WENDELL Painter (1867-1951)
HUNTLEY, DAVID C Painter, Administrator (1930-2004)
HUNTLEY, VICTORIA HUTSON Lithographer (1900-1970)
HUPY, ART Curator, Photographer (1924-2003)
HURD, PETER Painter, Writer (1904-)
HURLEY, EDWARD TIMOTHY Etcher, Painter (1869-1950)
HURST, RALPH N Sculptor, Educator (1918-2003)
HUTCHINSON, MAX Art Dealer, Gallery Director (1925-1999)
HUTCHISON, MARY ELIZABETH Painter (1904-1970)
HUTINGTON JOHN W Collector, Patron (1910-1976)
HUTTON, DOROTHY WACKERMAN Designer, Printmaker (1899-2001)
HUTTON, HUGH MCMILLEN Cartoonist (1897-1976)
HUTTON, WILLIAM Museum Curator (1926-2000)
IACURTO, FRANCESCO Painter (1908-2001)
IHLE, JOHN LIVINGSTON Printmaker, Educator (1925-2002)
ILIGAN, RALPH W Painter (1994-1960)
INGLE, TOM Painter, Lecturer (1920-1973)
INMAN, PAULINE WINCHESTER Printmaker, Illustrator (1904-1990)
INVERARITY, ROBERT BRUCE Museum Director, Painter (1908-1999)
IORIO, ADRIAN J Illustrator (1879-1957)
IPSEN ERNEST L Portrait Painter (1869-1950)
IREDELL, RUSSELL Painter (1889-1959)
IRVIN, REA Painter (1881-1972)
IRVING, ANNA DUER Painter (1873-1957)
ISAACS, BETTY LEWIS Sculptor (1894-1971)
ISAACS, CAROLE SCHAEFER Collector, Patron (1931-1980)
ISKOWITZ, GERSHON Painter (1921-1988)
ISRAEL, MARVIN Designer, Painter (1924-1985)
ISROFF, LOLA K Painter (-2000)
ITTLESON HENRY, JR Collector (1900-1973)
IVES, NORMAN S Painter, Printmaker, Graphic Designer (1924-1978)
IVINS, WILLIAM M, JR Curator (1881-1961)
IZUMI, KIYOSHI Architect, Educator (1921-1996)
JACK, RICHARD Painter (-1952)
JACKSON, A B Educator, Painter (1925-1981)
JACKSON, ALEXANDER YOUNG Painter (1882-1974)
JACKSON, ANN Painter (-1956)
JACKSON, ANNIE HURLBURT Painter (1877-)
JACKSON, BILLY MORROW Painter, Educator (1926-2006)
JACKSON, HAZEL BRILL Sculptor (-1991)
JACKSON, HENRY ALDEN Textile Designer (-1952)
JACKSON, JOHN EDWIN Painter, Designer (1875-)
JACKSON, LESLEY Painter (1866-1958)
JACKSON, MARTHA Gallery Director (-1969)
JACOBS, MICHEL Painter (1877-1951)
JACOBSSON, STEN WILHELM JOHN Painter, Sculptor (1899-1983)
JAFFE, WILLIAM B Collector (-1972)
JANELSINS, VERONICA Painter, Illustrator (1910-2001)
JANICKI, HAZEL (MRS WILLIAM SCHOCK) Painter, Instructor (1918-1976)
JANIS, SIDNEY Dealer, Writer (1896-1989)
JANKO, MAY Printmaker, Painter (1926-2003)
JANSON, HORST WOLDEMAR Art Historian (1913-1982)
JANSSEN, HANS Educator, Museum Curator
JARMAN, WALTON MAXEY Collector (1904-1980)
JARRELL, RANDALL Critic, Poet (1914-1965)
JAUSS, ANNE MARIE Painter, Illustrator (1907-)
JECT-KEY, DAVID Painter
JEFFE, HULDAH C Painter (1906-2001)
JEFFERSON, JACK ANDREW Painter, Printmaker (1920-2000)
JEFFERYS, CHARLES WILLIAM Illustrator (1869-1951)
JELINEK, HANS Printmaker, Educator (-1992)
JELLICO, JOHN ANTHONY Director, Painter (1914-2004)
JENKINS, DURPIS Cartoonist (1897-1966)
JENKINS, PAUL RIPLEY Sculptor, Painter (1904-1974)
JENNEWEIN, C PAUL Sculptor (1890-1978)
JENSEN, ALFRED Painter (1903-1991)
JENSEN, CECIL LEON Cartoonist (1902-1976)
JENSEN, JOHN EDWARD Painter, Designer (1921-1982)
JENSEN, MARIT Painter, Sculptor
JETER, RANDY JOE Drawer, Educator (1937-1997)
JEWELI,, WILLIAM M Educator, Painter (1905-1990)
JOHANSEN, JOHN C Portrait Painter (1876-1964)
JOHN, GRACE SPAULDING Painter Writer (1890-1972)
JOHNSON JAMES RALPH Painter, Writer (1922-)
JOHNSON, AVERY FISCHER Painter, Illustrator (1906-1990)
JOHNSON, BEN Painter (1902-1967)
JOHNSON, BRUCE Museum Director (1949-1976)
JOHNSON, CONTENT Portrait Painter (-1949)
JOHNSON, CROCKOT Painter, Writer (1906-1976)
JOHNSON, DORRIS MILLER Painter (1909-2001)
JOHNSON, ELLEN HULDA Historian, Critic (1910-1992)
JOHNSON, ERNEST (MELVIN) Painter, Inatmetor (1924-1996)
JOHNSON, FRIDOLE LESTER Designer, Writer (1905-1988)
JOHNSON, HERBERT FISK Patron (1901-1980)
JOHNSON, IVAN EARL Educator, Craftsman (1911-2003)
JOHNSON, JEANNE PAYNE (MRS LOUIS C) Painter (1887-1958)
JOHNSON, KATHERINE KING Administrator, Painter (1906-)
JOHNSON, MALVIN GRAY Painter (1896-1934)
JOHNSON, MARIAN WILLARD Dealer (1904-)
JOHNSON, RAY Painter (1927-1995)
JOHNSON, ROBERT JAY Dealer, Collector (1951-1990)
JOHNSON, SARGENT Sculptor (1888-1967)
JOHNSON, UNA E Curator, Writer (-1997)
JOHNSTON, HELEN HEAD Book Dealer
JOHNSTON, ROBERT HAROLD Administrator, Craftsman (1928-2005)
JOLLEY, GERALDINE FI(RIORRY) Painter, Sculptor (1910-)
JONES, ALBERTUS EUGENE Painter (1982-1951)
JONES, DEXTER CHARLES WEATHERBEE Sculptor, Designer (1926-)
JONES, HENRY WANTON Painter, Sculptor (1925-2003)
JONES, JACOBINE Sculptor
JONES, JOSEPH JOHN (JOE) Painter (1909-1963)
JONES, LOIS MAILOU (MRS V PIERRE-NOEL) Painter, Designer (1905-1998)
JONES, LOUIS C Museum Director (1908-1990)
JONES, MURRAY Painter
JONSON, JON M Sculptor (1893-1947)
JONSON, RAYMOND Painter, Gallery Director (1891-1982)
JORDAN, BARBARA SCHWINN Painter (1907-2005)

JORDAN, LENA E Painter
JORGENSEN, SANDRA Painter, Educator (1934-1999)
JORN, ASGER Painter, Writer (1904-1973)
JORNS, BYRON CHARLES Painter (1989-1958)
JOSIMOVICH, GEORGE Painter Designer (1894-)
JOSSET, RAOUL Sculptor (1900-1951)
JOVINE, MARCEL Medalist, Designer (1921-2003)
JUDD, DONALD CLARENCE Sculptor, Architect (1928-1994)
JUDSON ALICE Painter (-1948)
JULES, MERVIN M Painter, Educator (1912-1994)
JUNGWIRTH, LEONARD D Sculptor (1903-1964)
JUNKIN, MARION MONTAGUE Painter, Educator (1905-1977)
JUOSON, SYLVIA SHAW Sculptor (1897-1979)
JURECKA, CYRIL Educator (1884-)
JUSTUS, ROY BRAXTON Cartoonist (1901-1983)
KACERE, JOHN C Painter (1920-1999)
KACHADOORIAN, ZUBEL Painter, Educator (1924-2002)
KACHINSKY, ALEXANDER Painter (1888-1958)
KACHORGIS, GEORGE JOSEPH Painter, Educator (1907-1974)
KAD, RUTH (YU-HSIN) LEE Fiber Artist, Educator (-1985)
KAEP, LOUIS JOSEPH Painter (1903-1991)
KAGY, SHEFFIELD HAROLD Painter, Printmaker (1907-1989)
KAHILL JOSEPH B Painter (1882-1957)
KAHN, A MICHAEL Painter, Designer (1917-2000)
KAHN, GARY Sculptor (1947-1974)
KAHN, PETER Painter, Graphic Designer (1921-)
KAHN, RALPH Dealer, Lecturer (1920-1987)
KAJIWARA, TAKUMA Painter (1877-1960)
KALLEM, HENRY Painter (1912-)
KALLER, ROBERT JAMESON Dealer (-1959)
KALLIR, OTTO Art Dealer, Historian (1894-1978)
KAMIHIRA, BEN Painter (1925-2004)
KAMROWSKI, GEROME Painter, Sculptor (1914-2004)
KANAGA, CONSEULO Photographer (1894-1978)
KANEMITSU, MATSUMI Painter, Lecturer (1922-1992)
KANTACK, WALTER W Industrial Artist (1889-1953)
KANTOR, MORRIS Painter (1896-1974)
KAPLAN, GEORGE Printmaker (1920-1997)
KAPLAN, JOSEPH Painter (1900-1980)
KAPPEL, PHILIP Writer, Etcher (1901-1981)
KARASZ, MARISKA Craftsman (1898-1960)
KARFIOL, BERNARD Painter (1886-1952)
KARP, LEON Painter (-1951)
KARPEL, ELI Sculptor (1916-1998)
KARPICK, JOHN Painter (1884-1960)
KARWELIS, DONALD CHARLES Painter, Instructor (1934-2003)
KASS, JACOB JAMES Painter (1910-2000)
KASTOR, HUGO Painter
KATSOULIDIS, PANAGIOTIS Graphic Artist (1933-2002)
KATZ, (ALEXANDER) RAYMOND Painter (1895-1974)
KATZ, HILDA (HULDER WEBER) Painter, Writer (1909-1997)
KATZ, JOSEPH M Collector, Patron (1903-)
KATZ, SIDNEY L Architect (1915-1978)
KATZENBACH, WILLIAM E Designer, Lecturer (1904-1975)
KATZENELLENBOGEN, ADOLF EM Educator (1901-1964)
KATZENSTEIN, IRVING Painter (1902-)
KATZFN, LILA (PELL) Sculptor, Educator (1937-1998)
KATZMAN, HERBERT Painter, Instructor (1923-2004)
KATZMANN, HERBERT Painter
KAUFMAN, ENIT Painter (1898-1961)
KAUFMANN, ROBERT Painter (1914-1959)
KAYE, GEORGE Painter, Educator (1911-2000)
KAYN, HILDE B Painter (1903-1950)
KAZ, JOYCE ZICKERMAN Painter (1936-1979)
KEALLY, FRANCIS Architect, Sculptor (1889-1978)
KEATS, EZRA JACK Illustrator, Writer (1916-1983)
KECK, CHARLES Sculptor (1875-1951)
KECK, HARDU Painter, Administrator (1940-2003)
KECK, SHELDON WAUGH Educator, Conservator (1910-1993)
KEFAUVER, NANCY Art Advisor (-1967)
KELLEHER, PATRICK JOSEPH Historian, Musicologist (1917-1985)
KELLER, DEANE Educator, Painter (1901-1992)
KELLER, HENRY G Painter, Etcher (1870-1949)
KELLOGG, MAURICE DALE Painter, Lecturer (1919-1984)
KELPE, PAUL Painter (1902-1985)
KEMPER, JOHN GARNER Painter, Graphic Artist (1909-1991)
KEMPTON, GRETA Painter (1903-1991)
KENDA, JUANITA ECHEVERRIA Painter, Writer (1923-)
KENDERDINE, AUGUSTUS FREDERICK Painter (-1947)
KENNEDY, J WILLIAM Painter (1903-)
KENNEDY, JANET ROBSON Painter, Illustrator (1902-1974)
KENT, FRANK WARD Painter (1912-1977)
KENT, JACK Illustrator (1920-1985)
KENT, NORMAN Engraver, Book Designer (1903-1972)
KENT, ROCKWELL Painter (1882-1971)
KEPES, GYORGY Painter, Educator (1906-2001)
KERKAM, EARL Painter (1890-1965)
KERR, ARTHUR Director (1926-1979)
KERR, E COE Art Dealer (1914-1973)
KESTNBAUM, GERTRUDE DANA Collector (-1982)
KETCHAM, HENRY KING (HANK) Cartoonist (1920-2001)
KEVE, FLORENCE Educator
KEYES, BERNARD M Painter (1898-1973)
KEY-OBERB, ELLEN BURKE Sculptor (1905-)
KEY-OBERB, ROLF Ceramist (1900-1959)
KEYSER, ERNEST WISE Sculptor (1876-1959)
KHOURI, ALFRED Painter (-1962)
KIAH, VIRGINIA JACKSON Painter, Museum Director (1911-2001)
KIBBEY, ILAH MARIAN Painter (1883-1958)
KIENBUSCH, WILLIAM AUSTIN Painter (1914-1979)
KIESLER, FREDERICK J Architect (1892-1966)
KIHN, WILLIAM LANGDON Painter (1898-1957)
KIJANKA, STANLEY JOSEPH Painter (1937-1981)
KIKER, EVELYN COALSON Painter, Instructor (1932-)
KILENYI, JULIO Sculptor (1886-1959)
KILGORE, AL Cartoonist (1927-1983)
KILGORE, RUPERT Educator (1910-1971)
KILHAM, WALTER H Painter, Architect (1868-1948)
KILLAM, WALT Painter, Art Dealer (1907-1979)
KILLEBREW, BETTY RACKLEY Educator (1931-2002)
KILPATRICK, ADA ARILLA Painter (-1951)
KILPATRICK, ELLEN PERKINS Painter (1877-1951)
KIMAK, GEORGE Painter (1921-1972)
KIMBALL, YEFFE Painter (1914-1978)
KIMBROUGH, SARA DODGE Painter (-1990)
KING, CLINTON BLAIR Painter, Printmaker (1901-1979)
KING, ELEANOR (ELEANOR KING HOOKHAM) Painter, Patron (1909-2003)
KING, FRANK 0 Cartoonist (1883-1969)
KING, HAMILTON Illustrator (1871-1952)
KING, MABEL DEBRA Painter (1895-1950)
KING, PAUL Painter (1867-1947)
KING, WARREN THOMAS Cartoonist (1916-1978)
KINGHAN, CHARLES ROSS Painter (1895-1984)
KINGMAN, DONG Painter, Illustrator (1911-2000)
KINGMAN, EUGENE Painter, Art Administrator (1909-1975)
KIPPENBERGER, MARTIN Painter (1953-1997)
KIRBY, KENT BRUCE Printmaker, Photographer (-2005)
KIRK, FRANK C Painter (1889-1963)
KIRKBRIDE, EARLE R Painter (1891-1968)
KIRKLAND, VANCE HALL Painter (1904-1981)
KIRKWOOO, MARY BURNETTE Painter (1904-1995)
KIRSCHENBAUM, JULES Painter, Educator (1920-2000)
KISELEWSKI, JOSEPH Sculptor (1901-1986)
KISKADDEN, ROBERT MORGAN Painter (1918-2004)
KITNER, HAROLD Educator, Painter (1921-2004)
KITZINGER, ERNST Historian (1912-2003)
KLEBE, GENE (CHARLES EUGENE) Painter, Writer (1918-)
KLEINBARDT, ERNEST Painter (1875-1962)
KLETT, WALTER CHARLES Illustrator (1897-1966)
KLEY, ALFRED JULIUS Craftsman (1895-1957)
KLINE, ALMA Sculptor
KLINE, FRANZ Painter (1910-1962)
KLINE, GEORGE T Illustrator (1874-1956)
KLINE, RONALD WAYNE Printmaker, Publisher (1949-2005)
KLINKER, ORPHA Etcher (-1964)
KLONIS, BERNARD Painter (1906-1957)
KNAPP, SADIE MAGNET Painter, Sculptor (1909-2004)
KNATHS, (OTTO) KARL Painter (1891-1971)
KNIGHT, FREDERIC CHARLES Painter (1898-1979)
KNIGHT, TACK (BENJAMIN THACKSTON) Cartoonist (1895-1976)
KNIPSCHILD, ROBERT Painter, (1927-2004)
KNOWLTON, MAUDE BRIGGS Painter (1876-1956)
KO, ANTHONY Printmaker, Educator (1934-)
KOCH, BERTHA COUCH Painter (1899-1975)
KOCH, JOHN Painter, Collector (1909-1978)
KOCH, ROBERT Historian, Writer (1918-2003)
KOCH, WILLIAM EMERY Dealer, Collector (1922-1987)
KOENIG, CATHERINE CATANZARO Painter (1921-2004)
KOERNER, HENRY Painter, Lecturer (1915-1991)
KOGA, MARY Photographer (1920-)
KOGELNIK, KIKI Painter, Sculptor (1935-1997)
KOGER, IRA MCKISSICK Collector, Patron (1912-2004)

KOHLER, ROSE Sculptor, Painter (1873-1947)
KOHLHEPP, DOROTHY IRENE Painter (-1964)
KOHLHEPP, NORMAN Painter, Conservator (-1986)
KOHLMEYER, IDA (R) Painter, Sculptor (1912-1997)
KOHN, GABRIEL Sculptor (1910-1975)
KOHN, MISCH Painter, Printmaker (1916-2003)
KOHN, WILLIAM ROTH Painter, Educator (1931-2004)
KOLDE, FREDERICK WILLIAM Painter (1870-)
KOLIN, SACHA Sculptor, Painter (1911-1975)
KOLODNER, NATHAN K Dealer (1950-)
KOMAR, MATHIAS Dealer (1909-)
KONI, NICOLAUS Sculptor, Lecturer (1911-2000)
KONRAD, ADOLF FERDINAND Painter
KOOPMAN, JOHN R Painter (1881-1949)
KOPLOWITZ, BENJAMIN (BEN KOPEL) Painter (1893-)
KOPMAN, BENJAMIN Painter (1887-1965)
KOPPE, RICHARD Painter, Educator (1916-)
KORDA, VINCENT Director, Painter
KORMENDI, EUGENE Sculptor (1889-1959)
KORN, ELIZABETH P Painter, Illustrator (1900-)
KOSA, EMIL J, JR Painter (1903-1968)
KOTIN, ALBERT Painter, Educator (1907-1980)
KOTTLER, HOWARD WILLIAM Sculptor, Educator (1930-)
KOURSAROS, HARRY G Painter (1928-1986)
KOUWENHOVEN, JOHN A Writer, Educator (1909-1990)
KOWALEK, JON W Museum Director, Lecturer (1934-)
KRAMER, JACK N Painter, Educator (1923-1984)
KRAMRISCH, STELLA Curator, Educator (1896-1993)
KRANER, FLORIAN G Painter, Educator (1908-)
KRASNER, LEE Painter (1908-1984)
KRAUSZ, LASZLO Painter (1903-1979)
KRAUTH, HARALD Painter (1923-1997)
KREINDLER, DORIS BARSKY Painter, Lithographer (1901-1974)
KRIENSKY (MORRIS E) Painter, Writer (1917-1998)
KRIES, HENRY Sculptor (-1963)
KROLL, LEON Painter, Lithographer (1884-1974)
KRONBERG, LOUIS Painter (1872-1965)
KRUSHENICK, JOHN Painter, Consultant (1927-1998)
KRUSHENICK, NICHOLAS Painter (1929-1999)
KUEKES, EDWARD D Cartoonist (1901-1987)
KUH, KATHERINE Critic, Consultant (1904-1994)
KUHLER, OTTO AUGUST Etcher, Painter (1894-1977)
KUHN, MARYLOU Educator, Painter (1923-1999)
KUHN, WALT Painter (1880-1949)
KUJUNDZIC, ZELJKO D Ceramist, Sculptor (1920-2003)
KUMM, MARGUERITE ELIZABETH Painter, Printmaker (-1992)
KUNIYOSHI, YASUO Painter (1893-1953)
KUNTZ, ROGER EDWARD Painter, Sculptor (1926-1975)
KUPFERMAN, LAWRENCE Painter, Printmaker (1909-1982)
KUPFERMAN, MURRY Painter, Sculptor (1897-2002)
KURELEK, WILLIAM Painter (1927-1977)
KURTZ, BRUCE D Historian, Curator (1943-2003)
KURZ, GERTRUDE ALICE Craftsman (-1951)
KUSHNER, DOROTHY BROWDY Painter, Printmaker (1909-2000)
KUVSHINOFF, NICOLAI Sculptor, Painter (1910-1997)
L'ENGLE, WILLIAM JOHNSON Painter (1884-1957)
LA FON, JULIA ANNA Painter, Craftsman (1919-1981)
LA HOTAN, ROBERT Painter (1927-2002)
LA MORE, CHET HARMON Painter, Sculptor (1908-1980)
LAATSCH, GARY Sculptor (1956-)
LABICHE, WALTER ANTHONY Administrator, Instructor (1924-1979)
LABRIE, ROSE Painter, Writer (1916-1986)
LAFAYE, NELL MURRAY Painter, Educator (1937-1990)
LAGATTA, JOHN Illustrator (1894-1976)
LAGER, FANNIE Sculptor, Painter, Collector (1911-2004)
LAHEY, MARGUERITE DUPREZ Rare Book Binder (1880-1958)
LAHEY, RICHARD (FRANCIS) Painter, Lecturer (1893-1979)
LAKE, FREDERIC Art Dealer
LAM, JENNETTE (BRINSMADE) Painter, Educator (1911-1985)
LAMANNA, CARMEN Art Dealer, Gallery Director (1927-1991)
LAMB, ADRIAN S Painter (-1989)
LAMMEL, ROBERT C Painter, Architect (1913-2003)
LAMONT, FRANCES K Sculptor (-1975)
LANDACRE, PAUL Engraver (1893-1963)
LANDAU, JACOB Painter, Printmaker (1917-2001)
LANDECK, ARMIN Painter, Engraver (1905-)
LANDON, EDWARD AUGUST Printmaker, Painter (1910-1984)
LANDSMAN, STANLEY Sculptor (1930-)
LANGE, DOROTHEA Photographer (1895-1965)
LANGLAIS, BERNARD Sculptor, Painter (1921-1977)
LANGSNER, JULES Art Writer (-1967)
LANGSTON, MILDRED Art Dealer, Collector (1902-1976)
LANGTON, BERENICE Sculptor (1878-1959)
LANKES, JULIUS J Engraver (1884-1960)
LAPOSKY, BEN FRANCIS Designer, Video Artist (1914-2000)
LARCADA, RICHARD KENNETH Art Dealer (1935-)
LARK, RAYMOND Draftsman, Painter (1939-2004)
LARK, SYLVIA Painter, Printmaker (1847-)
LARKIN, OLIVER Educator (1896-1970)
LARKIN, WILLIAM Painter, Printmaker (1902-1969)
LARSEN, OLE Painter, Illustrator (-1984)
LARSEN, ROBERT WESLEY Painter (1923-2002)
LASH, KENNETH Educator, Writer (1908-1985)
LASKA, DAVID Designer, Painter (1910-2003)
LASSAW, IBRAM Sculptor, Painter (1913-2003)
LASSEN, BEN Painter (-1968)
LATHROP, GERTRUDE K Sculptor (1896-1986)
LAUFMAN, SIDNEY Painter (1911-1985)
LAUGHLIN, ALICE D Painter (1895-1952)
LAUGHLIN, THOMAS Painter, Publisher (-1965)
LAUNOIS, JOHN RENE Photographer
LAURENT, JOHN LOUIS Painter, Educator (1921-2005)
LAURENT, ROBERT Sculptor, Collector (1890-1970)
LAURITZ, PAUL Painter (1899-1975)
LAUTERER, ARCH Designer (1904-)
LAVANOUX, MAURICE Art Editor (-1974)
LAVENTHOL, HANK Painter, Printmaker (1927-2001)
LAW, MARGARET Painter
LAWRENCE, HELEN HUMPHREYS Painter (1879-)
LAWRENCE, JACOB Painter, Mosaic Artist (1917-2000)
LAWRIE, LEE Sculptor (1877-1963)
LAWSON, ROBERT Illustrator (1892-1957)
LAX, DAVID Painter (1910-1990)
LAYNOR, HAROLD ARTHUR Painter (1922-1991)
LAYTON, GLORIA (MRS HARRY GEWISS) Painter (1914-)
LAZARUS, MARVIN P Photographer (1918-1992)
LAZZARI, PIETRO Sculptor, Painter (1888-1979)
LAZZELL, BLANCHE Painter (1878-1956)
LE PRINCE, GABRIELLA Ceramist (-1953)
LE ROY, HAROLD M Painter, Graphic Artist (1905-)
LEA, TOM Painter, Writer (1907-2001)
LEACH, LOUIS LAWRENCE Sculptor (1885-1957)
LEADER, GARNET ROSAMONDE Administrator, Painter (-2002)
LEAF, MUNRO Illustrator (1906-1977)
LEAKE, EUGENE W Painter (1911-2005)
LEAKE, GERALD Painter (1885-1975)
LEAR, GEORGE Engraver (1879-1956)
LEBRUN, RICO (FREDERICO) Painter (1900-1964)
LECHAY, JAMES Painter (1907-2001)
LECOQUE Painter, Writer (1891-1981)
LEDGERWOOD, ELLA RAY Painter (-1951)
LEE, AMY FREEMAN Painter, Lecturer (1914-2004)
LEE, ARTHUR Sculptor (1880-1961)
LEE, CAROLINE D Fine Art Appraiser (1934-2003)
LEE, GEORGE J Art Administrator, Photographer (1919-1976)
LEE, RENSSELAER WRIGHT Historian, Educator (1888-1984)
LEE, RUSSELL W Photographer, Educator (1903-1986)
LEECH, HILTON Painter, Instructor (1906-1969)
LEEDS, ANNETTE Painter (1916-1998)
LEES, HARRY HANSON Illustrator
LEE-SMITH, HUGHIE Painter, Instructor (1915-1999)
LEFCOURT, IRWIN Dealer (1910-2004)
LEFEBRE, JOHN Art Dealer (1905-1986)
LEFEBVRE D'ARGENCE, RENE-YVON Museum Director, Writer (1928-1997)
LEFEVRE, LAWRENCE E Painter (1904-1960)
LEFEVRE, RICHARD JOHN Painter, Illustrator (1931-)
LEFF, JULIETTE Painter, Educator (1939-1987)
LEFRANC, MARGARET (MARGARET LEFRANC SCHOONOVER Painter, Illustrator (-1998)
LEHMAN, IRVING Painter, Sculptor (1900-1983)
LEHMAN, ROBERT Collector (-1969)
LEIGHTON, A C Painter (-1965)
LEIGHTON, THOMAS CHARLES Painter, Instructor (1913-1976)
LEIN, MALCOLM EMIL Administrator, Designer (1913-2003)
LEITES, SUSAN Painter, Educator (-1996)
LEITH-ROSS, HARRY Painter (1896-)
LEITMAN, SAMUEL Painter (1908-1981)
LEM, RICHARD DOUGLAS Painter (1933-2004)
LEMIEUX, JEAN PAUL Painter (1904 -)
LENNEY, ANNIE Painter (1900-)
LENSKI, LOIS Writer, Illustrator (1893-)

LENSON, MICHAEL Painter (1903-1971)
LENTELLI, LEO Sculptor (1892-1962)
LENTINE, JOHN Painter
LEON, RALPH BERNARD Painter, Illustrator (1932-2000)
LEONID (LEONID BERMAN) Painter (1886-1976)
LERMAN, DORIS (HARRIET) Painter, Sculptor (-2001)
LERMAN, ORA Painter, Sculptor (1938-1998)
LERNER, NATHAN BERNARD Photographer, Painter (1913-1997)
LERNER, RICHARD J Art Dealer (1929-1982)
LESHER, MARIE PALMISANO Sculptor (1919-2005)
LESTER, MICHELLE Illustrator, Tapestry Artist (1942-2002)
LEVENTHAL, RUTH LEE Sculptor, Painter (1923-1989)
LEVER, R HAYLEY Painter (1876-1968)
LEVI, CARLO Painter, Writer (1902-1975)
LEVI, JULIAN E Painter, Educator (1900-1982)
LEVINE, MELINDA (ESTHER) Critic, Editor (1947-2004)
LEVIT, HERSCHEL Photographer, Historian (1912-1986)
LEVITINE, GEORGE Historian (1916-)
LEVITT, ALFRED Painter, Prehistorian (1894-2000)
LEV-LANDAU (SAMUEL DAVID LANDAU) Painter (1895-1979)
LEVY, BEATRICE S Painter (1892-1974)
LEVY, FLORENCE N Writer, Editor (1870-1947)
LEVY, JULIEN Educator, Writer (1906-1981)
LEVY, LEON Administrator, Collector (1925-2003)
LEWANDOWSKI, EDMUND D Painter, Administrator (1914-1998)
LEWIN, MILTON J Historian (1929-1979)
LEWIS, ALLEN Etcher (1873-1957)
LEWIS, DON S, SR Art Dealer, Painter (1919-2004)
LEWIS, MARTIN Printmaker (1883-1962)
LEWIS, NORMAN WILFRED Painter, Instructor (-1979)
LEWITIN, LANDES Painter (-1966)
LEYDENFROST, ALEXANDER Illustrator (1889-1961)
LEYENDECKER, JOSEPH C Painter (1874-1951)
LIAS, THOMAS R Painter
LIBBY, WILLIAM C Painter, Writer (1919-)
LIBERI, DANTE Painter, Sculptor (1919-2004)
LIBERMAN, ALEXANDER Painter, Sculptor (1912-1999)
LIBERTE, JEAN Painter (1896-1965)
LIBERTS, LUDOLFS Painter (1895-1951)
LIBHART, MYLES LAROY Administrator, Writer (1931-1990)
LICHTEN FRANCES Writer (1889-1961)
LICHTENSTEIN ROY Painter, Sculptor (1923-1987)
LICHTENSTEIN, SARA Art Historian (1929-)
LICHTY, GEORGE M Cartoonist (1905-)
LIDDLE, NANCY HYATT Museum Director, Consultant (1931-2004)
LIEBER, FRANCE Printmaker, Painter
LIEBERMAN, HARRY Painter, Sculptor (1876-1983)
LIEBES, DOROTHY (MRS RELMAN MORIN) Textile Designer (1899-1972)
LILIENFIELD, KARL Scholar (-1966)
LINDNER RICHARD Painter (1911-1978)
LINTOTT, EDWARD BARNARD Painter (1875-1951)
LIPCHITZ, JACQUES Sculptor (1891-1973)
LIPMAN, HOWARD W Collector (1905-1992)
LIPMAN-WULF, PETER Sculptor, Printmaker (1905-1993)
LIPPERT, LEON Painter
LIPPOLD, RICHARD Sculptor (1915-2002)
LISSIM, SIMON Painter, Designer (1900-1981)
LIST, VERA G Patron, Collector (1908-2002)
LISTON, MRS, FLORENCE CARY Portraitist (-1964)
LITAKER, THOMAS (FRANKLIN) Painter (1904-1976)
LITTLE, JOHN Painter, Sculptor (1907-)
LIZER, HARLAN DE LOS Painter (1910-2003)
LO MEDICO, THOMAS GAETANO Sculptor, Designer (1904-1985)
LOBER, GEORGE J Sculptor (1892-1961)
LOCHRIE, ELIZABETH DAVEY Painter, Sculptor (1890-1981)
LOCKWOOD, WARD Painter (1894-1963)
LOEHR, MAX Curator, Educator (1903-1988)
LOGAN, MAURICE Painter, Illustrator (1856-1977)
LOGGIE, HELEN A Printmaker, Painter (-1976)
LOLOMA, CHARLES Jeweler, Silversmith (1921-1991)
LOMBARD, ANNETTE Painter, Instructor (1929-2002)
LOMBARDO, JOSEF VINCENT Art Historian, Writer (1908-1992)
LONDON, ELCA Dealer (1930-1990)
LONG, C CHEE Craftsman, Goldsmith (1942-)
LONG, HUBERT Sculptor (1907-1992)
LONG, SCOTT Cartoonist (1907-1991)
LONG, STANLEY M Painter (1892-1972)
LONG, WALTER KINSCELLA Museum Director, Painter (1904-1986)
LONGACRE, LYDIA E Miniature Painter (1870-1951)
LONGACRE, MARGARET GRUEN Printmaker, Lecturer (1910-1976)
LONGAKER, JON DASU Educator, Writer (1920-2002)
LONGLEY, BERNIQUE Painter, Sculptor (1923-1999)
LONGLEY, EVELYN LOUISE Painter (1911-1959)
LONGSTAFFE, JOHN RONALD Collector (1934-)
LOONEY, ROBERT FAIN Curator, Librarian (1925-)
LOPEZ, MICHAEL JOHN Ceramist (1937-2003)
LORAN, ERLE Painter, Writer (1905-1999)
LORD, HARRIET Painter (1879-1958)
LORENZANI, ARTHUR EMANUELE Sculptor (1886-1986)
LORIMER, AMY MCCLELLAN Painter
LOSCH, TILLY Painter (1904-1975)
LOTHROP, KRISTIN CURTIS Sculptor (1930-2004)
LOTTES, JOHN WILLIAM Educator, Administrator (1934-1996)
LOUGHLIN, JOHN LEO Painter (1931-2004)
LOUIS, MORRIS Painter (1912-1963)
LOURIE, HEBERT S Painter, Educator (1923-1981)
LOVATO, CHARLES FREDERIC Printmaker, Craftsperson (1937-1988)
LOVELL, TOM Painter, Illustrator (1909-1997)
LOVET-LORSKI, BORIS Sculptor (1894-1973)
LOW, SANFORD Museum Director, Painter (1905-1964)
LOWE, EMILY Painter (-1966)
LOWELL, ORSON BYRON Illustrator (1871-1956)
LOWENFELD, VIKTOR Educator (1903-1960)
LOWENGRUND, MARGARET Painter (1905-1957)
LOWRY, BATES Historian, Museum Director (1923-2004)
LOZOWICK, LOUIS Painter, Printmaker (1892-1973)
LUCA, MARK Printmaker (1918-2005)
LUDGIN, EARLE Collector (1898-1981)
LUDLAM, EUGENIE SHONNARD Sculptor (1936-1978)
LUKE, ALEXANDRA Painter (1901-)
LUKOSIUS, RICHARD BENEDICT Painter, Craftsman (1918-)
LUNA (ANTONIO RODRIGUEZ) Painter (1910-1984)
LUNDBORG, FLORENCE Painter (-1949)
LUNDEBERG, HELEN Painter (1908-1999)
LUNDIE, EDWIN HUGH Architect (1886-1972)
LUQUIENS, HUC-MAZELET Etcher (1882-1961)
LUTZ, DAN S Painter (1906-1979)
LYE, LEN Painter, Kinetic Artist (1901-1981)
LYMAN, JOHN Painter (-1967)
LYNCH, GERALD Sculptor (1944-2000)
LYNES, RUSSELL Writer, Critic (1910-1992)
LYTTON, BART Collector (-1968)
MABE, MANABU Painter (1924-1998)
MACAGY, DOUGLAS GUERNSEY Art Administrator (1913-1973)
MACAGY, JERMAYNE Educator
MACALISTER, PAUL RITTER Designer, Collector (1911-1990)
MACDONALD, GRANT Painter, Illustrator (1909-1987)
MACDONALD, HERBERT Painter (1898-1972)
MACDONALD, JAMES W A Painter (1824-1908)
MACDONALD, THOMAS REID Painter (1908-)
MACDONALD-WRIGHT, STANTON Painter (1890-1973)
MACGILLIS, ROBERT DONALD Painter, Printmaker (1936-2002)
MACGILVARY, NORWOOD Painter, Educator (1874-1949)
MACHAMER, JEFFERSON Cartoonist (1900-1960)
MACHETANZ, FRED Painter, Lithographer (1908-2002)
MACHLIN, SHELDON M Sculptor, Printmaker (1908-1975)
MACIUNAS, GEORGE Designer (1931-1979)
MACIVER, LOREN Painter (1909-1989)
MACK, RODGER ALLEN Sculptor, Educator (1938-2002)
MACKAY, DONALD CAMERON Painter, Historian (1906-1978)
MACKEOWN, IDA C Portrait Painter (1952)
MACKY, SPENCER Educator (1880-1958)
MACLAGGER, RICHARD JOSEPH Dealer, Collector (1947-1989)
MACLANE, JEAN Painter (1878-1964)
MACLEAD, YAN Sculptor (1899-1978)
MACLEOD, PEGI NICHOL Painter, Teacher
MACNELLY, JEFFREY KENNETH Cartoonist, Sculptor (1947-2000)
MACNUTT, GLENN GORDON Painter, Illustrator (1906-1997)
MACOMBER, ALLISON Painter, Sculptor (1916-1979)
MACOMBER, WILLIAM B Administrator (1921-2003)
MADSEN, VIGGO HOLM Printmaker, Craftsman (1925-1999)
MAGAFAN, ETHEL Painter, Muralist (1906-1983)
MAGAFAN, JENNE Painter, Lithographer (1916-1952)
MALBIN, LYDIA W Collector (1897-1999)
MALDARELLI, ORONZIO Sculptor (1892-1963)
MALICOAT, PHILIP CECIL Painter (1908-1981)
MALINA, FRANK JOSEPH Painter, Editor (1912-1981)
MALLARY, ROBERY W Sculptor, Educator (1917-1997)
MALLORY, MARGARET Collector, Filmmaker (1911-)
MALMAN, CHRISTINA Magazine Cover Artist (1902-1958)
MALONE, LEE H B Museum Director (1903-1989)
MALONE, NOLA LANGER Illustrator, Writer (1930-2003)

MALPASS, MICHAEL ALLEN Sculptor (1946-1992)
MALRAUX, ANDRE Writer (1900-1976)
MALSCH, ELLEN L Painter, Instructor (-1988)
MALVERN, CORINNE Illustrator (-1956)
MANARAY, THELMA ALBERTA Printmaker, Painter (1913-)
MANDEL, HOWARD Painter, Sculptor (1917-1999)
MANGRAVITE, PEPPINO GINO Painter, Lecturer (1896-1978)
MANKOWSKI, BRUNO Sculptor (1902-1990)
MANN, MARGERY (MARGARET MANN VASEY) Photographer, Curator (1919-1977)
MANNING, HILDA SCUDDER Sculptor (-1988)
MANNING, REG (REGINALD WEST) Designer (1905-1986)
MANO, TORU Curator (1945-2001)
MANRAY Artist, Photographer (1890-1976)
MANSHIP, PAUL Sculptor (1885-1966)
MANSO, LEO Painter, Educator (1914-1993)
MANVILLE, ELLA VIOLA GRAINGER Painter (1889-1979)
MAPPLETHORPE, ROBERT Photographer (1946-1989)
MARADIAGA, RALPH Director, Designer (1934-1985)
MARAGIRIOTTI, VINCENT Muralist (1888-1978)
MARANS, MOISSAYE Sculptor, Instructor (1902-1977)
MARANTZ, IRVING Painter (1912-1972)
MARBERGER, A ALDAR Dealer, Museum Director (1947-1988)
MARCUS, EDWARD S Collector (1910-1972)
MARCUS, STANLEY Collector (1905-2002)
MAREMONT, ARNOLD H Collector (1904-1978)
MARGULES, DEHIRSH Painter (1899-1965)
MARGULIES, HERMAN Painter (1922-2004)
MARGULIES, JOSEPH Painter, Printmaker (1896-1986)
MARGULIS, MARTHA (BOYER) Painter, Printmaker (1928-2003)
MARIL, HERMAN Painter, Printmaker (1908-1986)
MARIN, JOHN Painter (1870-1951)
MARINO, ALBERT JOSEPH Collector (1899-1975)
MARINO-MERLO, JOSEPH Painter (1906-1956)
MARKOW, JACK Cartoonist, Painter (1905-1993)
MARKS CEDRIC H Collector, Patron (-2000)
MARKS, CLAUDE Painter, Writer (1915-1991)
MARKS, GEORGE B Painter, Sculptor (1923-1983)
MARKS, ROYAL S Dealer, Collector (1927-1987)
MARKUS, HENRY A Collector
MARSH, (EDWIN) THOMAS Potter, Educator (1934-1991)
MARSH, FRED DANA Painter (1872-1911)
MARSH, REGINALD Painter (1898-1954)
MARSHALL, EDMUND Photographer (1938-1979)
MARSHALL, RALPH Educator, Photographer (1923-1984)
MARSTELLER, WILLIAM A Collector (1914-1987)
MARTIN, FLETCHER Painter (1904-1979)
MARTIN, KEITH MORROW Painter (1911-1983)
MARTIN, RICHARD (HARRISON) Historian, Curator (1946-1999)
MARTIN, THOMAS Painter, Educator (1943-2000)
MARTINELLO, EZIO Sculptor (1913-)
MARTINET, MARJORIED Painter (1886-1981)
MARTINO, GIOVANNI Painter (1908-1998)
MARTMER, WILLIAM PHILIP Painter (1939-1982)
MARTZ, KARL Ceramist, Educator (1912-1987)
MARYAN, MARYAN S Painter (1927-1977)
MASER, EDWARD ANDREW Historian, Museum (1923-1988)
MASON, ALICE FRANCES Lithographer, Painter (1895-)
MASON, ALICE TRUMBALL Painter (1904-1971)
MASON, MAUDE M Painter (1867-1951)
MASON, ROY MARTELL Painter (1886-1972)
MASSEY, ROBERT JOSEPH Painter, Educator (1911-1993)
MAST, GERALD Painter (1908-1971)
MATASSA, JOHN P Painter, Educator (1945-2004)
MATISSE, PIERRE Dealer (1900-1989)
MATLICK, GERALD ALLEN Painter, Historian (1947-1988)
MATTA-CLARK, GORDON Sculptor (1945-1978)
MATTERN, KARL Painter (1882-1969)
MATTISON, DONALD MANGUS Painter (1905-1975)
MATTISON, HENRY (ELIS) Painter (1887-1971)
MATULKA, JAN Painter (1890-1972)
MAULDIN, WILLIAM HENRY Cartoonist, Writer (1921-2003)
MAUNSBACH, GEORGE ERIC Painter (1890-)
MAURER, SASCHA Painter (1897-1961)
MAXON, JOHN Museum Director (1916-1977)
MAXWELL, JOHN Painter (-1997)
MAXWELL, WILLIAM JACKSON Sculptor, Environmental Artist (-2000)
MAYEN, PAUL Designer (1918-2000)
MAYER, BENA FRANK Painter (1898-1991)
MAYER, GRACE M Curator, Collector (-1996)
MAYER, RALPH Painter, Writer (1895-1979)
MAYHEW, EDGAR DE NOAILLES Educator, Museum Director (1913-1990)
MAYHEW, ELZA Sculptor (1916-2004)
MAYOR, A HYATT Curator (1901-1980)
MAYS, PAUL KIRTLAND Painter (1887-1961)
MAZZONE, DOMENICO Sculptor, Painter (1927-)
MCBEY, JAMES Painter (1884-1951)
MCBRIDE, HENRY Critic (1867-1962)
MCCARTHY, JUSTIN Painter (1892-)
MCCARTIN, WILLIAM FRANCIS (1905-2003)
MCCASLIN, WALTER WRIGHT Art Critic, Writer (1924-)
MCCAUSLAND, ELIZABETH Writer (1889-1965)
MCCLOSKEY, ROBERT Painter, Illustrator (1914-2003)
MCCORMICK, KATHARINE H Painter (1882-1960)
MCCOSH, DAVID J Painter (1903-1980)
MCCOUCH, GORDON MALLET Painter (1885-1962)
MCCOY, JOHN W Painter (1910-1999)
MCCREADY, KAREN (KAREN MCCREADY NOBLET) Art Dealer (1946-2000)
MCCREERY, FRANC ROOT (MRS) Painter (-1957)
MCCURRY, HARR ORR Museum Director (1889-1964)
MCDONALD, JOHN STANLEY Art Dealer (1943-1981)
MCDOO, DONALD ELDRIDGE Painter, Printer (1929-)
MCEWEN, JEAN Painter (1923-1999)
MCFEE, HENRY LEE Painter (1896-1953)
MCGEE, OLIVIA JACKSON Painter, Illustrator (1915-1987)
MCGILL, HAROLD A Cartoonist (-1952)
MCGLYNN, THOMAS Sculptor (1906-)
MCGREW, R BROWNELL Painter (1916-1994)
MCHUGH, ADELIZA SORENSON Dealer, Collector (1912-2003)
MCHUGH, JAMES FRANCIS Collector (-1969)
MCINTOSH, HAROLD Painter (1916-1996)
MCKAY, JOHN SANGSTER Administrator, Educator (1921-2003)
MCKEE, FRANCES BARRETT Illustrator (1909-1975)
MCKEEBY, BYRON GORDON Printmaker, Educator (1936-1984)
MCKENDRY, JOHN Curator (1933-1975)
MCKENZIE, VINNORMA SHAW Painter (1890-1952)
MCKESSON, MALCOLM FORBES Painter, Sculptor (1909-)
MCKIM, WILLIAM WIND Lithographer, Painter (1916-1895)
MCKININ, LAWRENCE Educator, Painter (1917-)
MCKINLEY, RUTH GOWDY Ceramist, Designer (1911-1981)
MCLAUGHLIN, DONAL Architect (1875-1978)
MCLAUGHLIN, JOHN Artist (1899-1976)
MCMAHON, A PHILIP Writer, Educator (1890-)
MCMANUS, JAMES Painter (1882-1955)
MCMEIN, NEYSA Painter, Designer (1890-)
MCMILLAN, ROBERT W Painter, Educator (1915-1991)
MCMLLLAN, MARY Painter (1885-)
MCMULLEN, E ORMOND Painter (1888-)
MCMURTRIE, EDITH Painter (1883-)
MCNEAR, EVERETT C Painter, Designer (1904-1984)
MCNETT, WILLIAM BROWN Illustrator (1896-1969)
MCNULTY, KNEELAND Curator, Writer (1921-1991)
MCNULTY, WILLIAM CHARLES Painter (1884-1963)
MCPHARLIN, PAUL Writer, Illustrator (1903-1948)
MCQUILLAN, FRANCES Painter, Instructor (-1996)
MCVEY, LEZA Ceramist, Weaver (1907-1984)
MCWHINNIE, HAROLD JAMES Printmaker, Collage Artist (1929-2004)
MEAD, KATHERINE HARPER Curator, Historian (1929-)
MEADMORE, CLEMENT L Sculptor (1929-2005)
MEADOWS, ALGUR H Patron (1899-1980)
MEANS, ELLIOTT Painter (1905-1962)
MECHLIN, LEILA Critic, Writer (1894-1949)
MECKLEM, AUSTIN MERRILL Painter (1894-1951)
MEDEARIS, ROGER Painter, Printmaker (1920-2001)
MEEHAN, WILLIAM DALE Painter, Educator (1930-1997)
MEEKER, DEAN JACKSON Printmaker, Sculptor (1920-2002)
MEGGS, PHILIP B Designer, Historian (1942-2002)
MEGIS, JOHN LIGGET Painter, Collector (1916-)
MEHRING, HOWARD WILLIAM Painter (1931-1978)
MEIERE, HILDRETH Painter (-1960)
MEIGS, JOHN LIGGETT Painter, Collector (1916-2003)
MEIGS, WALTER Painter (1918-1988)
MEISS, MILLARD Art Historian, Writer (1904-1975)
MEIXNER, MARY LOUISE Painter, Educator (1916-2004)
MELAMED, ABRAHAM Collector, Patron (1914-)
MELCARTH, EDWARD Painter, Sculptor
MELCHER, BETSY FLAGG Painter (1900-1991)
MELLON, PAUL Collector (1907-)
MELLOR, GEORGE EDWARD Educator, Sculptor (1928-1987)
MELVIN, GRACE WILSON Painter, Illustrator (-1977)
MENCONI, RALPH JOSEPH Sculptor (1915-1972)

MENDELOWITZ, DANIEL MARCUS Painter, Writer (1905-1980)
MENKES, SIGMUND J Painter (1896-1986)
MEOSSNER, LEO J Painter, Engraver (1885-1977)
MEREDITH, DOROTHY LAVERNE Weaver, Educator (1906-1986)
MERMIN, MILDRED (SHIRE) Painter (-1985)
MERRICK, JAMES KIRK Painter, Educator (1905-1985)
MERRITT, FRANCIS SUMNER Painter, Printmaker (1913-2000)
MERYMAN, HOPE Artist, Illustrator (-1975)
MESS, GEORGE JO Painter (1898-1962)
MESS, GORDON BENJAMIN Painter (1900-1959)
MESSEGUER, VILLORO BENITO Painter, Sculptor (1930-1982)
MESSICK, BEN (NEWTON) Painter, Instructor (1911-)
MESTROVIC, IVAN Sculptor (1884-1962)
MEYER, FRANK HILDBRIDGE Painter, Printmaker (1923-1996)
MEYER, FRED (ROBERT) Sculptor, Painter (-1986)
MEYER, FREDERICK H Educator (1873-1961)
MEYER, HERBERT Painter (1882-1960)
MEYEROWITZ, WILLIAM Painter (1896-1981)
MEYERS, LEONARD H Computer Art (1932-1979)
MEYERS, ROBERT WILLIAM Illustrator (1919-1970)
MICALE, ALBERT Painter, Sculptor (-1993)
MIDENER, WALTER Sculptor, Instructor (1912-1998)
MIDGETTE, WILLARD FRANKLIN Painter, Printmaker (1937-1978)
MIELZINER, JO Designer, Lecturer (1901-1976)
MIES VAN DER ROHE, LUDWIG Architect (1886-1969)
MILCH, HAROLD CARLTON Art Dealer (1908-)
MILES, JEANNE PATTERSON Painter, Sculptor (1908-1999)
MILHOLLAND, RICHARD ALEXANDER Painter, Instructor (1946-2004)
MILHOUS, KATHERINE Illustrator, Writer (1894-1977)
MILLER, BARSE Painter, Educator (1924-1973)
MILLER, BURR Sculptor (1904-1958)
MILLER, DONALD Critic, Writer (1934-2003)
MILLER, DONALD LLOYD Painter, Muralist (1923-1993)
MILLER, DONALD RICHARD Sculptor, Medallist (1925-1989)
MILLER, HELEN PENDELTON Etcher (1888-1957)
MILLER, JEAN JOHNSON Librarian, Historian (1918-)
MILLER, KENNETH HAYES Painter, Teacher (1876-1952)
MILLET, CLARENCE Painter (1897-1959)
MILLIKEN, WILLIAM M Museum Director, Curator (1889-1978)
MILLMAN, EDWARD Painter (1907-1964)
MILLS, PAUL CHADBOURNE Museum Director, Consultant (1924-2004)
MINA-MORA, DORISE OLSON Painter (1932-1991)
MINER, DOROTHY EUGENIA Museum Curator, Art Historian (1906-1973)
MINEWSKI, ALEX Painter, Educator (1917-1979)
MINNEGERODE, CUTHBERT POWELL Museum Director (1876-1951)
MINNICK, ESTHER TRESS Painter (-1999)
MISSAL, PEGGE Art Dealer, Consultant (1923-2001)
MITCHELL, ALFRED R Painter (1888-1972)
MITCHELL, BRUCE HANDISIDE Painter (1908-1963)
MITCHELL, CLIFFORD Architect, Painter (1925-2005)
MITCHELL, DANA COVINGTON Collector (1918-)
MITCHELL, ELEANOR Consultant, Librarian (1907-)
MITCHELL, GLEN Painter (1894-1972)
MITCHELL, HENRY (WEBER) Sculptor (1915-1990)
MITCHELL, JOAN Painter (1926-)
MITCHELL, THOMAS W Painter
MITCHELL, WALLACE (MACMAHON) Museum Director, Painter (1911-1977)
MITRA, GOPAL C Painter, Printmaker (1928-1992)
MIYASHITA, TAD Painter (1922-1979)
MOCHI, UGO Sculptor (1894-1977)
MOCHON, DONALD Graphic Artist, Educator (1916-)
MOCK, GEORGE ANDREW Painter (1886-)
MODEL, EVSA Artist (1900-1976)
MOE, HENRY ALLEN Art Administrator (1894-1975)
MOFFETT, ROSS E Painter (1888-1971)
MOLARSKY, MAURICE Painter, Educator (1885-1950)
MONAGHAN, KEITH Painter, Educator (1921-2001)
MONES, ARTHUR Photographer (1919-1998)
MONONGYE, PRESTON LEE Silversmith, Printmaker (1927-1988)
MONTAGUE, JAMES L Painter, Printmaker (1906-)
MONTANA, BOB Cartoonist (1920-1975)
MONTANA, PIETRO Sculptor, Painter (1890-1978)
MONTGOMERY, CHARLES FRANKLIN Art Administrator, Educator (1910-1978)
MONTGOMERY, CLAUDE Painter, Etcher (1912-1990)
MOON, CARL Illustrator (1879-1948)
MOOSE, PHILIP ANTHONY Painter, Illustrator (1921-2001)
MOOSE, TALMADGE BOWERS Painter, Illustrator (1933-2003)
MORANG, ALFRED GWYNNE Painter (1901-1951)
MORATH, INGE (INGE MORATH MILLER) Photographer (1923-2002)
MORDVINOFF, NICOLAS Painter, Illustrator (1911-1973)
MORE, HERMON Museum Director (1887-1968)
MORGAN, GLADYS B Painter, Lithographer (1899-1981)
MORGAN, MARITZA LESKOVAR Painter, Illustrator (1921-)
MORGAN, MYRA J Art Dealer (1938-2005)
MORGAN, WALLACE Illustrator (1873-1948)
MORISSET, GERARD Educator (1898-1970)
MORRIS, CARL Painter (1911-1993)
MORRIS, DONALD FISCHER Dealer (1925-2004)
MORRIS, DUDLEY H, JR Painter (1912-1966)
MORRIS, GEORGE FORD Painter (-1860)
MORRIS, GEORGE L K Painter, Sculptor (1905-1975)
MORRIS, HILDA Sculptor (-1990)
MORRIS, KYLE RANDOLPH Painter (1918-1979)
MORRISON, GEORGE Painter, Sculptor (1919-)
MORROW, BENJAMIN FRANCIS Painter (1891-1958)
MORROW, ROBERT EARL Designer, Muralist (1917-2004)
MORSE, DOROTHY B Illustrator, Educator (1906-1979)
MORSE, GLENN TILLEY Painter (1870-1950)
MORSE, ROSABELLE (JACQUELINE) Painter (-2002)
MORTON, REE Sculptor, Painter (1936-1977)
MORTON, RICHARD H Painter, Graphic Artist (1921-2003)
MOSBY, WILLIAM HARRY Painter (1898-1964)
MOSCA, AUGUST Painter, Printmaker (1907-2003)
MOSE, CARL C Sculptor, Lecturer (1903-1973)
MOSELSIO, SIMON Sculptor (1880-)
MOSER, FRANK H Painter (1886-1964)
MOSES, ANNA MARY ROBERTSON (GRANDMA) Painter (1860-1961)
MOSES, FORREST KING Painter (1893-1974)
MOSLEY, ZACK T Illustrator, Cartoonist (1906-1993)
MOTHERWELL, ROBERT Painter, Printmaker (1915-1991)
MOTT-SMITH, MAY Medallist, Painter (1879-1952)
MOUFARREGE, NICHOLAS A Painter, Critic (1947-)
MOY, MAY (WONG) Painter, Instructor (1913-2003)
MUEHSAM, GERD Librarian, Writer (1913-1979)
MUIR, WILLIAM HORACE Sculptor (1902-1965)
MULLER, GEORGE F Painter (1866-1958)
MULLER, HELEN B Painter, Gallery Director (1922-1999)
MULLER, JAN Painter (1922-1958)
MULLICAN, LEE Painter, Educator (1919-1978)
MULLIN, WILLARD Cartoonist (1902-1979)
MUNDY, ETHEL FRANCES Sculptor (-1964)
MUNDY, LOUISE EASTERDAY Painter (1870-1952)
MUNFORD, ROBERT WATSON Painter, Educator (1925-1991)
MUNOWOTZ, KEN Illustrator (1936-1978)
MUNRO, THOMAS Art Scholar (1897-1974)
MUOGE, EDMOND WEBSTER, JR Collector (1904-1984)
MURANYI, GUSTAVE Painter (1872-1961)
MURCH, WALTER Painter (1907-1967)
MURCHOSON, JOHN D Collector (1921-1978)
MURPHY, CHESTER GLENN Painter (1907-1997)
MURPHY, GLADYS WILKINS Painter, Craftsman (1907-1985)
MURPHY, ROWLEY WALTER Painter, Designer (1891-1975)
MURRAY, ALBERT (KETCHAM) Painter (1906-1992)
MURRAY, FLORETTA MAY Administrator, Painter (-2001)
MURRAY, FRANK WALDO Painter (1884-1956)
MURRAY, WILLIAM COLMAN Collector, Patron (1899-1977)
MUSGROVE, A J Museum Director
MYERS, ETHEL K Sculptor (1881-1960)
MYERS, FRANK HARMON Painter (1899-1951)
MYERS, FRED A Museum Director (1937-)
MYERS, GEORGE HEWITT Museum President (1865-1957)
MYRICK, KATHERINE S Painter
NADLER, HARRY Painter, Educator (1930-1990)
NAEGLE, STEPHEN HOWARD Painter, Sculptor (1938-1981)
NAGEL, STINA Painter (1918-1969)
NAGLER, EDITH KROGER Painter (1895-1986)
NAGLER, FRED Printmaker, Sculptor (1890-1983)
NAHA, RAYMOND Painter (-1975)
NAILOR, GERALD LLOYDE Painter, Illustrator (1917-1952)
NAKAMIZO, FUJI Painter (1889-)
NAMUTH, HANS Photographer, Filmmaker (1915-1990)
NASH, RAY Art Historian (1905-1982)
NASON, GERTRUDE Painter (1890-)
NASON, THOMAS W Engraver (1888-1971)
NATHAN, HELMUTH MAX Educator, Painter (1901-1979)
NATHANS, RHODA R Photographer (1940-1998)
NATZLER, GERTRUD Ceramic Craftsman (1908-1971)
NAVAS, ELIZABETH S Collector, Patron (1895-)
NAY, MARY SPENCER Painter, Educator (1913-1993)
NEAL, REGINALD H Painter, Printmaker (1909-1992)

NEANDROSS, SIGURD Sculptor (1869-1958)
NEBEL, BERTHOLD Sculptor (1889-1964)
NEDDEAU, DONALD FREDERICK PRICE Painter, Designer (1913-1998)
NEEL, ALICE Painter (1900-1984)
NEFF, JOSEPH Collector (1900-1969)
NEILL, BEN E Painter (1914-2001)
NEILSON, KATHERINE B Art Historian (1902-1977)
NEILSON, RAYMOND P R Painter (1891-1964)
NELSON, GEORGE LAURENCE Painter (1887-1975)
NELSON, JACK D Sculptor, Graphic Artist (1929-1997)
NEMEC, NANCY Printmaker, Painter (1923-2003)
NEMEROV, DAVID Painter (-1963)
NEPOTE, ALEXANDER Painter (1913-1986)
NESBERT, VINCENT Miniature Painter (-1976)
NESBITT, ALEXANDER JOHN Educator, Calligrapher (1801-1995)
NESBITT, LOWELL BLAIR Painter, Sculptor (1933-1993)
NESEMANN, ENNO Painter (1861-1949)
NESS, (ALBERT) KENNETH Painter, Designer (1903-2001)
NESS, EVALINE (MRS ARNOLD A BAYARD) Illustrator, Writer (1910-)
NEUGEBERGER, MARGOT Designer, Craftsman (1929-1996)
NEUMANN, J B Art Dealer, Critic (1887-1961)
NEUMANN, WILLIAM A Educator, Goldsmith (1924-1995)
NEUMEYER, ALFRED Art Historian (1901-1973)
NEUTRA, RICHARD Architect (1892-1970)
NEWBERRY, CLARE TURLAY Illustrator (1903-1970)
NEWBERRY, JOHN S Museum Curator (-1964)
NEWHALL, ADELAIDE MAY Painter (1894-1960)
NEWHALL, BEAUMONT Photographer, Educator (1908-)
NEWHOUSE, BERTRAM MAURICE Art Dealer (1888-1982)
NEWHOUSE, CLYDE MORTIMER Dealer, Historian (1920-1990)
NEWMAN, BARNETT Painter (1905-1970)
NEWMAN, ELIAS Painter (1903-1999)
NEWTON, DOUGLAS Administrator, Museum Director (1920-2001)
NEWTON, GRACE HAMILTON (MRS ARTHUR NEWTON) Painter (-1958)
NEWTON, MARGARET, Painter (1893-1960)
NICHOLS DONALD EDWARD Designer, Educator (1922-1987)
NICHOLS, ELEANOR CARY Designer, Mettalsmith (1903-1988)
NICHOLS HOBART Painter (1869-1962)
NICHOLS, JAMES WILLIAM Painter (1928-2004)
NICHOLS, SPENCER B Painter (1875-1950)
NICHOLSON, BEN Painter (1894-1952)
NICHOLSON, THOMAS D Director (1922-)
NICKLE, ROBERT W Painter, Educator (1919-1980)
NICOLOSI, JOSEPH Sculptor (1893-1961)
NIEMEYER, ARNOLD MATTHEW Collector, Patron (1913-1990)
NILES, ROSAMOND Painter (1891-)
NISBET, ROBERT H Painter (1879-1961)
NITZSCHE, ELSA KOENIG Portrait Painter (1880-1952)
NOA, FLORENCE Printmaker, Educator (1941-1989)
NOBLE, JOHN A Fainter, Lithographer (1903-1983)
NODEL, SOL Illuminator Designer (1912-1976)
NOFER, FRANK Painter, Graphic Artist (1929-2002)
NOGGLE, ANNE Photographer, Educator (1922-2005)
NOGUCHI, ISAMU Sculptor (1904-1989)
NOLTE, GUNTER Sculptor, Draftsman (1938-2000)
NOORDHOEK, HARRY CECIL Sculptor, Painter (1909-1992)
NORBURY, LOUISE H Painter (1878-1952)
NORDELL, EMMA PARKER (POLLY) Painter
NORTARO, ANTHONY Sculptor (1905-1984)
NORTON, ANN W Sculptor (-1982)
NOVOTNY, ELMER LADISLAW Painter, Educator (1909-1987)
NOWACK, WAYNE KENYON Painter, Graphic Artist (1923-2004)
NOWAK, LEO Illustrator, Cartoonist (1924-2001)
NOYES, ELIOT Architect, Designer (1910-1977)
NUDERSCHER, FRANK BERNARD Painter (1881-1951)
NUGENT, ARTHUR WILLIAM Cartoonist, Illustrator (1891-1975)
NUKI, (DANIEL MILLSAPS) Painter, Writer (1918-1984)
NUNN, FREDERIC Painter (1879-)
O'HANLON, RICHARD E Sculptor, Painter (1906-1985)
O'HARA, (JAMES) FREDERICK Printmaker (1904-1980)
O'HARA, ELIOT Painter (1890-1969)
O'KEEFFE, GEORGIA Painter (1887-1986)
OAKLEY, VIOLET Painter (1874-1960)
OBERHARDT, WILLIAM Illustrator (1892-1955)
OBRIEN, WILLIAM VINCENT Art Dealer (1902-)
OCHIKUBO, TETSUO Painter, Designer (1923-1975)
OCHS, RICHARD WAYNE Painter, Instructor (1938-2006)
OCHTMAN DOROTHY (MRS WA DEL MAR) Painter (1892-1971)
OENSLAGER DONALD MITCHELL Stage Designer (1902-1975)
OERI GEORGINE Critic (-1968)
OFFIN, CHARLES Z Collector, Critic (1899-1989)
OGDEN, RALPH E Collector, Patron (-1974)
OGG, OSCAR Designer, Writer (1908-1971)
OGILVIE, WILL (WILLIAM ABERNETHY) Painter (1901-1989)
OKADA, KENZO Painter (1902-1982)
OLINSKY, IVAN G Painter (1878-1962)
OLIVER, RICHARD BRUCE Architect (1942-1993)
OLMER, HENRY Sculptor (1887-1950)
OLSEN, HERB Painter, Writer (1905-1973)
O'NEIL, JOHN Painter, Educator (1915-2004)
O'NEIL, JOHN JOSEPH Administrator, Designer (1932-2004)
ONLEY, TONI Painter, Printmaker (1928-2004)
OPDYCKE, LEONARD Educator (1895-1977)
OPPENHEIM, SAMUEL EDMUND Painter (1901-1992)
OPPENHEIMER, SELMA L Painter (1898-)
ORDER, TRUDY Painter (1944-)
ORKIN, RUTH (MRS MORRIS ENGEL) Photographer, Filmmaker (1921-1985)
ORLING, ANNE Consultant, Painter (-1989)
ORLOFF, LILY Painter (1908-1957)
ORLOWSKY, LILLIAN Painter, Collage Artist (1914-2004)
ORME, LYDIA GARDNER Painter (-1963)
ORR, ARTHUR (Leslie) Painter, Graphic Artist (1938-2005)
ORR, ELLIOT Painter (1904-1997)
ORTLIP, MARY KRUEGER Painter (-2001)
OSBORNE, ROBERT LEE Painter, Educator (1928-2004)
OSGOOD, RUTH Painter (-1977)
OSSORIO, ALFONSO Painter, Sculptor (1916-1980)
OSTER, GERALD Painter, Kinetic Artist (1918-1993)
OSTUNI, PETER W Painter (1909-1992)
OTTIANO, JOHN WILLIAM Jeweler, Sculptor (1926-)
OWEN, FREDERICK Painter (1869-1959)
OZENFANT, AMEDEE J Painter (1886-1966)
PACH, MAGDA F Painter (1884-1950)
PACH, WALTER Writer (1883-1951)
PACKER, CLAIR LANGE Painter, Writer (1901-1978)
PACKER, FRANCIS H Sculptor (1873-1957)
PACKER, FRED L Cartoonist (1886-1956)
PADDOCK, WILLARD DRYDEN Painter (1873-1956)
PAEFF, BASHKA (BASHKA PAEFF WAXMAN) Sculptor (1893-1979)
PAGAN, RICHARD Painter, Sculptor (1954-1999)
PAGE, GROVER Cartoonist (1893-1958)
PAGENT-FREDERICKS, J ROUS-MARTEN Illustrator (1905-1963)
PAGES, JEAN Illustrator, Muralist (1907-1977)
PAINE, ROBERT T Museum Curator (1900-1965)
PALAZZOLA, GUY Administrator Educator (1919-1978)
PALEY, WILLIAM S (MRS) Collector
PALEY, WILLIAMS (MR) Collector (1901-1990)
PALMER, ALLEN INGELS Painter (1910-1950)
PALMER, DELOS Painter (1891-1961)
PAPASHVILY, GEORGE Sculptor, Writer (1898-1978)
PAPASIAN, JACK C Sculptor (1878-1957)
PARADISE, PHIL (HERSCHEL) Painter, Sculptor (1905-1997)
PARDI, JUSTIN A Painter (1898-1951)
PARDON, EARL B Craftsman, Educator (1926-1991)
PAREDES, LIMON MARIANO Engraver, Painter (1912-1878)
PARELLA, ALBERT LUCIAN Painter, Instructor (1909-1999)
PARIS, HAROLD PERSICO Sculptor (1925-1979)
PARK, MADELEINE F Sculptor (1891-1960)
PARKER, ALFRED Illustrator (1906-1985)
PARKER, GEORGE WALLER Painter (1888-1957)
PARKER, RAYMOND Painter (1922-1990)
PARKER, THOMAS Administrator (1904-1967)
PARRISH, MAXFIELD Painter (1870-1966)
PARSHALL, DEWITT Painter (1864-1956)
PARSONS, BETTY BIERNE Painter, Art Dealer (1900-1982)
PARSONS, DAVID GOODE Sculptor, Educator (1911-2005)
PARSONS, EDITH BARRETTO Sculptor (1878-1956)
PARSONS, ERNESTINE Painter (1884-1967)
PARSONS, LLOYD HOLMAN Painter (1883-1968)
PARTCH, VIRGIL FRANKLIN Cartoonist, Illustrator (1906-)
PARTRIDGE, ROI Printmaker (1889-1984)
PARTZ, FELIX (RON GABE) Painter (1945-1994)
PASCAL. DAVID Painter, Cartoonist (1918-2003)
PASCHKE, EDWARD Painter (1939-2004)
PASINSKI, IRENE Painter, Sculptor (1923-2002)
PATRICK, RANSOM R Educator (1906-1971)
PATTERSON, CHARLES ROBERT Painter (1875-1958)
PATTISON, ABBOTT Sculptor, Painter (1916-1999)
PATTY, WILLIAM A Painter (1898-1961)
PAUL, BORIS DUPONT Painter (1900-)
PAUL, SUZANNE Photographer (1945-2005)
PAULIN, RICHARD CALKINS Museum Director (1928-2004)

PAULSON, MICHAEL Artist
PAYNE, JOHN D Sculptor, Educator (1934-)
PEABODY, AMELIA Sculptor (1890-1984)
PEAK, CHANNING Painter, Muralist (1910-1991)
PEAK, ROBERT Painter, Illustrator (-1992)
PEARLMAN, HENRY Collector (1895-1974)
PEARMAN, KATHARINE K Painter (1893-1961)
PEARSON, JOSEPH T, JR Painter (1876-1951)
PEARSON, RALPH M Etcher (1883-1958)
PECK, EDWARD Gallery Director (-1970)
PECK, JAMES EDWARD Painter, Designer (1907-2002)
PEEBLES, ROY B Painter (1899-1951)
PEETS, ORVILLE Painter (1884-1968)
PEIRCE, WALDO Painter (1894-1970)
PELLICONE, WILLIAM Painter, Sculptor (1915-2004)
PENA, TONITA Painter (1895-1949)
PENNEY, JAMES Painter, Educator (1910-1982)
PENNOYER, A SHELDON Painter (1889-1957)
PENNY, AUBREY JOHN ROBERT Painter, Sculptor (1917-2000)
PEPPER, CHARLES HOVEY Painter (1864-1950)
PERARD, VICTOR S Etcher (1867-1957)
PEREIRA, I RICE Painter (1901-1971)
PERINE, ROBERT HEATH Painter, Writer (1922-2004)
PERKINS, ANN Historian, Educator (1915-2006)
PERKINS, CONSTANCE M Educator, Critic (1903-)
PERKINS, G HOLMES Architect, Educator (1904-2004)
PERKINS, MABLE H Collector (1880-1974)
PERKINS, MARION Sculptor (1908-1961)
PERKINS, PHILIP R Painter (-1968)
PERKINS, ROBERT EUGENE Administrator (1931-1997)
PERKINS-RIPLEY, LUCY FAIRFIELD O Painter
PERLS, FRANK (RICHARD) Art Dealer, Collector (1910-1975)
PERRET, FERDINAND Historian (1888-1960)
PERRET, NELL FOSTER Painter, Printmaker (1916-1986)
PERRETT, GALEN J Painter (1875-1949)
PERRIN, C ROBERT Painter, Illustrator (1915-1999)
PERRY, RAYMOND Painter (1876-1960)
PETERDI, GABOR F Painter, Printmaker (1915-)
PETERS, CARL W Painter (1897-1980)
PETERS, FRANCIS C Painter (1902-1977)
PETERSHAM, MISKA Illustrator (1888-1959)
PETERSON, A E S Painter, Printmaker (1908-1984)
PETERSON, JANE Painter (1876-1965)
PETERSON, JOHN P Craftsman (-1949)
PETERSON, PERRY Illustrator (1908-1958)
PETREMONT, CLARICE M Painter (-1949)
PETTUS, JANE M Painter (1908-)
PEYTON, BERTHA MENZLER Painter (1871-1947)
PFEIFFER FRITZ Painter (1889-1960)
PFEIFFER HEINRICH H Painter (1874-)
PFISTER, JEAN JACQUES Painter (1878-1949)
PHELAN, LINN LOVEJOY Designer (1906-1992)
PHELPS, EDITH CATLIN Painter (1875-1961)
PHELPS, NAN Painter (-1990)
PHILBRICK, OTIS Painter, Printmaker (1888-1973)
PHILIP, LOTTE BRAND Historian (1910-)
PHILIPP, ROBERT Painter (1895-1981)
PHILLIPS, DOROTHY W Art Administrator, Writer (1906-1977)
PHILLIPS, DUNCAN Museum Director (1886-1966)
PHILLIPS, J CAMPBELL Painter (1873-1949)
PHILLIPS, JAMES Historian, Painter (1929-)
PHILLIPS, MARJORIE Painter (1894-1995)
PHIPPS, DARLEEN (MARIE) Painter (1929-1999)
PICKEN, GEORGE Painter, Printmaker (1898-1971)
PICKENS, ALTON Painter, Instructor (1917-1991)
PICKHARDT, CARL Painter, Printmaker (1908-2004)
PIERCE, DELILAH W Painter, Educator (1904-1992)
PIERCE, GARY Painter (-1969)
PILGRIM, JAMES F Curator, Administrator (1941-2002)
PILLIN, POLIA Painter, Ceramist (1909-1992)
PIMENTEL, DAVID DELBERT Goldsmith, Educator (1943-2004)
PINCHBECK, PETER G Painter (1940-2000)
PINEDA, MARIANNA Sculptor (1925-1996)
PINTO, ANGELO RAPHAEL Painter, Printmaker (1908-1994)
PINTO, BIAGIO Painter (1911-1989)
PIPER, JANE Painter (1916-1991)
PITTMAN, HOBSON Painter (1900-1972)
PITTMAN, KATHRYN Painter, Instructor (1915-1979)
PITZ HENRY CLARENCE Painter, Writer (1895-1976)
PLATE, WALTER Painter, Educator (1925-1972)
PLATT, ELEANOR Sculptor (1910-1974)
PLAVCAN, JOSEPH MICHAEL Painter, Sculptor (1908-1981)
PLEASANTS, FREDERICK R Collector, Patron (1906-)
PLEISSNER OGDEN MINTON Painter (1905-1983)
PLUNGUIAN, GINA Painter (-1962)
POCCIRILLO, FURID Sculptor (1868-1949)
POGACH, GERALD Painter, Sculptor (-1996)
POHL, HUGO DAVID Painter (1878-1960)
POINIER, ARTHUR BEST Editorial Cartoonist (1911-)
POKE, JOHN Illustrator, Painter (1900-1979)
POLAN, LINCOLN M Collector, Patron (1909-1999)
POLAN, NANCY MOORE Painter, Printmaker
POLANSKY, LOIS B Printmaker, Painter (1939-2003)
POLKES, ALAN H Collector, Patron (1931-)
POLLACK, LOUIS Art Dealer (1921-1970)
POLLACK, PETER Photographer, Writer (1911-1978)
POLLACK, VIRGINIA MORRIS Sculptor
POLLAND, DONALD JACK Sculptor (1932-2003)
POLLET, JOSEPH Painter (1898-1979)
POLLEY, FREDERICK Painter (1875-)
POLLOCK, JACKSON Painter (1912-1956)
POLLOCK, JAMES ARLIN Painter (1898-1949)
POMEROY, JAMES CALOWELL Performance Artist, Photographer (1945-1992)
POMMER, RICHARD Educator, Historian (1930-1992)
POND, DANA Painter (1880-1962)
POND, WILLI BAZE (MRS CHARLES E) Painter (1896-1947)
POOLE, ABRAM Painter (1882-1961)
POOLE, EARL LINCOLN Illustrator, Art Administrator (1891-1972)
POOR, HENRY VARNUM Painter (1888-1970)
POPE, JOHN ALEXANDER Historian, Museum Director (1906-1992)
POPE, MARION HOLDEN Painter (-1958)
POPESCU, CARA Sculptor, Printmaker (-1991)
POPKIN, ELSIE DINSMORE Graphic Artist (1937-2005)
PORADA, EDITH Historian (1912-1994)
PORAY, STAN P Painter, Designer (1888-1948)
PORSMAN, FRANK O Painter (1905-)
PORTANOVA, JOSEPH DOMENICO Sculptor, Designer (1909-1979)
PORTER, ELIOT FURNESS Photographer, Writer (1901-1990)
PORTER, FAIRFIELD Painter, Lecturer (1907-1975)
PORTNOFF, ALEXANDER Sculptor (1887-1949)
POST, GEORGE BOOTH Painter (1906-1997)
POST, MARION (MARION POST WOLCOTT) Photographer (1910-1990)
POTTER, WILLIAM J Painter (1883-1964)
POTTS, CHARLES A Administrator (-1986)
POUSETTE-DART, NATHANIEL J Painter (1886-1965)
POUSETTE-DART, RICHARD Painter, Sculptor (1916-1992)
POWELL, DOANE Craftsman (1881-1951)
POWELL, LYDIA BOND Art Administrator, Consultant (1892-1978)
POWERS, MARILYN Painter (1925-1976)
POWERS, MARY SWIFT Painter (1885-1959)
POZITZ, SILVIA Collector, Patron (-1991)
PRAGER, DAVID A Collector (1913-1997)
PRATT, DUDLEY Sculptor (1897-1975)
PRATT, ELIZABETH SOUTHWOCK Painter (-1964)
PRATT, VERNON GAITHER Painter, Educator (1940-2000)
PREDERGAST, CHARLES E Painter (1868-1948)
PRESSER, JOSEF Painter (1907-1967)
PRESTINI, JAMES LIBERO Sculptor, Designer (1908-1993)
PRESTON, ALICE BOLAM (MRS FRANK I) Illustrator (1889-1958)
PRESTON, HARRIET BROWN Painter (1892-1961)
PRESTON, JAMES M Painter (1874-1961)
PRESTOPINO, GREGORIO Painter (1907-)
PREZZI, WILMA M Painter (1915-)
PRICE, CHESTER B Illustrator (1885-1962)
PRICE, CLAYTON S Painter (1874-1950)
PRICE, FREDERIC NEWLIN Museum Director (1884-1963)
PRICE, GARRETT Cartoonist (1897-1979)
PRICE, MARGARET E Illustrator, Painter (1888-)
PRICE, MINNIE Painter (1877-1951)
PRICE, NORMAN MILLS Illustrator (1877-1951)
PRICE, ROSALIE PETTUS Painter
PRICE, VINCENT Collector, Dealer (1927-1993)
PRIEBE, KARL Painter (1914-1976)
PRIEST, ALAN Museum Curator (1898-1969)
PRIEST, HARTWELL WYSE Painter, Printmaker (1901-2004)
PRINCE, WILLIAM MEADE Illustrator (1893-1951)
PRIOR, HARRIS KING Art Administrator, Educator (1911-1975)
PROCTOR, A PHIMISTER Sculptor (1862-1950)
PROHASKA, RAY Painter, Illustrator (1901-1981)
PROKOPOFF, STEPHEN Museum Director, Historian (1929-2001)
PUCCINELLI, RAIMONDO Sculptor, Graphic Artist (1904-1986)

PUFAHL, JOHN K Educator, Printmaker (1942-1998)
PULOS, ARTHUR JON Designer, Educator (1917-)
PURSER, STUART ROBERT Painter, Educator (1907-1986)
PUSHMAN, HOVSEP Painter (1877-1966)
PUTMAN, BRENDA Sculptor (1890-1975)
PUTMAN, JOHN B (MRS) Collector (1903-)
QUANDT, RUSSELL JEROME Museum Art Restorer (1919-1970)
QUATTROCCHI, EDMONDO Sculptor (1889-1966)
QUINN, NOEL JOSEPH Painter, Instructor (1915-1993)
QUINN, ROBERT HAYES Illustrator (1902-1962)
QUIRK, FRANCIS JOSEPH Painter, Museum Director (1907-1974)
QUIRT, WALTER Painter, Educator (1902-1868)
QUISTGAARD, JOHAN WALDEMAR DE REHLING Portrait Painter (1877-1962)
RAAB, ADA DENNETT (MRS S V) Painter (-1950)
RAHILL, MARGARET FISH Curator, Critic (1919-1998)
RAHMING NORRIS Painter (1886-1959)
RAINVILLE, PAUL Museum Director (-1952)
RALSTON, JAMES KENNETH Painter, Illustrator (1896-1987)
RANDALL, (LILLIAN) PAULA Sculptor, Designer (1885-1985)
RANDALL, RICHARD HARDING JR Curator, Historian (1926-1997)
RANES, CHRIS Painter, Designer (1929-2002)
RANEY, SUZANNE BRYANT Printmaker (-1967)
RANN, VOLLIAN BURR Painter (1897-1956)
RANNEY, GLEN ALLISON Painter (1896-1959)
RANSON, NANCY SUSSMAN Painter, Printmaker (1905-)
RASKO, MAXIMILIAN A Painter (1884-1961)
RATHBONE, PERRY TOWNSHEND Museum Director (1911-2000)
RATKAI, GEORGE Painter, Sculptor (1907-1999)
RATTNER, ABRAHAM Painter (1895-1978)
RATZKA, ARTHUR L Painter (1869-)
RAU, WILLIAM R Artist (1874-)
RAUCH, JOHN G Collector, Patron (1890-1976)
RAVENSCROFT, ELLEN Painter (1876-1949)
RAVESON, SHERMAN HAROLD Painter, Writer (1907-1974)
RAY, ROBERT (DONALD) Painter, Photographer (1924-2002)
RAY, RUTH (MRS JOHN REGINALD GRAHAM) Painter (1919-1977)
RAYMOND, ALEXANDER Cartoonist (1909-1956)
READ, HELEN APPLETON Art Historian, Art Critic (1887-1974)
READE, ROMA (MABEL KELLEY AUBREY) Painter (1877-1958)
READIO, WILFRED A Painter (1895-1961)
REALE, NICHOLAS ALBERT Painter, Instructor (1922-)
REASON, PATRICK Engraver (1817-1852)
REBAY, HILLA Painter (1885-1983)
RECCHIA RICHARD (HENRY) Sculptor (1885-1983)
REDEIN, ALEX S Painter, Instructor (1912-)
REDER, BERNARD Sculptor (1897-1963)
REDFIELD, EDWARD W Painter (1869-1965)
REED, DOEL Painter, Printmaker (1894-)
REEVES, J MASON Painter (1898-1973)
REFREGIER, ANTON Painter (1905-1979)
REGENSBURG, SOPHY P Painter, Collector (1885-1974)
REGENSTEINER, ELSE (FRIEDSAM) Designer, Weaver (1906-2003)
REGESTER, CHARLOTTE Painter
REICH, NATHANIEL E Painter, Collage Artist (1907-2004)
REICH, SHELDON Historian, Lecturer (1931-2002)
REICHARD, STEPHEN BRANTLEY Administrator (1949-)
REICHEK, JESSE Painter, Educator (1916-2005)
REICHMAN, FRED Painter (-2005)
REID, GEORGE AGNEW Painter (-1947)
REIFF, ROBERT FRANK Art Historian, Painter (1918-1982)
REILLY, ELVIRA Painter (1899-1958)
REINDEL, WILLIAM GEORGE Painter (1871-1948)
REINDORF, SAMUEL Painter (1914-1988)
REINHARDT, AD F Painter (1913-1967)
REISE, BARBARA Art Critic (-1978)
REISMAN, PHILIP Painter (1904-1992)
REISS, LIONEL S Painter, Writer (1929-)
REMENICK, SEYMOUR Painter, Instructor (1923-1999)
REMMEY, PAUL B Illustrator
RENIER, JOSEPH EMILE Sculptor (-1966)
RENNINGER, KATHARINE STEELE Painter (1925-2004)
RENOUF, EDWARD Painter, Sculptor (1906-1999)
RESNICK, MILTON Painter (1917-2004)
REVINGTON, GEORGE D, III Collector
REWALD, JOHN Curator, Writer (1912-1994)
REY, H A Illustrator, Writer (1898-1977)
REYNARD, GRANT T Painter (1887-1967)
REYNOLDS, LLOYD J Calligrapher (1887-1978)
REYNOLDS, RALPH WILLIAM Painter, Educator (1905-1991)
RIBA, PAUL F Painter (1912-1977)
RIBAK, LOUIS Painter (1902-1980)
RICCI, ULYSSES Sculptor (1888-1960)
RICE, HAROLD RANDOLPH Educator, Writer (1912-1987)
RICH, DANIEL CATTON Art Administrator, Lecturer (1904-1976)
RICH, LORIMER Architect (1892-1978)
RICHARDSON, EDGAR PRESTON Historian (1902-1995)
RICHARDSON, JAMES LEWIS Educator, Printmaker (1927-)
RICHMOND, LAWRENCE Collector (1909-1978)
RICHTER, GISELA MARIE AUGUSTA Museum Curator, Writer (1882-1972)
RICHTER, HANS Artist, Filmmaker (1888-1976)
RICKEY, GEORGE W Kinetic Artist, Sculptor (1907-2002)
RIDABOCK, RAY (BUDD) Painter, Instructor (1904-1970)
RIDLEY, GREGORY D, JR Painter, Sculptor (1925-2004)
RIEKER, ALBERT GEORGE Sculptor (1889-1959)
RIEPPEL, LUDWIG Sculptor (1861-1960)
RIGGS, ROBERT Lithographer (1896-1970)
RILEY, BERNARD JOSEPH Painter (1911-1984)
RINGIUS, CARL Painter (1879-1950)
RIPLEY, ALDEN LASSELL Painter (1896-1969)
RIPLEY, ROBERT L Illustrator (1893-1949)
RISHELL, ROBERT CLIFFORD Painter, Sculptor (1917-1976)
RIST, LOUIS G Printmaker (1888-1959)
RITCHIE, ANDREW C Administrator, Historian (1907-1978)
RITMAN, LOUIS Painter (1889-1963)
RITSCHEL, WILLIAM Painter (1864-1949)
RIU, VICTOR Sculptor (1887-1974)
RIVERON, ENRIQUE Painter, Sculptor (1902-1998)
RIVERS, LARRY Painter (1923-2002)
ROBBINS, FRANK Cartoonist, Illustrator (1907-)
ROBERTS, BILL Cartoonist (1914-1978)
ROBERTS, COLETTE (JACQUELINE) Critic, Administrator (1910-1971)
ROBERTS, MORTON Painter (1927-1964)
ROBERTS, PERCIVAL R Educator (1935-)
ROBERTS, TOM (THOMAS KEITH) Painter (1908-)
ROBERTS, VIOLET KENT Painter (1880-)
ROBERTSON, PAUL CHANDLER Painter (1902-1961)
ROBERTSON, SARAH M Painter (-1948)
ROBERTSON, TED WALTER Painter, Instructor (1942-2002)
ROBINSON, ARTHUR GROVE Painter, Printmaker (1935-2002)
ROBINSON, BOARDMAN Painter, Educator (1876-1952)
ROBINSON, MARIE RACHELLE Dealer, Painter (1919-1988)
ROBINSON, THEODORE Painter (1852-1896)
ROBUS, HUGO Sculptor (1885-1964)
ROCH, ERNST Graphic Designer (1928-2003)
ROCKEFELLER, JOHN DAVISON III Collector, Patron (1906-1978)
ROCKEFELLER, LAWRENCE S (MRS) Collector (1910-1997)
ROCKEFELLER, NELSON ALDRICH Collector, Patron (1908-1979)
ROCKEFELLER, WINTHROP Collector (1912-1973)
ROCKWELL, NORMAN Illustrator (1894-1978)
RODMAN, SELDEN Writer, Critic (1909-2002)
ROESCH, KURT (FERDINAND) Painter (1905-)
ROESLER, NORBERT LEONHARD HUGO Collector (1901-)
ROGERS, BRUCE Designer (1870-1957)
ROGERS, CHARLES B Painter, Museum Director (1911-1987)
ROGERS, JOHN Painter (1906-1985)
ROGERS, MARGARET ESTHER Painter (1873-1961)
ROGERS, MEYRIC REYNOLD Museum Curator (1893-1972)
ROGERS, ROBERT STOCKTON Painter (1896-)
ROGNAN, LLOYD NORMAN Illustrator, Painter (1923-2005)
ROHLAND, PAUL Painter, Serigrapher (1884-1953)
ROHLFING, CHRISTIAN Administrator, Curator (1916-2004)
ROJAN, KOVSKY, FEODOR STEPANOVICH Illustrator (1891-1970)
ROLAND, JAY Painter (1905-1960)
ROLLINS, JO LUTZ Dealer, Painter (1896-1989)
ROMANO, EMANUEL GLICEN Painter, Illustrator (1897-)
ROMANS, CHARLES JOHN Painter (1891-1973)
ROMBOUT, LUKE Consultant (1933-2000)
RONALD, WILLIAM Painter (1926-1998)
RONEY, HAROLD ARTHUR Painter, Lecturer (1899-1986)
RONNEBECK, ARNOLD H Sculptor (1885-1947)
ROOD, JOHN Sculptor, Painter (1906-1974)
ROODY, EDITH JEANNETTE Painter
ROOK, EDWARD F Painter (1870-1960)
ROOT, EDWARD WALES Art Authority, Collector (1884-1956)
ROOT, MRS EDWARD W Collector
RORIMER, JAMES J Museum Director (1905-1966)
ROSE, HANNA TOBY Art Administrator (1909-1976)
ROSE, IVER Painter (1899-1972)
ROSELAND, HARRY HERMAN Painter (1866-1950)
ROSEN, CHARLES Painter, Illustrator (1878-1950)
ROSEN, DAVID Restorer (1880-1960)

ROSEN, ESTHER YOVITS Painter, Sculptor (1916-1999)
ROSENBERG, HAROLD Writer, Educator (1906-1978)
ROSENBERG, JAKOB Writer (1893-1990)
ROSENBERG, SAEMY Art Dealer
ROSENBERG, SAMUEL Painter (1896-1972)
ROSENBLUM, JAY Painter, Printmaker (1933-1989)
ROSENBLUM, RICHARD STEPHEN Printmaker, Sculptor (1940-2000)
ROSENQUIT, BERNARD Painter, Printmaker (1923-1991)
ROSENTHAL, (MRS) ALAN H Collector (-1990)
ROSENTHAL, DAVID Painter, Restorer (1876-1949)
ROSENTHAL, DORIS Painter, Lithographer (-1971)
ROSENTHAL, GERTRUDE Historian, Administrator (1903-1989)
ROSENTHAL, LESSING JULIUS Collector, Patron (1891-1979)
ROSIN, HARRY Sculptor, Educator (1897-1973)
ROSOFSKY, SEYMOUR Painter, Printmaker (1924-)
ROSS, ALEXANDER Painter (1908-1990)
ROSS, ALVIN Painter, Educator (1920-1975)
ROSS, C CHANDLER Portrait Painter (-1952)
ROSS, LOUIS Mural Painter (1901-1963)
ROST, MILES ERNEST Painter (1891-1961)
ROSTAND, MICHEL Painter (1895-)
ROSZAK, THEODORE Painter, Sculptor (1907-1981)
ROTAN, WALTER Sculptor (1912-2001)
ROTH, BEN Cartoonist (1910-1960)
ROTHKO, MARK Painter (1903-1970)
ROTHMAN, SIDNEY Gallery Director, Critic (-1995)
ROTHROCK, ILSE SKOPSNA Librarian (1928-1981)
ROTHSCHILD, AMALIE (ROSENFELD) Sculptor, Painter (1916-2001)
ROTHSCHILD, HERBERT Art Collector (1892-1976)
ROTHSCHILD, JUDITH Painter, Collage Artist (-1993)
ROTHSCHILD, LINCOLN Sculptor, Writer (1902-1983)
ROTHSTEIN, ARTHUR Photographer (1915-1985)
ROTIER, PETER Painter (1888-)
ROUSSEAU, THEODORE, JR Museum Curator (1912-1974)
ROVELSTAD, TRYGUE A Sculptor (-1990)
ROWAN, EDWARD BEATTY Painter (1898-1946)
ROWE, CORINNE Painter (-1965)
ROWE, GUY Painter (1894-1969)
ROWLAND, BENJAMIN J R Educator (1904-1972)
ROWLAND, ELDEN HART Painter (1915-1982)
ROZZI, JAMES A Painter, Sculptor (1921-)
RUBEL, C ADRAIN Collector (1904-1978)
RUBEN, RICHARDS Painter, Educator (1925-1998)
RUBEN, LEONARD Designer, Educator (1921-2004)
RUBENSTEIN, LEWIS W Painter, Printmaker (1908-2003)
RUBIN, ARNOLD GARY Historian (1937-1988)
RUBIN, HY Illustrator (1905-1960)
RUBIN, SAMUEL Patrons (1901-1978)
RUBINS, DAVID KRESZ Sculptor (1902-1985)
RUELLAN, ANDRÉE Painter (1905-2006)
RUNGIUS, CARL, Painter (1869-1959)
RUSKIN, LEWIS Collector, Patron (1905-1981)
RUSSELL, BRUCE ALEXANDER Cartoonist (1903-1963)
RUSSELL, HELEN CROCKER Collector (1896-1966)
RUSSELL, HELEN DIANE Historian (1936-2004)
RUSSELL, MORGAN Painter (1886-1953)
RUSSO, MICHELE Painter (1909-2004)
RUSSOLI, FRANCO Art Critic (1923-1977)
RUTSCH, ALEXANDER Sculptor, Painter (-1997)
RUZICKA, RUDOLPH Illustrator, Designer (1883-1978)
RYDER, CHAUNCEY FOSTER Painter (1868-1949)
RYDER, MAHLER BESSINGER Collage Artist, Illustrator (1937-1991)
RYLAND, ROBERT KNIGHT Painter (1873-1951)
SAARJNEN, EERO Architect, Designer (1910-1961)
SABATINI, RAPHAEL Painter, Sculptor (1896-1985)
SABLER, HELEN GERTRUDE Painter (-1950)
SACHS, JAMES H Collector, Patron (1907-1971)
SACHS, PAUL J Educator (1878-1965)
SACHSE, JANICE R Painter, Printmaker (1908-1998)
SACKS, RAY Art Dealer, Consultant (-2001)
SAGE, BILL B Ceramist, Instructor (-1990)
SAGE, KAY (TANGUY) Painter (1898-1963)
SAIDENBERG, DANIEL Dealer (1906-1997)
SAINT, LAWRENCE Painter (1855-1961)
SALEMME, MARTHA Painter (1912-2004)
SALERNO, CHARLES Sculptor, Educator (1916-1999)
SALTER, GEORGE Book Designer (1907-1967)
SALTER, JOHN RANDALL Sculptor, Painter (1898-1978)
SALTONSTALL, ELIZABETH Painter (1900-1990)
SALVATORE, VICTOR Sculptor (1885-1965)
SAMERJAN, GEORGE E Designer, Painter (1915-2005)
SAMPLE, PAUL Painter (1896-1974)
SAMSTAG, GORDON Painter, Sculptor (1906-)
SAMUELS, GERALD Painter, Sculptor (1927-2004)
SANDER, LUDWIG Painter (1906-1975)
SANDERS, HERBERT HARVEY Ceramist, Writer (1909-)
SANDESON, WILLIAM SEYMOUR Cartoonist (1913-2003)
SANKOWSKY, ITZHAK Painter, Sculptor (1908-1994)
SARASON, HENRY Photographer (1896-1979)
SARDEAU, HELENE Sculptor (1889-1968)
SARKIS (SARKIS SARKISIAN) Painter (1909-1977)
SATO, TADASHI Painter, Designer (1923-2005)
SAUGSTAD, OLAF Craftsman, Educator (-1950)
SAUNDERS, AULUS WARD Painter, Educator (1904-1991)
SAUNDERS, CLARA ROSMAN Painter, Educator (-1951)
SAVAGE, AUGUSTA Sculptor (1900-1962)
SAVITZ, FRIEDA Painter, Instructor (1931-1985)
SAWYER, CHARLES HENRY Museum Director (1906-2005)
SAWYER, PHILIP AYER Painter (-1949)
SAWYER, WELLS M Painter (1863-)
SAXON, CHARLES DAVID Cartoonist, Illustrator (1920-1988)
SCANGA, ITALO Sculptor, Educator (1932-2001)
SCARAVAGLIONE, CONCETTA MARIA Sculptor (1900-1975)
SCHAFER, ALICE PAULINE Printmaker (1899-1980)
SCHAFFER, ROSE Painter, Lecturer (-1989)
SCHAN, BERNARDA BRYSON Painter (1903-2004)
SCHANKER, LOUIS Printmaker, Painter (1903-1981)
SCHARY, SAUL Illustrator, Painter (1904-1978)
SCHAUMBURG, DONALD ROLAND Educator, Ceramist (1919-2003)
SCHEIRER, GEORGE A Hand Bookbinder (1895-1959)
SCHELLSTEDE, RICHARD LEE Art Dealer (1948-2004)
SCHELLIN, ROBERT WILLIAM Painter, Craftsman (1910-1985)
SCHEYER ERNST Historian, Lecturer (1900-1985)
SCHIEFER, JOHANNES Painter, Curator
SCHIFF, GERT K A Historian (1926-1990)
SCHINDLER, R M Architect (1887-1953)
SCHLAIKJER JES (WILHELM) Painter, Illustrator (1897-1982)
SCHLICHER KARL THEODORE Painter, Historian (1905-1989)
SCHMECKEBIER, LAURENCE E Historian, Sculptor (1906-)
SCHMEIDLER, BLANCHE J Painter
SCHMIDT, FREDERICK LOUIS Painter, Illustrator (1922-2004)
SCHMIDT, KATHERINE (KATHERINE SCHMIDT SHUBERT) Painter (1898-1978)
SCHMITZ, CARL LUDWIG Sculptor (1900-1967)
SCHNAKENBERG, HENRY Painter (1892-1970)
SCHNEEBAUM, TOBIAS Painter (1921-2005)
SCHNIEWIND, CARL O Curator (1900-1957)
SCHNITTMANN, SASCHA S Sculptor (1913-)
SCHOELKOPF, ROBERT J JR Dealer (1927-1991)
SCHOEN, EUGENE Designer (1880-1957)
SCHOENER, JASON Painter, Lecturer (1919-1997)
SCHOLDER, FRITZ Painter, Sculptor (1937-2005)
SCHOLLE, HARDINGE Museum Director (-1969)
SCHONWALTER, JEAN FRANCES Sculptor, Painter
SCHORR, JUSTIN Painter, Educator (1928-2005)
SCHRACK, JOSEPH EARL Painter (1890-1973)
SCHREIBER, GEORGES Painter (1904-1977)
SCHREIBER, MARTIN Sculptor, Painter (1923-2005)
SCHREIVER, GEORGE AUGUST Curator, Art Historian (-1977)
SCHREYER, GRETA L Painter, Printmaker (1917-2005)
SCHROEDER, ERIC Museum Curator, Writer (1904-)
SCHUCKER, CHARLES Painter, Educator (1908-1998)
SCHUELER, JON R Painter (1916-1992)
SCHULE, CLIFFORD HAMILTON Painter, Sculptor (1918-2000)
SCHULLER, GRETE Sculptor
SCHULMAN, JACOB Collector (1915-1987)
SCHULMAN, ROBERT Painter, Director (1924-2004)
SCHULTZ, HAROLD A Painter, Educator (1907-2004)
SCHULZ ROBERT EMIL Illustrator, Painter (1929-1978)
SCHULZ, CHARLES MONROE Cartoonist (1922-2000)
SCHUPLINSKY, WALTER Painter (1921-1990)
SCHUSTER DONNA NORINE Painter (1883-1953)
SCHUSTER, CARL Art Historian, Art Writer (1904-)
SCHUTZ, ANTON Restorer, Writer (1894-1977)
SCHUTZ, ESTELLE Painter, Printmaker (1907-2005)
SCHUTZ, PRESCOTT DIETROCH Dealer (1948-1990)
SCHUYLER, PHILIP (GRIFFIN) Painter, Educator (1913-)
SCHWABACHER, ETHEL K Painter (1903-1984)
SCHWACHA, GEORGE Painter (1908-1986)
SCHWARTZ, MANFRED Painter (1909-1970)
SCHWARTZ, MARJORIE WATSON Painter (1905-)
SCHWARTZMAN, DANIEL Architect (1909-1977)

SCHWARZ, FELIX CONRAD Painter, Educator (1906-1990)
SCHWARZ, FRANK HENRY Painter (1894-1951)
SCHWARZ, HEINRICH Curator, Educator (1894-1974)
SCHWEDLER, WILLIAM A Painter (1942-1982)
SCHWEITZER, M R Dealer, Gallery Director (1911-)
SCHWIDDER, ERNST Sculptor, Designer (1931-1998)
SCHWIERING, CONRAD Painter (1916-)
SCOTT, BERTHA Portrait Painter (1884-1965)
SCOTT, C(HARLES) A(RTHUR) Sculptor (1940-2004)
SCOTT, CLYDE EUGENE Painter (1884-1959)
SCOTT, HENRY E Painter, Educator (1900-1990)
SCOTT, MARTHA F Printmaker, Sculptor (1916-1996)
SCOTT-GIBSON, HERBERT NATHANIEL Art Administrator, Educator (1928-1981)
SCRIVNER, (BOB) ROBERT MACFIE Sculptor, Curator (1914-1999)
SEAMES, CLARANN Painter, Illustrator (-1992)
SEARLES, STEPHEN Sculptor, Painter
SEAVER, ESTHER Educator (-1965)
SEGAL, GEORGE Sculptor (1924-2000)
SEGY, LADISLAS Dealer, Collector (1904-1998)
SEIBEL, FRED 0 Cartoonist (1886-1968)
SEIDE, CHARLES Painter, Educator (1915-1980)
SEIDEL, ALEXANDER CARL-VICTOR Painter, Designer (1897-1979)
SEITZ, WILLIAM CHAPIN Educator, Art Historian (1914-1974)
SELDIS, HENRY J Art Critic (1925-1978)
SELEY, JASON Sculptor (1919-1983)
SELIG, J DANIEL Museum Director, Curator (1938-)
SELIGMAN, CHARLES Art Dealer (1893-1978)
SELIGMANN, HERBERT J Writer (1891-1984)
SELIGMANN, KURT Painter, Printmaker (1900-1962)
SELLECK, MARGARET Painter (1892-)
SELLIN, DAVID Lecturer, Curator (1930-2006)
SELONKE, IRENE A Painter (-1981)
SEMANS, JAMES HUSTEAD Patron (1932-2004)
SENNHAUSER, JOHN Painter, Designer (-1978)
SERGER, FREDERICK B Painter (1889-1965)
SERGER, HELEN Art Dealer (1901-1989)
SERISAWA, SUEO Painter (1910-2004)
SESSLER, ALFRED A Painter (1909-1963)
SETTERBERG, CARL GEORG Painter, Illustrator (1897-)
SEWELL, HELEN MOORE Illustrator (1897-1957)
SEXTON, EMILY STRYKER Painter (1880-1948)
SEYFERT, RICHARD LEOPOLD Painter, Instructor (1915-1979)
SEYMOUR, CHARLES JR Art Historian, Curator (1912-1977)
SHACKELFORD, SHELBY Painter (1899-1987)
SHADBOLT, JACK LEONARD Painter (1909-1998)
SHAFER, BURR Cartoonist (-1965)
SHAFER, MARGUERITE (PHILLIPS) NEUHAUSER Artist (1888-1976)
SHAHN, BEN Painter (1898-1969)
SHANGRAW, CLARENCE FRANK Historian, Curator (1935-2004)
SHANGRAW, SYLVIA CHEN Historian, Curator (1937-)
SHAPIRO, DAVID Painter, Printmaker (1916-2005)
SHAPLEY, JOHN Historian (1890-1969)
SHAPSHAK, RENE Sculptor (-1985)
SHARON, MARY B Painter (1891-1961)
SHARP, WILLIAM Painter (1900-1961)
SHAVER, JAMES ROBERT Painter (1867-1949)
SHAW, CHARLES GREEN Painter, Writer (1892-1974)
SHAW, WILFRED B Painter (1881-)
SHEELER, CHARLES Painter (1883-1965)
SHEETS, MILLARD Designer, Painter (1907-1989)
SHEFFER, GLENN C Painter, Illustrator (1881-1948)
SHEFFERS, PETER WINTHROP Painter (1893-1949)
SHEPLER, DWIGHT (CLARK) Painter, Writer (1905-)
SHEPPARD, CARL DUNKLE Historian (1916-1998)
SHEPPARD, JOHN CRAIG Painter, Educator (1913-1978)
SHERMAN, JOHN K (URTZ) Critic (1898-1969)
SHERWOOD, ROSINA EMMET Painter (1854-1948)
SHERWOOD, SHERRY Designer (1902-)
SHERWOOD, WILLIAM ANDERSON Painter, Etcher (1875-1951)
SHINN, EVERETT Painter (1876-1953)
SHIPLEY, JAMES R Educator, Designer (1910-1990)
SHIRAI, AKIKO Painter, Printmaker (-2001)
SHOEMAKER, PETER Painter (1920-)
SHOEMAKER, PETER Painter (1920-1998)
SHOENFELT, JOSEPH FRANKLIN Painter (1918-1968)
SHOKLER, HARRY Painter, Serigrapher (1896-)
SHOOTER, TOM Painter (1941-2004)
SHOPE, IRVIN (SHORTY) Painter (1900-1977)
SHOPEN, KENNETH Painter (1902-1967)
SHORNEY, MARGO KAY (MCIVER) Art Dealer, Sculptor (1930-1996)
SHORTER, EDWARD SWIFT Painter, Collector (1902-)
SHOWELL, KENNETH L Painter (1939-1997)
SHRADY, FREDERICK Sculptor (1907-1990)
SHRYOCK, BURNETT HENRY, SR Painter (1904-1971)
SHUCK, KENNETH MENAUGH Museum Director, Painter (1921-1992)
SHULKIN, ANATOL Painter (1901-1961)
SHULL, JAMES MARION Painter (1872-1948)
SHUNNEY, ANDREW Painter (1921-)
SHUTE, BEN E Painter (1905-1986)
SIBLEY, CHARLES KENNETH Painter, Educator (1921-2005)
SICA Printmaker, Sculptor (1932-)
SIDERIS, ALEXANDER Painter (1898-1978)
SIEGEL, ADRIAN Photographer, Painter (1898-1978)
SIEGL, THEODOR Conservator, Lecturer (-1976)
SIEGRIST, LUNDY Painter (1925-1985)
SIEVAN, MAURICE Painter (1898-1981)
SIGLER, HOLLIS Painter (1948-2001)
SIHVONEN, OLI Painter (1921-1991)
SILKOTCH, MARY ELLEN Painter (1911-)
SILVA, WILLIAM POSEY Painter (1859-1948)
SILVER, PAT Graphic Artist, Painter (1922-1992)
SILVERCRUYS, SUSANNE (MRS EDWARD FORD STEVENSON) Sculptor, Lecturer (1899-1973)
SILVERMAN, MEL Painter (-1966)
SIMMONS, WILLIAM Etcher (1884-1949)
SIMON, BERNARD Sculptor, Instructor (1896-1980)
SIMON, ERIC M Illustrator, Designer (1892-1978)
SIMON, HOWARD Illustrator, Painter (1903-1979)
SIMON, NORTON Collector (1907-1993)
SIMON, SYDNEY Sculptor, Painter (1917-1997)
SIMONDS, JOHN ORMSBEE Architect (1913-2005)
SIMONET, SEBASTIAN Illustrator, Painter (1898-1948)
SIMONI, JOHN PETER Painter, Educator (1911-2003)
SIMONS, LOUIS BEDELL Painter (1912-1977)
SIMPSON, MARSHALL Painter (1900-1958)
SIMPSON, WILLIAM Painter (1818-1872)
SINAIKO, ARLIE Sculptor, Collector (1902-)
SINGER, ARTHUR B Illustrator, Painter (1917-1990)
SINGER, NANCY BARKHOUSE Dealer (1912-2003)
SINSABAUGH, ART Photographer, Educator (1924-1983)
SINTON, NELL (WALTER) Painter, Instructor (-1997)
SIPORIN, MITCHELL Painter, Educator (1910-1976)
SIQUEIROS, DAVID ALFARO Painter (1896-1974)
SISSON, JACQUELINE D Librarian, Educator (1925-1980)
SIUMMERS, DUDLEY GLOYNE Painter, Illustrator (1892-1975)
SIVARD, ROBERT PAUL Painter (1914-1990)
SKEGGS, DAVID POTTER Designer, Painter (1924-1973)
SKEMP, ROBERT OLIVER Painter (1910-1984)
SKILES, CHARLES Cartoonist (-1969)
SKINAS, JOHN CONSTANTINE Painter (-1966)
SKLAR, DOROTHY Painter
SKLAR, GEORGE Painter (1905-1968)
SKOOGFORS, OLAF Silversmith (-1975)
SLATER, FRANK Portrait Painter (-1965)
SLATKES, LEONARD J Historian (1930-2003)
SLATKIN, CHARLES E Art Dealer (1908-1977)
SLATKIN, YEFFE KIMBALL Painter (1914-1978)
SLAUGHTER, HAZEL BURNHAM Painter (1888-1979)
SLAUGHTER, LURLINE EDDY Painter (1919-1991)
SLICK, JAMES NELSON Painter, Sculptor (1901-1979)
SLOAN, JOHN Painter, Educator (1871-1951)
SLOANE, ERIC Painter (1910-1985)
SLOANE, JOSEPH CURTIS Historian (1909-)
SLOBODKIN, LOUIS Sculptor, Illustrator (1903-1975)
SMALLEY, JANET Illustrator (1893-)
SMEDLEY, WILL LARYMORE Painter (1871-)
SMITH, ALBERT DELMONT Portrait Painter (1886-1962)
SMITH, ANDRE Painter (1880-1959)
SMITH, BARBARA NEFF Patron (1908-1977)
SMITH, CECIL ALDEN Painter, Sculptor (1910-1984)
SMITH, DAVID Sculptor (1906-1965)
SMITH, EMILY GUTHRIE Painter (1909-1987)
SMITH, GORDON MACKINTOSH Museum Director (1906-1979)
SMITH, GREGORY Painter
SMITH, HELEN M Illustrator, Painter (1917-2005)
SMITH, HENRY HOLMES Photographer, Educator (1909-1986)
SMITH, HOWARD ROSS Curator (1910-)
SMITH, JACOB GETLAR Painter (1898-1958)
SMITH, JUDSON Painter (1880-1962)
SMITH, JUSTIN V Collector (1903-)
SMITH, LAWRENCE M C Collector, Patron (1902-1975)

SMITH, LEON POLK Painter, Cottage Artist (1906-1996)
SMITH, LYN WALL Writer, Painter (1909-1979)
SMITH, ROBERT C Educator (1912-1975)
SMITH, SAM Painter, Educator (1918-1999)
SMITH, TONY Sculptor (1902-)
SMITH, VINCENT D Painter, Printmaker (1929-2003)
SMITH, W HARRY Painter, Restorer (1875-1951)
SMITH, WALT ALLEN Sculptor, Designer (1910-1971)
SMITH, WILLIAM ARTHUR Painter, Printer (1918-)
SMITHSON, ROBERT Sculptor, Lecturer (1938-1974)
SMOLIN, NAT Sculptor, Painter (1890-1950)
SMONGESLI, JOSEPH LEON Painter, Designer (1914-2001)
SMYTH, ED Illustrator, Painter (1916-1996)
SNELOROVE, GORDON WILLIAM Educator
SOBY, JAMES THRALL Writer, Critic (1906-1979)
SOGLOW, OTTO Cartoonist (1900-1975)
SOLES, WILLIAM Sculptor (-1967)
SOLINGER, DAVID M Collector, Patron
SOLOMON, HOLLY Art Dealer, Collector (-2002)
SOLOMON, HYDE Painter (1911-)
SOLON, HARRY Painter (1873-1958)
SOLOWEY, BEN Cartoonist (1901-1978)
SOLTESZ, FRANK JOSEPH Painter (1912-1986)
SOMBERG, HERMAN Painter (1917-1991)
SOMMER, WASSILY Painter, Educator (1912-1979)
SOMMERBURG, MIRIAM Mosaic Artist, Sculptor (-1980)
SONED, WARREN Painter (1911-1966)
SONNENSCHEIN Patron, Historian (1917-1981)
SOPHER, AARON Painter, Illustrator (1905-1972)
SOPHER, BERNHARD D Sculptor (1879-1949)
SORBY, J RICHARD Painter, Designer (1911-2001)
SOREFF, HELEN Painter (1937-1998)
SORENSEN, JEAN Painter
SORENSEN, JOHN HJELMHOF Cartoonist (1923 1969)
SORIA, MARTIN SEBASTIAN Educator (1911-1961)
SOROKIN, DAVIS Art Dealer, Painter (1908-1977)
SOUTHWELL, WILLIAM JOSEPH Painter, Writer (1914-2002)
SOVIAK, HARRY Painter, Sculptor (1935-)
SOYER, ISAAC Painter, Instructor (1902-1981)
SOYER, MOSES Painter (1899-1974)
SOZID, ARMANDO Painter (-1966)
SPAETH, OTTO Collector (1897-1966)
SPANDORF, LILY GABRIELLA Painter, Muralist (-2000)
SPARK, VICTOR DAVID Dealer (1898-1991)
SPAVENTA, GEORGE Sculptor (1918-1978)
SPAYREGEN, MORRIS Collector
SPEAR, ARTHUR P Painter (1879-1959)
SPEICHER, EUGENE E Painter (1883-1962)
SPEIGHT, FRANCIS Painter, Educator (1896-1989)
SPENCER, HUGH Illustrator, Photographer (1887-1975)
SPENCER, LEONTINE G Painter (1882-1964)
SPENCER, NILES Painter (1893-1952)
SPERRY, ROBERT Ceramist (1927-1998)
SPICER-SIMPSON, THEODORE Sculptor (1871-1959)
SPIEGELMAN, LON HOWARD Painter, Publisher (1941-2002)
SPOHN, CLAY (EDGAR) Painter, Instructor (1898-1977)
SPRADLING, FRANK L Painter (1885-1972)
SPRAGUE-SMITH, ISABELLE DWIGHT (MRS CHARLES) (1861-1951)
SPRANG, ELIZABETH Painter, Sculptor (-1993)
SPRINGHORN, CARL Painter (1897-1971)
SPRINGWEILER, ERWIN FREDERICK Sculptor (1896-1968)
SPRUANCE, BENTON Lithographer (1904-1967)
SPURGEON, SARAH (EDNA M) Painter, Educator (1903-1985)
SQUIRE, ALLAN TAFT Designer
ST AMAND, JOSEPH Painter (1925-1992)
ST CLAIR, MICHAEL Art Dealer (1912-1999)
ST GAUDENS, HOMER Educator (1879-1958)
ST JOHN, BRUCE Administrator, Historian (1916-)
STACHELBERG, CHARLES G Collector, Patron
STACKS, WILLIAM LEON Painter, Restorer (1928-1991)
STADLER, ALBERT Painter (1923-2000)
STAEMPFLI, GEORGE W Dealer, Painter (1910-1999)
STAFFEL, RUDOLF HARRY Ceramist, Instructor (1911-2002)
STAGG, MRS JESSIE A Sculptor (1891-1958)
STALLMAN, EMMA S Craftsman (1888-1959)
STAMATS, PETER OWEN Collector, Patron (1929-2003)
STAMATY, STANLEY Cartoonist, Illustrator (1916-1979)
STAMOS, THEODOROS (S) Painter (1922-1997)
STAMPER, WILSON YOUNG Painter (1912-1988)
STAMPFLE, FELICE Curator, Writer (1912-2000)
STANDEN, EDITH APPLETON Historian (1905-1998)
STANKIEWICZ, RICHARD PETER Sculptor, Educator (1922-1983)
STANLEY, BOB Painter (1932-)
STAPLES, ROY HARVARD Painter (1905-1958)
STAPP, RAY VERYL Painter, Printmaker (1913-2000)
STARK, GEORGE KING Educator, Sculptor (1923-1992)
STARK, JACK GAGE Painter (1882-1950)
STARKWEATHER, WILLIAM E B Painter (1878-1969)
STARRS, MILDRED Painter
STARS, WILLIAM KENNETH Educator, Museum Director (1921-1985)
STAUFFER, EDNA PENNYPACKER Painter (1887-1956)
STAUFFER, RICHARD L Sculptor, Educator (1932-2005)
STAVENITZ, ALEXANDER RAQUL Etcher (1901-1960)
STEA, CESARE Sculptor (1893-1960)
STEAD, REXEORD ARTHUR Administrator, Historian (1923-)
STECHOW, WOLFGANG Art Historian (1896-1975)
STEDMAN, WILFRED HENRY Sculptor (1882-1950)
STEEGMULLER, BEATRICE STEIN Painter (-1961)
STEENE, WILLIAM Painter (1888-1965)
STEICHEN, EDWARD Photographer (1879-1979)
STEIG, WILLIAM Cartoonist, Sculptor (1907-2003)
STEIGER, FREDERIC Painter, Instructor (-1990)
STEINBERG, MRS MILTON (EDITH) Art Director (1910-1970)
STEINBERG, SAUL Cartoonist (1914-1999)
STEINER, RALPH Photographer (1899-1986)
STEINITZ, KATE TRAUMAN Writer, Historian (1893-)
STEINMETZ, GRACE ERNST TITUS Painter (1911-2004)
STELL, H KENYON Printmaker, Historian (1910-1990)
STEPPAT, LEO LUDWIG Sculptor, Educator (1910-1964)
STERN, ARTHUR LEWIS (MR) Collector (1911-)
STERN, ARTHUR LEWIS (MRS) Collector (1913-)
STERN, HAROLD PHILLIP Museum Director, Writer (1922-1977)
STERN, JAN PETER Sculpture (1926-2004)
STERNBERG, HARRY Graphic Artist, Painter (1904-2001)
STERNBERG, PAUL Collector (1917-2004)
STERNBERG, PAUL EDWARD, SR Curator, Consultant (1934-2003)
STERNE, MAURICE Painter (1878-1957)
STERRETT, CLIFF Cartoonist (1883-1964)
STEVENS, EDWARD JOHN JR Painter, Director (1923-1988)
STEVENS, LAWRENCE TENNY Sculptor, Educator (1896-1972)
STEVENS, WALTER HOLLIS Painter, Educator (1927-1980)
STEVENSON, BEULAH Painter (-1965)
STEWARD, DONN HORATIO Printmaker, Publisher (1921-1986)
STEWARD, JARVIS ANTHONY Educator, Painter (1914-1981)
STIEGELMEYER, NORMAN EARL Painter, Sculptor (1937-)
STILES, HELEN Painter, Printmaker (-1992)
STILL, CLYFFORD Painter (1904-1981)
STILLMAN, GEORGE Painter (1921-)
STILWELL, WILBUR MOORE Educator, Writer (1908-1974)
STITES, RAYMOND SOMMERS Historian, Writer (1899-1974)
STOESSEL, HENRY KURT Painter, Designer (1909-)
STOFFA, MICHAEL Instructor, Painter (-2001)
STONE, ANNA B Painter (1874-1949)
STONE, BEATRICE Sculptor (1900-1962)
STONE, EDWARD DURELL Architect (1902-1978)
STONE, FRED J Art Dealer, Consultant (1919-2003)
STONEHILL, MARY (MRS GEORGE) Painter (1900-1951)
STOOPS, HERBERT M Illustrator (1887-1948)
STORM, MARK (KENNEDY) Painter, Sculptor (1911-2002)
STORRS, JOHN Sculptor (1885-1956)
STORY, WILLIAM EASTON Painter, Museum Director (1925-1998)
STOUMEN, LOU Filmmaker, Photographer (1916-1991)
STOUT, GEORGE LESLIE Consultant (1897-1978)
STRALEM, DONALD S Collector, Patron (1903-1976)
STRATER, HENRY Painter (1896-1987)
STRAUSER, STERLING BOYD Painter (1907-)
STRAUSS, WALTER LEOPOLD Historian, Publisher (1932-1988)
STRAUTMANIS, EDVINS Painter, Sculptor (1933-1992)
STRISIK, PAUL Painter (1918-1998)
STROESSNER, ROBERT JOSEPH Curator, Historian (1942-1991)
STROSAHL, WILLIAM Painter (1910-2002)
STROTHMANN, FRED Illustrator (1880-1958)
STRUNK, HERBERT JULOAN Sculptor (1891-)
STUART, DAVID Dealer (-1984)
STUBBLEDINE, JAMES HARVEY Historian (1920-1987)
STUIDA, WILLIAM Art Authority (1877-1959)
STYKA, ADAM Painter (1890-1959)
STYLES, GEORGE WILLIAM Painter (1887-1949)
SUGARMAN, GEORGE Sculptor, Painter (1912-1999)
SULLINS, ROBERT M Painter (1926-1991)
SUMMY, ANNE TUNIS Painter, Printmaker (1912-1986)
SURREY, MILT Painter (1922-2004)

SURREY, PHILIP HENRY Painter (1910-1990)
SUSSMAN, RICHARD N Painter, Graphic Artist (1909-1971)
SUTHERLAND, SANDY Painter (1902-)
SUTTON, GEORGE MIKSCH Painter, Illustrator (1898-1982)
SUTTON, RUTH HAVILAND Painter (1898-1960)
SVENDSEN, LOUISE AVERILL Curator (1915-1994)
SVOBODA, VINCENT A Painter (1877-1961)
SWAN, BRADFORD F Art Critic, Painter (1907-1976)
SWANN, ERWIN Collector, Patron (1906-1973)
SWARTBURG, B ROBERT Architect (1895-1975)
SWARTZ, PHILIP SCOTT Painter, Collector (1936-1990)
SWARZENSKI, GEORG Research Fellow (1876-1957)
SWAY, ALBERT Painter, Etcher (1913-2003)
SWAZO, (PATRICK SWAZO HINDS) Painter, Illustrator (1924-1974)
SWENEY, FRED Illustrator, Painter (1912-1995)
SWENSON, HOWARD WILLIAM Sculptor (1901-1960)
SWIGGETT, JEAN DONALD Graphic Artist, Painter (1910-)
SWINDELL, BERTHA Painter (1874-1951)
SWINNERTON, EDNA HUESTIS Miniature Painter (-1964)
SWINNERTON, JAMES Cartoonist, Painter (1875-1974)
SYLVESTER, LUCILLE Painter, Writer (1909-)
SZABO, ZOLTAN Painter, Writer (1928-2003)
SZANTO, LOUIS P Painter (1889-1965)
SZASZ, FRANK V Painter, Printmaker (1925-1995)
SZYK, ARTHUR Illustrator (1894-1951)
TAIT, KATHARINE LAMB Painter, Designer (1895-1981)
TAKACH, MARY H Museum Director, Historian (1932-1997)
TAKIS, NICHOLAS Painter (1903-1965)
TALBOT, JAROLD DEAN Painter, Director (1907-1997)
TALBOT, WILLIAM (H M) Kinetic Artist, Sculptor (1918-1980)
TAM, REUBEN Painter, Poet (1916-1992)
TAMAYO, RUFINO Painter (1899-1991)
TAMOTZU, CHUZO Artist
TANGUY, YVES Painter (1900-1955)
TANNER, HENRY OSSAWA Painter (1859-1937)
TANNER, WARREN Painter, Administrator (1942-)
TARNOPOL, GREGOIRE Painter, Collector (1891-1979)
TATTI, BENEDICT MICHAEL Sculptor, Painter (1917-1993)
TAUBES, FREDERIC Painter, Writer (1900-1981)
TAUCH WALDINE AMANDA Sculptor, Collector (1892-1986)
TAYLOR, AL C Sculptor, Printmaker (1948-1999)
TAYLOR, ANNA HEYWARD Painter (1879-1956)
TAYLOR, DAVIDSON Director (1907-1979)
TAYLOR, EMILY (MRS J MADISON TAYLOR) Miniature Painter (1860-1952)
TAYLOR, FRANCIS HENRY Museum Director (1903-1857)
TAYLOR, FREDERICK BOURCHIER Painter, Sculptor (1906-)
TAYLOR, HARRY GEORGE Printmaker (1918-2002)
TAYLOR, JOHN (WILLIAMS) Painter, Printmaker (1897-1983)
TAYLOR, JOHN CE Painter, Educator (1902-1985)
TAYLOR, JOHN LLOYD Director, Consultant (1935-)
TAYLOR, JOSHUA CHARLES Museum Director, Historian (1917-1981)
TAYLOR, LISA Museums Director (1933-1991)
TAYLOR, PAUL Writer, Critic (1958-1992)
TAYLOR, PRENTISS (HOTTEL) Painter, Lithographer (1907-1991)
TAYLOR, RENE CLAUDE Museum Director, Historian (1916-1997)
TEAGUE, DONALD Painter (1897-1991)
TEAGUE, WALTER DORWIN Designer (1884-1960)
TEE-VAN, HELEN DAMROSCH Painter, Illustrator (1893-1976)
TEFET, CHARLES EUGENE Sculptor (1874-)
TEICHMAN, SABINA Painter, Sculptor (-1983)
TELLER, JANE (SIMON) Sculptor
TEMPLETON, ROBERT CLARK Painter (1929-1991)
TENGGREN, GUSTAV ADOLF Painter (1896-1970)
TEPPER, NATALIE ARRAS Painter (1895-1950)
TERRY, DUNCAN NILES Stained Glass Artist, Craftsman (1909-1989)
THAL, SAMUEL Etcher (1903-)
THALACKER, DONALD WILLIAM Administrator, Architect (1939-1987)
THEODORE, ION PAN Sculptor, Instructor (-1997)
THIELEN, GREG GLEN Curator (1940-1994)
THOMAS, ALMA WOODSEY Painter (1891-1978)
THOMAS, BYRON Painter (1902-1978)
THOMAS, H REYNOLDS Painter, Illustrator (1927-1991)
THOMAS, HELEN (DOANE) Writer, Painter (-2003)
THOMAS, JOHN Painter, Printmaker (1927-2001)
THOMAS, MARY LEATH Painter (1905-1959)
THOMAS, ROBERT CHESTER Sculptor (1924-1987)
THOMAS, STEFFEN WOLFGANG Sculptor, Painter (1906-1990)
THOMPSON, BOB Painter (-1966)
THOMPSON, ERNEST THORNE Educator, Painter (-1992)
THOMPSON, FREDERICK Painter (1904-1956)
THOMPSON, GEORGE LOUIS Designer (1913-1981)
THOMPSON, JULIET H Painter (-1956)
THOMPSON, KENNETH WEBSTER Illustrator, Painter (1907-)
THOMPSON, LESLIE P Painter (1880-1963)
THOMPSON, RICHARD EARL SR Painter (1914-1991)
THOMPSON, WALTER WHITCOMB Painter (1892-1948)
THORP, EARL NORWELL Sculptor (-1951)
THORPE, HILDA (SHAPIRO) Painter, Sculptor (1919-2000)
THURLOW, FEARN CUTLER Curator (1924-1982)
THWAITES, CHARLES WINSTANLEY Painter, Muralist (1904-2002)
TIBBS, THURLOW E Museum Director
TIBBS, THURLOW EVANS JR Writer, Collector (-1997)
TILLIM, SIDNEY Painter, Instructor (1925-2001)
TISCHLER, VICTOR Painter, Lithographer (1890-1951)
TISHMAN, JACK A Collector (-1966)
TOBEY, ALTON S Painter, Sculptor (1914-2005)
TOBEY, MARK Painter (1890-1976)
TOBIAS, JULIUS Sculptor, Painter (1915-1999)
TOBIAS, THOMAS J Collector, Museum Trustee (1906-1970)
TOFEL, JENNINGS Painter (1892-1959)
TOIGO, DANIEL JOSEPH Painter (1912-1992)
TOLGESY, VICTOR Sculptor, Writer (1928-1980)
TOMLIN, BRADLEY WALKER Painter (1899-1953)
TONEY, ANTHONY Painter, Educator (1913-2004)
TOO, OSMA GALLINGER Writer, Weaver (-1983)
TOPCHEVSKY, MORRIS Painter, Etcher (1899-)
TOPPING, JAMES Painter (1879-1949)
TORBERT, DONALD ROBERT Educator, Historian (1910-1985)
TORRES, HORACIO Painter (1924-1976)
TOWN, HAROLD BARLING Painter, Writer (1924-1990)
TOWNSEND, (ALVIN) NEAL Ceramist, Painter (1934-2002)
TOWNSEND, LEE Painter (1895-1965)
TRACY, BERRY BRYSON Curator, Administrator (1933-1984)
TRANK, LYNN EDGAR Educator, Painter (1918-2004)
TRAPHAGEN, ETHEL Designer (1882-1963)
TRAPIER, PIERRE PINCKNEY ALSTON Painter (1897-1957)
TRAPP, FRANK ANDERSON Museum Director, Historian (1922-2005)
TRAVERS, GWYNETH MABEL Printmaker (1911-1982)
TRAVIS, KATHRYNE HAIL Painter (1894-1972)
TRAVIS, OLIN (HERMAN) Painter (1888-1975)
TREASTER, RICHARD A Painter, Educator (1932-2002)
TREES, CLYDE C Numismatist (1885-1960)
TREIMAN, JOYCE WAHL Painter, Sculptor (1922-1991)
TRIMM, ADON Painter (1895-1959)
TROCHE, E GUNTER Museum Director (1909-1971)
TROFON, HARRIETTE Painter, Sculptor
TRUBNER, HENRY Curator, Museologist (1920-1999)
TRUEX, VAN DAY Painter, Designer (1904-)
TSCHACBASOV, NAHUM Painter, Printmaker (1899-1984)
TSEU, ROSITA HSU Administrator, Instructor (1916-2003)
TSUTAKAWA, GEORGE Sculptor, Painter (1910-1997)
TUBBY, JOSIAH THOMAS Painter (1875-1958)
TUCKER, CHARLES CLEMENT Painter (1913-1996)
TUCKER, CURTIS (DEE) Ceramist, Lecturer (1938-1992)
TUDOR, ROSAMOND Painter, Etcher (1878-1949)
TUFTS, ELEANOR M Historian, Educator (-1991)
TULLSEN, REX Painter, Instructor (1907-1991)
TUNIS, EDWIN Writer, Illustrator (1897-1973)
TUPPER, ALEXANDER GARFIELD Painter
TURANO, DON Sculptor, Medalist (1930-2002)
TURNBULL, GRACE HJLL Sculptor, Painter (1880-1976)
TURNBULL, JAMES B Painter (1906-1976)
TURNER SR, JAMES THOMAS Sculptor, Painter (1933-2001)
TURNER, HARRIET FRENCH Painter (-1967)
TURNER, JANET E Printmaker, Educator (1914-1988)
TURNER, JOSEPH Patron (1892-1973)
TURNER, RAYMOND Sculptor (1903-1985)
TURNER, ROBERT CHAPMAN Ceramist, Educator (1913-2005)
TURNER, THEODORE ROY Educator, Painter (1922-2002)
TWIGGS, RUSSELL GOULD Painter (1898-1991)
TWIGG-SMITH, LAILA Collector (1944-)
TWORKOV, JACK Painter (1900-1982)
TYSON, MARY (MRS KENNETH THOMPSON) Painter (1909-2001)
TYTELL, LOUIS Painter (1913-2001)
UCELLO, VINCENZA AGATHA Painter, Director (-2004)
UCHIMA, ANSEI Printmaker, Painter (1921-2000)
UCHIMA, TOSHIKO Painter, Assemblage Artist (1918-2000)
UHLER, RUTH PERSHING Painter (1898-)
UHRMAN, CELIA Painter, Writer (1927-1998)
UHRMAN, ESTHER Painter, Writer (1921-2004)
ULLMAN, HAROLD P Collector (1899-)
ULP, CLIFFORD McCORMICK Painter (1885-1957)

ULREOCH, NURA WOODSON Painter (-1950)
UNDERWOOD, ELISABETH (KENDALL) Artist (1896-1976)
UNDERWOOD, EVELYN NOTMAN Painter (1898-1983)
UNGER, MARY ANN Sculptor (1945-1999)
UNWIN, NORA SPICER Illustrator, Printmaker (-1982)
UPJOHN, EVERARD MILLER Historian (1903-1978)
URBACH, LES Sculptor (-1997)
URBAITIS, ELENA Painter, Sculptor (-2006)
URBAN, ALBERT Painter (1909-1959)
URBAN, REVA Painter, Sculptor (1925-1987)
USHER, DAVID Publisher, Art Dealer (1939-1997)
USHER, RUBY WALKER Painter (1889-1957)
USUI, KIICHI Curator (1931-2001)
VACCARO, NICK DANTE Educator, Painter (1931-2002)
VAIL, LAURENCE Collegiate (1857-1968)
VALENSTEIN, ALICE Painter, Collector (1904-2002)
VALENTINER, WILLIAM REINHOLD Museum Director (1880-1958)
VALINSKI, DENNIS JOHN Sculptor, Lecturer (1946-1979)
VALTMAN, EDMUND Cartoonist, Editor (1914-2005)
VAN BUREN, RAEBURN Illustrator, Cartoonist (1891-1987)
VAN DER BEEK, EDWARD STANLEY Filmmaker, Video Artist (1927-1984)
VAN DER POOL, JAMES GROTE Historian (1903-1979)
VAN DER ROHE, LUDWIG M Architect (-1969)
VAN DER VOORT, AMANDA VENELIA Painter (-1980)
VAN DOREN, HAROLD LIVINGSTON Designer (1896-1957)
VAN DRESSER, WILLIAM Portrait Painter (1871-1950)
VAN HOOK, DAVID H Painter, Administrator (1923-1986)
VAN LEER, W LEICESTER Collector (1905-)
VAN OORDT, PETER Painter, Graphic Artist (1903-1988)
VAN ROSEN, ROBERT E Industrial Designer (1904-1966)
VAN SOELEN, THEODORE Painter (1880-1964)
VAN TONGEREN, HERK Sculptor (1943-1988)
VAN WOLF, HENRY Sculptor (1898-1982)
VANDER SLUIS, GEORGE J Painter, Educator (1915-1984)
VANN, LOLI (MRS LILIAN VAN YOUNG) Painter (1913-1999)
VARGA, FERENC Sculptor (-1989)
VARGA, MARGIT Painter, Writer (1908-2005)
VARGIS, POLYGNOTIS Sculptor (1894-1965)
VARLEY, FREDERICK H Painter (-1969)
VASILIEFF, NICHOLAS Painter (1892-1970)
VASILS, ALBERT Painter, Illustrator (1915-)
VAWTER, MARY H MURRAY Painter (1871-)
VELSEY, SETH M Sculptor (1903-1967)
VERNER, ELIZABETH O'NEILL Etcher, Writer (1883-1979)
VERTES, MARCEL Painter (1895-1961)
VERZYL, KENNETH H Dealer, Draftsman (1922-1987)
VIAN, ORFEO Educator, Printmaker (1924-1989)
VICENTE, ESTEBAN Painter (1903-2001)
VICKERS, RUSS(ELL GERON) Painter, Conceptual Artist (1923-1997)
VIESULAS, ROMAS Printmaker, Educator (1918-)
VIGIL, VELOY JOSEPH Painter, Printmaker (1931-1997)
VILLON, VLADIMAR Exhibition Director (1905-1976)
VOGEL, EDWIN CHESTER Collector (1883-1973)
VOLKMAR, LEON Ceramist (1879-1959)
VOLLMER, RUTH Sculptor (-1982)
VON DER LANCKEN, FRANK Painter (1872-1950)
VON FUEHRER, OTTMAR F Painter (-1967)
VON JOST, ALEXANDER Painter (1889-1968)
VON SCHLEGELL, DAVID Sculptor (1920-1992)
VON WEISE, WENDA FRAKER Printmaker, Tapestry Artist (1941-)
VON WICHT, JOHN Painter, Graphic Designer (1888-1970)
VON WIEGAND, CHARMION Painter, Writer (1898 1993)
VORIS, MARK Educator, Painter (1907 974)
VORWERK, E CHARLSIE Painter, Illustrator (1934-2003)
VOSE, ROBERT C Art Dealer (1873-1965)
VOULKOS, PETER Sculptor, Educator (1924-2002)
VUILLEMENOT FRED A Designer, Sculptor (1890-1952)
VYTLACIL, VACLAV Painter, Educator (1892-)
WAALAND, JAMES BREARLEY, II Dealer, Gallery Director (1953-2005)
WAANO-GANO, JOE Painter, Lecturer (1906-1982)
WACHSTETER, GEORGE Illustrator (1911-2004)
WADDELL, RICHARD H Art Dealer (-1974)
WADDINGHAM, JOHN ALFRED Painter, Printmaker (1915-2002)
WAGNER, BLANCHE COLLET Lecturer (1873-)
WAGNER, GLADYS NOBLE Painter, Sculptor (1907-)
WAGNER, GORDON PARSONS Assemblage Artist, Environmental Artist (1915-1987)
WALCH, JOHN LEO Painter, Sculptor (1918-2003)
WALD, PALMER B Administrator (1930-1988)
WALDRON, JAMES MACKEILAR Painter (1909-1974)
WALINSKA, ANNA Painter, Lecturer (1916-1997)
WALKER, EVERETT Educator (-1968)
WALKER, HENRY BABCOCK JR Collector (1885-1966)
WALKER, HERSCHEL CAREY Collector
WALKER, HUDSON D Collector, Art Administrator (1907-1976)
WALKER, JAMES ADAMS Painter, Printmaker (1921-1987)
WALKER, LYDIA LE BARON Designer (1869-1958)
WALKEY, FREDERICK P Consultant (1922-2001)
WALKOWITZ ABRAHAM Painter (1890-1965)
WALL, MARGARET V Museum Director (1895-1958)
WALLACE, FREDERICK E Painter (1893-1958)
WALLEEN, HANS AXEL Illustrator (1902-1978)
WALLEN, BURR Historian, Curator (1941-)
WALMSLEY, WILLIAM AUBREY Printmaker, Collector (1923-2003)
WALTER, MARTHA Painter (1875-1976)
WALTER, WILLIAM F Artist (1904-1977)
WALTMANN, HARRY FRANKLIN Painter (1871-1951)
WANDS, ALFRED JAMES Painter, Graphic Artist (1904-1998)
WARD, EVELYN SVEC Tapestry Artist, Collage Artist (-1989)
WARD, LAURISTON Curator (1883-1960)
WARD, LYND (KENDALL) Illustrator, Writer (1905-1985)
WARD, PHILLIP A Ceramist, Educator (1927-)
WARD, WILLIAM EDWARD Designer, Painter (1922-2004)
WARDELL, ALLEN Museum Director, Consultant (1935-1999)
WARDER, WILLIAM Painter, Writer
WARING, LAURA WHEELER Portrait Painter (-1949)
WARNEKE, HEINZ Sculptor (1895-1983)
WARNER, EVERETT LONGLEY Painter (1877-1963)
WARNER, JO Painter (1931-1999)
WARREN, CALLIE Administrator (-1984)
WARREN, FERDINAND EARL Painter, Administrator (1899-1981)
WARREN, L D Cartoonist (1906-1992)
WARREN, MRS GEORGE HENRY Collector (1897-1976)
WARSHAW, HOWARD Painter (1920-)
WARSHAWSKY ABEL GEORGE Painter (1884-1962)
WASEY, JANE Sculptor (1912-)
WASHBURN CADWALLADER Painter (1866-1965)
WASHBURN, GORDON BAILEY Museum Director (1904-)
WASHBURN, LOUESE B Painter (1875-1959)
WATERMAN, DONALD CALVIN Designer, Educator (1928-1979)
WATERS, GEORGE FITE Sculptor (1894-1961)
WATERS, TERRANCE Architect (1920-2004)
WATKINS, FRANKLIN CHENAULT Painter (1894-1972)
WATROUS, JAMES SCALES Painter, Historian (1908-1999)
WATSON, HILDEGARDE LASELL Artist, Patron (-1976)
WATTS, DOROTHY BURT (TROUT) Artist (1892-1977)
WAUGH, COULTON Painter, Writer (1886-1973)
WAUGH, SIDNEY B Sculptor (1904-1963)
WEBB, AILEEN OSBORN Painter, Enamelist (1892-1979)
WEBB, TODD Photographer, Historian (1905-2000)
WEBER, ALBERT JACOB Painter, Educator (1919-2004)
WEBER, FREDERICK THEODORE Painter (1883-1956)
WEBER, HUGO Painter (1918-1971)
WEBER, JANET RUTH Painter (1925-)
WEBER, MAX Painter, Sculptor (1881-1961)
WEBER, SYBILLA MITTELL Painter (1892-1957)
WEBSTER, H T Cartoonist (1885-1952)
WEBSTER, STOKELY Painter, Printmaker (1912-2002)
WECHSIER, HERMAN J Art Consultant, Writer (1904-1976)
WEDDIGE, EMIL A Printmaker, Painter (1907-2001)
WEDOW, RUDY Sculptor (1906-1965)
WEEBER, GRETCHEN Painter
WEEKS, JAMES (DARRELL NORTHRUP) Painter, Art Dealer (1922-1998)
WEEKS, LEO ROSCO Painter, Illustrator (1903-1977)
WEEMS, KATHERINE LANE Sculptor (1899-)
WEHR, PAUL ADAM Illustrator, Designer (1914-1973)
WEHR, WESLEY CONRAD Painter, Paleontologist (1929-2004)
WEIDENAAR, REYNOLD HENRY Etcher, Painter (1915-1985)
WEIDNER, ROSWELL THEODORE Painter, Instructor (1911-1999)
WEILL, ERNA Sculptor, Instructor (1904-1996)
WEIN, ALBERT W Sculptor, Painter (1915-1991)
WEINBERG, BELLA Painter, Writer (1912-2002)
WEINBERG, LOUIS Sculptor (1918-)
WEINBERGER, MARTIN Educator, Scholar (-1965)
WEINER, ABE Painter, Instructor (1917-1993)
WEINER, TED Collector, Patron (1911-1979)
WEINGAERTNER HANS Painter (1896-1970)
WEINHARDT, CARL Museum Director, Historian (1922-)
WEINMAN, ADOLPH ALEXANDER Sculptor (1870-1952)
WEINMAN, ROBERT ALEXANDER Sculptor (1915-2003)
WEISBECKER CLEMENT Painter
WEISEL, DEBORAH DELP Painter (-1951)

WEISSBUCH, OSCAR Painter (-1948)
WEITZMANN, KURT Educator, Historian (1904-1993)
WELCH, LIVINGSTON Sculptor, Painter (1901-1976)
WELCH, MABEL R Painter (-1959)
WELCH, ROBERT G Collector (1915-)
WELLER, ALLEN STUART Educator, Historian (1907-1997)
WELLER, JOHN SIDNEY Painter, Printmaker (1928-1981)
WELLINGTON, DUKE Painter (1896-1987)
WELLIVER, NEIL G Painter (1929-2005)
WELLS, CADY Painter (1904-1954)
WELLS, THOMAS (WINCHESTER) Painter (1916-2004)
WENGENROTH, STOW Lithographer (1906-1978)
WENGER, MURIEL Dealer, Collector (1915-1989)
WENLEY, ARCHIBALD GIBSON Museum Director (1898-1962)
WENSLEY, WILLIAM CHARLES Painter, Instructor (-1984)
WERNER, (CHARLES GEORGE) Cartoonist (1909-1997)
WERNER, ALFRED Critic, Writer (1911-1979)
WERNER, NAT Sculptor (1907-1991)
WERTHEIM MRS MAURICE Collector (-1974)
WESCOTT, PAUL Painter (1904-1970)
WESSELS, GLENN ANTHONY Painter (1895-1982)
WEST, PENNERTON Painter (-1965)
WESTERMANN HORACE CLIFFORD Sculptor, Painter (1922-1981)
WESTON, HAROLD Painter (1894-1972)
WETHEY, HAROLD EDWIN Historian (1902-1984)
WHARTON, CAROL FORBES (MRS JAMES P) Painter (1907-1958)
WHARTON, JAMES PEARCE Educator (1893-1963)
WHEELER, ORSON SHOREY Sculptor, Lecturer (1902-)
WHEELOCK, WARREN F Painter (1880-1960)
WHIPPLE, BARBARA Graphic Artist, Gallery Director (-1989)
WHITAKER, FREDERIC Painter (1891-1980)
WHITE, ALBERT Dealer, Collector (-1991)
WHITE, CHARLES WILBERT Painter, Educator (1918-1979)
WHITE, EUGENE B Painter (-1966)
WHITE, MINOR Photographer (1908-1976)
WHITE, RALPH Painter, Educator
WHITE, ROBERT (WINTHROP) Sculptor, Educator (1921-2002)
WHITE, WALTER L Painter (-1963)
WHITEHILL, WALTER MUIR Writer, Historian (1905-1978)
WHITENER, PAUL A W Museum Director (1911-1959)
WHITNEY, CHARLES E Interior Designer, Publisher (1903-1977)
WHITNEY, EDGAR ALBERT Painter, Instructor (1891-)
WHITNEY, ISABEL LYDIA Painter (-1962)
WHITNEY, JOHN HAY Administrator, Collector (1904-1982)
WHITNEY, PHILIP RICHARDSON Painter (1878-)
WHITNEY, WILLIAM KUEBLER Painter, Historian (1921-1985)
WHITTEMORE, HELEN SIMPSON Painter
WHORF, JOHN Painter (1903-1959)
WHYTE, RAYMOND A Painter (1923-2003)
WIBSTROM EDWARD FREDERICK Sculptor (1903-1989)
WICKISER, RALPH LEWANDA Administrator, Painter (1910-1998)
WICKS, EUGENE CLAUDE Painter, Educator (1931-2005)
WIEGAND, ROBERT Painter (1934-1994)
WIEGHARDT PAUL Painter, Educator (1897-1969)
WIELAND, JOYCE Painter, Filmmaker (1931-1998)
WIENER, GEORGE Art Dealer
WIESENFELD, PAUL Painter (1942-1990)
WIGGINS, GUY C Painter (1883-1962)
WIGGINS, MYRA ALBERT Painter (1869-1956)
WIGGINS, WALTON WRAY Writer,, Photographer (1924-1992)
WIGHT, FREDERICK S Painter, Administrator (1902-1986)
WILBUR, LAWRENCE NELSON Painter, Printmaker (1897-1988)
WILCOX, LUCIA Painter
WILCOX, RUTH Librarian (1889-1958)
WILDENHAIN, FRANS Potter (1905-1980)
WILDENSTEIN, FELIX Gallery Director (-1952)
WILDENSTEIN, GEORGES Art Editor (1892-1963)
WILDER, MITCHELL ARMITAGE Administrator (1913-1979)
WILDER, NICHOLAS Artist
WILDMAN, CAROLINE LAX Painter (-1949)
WILE, ANDREW JEFFREY Painter (1949-1982)
WILES, IRVING R Portrait Painter (1861-1948)
WILFORD, LORAN Painter, Educator (1892-1972)
WILFRED, THOMAS Sculptor (1889-1968)
WILKE, HANNAH Sculptor, Instructor (1940-1993)
WILKE, ULFERT S Painter, Administrator (1907-1988)
WILKINSON, JOHN Painter (1913-1973)
WILLARD, FRANK H Cartoonist (1893-1958)
WILLARD, HELEN Curator (-1979)
WILLET, HENRY LEE Craftsman (1899-1983)
WILLETT, JACQUES Painter (1882-1958)
WILLIAMS, EDWARD K Painter (1870-)
WILLIAMS, FREDERIC ALLEN Sculptor (1899-1958)
WILLIAMS, FREDERICK BALLARD Painter (1871-1956)
WILLIAMS, HERMANN WARNER JR Art Administrator, Writer (1908-1975)
WILLIAMS, HIRAM DRAPER Painter (1917-2003)
WILLIAMS, JULIA TOCHIE Painter (1887-1948)
WILLIAMS, KEITH SHAW Painter, Etcher (1905-1951)
WILLIAMS, LEWIS WIt Historian, Educator (1918-1990)
WILLIAMS, NEIL Artist
WILLIAMS, WARNER Sculptor, Designer (1903-1982)
WILLIAMS, WHEELER Sculptor (1897-1972)
WILLIAMSON, ADA C Painter (1883-1958)
WILLIAMSON, CLARA McDONALD Painter (-1976)
WILLIS, ELIZABETH BAYLEY, Historian, Collector (-2003)
WILLIS, ROBERT E Painter, Printmaker (1922-)
WILSON, BEN Painter, Lecturer (1913-2001)
WILSON, EDWARD N (ED) Sculptor, Educator (1925-1997)
WILSON, GEORGE LEWIS Painter (1930-1987)
WILSON, HELEN Sculptor (1884-1974)
WILSON, ORME Patron (1885-1966)
WILSON, SOL Painter (1896-1974)
WILTON, ANNA KEENER Painter Educator (1895-)
WILWERS, EDWARD M (1918-2002)
WINCHESTER, ALICE Editor, Writer (1907-)
WINDELL, VIOLET BRUNER Graphic Artist, Cartoonist (1922-2005)
WINGERT, PAUL STOVER Writer, Art Historian (1900-1974)
WINKEL, NINA Sculptor, Lecturer (1905-1990)
WINOGRAND, GARRY Photographer, Lecturer (1928-1984)
WINSLOW, RALPH E Architect (1902-1978)
WINSTANLEY, JOHN BREYFOGLE Painter (1874-1947)
WINTER, ANDREW Painter (1892-1958)
WINTER, EZRA Painter (1886-1949)
WIRTSCHAFTER, BUD Filmmaker, Instructor (1924-1988)
WISA, LOUIS SR Cartoonist (-1953)
WISE, HOWARD Administrator (1903-1989)
WISE, LOUISE WATERMAN (MRS STEPHENS) Painter (-1947)
WITAKER, EILEEN MONAGHAN Painter (1911-2005)
WITTEN BORN, GEORGE Collector, Art Dealer (1905-1974)
WITTMACK, EDGAR FRANKLIN Illustrator (1894-1956)
WOELFFER, EMERSON Painter (1914-2003)
WOJNAROWICZ, DAVID Painter, Sculptor (1954-1992)
WOLFE, ANN (ANN WOLFE GRAUBARD) Sculptor
WOLFF, ROBERT J Painter, Writer (1905-1978)
WOLFF, WILLIAM H Dealer (1906-1991)
WOLFSON, SIDNEY Painter, Sculptor (1911-1973)
WOLINS, JOSEPH Painter (1915-)
WOLLE, MURIEL SIBELL Painter, Writer (1898-1977)
WONG, JASON Museum Director, Designer (1934-2002)
WONTERSTEEN, BERNICE McILHENNY Administrator, Collector (1903-1986)
WOOD, BEATRICE Ceramist, Educator (-1998)
WOOD, MARCIA JOAN Sculptor (1933-2001)
WOOD, ROBERT E Painter, Instructor (1926-1999)
WOODLOCK, ETHELYN HURD Painter (1907-2001)
WOODRUFF, HALE A Painter, Educator (1900-1980)
WOODS, SARAH LADD Collector, Patron (1895-1980)
WOODS, WILLIS FRANKLIN Consultant (1920-1988)
WOODWARD, ROBERT STRONG Painter (1885-1957)
WOODWARD, STANLEY Painter (1890-1970)
WOOLF, SAMUEL J Painter (1880-1948)
WORCESTER, EVA Painter (1892-1970)
WORTHAM, HAROLD Painter, Art Consultant (1909-1974)
WORTHMAN, DENYS Cartoonist (1886-1958)
WRAY, MARGARET MASLE Painter (-1988)
WRIGHT, CATHARINE MORRIS painter, Writer (1899-1988)
WRIGHT, G ALAN Sculptor (1927-)
WRIGHT, GEORGE HAND Etcher, Painter (1872-1951)
WRIGHT, LLOYD Architect (1890-1978)
WRIGHT, MILTON Painter, Educator (1920-2005)
WRIGHT, ROBERT A Cartoonist (1900-1958)
WRIGHT, RUSSEL Designer, Sculptor (1904-1976)
WRIGHT, STANLEY MARC Painter, Instructor (1911-)
WU, LINDA YEE CHAU Sculptor (1919-2004)
WUERPEL, EDMUND HENRY Painter (1886-1958)
WUNDER, RICHARD PAUL Historian, Administrator (1926-2002)
WUNDERLICH, RUDOLF G Dealer (1920-2004)
WURDEMANN, HELEN (BARONESS ELENA GUZZARDO) Administrator, Collector
WURTZBURGER, JANET E C Collector, Patron (1908-)
WYETH, HENRIETTE (MRS PETER HURD) Painter (1907-)
WYMAN, WILLIAM Sculptor (1922-1980)

XCERON, JEAN Painter (1890-1967)
YAEGER, EDGAR LOUIS Painter, Muralist (1904-1997)
YAFFEE, EDITH WIDING Painter (1895-1961)
YAGHJIAN, EDMUND Painter, Instructor (1903-1997)
YARDLEY, RICHARD QUINCY Cartoonist (1903-1979)
YEE, CHIANG Painter, Calligrapher (1903-1977)
YERBYSMITH, ERNEST ALFRED Sculptor (-1952)
YOORS, JAN Tapestry Artist, Photographer (1922-1977)
YORK, ROBERT Cartoonist (1919-1975)
YOSHIMURA, FUMIO Sculptor (1926-2002)
YOST, FRED J Painter (1888-1968)
YOUNG, CHIC (MURAT BERNARD YOUNG) Cartoonist (1901-1973)
YOUNG, CLIFF Painter, Muralist (1905-1985)
YOUNG, MAHONRI M Sculptor (1877-1957)
YUNKERS, ADJA Painter, Educator (1900-1983)
ZACHA, WILLIAM Painter, Sculptor (1920-1998)
ZACKS, SAMUEL JACOB Collector, Patron (1904-1970)
ZALLINGER, RUDOLPH FRANZ Painter, Educator (1919-1995)
ZEIGLER, LEE WOODWARD Illustrator (1896-1952)
ZEISLER, CLAIRE (BLOCK) Sculptor, Collector (1903-1991)
ZELLERBACH, HAROLD L Patron, Director (1895-1978)
ZERBE, KARL Painter, Educator (1903-1972)
ZILZER, GYULA Printmaker, Painter (1898-1969)
ZIMMER, FRITZ Sculptor
ZIMMERMAN, FREDERICK A Painter, Instructor (1886-1974)
ZIOLKOWSKI, KORCZAK Sculptor (1908-1982)
ZOGBAUM, WILFRED Painter (-1965)
ZOGROSSER, CARL Writer (1891-1975)
ZORACH, MARGUERITE T Painter (1887-1968)
ZORACH, WILLIAM Sculptor (1887-1966)
ZOROLI, ANGELO GERARDO Sculptor (1899-1948)
ZUCKER, JACQUES Painter (1900-1981)
ZUCKERMAN, RUTH VICTOR Sculptor, Photographer (1933-)
ZUEHLKE, CLARENCE EDGAR Painter (-1963)
ZUNIGA, FRANCISCO Sculptor, Graphic Artist (1912-1998)
ZWICK, ROSEMARY G Sculptor, Printmaker (1925-1995)